P9-AOJ-371

Analytical Concordance to the Bible

ON AN ENTIRELY NEW PLAN

CONTAINING ABOUT 311,000 REFERENCES, SUBDIVIDED
UNDER THE HEBREW AND GREEK ORIGINALS,
WITH THE LITERAL MEANING AND
PRONUNCIATION OF EACH

DESIGNED FOR THE SIMPLEST READER OF THE ENGLISH BIBLE

BY ROBERT YOUNG, LL. D.

AUTHOR OF "A NEW TRANSLATION OF THE BIBLE," "NEW CONCORDANCE TO THE GREEK NEW TESTAMENT," "DICTIONARY AND CONCORDANCE OF BIBLE WORDS AND SYNONYMS," "CONCISE CONCORDANCE TO EIGHT THOUSAND CHANGES OF THE REVISED TESTAMENT," AND NUMEROUS OTHER WORKS IN BIBLICAL AND ORIENTAL LITERATURE

ALSO

INDEX LEXICONS TO THE OLD AND NEW TESTAMENTS

BEING A GUIDE TO PARALLEL PASSAGES

AND

A COMPLETE LIST OF SCRIPTURE PROPER NAMES

SHOWING THEIR MODERN PRONUNCIATION

TWENTY-SECOND AMERICAN EDITION

REVISED

BY WM. B. STEVENSON, B.D. (EDIN.)

PROFESSOR OF HEBREW AND OLD TESTAMENT EXEGESIS AT BALA THEOLOGICAL COLLEGE,
EXAMINER IN THEOLOGY AT EDINBURGH UNIVERSITY

WITH A SUPPLEMENT ENTITLED

THE CANON OF SCRIPTURE

BY R. K. HARRISON, PROFESSOR OF OLD TESTAMENT, WYCLIFFE COLLEGE, UNIVERSITY OF TORONTO
AND EVERETT F. HARRISON, PROFESSOR OF NEW TESTAMENT, FULLER THEOLOGICAL SEMINARY

WM. B. EERDMANS PUBLISHING COMPANY

GRAND RAPIDS MICHIGAN

Analytical Concordance to the Bible

By ROBERT YOUNG

Library of Congress Catalog Card Number 55-5338

Reprinted 1975

ISBN 0-8028-2283-5

ISBN 0-8028-2284-3

EXCERPT FROM

PREFATORY NOTE TO THE FIRST EDITION

THE PRESENT WORK is the result of very many years' labour, and is designed to lead the simplest reader to a more correct understanding of the common English Bible, *by a reference to the original words* in Hebrew and Greek, *with their varied shades of meaning,* as explained by the most recent critics—Fürst, Robinson, &c. Every word in the English Bible is cast into proper alphabetical order, these are then arranged under their respective original words, all in their own proper alphabetical order. To each of these the *literal* meaning is prefixed, and the *pronunciation* appended, with certain figures which indicate the number of the Hebrew conjugation; which latter sign is of great value, since each conjugation has more or less a *definite* signification of its own. Thus Nos. 1, 3, 5 are *active,* Nos. 2, 4, 6 *passive,* and No. 7 *reflexive.* (The "conjugations" from 1 to 7 are: Kal, Niphal, Piel, Pual, Hiphil, Hophal, Hithpael.) So that if QATAL in the first conjugation is "he killed," the second is "he was killed," the third "he killed violently," the fourth "he was killed violently," the fifth "he caused to kill," the sixth "he was caused to kill," and the seventh "he killed himself." Though many exceptions are found, the general formula holds good very distinctly.

Nouns, Adjectives, Verbs, and Adverbs are here given generally at *full length,* with the exception of the phrase "The LORD," which it has been deemed unnecessary to insert, as it is uniformly printed in the Common Version in small capitals—"the LORD"—and is thus easily distinguished. It occurs no less than 5000 times, and, if printed in full, would alone have occupied above fifteen pages of this Concordance.

The Hebrew **Particles** (specially those inseparable) have few or no illustrations presented, but the Greek ones are more extended; yet in such cases as ἀλλά, δέ, &c., they are much too numerous for a separate exhibition at length.

The Italics of the English Bible are enclosed within *parentheses* ( ), while the **Various Readings of the Greek New Testament** are marked by brackets [ ], and amount to about 30,000 in all. Unfortunately, the entire lack of *ancient* HEBREW MSS. prevents the same course from being followed with the Old Testament quotations; but we are not without hopes that future excavations in the Temple Area in Jerusalem may yet provide us with MSS. of the age of Josiah, or of David, if not with the very Autographs once preserved with the Ark of the Tabernacle.

The Proper Names of Persons and Places are, in all existing Concordances (almost without a single exception), either omitted, or put at the end under a separate alphabet; they are here, for the first time, inserted in their proper alphabetical order, with the *literal* meaning of each, as far as can be at present ascertained. Their proper *syllables* are also marked and accented according to the *principles* of Hebrew and Greek—the accent being placed on the last or on the second last syllable of the word.

The Geographical, Historical, and Biographical remarks have been generally limited (after the first *ninety-six* pages) to Biblical details; and the modern names of ascertained Bible sites have been given in accordance with the researches of *Robinson, Baedeker,* the *Palestine Exploration Society,* &c. The thorough VERACITY of the Scriptures is thus incidentally confirmed by existing facts that cannot be denied or ignored, and are of priceless value.

In consulting this Work, the student is to bear in mind that it is **a Concordance of Words, not of Phrases** save in so far as any given Hebrew or Greek word may be translated in the English Bible not by a *word* merely, but by a *phrase*; thus the word "great" will be found not only under the *adjective,* but also under the words *"authority, deal, delight, desire, do, drops, drought, flame, forces, grasshopper, hailstones, how, lion, man, mercies, noise, owl, pain, power, price, shew, so, stature, swelling, teeth, toe, very, way, what, while to come, wonders,"* &c., in all which cases it is *not* a separate word in the original, but indicates simply what the Translators deemed to be necessary to express the *full* force of each of the words in question.

So with the Verbs. These are arranged under separate headings, e.g., "to come, come *in,* come *upon,*" &c. Yet, under the simple verb "to come," the student will find numerous cases where Come *in,* come *upon,* &c., occur. The explanation is, that in such cases the adverbs are *separate* particles, and are no part of the signification of the verb itself. Passives are *sometimes* to be found under Actives, especially in the Greek.

As Cruden's **Definitions,** though many of them interesting and good, often express too decidedly his own specific view of religious truth to be satisfactory, the present Work confines the definitions strictly to their literal or idiomatic force; which, after all, will be found to form the best (and indeed *the only safe and solid*) basis for theological deductions of any kind.

The present Work is thus an entirely independent one, and in no sense an edition of Cruden, either in its plan or its execution. **Its great object,** as Tyndale says of his New Testament, is to enable every "PLOUGH-BOY" to know more of the Scriptures than the "ancients," by enabling him at a glance to find out **Three Distinct Points**—*First,* What is the *original* Hebrew or Greek of any ordinary word in his English Bible: *Second,* What is the *literal* and primitive meaning of every such original word: and *Third,* What are thoroughly true and reliable *parallel passages.*

In carrying out these three important Points, the following plan has been adopted: *First,* One Hundred and Eighteen Thousand references have been given, which are not found in Cruden. *Second,* Every passage in the New Testament which critical investigators, like Griesbach and Tischendorf, have noted as doubtful, or as having a Various Reading, has been marked by brackets. *Third,* The Proper Name of every Person and Place has been given, with the literal meaning. *Fourth,* The date or era of every Person, so as to distinguish him from every other of the same name. *Fifth,* The location of every place in its tribe, with the modern name (if identified), so as to form a complete Scripture Geography and Gazetteer.

But the predominating feature of this work is the *Analytical arrangement* of each English word under its *own proper original* in Hebrew or Greek, with the literal meaning of the same. By this means the reader is enabled to *distinguish things that differ,* which are frequently confounded in the English Bible, and for the elucidation of which Cruden offers no real help at all, and which indeed have hitherto been the exclusive property of scholars. For our Translation often renders *one* Greek word by *ten* or *twenty* English ones; and, on the other hand, it sometimes employs *one* English word to translate *ten* or *twenty* Greek ones.

In sending forth this "ANALYTICAL CONCORDANCE" for the benefit of the Christian student of Holy Writ, the Author trusts that as it is only the practical outcome of all his previous Biblical Studies, many of his readers, lay as well as clerical, may give themselves more to the study of the ORIGINAL Scriptures, which have "God for their Author, Truth without mixture of Error for their Matter, and Salvation for their End."

ROBERT YOUNG.

PREFACE TO THE 21ST AMERICAN EDITION

THE 21st American Edition of Dr. Robert Young's widely known Concordance has been greatly improved in completeness and accuracy by the incorporation in it of new material drawn from the latest revised British Edition. The following extracts from the Preface to that Edition show the nature of the improvements made:

The most important additions are of two kinds. Forty-five entirely new headings or sub-headings have been printed, most of them on a supplementary page which immediately precedes the beginning of the Concordance. The number of references in the Concordance has also been substantially increased. About fifty new references are given on the supplementary page and about seventy have been included in the body of the Concordance.

During the revision some improvements have been introduced into the headings and sub-headings so as to show more precisely the Hebrew and Greek originals of the English words, and new cross references have been inserted to make it easier to find some of the words and verses of the English Bible. Users of the Concordance are asked to remember that two closely associated English words are often given only under one of them, because the two words together represent only one single Greek or Hebrew word.

Special attention may be called to the fact emphasized in Dr. Young's original preface, that particles (i.e. small words of no special significance or difficulty) are not considered to be of sufficient importance to require the printing of every verse in which they occur. Again, because of the great number of passages in which "the Lord," as a divine title, occurs, only a representative portion of them has been included, and the same selective treatment is given to some other classes of words, such as the adverb surely (for which see new supplementary page).

It may be noted also that the spelling of certain words, the use of capitals and the punctuation of sentences are not always the same in every Bible. It follows that many small differences may be found between the Concordance and the Bible used by some particular reader. Because of these differences alternative spellings have been somewhat increased in the headings of the new Edition (e.g., ax and axe, injoin and enjoin, hungered and hungred).

The special part taken by Emeritis Professor Wm. B. Stevenson in the preparation of the revised edition is also acknowledged and he is warmly thanked for his valuable co-operation and advice.

M. J. E. STUART.

PREFACE TO THE 22ND AMERICAN EDITION

THE objects and contents of this edition of Dr Young's Concordance continue to be best described by the original preface. The experience of Bible students has only confirmed the value of his work. Numerous corrections and improvements will be found in the present edition as compared even with that immediately preceding, but changes have been made only to secure accuracy, or when Dr Young's own principles seemed to suggest them.

An important addition has been made to the Concordance in the shape of the Index-lexicons printed at the end. These have been prepared in response to a widely expressed desire that there should be some means of finding parallel passages even when the original has not been rendered into English by one and the same word only. The indexes enable even those who are unacquainted with Greek or Hebrew to find every passage in the Bible in which the same original word is employed. The ability to find "true and reliable" parallel passages is in this way very largely increased. The indexes are also of the nature of lexicons, for they give under each word all its meanings according to the English version of 1611. Dictionaries of Biblical Greek and Hebrew have thus been provided in Roman characters for the "simplest reader."

The material used in the Index-lexicons has been taken from Dr Young's own Greek and Hebrew lexicons. The revision of that material has been incidental only, not systematic; but comparison will show that it has, nevertheless, been of a substantial character. The transliteration adopted in the indexes is necessarily that already used in the body of the Concordance.

The Concordance itself has been submitted to a more considerable revision than for several editions. The preparation of the Index-lexicons gave an unusual opportunity of increasing its accuracy and fulness. The number of references has been appreciably increased. In many cases the original words are now given with more exactness. Correction was particularly necessary when the English heading or rubric represented several original words in combination, and yet only one of these was given in the sub-heading.

The systematic revision of the Concordance has included three points:—

(1) Proper names spelled in various ways are now all placed in alphabetical order. To find Shamariah, it is no longer necessary to know that it is also spelled Shemariah.

(2) The double readings which appear in the Hebrew text (*k^etîb* and *k^erê*) have been printed as completely as possible. That which the English translators have rejected is enclosed in square brackets with V.L. (*varia lectio*) preceding. Previously either both readings were given, without indication of which was translated, or one only, and that not always the reading adopted by the translators.

(3) The transliterations of Hebrew words have been thoroughly revised so as to enable all readers to find any word in the Index-lexicons. A transliteration is now given which can always (it is hoped) be found as a rubric in the lexicons. When such a transliteration does not exactly correspond to the Hebrew form alongside of it, it is placed in square brackets. A dash dividing the transliteration in two (as *le-mishi*) denotes that the two parts are separate words, but written together in the Hebrew character. This part of the revision, from considerations of space, etc., has been carried out in the case of Greek words only partially. Sometimes only the commencement of a Greek word is transliterated.

It is believed that the successive revisions of the Concordance have confined merely accidental errors to very small compass. Where such were detected they have been corrected. A few texts which required to be cancelled, because they stood under a wrong sub-heading, have been enclosed in heavy square brackets instead of being completely deleted. Comparatively few changes have been made in the meanings assigned to the Greek and Hebrew words. With very few exceptions these are introducéd along with other changes only.

An addition to the supplements has been made in the shape of a complete list of proper names, which is intended to be a guide to their recognised pronunciation. The accentuation of these words in the body of the Concordance is not that of ordinary speech, and what is wanting in this respect is now supplied by the supplement. Those who consult pronouncing lists of Scripture names are aware that they differ in a most perplexing manner. The discussion of principles which has been prefixed to the Concordance list is intended to reduce somewhat the confusion which every new list, without such guidance, merely intensifies. The writer hopes that he has provided material which will help to make decision easier even in cases where his recommendations are not adopted. As the original Hebrew names often differ strikingly from their current English forms, an accurate transliteration of the originals is also given.

The valuable and interesting "Sketch of Recent Exploration in Bible Lands," contributed by Dr Nicol to the previous edition, has been thoroughly revised by him and brought up to date.*

WM. B. STEVENSON.

*PUBLISHER'S NOTE: For the current edition the supplement "The Canon of Scripture" by Professors R. K. Harrison and Everett F. Harrison replaces the earlier sketch by Dr. Nicol.

HINTS AND HELPS TO BIBLE INTERPRETATION.

Illustrations of Bible Idioms.

1. HUMAN feelings, actions, and parts are ascribed to GOD, not that they are really in Him, but because such effects proceed from Him as are like those that flow from such things in Men, *see*—Gen. 6. 3, 6; 11. 7; 18. 33; Psa. 60. 8; 78. 65; Isa. 1. 24; Jer. 7. 13; Heb. 10. 12; 12. 6; Jas. 5. 4; 2 Pe. 2. 9; Deut. 8. 2; Heb. 4. 13; Luke 1. 66; Psa. 4. 6; Josh. 7. 26; Lev. 26. 28.

(*b*.) God is frequently spoken of as dealing with MEN as they deal with HIM, *see*—Josh. 7. 12; Judg. 2. 20, 21; 2 Sa. 22. 26, 27; 2 Ch. 15. 2; Matt. 6. 15; 18. 35; John 15. 14.

2. Abstract and inanimate things are frequently PERSONIFIED, *e.g.* —*Ears* are attributed to the heavens, the earth, death, and destruction; *hands* to the deep; *eyes* to the sea and the mountains; a *voice* to the deep, wisdom, and understanding; a *will* to the flesh and mind; *witnessing* to an altar, a song, a stone, blood, and water; *speaking* to the ear, eye, foot, days, years, blood, law, righteousness, and blood of sprinkling; *knowing, rejoicing, rising*, and *going down* to the sun; *being roused from sleep* to the sword and arm of Jehovah; *skipping* and *leaping* to mountains and hills; *crying out* to the heart and flesh, wisdom and understanding; *seeing* and *preaching* to the Scripture; *judging* to the word; *teaching* to grace, the heaven, and the earth; *leading* and *guiding* to light, truth, and the commandments; *dominion* and *enmity* to death; *mastery* to sin; *comforting* to a rod and staff; *carrying a message* to anger, fear, mercy, light, and truth; and every *Christian virtue* to charity or love.

3. OPPOSITE statements are to be carefully compared, *e.g.*—Gen. 2. 2 and John 5. 17; Exod. 24. 10 and John 1. 18; 1 Sa. 15. 11 and 29; 1 Ki. 22. 20 and Isa. 40. 14; Psa. 51. 10 and Ezek. 18. 31; Prov. 6. 1 and Phile. 18, 19; Prov. 26. 4 and 5; Isa. 9. 21 and Luke 18. 1; Ezek. 18. 32 and Rom. 9. 18; Matt. 5. 11 and John 16. 4; Matt. 5. 16 and 6. 1; 5. 34 and Rev. 10. 6 and Rom. 9. 1; Matt. 6. 34 and 1 Ti. 5. 8; Matt. 7. 7, 8 and John 8. 21; Matt. 10. 9 and Mark 6. 9; Matt. 10. 37 and Luke 14. 26 and Eph. 5. 29; Matt. 12. 30 and Mark 9. 40; Matt. 20. 29 and Mark 10. 46 and Luke 18. 35; Matt. 26. 52 and Luke 22. 36; Luke 1. 33 and 1 Co. 15. 24; Luke 22. 36 and 2 Co. 10. 4; Luke 16. 8 and Mark 10. 19; Luke 18. 1 and John 9. 31; John 5. 23 and 41; 8. 51 and Heb. 9. 27; John 9. 39 and 12. 47; 10. 30 and 14. 28; Acts 16. 3 and Gal. 5. 2; Rom. 3. 28 and Jas. 2. 24; Col. 2. 20 and 1 Pe. 2. 13.

4. GENERAL statements are frequently to be LIMITED, *see*—Prov. 3. 16; 9. 11; 10. 27; 11. 14, 15; 12. 28; 16. 7, 10; 17. 6; 18. 22; 22. 6, 29; Mark 16. 17, 18; John 3. 22; 11. 9; Rom. 3. 10, 11; 9. 30; 1 Co. 7. 32.

5. POSITIVE statements are frequently to be understood COMPARATIVELY, *see*—Gen. 45. 8; Exod. 16. 8; 1 Sa. 8. 7; Prov. 8. 10; Jer. 7. 22, 23; Joel 2. 13; Hos. 6. 6; Matt. 9. 13; 11. 18, 19; 15. 24; 23. 2; Luke 14. 12; John 5. 22, 30; 6. 27; Rom. 9. 21; 1 Co. 1. 17; 3. 7; Col. 3. 2; 1 Ti. 1. 9; 6. 8.

6. GENERAL REASONINGS, of various kinds, are sometimes employed, *e.g.*—From the nature, attributes, and actions of God, the nature and social relations of Man, for analogy, contrast, cause and effect, the greater and the less, the less and the greater, the truthfulness of the senses, self consciousness, the truths of testimony, the works of nature and providence, from experience, &c.

7. The language of the MESSENGER frequently glides into that of the SENDER, *e.g.*—Gen. 16. 10; 18. 14; Exod. 7. 16, 17; 15. 25, 26; Deut. 11. 13–15; 29. 2–6; 31. 22, 23; Isa. 10. 4, 7, 25, 26; 50. 3, 4; Jer. 4. 19–27; 6. 22–30; 9. 1–3; Zech. 2. 8–11.

8. What a SERVANT says or does is ascribed to the MASTER, *e.g.*—Matt. 19. 4, 5.

9. Persons and things are spoken of according to what they ONCE were, or PROFESSED (or are presently THOUGHT) to be, though not really so, either formerly or at present, *e.g.*—1 Sa. 13. 14; 1 Ki. 13. 11; Jer. 28. 1, 5, 10; Ezek. 21. 4; Matt. 5. 13; 9. 12, 13; 10. 3; 12. 42; 26. 6; Luke 2. 1, 48; 15. 7, 24, 29; 16. 15; 19. 22; Acts 28. 2; Rom. 6. 2; 1 Co. 1. 21; 2. 6; Titus 1. 12; 2 Pe. 2. 1.

10. Words are frequently used in an IRONICAL manner, *e.g.*—Judg. 10. 14; 1 Ki. 18. 27; 22. 15; Job 12. 2; Eccl. 11. 9; Matt. 25. 26; Mark 7. 9; 1 Co. 4. 8.

11. TRANSPOSITION of clauses is frequently necessary, *e.g.*—Matt. 7. 6; Mark 9. 13; 11. 13; 15. 21; 16. 3, 4; Luke 4. 5; 5. 15, 17; Acts 4. 27, 28; 5. 12, 15, 38, 39; 28. 18; 1 Ti. 1. 13, 14; Rev. 13. 8.

12. HEBRAISMS, Latinisms, Syriacisms, &c., are frequently used, *e.g.*—Abba, aceldama, amen, corban, ephphatha, eloi, hallelujah, &c.—centurion, census, colony, legion, libertine, mile, prætorium, tavern, title, forum, &c.; to accept, *i.e.*, lift up the face of any one; to have compassion, *i.e.*, have the bowels moved for any one; flesh and blood, *i.e.*, a human being; to confess (in, with) one; one for first, &c., &c.

13. The SAME persons and places have frequently DIFFERENT names, *e.g.*—Abiathar and Ahimelech; Abiud and Meshallum; Abram and Abraham; Adah and Bashemath; Ahaziah, Azariah, and Jehoahaz; Amiel and Eliam; Azariah and Uzziah; Barachias, Jehoiada, and Johanan; Barnabas and Joses; Barsabas, Joseph, and Justus; Bartholomew and Nathaniel; Cæsarea, Dan, and Laish; Cephas, Peter, Simon, Simeon; Dalmanutha and Magdala; Didymus and Thomas; Eliseus and Elisha; Elias and Elijah; En-Mishpat and Kadesh; Gadarenes and Gergasenes; Gideon and Jerubbaal; Hadadezar and Hadarezar; Hermon, Shenir, and Sirion; Hobab and Jethro; Horeb and Sinai; Jebus and Jerusalem; Jedidiah and Solomon; Jehoahaz, Johanan, and Shallum; Jesus and Joshua; Judah, Judas, and Jude; Lebbaeus and Thaddeus; Levi and Matthew; Lucas and Luke; Sheshbazzar and Zerubbabel; Silas and Silvanus; Timotheus and Timothy; Nebuchadnezzar is spelt in seven different ways.

There were also *two* places named Bethlehem, Cana, &c.; *three* persons named Herod, and several named Abimelech, Agag, Artaxerxes, James, John, Mary, Moses, Pharaoh, Zachariah, &c.

14. The SAME word has frequently a DIFFERENT meaning even in the same verse, *e.g.*—Lev. 16. 8; Matt. 8. 22; 13. 12; Rom. 4. 25; 14. 13; 1 Co. 10. 2; 15. 51; 2 Co. 5. 21; 1 Jo. 5. 20.

15. The name of a BOOK or its WRITER is frequently omitted, *e.g.*—Acts 1. 4; Rom. 9. 7; Gal. 3. 11, 12; Heb. 1. 6; 2. 6.

(*b*.) The name of the WRITER is frequently put for his WRITINGS, *e.g.*—Luke 16. 29, 31; 24. 27; Acts 15. 21; 21. 21; 2 Co. 3. 15.

(*c*.) The SUBJECT treated of is frequently put for the BOOK or WRITER, *e.g.*—Mark 2. 26; 12. 26; Rom. 11. 2.

16. PARENTHESES are to be carefully attended to, *e.g.*—Gen. 13. 10; Isa. 52. 14; Mark 9. 13, 38, 39, 40; Luke 1. 27, 55, 70; Acts 1. 19, 25; 4. 27. 14. 2; Rom. 1. 2–6; 2. 13–16; 5. 7, 8, 12–18; 8. 20, 21; 1 Co. 8. 1–4; 15. 52; 2 Co. 5. 6–8.

17. A negative and an affirmative statement imply CERTAINTY, *e.g.*—2 Ki. 18. 36; Psa. 118. 17; Isa. 38. 1; Luke 1. 20; John 1. 3, 20; Rom. 4. 17; 9. 1; 1 Jo. 2. 27.

18. The REPETITION of a word denotes the SUPERLATIVE degree, *e.g.*—Gen. 9. 25; Exod. 36. 33; Deut. 10. 17; 1 Sa. 2. 3; 2 Ki. 10. 15; Psa. 79. 13; Eccl. 1. 1; 7. 24; Isa. 6. 3; Ezek. 32. 28; Mic. 2. 4.

19. Some words (nouns, pronouns, verbs, &c.) are EXPLETIVE, *e.g.*, account, begin, find, seem, &c. See Mat. 3. 9; 20. 25; Mark 10. 42; Luke 3. 8; 22. 24; John 5. 35; 7. 17; Acts 11. 15; Ro. 5. 7; 1 Co. 3. 18; 7. 40; 10. 12; 11. 16; 14. 37; Phil. 3. 4; Heb. 4. 1; 12. 11.

20. The denial of the ACT frequently implies denial of the POWER of acting, *e.g.*—Gen. 13. 6; Isa. 43. 13; Matt. 12. 25 (Mark 3. 25); Matt. 17. 21 (Mark 9. 29); Rom. 9. 19.

21. REFERENCES—are sometimes made to Non-Canonical Books, which yet were true and contemporary histories, *e.g.*, Num. 21. 14; Josh. 10. 12, 13; 1 Sa. 10. 25; 2 Sa. 1. 18; 1 Ki. 4. 32; 11. 41; 14. 19; 15. 7; 16. 5, 20, 27; 22. 39; 1 Ch. 29. 29; 2 Ch. 9. 29; 12. 15; 20. 34; 26. 22; 28. 26; 33. 18, 19; 35. 25, 27; 36. 8.

22 God's PROMISES and THREATS are frequently CONDITIONAL, *e.g.*—Gen. 2. 17; 15. 18; 17. 7; 1 Sa. 2. 30; Prov. 22. 6; Isa. 38. 1; Jon. 3. 4; Matt. 8. 21; 18. 32; 19. 28; John 3. 36; Acts 27. 24, 31.

(*b*.) Promises and threats are to be understood as referring to the PRESENT condition of man, *e.g.*—John 3. 18; 1 Co. 6. 9, 10.

23. DISTRIBUTION—is expressed in a variety of ways, *e.g.*—by repeating the cardinal number "*two, two*," as in Gen. 7. 9, 15; Mark 6. 7; or by repeating the noun "*heaps, heaps*," as in Exod. 8. 14; "*companies, companies*," Mark 6. 39. Compare also Mark 14. 19; John 8. 9; Rom. 12. 5; 2 Co. 4. 16; Rev. 21. 21.

24. VARIOUS READINGS—are to be duly studied and weighed, *e.g.*—Matt. 1. 25; 2. 18; 6. 4, 6, 18, 34; 23. 8; Mark 6. 20; 11. 13; Luke 2. 14; 10. 6; 12. 49; 14. 5; 16. 9; 18. 7; 21. 34, 35; John 1. 18; 5. 3; 13. 2; Acts 4. 25; 9. 31; 10. 30; 13. 19, 20; 18. 5; Rom. 4. 19; 5. 1; 8. 1; 1 Co. 3. 4; 6. 20; 9. 23; 11. 29; 15. 29; 2 Co. 5. 17; Gal. 4. 14; Eph. 1. 18; Phil. 3. 11; Col. 2. 18; 1 Ti. 3. 16; 6. 13, 19; 2 Ti. 4. 1, 14; Heb. 4. 2; Jas. 5. 9; 1 Pet. 3. 15, 21; 2 Pet. 1. 3; 2. 18; 1 Jo. 5. 7, 8, 13; 2 Jo. 9; Jude 1; Rev. 1. 5, 6; 2. 9, 13; 17. 8; 20. 14, &c.

25. INTERPOLATIONS—are never to be adduced as proof texts, *e.g.*—Matt. 6. 13; 10. 8; 17. 11; 21. 44; 23. 14; Mark 7. 16; 9. 44, 46; 11. 26; 15. 28; 16. 9–20; Luke 17. 36; 23 17; 24. 12, 40; John 5. 4; 7. 53–8. 11; Acts 8. 37; 15. 34; 24. 7; 28. 29; 1 John 5. 7, &c.

26. The ORDER OF EVENTS is frequently disregarded, *e.g.*—John 2. 13 when compared with Matt. 21. 12; Gen. 37. 1–30 with 36. 21; Judg. 17. 1 with 18. 31; also 19. 1–21, 25 with 1. 34.

27. The Scripture writers frequently use ROUND and common numbers, *e.g.*—Gen. 15. 13; Exod 12. 40; Acts 7. 6; Exod. 1. 5; Acts 7. 14; Matt. 17. 1; Mark 9. 2; Luke 9. 28.

28. A PART of a thing is frequently put for the WHOLE, *e.g.*—Gen. 1. 5; 12. 5; Matt. 6. 11; Luke 14. 14; Acts 2. 41; Rom. 1. 16; 10. 9, 13; 13. 1; Heb. 2. 16.

29. The WHOLE is frequently put for a PART, *e.g.*—The "world" for the Roman Empire or Palestine, Matt. 4. 8; 24. 14; Luke 2. 1; 4. 5; Acts 11. 28; 17. 6, 31; 19. 27; 24. 5; Rom. 10. 18; Rev. 3. 10; 12. 9; 16. 14. "Every creature" for the human race, Mark 16. 15; Col. 1. 15, 23; Rev. 5. 13; 8. 9. As also "all flesh," Gen. 6. 12; Psa. 145. 21; Isa. 40. 5, 6; 66. 23; Matt. 24. 22; Luke 3. 6; Rom. 3. 20.

30. A DEFINITE number is frequently used for an INDEFINITE, *e.g.*—Gen. 4. 15; 31. 7; Exod. 20. 6; Lev. 26. 18; 1 Sa. 18. 7; Eccl. 6. 3; Psa. 62. 11; Isa. 4. 1; 40. 2; Dan. 7. 10; Matt. 12. 45; 18. 21; 19. 29; Mark 16. 9; 1 Co. 14. 19; Rev. 1. 5; 2. 10; 3. 1; 4. 5; 5. 6; 20. 2, 7.

31. Supplements (from other passages, &c.) are frequently NECESSARY, *e.g.*—Num. 14. 30; Prov. 16. 13; Matt. 5. 34; Mark 16. 16; Luke 16. 18; John 4. 14; 6. 44; 9. 3; Rom. 9. 22–24; 13. 2; 1 Co. 7. 19; Gal. 3. 17; Eph. 4. 20; 1 Jo. 2. 18.

32. THE DEFINITE ARTICLE—is sometimes injuriously omitted, *e.g.*—Matt. 1. 23, the virgin; 4. 5, the pinnacle; 4. 21, the ship; 5. 1. the mountain; 5. 15, the bushel, the candlestick; 7. 17, the corrupt; 7. 24, the rock; 8. 23, the ship; 8. 32, the steep; 9. 1, the ship; 10. 12, the house; 12. 35, the good, the evil; 12. 43, the man; 15. 20, the man, the man; 18. 17, the heathen, the publican; 23. 24, the gnat, the camel; 24. 32, the parable; 25. 32, the shepherd; 26. 51, the servant; 28. 16, the mountain, &c. &c.

33. The DEFINITE ARTICLE—is sometimes injuriously inserted, *e.g.*—Matt. 1. 20; 2. 13; 28. 2; Luke 2. 9; Acts 5. 19; 7. 35; 8. 26; 12. 7, 23, an angel; Matt. 3. 3, a voice; 8. 8, a word; 15. 9, commandments; 22. 30, angels; Mark 1. 45, a city; 2. 1, a house; 7. 7, commandments; 12. 25, angels; Luke 1. 78, dayspring; 2. 12, a babe; 7. 3, elders; 22. 17, a cup; 22. 37, transgressors; Acts 7. 38, lively; 9. 5, pricks, &c. &c.

34. The COMING of God (or of Christ) frequently means a MANIFESTATION to assist, deliver, reward, or punish, *e.g.*—Psa. 50. 3; Hos. 6. 3; Matt. 16. 27; Luke 18. 8; Rom. 9. 9; Eph. 2. 17; Heb. 10. 37; Jas. 5. 8; Rev. 2. 5.

35. Things are spoken of as GIVEN, DONE, or POSSESSED, which are only PROMISED and PROPOSED, *e.g.*—Gen. 15. 18; 27. 37; 37. 21; Josh. 1. 3; 24. 9; Jer. 1. 10; Ezek. 24. 13; 1 Co. 10. 33; Eph. 1. 3, 4; 2 Ti. 1. 9; Rev. 13. 8.

36. That which is DIFFICULT is frequently spoken of as IMPOSSIBLE, *e.g.*—Matt. 17. 20; 19. 24 (Mark 10. 25; Luke 18. 25); Luke 17 1; Heb. 6. 4.

37. The RELATIVE pronoun frequently refers to a more *remote* antecedent, *e.g.*—Psa. 99. 8; Matt. 11. 1; 12. 9; Luke 5. 17, 26; John 6. 50; Acts 4. 11; 7. 19; 10. 6; 15. 11; 2 Th. 2. 9; Heb. 12. 17; 1 John 5. 20; 2 John 7.

38. Persons and things are reckoned CHILDREN of that which they imitate, or to which they are attached, *e.g.*—1 Sa. 18. 17; 20. 30; 25. 17; 1 Ki. 20. 35; 2 Ki. 6. 32; Psa. 89. 22; Isa. 57. 3; Eze. 16. 3; Mark 3. 17; Luke 10. 6; John 17. 12; Acts 4. 36; 13. 10; 2 Th. 2. 3; 1 Pe. 3. 6.

And in such expressions as "Children—of God, Abraham, Jacob, Israel; of faith, wisdom, wrath, disobedience, Satan, hell; the devil, the promise, the resurrection, the day, the light, the bridechamber, the bondswoman, the kingdom," &c.

39. The verb TO HATE is frequently used for to LOVE LESS, *e.g.*—Gen. 29. 31; Deut. 21. 15; Mal. 1. 3; Matt. 6. 24; Luke 14. 26; John 12. 25; Rom. 9. 13.

40. A PEOPLE is frequently called by the name of its FOUNDER, *e.g.*—Gen. 9. 25, 27; 49. 7; Num. 20. 21; Deut. 32. 9; 2 Ch. 25. 24; Psa. 14. 7; 24. 6; 83. 8; Amos 7. 9; 1 Co. 12. 12; Gal. 3. 16.

41. When two nouns are coupled by a conjunction, the SECOND is frequently equal to an ADJECTIVE, *e.g.*—Jer. 29. 11; Luke 21. 15; John 3. 5; 14. 6; Acts 1. 25; 23. 6; Col. 2. 8; 2 Ti. 1. 10; 2 Pe. 1. 3.

42. The name CHRIST is frequently used to denote the doctrine, subject, or spirit of His RELIGION, *e.g.*—Acts 5. 42; 8. 5, 35; Rom. 3. 26; 8. 10; 1 Co. 1. 24; 2 Co. 1. 19, 21; 4. 5; 5. 17; 11. 4; Gal. 1. 16; 4. 19; Eph. 3. 17; 4. 20; Phil. 1. 15, 16, 18; Col. 1. 27, 28; 2. 6, 7; 2 Ti. 3. 12.

43. The verb TO HAVE is frequently used for to HOLD FAST, USE, *e.g.*—Matt. 13. 12; 21. 26; Luke 19. 20; Rom. 1. 28; Phil. 2. 29; 1 Ti. 1. 19; 3. 9; 2 Ti. 1. 13; 1 Pe. 2. 16; Rev. 6. 9.

44. The NAME of a person is HIMSELF or his CHARACTER, *e.g.*—Ps. 5. 11; 75. 1; Matt. 10. 22; 12. 21; John 1. 12; 12. 28; 17. 6; Rev. 22. 4.

45. To be IN CHRIST is frequently simply to be a CHRISTIAN, *e.g.*—Rom. 9. 1; 12. 5; 16. 7, 9, 10; 1 Co. 3. 1; 4. 10, 15, 17; 15. 18, 19; 2 Co. 2. 17; 3. 14; 5. 17, 19; 12. 2, 19; Gal. 1. 22; Eph. 1. 3; Phil. 1. 13; 2. 1; Col. 1. 2; 2. 5; 1 Th. 4. 16; 1 Ti. 2. 7; Phm. 8.

46. The word ANSWERED is frequently used when no preceding statement appears, *e.g.*—Matt. 11. 25; 12. 38; 15. 15; 22. 1; 26. 63; Mark 9. 19; 10. 24.

47. The CAUSE or SOURCE is frequently used for the EFFECTS, *e.g.*—The *Spirit* for his operations, Matt. 1. 18, 20; Mark 1. 8; Luke 1. 35; 4. 1; John 3. 34; Acts 10. 38; Rom. 5. 5; 1 Co. 2. 13; 2 Co. 6. 6; Eph. 1. 13; 1 Th. 1. 5; 2 Ti. 1. 14; Titus 3. 5; Heb. 2. 4; 1 Pe. 1. 12; 2 Pe. 1. 21; Jude 20.

48. ABSTRACT words are frequently used for CONCRETE ones, *e.g.*—Gen. 15. 1; 46. 34; Judg. 5. 12; 1 Sa. 15. 29; Psa. 35. 3; Luke 2. 30; John 4. 22; 11. 25; 17. 3; Rom. 3. 30; 8. 7; 11. 7; 1 Co. 1. 30; 2 Co. 5. 21; Gal. 3. 13; Eph. 5. 8.

49. The phrase TO BE CALLED frequently indicates actual BEING, *e.g.*—Isa. 1. 26; 56. 7; 60. 18; Matt. 1. 23; 2. 23; 5. 9, 19; 21. 13; Mark 11. 17; Luke 19. 46; Rom. 9. 26; 1 Jo. 3. 1; Jas. 2. 23.

50. PLURAL nouns, pronouns, and verbs are frequently used for the SINGULAR, *e.g.*—Gen. 1. 1, 26; 3. 22; 8. 4; 11. 7; 19. 29; 21. 7; 46. 7; Judg. 12. 7; 2 Ch. 24. 25; Neh. 3. 8; Prov. 9. 10; Hos. 12. 8; Isa. 6. 8; Amos 6. 10; Jon. 1. 5; Zech. 9. 9; Matt. 2. 20; 12. 20; 21. 7; 20. 8; 27. 44; Mark 1. 2; 4. 30; 15. 32; John 3. 2, 11; 6. 45; 12. 4; 21. 24; Acts 13. 40; Rom. 7. 14; 1 Co. 15. 29; 2 Co. 10. 2; 1 Th. 2. 18; Heb. 9. 23; 11. 37; 1 Ti. 1. 8, 9; 1 Jo. 1. 1, 3, 4; 2. 1; 3 Jo. 12.

51. The word GOD is frequently used to denote GREATNESS, *e.g.*—Gen. 1. 2; 13. 10; 23. 6; 30. 8; 35. 5; Exod. 9. 28; Deut. 33. 1; 1 Sa. 14. 15; 2 Sa. 9. 3; 23. 20; Job 1. 16; 4. 9; Psa. 36. 6; 65. 9; 80. 2, 10; Song 8. 6; Jon. 3. 3; Mark 11. 22; Luke 2. 40; John 9. 3; Acts 7. 20; Rom. 1. 16, 18; 10. 2; 1 Co. 1. 18, 24; 2 Co. 1. 12; 10. 4; Col. 2. 19; 1 Th. 4. 16; Rev. 15. 2; 21. 11.

52. CANNOT, in Scripture idiom, frequently means WILL NOT, *e.g.*—Gen. 19. 22; 24. 50; 37. 4; 43. 32; 44. 22, 26; Exod. 7. 21, 24; Num. 22. 18; Deut. 12. 17; 16. 5; 17. 15; 22. 4; 24. 4; Josh. 9. 19; Judg. 21. 18; Neh. 6. 3; Psa. 78. 19, 20; Isa. 56. 10; Jer. 3. 5; 6. 10; 38. 5; Lam. 4. 14; Matt. 9. 15 (Mark 2. 19); 12. 34; 16. 3; Mark 3. 23; 6. 5; 9. 29, 39; 10. 38, 39; Luke 6. 42; 11. 7; 14. 20, 26; 16. 13; John 5. 19, 30, 44; 6. 44, 60, 65; 7. 7; 8. 43; 9. 4, 16; 10. 21; 13. 36; 14. 7; Acts 4. 30; 10. 47; Rom. 4. 21; 8. 7, 8; 11. 23; 14. 4; 16. 25; 1 Co. 2. 14; 12. 3; 2 Co. 9. 8; 13. 8; 2 Ti. 1. 12; 2. 13; Heb. 2. 18, 5. 2; 11. 19; 1 Jo. 3. 9; 4. 20; Rev. 2. 2.

53. NOUNS are frequently used for PERSONAL PRONOUNS, *e.g.*—Gen. 2. 3; 4. 23; 5. 1; 16. 16; 17. 23; 19. 24; Exod. 16. 7; 34. 35; Num. 6. 24–26; Josh. 9. 21; 1 Sa. 3. 21; 1 Ki. 2. 19; 8. 1; 10. 13; 12. 21; 2 Ki. 16. 11; 2 Ch. 7. 2; Neh. 8. 5, 6; Esth. 8. 8; Eccl. 8. 8; Isa. 14. 22; Ezek. 11. 24; Dan. 9. 17; Luke 11. 17; John 4. 1; Rom. 1. 28; 2 Ti. 1. 18; 1 Jo. 4. 7–9.

54. Some particles, such as ALL, are frequently used for SOME or MOST, *e.g.*—Exod. 9. 6, 20; Matt. 3. 5; 26. 52; Luke 11. 41; 23. 48; John 15. 15; 16. 13; 1 Co. 6. 12; 8. 1; 11. 2; 15. 51; Col. 3. 22; 2 Th. 3. 2; Titus 1. 12, 13, 15; 1 Jo. 2. 20.

55. The word SOME is frequently used for ALL, *e.g.*—Rom. 3. 3; 11. 17; 1 Ti. 4. 1; Heb. 3. 16.

56. The word MANY is frequently used for ALL, *e.g.*—Dan. 12. 2; Matt. 20. 28.

57. The ACTIVE voice in Greek is frequently used for the CAUSATIVE, *e.g.*—Matt. 5. 25, 45; Mark 14. 54; Luke 11. 53; 1 Co. 6. 4; 2 Co. 2. 14; 9. 8; 2 Pe. 3. 12.

58. NEUTER gender is frequently used for MASCULINE, *e.g.*—Matt. 11. 27; 18. 11, 14; Heb. 7. 19; 12. 13; 1 Jo. 5. 4; Rev. 21. 27.

59. The PRESENT tense is frequently used to express HABITUAL o: immediately future action, *e.g.*—Matt. 2. 4; 3. 10; 17. 11; 26. 2; Luke 12. 54; John 4. 21; 7. 42, 52; 10. 32; 12. 26; 13. 6, 27; 14. 3; 16. 2, 17; 17. 11, 24; 21. 3; Rom. 15. 25; 1 Co. 3. 13; 12. 31; 15. 2, 35; 2 Co. 5. 1; 13. 1; Eph. 5. 5; Col. 3. 6; Heb. 4. 3.

60. The PAST tense is frequently used to express the CERTAINTY of a future action, *e.g.*—John 13. 31; 15. 6; 17. 18; Jude 14; Rev. 10. 7.

61. The POSITIVE degree is frequently put for the COMPARATIVE or SUPERLATIVE, *e.g.*—Luke 9. 48.

62. SON and DAUGHTER are frequently used for a DESCENDANT, *e.g.*—Gen. 29. 5; 46. 21, 22; 2 Sa. 19. 24; Eccl. 1. 1; Matt. 1. 1; Luke 1. 5; 3. 23; 13. 16.

63. FATHER and MOTHER are frequently used for an ANCESTOR, *e.g.*—Gen. 37. 10; 1 Ki. 15. 10; Matt. 3. 9; Mark 11. 10; Luke 1. 31, 73; John 4. 12; Acts 7. 2; Rom. 4. 11.

64. BROTHER and SISTER are frequently used for a RELATIVE or COMPANION, *e.g.*—Gen. 14. 14; 2 Ki. 8. 26; Matt. 5. 22, 23, 24, 47; 7. 5; 12. 46; 23. 8; 25. 40; John 7. 3; Acts 1. 14; 3. 22; 9. 30; 11. 29; 1 Co. 1. 1; 5. 11; Gal. 1. 19; Heb. 2. 11, 12, 17; 7. 5; 8. 11; 2 Co. 1. 1; 2. 13; Rev. 6. 11; 19. 10; 22. 9.

65. GOD—is used of any one (professedly) MIGHTY, whether truly so or not, and is applied not only to the true God, but to false gods, magistrates, judges, angels, prophets, &c., *e.g.*—Exod. 7. 1; 15. 11; 21. 6; 22. 8, 9; 32. 8, 22, 31; Deut. 10. 17; Judg. 8. 33; 9. 9, 13; 13. 21, 22; 16. 23; 1 Sa. 2. 25; 28. 13; 1 Ki. 11. 33; 2 Ki. 1. 2, 3; 19. 37; Psa. 8. 5; 45. 6; 82. 1, 6; 97. 7, 9; 136. 2; Matt. 1. 23; John 1. 1; 10. 33, 34, 35; 20. 28; Acts 7. 40, 43, 59; 12. 22; 14. 11; 17. 18, 23; 19. 26; 20. 28; 28. 6; Rom. 9. 5; 1 Co. 8. 5; Phil. 3. 19; 2 Th. 2. 4; 1 Ti. 3. 16; Titus 2. 13; Heb. 1. 8; 2 Pe. 1. 1; 1 Jo. 3. 16; 5. 20.

66. SPIRIT—is used of God himself, or the Divine Mind, His energy, influence, gifts; of the vital principle of animals, and of breath, wind, or air in motion, &c., *e.g.*—Gen. 1. 1; 3. 8; 6. 3, 17; 8. 1; 26. 35, &c.

67. ANGEL—is used of a messenger (good or bad) from heaven or from men, and applied to spiritual intelligences, to the pillar of cloud and fire, to the (pestilential) winds, to priests, prophets, ministers, disembodied spirits, &c., *e.g.*—Gen. 16. 7; 32. 1, 3, 6; Ex. 14. 19; Judg. 2. 1; Psa. 97. 7; 104. 4; Eccl. 5. 6; Hag. 1. 13; Mal. 2. 7; Matt. 4. 6; 11. 10; 13. 39, 41, 49; 16. 27; 18. 10; 24. 31; Mark 1. 2; 13. 27; Luke 7. 24, 27; 9. 52; Acts 7. 53; 12. 15; 1 Co. 4. 9; 6. 3; 11. 10; Gal. 3. 19; Col. 2. 18; 2 Thess. 1. 17; 1 Ti. 3. 16; 5. 21; Heb. 1. 7; Jas. 2. 25; 1 Pe. 1. 12; Rev. 1. 20; 2. 1, 3, 8, 12; 3. 1, 7, 14; 14. 6.

68. PROPHET—is used of one who (professedly) announces the will or celebrates the works of God, whether these relate to things past, present, or future, and it is applied to patriarchs, orators, singers, and songstresses, priests, and preachers, *e.g.*—Gen. 20. 7; Ex. 7. 1; 15. 20; Num. 11. 29; 1 Sa. 10. 5; Matt. 10. 41; 23. 34; Luke 4. 24; 7. 28; John 4. 19; Acts 11. 27; 13. 1; 15. 32; 1 Co. 12. 28, 29; 14. 29, 32, 37; Eph. 2. 20; 3. 5; 4. 11; also Matt. 7. 22; 26. 68; Mark 14. 65; Luke 22. 64; Acts 2. 17; 21. 19; 1 Co. 11. 4, 5; 13. 9; 14. 1–6, 24, 31, 39; 1 Ti. 1. 18; 4. 14, &c.

69. NOUNS are frequently (in Hebrew *commonly*) used for ADJECTIVES, *e.g.*—John 6. 63; Rom. 3. 30; Eph. 5. 8.

70. Active verbs frequently express only an *attempt* to do the action, *e.g.*—Deut. 28. 68; Eze. 22. 13; Matt. 10. 39; 17. 11; John 1. 9, 29; 12. 32; Rom. 2. 4; 1 Co. 10. 33; Gal. 5. 4; Phil. 3. 15; 1 John 1. 10; 2. 26; 5. 4, 10; Rev. 12. 9.

(*b*) Active verbs frequently express a *permission* of it, *e.g.*—Exod. 4. 21; 5. 22; 2 Sa. 24. 1; Jer. 4. 10; 20. 7; Eze. 14. 9; Matt. 6. 13; 11. 25; 23. 32; Mark 5. 12; John 13. 27; Acts 13. 29; Rom. 9. 18; 11. 7; 2 Th. 2. 11.

(*c*) Active verbs frequently express an *announcement* of it, *e.g.*—Gen. 41. 13; Lev. 13. 6, 13; 2 Ki. 2. 24; Isa. 6. 10; Jer. 1. 10; Eze. 32. 2; 43. 3; Hos. 6. 5; Matt. 16. 19; John 8. 10, 11; Acts 10. 15; 1 Co. 6. 2.

(*d*) Active verbs frequently express *giving an occasion* for it, *e.g.*—Gen. 42. 38; 1 Sa. 23. 7; 2 Sa. 16. 10; 1 Ki. 14. 16; Jer. 38. 23; Amos 3. 6; Matt. 5. 32; 10. 21; Acts 1. 18; Rom. 2. 5; 14. 15; 1 Co. 7. 16; Jas. 5. 20.

(*e*) Active verbs frequently express a *direction* or *sanction* to it, *e.g.*—Gen. 3. 21; John 4. 1, &c.

(*f*) Active verbs frequently express a *promise* to do it, *e.g.*—Ezek. 13. 22, &c.

(*g*) Active verbs frequently express a *continuation* of it, *e.g.*—1 John 5. 13, &c.

(*h*) Active verbs frequently express what is done *by a deputy*, *e.g.*—Gen. 16. 13, &c.

71. PARONOMASIA, or a play upon words, to excite attention, is often observable in the original, *e.g.*—Gen. 9. 6, 27; 18. 27; 27. 36; 29. 34, 35; 31. 20, 52; 32. 24; 41. 51, 52; 42. 35; 48. 22; 49. 8, 16, 19; Exod. 23. 2; 32. 18; Num. 5. 18; 18. 2; 20. 1; 24. 21; 27. 14; Judg. 10. 4; 15. 16; Ruth 1. 20; 1 Sa. 1. 27, 28; 6. 14, 15; 6. 18, 19; 25. 25; 2 Sa. 22. 11, 42; 1 Ki. 8. 66 (2 Ch. 7. 10); 18. 21, 26; Neh. 9. 24; Job 11. 12; 24. 18; 29. 16; 30. 3, 19; 38. 27; Psa. 18. 7, 41; 25. 16; 32. 7; 39. 11; 40. 3; 52. 6; 56. 8; 64. 4; 68. 28; 96. 5; Prov. 6. 23; 12. 21; 13. 12; Eccl. 1. 2, 13; 7. 1, 6; Isa. 1. 23; 2. 19, 21; 5. 7; 7. 9; 10. 18, 30; 13. 4, 6 (Joel 1. 15); 14. 4; 15. 8, 9; 17. 1, 2; 21. 2; 22. 18; 24. 3, 4, 17, 18; 25. 6; 29. 9; 30. 16; 32. 6, 7, 8, 19; 41. 5; 54. 8; 56. 10; 57. 6; 61. 3; 65. 11, 12; Jer. 1. 11, 12, 17; 2. 5; 5. 23; 6. 1, 28; 7. 13; 10. 11; 19. 1, 2, 7; 22. 22; 23. 33, 36, 37, 38, 39; 30. 3; 48. 2; 49. 9; 51. 2, 20; Lam. 3. 47; Eze. 7. 6; 12. 10; 24. 21; 25. 18; 39. 9; Dan. 5. 26–28; Hos. 2. 23; 8. 7; 9. 15, 16; 10. 1; 12. 11; 13. 15; Amos 5. 5; 8. 1, 2; Jon. 4. 6; Mic. 1. 10, 13, 14; Nah. 2. 10; Hab. 2. 18; Zeph. 1. 2; 2. 4; 3. 1; Zech. 9. 3, 5; Matt. 16. 18; 21. 41; Luke 21. 11; John 2. 23; Acts 8. 30; 24. 3; Rom. 1. 20, 28, 29–31; 3. 3; 5. 19; 8. 23; 11. 17; 12. 3; 16. 2; 1 Co. 2. 13; 3. 17; 6. 2; 10. 12; 11. 29, 31; 14. 10; 2 Co. 3. 2; 4. 8; 5. 4, 21; 8. 22; 9. 8; 10. 3; Gal. 4. 17; 5. 7; Eph. 1. 23; 3. 14, 19; Phil. 1. 4: ; 2 Th. 3. 11; 1 Ti. 1. 8; 2 Ti. 3. 4; 4. 7; Phm. 11; 3 John

ADDITIONAL WORDS*

ABOUT —
3a. *At the hand of, at the beck of,* לְיַד *le-yad.*
1 Ch. 18. 17 sons of David (were) chief about the king
ANGRY, to be —
5a. *To be indignant,* זָעַם *zaam.*
Psa. 7. 11 God is angry (with the wicked) every day
ARMY —
5a. *An army force,* חַיִל צָבָא *[chayil].*
2 Ch. 26. 13 under their hand (was) an army
BETTER —
1. *Good, better, best,* טוֹב *tob.*
Add Psa. 37. 16, 118. 8, 9, Prov. 16. 8, 16, 19, 21. 9, 19.
BITTER —
6a. *Bitterness (bitter),* תַּמְרוּרִים *tamrurim.*
Jer. 31. 15 lamentation (and) bitter weeping
BROKEN down —
3. *To overthrow, ruin,* הָרַס *haras* [pass. partic.].
1 Ki. 18. 30 altar of the LORD (that was) broken down
CERTAINLY —
This word, like surely, expresses an emphasising repetition of any Hebrew verb. It is used with see (Gen. 26. 28), know (Gen. 43. 7), stone (Lev. 24. 16), hear (1 Sa. 23. 10), make (1 Sa. 25. 28), come (Dan. 11. 10, 13), etc. *See* SURELY.
CERTAINTY —
4a. *Truth,* קֹשְׁט *qosht.*
Prov. 22. 21 make thee know the certainty of
CONTINUAL weeping —
With weeping weeping, בִּבְכִי..בֶּכִי *[beki].*
Jer. 48. 5 continual weeping shall go up
DESTROYED, to be —
6a. *Be overthrown, ruined,* הָרַס *haras* 2.
Psa. 11. 3 If the foundations be destroyed, what can
DONE, to have —
1a. *To have sinned,* חָטָא *chata.*
Lev. 19. 22 for his sin which he hath done . . . hath done
EARNESTLY —
1. *To show heat, show diligence,* חָרָה *charah* 5.
Neh. 3. 20 earnestly repaired the other piece
2. *Well, thoroughly,* לְהֵיטִיב *[yatab 5, infin.].*
Mic. 7. 3 do evil with both hands earnestly.
[*See also* ask, desire, protest, remember, send.]
ELEAZAR —
6a. Son of Parosh, in time of Ezra.
Ezra. 10. 25 of the sons of Parosh; Ramiah . . . and Eleazar,
FAIR —
11. *Beauty (beautiful),* תִּפְאֶרֶת *tiphereth.*
Eze. 16. 17 Thou hast also taken thy fair jewels
16. 39 they . . . shall take thy fair jewels
23. 26 They shall . . . take away thy fair jewels.
FLINT —
3. *Rock* or *flint,* צַר *tsar* [=*tsor*].
Isa. 5. 28 horses' hoofs shall be counted like flint
FOR —
3a. *Into (by) the hand (power) of,* בְּיַד *be-yad.*
Job 8. 4 cast them away for their transgression
GOODLY —
16a. *Form, shape (shapely),* תֹּאַר *toar.*
Jer. 11. 16 A green olive tree . . . of goodly fruit
GROW, let —
Make great, let grow, גִּדֵּל *[gadal 3].*
Num. 6. 5 he . . . shall let . . . the hair of his head grow
HANDLE wisely —
Show skill in, pay heed to, הִשְׂכִּיל עַל *[sakal 5]*
Prov. 16. 20 He that handleth a matter wisely shall
HEAVY LADEN. *See* **LADEN.**
HEAVY LOADEN —
Loaded, עֲמֻסִים *amas* [pass. partic.].
Isa. 46. 1 your carriages (were) heavy loaden
KIND —
1. *Good,* טוֹב *tob.*
2 Ch. 10. 7 If thou be kind to this people,
MEAN, to — *See* **WHAT mean ye.**

MIGHTY —
24. *Great, mighty,* רַב *rab.*
Job. 35. 9 by reason of the arm of the mighty
Psa. 89. 50 (the reproach of) all the m. people
Isa. 63. 1 I that speak . . . mighty to save
Jer. 32. 19 Great in counsel and m. in work
Eze. 38. 15 a great company, and a mighty army
NEAR of kin —
Near, קָרוֹב *qarob.*
Ruth 2. 20 The man (is) near of kin unto us
2 Sam. 19. 42 the king (is) near of kin to us
OFFER —
15. *Do, make, prepare,* עָשָׂה *asah.*
Add Num. 8. 12, 15. 14, 24, 28. 4 (twice), 28. 8 (twice), 28, 20, 21, 23, 24 (twice), 28. 31, 29. 2, Deut. 12. 27.
ORDAIN —
5a. *Do, make, institute,* עָשָׂה *asah.*
Num. 28. 6 which was ordained in Mount Sinai
1 Ki. 12. 32 J. ordained a feast in the eighth month
33 ordained a feast unto the children of Is.
PLAY on an instrument —
Play on stringed instrument, נָגַן *nagan* 3.
Eze. 33. 32 and can play well on an instrument
REDEEMED again, to be —
Redemption is to, גְּאֻלָּה..לְ *[geullah].*
Lev. 25. 48 After . . . he is sold he may be redeemed again
SPIES —
2a. *Watchmen, sentries,* שֹׁמְרִים *[shamar].*
Judg. 1. 24 And the spies saw a man come forth
SUCH things as ye have —
Things in your power, things internal, τὰ ἐνόντα *[eneimi].*
Luke 11. 41 give alms of such things as ye have
SURELY —
In Hebrew often expressed by repeating a verb in an infinitive form (adverbial infinitive). So with come (Hab. 2. 3), deliver (2 Ki. 18. 30), die (Gen. 2. 17, Judg. 13. 22), be put to death (Exod. 19. 12, Judg. 21. 5), etc. The word surely occurs with die or be put to death about fifty times in the Old Testament and is then always a translation of an emphasising infinitive.
TAKE —
38a. *Take as witness,* הֵעִיד *[ud 5].*
Jer. 32. 10 I . . . sealed (it) and took witnesses
32. 25 thou hast said unto me . . . take witnesses
32. 44 take witnesses in the land of Benjamin
THROUGHLY —
§. *In every respect,* ἐν παντὶ *en panti [pas].*
2 Cor. 11. 6 we have been throughly made manifest
TO —
2a. *Into (by) the hand (agency) of,* בְּיַד *be-yad.*
2 Ch. 34. 16 All that was committed to thy servants,
Jer. 39. 11 Nebuchadrezzar . . . gave charge . . . to
TOWNS —
1. *Daughters, dependencies,* בָּנוֹת *[bath].*
Add Judg. 1. 27 (five times), 1 Ch. 5. 16, 18. 1.
VEHEMENT, most —
(Flame) from Jah, שַׁלְהֶבֶת יָהּ *shalhebeth-Yah.*
Song 8. 6 (which hath) a most vehement flame.
VOLUNTARY —
3. *Choose, prefer, delight in,* θέλω *thelo* [partic.].
Col. 2. 18 no man . . . in a v. humility (M. being a v. in hum.).
WELL pleased, to be — *See* **PLEASED, to be.**
WHAT mean ye —
What is to you? מָה..לָכֶם *mah . . . la-kem [la=le].*
Exod. 12. 26 What mean ye by this service?
WORKMANSHIP, manner of workmanship —
1. *Business, craft, craftsmanship,* מְלָאכָה *melakah.*
Exod. 31. 3 and in all manner of workmanship
5 to work in all manner of w.
35. 31 and in all manner of workmanship
1 Ch. 28. 21 with thee, for all manner of workmanship
Eze. 28. 13 w. of thy tabrets and of thy pipes
2. *Doing, making,* מַעֲשֶׂה *maaseh.*
2 Ki. 16. 10 according to all the w. thereof
3. *Making, thing made,* ποίημα *poiēma.*
Eph. 2. 10 For we are his w., created in Christ

* It is recommended that, before the Concordance is used, these words (headings only, such as ORDAIN) should be entered in their alphabetical place on the margins of the body of the Concordance.

ANALYTICAL CONCORDANCE.

AA'-RON, אַהֲרֹן *enlightened, illumined.*

He was the first high priest of Israel: of the family of Kohath the second son of Levi the third son of Jacob; he had Miriam for an elder sister, and Moses for a younger brother; his father's name was Amram, and his mother's Jochebed; he married Elisheba, daughter of Amminadab, and sister of Naashon; and by her had four sons, Nadab and Abihu, Eleazar and Ithamar, Exod. 6 16-23. He was an excellent speaker, and was appointed to be the prophet or spokesman of Moses: he was then directed by God to meet Moses, and did so at the Mount of God, and received the good news; he went in with Moses to Pharaoh, did the signs foretold, and the plagues commanded, iv.-xi.

He was murmured against along with Moses for the want of bread, and called on the people to come near before the LORD; was commanded to lay up a pot full of manna before the testimony; held up the hands of Moses during the battle with Amalek; eat bread with Jethro, father-in-law of Moses, xii.-xviii.; was called to come up into Sinai to the LORD; along with the elders he saw the God of Israel; tarried below with the people when Moses went up; was set apart with his whole family to the priesthood; had sacred garments prepared for him; was anointed and consecrated to his office by Moses, appointed to light the lamps, and burn incense and make atonement, to wash his hands and feet, xxx. He is persuaded by the people to make a molten image, and is reproved for it by Moses, XXXII.; he sees the shining of Moses face, and is afraid, xxxiv.; holy garments are made for him, xxxix.; he and his sons are sanctified, and wash their hands and feet, xl.

The priestly duties of Aaron and his sons are prescribed in Lev. i.-ix.; his two eldest sons being destroyed for offering strange fire, he is silent and submissive; he receives various prohibitions and regulations, x.; how he was to enter the holy place, xvi.; not to mourn for the dead, xxi.; nor touch the holy things in uncleanness, xxii. He was commanded to number the people with Moses and the twelve princes of Israel, Num. i.; he receives the tribe of Levi for helps, iii.; numbers the Kohathites, Gershonites, and Merarites, iv.; receives the form for blessing the people, vi.; lights the lamps, offers the Levites before the LORD, and makes atonement for them, viii. He and Miriam speak against Moses, and are reproved by God for it, xii.; spoken against by Korah, Dathan, and Abiram, also by the whole congregation of Israel, he intercedes with God for them, xvi.; his rod flourishes, and is preserved for a memorial, xvii.; he receives a charge from God of various duties and privileges, xviii.; the people again murmur against him and Moses; he dies on Mount Hor, in the land of Edom, and is buried there, xx. Born B.C. 1574, he dies B.C. 1451, aged 123 years.

Exod. 4. 14 (Is) not A. the Levite thy brother?
4. 27 the LORD said to A., Go into the wilderness
4. 28 And M. told A. all the words of the LORD
4. 29 And M. and A. went and gathered together
4. 30 And A. spake all the words which the LORD
5. 1 And afterward Moses and A. went in
5. 4 Wherefore do ye, M. and A., let the people
5. 20 And they met Moses and A., who stood in
6. 13 And the LORD spake unto M. and unto A.
6. 20 and she bare him A. and Moses
6. 23 And A. took him Elisheba, daughter of
6. 25 And Eleazar A.'s son took him (one) of the
6. 26 These (are) that A. and M., to whom the LORD
6. 27 these (are) that Moses and A.
7. 1 and A. thy brother shall be thy prophet
7. 2 and A. thy brother shall speak unto Pharaoh
7. 6 and A. did as the LORD commanded them
7. 7 A. [was] fourscore and three years old, when
7. 8 the LORD spake unto Moses and unto A.
7. 9 thou shalt say unto A., Take thy rod, and
7. 10 And M. and A. went in unto Pharaoh
7. 10 and A. cast down his rod before Pharaoh
Exod. 7. 12 but A.'s rod swallowed up their rods
7. 19 Say unto A., Take thy rod, and stretch
7. 20 And Moses and A. did so, as the LORD
8. 5 Say unto A., Stretch forth thine hand
8. 6 And A. stretched out his hand over the
8. 8 Then Pharaoh called for Moses and A. and
8. 12 And M. and A. went out from Pharaoh
8. 16 Say unto A., Stretch out thy rod, and
8. 17 for A. stretched out his hand with his rod
8. 25 Pharaoh called for M. and for A., and said
9. 8 the LORD said unto M. and unto A., Take
9. 27 and called for M. and A., and said unto
10. 3 And Moses and A. came in unto Pharaoh
10. 8 And Moses and A. were brought again unto
10. 16 Then Pharaoh called for M. and A. in haste
11. 10 M. and A. did all these wonders before Ph.
12. 1 the LORD spake unto M. and A. in the land
12. 28 as the LORD had commanded Moses and A.
12. 31 And he called for Moses and A. by night
12. 43 the LORD said unto Moses and A., This (is)
12. 50 as the LORD commanded M. and A., so did
15. 20 the sister of A., took a timbrel in her hand
16. 2 murmured against Moses and A. in the
16. 6 And A. said unto all the children of Israel
16. 9 Moses spake unto A., Say unto all the
16. 10 as A. spake unto the whole congregation
16. 33 And Moses said unto A., Take a pot
16. 34 so A. laid it up before the Testimony
17. 10 Moses, A., and Hur went up to the top of
17. 12 and A. and Hur stayed up his hands
18. 12 and A. came, and all the elders of Israel, to
19. 24 thou, and A. with thee: but let not the
24. 1 thou, and A., Nadab, and Abihu, and
24. 9 Then went up Moses, and A., Nadab
24. 14 and, behold, A. and Hur (are) with you
27. 21 A. and his sons shall order it from evening
28. 1 take thou unto thee A. thy brother, and
28. 1 (even) A., Nadab and Abihu, Eleazar and A.
28. 2 thou shalt make holy garments for A. thy
28. 3 they may make A.'s garments to consecrate
28. 4 they shall make holy garments for A. thy
28. 12 A. shall bear their names before the
28. 29 A. shall bear the names of the children of
28. 30 they shall be upon A.'s heart, when he
28. 30 A. shall bear the judgment of the children
28. 35 it shall be upon A. to minister: and his
28. 38 it shall be upon A.'s forehead
28. 38 that A. may bear the iniquity of the
28. 40 And for A.'s sons thou shalt make coats
28. 41 thou shalt put them upon A. thy brother
28. 43 they shall be upon A., and upon his sons
29. 4 A. and his sons thou shalt bring unto
29. 5 and put upon A. the coat, and the robe
29. 9 thou shalt gird them with girdles, A. and
29. 9 thou shalt consecrate A. and his sons
29. 10 A. and his sons shall put their hands
So in v. 15, 19.
29. 20 the tip of the right ear of A., and upon
29. 21 and sprinkle (it) upon A., and upon his
29. 24 thou shalt put all in the hands of A., and
29. 26 the breast of the ram of A.'s consecration
29. 27 (even) of (that) which (is) for A., and of (that)
29. 28 it shall be A.'s and his sons' by a statute
29. 29 the holy garments of A. shall be his sons'
29. 32 A. and his sons shall eat the flesh of
29. 35 thus shalt thou do unto A., and to his sons
29. 44 I will sanctify also both A. and his sons
30. 7 And A. shall burn thereon sweet incense
30. 8 when A. lighteth the lamps at even
30. 10 A. shall make an atonement upon
30. 19 For A. and his sons shall wash their
30. 30 thou shalt anoint A. and his sons
31. 10 the holy garments for A. the priest
32. 1 together unto A., and said unto him
32. 2 A. said unto them, Break off the
32. 3 in their ears, and brought (them) unto A.
32. 5 when A. saw (it), he built an altar
32. 5 and A. made proclamation, and said
32. 21 And Moses said unto A., What did
32. 22 And A. said, Let not the anger of my lord

AARON

Exod. 32. 25 for A. had made them naked unto
32. 35 because they made the calf, which A. made
34. 30 when A. and all the children of Israel
34. 31 A. and all the rulers of the congregation
35. 19 the holy garments for A. the priest, and the
38. 21 by the hand of Ithamar, son to A.
39. 1 and made the holy garments for A.
39. 27 fine linen (of) woven work for A.
39. 41 the holy garments for A. the priest
40. 12 thou shalt bring A. and his sons unto
40. 13 thou shalt put upon A. the holy garments
40. 31 A. and his sons washed their hands
Lev. 1. 5 the priests, A.'s sons, shall bring the blood
1. 7 the sons of A. the priest shall put fire
1. 8 the priests, A.'s sons, shall lay the parts
1. 11 the priests, A.'s sons, shall sprinkle his
2. 2 he shall bring it to A.'s sons the priests
2. 3, 10 of the meat offering (shall be) A.'s and
3. 2 and A.'s sons the priests shall sprinkle
3. 5 And A.'s sons shall burn it on the altar
3. 8 and A.'s sons shall sprinkle the blood
3. 13 and the sons of A. shall sprinkle the blood
6. 9 Command A. and his sons, saying
6. 14 the sons of A. shall offer it before the LORD
6. 16 the remainder thereof shall A. and his
6. 18 among the children of A. shall eat of it
6. 20 the offering of A. and of his sons
6. 25 Speak unto A. and to his sons, saying
7. 10 shall all the sons of A. have, one (as much)
7. 31 the breast shall be A.'s and his sons'
7. 33 He among the sons of A., that offereth
7. 34 and have given them unto A. the priest
7. 35 of the anointing of A., and of the
8. 2 Take A. and his sons with him
8. 6 Moses brought A. and his sons, and
8. 12 And he poured..oil upon A.'s head
8. 13 Moses brought A.'s sons, and put coats
8. 14 A. and his sons laid their hands
So in v. 18, 22.
8. 23 the tip of A.'s right ear, and upon the
8. 24 And he brought A.'s sons, and Moses
8. 27 he put all upon A.'s hands, and upon
8. 30 and sprinkled (it) upon A., (and) upon his
8. 30 and sanctified A., (and) his garments
8. 31 Moses said unto A. and to his sons
8. 31 saying, A. and his sons shall eat it
8. 36 So A. and his sons did all things which
9. 1 (that) Moses called A. and his sons, and
9. 2 he said unto A., Take thee a young
9. 7 Moses said unto A., Go unto the altar
9. 8 A. therefore went unto the altar, and
9. 9 the sons of A. brought the blood unto
9. 12, 18 and A.'s sons presented unto him
9. 21 the right shoulder A. waved (for)
9. 22 And A. lifted up his hand toward the
9. 23 Moses and A. went into the tabernacle
10. 1 the sons of A., took either of them his
10. 3 Moses said unto A., This (is it) that the
10. 3 I will be glorified. And A. held his peace
10. 4 the uncle of A., and said unto them, Come
10. 6 Moses said unto A., and unto Eleazar
10. 8 And the LORD spake unto A., saying
10. 12 M. spake unto A., and unto Eleazar, and
10. 16 the sons of A. (which were) left (alive),
10. 19 And A. said unto M., Behold, this day
11. 1 the LORD spake unto M. and to A., saying
13. 1 the LORD spake unto M. and A., saying
13. 2 he shall be brought unto A. the priest, or
14. 33 the LORD spake unto M. and unto A., saying
15. 1 the LORD spake unto M. and to A., saying
16. 1 of the two sons of A., when they offered
16. 2 Speak unto A. thy brother, that he come
16. 3 Thus shall A. come into the holy (place)
16. 6 A. shall offer his bullock of the sin
16. 8 And A. shall cast lots upon the two goats
16. 9 And A. shall bring the goat upon which
16. 11 And A. shall bring the bullock of the sin
16. 21 And A. shall lay both his hands upon
16. 23 And A. shall come into the tabernacle
17. 2 Speak unto A., and unto his sons, and

Lev. 21. 1 the sons of A., and say unto them, There
21. 17 Speak unto A., saying, Whosoever (he be)
21. 21 of the seed of A. the priest shall come nigh
21. 24 Moses told (it) unto A., and to his sons, and
22. 2, 18 Speak unto A. and to his sons
22. 4 of the seed of A.(is) a leper, or hath a running
24. 3 shall A. order it from the evening unto the
24. 9 And it shall be A.'s and his sons'; and
Num. 1. 3 thou and A. shall number them by their
1. 17 Moses and A. took these men which are
1. 44 which Moses and A. numbered, and the
2. 1 the LORD spake unto M. and unto A., saying
3. 1 the generations of A. and Moses in the day
3. 2, 3 these (are) the names of the sons of A.
3. 4 office in the sight of A. their father
3. 6 and present them before A. the priest
3. 9 the Levites unto A. and to his sons
3. 10 thou shalt appoint A. and his sons, and
3. 32 the son of A. the priest (shall be) chief over
3. 38 and A. and his sons, keeping the charge
3. 39 which Moses and A. numbered at the
3. 48 redeemed, unto A. and to his sons
3. 51 that were redeemed unto A. and to his sons
4. 1, 17 LORD spake unto M. and unto A., saying
4. 5 A. shall come, and his sons, and they shall
4. 15 when A. and his sons have made an end
4. 16 the son of A. the priest (pertaineth) the oil
4. 19 A. and his sons shall go in, and appoint
4. 27 the appointment of A. and his sons shall be
4. 28 of Ithamar the son of A. the priest
4. 33 under the hand of Ithamar the son of A.
4. 34 And M. and A. and the chief of the
4. 37 which Moses and A. did number according
4. 41 whom Moses and A. did number according
4. 45 whom Moses and A. numbered according
4. 46 whom Moses and A. and the chief of Israel
6. 23 Speak unto A. and unto his sons, saying
7. 8 the hand of Ithamar the son of A. the priest
8. 2 Speak unto A., and say unto him, When
8. 3 And A. did so; he lighted the lamps
8. 11 And A. shall offer the Levites before
8. 13 thou shalt set the Levites before A., and
8. 19 the Levites (as) a gift to A. and to his sons
8. 20 And M., and A., and all the congregation
8. 21 and A. offered them (as) an offering before
8. 21 and A. made an atonement for them
8. 22 before A., and before his sons: as the LORD
9. 6 they came before Moses and before A.
10. 8 And the sons of A., the priests, shall
12. 1 Miriam and A. spake against Moses
12. 4 the LORD spake..unto M., and unto A.
12. 5 and called A. and Miriam; and they both
12. 10 and A. looked upon Miriam, and, behold
12. 11 A. said unto Moses, Alas, my lord, I
13. 26 came to Moses, and to A., and to all the
14. 2 murmured against Moses and against A.
14. 5 Then Moses and A. fell on their faces
14. 26 the LORD spake unto Moses and unto A.
15. 33 brought him unto Moses and A., and
16. 3 against Moses and against A., and said
16. 11 and what (is) A., that ye murmur against him?
16. 16 thou, and they, and A., to morrow
16. 17 thou also, and A., each (of you) his censer
16. 18 of the congregation with Moses and A.
16. 20 the LORD spake unto Moses and unto A.
16. 37 the son of A. the priest, that he take up the
16. 40 which (is) not of the seed of A., come near
16. 41 murmured against M. and against A., saying
16. 42 was gathered against Moses and against A.
16. 43 Moses and A. came before the tabernacle
16. 46 Moses said unto A., Take a censer, and
16. 47 And A. took as Moses commanded, and
16. 50 And A. returned unto Moses unto the door
17. 3 thou shalt write A.'s name upon the rod
17. 6 and the rod of A. (was) among their rods
17. 8 the rod of A. for the house of Levi was
17. 10 Bring A.'s rod again before the testimony
18. 1 the LORD said unto A., Thou and thy
18. 8 the LORD spake unto A., Behold, I also
18. 20 the LORD spake unto A., Thou shalt have
18. 28 the LORD'S heave offering to A. the priest
19. 1 the LORD spake unto Moses and unto A.
20. 2 together against Moses and against A.
20. 6 And Moses and A. went from the presence
20. 8 thou, and A. thy brother, and speak ye
20. 10 and A. gathered the congregation together
20. 12, 23 And the LORD spake unto Moses and A.
20. 24 A. shall be gathered unto his people
20. 25 Take A. and Eleazar his son, and bring
20. 26 And strip A. of his garments, and put
20. 26 A. shall be gathered (unto his people)
20. 28 Moses stripped A. of his garments, and
20. 28 and A. died there in the top of the mount
20. 29 all the congregation saw that A. was dead
20. 29 they mourned for A. thirty days, (even) all
25. 7 the son of A. the priest, saw (it), he rose
25. 11 the son of A. the priest, hath turned my
26. 1 Eleazar the son of A. the priest, saying
26. 9 against Moses and against A. in the
26. 59 she bare unto Amram A. and Moses
26. 60 And unto A. was born, Nadab, and Abihu
26. 64 whom Moses and A. the priest numbered
27. 13 thy people, as A. thy brother was gathered
33. 1 armies under the hand of Moses and A.
33. 38 And A. the priest went up into mount
33. 39 And A. (was) an hundred and twenty
Deut. 9. 20 the LORD was very angry with A. to
9. 20 I prayed for A. also the same time
10. 6 there A. died, and there he was buried
32. 50 as A. thy brother died in mount Hor
Josh. 21. 4 and the children of A. the priest, (which
21. 10 Which the children of A., (being) of the
Josh. 21. 13 they gave to the children of A. the priest
21. 19 of the children of A., the priests, (were)
24. 5 I sent Moses also and A., and I plagued
24. 33 Eleazar the son of A. died; and they buried
Judg. 20. 28 Eleazar, the son of A., stood before it
1 Sa. 12. 6 that advanced Moses and A., and that
12. 8 the LORD sent Moses and A., which
1 Ch. 6. 3 the children of Amram; A., and Moses
6. 3 The sons also of A. Nadab, and Abihu
6. 49 But A. and his sons offered upon the
6. 50 these (are) the sons of A.; Eleazar his son
6. 54 of the sons of A. of the families of
6. 57 And to the sons of A. they gave the
15. 4 David assembled the children of A., and
23. 13 The sons of Amram; A. and Moses; and
23. 13 and A. was separated, that he should
23. 28 on the sons of A. for the service of the
23. 32 and the charge of the sons of A. their
24. 1 the divisions of the sons of A.
24. 1 The sons of A.; Nadab, and Abihu
24. 19 under A. their father, as the LORD
24. 31 the sons of A. in the presence of David
2 Ch. 13. 9 the sons of A., and the Levites, and have
13. 10 (are) the sons of A., and the Levites (wait)
26. 18 the sons of A., that are consecrated to
29. 21 the sons of A. to offer (them) on the
31. 19 Also of the sons of A. the priests, which
35. 14 the priests the sons of A. (were busied)
35. 14 themselves, and for the priests the sons of A.
Ezra 7. 5 Eleazar, the son of A. the chief priest
Neh. 10. 38 the priest the son of A. shall be with
12. 47 sanctified (them) unto the
Psa. 77. 20 like a flock by the hand of Moses and A.
99. 6 Moses and A. among his priests, and
105. 26 his servant, (and) A. whom he had chosen
106. 16 in the camp, (and) A. the saint of the LORD
115. 10 O house of A., trust in the LORD
115. 12 Israel; he will bless the house of A.
118. 3 Let the house of A. now say, that his
133. 2 down upon the beard, (even) A.'s beard
135. 19 bless the LORD, O house of A.
Mic. 6. 4 I sent before thee Moses, A., and Miriam
Luke 1. 5 (was) of the daughters of A., and her name
Acts 7. 40 Saying unto A., Make us gods to go before
Heb. 5. 4 but he that is called of God, as (was) A.
7. 11 and not be called after the order of A?
9. 4 and A.'s rod that budded, and the tables

AA-RO-NITES, לְאַהֲרֹן *lit. of or belonging to Aaron.*

The descendants of the preceding person are so called in 1 Ch. 12. 27, where we read that Jehoiada their leader with 3700 men, also Zadok and 22 captains, joined David in Ziklag; and in 27. 17, that this Zadok was their ruler afterwards; and in Luke 1. 5, that Zacharias's wife was of the daughters of Aaron.

From Josh. 21. 13-19, it appears that the *Aaronites* had thirteen cities assigned to them, viz., Hebron, Libnah, Jattir, Eshtemoa, Holon, Debir, Ain, Juttah, and Beth-shemesh, out of Judah and Simeon; Gibeon, Geba, Anathoth and Almon, out of Benjamin; while the *Kohathites* had ten, viz., Shechem, Gezer, Kibzaim, and Beth-horon, out of Ephraim; Eltekeh, Gibbethon, Aijalon, and Gath-rimmon, out of Dan; Taanach and Gath-rimmon, out of the half tribe of Manasseh; and the *Gershonites* had thirteen, viz., Golan in Bashan, and Beesh-terah, out of the other half tribe of Manasseh; Kishon, Dabareh, Jarmuth, and Engannim, out of Issachar; Mishal, Abdon, Helkath, and Rehob, out of Asher; Kedesh in Galilee, Hammoth-dor, and Kartan, out of Naphtali; and the *Merarites* had twelve, viz., Jokneam, Kartah, Dimnah, and Nahalal, out of Zebulun; Bezer, Jahazah, Kedemoth, and Mephaath, out of Reuben; Ramoth in Gilead, Mahanaim, Heshbon, and Jazer, out of Gad. In all forty-eight cities with their suburbs. The high-priesthood continued in the family of Eleazar, the third son of Aaron, till the time of Eli, B.C. 1200–1141, who was of the family of Ithamar, the younger son, but it was restored to the house of Eleazar in the person of Zadok, who received it when Abiathar was dismissed by Solomon, 1 Ki. 2. 35, thus fulfilling the prediction in 1 Sa. 2. 30.

1 Ch. 12. 27 Jehoiada (was) the leader of the A.
27. 17 [the ruler]..of the A., Zadok

A-BAD'-DON, Ἀβαδδών *destruction*, i.e., *destroyer.*

The king and angel (*or* messenger) of the abyss, whose name translated into Greek is APOLLYON (which see), who was manifested after the fifth angel (*or* messenger) had sounded.

Rev. 9. 11 whose name in the Hebrew tongue (is) A.

A-BAG'-THA, אֲבַגְתָא *happy, prosperous, felix.*

One of the seven chamberlains or eunuchs that served in the presence of Ahasuerus, also called Xerxes, king of Persia, B.C. 485–467. Compare other Persian names such as *Bigtha, Bigthan, Bigthana, Bigvai.*

Esth. 1. 10 the king..commanded..Bigtha and A.

A-BA'-NA, אֲבָנָה *permanent, perennial* [V.L. **AMANAH**]

A river rising at a height of 1149 feet on the top of Anti-Libanus, near *Zebdany*, and (along with the *Awaj* or Pharpar), flowing through the city and plain of Damascus, which is twenty-three miles off. It is now called *Barada* or *Chrysorrhoas*, and is the larger of the two rivers; it loses itself in the marsh *Bahret el Kibliyeh;* fourteen villages are more or less dependent on this river for water.

2 Ki. 5. 12 (Are) not A. and Pharpar..better than

A-BA'-RIM, עֲבָרִים *passages, fords, ridges.*

The two sides of a range of high and rugged mountains E. of the Jordan, in Moab, facing Jericho, stretching from Gilead to the Arnon; its highest point is Mount Nebo, now *Jebel Nebbeh*, the top of the "Pisgah," whence Moses viewed the land before his death; here Israel pitched after leaving Almon-Diblathaim.

Num. 27. 12 Get thee up into this mount A.
33. 47 in the mountains of A., before Nebo
33. 48 they departed from the mountains of A.
Deut. 32. 49 Get thee up into this mountain A.

ABASE, to—

To make low, שָׁפֵל *shaphel,* 5, שְׁפַל *shephal,* 5.

Job 40. 11 behold every one (that is) proud, and abase
Eze. 21. 26 exalt (him that is) low, and abase (him that
Dan. 4. 37 those that walk in pride he is able to abase

ABASED, to be—

To make low, humble, ταπεινόω *tapeinoō.*

Matt. 23. 12 whosoever shall exalt himself shall be ab.
Luke 14. 11 whosoever exalteth himself shall be ab.
18. 14 every one..exalteth himself shall be ab.
Phil. 4. 12 I know both how to be abased, and I know

ABASING—

To make low, humble, ταπεινόω *tapeinoō.*

2 Co. 11. 7 Have I committed an offence in abasing

ABASE one's self, to—

To be humble, to submit oneself, עָנָה *anah.*

Isa. 31. 4 (he) will not..abase himself for the noise

ABATE, to—

To flee, hasten away, נוּס *nus.*

Deut. 34. 7 not dim, nor his natural force abated

ABATED, to be—

1. *To cut off, diminish, withdraw,* גָּרַע *gara,* 2.
Lev. 27. 18 it shall be abated from thy estimation

2. *To be lacking, wanting,* חָסֵר *chaser.*
Gen. 8. 3 after the end..the waters were abated

3. *To become light, lightened, swift,* קָלַל *qalal.*
Gen. 8. 8 to see if the waters were abated from off
8. 11 So Noah knew that the waters were abated

4. *To be feeble, desist, fall,* רָפָה *raphah.*
Judg. 8. 3 Then their anger was abated toward him

AB-BA, Ἀββᾶ *Aramaic word signifying "father."*

Mark 14 36 Abba, Father, all things (are) possible unto
Rom. 8. 15 whereby we cry, Abba, Father
Gal. 4. 6 sent forth..into [your] hearts, crying, A.

AB'-DA, עַבְדָּא *servant, slave, worshipper.*

1. Father of Adoniram, Solomon's tribute officer.
1 Ki. 4. 6 Adoniram, the son of A. (was) over the

2. A chief Levite in Jerusalem after the exile, the son of Shammua, called Obadiah son of Shemaiah in 1 Ch. 9. 16.
Neh. 11. 17 A. the son of Shammua, the son of Galal

AB-DE'-EL, עַבְדְּאֵל *servant of God.*

The father of Shelemiah whom Jehoiakim, king of Judah, ordered to apprehend Baruch the scribe and Jeremiah the prophet.

Jer. 36. 26 Shelemiah the son of A., to take Baruch

AB'-DI, עַבְדִּי *servant of Jah.*

1. A Merarite, grandfather of Ethan, one of those whom David set over the service of song.
1 Ch. 6. 44 hand: Ethan the son of Kishi, the son of A.
2 Ch. 29. 12 of the sons of Merari, Kish the son of A.

2. A descendant of one of the two Elams, who had taken a strange wife during the exile, a thing forbidden by the law of Moses.
Ezra 10. 26 of the sons of Elam..A., and Jeremoth

AB-DI'-EL, עַבְדִּיאֵל *servant of God.*

The ancestor of a family of Gadites dwelling in Gilead in Bashan, as reckoned in the days of Jotham and Jeroboam, kings of Judah and Israel, B.C. 825–742.

1 Ch. 5. 15 Ahi the son of A., the son of Guni

AB'-DON, עַבְדּוֹן *service, servile.*

1. A Levitical city in Asher, now called *Abdeh*, at the N. of Acre, on the banks of the *Wady Kurn;* called Hebron (Ebron) in Josh. 19. 28.
Josh. 21. 30 A. with her suburbs
1 Ch. 6. 74 A. with her suburbs

2. A son of Hillel the Pirathonite (perhaps the same as Bedan in 1 Sa. 12. 11); he judged Israel eight years, B.C. 1120–1112, had forty sons and thirty grandsons, who rode on seventy ass colts, was buried in Pirathon in the land of Ephraim in what was called the mount of the Amalekites.
Judg. 12. 13 A., son of Hillel, a Pirathonite, judged
12. 15 A., son of Hillel the Pirathonite died

3. A Benjamite in Jerusalem.
1 Ch. 8. 23 And A., and Zichri, and Hanan

4. The firstborn son of Jehiel from Maachah, in Gibeon of Benjamin.
1 Ch. 8. 30 And his firstborn son A., and Zur, and
9. 36 And his firstborn son A., then Zur, and

5. A son of Micah, and sent with others by king Josiah to Huldah the prophetess to enquire of Jehovah regarding the words of the Book of the Law found

in the temple, B.C. 624. He is called ACHBOR in 2 Ki. 22. 12.

2 Ch. 34. 20 the king commanded..A. son of Micah

A-BED-NE'-GO, עֲבֵד נְגוֹא *servant of Nego.*

A name given by the prince of the eunuchs of Nebuchadnezzar, king of Babylon, to AZARIAH, one of the four young princes of Judah who were carried away B.C. 607. He was one of the three companions of Daniel that were cast into the burning fiery furnace for refusing to bow before the golden image set up by Nebuchadnezzar in the plain of Dura, in the province of Babylon.

Dan. 1. 7 for he gave unto..Azariah [the name] of A.
2. 49 and he set..A., over the affairs of
3. 12 whom thou hast set over the affairs..A.
3. 13 Nebuchadnezzar..commanded to bring A.
3. 14 (Is it) true, O Shadrach, Meshach, and A.
3. 16 Shadrach, Meshach, and A., answered and
3. 19 changed against Shadrach, Meshach, & A.
3. 20 his army to bind Shadrach, Meshach, & A.
3. 22 slew those men that took up..A.
3. 23 And these three men..A., fell down bound
3. 26 Shadrach, Meshach, and A., ye servants of
3. 26 Then Shadrach, Meshach, and A., came
3. 28 Blessed (be) the God of Shadrach, M., and A.
3. 29 speak anything amiss against..God of..A.
3. 30 Then the king promoted..A., in the

A'-BEL, אָבֵל *fresh, grassy, meadow.*

1. A stony place in the field of Joshua the Bethlehemite, in the N.W. of Judah, between Ekron and Beth-shemesh, whereon the ark was left by the Philistines, B.C. 1140.

1 Sa. 6. 18 the great (stone of) A., whereon they set

2. A city in Naphtali (now called *Abil*, three miles N.E. of Beth-rehob), where Joab besieged Sheba, whose head was given up to him at the suggestion of a wise woman of Abel of Beth-maachah.

2 Sa. 20. 14 And he went through..unto A., v. 15. 18.

A-BEL-BETH-MA-A'-CHAH, אָבֵל בֵּית הַמַּעֲכָה *meadow of the house of Maachah.*

A city in Manasseh or Naphtali, which is mentioned along with Ijon, and Dan, and Janoah, and Kedesh, and Hazor, as being taken by Tiglath-pileser B.C. 740, and the inhabitants carried off to Assyria.

1 Ki. 15. 20 Ben-hadad..smote..A., and all Cinneroth
2 Ki. 15. 29 Tiglath-pileser..took Ijon and A., and

A-BEL-KE-RA'-MIM, אָבֵל כְּרָמִים *meadow of the vineyards.*

A place E. of the Jordan beyond Aroer, and now called *Abila*, six or seven miles beyond Rabbah (or Philadelphia) of the Ammonites.

Judg. 11. 33 smote them..unto the plain of the v.-y.

A-BEL-MA'-IM, אָבֵל מַיִם *meadow of the waters.*

Apparently another name for Abel-beth-maachah; it was smitten by the armies of Benhadad B.C. 940, in the days of Asa.

2 Ch. 16. 4 they smote Ijon, and Dan, and A.

A-BEL-ME-HO'-LAH, אָבֵל מְחוֹלָה *meadow of the dance.*

A city in Issachar, at the N. of the Jordan Valley, and ten or twelve miles S. of Beth-shean; the birth-place of Elisha the prophet, son of Shaphat.

Judg. 7. 22 the host fled..to the border of A., unto
1 Ki. 4. 12 from Beth-shean to A., (even) unto (the
19. 16 and Elisha, the son of Shaphat of A.

A-BEL-MIZ-RA'-IM, אָבֵל מִצְרַיִם *meadow or mourning of the Egyptians.*

A place at the threshing floor at Atad, "beyond Jordan," probably on the W. between it and Hebron, at Beth-hogla, now *Ain-Hajla*; according to others, at *El-Haram*, near Hebron. See *Atad*.

Gen. 50. 11 wherefore the name of it was called A.

A-BEL-SHIT'-TIM, אָבֵל הַשִּׁטִּים *meadow of the acacias.*

A place in the plains (or deserts) of Moab E. of the Jordan, about seven miles off, opposite Jericho, and nearly W. of Heshbon. It was the extreme N. border of the last encampment of Israel before passing over the Jordan, B.C. 1451. See *Shittim*.

Num. 33. 49 pitched..unto A., in the plains of Moab

A'-BEL, הֶבֶל *transitoriness.*

The second son of Adam and Eve, and apparently the twin brother of Cain. He was a shepherd, and at the end of a certain time brought an offering to Jehovah of the best of his flock. Cain being displeased, slew him "in the field," as all the ancient versions declare. His blood is represented as "crying from the ground."

Gen. 4. 2 And she again bare his brother A. And A.
4. 4 A., he also brought..had respect unto A.
4. 8 And Cain talked with A...against A.
4. 9 said unto Cain, Where (is) A. thy brother?
4. 25 another seed instead of A., whom Cain
Matt 23. 35 from the blood of righteous A., unto the
Luke 11. 51 From the blood of A. unto the blood of
Heb. 11. 4 By faith A. offered unto God a more
12. 24 speaketh better things than (that of) A.

A'-BEZ, אֶבֶץ *white, shining.*

A city in Issachar, near Kishion or Remeth (perhaps the same as Thebez, now *Tubas*), near Engannin and Shunem.

Josh. 19. 20 [border was toward]..Kishion and A

ABHOR, to —

1. *To abhor,* בָּחַל *bachal.*
Zech. 11. 8 loathed them, and their soul also abhorred

2. *To separate, cast away, loathe,* גָּעַל *gaal.*
Lev. 26. 11 among you: and my soul shall not abhor
26. 15 or if your soul abhor my judgments, so
26. 30 I will destroy..and my soul shall abhor
26. 43 and because their soul abhorred my
26. 44 neither will I abhor them, to destroy

3. *To nauseate, abhor,* זָהַם *zaham,* 3.
Job 33. 20 So that his life abhorreth bread, and his

4. *To be indignant, defy, abhor,* זָעַם *zaam.*
Prov. 24. 24 the people curse, nations shall abhor

5. *To despise, reject, loath,* מָאַס *maas.*
Job 42. 6 Wherefore I abhor (myself), and repent
Psa. 36. 4 He deviseth..he abhorreth not evil
78. 59 he was wroth, and greatly abhorred Israel
89. 38 But thou hast cast off and abhorred, thou

6. *To despise, pierce, sting,* נָאַץ *naats,* 1, 3.
Deut. 32. 19 And when the LORD saw (it), he abhorred
1 Sa. 2. 17 for men abhorred the offering of the LORD
Psa. 10. 3 the covetous (whom) the LORD abhorreth
Jer. 14. 21 Do not abhor (us), for thy name's sake

7. *To reject, cast down,* נָאַר *naar,* 3.
Lam. 2. 7 the LORD..hath abhorred his sanctuary

8. *To be vexed, wearied with,* קוּץ *quts.*
Lev. 20. 23 these things, and therefore I abhorred
1 Ki. 11. 25 he abhorred Israel, and reigned over S.
Isa. 7. 16 the land that thou abhorrest shall be

9. *To have in abomination,* שָׁקַץ *shaqats,* 3.
Psa. 22. 24 not despised nor abhorred the affliction of

10. *To contemn, abhor, reject,* תָּאַב *taab,* 3.
Amos 6. 8 I abhor the excellency of Jacob, and hate

11. *To have in abomination, reject,* תָּעַב *taab,* 3.
Deut. 7. 26 and thou shalt utterly abhor it; for it (is)
23. 7 Thou shalt not abhor an Edomite; for he
23. 7 thou shalt not abhor an Egyptian; because
Job 9. 31 and mine own clothes shall abhor me
19. 19 All my inward friends abhorred me
30. 10 They abhor me, they flee far from me
Psa. 5. 6 the LORD will abhor the bloody and
106. 40 insomuch that he abhorred his own
107. 18 Their soul abhorreth all manner of meat
119. 163 I hate and abhor lying; (but) thy law do I
Isa. 49. 7 to him whom the nation abhorreth
Amos 5. 10 they abhor him that speaketh uprightly
Mic. 3. 9 ye..princes of..Israel, that abhor

12. *To shrink from,* ἀποστυγέω *apostugeō.*
Rom. 12. 9 Abhor that which is evil; cleave to that

13. *To abominate,* βδελύσσομαι *bdelussomai.*
Rom. 2. 22 thou that abhorrest idols, dost thou

ABHORRED, to be —

1. *To be or become stinking,* בָּאַשׁ *baash,* 2.
2 Sa. 16. 21 Israel shall hear that thou art abhorred

2. *To be indignant, defy, abhor,* זָעַם *zaam.*
Prov. 22. 14 he that is abhorred of the LORD

ABHORRED, to make to be —

1. *To cause to stink,* בָּאַשׁ *baash,* 5.
Exod. 5. 21 ye have made our savour to be abhorred
1 Sa. 27. 12 He hath made..utterly to abhor him

2. *To make abominable, reject,* תָּעַב *taab,* 3.
Eze. 16. 25 hast made thy beauty to be abhorred

ABHORRING —

An object of abhorrence, דֵּרָאוֹן *deraon.*
Isa. 66. 24 they shall be an abhorring unto all flesh

A'-BI, אֲבִי *Jah is father.*

The daughter of Zechariah, wife of Ahaz, and mother of Hezekiah, kings of Judah, (called *Abijah* in 2 Ch. 29. 1,) B.C. 726.

2 Ki. 18. 2 His mother's name also (was) A.

A-BI'-A, A-BI'-AH, אֲבִיָּה *Jah is father.*

1. The second son of Samuel the prophet and judge of Israel; with his brother Joel or Vashni, he judged in Beersheba, and did wickedly, so that Israel desired and obtained a king.

1 Sa. 8. 2 and the name of his second A...judges in
1 Ch. 6. 28 of Samuel; the first-born Vashni, and A.

2. The wife of Hezron grandson of Judah by Pharez, and mother of Ashur father of Tekoa.

1 Ch. 2. 24 then A. Hezron's wife bare him Ashur

3. A son of Rehoboam, called *Abijam* in 1 Ki. 14. 31; 15. 1, 7, 8.

1 Ch. 3. 10 Solomon's son (was) Rehoboam, A. his
Matt. 1. 7 and Roboam begat A.; and A. begat

4. The seventh son of Becher son of Benjamin.

1 Ch. 7. 8 And the sons of Becher; Zemira..and A.

5. A priest in the days of David, set over a particular course of service in the Tabernacle.

Luke 1. 5 priest..Zacharias, of the course of A.

A-BI-AL'-BON, אֲבִי עַלְבוֹן *father of strength.*

One of David's mighty men, from Arabah or Beth-arabah, a city in the N. of the country of the tribe of Judah, adjacent to the territory of the tribe of Benjamin. He is called ABIEL in 1 Ch. 11. 32.

2 Sa. 23. 31 A. the Arbathite

A-BI-A'-SAPH, אֲבִיאָסָף *father of gathering.*

The third son of Korah first-born of Izhar, second son of Kohath, second son of Levi third son of Jacob. See *Ebiasaph*.

Exod. 6. 24 And the sons of Korah; Assir..and A.

A-BI-A'-THAR, אֶבְיָתָר *father of superfluity.*

The eleventh high-priest in succession from Aaron: son of Ahimelech, son of Ahitub, priest at Nob. He escaped when Doeg the Edomite slew his father and 85 priests, and fled to David in the cave of Adullam; was sent back to Jerusalem with the ark when David fled from Absalom; was joint high-priest with Zadok; conspired to make Adonijah king; was banished to his birth place, Anathoth in Benjamin: and at last was expelled from his office by Solomon, B.C. 1014.

1 Sa. 22. 20 And..A., escaped, and fled after David
22. 21 And A. shewed David that Saul had
22. 22 And David said unto A., I knew (it) that
23. 6 when A...fled to David..he came down
23. 9 David..said to A. the priest, Bring
30. 7 And David said to A...bring me hither
30. 7 And A. brought thither the ephod to
2 Sa. 8. 17 And Zadok..and Ahimelech the son of A.
15. 24 and A. went up, until all the people
15. 27 two sons with you,..and..the son of A.
15. 29 Zadok therefore and A. carried the ark
15. 35 not there with thee Zadok and A. the
15. 35 thou shalt tell (it) to Zadok and A. the
15. 36 there with them..and Jonathan A.'s
17. 15 Then said Hushai unto Zadok and to A.
19. 11 David sent to Zadok and to A. the priests
20. 25 and Zadok and A. (were) the priests
1 Ki. 1. 7 he conferred with Joab..and with A.
1. 19 and hath called..A. the priest, and Joab
1. 25 and hath called all..and A. the priest
1. 42 Jonathan the son of A. the priest came
2. 22 even for him, and for A. the priest, and
2. 26 And unto A. the priest said the king
2. 27 So Solomon thrust out A. from being
2. 35 Zadok..the king put in the room of A.
4. 4 and Zadok and A. (were) the priests
1 Ch. 15. 11 David called for Zadok and A. the
18. 16 Zadok..and Abimelech the son of A.
24. 6 before the king, and..the son of A.
27. 34 after Ahithophel (was) Jehoiada..and A.
Mark 2. 26 into the house of God, in the days of A.

A'-BIB, אָבִיב *sprouting, budding.*

The first month of the sacred and seventh of the civil year of the Hebrews, on the 15th of which Israel left Egypt. It commenced at the new moon of April or March (according to the Rabbis), and was constituted the first month of the year in commemoration of the release from Egyptian slavery.

Exod. 13. 4 This day came ye out in the month A.
23. 15 in the time appointed of the month A.
34. 18 bread..in the time of the month A.
34. 18 in the month A. thou camest out from
Deut. 16. 1 Observe the month of A. and keep the
16. 1 for in the month of A. the LORD thy God

A-BI'-DA, A-BI'-DAH, אֲבִידָע *father of knowledge.*

The fourth son of Midian the fourth son of Keturah and Abraham. Comp. the city of *Eboda*, between Canaan and Sinai.

Gen. 25. 4 the sons of Midian; Ephah..and A.
1 Ch. 1. 33 the sons of Midian; Ephah..and A.

A-BI'-DAN, אֲבִידָן *father of judgment.*

The son of Gideoni, a chief Benjamite, who was appointed along with Moses and Aaron, and a chief man out of every tribe, to number the people.

Num. 1. 11 Of Benjamin; A. the son of Gideoni
2. 22 the captain of the sons of Benjamin..A.
7. 60 On the ninth day A. the son of Gideoni
7. 65 this (was) the offering of A. the son of
10. 24 And over the host..(was) A. the son of

ABIDE, to —

1. *To go in, enter, come,* בּוֹא *bo.*
Num. 31. 23 that may abide the fire..all that abideth

2. *To sojourn as a stranger,* גּוּר *gur.*
Psa. 15. 1 LORD, who shall abide in thy tabernacle?
61. 4 I will abide in thy tabernacle for ever

3. *To stay, wait for,* חוּל *chul.*
Hos. 11. 6 And the sword shall abide on his cities

4. *To encamp, incline downward,* חָנָה *chanah.*
Num. 9. 20 according to the..they abode in their
9. 22 children of Israel abode in their tents
31. 19 do ye abide without the camp seven
Ezra 8. 15 and there abode we in tents three days

5. *To sit, sit down, settle down, dwell,* יָשַׁב *yashab.*
Gen. 22. 5 Abide ye here with the ass; and I
24. 55 Let the damsel abide with us (a few)
29. 14 And he abode with him the space of a
29. 19 And Laban said,..abide with me
44. 33 let thy servant abide instead of the lad
49. 24 But his bow abode in strength, and
Exod 16. 29 See..abide ye every man in his place
Lev. 8. 35 Therefore shall ye abide (at) the door of
Num 20. 1 and the people abode in Kadesh
22. 5 and they abide over against me
22. 8 the princes of Moab abode with Balaam
25. 1 And Israel abode in Shittim
35. 25 he shall abide in it unto the death of
Deut. 1. 46 So ye abode in Kadesh many days
3. 19 your wives..shall abide in your cities
3. 29 So we abode in the valley over against
9. 9 then I abode in the mount forty days

Josh. 2. 22 and abode there three days, until the
5. 8 that they abode in their places in the
8. 9 and abode between Beth-el and Ai
Judg. 5. 16 Why abodest thou among the sheepfolds
11. 17 and Israel abode in Kadesh
19. 4 and he abode with him three days
20. 47 and abode in the rock Rimmon four
21. 2 and abode there till even before God
1 Sa. 1. 22 before the LORD, and there abide for
1. 23 So the woman abode, and gave her son
5. 7 The ark..shall not abide with us
7. 2 while the ark abode in Kirjath-jearim
13. 16 And Saul..abode in Gibeah of Benjamin
19. 2 and abide in a secret (place), and hide
22. 5 the prophet Gad said..abide not in the
22. 6 (now Saul abode in Gibeah under a tree
22. 23 Abide thou with me, fear not: for he
23. 14 And David abode in the wilderness
23. 18 and David abode in the wood, and
23. 25 and abode in the wilderness of Maon
25. 13 and two hundred abode by the stuff
26. 3 But David abode in the wilderness
2 Sa. 1. 1 and David had abode two days in
11. 11 The ark, and Israel, and Judah, abide
11. 12 So Uriah abode in Jerusalem that day
15. 8 thy servant vowed..while I abode at
15. 19 return to thy place, and abide with the
16. 3 Behold, he abideth at Jerusalem
16. 18 and with him will I abide
1 Ki. 8. 13 a settled place for thee to abide in for
17. 19 carried him up into a loft, where he a.
2 Ki. 19. 27 But I know thy abode, and thy going
2 Ch. 25. 19 abide now at home; why shouldest
32. 10 that ye abide in the siege in Jerusalem?
Ezra 8. 32 we came to Jerusalem, and abode there
Job 24. 13 nor abide in the paths thereof
38. 40 (and) abide in the covert to lie in wait?
Psa. 55. 19 even he that abideth of old
61. 7 He shall abide before God for ever
125. 1 (which) cannot be removed, (but) abideth
Isa. 37. 28 But I know thy abode, and thy going
Jer. 21. 9 He that abideth in this city shall die by
38. 28 So Jeremiah abode in the court of the
42. 10 If ye will still abide in this land
49. 18 no man shall abide there, neither shall
49. 33 there shall no man abide there, nor
50. 40 (so) shall no man abide there, neither
Hos. 3. 3 Thou shalt abide for me many days
3. 4 the children of Israel shall abide many
Mic. 5. 4 and they shall abide: for now shall he

6. *To bear, hold out, sustain,* כּוּל *kul,* 3a.
Mal. 3. 2 But who may abide the day of his

7. *To lodge, pass the night,* לוּן *lun,* 1, 7a.
Job 39. 9 Will the unicorn..abide by thy crib?
39. 28 She dwelleth and abideth on the rock
Psa. 49. 12 man (being) in honour abideth not
91. 1 He that dwelleth..shall abide under the
Prov. 15. 31 The ear that heareth..abideth among the
19. 23 and (he that hath it) shall abide satisfied

8. *To stand, stand still, remain,* עָמַד *amad.*
Josh. 18. 5 Judah shall abide in their coast on the
Psa. 119. 90 established the earth, and it abideth
Eccl. 1. 4 but the earth abideth for ever

9. *To rise, rise up, stand up, be fixed,* קוּם *qum.*
Nah. 1. 6 who can abide..fierceness of his anger?

10. *To recline, tabernacle,* שָׁכַן *shaken.*
Exod. 24. 16 the glory of the LORD abode upon mount
40. 35 because the cloud abode thereon
Num. 9. 17 and in the place where the cloud abode
9. 18 as long as the cloud abode upon the
24. 2 and he saw Israel abiding (in his tents)
Judg. 5. 17 Gilead abode beyond Jordan...Asher...a.
Prov. 7. 11 her feet abide not in her house

11. *To be, exist, continue,* הָיָה *hayah.*
Num. 9. 21 when the cloud abode from even unto
11. 35 the people journeyed..and abode at

12. *To turn up and down,* ἀναστρέφω *ana-strephō.*
Matt 17. 22 And while they abode in Galilee, Jesus

13. *To remain in a courtyard,* αὐλίζομαι *aulizomai.*
Luke 21. 37 and abode in the mount that is called

14. *To rub away, spend,* διατρίβω *dia-tribō.*
Acts 12. 19 from Judæa to Cæsarea, and (there) abode
14. 3 Long time therefore abode they
14. 28 there they abode long time with the
16. 12 and we were in that city abiding certain
20. 6 to Troas..where we abode seven days

15. *To remain in or on,* ἐπιμένω *epimenō.*
Acts 15. 34 Notwithstanding it pleased Silas to abide
Gal. 1. 18 to see Peter, and abode with him fifteen

16. *To place, cause to stand,* ἵστημι *histēmi.*
John 8. 44 and abode not in the truth, because there

17. *To remain steadily,* καταμένω *kata-menō.*
Acts 1. 13 an upper room, where abode both Peter

18. *To remain, continue,* μένω *menō.*
Matt. 10. 11 and there abide till ye go thence
Mark 6. 10 there abide till ye depart from that place
Luke 1. 56 And Mary abode with her about three
8. 27 neither abode in (any) house, but in the
9. 4 ye enter into, there abide, and thence
19. 5 for to-day I must abide at thy house
24. 29 Abide with us: for it is toward evening
John 1. 32 I saw the spirit..and it abode upon him
1. 39 they came..and abode with him that
3. 36 but the wrath of God abideth on him
John 4. 40 with them: and he abode there two days
5. 38 And ye have not his word abiding in you
7. 9 When he had said..he abode (still) in
8. 35 the servant abideth not..the Son abideth
10. 40 went away again..and there he abode
11. 6 he abode two days still in the same place
12. 24 Except a corn of wheat..die, it abideth
12. 34 We have heard..that Christ abideth for
12. 46 on me should not abide in darkness
14. 16 Comforter, that he may [abide] with you
15. 4 Abide in..except it abide..except ye a.
15. 5 He that abideth in me, and I in him
15. 6 If a man abide not in me, he is cast forth
15. 7 If ye abide in me, and my words abide in
15. 10 ye shall abide in my love..I..abide in
Acts 16. 15 come into my house, and abide (there)
18. 3 the same craft, he abode with them, and
20. 23 saying that bonds and afflictions abide
21. 7 the brethren, and abode with them one
21. 8 which was (one) of the seven; and abode
27. 31 Except these abide in the ship, ye
1 Co. 3. 14 If any man's work abide which he hath
7. 8 It is good for them if they abide even as
7. 20 Let every man abide in the same calling
7. 24 let every man..therein abide with God
7. 40 But she is happier if she so abide, after
13. 13 And now abideth faith, hope, charity
Phil. 1. 25 I know that I shall abide and continue
2 Ti. 2. 13 If we believe not, (yet) he abideth
4. 20 Erastus abode at Corinth; but Trophimus
Heb. 7. 3 Without father..abideth a priest
1 Pe. 1. 23 word of God, which liveth and abideth
1 Jo. 2. 6 He that saith he abideth in him ought
2. 10 He that loveth his brother abideth in
2. 14 strong, and the word of God abideth in
2. 17 he that doeth the will of God abideth for
2. 24 Let that [therefore] abide in you, which
2. 27 abideth in you, and..ye shall abide in him
2. 28 And now, little children, abide in him
3. 6 Whosoever abideth in him sinneth not
3. 14 He that loveth not..abideth in death
3. 15 no murderer hath eternal life abiding in
3. 24 we know that he abideth in us, by the
2 Jo. 9 abideth not in..doctrine..He that abideth

19. *To remain alongside,* παραμένω *para-menō.*
1 Co. 16. 6 And it may be that I will abide, yea

20. *To do, make,* ποιέω *poieō.*
Acts 20. 3 And (there) abode three months

21. *To remain behind,* ὑπομένω *hupo-menō.*
Acts 17. 14 but Silas and Timotheus abode there

ABIDE, to be able to —

To contain, bear, כּוּל *kul,* 5.
Jer. 10. 10 the nations shall not be able to abide his

ABIDE all night, to —

To lodge, pass the night, לוּן *lun.*
Gen. 19. 2 we will abide in the street all night
Lev. 19. 13 shall not abide with thee all night

ABIDE behind, to —

To stand, stand still, remain, עָמַד *amad.*
1 Sa. 30. 10 two hundred abode behind, which were

ABIDE, can —

To contain, bear, כּוּל *kul,* 5.
Joel 2. 11 the day of the LORD..who can abide it?

ABIDE fast, to —

To cleave, adhere, pursue, דָּבַק *dabeq.*
Ruth 2. 8 abide here fast by my maidens

ABIDE in, to —

To remain on, continue, ἐπιμένω *epi-menō.*
Rom. 11. 23 and they also, if they abide not still in
Phil. 1. 24 Nevertheless to abide in the flesh (is)

ABIDE in the field, to —

To be in a fold in the field, ἀγραυλέω *agrauleō.*
Luke 2. 8 were..shepherds abiding in the field

ABIDE, to make to —

To cause to sit or dwell, settle, יָשַׁב *yashab,* 5.
1 Sa. 30. 21 whom they had made also to abide

ABIDE still, to —

To remain towards, or on, προσμένω *pros-menō.*
1 Ti. 1. 3 As I besought thee to abide still at Eph.

ABIDE with, to —

To be joined, לָוָה *lavah.*
Eccl. 8. 15 for that shall abide with him of his labour

ABIDING —

1. *To sit, sit still, dwell,* יָשַׁב *yashab.*
Judg. 16. 9 Now (there were) men..abiding with her
16. 12 And (there were) liers in wait abiding in

2. *Hope, expectation,* מִקְוֶה *miqveh.*
1 Ch. 29. 15 and (there is) none abiding

3. *To be admitted, join oneself to,* סָפַח *saphach,* 7.
1 Sa. 26. 19 driven me out this day from abiding in

A-BI'-EL, אֲבִיאֵל *father of might.*

1. Son of Zeror, and father of Ner, and of Kish who was father of Saul the first king of Israel.
1 Sa. 9. 1 a man of Benjamin..Kish, the son of A.
14. 51 Ner the father of Abner (was)..son of A.

2. One of David's thirty mighty men, called ABI-ALBON in 2 Sa. 23. 31.
1 Ch. 11. 32 A. the Arbathite.

A-BI-E'-ZER, אֲבִיעֶזֶר *father of help.*

1. A descendant of Manasseh, probably the same as Jeezer, son of Gilead, Num. 26. 30.
Josh. 17. 2 was also (a lot) for..the children of A.
1 Ch. 7. 18 sister Hammoleketh bare Ishod, and A.

2. A district in Manasseh inhabited by the Abiezrites.
Judg. 6. 34 came upon Gideon..and A. was gathered
8. 2 gleaning of..better than the vintage of A.?

3. A native of Anathoth in Benjamin (now *Anata*), two miles E. of Gibeah, and one and a-half hours from Jerusalem, on the other side of the *Wady Selam.*
2 Sa. 23. 27 A. the Anethothite
1 Ch. 11. 28 A. the Antothite
27. 12 ninth (captain)..(was) A. the Anetothite

A-BI-EZ-RITE, אֲבִי הָעֶזְרִי *belonging to Abiezer.*

The Abiezrites were descendants of Manasseh the elder son of Joseph.
Judg. 6. 11 oak..that (pertained) unto Joash the A.
6. 24 altar..yet in Ophrah of the A.
8. 32 buried..in Ophrah of the A.

A-BI-GA'-IL, אֲבִיגַיִל *source or cause of delight.*

1. Wife of Nabal the Carmelite; she met and pacified David, and afterwards became his wife, and was the mother of Daniel *or* Chileab.
1 Sa. 25. 3 Nabal; and the name of his wife A.
25. 14 But one of the young men told A.
25. 18 Then A. made haste, and took two
25. 23 And when A. saw David, she hasted, and
25. 32 And David said to A., Blessed (be) the
25. 36 And A. came to Nabal; and, behold,
25. 39 David sent and communed with A., to
25. 40 the servants of David were come to A. to
25. 42 And A. hasted, and arose, and rode upon
27. 3 David dwelt with Achish..and A. the
30. 5 David's two wives were taken captives..A.
2 Sa. 2. 2 David went up..and A. Nabal's wife
3. 3 And his second, Chileab, of A. the wife of
1 Ch. 3. 1 the second Daniel, of A. the Carmelitess

2. A daughter of Nahash *or* Jesse, and sister or niece of Zeruiah. She was the mother of Amasa, whom Absalom made captain in place of Joab.
2 Sa. 17. 25 Ithra..went in to A. [Hebrew, Abigal].
1 Ch. 2. 16 [David]..whose sisters (were) Zeruiah & A.
2. 17 And A. bare Amasa: and the father of

A-BI-GIB-E'-ON, אֲבִי גִבְעוֹן *father of Gibeon.*

A descendant of Benjamin who dwelt at Gibeon; his family afterwards settled at Jerusalem. In the common version this name is translated as a patronymic; but as it occurs in a list of persons specially named, it seems to denote an individual. [*See* R.V.]
1 Ch. 8. 29 And at Gibeon dwelt the father of Gibeon

A-BI-HA'-IL, אֲבִיחַיִל *father of might.*

1. A Levite, father of Zuriel, the chief of the Merarites in the time of Moses.
Num. 3. 35 the chief..(was) Zuriel the son of A.

2. The wife of Abishur, a descendant of Hezron of Judah.
1 Ch. 2. 29 the name of the wife of Abishur (was) A.

3. Head of a family of the tribe of Gad
1 Ch. 5. 14 These (are) the children of A. the son of H.

4. A daughter of Eliab David's brother, and wife of Rehoboam.
2 Ch. 11. 18 Rehoboam took..A. the daughter of E.

5. Father of Esther, the cousin of Mordecai, who became queen of Persia as wife of Ahasuerus (*i.e.,* Xerxes), in the stead of Vashti.
Esth. 2. 15 the turn of Esther, the daughter of A.
9. 29 Esther..daughter of A., and Mordecai

A-BI'-HU, אֲבִיהוּא *he is my father.*

A son of Aaron, who was destroyed with his brother Nadab for offering strange fire.
Exod. 6. 23 Elisheba..bare him Nadab, and A., Eleaz.
24. 1 Come up unto the LORD, thou, and..A.
24. 9 Then went up Moses..and A., and
28. 1 take thou..that he may minister..A.
Lev. 10. 1 And Nadab and A., the sons of Aaron
Num. 3. 2 (are) the names of the sons of Aaron..A.
3. 4 And Nadab and A. died before the LORD
26. 60 And unto Aaron was born. A.
26. 61 And Nadab and A. died, when they
1 Ch. 6. 3 The sons also of Aaron; Nadab, and A.
24. 1 The sons of Aaron; Nadab, and A., E.
24. 2 But Nadab and A. died before their

A-BI'-HUD, אֲבִיהוּד *father of honour.*

A son of Bela, son of Benjamin.
1 Ch. 8. 3 And the sons of Bela..Addar,..and..A.

A-BI'-JAH, אֲבִיָּה *my father is Jah.*

1. A son of Jeroboam who died in youth.
1 Ki. 14. 1 At that time A. the son of Jeroboam fell

2. A priest in the time of David, to whom it fell by lot to be the head of the eighth course in the service of the temple. See *Abiah.*
1 Ch. 24. 10 the eighth (lot came forth) to A.
26. 20 And of the Levites, A. (was) over the

3. A son of Rehoboam. His mother was Maachah, a daughter of Absalom.
2 Ch. 11. 20 Maachah..daughter of Absalom..bare A.
11. 22 Rehoboam made A...the chief, (to be)

2 Ch. 12. 16 and A. his son reigned in his stead
13. 1 in the eighteenth year..began A. to reign
13. 2 And there was war between A. and J.
13. 3 And A. set the battle in array with an
13. 4 And A. stood up upon mount Zemaraim
13. 15 God smote..Israel before A. and Judah
13. 17 And A. and his people slew them with a
13. 19 And A. pursued after Jeroboam, and took
13. 20 Neither did Jeroboam..in the days of A.
13. 21 But A. waxed mighty, and married
13. 22 And the rest of the acts of A., and his
14. 1 So A. slept with his fathers, and they

4. Mother of Hezekiah, king of Judah.
2 Ch. 29. 1 And his mother's name (was) A., the

5. A priest that sealed the covenant made by Nehemiah and the people to serve the LORD.
Neh. 10. 7 Meshullam, Abijah, Mijamin

6. A priest that went up from Babylon with Zerubbabel. Perhaps the same as the preceding.
Neh. 12. 1–4 these (are) the priests..Iddo, G. and A.
12. 12–17 the chief of the fathers..of A., Zichri

A-BI'-JAM, אֲבִיָּם *father of light.*
The name of Rehoboam's son who succeeded his father as king of Judah; in 2 Chronicles he is called ABIJAH.
1 Ki. 14. 31 And A. his son reigned in his stead
15. 1 in the eighteenth year..reigned A. over
15. 7 Now the rest of the acts of A. and all that
15. 7 And there was war between A. and J.
15. 8 And A. slept with his fathers; and they

AB-I-LE'-NE, Ἀβιληνή *region of Abila.*
A province or tetrarchy, situated at the extreme N. of Palestine, and E. of the Jordan; it was so named from the city Abila or Abela (now *Abil*), which is about twenty miles N.W. of Damascus towards Baalbek or Heliopolis, lying among the mountains of Antilibanus, in lat. 33° 38′ N., long. 36° 18′ E. In the time of John the Baptist LYSANIAS was its tetrarch. It was given by Claudius to Herod Agrippa, A.D. 53.
Luke 3. 1 and Lysanias the tetrarch of Abilene

ABILITY—
1. *Power, strength, wealth,* כֹּחַ *koach.*
Ezra 2. 69 They gave after their ability unto the
Dan. 1. 4 and such as (had) ability in them to stand

2. *(His) hand reaches,* נָשַׂג יָד *nasag* (5) *yad.*
Lev. 27. 8 shall value him; according to his ability

3. *Sufficiency, fulness, abundance,* דַּי *dai.*
Neh. 5. 8 We after our ability have redeemed our

4. *Power, might, strength,* δύναμις *dunamis.*
Matt. 25. 15 to every man acco. to his several ability

5. *To go on well,* εὐπορέομαι *eu-poreomai.*
Acts 11. 29 disciples, every man acco. to his ability

6. *Strength, vigour,* ἰσχύς *ischus.*
1 Pe. 4. 11 if any man minister..as of the ability

AB-I-MA'-EL, אֲבִימָאֵל *my father is God.*
A son of Joktan of the family of Shem. The place where Abimael's descendants settled is still unknown, but it is supposed to have been in some part of Arabia-Petræa.
Gen. 10. 26–28 And Joktan begat Almodad..and A
1 Ch. 1. 20–22 And Joktan begat Almodad..and A.

A-BI-ME'-LECH, אֲבִימֶלֶךְ *father of the king.*
1. King of Gerar in the time of Abraham.
Gen. 20. 2 and A. king of Gerar sent, and took Sarah
20. 3 God came to A. in a dream by night
20. 4 But A. had not come near her: and he
20. 8 Therefore A. rose early in the morning
20. 9 Then A. called Abraham, and said
20. 10 And A. said unto Abraham, What
20. 14 And A. took sheep, and oxen, and men-
20. 15 And A. said, Behold, my land (is) before
20. 17 So Abraham prayed..and God healed A.
20. 18 closed up all the wombs of the house of A.
21. 22 A. and Phichol..spake unto Abraham
21. 25 Abraham reproved A. because of a well
21. 25 which A.'s servants had violently taken
21. 26 And A. said, I wot not who hath done
21. 27 Abraham took sheep..gave them unto A.
21. 29 And A. said unto Abraham, What (mean)
21. 32 then A. rose up, and..returned into the
26. 1 And Isaac went unto A. king of the
26. 8 A. king of the Philistines looked out at a
26. 9 And A. called Isaac, and said, Behold
26. 10 And A. said, What (is) this thou hast
26. 11 And A. charged all (his) people, saying
26. 16 And A. said unto Isaac, Go from us; for
26. 26 Then A. went to him from Gerar, and

2. Son of Gideon by a concubine in Shechem.
Judg. 8. 30–31 Gideon had..a son, whose name..A.
9. 1 And A...went to Shechem unto his
9. 3 their hearts inclined to follow A.; for
9. 4 A. hired vain and light persons, which
9. 6 made A. king, by the plain of the pillar
9. 16 have done truly..in that ye have made A.
9. 18 made A...king over the men of Shechem
9. 19 rejoice ye in A., and let him also rejoice
9. 20 let fire come out from A., and devour the
9. 20 let fire..men of Shechem..and devour A.
9. 21 And Jotham ran away..for fear of A. his
9. 22 A. had reigned three years over Israel
9. 23 God sent an evil spirit between A. and
9. 23 the men of S. dealt treacherously with A.
9. 24 and their blood be laid upon A. their
9. 25 the men of Shechem set liers..was told A.
Judg. 9. 27 they went..and did eat and drink, and..A.
9. 28 Gaal the son of Ebed said, Who (is) A.
9. 29 would I remove A. And he said to A.
9. 31 And he sent messengers unto A. privily
9. 34 And A. rose up, and all the people that
9. 35 and A. rose up, and the people that (were)
9. 38 Who (is) A., that we should serve him?
9. 39 And Gaal went out..and fought with A.
9. 40 And A. chased him, and he fled before
9. 41 And A. dwelt at Arumah: and Zebul
9. 42 people went..into the field; and..told A.
9. 44 And A., and the company that (was) with
9. 45 And A. fought against the city all that
9. 47 And it was told A., that all the men of
9. 48 And A. gat him up to mount Zalmon, he
9. 48 and A. took an ax in his hand, and cut
9. 49 and followed A., and put (them) to the
9. 50 Then went A. to Thebez, and encamped
9. 52 And A. came unto the tower, and fought
9. 53 And a certain woman cast..upon A.'s
9. 55 when the men of Israel saw that A. was
9. 56 Thus God rendered the wickedness of A.
10. 1 And after A. there arose to defend Israel
2 Sa. 11. 21 Who smote A. the son of Jerubbesheth?

3. Father or son of Abiathar the high priest in the time of David. In one passage he is called AHIMELECH.
1 Ch. 18. 16 and A. the son of Abiathar, (were) the

4. In the title of Psa. 34 this name is given apparently to Achish king of Gath, to whom David had fled, as stated in 1 Sa. 21. 10.
Psa. 34. *title.* of David..his behaviour before A.

A-BI-NA'-DAB, אֲבִינָדָב *father or source of liberality.*
1. An Israelite of the tribe of Judah, who lived near Kirjath-jearim, and in whose house the ark was placed after being sent back by the Philistines.
1 Sa. 7. 1 and brought it into the house of A. in the
2 Sa. 6. 3 out of the house of A...the sons of A.
6. 4 And they brought it out of the house of A.
1 Ch. 13. 7 carried the ark..out of the house of A.

2. Second son of Jesse, the father of David.
1 Sa. 16. 8 Then Jesse called A., and made him pass
17. 13 Eliab the first-born, and next unto him A.
1 Ch. 2. 13 Jesse begat his first-born Eliab, and A.

3. A son of king Saul slain at Gilboa by the Philistines, together with his brother Jonathan.
1 Sa. 31. 2 and the Philistines slew Jonathan, and A.
1 Ch. 8. 33 Saul..Jonathan, and Malchi-shua, and A.
9. 39 Saul..Jonathan, and Malchi-shua, and A.
10. 2 and the Philistines slew Jonathan, and A.

4. Father of one of Solomon's officers.
1 Ki. 4. 11 The son of A., in all the region of Dor

ABINER, אֲבִינֵר. *See* **ABNER.**

A-BI-NO'-AM, אֲבִינֹעַם *father of pleasantness.*
Father of Barak (of the tribe of Naphtali), an Israelite, who defeated the army of Jabin, B.C. 1296.
Judg. 4. 6 she sent and called Barak the son of A.
4. 12 shewed Sisera that Barak the son of A.
5. 1 sang Deborah and Barak the son of A.
5. 12 lead thy captivity captive, thou son of A.

A-BI'-RAM, אֲבִירָם *father of elevation.*
1. A son of Eliab, a Reubenite, who with Dathan his brother, Korah a Levite, and On a Reubenite, conspired against Moses and Aaron in the wilderness, and perished with his accomplices.
Num 16. 1 Now Korah..and Dathan and A...took
16. 12 And Moses sent to call Dathan and A., the
16. 24 the tabernacle of Korah, Dathan, and A.
16. 25 Moses rose up and went unto Dathan..A.
16. 27 they gat up from the tabernacle of..and A.
16. 27 and Dathan and A. came out, and stood
26. 9 sons of Eliab; Nemuel, and Dathan, and A.
26. 9 This (is that) Dathan and A., (which were)
Deut 11. 6 And what he did unto Dathan and A.
Psa. 106. 17 The earth..covered the company of A.

2. First-born son of Hiel the Bethelite, who began to rebuild Jericho. He died when his father laid the foundations of that city, as Joshua had foretold of him. (Josh. 6. 26).
1 Ki. 16. 34 he laid the foundation thereof in A. his

A-BI'-SHAG, אֲבִישַׁג *father of error,* i.e., *cause of wandering.*
A beautiful damsel of the town of Shunem in Issachar. She was employed to nurse David in his old age.
1 Ki. 1. 3 they..found A. a Shunammite, & brought
1. 15 and A. the Shunammite ministered unto
2. 17 Speak..unto Solomon..that he give me A.
2. 21 Let A. the Shunammite be given to A. thy
2. 22 why dost thou ask A. the Shunammite

A-BI'-SHAI, אֲבִישַׁי *source of wealth.*
A son of David's sister Zeruiah, and a brother of Joab. After numerous victories, and slaying the Philistine giant Ishbibenob, he obtained a place among David's thirty valiant men. In the margin of 1 Ch. 18. 12, he is called ABSHAI.
1 Sa. 26. 6 David..said to A...And A. said, I will
26. 7 So David and A. came to the people by
26. 8 Then said A. to David, God hath delivered
26. 9 And David said to A., Destroy him not
2 Sa. 2. 18 And there were..there, Joab, and A., and
2. 24 Joab also and A. pursued after Abner
3. 30 Joab and A. his brother slew Abner
10. 10 he delivered into the hand of A. his
10. 14 then fled they also before A., and entered
2 Sa. 16. 9 Then said A...Why should this dead dog
16. 11 David said to A...Behold, my son, which
18. 2 sent..a third part under the hand of A.
18. 5 And the king commanded Joab and A.
18. 12 the king charged thee and A. and Ittai
19. 21 But A...answered and said, Shall not S.
20. 6 David said to A., Now shall Sheba the
20. 10 Joab and A. his brother pursued after
21. 17 But A...succoured him, and smote the
23. 18 And A...was chief among three. And he
1 Ch. 2. 16 And the sons of Zeruiah; A., and Joab
11. 20 And A. the brother of Joab, he was chief
18. 12 Moreover, A...slew of the Edomites
19. 11 he delivered into the hand of A. his
19. 15 they likewise fled before A...and entered

A-BI-SHA'-LOM, אֲבִישָׁלוֹם *father of peace.*
Father of Maachah, wife of Jeroboam; in 2 Ch. 11. 20, 21, the name is Absalom.
1 Ki. 15. 2 his mother's name (was) Maachah..of Abi.
15. 10 his mother's name (was) Maachah..of Abi.

A-BI-SHU'-A, אֲבִישׁוּעַ *father of safety.*
1. Son of Phinehas, grandson of Aaron.
1 Ch. 6. 4 Eleazar begat Phinehas, Phinehas begat A.
6. 5 And A. begat Bukki, and Bukki begat
6. 50 these (are) the sons of Aaron; Eleazar..A.
Ezra 7. 5 A., the son of Phinehas, the son of Eleazar

2. A son of Bela the son of Benjamin.
1 Ch. 8. 4 [sons of Bela were, Addar]..And A. and

A-BI'-SHUR, אֲבִישׁוּר *father of oxen.*
A son of Shammai the grandson of Jerahmeel, the great-grandson of Judah.
1 Ch. 2. 28 the sons of Shammai; Nadab, and A.
2. 29 the name of the wife of A. (was) Abihail

A-BI'-TAL, אֲבִיטַל *source of dew.*
A wife of David and mother of his fourth son Shephatiah.
2 Sa. 3. 4 and the fifth, Shephatiah the son of A.
1 Ch. 3. 3 The fifth, Shephatiah of A.

A-BI'-TUB, אביטוב *source of good.*
A son of Shaharaim, a descendant of Benjamin. In the common version it is AHITUB.
1 Ch. 8. 11. And of Hushim he begat A., and Elpaal

A-BI'-UD, אֲבִיהוּד *father of honour.*
A son of Zerubbabel, omitted in 1 Ch. 3. 19.
Matt. 1. 13 And Zorobabel begat A.; and A. begat

ABJECTS, *smitten, stricken,* נֵכֶה *nekeh.*
Psa. 35. 15 the abjects gathered themselves together

ABLE—
1. *Sufficiency, fulness, abundance,* דַּי *dai.*
Lev. 5. 7 if he be not able to bring a lamb
12. 8 if she be not able to bring a lamb
25. 26 And if..himself be able to redeem it
25. 28 if he be not able to restore (it) to him

2. *Strength, might,* חַיִל *chayil.*
Exod 18. 21 shalt provide out of all the people able
18. 25 And Moses chose able men; 1 Ch. 26. 8.

2a. *Able man,* גִּבּוֹר *gibbor.*
1 Ch. 9. 13 very able men for the work

3. *Power, strength,* כֹּחַ *koach.*
1 Ch. 29. 14 we should be able to offer so willingly
2 Ch. 2. 6 who is able to build him an house, seeing
Ezra 10. 13 we are not able to stand without, neither

4. *Powerful, mighty, strong,* δυνατός *dunatos.*
Luke 14. 31 consulteth whether he be able with ten
Acts 25. 5 Let them therefore..among you are able
Rom. 4. 21 what he had promised, he was able also
11. 23 for God is able to graff them in again
14. 4 for God is able to make him stand
2 Co. 9. 8 God (is) able to make all grace abound
2 Ti. 1. 12 am persuaded that he is able to keep
Tit. 1. 9 that he may be able by sound doctrine
Heb. 11. 19 Accounting that God (was) able to raise
Jas. 3. 2 (and) able also to bridle the whole body

5. *Sufficient,* ἱκανός *hikanos.*
2 Tim 2. 2 who shall be able to teach others also

ABLE, be, *gift of (his) power,* מַתַּת יָד (מַתְּנַת יָד), *mattath (mattanah) yad.*
Deut 16. 17 Every man (shall give) as he is able
Eze. 46. 5 for the lambs as he shall be able to give
46. 11 and to the lambs as he is able to give

ABLE, to be—
1. *To be able,* יָכֹל *yakol.*
Gen. 15. 5 tell the stars, if thou be able to number
Exod 10. 5 that one cannot be able to see the earth
18. 18 thou art not able to perform it thyself
18. 23 thou shalt be able to endure, and all this
40. 35 And Moses was not able to enter into the
Num 11. 14 I am not able to bear all this people
13. 30 for we are well able to overcome it
13. 31 We be not able to go up against the people
14. 16 the LORD was not able to bring this people
22. 11 peradventure I shall be able to overcome
22. 37 am I not able indeed to promote thee
Deut. 1. 9 I am not able to bear you myself alone
9. 28 Because the LORD was not able to bring
14. 24 thou art not able to carry it
Judg. 8. 3 what was I able to do in comparison of
1 Sa. 6. 20 Who is able to stand before this holy LORD
17. 9 If he be able to fight with me, and to
17. 33 Thou art not able to go against this

1 Ki. 3. 9 who is able to judge this thy so great a
9. 21 were not able utterly to destroy
2 Ki. 18. 23 if thou be able on thy part to set riders
18. 29 he shall not be able to deliver you
2 Ch. 7. 7 the brasen altar..was not able to receive
32. 13 were the gods..any ways able to deliver
32. 14 that your God should be able to deliver
32. 15 no god..was able to deliver his people
Neh. 4. 10 so that we are not able to build the wall
Psa. 18. 38 wounded them that they were not able to
21. 11 a mischievous device..they are not able
36. 12 cast down, and shall not be able to rise
40. 12 so that I am not able to look up
Eccl. 8. 17 yet shall he not be able to find (it)
Isa. 36. 8 I will give thee..if thou be able on thy
36. 14 he shall not be able to deliver you
47. 11 thou shalt not be able to put it off
47. 12 if so be thou shalt be able to profit
Jer. 11. 11 they shall not be able to escape
49. 10 he shall not be able to hide himself
Lam. 1. 14 hands, (from whom) I am not able to rise
Eze. 7. 19 their gold shall not be able to deliver
33. 12 neither shall the righteous be able to live
Dan. 3. 17 our God,..is able to deliver us from the
4. 18 the wise (men) of my kingdom are not a. to
4. 37 those that walk in pride he is able to
6. 20 is thy God..able to deliver thee from the
Amos 7. 10 the land is not able to bear all his words
Zeph. 1. 18 nor their gold shall be able to deliver

2. *To be able,* כְּהַל *kehal.*
Dan. 2. 26 Art thou able to make known unto me
4. 18 thou (art) able; for the spirit of the holy

3. *To reach, attain,* נָשַׂג *nasag,* 5.
Lev 5. 11 if he be not able to bring two turtledoves
14. 22 And two turtledoves..such as he is able
14. 31 (Even) such as he is able to get
14. 32 whose hand is not able to get 25. 49

3*a*. *Reach and find sufficient* [Heb., Nos. 3 & 5 combined]
Lev 25 26 And if..himself be able to redeem it

4. *Keep, possess (strength)* (כֹּחַ) עָצַר *atsar (koach).*
1 Ch 29. 14 we should be able to offer so willingly
2 Ch. 2 6 but who is able to build him an house
20. 37 they were not able to go to Tarshish

5. *To find sufficient,* מָצָא כְּדֵי *matsa ke-de.*
Lev 25. 28 if he be not able to restore (it) to him
[*See also* Bear, bring, get, go, go forth, stand.]

6. *To be powerful, have power,* δύναμαι *dunamai.*
Matt. 3. 9 God is able of these stones to raise up
9. 28 Believe ye that I am able to do this?
10. 28 but are not able to kill the soul
10. 28 which is able to destroy both soul and
19. 12 He that is able to receive (it), let him
20. 22 Are ye able to drink..We are able
22. 46 And no man was able to answer him a
26. 61 I am able to destroy the temple of God
Mark 4. 33 they were able to hear (it)
Luke 1. 20 thou shalt be dumb, and not able to
3. 8 God is able of these stones to raise up
12. 26 If ye then be not able to do that
21. 15 your adversaries shall not be able to
John 10. 29 no (man) is able to pluck (them) out of my
Acts 20. 32 his grace, which is able to build you up
Rom. 8. 39 nor any other creature, shall be able to
15. 14 filled with all knowledge, able also to
1 Co. 3. 2 ye were not able..yet now are ye able
6. 5 no, not one that shall be able to judge
10. 13 you to be tempted above that ye are able
10. 13 that ye may be able to bear (it)
2 Co. 1. 4 that we may be able to comfort them
Eph. 3. 20 Now unto him that is able to do exceeding
6. 11 that ye may be able to stand against
6. 13 that ye may be able to withstand 6. 16.
Phil. 3. 21 the working whereby he is able even to
2 Ti. 3. 7 and never able to come to the knowledge
3. 15 scriptures, which are able to make thee
Heb. 2. 18 he is able to succour them that are
5. 7 unto him that was able to save him from
7. 25 Wherefore he is able also to save them
Jas. 1. 21 engrafted word, which is able to save
4. 12 one lawgiver, who is able to save and to
Jude 24 Now unto him that is able to keep you
Rev. 5. 3 And no man..was able to open the book
6. 17 and who shall be able to stand?
13. 4 the beast? who is able to make war with
15. 8 and no man was able to enter into the

7. *To have full power,* ἐξισχύω *exischuō.*
Eph. 3. 18 [that ye]..may be able to comprehend

8. *To have, hold, possess,* ἔχω *echō.*
2 Pe. 1. 15 that ye may be able after my decease

9. *To have power,* ἰσχύω *ischuō.*
Luke 13. 24 will seek to enter in, and shall not be able
14. 29 the foundation, and is not able to finish (it)
14. 30 to build, and was not able to finish
John 21. 6 and now they were not able to draw it
Acts 6. 10 And they were not able to resist 15. 10.

ABLE to bring—
1. *To find sufficient (for),* מָצָא דֵי, *matsa de.*
Lev. 12 8 if she be not able to bring a lamb
2. *To reach sufficient (for),* נגע די, *naga* (5) *de.*
Lev. 5 7 if he be not able to bring a lamb

ABLE to endure, to be —
The foot (lit. according to the foot of), רֶגֶל *regel.*
Gen. 33. 14 according as..the children be able to endure

ABLE, to make —
To make sufficient, ἱκανόω *hikanoō.*
2 Co. 3 6 Who also hath made us able ministers of

AB'-NER (1 Sa. 14. 50, ABINER), אַבְנֵר *father of light.*
Son of Saul's uncle Ner, and captain of Saul's army. From his relationship to the king, and his force of character, he exercised great influence during Saul's reign as well as afterwards.
1 Sa. 14. 50 the name of the captain of his host (was) A.
14. 51 and Ner the father of A. (was) the son
17. 55 Saul..said unto A...A., whose son (is)
17. 55 And A. said (As) thy soul liveth, O king
17. 57 A. took him, and brought him before
20. 25 and A. sat by Saul's side, and David's
26. 5 and A. the son of Ner, the captain of his
26. 7 but A. and the people lay round about
26. 14 David cried to the people, and to A. the
26. 14 saying, Answerest thou not, A.? Then A.
26. 15 David said to A. (Art) not thou a (valiant)
2 Sa. 2. 8 But A. the son of Ner, captain of Saul's
2. 12 And A. the son of Ner, and the servants
2. 14 And A. said to Joab, Let the young men
2. 17 there was a very sore battle..and A. was
2. 19 And Asahel pursued after A.; and in
2. 19 nor to the left from following A.
2. 20 Then A. looked behind him, and said
2. 21 And A. said to him, Turn thee aside
2. 22 And A. said again to Asahel, Turn thee
2. 23 he refused to turn aside: wherefore A.
2. 24 Joab also and Abishai pursued after A.
2. 25 gathered themselves together after A.,
2. 26 Then A. called to Joab, and said, Shall
2. 29 And A. and his men walked all that
2. 30 And Joab returned from following A.
2. 31 had smitten of Benjamin, and of A.'s men
3. 6 that A. made himself strong for the house
3. 7 and (Ishbosheth) said to A., Wherefore
3. 8 Then was A. very wroth for the words of
3. 9 So do God to A., and more also, except
3. 11 And he could not answer A. a word again
3. 12 And A. sent messengers to David on his
3. 16 Then said Abner unto him, Go, return
3. 17 And A. had communication with the
3. 19 And A. also spake in the ears of Benjamin
3. 19 and A. went also to speak in the ears of
3. 20 So A. came to David to Hebron, and
3. 20 And David made A. and the men that
3. 21 And A. said unto David, I will arise
3. 21 And David sent A. away; and he went
3. 22 but A. (was) not with David in Hebron
3. 23 A. the son of Ner came to the king, and
3. 24 behold, A. came unto thee; why (is) it
3. 25 Thou knowest A. the son of Ner, that he
3. 26 when Joab was come..he sent..after A.
3. 27 And when A. was returned to Hebron
3. 28 guiltless..for ever from the blood of A.
3. 30 So Joab and Abishai his brother slew A.
3. 31 and gird you with sackcloth, and m.b.A.
3. 32 And they buried A. in Hebron: and the
3. 32 the king..wept at the grave of Abner
3. 33 And the king lamented over A., and said
3. 33 the king..said, Died A. as a fool dieth?
3. 37 it was not of the king to slay A. the son of
4. 1 when Saul's son heard that A. was dead
4. 12 and buried (it) in the sepulchre of A. in
1 Ki. 2. 5 unto A. the son of Ner, and unto
2. 32 A. the son of Ner, captain of the host of
1 Ch. 26. 28 Saul the son of Kish, and A. the son of
27. 21 of Benjamin, Jaasiel the son of A.

ABOARD, to go—
To go on or upon, ἐπιβαίνω *epibainō.*
Acts 21. 2 finding a ship..we went aboard, and set

ABODE—
Home, mansion, permanent place, μονή *monē.*
John 14. 23 will come unto him, and make our abode

ABOLISH, to—
1. *To change, pass on or away,* חָלַף *chalaph.*
Isa. 2. 18 And the idols he shall utterly abolish
2. *To make thoroughly inactive,* καταργέω, *katargeō.*
2 Co. 3. 13 look to the end of that which is abolished
Eph. 2. 15 Having abolished in his flesh the enmity
2 Ti. 1. 10 Jesus Christ, who hath abolished death

ABOLISHED, to be —
1. *To be broken down, cast down,* חָתַת *chathath,* 2.
Isa. 51. 6 my righteousness shall not be abolished
2. *To wipe away, blot out,* מָחָה *machah,* 2.
Eze. 6. 6 and your works may be abolished

ABOMINABLE—
1. *Indignation (worthy of),* זַעַם *zaam.*
Mic. 6. 10 the scant measure (that is) abominable?
2. *Abominable, impure thing,* פִּגּוּל *piggul.*
Lev. 19. 7 on the third day, (it) is abominable
Isa. 65. 4 broth of abominable (things is in) their
Eze. 4. 14 neither came there abominable flesh into
3. *Abominable, detestable thing,* שֶׁקֶץ *sheqets.*
Lev. 7 21 unclean beast, or any abominable unclean
Eze. 8. 10 behold every form of..abominable beasts
4. *To be abominable,* תָּעַב *taab,* 2.
Job 15. 16 How much more abominable and filthy (is)
Isa. 14. 19 cast out of thy grave like an abominable
5. *Without law, unlawful,* ἀθέμιτος *a-themitos.*
1 Pe. 4. 3 we walked in..abominable idolatries
6. *Abominable, disgusting,* βδελυκτός *bdeluktos.*
Titus 1. 16 in works..deny (him), being abominable

ABOMINABLE, to be—
1. *To be abominable,* תָּעַב *taab,* 2.
1 Ch. 21. 6 for the king's word was abominable to
2. *To abominate,* βδελύσσομαι *bdelussomai.*
Rev. 21. 8 But the..abominable..shall have their

ABOMINABLE, to commit more—
To do abominably, תָּעַב *taab,* 5.
Eze. 16. 52 thou hast committed more abominable

ABOMINABLE CUSTOM—
Abomination, תּוֹעֵבָה *toebah.*
Lev. 18. 30 commit not..of these abominable customs

ABOMINABLE, to do—
To do abominably, תָּעַב *taab,* 5.
Psa. 14. 1 they have done abominable works
53. 1 and have done abominable iniquity

ABOMINABLE FILTH—
Abominable, detestable thing, שִׁקּוּץ *shiqquts.*
Nah. 3. 6 And I will cast abominable filth upon

ABOMINABLE IDOLS—
Abominable, detestable thing, שִׁקּוּץ *shiqquts.*
2 Ch. 15. 8 and put away the abominable idols out of

ABOMINABLE, to make—
To act abominably, שָׁקַץ *shaqats,* 3.
Lev. 11. 43 Ye shall not make yourselves abominable
20. 25 ye shall not make your souls abominable

ABOMINABLE thing—
1 *Abominable, impure thing,* פִּגּוּל *piggul.*
Isa. 65. 4 and broth of abominable (things is in) their
2. *Abomination,* תּוֹעֵבָה *toebah.*
Deut 14. 3 Thou shalt not eat any abominable thing
Jer. 16. 18 carcases of their..abominable things
44. 4 Oh, do not this abominable thing that I

ABOMINABLY, to do—
To do abominably, תָּעַב *taab,* 5.
1 Ki. 21. 26 And he did very abominably in following

ABOMINATION—
1. *Abominable, impure thing,* פִּגּוּל *piggul.*
Lev. 7. 18 it shall be an abomination, and the
2. *Abominable, detestable thing,* שִׁקּוּץ *shiqquts.*
Deut. 29. 17 And ye have seen their abominations
1 Ki. 11. 5 For Solomon went after..the ab. of
11. 7 the abomination of Moab, in the hill
11. 7 the abomination of the children of A.
2 Ki. 23. 13 the abomination of the..the abomination
23. 24 and all the abominations that were spied
Isa. 66. 3 their soul delighteth in their abominations
Jer. 4. 1 if thou wilt put away thine abominations
7. 30 they have set their abominations in the
13. 27 thine abominations on the hills in
32. 34 But they set their abominations in the
Eze. 5. 11 [and with all thine abominations, therefore]
20. 7 Cast ye away every man the abominations
20. 8 every man cast away the abominations of
20. 30 and commit ye whoredom after their ab.
Dan. 9. 27 for the overspreading of abominations he
11. 31 they shall place the abomination that
12. 11 and the abomination that maketh desolate
Hos. 9. 10 and (their) abominations were according
Zech. 9. 7 And I will take away..his abominations
3. *Abomination, detestation,* שֶׁקֶץ *sheqets.*
Lev. 11. 10 they (shall be) an abomination unto you
11. 11 abomination..ye shall have..in abomina.
11. 12 that (shall be) an abomination unto you
11. 13 and these..ye shall have in abomination
11. 20 All..that creep..(shall be) an abomination
11. 23 But all (other)..(shall be) an abomination
11. 41 every creeping thing..(shall be) an abom.
11. 42 for they (are) an abomination Isa. 66. 17.
4. *Abomination,* תּוֹעֵבָה *toebah.*
Gen. 43. 32 for that (is) an abomination unto the
46. 34 for every shepherd (is) an abomination
Exod. 8. 26 we shall sacrifice the abomination of the
8. 26 shall we sacrifice the abomination of the
Lev. 18. 22 Thou shalt not lie with mankind..abom.
18. 26 and shall not commit (any) of these ab.
18. 27 For all these abominations have the men
18. 29 whosoever shall commit any of these ab.
20. 13 both of them have committed an ab.
Deut. 7. 25 for it (is) an abomination to the LORD thy
7. 26 Neither shalt thou bring an abomination
12. 31 for every abomination to the LORD, which
13. 14 (that) such abomination is wrought
17. 1 for that (is) an abomination unto the LORD
17. 4 (that) such abomination is wrought in
18. 9 to do after the abominations of those
18. 12 all that do these things (are) an ab.
18. 12 because of these abominations the LORD
20. 18 not to do after all their abominations
22. 5 all that do so (are) abomination unto
23. 18 these (are) abomination unto the LORD
24. 4 for that (is) abomination before the LORD
25. 16 (are) an abomination unto the LORD thy
27. 15 Cursed (be) the man that maketh..an ab.
32. 16 with abominations provoked they him to
1 Ki. 14. 24 according to all the abominations of the
2 Ki. 16. 3 according to the abominations of the
21. 2 after the abominations of the heathen
21. 11 hath done these abominations, (and) hath
23. 13 the abomination of..the abomination of
2 Ch. 28. 3 after the abominations of the heathen
33. 2 like unto the abominations of the heathen
34. 33 And Josiah took away all the abominations
36. 8 and his abominations which he did, and

2 Ch. 36. 14 after all the abominations of the heathen
Ezra 9. 1 (doing) according to their abominations
9. 11 with their abominations, which have
9. 14 people of these abominations? wouldest
Psa. 88. 8 thou hast made me an abomination unto
Prov. 3. 32 For the froward (is) abomination to the
6. 16 seven (are) an abomination unto him
8. 7 and wickedness (is) an abomination to
11. 1 A false balance (is) abomination to the
11. 20 They..of a froward heart (are) ab. to the
12. 22 Lying lips (are) abomination to the LORD
13. 19 but (it is) abomination to fools to depart
15. 8 the wicked (is) an abomination to the
15. 9 The way of the wicked (is) an abomination
15. 26 The thoughts of the wicked (are) an ab.
16. 5 one (that is) proud in heart (is) an ab.
16. 12 (It is) an abomination to kings to
17. 15 even they both (are) abomination to the
20. 10 both of them (are) alike abomination to
20. 23 Divers weights (are) an abomination unto
21. 27 The sacrifice of the wicked (is) ab.
24. 9 the scorner (is) an abomination to men
26. 25 (there are) seven abominations in his
28. 9 even his prayer (shall be) abomination
29. 27 An unjust man (is) an abomination to the
29. 27 upright in the way (is) abomination to
Isa. 1. 13 incense is an abomination unto me
41. 24 an abomination (is he that) chooseth you
44. 19 shall I make the residue thereof an ab.?
Jer. 2. 7 and made mine heritage an abomination
6. 15 ashamed when they had committed ab.
7. 10 We are delivered to do all these ab.
8. 12 ashamed when they had committed ab.
32. 35 that they should do this abomination
44. 22 because of the abominations which ye
Eze. 5. 9 I will not..because of all thine ab.
5. 11 and with all thine abominations, therefore
6. 9 for the evils..in all their abominations
6. 11 Alas for all the evil abominations of the
7. 3 will recompense upon thee all thine ab.
7. 4 and thine abominations shall be in the
7. 8 will recompense thee for all thine ab.
7. 9 thine abominations (that) are in the
7. 20 but they made the images of their ab.
8. 6 (even) the great abominations that the
8. 6 thou shalt see greater abominations
8. 9 behold the wicked abominations that
8. 13 thou shalt see greater abominations
8. 15 thou shalt see greater abominations than
8. 17 a light thing..that they commit the ab.
9. 4 cry for all the abominations that be
11. 18 and all the abominations thereof from
11. 21 and their abominations, I will recompense
12. 16 that they may declare all their ab.
14. 6 turn away your faces from all your ab.
16. 2 cause Jerusalem to know her abominations
16. 22 And in all thine abominations and thy
16. 36 with all the idols of thy abominations
16. 43 lewdness above all thine abominations
16. 47 nor done after their abominations: but
16. 50 and committed abomination before me
16. 51 thine abominations..thine abominations
16. 58 Thou hast borne..thine abominations
18. 12 his eyes to the idols, hath committed ab.
18. 13 he hath done all these abominations; he
18. 24 doeth according to all the abominations
20. 4 cause them to know the abominations
22. 2 yea, thou shalt show her all her ab.
22. 11 And one hath committed abomination
23. 36 yea, declare unto them their abominations
33. 26 ye work abomination, and ye defile every
33. 29 because of all their abominations which
36. 31 your iniquities and for your abominations
43. 8 by their abominations that they have
44. 6 let it suffice you of all your abominations
44. 7 they have broken..because of all your ab.
44. 13 and their abominations which they have
Mal. 2. 11 and an abomination is committed in

5. *Abomination*, βδέλυγμα *bdelugma*.
Matt 24. 15 shall see the abomination of desolation
Mark 13. 14 ye shall see the abomination of
Luke 16. 15 esteemed among men is abomination
Rev. 17. 4 having a golden cup..full of abominations
17. 5 the mother of harlots and abominations
21. 27 that defileth, neither..worketh abomina.

ABOMINATION, to be had in—
To be stinking, abhorred, בָּאַשׁ *baash* 2.
1 Sa. 13. 4 (that) Israel also was had in abomination

ABOMINATION, to have in—
To make detestable, שָׁקַץ *shaqats*, 3.
Lev. 11. 11 shall have their carcases in abomination

ABOUND, to—
1. *Many, much, enough*, רַב *rab*.
Prov 28. 20 A faithful man shall abound with
29. 22 and a furious man aboundeth in

2. *To be, become, make more*, πλεονάζω *pleonazō*.
Rom. 5. 20 offence might abound. But where sin ab.
6. 1 continue in sin, that grace may abound?
Phil. 4. 17 fruit that may abound to your account
2 Th. 1. 3 the charity of..toward each other ab.
2 Pe. 1. 8 if these things be in you, and abound

3. *To be multiplied*, πληθύνω *plēthunō*.
Matt. 24. 12 And because iniquity shall abound, the

4. *To be over and above*, περισσεύω *perisseuō*.
Rom. 5. 15 the grace of God..hath abounded unto
15. 13 that ye may abound in hope, through the
1 Co. 15. 58 always abounding in the work of the
2 Co. 1. 5 For as the sufferings of Christ abound in
1. 5 consolation also aboundeth by Christ
8. 2 abounded unto the riches of their
8. 7 Therefore, as ye abound in every(thing, in)
8. 7 (see) that ye abound in this grace also
9. 8 that ye..may abound to every good work
Eph. 1. 8 Wherein he hath abounded toward us in
Phil. 1. 9 that your love may abound yet more and
4. 12 I know how to abound..both to abound
4. 18 But I have all, and abound: I am
Col. 2. 7 abounding therein with thanksgiving
1 Th. 4. 1 (so) ye would abound more and more

ABOUND, to make—
To be over and above, περισσεύω *perisseuō*.
2 Co. 9. 8 God (is) able to make all grace abound
1 Th. 3. 12 make you to..abound in love one

ABOUND, to more—
To be over and above, περισσεύω *perisseuō*.
Rom. 3. 7 if the truth of God hath more abounded

ABOUND, to much more—
To be over abundant, ὑπερπερισσεύω *hupcrperisseuō*.
Rom. 5 20 sin abounded, grace did much more ab.

ABOUNDING with—
To be, or become heavy, כָּבֵד *kabed*, 2.
Prov. 8. 24 when..no fountains abounding with

ABOUT (*Prep.*)—
1. *Unto, to*, אֶל *el*.
2 Ki. 11. 7 even they shall keep the watch..about

2. *For, in behalf of*, בְּעַד *bead*.
Job 1. 10 about him, and about his house, and about
Psa. 139. 11 even the night shall be light about me

3. *Before, in presence of*, נֶגֶד *neged*.
Neh. 13. 21 Why lodge ye about the wall? if ye do

4. *Round about, around*, סָבִיב *sabib*.
Num. 2. 2 far off about the tabernacle of the
16. 24 Get you up from about the tabernacle of
Deut. 17. 14 like as all the nations that (are) about
2 Sa. 24. 6 they came to Dan-jaan, and about to
1 Ki. 7. 23 round all about, and his height (was)
18. 32 he made a trench about the altar, as
Ezra 1. 6 they that (were) about them strengthened
Neh. 5. 17 from among the heathen that (are) about
6. 16 the heathen that (were) about us saw
Job 29. 5 with me, (when) my children (were) about
Psa. 89. 7 reverence of all..(that are) about him
Song 3. 7 threescore valiant men (are) about it, of
Jer. 17. 26 and from the places about Jerusalem,
32. 44 and in the places about Jerusalem, and
33. 13 and in the places about Jerusalem, and
48. 17 All ye that are about him, bemoan him
48. 39 so shall Moab be..to all them about him
49. 5 from all those that be about thee; and
Eze. 1. 4 and a brightness (was) about it, and out
5. 2 smite about it with a knife: and a
12. 14 I will scatter..all that (are) about him
32. 22 his graves (are) about him: all of them
36. 7 Surely the heathen that (are) about you
43. 17 and the border about it (shall be) half a
43. 17 bottom thereof (shall be) a cubit about
Dan. 9. 16 a reproach to all (that are) about us

5. *On, upon, over*, עַל *al*.
Dan. 5. 7 and (have) a chain of gold about his neck
5. 16 and (have) a chain of gold about thy neck
5. 29 and (put) a chain of gold about his neck
[*See also* Beset, bind, bounds, bring, carried, carry, cast, come, compass, fence, fetch, gad, give, go, go round, going, gone, lead, places, round, scatter, set, turn, turned, walk, whirl, winding, wrapped.]

6. *In among, by, with*, ἐν *en*.
Luke 2. 49 that I must be about my Father's business?

7. *On, upon, over*, ἐπί *epi* (*g. d. ac.*)
Matt 18. 6 a millstone were hanged about his neck
Mark 14. 51 a linen cloth cast about (his) naked (body)
John 20. 7 the napkin, that was about his head
Acts 11. 19 the persecution that arose about Stephen

8. *About*, κατά *kata*. (*ac.*)
Acts 2. 10 and in the parts of Libya about Cyrene
12. 1 Now about that time Herod the king
27. 27 about midnight the shipmen deemed that

9. *Around, about*, περί *peri* (*ac. g.*)
Matt. 3. 4 and a leathern girdle about his loins
8. 18 Jesus saw great multitudes about him
20. 3 And he went out about the third hour
20. 5 Again he went out about the sixth and
20. 6 And about the eleventh hour he went out
20. 9 that (were hired) about the eleventh hour
27. 46 And about the ninth hour Jesus cried
Mark 1. 6 with a girdle of a skin about his loins
3. 8 and they about Tyre and Sidon, a great
3. 32 And the multitude sat about him, and
3. 34 on them which sat about him, and said
6. 48 and about the fourth watch of the night
9. 14 he saw a great multitude about them
9. 42 a millstone were hanged about his neck
Luke 10. 40 Martha was cumbered about much serving
10. 41 careful and troubled about many things
13. 8 till I shall dig about it, and dung (it)
17. 2 a millstone were hanged about his neck
John 3. 25 of John's disciples and the Jews about
Acts 10. 9 went up..to pray about the sixth hour
Acts 15. 2 the apostles and elders about this question
19. 23 there arose no small stir about that way
22. 6 about noon..a great light round about
25. 15 About whom, when I was at Jerusalem
25. 24 about whom all the multitude of the Jews
1 Ti. 6. 4 but doting about questions and strifes
Jude 7 and the cities about them in like manner
9 he disputed about the body of Moses

(*About, they that were*, οἱ περί *hoi peri*).
Mark 4. 10 they that were about him with the twelve
Luke 22. 49 When they which were about him saw

10. *Towards*, πρός *pros* (*d. ac.*)
Mark 2. 2 not so much as about the door: and he
Rev. 1. 13 girt about the paps with a golden girdle

11. *From round about*, κυκλόθεν *kuklothen*.
Rev. 4. 8 had each of them six wings about (him)

ABOUT (*adv.*):—
1. *Somewhere*, πού *pou*.
Rom. 4. 19 when he was about an hundred years old

2. *As, so as*, ὡς *hōs*.
Mark 5. 13 (they were about two thousand;) and were
8. 9 that had eaten were about four thousand
Luke 2. 37 a widow of about fourscore and four years
8. 42 only daughter, about twelve years of age
John 1. 39 abode..for it was about the tenth hour
6. 19 rowed about five and twenty or thirty fur.
11. 18 Bethany was..about fifteen furlongs off
Acts 1. 15 together were about an hundred and
5. 7 about the space of three hours after, when
13. 18 And about the time of forty years suffered
13. 20 about the space of four hundred and fifty
19. 34 about the space of two hours cried out
Rev. 8. 1 silence..about the space of half an hour
16. 21 (every stone) about the weight of a talent

3. *As if, as though*, ὡσεί *hōsei*.
Matt 14. 21 were about five thousand men
Mark 6. 44 that did eat were [about] five thousand
Luke 1. 56 Mary abode with her about three months
3. 23 began to be about thirty years of age
9. 14 they were about five thousand men.
9. 28 about an eight days after these sayings
22. 41 withdrawn from them about a stone's cast
22. 59 about the space of one hour after another
23. 44 And it was about the sixth hour, and
John 4. 6 it was about the sixth hour
6. 10 the men sat down, in number about five
19. 14 it was..about the sixth hour, and he
19. 39 Nicodemus..brought..about an hundred
Acts 2. 41 there were added..about three thousand
4. 4 number of the men was about five
5. 36 a number of men, about four hundred
10. 3 He saw..about the ninth hour of the day
19. 7 And all the men were about twelve
[*See also* under Bear, bound, carry, cast, come, compass, country, gird, go, hang, lead, minister, put round, turn, walk.]

ABOUT, to go—
To go round about, surround, סָבַב *sabab*.
2 Ki. 3. 25 the slingers went about (it), and smote it
2 Ch. 17. 9 and went about throughout all the cities
23. 2 And they went about in Judah, and
Eccl. 2. 20 Therefore I went about to cause my
12. 5 and the mourners go about the streets
Song 3. 3 The watchmen that go about the city
5. 7 The watchmen that went about the city
Isa. 23. 16 Take an harp, go about the city, thou

ABOUT, to make—
To go round about, surround, סָבַב *sabab*, 5.
2 Ch. 14. 7 build these cities, and make about (them)

ABOUT on every side, to be—
To be round about, surround, סָבַב *sabab*.
1 Ki. 5. 3 wars which were about him on every side

ABOUT, to be—
To seek, desire, ζητέω *zēteō*.
Acts 27. 30 shipmen were about to flee out of the

ABOUT THE TIME—
Upon, on, over, ἐπί *epi* (*g.*)
Matt. 1. 11 about the time they were carried away to

ABOUT, (there)—
Concerning this, περὶ τούτου *peri toutou*.
Luke 24. 4 they were much perplexed thereabout

ABOUT, to be—
To be on the point of, delay, μέλλω *mellō*.
Acts 3. 3 seeing Peter and John about to go into
18. 14 Paul was now about to open (his) mouth
20. 3 as he was about to sail into Syria, he
Heb. 8. 5 when he was about to make the
Rev. 10. 4 I was about to write: and I heard a voice

ABOVE—
1. *From, out of*, מִן *min*.
Lev. 9. 10 the kidneys, and the caul above the liver

2. *At above* (adv.), מִמַּעַל, לְמַעְלָה, etc. [*maal*].
Gen. 6. 16 in a cubit shalt thou finish it above
Exod 20. 4 (of any thing) that (is) in heaven above
25. 21 thou shalt put the mercy seat above
26. 14 and a covering above (of) badgers' skins
28. 27 over against the (other) coupling..above
30. 14 one..from twenty years old and above
36. 19 a covering (of) badgers' skins above (that)
39. 20 over against the (other) coupling..above

Exod40. 19 put the covering of the tent above upon
40. 20 put the mercy seat above upon the ark
Lev. 11. 21 which have legs above their feet, to leap
27. 7 And if..from sixty years old and above
Num. 4. 25 the badgers' skins..above upon it
Deut. 4. 39 he (is) God in heaven above, and upon
5. 8 (of anything) that (is) in heaven above
28. 13 thou shalt be above only, and thou shalt
Josh. 2. 11 your God, he (is) God in heaven above
1 Ki. 7. 3 covered with cedar above upon the
7. 11 And above (were) costly stones, after the
7. 20 chapiters..(had pomegranates) also above
7. 25 and the sea (was set) above upon them
7. 29 upon the ledges..a base above: and
7. 31 within the chapiter and above (was) a
8. 7 covered the..staves thereof above
8. 23 no God like thee, in heaven above, or on
1 Ch. 23. 27 from twenty years old and above
2 Ch. 4. 4 and the sea (was set) above upon them
5. 8 covered the..staves thereof above
25. 5 from twenty years old and above
Job 18. 16 and above shall his branch be cut off
31. 28 have denied the God (that is) above
Prov. 8. 28 When he established the clouds above
15. 24 The way of life (is) above to the wise
Isa. 6. 2 Above it stood the seraphims: each one
7. 11 in the depth, or in the height above
14. 13 I will exalt my throne above the stars of
Jer. 4. 28 For this shall the..heaven above be
31. 37 Thus saith the LORD; If heaven above
35. 4 which (was) above the chamber of M.
52. 32 spake kindly..and set his throne above
Eze. 1. 22 stretched forth over their heads above
1. 26 And above the firmament that (was) over
1. 26 as the appearance of a man above upon it
10. 19 the God of Israel (was) over them above
11. 22 the God of Israel (was) over them above
37. 8 skin covered them above: but (there was)

3. *More,* πλείων *pleiōn.*
Acts. 4. 22 the man was above forty years old, on

4. *Above, up, upwards,* ἄνω *anō.*
John 8. 23 I am from above: ye are of this world; I
Acts 2. 19 I will show wonders in heaven above
Gal. 4. 26 Jerusalem which is above is free, which
Col. 3. 1 seek those things which are above, where
3. 2 Set your affection on things above, not on

5. *Above, superior to,* ἐπάνω *epanō.*
John 3. 31 He that cometh...is above all...above all
1 Co. 15. 6 seen of above five hundred breth. at once

6. *Higher up,* ἀνώτερον *anōteron.*
Heb. 10. 8 Above when he said, Sacrifice and offering

7. *Upon, on, over,* ἐπί *epi (g. d. ac.)*
Luke 3. 20 Added this yet above all, that he shut
Eph. 4. 6 who (is) above all, and through all, and
6. 16 [Above] all, taking the shield of faith
Col. 3. 14 And above all these things (put on)
2 Th. 2. 4 exalteth himself above all that is called

8. *Alongside of, beside,* παρά *para (ac.)*
Luke 13. 2 were sinners above all the Galileans
13. 4 sinners above all men that dwelt in
Rom 14. 5 One man esteemeth one day above another
Heb. 1. 9 God, hath anointed thee..above thy

9. *Around,* περί *peri (g.)*
3 Jo. 2 I wish above all things that thou

10. *Before,* πρό *pro.*
2 Co. 12. 2 a man in Christ above fourteen; Ja. 5. 12.
1 Pe. 4. 8 above all things have fervent charity

11. *Over, above, in behalf of,* ὑπέρ *huper (ac.)*
Matt 10. 24 disciple is not above..the servant above
Luke 6. 40 The disciple is not above his master: but
Acts 26. 13 above the brightness of the sun, shining
1 Co. 4. 6 not to think (of men) above that which is
10. 13 suffer you to be tempted above that ye
2 Co. 1. 8 were pressed out of measure, above
12. 6 think of me above that which he seeth
Gal. 1. 14 profited..above many my equals in
Eph. 3. 20 able to do..above all that we ask or think
Phil. 2. 9 a name which is above every name
Phm. 16 Not now as a servant, but above a servant
[*See also* Abundantly, far, measure.]

ABOVE, far —
A height, high place, מָרוֹם *marom.*
Psa. 10. 5 thy judgments (are) far above out of his

ABOVE, from —
1. *From above,* מִלְמַעְלָה, מִמַּעַל *mi-le-maalah, mim-maal*
Josh. 3. 13 the waters that come down from above
3. 16 the waters which came down from above
Job 3. 4 let not God regard it from above
31. 2 what portion of God (is there) from above?
Psa. 78. 23 he had commanded the clouds from above
Isa. 45. 8 Drop down, ye heavens, from above, and
Amos 2. 9 I destroyed his fruit from above, and his

2. *From a height, high place,* מִמָּרוֹם *mim-marom.*
2 Sa. 22. 17 He sent from above, he took me; he drew
Psa. 18. 16 He sent from above, he took me; he drew
144. 7 Send thine hand from above; rid me, and
Lam. 1. 13 From above hath he sent fire into my

3. *From above,* ἄνωθεν *anōthen.*
John 3. 31 He that cometh from above is above all
19. 11 except it were given thee from above
Jas. 1. 17 every perfect gift is from above, and
3. 15 This wisdom descendeth not from above
3. 17 the wisdom that is from above is first

AB-RA'HAM, אַבְרָהָם *father of a multitude.*

The name given to ABRAM when the promise of a numerous progeny was renewed to him by God. He was the youngest son of Terah, and born 1996 B.C., and died at the age of 175, B.C. 1821. A native of Ur of the Chaldees, and descended through Heber in the 9th generation from Shem the eldest son of Noah, he was the progenitor of the Hebrews, and of several cognate tribes.

Gen. 17. 5 thy name shall be A.; for a father of
17. 9 And God said unto A.; Thou shalt keep
17. 15 And God said unto A., As for Sarai
17. 17 Then A. fell upon his face, and laughed
17. 18 And A. said unto God, Oh that Ishmael
17. 22 and God went up from A.
17. 23 And A. took Ishmael his son, and all that
17. 23 every male among the men of A's house
17. 24 And A. (was) ninety years old and nine
17. 26 In the selfsame day was A. circumcised
18. 6 A. hastened into the tent unto Sarah
18. 7 And A. ran unto the herd, and fetcht a
18. 11 Now A. and Sarah (were) old (and) well
18. 13 the LORD said unto A., Wherefore did Sarah
18. 16 and A. went with them to bring them on the
18. 17 Shall I hide from A. that thing which I do
18. 18 Seeing that A. shall surely become a great
18. 19 that the LORD may bring upon A. that
18. 22 the men turned their faces..but A. stood
18. 23 And A. drew near, and said, Wilt thou
18. 27 And A. answered and said, Behold now
18. 33 as soon as he had left communing with A.
18. 33 and A. returned unto his place
19. 27 A. gat up early in the morning to the
19. 29 God remembered A., and sent Lot out of
20. 1 A. journeyed from thence toward the south
20. 2 A. said of Sarah his wife, She (is) my
20. 9 Then Abimelech called A., and said unto
20. 10 And Abimelech said unto A., What sawest
20. 11 And A. said, Because I thought, Surely the
20. 14 Abimelech took sheep..and gave..unto A.
20. 17 So A. prayed unto God: and God healed
20. 18 because of Sarah A.'s wife
21. 2 and bare A. a son in his old age
21. 3 A. called the name of his son that was born
21. 4 And A. circumcised his son Isaac
21. 5 A. was an hundred years old, when his
21. 7 Who would have said unto A., that Sarah
21. 8 A. made a great feast the (same) day that
21. 9 which she had born unto A., mocking
21. 10 Wherefore she said unto A., Cast
21. 11 the thing was very grievous in A.'s sight
21. 12 God said unto A., Let it not be grievous
21. 14 A. rose up early in the morning
21. 22 spake unto A., saying, God (is) with
21. 24 And A. said, I will swear
21. 25 And A. reproved Abimelech because
21. 27 A. took sheep and oxen, and gave
21. 28 And A. set seven ewe-lambs of the
21. 29 Abimelech said unto A., What (mean)
21. 33 And [A.] planted a grove in Beersheba
21. 34 A. sojourned in the Philistines' land
22. 1 God did tempt A. and said unto him, A.
22. 3 And A. rose up early in the morning
22. 4 Then on the third day A. lifted up
22. 5 A. said unto his young men, Abide
22. 6 A. took the wood of the burnt-offering
22. 7 Isaac spake unto A. his father, and said
22. 8 A. said, My son, God will provide himself
22. 9 and A. built an altar there, and laid the
22. 10 A. stretched forth his hand, and took
22. 11 and said, A., A.: and he said, Here (am) I
22. 13 And A. lifted up his eyes, and looked
22. 13 and A...took the ram, and offered him
22. 14 And A... called the name of that place
22. 15 the angel of the LORD called unto A. out of
22. 19 So A. returned unto his young men, and
22. 19 to Beersheba; and A. dwelt at Beersheba
22. 20 it was told A., saying, Behold, Milcah
22. 23 Milcah did bear to Nahor, A.'s brother
23. 2 and A. came to mourn for Sarah, and to
23. 3 And A. stood up from before his dead
23. 5 the children of Heth answered A., saying
23. 7 And A. stood up, and bowed himself to
23. 10 Ephron the Hittite answered A. in the
23. 12 And A. bowed down himself before the
23. 14 Ephron answered A., saying unto him
23. 16 And A. hearkened unto Ephron
23. 16 and A. weighed to Ephron the silver
23. 18 Unto A. for a possession in the presence of
23. 19 A. buried Sarah his wife in the cave of
23. 20 were made sure unto A. for a possession
24. 1 And A. was old, (and) well stricken in
24. 1 the LORD had blessed A. in all things
24. 2 And A. said unto his eldest servant of
24. 6 And A. said unto him, Beware thou
24. 9 put his hand under the thigh of A. his
24. 12 O LORD God of my master A., I pray
24. 12 shew kindness unto my master A.
24. 15 Milcah, the wife of Nahor, A.'s brother
24. 27 Blessed (be) the LORD God of my master A.
24. 34 And he said, I (am) A.'s servant
24. 42 O LORD God of my master A., if now
24. 48 and blessed the LORD God of my master A.
24. 52 when A.'s servant heard their words, he
24. 59 they sent away Rebekah..and A.'s servant,
25. 1 Then again A. took a wife, and her name
25. 5 And A. gave all that he had unto Isaac.
25. 6 unto the sons..which A. had, A. gave gifts
25. 7 these (are) the days..of A.'s life which he
25. 8 Then A. gave up the ghost, and died in a
25. 10 The field which A. purchased of the sons of

Gen. 25. 10 there was A. buried, and Sarah his wife
25. 11 it came to pass after the death of A.
25. 12 these (are) the generations of Ishmael, A.'s
25. 12 son, whom Hagar..bare unto A.
25. 19 these (are) the generations of Isaac, A.'s
26. 1 the first famine that was in the days of A.
26. 3 I will perform the oath which I sware unto A.
26. 5 Because that A. obeyed my voice, and kept
26. 15 father's servants had digged in the days of A.
26. 18 which they had digged in the days of A. his
26. 18 Philistines..stopped..after the death of A.
26. 24 I (am) the God of A. thy father: fear not
26. 24 will bless thee..for my servant A.'s sake
28. 4 give thee the blessing of A., to thee, and t
28. 4 mayest inherit the land..God gave unto A.
28. 9 Esau..took..the daughter of Ishmael A.'s
28. 13 I (am) the LORD God of A. thy father, and
31. 42 the God of my father, the God of A.
31. 53 The God of A., and the God of Nahor, the
32. 9 And Jacob said, O God of my father A.
35. 12 And the land which I gave A. and Isaac
35. 27 Hebron, where A. and Isaac sojourned
48. 15 before whom my fathers A. and Isaac did
48. 16 and the name of my fathers A. and Isaac
49. 30 which A. bought with the field of Ephron
49. 31 There they buried A. and Sarah his wife
50. 13 which A. bought with the field for a
50. 24 unto the land which he sware to A.
Exod. 2. 24 God remembered his covenant with A.
3. 6 I (am) the God of thy father, the God of A.
3. 15 The LORD God of your fathers, the God of A.
3. 16 the God of A...appeared unto me, saying
4. 5 the God of A...hath appeared unto thee
6. 3 And I appeared unto A., unto Isaac, to
6. 8 which I did swear to give it to A.
32. 13 Remember A., Isaac, and Israel, thy
33. 1 unto the land which I sware unto A.
Lev. 26. 42 Then will I remember..my covenant with A.
Num. 32. 11 shall see the land which I sware unto A.
Deut. 1. 8 the LORD sware unto your fathers, A.
6. 10 which he sware unto thy fathers, to A.
9. 5 which the LORD sware unto thy fathers, A.
9. 27 Remember thy servants, A., Isaac, and
29. 13 as he hath sworn unto thy fathers, to A.
30. 20 which the LORD sware unto thy fathers, to A.
34. 4 This (is) the land which I sware unto A.
Josh. 24. 2 Terah, the father of A., and the father of
24. 3 And I took your father A. from the other
1 Ki. 18. 36 Elijah the prophet..said, LORD God of A.
2 Ki. 13. 23 because of his covenant with A., Isaac, and
1 Ch. 1. 23-27 sons of Joktan..Abram; the same (is) A.
1. 28 The sons of A.; Isaac, and Ishmael
1. 32 Now the sons of Keturah, A.'s concubine
1. 34 And A. begat Isaac
16. 16 (Even of the covenant) which he made with A.
29. 18 O LORD God of A., Isaac, and of Israel, our
2 Ch. 20. 7 and gavest it to the seed of A. thy friend
30. 6 turn again unto the LORD God of A.,
Neh. 9. 7 Thou (art)..the God who didst choose A.
Psa. 47. 9 the people of the God of A.: for the shields
105. 6 O ye seed of A. his servant, ye children of
105. 9 Which (covenant) he made with A., and his
105. 42 remembered his holy promise, (and) A. his
Isa. 29. 22 thus saith the LORD, who redeemed A.
41. 8 But thou, Israel,..the seed of A. my friend
51. 2 Look unto A. your father, and unto Sarah
63. 16 Doubtless thou (art) our father, though A.
Jer. 33. 26 I will not..(to be) rulers over the seed of A.
Eze. 33. 24 A. was one, and he inherited the land
Mic. 7. 20 the mercy to A., which thou hast sworn
Matt. 1. 1 Jesus Christ, the son of David, the son of A.
1. 2 A. begat Isaac; and Isaac begat Jacob
1. 17 all the generations from A. to David (are)
3. 9 We have A. to our father: for I say unto
3. 9 God is able..to raise up children unto A.
8. 11 many..shall sit down with A., and Isaac
22. 32 I am the God of A., and the God of Isaac
Mark 12. 26 God spake..saying, I (am) the God of A.
Luke 1. 55 As he spake to our fathers, to A., and to
1. 73 The oath which he sware to our father A.
3. 8 We have A. to (our) father: for I say unto you
3. 8 God is able..to raise up children unto A.
3. 23-34 Jesus..being..son of Joseph..(son) of A.
13. 16 this woman, being a daughter of A., whom
13. 28 when ye shall see A., and Isaac, and
16. 22 carried by the angels into A.'s bosom
16. 23 lifted up his eyes..and seeth A. afar off
16. 24 he cried and said, Father A., have mercy
16. 25 But A. said, Son, remember that thou
16. 29 A. saith unto him, They have Moses and
16. 30 And he said, Nay, father A.: but if
19. 9 forsomuch as he also is a son of A.
20. 37 when he calleth the Lord the God of A.
John 8. 33 We be A.'s seed, and were never in
8. 37 I know that ye are A.'s seed; but
8. 39 They answered and said unto him, A. is
8. 39 Jesus saith..If ye were A.'s children
8. 39 Ye would do the works of A.
8. 40 Ye seek to kill me..this did not A.
8. 52 A. is dead, and the prophets; and thou
8. 53 Art thou greater than our father A.
8. 56 Your father A. rejoiced to see my day
8. 57 Thou art not yet..hast thou seen A.?
8. 58 Jesus said..Before A. was, I am
Acts 3. 13 The God of A...hath glorified his Son
3. 25 covenant which God made..saying unto A.
7. 2 God of glory appeared unto our father A.
7. 8 so [A.] begat Isaac, and circumcised him
7. 16 the sepulchre that A. bought for
7. 17 the promise..which God had sworn to A.
7. 32 the God of thy fathers, the God of A.
13. 26 children of the stock of A., and whosoever

Rom. 4. 1 What shall we then say that A., our father
4. 2 For if A. were justified by works, he hath
4. 3 A. believed God; and it was counted unto
4. 9 we say that faith was reckoned to A.
4. 12 in the steps of that faith of our father A.
4. 13 For the promise..not to A., or to his seed
4. 16 to that also which is of the faith of A.
9. 7 Neither, because they are the seed of A.
11. 1 I also am an Israelite, of the seed of A.
2 Co. 11. 22 Are they the seed of A.? so (am) I
Gal. 3. 6 Even as A. believed God, and it was ac.
3. 7 the same are the children of A.
3. 8 scripture..preached..the gospel unto A.
3. 9 which be of faith are blessed with..A.
3. 14 That the blessing of A. might come on the
3. 16 Now to A. and his seed were the promises
3. 18 but God gave (it) to A. by promise
3. 29 If ye (be) Christ's then are ye A.'s seed
4. 22 it is written, that A. had two sons, the one
Heb. 2. 16 he took on (him) the seed of A.
6. 13 For when God made promise to A., because
7. 1 Melchisedec..met A. returning from the
7. 2 To whom also A. gave a tenth part of all
7. 4 unto whom even the patriarch A. gave the
7. 5 though they come out of the loins of A.
7. 6 But he..received tithes of A., and blessed
7. 9 Levi..receiveth tithes, payed tithes in A.
11. 8 By faith A., when he was called to go out
11. 17 By faith A., when he was tried, offered up
Jas. 2. 21 Was not A. our father justified by works
2. 23 A. believed God, and it was imputed unto
1 Pe. 3. 6 Even as Sarah obeyed A., calling him lord

AB-RAM, אַבְרָם *father of height.*

The original name of *Abraham.*

Gen. 11. 26 Terah lived seventy years, and begat A.
11. 27 Terah begat A., Nahor, and Haran
11. 29 And A. and Nahor took them wives
11. 29 the name of A.'s wife (was) Sarai
11. 31 And Terah took A. his son, and Lot
11. 31 Sarai his daughter in law, his son A.'s
12. 1 the LORD had said unto A., Get thee
12. 4 So A. departed, as the LORD had spoken
12. 4 and A. (was) seventy and five years old
12. 5 And A. took Sarai his wife, and Lot
12. 6 And A. passed through the land unto
12. 7 And the LORD appeared unto A., and
12. 9 And A. journeyed, going on still toward
12. 10 and A. went down into Egypt to sojourn
12. 14 when A. was come into Egypt, the
12. 16 And he entreated A. well for her sake
12. 17 the LORD plagued P..because of Sarai A.'s
12. 18 And Pharaoh called A., and said, What (is)
13. 1 And A. went up out of Egypt, he, and
13. 2 And A. (was) very rich in cattle, in silver
13. 4 and there A. called on the name of the
13. 5 And Lot also, which went with A., had
13. 7 a strife between the herdmen of A.'s
13. 8 And A. said unto Lot, Let there be no
13. 12 A. dwelled in the land of Canaan, and L.
13. 14 And the LORD said unto A., after that
13. 18 Then A. removed (his) tent, and came and
14. 12 And they took Lot, A.'s brother's son
14. 13 came one that had escaped, and told A.
14. 13 and these (were) confederate with A.
14. 14 And when A. heard that his brother was
14. 19 Blessed (be) A. of the most high God
14. 21 the king of Sodom said unto A., Give me
14. 22 And A. said to the king of Sodom, I have
14. 23 lest thou shouldest say, I have made A.
15. 1 the word of the LORD came unto A. in a
15. 1 saying, Fear not, A.: I (am) thy shield
15. 2 And A. said, LORD God, what wilt thou
15. 3 And A. said, Behold, to me thou hast
15. 11 fowls came down upon the carcases, A.
15. 12 was going down, a deep sleep fell upon A.
15. 13 And he said unto A., Know of a surety
15. 18 day the LORD made a covenant with A.
16. 1 Now Sarai A.'s wife bare him no children
16. 2 And Sarai said unto A., Behold now, the
16. 2 And A. hearkened to the voice of Sarai
16. 3 And Sarai A.'s wife took Hagar her maid
16. 3 after A. had dwelt ten years in the land
16. 3 and gave her to her husband A. to be his
16. 5 And Sarai said unto A., My wrong (be)
16. 6 But A. said unto Sarai, Behold, thy maid
16. 15 And Hagar bare A. a son: and A. called
16. 16 And A. (was) fourscore and six years old
16. 16 when Hagar bare Ishmael to A.
17. 1 And when A. was ninety years old and
17. 1 the LORD appeared to A., and said unto
17. 3 And A. fell on his face: and God talked
17. 5 shall thy name any more be called A.
1 Ch. 1. 27 A.; the same (is) Abraham
Neh. 9. 7 Thou (art) the LORD..who didst choose A.

ABROAD —

1. *The outside, without,* חוּץ *chuts.*

Gen. 15. 5 And he brought him forth abroad, and
19. 17 they had brought them forth abroad
Exod. 12. 46 thou shalt not carry forth ought..abroad
21. 19 If he rise again, and walk abroad upon
Lev. 14. 8 after that he shall..tarry abroad
18. 9 (whether she be) born at home, or born ab.
Deut. 23. 10 then shall he go abroad out of the camp
23. 12 a place..whither thou shalt go..abroad
23. 13 when thou wilt ease thyself abroad, thou
24. 11 Thou shalt stand abroad, and the man to
24. 11 shall bring out the pledge abroad unto
Judg. 12. 9 thirty daughters, (whom) he sent abroad
12. 9 and took in thirty daughters from abroad
1 Sa. 9. 26 went out..he and Samuel, abroad
2 Ki. 4. 3 Go, borrow thee vessels abroad of all thy
2 Ch. 29. 16 Levites took (it), to carry (it) out abroad
Psa. 41. 6 (when) he goeth abroad, he telleth (it)
Prov. 5. 16 Let thy fountains be dispersed abroad
Jer. 6. 11 upon the children abroad, and upon the
Lam. 1. 20 abroad the sword bereaveth, at home
Eze. 34. 21 till ye have scattered them abroad

2. *To break forth,* פָּרַח *parach.*

Lev. 13. 12 if a leprosy break out abroad in the skin,

3. *To break forth or through,* פָּרַץ *parats.*

1 Ch. 13. 2 let us send abroad unto our brethren

[*See also* All, break out, cast, come, far, go, scattered, send, spread, walk, wander.]

4. *To manifest,* εἰς φανερόν *eis phaneron.*

Mark 4. 22 but that it should come abroad.
Luke 8. 17 shall not be known, and come abroad

5. *To become manifest,* φανερὸς γίνομαι [*ginomai*].

Mark 6. 14 for his name was spread abroad

[*See also* Blaze, come, disperse, go, noise, scatter, shed, spread, wander.]

AB-SA'-LOM, אַבְשָׁלוֹם *father of peace.*

Third son of David by his wife Maacah, daughter of Talmai, king of Geshur, B.C. 1000.

2 Sa. 3. 3 and the third, A. the son of Maacah the
13. 1 A. the son of David had a fair sister
13. 4 I love Tamar, my brother A.'s sister
13. 20 A. her brother said unto her, Hath Am.
13. 20 remained desolate in her brother A.'s
13. 22 And A. spake unto his brother Amnon
13. 22 for A. hated Amnon, because he had
13. 23 A. had sheepshearers in Baal-hazor
13. 23 A. invited all the king's sons
13. 24 And A. came to the king, and said
13. 25 the king said to A., Nay, my son, let us
13. 26 Then said A., If not, I pray thee, let my
13. 27 But A. pressed him, that he let Amnon
13. 28 Now A. had commanded his servants
13. 29 the servants of A. did unto Amnon as A.
13. 30 A. hath slain all the king's sons, and
13. 32 for by the appointment of A. this hath
13. 34 But A. fled
13. 37 But A. fled, and went to Talmai, the son
13. 38 So A. fled, and went to Geshur, and was
13. 39 (the soul of) king David longed to go..to A.
14. 1 the king's heart (was) toward A.
14. 21 go therefore, bring the young man A.
14. 23 So Joab arose..and brought A. to
14. 24 So A. returned to his own house, and saw
14. 25 none to be so much praised as A. for
14. 27 And unto A. there were born three sons
14. 28 So A. dwelt two full years in Jerusalem
14. 29 Therefore A. sent for Joab, to have sent
14. 30 And A.'s servants set the field on fire
14. 31 Joab arose, and came to A. unto (his) house
14. 32 And A. answered Joab, Behold, I sent
14. 33 when he had called for A., he came to
14. 33 and the king kissed A.
15. 1 A. prepared him chariots and horses
15. 2 And A. rose up early, and stood beside
15. 2 then A. called unto him, and said
15. 3 And A. said unto him, See, thy matters
15. 4 A. said moreover, Oh that I were made
15. 6 And on this manner did A. to all Israel
15. 6 so A. stole the hearts of the men of Israel
15. 7 A. said unto the king, I pray thee, let
15. 10 But A. sent spies throughout all the
15. 10 then ye shall say, A. reigneth in Hebron
15. 11 And with A. went two hundred men out
15. 12 and A. sent for Ahithophel the Gilonite
15. 12 people increased continually with A.
15. 13 hearts of the men of Israel are after A.
15. 14 for we shall not (else) escape from A.
15. 31 among the conspirators with A.
15. 34 say unto A., I will be thy servant, O king
15. 37 and A. came into Jerusalem
16. 8 LORD hath delivered..into the hand of A.
16. 15 And A., and all the people the men of
16. 16 when Hushai..was come unto A.
16. 16 that Hushai said unto A., God save the
16. 17 And A. said to Hushai, (Is) this thy
16. 18 And Hushai said unto A., Nay; but
16. 20 Then said A. to Ahithophel, Give
16. 21 And Ahithophel said unto A., Go in unto
16. 22 So they spread A. a tent upon the top of
16. 22 and A. went in unto his father's con.
16. 23 the counsel of Ahithophel..both with..A.
17. 1 Moreover Ahithophel said unto A., Let
17. 4 And the saying pleased A. well, and all
17. 5 Then said A., Call now Hushai the Archite
17. 6 when Hushai was come to A.. A. spake
17. 7 And Hushai said unto A., The counsel
17. 9 slaughter among the people..follow A.
17. 14 And A. and all the men of Israel said
17. 14 the LORD might bring evil upon A.
17. 15 thus did Ahithophel counsel A. and the
17. 18 a lad saw them, and told A.: but they
17. 20 And when A.'s servants came to the
17. 24 And A. passed over Jordan, he and all the
17. 25 And A. made Amasa captain of the host
17. 26 So Israel and A. pitched in the land of
18. 5 king comm. Joab..(Deal) gently..with A.
18. 5 gave all the captains charge concerning A.
18. 9 And A. met the servants of David
18. 9 And A. rode upon a mule, and the mule
18. 10 a certain man saw (it)..and said..I saw A.
18. 12 Beware that none (touch) the young man A.
18. 14 and thrust them through the heart of A.
18. 15 young men..compassed about..smote A.
2 Sa. 18. 17 And they took A., and cast him into a
18. 18 Now A. in his lifetime had taken and
18. 18 it is called unto this day, A.'s place
18. 29 the king said, Is the young man A. safe?
18. 32 king said..(Is) the young man A. safe?
18. 33 O my son A., my son, my son A.! would
18. 33 died for thee, O A., my son, my son!
19. 1 the king weepeth and mourneth for A.
19. 4 cried with a loud voice, O my son A., O A.
19. 6 this day I perceive, that if A. had lived
19. 9 now he is fled out of the land for A.
19. 10 And A., whom we anointed over us, is dead
20. 6 shall Sheba..do us more harm than..A.
1 Ki. 1. 6 and (his mother) bare him after A.
2. 7 when I fled because of A. thy brother
2. 28 Adonijah, though he turned not after A.
1 Ch. 3. 2 The third, A. the son of Maachah the
2 Ch. 11. 20 her he took Maachah the daughter of A.
11. 21 Rehoboam loved..the daughter of A.
Psa. 3. *title.* A Psalm of David, when he fled from A.

ABSENCE —

A being off from, ἀπουσία *apousia.*

Phil. 2. 12 but now much more in my absence

ABSENCE of—

Without, ἄτερ *ater.*

Luke 22. 6 to betray him..in the absence of

ABSENT, to be—

1. *To be hidden,* סָתַר *sathar,* 2.

Gen. 31. 49 The LORD watch..when we are absent

2. *To be away from,* ἄπειμι *apeimi.*

1 Co. 5. 3 I verily, as absent in body, but present
2 Co. 10. 1 but being absent am bold toward you
10. 11 in word by letters when we are absent
13. 2 being absent now I write to them
13. 10 I write these things being absent
Phil. 1. 27 whether I..see you, or else be absent
Col. 2. 5 though I be absent in the flesh, yet am I

3. *To be away from one's people,* ἐκδημέω *ekdēmeō.*

2 Co. 5. 6 in the body, we are absent from the LORD
5. 8 willing rather to be absent from the body
5. 9 whether present or absent, we may be

ABSTAIN, to—

To hold off from, ἀπέχομαι *apechomai.*

Acts 15. 20 we write unto them, that they abstain
15. 29 That ye abstain from meats offered to
1 Th. 4. 3 will of God..that ye should abstain
5. 22 Abstain from all appearance of evil
1 Ti. 4. 3 Forbidding to marry (and..) to abstain
1 Pe. 2. 11 I beseech..abstain from fleshly lusts

ABSTINENCE —

Want of food, ἀσιτία *asitia.*

Acts 27. 21 after long abstinence Paul stood forth

ABUNDANCE —

1. *Multitude,* הָמוֹן *hamon.*

1 Ki. 18. 41 for (there is) a sound of abundance of rain
Eccl. 5. 10 nor he that loveth abundance with
Isa. 60. 5 be enlarged; because the abundance of

2. *Brightness,* זִיז *ziz.*

Isa. 66. 11 delighted with the abundance of her

3. *Abundance, remnant,* יִתְרָה *yithrah.*

Isa. 15. 7 Therefore the abundance they have gotten

4. *Strength, substance,* עָצְמָה *otsmah.*

Isa. 47. 9 for the great abundance of thine

5. *Abundance, residue,* עֲתֶרֶת *athereth.*

Jer. 33. 6 and will reveal unto them the abundance

6. *Abundance, multitude,* רֹב *rob.*

Deut. 28. 47 for the abundance of all (things)
1 Sa. 1. 16 for out of the abundance of my complaint
1 Ki. 1. 19 he hath slain..sheep in abundance
1. 25 hath slain oxen..and sheep in abundance
10. 10 there came no more such abundance of
10. 27 that (are) in the vale, for abundance
1 Ch. 22. 3 David prepared iron in abundance for the
22. 3 and brass in abundance without weight
22. 14 without weight; for it is in abundance
22. 15 workmen with thee in abundance
29. 2 stones, and marble stones in abundance
29. 21 and sacrifices in abundance for all Israel
2 Ch. 1. 15 that (are) in the vale for abundance
2. 9 Even to prepare me timber in abundance
4. 18 all these vessels in great abundance
9. 1 bare spices, and gold in abundance
9. 9 and of spices great abundance, and
9. 27 that (are) in the low plains in abundance
11. 23 he gave them victual in abundance
14. 15 and carried away..camels in abundance
15. 9 for they fell to him..in abundance
17. 5 he had riches and honour in abundance
18. 1 had riches and honour in abundance
18. 2 killed sheep..for him in abundance
20. 25 they found among them in abundance
24. 11 Thus they..gathered money in abundance
29. 35 burnt-offerings (were) in abundance, with
32. 5 made darts and shields in abundance
32. 29 flocks and herds in abundance
Neh. 9. 25 and fruit trees in abundance
Psa. 37. 11 delight themselves in the abundance of
52. 7 but trusted in the abundance of his riches
72. 7 and abundance of peace so long as the
Isa. 7. 22 And..for the abundance of milk (that)
Zech. 14. 14 silver, and apparel, in great abundance

7. *To make abundant,* רָבָה *rabah,* 5.

2 Sa. 12. 30 spoil of the city in great abundance

8. *Satiety, plenty, fulness,* שָׂבָע *saba.*
Eccl. 5. 12 but the abundance of the rich will not

9. *Ease, rest,* שַׁלְוָה *shalvah.*
Eze. 16. 49 and abundance of idleness was in her and

10. *Abundance,* שֶׁפַע *shepha.*
Deut 33. 19 they shall suck (of) the abundance of the

11. *Abundance, company,* שִׁפְעָה *shiphah.*
Job 22. 11 Or darkness..and abundance of waters
38. 34 that abundance of waters may cover thee?
Eze 26. 10 By reason of the abundance of his horses

12. *Without number,* לְאֵין מִסְפָּר *le-en mispar.*
1 Ch. 22. 4 Also cedar trees in abundance: for the

13. *Abundance,* ἁδρότης *hadrotēs.*
2 Co. 8. 20 no man..blame us in this abundance

14. *Power, ability,* δύναμις *dunamis.*
Rev. 18. 3 the abundance of her delicacies

15. *Over-abundance,* περισσεία *perisseia.*
Rom. 5. 17 they which receive abundance of grace
2 Co. 8. 2 great trial of affliction the abundance of

16. *Superfluity,* περίσσευμα *perisseuma.*
Matt 12. 34 out of the abundance of the heart the
Luke 6. 45 of the abundance of the heart his mouth
2 Co. 8. 14 your abundance..that their abundance

17. *To be over and above,* περισσεύω *perisseuō.*
Mark 12. 44 all..did cast in of their abundance
Luke 12. 15 life consisteth not in the abundance of
21. 4 these have of their abundance cast in

18. *Excess, over-abundance,* ὑπερβολή *huperbolē.*
2 Co. 12. 7 exalted..through the abundance of the

ABUNDANCE, to have —
To be over and above, περισσεύω *perisseuō.*
Matt 25. 29 every one..and he shall have abundance

ABUNDANCE, to have more —
To be over and above, περισσεύω *perisseuō.*
Matt 13. 12 he shall have more abundance: but who

ABUNDANCE, to bring in —
To make abundant, רָבָה *rabah,* 5.
2 Ch. 31. 5 Israel brought in abundance the first

ABUNDANCE, in — [*See* **ABUNDANCE,** 12.]
1. *To make heavy, weighty,* כָּבַר *kabar,* 5.
Job 36. 31 he giveth meat in abundance

2. *Many, much,* רַב *rab.*
Esth. 1. 7 and royal wine in abundance, according

ABUNDANT —
1. *Many, much,* רַב *rab.*
Exod 34. 6 long-suffering, and abundant in goodness
Jer. 51. 13 abundant in treasures, thine end is come

2. *Great in superfluity,* גָּדוֹל יֶתֶר *gadol yether.*
Isa. 56. 12 as this day, (and) much more abundant

3. *To be over and above,* περισσεύω *perisseuō.*
2 Co. 9. 12 is abundant also by many thanksgivings

4. *To become more, increase,* πλεονάζω *pleonazō.*
2 Co. 4. 15 for your sakes, that the abundant grace

5. *Many, much,* πολύς *polus.*
1 Pe. 1. 3 which according to his abundant mercy

ABUNDANT, to be exceeding —
To become more abundant, ὑπερπλεονάζω.
1 Ti. 1. 14 the grace..was exceeding abundant with

ABUNDANT, to be more —
To be over and above, περισσεύω *perisseuō.*
Phil. 1. 26 your rejoicing may be more abundant

ABUNDANT, more —
1. *More abundant,* περισσότερος *perissoteros.*
1 Co. 12. 23 bestow more abundant..more abundant
12. 24 having given more abundant honour

2. *More abundantly,* περισσοτέρως *perissoterōs.*
2 Co. 7. 15 his inward affection is more abundant
11. 23 in labours more abundant, in stripes

ABUNDANTLY — [*See* **WEEP.**]
1. *To break forth,* פָּרַח *parach.*
Isa. 35. 2 It shall blossom abundantly, and rejoice

2. *Many, much,* רַב *rab.*
Num. 20. 11 and the water came out abundantly, and
Job 36. 28 clouds..distil upon man abundantly

3. *Multitude, abundance,* רֹב *rob.*
1 Ch. 12. 40 and oxen, and sheep abundantly; for
[*See also* 22. 5, 8; 2 Ch. 31. 5.]

4. *To make many,* רָבָה *rabah* 5.
Isa. 55. 7 he will abundantly (*lit.* multiply to) par.

5. *Into abundance,* εἰς περισσείαν *eis perisseian.*
2 Co. 10. 15 according to our rule abundantly

6. *Richly,* πλουσίως *plousiōs.*
Titus 3. 6 he shed on us abundantly through Jesus
2 Pe. 1. 11 entrance shall be ministered..abundantly

ABUNDANTLY above, exceeding —
Over, above, ὑπὲρ ἐκ περισσοῦ.
Eph. 3. 20 is able to do exceeding abundantly above

ABUNDANTLY, more —
1. *Above the common,* περισσός *perissos.*
John 10. 10 might have (it) more abundantly

2. *More abundant,* περισσότερος, -ως, *perissoteros.*
1 Co. 15. 10 I laboured more abund. than; Heb. 6. 17.
2 Co. 1. 12 more abundantly; 2. 4; 12. 15; 1 Th. 2. 17.
[*See also* Bread, bring forth, drink, increase, harden, satisfied, utter, water, weep.]

ABUSE, to —
1. *To do, roll oneself on or upon,* עָלַל *alal,* 7.
Judg 19. 25 they knew her, and abused her all the
1 Sa. 31. 4 lest these uncircumcised..abuse me
1 Ch. 10. 4 lest these uncircumcised..abuse me

2. *To use badly,* καταχράομαι *katachraomai.*
1 Co. 7. 31 that use this world, as not abusing
9. 18 that I abuse not my power in the gospel

ABUSERS of themselves with mankind —
Lying with a male, ἀρσενοκοίτης *arsenokoitēs.*
1 Co. 6. 9 abusers of themselves with mankind

AC'-CAD, אַכַּד *castle, fortress.*
A city in the land of Shinar (near Babel, Erech, and Calneh), supposed by the Targums to be Nisibis in Mesopotamia. In the LXX. it is called *Archad,* and in the Talmud, *Bashkar.*
Gen. 10. 10 begin. of his kingdom was Babel, and..A.

ACCEPT, to —
1. *To reduce to ashes,* דָּשֵׁן *dashen,* 3.
Psa. 20. 3 Remember all thy offerings, and accept

2. *To take, receive,* לָקַח *laqach.*
Exod 22. 11 and the owner of it shall accept (thereof)

3. *To lift up,* נָשָׂא *nasa.* [With *panim,* Job 42. 9].
Gen. 19. 21 See, I have accepted thee concerning this
32. 20 peradventure he will accept of me
1 Sa. 25. 35 and have accepted thy person
Job 13. 8 Will ye accept his person? will ye contend
13. 10 if ye do secretly accept persons
32. 21 Let me not, I pray you, accept any man's
34. 19 (How much less to him) that accepteth
42. 8 for him will I accept: lest I deal with you
42. 9 them: the LORD also accepted Job
Psa. 82. 2 and accept the persons of the wicked?
Prov 18. 5 (It is) not good to accept the person of the
Mal. 1. 8 will he..accept thy person? saith the L.

4. *To smell,* רוּחַ *ruach,* 5.
1 Sa. 26. 19 let him accept an offering: but if (they be)

5. *To be pleased,* רָצָה *ratsah.*
Lev. 26. 41 and they then accept of the punishment
26. 43 and they shall accept of the punishment
Deut 33. 11 and accept the work of his hands
2 Sa. 24. 23 Araunah said..The LORD thy God accept
Psa. 119. 108 Accept, I beseech thee, the free-will
Eccl. 9. 7 for God now accepteth thy works
Jer. 14. 10 therefore the LORD doth not accept them
14. 12 I will not accept them: but I will consume
Eze. 20. 40 there will I accept them, and there will I
20. 41 I will accept you with your sweet savour
43. 27 and I will accept you, saith the LORD God
Hos. 8. 13 (but) the LORD accepteth them not; now
Amos 5. 22 I will not accept (them): neither will I
Mal. 1. 10 neither will I accept an offering at your
1. 13 should I accept this of your hand?

6. *To receive off, from,* ἀποδέχομαι *apodechomai.*
Acts 24. 3 We accept (it) always, and in all places

7. *To receive,* δέχομαι *dechomai.*
2 Co. 8. 17 For indeed he accepted the exhortation
11. 4 or another..which ye have not accepted

8. *To receive, take hold of,* λαμβάνω *lambanō.*
Luke 20. 21 neither acceptest thou the person (of any)
Gal. 2. 6 God accepteth no man's person

9. *To receive to (oneself),* προσδέχομαι *prosdechomai.*
Heb. 11. 35 were tortured, not accepting deliverance

ACCEPTABLE —
1. *To be chosen, selected,* בָּחַר *bachar,* 2.
Prov. 21. 3 To do justice..(is) more acceptable to the

2. *Pleasure, delight,* חֵפֶץ *chephets.*
Eccl. 12. 10 sought to find out acceptable words: and

3. *Pleasure, good pleasure,* רָצוֹן *ratson.*
Lev. 22. 20 for it shall not be acceptable for you
Psa. 69. 13 (in) an acceptable time: O God, in the
Prov. 10. 32 the righteous know what is acceptable
Isa. 49. 8 In an acceptable time have I heard thee
58. 5 wilt thou call this..an acceptable day to
61. 2 To proclaim the acceptable year of the
Jer. 6. 20 burnt-offerings (are) not acceptable, nor

4. *Acceptable, receivable from,* ἀπόδεκτος *apodektos.*
1 Ti. 2. 3 this (is) good and acceptable in the sight
5. 4 their parents: for that is..acceptable

5. *Acceptable, receivable,* δεκτός *dektos.*
Luke 4. 19 To preach the acceptable year of the
Phil. 4. 18 a sacrifice acceptable, well-pleasing to

6. *Well-pleasing,* εὐάρεστος *euarestos.*
Rom. 12. 1 a living sacrifice, holy, acceptable
12. 2 what (is) that good, and acceptable, and
14. 18 he that..serveth Christ (is) acceptable
Eph. 5. 10 Proving what is acceptable unto the LORD

7. *Very acceptable,* εὐπρόσδεκτος *euprosdektos.*
Rom. 15. 16 the offering up..might be acceptable
1 Pe. 2. 5 spiritual sacrifices, acceptable to God

8. *Grace, kindness,* χάρις *charis.*
1 Pe. 2. 20 take it patiently, this (is) acceptable

ACCEPTABLE, to be —
1. *To be pleased,* רָצָה *ratsah.*
Deut 33. 24 let him be acceptable to his brethren, and

2. *Pleasure, good pleasure,* רָצוֹן *ratson.*
Psa. 19. 14 be acceptable in thy sight, O LORD, my
Prov. 10. 32 the righteous know what is acceptable

3. *To be fair,* שְׁפַר *shephar*
Dan. 4. 27 let my counsel be acceptable unto thee

ACCEPTABLY —
Pleasingly, εὐαρέστως *euarestōs.*
Heb. 12. 28 whereby we may serve God acceptably

ACCEPTANCE —
Pleasure, good pleasure, רָצוֹן *ratson.*
Isa. 60. 7 they shall come up with acceptance on

ACCEPTATION —
Full reception, ἀποδοχή *apodochē.*
1 Ti. 1. 15 faithful..and worthy of all acceptation
4. 9 faithful..and worthy of all acceptation

ACCEPTED (of) —
1. *Acceptable, receivable,* δεκτός *dektos.*
Luke 4. 24 No prophet is accepted in his own
Acts 10. 35 worketh righteousness, is accepted with
2 Co. 6. 2 I have heard thee in a time accepted

2. *Well pleasing,* εὐάρεστος *euarestos.*
2 Co. 5. 9 or absent, we may be accepted of him

3. *Very acceptable,* εὐπρόσδεκτος *euprosdektos.*
Rom. 15. 31 my service..may be accepted of the
2 Co. 6. 2 behold, now (is) the accepted time; behold
8. 12 accepted according to that a man hath

ACCEPTED, be —
Is there not a lifting up, שְׂאֵת, inf. of *nasa.*
Gen. 4. 7 doest well, shalt thou not be accepted?

ACCEPTED, to be —
1. *To be good,* יָטַב *yatab.*
Lev. 10. 19 should it have been accepted in the sight
1 Sa. 18. 5 and he was accepted in the sight of all

2. *To fall,* נָפַל *naphal.*
Jer. 37. 20 let my supplication..be accepted before
42. 2 Let..our supplication be accepted before

3. *To be pleased,* רָצָה *ratsah,* 2.
Lev. 1. 4 and it shall be accepted for him to make
7. 18 it shall not be accepted, neither shall it
[*See also* 19. 7; 22. 23, 25, 27.]

4. *To be pleasing, pleased with,* רָצָה *ratsah.*
Esth. 10. 3 and accepted of the multitude of his bre.

5. *Pleasure, good pleasure,* רָצוֹן *ratson.*
Exod 28. 38 that they may be accepted before the
Lev. 22. 21 it shall be perfect to be accepted; there
23. 11 before the LORD, to be accepted for you
Isa. 56. 7 their sacrifices (shall be) accepted upon

ACCEPTED, to make —
To make gracious or acceptable, χαριτόω *charitoō.*
Eph. 1. 6 he hath made us accepted in the beloved

ACCESS —
A leading unto, προσαγωγή *prosagōgē.*
Rom. 5. 2 By whom also we have access by faith
Eph. 2. 18 through him we both have access by one
3. 12 In whom we have boldness and access

AC'-CHO, עַכּוֹ *compressed.*
The city *Ptolemais,* in Asher, on the coast of the Mediterranean or Great Sea, now called *Akka* and *St Jean d'Acre,* in lat. 32° 54', long. 35° 6' E.
Judg. 1. 31 did Asher drive out the inhabitants of A.

ACCOMPANY, to —
1. *To come with,* ἔρχομαι σύν *erchomai sun.*
Acts 11. 12 these six brethren accompanied me, and

2. *To have, hold, keep,* ἔχω *echō.*
Heb. 6. 9 things that accompany salvation, though

3. *To send forward,* προπέμπω *propempō.*
Acts 20. 38 they accompanied him unto the ship

4. *To follow with,* συνέπομαι *sunepomai.*
Acts 20. 4 there accompanied him into Asia Sopate

5. *To come with,* συνέρχομαι *sunerchomai.*
Acts 10. 23 certain brethren from Joppa accompanied

ACCOMPANYING —
With, along with, עִם *im.*
2 Sa. 6. 4 they brought it..accompanying the ark

ACCOMPLISH, to —
1. *To be completed, finished,* כָּלָה *kalah,* 3.
Lam. 4. 11 The LORD hath accomplished his fury
Eze. 4. 6 And when thou hast accomplished them
6. 12 thus will I accomplish my fury upon them
7. 8 and accomplish mine anger upon thee
13. 15 Thus will I accomplish my wrath upon
20. 8 I will pour out my fury..to accomplish
20. 21 to accomplish my anger against them in
Dan. 12. 7 when he shall have accomplished to

2. *To make full, fulfil,* מָלֵא *male,* 3.
Dan. 9. 2 he would accomplish seventy years in the

3. *To do, execute, make,* עָשָׂה *asah.*
1 Ki. 5. 9 and thou shalt accomplish my Isa. 55. 11.

4. *To separate, distinguish,* פָּלָא *pala,* 3.
Lev. 22. 21 offereth..unto the LORD to accomplish

5. *To establish, confirm, raise up,* קוּם *qum,* 5.
Jer. 44. 25 ye will surely accomplish your vows, and
6. *To be pleased,* רָצָה *ratsah.*
Job 14. 6 till he shall accomplish, as an hireling
7. *To be perfected, finished,* תָּמַם *tamam.*
Psa. 64. 6 they accomplish a diligent search
8. *It came that we perfected,* ἐγένετο ἡμᾶς ἐξαρτίσαι.
Acts 21. 5 when we had accomplished [exartizo]
9. *To end fully,* ἐπιτελέω *epiteleō.*
Heb. 9. 6 into the first tabernacle, accomplishing
1 Pe. 5. 9 the same afflictions are accomplished in
10. *To be or become full,* πλήθω *plēthō.*
Luke 1. 23 of his ministration were accomplished
2. 6 the days were accomplished that she
2. 21 when eight days were accomplished for
2. 22 when the days were accomplished, they
11. *To make full, fill out,* πληρόω *plēroō.*
Luke 9. 31 his decease which he should accomplish
12. *To end, complete,* τελέω *teleō.*
Luke 12. 50 am I straitened till it be accomplished!
18. 31 all things..shall be accomplished
22. 37 this..must yet be accomplished in me
John 19. 28 that all things were now accomplished

ACCOMPLISHED, to be —
1. *To be, exist,* הָיָה *hayah,* 2.
Prov. 13. 19 The desire accomplished is sweet to the
2. *To be completed, finished,* כָּלָה *kalah.*
2 Ch. 36. 22 that the word..might be accomplished
Eze. 5. 13 Thus shall mine anger be accomplished
Dan. 11. 36 till the indignation be accomplished
3. *To be full, filled out,* מָלֵא *male.*
Esth. 2. 12 days of their purifications accomplished
Isa. 40. 2 cry..that her warfare is accomplished
Jer. 25. 12 when seventy years are accomplished
25. 34 days of .dispersions are accomplished
29. 10 That after seventy years be accomplished
4. *To be filled, completed,* מְלָא *male,* 2.
Job 15. 32 It shall be accomplished before his time
5. *To be perfected, consummated,* תָּמַם *tamam.*
Lam. 4. 22 punishment of thine..is accomplished

ACCOMPLISHMENT —
Entire fulfilment, ἐκπλήρωσις *ekplērōsis.*
Acts 21. 26 to signify the accomplishment of the

ACCORD —
1. *Mouth,* פֶּה *peh.*
Josh. 9 2 gathered..to fight..with one accord
2. *Joint-soul,* σύμψυχος *sumpsuchos.*
Phil. 2. 2 having the same love..of one accord

ACCORD, of one's own —
1. *Choosing of himself,* αὐθαίρετος *authairetos.*
2 Co. 8. 17 of his own accord he went unto you
2. *Moving of itself,* αὐτόματος *automatos.*
Acts 12 10 opened to them of his own accord

ACCORD, with one —
Like-minded, ὁμοθυμαδόν *homothumadon.*
Acts 1 14 all continued with one accord in prayer
2. 1 they were all with one accord in one
2. 46 they, continuing daily with one accord
4. 24 lifted up their voice..with one accord
5. 12 they were all with one accord in S.'s porch
7. 57 and ran upon him with one accord
8. 6 the people with one accord gave heed
12. 20 they came with one accord to him, and
15. 25 good..being assembled with one accord
18. 12 Jews made insurrection with one accord
19. 29 rushed with one accord into the theatre

ACCORDING as —
1. *The mouth,* פֶּה *peh.*
Mal. 2. 9 according as ye have not kept my
2. *Even as, because that,* καθότι *kathoti.*
Acts 4. 35 unto every man according as he had need
3. *Even as, like as,* καθώς *kathōs.*
Rom. 11. 8 According as it is written, God hath
1 Co. 1. 31 That, according as it is written, He that
2 Co. 9. 7 Every man according as he purposeth in
Eph. 1. 4 According as he hath chosen us in him
4. *As, that, in order that, on the ground that,* ὡς *hōs.*
Rom. 12. 3 but to think soberly, according as God
2 Pe. 1. 3 According as his divine power hath
Rev. 22. 12 (is) with me, to give every man accord. as
5. *Down, according to,* κατά *kata.*
2 Co. 4. 13 the same spirit of faith, according as it is

ACCORDING to —
1. *To, unto,* אֶל *el.*
Josh. 15. 13 according to the commandment of the
2. *Sufficiency, enough,* דַּי *dai.*
Deut. 25 2 to be beaten..according to his fault
3. *Even as,* כְּמוֹ *kemo.*
Zech. 5. 3 shall be cut off..according to it
4. *As on, as upon,* כְּעַל *ke-al.*
Isa. 59. 18 According to (their) deeds, accordingly he
5. *On, upon, over* עַל *al.*
Gen. 43. 7 we told him according to the tenor of
6. *According to the mouth of,* לְפִי *le-phi.*
Gen. 47 12 with bread, according to (their) families
Exod 12. 4 every man according to his eating
16. 16 Gather of it every man according to his
16 18 they gathered every man according to
16 21 every man according to his eating and
Lev. 25. 16 according to the multitude..according
25 51 according unto them he shall give again
25. 52 according unto his years shall he give
27 8 according to his ability that vowed shall
27. 16 thy estimation shall be according to the
27 18 shall reckon..according to the years
Num. 6 21 according to the vow which he vowed
7 5 to every man according to his service
7 7 sons of Gershon, according to their
7. 8 sons of Merari, according unto their
26 54 to every one shall..be given according to
26. 56 According to the lot shall the possession
35 8 according to his inheritance which
Deut 17. 10 And thou shalt do according to the
Josh. 18. 4 and describe it according to the
1 Ki 17. 1 there shall not be dew..but according to
1 Ch 12. 23 according to the word of the LORD
2 Ch. 31. 2 every man according to his service, the
7. *From, out of,* מִן *min.*
Ezra 6. 14 according to the..and according to the
8. *Before, over-against,* קֳבֵל *qobel.*
Ezra 6. 13 according to that which Darius the king
8a. *From with,* מֵעִם *me-im.*
Job. 34. 33 (should it be) according to thy mind
9. *According to, by,* κατά *kata* (ac.)
Matt. 2. 16; 9. 29; 16. 27; 25. 15.
Mark 7. 5 Why walk not thy disciples according to
Luke 1 9 According to the custom of the priest's
1. 38 be it unto me according to thy word
2. 22 when the days..according to the
2. 24 to offer a sacrifice according to that
2. 29 depart in peace, according to thy word
2. 39 performed all things according to the
23. 56 according to the commandment
John 7 24 Judge not according to the appearance
18. 31 and judge him according to your law
Acts 2. 30 [fruit of his loins, according to the flesh]
7. 44 make it according to the fashion that he
13. 23 hath God according to (his) promise
22. 3 taught according to the perfect manner
22. 12 Ananias, a devout man according to the
24. 6 [would have judged according to our law]
Rom. 1. 3 of the seed of David according to the
1. 4 Son of God..according to the spirit
2. 2 the judgment of God is according to
2. 6 render to every man according to his
2. 16 by Jesus Christ according to my gospel
4. 18 according to that which was spoken
8. 27 intercession..according to (the will of)
8. 28 who are the called according to (his)
9. 3 my kinsmen according to the flesh
9. 11 the purpose of God, according to election
10. 2 zeal..but not according to knowledge
11. 5 a remnant according to the election of
12. 3 according as God hath dealt to every
12. 6 according to the grace..according to the
15. 5 like minded..according to Christ Jesus
16. 25 according to my..according to the
16. 26 prophets, according to the commandment
1 Co. 3. 8 his own reward according to his own
3 10 According to the grace of God which is
15. 3 Christ died for our sins according to the
15. 4 rose again the third day according to the
2 Co. 1. 17 do I purpose according to the flesh
10. 2 as if we walked according to the flesh
10. 13 measure, but according to the measure
10. 15 enlarged by you according to our rule
11. 15 end shall be according to their works
13. 10 sharpness, according to the power which
Gal. 1. 4 according to the will of God and our
3. 29 seed, and heirs according to the promise
Eph. 1. 5 according to the good pleasure of his will
1. 7 forgiveness of sins, according to the riches
1. 9 the mystery of his will, according to his
1. 11 being predestinated according to the
1. 19 who believe, according to the working of
2. 2 in time past ye walked according to the
3. 7 Whereof I was made a minister accord. to
3. 11 According to the eternal purpose which
3. 16 grant you, according to the riches of his
3. 20 according to the power that worketh
4. 7 is given grace according to the measure
4. 16 according to the effectual working in the
4. 22 which is corrupt according to the
6 5 (your) masters according to the flesh
Phil. 1. 20 According to my earnest expectation and
3. 21 according to the working whereby he is
4. 19 supply all your need according to his
Col. 1. 11 might, according to his glorious power
1. 25 a minister, according to the dispensation
1. 29 I also labour, striving according to his
3. 22 Servants, obey..masters according to the
2 Th. 1. 12 according to the grace of our God and
1 Ti. 1. 11 According to the glorious gospel of the
1. 18 son Timothy, according to the prophecies
6 3 doctrine which is according to godliness
2 Ti. 1 1 according to the promise of life which is
1. 8 gospel according to the power of God
1. 9 not according to our works, but accord. to
2. 8 Jesus..was raised..according to my
4. 14 Lord reward him according to his works
Titus 1. 1 according to the faith of God's elect
Titus 1. 3 unto me according to the commandment
3. 5 according to his mercy he saved us, by
3. 7 be made heirs according to the hope of
Heb. 2. 4 gifts. according to his own will?
7 5 according to the law, that is, of their
8 4 that offer gifts according to the law
8 5 make all things according to the
8. 9 Not according to the covenant that I
9. 19 spoken to all the people according to
Jas. 2. 8 royal law according to the scripture
1 Pe. 1. 2 Elect according to the foreknowledge
1. 3 which according to his abundant mercy
1. 17 who..judgeth according to every man's
3. 7 dwell with (them) according to knowledge
4. 6 judged according to men..according to
4. 19 suffer according to the will of God
2 Pe. 3. 13 we, according to his promise, look for
3. 15 Paul also according to the wisdom
1 Jo. 5. 14 we ask anything according to his will
Rev 2. 23 I will give..according to your works
[*See also* 18. 6; 20. 12, 13.]
10. *According to,* καθώς *kathōs.*
Acts 11. 29 every man according to his ability
11. *Toward,* πρός *pros.* (ac.)
Luke 12. 47 neither did according to his will, shall
2 Co. 5 10 according to that he hath done, whether
Gal. 2. 14 walked not uprightly according to the

ACCORDING to that —
According to that, καθό *katho.*
2 Co 8. 12 accepted according to that a man hath

ACCORDINGLY —
As on, or upon, כְּעַל *ke-al.*
Isa. 59. 18 According to (their) deeds, accordingly he

ACCOUNT —
1. *Thought, device, reckoning,* חֶשְׁבּוֹן *cheshbon.*
Eccl. 7. 27 one by one, to find out the account
2. *Taste, reason,* טְעֵם *taam.*
Dan. 6. 2 that the princes might give accounts
3. *Number, account,* מִסְפָּר *mispar.*
1 Ch. 27. 24 neither was..put in the account of the
4. *Inspection, oversight,* פְּקֻדָּה *pequddah.*
2 Ch. 26. 11 the number of their account by the
5. *Word, reckoning,* λόγος *logos.*
Matt 12. 36 shall give account thereof in the day of
18. 23 king, which would take account of his
Luke 16. 2 give an account of thy stewardship; for
Acts 19. 40 we may give an account of this concourse
Rom. 14. 12 every one of us shall give account of
[*See also* Phil. 4. 17; Heb. 13. 17; 1 Pe. 4. 5.]

ACCOUNT, to —
1. *To reckon, account,* λογίζομαι *logizomai.*
Heb. 11. 19 Accounting that God (was) able to raise
2. *To go before, guide, think,* ἡγέομαι *hēgeomai.*
2 Pe. 3. 15 And account (that) the long-suffering of

ACCOUNT, to give —
To answer, respond, עָנָה *anah.*
Job 33. 13 he giveth not account of any of his

ACCOUNT of, to make —
1. *To think, devise, reckon,* חָשַׁב *chashab,* 3.
Psa. 144. 3 of man, that thou makest account of him!
2. *To make a reckoning,* λογίζομαι *logizomai.*
1 Co 4. 1 Let a man so account of us, as of the

ACCOUNTED, to be —
1. *To be thought, reckoned,* חָשַׁב *chashab,* 2.
Deut. 2. 11 Which also were accounted giants, as the
2 20 That also was accounted a land of giants
1 Ki. 10 21 it was nothing accounted of in the days
2 Ch. 9. 20 it was (not) anything accounted of in the
Isa. 2. 22 for wherein is he to be accounted of?
2. *To be numbered,* סָפַר *saphar,* 4.
Psa. 22. 30 it shall be accounted to the LORD for a
3. *To appear, have the appearance,* δοκέω *dokeō.*
Mark 10. 42 they which are accounted to rule over
Luke 22. 24 which of them should be accounted the
4. *To make an account of,* λογίζομαι *logizomai.*
Rom 8. 36 we are accounted as sheep for...Gal. 3. 6.

ACCURSED —
1. *A devoted thing,* חֵרֶם *cherem.*
Josh. 6 17 And the city shall be accursed, (even) it
7 12 their enemies, because they were accursed
7. 12 except ye destroy the accursed from
2. *A thing lightly esteemed,* קְלָלָה *qelalah.*
Deut. 21 23 for he that is hanged (is) accursed of God
3. *A thing put up, devoted,* ἀνάθεμα *anathema.*
Rom. 9. 3 that myself were accursed from Christ
1 Co 12. 3 no man..calleth Jesus accursed: and
Gal. 1. 8 preached unto you, let him be accursed
1. 9 ye have received, let him be accursed

ACCURSED, to be —
To be lightly esteemed, קָלַל *qalal,* 4.
Isa. 65 20 but the sinner..shall be accursed

ACCURSED, to make —
To devote (to God or destruction), חָרַם *charam,* 5.
Josh. 6 18 lest ye make (yourselves) accursed, when

ACCURSED THING —
A devoted thing, חֵרֶם *cherem.*
Josh. 6. 18 keep (yourselves) from the accursed thing

Josh. 6. 18 when ye take of the accursed thing
7. 1 committed a trespass in the accursed thing
7. 1 for Achan..took of the accursed thing
7. 11 have even taken of the accursed thing
7. 13 an accursed thing..the accursed thing
7. 15 he that is taken with the accursed thing
22. 20 commit a trespass in the accursed thing
1 Ch. 2. 7 Achar..who trans. in the thing accursed

ACCUSATION —

1.*Accusation*, שִׂטְנָה *sitnah*.
Ezra 4. 6 wrote they (unto him) an accusation

2.*Cause, matter*, αἰτία *aitia*.
Matt 27. 37 set up over his head his accusation
Mark 15. 26 the superscription of his accusation was
Acts 25. 18 they brought none accusation of such

3.*A speaking down*, κατηγορία *katēgoria*.
Luke 6. 7 that they might find an accusation
John 18. 29 What accusation bring ye against this
1 Ti. 5. 19 Against an elder receive not an accusation

4.*Judgment*, κρίσις *krisis*.
2 Pe. 2. 11 bring not railing accusation against
Jude 9 durst not bring..a railing accusation

ACCUSATION, to take by false —

To disclose about figs, συκοφαντέω *sukophanteō*.
Luke 19. 8 from any man by false accusation, I

ACCUSE, to —

1.*To eat pieces torn off*, אֲכַל קַרְצִין *akal-qaretsin*.
Dan. 3. 8 Chaldeans came near, and accused the
6. 24 brought those men which had accused D.

2.*To use the tongue freely*, לְשַׁן *lushan* 5.
Prov. 30. 10 Accuse not a servant unto his master

3.*To call in*, ἐγκαλέω *engkaleō*.
Acts 23. 28 wherefore they accused him, I brought
23. 29 Whom I perceived to be accused of
26. 2 touching all..whereof I am accused of
26. 7 For which hope's sake..I am accused of

4.*To speak down*, κατηγορέω *katēgoreō*.
Matt 12. 10 sabbath days? that they might accuse
27. 12 when he was accused of the chief priests
Mark 3. 2 sabbath day; that they might accuse
15. 3 the chief priests accused him of many
Luke 11. 54 something..[that they might accuse him]
23. 2 they began to accuse him, saying, We
23. 10 scribes stood and vehemently accused
23. 14 touching those things whereof ye accuse
John 5. 45 I will accuse you..that accuseth you
8. 6 [tempting..they might have to accuse]
Acts 22. 30 known..wherefore he was accused of the
24. 2 Tertullus began to accuse (him), saying
24. 8 knowledge of all..whereof we accuse
24. 13 prove the things whereof they now accuse
25. 5 go down with (me), and accuse this man
25. 11 whereof these accuse me, no man may
25. 16 before that he which is accused have the
28. 19 not that I had ought to accuse my nation
Rom. 2. 15 thoughts the mean while accusing or else
Rev. 12. 10 which accused them before our God day

ACCUSE falsely, to —

1.*To injure, harass, insult*, ἐπηρεάζω *epēreazō*.
1 Pe. 3. 16 may be ashamed that falsely accuse your

2.*To disclose about figs*, συκοφαντέω *sukophanteō*.
Luke 3. 14 no man, neither accuse (any) falsely

ACCUSED —

Under accusation, ἐν κατηγορίᾳ *en katēgoria*.
Titus 1. 6 having faithful children, not accused of

ACCUSED, be —

To be thrust through, διαβάλλομαι *diaballomai*.
Luke 16. 1 the same was accused unto him that he

ACCUSER —

One who speaks down, κατήγορος *katēgoros*.
John 8. 10 [where are those thine accusers? hath]
Acts 23. 30 gave commandment to his accusers also
23. 35 I will hear thee..when thine accusers
24. 8 [Commanding his accusers to come unto]
25. 16 have the accusers face to face, and have
25. 18 when the accusers stood up, they
Rev. 12. 10 for the accuser of our brethren is cast

ACCUSER, false —

A thruster through, διάβολος *diabolos*.
2 Ti. 3. 3 Without natural affection..false accusers
Titus 2. 3 not false accusers, not given to much

ACCUSTOMED —

Taught, trained, לִמּוּד *limmud*.
Jer. 13. 23 do good, that are accustomed to do evil

A-CEL-DA'-MA, Ἀκελδαμά *portion of blood*.

The piece of ground purchased with the thirty pieces of silver which Judas received for betraying Jesus, but which were afterwards thrown down by him in his remorse.
Acts 1. 19 that field is called..A., that is to say

A-CHAI'-A, Ἀχαΐα *land of Achaicus*.

Classic name of that part of Greece which lies along the S. coast of the Gulf of Corinth. This name is sometimes used for the whole of Greece, and *Corinth* was its capital.
Acts 18. 12 And when Gallio was the deputy of A.
18. 27 And when he was disposed to pass into A.
19. 21 he had passed through Macedonia and A.
Rom 15. 26 it hath pleased them of Macedonia and A.
16. 5 Epænetus..the firstfruits of [A.] unto
1 Co. 16. 15 Stephanas, that it is the firstfruits of A.
2 Co. 1. 1 with all the saints which are in all A.
9. 2 I boast..that A. was ready a year ago
11. 10 stop me of this boasting..regions of A
1 Th. 1. 7 So that ye were ensamples to all..in..A.
1. 8 sounded out the word..not only in..A.

A-CHAI'-CUS, Ἀχαϊκός *belonging to Achaia*.

A Corinthian who visited Paul at Philippi.
1 Co. 16. 17 glad of the coming of Stephanas..and A.

A'-CHAN, A'-CHAR, עָכָן, עָכָר *trouble*.

One of the tribe of Judah, who, at the destruction of Jericho by Joshua, stole part of the spoil and hid it, and was put to death in consequence, B.C. 1451.
Josh. 7. 1 for A. the son of Carmi..took of the
7. 18 and A., the son of Carmi..was taken
7. 19 And Joshua said unto A., My son, give
7. 20 And A. answered Joshua, and said
7. 24 And Joshua..took A. the son of Zerah
22. 20 Did not A. the son of Zerah commit a
1 Ch. 2. 7 And the sons of Carmi; Achar, the

A'-CHAZ, Ἄχαζ, אָחָז *he holds*.

The Greek form of *Ahaz*, one of the kings of Judah.
Matt. 1. 9 Joatham begat A.; and A. begat Ezekias

ACH'-BOR, עַכְבּוֹר *a mouse*.

1. Father of the seventh Edomite king.
Gen. 36. 38 Saul died, and Baal-hanan the son of A.
36. 39 And Baal-hanan the son of A. died, and
1 Ch. 1. 49 Baal-hanan the son of A. reigned in his

2. One of Josiah's messengers sent to inquire concerning the denunciation of wrath against the national sins, as found recorded in the book of the law discovered by Hilkiah in the temple, B.C. 641. In 2 Ch. 34. 20 *Abdon* is named in the place of *Achbor*.
2 Ki. 22. 12 the king commanded..A. the son of Mi.
22. 14 So Hilkiah the priest..and A...went unto

3. A Jew, whose son was sent by Jehoiakim to bring back Urijah the prophet out of Egypt, B.C 600.
Jer. 26. 22 the king sent..Elnathan the son of A.
36. 12 princes sat there Elnathan the son of A.

A'-CHIM, Ἀχείμ *woes*.

An ancestor of Joseph, husband of Mary, mother of Jesus.
Matt. 1. 14 Sadoc begat A.; and A. begat Eliud

A'-CHISH, אָכִישׁ *serpent-charmer*.

1. A king of Gath to whom David fled, B.C. 1060.
1 Sa. 21. 10 David arose..and went to A. the king of
21. 11 the servants of A. said unto him, (Is) not
21. 12 David..was sore afraid of A. the king of
21. 14 Then said A. unto his servants, Lo, ye
27. 2 David arose, and he passed over..unto A.
27. 3 David dwelt with A. at Gath, he and
27. 5 David said unto A., If I have now found
27. 6 Then A. gave him Ziklag that day
27. 9 David smote the land..returned..to A.
27. 10 And A. said, Whither have ye made a
27. 12 And A. believed David, saying, He hath
28. 1 And A. said unto David, Know thou
28. 2 David said to A., Surely thou shalt
28. 2 And A. said to David, Therefore will I
29. 2 David..passed on in the rereward with A.
29. 3 And A. said unto the princes of the Phil.
29. 6 Then A. called David, and said unto him
29. 8 David said unto A., But what have I
29. 9 And A. answered and said to David, I

2. A king of Gath, who reigned about forty-five years later than No. 1. in the time of Solomon, B.C. 1013.
1 Ki. 2. 39 the servants of Shimei ran away unto A.
2. 40 Shimei arose..and went to Gath to A. to

ACH-ME'-THA, אַחְמְתָא *a place of horses*.

A city of Media, perhaps the same as Ecbatana, *i.e.* the modern *Hamadan*. N. lat. 34° 47', E. long. 47° 52'.
Ezra 6. 2 there was found at A., in the palace

A'-CHOR, עָכוֹר *trouble*.

A valley near Jericho, in which Achan and his property was destroyed and buried, B.C. 1451.
Josh. 7. 24 they brought them unto the valley of A.
7. 26 name of that place was..The valley of A.
15. 7 border went up..from the valley of A.
Isa. 65. 10 the valley of A. a place for the herds to
Hos. 2. 15 and the valley of A. for a door of hope

ACH'-SA, ACH'-SAH, עַכְסָה *serpent-charmer*.

Daughter of Caleb, and wife of Othniel, B.C. 1440.
Josh. 15. 16 He that smiteth..to him will I give A.
15. 17 and he gave him A. his daughter to wife
Judg. 1. 12 He that smiteth..to him will I give A.
1. 13 and he gave him A. his daughter to wife
1 Ch. 2. 49 and the daughter of Caleb (was) A.

ACH'-SHAPH, אַכְשָׁף *dedicated*.

A Phenician city, at the foot of Carmel, allotted to Asher; now called *Khaifa*.
Josh. 11. 1 Jabin king of Hazor..sent to..king of A.
12. 7, 20 these (are) the kings..the king of A.
19. 24, 25 children of A...border..Helkath..A.

ACH'-ZIB, אַכְזִיב *a winter brook, a lie*.

1. A town in W. of Judah. Comp. Gen. 38. 5.
Josh. 15. 33, 44 in the valley..Keilah, and A., and M.
Mic. 1. 14 the houses of A. (shall be) a lie to the

2. A city of Asher by the sea of Galilee, and 19 miles from Accho, and now called *Es-zib*
Josh. 19. 29 are at the sea from the coast to A.
Judg. 1. 31 did Asher drive out the inhabitants..of A.

ACKNOWLEDGE, to —

1.*To know*, יָדַע *yada*.
Psa. 51. 3 For I acknowledge my transgressions
Prov. 3. 6 In all thy ways acknowledge him, and
Isa. 33. 13 ye (that are) near, acknowledge my might
Jer. 3. 13 Only acknowledge thine iniquity, that
14. 20 We acknowledge, O LORD, our wickedness.

2.*To make known*, יָדַע *yada*, 5.
Psa. 32. 5 I acknowledged my sin unto thee, and

3.*To make known, discern*, נָכַר *nakar*, 5.
Gen. 38. 26 And Judah acknowledged (them), and
Deut. 21. 17 But he shall acknowledge the son of the
33. 9 neither did he acknowledge his brethren
Isa. 61. 9 all that see them shall acknowledge
63. 16 though .be ignorant..Israel acknowledge
Jer. 24. 5 Like these..so will I acknowledge them
Dan. 11. 39 whom he shall acknowledge (and) increase

4.*To make known fully*, ἐπιγινώσκω *epiginōskō*.
1 Co. 14. 37 let him acknowledge that the things that
16. 18 therefore acknowledge ye them that are
2 Co. 1. 13 shall acknowledge..or acknowledge
1. 14 As also ye have acknowledged us in part

ACKNOWLEDGING —

Full knowledge, ἐπίγνωσις *epignōsis*.
2 Ti. 2. 25 give them repentance to the acknowled.
Titus 1. 1 the acknowledging of the truth which
Phm. 6 become effectual by the acknowledging

ACKNOWLEDGMENT —

Full knowledge, ἐπίγνωσις *epignōsis*.
Col. 2. 2 to the acknowledgment of the mystery of

ACQUAINT self, to —

To make profit, סָכַן *sakan*, 5.
Job 22. 21 Acquaint now thyself with him, and be at

ACQUAINTANCE —

1.*To know*, יָדַע *yada*.
Job 19. 13 and mine acquaintance are verily
42. 11 they that had been of his acquaintance

2.*To be known*, יָדַע *yada*, 4.
Psa. 31. 11 and a fear to mine acquaintance: they
55. 13 But (it was) thou, a man..acquaintance
88. 8 Thou hast put away mine acquaintance
88. 18 far from me, (and) mine acquaintance

3.*One known, discerned*, מַכָּר *makkar*.
2 Ki. 12. 5 every man of his acquaintance
12. 7 receive no..money of your acquaintance

4.*One known*, γνωστός *gnōstos*.
Luke 2. 44 they sought him among..acquaintance
23. 49 all his acquaintance, and the women that

ACQUAINTANCE, his —

One's own, ἴδιος *idios*.
Acts 24. 23 forbid none of his acquaintance to

ACQUAINTED, to be —

To make useful, acquainted, סָכַן *sakan*, 5.
Psa. 139. 3 and art acquainted (with) all my ways

ACQUAINTED with, to be —

To know, יָדַע *yada*.
Isa. 53. 3 man of sorrows, and acquainted with

ACQUAINTING —

To lead, drive, נָהַג *nahag*.
Eccl. 2. 3 yet acquainting mine heart with wisdom

ACQUIT, to —

To declare innocent, cut off, נָקָה *naqah*, 3.
Job 10. 14 and thou wilt not acquit me from mine
Nah. 1. 3 The LORD..will not at all acquit

ACRE —

1.*A yoke (of oxen)*, צֶמֶד *tsemed*.
Isa. 5. 10 ten acres of vineyard shall yield one bath

2.*A furrow*, מַעֲנָה *maanah*.
1 Sa. 14. 14 half acre of land, (which) a yoke (of oxen)

ACT —

1.*Word, thing*, דָּבָר *dabar*.
1 Ki. 10. 6 I heard in mine own land of thy acts and
11. 41 And the rest of the acts of Solomon, and
11. 41 in the book of the acts of Solomon?
14. 19 And the rest of the acts of Jeroboam
14. 29 Now the rest of the acts of Rehoboam
15. 7 Now the rest of the acts of Abijam, and
15. 23 The rest of all the acts of Asa, and all
15. 31 Now the rest of the acts of Nadab, and
16. 5 Now the rest of the acts of Baasha, and
16. 14 Now the rest of the acts of Elah, and all
16. 20 Now the rest of the acts of Zimri, and
16. 27 Now the rest of the acts of Omri which
22. 39 Now the rest of the acts of Ahab, and all
22. 45 Now the rest of the acts of Jehoshaphat
2 Ki. 1. 18 Now the rest of the acts of Ahaziah
8. 23 And the rest of the acts of Joram, and all
10. 34 Now the rest of the acts of Jehu, and all
12. 19 And the rest of the acts of Joash, and all
13. 8 Now the rest of the acts of Jehoahaz
13. 12 And the rest of the acts of Joash and all
14. 15 Now the rest of the acts of Jehoash
14. 18 And the rest of the acts of Amaziah, (are)

2 Ki. 14. 28 Now the rest of the acts of Jeroboam
15. 6 And the rest of the acts of Azariah, and
15. 11 And the rest of the acts of Zachariah
15. 15 And the rest of the acts of Shallum, and
15. 21 And the rest of the acts of Menahem
15. 26 And the rest of the acts of Pekahiah
15. 31 And the rest of the acts of Pekah, and
15. 36 Now the rest of the acts of Jotham, and
16. 19 Now the rest of the acts of Ahaz which
20. 20 And the rest of the acts of Hezekiah
21. 17 Now the rest of the acts of Manasseh
21. 25 Now the rest of the acts of Amon which
23. 28 Now the rest of the acts of Josiah, and
24. 5 Now the rest of the acts of Jehoiakim
1 Ch. 29. 29 Now the acts of David the king, first
2 Ch. 9. 5 I heard in mine own land of thine acts
9. 29 Now the rest of the acts of Solomon
12. 15 Now the acts of Rehoboam, first and last
13. 22 And the rest of the acts of Abijah, and
16. 11 And, behold, the acts of Asa, first and
20. 34 Now the rest of the acts of Jehoshaphat
25. 26 Now the rest of the acts of Amaziah
26. 22 Now the rest of the acts of Uzziah, first
27. 7 Now the rest of the acts of Jotham, and
28. 26 Now the rest of his acts and of all his
32. 32 Now the rest of the acts of Hezekiah
33. 18 Now the rest of the acts of Manasseh
35. 26 Now the rest of the acts of Josiah, and
36. 8 Now the rest of the acts of Jehoiakim

2. *Work,* מַעֲשֶׂה *maaseh.*
Deut. 11. 3 And his miracles, and his acts, which he
11. 7 But your eyes have seen all the great acts
2 Ki. 23. 19 according to all the acts that he had done
Esth. 10. 2 And all the acts of his power and of his

3. *Service, deed,* עֲבוֹדָה *abodah.*
Isa. 28. 21 and bring to pass his act, his strange

4. *Act, action,* עֲלִילָה *alilah.*
Psa. 103. 7 He made known his..acts unto the

5. *Act, deed, doing,* פֹּעַל *poal.*
2 Sa. 23. 20 Benaiah..who had done many acts, he
1 Ch. 11. 22 Benaiah..who had done many acts
Isa. 59. 6 the act of violence (is) in their hands

ACT, in the very —
In the very theft, ἐπαυτοφώρῳ *epautophōrō.*
John 8. 4 [this woman was taken..in the very act]

ACTION —
Act, action, עֲלִילָה *alilah.*
1 Sa. 2. 3 and by him actions are weighed

ACTIVITY —
Strength, force, חַיִל *chayil.*
Gen. 47. 6 if thou knowest (any) men of activity

AD-A'-DAH, עַדְעָדָה *bordering.*
A city in S. of Judah, near Dimonah.
Josh. 15. 21-22 the coast of Edom southward..A

A'-DAH, עָדָה *pleasure.*
1. One of the wives of Lamech, B.C. 3874.
Gen. 4. 19 the name of the one (was) A., and the
4. 20 And A. bare Jabal: he was the father of
4. 23 Lamech said unto his wives, A. and
2. One of the wives of Esau, B.C. 1750.
Gen. 36. 2 A. the daughter of Elon the Hittite, and
36. 4 And A. bare to Esau Eliphaz; and
36. 10 Eliphaz the son of A. the wife of Esau
36. 12 these (were) the sons of A. Esau's wife
36. 16 (are)..dukes..these (were) the sons of A.

A-DA'-IAH, עֲדָיָה *pleasing to Jah.*
1. Maternal grandfather of king Josiah, B.C. 641.
2 Ki. 22. 1 mother's name (was)..the daughter of A.
2. A Levite descended from Gershom.
1 Ch. 6. 41 the son of Zerah, the son of A.
3. A son of Shimhi the Benjamite.
1 Ch. 8. 12-21 The sons of Elpaal..A., and Beraiah
4. A Levite of the family of Aaron, and head of a family in Jerusalem.
1 Ch. 9. 10-12 of the priests..A. the son of Jeroham
5. The father of a captain that aided Jehoiada to put Joash on the throne of Judah.
2 Ch. 23. 1 Jehoiada..took..Maaseiah the son of A.
6. One of the family of Bani, who took a strange wife during the exile, B.C. 457.
Ezra 10. 29 of the sons of Bani; Meshullam..and A.
7. Another of a different family of Bani, who had also taken a strange wife, B.C. 445.
Ezra 10. 34-39 of the sons of Bani..Nathan, and A.
8. A descendant of Judah by Pharez.
Neh. 11. 5 [children of Judah]..Maaseiah..son of A.
9. A Levite of the family of Aaron, probably the same as No. 4.
Neh. 11. 12 and A. the son of Jeroham, the son of P.

A-DAL'-IA, אֲדַלְיָא *honour of Ized.*
One of the ten sons of Haman who were hanged along with their father, B.C. 510.
Esth. 9. 8 A...The ten sons of Haman the son of H.

AD'-AM, אָדָם *of the ground, firm.*
1. The man that God created and placed in the garden of Eden, B.C. 4004.
Gen. 2. 19 the LORD God..brought (them) unto A. to
Gen. 2. 19 whatsoever A. called every living creature
2. 20 And A. gave names to all cattle, and to the
2. 20 but for A. there was not found an help
2. 21 caused a deep sleep to fall upon A.
2. 23 A. said, This (is) now bone of my bones
3. 8 and A. and his wife hid themselves from
3. 9 And the LORD God called unto A., and
3. 17 And unto A. he said, Because thou hast
3. 20 And A. called his wife's name Eve
3. 21 Unto A. also and to his wife did the LORD
4. 1 And A. knew Eve his wife; and she
4. 25 And A. knew his wife again; and she bare
5. 1 the book of the generations of A.
5. 2 and called their name A., in the day when
5. 3 And A. lived an hundred and thirty years
5. 4 And the days of A. after he had begotten
5. 5 And all the days that A. lived were
Deut 32. 8 when he separated the sons of A., he set
1 Ch. 1. 1 A., Sheth, Enosh
Job 31. 33 If I covered my transgressions as A.
Luke 3. 38 Seth, which was..of A., which was..of
Rom. 5. 14 Nevertheless death reigned from A. to
5. 14 after the similitude of A.'s transgression
1 Co. 15. 22 For as in A. all die, even so in Christ
15. 45 The first man A. was made a living soul
15. 45 the last A. (was made) a quickening spirit
1 Ti. 2. 13 For A. was first formed, then Eve
2. 14 And A. was not deceived, but the woman
Jude 14 And Enoch also, the seventh from A.
2. A town on the E. of the Jordan, 12 miles from Zartan in Manasseh, and 36 miles N. of Jericho. In the LXX. it is called Kiriatharim, and the termination *arim* may be = *adam.* It would thus mean "the city (Kiriath) of Arim or Adam."
Josh. 3. 16 waters..rose up..very far from the city A.

A-DA'-MAH, אֲדָמָה *ground, fortress.*
A fenced city in Naphtali.
Josh. 19. 35-36 And the fenced cities..A., and Ramah

ADAMANT stone —
Brier, diamond point, שָׁמִיר *shamir.*
Eze. 3. 9 As an adamant harder than flint have I
Zech. 7. 12 made their hearts (as) an adamant stone

A-DA'-MI, אֲדָמִי *fortified.*
A city of Naphtali, the same as ADAMAH.
Josh. 19. 33 their coast was from Heleph..and A

A'-DAR, אֲדָר *fire god.*
The 12th month of the Jewish sacred year, from the new moon of March till the one of April, and was doubled seven times in nineteen years to synchronise the lunar and the solar years.
Ezra 6. 15 was finished on the third day of..A.
Esth. 3. 7 twelfth (month), that (is), the month A.
3. 13 twelfth month, which (is) the month A.
8. 12 twelfth month, which (is) the month A.
9. 1 the twelfth month, that (is) the month A.
9. 15 the fourteenth day also of the month A.
9. 17 the thirteenth day of the month A.
9. 19 made the fourteenth day of the month A.
9. 21 keep the fourteenth day of the month A.

A'-DAR or AD'-DAR, אַדָּר *height, honour.*
1. A city called also Hazar-Addar, in the S. of Judah, near Edom.
Josh. 15. 3 and went up to A., and fetched a compass
2. Son of Bela, and grandson of Benjamin, B.C. 1680.
1 Ch. 8. 3 And the sons of Bela were, A., and Gera.

AD-BE'-EL, אַדְבְּאֵל *languishing for God.*
Son of Ishmael, and grandson of Abraham, B.C. 1840.
Gen. 25. 13 firstborn of Ishmael, Nebajoth..and A.
1 Ch. 1. 29 firstborn of Ishmael, Nebajoth..and A.

ADD, to —
1. *To add, increase,* יָסַף *yasaph.*
Lev. 27. 13 then he shall add a fifth (part) thereof
27. 15 then he shall add the fifth (part) of the
27. 19 then he shall add the fifth (part) of the
27. 27 he shall redeem (it)..and shall add
Deut. 5. 22 and he added no more. And he wrote them
19. 9 then shalt thou add three cities more for
1 Sa. 12. 19 for we have added unto all our sins (this)
Isa. 38. 5 behold, I will add unto thy days fifteen
Jer. 45. 3 for the LORD hath added grief to my

2. *To add, increase, continue,* יָסַף *yasaph,* 5.
Gen. 30. 24 The LORD shall add to me another son
Lev. 5. 16 and shall add the fifth part thereto, and
6. 5 and shall add the fifth part more thereto
27. 31 shall add thereto the fifth (part) thereof
Num. 5. 7 and add unto it the fifth (part) thereof, and
Deut. 4. 2 Ye shall not add unto the word which I
12. 32 thou shalt not add thereto, nor diminish
2 Sa. 24. 3 Now the LORD thy God add unto the
1 Ki. 12. 11 I will add to your yoke: my father
12. 14 and I will add to your yoke: my father
2 Ki. 20. 6 And I will add unto thy days fifteen years
1 Ch. 22. 14 and thou mayest add thereto
2 Ch. 10. 14 but I will add thereto: my father chastised
28. 13 ye intend to add (more) to our sins and to
Job 34. 37 For he addeth rebellion unto his sin, he
Prov. 3. 2 length of days..shall they add to thee
10. 22 it maketh rich, and he addeth no sorrow
16. 23 The heart of the wise..addeth learning to
30. 6 Add thou not unto his words, lest he

3. *To give,* נָתַן *nathan.*
Num 35. 6 to them ye shall add forty and two cities
Psa. 69. 27 Add iniquity unto their iniquity: and

4. *To add,* סָפָה *saphah.*
Deut 29. 19 though I walk in the imagination..to add
Isa. 29. 1 add ye year to year; let them kill sacrifices
30. 1 not of my spirit, that they may add sin to

5. *To bear or bring upon,* ἐπιφέρω *epipherō.*
Phil. 1. 16 supposing to add affliction to my bonds

6. *To furnish abundantly,* ἐπιχορηγέω *epichorēgeō.*
2 Pe. 1. 5 giving all diligence, add to your faith

7. *To put to, or forward,* προστίθημι *prostithēmi.*
Matt. 6. 27 can add one cubit unto his stature?
6. 33 all these things shall be added unto you
Luke 3. 20 Added this yet above all, that he shut up
12. 25 with taking thought can add to his stature
12. 31 all these things shall be added unto you
19. 11 as they heard these things, he added and
Acts 2. 41 the same day there were added (unto
2. 47 the LORD added to the church daily such
5. 14 believers were the more added to the
11. 24 much people was added unto the LORD
Gal. 3. 19 It was added because of transgressions

ADD in conference, to —
To add up together, προσανατίθημι *prosanatithēmi.*
Gal. 2. 6 in conference added nothing to me, but

ADD (thereto), to —
To join in order, ἐπιδιατάσσομαι, *epidiatassomai.*
Gal. 3. 15 no man disannulleth, or addeth thereto

ADD unto, to —
To put on, or upon, ἐπιτίθημι *epitithēmi.*
Rev. 22. 18 If any man shall add unto...shall add un

AD-'DAN, אַדָּן *strong.*
The name of a place from which some of the inhabitants came with Zerubbabel to Jerusalem; others consider it the name of a man who was unable to show his genealogy to be of Israel, B.C. 536, Ezra 2. 59.

ADDAR. *See* ADAR.

ADDED, to be —
1. *To be added,* יָסַף *yasaph,* 2.
Jer. 36. 32 and there were added besides unto them
2. *To be added,* יְסַף *yesaph,* 6.
Dan. 4. 36 and excellent majesty was added unto me

ADDER —
1. *Adder,* עַכְשׁוּב *akshub.*
Psa. 140. 3 adders' poison (is) under their lips
2. *Asp,* פֶּתֶן *pethen.*
Psa. 58. 4 (they are) like the deaf adder (that)
91. 13 Thou shalt tread upon the lion and adder
3. *Basilisk, cockatrice,* צִפְעֹנִי *tsiphoni.*
Pro. 23. 32 At the last it..stingeth like an adder
4. *Adder, viper,* שְׁפִיפֹן *shephiphon.*
Gen. 49. 17 Dan shall be..an adder in the path, that

AD'-DI, Ἀδδί *(meaning uncertain).*
An ancestor of Joseph the husband of Mary mother of Jesus.
Luke 3. 28 which was (the son) of A., which was (the

ADDICT, to —
To arrange, set oneself, τάσσω *tassō.*
1 Co. 16. 15 and (that) they have addicted themselves

ADDITIONS —
Joinings, wreaths, לֹיוֹת *loyoth.*
1 Ki. 7. 29 (were) certain additions made of thin
7. 30 undersetters molten, at the side of every a.
7. 36 proportion of every one, and additions

AD'-DON, אַדּוֹן *strong.*
The same perhaps as Addan, B.C. 536.
Neh. 7. 61 these (were) they which went up..from..A.

A'-DER, עֶדֶר *a flock.*
A son of Berah, grandson of Shaharaim, a Benjamite.
1 Ch. 8. 15 And Zebadiah, and Arad, and A.

A-DI'-EL, עֲדִיאֵל *ornament of God.*
1. A descendant of Simeon.
1 Ch. 4. 36 and Jaakobah, and Jeshohaiah..and A.
2. A descendant of Aaron.
1 Ch. 9. 12 and Maasiai the son of A., the son of
3. Asmaveth's father, who was David's treasurer (perhaps the same as No. 2.), B.C. 1030.
1 Ch. 27. 25 the king's treasures (was)..the son of A.

A'-DIN, עָדִין *ornament.*
1. One whose descendants returned from Babylon with Zerubbabel, B.C. 445.
Ezra 2. 15 The children of A., four hundred fifty and
Neh. 7. 20 The children of A., six hundred fifty and
2. One whose posterity came up with Ezra.
Ezra 8. 6 Of the sons also of A.; Ebed the son of J.
3. The name of a family who with Nehemiah and the people sealed the covenant.
Neh. 10. 14-16 [The chief of the people]..A.

A-DI'-NA, עֲדִינָא *ornament.*
A Reubenite captain of David's, B.C. 1048.
1 Ch. 11. 42 A. the son of Shiza the Reubenite, a

A-DI'-NO, עֲדִינוֹ *ornament.*
One of David's thirty valiant men, B.C. 1048.
2 Sa. 23. 8 The Tachmonite..the same (was) A. the

A-DI-THA'-IM, עֲדִיתַיִם *two ways, or passages.*
A city in the plain of Judah.
Josh. 15. 33-36 in the valley..Sharaim, and A., and

ADJURE, to —
1. *To cause to take oath*, אָלָה *alah*, 5.
1 Sa. 14. 24 for Saul had adjured the people, saying
2. *To cause to swear*, שָׁבַע *shaba*, 5.
Jos. 6. 26 And Joshua adjured (them) at that time
1 Ki. 22. 16 How many times shall I adjure thee that
2 Ch. 18. 15 How many times shall I adjure thee that
3. *To adjure thoroughly*, ἐξορκίζω *exorkizō.*
Matt 26. 63 I adjure thee by the living God, that thou
4. *To adjure*, ὁρκίζω *horkizō.*
Mark 5. 7 I adjure thee by God, that thou torment
Acts 19. 13 We adjure you by Jesus whom Paul

AD'-LAI, עַדְלַי *lax, weary.*
Father of Shaphat, who was overseer of the herds in the lowlands in David's time, B.C. 1040.
1 Ch. 27. 29 over the herds..(was) Shaphat the son of A.

AD'-MAH, אַדְמָה *earthwork, fortress.*
A town in the vale of Siddim which was destroyed with Sodom, Gomorrah, Zeboim, B.C. 1897.
Gen. 10. 19 as thou goest unto..Gomorrah, and A.
14. 2 made war with..Shinab king of A., and
14. 8 there went out..the king of A., and the
Deut 29. 23 the overthrow of Sodom and Gomorrah, A.
Hos. 11. 8 how shall I make thee as A.?

AD-MA'-THA, אַדְמָתָא *God-given.*
One of the seven princes of Persia and Media in the reign of Ahasuerus, B.C. 510.
Esth. 1. 14 the next unto him (was) Carshena..A.

ADMINISTERED, to be —
To minister, διακονέω *diakoneō.*
2 Co. 8. 19 which is administered by us to the glory
8. 20 this abundance which is administered by

ADMINISTRATION —
Ministry, διακονία *diakonia.*
1 Co. 12. 5 there are differences of administrations
2 Co. 9. 12 For the administration of this service

ADMIRATION —
Wonder, θαῦμα *thauma.*
Rev. 17. 6 I wondered with great admiration

ADMIRATION, to have in —
To wonder, θαυμάζω *thaumazō.*
Jude 16 having men's persons in admiration

ADMIRED, to be —
To wonder, θαυμάζω *thaumazō.*
2 Th. 1. 10 and to be admired in all them that believe

ADMONISH, to —
1. *To testify, say again and again*, עוּד *ud*, 5.
Jer. 42. 19 know certainly that I have admonished
2. *To put in mind*, νουθετέω *noutheteō.*
Rom. 15. 14 able also to admonish one another
Col. 3. 16 teaching and admonishing one another
1 Th. 5. 12 we beseech you..and admonish you
2 Th. 3. 15 but admonish (him) as a brother
3. *To recommend*, παραινέω *paraineō.*
Acts 27. 9 was now already past, Paul admonished

ADMONISHED, to be —
To be shone on, זָהַר *zahar*, 2.
Eccl. 4. 13 king, who will no more be admonished
12. 12 further, by these, my son, be admonished

ADMONISHED of God, to be —
To have a divine oracle, χρηματίζω *chrēmatizō.*
Heb. 8. 5 as Moses was admonished of God when

ADMONITION —
A putting into the mind, νουθεσία *nouthesia.*
1 Co. 10. 11 they are written for our admonition
Eph. 6. 4 bring them up in the..admonition of the
Titus 3. 10 an heretick, after the..second admonition

AD'-NA, עַדְנָא *pleasure.*
1. One of the family of Pahath-moab who had taken a strange wife during the exile, B.C. 456.
Ezra 10. 30 of the sons of Pahath-moab; A., and
2. A priest in the time of Joiakim, grandson of Jozadak.
Neh. 12. 12-15 [the chief of the fathers]..Of Harim, A.

AD'-NAH, עַדְנָה *pleasure.*
1. A captain of Manasseh, who joined David in Ziklag, B.C. 1048.
1 Ch. 12. 20 there fell to him of Manasseh, A., and
2. The chief captain of the army of Jehoshaphat, B.C. 914.
2 Ch. 17. 14 Of Judah..A. the chief, and with him

ADO, to make an —
To be tumultuous, θορυβέομαι *thorubeomai.*
Mark 5. 39 he saith..Why make ye this ado, and

A-DO-NI-BE'-ZEK, אֲדֹנִי־בֶזֶק *lord of lightning.*
A king of Bezek, captured by the men of Judah and Simeon and taken to Jerusalem, where he was mutilated, and died, B.C. 1449.
Judg. 1. 5 And they found A. in Bezek: and they
1. 6 But A. fled; and they pursued after him
1. 7 And A. said, Threescore and ten kings

A-DO-NI'-JAH, אֲדֹנִיָּה *Jah is my lord.*
1. Fourth son of David, born in Hebron, and afterwards put to death by Solomon for aspiring to the throne, B.C. 1015.
2 Sa. 3. 4 [unto David were sons born]..fourth A.
1 Ki. 1. 5 Then A. the son of Haggith exalted
1. 7 and they following A. helped (him)
1. 8 Zadok the priest, and..were not with A.
1. 9 And A. slew sheep and oxen and fat cattle
1. 11 saying, Hast thou not heard that A. the
1. 13 Solomon..shall reign..why then doth A.
1. 18 And now, behold, A. reigneth; and now
1. 24 Nathan said..hast thou said, A. shall
1. 25 behold, they..say, God save king A.
1. 41 And A. and all the guests that (were) with
1. 42 And A. said unto him, Come in; for thou
1. 43 Jonathan answered and said to A., Verily
1. 49 all the guests that (were) with A. were
1. 50 And A. feared because of Solomon and
1. 51 it was told Solomon, saying, Behold, A.
2. 13 And A. the son of Haggith came to B.
2. 19 king Solomon, to speak unto him for A.
2. 21 And she said, Let Abishag..be given to A.
2. 22 why dost thou ask Abishag..for A.? ask
2. 23 God do so to me and more also, if A. have
2. 24 A. shall be put to death this day
2. 28 Joab hath turned after A., though he
1 Ch. 3. 1, 2 sons of David..third Absalom..fourth A.
2. One of the Levites sent by Jehoshaphat to teach the law, B.C. 914.
2 Ch. 17. 8 with them (he sent) Levites..A., and
3. A chief of the people that with Nehemiah sealed the covenant, B.C. 445.
Neh. 10. 14-16 The chief of the people..A., Bigvai

A-DO-NI'-KAM, אֲדֹנִיקָם *my lord has risen.*
1. An Israelite whose descendants came up from Babylon after the exile, B.C. 536.
Ezra 2. 13 the children of A., six hundred sixty and
Neh. 7. 18 the children of A., six hundred threescore
2. One, some of whose posterity came up from Babylon with Ezra, B.C. 457. This may be the same as No. 1.
Ezra. 8. 13 of the last sons of A., whose names (are)

A-DO-NI'-RAM, אֲדֹנִירָם *my lord is high.*
A tribute officer of Solomon's, B.C. 975.
1 Ki. 4. 6 and A. the son of Abda (was) over the
5. 14 and A. (was) over the levy

A-DO-NI-ZE'-DEK, אֲדֹנִי־צֶדֶק *lord of justice.*
A king of the Canaanites or Amorites in Jerusalem, and slain by Joshua, B.C. 1452.
Josh. 10. 1 when A. king of Jerusalem had heard
10. 3 Wherefore A. king of Jerusalem sent

ADOPTION —
Placing as a son, υἱοθεσία *huiothesia.*
Rom. 8. 15 ye have received the Spirit of adoption
8. 23 waiting for the adoption, (to wit), the
9. 4 to whom (pertaineth) the adoption, and

ADOPTION of sons or children —
Placing as a son, υἱοθεσία *huiothesia.*
Gal. 4. 5 we might receive the adoption of sons
Eph. 1. 5 predestinated us unto the adoption of c.

A-DO-RA'-IM, אֲדוֹרַיִם *double honour.*
A city in the S.W. of Judah, built by Rehoboam, son of Solomon, and now called Dura, 5 miles S.W. of Hebron.
2 Ch. 11. 5-9 Rehoboam dwelt in Jer., and built..A.

A-DO'-RAM, אֲדֹרָם *high honour.*
1. An officer of David's, set over the tribute: supposed to be the same as Adoniram, B.C. 975.
2 Sa. 20. 24 And A. (was) over the tribute: and
2. An officer of Solomon's and afterwards of Rehoboam's.
1 Ki 12. 18 Then king Rehoboam sent A., who (was)

ADORN, to —
1. *To pass on or over*, עָדָה *adah.*
Isa. 61. 10 ornaments, and as a bride adorneth
2. *To polish, adorn*, κοσμέω *kosmeō.*
Luke 21. 5 how it was adorned with goodly stones
1 Ti. 2. 9 also, that women adorn themselves
Titus 2. 10 that they may adorn the doctrine of God
1 Pe. 3. 5 holy women also..adorned themselves
Rev. 21. 2 as a bride adorned for her husband

ADORNED, to be —
To be passed on or over, עָדָה *adah.*
Jer. 31. 4 thou shalt again be adorned with thy

ADORNING —
Ornament, κόσμος *kosmos.*
1 Pe. 3. 3 Whose adorning let it not be that outward

A-DRAM-ME'-LECH, אַדְרַמֶּלֶךְ *honour of the king.*
1. An idol of the Sepharvites whom Shalmaneser brought to people the cities of Israel after carrying their inhabitants captive to Assyria.
2 Ki. 17. 31 Sepharvites burnt their children..to A.
2. A son of Sennacherib, king of Assyria, who, with his brother Sharezer, slew their father in the temple of Nisroch, B.C. 721.
2 Ki. 19. 37 A. and Sharezer his sons smote him with
Isa. 37. 38 it came to pass..that A...smote him with

AD-RA-MYT'-TIUM, Ἀδραμύττειον.
A seaport of Mysia in Asia Minor, colonised by the Athenians.
Acts 27. 2 entering into a ship of A., we launched

A-DRI'-A, Ἀδρίας.
The sea on the E. of Italy called the Adriatic, or Gulf of Venice. In Paul's time it embraced also the part of the Mediterranean between Greece and Sicily.
Acts 27. 27 we were driven up and down in A.

AD-RI'-EL, עַדְרִיאֵל *honour of God.*
A man of Issachar, to whom Merab (Saul's daughter) was given, B.C. 1064.
1 Sa. 18. 19 she was given unto A. the Meholathite
2 Sa. 21. 8 whom she brought up for A. the son of

A-DUL'-LAM, עֲדֻלָּם *resting place.*
1. A royal city S.W. of Jerusalem.
Josh. 12. 7-15 these (are) the kings..the king of A.
15. 33-35 in the valley..Jarmuth and A., Socoh
2 Ch. 11. 5-7 Rehoboam dwelt in Jer., and built..A.
Neh. 11. 25-30 the children of Judah dwelt at..A.
Mic. 1. 15 he shall come unto A. the glory of Israel
2. A large cave near the city (No. 1).
1 Sa. 22. 1 David..escaped to the cave A.: and
2 Sa. 23. 13 of the thirty..came..unto the cave of A.
1 Ch. 11. 15 three..went down..into the cave of A.

A-DUL-LAM-ITE, עֲדֻלָּמִי *a native of Adullam.*
Gen. 38. 1 Judah went..and turned in to a certain A.
38. 12 he and his friend Hirah the A.
38. 20 sent the kid by..his friend the A.

ADULTERER —
1. *To commit adultery*, נָאַף *naaph.*
Lev. 20. 10 the adulterer and the adulteress shall surely
Job 24. 15 The eye also of the adulterer waiteth for
2. *To commit adultery*, נָאַף *naaph*, 3.
Psa. 50. 18 and hast been partaker with adulterers
Isa. 57. 3 the seed of the adulterer and the whore
Jer. 9. 2 go from them! for they (be) all adulterers
23. 10 For the land is full of adulterers; for
Hos. 7. 4 They (are) all adulterers, as an oven
Mal. 3. 5 and I will be..against the adulterers
3. *Adulterer*, μοιχός *moichos.*
Luke 18. 11 I thank thee..I am not as..adulterers
1 Co. 6. 9 fornicators, nor idolaters, nor adulterers
Heb. 13. 4 whoremongers and adulterers God will
Jas. 4. 4 adulterers and adulteresses, know ye not

ADULTERESS —
1. *To commit adultery*, נָאַף *naaph.*
Lev. 20. 10 the adulterer and the adulteress shall
Eze. 23. 45 them after the manner of adulteresses, and
23. 45 because they (are) adulteresses, and blood
2. *To commit adultery*, נָאַף *naaph*, 3.
Hos. 3. 1 yet an adulteress, according to the love
3. *The wife of a man*, אֵשֶׁת אִישׁ *esheth ish.*
Prov. 6. 26 and the adulteress will hunt for the
4. *Adulteress*, μοιχαλίς *moichalis.*
Rom. 7. 3 called an adulteress..is no adulteress
Jas. 4. 4 Ye adulterers and adulteresses, know ye

ADULTERIES —
1. *Adulterous objects*, נַאֲפוּפִים *naaphuphim.*
Hos. 2. 2 therefore put away..her adulteries from
2. *Adulteries*, נִאֻפִים *niuphim.*
Jer. 13. 27 I have seen thine adulteries, and thy

ADULTERIES, in —
Adulterous acts, נִאֻפִים *niuphim.*
Eze. 23. 43 I unto (her that was) old in adulteries

ADULTEROUS —
1. *To commit adultery*, נָאַף *naaph*, 3.
Prov. 30. 20 such (is) the way of an adulterous woman
2. *Adulteress*, μοιχαλίς *moichalis.*
Matt 12. 39 An evil and adulterous generation seeketh
16. 4 wicked and adulterous generation seeketh
Mark 8. 38 in this adulterous and sinful generation

ADULTERY —
1. *Adulteress*, μοιχαλίς *moichalis.*
2 Pe. 2. 14 Having eyes full of adultery, and that
2. *Adultery*, μοιχεία *moicheia.*
Matt. 15. 19 For out of the heart proceed..adulteries
Mark 7. 21 of the heart of men, proceed..adulteries
John 8. 3 unto him a woman taken in adultery
Gal. 5. 19 works of the flesh are..Adultery

ADULTERY, to commit —
1. *To commit adultery*, נָאַף *naaph.*
Exod 20. 14 Thou shalt not commit adultery
Lev. 20. 10 And the man that committeth adultery
20. 10 (even he) that committeth adultery with
Deut. 5. 18 Neither shalt thou commit adultery
Prov. 6. 32 (But) whoso committeth adultery with a
Jer. 3. 9 committed adultery with stones and with
5. 7 they then committed adultery, and
7. 9 Will ye..murder, and commit adultery
23. 14 they commit adultery, and walk in lies
2. *To commit adultery*, נָאַף *naaph*, 3.
Jer. 3. 8 backsliding Israel committed adultery
29. 23 and have committed adultery with their
Eze. 16. 32 (But as) a wife that committeth adultery

Eze. 23. 37 That they have committed adultery, and
23. 37 with their idols..committed adultery
Hos. 4. 13 and your spouses shall commit adultery
4. 14 your spouses when they commit adultery
3.*To commit adultery, μοιχάομαι, moichaomai.*
Matt. 5. 32 causeth her to commit adultery: and
5. 32 shall marry her..committeth adultery
19. 9 committeth adultery..doth commit adul.
Mark10. 11 and marry another, committeth adultery
10. 12 and be married..she committeth adultery
4.*To commit adultery, μοιχεύω moicheuō.*
Matt. 5. 27 Thou shalt not commit adultery
5. 28 whosoever looketh..committed adultery
19. 18 Thou shalt not commit adultery
Mark10. 19 Thou knowest..Do not commit adultery
Luke16. 18 committeth adultery..committeth adul.
18. 20 Thou knowest..Do not commit adultery
Rom. 2. 22 commit adultery..dost thou..adultery
13. 9 For this, Thou shalt not commit adultery
Jas. 2. 11 not commit adultery..commit no adultery
Rev. 2. 22 and them that commit adultery with

ADULTERY, committing —
To commit adultery נָאַף *naaph.*
Hos. 4. 2 and stealing, and committing adultery

ADULTERY, in—
To commit adultery, μοιχεύω moicheuō.
John 8. 4 [Master, this woman..taken in adultery]

A-DUM'-MIM, אֲדֻמִּים *red places.*
A ridge of hills, W. of Gilgal, between Judah and Benjamin.
Josh.15. 7 Gilgal, that (is) before the going up to A.
18. 17 Geliloth..over against the going up of A.

ADVANCE, to —
1.*To make great,* גָּדַל *gadal,* 3.
Esth. 10. 2 whereunto the king advanced him, (are)
2.*To lift up,* נָשָׂא *nasa,* 3.
Esth. 3. 1 and advanced him, and set his seat above
5. 11 and how he had advanced him above the
3.*To do, make,* עָשָׂה *asah.*
1 Sa. 12. 6 (It is) the LORD that advanced Moses and

ADVANTAGE —
1.*Over and above, superfluity, περισσός perissos.*
Rom. 3. 1 What advantage then hath the Jew?
2.*Profit, advantage, ὠφέλεια ōpheleia.*
Jude 16 persons in admiration..of advantage

ADVANTAGE, to be of —
To profit, be useful, סָכַן *sakan.*
Job 35. 3 thou saidst, What advantage will it be

ADVANTAGE, to get an —
To get more than another, πλεονεκτέω pleonekteō.
2 Co. 2. 11 Lest Satan should get an advantage of us

ADVANTAGED, to be —
To profit, ὠφελέω ōpheleō.
Luke 9. 25 For what is a man advantaged, if he gain

ADVANTAGETH —
Profit, advantage, ὄφελος ophelos.
1 Co. 15 32 what advantageth it me, if the dead

ADVENTURE self, to —
To give, give up, δίδωμι didōmi.
Acts 19. 31 not adventure himself into the theatre

ADVENTURE, to —
1.*To try, attempt,* נָסָה *nasah,* 3.
Deut.28. 56 which would not adventure to set..her
2.*To send forth,* שָׁלַח *shalak,* 5.
Judg. 9 17 my father fought for you, and adventured

ADVERSARY —
1.*To bind, distress, straiten,* צוּר *tsur.*
Exod23. 22 an adversary unto thine adversaries
2.*Straitness, straitener,* צַר *tsar.*
Deut32. 27 lest their adversaries should behave
32. 43 will render vengeance to his adversaries
Josh. 5. 13 (Art) thou for us, or for our adversaries?
Ezra 4. 1 Now when the adversaries of Judah and
Neh 4. 11 And our adversaries said, They shall not
Esth. 7 6 And Esther said, The adversary and
Psa. 74. 10 how long shall the adversary reproach?
81. 14 turned my hand against their adversaries
89. 42 set up the right hand of his adversaries
Isa. 1. 24 I will ease me of mine adversaries, and
9. 11 LORD shall set up the adversaries of Rezin
59. 18 he will repay, fury to his adversaries
63. 18 our adversaries have trodden down thy
64. 2 to make..known to thine adversaries
Jer. 30. 16 and all thine adversaries, every one of
46. 10 may avenge him of his adversaries
50. 7 and their adversaries said, We offend not
Lam. 1. 5 Her adversaries are the chief her enemies
1. 7 the adversaries saw her, (and) did mock at
1. 10 The adversary hath spread out his hand
1 17 (that) his adversaries (should be) round
2. 4 he stood..as an adversary, and slew all
2. 17 hath set up the horn of thine adversaries
4. 12 not have believed that the adversary and
Amos 3. 11 An adversary (there shall be) even round
Mic. 5. 9 Thine hand..upon thine adversaries
Nah. 1. 2 will take vengeance on his adversaries
3.*Straitness,* צָרָה *tsarah.*
1 Sa. 1. 6 and her adversary also provoked her sore
4.*To straiten, distress,* צָרַר *tsarar.*
Exod23. 22 an adversary unto thine adversaries
Psa. 69. 19 mine adversaries (are) all before thee
Isa. 11 13 and the adversaries of Judah shall be cut
5.*To strive, plead,* רִיב *rib,* 5.
1 Sa. 2. 10. The adversaries of the LORD shall be
6.*Accuser, opponent,* שָׂטָן *satan.*
Num22. 22 angel of the LORD stood..an adversary
1 Sa. 29. 4 lest in the battle he be an adversary to us
2 Sa. 19 22 that ye should this day be adversaries
1 Ki. 5. 4 (so that there is) neither adversary nor
11. 14 And the LORD stirred up an adversary
11. 23 God stirred him up (another) adversary
11. 25 he was an adversary to Israel all the days
7.*To accuse, oppose,* שָׂטַן *satan.*
Psa. 71. 13 Let..be..consumed that are adversaries
109. 20 this (be) the reward of mine adversaries
109. 29 Let mine adversaries be clothed with
8.*Owner of a judgment,* בַּעַל מִשְׁפָּט *baal mishpat.*
Isa. 50. 8 who (is) mine adversary? let him come
9.*A man of strife,* אִישׁ רִיב *ish rib.*
Job 31. 35 and (that) mine adversary had written a
10.*Opponent in law, ἀντίδικος antidikos.*
Matt. 5. 25 Agree with thine adversary ...lest the a.
Luke12. 58 when thou goest with thine adversary to
18. 3 saying, Avenge me of mine adversary
1 Pe. 5. 8 because your adversary the devil
11.*To be laid in opposition, ἀντίκειμαι antikeimai.*
Luke 13. 17 all his adversaries were ashamed: and
21. 15 which all your adversaries shall not be
1 Co 16. 9 opened unto me, and..many adversaries
Phil. 1. 28 in nothing terrified by your adversaries
1 Tim.5. 14 give none occasion to the adversary to
12.*Over against, ὑπεναντίος hupenantios*
Heb 10. 27 which shall devour the adversaries

ADVERSARY, to be an —
To accuse, oppose, שָׂטַן *satan.*
Psa. 38 20 They also that..are mine adversaries
109. 4 For my love they are my adversaries: but

ADVERSITY —
1.*Halting, limping,* צֶלַע *tsela.*
Psa. 35 15 But in mine adversity they rejoiced, and
2.*Straitness, distress,* צָרָה *tsarah.*
2 Sa 4. 9 redeemed my soul out of all adversity
2 Ch. 15 6 for God did vex them with all adversity
Psa. 31. 7 thou hast known my soul in adversities
Prov.17. 17 and a brother is born for adversity
24. 10 (If) thou faint in the day of adversity
3.*Straitness, straitener,* צַר *tsar.*
Isa. 30 20 the Lord give you the bread of adversity
4.*Evil,* רַע *ra.*
1 Sa. 10 19 saved you out of all your adversities and
Psa. 10 6 for I (shall) never (be) in adversity
94. 13 give him rest from the days of adversity
Eccl. 7. 14 in the day of adversity consider

ADVERSITY, to suffer —
Held by evil, κακουχούμενος, pass. pt. of *kakoucheō.*
Heb. 13 3 them which suffer adversity, as being

ADVERTISE, to —
1.*To counsel,* יָעַץ *yaats.*
Num.24. 14 I will advertise thee what this people
2.*To uncover the ear,* גָּלָה אֹזֶן *galah ozen.*
Ruth 4. 4 I thought to advertise thee, saying

ADVICE —
1.*Word,* דָּבָר *dabar.*
Judg20. 7 give here your advice and counsel
2 Sa. 19. 43 advice should not be first had in bringing
2.*Taste, reason,* טַעַם *taam.*
1 Sa 25. 33 blessed(be)thy advice,and blessed(be)thou
3.*Counsel,* עֵצָה *etsah.*
2 Ch. 10. 14 and answered them after the advice of
4.*Opinion founded on knowledge, γνώμη gnōmē.*
2 Cor. 8. 10 And herein I give (my) advice: for this is

ADVICE, good —
Combinations, תַּחְבֻּלוֹת *tachbuloth.*
Prov.20. 18 and with good advice make war

ADVICE, to take or give —
1.*To give or take counsel,* יָעַץ *yaats,* 2.
2 Ch. 10. 9 What advice give ye that we may return
25. 17 Then Amaziah king of Judah took advice
2.*To take counsel,* עוּץ *uts.*
Judg 19. 30 consider of it, take advice, and speak

ADVISE, to —
1.*To know,* יָדַע *yada.*
2 Sa. 24. 13 now advise, and see what answer I shall
2.*To be counselled,* יָעַץ *yaats,* 2.
1 Ki. 12. 6 How do ye advise that I may answer this
3.*To give counsel, βουλὴν τίθημι boulēn tithēmi.*
Acts 27. 12 the more part advised to depart thence

ADVISE self, to —
To see, רָאָה *raah.*
1 Ch. 21. 12 advise thyself what word I shall bring

ADVISED, well —
To be counselled, יָעַץ *yaats,* 2.
Prov.13 10 but with the well advised (is) wisdom

ADVISEMENT —
Counsel, עֵצָה *etsah.*
1 Ch 12. 19 the Philistines upon advisement sent him

ADVOCATE —
One called alongside (to help), παράκλητος.
1 Jo. 2. 1 And if any man sin, we have an advocate

AE-NE'-AS, *Αἰνέας praise.*
A paralytic of Lydda healed by Peter.
Acts 9. 33 there he found a certain man named A.
9. 34 Peter said unto him, A., Jesus Christ

AE'-NON, *Αἰνών (natural) fountains.*
A place near Salim (a little N. of it, and now called *Aynun*), at the head of the valley of Shechem. Copious springs are still here, in a broad open valley called *Wady-Farah.*
John 3. 23 John also was baptising in A. near to S.

AFAR (off) —
1.*A place far off,* מֶרְחָק *merchaq.*
Psa. 138. 6 but the proud he knoweth afar off
Jer. 31. 10 nations, and declare..in the isles afar off
2. *Far off,* רָחוֹק *rachoq.*
Gen. 22. 4 Abraham lifted up..saw the place afar off
37. 18 they saw him afar off..before he came
Exod. 2. 4 And his sister stood afar off, to wit
20. 18 the people saw (it), they..stood afar off
20. 21 And the people stood afar off
24. 1 seventy of the elders..worship..afar off
Num. 9. 10 If any man..(be)..in a journey afar off
1 Sa. 26. 13 stood on the top of an hill afar off
2 Ki. 2. 7 fifty men..went, and stood to view afar off
Ezra 3. 13 people shouted..noise was heard afar off
Neh. 12. 43 joy of Jerusalem was heard even afar off
Job 2. 12 when they lifted up their eyes afar off
36. 25 Every man..may behold (it) afar off
39 25 Ha..he smelleth the battle afar off
39. 29 she seeketh..her eyes behold afar off
Psa. 10. 1 Why standest thou afar off, O LORD?
38. 11 My lovers..and my kinsmen stand afar off
65. 5 them that are afar off (upon) the sea
139. 2 thou understandest my thought afar off
Isa. 23. 7 her own feet shall carry her afar off
59. 14 And..justice standeth afar off
66. 19 (to) Tubal, and Javan, (to) the isles afar off
Jer. 23. 23 a God at hand..and not a God afar off?
46. 27 behold, I will save thee from afar off
51 50 go away..remember the LORD afar off
Mic. 4. 3 he shall..rebuke strong nations afar off
3.*To put or go far off,* רָחַק *rachaq,* 5.
Exod33. 7 and pitched it..afar off from the camp
4.*Far, distant, μακράν makran.*
Acts 2. 39 and to all that are afar off, (even) as many
Eph. 2. 17 peace to you which were afar off
5.*From far, μακρόθεν makrothen.*
Mark11. 13 seeing a fig tree afar off, having
Luke18, 13 the publican, standing afar off, would
16. 23; 22. 54; 23. 49; Matt. 26. 58; 27. 55;
Mark 5. 6; 14. 54; 15. 40; Rev. 18. 10, 15, 17.
6.*From afar, πόῤῥωθεν porrhōthen.*
Luke17. 12 that were lepers, which stood afar off
Heb 11. 13 but having seen them afar off

AFFAIR —
1.*Word, thing,* דָּבָר *dabar.*
1 Ch. 26 32 made rulers..for..affairs of the king
Psa.112 5 he will guide his affairs with discretion
2.*Service,* עֲבִידָה *abidah.*
Dan. 2. 49 he set..over the affairs of the province
3. 12 certain..thou hast set over the affairs
3.*The things concerning, τὰ περί ta peri. (gen.)*
Eph. 6. 22 that ye might know our affairs, and (that)
Phil. 1. 27 I may hear of your affairs, that ye stand
4.*The things concerning, τὰ κατά ta kata. (ac.)*
Eph. 6. 21 But that ye may know my affairs,
5.*Business, matter, πραγματεία pragmateia.*
2 Ti. 2. 4 entangleth himself with the affairs

AFFECT, to —
1.*To roll, move, act,* עָלַל *alal.* 3a.
Lam. 3. 51 Mine eye affecteth mine heart
2.*To be or make zealous, ζηλόω zēloō.*
Gal. 4. 17 exclude you, that ye might affect them

AFFECT, to zealously —
To be or make zealous, ζηλόω zēloō.
Gal. 4. 17 They zealously affect you, (but) not well
4. 18 good to be zealously affected always

AFFECTED, to make evil —
To make evil, κακόω kakoō.
Acts 14. 2 made their minds evil affected against

AFFECTION —
1.*Feeling, passion, πάθημα pathēma.*
Gal. 5. 24 the flesh with the affections and lusts
2.*Feeling, passion, πάθος pathos.*
Rom. 1. 26 God gave them up unto vile affections

AFFECTION, inordinate —
Feeling, passion, πάθος pathos.
Col. 3. 5 fornication, uncleanness, inordi. affection

AFFECTION, inward —
Bowels, σπλάγχνα *splangchna.*
2 Co. 7. 15 his inward affection is more abundant

AFFECTION on, to set the —
To mind, think, φρονέω *phroneō.*
Col. 3. 2 Set your affection on things above, not on

AFFECTION to, to set —
To be pleased, רָצָה *ratsah.*
1 Ch. 29. 3 have set my affection to the house of my

AFFECTION, without natural —
Without affection, ἄστοργος *astorgos.*
Rom. 1. 31 without natural affection; 2 Tim. 3. 3.

AFFECTIONED, kindly —
Lovingly affectioned, φιλόστοργος *philostorgos.*
Rom 12. 10 kindly affectioned one to another with

AFFECTIONATELY desirous of, be —
To long or yearn for, ἱμείρομαι *himeiromai.*
1 Th. 2. 8 So being affectionately desirous of you

AFFINITY, to join, join in, make —
To join oneself, חָתַן *chathan,* 7.
1 Ki. 3. 1 Solomon made affinity with Pharaoh king
2 Ch. 18. 1 Jehoshaphat..joined affinity with Ahab
Ezra 9. 14 Should we..join in affinity

AFFIRM confidently, to —
To asseverate, διϊσχυρίζομαι *diischurizomai.*
Luke 22. 59 another confidently affirmed, saying

AFFIRM constantly, to —
1. *Maintain strongly,* διαβεβαιόομαι *diabebaioomai.*
Titus 3. 8 I will that thou affirm constantly
2. *To asseverate,* διϊσχυρίζομαι *diischurizomai.*
Acts 12. 15 But she constantly affirmed that it was

AFFIRM, to —
1. *To maintain strongly,* διαβεβαιόομαι *diabebaioomai*
1 Ti. 1. 7 what they say, nor whereof they affirm
2. *To say frequently,* φάσκω *phaskō.*
Acts 25. 19 Jesus..whom Paul affirmed to be alive
3. *To say,* φήμι *phēmi.*
Rom. 3. 8 as..reported, and as some affirm

AFFLICT lightly, to —
To esteem lightly, קָלַל *qalal,* 5.
Isa. 9. 1 at the first he lightly afflicted the land

AFFLICT, to —
1. *To afflict, grieve,* יָגָה *yagah,* 5.
Isa. 51. 23 into the hand of them that afflict thee
Lam. 1. 5 for the LORD hath afflicted her
1. 12 wherewith the LORD hath afflicted (me)
2. *To press,* לָחַץ *lachats.*
Amos 6. 14 they shall afflict you from the entering
3. *To lower, afflict,* עָנָה *anah,* 3.
Gen. 15. 13 they shall afflict them four hundred years
31. 50 If thou shalt afflict my daughters
Exod. 1. 11 they did..afflict them with their burdens
1. 12 the more they afflicted them, the more
22. 22 Ye shall not afflict any widow
22. 23 If thou afflict them in any wise
Lev. 16. 29 the month, ye shall afflict your souls
16. 31 ye shall afflict your souls, by a statute
23. 27 and ye shall afflict your souls
23. 32 and ye shall afflict your souls
Num 24. 24 the coast of Chittim, and shall afflict
24. 24 and shall afflict Eber..he also shall
29. 7 and ye shall afflict your souls
30. 13 every binding oath to afflict the soul
Deut 26. 6 evil entreated us, and afflicted us
Judg 16. 5 we may bind him to afflict him
16. 6 thou mightest be bound to afflict thee
16. 19 and she began to afflict him
2 Sa. 7. 10 children of wickedness afflict them
1 Ki. 11. 39 And I will for this afflict the seed
2 Ki. 17. 20 all the seed of..afflicted them
Job 30. 11 hath loosed my cord, and afflicted me
37. 23 plenty of justice: he will not afflict
Psa. 88. 7 thou hast afflicted (me) with all thy
89. 22 nor the son of wickedness afflict him
90. 15 the days (wherein) thou hast afflicted us
94. 5 They break in pieces..and afflict thine
119. 75 thou in faithfulness hast afflicted me
Isa. 58. 3 (wherefore) have we afflicted our soul
58. 5 a day for a man to afflict his soul?
60. 14 The sons..that afflicted thee shall come?
64. 12 wilt thou hold thy peace, and afflict us
Lam. 3. 33 For he doth not afflict willingly
[*See also* Nah. 1. 12, 12; Zeph. 3. 19.]
4. *To lower, afflict,* עָנָה *anah.*
Psa. 55 19 God shall hear and afflict them, even he
5. *To lower, afflict,* עָנָה *anah,* 5.
1 Ki. 8. 35 their sin, when thou afflictest them
2 Ch. 6. 26 their sin, when thou dost afflict them
6. *To straiten,* צָרַר *tsarar.*
Psa. 129. 1 Many a time have they afflicted me v. 2,
143. 12 destroy all them that afflict my soul
Amos 5 12 they afflict the just, they take a bribe
7. *To do evil,* רָעַע *raa,* 5.
Num 11. 11 Wherefore hast thou afflicted thy servant?
Ruth 1. 21 and the Almighty hath afflicted me?
Psa. 44. 2 (how) thou didst afflict the people
Jer. 31. 28 and to destroy, and to afflict
Mic. 4. 6 and her that I have afflicted
8. *To press,* θλίβω *thlibō.*
2 Co. 1. 6 whether we be afflicted, (it is) for your
1 Ti. 5. 10 if she have relieved the afflicted, if she
Heb. 11. 37 wandered about..destitute, afflicted

AFFLICT, to more grievously —
To make heavy, כָּבַד *kabad,* 5.
Isa. 9. 1 did more grievously afflict

AFFLICT selves, to —
To lower, afflict oneself, עָנָה *anah* 7.
Ezra 8. 21 that we might afflict ourselves before

AFFLICTED —
1. *Bruised,* דַּךְ *dak.*
Prov. 26. 28 A lying tongue hateth (those..) afflicted
2. *Lowered, humbled,* עָנִי *ani.*
2 Sa. 22. 28 And the afflicted people thou wilt save
Job 34. 28 he heareth the cry of the afflicted
Psa. 18. 27 thou wilt save the afflicted people
22. 24 abhorred the affliction of the afflicted
25. 16 I (am) desolate and afflicted
82. 3 do justice to the afflicted and needy
88. 15 I (am) afflicted and ready to die from (my)
102. *title.* Prayer of the afflicted when he is
140. 12 will maintain the cause of the afflicted
Prov. 15. 15 all the days of the afflicted (are) evil
22. 22 neither oppress the afflicted in the gate
Isa. 49. 13 will have mercy upon his afflicted
51. 21 Therefore, hear now this, thou afflicted
54. 11 O thou afflicted, tossed with tempest
Zeph. 3. 12 I will..leave..an afflicted and poor
3. *Son of affliction,* בֶּן־עֳנִי *ben oni.*
Prov. 31. 5 pervert the judgment..of the afflicted
4. *Straitness,* צַר *tsar.*
Isa. 63. 9 In all their affliction he was afflicted
5. *To press,* θλίβω *thlibō.*
1 Tim. 5 10 if she have relieved the afflicted,

AFFLICTED, to be —
1. *To be afflicted, grieved,* יָגָה *yagah,* 2.
Lam. 1. 4 her priests sigh, her virgins are afflicted
2. *To be lowered, humbled,* עָנָה *anah.*
Psa. 116. 10 I believed..I was greatly afflicted
119. 67 Before I was afflicted I went astray
3. *To be lowered, humbled,* עָנָה *anah,* 2.
Psa. 119. 107 I am afflicted very much: quicken me
Isa. 53. 7 He was oppressed, and he was afflicted
58. 10 the hungry, and satisfy the afflicted soul
4. *To be lowered, humbled,* עָנָה *anah,* 4.
Lev. 23. 29 that shall not be afflicted in that same day
Psa. 119. 71 good for me that I have been afflicted
Isa. 53. 4 stricken, smitten of God, and afflicted
5. *To lower or afflict oneself,* עָנָה *anah,* 7.
1 Ki. 2. 26 been afflicted..my father was afflicted
Psa. 107. 17 because of their iniquities, are afflicted
6. *To press,* θλίβω *thlibō.*
2 Cor. 1. 6 whether we be afflicted..your consolation
Heb. 11. 37 being destitute, afflicted, tormented
7. *Pressure,* θλῖψις *thlipsis.*
Matt 24. 9 they deliver you up to be afflicted
8. *To suffer evil,* κακοπαθέω *kakopatheō.*
Jas. 5. 13 Is any among you afflicted? let him pray
9. *To bear labour,* ταλαιπωρέω *talaipōreō.*
Jas. 4. 9 Be afflicted, and mourn, and weep

AFFLICTED, him that is —
One that is melting away, מָס *mas.*
Job 6. 14 To him that is afflicted pity (should be

AFFLICTION —
1. *Iniquity, vanity,* אָוֶן *aven.*
Job 5. 6 Although affliction cometh not forth of
Jer. 4. 15 a voice..publisheth affliction from
Hab. 3. 7 I saw the tents of Cushan in affliction
2. *Pressure,* לַחַץ *lachats.*
1 Ki. 22. 27 bread of affliction and with water of a.
2 Ch. 18 26 bread of affliction and with water of a.
Isa. 30. 20 the LORD give you..the water of affliction
3. *Pressure, straitness,* מוּעָקָה *muaqah.*
Psa. 66. 11 thou laidst affliction upon our loins
4. *Eye, aspect,* עַיִן *ayin* [V. L. עָוֹן ? *avon*].
2 Sa. 16. 12 the LORD will look on mine affliction
5. *To be lowered, humbled,* עָנָה *anah,* 4.
Psa. 132. 1 remember David, (and) all his afflictions
6. *Lowered one, or state,* עֱנוּת *enuth.*
Psa. 22. 24 nor abhorred the affliction of the afflicted
7. *Affliction,* עֳנִי *oni.*
Gen. 16. 11 because the LORD hath heard..affliction
29. 32 the LORD hath looked upon my affliction
31. 42 God hath seen mine affliction
41. 52 be fruitful in the land of my affliction
Exod. 3. 7 I have..seen the affliction of my people
3. 17 I will bring you up out of the affliction
4. 31 he had looked upon their affliction
Deut 16. 3 seven days shalt thou eat..bread of afflict.
26. 7 the LORD..looked on our affliction
1 Sa. 1. 11 look on the affliction of thine handmaid
2 Ki. 14. 26 For the LORD saw the affliction of Israel
Neh. 9. 9 the affliction of our fathers in Egypt
Job 10. 15 of confusion; therefore see..mine afflict
30. 16 the days of affliction have taken hold
30. 27 the days of affliction prevented me
Job. 36. 8 (and) be holden in cords of affliction
36. 15 He delivereth the poor in his affliction
36 21 this hast thou chosen rather than afflict.
Psa. 25 18 Look upon mine affliction and my pain
44. 24 thou..forgettest our affliction and our
88. 9 Mine eye mourneth by reason of affliction
107. 10 sit in darkness..(being) bound in affliction
107. 41 setteth he the poor on high from affliction
119. 50 This (is) my comfort in my affliction
119 92 should then have perished in mine afflict
119. 153 Consider mine affliction, and deliver me
Isa 48. 10 have chosen thee in the furnace of afflict.
Lam. 1 3 because of affliction, and because of great
1. 7 Jerusalem remembered..her affliction
1 9 O LORD, behold my affliction
3. 1 I (am) the man (that) hath seen affliction
3. 19 Remembering mine affliction and my
8. *Straitness,* צַר *tsar.*
Psa. 106. 44 Nevertheless he regarded their affliction
Hos. 5. 15 and seek my face: in their affliction
Zech. 8. 10 there any) peace..because of the afflict.
9. *Straitness,* צָרָה *tsarah.*
2 Ch. 20. 9 we..cry unto thee in our affliction
Isa. 63. 9 In all their affliction he was afflicted
Jer. 15. 11 entreat thee (well)..in..time of affliction
16. 19 and my refuge in the day of affliction
Jon. 2. 2 I cried by reason of mine affliction
Nah. 1. 9 affliction shall not rise up the second
Zech. 10. 11 he shall pass through the sea..affliction
10. *Evil,* רַע *ra.*
Neh. 1. 3 the captivity..(are) in great affliction
Psa. 34. 19 Many (are) the afflictions of the righteous
107. 39 brought low through oppression, affliction
Jer. 48. 16 the calamity of Moab..his affliction
Obad. 13 not have looked on their affliction
Zech. 1. 15 and they helped forward the affliction
11. *Breach, breaking,* שֶׁבֶר *sheber.*
Jer. 30. 15 Why criest thou for thine affliction?
Amos 6. 6 but they are not grieved for the affliction
12. *Pressure,* θλῖψις *thlipsis.*
Mark 4. 17 afterward, when affliction or persecution
13. 19 For (in) those days shall be affliction
Acts 7. 10 delivered him out of all his afflictions
7. 11 Egypt and Chanaan, and great affliction
20. 23 that bonds and afflictions abide me
2 Co. 2. 4 out of much affliction and anguish of heart
4. 17 our light affliction, which is but for a
6. 4 of God, in much patience, in afflictions
8. 2 that in a great trial of affliction
Phil. 1. 16 supposing to add affliction to my bonds
4. 14 ye did communicate with my affliction
Col. 1. 24 and fill up..the afflictions of Christ
1 Th. 1. 6 received the word in much affliction
3. 3 no man should be moved by these afflict.
3. 7 we were comforted..in all our affliction
Heb. 10. 33 both by reproaches and afflictions; and
Jas. 1. 27 To visit the fatherless..in their affliction
13. *Evil treatment,* κάκωσις *kakōsis.*
Acts 7. 34 I have seen the affliction of my people
14. *Suffering, feeling,* πάθημα *pathēma.*
2 Ti. 3. 11 Persecutions, afflictions, which came unto
Heb 10. 32 ye endured a great fight of afflictions
1 Pe 5. 9 knowing that the same afflictions are

AFFLICTION, to be partaker of —
To suffer evil together, συγκακοπαθέω *sugkakopatheō*
2 Ti. 1. 8 be thou partaker of the afflictions of the

AFFLICTION with, to suffer —
To have evil together, συγκακουχέω *sugkakoucheō.*
Heb. 11. 25 Choosing rather to suffer affliction with

AFFLICTION, suffering —
Suffering evil, κακοπάθεια *kakopatheia.*
Jas. 5. 10 for an example of suffering affliction, and

AFFLICTION, to be in —
To straiten, send distress, צָרַר *tsarar,* 5.
2 Ch. 33. 12 when he was in affliction, he besought

AFFLICTIONS, to endure —
To suffer evil, κακοπαθέω *kakopatheō.*
2 Ti. 4. 5 watch thou in all..endure afflictions

AFFORDING —
To bring out, פּוּק *puq,* 5.
Psa. 144. 13 garners..full, affording all manner of

AFFRIGHT, to —
1. *To make afraid, terrify,* בָּעַת *baath,* 3.
Isa. 21. 4 My heart panted, fearfulness affrighted
2. *To make afraid,* יָרֵא *yare,* 3.
2 Ch. 32. 18 to affright them, and to trouble them

AFFRIGHTED —
In fear, ἔμφοβος *emphobos.*
Luke 24. 37 they were terrified and affrighted
Rev. 11. 13 the remnant were affrighted, and gave

AFFRIGHTED, to be —
1. *To be troubled,* בָּהַל *bahal,* 2.
Jer. 51. 32 and the men of war are affrighted
2. *To be broken down,* חָתַת *chathath,* 2.
Job 39. 22 He mocketh at fear, and is not affrighted
3. *To be terrified,* עָרַץ *arats.*
Deut. 7. 21 Thou shalt not be affrighted at them
4. *To lay hold on fear,* אָחַז שַׂעַר *achaz saar.*
Job 18. 20 as they that went before were affrighted

5. *To wonder greatly*, ἐκθαμβέω, *ekthambeō*.
Mark 16. 5 and they were affrighted
16. 6 he saith unto them, Be not affrighted

AFOOT —
On foot, πεζῇ *pezē*.
Mark 6. 33 ran afoot thither out of all cities

AFOOT, to go —
To be or go on foot, πεζεύω, *pezeuō*.
Acts 20. 13 minding himself to go afoot

AFORE —
1. *Face, front*, פָּנִים *panim*.
Isa. 18. 5 For afore the harvest, when the bud is
Eze. 33. 22 in the evening, afore he that was escaped
2. *Former state or time*, קַדְמָה *qadmah*.
Psa. 129. 6 which withereth afore it groweth

AFORE, to promise —
Announce before, προεπαγγέλλομαι *proepaggellomai*
Rom. 1. 2 Which he had promised afore by his

AFORE or aforetime, to write —
To write beforehand, προγράφω, *prographō*.
Eph. 3. 3 as I wrote afore in few words
Rom. 15. 4 whatsoever things.. written aforetime

AFOREHAND, to come —
To take beforehand, προλαμβάνω *prolambanō*.
Mark 14. 8 she is come aforehand to anoint my body

AFORETIME —
1. *Face, front*, פָּנִים *panim*.
Neh. 13. 5 where aforetime they laid the meat offer.
Job 17. 6 and aforetime I was as a tabret
2. *East, former, before*, קֶדֶם *qedem*.
Jer. 30. 20 Their children al o shall be as aforetime
3. *Once*, ποτέ, *pote*.
John 9. 13 They brought..him that aforetime was
Before this, מִן קַדְמַת דְּנָה *min qadmath denah*.
Dan. 6 10 gave thanks before his God, as.. aforetime

AFRAID —
1. *Trembling*, חָרֵד *chared*.
Judg. 7. 3 Whosoever (is) fearful and afraid, let him
2. *Fearing*, יָרֵא *yare*.
Deut. 7. 19 all the people of whom thou art afraid
1 Sa. 23. 3 Behold, we be afraid here in Judah
Jer. 42. 11 Be not afraid..are afraid..be not afraid
3. *In fear*, ἔμφοβος, *emphobos*.
Luke 24. 5 as they were afraid, and bowed down
Acts 10. 4 when he looked on him, he was afraid, and
22. 9 they..saw indeed the light..were afraid

AFRAID, to be —
1. *To be troubled*, בָּהַל *bahal*, 2.
Job 21. 6 Even when I remember I am afraid
Isa. 13. 8 And they shall be afraid
2. *To be terrified, afraid*, בָּעַת *baath*, 2.
1 Ch. 21. 30 to enquire of God: for he was afraid
Esth. 7. 6 Haman was afraid before the king
Dan. 8. 17 I was afraid, and fell upon my face
3. *To be afraid*, גּוּר *gur*.
Num 22. 3 And Moab was sore afraid of the people
Deut. 1. 17 ye shall not be afraid of the face of man
18. 22 thou shalt not be afraid of him
1 Sa. 18. 15 when Saul saw..he was afraid of him
Job 19. 29 Be ye afraid of the sword
41. 25 raiseth up himself, the mighty are afraid
4. *To be grieved, melted*, דָּאַג *daag*.
Isa. 57. 11 of whom hast thou been afraid
Jer. 38. 19 I am afraid of the Jews that are fallen
42. 16 the famine, whereof ye were afraid
5. *To be afraid, to creep*, זָחַל *zachal*.
Job 32. 6 ye (are) very old; wherefore I was afraid
6. *To be girded, restrained*, חָגַר *chagar*.
2 Sa. 22. 46 they shall be afraid out of their close
7. *To be pained*, חִיל, חוּל *chul, chil*.
Psa. 77. 16 the waters saw thee; they were afraid
8. *To be girded, restrained*, חָרַג *charag*.
Psa. 18. 45 and be afraid out of their close places
9. *To tremble*, חָרַד *charad*.
Gen. 42. 28 their heart failed..they were afraid
Ruth 3. 8 it came to pass..the man was afraid
1 Sa. 21. 1 Ahimelech was afraid at the meeting
28. 5 when Saul saw the host..he was afraid
1 Ki. 1. 49 the guests that (were) with A. were afraid
Isa 10. 29 Ramah is afraid; Gibeah of Saul is fled
19. 16 and it shall be afraid and fear
41. 5 the ends of the earth were afraid
Amos 3. 6 and the people not be afraid?
10. *To be cast down*, חָתַת *chathath*.
Isa. 20. 5 they shall be afraid and ashamed of E.
31. 9 his princes shall be afraid of the ensign
11. *To be cast down*, חָתַת *chathath*, 2.
Isa. 31. 4 will not be afraid of their voice
51. 7 neither be ye afraid of their revilings
Mal. 2. 5 wherewith he..was afraid before my name
12. *To be afraid*, יָגֹר *yagor*.
Deut. 9. 19 For I was afraid of the anger
28. 60 all the diseases..thou wast afraid of
Job 3. 25 that which I was afraid of is come
9. 28 I am afraid of all my sorrows
Jer. 39. 17 the men of whom thou (art) afraid
13. *To fear, reverence*, יָרֵא *yare*.
Gen. 3. 10 I was afraid, because I (was) naked
18. 15 I laughed not; for she was afraid
20. 8 and the men were sore afraid
28. 17 he was afraid, and said, How dreadful
31. 31 and said to Laban, Because I was afraid
32. 7 Then Jacob was greatly afraid and
42. 35 father saw the..money, they were afraid
43. 18 And the men were afraid
Exod. 3. 6 Moses hid his face; for he was afraid
14. 10 and they were sore afraid
34. 30 they were afraid to come nigh him
Num 12. 8 then were ye not afraid to speak
Deut. 1. 29 Dread not, neither be afraid of them
2. 4 and they shall be afraid of you
5. 5 for ye were afraid by reason of the fire
7 18 Thou shalt not be afraid of them
20. 1 and seest horses,..be not afraid of them
28. 10 and they shall be afraid of thee
Josh. 9. 24 we were sore afraid of our lives
11. 6 LORD said..Be not afraid because of them
1 Sa. 4. 7 And the Philistines were afraid, for they
7. 7 Israel heard (it), they were afraid
17. 11 they were dismayed, and greatly afraid
17. 24 all..fled from him, and were sore afraid
18. 12 And Saul was afraid of David
18. 29 Saul was yet the more afraid of David
21. 12 was sore afraid of Achish the king of
28. 5 he was afraid, and his heart greatly
28. 13 the king said unto her, Be not afraid
28. 20 was sore afraid, because of the words of S.
31. 4 would not; for he was sore afraid
2 Sa. 1. 14 wast thou not afraid to stretch forth thine
6. 9 David was afraid of the LORD that day
2 Ki. 1. 15 Go down with him: be not afraid of him
10. 4 But they were exceedingly afraid, and
19. 6 Be not afraid of the words which thou
25. 26 for they were afraid of the Chaldees
1 Ch. 10. 4 would not; for he was sore afraid
13. 12 David was afraid of God that day
2 Ch. 20. 15 Be not afraid nor dismayed by reason
32. 7 be not afraid nor dismayed for the king
Neh. 2. 2 Then I was very sore afraid
4. 14 Be not ye afraid of them: remember the
6. 13 that I should be afraid, and do so, and sin
Job 5. 21 neither shalt thou be afraid of destruction
5. 22 neither shalt thou be afraid of the beasts
6. 21 see (my) casting down, and are afraid
Psa. 3. 6 I will not be afraid of ten thousands of
49. 16 Be not thou afraid when one is made rich
56. 3 What time I am afraid, I will trust in thee
56. 11 I will not be afraid what man can do
65. 8 They also that dwell..are afraid at thy
91. 5 Thou shalt not be afraid for the terror by
112. 7 He shall not be afraid of evil tidings
112. 8 His heart (is) established, he..be afraid
119. 120 and I am afraid of thy judgments
Prov. 3. 25 Be not afraid of sudden fear
31. 21 She is not afraid of the snow for her
Eccl. 12. 5 they shall be afraid of (that which is)
Isa. 10. 24 O my people..be not afraid of the
37. 6 Be not afraid of the words that thou hast
40. 9 lift up thy voice..be not afraid
51. 12 that thou shouldest be afraid of a man
Jer. 1. 8 Be not afraid of their faces: for I (am)
10. 5 Be not afraid of them; for they cannot
26. 21 when Urijah heard it, he was afraid
41. 18 Chaldeans: for they were afraid of them
42. 11 Be not afraid of the king of Babylon
42. 11 be not afraid of him, saith the LORD
Eze. 2. 6 be not afraid of them..neither be afraid
2. 6 be not afraid of their words, nor be
Joel 2. 22 Be not afraid, ye beasts of the field
Jon. 1. 5 Then the mariners were afraid, and cried
1. 10 Then were the men exceedingly afraid
Hab. 3. 2 I..heard thy speech, (and) was afraid
14. *To be afraid, to tremble*, רָהָה *rahah*.
Isa. 44. 8 Fear ye not, neither be afraid: have not
15. *To be affrighted*, עָרַץ *arats*.
Deut 31. 6 fear not, nor be afraid of them
Josh. 1. 9 be not afraid, neither be thou dismayed
16. *To declare fearful*, עָרַץ *arats*, 5.
Isa. 8. 12 neither fear ye..nor be afraid
17. *To fear, be afraid, hasten*, פָּחַד *pachad*.
Job 23. 15 when I consider, I am afraid of him
Psa 27. 1 of whom shall I be afraid?
Prov. 3. 24 thou liest down, thou shalt not be afraid
Isa. 12. 2 I will trust, and not be afraid
19. 17 every one..shall be afraid in himself
33. 14 The sinners in Zion are afraid
Jer. 36. 16 they were afraid both one and other
36. 24 Yet they were not afraid, nor rent their
Mic. 7. 17 they shall be afraid of the LORD our God
18. *To be angry, tremble*, רָגַז *ragaz*.
Exod 15. 14 people shall hear, (and) be afraid
19. *To be afraid, to tremble*, רָהָה *rahah*.
Isa. 44. 8 Fear ye not, neither be afraid: have not
20. *To be whirled away*, שָׂעַר *saar*.
Eze. 27. 35 their kings shall be sore afraid, they shall
32. 10 their kings shall be horribly afraid for
21. *To be timid, shrinking*, δειλιάω, *deiliaō*.
John 14. 27 be troubled, neither let it be afraid
22. *To tremble*, τρέμω, *tremō*.
2 Pe. 2. 10 not afraid to speak evil of dignities
23. *To fear, be afraid*, φοβέομαι, *phobeomai*.
Matt. 2. 22 he was afraid to go thither
14. 27 Be of good cheer..be not afraid
14. 30 he was afraid; and beginning to sink
17. 6 fell on their face, and were sore afraid
17. 7 Jesus..said, Arise, and be not afraid
25. 25 I was afraid, and went and hid
28. 10 Then said Jesus unto them, be not afraid
Mark 5. 15 his right mind: and they were afraid
5. 36 he saith unto the ruler..Be not afraid
6. 50 Be of good cheer..be not afraid
9. 32 not that saying, and were afraid to ask him
10. 32 as they followed, they were afraid
16 8 anything to any (man)..they were afraid
Luke 8. 25 And they being afraid wondered, saying
8. 35 in his right mind: and they were afraid
12. 4 Be not afraid of them that kill the body
John 6 19 see Jesus walking..and they were afraid
6. 20 he saith unto them..be not afraid
19. 8 that saying, he was the more afraid
Acts 9 26 they were all afraid of him, and
18. 9 Be not afraid, but speak, and hold not
22. 29 and the chief captain also was afraid
Rom 13. 3 Wilt thou then not be afraid of the
13. 4 But if thou do that which is evil, be afraid
Gal. 4. 11 I am afraid of you, lest I have bestowed
Heb. 11. 23 and they were not afraid of the king's
1 Pe. 3. 6 and are not afraid with any amazement
3. 14 and be not afraid of their terror, neither

AFRAID, sore —
Greatly fearing, ἔκφοβος *ekphobos*.
Mark 9. 6 for they were sore afraid

AFRAID, to be sore —
They feared a great fear, ἐφοβήθησαν φόβον μέγαν.
Luke 2. 9 the glory..shone..they were sore afraid

AFRAID, to be horribly —
To be whirled away, שָׂעַר *saar*.
Jer. 2. 12 be horribly afraid, be ye Eze. 32. 10.

AFRAID, to make —
1. *To trouble, hasten*, בָּהַל *bahal*, 3.
Psa. 83. 15 make them afraid with thy storm
2. *To make afraid, terrify*, בָּעַת *baath*, 3.
2 Sa. 22. 5 floods of ungodly men made me afraid
Job 13. 11 Shall not his excellency make you afraid?
13. 21 and let not thy dread make me afraid
15. 24 anguish shall make him afraid
18. 11 Terrors shall make him afraid on every
33. 7 my terror shall not make thee afraid
Psa. 18. 4 floods of ungodly men made me afraid
3. *To make afraid*, דְּחַל *dechal*, 3.
Dan. 4. 5 I saw a dream which made me afraid
4. *To cause to tremble, trouble*, חָרַד *charad*, 5.
Lev. 26. 6 and none shall make (you) afraid
2 Sa. 17. 2 I will come..and will make him afraid
Job 11. 19 lie down, and none shall make..afraid
Isa. 17. 2 and none shall make (them) afraid
Jer. 30. 10 quiet, and none shall make (him) afraid
46. 27 Jacob..none shall make (him) afraid
Eze. 30. 9 to make the careless Ethiopians afraid
34. 28 safely, and none shall make..afraid
39. 26 safely..and none made (them) afraid
Mic. 4. 4 and none shall make (them) afraid
Nah. 2. 11 whelp, and none made (them) afraid?
Zeph. 3. 13 and none shall make (them) afraid
5. *To cast down*, חָתַת *chathath*, 5.
Hab. 2. 17 spoil of beasts..made them afraid
6. *To make afraid*, יָרֵא *yare*, 3.
2 Sa. 14. 15 because the people have made me afraid
Neh. 6. 9 For they all made us afraid, saying
7. *To cause to shake or tremble*, רָעַשׁ *raash*, 5.
Job 39. 20 Canst thou make..afraid as a grasshopper?

AFRESH, to crucify —
To crucify again, or anew, ἀνασταυρόω, *anastauroō*.
Heb. 6. 6 crucify to themselves the son of God afresh

AFTER, (that follow)—
1. *After*, אַחַר *achar*.
Gen. 5. 4 And the days of Adam after he had
5. 7 Seth lived after he begat Enos
5. 10 And Enos lived after he begat Cainan
2. *Last, latter end*, אַחֲרוֹן *acharon*.
Gen. 33. 2 he put..Leah and her children after
1 Ki. 17. 13 and after make for thee and for thy son
Job 18. 20 They that come after (him) shall be
Eccl. 1. 11 come with (those) that shall come after
4. 16 they..that come after shall not rejoice
3. *After*, אַחֲרֵי *achare*.
Dan. 7. 24 and another shall rise after them
4. *Unto, to*, אֶל *el*.
Lev. 20. 6 And the soul that turneth after such
5. *When*, כַּאֲשֶׁר *ka-asher*.
Judg 16. 22 hair..began to grow again after he was
6. *After, step, walk*, אֲתַר *athar*.
Dan. 2. 39 after thee shall arise another kingdom
7. *From (the time) that*, מִדֵּי *mid-de*.
1 Sa. 18. 30 it came to pass, after they went forth
8. *From*, מִן *min*.
1 Ch. 8. 8 (children)..after he had sent them away
Ezra 5. 12 after that our fathers had provoked the
Dan. 4. 26 after that thou shalt have known

9.*On, upon, in addition to,* עַל *al.*
Gen. 48. 6 shall be called after the name of their

10.*According to the mouth of* לְפִי *le-phi.*
Jer. 29. 10 That after seventy years be accomplished

11.*From the end,* מִקֵּץ *miq-qets.*
Gen. 16. 3 after Abram had dwelt ten years in the
Num 13. 25 returned from searching..after forty
2 Sa. 15. 7 And it came to pass after forty years
1 Ki. 17. 7 And it came to pass after a while
2 Ch. 18. 2 And after (certain) years he went down
Neh. 13. 6 and after certain days obtained I leave
Esth. 2. 12 after that she had been twelve months
Jer. 13. 6 And it came to pass after many days
42. 7 And it came to pass after ten days
Dan. 11. 13 shall certainly come after certain years

12.*From the end of,* מִקְצֵה [*miq-qatseh*].
Josh. 3. 2 And it came to pass after three days

13.*At the time of the going out of,* כְּעֵת צֵאת [*eth*].
2 Ch. 21. 19 it came to pass..after the end of two

14.*The foot,* רֶגֶל *regel.*
1 Sa. 25. 42 five damsels of her's that went after her
2 Sa. 15. 16 went forth, and all his household after
15. 17 went forth, and all the people after him
15. 18 six hundred men which came after him

15.*At the time,* לְעֵת *le-eth.*
1 Ch. 20. 1 it came to pass that after the year was

16.*Through, during, after,* διά *dia (gen.)*
Mark 2. 1 And..he entered into Capernaum after
Acts 24. 17 Now after many years I came to bring
Gal. 2. 1 Then fourteen years after I went up again

17.*In, by,* ἐν, *en.*
Heb. 4. 11 lest any man fall after the same example

18.*Upon, on account of,* ἐπί *(dat.) epi.*
Luke 1. 59 called him Zacharias, after Ro. 5. 14.

19.*Upon,* ἐπί *epi (acc.)* Luke 15. 4.

20.*Down towards, according to,* κατά *(acc.) kata.*
Matt 23. 3 but do not ye after their works: for they
Luke 2. 27 to do for him after the custom of the law
2. 42 they went up to Jerusalem after the
John 8. 15 Ye judge after the flesh; I judge no man
Acts 13. 22 the (son) of Jesse, a man after mine own
23. 3 for sittest thou to judge me after the
24. 14 I confess unto thee, that after the way
26. 5 that after the most straitest sect of our
Rom. 2. 5 But after thy hardness and impenitent
7. 22 in the law of God after the inward man
8. 1 [walk not after the flesh, but after the]
8. 4 walk not after the flesh, but after the
8. 5 are after the flesh..are after the Spirit
8. 12 not to the flesh, to live after the flesh
8. 13 if ye live after the flesh, ye shall die
1 Co. 1. 26 not many wise men after the flesh
7. 40 if she so abide after my judgment
10. 18 Behold Israel after the flesh: are not
2 Co. 5. 16 no man after the..Christ after the flesh
10. 3 we do not war after the flesh; 7. 9, 11.
10. 7 Do ye look on things after the outward
11. 17 I speak (it) not after the Lord, but as it
11. 18 seeing that many glory after the flesh
Gal. 1. 11 was preached of me is not after man
4. 23 of the bondwoman was born after the
4. 29 born after the flesh..after the Spirit
Eph. 1. 11 worketh all things after the counsel of
4. 24 after God is created in righteousness
Col. 2. 8 after..men, after the rudiments..after
2. 22 after the commandments and doctrines
3. 10 is renewed in knowledge after the image
2 Th. 2. 9 whose coming is after the working
3. 6 not after the tradition which he received
2 Ti. 4. 3 after their own lusts shall they heap
Titus 1. 1 acknowledging of the truth..after
1. 4 Titus, (mine) own son after the common
Heb. 5. 6 Thou (art) a priest for ever after the
5. 10 Called of God an high priest after the
6. 20 an high priest for ever after the order
7. 11 after the order of M...after the order of A.
7. 15 for that after the similitude of Melchisedec
7. 16 not after the law..but after the power
7. 17 Thou (art) a priest for ever after the order
7. 21 Thou (art) a priest for ever [after the order]
12. 10 For they verily..after their own pleasure
Jas. 3. 9 which are made after the similitude of
2 Pe. 3. 3 scoffers, walking after their own lusts
2 Jo. 6 this is love, that we walk after his
Jude 16 These are murmurers,..walking after
18 who should walk after their own ungodly

21.*After, upon,* μετά *(acc.) meta.*
Matt. 1. 12 after they were brought to Babylon
17. 1 after six days Jesus taketh Peter, James
24. 29 Immediately after the tribulation of those
25. 19 After a long time the lord of those
26. 2 Ye know that after two days is
26. 32 But after I am risen again, I will go
26. 73 And after a while came unto him
27. 53 came out of the graves after his
27. 63 After three days I will rise again
Mark 1. 14 after that John was put in prison
8. 31 be killed, and after three days rise again
9. 2 after six days Jesus taketh (with him)
13. 24 in those days, after that tribulation
14. 1 After two days was (the feast of) the
14. 28 after that I am risen, I will go
14. 70 And a little after, they that stood by
16. 12 [After that he appeared in another form]
16. 19 [So then after the Lord had spoken unto]
Luke 1. 24 And after those days his wife Elisabeth
Luke 2. 46 it came to pass, that after three days
5. 27 And after these things he went forth
9. 28 about an eight days after these sayings
10. 1 After these things the Lord appointed
12. 4 and after that have no more that they
12. 5 Fear him which after he hath killed hath
15. 13 And not many days after the younger son
22. 20 Likewise also the cup after supper, saying
22. 58 after a little while another saw him
John 2. 12 After this he went down to Capernaum
3. 22 After these things came Jesus and his
4. 43 after two days he departed thence, and
5. 1 after this there was a feast of the Jews
5. 4 [whosoever then first after the troubling]
6. 1 After these things Jesus went over the
7. 1 After these things Jesus walked in
11. 7 Then after that saith he to (his) disciples
11. 11 and after that he saith unto them, Our
13. 27 after the sop Satan entered into him
19. 28 After this, Jesus knowing that all things
19. 38 after this Joseph of Arimathea, being a
20. 26 after eight days again his disciples
21. 1 After these things Jesus shewed himself
Acts 1. 3 he shewed himself alive after his passion
5. 37 After this man rose up Judas of Galilee
7. 5 and to his seed after him, when (as yet)
7. 7 and after that shall they come forth, and
10. 37 and began from Galilee, after the baptism
10. 41 who did eat..after he rose from the dead
12. 4 intending after Easter to bring him forth
13. 15 And after the reading of the law and
13. 20 And after that he gave (unto them)
13. 25 But, behold, there cometh one after me
15. 13 And after they had held their peace
15. 16 After this I will return, and will build
15. 36 And some days after Paul said unto
18. 1 After these things Paul departed from
19. 4 on him which should come after him
19. 21 After these things were ended, Paul
20. 1 after the uproar was ceased, Paul called
20. 6 we sailed away from Philippi after the
20. 29 I know this, that after my departing
21. 15 after those days we took up our carriages
24. 1 after five days Ananias the high priest
24. 24 after certain days, when Felix came with
25. 1 after three days he ascended from
28. 11 after three months we departed in a ship
28. 13 after one day the south wind blew
28. 17 And it came to pass, that after three days
Gal. 1. 18 Then after three years I went up to
3. 17 was four hundred and thirty years after
Titus 3. 10 A man that is an heretick after the first
Heb. 4. 7 To day, after so long a time; as it is said
8. 10 this (is) the covenant..after those days
9. 3 after the second veil, the tabernacle
9. 27 but after this the judgment
10. 15 for after that he had said before
10. 16 This (is) the covenant that..after those
10. 26 if we sin wilfully after that we have
2 Pe. 1. 15 Moreover I will endeavour..after my
Rev. 4. 1 After this I looked, and, behold, a door
7. 1 after these things I saw four angels
7. 9 After this I beheld, and, lo, a great
11. 11 after three days and an half the Spirit
15. 5 And after that I looked, and, behold
18. 1 after these things I saw another angel
19. 1 after these things I heard a great voice
20. 3 after that he must be loosed a little

22.*The next in order,* ἑξῆς *hexes.*
Luke 7. 11 and it came to pass the day after, that

23.*According to order,* καθεξῆς *kathexes.*
Acts 3. 24 from Samuel and those that follow after

24.*From after, from behind,* ὄπισθεν *opisthen.*
Matt 15. 23 Send her way; for she crieth after us
Luke 23. 26 that he might bear (it) after Jesus

25.*After, behind,* ὀπίσω *opisō.*
Matt. 3. 11 he that cometh after me is mightier
10. 38 followeth after me, is not worthy of me
16. 24 If any (man) will come after me, let
Mark 1. 7 cometh one mightier than I after me
1. 17 Jesus said unto them, Come ye after me
1. 20 they left their father..and went after
8. 34 Whosoever will come after me, let him
Luke 9. 23 If any (man) will come after me, let
14. 27 bear his cross, and come after me
19. 14 and sent a message after him, saying
21. 8 go ye not therefore after them
John 1. 15 He that cometh after me is preferred
1. 27 He it is, who coming after me is preferred
1. 30 After me cometh a man which is preferred
12. 19 behold, the world is gone after him
Acts 5. 37 drew away much people after him: he also
20. 30 to draw away disciples after them
1 Ti. 5. 15 some are already turned aside after Satan
2 Pe. 2. 10 chiefly them that walk after the flesh
Jude 7 going after strange flesh, are set forth
Rev. 12. 15 the serpent cast out..after the wo. 13. 3.

26.*Containing,* περιέχω *periechō*; Acts 23. 25.

27.*When,* ὅτε *hote.*
John 13. 12 So after he had washed their feet, and

28.*As, that, when, after that,* ὡς *hōs.*
Acts 16. 10 And after he had seen the vision
19. 21 After I have been there, I must also see
21. 1 And it came to pass, that after we were

29.*To come through, pass,* διαγίνομαι *diaginomai.*
Acts 25. 13 after certain days king Agrippa and

30.*To fill, fulfil,* πληρόω *plēroō.*
Acts 24. 27 after two years Porcius Festus came into

31.*To be, begin,* ὑπάρχω *huparchō.*
Acts 27. 21 after long abstinence Paul stood forth in
[*See* Ask, come, covet, feel, follow, long, looking, lust, manner, seek, that.]

AFTER, here—
After these, μετὰ ταῦτα *meta tauta.*
John 13. 7 not now; but thou shalt know hereafter
Rev. 1. 19 and the things which shall be hereafter
4. 1 shew thee things which must be hereafter
9. 12 there come two woes more hereafter

AFTER our ability —
According to the measure in us, כְּדֵי בָנוּ [*ke-de be*]
Neh. 5. 8 We after our ability have redeemed our

AFTER should, that —
To be about to, μέλλω *mellō.*
Heb. 11. 8 a place which he should after receive for
2 Pe. 2. 6 those that after should live ungodly

AFTER that —
1.*After,* אַחַר *achar.*
Gen. 13. 14 after that Lot was separated from him
18. 5 hearts; after that ye shall pass on
24. 55 the damsel..after that she shall go
Lev. 13. 55 look on the plague, after that it is
14. 43 after that he hath taken away the stones
15. 28 and after that she shall be clean
25. 48 After that he is sold he may be redeemed
Num. 6. 20 after that the Nazarite may drink
12. 14 and after that let her be received in
30. 15 make them void after that he hath heard
Deut 24. 4 may not take her..after that she is
Judg 15. 7 and after that I will cease
2 Sa. 1. 10 he could not live after that he was
2 Ki 14. 22 after that the king slept with his fathers
1 Ch. 2. 24 And after that Hezron was dead
2 Ch. 25. 14 after that Amaziah was come from the
Eccl. 9. 3 and after that (they go) to the dead
Jer. 12. 15 after that I have plucked them out
24. 1 after that Nebuchadrezzar..had carried
28. 12 after that Hananiah..had broken the
29. 2 after that Jeconiah..and the queen..were
31. 19 Surely after that I was turned, I
34. 8 after that the king..had made a covenant
36. 27 after that the king had burned the roll
40. 1 after that Nebuzar-adan..had let him go
51. 46 and after that in (another) year (shall

2.*After that,* אַחֲרֵי־כֵן *achare ken.*
Gen. 6. 4 after that, when the sons of God came in

3.*Then, afterwards,* εἶτα *eita.*
Mark 4. 28 then the ear; after that the full corn in
8. 25 After that he put (his) hands again upon
John 13. 5 After that he poureth water into a bason

4.*When truly,* ἐπειδή *epeidē.*
1 Co. 1. 21 For after that in the wisdom of God

5.*Afterward,* ἔπειτα *epeita.*
1 Co. 12. 28 after that miracles, then gifts of healing
15. 6 After that, he was seen of above five
15. 7 After that he was seen of James; then
Heb. 7. 2 and after that also King of Salem, which

6.*Yet, still, any more,* ἔτι *eti.*
Luke 20. 40 And after that they durst not ask him any

7.*No more,* οὐκέτι *ouketi.*
Mark 12. 34 And no man after that durst ask him

8.*When,* ὅτε *hote.*
Matt 27. 31 And after that they had mocked, Ti. 3. 4.

9.*At the coming time,* εἰς τὸ μέλλον, Luke 13. 9.

10.*As, that, when, after that,* ὡς *hōs.*
Acts 9. 23 after that many days were fulfilled

AFTER that manner —
According to, thus, כָּכָה *kakah.*
2 Ch. 18. 19 and another saying after that manner

AFTER the manner of —
According to, down, κατά *(acc.) kata.*
John 2. 6 after the manner of the purifying of the

AFTER the same manner —
In the same manner, ὡσαύτως *hōsautōs.*
1 Co. 11. 25 After the same manner also..the cup

AFTER this manner —
1.*Thus,* כָּכָה *kakah.*
2 Ch. 18. 19 one spake saying after this manner

2.*To hold or have around,* περιέχω *periechō.*
Acts 23. 25 he wrote a letter after this manner

AFTER this sort —
According to this, כִּדְנָה *ki-denah.*
Dan. 3. 29 no other..can deliver after this sort

AFTERNOON —
The declining of the day, נְטוֹת הַיּוֹם *netoth hay-yom.*
Judg 19. 8 they tarried until afternoon, and they

AFTERWARD —
1.*After, afterward,* אַחַר *achar.*
Gen. 10. 18 afterward were the families of the
15. 14 afterward shall they come out with great
30. 21 And afterwards she bare a daughter
32. 20 and afterward I will see his face
38. 30 And afterward came out his brother
Exod. 5. 1 And afterward Moses and Aaron went in
Lev. 14. 19 and afterward he shall kill the burnt
14. 36 afterward the priest shall go in to see
22. 7 he..shall afterward eat of the holy things

Num. 5. 26 the priest..afterward shall cause the
12. 16 And afterward the people removed from
19. 7 and afterward he shall come into the
31. 2 afterward shalt thou be gathered unto
31. 24 and afterward ye shall come into the
32. 22 then afterward ye shall return, and be
Deut 24. 21 vineyard,..shalt not glean (it) afterward
Josh. 2. 16 hide yourselves..and afterward may ye
24. 5 I plagued Egypt..and afterward I
Judg. 1. 9 And afterward the children of Judah
7. 11 afterward shall thine hands be strength.
19. 5 Comfort thine heart..and afterward go
1 Ch. 2. 21 afterward Hezron went in to the daughter
2 Ch. 35. 14 And afterward they made ready for
Job 18. 2 mark, and afterwards we will speak
Psa. 73. 24 Thou shalt guide me..and afterward
Prov. 20. 17 afterwards his mouth shall be filled with
24. 27 Prepare thy work without..afterwards
28. 23 He that rebuketh a man afterwards shall
Hos. 3. 5 Afterward shall the children of Israel

2. *Last, latter, at last,* אַחֲרוֹן *acharon.*
Deut 13. 9 afterwards the hand of all the people
17. 7 afterward the hands of all the people
Isa. 9. 1 afterward did more grievously afflict her

3. *After it was so,* אַחֲרֵי־כֵן *achare ken.*
Gen. 15. 14 afterward shall they come out with great

4. *Second, secondly,* δεύτερος *deuteros.*
Jude 5 how that the Lord..afterward destroyed

5. *Then, afterwards,* εἶτα *eita.*
Mark 4. 17 afterward, when affliction or persecution

6. *Afterward,* ἔπειτα *epeita.*
1 Co. 15. 23 afterward they that are Christ's at his
15. 46 that which is natural; and afterward
Gal. 1. 21 Afterwards I came into the regions of

7. *The next in order,* καθεξῆς *kathexēs.*
Luke 8. 1 it came to pass afterward, that he

8. *After these,* μετὰ ταῦτα *meta tauta.*
Luke 17. 8 afterward thou shalt eat and drink?
18. 4 afterward he said within himself, Though
John 5. 14 Afterward Jesus findeth him in the
Heb. 4. 8 then would he not afterward have

9. *After then,* μετέπειτα *metepeita.*
Heb. 12. 17 ye know how that afterward, when he

10. *Afterwards,* ὕστερον *husteron.*
Matt. 4. 2 he had fasted..he was afterward an
21. 29 but afterward he repented, and went
21. 32 repented not afterward, that ye might
25. 11 Afterward came also the other virgins
Mark 16. 14 [Afterward he appeared unto the eleven]
Luke 4. 2 when they were ended, he afterward
John 13. 36 but thou shalt follow me afterwards
Heb. 12. 11 nevertheless afterward it yieldeth the

AFTERWARDS, till—
Behind, backwards, אָחוֹר *achor.*
Prov. 29. 11 wise..keepeth it in till afterwards

AG-AB'-US — Ἄγαβος.
1. A prophet from Jerusalem who went to Paul at Antioch and foretold a great famine.
Acts 11. 28 And there stood up one of them..A.
2. A disciple who went from Judea to Ptolemais and foretold the imprisonment of Paul. (Probably the same as No. 1.)
Acts 21. 10 there came down..a..prophet, named A.

A'-GAG, אֲגַג *high, warlike.*
A poetic name of Amalek, derived from a particular dynasty.
Num 24. 7 his king shall be higher than A., and his
1 Sa. 15. 8 And he took A. the king of the Amalek.
15. 9 Saul and the people spared A., and the
15. 20 Saul said..I have..brought A. the king
15. 32 Then said Samuel, Bring..to me A. the
15. 32 And A. came unto him delicately
15. 32 And A. said, Surely the bitterness of
15. 33 And Samuel hewed A. in pieces before

A-GA-GITE, אֲגָגִי, *belonging to Agag.*
The Agagites were an Amalekite tribe.
Esth. 3. 1 Haman the son of Hammedatha the A.
3. 10 Haman the son of Hammedatha the A.
8. 5 Haman the son of Hammedatha the A.
9. 24 Haman the son of Hammedatha the A.

AGAIN —
1. *Behind,* אַחַר *achar.*
Deut 24. 20 thou shalt not go over the boughs again

2. *Even, also,* גַּם *gam.*
Eccl. 4. 11 Again, if two lie together, then they have

3. *Again,* עוֹד *od.*
Gen. 4. 25 And Adam knew his wife again

4. *Second,* שֵׁנִי *sheni.*
Lev. 13. 6 the priest shall look on him again
13. 7 he shall be seen of the priest again [21.
2 Sa. 16. 19 And again, whom should I serve? Neh. 13.
Eze. 4. 6 lie again on thy right side, and thou shalt
Hag. 2. 20 again the word of the LORD came unto H.
Zech. 4. 12 And I answered again, and said unto him
Mal. 2. 13 And this have ye done again, covering

5. *Second,* תִּנְיָנוּת *tinyanuth.*
Dan. 2. 7 They answered again and said, Let the

6. *To go,* הָלַךְ *yalak.*
Eccl. 1. 7 whence the rivers come..they return again

7. *To add,* יָסַף *yasaph.*
Gen. 8. 12 which returned not again unto him any
Gen. 38. 26 And he knew her again no more
Num 32. 15 he will yet again leave them in the wild.
1 Sa. 27. 4 and he sought no more again for him
2 Ki. 19. 30 house of Judah shall yet again take root
Isa. 37. 31 the remnant..shall again take root

8. *To add,* יָסַף *yasaph,* 5.
Gen. 4. 2 And she again bare his brother Abel
8. 10 and again he sent forth the dove out of
8. 21 I will not again curse..again smite any
18. 29 And he spake unto him yet again
25. 1 again Abraham took a wife, and her name
38. 5 And she yet again conceived, and bare a
Exod 10. 29 I will see thy face again no more
14. 13 ye shall see them again no more for ever
Num 22. 15 And Balak sent yet again princes
22. 25 crushed Balaam's foot..smote her again
Deut 18. 16 Let me not hear again the voice 28. 68.
Judg. 3. 12 the children of Israel did evil again
4. 1 the children of Israel again did evil
9. 37 And Gaal spake again and said
10. 6 the children of Israel did evil again
11. 14 Jephthah sent messengers again unto the
13. 1 the children of Israel did evil again in
20. 22 and set their battle again in array
20. 23 Shall I go up again to battle against the
20. 28 Shall I yet again go out to battle against
1 Sa. 3. 6 the LORD called yet again, Samuel
3. 8 the LORD called Samuel again the third
3. 21 the LORD appeared again in Shiloh
9. 8 the servant answered Saul again, and
19. 8 there was war again: and David went out
19. 21 Saul sent messengers again the third time
20. 17 Jonathan caused David to swear again
23. 4 David enquired of the LORD yet again
27. 4 and he sought no more again for him
2 Sa. 2. 22 And Abner said again to Asahel
3. 34 all the people wept again over him
5. 22 the Philistines came up yet again 6. 1.
18. 22 Then said..the son of Zadok yet again
24. 1 again the anger of the LORD was kindled
2 Ki. 24. 7 the king of Egypt came not again
1 Ch. 14. 13 the Philistines yet again spread themselves
Esth. 8. 3 Esther spake yet again before the king
Prov. 19. 19 if thou deliver..thou must do it again
Isa. 7. 10 Moreover the LORD spake again unto A.
8. 5 The LORD spake also unto me again
11. 11 the LORD shall set his hand again
24. 20 it shall fall, and not rise again
Dan. 10. 18 Then there came again and touched me
Amos 7. 8 I will not again pass by them any more
7. 13 prophesy not again any more at Beth-el
8. 2 I will not again pass by them any more
Jon. 2. 4 I will look again toward thy holy temple

9. *To turn back,* שׁוּב *shub.*
Gen. 26. 18 Isaac digged again the wells of water
30. 31 I will again feed (and) keep thy flock
Num 11. 4 the children of Israel also wept again
Deut 24. 4 Her..husband,..may not take her again
30. 9 the LORD will again rejoice over thee for
Josh. 5. 2 circumcise again the children of Israel
Judg. 19. 7 therefore he lodged there again
1 Sa. 3. 5 he said, I called not; lie down again
3. 6 I called not, my son; lie down again
1 Ki. 13. 33 made again of the lowest of the people
19. 6 drink, and laid him down again
19. 20 Go back again: for what have I done to
2 Ki. 1. 11 Again also he sent unto him another
1. 13 And he sent again a captain of the third
13. 25 Jehoash the son of Jehoahaz took again
19. 9 he sent messengers again unto Hezekiah
21. 3 For he built up again the high places
2 Ch. 19. 4 he went out again through the people
33. 3 For he built again the high places
Ezra 9. 14 Should we again break thy command.
Neh. 9. 28 after they had rest, they did evil again
Job 10. 16 again thou shewest thyself marvellous
Psa. 71. 20 (Thou) shalt quicken me again
71. 20 and shalt bring me up again from the
85. 6 Wilt thou not revive us again
Jer. 18. 4 so he made it again another vessel
36. 28 Take thee again another roll
Dan. 9. 25 the street shall be built again, and the
Zech. 8. 15 So again have I thought in these days

10. *To cause to turn back,* שׁוּב *shub,* 5.
1 Sa. 17. 30 the people answered him again after the
[*See also* Answer, back, break, bring, brought, build, carry, circumcise, come, conceive, deliver, dig, doubtless, evil, feed, fetch, gathered, get, give, go, lay down, lie down, lift up, lodge, make, pay, place, pull in, put, rejoice, render, restored, return, ring, rise up, send, set, sounding, take, turn, turn back, vomit, weep.]

11. *A second time,* δεύτερον *deuteron.*
Rev. 19. 3 And again they said, Alleluia.

12. *A second time,* ἐκ δευτέρου *ek deuterou.*
John 9. 24 Then again called they the man that was
Acts 11. 9 the voice answered me again from heaven

13. *From above,* ἄνωθεν *anōthen.*
John 3. 3 Except a man be born again, he cannot
3. 7 that I said..Ye must be born again

14. *Twice,* δίς *dis.*
Phil. 4. 16 For..ye sent once and again unto my
1 Th. 2. 18 even I Paul, once and again; but Satan

15. *Again, on the other hand,* πάλιν *palin.*
Matt. 4. 7 Jesus said..It is written again
4. 8 Again, the devil taketh him up into an
5. 33 Again, ye have heard that it hath been
13. 44 [Again], the kingdom of heaven is like
Matt 13. 45 Again, the kingdom of heaven is like unto
13. 47 Again, the kingdom of heaven is like unto
18. 19 [Again], I say unto you, That if two of
19. 24 again I say unto you, It is easier
20. 5 Again he went out about the sixth and
21. 36 Again, he sent other servants more than
22. 1 Jesus answered..again by parables, and
22. 4 Again he sent forth other servants, saying
26. 42 He went away again the second time, and
26. 43 he came and found them asleep again
26. 44 he left them, and went away again
26. 72 again he denied with an oath
27. 50 Jesus, when he had cried again with a
Mark 2. 1 again he entered into Capernaum
2. 13 he went forth again by the sea side
3. 1 he entered again into the synagogue
3. 20 the multitude cometh together again
4. 1 he began again to teach by the sea-side
5. 21 when Jesus was passed over again by
7. 31 again, departing from the coasts of Tyre
8. 13 entering into the ship again departed to
8. 25 After that he put (his) hand again upon
10. 1 resort unto him again..he taught..again
10. 10 his disciples asked him again of the same
10. 24 Jesus answereth again, and saith unto
10. 32 he took again the twelve, and began
11. 27 they come again to Jerusalem: and as
12. 4 again he sent unto them another servant
12. 5 And [again] he sent another; and him they
14. 39 again he went away, and prayed
14. 40 he found them asleep again, (for their
14. 61 Again the high priest asked him, and said
14. 69 a maid saw him again, and began
14. 70 he denied it again..said again to Peter
15. 4 Pilate asked him again, saying
15. 12 Pilate answered and said again unto
15. 13 they cried out again, Crucify him
Luke 13. 20 again he said, Whereunto shall I liken
23. 20 Pilate..to release Jesus, spake again to
John 1. 35 Again the next day after John stood
4. 3 He left Judea, and departed [again] into
4. 13 Whosoever drinketh..shall thirst again
4. 46 So Jesus came again into Cana of Galilee
4. 54 This (is) again the second miracle (that)
6. 15 departed [again] into a mountain himself
8. 2 [early in the morning he came again into]
8. 8 again he stooped down, and wrote on
8. 12 Then spake Jesus again unto them, saying
8. 21 Then said Jesus again unto them, I go
9. 15 Then again the Pharisees also asked him
9. 17 They say unto the blind man again
9. 26 Then said they to him [again], What did
9. 27 wherefore would ye hear (it) again? will
10. 7 Then said Jesus unto them again, Verily
10. 17 my life, that I might take it again
10. 18 I have power to take it again
10. 19 There was a division therefore again
10. 31 the Jews took up stones again to stone
10. 39 Therefore they sought again to take him
10. 40 And went away again beyond Jordan into
11. 7 Let us go into Judæa again
11. 8 disciples say..goest thou thither again?
11. 38 Jesus therefore again groaning in himself
12. 22 again Andrew and Philip tell Jesus
12. 28 glorified (it), and will glorify (it) again
12. 39 because that Esaias said again
13. 12 was set down again, he said unto them
14. 3 I will come again, and receive you unto
16. 16, 17, 19 again, a little while, and ye shall
16. 22 I will see you again, and your heart
16. 28 again, I leave the world, and go to the
18. 7 Then asked he them again, Whom seek
18. 27 Peter then denied again: and immediately
18. 33 entered into the judgment hall again
18. 38 went out again unto the Jews, and saith
18. 40 Then cried they all again, saying, Not
19. 4 Pilate therefore went forth again, and
19. 9 went again into the judgment hall, and
19. 37 again another scripture saith, They shall
20. 10 Then the disciples went away again unto
20. 21 Then said Jesus to them again, Peace (be)
20. 26 after eight days again his disciples were
21. 1 Jesus shewed himself again to the
21. 16 He saith to him again the second time
Acts 10. 15 the voice (spake) unto him again the
10. 16 the vessel was received up [again] into
11. 10 all were drawn up again into heaven
17. 32 We will hear thee again of this (matter)
18. 21 I will return again unto you, if
27. 28 they sounded again, and found (it) fifteen
Rom. 8. 15 ye have not received..again to fear
11. 23 for God is able to graff them in again
15. 10 again he saith, Rejoice, ye Gentiles, with
15. 11 again, praise the Lord, all ye Gentiles
15. 12 again, Esaias saith, There shall be a root
1 Co. 3. 20 again, the Lord knoweth the thoughts
7. 5 and come together again, that Satan
12. 21 nor again the head to the feet, I have no
2 Co. 1. 16 to come again out of Macedonia unto
2. 1 that I would not come again to you in
3. 1 Do we begin again to commend ourselves?
5. 12 we commend not ourselves again unto you
10. 7 let him of himself think this again, that
11. 16 I say again, Let no man think me
12. 19 [Again], think ye that we excuse ourselves
12. 21 lest, when I come again, my God
Gal. 1. 9 As we said before, so say I now again, If
1. 17 I went into Arabia, and returned again
2. 1 I went up again to Jerusalem with
2. 18 For if I build again the things which I
4. 9 whereunto ye desire again to be in
4. 19 I travail in birth again until Christ be

Gal. 5. 1 be not entangled again with the yoke
5. 3 For I testify again to every man that
Phil. 1. 26 your rejoicing..my coming to you again
2. 28 that, when ye see him again, ye may
4. 4 Rejoice in the Lord alway: (and) again I
Heb. 1. 5 again, I will be to him a Father
1. 6 again, when he bringeth in the first-begot.
2. 13 again, I will put..trust in him. And again
4. 5 And in this (place) again, If they shall
4. 7 Again, he limiteth a certain day, saying
5. 12 ye have need that one teach you again
6. 1 not laying again the foundation of repent.
6. 6 to renew them again unto repentance
10. 30 again, The Lord shall judge his people
Jas. 5. 18 he prayed again, and the heaven gave
2 Pe. 2. 20 they are again entangled therein, and
1 Jo. 2. 8 Again, a new commandment I write unto
Rev. 10. 8 And the voice..spake unto me again
10. 11 Thou must prophesy again before many

16. *The second time*, εἰς τὸ πάλιν *eis to palin.*
2 Co. 13. 2 that, if I come again, I will not spare

17. *Again, anew*, πάλιν ἄνωθεν *palin anōthen.*
Gal. 4. 9 whereunto ye desire again to be in bondage?

AGAIN, to come —

To turn back, שׁוּב *shub.*
Gen. 15. 16 But..they shall come hither again
22. 5 I and the lad will go..and come again to
28. 21 So that I come again to my father's house
50. 5 Now..let me go up..I will come again
Exod 14. 26 that the waters may come again upon the
24. 14 Tarry ye..until we come again unto you
Lev. 14. 39 the priest shall come again the seventh
14. 43 And if the plague come again
Num 35. 32 he should come again to dwell in the
Josh 18. 8 walk through the land..and come again
Judg. 6. 18 I will tarry until thou come again
8. 9 saying, When I come again in peace
15. 19 when he had drunk, his spirit came again
21. 14 And Benjamin came again at that time
Ruth 4. 3 that is come again out of the country
1 Sa. 23. 23 come ye again to me with the certainty
30. 12 he had eaten, his spirit came again to him
1 Ki. 2. 41 Shimei had gone..and was come again
12. 5 (for) three days, then come again to me
12. 12 Come to me again the third day
12. 20 when..Jeroboam was come again
17. 21 let this child's soul come into him again
17. 22 the soul of the child came into him again
19. 7 And the angel of the LORD came again
20. 5 And the messengers came again
2 Ki. 2. 18 And when they came again to him
4. 22 run to the man of God, and come again
4. 38 And Elisha came again to Gilgal
5. 10 and thy flesh shall come again to thee
5. 14 and his flesh came again..and he was
7. 8 and went and hid (it); and came again
9. 18 came to them, but he cometh not again
9. 20 He came..them, and cometh not again
9. 36 Wherefore they came again, and told him
2 Ch. 10. 5 Come again unto me after three days
10. 12 Come again to me on the third day
30. 9 that they shall come again into this land
Ezra 2. 1 and came again unto Jerusalem
6. 21 which were come again out of captivity
Neh. 7. 6 came again to Jerusalem, and to Judah
8. 17 them that were come again out of the
Esth. 6. 12 And Mordecai came again to the..gate
Ps. 78. 39 passeth away, and cometh not again
Prov. 3. 28 Say not..Go, and come again
Jer. 31. 16 they shall come again from the land
31. 17 that thy children shall come again
37. 8 And the Chaldeans shall come again
Zech. 4. 1 angel that talked with me came again

AGAIN, to do, speak—

To repeat, שָׁנָה *shanah.*
Neh. 13. 21 if ye do (so) again, I will lay hands on you
Job. 29. 22 After my words they spake not again

AGAIN, to send—

To send besides, προσέθετο πέμψαι.
Luke 20. 11 again he sent another servant: and they
20. 12 again he sent a third: and they wounded
[*See also* Alive, answer, ask, beget, bid, born, bring, build, come, deliver, flourish, foam, give, go, live, measure, put up, raise, raise to life, remembrance, restore, return, rise, rising, send, set, that, turn, word.]

AGAINST, (you)—

1. *Unto, to*, אֶל *el.*
Gen. 4. 8 Cain rose up against Abel his brother

2. *With, near, even, by*, אֵת *eth.*
1 Ki. 16. 22 Omri prevailed against the people

3. *Over against*, מוּל *mul.*
Josh. 8. 33 half of them over against mount Gerizim
9. 1 coasts of the great sea over against Leba.
22. 11 an altar over against the land of
1 Ki. 7. 5 and light (was) against light (in) three

4. *Before, in front of*, נֶגֶד *neged.*
Num. 25. 4 hang them up before the LORD against
Judg 20. 34 there came against Gibeah ten thousand

5. *Over against*, נֹכַח *nokach.*
1 Ki. 22. 35 the king..in his chariot against the Syr.
2 Ch. 18. 34 the king..in (his) chariot against the Syr.

6. *Unto*, עַד *ad.*
Gen. 43. 25 And they made ready the present against

7. *On, upon, concerning*, עַל *al.*
Gen. 40. 2 Pharaoh was wroth against..his officers
Ezra 4. 8 the scribe wrote a letter against Jerusalem
4. 19 this city..hath made insurrection against
7. 23 why should there be wrath against the
Dan. 3. 19 form of his visage was changed against
3. 29 which speak anything amiss against the
5. 23 hast lifted up thyself against the LORD
6. 5 We shall not find..occasion against this

8. *With*, עִם *im.*
Deut. 9. 7 ye have been rebellious against the LORD

9. *With*, עִמָּד *immad.*
Job 23. 6 Will he plead against me with (his) great

10. *Over against, near, just as*, עֻמָּה *ummah.*
1 Ch. 25. 8 And they cast lots, ward against (ward)
26. 12 (having) wards one against another
26. 16 by the causeway..ward against ward
Eze. 3. 8 against their faces..against their foreh.

11. *Face, presence*, פָּנִים *panim.*
Deut 31. 21 this song shall testify against them
32. 49 that (is) over against Jericho
34. 1 that (is) over against Jericho
1 Sa. 15. 7 that (is) over against Egypt
2 Ch. 20. 12 we have no might against this great
Eze. 41. 15 he measured the length..over against
48. 15 in the breadth over against the five
48. 21 against the five..against the..against the

12. *Concerning*, צַד *tsad.*
Dan. 7. 25 he shall speak (great) words against the

13. *Over, beyond*, עֵבֶר *eber.*
Exod 25. 37 they may give light over against it

14. *To meet*, קָרָא *qara.*
Gen. 15. 10 laid each piece one against another
Exod 14. 27 and the Egyptians fled against it
Num 20. 18 lest I come out against thee with the
20. 20 Edom came out against him with..people
21. 23 he came to Jahaz and fought against
21. 33 the king of Bashan went out against
22. 34 I knew not that thou stoodest..against
Deut. 1. 44 the Amorites..came out against you
2. 32 Then Sihon came out against us
3. 1 the king of Bashan came out against us
29. 7 Sihon..came out against us unto battle
Josh. 8. 5 when they come out against us
8. 14 the men..went out against Israel to
8. 22 issued out of the city against them
11. 20 they should come against Israel in battle
Judg. 7. 24 Come down against the Midianites
14. 5 a young lion roared against him
15. 14 the Philistines shouted against him
20. 25 Benjamin went forth against them
20. 31 Benjamin went out against the people
1 Sa. 4. 1 Israel went out against the Philistines
4. 2 put themselves in array against
9. 14 Samuel came out against them
17. 2 set the battle..against the Philistines
17. 21 Philistines had put..army against army
17. 55 David go forth against the Philistine
23. 28 and went against the Philistines
25. 20 David and his men came down against
2 Sa. 10. 9 put (them) in array against the Syrians
10. 10 might put (them) in array against the
10. 17 Syrians set themselves..against David
18. 6 people went out into the field against I.
1 Ki. 20. 27 children of Israel..went against them
2 Ki. 9. 21 and they went out against Jehu
23. 29 and king Josiah went against him
1 Ch. 19. 10 put (them) in array against the Syrians
19. 11 they set..in array against the children
19. 17 and set..in array against them
19. 17 put the battle in array against the Syr.
2 Ch. 35. 20 and Josiah went out against him
Psa. 35. 3 and stop (the way) against them

15. *In reference to, with regard to*, εἰς *eis.*
Matt 18. 15 thy brother shall trespass [against] thee
18. 21 how oft shall my brother sin against me
Mark 3. 29 he that shall blaspheme against the Holy
Luke 7. 30 rejected the counsel of God against
12. 10 against the Son..against the Holy Ghost
15. 18, 21 Father, I have sinned against heaven
17. 3 If thy brother trespass [against] thee
17. 4 if he trespass against thee seven times
22. 65 things blasphemously spake they against
John 12. 7 Then said Jesus, Let her alone: against
13. 29 Buy..that we have need of [against] the
Acts 6. 11 We have heard him speak..against
9. 1 against the disciples of the Lord
25. 8 against the..against the..against Cæsar
Rom. 8. 7 the carnal mind (is) enmity against God
1 Co. 6. 18 committeth fornication sinneth against
8. 12 against the brethren..sin against Christ
1 Ti. 6. 19 a good foundation against the time to
2 Ti. 1. 12 which I..committed unto him against
Heb. 12. 3 such contradiction of sinners against
2 Pe. 3. 7 reserved unto fire against the day of

16. *Before, in the face of*, ἔμπροσθεν *emprosthen.*
Matt 23. 13 shut up the kingdom of heaven against

17. *In*, ἐν *en.*
Rom. 2. 5 against the day of wrath, and revelation

18. *On, upon*, ἐπί (*dat.*) *epi.*
Luke 12. 52 three against two, and two against three
12. 53 against..son..against..father..against
12. 53 against..mother..against her..against

19. *On, upon*, ἐπί (*acc.*) *epi.*
Matt 10. 21 and the children shall rise up against
[*See also* Matt. 12. 26; 24. 7, 7; 26. 55; Mark 3. 24, 25, 26; 10. 11; 13. 8, 8, 12; 14. 48; Luke 9. 5; 11. 17, 17, 18; 12. 53, 53; 14. 31; 21. 10, 10; 22. 52, 53; John 13. 18; Acts 4. 27; 8. 1; 13. 50, 51; Rom. 1. 18; 2. 2; 2 Co. 10. 2; 1 Pe. 3. 12.]

20. *Against*, κατά (*gen.*) *kata.*
Matt. 5. 11 shall say all manner of evil against you
5. 23 that thy brother hath ought against thee
10. 35 against his..against her..against her
12. 14 held a council against him, how they
12. 25 divided against itself..divided against
12. 30 He that is not with me is against me
12. 32 against the Son..against the Holy Ghost
20. 11 they murmured against the goodman of
26. 59 sought false witness against Jesus, to put
27. 1 counsel against Jesus to put him to death
Mark 3. 6 took counsel with the Herodians against
9. 40 For he that is not against us is on our
11. 25 forgive, if ye have ought against any
14. 55 sought for witness against Jesus to put
14. 56 many bare false witness against him, but
14. 57 bare false witness against him, saying
Luke 9. 50 for he that is not against us is for us
11. 23 He that is not with me is against me
John 18. 29 What accusation bring ye against this
19. 11 couldest have no power..against me
Acts 4. 26 against the Lord, and against his Christ
6. 13 ceaseth not to speak..against this holy
14. 2 made their minds evil affected against
16. 22 the multitude rose up together against
19. 16 overcame them, and prevailed against
21. 28 teacheth all..every where against the
24. 1 who informed the governor against Paul
25. 2 chief of the Jews informed him against
25. 3 desired favour against him, that he
25. 7 complaints [against Paul], which they
25. 15 desiring (to have) judgment against him
25. 27 not withal..the crimes (laid) against him
27. 14 not long after there arose against it a
Rom. 8. 31 If God (be) for us, who (can be) against
11. 2 he maketh intercession to God against
1 Co. 4. 6 that no one of you..one against another
2 Co. 10. 5 high thing that exalteth itself against
13. 8 For we can do nothing against the truth
Gal 3. 21 (Is) the law then against the promises of
5. 17 against the Spirit, and the Spirit against
5. 23 Meekness, temperance: against such
Col. 2. 14 the handwriting..that was against us
1 Ti. 5. 19 Against an elder receive not an accusation
Jas. 3. 14 and lie not against the truth
5. 9 Grudge not one against another, brethren
1 Pe. 2. 11 abstain from..lusts, which war against
2 Pe. 2. 11 bring not railing accusation against them
Jude 15 ungodly sinners have spoken against him
Rev. 2. 4 Nevertheless I have (somewhat) against
2. 14 I have a few things against thee, because
2. 20 I have a few things against thee, because
12. 7 Michael and his angels fought [against]

21. *With*, μετά (*g.a.*) *meta.*
Rev. 2. 16 will fight against them with the sword
11. 7 the beast..shall make war against them
19. 19 against him that sat..and against his

22. *Beside, alongside of*, παρά *para*, (*dat.*).
Rom. 1. 26 natural use into that which is against
4. 18 Who against hope believed in hope, that

23. *Around, concerning*, περί (*gen.*) *peri.*
Matt 20. 24 were moved with indignation against the
Acts 25. 18 Against whom when the accusers stood

24. *Towards*, πρός (*acc.*) *pros.*
Matt. 4. 6 thou dash thy foot against a stone
Mark 12. 12 that he had spoken the parable against
Luke 4. 11 thou dash thy foot against a stone
5. 30 scribes and Pharisees murmured against
20. 19 that he had spoken this parable against
Acts 6. 1 arose a murmuring of the Grecians against
9. 5 [hard for thee to kick against the pricks]
9. 29 disputed against the Grecians: but they
19. 38 have a matter against any man, the law
23. 30 to say before thee what (they had) against
24. 19 if they had ought against me
25. 19 But had certain questions againt him of
26. 14 hard for thee to kick against the pricks
1 Co. 6. 1 Dare any of you, having a matter against
Eph. 6. 11 that ye may be able to stand against the
6. 12 against flesh..against princ...against po.
6. 12 against the rulers..against spiritual wic.
Col. 3. 13 if any man have a quarrel against any
3. 19 love (your) wives..not bitter against them
Heb. 12. 4 resisted unto blood, striving a. Re. 13. 6.

25. *To you*, ὑμῖν *humin*, Luke 10. 11.

26. *Contrary to*, ἐναντίος *enantios.*
Acts 28. 17 though I have committed nothing against

AGAINST, as —

As against, כְּעַל *ke-al.*
2 Ch. 32. 19 as against the gods of the people of the

AGAINST he come —

To meet, קָרָא *qara.*
Exod. 7. 15 by the river's brink against he come

AGAINST, over —

1. *Over against*, מוֹאל *mol.*
Neh. 12. 38 the other..went over against (them)

2. *Over against*, מוֹל *mol.*
Deut 1. 1 in the plain over against the Red (sea)

3. *Over against*, מוּל *mul.*
Num. 8. 2 lamps shall give light over against the
8. 3 lighted the lamps..over against the
22. 5 and they abide over against me
Deut. 2. 19 thou comest..over against the children
3. 29 we abode in the valley over against
4. 46 in the valley over against Beth-peor

Deut 11. 30 which dwell..over against Gilgal
34. 6 he buried him..over against Beth-peor
Josh. 18. 18 passed..toward the side over against
1 Sa. 14. 5 over against Michmash..over against Gib
2 Sa. 5. 23 come upon them over against the..trees
1 Ki. 7. 39 the house eastward over against the south
1 Ch. 14. 14 come upon them over against the..trees
2 Ch. 4. 10 set the sea..over against the south

4. *Before, in the presence of,* נֶגֶד *neged.*
Gen. 21. 16 and sat her down over against (him)
1 Ch. 8. 32 these also dwelt..over against them
Neh. 3. 28 every one over against his house
Eze. 41. 16 the galleries..over against the door

5. *Straightforward, straight-before,* נֹכַח *nokach.*
Exod 26. 35 the candlestick over against the table
40. 24 put the candlestick..over against the
Josh. 18. 17 which (is) over against the going up of
Judg 19. 10 and came over against Jebus
20. 43 trode them down..over against Gibeah
1 Ki. 20. 29 they pitched one over against the other
Esth. 5. 1 over against the king's..over against the
Eze. 47. 20 till a man come over against Hamath

6. *Straight before,* נֶכַח *nekach.*
Eze. 46. 9 but shall go forth over against it

7. *Near, just as, over against,* עֻמָּה *ummah.*
Exod 25. 27 Over against the border shall the rings be
28. 27 over against the (other) coupling thereof
37. 14 Over against the border were the rings
39. 20 over against the (other) coupling thereof
2 Sa. 16. 13 Shimei went along..over against him
1 Ki. 7. 20 over against the belly which (was) by the
1 Ch. 24. 31 These likewise cast lots over against
24. 31 principal fathers over against their
Neh. 12. 24 David the man of God, ward over against
Eccl. 7. 14 hath set the one over against the other
Eze. 1. 20 the wheels were lifted up over against
1. 21 the wheels were lifted up over against
3. 13 the noise of the wheels over against them
40. 18 the pavement..over against the length of
42. 7 wall that (was) without over against the
45. 6 over against the oblation of the holy
45. 7 the length (shall be) over against one of
48. 13 over against the border of the priests
48. 18 over against the oblation of the holy
48. 18 over against the oblation of the holy
48. 21 over against the portions for the prince

8. *Over against,* ἀντικρύ *antikru.*
Acts 20. 15 came the next (day) over against Chios

9. *Over beyond,* ἀντιπέραν *antiperan.*
Luke 8. 26 Gadarenes, which is over against Galilee

10. *Over against,* ἀπέναντι *apenanti.*
Matt 21. 2 Go into the village [over against] you
27. 61 Mary, sitting over against the sepulchre

11. *Opposite, contrary,* ἐξ ἐναντίας *ex enantias.*
Mark 15. 39 centurion, which stood over against him

12. *Down, down by,* κατά (acc.) *kata.*
Acts 27. 7 when we had..come over against Cnidus
27. 7 we sailed under Crete, over against

13. *Over against,* κατέναντι *katenanti.*
Mark 11. 2 Go your way into the village over against
12. 41 Jesus sat [over against] the treasury
13. 3 mount of Olives over against the temple
Luke 19. 30 Go ye into the village over against (you)
[*See also* Beat, boast, bring, crime, cry, mad, murmur, over, prate, prevail, quarrel, rejoice, rise up, say, speak, spoken, strive, war, will.]

A'-GAR, Ἄγαρ.
Greek name of Sarah's handmaid *Hagar.*
Gal. 4. 24 Sinai, which gendereth to bondage..is A.
4. 25 For this A. is mount Sinai in Arabia, and

AGATE —
1. *Agate or ruby,* כַּדְכֹּד *kadkod.*
Isa. 54. 12 I will make thy windows of agates
Eze. 27. 16 fine linen, and coral, and agate

2. *Agate, achates,* שְׁבוֹ *shebu.*
Exod 28. 19 the third row..an agate, and an amethyst
39. 12 the third row..an agate, and an amethyst

AGE —
1. *Revolution,* דּוֹר *dor.*
Job 8. 8 enquire, I pray thee, of the former age
Isa. 38. 12 Mine age is departed, and is removed from

2. *Old age,* זֹקֶן *zoqen.*
Gen. 48. 10 the eyes of Israel were dim for age

3. *Lifetime,* חֶלֶד *cheled.*
Job 11. 17 (thine) age shall be clearer than the noon
Psa. 39. 5 mine age (is) as nothing before thee

4. *Day,* יוֹם *yom.*
Gen. 18. 11 (were) old..well stricken in age
24. 1 Abraham was..well stricken in age
Josh. 23. 1 Joshua waxed old (and) stricken in age
23. 2 I am old (and) stricken in age
Zech. 8. 4 his staff in his hand for very age

5. *Old age, greyheadness,* שֵׂיב *seb.*
1 Ki. 14. 4 his eyes were set by reason of his age

6. *A son,* בֵּן *ben.*
Num. 8. 25 from the age of fifty years they shall
1 Ch. 23. 3 from the age of thirty years and upward
23. 24 from the age of twenty years and upward

7. [*See* **WHOLE AGE.**]
Gen. 47. 28 the..age of Jacob, was an hundred forty
[*See also* Flower, great, old, pass, stoop for, whole.]

8. *Maturity,* ἡλικία *hēlikia.*
Heb. 11. 11 delivered of a child when she..past age

AGE, full —
1. *Full age,* כֶּלַח *kelach.*
Job 5. 26 shalt come to (thy) grave in a full age

2. *Complete, perfect,* τέλειος *teleios.*
Heb 5. 14 strong meat..to them that are of full age

AGE, old —
Full age, כֶּלַח *kelach.*
Job 30. 2 me, in whom old age was perished?

AGE, to be of —
1. *He has maturity,* ἡλικίαν ἔχει *hēlikian echei.*
John 9. 21 we know not: he is of age; ask him
9. 23 Therefore said his parents, He is of age

2. *Be advanced in days* προβεβηκὼς ἐν ἡμέραις
Luke 2. 36 daughter of Phanuel..was of a great age

AGE, whole —
Days of the years of the life, יְמֵי שְׁנֵי חַיֵּי. [*yom.*]
Gen. 47. 28 the whole age of Jacob was an hundred

AGED —
1. *Aged, bearded,* זָקֵן *zaqen.*
Job 12. 20 taketh..the understanding of the aged
32. 9 neither do the aged understand judgment
Jer. 6. 11 the aged, with (him that is) full of days

2. *One white, grey, old, dry,* יָשִׁישׁ *yashish.*
Job 29. 8 the aged arose (and) stood up

3. *Aged, advanced in days,* πρεσβύτης *presbutēs.*
Phm. 9 as Paul the aged..now also a prisoner

AGED man —
1. *Aged, bearded,* זָקֵן *zaqen.*
2 Sa. 19. 32 Barzillai was a very aged man

2. *Aged, advanced in days,* πρεσβύτης *presbutēs.*
Titus 2. 2 aged men be sober..in faith, in charity

AGED man, very —
One white, grey, old, dry, יָשִׁישׁ *yashish.*
Job 15. 10 very aged men, much elder than thy

AGED woman —
Aged female, πρεσβῦτις *presbutis.*
Titus 2. 3 The aged women likewise, that (they be)

A'-GEE, אָגֵא *fugitive.*
The father of Shammah, one of David's valiant men, B.C. 1080.
2 Sa. 23. 11 after him (was) Shammah the son of A.

AGES
1. *Age, dispensation,* αἰών *aiōn.*
Eph. 2. 7 That in the ages to come he might shew
Col. 1. 26 mystery which hath been hid from ages

2. *Generations,* γενεαί [*genea*]
Eph. 3. 5 Which in other ages was not made known
3. 21 throughout all ages, world without end

AGO—
1. *Before this* מִקַּדְמַת דְּנָה *miq-qadmath denah.*
Ezra 5. 11 house..was builded these many years ago

2. *To-day,* הַיּוֹם *hay-yom.*
1 Sa. 9. 20 asses that were lost three days ago

3. *From,* ἀπό *apo.*
Acts 10. 30 And Cornelius said, Four days ago I was
15. 7 ye know how that a good while ago
2 Co. 8. 10 but also to be forward a year ago
9. 2 that Achaia was ready a year ago

4. *Before,* πρό *pro.*
2 Co. 12. 2 I knew a man..above fourteen years ago

AGONE—
To-day, הַיּוֹם *hay-yom.*
1 Sa. 30. 13 because three days agone I fell sick

AGONY—
Agony, contest, ἀγωνία *agōnia.*
Luke 22. 44 And being in an agony he prayed more

AGREE—
1. *To be into or for,* εἰμὶ εἰς *eimi eis.*
1 Jo. 5. 8 and these three agree in one

2. *To be in good mind,* εὐνοέω *eunoeō.*
Matt. 5. 25 Agree with thine adversary quickly

3. *To be the same,* ἴσος εἰμί *isos eimi.*
Mark 14. 56 but their witness agreed not together
14. 59 But neither so did their witness agree

4. *To be like or similar,* ὁμοιάζω *homoiazō.*
Mark 14. 70 [and thy speech agreeth (thereto)]

5. *To persuade, prevail upon,* πείθω *peithō.*
Acts 5. 40 And to him they agreed: and when they

6. *To make one opinion,* ποιῆσαι μίαν γνώμην.
Rev. 17. 17 and to agree, and give their kingdom

7. *To sound or speak together,* συμφωνέω *sumphōneō.*
Matt 18. 19 That if two of you shall agree on earth
20. 2 And when he had agreed with the
Acts 15. 15 And to this agree the words of the

8. *To put together,* συντίθημι *suntithēmi.*
John 9. 22 for the Jews had agreed already, that if
Acts 23. 20 The Jews have agreed to desire thee that

AGREE together —
To sound or speak together, συμφωνέω *sumphōneō.*
Acts 5. 9 How is it that ye have agreed together

AGREE with —
To sound or speak together, συμφωνέω *sumphōneō.*
Matt 20. 13 didst not thou agree with me for a penny?
Luke 5. 36 the piece that was..agreeth not with

AGREED, to be —
To be met together (by appointment), יָעַד *yaad,* 2.
Amos 3 3 Can two walk..except they be agreed?

AGREED not —
Not sounding together, ἀσύμφωνος *asumphōnos.*
Acts 28. 25 when they agreed not among themselves

AGREEMENT —
1. *A seer, vision,* חֹזֶה *chozeh.*
Isa. 28. 15 with hell are we at agreement

2. *Vision,* חָזוּת *chazuth.*
Isa. 28. 18 your agreement with hell shall not stand

3. *Upright things,* מֵישָׁרִים *mesharim.*
Dan. 11. 6 come to the..north to make an agreement

4. *A putting down together,* συγκατάθεσις.
2 Co 6. 16 what agreement hath the temple of God

A-GRIP'-PA, Ἀγρίππας.
Great-grandson of Herod the Great. His father being eaten of worms, he, as Herod Agrippa, succeeded (A.D. 53) as tetrarch of Abilene, Galilee, Iturea, and Trachonitis.
Acts 25. 13 after certain days king A. and Bernice
25 22 Then A. said unto Festus, I would also
25. 23 on the morrow, when A. was come, and
25. 24 And Festus said, King A., and all men
25. 26 I have brought..before you..O king A.
26. 1 Then A. said unto Paul, Thou art
26. 2 I think myself happy, king A., because I
26. 7 For which hope's sake, king A., I am
26. 19 Whereupon, O king A., I was not
26. 27 King A. believest thou the prophets? I
26. 28 Then A. said unto Paul, Almost thou
26. 32 Then said A. unto Festus This man might

AGROUND, to run —
To force upon, ἐποκέλλω *epokellō.*
Acts 27 41 they ran the ship aground; and the

A'-GUR, אָגוּר *gatherer.*
The son of Jakeh. Jerome and others consider this name as symbolical of Solomon himself; but this is inconsistent with the designation "Son of Jakeh," and Solomon, in the same book, is expressly called "Son of David."
Prov. 30. 1 The words of A the son of Jakeh..the

AH! —
1. *Aha! (complaint),* אֲהָהּ *ahah.*
Jer. 1. 6 Ah, LORD God! behold, I cannot speak
4. 10 Ah, LORD God! surely thou hast..deceived
14. 13 Ah, LORD God! behold, the prophets
32. 17 Ah LORD God! behold, thou hast made
Eze. 4. 14 Ah LORD God! behold, my soul
9. 8 Ah LORD God! wilt thou destroy all the
11 13 Ah LORD God! wilt thou make a full end
20. 49 Ah LORD God!..Doth he not speak

2. *Ah! (grief),* אָח *ach.*
Eze. 21. 15 ah! (it is) made bright, (it is) wrapped up

3. *He! he-ah! (malicious joy),* הֶאָח *heach.*
Psa. 35. 25 Ah, so would we have it: let them not

4. *Ho! (threatening, grief, exhortation),* הוֹי *hoi.*
Isa. 1. 4 Ah sinful nation..laden with iniquity
1. 24 Ah, I will ease me of mine adversaries
Jer. 22. 18 saying, Ah my brother! or, Ah sister!
22. 18 saying, Ah Lord! or, Ah his glory!
34. 5 Ah, Lord! for I have pronounced the

5. *O, ah (derision, insult),* οὐά *oua.* [*Lat.*]
Mark 15. 29 Ah, thou that destroyest the temple

AHA —
He! (malicious joy), הֶאָח *heach.*
Psa. 35. 21 Aha, aha, our eye hath seen (it)
40. 15 Let them be desolate..that say..Aha
70. 3 Let them be turned..that say, Aha, aha
Isa. 44. 16 Aha, I am warm, I have seen the fire
Eze. 25. 3 thou saidst, Aha, against my sanctuary
26. 2 Aha, she is broken (that was) the gates
36. 2 Aha, even the ancient high places are

AH'-AB, אַחְאָב *father's brother* (= *uncle.*)
1. Son of Omri, and his successor as 7th king of Israel (919-897 B.C.) He married Jezebel, daughter of Eth-baal, king of the Zidonians, and was led by her into idolatry and incited to the persecution of the prophets of Jehovah. The most remarkable incidents in his life were his defeating Benhadad, whom he freely dismissed, and his seizing the vineyard of Naboth. During his reign appeared the great prophet Elijah, who came into direct collision with Jezebel when she attempted to introduce the worship of Baal and the goddess Astarte, of whom her father had been a priest before he usurped the sovereignty of Tyre, B.C. 900.
1 Ki. 16. 28 So Omri slept with his fathers..and A.
16. 29 in the thirty and eighth year..began A.
16. 29 and A. the son of Omri reigned over
16. 30 And A. the son of Omri did evil in the
16. 33 And A. made a grove
16. 33 and A. did more to provoke the LORD
17. 1 And Elijah..said unto A., (As) the LORD

1 Ki. 18. 1 Go, shew thyself unto A.; and I will send
18. 2 And Elijah went to shew himself unto A.
18. 3 And A. called Obadiah, which (was) the
18. 5 And A. said unto Obadiah, Go into the
18. 6 A. went one way by himself, and
18. 9 wouldst deliver..into the hand of A.
18. 12 when I come and tell A., and he cannot
18. 16 So Obadiah went to meet A., and told
18. 16 and A. went to meet Elijah
18. 17 it came to pass, when A. saw Elijah
18. 17 that A. said unto him, (Art) thou he that
18. 20 So A. sent unto all the children of Israel
18. 41 And Elijah said unto A., Get thee up, eat
18. 42 So A. went up to eat and to drink
18. 44 And he said, Go up, say unto A., Prepare
18. 45 And A. rode, and went to Jezreel
18. 46 Elijah..ran before A. to the entrance of
19. 1 And A. told Jezebel all that Elijah had
20. 2 And he sent messengers to A. king of
20. 13 behold, there came a prophet unto A.
20. 14 And A. said, By whom? And he said
21. 1 had a vineyard..hard by the palace of A.
21. 2 And A. spake unto Naboth, saying, Give
21. 3 And Naboth said to A., The LORD forbid
21. 4 And A. came into his house heavy and
21. 8 So she wrote letters in A.'s name, and
21. 15 Jezebel said to A., Arise, take possession
21. 16 And it came to pass, when A. heard that
21. 16 A. rose up to go down to the vineyard of
21. 18 Arise, go down to meet A. king of Israel
21. 20 And A. said to Elijah, Hast thou found
21. 21 Behold, I..will cut off from A. him that
21. 24 Him that dieth of A. in the city
21. 25 But there was none like unto A.
21. 27 And it came to pass, when A. heard those
21. 29 Seest thou how A. humbleth himself
22. 20 the LORD said, Who shall persuade A.
22. 39 Now the rest of the acts of A., and all that
22. 40 So A. slept with his fathers; and Ahaziah
22. 41 began to reign..in the fourth year of A.
22. 49 Then said Ahaziah the son of A. unto
22. 51 Ahaziah the son of A. began to
2 Ki. 1. 1 Moab rebelled..after the death of A.
3. 1 Now Jehoram the son of A. began to
3. 5 But it came to pass, when A. was dead
8. 16 in the fifth year of Joram the son of A.
8. 18 And he walked..as did the house of A.
8. 18 for the daughter of A. was his wife
8. 25 the twelfth year of Joram the son of A.
8. 27 he walked in the way of the house of A.
8. 27 the house of A...the h. of A...the h. of A.
8. 28 And he went with Joram the son of A.
8. 29 Ahaziah..went..to see..the son of A.
9. 7 And thou shalt smite the house of A.
9. 8 For the whole house of A. shall perish
9. 8 and I will cut off from A. him that pisseth
9. 9 And I will make the house of A. like the
9. 25 when I and thou rode together after A.
9. 29 eleventh year of Joram the son of A.
10. 1 And A. had seventy sons in Samaria
10. 1 wrote..to them that brought up A.'s
10. 10 which the LORD spake concerning the..A.
10. 11 Jehu slew all that remained of..A.
10. 17 slew all that remained unto A. in Samaria
10. 18 A. served Baal a little; (but) Jehu shall
10. 30 thou..hast done unto the house of A.
21. 3 and made a grove, as did A. king of Israel
21. 13 and the plummet of the house of A.
2 Ch. 18. 1 Now Jehoshaphat..joined affinity with A.
18. 2 after (certain) years he went down to A.
18. 2 And A. killed sheep and oxen for him in
18. 3 And A. king of Israel said unto Jehosha.
18. 19 the LORD said, Who shall entice A. king
21. 6 he walked..like as did the house of A.
21. 6 for he had the daughter of A. to wife
21. 13 like to the whoredoms of the house of A.
22. 3 He..walked in the ways of the house of A.
22. 4 Wherefore he did evil..like the house of A.
22. 5 He..went with Jehoram the son of A.
22. 6 Azariah..went down to see..the son of A.
22. 7 whom the LORD had anointed to cut off..A.
22. 8 Jehu was executing judgment upon..A.
Mic. 6. 16 and all the works of the house of A.

2. A false prophet who was in Babylon during the early part of the exile, but was put to death by Nebuchadnezzar, B.C. 600.

Jer. 29. 21 Thus saith the LORD of hosts..of A. the
29. 22 make thee like Zedekiah and like A.

A-HA'-RAH, אַחְרַח *brother of Rach, or after a brother.*

Third son of Benjamin, elsewhere called Ehi, Ahiram, and Aher, B.C. 1700.

1 Ch. 8. 1 begat Bela his firstborn..and A. the

A-HAR'-HEL, אֲחַרְחֵל *brother of Rachel, or after might.*

Son of Harum, a descendant of Judah through Caleb, son of Hur, B.C. 1430.

1 Ch. 4. 8 And Coz begat..the families of A. the

A-HA'-SAI, אַחְזַי *my holder, protector.*

A priest of the family of Immer, some of whom dwelt in Jerusalem after the exile, B.C. 445.

Neh. 11. 13 Amashai the son of Azareel, the son of A.

A-HAS'-BAI, אֲחַסְבַּי *blooming, shining.*

Father of one of David's valiant men, whose family had been early settled at Maachah, B.C. 1080.

2 Sa. 23. 34 [of the thirty]..Eliphelet..son of A.

A-HAS-U-E'-RUS, אֲחַשְׁוֵרוֹשׁ *king.*

1. A king of Persia (529-521 B.C); was the Cambyses of profane history.

Ezra 4. 6 And in the reign of A., in the beginning

2. The father of Darius the Mede, or Astyages (594 B.C.)

Dan. 9. 1 In the first year of Darius the son of A.

3. Xerxes, the son of Darius Hystaspis (485 B.C.)

Esth. 1. 1 came to pass in the days of A., (this (is) A.
1. 2 when the king A. sat on the throne of his
1. 9 royal house which (belonged) to king A.
1. 10 chamberlains that served..presence of A.
1. 15 not performed the commandment of..A.
1. 16 in all the provinces of the king A.
1. 17 The king A. commanded Vashti the
1. 19 that Vashti come no more before king A.
2. 1 when the wrath of king A. was appeased
2. 12 every maid's turn..to go in to king A.
2. 16 So Esther was taken unto king A. into
2. 21 Bigthan..sought to lay hand on..A.
3. 1 After these things did king A. promote
3. 6 throughout the whole kingdom of king A.
3. 7 in the twelfth year of king A., they cast
3. 8 And Haman said unto king A., There is a
3. 12 in the name of king A. was it written
6. 2 who sought to lay hand on the king A.
7. 5 Then the king A. answered and said unto
8. 1 On that day did the king A. give the
8. 7 Then the king A. said unto Esther the
8. 10 And he wrote in the king A.'s name
8. 12 one day in all the provinces of..A.
9. 2 throughout all the provinces of..A.
9. 20 in all the provinces of the king A.
9. 30 to the..provinces of the kingdom of A.
10. 1 And the king A. laid a tribute upon the
10. 3 Mordecai the Jew (was) next unto king A.

A-HA'-VA, אַהֲוָא *stream.*

A river in the N.E. of Media near the district of Casiphia; some think it the same as the *Adiaba* in Adiabene, or *Hit*, due E. of Damascus, on the Euphrates. On a tributary of this river Ezra assembled the Jews before starting on their journey to Jerusalem. Some consider the name as applying to a district in the plains of Babylon.

Ezra 8. 15 to the river that runneth to A.; and there
8. 21 proclaimed a fast there, at the river of A.
8. 31 Then we departed from the river of A. on

A'-HAZ, אָחָז *he holds.*

1. Son of Jotham, king of Judah, and father of Hezekiah. He succeeded his father as eleventh king of Judah, and reigned sixteen years (740-724 B.C.)

2 Ki. 15. 38 And Jotham slept..and A. his son reigned
16. 1 A. the son of Jotham king of Judah began
16. 2 Twenty years old (was) A. when he began
16. 5 and they besieged A., but could not
16. 7 So A. sent messengers to Tiglath-pileser
16. 8 And A. took the silver and gold that was
16. 10 And king A. went to Damascus to meet
16. 10 and king A. sent to Urijah the priest the
16. 11 an altar according to all that king A.
16. 11 the priest made (it) against king A. came
16. 15 And king A. commanded Urijah the priest
16. 16 according to all that king A. commanded
16. 17 And king A. cut off the borders of the
16. 19 Now the rest of the acts of A. which he
16. 20 And A. slept with his fathers, and was
17. 1 In the twelfth year of A. king of Judah
18. 1 Hezekiah the son of A. king of Judah
20. 11 which it had gone down in the dial of A.
23. 12 on the top of the upper chamber of A.
1 Ch. 3. 13 A. his son, Hezekiah his son, Manasseh
9. 42 And A. begat Jarah; and Jarah begat
2 Ch. 27. 9 Jotham slept..and A. his son reigned in
28. 1 A. (was) twenty years old when he began
28. 16 At that time did king A. send unto the
28. 19 the LORD brought Judah low because of A.
28. 21 For A. took away a portion (out) of the
28. 22 this (is that) king A.
28. 24 And A. gathered together the vessels of
28. 27 And A. slept with his fathers, and they
29. 19 Moreover all the vessels, which king A.
Isa. 1. 1 The vision of Isaiah..in the days of..A.
7. 1 And it came to pass in the days of A.
7. 3 Go forth now to meet A., thou, and
7. 10 Moreover the LORD spake again unto A.
7. 12 But A. said, I will not ask, neither will I
14. 28 In the year that king A. died was this
38. 8 which is gone down in the sun dial of A.
Hos. 1. 1 The word of the LORD..in the days of..A.
Mic. 1. 1 The word of the LORD..in the days of..A.

2. A Benjamite, of the family of Saul

1 Ch. 8. 35 And the sons of Micah (were)..A.
8. 36 And A begat Jehoadah; and Jehoadah
9. 41 And the sons of Micah (were..A.)
9. 42 And A. begat Jarah; and Jarah begat

A-HAZ-I'AH, אֲחַזְיָה אֲחַזְיָהוּ *Jah holds, possesses.*

1. A son of Ahab, who succeeded as eighth king of Israel and reigned two years (896 and 895 B.C.).

1 Ki. 22. 40 So Ahab slept..and A. his son reigned
22. 49 Then said A. the son of Ahab unto
22. 51 A. the son of Ahab began to reign over
2 Ki. 1. 2 And A. fell down through a lattice
1. 18 Now the rest of the acts of A. which he
1 Ch. 3. 11 [Joram his son, A. his son, Joash his]
2 Ch. 20. 35 did Jehoshaphat..join himself with A.
20. 37 Because thou hast joined thyself with A.

2. A son of Jehoram (or Joram), who succeeded as fifth king of Judah. He is also called Jehoahaz and Azariah, and reigned only one year (884 B.C.).

2 Ki. 8. 24 And Joram slept..and A. his son reigned
8. 25 twelfth year of Joram..did A...begin to
8. 26 Two and twenty years old (was) A. when
8. 29 And A...went down to see Joram the son
9. 16 And A. king of Judah was come down to
9. 21 Joram king of Israel and A. king of Judah
9. 23 Joram..said to A...treachery, O A.
9. 27 But when A. the king of Judah saw (this)
9. 29 in the eleventh year of Joram..began A.
10. 13 Jehu met with the brethren of A. king of
10. 13 they answered, We (are) the brethren of A.
11. 1 when Athaliah the mother of A. saw that
11. 2 the..sister of A., took Joash the son of A.
12. 18 hallowed things that Jehoshaphat..and A.
13. 1 three and twentieth year of..the son of A.
14. 13 Amaziah..son of Jehoash the son of A.
1 Ch. 3. 11 Joram his son, A. his son, Joash his son
2 Ch. 22. 1 the inhabitants of Jerusalem made A.
22. 2 Forty and two years old (was) A. when he
22. 7 And the destruction of A. was of God by
22. 8 of the brethren of A., that ministered to A.
22. 9 And he sought A.: and they caught him
22. 9 So the house of A. had no power to keep
22. 10 when Athaliah the mother of A. saw
22. 11 Jehoshabeath..took Joash the son of A.
22. 11 Jehoshabeath..was the sister of A.

AH'-BAN, אַחְבָּן *brother of intelligence.*

Son of Abishur, a descendant of Jerahmeel, grandson of Pharez, B.C. 1040.

1 Ch. 2. 29 Abihail..bare him A., and Molid

A'-HER, אַחֵר *one that is behind.*

A Benjamite (perhaps the same as Ahiram), B.C. 1700.

1 Ch. 7. 12 of Ir, (and) Hushim, the sons of A.

A'-HI, אֲחִי *my brother.*

1. A head of the families of Gad, B.C. 1360.

1 Ch. 5. 15 A. the son of Abdiel, the son of Guni

2. An Israelite of the tribe of Asher.

1 Ch. 7. 34 the sons of Shamer; A., and Rohgah

A-HI'-AH, אֲחִיָּה *Jah is a brother.*

1. Grandson of Phinehas son of Eli, B.C. 1080.

1 Sa. 14. 3 And A., the son of Ahitub, I-chabod's
14. 18 And Saul said unto A., Bring hither

2. One of Solomon's scribes.

1 Ki. 4. 3 Elihoreph and A., the sons of Shisha

3. A descendant of Benjamin, B.C. 1400.

1 Ch. 8. 7 And Naaman, and A., and Gera

A-HI'-AM, אֲחִיאָם *a mother's brother.*

One of David's thirty mighty men, and son of Sharar the Hararite, who, in 1 Ch. 11. 35, is called *Sacar*, B.C. 1048.

2 Sa. 23. 33 A. the son of Sharar the Hararite
1 Ch. 11. 35 A. the son of Sacar the Hararite

A-HI'-AN, אַחְיָן *brother of day.*

Son of Shemidah, a Manassehite, B.C. 1400.

1 Ch. 7. 19 the sons of Shemidah were, A., and

A-HI-EZ'-ER, אֲחִיעֶזֶר *helping brother.*

1. A prince of Dan, appointed to assist Moses in numbering the people, B.C. 1491.

Num. 1. 12 Of Dan; A. the son of Ammishaddai
2. 25 of Dan (shall be) A. the son of Ammisha.
7. 66 On the tenth day A. the son of Ammisha.
7. 71 this (was) the offering of A. the son of
10. 25 and over his host (was) A. the son of

2. A Danite chief who joined David when lying at Ziklag for fear of Saul.

1 Ch. 12. 3 The chief (was) A., then Joash, the sons of

A-HI'-HUD, אֲחִיהוּד *brother of honour.*

A prince of Asher, appointed to allocate the land W. of the Jordan, B.C. 1491.

Num 34. 27 of Asher, A., the son of Shelomi

A-HI'-HUD, אֲחִיחֻד *brother of mystery.*

A Benjamite of the family of Ehud, B.C. 1400.

1 Ch. 8. 7 he removed them, and begat Uzza, and A.

A-HI'-JAH, אֲחִיָּה *Jah is brother.*

This name, though variously expressed in the English version is the same in every passage in which it occurs in the original. See *Ahiah.*

1. A prophet, probably of Ephraim, who foretold to Jeroboam the revolt of the ten tribes, B.C. 980.

1 Ki. 11. 29 the prophet A. the Shilonite found him
11. 30 And A. caught the new garment that
12. 15 which the LORD spake by A. the Shilonite
14. 2 behold, there (is) A. the prophet, which
14. 4 to Shiloh, and came to the house of A.
14. 4 But A. could not see; for his eyes were
14. 5 And the LORD said unto A., Behold
14. 6 And it was (so), when A. heard the sound
14. 18 by the hand of his servant A. the prophet
15. 29 which he spake by his servant A. the
2 Ch. 9. 29 and in the prophecy of A. the Shilonite
10. 15 which he spake by the hand of A. the

2. Father of Baasha who conspired against Nadab son of Jeroboam and reigned in his stead, B.C. 953.

1 Ki. 15. 27 And Baasha the son of A., of the house of
15. 33 began Baasha the son of A. to reign over
21. 22 like the house of Baasha the son of A.
2 Ki. 9. 9 and like the house of Baasha the son of A.

3. Son of Jerahmeel, brother of Caleb (or Chelubai), of the tribe of Judah.

1 Ch. 2. 25 and Bunah, and Oren, and Ozem, (and) A.

4. One of David's thirty valiant men, B.C. 1050.

1 Ch. 11. 36 Hepher the Mecherathite, A. the Pelonite

5. A Levite set over the treasures of the house of God in the time of David, B.C. 1015.

1 Ch. 26. 20 And of the Levites, A. (was) over the

6. A Levite who, with Nehemiah, sealed the covenant B.C. 445.

Neh. 10. 26 And A., Hanan, Anan

A-HI'-KAM, אֲחִיקָם *my brother has risen.*

An officer in Josiah's court, the son of Shaphan, who was one of the king's officers, B.C. 641.

2 Ki. 22. 12 and A. the son of Shaphan, and Achbor
22. 14 So Hilkiah the priest, and A., and Achbor
25. 22 the son of A., the son of Shaphan, ruler
2 Ch. 34. 20 the king commanded Hilkiah, and A. the
Jer. 26. 24 the hand of A. the son of Shaphan was
39. 14 the son of A. the son of Shaphan, that
40. 5 the son of A. the son of Shaphan, whom
40. 6 the son of A. to Mizpah; and dwelt with
40. 7 the son of A. governor in the land, and
40. 9 the son of A. the son of Shaphan sware
40. 11 the son of A. the son of Shaphan
40. 14 Gedaliah the son of A. believed them not
40. 16 Gedaliah the son of A. said unto Johanan
41. 1 unto Gedaliah the son of A. to Mizpah
41. 2 smote Gedaliah the son of A. the son of
41. 6 Come to Gedaliah the son of A.
41. 10 had committed to Gedaliah the son of A.
41. 16, 18 had slain Gedaliah the son of A.
43. 6 with Gedaliah the son of A. the son of

A-HI'-LUD, אֲחִילוּד *a brother born.*

An Israelite whose son Jehoshaphat was appointed recorder by David, B.C. 1040.

2 Sa. 8. 16 Jehoshaphat the son of A. (was) recorder
20. 24 Jehoshaphat the son of A. (was) recorder
1 Ki. 4. 3 Jehoshaphat the son of A., the recorder
4. 12 Baana the son of A.; (to him pertained)
1 Ch. 18. 15 and Jehoshaphat the son of A., recorder

A-HI-MA'-AZ, אֲחִימַעַץ *powerful brother.*

1. Father of Ahinoam, wife of king Saul, B.C. 1090.

1 Sa. 14. 50 Ahinoam, the daughter of A.: and

2. A son of Zadok the priest, who carried tidings to David of the proceedings of Absalom, B.C. 1050.

2 Sa. 15. 27 your two sons with you, A. thy son, and
15. 36 with them their two sons, A. Zadok's (son)
17. 17 Jonathan and A. stayed by En-rogel
17. 20 Where (is) A. and Jonathan? And the
18. 19 Then said A. the son of Zadok, Let me
18. 22 Then said A. the son of Zadok yet again
18. 23 Then A. ran by the way of the plain
18. 27 is like the running of A. the son of Zadok
18. 28 And A. called, and said unto the king
18. 29 And A. answered, When Joab sent the
1 Ch. 6. 8 begat Zadok, and Zadok begat A.
6. 9 And A. begat Azariah, and Azariah begat
6. 53 Zadok his son, A. his son

3. One of Solomon's officers who had the charge of victualling the king's household for one month in the year. B.C. 1015.

1 Ki. 4. 15 A. (was) in Naphtali; he also took

A-HI'-MAN, אֲחִימַן *brother of Man.*

1. A son of Anak, who dwelt in Hebron, B.C. 1450.

Num 13. 22 where A., Sheshai, and Talmai, the
Josh. 15. 14 sons of Anak, Sheshai, and A., and
Judg. 1. 10 and they slew Sheshai, and A., and

2. A Levite porter in the temple, B.C. 1000.

1 Ch. 9. 17 and Talmon, and A., and their brethren

A-HI-ME'-LECH, אֲחִימֶלֶךְ *brother of the king.*

1. A priest slain in consequence of assisting David when he fled from Saul, B.C. 1060.

1 Sa. 21. 1 Then came David to Nob to A. the priest
21. 1 and A. was afraid at the meeting of David
21. 2 And David said unto A. the priest, The
21. 8 And David said unto A., And is there
22. 9 coming to Nob, to A. the son of Ahitub
22. 11 Then the king sent to call A. the priest
22. 14 Then A. answered the king, and said
22. 16 Thou shalt surely die, A., thou, and all
22. 20 And one of the sons of A. the son of
23. 6 when Abiathar the son of A. fled to David
30. 7 David said to Abiathar the priest, A.'s
2 Sa. 8. 17*and A. the son of Abiathar, (were) the
1 Ch. 24. 3 and A. of the sons of Ithamar
24. 6*and A. the son of Abiathar, and (before)
24. 31 and Zadok, and A., and the chief of the
Psa. 52. *title.* David is come to the house of A.

* [The names in these verses are supposed to have been transposed by a copyist.]

2. A Hittite officer in the service of David, B.C. 1048.

1 Sa. 26. 6 Then answered David and said to A. the

A-HI'-MOTH, אֲחִימוֹת *brother of death.*

Son of Elkanah, a descendant of Kohath son of Levi.

1 Ch. 6. 25 the sons of Elkanah; Amasai, and A.

A-HI-NA'DAB, אֲחִינָדָב *brother of liberality.*

Son of Iddo, and one of Solomon's twelve purveyors, B.C. 1015.

1 Ki. 4. 14 A. the son of Iddo (had) Mahanaim

A-HI-NO'-AM, אֲחִינֹעַם *pleasant brother.*

1. Wife of Saul first king of Israel, B.C. 1090.

1 Sa. 14. 50 the name of Saul's wife (was) A., the

2. A woman of Jezreel who became wife of David during his wandering, and went with him and his other wife, Abigail, to the court of Achish in Gath. She was mother of Amnon, David's eldest son, B.C. 1060.

1 Sa. 25. 43 David also took A. of Jezreel; and they
27. 3 with his two wives, A. the Jezreelitess, and
30. 5 were taken captives, A. the Jezreelitess
2 Sa. 2. 2 and his two wives also, A. the Jezreelitess
3. 2 his firstborn was Amnon, of A. the
1 Ch. 3. 1 the firstborn Amnon, of A. the Jezreelitess

A-HI'-O, אַחְיוֹ *his brother.*

1. Son of Abinadab, in whose house the ark of God remained for twenty years after being sent back by the Philistines, B.C. 1045.

2 Sa. 6. 3 And Uzzah and A., the sons of Abinadab
6. 4 the ark of God, and A. went before the
1 Ch. 13. 7 of Abinadab: and Uzza and A. drave the

2. An Israelite of the tribe of Benjamin.

1 Ch. 8. 14 And A., Shashak, and Jeremoth.

3. A Benjamite of the Gibeon family from which Saul sprang.

1 Ch. 8. 31 And Gedor, and A., and Zacher
9. 37 And Gedor, and A., and Zechariah

A-HI'-RA, אֲחִירַע *brother of evil.*

A chief of Naphtali when Moses took the census shortly after the exodus, B.C. 1491.

Num. 1. 15 Of Naphtali; A. the son of Enan
2. 29 of Naphtali (shall be) A. the son of Enan
7. 78 On the twelfth day A. the son of Enan
7. 83 this (was) the offering of A. the son of
10. 27 the children of Naphtali (was) A. the son

A-HI-RAM, אֲחִירָם *exalted brother.*

A Benjamite from whom a family was named. He is called *Ehi* in Gen. 46. 21, and is supposed to be the same as the *Aher* of 1. Ch. 7. 12. B.C. 1680.

Num 26. 38 of A., the family of the Ahiramites

A-HI-RAM'-ITE, אֲחִירָמִי *belonging to Ahiram.*

The Ahiramites were an Israelite family.

Num 26. 38 Ashbelites: of Ahiram, the family of the A.

A-HI-SA'-MACH, אֲחִיסָמָךְ *supporting brother.*

Father of Aholiab, a Danite B.C. 1500.

Exod 31. 6 with him Aholiab, the son of A., of the
35. 34 Aholiab the son of A., of the tribe of Dan
38. 23 Aholiab, son of A., of the tribe of Dan

A-HI-SHA'-HAR, אֲחִישַׁחַר *brother of the dawn.*

Son of Bilhan and grandson of Benjamin, B.C. 1400.

1 Ch. 7. 10 The sons also of Jediael..Zethan..and A.

A-HI'-SHAR, אֲחִישָׁר *brother of song.*

Controller of Solomon's household, B.C. 1015.

1 Ki. 4. 6 And A. (was) over the household: and

A-HI-THO'-PHEL, אֲחִיתֹפֶל *foolish brother.*

A native of Giloh in the highlands of Judah, and privy counsellor to David; but joined Absalom, and then hanged himself, B.C. 1023.

2 Sa. 15. 12 And Absalom sent for A. the Gilonite
15. 31 And (one) told David, saying, A. (is) among
15. 31 turn the counsel of A. into foolishness
15. 34 mayest thou..defeat the counsel of A.
16. 15 came to Jerusalem, and A. with him
16. 20 Then said Absalom to A., Give counsel
16. 21 And A. said unto Absalom, Go in unto
16. 23 And the counsel of A., which he
16. 23 so (was) all the counsel of A., both with
17. 1 Moreover A. said unto Absalom, Let
17. 6 saying, A. hath spoken after this manner
17. 7 The counsel that A. hath given (is) not
17. 14 counsel..(is) better than the counsel of A.
17. 14 to defeat the..counsel of A., to the intent
17. 15 Thus and thus did A. counsel Absalom
17. 21 for thus hath A. counselled against you
17. 23 And when A. saw that his counsel was
23. 34 Eliam the son of A. the Gilonite
1 Ch. 27. 33 And A. (was) the king's counsellor
27. 34 And after A. (was) Jehoiada the son of

A-HI'-TUB, אֲחִיטוּב *a good brother.*

1. Son of Phinehas, and grandson of Eli, B.C. 1100.

1 Sa. 14. 3 the son of A., I-chabod's brother, the son
22. 9 coming to Nob, to Ahimelech the son of A.
22. 11 to call Ahimelech the priest, the son of A.
22. 12 And Saul said, Hear now, thou son of A.
22. 20 of Ahimelech the son of A., named

2. Father of Zadok the high-priest in the time of David, B.C. 1060. Perhaps the same as No. 1.

2 Sa. 8. 17 And Zadok the son of A., and Ahimelech
1 Ch. 6. 7 and Amariah begat A.
6. 8 And A. begat Zadok, and Zadok begat
6. 52 Amariah his son, A. his son
18. 16 And Zadok the son of A., and
Ezra 7. 2 the son of Zadok, the son of A.

3. Another priest, in the 7th generation after No. 2, B.C. 758.

1 Ch. 6. 11 begat Amariah, and Amariah begat A.
6. 12 A. begat Zadok, and Zadok begat Shallum

4. Another priest, progenitor of Seraiah, and ruler of the house of God in the time of Nehemiah.

1 Ch. 9. 11 son of A., the ruler of the house of God
Neh. 11. 11 the son of Meraioth, the son of A.

AH'-LAB, אַחְלָב *fruitful place.*

A city of Asher from which the Canaanites were not driven out.

Judg. 1. 31 nor the inhabitants of Zidon, nor of A

AH'-LAI, אַחְלַי *Jah is staying.*

1. A daughter of Sheshan, a descendant of Pharez, B.C. 1430.

1 Ch. 2. 31 And the children of Sheshan; A.

2. Father of one of David's thirty valiant men, B.C. 1050.

1 Ch. 11. 41 Uriah the Hittite, Zabad the son of A

A-HO'-AH, אֲחוֹחַ *a brother's reed.*

Son of Bela and grandson of Benjamin, B.C. 1650.

1 Ch. 8. 4 Abishua, and Naaman, and A.

A-HO-HITE, אֲחוֹחִי *belonging to Ahoah.*

1. A patronymic derived from Ahoah, a grandson of Benjamin.

2 Sa. 23. 28 Zalmon the A., Maharai the Netophathite
1 Ch. 11. 12 Eleazar the son of Dodo, the A., who
11. 29 Ilai the A.
27. 4 the second month (was) Dodai an A.

2. This word occurs in the common version of 2 Sa. 23. 9, but in the original the expression used is *Ben Ahohi* "son of Ahohi," which thus seems to be a proper name, not a patronymic. B.C. 1650.

2 Sa. 23. 9 (was) Eleazar the son of Dodo the A.

A-HO'-LAH, אָהֳלָה *her own tent.*

A symbolic name for Samaria and the ten tribes.

Eze. 23. 4 And the names of them (were) A. the elder
23. 4 Thus (were) their names; Samaria (is) A.
23. 5 And A. played the harlot when she was
23. 36 Son of man, wilt thou judge A. and
23. 44 went they in unto A. and unto Aholibah

A-HO-LI'-AB, אָהֳלִיאָב *a father's tent.*

A Danite, in the time of Moses, appointed by God to work with Bezaleel in preparing the tabernacle, B.C. 1490.

Exod 31. 6 I have given with him A., the son of
35. 34 (both) he, and A., the son of Ahisamach
36. 1 Then wrought Bezaleel and A., and every
36. 2 And Moses called Bezaleel and A., and
38. 23 And with him (was) A., son of Ahisamach

A-HO-LI'-BAH, אָהֳלִיבָה *my tent (is) in her.*

A symbolic name for Judah and Jerusalem.

Eze. 23. 4 A. her sister: and they were mine
23. 4 Samaria (is) Aholah, and Jerusalem A.
23. 11 when her sister A. saw (this), she
23. 22 Therefore, O Aholibah, thus saith the Lord
23. 36 wilt thou judge Aholah and A.?
23. 44 so went they in unto Aholah and unto A

A-HO-LI-BA'-MAH, אָהֳלִיבָמָה *tent of the high place.*

1. Granddaughter of Gideon the Hivite, and wife of Esau. She is called Judith in Gen. 26. 34. B.C. 1760.

Gen. 36. 2 A. the daughter of Anah the daughter of
36. 5 And A. bare Jeush, and Jaalam, and
36. 14 these were the sons of A., the daughter of
36. 18 And these (are) the sons of A. Esau's wife
36. 18 these (were) the dukes (that) came of A.
36. 25 Dishon, and A. the daughter of Anah

2. A chief that sprang from Esau, B.C. 1470.

Gen. 36. 41 Duke A., duke Elah, duke Pinon
1 Ch. 1. 52 Duke A., duke Elah, duke Pinon

A-HU'-MAI, אֲחוּמַי *heated by Jah.*

Grandson of Shobal, son of Judah, B.C. 1380.

1 Ch. 4. 2 begat Jahath; and Jahath begat A.

A-HU'-ZAM, אֲחֻזָּם *a holding fast.*

A son of Ashur, a descendant of Judah through Caleb son of Hur, B.C. 1500.

1 Ch. 4. 6 And Naarah bare him A., and Hepher

A-HUZ'-ZATH, אֲחֻזַּת *holding fast.*

A friend of Abimelech, king of the Philistines in the time of Isaac, B.C. 1804.

Gen. 26. 26 Abimelech went to him..and A. one of

A'-I, עַי הָעַי *the heap.*

A city near Bethel, and about 10 miles N. of Jerusalem, within the territory of Benjamin. See *Aiath, Aija,* and *Hai,* other forms of the name. Its modern name is *Et Teel,* "the heap."

Josh. 7. 2 Joshua sent men from Jericho to A.
7. 2 And the men went up and viewed A.
7. 3 three thousand men, go up and smite A.
7. 4 they fled before the men of A.
7. 5 And the men of A. smote of them about
8. 1 go up to A.: see, I have given into thy
8. 1 the king of A., and his people, and his
8. 2 And thou shalt do to A. and her king
8. 3 So Joshua arose..to go up against A.
8. 9 and abode between Beth-el and A.
8. 9 on the west side of A.: but Joshua
8. 10 elders of Israel, before the people to A.
8. 11 side of A...a valley between them and A.
8. 12 in ambush between Bethel and A.
8. 14 when the king of A. saw (it), that they
8. 16*all the people that (were) in A. were
8. 17 there was not a man left in A. or
8. 18 spear that (is) in thy hand toward A.
8. 20 And when the men of A. looked
8. 21 turned again, and slew the men of A.
8. 23 And the king of A. they took alive, and
8. 24 slaying all the inhabitants of A.
8. 24 all the Israelites returned unto A.

[* The Hebrew text has "*in the city.*"]

Josh. 8. 25 twelve thousand..all the men of A.
8. 26 destroyed all the inhabitants of A
8. 28 And Joshua burnt A., and made it
8. 29 And the king of A. he hanged on a tree
9. 3 Joshua had done unto Jericho and to A.
10. 1 when..heard how Joshua had taken A.
10. 1 so he had done to A. and her king
10. 2 because it (was) greater than A., and all
12. 9 the king of A., which (is) beside Beth-el
Ezra 2. 28 The men of Beth-el and A., two hundred
Neh. 7. 32 The men of Beth-el and A., an hundred
Jer. 49. 3 *Howl, O Heshbon, for A. is spoiled: cry
[* Here the article is omitted.]

A'-IAH, A'-JAH, אַיָּה *a vulture.*

1. Son of Zibeon, son of Seir the Horite, B.C. 1500.
Gen. 36. 24 these (are) the children of Zibeon; both A.
1 Ch. 1. 40 And the sons of Zibeon; A., and Anah
2. The father of Rizpah, Saul's concubine, B.C. 1050.
2 Sa. 3. 7 name (was) Rizpah, the daughter of A.
21. 8 two sons of Rizpah the daughter of A.
21. 10 And Rizpah the daughter of A. took
21. 11 what Rizpah the daughter of A., the

AI'-ATH, עַיָּת *a heap, a ruin.*

The feminine form of Ai, but it is not certain that it applies to the same place.
Isa. 10. 28 He is come to A., he is passed to

AID, to —

To strengthen, חָזַק *chazeq,* 3.
Judg. 9. 24 men of Shechem..aided him in the

AI'-JA, עַיָּא *a heap, a ruin.*

One of the forms of Ai.
Neh. 11. 31 (dwelt) at Michmash, and A., and Beth-el

AI-JA'-LON, A-JA'-LON, אַיָּלוֹן.

1. The name of a valley in Dan.
Josh 10. 12 and thou, Moon, in the valley of A.
2. A Levitical town in Dan, so called from its situation in or near the valley of Ajalon.
Josh. 19. 42 And Shaalabbin, and A., and
21. 24 A. with her suburbs, Gath-rimmon with
Judg 1. 35 Amorites..dwell in mount Heres in A.
3. A place in the tribe of Zebulun.
Judg 12. 12 and was buried in A. in the country of
4. A town in Benjamin or Judah, or perhaps identical with Ajalon in Dan.
1 Sa. 14. 31 smote the Philistines that day..to A.
1 Ch. 8. 13 fathers of the inhabitants of A.
2 Ch. 11. 10 And Zorah, and A...which (are) in Judah
28. 18 and had taken Beth-shemesh, and A., and
5. A Levitical city in Ephraim, probably the same as No. 2.
1 Ch. 6. 69 A. with her suburbs, and Gath-rimmon

AI-JE-LETH SHA'-HAR —

Hind of the morning, אַיֶּלֶת שַׁחַר *ay-ye-leth Shachar.*
Psa. 22. *title.* To the chief musician upon A. S.

AIL, to —

What to thee? מַה־לְּךָ *mah-leka.*
Gen. 21. 17 What aileth thee, Hagar? fear
Judg 18. 23 What aileth thee, that thou comest with
1 Sa. 11. 5 What (aileth) the people that they weep?
2 Sa. 14. 5 What aileth thee? ..I (am) indeed a widow
2 Ki. 6. 28 What aileth thee?..she answered..Give
Psa. 114. 5 What (ailed) thee, O thou sea, that thou
Isa. 22. 1 What aileth thee now, that thou art

A'-IN, עַיִן עַיִן *a (natural) fountain.*

1. A place in the N.E. of Caanan, between Riblah and the Sea of Chinnereth.
Num. 34. 11 Shepham to Riblah, on the east side of A.
2. A Levitical city in Simeon, at first belonging to Judah.
Josh. 15. 32 Lebaoth, and Shilhim, and A., and
19. 7 A., Remmon, and Ether, and Ashan
21. 16 And A. with her suburbs, and Juttah
1 Ch. 4. 32 Etam, and A., Rimmon, and Tochen

AIR —

1. *Air, wind,* רוּחַ *ruach.*
Job. 41. 16 no air can come between them
2. *Heaven,* שָׁמַיִם *shamayim.*
Gen. 1. 26 have dominion over the..fowl of the air
1. 28 have dominion over the..fowl of the air
1. 30 to every fowl of the air
2. 19 LORD God formed every..fowl of the air
2. 20 gave names to..the fowl of the air
6. 7 I will destroy..the fowls of the air
7. 3 fowls also of the air by sevens..the male
9. 2 the fear..upon every fowl of the air
Deut. 4. 17 winged fowl that flieth in the air
28. 26 shall be meat unto all fowls of the air
1 Sa. 17. 44 give thy flesh unto the fowls of the air
17. 46 I will give..unto the fowls of the air
2 Sa. 21. 10 suffered neither the birds of the air to rest
1 Ki. 14. 11 him that dieth..the fowls of the air
16. 4 shall the fowls of the air eat
21. 24 Him that dieth..the fowls of the air eat
Job 12. 7 ask..the fowls of the air, and they shall
28. 21 it is..kept close from the fowls of the air
Psa. 8. 8 The fowl of the air, and the fish of the sea
Prov. 30. 19 The way of an eagle in the air
Eccl. 10. 20 a bird of the air shall carry the voice
3. *Air, atmosphere,* ἀήρ *aēr.*
Acts 22. 23 and threw dust into the [air]
1 Co. 9. 26 not as one that beateth the air
14. 9 for ye shall speak into the air
Eph. 2. 2 to the prince of the power of the air
1 Th. 4. 17 to meet the Lord in the air: and so shall
Rev. 9. 2 and the sun and the air were darkened
16. 17 poured out his vial into the air
4. *Heaven,* οὐρανός *ouranos.*
Matt. 6. 26 Behold the fowls of the air: for they sow
8. 20 and the birds of the air (have) nests
13. 32 so that the birds of the air come and lodge
Mark 4. 4 and the fowls of the [air]..and devoured it
4. 32 so that the fowls of the air may lodge
Luke 8. 5 and the fowls of the air devoured it
9. 58 Foxes have holes, and birds of the air
13. 19 and the fowls of the air lodged in the
Acts 10. 12 creeping things, and fowls of the air
11. 6 creeping things, and fowls of the air

A'-KAN or JA'-KAN, יַעֲקָן עֲקָן *acute, twisted.*

Son of Ezer, son of Seir the Horite, B.C. 1780.
Gen. 36. 27 (are) these; Bilhan, and Zaavan, and A.
1 Ch. 1. 42 sons of Ezer; Bilhan, and Zavan, (and) J.

AK'-KUB, עַקּוּב *lain in wait.*

1. Son of Elioenai, of the family of David.
1 Ch. 3. 24 and Eliashib, and Pelaiah, and A., and
2. A porter in the second temple.
1 Ch. 9. 17 the porters (were), Shallum, and A., and
Neh. 11. 19 Moreover the porters, A., Talmon, and
12. 25 Talmon, A., (were) porters keeping the
3. A family of hereditary porters in the temple.
Ezra 2. 42 children of A., the children of Hatita
Neh. 7. 45 children of A., the children of Hatita
4. The chief of a family of the Nethinim who came up to Jerusalem after the exile.
Ezra 2. 45 the children of Hagabah..children of A.
5. A priest employed by Ezra to make the people understand the law when it was read to them.
Neh. 8. 7 Jamin, A., Shabbethai, Hodijah, M.

AK-RAB'-BIM, עַקְרַבִּים *curves or scorpions.*

An ascent from the S. of the Salt Sea, curving eastward near Kadesh Barnea, along which the S. border of Canaan was traced, now called *Nuikes-Sufa.*
Num 34. 4. to the ascent of A., and pass on to Zin
Josh. 15. 3. it went out to the south side to M.-ac.

ALABASTER BOX —

Alabaster, ἀλάβαστρον *alabastron,*
Matt 26. 7 a woman having an alabaster box
Mark 14. 3 a woman having an alabaster box
Luke 7. 37 brought an alabaster box of ointment

A-LA'-METH, עָלֶמֶת *youthful vigour.*

Son of Becher, and grandson of Benjamin, B.C. 1650.
1 Ch. 7. 8 Jerimoth, and Abiah, and Anathoth..A.

A-LAM-ME'-LECH, אַלַּמֶּלֶךְ *the king's oak.*

A town in Asher, marked now by the *Wady-el-Melek,* a small stream running into the Kishon, 6 miles inland from *Hhaiffa.*
Josh. 19. 26 And A., and Amad, and Mishael; and

A-LA'-MOTH, עֲלָמוֹת *soprano or treble.*

A term derived from *Almah* "a virgin," in reference to the higher pitch of her voice when compared with that of an adult male's.
1 Ch. 15. 20 and Benaiah, with psalteries on A.
Psa. 46. *title.* for the sons of Korah, A Song upon A.

ALARM —

Shout (of jubilee or battle), תְּרוּעָה *teruah.*
Num 10. 5 When ye blow an alarm..parts shall go
10. 6 When ye blow an alarm the second time
10. 6 they shall blow an alarm for their
Jer. 4. 19 the sound of the trumpet, the alarm
49. 2 I will cause an alarm of war to be heard
Zeph. 1. 16 day of..alarm against the fenced cities
[*See also* Blow, cry, sound.]

ALAS —

1. *Aha! (complaint)* אֲהָהּ *ahah.*
Josh. 7. 7 Joshua said, Alas, O LORD God
Judg. 6. 22 Gideon said, Alas! O LORD God!
11. 35 Alas, my daughter! thou hast brought
2 Ki. 3. 10 Alas! that the LORD hath called these
6. 5 Alas, master! for it was borrowed
6. 15 Alas, my master! how shall we do?
Joel 1. 15 Alas..for the day of the LORD (is) at hand
2. *O, oh! (grief)* אוֹי *oy.*
Num 24. 23 Alas, who shall live when God doeth this!
3. *Ah! (grief)* אָח *ach.*
Eze. 6. 11 Alas for all the evil abominations of the
4. *I pray thee,* בִּי *bi.*
Num 12. 11 Alas, my lord..lay not the sin upon us
5. *Exhortation, grief, threatening,* הוֹ *ho.*
Amos 5. 16 say in all the highways, Alas! alas!
6. *Exhortation, grief, threatening,* הוֹי *hoi.*
1 Ki. 13. 30 they mourned over him, (saying), Alas, my
Jer. 30 7 Alas! for that day (is) great..none (is) like
7. *Wo,* οὐαί *ouai.* [*Lat.*]
Rev. 18. 10 saying, Alas, alas that great city Babylon
18. 16 And saying, Alas, alas that great city
18. 19 Alas, alas that great city, wherein were

ALBEIT —

That, ἵνα *hina.*
Phm. 19 albeit I do not say to thee how thou owest

A-LE'-METH, עָלֶמֶת עַלְמֶת *hiding place.*

1. A Levitical city of Benjamin.
1 Ch. 6. 60 and A. with her suburbs, and Anathoth
2. A descendant of Jonathan, son of Saul.
1 Ch. 8. 36 and Jehoadah begat A., and Azmaveth
9. 42 and Jarah begat A., and Azmaveth

A-LEX-AN'-DER, Ἀλέξανδρος *helper of man.*

1. Son of Simon the Cyrenian who was compelled to carry the cross of Jesus.
Mark 15. 21 the father of A. and Rufus, to bear his
2. A leading man in Jerusalem when Peter and John were apprehended, A.D. 33.
Acts 4. 6 and John, and A., and as many as were of
3. A convert who was with Paul when the Ephesians raised a tumult; perhaps the same as No. 1.
Acts 19. 33 And they drew A. out of..And A.
4. A convert who afterwards apostatised.
1 Ti. 1. 20 Of whom is Hymeneus and A.; whom I
5. A person who opposed Paul, perhaps the same as No. 4.
2 Ti. 4. 14 A. the coppersmith did me much evil

A-LEX-AN-DRI-A, Ἀλεξανδρεύς *of Alexander.*

A city in Egypt, founded by Alexander the Great, B.C. 332, near the W. branch of the Nile where it flows into the Mediterranean. It was long one of the most celebrated cities in the world, the metropolis of Egypt as well as a grand seat of commerce and wealth. Jews dwelt in it in great numbers. The modern city is built on the ruins of the ancient one, about 125 miles N. of Cairo. It is still the seat of extensive commerce, and has nearly 50,000 of a population.
Acts 6. 9 certain of the synagogue..of the..A.
18. 24 born at A., an eloquent man, (and) mighty
27. 6 the centurion found a ship of A. sailing
28. 11 we departed in a ship of A., which had

ALGUM trees —

A costly wood, אַלְגּוּמִּים *algummim.*
2 Ch. 2. 8 Send me also..algum trees, out of Leba.
9. 10 the servants..brought algum trees
9. 11 the king made (of) the algum trees

AL'-IAH, עַלְיָה *sublimity* [V. L. ALVAH].

A duke of Edom, descended from Esau.
[Gen. 36. 40 the names of the dukes..of Esau..duke A.]
1 Ch. 1. 51 dukes of Edom were; duke Timnah..A.

AL'-IAN, עַלְיָן *sublime.*

A son of Shobal, a descendant of Seir.
[Gen. 36. 23 the children of Shobal (were) these; A.]
1 Ch. 1. 40 The sons of Shobal; A., and Manahath

ALIEN —

1. *Sojourner,* גֵּר *ger.*
Exod 18. 3 I have been an alien in a strange land
2. *Unknown,* נֵכָר *nekar.*
Isa. 61. 5 sons of the alien (shall be) your plowmen
3. *Unknown,* נָכְרִי *nokri.*
Deut 14. 21 thou mayest sell it unto an alien
Job 19. 15 I am an alien in their sight
Psa. 69. 8 I am..an alien unto my mother's children
Lam. 5. 2 to strangers, our houses to aliens
4. *Belonging to others,* ἀλλότριος *allotrios.*
Heb. 11. 34 turned..the armies of the aliens

ALIEN, to be —

To alienate, ἀπαλλοτριόω *apallotrioō.*
Eph 2. 12 being aliens from the commonwealth of

ALIENATE, to—

1. *To pass over,* עָבַר *abar* [another reading for No. 2].
Eze. 48. 14 they shall not..alienate the first-fruits
2. *To cause to pass over,* עָבַר *abar,* 5.
Eze. 48. 14 they shall not..alienate the first-fruits
3. *To give to others,* ἀπαλλοτριόω *apallotrioō.*
Eph. 4. 18 the understanding..being alienated from
Col. 1. 21 you, that were sometime alienated

ALIENATED, to be —

1. *To be disjointed,* יָקַע *yaqa.*
Eze 23. 17 her mind was alienated from them
23. 18 my mind was alienated from her
2. *To be disjointed,* נָקַע *naqa.*
Eze. 23. 18 my mind was alienated from her sister
23. 22 from whom thy mind is alienated
23. 28 from whom thy mind is alienated

ALIKE —

1. *One,* אֶחָד *echad.*
Eccl. 11. 6 whether they both (shall be) alike good
2. *As, just as,* כַּאֲשֶׁר *ka-asher.*
Eccl. 9. 2 All (things come) alike to all
3. *Also, even,* גַּם *gam.*
Prov. 20. 10 both of them (are) alike abomination to
4. *Together,* יַחַד *yachad.*
Deut 12. 22 and the clean shall eat (of) them alike
15. 22 the clean (person shall eat it) alike
1 Sa. 30. 24 his part (be)..they shall part alike
Job 21. 26 They shall lie down alike in the dust
Psa. 33. 15 He fashioneth their hearts alike

ALIKE, to be —

To be or show oneself equal, שָׁוָה *shavah,* 8.
Prov. 27. 15 and a contentious woman are alike

ALIVE —

1. *Alive, living,* חַי *chai.*
Gen. 43. 7 (Is) your father yet alive? have ye
43. 27 the old man..(Is) he yet alive?
43. 28 in good health, he (is) yet alive
45. 26 Joseph (is) yet alive, and he (is) governor
45. 28 enough; Joseph my son (is) yet alive
46. 30 seen thy face, because thou (art) yet alive
Exod. 4. 18 and see whether they be yet alive
22. 4 be certainly found in his hand alive
Lev. 14. 4 that is to be cleansed two birds alive
16. 10 shall be presented alive before the LORD
Num 16. 33 went down alive into the pit
Deut. 5. 3 who (are) all of us here alive this, 4. 4
31. 27 I am yet alive with you this day
Josh 8. 23 The king of Ai they took alive, and
1 Sa. 15. 8 took..the king of the Amalekites alive
2 Sa. 12. 18 while the child was yet alive, we spake
12. 21 weep for the child, (while it was) alive
12. 22 While the child was yet alive, I fasted
18. 14 he (was) yet alive in the midst of the oak
1 Ki. 20. 18 come out for peace, take them alive
20. 18 come out for war, take them alive
20. 32 And he said, (Is) he yet alive?
21. 15 Naboth is not alive, but dead
2 Ki. 7. 12 we shall catch them alive and get into
10. 14 Take them alive..they took them alive
2 Ch. 25. 12 And (other) ten thousand (left) alive
Prov. 1. 12 Let us swallow them up alive
Eze. 7. 13 although they were yet alive

2. *Remaining one, remnant,* שָׂרִיד *sarid.*
Num 21. 35 smote him, and..none left him alive

3. *To live,* ζάω *zaō.*
Acts 1. 3 To whom also he shewed himself alive
9. 41 saints and widows, presented her alive
20. 12 they brought the young man alive, and
25. 19 Jesus..whom Paul affirmed to be alive
Rom. 6. 11 reckon ye also yourselves..alive unto God
Rev. 1. 18 and, behold, I am alive for evermore
19. 20 These both were cast alive into a lake of
[*See also* Preserve, save.]

ALIVE again, to be —

To live again, ἀναζάω *anazaō.*
Luke 15. 24 this my son was dead, and is alive again
15. 32 thy brother was dead, and is alive [again]

ALIVE, to be —

To live, be active, ζάω *zaō.*
Matt 27. 63 while he was yet alive, After three days I
Mark 16. 11 [they had heard that he was alive]
Luke 24. 23 which said that he was alive
Acts 25. 19 Jesus..whom Paul affirmed to be alive
Rom. 6. 13 as those that are alive from the dead
7. 9 For I was alive without the law once
1 Th. 4. 15 that we which are alive (and) remain
4. 17 Then we which are alive (and) remain
Rev. 2. 8 and the last, which was dead and is alive

ALIVE, to keep —

1. *To keep living or alive,* חָיָה *chayah,* 3.
Gen. 7. 3 keep seed alive upon the face of all the
Psa. 22. 29 none can keep alive his own soul
30. 3 thou hast kept me alive
33. 19 and to keep them alive in famine
41. 2 The LORD will..keep him alive

2. *To keep living, restore life,* חָיָה *chayah,* 5.
Gen. 6. 19 to keep (them) alive with thee
6. 20 shall come unto thee..keep (them) alive
Num 31. 18 with him, keep alive for yourselves
Josh. 14. 10 behold, the LORD hath kept me alive
2 Sa. 8. 2 with one full line to keep alive

3. *To keep living,* חָיָא *chaya,* 5.
Dan. 5. 19 whom he would he kept alive

ALIVE, to leave —

To keep living or alive, חָיָה *chayah,* 3.
1 Sa. 27. 9 left neither man nor woman alive

ALIVE, to make —

1. *To keep living or alive,* חָיָה *chayah,* 3.
Deut 32. 39 I kill, and I make alive
1 Sa. 2. 6 The LORD killeth, and maketh alive

2. *To keep living, restore life,* חָיָה *chayah,* 5.
2 Ki. 5. 7 (Am) I God, to kill and to make alive

3. *To make alive,* ζωοποιέω *zōopoieō.*
1 Co. 15. 22 in Christ shall all be made alive

ALL —

1. *All,* כֹּל *kol.*
Gen. 3. 17 in sorrow shalt thou eat (of) it all the

2. *All,* כֹּל *kol.*
Ezra 4. 20 mighty kings..have ruled over all
5. 7 written thus; Unto Darius the king, all
6. 12 destroy all kings and people, that shall
6. 17 lambs..for a sin offering for all Israel
7. 13 all they..will to go up to Jerusalem
7. 16 all the silver and gold that..in all
7. 21 I..make a decree to all the treasurers
7. 25 judges, which may judge all..all such
Dan. 2. 12 the king..commanded to destroy all the
2. 38 he..hath made thee ruler over them all
2. 39 which shall bear rule over all the earth
2. 40 subdueth all..as iron that breaketh all
2. 44 shall break in pieces and consume all
2. 48 the king made Daniel..chief..over all
3. 2, 3 all the rulers..were gathered together
3. 5, 7, 10, 15 the sound of..all kinds of music
Dan. 3. 7 all the people heard..all the people
4. 1 all people..that dwell in all the earth
4. 6 bring in all the wise (men) of Babylon
4. 11 to the end of all the earth
4. 12, 21 and in it (was) meat for all..all flesh
4. 18 all the wise (men) of my kingdom are not
4. 20 and the sight thereof to all the earth
4. 28 All this came upon the king
4. 35 all the inhabitants of the earth
4. 37 the King of heaven, all whose works (are)
5. 8 Then came in all the king's wise (men)
5. 19 he gave him, all people..and languages
5. 22 though thou knewest all this
5. 23 and whose (are) all thy ways
6. 7 All the presidents of the kingdom
6. 24 and brake all their bones in pieces
6. 25 Darius wrote unto all people..in all the
7. 7 it (was) diverse from all the beasts
7. 14 that all people..and languages, should
7. 16 and asked him the truth of all this
7. 19 which was diverse from all the others
7. 23 which shall be diverse from all kingdoms
7. 27 all dominions shall serve and obey him

3. *Complete, wholly,* כָּלִיל *kalil.*
Exod. 28. 31 the robe of the ephod all (of) blue
39. 22 the ephod (of) woven work, all (of) blue

4. *Multitude,* רֹב *rob.*
Deut. 28. 47 for the abundance of all (things)
Job 4. 14 which made all my bones to shake

5. *All together,* ἅπας *hapas.*
Matt. 6. 32 after all these things do the Gentiles
24. 39 until the flood came, and took them all
28. 11 shewed unto the chief priests all the
Mark 5. 40 But when he had put them all out
11. 32 for all (men) counted John, that he was
16. 15 Go ye into all the world, and preach
Luke 3. 16 John answered, saying unto (them) all, I
3. 21 Now when all the people were baptized
4. 6 All this power will I give thee, and
5. 11 they forsook all, and followed him
5. 26 they were all amazed, and they glorified
5. 28 he left all, rose up, and followed him
7. 16 there came a fear on all: and they
9. 15 they did so, and made them all sit down
15. 13 the younger son gathered all together
17. 27 the flood came, and destroyed them all
17. 29 it rained fire..and destroyed (them) all
19. 7 when they saw (it,) they all murmured
19. 48 all the people were very attentive to hear
21. 4 all these have of their abundance cast..all
21. 12 before all these, they shall lay their hands
Acts 2. 1 they were [all] with one accord in one place
2. 4 they were all filled with the Holy Ghost
2. 14 Ye men of Judea, and all (ye) that dwell
4. 31 they were all filled with the Holy Ghost
5. 12 they were all with one accord in Solomon's
6. 15 all that sat in the council, looking
11. 10 all were drawn up again into heaven
13. 29 when they had fulfilled all that was
16. 3 they knew all that his father was a Greek
16. 28 Do thyself no harm: for we are all here
27. 33 Paul besought (them) all to take meat
Eph. 6. 13 and having done all, to stand
Jas. 3. 2 For in many things we offend all

6. *The whole,* ὅλος *holos.*
Matt. 1. 22 all this was done, that it might be
4. 23 Jesus went about all Galilee, teaching
4. 24 his fame went throughout all Syria
9. 26 the fame hereof went abroad into all that
9. 31 spread abroad his fame in all that country
14. 35 they sent out into all that country round
20. 6 Why stand ye here all the day idle?
21. 4 [All] this was done; that it might be fulfilled
22. 37 all thy heart..all thy soul..all thy mind
22. 40 On these two commandments hang all
24. 14 shall be preached in all the world
26. 56 all this was done, that the scriptures
26. 59 the chief priests, and elders, and all the
Mark 1. 28 his fame spread abroad throughout all
1. 33 all the city was gathered together at the
1. 39 And he preached..throughout all Galilee
12. 30 all thy heart..all thy soul..all thy mind..all
12. 33 And to love him with all the heart
12. 33 and with all the understanding
12. 33 [with all the soul,] and with all the strength
12. 44 all (they) did cast in of their abundance
14. 55 the chief priests and all the council
Luke 1. 65 fear came on all that dwelt round
4. 14 a fame of him through all the region
5. 5 Master, we have toiled all the night, and
7. 17 this..went forth throughout all Judea
8. 43 which had spent all her living on physicians
10. 27 all thy heart..all thy soul..all thy stre...all
23. 5 He stirreth up..teaching throughout all
23. 44 there was a darkness over all the earth
Acts 2. 2 it filled all the house where they were
2. 47 Praising God, and having favour with all
5. 11 great fear came upon all the church
7. 10 delivered him out of all his afflictions
7. 11 Now there came a dearth over all the land
8. 37 If thou believest with [all] thine heart, thou
9. 31 throughout all Judea and G. and Samaria.
9. 42 It was known throughout all Joppa
10. 22 of good report among all the nation
10. 37 which was published throughout all Judea
11. 28 should be great dearth throughout all
13. 49 the word..throughout all the region
18. 8 believed on the Lord with all his house
19. 27 whom all Asia and the world worshippeth
21. 30 all the city was moved, and the people
Acts 21. 31 that all Jerusalem was in an uproar
22. 30 the chief priests and all, Ro. 8. 36; 10. 21.
2 Co. 1. 1 all the saints which are in all Achaia
Phil. 1. 13 bonds in Christ are manifest in all
1 Th. 4. 10 indeed ye do it toward all the brethren
Heb. 3. 2 as also Moses (was faithful) in all his house
3. 5 Moses verily (was) faithful in all his house
Rev. 3. 10 which shall come upon all the world
13. 3 all the world wondered after the beast

7. *How much, great, many, long,* ὅσος *hosos.*
2 Co. 1. 20 all the promises of God in him (are) yea

8. *All, any, every,* πᾶς *pas.*
Matt. 2. 3 he was troubled, and all Jerusalem with
3. 5 Jerusalem, and all Judea, and all the
3. 15 for thus it becometh us to fulfil all
6. 29 even Solomon in all his glory was not
18. 32 O thou wicked servant, I forgave thee all
18. 34 till he should pay all that was due unto
21. 10 when he was come into Jerusalem, all the
23. 27 are within full..of all uncleanness
23. 35 That upon you may come all the righteous
27. 25 Then answered all the people, and said
27. 45 there was darkness over all the land unto
28. 18 All power is given unto me in heaven and
Mark 1. 5 there went out unto him all the land
2. 13 all the multitude resorted unto him
5. 33 and told him all the truth
7. 14 when he had called [all] the people
9. 15 straightway all the people, when they
11. 18 all the people was astonished at his doctrine
Luke 2. 1 that all the world should be taxed
2. 10 great joy, which shall be to all people
3. 3 he came into all the country about Jordan
3. 6 all flesh shall see the salvation of God
4. 13 when the devil had ended all the tempta.
4. 25 great famine was throughout all the land
6. 17 multitude of people out of all Judea
7. 17 rumour..went forth throughout all Judea
7. 29 And all the people that heard (him)
8. 47 she declared unto him before all the
9. 13 and buy meat for all this people
10. 19 and over all the power of the enemy
12. 27 Solomon in all his glory was not
13. 17 all his adversaries were ashamed
18. 43 all the people, when they saw (it)
20. 6 [all] the people will stone us; for
20. 45 in the audience of all the people
21. 38 all the people came early in the morning
24. 19 a prophet mighty..before..all the people
John 5. 22 hath committed all judgment unto the Son
6. 37 All that the Father giveth me shall come
6. 39 that of all which he hath given me I should
8. 2 [and all the people came unto him]
16. 13 he will guide you into all truth
17. 2 As thou hast given him power over all flesh
Acts 1. 8 both in Jerusalem, and in all Judea
1. 21 which have companied with us all the time
2. 17 I will pour out of my Spirit upon all flesh
2. 36 let all the house of Israel know assuredly
3. 9 all the people saw him walking and
3. 11 all the people ran together unto them
4. 29 that with all boldness they may speak thy
5. 21 all the senate of the children of Israel
5. 34 a doctor of the law..among all the people
7. 14 all his kindred, threescore and fifteen souls
7. 22 And Moses was learned in all the wisdom
8. 27 who had the charge of all her treasure
10. 2 one that feared God with all his house
10. 41 Not to all the people, but unto witnesses
11. 14 whereby thou and all thy house shall be
12. 11 and (from) all the expectation of the people
13. 10 O full of all subtilty and all mischief..all
13. 24 the baptism of repentance to all the people
13. 39 And by him all that believe are justified
15. 12 all the multitude kept silence, and gave
17. 11 they received the word with all readiness of
17. 26 hath made of one blood all nations
17. 26 to dwell on all the face of the earth
19. 27 whom all Asia and the world worshippeth
20. 18 I have been with you at all seasons
20. 19 Serving the Lord with all humility of mind
20. 27 to declare unto you all the counsel of God
20. 28 Take heed..unto yourselves, and to all
21. 27 stirred up all the people, and laid hands
22. 5 and all the estate of the elders: from
23. 1 I have lived in all good conscience before
24. 3 We accept (it) always, and in all places
25. 24 Festus said, King Agrippa, and all men
26. 20 throughout all the coasts of Judea
27. 20 all hope that we should be saved was
28. 31 with all confidence, no man forbidding
Rom. 1. 18 the wrath of God..against all ungodliness
1. 29 Being filled with all unrighteousness
3. 19 all the world may become guilty before
4. 16 Abraham; who is the father of us all
9. 17 name might be declared throughout all
10. 18 their sound went into all the earth
11. 26 so all Israel shall be saved: as it is
15. 13 the God of hope fill you with all joy and
15. 14 filled with all knowledge, able also to
1 Co. 1. 5 in all utterance, and (in) all knowledge
13. 2 understand all mysteries, and all
15. 24 he shall have put down all rule and all
15. 39 All flesh (is) not the same flesh: but
2 Co. 1. 3 Father of mercies, and the God of all
1. 4 Who comforteth us in all our tribu. 6. 4.
7. 1 let us cleanse ourselves from all filthiness
7. 4 I am exceeding joyful in all our; v. 11.
8. 7 and knowledge, and (in) all diligence, and
9. 8 God (is) able to make all grace abound..all
9. 11 Being enriched in everything to all

2 Co. 10. 6 having in a readiness to revenge all, 11. 9.
12. 12 were wrought among you in all patience
Gal. 5. 14 all the law is fulfilled in one word
Eph 1. 3 who hath blessed us with all spiritual
1. 8 he hath abounded toward us in all wisdom
1. 21 Far above all principality, and power, and
2. 21 In whom all the building fitly framed
3. 19 that ye might be filled with all the fulness
4. 2 With all lowliness and meekness, with
4. 19 to work all uncleanness with greediness
4. 31 Let all bitterness, and wrath, and..all
5. 3 But fornication, and all uncleanness, or
5. 9 (For the fruit of the Spirit (is) in all
6. 18 with all prayer..all perseverance..for all
Phil. 1. 9 your love may abound..(in) all judgment
1. 20 but (that) with all boldness, as always
2. 29 Receive him..in the Lord with all gladness
4. 7 the peace of God, which passeth all
4. 19 But my God shall supply all your need
Col. 1. 6 Which is come unto you, as..in all the
1. 9 in all wisdom and spiritual understanding
1. 10 ye might walk worthy of the Lord unto all
1. 11 Strengthened with all might..all patience
1. 19 that in him should all fulness dwell
1. 28 and teaching every man in all wisdom; that
2. 2 and unto all riches of the full assurance of
2. 9 in him dwelleth all the fulness of the
2. 10 which is the head of all principality and
2. 19 from which all the body by joints and
3. 16 dwell in you richly in all wisdom; teaching
4. 12 that ye may stand..in all the will of God
1 Th. 3. 7 in all our affliction and distress, by your
3. 9 for all the joy wherewith we joy for your
5. 22 Abstain from all appearance of evil
2 Th. 1. 11 and fulfil all the good pleasure of (his)
2. 4 exalteth himself above all that is called
2. 9 with all power and signs and lying wonders
2. 10 with all deceivableness of unrighteousness
3. 16 The Lord (be) with you all
1 Ti. 1. 15 a faithful saying, and worthy of all accepta.
1. 16 Jesus Christ might shew forth all long-suff
2. 2 For kings, and (for) all that are in authority
2. 11 Let the woman learn in silence with all
3. 4 having his children in subjection with all
4. 9 a faithful saying and worthy of all accepta.
5. 2 the younger as sisters, with all purity
6. 1 count their own masters worthy of all
2 Ti. 3. 16 All scripture (is) given by inspiration of
3. 17 throughly furnished unto all good works
4. 2 reprove, rebuke, exhort with all long-suff.
Titus 2. 10 Not purloining, but shewing all good
2. 14 that he might redeem us from all iniquity
2. 15 These things speak..and rebuke with all
3. 2 gentle, shewing all meekness unto all men
Heb. 2. 15 deliver them who..were all their lifetime
6. 16 an oath..(is) to them an end of all strife
7. 7 without all contradiction the less is
9. 19 to all the people..and all the people
Jas. 1. 2 count it all joy when ye fall into
1. 21 lay apart all filthiness and superfluity
4. 16 ye rejoice in your boastings: all such
1 Pe. 1. 24 all flesh (is) as grass, and all the glory
2. 1 all malice..all guile..all evil-speakings
2. 18 (be) subject to (your) masters with all fear
5. 7 Casting all your care upon him; for he
5. 10 But the God of all grace, who hath called
2 Pe. 1. 5 beside this, giving all diligence, add to
1 Jo. 1. 7 and the blood..cleanseth us from all sin
1. 9 to cleanse us from all unrighteousness
2. 16 For all that (is) in the world, the lust
5. 17 All unrighteousness is sin: and there is a
Jude 3 when I gave all diligence to write to you
Rev. 5. 6 the seven..sent forth into all the earth
7. 4 there were) sealed..of all the tribes
7. 9 which no man could number, of all
7. 17 and God shall wipe away all tears from
8. 7 and all green grass was burnt up
11. 6 and to smite the earth with all plagues
12. 5 who was to rule all nations with a rod
13. 7 power was given him over all kindreds
13. 12 he exerciseth all the power of the first
18. 12 all thyine wood..all manner..all manner
18. 17 every shipmaster, and all the company in
21. 4 God shall wipe away all tears from

Plural.

Matt. 1. 17 So all the generations from Abraham to
2. 4 when he had gathered all the chief priests
2. 16 slew all the children that were in..all the
4. 8 sheweth him all the kingdoms of the
4. 9 All these things will I give thee, if
4. 24 they brought unto him all sick people
5. 15 it giveth light unto all that are
5. 18 one tittle..till all be fulfilled
6. 32 that ye have need of all these things
6. 33 all these things shall be added unto
8. 16 word, and healed all that were sick
9. 35 Jesus went about all the cities and
10. 30 hairs of your head are all numbered
11. 13 all the prophets and the law prophesied
11. 28 Come unto me, all (ye) that labour and
12. 15 great multitudes..and he healed them all
12. 23 all the people were amazed, and said
13. 32 Which indeed is the least of all seeds
13. 34 All these things spake Jesus unto the
13. 44 for joy thereof goeth and selleth all
13. 46 went and sold all that he had, and
13. 51 Have ye understood all these things?
13. 56 are they not all..whence..all these
14. 20 And they did all eat, and were filled
14. 35 brought unto him all that were diseased
15. 37 And they did all eat, and were filled
Matt. 18. 25 and all that he had, and payment to
18. 26 Lord, have patience..I will pay thee all
18. 29 Have patience..and I will pay thee [all]
18. 31 told unto their lord all that was done
19. 20 All these things have I kept from my
19. 27 Behold, we have forsaken all, and
21. 12 and cast out all them that sold and
21. 26 for all hold John as a prophet
22. 10 and gathered together all as many as
22. 27 And last of all the woman died also
22. 28 in the resurrection..for they all had
23. 3 All therefore whatsoever they bid you
23. 5 But all their works they do for to be seen
23. 8 (even) Christ; and all ye are brethren
23. 36 All these things shall come upon this
24. 2 See ye not all these things? verily I
24. 6 for [all] (these things) must come to pass
24. 8 All these (are) the beginning of sorrows
24. 9 and ye shall be hated of all nations
24. 14 this gospel..shall be preached in all the
24. 30 and then shall all the tribes of the earth
24. 33 when ye shall see all these things, know
24. 34 this generation shall not pass, till all these
24. 47 he shall make him ruler over all his goods
25. 5 While the bridegroom tarried, they all
25. 7 Then all those virgins arose, and trimmed
25. 31 and all the holy angels with him, then
25. 32 before him shall be gathered all nations
26. 1 when Jesus had finished all these sayings
26. 27 saying, Drink ye all of it
26. 31 Then saith Jesus unto them, All ye shall
26. 35 Likewise also said all the disciples
26. 52 for all they that take the sword, shall
26. 56 Then all the disciples forsook him, and fled
26. 70 But he denied before (them) all, saying
27. 1 When the morning was come, all the chief
27. 22 all say unto him, Let him be crucified
28. 19 Go ye therefore, and teach all nations
Mark 1. 5 there went out unto him all the land
1. 27 they were all amazed, insomuch that they
1. 32 they brought unto him all that were
2. 12 went forth before them all; insomuch..all
3. 28 Verily I say unto you, All sins shall be
4. 13 how then will ye know all parables? 4. 11.
4. 31 less than all the seeds that be in the earth
4. 32 it..becometh greater than all herbs
5. 12 [all] the devils besought him, saying, Send
5. 26 and had spent all that she had, and was
6. 33 ran afoot thither out of all cities
6. 39 he commanded them to make all sit
6. 41 two fishes divided he among them all
6. 42 And they did all eat, and were filled
6. 50 For they all saw him, and were troubled
7. 3 For the Pharisees, and all the Jews, except
7. 19 goeth out into the draught, purging all
7. 23 All these evil things come from within
9. 35 shall be last of all, and servant of all
10. 20 all these have I observed from my youth
10. 28 we have left all, and have followed thee
10. 44 the chiefest, shall be servant of all
11. 17 My house shall be called of all nations
12. 22 last of all the woman died also
12. 28 Which is the first commandment of all?
12. 29 The first [of all the commandments]..Hear
12. 33 all the heart..all the..all the soul..all the
12. 43 this poor widow hath cast more in than all
12. 44 For all (they) did cast in of their abundance
13. 4 what (shall be) the sign when all these
13. 10 gospel must first be published among all
13. 30 this generation shall not pass, till all these
13. 37 what I say unto you, I say unto all
14. 23 he took the cup..and they all drank
14. 27 And Jesus saith unto them, All ye shall
14. 29 Peter said unto him, Although all shall
14. 31 Likewise also said they all
14. 50 And they all forsook him, and fled
14. 53 with him were assembled all the chief
14. 64 they all condemned him to be guilty
Luke 1. 6 they were both righteous..walking in all
1. 48 behold, from henceforth all generations
1. 63 And they marvelled all
1. 65 on all..all these sayings..all the hill
1. 66 And all they that heard (them) laid (them)
1. 71 from the hand of all that hate us
1. 75 In holiness..before him, all the days
2. 3 all went to be taxed, every one into
2. 18 all they that heard (it) wondered at
2. 19 Mary kept all these things, and pondered
2. 31 thou hast prepared before the face of all
2. 38 spake of him to all them that looked
2. 47 all that heard him were astonished
2. 51 his mother kept all these sayings in
3. 15 all men mused in their hearts of John
3. 19 for all the evils which Herod had done
3. 20 Added yet this above all, that he shut
4. 5 the devil..shewed unto him all the
4. 7 If thou..wilt worship me, all shall
4. 15 And he taught..being glorified of all
4. 20 the eyes of all them that were in
4. 22 all bare him witness, and wondered at
4. 28 all they in the synagogue when they
4. 36 they were all amazed, and spake among
4. 40 all they that had any sick with divers
5. 9 he was astonished, and all that were
6. 10 looking round about upon them all, he
6. 19 went virtue out..and healed (them) all
6. 26 Woe unto you when [all] men shall speak
7. 1 Now when he had ended all his sayings
7. 18 the disciples..shewed him of all these
7. 35 Wisdom is justified of [all] her children
8. 40 for they were all waiting for him
8. 45 Jesus said, Who touched me? When all
Luke 8. 52 And all wept, and bewailed her: but he
8. 54 And he [put them all out, and] took
9. 1 gave them power and authority over all
9. 7 Herod the tetrarch heard of all that
9. 17 And they did eat, and were all filled
9. 23 And he said to (them) all, If any
9. 43 they were all amazed at the mighty
9. 48 for he that is least among you all
11. 50 That the blood of all the prophets, which
12. 7 very hairs of your head are all numbered
12. 18 there will I bestow all my fruits
12. 30 all these things do the nations of
12. 31 [all] these things shall be added
12. 41 this parable unto us, or even to all?
12. 44 that he will make him ruler over all
13. 2 these Galileans were sinners above all the
13. 3 except ye repent, ye shall all likewise
13. 4 think ye that they were sinners above all
13. 5 except ye repent, ye shall all likewise perish
13. 17 all his..all the people..for all the glorious
13. 27 depart from me, all (ye) workers of iniquity
13. 28 when ye shall see Abraham..and all the
14. 18 they all with one (consent) began to
14. 29 all that behold (it) begin to mock him
14. 33 whosoever he be..that forsaketh not all
15. 1 Then drew near unto him all the publicans
15. 14 when he had spent all, there arose
15. 31 and all that I have is thine
16. 14 the Pharisees also..heard all these things
16. 26 beside all this, between us and you
17. 10 when ye shall have done all those things
18. 12 I give tithes of all that I possess
18. 21 he said, All these have I kept from
18. 22 Yet lackest thou one thing: sell all
18. 28 Peter said, Lo, we have left [all,] and
19. 37 for all the mighty works that they
20. 32 Last [of all] the woman died also
20. 38 for all live unto him
21. 3 widow hath cast in more than they all
21. 15 I will give you a mouth..which all
21. 24 shall be led away captive into all
21. 29 Behold the fig tree, and all the trees
21. 32 generation shall not pass away till all
21. 35 as a snare shall it come on all
21. 36 ye may be accounted worthy to escape all
22. 70 Then said they all, Art thou then the
23. 48 all the people that came together to
23. 49 all his acquaintance, and the women
24. 9 and told all these things..to all the rest
24. 14 they talked together of all these things
24. 21 beside all this, to-day is the third day
24. 25 O fools, and slow of heart to believe all
24. 27 all the prophets..in all the scriptures the
24. 47 repentance..be preached..among all
John 1. 16 of his fulness have all we received
2. 15 he drove them all out of the temple
3. 31 He that cometh from above is above all
3. 31 he that cometh from heaven is above all
4. 39 He told me all that ever I did
5. 28 the hour is coming, in the which all
6. 45 they shall be all taught of God
7. 21 I have done one work, and ye all marvel
10. 8 All that ever came before me are thieves
10. 29 My Father..is greater than all; and no
13. 10 and ye are clean, but not all
13. 11 Ye are not all clean
13. 18 I speak not of you all: I know
15. 21 all these things will they do unto
17. 10 all mine are thine, and thine are
17. 21 That they all may be one; as thou
18. 40 Then cried they all again, saying, Not this
Acts 1. 1 The former treatise have I made..of all
1. 14 all continued with one accord in prayer
1. 18 and all his bowels gushed out
1. 19 it was known unto all the dwellers
2. 7 they were [all] amazed, and marvelled
2. 7 are not all these which speak Galileans?
2. 12 they were all amazed, and were in
2. 32 whereof we are all witnesses
2. 39 the promise is unto you..and to all
2. 44 all that believed were together, and had
3. 16 this..soundness in the presence of you all
3. 18 had shewed by the mouth of all his
3. 21 God hath spoken by the mouth of all
3. 22 him shall ye hear in all things whatsoever
3. 24 Yea, and all the prophets from Samuel, and
3. 25 in thy seed shall all the kindreds of
4. 10 Be it known unto you all, and to all
4. 16 a notable miracle..(is) manifest to all them
4. 24 thou (art) God, which hast made..all that
4. 33 great grace was upon them all
5. 5 great fear came on all them that
5. 11 great fear came upon all the church
5. 17 Then the high priest rose up, and all
5. 20 Go..stand and speak..to the people all
5. 23 The prison truly found we shut with all
5. 36 all, as many as obeyed him, were
5. 37 all, (even) as many as obeyed him
7. 10 delivered him out of all his afflictions
7. 50 Hath not my hand made all these things?
8. 1 they were all scattered abroad throughout
8. 10 To whom they all gave heed, from the least
8. 40 he preached in [all] the cities, till he came
9. 14 here he hath authority..to bind all
9. 21 all that heard (him) were amazed, and
9. 26 they were all afraid of him, and, v. 32.
9. 35 all that dwelt at Lydda and Saron
9. 39 all the widows stood by him weeping
9. 40 Peter put them all forth, and kneeled
10. 33 Now therefore are we all here present before
10. 36 Jesus Christ: (he is Lord of all)
10. 38 healing all that were oppressed of

Acts 10. 43 To him give all the prophets witness
10. 44 the Holy Ghost fell on all them which
11. 23 Who, when he came..exhorted them all
13. 22 a man..which shall fulfil all my will
14. 16 Who in times past suffered all nations to
15. 3 they caused great joy unto all
15. 17 the residue of men might seek..all the
15. 17 saith the Lord, who doeth [all these things]
15. 18 [Known unto God are all his works], from
16. 26 immediately all the doors were opened
16. 32 and to all that were in his house
16. 33 was baptized, he and all his, straightway
17. 7 Whom Jason hath received: and these all
17. 21 all the Athenians and strangers which
17. 25 seeing he giveth to all life..and all things
17. 30 now commandeth all men everywhere
17. 31 he hath given assurance unto all (men)
18. 2 that Claudius had commanded all Jews
18. 17 all the Greeks took Sosthenes, the chief
18. 23 he departed, and went over (all) the
19. 7 And all the men were about twelve
19. 10 so that all they which dwelt in Asia
19. 19 brought..books..and burned..before all
19. 34 all with one voice..cried out, Great (is)
20. 25 And now, behold, I know that ye all
20. 26 I (am) pure from the blood of all (men)
20. 32 to give you an inheritance among all
20. 36 he kneeled down, and prayed with them all
20. 37 they all wept sore, and fell on Paul's
21. 5 they all brought us on our way
21. 18 and all the elders were present
21. 20 and they are all zealous of the law
21. 21 thou teachest [all] the Jews which are
21. 24 and all may know that those things
22. 3 and was zealous toward God, as ye all
22. 12 having a good report of all the Jews
22. 15 thou shalt be his witness unto all men
24. 5 a mover of sedition among all the Jews
24. 8 thyself mayest take knowledge of all these
25. 24 King Agrippa and all men which are here
26. 3 (I know) thee to be expert in all customs
26. 4 My manner of life..know all the Jews
26. 14 when we were all fallen to the earth
26. 29 but also all that hear me this day
27. 24 and, lo, God hath given thee all them
27. 35 gave thanks to God in presence of them all
27. 36 Then were they all of good cheer
27. 37 And we were in all in the ship
27. 44 that they escaped all safe to land
28. 30 received all that came in unto him
Rom. 1. 5 for obedience to the faith among all
1. 7 To all that be in Rome, beloved of God
1. 8 First, I thank my God..for you all
3. 9 that they are all under sin
3. 12 They are all gone out of the way, they
3. 22 unto all and upon all them that believe
3. 22 by faith of Jesus Christ unto all
3. 23 all have sinned, and come short of the
4. 11 that he might be the father of all
4. 16 the promise might be sure to all the seed
5. 18 upon all men to..upon all men unto
5. 12 so death passed upon all men, for that all
8. 32 delivered him up for us all how shall
8. 37 Nay, in all these things we are more
9. 5 Christ (came), who is over all, God blessed
9. 6 they (are) not all Israel, which are of Israel
9. 7 Neither..are (they all) children; but
10. 12 the same Lord over all is rich unto all
10. 16 But they have not all obeyed the gospel
11. 32 concluded them all..have mercy upon all
12. 4 and all members have not the same office
12. 17 Provide things honest in the sight of all
12. 18 If it be possible..live peaceably with all
13. 7 Render therefore to all their dues
14. 10 we shall all stand before the judgment
15. 11 Praise..all ye Gentiles..laud..all ye people
15. 33 Now the God of peace (be) with you all
16. 4 but also all the churches of the Gentiles
16. 15 Salute Philologus..and all the saints which
16. 24 The grace of our Lord..(be) with you all
16. 26 made known to all nations for the obedience
1 Co. 1. 10 I beseech you..that ye all speak
3. 22 or things to come; all are your's
7. 7 For I would that all men were even
7. 17 And so ordain I in all churches
8. 1 we know that we all have knowledge
9. 19 For though I be free from all (men)
9. 24 that they which run in a race run all
10. 1 how that all our fathers..all passed
10. 2 were all baptized unto Moses in the
10. 3 did all eat the same spiritual meat
10. 4 did all drink the same spiritual drink
10. 11 [all] these things happened unto them
10. 17 we are all partakers of that one bread
10. 31 whatsoever ye do, do all to the glory of God
12. 6 the same God which worketh all in all
12. 11 all these worketh that one and the
12. 12 and all the members of that one body
12. 13 For by one Spirit are we all baptized..all
12. 19 if they were all one member, where
12. 26 all the members suffer..all the members
12. 29 all apostles..all prophets..all teachers..all
12. 30 Have all the gifts of healing? do all..do all
13. 2 understand all mysteries, and all knowledge
13. 3 though I bestow all my goods to feed
14. 5 I would that ye all spake with tongues
14. 18 I speak with tongues more than ye all
14. 23 and all speak with tongues, and there come
14. 24 But if all prophesy..he is judged of all
14. 31 For ye may all prophesy..all may..all may
14. 33 as in all churches of the saints
15. 7 he was seen of James; then of all the

1 Co. 15. 8 And last of all he was seen of me also
15. 10 I laboured more abundantly than they all
15. 19 we are of all men most miserable
15. 22 as in Adam all die, even so in Christ..all
15. 25 till he hath put all enemies under his feet
15. 28 all things..put all things..be all in all
15. 51 We shall not all sleep, but we shall all
16. 20 All the brethren greet you. Greet ye one
16. 24 My love (be) with you all in Christ
2 Co. 1. 1 with all the saints which are in all Achaia
2. 3 confidence in you all that..joy of..all
2. 5 that I may not overcharge you all
3. 2 Ye are our epistle..read of all men
3. 18 we all, with open face beholding as in
5. 10 we must all appear before the judgment
5. 14 if one died for all, then were all dead
5. 15 And (that) he died for all, that they
7. 13 because his spirit was refreshed by you all
7. 15 he remembereth the obedience of you all
8. 18 whose praise (is)..throughout all
11. 28 Beside..the care of all the churches
13. 2 and to all other, that, if I come again
13. 13 All the saints salute you
13. 14 The grace of the Lord..(be) with you all
Gal. 1. 2 all the brethren which are with me
2. 14 I said unto Peter before (them) all, If
3. 8 In thee shall all nations be blessed
3. 22 the scripture hath concluded all under
3. 26 For ye are all the children of God
3. 28 for ye are all one in Christ Jesus
4. 1 the heir..though he be lord of all
4. 26 which is the mother of us [all]
6. 6 communicate unto him..in all
Eph. 1. 15 and love unto all the saints
1. 23 fulness of him that filleth all in all
2. 3 Among whom also we all had our
3. 8 who am less than the least of all saints
3. 18 May be able to comprehend with all saints
3. 20 exceeding abundantly above all that we ask
3. 21 Unto him (be) glory..throughout all ages
4. 6 of all..above all..through all..in you all
4. 10 that he might fill all things
4. 13 Till we all come in the unity of
6. 16 [Above all], taking the shield of faith..all
6. 18 Praying always with all prayer and
6. 24 Grace (be) with all them that love our Lord
Phil. 1. 1 to all the saints in Christ Jesus which
1. 4 for you all making request with joy
1. 7 of you all..ye all are partakers of my grace
1. 8 how greatly I long after you all in
1. 13 my bonds in Christ are manifest in all
1. 25 I know that I shall abide..with you all
2. 17 I joy, and rejoice with you all
2. 21 For all seek their own, not the things
2. 26 For he longed after you all, and was
4. 5 Let your moderation be known unto all
4. 18 But I have all, and abound: I am
4. 22 All the saints salute you, chiefly they that
4. 23 The grace of our Lord..(be) with you all
Col. 1. 4 the love (which ye have) to all the saints
2. 3 In whom are hid all the treasures of
2. 13 having forgiven you all trespasses
2. 22 Which all are to perish with the using
3. 8 But now ye also put off all these
3. 11 but Christ (is) all, and in all
3. 14 above all these things (put on) charity
3. 17 whatsoever ye do..(do) all in the name
4. 7 All my state shall Tychicus declare unto
1 Th. 1. 2 We give thanks to God always for you all
1. 7 So that ye were ensamples to all that
2. 15 and are contrary to all men
3. 13 at the coming of our Lord..with all
4. 6 the Lord (is) the avenger of all such
4. 10 indeed ye do it toward all the brethren
5. 5 Ye are all the children of light, and
5. 26 Greet all the brethren with an holy kiss
5. 27 that this epistle be read unto all
2 Th. 1. 3 the charity of every one of you all toward
1. 4 for your patience and faith in all your
1. 10 and to be admired in all them that
2. 12 That they all might be damned who
3. 18 The grace of our Lord..(be) with you all
1 Ti. 2. 1 I exhort therefore, that, first of all..for all
2. 2 For kings, and (for) all that are in
2. 4 Who will have all men to be saved
2. 6 Who gave himself a ransom for all
4. 10 the living God, who is the saviour of all
4. 15 that thy profiting may appear to all
5. 20 Them that sin rebuke before all that
6. 10 the love of money is the root of all evil
2 Ti. 1. 15 This thou knowest, that all they which
3. 9 for their folly shall be manifest unto all
3. 11 but out of (them) all the Lord delivered
3. 12 Yea, and all that will live godly in
4. 8 unto [all] them also that love his appearing
4. 17 and (that) all the Gentiles might hear
4. 21 Eubulus greeteth thee..and all the
Titus 2. 11 the grace of God..hath appeared to all
3. 2 shewing all meekness unto all men
3. 15 All that are with me salute thee..you all
Phm. 5 Hearing of thy love and faith..toward all
Heb. 1. 6 let all the angels of God worship him
1. 11 they all shall wax old as doth a garment
1. 14 Are they not all ministering spirits, sent
2. 8 Thou hast put all things in subjection
2. 11 For both he that sanctifieth..(are) all of
3. 16 howbeit not all that came out of Egypt
4. 4 God did rest the seventh day from all
5. 9 he became the author of..salvation unto all
7. 2 Abraham gave a tenth part of all; first
8. 11 for all shall know me, from the least
9. 21 he sprinkled with blood..all the

Heb. 11. 13 These all died in faith, not having received
11. 39 these all, having obtained a good report
12. 8 if ye be without chastisement, whereof all
12. 23 to God the Judge of all, and to the
13. 4 Marriage (is) honourable in all, and the
13. 24 all them that have the rule over..and all
13. 25 Grace (be) with you all. Amen
Jas 1. 8 A double-minded man (is) unstable in all
2. 10 he is guilty of all
1 Pe. 2. 1 Wherefore laying aside all malice, and all
3. 8; 5. 5; 5. 14; 2 Pe. 3. 9, 11, 16; 1 Jo. 2. 19; 2 Jo. 1; 3 Jo. 12; Jude 15; Rev. 1. 7; 2. 23; 5. 13; 7. 11; 8. 3; 12. 5; 13. 8, 16; 14. 8; 15. 4; 18. 3, 19, 23, 24; 19. 5, 17, 21; 21. 8; 22. 21.
[*See also* Any, at, first, glorious here, house, in, most, no, places, put, sorts, speed, therein.]

9. *Number*, מִסְפָּר *mispar.*
Eccl. 2. 3 which they should do..all the days of
5. 18 under the sun all the days of his life
6. 12 all the days of his vain..which he spen.

ALL (men, points, things)—*All*, πᾶς *pas.*
Matt. 7. 12; 10. 22; 11. 27; 13. 41; 17. 11; 19. 11, 26; 21. 22; 22. 4; 23. 20; 26. 33; 28. 20; Mark 1. 37; 4. 34; 5. 20; 6. 30; 7. 37; 9. 12, 23; 10. 27; 11. 11; 13. 13, 23; 14. 36; Luke 1. 3; 2. 20; 9. 43; 10. 22; 11. 41; 14. 17; 18. 31; 21. 17, 22; 24. 14; John 1. 3, 7; 2. 24; 3. 26, 35; 4. 25, 29, 45; 5. 20, 23; 10. 41; 11. 48; 12. 32; 13. 3, 35; 14. 26, 26; 15. 15; 16. 15, 30; 17. 7; 18. 4; 19. 28; 21. 17; Acts 1. 24; 2. 45; 3. 21, 22; 4. 21; 10. 33, 39; 13. 39; 14. 15; 17. 22, 24, 25; 19. 19; 20. 35; 21. 28; 22. 10; 24. 14; 26. 2; Rom. 8. 28, 32; 11. 36; 14. 2, 20; 16. 19; 1 Co. 2. 10, 15; 3. 21; 4. 13; 6. 12, 12, 12; 8. 6, 6; 9. 12, 19, 22, 22, 25; 10. 23, 23, 23, 23, 33, 33; 11. 2, 12; 13. 7, 7, 7, 7; 14. 26, 40; 15. 27, 27, 27, 28, 28; 16. 14; 2 Co. 2. 9; 4. 15; 5. 17, 18; 6. 10; 7. 14; 9. 8, 13, 11. 6; 12. 19; Gal. 3. 10; 6. 10; Eph. 1. 10, 11, 22, 22; 3. 9, 9; 4. 10, 15; 5. 13, 20; 6. 21; Phil. 2. 14; 3. 8, 8, 21; 4. 12, 13; Col. 1. 16, 16, 17, 17, 18, 20; 3. 20, 22; 4. 9; 1 Th. 3. 12; 5. 14, 15, 21; 2 Th. 3. 2; 1 Ti. 3. 11; 4. 8; 6. 13, 17; 2 Ti. 2. 7, 10, 24; 4. 5, 16; Tit. 1. 15; 2. 7, 9, 10; Heb. 1 [illegible] 8, 10, 10, 17; 3. 4; 4. 13, 15; 8. 5; 9. 22; 12. 14; 13. 18; Jas. 1. 5; 5. 12; 1 Pe. 2. 17; 4. 7, 8, 11; 2 Pe. 1. 3; 3. 4; 1 Jo. 2. 20, 27; 3. 20; 3 Jo. 2; Rev. 4. 11; 18. 14; 19. 18; 21. 5, 7.

ALL abroad —
To spread out, שָׁטַח *shatach.*
Num 11. 32 and they spread (them) all abroad for

ALL along —
1. *To go, go on*, הָלַךְ *halak.*
Jer. 41. 6 to meet them, weeping all along as he
2. *Fulness of his stature* מְלֹא קוֹמָה *melo qomah.*
1 Sa. 28. 20 Saul fell straightway all along on the

ALL at— [*See* AT.]
Wholly, πάντως *pantōs.*
1 Co. 16. 12 but his will was not at all to come at

ALL at once —
All together, παμπληθεί *pamplēthei.*
Luke 23. 18 And they cried out all at once, saying

ALL gone, to be —
To be finished, תָּמַם *tamam.*
1 Ki. 14. 10 taketh away dung, till it be all gone

ALL here, to be —
To be finished, תָּמַם *tamam.*
1 Sa. 16. 11 Are here all (thy) children? And he said

ALL, in —
All, כֹּל *kol.*
Num 31. 35 thirty and two thousand persons in all

ALL life long —
Again, yet, עוֹד *od.*
Gen. 48 15 God which fed me all my life long

ALL manner (of) —
1. *All*, כֹּל *kol.*
Exod 35. 35 wisdom of heart, to work all manner of
2. *All, any, every*, πᾶς *pas.*
Matt. 4. 23 all manner of..and all manner of disease
5. 11 shall say all manner of evil against
10. 1 all manner of sickness and all manner
12. 31 Wherefore I say unto you, All manner of
Luke 11. 42 ye tithe mint and rue and all manner
Rom. 7. 8 sin..wrought in me all m. of Ac. 10. 12.
1 Pe. 1. 15 be ye holy in all manner of conversation
Rev. 21. 19 foundations..garnished with all m. 18. 12.

ALL day long—
The whole, ὅλος, *holos*, Rom. 8, 36; 10. 21.

ALL night—[*See* Abide, lie, lodge, tarry].

ALL that —
How much, great, long, many, ὅσος *hosos.*
Luke 9. 10 the apostles..told him all that they
Acts 4. 23 let go, they went..and reported all that
14. 27 they rehearsed all that God

ALL that is in —
Fulness, מְלֹא *melo.*
Isa. 34. 1 the earth...and all that is therein
42. 10 the sea, and all that is therein
Jer. 8. 16 the land, and all that is in it
47. 2 the land, and all that is therein
Eze. 12. 19 be desolate from all that is therein
30. 12 the land waste, and all that is therein
Amos 6. 8 up the city, with all that is therein
Mic. 1. 2 O earth, and all that therein is

ALL THINGS (that)—
1. *All together,* ἅπας *hapas.*
Luke 2. 39 when they had performed all things
Acts 2. 44 believed were together,and had all things
4. 32 they had all things common, 10. 8
2. *As many as,* ὅσα *hosa,* Acts 15. 4 ; Rev. 1. 2.
ALLEGE, to —
To put alongside, παρατίθημι *paratithēmi.*
Acts 17 3 Opening and alleging, that Christ must
ALLEGORY, to be a —
To speak otherwise, ἀλληγορέω *allēgoreō.*
Gal. 4. 24 Which things are an allegory : for these
ALLELUIA —
Praise Jah, ἀλληλούϊα (*Heb.*) *allēlouia.*
Rev. 19. 1 I heard a great voice..saying, Alleluia
19. 3 And again they said, Alleluia
19. 4 worshipped God..saying, Amen; Alleluia
19. 6 mighty thunderings, saying, Alleluia
ALLIED —
Near, קָרוֹב *qarob.*
Neh. 13. 4 the house of our God, (was) allied
AL'-LON, אַלּוֹן *an oak.*
1. A city near Kadesh Naphtali.
Josh. 19. 33 their coast was..from A. to Zaanannim
2. The chief of a family in Simeon, B.C. 715.
1 Ch. 4. 37 the son of Shiphi, the son of A., the son
AL-LON-BA'-CHUTH, אַלּוֹן בָּכוּת *oak of weeping.*
A place near Bethel where Deborah was buried.
Gen. 35. 8 and the name of it was called A. B.
ALLOW, to —
1. *To know, recognise,* γινώσκω *ginōskō.*
Rom. 7. 15 that which I do I allow not
2. *To make trial, test, proof,* δοκιμάζω *dokimazō.*
Rom. 14. 22 in that thing which he alloweth
1 Th. 2. 4 as we were allowed of God to be
3. *To receive to oneself,* προσδέχομαι *prosdechomai.*
Acts 24. 15 which they themselves also allow, that
4. *To think well of together,* συνευδοκέω *suneudokeō.*
Luke 11. 48 ye bear witness that ye allow the deeds
ALLOWANCE —
Customary or usual diet, אֲרֻחָה *aruchah.*
2 Ki. 25. 30 allowance (was) a continual allowance
ALLURE, to —
1. *To persuade, entice,* פָּתָה *pathah,* 3.
Hos. 2. 14 I will allure her, and bring her
2. *To lay a bait,* δελεάζω *deleazō.*
2 Pe. 2. 18 they allure through the lusts of the flesh
ALMIGHTY —
1. *Sufficient, mighty,* שַׁדַּי *shaddai.*
Gen. 17. 1 I (am) the Almighty God; walk before
28. 3 God Almighty bless thee, and make thee
35. 11 I (am) God Almighty: be fruitful and
43. 14 God Almighty give you mercy before the
48. 3 God Almighty appeared unto me at Luz
49. 25 by the Almighty who shall bless thee
Exod. 6. 3 by (the name of) God Almighty
Num 24. 4 which saw the vision of the Almighty
24. 16 (which) saw the vision of the Almighty
Ruth 1. 20 the Almighty hath dealt very bitterly
1. 21 the Almighty hath afflicted me?
Job. 5. 17 despise..the chastening of the Almighty
6. 4 the arrows of the Almighty (are) within
6. 14 he forsaketh the fear of the Almighty
8. 3 doth the Almighty pervert justice?
8. 5 make thy supplication to the Almighty
11. 7 canst thou find out the Almighty
13. 3 Surely I would speak to the Almighty
15. 25 he strengtheneth..against the Almighty
21. 15 What (is) the Almighty, that we should
21. 20 shall drink of the wrath of the Almighty
22. 3 (Is it) any pleasure to the Almighty
22. 17 what can the Almighty do for them?
22. 23 to the Almighty, thou shalt be built up
22. 25 the Almighty shall be thy defence
22. 26 thou have thy delight in the Almighty
23. 16 and the Almighty troubleth me
24. 1 times are not hidden from the Almighty
27. 2 the Almighty, (who) hath vexed my soul
27. 10 Will he delight himself in the Almighty?
27. 11 which (is) with the Almighty will I not
27. 13 they shall receive of the Almighty
29. 5 the Almighty (was) yet with me
31. 2 (what) inheritance of the Almighty from
31. 35 Oh..(that) the Almighty would answer
32. 8 the Almighty giveth them understanding
33. 4 the Almighty hath given me life
34. 10 far be it..(from) the Almighty, (that he)
34. 12 neither will the Almighty pervert
35. 13 neither will the Almighty regard it
37. 23 (Touching) the Almighty, we cannot find
40. 2 Shall he..with the Almighty instruct
Psa. 68. 14 the Almighty scattered kings in it
91. 1 abide under the shadow of the Almighty
Isa. 13. 6 come as a destruction from the Almighty
Eze. 1. 24 as the voice of the Almighty
10. 5 as the voice of the Almighty God
Joel 1. 15 as a destruction from the Almighty
2. *All-powerful,* παντοκράτωρ *pantokratōr.*
2 Co. 6. 18 be a Father..saith the Lord Almighty
Rev. 1. 8 and which is to come, the Almighty
4. 8 saying, Holy, holy, holy, Lord God Almighty
11. 17 give thee thanks, O Lord God Almighty
15. 3 marvellous..works, Lord God Almighty
16. 7 Even so, Lord God Almighty, true and
16. 14 gather them to the battle..God Almighty
19. 15 he treadeth the winepress..of Almighty
21. 22 the Lord God Almighty and the Lamb
AL-MO'-DAD, אַלְמוֹדָד *the agitator.*
Son of Joktan, of the family of Shem, B.C. 2210.
Gen. 10. 26 And Joktan begat A., and Sheleph, and
1 Ch. 1. 20 And Joktan begat A., and Sheleph, and
AL'-MON, עַלְמוֹן *hiding place.*
A Levitical town in Benjamin.
Josh. 21. 18 and A. with her suburbs; four cities
AL-MON-DIB-LA-THA'-IM, עַלְמֹן דִּבְלָתָיְמָה.
The 39th encampment of Israel after leaving Egypt, the 28th from Sinai, and the 8th from Eziongeber. It was in the territory of Sihon, and probably N. of the wilderness of Kedemoth. See *Beth-diblathaim.* N 1. 33. 46, 47.
ALMOND —
Almond, שָׁקֵד *shaqed.*
Gen. 43. 11 a little honey..nuts, and almonds
Num 17. 8 bloomed blossoms, and yielded almonds
ALMOND TREE —
Almond tree, שָׁקֵד *shaqed.*
Eccl. 12. 5 and the almond tree shall flourish
Jer. 1. 11 I see a rod of an almond tree
ALMONDS, made after the fashion of —
To be like almonds, שָׁקַד *shaqad,* 4.
Exod 37. 19 bowls made after the fashion of almonds
ALMONDS, made like —
To be like almonds, שָׁקַד *shaqad,* 4.
Exod 25. 33 three bowls made like almonds
37. 19 three bowls made like almonds in
37. 20 four bowls made like almonds
ALMONDS, made like unto —
To be like almonds, שָׁקַד *shaqad,* 4.
Exod 25. 33 Three bowls made like unto almonds
ALMOST —
1. *A little, few,* מְעַט *me'at.*
Exod 17. 4 they be almost ready to stone me
Psa. 73. 2 my feet were almost gone
94. 17 my soul had almost dwelt in silence
119. 87 They had almost consumed me upon
Prov. 5. 14 I was almost in all evil
2. *In or with a little,* ἐν ὀλίγῳ *en oligō.*
Acts 26. 28 Agrippa said unto Paul, Almost thou
26. 29 both almost, and altogether such as I am
3. *Almost, nearly,* σχεδόν *schedon.*
Acts 13. 44 the next sabbath-day came almost the
19. 26 almost throughout all Asia, this Paul
Heb. 9. 22 almost all things are by the law purged
ALMOST, to be —
To be about to, μέλλω *mellō.*
Acts 21. 27 when the seven days were almost ended
ALMS —
Kindness, kind act, ἐλεημοσύνη *eleēmosunē.*
Matt. 6. 1 Take heed that ye do not your [alms]
6. 2 Therefore when thou doest (thine) alms
6. 3 But when thou doest alms, let not thy
6. 4 That thine alms may be in secret
Luke 11. 41 rather give alms of such things as ye
12. 33 Sell that ye have, and give alms
Acts 3. 2 to ask alms of them that entered into
3. 3 seeing Peter and John..asked an alms
3. 10 it was he which sat for alms at the
10. 2 devout (man)..which gave much alms
10. 4 Thy prayers and thine alms are come
10. 31 and thine alms are had in remembrance
24. 17 I came to bring alms to my nation
ALMSDEED —
Kindness, kind act, ἐλεημοσύνη *eleēmosunē.*
Acts 9. 36 this woman was full of..almsdeeds
ALMUG-TREE —
Almug-trees, אַלְמֻגִּים *almuggim.*
1 Ki. 10. 11 from Ophir great plenty of almug trees
10. 12 the king made of the almug trees pillars
10. 12 there came no such almug trees
ALOES, (trees of lign)—
1. *Aloes, lign-aloes,* אֲהָלוֹת *ahaloth.*
Psa. 45. 8 garments (smell) of myrrh, and aloes
Song 4. 14 all trees of frankincense..and aloes
2. *Aloes, lign-aloes,* אֲהָלִים *ahalim.*
Num 24. 6 as the trees of lign aloes, which the LORD
Pro. 7. 17 I have perfumed my bed with..aloes
3. *Aloe,* ἀλόη *aloē.*
John 19. 39 brought a mixture of myrrh and aloes
ALONE —
1. *One,* אֶחָד *echad.*
Josh. 22. 20 and that man perished not alone
Isa. 51. 2 for I called him alone Eccl. 4. 10.
2. *Alone, separate,* בַּד *bad.*
Num 11. 14 not able to bear all this people alone
Deut. 1. 9 I am not able to bear you myself alone
3. *To be separate,* בָּדַד *badad.*
Psa. 102. 7 I watch, and am as a sparrow alone
Isa. 14. 31 none (shall be) alone in his appointed
Hos. 8. 9 a wild ass alone by himself
4. *Separate,* בָּדָד *badad.*
Lev. 13. 46 he (is) unclean; he shall dwell alone
Num 23. 9 lo, the people shall dwell alone
Deut 32. 12 the LORD alone did lead him
33. 28 then shall dwell in safety alone
Jer. 15. 17 I sat alone because of thy hand
49. 31 gates nor bars, (which) dwell alone
Lam. 3. 28 He sitteth alone and keepeth silence
5. *By itself* καθ' ἑαυτήν *kath heautēn.*
Jas. 2. 17 Even so faith..is dead, being alone
6. *By themselves,* κατ' ἰδίαν *kat' idian.*
Mark 4. 34 when they were alone, he expounded all
7. *Apart, in private,* καταμόνας *katamonas.*
Mark 4. 10 when he was alone, they that were
Luke 9. 18 it came to pass, as he was alone praying
8. *Alone,* μόνον *monon.*
John 17. 20 Neither pray I for these alone, but for
Acts 19. 26 Moreover ye see and hear that not alone
Rom. 4. 23 Now it was not written for his sake alone
9. *Alone,* μόνος *monos.*
Matt. 4. 4 Man shall not live by bread alone, but
14. 23 the evening was come, he was there alone
18. 15 go and tell him his fault..alone
Mark 6. 47 and he alone on the land
Luke 4. 4 man shall not live by bread alone
5. 21 Who can forgive sins, but God alone?
6. 4 but for the priests alone
9. 36 when the voice was past, Jesus was..alone
10. 40 my sister hath left me to serve alone?
John 6. 15 again into a mountain himself alone
6. 22 his disciples were gone away alone
8. 9 [Jesus was left alone, and the woman]
8. 16 for I am not alone, but I and the Father
8. 29 the Father hath not left me alone
12. 24 it abideth alone: but if it die, it
16. 32 and shall leave me alone..yet..not alone
Rom 11 3 and I am left alone, and they seek
Gal. 6. 4 shall he have rejoicing in himself alone
1 Th. 3. 1 thought it good to be left at Athens alone
Heb. 9. 7 into the second..the high priest alone
ALONG (by)—
1. *a, In,* בְּ *be.* 1 *b From the way of* מִדֶּרֶךְ [*derek*].
Judg. 9. 25 robbed all that came along that way
9. 37 another company come along by the plain
2. *To go on,* הָלַךְ *halak.*
1 Sa. 6. 12 And the kine..went along the highway
2 Sa. 3. 16 her husband went with her along weeping
Jer 41. 6 Ishmael..went forth..weeping all along
3. *The fulness of his stature,* מְלֹא קוֹמָתוֹ *melo qomatho.*
1 Sa. 28. 20 Saul fell straightway all along on the
[*See also* All along, draw, go, lay, pass, run.]
ALOOF —
From before, מִנֶּגֶד *min-neged.*
Psa. 38. 11 my friends stand aloof from my sore
A'-LOTH, עָלוֹת *ascents, steeps.*
A hilly region near Asher. But if the name is *Bealoth,* as some translate the original (making "in" the first letter of the root instead of a preposition), then it would be a town in the S.E. of Judah.
1 Ki. 4. 16 Baanah..(was) in Asher and in A.
ALOUD —
1. (*With*) *the throat,* גָּרוֹן *garon.*
Isa. 58. 1 Cry aloud, spare not, lift up thy voice
2. (*With*) *might,* חַיִל *chayil.*
Dan. 3. 4 an herald cried aloud, To you it is com.
4. 14 He cried aloud, and said thus, Hew down
5. 7 king cried aloud to bring in the astrologers
3. *Crying out, shouting,* רֵעַ *rea.*
Mic. 4. 9 Now why dost thou cry out aloud?
4. *With a great voice,* בְּקוֹל גָּדוֹל *be-qol gadol.*
1 Ki. 18. 27 Elijah mocked them, and said, Cry aloud
18. 28 And they cried aloud, and cut themselves
5. *Lifting up* (*the voice*), רוּם קוֹל *rum* (5) *qol.*
Ezra 3 12 and many shouted aloud for joy
[*See also* Cry, sing, weep.]
ALOUD for joy —
To sing or cry aloud, רָנַן *ranan,* 3.
Psa. 132. 16 her saints shall shout aloud for joy
AL'-PHA, Ἄλφα (*first letter of the Greek alphabet*).
A title of Christ, descriptive of his position in relation to the new economy, "the beginning." See also *Omega.*
Rev. 1. 8 I am A. and Omega, the beginning and
1. 11 Saying, [I am A. and Omega, the first]
21 6 I am A. and Omega, the beginning and
22. 13 I am A. and Omega, the beginning and
AL-PHE'-US, Ἀλφαῖος *leader, chief.*
1. Father of James, one of the twelve apostles.
Matt 10. 3 James (the son) of A., and Lebbeus, whose
Mark 3. 18 and James the (son) of A., and Thaddeus
Luke 6. 15 James the (son) of A., and Simon called
Acts 1. 13 James (the son) of A., and Simon Zelotes
2. Father of Levi (or Matthew) the apostle and evangelist. Perhaps the same as No. 1.
Mark 2. 14 he saw Levi the (son) of A. sitting at the
ALREADY —
1. *Already,* כְּבָר *kebar.*
Eccl. 1. 10 it hath been already of old time

Eccl. 2. 12 that which hath been already done
3. 15 that which is to be hath already been
4. 2 I praised the dead which are already dead
6. 10 That which hath been is named already

2. *Now, at, or by this time,* ἤδη *ēdē.*
Matt. 5. 28 committed adultery with her already
17. 12 That Elias is come already, and they
Mark 15. 44 Pilate marvelled if he were already
Luke 12. 49 what will I, if it be already kindled
John 3. 18 that believeth not is condemned already
4. 35 for they are white already to harvest
9. 22 the Jews had agreed already, that if
9. 27 answered them, I have told you already
11. 17 that he had (lain)..four days [already]
19. 33 and saw that he was dead already Ac. 27.9
1 Co. 5. 3 For I verily..have judged already, as
Phil. 3. 12 Not as though I had already..already
2 Th. 2. 7 mystery of iniquity doth already work
1 Ti. 5. 15 some are already turned aside after
2 Ti. 2. 18 that the resurrection is past already
1 Jo. 4. 3 even now already is it in the world
[*See also* Attain, now, sin.]

ALSO —

1. *Or, either, rather,* אוֹ.
Prov. 30. 31 A greyhound; an he-goat also; and a king

2. *Only,* אַךְ *ak.*
Lev. 23. 27 Also on the tenth (day) of this seventh

3. *Also,* אַף *aph.*
Gen. 40. 16 he said unto Joseph, I also (was) in my
1 Ch. 8. 32 these also dwelt with their brethren

4. *Also,* אַף *aph.*
Ezra 5. 10 We asked their names also, to certify thee
5. 14 the vessels also of gold and silver of the
6. 5 also let the golden and silver vessels
Dan. 6. 22 also before thee, O king, have I done no

5. *Even, also,* גַּם *gam.*
Gen. 3. 6 gave also unto her husband with her
1 Sa. 19. 24; Eccl. 1. 17; 2. 15; 8. 14.

6. *Also even,* ἀλλὰ καί *alla kai,* Rom. 6. 5.

7. *And, also, even,* καί *kai.*
Matt. 22. 26; Luke 23. 27; 1 Co. 7. 34; 15. 40; Ph. 4. 3.

8. *Thus,* כֹּה *koh.*
1 Sa. 25 22 So and more also do God unto the enemies

9. *And with this,* ἅμα δὲ καί *hama de kai.*
Acts 24. 26 He hoped also that money should have

10. *Truly, indeed,* δή *dē.*
Matt 13. 23 which also beareth fruit, and bringeth

11. *Any more, yet, still,* ἔτι *eti.*
Luke 14. 26 and his own life also, he cannot be my

12. *And truly indeed,* μέντοι καί *mentoi kai.*
Jude 8 Likewise also these (filthy) dreamers defile

13. *And, also,* τε *te.*
Heb. 11. 32 time would fail me to tell of..David also

ALSO, for that —

In that also, בְּשַׁגַּם *be-shag-gam.*
Gen. 6. 3 the LORD said..for that he also (is) flesh

ALSO if —

And if, κἄν = *kai an.*
Matt 21. 21 also if ye shall say unto this mountain

ALSO not —

Not even, οὐδέ *oude.*
Rom. 11. 21 (take heed) lest he also spare not thee

ALTAR —

1. *Hill of God,* הַרְאֵל *harel.*
Eze. 43. 15 So the altar (shall be) four cubits

2. *Lion of God,* אֲרִיאֵל *ariel.*
Eze. 43. 15 from the altar and upward (shall be) 43. 16

3. *Slaughter place,* מַדְבַּח *madbach.*
Ezra 7. 17 offer them upon the altar of the house of

4. *Slaughter place,* מִזְבֵּחַ *mizbeach.*
Gen. 8. 20 Noah builded an altar unto the LORD
8. 20 and offered burnt offerings on the altar
12. 7 there builded he an altar unto the LORD
12. 8 there he builded an altar unto the LORD
13. 4 Unto the place of the altar, which he had
13. 18 built there an altar unto the LORD
22. 9 Abraham built an altar there and laid the
22. 9 laid him on the altar upon the wood
26. 25 he builded an altar there, and called upon
33. 20 he erected there an altar, and called it
35. 1 make there an altar unto God, that
35. 3 I will make there an altar unto God
35. 7 he built there an altar, and called the place
Exod. 17. 15 Moses built an altar, and called the name
20. 24 An altar of earth thou shalt make unto
20. 25 if thou wilt make me an altar of stone
20. 26 Neither..go up by steps unto mine altar
21. 14 thou shalt take him from mine altar
24. 4 builded an altar under the hill, and twelve
24. 6 half of the blood he sprinkled on the altar
27. 1 thou shalt make an altar (of) shittim wood
27. 1 the altar shall be four square
27. 5 put it under the compass of the altar
27. 5 may be even to the midst of the altar
27. 6 thou shalt make staves for the altar
27. 7 shall be upon the two sides of the altar
28. 43 when they come near unto the altar to
29. 12 put (it) upon the horns of the altar
29. 12 the blood beside the bottom of the altar
29. 13 kidneys..and burn (them) upon the altar

Exod. 29. 16 sprinkle (it) round about upon the altar
29. 18 burn the whole ram upon the altar
29. 20 sprinkle the blood upon the altar round
29. 21 take of the blood that (is) upon the altar
29. 25 burn (them) upon the altar for a burnt off.
29. 36 thou shalt cleanse the altar, when thou
29. 37 shalt make an atonement for the altar
29. 37 the altar..shall be an altar most holy
29. 38 which thou shalt offer upon the altar
29. 44 sanctify the tabernacle..and the altar
30. 1 thou shalt make an altar to burn incense
30. 18 put it between the tabernacle..and the altar
30. 20 when they come near to the altar to minis.
30. 27 and his vessels..and the altar of incense
30. 28 the altar of burnt offering with all his
31. 8 And the table.. and the altar of incense
31. 9 the altar of burnt offering with all his
32. 5 Aaron saw (it) he built an altar before it
34. 13 ye shall destroy their altars, break their
35. 15 And the incense altar, and his staves
35. 16 The altar of burnt offering, with his brasen
37. 25 he made the incense altar (of) shittim wood
38. 1 he made the altar of burnt offering (of)
38. 3 he made all the vessels of the altar
38. 4 he made for the altar a brasen grate
38. 7 of the altar, to bear it withal: he made the
38. 30 therewith he made.. the brasen altar
38. 30 and all the vessels of the altar
39. 38 the golden altar, and the anointing oil
39. 39 The brasen altar, and his grate of brass
40. 5 thou shalt set the altar of gold for the
40. 6 shalt set the altar of the burnt offering
40. 7 laver between the tent..and the altar
40. 10 thou shalt anoint the altar of the burnt off.
40. 10 the altar..shall be an altar most holy
40. 26 he put the golden altar in the tent
40. 29 he put the altar of burnt offering (by) the
40. 30 laver between the tent..and the altar
40. 32 when they came near unto the altar, they
40. 33 the court round about..the altar
Lev. 1. 5 sprinkle the blood..upon the altar
1. 7 And..shall put fire upon the altar
1. 8 the fire which (is) upon the altar
1. 9 priest shall burn all on the altar
1. 11 on the side of the altar..upon the altar
1. 12 on the fire which (is) upon the altar
1. 13 priest shall burn..(it) upon the altar
1. 15, 15 priest shall bring it unto the altar
1. 15 off his head, and burn (it) on the altar
1. 16 cast it beside the altar on the east part
1. 17 priest shall burn it upon the altar
2. 2 burn the memorial of it upon the altar
2. 8 he shall bring it unto the altar
2. 9 and shall burn (it) upon the altar
2. 12 they shall not be burnt on the altar
3. 2 shall sprinkle the blood upon the altar
3. 5 Aaron's sons shall burn it on the altar
3. 8 shall sprinkle the blood..upon the altar
3. 11 the priest shall burn it upon the altar
3. 13 sprinkle the blood thereof upon the altar
3. 16 priest shall burn them upon the altar
4. 7 of the altar of sweet incense before the
4. 7 all the blood..at the bottom of the altar
4. 10 priest shall burn them upon the altar
4. 18 of the altar which (is) before the LORD
4. 18 all the blood at the bottom of the altar
4. 19 he shall..burn (it) upon the altar
4. 25 of the altar of burnt-offering
4. 26 shall burn all his fat upon the altar
4. 30 put (it) upon the horns of the altar
4. 30 all the blood..at the bottom of the altar
4. 31 priest shall burn (it) upon the altar
4. 34 put (it) upon the horns of the altar
4. 35 priest shall burn (them) upon the altar
5. 9 sprinkle..upon the side of the altar
5. 9 be wrung out at the bottom of the altar
5. 12 a memorial..and burn (it) on the altar
6. 9 because of the burning upon the altar all
6. 9 and the fire of the altar shall be burning
6. 10 the fire hath consumed..on the altar
6. 10 he shall put them beside the altar
6. 12 the fire upon the altar shall be burning in
6. 13 shall ever be burning upon the altar
6. 14 Aaron shall offer it..before the altar
6. 15 shall burn (it) upon the altar (for) a sweet
7. 2 blood..shall he sprinkle..upon the altar
7. 5 priest shall burn them upon the altar
7. 31 priest shall burn..upon the altar
8. 11 sprinkled thereof upon the altar seven times
8. 11 and anointed the altar and all his vessels
8. 15 horns of the altar..the altar..of the altar
8. 15 poured the blood at the bottom of the altar
8. 16 and Moses burned (it) upon the altar
8. 19 sprinkled the blood upon the altar round
8. 21 Moses burnt the whole ram upon the altar
8. 24 sprinkled the blood upon the altar round
8. 28 burnt (them) on the altar upon the burnt
8. 30 the blood which (was) upon the altar
9. 7 Go unto the altar, and offer thy sin offerin
9. 8 Aaron therefore went unto the altar
9. 9 put it upon the horns of the altar
9. 9 out the blood at the bottom of the altar
9. 10 But the fat..he burnt upon the altar
9. 12 sprinkled round about upon the altar
9. 13 and he burnt (them) upon the altar
9. 14 upon the burnt offering on the altar
9. 17 burnt (it) upon the altar, beside the burnt
9. 18 he sprinkled upon the altar round about
9. 20 and he burnt the fat upon the altar
9. 24 and consumed upon the altar the burnt off.
10. 12 and eat it without leaven beside the altar
14. 20 offer the burnt offering..upon the altar

Lev. 16. 12 take a censer full..from off the altar
16. 18 And he shall go out unto the altar
16. 18 put (it) upon the horns of the altar
16. 20 made an end of reconciling..the altar
16. 25 the fat..shall he burn upon the altar
16. 33 he shall make an atonement..for the altar
17. 6 shall sprinkle the blood upon the altar
17. 11 I have given it to you upon the altar
21. 23 he shall not..come nigh unto the altar
22. 22 an offering by fire of them upon the altar
Num. 3. 26 (is) by the tabernacle, and by the altar
3. 31 their charge (shall be) the..altars
4. 11 upon the golden altar they shall spread a
4. 13 they shall take away the ashes from the
4. 14 the censers.. all the vessels of the altar
4. 26 (is) by the tabernacle and by the altar
5. 25 shall wave..and offer it upon the altar
5. 26 memorial..and burn (it) upon the altar
7. 1 both the altar and all the vessels thereof
7. 10 offered for dedicating of the altar
7. 10 offered their offering before the altar
7. 11 prince..for the dedicating of the altar
7. 84 This (was) the dedication of the altar
7. 88 This (was) the dedication of the altar
16. 38 broad plates (for) a covering of the altar
16. 39 broad (plates for) a covering of the altar
16. 46 put fire therein from off the altar
18. 3 not come nigh the vessels..and the altar
18. 5 ye shall keep..the charge of the altar
18. 7 your..office for every thing of the altar
18. 17 sprinkle their blood upon the altar
23. 1 Build me here seven altars
23. 2 Balaam offered on (every) altar a bullock
23. 4 he said..I have prepared seven altars
23. 4 and I have offered upon (every) altar a
23. 14 built seven altars, and offered a bullock
23. 14 and a ram on (every) altar
23. 29 Balaam said..Build me here seven altars
23. 30 and offered a bullock..on (every) altar
Deut. 7. 5 ye shall destroy their altars, and break
12. 3 And ye shall overthrow their altars
12. 27 offer thy burnt offerings..upon the altar
12. 27 blood..shall be poured out upon the altar
16. 21 any trees near unto the altar of the LORD
26. 4 and set it down before the altar
27. 5 there shalt thou build an altar
27. 5 an altar of stones: thou shalt not lift
27. 6 Thou shalt build the altar of the LORD
33. 10 whole burnt sacrifice upon thine altar
Josh. 8. 30 Then Joshua built an altar unto the LORD
8. 31 an altar of whole stones, over which no
9. 27 for the altar of the LORD, even unto this
22. 10 Manasseh built there an altar..a great altar
22. 11 children of Reuben..have built an altar
22. 16 in that ye have builded you an altar
22. 19 in building you an altar beside the altar
22. 23 That we have built us an altar to turn
22. 26 Let us now prepare to build us an altar
22. 28 Behold the pattern of the altar of the LORD
22. 29 to build an altar..beside the altar
22. 34 children of Reuben..called the altar (*Ed*)
Judg. 2. 2 ye shall throw down their altars
6. 24 Gideon built an altar there unto the LORD
6. 25 and throw down the altar of Baal
6. 26 And build an altar unto the LORD thy God
6. 28 behold, the altar of Baal was cast down
6. 28 second bullock was offered upon the altar
6. 30 he hath cast down the altar of Baal
6. 31 because (one) hath cast down his altar
6. 32 because he hath thrown down his altar
13. 20 the flame went up..from off the altar
13. 20 angel..ascended in the flame of the altar
21. 4 that the people..built there an altar
1 Sa. 2. 28 I choose him..to offer upon mine altar
2. 33 I shall not cut off from mine altar
7. 17 and there he built an altar unto the LORD
14. 35 Saul built an altar..the first altar
2 Sa. 24. 18 Go up, rear an altar unto the LORD
24. 21 to build an altar unto the LORD
24. 25 David built there an altar unto the LORD
1 Ki. 1. 50 caught hold on the horns of the altar
1. 51 caught hold on the horns of the altar
1. 53 and they brought him down from the altar
2. 28 caught hold on the horns of the altar
2. 29 and, behold, (he is) by the altar
3. 4 thousand burnt offerings..upon that altar
6. 20 and (so) covered the altar (which was of)
6. 22 also the whole altar..he overlaid with gold
7. 48 the altar of gold, and the table of gold
8. 22 Solomon stood before the altar of the LORD
8. 31 and the oath come before thine altar in
8. 54 he arose from before the altar of the LORD
8. 64 because the brasen altar..(was) too little
9. 25 upon the altar which he built unto the
12. 32 and he offered upon the altar
12. 33 he offered upon the altar..the altar
13. 1 Jeroboam stood by the altar to burn
13. 2 he cried against the altar..altar, altar
13. 3 Behold, the altar shall be rent
13. 4 which had cried against the altar..altar
13. 5 The altar also was rent..from the altar
13. 32 saying which he cried..against the altar
16. 32 And he reared up an altar for Baal
18. 26 And they leaped upon the altar which was
18. 30 And he repaired the altar of the LORD
18. 32 And with the stones he built an altar
18. 32 and he made a trench about the altar
18. 35 And the water ran round about the altar
19. 10 Israel have..thrown down thine altars
19. 14 Israel have..thrown down thine altars
2 Ki. 11. 11 (along) by the altar and the temple
11. 18 his altars and his images..before the altar

2 Ki. 12. 9 set it beside the altar, on the right side
16. 10 an altar that (was) at Damascus..altar
16. 11 And Urijah the priest built an altar
16. 12 come..the king saw the altar..altar
16. 13 sprinkled the blood..upon the altar
16. 14 brought also the brasen altar..the altar
16. 14 and put it on the north side of the altar
16. 15 the great altar burn the morning..altar
18. 22 whose altars Hezekiah hath taken away
18. 22 shall worship before this altar in Jerusalem?
21. 3 he reared up altars for Baal, and made a
21. 4 he built altars in the house of the LORD
21. 5 he built altars for all the host of heaven
23. 9 the priests..came not up to the altar
23. 12 the altars that (were) on the top
23. 12 the altars which Manasseh had made
23. 15 Moreover the altar that (was)..that altar
23. 16 and burned (them) upon the altar
23. 17 thou hast done against the altar of Beth-el
23. 20 that (were) there upon the altars
1 Ch. 6. 49 Aaron and his sons offered upon the altar
6. 49 and on the altar of incense, (and were ap.)
16. 40 To offer burnt offerings..upon the altar
21. 18 David should go up, and set up an altar
21. 22 that I may build an altar therein unto the
21. 26 And David built there an altar unto the
21. 26 he answered him..by fire upon the altar
21. 29 the tabernacle of the LORD..and the altar
22. 1 this (is) the altar of the burnt offering
28. 18 for the altar of incense refined gold
2 Ch. 1. 5 brasen altar that Bezaleel..had made
1. 6 Solomon went up thither to the..altar
4. 1 Moreover he made an altar of brass
4. 19 the golden altar also, and the tables
5. 12 stood at the east end of the altar
6. 12 And he stood before the altar of the LORD
6. 22 and the oath come before thine altar
7. 7 because the brasen altar..was not able
7. 9 kept the dedication of the altar seven days
8. 12 offered burnt offerings..on the altar
14. 3 took away the altars of the strange (gods)
15. 8 and renewed the altar of the LORD
23. 10 set all the people..along by the altar
23. 17 brake his altars..before the altars
26. 16 and went..to burn incense upon the altar
26. 19 rose up..from beside the incense altar
28. 24 he made him altars in every corner
29. 18 We have cleansed..the altar of burnt off.
29. 19 they (are) before the altar of the LORD
29. 21 commanded..to offer (them) on the altar
29. 22 priests..sprinkled (it) on the altar
29. 22, 22 sprinkled the blood upon the altar
29. 24 made reconciliation..upon the altar
29. 27 offer the burnt offering upon the altar
30. 14 they arose and took away the altars that
31. 1 threw down the high places and the altars
32. 12 taken away his high places and his altars
32. 12 Ye shall worship before one altar
33. 3 he reared up altars for Baalim.
33. 4 he built altars in the house of the LORD
33. 5 he built altars for all the host
33. 15 all the altars that he had built
33. 16 he repaired the altar of the LORD
34. 4 they brake down the altars of Baalim
34. 5 burnt the bones..upon their altars
34. 7 when he had broken down the altars
35. 16 to offer burnt offerings upon the altar
Ezra 3. 2 and builded the altar of the God
3. 3 And they set the altar upon his bases
Neh. 10. 34 to burn upon the altar of the LORD our
Psa. 26. 6 so will I compass thine altar, O LORD
43. 4 Then will I go unto the altar of God
51. 19 shall they offer bullocks upon thine altar
84. 3 thine altars, O LORD of hosts, my King
118. 27 unto the horns of the altar
Isa. 6. 6 (which) he had taken..from off the altar
17. 8 And he shall not look to the altars
19. 19 In that day shall there be an altar
27. 9 he maketh all the stones of the altar
36. 7 whose altars Hezekiah hath taken away
36. 7 Ye shall worship before this altar
56. 7 sacrifices..accepted upon mine altar
60. 7 they shall come up..on mine altar
Jer. 11. 13 set up altars to (that) shameful..altars
17. 1 and upon the horns of your altars
17. 2 their children remember their altars
Lam. 2. 7 The LORD hath cast off his altar
Eze. 6. 4 And your altars shall be desolate
6. 5 scatter..bones round about your altars
6. 6 that your altars may be laid waste
6. 13 among their idols..about their altars
8. 5 northward at the gate of the altar
8. 16 between the porch and the altar (were)
9. 2 and stood beside the brasen altar
40. 46 the keepers of the charge of the altar
40. 47 and the altar..before the house
41. 22 The altar of wood (was) three cubits high
43. 13 (are) the measures of the altar..altar
43. 18 These (are) the ordinances of the altar in
43. 22 and they shall cleanse the altar
43. 26 Seven days shall they purge the altar
43. 27 make your burnt offerings upon the altar
45. 19 four corners of the settle of the altar
47. 1 at the south (side) of the altar
Hos. 8. 11 hath made many altars to sin, altars
10. 1 of his fruit he hath increased the altars
10. 2 he shall break down their altars
10. 8 thistle shall come up on their altars
12. 11 their altars (are) as heaps in the furrows
Joel 1. 13 howl, ye ministers of the altar
2. 17 weep between the porch and the altar
Amos 2. 8 clothes laid to pledge by every altar
Amos 3. 14 I will also visit the altars of Beth-el
3. 14 the horns of the altar shall be cut off
9. 1 I saw the LORD standing upon the altar
Zech. 9. 15 as the corners of the altar
14. 20 shall be like the bowls before the altar
Mal. 1. 7 Ye offer polluted bread upon mine altar
1. 10 neither do ye kindle (fire) on mine altar
2. 13 covering the altar of the LORD with tears

5. *A raised place*, βωμός *bōmos.*
Acts 17. 23 I found an altar with this inscription

6. *A place of sacrifice*, θυσιαστήριον *thusiastērion.*
Matt. 5. 23 if thou bring thy gift to the altar
5. 24 Leave there thy gift before the altar
23. 18 Whosoever shall swear by the altar
23. 19 or the altar that sanctifieth the gift
23. 20 Whoso therefore shall swear by the altar
23. 35 slew between the temple and the altar
Luke 1. 11 standing on the right side of the altar
11. 51 which perished between the altar and the
Rom. 11. 3 and digged down thine altars; and I am
1 Co. 9. 13 altar are partakers with the altar
10. 18 not they which eat..partakers of the altar
Heb. 7. 13 no man gave attendance at the altar
13. 10 We have an altar whereof they have no
Jas. 2. 21 had offered Isaac his son upon the altar
Rev. 6. 9 I saw under the altar the souls of them
8. 3 angel came and stood at the altar..altar
8. 5 and filled it with fire of the altar
9. 13 the golden altar which is before God
11. 1 measure the temple..and the altar
14. 18 another angel came out from the altar
16. 7 I heard another out of the altar say

ALTARS for incense —
Incense altars, מְקַטְּרוֹת *meqatteroth.*
2 Ch. 30. 14 all the altars for incense took they away

ALTARS of brick —
Brick altar, לְבֵנָה *lebenah.*
Isa. 65. 3 and burneth incense upon altars of brick

AL-TASCHITH —
Destroy or corrupt not, אַל תַּשְׁחֵת *al tashcheth.*
Psa. 57. *title.* To the chief Musician, A.-t., Michtam
58. *title.* To the chief Musician, A.-t., Michtam
59. *title.* To the chief Musician, A.-t., Michtam
75. *title.* To the chief Musician, A.-t., A Psalm

ALTER, to —
1. *To exchange*, חֲלַף *chalaph*, 5.
Lev. 27. 10 He shall not alter it, nor change it

2. *To pass on, or away*, עֲדָא *ada.*
Dan. 6. 8 the law of the Medes..which altereth
6. 12 the law of the Medes..which altereth

3. *To change*, שְׁנָא *shena*, 5.
Ezra 6. 11 a decree..whosoever shall alter this
6. 12 that shall put to their hand to alter

4. *To change*, שָׁנָה *shanah*, 3.
Psa. 89. 34 My covenant will I not break nor alter

ALTERED, to be —
1. *To pass over*, עָבַר *abar.*
Esth. 1. 19 commandment..that it be not altered

2. *Become another*, γίνομαι ἕτερος *ginomai heteros.*
Luke 9. 29 fashion of his countenance was altered

ALTHOUGH —
1. *That, because*, כִּי *ki.*
Exod 13. 17 land of the Philistines, although that

2. *Although*, אַף כִּי *aph ki.*
Job 35. 14 Although thou sayest thou shalt not see

3. *And if*, καὶ εἰ *kai ei.*
Mark 14. 29 Although all shall be offended, yet (will)

4. *And truly*, καίτοι *kaitoi.*
Heb. 4. 3 although the works were finished from

ALTOGETHER —
1. *One*, אֶחָד *echad.*
Jer. 10. 8 But they are altogether brutish and

2. *Together*, יַחַד *yachad.*
Psa. 19. 9 judgments..(are)..righteous altogether
53. 3 they are altogether become filthy
62. 9 they (are) altogether (lighter) than vanity
Isa. 10. 8 (Are) not my princes altogether kings
Jer. 5. 5 these have altogether broken the yoke

3. *All*, כֹּל *kol.*
Psa. 39. 5 his best state (is) altogether vanity

4. *Wholly*, כָּלָה *kalah.*
Gen. 18. 21 see whether they have done altogether
Exod 11. 1 shall..thrust you out hence altogether
2 Ch. 12. 12 he would not destroy (him) altogether

5. *Vanity*, הֶבֶל *hebel.*
Job 27. 12 why then are ye thus altogether vain?

6. *Wholly*, ὅλος *holos.*
John 9. 34 Thou wast altogether born in sins, and

7. *Altogether*, πάντως *pantōs.*
1 Co. 5. 10 Yet not altogether with the fornicators
9. 10 Or saith he (it) altogether for our sakes?

8. *In or with much*, ἐν πολλῷ *en pollō.*
Acts 26. 29 [altogether] such as I am, except these

A'-LUSH, אָלוּשׁ *wild place.*
The 9th encampment of Israel on the way from Sin to Sinai.
Num 33. 13 And they departed..and encamped in A.
33. 14 And they removed from A., and encamped

AL'-VAH, עַלְוָה *sublimity.* [*See* **ALIAH.**]
A duke of Edom, descended from Esau, B.C. 1740.
Gen. 36. 40 names of the dukes..of Esau..duke A.
[1 Ch. 1. 51 dukes of Edom..duke Timnah, duke A.]

AL'-VAN, עַלְוָן *sublime.*
Son of Shobal, a descendant of Seir, B.C. 1760.
Gen. 36. 23 the children of Shobal (were) these; A.
[1 Ch. 1. 40 The sons of Shobal, A. and Manahath]

ALWAY —
1. *(For) pre-eminence, perpetuity*, נֵצַח *netsach.*
Psa. 9. 18 the needy shall not alway be forgotten

2. *(For an) indefinite time*, עוֹלָם *olam.*
Job 7. 16 I loathe (it); I would not live alway

3. *Continually*, תָּמִיד *tamid.*
Exod 25. 30 set upon the table..before me alway
Num. 9. 16 it was alway: the cloud covered it (by day)
2 Sa. 9. 10 shall eat bread alway at my table
Prov. 28. 14 Happy (is) the man that feareth alway

4. *All the days*, כָּל הַיָּמִים *kol hay-yamim.*
Deut 11. 1 judgments, and his commandments, alway
28. 33 shalt be only oppressed and crushed alway
1 Ki. 11. 36 David my servant may have a light alway
2 Ki. 8. 19 promised him to give him alway a light

5. *Through all (time)*, διαπαντός *diapantos.*
Acts 10. 2 much alms..and prayed to God alway
Rom. 11. 10 and bow down their back alway

6. *All the days*, πάσας τὰς ἡμέρας. [*pas, hēmera*].
Matt 28. 20 and, lo, I am with you alway

7. *Always*, πάντοτε *pantote.*
John 7. 6 but your time is alway ready
Phil. 4. 4 rejoice in the Lord alway: (and) again I
Col. 4. 6 Let your speech (be) alway with grace
1 Th. 2. 16 to fill up their sins alway; for the wrath
2 Th. 2. 13 But we are bound to give thanks alway

8. *Ever, always*, ἀεί *aei.*
2 Co. 4. 11 For we which live are alway delivered
6. 10 As sorrowful, yet alway rejoicing; as poor
Titus 1. 12 Cretians (are) alway liars, evil beasts
Heb. 3. 10 They do alway err in (their) heart; and

ALWAYS —
1. *(For) pre-eminence, perpetuity*, נֵצַח *netsach.*
Psa. 103. 9 He will not always chide; neither
Isa. 57. 16 neither will I be always wroth

2. *(For an) indefinite time*, עוֹלָם *olam.*
Gen. 6. 3 My spirit shall not always strive with
1 Ch. 16. 15 Be ye mindful always of his covenant
Jer. 20. 17 her womb (to be) always great (with me)

3. *Continually*, תָּמִיד *tamid.*
Exod 27. 20 to cause the lamp to burn always
28. 38 it shall always be upon his forehead
Deut 11. 12 the eyes of the LORD..(are) always upon
Psa. 16. 8 I have set the LORD always before me
Prov. 5. 19 be thou ravished always with her love
Eze. 38. 8 mountains..which have been always

4. *All the days*, כָּל הַיָּמִים *kol hay-yamim.*
Deut. 5. 29 keep all my commandments always
6. 24 to fear the LORD..for our good always
14. 23 mayest learn to fear the LORD..always
2 Ch. 18. 7 he never prophesied good..but always

5. *In all time*, בְּכָל־עֵת *be-kol eth.*
Job 27. 10 will he always call upon God?
Psa. 10. 5 His ways are always grievous; thy
Prov. 8. 30 daily..delight, rejoicing always
Eccl. 9. 8 Let thy garment be always white, and

6. *Ever, always*, ἀεί *aei.*
Acts 7. 51 ye do always resist the Holy Ghost: as
1 Pe. 3. 15 ready always to (give) an answer to every
2 Pe. 1. 12 to put you always in remembrance of

7. *Through all (time)*, διὰ παντός, *dia pantos.*
Matt 18. 10 in heaven their angels do always behold
Acts 2. 25 I foresaw the Lord always before my face
2 Th. 3. 16 give you peace always by all means

8. *Through all (time)*, διαπαντός *diapantos.*
Mark 5. 5 always, night and day, he was in the
Acts 24. 16 to have always a conscience void of
Heb. 9. 6 priests went always into the first tabern.

9. *Each time*, ἑκάστοτε *hekastote.*
2 Pe. 1. 15 have these things always in remembrance

10. *In every season*, ἐν παντὶ καιρῷ [*pas, kairos*]
Luke 21. 36 Watch ye, therefore, and pray always
Eph. 6. 18 Praying always with all prayer and

11. *In every way*, πάντῃ *pantē.*
Acts 24. 3 We accept (it) always, and in all places

12. *Always*, πάντοτε *pantote.*
Matt 26. 11 poor always..me ye have not always
Mark 14. 7 you always..but me ye have not always
Luke 18. 1 men ought always to pray, and not to
John 8. 29 I do always those things that please him
11. 42 I knew that thou hearest me always: but
12. 8 poor always..but me ye have not always
18. 20 in the temple, whither the Jews [always]
Rom. 1. 9 I make mention of you always in my
1 Co. 1. 4 I thank my God always on your behalf

1 Co. 15. 58 always abounding in the work of the Lord
2 Co. 2. 14 which always causeth us to triumph in
4. 10 Always bearing about in the body the
5. 6 Therefore..always confident, knowing
9. 8 always having all sufficiency in all(things)
Gal. 4. 18 good to be zealously affected always in
Eph. 5. 20 Giving thanks always for all things unto
Phil. 1. 4 Always in every prayer of mine for you
1. 20 but..with all boldness, as always..now
2. 12 my beloved, as ye have always obeyed
Col. 1. 3 We give thanks..praying always for you
4. 12 always labouring fervently for you in
1 Th. 1. 2 We give thanks to God always for you all
3. 6 ye have good remembrance of us always
2 Th. 1. 3 We are bound to thank God always for you
1. 11 Wherefore also we pray always for you
Phm. 4 making mention of thee always in my

AM'-AD, עַמְעָד *a station.*
A town on the border of Asher, near Alammelech.
Josh. 19. 26 And Alammelech, and A., and Misheal

A'-MAL, עָמָל *labouring.*
A descendant of Asher through Beriah his son, B.C. 1600.
1 Ch. 7. 35 And the sons of his brother Helem..A.

A-MA'-LEK, עֲמָלֵק *warlike, dweller in the vale.*
1. Son of Eliphaz and grandson of Esau, B.C. 1680.
Gen. 36. 12 and she bare to Eliphaz A.: these (were)
36. 16 Duke Korah, duke Gatam, (and) duke A.
1 Ch. 1. 36 The sons of Eliphaz; Teman..and A.
2. The name is also applied to his descendants, who are, however, generally called Amalekites.
Exod 17. 8 Then came A., and fought with Israel
17. 9 Choose..men, and go out, fight with A.
17. 10 So Joshua..fought with A.: and Moses
17. 11 when he let down his hand, A. prevailed
17. 13 Joshua discomfited A. and his people
17. 14 I will..put out the remembrance of A.
17. 16 the LORD (will have) war with A. from
Num 24. 20 when he looked on A., he took up his
24. 20 and said, A. (was) the first of the nations
Deut 25. 17 Remember what A. did unto thee by the
25. 19 thou shalt blot out the remembrance of A.
Judg. 3. 13 he gathered unto him the children of..A.
5. 14 Out of Ephraim..a root of them against A.
1 Sa. 15. 2 I remember (that) which A. did to Israel
15. 3 Now go and smite A., and utterly
15. 5 Saul came to a city of A., and laid wait
15. 20 and have brought Agag the king of A.
28. 18 nor executedst his fierce wrath upon A.
2 Sa. 8. 12 of the Philistines, and of A., and of the
1 Ch. 18. 11 from the Philistines, and from A.
Psa. 83. 7 Gebal, and Ammon, and A.; the Philistines

A-MA-LE-KITE, עֲמָלֵקִי *belonging to Amalek.*
The name of a people and country smitten by Chedorlaomer and his confederates in the days of Abraham, B.C. 1917 (Gen. 14. 7), erroneously supposed by some to be the descendants of *Amalek*, the son of Eliphaz (eldest son of Esau, Gen. 36. 10–16; 1 Ch. 1. 36), by his concubine *Timna*. Without any provocation they came and attacked the rear of Israel as they were journeying through the wilderness, but were defeated by Joshua at Rephidim (Exod. 17. 8–16), and in consequence of this assault a perpetual war was declared against them by Jehovah; they dwelt in the land of the S. of Judah (Num. 13. 29), and in the valley (Num. 14. 25); along with the Canaanites they defeated the rash attack of Israel, and drove them even unto Hormah (Num. 14. 43–45); they are called by Balaam "the first of the nations" (or Goyim), either from their antiquity, or their warlike character, or from their being the first to attack Israel (Num. 24. 20), which was henceforth required to "remember" their treacherous attack (Deut. 25. 17–19). They, along with the children of Ammon, joined with Eglon, king of Moab (B.C. 1354), to attack Israel, and took Jericho, the city of palm-trees (Judg. 3. 13); they were successfully opposed by the Ephraimites in the conflict with Jabin, king of Hazor, B.C. 1296 (Judg. 5. 14); they joined with the Midianites and the children of the East (or Kedem) in the days of Gideon, the son of Joash the Abi-ezrite, B.C. 1256 (Judg. 6. 3), but were defeated by him in the valley of Jezreel (Judg. 6. 33, 7. 12–22); they are mentioned among the oppressors of Israel (Judg. 10. 12); they had once possession of a mountain in the land of Ephraim, in which Abdon, the son of Hillel the Pirathonite was buried, B.C. 1112 (Judg. 12. 15); they were smitten by Saul, B.C. 1086 (1 Sa. 14. 48); again by him, B.C. 1079, throughout their whole country "from Havilah to Shur," on the border of Egypt, when Agag their king was cut in pieces (1 Sa. 15. 2–33); they were invaded and destroyed by David (1 Sa. 27. 8–10); their previous non-destruction by Saul was the cause of his rejection (1 Sa. 28. 18); in David's absence they invaded and plundered Ziklag, B.C. 1056, and carried off his two wives and others as captives, but they were pursued, overtaken, and defeated by David (1 Sa. 30. 1–31); one of their nation accusing himself of Saul's death was put to death by David (2 Sa. 1. 1–16), by whom their silver and gold was dedicated to Jehovah (2 Sa. 8. 12; 1 Ch. 18. 11); they were again smitten in the days of Hezekiah, B.C. 726–693, by five hundred men of the tribe of Simeon, who thereafter dwelt in their place, at the east of the valley of Gedor, or Gerar (1 Ch. 4. 39–43); they are mentioned with Ammon and the Philistines as among the enemies of Israel (Psa. 83. 7). They are not again noticed in Scripture, except Haman the Agagite be reckoned one of their nation, which is not improbable (Esth. 3. 1), &c. Comp. Num 24. 7.
Gen. 14. 7 and smote all the country of the A.
Num 13. 29 The A. dwell in the land of the south
14. 25 Now the A...dwelt in the valley
Num 14. 43 the A...(are) there before you, and ye
14. 45 the A. came down, and the Canaanites
Judg. 6. 3 and the A...even they came up against
6. 33 the A...were gathered together, and went
7. 12 the A...lay along in the valley like
10. 12 the A...did oppress you; and ye cried to
12. 15 and was buried in..the mount of the A.
1 Sa. 14. 48 smote the A., and delivered Israel
15. 6 get you down from among the A., lest
15. 6 the Kenites departed from among the A.
15. 7 Saul smote the A. from Havilah (until)
15. 8 he took Agag the king of the A. alive
15. 15 They have brought them from the A.: for
15. 18 Go and utterly destroy..the A., and fight
15. 20 and have utterly destroyed the A.
15. 32 Bring ye..Agag the king of the A.
27. 8 and invaded..the A.: for those
30. 1 that the A. had invaded the south, and
30. 13 I (am) a..servant to an A.; and my master
30. 18 David recovered all that the A. had carried
2 Sa. 1. 1 was returned from the slaughter of the A.
1. 8 And I answered him, I (am) an A.
1. 13 I (am) the son of a stranger, an A.
1 Ch. 4. 43 they smote the rest of the A. that were

A'-MAM, אֲמָם *gathering place.*
A city near Shema and Moladah, probably in the south of Judah.
Josh. 15. 26 Amam, and Shema, and Moladah

A-MA'-NA, אֲמָנָה *permanent.*
The northern ridge of Antilibanus, as Hermon was the southern.
Song 4. 8 look from the top of A., from the top of

A-MAR-I'AH, אֲמַרְיָהוּ אֲמַרְיָה *Jah has said.*
1. Grandfather of Zadok, a high priest in the time of David, B.C. 1100.
1 Ch. 6. 7 Meraioth begat A., and A. begat Ahitub
6. 52 Meraioth his son, A. his son, Ahitub
Ezra 7. 3 The son of A. the son of Azariah, the son
2. The son of Azariah, a high priest in the time of Solomon, B.C. 1015.
1 Ch. 6. 11 And Azariah begat A., and A. begat
3. A descendant of Kohath, son of Levi, B.C. 1015.
1 Ch. 23. 19 the sons of Hebron..A. the second
24. 23 And the sons (of Hebron)..A. the second
4. Chief priest in the time of Jehoshaphat, B.C. 912.
2 Ch. 19. 11 behold, A. the chief priest (is) over you
5. A Levite appointed in the time of Hezekiah to distribute the tithes and oblations among his brethren B.C. 727.
2 Ch. 31. 15 And next him (were) Eden, and..A., and
6. A man of the family of Bani, who took a strange wife during the exile, B.C. 465.
Ezra 10. 42 Shallum, Amariah (and) Joseph
7. A priest who, with Nehemiah, sealed the covenant, B.C. 445.
Neh. 10. 3 Pashur, Amariah, Malchijah
12. 2 Amariah, Malluch, Hattush
12. 13 Of Ezra, Meshullam; of A., Jehohanan
8. A descendant of Judah by Pharez, some of whose posterity dwelt in Jerusalem after the exile, B.C. 465.
Neh. 11. 4 Of the children of Judah..A., the son of
9. An ancestor of Zephaniah the prophet in the time of Josiah, B.C. 630.
Zeph. 1. 1 which came unto..A., the son of Hizkiah

A-MA'-SA, עֲמָשָׂא *burden-bearer.*
1. David's nephew, whom Absalom made captain over his rebel army, B.C. 1023.
2 Sa. 17. 25 Absalom made A. captain of the host
17. 25 which A. (was) a man's son, whose name
19. 13 And say ye to A., (Art) thou not of my
20. 4 Then said the king to A., Assemble
20. 5 So A. went to assemble (the men of) Judah
20. 8 which (is) in Gibeon, A. went before them
20. 9 And Joab said to A., (Art) thou in health
20. 9 And Joab took A. by the beard with
20. 10 But A. took no heed to the sword that
20. 12 And A. wallowed in blood in the midst
20. 12 he removed A. out of the highway into
1 Ki. 2. 5 what Joab..did..unto A. the son of
2. 32 and slew..A. the son of Jether, captain
1 Ch. 2. 17 And Abigail bare A.: and the father of
2. 17 and the father of A. (was) Jether the
2. The name of an Ephraimite who with others resisted the bringing into Samaria of the Jews made prisoners in the time of Ahaz, B.C. 741.
2 Ch. 28. 12 and A. the son of Hadlai, stood up against

A-MA'-SAI, עֲמָשַׂי *burden-bearer.*
1. A descendant of Kohath, son of Levi, B.C. 1045.
1 Ch. 6. 25 And the sons of Elkanah, A., and Ahimoth
6. 35 Elkanah, the son of Mahath, the son of A.
2 Ch. 29. 12 the Levites arose, Mahath the son of A.
2. A captain who joined David at Ziklag.
1 Ch. 12. 18 Then the spirit came upon A...chief
3. A priest who assisted at the bringing up the ark to the house of Obed-edom, B.C. 1042.
1 Ch. 15. 24 A., and Zechariah..did blow with the

A-MASH'-AI, עֲמַשְׁסַי *carrying spoil.*
A priest of the family of Immer dwelling at Jerusalem B.C. 445.
Neh. 11. 13 A. the son of Azareel, the son of Ahasai

A-MAS-I'-AH, עֲמַסְיָה *Jah has strength.*
Chief captain of the army of Jehoshaphat.
2 Ch. 17. 16 next him (was) A...who willingly offered

AMAZED —
Amazement fell, ἐγένετο θάμβος *egeneto thambos.*
Luke 4. 36 they were all amazed, and spake among

AMAZED, be greatly or sore —
To be greatly amazed, ἐκθαμβέω *ekthambeō.*
Mark 9. 15 straightway all..were greatly amazed
14. 33 began to be sore amazed, and to be very

AMAZED, to be —
1. *To be troubled,* בָּהַל *bahal,* 2.
Exod 15. 15 the dukes of Edom shall be amazed
Judg 20. 41 the men of Benjamin were amazed
2. *To be cast down,* חָתַת *chathath.*
Job 32. 15 They were amazed, they answered no
3. *To be cast down,* תָּמַהּ *tamah.*
Isa. 13. 8 they shall be amazed one at another
4. *To be exceedingly struck,* ἐκπλήσσομαι *ekplēssomai*
Matt. 19. 25 they were exceedingly amazed, saying
Luke 2. 48 when they saw him, they were amazed
9. 43 they were all amazed at the mighty
5. *Wonder took them,* ἔκστασις ἔλαβεν or εἶχε [*ekstasis*]
Luke 5. 26 they were all amazed, and they Mr. 16. 8
6. *To be astonished,* ἐξίσταμαι *existamai.*
Matt 12. 23 all the people were amazed, and said
Mark 2. 12 insomuch that they were all amazed, and
6. 51 they were sore amazed in themselves
Acts 2. 7 they were all amazed, and marvelled
2. 12 they were all amazed, and were in doubt
9. 21 all that heard..were amazed, and said
7. *To be astonished, awed,* θαμβέομαι *thambeomai.*
Mark 1. 27 they were all amazed, insomuch that
10. 32 they were amazed; and as they followed

AMAZED, to make —
To make astonished, שָׁמֵם *shamem,* 5.
Eze. 32. 10 I will make many people amazed at thee

AMAZEMENT —
1. *Ecstasy,* ἔκστασις *ekstasis.*
Acts 3. 10 were filled with wonder and amazement
2. *Terror,* πτόησις *ptoēsis.*
1 Pe. 3. 6 and are not afraid with any amazement

A-MAZ-I'AH, אֲמַצְיָהוּ ,אֲמַצְיָה *Jah has strength.*
1. Son of Joash, king of Judah, who succeeded after the slaughter of his father, B.C. 839.
2 Ki. 12. 21 and A. his son reigned in his stead
13. 12 he fought against A. king of Judah
14. 1 reigned A. the son of Joash king of Judah
14. 8 Then A. sent messengers to Jehoash
14. 9 the king of Israel sent to A. king of
14. 11 But A. would not hear. Therefore Jeho.
14. 11 he and A. king of Judah looked one
14. 13 Jehoash king of Israel took A. king of
14. 15 how he fought with A. king of Judah
14. 17 A. the son of Joash king of Judah lived
14. 18 the rest of the acts of A. (are) they not
14. 21 made him king instead of his father A.
14. 23 In the fifteenth year of A. the son of Joash
15. 1 began Azariah the son of A. king of
15. 3 according to all that his father A. had
1 Ch. 3. 12 A. his son, Azariah his son, Jotham his
2 Ch. 24. 27 And A. his son reigned in his stead
25. 1 A. (was) twenty and five years old (when)
25. 5 Moreover A. gathered Judah together
25. 9 And A. said to the man of God, But
25. 10 Then A. separated them, (to wit), the
25. 11 A. strengthened himself, and led forth
25. 13 the soldiers of the army which A. sent
25. 14 after that A. was come from the slaughter
25. 15 anger of the LORD was kindled against A.
25. 17 Then A. king of Judah took advice, and
25. 18 Joash..sent to A. king of Judah, saying
25. 20 But A. would not hear; for it (came) of
25. 21 they saw one another..he and A. king of
25. 23 Joash..took A. king of Judah, the son of
25. 25 A. the son of Joash, king of Judah lived
25. 26 the rest of the acts of A., first and last
25. 27 after the time that A. did turn away
26. 1 made..king in the room of his father A.
26. 4 according to all that his father A. did
2. A man of the tribe of Simeon.
1 Ch. 4. 34 and Jamlech, and Joshah the son of A.
3. A Levite descended from Merari.
1 Ch. 6. 45 Hashabiah, the son of A., the son of
4. Priest of the idol set up in Bethel, B.C. 787.
Amos 7. 10 Then A. the priest of Beth-el sent to
7. 12 A. said unto Amos, O thou seer, go, flee
7. 14 and said to A., I (was) no prophet

AMBASSADOR —
1. *Interpreter,* לִיץ *luts,* 5.
2 Ch. 32. 31 in..ambassadors of the princes of Baby.
2. *Messenger, agent,* מַלְאָךְ *malak.*
2 Ch. 35. 21 he sent ambassadors to him, saying
Isa. 30. 4 and his ambassadors came to Hanes
33. 7 ambassadors of peace shall weep bitterly
Eze. 17. 15 against him in sending his ambassadors

AMBASSADOR, to be an —
To be elders, seniors, πρεσβεύω *presbeuō.*
2 Co. 5. 20 Now then we are ambassadors for Christ
Eph. 6. 20 For which I am an ambassador in bonds

AMBASSADOR, to make as if one had been —
To feign to be a wanderer, ציר *tsir,* 7.
Josh. 9. 4 made as if they had been ambassadors

AMBASSAGE —
Age, eldership, embassy, πρεσβεία *presbeia.*
Luke 14. 32 he sendeth an ambassage, and desireth

AMBER —
Amber, electrum, חַשְׁמַל *chashmal.*
Eze. 1. 4 the midst thereof as the colour of amber
1. 27 I saw as the colour of amber, as the
8. 2 the appearance..as the colour of amber

AMBUSH —
To be behind, to weave plots, אָרַב *arab.*
Josh. 8. 2 lay thee an ambush for the city behind it
8. 7 ye shall rise up from the ambush
8. 12 set them to lie in ambush between
8. 14 he wist not that..liers in ambush
8. 19 ambush arose quickly out of their place
8. 21 Joshua..saw that the ambush had taken
Jer. 51. 12 prepare the ambushes for the LORD

AMBUSH, lie in —
Ambush, מַאֲרָב *maarab.*
Josh. 8. 9 they went to lie in ambush, and abode

AMBUSHMENT —
1. *To put behind, weave plots,* אָרַב *arab,* 3.
2 Ch. 20. 22 LORD set ambushments against..Ammon
2. *Ambush,* מַאֲרָב *maarab.*
2 Ch. 13. 13 Jeroboam caused an ambushment to come
13. 13 and the ambushment (was) behind them

A'-MEN, אָמֵן, ἀμήν *it is steadfast.*
[Rev. 3. 14 These things saith the A., the faithful]

AMEN —
1. *Amen, so be it, so it is,* אָמֵן *amen.*
Num. 5. 22 And the woman shall say, Amen, amen
Deut 27. 15 the people shall answer and say, Amen
[So also in v. 16, 17, 18, 19, 20, 21, 22, 23, 24, 25, 26.]
1 Ki. 1. 36 answered the king, and said, Amen
1 Ch. 16. 36 people said, Amen, and praised the LORD
Neh. 5. 13 all the congregation said, Amen, and
8. 6 all the people answered, Amen, Amen
Psa. 41. 13 Blessed (be) the LORD..Amen, and Amen
72. 19 earth be filled..his glory; Amen, & Amen
89. 52 Blessed (be) the LORD for..Amen, & Amen
106. 48 and let all the people say, Amen
Jer. 28. 6 Jeremiah said, Amen: the LORD do so
2. *Amen, steadfast,* ἀμήν *amēn.*
Matt. 6. 13 [the power, and the glory, for ever. Amen]
28. 20 unto the end of the world. [Amen]
Luke 24. 53 praising and blessing God. [Amen]
John 21. 25 books that should be written. [Amen]
Rom. 1. 25 Creator, who is blessed for ever. Amen
9. 5 is over all, God blessed for ever. Amen
11. 36 to whom (be) glory, for ever. Amen
15. 33 God of peace (be) with you all. [Amen]
16. 20 The grace of..(be) with you. [Amen]
16. 24 The grace of..(be) with you all. [Amen]
16. 27 through Jesus Christ for ever. Amen
1 Co. 14. 16 say Amen at thy giving of thanks
16. 24 My love (be) with you all..[Amen]
2 Co. 1. 20 and in him Amen, unto the glory of God
13. 14 grace of the Lord..with you all. [Amen]
Gal. 1. 5 whom (be) glory for ever and ever. Amen
6. 18 Brethren..grace..with your spirit. Amen
Eph. 3. 21 (be) glory..world without end. Amen
6. 24 that love our Lord..in sincerity. [Amen]
Phil. 4. 20 (be) glory for ever and ever. Amen
4. 23 The grace..(be) with you all. [Amen]
Col. 4. 18 Grace (be) with you. [Amen]
1 Th. 5. 28 grace of our Lord..(be) with you. [Amen]
2 Th. 3. 18 The grace..(be) with you all. Amen
1 Ti. 1. 17 and glory for ever and ever. Amen
6. 16 honour and power everlasting. Amen
6. 21 Grace (be) with thee. [Amen.]
2 Ti. 4. 18 (be) glory for ever and ever. Amen
4. 22 Grace (be) with you. [Amen]
Titus 3. 15 Grace (be) with you all. [Amen]
Phm. 25 grace..(be) with your spirit. [Amen]
Heb. 13. 21 whom (be) glory for ever and ever. Amen
13. 25 Grace (be) with you all. [Amen]
1 Pe. 4. 11 to whom (be) praise and dominion..Amen
5. 11 To him (be) glory and dominion..Amen
5. 14 Peace (be) with you all..[Amen]
2 Pe. 3. 18 (be) glory both now and for ever. [Amen]
1 Jo. 5. 21 Little children, keep..from idols. [Amen]
2 Jo. 13 children of thy..sister greet thee. [Amen]
Jude 25 To..God..(be) glory..now and ever. Amen
Rev. 1. 6 (be) glory and dominion for ever..Amen
1. 7 he cometh with clouds..Even so, Amen
1. 18 behold, I am alive for evermore, [Amen]
3. 14 These things saith the Amen, the faithful
5. 14 And the four beasts said, Amen
7. 12 Saying, Amen: Blessing, and glory, and
7. 12 unto our God for ever and ever. [Amen]
19. 4 the four beasts fell down..saying, Amen
22. 20 Surely I come quickly; Amen. Even so
22. 21 The grace..(be) with you all. [Amen]

AMEND, to —
1. *To strengthen,* חָזַק *chazeq,* 3.
2 Ch 34. 10 gave it..to repair and amend the house
2. *To make good, do well,* יָטַב *yatab,* 5.
Jer. 7. 3 Amend your ways and your doings, and
7. 5 if ye throughly amend your ways and
26. 13 amend your ways and your doings
35. 15 Return ye..and amend your doings

AMEND, to begin to —
To have oneself better, ἔχω κομψότερον [*echō.*]
John 4. 52 Then enquired..when he began to amend

AMENDS, to make —
To complete, recompense, שָׁלַם *shalam,* 3.
Lev. 5. 16 he shall make amends for the harm

AMERCE, to —
To fine, עָנַשׁ *anash.*
Deut 22. 19 they shall amerce him in..silver

AMETHYST —
1. *Amethyst,* אַחְלָמָה *achlamah.*
Exod 28. 19 third row a ligure..and an amethyst
39. 12 third row, a ligure..and an amethyst
2. *Amethyst,* ἀμέθυστος *amethustos.*
Rev. 21. 20 a jacinth; the twelfth, an amethyst

A'-MI, אָמִי *(meaning uncertain.)*
A servant of Solomon, whose descendants came up with Zerubbabel from Babylon. In Neh. 7. 59 he is called *Amon* ("steadfast"), B.C. 536.
Ezra 2. 57 Pochereth of Zebaim, the children of A.

AMIABLE —
Beloved, יָדִיד *yadid.*
Psa. 84. 1 How amiable (are) thy tabernacles, O LORD

A-MIN-A'-DAB, Ἀμιναδάβ *my people is willing.*
Son of Aram (or Ram), son of Esrom.
Matt. 1. 4 Aram begat A.; and A. begat Naasson
Luke 3. 33 Which was (the son) of A., which was

AMISS —
1. *Out of place,* ἄτοπος *atopos.*
Luke 23. 41 but this man hath done nothing amiss
2. *Evilly, wickedly,* κακῶς *kakōs.*
Jas. 4. 3 ye ask amiss, that ye may consume (it)

AMISS, to do —
To do perversely, pervert, עָוָה *avah,* 5.
2 Ch. 6. 37 We have sinned, we have done amiss

AMISS, thing —
Error, rashness, שָׁלוּ, שָׁלָה *shalu, shalah.*
Dan. 3. 29 every people..which speak anything amiss

A-MIT'-TAI, אֲמִתַּי *truthful.*
A Zebulonite, father of the prophet Jonah, B.C. 890.
2 Ki. 14. 25 the hand of his servant Jonah..son of A.
Jon. 1. 1 came unto Jonah the son of A., saying

AM'-MAH, אַמָּה, *an aqueduct.*
A hill E. of Giah near Gibeon of Benjamin, where Abner was defeated, B.C. 1053.
2 Sa. 2. 24 they were come to the hill of A., that

AM'-MI, עַמִּי *my people.*
A symbolic name which the ransomed people are directed by the Lord to use.
Hos. 2. 1 Say ye unto your brethren, A.; and to

AM-MI'-EL, עַמִּיאֵל *my people is strong.*
1. One of the spies sent out by Moses, B.C. 1490.
Num 13. 12 Of the tribe of Dan, A. the son of Gemalli
2. A Manassehite of Lodebar, near Mahanaim, in the time of David, B.C. 1070.
2 Sa. 9. 4 the house of Machir, the son of A., in
9. 5 the house of Machir, the son of A., from
17. 27 and Machir the son of A. of Lo-debar, and
3. Father of Bathshua, a wife of David, B.C. 1070.
1 Ch. 3. 5 four, of Bathshua the daughter of A.
[These names in 2 Sa. 11. 2 are *Bathsheba* and *Eliam.*]
4. A Levite, a son of Obed-edom, and a porter in the tabernacle in the time of David, B.C. 1050.
1 Ch. 26. 5 A. the sixth, Issachar the seventh, Peulthai

AM-MI'-HUD, עַמִּיהוּד *my people is honourable.*
1. Father of Elishama, chief of Ephraim, B.C. 1510.
Num. 1. 10 of Ephraim; Elishama the son of A.
2. 18 of Ephraim..Elishama the son of A.
7. 48 Elishama the son of A...(offered)
7. 53 the offering of Elishama the son of A.
10. 22 over his host..Elishama the son of A.
1 Ch. 7. 26 Laadan his son, A. his son, Elishama his
2. A Simeonite whose son, Shemuel, was appointed for the divison of the land, B.C. 1492.
Num 34. 20 children of Simeon, Shemuel the son of A
3. A Naphtalite whose son, Pedahel, was appointed for the division of the land, B.C. 1492.
Num 34. 28 of..Naphtali, Pedahel the son of A.
4. Father of Talmai, king of Geshur, to whom Absalom fled after slaying his brother Amnon, B.C. 1045.
Sa. 13. 37 to Talmai, the son of A., king of Geshur
5. A man of Judah, descended from Pharez, B.C. 536.
1 Ch. 9. 4 Uthai the son of A., the son of Omri, the

AM-MI'-HUR, עַמִּיחוּר *my people is noble.*
Father of Talmai. (A various reading of the Hebrew: given in English margin.) B.C. 1045.
2 Sa. 13. 37 went to Talmai, the son of A., king of

AM-MI-NA'-DAB, עַמִּינָדָב *my people is willing.*
1. A Levite, Aaron's father-in-law, B.C. 1520
Exod. 6. 23 Aaron took him Elisheba, daughter of A.
2. A prince of Judah (perhaps the same as No. 1), B.C. 1510.
Num. 1. 7 Of Judah; Nahshon the son of A.
2. 3 and Nahshon the son of A. (shall be)..
7. 12 he that offered..was Nahshon the son of A.
7. 17 the offering of Nahshon the son of A.
10. 14 over his host (was) Nahshon the son of A.
Ruth 4. 19 Hezron begat Ram, and Ram begat A.
4. 20 A. begat Nahshon, and Nahshon
1 Ch. 2. 10 Ram begat A.; and A. begat Nahshon
3. A son of Kohath, son of Levi. Perhaps the same as No. 1.
1 Ch. 6. 22 The sons of Kohath; A. his son, Korah
4. A Levite of the family of Kohath, who assisted in bringing up the ark out of the house of Obed-edom, B.C. 1045.
1 Ch. 15. 10 Of the sons of Uzziel; A. the chief
15. 11 And David called for..the Levites..and A

AM-MI-NA'-DIB, עַמִּי נָדִיב *my people is liberal.*
Perhaps this is not an appellation.
Song 6. 12 Or ever I was aware..the chariots of A.

AM-MI-SHAD'-DAI, עַמִּישַׁדַּי *my people is mighty.*
Father of Ahiezer, captain of the tribe of Dan in the time of Moses, B.C. 1510.
Num 1. 12 Of Dan; Ahiezer the son of A.
2. 25 of the children..Ahiezer the son of A.
7. 66 On the tenth day Ahiezer the son of A.
7. 71 (was) the offering of Ahiezer the son of A.
10. 25 over his host (was) Ahiezer the son of A.

AM-MI-ZA'-BAD, עַמִּיזָבָד *my people is endowed.*
Son of Benaiah, third of David's captains, B.C. 1015.
1 Ch. 27. 6 Benaiah..and in his course (was) A. his son

AM'-MON, עַמּוֹן *a fellow-countryman.*
The name of the descendants of *Ben-Ammi,* the younger son of Lot by his younger daughter, born in a cave of a mountain near Zoar (now called *Zi'ara,* a few miles from Heshbon), B.C. 1897. Their country lay at the N.E. of Moab, and E. of the tribe of Reuben, between the Arnon and the Jabbok. Their border was strong (Num. 21. 24); they were not to be distressed or meddled with by Israel; the original inhabitants of their country were giants, and called Zamzummim (great, and tall, and many as the Anakim), who were destroyed by the Ammonites (Deut. 2. 19, 20, 37); their chief city was Rabbath-Ammon, and it contained the gigantic bedstead of Og, king of Bashan (Deut. 3. 11); the river Jabbok was their border (Deut. 3. 16); none of their nation was to be allowed to enter the congregation of Jehovah to the tenth generation (Deut. 23. 3); Jabbok is again mentioned as their border (Josh. 12. 2; 13. 10, 25); they, along with Amalek, joined Eglon, king of Moab, B.C. 1354, and smote Israel, and took Jericho, the city of palm-trees (Judg. 3. 13); their gods were served by the children of Israel, B.C. 1161, so that Jehovah sold the latter into their hands, and they served them eighteen years, on both sides of the Jordan. Israel crying to Jehovah, the Ammonites encamped in Gilead, but were defeated by Jephthah, who drove them from Aroer to Minnith (Judg. 10. 6–18; 11. 1–33); their chief national god was Chemosh (Judg. 11. 24); they besieged Jabesh-Gilead, when Nahash their king threatened its inhabitants with a severe penalty, but he was discomfited by Saul (1 Sa. 11. 1–11; 12. 12); they were accordingly vexed by Saul afterwards (1 Sa. 14. 47); their silver and gold taken in battle were dedicated to Jehovah by David (2 Sa. 8. 12; 1 Ch. 18. 11); Hanun their king, the son of Nahash, having insulted the messengers of David, hired the Syrians to help him, but they were defeated by Joab and Abishai (2 Sa. 10. 1–19; 1 Ch. 19. 1–19); who also besieged Rabbah his capital, and took it, whereon David went to complete the capture, and took all the spoil, and humbled the inhabitants (2 Sa. 11. 1; 12. 26–31; 1 Ch. 20. 1–3); Shobi, the son of Nahash, and brother of Hanun, of the city of Rabbah, however, brought provisions to support David at Mahanaim when he was fleeing from Absalom (2 Sa. 17. 27); Zelek, also an Ammonite, was one of David's thirty valiant men (2 Sa. 23. 37; 1 Ch. 11. 39); Solomon loved several women of that nation, and went after Milcom their abomination, and also built a high-place for Molech (1 Ki. 11. 1, 5, 7, 33); his wife, the mother of Rehoboam, was Naamah, an Ammonitess (1 Ki. 14. 21, 31; 2 Ch. 12. 13); along with the Moabites and the Edomites they attacked Jehoshaphat, but were defeated, B.C. 896, and destroyed each other (2 Ch. 20. 1–23); Zabad, the son of Shimeath an Ammonitess, conspired with Jehozabad, the son of Shimrith a Moabitess, against Joash, king of Judah, and slew him, B.C. 839 (2 Ch. 24. 26); the Ammonites gave gifts to Uzziah, B.C. 810 (2 Ch. 26. 8); Jotham again reduced them to tribute, B.C. 758 (2 Ch. 27. 5); Josiah, B.C. 624, defiled the high-place which Solomon had built in Jerusalem for Milcom (2 Ki. 23. 13); the Ammonites, along with others, invaded Judah in the days of Jehoiakim, B.C. 610–599.
Their abominable customs still infected the Jews in the time of Ezra, B.C. 457 (Ezra 9. 1); Tobiah an Ammonite, along with Sanballat the Horonite, B.C. 445, mocked, reviled, and tried to hinder Nehemiah in his work (Neh. 2. 10, 19; 4. 3, 7); the Jews, though acquainted with the law against admitting an Ammonite to the tenth generation, nevertheless married wives of that nation (Neh. 13. 1, 23); they are mentioned along with Amalek as among the enemies of Israel (Psa. 83. 7); yet

as becoming obedient to the people of God in the latter days (Isa. 11. 14); they cruelly used the women in Gilead, and were threatened with destruction, B.C. 878 (Amos 1. 13-16); and because of their reviling Judah, and magnifying themselves against Jehovah, they are again threatened with destruction, B.C. 630 (Zeph. 2. 8-11); they are described as being uncircumcised in flesh, and as punished with the uncircumcised in heart of the house of Israel (Jer. 9. 26); as receiving, along with the other nations, from Jeremiah the cup of the Lord's anger (Jer. 25. 21); as having a yoke sent to their king by Jeremiah in token of their subjection to Nebuchadnezzar (Jer. 27. 3); as having afforded shelter to the Jews who feared Nebuchadnezzar (Jer. 40. 11); their king Baalis is said to have sent Ishmael, son of Nethaniah, to slay Gedaliah, son of Ahikam (Jer. 40. 14); Ishmael tried to carry off his captives to the Ammonites (Jer. 41. 10), but being defeated escaped himself to them with only eight men (Jer. 41. 15); the destruction of Rabbah, Heshbon, and Ai, was foretold by Jeremiah, with their restoration (Jer. 1. 1-6); Ezekiel foretells the coming of the sword of Nebuchadnezzar to Rabbah and the people (Eze. 21. 20, 28); also the coming of the children of the East, *or* of Kedem (Eze. 25. 2-10), but they were to escape from Antiochus Epiphanes (Dan. 11. 41).

Gen. 19. 38 same (is) the father of the children of A.
Num 21. 24 the children of A...the children of A.
Deut. 2. 19 thou comest..against the children of A.
2. 19 for I will not give thee of the land of..A.
2. 37 Only unto the land of the children of A.
3. 11 (is) it not in Rabbath of the children of A.
3. 16 (which is) the border of the children of A.
Josh. 12. 2 (which is) the border of the children of A.
13. 10 unto the border of the children of A.
13. 25 and half the land of the children of A.
Judg. 3. 13 he gathered unto him the children of A.
10. 6 and the gods of the children of A.
10. 7 and into the hands of the children of A.
10. 9 Moreover the children of A. passed over
10. 11 (Did) not (I deliver you)..children of A.
10. 17 Then the children of A. were gathered
10. 18 What man (is he) that..the children of A.
11. 4 And it came to pass..the children of A.
11. 5 that when the children of A. made war
11. 6 that we may fight with the children of A.
11. 8 and fight against the children of A.
11. 9 Jephthah said..against the children of A
11. 12, 14 the king of the children of A.
11. 13 the king of the children of A. answered
11. 15 nor the land of the children of A.
11. 27 the children of Israel..the children of A.
11. 28 Howbeit the king of the children of A.
11. 29 he passed over (unto) the children of A.
11. 30 thou shalt without fail deliver the..of A
11. 31 when I return in peace from the..of A.
11. 32 passed over unto the children of A. to
11. 33 Thus the children of A. were subdued
11. 36 the LORD hath taken vengeance..of A.
12. 1 Wherefore passedst thou over..the..of A.
12. 2 at great strife with the children of A.
12. 3 passed over against the children of A.
1 Sa. 12. 12 Nahash the king of the children of A.
14. 47 So Saul took..against the children of A.
2 Sa. 8. 12 Of Syria..and of the children of A.
10. 1 that the king of the children of A. died
10. 2 David's servants.. of the children of A.
10. 3 And the princes of the children of A. said
10. 6 when the children of A. saw that they
10. 6 the children of A. sent and hired the Sy.
10. 8 And the children of A. came out
10. 10 in array against the children of A.
10. 11 but if the children of A. be too strong for
10. 14 when the children of A .returned fm...A.
10. 19 So the Syrians feared to help the..of A.
11. 1 and they destroyed the children of A.
12. 9 him with the sword of the children of A.
12. 26 against Rabbah of the children of A.
12. 31 unto all the cities of the children of A.
17. 27 Nahash of Rabbah of the children of A.
1 Ki. 11. 7 the abomination of the children of A.
11. 33 and Milcom the god of the children of A.
2 Ki. 23. 13 the abomination of the children of A.
24. 2 against him bands..of the children of A.
1 Ch. 18. 11 that he brought from..the children of A.
19. 1 the king of the children of A. died
19. 2 into the land of the children of A. to
19. 3 the princes of the children of A. said
19. 6 when the children of A. saw that they
19. 6 Hanum and the children of A. sent a
19. 7 the children of A. gathered themselves
19. 9 And the children of A. came out, and
19. 11 set (themselves) in array against..A.
19. 12 but if the children of A. be too str. v. 15.
19. 19 Syrians help the children of A. any more
20. 1 wasted the country of the children of A.
20. 3 the cities of the children of A.
2 Ch. 20. 1 and the children of A...came against
20. 10 now, behold, the children of A. and
20. 22 ambushments against the children of A.
20. 23 the children of A. and Moab stood up
27. 5 fought also with the king of the A.
27. 5 the children of A...the children of A.
Neh. 13. 23 Jews (that) had married wives..of A.
Psa. 83. 7 Gebal, and A., and Amalek; the Philistines
Isa. 11. 14 the children of A. shall obey them
Jer. 9. 26 Egypt, and Judah..and the children of A.
25. 21 and the children of A.
49. 6 again the captivity of the children of A.
Dan. 11. 41 and the chief of the children of A.
Amos 1. 13 three transgressions of the children of A.
Zeph. 2. 8 I have heard..the revilings of..A.
2. 9 the children of A. as Gomorrah, (even)

AM-MO-NITE, עַמּוֹנִי. See *Ammon.*

Deut. 2. 20 the A. call them Zamzummims
23. 3 An A. or Moabite shall not enter into
1 Sa. 11. 1 Then Nahash the A. came up, and
11. 2 And Nahash the A. answered them
11. 11 and slew the A. until the heat of the day
2 Sa. 23. 37 Zelek the A., Nahari the Beerothite
1 Ki. 11. 1 loved many strange women..of the..A.
11. 5 the abomination of the children of A.
14. 21 mother's name (was) Naamah an A.-ess
14. 31 mother's name (was) Naamah an A.-ess
1 Ch. 11. 39 Zelek the A., Naharai the Berothite
2 Ch. 12. 13 mother's name (was) Naamah an A.-ess
20. 1 with them (other) beside the A., came
24. 26 Zabad the son of Shimeath an A.-ess
26. 8 And the A. gave gifts to Uzziah
27. 5 He fought also with the king of the A.
Ezra 9. 1 according to their ab...of the..A.
Neh. 2. 10 and Tobiah the servant, the A., heard
2. 19 and Tobiah the servant, the A...heard
4. 3 Now Tobiah the A. (was) by him, and he
4. 7 and the A...heard that the walls of
13. 1 therein was found written, that the A.
Jer. 27. 3 send them..to the king of the A.
40. 11 that (were) in Moab, and among the A.
40. 14 that Baalis the king of the A. hath sent
41. 10 and departed to go over to the A.
41. 15 Ishmael..escaped..and went to the A.
49. 1 Concerning the A., thus saith the LORD
49. 2 cause..to be heard in Rabbah of the A.
Eze. 21. 20 Appoint a way..to Rabbath of the A.
21. 28 Thus saith the LORD God concerning the A.
25. 2 set thy face against the A.
25. 3 And say unto the A., Hear the word of
25. 5 And I will make..the A. a couching
25. 10 Unto the men of the east with the A.
25. 10 that the A. may not be remembered

AM'-NON, אַמְנוֹן אֲמִינוֹן *tutelage, up-bringing.*

1. Eldest son of David, by Ahinoam, and slain by Absalom, B.C. 1035.

2 Sa. 3. 2 his firstborn was A., of Ahinoam the
13. 1 Tamar; and A. the son of David loved her
13. 2 And A. was so vexed, that he fell sick for
13. 2 and A. thought it hard for him to do
13. 3 But A. had a friend, whose name (was)
13. 4 And A. said unto him, I love Tamar
13. 6 So A. lay down, and made himself sick
13. 6 A. said unto the king, I pray thee
13. 7 saying, Go now to thy brother A.'s house
13. 8 So Tamar went to her brother A.'s house
13. 9 And A. said, Have out all men from me
13. 10 And A. said unto Tamar, Bring the meat
13. 10 and brought (them) into the chamber to A
13. 15 Then A. hated her exceedingly
13. 15 And A. said unto her, Arise, be gone
13. 20 Hath A. thy brother been with thee?
13. 22 Absalom spake unto his brother A.
13. 22 for Absalom hated A., because he had
13. 26 I pray thee, let my brother A. go with us
13. 27 that he let A. and all the king's sons go
13. 28 saying, Mark ye now when A.'s heart is
13. 28 when I say unto you, Smite A.; then kill
13. 29 the servants of Absalom did unto A. as
13. 32 A. only is dead: for by the appointment
13. 33 let not my lord..think..for A. only is dead
13. 39 king David..was comforted concerning A.
1 Ch. 3. 1 the sons of David..the firstborn A., of

2. Son of Shimon, of the family of Caleb, son of Jephunneh, B.C. 1000.

1 Ch. 4. 20 And the sons of Shimon (were) A., and

A'-MOK, עָמוֹק *deep.*

A priest who came up with Zerubbabel, B.C. 536.

Neh. 12. 7 [these (are) the priests]..Sallu, A., Hilkiah
12. 20 [chief..fathers]..Of Sallai, Kallai; of A.

A'-MON, אָמֹן, אָמוֹן *workman.*

1. Governor of the city (of Samaria) in the time of Ahab, B.C. 900.

1 Ki. 22. 26 Take..and carry him back unto A.
2 Ch. 18. 25 Take..and carry him back to A.

2. Son of Manasseh, and fifteenth king of Judah, B.C. 643.

2 Ki. 21. 18 and A. his son reigned in his stead.
21. 19 A. (was) twenty and two years old when
21. 23 And the servants of A. conspired against
21. 24 that had conspired against king A.
21. 25 Now the rest of the acts of A. which he
1 Ch. 3. 14 A. his son, Josiah his son.
2 Ch. 33. 20 and A. his son reigned in his stead
33. 21 A. (was) two and twenty years old when
33. 22 for A. sacrificed unto all the carved
33. 23 but A. trespassed more and more
33. 25 that had conspired against king A.
Jer. 1. 2 Josiah the son of A. king of Judah, in the
25. 3 thirteenth year of Josiah the son of A.
Zeph. 1. 1 in the days of Josiah the son of A., king

3. A descendant of the servants of Solomon (called AMI in Ezra 2. 57), B.C. 536.

Neh. 7. 59 [of Solomon's servants]..children of A.

4. A son of Manasses, in Christ's ancestry.

Matt. 1. 10 Manasses begat A.; and A. begat Josias

AMONG —

1. *Unto, to,* אֶל *el.*

Josh. 13. 22 among them that were slain by them

2. *With, near,* אֵת *eth.*

Judg. 1. 16 they went and dwelt among the people

3. *Between,* בֵּין *ben.*

Judg. 5. 16 Why abodest thou among the sheepfolds
Dan. 7. 8 there came up among them another little

4. *In between,* בְּבֵין *be-ben.*

Isa. 44. 4 they shall spring up..among the grass

5. *From between,* מִבֵּין *mib-ben.*

Psa. 104. 12 the fowls..sing among the branches

6. *Midst,* גֵּו *gev.*

Job 30. 5 They were driven forth from among

7. *In the sufficiency of,* בְּדֵי *be-de.*

Job 39. 25 He saith among the trumpets, Ha, ha!

8. *From, out of,* מִן *min.*

Lev. 11. 13 (which) ye shall have..among the fowls

9. *On, upon, in addition to,* עַל *al.*

Exod. 30. 13, 14 one that passeth among them. Ecc. 6. 1.

10. *With,* עִם *im.*

Josh. 22. 7 gave Joshua among their brethren

11. *In the midst, heart of,* קֶרֶב *qereb.*

Gen. 24. 3 the Canaanites, among whom I dwell
Exod 17. 7 saying, Is the LORD among us, or not?
31. 14 shall be cut off from among his people
34. 9 let my Lord, I pray thee, go among us
34. 10 all the people among which thou (art)
Lev. 17. 4 shall be cut off from among his people
17. 10 the strangers that sojourn among you
18. 29 shall be cut off from among their people
20. 3 will cut him off from among his people
20. 5 will cut him off..from among their people
20. 6 will cut him off from among his people
20. 18 shall be cut off from among their people
23. 30 will I destroy from among his people
Num. 5. 27 the woman shall be a curse among her
11. 4 the mixt multitude that..among them
11. 20 the LORD which (is) among you, and have
11. 21 Moses said, The people, among whom I
14. 11 signs which I have shewed among them?
14. 13 thou broughtest up..from among them
14. 14 that thou LORD (art) among this people
14. 42 Go not up, for the LORD (is) not among
15. 30 shall be cut off from among his people
Deut. 1. 42 Go not up..for I (am) not among you
2. 14 were wasted out from among the host
2. 15 to destroy them from among the host
2. 16 men..were..dead from among the people
4. 3 LORD..hath destroyed them from among
6. 15 LORD thy God..a jealous God among you
7. 21 for the LORD thy God (is) among you
13. 1 If there arise among you a prophet
13. 11 do no..wickedness as this is among you
13. 13 men..are gone out from among you
13. 14 (that) such abomination is..among you
16. 11 and the fatherless..that (are) among you
17. 2 If there be found among you, within
17. 7 shalt put the evil away from among you
17. 15 from among thy brethren shalt thou set
18. 2 have no inheritance among their brethren
18. 18 a Prophet from among their brethren
19. 19 shalt thou put the evil..from among you
19. 20 henceforth commit no..evil among you
21. 9 put away the (guilt)..from among you
21. 21 thou put evil away from among you
22. 21, 24 thou put evil away from among you
23. 16 He shall dwell with thee..among you
24. 7 shalt put evil away from among you
26. 11 and the stranger that (is) among you
31. 16 whither they go..among them, and
31. 17 because our God (is) not among us?
Josh. 3. 5 the LORD will do wonders among you
3. 10 know..the living God (is) among you
4. 6 That this may be a sign among you
7. 12 ye destroy the accursed from among you
7. 13 take away the accursed thing from among
8. 35 the strangers that were..among them
9. 7 Peradventure ye dwell among us; and how
9. 16 they heard..(that) they dwelt among them
9. 22 far from you; when ye dwell among us?
10. 1 inhabitants of Gibeon..were among them
13. 13 Geshurites..dwell among the Israelites
16. 10 Canaanites dwell among the Ephraimites
18. 7 the Levites have no part among you
24. 5 according to that which I did among them
24. 23 the strange gods which (are) among you
Judg. 1. 29 Canaanites dwelt in Gezer among them
1. 30 Canaanites dwelt among them, and
1. 32 Asherites dwelt among the Canaanites
1. 33 he dwelt among the Canaanites, the
3. 5 children of Israel dwelt among the
10. 16 put away the strange gods from among
1 Sa. 4. 3 when it cometh among us, it may save us
Psa. 55. 15 for wickedness (is)..among them
82. 1 God..he judgeth among the gods
Prov. 15. 31 The ear that heareth..abideth among the
Mic. 3. 11 and say, (Is) not the LORD among us?

12. *In the midst of,* תָּוֶךְ *tavek.*

Gen. 23. 6 thou (art) a mighty prince among us
23. 10 Ephron dwelt among the children of Heth
35. 2 Put away the strange gods..among you
40. 20 the chief baker among his servants
42. 5 to buy..among those that came
Exod. 2. 5 she saw the ark among the flags
7. 5 bring out the children..from among them
12. 31 get you forth from among my people
12. 49 the stranger that sojourneth among you
25. 8 that I may dwell among them
28. 1 take thou..from among the children
29. 45 I will dwell among the children of
29. 46 that I may dwell among them
Lev. 15. 31 my tabernacle that (is) among them

Lev. 16. 29 a stranger that sojourneth among you
17. 8 the strangers which sojourn among you
17. 10, 13 of the strangers that sojourn among
17. 12 any stranger that sojourneth among you
18. 26 any stranger that sojourneth among you
20. 14 there be no wickedness among you
22. 32 I will be hallowed among the children of
24. 10 an Egyptian, went out among the children
25. 33 their possession among the children of
26. 11 I will set my tabernacle among you
26. 12 I will walk among you, and will be your
26. 25 I will send the pestilence among you
Num. 1. 47 their fathers were not numbered among
1. 49 the sum of them among the children of
2. 33 Levites were not numbered among the
3. 12 I have taken the Levites from among the
4. 2 Take the..sons..from among the sons of
4. 18 families of the Kohathites from among the
5. 21 a curse and an oath among thy people
8. 6, 14 the Levites from among the children of
8. 16 they (are) wholly..from among the
8. 19 to his sons from among the children of
9. 7 his appointed season among the children
15. 14 whosoever (be) among you in your
15. 26, 29 the stranger that sojourneth among
16. 3 every one..and the LORD (is) among them
16. 21 Separate yourselves from among this
16. 33 they perished from among the congrega.
16. 45 Get you up from among this congregation
17. 6 the rod of Aaron (was) among their rods
18. 6 I have taken..the Levites from among the
18. 20 neither shalt thou have any part among
18. 20 I (am) thy part and..inheritance among
18. 23 that among the children of Israel they
18. 24 Among the children of Israel they shall
19. 10 the stranger that sojourneth among them
19. 20 shall be cut off from among the congrega.
25. 7 he rose up from among the congregation
25. 11 he was zealous for my sake among them
26. 62 they were not numbered among the
26. 62 was no inheritance given them among the
27. 4 be done away from among his family
27. 4 possession among the brethren of our
27. 7 possession of an inheritance among their
32. 30 they shall have possessions among you
35. 15 for the sojourner among them: that
35. 34 the LORD dwell among the children of
Deut 32. 51 ye trespassed against me among the
Josh. 8. 9 Joshua lodged that night among the
14. 3 he gave none inheritance among them
15. 13 he gave a part among the children of Judah
16. 9 children of Ephraim (were) among the
17. 4 to give us an inheritance among our
17. 4 he gave them an inheritance among the
17. 6 Manasseh had an inheritance among his
17. 9 cities of Ephraim (are) among the cities
19. 49 to Joshua the son of Nun among them
20. 9 the stranger that sojourneth among them
22. 19 take possession among us: but rebel not
22. 31 we perceive that the LORD (is) among us
Judg 12. 4 among the Ephraimites..among the
18. 1 fallen unto them among the tribes of Israel
1 Sa. 7. 3 put away..Ashtaroth from among you
10. 10 and he prophesied among them
10. 23 when he stood among the people, he was
15. 6 get you down from among the Amalekites
15. 6 Kenites departed from among the Amale.
1 Ki. 6. 13 I will dwell among the children of Israel
11. 20 Genubath was..among the sons of Phara.
14. 7 I exalted thee from among the people
2 Ki. 4. 13 I dwell among mine own people
9. 2 arise up from among his brethren
11. 2 stole him from among the king's sons
23. 9 eat of the unleavened bread among their
1 Ch. 21. 6 Benjamin counted he not among them
2 Ch. 22. 11 stole him from among the king's sons
Neh. 4. 11 we come in the midst among them
Esth. 9. 28 should not fail from among the Jews
Job 1. 6 and Satan came also among them
2. 1 Satan came also among them to present
2. 8 and he sat down among the ashes
15. 19 and no stranger passed among them
42. 15 father gave them inheritance among their
Psa. 57. 4 My soul (is) among lions: (and) I lie
68. 25 among (them were) the damsels playing
109. 30 I will praise him among the multitude
136. 11 And brought out Israel from among them
Prov. 1. 14 Cast in thy lot among us; let us all
17. 2 of the inheritance among the brethren
27. 22 bray a fool in a mortar among wheat
Isa. 24. 13 in the midst of the land among the
61. 9 their seed shall be known among the
Jer. 12. 14 pluck out the house of Judah from among
29. 32 a man to dwell among this people
37. 4 came in and went out among the people
39. 14 so he dwelt among the people
40. 1 being bound in chains among all that
40. 5, 6 and dwelt with him among the people
41. 8 ten men were found among them that
Eze. 1. 1 as I (was) among the captives by the river
2. 5 there hath been a prophet among them
3. 15 remained there..among them seven days
3. 25 thou shalt not go out among them
6. 13 their slain..shall be among their idols
9. 2 one man among them..clothed with linen
11. 1 among whom I saw Jaazaniah the son
12. 10 the house of Israel that (are) among them
12. 12 the prince that (is) among them shall bear
18. 18 did (that) which (is) not good among his
19. 2 she nourished her whelps among young
19. 6 he went up and down among the lions
20. 9 before the heathen, among whom they
Eze. 22. 26 and I am profaned among them
29. 12 her cities among the cities..laid waste
33. 33 know that a prophet hath been among
34. 12 in the day that he is among his sheep
34. 24 my servant David a prince among them
44. 9 any stranger that is among the children
47. 22 among you..among you..among the
Hag. 2. 5 so my spirit remaineth among you

13. *Through, by means of,* διά *dia (gen.)*

2 Ti. 2. 2 the things that thou hast heard..among

14. *Into, toward, among,* εἰς *eis.*

Matt 13. 22 He..that received seed among the thorns
Mark 4. 7 some fell [among] thorns, and the thorns
4. 18 are they which are sown among thorns
8. 19 When I brake the five loaves among five
8. 20 when the seven among four thousand
13. 10 gospel must first be published among
Luke 8. 14 that which fell among thorns are they
10. 36 was neighbour unto him that fell among
24. 47 repentance..should be preached..among
John 6. 9 but what are they among so many?
21. 23 Then went this saying abroad among the
Acts 2. 22 a man approved of God among you by
4. 17 that it spread no further among the people
14. 14 they rent their clothes, and ran in among
20. 29 shall grievous wolves enter in among you
2 Co. 11. 6 we have been..made manifest among
1 Th. 5. 15 both among yourselves, and to all (men)
1 Pe. 4. 8 above all things have..charity among

15. *Out of,* ἐκ *ek.*

Matt 12. 11 What man shall there be among you, that
John 12. 20 there were certain Greeks among them
12. 42 among the chief rulers also many believed
Acts 6. 3 look ye out among you seven men of
27. 22 there shall be no loss of..life among

16. *In,* ἐν *en.*

Matt. 2. 6 thou Bethlehem..art not the least among
4. 23 all manner of disease among the people
9. 35 healing..every disease [among] the people
11. 11 Verily I say unto you, Among them that
16. 7 they reasoned among themselves, saying
16. 8 why reason ye among yourselves, because
20. 26 not be so among you..be great among
20. 27 whosoever will be chief among you, let
21. 38 they said among themselves, This is the
26. 5 lest there be an uproar among the people
27. 56 Among which was Mary Magdalene, and
Mark 5. 3 Who had (his) dwelling among the tombs
6. 4 in his own country, and among his own
10. 43 not be among you..be great among you
15. 40 among whom was Mary Magdalene, and
Luke 1. 1 those things which are..believed among
1. 25 to take away my reproach [among] men
1. 28, 42 [blessed (art) thou among women]
2. 44 they sought him among..kinsfolk and
7. 16 a great prophet is risen up among us
7. 28 Among those that are born of women
9. 46 there arose a reasoning among them
9. 48 he that is least among you all, the same
16. 15 that which is highly esteemed among men
22. 24 there was also a strife among them, which
22. 26 he that is greatest among you, let him be
John 1. 14 Word was made flesh, and dwelt among
7. 12 was much murmuring among the people
7. 43 So there was a division among the people
9. 16 And there was a division among them
10. 19 There was a division..among the Jews
11. 54 Jesus..walked no more openly among the
15. 24 If I had not done among them the works
Acts 4. 12 there is none other name..given among
4. 34 Neither was there any among them that
5. 12 signs and wonders wrought among the
6. 8 Stephen..did great wonders..among
12. 18 there was no small stir among the soldiers
13. 26 whosoever among you feareth God to
15. 7 God made choice among us, that the
15. 12 wonders God had wrought among the
15. 22 Silas, chief men among the brethren
17. 34 among the which (was) Dionysius the
18. 11 teaching the word of God among them
20. 25 among whom I have gone preaching the
20. 32 to give you an inheritance among all
21. 19 what things God had wrought among the
21. 34 some cried one thing, some..among the
24. 21 that I cried standing among them
25. 5 which among you are able, go down with
25. 6 when he had tarried among them more
26. 4 which was at the first among mine own
26. 18 and inheritance among them which are
28. 29 [had great reasoning among themselves]
Rom. 1. 5 obedience to the faith among all nations
1. 6 Among whom are ye also the called of
1. 13 fruit among you..as among other Gentiles
2. 24 the name of God is blasphemed among
8. 29 that he might be the firstborn among
11. 17 wild olive tree, wert graffed in among
12. 3 I say..to every man that is among you
15. 9 I will confess to thee among the Gentiles
16. 7 fellow-prisoners, who are of note among
1 Co. 1. 10 (that) there be no divisions among you
1. 11 that there are contentions among you
2. 2 I determined not to know any..among
2. 6 we speak wisdom among them that are
3. 3 whereas (there is) among you envying
3. 18 If any man among you seemeth to be
5. 1 fornication among you..among the
6. 5 that there is not a wise man among you?
6. 7 Now..there is utterly a fault [among] you
11. 18 I hear that there be divisions among you
1 Co. 11. 19 heresies among you..manifest among you
11. 30 many (are) weak and sickly among you
15. 12 how say some among you that there is
2 Co. 1. 19 Jesus Christ, who was preached among
10. 1 who in presence (am) base among you
11. 26 in the sea, (in) perils among false brethren
12. 12 signs of an apostle were wrought among
Gal. 1. 16 that I might preach him among the
2. 2 that gospel which I preach among the
3. 1 Christ hath been..set forth..[among] you
3. 5 and worketh miracles among you, (doeth)
Eph. 2. 3 Among whom also we all had our
3. 8 that I should preach [among] the Gentiles
5. 3 let it not be once named among you, as
Phil. 2. 15 among whom ye shine as lights in the
Col. 1. 27 the glory of this mystery among the
1 Th. 1. 5 men we were among you for your sake
5. 12 to know them which labour among you
5. 13 be at peace among yourselves
2 Th. 3. 7 we behaved not..disorderly among you
3. 11 there are some which walk among you
Jas. 1. 26 If any man [among] you seem to be
3. 6 so is the tongue among our members, that
3. 13 and endued with knowledge among you?
4. 1 whence (come) wars and fightings among
5. 13 Is any among you afflicted? let him
5. 14 Is any sick among you? let him call for
1 Pe. 2. 12 Having your conversation honest among
5. 1 The elders which are among you I exhort
5. 2 Feed the flock of God which is among you
2 Pe. 2. 1 among the people, even as..among you
2. 8 that righteous man dwelling among them

17. *On, upon,* ἐπί *epi (acc.)*

Matt 13. 7 some fell among thorns; and the thorns
Acts 1. 21 Lord Jesus went in and out among us
2 Th. 1. 10 (because our testimony among you was
Rev. 7. 15 sitteth on the throne shall dwell among

18. *At, in,* κατά *(acc.) kata*

Acts 21. 21 teachest all the Jews which are among
26. 3 and questions which are among the Jews

19. *In the midst,* μέσος, ἐν μέσῳ, ἀνὰ μέσον *[mesos].*

Luke 8. 7 some fell among thorns; Mt. 13, 25.
10. 3 I send you forth as lambs among wolves
22. 27 I am among you as he that serveth
22. 55 And..Peter sat down among them
John 1. 26 there standeth one among you, whom ye
1 Th. 2. 7 we were gentle among you, even as a

20. *With,* μετά *meta (gen.)*

Luke 22. 37 he was reckoned among the transgressors
24. 5 Why seek ye the living among the dead?
John 6. 43 Jesus..said..murmur not among
11. 56 sought they for Jesus, and spake among
16. 19 Do ye enquire among yourselves of that

21. *Alongside of,* παρά *para (dat.)*

Matt 28. 15 this saying is commonly reported among
Col. 4. 16 when this epistle is read among you
Rev. 2. 13 my faithful martyr..slain among you

22. *Toward,* πρός *pros (acc.)*

Mark 1. 27 insomuch that they questioned among
8. 16 they reasoned among themselves, saying
9. 33 What was it that ye disputed [among]
9. 34 by the way they had disputed among
10. 26 saying among themselves, Who then can
12. 7 those husbandmen said among themselves
15. 31 also the chief priests mocking..among
16. 3 they said among themselves, Who shall
Luke 4. 36 they were all amazed, and spake among
20. 14 they reasoned among themselves, saying
22. 23 they began to enquire among themselves
John 6. 52 The Jews therefore strove among
7. 35 Then said the Jews among themselves
12. 19 The Pharisees therefore said among
16. 17 Then said (some) of his disciples among
19. 24 They said therefore among themselves
Acts 4. 15 But..they conferred among themselves
28. 4 they said among themselves, No doubt
28. 25 when they agreed not among themselves
2 Co. 12. 21 my God will humble me among you

23. *By, under,* ὑπό *hupo (gen.)*

Acts 10. 22 a just man..and of good report among all

[*See also* Compare, dwell, fall, from, in, out, speak.]

A-MO-RITE, אֱמֹרִי *mountaineer.*

A race or tribe descended from Canaan, the fourth son of Ham, the younger son of Noah; it is mentioned after the Jebusite and before the Girgashite (Gen. 10. 16; 1 Ch. 1. 13); some of them dwelt in Hazezon-tamar, or Engedi, on the W. of the Salt Sea, and were smitten by Chedorlaomer, in the days of Abraham, B.C. 1913 (Gen. 14. 7); three of their chiefs, Mamre, Eschol, and Aner, were confederates of Abraham (Gen. 14. 13); the iniquity of the tribe (as the representative of the Canaanites generally) was not yet full (Gen. 15. 16, 21); they seem to have contended unsuccessfully with Jacob (48. 22); they are mentioned between the Hittites and Perizzites, as inhabitants of Canaan (Exod. 3. 8, 17; Judg. 3. 5; Neh. 9. 1); between the Hittites and the Hivites (Exod. 13. 5); before the other tribes (Exod. 23. 23); between the Canaanite and the Hittite (Exod. 33. 2; Josh. 11. 3); before the Canaanites and the other tribes (Exod. 34. 11); as dwelling in the mountains of Judah (Num. 13. 29); as having the river Arnon as their dividing line from Moab (Num. 21. 13); as having a king named Sihon, B.C. 1452, who not only refused to let Israel pass, but came and attacked them at Jahaz, when he was defeated and his land taken possession of by Israel (Num. 21. 21–32); it was given to the two-and-a-half tribes (Num. 32. 33); the chief city of the south portion of the tribe was Heshbon (Deut. 1. 4); the "mount of the Amorites" was apparently another name for Canaan (Deut. 1. 7, 19, 20); Israel was afraid of them (Deut. 1. 27); and was beaten by them in Seir, even unto Hormah (Deut. 1. 44); their land was to be possessed by Israel (Deut. 3. 2), even from the river Arnon to Mount Hermon, including the land of Og, who reigned in Edrei in Bashan (Deut. 3. 8, 9; 4. 46, 47); mentioned between the Girgashites and the Canaanites (Deut 7. 1); between the Hittites and the Canaanites (Deut. 20. 17; Josh. 9. 1; 12. 8); their fate seems to have terrified the other peoples (Josh. 2. 10; 9. 10); mentioned between the Girgashites and the Jebusites (Josh. 3. 10); mentioned along with the Canaanites as the sole inhabitants of the land W. of the Jordan (Josh. 5. 1); alone mentioned as such (Josh. 7. 7); five of their kings besiege Gibeon, but are defeated (Josh. 10. 5–12).

They had a variety of gods (Josh. 24. 15; Judg. 6. 10); they forced the children of Dan into the mountain (Judg. 1. 34); they were reduced to tribute by the house of Joseph (Judg. 1. 35); their border was from the ascent of Akrabbim northward (Judg. 1. 36); they were at peace with Israel in the days of Samuel, B.C. 1171–1061 (1 Sa. 7..14); the Gibeonites were a remnant of them (2 Sa. 21. 2); Geber, the son of Uri, was over their land E. of the Jordan in the days of Solomon, B.C. 1014 (1 Ki. 4. 19); their remnant was reduced to servitude by Solomon (1 Ki. 9. 20, 21; 2 Chron. 8. 7): their idol worship was followed by Ahab, B.C. 899 (1 Ki. 21. 26); also by Manasseh (2 Ki. 21. 11); their abominations by the Jews under Ezra (9. 8). The overthrow of Og and Sihon was celebrated (Psa. 135. 11; 136. 19); Judah, because of her sins, is represented as having an Amorite for a father, a Hittite for a mother, and Samaria and Sodom for sisters (Eze. 16. 3, 45); the Amorite is represented as tall and strong, yet destroyed before Israel, to whom his land was promised (Amos 2. 9, 10).

Gen. 10. 16 [Canaan begat]..the Jebusite, and the A.
14. 7 smote all the country of..the A., that
14. 13 he dwelt in the plain of Mamre the A.
15. 16 for the iniquity of the A. (is) not yet full
15. 21 [have I given this land]..And the A
48. 22 which I took out of the hand of the A.
Exod. 3. 8 to bring them..unto the place of the..A.
3. 17 I will bring you..unto the land of..the A.
13. 5 shall bring thee into the land of..the A.
23. 23 Angel shall..bring thee in unto the A.
33. 2 I will drive out the Caananite, the A.
34. 11 behold, I drive out before thee the A.
Num 13. 29 the Jebusites, and the A., dwell in the
21. 13 that cometh out of the coasts of the A.
21. 13 Arnon (is)..between Moab and the A.
21. 21 Israel sent..unto Sihon king of the A.
21. 25 Israel dwelt in all the cities of the A.
21. 26 Heshbon..the city of..the king of the A.
21. 29 into captivity unto Sihon..king of the A.
21. 31 Thus Israel dwelt in the land of the A.
21. 32 the villages thereof, and drove out the A.
21. 34 as thou didst unto Sihon king of the A.
22. 2 saw all that Israel had done to the A.
32. 33 the kingdom of Sihon king of the A.
32. 39 children of Machir..dispossessed the A.
Deut. 1. 4 After he had slain Sihon..king of the A.
1. 7 Turn you..and go to the mount of the A.
1. 19 by the way of the mountain of the A.
1. 20 Ye are come unto the mountain of the A.
1. 27 to deliver us into the hand of the A., to
1. 44 And the A., which dwelt in that mountain
2. 24 I have given into thine hand Sihon the A.
3. 2 as thou didst unto Sihon king of the A.
3. 8 out of the hand of the two kings of the A.
3. 9 Hermon..the A. call it Shenir
4. 46 in the land of Sihon king of the A.
4. 47 And they possessed..two kings of the A.
7. 1 the LORD thy God..hath cast out..the A.
20. 17 But thou shalt utterly destroy..the A.
31. 4 as..to Sihon and to Og, kings of the A.
Josh. 2. 10 what ye did unto the two kings of the A.
3. 10 he will without fail drive out..the A.
5. 1 to pass, when all the kings of the A.
7. 7 to deliver us into the hand of the A.
9. 1 when..the A., the Canaanite, the Perizz.
9. 10 he did to the two kings of the A.
10. 5 Therefore the five kings of the A., the
10. 6 all the kings of the A. that dwell in the
10. 12 when the LORD delivered up the A.
11. 3 [Jabin king of Hazor..sent to]..the A.
12. 2 Sihon king of the A. who dwelt in
12. 8 the Hittites, the A., and the Canaanites
13. 4 unto Aphek, to the borders of the A.
13. 10 all the cities of Sihon king of the A.
13. 21 all the kingdom of Sihon king of the A.
24. 8 I brought you into the land of the A.
24. 11 men of Jericho fought against you, the A.
24. 12 drave them out..the two kings of the A.
24. 15 the gods of the A., in whose land ye dwell
24. 18 the LORD drave out..the A. which dwelt
Judg. 1. 34 And the A. forced the children of Dan
1. 35 But the A. would dwell in mount Heres
1. 36 And the coast of the A. (was) from the
3. 5 children of Israel dwelt among the..A.
6. 10 fear not the gods of the A., in whose land
10. 8 in the land of the A., which (is) in Gilead
10. 11 (Did) not (I deliver you) from the..A.
11. 19 messengers unto Sihon king of the A.
11. 21 Israel possessed all the land of the A.
11. 22 they possessed all the coasts of the A.
11. 23 LORD God of Israel..dispossessed the A.
1 Sa. 7. 14 there was peace between Israel and the A.
2 Sa. 21. 2 Gibeonites..of the remnant of the A.
1 Ki. 4. 19 the country of Sihon king of the A.
1 Ki. 9. 20 all the people (that were) left of the A.
21. 26 the A., whom the LORD cast out before
2 Ki. 21. 11 abominations..above all that the A. did
1 Ch. 1. 14 The Jebusite also, and the A., and the Gir
2 Ch. 8. 7 (As for) all the people..left of..the A.
Ezra 9. 1 according to..abominations..of the..A.
Neh. 9. 8 a covenant..to give the land of..the A
Psa. 135. 11 Sihon king of the A., and Og king of
136. 19 Sihon king of the A.: for his mercy
Eze. 16. 3 thy father (was) an A., and thy mother
16. 45 mother..an Hittite, and your father an A.
Amos 2. 9 Yet destroyed I the A. before them
2. 10 led you..to possess the land of the A.

A'-MOS, עָמוֹס *burden-bearer.*

1. A native of Tekoa, a place about 6 miles S. of Bethlehem in Judah; originally he was a shepherd and dresser of sycamore trees, but was called to be a prophet, and exercised his office (about 808 B.C.) during the reign of Uzziah, while Isaiah and Hosea also prophesied.

Amos 1. 1 The words of A., who was among the
7. 8 And the LORD said unto me, A., what
7. 10 A. hath conspired against thee in the
7. 11 For thus A. saith, Jeroboam shall die by
7. 12 Also Amaziah said unto A., O thou seer
7. 14 Then answered A., and said to Amaziah
8. 2 And he said, A., what seest thou? And I

2. An ancestor of Joseph, husband of Mary.

Luke 3. 25 (the son) of A., which was (the son) of

A'-MOZ, אָמוֹץ *strong.*

Father of the prophet Isaiah, and apparently of the tribe of Judah, B.C. 800.

2 Ki. 19. 2 sent..to Isaiah the prophet the son of A.
19. 20 Then Isaiah the son of A. sent to Hezek.
20. 1 And the prophet Isaiah the son of A.
2 Ch. 26. 22 acts of Uzziah..did Isaiah..son of A.
32. 20 the prophet Isaiah the son of A., prayed
32. 32 vision of Isaiah the prophet, the son of A.
Isa. 1. 1 The vision of Isaiah the son of A., which
2. 1 The word that Isaiah the son of A. saw
13. 1 burden of..which Isaiah the son of A.
20. 2 spake the LORD by Isaiah the son of A.
37. 2 unto Isaiah the prophet the son of A.
37. 21 Then Isaiah the son of A. sent unto
38. 1 And Isaiah the prophet the son of A.

AM-PHI'-PO-LIS, Ἀμφίπολις *about the city.*

A city of Macedonia, on the river Strymon, which flows nearly round the town; whence its name. It was called Popolia under the Byzantine empire. Its site is now occupied by a village called Neokhoria, in Turkish, Jeni Keni, literally "new town."

Acts 17. 1 when they had passed through A.

AM-PLI'-AS, Ἀμπλίας.

A convert that dwelt at Rome.

Rom. 16. 8 Greet A. my beloved in the Lord

AM'-RAM, עַמְרָם *exalted people.*

1. A son of Kohath, Levi's son, and father of Aaron, Moses, and Miriam. He died in Egypt, aged 137 years, B.C. 1540.

Exod. 6. 18 And the sons of Kohath; A. and Izhar
6. 20 And A. took him Jochebed his father's
6. 20 and the years of the life of A. (were) an
Num. 3. 19 the sons of Kohath by their families; A.
26. 58 And Kohath begat A.
26. 59 And the name of A.'s wife (was) Jochebed
26. 59 and she bare unto A. Aaron and Moses
1 Ch. 6. 2 And the sons of Kohath; A., Izhar, and
6. 3 And the children of A.; Aaron, and Moses
6. 18 And the sons of Kohath (were), A., and
23. 12 the sons of Kohath; A., Izhar
23. 13 The sons of A.; Aaron and Moses, and
24. 20 Of the sons of A.; Shubael: of the sons

2. A son of Bani, who had taken a strange wife during the exile, B.C. 456.

Ezra 10. 34 Of the sons of Bani; Maadai, A., and

AM'-RAM, חַמְרָן *red.*

A son of Dishon, son of Anah, and great-grandson of Seir the Horite, B.C. 1709.

This name should be written Hamram or Hamran. It is given to Hemdan, "desirable," in Gen. 36. 26, which is probably correct. The form adopted in the common version is manifestly incorrect.

1 Ch. 1. 41 And the sons of Dishon; A., and Eshban

AM-RAM-ITE, עַמְרָמִי *belonging to Amram.*

Patronymic of the family of Amram, father of Miriam, Aaron, and Moses.

Num. 3. 27 of Kohath (was) the family of the A.
1 Ch. 26. 23 Of the A.,(and) the Izharites, the Hebron.

AM-RA'-PHEL, אַמְרָפֶל *powerful people.*

A king of Shinar in the time of Abraham, B.C. 1920.

Gen. 14. 1 it came to pass in the days of A. king of
14. 9 [they joined battle with]..A. king of Shinar

AM'-ZI, אַמְצִי *my strength.*

1. A descendant of Merari, son of Levi, and progenitor of Ethan, whom David set over the service of song, B.C. 1050.

1 Ch. 6. 46 The son of A., the son of Bani, the son of

2. Ancestor of Adaiah, a returned exile, B.C. 445.

Neh. 11. 12 Pelaliah, the son of A., the son of Zechar.

A'-NAB, עֲנָב *a hill.*

A city in the S. of Canaan, inhabited by Anakim. It is still called *Anab*, and is equidistant from Sochoh and Eshtemoa.

Josh 11. 21 Joshua..cut off the Anakims from..A.
15. 50 [in the mountains]..A., and Eshtemoh

A'-NAH, עֲנָה *answering.*

1. A daughter(?) of Zibeon, a Hivite, B.C. 1760.

Gen. 36. 2 Aholibamah the daughter of A. the
36. 14 sons of Aholibamah, the daughter of A.
36. 18 Aholibamah the daughter of A., Esau's
36. 25 the children of A. (were) these
36. 25 and Aholibamah the daughter of A.

2. A son of Seir the Horite, and one of the chiefs of the land.

Gen. 36. 20 These..the sons of Seir..Zibeon, and A.
36. 29 These..the dukes..duke Zibeon, duke A
1 Ch 1. 38 And the sons of Seir..Zibeon, and A.

3. A son of Zibeon, son of Seir, B.C. 1760.

Gen. 36. 24 children of Zibeon; both Ajah, and A.
36. 24 this (was that) A. that found the mules
1 Ch. 1. 40 And the sons of Zibeon: Aiah, and A.
1. 41 The sons of A.; Dishon. And the sons of

A-NA-HA'-RATH, אֲנָחֲרָת *narrow way.*

A town in Issachar.

Josh 19. 19 [border was toward]..Shihon, and A.

A-NA-I'AH, עֲנָיָה *Jah answers.*

1. A priest or prince that stood on the right hand of Ezra while he read the law to the people, B.C. 445.

Neh. 8. 4 Ezra the scribe stood..and A...on his

2. A Jew who, with Nehemiah, sealed the covenant, B.C. 445.

Neh. 10. 22 [The chief of the people]..Hanan, and A.

A'-NAK, עֲנָק, עֲנוֹק *giant, long-necked.*

Son of Arba, and ancestor of the Anakim.

Num 13. 22 Hebron; where..the children of A.,(were)
13. 28 moreover we saw the children of A. there
13. 33 there we saw the giants, the sons of A.
Deut. 9. 2 Who can stand before the children of A.
Josh 15. 13 the city of Arba the father of A., which
15. 14 Caleb drove thence the three sons of A.
15. 14 Ahiman, and Talmai, the children of A.
21. 11 the city of Arba the father of A.
Judg. 1. 20 expelled thence the three sons of A.

A-NA-KIMS, עֲנָקִים *giants.*

The descendants of the preceding Arba, one of the "sons of Heth" (Gen. 23. 3); who, seven years before the building of Zoar in Egypt (Gen. 23. 2; Num. 13. 22; Josh. 15. 13, 54), built Hebron, which was hence called Kirjath-arba, *i.e.*, the city of Arba. Anak, his son, had three distinguished descendants in the days of Moses and Joshua, B.C. 1490 (Num. 13. 22), whose names were Ahiman, Sheshai, and Talmai, and who dwelt in Hebron; in whose presence the Israelites reckoned themselves only as grasshoppers (Num. 13. 28, 33); this greatly disheartened Israel (Deut. 1. 28); the Anakim were like the Emim, who were great, and many, and tall, but who were dispossessed by Moab (Deut. 2. 10, 11, 21); it was a common saying, Who can stand before the sons of the Anakim? (Deut. 9. 2), but Joshua cut them off from the mountains, and from Hebron, Debir, and Anab, so that only a few were left in Gaza, Gath, and Ashdod, cities of the Philistines (Josh. 11. 21, 22); they had great and fenced cities, the chief of which was Hebron, which they had called Kirjath-arba, or the city of *Arba*, who had been a great man among them (Josh. 14. 12, 15); and who was also the father of Anak (Josh. 15. 13); this Anak had three leading descendants in Hebron (Josh. 15. 14), which city was afterwards assigned to the Kohathites for a possession (Josh. 21. 11). The tribe lost its separate existence among the Philistines.

Deut. 1. 28 we have seen the sons of the A. there
2. 10 great, and many, and tall, as the A.
2. 11 also were accounted giants, as the A.
2. 21 great, and many, and tall as the A.
9. 2 great and tall, the children of the A.
Josh. 11. 21 time came Joshua, and cut off the A.
11. 22 There was none of the A. left in the land
14. 12 heardest in that day how the A. (were)
14. 15 Arba was) a great man among the A.

A-NA'-MIM, עֲנָמִים *rockmen.*

A Mizraite people, of whose locale nothing certain is known; but it was most probably in Northern Egypt.

Gen. 10. 13 And Mizraim begat Ludim, and A.
1 Ch. 1. 11 And Mizraim begat Ludim, and A.

A-NAM-ME'-LECH, עֲנַמֶּלֶךְ *the king's rock.*

An idol whose worship among the Sepharvaim was transplanted to Israel when Shalmaneser peopled the cities of Israel with the Sepharvaim.

2 Ki. 17. 31 Sepharvites burnt..children in fire to..A.

A'-NAN, עָנָן *he beclouds.*

An exile who, with Nehemiah, signed the covenant, B.C. 445.

Neh. 10. 26 [chief of the people;] Ahijah, Hanan, A.

A-NA'-NI, עֲנָנִי *my cloud* (i.e., *protector*).

Son of Elioenai, of the family of David, B.C. 445.

1 Ch. 3. 24 sons of Elioenai (were)..Dalaiah, and A.

A-NAN-I'AH, עֲנַנְיָה *Jah is a cloud* (i.e., *protector*).

Grandfather of Azariah, a returned exile, B.C. 460.

Neh. 3. 23 repaired Azariah..the son of A. by his

A-NAN-I'AS, Ἀνανίας *Jah is gracious.*

1. A disciple whose wife conspired with him in attempting to deceive the apostles in regard to the value obtained for their property, A.D. 35.

Acts 5. 1 But a certain man named A., with Sapphira

Acts 5. 3 But Peter said, A., why hath Satan filled
5. 5 And A. hearing these words fell down, and

2. A disciple at Damascus to whom was made known the conversion of Saul of Tarsus, A.D. 35.

Acts 9. 10 there was a certain disciple..named A.
9. 10 to him said the Lord in a vision, A.
9. 12 hath seen in a vision a man named A.
9. 13 Then A. answered, Lord, I have heard by
9. 17 And A. went his way, and entered into
22. 12 And one A., a devout man according to

3. A high priest at Jerusalem, A.D. 60.

Acts 23. 2 And the high priest A. commanded them
24. 1 And after five days A. the high priest

A'-NATH, ענת, *answer.*

Father of Shamgar, third judge after Joshua, B.C. 1360.

Judg. 3. 31 after him was Shamgar the son of A.
5. 6 In the days of Shamgar the son of A.

A-NA'-THE-MA, ἀνάθεμα.

Any thing "put up" in the temple of a god, set apart or separated, consecrated, devoted.

1 Co. 16. 22 if any..love not..let him be A.

A-NA'-THOTH, ענתות, *answers.*

1. A Levitical city in Benjamin, 3 miles N. of Jerusalem, the birthplace of Jeremiah, now called *Anata*.

Josh. 21. 18 A. with her suburbs, and Almon with her
1 Ki. 2. 26 Get thee to A., unto thine own fields; for
1 Ch. 6. 60 out of the tribe of Benjamin..A. with her
Ezra 2. 23 The men of A., an hundred twenty and
Neh. 7. 27 The men of A., an hundred twenty and
11. 32 [children..of Benjamin..dwelt at]..A.
Isa. 10. 30 cause it to be heard unto Laish, O poor A.
Jer. 1. 1 the priests that (were) in A. in the land
11. 21 thus saith the LORD of the men of A., that
11. 23 I will bring evil upon the men of A.
29. 27 hast thou not reproved Jeremiah of A.
32. 7 Buy thee my field that (is) in A.: for the
32. 8 Buy my field, I pray thee, that (is) in A.
32. 9 I bought the field..that (was) in A.

2. The eighth of the nine sons of Becher, son of Benjamin, B.C. 1650.

1 Ch. 7. 8 And the sons of Becher..A. and Alemeth

3. One of the chiefs that signed the covenant with Nehemiah, B.C. 445.

Neh. 10. 19 Hariph, A., Nebai

ANCESTOR —

First, former, ראשון *rishon.*

Lev. 26. 45 remember the covenant of their ancestors

ANCHOR —

An anchor, ἄγκυρα *angkura.*

Acts 27. 29 they cast four anchors out of the stern
27. 30 they would have cast anchors out of the
27. 40 when they had taken up the anchors, they
Heb. 6. 19 Which..we have as an anchor of the soul

ANCIENT —

1. *Aged, senior,* זקן *zaqen.*

Psa. 119. 100 I understand more than the ancients
Isa. 3. 2 mighty man..prudent, and the ancient
3. 5 behave himself..against the ancient
3. 14 will enter into judgment with the ancients
9. 15 The ancient and honourable, he (is) the
24. 23 and before his ancients gloriously
47. 6 upon the ancient hast thou very heavily
Jer. 19. 1 ancients of the people..ancients of the
Eze. 7. 26 priest, and counsel from the ancients
8. 11 there stood..seventy men of the ancients
8. 12 hast thou seen what the ancients..do in
9. 6 Then they began at the ancient men
27. 9 The ancients of Gebal and the wise

2. *White, grey, old, dry,* ישיש *yashish.*

Job 12. 12 With the ancient (is) wisdom; and in

3. *Age, indefinite time,* עולם *olam.*

Prov. 22. 28 Remove not the ancient landmark, which
Isa. 44. 7 since I appointed the ancient people?
Jer. 5. 15 mighty nation, it (is) an ancient nation
18. 15 stumble in their ways..the ancient paths
Eze. 36. 2 Aha, even the ancient high places are our's

4. *Removed,* עתיק *attiq.*

1 Ch. 4. 22 And (these are) ancient things
Dan. 7. 9 the Ancient of days did sit, whose garment
7. 13 came to the Ancient of days, and they
7. 22 Until the Ancient of days came, and

5. *Ancient times,* קדומים *qedumim.*

Judg. 5. 21 that ancient river, the river Kishon

6. *East, that which is before,* קדם *qedem.*

Deut 33. 15 the chief things of the ancient mountains
2 Ki. 19. 25 Hast thou not heard..of ancient times
Isa. 19. 11 I (am) the son of..ancient kings?
23. 7 whose antiquity (is) of ancient days?
37. 26 Hast thou not heard..of ancient times
51. 9 awake, as in the ancient days, in the

7. *Eastern, what is before,* קדמוני *qadmoni.*

1 Sa. 24. 13 As saith the proverb of the ancients

ANCIENT man —

Aged, senior, elder, זקן *zaqen.*

Ezra 3. 12 many of the priests..ancient men

ANCIENT time —

1. *Indefinite time,* עולם *olam.*

Psa. 77. 5 I have considered..the years of ancient t.

2. *East, what is before,* קדם *qedem.*

Isa. 45. 21 who..declared this from ancient time
46. 10 Declaring the end from..ancient times

ANCLE —

Ancle, end, אפס *ephes.*

Eze. 47. 3 he brought me through..to the ancles

ANCLE-BONE —

Ancle-bone, σφυρόν *sphuron.*

Acts 3. 7 immediately his..ancle bones received

AND —

1. *Or,* או *o.*

Song 2. 7 by the roes, and by the hinds of the field
3. 5 by the roes, and by the hinds of the field

2. *Also,* אף *aph.*

1 Sa. 2. 7 The LORD bringeth low, and lifteth up

3. *When,* כי *ki.*

1 Sa. 2. 21 And the LORD visited Hannah, so that she

4. *Unto,* עד *ad.*

Gen. 6. 7 I will destroy..both man, and beast
Judg 20. 48 the beast and all that came to hand

5. *On, upon, in addition to,* על *al.*

Judg. 15. 8 he smote them hip and thigh with a great

6. *With,* עם *im.*

Judg. 20. 38 the men of Israel and the liers in wait

AND —

1. *But,* ἀλλά *alla,* ἀλλά γε *alla ge.*

Luke 17. 8 And will not rather say unto him
24. 21 and beside all this, to-day is the third day

2. *Together with,* ἅμα *hama.*

Acts 27. 40 to the sea, and loosed the rudder bands

3. *By (distributively),* ἀνά *ana.*

Luke 10. 1 sent them two and two before his face

4. *For, verily then,* γάρ *gar.*

John 4. 37 And herein is that saying true, One
Acts 8. 39 and he went on his way rejoicing
2 Ti. 2. 7 and the Lord give thee understanding

5. *And, then, now, so, but,* δέ *de.*

Mark 12. 5 beating some, and killing some
Luke 18. 9 And he spake this parable unto certain
1 Co. 15. 56 and the strength of sin (is) the law
Gal. 3. 17 And this I say, (that) the covenant, that

6. *Certainly, now,* δή *dē.*

Acts 15. 36 Let us go again and visit our brethren

7. *Or, than,* ἤ *ē.*

Mark 6. 11 more tolerable for Sodom [and] Gomorrha
1 Co. 11. 27 [and] drink (this) cup of the Lord unwor.
1 Pe. 1. 18 with corruptible things..silver and gold

8. *And, also,* καί *kai.*

Matt. 1. 2 Jacob begat Judas and his brethren

9. *With,* μετά *meta (gen.)*

John 3. 25 between..John's disciples and the Jews

10. *Whosoever,* ὅστις *hostis.*

Acts 9. 35 all..saw him, and turned to the Lord

11. *Therefore, then,* οὖν *oun.*

Matt 18. 29 And his fellow servant fell down at his
John 6. 62 and if ye shall see the Son of man
20. 11 and as she wept, she stooped down
Acts 15. 39 And the contention was so sharp between
25. 23 And on the morrow, when Agrippa was

12. *Therefore indeed, moreover,* μὲν οὖν *men oun.*

Luke 3. 18 And many other things in his exhortation
Acts 5. 41 And they departed from the presence of
8. 25 And they, when they had testified and
15. 3 And being brought on their way by the
17. 30 And the times of this ignorance God
28. 5 And he shook off the beast into the fire

13. *And, also,* τε *te.*

Matt 23 6 [And] love the uppermost rooms at feasts
27. 48 a spunge, and filled (it) with vinegar
28. 12 and had taken counsel, they gave large
Mark 15 36 spunge full of vinegar, [and] put (it) on
Luke 2. 16 came with haste, and found Mary, and
12. 45 and to eat and drink, and to be drunken
21. 11 And great earthquakes shall be in divers
21. 11 and fearful sights and great signs shall
22. 66 and the chief priests and the scribes came
24. 20 And how the chief priests and our rulers
John 2. 15 all out of the temple, and the sheep, and
4. 42 And said unto the woman, Now we
6. 18 And the sea arose by reason of a..wind
Acts 2. 3 as of fire, and it sat upon each of them
2. 9 And in Judea, and Cappadocia, in Pontus
2. 10 Phrygia, and Pamphylia..Jews and pros.
2. 33 and having received of the Father the
2. 37 and said unto Peter and to the rest of the
2. 40 and with many other words did he testify
2. 43 and many wonders and signs were done
2. 46 and they, continuing..and breaking bread
3. 10 And they knew that it was he which sat
4. 13 and they took knowledge of them, that
4. 33 and great grace was upon them all
5. 19 and brought them forth, and said
5. 35 And said unto them, Ye men of Israel
5. 42 And daily in the temple, and in every
6. 7 and a great company of the priests were
6. 12 and they stirred up the people, and the
6. 13 And set up false witnesses, which said
7. 26 [And] the next day he shewed himself unto
8. 1 [and] they were all scattered abroad
8. 3 and haling men and women..to prison
8. 6 And the people with one accord gave
8. 13 and wondered, beholding the miracles
8. 25 and preached the gospel in many villages
8. 31 And he desired Philip that he would come
9. 6 [And he trembling and astonished said]
9. 15 before..kings, and the children of Israel
9. 18 and he received sight forthwith, and arose
9. 24 [And] they watched the gates day and night
10. 22 and of good report among all the nation
10. 28 And he said unto them, Ye know how
10. 33 and thou hast well done that thou art
10. 48 And he commanded them to be baptized
11. 13 [And] he shewed us how he had seen an
11. 21 was with them: and a great number
11. 26 And the disciples were called Christians
12. 6 and the keepers before the door kept the
12. 8 [And] the angel said unto him, Gird thyself
12. 12 And when he had considered..he came to
13. 1 and Manaen, which had been brought up
13. 4 and from thence they sailed to Cyprus
14. 12 And they called Barnabas, Jupiter; and
14. 21 And when they had preached the gospel
15. 4 and they declared all things that God hat
15. 5 and to command..keep the law of Mose:
15. 39 one from the other: and so Barnabas took
16. 11 we came..to..and the next..to Neapolis
16. 12 [And] from thence to Philippi, which is the
16. 13 And on the sabbath we went out of the
16. 23 And when they had laid many stripes
16. 26 [and] immediately all..doors were opened
16. 34 And when he had brought them into his
17. 4 and of the devout Greeks a great
17. 4 and of the chief women not a few
17. 5 an uproar, and assaulted the house of
17. 19 and they took him, and brought him untc
17. 26 And hath made of one blood all nations
18. 4 and persuaded the Jews and the Greeks
18. 11 [And] he continued..a year and six months
18. 26 And he began to speak boldly in the
19. 3 And he said unto them, Unto what then
19. 6 and they spake with tongues, and prophe.
19. 11 And God wrought special miracles by
19. 12 and the evil spirits went out of them
19. 18 And many that believed came, and
19. 29 and having caught Gaius and Aristarchus
20. 3 And (there) abode three months. And
20. 7 and continued his speech until midnight
20. 11 [and] talked a long while, even till break
20. 35 and to remember the words of the Lord
21. 11 [and] bound his own hands and feet, and
21. 18 unto James; and all the elders were
21. 20 and said unto him, Thou seest, brother
21. 28 and further brought Greeks also into the
21. 30 And all the city was moved, and the
21. 37 And as Paul was to be led into the castle
22. 7 And I fell unto the ground, and heard a
22. 8 And he said unto me, I am Jesus of Naz.
22. 28 [And] the chief captain answered, With a
23. 10 take him..and to bring (him) into the
23. 24 And provide..beasts, that they may set
23. 35 And he commanded him to be kept in
24. 5 and a ringleader of the sect of..Nazarenes
24. 23 [And] he commanded..and to let (him) have
24. 27 and Felix, willing to shew the Jews a
26. 10 and when they were put to death, I gave
26. 11 and being exceedingly mad against them
26. 16 which thou hast seen, and of those things
26. 20 and throughout all the coasts of Judea
26. 30 thus spoken, the king rose up..and Bernice
27. 3 And the next..And Julius courteously
27. 5 And when we had sailed over the sea of
27. 8 And, hardly passing it, came unto a place
27. 17 and, fearing lest they should fall into the
27. 20 and no small tempest lay on (us), all hope
27. 21 and to have gained this harm and loss
27. 43 and commanded that they which could
Rom. 1. 27 [And] likewise also the men, leaving the
2. 19 And art confident that thou thyself art a
14. 8 and whether we die, we die unto the Lord
16. 26 and by the scriptures of the prophets
1 Co. 1. 30 made unto us wisdom, and righteousness
4. 21 in love, and (in) the spirit of meekness?
Eph. 3. 19 And to know the love of Christ, which
Heb. 1. 3 and upholding all things by the word of
4. 12 and of the joints and marrow, and (is) a
6. 2 and of laying on..and of resurrection of
6. 4 and have tasted of the heavenly gift, and
6. 5 and the powers of the world to come
9. 1 of divine service, and a worldly sanctuary
11. 32 to tell of Gideon, and (of) Barak, and (of)
12. 2 and is set down at the..throne of God
Jas. 3. 7 every kind of beasts, and of birds, and of
Jude 6 And the angels which kept not their first
Rev. 1. 2 Christ, and of all things that he saw
21. 12 [And] had a wall great and high

AND afterward —

And from thence, κἀκεῖθεν = *kai ekeithen.*

Acts 13. 21 And afterward they desired a king; and

AND even —

Nevertheless, ὅμως *homōs.*

1 Co. 14. 7 And even things without life giving sound

AND from thence —

And from thence, κἀκεῖθεν = *kai ekeithen.*

Mark 10. 1 And he arose from thence, and cometh
Acts 7. 4 and from thence, when his father was
21. 1 Rhodes, and from thence unto Patara

Acts 27. 4 And when we had launched from thence
28. 15 And from thence, when the brethren

AND I —

And I, κἀγώ *kagō.*

Matt 11. 28 Come unto me..and I will give you rest
26. 15 What..and I will deliver him unto you?
Luke 2. 48 father and I have sought thee sorrowing
11. 9 And I say unto you, Ask, and it shall be
16. 9 And I say unto you, Make to yourselves
22. 29 And I appoint unto you a kingdom, as
John 1. 31 And I knew him not: but that he should
1. 33 And I knew him not: but he that sent me
1. 34 And I saw, and bare record that this is
5. 17 My Father worketh hitherto, and I work
6. 56 He that..dwelleth in me, and I in him
6. 57 and I live by the Father: so he that eateth
8. 26 and I speak to the world those things
10. 27 My sheep hear my voice, and I know them
10. 28 And I give unto them eternal life; and
10. 38 that the Father (is) in me, and I in him
12. 32 And I, if I be lifted up from the earth
14. 20 in my Father, and ye in me, and I in you
15. 4 Abide in me, and I in you. As the branch
15. 5 He that abideth in me, and I in him, the
17. 21 as thou, Father, (art) in me, and I in thee
17. 26 the love..may be in them, and I in them
20. 15 hast laid him, and I will take him away
Acts 22. 10 And I said, What shall I do, Lord? And
22. 19 And I said, Lord, they know that I
Rom. 11. 3 and I am left alone, and they seek my
1 Co. 2. 1 And I, brethren, when I came to you
2 Co. 6. 17 touch not the unclean (thing); and I will
12. 20 and (that) I shall be found unto you such
Gal. 6 14 crucified unto me, and I unto the world
Phil. 2. 28 and that I may be the less sorrowful
Heb. 7. 9 And as I may so say, Levi also, who
Jas. 2. 18 and I have works..and I will shew

AND if —

And if, κἄν *kan.*

Mark 16. 18 [and if they drink any deadly thing]
Luke 13. 9 And if it bear fruit, (well): and if not
Jas. 5 15 and if he have committed sins, they shall

AND if so much as —

And if, κἄν *kan.*

Heb 12. 20 And if so much as a beast touch the

AND not, וְאִם *ve-im.*

Gen. 14. 23 and that I will not take anything that

AND so —

Then, οὖν *oun.*

Acts 16. 5 And so were the churches established in

AND there —

And there, κἀκεῖ = *kai ekei.*

Matt. 5. 23 and there rememberest that thy brother
10. 11 and there abide till ye go thence
28. 10 go into Galilee, and there shall they see
Mark 1. 35 into a solitary place, and there prayed
John 11. 54 and there continued with his disciples
Acts 14. 7 And there they preached the gospel
22. 10 go into Damascus, and there it shall be
25 20 and there be judged of these matters 27.6.

AND when — *Then*, τότε *tote*, Acts 13. 3.

AND they —

Who, ὅστις *hostis.*

Acts 5. 16 and they were healed every one
23. 14 And they came to the chief priests and

AND truly —

Then, οὖν *oun.*

John 20. 30 And many other signs truly did Jesus in

AND [two **AND** two] —

Two and two, ἀνὰ δύο *ana duo.*

Luke 10. 1 sent them two and two before his face

AND yet —

Although, καίπερ *kaiper.*

Rev. 17. 8 the beast that was, and is not, and yet is

AN'-DREW, Ἀνδρέας *manly.*

Brother of Simon Peter, and one of the apostles.

Matt. 4. 18 Simon called Peter, and A. his brother
10. 2 first, Simon, who is called Peter, and A.
Mark 1. 16 he saw Simon and A. his brother casting
1. 29 entered into the house of Simon and A.
3 18 And A. and Philip, and Bartholomew, and
13. 3 and A. asked him privately
Luke 6. 14 Simon (whom he also named Peter) and A.
John 1. 40 One of the two which heard..was A.
1. 44 Philip was of Bethsaida, the city of A.
6. 8 One of his disciples, A...saith unto him
12. 22 telleth A.: and again A. and Philip
Acts 1. 13 upper room, where abode..Peter..and A.

AN-DRO'-NI-CUS, Ἀνδρόνικος, *conqueror.*

A kinsman of Paul at Rome, A.D. 60.

Rom. 16. 7 Salute A. and Junia, my kinsmen

A'-NEM, עָנֵם *double fountain.*

A Levitical city of Issachar. It is omitted in the lists in Josh. 19. 21, and instead of it we find *En-gannim.* The one is probably a contraction of the other, as *Kartan* for *Kirjathaim.* It is now called *Jenin*, and is at the opening of the spreading valley into the plain.

1 Ch. 6. 73 Ramoth with her suburbs, and A. with

A'-NER, עָנֵר *sprout, waterfall.*

1. Brother of Mamre, the Amorite, Abraham's ally, B.C. 1912.

Gen. 14. 13 brother of Eshcol, and brother of A.
14. 24 the men which went with me, A., Eshcol

2. A Levitical city in Manasseh, W. of Jordan. It is the "Taanach" of Josh. 21. 25. The modern village of *Anim*, near *Ta'anik*, is probably the site of "Aner," which is substituted for "Taanach" in 1 Ch. 6. 70, as below.

1 Ch. 6. 70 out of the half tribe of Manasseh; A. with

A-NE-THO-THITE (ANETOTHITE), עַנְּתֹתִי עַנְתֹתִי.

A native of Anathoth, a place in Benjamin.

2 Sa. 23. 27 Abiezer the A., Mebunnai the
1 Ch. 27. 12 The ninth (captain..was) Abiezer the A.

ANGEL —

1. *Mighty*, אַבִּיר *abbir.*

Psa. 78. 25 Man did eat angels' food: he sent them

2. *Messenger, agent*, מַלְאָךְ *malak.*

Gen. 16. 7 the angel of the LORD found her by a
16. 9, 10, 11 the angel of the LORD said unto her
19. 1 there came two angels to Sodom at even
19. 15 when the morning arose, then the angels
21. 17 the angel of God called to Hagar out of
22. 11 the angel of the LORD called unto him
22. 15 the angel of the LORD called unto Abraham
24. 7 he shall send his angel before thee, and
24. 40 The LORD..will send his angel with thee
28. 12 and behold the angels of God..on it
31. 11 the angel of God spake unto me in a dream
32. 1 and the angels of God met him
48. 16 The Angel which redeemed me from all evil
Exod. 3. 2 the angel of the LORD appeared unto him
14. 19 the angel of God, which went before the
23. 20 I send an Angel before thee, to keep thee
23. 23 mine Angel shall go before thee, and bring
32. 34 behold, mine Angel shall go before thee
33. 2 I will send an angel before thee; and I
Num. 20. 16 heard our voice, and sent an angel, and
22. 22 the angel of the LORD stood in the way for an
22. 23, 25, 27 the ass saw the angel of the LORD
22. 24 the angel of the LORD stood in a path of the
22. 26 the angel of the LORD went further, and
22. 31 he saw the angel of the LORD standing in the
22. 32 And the angel of the LORD said unto him
22. 34 Balaam said unto the angel of the LORD, I
22. 35 the angel of the LORD said unto Balaam, Go
Judg. 2. 1 an angel of the LORD came up from Gilgal
2. 4 when the angel of the LORD spake these words
5. 23 Curse ye Meroz, said the angel of the LORD
6. 11 there came an angel of the LORD, and sat
6. 12 the angel of the LORD appeared unto him
6. 20 the angel of God said unto him, Take the
6. 21 the angel of the LORD put forth..the staff
6. 21 the angel of the LORD departed out of his
6. 22 Gideon perceived..he (was) an angel of the
6. 22 because I have seen an angel of the LORD
13. 3 the angel of the LORD appeared unto the
13. 6 his countenance..like..an angel of God
13. 9 the angel of God came again unto the
13. 13 the angel of the LORD said unto Manoah
13. 15 Manoah said unto the angel of the LORD
13. 16 the angel of the LORD..an angel of the LORD
13. 17 Manoah said unto the angel of the LORD
13. 18 the angel of the LORD said unto him
13. 20 the angel of the LORD ascended in the flame
13. 21 the angel of the LORD did no more appear
13. 21 Manoah knew that he (was) an angel of the
1 Sa. 29. 9 thou (art) good..as an angel of God
2 Sa. 14 17 for as an angel of God, so (is) my Lord the
14. 20 according to the wisdom of an angel of God
19. 27 my lord the king (is) as an angel of God
24. 16 when the angel stretched out his hand
24. 16 said to the angel that destroyed
24. 16 the angel of the LORD was by the threshing
24. 17 he saw the angel that smote the people
1 Ki. 13 18 an angel spake unto me by the word of
19. 5 an angel touched him, and said unto him
19. 7 the angel of the LORD came again the
2 Ki. 1. 3 the angel of the LORD said to Elijah the
1. 15 the angel of the LORD said unto Elijah
19. 35 the angel of the LORD went out, and smote
1 Ch. 21. 12 the angel of the LORD destroying
21. 15 sent an angel..the angel..the angel
21. 16 David..saw the angel of the LORD stand
21. 18 the angel of the LORD commanded Gad
21. 20 Ornan turned back, and saw the angel
21. 27 the LORD commanded the angel; and he
21. 30 afraid because..of the angel of the LORD
2 Ch. 32. 21 the LORD sent an angel, which cut off all
Job 4. 18 his angels he charged with folly
Psa. 34. 7 The angel of the LORD encampeth round
35. 5 let the angel of the LORD chase (them)
35. 6 let the angel of the LORD persecute them
78. 49 He cast..trouble, by sending evil angels
91. 11 he shall give his angels charge over thee
103. 20 Bless the LORD, ye his angels, that
104. 4 Who maketh his angels spirits; his
148. 2 Praise ye him, all his angels: praise
Eccl. 5. 6 neither say thou before the angel, that it
Isa. 37. 36 the angel of the LORD went forth, and
63. 9 the angel of his presence saved them
Dan. 3. 28 who hath sent his angel, and delivered
6. 22 My God hath sent his angel, and hath
Hos. 12. 4 he had power over the angel, and prevailed
Zech. 1. 9 the angel that talked with me said unto me
1. 11 they answered the angel of the LORD
1. 12 the angel of the LORD answered and said
1. 13 the LORD answered the angel that talked
1. 14 the angel that communed with me said
1. 19 I said unto the angel that talked with me
2. 3 the angel that talked with me went forth
Zech. 2. 3 and another angel went out to meet him
3. 1 Joshua..standing before the angel of the
3. 3 Now Joshua..stood before the angel
3. 5 And the angel of the LORD stood by
3. 6 the angel of the LORD protested unto
4. 1 the angel that talked with me came again
4. 4 I answered and spake to the angel
4. 5 the angel that talked with me answered
5. 5 the angel that talked with me went forth
5. 10 Then said I to the angel that talked with
6. 4 I answered and said unto the angel
6. 5 the angel answered and said unto me
12. 8 as the angel of the LORD before them

3. *Messenger, agent*, ἄγγελος *aggelos.*

Matt. 1. 20 the angel of the Lord appeared unto him
1. 24 Joseph..did as the angel of the Lord had
2. 13 the angel of the Lord appeareth to Joseph
2. 19 when Herod was dead, behold, an angel
4. 6 He shall give his angels charge concerning
4. 11 angels came and ministered unto him
13. 39 and the reapers are the angels
13. 41 Son of man shall send forth his angels
13. 49 angels shall come forth, and sever the
16. 27 Son of man shall come..with his angels
18. 10 in heaven their angels do always behold
22. 30 but are as the angels of God in heaven
24. 31 he shall send his angels with a great sound
24. 36 not the angels of heaven, but my Father
25. 31 all the holy angels with him, then shall
25. 41 prepared for the devil and his angels
26. 53 give me more than twelve legions of angels?
28. 2 the angel of the Lord descended from
28. 5 the angel answered and said unto the
Mark 1. 13 and the angels ministered unto him
8. 38 when he cometh..with the holy angels
12. 25 are as the angels which are in heaven
13. 27 then shall he send his angels, and shall
13. 32 not the angels which are in heaven
Luke 1. 11 there appeared unto him an angel of the
1. 13 the angel said unto him, Fear not
1. 18 Zacharias said unto the angel, Whereby
1. 19 the angel answering said unto him, I am
1. 26 in the sixth month the angel Gabriel
1. 28 [the angel] came in unto her, and said
1. 30 the angel said unto her, Fear not, Mary
1. 34 Then said Mary unto the angel, How shall
1. 35 the angel answered and said unto her
1. 38 And the angel departed from her
2. 9 the angel of the Lord came upon them
2. 10 the angel said unto them, Fear not: for
2. 13 And suddenly there was with the angel a
2. 15 as the angels were gone away from them
2. 21 Jesus, which was so named of the angel
4. 10 He shall give his angels charge over thee
9. 26 in his own glory..and of the holy angels
12. 8 also confess before the angels of God
12. 9 shall be denied before the angels of God
15. 10 there is joy in the presence of the angels
16. 22 the beggar..was carried by the angels into
22. 43 [there appeared an angel unto him from]
24. 23 they had also seen a vision of angels
John 1. 51 the angels of God ascending and descending
5. 4 [an angel went down at a certain season]
12. 29 others said, An angel spake to him
20. 12 seeth two angels in white sitting, the one
Acts 5. 19 the angel of the Lord by night opened
6. 15 as it had been the face of an angel
7. 30 there appeared to him..an angel of the Lord
7. 35 by the hand of the angel which appeared
7. 38 This is he, that was..with the angel which
7. 53 the law by the disposition of angels, and
8. 26 the angel of the Lord spake unto Philip
10. 3 He saw in a vision evidently..an angel
10. 7 when the angel which spake unto Cornelius
10. 22 was warned from God by an holy angel
11. 13 how he had seen an angel in his house
12. 7 the angel of the Lord came upon (him)
12. 8 the angel said unto him, Gird thyself, and
12. 9 which was done by the angel; but thought
12. 10 forthwith the angel departed from him
12. 11 that the Lord hath sent his angel, and
12. 15 Then said they, It is his angel
12. 23 immediately the angel of the Lord smote
23. 8 is no resurrection, neither angel nor spirit
23. 9 if a spirit or an angel hath spoken to him
27. 23 there stood by me this night the angel of
Rom. 8. 38 I am persuaded, that neither..angels, nor
1 Co. 4. 9 for we are made a spectacle unto..angels
6. 3 Know ye not that we shall judge angels?
11. 10 power on (her) head because of the angels
13. 1 Though I speak with the tongues..of angels
2 Co. 11. 14 Satan himself is transformed into an angel
Gal. 1. 8 though we, or an angel from heaven
3. 19 ordained by angels in the hand of a
4. 14 received me as an angel of God, (even) as
Col. 2. 18 humility and worshipping of angels
2 Th. 1. 7 shall be revealed..with his mighty angels
1 Ti. 3. 16 was manifest in the flesh..seen of angels
5. 21 I charge (thee) before..the elect angels, that
Heb. 1. 4 made so much better than the angels, as he
1. 5 unto which of the angels said he at any
1. 6 let all the angels of God worship him
1. 7 of the angels he saith..his angels a flaming
1. 13 to which of the angels said he at any
2. 2 if the word spoken by angels was stedfast
2. 5 unto the angels hath he not put in subjec.
2. 7 madest him a little lower than the angels
2. 9 was made a little lower than the angels
2. 16 took not on..angels; but took on the seed
12. 22 to an innumerable company of angels
13. 2 thereby some have entertained angels

1 Pe. 1. 12 which things the angels desire to look into
3. 22 angels and authorities and powers being
2 Pe. 2. 4 if God spared not the angels that sinned
2. 11 angels, which are greater in power and
Jude 6 angels which kept not their first estate
Rev. 1. 1 he sent and signified (it) by his angel
1. 20 The seven stars are the angels of the seven
2. 1 Unto the angel of the church of Ephesus
2. 8 unto the angel of the church in Smyrna
2. 12 to the angel of the church in Pergamos
2. 18 unto the angel of the church in Thyatira
3. 1 unto the angel of the church in Sardis
3. 5 I will confess his name..before his angels
3. 7 to the angel of the church in Philadelphia
3. 14 unto the angel of the church..Laodiceans
5. 2 I saw a strong angel proclaiming with a
5. 11 I heard the voice of many angels round
7. 1 I saw four angels standing on the four
7. 2 another angel..cried..to the four angels
7. 11 all the angels stood round about the
8. 2 I saw the seven angels which stood
8. 3 another angel came and stood at the
8. 4 up before God out of the angel's hand
8. 5 the angel took the censer, and filled
8. 6 the seven angels which had the seven
8. 7 The first [angel] sounded, and there followed
8. 8 the second angel sounded, and as it were a
8. 10 the third angel sounded, and there fell v.11.
8. 12 the fourth angel sounded, and the third
8. 13 I beheld, and heard an [angel]..saying
8. 13 voices of the trumpet of the three angels
9. 1 the fifth angel sounded, and I saw a star
9. 11 they had a king..the angel of the bottomless
9. 13 the sixth angel sounded, and I heard a voice
9. 14 Saying to the..angel..Loose the four angels
9. 15 the four angels were loosed, which were
10. 1 I saw another mighty angel come down
10. 5 the angel which I saw stand upon the
10. 7 in the days..of the seventh angel, when
10. 8 which is open in the hand of the angel
10. 9 I went unto the angel, and said unto
10. 10 I took the little book out of the angel's hand
11. 1 [the angel stood,] saying, Rise and measure
11. 15 the seventh angel sounded; and there were
12. 7 his angels fought against..his angels
12. 9 and his angels were cast out with him
14. 6 I saw another angel fly in the midst of
14. 8 there followed another angel, saying, B.
14. 9 the third angel followed them, saying with
14. 10 in the presence of the holy angels, and in
14. 15, 17 another angel came out of the temple
14. 18 another angel came out from the altar
14. 19 the angel thrust in his sickle into the
15. 1 I saw another sign..seven angels having
15. 6 the seven angels came out of the temple
15. 7 one..gave unto the seven angels seven
15. 8 the seven plagues of the seven angels
16. 1 I heard..saying to the seven angels
16. 3, 4, 8, 10, 12 [angel] poured out his vial upon
16. 5 I heard the angel of the waters say, Thou
16. 17 the seventh [angel] poured out his vial into
17. 1 there came one of the seven angels which
17. 7 the angel said unto me, Wherefore didst
18. 1 after these things I saw another angel come
18. 21 a mighty angel took up a stone like a
19. 17 I saw an angel standing in the sun; and
20. 1 I saw an angel come down from heaven
21. 9 there came..one of the seven angels which
21. 12 [at the gates twelve angels, and names]
21. 17 the measure of a man, that is, of the angel
22. 6 the Lord God..sent his angel to shew
22. 8 to worship before the feet of the angel
22. 16 I Jesus have sent mine angel to testify unto

ANGELS —

1. *God, a god, judge,* אֱלֹהִים *elohim.*
Psa. 8. 5 made him a little lower than the angels

2. *Repetition,* שִׁנְאָן *shinan.* [*Cf.* margin.]
Psa. 68. 17 chariots of God..thousands of angels

ANGELS, equal unto the—

Equal or like to the angels, ἰσάγγελος *isaggelos.*
Luke 20. 36 they are equal unto the angels; and are

ANGER —

1. *Anger, snorting,* אַף *aph.*
Gen. 27. 45 Until thy brother's anger turn away from
30. 2 Jacob's anger was kindled against Rachel
44. 18 let not thine anger burn against thy servant
49. 6 in their anger they slew a man, and in
49. 7 Cursed (be) their anger, for..fierce; and
Exod. 4. 14 the anger of the LORD was kindled against
11. 8 went out from Pharaoh in a great anger
32. 19 Moses' anger waxed hot, and he cast the
32. 22 Let not the anger of my lord wax hot
Num. 11. 1 the LORD heard (it); and his anger was
11. 10 the anger of the LORD was kindled greatly
12. 9 the anger of the LORD was kindled against
22. 22 God's anger was kindled because he went
22. 27 Balaam's anger was kindled, and he smote
24. 10 Balak's anger was kindled against Balaam
25. 3 the anger of the LORD was kindled against
25. 4 the fierce anger of the LORD may be turned
32. 10 the LORD's anger was kindled the same time
32. 13 the LORD's anger was kindled against Israel
32. 14 to augment yet the fierce anger of the LORD
Deut. 6. 15 lest the anger of the LORD thy God be
7. 4 so will the anger of the LORD be kindled
9. 19 I was afraid of the anger and hot displeasure
13. 17 that the LORD may turn from..his anger
29. 20 the anger of the LORD..shall smoke against
29. 23 which the LORD overthrew in his anger
Deut. 29. 24 what..the heat of this great anger?
29. 27 the anger of the LORD was kindled against
29. 28 rooted them out of their land in anger
31. 17 my anger shall be kindled against them
32. 22 a fire is kindled in mine anger
Josh. 7. 1 the anger of the LORD was kindled against
7. 26 So the LORD turned from..his anger
23. 16 shall the anger of the LORD be kindled
Judg. 2. 14 the anger of the LORD was hot against Israel
2. 20 the anger of the LORD was hot against Israel
3. 8 the anger of the LORD was hot against Israel
6. 39 Let not thine anger be hot against me
9. 30 when Zebul..heard..his anger was kindled
10. 7 the anger of the LORD was hot against Israel
14. 19 his anger was kindled, and he went up
1 Sa. 11. 6 and his anger was kindled greatly
17. 28 Eliab's anger was kindled against David
20. 30 Saul's anger was kindled against Jonathan
20. 34 Jonathan arose from the table in fierce anger
2 Sa. 6. 7 the anger of the LORD was kindled against
12. 5 David's anger was greatly kindled against
24. 1 again the anger of the LORD was kindled
2 Ki. 13. 3 the anger of the LORD was kindled against
23. 26 his anger was kindled against Judah
24. 20 through the anger of the LORD it came to
1 Ch. 13. 10 the anger of the LORD was kindled against
2 Ch. 25. 10 their anger was greatly kindled against
25. 10 and they returned home in great anger
25. 15 the anger of the LORD was kindled against
Neh. 9. 17 a God ready to pardon..slow to anger
Job 9. 5 which overturneth them in his anger
9. 13 God will not withdraw his anger
18. 4 He teareth himself in his anger
21. 17 distributeth sorrows in his anger
35. 15 he hath visited in his anger; yet he
Psa. 6. 1 O LORD, rebuke me not in thine anger
7. 6 Arise, O LORD, in thine anger, lift up
27. 9 put not thy servant away in anger
30. 5 his anger..a moment; in his favour (is) life
37. 8 Cease from anger, and forsake wrath
56. 7 in..anger cast down the people, O God
69. 24 let thy wrathful anger take hold of them
74. 1 doth thine anger smoke against the sheep
77. 9 hath he in anger shut up his tender mercies?
78. 21 and anger also came up against Israel
78. 38 many a time turned he his anger away
78. 49 He cast upon them..his anger, wrath
78. 50 He made a way to his anger; he spared
85. 3 thou hast turned..from..thine anger
85. 5 Wilt thou be angry with us for ever?
90. 7 we are consumed by thine anger, and by
90. 11 Who knoweth the power of thine anger?
103. 8 The LORD (is) merciful and..slow to anger
145. 8 The LORD (is) gracious..slow to anger, and of
Prov. 15. 1 but grievous words stir up anger
15. 18 (he that is) slow to anger appeaseth strife
16. 32 slow to anger (is) better than the mighty
19. 11 The discretion of a man deferreth his anger
21. 14 A gift in secret pacifieth anger
27. 4 Wrath (is) cruel, and anger (is) outrageous
Isa. 5. 25 Therefore is the anger of the LORD kindled
5. 25 For all this his anger is not turned away
7. 4 for the fierce anger of Rezin with Syria
9. 12, 17, 21 For all this his anger is not turned
10. 4 For all this his anger is not turned away
10. 5 O Assyrian, the rod of mine anger, and
10. 25 and mine anger in their destruction
12. 1 though thou wast angry with me, thine anger
13. 3 called my mighty ones for mine anger
13. 9 both with wrath and fierce anger
13. 13 and in the day of his fierce anger
14. 6 he that ruled the nations in anger
30. 27 Behold..burning..his anger, and the burden
30. 30 with the indignation of (his) anger
42. 25 poured upon him the fury of his anger
48. 9 my name's sake will I defer mine anger
63. 3 I will tread them in mine anger
63. 6 I will tread down the people in mine anger
66. 15 LORD will..render his anger with fury
Jer. 2. 35 surely his anger shall turn from me
4. 8 the fierce anger of the LORD is not turned
4. 26 were broken down..by his fierce anger
7. 20 mine anger..shall be poured out upon this
10. 24 O LORD, correct me..not in thine anger
12. 13 because of the fierce anger of the LORD
15. 14 for a fire is kindled in mine anger
17. 4 for ye have kindled a fire in mine anger
18. 23 with them in the time of thine anger
21. 5 I myself will fight..even in anger
23. 20 The anger of the LORD shall not return
25. 37 because of the fierce anger of the LORD
25. 38 desolate..because of his fierce anger
30. 24 fierce anger of the LORD shall not return
32. 31 a provocation of mine anger and of my
32. 37 I have driven them in mine anger, and in
33. 5 whom I have slain in mine anger and in
36. 7 great (is) the anger and the fury that the
42. 18 mine anger and my fury hath been poured
44. 6 my fury and mine anger was poured forth
49. 37 will bring..my fierce anger, saith the LORD
51. 45 deliver..from the fierce anger of the LORD
52. 3 through the anger of the LORD it came
Lam. 1. 12 LORD hath afflicted..in. his fierce anger
2. 1 covered the daughter of Zion..in his anger
2. 1 remembered not his footstool in..anger!
2. 3 He hath cut off in..fierce anger
2. 6 hath despised..in..his anger the king
2. 21 hast slain..in the day of thine anger
2. 22 so that in the day of the LORD's anger
3. 43 Thou hast covered with anger
3. 66 Persecute and destroy them in anger
4. 11 he hath poured out his fierce anger
Eze. 5. 13 Thus shall mine anger be accomplished
5. 15 I shall execute judgments in thee in anger
7. 3 I will send mine anger upon thee
7. 8 and accomplish mine anger upon thee
13. 13 and..an overflowing..in mine anger
20. 8 I will..accomplish my anger against them
20. 21 I would..accomplish my anger against
22. 20 so will I gather..in mine anger
25. 14 they shall do..according to mine anger
35. 11 I will even do according to thine anger
43. 8 I have consumed them in mine anger
Dan. 9. 16 let thine anger and thy fury be turned
11. 20 he shall be destroyed, neither in anger
Hos. 8. 5 mine anger is kindled against them
11. 9 I will not execute the..of mine anger
13. 11 I gave thee a king in mine anger
14. 4 mine anger is turned away from him
Joel 2. 13 gracious and merciful, slow to anger
Amos 1. 11 and his anger did tear perpetually
Jon. 3. 9 and turn away from his fierce anger
4. 2 gracious God, and merciful, slow to anger
Mic. 5. 15 I will execute vengeance in anger
7. 18 he retaineth not his anger for ever
Nah. 1. 3 The LORD (is) slow to anger, and great in
1. 6 who can..in the fierceness of his anger?
Hab. 3. 8 (was) thine anger against the rivers?
3. 12 thou didst thresh the heathen in anger
Zeph. 2. 2 fierce anger..before the..anger come
2. 3 shall be hid in the day of the LORD's anger
3. 8 to pour upon them..all my fierce anger
Zech. 10. 3 Mine anger was kindled against the

2. *Indignation,* זַעַם *zaam.*
Psa. 38. 3 no soundness..because of thine anger

3. *Fury, heat,* חֵמָה *chemah.*
Esth. 1. 12 the king..his anger burned in him

4. *Anger, sadness,* כַּעַס *kaas.*
Psa. 85. 4 and cause thine anger toward us to cease
Eccl. 7. 9 for anger resteth in the bosom of fools

5. *Passing over, transgression,* עֶבְרָה *ebrah.*
Prov. 22. 8 and the rod of his anger shall fail

6. *Face, countenance,* פָּנִים *panim.*
Psa. 21. 9 make them..in the time of thine anger
Jer. 3. 12 I will not cause mine anger to fall upon
Lam. 4. 16 The anger of the LORD hath divided them

7. *Spirit,* רוּחַ *ruach.*
Judg. 8. 3 their anger was abated toward him

8. *Anger,* ὀργή *orgē.*
Mark 3. 5 when he had looked..with anger, being
Eph. 4. 31 Let all bitterness, and wrath, and anger
Col. 3. 8 ye also put off all these; anger, wrath

ANGER to—

1. *To make wroth,* קָצַף *qatsaph,* 5.
Psa. 106. 32 They angered..at the waters of strife

2. *Make angry,* παροργίζω *parorgizō.*
Rom. 10. 19 by a foolish nation will I anger you

ANGLE—

Angle, hook, חַכָּה *chakkah.*
Isa. 19. 8 all they that cast angle into the brooks
Hab. 1. 15 They take up all of them with the angle

ANGRY—

1. *To be indignant,* זָעַם *zaam,* 2.
Prov. 25. 23 an angry countenance a backbiting tongue

2. *Anger, sadness,* כַּעַס *kaas.*
Prov. 21. 19 with a contentious and an angry woman

3. *Bitter of soul,* מַר נֶפֶשׁ *mar nephesh.*
Judg. 18. 25 lest angry fellows run upon thee

ANGRY, to be —

1. *To snort, be angry,* אָנַף *anaph.*
1 Ki. 8. 46 If they sin..and thou be angry with them
2 Ch. 6. 36 If they sin..and thou be angry with them
Ezra 9. 14 wouldst not thou be angry with us till
Psa. 2. 12 Kiss the Son, lest he be angry
79. 5 How long, LORD? wilt thou be angry
85. 5 Wilt thou be angry with us for ever?
Isa. 12. 1 though thou wast angry with me

2. *To show oneself angry,* אָנַף *anaph,* 7.
Deut. 1. 37 LORD was angry with me for your sakes
4. 21 LORD was angry with me for your sakes
9. 8 so that the LORD was angry with you
9. 20 the LORD was very angry with Aaron
1 Ki. 11. 9 the LORD was angry with Solomon
2 Ki. 17. 18 the LORD was very angry with Israel

3. *Anger,* אַף *aph.*
Psa. 76. 7 who may stand..when..thou art angry

4. *To be angry,* בְּנַס *benas.*
Dan. 2. 12 For this cause the king was angry

5. *To burn, be heated,* חָרָה *charah.*
Gen. 18. 30, 32 Oh let not the LORD be angry
45. 5 be not..angry with yourselves
2 Sa. 19. 42 wherefore then be ye angry for this
Neh. 5. 6 I was very angry when I heard their cry
Jon. 4. 1 Jonah exceedingly, and he was very angry
4. 4, 9 Doest thou well to be angry for the
4. 9 I do well to be angry..unto death

6. *To be burning, burnt,* חָרַר *charar,* 2.
Song 1. 6 my mother's children were angry with me

7. *To be angry, sad,* כָּעַס *kaas.*
Eccl. 7. 9 Be not hasty in thy spirit to be angry
Eze. 16. 42 be quiet, and will be no more angry

8. *To smoke,* עָשַׁן *ashan.*
Psa. 80. 4 wilt thou be angry against the prayer
9. *To be wroth,* קָצַף *qatsaph.*
Lev. 10. 16 he was angry with Eleazar and Ithamar
Eccl. 5. 6 wherefore should God be angry at thy
10. *To be angry,* ὀργίζομαι *orgizomai.*
Matt. 5. 22 I say unto you, That whosoever is angry
Luke 14. 21 the master of the house being angry said
15. 28 And he was angry, and would not go in
Eph. 4. 26 Be ye angry, and sin not: let not the
Rev. 11. 18 the nations were angry, and thy wrath is
11. *To be full of bile,* χολάω *cholaō.*
John 7. 23 are ye angry at me, because I have made

ANGRY, soon —
Prone to anger, ὀργίλος *orgilos.*
Titus 1. 7 a bishop must be..not soon angry

ANGUISH—
1. *Straitness, anguish,* מָצוֹק *matsoq.*
Psa. 119. 143 Trouble and anguish have taken hold on
2. *Straitness, anguish,* מְצוּקָה *metsuqah.*
Job 15. 24 Trouble and anguish shall make him
3. *Straitness, anguish,* צוּקָה *tsuqah.*
Prov. 1. 27 when distress and anguish cometh upon
Isa. 8. 22 behold trouble and..dimness of anguish
30. 6 into the land of trouble and anguish
4. *Straitness, distress,* צַר *tsar.*
Job 7. 11 I will speak in the anguish of my spirit
5. *Straitness, distress,* צָרָה *tsarah.*
Gen. 42. 21 in that we saw the anguish of his soul
Jer. 4. 31 the anguish as of her that bringeth forth
6. 24 anguish hath taken hold of us
49. 24 anguish and sorrows have taken her
50. 43 anguish took hold of him..pangs
6. *Straitness, distress,* קֹצֶר *qotser.*
Exod. 6. 9 they hearkened not..for anguish of spirit
7. *Confusion,* שָׁבָץ *shabats.*
2 Sa. 1. 9 anguish is come upon me, because
8. *Pressure,* θλῖψις *thlipsis.*
John 16. 21 she remembereth no more the anguish
9. *Straitness, strait place,* στενοχωρία *stenochōria.*
Rom. 2. 9 Tribulation and anguish, upon every soul
10. *Holding together, anguish,* συνοχή *sunochē.*
2 Co. 2. 4 out of much affliction and anguish of

ANGUISH, to be in —
To be pained, חוּל *chul.*
Deut. 2. 25 and be in anguish because of thee

A-NI'-AM, אֲנִיעָם *lamentation of the people.*
A son of Shemidah, a Manassehite, B.C. 1400.
1 Ch. 7. 19 And the sons of Shemidah were..A.

A'-NIM, עָנִים *fountains.*
A city among the mountains at the N.W. of Judah.
Josh. 15. 50 And Anab, and Eshtemoh, and A.

ANISE—
Anise, dill, ἄνηθον *anēthon.*
Matt 23. 23 ye pay tithe of mint and anise and

AN'-NA, Ἄννα *grace.*
A prophetess of the tribe of Asher at the time of the birth of Jesus.
Luke 2. 36 And there was one A., a prophetess, the

AN'-NAS, Ἄννας *grace of Jah.*
A Jewish high-priest, the son of Seth, and appointed high-priest in his 37th year (A.D. 7) by Quirinus, the imperial governor of Syria, after the battle of Actium, but was obliged to resign at the beginning of the reign of Tiberius (A.D. 14).
Luke 3. 2 A. and Caiaphas being the high priests
John 18. 13 And led him away to A. first
18. 24 Now A. had sent him bound unto Caiaphas
Acts 4. 6 And A. the high priest..were gathered

ANOINT, to —
1. *To fatten,* דָּשֵׁן *dashen,* 3.
Psa. 23. 5 thou anointest my head with oil
2. *To smear, anoint,* מָשַׁח *mashach.*
Gen. 31. 13 where thou anointedst the pillar
Exod 28. 41 his sons with him; and shall anoint them
29. 7 pour (it) upon his head, and anoint him
29. 36 thou shalt anoint it, to sanctify it
30. 26 thou shalt anoint the tabernacle
30. 30 thou shalt anoint Aaron and his sons
40. 9 thou shalt..anoint the tabernacle
40. 10 thou shalt anoint the altar of the burnt
40. 11 thou shalt anoint the laver and his foot
40. 13 thou shalt put upon Aaron..and anoint
40. 15 shalt anoint them, as thou didst anoint
Lev. 7. 36 in the day that he anointed them, (by) a
8. 10 Moses..anointed the tabernacle and all
8. 11 anointed the altar and all his vessels
8. 12 and anointed him, to sanctify him
16. 32 the priest, whom he shall anoint, and
Num. 7. 1 had anointed it, and sanctified it
7. 1 had anointed them, and sanctified them
Judg. 9. 8 The trees went forth..to anoint a king
9. 15 If in truth ye anoint me king over you
1 Sa. 9. 16 thou shalt anoint him (to be) captain
10. 1 (Is it) not because..LORD hath anointed
15. 1 LORD sent me to anoint thee (to be) king
15. 17 the LORD anointed thee king over Israel
16. 3 thou shalt anoint unto me..whom I name
16. 12 the LORD said, Arise, anoint him: for
16. 13 anointed him in the midst of his brethren
2 Sa. 2. 4 there they anointed David king over the
2. 7 the house of Judah have anointed me king
5. 3 they anointed David king over Israel
5. 17 heard that they had anointed David king
12. 7 I anointed thee king over Israel, and I
19. 10 Absalom, whom we anointed over us
1 Ki. 1. 34 let Zadok..anoint him there king
1. 39 Zadok the priest..anointed Solomon
1. 45 have anointed him king in Gihon
5. 1 heard that they had anointed him king
19. 15 anoint Hazael..king over Syria
19. 16 shalt thou anoint..shalt thou anoint
2 Ki. 9. 3, 6, 12, I have anointed thee king over
11. 12 made him king, and anointed him
23. 30 anointed him, and made him king
1 Ch. 11. 3 they anointed David king over Israel
29. 22 anointed..unto the LORD..the chief
2 Ch. 22. 7 whom the LORD had anointed to cut off
23. 11 Jehoiada and his sons anointed him
Psa. 45. 7 God, hath anointed thee with the oil of
89. 20 with my holy oil have I anointed him
Isa. 21. 5 arise, ye princes..anoint the shield
61. 1 the LORD hath anointed me to preach
Dan. 9. 24 and to anoint the most Holy
3. *To pour out,* סוּךְ *suk.*
Deut 28. 40 but thou shalt not anoint..with the oil
Ruth 3. 3 Wash thyself therefore, and anoint thee
2 Ch. 28. 15 gave them to eat..and anointed them
Eze. 16. 9 from thee, and I anointed thee with oil
Mic. 6. 15 but thou shalt not anoint thee with oil
4. *To anoint,* ἀλείφω *aleiphō.*
Matt. 6. 17 thou, when thou fastest, anoint thine head
Mark 6. 13 anointed with oil many that were sick
16. 1 that they might come and anoint him
Luke 7. 38 kissed his feet, and anointed (them) with
7. 46 thou didst not anoint..hath anointed
John 11. 2 It was (that) Mary which anointed the
12. 3 anointed the feet of Jesus, and wiped his
Jas. 5. 14 anointing him with oil in the name of
5. *To rub in,* ἐγχρίω *egchriō.*
Rev. 3. 18 anoint thine eyes with eyesalve, that thou
6. *To rub on,* ἐπιχρίω ἐπί *epichriō epi.*
John 9. 6 he anointed the eyes of the blind man with
9. 11 A man that is called Jesus..anointed mine
7. *To anoint with aromatics,* μυρίζω *murizō.*
Mark 14. 8 she is come aforehand to anoint my body
8. *To rub,* χρίω *chriō.*
Luke 4. 18 he hath anointed me to preach the
Acts 4. 27 child Jesus, whom thou hast anointed
10. 38 How God anointed Jesus of Nazareth with
2 Co. 1. 21 he which..hath anointed us, (is) God
Heb. 1. 9 thy God; hath anointed thee with the

ANOINT self, to —
1. *To pour out,* סוּךְ *suk.*
2 Sa. 14. 2 anoint not thyself with oil, but be as a
Dan. 10. 3 neither did I anoint myself at all, till
2. *To cause to pour out,* סוּךְ *suk,* 5.
2 Sa. 12. 20 and washed, and anointed (himself)
3. *To smear, anoint,* מָשַׁח *mashach.*
Amos 6. 6 anoint themselves with the chief ointms.

ANOINTED —
1. *Smeared, anointed,* מִמְשַׁח *mimshach.*
Eze. 28. 14 Thou (art) the anointed cherub that
2. *Smeared, anointed,* מָשִׁיחַ *mashiach.*
Lev. 4. 3 If the priest that is anointed do sin
4. 5, 16 And the priest that is anointed shall
6. 22 that is anointed in his stead shall offer it
1 Sa. 2. 10 and exalt the horn of his anointed
2. 35 he shall walk before mine anointed for
12. 3 here I (am)..and before his anointed
12. 5 and his anointed (is) witness this day
16. 6 Surely the LORD'S anointed (is) before him
24. 6 unto my master, the LORD'S anointed
24. 6 seeing he (is) the anointed of the LORD
24. 10 for he (is) the LORD'S anointed
26. 9 his hand against the LORD'S anointed
26. 11 mine hand against the LORD'S anointed
26. 16 ye have not kept..the LORD'S anointed
26. 23 mine hand against the LORD'S anointed
2 Sa. 1. 14 thine hand to destroy the LORD'S anointed
1. 16 saying, I have slain the LORD'S anointed
1. 21 the shield of Saul..not..anointed with oil
19. 21 because he cursed the LORD'S anointed
22. 51 sheweth mercy to his anointed, unto David
23. 1 the anointed of the God of Jacob, and the
1 Ch. 16. 22 Touch not mine anointed, and do my
2 Ch. 6. 42 turn not away the face of thine anointed
Psa. 2. 2 the LORD, and against his anointed
18. 50 sheweth mercy to his anointed, to David
20. 6 that the LORD saveth his anointed
28. 8 the saving strength of his anointed
84. 9 look upon the face of thine anointed
89. 38 hast been wroth with thine anointed
89. 51 reproached the footsteps of thine anointed
105. 15 Touch not mine anointed, and do my
132. 10 turn not away..thine anointed
132. 17 ordained a lamp for mine anointed
Isa. 45. 1 Thus saith the LORD to his anointed
Lam. 4. 20 the anointed of the LORD, was taken in
Hab. 3. 13 for salvation with thine anointed
3. *To anoint, smear,* מָשַׁח *mashach.*
Exod 29. 2 and wafers unleavened anointed with oil
Lev. 2. 4 or unleavened wafers anointed with oil
7. 12 and unleavened wafers anointed with oil
Num. 3. 3 the priests which were anointed, whom he
6. 15 wafers of unleavened bread anointed with
2 Sa. 3. 39 I (am) this day weak, though anointed king

ANOINTED one —
Son of the oil, shining one, בֶּן־הַיִּצְהָר *ben hay-yitshar.*
Zech. 4. 14 These (are) the two anointed ones, that

ANOINTED, to be —
1. *To mix, anoint,* בָּלַל *balal.*
Psa. 92. 10 I shall be anointed with fresh oil
2. *To smear, anoint,* מָשַׁח *mashach.*
Num 35. 25 which was anointed with the holy oil
3. *To be smeared, anointed,* מָשַׁח *mashach,* 2.
Lev. 6. 20 Aaron..in the day when he is anointed
Num. 7. 10 altar in the day that it was anointed
7. 84 altar, in the day when it was anointed
7. 88 altar, after that it was anointed
1 Ch. 14. 8 heard that David was anointed king over
4. *Smearing, anointing,* מָשְׁחָה *moshchah.*
Exod 29. 29 to be anointed therein, and to be consec.

ANOINTING —
1. *Smearing, anointing,* מִשְׁחָה *mishchah.*
Exod 25. 6 for the light, spices for anointing oil
29. 7 Then shalt thou take the anointing oil
29. 21 thou shalt take of the..anointing oil
30. 25 it shall be an holy anointing oil
30. 31 This shall be an holy anointing oil unto
31. 11 the anointing oil, and sweet incense
35. 8 spices for anointing oil, and for the
35. 15 the anointing oil, and the sweet
35. 28 for the anointing oil, and for the
37. 29 he made the holy anointing oil, and the
39. 38 the golden altar, and the anointing oil
40. 9 shalt take the anointing oil, and anoint
Lev. 7. 35 This..of the anointing of Aaron
7. 35 and of the anointing of his sons
8. 2 the garments, and the anointing oil
8. 10 Moses took the anointing oil, and anointed
8. 12 he poured of the anointing oil upon
8. 30 Moses took of the anointing oil, and of
10. 7 the anointing oil of the LORD (is) upon you
21. 10 upon whose head the anointing oil was
21. 12 crown of the anointing oil of his God (is)
Num. 4. 16 meat-offering, and the anointing oil
2. *Smearing,* מָשְׁחָה *moshchah.*
Exod 40. 15 their anointing shall surely be an everlg.
Num 18. 8 given them by reason of the anointing
3. *Oil,* שֶׁמֶן *shemen.*
Isa. 10. 27 destroyed because of the anointing
4. *Anointing, rubbing in,* χρίσμα *chrisma.*
1 Jo. 2. 27 But the anointing..the same anointing

ANON —
1. *Straightway, directly,* εὐθέως *eutheōs.*
Mark 1. 30 fever, and anon they tell him of her
2. *Straight, direct,* εὐθύς *euthus.*
Matt 13. 20 word, and [anon] with joy receiveth it

ANOTHER —
1. *A man, human being,* אָדָם *adam.*
Eccl. 8. 9 one man ruleth over another to his own
2. *One,* אֶחָד *echad.*
Exod 26. 19, 21, 25 two sockets under another board
36. 10 one unto another..one unto another
36. 12 the loops held one..to another
36. 13 coupled the curtains one unto another
36. 22 equally distant one from another
36. 24, 26 two sockets under another board
37. 8 another cherub on the..end on that side
37. 19 bowls made like almonds in another
Deut 21. 15 wives, one beloved, and another hated
Judg. 9. 37 another company come along by the plain
16. 7, 11 I be weak, and be as another man
1 Sa. 10. 3 another carrying three..another carrying
13. 18 another company..and another company
1 Ki. 18. 6 Obadiah went another way by himself
Job 41. 16 One is so near to another, that no
Eze. 10. 9 another wheel by another cherub: and
17. 7 There was also another great eagle with
19. 5 then she took another of her whelps
33. 30 speak one to another, every one to his
37. 16 take another stick, and write upon it
37. 17 join them one to another into one stick
40. 26, 49 one on this side, and another on that
41. 11 one door toward the north, and another
Dan. 8. 13 I heard one saint speaking, and another
Amos 4. 7 I caused it..not to rain upon another city
Zech. 8. 21 inhabitants of one ..shall go to another
3. *A brother,* אָח *ach.*
Gen. 26. 31 they rose up..and sware one to another
37. 19 said one to another, Behold, this dreamer
42. 21 said one to another, We (are) verily guilty
42. 28 saying one to another, What (is) this..God
Exod 10. 23 They saw not one another, neither rose
16. 15 said one to another, It (is) manna: for
25. 20 their faces (shall look) one to another
37. 9 seat, with their faces one to another
Lev. 7. 10 all the sons..have, one..as another

Lev. 25. 14 ye shall not oppress one another
25. 46 ye shall not rule one over another
26. 37 they shall fall one upon another, as it
Num 14. 4 said one to another, Let us make a
Deut 25. 11 When men strive..one with another
2 Ki. 7. 6 said one to another, Lo, the king of Israel
1 Ch. 26. 12 chief men..wards one against another
Neh. 4. 19 upon the wall, one far from another
Job 41. 17 They are joined one to another, they stick
Jer. 13. 14 I will dash them one against another
25. 26 far and near, one with another, and all
Eze. 4. 17 be astonied one with another, and
24. 23 away..and mourn one toward another
47. 14 ye shall inherit it, one as well as another
Joel 2. 8 Neither shall one thrust another; they

4. *A sister*, אָחוֹת *achoth.*
Exod 26. 3 one to another..one to another
26. 5 the loops may take hold one of another
26. 17 tenons..set in order one against another
Eze. 1. 9 Their wings..joined one to another
3. 13 living creatures that touched one another

5. *Another*, אַחֵר *acher.*
Gen. 4. 25 For God..hath appointed me another seed
26. 21 they digged another well, and strove for
26. 22 he removed..and digged another well
29. 19 than that I should give her to another man
30. 24 The LORD shall add to me another son
37. 9 he dreamed yet another dream, and told
Exod 21. 10 If he take him another..her food, her
Lev. 27. 20 if he have sold the field to another man
Num 14. 24 because he had another spirit with him
23. 13 Come..with me unto another place, from
23. 27 Come..I will bring thee unto another place
36. 9 remove from..tribe to another tribe
Deut 20. 5 in the battle, and another man dedicate
20. 6 in the battle, and another man eat of it
20. 7 in the battle, and another man take her
24. 2 she may go and be another man's
28. 30 a wife, and another man shall lie with her
28. 32 thy daughters..given unto another people
29. 28 cast them into another land, as..this day
Judg. 2. 10 there arose another generation after them
Ruth 2. 8 Go not to glean in another field, neither
1 Sa. 10. 6 and shalt be turned into another man
10. 9 God gave him another heart: and all those
17. 30 he turned from him toward another, and
2 Sa. 18. 20 thou shalt bear tidings another day: but
18. 26 the watchman saw another man running
1 Ki. 7. 8 (had) another court within the porch
13. 10 So he went another way, and returned
20. 37 Then he found another man, and said
2 Ki. 1. 11 sent unto him another captain of fifty
7. 8 came again, and entered..another tent
1 Ch. 2. 26 Jerahmeel had also another wife, whose
16. 20 and from (one) kingdom to another people
2 Ch. 32. 5 and built up..another wall without
Esth. 4. 14 arise to the Jews from another place; but
Job 31. 8 let me sow, and let another eat; yea, let
31. 10 let my wife grind unto another, and let
Psa. 16. 4 multiplied (that) hasten (after) another
105. 13 they went from one nation to another
109. 8 be few; (and) let another take his office
Prov. 25. 9 and discover not a secret to another
Isa. 28. 11 with stammering lips and another tongue
42. 8 my glory will I not give to another
48. 11 I will not give my glory unto another
65. 15 and call his servants by another name
65. 22 They shall not build and another inhabit
65. 22 they shall not plant and another eat
Jer. 3. 1 she go from him, and become another
18. 4 so he made it again another vessel, as
22. 26 I will cast thee out..into another country
36. 28 Take thee again another roll, and write
36. 32 Then took Jeremiah another roll, and
Eze. 12. 3 shalt remove from thy place to another
Joel 1. 3 and their children another generation
Zech. 2. 3 another angel went out to meet him

6. *Another*, אָחֳרִי *ochori.*
Dan. 2. 39 another kingdom..another third kingdom
7. 5 another beast, a second, like to a bear
7. 6 I beheld, and lo another, like a leopard
7. 8 there came up among them another little

7. *Another*, אָחֳרָן *ochoran.*
Dan. 5. 17 give thy rewards to another; yet I will
7. 24 another shall rise after them; and he

8. *A man, individual*, אִישׁ *ish.*
1 Sa. 2. 25 If one man sin against another, the judge
Isa. 3. 5 shall be oppressed, every one by another
Eze. 1. 11 wings..(were) joined one to another, v. 9.
22. 11 another hath lewdly defiled..and another
Hos. 4. 4 let no man strive, nor reprove another

9. *A mortal man*, אֱנוֹשׁ *enosh.*
Job 13. 9 as one man mocketh another, do ye

10. *Revolution, generation*, דּוֹר *dor.*
Psa. 145. 4 One generation shall praise..to another

11. *A stranger*, זוּר *zur* (partic.).
Job 19. 27 mine eyes shall behold, and not another

12. *New moon. Sabbath.* חֹדֶשׁ *chodesh.* שַׁבָּת *shabbath.*
Isa. 66. 23 new moon to another, and..to another

13. *Instrument, vessel*, כְּלִי *keli.*
Esth. 1. 7 (the vessels..diverse one from another)

14. *Wing*, כָּנָף *kanaph.*
1 Ki. 6. 27 their wings touched one another in the

15. *Runner*, רָץ [*ruts*] (partic.).
Jer. 51. 31 One post shall run to meet another, and

16. *Announcer*, מַגִּיד [*nagad*] (5, partic.).
Jer. 51. 31 one messenger to meet another.

17. *Fellow countryman*, עָמִית *amith.*
Lev. 19. 11 Ye shall not..neither lie one to another
25. 17 Ye shall not therefore oppress one another

18. *Friend*, רֵעַ *rea.*
Gen. 11. 3 they said one to another, Go to, let us
11. 7 may not understand one another's speech
15. 10 and laid each piece one against another
31. 49 when we are absent one from another
43. 33 and the men marvelled one at another
Exod 18. 16 I judge between one and another, and I
21. 18 one smite another with a stone, or with
21. 35 if one man's ox hurt another's, that he die
Judg. 6. 29 said one to another, Who hath done this
10. 18 princes of Gilead said one to another
Ruth 3. 14 she rose up before one could know another
1 Sa. 10. 11 then the people said one to another, What
20. 41 one another, and wept one with another
2 Ki. 3. 23 the kings..have smitten one another
7. 3 said one to another, Why sit we here
7. 9 said one to another, We do not well: this
2 Ch. 20. 23 and..every one helped to destroy another
Esth. 9. 19, 22 day..sending portions one to another
Isa. 13. 8 they shall be amazed one at another
Jer. 46. 16 yea, one fell upon another: and they said
Mal. 3. 16 feared the LORD spake..one to another

19. *A female friend*, רְעוּת *reuth.*
Esth. 1. 19 king give her royal estate unto another
Zech 11. 9 rest eat every one the flesh of another

20. *Second*, שֵׁנִי *sheni.*
Num. 8. 8 another young bullock shalt thou take for
Neh. 3. 19 another piece over against the going up
3. 21 After him repaired Meremoth..another
3. 24 After him repaired Binnui..another piece
3. 27 After them the Tekoites repaired another
3. 30 After him repaired Hananiah..another
Eccl. 4. 10 alone when he falleth; for..not another

21. *Other, not the same*, ἄλλος *allos.*
Matt. 2. 12 into their own country another way
8. 9 to another, Come, and he cometh; and to
10. 23 you in this city, flee ye into [another]
13. 24, 31 Another parable put he forth unto
13. 33 Another parable spake he unto them
19. 9 shall marry another, committeth adultery
21. 33 Hear another parable: There was a certain
26. 71 he was gone out..another (maid) saw
Mark 10. 11 shall put away his wife and marry another
10. 12 be married to another, she committeth
12. 4 again he sent unto them another servant
12. 5 again he sent another; and him they
14. 19 [it I? and another (said, Is) it I?]
14. 58 within three days I will build another
Luke 7. 8 to another, Come, and he cometh; and to
7. 19 Art thou he..or look we for [another]?
7. 20 Art thou he..or look we for another?
John 5. 7 while I am coming, another steppeth
5. 32 There is another that beareth witness of
5. 43 if another shall come in his own name
14. 16 he shall give you another Comforter, that
18. 15 Peter followed Jesus..(so did) [another]
21. 18 another shall gird thee, and carry
1 Co. 3. 10 I have laid the foundation, and another
12. 8 to another the word of knowledge by the
12. 9 to another the gifts of healing by the
12. 10 To another..miracles; to another proph.
12. 10 to another..to another the interpretation
14. 30 If..be revealed to another that sitteth by
15. 39 another flesh..another of..another of
15. 41 another glory of the moon, and another
2 Co. 11. 4 he that cometh preacheth another Jesus
Gal. 1. 7 Which is not another; but there be some
Heb. 4. 8 would he not..have spoken of another
Rev. 6. 4 there went out another horse (that was)
7. 2 I saw another angel ascending from the
8. 3 another angel came and stood at the
10. 1 I saw [another] mighty angel come down
12. 3 there appeared another wonder in heaven
13. 11 I beheld another beast coming up out
14. 6 I saw [another] angel fly in the midst
14. 8 there followed another angel, saying
14. 15 another angel came out of the temple
14. 17 another angel came out of the temple
14. 18 another angel came out from the altar
15. 1 I saw another sign in heaven, great
16. 7 I heard [another] out of the altar say
18. 1 after these things I saw another angel
18. 4 I heard another voice from heaven, saying
20. 12 another book was opened, which is

22. *Another, the other*, ἕτερος *heteros.*
Matt. 8. 21 another of his disciples said unto him
11. 3 Art thou he..or do we look for another?
Mark 16. 12 [After that he appeared in another form]
Luke 6. 6 it came to pass also on another sabbath
9. 56 And they went to another village
9. 59 And he said unto another, follow me
9. 61 another also said, Lord, I will follow thee
14. 19 another said, I have bought five yoke
14. 20 another said, I have married a wife, and
14. 31 going to make war against another king
16. 7 Then said he to another, And how much
16. 18 putteth away his wife..marrieth another
19. 20 And another came, saying, Lord, behold
20. 11 again he sent another servant: and they
22. 58 after a little while another saw him
John 19. 37 again another scripture saith, They shall
Acts 1. 20 and his bishopric let another take
7. 18 Till another king arose, which knew not
Acts 12. 17 he departed, and went into another 13. 35.
17. 7 saying that there is another king
Rom. 2. 1 for wherein thou judgest another, thou
2. 21 Thou therefore which teachest another
7. 3 to another man..be married to another
7. 4 that ye should be married to another
7. 23 I see another law in my members, warring
13. 8 Owe no man..but to love one another
1 Co. 3. 4 another, I (am) of Apollos; are ye not
4. 6 be puffed up for one against another
6. 1 Dare any..a matter against another
10. 24 seek his own, but every man another's
12. 9 To another faith by the same Spirit
12. 10 to another (divers) kinds of tongues 15. 40
2 Co. 11. 4 ye receive another spirit..or another
Gal. 1. 6 the grace of Christ unto another gospel
6. 4 rejoicing in himself..not in another
Heb. 7. 11 further need (was there) that ano. 5. 6
7. 13 things are spoken pertaineth to another
7. 15 after the similitude of..ariseth another
Jas. 2. 25 and had sent (them) out another way?
4. 12 who art thou that judgest [another]?
[*See also* As well as, compassion, feign, justle, look, one, other, performing, see.]

ANOTHER man —

1. *Another*, אַחֵר *acher.*
Exod 22. 5 shall feed in another man's field; of the
Neh. 5. 5 for other men have our lands and viney.

2. *A stranger*, זוּר *zur.* (partic.).
Prov. 27. 2 Let another man praise thee, and not

ANOTHER man's —

Belonging to another, ἀλλότριος *allotrios.*
Luke 16. 12 faithful in that which is another man's
Rom 14. 4 Who art thou that judgest another man's
15. 20 lest I should build upon another man's
2 Co. 10. 15 Not boasting..of other men's labours
10. 16 not to boast in another man's li. 1 Ti. 5. 22.

Another, other, ἄλλος *allos* 1 Co. 10. 29.

ANOTHER nation, one of —

Of another tribe, ἀλλόφυλος *allophulos.*
Acts 10. 28 or come unto one of another nation: but

ANOTHER place, that come from —

Strange, זוּר *zur.* (partic.).
Jer. 18. 14 waters that come from another place be

ANSWER —

1. *Saying*, אֵמֶר *emer.*
Judg. 5. 29 yea, she returned answer to herself

2. *Word*, דָּבָר *dabar.*
2 Sa. 24. 13 see what answer I shall return to him
2 Ch. 10. 6 What counsel give ye..to return answer
10. 9 What advice give ye that we may..answer
Prov 24. 26 kiss..lips that giveth a right answer
Jer. 44. 20 which had given him..answer, saying
[*See also* 1 Sa. 17. 30; 1 Ki. 12. 6, 9; Neh. 2. 20; Prov. 27. 11.]

3. *Answer*, מַעֲנֶה *maaneh.*
Job 32. 3 because they had found no answer, and
32. 5 no answer in the mouth of..three men
Prov. 15. 1 A soft answer turneth away wrath: but
15. 23 A man hath joy by the answer of his
16. 1 the answer of the tongue, (is) from the
29. 19 though he understand he will not answer
Mic. 3. 7 ashamed..for (there is) no answer of God

4. *Matter, word*, פִּתְגָם *pithgam.*
Ezra 4. 17 (Then) sent the king an answer unto Re.
5. 11 thus they returned us answer, saying, We

5. *Answer, response*, תְּשׁוּבָה *teshubah.*
Job 21. 34 seeing in your answers there remaineth
34. 36 Job may be tried..because of..answers

6. *Word*, מִלָּה *millah.*
Job 35. 4 I will answer thee, and thy companions

7. *An answer*, ἀπόκρισις *apokrisis.*
Luke 2. 47 And all..were astonished at his..answers
20. 26 they marvelled at his answer, and held
John 1. 22 Who art thou? that we may give an answer
19. 9 But Jesus gave him no answer

8. *An apology*, ἀπολογία *apologia.*
1 Co. 9. 3 Mine answer to them that do examine
2 Ti. 4. 16 At my first answer no man stood with me
1 Pe. 3. 15 ready always to (give) an answer to every

9. *An asking about*, ἐπερώτημα *eperōtēma.*
1 Pe. 3. 21 the answer of a good conscience toward

ANSWER, to —

1. *To say*, אָמַר *amar.*
Gen. 43. 28 they answered, Thy servant our father
Josh 2. 14 the men answered her, Our life for your's
4. 7 ye shall answer them, That the waters
15. 19 Who answered, Give me a blessing; for
17. 15 Joshua answered them, If thou (be) a
Judg. 8. 18 they answered, As thou..so..they; each
8. 25 they answered, We will willingly give
11. 13 the king..answered unto the messengers
15. 6 Who hath done this? And they answered
15. 10 they answered, To bind Samson are we
Ruth 2. 4 they answered him, The LORD bless thee
3. 9 she answered, I (am) Ruth thine handm.
1 Sa. 2. 16 he would answer him..but thou shalt
3. 4 LORD called Samuel: and he answered
3. 6 he answered, I called not, my son; lie
3. 10 Samuel answered, Speak; for thy servant
3. 16 Samuel, my son. And he answered, Here
5. 8 they answered, Let the ark of the God

1 Sa. 6. 4 They answered, Five golden emerods
10. 22 LORD answered, Behold, he hath hid
11. 2 Nahash the Ammonite answered them
12. 5 And they answered, (He is) witness
14. 44 Saul answered, God do so and more also
17. 27 the people answered him after this
17. 58 David answered, (I am) the son of thy
19. 17 Michal answered Saul, He said unto me
22. 12 And he answered, Here I (am), my lord
30. 8 he answered him, Pursue: for thou shalt
2 Sa. 1. 4 he answered, That the people are fled
1. 7 And I answered, Here (am) I
1. 8 And I answered him, I (am) an Amalekite
1. 13 he answered, I (am) the son of a stranger
2. 20 (Art) thou Asahel? And he answered, I
9. 6 And he answered, Behold thy servant!
13. 12 she answered him Nay, my brother, do
14. 5 she answered, I (am) indeed a widow
14. 32 Absalom answered Joab, Behold, I sent
18. 3 the people answered, Thou shalt not go
18. 29 Ahimaaz answered, When Joab sent the
18. 32 Cushi answered, The enemies of my lord
19. 26 he answered, My lord, O king, my servant
19. 38 the king answered, Chimham shall go
20. 17 And he answered.. And he answered
21. 1 the LORD answered, (It is) for Saul, and
21. 5 they answered the king, The man that
1 Ki. 9. 9 they shall answer, Because they forsook
11. 22 he answered, Nothing: howbeit let me
18. 8 he answered him, I (am): go, tell thy
18. 18 he answered, I have not troubled Israel
20. 14 Who shall order the battle? And he ans.
21. 6 he answered, I will not give thee my
21. 20 he answered, I have found.. because
22. 15 he answered him, Go, and prosper: for
2 Ki. 1. 8 they answered him.. an hairy man, and
2. 5 he answered, Yea, I know (it); hold ye
3. 8 he answered, The way through the
4. 13 she answered, I dwell among mine own
4. 14 Gehazi answered, Verily she hath no
4. 26 well with the child.. she answered, (It is)
6. 2 Let us go, we pray thee.. And he answered
6. 3 go with thy servants. And he answered
6. 16 he answered Fear not: for they that (be)
6. 22 he answered, Thou shalt not smite
6. 28 She answered, This woman said unto me
8. 12 he answered, Because I know the evil
8. 13 Elisha answered, The LORD hath shewed
8. 14 he answered, He told me.. thou shouldest
9. 19 Jehu answered, What hast thou to do
9. 22 (Is it) peace, Jehu? And he answered
10. 13 they answered, We (are) the brethren of
10. 15 Jehonadab answered, It is. If it be, give
20. 10 Hezekiah answered, It is a light thing
20. 15 Hezekiah answered, All.. that (are) in
1 Ch. 21. 3 Joab answered, The LORD make his
2 Ch. 2. 11 Huram the king of Tyre answered in
10. 10 Thus shalt thou answer the people that
18. 3 he answered him, I.. as thou.. and my
25. 9 the man of God answered, The LORD is
31. 10 Azariah the chief priest.. answered him
34. 23 she answered them, Thus saith the LORD
Esth. 1. 16 Memucan answered before the king and
5. 4 Esther answered, If.. good unto the king
6. 7 Haman answered the king, For the man
7. 5 Ahasuerus answered and said unto Esther
Isa. 6. 11 he answered, Until the cities be wasted
39. 4 Hezekiah answered, All that (is) in mine
Jer. 5. 19 then shalt thou answer them, Like as
22. 9 they shall answer, Because they have
36. 18 Baruch answered them, He pronounced
Eze. 21. 7 thou shalt answer, For the tidings
24. 20 I answered them, The word of the LORD
37. 3 And I answered, O Lord GOD, thou
Zech. 1. 19 he answered me, These (are) the horns
4. 13 he answered me and said, Knowest thou
5. 2 I answered, I see a flying roll; the length
13. 6 he shall answer, (Those) with which I

2. *To speak*, דָּבַר *dabar*, 3.
2 Ch. 10. 14 answered them after the advice of the

3. *To make known*, יָדַע *yada*, 5.
Job 38. 3 I will demand of thee, and answer thou

4. *To answer*, עָנָה *anah*.
Gen. 18. 27 Abraham answered and said, Behold now
23. 5 the children of Heth answered Abraham
23. 10 Ephron the Hittite answered Abraham
23. 14 Ephron answered Abraham, saying unto
24. 50 Laban and Bethuel answered and said
27. 37 Isaac answered and said unto Esau
27. 39 Isaac his father answered and said unto
30. 33 So shall my righteousness answer for me
31. 14 Rachel and Leah answered and said unto
31. 31 Jacob answered and said unto Laban
31. 36 Jacob answered and said unto Laban
31. 43 And Laban answered and said to Jacob
34. 13 the sons of Jacob answered Shechem and
35. 3 who answered me in the day of my
40. 18 Joseph answered and said, This (is) the
41. 16 Joseph answered Pharaoh, saying, (It is)
42. 22 Reuben answered them, saying, Spake I
45. 3 his brethren could not answer him; for
Exod. 4. 1 Moses answered and said, But, behold
15. 21 Miriam answered them, Sing ye to the
19. 8 all the people answered together, and
19. 19 Moses spake, and God answered him by
24. 3 all the people answered with one voice
Num. 11. 28 Joshua.. answered and said, My lord
22. 18 Balaam answered and said unto the
23. 12 he answered and said, Must I not take
23. 26 Balaam answered and said unto Balak

Num. 32. 31 the children of Gad.. answered, saying
Deut. 1. 14 ye answered me and said. The thing
1. 41 ye answered and said unto me, We have
21. 7 they shall answer and say, Our hands
25. 9 shall answer and say, So shall it be done
27. 15 all the people shall answer and say
Josh. 1. 16 they answered Joshua, saying, All that
7. 20 Achan answered Joshua, and said, Indeed
9. 24 they answered Joshua, and said, Because
22. 21 children of Reuben.. answered, and said
24. 16 the people answered and said, God forbid
Judg. 5. 29 Her wise ladies answered her, yea, she
7. 14 his fellow answered and said, This (is)
8. 8 the men of Penuel answered him as the
18. 14 Then answered the five men that went to
19. 28 Up, and.. be going. But none answered
20. 4 the Levite.. answered and said, I came
Ruth 2. 6 the servant.. answered and said, It (is)
2. 11 Boaz answered and said unto her, It hath
1 Sa. 1. 15 Hannah answered and said, No, my lord
1. 17 Eli answered and said, Go in peace: and
4. 17 the messenger answered and said, Israel
4. 20 she answered not, neither did she regard
9. 8 the servant answered Saul again, and said
9. 12 they answered them, and said, He is
9. 19 Samuel answered Saul, and said, I (am)
9. 21 Saul answered and said, (Am) not I a Benj.
10. 12 one of the same place answered and said
14. 12 the men of the garrison answered
14. 28 Then answered one of the people, and
14. 37 But he answered him not that day
14. 39 not a man among all.. people.. answered
16. 18 Then answered one of the servants, and
18. 7 women answered.. as they played.. Saul
20. 10 or what (if) thy father answer thee
20. 28 Jonathan answered Saul, David earnestly
20. 32 Jonathan answered Saul his father, and
21. 4 the priest answered David, and said
21. 5 David answered the priest, and said unto
22. 9 Then answered Doeg the Edomite which
22. 14 Then Ahimelech answered the king, and
23. 4 the LORD answered him and said, Arise
25. 10 Nabal answered David's servants, and
26. 6 Then answered David and said to Ahim.
26. 14 Answerest thou not.. Abner answered
26. 22 David answered and said, Behold the
28. 6 LORD answered him not, neither by
28. 15 Saul answered, I am sore distressed; for
29. 9 Achish answered and said to David, I
30. 22 Then answered all the wicked men and
2 Sa. 4. 9 David answered Rechab and Baanah his
13. 32 Jonadab, the son of Shimeah.. answered
14. 18 the king answered and said unto the
14. 19 the woman answered and said, (As) thy
15. 21 Ittai answered the king, and said, (As) the
19. 21 Abishai the son of Zeruiah answered and
19. 42 the men of Judah answered the men of I.
19. 43 the men of Israel answered the men of
20. 20 Joab answered and said, Far be it, far be
22. 42 unto the LORD, but he answered them
1 Ki. 1. 28 king David answered and said, Call me
1. 36 Benaiah the son of Jehoiada answered
1. 43 Jonathan answered and said to Adonijah
2. 22 Solomon answered and said unto his
2. 30 Thus said Joab, and thus he answered
3. 27 the king answered and said, Give her the
12. 7 If thou.. wilt serve them, and answer
12. 13 the king answered the people roughly
13. 6 king answered and said unto the man of
18. 21 And the people answered him not a word
18. 24 the God that answereth by fire, let him
18. 26 but.. no voice, nor any that answered
18. 29 that.. neither voice, nor any to answer
20. 4, 11 the king of Israel answered and said
2 Ki. 1. 10 Elijah answered and said to the captain
1. 11 he answered and said unto him, O man
1. 12 Elijah answered and said unto them, If
3. 11 one of the.. servants answered and said
4. 29 If any salute thee, answer him not
7. 2 Then a lord.. answered the man of God
7. 13 one of his servants answered and said
7. 19 that lord answered the man of God, and
18. 36 people held their peace, and answered
18. 36 king's commandment was, saying, Answer
1 Ch. 12. 17 David.. answered and said unto them, If
21. 26 he answered him from heaven by fire
21. 28 the LORD had answered him in the
2 Ch. 10. 13 the king answered them roughly; and
29. 31 Hezekiah answered and said, Now ye
34. 15 Hilkiah answered and said to Shaphan
Ezra 10. 2 Shechaniah.. answered and said unto
10. 12 all the congregation answered and said
Neh. 8. 6 all the people answered, Amen, Amen
Esth. 5. 7 Then answered Esther, and said, My pet.
7. 3 Esther the queen answered and said, If
Job 1. 7, 9 Satan answered the LORD, and said
2. 2, 4 Satan answered the LORD, and said
4. 1 Eliphaz the Temanite answered and said
5. 1 if there be any that will answer thee
6. 1 But Job answered and said, Oh that my
8. 1 Then answered Bildad the Shuhite, and
9. 1 Then Job answered and said, I know
9. 3 he cannot answer him one of a thousand
9. 14 How much less shall I answer him
9. 15 I were righteous, (yet) would I not answer
9. 16 If I had called, and he had answered me
9. 32 not a man.. (that) I should answer him
11. 1 Then answered Zophar the Naamathite
12. 1 And Job answered and said, No doubt
12. 4 who calleth upon God, and he answereth
13. 22 Then call thou, and I will answer: or let
14. 15 Thou shalt call, and I will answer thee

Job 15. 1 Then answered Eliphaz the Temanite
16. 1 Then Job answered and said, I have
16. 3 what emboldeneth.. that thou answerest?
18. 1 Then answered Bildad the Shuhite, and
19. 1 Then Job answered and said, How long
20. 1 Then answered Zophar the Naamathite
21. 1 But Job answered and said, Hear
22. 1 Then Eliphaz the Temanite answered and
23. 1 Then Job answered and said, Even to day
23. 5 know the words (which) he would answer
25. 1 Then answered Bildad the Shuhite, and
26. 1 But Job answered and said, How hast
31. 35 my desire.. the Almighty would answer
32. 1 So these three men ceased to answer Job
32. 6 Elihu.. answered and said, I (am) young
32. 12 none of you.. that answered his words
32. 15 They were amazed, they answered no
32. 16 they spake not.. answered no more
32. 17 I will answer also my part, I also will
32. 20 I will open my lips and answer
33. 12 I will answer thee, that God is greater
34. 1 Furthermore Elihu answered and said
38. 1 LORD answered Job out of the whirlwind
40. 1 Moreover the LORD answered Job, and
40. 2 he that reproveth God, let him answer it
40. 3 Then Job answered the LORD, and said
40. 5 Once have I spoken; but I will not answer
40. 6 Then answered the LORD unto Job out of
42. 1 Then Job answered the LORD, and said
Psa. 18. 41 They cried.. but he answered them not
27. 7 have mercy also upon me, and answer me
65. 5 wilt thou answer us, O God of our salvation
81. 7 I answered thee in the secret place of
86. 7 call upon thee: for thou wilt answer me
91. 15 shall call upon me, and I will answer him
99. 6 called upon the LORD, and he answered
99. 8 Thou answeredst them, O LORD our God
102. 2 in the day.. I call answer me speedily
108. 6 save (with) thy right hand, and answer
118. 5 the LORD answered me.. in a large place
119. 42 So shall I have wherewith to answer him
138. 3 the day when I cried thou answeredst me
143. 1 in thy faithfulness answer me.. in thy
Prov. 1. 28 they call upon me, but I will not answer
15. 28 heart of the righteous studieth to answer
18. 23 but the rich answereth roughly
26. 4 Answer not a fool according to his folly
26. 5 Answer a fool according to his folly
Eccl. 10. 19 but money answereth all
Isa. 14. 32 What shall (one) then answer the messen.
21. 9 he answered and said, Babylon is fallen
30. 19 when he shall hear it, he will answer
36. 21 they held their peace, and answered him
36. 21 commandment was, saying, Answer him
46. 7 shall cry unto him, yet can he not answer
50. 2 when I called, (was there) none to answer?
58. 9 thou call, and the LORD shall answer
65. 12 when I called, ye did not answer; when
65. 24 before they call, I will answer; and while
66. 4 because when I called, none did answer
Jer. 7. 13 and I called you, but ye answered not
7. 27 also call.. but they will not answer thee
11. 5 Then answered I, and said, So be it, O
23. 35 What hath the LORD answered? and
23. 37 What hath the LORD answered thee?
33. 3 Call unto me, and I will answer thee
35. 17 have called.. but they have not answered
42. 4 whatsoever thing the LORD shall answer
44. 15 all the people.. answered Jeremiah, saying
Joel 2. 19 LORD will answer and say unto his people
Amos 7. 14 Then answered Amos, and said to Amaz.
Mic. 6. 5 Balaam the son of Beor answered him
Hab. 2. 11 beam out of the timber shall answer it
Hag. 2. 12 And the priests answered and said, No
2. 13 The priests answered and said, It shall be
2. 14 Then answered Haggai, and said, So (is)
Zech. 1. 10 the man.. answered and said, These
1. 11 they answered the angel of the LORD that
1. 12 the angel of the LORD answered and said
1. 13 the LORD answered the angel that talked
3. 4 he answered and spake unto those that
4. 4 So I answered and spake to the angel that
4. 5 the angel.. answered and said unto me
4. 6 he answered and spake unto me, saying
4. 11 Then answered I, and said unto him, What
4. 12 I answered again, and said unto him
6. 4 I answered and said unto the angel that
6. 5 the angel answered and said unto me

5. *To be answered*, עָנָה *anah*, 2.
Eze. 14. 4 I the LORD will answer him that cometh
14. 7 I the LORD will answer him by myself

6. *To make or give an answer*, עָנָה *anah*, 5.
Eccl. 5. 20 God answereth (him) in the joy of his

7. *To make or give an answer*, עֲנָה *anah*.
Dan. 2. 5 king answered and said to the Chaldeans
2. 7 They answered again and said, Let the
2. 8 king answered and said, I know of certain.
2. 10 The Chaldeans answered before the king
2. 15 He answered and said to Arioch the
2. 20 Daniel answered and said, Blessed be the
2. 26 The king answered and said to Daniel
2. 27 Daniel answered in the presence of the
2. 47 The king answered unto Daniel, and said
3. 24 They answered and said unto the king
3. 25 He answered and said, Lo, I see four
4. 19 Belteshazzar answered and said, My lord
5. 17 Daniel answered and said before the
6. 12 The king answered and said, The thing
6. 13 Then answered they and said before the

8. *To turn back,* שׁוּב *shub,* 5.

2 Sa. 3. 11 he could not answer Abner a word again
2 Ch. 10. 16 the people answered the king, saying
Neh. 6. 4 I answered them after the same manner
Esth. 4. 13 Mordecai commanded to answer Esther
Job 13. 22 or let me speak, and answer thou me
31. 14 when he visiteth, what shall I answer
32. 14 neither will I answer him with your
33. 32 If thou hast anything to say, answer me
33. 5 If thou canst answer me, set..in order
40. 4 I am vile; what shall I answer thee?
Prov. 22. 21 that thou mightest answer the words of
Isa. 41. 28 that, when I asked of them, could answer a
Hab. 2. 1 what shall I answer when I am reproved

9. *To turn back a word,* שׁוּב דָּבָר *shub* (5) *dabar.*

1 Ki. 12. 6 How do ye advise that I may answer this
12. 9 What counsel give ye that we may answer
12. 16 the people answered the king, saying
Neh. 2. 20 Then answered I them, and said unto
Prov. 18. 13 He that answereth a matter before he
24. 26 shall kiss..that giveth a right answer
27. 11 that I may answer him that reproacheth

9a. *Return a word,* שׁוּב מִלָּה *shub* (5) *millah.*

Job. 35. 4 I will answer thee, and thy companions

10. *To turn back,* תּוּב *tub,* 5.

Dan. 2. 14 Daniel answered with counsel and wisdom

10a. *Return a word,* תּוּב פִּתְגָם *tub* (5) *pithgam.* 3. 16.

11. *To answer,* ἀποκρίνομαι *apokrinomai.*

Matt. 3. 15 Jesus answering said unto him, Suffer
4. 4 he answered and said, It is written, Man
8. 8 The centurion answered and said, Lord
11. 4 Jesus answered and said unto them, Go
11. 25 At that time Jesus answered and said, I
12. 38 the Pharisees answered, saying, Master
12. 39 he answered and said unto them, An evil
12. 48 he answered and said unto him that
13. 11 He answered and said unto them, Because
13. 37 He answered and said unto them, He
14. 28 Peter answered him and said, Lord, if it
15. 3 he answered and said unto them, Why
15. 13 he answered and said, Every plant, which
15. 15 Then answered Peter and said unto him
15. 23 But he answered her not a word. And
15. 24 he answered and said, I am not sent but
15. 26 he answered and said, It is not meet to
15. 28 Then Jesus answered and said unto her
16. 2 He answered and said unto them, When
16. 16 Simon Peter answered and said, Thou art
16. 17 Jesus answered and said unto him, Blessed
17. 4 Then answered Peter, and said unto
17. 11 Jesus answered and said unto them
17. 17 Jesus answered and said, O faithless and
19. 4 he answered and said unto them, Have
19. 27 Then answered Peter and said unto him
20. 13 But he answered one of them, and said
20. 22 Jesus answered and said, Ye know not
21. 21 Jesus answered and said unto them, Verily
21. 24 And Jesus answered and said unto them
21. 27 they answered Jesus, and said, We cannot
21. 29 He answered and said, I will not: but
21. 30 he answered and said, I (go,) sir: and
22. 1 Jesus answered and spake unto them
22. 29 Jesus answered and said unto them, Ye
22. 46 no man was able to answer him a word
24. 4 Jesus answered and said unto them
25. 9 the wise answered, saying, (Not so;) lest
25. 12 he answered and said, Verily I say unto
25. 26 His lord answered and said unto him
25. 37 Then shall the righteous answer him
25. 40 the King shall answer and say unto them
25. 44 Then shall they also answer him, saying
25. 45 Then shall he answer them, saying, Verily
26. 23 he answered and said, He that dippeth
26. 25 Judas, which betrayed him, answered
26. 33 Peter answered and said unto him
26. 62 high priest arose, and said..Answerest
26. 63 the high priest [answered and] said unto
26. 66 They answered and said, He is guilty of
27. 12 when he was accused..he answered
27. 14 And he answered him to never a word
27. 21 The governor answered and said unto
27. 25 Then answered all the people, and said
28. 5 the angel answered and said unto the
Mark 3. 33 he answered them, saying, Who is my
5. 9 [answered], saying, My name (is) Legion
6. 37 He answered and said unto them, Give
7. 6 He [answered and] said unto them, Well
7. 28 she answered and said unto him, Yes
8. 4 his disciples answered him, From whence
8. 28 [they answered,] John the Baptist: but
8. 29 Peter answereth and saith unto him
9. 5 Peter answered and said to Jesus, Master
9. 12 he answered and told them, Elias verily
9. 17 one of the multitude answered and said
9. 19 He answereth him, and saith, O faithless
9. 38 John [answered] him, saying, Master, we
10. 3 he answered and said unto them, What
10. 5 Jesus [answered and] said unto them, For
10. 20 he answered and said unto them, Master
10. 24 Jesus answereth again, and saith unto
10. 29 Jesus [answered and] said, Verily I say
10 51 Jesus answered and said unto him, What
11. 14 Jesus answered and said unto it, No
11. 22 Jesus [answering] saith unto them, Have
11. 29 Jesus [answered and] said unto them
11. 29 I will also ask..one question, and answer
11. 30 The baptism....from heaven..answer
11. 33 they answered and said unto Jesus, We
11. 33 Jesus [answering] saith unto them
12. 17 Jesus [answering] said unto them, Render
Mark 12. 24 Jesus [answering] said unto them, Do ye
12. 28 perceiving that he had answered them
12. 29 Jesus answered him, The first of all the
12. 34 when Jesus saw that he answered discre.
12. 35 Jesus answered and said, while he taught
13. 2 Jesus [answering] said unto him, Seest
13. 5 Jesus [answering] them began to say
14. 20 he [answered and] said unto them..one of
14. 40 neither wist they what to answer him
14. 48 Jesus answered and said unto them, Are
14. 60 asked Jesus, saying, Answerest thou
14. 61 he held his peace, and answered nothing
15. 2 he answering said unto him, Thou sayest
15. 4 Pilate asked him again, saying, Answerest
15. 5 Jesus yet answered nothing; so that
15. 9 Pilate answered them, saying, Will ye
15. 12 Pilate answered and said again unto
Luke 1. 19 the angel answering said unto him, I
1. 35 the angel answered and said unto her
1. 60 his mother answered and said, Not (so)
3. 11 He answereth and saith unto them, He
3. 16 John answered, saying unto (them) all, I
4. 4 Jesus answered him, saying, It is written
4. 8 Jesus answered and said unto him, Get
4. 12 Jesus, answering said unto him, It is
5. 5 Simon answering said unto him, Master
5. 22 But when Jesus perceived..[answering]
5. 31 Jesus answering said unto them, They
6. 3 Jesus answering them said, Have ye not
7. 22 Jesus answering said unto them, Go
7. 40 Jesus answering said unto him, Simon
7. 43 Simon answered and said, I suppose
8. 21 he answered and said unto them, My
8. 50 when Jesus heard (it), he answered him
9. 19 They answering said, John the Baptist
9. 20 Peter answering said, The Christ of
9. 41 Jesus answering said, O faithless and
9. 49 John answered and said, Master, we saw
10. 27 he answering said, Thou shalt love the
10. 28 he said unto him, Thou hast answered
10. 41 Jesus answered and said unto her, Martha
11. 7 he from within shall answer and say
11. 45 Then answered one of the lawyers, and
13. 2 Jesus answering said unto them, Suppose
13. 8 he answering said unto him, Lord, let
13. 14 the ruler of the synagogue answered
13. 15 The Lord then answered him, and said
13. 25 he shall answer and say unto you, I
14. 3 Jesus answering spake unto the lawyers
14. 5 And [answered] them, saying, Which of
15. 29 he answering said to (his) father, Lo
17. 17 Jesus answering said, Were there not ten
17. 20 he answered them and said, The kingdom
17. 37 they answered and said unto him, Where
19. 40 he answered and said unto them, I tell
20. 3 he answered and said unto them, I will
20. 7 they answered, that they could not tell
20. 24 They answered and said, Cesar's
20. 34 Jesus [answering] said unto them, The
20. 39 certain of the scribes answering said
22. 51 Jesus answered and said, Suffer ye thus
22. 68 if I also ask (you), ye will not answer me
23. 3 he answered him and said, Thou sayest
23. 9 words; but he answered him nothing
23. 40 the other answering rebuked him
24. 18 Cleopas, answering said unto him, Art
John 1. 21 Art thou that prophet? And he answered
1. 26 John answered them, saying, I baptize
1. 48 Jesus answered and said unto him, Before
1. 49 Nathanael answered and saith unto him
1. 50 Jesus answered and said unto him
2. 18 Then answered the Jews and said unto
2. 19 Jesus answered and said unto them
3. 3 Jesus answered and said unto him
3. 5 Jesus answered, Verily, verily, I say unto
3. 9 Nicodemus answered and said unto him
3. 10 Jesus answered and said unto him, Art
3. 27 John answered and said, A man can
4. 10 Jesus answered and said unto her, If
4. 13 Jesus answered and said unto her
4. 17 The woman answered and said, I have
5. 7 The impotent man answered him, Sir, I
5. 11 He answered them, He that made me
5. 17 Jesus answered them, My Father worketh
5. 19 Then answered Jesus and said unto them
6. 7 Philip answered him, Two hundred
6. 26 Jesus answered them and said, Verily
6. 29 Jesus answered and said unto them, This
6. 43 Jesus therefore answered and said unto
6. 68 Simon Peter answered him, Lord, to
6. 70 Jesus answered them, Have not I chosen
7. 16 Jesus answered them, and said, My
7. 20 The people answered and said, Thou
7. 21 Jesus answered and said unto them, I
7. 46 The officers answered, Never man spake
7. 47 Then answered them the Pharisees, Are
7. 52 They answered and said unto him, Art
8. 14 Jesus answered..said unto them, Though
8. 19 Jesus answered, Ye neither know me
8. 33 They answered him, We be Abraham's
8. 34 Jesus answered them, Verily, verily, I
8. 39 They answered..said unto him, Abraham
8. 48 Then answered the Jews, and said unto
8. 49 Jesus answered, I have not a devil; but
8. 54 Jesus answered, If I honour myself, my
9. 3 Jesus answered, Neither hath this man
9. 11 He answered and said, a man that is
9. 20 His parents answered them and said, We
9. 25 He answered and said, Whether he be a
9. 27 He answered them, I have told you already
9. 30 The man answered and said unto them
9. 34 They answered and said unto him, Thou
John 9. 36 He answered and said, Who is he, Lord
10. 25 Jesus answered them, I told you, and ye
10. 32 Jesus answered them, Many good works
10. 33 The Jews answered him, saying, For a
10. 34 Jesus answered them, Is it not written
11. 9 Jesus answered, Are there not twelve
12. 23 Jesus answered them, saying, The hour
12. 30 Jesus answered and said, This voice came
12. 34 The people answered him, We have heard
13. 7 Jesus answered and said unto him, What
13. 8 Jesus answered him, If I wash thee not
13. 26 Jesus answered, He it is, to whom I shall
13. 36 Jesus answered him, Whither I go, thou
13. 38 Jesus answered him, Wilt thou lay down
14. 23 Jesus answered and said unto him, If a
16. 31 Jesus answered them, Do ye now believe?
18. 5 They answered him, Jesus of Nazareth
18. 8 Jesus answered, I have told you that I
18. 20 Jesus answered him, I spake openly to
18. 22 Answerest thou the high priest so?
18. 23 Jesus answered him, If I have spoken
18. 30 They answered and said unto him, If he
18. 34 Jesus answered him, Sayest thou this
18. 35 Pilate answered, Am I a Jew? Thine own
18. 36 Jesus answered, My kingdom is not of
18. 37 Jesus answered, Thou sayest that I am a
19. 7 The Jews answered him, We have a law
19. 11 Jesus answered, Thou couldest have no
19. 15 The chief priests answered, We have no
19. 22 Pilate answered, What I have written I
20. 28 Thomas answered and said unto him
21. 5 have ye any meat? They answered him
Acts 3. 12 when Peter saw (it), he answered unto
4. 19 Peter and John answered and said
5. 8 Peter answered unto her, Tell me
5. 29 Peter and the (other) apostles answered
8. 24 Then answered Simon, and said, Pray ye
8. 34 the eunuch answered Philip, and said
8. 37 [he answered and said, I believe that]
9. 13 Ananias answered, Lord, I have heard
10. 46 Then answered Peter, Can any man
11. 9 the voice answered me again from heaven
15. 13 James answered, saying, Men..brethren
19. 15 And the evil spirit answered and said
21. 13 Paul answered, What mean ye to weep
22. 8 I answered, Who art thou, Lord? And
22. 28 the chief captain answered, With a great
24. 10 Paul..answered, Forasmuch as I know
24. 25 Felix trembled, and answered, Go thy
25. 4 Festus answered, that Paul should be
25. 9 Festus..answered Paul, and said, Wilt
25. 12 Festus..answered, Hast thou appealed
25. 16 To whom I answered, It is not the
Col. 4. 6 that ye may know how ye ought to answer
Rev. 7. 13 one of the elders answered, saying unto

12. *To speak off,* ἀπολογέομαι *apologeomai.*

Luke 12. 11 what thing ye shall answer, or what ye
21. 14 meditate before what ye shall answer
Acts 24. 10 I do the more cheerfully answer for

13. *To speak, say,* ἔπω, εἶπον *epō, eipon.*

Luke 20. 3 answer me: The baptism of John, was it

14. *To take up,* ὑπολαμβάνω *hupolambanō.*

Luke 10. 30 Jesus answering said, A certain (man)

ANSWER again, to —

1. *To turn back a word,* שׁוּב דָּבָר *shub,* (5) *dabar.*

1 Sa. 17. 30 the people answered him again after the

2. *To answer in return,* ἀνταποκρίνομαι.

Luke 14. 6 they could not answer him again to

3. *To speak in return,* ἀντιλέγω *antilegō.*

Titus 2. 9 servants..obedient..not answering again

ANSWER for one's self, to —

To speak off for himself, ἀπολογέομαι *apologeomai.*

Acts 25. 8 While he answered for himself, Neither
26. 1 Paul stretched forth..answered for him.
26. 2 because I shall answer for myself this

ANSWER for one's self —

A speaking off for oneself, ἀπολογία *apologia.*

Acts 25. 16 and have license to answer for himself

ANSWER of God —

A divine oracle, χρηματισμός *chrēmatismos.*

Rom 11. 4 what saith the answer of God unto

ANSWER, to give —

To answer, עָנָה *anah.*

Gen. 41. 16 God shall give Pharaoh an answer of
Job 19. 16 my servant, and he gave (me) no answer
35. 12 There they cry, but none giveth answer
Song 5. 6 I called him, but he gave me no answer
Jer. 44. 20 people which had given him (that) answer

ANSWER, to make or cause to —

1. *To answer,* עָנָה *anah,* Deut. 20. 11; Job 20. 3.

2. *To cause to turn back,* שׁוּב *shub,* 5, Job 20 2.

ANSWER, return —

To return, תּוּב *tub,* 5.

Ezra 5. 5 they returned answer by letter

ANSWER to, to —

To be in the same line, συστοιχέω *sustoicheō.*

Gal. 4. 25 answereth to Jerusalem which now is

ANSWERABLE to —

Companionship, עֻמָּה *ummah,* Exod. 38. 18.

ANSWERED, to be —
To be answered, עָנָה *anah,* 2.
2 Ch. 7. 22 it shall be answered, Because they
Job 11. 2 not the multitude of words be answered?

ANT —
Ant, נְמָלָה *nemalah.*
Prov. 6. 6 Go to the ant, thou sluggard: consider
30. 25 The ants (are) a people not strong

ANTI-CHRIST —
An opponent of Christ, Ἀντίχριστος *antichristos.*
1 Jo. 2. 18 antichrist shall come..are there many a.
2. 22 He is antichrist, that denieth the Father
4. 3 this is that (spirit) of antichrist, whereof
2 Jo. 7 This is a deceiver and an antichrist

AN-TI'-OCH, Ἀντιόχεια. *Meaning uncertain.*
1. Antioch was founded by Seleucus Nicator, B.C. 300, who named it after his father. It remained the capital of the dynasty till Syria was conquered by Pompey, and made a Roman province, B.C. 64. Christianity was planted in Antioch by Paul and Barnabas, and here the disciples were first called Christians, A.D. 42 (Acts 11. 26). This city, long known as "the Queen of the East," was captured by the Persian king Nushirvan, or Chosroes, A.D. 540. Chosroes II. wrested it from the empire in 611. Heraclius expelled the Persians, but it fell into the power of the Saracens in 638, and they degraded it to the rank of a provincial town. Nicephorus Phocas recovered it in 966; it was betrayed to the Turks in 1084. The crusaders laid siege to it in 1097, and captured it 1098. The citadel held out, but the Saracens, who made an effort to regain the prize, were defeated in a great battle under the walls of Antioch, 1098; and Antioch became the capital of a Christian principality. Bibars, sultan of Egypt, captured it, destroyed its churches, and completely ruined it, 1268. It was annexed to the Ottoman empire in 1516. Ibm Pasharahi seized it in 1832, but it was afterwards restored to the Porte. Antioch has frequently suffered from earthquakes; the most disastrous occurred A.D. 115, 340, 394, 396, 458, 526, and 588. Antioch was a patriarchate third after Rome and Alexandria. Thirty-one councils were held at Antioch, the first in 252, and the last in 1141.
Acts 6. 5 They chose..Nicolas a proselyte of A.
11. 19 were scattered..travelled as far as..A.
11. 20 when they were come to A., spake unto
11. 22 Barnabas, that he should go as far as A.
11. 26 had found him, he brought him unto A.
11. 26 disciples called Christians first in A.
11. 27 in these days came prophets..unto A.
13. 1 there were in the church that was at A.
14. 26 And thence sailed to A., from whence
15. 22 chosen men of their own company to A.
15. 23 brethren which are of the Gentiles in A.
15. 30 when they were dismissed, they came to A.
15. 35 Paul also and Barnabas continued in A.
18. 22 saluted the church, he went down to A.
Gal. 2. 11 when Peter was come to A., I withstood

2. A city in Pisidia, Asia Minor, W. of Iconium, now called *Galobatch.* Like the Syrian Antioch, this city was founded by Seleucus Nicator. Under the Romans it was called *Cæsarea.*
Acts 13. 14 when they departed..they came to A.
14. 19 And there came thither..Jews from A.
14. 21 preached..they returned again..to A.
2 Ti. 3. 11 afflictions, which came unto me at A.

AN-TI'-PAS, Ἀντίπας.
A martyr in Pergamos. The name is an abbreviation of *Antipater.*
Rev. 2. 13 even in those days wherein A. (was) my

AN-TI-PA'-TRIS, Ἀντιπατρίς *belonging to Antipater.*
A city of Palestine, not far from the Mediterranean, now called *Kefr-Saba.* Josephus says that the old name was Καφαρσαβα or Χαβαρζάβα, and that Herod when he rebuilt the city called it *Antipatris,* in honour of his father Antipater.
Acts 23. 31 took Paul, and brought (him)..to A.

ANTIQUITY —
Former state, קַדְמָה *qadmah.*
Isa. 23. 7 whose antiquity (is) of ancient days? her

AN-TO-THI'-JAH, עַנְתֹתִיָּה *answers of Jah.*
Son of Shashak, a Benjamite, B.C. 1340.
1 Ch. 8. 24 And Hananiah, and Elam, and A.

AN-TO-THITE, עַנְּתֹתִי *belonging to Anathoth.*
It is sometimes written Anethothite.
1 Ch. 11. 28 [men of the armies]..Abiezer the A.
12. 3 Berachah, and Jehu the A.

A'-NUB, עָנוּב *strong or high.*
A descendant of Judah through Caleb, son of Hur, B.C. 1430.
1 Ch. 4. 8 And Coz begat A., and Zobebah, and

ANVIL —
Step, stroke פַּעַם *paam.*
Isa. 41. 7 (with)the hammer him that smote the anvil

ANY —
1. *One,* אֶחָד *echad.*
Lev. 4. 2 If a soul shall sin..against any of
4. 13 have done..any of the commandments
4. 22 When a ruler hath..done..any of the
4. 27 And if any one of the common people
4. 27 he doeth..any of the commandments
5. 17 if a soul sin, and commit any of these
6. 3 in any of all these that a man doeth
Num 15. 27 if any soul sin through ignorance, then
36. 3 if they be married to any of the sons of
Deut 16. 5 within any of thy gates, which the LORD
17. 2 If there be found among you, within any
18. 6 if a Levite come from any of thy gates
28. 55 So that he will not give to any of them
2 Sa. 2. 1 Shall I go up into any of the cities of
7. 7 spake I a word with any of the tribes of
1 Ch. 17. 6 spake I a word to any of the judges of
Eze. 16. 5 None eye pitied thee, to do any of these

2. *A man, individual,* אִישׁ *ish.*
Exod 10. 23 They saw not one another, neither rose any
Lev. 21. 9 the daughter of any priest, if she profane
Judg 20. 8 We will not any..neither will we any
21. 1 There shall not any of us give his daughter
1 Sa. 30. 2 they slew not any, either great or small
2 Sa. 9. 3 (Is) there not yet any of the house of Saul
1 Ki. 3. 13 there shall not be any among the kings
5. 6 not among us any that can skill to
2 Ki. 4. 29 if any salute thee, answer him not again
10. 5 we will not make any king: do thou
10. 14 took them alive..neither left he any of
10. 24 (If) any of the men whom I have brought
18. 33 Hath any of the gods of the nations
Isa. 36. 18 Hath any of the gods of the nations
Jer. 23. 24 Can any hide himself in secret places
Eze. 7. 13 neither shall any strengthen himself
18. 7 hath not oppressed any..hath restored
18. 16 Neither hath oppressed any, hath not
46. 16 If the prince give a gift unto any of his
Zech 13. 3 to pass,(that) when any shall yet prophesy

3. *All, any,* כֹּל *kol.*
Deut. 4. 23 a graven image, (or) the likeness of any
Ezra 7. 24 touching any of the priests and Levites
Dan. 2. 10 asked such things at any magician, or
2. 30 is not revealed to me..more than any
3. 28 that they might not serve nor worship any
6. 4 neither was there any error or fault found
6. 5 We shall not find any occasion against
6. 12 that shall ask..of any God or man within

4. *Who? whom?* מִי *mi.*
Gen. 19. 12 Hast thou here any besides? son in law

5. *Soul, person,* נֶפֶשׁ *nephesh.*
Lev. 2. 1 when any will offer a meat offering
24. 17 he that killeth any man shall surely be
Num 19. 11 toucheth the dead body of any man shall
Deut 24. 7 If a man be found stealing any of his

6. *One,* εἷς *heis.*
Acts 4. 32 neither said any..that ought of the things

7. *Not,* μή *mē.*
Luke 20. 27 Sadducees, which deny that there is any

8. *Not one, no one,* μηδείς *mēdeis.*
Acts 25. 17 without any delay on the morrow I sat
2 Th. 2. 3 Let no man deceive you by any means
1 Pe. 3. 6 and are not afraid with any amazement

9. *Has any one?* μήτις *mētis.*
John 7. 48 Have any of the rulers or of the Pharisees

10. *Any thing,* μή τι *mē ti.*
John 21. 5 Jesus saith..have ye any meat?

11. *Not even one,* οὐδείς *oudeis.*
Mark 5. 4 broken..neither could any (man) tame
16. 8 neither said they anything to any (man)
Luke 8. 43 neither could be healed of any
9. 36 and told no man in those days any of
20. 40 after that they durst not ask him any
Acts 4. 12 [Neither is there salvation in any other]

12. *All, any, every,* πᾶς *pas.*
Matt 18. 19 as touching anything that they shall
2 Co. 1. 4 comfort them which are in any trouble
Heb. 4. 12 and sharper than any two-edged sword
Rev. 7. 1 not blow..on the sea, nor on [any] tree
7. 16 hunger no more, neither thirst any more
9. 4 neither any green thing, neither any tree

13. *Any one, any,* τις *tis.*
Mark 8. 26 nor tell (it) to any in the town
11. 25 forgive, if ye have ought against any
16. 18 [and if they drink any deadly thing]
Luke 24. 41 he said..Have ye here any meat? 11. 11.
John 1. 46 Can there any good thing come out of
2. 25 needed not that any should testify, 7. 48.
Acts 4. 34 Neither was there any among them that
9. 2 if he found any of this way, whether they
25. 16 the manner of the Romans to deliver any
27. 42 lest any of them should swim out, and
28. 21 neither any of the brethren..spake any
Rom. 8. 39 height, nor depth, nor any other creature
9. 11 neither having done any good or evil
15. 18 I will not dare to speak of any of
1 Co. 1. 15 Lest any should say that I had baptized
6. 1 Dare any of you, having a matter against
6. 12 not be brought under the power of any
7. 18 Is any man called being circumcised?
2 Co. 11. 21 Howbeit, whereinsoever any is bold, (I
12. 17 Did I make a gain of you by any of them
Eph. 5. 27 having spot, or wrinkle, or any such thing
Col. 2. 23 not in any honour to the satisfying of
3. 13 if any man have a quarrel against any
1 Th. 2. 9 we would not be chargeable unto any
5. 15 none render evil for evil unto any
2 Th. 3. 8 Neither did we eat any man's bread
Heb. 3. 12 Take heed..lest there be in any of you
3. 13 lest any of you be hardened through the
4. 1 lest, a promise being left..any of you
12. 15 Looking diligently lest any man fail of
12. 16 Lest there (be) any fornicator, or profane
Jas. 5. 12 swear not..neither by any other oath
Jas. 5. 13 Is any among you afflicted?..Is any merry?
5. 14 Is any sick among you? let him call for
5. 19 Brethren, if any of you do err from the
2 Pe. 3. 9 not willing that any should perish, but
[*See also* Kin, longer, means, more, never, nor, not, thing, time, whether, which, wise without.]

ANY at all —
1. *Pleasure,* חָפֵץ *chaphets.*
Eze. 18. 23 Have I any pleasure at all that the
2. *To be able,* יָכֹל *yakol.*
Num 22. 38 have I now any power at all to say any

ANY case, in —
To bring back, שׁוּב *shub,* 5. [adv. inf.]
Deut 22. 1 thou shalt in any case bring them again
24. 13 In any case thou shalt deliver him the

ANY further —
Yet, further, ἔτι *eti.*
Mark 5. 35 why troublest thou the Master any further
14. 63 What need we any further witnesses?
Luke 22. 71 What need we any further witness?

ANY longer —
1. *Yet, further,* ἔτι *eti.*
Rom 6. 2 How shall we..live any longer therein?
2. *No further,* μηκέτι *mēketi.*
Acts 25. 24 that he ought not to live any longer

ANY man, man's, (not)—
1. *A man, individual,* אִישׁ *ish.*
Gen. 24. 16 (was) very fair..neither had any man
Exod 34. 3 neither let any man be seen throughout
34. 24 neither shall any man desire thy land
Lev. 7. 8 the priest that offereth any man's burnt
15. 16 if any man's seed of copulation go out
15. 24 if any man lie with her at all
Num. 5. 10 whatsoever any man giveth the priest
21. 9 if a serpent had bitten any man, when
Deut 19. 11 if any man hate his neighbour, and lie in
19. 16 If a false witness rise up against any man
22. 13 If any man take a wife, and go in unto
23. 10 If there be among you any man, that is
Josh. 1. 5. There shall not any man be able to stand
2. 11 remain any more courage in any man
Judg. 4. 20 when any man doth come and enquire of
1 Sa. 2. 13 when any man offered sacrifice, the
2. 16 if any man said unto him, Let them, 12. 4.
2 Sa. 15. 2 it was (so), that when any man that had
15. 5 it was (so), that when any man came nigh
19. 22 shall there any man be put to death this
21. 4 neither for us shalt thou kill any man
2 Ki. 4. 29 if thou meet any man, salute him not
1a. *A man, a man,* אִישׁ אִישׁ *ish ish.*
Lev. 15. 2 When any man hath a running issue
Num. 5. 12 If any man's wife go aside, and commit a
9. 10 If any man of you or of your posterity
2. *Whoso,* מִי *mi.*
Exod 24. 14 if any man have any matters to do, let
3. *Each one,* ἕκαστος *hekastos.*
Eph. 6. 8 that whatsoever good thing any man
4. *Not one, no one,* μηδείς *mēdeis.*
Mark 1. 44 See thou say nothing to any man
Acts 10. 28 that I should not call any man common
5. *Has any one?* μήτις *mētis.*
John 4. 33 Hath any man brought him (ought) to
6. *Not even one,* οὐδείς *oudeis.*
Matt 22. 16 neither carest thou for any..for thou
Mark 16. 8 said they any thing to any..for they were
John 8. 33 and were never in bondage to any man
18. 31 It is not lawful for us to put any man to
Jas. 1. 13 neither tempteth he any man: but every
7. *Any, any one,* τις *tis.*
Matt 11. 27 neither knoweth any man the Father
12. 19 neither shall any man hear his voice in
21. 3 if any..say ought unto you, ye shall
22. 46 neither durst any..from that day forth
24. 23 if any man shall say unto you, Lo, here
Mark 9. 30 he would not that any man should know
11. 3 if any man say unto you, Why do ye
11. 16 would not suffer that any man should
13. 5 Take heed lest any..deceive you
13. 21 then if any man shall say to you, Lo
Luke 14. 8 When thou art bidden of any (man) to a
19. 8 if I have taken any thing from any man
19. 31 if any man ask you, Why do ye loose
20. 28 If any man's brother die, having a wife
John 4. 33 Hath any man brought him (ought) to eat?
6. 46 Not that any man hath seen the Father
6. 51 if any man eat of this bread, he shall
7. 17 If any man will do his will, he shall
7. 37 If any man thirst, let him come unto me
9. 22 that if any man did confess that he was
9. 31 if any man be a worshipper of God, and
9. 32 that any man opened the eyes of one that
10. 9 I am the door: by me if any man
10. 28 neither shall any..pluck them out of
11. 9 If any man walk in the day, he stumbleth
11. 57 that, if any man knew where he were
12. 26 If any man serve me..if any man serve
12. 47 if any man hear my words, and believe
16. 30 and needest not that any man should
Acts 10. 47 Can any man forbid water, that these
19. 38 if Demetrius..have a matter against any m.
24. 12 neither found me..disputing with any m.
Rom. 8. 9 Now if any man have not the Spirit of
1 Co. 5. 11 if any man that is called a brother be a
7. 18 Is any man called being circumcised? let

1 Co. 8. 10 For if any man see thee which hast
9. 15 than that any man should make my
10. 28 if any man say unto you, This is offered
14. 27 If any man speak in an..tongue..by two
2 Co. 12. 6 lest any man should think of me above
Eph. 2. 9 Not of works, lest any man should boast
Col. 2. 4 this I say, lest any man should beguile
2. 8 Beware lest any man spoil you
3. 13 if any man have a quarrel against any
2 Th. 3. 8 Neither did we eat any man's bread for
Heb. 4. 11 lest any man fall after the same example
12. 15 lest any man fail of the grace of God
1 Jo. 2. 1 if any man sin, we have an advocate with
2. 15 If any man love the world, the love of
2. 27 ye need not that any man teach you; but
5. 16 If any man see his brother sin a sin..not
Rev. 3. 20 if any man hear my voice, and open the
22. 18 If any man shall add unto these things
22. 19 if any man shall take away from the
[*See also* If, by, lest, neither, not.]

ANY manner —
Any, כֹּל *kol.*
Exod 22. 9 for any manner of lost thing which
Lev. 7. 27 soul..that eateth any manner of blood
Deut 27. 21 he that lieth with any manner of beast

ANY marks —
Writing, כְּתֹבֶת *kethobeth.*
Lev. 19. 28 nor print any marks upon you: I (am)

ANY more —
1. *To add,* יָסַף *yasaph.*
Deut. 5. 25 hear the voice of the LORD..any more
2. *To add,* יָסַף *yasaph,* 5.
Exod. 8. 29 not Pharaoh deal deceitfully any more
11. 6 nor shall be like it any more
Josh. 7. 12 neither will I be with you any more
2 Sa. 7. 10 neither shall..afflict them any more
14. 10 he shall not touch thee any more
2 Ki. 21. 8 Neither will I make..Israel..any more
1 Ch. 17. 9 children of wickedness waste..any more
2 Ch. 33. 8 Neither will I any more remove the foot
Jer. 31. 12 they shall not sorrow any more at all
Joel 2. 2 neither shall be any more after it
3. *Still, yet, again,* עוֹד *od.*
Gen. 8. 12 returned not again unto him any more
4. *(For an) indefinite time,* עוֹלָם *olam.*
Eze. 27. 36 and never (shalt be) any more
28. 19 and never (shalt) thou (be) any more
5. *Yet, further,* ἔτι *eti.*
Luke 20. 36 Neither can they die any more: for they
Rev. 7. 16 neither thirst any more; neither shall
12. 8 neither was their place found any more
18. 22 no craftsman..shall be found any more
21. 4 neither shall there be any more pain, for
6. *No more,* μηκέτι *mēketi.*
Rom 14. 13 let us not..judge one another any more
7. *No further,* οὐκέτι *ouketi.*
Matt 22. 46 from that day forth ask him any more
Mark 9. 8 they saw no man any more, save Jesus
Luke 22. 16 I will not [any more] eat thereof, until
Rev. 18. 11 no man buyeth..merchandise any more

ANY of their's —
מֶהֱמֵהֶם [*probably error*].
Eze. 7. 11 their multitude, nor of any of their's

ANY one —
All, any, every, πᾶς *pas.*
Matt 13. 19 When any one heareth the word of the

ANY person —
Soul, person, נֶפֶשׁ *nephesh.*
Num 31. 19 whosoever hath killed any person, and
35. 11 which killeth any person at unawares
35. 15 everyone that killeth any person unawares
35. 30 Whoso killeth any person, the murderer
35. 30 one..shall not testify against any person

ANY such —
Matter, word, דָּבָר *dabar.*
Deut 13. 11 shall do no more any such wickedness
19. 20 henceforth commit no more any such

ANY thing —
1. *One,* אֶחָד *echad.*
Lev. 6. 7 it shall be forgiven him for any thing
2. *Word, thing,* דָּבָר *dabar.*
Gen. 18. 14 Is any thing too hard for the LORD?
Num 20. 19 I will only, without..any thing..go
3. *What and what,* מְאוּמָה *meumah.*
Gen. 22. 12 neither do thou any thing unto him: for
30. 31 Thou shalt not give me any thing: if thou
39. 9 neither hath he kept back any thing from
39. 23 of the prison looked not to any thing
Num 22. 38 have I..any power at all to say any thing?
Deut 24. 10 thou dost lend thy brother any thing
1 Sa. 20. 26 Saul spake not any thing that day: for
20. 39 the lad knew not any thing: only Jonathan
21. 2 Let no man know any thing of the
25. 15 neither missed we any thing, as long as
2 Sa. 13. 2 thought it hard for him to do any thing
2 Ch. 9. 20 it was (not) any thing accounted of in
Eccl. 9. 5 the dead know not any thing, neither
Jon. 3. 7 neither..herd nor flock, taste any thing
4. *Not one, no one,* μηδείς, *mēdeis.*
Rom. 13. 8 Owe no man any thing, but to love one
2 Co. 6. 3 Giving no offence in any thing, that the
5. *Not even one,* οὐδείς *oudeis.*
Mark 16. 8 neither said they any thing to any (man)
6. *Any, anything,* τις *tis,* τι *ti.*
Matt 24. 17 Let him..come down to take any thing
Mark 11. 13 came, if haply he might find any thing
13. 15 neither enter..to take any thing out of
Luke 19. 8 if I have taken any thing from any man
22. 35 when I sent you..lacked ye any thing?
John 7. 4 no man (that) doeth any thing in secret
14. 14 If ye shall ask any thing in my name
Acts 17. 25 as though he needed any thing, seeing
19. 39 if ye enquire any thing concerning other
25. 11 or have committed any thing worthy of
Rom 14. 14 but to him that esteemeth any thing to
1 Co. 2. 2 For I determined not to know any thing
3. 7 neither is he that planteth any thing
8. 2 if any man think..he knoweth any thing
10. 19 [say I then? that the idol is any thing]
10. 19 that which is offered..idols is any thing?
14. 35 if they will learn any thing, let them
2 Co. 2. 10 To whom ye forgive any thing, I (forgive)
3. 5 to think any thing as of ourselves; but
Gal. 5. 6 neither circumcision availeth any thing
6. 15; 1 Th. 1. 8; Jas. 1. 7; 1 Jo. 5. 14.
7. *One,* ἕν *hen,* John 1. 3.
8. *All,* πᾶς *pas,* Acts 10. 14; Rev. 21. 27.
[*See also* Not, superfluous, sweat.]

ANY thing at all —
Any one, any thing, τις *tis,* τι *ti.*
Acts 25. 8 Cesar, have I offended any thing at all

ANY whither —
Whither, אָנָה וָאָנָה *aneh va-anah.*
1 Ki. 2. 36 and go not forth thence any whither
2. 42 walkest abroad any whither, that thou

ANY wise, in —
1. *Only,* אַךְ *ak.*
Psa. 37. 8 fret not thyself in any wise to do evil
2. *Only, surely,* רַק *raq.*
Josh. 6. 18 ye, in any wise keep..from the accursed
[*See also* Exod. 22. 23; Lev. 19. 17; 27. 19; Deut. 17. 15; 21. 23; 22. 7; Josh. 23. 12; 1 Sa. 6. 3; 1 Ki. 11. 22.]

APACE —
1. *To go on,* הָלַךְ *halak.*
2 Sa. 18. 25 And he came apace, and drew near
2. *Refuge, flight,* מָנוֹס *manos.*
Jer 46. 5 and are fled apace, and look not back

APART —
1. *Apart,* בַּד *bad.*
Zech. 12. 12 the land shall mourn, every family apart
[This particle occurs eleven times in v. 12, 13, 14.]
2. *By themselves,* κατ' ἰδίαν *kat' idian.*
Matt 14. 13 he departed..into a desert place apart
14. 23 went up into a mountain apart to pray
17. 1 bringeth..into an high mountain apart
17. 19 Then came the disciples to Jesus apart
20. 17 Jesus..took the twelve disciples apart in
Mark 6. 31 Come ye yourselves apart into a desert
9. 2 and leadeth them up..apart by themselves

APART, to put or set —
Separation, נִדָּה *niddah.*
Lev. 15. 19 she shall be put apart seven days
18. 19 as she is put apart for her uncleanness
Eze. 22. 10 that was set apart for pollution

APE —
Ape, marmoset, קוֹף *qoph.*
1 Ki. 10. 22 silver, ivory, and apes, and peacocks
2 Ch. 9. 21 silver, ivory, and apes, and peacocks

A-PEL'-LES, Ἀπελλῆς.
A disciple at Rome, to whom Paul sends salutation
Rom. 16 10 Salute A. approved in Christ

A-PHAR-SA'-CHITES, אֲפַרְסְכָיֵא. *Meaning uncertain.*
An unknown Assyrian tribe.
Ezra 5. 6 Tatnai..and his companions the A.
6. 6 Tatnai..and your companions the A.

A-PHAR-SATH'-CHITES, אֲפַרְסַתְכָיֵא
Perhaps the same as the preceding.
Ezra 4. 9 Then..Rehum the chancellor, and..A.

A-PHAR'-SITES, אֲפָרְסָיֵא. *Meaning uncertain.*
Perhaps the same as the preceding.
Ezra 4. 9 Then..Rehum the chancellor, and..A.

A'-PHEK, אֲפֵק *fortress.* [*See* **APHIK.**]
1. A royal city of the Canaanites, taken by Joshua and assigned to Issachar. Probably the same as the Aphekah of Josh. 15. 53.
Josh. 12. 18 [these are the kings]..The king of A.;
1 Sa. 4. 1 and the Philistines pitched in A.
29. 1 Philistines gathered..their armies to A.
2. A city E. of Cinneroth, where Benhadad was defeated by Ahab.
1 Ki. 20. 26 came to pass..Ben-hadad..went up to A
20. 30 But the rest fled to A., into the city
2 Ki. 13. 17 thou shalt smite the Syrians in A., till
3. With the article "*the* Aphek," a place where the Philistines encamped while the Israelites were at Ebenezer. This was N.W. and not far from Jerusalem.
1 Sa. 4. 1 and the Philistines pitched in A.
4. The scene of a battle wherein Saul was defeated and slain.
1 Sa. 29. 1 Philistines gathered..their armies to A.

A-PHE'-KAH, אֲפֵקָה *fortress.* [*See* **APHEK** 1.]
A city in the hill-country of Judah, near Beth-tappuah.
Josh. 15. 53 And Janum, and Beth-tappuah, and A.

A-PHI'-AH, אֲפִיחַ *striving.*
One of Saul's ancestors, B.C. 1225.
1 Sa. 9. 1 Zeror, the son of Bechorath, the son of A.

A'-PHIK, אֲפִיק אֲפֵקָה אֲפֵק *fortress.*
A city of Asher in the N. of Canaan. It is the *Aphaka* on the river Adonis. The Canaanites kept possession of this stronghold.
Josh. 13. 4 unto A., to the borders of the Amorites
19. 30 Ummah also, and A., and Rehob, twenty
Judg. 1. 31 did Asher drive out the inhabitants of A.
[In Joshua Aphek].

APH'-RAH, עַפְרָה *hamlet.*
A city in Benjamin, near Philistia. It is perhaps the same as *Ophrah,* but this is uncertain, as all the towns named in the context are in the low country, while Ophrah would seem to be E. of Bethel.
Mic. 1. 10 in the house of A. roll thyself in the dust

APH'-SES, הַפִּצֵּץ *the dispersed.*
A Levite chief of the 18th of the 24 courses in the service of the temple, B.C. 1015.
1 Ch. 24. 15 seventeenth to Hezir..eighteenth to A.

APIECE —
1. *The one pillar,* הָעַמּוּד הָאֶחָד *ha-ammud ha-echad.*
1 Ki. 7. 15 pillars..of eighteen cubits high apiece.
2. *The spoon,* הַכַּף *hak-kaph.*
Num. 7. 86 spoons..(weighing) ten (shekels) apiece
3. *Up to, up by, apiece,* ἀνά *ana.*
Luke 9. 3 journey..neither have two coats [apiece]
John 2. 6 containing two or three firkins apiece
4. *For one prince,* לְנָשִׂיא אֶחָד *le-nasi echad.*
Num. 17. 6 a rod apiece, for each prince one

A-POL-LO-NI'-A, Ἀπολλωνία, *place of Apollo.*
A city of Macedonia, in the district of Mygdonia, 28 miles from Amphipolis, and 35 from Thessalonica. This city must not be confounded with the more celebrated Apollonia in Illyria, Acts 17. 1.

A-POL'-LOS, Ἀπολλώς *a destroyer.*
An eloquent Jew from Alexandria, who came to Ephesus during the absence of Paul (A.D. 54), and was there more perfectly taught in Christian doctrine by Aquila and Priscilla.
Acts 18. 24 a certain Jew named A...came to Ephesus
19. 1 And it came to pass, that, while A. was
1 Co. 1. 12 every one of you saith, I am of..A.
3. 4 and another, I (am) of A.; are ye not
3. 5 Who then is Paul, and who (is) A., but
3. 6 I have planted, A. watered; but God gave
3. 22 Whether Paul, or A., or Cephas, or the
4. 6 I have..transferred to myself and to A.
16. 12 As touching (our) brother A., I greatly
Titus 3. 13 Bring..and A. on their journey diligently

A-POL-LY'-ON, Ἀπολλύων, *destruction, destroyer.*
The Greek translation of the Hebrew "Abaddon."
Rev. 9. 11 in the Greek tongue hath (his) name A.

APOSTLE —
One sent forth, ἀπόστολος, *apostolos.*
Matt 10. 2 Now the names of the twelve apostles
Mark 6. 30 And the apostles gathered themselves
Luke 6. 13 chose twelve, whom..he named apostles
9. 10 the apostles, when they were returned
11. 49 I will send them prophets and apostles
17. 5 the apostles said unto the Lord, Increase
22. 14 he sat down, and the twelve apostles
24. 10 which told these things unto the apostle
Acts 1. 2 given commandments unto the apostles
1. 26 was numbered with the eleven apostles
2. 37 and said..to the rest of the apostles
2. 42 continued stedfastly in the apostles'
2. 43 many wonders..done by the apostles
4. 33 with great power gave the apostles
4. 35 laid..down at the apostles' feet: and
4. 36 Joses, who by the apostles was surnamed
4. 37 sold..and laid (it) at the apostles' feet
5. 2 part, and laid (it) at the apostles' feet
5. 12 by the hands of the apostles were many
5. 18 laid their hands on the apostles, and put
5. 29 Peter and the..apostles answered and
5. 34 commanded to put the [apostles] forth a
5. 40 when they had called the apostles, and
6. 6 Whom they set before the apostles: and
8. 1 were all scattered..except the apostles
8. 14 when the apostles which were at Jerusa.
8. 18 through laying on of the apostles' hands
9. 27 took..and brought (him) to the apostles
11. 1 the apostles and brethren that were in
14. 4 with the Jews, and part with the apostles
14. 14 (which) when the apostles, Barnabas and
15. 2 go up to Jerusalem unto the apostles
15. 4 they were received..(of) the apostles and
15. 6 the apostles and elders came together
15. 22 Then pleased it the apostles and elders
15 23 The apostles and elders and brethren
15. 33 were let go in peace..unto the apostles
16. 4 that were ordained of the apostles and
Rom. 1. 1 Paul..called (to be) an apostle, separated
11. 13 inasmuch as I am the apostle of the
16. 7 who are of note among the apostles, who

1 Co. 1. 1 Paul, called..an apostle of Jesus Christ
4. 9 God hath set forth us the apostles last
9. 1 Am I not an apostle? am I not free?
9. 2 If I be not an apostle unto others, yet
9. 5 a wife, as well as other apostles, and
12. 28 hath set some in the church, first apostles
12. 29 (Are) all apostles? (are) all prophets?
15. 7 seen of James; then of all the apostles
15. 9 least..apostles..to be called an apostle
2 Co. 1. 1 Paul, an apostle of Jesus Christ by the
11. 5 not a whit behind the very chiefest apostle
11. 13 transforming themselves into the apostles
12. 11 am I behind the very chiefest apostles
12. 12 the signs of an apostle were wrought
Gal. 1. 1 Paul, an apostle, (not of men, neither by
1. 17 Neither went..them which were apostles
1. 19 other of the apostles saw I none, save
Eph. 1. 1 Paul, an apostle of Jesus Christ by the
2. 20 built upon the foundation of the apostles
3. 5 now revealed unto his holy apostles and
4. 11 gave some apostles; and some, prophets
Col. 1. 1 Paul, an apostle of Jesus Christ by the
1 Th. 2. 6 have been burdensome, as the apostles of
1 Ti. 1. 1 Paul, an apostle of Jesus Christ by the
2. 7 I am ordained a preacher, and an apostle
2 Ti. 1. 1 Paul, an apostle of Jesus Christ by the
1. 11 I am appointed a preacher, and an apostle
Titus 1. 1 Paul, a servant of God, and an Apostle of
Heb. 3. 1 holy brethren..consider the apostle and
1 Pe. 1. 1 Peter, an apostle of Jesus Christ, to the
2 Pe. 1. 1 Simon Peter, a servant and an apostle of
3. 2 of the commandment of us the apostles
Jude 17 which were spoken before of the apostles
Rev. 2. 2 tried them which say they are apostles, and
18. 20 Rejoice..holy apostles and prophets; for
21. 14 the names of the twelve apostles of the

APOSTLE, false —
False apostle, ψευδαπόστολος *pseudapostolos.*
2 Co. 11. 13 For such (are) false apostles, deceitful

APOSTLESHIP —
A sending forth, ἀποστολή *apostolē.*
Acts 1. 25 part of this ministry and apostleship
Rom. 1. 5 we have received grace and apostleship
1 Co. 9. 2 for the seal of mine apostleship are ye in
Gal. 2. 8 to the apostleship of the circumcision

APOTHECARIES' ART, prepared by the —
Perfumes, מִרְקַחַת *mirqachath.*
2 Ch. 16. 14 (spices) prepared by the apothecaries' art

APOTHECARY —
1. *To mix, compound, perfume*, רָקַח *raqach.*
Exod 30. 25 compound after the art of the apothecary
30. 35 confection after the art of the apothecary
37. 29 according to the work of the apothecary
Eccl. 10. 1 cause the ointment of the apothecary
2. *Mixture, spices*, רַקָּח *raqqach.*
Neh. 3. 8 Hananiah..son of (one of)..apothecaries

AP-PA'-IM, אַפַּיִם *face, presence.*
Son of Nadab, great-grandson of Jerahmeel, son of Hezron, B.C. 1400.
1 Ch. 2. 30 And the sons of Nadab; Seled, and A.
2. 31 And the sons of A.; Ishi. And the sons

APPAREL —
1. *Garment*, בֶּגֶד *beged.*
Judg 17. 10 I will give thee..a suit of apparel, and
1 Sa. 27. 9 took away the sheep..and the apparel
2 Sa. 14. 2 put on now mourning apparel, and
Zech. 14. 14 silver, and apparel, in great abundance
2. *Clothing*, לְבוּשׁ *lebush.*
2 Sa. 1. 24 on ornaments of gold upon your apparel
Esth. 6. 8 Let the royal apparel be brought which
6. 9 let this apparel and horse be delivered to
6. 10 Make haste..take the apparel and the
6. 11 Then took Haman the apparel and the
8. 15 Mordecai went out..in royal apparel of
Isa. 63. 1 this..glorious in his apparel, travelling
63. 2 Wherefore..red in thine apparel, and thy
3. *Clothing*, מַלְבּוּשׁ *malbush.*
1 Ki. 10. 5 of his ministers, and their apparel
2 Ch. 9. 4 of his ministers, and their apparel
9. 4 his cup-bearers also, and their apparel
Zeph. 1. 8 are clothed with strange apparel
4. *Raiment*, שִׂמְלָה *simlah.*
2 Sa. 12. 20 David arose..and changed his apparel
Isa. 4. 1 We will..wear our own apparel
5. *Robe, garment*, ἐσθής *esthēs.*
Acts 1. 10 two men stood by them in white apparel
12. 21 Herod, arrayed in royal apparel, sat upon
Jas. 2. 2 a man with a gold ring, in goodly apparel
6. *Garment*, ἱμάτιον *himation.*
1 Pe. 3. 3 or of putting on of apparel
7. *Garment*, ἱματισμός, *himatismos.*
Acts 20. 33 I have coveted no man s silver..or apparel
8. *Long robe*, καταστολή *katastolē.*
1 Ti. 2. 9 adorn themselves in modest apparel

APPAREL, changeable suits of —
Costly apparel, mantle, מַחֲלָצוֹת *machalatsoth.*
Isa. 3. 22 changeable suits of apparel, and the

APPAREL in —
To be clothed, לָבֵשׁ *labesh*, 4.
Ezra 3. 10 they set the priests in their apparel with

APPAREL, rich —
Rich apparel, בְּרֹמִים *beromim.*
Eze. 27. 24 work, and in chests of rich apparel

APPARELLED —
In apparel, ἐν ἱματισμῷ *en himatismō.*
Luke 7. 25 they which are gorgeously apparelled

APPARELLED, to be —
To be clothed, לָבֵשׁ *labesh.*
2 Sa. 13. 18 king's daughters..virgins apparelled

APPARENTLY —
(And) appearance, מַרְאֶה *mareh.*
Num 12. 8 With him will I speak..even apparently

APPEAL to or unto, to —
To call upon, ἐπικαλέομαι *epikaleomai.*
Acts 25. 11 but if there be none..I appeal unto Cesar
25. 12 Hast thou appealed unto Cesar unto
25. 21 when Paul had appealed to be reserved
25. 25 he himself hath appealed to Augustus
26. 32 if he had not appealed unto Cesar
28. 19 I was constrained to appeal unto Cesar

APPEAR, (things which do), to—
1. *To reveal (itself)*, גָּלָה *galah.*
Prov. 27. 25 hay appeareth, and the tender grass
2. *To be revealed, uncovered*, גָּלָה *galah*, 2.
Gen. 35. 7 there God appeared unto him, when he
1 Sa. 2. 27 Did I plainly appear unto the house of
3. *To lie down, be white, shine*, גָּלַשׁ *galash.*
Song 4. 1 flock of goats..appear from mt. Gilead
6. 5 flock of goats..appear from Gilead
4. *To go forth*, יָצָא *yatsa.*
Neh. 4. 21 of the morning till the stars appeared
5. *To turn or shew the face, front*, פָּנָה *panah.*
Exod 14. 27 when the morning appeared..the Egypt.
6. *To open*, פָּתַח *pathach*, 3.
Song 7. 12 the tender grape appear..the pomegran.
7. *To be seen*, רָאָה *raah*, 2.
Gen. 1. 9 let the dry (land) appear: and it was so
12. 7 the LORD appeared unto Abram, and said
12. 7 altar unto the LORD, who appeared unto
17. 1 LORD appeared to Abram, and said unto
18. 1 LORD appeared unto him in the plains of
26. 2 the LORD appeared unto him, and said
26. 24 LORD appeared unto him the same night
35. 1 appeared unto thee when thou fleddest
35. 9 God appeared unto Jacob again, when he
48. 3 Jacob said..God Almighty appeared unto
Exod. 3. 2 LORD appeared unto him in a flame of
3. 16 LORD God of your fathers..appeared unto
4. 1 LORD hath not appeared unto thee
4. 5 God of Jacob, hath appeared unto thee
6. 3 I appeared unto Abraham..and unto J.
16. 10 glory of the LORD appeared in the cloud
23. 15 and none shall appear before me empty
23. 17 thy males shall appear before the LORD
34. 20 And none shall appear before me empty
34. 23 shall all your men children appear
34. 24 thou shalt go up to appear before the
Lev. 9. 4 to-day the LORD will appear unto you
9. 6 the glory of the LORD shall appear unto
9. 23 the glory of the LORD appeared unto all
13. 14 when raw flesh appeareth..he shall be
13. 57 if it appear still in the garment, either
16. 2 I will appear in the cloud upon the mercy
Num 14. 10 LORD appeared in the tabernacle of the
16. 19 LORD appeared unto all the congregation
16. 42 and the glory of the LORD appeared
20. 6 glory of the LORD appeared unto them
Deut 16. 16 shall all thy males appear before the LORD
16. 16 they shall not appear before the LORD
31. 11 Israel is come to appear before the LORD
31. 15 the LORD appeared in the tabernacle
Judg. 6. 12 the angel of the LORD appeared unto him
13. 3 the angel of the LORD appeared unto the
13. 10 the man hath appeared unto me, that
13. 21 LORD did no more appear to Manoah
1 Sa. 1. 22 I will bring him, that he may appear
3. 21 the LORD appeared again in Shiloh
2 Sa. 22. 16 the channels of the sea appeared, the
1 Ki. 3. 5 LORD appeared to Solomon in a dream
9. 2 LORD appeared to Solomon the second
11. 9 which had appeared unto him twice
2 Ch. 1. 7 that night did God appear unto Solomon
3. 1 appeared unto David his father, in the
7. 12 LORD appeared to Solomon by night
Psa. 42. 2 when shall I come and appear before God?
84. 7 (everyone of them)..appeareth before God
90. 16 Let thy work appear unto thy servants
102. 16 when.. he shall appear in his glory
Song 2. 12 The flowers appear on the earth; the
Isa. 1. 12 When ye come to appear before me
66. 5 he shall appear to your joy, and they
Jer. 13. 26 upon thy face, that..shame may appear
31. 3 LORD hath appeared of old unto me
Eze. 10. 1 appeared over them..a sapphire stone
10. 8 appeared..a man's hand under their
19. 11 appeared in her height with the multitude
21. 24 in all your doings your sins do appear
Dan. 1. 15 their countenances appeared fairer and
8. 1 a vision appeared unto me..me Daniel
8. 1 which appeared unto me at the first
Mal. 3. 2 who shall stand when he appeareth?
8. *To be seen, look out*, שָׁקַף *shaqaph*, 2.
Jer. 6. 1 evil appeareth out of the north, and
9. *To shine again*, ἀναφαίνομαι *anaphainomai.*
Luke 19. 11 kingdom..should immediately appear
10. *To manifest (one's self)*, ἐμφανίζω *emphanizō.*
Matt 27. 53 after his resurrection..appeared unto
Heb. 9. 24 now to appear in the presence of God for
11. *To shine upon*, ἐπιφαίνω *epiphainō.*
Acts 27. 20 when neither sun nor stars..appeared
Titus 2. 11 For the grace of God..hath appeared to
3. 4 that the kindness and love..appeared
12. *To come*, ἔρχομαι *erchomai.*
Acts 22. 30 commanded the chief priests..to [appear]
13. *To see, be seen*, ὄπτομαι *optomai.*
Matt 17. 3 there appeared unto them Moses and
Mark 9. 4 there appeared unto them Elias with
Luke 1. 11 there appeared unto him an angel of the
9. 31 who appeared in glory, and spake of his
22. 43 [there appeared an angel unto him from]
24. 34 The Lord is risen..and hath appeared to
Acts 2. 3 there appeared unto them cloven tongues
7. 2 The God of glory appeared unto our
7. 30 when forty years were expired..appeared
7. 35 the angel which appeared to him in the
9. 17 Jesus, that appeared unto thee in the way
16. 9 a vision appeared to Paul in the night
26. 16 I have appeared..the which I will appear
Heb. 9. 28 them that look for him shall he appear
Rev. 12. 1 there appeared a great wonder in heaven
12. 3 there appeared another wonder in heaven
14. *To shine, appear, be seen*, φαίνομαι *phainomai.*
Matt. 1. 20 the angel of the Lord appeared unto him
2. 7 enquired..what time the star appeared
2. 13 the angel of the Lord appeareth to Joseph
2. 19 an angel of the Lord appeareth in a dream
6. 16 that they may appear unto men to fast
6. 18 That thou appear not unto men to fast
13. 26 brought forth..then appeared the tares
23. 27 which indeed appear beautiful outward
23. 28 Even so ye also outwardly appear
24. 30 then shall appear the sign of the Son of
Mark 16. 9 [when (Jesus) was risen..appeared first]
Luke 9. 8 And of some, that Elias had appeared
Rom. 7. 13 But sin, that it might appear sin, working
2 Co. 13. 7 not that we should appear approved, but
Heb. 11. 3 were not made of things which do appear
Jas. 4. 14 It is even a vapour, that appeareth for a
1 Pe. 4. 18 shall the ungodly and the sinner appear?
15. *To be manifest*, εἰμὶ φανερός *eimi phaneros.*
1 Ti. 4. 15 that thy profiting may appear to all
16. *To make manifest*, φανερόω *phaneroō.*
Mark 16. 12 [After that he appeared in another form]
16. 14 [Afterward he appeared unto the eleven]
2 Co. 5. 10 we must all appear before the judgment
7. 12 that our care for you..might appear unto
Col. 3. 4 Christ..shall appear..ye shall also appear
Heb. 9. 26 he appeared to put away sin by the
1 Pe. 5. 4 when the chief Shepherd shall appear, ye
1 Jo. 2. 28 that, when he shall appear, we may have
3. 2 it doth not yet appear..he shall appear
Rev. 3. 18 shame of thy nakedness do not appear

APPEAR, made —
Making bare, מַחְשֹׂף *machsoph.*
Gen. 30. 37 and made the white appear..in the rod

APPEARANCE —
1. *Appearance*, מַרְאֶה *mareh.*
Num. 9. 15 upon the tabernacle..the appearance of
9. 16 and the appearance of fire by night
Eze. 1. 5 And this (was) their appearance; they had
1. 13 their appearance..like the appearance of
1. 14 as the appearance of a flash of lightning
1. 16 the appearance of the wheels and their
1. 16 their appearance and their work..as it
1. 26 as the appearance of a sapphire stone
1. 26 as the appearance of a man above upon it
1. 27 appearance of fire..from the appearance
1. 27 from the appearance..the appearance of
1. 28 as the appearance of the bow that is
1. 28 so (was) the appearance of the brightness
1. 28 This (was) the appearance of the likeness
8. 2 the app. of fire..from the app...the app.
10. 1 as the appearance of the likeness of a
10. 9 the appearance of the wheels..as the
10. 10 their appearances, they four had one
10. 22 their appearances and themselves: they
40. 3 whose appearance..like the appearance
41. 21 the appearance..as the appearance
42. 11 the way..(was) like the appearance of the
43. 3 according to the appearance of the vision
Dan. 8. 15 there stood..the appearance of a man
10. 6 his face as the appearance of lightning
10. 18 like the appearance of a man, and he
Joel 2. 4 The appearance..as the appearance
2. *Sight*, εἶδος *eidos.*
1 Th. 5. 22 Abstain from all appearance of evil
3. *Sight*, ὄψις *opsis.*
John 7. 24 Judge not according to the appearance
4. *Face, countenance*, πρόσωπον *prosōpon.*
2 Co. 5. 12 them which glory in appearance, and not

APPEARANCE, outward —
1. *Eye*, עַיִן *ayin.*
1 Sa. 16. 7 man looketh on the outward appearance

2. *Face, countenance,* πρόσωπον *prosōpon.*
2 Co. 10. 7 on things after the outward appearance?

APPEARETH —
Appearance, מַרְאֶה *mareh.*
Lev. 13. 43 leprosy appeareth in the skin of the

APPEARING —
1. *Uncovering,* ἀποκάλυψις *apokalupsis.*
1 Pe. 1. 7 and glory at the appearing of Jesus Christ
2. *Manifestation,* ἐπιφάνεια *epiphaneia.*
1 Ti. 6. 14 the appearing of our Lord Jesus Christ
2 Ti. 1. 10 the appearing of our Saviour Jesus Christ
4. 1 judge..at his appearing and his kingdom
4. 8 unto all them also that love his appearing
Titus 2. 13 Looking for..the glorious appearing of

APPEAR, not —
Not evident, ἄδηλος *adēlos.*
Luke 11. 44 for ye are as graves which appear not

APPEASE, to —
1. *To cover, pacify,* כָּפַר *kaphar,* 3
Gen. 32. 20 I will appease him with the present
2. *To quiet,* שָׁקַט *shaqat,* 5.
Prov. 15. 18 (he that is) slow to anger appeaseth strife
3. *To let or send down,* καταστέλλω *katastellō.*
Acts 19. 35 the town-clerk had appeased the people

APPEASED, to be —
To cease, settle down, שָׁכַךְ *shakak.*
Esth. 2. 1 wrath of king Ahasuerus was appeased

APPERTAIN, to —
To be becoming, יָאָה *yaah.*
Jer. 10. 7 O King..to thee doth it appertain

APPETITE —
1. *Life,* חַיָּה *chaiyah.*
Job 38. 39 or fill the appetite of the young lions
2. *Soul,* נֶפֶשׁ *nephesh.*
Prov. 23. 2 if thou (be) a man given to appetite
Eccl. 6. 7 and yet the appetite is not filled

APPETITE, to have —
To go or run to and fro, שָׁקַק *shaqaq.*
Isa. 29. 8 faint, and his soul hath appetite

AP-PHI'-A, Ἀπφία.
A female disciple to whom, with Philemon and Archippus, Paul wrote an epistle.
Phm. 2 to (our) beloved A., and Archippus

AP-PII FO'-RUM, *market of Appius (Claudius).*
A well-known station, 43 miles from Rome, on the Appian Way, the great road from Rome to the Bay of Naples. The site is near *Treponti,* where the forty-third mile stone is still preserved.
Acts 28. 15 they came to meet us as far as A. forum

APPLE —
Apple, quinces, תַּפּוּחַ *tappuach.*
Prov. 25. 11 A word fitly spoken..apples of gold in
Song 2. 5 comfort me with apples: for I (am) sick
7. 8 and the smell of thy nose like apples

APPLE of the eye —
1. *Little man,* אִישׁוֹן *ishon* (Ps. 17. 8 with *bath*).
Deut 32. 10 he kept him as the apple of his eye
Psa. 17. 8 Keep me as the apple of the eye, hide
Prov. 7. 2 Keep..my law as the apple of thine eye
2. *The pupil, or gate,* בָּבָה *babah.*
Zech. 2. 8 toucheth you toucheth the apple of his e.
3. *Daughter,* בַּת *bath.*
Lam. 2. 18 let not the apple of thine eye cease

APPLE TREE —
Apple-tree, תַּפּוּחַ *tappuach.*
Song 2. 3 As the apple-tree among the trees of the
8. 5 I raised thee up under the apple-tree
Joel 1. 12 the apple-tree..is withered away

APPLY, to —
1. *To cause to go in,* בּוֹא *bo,* 5.
Psa. 90. 12 we may apply (our) hearts unto wisdom
Prov 23. 12 Apply thine heart unto instruction
2. *To incline,* נָטָה *natah,* 5.
Prov. 2. 2 apply thine heart to understanding
3. *To give,* נָתַן *nathan.*
Eccl. 8. 9 All this have I seen, and applied my heart
8. 16 I applied mine heart to know wisdom
4. *To go round,* סָבַב *sabab.*
Eccl. 7. 25 I applied mine heart to know..wisdom
5. *To set, place, put,* שִׁית *shith.*
Prov 22. 17 apply thine heart unto my knowledge

APPOINT, to —
1. *To say,* אָמַר *amar.*
1 Ki. 5. 6 according to all that thou shalt appoint
11. 18 Pharaoh..appointed him victuals and
Esth. 2. 15 Hegai..keeper of the women, appointed
2. *To choose,* בָּחַר *bachar.*
2 Sa. 15. 15 whatsoever..the king shall appoint
3. *To speak,* דָּבַר *dabar,* 3.
1 Ki. 12. 12 the third day, as the king had appointed
4. *To decree, engrave,* חָקַק *chaqaq.*
Prov. 8. 29 he appointed the foundations of the earth
5. *To cause to know,* יָדַע *yada,* 5.
1 Sa. 21. 2 I have appointed (my) servants to such
6. *To decide, manifest,* יָכַח *yakach,* 5.
Gen. 24. 14 thou hast appointed for thy servant
24. 44 hath appointed out for my master's son
7. *To found, appoint,* יָסַד *yasad,* 3.
Esth. 1. 8 king had appointed to all the officers
8. *To appoint,* יָעַד *yaad.*
2 Sa. 20. 5 the set time which he had appointed
Jer. 47. 7 shore? there hath he appointed it
Mic. 6. 9 hear ye the rod, and who hath appointed
9 *To number,* מָנָה *manah,* 3.
Job 7. 3 wearisome nights are appointed to me
Dan. 1. 5 king appointed them a daily provision
1. 10 the king, who hath appointed your
10. *To point out, indicate, define,* נָקַב *naqab.*
Gen. 30. 28 Appoint me thy wages, and I will give it
11. *To give,* נָתַן *nathan.*
Exod 30. 16 appoint it for the service of the
Num 35. 6 six cities..which ye shall appoint for the
Josh. 20. 2 Appoint out for you cities of refuge
2 Ki. 8. 6 the king appointed unto her a certain
1 Ch. 16. 4 appointed (certain) of the Levites to
Ezra 8. 20 David..had appointed for the service
Neh. 9. 17 in their rebellion appointed a captain
Eze. 4. 6 I have appointed thee each day for a year
36. 5 the heathen..have appointed my land
45. 6 ye shall appoint the possession of the
12. *To cause to stand,* עָמַד *amad,* 5.
1 Ch. 15. 16 appoint their brethren..the singers
15. 17 Levites appointed Heman the son of Joel
2 Ch. 8. 14 he appointed, according to the order of
20. 21 he appointed singers unto the LORD, and
31. 2 Hezekiah appointed the courses of the
33. 8 I have appointed for your fathers
Ezra 3. 8 Zerubbabel..appointed the Levites, from
Neh. 6. 7 thou hast also appointed prophets to
7. 3 appoint watches of the inhabitants of
12. 31 I..appointed two great (companies of
13. 30 I..appointed the wards of the priests
Esth. 4. 5 Hatach..whom he had appointed to
13. *To do, make,* עָשָׂה *asah.*
Job 14. 5 thou hast appointed his bounds that he
Psa. 104. 19 he appointed the moon for seasons
14. *To inspect, overlook,* פָּקַד *paqad.*
Num. 3. 10 thou shalt appoint Aaron and his sons
4. 27 ye shall appoint unto them in charge
Jer. 15. 3 I will appoint over them four kinds
49. 19 a chosen (man, that) I may appoint over
50. 44 a chosen (man, that) I may appoint over
51. 27 Ashchenaz; appoint a captain against
15. *To charge,* פָּקַד *paqad,* 5.
Gen. 41. 34 let him appoint officers over the land
Lev. 26. 16 I will even appoint over you terror
Num. 1. 50 thou shalt appoint the Levites over the
1 Sa. 29. 4 thou hast appointed him, and let him not
2 Ki. 7. 17 the king appointed the lord on whose
Esth. 2. 3 let the king appoint officers in all the
16. *To command,* צָוָה *tsavah,* 3.
1 Sa. 25. 30 the LORD..shall have appointed thee
2 Sa. 6. 21 to appoint me ruler over the people of
17. 14 the LORD had appointed to defeat the
1 Ki. 1. 35 I have appointed him to be ruler 20. 42
Neh. 5. 14 I was appointed to be their governor in
17. *To set apart,* קָדַשׁ *qadesh,* 5.
Josh 20. 7 they appointed Kedesh in Galilee in
18. *To raise up,* קוּם *qum,* 5.
Dan. 5. 21 he appointeth over it whomsoever he will
19. *To cause to meet, prepare,* קָרָה *qarah,* 5.
Num 35. 11 ye shall appoint you cities to be cities of
20. *To set,* שׂוּם *sum.*
Exod. 9. 5 LORD appointed a set time, saying
21. 13 I will appoint thee a place whither he
Num. 4. 19 appoint them every one to his service
1 Sa. 8. 11 He will..appoint..for himself, for his
8. 12 he will appoint him captains over
2 Sa. 7. 10 I will appoint a place for my people
2 Ki. 10. 24 Jehu appointed fourscore men without
11. 18 the priest appointed officers over the
18. 14 king of Assyria appointed..three hundred
2 Ch. 23. 18 Jehoiada appointed the officers of the
Psa. 78. 5 he..appointed a law in Israel which
Isa. 44. 7 since I appointed the ancient people
61. 3 To appoint unto them that mourn in
Jer. 33. 25 I have not appointed the ordinances of
Eze. 21. 19 thou son of man, appoint thee two ways
21. 20 Appoint a way that the sword may come
21. 22 to appoint captains..to appoint..rams
Hos. 1. 11 the children..appoint themselves one
21. *To set, place, put,* שִׁית *shith.*
Job 14. 13 thou wouldest appoint me a set time
Isa. 26. 1 salvation will (God) appoint..walls and
22. *To send,* שָׁלַח *shalach.*
1 Ki. 5. 9 unto the place that thou shall appoint
23. *To shew, point out,* ἀναδείκνυμι *anadeiknumi.*
Luke 10. 1 After these things the Lord appointed
24. *To be laid off or aside,* ἀπόκειμαι *apokeimai.*
Heb. 9. 27 as it is appointed unto men once to die
25. *To arrange throughout,* διατάσσω *diatassō.*
Luke 3. 13 Exact no more than that..appointed you
Acts 7. 44 tabernacle..as he had appointed
20. 13 for so had he appointed, minding himself
Tit. 1. 5 ordain elders..as I had appointed thee
26. *To put throughout,* διατίθημι *diatithēmi.*
Luke 22. 29 I appoint unto you..hath appointed..me
27. *To put, place,* ἵστημι *histēmi.*
Acts 1. 23 they appointed two, Joseph called
17. 31 Because he hath appointed a day, in the
28. *To set down,* καθίστημι *kathistēmi.*
Acts 6. 3 whom we may appoint over this business
29. *To do, make,* ποιέω *poieō.*
Heb. 3. 2 was faithful to him that appointed him
30. *To arrange together,* συντάσσω *suntassō.*
Matt 26. 19 the disciples did as Jesus had appointed
27. 10 the potter's field, as the Lord appointed
31. *To arrange, set in order,* τάσσω *tassō.*
Matt 28. 16 where Jesus had appointed them
Acts 22. 10 things which are appointed for thee to do
28. 23 when they had appointed him a day
32. *To put, place,* τίθημι *tithēmi.*
Matt 24. 51 and appoint (him) his portion with the
Luke 12. 46 and will appoint him his portion with
1 Th. 5. 9 God hath not appointed us to wrath, but
2 Ti. 1. 11 Whereunto I am appointed a preacher
Heb. 1. 2 Son, whom he hath appointed heir of all
1 Pe. 2. 8 whereunto also they were appointed

APPOINT before, to —
To arrange before hand, προτάσσομαι *protassomai.*
Acts 17. 26 determined the times before appointed

APPOINT a time, to —
To cause to meet, convene, יָעַד *yaad,* 5.
Jer. 49. 19 and who will appoint me the time?
50. 44 and who will appoint me the time?

APPOINTED —
1. *Sons of death,* בְּנֵי תְמוּתָה *bene temuthah.*
Psa. 79. 11 preserve thou those that are app: to die
2. *To be at a set season,* זָמַן *zaman,* 4.
Ezra 10. 14 wives in our cities come at appointed
Neh. 10. 34 at times appointed year by year, to burn
13. 31 at times appointed, and for the first-fruits
3. *To gird on,* חָגַר *chagar.*
Judg 18. 11, 16 six hundred men appointed with
18. 17 six hundred men..appointed with
4. *Statute,* חֹק *choq.*
Job 23. 14 For he performeth..appointed for me
5. *Statute, decreed thing,* חֻקָּה *chuqqah.*
Jer. 5. 24 he reserveth unto us the appointed weeks
6. *New or full moon,* כֶּסֶא *kese.*
Prov. 7. 20 will come home at the day appointed
7 *Appointed place or time,* מוֹעֵד *moed.*
Gen. 18. 14 At the time appointed I will return
Exod 23. 15 in the time appointed of the month Abib
Num. 9. 2 keep the passover at his appointed season
9. 3 ye shall keep it in his appointed season
9. 7 in his appointed season among the
9. 13 in his appointed season, that man..bear
Josh. 8. 14 all his people, at a time appointed
1 Sa. 13. 11 camest not within the days appointed
20. 35 went..into the field, at the..appointed
2 Sa. 24. 15 the morning even to the time appointed
Job 30. 23 the house appointed for all living
Isa. 1. 14 Your new moons and your appointed
Jer. 46. 17 he hath passed the time appointed
Dan. 8. 19 at the time appointed the end (shall be)
11. 27 the end..at the time appointed
11. 29 At the time appointed he shall return
11. 35 because (it is) yet for a time appointed
8. *Appointed place,* מוּעָדָה *muadah.*
Josh 20. 9 These were the cities appointed for all
9. *To be set up,* נָצַב *natsab,* 2.
1 Sa. 19. 20 Samuel standing (as) appointed over them
10. *To be marked out or off,* סָמַן *saman,* 2.
Isa. 28. 25 cast in the..appointed barley..the rye
[*See also* Destruction, season, time.]

APPOINTED, to be —
1. *To number,* מָנָה *manah,* 3.
Job 7. 3 wearisome nights are appointed to me
2. *To be numbered,* מָנָה *manah,* 4.
1 Ch. 9. 29 of them also (were) appointed to oversee
3. *To be appointed,* פָּקַד *paqad,* 2.
Neh. 7. 1 singers and the Levites were appointed
12. 44 were some appointed over the chambers
4. *To be laid,* κεῖμαι *keimai.*
1 Th. 3. 3 yourselves know that we are appointed

APPOINTED place —
Appointed place, appointment, מִפְקָד *miphqad.*
Eze. 43. 21 the appointed place of the house, without

APPOINTED sign —
Appointed sign, מוֹעֵד *moed.*
Judg 20. 38 there was an appointed sign between

APPOINTED time —
1. *Appointed time,* מוֹעֵד *moed.*
Jer. 8. 7 the stork..knoweth her appointed times
Hab 2. 3 the vision (is) yet for an appointed time

2. *Warfare*, צָבָא *tsabah.*
Job 7. 1 (Is there) not an appointed time to man
14. 14 all the days of my appointed time will I
Dan. 10. 1 true, but the time appointed (was) long

APPOINTED unto him —
Saying, אֵמֶר *emer.*
Job 20. 29 heritage appointed unto him by God

APPOINTMENT —
1. *Saying*, מַאֲמַר *memar.*
Ezra 6. 9 according to the appointment of the
2. *Mouth*, פֶּה *peh.*
Num. 4. 27 At the appointment of Aaron and his sons
2 Sa. 13. 32 by the appointment of Absalom this hath

APPOINTMENT, to make an —
To meet together by appointment, יָעַד *yaad*, 2.
Job 2. 11 they had made an appointment together

APPREHEND, to —
1. *To receive thoroughly*, καταλαμβάνω *katalambanō.*
Phil. 3. 12 I may apprehend..I am apprehended
3. 13 I count not myself to have apprehended
2. *To press, seize*, πιάζω *piazō.*
Acts 12. 4 when he had apprehended him, he put
2 Co. 11. 32 the governor..desirous to apprehend me

APPROACH —
1. *To draw near*, קָרַב *qareb.*
Deut 20. 3 ye approach this day unto battle against
2. *Near*, קָרוֹב *qarob.*
Eze. 42. 13 the priests that approach..shall eat
43. 19 approach unto me, to minister unto me,

APPROACH, to —
1. *To draw nigh*, נָגַשׁ *nagash.*
Num. 4. 19 when they approach unto the most holy
Jer. 30. 21 engaged his heart to approach unto me ?
2. *To be nigh*, נָגַשׁ *nagash*, 2.
Deut 20. 2 the priests shall approach and speak
Jer. 30. 21 he shall approach unto me : for who
3. *To draw near*, קָרַב *qareb.*
Lev. 18. 6 None of you shall approach to any
18. 14 thou shalt not approach to his wife
18. 19 thou shalt not approach unto a woman
20. 16 if a woman approach unto any beast
21. 17 let him not approach to offer the bread
21. 18 that hath a blemish..shall not approach
Deut 31. 14 thy days approach that thou must die
Josh. 8. 5 the people..will approach unto the city
2 Ki. 16. 12 the king approached to the altar, and
Eze. 42. 14 shall approach to (those things) which
4. *To draw nigh*, ἐγγίζω *eggizo.*
Luke 12. 33 where no thief approacheth, neither moth
Heb. 10. 25 the more, as ye see the day approaching

APPROACH nigh, to —
To be drawn nigh, נָגַשׁ *nagash*, 2.
2 Sa. 11. 20 Wherefore approached ye so nigh unto

APPROACH, to cause to —
To cause to draw near, קָרַב *qareb*, 3.
Psa. 65. 4 thou choosest, and causest to approach

APPROACH, to make to —
To cause to draw nigh, נָגַשׁ *nagash*, 5.
Job 40. 19 can make his sword to approach (unto)

APPROACH unto, which no man—
Unapproached, ἀπρόσιτος *aprositos.*
1 Ti. 6. 16 light which no man can approach unto

APPROACHING —
A drawing near, קִרְבָה *qerabah.*
Isa. 58. 2 they take delight in approaching to God

APRON —
1. *Anything girded on*, חֲגוֹרָה *chagorah.*
Gen. 3. 7 sewed fig leaves..and made..aprons
2. *Handkerchief or apron*, σιμικίνθιον *simikinthion.*
Acts 19. 12 unto the sick handkerchiefs or aprons

APPROVE, to —
1. *To see*, רָאָה *raah.*
Lam. 3. 36 To subvert a man..the LORD approveth
2. *To be pleased*, רָצָה *ratsah.*
Psa. 49. 13 yet their posterity approve their sayings
3. *To show off*, ἀποδείκνυμι *apodeiknumi.*
Acts 2. 22 a man approved of God among you by
4. *To test, make proof of*, δοκιμάζω *dokimazō.*
Rom. 2. 18 knowest (his) will, and approvest the
1 Co. 16. 3 whomsoever ye shall approve by
Phil. 1. 10 That ye may approve things that are
5. *To place together*, συνιστάω *sunistaō.*
2 Co. 6. 4 in all (things) approving ourselves as the
7. 11 ye have approved yourselves to be clear

APPROVED —
Tested, tried, δόκιμος *dokimos.*
Rom 14. 18 he that..serveth Christ (is)..approved of
16. 10 Salute Apelles approved in Christ
1 Co. 11. 19 that they which are approved may be
2 Co. 10. 18 not he that commendeth..is approved
13. 7 not that we should appear approved, but
2 Ti. 2. 15 Study to shew thyself approved unto God

APT —
To do, (lit. *doers*), עָשָׂה *asah.*
2 Ki. 24. 16 all (that were) strong (and) apt for war

APT to teach —
Apt to teach, διδακτικός *didaktikos.*
1 Ti. 3. 2 A bishop then must be..apt to teach
2 Ti. 2. 24 but be gentle unto all..apt to teach

A-QUI'-LA, Ἀκύλας *eagle.*
A Jew whom Paul found at Corinth on his arrival from Athens.
Acts 18. 2 And found a certain Jew named A., born
18. 18 sailed thence..with him Priscilla and A.
18. 26 whom when A. and Priscilla had heard
Rom. 16. 3 Greet Priscilla and A. my helpers in Christ
1 Co. 16. 19 A. and Priscilla salute you much in the
2 Ti. 4. 19 Salute Prisca and A., and the household

AR, עָר *city.*
The capital of Moab, on the left bank of the river Arnon. It was in Jerome's time known as Areopolis and Rabbath Moab. The site is still called *Rabba*, between *Kerek* and the *Wady Mojeb*, about 11 miles from each.
Num 21. 15 brook that goeth..to the dwelling of A.
21. 28 it hath consumed A. of Moab, (and) the
Deut. 2. 9 because I have given A. unto the children
2. 18 Thou art to pass over through A., the
2. 29 As..the Moabites which dwell in A., did
Isa. 15. 1 Because in the night A. of Moab is laid

A'-RA, אָרָא *strong.*
Son of Jether, of the tribe of Asher, B.C. 1540.
1 Ch. 7. 38 And the sons of Jether..Pispah, and A.

A'-RAB, אֲרָב *a court.*
A city in the hill country of Judah, near Hebron.
Josh. 15. 48-52 And in the mountains..A., and Dumah

A-RA'-BAH, הָעֲרָבָה *the plain, wilderness.*
The valley on both sides of the Jordan from the Sea of Galilee to the southern extremity of the Salt Sea. This word is translated "plain" in many places, but seems to denote a particular place in Josh. xviii. The description of an *arabah* is beautifully given in Jer. 51. 43.
Josh. 18. 18 And passed along..over against A.
18. 18 northward, and went down unto A.

A-RA-BI-A, עֲרָב, הָעֲרָב, עֲרָב *wilderness.*
Generally in the Scriptures this name is applied to Arabia Petræa, or that portion of the great Arabian Peninsula which consists of that of Sinai, Idumea, and the region of Mount Seir, being bounded by Egypt and the upper part of the Red Sea, the Land of Canaan, and Northern Arabia. Its oldest inhabitants were called Horim or Horites, because of their living in "holes or caves;" these were supplanted by the Edomites, and the Ishmaelites, and the Amalekites. The first mention of the name occurs in the reign of Solomon, B.C. 1014–975, when he is represented as receiving gold from "all the kings of Arabia," but whether as tribute or as a present is not mentioned (1 Ki. 10. 15; 2 Ch. 9. 14); Jehoshaphat, B.C. 941, is also represented as receiving from the Arabians 1700 rams, and 7700 he-goats (2 Ch. 17. 11); the Arabians, who are represented as "near the Ethiopians," came up against Judah in the days of Jehoram, B.C. 887, plundered his house, carried away his wives and his sons (whom they afterwards slew) except Jehoahaz (*or* Ahaziah, *or* Azariah), his youngest son (2 Ch. 21. 17; 22. 1); they are said to dwell in Gurbaal, a place unknown, and to have been defeated by Uzziah, B.C. 810 (2 Ch. 26. 7); Geshem the Arabian, joined with Sanballat the Horonite and Tobiah the Ammonite, to mock and intimidate Nehemiah (Neh. 2. 19; 4. 7; 6. 1); the woe denounced against Babylon was, that "neither shall the Arabian pitch tent there" (Isa. 13. 20); a woe was denounced against Arabia itself, against a forest there, and against the travelling companies of Dedanim, the land of Tema, and the glory of Kedar (Isa. 21. 13–17); lust for idolatry is represented as that of the Arabian in the wilderness watching for prey (Jer. 3. 2); their kings, distinct from those of Dedan, and Tema, and Buz, had to drink of the cup of the Lord from the hand of Jeremiah (Jer. 25. 24).

Arabia and the princes of Kedar traded with Tyre, B.C. 588 (Eze. 27. 21); some of its inhabitants were among the hearers of the Apostles on the day of Pentecost (Acts 2. 11); and were perhaps converted, and with these Paul may have associated himself when he went to Arabia after his conversion (Gal. 1. 17; 4. 25). It is sometimes referred to as "Kedem," *or* "the East," as in Gen. 10. 30; 25. 6; 29. 1; Num. 23. 7, &c. This would seem to have been the name given to it by the inhabitants of Egypt and Canaan, as being to the East of these countries, as "*Arab*," or the "West," may have been given to it by the people of Babylonia. The principal tribes in Arabia Petræa, with which the Bible principally deals, were the Amalekites, Edomites, Geshurites, Gezerites, Hagarites, Horites, Ishmaelites, Kadmonites, Kenites, Kenizzites, Kederenes, Midianites, Nabathæans, with the Moabites and Ammonites. The chief places mentioned are Almon-Diblathaim, Alush, Baal-Zephon, Bemoth, Beeroth, Bene-jaakan Beer-lahai-roi, Bozrah (in Edom), Buz, Diklah, Dinhabah, Dizahab, Dophkah, Ebronah, Elath, Elim, Eneglaim, En-mishpat, Ezion-geber, Gebal, &c.
1 Ki. 10. 15 Beside..of all the kings of A., and of the
2 Ch. 9. 14 And all the kings of A. and governors
Isa. 21. 13 burden upon A. In the forest in A.
Jer. 25. 24 And all the kings of A., and all the kings
Eze. 27. 21 A., and all the princes of Kedar, they
Gal. 1. 17 but I went into A., and returned again
4. 25 For this Agar is mount Sinai in A., and

A-RA-BI-AN, עַרְבִי, עֲרָבִי.
The Gentile appellation of the inhabitants of Arabia.
2 Ch. 17. 11 and the A. brought him flocks, seven
21. 16 LORD stirred up..the spirit of the..A.
22. 1 for the band..that came with the A. to
26. 7 And God helped him..against the A.
Neh. 2. 19 But when..Geshem the A., heard (it), they
4. 7 when Sanballat, and Tobiah, and the A.
6. 1 Sanballat, and Tobiah, and Gesham the A.
Isa. 13. 20 neither shall the A. pitch tent there
Jer. 3. 2 In the ways hast thou sat..as the A. in
Acts 2. 11 Cretes and A., we do hear them speak

A'-RAD, עֲרָד *fugitive.*
1. A king who attacked the Israelites near Mount Hor, and was defeated, B.C. 1452.
Num 21. 1 And (when) king A. the Canaanite, which
33. 40 And king A. the Canaanite, which dwelt
2. A Benjamite, son of Beriah, one of the principal inhabitants of Aijalon, B.C. 1400.
1 Ch. 8. 15 [sons of Elpaal]..Zebadiah, and A., and
3. A town or district in the S. of Judah, N. of the wilderness.
Josh. 12. 14 [These (are) the kings]..the king of A.
Judg 1. 16 wilderness of Judah..in the south of A.

A'-RAH, אָרַח *wayfarer.*
1. An Asherite, and son of Ulla, B.C. 1500.
1 Ch. 7. 39 And the sons of Ulla; A. and Haniel, and
2. The father of a family that came up from exile, B.C. 536.
Ezr. 2. 5 The children of A., seven hundred seventy
Neh. 7. 10 The children of A., six hundred fifty
3. A Jew whose granddaughter became the wife of Tobiah the Ammonite, who attempted to hinder Nehemiah in the rebuilding of Jerusalem, B.C. 536.
Neh. 6. 18 son in law of Shechaniah the son of A.

A'-RAM, אֲרָם *high, exalted.*
1. A son of Shem, B.C. 2280.
Gen. 10. 22 children of Shem; Elam..Lud, and A.
10. 23 And the children of A.; Uz, and Hul, and
1 Ch. 1. 17 The sons of Shem; Elam..Lud, and A.
2. Son of Kemuel Abraham's nephew, B.C. 1838.
Gen. 22. 21 Kemuel the father of A.
3. This term is used to denote the whole country of Syria, but especially the hilly districts. In such cases it is generally translated *Syria* or *Mesopotamia.*
Num 23. 7 Balak..hath brought me from A.
4. A district of the hill country N. of Canaan.
1 Ch. 2. 23 And he took Geshur, and A., with the
5. Son of Shamer, of the tribe of Asher.
1 Ch. 7. 34 And the sons of Shamer; Ahi..and A.
Matt. 1. 3 Phares begat Esrom; and Esrom begat A
1. 4 And A. begat Aminadab; and Aminadab
Luke 3. 33 Aminadab, which was (the son) of A.
Aram is used in the Hebrew to denote the nation of which *Aram*, son of Shem, was the founder, or that dwelt in the country called *Aram.* In such cases the English version has it always rendered *Syrians.*

A-RA-MI-TESS, הָאֲרַמִּיָּה *the female Aramite.*
Manasseh's concubine.
1 Ch. 7. 14 his concubine the A. bare Machir the

A-RAM NA-HA-RA'-IM, אֲרַם נַהֲרַיִם *Aram of two rivers.*
The country between the Tigris and the Euphrates, called in Greek *Mesopotamia.*
Psa. 60. *title.* when he strove with A. Naharaim, and

A-RAM ZO'-BAH, אֲרַם צוֹבָה *Aram of Tsobah.*
The land between the Orontes and the Euphrates, N.E of Damascus, and S. of Hamath.
Psa. 60. *title.* when he strove with..A. Zobah

A'-RAN, אֲרָן *firmness.*
Son of Seir the Horite, B.C. 1700.
Gen. 36. 28 children of Dishan (are) these; Uz, and A
1 Ch. 1. 42 The sons of Dishan; Uz, and A.

A-RA'-RAT, אֲרָרָט *creation, holy land.*
A district of Armenia, between the river Araxes and the lakes Van and Urumia.
Gen. 8. 4 the ark rested..upon the mountains of A.
Jer. 51. 27 call..against her the kingdoms of A.

A-RAU'-NAH, אֲרַוְנָה,(אֲרַנְיָה) *Jah is firm.*
A Jebusite from whom David purchased the site of an altar to the Lord. (In 1 Ch. 21. 15, it is *Ornan.*) B.C. 1040.
2 Sa. 24. 16 angel..was by the threshing-place of A.
24. 18 an altar..in the threshing-floor of A.
24. 20 And A. looked, and saw the king and his
24. 20 and A. went out, and bowed himself
24. 21 And A. said, Wherefore is my lord the
24. 22 And A. said unto David, Let my lord the
24. 23 All these (things) did A., as a king, give
24. 23 And A. said unto the king, The LORD thy
24. 24 And the king said unto A., Nay; but I

AR'-BA, אַרְבַּע *strength of Baal.*
Father of the Anakim (Hivites) and Nephilim (giants). The name Arba occurs in the Hebrew in connection with Kirjath "city" only, which is left untranslated in the English version, so that "Kirjath-arba" appears as the name of the city which is elsewhere called the "City of Arba."

Gen. 35. 27 And Jacob came..unto the city of A.
Josh 15. 13 unto Caleb..he gave..the city of A. the
21. 11 And they gave them the city of A. the

AR-BA-THITE, עַרְבָתִי *belonging to Arabah.*
The patronymic of Abialbon and of Abiel.

2 Sa. 23. 31 [one of the thirty]..Abi-albon the A.
1 Ch. 11. 32 Hurai of the brooks of Gaash, Abiel the A.

AR-BITE, אַרְבִּי *a native of Arab.*
Paarai was one of David's guard; in the parallel list of Chronicles it is given as *Ben-ezbai*, by a change in letters not unfrequent.

2 Sa. 23. 35 [One of the thirty]..Paarai the A.

ARCHANGEL —
Chief messenger, ἀρχάγγελος *archaggelos.*
1 Th. 4. 16 with the voice of the archangel, and with
Jude 9 Michael the archangel, when contending

AR-CHE-LA'-US, Ἀρχέλαος *people's chief.*
A son of Herod the Great, who succeeded his father as ruler of Idumea, Judea, and Samaria.

Matt. 2. 22 But when he heard that A. did reign in

ARCHER —
1. *To tread (a bow),* (קֶשֶׁת) דָּרַךְ *darak (qesheth).*
1 Ch. 8. 40 the sons of Ulam were mighty..archers
Jer. 51. 3 let the archer bend his bow, and against

2. *To shoot, shoot arrows,* חָצַץ *chatsats,* 3.
Judg. 5. 11 (are delivered) from the noise of archers

3. *To shoot,* יָרָה *yarah.*
1 Ch. 10. 3 the archers hit him, and he was wounded
2 Ch. 35. 23 the archers shot at king Josiah; and

4. *Archer,* רַב *rab.*
Job 16. 13 His archers compass me round about, he

5. *Bow,* קֶשֶׁת *qesheth.*
Isa. 21. 17 the residue of the number of archers
22. 3 they are bound by the archers: all that

6. *Shooters with a bow,* מוֹרִים (אֲנָשִׁים) בַּקֶּשֶׁת [*yarah* 5].
1 Sa. 31. 3 and he was sore wounded of the archer
1 Ch. 10. 3 and he was wounded of the archers

7. *A bowman shooter,* רֹבֵה קַשָּׁת [*rabah*].
Gen. 21. 20 and he grew..and became an archer

8. *Owner of arrows,* בַּעַל חֵץ *baal chets.*
Gen. 49. 23 The archers have sorely grieved him

ARCHES —
1. *Arches, porches,* אֵילַמִּים *elammim.*
Eze. 40. 21 the arches..were after the measure of the
40. 22 their arches, and their palm trees,
40. 22, 26 the arches thereof (were) before them
40. 24, 29, 33 arches thereof..according to those
40. 25, 29, 33 in the arches thereof round about
40. 31 the arches thereof (were) toward the utter
40. 34 the arches thereof (were) toward the
40. 36 the arches thereof, and the windows to it

2. *Arches, porches,* אֵלַמּוֹת *elammoth.*
Eze. 40. 16 And..narrow windows..to the arches
40. 30 the arches round about (were) five

AR-CHE-VITES, אַרְכְּוָיֵא. *Meaning uncertain.*
The inhabitants of Orchæ in Chaldea removed to Samaria to colonise the land after the Israelites were carried away.

Ezra 4. 9 Then..Rehum the chancellor and..the A.

AR'-CHI, הָאַרְכִּי *the long.*
A city on the border of Ephraim, between Luz and Ataroth.

Josh. 16. 2 passeth along unto the borders of A. to A.

ARCH-IP'-PUS, Ἄρχιππος *chief groom.*
One whom Paul exhorts to fidelity.

Col. 4. 17 And say to A., Take heed to the ministry
Phm. 2 to (our) beloved Apphia, and A. our

AR-CHITE, הָאַרְכִּי *the long.*
The patronymic of Hushai, David's friend, B.C. 1050.

2 Sa. 15. 32 Hushai the A. came to meet him with his
16. 16 And it came to pass, when Hushai the A.
17. 5 Call now Hushai the A. also, and let us
17. 14 The counsel of Hushai the A. (is) better
1 Ch. 27. 33 Hushai the A. (was) the king's companion

ARC-TU'-RUS, עָשׁ, עַיִשׁ *group, crowd.*
A constellation commonly called the Great Bear, of which the principal star is Dubbhe.

Job 9. 9 Which maketh A., Orion, and Pleiades
38. 32 canst thou guide A. with his sons?

ARD, אַרְדְּ *sprout, descent.*
1. A son of Benjamin, B.C. 1700.
Gen. 46. 21 sons of Benjamin (were) Belah and A.
2. A son of Bela, son of Benjamin, B.C. 1660.
Num 26. 40 the sons of Bela were A. and Naaman

AR-DITES, הָאַרְדִּי *the Ardite, belonging to Ard.*
Patronymic of the grandsons of Bela.

Num 26. 40 (of Ard), the family of the A.

AR'-DON, אַרְדּוֹן *descendant.*
Son of Caleb, son of Hezron, B.C. 1560.

1 Ch. 2. 18 her sons (are) these; Jesher..and A.

ARE there —
1. *Are there? there are or is,* אִישׁ *ish.*
Mic. 6. 10 Are there yet the treasures of wickedness

2. *There is or are,* יֵשׁ *yesh.*
Jer. 14. 22 Are there (any) among the vanities of

AR-E'-LI, אַרְאֵלִי *valiant, heroic.*
A son of Gad, B.C. 1700.

Gen. 46. 16 And the sons of Gad; Zephion..and A.
Num 26. 17 of A. the family of the Arelites

AR-E-LITES, אַרְאֵלִי *the patronymic of Areli's family.*
Num 26. 17 of Areli the family of the A.

A-RE-O-PA-GITE, Ἀρεοπαγίτης *of the Areopagus.*
Dionysius, a convert, is designated thus.

Acts 17 34 among the which (was) Dionysius the A.

A-RE-O-PA'-GUS, Ἄρειος Πάγος *Mars' Hill.*
This institution is attributed to Cecrops, the founder of Athens, B.C. 1556; Solon, B.C. 594, extended its jurisdiction. The guardianship of the laws and the power of enforcing them was intrusted by Solon to this court. Religion and the education of youth were placed under its control. Its constitution was preserved until Pericles, B.C. 461, caused himself to be elected without having previously received the appointment of archon. Paul was brought before this court A.D. 51 (Acts 17. 19).

Acts 17. 19 they took him, and brought him unto A.

A-RE'-TAS, Ἀρέτας *pleasing.*
An ethnarch in N. Arabia, whose deputy sought to apprehend Paul in Damascus.

2 Cor 11. 32 In Damascus the governor under A. the

AR'-GOB, אַרְגֹּב *strong.*
1. A district of the kingdom of Og in Bashan, afterwards called "Trachonitis,"..and now El-lejeh; it had no less than sixty cities.
Deut. 3. 4 all the region of A., the kingdom of Og
3. 13 all the region of A., with all Bashan
3. 14 all the country of A. unto the coasts of G.
1 Ki. 4. 13 the region of A., which (is) in Bashan
2. A man of rank under Pekah, son of Remaliah, B.C. 761.
2 Ki. 15. 25 palace of the king's house, with A. and

ARGUE, to —
To reason, יָכַח *yakach,* 5.
Job 6. 25 but what doth your arguing reprove?

ARGUMENT —
Reasoning, תּוֹכַחַת *tokachath.*
Job 23. 4 I would..fill my mouth with arguments

A-RI'-DAI, אֲרִידַי. *Meaning uncertain.*
A son of Haman, hanged along with his father.

Esth. 9. 9 Parmashta and Arisai, and A., and V.

A-RI-DA'-THA, אֲרִידָתָא.
Son of Haman, one of the ten who were hanged along with their father, B.C. 510.

Esth. 9. 8 Poratha, and Adalia, and A.

A-RI'-EH, הָאַרְיֵה *lion of Jah.*
A companion of Argob, B.C. 761.

2 Ki. 15. 25 Pekah..conspired..with Argob and A.

A-RI-EL, אֲרִיאֵל *lion of God.*
1. A person whom Ezra sent along with others to Iddo at Casiphia, B.C. 457.
Ezra 8. 16 Then sent I for Eliezer, for A., for
2. A symbolic name for Jerusalem.
Isa. 29. 1 Woe to A., to A., the city (where) David
29. 2 yet I will distress A., and there shall be
29. 2 and it shall be unto me as A.
29. 7 the nations that fight against A.

ARIGHT —
1. *Right,* כֵּן *ken.*
Jer. 8. 6 I hearkened..they spake not aright

2. *Upright thing,* מֵישָׁרִים *mesharim.*
Prov. 23. 31 when it is red..it moveth itself aright

ARIGHT, to set —
To prepare, set aright, כּוּן *kun,* 5.
Psa. 78. 8 (that) set not their heart aright

ARIGHT, to use —
To make good, use well, יָטַב *yatab,* 5.
Prov. 15. 2 tongue of the wise useth knowledge aright

A-RI-MA-THE'-A, Ἀριμαθαία *a height.*
Another name for Ramah, where Samuel dwelt, 5 miles N. of Jerusalem, on the borders of Ephraim and Benjamin. The LXX. call it *Armathaim,* and Josephus *Armatha.* It is now called *Rameh.*

Matt 27. 57 there came a rich man of A., named
Mark 15. 43 Joseph of A., an honourable counsellor
Luke 23. 51 (he was) of A., a city of the Jews: who
John 19. 38 And after this Joseph of A., being a

AR-I'-OCH, אַרְיוֹךְ *lion-like.*
1. A king of Ellasar in Assyria, B.C. 1926.
Gen. 14. 1 it came to pass in the days of..A. king of
14. 9 With..A. king of Ellasar; four kings with
2. Captain of the guard of Nebuchadnezzar.
Dan. 2. 14 Daniel answered with..wisdom to A.
2. 15 He anwered and said to A. the king's
2. 15 Then A. made the thing known to Daniel
2. 24 Therefore Daniel went in unto A., whom
2. 25 Then A. brought in Daniel before the king

A-RI'-SAI, אֲרִיסַי. *Meaning uncertain.*
A son of Haman the Agagite, B.C. 510.

Esth. 9. 9 Parmashta, and A., and Aridai, and

ARISE, to —
1. *To rise, burst forth,* זָרַח *zarach.*
Psa. 104. 22 The sun ariseth, they gather themselves
112. 4 Unto the upright there ariseth light
Eccl. 1. 5 The sun also ariseth, and the sun goeth
1. 5 hasteth to his place where he arose
Isa. 60. 2 the LORD shall arise upon thee, and his
Jon. 4. 8 when the sun did arise, that God
Nah. 3. 17 when the sun ariseth they flee away
Mal 4. 2 shall the Sun of righteousness arise

2. *To lift up oneself,* נָשָׂא *nasa.*
Psa. 89. 9 when the waves thereof arise

3. *To go up,* עָלָה *alah.*
Gen. 19. 15 And when the morning arose, then the an.
2 Sa. 11. 20 if so be that the king's wrath arise
1 Ki. 18. 44 there ariseth a little cloud out of the sea
2 Ch. 36. 16 the LORD arose against his people

4. *To stand up,* עָמַד *amad.*
Esth. 4. 14 and deliverance arise to the Jews 1 Ch. 20. [4

5. *To rise up,* קוּם *qum.*
Gen 13. 17 Arise, walk through the land in the length
19. 15 Arise, take thy wife, and thy..daughters
19. 33 when she lay down, nor when she arose
19. 35 the younger arose, and lay with him
21. 18 Arise, lift up the lad, and hold him
24. 10 he arose, and went to Mesopotamia
24. 61 Rebekah arose, and her damsels, and
27. 19 arise, I pray thee, sit..eat of my venison
27. 31 Let my father arise, and eat of his son's
27. 43 arise, flee thou to Laban my brother
28. 2 Arise, go to Padan-aram, to the house of
31. 13 arise, get thee out from this land
35 1 Arise, go up to Beth-el, and dwell there
35. 3 let us arise, and go up to Beth-el
37. 7 my sheaf arose, and also stood upright
38. 19 she arose, and went away, and laid by
41. 30 there shall arise..seven years of famine
43. 8 we will arise and go; that we may live
43. 13 Take..your brother, and arise, go again
Exod. 1. 8 there arose up a new king over Egypt
Deut. 9. 12 Arise, get thee down quickly from hence
10. 11 Arise, take (thy) journey before the people
13. 1 there arise among you a prophet
17. 8 If there arise a matter too hard for thee
34. 10 there arose not a prophet since in Israel
Josh. 1. 2 arise, go over this Jordan, thou, and
8. 1 take all the people of war..and arise
8. 3 Joshua arose, and all the people of war
8. 19 the ambush arose quickly out of their
18. 8 the men arose, and went away: and
24. 9 Then Balak..arose and warred against
Judg. 2. 10 there arose another generation after them
3. 20 And he arose out of (his) seat
4. 9 Deborah arose, and went
5. 7 until that I Deborah arose, that I arose
5. 12 arise, Barak, and lead thy captivity captive
7. 9 Arise, get thee down unto the host; for I
7. 15 Arise; for the LORD hath delivered into
8. 21 Gideon arose, and slew Zeba and Zalmunna
10. 1 there arose to defend Israel Tola the son
10. 3 after him arose Jair, a Gileadite, and
13. 11 Manoah arose, and went after his wife
16. 3 Samson..arose at midnight, and took the
18. 9 Arise, that we may go up against them
19. 3 her husband arose, and went after her
20. 8 all the people arose as one man, saying
20. 18 the children of Israel arose, and went up
Ruth 1. 6 Then she arose with her daughters-in-law
1 Sa. 3. 6 Samuel arose and went to Eli, and
3. 8 he arose and went to Eli, and said
9. 3 Kish said to Saul..arise, go seek the asses
9. 26 Saul arose, and they went out both of them
13. 15 Samuel arose, and gat him up from Gilgal
16. 12 Arise, anoint him: for this (is) he
17. 35 when he arose against me, I caught (him)
17. 52 the men of Israel and of Judah arose, and
17. 48 the Philistine arose, and came and drew
18. 27 David arose and went, he and his men
20. 25 Jonathan arose, and Abner sat by Saul's
20. 34 Jonathan arose from the table in fierce
20. 41 David arose out of (a place) toward the
20. 42 he arose..and Jonathan went into the
21. 10 David arose and fled that day for fear
23. 4 Arise, go down to Keilah; for I will
23. 13 David and his men..arose and departed
23. 16 Saul's son arose, and went to David
23. 24 they arose, and went to Ziph before Saul
24. 4 David arose, and cut off the skirt of Saul's
24. 8 David..arose afterward, and went out of
25. 1 David arose, and went down to..Paran
25. 41 she arose, and bowed herself on (her) face
25. 42 Abigail..arose and rode upon an ass
26. 2 Saul arose, and went down to..Ziph
26. 5 David arose, and came to the place where
27. 2 David arose, and he passed over with
28. 23 he arose from the earth, and sat upon the
31. 12 the valiant men arose, and went all night
2 Sa. 2. 14 Let the young men now arise, and play
2. 15 there arose and went over by number
3 21 I will arise and go, and will gather all
6. 2 David arose, and went with all the people
11. 2 David arose from off his bed, and walked
12. 17 And the elders of his house arose
12. 20 David arose from the earth, and washed
13. 15 Amnon said unto her, Arise, be gone

2 Sa. 13. 29 all the king's sons arose, and every man
13. 31 the king arose, and tare his garments
14. 23 Joab arose and went to Geshur, and
14. 31 Joab arose, and came to Absalom
15. 9 he arose, and went to Hebron
15. 14 Arise, and let us flee; for we shall
17. 1 I will arise and pursue after David
17. 21 Arise, and pass quickly over the water
17. 22 David arose, and all the people that
17. 23 he saddled (his) ass, and arose, and gat
19. 7 arise, go forth, and speak comfortably
19. 8 the king arose, and sat in the gate
22. 39 they could not arise..they are fallen
23. 10 He arose, and smote the Philistines until
1 Ki. 1. 50 arose, and went, and caught hold on the
2. 40 Shimei arose, and saddled his ass, and
3. 12 neither after thee shall any arise like
3. 20 she arose at midnight, and took my son
8. 54 he arose from before the altar of the LORD
11. 18 they arose out of Midian, and came to
11. 40 Jeroboam arose, and fled into Egypt, unto
14. 2 Arise, I pray thee, and disguise thyself
14. 4 Jeroboam's wife..arose, and went to
14. 12 Arise thou..get thee to thine own house
14. 17 Jeroboam's wife arose, and departed, and
17. 9 Arise, get thee to Zarephath, which
17. 10 So he arose and went to Zarephath
19. 3 he arose and went for his life, and came
19. 5 an angel..said unto him, Arise..eat
19. 7 and said, Arise..eat, because the journey
19. 8 he arose, and did eat and drink, and went
19. 21 he arose, and went after Elijah and
21. 7 arise, (and) eat bread, and let thine heart
21. 15 Arise, take possession of the vineyard of
21. 18 Arise, go down to meet Ahab king of
2 Ki. 1. 3 Arise, go up to meet the messengers of
1. 15 he arose, and went down with him unto
4. 30 And he arose, and followed her
7. 7 they arose and fled in the twilight, and
7. 12 the king arose in the night, and said unto
8. 1 Arise, and go thou and thine household
8. 2 the woman arose..and she went with
9. 6 he arose, and went into the house; and he
10. 12 And he arose and departed, and came to
11. 1 she arose and destroyed all the seed royal
12. 20 his servants arose, and made a conspiracy
23. 25 neither after him arose there..like him
25. 26 all..arose, and came to Egypt: for they
1 Ch. 10. 12 They arose, all the valiant men, and took
22. 16 Arise..and be doing, and the LORD be
22. 19 arise therefore, and build ye the sanctuary
2 Ch. 6. 41 arise, O LORD God, into thy resting place
22. 10 she arose and destroyed all the seed
29. 12 the Levites arose, Mahath
30. 14 they arose and took away the altars
30. 27 the Levites arose and blessed the people
Ezra 9. 5 I arose up from my heaviness; and having
10. 4 Arise; for (this) matter (belongeth) unto
10. 5 Then arose Ezra, and made the chief
Neh. 2. 12 I arose in the night, I and some few men
2. 20 we his servants will arise and build: but
Esth. 7. 7 the king arising from the banquet of
8. 4 Esther arose, and stood before the king
Job 1. 20 Job arose, and rent his mantle, and
7. 4 When shall I arise, and the night be
19. 18 Yea..I arose, and they spake against me
25. 3 upon whom doth not his light arise?
29. 8 and the aged arose..stood up
Psa. 3. 7 Arise, O LORD; save me, O my God: for
7. 6 Arise, O LORD, in thine anger, lift up
9. 19 Arise, O LORD; let not man prevail
10. 12 Arise, O LORD; O God, lift up thine hand
12. 5 now will I arise, saith the LORD; I will
17. 13 Arise, O LORD, disappoint him, cast him
44. 26 Arise, for our help, and redeem us for thy
68. 1 Let God arise, let his enemies be scattered
74. 22 Arise, O God, plead thine own cause
76. 9 God arose to judgment, to save all the
78. 6 should arise and declare..to their
82. 8 Arise, O God, judge the earth: for thou
88. 10 shall the dead arise (and) praise thee?
102. 13 Thou shalt arise, (and) have mercy upon
109. 28 when they arise, let them be ashamed
132. 8 Arise, O LORD, into thy rest; thou, and
Prov. 6. 9 when wilt thou arise out of thy sleep?
Song 2. 13 Arise, my love, my fair one, and come
Isa. 2. 19, 21 he ariseth to shake terribly the earth
21. 5 arise, ye princes..anoint the shield
23. 12 daughter of Zidon: arise, pass over to
26. 19 shall live..(with) my dead body..arise
31. 2 he..will arise against the house of the
49. 7 Kings shall see and arise, princes also
52. 2 arise..sit down, O Jerusalem: loose
60. 1 Arise, shine; for thy light is come, and
Jer. 1. 17 arise, and speak unto them all that I
2. 27 but..they will say, Arise, and save us
2. 28 let them arise, if they can save thee in
6. 4 arise, and let us go up at noon. Woe
6. 5 Arise, and let us go by night, and let us
8. 4 Shall they fall, and not arise? shall he
13. 4 Take the girdle..and arise, go to Euphr.
13. 6 Arise, go to Euphrates, and take the
18. 2 Arise, and go down to the potter's house
31. 6 Arise ye, and let us go up to Zion unto
41. 2 Then arose Ishmael the son of Nethaniah
46. 16 Arise, and let us go again to our own
49. 28 Arise ye, go up to Kedar, and spoil the men
49. 31 Arise, get you up unto the wealthy nation
Lam. 2. 19 Arise, cry out in the night: in the
Eze. 3. 22 Arise, go forth into the plain, and I will
3. 23 I arose, and went forth into the plain
Hos. 10. 14 shall a tumult arise among thy people

Amos 7. 2 by whom shall Jacob arise? for he (is)
7. 5 by whom shall Jacob arise? for he (is)
Obad. 1 Arise ye, and let us rise up against her
Jon. 1. 2 Arise, go to Nineveh, that great city
1. 6 O sleeper? arise, call upon thy God, if so
3. 2 Arise, go unto Nineveh, that great city
3. 3 So Jonah arose, and went unto Nineveh
3. 6 he arose from his throne, and he laid
Mic. 2. 10 Arise ye, and depart..this (is) not (your)
4. 13 Arise and thresh, O daughter of Zion
6. 1 Arise, contend thou before the mountains
7. 8 O mine enemy: when I fall, I shall arise

6. *To rise up*, קוּם *qum.*
Dan. 2. 39 after thee shall arise another kingdom
6. 19 the king arose very early in the morning
7. 5 said thus unto it, Arise, devour much flesh
7. 17 great beasts..shall arise out of the earth
7. 24 the ten horns..(are) ten kings..shall arise

7. *To awake*, קוּץ *quts*, 5.
Psa. 44. 23 Awake..arise, cast (us) not off for ever

8. *To stir up*, עוּר *ur.*
Hab. 2. 19 Woe unto him that saith to..stone, Arise

9. *To go or come up*, ἀναβαίνω *anabainō.*
Luke 24. 38 said unto them..why do thoughts arise
Rev. 9. 2 there arose a smoke out of the pit, as the

10. *To (make) rise up*, ἀνατέλλω *anatellō.*
2 Pe. 1. 19 and the day star arise in your hearts

11. *To make to stand up*, ἀνίστημι *anistēmi.*
Matt. 9. 9 And he arose, and followed him
26. 62 the high priest arose, and said unto him
Mark 2. 14 And he arose and followed him
5. 42 straightway the damsel arose, and walked
7. 24 from thence he arose, and went into the
9. 27 But Jesus..lifted him up; and he arose
10. 1 he arose from thence, and cometh into
14. 57 there arose certain, and bare false witness
Luke 1. 39 Mary arose in those days, and went
4. 38 he arose out of the synagogue, and
4. 39 immediately she arose and ministered
6. 8 And he arose and stood forth
8. 55 her spirit came again, and she arose
15. 18 I will arise and go to my father, and will
15. 20 And he arose, and came to his father
17. 19 he said unto him, Arise, go thy way: thy
23. 1 the whole multitude of them arose, and
24. 12 [Then arose Peter, and ran unto the]
Acts 5. 6 the young men arose, wound him up, and
6. 9 Then there arose certain of the synagogue
7. 18 Till another king arose, which knew not J.
8. 26 Arise, and go toward the south unto the
8. 27 he arose and went: and, behold, a man of
9. 6 the Lord (said) unto him, Arise, and go
9. 11 the Lord (said) unto him, Arise, and go
9. 18 he received sight forthwith, and arose
9. 34 arise, and make thy bed. And he arose
9. 39 Then Peter arose and went with them
9. 40 put them all forth..said, Tabitha, arise
10. 20 Arise therefore, and get thee down, and
11. 7 I heard a voice saying..Arise, Peter; slay
20. 30 Also of your own selves shall men arise
22. 10 the Lord said unto me, Arise, and go into
22. 16 And now why tarriest thou? arise, and be
23. 9 (that were) of the Pharisees' part arose,
Eph. 5. 14 Awake thou that sleepest, and arise from
Heb. 7. 15 after the similitude of..there ariseth

12. *To cast*, βάλλω *ballō.*
Acts 27. 14 there arose against it a tempestuous

13. *To come, become*, γίνομαι *ginomai.*
Matt. 8. 24 there arose a great tempest in the sea
13. 21 when tribulation or persecution ariseth
Mark 4. 17 when affliction or persecution ariseth for
4. 37 there arose a great storm of wind, and
Luke 6. 48 when the flood arose, the stream beat
15. 14 there arose a mighty famine in that land
John 3. 25 Then there arose a question between
Acts 6. 1 there arose a murmuring of the Grecians
11. 19 the persecution that arose about Stephen
19. 23 the same time there arose no small stir
23. 7 when he had so said, there arose a
23. 9 there arose a great cry: and the scribes
23. 10 when there arose a great dissension, the

14 *To wake up thoroughly*, διεγείρω *diegeirō.*
Mark 4. 39 he arose, and rebuked the wind, and said
John 6. 18 the sea arose by reason of a great wind

15. *To wake up*, ἐγείρω *egeirō.*
Matt. 2. 13 Arise and take the young child and his
2. 14 When he arose, he took the young child
2. 20 Arise, and take the young child and his
2. 21 he arose, and took the young child and
8. 15 he touched her hand..and she arose, and
8. 26 Then he arose, and rebuked the winds
9. 5 forgiven thee; or to say, [Arise,] and walk?
9. 6 [Arise,] take up thy bed, and go unto thine
9. 7 he arose, and departed to his house
9. 19 Jesus arose, and followed him, and
9. 25 took her by the hand, and the maid arose
17. 7 Jesus..said, Arise, and be not afraid
24. 24 there shall arise false Christs, and false
25. 7 all those virgins arose, and trimmed their
27. 52 bodies of the saints which slept arose
Mark 2. 9 or to say, [Arise,] and take up thy bed, and
2. 11 I say unto thee, [Arise,] and take up thy
2. 12 immediately he arose, took up the bed
5. 41 and said..Damsel, I say unto thee, [arise]
Luke 5. 24 I say unto thee, [Arise,] and take up thy
7. 14 said, Young man, I say unto thee, Arise

Luke 8. 24 Then he [arose,] and rebuked the wind
8. 54 the hand, and called, saying, Maid, [arise]
John 7. 52 look: for out of Galilee ariseth no
11. 29 As soon as she heard..she arose quickly
14. 31 even so I do. Arise, let us go hence
Acts 9. 8 Saul arose from the earth; and when his

16. *To come into*, εἰσέρχομαι *eiserchomai.*
Luke 9. 46 there arose a reasoning among them

ARISE early, to —

To rise or go early, שָׁכַם *shakam*, 5.
Judg 6. 28 the men..arose early in the morning
19. 5 when they arose early in the morning
19. 8 he arose early in the morning on the
1 Sa. 5. 3 they of Ashdod arose early on the morrow
5. 4 they arose early on the morrow morning
9. 26 And they arose early: and it came to
2 Ki. 19. 35 when they arose early in the morning
Isa. 37. 36 when they arose early in the morning

ARISE up, to —

1. *To go up*, עָלָה *alah.*
Judg 20. 40 the flame began to arise up out of the

2. *To rise up*, קוּם *qum.*
Exod. 1. 8 there arose up a new king over 2 Ki 9. 2
Ezra 9. 5 I arose up from my heaviness; and
Prov. 31. 28 Her children arise up, and call her

3. *To place up*, ἀνίστημι *anistēmi.*
Acts 12. 7 he smote Peter on the side..saying, A. up

A-RIST'-AR-CHUS, Ἀρίσταρχος *the best ruler.*

One who accompanied Paul on his third missionary journey through Asia Minor.
Acts 19. 29 and having caught Gaius and A., men of
20. 4 and of..Thessalonians, A. and Secundus
27. 2 A., a Macedonian of Thessalonica, being
Col. 4. 10 A. my fellow prisoner saluteth you, and
Phm. 24 Marcus, A., Demas, Lucas, my fellow

A-RIST-O'-BU-LUS, Ἀριστόβουλος *the best counsellor.*

A person in Rome, whose household Paul saluted. Some say that he was one of the seventy disciples, and preached in Britain.
Rom 16. 10 Salute them which are of A.'s (household)

ARK—

1. *An ark, chest, coffin*, אָרֹן, אֲרוֹן *aron.*
Exod 25. 10 they shall make an ark (of) shittim wood
25. 14 by the sides of the ark, that the ark
25. 15 staves shall be in the rings of the ark
25. 16 thou shalt put into the ark the testimony
25. 21 above upon the ark; and in the ark
25. 22 two cherubims..upon the ark of the
26. 33 bring..within the vail the ark of the
26. 34 put the mercy seat upon the ark of the
30. 6 by the ark of the testimony, before the
30. 26 thou shalt anoint..the ark of the
31. 7 the ark of the testimony, and the mercy
35. 12 The ark, and the staves thereof, (with)
37. 1 Bezaleel made the ark (of) shittim wood
37. 5 into the rings by the sides of the ark, to
39. 35 The ark of the testimony, and the staves
40. 3 put therein the ark..and cover the ark
40. 5 the incense before the ark of the testimony
40. 20 took and put the testimony into the ark
40. 20 the staves on the ark, and put..the ark
40. 21 he brought the ark into the tabernacle
40. 21 covered the ark of the testimony; as the
Lev. 16. 2 the mercy seat, which (is) upon the ark
Num. 3. 31 their charge (shall be) the ark, and the
4. 5 cover the ark of testimony with it
7. 89 off the mercy seat..upon the ark of
10. 33 the ark of the covenant..went before them
10. 35 when the ark set forward..Moses said
14. 44 nevertheless the ark of the covenant of
Deut 10. 1 come up..and make thee an ark
10. 2 and thou shalt put them in the ark
10. 3 I made an ark (of) shittim wood, and
10. 5 put the tables in the ark which I had
10. 8 bear the ark of the covenant of the LORD
31. 9, 25 bare the ark of the covenant of the
31. 26 and put it in the side of the ark of the
Josh. 3. 3 When ye see the ark..go after it
3. 6 Take up the ark of the covenant, and pass
3. 6 they took up the ark of the covenant, and
3. 8 priests that bear the ark of the covenant
3. 11 the ark of the covenant of the Lord of
3. 13 the priests that bear the ark of the LORD
3. 14 the ark of the covenant before the people
3. 15 they that bare the ark were come unto
3. 15, 17 the priests that bare the ark
4. 5 Pass over before the ark of the LORD
4. 7 the waters..were cut off before the ark
4. 9 the feet of the priests which bare the ark
4. 10 the priests which bare the ark stood in
4. 11 the ark of the LORD passed over, and the
4. 16 Command the priests that bear the ark
4. 18 the priests that bare the ark of the
6. 4 priests shall bear before the ark seven
6. 6 Take up the ark of the covenant, and let
6. 7, 13 pass on before the ark of the LORD
6. 8 and the ark of the covenant..followed
6. 9 and the rereward came after the ark
6. 11 the ark of the LORD compassed the city
6. 12 the priests took up the ark of the LORD
6. 13 bearing seven trumpets..before the ark
7. 6 fell..upon his face before the ark of the
8. 33 the Levites..bare the ark of the covenant
8. 33 stood on this side the ark and on that
Judg 20. 27 for the ark of the covenant of God

1 Sa. 3. 3 where the ark of God (was), and Samuel
4. 3 Let us fetch the ark of the covenant of
4. 4 bring from thence the ark of the covenant
4. 4 Phinehas..there with the ark
4. 5 the ark of the covenant..came into the
4. 6 they understood that the ark..was come
4. 11 And the ark of God was taken
4. 13 his heart trembled for the ark of God
4. 17 and the ark of God is taken
4. 18 when he made mention of the ark
4. 19 she heard the tidings that the ark..was
4. 21 because the ark of God was taken
4. 22 glory is departed..for the ark..is taken
5. 1, 2 the Philistines took the ark of God
5. 3 upon his face to the earth before the ark
5. 4 upon his face to the ground before the ark
5. 7 The ark..shall not abide with us: for
5. 8 What shall we do with the ark of the
5. 8 Let the ark .. and they carried the ark
5. 10 Therefore they sent the ark of God to
5. 10 as the ark of God came to Ekron, that
5. 10 They have brought..the ark..to us, to
5. 11 Send away the ark of the God of Israel
6. 1 the ark of the LORD was in the country
6. 2 What shall we do to the ark of the LORD?
6. 3 send away the ark..send it not empty
6. 8 take the ark..and lay it upon the cart
6. 11 And they laid the ark..upon the cart
6. 13 lifted up their eyes and saw the ark
6. 15 the Levites took down the ark of the
6. 18 whereon they set down the ark of the
6. 19 because they had looked into the ark
6. 21 Philistines have brought again the ark
7. 1 And the men..fetched up the ark of the
7. 1 Eleazar his son to keep the ark of the
7. 2 the ark abode at Kirjath-jearim
14. 18 Bring..the ark of God. For the ark
2 Sa. 6. 2 bring up from thence the ark of God
6. 3 they set the ark of God upon a new
6. 4 the ark..and Ahio went before the ark
6. 6 Uzzah put forth..to the ark of God, and
6. 7 and there he died by the ark of God
6. 9 How shall the ark of the LORD come
6. 10 So David would not remove the ark of
6. 11 the ark of the LORD continued in the
6. 12 The LORD hath..because of the ark of
6. 12 David went and brought up the ark of
6. 13 when they that bare the ark..had gone
6. 15 all the house of Israel brought up the ark
6. 16 as the ark of the LORD came into the city
6. 17 they brought in the ark of the LORD
7. 2 the ark of God dwelleth within curtains
11. 11 The ark, and Israel, and Judah, abide in
15. 24 bearing the ark..set down the ark
15. 25 Carry back the ark of God into the city
15. 29 Zadok..carried the ark of God again to
1 Ki. 2. 26 thou barest the ark of the LORD God
3. 15 stood before the ark of the covenant of
6. 19 to set there the ark of the covenant of
8. 1 that they might bring up the ark of the
8. 3 came, and the priests took up the ark
8. 4 they brought up the ark of the LORD
8. 5 congregation..(were)with..before the ark
8. 6 the priests brought in the ark of the
8. 7 the ark, and the cherubims covered the a.
8. 9 nothing in the ark save the two tables of
8. 21 And I have set there a place for the ark
1 Ch. 6. 31 David set over..after that the ark had
13. 3 let us bring again the ark of our God to
13. 5 to bring the ark of God from Kirjath-jear
13. 6 to bring up thence the ark of God the
13. 7 they carried the ark of God in a new cart
13. 9 Uzza put forth his hand to hold the ark
13. 10 because he put his hand to the ark: and
13. 12 How shall I bring the ark of God..to me?
13. 13 David brought not the ark..to himself
13. 14 the ark of God remained with the family
15. 1 and prepared a place for the ark of God
15. 2 None ought to carry the ark..but the
15. 2 hath the LORD chosen to carry the ark
15. 3 to bring up the ark of the LORD unto his
15. 12 that ye may bring up the ark of the LORD
15. 14 to bring up the ark of the LORD God of
15. 15 And the children..bare the ark of God
15. 23 and Elkanah..doorkeepers for the ark
15. 24 did blow with the trumpets before the ark
15. 24 and Jehiah (were) doorkeepers for the ark
15. 25 David..went to bring up the ark of the
15. 26 the Levites that bare the ark of the
15. 27 and all the Levites that bare the ark, and
15. 28 Thus all Israel brought up the ark of the
15. 29 the ark of the covenant of the LORD came
16. 1 So they brought the ark of God, and set
16. 4 to minister before the ark of the LORD
16. 6 before the ark of the covenant of God
16. 37 he left there before the ark of the
16. 37 to minister before the ark continually
17. 1 but the ark of the covenant..under
22. 19 to bring the ark of the covenant of the
28. 2 to build an house of rest for the ark
28. 18 and covered the ark of the covenant of
2 Ch. 1. 4 But the ark of God had David brought
5. 2 to bring up the ark of the covenant of the
5. 4 came; and the Levites took up the ark
5. 5 And they brought up the ark, and the
5. 6 were assembled unto him before the ark
5. 7 And the priests brought in the ark of the
5. 8 the ark, and the cherubims covered the ark
5. 9 the staves were seen from the ark before
5. 10 nothing in the ark save the two tables
6. 11 And in it have I put the ark, wherein
6. 41 arise..thou, and the ark of thy strength
2 Ch. 8. 11 whereunto the ark of the LORD hath come
35. 3 Put the holy ark in the house which
Psa. 132. 8 Arise..thou, and the ark of thy strength
Jer. 3. 16 say no more, The ark of the covenant of

2. *Ark*, κιβωτός *kibōtos.*
Matt 24. 38 the day that Noe entered into the ark
Luke 17. 27 the day that Noe entered into the ark
Heb. 9. 4 the ark of the covenant overlaid round
11. 7 By faith Noah..prepared an ark to the
1 Pe. 3. 20 while the ark was a preparing, wherein
Rev. 11. 19 there was seen in his temple the ark of

3. *An ark, boat, vessel*, תֵּבָה *tebah.*
Gen. 6. 14 Make thee an ark of gopher wood
6. 14 rooms shalt thou make in the ark
6. 15 length of the ark (shall be) three hundred
6. 16 window shalt thou make to the ark
6. 16 the door of the ark shalt thou set in the
6. 18 thou shalt come into the ark, thou, and
6. 19 every (sort) shalt thou bring into the ark
7. 1 Come thou and all thy house into the ark
7. 7 Noah went .into the ark, because of the
7. 9 There went in two and two..into the ark
7. 13 wives of his sons..into the ark
7. 15 they went in unto Noah into the ark, two
7. 17 the waters increased, and bare up the ark
7. 18 the ark went upon the face of the waters
7. 23 and they that (were) with him in the ark
8. 1 all the cattle..(was) with him in the ark
8. 4 the ark rested in the seventh month, on
8. 6 Noah opened the window of the ark
8. 9 she returned unto him into the ark, for
8. 9 and pulled her in unto him into the ark
8. 10 he sent forth the dove out of the ark
8. 13 Noah removed the covering of the ark
8. 16 Go forth of the ark, thou, and thy wife
8. 19 every beast..went forth out of the ark
9. 10 from all that go out of the ark, to every
9. 18 sons of Noah, that went forth of the ark
Exod. 2. 3 she took for him an ark of bulrushes, and
2. 5 when she saw the ark among the flags

AR-KITE, עַרְקִי *fugitive, belonging to Arka.*
The patronymic of a tribe descended from Canaan, son of Ham, residing in Arca, about 12 miles N. of Tripoli in Syria. Its ruins are now called *Tell Arka.*
Gen. 10. 17 [Canaan begat]..the Hivite, and the A.
1 Ch. 1. 15 [Canaan begat]..the Hivite, and the A.

ARM — [*See* **ARMS.**]

1. *Arm*, אֶזְרוֹעַ *ezroa.*
Job 31. 22 let.. mine arm be broken from the bone
Jer. 32. 21 with a stretched out arm, and with

2. *Arm*, דְּרָע *dera.*
Dan. 2. 32 his breast and his arms of silver, his

3. *Arm*, זְרוֹעַ *zeroa.*
Gen. 49. 24 the arms of his hands were made strong
Exod. 6. 6 redeem you with a stretched out arm
15. 16 by the greatness of thine arm they shall
Deut. 4. 34 by a stretched out arm, and by great
5. 15 God brought..by a stretched out arm
7. 19 hand, and the stretched out arm
9. 29 broughtest..by thy stretched out arm
11. 2 hand, and his stretched out arm
26. 8 brought..with an outstretched arm
33. 20 teareth the arm with the crown of the
33. 27 underneath (are) the everlasting arms
Judg 15. 14 the cords that (were) upon his arms
16. 12 he brake them from off his arms
1 Sa. 2. 31 I will cut off thine arm, and the arm of
2 Sa. 1. 10 the bracelet that (was) on his arm
22. 35 a bow of steel is broken by mine arms
1 Ki. 8. 42 shall hear..of thy stretched out arm
2 Ki. 9. 24 Jehu..smote Jehoram between his arms
17. 36 with great power and a stretched out arm
2 Ch. 6. 32 mighty hand, and thy stretched out arm
32. 8 With him (is) an arm of flesh; but with
Job 22. 9 the arms of the fatherless..been broken
26. 2 (how) savest thou the arm (that hath) no
35. 9 they cry out by reason of the arm of the
38. 15 and the high arm shall be broken
40. 9 Hast thou an arm like God? or canst
Psa. 10. 15 Break thou the arm of the wicked and
18. 34 a bow of steel is broken by mine arms
37. 17 the arms of the wicked shall be broken
44. 3 neither did their own arm save them
44. 3 but thy right hand, and thine arm
77. 15 Thou hast with (thine) arm redeemed thy
89. 10 thou hast scattered..with thy strong arm
89. 13 Thou hast a mighty arm: strong is thy
89. 21 mine arm also shall strengthen him
98. 1 his right hand, and his holy arm
136. 12 strong hand, and with a stretched out arm
Prov. 31. 17 girdeth her loins..strengtheneth her arms
Song 8. 6 Set me..as a seal upon thine arm
Isa. 9. 20 they shall eat..the flesh of his own arm
17. 5 and reapeth the ears with his arm
30. 30 shall shew the lighting down of his arm
33. 2 be thou their arm every morning
40. 10 Behold..his arm shall rule for him
40. 11 he shall gather the lambs with his arm
44. 12 worketh it with the strength of his arms
48. 14 and his arm (shall be on) the Chaldeans
51. 5 and mine arms shall judge the people
51. 5 and on mine arm shall they trust
51. 9 awake, put on strength, O arm of the LORD
52. 10 The LORD hath made bare his holy arm
53. 1 to whom is the arm of the LORD revealed?
59. 16 therefore his arm brought salvation unto
62. 8 The LORD hath sworn..by the arm of his
63. 5 therefore mine own arm brought salvation
Isa. 63. 12 led..by..Moses with his glorious arm
Jer. 17. 5 and maketh flesh his arm, and whose
21. 5 I myself will fight..with a strong arm
27. 5 great power and by my outstretched arm
32. 17 thy great power and stretched out arm
48. 25 Moab is cut off, and his arm is broken
Eze. 4. 7 and thine arm..uncovered, and thou shalt
13. 20 and I will tear them from your arms
20. 33 (As) I live..with a stretched out arm
20. 34 gather you..with a stretched out arm
30. 21 I have broken the arm of Pharaoh king
30. 22 against Pharaoh..and will break his arms
30. 24, 25 I will strengthen the arms of the king
30. 24 I will break Pharaoh's arms, and he
30. 25 the arms of Pharaoh shall fall down
31. 17 (they that were) his arm, (that) dwelt
Dan. 10. 6 his arms and his feet like..polished brass
11. 6 the power of the arm..nor his arm
11. 15 the arms of the south shall not withstand
11. 22 with the arms of a flood shall they be
11. 31 And arms shall stand on his part
Hos. 7. 15 Though I have..strengthened their arms
11. 3 taking them by their arms; but they
Zech. 11. 17 the sword (shall be) upon his arm, and
11. 17 his arm shall be clean dried up, and his

4. *Bosom, lap*, חֹצֶן *chotsen.*
Isa. 49. 22 shall bring thy sons in (their) arms

5. *Shoulder*, כָּתֵף *katheph.*
Job 31. 22 let mine arm fall from my shoulder

6. *Arm*, βραχίων *brachiōn.*
Luke 1. 51 He hath shewed strength with his arm
John 12. 38 to whom hath the arm of the Lord been
Acts 13. 17 with an high arm brought he them out

ARM, to —
1. *To clothe*, לָבֵשׁ *labesh*, 5.
1 Sa. 17. 38 Saul armed David..also he armed him
2. *To draw out*, רוּק *ruq*, 5.
Gen. 14. 14 he armed his trained..born in his

ARM self, to —
1. *To be drawn out or off*, חָלַץ *chalats*, 2.
Num 31. 3 Arm some of yourselves unto the war
2. *To arm self*, ὁπλίζομαι *hoplizomai.*
1 Pe. 4. 1 arm yourselves likewise with the same

ARMED —
1. *To arm*, חָלַץ *chalats.*
Num 31. 5 twelve thousand armed for war
32. 21 will go all of you armed over Jordan
32. 27 will pass over, every man armed for war
32. 29 every man armed to battle, before the
32. 30 will not pass over with you armed
32. 32 We will pass over armed before the LORD
Deut. 3. 18 ye shall pass over armed before your
Josh. 6. 7 let him that is armed pass on before the
2. *By fifties, armed*, חֲמֻשִׁים *chamushim.*
Josh. 1. 14 pass before your brethren armed
4. 12 Manasseh, passed over armed before the
3. *To clothe oneself*, לָבֵשׁ *labesh.*
1 Sa. 17. 5 he (was) armed with a coat of mail
4. *Shield*, מָגֵן *magen.*
Prov. 6. 11 and thy want as an armed man
24. 34 and thy want as an armed man
5. *To clasp, arm oneself*, נָשַׁק *nashaq.*
1 Ch. 12. 2 (They were) armed with bows, and could
Psa. 78. 9 The children of Ephraim, (being) armed

ARMED, to be —
To arm one's self, καθοπλίζομαι *kathoplizomai.*
Luke 11. 21 a strong man armed keepeth his palace

ARMED, to go —
To be armed, drawn out, חָלַץ *chalats*, 2.
Num 32. 17 But we ourselves will go ready armed
32. 20 if ye will go armed before the LORD to

ARMED men —
1. *Armed, drawn out*, חָלוּץ *chaluts.*
Josh. 6. 9 the armed men went before the priests
6. 13 and the armed men went before them
2 Ch. 28. 14 So the armed men left the captives and
2. *Armed, fifties*, חֲמֻשִׁים *chamushim.*
Judg. 7. 11 Then went he..outside of the armed men
3. *To kiss, clasp, arm oneself*, נָשַׁק *nashaq.*
2 Ch. 17. 17 and with him armed men with bow and
4. *Armour*, נֶשֶׁק *nesheq.*
Job 39. 21 he goeth on to meet the armed men

ARMED, ready —
To be drawn out, armed חָלַץ *chalats.*
1 Ch. 12. 23 the numbers..ready armed to the war
12. 24 of Judah..ready armed to the war

ARMED soldier —
To arm, draw out, חָלַץ *chalats.*
Isa. 15. 4 the armed soldiers of Moab shall cry out

AR-MA-GED'-DON, 'Αρμαγεδδών *hill of Megiddo.*
A symbolic name (derived from 2 Ch. 35. 22) for the scene of some great spiritual contest.
Rev. 16. 16 place called in the Hebrew tongue A.

AR-ME'-NI-A, *the Greek form of Ararat.*
Armenia, according to tradition, was settled by Haik, son of Togarmah, and grandson of Japhet (Gen. 10. 3);

it is noticed in Scripture under the names Togarmah and Ararat. The country, afterwards divided into Lesser and Greater Armenia, was frequently invaded by the Assyrians, the Babylonians, the Medes and Persians, and for many years remained in subjection to one or other of these empires. The accounts given by Greek and Roman writers are at variance with those of the Armenian historians. M. St Martin has investigated the subject with diligence, and upon his work the following chronological table is based :—

In B.C. 2107, Haik, fleeing from Belus king of Assyria, settles in Armenia, and becomes its first ruler: 1827, accession of Aram, who carries his arms into Asia Minor and founds Mazaca, *i.e.* Cæsareia of Cappadocia; 1725, Armenia becomes subject to Assyria; 743, Baroïr renders it independent; 565, accession of Tigranes, who restores it to its ancient position; 323, on the death of Alexander it falls under the sway of Greek governors; 317, under Ardoates it throws off the Grecian yoke; 149, Valarsaces, or Wagharshag I., founds the dynasty of the Arsacidæ; 34, Antony leads its sovereign captive to Alexandria; 30, on the death of Antony, Artaxes expels the Romans, and is crowned king. In A.D. 16, Vonones, king of the Parthians, seeks shelter in Armenia, and is made king; 18, Germanicus makes Zeno king under the name of Artaxias; 62, Tiridates king, by order of Nero; 115, invaded and conquered by Trajan; 232, subjected by Ardashir, king of Persia; 276, Tiridates is converted to Christianity by Gregory; 387, Armenia divided between the Romans and the Persians: 428, end of the kingdom of the Arsacidæ.

2 Ki. 19. 37 and they escaped into the land of A.
Isa. 37. 38 and they escaped into the land of A.

ARM HOLE —

Arm-hole, אַצִּיל יָד *atstsil yad.*

Jer. 38. 12 Put now (these)..under thine armholes
Eze. 13. 18 Woe to..that sew pillows to all armholes

ARMIES —

Bare, open spaces, מַעֲרוֹת *maaroth.*

1 Sa. 17. 23 came up..out of the armies of the

AR-MO'-NI, אַרְמֹנִי *of the palace.*

A son of Saul, by Rizpah, B.C. 1050

2 Sa. 21. 8 But the king took..A. and Mephibosheth

ARMOUR —

1. *Pieces of armour, pointed weapons,* זוֹנוֹת *zonoth.*

1 Ki. 22. 38 and they washed his armour

2. *A thing to gird on,* חֲגוֹרָה *chagorah.*

2 Ki. 3. 21 all that were able to put on armour

3. *A thing to draw on,* חֲלִיצָה *chalitsah.*

2 Sa. 2. 21 young men, and take thee his armour

4. *Instrument, vessel,* כְּלִי *keli.*

1 Sa. 14. 1 unto the young man that bare his armour
14. 6 to the young man that bare his armour
17. 54 but he put his armour in his tent
31. 9 they..stripped off his armour
31. 10 they put his armour in the house of Asht.
2 Sa. 18. 15 ten young men that bare Joab's armour
2 Ki. 20. 13 and (all) the house of his armour
1 Ch. 10. 9 they took his head, and his armour, and
10. 10 they put his armour in the house of their
Isa. 39. 2 and all the house of his armour

5. *Long robe,* מַד *mad.*

1 Sa. 17. 38 Saul armed David with his armour
17. 39 David girded his sword upon his armour

6. *Armour, thing joined together,* נֶשֶׁק *nesheq.*

1 Ki. 10. 25 brought every man his present..armour
2 Ki. 10. 2 with you..a fenced city also, and armour
Isa. 22. 8 thou didst look..to the armour of the

7. *Arms, armour,* ὅπλα *hopla.*

Rom 13. 12 let us put on the [armour] of light
2 Co. 6. 7 by the armour of righteousness on the

ARMOUR, (all) —

Whole armour, πανοπλία *panoplia.*

Luke 11. 22 he taketh from him all his armour wherein

ARMOUR (whole) —

Whole armour, πανοπλία *panoplia.*

Eph. 6. 11 Put on the whole armour of God, that
6. 13 take unto you the whole armour of God

ARMOUR BEARER —

Bearer of weapon, נֹשֵׂא כְלִי *nose keli.* [*nasa*]

Judg. 9. 54 called..the young man his armourbearer
1 Sa. 14. 7 his armourbearer said unto him, Do all
14. 12 answered Jonathan and his armourbearer
14. 12 Jonathan said unto his armourbearer
14. 13 climbed up..and his armourbearer
14. 13 and his armourbearer slew after him
14. 14 which Jonathan and his armourbearer
14. 17 Jonathan and his armourbearer (were)
16. 21 and he became his armourbearer
31. 4 Then said Saul unto his armourbearer
31. 4 his armourbearer would not; for he was
31. 5 when his armourbearer saw that Saul
31. 6 So Saul died..and his armourbearer
2 Sa. 23. 37 Zelek..armourbearer to Joab the son of
1 Ch. 10. 4 Then said Saul to his armourbearer
10. 4 his armourbearer would not; for he was
10. 5 his armourbearer saw that Saul was dead
11. 39 Zelek..the armourbearer of Joab

ARMOURY —

1. *Treasury,* אוֹצָר *otsar.*

Jer. 50. 25 The LORD hath opened his armoury

2. *Thing joined on or together,* נֶשֶׁק *nesheq.*

Neh. 3. 19 over against the going up to the armoury

3. *Armoury, heap of swords,* תַּלְפִּיּוֹת *talpiyyoth.*

Song 4. 4 Thy neck (is) like..for an armoury

ARMS —

Arms (as bent or crooked), ἀγκάλαι *agkalai.*

Luke 2. 28 Then took he him up in his arms.

ARMS, to take (up) in —

To take in arms, ἐναγκαλίζομαι *enagkalizomai.*

Mark 9. 36 and when he had taken him in his arms
10. 16 took them up in his arms, put (his) hands

ARMY —

1. *Troop,* גְּדוּד *gedud.*

2 Ch. 25. 9 I have given to the army of Israel?
25. 10 the army that was come to him out of
25. 13 the soldiers of the army which Amaziah
Job 25. 3 Is there any number of his armies, 29. 25.

2. *An army force,* חֵיל צָבָא *chel* (=*chayil*) *tsaba.*

2 Ch. 26. 13 under their hand (was) an army, three

2a. *Strength, might, force,* חַיִל *chayil.*

Exod. 14. 9 Pharaoh, and his horsemen, and his army
Deut 11. 4 what he did unto the army of Egypt
1 Ki. 20. 19 and the army which followed them
20. 25 number thee an army, like the army that
2 Ki. 25. 5 the army of the Chaldees pursued after
25. 5 all his army were scattered from him
25. 10 all the army of the Chaldees, that
25. 23 when all the captains of the armies
25. 26 all the people..the captains of the armies
1 Ch. 11. 26 the valiant men of the armies..Asahel
2 Ch. 13. 3 Abijah..with an army of valiant men of
14. 8 Asa had an army..that bare targets and
16. 4 Ben-hadad..sent the captains of..armies
24. 24 the army of the Syrians came with a
26. 13 under their hand (was) an army, three
Neh. 2. 9 king had sent captains of the army
4. 2 he spake before..the army of Samaria
Isa. 43. 17 Which bringeth forth..the army and the
Jer. 32. 2 the king of Babylon's army besieged Jer.
34. 1 when Nebuchadnezzar..and all his army
34. 7 king of Babylon's army fought against J.
34. 21 the hand of the king of Babylon's army
35. 11 for fear of the army of the Chaldeans
35. 11 for fear of the army of the Syrians
37. 5 Pharaoh's army was come forth out of E.
37. 7 Pharaoh's army..shall return to Egypt
37. 10 though ye had smitten the..army of the
37. 11 army..for fear of Pharaoh's army
38. 3 the hand of the king of Babylon's army
39. 1 came Nebuchadrezzar..and all his army
39. 5 the Chaldeans' army pursued after them
46. 2 against the army of Pharaoh-necho king
46. 22 for they shall march with an army
52. 4 Nebuchadrezzar..he and all his army
52. 8 the army of the Chaldeans pursued after
52. 8 all his army was scattered from him
52. 14 all the army of the Chaldeans
Eze. 17. 17 shall Pharaoh with (his) mighty army
27. 10 They of Persia..were in thine army, thy
27. 11 The men of Arvad with thine army
29. 18 Nebuchadrezzar..caused his army to
29. 18 yet had he no wages, nor his army, for
29. 19 and it shall be the wages for his army
32. 31 and all his army slain by the sword
37. 10 they lived..an exceeding great army
38. 4 I will bring thee..and all thine army
38. 15 a great company, and a mighty army
Dan. 11. 7 which shall come with an army, and shall
11. 13 shall certainly come..with a great army
11. 25 stir up his power..with a great army
11. 25 with a very great and mighty army
11. 26 destroy him, and his army shall overflow
Joel 2. 11 shall utter his voice before his army
2. 25 my great army which I sent among you

3. *Might, strength, force,* חַיִל *chayil.*

Dan. 3. 20 mighty men that (were) in his army
4. 35 doeth according to his will in the army

4. *Might, strength, force,* חֵיל *chel.*

Isa. 36. 2 unto king Hezekiah with a great army

5. *Camp,* מַחֲנֶה *machaneh.*

1 Sa. 17. 1 Philistines gathered together their armies
28. 1 Philistines gathered their armies together
29. 1 the Philistines gathered..all their armies
Song 6. 13 As it were the company of two armies

6. *Arrangement,* מַעֲרָכָה *maarakah.*

1 Sa. 4. 2 they slew of the army in the field
4. 12 a man of Benjamin out of the army
4. 16 came out of the army..out of the army
17. 8 he..cried unto the armies of Israel
17. 10 I defy the armies of Israel this day; give
17. 21 put the battle in array, army against army
17. 22 David left..and ran into the army, and
17. 23 came up the champion..out of the armies
17. 26 should defy the armies of the living God?
17. 36 hath defied the armies of the living God
17. 45 God of the armies of Israel, whom thou
17. 48 David hasted, and ran toward the army
23. 3 if we come to Keilah against the armies

7. *Army,* צָבָה *tsabah.*

Zech. 9. 8 I will encamp about..because of the army

8. *Host (as joined together),* צָבָא *tsaba.*

Gen. 26. 26 Phichol the chief captain of his army
Exod. 6. 26 Bring out..according to their armies
7. 4 that I may..bring forth mine armies
12. 17 have I brought your armies out of the
12. 51 the LORD did bring..by their armies
Num. 1. 3 Aaron shall number them by their armies
Num. 2. 3 shall..pitch throughout their armies
2. 9 of Judah..throughout their armies
2. 10 the standard..according to their armies
2. 16 of Reuben..throughout their armies
2. 18 the standard..according to their armies
2. 24 of Ephraim..throughout their armies
2. 25 The standard..by their armies
10. 14, 22 standard..according to their armies
10. 28 journeyings of..according to their armies
33. 1 which went forth out..with their armies
Deut 20. 9 they shall make captains of the armies
Judg. 4. 7 I will draw..the captain of Jabin's army
8. 6 we should give bread unto thine army?
9. 29 Increase thine army, and come out
1 Ch. 20. 1 Joab led forth the power of the army, and
27. 34 the general of the king's army (was) Joab
2 Ch. 25. 7 O king, let not the army of Israel go with
26. 13 under their hand (was) an army, three
Psa. 44. 9 But thou..goest not forth with our armies
60. 10 didst not go out with our armies?
68. 12 Kings of armies did flee apace: and she
Isa. 34. 2 and..fury upon all their armies: he hath

9. *An encampment,* παρεμβολή *parembolē.*

Heb. 11. 34 turned to flight the armies of the aliens

10. *Armament,* στράτευμα *strateuma.*

Matt 22. 7 he sent forth his armies, and destroyed
Acts 23. 27 then came I with an army, and rescued
Rev. 9. 16 the number of the army of the horsemen
19. 14 the armies..in heaven followed him upon
19. 19 and their armies..against his army

11. *A camp, army,* στρατόπεδον *stratopedon.*

Luke 21. 20 ye shall see..compassed with armies

AR'-NAN, אַרְנָן *strong.*

Patronymic of a family descended from David, B.C. 500

1 Ch. 3. 21 the sons of Rephaiah, the sons of A., the

AR'-NON, אַרְנוֹן *rushing stream.*

A river and valley forming the S. boundary of Canaan towards Moab. Rising in the mountains of Arabia, it flows into the Salt Sea, opposite *Ain-gidy.* Now *Mojeb.*

Num 21. 13 pitched on the other side of A., which
21. 13 for A. (is) the border of Moab, between
21. 14 and in the brooks of A.
21. 24 possessed his land from A. unto Jabbok
21. 26 taken all his land..even unto A.
21. 28 the lords of the high places of A.
22. 36 Moab, which (is) in the border of A.
Deut. 2. 24 your journey, and pass over the river A.
2. 36 Aroer..(is) by the brink of the river of A.
3. 8 from the river of A. unto mount Hermon
3. 12 from A., which (is) by the river A., and
3. 16 from Gilead even unto the river A. half
4. 48 Aroer, which (is) by the bank of..river A.
Josh. 12. 1 from the river A. unto mount Hermon
12. 2 Aroer..upon the bank of the river A.
13. 9, 16 Aroer..upon the bank of the river A.
Judg 11. 13 they came up out of Egypt, from A. even
11. 18 and pitched on the other side of A., but
11. 18 for A. (was) the border of Moab
11. 22 from A. even unto Jabbok and from the
11. 26 cities that (be) along by the coasts of A.
2 Ki. 10. 33 from Aroer, which (is) by the river A.
Isa. 16. 2 Moab shall be at the fords of A.
Jer. 48. 20 tell ye it in A., that Moab is spoiled

A'-ROD, אֲרוֹד *descent, posterity.*

One of Gad's sons, whence came the Arodi, B.C. 1700.

Num 26. 17 Of A., the family of the Arodites

A-RO'-DI, אֲרוֹדִי *my posterity.*

The Arodites, descendants of Arod.

Gen. 46. 16 sons of Gad; Ziphion..and A., and

A-RO-DITES, הָאֲרוֹדִי.

The same as the preceding Arodi.

Num. 26. 17 Of Arod, the family of the A.

A-RO'-ER, עֲרֹעֵר, עֲרוֹעֵר *enclosed.*

1. A city near Rabbath Ammon, in the valley of Jabbok, now called *Arieh.*

Num 32. 34 the children of Gad built Dibon..and A.
Josh 13. 25 land of the children of Ammon, unto A.
2 Sa. 24. 5 passed over Jordan, and pitched in A.
Isa. 17. 2 The cities of A. (are) forsaken: they shall

2. A city of the Amorites, on the bank of the Arnon, and now called *Arair.*

Deut. 2. 36 From A., which (is) by the brink of the
3. 12 from A., which (is) by the river Arnon
4. 48 From A., which is by the bank of the
Josh 12. 2 Sihon..in Heshbon, (and) ruled from A.
13. 9 From A., that (is) upon the bank of the
13. 16 And their coast was from A., that (is) on
Judg 11. 26 While Israel dwelt in..A. and her towns
11. 33 And he smote them from A., even till
2 Ki. 10. 33 from A., which (is) by the river Arnon
1 Ch. 5. 8 Shema, the son of Joel, who dwelt in A.
Jer. 48. 19 O inhabitant of A., stand by the way

3. A city in the S. of Judah. Now called *Ararah.*

1 Sa. 30. 28 And to (them) which (were) in A., and

A-RO-E-RITE, עֲרֹעֵרִי *of Aroer.*

The patronymic of one Hothan.

1 Ch. 11. 44 and Jehiel the sons of Hothan the A.

AR'-PAD, AR'-PHAD, אַרְפָּד *a couch, resting place.*

A fortified city near Hamath, perhaps the same as Arvad, now called *Ruad.*

2 Ki. 18. 34 Where (are) the gods of Hamath and of A.

2 Ki. 19. 13 the king of Hamath, and the king of A.
Isa. 10. 9 (is) not Hamath as A? (is) not Samaria as
36. 19 Where (are) the gods of Hamath and A.?
37. 13 the king of Hamath, and the king of A.
Jer. 49. 23 Hamath is confounded, and Arpad: for

AR-PHAX'-AD, אַרְפַּכְשַׁד. *Meaning uncertain.*
A son of Shem, and a tribe E. of the Tigris near Elam and Asshur, in the N. of Assyria, with Media on the E. and Armenia on the N. B.C. 2348–1904.
Gen. 10. 22 The children of Shem; Elam..and A.
10. 24 And A. begat Salah; and Salah begat
11. 10 an hundred years old, and begat A
11. 11 And Shem lived after he begat A. five
11. 12 And A. lived five and thirty years, and
11. 13 And A. lived after he begat Salah four
1 Ch. 1. 17 sons of Shem; Elam, and Ashur, and A.
1. 18 And A. begat Shelah, and Shelah begat
1. 24 Shem, A., Shelah
Luke 3. 36 Cainan, which was (the son) of A

ARRAY —
Clothing, ἱματισμός *himatismos.*
1 Ti. 2. 9 not with broidered hair..or costly array

ARRAY, to —
To clothe, לָבֵשׁ *labesh,* 5.
Gen. 41. 42 arrayed him in vestures of fine linen
2 Ch. 28. 15 all that were naked..and arrayed them
Esth. 6. 9 that they may array the man..whom the
6. 11 Then took Haman..and arrayed Mordecai

ARRAY, in —
To set, place, שִׁית *shith.*
Isa. 22. 7 horsemen shall set themselves in array

ARRAY, put in —
To array, עָרַךְ *arak.*
Jer. 50. 42 (every one) put in array, like a man

ARRAY, to put in —
To array, עָרַךְ *arak.*
2 Sa. 10. 9 and put..in array against the Syrians
10. 8 and put the battle in array at the
10. 10 that he might put (them) in array against
1 Ch. 19. 9 put the battle in array before the gate of
19. 10 and put..in array against the Syrians
19. 17 when David had put the battle in array

ARRAY, to put selves in —
To array, עָרַךְ *arak.*
Judg 20. 20 Israel put themselves in array to fight
20. 22 where they put themselves in array
20. 30 put themselves in array against Gibeah
20. 33 put themselves in array at Baal-tamar
1 Sa. 4. 2 Philistines put themselves in array
Jer. 50. 14 Put yourselves in array against Babylon

ARRAY, to put the battle in —
To array, עָרַךְ *arak.*
1 Sa. 17. 21 For Israel..had put the battle in array

ARRAY self, to —
1. *To clothe,* לָבֵשׁ *labesh.*
Job 40. 10 array thyself with glory and beauty
2. *To cover, wrap up, veil,* עָטָה *atah.*
Jer. 43. 12 he shall array himself with the land of

ARRAY, set in —
To array, עָרַךְ *arak.*
Jer. 6. 23 they ride upon horses, set in array
Joel 2. 5 as a strong people set in battle array

ARRAY, to set in —
To array, עָרַךְ *arak.*
Judg 20. 22 set their battle again in array in the
1 Sa. 17. 2 set the battle in array against the
17. 8 come out to set..battle in array?
1 Ch. 19. 11 they set..in array against the children
19. 17 and set..in array against them
2 Ch. 13. 3 Abijah set the battle in array with an
14. 10 they set the battle in array in the valley

ARRAY, to set selves in —
To array, עָרַךְ *arak.*
2 Sa. 10. 17 the Syrians set themselves in array
Job 6. 4 terrors of God do set themselves in array
Jer. 50. 9 they shall set themselves in array against

ARRAY in, to —
To cast around, περιβάλλω *periballō.*
Luke 23. 11 and arrayed him in a gorgeous robe, and

ARRAYED, to be —
1. *Be clothed,* לָבֵשׁ *labesh,* 4.
2 Ch. 5. 12 their brethren..arrayed in white linen
2. *Be clothed,* περιβάλλομαι [*periballō*].
Mat. 6. 29, Lu. 12. 27, Rev. 7. 13, 17. 4, 19. 8.
3. *Be entered in, be put on,* ἐνδύομαι [*enduō*].
Acts 12. 21 Herod, arrayed in royal apparel

ARRIVE, to —
1. *To sail down,* καταπλέω *katapleō.*
Luke 8. 26 they arrived at the country of the Gad.
2. *To cast alongside,* παραβάλλω *paraballō.*
Acts 20. 15 next (day) we arrived at Samos, and

ARROGANCY —
1. *Pride, rising, excellency,* גָּאוֹן *gaon.*
Prov. 8. 13 pride, and arrogancy..do I hate
Isa. 13. 11 cause the arrogancy of the proud to cease
Jer. 48. 29 the pride of Moab..and his arrogancy
2. *Stiffness, insolence,* עָתָק *athaq.*
1 Sa. 2. 3 let (not) arrogancy come out of your

ARROW —
1. *Arrow,* חֵץ *chets.*
Num 24. 8 pierce..through with his arrows
Deut 32. 23 I will spend mine arrows upon them
32. 42 I will make mine arrows drunk with
1 Sa. 20. 20 I will shoot three arrows on the side
20. 21 find out the arrows..the arrows (are)
20. 22 Behold, the arrows (are) beyond thee; go
20. 36 find out now the arrows which I shoot
20. 38 Jonathan's lad gathered up the arrows
2 Sa. 22. 15 he sent out arrows, and scattered them
2 Ki. 13. 15 Elisha said unto..Take bow and arrows
13. 15 And he took unto him bow and arrows
13. 17 The arrow of the LORD'S deliverance
13. 17 the arrow of deliverance from Syria
13. 18 he said, Take the arrows. And he took
19. 32 He shall not..shoot an arrow there
1 Ch. 12. 2 (hurling) stones, and..arrows out of a
2 Ch. 26. 15 to shoot arrows and great stones withal
Job 6. 4 the arrows of the Almighty (are) within
Psa. 7. 13 he ordaineth his arrows against the
11. 2 they make ready their arrow upon the
18. 14 he sent out his arrows, and scattered
38. 2 thine arrows stick fast in me, and thy
45. 5 Thine arrows (are) sharp in the heart of
57. 4 sons of men, whose teeth (are)..arrows
58. 7 he bendeth (his bow to shoot) his arrows
64. 3 bend (their bows to shoot) their arrows
64. 7 God shall shoot at them (with) an arrow
91. 5 Thou shalt not be afraid for the..arrow
120. 4 Sharp arrows..with coals of juniper
127. 4 As arrows (are) in the hand of a mighty
144. 6 shoot out thine arrows, and destroy them
Prov. 25. 18 a maul, and a sword, and a sharp arrow
26. 18 As a mad (man) who casteth..arrows
Isa. 5. 28 Whose arrows (are) sharp, and all their
7. 24 With arrows and with bows shall (men)
37. 33 He shall not..shoot an arrow there
Jer. 9. 8 Their tongue (is as) an arrow shot out
50. 9 their arrows..as of a mighty expert man
50. 14 shoot at her, spare no arrows: for she
51. 11 Make bright the arrows; gather the
Lam. 3. 12 and set me as a mark for the arrow
Eze. 5. 16 I shall send..the evil arrows of famine
21. 21 he made (his) arrows bright, he consulted
39. 3 I will..cause thine arrows to fall out of
39. 9 shall go forth..and burn..the arrows, and
Hab. 3. 11 at the light of thine arrows they went
Zech. 9. 14 his arrow shall go forth as the lightning
2. *Arrow,* חֵצִי *chetsi.*
1 Sa. 20. 36 he shot an arrow beyond him
20. 37 place of the arrow which Jonathan had
20. 37 Jonathan cried..(Is) not the arrow beyond
20. 38 Jonathan's lad gathered up the arrows
2 Ki. 9. 24 the arrow went out at his heart
3. *Arrow (as piercing, cutting in),* חָצָץ *chatsats.*
Psa. 77. 17 thine arrows also went abroad
4. *Arrow (as flashing, rushing forth),* רֶשֶׁף *resheph.*
Psa. 76. 3 There brake he the arrows of the bow
5. *Son of the bow,* בֶּן־קֶשֶׁת *ben qesheth.*
Job 41. 28 The arrow cannot make him flee
6. *Son,* בֵּן *ben.*
Lam. 3. 13 caused the arrows of his quiver to enter.

ART —
1. *Work,* מַעֲשֶׂה *maaseh.*
Exod 30. 25 an ointment..after the art of the, 30. 35.
2 Ch. 16. 14 prepared by the apothecaries' art
2. *Art, handicraft, skill,* τέχνη *technē.*
Acts 17. 29 stone, graven by art and man's device

ARTS, curious —
Works of care, τὰ περίεργα [*periergon*], Acts 19. 19.

AR-TA-XER'-XES, אַרְתַּחְשַׁשְׂתָּא *great king.*
1. A Persian king, the Longimanus of profane history. In 7th year of his reign Ezra went up to Jerusalem, B.C. 418.
Ezra 7. 1 after these things, in the reign of A king
7. 7 there went up..in the seventh year of A.
7. 11 the copy of the letter that the king A.
7. 12 A., king of kings, unto Ezra the priest, a
7. 21 And I, (even) I A. the king, do make a
8. 1 These..went up with me..reign of A.
Neh. 2. 1 to pass..in the twentieth year of A. the
5. 14 unto the two and thirtieth year of A.
13. 6 for in the two and thirtieth year of A.
2. A king of Persia, the Cambyses of profane history, B.C. 521.
Ezra 4. 7 And in the days of A.
4. 7 the rest of their companions, unto A.
4. 8 Rehum..wrote..against Jerusalem to A.
4. 11 the copy of the letter..unto A. the king
4. 23 when the copy of king A.'s letter (was)
3. Another king of Persia, contemporary with Darius, or subsequent to him.
Ezra 6. 14 according to the commandment of..A.

AR-TE'-MAS, Ἀρτεμᾶς *whole, sound.*
A companion of Paul at Nicopolis.
Tit. 3. 12 When I..send A. unto thee, or Tychicus

ARTIFICER —
1. *Engraver, carver,* חָרָשׁ *charash.*
1 Ch. 29. 5 all manner of work..(made) by..artificers
2 Ch. 34. 11 to the artificers and builders gave they
2. *Engraver, carver,* חֹרֵשׁ *choresh.*
Gen. 4. 22 Tubal-cain, an instructer of every artificer
3. *Engraving, carving,* חֶרֶשׁ *cheresh.*
Isa. 3. 3 The counsellor, and the cunning artificer

ARTILLERY —
Instrument, כְּלִי *keli.*
1 Sa. 20. 40 Jonathan gave his artillery unto his lad

A-RU'-BOTH, אֲרֻבּוֹת *courts.*
The third of Solomon's commissariat districts, including Sochoh; it was therefore probably a name for the rich corn-growing country of the Shefelah or "plain" of Judah.
1 Ki. 4. 10 son of Hesed, in A.; to him (pertained)

A-RU'-MAH, אֲרוּמָה *height.*
A place near Shechem, in Ephraim, perhaps the same as Rumah (now called *El-Ormah*, N.E. of Nablus).
Judg. 9. 41 And Abimelech dwelt at A.: and Zebul

AR'-VAD, אַרְוַד *refuge.*
An island near Zidon, whence probably it was colonised It is now called *Ruad*, but formerly *Antaradus.*
Eze. 27. 8 The inhabitants of..A. were thy mariners
27. 11 The men of A. with thine army (were)

AR-VAD-ITES, אַרְוָדִי *inhabiting Arvad.*
The patronymic of the descendants of the 9th son of Canaan, son of Ham.
Gen. 10. 18 the A., and the Zemarite, and the
1 Ch. 1. 16 the A., and the Zemarite, and the

AR'-ZA, אַרְצָא *firm.*
A steward of Elah, king of Israel, B.C. 930.
1 Ki. 16. 9 in the house of A. steward of (his) house

AS —
1. *Who, that, as,* אֲשֶׁר *asher.*
Gen. 22. 14 Jehovah-jireh: as it is said (to) this day
2. *Even as,* כַּאֲשֶׁר *ka-asher.*
Gen. 7. 9 the male and the female, as God had
3. *Also,* גַּם *gam.*
Jer. 51. 49 As Babylon..the slain of Israel to fall
4. *As a sufficiency,* כְּדֵי *ke-de.*
Judg. 6. 5 For they came up..as grasshoppers for
5. *That, though,* כִּי *ki.*
Job 22. 2 as he that is wise may be
6. *Even as,* כְּמוֹ *kemo.*
Exod 15. 5 they sank into the bottom as a stone
7. *Unto,* עַד *ad.*
Judg 20. 48 the men of (every) city, as the beast, and
8. *With,* עִם *im.*
Job 9. 26 They are passed away as the swift ships
9. *Under, instead of,* תַּחַת *tachath.*
Job 34. 26 He striketh them as wicked men
10. *On, upon, in addition to,* עַל *al.*
Job 22. 24 shalt thou lay up gold as dust
10a. *On the surface of,* עַל־פְּנֵי *al pene.*
Job 24. 18 He is swift as the waters
11. *Verily, then, for,* γάρ *gar,* Matt. 1. 18.
12. *With a view to,* εἰς *eis,* Phil. 4. 15.
13. *In, during,* ἐν, Luke 8. 5.
14. *Even, as,* καθάπερ *kathaper.*
Rom 12. 4 For as we have many members in one
1 Co. 12. 12 For as the body is one, and hath many
2 Co. 3. 13 not as Moses..put a veil over his face
8. 11 that as..to will, so..a performance
1 Th. 2. 11 As ye know how we exhorted, and
3. 6 desiring greatly to see us, as we also
Heb. 5. 4 he that is called of God, [as]..Aaron
15. *According to which,* καθά *katha.*
Matt 27. 10 the potter's field, as the Lord appointed
16. *According to what,* καθό *katho.*
Rom. 8. 26 Know not what we should pray for as we
17. *Even or according as,* καθότι *kathoti.*
Acts 2. 45 parted them to all..as every man had
18. *Even or according as,* καθώς *kathōs.*
Matt 21. 6 disciples went, and did as Jesus
26. 24 The Son of man goeth as it is written of
28. 6 for he is risen, as he said. Come, see the
Mark 4. 33 spake he the word unto them, as they were
9. 13 whatsoever they listed, as it is written of
14. 16 his disciples went forth..and found as he
14. 21 The Son of man..goeth, as it is written
15. 8 multitude..began to desire..as he had
16. 7 there shall ye see him, as he said unto
Luke 1. 55 As he spake to our fathers, to Abraham
1. 70 As he spake by the mouth of his holy
2. 20 heard and seen, as it was told unto them
2. 23 As it is written in the law of the Lord
5. 14 according as Moses commanded, for a
6. 31 as ye would that men should do to you
6. 36 Be ye therefore merciful, as your Father
11. 1 teach us to pray, as John also taught his
11. 30 as Jonas was a sign unto the Ninevites
17. 26 as it was in the days of Noe, so shall it
22. 13 they went, and found as he had said unto
22. 29 as my Father hath appointed unto me
24. 24 found (it) even so as the women had said
24. 39 hath not flesh and bones as ye see me
John 1. 23 Make straight the way..as said the pro.

John 3. 14 as Moses lifted up the serpent in the
5. 30 as I hear, I judge: and my judgment
6. 31 as it is written, He gave them bread from
6. 57 As the living Father hath sent me, and
6. 58 not as your fathers did eat manna, and
7. 38 He that believeth on me, as the scripture
8. 28 as my Father hath taught me, I speak
10. 15 As the Father knoweth me, even so know
10. 26 [ye are not of my sheep, as I said unto you]
12. 14 Jesus..sat thereon; as it is written
13. 15 that ye should do as I have done to you
13. 33 Ye shall seek me: and as I said unto the
13. 34 ye love one another; as I have loved you
14. 27 not as the world giveth, give I unto you
14. 31 as the Father gave me commandment
15. 4 As the branch cannot bear fruit of itself
15. 9 As the Father hath loved me, so have I
15. 12 ye love one another, as I have loved you
17. 2 As thou hast given him power over all
17. 11 keep..that they may be one, as we (are)
17. 18 As thou hast sent me into the world, even
17. 21 That they all may be one; as thou, Father
17. 23 hast loved them, as thou hast loved me
19. 40 as the manner of the Jews is to bury
20. 21 Peace..unto you: as..Father hath sent
Acts 2. 4 tongues, as the Spirit gave them utterance
2. 22 midst of you, as ye yourselves also know
7. 42 as it is written in the book of the prophets
7. 44 as he had appointed, speaking unto Moses
7. 48 most High dwelleth..in temples..as saith
10. 47 received the Holy Ghost as well as we?
15. 8 giving them the Holy Ghost, even as
15. 15 to this agree the words..as it is written
22. 3 was zealous toward God, as ye all are this
Rom. 1. 13 you also, even as among other Gentiles
1. 17 as it is written, The just shall live by faith
2. 24 name..is blasphemed..as it is written
3. 4 as it is written, That thou mightest be
3. 8 as we be slanderously reported, and as
3. 10 As it is written, There is none righteous
4. 17 As it is written, I have made thee a father
8. 36 As it is written, For thy sake we are
9. 13 As it is written, Jacob have I loved, but
9. 29 And as Esaias said before, Except the
9. 33 As it is written, Behold, I lay in Sion
10. 15 as it is written, How beautiful are the
11. 26 as it is written, There shall come out of
15. 3 but, as it is written, The reproaches of
15. 7 receive ye one another, as Christ also
15. 9 as it is written, For this cause I will
15. 21 as it is written, To whom he was not
1 Co. 2. 9 as it is written, Eye hath not seen, nor
4. 17 as I teach every where in every church
5. 7 may be a new lump, as ye are unleavened
8. 2 knoweth nothing yet as he ought to know
10. 6 we should not lust after evil things, as they
10. 7 Neither be ye idolators, as..some of them
10. 8 Neither..commit fornication, as some of
10. 9 Neither..tempt Christ, as some of them
10. 10 Neither murmur ye, as some of them also
10. 33 Even as I please all (men) in all (things)
11. 2 keep the ordinances, as I delivered..to
12. 11 dividing to every man severally as he will
12. 18 set..in the body, as it hath pleased him
14. 34 to be under obedience, as..saith the law
15. 38 God giveth it a body as it hath pleased
15. 49 as we have borne the image of the earthy
2 Co. 1. 5 as the sufferings of Christ abound in us
1. 14 As also ye have acknowledged us in part
4. 1 as we have received mercy, we faint not
6. 16 as God hath said, I will dwell in them
8. 5 and..not as we hoped, but first gave their
8. 6 Insomuch that we desired Titus, that as
8. 15 As it is written, He that (had gathered)
9. 3 I sent..that, as I said, ye may be ready
9. 9 As it is written, He hath dispersed abroad
10. 7 as he (is) Christ's, even so (are) we Christ's
11. 12 they glory, they may be found even as we
Gal. 2. 7 committed unto me, as..the circumcision
5. 21 as I have also told..in time past, that
Eph. 3. 3 mystery; as I wrote afore in few words
4. 4 even as ye are called in one hope of your
4. 17 that ye henceforth walk not as other
4. 21 and have been taught by him, as the
4. 32 as God for Christ's sake, hath forgiven
5. 2 walk in love, as Christ also hath loved
5. 3 let it not be once named..as becometh
5. 25 Husbands, love your wives, even as Christ
5. 29 nourisheth and cherisheth it, even as the
Phil. 2. 12 Wherefore, my beloved, as ye have always
3. 17 mark them which walk so as ye have us
Col. 1. 6 as..in all the world..as..also in you
1. 7 As ye also learned of Epaphras our dear
2. 7 and stablished in the faith, as ye have
3. 13 as Christ forgave you, so also..ye
1 Th. 1. 5 as ye know what manner of men we were
2. 2 and were shamefully entreated, as ye know
2. 4 as we were allowed of God to be put in
2. 5 as ye know, nor a cloak of covetousness
2. 13 ye received..not..the word of men, but as
2. 14 countrymen, even as they..of the Jews
3. 4 even as it came to pass, and ye know
4. 1 that as ye have received of us how ye
4. 6 as we also have forewarned you and
4. 11 with your own hands, as we commanded
4. 13 not, even as others which have no hope
2 Th. 1. 3 We are bound to thank God..as it is meet
3. 1 and be glorified, even as..with you
1 Ti. 1. 3 As I besought thee to abide still at Eph.
Heb. 3. 7 Wherefore, as the Holy Ghost saith
4. 3 as he said.... I have sworn in my wrath
4. 7 as it is said, To day if ye will hear his
Heb. 5. 3 by reason hereof he ought, as for the
5. 6 As he saith also in another (place), Thou
8. 5 as Moses was admonished of God when
10. 25 Not forsaking the assembling..as the
11. 12 as the stars of the sky in multitude
1 Pe. 4. 10 as every man hath received the gift
2 Pe. 1. 14 as our Lord Jesus Christ hath shewed me
3. 15 even as our beloved brother Paul also
1 Jo. 2. 18 as ye have heard that antichrist
3. 2 like him; for we shall see him as he is
3. 12 Not as Cain, (who) was of that wicked one
3. 23 love one another, as he gave us
4. 17 because as he is, so are we in this world
2 Jo. 4 as we have received a commandment
6 This is the commandment, That, as ye

19. *According to,* κατά *kata* [Heb. 9. 27 *kath hoson*]

Luke 4. 16 as his custom was, he went into the
22. 22 truly the Son of man goeth, as it was
22. 39 he came out, and went, as he was wont
Acts 17. 2 Paul, as his manner was, went in unto
23. 31 the soldiers, as it was commanded them
Rom. 1. 15 So, as much as in me is, I am ready
3. 5 who taketh vengeance? I speak as a man
1 Co. 3. 3 are ye not carnal, and walk as men?
9. 8 Say I these things as a man? or saith not
Gal. 4. 28 Now we, brethren, as Isaac was, are the
Titus 1. 9 Holding fast the faithful word as he hath
Heb. 9. 27 as it is appointed unto men once to die
1 Pe. 1. 15 as he which hath called you is holy, so be

20. *Of what kind or sort,* οἷος *hoios.*

1 Co. 15. 48 As (is) the earthy..as is the heavenly

21. *How much, many, long,* ὅσος *hosos.*

Heb. 1. 4 as he hath by inheritance obtained a
10. 25 so much the more, as ye see the day ap.

22. *Whosoever,* ὅστις *hostis.*

1 Co. 16. 2 lay by him in store, as (God) hath

23. *Thus, so,* οὕτω *houtō.*

2 Pe. 3. 4 all things continue as..from the

24. *What manner,* ὃν τρόπον [*hos, tropos*].

Luke 13. 34 as a hen..her brood under (her) wings
Acts 7. 28 Wilt thou kill me, as thou diddest the E.
2 Ti. 3. 8 as Jannes and Jambres withstood Moses

25. *As, that, in order to, for,* ὡς *hōs.*

Matt. 1. 24 Joseph..did as the angel of the Lord had
6. 10 Thy will be done in earth, as (it is) in
6. 12 forgive us our debts, as we forgive our
7. 29 as (one) having authority, and not as
8. 13 Go thy way; and as thou hast believed
10. 16 as sheep..wise as serpents..as doves
10. 25 be as his master..as his lord
13. 43 Then shall the righteous shine forth as
14. 5 because they counted him as a prophet
17. 2 shine as the sun..white as the light
17. 20 If ye have faith as a grain of mustard
18. 3 Except ye be converted, and become as
18. 4 whosoever..shall humble himself as this
18. 33 compassion..even as I had pity on thee?
19. 19 Thou shalt love thy neighbour as thyself
20. 14 I will give unto this last, even as unto
21. 26 people; for all hold John as a prophet
22. 30 but are as the angels of God in heaven
22. 39 Thou shalt love thy neighbour as thyself
26. 19 the disciples did as Jesus had appointed
26. 39 nevertheless not as I will, but as thou
26. 55 Are ye come out as against a thief with
27. 65 go your way, make (it) as sure as ye can
28. 9 [as they went to tell his disciples, behold]
28. 15 So they took the money, and did as they
Mark 1. 2 [As] it is written in the prophets, Behold
1. 22 as one that had authority, and not as
3. 5 his hand was restored whole [as] the
4. 26 as if a man should cast seed into the
6. 15 it is a prophet, or as one of the prophets
6. 34 because they were as sheep not having a
7. 6 as it is written, This people honoureth me
8. 24 and said, I see men as trees, walking
9. 3 became shining, exceeding white [as]
10. 1 as he was wont, he taught them again
10. 15 Whosoever shall..receive..kingdom..as
12. 26 as touching the dead, that they rise
12. 31 Thou shalt love thy neighbour as thyself
12. 33 and to love (his) neighbour as himself
13. 34 For the Son of man is) as a man taking
14. 48 Are ye come out, as against a thief, with
Luke 2. 15 it came to pass, as the angels were gone
3. 4 As it is written in the book of the words
3. 23 Jesus..being (as was supposed) the son
6. 10 [his hand was restored whole as..other]
6. 22 cast out your name as evil, for the Son of
6. 40 every one that is perfect shall be as his
9. 54 [and consume them, even as Elias did?]
10. 3 I send you forth as lambs among wolves
10. 18 I beheld Satan as lightning fall from
10. 27 Thou shalt love..thy neighbour as thyself
11. 2 [Thy will be done, as in heaven, so in]
11. 36 as when the bright shining of a candle
11. 44 for ye are as graves which appear not
14. 22 Lord, it is done as thou hast commanded
15. 19 make me as one of thy hired servants
15. 25 as he came and drew nigh to the house
17. 6 If ye had faith as a grain of mustard seed
17. 28 Likewise also [as] it was in the days of Lot
18. 11 that I am not..even as this publican
18. 17 shall not receive the kingdom..as a
21. 35 as a snare shall it come on all them
22. 26 let him be as the younger..as he that
22. 27 I am among you as he that serveth
Luke 22. 31 desired..that he may sift..as wheat
22. 52 Be ye come out, as against a thief, with
23. 14 Ye have brought this man unto me, as
23. 26 as they led him away, they laid hold
John 1. 14 and we beheld his glory, the glory as of
15. 6 he is cast forth as a branch, and is
20. 11 and as she wept, she stooped down
Acts 2. 15 these are not drunken, as ye suppose
3. 12 why look ye so earnestly on us, as though
7. 51 ye do always resist the Holy Ghost: [as]
8. 32 He was led as a sheep to the slaughter
8. 36 as they went on..way, they came unto
10. 25 as Peter was coming in, Cornelius met
11. 17 Forasmuch then as God gave them the
13. 25 as John fulfilled his course, he said
13. 33 as it is also written in the second psalm
16. 4 as they went through the cities, they
17. 28 For in him we live..as certain also of your
22. 5 As also..high priest doth bear me witness
22. 25 as they bound him with thongs, Paul
23. 11 Be of good cheer, Paul: for as thou hast
23. 15 as though ye would inquire something
23. 20 as though they would inquire somewhat
25. 10 to the Jews have I done no wrong, as
27. 30 as the shipmen were about to flee out of
Rom. 1. 21 they glorified (him) not as God, neither
3. 7 why yet am I also judged as a sinner?
4. 17 things which be not as though they were
5. 15 not as the offence, so also (is) the free
5. 16 And not as..by one that sinned..the gift
5. 18 Therefore, as by the offence of one
6. 13 Neither yield ye your members..[as] those
8. 36 are accounted as sheep for the slaughter
9. 27 the number of the children..be as..sand
9. 29 we had been as Sodoma, and been made
13. 9 Thou shalt love thy neighbour as thyself
13. 13 Let us walk honestly, as in the day; not
15. 15 as putting you in mind, because of..grace
1 Co. 3. 1 as unto spiritual..as unto carnal..as unto
3. 10 the grace..which is given unto me, as a
3. 15 he..shall be saved; yet so as by fire
4. 1 Let a man so account of us, as of the
4. 7 why dost thou glory, as if thou hadst not
4. 13 we are made as the filth of the world
4. 14 you, but as my beloved sons I warn
4. 18 Now some are puffed up, as though I
5. 3 as absent..as though I were present
7. 7 I would that all men were even as I
7. 8 It is good..if they abide even as I
7. 17 as God hath..as the Lord hath called every
7. 25 yet I give my judgment, as one that hath
7. 29 they that have wives be as..they had none
7. 30 as though they..as though they..as
7. 31 they that use this world, as not abusing
8. 7 some..eat (it) as a thing offered unto an
9. 20 I became as a Jew..as under the law
9. 21 To them that are without law, as without
9. 22 To the weak became I [as] weak, that I
9. 26 not as uncertainly..not as one..beateth
10. 7 Neither be ye idolaters, [as] (were) some
10. 15 I speak as to wise men; judge ye what I
13. 11 spake as..understood as..thought as
14. 33 peace, as in all churches of the saints
16. 10 he worketh the work of the Lord, as I
2 Co. 2. 17 not as many..as of sincerity..as of God
3. 1 or need we, as some..epistles of
3. 5 to think anything as of ourselves; but
5. 20 as though God did beseech..by us: we
6. 4 in all..approving ourselves as..ministers
6. 8 evil report and good report: as deceivers
6. 9 As unknown..as dying..as chastened
6. 10 As sorrowful..as poor..as having nothing
6. 13 I speak as unto..children, be ye also
7. 14 as we spake all things to you in truth
9. 5 as..bounty, and not ....covetousness
10. 2 some, which think of us as if we walked
10. 14 we are come as far as to you also in..the
11. 3 as the serpent beguiled Eve through his
11. 15 if his ministers also be transformed as the
11. 16 if otherwise, yet as a fool receive me
13. 2 foretell you, as if I were present, the
13. 7 do that which is honest, though we be as
Gal. 1. 9 As we said before, so say I now again
3. 16 to seeds, as of many; but as of one
4. 12 I beseech you, be as I (am); for I (am) as
4. 14 received me as an angel of God, (even) as
5. 14 Thou shalt love thy neighbour as thyself
6. 10 As we have therefore opportunity, let us
Eph. 2. 3 by nature the children of wrath, even as
3. 5 as it is now revealed unto his holy
5. 1 Be ye..followers of God, as dear children
5. 8 in the Lord: walk as children of light
5. 15 circumspectly, not as fools, but as wise
5. 22 Wives submit yourselves..as unto the
5. 23 even as Christ is the head of the church
5. 28 So ought men to love their wives as their
6. 5 in singleness of your heart, as unto Christ
6. 6 with eye service, as men pleasers; but as
6. 7 With good will doing service, [as] to the
6. 20 I may speak boldly, as I ought to speak
Phil. 1. 20 but (that) with all boldness, as always
2. 8 And being found in fashion as a man
2. 12 ye have always obeyed, not as in my
2. 15 among whom ye shine as lights in the
2. 22 that, as a son with the father, he hath
Col. 2. 6 As ye have therefore received Christ
2. 20 why, as though living in the world, are
3. 12 Put on therefore, as the elect of God
3. 18 Wives, submit yourselves..as it is fit in
3. 22 Servants, obey..not with eye service, as
3. 23 whatsoever ye do, do (it) heartily, as to
4. 4 I may make it manifest, as I ought to

1 Th. 2. 4 not as pleasing men, but God, which trieth
2. 7 we were gentle among you, even as a
2. 11 and charged every one of you, as a father
2. 13 (it) not (as) the word of men, but [as] it
5. 2 the day of the Lord so cometh as a thief
5. 4 that day should overtake you as a thief
5. 6 Therefore let us not sleep, as (do) others
2 Th. 2. 2 as from us, as that the day of Christ
2. 4 so that he [as] God sitteth in the temple
3. 15 but admonish (him) as a brother
1 Ti. 5. 1 as a father.. younger men as brethren
5. 2 elder women as mothers; the younger as
2 Ti. 2. 3 Thou therefore endure hardness, as a
2. 9 Wherein I suffer trouble, as an evil doer
2. 17 their word will eat as doth a canker
3. 9 their folly shall be manifest..as their's
Titus 1. 5 ordain elders in every city, as I had
1. 7 a bishop must be blameless, as the
Phm. 9 I rather beseech (thee), being..as Paul
16 Not now as a servant, but above a servant
17 If thou count me..receive him as myself
Heb. 1. 11 they all shall wax old as doth a
3. 2 as also Moses (was faithful) in all his
3. 5 Moses verily (was) faithful..as a servant
3. 6 But Christ as a son over his own house
3. 8 Harden not your hearts, as in the prov.
3. 15 harden not your hearts, as in the prov.
4. 3 As I have sworn in my wrath, if they
6. 19 Which (hope) we have as an anchor of
7. 9 And as I may so say, Levi also, who
11. 9 By faith he sojourned..as (in) a strange
11. 27 he endured, as seeing him who is invisible
11. 29 By faith they passed through..as by dry
12. 5 exhortation which speaketh unto you as
12. 7 God dealeth with you as with sons
12. 16 Lest there (be)..or profane person, as
12. 27 as of things that are made, that those
13. 3 as bound with them..as being yourselves
13. 17 for they watch for your souls, as they
Jas. 1. 10 because as the flower of the grass he shall
2. 8 Thou shalt love thy neighbour as thyself
2. 9 are convinced of the law as transgressors
2. 12 So speak ye, and so do, as they that
5. 3 shall eat your flesh as it were fire
5. 5 ye have nourished your hearts, [as] in a
1 Pe. 1. 14 As obedient children, not fashioning
1. 19 with the precious blood of Christ, as of a
1. 24 all flesh (is) as grass..[as] the flower of
2. 2 As new born babes, desire the sincere
2. 5 Ye also, as lively stones, are built up
2. 11 Dearly beloved, I beseech (you) as
2. 12 that, whereas they speak against you as
2. 14 Or unto governors, as unto them that are
2. 16 As free..but as the servants of God
2. 25 ye were as sheep going astray; but are
3. 7 as unto the weaker vessel, and as being
3. 16 [whereas they speak evil of you, as of evil]
4. 10 as good stewards of the manifold grace of
4. 11 as the oracles of God..as of the ability
4. 12 as though some strange thing happened
4. 15 as a murderer..or as a busybody
4. 16 Yet if..as a Christian, let him not be ash.
4. 19 in well-doing, [as] unto a faithful Creator
5. 3 Neither as being lords over (God's) heritage
5. 8 your adversary the devil, as a roaring
5. 12 By Silvanus, a faithful brother..as I
2 Pe. 1. 19 take heed, as unto a light that shineth
2. 1 as there shall be false teachers among
2. 12 these, as natural brute beasts, made
3. 8 as a thousand years..as one day
3. 9 The Lord is not slack..as some men count
3. 10 the day of the Lord will come as a thief in
3. 16 As also in all..as..the other scriptures
1 Jo. 1. 7 if we walk in the light, as he is in the
2. 27 as the same anointing teacheth you
2 Jo. 5 now I beseech thee, lady, not as though I
Jude 10 what they know naturally, as brute beasts
Rev. 1. 10 behind me a great voice, as of a trumpet
1. 14 white as snow..eyes..as a flame of fire
1. 15 as if they burned..his voice as the sound
1. 16 his countenance (was) as the sun shineth
1. 17 when I saw him, I fell at his feet as dead
2. 24 known the depths of Satan, as they speak
2. 27 as the vessels of..even as I received
3. 3 I will come on thee as a thief, and thou
3. 21 even as I also overcame, and am set down
4. 7 the third beast had a face [as] a man
5. 6 a Lamb as it had been slain, having
6. 11 their brethren, that should be killed as
6. 12 black as sackcloth of hair..as blood
6. 13 even as a fig tree casteth her untimely figs
6. 14 the heaven departed as a scroll when
9. 2 there arose a smoke out of the pit, as the
9. 3 them was given power, as the scorpions of
9. 5 torment..as the torment of a scorpion
9. 7 their faces..as the faces of men
9. 8 hair as the hair of women ..teeth..as
9. 9 as the sound of chariots of many horses
9. 17 heads of the horses..as the heads of lions
10. 1 and his feet as pillars of fire
10. 7 as he hath declared to his servants the
10. 9 it shall be in thy mouth sweet as honey
10. 10 and it was in my mouth sweet as honey
12. 15 the serpent cast out..water as a flood
13. 2 were as..of a bear, and his mouth as
13. 11 like a lamb, and he spake as a dragon
14. 2 as the voice of..as the voice of a great
16. 3 it became as the blood of a dead (man)
16. 15 Behold, I come as a thief. Blessed is he
17. 12 receive power as kings one hour with the
18. 6 Reward her even as she rewarded you
19. 6 as..the voice of..[as] the voice..and as
Rev. 19. 12 His eyes..[as] a flame of fire, and
20. 8 the number of whom (is) as the sand of
21. 2 new Jerusalem..prepared as a bride
22. 1 pure river of water of life, clear as crystal

26. *As if*, ὡσεί *hōsei.*
Matt. 9. 36 were scattered abroad, [as] sheep having
28. 3 and his raiment white [as] snow
28. 4 the keepers did shake, and became [as]
Mark 9. 26 he was as one dead; insomuch that
Luke 24. 11 their words seemed to them as idle tales
Heb. 1. 12 as a vesture shalt thou fold them up
11. 12 and [as] the sand which is by the sea

27. *Even as*, ὥσπερ *hōsper.*
Matt. 6. 2 as the hypocrites do in the synagogues
6. 5 when thou prayest, thou shalt not be [as]
6. 7 use not vain repetitions, as the heathen
6. 16 Moreover when ye fast, be not, [as] the
12. 40 as Jonas was three days and three nights
13. 40 As therefore the tares are gathered and
18. 17 let him be unto thee as an heathen man
24. 27 as the lightning cometh out of the east
24. 37 as the days of Noe..so shall also the
24. 38 [as] in the days that were before the flood
25. 14 For..(is) as a man travelling into a far
25. 32 he shall separate them..as a shepherd
Luke 17. 24 as the lightning, that lighteneth out of
18. 11 I thank thee, that I am not [as] other men
John 5. 21 as the Father raiseth up the dead, and
5. 26 as the Father hath life in himself; so hath
Acts 2. 2 there came a sound from heaven as of a
3. 17 wot that through ignorance ye did (it,) as
11. 15 fell on them, as on us at the beginning
Rom. 5. 12 as by one man sin entered into the
5. 19 as by one man's disobedience many were
5. 21 That as sin hath reigned unto death
6. 19 for as ye have yielded your members
11. 30 as ye in times past have not believed God
1 Co. 8. 5 as there be gods many, and lords many
11. 12 as the woman (is) of the man, even so
15. 22 For as in Adam all die, even so in Christ
16. 1 as I have given order to the churches of
2 Co. 1. 7 knowing, that [as] ye are partakers of the
8. 7 Therefore, as ye abound in every..faith
9. 5 bounty, and not [as] (of) covetousness
Gal. 4. 29 But as then he that was born after the
Eph. 5. 24 Therefore [as] the church is subject unto
1 Th. 5. 3 sudden destruction cometh upon them, as
Heb. 4. 10 also hath ceased from his..works, as God
7. 27 needeth not daily, as those high priests
9. 25 as the high priest entereth into the holy
Jas. 2. 26 as the body without the spirit is Rev. 10. 3.

28. *As if it were*, ὡσπερεί *hōsperei.*
1 Co. 15. 8 he was seen of me also, as of one born out

29. *So that*, ὥστε *hōste.*
Matt 15. 33 Whence should we have..bread..as to fill

[*See also*, According as, becometh, concerning, crystal, even, forasmuch, friend, hurl, inasmuch, light, like, long as, power, so, such.]

AS...as —
As...so, כְּ...כֵּן *ke...ken.*
Eze. 42. 11 as long as they..as broad as they: and all

AS for —
1. *But, truly, yet*, אוּלָם *ulam.*
Job 17. 10 as for you all, do ye return, and come
2. *Unto, to*, אֶל *el.*
2 Ch. 34. 26 as for the king of Judah, who sent you

AS concerning —
Even or according to, κατά *kata.*
Rom. 9. 5 and of whom as concerning the flesh
11. 28 As concerning the gospel..for your
2 Co. 11. 21 I speak as concerning reproach, as

AS concerning that —
That because, ὅτι *hoti.*
Acts 13. 34 And as concerning that he raised him up

AS far as (to) —
1. *Unto, even unto*, ἄχρι *achri.*
Acts 28. 15 came to meet us as far as Appii forum
2 Co. 10. 14 we are come as far as to you also
2. *Unto, up to*, ἕως *heōs.*
Luke 24. 50 he led them out as far as to Bethany
Acts 11. 19 Now they..travelled as far as Phenice
11. 22 that he should go as far as Antioch

AS hast served —
Recompense, deed, גְּמוּל *gemul.*
Psa. 137. 8 rewardeth thee as thou hast served us

AS it had been —
1. *As, that, in order to, for*, ὡς *hōs.*
Acts 10. 11 a certain vessel descending..as it had b.
11. 5 A certain vessel descend, as it had been
2. *As if*, ὡσεί *hōsei.*
Acts 6. 15 all..saw his face as it had been the face
9. 18 there fell from his eyes [as it had been]

AS it were —
1. *Even as*, כְּמוֹ *kemo.*
Isa. 26. 18 we have as it were brought forth wind
2. *As, that, in order to, for*, ὡς *hōs.*
John 7. 10 not openly, but as it were in secret
21. 8 not far from land, but as it were two
Acts 17. 14 brethren sent away Paul to go [as it were]
Rom. 9. 32 not by faith, but as it were by the works
1 Co. 4. 9 the apostles last, as it were appointed to
2 Co. 11. 17 I speak (it)..as it were foolishly, in this
Phm. 14 thy benefit should not be as it were of
Jas. 5. 3 shall eat your flesh as it were fire
Rev. 4. 1 the first voice which I heard..as it were
6. 1 I heard, as it were the noise of thunder
8. 8 the second angel sounded, and as it were
8. 10 a great star..burning as it were a lamp
9. 7 on their heads..as it were crowns like
9. 9 they had breastplates, as it were
10. 1 his face..as it were the sun, and his feet
13. 3 I saw one of his heads as it were
14. 3 they sung [as it were] a new song
15. 2 I saw as it were a sea of glass mingled
19. 6 I heard as it were the voice of a great
21. 21 the street of the city..as it were transp.
3. *As if*, ὡσεί *hōsei.*
Luke 22. 44 [his sweat was as it were great drops of
Acts 9. 18 from his eyes as it had been scales

AS large as —
So great, long, much, τοσοῦτος *tosoutos.*
Rev. 21. 16 the length is [as large] as the breadth

AS long as —
1. *With..and before* עִם..וְלִפְנֵי *im..ve-li-phene.*
Psa. 72. 5 They..fear thee as long as the sun and
2. *As long as*, ἐφ' ὅσον *eph hoson.*
Matt. 9. 15 Can the children..mourn, as long as
2 Pe. 1. 13 I think it meet, as long as I am in this
3. *When, while*, ὅταν *hotan.*
John 9. 5 As long as I am in the world, I am the

AS many as —
1. *All*, כֹּל *kol.*
Exod 35. 22 both..women, as many as were willing
2. *How much, long, many*, ὅσος *hosos.*
Matt 14. 36 as many as touched were made perfectly
22. 10 as many as they found, both bad and v. 9
Mark 3. 10 they pressed upon him..as many as 6. 56
Luke 11. 8 will rise and give him as many as
John 1. 12 as many as received him, to them gave
Acts 3. 24 as many as have spoken, 2. 39.
4. 6 as many as were of the kindred of the
4. 34 as many as were possessors of lands
5. 36 as many as obeyed him, were scattered
5. 37 as many as obeyed him, were dispersed
10. 45 [as many as] came with Peter, because
13. 48 as many as were ordained to eternal life
Rom. 2. 12 as many as have..as many as have sinned
8. 14 as many as are led by the Spirit of
Gal. 3. 10 as many as are of the works of the law
3. 27 as many of you as have been baptized
6. 12 As many as desire to make a fair shew in
6. 16 as many as walk according to this rule
Phil. 3. 15 Let us therefore, as many as be perfect
Col. 2. 1 as many as have not seen my face in
1 Ti. 6. 1 Let as many servants as are under the
Rev. 2. 24 as many as have not this doct. 3. 19; 13. 15.
18. 17 as many as trade by sea, stood afar off
3. *All who*, πᾶς ὅς *pas hos.*
John 17. 2 he should give eternal life to as many as

AS much —
The equal, τὰ ἴσα *ta isa.*
Luke 6. 34 sinners also lend..to receive as much

AS much as —
How much, long, many, ὅσος *hosos.*
John 6. 11 and likewise of the fishes as much as

AS oft as —
From the sufficiency, מִדֵּי *mid-de.*
2 Ki. 4. 8 it was..as oft as he passed by, he turned

AS oft or often as —
How many times, ὁσάκις ἄν or ἐάν *hosakis an.*
1 Co. 11. 25 this do ye, as oft as ye drink (it,) in
11. 26 as often as ye eat this bread, and drink
Rev. 11. 6 have power over..as often as they will

As pertaining to —
Down according to, κατά (acc.) *kata.*
Rom. 4. 1 Abraham, our father as pertaining to
Heb. 9. 9 did the service perfect, as pertaining to

AS soon —
Also, גַּם *gam.*
Isa. 66. 8 as soon as Zion travailed, she brought

AS soon as —
1. *Even as*, כַּאֲשֶׁר *ka-asher.*
Gen. 18. 33 as soon as he had left communing with
2. *As, that, in order to, for*, ὡς *hōs.*
Luke 1. 23 it came to pass, that, as soon as the days
1. 44 as soon as the voice of thy salutation
22. 66 as soon as it was day, the elders of the
John 11. 20 Then Martha, as soon as she heard that
11. 29 As soon as she heard..she arose quickly
18. 6 As soon then as he had said unto them
21. 9 As soon then as they were come to land
Phil. 2. 23 so soon as I shall see how it will go
3. *Whenever*, ὅταν *hotan.*
John 16. 21 as soon as she is delivered of the child
Rev. 12. 4 for to devour her child as soon as it was
4. *When*, ὅτε *hote.*
Luke 15. 30 But as soon as this thy son Re. 10. 10.
5. *Straightway*, εὐθέως *eutheōs*, Mark 5. 36; 11. 2.

AS though, not —

As not, כְּלֹא *ke-lo.*
Obad. 16 shall be as though they had not been

AS though —

1. *That, because,* ὅτι *hoti.*
Phil. 3. 12 Not as though I had already attained

2. *As that,* οἷον ὅτι *hoion hoti,* ὡς ὅτι *hōs hoti.*
2 Co. 11 21 concerning reproach, as though, Ro. 9. 6.

AS touching —

1. *Upon,* ἐπί *epi (dat.)*
Acts 5. 35 what ye intend to do as touching these

2. *Down, according to,* κατά *kata (acc.)*
Rom. 11. 28 as touching the election..beloved for the
Phil. 3. 5 as touching the law, a Pharisee

3. *About, concerning,* περί *peri (gen.)*
Matt 18. 19 if two of you shall agree..as touching any
22. 31 as touching the resurrection of the dead
Mark 12. 26 as touching the dead, that they rise
Acts 21. 25 As touching the Gentiles which believe
1 Co. 8. 1; 16. 12; 2 Co. 9. 1; 1 Th. 4. 9.

AS well as—

1. *Even as also,* καθὼς καί *kathōs kai,* Acts 10. 47.
2. *As also,* ὡς καί *hōs kai,* 1 Co. 9. 5.
3. *According as, even as,* καθάπερ *kathaper.*
Heb. 4. 2 the gospel preached, as well as unto them

AS well as another —

Like this, כָּזֶה *ka-zeh.*
2 Sa. 11. 25 sword devoureth one as well as another

AS when —

As the day, כְּיוֹם *ke-yom.*
Zech. 14. 3 fight against those nations, as when he

AS they would —

According to their pleasure, כִּרְצוֹנָם *[ratson].*
Neh. 9. 24 they might do with them as they would

AS yet —

1. *Until so, hitherto,* עַד־כֵּן *ad ken.*
Neh. 2. 16 neither had I as yet told (it) to

2. *Yet, still,* עוֹד *od.*
2 Ki. 14. 4 as yet the people did sacrifice and burnt

3. *Till now,* עַד עַתָּה *ad attah.*
2 Ki. 13. 23 cast he them from his presence as yet

4. *Not yet,* οὔπω *oupō.*
Acts 8. 16 [as yet] he was fallen upon none of them
Rev. 17. 12 which have received no kingdom as yet

AS yet..not —

Not yet, οὐδέπω *oudepō.*
John 20. 9 [as yet] they knew not the scripture, that

A'-SA, אָסָא *physician.*

1. The great grandson of Solomon, B.C. 914.
1 Ki. 15. 8 and A. his son reigned in his stead
15. 9 twentieth year of Jeroboam..reigned A.
15. 11 And A. did (that which was) right in the
15. 13 A. destroyed her idol, and burnt (it) by
15. 14 nevertheless A.'s heart was perfect with
15. 16 there was war between A. and Baasha
15. 17 to go out or come into A. king of Judah
15. 18 Then A. took all the silver and the gold
15. 18 and king A. sent them to Ben-hadad, the
15. 20 Ben-hadad hearkened unto king A., and
15. 22 Then king A. made a proclamation
15. 22 and king A. built with them Geba of
15. 23 The rest of all the acts of A., and all his
15. 24 And A. slept with his fathers, and was
15. 25 in the second year of A. king of Judah
15. 28 in the third year of A. king of Judah
15. 32 there was war between A. and Baasha
15. 33 In the third year of A. king of Judah
16. 8 In the twenty and sixth year of A. king
16. 10, 15 in the twenty and seventh year of A.
16. 23 In the thirty and first year of A. king of
16. 29 in the thirty and eighth year of A. king of
22. 41 Jehoshaphat the son of A. began to reign
22. 43 he walked in all the ways of A. his father
22. 46 which..in the days of his father A.
1 Ch. 3. 10 Abia, his son, A. his son, Jehoshaphat his
2 Ch. 14 1 and A. his son reigned in his stead
14. 2 A. did (that which was) good and right in
14. 8 And A. had an army (of men) that bare
14. 10 Then A. went out against him, and they
14. 11 And A. cried unto the LORD his God, and
14. 12 the LORD smote the Ethiopians before A.
14. 13 And A. and the people that (were) with
15. 2 he went out to meet A., and said unto
15. 2 Hear ye me, A., and all Judah and
15. 8 when A. heard these words, and the
15. 10 in the fifteenth year of the reign of A.
15. 16 the mother of A. the king, he removed
15. 16 and A. cut down her idol, and stamped
15. 17 nevertheless the heart of A. was perfect all
15. 19 there was no (more) war unto..reign of A.
16. 1 In the..year of the reign of A., Baasha
16. 1 he might let none..to A. king of Judah
16. 2 Then A. brought out silver and gold out
16. 4 Ben-hadad hearkened unto king A., and
16. 6 Then A. the king took all Judah; and
16. 7 Hanani the seer came to A. king of Judah
2 Ch. 16. 10 Then A. was wroth with the seer, and
16. 10 And A. oppressed (some) of the people the
16. 11 behold, the acts of A., first and last, lo
16. 12 And A. was diseased in his feet, until
16. 13 And A. slept with his fathers, and died
17. 2 in the cities..which A. his father had
20. 32 he walked in the way of A. his father
21. 12 thou hast not walked in the ways of..A.
Jer. 41. 9 it which A. the king had made for fear
Matt. 1. 7 Roboam begat Abia; and Abia begat A.
1. 8 And A. begat Josaphat; and Josaphat begat

2. A Levite, head of a family in the villages of the Netophathites, near Jerusalem.
1 Ch. 9. 16 the son of A., the son of Elkanah, that

A-SAH'-EL, עֲשָׂהאֵל *God is doer.*

1. A son of Zeruiah, David's sister. He was slain by Abner unwillingly, B.C. 1053.
2 Sa. 2. 18 and A.: and A (was as) light of foot as a
2. 19 A. pursued after Abner; and in going he
2. 20 and said (Art) thou A.? And he answered
2. 21 But A. would not turn..from following
2. 22 Abner said again to A., Turn thee aside
2. 23 came to the place where A. fell down and
2. 30 there lacked of David's servants..and A.
2. 32 they took up A., and buried him in the
3. 27 that he died, for the blood of A. his
3. 30 he had slain their brother A. at Gibeon
23. 24 A. the brother of Joab (was) one of the
1 Ch. 2. 16 the sons of Zeruiah..and A., three
11. 26 the valiant men..(were), A., the brother of
27. 7 The fourth (captain..was) A. the brother

2. A Levite sent by Jehoshaphat to teach the law to the people in Judah, B.C. 914.
2 Ch. 17. 8 with them (he sent)..A., and Shemi

3. A Levite employed under Hezekiah as an officer of the offerings and tithes and dedicated things, B.C. 727.
2 Ch. 31. 13 Jehiel..and A...(were) overseers under

4. Father of Jonathan whom Ezra appointed to take a census of the Jews who had taken strange wives during the exile, B.C. 536.
Ezra 10. 15 Jonathan the son of A...were employed

A-SAH-I'AH, עֲשָׂיָה *Jah is doer.*

An officer of king Josiah's, sent with others to inquire of the Lord in consequence of the reading of the book of the law found by Shaphan, B.C. 641.
2 Ki. 22. 12 the king commanded..A. a servant of the
22. 14 So..A., went unto Huldah the prophetess
2 Ch. 34. 20 the king commanded..A. a servant of the

A-SA-I'AH, עֲשָׂיָה *Jah is doer.*

1. A descendant of Simeon, B.C. 800.
1 Ch. 4. 36 and A., and Adiel, and Jesimiel, and Ben.

2. A descendant of Libni, grandson of Merari.
1 Ch. 6. 30 Shimei his son, Haggiah his son, A. his

3. A Shilonite, dwelling in Jerusalem, B.C 536.
1 Ch. 9. 5 of the Shilonites; A. the firstborn, and

4. A descendant of Merari, who assisted in bringing up the ark from the house of Obed-edom in the time of David, B.C. 1040. [This may be the same as No. 2.]
1 Ch. 15. 6 Of the sons of Merari; A. the chief, and
15. 11 David called for Zadok and..A., and Joel

A'-SAPH, אָסָף *collector, gatherer.*

1. Father of Joah recorder to Hezekiah, B.C. 727.
2 Ki. 18 18 and Joah the son of A. the recorder
18. 37 the scribe, and Joah the son of A. the
2 Ch. 29. 13 of the sons of A.; Zechariah, and Matta.
Isa. 36. 3 the scribe, and Joah, A.'s son, the recor
36. 22 the scribe, and Joah, the son of A., the

2. One appointed by David over the service of song; and by Solomon in the temple service, B.C. 1040.
1 Ch. 6. 39 his brother A., who stood on his right
6. 39 A. the son of Berachiah, the son of
15. 17 the Levites appointed..A. the son of
15. 19 So the singers..A...(were appointed) to
16. 5 A. the chief, and next to him Zechariah
16. 5 with harps; but A made a sound with
16. 7 into the hand of A. and his brethren
16. 37 he left there..A. and his brethren, to
25. 1 separated to the service of the sons of A.
25. 2 Of the sons of A., Zaccur and Joseph
25. 2 the sons of A.; under the hands of A.
25. 6 according to the king's order to A.
25. 9 the first lot came forth for A to Joseph
2 Ch. 5. 12 (which were)..singers, all of them of A.
20. 14 a Levite of the sons of A. came the spirit
29. 13 and of the sons of A.; Zechariah, and
29. 30 with the words of David, and of A. the
35. 15 the singers the sons of A. (were) in their
35 15 according to the commandment of..A.
Ezra 2. 41 The singers: the children of A., an
3. 10 the Levites the sons of A. with cymbals
Neh. 7. 44 The singers: the children of A., an
11. 17 Mattaniah..the son of A., (was) the
11. 22 Of the sons of A., the singers (were) over
12. 35 Michaiah, the son of Zaccur..son of A.
12. 46 in the days of David and A. of old
Psa. 50. *title.* A Psalm of A. The mighty God
73. A Psalm of A. Truly God (is) good
74. Maschil of A. O God, why hast thou
75. Al-taschith, A Psalm (or) Song of A.
76. on Neginoth, A Psalm (or) Song of A.
77. Musician, to Jeduthun, A Psalm of A.
78. Maschil of A. Give ear, O my people
Psa. 79. A Psalm of A. O God, the heathen are
80. upon Shoshannim-Eduth, A Psalm of A.
81. the..Musician upon Gittith, (A Psalm) of A.
82. A Psalm of A. God standeth in the
83. A Song (or) Psalm of A. Keep not thou

3. A Levite, whose posterity dwelt in Jerusalem after the exile, B.C. 444.
1 Ch. 9. 15 Micah, the son of Zichri, the son of A.

4. A descendant of Kohath, son of Levi. His descendants were porters in the service of the tabernacle in the time of David.
1 Ch. 26. 1 Meshelemiah..of the sons of A.

5. An officer (probably a Jew) appointed by the king of Persia as keeper of the royal forests in Judah, B.C. 444.
Neh. 2. 8 a letter unto A. the keeper of the king's

A-SAR-E'EL, אֲשַׂרְאֵל *God is joined.*

A son of Jehaleleel, a descendant of Judah through Caleb, son of Jephunneh, B.C. 1400.
1 Ch. 4. 16 the sons of Jehaleleel; Ziph..and A.

A-SAR-E'-LAH, אֲשַׂרְאֵלָה *Jah is joined.*

A son of Asaph, appointed by David for the service of song in the sanctuary, B.C. 1040.
1 Ch. 25. 2 Of the sons of Asaph; Zaccur..and A.
[*Azareel* in verse 18 is perhaps the same.]

ASCEND, to —

To go or come up, ἀναβαίνω *anabainō.*
John 1. 51 the angels of God ascending and descend.
20. 17 I am not yet ascended..I ascend unto
Acts 2. 34 For David is not ascended into the
25. 1 when Festus was come..he ascended from
Rom. 10. 6 Who shall ascend into heaven? that is, to
Eph. 4. 9 Now that he ascended, what is it but
Rev. 7. 2 I saw another angel ascending from the
11. 7 the beast that ascendeth out of the..pit
17. 8 The beast..shall ascend out of the

ASCEND, to cause to —

To cause to go up, עָלָה *alah,* 5.
Psa. 135. 7 He causeth the vapours to ascend from
Jer. 10. 13 he causeth the vapours to ascend from
51. 16 he causeth the vapours to ascend from

ASCEND (up), to —

1. *To go up, climb,* נָסַק *nasaq.*
Psa. 139. 8 If I ascend up into heaven, thou art

2. *To go up,* עָלָה *alah.*
Gen. 28. 12 the angels of God ascending and descend.
Exod 19. 18 the smoke thereof ascended as the smoke
Num 13. 22 they ascended by the south, and came
Josh. 6. 5 people shall ascend up every man
8. 20 the smoke of the city ascended up to
8. 21 the smoke of the city ascended, then
10. 7 Joshua ascended from Gilgal, he, and all
15. 3 it went out..and ascended up on the
Judg 13. 20 the LORD ascended in the flame of the
20. 40 the flame of the city ascended up to
1 Sa. 28. 13 I saw gods ascending out of the earth
Psa. 24. 3 Who shall ascend into the hill of the
68. 18 Thou hast ascended on high, thou hast
Prov. 30. 4 Who hath ascended up into heaven, or
Isa. 14. 13 I will ascend into heaven, I will exalt
14. 14 I will ascend above the heights of the
Eze 38. 9 Thou shalt ascend and come like a storm

3. *To go or come up,* ἀναβαίνω *anabainō.*
Luke 19. 28 he went before, ascending up to Jerus.
John 3. 13 no man hath ascended up to heaven, but
6. 62 if ye shall see the Son of man ascend up
Eph. 4. 8 When he ascended up on high, he led
4. 10 the same also that ascended up far above
Rev. 8. 4 the smoke..ascended up before God out
11. 12 they ascended up to heaven in a cloud
14. 11 the smoke of their torment ascendeth up

ASCENT —

1. *Going up,* מַעֲלֶה *maaleh.*
Num 34. 4 from the south to the ascent of Akrabbim
2 Sa. 15 30 David went up by the ascent of..Olivet

2. *Going up, (burnt) offering,* עֹלָה *olah.*
1 Ki. 10. 5 his ascent by which he went up unto the

3. *Uppermost place,* עֲלִיָּה *aliyyah.*
2 Ch. 9. 4 his ascent by which he went up into the

ASCRIBE, to —

1. *To give,* יָהַב *yahab.*
Deut 32. 3 ascribe ye greatness unto our God

2. *To give,* נָתַן *nathan.*
1 Sa. 18. 8 They have ascribed unto David ten
18. 8 and to me they have ascribed..thousands
Job 36. 3 will ascribe righteousness to my Maker
Psa. 68. 34 Ascribe ye strength unto God: his

A-SE'-NATH, אָסְנַת *dedicated to Neit.*

Daughter of Poti-pherah, priest of On, and wife of Joseph, B.C. 1715.
Gen. 41. 45 he gave him to wife A. the daughter of
41. 50 which A. the daughter of Poti-pherah
46. 20 which A. the daughter of Poti-pherah

AS'-ER, Ἀσήρ.

The Greek form of *Asher.*
Luke 2. 36 the daughter of Phanuel, of the tribe of A.
Rev. 7. 6 Of the tribe of A. (were) sealed twelve

ASH —
Ash or pine, אֹרֶן *oren.*
Isa. 44. 14 he planteth an ash, and the rain doth
ASHAMED, (of), to be—
1. *Shame*, בֹּשֶׁת *bosheth.*
Jer. 2. 26 As the thief is ashamed when he is found
2. *To be ashamed, become pale*, בּוֹשׁ *bosh.*
Judg. 3. 25 they tarried till they were ashamed
2 Ki. 2. 17 they urged him till he was ashamed
8. 11 stedfastly, until he was ashamed
Ezra 8. 22 I was ashamed to require of the king a
9. 6 I am ashamed and blush to lift up my
Job 19. 3 ye are not ashamed..ye make yourselves
Psa. 6. 10 Let all mine enemies be ashamed and
6. 10 let them return..be ashamed suddenly
25. 2 let me not be ashamed, let not mine
25. 3 let none that wait on thee be ashamed
25. 3 let them be ashamed which transgress
25. 20 let me not be ashamed; for I put my
31. 1 let me never be ashamed: deliver me in
31. 17 Let me not be ashamed, O LORD
31. 17 let the wicked be ashamed..let them be
35. 26 Let them be ashamed and brought to
37. 19 They shall not be ashamed in the evil
40. 14 Let them be ashamed and confounded
69. 6 Let not them..be ashamed for my sake
70. 2 Let them be ashamed and confounded
86. 17 they which hate me may..be ashamed
109. 28 when they arise, let them be ashamed
119. 6 Then shall I not be ashamed, when
119. 46 I will speak..and will not be ashamed
119. 78 Let the proud be ashamed; for they
119. 80 heart be sound..that I be not ashamed
127. 5 they shall not be ashamed, but they shall
Isa. 1. 29 they shall be ashamed of the oaks
20. 5 they shall be..ashamed of Ethiopia
23. 4 Be thou ashamed, O Zidon: for the sea
24. 23 and the sun ashamed, when the LORD of
26. 11 they shall see, and be ashamed for
29. 22 Jacob shall not now be ashamed, neither
41. 11 all..shall be ashamed and confounded
42. 17 they shall be greatly ashamed, that trust
44. 9 they see not..that they may be ashamed
44. 11 all his fellows shall be ashamed
44. 11 they shall fear..they shall be ashamed
45. 16 They shall be ashamed, and also
45. 17 ye shall not be ashamed nor confounded
45. 24 all..against him shall be ashamed
49. 23 they shall not be ashamed that wait for
50. 7 I know that I shall not be ashamed
54. 4 Fear not..thou shalt not be ashamed
65. 13 shall rejoice, but ye shall be ashamed
66. 5 your joy, and they shall be ashamed
Jer. 2. 36 thou also shalt be ashamed of Egypt
6. 15 Were they ashamed when they had
6. 15 nay, they were not at all ashamed
8. 12 Were they ashamed when they had
8. 12 nay, they were not at all ashamed
12. 13 they shall be ashamed of your revenues
14. 3 they were ashamed and confounded
14. 4 the plowmen were ashamed, they covered
15. 9 she hath been ashamed and confounded
17. 13 all that forsake thee shall be ashamed
20. 11 they shall be greatly ashamed; for they
22. 22 then shalt thou be ashamed and
31. 19 I was ashamed, yea, even confounded
48. 13 the house of Israel was ashamed of
48. 13 Moab shall be ashamed of Chemosh
Eze. 32. 30 with their terror they are ashamed of
36. 32 be ashamed and confounded for your
Hos. 4. 19 they shall be ashamed because of their
10. 6 Israel shall be ashamed of his own counsel
Joel 2. 26, 27 my people shall never be ashamed
Mic. 3. 7 Then shall the seers be ashamed, and the
Zeph. 3. 11 In that day shalt thou not be ashamed
Zech 13. 4 prophets shall be ashamed every one of
3. *To put to shame*, בּוֹשׁ *bosh*, 5.
Psa. 119. 116 let me not be ashamed of my hope
4. *To be ashamed of one's self*, בּוֹשׁ *bosh*, 7*a*.
Gen. 2. 25 were both naked..and were not ashamed
5. *To be ashamed, become red*, חָפֵר *chapher.*
Job 6. 20 they came thither, and were ashamed
Psa. 34. 5 and their faces were not ashamed
Jer. 50. 12 she that bare you shall be ashamed.
6. *To be dried up*, יָבֵשׁ *yabash*, 5.
Isa. 30. 5 They were all ashamed of a people (that)
Jer. 2. 26 so is the house of Israel ashamed
8. 9 The wise..are ashamed, they are
Joel 1. 11 Be ye ashamed, O ye husbandmen
Zech. 9. 5 her expectation shall be ashamed
7. *To be made ashamed, red*, חָפֵר *chapher*, 5.
Isa. 33. 9 Lebanon is ashamed..hewn down
8. *To be ashamed, blush*, כָּלַם *kalam*, 2.
Num 12. 14 should she not be ashamed seven days?
2 Sa. 10. 5 the men were greatly ashamed: and the
19. 3 people being ashamed steal away when
1 Ch. 19. 5 for the men were greatly ashamed
2 Ch. 30. 15 Levites were ashamed, and sanctified
Psa. 74. 21 let not the oppressed return ashamed
Jer. 3. 3 thou refusedst to be ashamed
Eze. 16. 27 daughters..are ashamed of thy lewd way
16. 61 shalt remember thy ways, and be ashamed
43. 10 they may be ashamed of their iniquities
43. 11 if they be ashamed..shew them the form
9. *To be ashamed*, αἰσχύνομαι *aischunomai.*
Luke 16. 3 I cannot dig; to beg I am ashamed
2 Co. 10. 8 I should boast..I should not be ashamed
Phil. 1. 20 that in nothing I shall be ashamed, but
1 Pe. 4. 16 if..as a Christian, let him not be ashamed
1. Jo. 2. 28 and not be ashamed before him at his
10. *To be ashamed of*, ἐπαισχύνομαι *epaischunomai.*
Mark 8. 38 shall be ashamed of..shall..be ashamed
Luke 9. 26 shall be ashamed of..shall..be ashamed
Rom. 1. 16 I am not ashamed of the gospel of Christ
6. 21 those things whereof ye are now ashamed?
2 Ti. 1. 8 Be not thou therefore ashamed of the
1. 12 nevertheless I am not ashamed: for I
1. 16 and was not ashamed of my chain
Heb. 2. 11 for which cause he is not ashamed to call
11. 16 wherefore God is not ashamed to be
11. *To be utterly ashamed*, καταισχύνομαι.
Luke 13. 17 all his adversaries were ashamed: and all
Rom. 9. 33 whosoever believeth..shall not be asham.
10. 11 believeth on him shall not be ashamed
2 Co. 7. 14 if I have boasted..I am not ashamed
9. 4 Lest..we..should be ashamed, 1 Pe. 3. 16.
12. *To be turned in*, ἐντρέπομαι, 2 Th. 3. 14; Tit. 2. 8.
ASHAMED, to make —
1. *To make ashamed, pale*, בּוֹשׁ *bosh*, 5.
Prov. 12. 4 she that maketh ashamed (is) as
2. *To cause to blush*, כָּלַם *kalam*, 5.
Job 11. 3 shall no man make thee ashamed?
3. *To shame utterly*, καταισχύνω *kataischunō.*
Rom. 5. 5 And hope maketh not ashamed; because
ASHAMED, needeth not to be —
Not ashamed of, ἀνεπαίσχυντος *anepaischuntos.*
2 Ti. 2. 15 workman that needeth not to be ashamed
A'-SHAN, עָשָׁן *smoke.*
A Levitical city in Judah, afterwards given to Simeon.
Josh. 15. 42 Libnah, and Ether, and A.
19. 7 Ain..and A.; four cities and their
1 Ch. 4. 32 their villages (were), Etam..and A., five
6. 59 And A. with her suburbs, and Beth
ASH-BE'-A, אַשְׁבֵּעַ *man of Baal.*
The patronymic of a family that sprang from Shelah son of Judah, B.C. 1400.
1 Ch. 4. 21 that wrought fine linen, of the house of A.
ASH'-BEL, אַשְׁבֵּל *man of Baal.*
A son of Benjamin, B.C. 1700.
Gen. 46. 21 the sons of Benjamin (were) Belah..and A.
Num 26. 38 sons of Benj. after their families..of A.
1 Ch. 8. 1 Benjamin begat..A. the second, and Ah.
ASH-BE-LITE, הָאַשְׁבֵּלִי *belonging to Ashbel.*
A family that sprang from Ashbel, Num. 26. 38.
ASHCHENAZ. *See* **ASHKENAZ.**
ASH'-DOD, אַשְׁדּוֹד *fortress, castle.*
One of the five chief cities of the Philistines. It was strongly fortified, and stood on the border at the N. extremity of what afterwards belonged to Simeon towards Egypt. It is now called *Asdud*, and in the New Testament and LXX. *Azotus.* It is about 30 miles from the southern frontier of Canaan, 3 from the Mediterranean, and midway between Gaza and Joppa.
Josh. 11. 22 in Gaza, in Gath, and in A...remained
15. 46 all that (lay) near A., with their villages
15. 47 A. with her towns and her villages, Gaza
1 Sa. 5. 1 took the ark..and brought it..unto A.
5. 3 when they of A. arose early on the morrow
5. 5 on the threshold of Dagon in A. unto this
5. 6 was heavy upon them of A., and he
5. 6 and smote them with emerods, (even) A.
5. 7 when the men of A. saw that (it was) so
6. 17. for A. one, for Gaza one, for Askelon one
2 Ch. 26. 6 and brake down the wall of..A., and built
26. 6 and built cities about A., and among the
Neh. 13. 23 Jews (that) had married wives of A., of
13. 24 children spake half in the speech of A.
Isa. 20. 1 In the year that Tartan came unto A
20. 1 and fought against A., and took it
Jer. 25. 20 Azzah, and Ekron, and the remnant of A.
Amos 1. 8 I will cut off the inhabitant from A.
3. 9 Publish in the palaces at A., and in the
Zeph. 2. 4 they shall drive out A. at the noon day
Zech. 9. 6 a bastard shall dwell in A., and I will
ASH-DO-DITES, ASH-DO-THITES, אַשְׁדּוֹדִי.
The inhabitants of Ashdod.
Josh. 13. 3 the Gazathites..the A., the Eshkalonites
Neh. 4. 7 when..the A., heard that the walls of
ASH-DOTH PIS'-GAH, אַשְׁדּוֹת הַפִּסְגָּה *springs of Pisgah.*
The spurs and ravines of Pisgah, the top of which is Mount Nebo. Now *Ain Musa.*
Deut. 3. 17 of the plain..the salt sea, under A.-p
4. 49 of the plain, under the springs of P.
Josh 12. 3 and from the south, under A.-p
13. 20 Beth-peor, and A.-p. and Beth-jeshimoth
A'-SHER, אָשֵׁר *happy.*
1. Eighth son of Jacob, and second by Zilpah, Leah's maid. (See *Aser*, the N.T. form.) B.C. 1730.
Gen. 30. 13 And Leah..called his name A.
35. 26 the sons of Zilpah..Gad, and A.
46. 17 the sons of A.; Jimnah, and Ishuah, and
49. 20 Out of A. his bread (shall be) fat, and he
Exod. 1. 4 Dan. and Naphtali, Gad, and A.
Num 26. 46 the name of the daughter of A. (was) Sar.
Josh. 17. 10 they met together in A. on the north, and
17. 11 Manasseh had in..A. Beth-shean and her
1 Ch. 2. 2 Benjamin, Naphtali, Gad, and A.
7. 30 sons of A.; Imnah, and Isuah, and Ishuai
7. 40 All these (were) the children of A., heads
2. Asher is used also as the name of the tribe descended from Asher, and of that part of Canaan in which they dwelt.
Num. 1. 13 Of A.; Pagiel the son of Ocran
1. 40 Of the children of A., by their generations
1. 41 that were numbered of..the tribe of A.
2. 27 that encamp..(shall be) the tribe of A.
2. 27 the captain of the children of A. (shall be)
7. 72 Pagiel..prince of the children of A.
10. 26 And over..the children of A. (was) Pagiel
13. 13 Of the tribe of A., Sethur the son of M.
26. 44 (Of) the children of A. after their families
26. 47 These (are) the families..of A. according
34. 27 the prince of the tribe..of A., Ahihud
Deut 27. 13 shall stand..to curse; Reuben..and A.
33. 24 of A. he said, (Let) A. (be) blessed with
Josh 19. 24 fifth lot came out for the tribe..of A.
19. 31 (is) the inheritance of the tribe..of A.
19. 34 the coast..reacheth to A. on the west
21. 6 of Gershon (had)..out of the tribe of A.
21. 30 out of the tribe of A., Mishal with her
Judg. 1. 31 Neither did A. drive out the inhabitants
5. 17 A. continued on the sea shore, and abode
6. 35 he sent messengers unto A., and unto
7. 23 Israel gathered themselves..out of A.
1 Ki. 4. 16 Baanah the son of Hushai (was) in A. and
1 Ch. 6. 62 to the sons of Gershom..out of..A.
6. 74 out of the tribe of A.; Mashal with her
12. 36 of A., such as went forth to battle..forty
2 Ch. 30. 11 Nevertheless divers of A...humbled
Eze. 48. 2 by the border of Dan.. a (portion for) A.
48. 3 by the border of A...a (portion for) N.
48. 34 one gate of Gad, one gate of A., one gate
3. A town E. of Shechem, on the road to Beth-shean, in Manasseh, W. of the Jordan. Now *Asirah.*
Josh. 17. 7 the coast of Manasseh was from A. to M.
[The following localities were in the territory of Asher:—Abdon, Accho, Achshaph, Achzib, Ahlab, Amad, Aphek, Beten, Beth-Dagon, Beth-Emek, Beth-Rehob, Carmel, Ebron, Hali, Hammon, Helbah, Helkath, Hosah, Hukkok, Jiphtah-el, Kanah, Mearah, Mishal, Neiel, Sidon, Ummah, &c.]
A-SHE-RITE, הָאָשֵׁרִי *the (one of) Asher.*
Patronymic of the tribe of Asher.
Judg. 1. 32 But the A. dwelt among the Canaanites
ASHES —
1. *Dust, (bruised, fine)*, אֵפֶר *epher.*
Gen. 18. 27 I..(am but) dust and ashes
Num 19. 9 a man..shall gather up the ashes
19. 10 he that gathereth the ashes..shall wash
2 Sa. 13. 19 Tamar put ashes on her head, and rent
1 Ki. 20. 38 prophet..disguised himself with ashes
20. 41 he..took the ashes away from his face
Esth. 4. 1 Mordecai..put on sackcloth with ashes
4. 3 great mourning..many lay in..ashes
Job 2. 8 and he sat down among the ashes
13. 12 Your remembrances (are) like unto ashes
30. 19 and I am become like dust and ashes
42. 6 I abhor..and repent in dust and ashes
Psa. 102. 9 For I have eaten ashes like bread
147. 16 he scattereth the hoar frost like ashes
Isa. 44. 20 He feedeth on ashes: a deceived heart
58. 5 spread sackcloth and ashes (under him)?
61. 3 give unto them beauty for ashes, the oil
Jer. 6. 26 sackcloth, and wallow thyself in ashes
Lam. 3. 16 stones, he hath covered me with ashes
Eze. 27. 30 they shall wallow themselves in the ashes
28. 18 I will bring thee to ashes upon the earth
Dan. 9. 3 by prayer..with fasting..and ashes
Jon. 3. 6 covered..with sackcloth, and sat in ashes
Mal. 4. 3 they shall be ashes under the soles of
2. *Ashes (fat)*, דֶּשֶׁן *deshen.*
Lev. 1. 16 the altar..by the place of the ashes
4. 12 ashes are poured out..ashes are poured
6. 10 take up the ashes which the fire hath
6. 11 carry forth the ashes without the camp
1 Ki. 13. 3 ashes that (are) upon it shall be poured
13. 5 and the ashes poured out from the altar
Jer. 31. 40 valley of the dead bodies, and of the ashes
3. *Dust, (bruised, fine)*, עָפָר *aphar.*
Num 19. 17 take of the ashes of the burnt heifer
2 Ki. 23. 4 carried the ashes of them unto Beth-el
4. *Dust, ashes*, פִּיחַ *piach.*
Exod. 9. 8 Take to you handfuls of ashes of the
9. 10 they took ashes of the furnace, and stood
5. *Ashes, embers*, σποδός *spodos.*
Matt 11. 21 have repented..in sackcloth and ashes
Luke 10. 13 repented, sitting in sackcloth and ashes
Heb. 9. 13 ashes of an heifer sprinkling the unclean
ASHES from, to receive or take away the, turn into—
To remove or cleanse from ashes, דָּשַׁן *dashen*, 3.
Exod 27. 3 make..pans to receive his ashes, Nu. 4. 13.
To turn into ashes, τεφρόω *tephroō*, 2 Pe. 2. 6.
A-SHI'-MA, אֲשִׁימָא *heaven.*
An idol worshipped by the people of Hamath, and introduced into Samaria by the colonists whom Shalmaneser settled therein.
2 Ki. 17. 30 and the men of Hamath made A

ASH-KE'-LON, AS-KE'-LON, אַשְׁקְלוֹן *holm-oak.*

Askalon is mentioned as a city of the Philistines, Josh. 13. 3, and 1 Sam. 6. 17. The tribe of Judah captured it B.C. 1425 (Judges 1. 18), but it was retaken by the Philistines, and is frequently denounced by the prophets. It fell successively into the hands of the Egyptians, the Greeks, and the Romans. It became a bishop's see in the 4th century. It was besieged by the Crusaders in 1100, and again in 1148, without success. Baldwin III. captured it in 1157. Saladin re-took it in 1187, and burnt it in 1191. Richard I. of England obtained possession the same year, and restored the fortifications in 1192. Sultan Bibars destroyed its fortifications and filled up its harbour in 1270. (*Askulan.*)

Judg. 1. 18 Also Judah took..A. with the coast
14. 19 he went down to A., and slew thirty men
1 Sa. 6. 17 these (are) the golden emerods..for A.
2 Sa. 1. 20 publish (it) not in the streets of A.; lest
Jer. 25. 20 the land of the Philistines, and A., and
47. 5 A. is cut off (with) the remnant of their
47. 7 LORD hath given it a charge against A.
Amos 1. 8 I will cut off..him that holdeth..from A.
Zeph. 2. 4 Gaza shall be forsaken, and A. a desolation
2. 7 in the houses of A. shall they lie down in
Zech. 9. 5 A. shall see (it), and fear..and A. shall

ASH-KE'-NAZ, ASH-CHE'-NAZ, אַשְׁכְּנַז.

1. Son of Gomer, son of Japheth.
Gen. 10. 3 the sons of Gomer; A., and Riphath, and
1 Ch. 1. 6 the sons of Gomer; A., and Riphath, and

2. The people or tribe whose original seat was in the neighbourhood of Armenia, along with the kingdoms of Ararat and Minni.
Jer. 51. 27 call together..the kingdoms of..A.

ASH'-NAH, אַשְׁנָה *fortification.*

1. A town in W. of Judah, near Dan.
Josh 15 33 the valley, Eshtaol, and Zoreah, and A.

2. Another town in the plains of Judah.
Josh. 15. 43 And Jiphtah, and A., and Nezib

ASH-PE'-NAZ, אַשְׁפְּנַז. *Meaning uncertain.*

The prince of the eunuchs under Nebuchadnezzar
Dan 1. 3 the king spake unto A. the master of his

ASHRIEL. *See* **ASRIEL.**

ASH-TAR'-OTH, ASH-TOR'-ETH, AS-TAR'-OTH, עַשְׁתֹּרֶת, עַשְׁתָּרוֹת *a wife.*

1. An idol of the Philistines, Phoenicians, and Zidonians, worshipped by Israel soon after the death of Joshua, and also by Solomon.
Judg. 2. 13 forsook the LORD, and served Baal and A.
10. 6 the children of Israel..served..A., and
1 Sa. 7. 3 put away A. from among you, and
7. 4 the children of Israel did put away..A.
12. 10 forsaken the LORD, and have served..A.
31. 10 they put his armour in the house of A.
1 Ki. 11. 5 Solomon went after A. the goddess of
11. 33 and have worshipped A. the goddess of
2 Ki. 23. 13 high places..Solomon..builded for A.

2. A city on the E. of the Jordan, in Bashan.
Deut. 1. 4 After he had slain..Og..dwelt at A.
Josh. 9. 10 all that he did..to Og..which (was) at A.
12. 4 the giants, that dwelt at A. and at Edrei
13. 12 the kingdom of Og which reigned in A.
13. 31 A., and Edrei, cities of the kingdom of

3. A Levitical town of Manasseh, beyond Jordan.
1 Ch. 6. 71 Unto the sons of Gershom..A. with

ASH-TE-RA-THITE, עַשְׁתְּרָתִי *of Ashteroth.*

Patronymic of one of David's worthies.
1 Ch. 11. 44 Uzzia the A., Shama and Jehiel the sons

ASH-TER'-OTH KAR-NA'-IM, עַשְׁתְּרֹת קַרְנַיִם.

A city of the Rephaim, in the kingdom of Og, in Manasseh beyond Jordan. It was an abode of the Rephaim at the time of Chedorlaomer, B.C. 1912. (*Ashterah.*)
Gen. 14. 5 and smote the Rephaims in A. K., and

ASH'-UR, אַשְׁחוּר *freeman.*

A son of Hezron, son of Pharez, B.C. 1560.
1 Ch. 2. 24 Abiah Hezron's wife bare him A. the
4. 5 A. the father of Tekoa had two wives

ASH-UR-ITES. אֲשׁוּרִי *belonging to Ashur.*

A tribe occupying the whole country W. of the Jordan above Jezreel, the district of the plain of Esdraelon. (Asherite occurs in Judg. 1. 32.)
2 Sa. 2. 9 made him king over Gilead..over the A.
Eze. 27. 6 the company of the A. have made thy

ASH'-VATH, עַשְׁוָת *made, wrought.*

A son of Japhlet, a descendant of Asher, B.C. 1660.
1 Ch. 7. 33 the sons of Japhlet; Pasach..and A.

A-SI'-A, Ἀσία.

This name was first applied in the 4th century to the north-western peninsula of the Asiatic continent. It is also called Anatolia, although the latter term is more correctly used for a particular portion. "Asia Minor was the theatre of the earliest remarkable events recorded in profane history; as the Argonautic expedition, the Trojan war, in which the gods are said to have descended from Olympus and joined battle with mortals; the conquests of the Persians, the overthrow of their empire by Alexander, and the settlement in this part of Asia of his successors. It subsequently fell under the Roman sway, and suffered severely in after-ages in the wars of the Saracens, Turks, Tartars, &c. It is also intimately connected with the early history of Christianity, and the first Christian churches were planted here." Its chief political divisions in ancient times were Bithynia, Cappadocia, Caria, Cilicia, Galatia, Lydia, Lycaonia and Isauria, Lycia, Mysia, Pamphylia, Paphlagonia, Phrygia, Pisidia, and Pontus.

Acts 2. 9 the dwellers in Mesopotamia, and in..A.
6. 9 (the synagogue) of the Libertines..of A.
16. 6 were forbidden..to preach the word in A.
19. 10 all they which dwell in A. heard the word
19. 22 but he himself stayed in A. for a season
19. 26 almost throughout all A., this Paul hath
19. 27 whom all A. and the world worshippeth
19. 31 certain of the chief of A...sent unto him
20. 4 there accompanied him into A. Sopater
20. 4 and of A., Tychicus and Trophimus.
20. 16 because he would not spend the time in A.
20. 18 from the first day that I came into A.
21. 27 the Jews which were of A., when they
24. 18 certain Jews from A. found me purified
27. 2 we launched, meaning to sail by..A.
1 Co. 16. 19 The churches of A. salute you. Aquila
2 Co. 1. 8 have you ignorant of our trouble..in A.
2 Ti. 1. 15 all they which are in A. be turned away
1 Pe. 1. 1 the strangers scattered throughout..A.
Rev. 1. 4 John to the seven churches which are in A.
1. 11 send (it) unto the seven churches..in A.

ASIDE —

By oneself, κατ' ἰδίαν *kat idian.*
Mark 7. 33 took him aside from the multitude
[*See also* Carry, go, gone, lay, set, take, turn, turned.]

ASIDE, to go or turn —

To retire, withdraw, ἀναχωρέω *anachōreō.*
Matt. 2. 22 he turned aside into the parts of Galilee
Acts 23. 19 and went..aside privately, and asked
26. 31 when they were gone aside, they talked

A-SI'-EL, עֲשִׂיאֵל *God is doer.*

A Simeonite, grandfather of Jehu, B.C. 800.
1 Ch. 4. 35 Josibiah, the son of Seraiah, the son of A.

ASK (earnestly), to —

1. *To inquire,* (בְּעָה) בְּעָא *bea.*
Dan. 6. 7 ask a petition of any God or man for
6. 12 ask..of any God or man within thirty
7. 16 I..asked him the truth of all this

2. *To seek, inquire,* בָּקַשׁ *baqash,* 3.
Judg. 6. 29 when they enquired and asked, they said
2 Ch. 20. 4 Judah gathered..to ask..of the LORD

3. *To seek, search,* דָּרַשׁ *darash.*
1 Ki. 14. 5 the wife..cometh to ask a thing of thee

4. *To ask,* שָׁאַל *shaal.*
Gen. 24. 47 I asked her, and said, Whose daughter
26. 7 the men..asked..of his wife; and he
32. 17 and asketh thee, saying, Whose (art) thou?
32. 29 Jacob asked..and said, Tell (me)
32. 29 Wherefore (is) it (that) thou dost ask
37. 15 the man asked him..What seekest thou?
38. 21 he asked the men of that place..Where
40. 7 he asked Pharaoh's officers that (were)
43. 7 The man asked us straitly of our state
43. 27 he asked them of..welfare, and said
44. 19 My lord asked his servants Have ye a
Exod 13. 14 it shall be when thy son asketh thee
18. 7 they asked each other of..welfare
Num 27. 21 Eleazar..shall ask..for him
Deut. 4. 32 ask now of the days that are past, which
6. 20 when thy son asketh thee in time to come
13. 14 and make search, and ask diligently
32. 7 ask thy father, and he will shew thee
Josh. 4. 6, 21 when your children ask..in time to
9. 14 the men..asked not..at the mouth
15. 18 she moved him to ask of her father a field
19. 50 they gave him the city which he asked
Judg. 1. 1 the children of Israel asked the LORD
1. 14 she moved him to ask of her father a field
5. 25 He asked water..she gave (him) milk
13. 6 I asked him not whence he (was), neither
13. 18 Why askest thou thus after my name
1 Sa. 1. 17 thy petition that thou hast asked of him
1. 20 Because I have asked him of the LORD
1. 27 given me my petition which I asked..him
8. 10 unto the people that asked of him a king
12. 17 which ye have done..in asking you a king
12. 19 we have added..evil, to ask us a king
19. 22 asked and said, Where (are) Samuel and
25. 8 Ask thy young men, and they will shew
28. 16 Wherefore then dost thou ask of me
2 Sa. 14. 18 Hide not..the thing that I shall ask thee
1 Ki. 2. 16 I ask one petition of thee, deny me not
2. 22 why dost thou ask Abishag..for Adonijah?
2. 22 ask for him the kingdom also; for he (is)
3. 5 God said, Ask what I shall give thee
3. 10 LORD, that Solomon had asked this thing
3. 11 thou hast asked..hast not asked..neither
3. 13 given thee that which thou hast not asked
10. 13 king Solomon gave..whatsoever she asked
2 Ki. 2. 9 Ask what I shall do for thee, before I be
2. 10 he said, Thou hast asked a hard thing
8. 6 when the king asked the woman, she told
2 Ch. 1. 7 said unto him, Ask what I shall give thee
1. 11 thou hast not asked riches, wealth, or
1. 11 hast asked long life; but hast asked
9. 12 king Solomon gave..whatsoever she asked
Neh. 1. 2 I asked them concerning the Jews that
Job 12. 7 ask now the beasts, and they shall teach
21. 29 Have ye not asked them that go by the
Psa. 2. 8 Ask of me, and I shall give..the heathen
21. 4 He asked life of thee..thou gavest (it)
78. 18 tempted..by asking meat for their lust
105. 40 (The people) asked, and he brought quails
Isa. 7. 11 Ask thee a sign of the LORD thy God
7. 11 ask it either in the depth, or in the height
7. 12 Ahaz said, I will not ask, neither will I
30. 2 walk..and have not asked at my mouth
41. 28 no counsellor, that, when I asked of them
45. 11 Ask me of things to come concerning my
58. 2 they ask of me the ordinances of justice
65. 1 I am sought of (them that) asked not
Jer. 6. 16 Stand ye..and ask for the old paths
15. 5 who shall go aside to ask how thou doest?
18. 13 Ask ye now among the heathen, who hath
23. 33 when this people..shall ask thee, saying
30. 6 Ask ye now, and see whether a man doth
36. 17 they asked Baruch, saying, Tell us now
37. 17 the king asked him secretly in his house
38. 14 I will ask thee a thing; hide nothing from
38. 27 Then came all the princes..and asked
48. 19 ask him that fleeth, and her that escapeth
50. 5 They shall ask the way to Zion with their
Lam. 4. 4 the young children ask bread..no man
Mic. 7. 3 the prince asketh, and the judge..for a
Hag. 2. 11 Ask now the priests..the law, saying
Zech 10. 1 Ask ye of the LORD rain in the time of the

5. *To ask (for oneself),* שָׁאַל *shaal,* 2.
1 Sa. 20. 6, 28 say David earnestly asked..of me

6. *To ask (earnestly),* שָׁאַל *shaal,* 3.
2 Sa. 20. 18 They shall surely ask..at Abel

7. *To ask (earnestly).* שְׁאֵל *sheel,* 3.
Ezra 5. 9 Then asked we those elders, (and) said
5. 10 We asked their names also, to certify
Dan. 2. 10 asked such things at any magician, or

8. *To ask, crave,* αἰτέω *aiteō.*
Matt. 5. 42 Give to him that asketh thee, and from
6. 8 what..ye have need of, before ye ask him
7. 7 Ask, and it shall be given you; seek, and
7. 8 every one that asketh receiveth; and he
7. 9 if his son ask bread, will he give him a
7. 10 if he ask a fish, will he give him a serpent
7. 11 give good things to them that ask him?
14. 7 to give her whatsoever she would ask
18 19 as touching anything that they shall ask
20. 22 Jesus answered..Ye know not what ye ask
21 22 all things, whatsoever ye shall ask in
27. 20 that they should ask Barabbas and
Mark 6. 22 Ask of me whatsoever thou wilt, and I
6. 23 Whatsoever thou shalt ask of me, I will
6. 24 went forth, and said..What shall I ask?
6. 25 she came in..with haste..and asked
10. 38 Jesus said..Ye know not what ye ask
Luke 1. 63 he asked for a writing-table, and wrote
6 30 Give to every man that asketh of thee
11. 9 I say unto you, Ask, and it shall be given
11. 10 every one that asketh receiveth; and he
11. 11 If a son shall ask bread of any of you that
11. 12 Or if he shall ask an egg, will he offer him
11. 13 give the Holy Spirit to them that ask him?
12. 48 to whom men..committed..they will ask
John 4. 9 How is it that thou, being a Jew, askest
4. 10 thou wouldest have asked of him, and he
11. 22 whatsoever thou wilt ask of God, God
14. 13 whatsoever ye shall ask in my name
14. 14 If ye shall ask anything in my name
15. 7 ye shall ask what ye will, and it shall
15. 16 that whatsoever ye shall ask of the Father
16. 23 whatsoever ye shall ask the Father
16. 24 Hitherto have ye asked nothing..ask, and
16. 26 At that day ye shall ask in my name: and
Acts 3. 2 to ask alms of them that entered into
Eph. 3. 20 to do..above all that we ask or think
Jas. 1. 5 If any of you lack wisdom, let him ask
1. 6 let him ask in faith, nothing wavering
4. 2 yet ye have not, because ye ask not
4. 3 Ye ask, and receive not, because ye ask
1 Pe. 3. 15 an answer to every man that asketh
1 Jo. 3. 22 whatsoever we ask, we receive of him
5. 14 that, if we ask anything according to his
5. 15 whatsoever we ask, we know that we have
5. 16 he shall ask, and he shall give him life

9. *To search out,* ἐξετάζω *exetazō.*
Jo. 21. 12 none of the disciples durst ask him

10. *To inquire, ask,* ἐπερωτάω *eperōtaō.*
Matt 12. 10 they asked him, saying, Is it lawful to heal
17. 10 his disciples asked him, saying, Why then
22 23 same day came..Sadducees..and asked
22. 35 Then one of them..a lawyer, asked
22. 41 the Pharisees were..together, Jesus asked
22. 46 neither durst any (man)..ask him
27. 11 the governor asked him, saying, Art
Mark 5. 9 he [asked] him, What (is) thy name? And
7. 5 the Pharisees and scribes asked him, Why
7. 17 his disciples asked him concerning the
8. 5 he asked them, How many loaves have
8. 23 he asked him if he saw ought
8. 27 by the way he asked his disciples, saying
9. 11 they asked him, saying, Why say the
9. 16 he asked the scribes, What question ye
9. 21 he asked his father, How long is it ago
9. 28 his disciples asked him privately, Why
9. 32 understood not..and were afraid to ask
9. 33 he asked them, What was it that ye
10. 2 the Pharisees came to him, and asked
10. 10 in the house his disciples asked him again
10. 17 there came one running..and asked him
12. 18 the Sadducees..asked him, saying

Mark12. 28 one of the scribes..asked him, Which
12. 34 no man after that durst ask him
13. 3 Peter and James..John..Andrew asked
14. 60 the high priest..asked Jesus, saying
14. 61 the high priest asked him, and said
15. 2 Pilate asked him, Art thou the King of
15. 4 Pilate asked him again, saying
15. 44 calling..the centurion, he asked him
Luke 3. 10 the people asked him, saying, What shall
6. 9 Then said Jesus unto them, I will ask you
8. 9 his disciples asked him, saying, What
8. 30 Jesus asked him, saying, What is thy
9. 18 he asked them, saying, Whom say the
18. 18 a certain ruler asked him, saying, Good
18. 40 when he was come near, he asked him
20. 21 they asked him, saying, Master, we know
20. 27 certain of the Sadducees..asked him, 20 40.
21. 7 they asked him, saying, Master, but
22. 64 they struck him on the face, and asked
23. 3 Pilate [asked] him, saying, Art thou the
23. 6 When Pilate heard of Galilee, he asked
John18. 7 Then asked he them again, Whom seek
18. 21 Why [askest] thou me? [ask] them which
Acts 5. 27 and the high priest asked them
23. 34 he asked of what province he was
1 Co. 14. 35 let them ask their husbands at home

11. *To ask of,* ἐρωτάω *erōtaō.*
Matt 16. 13 he a ked his disciples, saying, Whom do
21. 24 I also will ask you one thing, which
Mark 4. 10 they that were about him..asked of him
Luke 9. 45 they feared to [ask] him of that saying
19. 31 if any man ask you, Why do ye loose
20. 3 I will also ask you one thing; and answer
22. 68 if I also ask (you), ye will not answer
John 1. 19 when the Jews sent priests..to ask him
1. 21 they asked him, What then? Art thou
1. 25 they asked him, and said unto him
5. 12 Then asked they him, What man is that
8. 7 [So when they continued asking him]
9. 2 his disciples asked him, saying, Master
9. 15 Then again the Pharisees also asked him
9. 19 they asked them, saying, Is this your
9. 21 ask him: he shall speak for himself
9. 23 said his parents, He is of age; ask him
16. 5 none of you asketh me, Whither goest
16. 19 Jesus knew..they were desirous to ask
16. 23 in that day ye shall ask me nothing
16. 30 needest not that any man should ask
18. 19 The high priest then asked Jesus of his
Acts 3. 3 who seeing Peter and John..asked an

12. *To collect, lay together, speak,* λέγω *legō.*
Acts 25. 20 I asked (him) whether he would go to

13. *To ask information,* πυνθάνομαι *punthanomai.*
Luke15. 26 and asked what these things meant
18. 36 hearing the multitude pass by, he asked
John 13. 24 [that he should ask who it should be]
Acts 4. 7 they asked, By what power, or by what
10. 18 And called, and asked whether Simon
10. 29 I ask therefore for what intent ye have
23. 19 asked..What is that thou hast to tell me?

ASK after or of, to —
To inquire of, ask, ἐπερωτάω *eperōtaō.*
Mark11. 29 I will also ask of you one question
Acts 1. 6 they asked of him, saying, Lord, wilt
Rom 10. 20 manifest unto them that asked not after

ASK again, to —
To ask (back, beside), ἀπαιτέω *apaiteō.*
Luke 6. 30 of him that taketh away..ask..not again

ASK counsel, to —
To ask, שָׁאַל *shaal.*
Judg18. 5 Ask counsel, we pray thee, of God, that
20. 18 asked counsel of God, and said, Which of
20. 23 Israel..asked counsel of the LORD
1 Sa 14. 37 Saul asked counsel of God, Shall I go
Hos. 4. 12 My people ask counsel at their stocks

ASK questions, to —
1. *To ask about,* ἐπερωτάω *eperōtaō.*
Matt22. 35 Then one..asked (him a question)
Luke 2. 46 him in..temple..asking..questions

2. *To examine, ask questions,* ἀνακρίνω *anakrinō.*
1 Co. 10. 25 asking no question for conscience, 10. 27.

ASK on, to —
To ask, שָׁאַל *shaal.*
1 Ki. 2. 20 the king said unto her, Ask on, my mother

ASKELON. *See* **ASHKELON.**

ASKING —
To ask, שָׁאַל *shaal.*
1 Ch. 10. 13 for asking.. familiar spirit, to enquire

ASLEEP —
1. *Asleep, sleeping,* יָשֵׁן *yashen.*
1 Sa 26. 12 no man saw..for they (were) all asleep
Song 7. 9 causing the lips of those that are asleep

2. *To lie down to sleep,* καθεύδω *katheudō.*
Matt26. 40 the disciples, and findeth them asleep
26. 43 he came and found them asleep again
Mark 4. 38 was in the hinder part of the ship, asleep
14. 40 when he returned, he found them asleep

ASLEEP, to be —
1. *To lie down to sleep,* καθεύδω *katheudō.*
Matt. 8. 24 the ship was covered..but he was asleep

2. *To be laid down in death,* κοιμάομαι *koimaomai.*
1 Th. 4. 13 concerning them which are asleep, that
4. 15 shall not prevent them which are asleep

ASLEEP, to be fast —
To be in a deep sleep, רָדַם *radam,* 2.
Judg. 4. 21 for he was fast asleep and weary
Jon. 1. 5 Jonah was gone down..and was fast asleep

ASLEEP, to fall —
1. *To fall fast asleep,* ἀφυπνόω *aphupnoō.*
Luke 8. 23 But as they sailed he fell asleep

2. *to lie down in sleep,* κοιμάομαι *koimaomai.*
Acts 7. 60 when he had said this, he fell asleep
1 Co. 15. 6 part remain..but some are fallen asleep
15. 18 they..which are fallen asleep in Christ
2 Pe. 3. 4 since the fathers fell asleep, all things

AS'-NAH, אַסְנָה *dweller in the thornbush.*
A Nethinim, whose descendants came up with Zerubbabel from Babylon, B.C. 536.
Ezra 2. 50 The children of A., the children of Meh.

A-SNAP'-PER, אָסְנַפַּר *Asnap the great.*
An Assyrian satrap who settled Cuthæans in the cities of Samaria. Perhaps he was Esar-haddon, or one of his chief captains, B.C. 678.
Ezra 4. 10 nations whom the great and noble A.

ASP —
1. *Asp, adder,* פֶּתֶן *pethen.*
Deut32. 33 Their wine..the cruel venom of asps
Job 20. 14 (Yet) his meat..(is) the gall of asps
20. 16 He shall suck the poison of asps
Isa. 11. 8 child shall play on the hole of the asp

2. *An asp, kind of viper,* ἀσπίς *aspis.*
Rom. 3. 13 the poison of asps..under their lips

AS-PA'-THA, אַסְפָּתָא *horse-given.*
Third son of Haman the Agagite, B.C. 510.
Esth. 9. 7 And Parshandatha, and Dalphon, and A.

AS-RI'-EL, ASH-RI'-EL, אַשְׂרִיאֵל *God is joined.*
1. Son of Gilead, grandson of Manasseh, B.C. 1660.
Num26. 31 And (of) A., the family of the Asrielites
Josh 17. 2 There was also..for the children of A.
2. A son of Manasseh, B.C. 1660.
1 Ch. 7. 14 sons of Manasseh; A., whom she bare

AS-RI-E-LITES, הָאַשְׂרִאֵלִי *the (one of) Asriel.*
The family or descendants of Asriel.
Num26. 31 (of) Asriel, the family of the A.: and (of)

ASS —
1. *Ass, (so called from its endurance),* אָתוֹן *athon.*
Gen. 49. 11 Binding..his ass's colt..he washed his
Num22. 21 Balaam rose up..and saddled his ass
22. 22 Now he was riding upon his ass, and his
22. 23, 25, 27 the ass saw the angel of the LORD
22. 23 the ass turned aside out of the way
22. 23 Balaam smote the ass, to turn her
22. 27 and he smote the ass with a staff
22. 28 the LORD opened the mouth of the ass
22. 29 Balaam said unto the ass, Because thou
22. 30 ass said unto Balaam, (Am) not I thine ass
22. 32 Wherefore hast thou smitten thine ass
22. 33 the ass saw me, and turned from me
Judg. 5. 10 Speak, ye that ride on white asses
1 Sa. 9. 3 the asses of Kish Saul's father were lost
9. 3 one of the servants..go seek the asses
9. 5 my father leave (caring) for the asses
9. 20 thine asses that were lost three days ago
10. 2 The asses which thou wentest to seek
10. 2 thy father hath left the care of the asses
10. 14 Whither went ye?..To seek the asses
10. 16 told us plainly that the asses were found
2 Ki. 4. 22 Send me, I pray thee..one of the asses
4. 24 she saddled an ass, and said to her
1 Ch. 27. 30 over the asses..Jehdeiah the Meronothite
Job 1. 14 oxen were plowing, and the asses feeding
Zech. 9. 9 and upon a colt the foal of an ass

2. *Ass (so called from its ruddy colour),* חֲמוֹר *chamor.*
Gen. 22. 3 Abraham..saddled his ass, and took two
22. 5 Abide ye here with the ass; and I and
24. 35 the LORD..hath given..camels, and asses
30. 43 the man..had..camels, and asses
32. 5 I have oxen, and asses, flocks, and men
34. 28 They took their sheep..and their asses
36. 24 as he fed the asses of Zibeon his father
42. 26 they laded their asses with the corn
42. 27 to give his ass provender in the inn
43. 18 take us for bondmen, and our asses
43. 24 and he gave their asses provender
44. 3 men were sent away, they and their asses
44. 13 laded every man his ass, and returned to
45. 23 ten asses laden with the good things of
47. 17 Joseph gave them bread..for the asses
49. 14 Issachar..a strong ass couching down
Exod. 4. 20 set them upon an ass, and he returned
9. 3 the hand of the LORD is..upon the asses
13. 13 every firstling of an ass thou shalt
20. 17 Thou shalt not covet thy neighbour's..ass
21. 33 if..an ox or an ass fall therein
22. 4 whether it be ox, or ass, or sheep; he shall
22. 9 For all manner of trespass..for ass, for
22. 10 If a man deliver..an ass..to keep
23. 4 If thou meet thine enemy's ox or his ass
23. 5 If thou see the ass of him that hateth
23. 12 that thine ox and thine ass may rest
34. 20 the firstling of an ass thou shalt redeem

Num16. 15 I have not taken one ass from them
31. 28 levy a tribute..of the asses, and of the
31. 30 one portion of fifty..of the asses, and of
31. 34 threescore and one thousand asses
31. 39 the asses..thirty thousand and five
31. 45 thirty thousand asses and five hundred
Deut. 5. 14 thou shalt not do any work..nor thine ass
5. 21 neither shalt thou covet..his ass, or any
22. 3 In like manner shalt thou do with his ass
22. 4 Thou shalt not see thy brother's ass or his
22. 10 Thou shalt not plow with an ox and an ass
28. 31 thine ass..violently taken away from
Josh 6. 21 they utterly destroyed all..sheep,and ass
7. 24 Joshua..took Achan..and his asses
9. 4 took old sacks upon their asses, and wine
15. 18 she lighted off (her) ass; and Caleb said
Judg. 1. 14 she lighted from off (her) ass; and Caleb
6. 4 left no sustenance..neither..ox, nor ass
15. 15 he found a new jawbone of an ass, and
15. 16 With the jawbone of an ass, heaps upon
15. 16 with the jaw of an ass have I slain
19. 3 having his servant..and a couple of asses
19. 10 and..with him two asses saddled, his
19. 19 Yet there is..provender for our asses
19. 21 gave provender unto the asses: and they
19. 28 Then the man took her (up) upon an ass
1 Sa. 8. 16 he will take..your asses, and put..to his
12. 3 whose ass have I taken? or whom have I
15. 3 slay..man and woman..camel and ass
16. 20 Jesse took an ass..with bread, and
22. 19 smote he..both..oxen, and asses, and
25. 18 Abigail..took..loaves..and laid..asses
25. 20 it was..she rode on the ass, that she
25. 23 she hasted, and lighted off the ass, and
25. 42 And Abigail hasted..and rode upon an ass
27. 9 David..took..the oxen, and the asses
2 Sa. 16. 1 Ziba..met him, with a couple of asses
16. 2 The asses (be) for the king's household
17. 23 he saddled (his) ass, and arose, and gat
19. 26 I will saddle me an ass, that I may
1 Ki. 2. 40 Shimei arose, and saddled his ass, and
13. 13 said unto his sons, Saddle me the ass
13. 13 So they saddled him the ass: and he
13. 23 that he saddled for him the ass
13. 24 and the ass stood by it, the lion also
13. 27 saying, Saddle me the ass. And they
13. 28 and the ass and the lion standing by the
13. 28 the lion had not..nor torn the ass
13. 29 and laid it upon the ass, and brought
2 Ki. 6. 25 until an ass's head was..for fourscore
7. 7 and left their tents..and their asses
7. 10 but horses tied, and asses tied, and the
1 Ch. 5. 21 they took away..of asses two thousand
12. 40 Moreover they..brought bread on asses
2 Ch. 28. 15 carried all the feeble of them upon asses
Ezra 2. 67 asses, six thousand seven hundred and
Neh. 7. 69 thousand seven hundred..twenty asses
13. 15 bringing in sheaves, and lading asses
Job 24. 3 They drive away the ass of the fatherless
Prov. 26. 3 A whip for the horse, a bridle for the ass
Isa. 1. 3 The ox knoweth his owner, and the ass
21. 7 And he saw..a chariot of asses..a chariot
32. 20 that send forth..the feet of..the ass
Jer. 22. 19 shall be buried with the burial of an ass
Eze. 23. 20 whose flesh..the flesh of asses, and whose
Zech. 9. 9 lowly, and riding upon an ass, and upon
14. 15 so shall be the plague of..the ass, and of

3. *An ass, (male or female),* ὄνος *onos.*
Matt 21. 2 straightway ye shall find an ass tied
21. 5 thy King cometh..sitting upon an ass
21. 7 brought the ass..and put on them their
Luke13. 15 doth not each one..loose his..ass
14. 5 Which of you shall have an [ass] Jo. 12. 15.

4. *An ass (of burden),* ὑποζύγιον, Mt. 21. 5; 2 Pe. 2. 16.

ASS colt —
A young ass, עַיִר *ayir.*
Judg 10. 4 thirty sons that rode on thirty ass colts
12. 14 thirty nephews, that rode on..ten ass colts

ASS, he —
An ass, (from its ruddy colour), חֲמוֹר *chamor.*
Gen. 12. 16 he had sheep, and oxen, and he asses

ASS, young —
1. *A young ass,* עַיִר *ayir.*
Isa. 30. 6 riches upon the shoulders of young asses
30. 24 young asses that ear the ground shall

2. *A little ass, a colt,* ὀνάριον *onarion.*
John 12. 14 Jesus, when he had found a young ass

ASS, wild —
1. *A wild or free ass,* עֲרָד *arad.*
Dan. 5. 21 and his dwelling..with the wild asses

2. *A wild or free ass,* עָרוֹד *arod.*
Job 39. 5 hath loosed the bands of the wild ass?

3. *A free or wild ass,* פֶּרֶא *pere.*
Job 6. 5 Doth the wild ass bray when he hath
11. 12 though man be born..a wild ass's colt
24. 5 wild asses in the desert, go they forth
39. 5 Who hath sent out the wild ass free?
Psa. 104. 11 the wild asses quench their thirst
Isa. 32. 14 for dens for ever, a joy of wild asses
Jer. 2. 24 A wild ass..snuffeth up the wind at her
14. 6 the wild asses did stand in the high
Hos. 8. 9 a wild ass alone by himself: Ephraim

ASSAULT —
An assault, pressure, ὁρμή *hormē.*
Acts 14. 5 there was an assault made both of the

ASSAULT, to —

1. *To press,* צוּר *tsur.*
Esth. 8. 11 all the power..that would assault them

2. *To place oneself against,* ἐφίστημι *ephistēmi.*
Acts 17. 5 But the Jews.. assaulted the house of

ASSAY, to —

1. *To begin, be desirous,* יָאַל *yaal,* 5.
1 Sa. 17. 39 David girded his sword..and he assayed to

2. *To try, prove,* נָסָה *nasah,* 3.
Deut. 4. 34 hath God assayed to go (and) take him a
Job 4. 2 (If) we assay to commune with thee, wilt

3. *To make trial,* πειράζω *peirazō.*
Acts 16. 7 they assayed to go into Bithynia: but

4. *To try or attempt,* πειράομαι *peiraomai.*
Acts 9. 26 he assayed to join himself to the disciples

ASSAYING —

To make an attempt, πεῖραν λαμβάνειν. [*lambanō*].
Heb 11. 29 the Egyptians assaying to do were

ASSEMBLE, to —

1. *To gather,* אָסַף *asaph.*
1 Ch. 15 4 David assembled the children of Aaron
Isa 11 12 he..shall assemble the outcasts of Israel
Jer. 12. 9 come ye, assemble all the beasts of the
21. 4 I will assemble them into the midst of
Eze. 11. 17 I will..assemble you out of the countries
Dan. 11 10 his sons..shall assemble a multitude of
Mic. 2. 12 I will surely assemble, O Jacob, all of
4. 6 In that day..will I assemble her that

2. *To cry, call, summon,* זָעַק *zaaq,* 5.
2 Sa. 20 4 Assemble me the men of Judah within
20. 5 Amasa went to assemble..Judah: but he

3. *To be in the host, or to serve it,* צָבָא *tsaba.*
Exod 38. 8 assembling, which assembled (at) the door
1 Sa. 2. 22 they lay with the women that assembled

4. *To press,* קָבַץ *qabats.*
Joel 2 16 assemble the elders, gather the children

5. *To be pressed, gathered,* קָבַץ *qabats,* 2.
Ezra 10. 1 there assembled unto him out of Israel

6. *To call together,* קָהַל *qahal,* 5.
Num. 1. 18 they assembled all the congregation
1 Ki 8. 1 Then Solomon assembled the elders of
12 21 he assembled all the house of Judah
1 Ch 28 1 David assembled all the princes of Israel
2 Ch 5 2 Then Solomon assembled the elders of Is.

7. *To meet tumultuously,* רָגַשׁ *regash,* 5.
Dan. 6 11 these men assembled, and found Daniel
6. 15 Then these men assembled unto the king

ASSEMBLE selves, to —

1. *To be gathered,* אָסַף *asaph,* 2.
Judg 10. 17 children of Israel assembled themselves
Jer. 4. 5 Assemble yourselves, and let us go into
8. 14 assemble yourselves, and let us enter into
Amos 3. 9 Assemble yourselves upon the mountains

2. *To gather themselves, turn in,* גּוּר *gur,* 7a.
Hos. 7 14 they assemble themselves for corn and

3. *To be cried, called, summoned,* זָעַק *zaaq,* 2.
1 Sa. 14. 20 all the people..assembled themselves

4. *To be met by appointment,* יָעַד *yaad,* 2.
Num 10 3 the assembly shall assemble themselves

5. *To hasten,* עוּשׁ *ush.*
Joel 3. 11 Assemble yourselves, and come, all ye

6. *To be pressed together,* קָבַץ *qabats,* 2.
Isa. 45 20 Assemble yourselves and come; draw
48 14 All ye, assemble yourselves, and hear
Eze. 39. 17 Assemble yourselves, and come; gather

7. *To be called, invited,* קָהַל *qahal,* 2.
1 Ki 8. 2 all the men of Israel assembled themselves
2 Ch. 5 3 all the men of Israel assembled themselves
20 26 on the fourth day they assembled themsel.

8. *To go or lead together,* συνάγω *sunagō.*
Acts 11 26 they assembled themselves with the

ASSEMBLE selves by troops, to —

To gather together in troops, גָּדַד *gadad,* 7a.
Jer. 5. 7 they..assembled..by troops in the harlots'

ASSEMBLE together, to —

1. *To be called, invited,* קָהַל *qahal,* 2.
Josh 18. 1 whole congregation..assembled together
Esth 9. 18 the Jews..at Shusan assembled together

2. *To meet tumultuously,* רָגַשׁ *regash,* 5.
Dan. 6. 6 these presidents and princes assembled t.

3. *To lead or go together,* συνάγω *sunagō.*
Matt 26. 3 Then assembled together the chief priests

ASSEMBLED, to be —

To be gathered, added, אָסַף *asaph,* 2.
Ezra 9 4 Then were assembled unto me every one
Neh 9. 1 the children of Israel were assembled
Isa. 43. 9 let the people be assembled: who among

2. *To be met by appointment,* יָעַד *yaad,* 2.
1 Ki. 8 5 congregation..that were assembled unto
2 Ch. 5 6 that were assembled unto him before the
Psa. 48 4 kings were assembled, they passed by

3. *To be called, invited,* קָהַל *qahal,* 2.
Eze. 38. 7 thy company that are assembled unto

4. *To bring or lead together,* συνάγω *sunagō.*
Matt 26. 57 the scribes and the elders were assembled
28. 12 when they were assembled with the elders
John 20. 19 the disciples [were assembled] for fear of

5. *To become, be,* γίνομαι *ginomai.*
Acts 15. 25 It seemed good unto us, being assembled

ASSEMBLED together (with,) to be —

1. *To bring or lead together,* συνάγω *sunagō.*
Acts 4. 31 where they were assembled together

2. *To throng together,* συναλίζομαι *sunalizomai.*
Acts 1. 4 being assembled together with (them)

ASSEMBLED with, to be —

To come together, συνέρχομαι *sunerchomai.*
Mark 14. 53 with him were assembled all the chief

ASSEMBLIES —

Gatherings, אֲסֻפּוֹת *asuppoth.*
Eccl. 12. 11 fastened (by) the masters of assemblies

ASSEMBLING together —

Gathering together, ἐπισυναγωγή *episunagōgē.*
Heb. 10. 25 Not forsaking the assembling..together

ASSEMBLY —

1. *An appointed gathering,* מוֹעֵד *moed.*
Lam. 1. 15 he hath called an assembly against me
Eze. 44. 24 they shall keep..in all mine assemblies

2. *Seat,* מוֹשָׁב *moshab.*
Psa. 107. 32 praise him in the assembly of the elders

3. *Convocation,* מִקְרָא *miqra.*
Isa. 1. 13 the calling of assemblies, I cannot away
4. 5 the LORD will create..upon her assemblies

4. *Secret assembly,* סוֹד *sod.*
Psa. 89. 7 greatly to be feared in the assembly
111. 1 in the assembly of the upright, and (in)
Jer. 6. 11 I will pour it out..upon the assembly
15. 17 I sat not in the assembly of the mockers
Eze. 13. 9 they shall not be in the assembly

5. *An appointed meeting,* עֵדָה *edah.*
Lev. 8. 4 the assembly was gathered together unto
Num. 8. 9 the whole assembly of the children of Is.
10. 2 use them for the calling of the assembly
10. 3 the assembly shall assemble themselves
16. 2 fifty princes of the assembly, famous
20 8 gather thou the assembly together, thou
Psa. 22. 16 the assembly of the wicked have inclosed
86. 14 the assemblies of violent (men) have
Prov. 5. 14 midst of the congregation and assembly

6. *A gathering, restraint,* עֲצֶרֶת *atsereth.*
Jer. 9. 2 they (be)..an assembly of treacherous

7. *Called or invited gathering,* קָהָל *qahal.*
Gen. 49. 6 unto their assembly, mine honour, be not
Exod 12. 6 whole assembly of the congregation of
16. 3 to kill this whole assembly with hunger
Lev. 4. 13 be hid from the eyes of the assembly
Num 14. 5 fell on their faces before all the assembly
20. 6 went from the presence of the assembly
Deut. 5. 22 the LORD spake unto all your assembly
9. 10 the LORD spake..the day of the assembly
10. 4 the LORD spake..the day of the assembly
18. 16 thou desiredst..the day of the assembly
Judg 20. 2 presented themselves in the assembly
21. 8 none..from Jabesh-gilead to the assembly
1 Sa. 17. 47 all this assembly shall know that the
2 Ch. 30 23 the whole assembly took counsel to keep
Jer. 26. 17 of the elders..spake to all the assembly
50. 9 I will raise..up..an assembly of
Eze. 23 24 come against thee..with an assembly of

8. *Called or invited assembly,* קְהִלָּה *qehillah.*
Neh. 5 7 And I set a great assembly against them

9. *What is called out or forth,* ἐκκλησία *ekklēsia.*
Acts 19 32 the assembly was confused; and the
19. 39 shall be determined in a lawful assembly
19. 41 had..spoken, he dismissed the assembly

10. *A coming together,* συναγωγή *sunagōgē.*
Jas. 2. 2 if there come unto your assembly a man

ASSEMBLY, general —

A whole assembly, πανήγυρις *panēguris.*
Heb. 12. 23 To the general assembly and church of

ASSEMBLY, places of —

An appointed meeting, מוֹעֵד *moed.*
Lam. 2. 6 hath destroyed his places of..assembly

ASSEMBLY, solemn —

An appointed meeting, מוֹעֵד *moed.*
Zeph. 3. 18 I will gather..for the solemn assembly

ASSENT —

Mouth, פֶּה *peh.*
2 Ch. 18. 12 prophets (declare) good..with one assent

ASSENT, to —

To put together, agree, συντίθημι *suntithēmi.*
Acts 24. 9 the Jews also [assented], saying that

AS'-SHUR, AS'-SUR, אַשּׁוּר *level plain.*

1 The builder of Nineveh, apparently one of the descendants of Ham, or Assyria itself.
Gen. 10. 11 Out of that land went forth A., and

2. A son of Shem, and brother of Elam.
Gen 10. 22 children of Shem; Elam, and A., and
1 Ch. 1. 17 sons of Shem; Elam, and A., and

3. This word is sometimes left untranslated when it denotes *Assyria*, or the Assyrians.
Num 24. 22 until A. shall carry thee away captive
24. 24 ships..shall afflict A., and shall afflict
Ezra 4. 2 Esar-haddon king of A., which brought
Psa. 83. 8 A. also is joined with them: they have
Eze. 27. 23 the merchants of Sheba, A., and Chilmad
32. 22 A. (is) there and all her company: his
Hos. 14. 3 A. shall not save us; we will not ride

AS-SHU'-RIM, אַשּׁוּרִם *mighty ones.*

A son of Dedan, or his descendants.
Gen. 25. 3 sons of Dedan were A., and Letushim

ASSIGN, to —

To give, נָתַן *nathan.*
Josh 20. 8 other side Jordan..they assigned Bezer
2 Sa. 11. 16 Joab..assigned Uriah unto a place where

AS'-SIR, אַסִּיר *prisoner.*

1. A son of Korah, grandson of Kohath, B.C. 1530.
Exod. 6. 24 sons of Korah; A. and Elkanah, and
1 Ch. 6. 22 Amminadab his son, Korah his son, A.

2. A son of Ebiasaph, grandson of Assir, B.C. 1520.
1 Ch. 6. 23 Ebiasaph his son, and A. his son
6. 37 Tahath, the..son of A. the son of Ebiasaph

3. A son of Jeconiah, son of Jehoiakim, B.C. 588.
1 Ch. 3. 17 sons of Jeconiah; A., Salathiel his son

ASSIST, to —

To place alongside of, παρίστημι *paristēmi.*
Rom. 16. 2 assist her in whatsoever business she

ASSOCIATE selves, to —

[*Be comrades*], רָעַע *raa,* 3.
Isa. 8. 9 Associate yourselves, O ye people, and ye

AS'-SOS, *also called Apollonia,* Ἄσσος.

A seaport of Mysia, in Asia Minor, 9 miles from Troas, on the northern shore of the Gulf of Adramyttium.
Acts 20. 13 And we..sailed unto A., there intending
20. 14 when he met with us at A., we took him

ASSUR. *See* **ASSHUR.**

ASSURANCE —

1. *Confidence, trust,* בֶּטַח *betach.*
Isa. 32. 17 the effect of righteousness..assurance for

2. *Faith, trust, conviction,* πίστις *pistis.*
Acts 17. 31 he hath given assurance unto all (men)

3. *Full conviction,* πληροφορία *plērophoria.*
1 Th. 1. 5 the Holy Ghost, and in much assurance

ASSURANCE, full —

Full conviction, πληροφορία *plērophoria.*
Col. 2. 2 unto all riches of the full assurance of
Heb. 6. 11 shew..diligence to the full assurance of
10. 22 Let us draw near..in full assurance of

ASSURANCE, to have —

To hold stedfast, אָמַן *aman,* 5.
Deut 28. 66 thou..shalt have none assurance of..life

ASSURE, to —

To persuade, πείθω *peithō.*
1 Jo. 3. 19 and shall assure our hearts before him

ASSURED —

Truth, אֱמֶת *emeth.*
Jer. 14. 13 I will give you assured peace in this place

ASSURED, to be —

To rise up, stand firm, קוּם *qum.*
Lev. 27. 19 he shall add..and it shall be assured to

ASSURED of, to be —

To be made steady, πιστόομαι *pistoomai.*
2 Ti. 3 14 hast learned and hast been assured of

ASSUREDLY —

1. *Truth,* אֱמֶת *emeth.*
Jer. 32. 41 I will plant them in this land assuredly

2. *To know,* יָדַע *yada.*
1 Sa. 28. 1 Know thou assuredly, that thou shalt go

3. *To go forth,* יָצָא *yatsa.*
Jer. 38. 17 thou wilt assuredly go forth unto the king

4. *To drink,* שָׁתָה *shathah.*
Jer. 49. 12 drink of the cup have assuredly drunken

5. *Safely, surely, certainly,* ἀσφαλῶς *asphalōs.*
Acts 2. 36 all the house of Israel know assuredly

6. *That, because,* כִּי *ki.*
1 Ki. 1. 13 Assuredly Solomon thy son shall reign

ASSUREDLY gathering —

To put firmly together, συμβιβάζω *sumbibazō.*
Acts 16. 10 assuredly gathering that the Lord had

ASSWAGE, to —

1. *To restrain, hold back, dim,* חָשַׂךְ *chasak.*
Job 16. 5 the moving of my lips should asswage

2. *To subside, sink down,* שָׁכַךְ *shakak.*
Gen. 8. 1 a wind to pass..and the waters asswaged

ASSWAGED, to be —

To be restrained, חָשַׂךְ *chasak,* 2.
Job 16. 6 I speak, my grief is not asswaged

AS-SYR'-IA, אַשּׁוּר *plain, level.*

Assyria is the narrow tract of country inclosed between Mesopotamia, Babylonia, Armenia, Susiana, and Media, called by the ancients Assyria, or Asturia, and was the original seat of that extended dominion known as the Assyrian empire. From the 10th chapter of Genesis we learn that Nimrod, leaving Babylon, which he had founded, went forth into Assyria, where he built Nineveh, Rehoboth, Calah, and Resen, about B.C. 2218. Such is the interpretation given in the margin of the Bible, though some authors prefer the reading, that Assur went forth and built these cities. The next notice of this empire that occurs in the Old Testament is the invasion of Palestine in the reign of Uzziah, by Pul (2 Kings 15. 19), king of Assyria, B.C. 769. Menahem, king of Israel, induced him to retire by a bribe of 1000 talents. Tiglath-pileser, successor of Pul, at the solicitation of Ahaz, king of Judah, invaded Syria, and took many of its people away captive (2 Kings 16. 5-9), B.C. 738. Shalmanassar besieged Samaria three years, captured it, put an end to the kingdom of Israel B.C. 722 (2 Kings 17. 5, 6), and carried away its people into captivity. Another king, Sennacherib, came up against all the fenced cities of Judah, and took them (2 Kings 18. 13, and 2 Chron. 32.), B.C. 714, but failed in an attack upon Jerusalem, having 185,000 men slain in one night, B.C. 712 (2 Kings 18. 13; 19. 35, 36, and 2 Chron. 32. 21). On his return to Nineveh, Sennacherib was slain by two of his own sons, and another king, named Esarhaddon, assumed the Assyrian sceptre, B.C. 711 (2 Kings 19. 37). The last king of Assyria mentioned in Scripture is Nebuchadnezzar, who is supposed to have ascended the throne B.C. 650. It is evident that the Assyrian empire existed at a very early period in the history of the world; that its rulers obtained extensive dominion; and that, after a partial dismemberment, it continued to exist for many years. The theory of an Assyrian empire that terminated at the revolt of the Medes, about B.C. 711, followed by an Assyrian monarchy that continued till the destruction of Nineveh, B.C. 606, though supported by high authorities, is now generally rejected. Clinton (Fasti Hellenici, i. 268) remarks, with reference to the duration of the Assyrian monarchy: The period delivered by Ctesias seems to have been 1306 years. He placed its commencement 1000 years before the Trojan war, and its termination at B.C. 876. But in assigning the termination of the Assyrian monarchy, Ctesias, and those that followed him, confounded two events,—the revolt of the Medes and the destruction of Nineveh, which they made to happen together. These two events, however, were divided by a considerable interval of time, and the conclusion of the term of 1306 years assigned to that monarchy did not occur at the Median revolt, but at the final capture of Nineveh. The date of this event we are enabled to fix with precision, on the concurrent authority of Scripture and Herodotus. (B.C. 606.)

Clinton gives the following summary:—*Ninus*, B.C. 2182; Assyrian monarchy, 1306 years before the empire, 675 years, B.C. 1912; during the empire, 24 kings, 526 years, B.C. 1237. *Sardanapalus*, B.C. 876; after the empire, 6 kings, 105 years, B.C. 711. Capture of Nineveh, B.C. 606.

Vaux (Nineveh and Persepolis, p. 508) gives, on the authority of Rawlinson, the following list of Assyrian monarchs:—First Assyrian empire: Belukh, B.C. 1273; Pudil, 1255; Phulukh I., 1240; Silima-Rish I., 1220; Sanda-pal-imat, 1200; Asshur-capal-il, 1185; Mutaggil-Nebo, 1165; Asshur-Rish-ipan, 1140; Tiglath-Pileser I., 1120; Asshur-bani-pal I., 1100; Asshur-adan-akhi, 950; Asshur-danin-il, 925; Phulukh II., 900; Tigulti-Sanda, 880; Sardanapalus, 850; Silima-Rish II. (Asshur-danin-pal), 815; Shamasphul, 780; Phulukh III. (Pul), and Semiramis, 760. Second Assyrian empire: Tiglath-Pileser II., B.C. 747; Shalmaneser, 730; Sargon, 721; Sennacherib, 702; Esarhaddon, 680; Asshur-bani-pal II., 660; Asshur-Emit-Ilut, 640; final overthrow of Nineveh, 625.

Gen. 2. 14 it which goeth toward the east of A.
25. 18 before Egypt, as thou goest toward A.
2 Ki. 15. 19 Pul the king of A. came against the land
15. 20 exacted the money..give to the king of A.
15. 20 the king of A. turned back, and stayed
15. 29 came Tiglath-pileser king of A., and
15. 29 took Ijon..and carried them captive to A.
16. 7 Ahaz sent..to Tiglath-pileser king of A.
16. 8 and sent..a present to the king of A.
16. 9 the king of A. hearkened unto him: for
16. 9 the king of A. went up against Damascus
16. 10 went..to meet Tiglath-pileser king of A.
16. 18 the house of the LORD for the king of A.
17. 3 Against him..Shalmaneser king of A.
17. 4 king of A. found conspiracy in Hoshea
17. 4 brought no present to the king of A.
17. 4 therefore the king of A. shut him up, and
17. 5 the king of A. came up throughout all
17. 6 the ninth year of Hoshea the king of A.
17. 6 carried Israel away into A., and placed
17. 23 So was Israel carried away..to A. unto
17. 24 the king of A. brought..from Babylon
17. 26 Wherefore they spake to the king of A.
17. 27 Then the king of A. commanded, saying
18. 7 he rebelled against the king of A.
18. 9 Shalmaneser king of A. came up against
18. 11 the king of A. did carry away..unto A.
18. 13 did Sennacherib king of A. come up
18. 14 Hezekiah..of Judah sent to the king of A.
18. 14 the king of A. appointed unto Hezekiah
18. 16 and gave it to the king of A.
18. 17 the king of A. sent Tartan and
18. 19 Thus saith the great king, the king of A.
18. 23 give pledges to my lord the king of A.
18. 28 Hear the word of the great king..of A.
18. 30 delivered into the hand of the king of A.
2 Ki. 18. 31 for thus saith the king of A., Make
18. 33 land out of the hand of the king of A.
19. 4 whom the king of A. his master hath
19. 6 servants of the king of A. have
19. 8 found the king of A. warring against
19. 10 delivered into the hand of the king of A.
19. 11 heard what the kings of A. have done to
19. 17 the kings of A. have destroyed the nations
19. 20 against Sennacherib king of A. I have
19. 32 concerning the king of A., He shall not
19. 36 Sennacherib, king of A. departed
20. 6 out of the hand of the king of A.
23. 29 went up against the king of A. to the
1 Ch. 5. 6 whom Tilgath-pilneser king of A. carried
5. 26 stirred up the spirit of Pul king of A.
5. 26 the spirit of Tilgath-pilneser king of A.
2 Ch. 28. 16 did king Ahaz send unto the kings of A.
28. 20 Tilgath-pilneser king of A. came unto
28. 21 gave (it) unto..king of A.: but he helped
30. 6 out of the hand of the kings of A.
32. 1 Sennacherib king of A. came and
32. 4 Why should the kings of A. come, and
32. 7 nor dismayed for the king of A., nor for
32. 9 After this did Sennacherib king of A.
32. 10 Thus saith Sennacherib king of A.
32. 11 us out of the hand of the king of A.
32. 21 cut off..captains in the camp of..A.
32. 22 the hand of Sennacherib the king of A.
33. 11 captains of the host of the king of A.
Ezra 6. 22 turned the heart of the king of A. unto
Neh. 9. 32 since the time of the kings of A. unto
Isa. 7. 17 shall bring upon thee..the king of A.
7. 18 for the bee that (is) in the land of A.
7. 20 them beyond the river, by the king of A.
8. 4 shall be taken away before the king of A.
8. 7 the king of A., and all his glory
10. 12 punish..the stout heart of the king of A.
11. 11 which shall be left, from A., and from
11. 16 which shall be left, from A.; like as
19. 23 shall..be a highway out of Egypt to A.
19. 23 and the Egyptian into A., and the Egypt.
19. 24 the third with Egypt and with A.
19. 25 Blessed (be) Egypt my people, and A.
20. 1 when Sargon the king of A. sent him
20. 4 So shall the king of A. lead away the
20. 6 to be delivered from the king of A.: and
27. 13 were ready to perish in the land of A.
36. 1 Sennacherib king of A. came up against
36. 2 the king of A. sent Rabshakeh from
36. 4 Thus saith the great king, the king of A.
36. 8 I pray thee, to my master the king of A.
36. 13 words of the great king, the king of A.
36. 15 delivered into the hand of the king of A.
36. 16 for thus saith the king of A., Make
36. 18 land out of the hand of the king of A.
37. 4 whom the king of A. his master hath
37. 6 servants of the king of A. have
37. 8 found the king of A. warring against
37. 10 be given into the hand of the king of A.
37. 11 thou hast heard what the kings of A.
37. 18 the kings of A. have laid waste all the
37. 21 hast prayed to me against..the king of A.
37. 33 saith the LORD concerning the king of A.
37. 37 Sennacherib king of A. departed, and
38. 6 out of the hand of the king of A.: and I
Jer. 2. 18 what hast thou to do in the way of A.
2. 36 of Egypt, as thou wast ashamed of A.
50. 17 first the king of A. hath devoured him
50. 18 as I have punished the king of A.
Eze. 23. 7 all them..the chosen men of A., and
Hos. 7. 11 they call to Egypt, they go to A.
8. 9 For they are gone up to A., a wild ass
9. 3 they shall eat unclean (things) in A.
10. 6 It shall be also carried unto A. (for) a
11. 11 as a dove out of the land of A.: and
Mic. 5. 6 they shall waste the land of A. with
7. 12 he shall come even to thee from A.
Nah. 3. 18 Thy shepherds slumber, O king of A.
Zeph. 2. 13 he will stretch out..and destroy A., and
Zech. 10. 10 I will..gather them out of A., and I will
10. 11 the pride of A. shall be brought down

AS'-SYRIAN, אַשּׁוּר *Ashur*.

The same name is used to denote both the people and the country in which they dwell.

2 Ki. 19. 35 the angel..smote in the camp of the A.
Isa. 10. 5 O A., the rod of mine anger and the staff
10. 24 O my people..be not afraid of the A.: he
14. 25 That I will break the A. in my land, and
19. 23 the A. shall come..shall serve with the A.
23. 13 this people was not..the A. founded it
30. 31 through the voice of the LORD shall the A.
31. 8 Then shall the A. fall with the sword,
37. 36 the angel..smote in the camp of the A. an
52. 4 and the A. oppressed them without cause
Lam. 5. 6 We have given the hand (to)..the A., to
Eze. 16. 28 hast played the whore also with the A.
23. 5 and she doted on her lovers, on the A.
23. 9 into the hand of the A., upon whom she
23. 12 She doted upon the A. (her) neighbours
23. 23 Shoa, and Koa, (and) all the A. with them
31. 3 Behold, the A. (was) a cedar in Lebanon
Hos. 5. 13 then went Ephraim to the A., and sent to
11. 5 the A. shall be his king, because they
12. 1 they do make a covenant with the A., and
Mic. 5. 5 when the A. shall come into our land: and
5. 6 thus shall he deliver (us) from the A.

ASTONIED —

To be silent, astonished, שָׁמֵם *shamem*.

Ezra 9. 3 I rent..and sat down astonied
9. 4 I sat astonied until the evening sacrifice

ASTONIED, to be —

1. *To remain dumb*, דָּהַם *daham*, 2.
Jer. 14. 9 shouldest thou be as a man astonied

2. *To be perplexed*, שְׁבַשׁ *shebash*, 2.
Dan. 5. 9 Belshazzar..and his lords were astonied

3. *To be silent, astonished*, שָׁמֵם *shamem*.
Job 17. 8 Upright (men) shall be astonied at

4. *To remain silent, astonished*, שָׁמֵם *shamem*, 2.
Job 18. 20 that come after (him) shall be astonied
Eze. 4. 17 and be astonied one with another

5. *To be silent, astonished*, שְׁמַם *shemam*.
Dan. 4. 19 Then Daniel..was astonied for one hour

6. *To be vexed*, תְּוַהּ *tevah*.
Dan. 3. 24 Nebuchadnezzar the king was astonied

ASTONISHED —

To be silent, astonished, שָׁמֵם *shamem*, 5.
Eze. 3. 15 remained there astonished among them

ASTONISHED, to be —

1. *To be silent, astonished*, שָׁמֵם *shamem*.
Lev. 26. 32 your enemies..shall be astonished at it
1 Ki. 9. 8 one that passeth by it shall be astonished
Jer. 2. 12 Be astonished, O ye heavens, at this
18. 16 that passeth thereby shall be astonished
19. 8 that passeth thereby shall be astonished
49. 17 one that goeth by it shall be astonished
50. 13 goeth by Babylon shall be astonished
Eze. 26. 16 and shall..be astonished at thee
27. 35 the isles shall be astonished at thee
28. 19 the people shall be astonished at thee

2. *To be silent, astonished*, שָׁמֵם *shamem*, 2.
Jer. 4. 9 the priests shall be astonished, and the

3. *To be made silent, astonished*, שָׁמֵם *shamem*, 6.
Job 21. 5 Mark me, and be astonished, and lay

4. *To make silent or astonished*, שָׁמֵם *shamem*, 5.
Dan. 8. 27 and I was astonished at the vision

5. *To wonder, marvel*, תָּמַהּ *tamah*.
Job 26. 11 The pillars..are astonished at his reproof

6. *To be greatly struck*, ἐκπλήσσομαι *ekplēssomai*.
Matt. 7. 28 the people were astonished at his doctrine
13. 54 he taught them..they were astonished
22. 33 they were astonished at his doctrine
Mark 1. 22 they were astonished at his doctrine
6. 2 many hearing..were astonished, saying
7. 37 were beyond measure astonished, saying
10. 26 they were astonished out of measure
11. 18 the people was astonished at his doctrine
Luke 4. 32 they were astonished at his doctrine: for
Acts 13. 12 being astonished at the doctrine of the

7. *Be put out of one's self*, ἐξίστημι *existēmi*.
Mark 5. 42 they were astonished with a great aston.
Luke 2. 47 all that heard him were astonished at his
8. 56 her parents were astonished: but he
Acts 10. 45 they..which believed were astonished
12. 16 they had opened..they were astonished

8. *To be astonished*, θαμβέω *thambeō* (also pass.).
Mark 10. 24 the disciples were astonished at his words
Acts 9. 6 [he trembling and astonished said, Lord]

9. *Wonder surrounds*, θάμβος περιέχει [*thambos*].
Luke 5. 9 he was astonished, and all that were with

ASTONISHED, to make —

To amaze, expel, ἐξίστημι *existēmi*.
Luke 24. 22 and certain women..made us astonished

ASTONISHMENT —

1. *Astonishment (cause of)*, מְשַׁמָּה *meshammah*.
Eze. 5. 15 it shall be..an astonishment unto the

2. *Astonishment*, שַׁמָּה *shammah*.
Deut. 28. 37 thou shalt become an astonishment
2 Ch. 29. 8 the LORD..delivered them..astonishment
Jer. 8. 21 astonishment hath taken hold on me
25. 9 and make them an astonishment
25. 11 this whole land shall be..an astonishment
25. 18 a desolation, an astonishment, an hissing
29. 18 to be a curse, and an astonishment
42. 18 be an execration, and an astonishment
44. 12 be an execration, (and) an astonishment
44. 22 therefore is your land..an astonishment
51. 37 Babylon shall become..an astonishment
51. 41 how is Babylon become an astonishment
Eze. 23. 33 be filled..with the cup of astonishment

3. *Astonishment, desolation*, שִׁמָּמוֹן *shimmamon*.
Eze. 4. 16 drink water by measure..astonishment
12. 19 shall..drink..water with astonishment

4. *Wonder*, תִּמָּהוֹן *timmahon*.
Deut. 28. 28 LORD shall smite thee with..astonishm.
Zech. 12. 4 I will smite..horse with astonishment

5. *Trembling*, תַּרְעֵלָה *tarelah*.
Psa. 60. 3 to drink the wine of astonishment

6. *A standing out from*, ἔκστασις *ekstasis*.
Mark 5. 42 astonished with a great astonishment

ASTONISHMENT, to be an —

To be silent, astonished, שָׁמֵם *shamem*.
2 Ch. 7. 21 this house..shall be an astonishment

ASTRAY, to go —

1. *To err, wander*, תָּעָה *taah*.
Exod. 23. 4 If thou meet..his ass going astray, thou

Psa. 58. 3 they go astray as soon as they be born
119. 176 I have gone astray like a lost sheep
Prov. 7. 25 to her ways, go not astray in her paths
Isa. 53. 6 All we like sheep have gone astray
Eze. 14. 11 the house of Israel may go no more astray
44. 10 Israel went astray, which went astray
44. 15 when the children of Israel went astray
48. 11 went not astray..Israel went astray

2. *To go astray*, πλανάομαι *planaomai*.
Matt 18. 12 be gone astray..which is gone astray?
18. 13 the ninety and nine..went not astray
1 Pe. 2. 25 ye were as sheep going astray; but are
2 Pe. 2. 15 are gone astray, following the way of

ASTRAY, to cause to go —
To cause to go astray, err, wander, תָּעָה *taah*, 5.
Jer. 50. 6 shepherds have caused them to go astray

ASTROLOGER —
Enchanter, magician, אַשָּׁף *ashshaph*.
Dan. 2. 10 asked such things at any..astrologer
2. 27 the wise (men), the astrologers, the
4. 7 came in the magicians, the astrologers
5. 7 king cried..to bring in the astrologers
5. 11 thy father, made master of..astrologers
5. 15 the wise (men), the astrologers, have

ASTROLOGERS —
1. *Enchanters, magicians*, אַשָּׁפִים *ashshaphim*.
Dan. 1. 20 ten times better than all the..astrologers
2. 2 call the magicians, and the astrologers

2. *To view the heavens*, הָבַר שָׁמַיִם *habar shamayim*.
Isa. 47. 13 Let now the astrologers, the stargazers

ASUNDER —
Between, בֵּין *ben*.
2 Ki. 2. 11 parted them both asunder; and Elijah
[*See also* Break, burst, cleave, cut, depart, divide, drive, pluck, put, rend, saw.]

A-SUP'-PIM, הָאֲסֻפִּים *gatherings*.
This word, left untranslated in the English version, denotes not a proper name, but *granaries, storehouses, collections*.
1 Ch. 26. 15 and to his sons the house of A.
26. 17 southward four a day, and toward A. two

A-SYN-CRI'-TUS, Ἀσύγκριτος *incomparable*.
One to whom Paul sends salutation.
Rom. 16. 14 Salute A., Phlegon, Hermas, Patrobas

AT —
1. *After, behind*, אַחַר *achar*.
2 Ki. 19. 21 the daughter..hath shaken her head at

2. *Unto, to*, אֶל *el*.
Gen. 6. 6 the LORD..and it grieved him at his heart

3. *Near, by*, אֵצֶל *etsel*.
Prov. 7. 12 and lieth in wait at every corner
Isa. 19. 19 a pillar at the border thereof to the LORD

4. *Between*, בֵּין *ben*.
Exod. 16. 12 At even ye shall eat flesh, and in the

5. *Through*, בְּעַד *bead*.
Gen. 26. 8 Abimelech..looked out at a window, and

6. *Hand*, יָד *yad*.
Prov. 8. 3 She crieth at the gates, at the entry of

7. *To, for, with a view to*, לְמוֹ *lemo*.
Job 29. 21 waited, and kept silence at my counsel

8. *From, because of*, מִן *min*.
Psa. 104. 7 At thy rebuke they fled; at the voice

9. *Up to, till*, עַד *ad*.
Neh. 6. 1 at that time I had not set up the doors
Dan. 4. 8 But at the last Daniel came in before me

10. *On, upon, by*, עַל *al*.
Gen. 24. 30 behold, he stood by the camels at the well

11. *Over against*, עֻמָּה *ummah*.
2 Sa. 16. 13 Shimei..threw stones at him, and cast

12. *From, away from*, ἀπό *apo*.
Matt 19. 4 he which made (them) at the beginning
Luke 24. 27 beginning at Moses and all the prophets
24. 47 among all nations, beginning at Jerusalem
John 8. 9 [they..went out one by one, beginning at]
Acts 8. 35 Then Philip..began at the same scripture
23. 23 two hundred, at the third hour of..night
26. 4 My manner..which was at the first
1 Pe. 4. 17 at the house of God: and if..at us

13. *Through, by means of*, διά (*gen.*) *dia*.
Matt. 7. 13 Enter ye in at the strait gate: for wide
Luke 13. 24 Strive to enter in at the strait gate: for

14. *With a view to, at*, εἰς *eis*.
Matt 12. 41 because they repented at the preaching
18. 29 his fellow servant fell down [at] his feet
Luke 8. 26 they arrived at the country..Gadarenes
9. 61 farewell, which are at home at my house
11. 32 they repented at the preaching of Jonas
John 11. 32 she fell down at his feet, saying unto him
Acts 4. 6 were gathered together [at] Jerusalem
8. 40 Philip was found at Azotus: and passing
18. 22 he had landed at Cesarea, and gone up
20. 14 And when he met with us at Assos, we
20. 15 and the next (day) we arrived at Samos
20. 16 to be at Jerusalem the day of Pentecost
21. 3 sailed into Syria, and landed at Tyre
21. 13 but also to die at Jerusalem for the name
23. 11 so must thou bear witness also at Rome
Acts 25. 15 when I was at Jerusalem, the chief priests
27. 3 And the next (day) we touched at Sidon
28. 12 landing at Syracuse, we tarried (there)
Rom. 4. 20 staggered not at the promise of God
2 Ti. 2. 26 who are taken captive by him at his will

15. *Out of, from*, ἐκ *ek*.
John 16. 4 these..I said not unto you at the beginning
Jas. 3. 11 Doth a fountain send forth at the same
Rev. 19. 2 avenged the blood of his servants at her

16. *In front of*, ἔμπροσθεν *emprosthen*.
Rev. 19. 10 And I fell at his feet to worship him

17. *In, among*, ἐν *en*.
Matt. 8. 6 my servant lieth at home sick of the
11. 22 It shall be more tolerable..at the day of
11. 25 At that time Jesus answered and said
12. 1 At that time Jesus went on the sabbath
13. 49 So shall it be at the end of the world
14. 1 At that time Herod the tetrarch heard of
18. 1 At the same time came the disciples unto
23. 6 And love the uppermost rooms at feasts
24. 41 Two..grinding at the mill; the one shall
Mark 6. 3 with us? And they were offended at him
12. 39 and the uppermost rooms at feasts
Luke 4. 18 he hath sent me..to set at liberty them
9. 31 which he should accomplish at Jerusalem
10. 14 it shall be more tolerable..at the judgment
12. 46 at an hour when he is not aware, and will
13. 1 There were present at that season some
14. 14 thou shalt be recompensed at the
19. 5 Zaccheus..to day I must abide at thy
20. 10 [at] the season he sent a servant to the
20. 46 which..love..the chief rooms at feasts
23. 7 himself also was at Jerusalem at that time
23. 12 before they were at enmity between
John 4. 21 nor yet at Jerusalem, worship the Father
4. 45 things..he did at Jerusalem at the feast
4. 46 nobleman, whose son was sick at Caper.
4. 53 the father knew that..[at] the same hour
6. 39 but should raise it up again [at] the last
7. 11 the Jews sought him at the feast, and said
10. 22 it was at Jerusalem the feast of the
11. 24 rise again in the resurrection at the last
12. 20 Greeks..that came up to worship at the
14. 20 At that day ye shall know that I (am) in
16. 26 At that day ye shall ask in my name: and
18. 39 I should release unto you one at the
21. 20 which also leaned on his breast at supper
Acts 1. 6 wilt thou at this time restore again the
2. 5 there were dwelling at Jerusalem Jews
7. 13 at the second (time) Joseph was made
7. 29 Then fled Moses at this saying, and was
8. 1 at that time there was a great persecution
8. 14 the apostles which were at Jerusalem
9. 10 there was a certain disciple at Damascus
9. 13 how much evil he hath done..at Jerusalem
9. 19 with..disciples which were at Damascus
9. 22 confounded the Jews which dwelt at Da.
9. 27 how he had preached boldly at Damascus
9. 28 he was with them..going out [at] Jerus.
9. 36 there was at Joppa a certain disciple
11. 15 Holy Ghost fell..as on us at the beginning
13. 1 there were in the church that was at A.
13. 5 when they were at Salamis, they preached
13. 27 they that dwell at Jerusalem, and their
14. 8 there sat a..man at Lystra, impotent
16. 2 the brethren that were at Lystra and
16. 4 of the apostles..which were at Jerusalem
17. 13 the word of God was preached of Paul at
17. 16 Now while Paul waited for them at Athens
19. 1 while Appollos was at Corinth, Paul having
20. 5 These going before tarried for us at Troas
20. 14 when he met with us at Assos, we took
20. 15 [tarried at Trogyllium;] and the next (day)
21. 11 So shall the Jews at Jerusalem bind the
25. 4 that Paul should be kept [at] Cesarea
25. 24 the multitude..both at Jerusalem, and
26. 4 among mine own nation at Jerusalem
Rom. 1. 15 to preach..to you that are at Rome also
8. 34 who is even at the right hand of God
11. 5 Even so then at this present time also
15. 26 the poor saints which are at Jerusalem
16. 1 of the church which is at Cenchrea
1 Co. 1. 2 the church of God which is at Corinth
11. 34 if any man hunger, let him eat at home
14. 35 let them ask their husbands at home
15. 23 afterward they that are Christ's at his
15. 32 If..I have fought with beasts at Ephesus
15. 52 In a moment..at the last trump: for the
16. 8 I will tarry at Ephesus until Pentecost
2 Co. 1. 1 the church of God which is at Corinth
8. 14 now at this time your abundance
Eph. 1. 1 to the saints which are [at] Ephesus, and
2. 12 That [at] that time ye were without Christ
3. 13 desire that ye faint not at my tribulations
Phil. 1. 1 to all the saints..which are at Philippi
2. 10 That at the name of Jesus every knee
Col. 1. 2 To the saints..which are at Colosse
2. 1 have for you, and (for) them at Laodicea
1 Th. 2. 2 were shamefully entreated..at Philippi
2. 19 the presence of our Lord..at his coming?
3. 1 we thought it good to be left at Athens
3. 13 at the coming of our Lord Jesus Christ
1 Ti. 1. 3 I besought thee to abide still at Ephesus
2 Ti. 1. 18 things he ministered unto me at Ephesus
3. 11 at Antioch, at Iconium, at Lystra
4. 8 the Lord..shall give me at that day
4. 13 The cloak that I left at Troas with
4. 16 At my first answer no man stood with
4. 20 at Corinth: but Trophimus have I left at
Heb. 12. 2 Jesus..set down at the right hand of
1 Pe. 1. 7 glory at the appearing of Jesus Christ
1. 13 grace..at the revelation of Jesus Christ
5. 13 The (church that is) at Babylon, elected
1 Jo. 2. 28 and not be ashamed..at his coming

18. *Upon, over*, ἐπί (*gen.*) *epi*.
Luke 20. 37 dead are raised, even Moses shewed at the
22. 30 That ye may eat and drink at my table
22. 40 And when he was at the place, he said
John 6. 21 immediately the ship was at the land
21. 1 shewed himself..to the disciples at the
Acts 25. 10 Then said Paul, I stand at Cesar's

19. *Upon, over*, ἐπί (*dat.*) *epi*.
Matt. 7. 28 people were astonished at his doctrine
22. 33 they were astonished at his doctrine
24. 33 know that it is near, (even) at the doors
Mark 1. 22 they were astonished at his doctrine
10. 22 he was sad at that saying, and went
10. 24 the disciples were astonished at his words
11. 18 people was astonished at his doctrine
12. 17 And they marvelled at him
13. 29 know that it is nigh, (even) at the doors
Luke 1. 14 many shall rejoice at his birth
1. 29 she saw (him), she was troubled [at] his
2. 33 and his mother marvelled at those things
2. 47 all..were astonished at his understanding
4. 22 witness, and wondered at the gracious
4. 32 they were astonished at his doctrine
5. 5 at thy word I will let down the net
5. 9 he was astonished..at the draught of
5. 27 Levi, sitting at the receipt of custom
9. 43 at the mighty power of God..at all things
20. 26 and they marvelled at his answer
John 8. 7 [let him first cast a stone at her]
Acts 3. 10 at the Beautiful..at that which had
3. 12 men of Israel, why marvel ye at this?
5. 9 behold, the feet of them..(are) at the door
13. 12 deputy..being astonished at the doctrine
1 Co. 14. 16 say Amen at thy giving of thanks
Rev. 21. 12 [at the gates twelve angels, and names]

20. *Upon, over*, (*acc.*) ἐπί. *epi*.
Matt. 9. 9 Matthew, sitting at the receipt of custom
Mark 2. 14 sitting at the receipt of custom, and said
Luke 5. 27 a publican, named Levi, sitting at the
24. 22 women..which were early at the
John 8. 59 Then took they up stones to cast at him
Acts 3. 1 into the temple at the hour of prayer
10. 25 Cornelius..fell down at his feet
Rev. 3. 20 Behold, I stand at the door, and knock
8. 3 another angel came and stood at the

21. *Down, during*, κατά, (*acc.*) *kata*.
Matt 27. 15 at (that) feast the governor was wont to
Mark 15. 6 at (that) feast he released unto them one
Luke 10. 32 when he was at the place, came and
23. 17 [he must release one unto them at the]
John 5. 4 an angel went down at a certain season
Acts 16. 25 at midnight Paul and Silas prayed
Rom. 9. 9 At this time will I come, and Sarah shall
2 Ti. 4. 1 judge the quick and the dead at his

22. *Beside, alongside of*, παρά (*acc.*) *para*.
Matt 15. 30 cast them down at Jesus feet; and he
Luke 7. 37 sat at meat in the Pharisee's house
8. 35 sitting at the feet of Jesus, clothed, and
8. 41 named Jairus..fell down [at] Jesus' feet
10. 39 Mary..sat [at] Jesus' feet, and heard his
17. 16 fell down on (his) face at his feet, giving
Acts 4. 35 laid..down at the apostles' feet: and
4. 37 sold (it)..and laid (it) at the apostles' feet
5. 2 a certain part, and laid (it) at the apostles'
5. 10 Then fell she down straightway [at] his
7. 58 laid down their clothes at a young man's
22. 3 brought up in this city at the feet of Gam.

23. *Around, concerning*, περί (*gen.*) *peri*.
Luke 2. 18 they that heard (it) wondered at those
John 6. 41 The Jews then murmured at him, because
6. 61 that his disciples murmured at it, he

24. *Towards*, πρός (*dat.*) *pros*.
Luke 19. 37 at the descent of the Mount of Olives
John 18. 16 Peter stood at the door without. Then
20. 12 one at the head, and the other at the

25. *Towards*, πρός (*acc.*) *pros*.
Matt 26. 18 My time is at hand; I will keep
Mark 1. 33 the city was gathered together at the
5. 22 when he saw him, he fell at his feet
7. 25 of him, and came and fell at his feet
11. 1; 14. 54; Lu. 16. 20; 19. 29; Jo. 20. 11;
Acts 3. 2; Rev. 1. 17.
[*See also* Any, attendance, beginning, charges come, death, dwell, dweller, ease, fall, first, hand, home, last, law, least, length, liberty, look, marvel, most, not, nought, once, one, peace, piety, set, sit, stand, strain, stumble, time, wait, wink, wonder.]

AT, to be —
To do, make, עָשָׂה *asah*.
Isa. 28. 15 with death, and with hell are we at

AT, all —
1. *Together*, יַחַד *yachad*, Hos. 11. 7.
2. *Still, yet, again*, עוֹד *od*. Eze. 37. 22.
3. *In general*, καθόλου *katholou*, Acts 4. 18.
4. *The whole*, ὅλως *holōs*, Matt. 5 34; 1 Co. 15. 29.
5. οὐ μή, *ou mē* Rev. 18. 14, 21, 22, 22, 23, 23.
6. *Altogether*, πάντως *pantōs*, 1 Co. 16. 12.
[*Note.*—Also translates adv. infin. of many verbs *e.g.* Jos. 7. 7; 2 Sam. 19. 42, &c., &c.]

AT eventide —
At the turning of the evening, לִפְנוֹת עֶרֶב *[panah].*
Gen. 24. 63 went out..in the field at the eventide

AT least —
Only, אַךְ *ak.*
1 Sa. 21. 4 have kept themselves at least from women

AT once, at one—
1. *Together,* יַחַד *yachad.*
Psa. 74. 6 break down the carved work..at once
Isa. 42. 14 I will destroy and devour at once

2. *To go up,* עָלָה *alah.*
Num. 13. 30 Let us go up at once, and possess it

A'-TAD, אָטָד *thornbush.*
A spot "beyond Jordan" at which Joseph and his brethren, in their way from Egypt to Hebron, made their "seven days great and very sore mourning" over the body of Jacob, B.C. 1689.
Gen. 50. 10 they came to the threshing floor of A.
50. 11 saw the mourning in the floor of A., they

A-TA'-RAH, עֲטָרָה *crown, ornament.*
One of Jerahmeel's wives. He was grandson of Pharez, son of Judah, B.C. 1520.
1 Ch. 2. 26 (was) A.; she (was) the mother of Onam

A-TA'-ROTH, AT'-ROTH, עֲטָרוֹת עֲטָרֹת *crowns.*
1. A city on the E. of Jordan; having been destroyed in the war with Sihon, it was rebuilt by the Gadites.
Num 32. 3 A., and Dibon, and Jazer, and Nimrah
32. 34 the children of Gad built Dibon, and A.
2. A city in Ephraim, perhaps the same as *Ataroth-Adar,* on the W. border of Benjamin.
Josh. 16. 5 the border of their inheritance..A. 18. 13.
3. Another city in Ephraim, Josh. 16. 2. 7.
4. Ataroth, the house of Joab, occurs in the genealogy of Judah.
1 Ch. 2. 54 sons of Salma: Beth-lehem, and..A.
5. Atroth-Shophan, a city in Gad. Now *Attarus.*
Num 32. 35 [the children of Gad built]..A. Sh., and

A'-TER, אָטֵר *bound, lame.*
1. The ancestor of an exiled family.
Ezra 2. 16 children of A. of Hezekiah, ninety and
Neh. 7. 21 children of A. of Hezekiah, ninety and
2. Ancestor of a family of gatekeepers which came up with Zerubbabel, B.C. 536.
Ezra 2. 42 children of the porters..children of A.
Neh. 7. 45 The porters..the children of A.
3. A chief of the people that, with Nehemiah, sealed the covenant, B.C. 445.
Neh. 10. 17 [chief of the people]..A., Hizkijah, Azzur

A'-THACH, עֲתָךְ *lodging, inn.*
A city in the S. of Judah.
1 Sa. 30. 30 and to (them) which (were) in A.

A-THA'-IAH, עֲתָיָה *Jah is helper.*
A Jew in Jerusalem in Nehemiah's time, B.C. 445.
Neh. 11. 4 Of the children of Judah; A. the son of

A-THAL'-IAH, עֲתַלְיָה עֲתַלְיָהוּ *Jah is strong.*
1. Daughter of Jezebel wife of Ahab king of Israel, who became the wife of Jehoram, king of Judah, and ruled in Judah after the death of her son Ahaziah, B.C. 884.
2 Ki. 8. 26 his mother's name (was) A., the daughter
11. 1 when A. the mother of Ahaziah saw that
11. 2 they hid him..in the bedchamber from A.
11. 3 A. did reign over the land
11. 13 And when A. heard the noise of the guard
11. 14 A. rent her clothes, and cried, Treason
11. 20 they slew A. with the sword (beside) the
2 Ch. 22. 2 His mother's name also (was) A. the
22. 10 when A. the mother of Ahaziah saw that
22. 11 Jehoshabeath..hid him from A., so that
22. 12 A. reigned over the land
23. 12 when A. heard the noise of the people
23. 13 A. rent her clothes, and said, Treason
23. 21 was quiet, after that they had slain A.
24. 7 For the sons of A., that wicked woman
2. A son of Jeroham, a Benjamite.
1 Ch. 8. 26 [The sons of Elpaal]..Shehariah, and A.
3. The father of Jeshiah, a returned exile.
Ezra 8. 7 the sons of Elam; Jeshaiah the son of A.

A-THE-NI-ANS, Ἀθηναῖος *belonging to Athens.*
The dwellers in Athens.
Acts 17. 21 For all the A.s and strangers which were

A'-THENS, Ἀθῆναι.
Athens, capital of Attica, and the most celebrated city of ancient Greece, is said to have been first called Cecropia, from Cecrops, an Egyptian who built the original city on the Acropolis, according to Hales, B.C. 1558; Usher, B.C. 1556; and Clinton, B.C. 1433. It received the name of Athens from the worship of Athenæ or Minerva, said to have been established by Erechtheus, B.C. 1383. Theseus ascended the throne, according to Hales, B.C. 1236; Usher, B.C. 1235; and Clinton, B.C. 1234. He united into one body the twelve states into which Cecrops had divided Attica, and made Athens the capital. Codrus the last king of the dynasty, sacrificed himself for the safety of Athens, B.C. 1070 according to Hales, or B.C. 1044 according to Clinton. Seventeen kings reigned during the monarchical period, and these were followed by perpetual, by decennial, and finally by annual archons.
In B.C. 1069 Medon made the first perpetual archon; 754, Alcmæon the last; 752, Charops first decennial archon; 684, Erixias, the seventh and last, dies; 683, nine annual archons appointed, the title being given only to the first—Creon first annual archon; 621, legislation of Draco; 612, Cylon attempts to make himself master of Athens; 594, Solon remodels the constitution; 560, Pisistratus usurps the government—death of Solon; 554, Pisistratus expelled; 527, death of Pisistratus; 514, assassination of Hipparchus by Harmodius and Aristogiton; 510, Ostracism established; 505, war between Athens and Sparta; 490, battle of Marathon; 483, banishment of Aristides; 481, fleet of 200 ships built at Athens—ascendency of Themistocles; 480, Athens taken by Xerxes; 479, Mardonius burns Athens; 478, Themistocles rebuilds it; 477, commencement of Athenian supremacy; 471, banishment of Themistocles; 461, Ostracism of Cymon; 459, Athens asserts supremacy over the other states of Greece; 457, "long walls" of Athens commenced; 456, Athenians defeat the Thebans at Œnophyta; 449, Athenians defeat the Persians; 448, Athenians assist the Phocians in the Sacred War; 447, Bœotians defeat the Athenians at Chæronea; 445, thirty years' truce between Sparta and Athens; 444, Pericles at the head of affairs; 440, Samos subdued by Pericles; 433, alliance between Athenians and the Corcyræans; 431, Peloponnesian war begins, and Attica is invaded; 429, Pericles dies of the plague; 415, first Athenian campaign in Sicily; 411, government of the "four hundred;" 407, second and last banishment of Alcibiades—Lysander defeats Athenians; 404, end of the Peloponnesian war—rule of the "Thirty Tyrants," who are replaced by the "Ten;" 403, Thrasybulus overthrows "the Ten;" 399, death of Socrates; 394, Xenophon banished from Athens; 393, Conon rebuilds the walls of Athens; 388, Plato founds the Academy; 378, the Thebans and Athenians allied against Sparta; 371, general peace; 360, war between Athenians and Olynthians respecting Amphipolis; 359, Philip of Macedon makes peace with Athens; 357, commencement of Social War; 352, Philip takes Methoné, and enters Thessaly—stopped at Thermopylæ by the Athenians; 346, peace between Athens and Macedon; 339, war between Philip and the Athenians; 322, end of Samian War—submission of Athens to Macedon—death of Demosthenes; 317, Cassander conquers Athens; 307, Demetrius restores its ancient constitution; 287, it revolts from Demetrius; 277, Athens, Sparta, and Egypt allied; 268, surrenders to Antigonus Gonatus, king of Sparta; 229, Athens joins the Achæan league; 215, Athenians and Ætolians unite against Macedon; 211, a Roman fleet arrives at Athens; 200, Athens and other Greek states join Rome against Philip; 196, Romans proclaim Athens free from Macedonian power; 146, Romans subdue Greece; 86, Athens stormed by Sylla. In A.D. 267, Athens was besieged by the Goths; 395, taken by Alaric; 532, walls restored by Justinian.
Acts 17. 15 that conducted Paul brought him unto A.
17. 16 Now while Paul waited for them at A.
17. 22 Then Paul..said, (Ye) men of A., I perc.
18. 1 After these things Paul departed from A.
1 Th. 3. 1 we though it good to be left at A. alone

ATHIRST, to be —
1. *To be thirsty,* צָמֵא *tsame.*
Judg 15. 18 And he was sore athirst, and called
Ruth 2. 9 when thou art athirst, go unto the vessels
2. *To be thirsty,* διψάω *dipsaō.*
Matt 25. 44 when saw we thee an hungered, or athirst
Rev. 21. 6 I will give unto him that is athirst
22. 17 Come. And let him that is athirst come

ATH'-LAI, עַתְלַי *Jah is strong.*
One who married a strange woman, B.C. 456.
Ezra 10. 28 sons also of Bebai; Jehohanan..(and) A.

ATONEMENT —
1. *Coverings,* כִּפֻּרִים *kippurim.*
Exod 29. 36 a bullock (for) a sin offering..atonement
30. 10 blood of the sin offering of atonements
30. 16 thou shalt take the atonement money
30. 16 to make an atonement for your souls
Lev. 23. 27 seventh month..a day of atonement
23. 28 for it (is) a day of atonement, to make an
25. 9 day of atonement..make the trumpet
Num. 5. 8 priest; beside the ram of the atonement
29. 11 beside the sin offering of atonement
2. *Reconciliation,* καταλλαγή *katallagē.*
Rom. 5. 11 by whom we..received the atonement

ATONEMENT, to make —
To cover, כָּפַר *kaphar,* 3.
Exod 29. 36 when thou hast made an atonement for
29. 37 thou shalt make an atonement for the
30. 10 Aaron shall make an atonement upon the
30. 10 once in the year shall he make atonement
30. 15, 16 to make an atonement for your souls
32. 30 I shall make an atonement for your sin
Lev. 1. 4 for him to make atonement for him
4. 20 the priest shall make an atonement for
[So in v. 26, 31, 35; 5. 6, 10, 13, 16, 18; 6. 7.]
7. 7 priest that maketh atonement therewith
8. 34 LORD..commanded..make an atonement
9. 7 and make an atonement for thyself
9. 7 and make an atonement for them
10. 17 make atonement for them before the LORD?
12. 7 Who shall..make an atonement for her
Lev. 12. 8 priest shall make an atonement for her
14. 18 priest shall make an atonement for him
14. 19, 31 and make an atonement for him that
14. 20 the priest shall make an atonement for
14. 21, 29 to make an atonement for him
14. 53 and make an atonement for the house
15. 15, 30 make an atonement for him before
16. 6, 11, 24 and make an atonement for himself
16. 10 to make an atonement with him
16. 16 make an atonement for the holy (place)
16. 17 to make an atonement in the holy (place)
16. 17 and have made an atonement for himself
16. 18 and make an atonement for it; and shall
16. 27 blood..brought in to make atonement in
16. 30 shall..make an atonement for you, to
16. 32 shall make the atonement, and shall put
16. 33 shall make an atonement for the holy
16. 33 shall make an atonement for the priests
16. 34 to make an atonement for the children of
17. 11 to make an atonement for your souls
17. 11 blood..maketh an atonement for the
19. 22 priest shall make an atonement for him
23. 28 for it (is)..to make an atonement for you
Num. 5. 8 whereby an atonement shall be made for
6. 11 and make an atonement for him, for that
8. 12, 19 to make an atonement for the
8. 21 Aaron made an atonement for them to
15. 25 priest shall make an atonement for all
15. 28 the priest shall make an atonement for
15. 28 to make an atonement for him; and it
16. 46 make an atonement for them: for there
16. 47 and made an atonement for the people
25. 13 and made an atonement for the children
28. 22, 30 to make an atonement for you
29. 5 kid..to make an atonement for you
31. 50 an atonement for our souls before the
2 Sa. 21. 3 wherewith shall I make the atonement
1 Ch. 6. 49 to make an atonement for Israel
2 Ch. 29. 24 to make an atonement for all Israel
Neh. 10. 33 to make an atonement for Israel

ATONEMENT, to be made —
1. *To cover, make a covering,* כָּפַר *kaphar,* 3.
Num. 5. 8 whereby an atonement shall be made for
2. *To be covered,* כָּפַר *kaphar,* 4.
Exod 29. 33 things wherewith the atonement was made

ATROTH. *See* **ATAROTH.**

AT'-TAI, עַתַּי *seasonable.*
1. Grandson of Sheshan, descended from Pharez.
1 Ch. 2. 35 and she bare him A.
2. 36 A. begat Nathan, and Nathan begat
2. A Gadite who joined David at Ziklag, B.C. 1058.
1 Ch. 12. 11 A. the sixth, Eliel the seventh
3. A son of Rehoboam son of Solomon, B.C. 974.
2 Ch. 11. 20 he took Maachah..which bare him..A.

ATTAIN to or unto, to —
1. *To come,* בּוֹא *bo.*
2 Sa. 23. 19 he attained not unto the (first) three
23. 23 but he attained not to the (first) three
1 Ch. 11. 21 he attained not to the (first) three
11. 25 but attained not to the (first) three
2. *To be able,* יָכֹל *yakol.*
Hos. 8. 5 how long..ere they attain to innocency?
3. *To reach, cause to reach,* נָשַׂג *nasag,* 5.
Gen. 47. 9 have not attained unto the days of the
Eze. 46. 7 according as his hand shall attain
4. *To get, obtain,* קָנָה *qanah.*
Prov. 1. 5 a man of understanding shall attain
5. *To come, arrive,* καταντάω *katantaō.*
Acts 27. 12 if by any means..might attain to Phenice
Phil. 3. 11 I might attain unto the resurrection of
6. *To receive, take,* λαμβάνω *lambanō.*
Phil. 3. 12 Not as though I had already attained
7. *To come before another,* φθάνω *phthanō.*
Rom. 9. 31 not attained to the law of righteousness
8. *To go alongside of,* παρακολουθέω *parakoloutheō.*
1 Ti. 4. 6 doctrine, whereunto thou hast attained
9. *To lay hold of,* καταλαμβάνω *katalambanō.*
Rom. 9. 30 after righteousness, have attained to

ATTAIN already, to —
To come before (another), φθάνω *phthanō.*
Phil. 3. 16 whereto we have already attained

AT-TA'-LI-A Ἀττάλεια.
A seaport of Pamphylia, near Perga.
Acts 14. 25 had preached..they went down into A.

ATTEND, to —
1. *To understand,* בִּין *bin,* 7a.
Job 32. 12 Yea, I attended unto you, and, behold
2. *To give attention,* קָשַׁב *qashab,* 5.
Psa. 17. 1 attend unto my cry, give ear unto my
55. 2 Attend unto me, and hear me: I mourn
61. 1 Hear my cry..attend unto my prayer
66. 19 he hath attended to the voice of my
86. 6 attend to the voice of my supplications
142. 6 Attend unto my cry; for I am brought
Prov. 4. 1 and attend to know understanding
4. 20 attend to my words; incline thine ear
5. 1 attend unto my wisdom..bow thine ear
7. 24 attend to the words of my mouth

3. *Well-seated toward, εὐπρόσεδρος eupro edros.*
1 Co. 7. 35 that ye may [attend upon] the Lord

ATTEND continually upon, to —
Be strong toward, προσκαρτερέω proskartereō.
Rom. 13. 6 attending continually upon this very

ATTEND unto, to —
To hold toward, προσέχω prosechō.
Acts 16. 14 she attended unto the things which were

ATTENDANCE —
Standing, מַעֲמָד maamad.
1 Ki. 10. 5 attendance of his ministers, and their
2 Ch. 9. 4 attendance of his ministers, and their

ATTENDANCE at, to give —
To hold toward, προσέχω prosechō.
Heb. 7. 13 no man gave attendance at the altar

ATTENDANCE to, to give —
To hold toward, προσέχω prosechō.
1 Ti. 4. 13 Till I come, give attendance to reading

ATTENT —
Attentive, קַשָּׁב qashshub.
2 Ch. 6. 40 (let) thine ears (be) attent unto the prayer
7. 15 and mine ears attent unto the prayer

ATTENTIVE —
1. *Attentive, קַשֻּׁב qashshab.*
Neh. 1. 6 Let thine ear now be attentive, and
1. 11 let now thine ear be attentive to the
2. *Attentive, קַשָּׁב qashshub.*
Psa. 130. 2 hear my voice: let thine ears be attentive

ATTENTIVE, to be very —
To hang on exceedingly, ἐκκρέμαμαι ekkremamai.
Luke 19. 48 the people were very attentive to hear

ATTENTIVELY —
To hear, hearken, שָׁמַע shamea.
Job 37. 2 Hear attentively the noise of his voice

ATTIRE —
1. *Things bound on, קִשֻּׁרִים qishshurim.*
Jer. 2. 32 her ornaments, (or) a bride her attire?
2. *Something put on, שִׁית shith.*
Prov. 7. 10 a woman (with) the attire of an harlot

ATTIRED, to be —
To be wrapped round, צָנַף tsanaph.
Lev. 16. 4 with the linen mitre shall he be attired

AUDIENCE —
1. *Ear, אֹזֶן ozen.*
Gen. 23. 10 in the audience of the children of Heth
23. 13 he spake unto Ephron in the audience
23. 16 in the audience of the sons of Heth
Exod 24. 7 read in the audience of the people
1 Sa. 25. 24 I pray thee, speak in thine audience
1 Ch. 28. 8 and in the audience of our God, keep
Neh. 13. 1 On that day they read..in the audience
2. *Hearing, ear, ἀκοή akoē.*
Luke 7. 1 had ended all his sayings in the audience

AUDIENCE, to give —
To give ear, ἀκούω akouō.
Acts 13. 16 and ye that fear God, give audience
15. 12 multitude kept silence, and gave audience
22. 22 they gave him audience unto this word

AUDIENCE of, in the —
To give ear, ἀκούω akouō.
Luke 20. 45 in the audience of all the people he said

AUGHT or OUGHT —
1. *Not even one (thing), οὐδείς oudeis.*
Mark 7. 12 suffer him..to do ought for his father
2. *Any one or thing, τις tis.*
Matt. 5. 23 that thy brother hath ought against thee
21. 3 if any..say ought unto you, ye shall
Acts 4. 32 neither said any..that ought of..things
28. 19 I had ought to accuse my nation of
Phm. 18 If he..oweth..ought, put that on mine

AUGHT, if —
If any (one or thing), εἴ τις ei tis.
Mark 8. 23 upon him, he asked him if he saw ought
11. 25 forgive, if ye have ought against any
Acts 24. 19 have been here..if they had ought against

AUGHT to eat —
To eat, φαγεῖν [phagō].
John 4. 33 Hath any man brought him (ought) to eat?

AUGMENT, to —
To add, סָפָה saphah.
Num 32. 14 to augment yet..fierce anger of the LORD

AU-GUS'-TUS, Αὔγουστος, Σεβαστός *sacred, kingly.*
Augustus Cæsar became emperor of Rome after the death of his uncle, Julius Cæsar. B.C. 20.
Luke 2. 1 there went out a decree from Cesar A.
Acts 25. 21 Paul had appealed..unto the hearing of A.
25. 25 that he himself hath appealed to A., I
27. 1 named Julius, a centurion of A.'s band

AUL —
An awl, מַרְצֵעַ martsea.
Exod 21. 6 shall bore his ear through with an aul
Deut. 15. 17 thou shalt take an aul, and thrust

AUNT —
Father's sister, uncle's wife, דּוֹדָה dodah.
Lev. 18. 14 not approach to his wife: she..thine aunt

AUSTERE —
Rough, harsh, austere, αὐστηρός austēros.
Luke 19. 21 feared thee, because thou art an austere
19. 22 Thou knewest that I was an austere man

AUTHOR —
1. *Cause, occasion, αἴτιος aitios.*
Heb. 5. 9 he became the author of eternal salvation
2. *Beginner, chief leader, ἀρχηγός archēgos.*
Heb. 12. 2 unto Jesus the author and finisher of

AUTHORITY —
1. *Strength, תֹּקֶף toqeph.*
Esth. 9. 29 Mordecai the Jew, wrote with..authority
2. *Privilege, authority, ἐξουσία exousia.*
Matt. 7. 29 he taught them as..having authority
8. 9 For I am a man under authority, having
21. 23 By what authority doest thou these things?
21. 23 and who gave thee this authority?
21. 24 I..will tell you by what authority I do
21. 27 Neither tell I you by what authority I do
Mark 1. 22 taught them as one that had authority
1. 27 for with authority commandeth he even
11. 28 By what authority doest thou these things
11. 28 who gave thee this authority to do
11. 29 I will tell you by what authority I do
11. 33 Neither do I tell you by what authority
13. 34 who left his house, and gave authority
Luke 4. 36 with authority and power he commandeth
7. 8 I also am a man set under authority
9. 1 gave them power and authority over all
19. 17 have thou authority over ten cities
20. 2 by what authority doest thou these things?
20. 2 who is he that gave thee this authority?
20. 8 Neither tell I you by what authority I do
20. 20 unto the power and authority of the
John 5. 27 hath given him authority to execute
Acts 9. 14 he hath authority from the chief priests
26. 10 I shut up..having received authority from
26. 12 as I went to Damascus with authority
1 Co. 15. 24 he shall have put down all..authority
2 Co. 10. 8 boast somewhat more of our authority
1 Pe. 3. 22 angels and authorities and powers being
Rev. 13. 2 gave him..his seat, and great authority
3. *An injunction, ἐπιταγή epitagē.*
Titus 2. 15 things speak..and rebuke..all authority
4. *A holding over, ὑπεροχή huperochē.*
1 Ti. 2. 2 For kings, and..all that are in authority

AUTHORITY, to be in —
To be great, many, mighty, רָבָה rabah.
Prov. 29. 2 When the righteous are in authority, the

AUTHORITY upon, to exercise —
1. *To use or take privilege, ἐξουσιάζω exousiazō.*
Luke 22. 25 they that exercise authority upon them
2. *To use privilege over, κατεξουσιάζω katexousiazō.*
Matt. 20. 25 they that..exercise authority upon them
Mark 10. 42 their great ones exercise authority upon

AUTHORITY, of great —
Powerful one, δυνάστης dunastēs.
Acts 8. 27 an eunuch of great authority under Cand.

AUTHORITY over, to usurp —
To use one's own armour, αὐθεντέω authenteō.
1 Ti. 2. 12 nor to usurp authority over the man

A'-VA, עַוָּא *region.*
A district near Babylon and Cuthah, whose inhabitants were transported to Samaria. Perhaps the same as *Iva*.
2 Ki. 17. 24 the king of Assyria brought..from A.

AVAIL, to —
1. *To be equal, even, שָׁוָה shavah.*
Esth. 5. 13 Yet all this availeth me nothing, so long
2. *To be strong, ἰσχύω ischuō.*
Gal. 5. 6 neither circumcision availeth anything
6. 15 neither circumcision [availeth] anything
Jas. 5. 16 prayer of a righteous man availeth much

A'-VEN, אָוֶן *vanity.*
Egyptian city of On *or* Heliopolis.
Eze. 30. 17 The young men of A. and of Pibeseth
Hos. 10. 8 The high places also of A., the sin of
Amos 1. 5 the inhabitant from the plain of A.

AVENGE, to —
1. *To give ease, safety, יָשַׁע yasha, 5.*
1 Sa. 25. 31 or that my lord hath avenged himself
2. *To avenge the vengeance of, נָקַם נְקָמָה [naqam]*
Num. 31. 2 Avenge the children of Israel..Midianites
3. *To give out vengeance, נָתַן נְקָמָה nathan neqamah.*
Num 31. 3 go against..Midianites..avenge the LORD
2 Sa. 4. 8 LORD hath avenged my lord the king
22. 48 It (is) God that avengeth me, and that
Psa. 18. 47 God that avengeth me, and subdueth
4. *To breathe out, avenge, נָקַם naqam.*
Lev. 19. 18 Thou shalt not avenge, nor bear..grudge
26. 25 I will bring a sword..that shall avenge
Deut 32. 43 he will avenge the blood of his servants
1 Sa. 24. 12 the LORD avenge me of thee
5. *To avenge (earnestly), נָקַם naqam, 3.*
2 Ki. 9. 7 I may avenge the blood of my servants
6. *To look over or after, פָּקַד paqad.*
Hos. 1. 4 a little (while), and I will avenge the
7. *To judge, adjudicate, שָׁפַט shaphat.*
2 Sa. 18. 19 LORD hath avenged him of his enemies
18. 31 LORD hath avenged thee this day of
8. *To give full justice, ἐκδικέω ekdikeō.*
Luke 18. 3 saying, Avenge me of mine adversary
18. 5 I will avenge her, lest..she weary me
Rom 12. 19 Dearly beloved, avenge not yourselves
Rev. 6. 10 dost thou not judge and avenge our blood
19. 2 hath avenged the blood of his servants
9. *To judge judgment, κρίνω κρίμα krinō krima.*
Rev. 18. 20 Rejoice..for God hath avenged you on
10. *To do full justice, ποιέω ἐκδίκησιν. [poieo]*
Luke 18. 7 shall not God avenge his own elect
18. 8 I tell you that he will avenge..speedily
Acts 7. 24 he defended (him), and avenged him that

AVENGE selves, to —
1. *To avenge, נָקַם naqam.*
Josh 10. 13 until the people had avenged themselves
2. *To be avenged, נָקַם naqam, 2.*
Esth. 8. 13 to avenge themselves on their enemies
Isa. 1. 24 and avenge me of mine enemies
Jer. 46. 10 he may avenge him of his adversaries

AVENGED, to be —
1. *To be avenged, נָקַם naqam, 2.*
Judg 15. 7 yet will I be avenged of you, and after
16. 28 be at once avenged of the Philistines for
1 Sa. 14. 24 that I may be avenged on mine enemies
18. 25 but..to be avenged of the king's enemies
2. *To be avenged, נָקַם naqam, 6.*
Gen. 4. 24 If Cain shall be avenged sevenfold
3. *To avenge oneself, נָקַם naqam, 7.*
Jer. 5. 9, 29 shall not my soul be avenged on such
9. 9 shall not my soul be avenged on such a

AVENGER —
1. *To loose, set free (from blood), גָּאַל gaal.*
Num 35. 12 cities for refuge from the avenger
Deut 19. 6 Lest the avenger of the blood pursue the
19. 12 deliver him into the hand of the avenger
Josh 20. 3 shall be your refuge from the avenger of
20. 5 And if the avenger of blood pursue after
20. 9 and not die by the hand of the avenger
2. *To avenge oneself, נָקַם naqam, 7.*
Psa. 8. 2 mightest still the enemy and the avenger
44. 16 by reason of the enemy and avenger
3. *Doing full justice, ἔκδικος ekdikos.*
1 Th. 4. 6 the Lord (is) the avenger of all such

AVENGING —
1. *To give ease, יָשַׁע yasha, 5.*
1 Sa. 25. 26 from avenging thyself with thine own
25. 33 from avenging myself with mine own
2. *To free the free, פָּרַע פְּרָעוֹת para peraoth.*
Judg. 5. 2 Praise ye the LORD for the avenging of

AVERSE —
To turn back, שׁוּב shub.
Mic. 2. 8 pass by securely as men averse from war

AV-IM, AV-ITES, עַוִּים *villagers.*
1. A tribe destroyed before the time of Moses.
Deut. 2. 23 the A.s which dwelt in Hazerim.
Josh 13. 3 Gittites, and the Ekronites; also the A.s
2. A city of Benjamin, near Beth-el. (The definite article is here prefixed in the Hebrew). Now *Et-tell.*
Josh 18. 23 A., and Parah, and Ophrah
3. A tribe transported to Samaria, B.C. 678.
2 Ki. 17. 31 the A.s made Nibhaz and Tartak, and

A-VITH, עֲוִית, *hut, village.*
The capital of Hadad, 4th Edomite king.
Gen. 36. 35 and the name of his city (was) A.
1 Ch. 1. 46 and the name of his city (was) A.

AVOID, to —
1. *To go round about, סָבַב sabab, 2.*
1 Sa. 18. 11 David avoided out of his presence twice
2. *To be or keep free, פָּרַע para.*
Prov. 4. 15 Avoid it, pass not by it, turn from it
3. *Through, on account of, διά dia (acc.)*
1 Co. 7. 2 (to avoid) fornication, let every man have
4. *To incline or bend from, ἐκκλίνω ekklinō.*
Rom. 16. 17 doctrine which ye have learned..avoid
5. *To turn off from, ἐκτρέπομαι ektrepomai.*
1 Ti. 6. 20 avoiding profane (and) vain babblings
6. *To ask off from, παραιτέομαι paraiteomai.*
2 Ti. 2. 23 avoid, knowing that they do gender strifes
7. *To beware of, περιΐστημι periistēmi.*
Titus 3. 9 avoid foolish questions, and genealogies
8. *To set, place, στέλλω stellō.*
2 Co. 8. 20 Avoiding this, that no man should blame

AVOUCH, to —
To say, אָמַר amar, 5.
Deut 26. 17 Thou hast avouched the LORD this day
26. 18 the LORD hath avouched thee this day

AWAIT, laying —
Counsel against, ἐπιβουλή *epiboulē.*
Acts 9. 24 their laying await was known of Saul

AWAKE —
1. *To wake, be stirring,* יָקַץ *yaqats.*
Gen. 9. 24 Noah awoke from his wine, and knew
28. 16 Jacob awaked out of his sleep, and he
41. 4 and fat kine. So Pharaoh awoke
41. 7 Pharaoh awoke, and, behold..a dream
41. 21 as at the beginning. So I awoke
Judg 16. 14 he awaked out of his sleep, and went
16. 20 he awoke out of his sleep, and said
1 Ki. 3. 15 Solomon awoke; and, behold, (it was) a
Psa. 78. 65 the LORD awaked as one out of sleep
Hab. 2. 7 Shall they not..awake that shall vex

2. *To be stirring, awake,* עוּר *ur.*
Judg 5. 12 Awake, awake, Deborah: awake, awake
Psa. 7. 6 awake for me (to) the judgment (that)
44. 23 Awake, why sleepest thou, O LORD? arise
57. 8 Awake up, my glory; awake, psaltery
59. 4 without (my) fault: awake to help me
108. 2 Awake, psaltery and harp: I (myself) will
Song 4. 16 Awake, O north wind; and come, thou
Isa. 51. 9 Awake, awake, put on strength, O arm
51. 9 awake, as in the ancient days, in the
52. 1 Awake, awake; put on thy strength, O
Zech 13. 7 Awake, O sword, against my shepherd

3. *To awake, stir up,* עוּר *ur, 3a.*
Song 2. 7 that ye stir not up, nor awake (my) love
3. 5 that ye stir not up, nor awake (my) love
8. 4 that ye stir not up, nor awake (my) love

4. *To stir up, awake,* עוּר *ur, 5.*
Job 8. 6 surely now he would awake for thee, and
Psa. 57. 8 I (myself) will awake early
108. 2 Awake, psaltery and harp: I..will awake

5. *To stir oneself up,* עוּר *ur, 7a.*
Isa. 51. 17 Awake, awake, stand up, O Jerusalem

6. *To awake (from sleep)* קוּץ *quts, 5.*
1 Sa. 26. 12 no man saw (it)..neither awaked
Job 14. 12 they shall not awake, nor be raised out
Psa. 3. 5 I awaked; for the LORD sustained me
17. 15 I shall be satisfied, when I awake
35. 23 Stir up..and awake to my judgment
59. 5 God of Israel, awake to visit all the
73. 20 As a dream when (one) awaketh
139. 18 when I awake, I am still with thee
Prov. 23. 35 when shall I awake? I will seek it yet
Isa. 26. 19 Awake and sing, ye that dwell in dust
29. 8 but he awaketh..but he awaketh
Jer. 31. 26 I awaked, and beheld; and my sleep was
Dan. 12. 2 in the dust of the earth shall awake
Joel 1. 5 Awake, ye drunkards, and weep; and
Hab. 2. 19 to the wood, Awake; to the dumb stone

7. *To stir up, awake* עִיר *ir.*
Psa. 73. 20 O LORD, when thou awakest, thou

8. *To awake thoroughly,* διεγείρω *diegeirō.*
Mark 4. 38 they [awake] him, and say unto him
Luke 8. 24 they came to him, and awoke him

9. *To wake up,* ἐγείρω *egeirō.*
Matt. 8. 25 awoke him, saying, Lord, save us: we
Rom. 13. 11 (it is) high time to awake out of sleep
Eph. 5. 14 [Awake] thou that sleepest, and arise

10. *To be very sober,* ἐκνήφω *eknēphō.*
1 Co. 15. 34 Awake to righteousness, and sin not

AWAKE, to be —
1. *To awake,* קוּץ *quts, 5.*
2 Ki. 4. 31 told him, saying, The child is not awaked

2. *To wake thoroughly,* διαγρηγορέω *diagrēgoreō.*
Luke 9. 32 when they were awake, they saw his glory

AWAKE out of sleep, to —
1. *To wake out of sleep,* ἐξυπνίζω *exupnizō.*
John 11. 11 I go, that I may awake him out of sleep

2. *To become awake out of sleep,* γίνομαι ἔξυπνος.
Acts 16. 27 the keeper of the prison awaking out of s.

AWAKED, to be —
To awake, יָקַץ *yaqats.*
1 Ki. 18. 27 Cry..he sleepeth, and must be awaked

AWARE, to be —
1. *To know,* יָדַע *yada.*
Song 6. 12 Or ever I was aware, my soul made me
Jer. 50. 24 O Babylon, and thou wast not aware

2. *To know, have acquaintance with,* γινώσκω.
Luke 12. 46 at an hour when he is not aware

3. *To see, know,* οἶδα *oida.*
Luke 11. 44 men that walk over..are not aware

AWARE of, to be —
To know, γινώσκω *ginōskō.*
Matt. 24. 50 and in an hour that he is not aware of

AWAY —
1. *On a road,* בְּדֶרֶךְ *be-derek.*
1 Sa. 24. 19 his enemy, will he let him go well away?

2. *To go on,* יָלַךְ *yalak.*
Exod. 19. 24 Away, get thee down, and thou shalt

3. *To flee,* נוּס *nus.*
2 Sa. 18. 3 if we flee away, they will not care for us

4. *To turn aside,* סָרַר *sarar.*
Zech. 7. 11 refused to hearken, and pulled away the

5. *Without, outside* ἔξω *exō.*
Matt 13. 48 into vessels, but cast the bad away
[*See also* Ashes, break, bring, captive, carried, carry, carrying, cast, casting, catch, chase, chased, consume, convey, departing, do, done, draw, drawn, dried, drive, driven, fade, fadeth, fall, falling, far, flee, flood, flow, fly, gray, get, go, gone, haste, have, have taken, lay, lead, led, look, melt, move, pass, passed, pine, pluck, plucked, portion, purged, push, put, put far, putting, remove, roll, run, scatter, sell, sail, send, sending, slip, steal, stolen, sweep, swept, take, taken, thrust, turn, turned, turning, untaken, utterly, vanish, vilely cast, violently take, wash, waste, wear, wipe, wiped, wither, withered.]

AWAY far, to put —
To put far off, רָחַק *rachaq, 5.*
Job 11. 14 If iniquity..put it far away, and let not

AWAY from —
From after, מֵאַחֲרֵי *me-achare.*
Num 14. 43 ye are turned away from 32. 15
Jer. 32. 40 that I will not turn away from them

AWAY with, to —
1. *To be able,* יָכֹל *yakol.*
Isa. 1. 13 calling of assemblies, I cannot away with

2. *To lift up, bear away,* αἴρω *airō.*
Luke 23. 18 Away with this (man), and release unto
John 19. 15 Away with (him), away with (him), crucify
Acts 21. 36 multitude..followed after, crying, Away
22. 22 Away with such a (fellow) from the earth

AWE, to stand in —
1. *To shrink, be afraid,* גּוּר *gur*
Psa. 33. 8 inhabitants of the world stand in awe

2. *To fear,* פָּחַד *pachad.*
Psa. 119. 161 my heart standeth in awe of thy word

3. *To be angry,* רָגַז *ragaz.*
Psa. 4. 4 Stand in awe, and sin not: commune with

AX or AXE —
1. *An Axe,* גַּרְזֶן *garzen.*
Deut 19. 5 his hand fetcheth a stroke with the ax
20. 19 the trees thereof by forcing an ax against
1 Ki. 6. 7 that there was neither hammer nor ax
Isa. 10. 15 Shall the ax boast itself against him

2. *A destroying weapon, sword,* חֶרֶב *chereb.*
Eze. 26. 9 with his axes he shall break down thy

3. *A maul, great hammer,* כַּשִּׁיל *kashshil.*
Psa. 74. 6 break down the carved work..with axes

4. *A cutting or sawing instrument,* מַגְזֵרָה *magzerah.*
2 Sa. 12. 31 under harrows of iron, and under axes of

5. *Saw, axe,* מְגֵרָה *megerah.*
1 Ch. 20. 3 with harrows of iron, and with axes

6. *Ax, hatchet,* מַעֲצָד *maatsad.*
Jer. 10. 3 cutteth..out of the forest..with the ax

7. *Axe,* קַרְדֹּם *qardom.*
Judg. 9. 48 Abimelech took an ax in his hand, and cut
1 Sa. 13. 20 to sharpen every man..his ax, and his
13. 21 Yet they had a file..for the axes, and to
Psa. 74. 5 according as he had lifted up axes
Jer. 46. 22 come against her with axes, as hewers

8. *An axe,* ἀξίνη *axinē.*
Matt. 3. 10 now also the ax is laid unto the root
Luke 3. 9 now also the ax is laid unto the root

AX HEAD —
Iron, בַּרְזֶל *barzel,*
2 Ki. 6. 5 the ax head fell into the water: and

AXLE TREE —
Hand, cross-bar, יָד *yad.*
1 Ki. 7. 32 the axletrees of the wheels (were joined)
7. 33 their axletrees, and their naves, and their

A'-ZAL, אָצַל *declivity, slope.*
A place near Jerusalem.
Zech. 14. 5 valley of the mountains..shall reach..A.

A-ZAL'-IAH, אֲצַלְיָהוּ *Jah is noble.*
Father of Shaphan the scribe, B.C. 624.
2 Ki. 22. 3 the king sent Shaphan the son of A.
2 Ch. 34. 8 he sent Shaphan the son of A., and M.

A-ZAN'-IAH, אֲזַנְיָה *Jah is hearer.*
One whose son signed the covenant, B.C. 470.
Neh. 10. 9 the Levites: both Jeshua the son of A.

A-ZAR'-AEL, A-ZAR'-EEL, עֲזַרְאֵל *God is helper.*
1. An Aaronite of the family of Korah, who joined David at Ziklag, B.C. 1058.
1 Ch. 12. 6 Elkanah, and Jesiah, and A., and Joezer
2. A priest appointed by lot to minister in the service of song in the sanctuary in time of David, B.C. 1015. He seems to have been the same as *Asarelah* the son of Asaph.
1 Ch. 25. 18 The eleventh to A., (he,) his sons, and his
3. A Danite prince in the time of David, B.C. 1015.
1 Ch. 27. 22 Of Dan, A. the son of Jeroham
4. One of the family of Bani, who took strange wives during the exile, B.C. 456.
Ezra 10. 41 [Of the sons of Bani]..A., and Shelemiah
5. A priest of the family of Immer, B.C. 445.
Neh. 11. 13 Amashai the son of A., the son of Ahasai
12. 36 his brethren, Shemaiah, and A., Milalai

A-ZAR'-IAH, עֲזַרְיָה *Jah is keeper.*
A very common name in Hebrew, and especially in the family of *Eleazar,* whose name has a similar meaning. It is nearly identical with *Ezra,* as well as with *Zerahiah* and *Seraiah.*
1. A descendant of David's high priest, B.C. 1014.
1 Ki. 4. 2 These (were) the princes..A. the son of Z.
2. Son of Nathan, ruler of Solomon's officers, B.C. 1014.
1 Ki. 4. 5 A. the son of Nathan..over the officers
3. Son of Amaziah, who was made king of Judah after his father, B.C. 809.
2 Ki. 14. 21 all the people of Judah took A.
15. 1 began A. son of Amaziah king of Judah
15. 6 the rest of the acts of A., and all that
15. 7 So A. slept with his fathers; and they
15. 8 In the thirty and eighth year of A. king of
15. 17 In the nine and thirtieth year of A. king
15. 23 In the fiftieth year of A. king of Judah
15. 27 In the two and fiftieth year of A. king of
1 Ch. 3. 12 Amaziah his son, A. his son, Jotham
4. A descendant of Judah, through *Zerah,* B.C. 1660.
1 Ch. 2. 8 And the sons of Ethan; A.
5. A descendant of Jerahmeel, grandson of Pharez, B.C. 1330.
1 Ch. 2. 38 Obed begat Jehu, and Jehu begat A.
2. 39 A. begat Helez, and Helez begat
6. A son of Ahimaaz, and grandson of Zadok, B.C. 914.
1 Ch. 6. 9 Ahimaaz begat A., and A. begat Johanan
7. A grandson of the preceding, under Solomon, B.C. 840.
1 Ch. 6. 10 And Johanan begat A.
6. 11 A. begat Amariah, and Amariah
8. A son of Hilkiah, the high-priest in the reign of Josiah, B.C. 641–610.
1 Ch. 6. 13 Shallum begat Hilkiah..Hilkiah begat A.
6. 14 A. begat Seraiah, and Seraiah begat
9. 11 A. the son of Hilkiah, the son of
Ezra 7. 1 Ezra the son of Seraiah, the son of A.
9. A descendant of Kohath, from whom sprang the prophet Samuel, B.C. 1100.
1 Ch. 6. 36 Joel, the son of A., the son of Zephaniah
10. A prophet sent to encourage Asa to destroy the idols in Judah, B.C. 941.
2 Ch. 15. 1 the Spirit of God came upon A. the
11. A son of king Jehoshaphat, B.C. 890.
2 Ch. 21. 2 he had brethren..A., and Jehiel
12. Another son of Jehoshaphat, B.C. 890.
2 Ch. 21. 2 he had brethren..A. and Michael
13. Son of Jehoram, called also Ahaziah, B.C. 885
2 Ch. 22. 6 A. the son of Jehoram king of
14. A captain who aided in elevating Joash to the throne of Judah, B.C. 878.
2 Ch. 23. 1 Jehoiada..took..A. the son of
15. Another who assisted in the same work.
2 Ch. 23. 1 Jehoiada..took..A. the son of Obed
16. The high priest that hindered Uzziah from burning incense on the altar, B.C. 765.
2 Ch. 26. 17 A. the priest went in after him
26. 20 And A. the chief priest, and all the
17. A chief of the tribe of Ephraim, B.C. 741.
2 Ch. 28. 12 A. the son of Johanan, Berechiah the
18. A Kohathite and father of Joel, B.C. 726.
2 Ch. 29. 12 the Levites arose..and Joel the son of A.
19. A Merarite who assisted in cleansing the temple in the time of Hezekiah, B.C. 726,
2 Ch. 29. 12 Then the Levites arose..and A. the son
20. A priest (of the family of Zadok) who became chief priest in Hezekiah's time, B.C. 726.
2 Ch. 31. 10 A. the chief priest of the house of Zadok
31. 13 and A. the ruler of the house of God
21. Great-grandfather of Zadok the priest, and an ancestor of Ezra.
Ezra 7. 3 Amariah, the son of A., the son of Meraioth
22. One of the family of Ananiah. He repaired a portion of the wall of Jerusalem after the exile, B.C. 445.
Neh. 3. 23 After him repaired A. the son of
3. 24 from the house of A. unto the turning
23. In one passage this name is given to *Seraiah* who came up to Jerusalem with Zerubbabel, or perhaps *Seraiah* is here omitted, B.C. 590.
Neh. 7. 7 Nehemiah, A., Raamiah, Nahamani
24. A priest who explained the law to the people while Ezra was reading it, B.C. 445. Perhaps the same as No. 22.
Neh. 8. 7 A...caused the people to understand the
25. A priest who, with Nehemiah, sealed the covenant, B.C. 445.
Neh. 10. 2 [Now those that sealed (were)]..A., Jer.
26. A prince of Judah who joined in the procession with Nehemiah, B.C. 445.
Neh. 12. 33 [after them went]..A., Ezra, and M.
27. A son of Hoshaiah who charged Jeremiah with prophesying falsely, B.C. 587.
Jer. 43. 2 Then spake A. the son of Hoshaiah, and

8. A young man carried away to Babylon along with Daniel, B.C. 560.

Dan. 1. 6 of the children of Judah, Daniel..and A.
1. 7 and to A., of Abed-nego
1. 11 had set over Daniel, Hananiah..and A.
1. 19 among them all was found none like..A.
2. 17 Daniel..made the thing known to..A., his

A'-ZAZ, עָזָז *strong.*
Father of a chief of Reuben, in the time of Jeroboam II., B.C. 1200.

1 Ch. 5. 8 Bela the son of A., the son of Shema.

A-ZAZ-I'AH, עֲזַזְיָהוּ *Jah is strong.*
1. A Levite appointed for the musical service when the ark was brought up from the house of Obed-edom, B.C. 1040.

1 Ch. 15. 21 Jeiel, and A., with harps on the Sheminith

2. Father of Hoshea, prince of Ephraim, in the time of David, B.C. 1040.

1 Ch. 27. 20 children of Ephraim, Hoshea the son of A.

3. A Levite who had the oversight of the dedicated things in Hezekiah's reign, B.C. 726.

2 Ch. 31. 13 Jehiel, and A...(were) overseers under

AZ'-BUK, עַזְבּוּק *pardon.*
Father of Nehemiah who repaired a portion of the wall of Jerusalem after the return from Babylon, B.C. 445.

Neh. 3. 16 After him repaired..the son of A.

A-ZE'-KAH, עֲזֵקָה *breach.*
A town of Judah with dependant villages lying in the Shephelah or low agricultural plain. Near the northern Shochoh and Beth-horon, not far from the modern *Ain-shems;* or the modern *Tel Zakariya* on the *Wady Sumt*, the Vale of Elah.

Josh. 10. 10 smote them to A., and unto Makkedah
10. 11 stones from heaven upon them unto A.
15. 35 [in the valley]..Socoh, and A.
1 Sa. 17. 1 pitched between Shocoh and A., in
2 Ch. 11. 9 [He built even]..Lachish, and A.
Neh. 11. 30 the fields thereof, at A., and (in) the
Jer. 34. 7 king of Babylon's army fought against..A.

A'-ZEL, אָצֵל *noble.*
A Benjamite of the family of Saul, B.C. 860.

1 Ch. 8. 37 Rapha (was) his son, Eleasah his son, A.
8. 38 A. had six sons, whose names (are) these
8. 38 All these (were) the sons of A.
9. 43 Rephaiah his son, Eleasah his son, A. his
9. 44 A. had six sons, whose names (are) these
9. 44 Hanan: these (were) the sons of A.

A'-ZEM, עֶצֶם *fortress.*
A city in the extreme S. of Judah, assigned to Simeon, also spelled *Ezem.* (Now *El-Aujeh.*)

Josh. 15. 29 [cities of the tribe]..were Kabzeel..and A.
19. 3 [in their inheritance Beersheba]..and A.
1 Ch. 4. 29 [they dwelt at]..Bilhah, and at E.; and at

AZ'-GAD, עַזְגָּד *worship, supplication.*
1. One whose posterity came up with Zerubbabel, B.C. 536.

Ezra 2. 12 children of A., a thousand two hundred
Neh. 7. 17 children of A., two thousand three

2. One who came up from exile with Ezra, B.C. 458.

Ezra 8. 12 of the sons of A.; Johanan the son of

3. A chief, or the name of a family of Jews who, with Nehemiah, sealed the covenant, B.C. 536.

Neh. 10. 15 [chief of the people]..Bunni, A., Bebai

A-ZI'-EL, עֲזִיאֵל *God is might.*
A Levite in the choral service of the tabernacle at the time the ark was brought up from the house of Obed-edom, B.C. 1042. In v. 18 it is *Jaaziel.*

1 Ch. 15. 20 Zechariah, and A...with psalteries on

A-ZI'-ZA, עֲזִיזָא *strong.*
One of the family of Zattu who had taken a strange wife, B.C. 457.

Ezra 10. 27 of the sons of Zattu..Zabad and A.

AZ-MA'-VETH, עַזְמָוֶת *counsel or strength of death.*
1. One of David's thirty valiant men, B.C. 1050.

2 Sa. 23. 31 [one of the thirty] A. the Barhumite
1 Ch. 11. 33 A. the Baharumite, Eliahba the Shaalbon.

2. A descendant of Jonathan, Saul's son, B.C. 940.

1 Ch. 8. 36 Jehoada begat Alemeth, and A., and
9. 42 Jarah begat Alemeth, and A., and Zimri

3. One whose two sons joined David at Ziklag, B.C. 1050.

1 Ch. 12. 3 Jeziel, and Pelet, the sons of A.; and

4. A village called also *Beth-azmaveth*, lying on the confines of Judah and Benjamin. (Now *Hizmeh.*)

Ezra 2. 24 children of A., forty and two
Neh. 12. 29 out of the fields at Geba and A.: for the

5. One of David's treasury officers, B.C. 1015.

1 Ch. 27. 25 over the king's treasures..A. the son of

AZ'-MON, עַצְמוֹן *fortress.*
A place on the S. of Canaan, near the torrent of Egypt, *Wady-el-arish.*

Num 34. 4 your border shall..pass on to A.
34. 5 the border shall fetch a compass from A.
Josh 15. 4 it passed toward A.. and went out unto

AZ-NOTH TA'-BOR, אַזְנוֹת תָּבוֹר *ears or peaks of Tabor.*
A pair of hills on the border of Naphtali.

Josh. 19. 34 the coast turneth westward to A., and

A'-ZOR, Ἀζώρ *helper.*
Great grandson of Zorobabel, B.C. 400.

Matt. 1. 13 Abiud begat Eliakim..Eliakim begat A.
1. 14 And A. begat Sadoc; and Sadoc begat

A-ZO'-TUS, Ἄζωτος *fortress, castle.*
Another form of Ashdod, now called *Esdud.*

Acts 8. 40 Philip was found at A.: and passing

AZ-RI'-EL, עַזְרִיאֵל *God is helper.*
1. The head of a family of the half tribe of Manasseh, E. of the Jordan, B.C. 1300.

1 Ch. 5. 24 these..the heads..Eliel, and A., and

2. Father of the ruler of Naphtali in David's time, B.C. 1015.

1 Ch. 27. 19 Of Naphtali, Jerimoth the son of A.

3. The father of an officer sent to take Baruch, B.C. 606.

Jer. 36. 26 king commanded..Seraiah the son of A.

AZ-RI'-KAM, עַזְרִיקָם *my help has risen.*
1. Son of Neraiah, of the family of David, B.C. 460.

1 Ch. 3. 23 the sons of Neariah..Hezekiah, and A.

2. A son of Azel, of the family of Saul, B.C. 860.

1 Ch. 8. 38 Azel had six sons..A., Bocheru, and
9. 44 Azel had six sons..A., Bocheru, and

3. A Levite, a descendant of Merari, B.C. 470.

1 Ch. 9. 14 of the Levites..Hasshub, the son of A.
Neh. 11. 15 of the Levites..A., the son of Hashabiah

4. Governor of the house of king Ahaz, B.C. 741.

2 Ch. 28. 7 Zichri..slew..A. the governor of the house

A-ZU'-BAH, עֲזוּבָה *forsaken.*
1. The mother of king Jehoshaphat, B.C. 914.

1 Ki. 22. 42 his mother's name (was) A. the daughter
2 Ch. 20. 31 his mother's name (was) A. the daughter

2. The wife of Caleb, son of Hezron, B.C. 1540.

1 Ch. 2. 18 Caleb..begat..of A. (his) wife, and of Jer.
2. 19 when A. was dead, Caleb took unto him

A'-ZUR, עַזּוּר *helper.*
Father of Jaazaniah, a prince seen in vision, B.C. 594.

Eze. 11. 1 among whom I saw Jaazaniah..son of A.

AZ'-ZAH, עַזָּה *fortress.*
A city of the Philistines assigned to Judah, and commonly called *Gaza*, and now *Ghuzzeh.*

Deut. 2. 23 the Avims which dwelt..unto A., the
1 Ki. 4. 24 he had dominion..from Tiphsah..to A.
Jer. 25. 20 And all the mingled people..and A.

AZ'-ZAN, עַזָּן *sharp.*
Father of Paltiel, a prince of Issachar, chosen to apportion the land W. of the Jordan, B.C. 1540.

Num 34. 26 prince of the tribe..Paltiel the son of A.

AZ'-ZUR, עַזּוּר *helper.*
1. A man who, with Nehemiah, sealed the covenant, B.C. 445.

Neh. 10. 17 [chief of the people]..Ater, Hizkijah, A.

2. A Gibeonite, father of Hananiah, who withstood Jeremiah, B.C. 596.

Jer. 28. 1 Hananiah the son of A. the prophet

B

BA'-AL, BA-A-LIM, הַבַּעַל *master, possessor.*
The chief male deity of the Phœnicians and Canaanites, as *Ashtoreth* was their chief female deity. Both these names have the peculiarity of being used in the plural, and of *always* having the definite article prefixed, *e.g. the* Baalim.

1. An idol of the Phœnicians and Tyrians.

Num 22. 41 brought him up into the high places of B.
Judg. 2. 11 And the children of Israel..served B.
2. 13 they forsook the LORD, and served B.
3. 7 of Israel did evil..and served B.
6. 31 Joash said..Will ye plead for B.? will ye
6. 32 Let B. plead against him, because he hath
8. 33 children of Israel..went a whoring after B.
10. 6 of Israel did evil..and served B.
10. 10 have forsaken our God, and also served B.
1 Sa. 7. 4 children of Israel did put away B. and
12. 10 forsaken the LORD, and have served B.
1 Ki. 16. 31 went and served B., and worshipped him
16. 32 an altar for B. in the house of B.
18. 18 and thou hast followed B.
18. 19 the prophets of B. four hundred and fifty
18. 21 if the LORD (be) God, follow him: but if B.
18. 22 B.'s prophets (are) four hundred and fifty
18. 25 Elijah said unto the prophets of B., Choose
18. 26 the name of B...saying, O B., hear us
18. 40 Elijah said..Take the prophets of B.
19. 18 knees which have not bowed unto B.
22. 53 For he served B., and worshipped him
2 Ki. 3. 2 he put away the image of B. that his
10. 18 Ahab served B. a little..Jehu shall serve
10. 19 call unto me all the prophets of B.
10. 19 for I have a great sacrifice..to B.
10. 19 he might destroy the worshippers of B.
10. 20 Proclaim a solemn assembly for B.
10. 21 worshippers of B...into the house of B.
10. 21 the house of B. was full from one end to
10. 22 vestments for all the worshippers of B.
10. 23 And Jehu went..into the house of B.
10. 23 said unto the worshippers of B., Search
10. 23 none..but the worshippers of B. only
10. 25 and went to the city of the house of B.
2 Ki. 10. 26 forth the images out of the house of B.
10. 27 brake..the image of B...the house of B.
10. 28 Thus Jehu destroyed B. out of Israel
11. 18 the people..went into the house of B.
11. 18 slew Mattan the priest of B. before the
17. 16 all the host of heaven, and served B.
23. 4 all the vessels that were made for B.
23. 5 them also that burned incense unto B.
2 Ch. 17. 3 because he..sought not unto B.
23. 17 all the people went to the house of B.
23. 17 slew Mattan the priest of B. before the
24. 7 dedicated things..they bestow upon B.
28. 2 and made also molten images for B.
34. 4 they brake down the altars of B.
Jer. 2. 8 the prophets prophesied by B., and
2. 23 not polluted, I have not gone after B.?
7. 9 swear falsely, and burn incense unto B.
9. 14 But have walked..after B., which their
11. 13 set up altars..to burn incense unto B.
11. 17 to provoke me..offering incense unto B.
12. 16 taught my people to swear by B.; then
19. 5 have built also the high places of B., to
19. 5 their sons..(for) burnt offerings unto B.
23. 13 they prophesied in B., and caused my
32. 29 they have offered incense unto B.
32. 35 they built the high places of B., which
Hos. 2. 8 silver and gold..they prepared for B.
2. 13 I will visit upon her the days of B.
2. 17 For I will take away the names of B. out
11. 2 they sacrificed unto B., and burned inc.
13. 1 but when he offended in B., he died
Zeph. 1. 4 I will cut off the remnant of B. from
Rom. 11. 4 who have not bowed the knee to..B.

2. A city in the tribe of Simeon.

1 Ch. 4. 33 And all their villages..unto B.

3. A descendant of Reuben, B.C. 1300.

1 Ch. 5. 5 [sons of Joel]..Reaia his son, B. his son

4. A descendant of Benjamin, B.C. 1180.

1 Ch. 8. 30 his firstborn son Abdon..and B., and
9. 36 his firstborn son Abdon..and B., and

BA-AL BE'-RITH, בַּעַל בְּרִית *lord of the covenant.*
An idol worshipped by Israel, B.C. 1200.

Judg. 8. 33 children of Israel..made B. their god
9. 4 gave..silver out of the house of B.

BA-AL GAD, בַּעַל גָּד *lord of fortune.*
A place near Hermon, the northern limit of Joshua's conquests. *Banias* is probably on its site now. This place had long a great reputation as the sanctuary of *Pan.* (Now *Hasbeya.*)

Josh. 11. 17 even unto B. in the valley of Lebanon
12. 7 from B. in the valley of Lebanon even
13. 5 from B. under mount Hermon unto the

BA-AL HA'-MON, בַּעַל הָמוֹן *lord of the multitude.*
A place in mount Ephraim, near Samaria.

Song 8. 11 Solomon had a vineyard at B.; he let out

BA-AL HA'-NAN, בַּעַל חָנָן *the lord is gracious.*
1. The seventh of the kings of Edom, B.C. 1500.

Gen. 36. 38 Saul died, and B. the son of Achbor
36. 39 B. the son of Achbor died, and Hadar
1 Ch. 1. 49 when Shaul was dead, B. the son of A.
1. 50 when B. was dead, Hadad reigned in his

2. One of David's superintendents, B.C. 1015.

1 Ch. 27. 28 And over the olive trees..B. the Gederite

BA-AL HA'-ZOR, בַּעַל חָצוֹר *lord of Hazor.*
A place near Ephraim where Amnon was slain, B.C. 1035.

2 Sa. 13. 23 Absalom had sheepshearers in B., which

BA-AL HER'-MON, בַּעַל חֶרְמוֹן *lord of Hermon.*
This name occurring alone denotes a town near Mount Hermon. When coupled with "mount" it seems to denote the mountainous district. (Now *Jebel-es-Sheikh.*)

Judg. 3. 3 from mount B. unto the entering in of
1 Ch. 5. 23 they increased from Bashan unto B. and

BA-AL ME'-ON, בַּעַל מְעוֹן *lord of the habitation.*
A town built by the Reubenites. Supposed to be the same as the *Beth-baal-meon* of Josh. 13. 17, the *Beth-meon* of Jer. 48. 23, and the *Beon* of Num. 32. 3. (*Main.*)

Num 32. 38 [children of Reuben built]..Nebo, and B.
1 Ch. 5. 8 dwelt in Aroer, even unto Nebo and B.
Eze. 25. 9 glory of the country, Beth-jeshimoth, B.

BA-AL PE'-OR, בַּעַל פְּעוֹר *lord of the opening.*
An idol of Moab which Israel, by the counsel of Balaam to the Midianites, was enticed to worship. In several passages it is simply *Peor.*

Num 25. 3 Israel joined himself unto B.: and the
25. 5 Slay ye every one..joined unto B.-p.
Deut. 4. 3 what the LORD did because of B.-p.
4. 3 for all the men that followed B.-p., the
Psa. 106. 28 They joined themselves also unto B., and
Hos. 9. 10 they went to B., and separated themselves

BA-AL PE-RA'-ZIM, בַּעַל פְּרָצִים *lord of breaches.*
A place near the valley of Rephaim.

2 Sa. 5. 20 David came to B., and David smote them
5. 20 he called the name of that place B.
1 Ch. 14. 11 So they came up to B.; and David smote
14. 11 they called the name of that place B.

BA-AL SHA-LI'-SHA, בַּעַל שָׁלִשָׁה *lord of Shalisha.*
A place near Gilgal in Ephraim.

2 Ki. 4. 42 there came a man from B., and brought

BA-AL TA'-MAR, בַּעַל תָּמָר *lord of the palm.*
A place near Gibeah of Benjamin.
Judg.20. 33 Israel..put themselves in array at B.

BA-AL ZE-'BUB, בַּעַל זְבוּב *lord of the fly.*
An idol of the Philistines at Ekron.
2 Ki. 1. 2 Go, enquire of B. the god of Ekron
1. 3 ye go to enquire of B. the god of Ekron?
1. 6 (that) thou sendest to enquire of B. the
1. 16 thou hast sent messengers to enquire of B.

BA-AL ZE'-PHON, בַּעַל צְפוֹן *lord of Typhon.*
A place near where Israel crossed the Red Sea.
Exod14. 2 between Migdol and the sea..against B
14. 9 beside Pi-hahiroth, before B.
Num 33. 7 again unto Pi-hahiroth, which..before B.

BA-A'-LAH, בַּעֲלָה *mistress, possessor.*
1. A city of Judah, sometimes identical with *Kirjath-jearim* or *Kirjath-baal.*
Josh.15. 9 the border was drawn to B., which (is)
15. 10 the border compassed from B. westward
1 Ch. 13. 6 David went up, and all Israel, to B.
2. A hill on the S. border of Judah.
Josh.15. 11 the border..passed along to mount B.
3. A city in the S. of Judah, called *Balah* in Josh. 19. 3, and in 1 Ch. 4. 29 *Bilhah.* In 1 Ch. 4. 33 it is *Baal.*
Josh.15. 29 [the uttermost cities..were]..B., and Iim

BA-A'-LATH, בַּעֲלָת *belonging to Baal.*
A town in Dan. (Now *Balut.*)
Josh.19. 44 Eltekeh, and Gibbethon, and B.
1 Ki. 9. 18 [Solomon built]..B., and Tadmor in
2 Ch. 8. 6 B., and all the store cities that Solomon

BA-A-LATH BE'-ER, בַּעֲלַת בְּאֵר *lady of the well.*
A town, called also *Ramath-negeb* (or "heights of the south"), among those in the S. of Judah given to Simeon.
Josh.19. 8 the villages..about these cities to B.-b.

BA-A'-LE (*of Judah*), בַּעֲלֵי *possessors of* (or *in*).
Another form of Baalah, now *Kuriet el-Enab.*
2 Sa. 6. 2 the people that (were) with him from B.

BA-A'-LI, בַּעְלִי *my lord.*
A title rejected by God.
Hos. 2. 16 call me Ishi, and shalt call me no more B.

BA-A'-LIS, בַּעֲלִיס *lord of joy.*
King of the Ammonites when Jerusalem was taken by Nebuchadnezzar, B.C. 588.
Jer. 40. 14 Dost thou certainly know that B. the king

BA-A'-NA, BA-A'-NAH, בַּעֲנָא *son of grief, patient.*
1. Solomon's commissariat officer in Jezreel and the N. of the Jordan valley, B.C. 1015.
1 Ki. 4. 12 B. the son of Ahilud; (to him pertained)
2. Solomon's commissariat officer in Asher, B.C. 1015.
1 Ki. 4. 16 B. the son of Hushai..in Asher and in
3. The father of Zadok, who came up with Zerubbabel and helped to repair the wall, B.C. 470.
Neh. 3. 4 next unto them repaired..the son of B.

BA-A'-NAH, בַּעֲנָה *son of grief.*
1. Father of Heleb, one of David's thirty valiant men, B.C. 1075.
2 Sa. 23. 29 [one of the thirty]..Heleb the son of B.
1 Ch. 11. 30 Heled the son of B. the Netophathite
2. A captain of Ishbosheth's army, B.C. 1048.
2 Sa. 4. 2 the name of the one..B., and the name
4. 5 Rimmon the Beerothite, Rechab and B
4. 6 Rechab and B. his brother escaped
4. 9 David answered Rechab and B. his brother
3. One who came up with Zerubbabel, B.C. 536.
Ezra 2. 2 [are the children]..Bigvai, Rehum, B.
Neh. 7. 7 [are the children]..Bigvai, Nehum, B.
10. 27 [chief of the people]..Malluch, Harim, B.

BA-A'-RA, בַּעֲרָא *a wood, or daughter of the fresh.*
One of Shaharaim's wives, B.C. 1400.
1 Ch. 8. 8 Shaharaim..Hushim and B...his wives

BA-A-SE'-IAH, בַּעֲשֵׂיָה *Jah is bold.*
A Gershonite, ancestor of Asaph the musician, B.C. 1100.
1 Ch. 6. 40 Michael, the son of B., the son of

BA-A'-SHA, בַּעְשָׁא *boldness.*
A man of Issachar, who conspired against Nadab son of Jeroboam I., and slew all his posterity, B.C. 953.
1 Ki. 15. 16 there was war between Asa and B. king
15. 17 B. king of Israel went up against Judah
15. 19 break thy league with B. king of Israel
15. 21 when B. heard..he left off building of
15. 22 took away..the timber..wherewith B.
15. 27 B. the son of Ahijah..conspired against
15. 27 and B. smote him at Gibbethon, which
15. 28 in the third year of Asa..did B. slay him
15. 32 there was war between Asa and B. king
15. 33 In the third year of Asa..began B...to
16. 1 the word of the LORD came..against B.
16. 3 I will take away the posterity of B., and
16. 4 Him that dieth of B. in the city shall the
16. 5 the rest of the acts of B...(are) they not
16. 6 So B. slept with his fathers, and was
16. 7 came the word of the LORD against B.
16. 8 began Elah the son of B. to reign over
1 Ki. 16. 11 he slew all the house of B.: he left him
16. 12 did Zimri destroy all the house of B.
16. 12 which he spake against B. by Jehu the
16. 13 For all the sins of B., and the sins of Elah
21. 22 like the house of B. the son of Ahijah, for
2 Ki. 9. 9 like the house of B. the son of Ahijah
2 Ch.16. 1 B. king of Israel came up against Judah
16. 3 break thy league with B. king of Israel
16. 5 when B. heard (it), that he left..building
16. 6 carried away..the timber..wherewith B.
Jer. 41. 9 which Asa..had made for fear of B.

BABBLER —
1. *Master of (the) tongue,* בַּעַל לָשׁוֹן *baal lashon.*
Eccl. 10. 11 enchantment; and a babbler is no better
2. *A seed-picker,* σπερμολόγος *spermologos.*
Acts 17. 18 some said, What will this babbler say?

BABBLING —
1. *Meditation,* שִׂיחַ *siach.*
Prov.23. 29 hath contentions? who hath babbling?
2. *Empty sound,* κενοφωνία *kenophōnia.*
1 Ti. 6. 20 avoiding profane..vain babblings, and
2 Ti. 2. 16 shun profane..vain babblings: for they

BABE —
1. *Boy, lad,* נַעַר *naar.*
Exod. 2. 6 saw the child: and, behold, the babe
2. *Suckling, growing youth,* עוֹלֵל *olel.*
Psa. 8. 2 Out of the mouth of babes and sucklings
17. 14 leave the rest of their..to their babes
3. *Babe (new born, or unborn),* βρέφος *brephos.*
Luke 1. 41 it came to pass, that..the babe leaped
1. 44 the babe leaped in my womb for joy
2. 12 Ye shall find the babe wrapped in
2. 16 and found..the babe lying in a manger
1 Pe. 2. 2 As new born babes, desire the sincere milk
4. *Babe (without speech),* νήπιος *nēpios.*
Matt11. 25 and hast revealed them unto babes
21. 16 Out of the mouth of babes and sucklings
Luke10. 21 and hast revealed them unto babes
Rom. 2. 20 instructor of..foolish, a teacher of babes
1 Cor. 3. 1 as unto carnal..as unto babes in Christ
Heb. 5. 13 useth milk (is) unskilful..for he is a babe

BABES —
Mischief, mischievous (?), תַּעֲלוּלִים *taalulim.*
Isa. 3. 4 children..and babes shall rule over them

BA'-BEL, בָּבֶל (Bab-il, *gate of God*).
A city in the plain of Shinar.
Gen. 10. 10 the beginning of his kingdom was B., and
11. 9 Therefore is the name of it called B.

BABYLON, בָּבֶל *confusion, gate of Bel,* **Βαβυλών.**
The Greek mode of spelling what in the Hebrew is uniformly *Babel.* Perhaps when Nimrod founded the city he gave it the name *Bab-il,* "gate of IL" or "gate of God." After the "confusion" of tongues, the name was connected by the Hebrews with the root *balal,* "to confound." It was latterly the capital of the country called in Genesis *Shinar,* and in the later Scriptures "*Chaldea,*" or the "Land of the Chaldeans." The original city was built about 2230 B.C. Erech, Ur, and Ellasar seem to have been all older than it, and were cities when *Babil* was a village. But about 1700 B.C. the seat of government was fixed at the latter. Its enormous walls, iron gates, and hanging gardens, were among the greatest artificial wonders in the world. The modern *Birs-Nimrud* (anciently the temple of Nebo at Borsippa), and *Babil,* near *Hillah,* have both been taken for the site of the proposed Tower. Its history is naturally mixed up with that of the state to which it gave its name. "The Babylonian and Assyrian empires," says Sir John Stoddart, "in all historical records, are much blended together. These empires, whether distinct or united, possessed in very early times two vast cities—Babylon on the Euphrates, and Nineveh on the Tigris. The country on the Tigris was called Assyria; that on the Euphrates Babylonia; and the large intervening space was commonly termed Mesopotamia, or 'between the rivers': and this, together with Babylonia, seems to be meant in Scripture by the land of Shinar." In B.C. 747 Babylon is independent of Assyria—Nabonassar king; 699, Esarhaddon, or Sennacherib, king of Assyria, takes Babylon; 677 or 675, Asaridinus, king of Babylon, invades Judah, and makes prisoner its king, Manasseh; 625, Nabopolassar asserts his independence of the king of Assyria; 604, Nebuchadnezzar succeeds his father Nabopolassar; during his reign the Babylonian empire attains its highest splendour; 569, Nebuchadnezzar sets up the "golden image," and becomes insane the same year; 558, Neriglissar, the Belshazzar of Scripture, king; 538, Babylon taken, and the kingdom annexed to the Persian empire by Cyrus; 518, Babylon revolts from Darius Hystaspes; it is besieged and taken the following year; 331, Babylon surrenders to Alexander the Great; 324, Alexander enters it, and commences the restoration of its architectural greatness; 323, Alexander dies in Babylon; 321, Seleucus Nicator is made governor; 315, Antigonus expels Seleucus, and establishes Python, son of Agenor, in his dignities; 312, Seleucus returns to Babylon, which he recovers, and founds the kingdom and dynasty of the Seleucidæ; 240, invaded by the Gauls under Hierax—they are repulsed by Seleucus II.; 64, on the conquest of Syria by Pompey, Babylon falls into the hands of the Romans; 62, Babylon forms part of the Roman province of Syria. Many travellers, amongst whom may be mentioned Rich, Ker Porter, Layard, Frazer, Chesney, Botta, Loftus, and Rawlinson, have, by their explorations amongst the ruins of the ancient city, thrown light upon the history of Babylon. Sir Henry Rawlinson has interpreted many of the inscriptions found on various relics brought to this country. Babylonian sovereigns were: B.C. 747, Nabonassar; 733, Nadius; 731, Chinzirus; 725, Jugæus; 721, Mardocempadus; 709, Archianus; 704 (interregnum); 702, Belibus; 699, Apronadius; 693, Regibalus; 692, Mesesimordachus; 688 (interregnum); 680, Asaridinus; 667, Saosduchinus; 647, Chinaladanus; 625, Nabopolassar; 604, Nebuchadnezzar; 561, Evil Merodach; 558, Belshazzar; 553, Nabonadius; 538, Cyrus takes Babylon.
2 Ki. 17. 24 king of Assyria brought..from B.
17. 30 the men of B. made Succoth-benoth, and
20. 12 Baladan, king of B., sent letters and a
20. 14 They..come from a far country..from B.
20. 17 that..in thine house..be carried into B.
20. 18 eunuchs in the palace of the king of B.
24. 1 Nebuchadnezzar king of B. came up, and
24. 7 for the king of B. had taken from the river
24. 10 servants of Nebuchadnezzar king of B.
24. 11 Nebuchadnezzar king of B. came against
24. 12 Jehoiachin..went out to the king of B.
24. 12 the king of B. took him in the eighth
24. 15 he carried away Jehoaichin to B., and
24. 15 (those) carried he into captivity..to B.
24. 16 them the king of B. brought captive to B.
24. 17 the king of B. made Mattaniah..king
24. 20 Zedekiah rebelled against the king of B.
25. 1 Nebuchadnezzar king of B. came, he
25. 6 brought him up to the king of B.
25. 7 eyes of Zedekiah..and carried him to B.
25. 8 the nineteenth year of king..of B.
25. 8 came..a servant of the king of B., unto J
25. 11 fugitives that fell away to the king of B.
25. 13 and carried the brass of them to B.
25. 20 brought them to the king of B. to Riblah
25. 21 the king of B. smote them, and slew
25. 22 whom Nebuchadnezzar king of B. had
25. 23 the captains..heard that the king of B.
25. 24 dwell in the land and serve the king of B.
25. 27 Evil-merodach king of B. in the year that
25. 28 of the kings that (were) with him in B.
1 Ch. 9. 1 were carried away to B. for their trans.
2 Ch. 32. 31 the ambassadors of the princes of B., who
33. 11 bound..with fetters, and carried him to B.
36. 6 came up Nebuchadnezzar king of B.
36. 6 bound him in fetters, to carry him to B.
36. 7 Nebuchadnezzar..carried of the..to B.
36. 7 and put them in his temple at B.
36. 10 Nebuchadnezzar sent, and brought..to B.
36. 18 his princes; all (these) he brought to B.
36. 20 that had escaped..carried he away to B.
Ezra 1. 11 that were brought up from B. unto Jer.
2. 1 the king of B. had carried away unto B.
5. 12 them into the hand of..the king of B.
5. 12 who..carried the people away into B.
5. 13 the first year of Cyrus the king of B.
5. 14 brought them into the temple of B.
5. 14 did Cyrus..take out of the temple of B.
5. 17 king's treasure house, which (is) there at B.
6. 1 where the treasures were laid up in B.
6. 5 which Nebuchadnezzar..brought unto B.
7. 6 This Ezra went up from B.; and he (was)
7. 9 began he to go up from B., and on the
7. 16 all the silver..in all the province of B.
8. 1 them that went up with me from B. in
Neh. 7. 6 whom..the king of B. had carried away
13. 6 and thirtieth year of Artaxerxes king of B.
Esth. 2. 6 whom..the king of B. had carried away
Psa. 87. 4 I will make mention of..B. to them that
137. 1 By the rivers of B., there we sat down
137. 8 O daughter of B., who art to be destroyed
Isa. 13. 1 The burden of B., which Isaiah the son of
13. 19 B., the glory of kingdoms, the beauty of
14. 4 take up..proverb against..king of B.
14. 22 cut off from B. the name, and remnant
21. 9 he answered and said, B. is fallen, is
39. 1 Baladan, king of B., sent letters..to Hez.
39. 3 They are come from a far country..B.
39. 6 all..shall be carried to B.: nothing shall
39. 7 eunuchs in the palace of the king of B.
43. 14 For your sake I have sent to B., and have
47. 1 O virgin daughter of B., sit on the ground
48. 14 he will do his pleasure on B., and his arm
48. 20 Go ye forth of B., flee ye from the Chal.
Jer. 20. 4 into the hand of the king of B., and he
20. 4 shall carry them captive into B., and
20. 5 and take them and carry them to B.
20. 6 thou shalt come to B. and there thou
21. 2 Nebuchadrezzar king of B. maketh war
21. 4 wherewith ye fight against the king of B.
21. 7 the hand of Nebuchadrezzar king of B.
21. 10 be given into the hand of the king of B.
22. 25 the hand of Nebuchadrezzar king of B.
24. 1 Nebuchadrezzar king of B. had carried
24. 1 Jerusalem, and had brought them to B
25. 1 first year of Nebuchadrezzar king of B.
25. 9 Nebuchadrezzar the king of B., my
25. 11 these nations shall serve the king of B.
25. 12 I will punish the king of B., and that
27. 6 into the hand of..the king of B., my
27. 8 which will not serve the..king of B.
27. 8 under the yoke of the king of B., that
27. 9, 14 Ye shall not serve the king of B.
27. 11, 12 under the yoke of the king of B., and
27. 13 nation that will not serve the king of B.?
27. 16 now shortly be brought again from B.
27. 17 serve the king of B., and live: wherefore
27. 18 vessels which are left..go not to B.

Jer. 27. 20 Which Nebuchadnezzar king of B. took
27. 20 he carried away captive Jeconiah..to B.
27. 22 They shall be carried to B., and there
28. 2 I have broken the yoke of the king of B.
28. 3 that Nebuchadnezzar king of B. took
28. 3 took away..and carried them to B.
28. 4 the captives of Judah, that went into B.
28. 4 I will break the yoke of the king of B.
28. 6 to bring again the vessels..from B. into
28. 11 will I break the yoke of..king of B. from
28. 14 may serve Nebuchadnezzar king of B.
29. 1 had carried away..from Jerusalem to B.
29. 3 Zedekiah king of Judah sent unto B.
29. 3 to Nebuchadnezzar king of B. saying
29. 4 I have caused to be carried away..unto B.
29. 10 after seventy years be accomplished at B.
29. 15 LORD hath raised us up prophets in B.
29. 20 whom I have sent from Jerusalem to B.
29. 21 the hand of Nebuchadrezzar king of B.
29. 22 the captivity of Judah which (are) in B.
29. 22 like Ahab, whom the king of B. roasted
29. 28 therefore he sent unto us (in) B., saying
32. 2 then the king of B.'s army besieged Jeru.
32. 3, 4, 36 into the hand of the king of B., and
32. 5 he shall lead Zedekiah to B., and there
32. 28 the hand of Nebuchadrezzar king of B.
34. 1 when Nebuchadnezzar king of B...fought
34. 2 into the hand of the king of B., and he
34. 3 shall behold the eyes of the king of B.
34. 3 speak with thee..thou shalt go to B.
34. 7 When the king of B.'s army fought against
34. 21 the hand of the king of B.'s army, which
35. 11 when Nebuchadrezzar king of B. came up
36. 29 The king of B. shall certainly come and
37. 1 whom Nebuchadrezzar king of B. made
37. 17 delivered into the hand of the king of B.
37. 19 The king of B. shall not come against you
38. 3 into the hand of the king of B.'s army
38. 17 go forth unto the king of B.'s princes
38. 18 go forth to the king of B.'s princes, then
38. 22 brought forth to the king of B.'s princes
38. 23 thou..shalt be taken by..the king of B.
39. 1 Nebuchadrezzar king of B. and all his
39. 3 all the princes of the king of B. came in
39. 3 residue of the princes of the king of B.
39. 5 to Nebuchadnezzar king of B. to Riblah
39. 6 the king of B. slew the sons of Zedekiah
39. 6 the king of B. slew all the nobles of Jud.
39. 7 bound him with chains, to carry him to B.
39. 9 Nebuzar-adan..carried away captive..B.
39. 11 Nebuchadrezzar king of B. gave charge
39. 13 Rab-mag, and all the king of B.'s princes
40. 1 which were carried away captive unto B.
40. 4 If..good unto thee to come with me..B.
40. 4 if..ill unto thee to come with me into B.
40. 5 whom the king of B. hath made governor
40. 7 the captains..heard that the king of B.
40. 7 them that were not carried away..to B.
40. 9 serve the king of B., and it shall be well
40. 11 heard that the king of B. had left a
41. 2 whom the king of B. had made governor
41. 18 whom the king of B. made governor in
42. 11 Be not afraid of the king of B., of whom
43. 3 might..carry us away captives into B.
43. 10 I will send and take..the king of B., my
44. 30 the hand of Nebuchadrezzar king of B.
46. 2 which Nebuchadrezzar king of B. smote
46. 13 how Nebuchadrezzar king of B. should
46. 26 the hand of Nebuchadrezzar king of B.
49. 28 which Nebuchadrezzar king of B. shall
49. 30 Nebuchadrezzar king of B. hath taken
50. 1 The word that the LORD spake against B.
50. 2 say, B. is taken, Bel is confounded
50. 8 Remove out of the midst of B., and go
50. 9 I will..cause to come up against B. an
50. 13 every one that goeth by B. shall be
50. 14 Put yourselves in array against B. round
50. 16 Cut off the sower from B., and him that
50. 17 Nebuchadrezzar king of B. hath broken
50. 18 I will punish the king of B. and his land
50. 23 how is B. become a desolation among the
50. 24 thou art also taken, O B., and thou wast
50. 28 flee and escape out of the land of B., to
50. 29 Call together the archers against B.
50. 34 may..disquiet the inhabitants of B.
50. 35 A sword (is) upon..the inhabitants of B.
50. 42 against thee, O daughter of B.
50. 43 The king of B. hath heard the report of
50. 45 the counsel..he hath taken against B.
50. 46 At the noise of the taking of B. the earth
51. 1 Behold, I will raise up against B. and
51. 2 will send unto B. fanners, that shall
51. 6 Flee out of the midst of B., and deliver
51. 7 B. (hath been) a golden cup in the LORD'S
51. 8 B. is suddenly fallen and destroyed
51. 9 We would have healed B., but she is not
51. 11 for his device (is) against B., to destroy it
51. 12 the standard upon the walls of B.
51. 12 spake against the inhabitants of B.
51. 24 I will render unto B. and to all the
51. 29 performed against B., to make the..of B.
51. 30 The mighty men of B. have forborne to
51. 31 to shew the king of B. that his city is
51. 33 The daughter of B. (is) like a threshing
51. 34 Nebuchadrezzar the king of B. hath
51. 35 The violence done to me..(be) upon B.
51. 37 B. shall become heaps, a dwelling place
51. 41 how is B. become an astonishment among
51. 42 The sea is come up upon B.: she is
51. 44 I will punish Bel in B., and I will bring
51. 44 yea, the wall of B. shall fall
51. 47 do judgment upon the..images of B.

Jer. 51. 48 all that (is) therein, shall sing for B.
51. 49 As B. (hath caused) the slain of Israel to
51. 49 at B. shall fall the slain of all the earth
51. 53 Though B. should mount up to heaven
51. 54 A sound of a cry..from B., and great
51. 55 Because the LORD hath spoiled B., and
51. 56 because the spoiler is come upon..B., and
51. 58 The broad walls of B. shall be utterly
51. 59 when he went with Zedekiah..into B. in
51. 60 all the evil that should come upon B.
51. 60 these words that are written against B.
51. 61 When thou comest to B., and shalt see
51. 64 Thus shall B. sink, and shall not rise from
52. 3 Zedekiah rebelled against the king of B.
52. 4 Nebuchadrezzar king of B. came, he and
52. 9 carried him up unto the king of B. to Rib.
52. 10 the king of B. slew the sons of Zedekiah
52. 11 the king of B. bound him in chains, and
52. 11 carried him to B. and put him in prison
52. 12 nineteenth..Nebuchadrezzar king of B.
52. 12 served the king of B., into Jerusalem
52. 15 that fell to the king of B., and the rest of
52. 17 Chaldeans..carried all the brass..to B.
52. 26 and brought them to the king of B. to
52. 27 the king of B. smote them, and put them
52. 31 Evil-merodach king of B. in the (first) year
52. 32 above the throne of the kings..in B.
52. 34 a..diet given him of the king of B.
Eze. 12. 13 I will bring him to B. (to) the land of the
17. 12 Behold, the king of B. is come to Jerus.
17. 12 taken..and led them with him to B.
17. 16 with him in the midst of B. he shall die
17. 20 I will bring him to B., and will plead with
19. 9 they..brought him to the king of B.
21. 19 that the sword of the king of B. may come
21. 21 the king of B. stood at the parting of the
24. 2 the king of B. set himself against Jerus.
26. 7 bring..Nebuchadrezzar king of B., a king
29. 18 Nebuchadrezzar king of B. caused his army
29. 19 the land..unto Nebuchadrezzar king of B.
30. 10 the hand of Nebuchadrezzar king of B.
30. 24 strengthen the arms of the king of B.
30. 25 strengthen the arms of the king of B.
30. 25 my sword into the hand of the king of B.
32. 11 The sword of the king of B. shall come
Dan. 1. 1 came Nebuchadnezzar king of B. unto Jer.
2. 12 and..to destroy all the wise (men) of B.
2. 14 gone forth to slay the wise (men) of B.
2. 18 should not perish with the..(men) of B.
2. 24 ordained to destroy the wise (men) of B.
2. 24 Destroy not the wise (men) of B.: bring me
2. 48 ruler over the whole province of B.
2. 48 governors over all the wise (men) of B.
2. 49 he set Shadrach..over..the province of B.
3. 1 the plain of Dura, in the province of B.
3. 12 thou hast set over..the province of B.
3. 30 promoted Shadrach..in the province of B.
4. 6 bring in all the wise (men) of B. before me
4. 29 walked in the palace of the kingdom of B.
4. 30 Is not this great B., that I have built for
5. 7 spake, and said to the wise (men) of B.
7. 1 the first year of Belshazzar king of B.
Mic. 4. 10 thou shalt go..to B.; there shalt thou
Zech. 2. 7 Zion..dwellest (with) the daughter of B.
6. 10 Take of (them)..which are come from B.
Matt. 1. 11 the time they were carried away to B.
1. 12 after they were brought to B., Jechonias
1. 17 David until the carrying away into B.
1. 17 from the carrying away into B. unto Christ
Acts 7. 43 and I will carry you away beyond B.
1 Pe. 5. 13 The (church that is) at B., elected together
Rev. 14. 8 followed another angel, saying, B. is fallen
16. 19 great B. came in remembrance before God
17. 5 upon her forehead..a name..B. the Great
18. 2 he cried..saying, B. the great is fallen
18. 10 Alas, alas that great city B., that mighty
18. 21 with violence shall that great city B.

BA-BY-LO-NI-ANS, בְּנֵי בָבֶל, בַּבְלָיֵא *sons of Babel.*
The inhabitants of Babylonia, a district of country along the Euphrates.
Ezra 4. 9 Then (wrote) Rehum..the B., the Susan.
Eze. 23. 15 after the manner of the B. of Chaldea
23. 17 the B. came to her into the bed of love
23. 23 the B., and all the Chaldeans, Pekod

BA-BY-LON-ISH, שִׁנְעָר *belonging to Shinar.*
Anything pertaining to Shinar.
Josh. 7. 21 I saw among the spoils a goodly B. garment

BA'-CA, בָּכָא *weeping.*
A valley near Jerusalem, and the valley of Rephaim, whose exact locality is uncertain. A valley of the same name may still be found in the Sinaitic district—the *Wady-el-Baka.* The Targum renders it "Gehenna," that is, the "Ge-Hinnom" or ravine below Mount Zion. This locality accords well with the mention of Bacaim "tears," in 2 Sa. 5. 23.
Psa. 84. 6 passing through the valley of B. make

BACH-RITE, בַּכְרִי *belonging to Becher.*
Patronymic of the family of Becher, son of Ephraim, B.C. 1700.
Num 26. 35 sons of Ephraim..the family of the B.

BACK —
1. *Back, backward, behind,* אָחוֹר *achor.*
2 Sa. 1. 22 the bow of Jonathan turned not back
Psa. 9. 3 When mine enemies are turned back
35. 4 let them be turned back and brought to
44. 10 Thou makest us to turn back from the
44. 18 Our heart is not turned back, neither
56. 9 then shall mine enemies turn back

Psa. 114. 3 The sea..fled: Jordan was driven back
114. 5 thou Jordan, (that) thou wast driven back
129. 5 them all be confounded and turned back
Isa. 42. 17 They shall be turned back, they
50. 5 not rebellious, neither turned away back
Jer. 38. 22 mire, (and) they are turned away back
46. 5 dismayed (and) turned away back?
Lam. 1. 13 hath spread a net..hath turned me back
2. 3 he hath drawn back his right hand
Eze. 8. 16 with their backs toward the temple of

2. *Behind,* אַחַר *achar.* [*See* BACK from.]
Zeph. 1. 6 And them that are turned back from the

3. *The back,* גַּב *gab.*
Psa. 129. 3 The plowers plowed upon my back
Eze. 10. 12 and their backs, and their hands, and their
Dan. 7. 6 which had upon the back of it four wings

4. *The back* (*of a person*), גֵּו *gav.*
1 Ki. 14. 9 and hast cast me behind thy back
Neh. 9. 26 and cast thy law behind their backs
Prov. 10. 13 but a rod (is) for the back of him that is
19. 29 and stripes for the back of fools
26. 3 for the ass, and a rod for the fool's back
Isa. 38. 17 hast cast all my sins behind thy back
50. 6 I gave my back to the smiters
Eze. 23. 35 and cast me behind thy back

5. *Hence! yonder! beyond!* הָלְאָה *haleah.*
Gen. 19. 9 And they said, Stand back. And they

6. *The neck,* עֹרֶף *oreph.*
Exod 23. 27 make all thine enemies turn (their) backs
Josh. 7. 8 when Israel turneth their back before
7. 12 (but) turned (their) backs before their
2 Ch. 29. 6 away their faces..turned (their) backs
Jer. 2. 27 for they have turned (their) back unto
18. 17 I will shew them the back, and not the
32. 33 And they have turned unto me the back
48. 39 how hath Moab turned the back

7. *The shoulder,* שְׁכֶם *shekem.*
1 Sa. 10. 9 when he had turned his back to go from
Psa. 21. 12 shalt thou make them turn (their) back

8. *The back* (*of a person*), νῶτος *nōtos.*
Rom. 11. 10 and bow down their back alway

9. *Back, backward, behind,* (εἰς τὸ) ὀπίσω *opisō.*
Matt 24. 18 which is in the field return back to
Mark 13. 16 let him that is in the field not turn back
Luke 9. 62 No man..looking back, is fit for the
17. 31 let him likewise not return back
John 6. 66 (time) many of his disciples went back
20. 14 she turned herself back, and saw Jesus
[*See also,* Bring, bringing, brought, colt, carry, come, draw, drive, go, gone, hold, horseback, keep, kept, look, return, scroll, send, sent, slide, take, turn, turned.]

BACK again —
Backward, אֲחֹרַנִּית *achorannith.*
1 Ki. 18. 37 thou hast turned their heart back again

BACK from —
From behind, מֵאַחֲרֵי *me-achare.*
Zeph. 1. 6 And them that are turned back from the

BACK part —
Back part, אָחוֹר *achor.*
Exod. 33. 23 and thou shalt see my back parts

BACKBITE, to —
To use the feet (*as a talebearer*), רָגַל *ragal.*
Psa. 15. 3 He (that) backbiteth not with his tongue

BACKBITER —
One who speaks against, κατάλαλος *katalalos.*
Rom. 1. 30 Backbiters, haters of God, despiteful

BACKBITING —
1. *A secret thing,* סֵתֶר *sether.*
Prov. 25. 23 (doth) an angry countenance a backbiting
2. *A talking against,* καταλαλία *katalalia.*
2 Co. 12. 20 lest (there be) debates..backbitings

BACKBONE —
Wood, spine, firm part, עָצֶה *atseh.*
Lev. 3. 9 shall he take off hard by the backbone

BACKSIDE —
1. *Back part,* אָחוֹר *achor.*
Exod 26. 12 shall hang over the backside of the
2. *Behind, back part,* אַחַר *achar.*
Exod. 3. 1 he led the flock to the backside of the

BACKSIDE, on the —
From the back, from behind, ὄπισθεν *opisthen.*
Rev. 5. 1 book written within and [on the backside]

BACKSLIDER —
To go back, סוּג *sug.*
Prov. 14. 14 The backslider in heart shall be filled

BACKSLIDING —
1. *A turning back or away,* מְשׁוּבָה *meshubah.*
Jer. 2. 19 and thy backsliding shall reprove thee
3. 6 Hast thou seen (that) which backsliding
3. 8 whereby backsliding Israel committed
3. 11 The backsliding Israel hath justified
3. 12 Return, thou backsliding Israel, saith the
3. 22 ye backsliding..I will heal..backslidings
5. 6 (and) their backslidings are increased
8. 5 slidden back by a perpetual backsliding?

Jer. 14. 7 for our backslidings are many; we have
Hos. 11. 7 And my people are bent to backsliding
14. 4 I will heal their backsliding, I will love

2. *One turning back*, שׁוֹבָב, שׁוֹבֵב, *shobab, shobeb.*
Jer. 3. 14 Turn, O backsliding children, saith the
3. 22 Return, ye backsliding children, (and) I
31. 22 How long wilt thou..O thou backsliding
49. 4 O backsliding daughter? that trusted in

3. *To turn round, be refractory*, סָרַר *sarar.*
Hos. 4. 16 Israel slideth back as a backsliding heifer

BACKWARD —

1. *Backward*, אָחוֹר *achor.*
Gen. 49. 17 so that his rider shall fall backward
Job 23. 8 and backward, but I cannot perceive him
Psa. 40. 14 let them be driven backward and put to
70. 2 let them be turned backward, and put to
Isa. 1. 4 a people..they are gone away backward
28. 13 that they might go, and fall backward
44. 25 that turneth wise (men) backward, and
59. 14 And judgment is turned away backward
Jer. 7. 24 and went backward, and not forward
15. 6 hast forsaken me..art gone backward
Lam. 1. 8 yea, she sigheth, and turneth backward

2. *Backward*, אֲחֹרַנִּית *achorannith.*
Gen. 9. 23 and went backward, and covered the
9. 23 and their faces (were) backward, and they
1 Sa. 4. 18 he fell from off the seat backward
2 Ki. 20. 10 let the shadow return backward ten
20. 11 brought the shadow ten degrees backward
Isa. 38. 8 I will bring again the shadow..backward

3. *To the back parts*, εἰς τὰ ὀπίσω *eis ta opisō.*
John 18. 6 I am (he), they went backward, and fell to

BAD —

1. *Base, bad*, בְּאוּשׁ *biush* (true reading בְּאִישׁ).
Ezra 4. 12 building the rebellious and the bad city

2. *Evil*, רַע *ra.*
Gen. 24. 50 we cannot speak unto thee bad or good
31. 24 that thou speak not..either good or bad
31. 29 that thou speak not..either good or bad
Lev. 27. 10 a good for a bad, or a bad for a good
27. 12 shall value it, whether it be good or bad
27. 14 estimate it, whether it be good or bad
27. 33 shall not search whether it be good or bad
Num 13. 19 the land (is)..whether it (be) good or bad
24. 13 to do (either) good or bad of mine own
2 Sa. 13. 22 Absalom spake..neither good nor bad
14. 17 so (is)..the king to discern good and bad
1 Ki. 3. 9 that I may discern between good and bad

3. *Bad*, κακός *kakos.*
2 Co. 5. 10 according to that..whether..good or [bad]

4. *Evil*, πονηρός *ponēros.*
Matt 22. 10 as they found, both bad and good: and

5. *Rotten, putrid*, σαπρός *sapros.*
Matt 13. 48 good into vessels, but cast the bad away

BAD, to be so —

From badness, מֵרֹעַ *me-roa.*
Jer. 24. 2 could not be eaten, they were so bad

BADGER —

Badger or dark red coloured object, תַּחַשׁ *tachash.*
Exod 25. 5 rams' skins dyed red, and badgers' skins
26. 14 and a covering above (of) badgers' skins
35. 7 rams' skins dyed red, and badgers' skins
35. 23 and red skins of rams, and badgers' skins
36. 19 and a covering (of) badgers' skins above
39. 34 the covering of badgers' skins, and the
Num. 4. 6 put thereon..covering of badgers' skins
4. 8 cover..with a covering of badgers' skins
4. 10 within a covering of badgers' skins, and
4. 11 cover it with a covering of badgers' skins
4. 12 cover..with a covering of badgers' skins
4. 14 spread..a covering of badgers' skins
4. 25 the covering of the badgers' skins that (is)
Eze. 16. 10 and shod thee with badgers' skin, and I

BADNESS —

Evil, badness, רֹעַ *roa.*
Gen. 41. 19 such as I never saw..for badness

BAG —

1. *Bag, purse*, חֲרִיטִים *charitim.*
2 Ki. 5. 23 bound two talents of silver in two bags

2. *Cup*, כִּיס *kis.*
Deut 25. 13 Thou shalt not have in thy bag divers
Prov. 16. 11 all the weights of the bag (are) his work
Isa. 46. 6 They lavish gold out of the bag, and
Mic. 6. 11 and with the bag of deceitful weights?

3. *Vessel, instrument*, כְּלִי *keli.*
1 Sa. 17. 40 and put them in a shepherd's bag which
17. 49 And David put his hand in his bag

4. *Bundle*, צְרוֹר *tseror.*
Job 14. 17 My transgression (is) sealed up in a bag
Prov. 7. 20 He hath taken a bag of money with him
Hag. 1. 6 earneth wages (to put it) into a bag with

5. *That into which a thing is cast*, βαλάντιον.
Luke 12. 33 provide yourselves bags which wax not

6. *Where the tongues of wind instruments are put*, γλωσσόκομον *glōssokomon.*
John 12. 6 because he was a thief, and had the bag
13. 29 some..thought, because Judas had the bag

BAGS, to put up in —

To bind up, צוּר *tsur.*
2 Ki. 12. 10 they put up in bags, and told the money

BA-HA-RU-MITE, בַּחֲרוּמִי. [*See* **BARHUMITE.**]

Patronymic of one of David's thirty valiant men.
1 Ch. 11. 33 Azmaveth the B., Eliahba the Shaalbonite

BA-HU'-RIM, בַּחוּרִים *low grounds.*

A village on the road leading up from the valley of the Jordan to Jerusalem.
2 Sa. 3. 16 her husband went..behind her to B.
16. 5 when king David came to B., behold
17. 18 they..came to a man's house in B., which
19. 16 a Benjamite, which (was) of B., hasted
1 Ki. 2. 8 a Benjamite of B., which cursed me with

BA'-JITH, הַבַּיִת *house.*

This word occurs frequently in the names of towns, but is in this one passage used absolutely, and left *un*translated as the name of a place. In the original text it has the article, "the house," not referring to a place of this name, but to "The House" or temple of the gods of Moab, as opposed to the "high places" in the same sentence.
Isa. 15. 2 He is gone up to B., and to Dibon, the

BAK-BAK'-KAR, בַּקְבַּקַּר *diligent searcher.*

A Levite who came up from exile, B.C. 445.
1 Ch. 9. 15 [of the Levites]..B., Heresh, and Galal

BAK'-BUK, בַּקְבּוּק *waste, hollow.*

Ancestor of the Nethinims who returned from exile, B.C. 536.
Ezra 2. 51 children of B., the children of Hakupha
Neh. 7. 53 children of B., the children of Hakupha

BAK-BUK'-IAH, בַּקְבֻּקְיָה *wasted by Jah.*

A Levite of Asaph's family, and second leader in the temple worship of the exile, B.C. 445.
Neh. 11. 17 B the second among his brethren, and
12. 9 B. and Unni, their brethren, (were) over
12. 25 Mattaniah, and B...porters keeping the

BAKE, to —

1. *To bake*, אָפָה *aphah.*
Gen. 19. 3 and did bake unleavened bread
Exod 12. 39 they baked unleavened cakes of the dough
16. 23 bake (that) which ye will bake..and seethe
Lev. 24. 5 take fine flour, and bake twelve cakes
26. 26 ten women shall bake your bread in one
1 Sa. 28. 24 and did bake unleavened bread thereof
Isa. 44. 15 he kindleth (it), and baketh bread; yea
44. 19 also I have baked bread upon the coals
Eze. 46. 20 where they shall bake the meat offering

2. *To boil, cook*, בָּשַׁל *bashal*, 3.
Num 11. 8 and baked (it) in pans, and made cakes of
2 Sa. 13. 8 and made cakes..and did bake the cakes

3. *To bake cakes*, עוּג *ug.*
Eze. 4. 12 thou shalt bake it with dung that cometh

BAKE MEATS —

Food, work of a baker, מַאֲכָל מַעֲשֵׂה אֹפֶה. [*maakal*].
Gen. 40. 17 of all manner of bakemeats for Pharaoh

BAKEN —

1. *Anything baken*, מַאֲפֶה *maapheh.*
Lev. 2. 4 an oblation..baken in the oven

2. *To mingle, dip*, רָבַךְ *rabak*, 6.
Lev. 6. 21 (when it is) baken, thou shalt bring it in

BAKEN, to be —

To be baken, אָפָה *aphah*, 2.
Lev. 6. 17 It shall not be baken with leaven. I have
7. 9 all the meat offering that is baken in the
23. 17 they shall be baken with leaven..the first.

BAKEN pieces —

Baken or dried pieces, תֻּפִינֵים פִּתִּים [*tuphinim*].
Lev. 6. 21 the baken pieces of the meat offering

BAKEN on the coals —

Burning coals, hot stones, רְצָפִים *retsaphim.*
1 Ki. 19. 6 and, behold..a cake baken on the coals

BAKER —

To bake, אָפָה *aphah.*
Gen. 40. 1 (his) baker had offended their lord the
40. 2 was wroth..against the chief of the bakers
40. 5 the butler and the baker of the king of
40. 16 When the chief baker saw that the
40. 20 lifted up the head..of the chief baker
40. 22 But he hanged the chief baker: as Joseph
41. 10 put me in ward..me and the chief baker
1 Sa. 8. 13 will take your daughters..(to be) bakers
Jer. 37. 21 a piece of bread out of the bakers' street
Hos. 7. 4 as an oven heated by the baker, (who)
7. 6 their baker sleepeth all the night; in the

BAL'-AAM, בִּלְעָם *a pilgrim or lord of the people.*

Son of Beor, a Midianite prophet. He resided at Pethor, a city of Mesopotamia, as he himself tells us, he was "brought from Aram out of the mountains of the East." B.C. 1452.
Num 22. 5 He sent messengers therefore unto B.
22. 7 they came unto B., and spake unto him
22. 8 the princes of Moab abode with B.
22. 9 God came unto B., and said, What men
22. 10 B. said unto God, Balak the son of
Num 22. 12 God said unto B., Thou shalt not go
22. 13 B. rose up in the morning, and said
22. 14 the princes of Moab..said, B. refuseth to
22. 16 they came to B., and said to him, Thus
22. 18 B. answered and said unto the servants
22. 20 God came unto B. at night, and said
22. 21 B. rose up in the morning, and saddled
22. 23 B. smote the ass, to turn her into the way
22. 25 crushed B.'s foot against the wall: and
22. 27 she fell down under B.: and B.'s anger
22. 28 she said unto B., What have I done unto
22. 29 B. said unto the ass, Because thou hast
22. 30 the ass said unto B., (Am) not I thine ass
22. 31 Then the LORD opened the eyes of B., and
22. 34 And B. said unto the angel of the LORD, I
22. 35 the angel of the LORD said unto B., Go
22. 35 So B. went with the princes of Balak
22. 36 And when Balak heard that B. was come
22. 37 And Balak said unto B., Did I not
22. 38 And B. said unto Balak, Lo, I am come
22. 39 And B. went with Balak, and they came
22. 40 Balak offered oxen..and sent to B., and
22. 41 Balak took B., and brought him up into
23. 1 And B. said unto Balak, Build me here
23. 2 And Balak did as B. had spoken; and
23. 2 B. offered on (every) altar a bullock and
23. 3 B. said unto Balak, Stand by thy burnt
23. 4 God met B.: and he said unto him, I have
23. 5 And the LORD put a word in B.'s mouth
23. 11 And Balak said unto B., What hast thou
23. 16 And the LORD met B., and put a word in
23. 25 And Balak said unto B., Neither curse
23. 26 But B. answered and said unto Balak
23. 27 And Balak said unto B., Come, I pray
23. 28 And Balak brought B. unto the top of P.
23. 29 B. said unto Balak, Build me here seven
23. 30 And Balak did as B. had said, and offered
24. 1 when B. saw that it pleased the LORD to
24. 2 B. lifted up his eyes, and he saw Israel
24. 3, 15 B. the son of Beor hath said, and the
24. 10 Balak's anger was kindled against B.
24. 10 Balak said unto B., I called thee to curse
24. 12 B. said unto Balak, Spake I not also
24. 25 B. rose up, and went and returned to his
31. 8 B. also the son of Beor they slew with
31. 16 caused..Israel, through the counsel of B.
Deut 23. 4 because they hired against thee B. the
23. 5 LORD thy God would not hearken unto B.
Jos. 13. 22 B. also the son of Beor, the soothsayer
24. 9 Balak..sent and called B. the son of
24. 10 But I would not hearken unto B.; there
Neh. 13. 2 Because they..hired B. against them
Mic. 6. 5 O my people, remember..what B. the
2 Pe. 2. 15 are..following the way of B. (the son) of
Jude 11 ran greedily after the error of B. for
Rev. 2. 14 there them that hold the doctrine of B.

BA'-LAC, βαλάκ, *the Greek form of* בָּלָק.
Rev. 2. 14 Balaam who taught B. to cast a stumbling

BA-LA'-DAN, בַּלְאֲדָן *having power.*

Father of Merodach (or Berodach) Baladan, king of Babylon in the time of Hezekiah king of Judah.
2 Ki. 20. 12 Berodach-baladan, the son of B., king of
Isa. 39. 1 Merodach-baladan, the son of B., king of

BA'-LAH, בָּלָה *withered, old.*

A city of Simeon, called *Bilhah* in 1 Ch. 4. 29.
Josh 19. 3 [they had in their inheritance]..B., and

BA'-LAK, בָּלָק *void, empty, waster.*

King of Moab, and son of Zippor, at the time Israel were bringing their journeyings to a close. He hired Balaam to curse Israel when they were in his territory. B.C. 1452.
Num 22. 2 B. the son of Zippor saw all that
22. 4 B. the son of Zippor..king of the Moab.
22. 7 spake unto him the words of B.
22. 10 B. the son of Zippor, king of Moab, hath
22. 13 Balaam..said unto the princes of B.
22. 14 the princes of Moab..went unto B., and
22 15 B. sent yet again princes, more, and
22. 16 Thus saith B. the son of Zippor, Let
22. 18 Balaam answered..unto the serv. of B. If B
22. 35 So Balaam went with the princes of B.
22. 36 when B. heard that Balaam was
22. 37 B. said unto Balaam, Did I not
22. 38 Balaam said unto B., Lo, I am come
22. 39 Balaam went with B., and they came
22. 40 B. offered oxen and sheep, and sent
22. 41 B. took Balaam, and brought him up
23. 1 Balaam said unto B., Build me here seven
23. 2 B. did as Balaam had spoken; an
23. 2 B. and Balaam offered on (every) altar a
23. 3 Balaam said unto B., Stand by thy
23. 5 Return unto B., and thus thou shalt
23. 7 B. the king of Moab hath brought me
23. 11 B. said unto Balaam, What hast thou
23. 13 B. said unto him, Come, I pray thee
23. 15 he said unto B., Stand here by thy burnt
23. 16 Go again unto B., and say thus
23. 17 B. said unto him, What hath the LORD
23. 18 Rise up, B., and hear; hearken unto me
23. 25 B. said unto Balaam, Neither cause them
23. 26 Balaam answered and said unto B.
23. 27 B. said unto Balaam, Come, I pray thee
23. 28 B. brought Balaam unto the top of Peor
23. 29 Balaam said unto B., Build me here
23. 30 B. did as Balaam had said, and offered
24. 10 B.'s anger was kindled against Balaam
24. 10 B. said unto Balaam, I called thee to

Num 24. 12 Balaam said unto B., Spake I not also
24. 13 If B. would give me his house full of
24. 25 to his place: and B. also went his way
Josh.24. 9 Then B. the son of Zippor, king of Moab
Judg11. 25 And now (art) thou any thing better than B.
Mic. 6. 5 O my people, remember now what B.

BALANCE —
Stalk, cane, קָנֶה *qaneh.*
Isa. 46. 6 and weigh silver in the balance, (and)

BALANCES —
Pair of balances, מֹאזְנַיִם *moznayim.*
Lev 19. 36 Just balances, just weights, a just
Job 6. 2 calamity laid in the balances together!
31. 6 Let me be weighed in an even balance
Psa. 62. 9 to be laid in the balance, they (are)
Prov.11. 1 A false balance (is) abomination to the
16. 11 A just weight and balance (are) the
20. 23 and a false balance (is) not good
Isa. 40. 12 weighed the mountains..in a balance?
40. 15 counted as the small dust of the balance
Jer. 32. 10 weighed..the money in the balances
Eze. 5. 1 then take thee balances to weigh, and
45. 10 Ye shall have just balances, and a just
Dan. 5. 27 Thou art weighed in the balances, and
Hos. 12. 7 the balances of deceit (are) in his hand
Amos 8. 5 and falsifying the balances by deceit?
Mic. 6. 11 count (them) pure with the..balances

BALANCES, pair of —
Yoke, cross bar, ζυγός *zugos.*
Rev. 6. 5 and he..had a pair of balances in his

BALANCINGS —
Poisings, balancings, מִפְלָשׂ *miphlas.*
Job 37. 16 Dost thou know the balancings of the

BALD —
1. *Bald (in the back of head),* קֵרֵחַ *qereach.*
Lev. 13. 40 hair is fallen off his head, he (is) bald
2. *Baldness,* קָרְחָה *qorchah.*
Jer. 48. 37 every head (shall be) bald, and every

BALD forehead —
Bald (in front of head), גַּבַּחַת *gabbachath.*
Lev. 13. 42 or bald forehead, a white reddish sore
13. 42 leprosy sprung up in..his bald forehead
13. 43 or in his bald forehead, as the leprosy

BALD head —
1. *Bald (in back of head),* קֵרֵחַ *qereach.*
2 Ki. 2. 23 thou bald head; go up, thou bald head
2. *Bald spot, baldness,* קָרַחַת *qarachath.*
Lev. 13. 42 And if there be in the bald head, or
13. 42 a leprosy, sprung up in his bald head
13. 43 (be) white reddish in his bald head

BALD, made —
To be made bald, קָרַח *qarach,* 6.
Eze. 29. 18 every head..made bald..every shoulder

BALD, to make —
To make bald, קָרַח *qarach.*
Mic. 1. 16 Make thee bald, and poll thee for thy

BALD, to make (one's) self —
1. *To become bald,* קָרַח *qarach,* 2.
Jer. 16. 6 nor make themselves bald for them
2. *To be made bald,* קָרַח *qarach,* 6.
Eze. 27. 31 they shall make themselves utterly bald

BALDNESS —
Baldness (in back of head), קָרְחָה *qorchah.*
Lev. 21. 5 They shall not make baldness upon their
Deut 14. 1 nor make any baldness between your
Isa. 3. 24 and instead of well set hair baldness
15. 2 on all their heads..baldness
22. 12 and to baldness, and to girding with
Jer. 47. 5 Baldness is come upon Gaza; Ashkelon
Eze. 7. 18 and baldness upon all their heads
Amos 8. 10 I will bring up sackcloth..baldness
Mic. 1. 16 enlarge thy baldness as the eagle

BALL —
Ball, any thing round, דּוּר *dur.*
Isa. 22. 18 violently turn and toss thee (like) a ball

BALM —
Balsam, a medicinal gum, צְרִי, צֳרִי *tsori, tseri.*
Gen. 37. 25 their camels bearing spicery and balm
43. 11 carry..the man a present, a little balm
Jer. 8. 22 no balm in Gilead; (is there) no physician
46. 11 Go up into Gilead, and take balm, O
51. 8 howl for her; take balm for her pain, if
Eze. 27. 17 Pannag, and honey, and oil, and balm

BA'-MAH, בָּמָה *high place.*
Used in Ezekiel as the *name* of the places in which Israel offered sacrifices to idols.
Eze. 20. 29 the name thereof (is) called B. unto this

BA'-MOTH, בָּמוֹת *high places.*
A city on the N. side of the Arnon, which had belonged to the Moabites, but was taken from them by Sihon. It is thought to be the *Bamoth-baal* of Josh. 13. 17.
Num 21. 19 and from Nahaliel to B.
21. 20 from B. (in) the valley, that (is) in the

BA-MOTH BA'-AL, בָּמוֹת בַּעַל *high places of Baal.*
A town of Moab taken by Sihon, but afterwards a city of Reuben. It is probably the *Bamoth* of Num. 21. 19.
Josh.13. 17 Dibon, and B., and Beth-baal-meon

BAND —
1. *Band, bond, fetter,* אֱסוּר *esur.*
Judg 15. 14 and his bands loosed from off his hands
Eccl. 7. 26 heart (is) snares..her hands..bands
Dan. 4. 15 even with a band of iron and brass
4. 23 even with a band of iron and brass
2. *A troop (of men),* גְּדוּד *gedud.*
2 Sa. 4. 2 two men (that were) captains of bands
1 Ki. 11. 24 became captain over a band, when David
2 Ki. 6. 23 So the bands of Syria came no more into
13. 20 And the bands of the Moabites invaded
13. 21 that, behold, they spied a band
24. 2 And the LORD sent against him bands of
24. 2 and bands of the children of Ammon, and
1 Ch. 7. 4 And with them..bands of soldiers
12. 18 and made them captains of the band
12. 21 they helped David against the band
3. *Cord, rope,* חֶבֶל *chebel.*
Psa.119. 61 The bands of the wicked have robbed me
4. *Thick bands, wreathen cords,* עֲבֹת *aboth.*
Job 39. 10 Canst thou bind the unicorn with his band
Eze. 3. 25 But thou..behold, they shall put bands
4. 8 And, behold, I will lay bands upon thee
Hos. 11. 4 I drew them with cords..with bands of
5. *Head, detachment,* רֹאשׁ *rosh.*
1 Ch. 12. 23 these..the numbers of the bands
Job 1. 17 The Chaldeans made out three bands, and
6. *Lip, edge,* שָׂפָה *saphah.*
Exod 39. 23 a band round about the hole
7. *A band, body of men at arms,* σπεῖρα *speira.*
Matt 27. 27 and gathered unto him the whole band
Mark 15. 16 and they call together the whole band
John 18. 12 Then the band and the captain..took J
Acts 10. 1 centurion of the band called the Italian
21. 31 came unto the chief captain of the band
27. 1 Julius, a centurion of Augustus' band

BAND of men —
1. *A troop (of men),* גְּדוּד *gedud.*
2 Ch. 22. 1 for the band of men..had slain all the
2. *Strength, might, force,* חַיִל *chayil.*
1 Sa. 10. 26 there went with him a band of men
3. *Band, body of men at arms,* σπεῖρα *speira.*
John 18. 3 having received a band..and officers

BAND of soldiers —
Strength, might, force, חַיִל *chayil.*
Ezra 8. 22 to require of the king a band of soldiers

BAND together, to —
To make a gathering, ποιέω συστροφήν [*poieō*].
Acts 23. 12 certain of the Jews banded together

BANDS, חֹבְלִים *chobelim.*
Symbolic name given to one of two staves which symbolised the Lord's covenant with the seed of Jacob, and the brotherhood of Israel and Judah.
Zech.11. 7 one I called Beauty..the other I called B.
11. 14 I cut asunder mine other staff..B., that I

BANDS —
1. *Wings, corps,* אֲגַפִּים *agappim.*
Eze. 12. 14 I will scatter..all his bands
17. 21 all his fugitives with all his bands shall
38. 6 Gomer, and all his bands; the house of
38. 6 house of Togarmah..and all his bands
38. 9 thou, and all thy bands, and many people
38. 22 I will rain upon him, and upon his bands
39. 4 thou, and all thy bands, and the people
2. *Bands, pains,* חַרְצֻבּוֹת *chartsubboth.*
Psa. 73. 4 For..no bands in their death: but their
Isa. 58. 6 to loose the bands of wickedness, to undo
3. *Bar,* מוֹטָה *motah.*
Lev. 26. 13 I have broken the bands of your yoke
Eze. 34. 27 I have broken the bands of their yoke
4. *Band, fetter,* מוֹסֵר *moser.*
Job 39. 5 who hath loosed the bands of the wild ass?
Psa. 2. 3 Let us break their bands asunder, and
107. 14 and brake their bands in sunder
Isa. 28. 22 lest your bands be made strong: for I
52. 2 loose thyself from the bands of thy neck
Jer. 2. 20 broken thy yoke..burst thy bands
5. *Drawings together,* מוֹשְׁכוֹת *moshekoth.*
Job 38. 31 Canst thou..loose the bands of Orion?
6. *Camp,* מַחֲנֶה *machaneh.*
Gen. 32. 7 he divided the people..into two bands
32. 10 and now I am become two bands
7. *Band, fetter,* δεσμός *desmos.*
Luke 8. 29 he brake the bands, and was driven of
Acts 16. 26 and every one's bands were loosed
22. 30 he loosed him from (his) [bands]
8. *Band for yoking together,* ζευκτηρία *zeuktēria.*
Acts 27. 40 loosed the rudder bands, and hoisted up
9. *What binds together,* σύνδεσμος *sundesmos.*
Col. 2. 19 the body by joints and bands having
10. *To halve, divide,* חָצַץ *chatsats.*
Prov.30. 27 yet go they forth all of them by bands

BA'-NI, בָּנִי *posterity.*
1. A Gadite, and one of David's thirty valiant men, B.C 1048.
2 Sa. 23. 36 B. the Gadite
2. A Levite, a descendant of Merari, B.C. 1440.
1 Ch. 6. 46 Amzi, the son of B., the son of Shamer
3. A descendant of Pharez, son of Judah, B.C. 536.
1 Ch. 9. 4 Imri, the son of B., of the children of P.
4. Father of some of those who went up from Babylon with Zerubbabel, B.C. 536.
Ezra 2. 10 children of B., six hundred forty and two
(In Neh. 7. 15, the name is given as *Binnui.*)
Ezra 10. 29 of the sons of B., Meshullam, Malluch
5. One whose descendants had taken strange wives during the exile, B.C. 445.
Ezra 10. 34 Of the sons of B.; Maadai, Amram, and
6. A descendant of No. 5, who had taken a strange wife, B.C. 445.
Ezra 10. 38 And B., Binnui, Shimei.
7. A Levite whose son repaired part of the wall of Jerusalem, B.C. 445.
Neh. 3. 17 After him repaired..the son of B.
8. 7 Also Jeshua, and B., and Sherebiah
9. 4 Then stood up upon the stairs..B.
9. 5 the Levites, Jeshua, and Kadmiel, B.
8. A Levite who regulated the devotions of the people after Ezra had read the book of the law to them, B.C. 445.
Neh. 9. 4 of the Levites. Bunni, Sherebiah, B., and
10. 13 [And their brethren]..Hodijah, B., Beninu
9. A chief man or family that, with Nehemiah, sealed the covenant, B.C. 445.
Neh.10. 14 The chief of the people..Zatthu, B.
10. A Levite whose son was overseer of the Levites at Jerusalem after the exile. [The same perhaps as No. 7 or 8], B.C. 445.
Neh. 11. 22 The overseer..Uzzi the son of B.

BANISHED —
To be driven or forced away, נָדַח *nadach,* 2.
2 Sa. 14. 13 doth not fetch home again his banished
14. 14 that his banished be not expelled from

BANISHMENT —
Rooting out, שְׁרשׁוּ *sheroshu.*
Ezra 7. 26 whether..unto death, or to banishment

BANISHMENT, causes of —
Causes of being driven away, מַדּוּחִים *madduchim.*
Lam. 2. 14 false burdens and causes of banishment

BANK —
1. *Banks or cuttings out by water,* גָּדָה *gadah.*
Josh. 3. 15 Jordan overfloweth all his banks all the
4. 18 and flowed over all his banks, as..before
Isa. 8. 7 channels, and go over all his banks.
2. *Banks, cuttings,* גָּדָה *or* גִּדְיָה *gidyah (gadah).*
1 Ch. 12. 15 when it had overflown all his banks
3. *Any thing raised up on high,* סֹלְלָה *solelah.*
2 Sa. 20. 15 they cast up a bank against the city
2 Ki. 19. 32 He shall not..cast a bank against it
Isa. 37. 33 He shall not..cast a bank against it
4. *Lip, edge,* שָׂפָה *saphah.*
Gen. 41. 17 I stood upon the bank of the river
Deut. 4. 48 by the bank of the river Arnon
Josh.12. 2 upon the bank of the river Arnon
13. 9 upon the bank of the river Arnon
13. 16 on the bank of the river Arnon
2 Ki. 2. 13 and stood by the bank of Jordan
Eze. 47. 7 at the bank of the river..very many trees
47. 12 by the river upon the bank thereof
Dan. 12. 5 the one on this side of the bank
12. 5 the other on that side of the bank
5. *Table (for dining or business),* τράπεζα *trapeza.*
Luke 19. 23 gavest not thou my money into the bank

BANNER —
1. *Banner, standard,* דֶּגֶל *degel.*
Song 2. 4 and his banner over me (was) love
2. *Sign, ensign,* נֵס *nes.*
Psa. 60. 4 Thou hast given a banner to them that
Isa. 13. 2 Lift ye up a banner upon the high

BANNERS, to set up —
To set up a banner, דָּגַל *dagal.*
Psa. 20. 5 we will set up..banners: the LORD

BANNERS, with —
To have banners, דָּגַל *dagal,* 2.
Song 6. 4, 10 terrible as (an army) with banners

BANQUET —
1. *A shouting (for joy or sorrow),* מַרְזֵחַ *marzeach.*
Amos 6. 7 the banquet of them that stretched
2. *A drinking,* מִשְׁתֶּה *mishteh.*
Esth. 5. 4 let the king..come..unto the banquet
5. 5 So the king..came to the banquet that E.
5. 6 king said unto Esther at the banquet of
5. 8 let the king..come to the banquet that
5. 12 come in with the king unto the banquet
5. 14 then go thou in..unto the banquet
6. 14 hasted to bring Haman unto the banquet
7. 2 on the second day at the banquet of wine
7. 7 And the king arising from the banquet
7. 8 into the place of the banquet of wine
Dan. 5. 10 the queen..came into the banquet house

BANQUET, to —
To drink, שָׁתָה *shathah.*
Esth. 7. 1 So the king..came to banquet with Esther

BANQUET, to make a —
To dig, pierce, prepare, כָּרָה *karah.*
Job 41. 6 Shall thy companions make a banquet of

BANQUETING —
Wine, (what is pressed out, juice), יַיִן *yayin.*
Song 2. 4 He brought me to the banqueting house

BANQUETINGS —
A drinking, πότος *potos.*
1 Pe. 4. 3 when we walked in..banquetings, and

BAPTISM —
1. *Baptism (as a state),* βάπτισμα *baptisma.*
Matt. 3. 7 he saw..Sadducees come to his baptism
20. 22 [to be baptized with the baptism that I]
20. 23 [and be baptized with the baptism that I]
21. 25 The baptism of John, whence was it?
Mark 1. 4 and preach the baptism of repentance
10. 38 and be baptized with the baptism that
10. 39 with the baptism that I am baptized
11. 30 The baptism of John, was (it) from
Luke 3. 3 preaching the baptism of repentance
7. 29 being baptized with the baptism of John
12. 50 But I have a baptism to be baptized with
20. 4 The baptism of John, was it from heaven
Acts 1. 22 Beginning from the baptism of John, unto
10. 37 after the baptism which John preached
13. 24 John had first preached..the baptism of
18. 25 knowing only the baptism of John
19. 3 And they said, Unto John's baptism
19. 4 John verily baptized with the baptism of
Rom. 6. 4 we are buried with him by baptism into
Eph. 4. 5 One Lord, one faith, one baptism
Col. 2. 12 Buried with him in [baptism,] wherein
1 Pe. 3. 21 baptism doth also now save us, not the
2. *Baptism (as an act),* βαπτισμός *baptismos.*
Heb. 6. 2 Of the doctrine of baptisms

BAP'-TIST, βαπτιστής *baptistēs.*
Designation of the forerunner of Christ; *see below.*

BAPTIST —
1. *One that baptizes,* βαπτιστής *baptistēs.*
Matt. 3. 1 In those days came John the Baptist
11. 11 a greater than John the Baptist
11. 12 And from the days of John the Baptist
14. 2 This is John the Baptist; he is risen
14. 8 Give me here John Baptist's head
16. 14 Some..John the Baptist: some, Elias
17. 13 he spake unto them of John the Baptist
Mark 6. 24 she said, The head of John the [Baptist]
6. 25 give me..the head of John the Baptist
8. 28 they answered, John the Baptist
Luke 7. 20 John Baptist hath sent us unto thee
7. 28 a greater prophet than John [the Baptist]
7. 33 John the Baptist came neither eating
9. 19 They answering said, John the Baptist
2. *To baptize,* βαπτίζω *baptizō.*
Mark 6. 14 That John the Baptist was risen from

BAPTIZE, to —
To consecrate (by pouring out on, or putting into), βαπτίζω *baptizō.*
Matt. 3. 11 I indeed baptize..he shall baptize you
Mark 1. 4 John did baptize in the wilderness
1. 8 I..have baptized..he shall baptize you
Luke 3. 16 I indeed baptize you with water; but
3. 16 he shall baptize you with the Holy Ghost
John 1. 25 Why baptizest thou then, if thou be not
1. 26 John answered..I baptize with water
1. 33 he that sent me to baptize with water
1. 33 the same is he which baptizeth with the
3. 22 there he tarried with them, and baptized
3. 26 behold, the same baptizeth, and all (men)
4. 1 Jesus made and baptized more disciples
4. 2 Though Jesus himself baptized not, but
10. 40 went..where John at first baptized
Acts 1. 5 John truly baptized with water
8. 38 they went down..and he baptized him
11. 16 John indeed baptized with water; but
19. 4 John verily baptized with the baptism of
1 Co. 1. 14 I thank God..I baptized none of you
1. 15 Lest any should say that I had baptized
1. 16 I baptized also..household of Stephanas
1. 16 I know not whether I baptized any other
1. 17 Christ sent me not to baptize, but to

BAPTIZED, to be —
To baptize, βαπτίζω *baptizō.*
Matt. 3. 6 And were baptized of him in Jordan
3. 13 Then cometh Jesus..to be baptized of
3. 14 I have need to be baptized of thee, and
3. 16 Jesus, when he was baptized, went up
20. 22 and to be baptized with the baptism
20. 22 that I am baptized with? They say unto
20. 23 and be baptized with the baptism
20. 23 that I am baptized with
Mark 1. 5 and were all baptized of him in the
1. 9 and was baptized of John in Jordan
10. 38 and be baptized with the baptism
10. 38 that I am baptized with? And they said
10. 39 with the baptism that I am baptized
10. 39 withal shall ye be baptized; but to sit
16. 16 [He that believeth and is baptized shall]
Luke 3. 7 said he to the multitude..to be baptized
3. 12 Then came also publicans to be baptized
3. 21 Now when all the people were baptized
3. 21 Jesus also being baptized, and praying
7. 29 being baptized with the baptism of John
7. 30 rejected..being not baptized of him
12. 50 I have a baptism to be baptized with
John 3. 23 they came, and were baptized
Acts 1. 5 ye shall be baptized with the Holy Ghost
2. 38 Repent, and be baptized every one of
2. 41 they that gladly received..were baptized
8. 12 they were baptized, both men and women
8. 13 when he was baptized, he continued with
8. 16 they were baptized in the name of the
8. 36 what doth hinder me to be baptized?
9. 18 forthwith, and arose, and was baptized
10. 47 that these should not be baptized
10. 48 And he commanded them to be baptized
11. 16 ye shall be baptized with the Holy Ghost
16. 15 when she was baptized, and her household
16. 33 was baptized, he and all his, straightway
18. 8 hearing believed, and were baptized
19. 3 Unto what then were ye baptized?
19. 5 they were baptized in the name of the
22. 16 be baptized, and wash away thy sins
Rom. 6. 3 so many of us as were baptized into
6. 3 were baptized into his death?
1 Cor. 1. 13 were ye baptized in the name of Paul?
10. 2 were all baptized unto Moses in the
12. 13 For by one Spirit are we all baptized
15. 29 they do which are baptized for the dead
15. 29 why are they then baptized for the dead?
Gal. 3. 27 For as many of you as have been baptized

BAPTIZING —
To baptize, βαπτίζω *baptizō.*
Matt. 28. 19 baptizing them in the name of the
John 1. 28 were done..where John was baptizing
1. 31 therefore am I come baptizing with water
3. 23 John also was baptizing in Ænon near

BAR —
1. *Separate part,* בַּד *bad.*
Job 17. 16 They shall go down to the bars of the pit
2. *Flying or piercing object, bar,* בְּרִיחַ *beriach.*
Exod. 26. 26 thou shalt make bars (of) shittim wood
26. 27 five bars for the boards of the other side
26. 27 five bars for the boards of the
26. 28 the middle bar in the midst of the boards
26. 29 make their rings..places for the bars
26. 29 thou shalt overlay the bars with gold
35. 11 The tabernacle..and his boards, his bars
36. 31 he made bars of shittim wood; five for
36. 32 five bars for the boards of the other side
36. 32 five bars for the boards of the tabernacle
36. 33 the middle bar to shoot through the
36. 34 made their rings..places for the bars
36. 34 and overlaid the bars with gold
39. 33 they brought the tabernacle..his bars
40. 18 put in the bars thereof, and reared up
Num. 3. 36 the bars thereof, and the pillars thereof
4. 31 the bars thereof, and the pillars thereof
Deut. 3. 5 cities..fenced with high walls..and bars
Judg. 16. 3 went away with them, bar and all
1 Sa. 23. 7 entering..a town..hath gates and bars
1 Ki. 4. 13 great cities with walls and brasen bars
2 Ch. 8. 5 Beth-horon..with walls, gates, and bars
14. 7 Let us..make about (them) walls..bars
Neh. 3. 3, 6, 13, 14, 15, and set up..bars thereof
Job 38. 10 brake up..and set bars and doors
Psa. 107. 16 and cut the bars of iron in sunder
147. 13 hath strengthened the bars of thy gates
Prov. 18. 19 contentions..like the bars of a castle
Isa. 45. 2 and cut in sunder the bars of iron
Jer. 49. 31 which have neither gates nor bars
51. 30 they have burned her..her bars are
Lam. 2. 9 he hath destroyed and broken her bars
Eze. 38. 11 without walls..having neither bars nor
Amos 1. 5 I will break also the bar of Damascus
Jon. 2. 6 the earth with her bars (was) about me
Nah. 3. 13 Behold..the fire shall devour thy bars
3. *Bar, pole,* מוֹט *mot.*
Num. 4. 10, 12 and shall put..upon a bar
4. *Anything stretched out,* מְטִיל *metil.*
Job 40. 18 his bones..like bars of iron

BAR, to —
To hold fast, אָחַז *achaz.*
Neh. 7. 3 let them shut the doors, and bar (them)

BAR-AB'-BAS, Βαραββᾶς *father's son.*
A murderer preferred to Christ.
Matt 27. 16 had then a notable prisoner, called B.
27. 17 B., or Jesus which is called Christ?
27. 20 they should ask B., and destroy Jesus
27. 21 release unto you? They said, B.
27. 26 Then released he B. unto them: and when
Mark 15. 7 there was (one) named B...bound with
15. 11 that he should rather release B. unto
15. 15 Pilate..released B. unto them, and
Luke 23. 18 Away with this..release unto us B.
John 18. 40 Not this man, but B. Now B. was a robber

BA-RACH'-EL, בַּרַכְאֵל *blessed of God.*
Father of Elihu, who reasoned with Job after his three friends were silent, B.C. 1550.
Job 32. 2 the wrath of Elihu the son of B. the
32. 6 Elihu the son of B. the Buzite answered

BA-RACH'-IAH, בֶּרֶכְיָה *blessed of Jah* = BERECHIAH]
Father of Zechariah the prophet, B.C. 520.
Zech. 1. 1 Zechariah, the son of B., the son of Iddo
1. 7 Zechariah, the son of B., the son of Iddo

BAR-ACH-I'AS, Βαραχίας.
The Greek form of *Barachiah.*
Matt. 23. 35 the blood of Zacharias son of B., whom

BA'-RAK, בָּרָק *lightning,* Βαράκ.
A Naphtalite who, with Deborah, defeated Sisera, the leader of the Canaanites, and obtained a great victory over him, B.C. 1296.
Judg. 4. 6 she sent and called B. the son of Abin.
4. 8 B. said unto her, If thou wilt go with me
4. 9 Deborah arose..went with B. to Kedesh
4. 10 B. called Zebulun and Naphtali to
4. 12 they shewed Sisera that B. the son of A.
4. 14 Deborah said unto B., Up; for this (is)
4. 14 So B. went down from mount Tabor, and
4. 15 the LORD discomfited Sisera..before B.
4. 16 B. pursued after the chariots, and after
4. 22 behold, as B. pursued Sisera, Jael came
5. 1 Then sang Deborah and B. the son of Ab.
5. 12 arise, B., and lead thy captivity captive
5. 15 even Issachar, and also B.: he was sent
Heb. 11. 32 time would fail me to tell of..B.

BARBARIAN —
Foreigner, alien, βάρβαρος *barbaros.*
Acts 28. 4 And when the barbarians saw the
Rom. 1. 14 I am debtor both..to the Barbarians
1 Co. 14. 11 I shall be unto him..a barbarian, and he
14. 11 he that speaketh..a barbarian unto me
Col. 3. 11 there is neither Greek nor..Barbarian

BARBAROUS —
Foreign, alien, βάρβαρος *barbaros.*
Acts 28. 2 the barbarous people shewed us no little

BARBED irons —
A pointed weapon, dart, שֻׂכָּה *sukkah.*
Job 41. 7 Canst..fill his skin with barbed irons?

BARBER —
A barber, גַּלָּב *gallab.*
Eze. 5. 1 son of man..take thee a barber's razor

BARE —
1. *Bare, uncovered,* עֶרְיָה *eryah.*
Eze. 16. 7 grown, whereas thou (wast) naked and bare
16. 22 when thou wast naked and bare
16. 39 and leave thee naked and bare
23. 29 and shall leave thee naked and bare: and
2. *To bare,* פָּרַע *para.*
Lev. 13. 45 his clothes shall be rent..his head bare
3. *Naked,* γυμνός *gumnos.*
1 Co. 15. 37 but bare grain, it may chance of wheat

BARE, to make —
1. *To be used with violence,* חָמָס *chamas,* 2.
Jer. 13. 22 skirts discovered..thy heels made bare
2. *To draw or strip off,* חָשַׂף *chasaph.*
Isa. 47. 2 uncover thy locks, make bare the leg
52. 10 LORD hath made bare his holy arm
Jer. 49. 10 But I have made Esau bare, I have
Joel 1. 7 he hath made it clean bare, and cast (it)
3. *To be or become bare,* עָרַר *arar.*
Isa. 32. 11 strip you, and make you bare, and gird

BARE, within —
Bald (behind), קָרַחַת *qarachath.*
Lev. 13. 55 fret inward..bare within or without

BAREFOOT —
To be unshod, יָחֵף *yacheph.*
2 Sa. 15. 30 his head covered, and he went barefoot
Isa. 20. 2 he did so, walking naked and barefoot
20. 3 Isaiah hath walked naked and barefoot
20. 4 lead..the Ethiopians..naked and barefoot

BAR-HU'-MITE, בַּרְחֻמִי *belonging to young men.*
Patronymic of one of David's worthies, B.C. 1058.
2 Sa. 23. 31 [one of the thirty]..Azmaveth the B.
In 1 Ch. 11. 33 the epithet is *Baharumite,* the correct reading; denoting a person of *Bahurim,* a town of Benjamin.

BA-RI'-AH, בָּרִיחַ *fugitive.*
Grandson of Shechaniah, of the family of David, B.C. 460.
1 Ch. 3. 22 the sons of Shechaniah; Shemaiah..B.

BAR JE'-SUS, Βαριησοῦς *son of Joshua.*
Otherwise called *Elymas,* a false prophet who opposed Barnabas and Paul at Paphos,
Acts 13. 6 they found..a Jew, whose name (was) B.

BAR JO-NA, βὰρ Ἰωνᾶ *son of Johanan.*
A surname of Simon Peter.
Matt 16. 17 Blessed art thou, Simon B.-j.: for flesh

BARK, to —
To bark, lift up the voice, נָבַח *nabach.*
Isa. 56. 10 all dumb dogs, they cannot bark; sleeping

BARKED —
Make stripped off (?), שִׂים לִקְצָפָה *sim li-qetsaphah.*
Joel 1. 7 He hath laid..waste, and barked my

BAR'-KOS, בַּרְקוֹס *party-coloured.*
A Nethinim, whose descendants returned from exile with Zerubbabel, B.C. 536.
Ezra 2. 53 children of B., the children of Sisera,
Neh. 7. 55 children of B., the children of Sisera

BARLEY —

1.*Barley (long hair)*, שְׂעֹרָה *seorah.*
Exod. 9. 31 And the flax and the barley was smitten
9. 31 for the barley (was) in the ear, and the
Lev 27. 16 an homer of barley seed..at fifty shekels
Num. 5. 15 the tenth..of an ephah of barley meal
Deut. 8. 8 A land of wheat, and barley, and vines
Judg. 7. 13 a cake of barley bread tumbled into the
Ruth 1. 22 to Beth-lehem in the..barley harvest
2. 17 it was about an ephah of barley
2. 23 to glean unto the end of barley harvest
3. 2 Behold, he winnoweth barley to night
3. 15 he measured six..of barley, and laid (it)
3. 17 these six..of barley gave he me; for he
2 Sa. 14. 30 Joab's field..hath barley there
17 28 Brought beds..and wheat, and barley
21. 9 in the beginning of barley harvest
1 Ki. 4. 28 Barley also and straw for the horses
2 Ki. 4. 42 twenty loaves of barley, and full ears of
7. 1 two measures of barley for a shekel
7. 16 two measures of barley for a shekel
7. 18 Two measures of barley for a shekel, and
1 Ch. 11. 13 was a parcel of ground full of barley
2 Ch. 2. 10 twenty thousand measures of barley
2. 15 Now therefore the wheat, and the barley
27. 5 gave him..ten thousand of barley
Job 31. 40 cockle instead of barley. The words of
Isa. 28. 25 and the appointed barley and the rye
Jer. 41. 8 we have treasures in the field..of barley
Eze. 4. 9 Take..also unto thee wheat, and barley
4. 12 And thou shalt eat it (as) barley cakes
13. 19 And will ye..for handfuls of barley
45. 13 the sixth part of an ephah..of barley
Hos. 3. 2 homer of barley, and an half homer of b.
Joel 1. 11 for the wheat and for the barley

2.*Barley (pointed, piercing)*, κριθή *krithē.*
Rev. 6. 6 three measures of barley for a penny

3.*Made of barley*, κρίθινος *krithinos.*
John 6. 9 a lad here, which hath five barley loaves
6. 13 the fragments of the five barley loaves

BARN —

1.*An open threshing floor*, גֹּרֶן *goren.*
Job 39. 12 thy seed, and gather (it into) thy barn

2.*A place for collecting anything*, מְגוּרָה *megurah.*
Hag 2. 19 Is the seed yet in the barn? yea, as yet

3.*A place for putting away*, ἀποθήκη *apothēkē.*
Matt. 6. 26 neither..reap, nor gather into barns
13. 30 but gather the wheat into my barn
Luke 12. 18 This will I do. I will pull down my barns
12. 24 which neither have store house nor barn

BARN FLOOR —

An open threshing floor, גֹּרֶן *goren.*
2 Ki. 6. 27 shall I help thee? out of the barnfloor

BARNS —

1.*Places for heaping together*, אֲסָמִים *asamim.*
Prov. 3. 10 So shall thy barns be filled with plenty

2.*Places for collecting*, מַמְּגֻרוֹת *mammeguroth.*
Joel 1. 17 the barns are broken down; for the corn

BAR-NA'-BAS, Βαρνάβας *son of consolation.*

A Levite, Paul's companion in several of his journeys; otherwise called *Joses.*
Acts 4 36 Joses, who by the apostles..surnamed B.
9 27 B. took him, and brought (him) to the
11 22 they sent forth B., that he should go as
11 25 Then departed B to Tarsus, for to seek
11 30 sent it to the elders by the hands of B.
12. 25 B. and Saul returned from Jerusalem
13 1 certain prophets and teachers; as B., and
13. 2 Separate me B. and Saul for the work
13. 7 who called for B. and Saul, and desired
13. 43 many of the Jews..followed Paul and B
13. 46 Then Paul and B waxed bold, and said
13. 50 the Jews..raised persecution against..B
14. 12 they called B., Jupiter; and Paul Mer.
14. 14 when the apostles, B. and Paul, heard
14. 20 the next day he departed with B. to Derbe
15. 2 when therefore Paul and B. had no small
15. 2 they determined that Paul and B.
15 12 all the multitude..gave audience to B
15 22 to send chosen men..with Paul and B.
15. 25 to send chosen men..with our beloved B
15. 35 Paul also and B. continued in Antioch
15. 36 And some days after Paul said unto B.
15. 37 And B determined to take with them John
15. 39 so B. took Mark, and sailed unto Cyprus
1 Co. 9. 6 Or I only and B, have not we power to
Gal. 2. 1 I went up again to Jerusalem with B
2. 9 they gave to me and B. the right hands
2. 13 insomuch that B. also was carried away
Col. 4. 10 Marcus, sister's son to B., touching whom

BARREL —

An earthen jar, כַּד *kad.*
1 Ki. 17. 12 but an handful of meal in a barrel, and
17. 14 The barrel of meal shall not waste
17. 16 the barrel of meal wasted not, neither
18. 33 and said, Fill four barrels with water

BARREN —

1.*Restraining, restrained*, עֹצֶר *otser.*
Prov 30. 16 The grave; and the barren womb

2.*Rooted, sterile*, עָקָר *aqar.*
Gen. 11 30 But Sarai was barren: she (had) no child
25. 21 Isaac intreated..because she (was) barren
29. 31 opened her womb: but Rachel (was) bar.
Exod 23. 26 There shall nothing cast..nor be barren
Deut. 7. 14 there shall not be male or female barren
Judg 13. 2 and his wife (was) barren, and bare not
13. 3 Behold now, thou (art) barren, and
1 Sa. 2. 5 so that the barren hath born seven
Job 24. 21 He evil entreateth the barren (that)
Isa. 54. 1 Sing, O barren, thou (that) didst not bear

3.*Dry, drought*, צִיָּה *tsiyyah.*
Joel 2. 20 and will drive him into a land barren

4.*Bereaved*, שַׁכּוּל *shakkul.*
Song 4. 2 and none (is) barren among them
6. 6 and (there is) not one barren among them

5.*To bereave*, שָׁכֹל *shakol*, 3.
2 Ki. 2. 19 water (is) naught, and the ground barren
2. 21 shall not be..any more death or barren

6.*Not working*, ἀργός *argos.*
2 Pe. 1. 8 they..neither..barren nor unfruitful

7.*Barren, without seed*, στεῖρος *steiros.*
Luke 1. 7 no child, because..Elizabeth was barren
1. 36 month with her, who was called barren
23. 29 Blessed (are) the barren and the wombs
Gal. 4. 27 Rejoice, (thou) barren that bearest not

BARREN land —

Salt place, מְלֵחָה *melechah.*
Job 39. 6 and the barren land his dwellings

BARREN woman —

Rooted, sterile, עָקָר *aqar.*
Psa. 113. 9 He maketh the barren woman to keep

BARRENNESS —

Salt place, מְלֵחָה *melechah.*
Psa. 107. 34 A fruitful land into barrenness, for the

BAR-SA'-BAS, Βαρσαβᾶς *son of Saba.*

1. One nominated with Matthias to succeed Judas.
Acts 1. 23 they appointed two, Joseph called B.

2. A disciple sent with Silas to Antioch with letters from the apostles.
Acts 15 22 Judas surnamed B., and Silas, chief men

BAR-THO-LO-MEW. Βαρθολομαῖος *son of Tolmai.*

One of the apostles of Christ.
Matt 10. 3 [apostles are these]..Philip and B.
Mark 3. 18 Andrew, and Philip, and B, and Matthew
Luke 6. 14 brother, James and John, Philip and B.
Acts 1. 13 where abode both..Philip and Thomas, B.

BAR-TI-MÆ-US Βαρτίμαιος *son of Timæus.*

A beggar in Jericho who received sight.
Mark 10. 46 blind B, the son of Timæus, sat by the

BA'RUCH בָּרוּךְ *blessed.*

1. Son of Zabbai who helped to build the wall, B.C. 445.
Neh. 3 20 After him B the son of Zabbai earnestly
10. 6 [those that sealed (were)]..Ginnethon, B.

2. A descendant of Phares, a returned exile, B C. 445.
Neh 11 5 Maaseiah the son of B., the son of

3. The amanuensis of Jeremiah in prison, B.C 590
Jer. 32 12 the evidence of the purchase unto B.
32 13 And I charged B before them saying
32. 16 I had delivered the evidence..unto B.
36. 4 Then Jeremiah called B the son of Ner
36 4 and B. wrote from the mouth of Jeremiah
36 5 Jeremiah commanded B saying, I (am)
36. 8 B the son of Neriah did according to all
36 10 Then read B in the book the words of J
36 13 when B read the book in the ears of the
36. 14 Therefore all the princes sent..unto B.
36 14 So B the son of Neriah took the roll
36 15 So B. read (it) in their ears
36 16 they were afraid..and said unto B, We
36. 17 they asked B. saying, Tell us now, How
36. 18 B. answered them He pronounced all
36 19 Then said the princes unto B., Go, hide
36. 26 king commanded Jerahmeel..to take B.
36 27 the words which B wrote at the mouth
36 32 gave it to B the scribe, the son of Neriah
43. 3 B the son of Neriah setteth thee on
43 6 Jeremiah the prophet, and B the son of
45. 1 The word that Jeremiah..spake unto B.
45. 2 Thus saith the LORD..unto thee, O B.

BAR-ZIL'-LAI, בַּרְזִלַּי *strong, iron.*

1 A Gileadite friend of David in his flight from Absalom, B.C 1103–1023.
2 Sa. 17 27 it came to pass..that Shobi..and B. the
19. 31 B. the Gileadite came down from
19. 32 B. was a very aged man (even) fourscore
19. 33 the king said unto B., Come thou over
19. 34 B. said unto the king How long have I
19. 39 the king kissed B and blessed him; and
1 Ki. 2 7 shew kindness unto the sons of B the
Ezra 2. 61 children of the priests..children of B.
Neh. 7 63 of the priests..children of B

2 Father of Adriel, husband of Merab Saul's eldest daughter, B C. 1060.
2 Sa. 21 8 she brought up for Adriel the son of B.

3 A priest whose genealogy was lost, the father of some exiles who returned with Ezra, B C 600.
Ezra 2. 61 which took a wife of the daughter of B.
Neh. 7 63 which took (one) of the daughters of B.

BASE —

1 *Stand, pedestal*, כֵּן *ken.*
1 Ki. 7. 29 upon the ledges..a base above: and
7. 31 the work of the base, a cubit and a half

2.*Base, place for setting on*, מְכוֹנָה *mekonah.*
1 Ki. 7 27 bases..four cubits..length of one base
7. 28 the work of the bases (was) on this
7. 30 every base had four brasen wheels, and
7. 32 the axletrees of the wheels..to the base
7 34 to the four corners of one base
7 34 the undersetters (were) of the very base
7. 35 And in the top of the base..a round
7. 35 on the top of the base the ledges thereof
7 37 After this..he made the ten bases: all of
7. 38 upon every one of the ten bases one laver
7. 39 he put five bases on the right side
7. 43 the ten bases, and ten lavers on the bases
2 Ki. 16. 17 Ahaz cut off the borders of the bases
25. 13 and the bases, and the brasen sea
25. 16 and the bases which Solomon had made
2 Ch. 4. 14 bases, and lavers made he upon the bases
Ezra 3. 3 And they set the altar upon his bases
Jer. 27 19 concerning the bases, and concerning the
52. 17 and the bases, and the brasen sea that
52. 20 twelve brasen bulls..under the bases

3.*A base, place for setting on*, מְכֻנָה *mekunah.*
Zech. 5 11 it shall be..set there upon her own base

4.*To be or become light*, קָלָה *qalah*, 2.
Isa. 3. 5 and the base against the honourable

5.*Humble*, שָׁפָל *shaphal.*
2 Sa. 6. 22 and will be base in mine own sight
Eze. 17. 14 That the kingdom might be base, that
29 14 and they shall be there a base kingdom
Mal. 2. 9 I also made you contemptible and base

6.*Humble*, ταπεινός *tapeinos.*
2 Co. 10. 1 who in presence (am) base among you

7.*Without name*, בְּלִי־שֵׁם *beli shem.*
Job 30. 8 children of base men: they were viler

BASE things —

Ignoble, ἀγενής *agenēs.*
1 Co 1 28 base things of the world, and things which

BASER sort, of the —

Belonging to the market place, ἀγοραῖος *agoraios.*
Acts 17. 5 certain lewd fellows of the baser sort

BASEST —

1.*Humble*, שָׁפָל *shaphal.*
Eze. 29 15 It shall be the basest of the kingdoms

2.*Humble*, שְׁפַל *shephal.*
Dan. 4. 17 and setteth up over it the basest of men

BA-SHAN, הַבָּשָׁן *the fruitful.*

A district on the E. of Jordan, almost always written with the *definite article* in the original. It is sometimes called "The land of Bashan" It was the kingdom of Og, the Amorite, and extended from the "border of Gilead" on the S to mount Hermon on the N., and from the Arabah or Jordan valley on the W. to Salchah (*Sulkhad*) and the border of the Geshurites and the Maacathites on the E Bashan or "*the* Bashan" was the lot of the half tribe of Manasseh together with "half of Gilead."
Num 21. 33 they turned and went up by the way of B.
21 33 Og the king of B. went out against them
32. 33 the kingdom of Og king of B., the land
Deut. 1. 4 Og the king of B...dwelt at Ashtaroth
3. 1 we turned, and went up the way to B.
3. 1 Og the king of B came out against us
3. 3 the king of B, and all his people: and
3. 4 of Argob, the kingdom of Og in B.
3. 10 all Gilead, and all B., unto Salchah
3. 10 cities of the kingdom of Og in B.
3. 11 only Og king of B. remained of the
3. 13 the rest of Gilead, and all B., the
3. 13 all the region of Argob, with all B., which
4. 43 and Golan in B., of the Manassites.
4 47 his land, and the land of Og king of B.
29. 7 Og the king of B. came out against
32. 14 rams of the breed of B., and goats
33. 22 a lion's whelp: he shall leap from B.
Josh. 9 10 to Og king of B., which..at Ashtaroth
12. 4 And the coast of Og king of B...of the
12. 5 in all B, unto the border of the Geshurites
13. 11 mount Hermon, and all B. unto Salcah
13. 12 All the kingdom of Og in B., which
13. 30 their coast was from Mahanaim, all B.
13. 30 all the kingdom of Og king of B., and
13. 30 the towns..which (are) in B., threescore
13. 31 Edrei, cities of the kingdom of Og in B.
17. 1 a man of war, therefore he had..B.
17. 5 beside the land of Gilead and B., which
20. 8 Golan in B. out of the tribe of Manasseh
21. 6 half tribe of Manasseh in B, thirteen
21 27 Golan in B with her suburbs..a city of
22. 7 to..Manasseh Moses had given..in B.
1 Ki. 4. 13 the region of Argob, which (is) in B.
4. 19 and of Og king of B; and..the only
2 Ki. 10. 33 by the river Arnon, even Gilead and B.
1 Ch. 5. 11 dwelt..in the land of B. unto Salcah
5. 12 Joel the chief..and Shaphat in B.
5. 16 they dwelt in Gilead in B, and in her
5. 23 they increased from B. unto Baal-hermon
6. 62 out of the tribe of Manasseh in B.
6. 71 half tribe of Manasseh, Golan in B. with
Neh. 9. 22 Heshbon and the land of Og king of B.
Psa. 22 12 strong (bulls) of B. have beset me round
68 15 the hill of B..the hill of B.
68. 22 LORD said, I will bring again from B.
135. 11 Og king of B., and all the kingdoms
136. 20 Og the king of B.: for his mercy..for

Isa. 2. 13 lifted up, and upon all the oaks of B.
33. 9 and B. and Carmel shake off (their fruits)
Jer. 22. 20 lift up thy voice in B., and cry from the
50. 19 he shall feed on Carmel and B. and his
Eze. 27. 6 (Of) the oaks of B. have they made thine
39. 18 of bullocks, all of them fatlings of B.
Amos 4. 1 Hear this word, ye kine of B., that (are)
Mic. 7. 14 let them feed (in) B. and Gilead, as in
Nah. 1. 4 B. languisheth, and Carmel, and the
Zech. 11. 2 howl, O ye oaks of B.; for the forest of the

BA-SHAN HA-VOTH JA'-IR, בָּשָׁן חַוֹּת יָאִיר.
A name given to Argob after its conquest by Jair, a descendant of Manasseh, B.C. 1451.
Deut. 3. 14 called them after his own name, B.

BA-SHE'-MATH or BAS'-MATH, בָּשְׂמַת *fragrant.*
1. One of the wives of Esau, and daughter of Elon the Hittite, B. C. 1796.
Gen. 26. 34 and B. the daughter of Elon the Hittite
2. Another wife of Esau and daughter of Ishmael. B.C. 1796.
Gen. 36. 3 B. Ishmael's daughter, sister of Nebajoth
36. 4 Adah bare to Esau Eliphaz; and B. bare
36. 10 Reuel the son of B. the wife of Esau
36. 13 these were the sons of B. Esau's wife
36. 17 these (are) the sons of B. Esau's wife

BASIN, BASON —
1. *Bason, bowl, cup,* אַגָּן *aggan.*
Exod 24. 6 half of the blood, and put (it) in basons
2. *Cup, goblet,* כְּפוֹר *kephor.*
1 Ch. 28. 17 golden basons..every bason..every bason
Ezra 1. 10 Thirty basons of gold, silver basons of a
8. 27 twenty basons of gold, of a thousand
3. *Large bowl for sprinkling,* מִזְרָק *mizraq.*
Exod 27. 3 thou shalt make his pans..his basons
38. 3 he made all the vessels..and the basons
Num. 4. 14 they shall put upon it..the basons, all
1 Ki. 7. 40 Hiram made the lavers..and the basons
7. 45 basons..Hiram made..(of) bright brass
7. 50 the basons..and the censers (of) pure gold
2 Ki. 12. 13 not made..bowls of silver, snuffers, basons
2 Ch. 4. 8 And he made an hundred basons of gold
4. 11 Huram made the pots..and the basons
4. 22 basons..and the censers, (of) pure gold
Neh. 7. 70 The Tirshatha gave..fifty basons
4. *Dish, bowl,* סַף *saph.*
Exod 12. 22 dip (it) in the blood that (is) in the bason
12. 22 with the blood that (is) in the bason
2 Sa. 17. 28 Brought beds, and basons, and earthen
Jer. 52. 19 the basons, and the fire pans, and the
5. *Large vessel or ewer,* νιπτήρ *niptēr.*
John 13. 5 After that he poureth water into a bason

BASKET —
1. *Basket, pot, kettle,* דּוּד *dud.*
2 Ki. 10. 7 slew..and put their heads in baskets
Jer. 24. 2 One basket (had) very good figs..the
2. *Basket, pot, kettle,* דּוּדַי *dudai.*
Jer. 24. 1 two baskets of figs..set before the temple
3. *Basket of woven or twisted work,* טֶנֶא *tene.*
Deut 26. 2 shalt put (it) in a basket, and shalt go
26. 4 the priest shall take the basket out of
28. 5 Blessed (shall be) thy basket and thy store
28. 17 Cursed (shall be) thy basket and thy store
4. *Cage, basket,* כְּלוּב *kelub.*
Amos 8. 1 and behold a basket of summer fruit
8. 2 And I said, A basket of summer fruit
5. *Basket (wicker),* סַל *sal.*
Gen. 40. 16 (I had) three white baskets on my head
40. 17 in the uppermost basket..of all manner of
40. 17 birds did eat them out of the basket
40. 18 The three baskets (are) three days
Exod 29. 3 thou shalt put them into one basket
29. 3 bring them in the basket, with the bullock
29. 23 one wafer out of the basket of the
29. 32 shall eat..the bread that (is) in the basket
Lev. 8. 2 rams, and a basket of unleavened bread
8. 26 out of the basket of unleavened bread
8. 31 with the bread that (is) in the basket
Num. 6. 15 a basket of unleavened bread, cakes of
6. 17 with the basket of unleavened bread
6. 19 one unleavened cake out of the basket
Judg. 6. 19 the flesh he put in a basket, and he put
6. *Wicker basket,* σαργάνη *sarganē.*
2 Co. 11. 33 in a basket was I let down by the wall
7. *A hamper,* σπυρίς *spuris.*
Acts 9. 25 and let..down by the wall in a basket

BASKETS —
1. *Wicker baskets,* סַלְסִלּוֹת *salsilloth.*
Jer. 6. 9 turn back thine hand..into the baskets
2. *A wicker travelling basket,* κόφινος *kophinos.*
Matt 14. 20 took up..that remained twelve baskets
16. 9 and how many baskets ye took up?
Mark 6. 43 And they took up twelve baskets full
8. 19 how many baskets full of fragments
Luke 9. 17 there..remained to them twelve baskets
John 6. 13 filled twelve baskets with the fragments
3. *A hamper,* σπυρίς *spuris.*
Matt 15. 37 took up..that was left seven baskets full
16. 10 and how many baskets ye took up?
Mark 8. 8 took up..that was left seven [baskets]
8. 20 how may baskets full..took ye up?

BAS'-MATH, בָּשְׂמַת *fragrant, spicy.*
Solomon's daughter, who became wife of Ahimaaz, a purveyor for Solomon, B.C. 1014. [*See* **BASHEMATH.**]
1 Ki. 4. 15 he also took B. the daughter of Solomon

BASTARD —
1. *Mixed, spurious,* מַמְזֵר *mamzer.*
Deut 23. 2 A bastard shall not enter into the cong.
Zech. 9. 6 And a bastard shall dwell in Ashdod
2. *Bastard,* νόθος *nothos.*
Heb. 12. 8 then are ye bastards, and not sons

BAT —
Bat, night-bird, עֲטַלֵּף *atalleph.*
Lev. 11. 19 her kind, and the lapwing, and the bat
Deut 14. 18 the stork..and the lapwing, and the bat
Isa. 2. 20 shall cast..to the moles and to the bats

BATH —
A measure for fluids, about 8 gallons, בַּת *bath.*
1 Ki. 7. 26 of lilies: it contained two thousand baths
7. 38 lavers of brass: one..contained forty baths
2 Ch. 2. 10 thousand baths of wine..baths of oil
4. 5 received and held three thousand baths
Ezra 7. 22 baths of wine..baths of oil, and salt
Isa. 5. 10 acres of vineyard shall yield one bath
Eze. 45. 10 a just ephah, and a just bath
45. 11 The ephah and the bath..that the bath
45. 14 bath of oil..tenth part of a bath
45. 14 an homer of ten baths; for ten baths

BATH RAB'-BIM, בַּת־רַבִּים *daughter of many.*
A gate of the ancient city of Heshbon, near which were two pools to which the spouse compares the eyes of his "beloved."
Song 7. 4 fishpools in Heshbon, by the gate of B.

BATH SHE'-BA, בַּת־שֶׁבַע *daughter of an oath.*
Daughter of Eliam or Ammiel, wife of Uriah, and mother of Solomon by David. She is also called *Bathshua.* Jewish tradition has it that she composed and recited Proverbs 31st as an admonition to her son Solomon on his marriage with Pharaoh's daughter, B C. 1035.
2 Sa. 11. 3 (Is) not this B.-Sh., the daughter of Eliam
12. 24 David comforted B. his wife, and went
1 Ki. 1. 11 Wherefore Nathan spake unto B.-Sh. the
1. 15 B.-Sh. went in unto the king into the
1. 16 B.-Sh. bowed, and did obeisance unto
1. 28 David answered and said, Call me B.-Sh.
1. 31 B.-Sh. bowed with (her) face to the earth
2. 13 Adonijah..came to B.-Sh. the mother of
2. 18 B.-Sh. said, Well; I will speak for thee
2. 19 B.-Sh. therefore went unto king Solomon
Psa. 51. (*title*) A..after he had gone into B.-Sh.

BATH SHU'-A, בַּת־שׁוּעַ *daughter of prosperity.*
This name is translated "daughter of Shua" in Gen. 38. 12 and in 1 Ch. 2. 3; but in 1 Ch. 3. 5, it is employed as the name of the mother of Solomon, and she is called the daughter of Ammiel (elsewhere *Eliam*). In Gen. 38. 2, 12, Bathshua is really the name of Judah's wife, B.C. 1035.
1 Chron 3. 5 these were born unto him..of B.-Sh. the

BATHE, to —
To wash, rub, רָחַץ *rachats.*
Lev. 15. 13 and bathe his flesh in running water
16. 26 wash his clothes, and bathe his flesh in
16. 28 he that burneth them shall..bathe his
17. 16 But if he wash..not, nor bathe his
Num 19. 7 Then the priest..shall bathe his flesh in
19. 8 wash his clothes in water, and bathe his

BATHE (self), to —
To wash, rub, רָחַץ *rachats.*
Lev. 15. 5 shall wash his clothes and bathe (himself)
15. 6 bathe (himself) in water, and be unclean
15. 7 he that toucheth the flesh..and bathe
15. 8 then he shall..bathe (himself) in water
15. 10 and bathe (himself) in water, and be
15. 11 he shall wash his clothes, and bathe
15. 18 they shall (both) bathe (themselves) in
15. 21 bathe (himself) in water, and be unclean
15. 22 bathe (himself) in water, and be unclean
15. 27 and bathe (himself) in water..until the
17. 15 and bathe (himself)..then shall he be
Num 19. 19 wash his clothes, and bathe himself in

BATHED, to be —
To be satiated, רָוָה *ravah,* 3.
Isa. 34. 5 For my sword shall be bathed in heaven

BATTER, to —
To destroy, שָׁחַת *shachath,* 5.
2 Sa. 20. 15 the people that (were) with Joab battered

BATTLE —
1. *Circumvallation,* כִּידוֹר *kidor.*
Job 15. 24 prevail..as a king ready to the battle
2. *A camp,* מַחֲנֶה *machaneh.*
1 Sa. 28. 1 thou shalt go out with me to battle, thou
3. *Battle, conflict, eating up,* מִלְחָמָה *milchamah.*
Gen. 14. 8 joined battle with them in the vale of
Num 21. 33 he, and all his people, to the battle
31. 21 the men of war which went to the battle
32. 27 armed for war, before the LORD to battle
32. 29 every man armed to battle, before the
Deut. 2. 9 neither contend with them in battle
2. 24 possess (it), and contend..him in battle
3. 1 he and all his people, to battle at Edrei
20. 1 thou goest out to battle against thine
20. 2 when ye are come nigh unto the battle
20. 3 O Israel, ye approach this day unto battle
20. 5 return to his house, lest he die in..battle
20. 6 lest he die in the battle, and another
20. 7 return..lest he die in the battle, and
29. 7 the king..came out against us unto battle
Josh. 4. 13 passed over before the LORD unto battle
8. 14 the city went out against Israel to battle
11. 19 the Hivites..all (other) they took in battle
11. 20 they should come against Israel in battle
Judg. 8. 13 Gideon..returned from battle before
20. 14 go out to battle against the children of I.
20. 18 Which of us shall go up first to the battle
20. 20 the men of Israel went out to battle
20. 22 and set their battle again in array in the
20. 23 Shall I go up again to battle against the
20. 28 Shall I yet again go out to battle against
20. 34 out of all Israel, and the battle was sore
20. 39 the men of Israel retired in the battle
20. 42 but the battle overtook them; and them
1 Sa. 4. 1 went out against the Philistines to battle
4. 2 when..joined battle, Israel was smitten
7. 10 the Philistines drew near to battle
8. 20 go out before us, and fight our battles
13. 22 it came to pass in the day of battle, that
14. 20 Saul and all..came to the battle
14. 22 followed hard after them in the battle
14. 23 the battle passed over unto Beth-aven
17. 1 the Philistines gathered..armies to battle
17. 2 set the battle in array against the
17. 8 Why are ye come out to set (your) battle
17. 13 eldest sons..followed Saul to the battle
17. 13 of his three sons that went to the battle
17. 20 to the fight, and shouted for the battle
17. 28 down that thou mightest see the battle
17. 47 for the battle (is) the LORD'S, and he
18. 17 for me, and fight the LORD'S battles
25. 28 my lord fighteth the battles of the LORD
26. 10 he shall descend into battle, and perish
29. 4 let him not go down with us to battle
29. 9 He shall not go up with us to the battle
30. 24 part (is) that goeth down to the battle
31. 3 And the battle went sore against Saul
2 Sa. 1. 4 the people are fled from the battle
1. 25 mighty fallen in the midst of the battle!
2. 17 there was a very sore battle that day
3. 30 slain their brother Asahel..in the battle
10. 8 put the battle in array at the..gate
10. 9 the front of the battle was against him
10. 13 And Joab drew nigh..unto the battle
11. 15 Uriah in the forefront of the hottest battle
11. 25 make thy battle more strong against the
18. 6 the battle was in the wood of Ephraim
18. 8 For the battle was there scattered over
19. 3 ashamed steal away when..flee in battle
19. 10 And Absalom..is dead in battle
21. 17 Thou shalt go no more out..to battle
21. 18 there was again a battle with the Phil.
21. 19 And there was again a battle in Gob
21. 20 And there was yet a battle in Gath
22. 40 hast girded me with strength to battle
23. 9 the Philistines..gathered..to battle
1 Ki. 8. 44 thy people go out to battle against their
20. 14 he said, Who shall order the battle?
20. 29 in the seventh day the battle was joined
20. 39 Thy servant went out into..the battle
22. 4 Wilt thou go with me to battle to R.-G.?
22. 6 I go against Ramoth-gilead to battle
22. 15 we go against Ramoth-gilead to battle
22. 30 disguise myself, and enter into the battle
22. 30 the king of Israel..went into the battle
22. 35 And the battle increased that day: and
2 Ki. 3. 7 wilt thou go..against Moab to battle?
3. 26 Moab saw that the battle was too sore
1 Ch. 5. 20 for they cried to God in the battle
7. 11 fit to go out for war (and) battle
7. 40 that were apt to the war (and) to battle
10. 3 And the battle went sore against Saul
11. 13 were gathered together to battle
12. 8 (and) men of war (fit) for the battle
12. 19 with the Philistines against Saul to battle
12. 37 with all..instruments..for the battle
14. 15 then thou shalt go out to battle: for
19. 7 from their cities, and came to battle
19. 9 put the battle in array before the gate of
19. 10 saw that the battle; [*peneham-milchamah*]
19. 14 Joab..drew nigh..unto the battle
19. 17 David had put the battle in array against
26. 27 Out of the spoils won in battles did they
2 Ch. 13. 3 set the battle in array with an army of
13. 3 set the battle in array against him with
13. 14 behold, the battle (was) before and
14. 10 they set the battle in array in the valley
18. 5 Shall we go to Ramoth-gilead to battle
18. 14 shall we go to Ramoth-gilead to battle
18. 29 disguise myself, and will go to the battle
18. 29 disguised himself; and..went to..battle
18. 34 And the battle increased that day: how
20. 1 came against Jehoshaphat to battle
20. 15 for the battle (is) not your's, but God's
25. 8 do (it), be strong for the battle: God
25. 13 they should not go with him to battle
32. 8 with us (is) the LORD..to fight our battles
Job 39. 25 and he smelleth the battle afar off
41. 8 remember the battle, do no more
Psa. 18. 39 girded me with strength unto the battle
24. 8 The LORD strong and mighty..in battle
76. 3 the shield, and the sword, and the battle
89. 43 hast not made him to stand in the battle
Prov 21. 31 (is) prepared against the day of battle
Eccl. 9. 11 nor the battle to the strong, neither yet

Isa. 13. 4 LORD..mustereth the host of the battle
22. 2 slain with the sword, nor dead in battle
27. 4 set the..thorns against me in battle
28. 6 to them that turn the battle to the gate
30. 32 in battles of shaking will he fight with it
42. 25 his anger, and the strength of battle
Jer. 8. 6 as the horse rusheth into the battle
18. 21 young men (be) slain by the sword in battle
46. 3 and shield, and draw near to battle
49. 14 come against her, and rise up to..battle
50. 22 A sound of battle (is) in the land, and of
50. 42 put in array, like a man to the battle
Eze. 7. 14 none goeth to the battle: for my wrath
13. 5 stand in the battle in the day of the LORD
Dan. 11. 20 neither in anger, nor in battle
11. 25 the south shall be stirred up to battle
Hos. 1. 7 will not save..by bow..nor by battle
2. 18 the sword and the battle out of the earth
10. 9 there they stood: the battle in Gibeah
10. 14 spoiled Betharbel in the day of battle
Joel 2. 5 as a strong people set in battle array
Amos 1. 14 with shouting in the day of battle, with
Obad. 1 Arise..let us rise up against her in battle
Zech. 9. 10 and the battle bow shall be cut off: and
10. 3 made them as his goodly horse in..battle
10. 4 him the nail..out of him the battle bow
10. 5 in the mire of the streets in the battle
14. 2 all nations against Jerusalem to battle

4. *Armour, arms,* נֶשֶׁק *nesheq.*
Psa. 140. 7 covered my head in the day of battle

5. *Equipment,* סְאוֹן *seon.*
Isa. 9. 5 For every battle of the warrior (is) with

6. *The host, army,* צָבָא *tsaba.*
Num 31. 27 upon them, who went out to battle
31. 28 men of war which went out to battle
Josh 22. 33 intend to go up against them in battle
1 Ch. 12. 33 such as went forth to battle, expert
12. 36 such as went forth to battle, expert

7. *Host of the battle,* צְבָא הַמִּלְחָמָה. [*tsaba*].
Num 31. 14 the officers..which came from the battle

8. *A drawing near,* קְרָב *qerab.*
2 Sa. 17. 11 go to battle in thine own person
Job 38. 23 reserved against..the day of battle
Psa. 55. 18 hath delivered my soul..from the battle
78. 9 Ephraim..turned back in the day of battle
Zech 14. 3 as when he fought in the day of battle

9. *A battle, fight,* πόλεμος *polemos.*
1 Co. 14. 8 who shall prepare himself to the battle?
Rev. 9. 7 like unto horses prepared unto battle
9. 9 sound of..many horses running to battle
16. 14 go forth..to gather them to the battle
20. 8 go out..to gather them together to battle

BATTLE AXE—
Hammer, battle-axe, מַפֵּץ *mappets.*
Jer. 51. 20 Thou (art) my battle axe (and) weapons of

BATTLEMENT —
A restraint, מַעֲקֶה *maaqeh.*
Deut. 22. 8 thou shalt make a battlement for thy roof

BATTLEMENTS —
Any things stretched out, נְטִישׁוֹת *netishoth.*
Jer. 5. 10 take away her battlements; for they (are)

BA'-VAI, בַּוַּי *wisher.*
Descendant of Henadad who helped to rebuild the wall of Jerusalem, B.C. 445.
Neh. 3. 18 After him repaired their brethren, B.

BAY —
1. *The tongue,* לָשׁוֹן *lashon.*
Josh. 15. 2 from the bay that looketh southward
15. 5 north quarter (was) from the bay of the
18. 19 of the border were at the north bay

2. *Strong, deep red,* אֲמֻצִּים *amutstsim.*
Zech. 6. 3 in the fourth chariot grisled and bay
6. 7 And the bay went forth, and sought to go

BAY TREE —
Native born, אֶזְרָח *ezrach.*
Psa. 37. 35 spreading himself like a green bay tree

BAZ'-LITH, BAZ'-LUTH, בַּצְלִית בַּצְלוּת, *asking.*
One of the Nethinim whose posterity returned from exile, B.C. 536.
Ezra 2. 52 children of B., the children of Mehida
Neh. 7. 54 children of B., the children of Mehida

BDELLIUM —
An oily gum, or a white pearl, בְּדֹלַח *bedolach.*
Gen. 2. 12 there (is) bdellium and the onyx stone
Num 11. 7 the colour..as the colour of bdellium

BE, to (am, art, is, are, was, were, &c.) —
When this word is printed in *italics* in the common English version, there is no corresponding word in the original text; when it occurs in common type, it is *generally* the representative of הָיָה הָוָה הָוֵא *hayah, havah, hava,* "to be" in Hebrew; and of εἰμί, "to be" in Greek. Otherwise it is the translation of such words as the following:—

1. *To come, come in,* בּוֹא *bo.*
2 Ki. 24. 10 against Jerusalem, and..city was besieged
25. 2 And the city was besieged unto the
Jer. 52. 5 So the city was besieged unto the
Lam. 5. 4 our wood is sold unto us

2. *To give,* נָתַן *nathan.* [*See* 0].
Job 29. 2 Oh that I were as (in) months past
Jer. 9. 1 Oh that my head were waters, and mine

3. *Stand,* עָמַד *amad.*
Num. 7. 2 and were over them that were numbered

4. *There is, there are,* יֵשׁ *yesh.*
Gen. 18. 24 Peradventure there be fifty righteous
23. 8 If it be your mind that I should bury my
24. 23 is there room in (thy) father's house for
28. 16 Surely the LORD is in this place, and I
42. 1 Jacob saw that there was corn in Egypt
42. 2 I have heard that there is corn in Egypt
44. 26 if our youngest brother be with us
Exod 17. 7 saying, Is the LORD among us or not?
Num. 9. 20, 21 And (so) it was, when the cloud was
13. 20 whether there be wood therein, or not
22. 29 I would there were a sword in mine hand
Deut 29. 18 Lest there should be among you man or
29. 18 lest there should be among you a root
Judg. 4. 20 Is there any man here? that thou shalt
6. 13 Oh my Lord, if the LORD be with us
18. 14 there is in these houses an ephod, and
19. 19 yet there is..and there is bread and
Ruth 3. 12 there is a kinsman nearer than I
1 Sa. 9. 11 and said unto them, Is the seer here?
9. 12 they answered them, and said, He is
14. 39 though it be in Jonathan my son, he
17. 46 may know that there is a God in Israel
20. 8 if there be in me iniquity, slay me thyself
21. 3 Now therefore what is under thine hand?
21. 4 but there is hallowed bread; if the young
21. 8 is there not here under thine hand spear
23. 23 it shall come to pass, if he be in the land
2 Sa. 9. 1 Is there yet any that is left of the house
14. 32 if there be..iniquity in me, let him kill
1 Ki. 18. 10 there is no nation or kingdom, whither
2 Ki. 2. 16 there be with thy servants fifty strong
3. 12 The word of the LORD is with him. So
5. 8 shall know that there is a prophet in
9. 15 Jehu said, If it be your minds..let none
10. 15 Is thine heart right..It is. If it be, give
10. 23 look that there be here with you none of
2 Ch. 15. 7 for your work shall be rewarded
25. 9 The LORD is able to give thee much more
Ezra 10. 2 there is hope in Israel concerning this
Neh. 5. 2 For there were that said, We, our sons
5. 3 also there were that said, We have
5. 4 There were also that said, We have
5. 5 of our daughters are brought unto
Esth. 3. 8 There is a certain people scattered abroad
Job 5. 1 if there be any that will answer
6. 6 is there (any) taste in the white of an egg
6. 30 Is there iniquity in my tongue? cannot
9. 33 Neither is there any daysman betwixt us
11. 18 thou shalt be secure, because there is
14. 7 For there is hope of a tree, if it be cut
16. 4 if your soul were in my soul's stead, I
25. 3 Is there any number of his armies? and
28. 1 Surely there is a vein for the silver, and
33. 23 If there be a messenger with him, an
Psa. 7. 3 if there be iniquity in my hands
14. 2 if there were any that did understand
53. 2 if there were..that did understand, that
58. 11 he is a God that judgeth in the earth
73. 11 is there knowledge in the most high?
135. 17 neither is there (any) breath in their
Prov. 11. 24 There is that scattereth, and yet
12. 18 There is that speaketh like the piercings
13. 7 There is that maketh himself rich, yet
13. 23 but there is..destroyed for want of
14. 12 There is a way which seemeth right unto a
16. 25 There is a way that seemeth right unto a
18. 24 there is a friend..sticketh closer than a
19. 18 Chasten thy son while there is hope, and
20. 15 There is gold, and a multitude of rubies
23. 18 surely there is an end; and thine
24. 14 then there shall be a reward, and thy
Eccl. 1. 10 Is there (any) thing whereof it may be
2. 21 there is a man whose labour (is) in
4. 8 There is one..and..not a second; yea, he
5. 13 There is a sore evil..I have seen under
6. 1 There is an evil which I have seen under
6. 11 Seeing there be many things that increase
7. 15 there is a just..and there is a wicked
8. 6 to every purpose there is time and
8. 14 There is a vanity..that there be just
8. 14 there be wicked..to whom it happeneth
9. 4 joined to all the living there is hope: for
10. 5 There is an evil..I have seen under the
Isa. 44. 8 Is there a God beside me? yea..I know
Jer. 5. 1 if there be..that executeth judgment
14. 22 Are there..among the vanities of the G.
23. 26 How long shall (this) be in the heart of
27. 18 and if the word of the LORD be with
31. 6 there shall be a day, (that) the watchmen
31. 16 for thy work shall be rewarded, saith the
31. 17 there is hope in thine end, saith the LORD
37. 17 Is there..word..There is: for, said he
Lam. 1. 12 see if there be any sorrow like unto my
3. 29 in the dust; if so be there may be hope
Jon. 4. 11 wherein are more than sixscore thousand
Mic. 2. 1 because it is in the power of their hand

5. *To hold off,* ἀπέχω *apechō.*
Matt 15. 8 This people..their heart is far from me
Mark 7. 6 This people..their heart is far from me
Luke 7. 6 when he was now not far from the house
15. 20 when he was yet a great way off, his
24. 13 which was from Jerusalem..threescore

6. *To lead on or away,* ἄγω, *agō.*
Luke 24. 21 to day is the third day since these things

7. *To rub through, pass the time,* διατρίβω.
Acts 25. 14 when they had been there many days

8. *With a view to, for,* εἰς *eis.*
Acts 13. 22 he raised up unto them David to be, v. 47.

9. *To be,* εἰμί *eimi,* Luke 20. 6; 1 Pe. 4. 11.

10. *To have,* ἔχω *echō.*
John 8. 57 Thou art not yet fifty years old, and hast
9. 21, 23 he is of age; ask him; 5. 6; 11. 17.
Acts 7. 1 Then said the high priest, Are th. Ac. 1. 12.
12. 15 she constantly affirmed that it was even so
17. 11 searched..whether those things were so
24. 9 assented, saying that these things were so
1 Ti. 5. 25 they that are otherwise cannot be hid

11. *To become,* γίνομαι *ginomai.*
Matt. 5. 45 That ye may be the children of your
6. 16 when ye fast, be not, as the hypocrites, of
8. 26 the sea; and there was a great calm
9. 29 According to your faith be it unto you
10. 16 be ye therefore wise as serpents, and
10. 25 It is enough..that he be as his master
12. 45 the last..of that man is worse than the
14. 15 when it was evening, his disciples came
15. 28 be it unto thee even as thou wilt
16. 2 said unto them, When it is evening, ye
17. 2 and his raiment was white as the light
18. 13 if so be that he find it, verily I say unto
19. 8 but from the beginning it was not so
20. 26 whosoever will be great among you, let
23. 26 the outside of them may be clean also
24. 20 pray ye that your flight be not in the
24. 21 such as was not since the beginning
24. 21 to this time, no, nor ever shall be
24. 32 When his branch is yet tender, and
24. 44 Therefore be ye also ready: for in such
26. 2 Ye know that after two days is..the
26. 5 Not on the feast..lest there be an uproar
26. 6 Now when Jesus was in Bethany, in the
26. 54 scriptures be fulfilled, that thus it must be
27. 45 there was darkness over all the land
28. 2 there was a great earthquake: for the
Mark 4. 10 when he was alone, they that were about
4. 39 the wind ceased, and there was a great
6. 14 for his name was spread abroad: and he
6. 26 the king was exceeding sorry; (yet) for
6. 35 when the day was..far spent, his disciples
9. 7 there was a cloud that overshadowed
9. 26 came out of him: and he was as one dead
9. 33 being in the house he asked them, What
10. 43 but whosoever will be great among you
10. 44 whosoever of you [will be] the chiefest
13. 7 for (such things) must needs be; but the
13. 18 pray ye that your flight be not in the
13. 19 such as was not..neither shall be
13. 28 When her branch is yet tender, and
15. 33 there was darkness over the whole land
16. 10 [went and told them that had been with]
Luke 1. 2 which from the beginning were eyewitness
1. 5 There was in the days of Herod, the
1. 38 be it unto me according to thy word
2. 2 was first made when Cyrenius was
2. 6 so it was, that, while they were there
2. 13 suddenly there was with the angel a
2. 42 when he was twelve years old, they went
4. 25 great famine was throughout all the land
4. 36 they were all amazed, and spake among
4. 42 when it was day, he departed and went
6. 13 when it was day, he called..his disciples
6. 16 Judas Iscariot, which also was the traitor
6. 36 Be ye therefore merciful, as your Father
6. 49 it fell; and the ruin of that house was
8. 24 and they ceased, and there was a calm
9. 29 the fashion of his countenance was
10. 32 likewise a Levite, when [he was] at the
10. 36 Which now of these..was neighbour unto
11. 26 last (state) of that man is worse than the
11. 30 as Jonas was a sign unto the Ninevites, so
12. 40 Be ye therefore ready also: for the Son
12. 54 ye say, There cometh a shower; and so it
13. 2 Suppose ye that these Galileans were
13. 4 think ye that they were sinners above all
15. 10 there is joy in the presence of the angels
16. 11 ye have not been faithful in the
16. 12 if ye have not been faithful in that
17. 26 And as it was in the days of Noe, so
17. 28 Likewise also as it was in the days of Lot
18. 23 when he heard this, he was very
18. 24 when Jesus saw that [he was] very
19. 17 because thou hast been faithful in a very
19. 19 And he said..Be thou also over five
20. 14 kill him, that the inheritance [may be]
20. 33 in the resurrection whose wife..is she?
22. 24 And there was also a strife among them
22. 26 let him be as the younger; and he that
22. 40 when he was at the place, he said unto
22. 44 [being in an agony..his sweat was as it]
22. 66 as soon as it was day, the elders..came
23. 24 that it should be as they required
23. 44 there was a darkness over all the earth
24. 5 And as they were afraid, and bowed
24. 19 which was a prophet mighty in deed and
24. 22 women..which were early at the sepulchre
24. 37 But they were terrified and affrighted
John 1. 6 There was a man sent from God, whose
1. 15 cometh after me is preferred before me
1. 27 coming after me is preferred before me
1. 30 a man which is preferred before me
2. 1 the third day there was a marriage in
3. 9 said unto him, How can these things be?
4. 14 shall be in him a well of water springing
6. 17 it was now dark, and Jesus was not come

John 6. 21 immediately the ship was at the land
7. 43 So there was a division among the people
8. 58 I say unto you, Before Abraham was, I
9. 22 he should be put out of the synagogue
9. 27 wherefore..will ye also be his disciples?
10. 16 there shall be one fold,(and) one shepherd
10. 19 There was a division therefore again
10. 22 it was at Jerusalem the feast of the
12. 36 that ye may be the children of light
12. 42 lest they should be put out of the
14. 22 how is it that thou wilt manifest thyself
15. 8 much fruit; so shall ye be my disciples
20. 27 Then saith he..be not faithless, but
Acts 1. 16 which was guide to them that took
1. 19 it was known unto all the dwellers at
1. 20 Let his habitation be desolate, and let no
4. 4 the number of the men was about five th.
5. 7 it was about the space of three hours
7. 29 was a stranger in the land of Madian
7. 38 This is he, that was in the church in the
7. 52 of whom ye have been now the betrayers
8. 1 at that time there was a great persecution
8. 8 And there was great joy in that city
9. 19 Then was Saul certain days with the
9. 42 it was known throughout all Joppa; and
10. 4 when he looked on him, he was afraid
10. 25 Peter was coming in, Cornelius met him
12. 18 as soon as it was day, there was no small
12. 23 he was eaten of worms, and gave up the
13. 5 when they were at Salamis, they preached
15. 7 when there had been much disputing
15. 39 the contention was so sharp between
16. 26 suddenly there was a great earthquake
16. 35 when it was day, the magistrates sent the
19. 17 this was known to all the Jews and Greeks
19. 21 After I have been there I must also see
19. 28 they were full of wrath, and cried out
20. 16 hasted, if it were possible for him, to be at
20. 18 I have been with you at all seasons
22. 9 with me saw..the light, and were afraid
22. 17 I prayed in the temple, I [was] in a trance
23. 12 it was day, certain of the Jews banded
25. 15 when I was at Jerusalem, the chief priests
26. 4 which was at the first among mine own
26. 19 I was not disobedient unto the heavenly
26. 28 almost thou persuadest me [to be] a Chris.
26. 29 were both almost and altogether such as
27. 36 Then were they all of good cheer, and
27. 39 when it was day, they knew not the land
27. 42 the soldiers' counsel was to kill the
Rom. 3. 4 let God be true, but every man a liar
6. 5 if we have been planted together in the
9. 29 we had been as Sodoma, and been made
11. 5 there is a remnant according to the
11. 6 otherwise grace is no more grace. But
11. 34 or who hath been his counsellor?
12. 16 Be not wise in your own conceits
15. 8 Jesus Christ was a minister of the circum.
15. 16 offering up of the Gentiles might be
15. 31 my service..may be accepted of the saints
16. 2 for she hath been a succourer of many
16. 7 who also were in Christ before me
1 Co. 2. 3 I was with you in weakness, and in fear
3. 18 let him become a fool, that he may be
4. 16 I beseech you, be ye followers of me
7. 23 with a price; be not ye the servants of
9. 23 that I might be partaker thereof with
9. 27 lest..I myself should be a castaway
10. 6 Now these things were our examples, to
10. 7 Neither be ye idolaters, as..some of them
11. 1 Be ye followers of me, even as I also..of
14. 20 be not children in understanding..be men
15. 10 which (was bestowed) upon me was not in
15. 37 thou sowest not that body that shall be
15. 58 Therefore, my beloved brethren, be ye
16. 2 that there be no gatherings when I come
16. 10 see that he may be with you without fear
2 Co. 1. 18 our word toward you [was] not yea and nay
1. 19 was not yea and nay, but in him was yea
3. 7 the ministration of death..was glorious
6. 14 Be ye not unequally yoked together with
8. 14 abundance also may be..that there may
Gal. 3. 17 the law, which was four hundred and
3. 24 Wherefore the law was our schoolmaster
4. 12 Brethren, I beseech you, be as I..for I am
5. 26 Let us not be desirous of vain glory
Eph. 4. 32 be ye kind one to another, tenderhearted
5. 1 Be ye therefore followers of God, as dear
5. 7 Be ye not therefore partakers with them
5. 17 Wherefore be ye not unwise, but underst.
6. 3 That it may be well with thee, and thou
Phil. 1. 13 So that my bonds in Christ are manifest
2. 15 That [ye may be] blameless and harmless
3. 17 Brethren, be followers together of me
3. 21 [that it may be fashioned like unto his]
Col. 3. 15 called in one body; and be ye thankful
4. 11 which have been a comfort unto me
1 Th. 1. 5 what manner of men we were among you
1. 7 So that ye were ensamples to all that
2. 1 know our entrance..that it was not in
2. 7 But we were gentle among you, even as
2. 8 our own souls, because ye were dear unto
3. 5 have tempted you, and our labour be in
1 Ti. 2. 14 the woman being deceived was in the
4. 12 but be thou an example of the believers
5. 9 a widow..having been the wife of one
2 Ti. 1. 17 But, when he was in Rome, he sought me
3. 9 manifest unto all..as their's also was
Heb. 2. 2 if the word spoken by angels was stedfast
2. 17 that he might be a merciful and faithful
5. 11 hard to be uttered, seeing ye are dull of
6. 12 That ye be not slothful, but followers of

Heb. 7. 18 For there is verily a disannulling v. 23
9. 22 without shedding of blood is no remission
11. 6 he is a rewarder of them that diligently
12. 8 all are partakers, then are ye bastards
Jas. 1. 12 for when he is tried, he shall receive the
1. 22 be ye doers of the word, and not hearers
1. 25 he being not a forgetful hearer, but a
2. 10 and yet offend in one (point), he is guilty
3. 1 My brethren, be not many masters
3. 10 brethren, these things ought not so to be
5. 2 and your garments are moth eaten
1 Pe. 1. 15 be ye holy in all manner of conversation
1. 16 Because it is written, [Be ye] holy; for I
3. 6 whose daughters ye are, as long as ye do
3. 13 if ye be followers of that which is good?
4. 12 concerning the fiery trial which is to try
5. 3 but being ensamples to the flock
2 Pe. 1. 4 by these ye might be partakers of the
1. 16 but were eyewitnesses of his majesty
1. 20 no prophecy of the scripture is of any
2. 1 there were false prophets also among
2. 20 the latter end is worse with them than
1 Jo. 2. 18 even now are there many antichrists
3 Jo. 8 that we might be fellowhelpers to the
Rev. 1. 9 was in the isle that is called Patmos, for
1. 10 I was in the Spirit on the Lord's day
1. 18 I (am) he that liveth, and was dead; and
1. 19 and the things which shall be hereafter
2. 8 the first and the last, which was dead
2. 10 be thou faithful unto death, and I will
3. 2 Be watchful, and strengthen the things
4. 1 will shew thee things which must be
4. 2 And immediately I was in the spirit
6. 12 and, lo, there was a great earthquake
8. 1 there was silence in heaven about the
8. 5 there were voices, and thunderings, and
11. 13 same hour was there a great earthquake
11. 13 and the remnant were affrighted, and
11. 15 there were great voices in heaven, saying
11. 19 there were lightnings, and voices, and
12. 7 And there was war in heaven: Michael
16. 10 and his kingdom was full of darkness
16. 18 there were voices, and thunders, and
16. 18 [there was] a great earthquake, such as
16. 18 not since men were upon the earth, so

12. *To place down, or fast*, καθίστημι *kathistēmi.*
Jas. 3. 6 so is the tongue among our members
4. 4 a friend of the world is the enemy of God

13. *To lie, be laid*, κεῖμαι *keimai.*
2 Co. 3. 15 Moses is read, the vail is upon their

14. *To be about to*, μέλλω *mellō.*
Matt 11. 14 This is Elias, which was for to come
Luke 19. 4 to see him, for he was to pass that (way)
Acts 21. 27 when the seven days were almost ended
Rev. 12. 5 who was to rule all nations with a rod of

15. *To do, spend*, ποιέω *poieō.*
2 Co. 11. 25 a night and a day I have been in the

16. *To go up with*, συμβαίνω *sumbainō.*
Acts 21. 35 so it was, that he was borne of the

17. *To hit, chance*, τυγχάνω *tugchanō.*
1 Co. 14. 10 There are, it may be, so many kinds of
16. 6 And it may be that I will abide, yea, and

18. *To begin gradually, be*, ὑπάρχω *huparchō.*
Luke 8. 41 he was a ruler of the synagogue: and he
9. 48 he that is least among you all, the same
11. 13 If ye..being evil, know how to give good
16. 14 And the Pharisees also, who were covetous
16. 23 he lifted up his eyes, being in torments
Acts 2. 30 being a prophet, and knowing that God
4. 34 Neither [was there] any among them that
4. 34 for as many as were possessors of lands
5. 4 Whiles it remained, was it not thine own?
7. 55 But he, being full of the Holy Ghost
8. 16 only they were baptized in the name of
10. 12 Wherein were all manner of four footed
14. 8 [being] a cripple from his mother's womb
16. 3 for they knew all that his father was a
16. 20 These men, being Jews, do exceedingly
16. 37 being Romans, and have cast (us) into
17. 24 seeing that he is Lord of heaven and
17. 27 though he be not far from every one of
17. 29 Forasmuch then as we are the offspring
19. 36 ye ought to be quiet, and to do nothing
19. 40 there being no cause whereby we may
21. 20 believe; and they are all zealous of the
22. 3 was zealous toward God, as ye all are
27. 12 the haven was not commodious to winter
27. 34 for this is for your health: for there
28. 7 In the same quarters were possessions of
28. 18 because there was no cause of death in
Rom. 4. 19 when he was about an hundred years old
1 Co. 7. 26 I suppose therefore that this is good for
11. 7 forasmuch as he is the image and glory
11. 18 I hear that there be divisions among you
12. 22 the body, which seem to be more feeble
2 Co. 8. 17 being more forward, of his own accord
12. 16 being crafty, I caught you with guile
Gal. 1. 14; 2. 14; Phil. 2. 6; 3. 20; Jas. 2. 15; 2 Pe. 1. 8; 2. 19; 3. 11.

19. *To be a sojourner*, ἐπιδημέω *epidēmeō*, Acts 17. 21.

20. *To remain*, μένω *menō*, Acts 5. 4.

21. *To bear*, φέρω *pherō*, Heb. 9. 16.

BE SO, to —*To will*, θέλω *thelō*, 1 Pe. 3. 17.

BE, to be ordained to —
To become, γίνομαι *ginomai.*
Acts 1. 22 must one be ordained to be a witness

BE with, to —
1. *To remain toward*, προσμένω *prosmenō.*
Mark 8. 2 because they have now been with me

2. *To be with (a thing)*, σύνειμι *suneimi.*
Luke 9. 18 he was..praying, his disciples were with
Acts 22. 11 led by the hand of them that were with

BEACON —
A signal, pole, mast, תֹּרֶן *toren.*
Isa. 30. 17 as a beacon upon the top of a mountain

BE-AL'-IAH, בְּעַלְיָה *Jah is lord.*
A man who joined David at Ziklag, B.C. 1058.
1 Ch. 12. 5 Eluzai, and Jerimoth, and B., and

BE-A'-LOTH, בְּעָלוֹת *ladies, mistresses.*
A city in the S.E. of Judah, near Salem. It is now called *Kurnub*, and is S. W. of *Dhullam.*
Josh. 15. 24 [uttermost cities..were]..Telem, and B.

BEAM —
1. *A weaver's beam*, אֶרֶג *ereg.*
Judg 16. 14 went away with the pin of the beam

2. *A board*, גֵּב *geb.*
1 Ki. 6. 9 and covered the house with beams

3. *Cross beam, splinter*, כָּפִיס *kaphis.*
Hab. 2. 11 the beam out of the timber shall answer

4. *A weaver's beam, yoke*, מָנוֹר *manor.*
1 Sa. 17. 7 his spear (was) like a weaver's beam
2 Sa. 21. 19 whose spear (was) like a weaver's beam
1 Ch. 11. 23 hand (was) a spear like a weaver's beam
20. 5 spear-staff (was) like a weaver's beam

5. *A rib*, צֵלָע *tsela.*
1 Ki. 7. 3 covered with cedar above upon..beams

6. *A cross beam*, קוֹרָה *qurah.*
2 Ki. 6. 2 and take thence every man a beam
6. 5 as one was felling a beam, the ax head
2 Ch. 3. 7 the beams, the posts, and the walls
Song 1. 17 The beams of our house (are) cedar..our

7. *A beam, rafter*, δοκός *dokos.*
Matt. 7. 3 the beam that is in thine own eye?
7. 4 behold, a beam (is) in thine own eye?
7. 5 first cast out the beam out of thine own
Luke 6. 41 the beam that is in thine own eye?
6. 42 the beam that is in thine own eye?
6. 42 first the beam out of thine own eye

BEAM, thick —
A thick beam, עָב *ab.*
1 Ki. 7. 6 the (other) pillars and the thick beam

BEAMS —
Hewed beams, כְּרֻתוֹת *keruthoth.*
1 Ki. 6. 36 hewed stone, and a row of cedar beams
7. 2 with cedar beams upon the pillars
7. 12 hewed stones, and a row of cedar beams

BEAMS, to lay —
To cause (beams) to meet, קָרָה *qarah*, 3.
Psa. 104. 3 Who layeth the beams of his chambers
Neh. 3. 3 who..laid the beams thereof, and set
3. 6 they laid the beams thereof, and set up

BEAMS, to make —
To cause (beams) to meet, קָרָה *qarah*, 3.
Neh. 2. 8 he may give me timber to make beams

BEANS —
Bean, pea, פּוֹל *pol.*
2 Sa. 17. 28 and flour, and parched (corn), and beans
Eze. 4. 9 Take..wheat, and barley, and beans

BEAR —
1. *A bear (hairy, shaggy animal)*, דֹּב, דּוֹב *dob.*
1 Sa. 17. 34 there came a lion, and a bear, and took
17. 36 Thy servant slew both..lion and..bear
17. 37 delivered me..out of the paw of the bear
2 Sa. 17. 8 as a bear robbed of her whelps in the
Prov. 17. 12 Let a bear robbed of her whelps meet a
28. 15 (As) a roaring lion, and a ranging bear
Isa. 11. 7 And the cow and the bear shall feed
59. 11 We roar all like bears, and mourn sore
Lam. 3. 10 He (was) unto me (as) a bear lying in
Dan. 7. 5 another beast, a second, like to a bear
Hos. 13. 8 as a bear..bereaved..and will rend the
Amos 5. 19 As if a man did flee..and a bear met

2. *A bear*, ἄρκτος *arktos.*
Rev. 13. 2 his feet were as..of a bear, and his

BEARS, she —
A bear, דּוֹב *dob.*
2 Ki. 2. 24 there came forth two she bears out of the

BEAR, to —
1. *To conceive*, הָרָה *harah.*
1 Ch. 4. 17 she bare Miriam, and Shammai, and

2. *To sow*, זָרַע *zara.*
Gen. 1. 29 I have given you every herb bearing seed

3. *To be pained*, חוּל *chul*, 3a.
Isa. 51. 2 Abraham..and unto Sarah (that) bare

4. *To bear, yield, bring forth, beget*, יָלַד *yalad.*
Gen. 4. 1 she conceived, and bare Cain, and said
4. 2 she again bare his brother Abel. And
4. 17 she conceived, and bare Enoch: and he
4. 20 Adah bare Jabal: he was the father of
4. 22 Zillah, she also bare Tubal-cain, an
4. 25 she bare a son, and called his name Seth

Gen. 6. 4 they bare..to them, the same..mighty
16. 1 Sarai Abram's wife bare him no children
16. 2 the LORD..restrained me from bearing
16. 11 thou (art) with child, and shalt bear a
16. 15 Hagar bare Abram a son: and Abram
16. 15 his son's name, which Hagar bare, Ishm.
16. 16 when Hagar bare Ishmael to Abram
17. 19 Sarah thy wife shall bear thee a son
17. 21 which Sarah shall bear unto thee at this
18. 13 Shall I of a surety bear a child, which
19. 37 the firstborn bare a son, and called his
19. 38 she also bare a son, and called his name
20. 17 wife, and..maidservants; and they bare
21. 2 Sarah conceived, and bare Abraham a son
21. 3 unto him, whom Sarah bare to him, Isaac
21. 7 for I have born..a son in his old age
21. 9 she had born unto Abraham, mocking
22. 20 she hath also born children unto thy
22. 23 these eight Milcah did bear to Nahor
22. 24 his concubine..bare also Tebah, and
24. 24 son of Milcah, which she bare unto
24. 36 my master's wife bare a son to my
24. 47 Nahor's son, whom Milcah bare unto
25. 2 And she bare him Zimran, and Jokshan
25. 12 Sarah's handmaid, bare unto Abraham
25. 26 threescore years old when she bare them
29. 32 And Leah conceived, and bare a son
29. 33, 34, she conceived again, and bare a son
29. 34 because I have born him three sons
29. 35 she conceived again, and bare a son
29. 35 called his name Judah; and left bearing
30. 1 Rachel saw that she bare Jacob no
30. 3 and she shall bear upon my knees, that I
30. 5 Bilhah conceived, and bare Jacob a son
30. 7 Rachel's maid conceived again, and bare
30. 9 Leah saw that she had left bearing
30. 10 Zilpah Leah's maid bare Jacob a son
30. 12 Zilpah Leah's maid bare Jacob a second
30. 17 she conceived, and bare Jacob the fifth
30. 19 Leah conceived again, and bare Jacob
30. 20 because I have born him six sons: and
30. 21 afterwards she bare a daughter, and
30. 23 she conceived, and bare a son; and said
30. 25 it came to pass, when Rachel had born J.
31. 8 then all the cattle bare speckled
31. 8 then bare all the cattle ringstraked
31. 43 their children which they have born?
34. 1 Dinah..which she bare unto Jacob
36. 4 Adah bare to Esau..Bashemath bare Reuel
36. 5 Aholibamah bare Jeush, and Jaalam, and
36. 12 Timna..she bare to Eliphaz Amalek
36. 14 she bare to Esau Jeush, and Jaalam
38. 3 she conceived, and bare a son; and he
38. 4 she conceived again, and bare a son
38. 5 she yet again conceived, and bare a son
38. 5 he was at Chezib, when she bare him
41. 50 two sons..which Asenath..bare unto
44. 27 Ye know that my wife bare me two (sons)
46. 15 These (be) the sons of Leah, which she bare
46. 18 these she bare unto Jacob, (even) sixteen
46. 20 daughter of Poti-pherah priest of On bare
46. 25 and she bare these unto Jacob..seven
Exod. 2. 2 the woman conceived, and bare a son
2. 22 she bare..a son, and he called his name
6. 20 and she bare him Aaron and Moses
6. 23 she bare him Nadab, and Abihu, Eleazar
6. 25 she bare him Phinehas: these (are) the
21. 4 she have born him sons or daughters
Lev. 12. 2 conceived seed, and born a man child
12. 5 But if she bear a maid child, then she
12. 7 that hath born a male or a female
Num 26. 59 bare to Levi in Egypt: and she bare
Deut 21. 15 they have born him children..the
25. 6 the first-born which she beareth shall
28. 57 toward her children which she shall bear
Judg. 8. 31 she also bare him a son, whose name he
11. 2 Gilead's wife bare him sons; and his
13. 2 Manoah..his wife (was) barren, and bare
13. 3 now, thou (art) barren, and bearest not
13. 3, 5, 7 thou shalt conceive, and bear a son
13. 24 the woman bare a son, and called his
Ruth 1. 12 also to night, and should also bear sons
4. 12 Pharez, whom Tamar bare unto Judah
4. 13 the LORD gave..conception, and she bare
4. 15 thy daughter in law..hath born him
1 Sa. 1. 20 she bare a son, and called his name
2. 5 so that the barren hath born seven
2. 21 that she conceived, and bare three sons
4. 20 Fear not; for thou hast born a son
2 Sa. 11. 27 she became his wife, and bare him a son
12. 15 struck the child that Uriah's wife bare
12. 24 she bare a son, and he called his name S.
21. 8 the daughter of Aiah, whom she bare
1 Ki. 1. 6 and (his mother) bare him after Absalom
3. 21 it was not my son, which I did bear
11 20 the sister of Tahpenes bare him Genubath
2 Ki. 4. 17 the woman conceived, and bare a son
1 Ch. 1. 32 she bare Zimram, and Jokshan, and
2. 4 Tamar his daughter in law bare him
2. 17 And Abigail bare Amasa: and the
2. 19 Caleb took unto him Ephrath, which bare
2. 21 Hezron..and she bare him Segub
2. 24 Abiah; Hezron's wife bare him Ashur the
2. 29 and she bare him Ahban, and Molid
2. 35 gave his daughter..she bare him Attai
2. 46 Caleb's concubine, bare Haran, and
2. 48 Caleb's concubine, bare Sheber, and
2. 49 She bare also Shaaph the father of
4. 6 And Naarah bare him Ahuzam, and
4. 9 saying, Because I bare him with sorrow
4. 18 his wife Jehudijah bare Jered the father
7. 14 sons of Manasseh; Ashriel..she bare

1 Ch. 7. 14 his concubine the Aramitess bare Machir
7. 16 Maachah the wife of Machir bare a son
7. 18 his sister Hammoleketh bare Ishod, and
7. 23 she conceived, and bare a son, and he
2 Ch. 11. 19 Which bare him children; Jeush and
11. 20 the daughter of Absalom..bare him
Job 24. 21 He evil entreateth..barren (that) beareth
Prov. 17. 25 and bitterness to her that bare him
23. 25 and she that bare thee shall rejoice
Eccl. 3. 2 A time to be born, and a time to die
Song 6. 9 she (is) the choice (one) of her that bare
8. 5 she brought thee forth (that) bare thee
Isa. 7. 14 a virgin shall conceive, and bear a son
8. 3 and she conceived, and bare a son
54. 1 Sing, O barren, thou (that) didst not bear
Jer. 15. 9 She that hath borne seven languisheth
15. 10 thou hast borne me a man of strife
16. 3 their mothers that bare them
20. 14 the day wherein my mother bare me
22. 26 thee out, and thy mother that bare thee
29. 6 that they may bear sons and daughters
50. 12 she that bare you shall be ashamed
Eze. 16. 20 thy daughters, whom thou hast borne
23. 4 and they were mine, and they bare sons
23. 37 caused their sons, whom they bare unto
Hos. 1. 3 which conceived, and bare him a son
1. 6 she conceived again, and bare a daughter
1. 8 Lo ruhamah, she conceived, and bare a

5. *To cause to go*, יָלַךְ *yalak*, 5.
Zech. 5. 10 Whither do these bear the ephah?

6. *To contain*, כּוּל *kul*, 5.
Amos 7. 10 the land is not able to bear all his words

7. *To lift up*, נָטַל *natal.*
Lam. 3. 28 because he hath borne (it) upon him

8. *To lift up*, נָטַל *natal*, 3.
Isa. 63. 9 he bare them, and carried them all the

9. *To lift up, bear, bear away*, נָשָׂא *nasa.*
Gen. 4. 13 My punishment (is) greater than I can b.
7. 17 the waters increased, and bare up the ark
13. 6 the land was not able to bear them, that
36. 7 could not bear them because of their
Exod 18. 22 be easier for thyself, and they shall bear
19. 4 I bare you on eagles' wings, and brought
25. 14 that the ark may be borne with them
25. 27 places of the staves to bear the table
25. 28 that the table may be borne with them
27. 7 and the staves shall be..to bear it
28. 12 Aaron shall bear their names before the
28. 29 Aaron shall bear the names of the child.
28. 30 Aaron shall bear the judgment of the
28. 38 Aaron may bear the iniquity of the holy
28. 43 that they bear not iniquity, and die
30. 4 places for the staves to bear it withal
37. 5 he put the staves..to bear the ark
37. 14 places for the staves to bear the table
37. 15 he made the staves..to bear the table
37. 27 places for the staves to bear it withal
38. 7 he put the staves..to bear it withal
Lev. 5. 1 if he do not utter (it), then he shall bear
5. 17 yet is he guilty, and shall bear his
7. 18 the soul that eateth of it shall bear his
10. 17 hath given it you to bear the iniquity
11. 25 whosoever beareth..of the carcase of
11. 28 he that beareth the carcase of them shall
11. 40 he also that beareth the carcase of it
15. 10 he that beareth (any of) those things
16. 22 And the goat shall bear upon him all
17. 16 nor bathe..then he shall bear his iniquity
19. 8 that eateth it shall bear his iniquity
20. 17 a wicked thing..he shall bear his iniquity
20. 19 near kin: they shall bear their iniquity
20. 20 they shall bear their sin; they shall die
22. 9 lest they bear sin for it, and die therefore
22. 16 Or suffer them to bear the iniquity of
24. 15 Whosoever curseth his God shall bear his
Num. 1. 50 they shall bear the tabernacle, and all
4. 15 the sons of Kohath shall come to bear (it)
4. 25 they shall bear the curtains of the
5. 31 and this woman shall bear her iniquity
7. 9 they should bear upon their shoulders
9. 13 that man shall bear his sin
11. 12 as a nursing father beareth the sucking
11. 14 I am not able to bear all this people
11. 17 they shall bear the burden of the people
11. 17 that thou bear (it) not thyself alone
13. 23 they bare it between two upon a staff
14. 33 bear your whoredoms, until your carcases
14. 34 each day for a year, shall ye bear your
18. 1 shall bear the iniquity of the sanctuary
18. 1 thy sons with thee shall bear the iniquity
18. 22 Neither must..lest they bear sin, and
18. 23 they shall bear their iniquity: (it shall be)
18. 32 ye shall bear no sin by reason of it, when
30. 15 then he shall bear her iniquity
Deut. 1. 9 saying, I am not able to bear you myself
1. 12 How can I myself alone bear your
1. 31 how that the LORD thy God bare thee, as
1. 31 man doth bear his son, in all the way
10. 8 to bear the ark of the covenant of the
31. 9, 25 which bare the ark of the covenant of
32. 11 As an eagle..beareth them on her wings
Josh. 3. 8 the priests that bare the ark of the
3. 13 of the priests that bear the ark of the
3. 15 as they that bare the ark were come unto
3. 15 the feet of the priests that bare the ark
3. 17 the priests that bare the ark of the
4. 9 the feet of the priests which bare the ark
4. 10 For the priests which bare the ark stood

Josh. 4. 16 Command the priests that bear the ark
4. 18 when the priests that bare the ark of the
6. 4 seven priests shall bear before the ark
6. 6 let seven priests bear seven trumpets of
8. 33 which bare the ark of the covenant of
Judg. 3. 18 he sent away the people that bare the
1 Sa. 14. 1 said unto the young man that bare his
14. 6 said to the young man that bare his
17. 41 the man that bare the shield (went) before
2 Sa. 6. 13 when they that bare the ark of the LORD
18. 15 ten young men that bare Joab's armour
1 Ki. 2. 26 because thou barest the ark of the LORD
5. 15 ten thousand that bare burdens, and
10. 2 she came..with camels that bare spices
14. 28 that the guard bare them, and brought
2 Ki. 5. 23 servants: and they bare (them) before him
18. 14 that which thou puttest on me will I bear
1 Ch. 5. 18 men able to bear buckler and sword, and
12. 24 children of Judah that bare shield and
15. 15 children of the Levites bare the ark of
15. 26 God helped the Levites that bare the ark
15. 27 and all the Levites that bare the ark
2 Ch. 9. 1 and camels that bare spices, and gold in
14. 8 an army (of men) that bare targets and
14. 8 that bare shields and drew bows, two
Neh. 4. 17 and they that bare burdens, with those
Job 34. 31 I have borne (chastisement), I will not
Psa. 55. 12 then I could have borne (it): neither (was)
69. 7 for thy sake I have borne reproach; shame
89. 50 I do bear in my bosom (the reproach of)
91. 12 They shall bear thee up in (their) hands
Prov. 9. 12 (if) thou scornest, thou alone shalt bare
18. 14 but a wounded spirit who can bear?
30. 21 and for four (which) it cannot bear
Isa. 1. 14 a trouble unto me; I am weary to bear
22. 6 Elam bare the quiver with chariots of
46. 4 I have made, and I will bear; even I will
46. 7 They bear him upon the shoulder, they
52. 11 be ye clean, that bear the vessels of the
53. 4 he hath borne our griefs, and carried our
53. 12 and he bare the sin of many, and made
Jer. 10. 5 they must needs be borne, because they
10. 19 Truly this (is) a grief, and I must bear it
17. 21 bear no burden on the sabbath day, nor
17. 27 not to bear a burden, even entering in at
31. 19 I did bear the reproach of my youth
44. 22 the LORD could no longer bear, because
Lam. 3. 27 good for a man that he bear the yoke in
Eze. 4. 4 that thou shalt lie upon it thou shalt bear
4. 5 so shalt thou bear the iniquity of the
4. 6 and thou shalt bear the iniquity of the
12. 6 shalt thou bear (it) upon (thy) shoulders
12. 7 I bare (it) upon (my) shoulder in their
12. 12 the prince that (is) among them shall bear
14. 10 they shall bear the punishment of their
16. 52 bear thine own shame for thy sins that
16. 52 yea, be thou confounded also, and bear
16. 54 That thou mayest bear thine own shame
16. 58 Thou hast borne thy lewdness and thine
17. 8 that it might bear fruit, that it might be
18. 19 doth not the son bear the iniquity of the
18. 20 The son shall not bear the iniquity of the
18. 20 shall the father bear the iniquity of the
23. 35 therefore bear thou also thy lewdness
23. 49 ye shall bear the sins of your idols: and
32. 24 yet have they borne their shame with
32. 25 yet have they borne their shame with
32. 30 and bear their shame with them that go
34. 29 neither bare the shame of the heathen
36. 6 ye have borne the shame of the heathen
36. 7 about you, they shall bear their shame
36. 15 neither shalt thou bear the reproach of
39. 26 that they have borne their shame, and all
44. 10 they shall even bear their iniquity
44. 12 and they shall bear their iniquity
44. 13 they shall bear their shame, and their
Joel 2. 22 the tree beareth her fruit, the fig tree
Amos 5. 26 ye have borne the tabernacle of your
Mic. 6. 16 ye shall bear the reproach of my people
7. 9 I will bear the indignation of the LORD
Hag. 2. 12 If one bear holy flesh in the skirt of his
Zech. 6. 13 he shall bear the glory, and shall sit and

10. *To bear, carry away*, סָבַל *sabal.*
Gen. 49. 15 and bowed his shoulder to bear, and
Isa. 53. 11 many; for he shall bear their iniquities
Lam. 5. 7 and we have borne their iniquities

11. *To do, make*, עָשָׂה *asah.*
2 Ki. 19. 30 take root downward, and bear fruit
Isa. 37. 31 take root downward, and bear fruit
Eze. 17. 23 shall bring forth boughs, and bear fruit
Hos. 9. 16 their root is dried up, they shall bear no

12. *To be fruitful*, פָּרָה *parah.*
Deut 29. 18 a root that beareth gall and wormwood

13. *To cause to sprout*, צָמַח *tsamach*, 5.
Deut 29. 23 burning..it is not sown, nor beareth

14. *To lift up, bear on, or away*, αἴρω *airō.*
Matt 27. 32 him they compelled to bear his cross
Mark 2. 3 sick of the palsy, which was borne of four
15. 21 the father of Alexander..to bear his cross

15. *To bear upward*, ἀναφέρω *anapherō.*
Heb. 9. 28 Christ was once offered to bear the sins
1 Pe. 2. 24 Who his own self bare our sins in his own

16. *To bear, take up, carry*, βαστάζω *bastazō.*
Matt. 3. 11 whose shoes I am not worthy to bear
8. 17 Himself took our infirmities, and bare
20. 12 which have borne the burden..of the day
Luke 7. 14 and they that bare (him) stood still
11. 27 Blessed (is) the womb that bare thee

Luke 14. 27 whosoever doth not bear his cross..cannot
John 12. 6 and had the bag, and bare what was put
16. 12 but ye cannot bear them now
20. 15 if thou have borne him hence, tell me
Acts 9. 15 to bear my name before the Gentiles
15. 10 our fathers nor we were able to bear?
21. 35 was borne of the soldiers for the violence
Rom 11. 18 thou bearest not the root, but the root
15. 1 We then that are strong ought to bear
Gal. 5. 10 he that troubleth you shall bear his
6. 2 Bear ye one another's burdens
6. 5 For every man shall bear his own burden
6. 17 I bear in my body the marks of the Lord
Rev. 2. 2 thou canst not bear them which are evil
2. 3 And hast borne, and hast patience, and

17. *To bear or beget (children)*, *γεννάω gennaō.*
Luke 1. 13 thy wife Elisabeth shall bear thee a son
23. 29 Blessed (are) the..wombs that never bare

18. *To bear out*, *ἐκφέρω ekpherō.*
Heb. 6. 8 But that which beareth thorns and briers

19. *To do, make*, *ποιέω poieō.*
Luke 8. 8 and sprang up, and bare fruit an hundred
13. 9 And if it bear fruit, (well): and if not
Jas. 3. 12 Can the fig tree, my brethren, bear o. b.
Rev. 22. 2 the tree of life, which bare twelve

20. *To cover closely, endure*, *στέγω stegō.*
1 Co. 13. 7 Beareth all things, believeth all things

21. *To beget, bring forth*, *τίκτω tiktō.*
Gal. 4. 27 Rejoice, (thou) barren that bearest not

22. *To bear, carry*, *φέρω pherō.*
Luke 23. 26 that he might bare (it) after Jesus
John 2. 8 Draw out now, and bear..And they bare
15. 2 Every branch in me that beareth not
15. 2 every (branch) that beareth fruit, he
15. 4 As the branch cannot bear fruit of itself
15. 8 is my Father glorified, that ye bear

23. *To bear habitually, wear*, *φορέω phoreō.*
Rom 13. 4 for he beareth not the sword in vain
1 Co. 15. 49 as we have borne the image of the earthy
15. 49 we shall also bear the image of the

24. *To bear up under*, *ὑποφέρω hupopherō.*
1 Co 10. 13 that ye may be able to bear (it)

BEAR, to be able to —
To lift up, bear, endure, נָשָׂא *nasa.*
Gen. 4. 13 punishment (is) greater than I can bear
13. 6 the land was not able to bear them
Psa. 55. 12 an enemy..then I could have borne (it)

BEAR, to suffer to —
To cause to lift up, נָשָׂא *nasa*, 5.
Lev 22. 16 suffer them to bear the iniquity of

BEAR long, to —
To suffer long, *μακροθυμέω makrothumeō.*
Luke 18. 7 unto him, though he bear long with

BEAR out, to —
To cause to go forth, יָצָא *yatsa*, 5.
Eze. 46. 20 they bear (them) not out into the utter

BEAR, that—
A lifter up, נָטִיל *natil.*
Zeph. 1. 11 Howl..all they that bear silver are cut

BEAR up, to —
1. *To lift up*, נָשָׂא *nasa.*
Gen. 7. 17 the waters increased, and bare up the

2. *To rectify, fix, establish*, תָּכַן *takan*, 3.
Psa. 75. 3 are dissolved; I bear up the pillars of it

3. *To lift up*, *αἴρω airō.*
Matt. 4. 6 in (their) hands they shall bear thee up
Luke 4. 11 in (their) hands they shall bear thee up

BEAR up into, to —
To look eye to eye, *ἀντοφθαλμέω antophthalmeō.*
Acts 27. 15 could not bear up into the wind

BEAR with, to —
To hold up, *ἀνέχομαι anechomai.*
Acts 18. 14 reason would that I should bear with you
2 Co. 11. 1 Would to God ye could bear with me
11 1 in (my) folly: and indeed bear with me
11 4 accepted, ye might well bear with (him)

BEAR witness, to — [*See* **WITNESS.**]
To answer, respond, עָנָה *anah.*
Job 16. 8 leanness rising up in me beareth witness

BEARD —
1. *The beard*, זָקָן *zaqan.*
Lev. 13. 29 a plague upon the head or the beard
13. 30 (even) a leprosy upon the head or beard
14. 9 his hair off his head and his beard
19. 27 shalt thou mar the corners of thy beard
21 5 they shave off the corner of their beard
1 Sa. 17 35 I caught..by his beard, and smote him
21 13 let his spittle fall down upon his beard
2 Sa. 10. 4 shaved off the one half of their beards
10. 5 Tarry at Jericho until your beards be
20. 9 Joab took Amasa by the beard with the
1 Ch 19. 5 Tarry at Jericho until your beards be
Ezra 9. 3 plucked off the hair of..my beard
Psa 133. 2 the head, that ran down upon the beard
133 2 Aaron's beard: that went down to..his
Isa. 7. 20 it shall also consume the beard
15. 2 on..their heads..baldness..every beard
Jer. 41. 5 having their beards shaven, and their
48. 37 For every head..bald, and every beard
Eze. 5. 1 upon thine head and upon thy beard

2. *The chin or upper lip*, שָׂפָם *sapham.*
2 Sa. 19. 24 dressed his feet, nor trimmed his beard

BEARING —
1. *To lift up, bare, carry away*, נָשָׂא *nasa.*
Gen. 37. 25 their camels bearing spicery and balm
Num 10. 17 sons of Merari set forward, bearing the
10. 21 Kohathites set forward, bearing the
Josh. 3. 3 the priests the Levites bearing it, then
3. 14 priests bearing the ark of the covenant
6. 8 seven priests bearing the seven trumpets
6. 13 seven priests bearing seven trumpets of
1 Sa. 17. 7 and one bearing a shield went before
2 Sa. 15. 24 bearing the ark of the covenant of God

2. *To carry*, *βαστάζω bastazō.*
Mark 14. 13 a man bearing a pitcher of water
Luke 22. 10 a man meet you, bearing a pitcher of
John 19. 17 he bearing his cross went forth into a

3. *To bear*, *φέρω pherō.*
Heb. 13. 13 without the camp, bearing his reproach

BEARING about —
To bear about, *περιφέρω peripherō.*
2 Co. 4. 10 Always bearing about in the body the
[*See also* Armour, blame, burdens, children, fruit, grudge, loss, record, rule, take, testimony, tidings, twins, witness.]

BEAST —
1. *Cattle, quadruped*, בְּהֵמָה *behemah.*
Gen. 6. 7 both man, and beast, and the creeping
7. 2 every clean beast thou shalt take to thee
7. 2 and of beasts that (are) not clean by two
7. 8 clean beasts, and of beasts that (are) not
8. 20 took of every clean beast, and of every
34. 23 their substance and every beast of their's
36. 6 his cattle, and all his beasts, and all
Exod. 8. 17 it became lice in man, and in beast; all
8. 18 there were lice upon man, and upon b.
9. 9 a boil..blains upon man, and upon beast
9. 10 (with) blains upon man, and upon beast
9. 19 every man and beast which shall be found
9. 22 upon man, and upon beast, and upon
9. 25 all..in the field, both man and beast
11. 5 shall die..and all the firstborn of beasts
11. 7 move his tongue, against man or beast
12. 12 smite all the firstborn..man and beast
13. 2 firstborn..of man and of beast: it (is)
13. 12 every firstling that cometh of a beast
13. 15 of man, and the firstborn of beast
19. 13 shot through; whether (it be) beast or
22. 10 an ox, or a sheep, or any beast to keep
22. 19 Whosoever lieth with a beast shall
Lev. 7. 21 uncleanness of man, or (any) unclean b.
7. 25 For whosoever eateth the fat of the beast
7. 26 blood..of fowl or of beast, in any of your
11. 2 among all the beasts that (are) on
11. 3 (and) cheweth the cud, among the beasts
11. 26 (The carcases) of every beast which
11. 39 And if any beast, of which ye may eat
11. 46 This (is) the law of the beasts, and of the
18. 23 Neither shalt thou lie with any beast
18. 23 shall any woman stand before a beast
20. 15 lie with a beast..ye shall slay the beast
20. 16 And if a woman approach unto any beast
20. 16 thou shalt kill the woman, and the beast
20. 25 therefore put difference between..beasts
20. 25 not make your souls abominable by beast
24. 21 And he that killeth a beast, he shall
27. 9 if (it be) a beast, whereof men bring
27. 10 he shall at all change beast for beast
27. 11 And if..any unclean beast, of which they
27. 11 he shall present the beast before the
27. 26 Only the firstling of the beasts, which
27. 27 And if..of an unclean beast, then he
27. 28 all that he hath, (both) of man and beast
Num. 3. 13 the first born in Israel, both man and beast
8. 17 of Israel (are) mine..man and beast: on
18. 15 of men or beasts, shall be thine
18. 15 the firstling of unclean beasts shalt thou
31. 11 all the prey, (both) of men and of beasts
31 26 that was taken, (both) of man and of beast
31. 30 take..of the flocks, of all manner of beasts
31. 47 one portion..(both) of man and of beast
Deut. 4. 17 The likeness of any beast that (is) on the
14. 4 These (are) the beasts which ye shall eat
14. 6 And every beast that parteth the hoof
14. 6 cheweth the cud among the beasts, that
27. 21 he that lieth with any manner of beast
28. 26 be meat..unto the beasts of the earth, and
32. 24 I..send the teeth of beasts upon them
Judg 20. 48 as the beast, and all that came to hand
1 Sa. 17. 44 I will give thy flesh..to the beasts
1 Ki. 4. 33 he spake also of beasts, and of fowl
18. 5 find grass..that we loose not all the beasts
2 Ki. 3. 17 ye, and your cattle, and your beasts
2 Ch. 32. 28 and stalls for all manner of beasts
Ezra 1. 4, 6 with gold, and with goods..with beasts
Neh. 2. 12 neither (was there any) beast with me
2. 14 for the beast (that was) under me to pass
Job 12. 7 But ask now the beasts, and they shall
18. 3 Wherefore are we counted as beasts
35 11 Who teacheth us more than the beasts
Psa. 8. 7 oxen, yea, and the beasts of the field
36. 6 O LORD, thou preservest man and beast
49. 12, 20 man..he is like the beasts (that)
73. 22 ignorant: I was (as) a beast before thee
135. 8 firstborn of Egypt, both of man and beast
147. 9 He giveth to the beast his food, (and) to
Prov. 12. 10 regardeth the life of his beast: but the
30. 30 A lion..strongest among beasts, and
Eccl. 3. 18 might see that they themselves are beasts
3. 19 befalleth the sons of men befalleth beasts
3. 19 man hath no preeminence above a beast
3. 21 and the spirit of the beast that goeth
Isa. 18. 6 beasts of the earth..beasts of the earth
30. 6 The burden of the beasts of the south
63. 14 As a beast goeth down into the valley
Jer. 7. 20 this place, upon man, and upon beast
7. 33 shall be meat..for the beasts of the
9. 10 of the heavens and the beast are fled
12. 4 the beasts are consumed, and the birds
15. 3 of the heaven, and the beasts of the earth
16. 4 shall be meat..for the beasts of the earth
19. 7 to be meat..for the beasts of the earth
21. 6 will smite..this city, both man and beast
27. 5 the beast that (are) upon the ground
31. 27 seed of man, and with the seed of beast
32. 43 (It is) desolate without man or beast
33. 10 desolate without man and without beast
33. 10 without inhabitant, and without beast
33. 12 desolate without man and without beast
34. 20 be for meat..to the beasts of the earth
36. 29 to cease from thence man and beast?
50. 3 they shall depart, both man and beast
51. 62 shall remain in it, neither man nor beast
Eze. 8. 10 every form of creeping things, and..beasts
14. 13, 17 cut off man and beast from it
14. 19, 21 to cut off from it man and beast
25. 13 I..will cut off man and beast from it
29. 8 cut off man and beast out of thee
29. 11 nor foot of beast shall pass through it
32. 13 the beasts thereof..the hoofs of beasts
36. 11 I will multiply upon you man and beast
44. 31 that is dead of itself..fowl or beast
Joel 1. 18 How do the beasts groan! the herds
1. 20 The beasts of the field cry also unto thee
2. 22 Be not afraid, ye beasts of the field
Jon. 3. 7 Let neither man nor beast, herd nor flock
3. 8 let man and beast be covered with
Mic. 5. 8 as a lion among the beasts of the forest
Hab. 2. 17 shall cover thee, and the spoil of beasts
Zeph. 1. 3 I will consume man and beast; I will
Zech. 8. 10 hire for man, nor any hire for beast
14. 15 of all the beasts that shall be in these

2. *Beast, brute*, בְּעִיר *beir.*
Gen. 45. 17 This do ye; lade your beasts, and go, get
Exod 22. 5 shall put in his beast, and shall feed
Num 20. 8 give..congregation and their beasts drink
20. 11 the congregation drank, and their beasts

3. *A living creature*, חַיָּה (Dan. חֵיוָא) *chaiyah, cheva.*
Gen. 1. 24 beast of the earth after his kind
1. 25 God made the beast of the earth after
1. 30 to every beast of the earth, and to every
2. 19 God formed every beast of the field, and
2. 20 to every beast of the field; but for Adam
3. 1 serpent was more subtile than any beast
3. 14 above every beast of the field; upon thy
7. 14 They, and every beast after his kind, and
7. 21 both of fowl, and of cattle, and of beast
8. 19 Every beast, every creeping thing, and
9. 2 of you shall be upon every beast of the
9. 5 at the hand of every beast will I require
9. 10 of every beast of the earth with you
9. 10 all that go out of the ark, to every beast
37. 20 Some evil beast hath devoured him: and
37. 33 an evil beast hath devoured him; Joseph
Exod 23. 11 what they leave the beasts of the field
23. 29 the beast of the field multiply against
Lev. 5. 2 whether..a carcase of an unclean beast
11. 2 These (are) the beasts which ye shall eat
11. 27 all manner of beasts that go on (all) four
11. 47 between the beast that may be eaten
11. 47 and the beast that may not be eaten
17. 13 which hunteth and catcheth any beast
25. 7 for the beast that (are) in thy land, shall
26. 6 I will rid evil beasts out of the land
26. 22 I will also send wild beasts among you
Num 35. 3 for their goods, and for all their beasts
Deut. 7. 22 lest the beasts of the field increase upon
1 Sa. 17. 46 and to the wild beasts of the earth
2 Sa. 21. 10 nor the beasts of the field by night
2 Ki. 14. 9 and there passed by a wild beast
2 Ch. 25. 18 and there passed by a wild beast
Job 5. 22 shalt thou be afraid of the beasts
5. 23 the beasts of the field shall be at peace
37. 8 Then the beasts go into dens, and remain
39. 15 crush them..the wild beast may break
40. 20 where all the beasts of the field play
Psa. 50. 10 For every beast of the forest (is) mine
79. 2 the flesh of thy saints unto the beasts
104. 11 They give drink to every beast of the
104. 20 all the beasts of the forest do creep
104. 25 wherein (are)..small and great beasts
148. 10 Beasts, and all cattle..and flying fowl
Isa. 35. 9 No..ravenous beast shall go up thereon
40. 16 beasts thereof sufficient for a burnt-off.
43. 20 The beast of the field shall honour me
46. 1 idols were upon the beasts, and upon the
56. 9 beasts of the field..beasts in the forest
Jer. 12. 9 come ye, assemble all the beasts of the
27. 6 the beasts of the field have I given him
28. 14 I have given him the beasts of the field
Eze. 5. 17 will I send upon you famine..evil beasts
14. 15 I cause noisome beasts to pass through
14. 15 may pass through because of the beasts
14. 21 the famine, and the noisome beast, and
29. 5 I have given thee for meat to the beasts
31. 6 the beasts of the field bring forth their

Eze. 31. 13 the beasts of the field shall be upon his
32. 4 I will fill the beasts of the whole earth
33. 27 will I give to the beasts to be devoured
34. 5 they became meat to all the beasts of the
34. 8 my flock became meat to every beast of
34. 25 cause the evil beasts to cease out of the
34. 28 shall the beast of the land devour them
38. 20 the beasts of the field, and all creeping
39. 4 (to) the beasts of the field to be devoured
39. 17 Speak unto..every beast of the field
Dan. 2. 38 the beasts of the field..hath he given
4. 12 the beasts of the field had shadow under
4. 14 let the beasts get away from under it
4. 15 and (let) his portion (be) with the beasts
4. 16 let a beast's heart be given unto him
4. 21 under which the beasts of the field dwelt
4. 23 (let) his portion (be) with the beasts of
4. 25 thy dwelling shall be with the beasts
4. 32 thy dwelling..with the beasts of the field
5. 21 his heart was made like the beasts, and
7. 3 four great beasts came up from the sea
7. 5 another beast, a second, like to a bear
7. 6 the beast had also four heads; and
7. 7 behold a fourth beast, dreadful and
7. 7 it (was) diverse from all the beasts that
7. 11 I beheld..till the beast was slain, and
7. 12 As concerning the rest of the beasts they
7. 17 These great beasts..shall arise out of the
7. 19 I would know the truth of..fourth beast
7. 23 The fourth beast shall be the fourth
8. 4 no beasts might stand before him
Hos. 2. 12 the beasts of the field shall eat them
2. 18 a covenant for them with the beasts of
4. 3 the beasts of the field, and with the
13. 8 the wild beast shall tear them
Zeph. 2. 14 all the beasts of the nations: both the
2. 15 a place for beasts to lie down in!

4. *Life (of an animal)*, (בְּהֵמָה) נֶפֶשׁ *nephesh (behemah)*.
Lev. 24. 18 a beast shall make it good; beast for b.

5. *Slaughtered animal*, טֶבַח *tebach*.
Prov. 9. 2 She hath killed her beasts; she hath

6. *A living creature*, ζῶον *zōon*.
Heb. 13. 11 the bodies of those beasts..are burned
2 Pe. 2. 12 But these, as natural brute beasts
Jude 10 what they know naturally, as..beasts
Rev. 4. 6 round about the throne..four beasts
4. 7 beast (was) like a lion, and..second beast
4. 7 third beast had a face..the fourth beast
4. 8 the four beasts had each of them six
4. 9 when those beasts give glory and honour
5. 6 midst of the throne and of the four beasts
5. 8 the four beasts..fell down before the
5. 11 round about the throne and the beasts
5. 14 And the four beasts said, Amen. And
6. 1 one of the four beasts saying, Come
6. 3 I heard the second beast say Come and
6. 5 I heard the third beast say Come and
6. 6 a voice in the midst of the four beasts
6. 7 I heard the..fourth beast say, Come and
7. 11 the elders and the four beasts, and fell
14. 3 before the four beasts and the elders
15. 7 And one of the four beasts gave unto
19. 4 the four beasts fell down and worshipped

7. *A wild beast*, θηρίον *thērion*.
Acts 28. 5 And he shook off the beast into the fire
Titus 1. 12 The Cretians (are) alway liars evil beasts
Heb. 12. 20 so much as a beast touch the mountain
Jas. 3. 7 For every kind of beasts, and of birds
Rev. 6. 8 to kill..with the beasts of the earth
11. 7 the beast that ascendeth out of the
13. 1 I..saw a beast rise up out of the sea
13. 2 And the beast which I saw was like
13. 3 all the world wondered after the beast
13. 4 beast..worshipped the beast..the beast
13. 11 I beheld another beast coming up
13. 12 the power of the first beast before him
13. 12 the first beast, whose deadly wound was
13. 14 he had power..in the sight of the beast
13. 14 they should make an image to the beast
13. 15 give life unto the image of the beast
13. 15 image of the beast..image of the beast
13. 17 the name of the beast, or the number of
13. 18 Let him..count the number of the beast
14. 9 If any man worship the beast and his
14. 11 who worship the beast and his image
15. 2 that had gotten the victory over the beast
16. 2 men which had the mark of the beast
16. 10 poured..upon the seat of the beast
16. 13 out of the mouth of the beast, and out
17. 3 I saw a woman sit upon a..beast
17. 7 mystery of the woman and of the beast
17. 8 The beast that thou sawest was and is
17. 8 when they behold the beast that was
17. 11 And the beast that was, and is not
17. 12 power as kings one hour with the beast
17. 13 their power and strength unto the beast
17. 16 horns which thou sawest upon the beast
17. 17 give their kingdom unto the beast
19. 19 I saw the beast, and the kings of the
19. 20 And the beast was taken, and with him
19. 20 had received the mark of the beast
20. 4 which had not worshipped the beast
20. 10 where the beast and the false prophet

8. *Beast of burden, or for food*, κτῆνος *ktēnos*.
Luke 10. 34 set him on his own beast, and brought
Acts 23. 24 provide (them) beasts, that they may set
1 Co. 15 39 another flesh of beasts, another of fishes
Rev. 18. 13 and fine flour, and wheat, and beasts

BEAST, wild or venomous —
1. *A living creature*, חַיָּה *chaiyah*.
1 Sa. 17. 46 I will give..to the wild beasts of the
2. *A wild animal*, θηρίον, *thērion*.
Mark 1 13 in the wilderness..with the wild beasts
Acts 10. 12 [wild beasts], and creeping things, and
11. 6 wild beasts, and creeping things, and
28. 4 the barbarians saw the (venomous) beast

BEAST, swift —
A dromedary, כִּרְכָּרוֹת *kirkaroth*.
Isa. 66. 20 upon mules, and upon swift beasts
[*See also* Desert, fat, fed, fight with, fourfooted, slain, torn of, wild.]

BEAST that dieth of itself —
Carcase, נְבֵלָה *nebelah*.
Lev. 7. 24 the fat of the beast that dieth of itself

BEAT, to —
1. *To pound in a mortar*, דּוּךְ *duk*.
Num. 11. 8 ground (it) in mills, or beat..in a mortar
2. *To knock*, דָּפַק *daphaq*, 7.
Judg. 19. 22 beat at the door, and spake to the master
3. *To smite (as with a hammer)*, הָלַם *halam*.
Prov. 23. 35 they have beaten me, (and) I felt (it) not
4. *To beat out or off*, חָבַט *chabat*.
Deut. 24. 20 When thou beatest thine olive tree
5. *To crush, bruise*, כָּתַת *kathath*.
Joel 3. 10 Beat your plowshares into swords, and
6. *To beat down or out*, כָּתַת *kathath*, 3.
2 Ch. 34. 7 had beaten the graven images into powder
Isa. 2. 4 they shall beat their swords into plowsh.
Mic. 4. 3 they shall beat their swords into plowsh.
7. *To smite, cause to smite*, נָכָה *nakah*, 5.
Deut 25. 3 beat him above these with many stripes
2 Ki. 13. 25 Three times did Joash beat him, and
Prov. 23. 13 (if) thou beatest him with the rod, he
23. 14 Thou shalt beat him with the rod, and
Jon. 4. 8 the sun beat upon the head of Jonah
8. *To stamp, beat out*, רָקַע *raqa*, 3.
Exod 39. 3 they did beat the gold into thin plates
9. *To beat, wear away*, שָׁחַק *shachaq*.
Exod 30. 36 thou shalt beat (some) of it very small
2 Sa. 22. 43 I beat them as small as the dust
Psa. 18. 42 Then did I beat them small as the dust
10. *To skin, flay, thrash*, δέρω *derō*.
Matt 21. 35 beat one, and killed another, and stoned
Mark 12. 3 they caught..and beat him, and sent
Luke 20. 10 the husbandmen beat him, and sent (him)
20. 11 they beat him also, and entreated (him)
Acts 5. 40 when they had called..and beaten..they
16. 37 They have beaten us openly uncondemned
22. 19 beat in every synagogue them that
1 Co. 9. 26 not as one that beateth the air
11. *To beat with a rod*, ῥαβδίζω *rhabdizō*.
Acts 16. 22 the magistrates..commanded to beat
12. *To strike, smite*, τύπτω *tuptō*.
Luke 12. 45 begin to beat the men servants and
Acts 18. 17 took..and beat..before the judgment

BEAT into, to —
To cast or throw upon, ἐπιβάλλω *epiballō*.
Mark 4. 37 the waves beat into the ship, so that it

BEAT upon, to —
1. *To strike toward*, προσκόπτω *proskoptō*.
Matt. 7. 27 [beat upon] that house; and it fell: and
2. *To fall toward*, προσπίπτω *prospiptō*.
Matt. 7. 25 [beat upon] that house; and it fell not

BEAT vehemently against or upon, to —
To break against, προσρήγνυμι *prosrēgnumi*.
Luke 6. 48 the stream beat vehemently upon that
6. 49 against which the stream did beat vehem.

BEAT with rods, to —
To beat with rods, ῥαβδίζω *rhabdizō*.
2 Co. 11. 25 Thrice was I beaten with rods, once was

BEAT down, to —
1. *To smite (as with a hammer)*, הָלַם *halam*.
1 Sa. 14. 16 the multitude..went on beating down
2. *To break down or through*, הָרַס *haras*.
2 Ki. 3. 25 they beat down the cities, and on every
3. *To crush, bruise*, כָּתַת *kathath*.
Psa. 89. 23 I will beat down his foes before his face
4. *To break down*, נָתַץ *nathats*.
Judg. 8. 17 he beat down the tower of Penuel, and
9. 45 beat down the city, and sowed it with salt
2 Ki. 23. 12 did the king beat down, and brake

BEAT in pieces —
To beat small, דָּקַק *daqaq*, 5.
Mic. 4. 13 thou shalt beat in pieces many people

BEAT off, to —
To beat out or off, חָבַט *chabat*.
Isa. 27 12 the LORD shall beat off from the channel

BEAT out, to —
To beat out or off, חָבַט *chabat*.
Ruth 2. 17 beat out that she had gleaned: and it

BEAT to pieces, to —
To bruise, דָּכָא *daka*, 3.
Isa. 3. 15 What mean ye..ye beat my people to p.

BEATEN —
1. *Beaten down or out*, כָּתִית *kathith*.
Exod 27. 20 pure oil olive beaten for the light, to
29. 40 with the fourth part of an hin of beaten
Lev. 24. 2 pure oil olive beaten for the light, to
Num 28. 5 with the fourth..of an hin of beaten oil
2. *Beaten out work*, מִקְשָׁה *miqshah*.
Num. 8. 4 the candlestick..beaten gold, unto the
3. *To slaughter, beat out*, שָׁחַט *shachat*.
1 Ki. 10. 16 Solomon made..targets (of) beaten gold
10. 17 And..three hundred shields (of) beaten
2 Ch. 9. 15 two hundred targets (of) beaten gold: six
9. 15 hundred (shekels) of beaten gold went to
9. 16 And three hundred shields..beaten gold

BEATEN, to be —
1. *To be come upon, plagued*, נָגַע *naga*, 2.
Josh. 8. 15 as if they were beaten before them and
2. *To be smitten, plagued*, נָגַף *nagaph*, 2.
2 Sa. 2. 17 sore battle that day..Abner was beaten
3. *To smite*, נָכָה *nakah*, 5.
Deut. 25. 2 worthy to be beaten..to be beaten
4. *To be smitten*, נָכָה *nakah*, 6.
Exod. 5. 14 the officers..were beaten, (and) demanded
5. 16 Make brick: and, behold..(are) beaten
5. *To skin, flay, thrash*, δέρω *derō*.
Mark 13. 9 in the synagogues ye shall be beaten
Luke 12. 47 that servant..shall be beaten with many
12. 48 But he..shall be beaten with few (stripes)

BEATEN corn —
Beaten out corn, גֶּרֶשׂ *geres*.
Lev. 2. 14 corn dried..corn beaten out of full ears

BEATEN down, to be —
1. *To be cast down, affrighted*, חָתַת *chathath*, 2.
Isa. 30. 31 shall the Assyrian be beaten down
2. *To be beaten down or out*, כָּתַת *kathath*, 6.
Jer. 46. 5 their mighty ones are beaten down, and

BEATEN in sunder, to be —
To be dashed to pieces, נָפַץ *naphats*, 4.
Isa. 27. 9 as chalk stones that are beaten in sunder

BEATEN out, to be —
To be beaten out or off, חָבַט *chabat*, 2.
Isa. 28. 27 the fitches are beaten out with a staff

BEATEN out of one piece —
Beaten out work, מִקְשָׁה *miqshah*.
Exod 37. 7 beaten out of one piece made he them

BEATEN to pieces, to be —
To be beaten down or out, כָּתַת *kathath*, 6.
Mic. 1. 7 graven images..shall be beaten to pieces

BEATEN work —
Beaten out work, מִקְשָׁה *miqshah*.
Exod 25. 18 (of) beaten work shalt thou make them
25. 31 (of) beaten work shall the candlestick be
25. 36 it (shall be) one beaten work of pure gold
37. 17 (of) beaten work made he the candlestick
37. 22 all of it (was) one beaten work
Num. 8. 4 And this work..(was) beaten work

BEATING —
1. *To skin, flay, thrash*, δέρω *derō*.
Mark 12 5 beating some, and killing some
2. *To strike*, τύπτω *tuptō*.
Acts 21. 32 the soldiers, they left beating of Paul

BEAUTIFUL —
1. *Good of form*, טוֹבַת מַרְאֶה *tobath mareh*.
2 Sa. 11. 2 the woman (was) very beautiful to look
Esth. 2. 7 the maid (was) fair and beautiful; whom
2. *Beauty, desire, roe buck*, צְבִי *tsebi*.
Isa. 4. 2 the branch of the LORD be beautiful and
3. *Beauty, glory*, תִּפְאָרָה תִּפְאֶרֶת *tipharah, tiphereth*.
Isa. 52. 1 O Zion; put on thy beautiful garments
64. 11 Our holy and our beautiful house, where
Jer. 13. 20 (that) was given thee, thy beautiful flock?
48. 17 the strong staff broken..the beautiful
Eze. 16. 12 I put..a beautiful crown upon thine head
23 42 put..beautiful crowns upon their heads
4. *Fair, beautiful*, יָפֶה *yapheh*.
1 Sa. 16. 12 a beautiful countenance, and goodly to
Psa. 48. 2 Beautiful for situation, the joy of the
Eccl. 3. 11 He hath made every (thing) beautiful in
Song 6. 4 Thou (art) beautiful, O my love, as
5. *Fair of form*, יְפַת תֹּאַר *yephath toar*.
Gen. 29. 17 Rachel was beautiful and well favoured
Deut 21. 11 seest among the captives a beautiful
6. *Fair*, יָפֶה *yapheh*.
1 Sa. 16. 12 a beautiful countenance, and goodly to
7. *Opportune, ripe, fit*, ὡραῖος *hōraios*.
Matt 23. 27 which indeed appear beautiful outward
Acts 3. 2 the gate of the temple..called Beautiful
3. 10 he which sat for alms at the Beautiful
Rom 10. 15 beautiful are the feet of them that preach

BEAUTIFUL, to be —
1. *To be fair, beautiful*, יָפָה *yaphah*.
Song 7. 1 How beautiful are thy feet with shoes
Eze. 16. 13 thou wast exceeding beautiful, and thou

2. *To be comely*, נָאָה *naah*, 3a.
Isa. 52. 7 How beautiful upon the mountains are

BEAUTIFY, to —

To make beautiful, פָּאַר *paar*, 3.
Ezra 7. 27 to beautify the house of the LORD which
Psa. 149. 4 he will beautify the meek with salvation
Isa. 60. 13 to beautify the place of my sanctuary

BEAUTY —

1. *Honour, beauty*, הָדָר *hadar*.
Job 40. 10 array thyself with glory and beauty
Psa. 110. 3 thy power, in the beauties of holiness
Prov. 20. 29 the beauty of old men (is) the grey head
Lam. 1. 6 all her beauty is departed: her princes

2. *Honour, beauty*, הֲדָרָה *hadarah*.
1 Ch. 16. 29 worship the LORD in the beauty of
2 Ch. 20. 21 that should praise the beauty of holiness
Psa. 29. 2 worship the LORD in the beauty of
96. 9 O worship the LORD in the beauty of

3. *Honour, beauty, majesty*, הוֹד *hod*.
Hos. 14. 6 his beauty shall be as the olive tree, and

4. *To desire*, חָמַד *chamad*.
Psa. 39. 11 thou makest his beauty to consume away

5. *Fair, beautiful*, יָפֶה *yapheh*.
2 Sa. 14. 25 so much praised as Absalom for..beauty

6. *Fairness, beauty*, יְפִי *yephi*.
Eze. 28. 7 draw their swords against the beauty of

7. *Fairness, beauty*, יֳפִי *yophi*.
Esth. 1. 11 shew the people and the princes..beauty
Psa. 45. 11 So shall..king greatly desire thy beauty
50. 2 the perfection of beauty, God hath
Prov. 6. 25 Lust not after her beauty in thine heart
31. 30 Favour (is) deceitful, and beauty (is) vain
Isa. 3. 24 come to pass..burning instead of beauty
33. 17 Thine eyes shall see the king in..beauty
Lam. 2. 15 (Is) this the city..perfection of beauty
Eze. 16. 14 went forth among..heathen for..beauty
16. 15 thou didst trust in thine own beauty
16. 25 Thou..hast made thy beauty..abhorred
27. 3 thou hast said, I (am) of perfect beauty
27. 4 thy builders have perfected thy beauty
27. 11 they have made thy beauty perfect
28. 12 full of wisdom, and perfect in beauty
28. 17 was lifted up because of thy beauty
31. 8 tree..was like unto him in his beauty
Zech. 9. 17 how great (is) his beauty! corn shall

8. *Appearance, sight*, מַרְאֶה *mareh*.
Isa. 53. 2 no beauty that we should desire him

9. *Pleasantness*, נֹעַם *noam*.
Psa. 27. 4 to behold the beauty of the LORD
90. 17 let the beauty of the LORD our God be
Zech 11. 7 one I called Beauty..the other I called
11. 10 I took my staff, (even) Beauty, and cut

10. *Beauty, ornament, head-dress*, פְּאֵר *peer*.
Isa. 61. 3 to give unto them beauty for ashes

11. *Beauty, desire, roebuck*, צְבִי *tsebi*.
2 Sa. 1 19 The beauty of Israel is slain upon thy
Eze. 7 20 As for the beauty of his ornament

12. *Form*, צִיר [V.L. צוּר] *tsir*.
Psa. 49. 14 their beauty shall consume in the grave

13. *Beauty*, תִּפְאָרָה, תִּפְאֶרֶת *tipharah, tiphereth*.
Exod 28. 2 Aaron thy brother for glory and..beauty
28. 40 make for them, for glory and for beauty
2 Ch. 3. 6 house with precious stones for beauty
Psa. 96. 6 strength and beauty (are)..his sanctuary
Isa. 13. 19 the beauty of the Chaldees' excellency
28. 1 whose glorious beauty (is) a fading flower
28. 4 the glorious beauty, which (is) on the
28. 5 of glory, and for a diadem of beauty
44. 13 according to the beauty of a man; that
Lam. 2. 1 cast down from heaven..the beauty of

BEAUTY, to pass in —

To be pleasant, נָעֵם *naem*.
Eze. 32. 19 Whom dost thou pass in beauty? go

BE' BAI, בֵּבַי *fatherly*.

1. A man whose descendants came up with Zerubbabel, B.C. 445
Ezra 2. 11 children of B., six hundred twenty and
Neh. 7. 16 children of B., six hundred twenty and

2. One whose posterity came up with Ezra in the time of Artaxerxes [perhaps the same as No 1], B.C. 445.
Ezra 8. 11 of the sons of B.; Zechariah the son of B.
10. 28 Of the sons also of B.; Jehohanan

3. One that sealed the covenant, B.C. 445.
Neh. 10. 15 [chief of the people]..Bunni, Azgad, B.

BECAUSE —

1. *In regard to*, אֶל *el*.
1 Sa. 4. 21 because the ark of God was taken, and

2. *That*, אֲשֶׁר *asher*.
Gen. 30. 18 because I have given my maiden to my

3. *In that*, בַּאֲשֶׁר *ba-asher*.
Gen. 39. 9 from me but thee, because thou (art) his

4. *Even as*, כַּאֲשֶׁר *ka-asher*.
1 Sa. 28. 18 Because thou obeyedst not the voice of

5. *Because that*, יַעַן אֲשֶׁר *yaan asher*.
Gen. 22. 16 for because thou hast done this thing
Deut. 1. 36 because..hath wholly followed the LORD

6. *Because that*, עַל אֲשֶׁר *al asher*.
Exod 32. 35 plagued the people, because they made

7. *Because that*, עֵקֶב אֲשֶׁר *eqeb asher*.
Gen. 22. 18 because thou hast obeyed my voice
2 Sa. 12. 6 fourfold, because he did this thing, and

8. *From the face that*, מִפְּנֵי אֲשֶׁר *mip-pene asher*.
Exod 19. 18 because the LORD descended upon it in
Jer. 44. 23 Because ye have burned incense, and

9. *Under that*, תַּחַת אֲשֶׁר *tachath asher*.
Num 25. 13 because he was zealous for his God, and
Deut 21. 14 because thou hast humbled her

10. *Concerning the matter that*, עַל דְּבַר אֲשֶׁר. [*al*].
Deut 22. 24 because she cried not..because he hath

11. *In answer to, because*, יַעַן *yaan*.
Lev. 26. 43 because, even because they despised my
Num 11. 20 because that ye have despised the LORD
Eze. 25. 8 Because that Moab and Seir do say

12. *In answer that*, יַעַן כִּי *yaan ki*.
1 Ki. 21. 29 because he humbleth himself before me
Isa. 3. 16 Because the daughters of Zion are

13. *The heel, end, consequence*, עֵקֶב *eqeb*.
Num 14. 24 because he had another spirit with him
Deut 8. 20 because ye would not be obedient unto

14. *The consequence that*, עֵקֶב כִּי *eqeb ki*.
2 Sa. 12. 10 because thou hast despised me, and hast
Amos 4. 12 because I will do this unto thee, prepare

15. *Wholly over-against this*, כָּל־קֳבֵל דִּי *kol qebel di*.
Ezra 4. 14 because we have maintenance from
Dan. 2. 8 because ye see the thing is gone from me
3. 29 because there is no other God that can
6. 3 because an excellent spirit (was) in him

16. *On so, over so*, עַל־כֵּן *al ken*.
Judg. 6. 22 because I have seen an angel of the LORD

17. *From that*, מִן־דִּי *min di*.
Dan. 3. 22 because the king's commandment was

18. *From the face of*, מִפְּנֵי *mip-pene*.
Jer. 44. 23 Because ye have burned incense..because

19. *For, wherefore*, γάρ *gar*.
John 3. 19 than light, because their deeds were evil
10. 26 because ye are not of my sheep, as I said
Rom. 4. 15 Because the law worketh wrath: for

20. *In return for which things*, ἀνθ' ὧν *anth' hōn*.
Luke 1. 20 because thou believest not my words
19. 44 because thou knewest not the time of thy
Acts 12. 23 because he gave not God the glory: and
2 Th. 2. 10 because they received not the love of the

21. *Through, on account of*, διά (acc.) *dia*.
Matt 13. 5 because they had no deepness of earth
13. 6 because they had no root, they withered
24. 12 because iniquity shall abound, the love
Mark 4. 5 because it had no depth of earth
4. 6 because it had no root, it withered away
Luke 2. 4 because he was of the house..of David
8. 6 it withered away, because it lacked mois.
11. 8 because he is his friend..he will rise
18. 5 because this widow troubleth me, I will
19. 11 spake a parable, because he was nigh to J.
23. 8 because he had heard many things of him
John 2. 24 Jesus..because he knew all (men)
Acts 12. 20 because their country was nourished by
18. 3 because he was of the same craft, he
27. 4 Cyprus, because the winds were contrary
27. 9 because the fast was now already past
28. 18 because there was no cause of death in
Phil. 1. 7 Even..because I have you in my heart
Heb. 7. 23 because they were not suffered to continue
7. 24 because he continueth ever, hath an
Jas. 4. 2 yet ye have not, because ye ask not

22. *For this reason*, διότι *dioti*.
Luke 2. 7 because there was no room for them in
Acts 17. 31 [Because] he hath appointed a day, in
Rom. 8. 7 Because the carnal mind (is) enmity 1.19.
1 Co. 15. 9 because I persecuted the church of God
1 Th. 2. 8 our own souls, because ye were dear unto
Heb. 11. 5 because God..translated him: for before
11. 23 because they saw (he was) a proper child
Jas. 4. 3 and receive not, because ye ask amiss
1 Pe. 1. 16 Because it is written, Be ye holy; for I

23. *Since, after that*, ἐπεί *epei*.
Matt 18. 32 all that debt, because thou desiredst me
27. 6 treasury, because it is the price of blood
Mark 15. 42 because it was the preparation, that is
John 13. 29 some..thought, because Judas had the
19. 31 The Jews therefore, because it was the
Heb. 6. 13 because he could swear by no greater
11. 11 because she judged him faithful who had

24. *Since truly*, ἐπειδή *epeidē*.
Matt 21. 46 [because] they took him for a prophet
Acts 14. 12 because he was the chief speaker

25. *On account of which*, οὗ ἕνεκεν *hou heneken*.
Luke 4. 18 because he hath anointed me to preach

26. *In order that*, ἵνα *hina*.
Matt 20. 31 because they should hold their peace

27. *In as much as*, καθότι *kathoti*.
Acts 2. 24 because it was not possible that he should

28. *That, seeing that*, ὅτι *hoti*.
Matt. 2. 18 Rachel..would not be comforted, because
5. 36 Neither shalt thou swear..because thou
7. 14 [Because] strait (is) the gate, and narrow

Matt. 9. 36 he was moved with compassion..because
11. 20 Then began he to upbraid..because they
12. 41 The men..shall rise..because they rep.
13. 11 Because it is given unto you to know the
13. 13 speak I to them in parables: because they
14. 5 he feared the multitude, because they
15. 32 I have compassion..because they continue
16. 7 (It is) because we have taken no bread
16. 8 why reason ye among yourselves, because
20. 7 They say unto him, Because no man
20. 15 Is thine eye evil, because I am good?
23. 29 Woe unto you..because ye build..tombs
Mark 1. 34 suffered not the devils to speak, because
3. 30 Because they said, He hath an unclean
4. 29 he putteth in the sickle, because the har.
6. 34 Jesus..moved with compassion..because
7. 19 Because it entereth not into his heart
8. 2 I have compassion..because they have
8. 16 saying, (It is) because we have no bread
8. 17 Why reason ye, because ye have no bread?
9. 38 and..forbad him, [because he followeth]
9. 41 whosoever shall give you..because ye 11.11
16. 14 [because they believed not them which]
Luke 8. 30 because many devils were entered into
9. 49 we forbad him, because he followeth not
9. 53 because his face was as though he would
10. 20 because your names are written in heav.
11. 18 because ye say..I cast out devils through
12. 17 What shall I do, because I have no room
13. 2 these..were sinners above all..because
15. 27 thy father hath killed..because he hath
19. 3 and could not for the press, because he
19. 17 because thou hast been faithful in a very
19. 21 For I feared thee, because thou art an
John 1. 50 Because I said unto thee, I saw thee under
3. 18 is condemned already, because he hath
3. 23 John also was baptizing..because there
5. 16 sought to slay him, because he had done
5. 18 sought..to kill him, because he not only
5. 27 hath given him authority..because he is
5. 30 because I seek not mine own will, but the
6. 2 a great multitude followed him, because
6. 26 Ye seek me, not because ye saw the mir.
6. 26 Ye seek me..because ye did eat of the
6. 41 Jews then murmured at him, because he
7. 1 he would not walk..because the Jews
7. 7 but me it hateth, because I testify of it
7. 22 not because it is of M., but of the fathers
7. 30 no man laid hands on him, because his
8. 22 because he saith, Whither I go, ye
8. 37 ye seek to kill me, because my word hath
8. 43 because ye cannot hear my word
8. 44 abode not in the truth, because there is
8. 47 ye..hear (them) not, because ye are not
9. 16 because he keepeth not the sabbath day
9. 22 These (words) spake his parents, because
10. 13 The hireling fleeth, because he is an
10. 17 Therefore..my Father love me, because
10. 36 because I said, I am the Son of God?
11. 9 he stumbleth not, because he seeth
11. 10 he stumbleth, because there is no light
12. 6 but because he was a thief, and had the
14. 12 greater..than these shall he do because
14. 17 whom the world cannot receive, because
14. 19 because I live, ye shall live also
15. 19 but because ye are not of the world
15. 21 because they know not him that sent me
15. 27 ye also shall bear witness, because ye
16. 3 because they have not known the Father
16. 4 these things I said not unto you..because
16. 6 But because I have said these things unto
16. 9 Of sin, because they believe not on me
16. 10 Of righteousness, because I go to my Fa.
16. 11 Of judgment, because the prince of this
16. 16 [ye shall see me, because I go to the]
16. 21 A woman..hath sorrow, because her
16. 27 For the Father..loveth you, because ye
16. 32 I am not alone, because the Father is
17. 14 because they are not of the world
19. 7 because he made himself the Son of God
20. 13 Because they have taken away my Lord
20. 29 Thomas, because thou hast seen me
Acts 2. 27 Because thou wilt not leave my soul in
6. 1 because their widows were neglected
8. 20 because thou hast thought that the gift
17. 18 [because he preached unto them Jesus]
Rom 5. 5 because the love of God is shed abroad
6. 15 because we are not under the law, but
8. 27 because he maketh intercession for the
9. 7 Neither, because they are the seed of A.
9. 28 [because a short work will the Lord make]
9. 32 Because..not by faith, but as it were
1 Co. 1. 25 Because the foolishness of God is wiser
2. 14 because they are spiritually discerned
3. 13 because it shall be revealed by fire; and
12. 15 If the foot shall say, Because I am not the
12. 16 if the ear shall say, Because I am not the
15. 15 because we have testified of God that he
2 Co. 11. 11 Wherefore? because I love you not? God
Gal. 2. 11 I withstood him..because he was to be
4. 6 And because ye are sons, God hath sent
Eph. 5. 16 Redeeming the time, because the days
Phil. 2. 30 Because for the work of Christ he was
4. 17 Not because I desire a gift: but I desire
2 Th. 1. 10 because our testimony among you was
3. 9 Not because we have not power, but to
1 Ti. 1. 13 I obtained mercy, because I did (it)
4. 10 we both labour..because we trust in
5. 12 Having damnation, because they have
6. 2 because they are brethren..because they
Phm. 7 we have great joy..because the bowels
Heb. 8. 9 because they continued not in my coven.

Jas. 1. 10 because as the flower of the grass he shall
1 Pe. 2 21 because Christ also suffered for us, leaving
5. 8 be vigilant; [because your adversary the]
1 Jo. 2. 8 which thing is true..because the darkness
2. 12 I write..because your sins are forgiven
2. 13 because ye..because ye..because ye have
2. 14 because ye have..because ye are strong
2. 21 because ye know..but because ye know
3. 1 the world knoweth us not, because it
3. 9 he cannot sin, because he is born of God
3. 12 Because his own works were evil, and
3. 14 We know that we have passed..because
3. 22 we receive of him, because we keep his
4. 1 because many false prophets are gone out
4. 4 Ye are of God..because greater is he that
4. 18 perfect love casteth out fear: because fear
4. 19 We love him, because he first loved us
5. 10 hath made him a liar; because he believeth
Rev. 3. 10 Because thou hast kept the word of my
3. 16 So then because thou art lukewarm, and
3. 17 Because thou sayest, I am rich, and incr.
5. 4 I wept much, because no man was found
8. 11 men died of the waters, because they were
11. 10 shall rejoice over them..because these
14 8 Babylon is fallen..[because] she made all
16 5 which art, and wast..because thou hast

29. *As a demonstrative,* ὅτι *hoti.*
Matt 11. 25 because thou hast hid these things from
Luke 11 18 because ye say that I cast out devils
13. 14 because that Jesus had healed on the
16. 8 because he had done wisely: for the
17 9 because he did the things that were
19. 11 because they thought that the kingdom
19. 31 Because the Lord hath need of him
John 7 23 because I have made a man every whit
8. 45 because I tell (you) the truth, ye believe
14. 28 because I said, I go unto the Father: for
16. 17 he saith..Because I go to the Father?
21 17 because he said unto him the third time
Acts 2. 6 because that every man heard them
22. 29 a Roman, and because he had bound
Rom. 8. 21 Because the creature itself also shall be
14. 23 because (he eateth) not of faith: for
1 Co. 6. 7 because ye go to law one with another
2 Co. 7. 13 because his spirit was refreshed by you
11 7 because I have preached to you the
1 Th. 2. 13 because, when ye received the word of
2 Th. 2 13 because God hath from the beginning
1 Jo. 3. 16 because he laid down his life for us: and
4. 13 because he hath given us of his Spirit
4. 17 because as he is, so are we in this world
5. 6 beareth witness, because the Spirit is
Rev. 2. 4 because thou hast left thy first love
2 14 [because] thou hast there them that hold
2. 20 because thou sufferest that woman Jezeb.
11 17 because thou hast taken to thee thy

30. *In order that,* ὅπως *hopōs.*
Acts 20 16 because he would not spend the

BECAUSE of —

1. *On account of the causes of,* על אודת *al odoth.*
Gen. 21 11 thing was very grievous..because of his
21 25 Abraham reproved Abimelech because of
Num 12. 1 Aaron spake against Moses because..the
13. 24 because of the cluster of grapes which
Judg. 6. 7 Israel cried unto the LORD because of the

2. *Turning, circumstance, opportunity,* גָּלָל *galal.*
Gen 12. 13 and my soul shall live because of thee
Deut 18. 12 because of these abominations the LORD
1 Ki. 14. 16 because of the sins of Jeroboam, who
Jer. 15. 4 because of Manasseh the son of Hezekiah

3. *From the way,* מִדֶּרֶךְ *mid-derek.*
Psa 107. 17 Fools because of their transgression, and

4. *On account of the matter,* עַל דָּבָר *al dabar.*
Gen. 12. 17 with great plagues because of Sarai
20. 18 the house of Abimelech, because of
Exod. 8 12 because of the frogs which he had brought
Psa. 45 4 because of truth and meekness (and)

5. *By the hand of,* בְּיַד *be-yad.*
Jer. 41. 9 whom he had slain because of Gedaliah

6. *To answer to,* לְמַעַן *le-maan.*
2 Ki. 13. 23 because of his covenant with Abraham

7. *In going over,* בַּעֲבוּר *ba-abur.*
Exod 13. 8 because of that (which) the LORD did

8. *On, upon,* עַל *al.*
Gen. 27. 41 because of the blessing wherewith his

9. *From,* מִן *min.*
Gen. 5. 29 because of the ground which the LORD

10. *From,* מִן *min.*
Dan. 7. 11 because of the voice of the great words

11. *From the face of,* מִפְּנֵי *mip-pene.*
Gen. 7 7 went in..because of the waters of the
27. 46 because of the daughters of Heth: if Jac.
36. 7 could not bear them because of their
Exod. 1. 12 grieved because of the children of Israel
9. 11 could not stand before Moses because of
Num 32. 17 because of the inhabitants of the land
Deut. 2. 25 and be in anguish because of thee
20. 3 neither be ye terrified because of them
Josh. 6. 1 because of the children of Israel: none
9. 24 were sore afraid of our lives because of
11. 6 Be not afraid because of them: for
23. 3 unto all these nations because of you
Judg. 2. 18 because of their groanings by reason of
6. 2 because of the Midianites the children of
6. 6 greatly impoverished because of the

1 Sa. 8. 18 because of your king which ye shall
1 Ki. 1. 50 Adonijah feared because of Solomon
2. 7 I fled because of Absalom thy brother
8. 11 priests could not..minister because of
2 Ki. 9. 14 Joram had kept..because of Hazael king
2 Ch. 12. 5 princes..were gathered..because of
Neh. 4. 9 set a watch against them..because of
5. 15 so did not I, because of the fear of God
Job 35. 12 none giveth answer, because of..evil men
Psa. 38. 3 no soundness..because of thine anger
38. 3 neither..rest in my bones because of my
38. 5 My wounds stink..because of my
60. 4 it may be displayed because of the truth
102. 10 Because of thine indignation and thy
Isa. 10. 27 the yoke shall be destroyed because of
17. 9 which they left because of the children of
19. 16 it shall be afraid..because of the shaking
19. 17 because of the counsel of the LORD of
19. 20 they shall cry unto the LORD because of
Jer. 4. 4 because of the evil of your doings
14. 16 the people..shall be cast out..because of
15. 17 I sat alone because of thy hand: for thou
21. 12 because of the evil of your doings
23. 9 I am like a drunken man..because of
23. 10 because of swearing the land mourneth
25. 16 And they shall drink..because of the
25. 27 Drink ye..because of the sword which
25. 37 the..habitations are cut down because of
25. 38 their land is desolate because of..the
26. 3 which I purpose..because of the evil of
32. 24 and the city is given..because of the
41. 18 Because of the Chaldeans: for they were
44. 3 Because of their wickedness which they
44. 22 because of the evil of your doings
Lam. 5. 9 We gat our bread..because of the sword
5. 10 Our skin was black..because of the
Eze. 16. 63 never open thy mouth..because of thy
Hos. 10. 15 So shall Beth-el do unto you because of

12. *From,* ἀπό *apo.*
Matt 18. 7 Woe unto the world because of offences!

13. *Through, on account of,* διά (acc.) *dia.*
Matt. 13. 21 when tribulation..ariseth because of the
13. 58 did not many mighty works..because of
17. 20 Jesus said unto them, Because of your
27. 19 I have suffered..in a dream because of
Mark. 3. 9 small ship should wait on him because of
6. 6 And he marvelled because of their
Luke 5. 19 they might bring him in because of the
11. 8 yet because of his importunity he will
John 3. 29 the friend..rejoiceth greatly because of
4. 41 And many more believed because of his
4. 42 Now we believe, not because of thy saying
7. 43 there was a division..because of him
11. 42 because of the people which stand by
12. 30 This voice came not because of me, but
12. 42 because of the Pharisees they did not
19 42 There laid they Jesus..because of the
Acts 4. 21 they let them go..because of the people
16. 3 took and circumcised him because of the
28. 2 for they..received us..because of the
Rom. 6. 19 I speak..because of the infirmity of your
8. 10 the body (is) dead because of sin; but
8. 10 Spirit (is) life because of righteousness
15. 15 because of the grace that is given
1 Co. 11. 10 to have power on (her) head because of
Gal. 2. 4 And that because of false brethren
Eph. 4. 18 because of the blindness of their heart
5. 6 because of these things cometh the
Heb. 3. 19 they could not enter in because of
4. 6 they..entered not in because of unbelief

14. *Out of,* ἐκ *ek.*
Rev. 16. 11 because of their pains and their sores
16. 21 men blasphemed God because of the

15. *In, with,* ἐν *en.*
Matt 26. 31 All ye shall be offended because of me
26. 33 (men) shall be offended because of thee
Mark 14. 27 All ye shall be offended [because of] me

16. *On, upon,* ἐπί (acc.) *epi.*
Rev. 1. 7 all kindreds..shall wail because of him

17. *Towards,* πρός (acc.) *pros.*
Matt 19. 8 Moses because of the hardness of your

18. *For or on account of,* χάριν *charin.*
Gal. 3. 19 It was added because of transgressions
Jude 16 persons in admiration because of

BECAUSE that —

1. *Because,* יַעַן *yaan.*
Eze. 25. 8 Because that Moab and Seir do say

2. *Because,* כִּי *ki.*
Gen. 2. 3 because that in it he had rested from all

3. *For, verily, then,* γάρ *gar.*
Acts 28. 20 because that for the hope of Israel I am
3 Jo. 7 Because that for his name's sake they

4. *Through, on account of,* διά (acc.) *dia* (with *inf.*)
Mark 5. 4 Because that he had been often bound
Luke 9. 7 because that it was said of some, that J.
Acts 8. 11 because that of long time he had
18. 2 because that Claudius had commanded

5. *For this reason,* διότι *dioti.*
Rom. 1. 21 Because that, when they knew God, they
Phil. 2. 26 because that ye had heard that he had
1 Th. 4. 6 because that the Lord (is) the avenger of

6. *That, seeing that,* ὅτι *hoti.*
John 7. 39 because that Jesus was not yet glorified
10. 33 and because that thou, being a man

John 12. 11 Because that by reason of him many of
12. 39 they could not believe, because that E.
Acts 10. 45 And they..were astonished..because th.
2 Th. 1. 3 as it is meet, because that your faith
1 Jo. 2. 11 because that darkness hath blinded his
4. 9 because that God sent his only begotten

7. *In as much as,* καθότι *kathoti.*
Luke 1. 7 they had no child, because that Elisabeth

BECAUSE —
From, מִן *min.*
Eze. 16. 28 because thou wast unsatiable; Job 18. 15

BECAUSE...would —
Toward, in order to, πρός (acc.) *pros* (with *inf.*)
1 Th. 2. 9 because we would not be chargeable

BECAUSE he would not —
That it might not happen to him, ὅπως μὴ γένηται αὐτῷ.
Acts 20. 16 determined to sail..because he would not

BECAUSE...yet —
Yet, still, while, עוֹד *od.*
Gen. 46. 30 Now let me die..because thou (art) yet

BE'-CHER, בֶּכֶר *youth, first-born.*
1. A son of Benjamin, B.C. 1700.
Gen. 46. 21 the sons of Benjamin..Belah, and B., and
1 Ch. 7. 6 of Benjamin; Bela, and B., and Jediael
7. 8 sons of B...All these (are) the sons of B.

2. A son of Ephraim (called *Berad* in 1 Ch. 7. 20), B.C. 1680.
Num 26. 35 of B., the family of the Bachrites: of

BE-CHO'-RATH, בְּכוֹרַת *first birth.*
Son of Aphiah or Abiah, and grandson of Becher son of Benjamin, also an ancestor of Saul the first king of Israel, B.C. 1225.
1 Sa. 9. 1 Zeror, the son of B., the son of Aphiah

BECKON to or unto, to —

1. *To nod through,* διανεύω *dianeuō.*
Luke 1. 22 he beckoned unto them, and remained

2. *To nod downward,* κατανεύω *kataneuō.*
Luke 5. 7 they beckoned unto..partners, which

3. *To wave downward,* κατασείω *kataseiō.*
Acts 19. 33 Alexander beckoned with the hand and
21. 40 Paul..beckoned with the hand unto the

4. *To nod, make signs,* νεύω *neuō.*
John 13. 24 Simon Peter therefore beckoned to him
Acts 24. 10 Paul, after..the governor had beckoned

BECKONING —
To wave downward, κατασείω *kataseiō.*
Acts 12. 17 But he beckoning unto them with the
13. 16 Paul stood up, and beckoning with (his)

BECOME, to —

1. *To be, exist,* הֲוָה, הֲוָא *hava, havah.*
Dan. 2. 35 became like the chaff..image became a

2. *To be, exist,* הָיָה *hayah.*
2 Sa. 7. 24 and thou, LORD, art become their God

3. *To be comely,* נָאָה *naah, 3a.*
Psa. 93. 5 holiness becometh thine house, O LORD

4. *To do,* עָשָׂה *asah, 2.*
Esth. 2. 11 how Esther did, and what should become

5. *To be, become,* הָיָה *hayah, 2.*
Deut 27. 9 thou art become the people of the LORD

6. *To be turned,* הָפַךְ *haphak, 2.*
Job 30. 21 Thou art become cruel to me: with thy

7. *To become,* γίνομαι *ginomai.*
Matt 13. 22 He also that received seed..becometh
13. 32 when it is grown, it..becometh a tree
18. 3 Except ye..become as little children, ye
28. 4 the keepers did shake, and became as
Mark 1. 17 I will make you to become fishers of
4. 19 cares..choke the word, and it becometh
4. 32 it groweth up, and becometh greater
9. 3 And his raiment became shining..white
John 1. 12 to them gave he power to become the
Acts 7. 40 Moses..we wot not what is become of
10. 10 he became very hungry, and would have
12. 18 stir among the soldiers, what was become
Rom. 3. 19 all the world may become guilty before
4. 18 that he might become the father of many
7. 13 that sin..might become exceeding sinful
1 Co. 3. 18 let him become a fool, that he may be
8. 9 lest..this liberty of your's become a
9. 20 unto the Jews I became as a Jew, that I
9. 22 To the weak became I as weak, that I
13. 1 I am become (as) sounding brass, or
13. 11 when I became a man, I put away childish
15. 20 now is Christ..[become] the firstfruits of
2 Co. 5. 17 behold, all things are become new
12. 11 I am become a fool in glorying; ye have
Gal. 4. 16 Am I therefore become your enemy
Phil. 2. 8 humbled himself, and became obedient
1 Th. 1. 6 And ye became followers of us, and of
2. 14 For ye..became followers of the churches
Phm. 6 communication of thy faith may become
Heb. 5. 9 became the author of eternal salvation
5. 12 and are become such as have need of
10. 33 and partly, whilst ye became companions
11. 7 by the which he..became heir of the
Jas. 2. 4 and are become judges of evil thoughts?
2. 11 thou art become a transgressor of the

Rev. 6. 12 the sun became black as sackcloth of
6. 12 and, lo..the moon became as blood
8. 8 the third part of the sea became blood
11. 15 The kingdoms of this world are become
16. 3 the sea; and it became as the blood of a
16. 4 rivers and fountains of waters..became
18. 2 Babylon..is become the habitation of

8. *To become for or into*, γίνομαι εἰς *ginomai eis.*
Matt 21. 42 the same is become the head of the
Mark 12. 10 The stone..is become the head of the
Luke 20. 17 the same is become the head of the
Acts 4. 11 which is become the head of the corner
Rev. 8. 11 third part of the waters became wormwd.

BECOME surety, to —
To mix, traffic, עָרַב *'arab.*
Gen. 44. 32 thy servant became surety for the lad
Prov. 17. 18 becometh surety in the presence of his
[*See also* Brutish, dead, destitute, dim, dry, effect, fat, fool, full, glorious, great, great estate, guilty, Jews, lame, like, loathsome, long, mighty, old, poor, ready, rich, servant, stranger, strong, surety, uncircumcised, unprofitable, vain, weak.]

BECOME, to —
1. *Worthily,* ἀξίως *axiōs.*
Rom 16. 2 That ye receive her..as becometh saints
Phil. 1. 27 let your conversation be as it becometh
2. *It is proper,* πρέπει *prepei,* πρέπω *prepō.*
Matt. 3. 15 for thus it becometh us to fulfil all
Eph. 5. 3 let it not be once named..as becometh
1 Ti. 2. 10 which becometh women professing
Titus 2. 1 Speak thou the things which become
Heb. 2. 10 For it became him, for whom (are) all
7. 26 For such an high priest became us..holy
3. *Comely, comeliness,* נָאוֶה *naveh.*
Prov. 17. 7 Excellent speech becometh not a fool

BECOMETH holiness, as —
Proper to a sacred person or thing, ἱεροπρεπής.
Titus 2. 3 (they be) in behaviour as becometh h.

BED —
1. *Any thing spread out,* יָצוּעַ (עֶרֶשׂ) *(eres) yatsua.*
1 Ch. 5. 1 forasmuch as he defiled his father's bed
Job 17. 13 I have made my bed in the darkness
Psa. 63. 6 When I remember thee upon my bed
132. 3 I will not come..nor go up into my bed
2. *Place of reclining,* מִטָּה *mittah.*
Gen. 47. 31 Israel bowed himself upon the bed's
48. 2 Israel strengthened himself..upon..bed
49. 33 he gathered up his feet into the bed, and
Exod. 8. 3 into thy bedchamber, and upon thy bed
1 Sa. 19. 13 took an image, and laid (it) in the bed
19. 15 Bring him up to me in the bed, that I
19. 16 an image in the bed, with a pillow of
28. 23 arose from the earth, and sat upon the bed
2 Sa. 4. 7 he lay on his bed in his bedchamber
1 Ki. 17. 19 he abode, and laid him upon his own bed
21. 4 And he laid him down upon his bed
2 Ki. 1. 4 Thou shalt not come down from that bed
1. 6 thou shalt not come down from that bed
1. 16 thou shalt not come down off that bed
4. 10 and let us set for him there a bed
4. 21 and laid him on the bed of the man of God
4. 32 child was dead..laid upon his bed
2 Ch. 24. 25 and slew him on his bed, and he died
Esth. 1. 6 the beds..gold and silver, upon a
7. 8 and Haman was fallen upon the bed
Psa. 6. 6 all the night make I my bed to swim
Prov. 26. 14 hinges, so (doth) the slothful upon his bed
Song 3. 7 Behold his bed, which (is) Solomon's
Eze. 23. 41 And satest upon a stately bed, and a
Amos 3. 12 dwell in Samaria in the corner of a bed
6. 4 That lie upon beds of ivory, and stretch
3. *Anything spread out,* מַצָּע *matstsa.*
Isa. 28. 20 For the bed is shorter than that
4. *Place for lying down,* מִשְׁכָּב *mishkab.*
Gen. 49. 4 because thou wentest up to thy..bed
Exod 21. 18 fist, and he die not, but keepeth (his) bed
Lev. 15. 4 Every bed, whereon he lieth that hath
15. 5 whosoever toucheth his bed shall wash
15. 21 whosoever toucheth her bed shall wash
15. 23 And if it (be) on (her) bed, or on any thing
15. 24 all the bed whereon he lieth shall be
15. 26 Every bed whereon she lieth all the days
15. 26 shall be unto her as the bed of her separ
2 Sa. 4. 5 Ish-bosheth, who lay on a bed at noon
4. 11 have slain a righteous person..upon..bed
11. 2 David arose from off his bed, and walked
11. 13 he went out to lie on his bed with the
13. 5 Jonadab said..Lay thee down on thy bed
17. 28 Brought beds, and basons, and earthen
1 Ki. 1. 47 And the king bowed himself upon the bed
2 Ch. 16. 14 they..laid him in the bed which was
Job 33. 15 sleep falleth..in slumberings upon..bed
33. 19 chastened also with pain upon his bed
Psa 4. 4 commune with your..heart upon your bed
36. 4 He deviseth mischief upon his bed
41. 3 wilt make all his bed in his sickness
149. 5 let them sing aloud upon their beds
Prov. 7. 17 I have perfumed my bed with myrrh
22. 27 why should he take away thy bed
Song 3. 1 By night on my bed I sought him
Isa. 57. 2 they shall rest in their beds, (each one)
57. 7 Upon a..mountain hast thou set thy bed
57. 8 thou hast enlarged thy bed, and made
57. 8 thou lovedst their bed where thou
Eze. 23. 17 came to her into the bed of love
32. 25 They have set her a bed in the midst of
Dan. 2. 28 the visions of thy head upon thy bed
2. 29 thy thoughts came..upon thy bed, what
4. 5 the thoughts upon my bed and the
4. 10 the visions of mine head in my bed
4. 13 in the visions of my head upon my bed
7. 1 and visions of his head upon his bed
Hos. 7. 14 when they howled upon their beds
Mic. 2. 1 and work evil upon their beds!
5. *Furrow,* עֲרוּגָה *arugah.*
Song 5. 13 His cheeks (are) as a bed of spices..sweet
6. 2 gone down into his garden, to the beds of
6. *Couch,* עֶרֶשׂ *eres.*
Job 7. 13 When I say, My bed shall comfort me
Psa. 41. 3 The LORD will strengthen him upon..bed
Prov. 7. 16 I have decked my bed with coverings
Song 1. 16 yea, pleasant: also our bed (is) green
7. *Place for reclining,* κλίνη *klinē.*
Matt. 9. 2 a man sick of the palsy, lying on a bed
9. 6 Arise, take up thy bed, and go unto thine
Mark 4. 21 put under a bushel, or under a bed?
7. 30 and her daughter laid upon the bed.
Luke 5. 18 men brought in a bed a man which was
8. 16 with a vessel, or putteth (it) under a bed
17. 34 there shall be two (men) in one bed; the
Acts 5. 15 laid..on [beds] and couches, that at the
Rev. 2. 22 I will cast her into a bed, and them that
8. *A lying, bed,* κοίτη *koitē.*
Luke 11. 7 my children are with me in bed; I
Heb. 13. 4 honourable in all, and the bed undefiled
9. *A mattress,* κράββατος *krabbatos,* κράβαττος.(*Lat.*)
Mark 2. 4 they let down the bed wherein the sick
2. 9 Arise, and take up thy bed, and walk?
2. 11 Arise, and take up thy bed, and go thy
2. 12 he arose, took up the bed, and went
6. 55 to carry about in beds those that were
John 5. 8 Rise, take up thy bed, and walk
5. 9 the man..took up his bed, and walked
5. 10 it is not lawful for thee to carry (thy) bed
5. 11 the same said..Take up thy bed, and
5. 12 What man..said..Take up [thy bed,] and
Acts 9. 33 Æneas, which had kept his bed eight

BED, to make —
1. *To strew (a place for reposing in),* יָצַע *yatsa,* 5.
Psa 139. 8 If I make my bed in hell, behold, thou
2. *To strew,* στρωννύω *strōnnuō.*
Acts 9. 34 maketh thee whole: arise..make thy bed

BED CHAMBER —
1. *Inner reclining place,* חֲדַר מִשְׁכָּב *cheder mishkab.*
Exod. 8. 3 into thy bedchamber, and upon thy bed
2 Sa. 4. 7 he lay on his bed in his bedchamber
2 Ki. 6. 12 words..thou speakest in thy bedchamber
Eccl. 10. 20 curse not the rich in thy bedchamber
2. *Inner bed room,* חֲדַר מִטָּה *cheder mittah.*
2 Ki. 11. 2 hid..him and his nurse, in..bedchamber
2 Ch. 22. 11 put him and his nurse in a bedchamber

BE'-DAD, בְּדַד *son of Adad.*
Father of the fourth king of Edom, "Hadad-ben-Bedad," B.C. 1500.
Gen. 36. 35 Hadad the son of B., who smote Midian
1 Ch. 1. 46 Hadad the son of B., which smote Midian

BE'-DAN, בְּדָן *son of judgment.*
1. A judge of Israel between Jerubbaal (*i.e.* Gideon) and Jephthah. His name is omitted in the history of the Book of Judges. The LXX., Syriac and Arabic, have *Barak.* His name may be compared with that of *Jael* in Judg. 5. 6, who was probably also a judge, though we know nothing of him except from Deborah's song, B.C. 1112.
1 Sa. 12. 11 LORD sent Jerubbaal, and B., and
2. Descendant of Machir son of Manasseh, B.C. 1369.
1 Ch. 7. 17 the sons of Ulam; B. These (were) the

BE-DE'-IAH, בֵּדְיָה *servant of Jah.*
One of the family of Bani who had married a strange wife, B.C. 445.
Ezra 10. 35 [Of..sons of Bani; Maadai]..B., Chelluh

BED STEAD —
An arched bed, עֶרֶשׂ *eres.*
Deut. 3. 11 behold, his bedstead (was) a bedstead of

BEE —
A bee, דְּבוֹרָה *deborah.*
Deut. 1. 44 the Amorites..chased you, as bees do
Judg 14. 8 behold..a swarm of bees and honey in
Psa 118. 12 They compassed me about like bees; they
Isa. 7. 18 for the bee that (is) in the land of Assyria

BE-EL-IA'-DA, בְּעֶלְיָדָע *the lord knows.*
A son of David, called *Eliada* in 2 Sa. v. and 1 Ch. iii., B.C. 1020.
1 Ch. 14. 7 And Elishama, and B., and Eliphalet

BE-EL-ZE'-BUB, Βεελζεβούλ *lord of the fly.*
A heathen deity to whom the Jews ascribed supremacy among evil spirits. The correct orthography is *Beelzebul.*
Matt 10. 25 they have called the master of the house B.
12. 24 but by B. the prince of the devils
12. 27 if I by B. cast out devils, by whom do
Mark 3. 22 He hath B., and by the prince of the
Luke 11. 15 He casteth out devils through B. the
11. 18 ye say that I cast out devils through B.
11. 19 if I by B. cast out devils, by whom do

BE'-ER, בְּאֵר *a well (artificial).*
1. A station of the Israelites beyond the Arnon, and so called because of the "well" dug by the princes and nobles of the people. This is probably the *Beer-Elim* ("well of heroes") of Isa. 15. 8.
Num 21. 16 from thence..to B.: that (is) the well
2. A place to which Jotham son of Gideon fled for fear of his brother Abimelech, 8 miles W. of Hebron.
Judg. 9. 21 Jotham ran away, and fled..to B., and

BE-E'-RA, בְּאֵרָא *expounder.*
Son of Zophah of the tribe of Asher, B.C. 1570.
1 Ch. 7. 37 [sons of Zophah,] Suah..and B.

BE-E'-RAH, בְּאֵרָה *expounder.*
A prince of the Reubenites, carried captive to Assyria by Tilgath-pilneser, B.C. 740.
1 Ch. 5. 6 [sons of Joel]..B. his son, whom Tilgath.

BE-ER E'-LIM, בְּאֵר אֵלִים *well of Elim.*
In the S. confines of Moab, Eglaim being at the N. of the Salt Sea. The name points to the well dug by the chiefs (*Elim*) of Israel on their nearing the promised land.
Isa. 15. 8 and the howling thereof unto B.-e.

BE-E'-RI, בְּאֵרִי *expounder.*
1. A Hittite, father of Judith, wife of Esau, B.C. 1810.
Gen. 26. 34 took to wife Judith the daughter of B.
2. Father of Hosea the prophet, B.C. 800.
Hos. 1. 1 The word..came unto..the son of B.

BE-ER LA-HAI'-ROI, בְּאֵר לַחַי רֹאִי *well of the living one that beholds me.*
Between Kadesh and Bered, "in the way to Shur," and therefore in the S.
Gen. 16. 14 Wherefore the well was called B.-l.-r.
24. 62 Isaac came from the way of the well L.-r.
25. 11 and Isaac dwelt by the well L.-r.

BE-E'-ROTH, בְּאֵרֹת *wells.*
1. A station of Israel belonging to Jaakan.
Deut 10. 6 children of Israel took..journey from B.
2. One of the four cities of the Hivites that drew Joshua into a treaty of peace. It is 7 miles from Jerusalem on the way to Nicopolis. Now El-Bireh.
Josh. 9. 17 their cities (were) Gibeon..and B., and
18. 25 Gibeon, and Ramah, and B.
2 Sa. 4. 2 for B. also was reckoned to Benjamin
Ezra 2. 25 children of Kirjath-arim..and B., seven
Neh. 7. 29 men of Kirjath-jearim..and B., seven

BE-ER-O-THITE, בְּאֵרֹתִי *belonging to Beeroth.*
An inhabitant of Beeroth in Benjamin.
2 Sa. 4. 2 Rechab, the sons of Rimmon a B.
4. 3 the B.s fled to Gittaim, and were
4. 5 the sons of Rimmon the B., Rechab and
4. 9 David answered..sons of Rimmon the B.
23. 37 Naharai the B., armourbearer to Joab
1 Ch. 11. 39 Naharai the B..armourbearer of Joab

BE-ER SHE'-BA, בְּאֵר שֶׁבַע *well of the oath.*
One of the oldest places in Canaan at the extreme south.
Gen. 21. 14 Hagar..wandered in the wilderness of B.
21. 31 Wherefore he called that place B.
21. 32 Thus they made a covenant at B.: then
21. 33 And..planted a grove in B., and called
22. 19 they rose up and went together to B.
22. 19 and Abraham dwelt at B.
26. 23 And he went up from thence to B.
26. 33 the name of the city (is) B. unto this day
28. 10 Jacob went out from B., and went
46. 1 Israel took his journey..and came to B.
46. 5 Jacob rose up from B.: and the sons of
Josh. 15. 28 Hazar-shual, and B., and Bizjothjah
19. 2 they had in their inheritance B., and
Judg 20. 1 congregation was gathered..from Dan to B
1 Sa. 3. 20 all Israel from Dan even to B. knew that
8. 2 Joel..Abiah..judges in Beer-sheba
2 Sa. 3. 10 throne of David..from Dan even to B.
17. 11 Israel..gathered..from Dan even to B.
24. 2 Go now..from Dan even to B., and
24. 7 they went out to the south of Judah to B.
24. 15 died of the people from Dan even to B.
1 Ki. 4. 25 Israel dwelt safely..from Dan even to B.
19. 3 when he saw..he..came to B.
2 Ki. 12. 1 his mother's name (was) Zibiah of B.
23. 8 defiled the high places..from Geba to B
1 Ch. 4. 28 they dwelt at B., and Moladah, and
21. 2 Go, number Israel from B. even to Dan
2 Ch. 19. 4 he went out again..from B. to mount
24. 1 His mother's name also (was) Zibiah of B
30. 5 to make proclamation..from B. even to
Neh. 11. 27 at Hazar-shual, and at B., and (in) the
11. 30 they dwelt from B. unto the valley of
Amos 5. 5 seek not Beth-el..and pass not to B.: for
8. 14 and, The manner of B. liveth; even they

BE-ESH-TE'-RAH, בְּעֶשְׁתְּרָה *house of Ashterah.*
A Levitical city in Manasseh, W. of the Jordan. It was allotted to the Gershomites, and is identical with *Ashtaroth* or *Ashterah.*
Josh. 21. 27 tribe of Manasseh..B. with her suburbs

BEETLE —
A beetle, חַרְגֹּל *chargol.*
Lev. 11. 22 the beetle after his kind, and the

BEEVES —

Herd, ox, heifer, בָּקָר *baqar.*

Lev. 22. 19 a male without blemish, of the beeves
22. 21 a freewill offering in beeves or sheep
Num 31. 28 of the persons, and of the beeves, and of
31. 30 of the persons, of the beeves, of the asses
31. 33 threescore and twelve thousand beeves
31. 38 the beeves..thirty and six thousand; of
31. 44 And thirty and six thousand beeves

BEFALL, to —

1. *To meet,* אָנָה *anah,* 4.
Psa. 91. 10 There shall no evil befall thee, neither

2. *To come,* בּוֹא *bo.*
2 Sa. 19. 7 worse unto thee than all the evil..befell

3. *To find,* מָצָא *matsa.*
Num 20. 14 all the travail that hath befallen us
Deut 31. 17 many evils and troubles shall befall them
31. 21 when many evils..are befallen them
Josh. 2. 23 told him all (things) that befell them
Judg. 6. 13 why then is all this befallen us? and

4. *To meet, chance,* קָרָא *qara.*
Gen. 42. 4 Lest peradventure mischief befall him
42. 38 if mischief befall him by the way in the
49. 1 which shall befall you in the last days
Lev. 10. 19 and such things have befallen me
Deut 31. 29 evil will befall you in the latter days

5. *To meet, chance,* קָרָה *qarah.*
Gen. 42. 29 told him all that befell unto them
44. 29 if ye take..from me, and mischief befall
Esth. 6. 13 Haman told.. every (thing)..befallen
Dan. 10. 14 what shall befall thy people in the latter

6. *To become, come into being,* γίνομαι *ginomai.*
Mark 5. 16 they..told them how it befell to him

7. *To come together,* συμβαίνω *sumbainō.*
Acts 20. 19 temptations, which befell me by the lying

8. *To meet together,* συναντάω *sunantaō.*
Acts 20. 22 knowing the things that shall befall me

9. *The things of,* τὰ τῶν *ta tōn.*
Matt. 8. 33 what was befallen to the possessed of the

10. *Chance, occurrence,* מִקְרֶה *miqreh.*
1 Sa. 20. 26 Something hath befallen him, he (is) not
Eccl. 3. 19 that which befalleth the sons of men
3. 19 befalleth beasts; even one thing befalleth

BEFORE, (the presence of) —

1. *Unto, to,* אֶל *el.*
Gen. 12. 15 saw her, and commended her before Pha.

2. *Nose,* אַף *aph.*
Deut 33. 10 they shall put incense before thee, and

3. *With,* אֵת *eth.*
Gen. 19. 13 is waxen great before the face of the LORD

4. *Expectation,* טֶרֶם [V.L. טרום].
Ruth 3. 14 she rose up before one could know

5. *Expectation,* טֶרֶם *terem.*
Gen. 2. 5 before it was in the earth..before it grew

6. *In or with expectation,* בְּטֶרֶם *be-terem.*
Gen. 27. 4 that my soul may bless thee before I die
Jer. 1. 5 Before I formed thee..before thou came.

7. *In not, without,* בְּלֹא *be-lo.*
Job 15. 32 It shall be accomplished before his time

8. *Over against,* מוּל *mul.*
Exod 34. 3 flocks nor herds feed before that mount
Josh. 19. 46 and Rakkon, with the border before J.

9. *Over against the face,* מוּל פָּנִים *mul panim.*
Exod 28. 25 the shoulder pieces of the ephod, before
39. 18 the shoulder pieces of the ephod, before

10. *Ascent, up-going,* מַעֲלֶה *maaleh.*
Judg. 8. 13 returned from battle before the sun

11. *The front,* נֶגֶד *neged.*
Gen. 31. 32 before our brethren discern thou what

12. *At the front,* לְנֶגֶד *le-neged.*
2 Ki. 1. 13 came and fell on his knees before Elijah

13. *From the front,* מִנֶּגֶד *min-neged.*
Deut 28. 66 thy life shall hang in doubt before thee

14. *The front, over-against,* נֹכַח *nokach.*
Gen. 30. 38 the rods which he had pilled before the
Josh. 15. 7 that (is) before the going up to Adummim
Judg 18. 6 Go in peace: before the LORD (is) your
Prov. 5. 21 the ways of man (are) before the eyes of
Lam. 2. 19 like water before the face of the LORD
Eze. 14. 3 stumbling block of their iniquity before
14. 4 stumbling block of his iniquity before his
14. 7 stumbling block of his iniquity before his

15. *The front,* נֶכַח *nekach.*
Exod 14. 2 before it shall ye encamp by the sea

16. *Until,* עַד *ad.*
Gen. 48. 5 born..before I came unto thee into E.

17. *In the eye of,* בְּעֵין *be-en.*
1 Sa. 21. 13 changed his behaviour before; Jer. 32. 30.

17a. *To the eye of,* לְעֵין *le-en.*
1 Chr. 29. 10; Jer. 32. 12, 13; Eze. 20. 9, 14, 41.

18. *With,* עִם *im.*
1 Sa. 2. 21 the child Samuel grew before the LORD

19. *In face of,* לִפְנֵי *li-phene.*
Gen. 6. 11 was corrupt before God; 6 13; 7. 1.

Gen. 10. 9 He was a mighty hunter before the LORD
10. 9 the mighty hunter before the LORD
13. 9 (Is) not the whole land before thee?
13. 10 well watered every where, before the LORD
17. 1 walk before me, and be thou perfect
17. 18 O that Ishmael might live before thee!
18. 8 which he had dressed, and set (it) before
18. 22 Abraham stood yet before the LORD
19. 27 place where he stood before the LORD
20. 15; 23. 19; 25. 9, 18, 18; 49. 30; 50. 13 Ex. 20. 3; [34. 6.

20. *On the face,* עַל פָּנִים *al panim.*
Gen. 11. 28 Haran died before his father Terah in the

21. *Over-against,* קֳבֵל *qobal.*
2 Ki. 15. 10 smote him before the people, and slew

22. *Over-against,* קֳבֵל *qebel.*
Dan. 2. 31 brightness (was) excellent, stood before
3. 3 they stood before the image that N.
5. 1 Belshazzar..drank wine before the

23. *The east, what is before,* קֶדֶם *qedem.*
Psa. 139. 5 Thou hast beset me behind and before
Prov. 8. 22 of his way, before his works of old
Isa. 9. 12 The Syrians before, and the Philistines

24. *The east, what is before,* קֳדָם *qodam.*
Ezra 4. 18 The letter..hath been plainly read before
4. 23 Now when the copy..(was) read before
7. 19 (those) deliver thou before the God of
Dan. 2. 9 speak before me, till the time be changed
2. 10 The Chaldeans answered before the king
2. 11 none other that can show it before the
2. 24 bring me in before the king, and I will
2. 25 Arioch brought in Daniel before the king
2. 36 the interpretation thereof before the king
3. 13 they brought these men before the king
4. 6 the wise (men) of Babylon before me
4. 7 and I told the dream before them; but
4. 8 at the last Daniel came in before me
4. 8 and before him I told the dream, (saying)
5. 13 Then was Daniel brought in before the
5. 15 astrologers, have been brought in before
5. 17 Then Daniel answered..before the king
5. 23 they have brought the vessels..before
6. 10 he kneeled..gave thanks before his God
6. 11 found Daniel..making supplication before
6. 12 they..spake before the king concerning
6. 13 Then answered they, and said before the
6. 18 instruments of musick brought before
6. 22 and also before thee, O king, have I done
6. 26 men tremble and fear before the God of
7. 7 all the beasts that (were) before it
7. 8 before whom there were three of the first
7. 10 A fiery stream..came forth from before
7. 10 ten thousand times ten thousand..before
7. 13 and they brought him near before him

25. *The heart, inner part,* קֶרֶב *qereb.*
Exod 10. 1 that I might shew these my signs before

26. *First, former,* רִאשׁוֹן *rishon.*
Num. 6. 12 but the days that were before shall be
Josh. 8. 33 as Moses..had commanded before
1 Ki. 13. 6 the king's hand..became as..before

27. *From the east,* מִן קֳדָם *min qodam.*
Dan. 5. 19 all people..feared before him
6. 26 tremble and fear before the God of Daniel
7. 8 before whom there were three of the first
7. 20 and (of) the other..before whom three fell

28. *Yesterday, third day,* תְּמוֹל שִׁלְשׁוֹם *temol shilshom*
Gen. 31. 2 behold, it (was) not toward him as before
31. 5 that it (is) not toward me as before; but
Josh. 4. 18 the waters..flowed..as (they did) before

29. *From,* ἀπό *apo.*
Acts 7. 45 whom God drave out before the face of
1 Jo. 2. 28 we may..not be ashamed before him

30. *If..not first,* ἐὰν μὴ πρότερον *ean mē proteron.*
John 7. 51 Doth our law judge..man before it hear

31. *To, towards,* εἰς *eis.*
Acts 22. 30 brought Paul..and set him before them
Jas. 2. 6 rich men..draw you before the judgment

32. *To the face,* εἰς πρόσωπον *eis prosōpon.*
2 Co. 8. 24 Wherefore shew ye to them, and before

33. *From over-against,* ἀπέναντι *apenanti.*
Matt 27. 24 Pilate..washed (his) hands [before] the
Rom. 3. 18 There is no fear of God before their eyes

34. *In front of,* ἔμπροσθεν *emprosthen.*
Matt. 5. 16 Let your light so shine before men
5. 24 Leave there thy gift before the altar
6. 1 that ye do not your alms before men
6. 2 do not sound a trumpet before thee
7. 6 neither cast ye your pearls before swine
10. 32 Whosoever..shall confess me before men
10. 32 him will I confess also before my Father
10. 33 But whosoever shall deny me before men
10. 33 him will I also deny before my Father
11. 10 I send my messenger before thy face
17. 2 was transfigured before them: and his
25. 32 before him shall be gathered all nations
26. 70 he denied before (them) all, saying, I
27. 11 Jesus stood before the governor: and the
27. 29 they bowed the knee before him, and
Mark 1. 2 I send my messenger [before] thy face
9. 2 and he was transfigured before them
Luke 5. 19 they..let him down..before Jesus
7. 27 which shall prepare thy way before thee
12. 8 Whosoever shall confess me before men
12. 8 him shall the Son..confess before the
14. 2 there was a certain man before him

Luke 19. 4 he ran before, and climbed up into a
19. 27 bring hither, and slay (them) before me
19. 28 he went before, ascending up to Jerusalem
21. 36 and to stand before the Son of man
John 1. 15 preferred before me: for he was
1. 27 coming after me is preferred before me
1. 30 cometh a man..preferred before me
3. 28 not the Christ, but that I am sent before
10. 4 he putteth forth..he goeth before them
12. 37 he had done so many miracles before
Acts 18. 17 Greeks..beat him before the judgment
2 Co. 5. 10 we must all appear before the judgment
Gal. 2. 14 I said unto Peter before (them) all, If
Phil. 3. 13 unto those things which are before
1 Th. 3. 9 we joy for your sakes before our God
3. 13 unblameable in holiness before God
1 Jo. 3. 19 we..shall assure our hearts before him
Rev. 4. 6 full of eyes before and behind
22. 8 I fell down to worship before the feet of

35. *In the midst,* ἐν (τῷ μέσῳ) *en tō mesō.*
Matt 14. 6 the daughter of Herodias danced before
Acts 5. 27 they set..before the council: and the

36. *In before,* ἔναντι *enanti.*
Luke 1. 8 he executed the priest's office [before] God

37. *In before,* ἐναντίον *enantion.*
Mark 2. 12 went forth before them all; insomuch
Luke 20. 26 could not take hold..before the people
24. 19 mighty in deed and word before God and
Acts 8. 32 and like a lamb dumb before his shearer

38. *In the face,* ἐνώπιον *enōpion.*
Luke 1. 6 And they were both righteous [before]
1. 17 he shall go before him in the spirit and
1. 75 In holiness and righteousness before
5. 18 to bring him in, and to lay (him) before
5. 25 he rose up before them, and took up
8. 47 and falling down before him, she
12. 6 not one of them is forgotten before God
12. 9 denieth me [before]..be denied before
15. 18 I have sinned against heaven, and before
16. 15 which justify yourselves before men
23. 14 I, having examined (him) before you
24. 43 And he took (it), and did eat before them
Acts 2. 25 I foresaw the Lord always before my face
4. 10 doth this man stand here before you
6. 6 they set before the apostles: and when
7. 46 found favour before God, and desired to
9. 15 to bear my name before the Gentiles
10. 4 are come up for a memorial [before] God
10. 30 a man stood before me in bright clothing
10. 33 are we all here present before God, to
19. 9 but spake evil of that way before the
19. 19 and burned them before all (men): and
Rom 14. 22 Hast thou faith? have (it) to thyself before
Gal. 1. 20 I write unto you, behold, before God, I
1 Ti. 5. 4 that is good and acceptable before God
5. 20 Them that sin rebuke before all, that
5. 21 I charge (thee) before God, and the Lord
6. 12 professed a good profession before
2 Ti. 2. 14 charging (them) before the Lord that
4. 1 I charge (thee) therefore before God
3 Jo. 6 borne witness of thy charity before
Rev. 1. 4 Spirits which are before his throne
2. 14 to cast a stumbling block before the
3. 2 have not found thy works perfect before
3. 5 I will confess his name before my Father
3. 8 I have set before thee an open door, and
3. 9 to come and worship before thy feet
4. 5 lamps of fire burning before the throne
4. 6 And before the throne (there was) a sea
4. 10 down before him..before the throne
5. 8 four (and) twenty elders fell down before
7. 9 stood before the throne, and before the
7. 11 and fell before the throne on their faces
7. 15 are they before the throne of God, and
8. 2 seven angels which stood before God
8. 3 golden altar which was before the throne
8. 4 ascended up before God out of the
9. 13 of the golden altar which is before God
11. 4 standing before the God of the earth
11. 16 elders, which sat before God on their
12. 4 and the dragon stood before the woman
12. 10 accused them before our God day and
13. 12 the power of the first beast before him
14. 3 a new song before the throne, and before
14. 5 [without fault before the throne of God]
15. 4 shall come and worship before thee
16. 19 in remembrance before God, to give
19. 20 wrought miracles before him, with
20. 12 small and great, stand before God: and

39. *In presence of,* ἐπί (gen.) *epi.*
Mark 13. 9 ye shall be brought before rulers and
Acts 23. 30 say before thee what (they had) against
24. 19 Who ought to have been here before thee
24. 20 in me, while I stood before the council
25. 9 there be judged of these things before
25. 26 brought him forth before you..before
26. 2 I shall answer for myself this day before
1 Co. 6. 1 go to law before the unjust..not before
2 Co. 7. 14 our boasting, which (I made) before
1 Ti. 5. 19 accusation, but before two or three wit.
6. 13 Christ Jesus, who before Pontius Pilate

40. *On, upon, over,* ἐπί (dat.) *epi.*
Rev. 10. 11 Thou must prophesy again before many

41. *In presence of,* ἐπί (acc.) *epi.*
Matt 10. 18 And ye shall be brought before governors
Luke 21. 12 brought before kings and rulers for my
Acts 10. 17 men which were sent..stood before the

42. *Down toward*, κατά (acc.) *kata.*
Luke 2. 31 Which thou hast prepared before the face
Gal. 3. 1 O foolish Galatians..before whose eyes

43. *Down over against*, κατέναντι *katenanti.*
Rom. 4. 17 before him whom he believed, (even) God

44. *Down in face of*, κατενώπιον *katenōpion.*
2 Co. 12. 19 think..we speak [before] God in Christ
Eph. 1. 4 and without blame before him in love
Jude 24 to present (you) faultless before the p. of

45. *Alongside*, παρά (dat.) *para.*
Rom. 2. 13 the hearers of the law (are) just before
Jas. 1. 27 Pure religion and undefiled before God
2 Pe. 2. 11 accusation against them..[before] the

46. *Before, in front of*, πρό *pro.*
Matt. 5. 12 they the prophets which were before you
8. 29 art thou come..to torment us before the
11. 10 I send my messenger before thy face
24. 38 For as in the days that were [before] the
Mark 1. 2 I send my messenger before thy face
Luke 1. 76 for thou shalt go before the face of the
7. 27 Behold..my messenger before thy face
9. 52 And sent messengers before his face
10. 1 sent them two and two before his face
11. 38 he had not first washed before dinner
21. 12 But before all these, they shall lay their
John 5. 7 am coming, another steppeth down before
10. 8 All that ever came before me are thieves
11. 55 and many went out..before the passover
12. 1 Jesus, six days before the passover came
13. 1 Now before the feast of the passover
17. 5 which I had with thee before the world
17. 24 for thou lovedst me before the foundation
Acts 5. 23 the keepers standing without [before] the
5. 36 before these days rose up Theudas
12. 6 the keepers before the door kept the
12. 14 she..told how Peter stood before the
13. 24 When John had first preached before his
14. 13 Then the priest..which was before their
21. 38 which before these days madest an
Rom. 16. 7 who also were in Christ before me
1 Co. 2. 7 which God ordained before the world
4. 5 Therefore judge nothing before the time
Gal. 1. 17 them which were apostles before me
Eph. 1. 4 he hath chosen us in him before the
Col. 1. 17 And he is before all things, and by him
2 Ti. 4. 21 Do thy diligence to come before winter
Heb. 11. 5 for before his translation he had this
Jas. 5. 9 behold, the judge standeth before the
1 Pe. 1. 20 Who verily was foreordained before the

47. *Before*, πρό (adv.) *pro.*
Matt. 6. 8 your Father knoweth..before ye ask him
Luke 2. 21 named of the angel before he was
22. 15 I have desired to eat..before I suffer
John 1. 48 Jesus..said unto him, Before that Philip
13. 19 Now I tell you before it come, that
Gal. 2. 12 For before that certain came from James
3. 23 But before faith came, we were kept
2 Ti. 1. 9 which was given..before the world began
Titus 1. 2 which God..promised before the world

48. *Towards*, πρός (acc.) *pros.*
Acts 26. 26 before whom also I speak freely
Rom. 4. 2 he hath..to glory; but not before God

49. *Before the face of*, πρὸ προσώπου [*pro, prosōpon*].
Acts 13. 24 When John had first preached before his

50. *Formerly, before*, πρότερον (adv.) *proteron.*
John 6. 62 Son of man ascend up where he was before?
9. 8 and they which before had seen him
2 Co. 1. 15 I was minded to come unto you before
1 Ti. 1. 13 Who was before a blasphemer, and a

51. *Formerly, erst, before*, πρίν *prin.*
Matt 26. 34 That this night, before the cock crow
26. 75 Before the cock crow, thou shalt deny
Mark 14. 72 Before the cock crow twice, thou shalt
Luke 22. 61 Before the cock crow, thou shalt deny
John 8. 58 I say unto you, Before Abraham; 14. 29.

52. *If not first*, ἐὰν μὴ πρότερον [*ean*]; John 7. 51.

53. *Before that*, πρὶν ἤ *prin ē.*
Matt 1. 18 before they came together, she was found
Mark 14. 30 before the cock crow twice, thou shalt
Luke 2. 26 before he had seen the Lord's Christ
Acts 2. 20 [before] that great and notable day of the
7. 2 God..appeared unto..Abraham before he

54. *First, foremost*, πρῶτος *prōtos.*
John 1. 15, 30 for he was before me.

55. *First, before*, πρῶτον (adv.) *prōton.*
John 15. 18 ye know that it hated me before..you

BEFORE, to be —
To be formerly, προϋπάρχω *prouparchō.*
Luke 23. 12 for before they were at enmity between

BEFORE that —
Before that, πρὶν ἤ *prin ē.*
Luke 22. 34 [before that] thou shalt thrice deny that
Acts 25. 16 before that he which is accused have the

BEFORE that time —
Yesterday, third day, אתמול שלשום *ethmol shilshom.*
1 Sa. 14. 21 were with the Philistines before that

BEFORE, that were —
The former, הראשנים *ha-rishonim.*
Num. 6. 12 the days that were before shall be lost

BEFORE, they that went —
The former, קדמוני *qadmoni.*
Job 18. 20 as they that went before were affrighted.
[*See also* Appoint, begin, brought, choose, confirm, day, determine, fall, go, gospel, hear, instruct, know, meditate, never, notice, ordain, preach, preferring, presence, prove, run, sabbath, say, see, set, show, speak, spoken, stand, suffer, take, tell, world.]

BEFOREHAND —
[*See* Make, manifest, open, testify, thought.]

BEFORETIME —

1. *Formerly*, לפנים *le-phanim.*
Deut. 2. 12 Horims also dwelt in Seir beforetime

2. *In the former*, בראשנה *ba-rishonah.*
2 Sa. 7. 10 children of wickedness..as beforetime

3. *Yesterday third day*, אתמול שלשום *ethmol shilshom.*
1 Sa. 10. 11 when all that knew him beforetime saw

4. *Yesterday third day*, תמול שלשם *temol shilshom.*
Josh 20. 5 neighbour..hated him not beforetime
2 Ki. 13. 5 children of Israel dwelt..as beforetime

5. *To be before*, προϋπάρχω *prouparchō.*
Acts 8. 9 Simon, which beforetime in the same city

BEG, to —

1. *To seek, inquire*, בקש *baqash*, 3.
Psa. 37. 25 have I not seen..his seed begging bread

2. *To ask, demand*, שאל *shaal.*
Prov 20. 4 shall he beg in harvest, and (have)

3. *To ask earnestly*, שאל *shaal*, 3.
Psa. 109. 10 Let his children be..vagabonds, and beg

4. *To ask, entreat, supplicate*, αἰτέω *aiteō.*
Matt 27. 58 He went to Pilate, and begged the body
Luke 23. 52 This (man) went unto Pilate, and begged

5. *To ask more, or beside*, ἐπαιτέω *epaiteō.*
Luke 16. 3 I cannot dig; to beg I am ashamed

6. *To ask at*, προσαιτέω *prosaiteō.*
Mark 10. 46 Bartimæus..by the highway side [begging]
Luke 18. 35 blind man sat by the wayside [begging]
John 9. 8 Is not this he that sat and begged?

BEGAN —
Foundation, יסד *yesud.*
Ezra 7. 9 upon the first (day)..began he to go up

BEGAN, men —
To be begun, חלל *chalal*, 6.
Gen 4. 26 then began men to call upon the name of

BEGET, to —

1. *To beget, bring forth*, ילד *yalad.*
Gen. 4. 18 Irad begat M..M. begat M...M begat
10. 8 Cush begat Nimrod: he began to be a
10. 13 Mizraim begat Ludim, and Anamim
10. 15 Canaan begat Sidon his firstborn, and
10. 24 Arphaxad begat Salah, and Salah begat
10. 26 Joktan begat Almodad, and Sheleph
22. 23 Bethuel begat Rebekah: these eight
25. 3 Jokshan begat Sheba and Dedan
Num 11. 12 all this people? have I begotten them
Deut 32. 18 Of the Rock (that) begat thee thou art
1 Ch. 1. 10 Cush begat Nimrod: he began to be
1. 11 Mizraim begat Ludim, and Anamim
1. 13 Canaan begat Zidon his firstborn, and
1. 18 Arphaxad begat Shelah, and Shelah begat
1. 20 Joktan begat Almodad, and Sheleph
Psa. 2. 7 Thou (art) my son..have I begotten thee
Prov. 17. 21 He that begetteth a fool (doeth it) to his
23. 22 Hearken unto thy father that begat thee
23. 24 he that begetteth a wise (child) shall have
Isa. 49. 21 Who hath begotten me these, seeing I
Dan. 11. 6 and he that begat her, and he that
Hos. 5. 7 for they have begotten strange children
Zech 13. 3 his mother that begat him..that begat

2. *To cause to yield or bring forth*, ילד *yalad*, 5.
Gen. 5. 3 and begat (a son) in his own likeness
5. 4 after he had begotten..and he begat
5. 6 an hundred and five years, and begat
5. 7 after he begat Enos..begat sons and
5. 9 Enos lived ninety years, and begat
5. 10 after he begat Cainan..begat sons and
5. 12 Cainan lived seventy years, and begat
5. 13 after he begat Mahalaleel. begat sons
5. 15 Mahalaleel lived..and begat Jared
5. 16 after he begat Jared..begat sons and
5. 18 Jared lived an..and he begat Enoch
5. 19 after he begat Enoch..begat sons and
5. 21 Enoch lived sixty..and begat Methuselah
5. 22 after he begat Methuselah..begat sons
5. 25 Methuselah lived..and begat Lamech
5. 26 Methuselah..begat Lamech..and begat
5. 28 Lamech lived an hundred..and begat a
5. 30 after he begat Noah..begat sons and
5. 32 Noah begat Shem, Ham, and Japheth
6. 10 Noah begat three sons, Shem, Ham, and
11. 10 and begat Arphaxad two years after the
11. 11 Shem..begat Arphaxad..and begat sons
11. 12 Arphaxad lived five..and begat Salah
11. 13 after he begat Salah..begat sons and
11. 14 Salah lived thirty years, and begat Eber
11. 15 after he begat Eber..begat sons and
11. 16 Eber lived four and..and begat Peleg
11. 17 after he begat Peleg..begat sons and
11. 18 Peleg lived thirty years, and begat Reu
11. 19 after he begat Reu..and begat sons and
11. 20 Reu lived two and..and begat Serug
Gen. 11. 21 after he begat Serug..begat sons and
11. 22 Serug lived thirty years, and begat Nahor
11. 23 after he begat Nahor..begat sons and
11. 24 Nahor lived nine and..and begat Terah
11. 25 after he begat Terah..begat sons and
11. 26 Terah lived..begat Abram, Nahor, and
11. 27 Terah begat Abram..and Haran begat
17. 20 twelve princes shall he beget, and 25. 19
48. 6 which thou begettest after them, shall
Lev. 25. 45 which they begat in your land: and they
Num 26. 29 and Machir begat Gilead: of Gilead
26. 58 the Korathites. And Kohath begat
Deut. 4. 25 thou shalt beget children, and children's
28. 41 Thou shalt beget sons and daughters
Judg 11. 1 son of an harlot: and Gilead begat
Ruth 4. 18 the generations of Pharez: Pharez begat
4. 19 Hezron begat Ram, and Ram begat
4. 20 Amminadab begat Nahshon, and N. begat
4. 21 Salmon begat Boaz, and Boaz begat Obed
4. 22 Obed begat Jesse, and Jesse begat David
2 Ki. 20. 18 of thy sons..which thou shalt beget
1 Ch. 1. 34 Abraham begat Isaac. The sons of Isaac
2. 10 Ram begat Amminadab; and A. begat
2. 11 Nahshon begat Salma..Salma begat Boaz
2. 12 Boaz begat Obed, and Obed begat Jesse
2. 13 Jesse begat his firstborn Eliab, and
2. 18 Caleb..begat (children) of Azubah (his)
2. 20 Hur begat Uri, and Uri begat Bezaleel
2. 22 Segub begat Jair, who had three and
2. 36 Attai begat Nathan, and Nathan begat
2. 37 Zabad begat Ephlal, and Ephlal begat
2. 38 Obed begat Jehu, and Jehu begat Azariah
2. 39 Azariah begat Helez, and Helez begat
2. 40 Eleasah begat Sisamai, and Sisamai begat
2. 41 Shallum begat Jekamiah, and J..begat
2. 44 Shema begat Raham..Rekem begat
2. 46 Ephah..bare Haran..Haran begat
4. 2 Reaiah..begat Jahath; and Jahath begat
4. 8 Coz begat Anub, and Zobebah, and the
4. 11 Chelub the brother of Shuah begat Mehir
4. 12 Eshton begat Beth-rapha, and Paseah
4. 14 Meonothai begat Ophrah..Seraiah begat
6. 4 Eleazar begat Phinehas, Phinehas begat
6. 5 Abishua begat Bukki, and Bukki begat
6. 6 Uzzi begat Zerahiah, and Zerahiah begat
6. 7 Meraioth begat Amariah, and A. begat
6. 8 Ahitub begat Zadok, and Zadok begat
6. 9 Ahimaaz begat Azariah, and A. begat
6. 10 Johanan begat Azariah, he (it is) that
6. 11 Azariah begat Amariah, and A. begat
6. 12 Ahitub begat Zadok..Zadok begat Shall.
6. 13 Shallum begat Hilkiah..Hilkiah begat
6. 14 Azariah begat Seraiah..Seraiah begat
7. 32 Heber begat Japhlet, and Shomer, and
8. 1 Benjamin begat Bela his firstborn, Ashbel
8. 7 he removed them, and begat Uzza and
8. 8 Shaharaim begat (children) in the country
8. 9 he begat of Hodesh his wife, Jobab, and
8. 11 of Hushim he begat Ahitub, and Elpaal
8. 32 Mikloth begat Shimeah. And these also
8. 33 Ner begat Kish..Kish begat Saul..Saul b.
8. 34 Merib-baal; and Merib-baal begat Micah
8. 36 Ahaz begat J..Jehoadah begat A...Z. b.
8. 37 Moza begat Binea: Rapha (was) his son
9. 38 Mikloth begat Shimeam. And they also
9. 39 Ner begat Kish..Kish begat Saul..Saul b
9. 40 Merib-baal; and Merib-baal begat Micah
9. 42 Ahaz begat J..Jarah begat Alemeth..Z. b
9. 43 Moza begat Binea; and Rephaiah his son
14. 3 David begat more sons and daughters
2 Ch. 11. 21 Rehoboam..begat twenty and eight sons
13. 21 Abijah..begat twenty and two sons
24. 3 Jehoiada..begat sons and daughters
Neh. 12. 10 Jeshua begat J...J...begat E..E. begat
12. 11 Joiada begat Jonathan..Jonathan begat
Job 38. 28 who hath begotten the drops of dew?
Eccl. 5. 14 and he begetteth a son, and (there is)
6. 3 If a man beget an hundred (children)
Isa. 39. 7 of thy sons..which thou shalt beget
45. 10 What begettest thou? or to the woman
Jer. 16. 3 concerning their fathers that begat them
29. 6 Take ye wives, and beget sons and
Eze. 18. 10 If he beget a son..a robber, a shedder
18. 14 Now, lo, (if) he beget a son, that seeth all
47. 22 which shall beget children among you

3. *To beget, bring forth*, ἀποκυέω *apokueō.*
Jas 1. 18 Of his own will begat he us with the word

4. *To beget, bring forth*, γεννάω *gennaō.*
Matt. 1. 2 Abraham begat Isaac; and Isaac begat
Jacob; and Jacob begat Judas and his
brethren: 3 And Judas begat Phares
and Zara of Thamar; and Phares begat
Esrom; and Esrom begat Aram; 4 And
Aram begat Aminadab; and Aminadab
begat Naasson; and Naasson begat
Salmon; 5 And Salmon begat Booz of
Rachab: and Booz begat Obed of Ruth;
and Obed begat Jesse; 6 And Jesse begat
David the king; and David the king
begat Solomon of her..of Urias; 7 And
Solomon begat Roboam; and Roboam
begat Abia; and Abia begat Asa; 8
And Asa begat Josaphat; and Josaphat
begat Joram; and Joram begat Ozias; 9
And Ozias begat Joatham; and Joatham
begat Achaz; and Achaz begat Ezekias;
10 And Ezekias begat Manasses; and
Manasses begat Amon; and Amon begat
Josias; 11 And Josias begat Jechonias
and his brethren.
1. 12 Jechonias begat Salathiel; and Salathiel

Matt. 1. 12 begat Zorobabel; 13 And Zorobabel begat Abiud; and Abiud begat Eliakim; and Eliakim begat Azor; 14 And Azor begat Sadoc; and Sadoc begat Achim; and Achim begat Eliud; 15 And Eliud begat Eleazar; and Eleazar begat Matthan; and Matthan begat Jacob; 16 And Jacob begat Joseph
Acts 7. 8 so (Abraham) begat Isaac, and circumc.
7. 29 Moses..was..in..Madian, where he begat
13. 33 Thou art my Son, this day have I begotten
1 Co. 4. 15 I have begotten you through the gospel
Phm. 10 whom I have begotten in my bonds
Heb. 1. 5 Thou art my Son this day have I begotten
5. 5 Thou art my Son, to day have I begotten
1 Jo. 5. 1 him that begat loveth him..is begotten
5. 18 he that is begotten of God keepeth him.

BEGET again, to —
To beget again or anew, ἀναγεννάω *anagennaō.*
1 Pe. 1. 3 God and Father..hath begotten us again

BEGGAR —
1. *Needy, desirous*, אֶבְיוֹן *ebyon.*
1 Sa. 2. 8 He..lifteth up the beggar from the
2. *Crouching, cringing*, πτωχός *ptōchos.*
Luke 16. 20 there was a certain beggar named Lazarus
16. 22 And it came to pass, that the beggar died

BEGGARLY —
Crouching, cringing, πτωχός *ptōchos.*
Gal. 4. 9 turn ye again to the weak and beggarly

BEGIN —
Beginning, commencement, תְּחִלָּה *techillah.*
Neh. 11. 17 Mattaniah..(was) the principal to begin

BEGIN, to —
1. *To begin*, חָלַל *chalal*, 5.
Gen. 6. 1 when men began to multiply on the face
9. 20 And Noah began..an husbandman, and
10. 8 he began to be a mighty one in the earth
11. 6 And the LORD said..this they begin to do
41. 54 the seven years of dearth began to come
44. 12 And he searched, (and) began at the
Num 16. 46 Take a censer..the plague is begun
16. 47 behold the plague was begun among the
25. 1 the people began to commit whoredom
Deut. 2. 24 begin to possess (it), and contend with
2. 25 This day will I begin to put the dread of
2. 31 I have begun to give..begin to possess
3. 24 thou hast begun to show thy servant thy
16. 9 begin to number the seven weeks from
Josh. 3. 7 This day will I begin to magnify thee
Judg 10. 18 What man (is he) that will begin to fight
13. 5 and he shall begin to deliver Israel out of
13. 25 the Spirit of the LORD began to move him
16. 19 she began to afflict him, and his strength
16. 22 the hair of his head began to grow again
20. 31 they began to smite of the people, (and)
20. 39 Benjamin began to smite (and) kill of the
20. 40 But when the flame began to arise up
1 Sa. 3. 2 his eyes began to wax dim, (that) he
3. 12 when I begin, I will also make an end
22. 15 Did I then begin to enquire of God for
2 Ki. 10. 32 In those days the LORD began to cut
15. 37 In those days the LORD began to send
1 Ch. 1. 10 he began to be mighty upon the earth
27. 24 Joab the son of Zeruiah began to number
2 Ch. 3. 1 Then Solomon began to build the house
3. 2 And he began to build in the second
20. 22 And when they began to sing and to
29. 17 Now they began on the first (day) of the
29. 27 the burnt offering began, the song..began
31. 7 In the third month they began to lay
31. 10 Since (the people) began to bring the
31. 21 And in every work that he began in the
34. 3 he began to seek after the God of David
Ezra 3. 6 From the first day..began they to offer
3. 8 Now in..second year..began Zerubbabel
Neh. 4. 7 that the breaches began to be stopped
Esth. 6. 13 before whom thou hast begun to fall
9. 23 the Jews undertook to do as they..begun
Jer. 25. 29 I begin to bring evil on the city which is
Eze. 9. 6 begin at my sanctuary Then they began
Jon. 3. 4 And Jonah began to enter into the city
2. *To be begun*, חָלַל *chalal*, 6.
Gen. 4. 26 then began (men) to call upon the name
3. *To begin, be pleased*, יָאַל *yaal*, 5.
Deut. 1. 5 On this side Jordan..began Moses to
4. *To begin, solve, loose*, שְׁרָא *shere*, 3.
Ezra 5. 2 Zerubbabel..and began to build the
5. *To begin, commence*, ἄρχομαι *archomai.*
Matt. 4. 17 Jesus began to preach, and to say
11. 7 Jesus began to say unto the multitudes
11. 20 Then began he to upbraid the cities
12. 1 his disciples..began to pluck the ears of
14. 30 beginning to sink, he cried..Lord, save
16. 21 From that time forth began Jesus to
16. 22 Peter took him, and began to rebuke
18. 24 when he had begun to reckon, one was
20. 8 Call the labourers..beginning from the
24. 49 And shall begin to smite (his) fellow
26. 22 they..began every one of them to say
26. 37 he..began to be sorrowful and very
26. 74 Then began he to curse and to swear
Mark 1. 45 he went out, and began to publish (it)
2. 23 his disciples began, as they went, to
4. 1 he began again to teach by the seaside
5. 17 they began to pray him to depart out
Mark. 5. 20 he departed, and began to publish in
6. 2 he began to teach in the synagogue
6. 7 he..began to send them forth by two and
6. 34 he began to teach them many things
6. 55 began to carry about in beds those that
8. 11 the Pharisees..began to question with
8. 31 he began to teach them, that the Son of
8. 32 Peter took him, and began to rebuke
10. 28 Then Peter began to say unto him, Lo
10. 32 he..began to tell them what things
10. 41 they began to be much displeased with
10. 47 he began to cry out, and say, Jesus
11. 15 Jesus..began to cast out them that sold
12. 1 he began to speak unto them by parables
13. 5 Jesus answering them began to say, Take
14. 19 they began to be sorrowful, and to say
14. 33 he..began to be sore amazed, and
14. 65 some began to spit on him, and to cover
14. 69 a maid..began to say to them that stood
14. 71 he began to curse and to swear..I know
15. 8 the multitude, crying aloud, began to
15. 18 began to salute him, Hail, King of..Jews
Luke 3. 8 begin not to say within yourselves, v. 23
4. 21 he began to say unto them, This day is
5. 21 the scribes and the Pharisees began to
7. 15 he that was dead sat up, and began to
7. 24 he began to speak unto the people
7. 38 began to wash his feet with tears, and
7. 49 they that sat..began to say within
9. 12 when the day began to wear away, then
11. 29 he began to say, This is an evil generation
11. 53 the scribes and the Pharisees began to
12. 1 he began to say unto his disciples first of
12. 45 shall begin to beat the men servants and
13. 25 ye begin to stand without, and to knock
13. 26 Then shall ye begin to say, We have
14. 9 thou begin with shame to take the lowest
14. 18 all with one (consent) began to make
14. 29 Lest..all that behold (it) begin to mock
14. 30 This man began to build, and was not
15. 14 when he had spent..he began to be in
15. 24 lost..And they began to be merry
19. 37 the whole multitude..began to rejoice
19. 45 began to cast out them that sold therein
20. 9 Then began he to speak to the people
21. 28 when these things begin to come to pass
22. 23 they began to enquire among themselves
23. 2 they began to accuse him, saying, We
23. 5 beginning from Galilee to this place
23. 30 Then shall they begin to say to the
24. 27 beginning at Moses and all the Prophets
24. 47 among all nations, beginning..Jerusalem
John 8. 9 [they..went out one by one, beginning at]
13. 5 he..began to wash the disciples' feet
Acts 1. 1 of all that..began both to do and teach
1. 22 Beginning from the baptism of John
2. 4 they..began to speak with other tongues
8. 35 Philip..began at the same scripture, and
10. 37 That word..began from Galilee, after the
11. 15 as I began to speak, the Holy Ghost fell
18. 26 he began to speak boldly in the synagogue
24. 2 Tertullus began to accuse (him), saying
27. 35 when he had broken (it), he began to eat
2 Co. 3. 1 Do we begin again to commend ourselves?
1 Pe. 4. 17 judgment must begin at the house of God
6. *To begin in*, ἐνάρχομαι *enarchomai.*
Gal. 3. 3 Are ye so foolish? having begun in the
Phil. 1. 6 he which hath begun a good work in you
7. *To begin before*, προενάρχομαι *proenarchomai.*
2 Co. 8. 6 that as he had begun, so he would also
8. *To be about to*, μέλλω *mellō.*
Rev. 10. 7 when he shall begin to sound, the

BEGIN at the first, to —
To receive a beginning, λαμβάνω ἀρχήν. [*lambanō*].
Heb. 2. 3 which at the first began to be spoken by

BEGIN before, to —
To begin before, προενάρχομαι *proenarchomai.*
2 Co. 8. 10 who have begun before, not only to do

BEGIN to be, to —
Was beginning, ἦν ἀρχόμενος *ēn archomenos.*
Luke 3. 23 Jesus himself began to be about thirty
[*See also* Amend, build, dark, dawn, reign, sink spring, wanton, world.]

BEGINNING —
1. *Then*, אָז *az.*
Isa. 48. 3 declared the former things from the b.
48. 5 I have even from the beginning v. 7.
2. *Head*, רֹאשׁ *rosh.*
Exod 12. 2 This month..unto you the beginning of
Num 10. 10 in the beginnings of your months, ye
28. 11 in the beginnings of your months ye shall
Deut 32. 42 from the beginning of revenges upon the
Judg 7. 19 came unto..in the beginning of the
Psa 119. 160 Thy word (is) true (from) the beginning
Prov. 8. 23 I was set up from..from the beginning
Eccl. 3. 11 that God maketh from the beginning to
Isa. 40. 21 hath it not been told you from the beg.
41. 4 calling the generations from the beg.
41. 26 Who hath declared from the beginning
48. 16 not spoken in secret from the beginning
Lam. 2. 19 in the beginning of the watches pour out
Eze. 40. 1 in the beginning of the year, in the tenth
3. *Head*, רֵאשָׁה *rishah.*
Eze. 36. 11 do better (unto you) than at your begin.
4. *First, former*, רִאשׁוֹן *rishon.*
Ruth 3. 10 more kindness..than at the beginning
1 Ch. 17. 9 waste them any more, as at the beginning
Prov. 20. 21 inheritance..gotten hastily at the begin.
Jer. 17. 12 A glorious high throne from the beginning
5. *First, former*, רֵאשִׁית *reshith.*
Gen. 1. 1 In the beginning God created the heaven
10. 10 the beginning of his kingdom was Babel
49. 3 my might, and the beginning of my
Deut 11. 12 from the beginning of the year even unto
21. 17 for he (is) the beginning of his strength
Job 8. 7 Though thy beginning was small, yet thy
42. 12 latter end of Job more than his beg
Psa. 111. 10 The fear of the LORD (is) the beginning
Prov. 1. 7 The fear of the LORD (is) the beginning
8. 22 The LORD possessed me in the beginning
17. 14 The beginning of strife (is as) when one
Eccl. 7. 8 Better (is) the end..than the beginning
Isa. 46. 10 Declaring the end from the beginning
Jer. 26. 1 In the beginning of the reign of Jehoiakim
27. 1 In the beginning of the reign of Jehoiakim
28. 1 in the beginning of the reign of Zedekiah
49. 34 in the beginning of the reign of Zedekiah
Mic. 1. 13 she (is) the beginning of the sin to the
6. *Beginning, commencement*, תְּחִלָּה *techillah.*
Gen. 13. 3 where his tent had been at the beginning
41. 21 they (were) still ill favoured, as at the beg.
Ruth 1. 22 came to B. in the beginning of barley
2 Sa. 21. 9 the first (days) in the beginning of barley
21. 10 from the beginning of harvest until water
2 Ki. 17. 25 it was at the beginning of their dwelling
Ezra 4. 6 in the beginning of his reign, wrote they
Neh. 11. 17 the principal to begin the thanksgiving
Prov. 9. 10 The fear of the LORD (is) the beginning of
Eccl. 10. 13 The beginning of the words of his mouth
Isa. 1. 26 restore..thy counsellors as at the beg.
Dan. 9. 21 whom I had seen in the vision at the beg.
9. 23 At the beginning of thy supplications the
Hos. 1. 2 The beginning of the word of the LORD
Amos 7. 1 in the beginning of the shooting up of the
7. *Beginning*, ἀρχή *archē.*
Matt 19. 4 he which made..at the beginning made
19. 8 but from the beginning it was not so
24. 8 All these (are) the beginning of sorrows
24. 21 such as was not since the beginning of
Mark 1. 1 The beginning of the gospel of Jesus
10. 6 from the beginning of the creation God
13. 8 These (are) the beginnings of sorrows
13. 19 such as was not from the beginning of
Luke 1. 2 which from the beginning were eye witn.
John 1. 1 In the beginning was the Word, and the
1. 2 The same was in the beginning with God
2. 11 This beginning of miracles did Jesus
6. 64 Jesus knew from the beginning who they
8. 25 that I said unto you from the beginning
8. 44 He was a murderer from the beginning
15. 27 ye have been with me from the beginning
16. 4 these things I said not..at the beginning
Acts 11. 15 fell on them, as on us at the beginning
Phil. 4. 15 that in the beginning of the gospel, when
Col. 1. 18 who is the beginning, the firstborn from
2 Th. 2. 13 because God hath from the beginning
Heb. 1. 10 Thou, Lord, in the beginning hast laid
3. 14 if we hold the beginning of our confidence
7. 3 having neither beginning of days, nor
2 Pe. 3. 4 continue as..from the beginning of the
1 Jo. 1. 1 which was from the beginning, which we
2. 7 old commandment..from the beginning
2. 7 word..have heard from the [beginning]
2. 13, 14 ye have known him..from the beg.
2. 24 heard from the beginning..from the beg.
3. 8 for the devil sinneth from the beginning
3. 11 message that ye heard from the beginning
2 Jo. 5 that which we had from the beginning
6 That, as ye have heard from the beg.
Rev. 1. 8 I am Alpha and Omega, [the beginning]
3. 14 true witness, the beginning of the
21. 6 I am Alpha and Omega, the beginning
22. 13 beginning and the end, the first and the
8. *First, former*, πρῶτος *prōtos.*
2 Pe. 2. 20 the latter end is worse..than the beg.

BEGINNING, at the —
First, former, πρῶτον *prōton.*
John 2. 10 Every man at the beginning doth set

BEGINNING, from the —
From above, ἄνωθεν *anōthen.*
Acts 26. 5 Which knew me from the beginning, if
[*See also* Rehearse, world.]

BEGOTTEN —
1. *Birth*, מוֹלֶדֶת *moledeth.*
Lev. 18. 11 begotten of thy father, she (is) thy sister
2. *To go out*, יָצָא *yatsa.*
Judg. 8. 30 Gideon had..sons of his body begotten

BEGOTTEN (Son), only
Only-born, chief, μονογενής *monogenēs.*
John 1. 14 glory as of the only begotten of the F.
1. 18 the only begotten Son, which is in the
3. 16 that he gave his only begotten Son, that
3. 18 in the name of the only begotten Son of
Heb. 11. 17 and he offered up his only begotten (son)
1 Jo. 4. 9 that God sent his only begotten Son into

BEGOTTEN, first —
First-born, πρωτότοκος *prōtotokos.*
Heb. 1. 6 when he bringeth in the first begotten into
Rev. 1. 5 the first begotten of the dead, and the

BEGOTTEN, to be —
To be born, יָלַד *yalad,* 2.
Deut23. 8 The children that are begotten of them

BEGUILE, to —
1. *To deceive,* נָכַל *nakal,* 3.
Num25. 18 wherewith they have beguiled you in the
2. *To beguile, lift up,* נָשָׁא *nasha,* 5.
Gen. 3. 13 The serpent beguiled me, and I did eat
3. *To throw, cast down,* רָמָה *ramah,* 3.
Gen. 29. 25 wherefore then hast thou beguiled me?
Josh. 9. 22 Wherefore have ye beguiled us, saying
4. *To entrap,* δελεάζω *deleazō.*
2 Pe. 2. 14 cannot cease from sin; beguiling unstable
5. *To deceive greatly,* ἐξαπατάω *exapataō.*
2 Co. 11. 3 as the serpent beguiled Eve through his
6. *To reason wrongly,* παραλογίζομαι *paralogizomai.*
Col. 2. 4 this I say, lest any man should beguile you

BEGUILE of one's reward, to —
Arbitrate against, καταβραβεύω *katabrabeuō.*
Col. 2. 18 Let no man beguile you of your reward

BEHALF —
Part, share, portion, μέρος *meros.*
2 Co. 9. 3 boasting..should be in vain in this behalf
1 Pe. 4. 16 but let him glorify God on this [behalf]

BEHALF of, in the —
On behalf of, for, ὑπέρ *(gen.) huper.*
Phil. 1. 29 unto you it is given in the behalf of Christ

BEHALF, on —
1. *In addition to, on account of,* ἐπί *(dat.) epi.*
Rom.16. 19 I am glad therefore on your behalf: but
2. *Concerning, about,* περί *(gen.) peri.*
1 Co. 1. 4 I thank my God always on your behalf
3. *On behalf of, for,* ὑπέρ *(gen.) huper.*
2 Co. 1. 11 thanks may be given..on our behalf
5. 12 give you occasion to glory on our b. 8. 24.
4. *Upon,* τὸ ἐπί *to epi,* Rom. 16. 19.

BEHAVE, to —
To compare, equal, שָׁוָה *shavah,* 3.
Psa. 131. 2 I have behaved and quieted myself, as a

BEHAVE self, (seemly, uncomely), to —
1. *To go on for one's self,* הָלַךְ *halak,* 7.
Psa. 35. 14 I behaved myself as though..my friend
2. *To turn round again,* ἀναστρέφω *anastrephō.*
1 Ti. 3. 15 know how thou oughtest to behave thyself
3. *To become,* γίνομαι *ginomai,* 1 Thes. 2. 10.
4. *Behave disgracefully, fear disgrace,* ἀσχημονέω *aschēmoneō.*
1 Cor. 7. 36 behaveth himself uncomely towards
13. 5 Doth not behave itself unseemly
[*See* Disorderly, ill, proudly, strangely, &c.]
1. *Taste, reason,* טַעַם *taam.*
1 Sa. 21. 13 he changed his behaviour before them
Psa. 34. *title.* when he changed his behaviour before
2. *Constitution,* κατάστημα *katastēma.*
Titus 2. 3 that..in behaviour as becometh holiness

BEHAVIOUR, of good —
Orderly, κόσμιος *kosmios.*
1 Ti. 3. 2 A bishop then must be . . of g. behaviour

BEHEAD, to —
1. *To turn aside the head,* סוּר רֹאשׁ *sur rosh,* 5.
2 Sa. 4. 7 beheaded him, and took his head, and gat
2. *To behead,* ἀποκεφαλίζω *apokephalizō.*
Matt14. 10 he sent, and beheaded John in the prison
Mark 6. 16 It is John, whom I beheaded: he is risen
6. 27 he went and beheaded him in the prison
Luke 9. 9 Herod said, John have I beheaded: but
3. *To cut away with an axe,* πελεκίζω *pelekizō.*
Rev.20. 4 (I saw) the souls of them..were beheaded

BEHEADED, that is —
To (cause to) drop, break down, עָרַף *araph*
Deut21. 6 over the heifer that is beheaded in the

BEHELD —
To see, view, חָזָה *chazah.*
Dan. 7. 4 I beheld till the wings thereof were pl.
7. 6 After this I beheld, and lo another, like
7. 9 I beheld till the thrones were cast down
7. 11 I beheld..because of..I beheld..till
7. 21 I beheld, and the same horn made war

BE-HE'-MOTH, בְּהֵמוֹת *a large beast.*
It is uncertain whether this is the elephant or the hippopotamus; but the weight of argument seems on the side of the latter.
Job 40. 15 Behold now b., which I made with thee

BEHIND —
1. *Behind,* אָחוֹר *achor.*
2 Sa. 10. 9 battle was against him before and behind
1 Ch. 19. 10 battle was..against him before and
2 Ch. 13. 14 the battle (was) before and behind: and
Psa.139. 5 Thou hast beset me behind and before
Isa. 9. 12 Syrians before, and the Philistines behind
2. *Behind,* אַחַר *achar.*
Gen. 18. 10 in the tent door, which (was) behind him
19. 17 Escape for thy life; look not behind thee
19. 26 his wife looked back from behind him
22. 13 behold, behind (him) a ram caught in a
32. 18 and, behold, also he (is) behind us
32. 20 Behold, thy servant Jacob (is) behind us
Exod14. 19 the angel of God..went behind them
Deut25. 18 smote..all..feeble behind thee, when
Josh. 8. 14 liers in ambush against him behind the
8. 20 when the men of Ai looked behind them
Judg18. 12 behold, (it is) behind Kirjath-jearim
20. 40 the Benjamites looked behind them, and
1 Sa. 21. 9 wrapped in a cloth behind the ephod: if
24. 8 when Saul looked behind him, David
2 Sa. 1. 7 when he looked behind him, he saw me
2. 20 Abner looked behind him, and said
2. 23 that the spear came out behind him
3. 16 her husband went..along weeping behind
5. 23 fetch a compass behind them, and come
13. 34 behold, there came much people..behind
1 Ki. 14. 9 thou..hast cast me behind thy back
2 Ki. 6. 32 the sound of his master's feet behind
9. 18 turn thee behind me. And the watchman
9. 19 What hast thou to do..turn thee behind
11. 6 a third part at the gate behind the guard
2 Ch. 13. 13 ambushment to come about behind them
13. 13 and the ambushment (was) behind them
Neh. 4. 16 the rulers (were) behind all the house of
9. 26 and cast thy law behind their backs, and
Psa. 50. 17 Seeing thou..castest my words behind
Song 2. 9 he standeth behind our wall, he looketh
Isa. 30. 21 thine ears shall hear a word behind thee
38. 17 thou hast cast all my sins behind thy
57. 8 Behind the doors also and the posts
66. 17 purify themselves in the gardens behind
Eze. 3. 12 I heard behind me a voice of a great
23. 35 Because thou hast..cast me behind thy
41. 15 the separate place which (was) behind
Joel 2. 3 behind them a flame..behind them a
2. 14 repent, and leave a blessing behind him
Zech. 1. 8 behind him..red horses, speckled, and
3. *Behind, backward,* ὀπίσω *opisō.*
Matt16. 23 Get thee behind me, Satan: thou art
Mark 8. 33 saying, Get thee behind me, Satan: for
Luke 4. 8 Get thee [behind] me, Satan: for it is
7. 38 stood at his feet behind (him) weeping
Rev. 1. 10 heard behind me a great voice, as of a
4. *From behind,* ὄπισθεν *opisthen.*
Matt. 9. 20 behold, a woman..came behind..and
Mark 5. 27 came in the press behind, and touched
Luke 8. 44 Came behind..and touched the border of
Rev. 4. 6 four beasts, full of eyes before and behind

BEHIND, to be —
To be behind, ὑστερέω *hustereō.*
2 Co.11. 5 I suppose I was not a whit behind the
12. 11 in nothing am I behind the very chiefest

BEHIND, to come —
To be behind, ὑστερέω *hustereō.*
1 Co. 1. 7 So that ye come behind in no gift

BEHIND, those things which are —
The things behind, τὰ ὀπίσω *ta opisō.*
Phil. 3. 13 forgetting those things which are behind

BEHIND, which is —
What is behind, ὑστέρημα *husterēma.*
Col. 1. 24 fill up that which is behind of the
[*See also* Abide, left, tarry.]

BEHOLD —
1. *Lo,* אֲלוּ *alu.*
Dan. 2. 31 Thou, O king, sawest, and behold, a great
4. 10 I saw, and behold a tree in the midst of
4. 13 behold, a watcher and an holy one came
7. 8 I considered the horns, and, behold
7. 8 behold, in this horn (were) eyes like the
2. *Lo, see!* אֲרוּ *aru.*
Dan. 7. 2 behold, the four winds of the heaven
7. 5 behold another beast, a second, like to
7. 7 behold a fourth beast, dreadful and
7. 13 behold, (one) like the Son of man came
3. *Lo, he!* הָא *he.*
Eze. 16. 43 behold, therefore I also will recompense
4. *Lo,* הֵן *hen.*
Gen. 3. 22 Behold, the man is become as one of us
5. *Lo,* הִנֵּה *hinneh.*
Gen. 1. 29 Behold, I have given you every herb
6. *See!* ἴδε *ide.*
Matt25. 20 behold, I have gained beside them five
25. 22 behold, I have gained two other talents
26. 65 behold, now ye have heard his blasphemy
Mark 2. 24 Behold, why do they on the sabbath day
3. 34 said, [Behold] my mother and my brethren
11. 21 behold, the fig tree..is withered away
15. 4 behold how many things they witness
16. 6 behold the place where they laid him
John 1. 29 Behold the Lamb of God, which taketh
1. 36 looking..he saith, Behold the Lamb of
1. 47 Behold an Israelite indeed, in whom is
3. 26 behold, the same baptizeth, and all..come
5. 14 Behold, thou art made whole: sin no
11. 3 Lord, behold, he whom thou lovest is sick
11. 36 Then said the Jews, Behold how he
12. 19 behold, the world is gone after him
18. 21 ask..behold, they know what I said
19. 4 Behold, I bring him forth to you, that ye
19. 5 And (Pilate) saith unto them, [Behold]
19. 14 he saith unto the Jews, Behold your
20. 27 Reach hither thy finger, and behold my
Rom. 2. 17 [Behold,] thou art called a Jew, and
Gal. 5. 2 [Behold,] I Paul say unto you, that if ye
7. *See! lo!* ἰδού *idou.*
Matt. 1. 20 behold, the angel of the Lord appeared
1. 23 Behold, a virgin shall be with child
2. 1 behold, there came wise men from the
2. 13 behold, the angel of the Lord appeareth
2. 19 behold, an angel of the Lord appeareth
4. 11 behold, angels came and ministered unto
7. 4 and, behold, a beam..in thine own eye?
8. 2 behold, there came a leper and worshipped
8. 24 behold, there arose a great tempest in
8. 29 behold, they cried out, saying, What
8. 32 behold, the whole herd of swine ran
8. 34 behold, the whole city came out to meet
9. 2 behold, they brought to him a man sick of
9. 3 behold, certain of the scribes said within
9. 10 behold, many publicans..came and sat
9. 18 behold, there came a certain ruler, and
9. 20 behold, a woman..came behind..and
9. 32 behold, they brought to him a dumb man
10. 16 Behold, I send you forth as sheep in the
11. 8 Behold, they that wear soft (clothing) are
11. 10 Behold, I send my messenger before thy
11. 19 Behold a man gluttonous..a wine bibber
12. 2 Behold, thy disciples do that which is
12. 10 behold, there was a man which had his
12. 18 Behold my servant, whom I have chosen
12. 41 and, behold, a greater than Jonas (is) here
12. 42 and, behold, a greater than Solomon (is)
12. 46 behold, (his) mother and his brethren
12. 47 Behold, thy mother and thy brethren
12. 49 he..said, Behold my mother and my
13. 3 saying, Behold, a sower went forth to sow
15. 22 behold, a woman of Canaan came out of
17. 3 behold, there appeared unto them Moses
17. 5 behold, a bright cloud..and behold a
19. 16 behold, one came and said unto him
19. 27 Behold, we have forsaken all, and
20. 18 Behold, we go up to Jerusalem; and the
20. 30 behold, two blind men sitting by the way
21. 5 Behold, thy king cometh unto thee, meek
22. 4 Behold, I have prepared my dinner: my
23. 34 behold, I send unto you prophets, and
23. 38 Behold, your house is left unto you
24. 25 Behold, I have told you before
24. 26 Behold, he is in the desert..behold, (he is)
25. 6 Behold the bridegroom cometh; go ye
26. 45 behold, the hour is at hand, and the Son
26. 46 behold, he is at hand that doth betray me
26. 51 behold, one of them..stretched out (his)
27. 51 behold, the veil of the temple was rent
28. 2 behold, there was a great earthquake: for
28. 7 behold, he goeth before you into Galilee
28. 9 behold, Jesus met them, saying, All hail!
28. 11 behold, some of the watch came into the
Mark 1. 2 Behold, I send my messenger before thy
3. 32 Behold, thy mother and thy brethren
4. 3 Hearken; Behold, there went out a sower
5. 22 [behold,] there cometh one of the rulers
10. 33 Behold, we go up to Jerusalem; and the
13. 23 [behold,] I have foretold you all things
14. 41 behold, the Son of man is betrayed into
15. 35 some of them..said, [Behold,] he calleth
Luke 1. 20 behold, thou shalt be dumb, and not able
1. 31 behold, thou shalt conceive in thy womb
1. 36 behold, thy cousin Elisabeth, she hath
1. 38 Mary said, Behold the handmaid of the
1. 48 behold, from henceforth all generations
2. 10 behold, I bring you good tidings of great
2. 25 behold, there was a man in Jerusalem
2. 34 Behold, this..is set for the fall and rising
2. 48 behold, thy father and I have sought thee
5. 12 behold a man full of leprosy; who, seeing
5. 18 behold, men brought in a bed a man
6. 23 for, behold, your reward (is) great in
7. 12 behold, there was a dead man carried out
7. 25 Behold, they which are gorgeously
7. 27 Behold, I send my messenger before thy
7. 34 Behold a gluttonous man, and a wine b.
7. 37 behold, a woman in the city, which was
8. 41 behold, there came a man named Jairus
9. 30 behold, there talked with him two men
9. 38 behold, a man of the company cried out
10. 3 behold, I send you forth as lambs among
10. 19 Behold, I give unto you power to tread
10. 25 behold, a certain lawyer stood up, and
11. 31 behold, a greater than Solomon (is) here
11. 32 behold, a greater than Jonas (is) here
11. 41 and, behold all things are clean unto you
13. 7 Behold, these three years I come seeking
13. 11 behold, there was a woman which had a
13. 30 behold, there are last which shall be first
13. 32 Behold, I cast out devils, and I do cures
13. 35 Behold, your house is left unto you des.
14. 2 Behold, there was a certain man before
17. 21 behold, the kingdom of God is within you
18. 31 Behold, we go up to Jerusalem, and all

Luke 19. 2 behold,(there was) a man named Zaccheus
19. 8 Behold, Lord, the half of my goods I give
19. 20 Lord, behold..thy pound, which I have
22. 10 Behold, when ye are entered into the city
22. 21 behold, the hand of him that betrayeth
22. 31 behold, Satan hath desired..you, that he
22. 38 they said, Lord, behold, here (are) two
22. 47 And while he yet spake, behold a
23. 14 behold, I..have found no fault in this
23. 29 For, behold, the days are coming, in the
23. 50 behold..a man named Joseph, a
24. 4 behold, two men stood by them in
24. 13 behold, two of them went that same day
24. 49 behold, I send the promise of my Father
John 4. 35 behold, I say unto you, Lift up your eyes
12. 15 Behold, thy King cometh, sitting on an
16. 32 Behold, the hour cometh, yea, is now
19. 26 he saith unto his mother, Woman,[behold]
19. 27 Then saith he to the disciple, [Behold] thy
Acts 1. 10 behold, two men stood by them in white
2. 7 Behold, are not all these which speak
5. 9 Behold, the feet of them which have
5. 25 Behold, the men..are standing in the
5. 28 behold, ye have filled Jerusalem with
7. 56 And said, Behold, I see the heavens
8. 27 he..went: and, behold, a man of
9. 10 And he said, Behold, I (am here) Lord
9. 11 enquire..for (one) called Saul..for, behold
10. 17 behold, the men..had made enquiry for
10. 19 the Spirit said unto him, Behold, three
10. 21 and said, Behold, I am he whom ye seek
10. 30 behold, a man stood before me in bright
11. 11 behold, immediately there were three
12. 7 behold, the angel of the Lord came upon
13. 11 behold, the hand of the Lord (is) upon
13. 25 behold, there cometh one after me, whose
16. 1 behold, a certain disciple was there
20. 22 behold, I go bound in the spirit unto
20. 25 behold, I know that ye all..shall see my
Rom. 9. 33 Behold, I lay in Sion a stumbling-stone
1 Co. 15. 51 Behold, I show you a mystery; We shall
2 Co. 5. 17 behold, all things are become new
6. 2 behold, now (is) the accepted time; behold
6. 9 as dying, and, behold, we live; as
7. 11 behold this selfsame thing, that ye
12. 14 Behold, the third time I am ready to
Gal. 1. 20 behold, before God, I lie not
Heb. 2. 13 Behold I and the children which God
8. 8 Behold, the days come, saith the Lord
Jas. 3. 3 [Behold,] we put bits in the horses' mouths
3. 4 Behold also the ships..yet are they turned
3. 5 Behold how great a matter a little fire
5. 4 Behold, the hire of the labourers..crieth
5. 7 Behold, the husbandman waiteth for the
5. 9 behold, the Judge standeth before the
5. 11 Behold, we count them happy which
1 Pe. 2. 6 Behold, I lay in Sion a chief corner stone
Jude 14 Behold..Lord cometh with ten thousand
Rev. 1. 7 Behold, he cometh with clouds; and every
1. 18 and, behold, I am alive for evermore
2. 10 behold, the devil shall cast..you into
2. 22 Behold, I will cast her into a bed, and
3. 8 behold, I have set before thee an open
3. 9 Behold, I will make them of the syna.
3. 9 behold, I will make them to come and
3. 11 [Behold,] I come quickly: hold that fast
3. 20 Behold, I stand at the door and knock
4. 1 behold, a door (was) opened in heaven
4. 2 behold, a throne was set in heaven, and
5. 5 behold, the Lion of the tribe of Juda
6. 2 And I saw, and behold a white horse
6. 8 And I looked, and behold a pale horse
9. 12 behold, there come two woes more here.
11. 14 behold, the third woe cometh quickly
12. 3 behold a great red dragon, having seven
14. 14 I looked, and behold a white cloud, and
15. 5 [behold,] the temple of the tabernacle of
16. 15 Behold, I come as a thief. Blessed (is) he
19. 11 I saw heaven opened, and behold a white
21. 3 Behold, the tabernacle of God (is) with
21. 5 he..said, Behold, I make all things new
22. 7 Behold, I come quickly: blessed (is) he
22. 12 behold, I come quickly; and my reward

BEHOLD, to —

1. *To view, see,* חָזָה *chazah.*
Job 23. 9 where he doth work, but I cannot behold
Psa. 11. 4 his eyes behold, his eyelids try, the
11. 7 his countenance doth behold the upright
17. 2 let thine eyes behold the things that are
17. 15 As for me, I will behold thy face in
27. 4 to behold the beauty of the LORD, and
46. 8 Come, behold the works of the LORD

2. *To (cause to) behold attentively,* נָבַט *nabat,* 5.
Num 12. 8 similitude of the LORD shall he behold
21. 9 when he beheld the serpent of brass, he
23. 21 He hath not beheld iniquity in Jacob
Job 36. 25 Every man may see it; man may behold
39. 29 From thence..her eyes behold afar off
Psa. 10. 14 for thou beholdest mischief and spite, to
91. 8 Only with thine eyes shalt thou behold
102. 19 from heaven did the LORD behold the
119. 18 that I may behold wondrous things out
Isa. 38. 11 I shall behold man no more with the
Lam. 1. 12 behold, and see if there be any sorrow
3. 63 Behold their sitting down, and their

3. *To face, front,* פָּנָה *panah.*
Job 24. 18 he beholdeth not the way of the vineyds.

4. *To look out, watch,* צָפָה *tsaphah.*
Psa. 66. 7 his eyes behold the nations: let not the
Prov 15. 3 beholding the evil and the good

5. *To see, look, consider,* רָאָה *raah.*
Gen. 12. 14 the Egyptians beheld the woman, that she
13. 10 Lot lifted up his eyes, and beheld all the
19. 28 and beheld, and, lo, the smoke of the
31. 2 Jacob beheld the countenance of Laban
48. 8 Israel beheld Joseph's sons, and said
Deut. 1. 8 Behold, I have set the land before you
1. 21 Behold, the LORD..hath set the land
2. 24 behold, I have given into thine hand Sih.
2. 31 Behold, I have begun to give Sihon and
3. 27 Get thee up into the top of..and behold
4. 5 Behold, I have taught you statutes and
11. 26 Behold, I set before you this day a
32. 49 behold the land of Canaan, which I give
Josh. 8. 4 Behold, ye shall lie in wait against the
22. 28 Behold the pattern of the altar of the
23. 4 Behold, I have divided unto you by lot
Judg 16. 27 men and women, that beheld while
1 Sa. 26. 5 David beheld the place where Saul lay
2 Sa. 24. 22 behold..oxen for burnt sacrifice, and
1 Ch. 21. 15 as he was destroying, the LORD beheld
Job 19. 27 mine eyes shall behold, and not another
22. 12 behold the height of the stars, how high
31. 26 If I beheld the sun when it shined, or
40. 11 behold every one..proud, and abase him
41. 34 He beholdeth all..he (is) a king over all
Psa. 33. 13 The LORD..beholdeth all the sons of men
37. 37 Mark the perfect..and behold the
59. 4 awake to help me, and behold
80. 14 look down from heaven, and behold
84. 9 Behold, O God our shield, and look upon
113. 6 Who humbleth..to behold..in heaven
119. 37 Turn away mine eyes from beholding
119. 158 I beheld the transgressors, and was
142. 4 I looked on (my) right hand, and beheld
Prov. 7. 7 And beheld among the simple ones, I
23. 33 Thine eyes shall behold strange women
Eccl. 1. 14 behold, all..vanity and vexation of
7. 27 Behold, this have I found, saith the
8. 17 Then I beheld all the work of God, that
11. 7 pleasant..for the eyes to behold the sun
Song 3. 11 behold king Solomon with the crown
Isa. 26. 10 will not behold the majesty of the LORD
33. 17 they shall behold the land that is very
40. 26 and behold who hath created these
41. 23 that we may be dismayed, and behold
41. 28 For I beheld, and..no man; even among
49. 18 Lift up thine eyes round about, and beho.
63. 15 Look down from heaven, and behold from
Jer. 4. 23 I beheld the earth, and, lo..without form
4. 24 I beheld the mountains, and, lo, they
4. 25 I beheld, and, lo..no man, and all the
4. 26 I beheld, and, lo, the fruitful place (was)
13. 20 Lift up your eyes, and behold them that
20. 4 thine eyes shall behold (it): and I will give
29. 32 Behold, I will punish Shemaiah the
31. 26 Upon this I awaked, and beheld; and my
32. 4 and his eyes shall behold his eyes
34. 3 thine eyes shall behold the eyes of the
40. 4 behold, all the land (is) before thee 42.2
Lam. 1. 9 O LORD, behold my affliction; for the
1. 18 hear, I pray you, all people, and behold
1. 20 Behold, O LORD, for I (am) in distress
2. 20 Behold, O LORD, and consider to whom
3. 50 the LORD look down, and behold from
5. 1 O LORD..consider, and behold our
Eze. 1. 15 as I beheld the living creatures, behold
8. 2 Then I beheld, and, lo, a likeness as the
8. 9 Go in, and behold the wicked abomin.
28. 17 I will lay thee..that they may behold
28. 18 in the sight of all them that behold thee
37. 8 And when I beheld, lo, the sinews 40. 4
44. 4 I looked, and, behold, the glory of the
44. 5 Son of man..behold with thine eyes, and
Dan. 9. 18 open thine eyes, and behold our desola.
Amos 3. 9 behold the great tumults in the midst
Mic. 7. 9 LORD..I shall behold his righteousness
7. 10 Where is the LORD thy God?..eyes shall b.
Hab. 1. 5 Behold ye among the heathen, and regard
1. 13 of purer eyes than to behold evil, and
3. 6 he beheld, and drove asunder the nations
Zech. 3. 4 Behold, I have caused thine iniquity to
6. 8 Behold, these..have quieted my spirit in

6. *To behold, look,* שׁוּר *shur.*
Num 23. 9 from the hills I behold him: lo, the
24. 17 I shall behold him, but not nigh: there
Job 20. 9 neither shall his place any more behold
34. 29 he hideth (his) face, who then can behold
35. 5 and behold the clouds..are higher than

7. *To look upon,* שִׁיר *shir,* 3a.
Job 36. 24 magnify his work, which men behold

8. *To view again,* ἀναθεωρέω *anatheōreō.*
Acts 17. 23 For as I passed by, and beheld your

9. *To behold, see, look,* βλέπω *blepō.*
Matt. 7. 3 why beholdest thou the mote that is in
18. 10 their angels do always behold the face of
Luke 6. 41 why beholdest thou the mote that is in
6. 42 when thou thyself beholdest not the
24. 12 [he beheld the linen clothes laid by]
Acts 1. 9 while they beheld, he was taken up; and
1 Co. 10. 18 Behold Israel after the flesh: are not
Rev 17. 8 when they behold the beast that was, and

10. *To see,* εἰδέω, εἶδον *eideō, eidon.*
Mark 9. 15 the people, when they beheld him, were
Luke 19. 41 he beheld the city, and wept over it
21. 29 Behold the fig tree, and all the trees
22. 56 a certain maid beheld him as he sat by

Luke 24. 39 Behold my hands and my feet, that it is
John 20. 27 Reach hither thy finger, and behold my
Acts 13. 41 Behold, ye despisers, and wonder, and
Rom 11. 22 Behold therefore the goodness and
1 Jo. 3. 1 Behold what manner of love the Father
Rev. 5. 6 I beheld, and, lo, in the midst of the
5. 11 I beheld, and I heard the voice of many
6. 5 I beheld, and lo a black horse: and he
6. 12 I beheld when he had opened the sixth
7. 9 After this I beheld, and, lo, a great
8. 13 I beheld, and heard an angel flying
13. 11 I beheld another beast coming up out of

11. *To look on or upon,* ἐμβλέπω *emblepō.*
Matt 19. 26 But Jesus beheld..and said unto 6. 26.
Luke 20. 17 he beheld them, and said, What is this
John 1. 42 when Jesus beheld him, he said, Thou

12. *To look over, or upon,* ἐποπτεύω *epopteuō.*
1 Pe. 2. 12 good works, which they shall behold
3. 2 While they behold your chaste conversa.

13. *To look upon,* ἐπεῖδον ἐπί *epeidon epi.*
Acts 4. 29 now, Lord, [behold] their threatenings

14. *To view,* θεάομαι *theaomai.*
Luke 23. 55 the women also..beheld the sepulchre
John 1. 14 we beheld his glory, the glory as of the

15. *To view,* θεωρέω *theōreō.*
Mark 12. 41 beheld how the people cast money into
15. 47 Mary Magdalene..beheld where he was
Luke 10. 18 I beheld Satan as lightning fall from
14. 29 Lest..all that behold (it) begin to mock
21. 6 these things which ye behold, the day
John 17. 24 they may behold my glory, which thou
Rev 11. 12 ascended..and their enemies beheld them

16. *To observe fully,* κατανοέω *katanoeō.*
Acts 7. 31 as he drew near to behold (it), the voice
7. 32 Moses trembled, and durst not behold
Jas. 1. 24 he beholdeth himself, and goeth his way

BEHOLD as in a glass, to —

To see in a mirror, κατοπτρίζομαι *katoptrizomai.*
2 Co. 3. 18 beholding as in a glass the glory of the

BEHOLD, to cause to —

To (cause to) look attentively, נָבַט *nabat,* 5.
Hab. 1. 3 Why dost thou..cause (me) to behold

BEHOLDING —

1. *To see,* רָאָה *raah.*
Psa 119. 37 Turn away mine eyes from beholding

2. *Seeing, sight,* רְאוּת *reuth.*
Eccl. 5. 11 saving the beholding..with their eyes?

3. *To view,* θεωρέω *theōreō.*
Matt 27. 55 many women were there beholding afar
Luke 23. 35 the people stood beholding. And the
23. 48 all the people..beholding the things
Acts 8. 13 beholding the miracles and signs which

4. *To behold,* βλέπω *blepō.*
Acts 4. 14 beholding the man which was healed
Col. 2. 5 joying and beholding your order, and the

5. *To behold intensely,* ἐμβλέπω *emblepō.*
Mark 10. 21 Then Jesus beholding him, loved him

6. *To observe fully,* κατανοέω *katanoeō.*
Jas. 1. 23 like unto a man beholding his natural

7. *To see,* ὁράω *horaō.*
Luke 23. 49 his acquaintance..stood afar..beholding
[*See also* Earnestly, steadily.]

BEHOVE, to —

To be binding on, δεῖ (acc.), *dei.*
Luke 24. 46 thus [it behoved] Christ to suffer, and to

BEHOVETH one, it —

To owe, ὀφείλω *opheilō.*
Heb. 2. 17 it behoved him to be made like unto (his)

BEING, while I have —

In my being, בְּעוֹדִי *be-od-i.*
Psa 104. 33 I will sing praise..while I have my being

BEING —

1. *To be,* εἰμί *eimi.*
Matt. 1. 19 Then Joseph her husband, being a just
7. 11 If ye then, being evil, know how to give
12. 34 how can ye, being evil, speak good
Mark 8. 1 In those days the multitude being very
14. 3 being in Bethany, in the house of Simon
Luke 2. 5 To be taxed with Mary..being great with
3. 23 being (as was supposed) the son of Joseph
13. 16 ought not this woman, being a daughter
20. 36 the children of God, being the children
22. 3 Judas..being of the number of the twelve
John 4. 9 How is it that thou, being a Jew, askest
5. 13 conveyed himself away, a multitude being
6. 71 that should betray him, [being] one of the
7. 50 he that came to Jesus by night, being one
10. 33 that thou, being a man, makest thyself
11. 49 one of them..being the high priest that
11. 51 being high priest that year, he prophesied
18. 26 One of the servants of..high priest, being
19. 38 Joseph of Arimathea, being a disciple of
Acts 15. 32 Judas and Silas, being prophets also
16. 21 teach customs..not lawful for us..being
27. 2 (one) Aristarchus, a Macedonian..being
Rom 11. 17 thou, being a wild olive tree, wert graffed
1 Co. 8. 7 and their conscience being weak is
9. 21 being not without law to God, but under
12. 12 all the members of that one body, being

Gal. 2. 3 neither Titus, who was with me, being a
Eph. 2. 20 Jesus Christ himself being the chief
4. 18 being alienated from the life of God
Col. 2. 13 you, being dead in your sins..hath he
1 Ti. 3. 10 use the office of a deacon, being..blameless
Titus 1. 16 in works they deny..being abominable
3. 11 and sinneth, being condemned of himself
Phm. 9 being such an one as Paul the aged, and
Heb. 1. 3 Who being the brightness of (his) glory
13. 3 as being yourselves also in the body

2. *To become, γίνομαι ginomai.*
Mark 9. 33 being in the house, he asked them, What
Luke 22. 44 being in an agony he prayed..earnestly
Jas. 1. 25 he being not a forgetful hearer, but a
1 Pe. 5. 3 Neither as being lords over..heritage

3. *To be, exist, ὑπάρχω huparchō.*
Luke 11. 13 If ye then, being evil, know how to give
16. 23 being in torments, and seeth Abraham
Acts 7. 55 But he, being full of the Holy Ghost
14. 8 [being] a cripple from his mother's womb
16. 20 These men, being Jews, do exceedingly
16. 37 being Romans, and have cast (us) into
19. 40 there being no cause whereby we may give
2 Co 8. 17 but being more forward..he went unto
12. 16 being crafty, I caught you with guile
Gal. 1. 14 being more exceedingly zealous of the
2. 14 If thou, being a Jew, livest after, **Ph. 2. 6**

4. *Upon, ἐπί (gen.) epi,* Luke 3. 2.

BEING, we have our —
We are, ἐσμέν esmen.
Acts 17. 28 we live, and move, and have our being

BEKAH —
A bekah, בֶּקַע beqa.
Exod 38. 26 A bekah for every man..half a shekel

BEL, בֵּל *lord.*
The Babylonian name of *Baal,* though some critics doubt their identity.
Isa. 46. 1 B boweth down, Nebo stoopeth; their
Jer. 50. 2 Babylon is taken, B is confounded
51. 44 I will punish B. in Babylon, and I will

BE'-LA, BE'-LAH, בֶּלַע *consumption.*
1. A place near the S. of the vale of Siddim, called also Zoar.
Gen. 14. 2 made war with..the king of B., which
14. 8 there went out..the king of B., the same
2. The first king of Edom mentioned in scripture, B.C. 1600.
Gen. 36. 32 B. the son of Beor reigned in Edom: and
36. 33 B died, and Jobab the son of Zerah of
1 Ch. 1. 43 these..the kings that reigned..B the son
1. 44 when B. was dead, Jobab the son of
3. Eldest son of Benjamin, and head of the Belaites, of whom the house of Ehud was most remarkable. He was one of the left-handed heroes, B.C. 1700.
Gen. 46 21 the sons of Benjamin.. Belah, and
Num 26. 38 of B., the family of the Belaites: of Ash.
26. 40 the sons of B. were Ard and Naaman
1 Ch. 7 6 of Benjamin; B. and Becher, and Jediael
7 7 the sons of Bela; Ezbon, and Uzzi, and
8. 1 Benjamin begat B. his firstborn, Ashbel
8. 3 the sons of B. were, Addar, and Gera and
4. A son of Azaz of the tribe of Reuben.
1 Ch. 5. 8 Bela the son of Azaz, the son of Shema

BE-LA-ITES. בַּלְעִי *belonging to Bela.*
Descendants of the preceding Bela.
Num 26. 38 of Bela, the family of the Belaites: of

BELCH out, to —
To cause to flow, utter, send forth, נָבַע *naba,* 5.
Psa. 59. 7 Behold, they belch out with their mouth

BE-LI'-AL, בְּלִיַּעַל *worthless, reckless, lawless.*
This should not be regarded as a proper name. It is generally associated with the words "man," "son," "daughter," or "chilren." Hence "son" or "man" of Belial, simply means "a worthless person." In the New Testament the form of the word is *Beliar* (*βελίαρ* not *βελίαλ* as given in the common version).
Deut 13 13 men the children of B., are gone out
Judg 19 22 certain sons of B., beset the house round
20. 13 deliver (us) the men, the children of B.
1 Sa. 1. 16 Count not thine handmaid for a dau. of B.
2. 12 Now the sons of Eli (were) sons of B.
10. 27 the children of B. said, How shall this
25 17 for he (is such) a son of B., that (a man)
25. 25 Let not my Lord..regard this man of B.
30. 22 Then answered all the wicked men...of B.
2 Sa. 16 7 Come out, come out..thou man of B.
20. 1 there happened to be there a man of B.
23. 6 But (the sons) of B...all of them as thorns
1 Ki. 21. 10 set two men. sons of B., before him, to
21. 13 there came in two men, children of B.
21. 13 the men of B. witnessed against him
2 Ch. 13. 7 there are gathered unto him..child. of B.
2 Cor. 6. 15 what concord hath Christ with B.?

BELIE, to —
To lie to, be false, כָּחַשׁ *kachash,* 3.
Jer. 5. 12 They have belied the LORD, and said

BELIEF —
Confidence, trust, πίστις pistis.
2 Th. 2. 13 through sanctification of the Spirit, & b.

BELIEVE, to —
1. *To remain stedfast,* אָמַן *aman,* 5.
Gen. 15. 6 he believed in the LORD; and he counted
45 26 Jacob's heart fainted, for he believed
Exod. 4. 1 they will not believe me, nor hearken
4. 5 That they may believe that the LORD God
4. 8 it shall come to pass, if they will not be.
4. 8 they will believe the voice of the latter
4. 9 if they will not believe also these two
4. 31 the people believed: and when they heard
14. 31 believed the LORD, and his servant Moses
19. 9 that the people may hear..and believe
Num 14. 11 how long will it be ere they believe me
20. 12 Because ye believed me not, to sanctify
Deut. 1 32 in this thing ye did not believe the LORD
9. 23 ye believed him not, nor hearkened to his
1 Sa. 27. 12 Achish believed David, saying, He hath
1 Ki. 10. 7 Howbeit I believed not the words, until
2 Ki. 17. 14 that did not believe in the LORD their God
2 Ch. 9. 6 Howbeit I believed not their words, until
20. 20 Believe in the LORD..believe his prophets
32. 15 nor persuade you..neither yet believe
Job. 9. 16 would I not believe that he..hearkened
15. 22 He believeth not that he shall return out
29. 24 (If) I laughed on them, they believed (it)
39. 12 Wilt thou believe him, that he will bring
39. 24 neither believeth he that (it is) the sound
Psa. 27. 13 unless I had believed to see the goodness
78. 22 Because they believed not in God, and
78. 32 and believed not for his wondrous works
106. 12 Then believed they his words; they sang
106 24 they despised the pleasant land; they be.
116. 10 I believed, therefore have I spoken: I
119. 66 for I have believed thy commandments
Prov. 14 15 The simple believeth every word: but the
26. 25 When he speaketh fair, believe him not
Isa. 7. 9 If ye will not believe, surely ye shall not
28. 16 he that believeth shall not make haste
43. 10 that ye may know and believe me, and
53. 1 Who hath believed our report? and to
Jer. 12. 6 believe them not, though they speak fair
40. 14 Gedaliah the son of Ahikam believed..not
Lam. 4. 12 The kings..would not have believed that
Dan. 6. 23 taken up out..because he believed in his
Jon 3. 5 So the people of Nineveh believed God
Hab. 1. 5 ye will not believe, though it be told

2. *To be persuaded, πείθομαι peithomai.*
Acts 17. 4 some of them believed, and consorted
27. 11 Nevertheless the centurion believed the
28. 24 some believed the things which were

3. *To adhere to, trust, rely on, πιστεύω pisteuō.*
Matt 8. 13 as thou hast believed, (so) be it done unto
9. 28 Believe ye that I am able to do this?
18 6 one of these little ones which believe in
21. 22 whatsoever ye shall ask in prayer, believ.
21 25 Why did ye not then believe him?
21. 32 believed him not..believed him..might b.
24. 23 Lo, here (is) Christ, or there; believe (it)
24. 26 (he is) in the secret chambers; believe (it)
27. 42 let him..come down..and we will believe
Mark 5 36 unto the ruler..Be not afraid, only believe
9. 23 If thou canst [believe]..him that believeth
9. 24 Lord I believe; help thou mine unbelief
9. 42 offend one of..little ones that [believe] in
11. 23 shall believe that those things which he
11. 24 when ye pray, believe that ye receive
11. 31 will say, Why then did ye not believe him?
13. 21 or, lo, (he is) there; believe (him) not
15. 32 descend..that we may see and believe
16. 13 [they went and told..neither believed]
16. 14 [because they believed not them which]
16. 16 [He that believeth..shall be saved; but]
16. 17 [these signs shall follow them that believe]
Luke 1. 20 because thou believest not my words
1. 45 blessed (is) she that believed: for there
8. 12 lest they should believe and be saved
8. 13 have no root, which for a while believe
8. 50 believe only, and she shall be made whole
20. 5 he will say, Why then believed ye him
22. 67 he said..If I tell you, ye will not believe
John 1. 7 that all (men) through him might believe
1. 12 power..to them that believe on his name
1. 50 I saw thee under the fig tree, believest
2. 11 miracles..and his disciples believed on
2. 22 they believed the Scripture, and the word
2. 23 many believed in his name, when they saw
3. 12 and ye believe not, how shall ye believe
3. 15 That whosoever believeth in him should
3. 16 that whosoever believeth in him should
3. 18 He that believeth on him is not condemn.
3. 18 he that believeth not is condemned al.
3. 18 because he hath not believed in the name
3. 36 He that believeth on the Son of man hath
4. 21 Woman, believe me, the hour cometh
4. 39 many of the Samaritans..believed on Him
4. 41 many more believed because of his own
4. 42 Now we believe, not because of thy saying
4. 48 Except ye see signs..ye will not believe
4. 50 the man believed the word that Jesus
4. 53 and himself believed, and his whole house
5. 24 believeth on him that sent me, hath ever.
5. 38 whom he hath sent, him ye believe not
5. 44 How can ye believe. which receive honour
5. 46 had ye believed Moses, ye would have b.
5. 47 if ye believe not his writings
5. 47 how shall ye believe my words?
6. 29 that ye believe on him whom he hath
6. 30 that we may see, and believe thee? what
6. 35 he that believeth on me shall never thirst
6. 36 That ye also have seen me, and believe
John 6. 40 which seeth the Son, and believeth on
6. 47 He that believeth on me hath everlasting
6. 64 some of you that believe not..believed
6. 69 we believe and are sure that thou art that
7. 5 For neither did his brethren believe in
7. 31 many of the people believed on him, and
7. 38 He that believeth on me, as the Scripture
7. 39 which they that believe on him should
7. 48 Have any of the rulers..believed on him?
8. 24 if ye believe not that I am (he), ye shall
8. 30 As he spake these words many believed
8. 31 said..to those Jews which believed on
8. 45 because I tell..the truth, ye believe me
8. 46 if I say the truth, why do ye not believe
9. 18 the Jews did not believe concerning him
9. 35 Dost thou believe on the Son of God?
9. 36 Who is he..that I might believe on him?
9. 38 he said, Lord, [I believe.] And he
10. 25 I told you, and ye believed not
10. 26 ye believe not, because ye are not of my
10. 37 If I do not the works..believe me not
10. 38 though ye believe not me, believe the
10. 38 that ye may know and [believe,] that the
10. 42 And many believed on him there
11. 15 to the intent ye may believe; nevertheless
11. 25 he that believeth in me, though he were
11. 26 whosoever..believeth in me shall ...Be.
11. 27 Believest thou this? I believe that thou
11. 40 if thou wouldest believe, thou shouldest
11. 42 that they may believe that thou hast sent
11. 45 Then many of the Jews..believed on him
11. 48 If we let him thus alone, all..will believe
12. 11 of the Jews went away, and believed on J.
12. 36 While ye have light, believe in the light
12. 37 done..many miracles..yet they believed
12. 38 Lord, who hath believed our report? and
12. 39 Therefore they could not believe, because
12. 42 among the chief rulers also many believed
12. 44 He that believeth on me, believeth not
12. 46 whosoever believeth on me should not
12. 47 if any man hear my words, and [believe]
13. 19 that..ye may believe that I am (he)
14. 1 ye believe in God, believe also in me
14. 10 Believest thou not that I am in the Father
14. 11 Believe me that I (am) in the Father, and
14. 11 or else believe me for the very works'
14. 12 I say unto you, He that believeth on me
14. 29 when it is come to pass, ye might believe
16. 9 Of sin, because they believe not on me
16. 27 and have believed that I came out from
16. 30 by this we believe that thou camest forth
16. 31 Jesus answered them, Do ye now believe?
17. 8 they have believed that thou didst send
17. 20 which shall believe on me through their
17. 21 that the world may believe that thou hast
19. 35 that he saith true, that ye might believe
20. 8 went in also that other..and believed
20. 25 thrust..into his side, I will not believe
20. 29 thou hast believed..and..have believed
20 31 that ye might believe..and that believing
Acts 2. 44 all that believed were together, and had
4. 4 many of them..heard the word believed
4. 32 the multitude of them that believed were
8. 12 when they believed Philip preaching the
8. 13 Simon himself believed also: and when
8. 37 [If thou believest..I believe]
9. 26 and believed not that he was a disciple
9. 42 it was known..and many believed in the
10. 43 whosoever believeth in him shall receive
11. 17 unto us, who believed on the Lord Jesus
11. 21 a great number believed, and turned unto
13. 12 when he saw what was done, believed
13. 39 by him all that believe are justified from
13. 41 a work which ye shall in no wise believe
13. 48 as..were ordained to eternal life believed
14. 1 a..multitude both of the Jews..believed
14. 23 to the Lord, on whom they believed
15. 5 there rose up certain of..which believed
15. 7 Gentiles..word of the gospel, and believe
15. 11 we believe that through the grace of the
16. 31 they said, Believe on the Lord Jesus
16. 34 believing in God with all his house
17. 12 Therefore many of them believed; also
17 34 men clave unto him, and believed
18. 8 believed on the Lord..hearing believed
18. 27 helped them much which had believed
19. 2 received the Holy Ghost since ye believed?
19. 4 they should believe on him which should
19. 18 many that believed came, and confessed
21. 20 thousands of Jews there are which believe
21. 25 As touching the Gentiles which believe
22. 19 beat in every synagogue..that believed
24. 14 believing all things which are written
26. 27 believest thou..I know. thou believest
27. 25 be of good cheer. for I believe God
Rom. 1. 16 power of God..every one that believeth
3. 22 unto all and upon all them that believe
4. 3 Abraham believed God, and it was
4. 5 believeth on him that justifieth the
4. 11 he might be the father of all them that be.
4. 17 before him whom he believed, (even) God
4. 18 Who against hope believed in hope, that
4. 24 if we believe on him that raised up Jesus
6. 8 we believe that we shall also live with
9. 33 whosoever believeth on him shall not be
10. 4 for righteousness to..one that believeth
10. 9 shalt believe in thine heart that God hath
10. 10 with the heart man believeth unto
10. 11 Whosoever believeth on him shall not be
10. 14 they have not believed..shall they believe
10. 16 Lord, who hath believed our report?
13. 11 now (is) our salvation..when we believed

Rom 14. 2 one believeth that he may eat all things
1 Co. 1. 21 it pleased God..to save them that believe
3. 5 but ministers by whom ye believed
11. 18 be divisions among you..partly believe it
13. 7 Beareth all things, believeth all things
14. 22 not to them that believe..that believe
15. 2 are saved..unless ye have believed in
15. 11 they, so we preach, and so ye believed
2 Co. 4. 13 I believed..we also believe, and therefore
Gal. 2. 16 even we have believed in Jesus Christ
3. 6 Even as Abraham believed God, and it
3. 22 promise..be given to them that believe
Eph. 1. 13 in whom also, after that ye believed, ye
1. 19 who believe, according to..his mighty
Phil. 1. 29 not only to believe on him, but also to
1 Th. 1. 7 to all that believe in Macedonia and
2. 10 behaved ourselves among you that believe
2. 13 effectually worketh..in you that believe
4. 14 if we believe that Jesus died and rose
2 Th. 1. 10 that believe..our testimony..believed
2. 11 delusion, that they should believe a lie
2. 12 might be damned who believed not the
1 Ti. 1. 16 which should hereafter believe on him
3. 16 believed on in the world, received up
2 Ti. 1. 12 I know whom I have believed, and am
Titus 3. 8 they which have believed in God might
Heb. 4. 3 we which have believed do enter into rest
11. 6 he that cometh to God must believe that
Jas. 2. 19 Thou believest..the devils also believe
2. 23 Abraham believed God, and it was
1 Pe. 1. 8 believing, ye rejoice with joy unspeakable
1. 21 Who by him do [believe] in God, that
2. 6 he that believeth on him shall not be
2. 7 Unto you therefore which believe (he is)
1 Jo. 3. 23 That we should believe on the name of
4. 1 believe not every spirit, but try the spirits
4. 16 we have known and believed the love
5. 1 Whosoever believeth that Jesus is the
5. 5 he that believeth that Jesus is the S.v.10
Jude 5 afterward destroyed them that believed

4. *To remain stedfast to,* πιστεύω εἰς *pisteuō eis.*
1 Jo. 5. 10 He that believeth on the Son of God
5. 10 he believeth not the record that God
5. 13 [that believe on..that ye may believe on]

5. *To remain stedfast in,* πιστεύω ἐν *pisteuō en.*
Mark 1. 15 saying..repent ye, and believe the Gospel

6. *To remain stedfast on,* πιστεύω ἐπί *pisteuō epi.*
Luke 24. 25 O fools, and slow of heart to believe all

BELIEVE not, to —

1. *To be unpersuaded,* ἀπειθέω *apeitheō.*
John 3. 36 he that believeth not the Son shall not see
Acts 17. 5 the Jews [which believed not,] moved
19. 9 when divers were hardened, and beli. not
Rom 11. 30 as ye in times past have not believed God
11. 31 Even so have these also now not believed
15. 31 from them that do not believe in Judea
Heb. 3. 18 sware he..to them that believed not?
11. 31 Rahab perished not with them that bel.n.

2. *To be without trust,* ἀπιστέω *apisteō.*
Mark16. 11 [they, when they had heard..believed not]
16. 16 [he that believeth not shall be damned]
Luke24. 11 as idle tales, and they believed them not
24. 41 while they yet believed not for joy, and
Acts 28. 24 which were spoken, and some believed n.
Rom. 3. 3 what if some did not believe? shall their
2 Ti. 2. 13 If we believe not..he abideth faithful

BELIEVE, them that —

Faith, πίστις *pistis.*
Heb. 10. 39 but of them that believe to the saving of

BELIEVED, most surely —

To bear, carry fully, πληροφορέω *plērophoreō.*
Luke 1. 1 which are most surely believed among us

BELIEVED, which —

Trusting, trusty, πιστός *pistos.*
Acts 10. 45 they of the circumcision which believed
16. 1 woman, which was a Jewess, and believed

BELIEVER —

1. *To trust, rely on,* πιστεύω *pisteuō.*
Acts 5. 14 believers were the more added to the

2. *Trusting, trusty,* πιστός *pistos.*
1 Ti. 4. 12 be thou an example of the believers, in

BELIEVETH, he that —

Who is of the faith of, ὁ ἐκ πίστεως. [*ho,ek,pistis*].
Rom. 3. 26 the justifier of him which believeth in J.

BELIEVETH, that or which —

Trusting, trusty, πιστός *pistos.*
2 Co. 6. 15 what part hath he that believeth with an
1 Ti. 4. 3 of them which believe and know the
4. 10 the Saviour..specially of those that believe
5. 16 If any man or woman that [believeth].

BELIEVETH not, that or which —

Untrusting, ἄπιστος *apistos.*
1 Co. 7. 12 If any brother hath a wife that beli. not
7. 13 woman..hath an husband that beli. not
10. 27 If any of them that believe not bid you
14. 22 are for a sign..to them that believe not
14. 22 not for them that believe not, but for
14. 24 there come in one that believeth not, or
2 Co. 4. 4 blinded the minds of them which bel. not

BELIEVING —

1. *To trust, rely on,* πιστευω *pisteuō.*
Rom 15. 13 God of hope fill you with..joy..believing

2. *Trusting,* πιστός *pistos.*
John 20. 27 saith he..be not faithless, but believing
1 Ti. 6. 2 they that have believing masters, let

BELL —

1. *A little bell,* מְצִלּוֹת *metsilloth.*
Zech 14. 20 In that day shall there be upon the bells

2. *A clock, bell,* פַּעֲמוֹן *paamon.*
Exod 28. 33 bells of gold between them round about
28. 34 A..bell and a pomegranate..a..bell
39. 25 they made bells..and put the bells
39. 26 A bell and a pomegranate, a bell and a

BELLOW, to —

To sound, צָהַל *tsahal.*
Jer. 50. 11 ye are grown fat..and bellow as bulls

BELLOWS —

Bellows, מַפֻּחַ *mappuach.*
Jer. 6. 29 the bellows are burnt, the lead is

BELLY —

1. *Belly,* בֶּטֶן *beten.*
Num. 5. 21 the LORD doth make..thy belly to swell
5. 22 make (thy) belly to swell..(thy) thigh to
5. 27 her belly shall swell..her thigh shall rot
Judg. 3. 21 Ehud..thrust it into his belly
3. 22 could not draw the dagger out of his belly
1 Ki. 7. 20 over against the belly which (was) by the
Job 3. 11 give up..when I came out of the belly?
15. 2 and fill his belly with the east wind?
15. 35 vanity, and their belly prepareth deceit
20. 15 God shall cast them out of his belly
20. 20 he shall not feel quietness in his belly
20. 23 he is about to fill his belly, (God) shall
32. 19 Behold, my belly (is) as wine (which) hath
40. 16 his force (is) in the navel of his belly
Psa. 17. 14 whose belly thou fillest with thy hid
22. 10 thou (art) my God from my mother's belly
31. 9 is consumed..my soul and my belly
44. 25 our belly cleaveth unto the earth
Prov. 13. 25 the belly of the wicked shall want
18. 8 go..into the innermost parts of the belly
18. 20 A man's belly shall be satisfied with the
20. 27 searching all the inward parts of the belly
20. 30 (do) stripes the inward parts of the bell
26. 22 go..into the innermost parts of the belly
Song 7. 2 thy belly (is like) an heap of wheat set
Isa. 46. 3 Israel, which are borne (by me) from t. b.
Jer. 1. 5 Before I formed thee in the belly, I knew
Eze. 3. 3 Son of man, cause thy belly to eat, and
Jon. 2. 2 out of the belly of hell cried I..thou
Hab. 3. 16 When I heard, my belly trembled; my

2. *Belly (of reptiles),* גָּחוֹן *gachon.*
Gen. 3. 14 upon thy belly shalt thou go, and dust
Lev. 11. 42 Whatsoever goeth upon the belly..ye

3. *Paunch,* כְּרֵשׂ *keres.*
Jer. 51. 34 he hath filled his belly with my delicates

4. *Bowels,* מֵעִים *meim.*
Song 5. 14 his belly (is as) bright ivory overlaid
Dan. 2. 32 his belly and his thighs of brass
Jon. 1. 17 Jonah was in the belly of the fish three
2. 1 Jonah prayed..out of the fish's belly

5. *Hollow place,* קֳבָה *qobah.*
Num 25. 8 thrust..the woman through her belly

6. *Belly,* γαστήρ *gastēr.*
Titus 1. 12 Cretians (are) alway liars..slow bellies

7. *Belly, inward parts,* κοιλία *koilia.*
Matt 12. 40 as Jonas was three days..whale's belly
15. 17 entereth in at the mouth..into the belly
Mark 7. 19 not into his heart, but into the belly
Luke 15. 16 he would fain have filled his belly with
John 7. 38 out of his belly shall flow rivers of living
Rom 16. 18 they that are such serve..their own belly
1 Co. 6. 13 Meats for the belly, and the belly for
Phil. 3. 19 Whose end (is) destruction, whose..belly
Rev. 10. 9 it shall make thy belly bitter, but it shall
10. 10 as soon as I had eaten it, my belly was

BELONG to or unto, to —

To be, εἰμί *eimi.*
Mark 9. 41 because ye belong to Christ, verily I say
Luke 23. 7 as soon as he knew that he belonged unto
Heb. 5. 14 strong meat belongeth to them that are

BELONG to, things that —

1. *Portion,* מָנָה *manah,*
Esth. 2. 9 with such things as belonged to her, and

2. *The things of,* τά *or* πρός, *also gen.*
Luke 9. 10 a desert place belonging to the 19. 42.
1 Co. 7. 32 He..careth for the things that belong to

[*See also* Gen. 40. 8; Lev. 27. 24; Deut. 29. 29; 32. 35; Judg. 19. 14; 20. 4; 1 Ki. 1. 8; Ezra 10 4; Psa. 3. 8; 47. 9; 62. 11, 12; 68. 20; Prov. 24. 23; Dan. 9. 7, 8, 9; Heb. 10. 30.]

BELOVED —

1 *To love,* אָהֵב *aheb.*
Deut 21. 15 If a man have two wives, one beloved, and
21. 15 have born him children..the beloved and
21. 16 he may not make the son of the beloved
Neh. 13. 26 who was beloved of his God, and God
Song 1. 14 My beloved (is) unto me (as) a cluster of
Hos. 3. 1 Go yet, love a woman beloved of (her)
Song 1. 16 thou (art) fair, my beloved, yea, pleasant

2. *Loved,* דּוֹד *dod.*
Song 2. 3 so (is) my beloved among the sons
2. 8 The voice of my beloved! behold, he
2. 9 My beloved is like a roe or a young hart
2. 10 My beloved spake, and said unto me, Rise
2. 16 My beloved (is) mine, and I (am) his: he
2. 17 turn, my beloved, and be thou like a roe
4. 16 Let my beloved come into his garden
5. 1 drink, yea, drink abundantly, O beloved
5. 2 the voice of my beloved that knocketh
5. 4 My beloved put in his hand by the hole
5. 5 I rose up to open to my beloved; and my
5. 6 I opened to my beloved; but my beloved
5. 8 O daughters of Jerusalem..my beloved
5. 9 What..thy beloved more than (another) b.
5. 9 what..thy beloved more than (another) b.
5. 10 My beloved (is) white and ruddy, the
5. 16 This (is) my beloved, and this (is) my
6. 1 is thy beloved gone..thy beloved turned
6. 2 My beloved is gone down into his garden
6. 3 I (am) my beloved's, and my beloved
7. 9 like the best wine for my beloved, that
7. 10 I (am) my beloved's, and his desire (is)
7. 11 Come, my beloved, let us go forth into
7. 13 (which) I have laid up for thee..beloved
8. 5 Who (is) this..leaning upon her beloved?
8. 14 Make haste, my beloved, and be thou
Isa. 5. 1 a song of my beloved touching his viney.

3. *Beloved,* יָדִיד *yadid.*
Deut 33. 12 The beloved of the LORD shall dwell in
Psa. 60. 5 That thy beloved may be delivered, save
108. 6 That thy beloved may be delivered save
127. 2 (for) so he giveth his beloved sleep
Jer. 11. 15 What hath my beloved to do in mine

4. *Desire,* מַחְמָד *machmad.*
Hos. 9. 16 yet will I slay..the beloved..of their

5. *To love dearly,* ἀγαπάω *agapaō.*
Rom. 9. 25 call..her beloved, which was not beloved
Eph. 1. 6 he hath made us accepted in the beloved
Col. 3. 12 as the elect of God, holy and beloved
1 Th. 1. 4 Knowing, brethren beloved, your election
2 Th. 2. 13 brethren beloved of the Lord, because
Rev. 20. 9 camp of the saints about..beloved city

6. *Dearly beloved,* ἀγαπητός *agapētos.*
Matt. 3. 17 This is my beloved Son, in whom I am
12. 18 my beloved, in whom my soul is well
17. 5 This is my beloved Son, in whom I am
Mark 1. 11 Thou art my beloved Son, in whom I am
9. 7 saying, This is my beloved Son: hear him
Luke 3. 22 Thou art my beloved Son; in thee I am
9. 35 saying, This is my [beloved] Son: hear him
20. 13 What shall I do? I will send my beloved
Acts 15. 25 to send chosen men..with our beloved
Rom. 1. 7 To all that be in Rome, beloved of God
11. 28 the election..beloved for the fathers'
16. 8 Greet Amplias my beloved in the Lord
16. 9 Salute Urbane..and Stachys my beloved
16. 12 [Salute the beloved Persis, which laboured]
1 Co. 4. 14 but, as my beloved sons, I warn (you)
4. 17 Timotheus, who is my beloved son
15. 58 Therefore, my beloved brethren, be ye
Eph. 6. 21 a beloved brother and faithful minister
Phil. 2. 12 my beloved, as ye have always obeyed
Col. 4. 7 Tychicus..beloved brother, and a
4. 9 Onesimus, a faithful and beloved brother
4. 14 Luke, the beloved physician, and Demas
1 Ti. 6. 2 because they are faithful and beloved
Phm. 2 to (our) [beloved] Apphia, and Archippus
16 but above a servant, a brother beloved
Heb. 6. 9 But, beloved, we are persuaded..of you
Jas. 1. 16 Do not err, my beloved brethren
1. 19 my beloved brethren, let every man be
2. 5 Hearken, my beloved brethren, Hath not
1 Pe. 4. 12 Beloved, think it not strange concerning
2 Pe. 1. 17 This is my beloved Son, in whom I am
3. 1 This second epistle, beloved, I now write
3. 8 beloved, be not ignorant of this one thing
3. 14 beloved, seeing that ye look for such
3. 15 even as our beloved brother Paul also
3. 17 beloved, seeing ye know..before, beware
1 Jo. 3. 2 Beloved, now are we the sons of God
3. 21 Beloved, if our heart condemn us not
4. 1 Beloved, believe not every spirit, but try
4. 7 Beloved, let us love one another: for love
4. 11 Beloved, if God so loved us, we ought also
3 Jo. 2 Beloved, I wish..thou mayest prosper
5 Beloved, thou doest faithfully whatsoever
11 Beloved, follow not that which is evil
Jude 3 Beloved, when I gave all diligence to
17 beloved, remember ye the words..of the
20 beloved, building up yourselves on your

BELOVED, dearly —

1. *Dearly beloved,* יְדִדוּת *yediduth.*
Jer. 12. 7 dearly beloved of my soul into the hand

2. *Dearly beloved,* ἀγαπητός *agapētos.*
Rom 12. 19 Dearly beloved, avenge not yourselves
1 Co. 10. 14 Wherefore, my dearly beloved, flee from
2 Co. 7. 1 dearly beloved, let us cleanse ourselves
12. 19 but..all things, dearly beloved, for your
Phil. 4. 1 my brethren dearly beloved and longed
4. 1 stand fast in the Lord, (my) dearly beloved
2 Ti. 1. 2 To Timothy, (my) dearly beloved son
Phm. 1 Philemon our dearly beloved, and fellow
1 Pe. 2. 11 Dearly beloved, I beseech (you) as

BELOVED, well —

Dearly beloved, ἀγαπητός *agapētos.*
Mark 12. 6 Having yet..one son, his well beloved

Rom 16. 5 Salute my well beloved Epenetus, who is
3 Jo. 1 The elder unto the well beloved Gaius

BELOVED, greatly —
Very desirable, חֲמוּדוֹת *chamudoth.*
Dan. 9. 23 for thou (art) greatly beloved : therefore
10. 11 O Daniel, a man greatly beloved
10. 19 And said, O man greatly beloved, fear not

BEL-SHAZ'-ZAR, בֵּלְשַׁאצַּר *the lord's leader.*
Son of Nebuchadnezzar and last of the kings of Babylon, slain B.C. 550.
Dan. 5. 1 B. the king made a great feast to a
5. 2 B., whiles he tasted the wine, commanded
5. 9 Then was king B. greatly troubled, and
5. 22 thou his son, O B., hast not humbled
5. 29 Then commanded B., and they clothed
5. 30 In that night was B. the king of the Chal.
7. 1 In the first year of B. king of Babylon
8. 1 In the third year of the reign of king B.

BEL-TE-SHAZ'-ZAR, בֵּלְטְשַׁאצַּר *the lord's leader.*
The name given to Daniel by the prince of Nebuchadnezzar's eunuchs, B.C. 550.
Dan. 1. 7 for he gave unto Daniel (the name) of B.
2. 26 said to Daniel whose name (was) B., Art
4. 8 at the last Daniel..whose name (was) B.
4. 9 O B., master of the magicians, because I
4. 18 Now thou, O B. declare the interpretation
4. 19 Then Daniel, whose name (was) B., was
4. 19 The king spake, and said, B., let not the
4. 19 B. answered and said, My Lord, the dream
5. 12 Daniel, whom the king named B. : now
10. 1 revealed unto Daniel, whose name was B.

BEMOAN, to —
To nod, move, נוּד *nud.*
Job 42. 11 they bemoaned him, and comforted him
Jer. 15. 5 O Jerusalem? or who shall bemoan thee?
16. 5 neither go to lament nor bemoan them
22. 10 Weep ye not for the dead, neither bemoan
48. 17 All ye that are about him, bemoan him
Nah. 3. 7 Nineveh is laid waste : who will bemoan

BEMOAN self, to —
To nod or move oneself, נוּד *nud, 7a.*
Jer. 31. 18 I have..heard Ephraim bemoaning h.

BEN, בֵּן *son, intelligent.*
A Levite set over the service of song in the time of David, B.C. 1042.
1 Ch. 15. 18 with them their brethren..B., and Jaaziel

BE-NA'-IAH, בְּנָיָהוּ, בְּנָיָה *Jah is intelligent.*
1. Son of Jehoiada, one of David's officers, B.C. 1042.
2 Sa. 8. 18 B. the son of Jehoiada (was over) both
20. 23 B. the son of Jehoiada (was) over the
23. 20 B. the son of Jehoiada, the son of a
23. 22 These (things) did B. the son of Jehoiada
1 Ki. 1. 8 Zadok the priest, and B. the son of Jehoia.
1. 10 Nathan the prophet, and B., and the
1. 26 Zadok the priest, and B. the son of Jeh.
1. 32 David said, Call me Zadok the priest..& B.
1. 36 B. the son of Jehoiada answered the king
1. 38 So Zadok the priest..and B. the son of
1. 44 the king hath sent..B., the son of Jehoiada
2. 25 king Solomon sent by the hand of B. the
2. 29 Then Solomon sent B. the son of Jehoiada
2. 30 B. came to the tabernacle of the LORD
2. 30 B. brought the king word again, saying
2. 34 So B. the son of Jehoiada went up, and
2. 35 the king put B. the son of Jehoiada
2. 46 So the king commanded B. the son of
4. 4 B. the son of Jehoiada (was) over the
1 Ch. 11. 22 B. the son of Jehoiada, the son of a
11. 24 These (things) did B. the son of Jehoiada
18. 17 B. the son of Jehoiada (was) over the
27. 5 The third captain of the host..(was) B. the
27. 6 This (is that) B., (who was) mighty (among)
2. One of David's valiant men from Pirathon, B.C. 1042.
2 Sa. 23. 30 [one of the thirty]..B. the Pirathonite
1 Ch. 11. 31 children of Benjamin, B. the Pirathonite
27. 14 The eleventh (captain..was) B. the Pira.
3. Head of a family of Simeon, B.C. 1050.
1 Ch. 4. 36 Asaiah, and Adiel, and Jesimiel, and B.
4. One of David's priests in Jerusalem, B.C. 1042.
1 Ch. 15. 18 with them their brethren..B., and Maas.
15. 20 Maaseiah, and B., with psalteries on
15. 24 B., and Eliezer, the priests, did blow with
16. 5 Mattithiah, and Eliab, and B., and Obed.
16. 6 B. also and Jahaziel the priests with
5. Father of one of David's counsellors, B.C. 1040.
1 Ch. 27. 34 Ahithophel (was) Jehoiada the son of B.
6. The grandfather of Jahaziel, B.C. 896.
2 Ch. 20. 14 Then upon Jahaziel..the son of B., the
7. A Levite overseer of the temple and the offerings in Hezekiah's reign, B.C. 725.
2 Ch. 31. 13 Mahath, and B...overseers under the hand
8. One of the family of Parosh, B.C. 456.
Ezra 10. 25 the sons of Parosh..Malchijah, and B.
9. A son of Pahath-moab, B.C. 456.
Ezra 10. 30 sons of Pahath-moab; Adna..Chelal, B.
10. A son of Bani, B.C. 456.
Ezra 10. 35 [Of the sons of Bani; Maadai]..B.
11. A son of Nebo, B.C. 456.
Ezra 10. 43 Of the sons of Nebo; Jeiel..and Joel, B.
12. Father of Pelatiah, a prince of Judah, B.C. 594.
Eze. 11. 1 among whom..Pelatiah the son of B.
11. 13 that Pelatiah the son of B. died. Then

BEN AM'-MI, בֶּן־עַמִּי *son of my people.*
The son whom Lot's younger daughter bore to him. He was father of the Ammonites, B.C. 1819.
Gen. 19. 38 also bare a son, and called his name B.

BENCH —
Board, bench, קֶרֶשׁ *qeresh.*
Eze. 27. 6 the Ashurites have made thy benches

BEND, to —
1. *To tread,* דָּרַךְ *darak.*
Psa. 7. 12 he hath bent his bow, and made it ready
11. 2 For, lo, the wicked bend..bow, they make
37. 14 The wicked..have bent their bow, to cast
58. 7 he bendeth..his arrows, let them be as
64. 3 bend..their arrows..bitter words
Isa. 5. 28 their bows bent, their horses' hoofs shall
21. 15 they fled..from the bent bow, and from
Jer. 46. 9 Lydians, that handle (and) bend the bow
50. 14 all ye that bend the bow, shoot at her
50. 29 all ye that bend the bow, camp against it
51. 3 Against (him that) bend. let the archer b.
Lam. 2. 4 He hath bent his bow like an enemy
3. 12 He hath bent his bow, and set me as a
Zech. 9. 13 When I have bent Judah for me
2. *To cause to tread,* דָּרַךְ *darak, 5.*
Jer. 9. 3 they bend their tongues (like) their bow
3. *To bend, bow,* כָּפַן *kaphan.*
Eze. 17. 7 this vine did bend her roots toward him

BENDING —
To bow down, שָׁחַח *shachach.*
Isa. 60. 14 sons also..shall come bending unto thee

BENEATH —
1. *Beneath, below,* מַטָּה *mattah.*
Exod 26. 24 they shall be coupled together beneath
27. 5 thou shalt put it under..the altar beneath
36. 29 they were coupled beneath, and coupled
38. 4 under the compass thereof beneath unto
Deut 28. 13 thou shalt not be beneath ; if that thou
Prov. 15. 24 that he may depart from hell beneath
Jer. 31. 37 the foundations..searched out beneath
2. *Under,* תַּחַת *tachath.*
Exod 32. 19 and brake them beneath the mount
Deut 33. 13 Blessed..for the deep that coucheth be.
3. *From under,* מִתַּחַת *mit-tachath.*
Exod 20. 4 heaven above, or..in the earth beneath
Deut. 4. 18 fish that (is) in the waters beneath the
4. 39 heaven above, and upon the earth beneath
5. 8 beneath, or in that (is) in the waters b.
Job 18. 16 His roots shall be dried up beneath
4. *Downwards, down,* κάτω *katō.*
Mark 14. 66 as Peter was beneath in the palace, there
John 8. 23 Ye are from beneath ; I am from above
Acts 2. 19 I will shew..signs in the earth beneath

BE-NE BE'-RAK, בְּנֵי־בְרַק *sons of lightning.*
A city in Dan, near Ashdod.
Josh. 19. 45 [coast of their inheritance]..Jehud..B.

BENEFACTOR —
Well-doer, εὐεργέτης *euergetēs.*
Luke 22. 25 exercise authority..are called benefactors

BENEFIT —
1. *Deed,* גְּמוּל *gemul.*
2 Ch. 32. 25 according to the benefit (done) unto him
Psa. 103. 2 Bless the LORD..forget not all his benefits
2. *Deed,* תַּגְמוּל *tagmul.*
Psa. 116. 12 I render unto the LORD..all his benefits
3. *Good,* ἀγαθός *agathos.*
Phm. 14 that thy benefit should not be as it were
4. *Good work, well-doing,* εὐεργεσία *euergesia.*
1 Ti. 6. 2 because they are..partakers of the benefit
5. *Grace,* χάρις *charis.*
2 Co. 1. 15 that ye might have a second benefit

BENEFIT, to —
To do good, יָטַב *yatab, 5.*
Jer. 18. 10 wherewith I said I would benefit them

BE-NE JA-A'-KAN, בְּנֵי יַעֲקָן *sons of intelligence.*
A tribe that gave its name to several wells around the 27th station of the Israelites, and 16th from Sinai. It lay between Moseroth and Horagidgad.
Num 33. 31 they departed..& pitched in B.
33. 32 they removed from B., and encamped at

BENEVOLENCE —
Good mind, εὔνοια *eunoia.*
1 Co. 7. 3 render unto the wife due benevolence

BEN HA'-DAD, בֶּן־הֲדַד *son of Hadad.*
1. A king of Syria, son of Tabrimon. He made a league with Asa, king of Judah, and invaded Israel, B.C. 951.
1 Ki. 15. 18 king Asa sent them to B., the son of
15. 20 So B. hearkened unto king Asa, and sent
2 Ch. 16. 2 sent to B. king of Syria, that dwelt at
16. 4 B. hearkened unto king Asa, and sent
2. Another king of Syria, who reigned in the time of Ahab king of Israel, B.C. 901.
1 Ki. 20. 1 B. the king of Syria gathered all his
20. 2 said unto him, Thus said B.
20. 5 Thus speaketh B., saying, Although I
20. 9 he said unto the messengers of B., Tell
20. 10 B. sent unto him, and said, The gods
20. 16 B. (was) drinking himself drunk in
20. 17 B. sent out, and they told him, saying
20. 20 B. the king of Syria escaped on an
20. 26 it came to pass..that B. numbered
20. 30 B. fled, and came into the city, into
20. 32 Thy servant B. saith, I pray thee, let me
20. 33 they said, Thy brother B. Then he said
20. 33 Then B. came forth to him ; and he
2 Ki. 6. 24 it came to pass after this, that B. king of
8. 7 B. the king of Syria was sick : and
8. 9 Thy son B. king of Syria hath sent me
3. Son of Hazael, who succeeded him, B.C. 842.
2 Ki. 13. 3 into the hand of B. the son of Hazael
13. 24 and B. his son reigned in his stead
13. 25 Jehoash..again out of the hand of B.
Amos 1. 4 which shall devour the palaces of B.
4. A general title of the kings of Damascus.
Jer. 49. 27 it shall consume the palaces of B.

BEN HA'-IL, בֶּן־חַיִל *strong, valiant.*
A prince of Judah under Jehoshaphat, B.C. 912.
2 Ch. 17. 7 he sent to his princes..to B., and to O

BEN HA'-NAN, בֶּן־חָנָן *very gracious.*
A son of Shimon, descended from Jephunneh, B.C. 1400
1 Ch. 4. 20 the sons of Shimon..B., and Tilon

BE-NI'-NU, בְּנִינוּ *posterity.*
A Levite who, with Nehemiah, sealed the covenant.
Neh. 10. 13 [And their brethren]..Hodijah, Bani, B.

BEN-JA-'MIN, בִּנְיָמִין *son of the right hand.*
1. The youngest son of Jacob, and the only one born in Canaan. His birth occurred a short distance from Bethlehem, and where his mother Rachel died, naming him with her last breath *Benoni* "son of my sorrow." This name was changed by Jacob into Benjamin or *Binyamin*, B.C. 1732.
Gen. 35. 18 but his father called him B.
35. 24 The sons of Rachel ; Joseph and B.
42. 4 B., Joseph's brother, Jacob sent not with
42. 36 Simeon (is) not, and ye will take B.
43. 14 may send away your other brother, and B.
43. 15 took double money in their hand, and B.
43. 16 when Joseph saw B. with them, he said
43. 29 he lifted up his eyes, and saw..B.
43. 34 B.'s mess was five times so much as any
44. 12 and the cup was found in B.'s sack
45. 12 your eyes see, and the eyes of my brother B
45. 14 he fell upon his brother B.'s neck, and
45. 14 and B. wept upon his neck
45. 22 but to B. he gave three hundred (pieces)
46. 19 of Rachel, Jacob's wife ; Joseph and B.
46. 21 the sons of B. (were) Belah, and Becher
49. 27 B. shall ravin (as) a wolf : in the morning
Exod. 1. 3 [children of Israel]..Issachar, Zebulun..B.
Deut 33. 12 of B. he said, The beloved of the LORD
1 Ch. 2. 2 [sons of Israel]..Dan, Joseph, and B.
7. 6 of B. ; Bela, and Becher, and Jediael
2. The tribe springing from Benjamin as well as the district occupied by it are frequently spoken of by this name.
Num. 1. 11 of B. ; Abidan the son of Gideoni
1. 36 Of the children of B., by their generations
1. 37 of the tribe of B...thirty and five thous.
2. 22 the tribe of B. : and the captain of the
2. 22 sons of B. (shall be) Abidan the son of
7. 60 Abidan..prince of the children of B.
10. 24 over the host of the tribe of..B. (was)
13. 9 of the tribe of B., Palti the son of Raphu
26. 38 The sons of B. after their families : of
26. 41 These..the sons of B. after their families
34. 21 of the tribe of B., Elidad the son of Chis.
Deut 27. 12 These shall stand..Joseph, and B.
Josh. 18. 11 the lot of the tribe of the children of B.
18. 20 This..the inheritance of the children of B.
18. 21 the cities of the tribe of the children of B.
18. 28 (is) the inheritance of the children of B.
21. 4 out of the tribe of B., thirteen cities
21. 17 out of the tribe of B., Gibeon with her
Judg. 1. 21 the children of B. did not drive out
1. 21 Jebusites dwell with the children of B.
5. 14 after thee, B., among thy people : out of
10. 9 Ammon passed..to fight also against..B.
19. 14 them..by Gibeah, which (belongeth) to B.
20. 3 Now the children of B. heard that the
20. 4 I came into Gibeah that (belongeth) to B.
20. 10 may do, when they come to Gibeah of B
20. 12 sent men through all the tribe of B.
20. 13 the children of B. would not hearken
20. 14 the children of B. gathered themselves
20. 15 the children of B. were numbered at
20. 17 the men of Israel, besides B., were
20. 18 to the battle against the children of B.?
20. 20 men of Israel went out to battle against B.
20. 21 the children of B. came forth out of
20. 23 shall I go..against the children of B.
20. 24 came near against the children of B.
20. 25 B. went forth against them out of Gibeah
20. 28 shall I..go out to battle against..B.
20. 30 Israel went up against the children of B.
20. 31 the children of B. went out against the
20. 32 the children of B. said, They (are) smitten
20. 35 the LORD smote B. before Israel: and
20. 36 the children of B. saw that they were
20. 39 B. began to smite (and) kill of the men

Judg 20. 41 the men of B. were amazed: for they saw
20. 44 there fell of B. eighteen thousand men
20. 46 So that all which fell that day of B.
20. 48 turned again upon the children of B.
21. 1 There shall not any of us give..unto B.
21. 6 Israel repented them for B. their brother
21. 13 to speak to the children of B. that (were)
21. 14 B. came again at that time; and
21. 15 the people repented them for B, because
21. 16 seeing the women are destroyed out of B.?
21. 17 inheritance for them that be escaped of B.
21. 18 Cursed (be) he that giveth a wife to B.
21. 20 they commanded the children of B.
21. 21 daughters of Shiloh, and go to..land of B.
21. 23 the children of B. did so, and took
1 Sa. 4. 12 there ran a man of B. out of the army
9. 1 there was a man of B., whose name
9. 16 send thee a man out of the land of B.
9. 21 least of all the families of the tribe of B.?
10. 2 Rachel's sepulchre, in the border of B. at
10. 20 Israel to come near, the tribe of B. was
10. 21 When he had caused the tribe of B. to
13. 2 were with Jonathan in Gibeah of B.
13. 15 gat him up from Gilgal unto Gibeah of B.
13. 16 Saul, and Jonathan..abode in Gibeah of B.
14. 16 the watchmen of Saul in Gibeah of B.
2 Sa. 2. 9 made him king over Gilead..and over B.
2. 15 there..went over by number twelve of B.
2. 25 the children of B. gathered themselves
2. 31 the servants of David had smitten of B.
3. 19 Abner also spake in the ears of B.
3. 19 that seemed good to the whole house of B.
4. 2 Rimmon a Beerothite, of the children of B.
4. 2 for Beeroth also was reckoned to B.
19. 17 And..a thousand men of B. with him
21. 14 buried they in the country of B. in Zelah
23. 29 Ribai out of Gibeah of the children of B.
1 Ki. 4. 18 Shimei the son of Elah in B.
12. 21 Rehoboam..assembled all..with..B.
12. 23 Speak..unto all the house of Judah and B.
15. 22 king Asa built with them Geba of B.
1 Ch. 6. 60 out of the tribe of B.; Geba with her
6. 65 they gave..out of the tribe..of B., these
8. 1 B. begat Bela his first born, Ashbel the
8. 40 All these (are) of the sons of B.
9. 3 in Jerusalem dwelt..of the children of B.
9. 7 of the sons of B.; Sallu the son of Mes.
11. 31 of Gibeah..to the children of B., Benaiah
12. 2 armed with bows..of Saul's brethren of B.
12. 16 there came of the children of B...unto
12. 29 of the children of B...three thousand
21. 6 Levi and B. counted he not among them
27. 21 of B.; Jaasiel the son of Abner
2 Ch. 11. 1 Rehoboam..gathered of the house of..B.
11. 3 Speak..to all Israel in Judah and B.
11. 10 which (are) in Judah and in B. fenced
11. 12 made them..strong, having..B. on his
11. 23 dispersed..his children throughout..B.
14. 8 out of B...two hundred and fourscore th.
15. 2 Hear ye me, Asa, and all Judah and B.
15. 8 put away the..idols out of..Judah and B.
15. 9 he gathered all Judah and B., and the
17. 17 of B.; Eliada a mighty man of valour
25. 5 captains over thousands..throughout..B.
31. 1 threw down..the altars out of all..B.
34. 9 the Levites..had gathered..of all..B.
34. 32 he caused all that were..in..B. to stand
Ezra 1. 5 Then rose up..chief of the fathers of..B.
4. 1 when the adversaries of Judah and B.
10. 9 the men of..B. gathered themselves
Neh. 11. 4 at Jerusalem dwelt..of..children of B.
11. 7 these (are) the sons of B.; Sallu the son
11. 31 The children also of B...at Michmash
11. 36 And of the Levites (were) divisions..in B.
Psa. 68. 27 There (is) little B...their ruler, the princes
80. 2 Before Ephraim and B...stir up thy
Jer. 1. 1 of the priests that (were)..in the land of B.
6. 1 O ye children of B., gather yourselves to
17. 26 they shall come..from the land of B.
32. 8 Buy my field..which (is) in..B.: for the
32. 44 and take witnesses in the land of B.
33. 13 in the land of B...shall the flocks pass
37. 12 Jeremiah went..into the land of B.
Eze. 48. 22 the border of Judah and the border of B.
48. 23 from the east side unto the west side, B.
48. 24 by the border of B...Simeon (shall have)
48. 32 one gate of B., one gate of Dan
Hos. 5. 8 cry aloud (at) Beth-aven, after thee, O B.
Obad. 19 of Samaria; and B. (shall possess) Gilead
Acts 13. 21 S. the son of C., a man of the tribe of B.
Rom. 11. 1 I also am an Israelite..(of) the tribe of B.
Phil. 3. 5 Circumcised the eighth day..tribe of B.
Rev. 7. 8 of the tribe of B. (were) sealed twelve

The following localities were in the territory of Benjamin:—Ai, Aja, Aiath, Ajalon, Alemeth, Allon-bachuth, Almon, Ammah, Ananiah, Anathoth, Aphrah, Avim, Baaltamar, Bahurim, Beeroth, Beth-Arabah, Beth-Aven, Beth-el, Beth-Haccerem, Beth-Hoglah, Beth-Horon (the lower), Beth-Phage, Bethany, Charashim, Chepar Haamonai, Chephirah, Eleph, En-rogel, En-shemesh, Emmaus, Ephraim, Gaba, Gallim, Gareb, Gebim, Giah, Gibeah, Gibeon, Gidom, Gihon, Gilgal, Gittaim, Goath, Hadid, Hazor, Helkath-hazzurim, Jebus, Jericho, Jerusalem, Keziz, Kirioth, Luz, Madmen, Maktesh, Michmas, Migron, Millo, Mizpah, Moza, Naioth, Neballat, Nephtoah, Nob, Ono, Ophel, Ophni, Ophrah, Parah, Ramah, Rekem, Sechu, Shaveh, Shen, Shual, Silla, Taralah, Zalmon, Zeboim, Zelah, Zelzah, Zemaraim, &c.

3. Great grandson of Benjamin.
1 Ch. 7. 10 The sons also of..Jeush, and B., and

4. A descendant of Harim.
Ezra 10. 32 B., Malluch, (and) Shemariah
5. One who took part in repairing the wall, B.C. 550.
Neh. 3. 23 After him repaired B. and Hashub
6. One who took part in purifying the wall. B.C. 550.
Neh. 12. 34 Judah, and B., and Shemaiah, and Jer.
7. One of the gates of Jerusalem.
Jer. 20. 2 the stocks that (were) in the..gate of B.
37. 13 And when he was in the gate of B., a
38. 7 the king then sitting in the gate of B.
Zech. 14. 10 from B's. gate unto the place of the first

BEN-JA-MITE, בֶּן־הַיְמִינִי *belonging to Benjamin.*
Patronymic of the tribe of Benjamin.
Judg. 3. 15 Ehud the son of Gera, a B., a man left
19. 16 but the men of the place (were) B.
20. 35 the children of Israel destroyed of the B.
20. 36 the men of Israel gave place to the B.
20. 40 the B. looked behind them, and, behold
20. 43 (Thus) they inclosed the B. round about
1 Sa. 9. 1 a B., a mighty man of power
9. 4 he passed through the land of the B.
9. 21 (Am) not I a B., of the smallest of the
22. 7 Hear now, ye B.; will the son of Jesse
2 Sa. 16. 11 how much more now (may this) B. (do it)?
19. 16 Shimei the son of Gera, a B...came down
20. 1 Sheba, the son of Bichri, a B.; and he
1 Ki. 2. 8 Shimei the son of Gera, a B. of Bahurim
1 Ch. 27. 12 ninth..Abiezer the Anetothite, of the B.
Esth. 2. 5 Shimei, the son of Kish, a B.
Psa. 7. *title.* concerning the words of Cush the B

BE'-NO, בְּנוֹ *his son.*
A descendant of Merari, son of Levi, B.C. 1000.
1 Ch. 24. 26 the sons of Jaaziah; B.
24. 27 The sons of Merari by Jaaziah; B., and

BEN O'-NI, בֶּן־אוֹנִי *son of my sorrow.*
The name given by Rachel to her second son, B.C. 1732.
Gen. 35. 18 it came to pass..she called his name B.

BENT, to be —
To hang, תָּלָא *tala.*
Hos. 11. 7 my people are bent to backsliding from

BEN ZO'-HETH, בֶּן־זוֹחֵת *corpulent, strong.*
A son of Ishi, a descendant of Judah through Caleb the son of Jephunneh, B.C. 1400.
1 Ch. 4. 20 the sons of Ishi (were) Zoheth, and B.

BE'-ON, בְּעֹן *lord or house of On.*
A place E. of the Jordan, doubtless a contraction of *Baal-meon.* Compare verse 38. Now *Main.*
Num 32. 3 Elealeh, and Shebam, and Nebo, and B.

BE'-OR, בְּעוֹר *shepherd.*
1. Father of Bela the first king of Edom, B.C. 1600.
Gen. 36. 32 Bela the son of B. reigned in Edom
1 Ch. 1. 43 Bela the son of B.: and the name of his
2. Father of Balaam the prophet, B.C. 1510.
Num 22. 5 messengers..unto Balaam the son of B.
24. 3 Balaam the son of B. hath said, and the
24. 15 Balaam the son of B. hath said, and the
31. 8 Balaam also the son of B. they slew with
Deut 23. 4 hired against thee Balaam the son of B.
Josh. 13. 22 Balaam also the son of B., the soothsayer
24. 9 called Balaam the son of B. to curse you
Mic. 6. 5 remember now..what Balaam..son of B.

BE'-RA, בֶּרַע *gift.*
A king of Sodom in the time of Abram, B.C. 1917.
Gen. 14. 2 made war with B. king of Sodom, and

BE-RA'-CHAH, בְּרָכָה *blessing.*
1. One who joined David at Ziklag, B.C. 1040.
1 Ch. 12. 3 The chief (was) Ahiezer, then Joash..B.
2. A valley near Tekoah, in the S. of Judah (in 2 Ch. 20. 26 the origin of the name "valley of blessing" is given). The name *Bereikût* still survives in a valley near Tekua.
2 Ch. 20. 26 they assembled..in the valley of B.
20. 26 the same place was called, The valley of B.

BERACHIAH. *See* **BERECHIAH** (No. 2).

BE-RA'-IAH, בְּרָאיָה *Jah is maker.*
A son of Shimhi, a Benjamite, B.C. 1340.
1 Ch. 8. 21 B., and Shimrath, the sons of Shimhi

BE-RE'-A, Βέροια.
A city in the S. of Macedonia, now called *Verria* or *Kara-verria,* and situated on the E. slope of the Olympian range.
Acts 17. 10 brethren..sent away..Silas by night..B.
17. 13 the word of God was preached of Paul at B.
20. 4 accompanied him into Asia, Sopater of B.

BEREAVE, to —
1. *To cause to lack,* חָסֵר *chaser,* 3.
Eccl. 4. 8 I labour, and bereave my soul of good
2. *To enfeeble, cause to stumble,* כָּשַׁל *kashal,* 3.
Eze. 36. 14 neither bereave thy nations any more
3. *To bereave, make childless,* שָׁכֹל *shakol,* 3.
Gen. 42. 36 Me have ye bereaved..Joseph (is) not
Lam. 1. 20 abroad the sword bereaveth, at home
Eze. 5. 17 evil beasts, and they shall bereave thee
36. 12 thou shalt no more henceforth bereave
36. 13 thou..hast bereaved thy nations
36. 14 neither bereave thy nations any more
Hos. 9. 12 they bring up..yet will I bereave

BEREAVE of children, to —
To bereave, make childless, שָׁכֹל *shakol,* 3.
Jer. 15. 7 I will bereave..of children, **I will destroy**

BEREAVED, to be —
To be bereaved, שָׁכֹל *shakol.*
Gen. 43. 14 If I be bereaved..I am **bereaved**

BEREAVED (of children) —
Bereaved, שַׁכּוּל *shakkul.*
Jer. 18. 21 let their wives be bereaved of **their child.**
Hos. 13. 8 a bear (that is) bereaved..and will rend

BE-RECH'-IAH, בֶּרֶכְיָהוּ, בֶּרֶכְיָה, *Jah is blessing.*
1. A descendant of Jehoiakim king of Judah, B.C. 520.
1 Ch. 3. 20 And Hashubah, and Ohel, and B.
2. Father of Asaph the chief singer, B.C. 1070.
1 Ch. 6. 39 (even) A. the son of Berachiah.
15. 17 of his brethren, A. the son of B.; **and of**
3. A Levite who lived near Jerusalem, B.C. 445.
1 Ch. 9. 16 B. the son of Asa, the son of Elkanah
4. A Levite, one of the tabernacle doorkeepers.
1 Ch. 15. 23 B. and Elkanah (were) doorkeepers for
5. An Ephraimite in the time of Pekah, B.C. 741.
2 Ch. 28. 12 certain of the heads..B. the son of Mes.
6. Father of Meshullam who assisted in repairing the wall of Jerusalem, B.C. 520.
Neh. 3. 4 next..repaired Meshullam the son of B.
3. 30 After..repaired Meshullam the son of B.
6. 18 the daughter of Meshullam the son of B.

BE'-RED, בֶּרֶד *seed place.*
1. A place in S. of Canaan, between which and Kadesh lay the well *La-hai-roi.* The Peshito gives Gadar= Gerar (?); the Arabic, Yarad; Onkelos, Chagra. It is perhaps *el-Khŭlasah,* 12 miles S. of Beersheba.
Gen. 16. 14 behold, (it is) between Kadesh and B.
2. An Ephraimite, perhaps the same as Becher, B.C. 1680.
1 Ch. 7. 20 the sons of Ephraim; Shuthelah, and B.

BE'-RI, בֵּרִי *expounder.*
A son of Zophah, an Asherite, B.C. 1570.
1 Ch. 7. 36 sons of Zophah; Suah..and **B., and Imrah**

BE-RI'-AH, בְּרִיעָה *unfortunate.*
1. A son of Asher, B.C. 1700.
Gen. 46. 17 Jimnah, and Ishuah, and Isui, **and B.**
46. 17 the sons of B.; Heber, and Malchiel
Num 26. 44 of B., the family of the Beriites.
26. 45 Of the sons of B.: of Heber, the **family**
1 Ch. 7. 30 Imnah, and Isuah, and Ishuai, and B.
7. 31 the sons of B.; Heber, and Malchiel
2. A son of Ephraim, B.C. 1670.
1 Ch. 7. 23 he called his name B., because
3. A son of Elpaal, a Benjamite, B.C. 1400.
1 Ch. 8. 13 B. also, and Shema..heads **of the fathers**
8. 16 Michael..Ispah, and Joha the sons of B.
4. A Levite, a Gershomite, B.C. 1015.
1 Ch. 23. 10 the sons of Shimei..Jahath, Zina..and **B.**
23. 11 but Jeush and B. had not many sons

BE-RI-ITE, בְּרִיעִי *unfortunate.*
A family of Asherites sprung from Beriah.
Num 26. 44 children of..Beriah, the family of **the B.**

BE-RITES, בֵּרִים *belonging to Beri.*
Descendants of Beri in the N. of Canaan, visited by Joab in his pursuit after Sheba.
2 Sa. 20. 14 And he went through all..the B.

BE'-RITH, בְּרִית *a covenant.*
An idol (Baal-berith) worshipped in Shechem.
Judg. 8. 33 children of Israel..made B. B. their god
9. 46 they entered into..the house of the god **B.**

BER-NI'-CE, Βερνίκη.
A daughter of Herod Agrippa, grandson of Herod the Great, and sister of Agrippa II., A.D. 50.
Acts 25. 13 B. came unto Cesarea to salute Festus
25. 23 B...was entered into the place of hearing
26. 30 king rose up, and the governor, and B.

BE-RO-DACH BAL-A'-DAN, בְּרֹאדַךְ בַּלְאֲדָן *bold.*
A king of Babylon, B.C. 713. The name is more accurately written Merodach Baladan.
2 Ki. 20. 12 At that time B. B...sent letters..unto H.
Isa. 39. 1 At that time M. B...sent letters..to Hez.

BE-RO'-THAH, בֵּרֹתָה *food.*
A city near Hamath on N. of Canaan, and considered by some as the same as *Berothai.* Ezekiel places Berothah between Hamath and Damascus; hence it cannot be *Beirût* (the classical Berytus); nor can it be *Beirût* in the form Berothai, for David's war with the king of Zobah led him from the sea coast towards the Euphrates. Besides, in the latter case, the Hebrew text reads *Chun* (instead of Berothai) in 1 Ch. 18. 8. Fürst regards Berothah and Berothai as distinct places, but identifies the former with Berytus. Mislin derives the name from the "wells" (Beeroth) which may still be seen bored in the solid rock at *Beirût.*
Beyrout, the ancient Berytus, was the seat of a famous school of jurisprudence from the third to the middle of the 6th century. The city having been destroyed by an earthquake 551 A.D., the school was removed to Sidon. Beyrout suffered severely during the crusades, and having been taken by the Saracens, was wrested from them by Baldwin in 1110. The Saracens, however,

regained possession in 1187. Ibrahim Pasha seized it in 1832; and it was bombarded by the combined fleets of England and Turkey, 1840, and being captured, was restored to the Porte. Beyrout was made a bishopric by Theodosius the Younger, and after its capture by Baldwin I. it became the seat of a Latin bishop about 1136.

Eze. 47. 16 B., Sibraim, which (is) between the border

BE-RO'-THAI, בֵּרֹתַי *cypresses of Jah.*
A city belonging to Hadadezer king of Zobah. See Berothah.
2 Sa. 8. 8 from B...king David took exceeding

BE-RO-THITE, בֵּרֹתִי *belonging to Beroth.*
A patronymic of Naharai Joab's armourbearer. Perhaps it ought to be *Beerothite*, as in 2 Sa. 23. 37.
1 Ch. 11. 39 Naharai the B., the armour bearer of Joab

BERRIES —
Berry, גַּרְגַּר *gargar.*
Isa. 17. 6 two (or) three berries in the top of the

BERRIES, olive —
Olive (tree or fruit), ἐλαία *elaia.*
Jas. 3. 12 Can the fig tree..bear olive berries?

BERYL —
1. *Beryl, chrysolite, topaz*, תַּרְשִׁישׁ *tarshish.*
Exod 28. 20 the fourth row a beryl, and an onyx, and
39. 13 the fourth row, a beryl, an onyx, and a
Song 5. 14 His hands..gold rings set with the beryl
Eze. 1. 16 their work..like unto the colour of a beryl
10. 9 appearance..as the colour of a beryl
28. 13 precious stone..thy covering..the beryl
Dan. 10. 6 His body also (was) like the beryl, and
2. *A jewel of sea green colour*, βήρυλλος *bērullos.*
Rev. 21. 20 the eighth, beryl; the ninth, a topaz; the

BE'-SAI, בֵּסַי *treading down.*
A Nethinim who returned with Zerubbabel, B.C. 550.
Ezra 2. 49 the children of Paseah, the children of B.
Neh. 7. 52 children of B., the children of Meunim

BESEECH, to —
1. *To seek, inquire*, בָּקַשׁ *baqash*, 3.
2 Sa. 12. 16 David therefore besought God for the
Ezra 8. 23 So we fasted, and besought our God for
2. *To smooth the face of*, חָלָה פָּנִים *chalah* (3) *panim.*
Exod 32. 11 Moses besought the LORD his God, and
1 Ki. 13. 6 the man of God besought the LORD, and
2 Ki. 13. 4 Jehoahaz besought the LORD, and the
2 Ch. 33. 12 when..in affliction, he besought the LORD
Jer. 26. 19 fear the LORD, and besought the LORD
Mal. 1. 9 beseech God that he will be gracious unto
3. *To incline, be gracious*, חָנַן *chanan*, 7.
Gen. 42. 21 when he besought us, and we would not
Deut. 3. 23 I besought the LORD at that time, saying
2 Ki. 1. 13 besought him, and said unto him, O man
Esth. 8. 3 besought him with tears to put away the
4. *To be in want*, δέομαι *deomai.*
Luke 5. 12 seeing Jesus, fell on..face, and besought
8. 28 Jesus..I beseech thee, torment me not
8. 38 the man..besought him that he might
9. 38 Master, I beseech thee, look upon my son
9. 40 I besought thy disciples to cast him out
Acts 21. 39 I beseech thee, suffer me to speak unto
26. 3 I beseech thee to hear me patiently
2 Co. 10. 2 I beseech (you), that I may not be bold
Gal. 4. 12 Brethren, I beseech you, be as I..for I
5. *To question, ask about*, ἐρωτάω *erōtaō.*
Matt 15. 23 his disciples came and besought him
Mark 7. 26 she besought him that he would cast
Luke 4. 38 wife's mother..they besought him for her
7. 3 sent..the elders of the Jews, beseeching
8. 37 whole multitude..besought him to depart
11. 37 a certain Pharisee besought him to dine
John 4. 40 besought him that he would tarry with
4. 47 besought him that he would come down
19. 31 besought Pilate that their legs might be
19. 38 besought Pilate that he might take away
1 Th. 4. 1 Furthermore then we beseech you
5. 12 we beseech you, brethren, to know them
2 Th. 2. 1 we beseech you, brethren, by the coming
2 Jo. 5 now I beseech thee, lady, not as though
6. *To call to one's side*, παρακαλέω *parakaleō.*
Matt. 8. 5 there came..a centurion, beseeching him
8. 31 So the devils besought him, saying, If thou
8. 34 they besought..that he would depart out
14. 36 besought him that they might only touch
18. 29 his fellow servant..besought him, saying
Mark 1. 40 there came a leper to him, beseeching him
5. 10 he besought him much that he would not
5. 12 all the devils besought him, saying, Send
5. 23 besought him greatly, saying, My little
6. 56 they laid the sick..and besought him
7. 32 they beseech him to put his hand upon
8. 22 a blind..and besought him to touch him
Luke 7. 4 they besought him instantly, saying
8. 31, 32, 41 they besought him that he
Acts 13. 42 the Gentiles besought that these words
16. 15 she besought..saying, If ye have judged
16. 39 they came and besought them, and
21. 12 we..besought him not to go up to Jeru.
25. 2 informed him against Paul, and besought
27. 33 Paul besought..all to take meat, saying
Rom. 12. 1 I beseech you therefore, brethren, by the
15. 30 I beseech you, brethren, for the Lord
16. 17 I beseech you, brethren, mark them
1 Co. 1. 10 I beseech you, brethren, by the name of
4. 16 I beseech you, be ye followers of me
16. 15 I beseech you, brethren, ye know the
2 Co. 2. 8 I beseech you that ye would confirm..love
5. 20 as though God did beseech..by us
6. 1 We then, (as) workers together..beseech
10. 1 I Paul myself beseech you by the meek.
12. 8 For this thing I besought the Lord thrice
Eph. 4. 1 I therefore..beseech you that ye walk
Phil. 4. 2 I beseech Euodias, and beseech Syntyche
1 Th. 4. 10 we beseech you, brethren, that ye
1 Ti. 1. 3 As I besought thee to abide still at Eph.
Phm. 9 Yet for love's sake I rather beseech
10 I beseech thee for my son Onesimus
Heb. 13. 19 I beseech..the rather to do this, that I
13. 22 I beseech you, brethren, suffer the word
1 Pe. 2. 11 I beseech (you) as strangers and pilgrims

BESEECH (I) thee —
1. *Pray*, אָנָּא, אָנָּה *ana, anah.*
2 Ki. 20. 3 I beseech thee, O LORD, remember now
Neh. 1. 5 I beseech thee, O LORD God of heaven
1. 11 O LORD, I beseech thee, let now thine ear
Psa. 116. 4 O LORD, I beseech thee, deliver my soul
118. 25 I beseech thee, O LORD: O LORD, I b.
Isa. 38. 3 Remember now, O LORD, I beseech thee
Jon. 1. 14 We beseech thee, O LORD, we beseech th.
2. *Pray*, נָא *na.*
Exod 33. 18 he said, I beseech thee, show me thy glory

BESET, to —
1. *To go round about*, סָבַב *sabab.*
Judg 20. 5 beset the house round about upon me by
2. *To bind, straiten*, צוּר *tsur.*
Psa. 139. 5 Thou hast beset me behind and before

BESET about, to —
To go round about, סָבַב *sabab.*
Hos. 7. 2 their own doings have beset them about

BESET round about, to —
To be round about, סָבַב *sabab*, 2.
Judg 19. 22 sons of Belial, beset the house round a.

BESET round, to —
To surround, כָּתַר *kathar*, 3.
Psa. 22. 12 (bulls) of Bashan have beset me round

BESET, which doth so easily —
Standing well around, εὐπερίστατος, *euperistatos.*
Heb. 12. 1 the sin which doth so easily beset (us)

BESIDE —
1. *Behind, after*, אַחַר *achar.*
Neh. 5. 15 bread and wine, beside forty shekels of
2. *Unto, to*, אֶל *el.*
Exod 29. 12 pour all the blood beside the bottom of
3. *Near*, אֵצֶל *etsel.*
Lev. 1. 16 cast it beside the altar on the east part
6. 10 and he shall put them beside the altar
10. 12 eat it without leaven beside the altar: for
Deut 11. 30 other side..beside the plains of Moreh?
1 Ki. 3. 20 took my son from beside me, while thine
10. 19 and two lions stood beside the stays
13. 31 buried; lay my bones beside his bones
2 Ki. 12. 9 set it beside the altar, on the right side
Neh. 8. 4 beside him stood Mattithiah, and Shema
Eze. 9. 2 they went in, and stood beside the brasen
10. 6 he went in, and stood beside the wheels
10. 16 same wheels also turned not from beside
4. *Apart from*, לְבַד מִן *le-bad min.*
Exod 12. 37 six hundred thousand..men, beside
2 Ki. 21. 16 beside his sin wherewith he made Judah
5. *Apart from*, מִלְּבַד *mi-le-bad.*
Gen. 26. 1 beside the first famine..in the days of
Lev. 9. 17 beside the burnt sacrifice of the morning
23. 38 Beside the sabbaths..beside your gifts
23. 38 beside all your vows, and beside all
Num. 6. 21 beside (that) that his hand shall get
28. 23 Ye shall offer these beside the burnt
29. 6 Beside the burnt offering of the month
Deut. 4. 35 the LORD he (is) God..none else beside
29. 1 words of the covenant..beside the cov.
Josh. 22. 29 beside the altar of the LORD our God
1 Ki. 10. 13 whatsoever she asked, beside (that) which
6. *Apart from*, בִּלְעֲדֵי *bilade.*
Num. 5. 20 some man have lain with thee beside
Josh. 22. 19 an altar beside the altar of the LORD our
Isa. 43. 11 I..I..the LORD; and beside me..no
44. 6 I (am) the last; and beside me..no God
44. 8 Is there a God beside me? yea..no God
45. 6 that..none beside me, I (am) the LORD
45. 21 and..no God else beside me..none
7. *Without*, בִּלְתִּי *bilti.*
Num 11. 6 nothing at all, beside this manna,(before)
1 Sa. 2. 2 none holy as the LORD..none beside thee
Hos. 13. 4 no god but me; for..no saviour beside
8. *Save, except, beside, only*, זוּלָה *zulah.*
Ruth 4. 4 none to redeem (it) beside thee; and I
2 Sa. 7. 22 neither..God beside thee, according to
1 Ch. 17. 20 neither..God beside thee, according to
Isa. 26. 13 lords beside thee have had dominion
45. 5 no God beside me: I girded thee, though
45. 21 and a Saviour (there is) none beside me
64. 4 neither hath the eye seen, O God, beside
9. *At the hand of*, לְיַד *leyad.*
1 Sa. 19. 3 I will go out and stand beside my father
2 Sa. 15. 2 Absalom..stood beside the way of the
15. 18 all his servants passed on beside him
10. *Yet, still*, עוֹד *od.*
Gen. 19. 12 Hast thou here any besides? son in law
1 Ki. 22. 7 not here a prophet of the LORD besides
2 Ch. 18. 6 not here a prophet of the LORD besides
11. *On, upon, above*, עַל *al.*
Gen. 31. 50 if thou shalt take..wives beside my
Lev. 18. 18 to uncover her nakedness, beside the
Psa. 23. 2 he leadeth me beside the still waters
Song 1. 8 feed thy kids beside the shepherds' tents
Isa. 32. 20 Blessed (are) ye that sow beside all waters
12. *From on*, מֵעַל *me-al.*
Jer. 36. 21 the princes which stood beside the king
Eze. 32. 13 the beasts thereof from beside the great
13. *With*, עִם *im.*
Josh. 7. 2 Ai, which (is) beside Beth-aven, on the
14. *Over, against, near, just as*, עֻמָּה *ummah.*
Eze. 10. 19 the wheels also (were) beside them; and
11. 22 and the wheels beside them; and the
15. *From the side of*, מִצַּד *mits-tsad.*
Josh. 3. 16 the city Adam, that (is) beside Zaretan
12. 9 the king of Ai, which (is) beside Beth-el
Ruth 2. 14 And she sat beside the reapers: and he
16. *On, upon*, ἐπί (dat.) *epi.*
Matt 25. 20 I have gained beside them five talents
25. 22 I have gained two other talents [beside]
Luke 16. 26 [beside] all this, between us and you
17. *With*, σύν *sun.*
Luke 24. 21 beside all this, to day is the third day
18. *Apart from*, χωρίς *chōris.*
Matt 14. 21 they that had eaten..beside women and
15. 38 they that did eat..beside women and
2 Co. 11. 28 Beside those things that are without
19. *The rest, that left*, λοιπόν *loipon.*
1 Co. 1. 16 besides, I know not whether I baptized

BESIDE, and —
But with, ἀλλά γε σύν *alla ge sun.*
Luke 24. 21 and beside all this, to-day is the third

BESIDE the rest of —
On, upon, above, עַל *al.*
Num 31. 8 beside the rest of them that were slain

BESIDE one self, to be —
1. *To place out*, ἐξίστημι *existēmi.*
Mark 3. 21 for they said, He is beside himself
2 Co. 5. 13 whether we be beside ourselves, (it is)
2. *To be eager, mad*, μαίνομαι *mainomai.*
Acts 26. 24 Paul, thou art beside thyself; much

BESIDE this —
Also this very thing, καὶ αὐτὸ τοῦτο [*auto*].
2 Pe. 1. 5 beside this, giving all diligence, add to

BESIDES, to owe —
To owe in addition, προσοφείλω *prosopheilō.*
Phm. 19 owest unto me even thine own self besides

BESIEGE, to —
1. *To go round*, סָבַב *sabab.*
Eccl. 9. 14 there came a great king..and besieged it
2. *To press, straiten*, צוּר *tsur.*
Deut 20. 12 against thee, then thou shalt besiege it
20. 19 When thou shalt besiege a city a long
1 Sa. 23. 8 to Keilah, to besiege David and his men
2 Sa. 11. 1 they destroyed the children..besieged
20. 15 they came and besieged him in Abel of B.
1 Ki. 16. 17 Israel with him, and they besieged Tirzah
20. 1 Ben-hadad..went up..besieged Samaria
2 Ki. 6. 24 Ben-hadad..went up..besieged Samaria
6. 25 behold, they besieged it, until an ass's
16. 5 they besieged Ahaz, but could not over.
17. 5 went up to Samaria, and besieged it
18. 9 came up against Samaria, and besieged it
24. 11 the city, and his servants did besiege it
1 Ch. 20. 1 came and besieged Rabbah. But David
Isa. 21. 2 Go up, O Elam: besiege, O Media: all the
Jer. 21. 4 which besiege you without the walls
21. 9 falleth to the Chaldeans that besiege you
32. 2 king of Babylon's army besieged Jerus.
37. 5 the Chaldeans that besieged Jerusalem
39. 1 against Jerusalem, and they besieged it
Dan. 1. 1 came Nebuchadnezzar..and besieged it
3. *To straiten*, צָרַר *tsarar*, 5.
Deut 28. 52 he shall besiege thee in all thy gates
28. 52 besiege thee in all thy gates, throughout
1 Ki. 8. 37 if their enemy besiege them in the land
2 Ch. 6. 28 if their enemies besiege them in the cities

BESIEGED —
1. *Straitness*, מָצוֹר *matsor.*
Eze. 4. 3 thy face against it, and it shall be besieged
2. *To keep, watch, besiege*, נָצַר *natsar.*
Isa. 1. 8 daughter of Zion is left..as a besieged
Eze. 6. 12 he that..is besieged shall die by the

BESIEGED, to be —
To go into siege, בּוֹא בַּמָּצוֹר *bo bam-matsor*
2 Ki. 24. 10 against Jerusalem, and the city was be.
25. 2 the city was besieged unto the..year
Jer. 52. 5 the city was besieged unto the..year

BESIEGED place —
Straitened place, מָצוֹר *matsor*.
2 Ki. 19. 24 I dried up all..besieged places
Isa. 37. 25 I dried up all..the besieged places

BE-SO-DE'-IAH, בְּסוֹדְיָה *given to trust in Jah.*
One of the repairers of the old gate, B.C. 470.
Neh. 3. 6 the old gate repaired..the son of B.

BESOM —
Besom, broom, מַטְאֲטֵא *matate*.
Isa. 14. 23 I will sweep it with the besom of destr.

BE'-SOR, בְּשׂוֹר *cool brook.*
A brook which falls into the sea near S. of Gaza. It is now called *el-Sheria*, and rises at *Debir*.
1 Sa. 30. 9 David went..and came to the brook B.
30. 10 they could not go over the brook B.
30. 21 they had..to abide at the brook B.: and

BEST —
1. *Good*, טוֹב *tob*.
Num 36. 6 Let them marry to whom they think best
Deut 23. 16 in that place..where it liketh him best
1 Sa. 8. 14 And he will take your fields..the best
2 Ki. 10. 3 best and meetest of your master's sons
Esth. 2. 9 he preferred her..unto the best..of the
Song 7. 9 the roof of thy mouth like the best wine
Eze. 31. 16 the choice and best of Lebanon, all that
Mic. 7. 4 The best of them (is) as a brier; the most
2. *Good, good part*, מֵיטָב *metab*.
Gen. 47. 6 in the best of the land make thy father
47. 11 in the best of the land, in the land of R.
Exod 22. 5 best of his own field..best of his own
1 Sa. 15. 9 the best of the sheep, and of the oxen
15. 15 the people spared the best of the sheep
3. *Fat*, חֵלֶב *cheleb*.
Num 18. 12 All the best of the oil, and all the best of
18. 29 of all the best thereof..the hallowed
18. 30 When ye have heaved the best thereof
18. 32 when ye have heaved from it the best of
4. *Stronger, more powerful*, κρεῖττον *kreitton*.
1 Co. 12. 31 covet earnestly the [best] gifts: and yet
5. *First, foremost*, πρῶτος *prōtos*.
Luke 15. 22 Bring forth the best robe, and put (it) on

BEST fruits —
Praised thing, זִמְרָה *zimrah*.
Gen. 43. 11 take of the best fruits in the land in your

BEST gold —
Refined (gold), פָּז *pazaz*, 6.
1 Ki. 10. 18 of ivory, and overlaid it with the best g.

BEST, to seem —
To be good, יָטַב *yatab*.
2 Sa. 18. 4 said..What seemeth you best I will do

BEST, to think —
To be good in the eyes, טוֹב בְּעַיִן *tob be-ayin*.
Num 36. 6 Let them marry to whom they think best

BEST state —
To be set up, נָצַב *natsab*, 2.
Psa. 39. 5 every man at his best state (is)..vanity

BESTEAD, hardly —
Oppressed, נִקְשָׁה [*qashah*, 2].
Isa. 8. 21 they shall pass through it hardly bestead

BESTIR oneself, to —
To move sharply, חָרַץ *charats*.
2 Sa. 5. 24 that then thou shalt bestir thyself: for

BESTOW, to —
1. *To make to rest, place*, נוּחַ *nuach*, 5.
2 Ch. 9. 25 whom he bestowed in the chariot cities
2. *To put*, נָחָה *nachah*, 5.
1 Ki. 10. 26 whom he bestowed in the cities for
3. *To give*, נָתַן *nathan*.
Exod. 32. 29; Deut. 14. 26; 2 Ki. 12. 15; 1 Ch. 29. 25; Ezra 7. 20; 7. 20.
4. *To do*, עָשָׂה *asah*.
2 Ch. 24. 7 of the LORD did they bestow upon B.
5. *To lay up*, פָּקַד *paqad*.
2 Ki. 5. 24 bestowed..in the house: and he let the
6. *To give*, δίδωμι *didōmi*.
2 Co. 8. 1 the grace..God bestowed on the churches
1 Jo. 3. 1 what manner of love..hath bestowed
7. *To bring together*, συνάγω *sunagō*.
Luke 12. 17 I have no room where to bestow my
12. 18 there will I bestow all my fruits and my

BESTOW labour (on), to —
To toil, κοπιάω *kopiaō*.
John 4. 38 reap that whereon ye bestowed no labour
Rom. 16. 6 Mary, who bestowed much labour on us
Gal. 4. 11 I have bestowed upon you labour in vain

BESTOW to feed, to —
To give morsels, fatten, ψωμίζω *psōmizō*.
1 Co. 13. 3 though I bestow all my goods to feed

BESTOW on or upon, to —
1. *To do, perform*, גָּמַל *gamal*.
Isa. 63. 7 according to all that..hath bestowed on
63. 7 he hath bestowed on them according to
2. *To put around*, περιτίθημι *peritithēmi*.
1 Co. 12. 23 upon these we bestow more abundant

BE'-TAH, בֶּטַח *confidence.*
A city of Hadadezer.
2 Sa. 8. 8 from B...king David took exceeding

BE'-TEN, בֶּטֶן *height.*
A city of Asher, 8 miles E. of Ptolemais.
Josh. 19. 25 border was Helkath, and Hali, and B.

BETH A-BA'-RA, Βηθαβαρά *place of passage.*
A place E. of the Jordan, perhaps *Bethbarah*, or rather *Bethany*.
John 1. 28 These things were done in B. beyond Jor.

BETH A'-NATH, בֵּית עֲנָת *house of echo.*
A city of Naphtali, 15 miles from *Diacæsaræa*. (Anata.)
Josh. 19. 38 Iron, and Migdal-el, Horem, and B.
Judg. 1. 33 did Naphtali drive out..inhabitants of B.
1. 33 the inhabitants of..B. became tributaries

BETH A'-NOTH, בֵּית עֲנוֹת *house of echo.*
A city of Judah, 4 miles from Hebron, near Maaroth. The modern *Beit-ainun*, near *Halhûl* and *Beit-Sûr*, the ancient Halhul and Bethzur.
Josh. 15. 59 Maarath, and B., and Eltekon

BETH'-ANY, Βηθανία *house of dates or figs.*
A village at the Mount of Olives. Its modern name *el-Azariyeh*, or *Lazarieh*, is derived from Lazarus. It is about 2 miles E. of Jerusalem, near the road from Jericho to the city.
Matt 21. 17 went out of the city into B.; and he
26. 6 when Jesus was in B., in the house of
Mark 11. 1 they came nigh to..Bethphage and B.
11. 11 he went out unto B. with the twelve
11. 12 when they were come from B., he was
14. 3 being in B., in the house of Simon the leper
Luke 19. 29 he was come nigh to Bethphage and B.
24. 50 he led them out as far as to B.; and he
John 11. 1 a certain (man) was sick..Lazarus, of B.
11. 18 B. was nigh unto Jerusalem, about fifteen
12. 1 Jesus..came to B., where Lazarus was

BETH A-RA'-BAH, בֵּית הָעֲרָבָה *house of the desert.*
One of the six cities of Judah that were in the *Arabah* or sunk valley of the Jordan and Salt Sea, the "wilderness" on the N. border of the tribe, and between Beth-hoglah and the high land on the W. of the Jordan. It is also included among the towns of Benjamin.
Josh. 15. 6 passed along by the north of B.; and the
15. 61 the wilderness, B., Middin, and Secacah
18. 22 B., and Zemaraim, and Beth-el

BETH A'-RAM, בֵּית הָרָם *house or place of the height.*
A city of Gad, E. of the Jordan, between Succoth and Debir, the same as Beth-haran, and now called *Beit-el-ramah*.
Josh. 13. 27 B...and Zaphon..of..kingdom of Sihon

BETH AR'-BEL, בֵּית אַרְבֵאל *house of God's court.*
A city destroyed by the king of Assyria, and supposed to be the *Arbela* of the Maccabees and Josephus. Now *Irbid*.
Hos. 10. 14 Shalman spoiled B. in the day of battle

BETH A'-VEN, בֵּית אָוֶן *house of iniquity.*
A town in Benjamin near Bethel.
Josh. 7. 2 Joshua sent men..to Ai, which..beside B.
18. 12 goings out..were at the wilderness of B.
1 Sa. 13. 5 they..pitched..Michmash, eastward..B.
14. 23 the battle passed over unto B.
Hos. 4. 15 neither go ye up to B., nor swear, The
5. 8 cry aloud (at) B., after thee, O Benjamin
10. 5 Samaria shall..because of the calves of B.

BETH AZ-MA'-VETH, בֵּית עַזְמָוֶת *house of Azmaveth.*
A village of Judah or Benjamin. In Ezra 2. 24 it is called *Azmaveth*.
Neh. 7. 28 The men of B., forty and two

BETH BA-AL ME'-ON, בֵּית בַּעַל מְעוֹן.
A town of Moab, given to Reuben; it was on the W. of the Arnon, not far from Jahaza.
Josh. 13. 17 Dibon, and Bamoth-baal, and B.

BETH BA'-RAH, בֵּית בָּרָה *fording place.*
A place on the E. of the Jordan, in Gad.
Judg. 7. 24 take before them the waters unto B.
7. 24 took the waters unto B. and Jordan

BETH BIR'-EI, בֵּית בִּרְאִי *place of the city.*
A town of Simeon, same as Beth-lebaoth.
1 Ch. 4. 31 Hazar-susim, and at B., and at Shaaraim

BETH CAR, בֵּית כָּר *place of pasture.*
A stronghold of the Philistines in Judah near Mizpeh.
1 Sa. 7. 11 Israel..smote them, until..under Beth-c.

BETH DA'-GON, בֵּית־דָּגוֹן *house of Dagon.*
1. A town of Judah near Gederoth. Now *B. Dejan*.
Josh. 15. 41 Gederoth, B., and Naamah, and Mak.
2. A town in the tribe of Asher, on the coast.
Josh. 19. 27 And turneth toward the sun rising to B.

BETH DIB-LA-THA'-IM, בֵּית דִּבְלָתַיִם.
A Moabite town, elsewhere called Almon-Diblathaim. The "circles" here likely means "cakes" (of figs).
Jer. 48. 22 [judgment is come] upon Nebo, and..B.

BETH'-EL, בֵּית־אֵל *house of God.*
A well-known holy place of Central Canaan. Two accounts are given of the origin of the name: 1. It was bestowed on the spot by Jacob under the awe inspired by the vision of God (Gen. 28. 19); 2. It received its name on the occasion of a blessing bestowed by God upon Jacob after his return from Padan-aram, at which time his name was changed to Israel (Gen. 35. 14, 15). Luz was the ancient name. Bethel was in the tribe of Benjamin. It is 12 miles N. of Jerusalem on the way to Shechem, and was the seat of one of Jeroboam's golden calves. It is now called *Beitin*. Luz was perhaps the city, and Bethel the holy place close by it.
Gen. 12. 8 unto a mountain on the east of B.
12. 8 pitched his tent..B. on the west
13. 3 on his journeys from the south even to B.
13. 3 his tent had been..between B. and Hai
28. 19 he called the name of that place B.
31. 13 I (am) the God of B., where thou
35. 1 God said unto Jacob, Arise, go up to B.
35. 3 let us arise, and go up to B.; and I will
35. 6 in the land of Canaan, that (is), B.
35. 8 she was buried beneath B. under an oak
35. 15 Jacob called the name of the place..B.
35. 16 they journeyed from B.; and there
Josh. 7. 2 Joshua sent..to Ai..on the east side of B.
8. 9 went to lie in ambush, and abode b. B.
8. 12 to lie in ambush between B. and Ai, on
8. 17 And there was not a man left in Ai or B.
12. 9 the king of Ai, which (is) beside B., one
12. 16 king of Makkedah, one; the king of B.
16. 1 up from Jericho, throughout mount B.
16. 2 goeth out from B. to Luz, and passeth
18. 13 border went..toward Luz..which (is) B.
18. 22 [cities of the tribe]..Zemaraim, and B.
Judg. 1. 22 house of Joseph..went up against B.
1. 23 the house of Joseph sent to descry B.
4. 5 she dwelt..between Ramah and B. in
21. 19 Shiloh..which (is) on the north of B.
21. 19 the highway that goeth up from B. to
1 Sa. 7. 16 he went from year to year in circuit to B.
10. 3 three men going up to God to B., one
13. 2 with Saul in Michmash and in mount B.
30. 27 which (were) in B., and to (them) which
1 Ki. 12. 29 he set the one in B., and the other
12. 32 So did he in B., sacrificing unto the
12. 32 he placed in B. the priests of the high pl.
12. 33 offered upon the altar which he had m. in B
13. 1 out of Judah by the word of the L. u. B.
13. 4 which had cried against the altar in B.
13. 10 returned not by the way he came to B.
13. 11 there dwelt an old prophet in B.; and
13. 11 that the man of God had done..in B.
13. 32 For the saying..against the altar in B.
2 Ki. 2. 2 sent me to B...they went down to B.
2. 3 the sons of the prophets that (were) at B.
2. 23 he went up from thence unto B.
10. 29 the golden calves that (were) in B.
17. 28 one of the priests..came and dwelt in B.
23. 4 carried the ashes of them unto B.
23. 15 moreover the altar that (was) at B., (and)
23. 17 that thou hast done against the altar of B.
23. 19 according to all..that he had done in B.
1 Ch. 7. 28 their possessions..(were) B. and the
2 Ch. 13. 19 Abijah..took cities from him; B. with the
Ezra 2. 28 The men of B...Ai, two hundred twenty
Neh. 7. 32 The men of B. and Ai, an hundred twenty
11. 31 children also of Benjamin..(dwelt) at B.
Jer. 48. 13 as the house of Israel was ashamed of B.
Hos. 10. 15 So shall B. do unto you because of your
12. 4 he found him (in) B., and there he spake
Amos 3. 14 I will also visit the altars of B.; and the
4. 4 Come to B., and transgress; at Gilgal
5. 5 seek not B., nor enter into Gilgal
5. 5 B. shall come to nought
5. 6 devour (it)..none to quench (it) in B.
7. 10 Amaziah the priest of B. sent to
7. 13 But prophesy not again any more at B.

BETH-EL-ITE, בֵּית הָאֱלִי *belonging to Bethel.*
The patronymic of Hiel who rebuilt Jericho.
1 Ki. 16. 34 In his days did Hiel the B. build Jericho

BETH E'-MEK, בֵּית הָעֵמֶק *house of the valley.*
A town in Asher on or near the border, on the N. side of which was the ravine of Jiphthah-el. It is now called *Amkah*, in a plain at the foot of the hills.
Josh. 19. 27 toward the north side of B., and Neiel

BE'-THER, בֶּתֶר *depth, separation.*
Perhaps a poetical form of *Bithron* in Gad, E. of the Jordan. Now *Bittir*.
Song 2. 17 be..like a roe..upon the mountains of B.

BETH ES'-DA, Βηθεσδά *house of mercy.*
A pool in Jerusalem near the sheep market gate. The large reservoir called the *Birket-Israil*, within the walls of the city, close by the St Stephen's gate, and under the N.E. wall of the Haram area, is generally considered the modern representative of "Bethesda."
John 5. 2 which is called in the Hebrew tongue B.

BETH EZ'-EL, בֵּית־הָאֵצֶל *place of declivity.*
A city near Zaanan in the N. of Judah.
Mic. 1. 11 came not forth in the mourning of B.

BETH GA'-DER, בֵּית גָּדֵר *walled place.*
A descendant of Caleb son of Hur.
1 Ch. 2. 51 Hareph the father of B. G.

BETH GA'-MUL, בֵּית־גָּמוּל *place of the camel.*
A town of Moab in the *mishor* or downs. Now *Jemal*.
Jer. 48. 23 upon Kiriathaim, and upon B., and upon

BETH HAC-CE'-REM, בֵּית הַכֶּרֶם *place of the vineyard.*
A town of Judah S.E. from Jerusalem, between it and Tekoah. Now *Fureideis*.

Neh. 3. 14 the son of Rechab, the ruler of part of B.
Jer. 6. 1 Gather..and set up a sign of fire in B.

BETH HA'-RAN, בֵּית הָרָן *high or strong place.*
A city of Gad in the region of Gilead. Perhaps the same called in Josh. 13. 37 *Betharam*; in the original "Beth-haram."

Num32. 36 And Beth-nimrah, and B., fenced cities

BETH HOG'-LAH, בֵּית חָגְלָה *place of magpies.*
A city of Benjamin 3 miles from Jericho. Now *Hajlah.*

Josh.15. 6 And the border went up to B., and
18. 19 the border passed along to the side of B.
18. 21 the cities..were Jericho, and B., and the

BETH HO'-RON, בֵּית־חוֹרוֹן *place of hollows.*
Two places (Upper and Lower) in Ephraim near Benjamin. The Lower was the more important.

Josh 10. 10 the LORD..chased them along..to B.
10. 11 as they..were in the going down to B.
18. 14 border was drawn..from..hill..before B.
21. 22 Kibzaim with her suburbs, and B. with
1 Sa. 13. 18 another company turned the way (to) B.
1 Ch. 6. 68 Jokmeam with her suburbs, and B. with
2 Ch.25. 13 fell upon..cities..from Samaria..unto B.

Bethhoron the Upper.

Josh.16. 5 the border..was..unto B. the upper
2 Ch. 8. 5 he built B. the upper, and B. the nether

Bethhoron the Nether.

Josh 16. 3 goeth down..unto..B. the nether
18 13 border descended to..south side of n. B.
1 Ki. 9. 17 Solomon built Gezer, and B the nether
2 Ch. 8. 5 he built B. the upper, and B. the nether

BETHINK themselves, to —
Take back to heart, חָשַׁב אֶל־לֵב [*shub* (5) *el leb* (*lebab*)].

1 Ki. 8. 47 if they shall bethink themselves in the
2 Ch. 6. 37 Yet (if) they bethink themselves in the

BETIMES, to rise —
1. *To be with the dawn,* שָׁחַר *shachar,* 3.

Job 24. 5 wild asses..rising betimes for a prey: the

2. *To take on one's shoulder,* שָׁכַם *shakam,* 5.

Gen. 26. 31 they rose up betimes in the morning, and
2 Ch. 36. 15 God..sent..rising up betimes, and sending

BETIMES —
To be with the dawn, שָׁחַר *shachar,* 3.

Job 8. 5 If thou wouldest seek unto God betimes
Prov.13. 24 that loveth him chasteneth him betimes

BETH JE-SHI'-MOTH, בֵּית הַיְשִׁמוֹת *place of desolations.*
A city of Moab, near where the Jordan falls into the Salt Sea. Now *Ramah.*

Num33. 49 they pitched by Jordan, from B . unto
Josh.12. 3 the salt sea on the east, the way to B.
13. 20 Beth-peor, and Ashdoth-pisgah, and B.
Eze. 25. 9 the glory of the country, B., Baal-meon

BETH LE-BA'-OTH, בֵּית־לְבָאוֹת *place of lionesses.*
A town in Simeon.

Josh 19. 6 B., and Sharuhen; thirteen cities and

BETH LE'-HEM, בֵּית לֶחֶם *place of food.*
1. This town, about 6 miles south of Jerusalem, is celebrated as the birthplace of the Saviour. It was called Ephrath, and is mentioned as the place at which Rachel died and was buried, B.C. 1729. Rehoboam fortified or rebuilt it, B.C. 973. David was born here (circ. B.C. 1085), and hence it was called the city of David. Helena, the mother of Constantine, A.D. 325, erected a church, which remains to this day, on the place of the Nativity. It was ceded, with other towns, to Frederick II. by the sultan of Egypt in 1229. It was called Bethlehem-Judah to distinguish it from Bethlehem in Zebulon (Josh. 19 15, 16). Bethlehem was made a bishopric in 1110.

Gen. 35. 19 buried in the way to Ephrath. which (is) B.
48. 7 the way of Ephrath; the same (is) B.
Judg17. 7 there was a young man out of B
17. 8 And the man departed out of..B. to
17. 9 he said..I (am) a Levite of B., and I go
19. 1 a..Levite..took..a concubine out of B.
19. 2 his concubine..went away from him..to B.
19. 18 We (are) passing from B. toward..mount
19. 18 I went to B., but I (am now) going to the
Ruth 1. 1 a certain man of B. went to sojourn in
1 2 Mahlon and Chilion, Ephrathites of B.
1. 19 they two went until they came to B.
1. 19 when they were come to B...they said
1. 22 they came to B. in the beginning of..har.
2. 4 Boaz came from B., and said unto the
4. 11 worthily in Ephratah..be famous in B.
1 Sa. 16. 4 Samuel..came to B...And the elders of
17. 12 David..son of that Ephrathite of B.
17. 15 David went..to feed his..sheep at B.
20. 6 David..asked..that he might run to B.
20. 28 David earnestly asked (leave..to go) to B.
2 Sa. 2. 32 buried him in the sepulchre..(in) B.
23. 14 the garrison of the Philistines (was..in) B.
23. 15 the water of the well of B...by the gate!
23. 16 and drew water out of the well of B.
23. 24 Elhanan the son of Dodo of B.
1 Ch. 11. 16 the Philistines' garrison (was) then at B.
11. 17 the water of the well of B...at the gate
11. 18 and drew water out of the well of B.
11. 26 Elhanan the son of Dodo of B.
2 Ch. 11. 6 He built even B., and Etam, and Tekoa
Ezra 2. 21 children of B., an hundred twenty and
Neh. 7. 26 of B. and Netophah, an hundred fourscore
Jer. 41. 17 Chimham, which is by B., to go to..Egyp.
Mic. 5. 2 But thou, B... (though) thou be little
Matt. 2. 1 Jesus was born in B. of Judea, in the
2. 5 they said unto him, In B. of Judea
2. 6 And thou, B...art not the least among the
2. 8 he sent them to B., and said, Go and
2. 16 Then Herod..slew all the children..in B.
Luke 2. 4 Joseph..went..unto the city..called B.
2. 15 the shepherds said..Let us now go..u. B.
John 7. 42 Christ cometh..out of the town of B.

2. A town in Zebulon. Now *Beit-lahm.*

Josh.19. 15 Nahallal, and Shimron, and Idalah..B.

3. The following passages refer to Nos. 1 or 2.

Judg12. 8 And after him Ibzan of B. judged Israel
12. 10 Then died Ibzan, and was buried at B.

4. A descendant of Caleb, son of Hur.

1 Ch. 2. 51 Salma the father of B., Hareph the father
2. 54 sons of Salma; B., and the Netophathites
4. 4 the firstborn of Ephratah, the father of B.

BETH-LE-HE-MITE, בֵּית הַלַּחְמִי *belonging to Bethlehem.*
Patronymic of an inhabitant of Bethlehem.

1 Sa. 16. 1 I will send thee to Jesse the B.: for I
16. 18 I have seen a son of Jesse the B., (that is)
17. 58 (I am) the son of..Jesse the B.
2 Sa. 21. 19 Elhanan the son of Jaare-oregim, a B.

BETH MA-A'-CHAH, בֵּית מַעֲכָה *place of oppression.*
A city of Manasseh at the foot of Hermon, near Dan, E. of the Jordan. It sometimes occurs as *Abel-beth-maachah*, and occasionally as *Abel.*

2 Sa. 20. 14 he went through all..Israel..to B.
20. 15 And they..besieged him in Abel of B.
20. 18 They shall surely ask..at Abel: and so
2 Ki. 15. 29 Tiglath-pileser king of Assyria..took.. A.

BETH MAR-CA'-BOTH, בֵּית הַמַּרְכָּבוֹת *place of chariots.*
A city of Simeon at the extreme S. of Judah, with Ziklag and Hormah.

Josh.19. 5 Ziklag, and B., and Hazar-susah
1 Ch. 4. 31 at B., and Hazar-susim, and at Beth-birei

BETH ME'-ON, בֵּית מְעוֹן *place of habitation.*
A city of Moab, near Beth-gamul [See *Beth-baal-meon*, the full form].

Jer. 48. 23 Kiriathaim, and upon Beth-gamul,..B.

BETH NIM'-RAH, בֵּית נִמְרָה *place of flowing water.*
A city of Gad, the same as *Nimrah* (Num. 32. 3), and *Nimrim* (Isa. 15. 6).

Num32. 36 B., and Beth-haran, fenced cities: and
Josh.13. 27 in the valley, Beth-aram, and B., and

BETH PA'-LET or BETH PHE-'LET, בֵּית פֶּלֶט.
A town in the S. of Judah.

Josh.15. 27 Hazar-gaddah, and Heshmon, and B.
Neh. 11. 26 at Jeshua, and at Moladah, and at B.

BETH PAZ'-ZEZ, בֵּית פַּצֵּץ *a place of destruction.*
A town of Issachar.

Josh.19. 21 and En-gannim, and En-haddah, and B.

BETH PE'-OR, בֵּית פְּעוֹר *house of the opening.*
A city of Moab, near mount Peor, E. of the Jordan, opposite Jericho, and 6 miles above Libias or Beth-haran. It was in the allotment of Reuben.

Deut. 3. 29 we abode in the valley over against B.
4. 46 this side Jordan, in..valley over against B.
34. 6 he buried him in a valley..over against B.
Josh 13. 20 And B. and Ashdoth-pisgah, and Beth.

BETH PHA'-GE, Βηθφαγή *house of figs.*
A village on the Mount of Olives, near Bethany, on the road between Jericho and Jerusalem.

Matt21. 1 when..drew nigh..and were come to B.
Mark11. 1 when they came nigh to Jerusalem..B.
Luke19. 29 when he was come nigh to B. and Beth.

BETH RA'-PHA, בֵּית רָפָא *place of fear.*
A name which occurs in the genealogy of Judah as the son of Eshton and grandson of Chelub through Caleb son of Hur. There is a Rapha in the line of Benjamin and elsewhere, but no connection can be traced between those and this Beth-rapha, B.C. 1450.

1 Ch. 4. 12 Eshton begat B., and Paseah, and Tehin.

BETH RE'-HOB, בֵּית רְחוֹב *roomy place.*
A place in the N. of Canaan near the valley in which lay the town of Laish or Dan; the place is now represented by *Hunin*, a fortress commanding the plain of *Huleh*, in which lay the city of Dan or *Tell-el-Kady.*

Judg18. 28 it was in the valley that (lieth) by B.
2 Sa. 10. 6 children of Ammon..hired..Syrians of B.

BETH SAI'-DA, Βηθσαϊδά *place of nets.*
1. "Bethsaida of Galilee" (the native city of Andrew, Peter, and Philip) in the land of Gennesareth, on the west side of the lake.

Matt 11. 21 Woe..thee, Chorazin! woe unto thee, B.!
Mark 6. 45 to go to the other side before unto B.
Luke10. 13 unto thee, Chorazin! woe unto thee, B.!
John 1. 44 Philip was of B., the city of Andrew and
12. 21 same..came..to Philip, which was of B.

2. Bethsaida at which the 5000 were fed, a place on the east of the Lake of Gennesareth. Such a place there was at the N.E. extremity, formerly a village, but rebuilt and adorned by Philip the Tetrarch, and raised to the dignity of a town under the name *Julias*, after the daughter of the emperor.

Mark 8. 22 he cometh to B.; and they bring a blind
Luke 9. 10 a desert place belonging to..city called B.

BETH SHAN, בֵּית שָׁן *house of security.*
A city of Manasseh W. of Jordan. Perhaps the same as Bethshean. It was the S. border town in Galilee and belonged to Decapolis.

1 Sa. 31. 10 they fastened his body to the wall of B.
31. 12 took the body of Saul..from the wall of B.
2 Sa. 21. 12 had stolen them from the street of B.

BETH SHE'-AN, בֵּית שְׁאָן *house of security.*
Probably the same as *Bethshan.* The Canaanites were not driven out from this town. In the time of Solomon it formed a commissariat district extending from the town itself to Abel-meholah (1 Ki. 4. 12). Its modern name is *Beisan.* It lies in the Ghor or Jordan valley, about 12 miles S. of the sea of Galilee and 4 W. of the Jordan.

Josh.17. 11 Manasseh had in Issachar and in Asher, B.
17. 16 who (are) of B. and her towns, and (they)
Judg. 1. 27 Neither did Manasseh drive out..B. and
1 Ki. 4. 12 Taanach..all B., which (is) by Zartanah
4. 12 from B. to Abel-meholah, (even) unto
1 Ch. 7. 29 by the borders of..Manasseh, B. and her

BETH SHE'-MESH, בֵּית שֶׁמֶשׁ *house of the sun.*
1. One of the towns marking the N. border of Judah, though not named among the cities of that tribe. It is now called *Ain-shems*, which is on the N.W. slope of the mountains of Judah, a low plateau at the junction of two plains, about 2 miles from the great Philistine plain, and 7 from Ekron.

Josh.15. 10 went down to B., and passed on to Tim.
21. 16 Juttah with her suburbs, (and) B. with
Judg. 1. 33 did Naphtali drive out..inhabitants of B.
1. 33 nevertheless..inhabitants of B...became
1 Sa. 6. 9 goeth up by..way of his own coast to B.
6. 12 kine took..straight way to the way of B.
6. 12 went after them unto the border of B.
6 13 (they of) Beth-shemesh (were) reaping
6. 15 the men of B. offered burnt offerings and
6. 19 he smote the men of B., because they
6. 20 the men of B. said, Who is able to stand
1 Ki. 4. 9 The son of Dekar..in Shaalbim, and B.
2 Ki. 14. 11 he and Amaziah..looked one a...at B.
14. 13 Jehoash king of Israel..Amaziah..at B.
1 Ch. 6. 59 Ashan with her suburbs, and B. with her
2 Ch. 25. 21 Joash..saw..Amaziah king of Judah, at B.
25. 23 Joash..took Amaziah..of Judah..at B.
28. 18 The Philistines..had taken B., and Ajalon

2. A city on the border of Issachar.

Josh. 19. 22 the coast reacheth to Tabor..and B., and

3. A fenced city of Naphtali.

Josh. 19.38 Iron, and Migdal-el, Horem, and B.

4. An idolatrous temple in Egypt, supposed to be On or Heliopolis, which in the middle ages was still called *Ain-Shems.*

Jer. 43. 13 break also the images of B., that (is) in..Eg.

BETH SHEM-ITE, בֵּית הַשִּׁמְשִׁי.
An inhabitant of Bethshemesh, B.C. 1140.

1 Sa. 6. 14 the cart came into..field of Joshua, a B.
6. 18 (stone remaineth)..in..field of Josh. the B.

BETH SHIT'-TAH, בֵּית הַשִּׁטָּה *place of acacia.*
The narrative and the name both require this place to be near the Jordan where Zererath and Abel-meholah also lay. The Shuttah of Robinson is too far to the W.

Judg. 7 22 and the host fled to B. in Zererath, (and) to

BETH TAP-PU'-AH, בֵּית־תַּפּוּחַ *place of fruit trees.*
A city in the mountainous district of Judah, near Hebron. This is a different place from *Tappuah.* The modern name is *Teffuh*, 5 miles W. of Hebron, on a ridge of high table land.

Josh. 15. 53 And Janum, and B., and Aphekah

BE-THU'-EL, בְּתוּאֵל *dweller in God.*
1. A son of Nahor, Abraham's brother, B.C. 1872.

Gen. 22. 22 Hazo, and Pildash, and Jidlaph, and B.
22. 23 B. begat Rebekah..eight Milcah did bear
24. 15 Rebekah came out, who was born to B.
24. 24 I (am) the daughter of B...son of Milcah
24. 47 The daughter of B., Nahor's son, whom
24. 50 Then Laban and B. answered and said
25. 20 Rebekah..the daughter of B. the Syrian
28. 2 Arise, go to Padan-aram, to..house of B.
28. 5 he went to Padan-aram..Laban, son of B.

2. A town in the tribe of Simeon, (the Bethul of Josh. 19. 4.)

1 Ch. 4. 30 And at B., and at Hormah, and at Ziklag

BE'-THUL, בְּתוּל *dweller in God.*
A city in Simeon, the same as *Bethuel.*

Josh. 19. 4 And Eltolad, and B., and Hormah

BETH ZUR, בֵּית־צוּר *place of rock.*
1. A city in the mountains of Judah towards Idumea. It was founded by the people of Maon, which had derived its origin from Hebron. Bethzur was fortified by Rehoboam for the defence of his new kingdom It is now called *Beit-sur.*

Josh.15. 58 Halhul, B., and Gedor
2 Ch. 11. 7 B., and Shoco, and Adullam.
Neh. 3. 16 Azbuk, the ruler of the half part of B.

2. Patronymic of the son of Maon, a descendant of Hebron, one of the posterity of Caleb, brother of Jerahmeel.

1 Ch. 2. 45 and Maon..the father of B

BE-TO'-NIM, בְּטֹנִים *heights.*
A town in the N. of Gad, on the E. of the Jordan.

Josh. 13. 26 from Heshbon..Ramath-mizpeh, and B.

BETRAY, to —
1. *To cast, throw,* רָמָה *ramah,* 3.
1 Ch. 12. 17 but if..to betray me to mine enemies
2. *To give over to,* παραδίδωμι *paradidōmi.*
Matt 10. 4 Judas Iscariot, who also betrayed him
17. 22 The Son of man shall be betrayed into
20. 18 the Son of man shall be betrayed unto the
24. 10 shall betray one another, and shall hate
26. 2 the Son of man is betrayed to be crucified
26. 16 he sought opportunity to betray him
26. 21 Verily I say..That one of you shall betray
26. 23 He that dippeth..the same shall betray
26. 24 by whom the Son of man is betrayed
26. 25 Then Judas, which betrayed him
26. 45 the Son of man is betrayed into the hands
26. 46 he is at hand that doth betray me
26. 48 he that betrayed him gave them a sign
27. 3 Then Judas, which had betrayed him
27. 4 I have betrayed the innocent blood
Mark 3. 19 Judas Iscariot, which also betrayed him
13. 12 the brother shall betray the brother to
14. 10 Iscariot..went..to betray him unto them
14. 11 he sought how he might..betray him
14. 18 One..which eateth with me shall betray
14. 21 by whom the Son of man is betrayed
14. 41 the Son of man is betrayed into the hands
14. 42 lo, he that betrayeth me is at hand
14. 44 he that betrayed him had given them a
Luke 21. 16 ye shall be betrayed both by parents
22. 4 how he might betray him unto them
22. 6 sought opportunity to betray him unto
22. 21 the hand of him that betrayeth me (is)
22. 22 unto that man by whom he is betrayed
22. 48 betrayest thou the Son of man with a
John 6. 64 For Jesus knew..who should betray him
6. 71 for he it was that should betray him
12. 4 Judas Iscariot..which should betray him
13. 2 the devil having now put..to betray him
13. 11 For he knew who should betray him
13. 21 verily, I say..one of you shall betray me
18. 2 Judas also, which betrayed him, knew
18. 5 Judas also, which betrayed him, stood
21. 20 Lord, which is he that betrayeth thee?
1 Co. 11. 23 the..night in which he was betrayed

BETRAYERS —
One betraying, προδότης *prodotēs.*
Acts 7. 52 of whom ye have been now the betrayers

BETROTH, to —
1. *To betroth, espouse,* אָרַשׂ *aras,* 3.
Deut 20. 7 what man..that hath betrothed a wife
28. 30 Thou shalt betroth a wife, and another
Hos. 2. 19 I will betroth thee..yea, I will betroth
2. 20 I will even betroth thee unto me in
2. *To appoint,* יָעַד *yaad.*
Exod 21. 8 master, who hath betrothed her to himself
21. 9 if he have betrothed her unto his son, he

BETROTHED, to be —
1. *To be prepared, exposed* חָרַף *charaph,* 2.
Lev. 19. 20 a bondmaid, betrothed to an husband
2. *To be betrothed, espoused* אָרַשׂ *aras,* 4.
Exod 22. 16 a man entice a maid that is not betrothed
Deut 22. 23 If a damsel..a virgin be betrothed unto
22. 25 if a man find a betrothed damsel in the
22. 27 the betrothed damsel cried, and..none
22. 28 which is not betrothed, and lay hold on

BETTER —
1. *Good,* טוֹב *tob.*
Gen. 29. 19 better that I give her to thee, than that
Exod 14. 12 better for us to serve the Egyptians
Num 14. 3 Were it not better for us to return into
Judg. 8. 2 (Is) not the gleaning of..better than the
9. 2 Speak, I pray you..Whether (is) better
11. 25 now (art) thou anything better than
Ruth 4. 15 which is better to thee than seven sons
1 Sa. 1. 8 (am) not I better to thee than ten sons?
15. 22 Behold, to obey (is) better than sacrifice
15. 28 a neighbour of thine..better than thou
27. 1 nothing better for me than that I should
2 Sa. 17. 14 The counsel of Hushai..(is) better than
18. 3 better that thou succour us out of the
1 Ki. 2. 32 two men more righteous and better than
19. 4 for I (am) not better than my fathers
21. 2 I will give thee for it a better vineyard
2 Ki. 5. 12 better than all the waters of Israel?
2 Ch. 21. 13 hast slain thy brethren..better than
Esth. 1. 19 give..unto another that is better than
Psa. 63. 3 thy loving kindness (is) better than life
119. 72 The law of thy mouth (is) better unto me
Prov. 3. 14 the merchandise of it (is) better than the
8. 11 wisdom (is) better than rubies; and all the
8. 19 My fruit (is) better than gold, yea, than
12. 9 better than he that honoureth himself
15. 16 Better (is) little with the fear of the
15. 17 Better (is) a dinner of herbs where love
16. 32 slow to anger (is) better than the mighty
17. 1 Better (is) a dry morsel, and quietness
19. 1 Better (is) the poor that walketh in his
19. 22 a poor man (is) better than a liar
25. 7 better..that it be said unto thee, Come
25. 24 better to dwell in the corner of the house
27. 5 Open rebuke (is) better than secret love
27. 10 better (is) a neighbour..near, than a
28. 6 Better (is) the poor that walketh in his
Eccl. 2. 24 nothing better for a man, (than) that he
3. 22 I perceive that..nothing better, than
4. 3 Yea, better..than both they, which hath
Eccl. 4. 6 Better (is) an handful (with) quietness
4. 9 Two (are) better than one; because they
4. 13 Better (is) a poor and a wise child than
5. 5 Better..that thou shouldest not vow
6. 3 I say..an untimely birth (is) better than
6. 9 Better (is) the sight of the eyes than the
7. 1 A (good) name (is) better than precious
7. 2 better to go to the house of mourning
7. 3 Sorrow (is) better than laughter: for by
7. 5 better to hear the rebuke of the wise
7. 8 Better (is) the end of a thing than the
7. 8 the patient in spirit (is) better than the
7. 10 the former days were better than these?
8. 15 a man hath no better thing under the
9. 4 for a living dog is better than a dead lion
9. 16 Then said I, Wisdom (is) better than
9. 18 Wisdom (is) better than weapons of war
Song 1. 2 for thy love (is) better than wine
Isa. 56. 5 name better than of sons and..daughters
Lam. 4. 9 slain with the sword are better than
Hos. 2. 7 for then (was it) better with me than now
Amos 6. 2 better than these kingdoms? or their
Jon. 4. 3, 8 (it is) better for me to die than to live
2. *More,* יוֹתֵר *yother.*
Eccl. 6. 11 increase vanity, what (is) man the better?
3. *Advantage, abundance,* יִתְרוֹן *yithron.*
Eccl. 10. 11 enchantment; and a babbler is no better
4. *Beautiful, honourable,* καλός *kalos.*
Matt 18. 8, 9 it is better for thee to enter into life
Mark 9. 43, 45, 47 it is better for thee to enter into
5. *Good...than,* καλόν...μᾶλλον *kalon...mallon.*
Mark 9. 42 it is better for him that a millstone
1 Co. 9. 15 better for me to die, than that any man
6. *Stronger, more powerful,* κρείσσων *kreissōn.*
1 Co. 7. 9 for it is better to marry than to burn
7. 38 he that giveth (her) not..doeth better
11. 17 ye come together not for the better, but
Phil. 1. 23 to be with Christ; which is far better
Heb. 1. 4 Being made so much better than the
7. 7 the less is blessed of the better
7. 19 but the bringing in of a better hope..by
7. 22 Jesus made a surety of a better testament
8. 6 a better covenant..upon better promises
9. 23 heavenly things..with better sacrifices
10. 34 ye have in heaven a better and an endur.
11. 35 they might obtain a better resurrection
1 Pe. 3. 17 better, if the will of God be so, 2 Pe. 2. 21.
7. *To be above, higher,* ὑπερέχω *huperechō,* Phil. 2. 3.
8. *Better, kindlier,* χρηστότερος [*chrēstos*].
Luke 5. 39 desireth new..he saith, The old is better

BETTER, to be —
1. *To be good,* טוֹב *tob.*
Song 4. 10 how much better is thy love than wine!
2. *To do good, or well,* יָטַב *yatab,* 5.
Nah. 3. 8 Art thou better than populous No, that
3. *To be different, bear diversely,* διαφέρω *diapherō.*
Matt. 6. 26 Are ye not much better than they?
12. 12 How much..is a man better than a sheep?
Luke 12. 24 how much more are ye better than the
4. *To be advantageous,* λυσιτελέω *lusiteleō.*
Luke 17. 2 It were better..that a millstone were
5. *To be profitable,* συμφέρω *sumpherō.*
Matt 18. 6 it were better..that a millstone were
6. *To hold forward, or before,* προέχομαι *proechomai.*
Rom. 3. 9 What then? are we better..No, in no

BETTER, to do —
To do good, טוֹב *tob,* 5.
Eze. 36. 11 will do better..than at your beginnings

BETTER, to make —
To do or make good, יָטַב *yatab,* 5.
1 Ki. 1. 47 make the name of Solomon better than

BETTER, to be made —
To be good יָטַב *yatab.*
Eccl. 7. 3 by the sadness..the heart is made better

BETTER, to be the —
To be over and above, περισσεύω *perisseuō.*
1 Co. 8. 8 for neither, if we eat, are we the better

BETTER (country) or thing —
Stronger, more powerful, κρείσσων *kreissōn.*
Heb. 6. 9 we are persuaded better things of you
11. 16 now they desire a better (country), that
11. 40 God having provided some better thing
12. 24 that speaketh better things than..Abel

BETTERED, to be —
To profit, ὠφελέω *ōpheleō.*
Mark 5. 26 had spent all..and was nothing bettered

BETWEEN —
1. *Between,* בֵּין *ben.*
Gen. 15. 17 a burning lamp that passed between
2. *Between,* בֵּינוֹת *benoth.*
Eze. 10. 2 Go in between the wheels..under the
3. *On, upon,* עַל *al.*
1 Ki. 18. 21 How long halt ye between two opinions
4. *Middle, midst,* תָּוֶךְ *tavek.*
Exod 28. 33 bells of gold between them round about
39. 25 put the bells between the pomegranates
39. 25 round about between the pomegranates
5. *In the midst,* ἀνὰ μέσον *ana meson.*
1 Co. 6. 5 not one..able to judge between his br.?
6. *In, among,* ἐν *en.*
Rom. 1. 24 dishonour their own bodies between
7. *In between,* μεταξύ *metaxu.*
Matt 18. 15 tell him his fault between thee and him
23. 35 whom ye slew between the temple and
Luke 11. 51 which perished between the altar and
16. 26 between us and you there is a great gulf
Acts 12. 6 Peter was sleeping between two soldiers
15. 9 put no difference between us and them
8. *Toward,* πρός *(acc.) pros.*
Luke 23. 12 they were at enmity between themselves
Acts 26. 31 they talked between themselves, saying

BETWEEN, to differ —
To make a parting, division, μερίζω *merizō.*
1 Co. 7. 34 There is difference (also) between a wife

BETWEEN (some) of..and —
From the...with, ἐκ τῶν...μετά *ek tōn...meta.*
John 3. 25 between (some) of John's disciples and

BETWIXT —
1. *Between,* בֵּין *ben.*
Gen. 31. 37 that they may judge betwixt; 32. 16, &c.
2. *Out of,* ἐκ *ek.*
Phil. 1. 23 I am in a strait betwixt two, having a des.

BETWIXT, to come —
To strike on, פָּגַע *paga,* 5.
Job 36. 32 by (the cloud) that cometh betwixt

BE-U'-LAH, בְּעוּלָה *married.*
A symbolic name which the land of Israel is to bear in its future prosperity.
Isa. 62. 4 thou shalt be called..and thy land B.

BEWAIL self, to —
To breathe one's self out, יָפַח *yaphach,* 7.
Jer. 4. 31 the daughter of Zion..bewaileth herself

BEWAIL, to —
1. *To weep,* בָּכָה *bakah.*
Lev. 10. 6 bewail the burning which the LORD hath
Deut 21. 13 bewail her father and her mother a full
Judg 11. 37 I may..bewail my virginity, I and my
11. 38 bewailed her virginity upon the mount.
Isa. 16. 9 I will bewail with the weeping of Jazer
2. *To wail,* κλαίω *klaiō.*
Rev. 18. 9 kings of the earth..shall bewail her
3. *To strike (the breast),* κόπτω *koptō.*
Luke 8. 52 all wept, and bewailed her: but he said
23. 27 which also bewailed and lamented him
4. *To lament, mourn,* πενθέω *pentheō.*
2 Co 12. 21 I shall bewail many which have sinned

BEWARE, to —
1. *To become subtile,* עָרַם *aram,* 5.
Prov. 19. 25 Smite..and the simple will beware
2. *To watch,* שָׁמַר *shamar.*
2 Sa. 18. 12 Beware that none..the young man Ab.
3. *To be watchful,* שָׁמַר *shamar,* 2.
Gen. 24. 6 Beware thou that..bring not my son
Exod 23. 21 Beware of him, and obey his voice
Deut. 6. 12 beware lest thou forget the LORD, which
8. 11 Beware that thou forget not the LORD thy
15. 9 Beware that there be not a thought in
Judg 13. 4 beware, I pray thee, and drink not wine
13. 13 that I said unto the woman let her beware
2 Ki. 6. 9 Beware that thou pass not such a place
4. *To behold,* βλέπω *blepō.*
Mark 8. 15 beware of the leaven of the Pharisees
12. 38 Beware of the scribes, which love to go
Acts 13. 40 Beware therefore, lest that come upon
Col. 2. 8 Beware lest any man spoil you through
5. *To guard,* φυλάσσω *phulassō.*
Luke 12. 15 beware of covetousness: for a man's life
2 Pe. 3. 17 seeing ye know..beware lest ye also

BEWARE of, to —
1. *To behold,* βλέπω *blepō.*
Phil. 3. 2 Beware of dogs, beware of evil workers
3. 2 beware of the concision
2. *To hold toward oneself,* προσέχω *prosechō.*
Matt. 7. 15 Beware of false prophets, which come to
10. 17 beware of men; for they will deliver you
16. 6 beware of the leaven of the Pharisees
16. 11 ye should beware of the leaven of the
16. 12 not beware of the leaven of bread, but of
Luke 12. 1 Beware ye of the leaven of the Pharisees
20. 46 Beware of the scribes, which desire to
3. *To guard,* φυλάσσω *phulassō.*
2 Ti. 4. 15 Of whom be thou ware also; for he hath

BEWITCH, to —
1. *To smite with the eye,* βασκαίνω *baskainō.*
Gal 3. 1 Galatians, who hath bewitched you, that
2. *To cause to stand out,* ἐξίστημι *existēmi.*
Acts 8. 9 bewitched the people of Samaria, giving
8. 11 he had bewitched them with sorceries

BEWRAY, to —
1. *To reveal, uncover,* גָּלָה *galah,* 3.
Isa. 16. 3 outcasts; bewray not him that wandereth

2. *To set before,* נָגַד *nagad,* 5.
Prov.29. 24 he heareth cursing, and bewrayeth (it)
3. *To call,* קָרָא *qara.*
Prov.27. 16 ointment of his right..bewrayeth
4. *To make evident,* ποιέω δῆλον *poieō dēlon.*
Matt.26. 73 of them; for thy speech bewrayeth thee

BEYOND —
1. *Yonder, beyond, henceforth,* הָלְאָה *haleah.*
Gen. 35. 21 spread his tent beyond the tower of Edar
1 Sa. 20. 22 Behold, the arrows (are) beyond thee; go
20. 37 said, (Is) not the arrow beyond thee?
Jer. 22. 19 cast forth beyond the gates of Jerusalem
Amos 5. 27 I cause you to go into captivity beyond
2. *To cause to pass over,* עָבַר *abar,* 5.
1 Sa. 20. 36 as the lad ran, he shot an arrow beyond
3. *Over,* עֵבֶר *eber.*
Gen. 50. 10 which (is) beyond Jordan, and there they
50. 11 Abel-mizraim, which (is) beyond Jordan
Deut. 3. 20 land..God hath given them beyond Jord.
3. 25 see the good land that (is) beyond Jordan
30. 13 Neither (is) it beyond the sea, that thou
Josh. 9. 10 that he did to the two kings..beyond
13. 8 which Moses gave them, beyond Jordan
18. 7 received their inheritance beyond Jordan
Judg. 5. 17 Gilead abode beyond Jordan: and why
2 Sa. 10. 16 the Syrians that (were) beyond the river
1 Ki. 4. 12 Abel-meholah..unto..beyond Jokneam
14. 15 shall scatter them beyond the river
1 Ch. 19. 16 the Syrians that (were) beyond the river
2 Ch. 20. 2 from beyond the sea on this side Syria
Neh. 2. 7 to the governors beyond the river, that
2. 9 I came to the governors beyond the river
Isa. 7. 20 by them beyond the river, by the king of
9. 1 the way of the sea, beyond Jordan, in
18. 1 which (is) beyond the rivers of Ethiopia
Jer. 25. 22 kings of the isles which (are) beyond the
Zeph. 3. 10 From beyond the rivers of Ethiopia my
4. *Over, beyond,* עֲבַר *abar.*
Ezra 4. 17 and (unto) the rest beyond the river
4. 20 have ruled over all..beyond the river
6. 6 Now..Tatnai, governor beyond the river
6. 6 Apharsachites, which (are) beyond the
6. 8 of the tribute beyond the river, forthwith
7. 21 the treasurers which (are) beyond the
7. 25 all the people that (are) beyond the river
5. *On yonder side of,* ἐπέκεινα *epekeina.*
Acts 7. 43 I will carry you away beyond Babylon
6. *Over, beyond,* πέραν *peran.*
Matt. 4. 15 the way of the sea, beyond Jordan
4. 25 multitudes of people..(from) beyond
19. 1 into the coasts of Judea beyond Jordan
Mark 3. 8 from Jerusalem, and..beyond Jordan
John 1. 28 were done in Bethabara beyond Jordan
3. 26 he that was with thee beyond Jor., 10. 40.
7. *The places beyond,* τὰ ὑπερέκεινα, 2 Co. 10. 16.
8. *Over,* ὑπέρ *(acc.) huper.*
2 Co. 8. 3 [beyond] (their) power..willing of thems.
[*See also* Go, measure, pass, regions, stretch.]

BEYOND the time —
Over, עַל *al.*
Lev. 15. 25 if it run beyond the time of her separation

BE'-ZAI, בֵּצָי *shining, high.*
1. One whose posterity to the number of 323 returned from exile with Zerubbabel, B.C. 536.
Ezra 2. 17 children of B., three hundred twenty and
Neh. 7. 23 children of B., three hundred twenty and
2. A family that, with Nehemiah, sealed the covenant, B.C., 445.
Neh. 10. 18 Hodijah, Hashum, B.

BE-ZAL'-EEL, בְּצַלְאֵל *God is protection.*
1. The artificer to whom was confided the design and execution of the works of art required for the tabernacle in the wilderness. His charge was chiefly in all works of metal, wood, and stone, Aholiab having charge of the textile fabrics. Bezaleel, however, was chief in both departments, B.C. 1491.
Exod31. 2 See, I have called by name B. the son of
35. 30 the LORD hath called by name B. the son
36. 1 Then wrought B. and Aholiab, and every
36. 2 Moses called B...unto the work to do it
37. 1 B. made the ark of shittim wood
38. 22 B...made all..LORD commanded Moses
1 Ch. 2. 20 Hur begat Uri, and Uri begat B.
2 Ch. 1. 5 Moreover the brasen altar..B...had
Son of Pahath-moab, and one of those who had taken a strange wife, B.C. 445.
Ezra 10. 30 of..sons of Pahath-moab..B., and Binn.

BE'-ZEK, בֶּזֶק *breach.*
. The residence of Adonibezek ("lord of Bezek") in Judah, inhabited by Canaanites and Perizzites.
Judg. 1. 4 and they slew..in B. ten thousand men
1. 5 And they found Adoni-bezek in B.
2. The place where Saul numbered his forces before going to the relief of Jabesh Gilead, somewhere in the centre of the country near the Jordan valley, a day's march from Jabesh. There were two places of this name 17 miles from Neapolis (Shechem), on the road to Bethshean.
1 Sa 11. 8 And when he numbered them in B.

BE'-ZER, בֶּצֶר *strong.*
1. A city of Reuben, in the downs, or *mishor,* one of the three cities of refuge on the E. of the Jordan, and allotted to the Merarites. Now *Besheir.*
Deut. 4. 43 B. in the wilderness, in the plain country
Josh.20. 8 they assigned B. in the wilderness upon
21. 36 of the tribe of Reuben, B. with her suburbs
1 Ch. 6. 78 of the tribe of Reuben, B...with her sub.
2. A son of Liph, one of the heads of Asher, B.C. 1540.
1 Ch. 7. 37 B., and Hod, and Shamma, and Shilshah

BICH'-RI, בִּכְרִי *youth, first born.*
Ancestor of Sheba who rose against David, B.C. 1022.
2 Sa. 20. 1 Sheba, the son of B., a Benjamite
20. 2 every man of Israel..followed..son of B.
20. 6 Now shall..the son of B. do us more harm
20. 7, 13 to pursue after Sheba the son of B.
20. 10 Joab..pursued after Sheba the son of B.
20. 21 the son of B...hath lifted up his hand
20. 22 they cut off the head of..the son of B.

BID, to —
1. *To say,* אָמַר *amar.*
Gen. 43. 17 the man did as Joseph bade; and the
Num 14. 10 the congregation bade stone them with
15. 38 bid them that they make them fringes
Josh. 6. 10 until the day I bid you shout; then shall
11. 9 did unto them as the LORD bade him
1 Sa. 9. 27 Bid the servant pass on before us
24. 10 and..bade..kill thee; but..spared thee
2 Sa. 1. 18 he bade them teach the children of Judah
2. 26 how long..ere thou bid the people return
16. 11 let..curse; for the LORD hath bidden him
2 Ki. 4. 24 slack not (thy) riding..except I bid thee
10. 5 we..will do all that thou shalt bid us
Esth. 4. 15 Esther bade..return Mordecai (this ans.)
2. *To speak,* דָּבַר *dabar.*
Jon. 3. 2 preach..the preaching that I bid thee
3. *To speak,* דָּבַר *dabar,* 3.
Gen. 27. 19 I have done according as thou badest me
2 Ki. 5. 13 the prophet had bid thee..great thing
2 Ch. 10. 12 came..as the king bade, saying, Come
4. *To set up, command,* צָוָה *tsavah,* 3.
Exod 16. 24 laid it up till the morning, as Moses bade
Ruth 3. 6 according to all..her mother-in-law bade
2 Sa. 14. 19 thy servant Joab, he bade me, and he put
5. *To separate, sanctify,* קָדַשׁ *qadash,* 5.
Zeph. 1. 7 prepared a sacrifice, he hath bid his
6. *To say,* εἶπον *eipon.*
Matt 16. 12 Then understood they how that he bade
23. 3 All..whatsoever they bid you observe
Luke 10. 40 sister..bid her therefore that she help me
Acts 11. 12 the Spirit bade me go with them, nothing
22. 24 bade that he should be examined by
7. *To call,* καλέω *kaleō.*
Matt 22. 3 call them that were bidden to the wedding
22. 4 Tell them which are bidden, Behold, I
22. 8 they which were bidden were not worthy
22. 9 as many as ye shall find, bid to the mar.
Luke 7. 39 the Pharisee which had bidden him saw
14. 7 put forth a parable to those..were bidden
14. 8 When thou art bidden of any..to a wed.
14. 8 honourable man than thou be bidden of
14. 9 he that bade thee and him come and say
14. 10 when thou art bidden, go and sit down
14. 10 when he that bade thee cometh, he may
14. 12 Then said he also to him that bade him
14. 16 A..man made a great supper, and bade
14. 17 to say to them that were bidden, Come
14. 24 none of those men which were bidden
1 Co. 10. 27 If any of them that believe not bid you
8. *To command,* κελεύω *keleuō.*
Matt 14. 28 bid me come unto thee on the water
9. *To say,* λέγω *legō.*
2 Jo. 10 receive..not..neither bid him God speed
11 he that biddeth him God speed is
10. *To put toward,* προστάσσω *prostassō.*
Matt. 1. 24 the angel of the Lord had bidden him

BID again, to —
To call in return, ἀντικαλέω *antikaleō.*
Luke 14. 12 lest they also bid thee again, and a

BID farewell, to —
To arrange off from, ἀποτάσσομαι *apotassomai.*
Luke 9. 61 let me first go bid them farewell which
Acts 18. 21 bade them farewell, saying, I must by all

BIDDEN, that are —
To call, invite, קָרָא *qara.*
1 Sa. 9. 13 afterwards they eat that be bidden
9. 22 place among them that were bidden

BIDDING —
Hearing, hearkening, מִשְׁמַעַת *mishmaath.*
1 Sa. 22. 14 who (is so) faithful..goeth at thy bidding

BID'-KAR, בִּדְקַר *servant of Kar.*
A captain of Jehu, originally his fellow-officer, who executed the sentence on Jehoram, son of Ahab, B.C. 884.
2 Ki. 9. 25 Then said (Jehu) to B. his captain, Take up

BIER —
1. *Bier,* מִטָּה *mittah.*
2 Sa. 3. 31 And king David (himself) followed the bier
2. *Bier,* σορός *soros.*
Luke 7. 14 he came and touched the bier: and they

BIG'-THA, בִּגְתָא *given by fortune.*
One of the chamberlains of Ahasuerus, B.C. 519.
Esth. 1. 10 B...served in the presence of Ahasuerus

BIG'-THAN, BIG-THA'-NA, בִּגְתָן, בִּגְתָנָא.
A chamberlain who conspired against Ahasuerus, B.C. 519.
Esth. 2. 21 B...sought to lay hand on..Ahasuerus
6. 2 B...sought to lay hand on..Ahasuerus

BIG'-VAI, בִּגְוַי *happy, or of the people.*
1. A chief who came up with Zerubbabel, B.C. 536.
Ezra 2. 2 Which came with Zerubbabel..B., Rehu.
Neh. 7. 7 Who came with Zerubbabel..B., Nehum
2. One whose posterity came up with Zerubbabel, B.C. 536.
Ezra 2. 14 children of B., two thousand fifty and six
Neh. 7. 19 children of B., two thousand threescore
3. One whose descendants came up with Ezra, B.C. 536.
Ezra 8. 14 Of the sons also of B.; Uthai, and Zabbud
4. Patronymic of a family that, with Nehemiah, sealed the covenant, B.C. 445.
Neh. 10. 16 Adonijah, B., Adin

BIL'-DAD, בִּלְדַּד *lord Adad, or son of contention.*
One of Job's three friends, a Shuhite, descended from Shuah, Abraham's son by Keturah, and dwelling in the E. of Arabia, B.C. 1520.
Job 2. 11 they came every one..B. the Shuhite
8. 1 Then answered B. the Shuhite, and said
18. 1 Then answered B. the Shuhite, and said
25. 1 Then answered B. the Shuhite, and said
42. 9 B. the Shuhite..Zophar the Naamathite

BIL'-EAM, בִּלְעָם *place of conquest.*
Levitical city in Manasseh, W. of Jordan. (*Belameh.*)
1 Ch. 6. 70 out of..Manasseh..B. with her suburbs

BIL'-GAH, בִּלְגָּה *bursting forth,* i.e., *firstborn.*
1. A priest in David's time, the head of the 15th course in the tabernacle service, B.C. 1015.
1 Ch 24. 14 The fifteenth to B...sixteenth to Immer
2. A priest who came up with Zerubbabel, B.C. 536.
Neh. 12. 5 Miamin, Maadiah, B.
12. 18 Of B., Shammua; of Shemaiah, Jehonath.

BIL'-GAI, בִּלְגַּי *bursting forth.*
Perhaps the same as Bilgah, No. 2.
Neh. 10. 8 Maaziah, B., Shemaiah: these (were) the

BIL'-HAH, בִּלְהָה *tender.*
1. The handmaid of Laban's younger daughter Rachel, and mother of Dan and Naphtali, B.C. 1753.
Gen. 29. 29 Laban gave to Rachel..B..to be her maid
3 3 Behold my maid B., go in unto her
30. 4 she gave him B. her handmaid to wife
30. 5 B. conceived, and bare Jacob a son
30. 7 B., Rachel's maid, conceived again, and
35. 22 Reuben..lay..B. his father's concubine
35. 25 sons of B., Rachel's handmaid; Dan, and
37. 2 the lad (was) with the sons of B., and
46. 25 These (are) the sons of B., which Laban
1 Ch. 7. 13 Jezer, and Shallum, the sons of B.
2. A town in Simeon, apparently that called *Balah* in Josh. 19. 3.
1 Ch. 4. 29 And at B., and at Ezem, and at

BIL'-HAN, בִּלְהָן *tender.*
From the same root as *Bilhah.* The final *n* is a Horite termination, as in Akan, Alvan, Aran, Dishan, Eshban, Hemdan, &c. Compare these with the Etruscan *ena.* Gr. *α (γ)s, α, ν,* &c.
1. A son of Ezer, son of Seir the Horite, B.C. 1680.
Gen. 36. 27 children of Ezer (are) these; B...Zaavan
1 Ch. 1. 42 sons of Ezer; B., and Zavan
2. A son of Jediael, son of Benjamin, B.C. 1650.
1 Ch. 7. 10 sons also of Jediael; B.: and
7. 10 the sons of B.; Jeush, and Benjamin

BILL —
1. *Book, writing,* סֵפֶר *sepher.*
Deut 24. 1 let him write her a bill of divorcement
24. 3 write her a bill of divorcement, and
Isa. 50. 1 Where (is) the bill of your mother's div.
Jer. 3. 8 I had..given her a bill of divorce; yet
2. *A little book or scroll,* βιβλίον *biblion.*
Mark10. 4 Moses suffered to write a bill of divorce
3. *Writing,* γράμμα *gramma.*
Luke 16. 6 Take thy bill, and sit down quickly, and
16. 7 he said..Take thy bill, and write foursco.

BILLOW —
1. *A heap,* גַּל *gal.*
Psa. 42. 7 thy waves and thy billows are gone over
2. *A breaker,* מִשְׁבָּר *mishbar.*
Jon. 2. 3 thy billows and thy waves passed over

BIL'-SHAN, בִּלְשָׁן *searcher.*
A prince of the Jews who came up with Zerubbabel, B.C. 536.
Ezra 2. 2 came with Zerubbabel..Mordecai, B.
Neh. 7. 7 Who came..Zerubbabel..Mordecai, B.

BIM'-HAL, בִּמְהָל *circumcised.*
A son of Japhlet, in the line of Asher, B.C. 1600.
1 Ch. 7. 33 sons of Japhlet; Pasach..B.., Ashvath

BIND, to —

1. *To bind,* אָלַם *alam,* 3.
Gen. 37. 7 we..binding sheaves in the field, and, lo

2. *To bind, gird,* אָסַר *asar.*
Gen. 42. 24 Simeon, and bound him before their eyes
49. 11 Binding his foal unto the vine, and his
Num 30. 2 swear..oath to bind his soul with a bond
30. 3 bind..by a bond..in her father's house
30. 4, 5 bond wherewith she hath bound her
30. 6, 8 of her lips, wherewith she bound her
30. 7, 11 her bonds wherewith she bound her
30. 9 vow..wherewith they have bound their
30. 10 or bound her soul by a bond with an oath
Judg 15. 10 To bind Samson are we come up, to do to
15. 12 We are come down to bind thee, that we
15. 13 we will bind thee fast, and deliver thee
15. 13 they bound him with two new cords
16. 5 that we may bind him to afflict him
16. 7 If they bind me with seven green withs
16. 8 withs..and she bound him with them
16. 11 If they bind me fast with new ropes
16. 12 Delilah..bound him therewith, and said
16. 21 bound him with fetters of brass; and he
2 Ki. 17. 4 king of Assyria..bound him in prison
25. 7 bound him with fetters of brass, and
2 Ch. 33. 11 bound him with fetters, and carried him
36. 6 bound him..fetters, to carry him to Bab.
Job 36. 13 wrath; they cry not when he bindeth
Psa 105. 22 To bind his princes at his pleasure, and
118. 27 bind the sacrifice with cords..unto the
149. 8 To bind their kings with chains, and
Jer. 39. 7 bound him with chains, to carry him to
52. 11 king of Babylon bound him in chains
Eze. 3. 25 shall bind thee with them, and thou
Hos. 10. 10 when they shall bind themselves in their

3. *To gird,* אָפַד *aphad.*
Lev. 8. 7 the ephod, and bound (it) unto him

4. *To wrap round,* חָבַשׁ *chabash.*
Job 40. 13 Hide them..bind their faces in secret
Eze. 24. 17 bind the tire of thine head upon thee
30. 21 to put a roller to bind it, to make it

5. *To wrap round,* חָבַשׁ *chabash,* 3.
Job 28. 11 He bindeth the floods from overflowing

6. *To gird,* יָסַר *yasar,* 3.
Hos. 7. 15 I have bound (and) strengthened their

7. *To bind, fetter,* כְּפַת *kephath,* 3.
Dan. 3. 20 most mighty men..to bind Shadrach
3. 21 these men were bound in their coats
3. 23 these three men..fell down bound into
3. 24 Did not we cast three men bound into

8. *To tie, bind,* עָנַד *anad.*
Job 31. 36 Surely I would..bind it..a crown to me

9. *To bind,* עָקַד *aqad.*
Gen 22. 9 bound Isaac his son, and laid him on the

10. *To press, compress,* צוּר *tsur.*
2 Ki. 5. 23 bound two talents of silver in two bags
Eze. 5. 3 Thou shalt also..bind them in thy skirts

11. *To compress, press,* צָרַר *tsarar.*
Prov 26. 8 As he that bindeth a stone in a
30. 4 who hath bound the waters in a garment?

12. *To bind (as a conspirator),* קָשַׁר *qashar.*
Deut. 6. 8 bind them for a sign upon thine hand
11. 18 bind them for a sign upon your hand
Josh. 2. 18 bind this line of scarlet thread in the
2. 21 she bound the scarlet line in the window
Job 39. 10 Canst thou bind the unicorn with..band
41. 5 or wilt thou bind him for thy maidens?
Prov. 3. 3 bind them about thy neck; write them
6. 21 Bind them continually upon thine heart
7. 3 Bind them upon thy fingers, write them
Jer. 51. 63 thou shalt bind a stone to it, and cast it

13. *To bind,* קָשַׁר *qashar,* 3.
Job 38. 31 Canst thou bind the sweet influences of
Isa. 49. 18 thou shalt surely..bind them (on thee)

14. *To entangle, bind,* רָכַס *rakas.*
Exod 28. 28 they shall bind the breastplate by the
39. 21 they did bind the breastplate by his

15. *To yoke, bind,* רָתַם *ratham.*
Mic. 1. 13 bind the chariot to the swift beast: she

16. *To fetter,* δεσμεύω *desmeuō.*
Matt 23. 4 they bind heavy burdens and grievous to
Acts 22. 4 binding and delivering into prisons both

17. *To fetter,* δεσμέω *desmeō.*
Luke 8. 29 was kept bound with chains and..fetters

18. *To bind, fasten, tie,* δέω *deō.*
Matt 12. 29 except he first bind the strong man?
13. 30 bind them in bundles to burn them; but
14. 3 Herod had laid hold on John, and bound
16. 19 thou shalt bind on earth shall be bound
18. 18 ye shall bind on earth shall be bound in
22. 13 Bind him hand and foot, and take him
27. 2 when they had bound him, they led
Mark 3. 27 except he will first bind the strong man
5. 3 no man could bind him, no, not with
5. 4 he had been often bound with fetters
6. 17 bound him in prison for Herodias' sake
15. 1 bound Jesus, and carried..away, and
15. 7 bound with them that had made insur.
Luke 13. 16 whom Satan hath bound, lo, these..years
John 11. 44 bound hand and foot with grave clothes
18. 12 Then the band..took Jesus, and bound
18. 24 Annas had sent him bound unto Caiaphas
Acts 9. 2 might bring them bound unto Jerusalem
9. 14 authority..to bind all that call on thy
9. 21 might bring them bound unto the chief
12. 6 Peter was sleeping..bound with two
20. 22 I go bound in the spirit unto Jerusalem
21. 11 bound his own hands and feet, and said
21. 11 So shall the Jews at Jerusalem bind the
21. 13 I am ready not to be bound only, but also
21. 33 commanded..to be bound with..chains
22. 5 to bring them..bound unto Jerusalem
22. 29 was afraid..because he had bound him
24. 27 Felix, willing to show..a..left Paul bound
Rom. 7. 2 the woman..is bound by the law to..hus.
1 Co. 7. 27 Art thou bound unto a wife? seek not to
7. 39 The wife is bound by the law as long as
2 Ti. 2. 9 bonds; but the word of God is not bound
Rev. 9. 14 are bound in the great river Euphrates
20. 2 Satan, and bound him a thousand years

19. *To stretch out before,* προτείνω *proteinō.*
Acts 22. 25 as they bound him with thongs, Paul

BIND about, to —

1. *To gird,* אָזַר *azar.*
Job 30. 18 it bindeth me about as the collar of my

2. *To bind around,* περιδέω *perideō.*
John 11. 44 his face was bound about with a napkin

BIND on, to —

To bind under, ὑποδέω *hupodeō.*
Acts 12. 8 Gird thyself, and bind on thy sandals

BIND sheaves, to —

To bind, עָמַר *amar,* 3.
Psa. 129. 7 nor he that bindeth sheaves his bosom

BIND up, to —

1. *To bind up, gird,* חָבַשׁ *chabash.*
Job 5. 18 For he maketh sore, and bindeth up; he
Isa. 30. 26 LORD bindeth up the breach of his people
61. 1 sent me to bind up the broken hearted
Eze. 34. 4 have ye bound up (that which was) broken
34. 16 will bind up (that which was) broken
Hos. 4. 19 The wind..bound her up in her wings

2. *To bind up, gird,* חָבַשׁ *chabash,* 3.
Psa. 147. 3 He healeth..and bindeth up their wounds

3. *To straiten, compress,* צוּר *tsur.*
Deut 14. 25 Then shalt thou..bind up the money in

4. *To straiten, compress,* צָרַר *tsarar.*
Job 26. 8 He bindeth up the waters in his thick
Isa. 8. 16 Bind up the testimony, seal the law among

5. *To bind fast,* καταδέω *katadeō.*
Luke 10. 34 went..and bound up his wounds, pouring

BIND with, to —

To bind along with, συνδέω *sundeō.*
Heb. 13. 3 them that are in bonds, as bound with

BINDING —

1. *Binding, obliging,* אֱסָר, אִסָּר *issar, esar.*
Num 30. 13 every binding oath to afflict the soul, her

2. *Lip, edge,* שָׂפָה *saphah.*
Exod 28. 32 it shall have a binding of woven work

[*See also* Curse, execration, oath.]

BI'-NEA, בִּנְעָה, בִּנְעָא *wanderer.*
A son of Moza, a descendant of Saul, B.C. 900.
1 Ch. 8. 37 Moza begat B.: Rapha (was) his son
9. 43 Moza begat B.; and Rephaiah his son

BIN-NU'-I, בִּנּוּי *familyship.*
1. A Levite appointed to the oversight of the weighing of the gold and silver vessels that Ezra brought up from Babylon, B.C. 536.
Ezra 8. 33 with them (was)..Noadiah the son of B.
2. One of the family of Pahath-moab, B.C. 445.
Ezra 10. 30 of the sons of Pahath-moab; Bezaleel..B.
3. One of the family of Bani, B.C. 445.
Ezra 10. 38 And Bani, and B., Shimei.
4. One of the family of Henadad, B.C. 460.
Neh. 3. 24 After him repaired B...another piece
10. 9 B. of the sons of Henadad, Kadmiel
5. One whose descendants came up with Zerubbabel. He is called Bani in Ezra 2. 10, B.C. 536.
Neh. 7. 15 The children of B..six hundred forty and
6. A Levite who came up with Zerubbabel, B.C. 536.
Neh. 12. 8 Moreover the Levites: Jeshua, B.

BIRD —

1. *Fowl, bird,* עוֹף *oph.*
Gen. 40. 17 the birds did eat them out of the basket
40. 19 the birds shall eat thy flesh from off thee
2 Sa. 21. 10 neither the birds of the air to rest on
Eccl. 10. 20 a bird of the air shall carry the voice, and
Isa. 16. 2 as a wandering bird cast out of the nest
Jer. 4. 25 all the birds of the heavens were fled
5. 27 As a cage is full of birds, so (are) their
12. 4 the beasts are consumed, and the birds
Hos. 9. 11 their glory shall fly away like a bird

2. *A ravenous bird,* עַיִט *ayit.*
Jer. 12. 9 speckled bird, the birds round about (are)

3. *A sparrow,* צִפּוֹר *tsippor.*
Gen. 7. 14 every fowl after his kind, every bird of
15. 10 divided them..the birds divided he not
Lev. 14. 4 that is to be cleansed two birds alive
14. 5 one of the birds be killed in an..vessel
14. 6 As for the living bird, he shall take it
Lev. 14. 6 dip..the living bird in the blood of the b
14. 7 shall let the living bird loose into the
14. 49 shall take to cleanse the house two birds
14. 50 he shall kill the one of the birds in an
14. 51 living bird..in the blood of the slain bird
14. 52 shall cleanse..with the blood of the bird
14. 52 running water, and with the living bird
14. 53 shall let go the living bird out of the city
Deut 14. 11 (Of) all clean birds ye shall eat
22. 6 If a bird's nest chance to be..in any tree
Job 41. 5 Wilt thou play with him as..a bird?
Psa. 11. 1 say ye..Flee (as) a bird to your mountain?
104. 17 Where the birds make their nests
124. 7 Our soul is escaped as a bird out of the
Prov. 6. 5 as a bird from the hand of the fowler
7. 23 as a bird hasteth to the snare, and
26. 2 As the bird by wandering, as the swallow
27. 8 As a bird that wandereth from her nest
Eccl. 9. 12 as the birds that are caught in the snare
12. 4 he shall rise up at the voice of the bird
Isa. 31. 5 As birds flying, so will the LORD of hosts
Lam. 3. 52 Mine enemies chased me sore, like a bird
Eze. 39. 4 I will give thee unto the ravenous birds
Hos. 11. 11 They shall tremble as a bird out of
Amos 3. 5 Can a bird fall in a snare upon the earth

4. *Bird,* צְפַר *tsephar.*
Dan. 4. 33 and his nails like birds' (claws)

5. *Owner of a wing,* בַּעַל כָּנָף *baal kanaph.*
Prov. 1. 17 the net is spread in the sight of any bird

6. *Bird (domestic or wild),* ὄρνεον *orneon.*
Rev. 18. 2 cage of every unclean and hateful bird

7. *Flying, winged animal,* πετεινόν *peteinon.*
Matt. 8. 20 the birds of the air..nests; but the Son
13. 32 that the birds of the air come and lodge
Luke 9. 58 birds of the air..nests; but the Son of
Rom. 1. 23 to birds, and fourfooted beasts, and
Jas. 3. 7 every kind of beasts, and of birds, and

8. *Feathered, winged animal,* πτηνόν *ptēnon.*
1 Co. 15. 39 one..flesh of men..another of birds

BIRD, ravenous —

A ravenous bird, (צִפּוֹר) עַיִט *ayit (tsippor).*
Isa. 46. 11 Calling a ravenous bird from the east
Eze. 39. 4 I will give thee unto the ravenous birds

BIR'-SHA, בִּרְשַׁע *thick, strong.*
A king of Gomorrah in the time of Abram, B.C. 1917.
Ge. 14. 2 made war with..B. king of Gomorrah

BIRTH —

1. *To bear, bring forth, yield,* יָלַד *yalad.*
Hos. 9. 11 glory shall fly away..from the birth

2. *Cutting out,* מְכוּרָה *mekurah.*
Eze. 16. 3 Thy birth and thy nativity (is) of the

3. *Breaking forth,* מַשְׁבֵּר *mashber.*
2 Ki. 19. 3 for the children are come to the birth
Isa. 37. 3 for the children are come to the birth

4. *Generations,* תּוֹלְדוֹת *toledoth.*
Exod 28. 10 their names..according to their birth

5. *Birth, a being born,* γενετή *genetē.*
John 9. 1 he saw a man which was blind..birth

6. *Birth, nativity,* γέννησις *gennēsis.*
Matt. 1. 18 the [birth] of Jesus Christ was on this wise
Luke 1. 14 and many shall rejoice at his [birth]

BIRTH, bring to the —

To break forth, שָׁבַר *shabar,* 5.
Isa. 66. 9 Shall I bring to the birth, and not cause

BIRTH, one's —

To be born, brought forth, יָלַד *yalad,* 2.
Eccl. 7. 1 the day of death than..of one's birth

BIRTH, untimely —

Fallen thing, נֵפֶל *nephel.*
Job 3. 16 Or as an hidden untimely birth I had not
Psa. 58. 8 the untimely birth of a woman..may
Eccl. 6. 3 an untimely birth (is) better than he

BIRTH DAY —

1. *Day of the birth,* יוֹם הֻלֶּדֶת *yom hulledeth.* [*yalad*].
Gen. 40. 20 third day..Pharaoh's birthday, that he

2. *Natal festivities,* γενέσια *genesia.*
Matt 14. 6 when Herod's birth day was kept, the
Mark 6. 21 Herod, on his birth day, made a supper to

BIRTH RIGHT —

1. *Status of a first born,* בְּכוֹרָה *bekorah.*
Gen. 25. 31 said, Sell me this day thy birthright
25. 32 what profit shall this birthright do to
25. 33 and he sold his birthright unto Jacob
25. 34 thus Esau despised (his) birthright
27. 36 said..he took away my birthright; and
43. 33 firstborn according to his birthright
1 Ch. 5. 1 his birthright was given unto the sons
5. 1 not to be reckoned after the birthright
5. 2 but the birthright (was) Joseph's

2. *Rights of a first born,* πρωτοτόκια *prōtotokia.*
Heb. 12. 16 who for..meat sold his birthright

BIR-ZA'-VITH, בִּרְזָוִת *olive well.*
A grandson of Beriah son of Asher.
1 Ch. 7. 31 Heber, and Malchiel..the father of B.

BISH'-LAM, בִּשְׁלָם *in peace.*
A commissioner of Artaxerxes in Canaan at the time of Zerubbabel's return from exile. He wrote against the rebuilders of the temple, B.C. 536.
Ezra 4. 7 in the days of A. wrote B., Mithredath

BISHOP —
Overseer, superintendent, ἐπίσκοπος *episkopos.*
Phil. 1. 1 Paul..to..the bishops and deacons
1 Ti. 3. 2 A bishop then must be blameless, the
Titus 1. 7 For a bishop must be blameless as the
1 Pe. 2. 25 are now returned unto the..Bishop of

BISHOP, office of a —
Oversight, ἐπισκοπή *episkopē.*
1 Ti. 3. 1 If a man desire the office of a bishop, he

BISHOPRIC —
Oversight, ἐπισκοπή *episkopē.*
Acts 1. 20 and, His bishopric let another take

BIT —
1. *Bridle, curb,* מֶתֶג *metheg.*
Psa. 32. 9 whose..be held in with bit and bridle
2. *The bit of a bridle, curb,* χαλινός *chalinos.*
Jas. 3. 3 Behold, we put bits in the horses' mouths

BITE, to —
1. *To bite,* נָשַׁךְ *nashak.*
Gen. 49. 17 Dan..a serpent..that biteth the horse
Num 21. 9 if a serpent had bitten any man, when
Prov. 23. 32 At the last it biteth like a serpent, and
Eccl. 10. 8 breaketh an hedge, a serpent shall bite
10. 11 serpent will bite without enchantment
Amos 5. 19 if a man did flee..and a serpent bit him
9. 3 I command the serpent, and he shall bite
Mic. 3. 5 my people err, that bite with their teeth
2. *To bite (violently),* נָשַׁךְ *nashak,* 3.
Num 21. 6 fiery serpents..they bit the people
Jer. 8. 17 and they shall bite you, saith the LORD
3. *To bite, irritate,* δάκνω *daknō.*
Gal. 5. 15 But if ye bite and devour one another

BITH'-IAH, בִּתְיָה *daughter of Jah, worshipper.*
Daughter of Pharaoh and wife of Mered, a descendant of Judah, about the time of the Exodus. Her name seems to imply her conversion, as Mered's other wife is called "the Jewess," B.C. 1400.
1 Ch. 4. 18 these (are) the sons of B...which Mered

BITH'-RON, הַבִּתְרוֹן *(the) broken or divided place.*
A district in the Arabah or Jordan valley on the E side. It was in Gad between Mahanaim and the Jordan.
2 Sa. 2. 29 Abner and his men..went through all B.

BI-THYN'-IA, Βιθυνία.
The original inhabitants of this ancient province were, according to the traditional account, expelled by some Thracian tribes, of which the Bithyni were the most numerous. The Megarians formed a colony at Astacus, B.C. 712, which became a flourishing city. Bithynia was incorporated with the Lydian empire by Croesus about B.C. 560. (Bithynia is included in the modern Anatolia.) In 541 B.C. it succumbs with Lydia to Persia; 431 or 436, Dydalsus, or Daedalsus, chief of the Bithynia, seizes Astacus, and founds the kingdom of Bithynia; 409, the Bithynians deliver to Alcibiades the property of the Chalcedonians intrusted to their safe keeping; 401, they vigorously oppose the retreat of the Ten Thousand: 333, they defeat Calas, one of the generals of Alexander the Great; 315, Zipoetes wars with Astacus and Chalcedon; 81, Lysimachus, the Thracian, sends an army to subdue Bithynia, but his troops are defeated and his generals slain; 278, Nicomedes, king of Bithynia, invites the Gauls into Asia, and assigns Galatia as their teritory, 264, Nicomedes I. founds Nicomedia; 228, Zielas having planned the massacre of the chiefs of Galatia, is detected and slain by them; 216, Prusias I. defeats the Gauls; 167, Prusias II. visits Rome; 156, war between the kings of Bithynia and Pergamus; 88, war between Nicomedes III., of Bithynia, and Mithridates, king of Pontus; 74, death of Nicomedes III., who bequeaths Bithynia to the Roman people. In A.D. 63. Bithynia and Pontus are united; 103, Pliny becomes governor; 104, complains of the Christians in his province; 260, ravaged by the Goths; 1074, seized by the Seljukian Turks; 1231, first settlement of the Tartars in Bithynia; 1298, the Ottomans found a new empire in Bithynia; 1339, Orchan conquers Nicomedia, and subdues the whole of Bithynia.
Acts 16. 7 they assayed to go into B.
1 Pe. 1. 1 to the strangers scattered throughout..B.

BITTEN, is —
To bite, נָשַׁךְ *nashak.*
Num 21. 8 every one that is bitten..shall live

BITTEN, hunger —
Hungry, רָעֵב *raeb.*
Job 18. 12 His strength shall be hunger bitten

BITTER —
1. *Bitter,* מַר *mar.*
Gen. 27. 34 he cried with a..exceeding bitter cry
Exod 15. 23 of the waters..for they (were) bitter
Num. 5. 18 shall have in his hand the bitter water
5. 19 be thou free from this bitter water
5. 23 shall blot (them) out with the bitter water
5. 24 cause the woman to drink the bitter
5. 27 shall enter into her, (and become) bitter
Esth. 4. 1 and cried with a loud and a bitter cry
Job 3. 20 misery, and life unto the bitter (in) soul
Psa. 64. 3 to shoot) their arrows, (even) bitter words
Prov. 5. 4 But her end is bitter as wormwood
27. 7 to the hungry soul every bitter thing is
Eccl. 7. 26 And I find more bitter than death the
Isa. 5. 20 put bitter for sweet, and sweet for bitter!
Jer. 2. 19 see that (it is) an evil..and bitter, that
4. 18 this (is) thy wickedness, because it is b
Eze. 27. 31 bitterness of heart (and) bitter wailing
Amos 8. 10 and the end thereof as a bitter day
Hab. 1. 6 the Chaldeans, (that) bitter and hasty
2. *To be bitter,* מָרָה *marah.*
2 Ki. 14. 26 the LORD saw..(that it was) very bitter
3. *Bitterness,* מְרִי *meri.*
Job 23. 2 Even to-day (is) my complaint bitter: my
4. *Very bitter,* מְרִירִי *meriri.*
Deut 32. 24 with burning heat, and with bitter
5. *Bitterness,* מְרֹרָה *merorah.*
Deut 32. 32 grapes of gall, their clusters (are) bitter
6. *Bitternesses,* מְרֹרִים *merorim.*
Exod 12. 8 with bitter (herbs) they shall eat it
Num. 9. 11 with unleavened bread and bitter (herbs)
7. *Pointed, sharp,* πικρός *pikros.*
Jas. 3. 11 at the same place sweet (water) and bitter
3. 14 if ye have bitter envying and strife

BITTER, to be —
1. *To be bitter,* מָרַר *marar.*
Isa. 24. 9 strong drink shall be bitter to them
2. *To make sharp, pointed,* πικραίνω *pikrainō.*
Col. 3. 19 love (your) wives, and be not bitter
Rev. 10. 10 as I had eaten it, my belly was bitter

BITTER, to make —
1. *To embitter,* מָרַר *marar,* 3.
Exod. 1. 14 they made their lives bitter with hard
2. *To make sharp, pointed,* πικραίνω *pikrainō.*
Rev. 8. 11 waters, because they were made bitter
10. 9 it shall make thy belly bitter, but it

BITTER, most —
Bitternesses, תַּמְרוּרִים *tamrurim.*
Jer. 6. 26 for) an only son, most bitter lamentation

BITTER things —
Bitterness, מְרֹרָה *merorah.*
Job 13. 26 For thou writest bitter things against me

BITTERLY, weep —
1. *To curse,* אָרַר *arar.*
Judg. 5. 23 curse ye bitterly the inhabitants thereof
2. *Bitter,* מַר *mar.*
Isa. 33. 7 ambassadors..shall weep bitterly
Eze. 27. 30 shall cry bitterly, and shall cast up
3. *To embitter with weeping,* מָרַר בְּבֶכִי [*marar*].
Isa. 22. 4 Look away from me; I will weep bitterly
4. *Pointedly, sharply,* πικρῶς *pikrōs.*
Matt 26. 75 And he went out, and wept bitterly
Luke 22. 62 And Peter went out, and wept bitterly

BITTERLY, to deal —
To embitter, make bitter, מָרַר *marar,* 5.
Ruth 1. 20 the Almighty hath dealt very bitterly

BITTERLY, most —
Bitternesses, תַּמְרוּרִים *tamrurim.*
Hos. 12. 14 Ephraim provoked..anger most bitterly

BITTERN —
Hedgehog, porcupine, קִפּוֹד *qippod.*
Isa. 14. 23 make it a possession for the bittern
34. 11 the cormorant and the bittern shall
Zeph. 2. 14 the bittern shall lodge in the upper

BITTERNESS —
1. *Bitterness,* מֶמֶר *memer.*
Prov. 17. 25 and bitterness to her that bare him
2. *Bitternesses,* מַמְרֹרִים *mammerorim.*
Job 9. 18 but filleth me with bitterness
3. *Bitter,* מַר *mar.*
1 Sa. 1. 10 And she (was) in bitterness of soul, and
15. 32 Surely the bitterness of death is passed
2 Sa. 2. 26 it will be bitterness in the latter end?
Job 7. 11 I will complain in the bitterness of my
10. 1 I will speak in the bitterness of my soul
21. 25 another dieth in the bitterness of his
Isa. 38. 15 all my years in the bitterness of my soul
Eze. 3. 14 I went in bitterness, in the heat of my
27. 31 they shall weep for thee with bitterness
4. *Bitterness,* מָרָה *marah.*
Prov. 14. 10 The heart knoweth his own bitterness
5. *Bitterness,* מְרִירוּת *meriruth.*
Eze. 21. 6 with bitterness sigh before their eyes
6. *Bitternesses,* מְרֹרִים *merorim.*
Lam. 3. 15 He hath filled me with bitterness, he
7. *Sharpness, bitterness,* πικρία *pikria.*
Acts 8. 23 that thou art in the gall of bitterness
Rom. 3. 14 mouth (is) full of cursing and bitterness
Eph. 4. 31 Let all bitterness, and wrath, and anger
Heb. 12. 15 lest any root of bitterness springing up

BITTERNESS, to be in —
1. *To be bitter,* מָרַר *marar.*
Lam. 1. 4 her virgins are afflicted..(is) in bitterness
2. *To make bitter,* מָרַר *marar,* 5.
Zech 12. 10, 10 shall be in bitterness for him, as one

BITTERNESS, to have —
To become bitter, מָרַר *marar,* 5.
Isa. 38. 17 Behold, for peace I had great bitterness

BIZ-JOTH'-JAH, בִּזְיוֹתְיָה *place of Jah's olives.*
A town in the S. of Judah, near Beer-sheba.
Josh. 15. 28 Hazar-shual, and Beer-sheba, and B.

BIZ'-THA, בִּזְתָא *eunuch.*
The second of the seven eunuchs of Ahasuerus, B.C. 519.
Esth. 1. 10 B...that served in the presence of..king

BLACK —
1. *Middle,* אִישׁוֹן *ishon.*
Prov. 7. 9 in the evening, in the black and dark
2. *Black, swarthy,* שָׁחוֹר *shachor.*
Lev. 13. 31 and..no black hair in it; then the priest
13. 37 (that) there is black hair grown up therein
Song 1. 5 I (am) black, but comely, O ye daughters
5. 11 his locks (are) bushy..black as a raven
Zech. 6. 2 in the second chariot black horses
6. 6 The black horses which (are) therein
3. *Very brown, blackish,* שְׁחַרְחֹרֶת *shecharchoreth.*
Song 1. 6 Look not upon me, because I (am) black
4. *Black,* μέλας *melas.*
Matt. 5. 36 thou canst not make one hair..black
Rev. 6. 5 I beheld, and lo a black horse: and he
6. 12 the sun became black as sackcloth of hair

BLACK, to be —
1. *To be dark,* חָשַׁךְ *chashak.*
Lam. 4. 8 Their visage is blacker than a coal; they
2. *To be contracted, dark,* כָּמַר *kamar,* 2.
Lam. 5. 10 Our skin was black like an oven because
3. *To be covered, dark,* קָדַר *qadar.*
Jer. 4. 28 For this shall..the heavens..be black
8. 21 I am black; astonishment hath taken
14. 2 they are black unto the ground; and the
4. *To become dark, covered,* קָדַר *qadar,* 7.
1 Ki. 18. 45 the heaven was black with clouds and
5. *To burn, be brown,* שָׁחַר *shachar.*
Job 30. 30 My skin is black upon me, and my bones

BLACK marble —
Glowing substance, סֹחֶרֶת *sochereth.*
Esth. 1. 6 upon a pavement of red..black marble

BLACKISH, to be —
To be covered, dark, קָדַר *qadar.*
Job 6. 16 Which are blackish by reason of the ice

BLACKNESS —
1. *Obscurations, bitternesses,* כִּמְרִירִים *kimririm.*
Job 3. 5 let the blackness of the day terrify it
2. *Redness, flame,* פָּארוּר *parur.*
Joel 2. 6 all faces shall gather blackness
Nah. 2. 10 the faces of them all gather blackness
3. *Darkness,* קַדְרוּת *qadruth.*
Isa. 50. 3 I clothe the heavens with blackness, and
4. *A thick cloud,* γνόφος *gnophos.*
Heb. 12. 18 that burned with fire, nor unto blackness
5. *Thick darkness,* ζόφος *zophos.*
Jude 13 to whom is reserved the blackness of

BLADE —
1. *Flaming weapon,* לַהַב *lahab.*
Judg. 3. 22 the haft also went in after the blade; and
3. 22 the fat closed upon the blade, so that he
2. *Blade, stalk,* χόρτος *chortos.*
Matt 13. 26 But when the blade was sprung up, and
Mark 4. 28 first the blade, then the ear after that

BLADE, shoulder —
Shoulder, שִׁכְמָה *shikmah.*
Job 31. 22 let mine arm fall from my shoulder blade

BLAINS —
A swelling, אֲבַעְבֻּעֹת *ababuoth.*
Exod. 9. 9, 10 a boil breaking forth (with) blains

BLAME, without —
Blameless, ἄμωμος *amōmos.*
Eph. 1. 4 that we should be holy and without blame

BLAME, to —
To blame, μωμάομαι *mōmaomai,* μωμέομαι.
2 Co. 8. 20 no man should blame us in this abund.

BLAME, to bear the —
To miss the mark, err, sin, חָטָא *chata.*
Gen. 43. 9 then let me bear the blame for ever
44. 32 I shall bear the blame to my father for

BLAMED, to be —
1. *To know (something) against one,* καταγινώσκω.
Gal. 2. 11 withstood him..because he was to be bl.
2. *To blame,* μωμάομαι *mōmaomai,* μωμέομαι.
2 Co. 6. 3 no offence..that the ministry be not bl.

BLAMELESS —
1.*Innocent, free,* נָקִי *naqi.*
Gen. 44. 10 my servant; and ye shall be blameless
Josh. 2. 17 We (will be) blameless of this thine oath
2.*Blameless,* ἄμεμπτος *amemptos.*
Luke 1. 6 walking in all..the ordinances..blameless
Phil. 2. 15 That ye may be blameless and harmless
3. 6 the righteousness..in the law, blameless
3.*Blamelessly,* ἀμέμπτως *amemptōs.*
1 Th. 5. 23 soul and body be preserved blameless
4.*Blameless,* ἀμώμητος *amōmētos.*
2 Pe. 3. 14 that ye may be found of him..blameless
5.*Causeless, guiltless,* ἀναίτιος *anaitios.*
Matt 12. 5 profane the sabbath, and are blameless?
6.*Not accused or called in,* ἀνέγκλητος *anegklētos.*
1 Co. 1. 8 blameless in the day of our Lord Jesus C.
1 Ti. 3. 10 the office of a deacon, being..blameless
Tit. 1. 6 If any be blameless, the husband of one
1. 7 a bishop must be blameless, as the
7.*Not laid hold on,* ἀνεπίληπτος *anepilēptos.*
1 Ti. 3. 2 A bishop then must be blameless, the
5. 7 give in charge, that they may be blameless

BLAMELESS, to be —
To be innocent, free, נָקָה *naqah,* 2.
Judg 15. 3 Now shall I be more blameless than the

BLASPHEME, to —
1.*To bless, declare blessed,* בָּרַךְ *barak,* 3.
1 Ki. 21. 10 Thou didst blaspheme God and the king
21. 13 Naboth did blaspheme God and the king
2.*To revile, cut into,* גָּדַף *gadaph,* 3.
2 Ki. 19. 6 which the servants..have blasphemed
19. 22 Whom hast thou reproached and blas.
Psa. 44. 16 him that reproacheth and blasphemeth
Isa. 37. 6 wherewith the servants..blasphemed
37. 23 Whom hast thou reproached and blas.
Eze. 20. 27 in this your fathers have blasphemed
3.*To cut into, expose,* חָרַף *charaph,* 3.
Isa. 65. 7 and blasphemed me upon the hills
4.*To pierce,* נָקַב *naqab.*
Lev. 24. 11 Israelitish woman's son blasphemed the
24. 16 that blasphemeth the name of the LORD
24. 16 when he blasphemeth the name..shall be
5.*To speak injuriously,* βλασφημέω *blasphēmeō.*
Matt. 9. 3 the scribes said..This (man) blasphemeth
Mark. 3. 28 wherewith soever they shall blaspheme
3. 29 he that shall blaspheme against the Holy
Luke 12. 10 unto him that [blasphemeth] against the
John 10. 36 Say ye of him..Thou blasphemest; because
Acts 13. 45 by Paul, contradicting and blaspheming
18. 6 they opposed themselves, and blasphemed
26. 11 punished..and compelled..to blaspheme
Rom. 2. 24 for the name of God is blasphemed among
1 Ti. 1. 20 that they may learn not to blaspheme
6. 1 that the name of God..be not blasphemed
Titus 2. 5 that the word of God be not blasphemed
Jas. 2. 7 Do not they blaspheme that worthy name
Rev. 13. 6 he opened his mouth..to blaspheme his
16. 9 men were scorched..and blasphemed the
16. 11 blasphemed the God of heaven because
16. 21 men blasphemed God because of the

BLASPHEME, (to give occasion) to —
To pierce, sting, נָאַץ *naats,* 3.
2 Sa. 12. 14 thou hast given..occasion..to blaspheme
Psa. 74. 10 shall the enemy blaspheme thy name for
74. 18 the foolish people have blasphemed thy

BLASPHEMED —
To pierce, sting, נָאַץ *naats,* 7.
Isa. 52. 5 my name..every day (is) blasphemed

BLASPHEMER —
1.*To speak injuriously,* βλασφημέω *blasphēmeō.*
Acts 19. 37 nor yet blasphemers of your goddess
2.*Injurious speaker,* βλάσφημος *blasphēmos.*
1 Ti. 1. 13 Who was before a blasphemer, and a
2 Ti. 3. 2 lovers of their own selves..blasphemers

BLASPHEMIES —
Piercings, נֶאָצוֹת *neatsoth.*
Eze. 35. 12 I have heard all thy blasphemies

BLASPHEMOUS —
Speaking injuriously, βλάσφημος *blasphēmos.*
Acts 6. 11 We..heard him speak blasphemous words
6. 13 This man..to speak [blasphemous] words

BLASPHEMOUSLY —
To speak injuriously, βλασφημέω *blasphēmeō.*
Luke 22. 65 many other things blasphemously spake

BLASPHEMY —
1.*Piercing,* נְאָצָה *neatsah.*
2 Ki. 19. 3 This day (is) a day of trouble..and blas.
Isa. 37. 3 This day (is) a day of trouble..and of bl.
2.*Injurious speaking,* βλασφημία *blasphēmia.*
Matt 12. 31 All manner of sin and blasphemy shall
12. 31 the blasphemy (against) the (Holy) Ghost
15. 19 out of the heart proceed..blasphemies
26. 65 now ye have heard his blasphemy
Mark 2. 7 Why doth this (man) thus speak [blasph.]?
3. 28 blasphemies..they shall blaspheme
7. 22 an evil eye, blasphemy, pride, foolishness
14. 64 Ye have heard the blasphemy: what think
Luke 5. 21 Who is this which speaketh blasphemies?
John 10. 33 we stone thee not; but for blasphemy
Col. 3. 8 anger, wrath, malice, blasphemy, filthy
Rev. 2. 9 the blasphemy of them, which say they
13. 1 upon his heads the name of blasphemy
13. 5 speaking great things and [blasphemies]
13. 6 he opened his mouth in blasphemy
17. 3 a woman..full of names of blasphemy

BLASPHEMY, to speak —
To speak injuriously, βλασφημέω *blasphēmeō.*
Matt 26. 65 He hath spoken blasphemy; what further

BLAST —
1.*Breath, blast,* נְשָׁמָה *neshamah.*
2 Sa. 22. 16 at the blast of the breath of his nostrils
Job 4. 9 By the blast of God they perish, and by
Psa. 18. 15 at the blast of the breath of thy nostrils
2.*Wind, spirit,* רוּחַ *ruach.*
Exod 15. 8 with the blast of thy nostrils the waters
2 Ki. 19. 7 Behold, I will send a blast upon him, and
Isa. 25. 4 when the blast of the terrible ones (is) as
37. 7 I will send a blast upon him, and he

BLASTED —
1.*Grain, young seed,* שְׁדֵמָה *shedemah.*
Isa. 37. 27 and..blasted before it be grown up
2.*To blight, blast,* שָׁדַף *shadaph.*
Gen. 41. 6 seven thin ears and blasted with the east
41. 23 seven ears..blasted with the east wind
41. 27 the seven empty ears, blasted with the
3.*Blighted, blasted,* שְׁדֵפָה *shedephah.*
2 Ki. 19. 26 and..blasted before it be grown up

BLASTING —
Blight, blasting, שִׁדָּפוֹן *shiddaphon.*
Deut 28. 22 with the sword, and with blasting, and
1 Ki. 8. 37 if there be pestilence, blasting, mildew
2 Ch. 6. 28 if there be pestilence, if there be blasting
Amos 4. 9 I have smitten you with blasting and
Hag. 2. 17 I smote you with blasting and with

BLAS'-TUS, Βλάστος *a bud.*
A chamberlain of Herod Agrippa I., A.D. 35.
Acts 12. 20 having made B. the king's chamberlain

BLAZE abroad, to —
To speak throughout, διαφημίζω *diaphēmizō.*
Mark 1. 45 he went out..to blaze abroad the matter

BLEATING —
Voice, sound, קוֹל *qol.*
1 Sa. 15. 14 What..then this bleating of the sheep

BLEATINGS —
Shriekings, pipings, שְׁרִיקוֹת *sheriqoth.*
Judg. 5. 16 Why abodest thou..to hear the bleatings

BLEMISH —
1.*Spot,* מאוּם *mum.*
Dan. 1. 4 Children in whom (was) no blemish, but
2.*Spot,* מוּם *mum.*
Lev. 21. 17 Whosoever (he be)..that hath..blemish
21. 18 whatsoever man..that hath a blemish
21. 21 that hath a blemish..he hath a blemish
21. 23 nor come nigh..because he hath a blemish
22. 20 whatsoever hath a blemish..shall ye
22. 21 perfect..there shall be no blemish
22. 25 their corruption (is) in them..blemishes
24. 19 if a man cause a blemish in his neighbour
24. 20 as he hath caused a blemish in a man, so
Num 19. 2 heifer without spot, wherein..no blemish
Deut 15. 21 if there be..blemish therein..ill blemish
17. 1 wherein is blemish, (or) any evil favoured.
2 Sa. 14. 25 from the sole of his foot..no blemish in
3.*White spots,* תְּבַלֻּל *teballul.*
Lev. 21. 20 that hath a blemish in his eye, or be
4.*Spot, blemish,* μῶμος *mōmos.*
2 Pe. 2. 13 Spots..and blemishes, sporting themsel.

BLEMISH, without —
1.*Perfect, complete,* תָּמִים *tamim.*
Exod 12. 5 Your lamb shall be without blemish, a
29. 1 Take one young bullock..without blemish
Lev. 1. 3 let him offer a male without blemish
1. 10 he shall bring it a male without blemish
3. 1, 6 he shall offer it without blemish
4. 3 bring..a young bullock without blemish
4. 23 kid of the goats, a male without blemish
4. 28 kid of the goats, a female without blemish
4. 32 he shall bring it a female without blemish
5. 15, 18 shall bring..a ram without blemish
6. 6 he shall bring..a ram without blemish
9. 2 Take thee a young calf..without blemish
9. 3 a calf and a lamb..without blemish
14. 10 shall take two he lambs without blemish
14. 10 lamb of the first year without blemish
22. 19 at your own will a male without blemish
23. 12 offer..an he lamb without blemish
23. 18 offer..seven lambs without blemish
Num. 6. 14 lamb of the first year without blemish
6. 14 ram without blemish..without blemish
28. 19, 31 they shall be..you without blemish
29. 2 seven lambs of the first..without blemish
29. 8 they shall be unto you without blemish
29. 13 lambs..they shall be without blemish
29. 20, 23, 29, 32, 36 first year, without blemish
Eze. 43. 22 thou shalt offer a kid..without blemish
43. 23 offer a young bullock without blemish
43. 23, 25 a ram out of the flock without blemish
45. 18 take a young bullock without blemish
Eze. 45. 23 seven bullocks..rams without blemish
46. 4 lambs without blemish..ram without bl.
46. 6 without blemish..be without blemish
46. 13 lamb of the first year without blemish
2.*Spotless, blameless,* ἄμωμος *amōmos.*
Eph. 5. 27 should be holy and without blemish
1 Pe. 1. 19 a lamb without blemish and without

BLESS, to —
1.*To declare happy,* אָשַׁר *ashar,* 3.
Job 29. 11 When the ear heard (me),..it blessed me
Song 6. 9 The daughters saw her and blessed her
2.*To declare blessed,* בָּרַךְ *barak,* 3.
Gen. 1. 22 God blessed them, saying, Be fruitful
1. 28 God blessed them, and God said unto
2. 3 God blessed the seventh day, and
5. 2 blessed them, and called their name
9. 1 God blessed Noah and his sons, and said
12. 2 I will bless thee, and make thy name
12. 3 I will bless them that bless thee, and
14. 19 And he blessed him, and said
17. 16 I will bless her..yea, I will bless her
17. 20 I have blessed him, and will make him
22. 17 That in blessing I will bless thee, and in
24. 1 the LORD had blessed Abraham in all
24. 35 the LORD hath blessed my master greatly
24. 48 blessed the LORD God of my master Abr.
24. 60 they blessed Rebekah, and said unto her
25. 11 after the death of A., that God blessed
26. 3 I will be with thee, and will bless thee
26. 12 Isaac sowed..and the LORD blessed him
26. 24 fear not, for I (am) with thee, and..bless
27. 4 that my soul may bless thee before I die
27. 7 that I may eat, and bless thee before the
27. 10 that he may bless thee before his death
27. 19 eat of my venison, that thy soul..bless
27. 23 And he discerned him not..so he blessed
27. 25 I will eat..that my soul may bless thee
27. 27 blessed him..which the LORD..blessed
27. 29 that curseth thee..that blesseth thee
27. 30 Isaac had made an end of blessing Jacob
27. 31 eat of..venison, that thy soul may bless
27. 33 before thou camest, and have blessed
27. 34, 38 Bless me, (even) me also, O my father!
27. 41 blessing wherewith his father blessed
28. 1 blessed him, and charged him, and said
28. 3 God Almighty bless thee, and make thee
28. 6 When Esau saw that Isaac had blessed
30. 27 learned..that the LORD hath blessed me
30. 30 the LORD hath blessed thee since my
31. 55 his sons and his daughters, and blessed
32. 26 I will not let thee go, except thou bless
32. 29 And he blessed him there
35. 9 God appeared unto Jacob..and blessed
39. 5 the LORD blessed the Egyptian's house
47. 7 brought in Jacob..and Jacob blessed
47. 10 Jacob blessed Pharaoh, and went out
48. 3 God Almighty appeared..and blessed me
48. 9 Bring them..unto me, and I will bless
48. 15 he blessed Joseph, and said, God, before
48. 16 The Angel which redeemed me..bless
48. 20 blessed them..In thee shall Israel bless
49. 25 the Almighty who shall bless thee with
49. 28 their father spake unto them..blessed
Exod 12. 32 as ye have said, and be gone; and bless
20. 11 wherefore the LORD blessed the sabbath
20. 24 I will come unto thee, and I will bless
23. 25 he shall bless thy bread, and thy water
39. 43 so had they done it: and Moses blessed
Lev. 9. 22 Aaron lifted up his hand..and blessed
9. 23 Aaron..came out, and blessed the people
Num. 6. 23 On this wise ye shall bless the children
6. 24 The LORD bless thee, and keep thee
6. 27 children of Israel; and I will bless them
22. 6 I wot that he whom thou blessest
23. 11 behold, thou hast blessed (them) altog.
23. 20 I have received..to bless: and..blessed
23. 25 Neither curse them at all, nor bless them
24. 1 saw that it pleased the Lord to bless Isr
24. 9 he that blesseth thee, and cursed (is) he
24. 10 thou hast altogether blessed..these three
Deut. 1. 11 the LORD..bless you, as he hath promised
2. 7 For the LORD thy God hath blessed thee
7. 13 he will..bless thee..he will also bless
8. 10 thou shalt bless the LORD thy God for
10. 8 and to bless in his name, unto this day
12. 7 wherein the LORD thy God hath blessed
14. 24 when the LORD thy God hath blessed
14. 29 that the LORD thy God may bless thee in
15. 4 for the LORD shall greatly bless thee in
15. 6 the LORD thy God blesseth thee, as he
15. 10 the LORD thy God shall bless thee in all
15. 14 the LORD thy God hath blessed thee thou
15. 18 the LORD thy God shall bless thee in all
16. 10 as the LORD thy God hath blessed thee
16. 15 the LORD thy God shall bless thee in all
21. 5 chosen..to bless in the name of the LORD
23. 20 that the LORD thy God may bless thee in
24. 13 sleep in his own raiment, and bless thee
24. 19 that the LORD thy God may bless thee in
26. 15 Look down..and bless thy people Israel
27. 12 stand upon mount Gerizim to bless the
28. 8 he shall bless thee in the land which the
28. 12 and to bless all the work of thine hand
30. 16 the LORD thy God shall bless thee in the
33. 1 wherewith Moses..blessed the children
33. 11 Bless, LORD, his substance, and accept
Josh. 8. 33 that they should bless the people of Isr.
14. 13 Joshua blessed him, and gave unto Caleb
17. 14 forasmuch as the LORD hath blessed me
22. 6 Joshua blessed them, and sent them

Josh 22. 7 when Joshua sent them away..he blessed
22. 33 the children of Israel blessed God, and
24. 10 therefore he blessed you still: so I
Judg. 5. 9 among the people. Bless ye the LORD
13. 24 the child grew, and the LORD blessed
Ruth 2. 4 they answered him, The LORD bless thee
1 Sa. 2. 20 Eli blessed Elkanah and his wife, and
9. 13 because he doth bless the sacrifice
2 Sa. 6. 11 LORD blessed Obed-edom, and all his
6. 12 LORD hath blessed..house of Obed-edom
6. 18 he blessed the people in the name of the
6. 20 David returned to bless his household
7. 29 let it please thee to bless the house of thy
8. 10 to salute him, and to bless him, because
13. 25 howbeit he would not go, but blessed him
19. 39 the king kissed Barzillai, and blessed
21. 3 that ye may bless the inheritance of the
1 Ki. 1. 47 the king's servants came to bless our lord
8. 14, 55 blessed all the congregation of Israel
8. 66 they blessed the king, and went unto
1 Ch. 4. 10 Oh that thou wouldest bless me indeed
13. 14 the LORD blessed the house of Obed-edom
16. 2 blessed the people in the name of the
17. 27 to bless the house..for thou blessest
23. 13 separated..to bless in his name for ever
26. 5 Peulthai the eighth: for God blessed him
29. 10 David blessed the LORD before all the
29. 20 bless the LORD .. congregation blessed
2 Ch. 6. 3 and blessed the whole congregation of
20. 26 for there they blessed the LORD: therefore
30. 27 priests the Levites arose and blessed the
31. 8 they blessed the LORD, and his people
31. 10 for the LORD hath blessed his people; and
Neh. 8. 6 And Ezra blessed the LORD, the great
9. 5 Stand up..bless the LORD your God for
9. 5 and blessed be thy glorious name
11. 2 And the people blessed all the men, that
Job 1. 10 Thou hast blessed the work of his hands
31. 20 If his loins have not blessed me, and (if)
42. 12 So the LORD blessed the latter end of Job
Psa. 5. 12 For thou, LORD, wilt bless the righteous
10. 3 blesseth the covetous, (whom) the LORD
16. 7 I will bless the LORD, who hath given me
26. 12 in the congregations will I bless the LORD
28. 9 Save thy people, and bless thine inherit.
29. 11 the LORD will bless his people with peace
34. 1 I will bless the LORD at all times: his
45. 2 therefore God hath blessed thee for ever
49. 18 Though while he lived he blessed his soul
62. 4 they bless with their mouth, but they
63. 4 Thus will I bless thee while I live: I will
65. 10 thou blessest the springing thereof
66. 8 O bless our God, ye people, and make the
67. 1 God be merciful unto us, and bless us
67. 6 God..our own God, shall bless us
67. 7 God shall bless us; and all the ends of
68. 26 Bless ye God in the congregations..the
96. 2 Sing unto the LORD, bless his name; shew
100. 4 be thankful unto him, (and) bless his
103. 1, 2, 22 Bless the LORD, O my soul
103. 20 Bless the LORD, ye his angels, that excel
103. 21 Bless ye the LORD, all (ye) his hosts; (ye)
103. 22 Bless the LORD, all his works in all places
104. 1 Bless the LORD, O my soul. O LORD my
104. 35 Bless thou the LORD, O my soul
107. 38 He blesseth them also, so that they are
109. 28 Let them curse, but bless thou: when
115. 12 he will bless (us); he will bless..he will
115. 13 He will bless them that fear the LORD
115. 18 we will bless the LORD from this time
118. 26 we have blessed you out of the house of
128. 5 The LORD shall bless thee out of Zion
129. 8 we bless you in the name of the LORD
132. 15 I will abundantly bless her provision
134. 1 bless ye the LORD, all (ye) servants of the
134. 2 Lift up your hands..and bless the LORD
134. 3 The LORD..bless thee out of Zion
135. 19, 20 bless the LORD..bless the LORD
145. 1 I will bless thy name for ever and ever
145. 2 Every day will I bless thee; and I will
145. 10 and thy saints shall bless thee
145. 21 let all flesh bless his holy name for ever
147. 13 he hath blessed thy children within thee
Prov. 3. 33 but he blesseth the habitation of the just
27. 14 He that blesseth his friend with a loud
30. 11 and doth not bless their mother
Isa. 19. 25 Whom the LORD of hosts shall bless
51. 2 I called him alone, and blessed him
61. 9 the seed (which) the LORD hath blessed
66. 3 he that burneth..(as if) he blessed an idol
Jer. 31. 23 The LORD bless thee, O habitation of
Hag. 2. 19 brought forth: from this day will I bless

3. *To declare blessed,* בָּרַךְ *berak,* 3.
Dan. 2. 19 Then Daniel blessed the God of heaven
2. 20 Blessed be the name of God for ever and
4. 34 I blessed the most high, and I praised

4. *To speak well of,* εὐλογέω *eulogeō.*
Matt. 5. 44 Love your enemies, [bless] them that
14. 19 looking up to heaven, he blessed, and
26. 26 Jesus took bread, and [blessed] (it), and
Mark 6. 41 blessed, and brake the loaves, and gave
8. 7 he blessed, and commanded to set them
10. 16 put (his) hands upon them, and [blessed]
14. 22 Jesus took bread, and blessed, and brake
Luke 2. 28 Then took he him up..and blessed God
2. 34 Simeon blessed them, and said unto Mary
6. 28 Bless them that curse you, and pray for
9. 16 looking up to heaven, he blessed them
24. 30 took bread, and blessed (it), and brake
24. 50 he lifted up his hands, and blessed them
24. 51 it came to pass, while he blessed them
Luke 24. 53 [continually..praising and blessing God]
Acts 3. 26 his Son Jesus, sent him to bless you, in
Rom 12. 14 Bless them which persecute you: bless
1 Co. 4. 12 being reviled, we bless; being persecuted
10. 16 The cup..which we bless, is it not the
14. 16 Else, when thou shalt bless with the spirit
Gal. 3. 9 they which be of faith are blessed with
Eph. 1. 3 Father of our Lord..who hath blessed us
Heb. 6. 14 blessing I will bless thee, and multiplying
7. 1 met Abraham returning..and blessed
7. 6 and blessed him that had the promises
7. 7 the less is blessed of the better
11. 20 By faith Isaac blessed Jacob and Esau
11. 21 By faith Jacob..blessed both the sons of
Jas. 3. 9 Therewith bless we God, even the Father
1 Pe. 3. 9 but contrariwise blessing; knowing that

BLESS self, to —
To bless oneself, think oneself blessed, בָּרַךְ *barak,* 7.
Deut 29. 19 that he bless himself in his heart, saying
Isa. 65. 16 who blesseth himself..shall bless himself
Jer. 4. 2 the nations shall bless themselves in him

BLESSED, (most) —
1. *Happy, very happy,* אַשְׁרֵי *ashere.*
Psa. 1. 1 Blessed (is) the man that walketh not in
2. 12 Blessed (are) all they that put their trust
32. 1 Blessed (is he whose) transgression (is)
32. 2 Blessed (is) the man unto whom the LORD
33. 12 Blessed (is) the nation whose God (is) the
34. 8 blessed (is) the man (that) trusteth in him
40. 4 Blessed (is) that man that maketh the
41. 1 Blessed (is) he that considereth the poor
65. 4 Blessed (is the man whom) thou choosest
84. 4 Blessed (are) they that dwell in thy house
84. 5 Blessed (is) the man whose strength (is)
84. 12 blessed (is) the man that trusteth in thee
89. 15 Blessed (is) the people that know the
94. 12 Blessed (is) the man whom thou chasten.
106. 3 Blessed (are) they that keep judgment
112. 1 Blessed (is) the man (that) feareth the
119. 1 Blessed (are) the undefiled in the way
119. 2 Blessed (are) they that keep his testimon.
128. 1 Blessed (is) every one that feareth the
Prov. 8. 32 blessed (are they that) keep my ways
8. 34 Blessed (is) the man that heareth me
20. 7 The just..his children (are) blessed after
Eccl. 10. 17 Blessed (art) thou, O land, when thy king
Isa. 30. 18 blessed (are) all they that wait for him
32. 20 Blessed (are) ye that sow beside all waters
56. 2 Blessed (is) the man (that) doeth this
Dan. 12. 12 Blessed (is) he that waiteth, and cometh

2. *To bless,* בָּרַךְ *barak.*
Gen. 9. 26 Blessed (be) the LORD God of Shem; and
14. 19 Blessed (be) Abram of the most high God
14. 20 blessed (be) the most high God, which
24. 27 Blessed (be) the LORD God of my master
24. 31 Come in, thou blessed of the LORD
26. 29 thou (art) now the blessed of the LORD
27. 29 and blessed (be) he that blesseth thee
27. 33 I have eaten..yea..he shall be blessed
Exod 18. 10 Jethro said, Blessed (be) the LORD, who
Num 22. 12 thou shalt not curse..they (are) blessed
24. 9 Blessed (is) he that..and cursed (is) the
Deut. 7. 14 Thou shalt be blessed above all people
28. 3 Blessed (shalt) thou (be)..blessed (shalt)
28. 4 Blessed (shall be) the fruit of thy body
28. 5 Blessed (shall) be thy basket and thy
28. 6 Blessed (shalt) thou (be)..blessed (shalt)
33. 20 Blessed (be) he that enlargeth Gad: he
33. 24 (Let) Asher (be) blessed with children; let
Judg 17. 2 said, Blessed (be thou) of the LORD, my
Ruth 2. 19 blessed be he that did take knowledge of
2. 20 Blessed (be) he of the LORD, who hath
3. 10 Blessed (be) thou of the LORD, my
4. 14 the women said..Blessed (be) the LORD
1 Sa. 15. 13 Saul said unto him, Blessed (be) thou of
23. 21 Saul said, Blessed (be) ye of the LORD
25. 32 Blessed (be) the LORD God of Israel
25. 33 blessed (be) thy advice, and blessed (be)
25. 39 Blessed (be) the LORD, that hath pleaded
26. 25 Blessed (be) thou, my son David: thou
2 Sa. 2. 5 Blessed (be) ye of the LORD, that ye have
18. 28 Blessed (be) the LORD thy God, which
22. 47 The LORD liveth; and blessed (be) my
1 Ki. 1. 48 Blessed (be) the LORD God of Israel
2. 45 king Solomon (shall be) blessed, and the
5. 7 rejoiced greatly, and said, Blessed (be)
8. 15 Blessed (be) the LORD God of Israel
8. 56 Blessed (be) the LORD, that hath given
10. 9 Blessed be the LORD thy God, which
1 Ch. 16. 36 Blessed (be) the LORD God of Israel for
29. 10 Blessed (be) thou, LORD God of Israel
2 Ch. 2. 12 Blessed (be) the Lord God of Israel, that
6. 4 Blessed (be) the Lord God of Israel, who
9. 8 Blessed be the LORD thy God, which
Ezra 7. 27 Blessed (be) the LORD God of our fathers
Psa. 18. 46 The LORD liveth; and blessed (be) my
28. 6 Blessed (be) the LORD, because he hath
31. 21 Blessed (be) the LORD: for he hath
41. 13 Blessed (be) the LORD God of Israel from
66. 20 Blessed (be) God, which hath not turned
68. 19 Blessed (be) the LORD, (who) daily loadeth
68. 35 unto (his) people. Blessed (be) God
72. 18 Blessed (be) the LORD God, the God
72. 19 blessed (be) his glorious name for ever
89. 52 Blessed (be) the LORD for evermore
106. 48 Blessed (be) the LORD God of Israel from
115. 15 Ye (are) blessed of the LORD which made
118. 26 Blessed (be) he that cometh in the name
119. 12 Blessed (art) thou, O LORD: teach me
124. 6 Blessed (be) the LORD, who hath not
Psa. 135. 21 Blessed be the LORD out of Zion, which
144. 1 Blessed (be) the LORD my strength, which
Prov. 5. 18 Let thy fountain be blessed: and rejoice
Isa. 19. 25 Blessed (be) Egypt my people, and Assyr.
65. 23 they (are)..of the blessed of the LORD
Jer. 17. 7 Blessed (is) the man that trusteth in the
20. 14 was born: let not the day..be blessed
Eze. 3. 12 Blessed (be) the glory of the LORD from
Zech 11. 5 they that sell them say, Blessed (be) the

3. *To bless,* בְּרַךְ *berak.*
Dan. 3. 28 Blessed (be) the God of Shadrach

4. *To speak well of,* εὐλογέω *eulogeō.*
Matt 21. 9 Blessed (is) he that cometh in the name
23. 39 Blessed (is) he that cometh in the name
25. 34 Come, ye blessed of my Father, inherit
Mark 11. 9 Blessed (is) he that cometh in the name of
11. 10 Blessed (be) the kingdom of our father
Luke 1. 28 with thee: [blessed (art) thou among]
1. 42 women, and blessed is the fruit of thy
13. 35 Blessed (is) he that cometh in the name
19. 38 Blessed (be) the King that cometh in the
John 12. 13 Blessed (is)..King of Israel that cometh

5. *Well-spoken of,* εὐλογητός *eulogētos.*
Mark 14. 61 Art thou the Christ..Son of the Blessed?
Luke 1. 68 Blessed (be) the Lord God of Israel; for
Rom. 1. 25 than the Creator, who is blessed for ever
9. 5 who is over all, God blessed for ever
2 Co. 1. 3 Blessed (be) God, even the Father of our
11. 31 The God and Father..which is blessed
Eph. 1. 3 Blessed (be) the God and Father of our
1 Pe. 1. 3 Blessed (be) the God and Father of our

6. *Happy,* μακάριος *makarios.*
Matt. 5. 3 Blessed (are) the poor in spirit: for
5. 4 Blessed (are) they that mourn; for they
5. 5 Blessed (are) the meek: for they shall
5. 6 Blessed (are) they which do hunger and
5. 7 Blessed (are) the merciful: for they shall
5. 8 Blessed (are) the pure in heart: for they
5. 9 Blessed (are) the peacemakers: for they
5. 10 Blessed (are) they which are persecuted
5. 11 Blessed are ye when (men) shall revile
11. 6 blessed is (he), whosoever shall not be
13. 16 blessed (are) your eyes, for they see; and
16. 17 Blessed art thou, Simon Bar-jona: for
24. 46 Blessed (is) that servant whom his lord
Luke 1. 45 And blessed (is) she that believed: for
6. 20 Blessed (be ye) poor: for yours is the
6. 21 Blessed (are ye) that hunger now: for ye
6. 21 Blessed (are ye) that weep now: for ye
6. 22 Blessed are ye when men shall hate you
7. 23 blessed is (he), whosoever shall not be
10. 23 Blessed (are) the eyes which see the
11. 27 Blessed (is) the womb that bare thee, and
11. 28 blessed (are) they that hear the word of
12. 37 Blessed (are) those servants, whom the
12. 38 and find (them) so, blessed are those
12. 43 Blessed (is) that servant, whom his lord
14. 14 thou shalt be blessed; for they cannot
14. 15 Blessed (is) he that shall eat bread in the
23. 29 Blessed (are) the barren, and the wombs
John 20. 29 blessed (are) they that have not seen
Acts 20. 35 It is more blessed to give than to receive
Rom. 4. 7 Blessed (are) they whose iniquities are
4. 8 Blessed (is) the man to whom the Lord
1 Ti. 1. 11 the glorious gospel of the blessed God
6. 15 (who is) the blessed and only Potentate
Titus 2. 13 Looking for that blessed hope, and the
Jas. 1. 12 Blessed (is) the man that endureth
1. 25 this man shall be blessed in his deed
Rev. 1. 3 Blessed (is) he that readeth, and they
14. 13 Blessed (are) the dead which die in the
16. 15 Blessed (is) he that watcheth, and keepeth
19. 9 Blessed (are) they which are called unto
20. 6 Blessed and holy (is) he that hath part in
22. 7 blessed (is) he that keepeth the sayings
22. 14 Blessed (are) they that do his command.

7. *For a blessing,* לִבְרָכָה *li-berakah.*
Psa. 21. 6 hast made him most blessed for ever
37. 26 and lendeth; and his seed (is) blessed
Prov 10. 7 memory of the just (is) blessed: but the

BLESSED, to be —
1. *To be happy,* אָשַׁר *ashar,* 4.
Psa. 41. 2 he shall be blessed upon the earth: and

2. *To be blessed,* בָּרַךְ *barak,* 2.
Gen. 12. 3 in thee shall all families..be blessed
18. 18 nations of the earth shall be blessed in
28. 14 in thy seed shall all..families..be blessed

3. *To be (declared) blessed,* בָּרַךְ *barak,* 4.
Num 22. 6 I wot..he whom thou blessest (is) blessed
Deut 33. 13 Blessed of the LORD (be) his land, for
Judg 5. 24 Blessed above women..blessed shall she be
2 Sa. 7. 29 let the house of thy servant be blessed
1 Ch. 17. 27 LORD, and (it shall be) blessed for ever
Job 1. 21 blessed be the name of the LORD
Psa. 37. 22 blessed of him shall inherit the earth
112. 2 generation of the upright shall be blessed
113. 2 Blessed be the name of the LORD from
128. 4 thus shall the man be blessed that feareth
Prov. 20. 21 but the end thereof shall not be blessed
22. 9 that hath a bountiful eye shall be blessed

4. *To bless oneself,* בָּרַךְ *barak,* 7.
Gen. 22. 18 in thy seed shall all..be blessed
26. 4 in thy seed shall all..be blessed
Psa. 72. 17 shall be blessed in him: all nations

5. *Be well spoken of by,* ἐνευλογέομαι *eneulogeomai.*
Acts 3. 25 shall all the kindreds..be blessed
Gal. 3. 8 In thee shall all nations be blessed

BLESSED, to call —

1. *To declare happy,* אָשַׁר *ashar,* 3.

Gen. 30. 13 for the daughters will call me blessed
Psa. 72. 17 all nations shall call him blessed
Prov. 31. 28 children arise up, and call her blessed
Mal. 3. 12 all nations shall call you blessed : for ye

2. *To make or declare happy,* μακαρίζω *makarizō.*

Luke 1. 48 all generations shall call me blessed

BLESSEDNESS —

Happiness, μακαρισμός *makarismos.*

Rom. 4. 6 David also describeth the blessedness of
4. 9 (Cometh) this blessedness then upon the
Gal. 4. 15 Where is then the blessedness ye spake

BLESSING —

1. *Blessing,* בְּרָכָה *berakah.*

Gen. 12. 2 name great; and thou shalt be a blessing
27. 12 bring a curse upon me, and not a blessing
27. 35 brother..hath taken away thy blessing
27. 36 now he hath taken away my blessing
27. 36 Hast thou not reserved a blessing for me?
27. 38 Hast thou but one blessing, my father?
27. 41 Esau hated Jacob because of the blessing
28. 4 give thee the blessing of Abraham, to
33. 11 Take, I pray thee, my blessing that is
39. 5 the blessing of the LORD was upon all
49. 25 shall bless thee with blessings of heaven
49. 25 blessings of the deep that lieth under
49. 25 blessings of the breasts, and of the womb
49. 26 blessings of thy father have prevailed
49. 26 above the blessings of my progenitors
49. 28 every one according to his blessing he
Exod 32. 29 that he may bestow upon you a blessing
Lev. 25. 21 I will command my blessing upon you in
Deut 11. 26 I set before you this day a blessing and a
11. 27 A blessing, if ye obey the commandments
11. 29 thou shalt put the blessing upon mount
12. 15 according to the blessing of the LORD thy
16. 17 according to the blessing of the LORD thy
23. 5 thy God turned the curse into a blessing
28. 2 all these blessings shall come on thee
28. 8 LORD shall command the blessing upon
30. 1 come upon thee, the blessing and the
30. 19 set before you..blessing and cursing
33. 1 And this (is) the blessing, wherewith
33. 23 and full with the blessing of the LORD
Josh. 8. 34 all the words of the law, the blessings
15. 19 Who answered, Give me a blessing; for
Judg. 1. 15 she said unto him, Give me a blessing
1 Sa. 25. 27 this blessing..let it even be given unto
2 Sa. 7. 29 with thy blessing let the house of thy
2 Ki. 5. 15 therefore..take a blessing of thy servant
Neh. 9. 5 is exalted above all blessing and praise
13. 2 our God turned the curse into a blessing
Job 29. 13 blessing of him that was ready to perish
Psa. 3. 8 the LORD: thy blessing (is) upon thy
21. 3 thou preventest him with the blessings
24. 5 He shall receive the blessing from the
109. 17 as he delighted not in blessing, so let it
129. 8 The blessing of the LORD (be) upon you
133. 3 there the LORD commanded the blessing
Prov. 10. 6 Blessings (are) upon the head of the just
10. 22 The blessing of the LORD, it maketh rich
11. 11 By the blessing of the upright the city
11. 26 blessing (shall be) upon the head of him
24. 25 and a good blessing shall come upon
28. 20 faithful..shall abound with blessings
Isa. 19. 24 a blessing in the midst of the land
44. 3 my blessing upon thine offspring
65. 8 Destroy it not; for a blessing (is) in it: so
Eze. 34. 26 a blessing..shall be showers of blessing
44. 30 that he may cause the blessing to rest in
Joel 2. 14 repent, and leave a blessing behind him
Zech. 8. 13 I save you, and ye shall be a blessing
Mal. 2. 2 I will curse your blessings; yea, I have
3. 10 heaven, and pour you out a blessing

2. *Good speech or utterance,* εὐλογία *eulogia.*

Rom 15. 29 I..come in the fulness of the blessing
1 Co. 10. 16 The cup of blessing which we bless, is it
Gal. 3. 14 That the blessing of Abraham might
Eph. 1. 3 all spiritual blessings in heavenly
Heb. 6. 7 the earth..receiveth blessing from God
12. 17 he would have inherited the blessing
Jas. 3. 10 Out of the same..proceedeth blessing
1 Pe. 3. 9 that ye should inherit a blessing
Rev. 5. 12 receive..honour, and glory, and blessing
5. 13 that are in them, heard I saying, Blessing
7. 12 Amen: Blessing, and glory, and wisdom

BLIND —

1. *Closed, contracted,* עִוֵּר *ivver.*

Exod. 4. 11 who maketh the dumb..or the blind?
Lev. 19. 14 put a stumbling block before the blind
21. 18 a blind man, or a lame, or he that hath
Deut. 15. 21 lame, or blind, (or have) any ill blemish
27. 18 Cursed (be) he that maketh the blind to
28. 29 as the blind gropeth in darkness, and
2 Sa. 5. 6 Except thou take away the blind and
5. 8 smiteth the Jebusites..and the blind
5. 8 The blind and the lame shall not come
Job 29. 15 I was eyes to the blind, and feet (was) I
Psa. 146. 8 The LORD openeth (the eyes of) the blind
Isa. 29. 18 the eyes of the blind shall see out of
35. 5 the eyes of the blind shall be opened, and
42. 7 To open the blind eyes, to bring out the
42. 16 I will bring the blind by a way (that) they
42. 18 ye deaf..look, ye blind, that ye may see
42. 19 Who (is) blind, but my servant? or deaf
42. 19 who (is) blind as..perfect, and blind as
56. 10 His watchmen (are) blind: they are all
Isa. 59. 10 We grope for the wall like the blind, and
Jer. 31. 8 with them the blind and the lame, the
Lam. 4. 14 They have wandered (as) blind (men) in
Mal. 1. 8 if ye offer the blind for sacrifice..not evil

2. *Blindness,* עַוֶּרֶת *avvereth.*

Lev. 22. 22 Blind, or broken, or maimed, or having a

3. *Blind,* τυφλός *tuphlos.*

Matt 11. 5 The blind receive their sight, and the
12. 22 one possessed with a devil, blind and
12. 22 the [blind] and dumb both spake and saw
15. 14 they be blind leaders of the blind. And
15. 14 if the blind lead the blind, both shall fall
15. 30 having with them..lame, blind, dumb
15. 31 the lame to walk, and the blind to see
21. 14 the blind and the lame came to him in
23. 16 Woe unto you, (ye) blind guides, which
23. 17 fools, and blind! for whether is greater
23. 19 fools, and blind! for whether (is) greater
23. 24 blind guides, which strain at a gnat, and
23. 26 blind Pharisee, cleanse first that..within
Mark 10. 46 blind Bartimeus..sat by the highway
Luke 4. 18 recovering of sight to the blind, to set at
6. 39 Can the blind lead the blind? shall they
7. 21 and unto many..blind he gave sight
7. 22 how that the blind see, the lame walk
14. 13 call the poor, the maimed..the blind
14. 21 bring in hither the poor..and the blind
John 5. 3 In these lay a great multitude..of blind
9. 1 he saw a man which was blind from
9. 2 or his parents, that he was born blind?
9. 8 which..had seen him that he was [blind]
9. 18 that he had been blind, and received his
9. 19 Is this your son, who..was born blind?
9. 20 is our son, and that he was born blind
9. 24 Then..called they the man that was blind
9. 25 I know, that, whereas I was blind, now I
9. 32 opened the eyes of one..born blind
9. 39 that they which see might be made blind
9. 40 and said unto him, Are we blind also?
9. 41 If ye were blind, ye should have no sin
10. 21 Can a devil open the eyes of the blind?
11. 37 man, which opened the eyes of the blind
Acts 13. 11 thou shalt be blind, not seeing the sun
Rom. 2. 19 thou thyself art a guide of the blind, a
2 Pe. 1. 9 But he that lacketh these things is blind
Rev. 3. 17 knowest not that thou art..blind, and

BLIND, to —

1. *To blind, close,* עָוַר *avar,* 3.

Exod 23. 8 the gift blindeth the wise, and perverteth
Deut 16. 19 for a gift doth blind the eyes of the wise

2. *To veil, conceal,* עָלַם *alam,* 5.

1 Sa. 12. 3 have I received..bribe to blind mine eyes

3. *To blind,* τυφλόω *tuphloō.*

John 12. 40 He hath blinded their eyes, and hardened
2 Co. 4. 4 the god of this world hath blinded the
1 Jo. 2. 11 because..darkness hath blinded his eyes

4. *To harden,* πωρόω *pōroō.*

Rom. 11. 7 obtained it, and the rest were blinded
2 Co. 3. 14 But their minds were blinded: for until

BLIND man —

Blind, τυφλός *tuphlos.*

Matt. 9. 27 two blind men followed him, crying, and
9. 28 the blind men came to him: and Jesus
20. 30 two blind men sitting by the way side
Mark 8. 22 and they bring a blind man unto him
8. 23 And he took the blind man by the hand
10. 49 they call the blind man, saying unto him
10. 51 The blind man said unto him, Lord, that
Luke 18. 35 a certain blind man sat by the way side
John 9. 6 he anointed the eyes of the [blind] man
9. 17 They say unto the blind man again

BLIND men —

Blind, עִוֵּר *ivver.*

Zeph. 1. 17 that they shall walk like blind men

BLIND people —

Blind, עִוֵּר *ivver.*

Isa. 43. 8 Bring forth the blind people that have

BLIND, he that was —

The blind one, ὁ τυφλός *ho tuphlos.*

John 9. 13 They brought..him that..was blind

BLINDFOLD, to —

To cover round about, περικαλύπτω *perikaluptō.*

Luke 22. 64 when they had blindfolded him, they

BLINDNESS —

1. *Coverings, veilings,* סַנְוֵרִים *sanverim.*

Gen. 19. 11 that (were) at the door..with blindness
2 Ki. 6. 18 Smite this people..with blindness
6. 18 And he smote them with blindness acc.

2. *Closing,* עִוָּרוֹן *ivvaron.*

Deut 28. 28 LORD shall smite thee with..blindness
Zech 12. 4 will smite every horse..with blindness

3. *Hardness,* πώρωσις *pōrōsis.*

Rom 11. 25 blindness in part is happened to Israel
Eph. 4. 18 because of the blindness of their heart

BLOOD —

1. *Blood,* דָּם *dam.*

Gen 4. 10 the voice of thy brother's blood crieth
4. 11 to receive thy brother's blood from thy
9. 4 the life thereof, (which is) the blood
9. 5 surely your blood of your lives will I
9. 6 sheddeth man's blood..shall his blood be
Gen. 37. 22 Reuben said unto them, Shed no blood
37. 26 if we slay..and conceal his blood?
37. 31 goats, and dipped the coat in the blood
42. 22 behold, also his blood is required
49. 11 and his clothes in the blood of grapes
Exod. 4. 9 the water..shall become blood upon the
7. 17 waters..and they shall be turned to blood
7. 19 waters..that they may become blood
7. 19 there may be blood throughout all the
7. 20 all the waters..were turned to blood
7. 21 there was blood throughout all the land
12. 7 they shall take of the blood, and strike
12. 13 the blood shall be to you for a token upon
12. 13 when I see the blood, I will pass over you
12. 22 dip (it) in the blood that (is) in the basin
12. 22 strike the lintel..with the blood that
12. 23 when he seeth the blood upon the lintel
22. 2 smitten that he die..no blood..for him
22. 3 blood..for him; (for) he should make
23. 18 Thou shalt not offer the blood of my
24. 6 And Moses took half of the blood, and
24. 6 half of the blood he sprinkled on the altar
24. 8 Moses took the blood, and sprinkled (it)
24. 8 and said, Behold the blood of the coven.
29. 12 thou shalt take..the blood of the bullock
29. 12 pour all the blood beside the bottom of
29. 16 thou shalt take his blood, and sprinkle
29. 20 take of his blood..sprinkle the blood
29. 21 thou shalt take of the blood that
30. 10 with the blood of the sin offering of
34. 25 Thou shalt not offer the blood of my
Lev. 1. 5 bring the blood, and sprinkle the blood
1. 11 Aaron's sons, shall sprinkle his blood
1. 15 the blood thereof shall be wrung out at
3. 2 the priests shall sprinkle the blood upon
3. 8 Aaron's sons shall sprinkle the blood
3. 13 sons of Aaron shall sprinkle the blood
3. 17 that ye eat neither fat nor blood
4. 5 priest..shall take of the bullock's blood
4. 6 the priest shall dip his finger in the blood
4. 6 sprinkle of the blood seven times before
4. 7 the priest shall put..of the blood upon
4. 7 pour all the blood of the bullock at the
4. 16 priest..shall bring of the bullock's blood
4. 17 shall dip his finger (in some) of the blood
4. 18 he shall put..of the blood upon the horns
4. 18 pour out all the blood at the bottom of
4. 25, 30, 34 the priest shall take of the blood
4. 25 shall pour out his blood at the bottom of
4. 30, 34 shall pour out all the blood thereof
5. 9 he shall sprinkle of the blood of the sin
5. 9 the rest of the blood shall be wrung out
6. 27 when there is sprinkled of the blood
6. 30 whereof (any) of the blood is brought
7. 2 the blood thereof shall he sprinkle
7. 14 that sprinkleth the blood of the peace
7. 26 Moreover ye shall eat no manner of blood
7. 27 that eateth any manner of blood, even
7. 33 that offereth the blood of the peace off.
8. 15 he slew (it); and Moses took the blood
8. 15 poured the blood at the bottom of the alt.
8. 19, 24 Moses sprinkled..blood upon the altar
8. 23 he slew (it); and Moses took of the blood
8. 24 Moses put of the blood upon the tip of
8. 30 of the blood which (was) upon the altar
9. 9 sons of Aaron brought the blood unto
9. 9 he dipped his finger in the blood, and put
9. 9 poured out the blood at the bottom of the
9. 12, 18 Aaron's sons presented..the blood
10. 18 the blood of it was not brought in within
12. 4 she shall then continue in the blood of
12. 5 she shall continue in the blood of her
12. 7 cleansed from the issue of her blood
14. 6 shall dip..the living bird in the blood
14. 14, 25 the priest shall take..of the blood
14. 17 upon the blood of the trespass offering
14. 28 upon the place of the blood of the
14. 51 dip them in the blood of the slain bird
14. 52 cleanse the house with the blood of the
15. 19 her issue in her flesh be blood, she shall
15. 25 if a woman have an issue of her blood
16. 14, 18 shall take of the blood of the bullock
16. 14 mercy seat shall he sprinkle of the blood
16. 15 bring his blood within the veil, and
16. 15 do with that blood as..with the blood
16. 18 of the blood of the goat, and put (it) upon
16. 19 he shall sprinkle of the blood upon it
16. 27 whose blood was brought in to make
17. 4 blood shall be imputed unto that man
17. 4 he hath shed blood; and that man shall
17. 6 the priest shall sprinkle the blood
17. 10 that eateth any manner of blood
17. 10 against that soul that eateth blood
17. 11 the life of the flesh (is) in the blood
17. 11 it (is) the blood (that) maketh..atonement
17. 12 No soul of you shall eat blood
17. 12 neither shall any stranger..eat blood
17. 13 shall even pour out the blood thereof
17. 14 the blood of it (is) for the life thereof
17. 14 Ye shall eat the blood of no manner of
17. 14 the life of all flesh (is) the blood thereof
19. 16 neither shalt thou stand against the blood
19. 26 Ye shall not eat (any thing) with the blood
20. 9 his blood (shall be) upon him
20. 11, 12, 13, 16, 27 their blood (shall be) upon
20. 18 hath uncovered the fountain of her blood
Num 18. 17 thou shalt sprinkle their blood upon the
19. 4 take of her blood..and sprinkle of her b.
19. 5 her blood, with her dung, shall he burn
23. 24 eat..and drink the blood of the slain
35. 19 the revenger of blood himself shall slay
35. 21 the revenger of blood shall slay the mur.

Num 35. 24 between..slayer and the revenger of blood
35. 25 out of the hand of the revenger of blood
35. 27 the revenger of blood find him without
35. 27 and the revenger of blood kill the slayer
35. 27 he shall not be guilty of blood
35. 33 for blood it defileth the land: and
35. 33 the land cannot be cleansed of the blood
35. 33 but by the blood of him that shed it
Deut 12. 16 Only ye shall not eat the blood
12. 23 be sure that thou eat not the blood
12. 23 for the blood (is) the life
12. 27 the flesh and the blood, upon the altar of
12. 27 the blood of thy sacrifices shall be
15. 23 thou shalt not eat the blood thereof
17. 8 between blood and blood, between plea
19. 6 Lest the avenger of the blood pursue the
19. 10 That innocent blood be not shed in thy
19. 10 an inheritance, and (so) blood be upon
19. 12 into the hand of the avenger of blood
19. 13 thou shalt put away..innocent blood
21. 7 say, Our hands have not shed this blood
21. 8 lay not innocent blood unto thy people
21. 8 And the blood shall be forgiven them
21. 9 shalt thou put away the..innocent blood
22. 8 that thou bring not blood upon thine
32. 14 didst drink the pure blood of the grape
32. 42 I will make mine arrows drunk with blood
32. 42 with the blood of the slain and of the
32. 43 he will avenge the blood of his servants
Josh. 2. 19 his blood (shall be) upon his head, and
2. 19 his blood (shall be) on our head, if (any)
20. 3 your refuge from the avenger of blood
20. 5 if the avenger of blood pursue after him
20. 9 die by the hand of the avenger of blood
Judg. 9. 24 their blood be laid upon Abimelech their
1 Sa. 14. 32 the people did eat (them) with the blood
14. 33 the LORD, in that they eat with the blood
14. 34 sin not..in eating with the blood. And
19. 5 wilt thou sin against innocent blood, to
25. 26 withholden thee from coming to..blood
25. 31 either that thou hast shed blood causeless
25. 33 kept me..from coming to..blood, and
26. 20 let not my blood fall to the earth before
2 Sa. 1. 16 David said..Thy blood (be) upon thy
1. 22 From the blood of the slain, from the
3. 27 died, for the blood of Asahel his brother
3. 28 ever from the blood of Abner the son of
4. 11 shall I not..now require his blood of
14. 11 the revengers of blood to destroy any
16. 8 hath returned upon thee all the blood
20. 12 Amasa wallowed in blood in the midst of
23. 17 blood of the men that went in jeopardy
1 Ki. 2. 5 and shed the blood of war in peace, and
2. 5 and put the blood of war upon his girdle
2. 9 bring thou down to the grave with blood
2. 31 mayest take away the innocent blood
2. 32 LORD shall return his blood upon his own
2. 33 Their blood shall therefore return upon
2. 37 thy blood shall be upon thine own head
18. 28 till the blood gushed out upon them
21. 19 the blood..shall dogs lick thy blood
22. 35 the blood ran out of the wound into the
22. 38 the dogs licked up his blood; and they
2 Ki. 3. 22 Moabites saw the water..red as blood
3. 23 they said, This (is) blood: the kings are
9. 7 I may avenge the blood of my servants
9. 7 the blood of all the servants of the LORD
9 26 I have seen yesterday the blood of Naboth
9. 26 the blood of his sons, saith the LORD
9. 33 of her blood was sprinkled on the wall
16. 13 sprinkled the blood of his peace offerings
16. 15 sprinkle upon it all the blood of the
16. 15 and all the blood of the sacrifice: and
21. 16 Manasseh shed innocent blood very much
24. 4 the innocent blood..with innocent blood
1 Ch. 11. 19 shall I drink the blood of these men that
22. 8 Thou hast shed blood abundantly, and
22. 8 because thou hast shed much blood upon
28. 3 thou..a man of war, and hast shed blood
2 Ch. 19. 10 between blood and blood, between law
24. 25 for the blood of the sons of Jehoiada
29. 22 the priests received the blood, and
29. 22 sprinkled the blood..sprinkled the blood
29. 24 made reconciliation with their blood
30. 16 the priests sprinkled the blood..of the
Job 16. 18 O earth, cover not thou my blood, and let
39. 30 Her young ones also suck up blood: and
Psa. 9. 12 When he maketh inquisition for blood
16. 4 their drink offerings of blood will I not
30. 9 What profit..in my blood, when I go..to
50. 13 flesh of bulls, or drink the blood of goats?
58. 10 wash his feet in the blood of the wicked
68. 23 That thy foot may be dipped in the blood
72. 14 precious shall their blood be in his sight
78. 44 had turned their rivers into blood; and
79. 3 Their blood have they shed like water
79 10 the revenging of the blood of thy servants
94. 21 They..condemn the innocent blood
105. 29 He turned their waters into blood
106. 38 shed innocent blood..blood of their sons
106. 38 and the land was polluted with blood
Prov. 1. 11 let us lay wait for blood, let us lurk
1. 16 their feet..make haste to shed blood
1. 18 they lay wait for their (own) blood
6. 17 and hands that shed innocent blood
12. 6 The words..(are) to lie in wait for blood
28. 17 A man that doeth violence to the blood
30. 33 wringing of the nose bringeth forth blood
Isa. 1. 11 I delight not in the blood of bullocks
1. 15 will not hear: your hands are full of blood
4. 4 shall have purged the blood of Jerusalem
9. 5 noise, and garments rolled in blood; but

Isa. 15. 9 waters of Dimon shall be full of blood
26. 21 the earth also shall disclose her blood
33. 15 stoppeth his ears from hearing of blood
34. 3 mountains shall be melted with their bl.
34. 6 sword of the LORD is filled with blood
34. 6 with the blood of lambs and goats, with
34. 7 their land shall be soaked with blood
49. 26 shall be drunken with their own blood
59. 3 For your hands are defiled with blood
59. 7 they make haste to shed innocent blood
66. 3 (as if he offered) swine's blood; he that
Jer. 2. 34 Also in thy skirts is found the blood of
7. 6 shed not innocent blood in this place
19. 4 have filled this place with the blood of
22. 3 neither shed innocent blood in this place
22. 17 for to shed innocent blood, and for
26. 15 shall surely bring innocent blood upon
46. 10 made drunk with their blood: for the
48. 10 that keepeth back his sword from blood
51. 35 blood upon the inhabitants of Chaldea
Lam. 4. 13 that have shed the blood of the just in
4. 14 have polluted themselves with blood, so
Eze. 3. 18, 20 his blood will I require at thine hand
5. 17 pestilence and blood shall pass through
9. 9 the land is full of blood, and the city full
14. 19 pour out my fury upon it in blood, to cut
16. 6 saw thee polluted in thine own blood, I
16. 6 in thy blood, Live..in thy blood
16. 9 I throughly washed away thy blood from
16. 22 when thou..wast polluted in thy blood
16. 36 by the blood of thy children, which thou
16. 38 women that break wedlock and shed bl.
16. 38 will give thee blood in fury and jealousy
18. 10 If he beget a son..a shedder of blood
18. 13 surely die; his blood shall be upon him
19. 10 Thy mother (is) like a vine in thy blood
21. 32 thy blood shall be in the midst of the
22. 3 The city sheddeth blood in the midst of
22. 4 Thou art become guilty in thy blood that
22. 6 every one were in thee..to shed blood
22. 9 are men that carry tales to shed blood
22. 12 have they taken gifts to shed blood; thou
22. 13 at thy blood which hath been in the midst
22. 27 wolves ravening the prey, to shed blood
23. 37 blood (is) in their hands, and with their
23. 45 after the manner of women that shed bl.
23. 45 adulteresses, and blood (is) in their hands
24. 7 her blood is in the midst of her; she set
24. 8 have set her blood upon the top of a rock
28. 23 I will send into her pestilence, and blood
32. 6 I will also water with thy blood the land
33. 4 his blood shall be upon his own head
33. 5 not warning; his blood shall be upon him
33. 6 his blood will I require at the watchman's
33. 8 his blood will I require at thine hand
33. 25 Ye eat with the blood..and shed blood
35. 6 prepare thee unto blood, and blood shall
35. 6 sith thou hast not hated blood, even bl.
36. 18 poured my fury upon them for the blood
38. 22 I will plead against him..with blood
39. 17 that ye may eat flesh, and drink blood
39. 18 drink the blood of the princes of the
39. 19 drink blood till ye be drunken, of my
43. 18 make it..to sprinkle blood thereon
43. 20 thou shalt take of the blood thereof, and
44. 7 offer my bread, the fat and the blood, and
44. 15 to offer unto me the fat and the blood
45. 19 the priest shall take of the blood of the
Hos. 1. 4 I will avenge the blood of Jezreel upon
4. 2 they break out, and blood toucheth blood
6. 8 Gilead (is) a city..polluted with blood
12. 14 therefore shall he leave his blood upon
Joel 2. 30 in the earth, blood, and fire, and pillars
2. 31 the moon into blood, before the great and
3. 19 they have shed innocent blood in their
3. 21 I will cleanse their blood (that) I have
Jon. 1. 14 and lay not upon us innocent blood: for
Mic. 3. 10 build up Zion with blood, and Jerusalem
7. 2 they all lie in wait for blood; they hunt
Hab. 2. 8 because of men's blood, and (for) the
2. 12 Woe to him that buildeth a town with bl.
2. 17 made them afraid, because of men's blood
Zeph. 1. 17 their blood shall be poured out as dust
Zech. 9. 7 will take away his blood out of his mouth
9. 11 for thee also, by the blood of thy covenant

2. *Strength*, נֵצַח *netsach.*
Isa. 63. 3 their blood shall be sprinkled upon my

3. *Blood*, αἷμα *haima.*
Matt 16. 17 flesh and blood hath not revealed (it)
23. 30 not have been partakers..in the blood
23. 35 upon you may come all the righteous bl.
23. 35 blood of righteous Abel unto the blood
26. 28 For this is my blood of the new testament
27. 4 I have betrayed the innocent blood. And
27. 6 to put..because it is the price of blood
27. 8 called, The field of blood, unto this day
27. 24 I am innocent of the blood of this just
27. 25 His blood (be) on us, and on our children
Mark 5. 25 which had an issue of blood twelve years
5. 29 the fountain of her blood was dried up
14. 24 This is my blood of the new testament
Luke 8. 43 a woman, having an issue of blood twelve
8. 44 immediately her issue of blood stanched
11. 50 That the blood of all the prophets..may
11. 51 From the blood of Abel, unto the blood
13. 1 whose blood Pilate had mingled with
22. 20 cup (is) the new testament in my blood
22. 44 [his sweat was as it were..blood]
John 1. 13 Which were born, not of blood, nor of
6. 53 and drink his blood, ye have no life in you
6. 54 eateth my flesh and drinketh my blood

John 6. 55 For..my blood is drink indeed
6. 56 eateth my flesh, and drinketh my blood
19. 34 forthwith came there out blood and
Acts 1. 19 that is to say, The field of blood
2. 19 blood, and fire, and vapour of smoke
2. 20 the moon into blood, before that great
5. 28 intend to bring this man's blood upon us
15. 20 (from) things strangled, and (from) blood
15. 29 from meats offered to idols, and from bl.
17. 26 And hath made of one [blood] all nations
18. 6 Your blood (be) upon your own heads
20. 26 that I (am) pure from the blood of all
20. 28 he hath purchased with his own blood
21. 25 from blood, and from strangled, and from
22. 20 when the blood of thy martyr Stephen
Rom. 3. 15 Their feet (are) swift to shed blood
3. 25 propitiation through faith in his blood
5. 9 being now justified by his blood
1 Co. 10. 16 is it not the communion of the blood of
11. 25 cup is the new testament in my blood
11. 27 shall be guilty of the body and blood
15. 50 that flesh and blood cannot inherit
Gal. 1. 16 I conferred not with flesh and blood
Eph. 1. 7 we have redemption through his blood
2. 13 are made nigh by the blood of Christ
6. 12 we wrestle not against flesh and blood
Col. 1. 14 [we have redemption through his blood
1. 20 made peace through the blood of his cross
Heb. 2. 14 children are partakers of flesh and blood
9. 7 high priest..not without blood, which
9. 12 blood of goats..by his own blood
9. 13 if the blood of bulls and of goats, and the
9. 14 How much more shall the blood of Christ
9. 18 the first..was dedicated without blood
9. 19 he took the blood of calves and of goats
9. 20 This (is) the blood of the testament which
9. 21 he sprinkled with blood both the taber.
9. 22 things are by the law purged with blood
9. 25 high priest entereth..with blood of
10. 4 that the blood of bulls and of goats
10. 19 to enter into the holiest by the blood of
10. 29 hath counted the blood of the covenant
11. 28 passover, and the sprinkling of blood
12. 4 Ye have not yet resisted unto blood
12. 24 the blood of sprinkling, that speaketh
13. 11 whose blood is brought into the sanctuary
13. 12 sanctify the people with his own blood
13. 20 through the blood of the everlasting cov.
1 Pe. 1. 2 sprinkling of the blood of Jesus Christ
1. 19 with the precious blood of Christ, as of
1 Jo. 1. 7 the blood of Jesus Christ..cleanseth us
5. 6 by water and blood..by water and blood
5. 8 the spirit, and the water, and the blood
Rev. 1. 5 washed us from our sins in his own blood
5. 9 hast redeemed us to God by thy blood
6. 10 dost thou not..avenge our blood on
6. 12 and the moon became as blood
7. 14 made them white in the blood of the
8. 7 hail and fire mingled with blood, and
8. 8 the third part of the sea became blood
11. 6 have power..to turn them to blood
12. 11 overcame him by the blood of the Lamb
14. 20 blood came out of the winepress, even
16. 3 and it became as the blood of a dead
16. 4 upon the rivers..and they became blood
16. 6 they have shed the blood..blood to drink
17. 6 blood of the saints, and with the blood
18. 24 in her was found the blood of prophets
19. 2 hath avenged the blood of his servants
19. 13 clothed with a vesture dipped in blood

BLOOD, diseased with an issue of —

To run with blood, αἱμοῤῥοέω *haimorrhoeō.*
Matt. 9. 20 which was diseased with an issue of blood

BLOOD, shedding of —

Outpouring of blood, αἱματεκχυσία *haimatekchusia.*
Heb. 9. 22 without shedding of blood is no remission

BLOOD guiltiness —

Blood, דָּם *dam.*
Psa. 51. 14 Deliver me from blood guiltiness, O God

BLOOD thirsty —

Man of blood, אֱנוֹשׁ דָּם *enosh dam.*
Prov. 29. 10 The blood thirsty hate the upright

BLOODY —

Of blood, דָּם *dam.*
Exod. 4. 25 a bloody husband (art) thou to me
4. 26 then she said, A bloody husband (thou art)
2 Sa. 16. 8 because thou (art) a bloody man. 16. 7
21. 1 for Saul, and for (his) bloody house
Psa. 5. 6 LORD will abhor the bloody and deceitful
26. 9 Gather not..my life with bloody men
55. 23 bloody and deceitful men shall not live
59. 2 and save me from bloody men
139. 19 depart from me therefore, ye bloody
Eze. 7. 23 the land is full of bloody crimes, and
22. 2 wilt thou judge the bloody city? yea
24. 6 Woe to the bloody city, to the pot whose
24. 9 saith the LORD God; Woe to the bloody
Nah. 3. 1 Woe to the bloody city! it (is) all full of

BLOODY flux —

Dysentery, δυσεντερία *dusenteria.*
Acts 28. 8 lay sick of a fever and of a bloody flux

BLOOM, to —

To shine, sprout, צוּץ *tsuts*, 5.
Num 17. 8 bloomed blossoms, and yielded almonds

BLOSSOM —
1. *Blossom, flower,* נֵץ *nets.*
Gen. 40. 10 blossoms shot forth; and the clusters
2. *Sprout, blossom,* פֶּרַח *perach.*
Isa. 5. 24 their blossom shall go up as dust
3. *Shining, sprouting,* צִיץ *tsits.*
Num 17. 8 brought forth buds, and bloomed blossoms

BLOSSOM, to —
1. *To break forth,* פָּרַח *parach.*
Num 17. 5 man's rod, whom I..choose, shall blossom
Isa. 35. 1 desert shall rejoice, and blossom as the
35. 2 It shall blossom abundantly, and rejoice
Hab. 3. 17 Although the fig tree shall not blossom
2. *To shine, sprout,* צוּץ *tsuts.*
Eze. 7. 10 the rod hath blossomed, pride hath bud.
3. *To cause to sprout,* צוּץ *tsuts,* 5.
Isa. 27. 6 Israel shall blossom and bud, and fill

BLOT —
1. *Spot,* מאוּם *mum.*
Job 31. 7 if any blot hath cleaved to mine hands
2. *Spot,* מוּם *mum.*
Prov. 9. 7 rebuketh a wicked (man getteth)..a blot

BLOT out, to —
1. *To rub or wipe off,* מָחָה *machah.*
Exod 32. 32 if not, blot me, I pray thee, out of thy
32. 33 him will I blot out of my book
Num. 5. 23 he shall blot (them) out with the bitter
Deut. 9. 14 blot out their name from under heaven
25. 19 shalt blot out the remembrance of Amalek
29. 20 shall blot out his name from under
2 Ki. 14. 27 said not that he would blot out the name
Psa. 51. 1 multitude..blot out my transgressions
51. 9 and blot out all mine iniquities
Isa. 43. 25 I, (even) I, (am) he that blotteth out thy
44. 22 I have blotted out, as a thick cloud, thy
2. *To cause to be wiped away,* מָחָה *machah,* 5.
Jer. 18. 23 neither blot out their sin from thy sight
3. *To smear out,* ἐξαλείφω *exaleiphō.*
Acts 3. 19 that your sins may be blotted out
Col. 2. 14 Blotting out..handwriting of ordinances
Rev. 3. 5 I will not blot out his name out of the

BLOTTED out, to be —
To be wiped away, מָחָה *machah,* 2.
Neh. 4. 5 let not their sin be blotted out from
Psa. 69. 28 Let them be blotted out of the book of
109. 13 posterity..let their name be blotted out
109. 14 not the sin of his mother be blotted out

BLOW —
1. *Smiting,* מַכָּה *makkah.*
Jer. 14. 17 broken..with a very grievous blow
2. *Strife,* תִּגְרָה *tigrah.*
Psa. 39. 10 I am consumed by the blow of thine

BLOW, to —
Shouting, תְּרוּעָה *teruah.*
Num 31. 6 and the trumpets to blow in his hand

BLOW, to —
1. *To sound shrill,* חֲצֹצֵר *chatsotser, 3a.* [V.L. חָצַר *chatsar,* 5.]
1 Ch. 15. 24 did blow with the trumpets before the
2. *To blow or breathe,* נָפַח *naphach.*
Isa. 54. 16 the smith that bloweth the coals in the
Eze. 22. 20 to blow the fire upon it, to melt (it)
22. 21 blow upon you in the fire of my wrath
Hag. 1. 9 brought (it) home, I did blow upon it
3. *To breathe, blow,* נָשַׁב *nashab.*
Isa. 40. 7 the spirit of the LORD bloweth upon it
4. *To breathe, blow,* נָשַׁף *nashaph.*
Exod 15. 10 Thou didst blow with thy wind, the sea
Isa. 40. 24 he shall also blow upon them, and they
5. *To breathe, blow,* פּוּחַ *puach,* 5.
Eze. 21. 31 I will blow against thee in the fire of my
6. *To come upon,* ἐπιγίνομαι *epiginomai.*
Acts 28. 13 after one day the south wind blew, and
7. *To blow, breathe,* πνέω *pneō.*
Matt. 7. 25 the floods came, and the winds blew
7. 27 the winds blew, and beat upon that house
Luke 12. 55 when (ye see) the south wind blow
John 3. 8 The wind bloweth where it listeth
6. 18 arose, by reason of a great wind that blew
Rev. 7. 1 the wind should not blow on the earth

BLOW an alarm, to —
To cry out, make a noise, רוּעַ *rua,* 5.
Num 10. 9 ye shall blow an alarm with the trumpets

BLOW, to cause to —
1. *To journey,* נָסַע *nasa,* 5.
Psa. 78. 26 He caused an east wind to blow in the
2. *To cause to blow,* נָשַׁב *nashab,* 5.
Psa. 147. 18 he causeth his wind to blow..the waters

BLOW (a trumpet), to —
To strike, strike up, תָּקַע *taqa.*
Num 10. 3 when they shall blow with them, all the
10. 4 if they blow (but) with one (trumpet)
10. 5 When ye blow an alarm, then the camps
10. 6 When ye blow an alarm
Num 10. 6 shall blow an alarm for their journeys
10. 7 ye shall blow, but ye shall not sound an
10. 8 sons of Aaron..shall blow with the trum.
10. 10 ye shall blow with the trumpets over
Josh. 6. 4 the priests shall blow with the trumpets
6. 8 passed on..and blew with the trumpets
6. 9 before the priests that blew with the tr.
6. 13 went on continually, and blew with the tr.
6. 16 when the priests blew with the trumpets
6. 20 when (the priests) blew with the trumpets
Judg. 3. 27 he blew a trumpet in the mountain of E.
6. 34 came upon Gideon, and he blew a trumpet
7. 18 When I blow..then blow ye..also on every
7. 19 they blew the trumpets, and brake the
7. 20 the three companies blew the trumpets
7. 22 the three hundred blew the trumpets
1 Sa. 13. 3 Saul blew the trumpet throughout all the
2 Sa. 2. 28 Joab blew a trumpet, and all the people
18. 16 Joab blew the trumpet and the people
20. 1 he blew a trumpet, and said, We have
20. 22 he blew a trumpet, and they retired from
1 Ki. 1. 34 and blow ye with the trumpet, and say
1. 39 they blew the trumpet; and all the
2 Ki. 9. 13 blew with trumpets, saying, Jehu is king
11. 14 the people of the land..blew with trum.
Psa. 81. 3 Blow up the trumpet in the new moon
Isa. 18. 3 when he bloweth a trumpet, hear ye
Jer. 4. 5 say, Blow ye the trumpet in the land
6. 1 blow the trumpet in Tekoa, and set up a
51. 27 blow the trumpet among the nations
Eze. 7. 14 They have blown the trumpet, even to
33. 3 blow the trumpet, and warn the people
33. 6 and blow not the trumpet, and the people
Hos. 5. 8 Blow ye the cornet in Gibeah..the trum.
Joel 2. 1 Blow ye the trumpet in Zion, and
2. 15 Blow the trumpet in Zion, sanctify a fast
Zech. 9. 14 the Lord GOD shall blow the trumpet

BLOW softly, to —
To blow by degrees, ὑποπνέω *hupopneō.*
Acts 27. 13 the south wind blew softly, supposing

BLOW upon, to —
To cause to breathe, blow, פּוּחַ *puach,* 5.
Song 4. 16 come, thou south; blow upon my garden

BLOWING —
To strike, strike up, תָּקַע *taqa.*
Josh. 6. 9, 13 going on, and blowing with the trum.

BLOWING of trumpets —
Shouting, תְּרוּעָה *teruah.*
Lev. 23. 24 a memorial of blowing of trumpets, an

BLOWING the trumpets —
Shouting, תְּרוּעָה *teruah.*
Num 29. 1 it is a day of blowing the trumpets unto

BLOWN —
To be breathed on, נָפַח *naphach,* 4.
Job 20. 26 a fire not blown shall consume him

BLOWN, to be —
To be struck, תָּקַע *taqa,* 2.
Isa. 27. 13 the great trumpet shall be blown
Amos 3. 6 Shall a trumpet be blown in the city

BLUE —
Blue or violet, תְּכֵלֶת *tekeleth.*
Exod 25. 4 blue, and purple, and scarlet, and fine
26. 1 (of) fine twined linen, and blue, and
26. 4 thou shalt make loops of blue upon the
26. 31 thou shalt make a veil (of) blue, and purple
26. 36 thou shalt make an hanging ..(of) blue
27. 16 an hanging of twenty cubits, (of) blue, and
28. 5 they shall take gold, and blue, and purple
28. 6 shall make the ephod (of) gold, (of) blue
28. 8 of gold, (of) blue and purple, and scarlet
28. 15 gold, (of) blue, and (of) purple, and (of)
28. 28 bind the breastplate..with a lace of blue
28. 31 make the robe of the ephod all (of) blue
28. 33 thou shalt make pomegranates (of) blue
28. 37 thou shalt put it on a blue lace, that it
35. 6 blue and purple, and scarlet, and fine
35. 23 with whom was found blue, and purple
35. 25 of blue, and of purple, (and) of scarlet
35. 35 of the embroiderer, in blue, and in purple
36. 8 (of) fine twined linen, and blue, and
36. 11 he made loops of blue on the edge of one
36. 35 he made a veil (of) blue, and purple, and
36. 37 an hanging for the tabernacle..(of) blue
38. 18 the hanging..(was) needlework, (of) blue
38. 23 an embroiderer in blue, and in purple
39. 1 of the blue, and purple, and scarlet
39. 2 he made the ephod (of) gold, blue, and
39. 3 to work (it) in the blue, and in the purple
39. 5, 8 (of) gold, blue, and purple, and scarlet
39. 21 bind the breastplate..with a lace of blue
39. 22 made the robe of the ephod..all (of) blue
39. 24 made..pomegranates (of) blue, and purple
39. 29 a girdle (of) fine twined linen, and blue
39. 31 they tied unto it a lace of blue, to fasten
Num. 4. 6 spread over (it) a cloth wholly of blue
4. 7 table..they shall spread a cloth of blue
4. 9 they shall take a cloth of blue, and cover
4. 11 altar they shall spread a cloth of blue
4. 12 put (them) in a cloth of blue, and cover
15. 38 put upon the fringe ..a ribband of blue
2 Ch. 2. 7 iron, and in purple, and crimson, and blue
2. 14 in blue, and in fine linen, and in crimson
3. 14 he made the veil (of) blue, and purple
Esth. 1. 6 white, green, and blue (hangings), fasten.
8. 15 in royal apparel of blue and white, and
Jer. 10. 9 blue and purple (is) their clothing: they
Eze. 23. 6 clothed with blue, captains and rulers
27. 7 blue and purple from the isles of Elishah
27. 24 in blue clothes, and broidered work, and

BLUE (marble) —
White (marble), שֵׁשׁ *shesh.*
Esth. 1. 6 pavement of..blue, and white, and black

BLUENESS —
Stripe, wound, חַבּוּרָה *chabburah.*
Prov. 20. 30 the blueness of a wound cleanseth away

BLUNT, to be —
To be weak, blunt, קָהָה *qahah,* 3.
Eccl. 10. 10 If the iron be blunt, and he do not whet

BLUSH, to —
1. *To be cut into, caused to blush,* כָּלַם *kalam,* 2.
Ezra 9. 6 I am ashamed and blush to lift up my
Jer. 8. 12 at all ashamed, neither could they blush
2. *To cut in, cause to blush,* כָּלַם *kalam,* 5.
Jer. 6. 15 at all ashamed, neither could they blush

BO-AN-ER'-GES, Βοανεργές *sons of rage, soon angry.*
Surname of the two sons of Zebedee, James and John. It had reference to their fiery zeal, signs of which may be seen in Luke 9. 54, and Mark 9. 38.
Mark 3. 17 he surnamed them B., which is, The sons

BOAR —
Boar, swine, חֲזִיר *chazir.*
Psa. 80. 13 boar out of the wood doth waste it, and

BOARD —
1. *Board,* לוּחַ *luach.*
Exod 27. 8 Hollow with boards shalt thou make it
38. 7 he made the altar hollow with boards
Song 8. 9 we will enclose her with boards of cedar
Eze. 27. 5 They have made all thy (ship) boards of
2. *Rib, side, slope,* צֶלַע *tsela.*
1 Ki. 6. 15 he built the walls..with boards of cedar
6. 16 both the floor and the walls with boards
3. *Board, plank,* קֶרֶשׁ *qeresh.*
Exod 26. 15 thou shalt make boards for the tabernacle
26. 16 length of a board..breadth of one board
26. 17 in one board..for all the boards of the
26. 18 make the boards ..twenty boards on the
26. 19 sockets of silver under the twenty boards
26. 19 under one board..under another board
26. 20 on the north side..twenty boards
26. 21 under one board..under another board
26. 22 for the sides..thou shalt make six boards
26. 23 two boards shalt thou make for the
26. 25 eight boards..one board..another board
26. 26 five for the boards of the one side of the
26. 27 bars for the boards..bars for the boards
26. 28 the middle bar in the midst of the boards
26. 29 thou shalt overlay the boards with gold
35. 11 his boards, his bars, his pillars, and his
36. 20 he made boards for the tabernacle
36. 21 length of a board..breadth of a board
36. 22 One board had ..make for all the boards
36. 23 he made boards..twenty boards for the
36. 24 twenty boards..one board..another board
36. 25 the other . . . he made twenty boards
36. 26 sockets under one board..another board
36. 27 for the sides..he made six boards
36. 28 two boards made he for the corners of
36. 30 there were eight boards..every board
36. 31 five for the boards of the one side of the
36. 32 five bars for the boards..for the boards
36. 33 middle bar to shoot through the boards
36. 34 he overlaid the boards with gold, and
39. 33 his taches, his boards, his bars, and his
40. 18 set up the boards thereof, and put in
Num. 3. 36 custody and charge..(shall be) the boards
4. 31 boards of the tabernacle, and the bars
4. *A row,* שְׂדֵרָה *sederah.*
1 Ki. 6. 9 covered the house with beams and boards
5. *Board, plank,* σανίς *sanis.*
Acts 27. 44 And the rest, some on boards, and some

BOAST —
To make great, גָּדַל *gadal,* 5.
Eze. 35. 13 Thus with your mouth ye have boasted

BOAST (against), to —
1. *To praise greatly,* הָלַל *halal,* 3.
Psa. 10. 3 the wicked boasteth of his heart's desire
44. 8 In God we boast all the day long, and
2. *To praise oneself,* הָלַל *halal,* 7.
1 Ki. 20. 11 Let not him..boast himself as he that
Psa. 49. 6 boast themselves in the multitude of
52. 1 Why boasteth thou thyself in mischief
Prov. 20. 14 he is gone his way, then he boasteth
3. *To make heavy, or honourable,* כָּבַד *kabad,* 5.
2 Ch. 25. 19 thine heart lifteth thee up to boast
4. *To boast against,* κατακαυχάομαι *katakauchaomai.*
Rom. 11. 18 Boast not against..if thou boast, thou
5. *To boast,* καυχάομαι *kauchaomai.*
2 Co. 7. 14 if I have boasted any thing to him of you
9. 2 for which I boast of you to them of M.
10. 8 though I should boast somewhat more
10. 13 we will not [boast] of things without (our)
10. 15 Not boasting of things without (our)
10. 16 not to boast in another man's line of
Eph. 2. 9 Not of works, lest any man should boast

6. *To say, lay out, allege,* λέγω *legō.*
Acts 5. 36 Theudas, boasting himself..somebody

BOAST great things, to —
To boast great things, μεγαλαυχέω *megalaucheō.*
Jas. 3. 5 is a little member, and boasteth great th.

BOAST, to make —
To praise oneself, הָלַל *halal,* 7.
Psa. 34. 2 My soul shall make her boast in the LORD

BOAST self, to —
1. *To say or speak of oneself,* אָמַר *amar,* 7.
Psa. 94. 4 the workers of iniquity boast themselves?

2. *To praise oneself,* הָלַל *halal,* 7.
Psa. 49. 6 boast themselves in the multitude of
52. 1 Why boastest thou thyself in mischief
97. 7 Confounded be all..that boast themselv.
Prov 25. 14 Whoso boasteth himself of a false gift
27. 1 Boast not thyself of tomorrow

3. *To speak of oneself, lift oneself up,* יָמַר *yamar,* 7.
Isa. 61. 6 in their glory shall ye boast yourselves

4. *To beautify oneself,* פָּאַר *paar,* 7.
Isa. 10. 15 Shall the ax boast itself against him

5. *To boast,* καυχάομαι *kauchaomai.*
2 Co. 11. 16 that I may boast myself a little

BOAST, to make one's —
To boast, καυχάομαι *kauchaomai.*
Rom. 2. 17 in the law, and makest thy boast of God
2. 23 Thou that makest thy boast of the law

BOASTER —
Taking on great airs, ἀλαζών *alazōn.*
Rom. 1. 30 proud, boasters, inventors of evil things
2 Ti. 3. 2 lovers of their own selves..boasters

BOASTING —
1. *A taking on of great airs,* ἀλαζονεία *alazoneia.*
Jas. 4. 16 ye rejoice in your boastings: all such

2. *Boasting,* καύχημα *kauchēma.*
2 Co. 9. 3 lest our boasting of you should be in

3. *Boasting (act of),* καύχησις *kauchēsis.*
Rom. 3. 27 Where (is) boasting then? It is excluded
2 Co. 7. 14 even so our boasting, which
8. 24 show..the proof..of our boasting on
9. 4 ashamed in this same confident [boasting]
11. 10 no man shall stop me of this boasting
11. 17 foolishly, in this confidence of boasting

BOAT —
1. *A (little) boat,* πλοιάριον *ploiarion.*
John 6. 22 saw that there was none other boat there
6. 22 went not with his disciples into the [boat]
6. 23 there came other [boats] from Tiberias

2. *A skiff,* σκάφη *skaphē.*
Acts 27. 16 we had much work to come by the boat
27. 30 when they had let down the boat into
27. 32 cut off the ropes of the boat

BOAT, ferry —
Ferry boat, עֲבָרָה *abarah.*
2 Sa. 19. 18 there went over a ferry boat to carry

BO'-AZ, בֹּעַז *fleetness, strength.*

1. A Bethlehemite, of the tribe of Judah, who became the husband of Ruth the Moabitess, and was an ancestor of David, B.C. 1312. In the N.T. he is called *Booz.*
Ruth 2. 1 Naomi..kinsman..and his name (was) B.
2. 3 part of the field (belonging) unto B., who
2. 4 behold, B. came from Beth-lehem, and
2. 5 Then said B..Whose damsel (is) this?
2. 8 Then said B..abide here..by my maidens
2. 11 B..said unto her, It hath fully been showed
2. 14 B. said..come thou..and eat of the bread
2. 15 B. commanded his young men, saying
2. 19 man's name with whom I wrought..(is) B.
2. 23 she kept fast by the maidens of B.
3. 2 now (is)..B. of our kindred, with whose
3. 7 when B. had eaten and drunk..he went
4. 1 Then went B. up to the gate, and sat
4. 1 the kinsman of whom B. spake came by
4. 5 Then said B...thou buyest the field of the
4. 8 the kinsman said unto B., Buy (it) for thee
4. 9 B. said..I have bought all that (was)
4. 13 B. took Ruth, and she was his wife
4. 21 Salmon begat B., and B. begat Obed
1 Ch. 2. 11 Nashon begat Salma, and Salma begat B.
2. 12 B. begat Obed, and Obed begat Jesse
Matt. 1. 5 Salmon begat B. of Rachab
Luke 3. 32 B., which was..of Salmon, which was..of

2. One of Solomon's brasen pillars erected at the temple porch. It stood on the left side, and was 17½ cubits high.
1 Ki. 7. 21 set up the..pillar, and..the name..B.
2 Ch. 3. 17 he..called the name of that on..left B.

BO-CHE'-RU, בֹּכְרוּ *youth.*
Son of Azel, a Benjamite of the family of Saul the son of Kish. The LXX. render it πρωτότοκος, firstborn, in both passages. B.C. 860.
1 Ch. 8. 38 Azel had six sons..Azrikam, B., and
9. 44 Azel had six sons..Azrikam, B., and

BO'-CHIM, הַבֹּכִים *the weepers.*
A place W. of the Jordan, above Gilgal.
Judg. 2. 1 an angel..came up from Gilgal to B.
2. 5 they called the name of that place B.

BODILY —
1. *Body,* σῶμα *sōma.*
2 Co. 10. 10 bodily presence (is) weak, and (his)

2. *Bodily,* σωματικός *sōmatikos.*
Luke 3. 22 the Holy Ghost descended in a bodily
1 Ti. 4. 8 bodily exercise profiteth little; but

3. *Bodily,* σωματικῶς *sōmatikōs.*
Col. 2. 9 all the fulness of the Godhead bodily

BODY —
1. *Belly,* בֶּטֶן *beten.*
Deut 28. 4 Blessed (shall be) the fruit of thy body
28. 11 plenteous..in the fruit of thy body
28. 18 Cursed (shall be) the fruit of thy body
28. 53 thou shalt eat the fruit of thine..body
30. 9 fruit of thy body, and in the fruit of thy
Job 19. 17 the children's (sake) of mine own body
Psa. 132. 11 Of the fruit of thy body will I set
Mic. 6. 7 fruit of my body (for) the sin of my soul?

2. *Flesh,* בָּשָׂר *basar.*
Isa. 10. 18 of his fruitful field, both soul and body
Eze. 10. 12 their whole body, and their backs, and

3. *Back,* גַּב *gab.*
Job 13. 12 ashes, your bodies to bodies of clay

4. *Back,* גֵּו *gev.*
Isa. 51. 23 thou hast laid thy body as the ground

5. *Back,* גֵּוָה *gevah.*
Job 20. 25 It is drawn, and cometh out of the body

6. *Back,* גְּוִיָּה *geviyyah.*
Gen. 47. 18 there is not ought left..but our bodies
1 Sa. 31. 10 they fastened his body to the wall
31. 12 went all night, and took the body of Saul
31. 12 the bodies of his sons from the wall
Neh. 9. 37 also they have dominion over our bodies
Eze. 1. 11 their wings..two covered their bodies
1. 23 which covered, on that side, their bodies
Dan. 10. 6 His body also (was) like the beryl

7. *Back,* גּוּפָה *guphah.*
1 Ch. 10. 12 They..the body of Saul..the bodies of his

8. *What is palpable, material,* גְּשֵׁם *geshem.*
Dan 3. 27 upon whose bodies the fire had no power
3. 28 the king's word, and yielded their bodies
4. 33 his body was wet with the dew of heaven
5. 21 his body was wet with the dew of heaven
7. 11 his body destroyed, and given to the

9. *Carcase, fallen object,* נְבֵלָה *nebelah.*
Deut 21. 23 His body shall not remain all night

10. *Soul, breathing creature,* נֶפֶשׁ *nephesh.*
Lev. 21. 11 Neither shall he go in to any dead body
Num. 6. 6 he shall come at no dead body
19. 13 Whosoever toucheth the dead body of any
Hag. 2. 13 If (one that is) unclean by a dead body

11. *Bone, substance,* עֶצֶם *etsem.*
Exod 24. 10 as it were the body of heaven in (his)
Lam. 4. 7 they were more ruddy in body than

12. *Flesh, that which is thick,* שְׁאֵר *sheer.*
Prov. 5. 11 when thy flesh and thy body are consumed

13. *Thigh,* יָרֵךְ *yarek.*
Judg. 8. 30 threescore and ten sons of his body

14. *Sheath,* נִדְנֶה *nidneh.*
Dan. 7. 15 in my spirit in the midst of (my) body

15. *Body,* σῶμα *sōma.*
Matt. 5. 29, 30 thy whole body should be cast into
6. 22 The light of the body is the eye
6. 22 thy whole body shall be full of light
6. 23 thy whole body shall be full of darkness
6. 25 nor yet for your body, what ye shall put
6. 25 and the body than raiment?
10. 28 fear not them which kill the body
10. 28 to destroy both soul and body in hell
14. 12 his disciples came, and took up the [body]
26. 12 hath poured this ointment on my body
26. 26 and said, Take, eat; this is my body
27. 52 many bodies of the saints which slept
27. 58 went to Pilate, and begged the body of
27. 58 Pilate commanded the [body] to be deliv.
27. 59 when Joseph had taken the body, he
Mark 5. 29 felt in (her) body that she was healed
14. 8 she is come aforehand to anoint my body
14. 22 Jesus..said, Take, eat: this is my body
15. 43 Joseph..craved the body of Jesus
15. 45 centurion, he gave the [body] to Joseph
Luke 11. 34 The light of the body is the eye
11. 34 thy whole body also is full of light
11. 34 thy body also (is) full of darkness
11. 36 If thy whole body..(be) full of light
12. 4 Be not afraid of them that kill the body
12. 22 neither for the body, what ye shall put
12. 23 and the body (is more) than raiment
17. 37 Wheresoever the body (is), thither will the
22. 19 This is my body, which is given for you
23. 52 This (man)..begged the body of Jesus
23. 55 beheld the sepulchre, and how his body
24. 3 found not the body of the Lord Jesus
24. 23 when they found not his body
John 2. 21 he spake of the temple of his body
19. 31 that the bodies should not remain upon
19. 38 that he might take away the body of
19. 38 and took the body of Jesus
19. 40 Then took they the body of Jesus
20. 12 feet, where the body of Jesus had lain
Acts 9. 40 turning (him) to the body, said, Tabitha
Rom. 1. 24 to dishonour their own bodies between
4. 19 considered not his own body now dead
6. 6 that the body of sin might be destroyed
6. 12 Let not sin..reign in your mortal body
7. 4 are become dead to the law by the body
7. 24 who shall deliver me from the body of
8. 10 the body (is) dead because of sin; but the
8. 11 shall also quicken your mortal bodies
8. 13 if ye..mortify the deeds of the body
8. 23 adoption..the redemption of our body
12. 1 that ye present your bodies a living
12. 4 as we have many members in one body
12. 5 we, (being) many, are one body in Christ
1 Co. 5. 3 I..as absent in body, but present in
6. 13 the body (is) not for fornication, but for
6. 13 and the Lord for the body
6. 15 Know ye not that your bodies are the
6. 16 know ye not that he..is one body?
6. 18 Every sin..is without the body: but he
6. 18 sinneth against his own body
6. 19 know ye not that your body is the temple
6. 20 glorify God in your body, and in your
7. 4 The wife hath not power of her own body
7. 4 husband hath not power of his own body
7. 34 that she may be holy both in body and in
9. 27 I keep under my body, and bring (it) into
10. 16 is it not the communion of the body of
10. 17 For we..are one bread, (and) one body
11. 24 Take, eat: this is my body, which is
11. 27 shall be guilty of the body and blood of
11. 29 himself, not discerning the Lord's body
12. 12 as the body is one, and hath many memb.
12. 12 members of that one body..are one body
12. 13 Spirit are we all baptized into one body
12. 14 the body is not one member, but many
12. 15 I am not the hand, I am not of the body
12. 15 is it therefore not of the body?
12. 16 I am not the eye, I am not of the body
12. 16 is it therefore not of the body?
12. 17 If the whole body (were) an eye, where
12. 18 set..every one of them in the body
12. 19 all one member, where (were) the body?
12. 20 many members, yet but one body
12. 22 much more those members of the body
12. 23 those (members) of the body, which we
12. 24 God hath tempered the body together
12. 25 there should be no schism in the body
12. 27 Now ye are the body of Christ, and
13. 3 though I give my body to be burned
15. 35 and with what body do they come?
15. 37 thou sowest not that body that shall be
15. 38 God giveth it a body as it hath pleased
15. 38 and to every seed his own body
15. 40 celestial bodies, and bodies terrestrial
15. 44, 44 natural body..spiritual body
2 Co. 4. 10 Always bearing about in the body
4. 10 might be made manifest in our body
5. 6 whilst we are at home in the body
5. 8 willing..to be absent from the body, and
5. 10 may receive the things..in (his) body
12. 2 whether in the body..or..out of the body
12. 3 whether in the body, or out of the body
Gal. 6. 17 I bear in my body the marks of the Lord
Eph. 1. 23 Which is his body, the fulness of him
2. 16 reconcile both unto God in one body by
4. 4 one body, and one Spirit, even as ye are
4. 12 for the edifying of the body of Christ
4. 16 body fitly joined..increase of the body
5. 23 Christ..he is the saviour of the body
5. 28 to love their wives as their own bodies
5. 30 For we are members of his body, of his
Phil. 1. 20 Christ shall be magnified in my body
3. 21 Who shall change our vile body, that
3. 21 like unto his glorious body
Col. 1. 18 he is the head of the body, the church
1. 22 In the body of his flesh through death
1. 24 afflictions of Christ..for his body's sake
2. 11 in putting off the body of the sins of
2. 17 a shadow..but the body (is) of Christ
2. 19 from which all the body by joints and
2. 23 humility, and neglecting of the body
3. 15 to the which..ye are called in one body
1 Th. 5. 23 (I pray God) your whole..body be preserd.
Heb. 10. 5 but a body hast thou prepared me
10. 10 through the offering of the body of Jesus
10. 22 having..our bodies washed with pure
13. 3 as being yourselves also in the body
13. 11 the bodies of those beasts, whose blood
Jas. 2. 16 things which are needful to the body
2. 26 as the body without the spirit is dead
3. 2 able also to bridle the whole body
3. 3 and we turn about their whole body
3. 6 the tongue..defileth the whole body
1 Pe. 2. 24 Who..bare our sins in his own body
Jude 9 he disputed about the body of Moses

16. *Surface of a body, frame, person,* χρώς *chrōs.*
Acts 19. 12 So that from his body were brought unto

BODY, dead —
1. *Carcase,* נְבֵלָה *nebelah.*
Psa. 79. 2 The dead bodies of thy servants have
Isa. 26. 19 (together with) my dead body shall they
Jer. 26. 23 cast his dead body into the graves
34. 20 their dead bodies shall be for meat
36. 30 his dead body shall be cast out

2. *Fallen thing, carcase,* πτῶμα *ptōma.*
Rev. 11. 8 And their dead bodies..in the street
11. 9 they..shall see their dead bodies
11. 9 they..shall not suffer their dead bodies

BODY, of the same —
Joined in one body, σύσσωμος *sussōmos.*
Eph. 3. 6 Gentiles should be..of the same body

BO'-HAN, בֹּהַן *stumpy.*
A Reubenite, after whom a stone was named which formed part of the boundary between Judah and Benjamin, B.C. 1714.
Josh.15. 6 the border went up to the stone of B.
18. 17 and descended to the stone of B.

BOIL —
Burning, inflammation, שְׁחִין *shechin.*
Exod. 9. 9 it..shall be a boil breaking forth
9. 10 it became a boil breaking forth (with)
9. 11 could not stand..because of the boils
9. 11 the boil was upon the magicians
Lev. 13. 18 The flesh also, in which..was a boil
13. 19 in the place of the boil there be a
13. 20 plague of leprosy broken out of the boil
13. 23 if the bright spot stay..it (is) a..boil
2 Ki. 20. 7 they took and laid (it) on the boil
Job 2. 7 Satan..smote Job with sore boils
Isa. 38. 21 lay (it) for a plaister upon the boil

BOIL, to —
1. *To boil,* בָּשַׁל *bashal,* 3.
Lev. 8. 31 Boil the flesh (at) the door of the tabernacle
1 Ki. 19. 21 boiled their flesh with the instruments
2 Ki. 6. 29 we boiled my son, and did eat him
Eze. 46. 20 the place where the priests shall boil
46. 24 These (are) the places of them that boil
46. 24 the ministers of the house shall boil
2. *To bubble up,* רָתַח *rathach,* 4.
Job 30. 27 My bowels boiled, and rested not

BOIL, to make to —
1. *To (cause to) bubble up,* רָתַח *rathach,* 3.
Eze. 24. 5 Take the choice..make it boil well
2. *To cause to bubble up,* רָתַח *rathach,* 5.
Job 41. 31 He maketh the deep to boil like a pot

BOILING places —
Cooking hearths, מְבַשְּׁלוֹת *mebashsheloth.*
Eze. 46. 23 (it was) made with boiling places under

BOISTEROUS —
Strong, ἰσχυρός *ischuros.*
Matt14. 30 when he saw the wind boisterous

BOLD, to be —
1. *To be confident,* בָּטַח *batach.*
Prov.28. 1 the righteous are bold as a lion
2. *To be warm, zealous, daring,* θαῤῥέω *tharrheō.*
2 Co. 10. 1 being absent am bold toward you
10. 2 that I may not be bold when I am present
3. *To use free utterance,* παῤῥησιάζομαι.
1 Th. 2. 2 we were bold in our God to speak
4. *To be bold,* τολμάω *tolmaō.*
2 Co. 10. 2 wherewith I think to be bold against some
11. 21 whereinsoever any is bold..I am bold
Phil. 1. 14 many..are much more bold to speak

BOLD, to be much —
To have much free utterance, ἔχω πολλὴν παῤῥησίαν.
Phm. 8 I might be much bold in Christ to enjoin

BOLD, to be very —
To be very bold, ἀποτολμάω *apotolmaō.*
Rom 10. 20 Esaias is very bold, and saith, I was found

BOLD, to wax —
To use free utterance, παῤῥησιάζομαι *parrhēsiazomai.*
Acts 13. 46 Paul and Barnabas waxed bold, and said

BOLDLY —
1. *Confidence,* בֶּטַח *betach.*
Gen. 34. 25 Simeon..Levi..came upon the city boldly
2. *To be warm, zealous, daring,* θαῤῥέω *tharrheō.*
Heb. 13. 6 So that we may boldly say, The Lord (is)
3. *Free utterance,* παῤῥησία *parrhēsia.*
John 7. 26 he speaketh boldly, and they say nothing
Eph. 6. 19 that I may open my mouth boldly
Heb. 4. 16 Let us therefore come boldly unto the
4. *To be bold,* τολμάω *tolmaō.*
Mark15. 43 Joseph..came, and went in boldly unto

BOLDLY, to preach —
To use free utterance, παῤῥησιάζομαι *parrhēsiazomai.*
Acts 9. 27 how he had preached boldly at Damascus

BOLDLY, to speak —
To use free utterance, παῤῥησιάζομαι *parrhēsiazomai.*
Acts 9. 29 he spake boldly in the name of the Lord
14. 3 abode they speaking boldly in the Lord
18. 26 he began to speak boldly in the synagogue
19. 8 spake boldly for the space of three months
Eph. 6. 20 that therein I may speak boldly, as I ought

BOLDLY, the more —
The more boldly, τολμηρότερον *tolmēroteron.*
Rom 15. 15 I have written the more boldly unto you

BOLDNESS —
1. *Strength,* עֹז *oz.*
Eccl. 8. 1 the boldness of his face shall be changed
2. *Free utterance,* παῤῥησία *parrhēsia.*
Acts 4. 13 when they saw the boldness of Peter and
4. 29 with all boldness they speak
Acts 4. 31 they spake the word of God with boldness
Eph. 3. 12 In whom we have boldness and access
Phil. 1. 20 (that) with all boldness, as always
1 Ti. 3. 13 great boldness in the faith which is in
Heb. 10. 19 Having therefore, brethren, boldness to
1 Jo. 4. 17 that we may have boldness in the day of

BOLDNESS of speech —
Free utterance, παῤῥησία *parrhēsia.*
2 Co. 7. 4 Great (is) my boldness of speech toward

BOLLED —
The calix of flowers, גִּבְעֹל *gibol.*
Exod. 9. 31 barley..in the ear..the flax..bolled

BOLSTER —
1. *Place of the head,* מְרַאֲשׁוֹת *meraashoth.*
1 Sa. 19. 13 put a pillow of goats' (hair) for his bolster
19. 16 a pillow of goats' (hair) for his bolster
26. 7 Saul lay..and his spear..at his bolster
26. 11 take thou now the spear..at his bolster
26. 16 cruse of water that (was) at his bolster
2. *Place of the head,* רַאֲשׁוֹת *raashoth.*
1 Sa. 26. 12 took the spear..from Saul's bolster

BOLT, to —
To bind up, נָעַל *naal.*
2 Sa. 13. 17 Put now this..out. and bolt the door
13. 18 Then his servant..bolted the door after

BOND —
1. *Bond,* אִסָּר, אֱסָר *issar, esar.*
Num 30. 2 If a man..bind his soul with a bond
30. 3 If a woman..bind (herself) by a bond
30. 4 her father hear..her bond..every bond
30. 5 not any of her vows, or of her bonds
30. 7 her vows shall stand, and her bonds
30. 10 if she..bound her soul by a bond
30. 11 all her vows shall stand, and every bond
30. 12 or concerning the bond of her soul
30. 14 then he establisheth all her..bonds
2. *Bond,* מוּסָר *musar.*
Job 12. 18 He looseth the bond of kings, and girdeth
3. *Bond,* מוֹסֵר *moser.*
Psa.116. 16 thy servant..thou hast loosed my bonds
Jer. 5. 5 these have altogether..burst the bonds
27. 2 Make thee bonds and yokes, and put
30. 8 I will..burst thy bonds, and strangers
Nah. 1. 13 now will I..burst thy bonds in sunder
4. *Tradition,* מָסֹרֶת *masoreth.*
Eze. 20. 37 I will bring you into the bond of the
5. *What is unloosed, a chain,* ἅλυσις *halusis.*
Eph. 6. 20 For which I am an ambassador in bonds
6. *Band, bond, fetter,* δεσμός *desmos.*
Luke13. 16 be loosed from this bond on the
Acts 20. 23 saying that bonds and afflictions abide
23. 29 to have nothing laid..worthy..of bonds
26. 29 altogether..as I am, except these bonds
26. 31 This man doeth nothing worthy..of bonds
Phil. 1. 7 as both in my bonds, and in the defence
1. 13 So that my bonds in Christ are manifest
1. 14 many..waxing confident by my bonds
1. 16 supposing to add affliction to my bonds
Col. 4. 18 Remember my bonds. Grace (be) with you
2 Ti. 2. 9 Wherein I suffer trouble..unto bonds
Phm. 10 whom I have begotten in my bonds
13 have ministered unto me in the bonds
Heb. 10. 34 had compassion of me in my [bonds]
11. 36 others had trial..of bonds and imprison.
7. *Joint bond,* σύνδεσμος *sundesmos.*
Acts 8. 23 I perceive..thou art..(in) the bond of
Eph. 4. 3 unity of the Spirit in the bond of peace
Col. 3. 14 charity, which is the bond of perfectness
8. *Slave, servant,* δοῦλος *doulos.*
1 Co. 12. 13 Jews or Gentiles, whether..bond or free
Gal. 3. 28 there is neither bond nor free, there
Eph. 6. 8 receive of the Lord, whether (he be) bond
Col. 3. 11 Barbarian, Scythian, bond (nor) free
Rev. 13. 16 he causeth all, both..free and bond
19. 18 flesh of all..free and bond, both small

BONDS, to be in —
1. *To bind,* δέω *deō.*
Col. 4. 3 Christ, for which I am also in bonds
2. *One bound,* δέσμιος *desmios.*
Acts 25. 14 There is a certain man left in bonds by
Heb. 13. 3 Remember them that are in bonds

BONDAGE —
1. *Servitude,* עַבְדוּת *abduth.*
Ezra 9. 8 give us a little reviving in our bondage
9. 9 God hath not forsaken us in our bondage
Neh. 9. 17 a captain to return to their bondage
2. *Service,* עֲבֹדָה *abodah.*
Exod. 1. 14 made their lives bitter with hard bondage
2. 23 Israel sighed by reason of the bondage
2. 23 came..unto God by reason of the bondage
6. 6 I will rid you out of their bondage
6. 9 they hearkened not..for cruel bondage
Deut26. 6 Egyptians..laid upon us hard bondage
Neh. 5. 18 the bondage was heavy upon this people
Isa. 14. 3 give thee rest..from the hard bondage
3. *Servant,* עֶבֶד *ebed.*
Exod13. 3 ye came..out of the house of bondage
13. 14 brought us..from the house of bondage
20. 2 brought..out of the house of bondage
Deut. 5. 6 brought thee..from the house of bondage
6. 12 brought thee..from the house of bondage
8. 14 brought thee..from the house of bondage
13. 5, 10 brought you..of the house of bondage
Josh 24. 17 land of Egypt, from the house of bondage
Judg. 6. 8 brought you..out of the house of bondage
4. *Slavery, service, bondage,* δουλεία *douleia.*
Rom. 8. 15 have not received the spirit of bondage
8. 21 creature..be delivered from the bondage
Gal. 4. 24 gendereth to bondage, which is Agar
5. 1 entangled again with the yoke of bondage
Heb. 2. 15 were all their lifetime subject to bondage

BONDAGE, to be in —
To be in slavery, δουλεύω *douleuō.*
John 8. 33 We..were never in bondage to any man
Acts 7. 7 to whom they shall be in bondage
Gal. 4. 9 ye desire again to be in bondage?
4. 25 and is in bondage with her children

BONDAGE, to be under —
To enslave, δουλόω *douloō.*
1 Co. 7. 15 A brother or a sister is not under bondage

BONDAGE, to bring into —
1. *To tread down,* כָּבַשׁ *kabash.*
Neh. 5. 5 we bring into bondage our sons and our
2. *To enslave,* δουλόω *douloō.*
Acts 7. 6 that they should bring them into bondage
2 Pe. 2. 19 of the same is he brought in bondage
3. *To enslave thoroughly,* καταδουλόω *katadouloō.*
2 Co. 11. 20 if a man bring you into bondage, if a
Gal. 2. 4 that [they might bring us into bondage]

BONDAGE, to be brought unto —
To be trodden down, כָּבַשׁ *kabash,* 2.
Neh. 5. 5 daughters are brought unto bondage

BONDAGE, in —
To enslave, δουλόω *douloō.*
Gal. 4. 3 Even so we..were in bondage under the

BONDAGE, to keep in —
To enslave, עָבַד *abad,* 5.
Exod. 6. 5 whom the Egyptians keep in bondage

BOND MAID —
1. *Handmaid,* אָמָה *amah.*
Lev. 25. 44 Both thy bond men and thy bond maids
25. 44 ye buy bond men and bond maids
2. *Maid-servant,* שִׁפְחָה *shiphchah.*
Lev. 19. 20 whosoever lieth..with..a bond maid
3. *A young female slave,* παιδίσκη *paidiskē.*
Gal. 4. 22 A. had two sons; the one by a bond maid

BOND MAN —
1. *Slave, servant,* עֶבֶד *ebed.*
Gen. 43. 18 take us for bond men, and our asses
44. 9 we also will be my lord's bond men
44. 33 let thy servant abide..a bond man
Lev. 25. 42 they shall not be sold as bond men
25. 44 thy bond men and thy bond maids
25. 44 shall ye buy bond men and bond maids
26. 13 that ye should not be their bond men
Deut. 6. 21 We were Pharaoh's bond men in Egypt
7. 8 redeemed..out of the house of bond men
15. 15 remember that thou wast a bond man
16. 12 remember that thou wast a bond man
24. 18 remember that thou wast a bond man
24. 22 remember that thou wast a bond man
28. 68 sold..for bond men and bond women
Josh. 9. 23 none of you..freed from being bond men
1 Ki. 9. 22 of Israel did Solomon make no bond men
2 Ki. 4. 1 to take..my two sons to be bond men
2 Ch. 28. 10 to keep..for bond men and bond women
Ezra 9. 9 For we (were) bond men; yet our God
Esth. 7. 4 But if we had been sold for bond men
Jer. 34. 13 forth..out of the house of bond men
2. *Slave, servant,* δοῦλος *doulos.*
Rev. 6. 15 every bond man, and every free man

BOND MEN, to be —
To be a slave, serve, עָבַד *abad.*
Lev. 25. 46 they shall be your bond men for ever

BOND SERVANT —
Service of a servant, עֲבֹדַת עֶבֶד *abodath ebed.*
Lev. 25. 39 compel him to serve as a bond servant

BOND SERVICE —
Forced service of a bondman, מַס עֹבֵד *mas obed [abad].*
1 Ki. 9. 21 did..levy a tribute of bond service

BOND WOMAN —
1. *Handmaid,* אָמָה *amah.*
Gen. 21. 10 Cast out this bond woman and her son
21. 10 the son of this bond woman shall not be
21. 12 grievous..because of thy bond woman
21. 13 And also of the son of the bond woman
2. *Maid servant,* שִׁפְחָה *shiphchah.*
Deut 28. 68 sold ..for bond men and bond women
2 Ch. 28. 10 to keep..bond men and bond women
Esth. 7. 4 been sold for bond men and bond women
3. *A young female slave,* παιδίσκη *paidiskē.*
Gal. 4. 23 he (who was) of the bond woman was
4. 30 Cast out the bond woman and her son
4. 30 son of the bond woman shall not be heir
4. 31 we are not children of the bond woman

BONE —

1. *Skin, bone, body, substance,* גֶּרֶם *gerem.*
Job 40. 18 His bones (are) like bars of iron.
Prov. 17. 22 a broken spirit drieth the bones
25. 15 a soft tongue breaketh the bone
Dan. 6. 24 and the lions..brake all their bones

2. *Bone, substance,* עֶצֶם *etsem.*
Gen. 2. 23 This (is) now bone of my bones
29. 14 Surely thou (art) my bone and my flesh
50. 25 ye shall carry up my bones from hence
Exod 12. 46 neither shall ye break a bone thereof
13. 19 Moses took the bones of Joseph with
13. 19 ye shall carry up my bones away hence
Num. 9. 12 leave none..nor break any bone of it
19. 16 whosoever toucheth..a bone of a man
19. 18 upon him that touched a bone, or one
24. 8 shall break their bones, and pierce
Josh. 24. 32 the bones of Joseph, which..Israel
Judg. 9. 2 remember also that I (am) your bone
19. 29 he..divided her..with her bones, into
1 Sa. 31. 13 they took their bones, and buried (them)
2 Sa. 5. 1 we (are) thy bone and thy flesh
19. 12 ye (are) my bones and my flesh
19. 13 (Art) thou not of my bone, and of my
21. 12 the bones of Saul and the bones of Jona.
21. 13 the bones of Saul, and the bones of Jona.
21. 13 the bones of them that were hanged
21. 14 the bones of Saul and Jonathan
1 Ki. 13. 2 men's bones shall be burnt upon thee
13. 31 lay my bones beside his bones
2 Ki. 13. 21 the man..touched the bones of Elisha
23. 14 filled their places with the bones of men
23. 16 took the bones out of the sepulchres
23. 18 Let him alone, let no man move his bones
23. 18 they let his bones alone, with the bones
23. 20 he..burned men's bones upon them
1 Ch. 10. 12 They..buried their bones under the oak
11. 1 Behold, we (are) thy bone and thy flesh
2 Ch. 34. 5 he burnt the bones of the priests upon
Job 2. 5 touch his bone and his flesh, and he
4. 14 which made all my bones to shake
10. 11 hast fenced me with bones and sinews
19. 20 My bone cleaveth to my skin and to my
20. 11 His bones are full (of the sin) of his
21. 24 his bones are moistened with marrow
30. 17 My bones are pierced in me in the night
30. 30 my bones are burned with heat.
33. 19 the multitude of his bones with strong
33. 21 his bones (that) were not seen stick out
40. 18 His bones (are as) strong pieces of brass
Psa. 6. 2 O LORD, heal me; for my bones are
22. 14 all my bones are out of joint: my
22. 17 I may tell all my bones: they look
31. 10 iniquity, and my bones are consumed
32. 3 my bones waxed old through my roaring
34. 20 He keepeth all his bones: not one of
35. 10 All my bones shall say, LORD, who (is)
38. 3 neither (is there any) rest in my bones
42. 10 (As) with a sword in my bones, mine
51. 8 the bones..thou hast broken may rejoice
53. 5 God hath scattered the bones of him
102. 3 my bones are burned as an hearth
102. 5 By reason..my bones cleave to my skin
109. 18 so let it come..like oil into his bones
141. 7 Our bones are scattered at the grave's
Prov. 3. 8 It shall be..marrow to thy bones
12. 4 she..(is) as rottenness in his bones
14. 30 but envy the rottenness of the bones
15. 30 a good report maketh the bones fat
16. 24 Pleasant words (are)..health to the bones
Eccl. 11. 5 thou knowest not..how the bones
Isa. 38. 13 so will he break all my bones
58. 11 the LORD shall..make fat thy bones
66. 14 your bones shall flourish like an herb
Jer. 8. 1 bring out the bones of the kings
8. 1 bring out..the bones of his princes
8. 1 bring out..the bones of the priests
8. 1 bring out..the bones of the prophets
8. 1 and the bones of the inhabitants
20. 9 burning fire shut up in my bones
23. 9 my bones shake: I am like a drunken man
Lam. 1. 13 From above..he sent fire into my bones
3. 4 made old; he hath broken my bones
4. 8 their skin cleaveth to their bones
Eze. 6. 5 I will scatter your bones round about
24. 4 fill (it) with the choice bones
24. 5 burn also the bones under it
24. 5 let them seethe the bones of it therein
24. 10 flesh..and let the bones be burned
32. 27 their iniquities shall be upon their bones
37. 1 midst of the valley..(was) full of bones
37. 3 Son of man, can these bones live?
37. 4 Prophesy upon these bones, and say
37. 4 O ye dry bones, hear the word of the
37. 5 saith the Lord GOD unto these bones
37. 7 the bones came together, bone to his bone
37. 11 these bones are the whole house of Israel
37. 11 Our bones are dried, and our hope is lost
39. 15 when (any) seeth a man's bone, then
Amos 2. 1 because he burned the bones of the king
6. 10 to bring out the bones out of the house
Mic. 3. 2 and their flesh from off their bones
3. 3 they break their bones, and chop them in
Hab. 3. 16 rottenness entered into my bones

3. *Reed, cane,* קָנֶה *qaneh.*
Job 31. 22 and mine arm be broken from the bone

4. *Bone,* ὀστέον *osteon.*
Matt 23. 27 are within full of dead (men's) bones
Luke 24. 39 for a spirit hath not flesh and bones
John 19. 36 A bone of him shall not be broken
Eph. 5. 30 [For we are members of..his bones]
Heb. 11. 22 gave commandment concerning his bones

BONE, ancle —

Ancle-bone, σφυρόν *sphuron.*
Acts 3. 7 his feet and ancle bones received strength
[*See also* Cheek, gnaw, break.]

BONES, to break —

To break the bone, עָצַם *atsam,* 3.
Jer. 50. 17 king of Babylon hath broken his bones

BONNET —

1. *Turbans, hilt-shaped,* מִגְבָּעוֹת *migbaoth.*
Exod 28. 40 thou shalt make for them girdles, and b.
29. 9 and put the bonnets on them
39. 28 and goodly bonnets (of) fine linen
Lev. 8. 13 Moses..put bonnets upon them; as the

2. *Tires, ornaments,* פְּאֵר *peer.*
Isa. 3. 20 The bonnets, and the ornaments of the
Eze. 44. 18 They shall have linen bonnets upon their

BOOK —

Books must have been co-eval with the commencement of writing, and the "Preacher" complained that, in his day, of making many books there was no end. Among those *mentioned* in Scripture, but which have not been preserved, are:—The Wars of the Lord, Jasher or the Upright, Samuel on the Kingdom, Chronicles of David, Acts of Solomon, Solomon's Natural History, History of the Kings, Samuel the Seer, Nathan the Seer, Shemaiah the Seer, Gad the Seer, Ahijah the Shilonite, Visions of Iddo, Jehu the Son of Hanani, Sayings of the Seers, and doubtless many others, which were genuine and authentic works, though not perhaps inspired.

1. *Words,* דָּבָר *dabar.*
1 Ch. 29. 29 book of Samuel..book of Nathan..book
2 Ch. 9. 29 (are) they not written in the book of N.
12. 15 (are) they not written in the book of S.
20. 34 they (are) written in the book of Jehu
33. 18 they (are written) in the book of the kings

2. *Book, writing,* סֵפֶר *sepher.*
Gen. 5. 1 This (is) the book of the generations of
Exod 17. 14 Write this (for) a memorial in a book
24. 7 took the book of the covenant, and read
32. 32 blot me, I pray thee, out of thy book
32. 33 him will I blot out of my book
Num. 5. 23 priest shall write these curses in a book
21. 14 it is said in the book of the wars of the
Deut 17. 18 write him a copy of this law in a book
28. 58 all the words of this law..in this book
28. 61 which (is) not written in the book of this
29. 20 the curses that are written in this book
29. 21 that are written in this book of the law
29. 27 the curses that are written in this book
30. 10 written in this book of the law
31. 24 made an end of writing..in a book
31. 26 Take this book of the law, and put it
Josh. 1. 8 This book of the law shall not depart
8. 31 as it is written in the book of the law of
8. 34 all that is written in the book of the law
10. 13 (Is) not this written in the book of Jasher
18. 9 described it..into seven parts in a book
23. 6 to do all that is written in the book of the
24. 26 Joshua wrote these words in the book
1 Sa. 10. 25 Then Samuel..wrote (it) in a book, and
2 Sa. 1. 18 behold, (it is) written in the book of J.
1 Ki. 11. 41 written in the book of the acts of Solomon
14. 19, 29 written in the book of the Chronicles
15. 7, 23, 31 (are) they not written in the book of
16. 5, 14, 20, 27 written in the book of the Chro.
22. 39, 45 written in the book of the Chronicles
2 Ki. 1. 18 (are) they not written in the book of the
8. 23 (are) they not written in the book of the
10. 34 (are) they not written in the book of the
12. 19 (are) they not written in the book of the
13. 8, 12 written in the book of the Chronicles
14. 6 which is written in the book of the law
14. 15, 18, 28 written in the book of the Chroni.
15. 6, 31 the book of the Chronicles of
16. 19 (are) they not written in the book of the
20. 20 (are) they not written in the book of the
21. 17, 25 (are) they not written in the book of
22. 8 I have found the book of the law in the
22. 8 Hilkiah gave the book to Shaphan, and
22. 10 the priest hath delivered me a book
22. 11 the king had heard the words of the book
22. 13 enquire..concerning the words of..book
22. 13 hearkened unto the words of this book
22. 16 all the words of the book which the king
23. 2 he read..the words of the book of the
23. 3 the words..that were written in this book
23. 21 (it is) written in the book of this covenant
23. 24 (which were) written in the book that
23. 28 (are) they not written in the book of the
24. 5 (are) they not written in the book of the
1 Ch. 9. 1 written in the book of the kings of Israel
2 Ch. 16. 11 they (are) written in the book of the
17. 9 the book of the law of the LORD with
20. 34 mentioned in the book of the kings
24. 27 they (are) written in the story of..book
25. 4 as (it is) written in the law in the book
25. 26 (are) they not written in the book of
27. 7 they (are) written in the book of the
28. 26 they (are) written in the book of the
32. 32 in the book of the kings of Judah and
34. 14 the priest found a book of the law of the
34. 15 I have found the book of the law in the
34. 15 Hilkiah delivered the book to Shaphan
2 Ch. 34. 16 Shaphan carried the book to the king
34. 18 Hilkiah the priest hath given..a book
34. 21 enquire..concerning the words of..book
34. 21 after all that is written in this book
34. 24 the curses that are written in the book
34. 30 he read..all the words of the book
34. 31 words..which are written in this book
35. 12 as (it is) written in the book of Moses
35. 27 they (are) written in the book of the
36. 8 they (are) written in the book of the
Neh. 8. 1 they spake..to bring the book of the law
8. 3 the people (were attentive) unto the book
8. 5 Ezra opened the book, in the sight of all
8. 8 So they read in the book, in the law of
8. 18 he read in the book of the law of God
9. 3 read in the book of the law of the LORD
12. 23 The sons of Levi..(were) written in..book
13. 1 read in the book of Moses in..audience
Esth. 2. 23 it was written in the book of the
6. 1 he commanded to bring the book of
9. 32 confirmed..and it was written in..book
10. 2 (are) they not written in the book of the
Job 19. 23 oh that they were printed in a book!
31. 35 (that) mine adversary had written a book
Psa. 40. 7 in the volume of the book (it is) written
69. 28 Let them be blotted out of the book of
139. 16 in thy book all (my members)..written
Ecc. 12. 12 of making many books (there is) no end
Isa. 29. 11 is become unto you as..words of a book
29. 12 the book is delivered to him that
29. 18 shall the deaf hear the words of the book
30. 8 note it in a book, that it may be for the
34. 16 Seek ye out of the book of the LORD
Jer. 25. 13 all that is written in this book, which
30. 2 Write thee all the words..in a book
32. 12 the witnesses that subscribed the book
36. 2 Take thee a roll of a book, and write
36. 4 Baruch wrote..upon a roll of a book
36. 8 reading in the book the words of the
36. 10 Then read Baruch in the book the words
36. 11 When Michaiah..had heard out..book
36. 13 Baruch read the book in the ears of the
36. 18 I wrote (them) with ink in the book
36. 32 wrote therein..all the words of the book
45. 1 he had written these words in a book
51. 60 Jeremiah wrote in a book all the evil
51. 63 hast made an end of reading this book
Eze. 2. 9 and, lo, a roll of a book (was) therein
Dan. 9. 2 I Daniel understood by books the number
12. 1 that shall be found written in the book
12. 4 shut up the words, and seal the book
Nah. 1. 1 The book of the vision of Nahum the E.
Mal. 3. 16 a book of remembrance was written

3. *Book, writing,* סְפַר *sephar.*
Ezra 4. 15 That search may be made in the book
4. 15 so shalt thou find in the book of the
6. 18 as it is written in the book of Moses
Dan. 7. 10 was set, and the books were opened

4. *Book, writing,* סִפְרָה *siphrah.*
Psa. 56. 8 wanderings..(are they) not in thy book?

5. *A (little) book, roll, scroll,* βιβλίον *biblion.*
Luke 4. 17 there was delivered unto him the book
4. 17 when he had opened the book, he
4. 20 he closed the book, and he gave (it) again
John 20. 30 which are not written in this book
21. 25 world..could not contain the books
Gal. 3. 10 all things which are written in the book
2 Ti. 4. 13 bring (with thee)..the books, (but)
Heb. 9. 19 sprinkled both the book, and..the people
10. 7 (in the volume of the book it is written
Rev. 1. 11 What thou seest, write in a book, and
5. 1 I saw..a book written within and on the
5. 2 Who is worthy to open the book, and to
5. 3 no man..was able to open the book
5. 4 no man was found..to open..the book
5. 5 Lion..hath prevailed to open the book
5. 7 he came and took the [book] out of the
5. 8 when he had taken the book, the four
5. 9 Thou art worthy to take the book, and to
17. 8 whose names were not written in the book
20. 12 books were opened; and another book
20. 12 which were written in the books
21. 27 which are written in the Lamb's book
22. 7 that keepeth the sayings..of this book
22. 9 which keep the sayings of this book
22. 10 Seal not the sayings..of this book
22. 18 that heareth the words..of this book
22. 18 plagues that are written in this book
22. 19 things which are written in this book

6. *Book, roll,* βίβλος *biblos.*
Matt. 1. 1 The book of the generation of Jesus
Mark 12. 26 have ye not read in the book of Moses
Luke 3. 4 As it is written in the book of the words
20. 42 David himself saith in the book of Psalms
Acts 1. 20 it is written in the book of Psalms, Let
7. 42 as it is written in the book of the Prophets
19. 19 which used curious arts brought..books
Phil. 4. 3 whose names (are) in the book of life
Rev. 3. 5 not blot out his name out of the book
13. 8 whose names are not written in the [book]
20. 15 who..was not found written in the book
22. 19 man shall take away from..the [book] of
22. 19 take away his part out of the [book] of

BOOK, little —

A little book, βιβλαρίδιον *biblaridion.*
Rev. 10. 2 he had in his hand a [little book] open
10. 8 Go..take the [little book] which is open
10. 9 I..said..Give me the little book
10. 10 I took the little book out of the angel's

BOOTH —

Booth, סֻכָּה *sukkah.*

Gen. 33. 17 Jacob..made booths for his cattle
Lev. 23. 42 Ye shall dwell in booths seven days
23. 42 all..Israelites born shall dwell in booths
23. 43 I made the children..to dwell in booths
Neh. 8. 14 children of Israel should dwell in booths
8. 15 Go forth unto the mount..make booths
8. 16 So the people went forth..made..booths
8. 17 made booths, and sat under the booths
Job 27. 18 as a booth (that) the keeper maketh
Jon. 4. 5 Jonah..there made him a booth, and sat

BOOTY —

1. *Prey, spoil,* בַּז, בָּז *baz.*
Jer. 49. 32 their camels shall be a booty, and the

2. *Prey,* מַלְקוֹחַ *malqoach.*
Num 31. 32 the booty..the rest of the prey which

3. *Spoil,* מְשִׁסָּה *meshissah.*
Hab. 2. 7 thou shalt be for booties unto them?
Zeph. 1. 13 their goods shall become a booty, and

BO'-OZ, Βοόζ.

The Greek mode of writing Boaz.
Matt. 1. 5 Salmon begat B. of Rachab, and B.
Luke 3. 32 Obed, which was (the son) of B., which

BORDER —

1. *Enclosure, enclosed place,* גְּבוּל *gebul.*
Gen. 10. 19 the border of the Canaanites was from
23. 17 the borders round about, were made
47. 21 the borders of Egypt even to the (other)
Exod. 8. 2 I will smite all thy borders with frogs
34. 24 and enlarge thy borders: neither shall
Num 20. 16 a city in the uttermost of thy border
20. 17 left, until we have passed thy borders
20. 21 passage through his border: wherefore
21. 13 the border of Moab, between Moab and
21. 15 of Ar, and lieth upon the border of
21. 22 (high) way, until we be past thy borders
21. 23 to pass through his border; but Sihon
21. 24 the border of the children of Ammon
22. 36 border of Arnon, which (is) in the utmost
33. 44 in Ije-abarim, in the border of Moab
34. 3 south border shall be the outmost coast
34. 4 your border shall turn from the south to
34. 5 the border shall fetch a compass from
34. 6 western border..for a border..west border
34. 7, 9 this shall be your north border
34. 8 goings forth of the border shall be to
34. 9 the border shall go on to Ziphron, and
34. 10 east border from Hazar-enan to Shepham
34. 11 the border shall descend, and shall reach
34. 12 the border shall go down to Jordan, and
35. 26 the border of the city of his refuge
35. 27 the borders of the city of his refuge, and
Deut. 3. 16 the border even unto..(is) the border
12. 20 God shall enlarge thy border, as he hath
Josh 12. 2 (is) the border of the children of Ammon
12. 5 the border of the..the border of Sihon
13. 3 unto the borders of Ekron northward
13. 4 unto Aphek, to the borders of the Am.'s
13. 10 unto the border of the children of Am.
13. 11 Gilead, and the border of the Geshurites
13. 23 border of the..and the border (thereof)
13. 26 from Mahanaim unto the border of Debir
13. 27 Jordan and (his) border, (even) unto the
15. 1 to the border of Edom the wilderness
15. 2 And their south border was from the
15. 5 east border (was)..(their) border in the
15. 6 the border went up..the border went up
15. 7 the border went up..the border passed
15. 8 the border went up..the border went up
15. 9 the border was drawn..the border was
15. 10 the border compassed from Baalah west.
15. 11 the border went out..the border was
15. 11 the goings out of the border were at the
15. 12 the west border (was) to the great sea
15. 47 and the great sea, and the border (thereof)
16. 2 along unto the borders of Archi to Atar.
16. 5 the border of the..even the border of
16. 6 the border went out..the border went
16. 8 The border went out from Tappuah
17. 7 and the border went along on the right
17. 8 but Tappuah on the border of Manasseh
17. 10 and the sea is his border; and they met
18. 12 their border on the..and the border went
18. 13 the border went..the border descended
18. 14 the border was drawn (thence), and
18. 15 and the border went out on the west, and
18. 16 the border came down to the end of the
18. 19 the border passed..the border were at
19. 10 and the border of their inheritance was
19. 11 their border went up toward the sea
19. 12 unto the border of Chisloth-tabor, and
19. 14 the border compasseth it on the north
19. 18 their border was toward Jezreel, and
19. 22 outgoings of their border were at Jordan
19. 25 their border was Helkath, and Hali, and
19. 46 and Rakkon, with the border before
22. 25 made Jordan a border between us and
24. 30 they buried him in the border of his
Judg. 2. 9 they buried him in the border of his
11. 18 the border of Moab..the border of Moab
1 Sa. 6. 12 after them unto the border of Beth-she.
10. 2 in the border of Benjamin, at Zelzah; and
13. 18 the way of the border that looketh to
1 Ki. 4. 21 and unto the border of Egypt: they
2 Ki. 3. 21 armour..upward, and stood in the border
18. 8 Gaza, and the borders thereof, from the
2 Ch. 9. 26 Philistines, and to the border of Egypt

Psa. 78. 54 them to the border of his sanctuary
147. 14 peace (in) thy borders, (and) filleth thee
Prov. 15. 25 will establish the border of the widow
Isa. 15. 8 gone round about the borders of Moab
19. 19 pillar at the border thereof to the LORD
54. 12 and all thy borders of pleasant stones
60. 18 within thy borders: but thou shalt
Jer. 15. 13 for all thy sins, even in all thy borders
17. 3 for sin, throughout all thy borders
31. 17 shall come again to their own border
Eze. 11. 10 judge you in the border of Israel; and
11. 11 I will judge you in the border of Israel
27. 4 Thy borders (are) in the midst of the
29. 10 Syene even unto the border of Ethiopia
43. 13 a cubit..and the border thereof by the
43. 17 thereof; and the border about it (shall be)
43. 20 and upon the border round about: thus
45. 1 in all the borders thereof round about
45. 7 from the west border unto..east border
47. 13 This (shall be) the border whereby ye
47. 15 this (shall be) the border of the land
47. 16 the border of Damascus and the border
47. 17 the border from the sea..the border of
47. 17 northward, and the border of Hamath
47. 18 Jordan, from the border unto the east
47. 20 sea from the border, till a man come over
48. 1 the border of Damascus northward, to
48. 2 the border of Dan, from the east side unto
48. 3 the border of Asher, from the east side
48. 4 the border of Naphtali, from the east side
48. 5 the border of Manasseh, from the east side
48. 6 the border of Ephraim, from the east side
48. 7 the border of Reuben, from the east side
48. 8 the border of Judah, from the east side
48. 12 most holy by the border of the Levites
48. 13 the border of the priests the Levites
48. 21 the east border..toward the west border
48. 22 the border of Judah, and the border
48. 24 the border of Benjamin, from the east side
48. 25 the border of Simeon, from the east side
48. 26 the border of Issachar, from the east side
48. 27 the border of Zebulun, from the east side
48. 28 And by the border of Gad, at..the border
Joel 3. 6 might remove them far from their border
Amos 1. 13 that they might enlarge their border
6. 2 their border greater than your border?
Obad. 7 thee (even) to the border: the men that
Mic. 5. 6 and when he treadeth within our borders
Zeph. 2. 8 (themselves) against their border
Mal. 1. 4 The border of wickedness, and, The people
1. 5 be magnified from the border of Israel

2. *Enclosed place,* גְּבוּלָה *gebulah.*
Psa. 74. 17 Thou hast set all the borders of the earth

3. *Circle, circuit,* גְּלִילָה *gelilah.*
Josh. 13. 2 all the borders of the Philistines, and
22. 10 they came unto the borders of Jordan
22. 11 land of Canaan, in the borders of Jordan

4. *Hand, space, power,* יָד *yad.*
2 Sa. 8. 3 went to recover his border at the river
1 Ch. 7. 29 by the borders of the children of Man.

5. *Thigh,* יַרְכָה *yarekah.*
Gen. 49. 13 and his border (shall be) unto Zidon

6. *Wing,* כָּנָף *kanaph.*
Num 15. 38 make them fringes in the border of their
15. 38 upon the fringe of the borders

7. *Enclosing,* מִסְגֶּרֶת *misgereth.*
Exod 25. 25 thou shalt make unto it a border of
25. 25 shalt make a golden crown to the border
25. 27 Over against the border shall the rings
37. 12 he made thereunto a border of an
37. 12 a crown of gold for the border thereof
37 14 Over against the border were the rings
1 Ki. 7. 28 the work of the bases..had borders
7. 28 the borders (were) between the ledges
7. 29 on the borders that (were) between the
7. 31 upon the mouth of it (were)..borders
7. 32 under the borders (were) four wheels
7. 35 the ledges thereof and the borders
7. 36 on the borders thereof, he graved cherub.
2 Ki. 16. 17 king Ahaz cut off the borders of the

8. *Height, hill,* נָפָה *naphah.*
Josh 11. 2 in the borders of Dor on the west

9. *End, extremity,* קֵץ *qets.*
2 Ki. 19. 23 enter into the lodgings of his borders
Isa. 37. 24 I will enter into the height of his border
Jer. 50. 26 Come against her from the utmost border

10. *End, extremity,* קָצֶה *qatseh.*
Exod 16. 35 they came unto the borders of the land
19. 12 into the mount, or touch the border
Josh. 4. 19 in Gilgal, in the east border of Jericho

11. *Lip, edge,* שָׂפָה *saphah.*
Exod 28. 26 thou shalt put them..in the border
39. 19 and put (them)..upon the border of it
Judg. 7. 22 the host fled..to the border of Abel-M.

12. *Outgoings,* תּוֹצָאוֹת *totsaoth.*
1 Ch. 5. 16 they dwelt in Gilead..upon their borders

13. *A row,* תּוֹר *tor.*
Song 1. 11 We will make thee borders of gold

14. *Frontier, marches, borders,* μεθόριον *methorion.*
Mark 7. 24 went into the [borders] of Tyre and Sidon

15. *Tassel, fringe, extremity,* κράσπεδον *kraspedon.*
Matt 23. 5 they..enlarge the borders of their garm.
Mark 6. 56 that they might touch..but the border
Luke 8. 44 came behind..and touched the border

16. *Goal, boundary, border, limit,* ὅριον *horion.*
Matt 4. 13 which is..in the borders of Zabulon and

BORDER, utmost —

End, extremity, קֵץ *qets.*
Jer. 50. 26 Come against her from the utmost border

BORDER, to (be) —

To be an enclosure, גָּבַל *gabal.*
Josh 18. 20 Jordan was the border of it on the east
Zech. 9. 2 Hamath also shall border thereby

BORE, to —

1. *To bore, pierce,* נָקַב *naqab.*
2 Ki. 12. 9 the priest took a chest, and bored a hole
Job 41. 2 or bore his jaw through with a thorn?

2. *To perforate,* רָצַע *ratsa.*
Exod 21. 6 his master shall bore his ear through with

BORN —

1. *To beget, bear, bring forth,* יָלַד *yalad.*
Job 14. 1 Man (that is) born of a woman (is) of few
15. 14 and (he which is) born of a woman, that
25. 4 can he be clean (that is) born of a woman?

2. *One born,* יָלִיד *yalid.*
Gen. 14. 14 trained (servants), born in his own house
17. 12 he that is born in the house, or bought
17. 13 He that is born in thy house, and he
17. 23 Abraham took..all that were born in his
17. 27 the men of his house, born in the house
Lev. 22. 11 and he that is born in his house

3. *One born,* יִלּוֹד *yillod.*
Exod. 1. 22 Every son that is born ye shall cast
Josh. 5. 5 the people (that were) born in the wild.
2 Sa. 5. 14 that were born unto him in Jerusalem
12. 14 the child also (that is) born..shall surely
Jer. 16. 3 concerning the daughters that are born

4. *Birth,* מוֹלֶדֶת *moledeth.*
Lev. 18. 9 born at home, or born abroad..their

BORN at or in —

By birth, τῷ γένει *tō genei.*
Acts 18. 2 found a certain Jew..born in Pontus
18. 24 a certain Jew..born at Alexandria

[*See also* Country, firstborn, land, new, servant.]

BORN, to be —

1. *To be born, begotten, brought forth,* יָלַד *yalad,* 2.
Gen. 21. 5 when his son Isaac was born unto him
Num 26. 60 unto Aaron was born Nadab and Abihu
2 Sa. 3. 2 unto David were sons born in Hebron
5. 13 there were..sons and daughters born
14. 27 unto Absalom there were born three sons
1 Ki. 13. 2 a child shall be born unto the house of
1 Ch. 2. 3 three were born unto him of the daughter
2. 9 The sons also of Hezron, that were born
3. 1 which were born unto him in Hebron
3. 4 six were born unto him in Hebron
3. 5 these were born unto him in Jerusalem
7. 21 whom the men of Gath (that were) born
20. 8 These were born unto the giant in Gath
22. 9 Behold, a son shall be born to thee
26. 6 unto Shemaiah his son were sons born
Ezra 10. 3 the wives, and such as are born of them
Job 1. 2 there were born unto him seven sons
3. 3 Let the day perish wherein I was born
11. 12 though man be born (like) a wild ass's
15. 7 thou the first man (that) was born?
38. 21 Knowest thou..because thou wast..born
Psa. 22. 31 They shall come..that shall be born
78. 6 the children (which) should be born
Prov. 17. 17 and a brother is born for adversity
Eccl. 4. 14 also (he that is) born..becometh poor
Isa. 66. 8 shall a nation be born at once?
Hos. 2. 3 set her as in the day that she was born

2. *To be born or begotten,* יָלַד *yalad,* 4.
Gen. 4. 26 to Seth, to him also there was born a son
6. 1 daughters were born unto them
10. 21 elder, even to him were (children) born
10. 25 unto Eber were born two sons: the name
24. 15 Rebekah came out, who was born to B.
35. 26 which were born to him in Padan-aram
36. 5 were born unto him in the land of Canaan
41. 50 unto Joseph were born two sons before the
46. 22 which were born to Jacob: all the souls
46. 27 which were born him in Egypt..two souls
Judg 18. 29 Dan their father, who was born unto Is.
Ruth 4. 17 There is a son born to Naomi; and they
2 Sa. 3. 5 There were born to David in Hebron.
21. 20 and he also was born to the giant.
21. 22 These four were born to the giant in Gath
1 Ch. 1. 19 unto Eber were born two sons: the name
Job 5. 7 man is born unto trouble, as the sparks
Psa. 87. 4 behold Philistia..this..was born there.
87. 5 This and that man was born in her: and
87. 6 (that) this (man) was born there
Isa. 9. 6 unto us a child is born, unto us a son
Jer. 20. 14 Cursed (be) the day wherein I was born
20. 15 saying, A man child it born unto thee
22. 26 I will cast thee..where ye were not born

3. *To be brought forth,* יָלַד *yalad,* 6.
Eze. 16. 4 in the day thou wast born thy navel
16. 5 person, in the day that thou wast born.

4. *To beget, bring forth,* γεννάω *gennaō.*
Matt. 1. 16 of whom was born Jesus..called Christ.
2. 1 when Jesus was born in Bethlehem of

Matt. 2. 4 of them where Christ should be born
19. 12 were so born from (their) mother's womb
26. 24 been good..if he had not been born
Mark 14 21 good were it..if he had never been born
Luke 1. 35 that holy thing which shall be born of
John 1. 13 Which were born, not of blood, nor of the
3. 3 Except a man be born again, he cannot
3. 4 can a man be born..and be born?
3. 5 Except a man be born of water and
3. 6 is born of the flesh..born of the spirit
3. 7 I said unto thee, Ye must be born again
3. 8 so is every one that is born of the Spirit
8. 41 We be not born of fornication; we have
9. 2 who did sin..that he was born blind?
9. 19 Is this your son, who ye say was born
9. 20 We know..that he was born blind
9. 32 opened the eyes of one that was born
9. 34 Thou wast altogether born in sins, and
16. 21 for joy that a man is born into the world
18. 37 To this end was I born, and for this cause
Acts 2. 8 in our own tongue, wherein we were born?
7. 20 In which time Moses was born, and was
22. 3 I am verily a man..a Jew, born in Tarsus
22. 28 And Paul said, But I was (free) born
Rom. 9. 11 (the children) being not yet born, neither
Gal. 4. 23 he..was born after the flesh; but he of
4. 29 he that was born after the flesh persecuted
Heb. 11. 23 By faith Moses, when he was born
1 Jo. 2. 29 every one that doeth righteousness is born
3. 9 is born of God..because he is born
4. 7 every one that loveth is born of God, and
5. 1 Whosoever believeth..is born of God: and
5. 4 whatsoever is born of God overcometh
5. 18 whosoever is born of God sinneth not

5. *To bring forth children*, τίκτω *tiktō.*
Matt. 2. 2 Where is he that is born king of the Jews?
Luke 2. 11 unto you is born this day, in the city of
Rev. 12. 4 to devour her child as soon as it was born

BORN again, to be —
To beget anew, ἀναγεννάω *anagennaō.*
1 Pe. 1. 23 Being born again, not of corruptible seed

BORN out of due time, one —
Abortion, an untimely birth, ἔκτρωμα *ektrōma.*
1 Co. 15. 8 as of one born out of due time

BORN, that is —
Begotten, born, γεννητός *gennētos.*
Matt 11. 11 Among them that are born of women
Luke 7. 28 Among those that are born of women

BORN, as they be —
From the belly, מִבֶּטֶן *mibbeten.*
Psa. 58. 3 they go astray as soon as they be born

BORN (in the land) —
An aboriginal, inborn, native, אֶזְרָח *ezrach.*
Exod 12. 19 whether..a stranger, or born in the land
12. 48 shall be as one that is born in the land
Lev. 23. 42 Israelites born shall dwell in booths
24. 16 stranger, as he that is born in the land
Num. 9. 14 for him that was born in the land
15. 30 born in the land, or a stranger, the same

BORN of or in the country —
An aboriginal, inborn, native, אֶזְרָח *ezrach.*
Num 15. 13 All that are born of the country shall do
Eze. 47. 22 shall be unto you as born in the country

BORN among you or home born —
Aboriginal, inborn, native, אֶזְרָח *ezrach.*
Exod 12. 49 One law shall be to him that is homeborn
Lev. 19. 34 be unto you as one born among you
Num 15. 29 him that is born among the children of
Josh. 8. 33 stranger, as he that was born among them

BORN (one) —
A son, בֵּן *ben.*
Gen. 15. 3 lo, one born in my house is mine heir
Eccl. 2. 7 and had servants born in my house

BORNE, to be —
To be lifted up, borne, נָשָׂא *nasa*, 2 or 1.
Exod 25. 14 that the ark may be borne with them
25. 28 that the table may be borne with them
Isa. 66. 12 ye shall be borne upon (her) sides
Jer. 10. 5 they must needs be borne, because they

BORNE, are —
To bear, carry, עָמַס *amas.*
Isa. 46. 3 which are borne (by me) from the belly

BORNE, grievous to be —
Hard to be borne, δυσβάστακτος *dusbastaktos.*
Matt 23. 4 heavy burdens and [grievous to be borne]
Luke 11. 46 lade..with burdens grievous to be borne

BORNE up, to be —
To be supported, סָמַךְ *samak*, 2.
Judg 16. 29 and on which it was borne up

BORROW, to —
1. *To be joined (to another)*, לָוָה *lavah.*
Deut 28. 12 thou shalt lend..thou shalt not borrow
Neh. 5. 4 We have borrowed money for the king's
Psa. 37. 21 The wicked borroweth, and payeth not

2. *To interweave*, עָבַט *abat.*
Deut 15. 6 thou shalt lend..thou shalt not borrow

3. *To ask*, שָׁאַל *shaal.*
Exod. 3. 22 every woman shall borrow of her
11. 2 let every man borrow of his neighbour
12. 35 they borrowed of the Egyptians jewels
22. 14 if a man borrow (ought) of his neighbour
2 Ki. 4. 3 said, Go, borrow thee vessels abroad

4. *To put out at usury*, δανείζω *daneizō.*
Matt. 5. 42 from him that would borrow of thee

BORROW a few, to —
To make few, מָעַט *maat*, 5.
2 Ki. 4. 3 empty vessels; borrow not a few

BORROWED, to be —
To ask, שָׁאַל *shaal.*
2 Ki. 6. 5 Alas, master! for it was borrowed

BORROWER —
To be joined, לָוָה *lavah.*
Prov. 22. 7 the borrower (is) servant to; Isa. 24. 2

BOSCATH. *See* **BOZKATH.**

BOSOM —
1. *Hidden place*, חֹב *chob.*
Job 31. 33 hiding mine iniquity in my bosom

2. *Inlet*, חֵיק *cheq.* [V.L. חוֹק *choq*].
Psa. 74. 11 pluck (it) out of thy bosom

3. *Inlet*, חֵיק *cheq.*
Gen. 16. 5 I have given my maid into thy bosom
Exod. 4. 6 Put now thine hand into thy bosom
4. 6 he put his hand into his bosom
4. 7 Put thine hand into thy bosom again
4. 7 he put his hand into his bosom again
4. 7 plucked it out of his bosom, and, behold
Num 11. 12 Carry them in thy bosom, as a..father
Deut 13. 6 the wife of thy bosom, or thy friend
28. 54 be evil toward..the wife of his bosom
28. 56 evil toward the husband of her bosom
Ruth 4. 16 Naomi took the child..in her bosom
2 Sa. 12. 3 one little ewe lamb..lay in his bosom
12. 8 thy master's wives into thy bosom
1 Ki. 1. 2 let her lie in thy bosom, that my lord
3. 20 and laid it in her bosom
3. 20 laid her dead child in my bosom
17. 19 he took him out of her bosom..and laid
Psa. 35. 13 my prayer returned into mine own bosom
79. 12 unto our neighbours..into their bosom
89. 50 I do bear in my bosom..all the mighty
Prov. 5. 20 and embrace the bosom of a stranger?
6. 27 Can a man take fire in his bosom, and
17. 23 wicked..taketh a gift out of the bosom
21. 14 a reward in the bosom strong wrath
Eccl. 7. 9 anger resteth in the bosom of fools
Isa. 40. 11 he shall..carry..in his bosom..shall
65. 6 but..even recompense into their bosom
65. 7 will I measure..work into their bosom
Jer. 32. 18 Thou..recompensest..into the bosom of
Lam. 2. 12 poured out into their mothers' bosom
Mic. 7. 5 keep..from her that lieth in thy bosom

4. *Lap*, חֹצֶן *chetsen.*
Psa. 129. 7 nor he that bindeth sheaves his bosom

5. *Lap, hollow thing*, צַלַּחַת *tsallachath.*
Prov. 19. 24 slothful..hideth his hand in..bosom
26. 15 slothful hideth his hand in..bosom

6. *Bosom, hollow thing*, κόλπος *kolpos.*
Luke 6. 38 good..shall men give into your bosom
16. 22 beggar..carried..into Abraham's bosom
16. 23 seeth Abraham..and Lazarus in his bosom
John 1. 18 which is in the bosom of the Father, he
13. 23 there was leaning on Jesus' bosom one of

BO'-SOR, Βοσόρ *the father of Balaam.*
The Greek form of writing Beor.
2 Pe. 2. 15 Balaam (the son) of B., who loved

BOSS —
Arch, protuberance, גַּב *gab.*
Job 15. 26 He runneth..upon the thick bosses of his

BOTCH —
Inflammation, שְׁחִין *shechin.*
Deut 28. 27 The LORD will smite thee with the botch
28. 35 LORD shall smite..with a sore botch

BOTH —
1. *Together*, יַחַד *yachad.*
Psa. 4. 8 I will both lay me down in peace

2. *Two*, שְׁנַיִם *shenayim.*
Gen. 2. 25 they were both naked, the man and his
3. 7 the eyes of them both were opened, and
9. 23 laid (it) upon both their shoulders
19. 36 Thus were both the daughters of Lot
21. 27 and both of them made a covenant
21. 31 because there they sware both of them
22. 6 and they went both of them together
22. 8 so they went both of them together
27. 45 why should I be deprived also of you both
31. 37 that they may judge betwixt us both
40. 5 they dreamed a dream both of them
48. 13 Joseph took them both, Ephraim
Exod 22. 11 oath of the LORD be between them both
26. 24 thus shall it be for them both; they
32. 15 tables (were) written on both their sides
36. 29 thus he did to both of them in both the
Lev. 16. 21 Aaron shall lay both his hands upon the
20. 11, 12 both of them shall surely be put to
20. 13 both of them have committed an abom.
20. 18 both of them shall be cut off from
Num. 7. 13 both..full of fine flour mingled
7. 19, 25 both of them full of fine flour
So in v. 31, 37, 43, 49, 55, 61, 67, 73, 79.
12. 5 LORD..called..and they both came forth
25. 8 thrust both of them through, the man of
Deut 19. 17 Then both the men, between whom the
22. 22 then they shall both of them die
22. 24 ye shall bring them both out unto the
23. 18 both these (are) abomination unto the
Judg 19. 6 did eat and drink both of them together
19. 8 afternoon, and they did eat both of them
Ruth 1. 5 Mahlon and Chilion died also both of
1 Sa. 2. 34 in one day they shall die both of them
3. 11 both the ears of every one that heareth
5. 4 both the palms of his hands (were) cut off
9. 26 they went..both of them, he and Samuel
14. 11 both of them discovered themselves unto
20. 11 they went out both of them into the field
20. 42 forasmuch as we have sworn both of us
25. 43 they were also both of them his wives
2 Sa. 9. 13 Mephibosheth..was lame on both his feet
17. 18 they went both of them away quickly
1 Ki. 6. 25 both the cherubim (were) of one measure
2 Ki. 2. 11 parted them both asunder; and Elijah
21. 12 whosoever heareth of it, both his ears
Esth. 2. 23 they were both hanged on a tree: and it
Job 9. 33 daysman. might lay his hand upon us both
Prov. 17. 15 they both (are) abomination to the LORD
20. 10 both of them (are) alike abomination to
20. 12 LORD hath made even both of them
24. 22 who knoweth the ruin of them both?
27. 3 fool's wrath (is) heavier than them both
29. 13 the LORD lighteneth both their eyes
Eccl. 4. 3 better (is he) than both they, which hath
11. 6 whether they both (shall be) alike good
Isa. 1. 31 they shall both burn together, and none
7. 16 shall be forsaken of both her kings
8. 14 a rock of offence to both the houses of
Jer. 46. 12 mighty..they are fallen both together
Eze. 15. 4 the fire devoureth both the ends of it
23. 13 I saw that..they (took) both one
Dan. 11. 27 both these kings' hearts..to do mischief
Zech. 6. 13 the counsel of peace..between them both

3. *Both (of two)*, ἀμφότεροι *amphoteroi.*
Matt. 9. 17 into new bottles, and both are preserved
13. 30 Let both grow together until the harvest
15. 14 if the blind lead..both shall fall into the
Luke 1. 6 they were both righteous before God
1. 7 they both were..well stricken in years
5. 7 filled both the ships, so that they began
5. 38 into new bottles; and [both] are preserved
6. 39 shall they not both fall into the ditch?
7. 42 to pay, he frankly forgave them both
Acts 8. 38 they went down both into the water
23. 8 spirit; but the Pharisees confess both
Eph. 2. 14 he is our peace, who hath made both one
2. 16 that he might reconcile both unto God
2. 18 through him we both have access by one

4. *Two*, δύο *duo.*
John 20. 4 they ran both together: and the other
Rev. 19. 20 both were cast alive into a lake of fire

5. *Each of the*, ἕκαστος τῶν *hekastos tōn.*
Heb. 11. 21 Jacob..blessed both the sons of Joseph

BOTH...and, (also) —
1. *Unto*, אֶל *el.*
Jer. 36. 16 they were afraid, both one and other

2. *Also...also*, גַּם...גַּם *gam...gam.*
Gen. 24. 25 We have both straw and provender
44. 16 both we, and (he) also with whom the cup

3. *And...and*, וְ...וְ *ve...ve.*
Num. 9. 14 one ordinance, both for the stranger, and
Psa. 76. 6 both the chariot and horse are cast into

4. *On, upon*, עַל *al.*
Exod 35. 22 they came, both men and women, as many

5. *And...and*, καί ..καί *kai...kai.*
Matt 10. 28 is able to destroy both soul and body in
12. 22 blind and dumb both spake and saw
Mark 6. 30 [both] what they had done, and what they
7. 37 he maketh both the deaf to hear, and
Luke 2. 46 both hearing them, and asking them
5. 36 then both the new maketh a rent, and
21. 16 shall be betrayed both by parents, and
22. 33 with thee, both into prison, and to death
John 2. 2 And both Jesus was called, and his
4. 36 both he that soweth and he that reapeth
7. 28 Ye both know me, and ye know whence
9. 37 Thou hast both seen him, and it is he
11. 48 take away both our place and nation
11. 57 Now [both] the chief priests and the Ph.
12. 28 I have both glorified (it), and will glorify
15. 24 they both seen and hated both me and
Acts 2. 29 that he is both dead and buried, and
26. 29 were both almost, and altogether such as
Rom 11. 33 both of the wisdom and knowledge of God!
14. 9 to this end Christ both died, and rose
14. 9 be Lord both of the dead and living.
1 Co. 4. 11 unto..present hour we both hunger and
6. 13 God shall destroy both it and them v. 14
7. 29 that both they that have wives
7. 34 may be holy both in body and in spirit
Phil. 2. 13 which worketh in you both to will and
4. 9 things, which ye have both learned and
4. 12 I am instructed [both] to be full and to be
4. 12 both to abound and to suffer need
1 Th. 2. 15 Who both killed the Lord Jesus and
5. 15 good, [both] among yourselves, and to all
2 Th. 3. 4 that ye both do and will do the things

1 Ti. 4. 10 For..we [both] labour and suffer reproach
4. 16 in doing this thou shalt both save thyself
Titus 1. 9 by sound doctrine both to exhort and to
Phm. 16 both in the flesh, and in the Lord?
2 Pe. 3. 18 To him (be) glory both now and for ever
2 Jo. 9 he hath both the Father and the Son
Rev. 13. 15 the image of the beast should both speak

6. *And.. and,* τε...καί *te...kai.*
Matt22. 10 as many as they found, both bad and
Acts 1. 1 all that Jesus began both to do and teach
1. 8 be witnesses unto me both in Jer. and
1. 13 where abode both Peter and James, and
4. 27 both Herod and Pontius Pilate, with
8. 12 were baptized, both men and women
8. 38 into the water, both Philip and the
10. 39 he did both in the land of the Jews and
14. 1 both of the Jews and also of the Greeks
14. 5 both of the Gentiles, and also of the
19. 10 word of the Lord..both Jews and Greeks
20. 21 Testifying both to the Jews, and also to
21. 12 both we, and they of that place, besought
22. 4 delivering into prisons both men and
24. 15 resurrection..both of the just and unjust
25. 24 both at Jerusalem, and..here, crying
26. 22 witnessing both to small and great
28. 23 both out of the law of Moses, and..the
Rom. 1. 12 by the mutual faith both of you and me
1. 14 I am debtor both to the Greeks and
1. 14 both to the wise, and to the unwise
3. 9 we have before proved both Jews and
1 Co. 1. 2 Christ our Lord, both theirs and our's
1. 24 them which are called, both Jews and
Eph. 1. 10 [both] which are in heaven, and which are
Phil. 1. 7 both in my bonds, and in the defence
Heb. 2. 4 both with signs and wonders, and with
2. 11 both he that sanctifieth and they who
5. 1 may offer both gifts and sacrifices for
5. 14 exercised to discern both good and evil
6. 19 Which..we have..both sure and stedfast
9. 9 in which were offered both gifts and
9. 19 sprinkled both the book, and all the
10. 33 both by reproaches and afflictions

7. *And...and,* τε...τε *te...te.*
Acts 26. 16 minister and a witness both of these

8. *And...and,* τε...δέ *te...de.*
Acts 5. 14 multitudes both of men and women

BOTH the hands —
The two fists, חָפְנַיִם *chophnayim.*
Eccl. 4. 6 than both the hands full (with) travail

BOTH parties —
Two, שְׁנַיִם *shenayim.*
Exod22. 9 the cause of both parties shall come

BOTH twain —
Two, שְׁנַיִם *shenayim.*
Eze. 21. 19 both twain shall come forth out of one

BOTTLE —
1. *Hollow thing, bottle,* אוֹב *ob.*
Job 32. 19 it is ready to burst like new bottles

2. *Hollow thing, bottle,* בַּקְבֻּק *baqbuq.*
Jer. 19. 1 Go and get a potter's earthen bottle, and
19. 10 Then shalt thou break the bottle in

3. *Heat,* חֵמָה *chemah.*
Hos. 7. 5 have made (him) sick with bottles of

4. *Bottle, thing shut up,* חֵמֶת *chemeth.*
Gen. 21. 14 took bread and a bottle of water, and
21. 15 the water was spent in the bottle, and
21. 19 she went, and filled the bottle with
Hab. 2. 15 Woe unto him..that puttest thy bottle

5. *Bottle,* נֹאד *nod.*
Josh. 9. 4 wine bottles, old, and rent, and bound
9. 13 these bottles of wine which we filled
Judg. 4. 19 she opened a bottle of milk, and gave
1 Sa. 16. 20 a bottle of wine, and a kid, and sent
Psa. 56. 8 put thou my tears into thy bottle
119. 83 I am become like a bottle in the smoke

6. *Bottle,* נֵבֶל *nebel.*
1 Sa. 1. 24 one ephah of flour, and a bottle of wine
10. 3 and another carrying a bottle of wine
25. 18 two hundred loaves, and two bottles of
2 Sa. 16. 1 summer fruits, and a bottle of wine
Job 38. 37 who can stay the bottles of heaven
Jer. 13. 12, 12 Every bottle shall be filled with wine
48. 12 I will send..and break their bottles

7. *Bottle of skin,* ἀσκός *askos.*
Matt. 9. 17 new wine into old bottles: else the bottles
9. 17 bottles perish..new wine into new bottles
Mark 2. 22 old bottles..wine doth burst the bottles
2. 22 bottles will be marred..[new bottles]
Luke 5. 37 no man putteth new wine into old bottles
5. 37 burst the bottles..the bottles shall perish
5. 38 new wine must be put into new bottles

BOTTOM —
1. *Lower part,* אַרְעִית *arith.*
Dan. 6. 24 or ever they came at the bottom of the

2. *Lap, hollow part,* חֵיק *cheq.*
Eze. 43. 13 even the bottom..a cubit, and..breadth
43. 14 from the bottom (upon) the ground..to
43. 17 the bottom thereof..a cubit about; and

3. *Foundation,* יְסוֹד *yesod.*
Exod29. 12 pour all the blood beside the bottom of
Lev. 4. 7 the blood of the bullock at the bottom of
4. 18, 25 blood at the bottom of the altar of
4. 30, 34 blood thereof at the bottom of the al.
5. 9 the rest of the blood..at the bottom of
8. 15 poured the blood at the bottom of the
9. 9 poured out the blood at the bottom of

4. *Depth, place of shadows,* מְצוֹלָה *metsolah.*
Exod15. 5 they sank into the bottom as a stone

5. *Depth, shadowy place,* מְצֻלָּה *metsullah.*
Zech. 1. 8 the myrtle trees that (were) in the bottom

6. *Cutting, extremity,* קֶצֶב *qetseb.*
Jon. 2. 6 I went down to the bottoms of the

7. *Soil, pavement,* קַרְקַע *qarqa.*
Amos 9. 3 though they be..in the bottom of the sea

8. *Couch covering,* רְפִידָה *rephidah.*
Song 3. 10 He made..the bottom thereof (of) gold

9. *Root,* שֹׁרֶשׁ *shoresh.*
Job 36. 30 and covereth the bottom of the sea

10. *Downward, beneath,* κάτω *katō.*
Matt27. 51 rent in twain from the top to the bottom
Mark15. 38 from the top to the bottom

BOTTOMLESS —
Very deep, ἄβυσσος *abussos.*
Rev. 9. 1 was given the key of the bottomless
9. 2 [he opened the bottomless pit; and there]

BOTTOMLESS pit —
Very deep place, ἄβυσσος *abussos.*
Rev. 9. 11 a king..the angel of the bottomless pit
11. 7 that ascendeth out of the bottomless pit
17. 8 shall ascend out of the bottomless pit
20. 1 having the key of the bottomless pit and
20. 3 cast him into the bottomless pit, and shut

BOUGH —
1. *Summit,* אָמִיר *amir.*
Isa. 17. 6 berries in the top of the uppermost bough

2. *Son,* בֵּן *ben.*
Gen. 49. 22 (is) a fruitful bough..a fruitful bough

3. *Thicket, forest,* חֹרֶשׁ *choresh.*
Isa. 17. 9 strong cities be as a forsaken bough

4. *Twig, shoot,* סְעַפָּה *seappah.*
Eze. 31. 6 fowls..made their nests in his boughs
31. 8 fir trees were not like his boughs, and the

5. *Twig, shoot,* סַרְעַפָּה *sarappah.*
Eze. 31. 5 his boughs were multiplied, and his

6. *Branch,* עָנָף *anaph.*
Lev. 23. 40 and the boughs of thick trees
Psa. 80. 10 the boughs thereof (were like) the goodly
Eze. 17. 23 it shall bring forth boughs, and bear
Dan. 4. 12 fowls of the heaven dwelt in the boughs

7. *Branch, ornament,* פֹּארָה *porah.*
Eze. 31. 12 his boughs are broken by all the rivers

8. *Branch, ornament,* פֻּארָה *purah.*
Isa. 10. 33 the LORD..shall lop the bough with terror

9. *Fruit,* פְּרִי *peri.*
Lev. 23. 40 ye shall take..the boughs of goodly trees

10. *A cutting, branch,* קָצִיר *qatsir.*
Job 14. 9 bud, and bring forth boughs like a plant
Psa. 80. 11 She sent out her boughs unto the sea
Isa. 27. 11 When the boughs thereof are withered

11. *Interwoven twig,* שׂוֹךְ *sok.*
Judg. 9. 49 people..cut down every man his bough

12. *Interwoven twig,* שׂוֹכָה *sokah.*
Judg. 9. 48 cut down a bough from the trees, and

BOUGH, thick —
1. *Thick, dense object,* עָבֹת *aboth.*
Eze. 31. 3 and his top was among the thick boughs
31. 10 shot up his top among the thick boughs
31. 14 shoot up their top among the thick boughs

2. *Outspread, entangled bough,* שׂוֹבֶךְ *sobek.*
2 Sa. 18. 9 the mule went under the thick boughs

BOUGHS —
Pointed twigs, סַנְסִנִּים *sansinnim.*
Song 7. 8 I will take hold of the boughs thereof

BOUGHS, to go over the —
To glean thoroughly, פָּאַר *paar,* 3.
Deut24. 20 thou shalt not go over the boughs

BOUGHT —
A purchase, acquisition, מִקְנָה *miqnah.*
Gen. 17. 12 or bought with money of any stranger
17. 27 bought with money of the stranger, were
Lev. 25. 51 out of the money that he was bought for
27. 22 a field which he hath bought, which

BOUGHT, to be —
To be gained, acquired, קָנָה *qanah,* 2.
Jer. 32. 43 fields shall be bought in this land, whereof

BOUGHT, he that is —
A purchase, acquisition, מִקְנָה *miqnah.*
Gen. 17. 13 he that is bought with thy money, must
17. 23 all that were bought with his money
Exod12. 44 every man's servant that is bought for

BOUND —
1. *Bound, girded,* אָסִיר *asir.*
Psa. 107. 10 Such as sit..bound in affliction and iron

2. *Enclosed place,* גְּבוּל *gebul.*
Exod23. 31 I will set thy bounds from the Red sea
Job 38. 20 thou shouldest take it to the bound thereof
Psa. 104. 9 hast set a bound that they may not pass
Jer. 5. 22 have placed the sand (for) the bound of
Hos. 5. 10 were like them that remove the bound

3. *Enclosed place,* גְּבוּלָה *gebulah.*
Deut32. 8 he set the bounds of the people according
Isa. 10. 13 I have removed the bounds of the people

4. *Statute, limit,* חֹק *choq.*
Job 14. 5 thou hast appointed his bounds that he
26. 10 He..compassed the waters with bounds

5. *Bent, bending, bowed down,* כְּפַת *kephath,* 3.
Dan. 3. 23 fell down bound into the midst..burning
3. 24 Did not we cast three men bound into

6. *Thread, cord; bound to,* פָּתִיל *pathil.*
Num 19. 15 which hath no covering bound upon it

7. *To bind, tie,* קָשַׁר *qashar.*
Prov.22. 15 Foolishness (is) bound in the heart of a

BOUND, to be —
1. *To be bound,* אָסַר *asar,* 2.
Gen. 42. 19 let one of your brethren be bound in the
Judg16. 6 wherewith thou mightest be bound to
16. 10, 13 wherewith thou mightest be bound

2. *To be bound,* אָסַר *asar,* 4.
Isa. 22. 3 thy rulers..are bound by the archers

3. *To be bound, bent,* כְּפַת *kephath.*
Dan. 3. 21 these men were bound in their coats, and

4. *To fetter,* רָתַק *rathaq,* 4.
Nah. 3. 10 all her great men were bound in chains

5. *To press,* צָרַר *tsarar.*
1 Sa. 25. 29 the soul of my lord shall be bound in the

6. *To be twisted together,* שָׂקַד *saqad,* 2.
Lam. 1. 14 The yoke of my transgressions is bound

7. *To owe,* ὀφείλω *opheilō.*
2 Th. 1. 3 We are bound to thank God always for
2. 13 we are bound to give thanks alway to

BOUND, to be kept —
To bind, δεσμέω *desmeō.*
Luke 8. 29 he was kept bound with chains and in

BOUND, those which are —
One bound, אָסִיר *asir.*
Psa. 68. 6 he bringeth out those which are bound

BOUND up —
1. *To be straitened, pressed together,* צָרַר *tsarar,* 4.
Josh. 9. 4 wine bottles, old, and rent, and bound up

2. *To bind, tie,* קָשַׁר *qashar.*
Gen. 44. 30 his life is bound up in the lad's life

BOUND up, be —
For the wound (or *binding up*), לְמָזוֹר *le-mazor.*
Jer. 30. 13 that thou mayest be bound up: thou hast

BOUND up, to be —
1. *To be wrapped around,* חָבַשׁ *chabash,* 4.
Isa. 1. 6 have not been closed, neither bound up
Eze. 30. 21 it shall not be bound up to be healed, to

2. *To press,* צָרַר *tsarar.*
Exod12. 34 their kneading troughs being bound up
Hos. 13. 12 The iniquity of Ephraim (is) bound up

BOUND about, to be —
To bind around, περιδέω *perideō.*
John11. 44 his face was bound about with a napkin

BOUND with, to be —
1. *To be laid round about,* περίκειμαι *perikeimai.*
Acts 28. 20 for the hope of Israel I am bound with

2. *To be bound with,* συνδέομαι *sundeomai.*
Heb. 13. 3 that are in bonds, as bound with them

BOUND, utmost —
Mark, limit, תַּאֲוָה *taavah.*
Gen. 49. 26 the utmost bound of the everlasting hills

BOUNDS —
Set limit, ὁροθεσία *horothesia.*
Acts 17. 26 determined..the bounds of their habits.

BOUNDS (about), to set —
To make an enclosure, גָּבַל *gabal,* 5.
Exod 19. 12 set bounds unto the people round about
19. 23 Set bounds about the mount, and sanctify

BOUNTIFUL —
1. *Good,* טוֹב *tob.*
Prov.22. 9 He that hath a bountiful eye shall be

2. *Rich, easy, free,* שׁוֹעַ *shoa.*
Isa. 32. 5 nor the churl said (to be) bountiful

BOUNTIFULLY —
Good or fair speech, blessing, εὐλογία *eulogia.*
2 Co. 9. 6 soweth bountifully shall reap..bountifully

BOUNTIFULLY, to deal —
To deal (with any one), גָּמַל *gamal.*
Psa. 13. 6 he hath dealt bountifully with me
116. 7 LORD hath dealt bountifully with thee
119. 17 Deal bountifully with thy servant
142. 7 thou shalt deal bountifully with me

BOUNTIFULNESS —
Simplicity, ἁπλότης *haplotēs*.
2 Co. 9. 11 enriched..every thing to all bountifulness
BOUNTY —
1. *Hand, power*, יָד *yad*.
1 Ki. 10. 13 Solomon gave her of his royal bounty
2. *Good speech, blessing*, εὐλογία *eulogia*.
2 Co. 9. 5 make up beforehand your bounty
BOUNTY (matter of) —
Good speech, blessing, εὐλογία *eulogia*.
2 Co. 9. 5 might be ready, as (a matter of) bounty
BOW —
1. *Bow*, קֶשֶׁת *qesheth*.
Gen. 9. 13 I do set my bow in the cloud, and it
9. 14 that the bow shall be seen in the cloud
9. 16 the bow shall be in the cloud; and I
27. 3 take..thy quiver and thy bow
48. 22 with my sword and with my bow
49. 24 his bow abode in strength, and the arms
Josh 24. 12 not with thy sword, nor with thy bow
1 Sa. 2. 4 The bows of the mighty men (are) broken
18. 4 even to his sword, and to his bow
2 Sa. 1. 18 teach the children of Judah..the bow
1. 22 the bow of Jonathan turned not back
22. 35 a bow of steel is broken by mine arms
1 Ki. 22. 34 a..man drew a bow at a venture, and
2 Ki. 6. 22 wouldest thou smite..with thy bow?
9. 24 Jehu drew a bow with his full strength
13. 15 Elisha said unto him, Take bow and arrows
13. 15 and he took unto him bow and arrows
13. 16 Put thine hand upon the bow; and he
1 Ch. 5. 18 to shoot with bow, and skilful in war
12. 2 armed with bows, and could use both
12. 2 stones and (shooting) arrows out of a bow
2 Ch. 14. 8 that bare shield and drew bows, two
17. 17 with him armed men with bow and shield
18. 33 a..man drew a bow at a venture, and
26. 14 Uzziah prepared..bows, and slings (to)
Neh. 4. 13 I even set the people..with..their bows
4. 16 the other half of them held..the bows
Job 20. 24 the bow of steel shall strike him through
29. 20 my bow was renewed in my hand
Psa. 7. 12 he hath bent his bow, and made it ready
11. 2 the wicked bend (their) bow, they make
18. 34 a bow of steel is broken by mine arms
37. 14 The wicked have..bent their bow, to cast
37. 15 heart, and their bows shall be broken
44. 6 I will not trust in my bow, neither
46. 9 breaketh the bow, and cutteth the spear
76. 3 There brake he the arrows of the bow
78. 9 armed..carrying bows, turned back in
78. 57 were turned aside like a deceitful bow
Isa. 5. 28 Whose arrows..sharp, and all their bows
7. 24 With arrows and with bows shall (men)
13. 18 bows also shall dash the young men to
21. 15 drawn sword, and from the bent bow
41. 2 he gave..as driven stubble to his bow
66. 19 that draw the bow, (to) Tubal, and Javan
Jer. 6. 23 They shall lay hold on bow and spear
9. 3 they bend their tongues (like) their bow
46. 9 Lydians, that handle (and) bend the bow
49. 35 I will break the bow of Elam, the chief
50. 14 all ye that bend the bow, shoot at her
50. 29 all ye that bend the bow, camp against
50. 42 They shall hold the bow and the lance
51. 3 let the archer bend his bow, and against
51. 56 every one of their bows is broken: for
Lam. 2. 4 He hath bent his bow like an enemy
3. 12 He hath bent his bow, and set me as a
Eze. 1. 28 the bow that is in the cloud in the day of
39. 3 I will smite thy bow out of thy left hand
39. 9 the shields..the bows and the arrows
Hos. 1. 5 I will break the bow of Israel in the
1. 7 will not save them by bow, nor by sword
2. 18 I will break the bow and the sword and
7. 16 they are like a deceitful bow: their
Amos 2. 15 shall he stand that handleth the bow
Hab. 3. 9 Thy bow was made quite naked..to the
Zech. 9. 10 and the battle bow shall be cut off
9. 13 filled the bow with Ephraim, and raised
10. 4 Out of him came forth..the battle bow
2. *A bow*, τόξον *toxon*.
Rev. 6. 2 he that sat on him had a bow; and a
BOW, to —
1. *To bend*, כָּרַע *kara*.
Judg. 5. 27 he bowed..he bowed..where he bowed
1 Ki. 19. 18 the knees which have not bowed unto
Esth. 3. 2 the king's servants..bowed, Mordecai b.
3. 5 Haman saw that Mordecai bowed not
Psa. 22. 29 they that go down to the dust shall bow
72. 9 They that dwell..shall bow before him
Isa. 45. 23 unto me every knee shall bow, every
2. *To incline*, נָטָה *natah*.
Gen. 49. 15 bowed his shoulder to bear, and became
Judg 16. 30 he bowed himself with (all his) might
2 Sa. 22. 10 He bowed the heavens also, and came
Psa. 18. 9 He bowed the heavens also, and came
3. *To cause to incline*, נָטָה *natah*, 5.
2 Sa. 19. 14 he bowed the heart of all the men of
Psa. 144. 5 Bow thy heavens, O LORD, and come
Prov. 5. 1 bow thine ear to my understanding
4. *To bow the head*, קָדַד *qadad*.
1 Ki. 1. 16 Bath-sheba bowed, and did obeisance
1. 31 Bath-sheba bowed with (her) face to the
5. *To bow down*, שָׁחַח *shachach*.
Prov. 14. 19 The evil bow before the good; and the
Hab. 3. 6 the perpetual hills did bow: his ways
6. *To bend*, κάμπτω *kamptō*.
Rom 11. 4 who have not bowed the knee to..Baal
14. 11 it is written..every knee shall bow to me
Eph. 3. 14 I bow my knees unto the Father of our
Phil. 2. 10 the name of Jesus every knee should bow
7. *To incline*, κλίνω *klinō*.
John 19. 30 he bowed his head, and gave up the ghost
8. *To put, place, set*, τίθημι *tithēmi*.
Mark 15. 19 and bowing..knees worshipped him
BOW down, to —
1. *To bend, double*, כָּפַף *kaphaph*.
Isa. 58. 5 to bow down his head as a bulrush
2. *To bend down*, כָּרַע *kara*.
Judg. 7. 5 every one that boweth down upon his
7. 6 the rest of the people bowed down upon
Job 31. 10 and let others bow down upon her
Psa. 95. 6 O come, let us worship and bow down
Isa. 10. 4 Without me they shall bow down under
46. 1 Bel boweth down, Nebo stoopeth, their
46. 2 They stoop, they bow down together
65. 12 ye shall all bow down to the slaughter
3. *To cause to incline*, נָטָה *natah*, 5.
2 Ki. 19. 16 LORD, bow down thine ear, and hear
Psa. 31. 2 Bow down thine ear to me; deliver me
86. 1 Bow down thine ear, O LORD, hear me
Prov. 22. 17 Bow down thine ear, and hear the words
4. *To bow down*, שָׁחָה *shachah*.
Isa. 51. 23 Bow down, that we may go over: and
5. *To bow oneself down*, שָׁחָה *shachah*, 7.
Gen. 27. 29 Let people serve..nations bow down to
27. 29 let thy mother's sons bow down to thee
49. 8 thy father's children shall bow down
Exod 23. 24 Thou shalt not bow down to their gods
Lev. 26. 1 neither..set up..image..bow down unto
Num 25. 2 the people did eat, and bowed down to
Deut. 5. 9 Thou shalt not bow down thyself unto
Judg. 2. 19 to bow down unto them; they ceased
Isa. 49. 23 they shall bow down to thee with (their)
6. *To bow down*, שָׁחַח *shachach*.
Psa. 35. 14 I bowed down heavily, as one that
7. *To be bowed down*, שָׁחַח *shachach*, 2.
Isa. 2. 9 the mean man boweth down, and the
8. *To incline*, κλίνω *klinō*.
Luke 24. 5 bowed down (their) faces to the earth
9. *To bend together*, συγκάμπτω *sugkamptō*.
Rom 11. 10 and bow down their back alway
BOW down the head, to —
To stoop down, קָדַד *qadad*.
Gen. 24. 26 the man bowed down his head, and
24. 48 I bowed down my head, and worshipped
43. 28 they bowed down their heads, and made
Num 22. 31 he bowed down his head, and fell flat
1 Ch. 29. 20 bowed down their heads, and worshipped
BOW down self, to —
To bow oneself (to God or man), שָׁחָה *shachah*, 7.
Gen. 23. 12 Abraham bowed down himself before the
37. 10 come to bow down ourselves to
42. 6 bowed down themselves before him
Exod 11. 8 bow down themselves unto me, saying
20. 5 Thou shalt not bow down thyself to them
2 Ki. 5. 18 I bow down myself in the house of Rim.
2 Ch. 25. 14 bowed down himself before them, and
Isa. 60. 14 despised thee shall bow themselves down
BOW self, to —
1. *To be bent double*, כָּפַף *kaphaph*, 2.
Mic. 6. 6 bow myself before the high God? shall I
2. *To bow down*, כָּרַע *kara*.
1 Sa. 4. 19 bowed herself and travailed; for her pains
2 Ch. 7. 3 bowed themselves with their faces to the
29. 29 all..present with him bowed themselves
Job 39. 3 bow themselves..they cast out their sor.
3. *To bend or curve oneself*, עָוַת *avath*, 7.
Eccl. 12. 3 strong men shall bow themselves, and
4. *To bow oneself (to God or man)*, שָׁחָה *shachah*, 7.
Gen. 18. 2 and bowed himself toward the ground
19. 1 bowed himself with his face toward the
23. 7 Abraham stood up, and bowed himself to
33. 3 bowed himself to the ground seven times
33. 6 their children, and they bowed themselves
33. 7 Leah..with her children..bowed them.
33. 7 came..near..and they bowed themselves
43. 26 bowed themselves to him to the earth
47. 31 Israel bowed himself upon the bed's
48. 12 bowed himself with his face to the earth
Josh 23. 7 serve..nor bow yourselves unto them
23. 16 served other gods, and bowed yourselves
Judg. 2. 12, 17 and bowed themselves unto them
Ruth 2. 10 she..bowed herself to the ground, and
1 Sa. 20. 41 bowed himself three times: and they
24. 8 David stooped..and bowed himself
25. 23 fell..and bowed herself to the ground
25. 41 bowed herself on (her) face to the earth
28. 14 stooped with (his) face..and bowed him.
2 Sa. 9. 8 he bowed himself, and said, What (is) thy
14. 22 Joab fell..on his face, and bowed himself
14. 33 bowed himself on his face to the ground
18. 21 Cushi bowed himself unto Joab, and ran
2 Sa. 24. 20 bowed himself before the king on his
1 Ki. 1. 23 bowed himself before the king with his
1. 47 the king bowed himself upon the bed
1. 53 came and bowed himself to king Solomon
2. 19 king rose..and bowed himself unto her
2 Ki. 2. 15 bowed themselves to the ground before
4. 37 bowed herself to the ground, and took
5. 18 I bow myself in the house of Rimmon
17. 35 nor bow yourselves to them, nor serve
1 Ch. 21. 21 bowed himself to David with (his) face
BOW the head, to —
To stoop down, bow the head קָדַד *qadad*.
Exod. 4. 31 they bowed their heads and worshipped
12. 27 people bowed the head and worshipped
34. 8 bowed his head toward the earth, and
2 Ch. 20. 18 Jehoshaphat bowed his head..to the
29. 30 they bowed their heads and worshipped
Neh. 8. 6 bowed their heads, and worshipped the
BOW the knee, to —
1. *Salute! give a blessing!* אַבְרֵךְ *abrek*.
Gen. 41. 43 they cried before him, Bow the knee
2. *To fall on the knees*, γονυπετέω *gonupeteō*.
Matt 27. 29 they bowed the knee before him
BOWED down, to be —
1. *To be bent double*, כָּפַף *kaphaph*.
Psa. 57. 6 my soul is bowed down: they have
145. 14 and raiseth up all..bowed down
146. 8 LORD raiseth them that are bowed down
2. *To be bent*, עָוָה *ivah*, 2.
Isa. 21. 3 I was bowed down at the hearing..I was
3. *To be bowed down*, שׁוּחַ *shuach*.
Psa. 44. 25 our soul is bowed down to the dust
4. *To bow down*, שָׁחַח *shachach*.
Psa. 38. 6 I am troubled; I am bowed down greatly
Isa. 2. 11 haughtiness of men shall be bowed down
2. 17 loftiness of man shall be bowed down
BOWED together, to be —
To bow together, συγκύπτω *sugkuptō*.
Luke 13. 11 there was a woman..bowed together
BOWELS —
1. *Bowels*, מֵעִים *meim*.
Gen. 15. 4 shall come forth out of thine own bowels
25. 23 people shall be separated from thy bowels
Num. 5. 22 this water..shall go into thy bowels
2 Sa. 7. 12 which shall proceed out of thy bowels
16. 11 my son, which came forth of my bowels
20. 10 shed out his bowels to the ground, and
2 Ch. 21. 15 of thy bowels, until thy bowels fall out
21. 18 LORD smote him in his bowels with an
21. 19 his bowels fell out by reason of his
32. 21 they that came forth of his own bowels
Job 20. 14 his meat in his bowels is turned
30. 27 My bowels boiled, and rested not: the
Psa. 22. 14 melted in the midst of my bowels
71. 6 took me out of my mother's bowels
Song 5. 4 and my bowels were moved for him
Isa. 16. 11 my bowels shall sound like an harp
48. 19 the offspring of thy bowels like the gravel
49. 1 from the bowels of my mother hath he
63. 15 the sounding of thy bowels and of thy
Jer. 4. 19 My bowels, my bowels! I am pained
31. 20 therefore my bowels are troubled for him
Lam. 1. 20 my bowels are troubled; mine heart
2. 11 my bowels are troubled, my liver is
Eze. 3. 3 fill thy bowels with this roll that I give
7. 19 they shall not..fill their bowels
2. *Heart*, קֶרֶב *qereb*.
Psa. 109. 18 let it come into his bowels like water
3. *Womb, feelings of pity*, רַחֲמִים *rachamim*.
Gen. 43. 30 his bowels did yearn upon his brother
1 Ki. 3. 26 her bowels yearned upon her son, and
4. *Bowels*, σπλάγχνα *splagchna*.
Acts 1. 18 he burst..and all his bowels gushed out
2 Cor. 6. 12 ye are straitened in your own bowels
Phil. 1. 8 I long after you all in the bowels of Jesus
2. 1 of the Spirit, if any bowels and mercies
Col. 3. 12 Put on therefore..bowels of mercies
Phm. 7 the bowels of the saints are refreshed by
12 receive him that is mine own bowels
20 the Lord: refresh my bowels in the Lord
BOWELS (of compassion) —
Bowels, σπλάγχνα *splagchna*.
1 Jo. 3. 17 shutteth up his bowels (of compassion)
BOWING —
To incline, נָטָה *natah*.
Psa. 62. 3 as a bowing wall..a tottering fence
BOWING down —
To incline, נָטָה *natah*.
Psa. 17. 11 set their eyes bowing down to the earth
BOWL —
1. *Bowl, calix*, גָּבִיעַ *gabia*.
Exod 25. 31 his bowls, his knops..shall be of the
25. 33 Three bowls made like unto almonds
25. 34 in the candlestick..four bowls made like
37. 17 his bowls, his knops..were of the same
37. 19 Three bowls made after the fashion of
37. 19 and three bowls made like almonds
37. 20 in the candlestick..four bowls made like
2. *Cruse*, גֹּל *gol*.
Zech. 4. 2 with a bowl upon the top of it, and his

3.*Cruise*, גֻּלָּה *gullah.*
1 Ki. 7. 41 bowls of the chapiters that (were) v. 41.
7. 42 to cover the two bowls of the chapiters
Eccl. 12. 6 or the golden bowl be broken, or the
Zech. 4. 3 one upon the right..of the bowl, and the

4.*Sprinkling pan*, מִזְרָק *mizraq.*
Num. 7. 13 one silver bowl of seventy shekels, after
So in v. 19, 25, 31, 37, 43, 49, 55, 61, 67, 73, 79.
7. 84 twelve silver bowls, twelve spoons of
7. 85 each bowl seventy: all the silver vessels
2 Ki. 25. 15 fire pans, and the bowls..such things as
1 Ch. 28. 17 the bowls, and the cups; and for the
Jer. 52. 18 the bowls, and the spoons, and all the
52. 19 the bowls, and the caldrons, and the
Amos 6. 6 That drink wine in bowls, and anoint
Zech. 9. 15 they shall be filled like bowls..as the
14. 20 shall be like the bowls before the altar

5.*Basin, dish*, סַף *saph.*
1 Ki. 7. 50 the bowls, and the snuffers, and the
2 Ki. 12. 13 for the house of the LORD bowls of silver

6.*A little cup or bowl*, סֵפֶל *sephel.*
Judg. 6. 38 it was so..a bowl full of water

BOWLS —
Sacrificial bowls, מְנַקִּיּוֹת *menaqqiyyoth.*
Exod. 25. 29 thou shalt make the..bowls thereof, to
37. 16 his bowls, and his covers to cover withal
Num. 4. 7 the bowls, and covers to cover withal

BOWMAN —
To cast (with) the bow, רָמָה קֶשֶׁת *ramah qesheth.*
Jer. 4. 29 noise of the horsemen and bowmen

BOW SHOT —
Stretchings of a bow, מְטַחֲוֵי קֶשֶׁת *metachave qesheth.*
Gen. 21. 16 as it were a bow shot; for she said, Let

BOX —
Cruet, flask, פַּךְ *pak.*
2 Ki. 9. 1 take this box of oil in thine hand
9. 3 take the box of oil, and pour (it) on his

BOX (tree) —
The sherbin cedar, תְּאַשּׁוּר *teashshur.*
Isa. 41. 19 I will set in the desert..the box tree
60. 13 the pine tree, and the box together, to

BOX, (alabaster) —
Alabaster box, ἀλάβαστρον *alabastron.*
Matt 26. 7 a woman having an alabaster box of very
Mark 14. 3 a woman having an alabaster box of
14. 3 she brake the box, and poured (it)
Luke 7. 37 brought an alabaster box of ointment

BOY —
1. *One born*, יֶלֶד *yeled.*
Joel 3. 3 have given a boy for an harlot, and sold
Zech 8. 5 streets of the city shall be full of boys

2.*A youth*, נַעַר *naar.*
Gen. 25. 27 the boys grew: and Esau was a cunning

BO'-ZEZ, בּוֹצֵץ *height, shining.*
A rock near the ravine of Michmash, not far from Gibeah of Benjamin. It was one of the two sharp rocks ("teeth of the cliff") between which Jonathan entered the garrison of the Philistines. It lay on the N. side, and may be the hills at the bottom of the *Wady Sweinit* just below *Mukmâs.*
1 Sa. 14. 4 and the name of the one (was) B.

BOZ'-KATH, בָּצְקַת *height.*
A city of Judah, in the Shephelah or plain. In 2 Ki. 22. 1 it is spelt *Boscath.*
Josh. 15. 39 Lachish, and B., and Eglon
2 Ki. 22. 1 mother..the daughter of Adaiah of B.

BOZ'-RAH, בָּצְרָה *fortification, restraint, sheepfold.*
1. The city of Jobab, son of Zerah, one of the early kings of Edom. Now called *el-Basaireh.*
Gen. 36. 33 Jobab the son of Zerah of B. reigned
1 Ch. 1. 44 Jobab the son of Zerah of B. reigned
Isa. 34. 6 for the LORD hath a sacrifice in B.
63. 1 cometh from Edom, with..garments..B.?
Jer. 49. 13 B. shall become a desolation..and a curse
49. 22 Behold, he shall..spread his wings over B.
Amos 1. 12 a fire..shall devour the palaces of B.
Mic. 2. 12 I will put them together as the sheep of B.
2. Bozrah, in the plain country of Moab.
Jer. 48. 24 upon Kerioth, and upon B., and upon

BRACELET —
1.*Arm band*, אֶצְעָדָה *etsadah.*
2 Sa. 1. 10 the bracelet that (was) on his arm, and

2.*Hook, ring*, חָח *chach.*
Exod 35. 22 brought bracelets, and ear rings

3.*Thread, cord*, פָּתִיל *pathil.*
Gen. 38. 18 Thy signet, and thy bracelets, and thy
38. 25 these, the signet, and bracelets, and staff

4.*Bracelet*, צָמִיד *tsamid.*
Gen. 24. 22 two bracelets for her hands of ten
24. 30 saw the..bracelets upon his sister's hands
24. 47 I put..the bracelets upon her hands
Num 31. 50 jewels of gold, chains, and bracelets
Eze. 16. 11 I put bracelets upon thy hands
23. 42 which put bracelets upon their hands

5.*Twisted ornaments*, שֵׁרוֹת *sheroth.*
Isa. 3. 19 The chains, and the bracelets, and the

BRAMBLE —
1.*Buck thorn*, אָטָד *atad.*
Judg. 9. 14 Then said all the trees unto the bramble
9. 15 the bramble said unto the trees, If in
9. 15 let fire come out of the bramble, and

2.*Thistle, thorn bush*, חוֹחַ *choach.*
Isa. 34. 13 nettles and brambles in the fortresses

BRAMBLE bush —
The bramble bush, ἡ βάτος *hē batos.*
Luke 6. 44 nor of a bramble bush gather they grapes

BRANCH —
1.*Summit*, אָמִיר *amir.*
Isa. 17. 9 an uppermost branch, which they left

2.*Branch*, בַּד *bad.*
Eze. 17. 6 brought forth branches, and shot forth
19. 14 fire is gone out of a rod of her branches
Hos. 11. 6 shall consume his branches, and devour

3.*Son*, בֵּן *ben.*
Psa. 80. 15 the branch..thou madest strong for thy

4.*Daughter*, בַּת *bath.*
Gen. 49. 22 (whose) branches run over the wall

5.*Twig, shoot*, זְמוֹרָה *zemorah.*
Num. 13. 23 a branch with one cluster of grapes
Eze. 8. 17 lo, they put the branch to their nose
15. 2 a branch which is among the trees of

6.*Twig, shoot*, זָמִיר *zamir.*
Isa. 25. 5 the branch of the terrible ones shall be

7.*Suckling*, יוֹנֶקֶת *yoneqeth.*
Job 8. 16 his branch shooteth forth in his garden
15. 30 the flame shall dry up his branches
Psa. 80. 11 She sent out..her branches unto the
Hos. 14. 6 His branches shall spread, and his

8. *Bending branch*, כַּף *kaph.*
Lev. 23. 40 ye shall take..branches of palm trees

9. *Bending branch*, כִּפָּה *kippah.*
Job 15. 32 and his branch shall not be green
Isa. 9. 14 head and tail, branch and rush
19. 15 which the head or tail, branch or rush

10.*Shoot*, נֵצֶר *netser.*
Isa. 11. 1 a Branch shall grow out of his roots
14. 19 cast out..like an abominable branch
60. 21 the branch of my planting, the work
Dan. 11. 7 out of a branch of her roots shall (one)

11. *Twig*, סְעִיף *saiph.*
Isa. 27. 10 shall he..consume the branches thereof

12.*Leaf, ascending sprout*, עָלֶה *aleh.*
Neh. 8. 15 fetch olive branches, and pine branches, and myrtle branches, and palm branches, and branches
Prov. 11. 28 righteous shall flourish as a branch

13. *Bough, branch*, עָנָף, עֲנַף *anaph.*
Eze. 17. 8 that it might bring forth branches
31. 3 the Assyrian..a cedar..with..branches
36. 8 ye shall shoot forth your branches, and
Mal. 4. 1 shall leave them neither root nor branch
Dan. 4. 14 Hew down..and cut off his branches
4. 14 and the fowls from his branches
4. 21 upon whose branches the fowls..had

14.*A leafy sapling*, פֹּארָה *porah.*
Eze. 31. 5 his branches became long, because of
31. 6 under his branches did all the beasts of
31. 8 chesnut trees were not like his branches
31. 13 all the beasts..shall be upon his branches

15.*A sprout*, צֶמַח *tsemach.*
Isa. 4. 2 In that day shall the branch of the LORD
Jer. 23. 5 I will raise unto..a righteous Branch
33. 15 will I cause the Branch of righteousness
Zech. 3. 8 I will bring forth my servant the BRANCH
6. 12 Behold..whose name (is) The BRANCH

16.*A reed, cane*, קָנֶה *qaneh.*
Exod 25. 31 his branches, his bowls, his knops, and
25. 32 six branches shall come out of the sides
25. 32 three branches..and three branches
25. 33 a knop and a flower in one branch
25. 33 three bowls..in the other branch
25. 33 so in the six branches that come out of
25. 35 a knop under two branches of the same
25. 35 a knop under two branches of the same
25. 35 a knop under two branches of the same
25. 35 according to the six branches that
25. 36 Their knops and their branches shall be
37. 17 his branch, his bowls, his knops, and his
37. 18 six branches going out of the sides
37. 18 three branches..out of the one side
37. 18 three branches..out of the other side
37. 19 Three bowls made..in one branch
37. 19 three bowls made..in another branch
37. 19 so throughout the six branches going out
37. 21 a knop under two branches of the same
37. 21 a knop under two branches of the same
37. 21 a knop under two branches of the same
37. 21 according to the six branches going out
37. 22 Their knops and their branches were of

17.*A cutting, branch*, קָצִיר *qatsir.*
Job 18. 16 and above shall his branch be cut off
29. 19 dew lay all night upon my branch

18.*A twig*, שִׁבֹּלֶת *shibboleth.*
Zech. 4. 12 What..two olive branches which through

19.*A branch of a palm tree*, βαΐον *baion.*
John 12. 13 Took branches of palm trees, and went

20.*A young slip or shoot*, κλάδος *klados.*
Matt 13. 32 birds..come and lodge in the branches
21. 8 others cut down branches from the trees
24. 32 When his branch is yet tender, and
Mark 4. 32 shooteth out great branches, so that the
13. 28 When her branch is yet tender, and
Luke 13. 19 the fowls..lodged in the branches of it
Rom. 11. 16 if the root (be) holy, so (are) the branches
11. 17 if some of the branches be broken off, and
11 18 Boast not against the branches. But if
11. 19 Thou wilt say then, The branches were
11. 21 if God spared not the natural branches

21.*A cutting, slip*, κλῆμα *klēma.*
John 15. 2 Every branch in me that beareth not
15. 4 As the branch cannot bear fruit of itself
15. 5 I am the vine, ye (are) the branches
15. 6 he is cast forth as a branch, and is withered

22.*Branch, leaves*, στοιβάς *stoibas.*
Mark 11. 8 others cut down [branches] off the trees

BRANCH, highest —
A high branch, צַמֶּרֶת *tsammereth.*
Eze. 17. 3 and took the highest branch of the cedar
17. 22 I will also take of the highest branch of

BRANCH, vine —
Twig, shoot, זְמוֹרָה *zemorah.*
Nah. 2. 2 and marred their vine branches

BRANCH, outmost —
A branch, sprout, סְעִיף *saiph.*
Isa. 17. 6 in the outmost fruitful branches thereof

BRANCH, tender —
Suckling, יוֹנֶקֶת *yoneqeth.*
Job 14. 7 the tender branch thereof will not cease

BRANCH, thick —
Thick branches, עֲבֹת *aboth.*
Eze. 19. 11 her stature was..among..thick branches

BRANCHES —
1. *Waving branches*, דָּלִיּוֹת *daliyyoth.*
Jer. 11. 16 olive tree..the branches of it are broken
Eze. 17. 6 whose branches turned toward him, and
17. 7 shot forth her branches toward him, that
17. 23 in the shadow of the branches thereof
19. 11 the multitude of her branches
31. 7 fair..in the length of his branches
31. 9 I have made him fair by..his branches
31. 12 in all the valleys his branches are fallen

2.*Tendrils, twigs*, נְטִישׁוֹת *netishoth.*
Isa. 18. 5 and take away..cut down the branches

3. *Twigs, branches, shoots*, עֳפָאִים *ophaim.*
Psa 104. 12 the fowls..sing among the branches!

4. *Shoots of a vine*, שָׂרִיגִים *sarigim.*
Gen. 40. 10 And in the vine (were) three branches
40. 12 The three branches (are) three days
Joel 1. 7 the branches thereof are made white

5.*Stretching out, sending forth*, שְׁלֻחוֹת *sheluchoth.*
Isa. 16. 8 her branches are stretched out, they are

BRANCHES, full of —
To abound in branches, עָנֵף *aneph.*
Eze. 19. 10 she was fruitful and full of branches

BRAND —
1. *Burning brand*, אוּד *ud.*
Zech. 3. 2 not this a brand plucked out of the fire?

2.*Burning torch*, לַפִּיד *lappid.*
Judg 15. 5 when he had set the brands on fire, he

BRANDISH, to —
To cause to fly or move swiftly, עוּף *uph*, 3a.
Eze. 32. 10 when I shall brandish my sword before

BRASEN —
Brass, copper, נְחֹשֶׁת *nechosheth.*
Exod 27. 4 make four brasen rings in the four corners
35. 16 The altar..with his brasen grate, his
38. 4 he made for the altar a brasen grate of
38. 10 their brasen sockets twenty: the hooks
38. 30 the brasen altar, and the brasen grate for
39. 39 The brasen altar, and his grate of brass
Lev. 6. 28 if it be sodden in a brasen pot, it shall
Num 16. 39 Eleazar the priest took the brasen censers
1 Ki. 4. 13 great cities with walls and brasen bars
7. 30 every base had four brasen wheels, and
8. 64 the brasen altar that (was) before the LORD
14. 27 made in their stead brasen shields, and
2 Ki. 16. 14 he brought also the brasen altar, which
16. 15 the brasen altar shall be for me to enquire
16. 17 took down the sea from off the brasen
18. 4 brake in pieces the brasen serpent that
25. 13 the brasen sea that (was) in the house of
1 Ch. 18. 8 Solomon made the brasen sea, and the
2 Ch. 1. 5 the brasen altar, that Bezaleel the son of
1. 6 went up thither to the brasen altar
6. 13 Solomon had made a brasen scaffold, of
7. 7 the brasen altar..was not able to receive
Jer. 1. 18 brasen walls against the whole land
15. 20 I will make thee..a fenced brasen wall
52. 17 the brasen sea that (was) in the house of
52. 20 twelve brasen bulls that (were) under the
Eze. 9. 2 went in, and stood beside..brasen altar

BRASEN vessel —

Copper or bronze vessel, χαλκίον *chalkion.*

Mark 7. 4 cups and pots, brasen vessels, and of

BRASS —

Brass was much used by the ancient Hebrews, and made into altars, bars, fetters, gates, greaves, helmets, household vessels, idols, instruments of music, lavers, mirrors, pillars, sacred vessels, shields, sockets for pillars, &c.

1. *Brass, copper,* נְחוּשׁ *nachush.*

Job 6. 12 (Is) my strength..(is) my flesh of brass

2. *Brass, copper,* נְחוּשָׁה *nechushah.*

Lev. 26. 19 heaven as iron, and your earth as brass
Job. 28. 2 and brass (is) molten (out of) the stone
40. 18 His bones(are as) strong pieces of brass
41. 27 He esteemeth..brass as rotten wood
Isa. 45. 2 I will break in pieces the gates of brass
48. 4 an iron sinew, and thy brow brass
Mic. 4. 13 I will make thy hoofs brass; and

3. *Brass, copper,* נְחָשׁ *nechash.*

Dan. 2. 32 his belly and his thighs of brass
2. 35 Then was..the brass..broken to pieces
2. 39 another third kingdom of brass, which
2. 45 it brake in pieces the iron, the brass, the
4. 15, 23 with a band of iron and brass, in the
5. 4 gods..of brass, of iron, of wood, and of
5. 23 gods of silver, and gold, of brass, iron
7. 19 whose teeth..iron, and his nails (of) brass

4. *Brass, copper,* נְחֹשֶׁת *nechosheth.*

Gen. 4. 22 an instructor of every artificer in brass
Exod 25. 3 take of them; gold, and silver, and brass
26. 11 thou shalt make fifty taches of brass, and
26. 37 thou shalt cast five sockets of brass for
27. 2 and thou shalt overlay it with brass
27. 3 the vessels..thou shalt make (of) brass
27. 4 make for it a grate of network (of) brass
27. 6 make staves..overlay them with brass
27. 10, 11 and their twenty sockets (of) brass
27. 17 hooks..of silver, and their sockets of brass
27. 18 twined linen, and their sockets (of) brass
27. 19 all the pins of the court, (shall be of) brass
30. 18 Thou shalt also make a laver (of) brass
30. 18 his foot (also of) brass, to wash (withal)
31. 4 work in gold, and in silver, and in brass
35. 5 let him bring..gold, and silver, and brass
35. 24 did offer an offering of silver and brass
35. 32 work in gold, and in silver, and in brass
36. 18 he made fifty taches (of) brass to couple
36. 38 but their five sockets (were of) brass
38. 2 and he overlaid it with brass
38. 3 the vessels thereof made he (of) brass
38. 5 for the four ends of the grate of brass
38. 6 and overlaid them with brass
38. 8 And he made the laver (of) brass
38. 8 and the foot of it (of) brass
38. 11 their sockets of brass twenty; the hooks
38. 17 the sockets for the pillars (were of) brass
38. 19 their sockets (of) brass four; their hooks
38. 20 all the pins of the tabernacle..brass
38. 29 the brass of the offering (was) seventy
Num 21. 9 Moses made a serpent of brass, and put
21. 9 when he beheld the serpent of brass
31. 22 Only the gold, and the silver, the brass
Deut. 8. 9 out of whose hills thou mayest dig brass
28. 23 heaven..over thy head shall be brass
33. 25 Thy shoes..iron and brass; and as thy
Josh. 6. 19 vessels of brass and iron, (are) consecrated
6. 24 the vessels of brass and of iron, they put
22. 8 with silver, and with gold, and with brass
1 Sa. 17. 5 an helmet of brass upon his head, and
17. 5 coat (was) five thousand shekels of brass
17. 6 greaves of brass upon his legs
17. 6 a target of brass between his shoulders,
17. 38 put an helmet of brass upon his head
2 Sa 8. 8 king David took exceeding much brass
8. 10 vessels of gold, and vessels of brass
21. 16 three hundred(shekels)of brass in weight
1 Ki. 7. 14 worker in brass..to work..in brass
7. 15 he cast two pillars of brass, of eighteen
7. 16 he made two chapiters (of) molten brass
7. 27 he made ten bases of brass; four cubits
7. 30 every base had..wheels..plates of brass
7. 38 Then made he ten lavers of brass
7. 45 vessels..for the house of the LORD..brass
7. 47 neither was the weight of the brass found
2 Ki. 25. 13 the pillars of brass that (were) in the
25. 13 carried the brass of them to Babylon
25. 14 and all the vessels of brass wherewith
25. 16 the brass of all these vessels was without
25. 17 the chapiter upon it (was) brass; and the
25. 17 the chapiter round about, all of brass
1 Ch. 15. 19 the singers..to sound..cymbals of brass
18. 8 brought David very much brass
18. 8 and the pillars, and the vessels of brass
18. 10 of vessels of gold and silver and brass
22. 3 and brass in abundance without weight
22. 14 brass and iron without weight; for it is
22. 16 Of the gold, the silver, and the brass, and
29. 2 and the brass for (things) of brass, the
29. 7 of brass eighteen thousand talents, and
2 Ch. 2. 7 in gold, and in silver, and in brass
2. 14 in gold, and in silver, in brass, in iron
4. 1 he made an altar of brass, twenty
4. 9 overlaid the doors of them with brass
4. 16 for the house of the LORD, of bright brass
4. 18 weight of the brass could not be found
12. 10 king Rehoboam made shields of brass
24. 12 brass to mend the house of the LORD
Psa. 107. 16 he hath broken the gates of brass, and
Isa. 60. 17 For brass I will bring gold, and for
Isa. 60. 17 and for wood brass, and for stones iron
Jer. 6. 28 brass and iron; they (are) all corrupters
52. 17 pillars of brass that (were) in the house
52. 17 carried all the brass of them to Babylon
52. 18 the spoons, and all the vessels of brass
52. 20 brass of all these vessels was without
52. 22 a chapiter of brass (was) upon it; and the
52. 22 the chapiters round about, all (of) brass
Eze. 1. 7 sparkled like the colour of burnished brass
22. 18 all they (are) brass, and tin, and iron
22. 20 they gather silver, and brass, and iron
24. 11 that the brass of it may be hot, and may
27. 13 and vessels of brass in thy market
40. 3 man..like the appearance of brass
Dan. 10. 6 his feet like in colour to polished brass
Zech. 6. 1 the mountains (were) mountains of brass

5. *Copper, bronze,* χαλκός *chalkos.*

Matt 10. 9 Provide neither gold..silver, nor brass
1 Co. 13. 1 I am become (as) sounding brass, or a
Rev. 18. 12 vessels of..precious wood, and of brass

BRASS, fine —

White copper, χαλκολίβανον *chalkolibanon.*

Rev. 1. 15 his feet like unto fine brass, as if
2. 18 and his feet (are) like fine brass

BRASS, of —

Of copper, χάλκεος *chalkeos,* χαλκοῦς.

Rev. 9. 20 idols of gold, and silver, and brass

BRASS, fetters of —

Brass, copper, נְחֹשֶׁת *nechosheth.*

Judg 16. 21 bound him with fetters of brass; and
2 Ki. 25. 7 bound him with fetters of brass, and

BRAVERY —

Beauty, תִּפְאָרָה (תִּפְאֶרֶת *tipharah*), *tiphereth.*

Isa. 3. 18 take away the bravery of..tinkling orn.

BRAWLER, not a —

Not fighting, not striving, ἄμαχος *amachos.*

1 Ti. 3. 3 patient, not a brawler, not covetous
Titus 3. 2 speak evil of no man, to be no brawlers

BRAWLING —

Contention, strife, מָדוֹן *madon* [V.L. מִדְיָנִים *midyanim*].

Prov. 21. 9 than with a brawling woman in a wide
25. 24 than with a brawling woman and in a

BRAY, to —

To bray, נָהַק *nahaq.*

Job 6. 5 Doth the wild ass bray when he hath
30. 7 Among the bushes they brayed; under

BRAY (in a mortar), to —

To butt, pound, כָּתַשׁ *kathash.*

Prov. 27. 22 Though thou shouldest bray a fool in a m.

BREACH —

1. *Breach, rent, leak,* בֶּדֶק *bedeq.*

2 Ki. 12. 5 let them repair the breaches of the house
12. 5 wheresoever any breach shall be found
12. 6 the priests had not repaired the breaches
12. 7 Why repair ye not the breaches of the
12. 7 deliver it for the breaches of the house
12. 8 neither to repair the breaches of the
12. 12 hewed stone to repair the breaches of the
22. 5 to repair the breaches of the house

2. *Cleft, valley,* בָּקִיעַ *baqia.*

Isa. 22. 9 the breaches of the city of David

3. *Gulf, incision,* מִפְרָץ *miphrats.*

Judg. 5. 17 Asher..abode in his breaches

4. *To break through,* פָּרַץ *parats* (pass. part.).

Neh. 4. 7 that the breaches began to be stopped

5. *A breaking forth,* פֶּרֶץ *perets.*

Gen. 38. 29 hast thou broken forth? (this) breach
Judg 21. 15 the LORD had made a breach in the tribes
2 Sa. 5. 20 upon mine enemies..as the breach of
6. 8 LORD had made a breach upon Uzzah
1 Ki. 11. 27 Solomon..repaired the breaches of the
1 Ch. 13. 11 LORD had made a breach upon Uzzah
Neh. 6. 1 there was no breach left therein
Job 16. 14 breaketh me with breach upon breach
Psa. 106. 23 stood before him in the breach, to
Isa. 30. 13 this iniquity shall be to you as a breach
58. 12 be called, The repairer of the breach
Amos 4. 3 ye shall go out at the breaches, every
9. 11 close up the breaches thereof; and I will

6. *Breach,* שֶׁבֶר *sheber.*

Lev. 24. 20 Breach for breach, eye for eye, tooth for
Psa. 60. 2 heal the breaches thereof; for it shaketh
Prov. 15. 4 perverseness therein (is) a breach in the
Isa. 30. 26 LORD bindeth up the breach of his people
Jer. 14. 17 great breach, with a very grievous blow
Lam. 2. 13 for thy breach (is) great like the sea

BREACH, to be made a —

To be cleft, בָּקַע *baqa,* 4.

Eze. 26. 10 into a city wherein is made a breach

BREACH, to make a —

1. *Cleave through,* בָּקַע *baqa,* 5; Isa. 7. 6.

2. *Break through,* פָּרַץ *parats;* 1 Ch. 15. 13.

BREACH of promise —

Removal, alienation, תְּנוּאָה *tenuah.*

Num 14. 34 ye shall know my breach of promise

BREACHES —

Droppings, רְסִיסִים *resisim.*

Amos 6. 11 will smite the great house with breaches

BREAD —

1. *Food, bread, sustenance,* לֶחֶם *lechem.*

Gen. 3. 19 sweat of thy face shalt thou eat bread
14. 18 Melchizedek..brought forth bread and
18. 5 I will fetch a morsel of bread, and
21. 14 took bread, and a bottle of water, and
25. 34 Jacob gave Esau bread and pottage of
27. 17 she gave the savoury meat and the bread
28. 20 give me bread to eat, and raiment to put
31. 54 and called his brethren to eat bread
31. 54 they did eat bread, and tarried all night
37. 25 they sat down to eat bread: and they
39. 6 ought..save the bread which he did eat
41. 54 in all the land of Egypt there was bread
41. 55 people cried to Pharaoh for bread: and
43. 25 heard that they should eat bread there
43. 31 refrained himself, and said, Set on bread
43. 32 the Egyptians might not eat bread with
45. 23 laden with corn and bread and meat
47. 12 all his father's household, with bread
47. 13 no bread in all the land; for the famine
47. 15 Give us bread: for why should we die
47. 17 Joseph gave them bread (in exchange)
47. 17 he fed them with bread for all their
47. 19 buy us and our land for bread, and we
49. 20 Out of Asher his bread (shall be) fat, and
Exod. 2. 20 call him, that he may eat bread
16. 3 when we did eat bread to the full!
16. 4 I will rain bread from heaven for you
16. 8 in the morning bread to the full; for
16. 12 the morning ye shall be filled with bread
16. 15 This (is) the bread which the LORD hath
16. 22 they gathered twice as much bread
16. 29 on the sixth day the bread of two days
16. 32 they may see the bread wherewith I
18. 12 to eat bread with Moses' father-in-law
23. 25 he shall bless thy bread, and thy water
29. 2 unleavened bread, and cakes unleavened
29. 23 loaf of bread, and one cake of oiled bread
29. 32 the bread that (is) in the basket, (by) the
29. 34 if ought..of the bread, remain unto the
34. 28 he did neither eat bread, nor drink
40. 23 he set the bread in order upon it before
Lev. 7. 13 he shall offer..his offering leavened bread
8. 26 out of the basket of unleavened bread
8. 31 there eat it with the bread that (is) in
8. 32 that which remaineth..of the bread shall
21. 6 the bread of their God, they do offer
21. 8 he offereth the bread of thy God: he shall
21. 17 approach to offer the bread of his God
21. 21 come nigh to offer the bread of his God
21. 22 He shall eat the bread of his God..of the
22. 25 shall ye offer the bread of your God of
23. 14 ye shall eat neither bread, nor parched
23. 18 ye shall offer with the bread seven lambs
23. 20 with the bread of the firstfruits..a wave
24. 7 it may be on the bread for a memorial
26. 5 ye shall eat your bread to the full, and
26. 26 I have broken the staff of your bread
26. 26 ten women shall bake your bread in one
26. 26 they shall deliver (you) your bread again
Num. 4. 7 and the continual bread shall be thereon
14. 9 they (are) bread for us: their defence is
15. 19 when ye eat of the bread of the land, ye
21. 5 no bread, neither (is there any) water
21. 5 and our soul loatheth this light bread
28. 2 my bread for my sacrifices made by fire
Deut. 8. 3 man doth not live by bread only, but by
8. 9 thou shalt eat bread without scarceness
9. 18 I did neither eat bread nor drink water
16. 3 Thou shalt eat no leavened bread with it
23. 4 Because they met you not with bread
29. 6 Ye have not eaten bread, neither have
Josh. 9. 5 all the bread of their provision was dry
9. 12 our bread we took hot (for) our provision
Judg. 7. 13 a cake of barley bread tumbled into the
8. 5 Give, I pray you, loaves of bread unto
8. 6 we should give bread unto thine army?
8. 15 give bread unto thy men (that are) weary?
13. 16 I will not eat of thy bread: and if thou
19. 5 Comfort thine heart with a morsel of b.
19. 19 there is bread and wine also for me, and
Ruth 1. 6 had visited his people in giving them b.
2. 14 come thou hither, and eat of the bread
1 Sa. 2. 5 full have hired out themselves for bread
2. 36 a piece of silver and a morsel of bread
2. 36 that I may eat a piece of bread
9. 7 for the bread is spent in our vessels
10. 3 another carrying three loaves of bread
10. 4 give thee two (loaves) of bread; which
16. 20 an ass (laden) with bread, and a bottle
21. 3 give (me) five (loaves of) bread in mine
21. 4 common bread..there is hallowed bread
21. 6 was no bread there but the shewbread
21. 6 to put hot bread in the day when it
22. 13 thou hast given him bread, and a sword
25. 11 Shall I then take my bread, and my water
28. 20 he had eaten no bread all the day, nor all
28. 22 let me set a morsel of bread before thee
30. 11 gave him bread, and he did eat; and
30. 12 for he had eaten no bread, nor drunk
2 Sa. 3. 29 falleth on the sword, or that lacketh b.
3. 35 if I taste bread, or ought else, till the
6. 19 a cake of bread, and a good piece (of flesh)
9. 7 thou shalt eat bread at my table contin.
9. 10 thy master's son shall eat bread..at my
12. 17 neither did he eat bread with them
12. 20 they set bread before him, and he did

2 Sa. 12. 21 was dead, thou didst rise and eat bread
16. 1 upon them two hundred (loaves) of bread
16. 2 bread and summer fruit for the young
1 Ki. 13. 8 neither will I eat bread nor drink water
13. 9 Eat no bread, nor drink water, nor turn
13. 15 Come home with me, and eat bread
13. 16 neither will I eat bread nor drink water
13. 17 Thou shalt eat no bread nor drink water
13. 18 that he may eat bread and drink water
13. 19 he went back..and did eat bread
13. 22 hast eaten bread and drunk water in
13. 22 Eat no bread, and drink no water; thy
13. 23 to pass, after he had eaten bread, and
17. 6 ravens brought him bread and flesh
17. 6 bread and flesh in the evening; and he
17. 11 Bring me, I pray thee, a morsel of bread
18. 4, 13 fed them with bread and water
21. 4 turned away..and would eat no bread
21. 5 so sad, that thou eatest no bread?
21. 7 Arise..eat bread, and let thine heart be
22. 27 feed him with bread of affliction, and
2 Ki. 4. 8 she constrained him to eat bread
4. 8 he turned in thither to eat bread
4. 42 brought the man of God bread of the
6. 22 Set bread and water before them, that
18. 32 a land of bread and vineyards, a land of
25. 3 there was no bread for the people of the
25. 29 he did eat bread continually before him
1 Ch. 12. 40 brought bread on asses, and on camels
16. 3 to every one a loaf of bread, and a good
2 Ch. 18. 26 feed him with bread of affliction and
Ezra 10. 6 he came thither, he did eat no bread, nor
Neh. 5. 14 my brethren have not eaten the bread of
5. 15 had taken of them bread and wine
5. 18 for all this required not I the bread
9. 15 gavest them bread from heaven for
13. 2 they met not..with bread and with water
Job 15. 23 He wandereth abroad for bread, (saying)
22. 7 thou hast withholden bread from the
27. 14 offspring shall not be satisfied with bread
28. 5 the earth, out of it cometh bread; and
33. 20 So that his life abhorreth bread, and
42. 11 did eat bread with him in his house
Psa. 14. 4 who eat up my people..they eat bread
37. 25 have I not seen..his seed begging bread
41. 9 familiar friend..did eat of my bread
53. 4 who eat up my people..they eat bread
78. 20 can he give bread also? can he provide
80. 5 Thou feedest them with the bread of
102. 4 grass; so that I forget to eat my bread
102. 9 I have eaten ashes like bread, and
104. 15 bread..strengtheneth man's heart
105. 16 land: he brake the whole staff of bread
105. 40 satisfied them with the bread of heaven
127. 2 sit up late, to eat the bread of sorrows
132. 15 I will satisfy her poor with bread
Prov. 4. 17 they eat the bread of wickedness, and
6. 26 (a man is brought) to a piece of bread
9. 5 Come, eat of my bread, and drink of the
9. 17 and bread..in secret is pleasant
12. 9 honoureth himself, and lacketh bread
12. 11 his land shall be satisfied with bread
20. 13 thou shalt be satisfied with bread
20. 17 Bread of deceit (is) sweet to a man; but
22. 9 for he giveth of his bread to the poor
23. 6 Eat thou not the bread of..an evil eye
25. 21 If..enemy be hungry, give him bread
28. 19 He that tilleth..land shall have..bread
28. 21 for a piece of bread..man will
31. 27 and eateth not the bread of idleness
Eccl. 9. 7 Go thy way, eat thy bread with joy
9. 11 neither yet bread to the wise
11. 1 Cast thy bread upon the waters: for thou
Isa. 3. 1 the staff, the whole stay of bread
3. 7 in..house (is) neither bread nor clothing
4. 1 We will eat our own bread, and wear
21. 14 prevented with their bread him that fled
28. 28 Bread..is bruised; because he will not
30. 20 LORD give you the bread of adversity
30. 23 bread of the increase of the earth, and
33. 16 bread shall be given him, his waters
36. 17 to a land..of bread and vineyards
44. 15 he kindleth (it), and baketh bread; yea
44. 19 I have baked bread upon the coals
51. 14 not die..nor that his bread should fail
55. 2 do ye spend money for..not bread?
55. 10 seed to the sower, and bread to the eater
58. 7 (Is it) not to deal thy bread to the hungry
Jer. 5. 17 eat up thine harvest, and thy bread
37. 21 should give him daily a piece of bread
37. 21 until all the bread..were spent
38. 9 for (there is) no more bread in the city
41. 1 they did eat bread together in Mizpah
42. 14 see no war..nor have hunger of bread
52. 6 there was no bread for the people of
52. 33 he did continually eat bread before him
Lam. 1. 11 All her people sigh, they seek bread
4. 4 young children ask bread..no man
5. 6 the Assyrians, to be satisfied with bread
5. 9 We gat our bread with..our lives
Eze. 4. 9 vessel, and make thee bread thereof
4. 13 eat their defiled bread among the Gentiles
4. 15 thou shalt prepare thy bread therewith
4. 16 I will break the staff of bread in Jerus.
4. 16 they shall eat bread by weight, and with
4. 17 That they may want bread and water
5. 16 and will break your staff of bread
12. 18 Son of man, eat thy bread with quaking
12. 19 shall eat their bread with carefulness
13. 19 handfuls of barley and for..bread
14. 13 will break the staff of the bread thereof
16. 49 fulness of bread, and abundance of idle.
Eze. 18. 7, 16 hath given his bread to the hungry
24. 17 Forbear..eat not the bread of men
24. 22 cover..lips, nor eat the bread of men
44. 3 the prince, he shall sit in it to eat bread
44. 7 ye offer my bread, the fat and the blood
Dan. 10. 3 I ate no pleasant bread, neither came
Hos. 2. 5 that give (me) my bread and my water
9. 4 unto them as the bread of mourners
9. 4 their bread for their soul shall not come
Amos 4. 6 want of bread in all your places: yet
7. 12 there eat bread, and prophesy there
8. 11 in the land, not a famine of bread
Obad. 7 (they that eat) thy bread have laid a
Hag. 2. 12 with his skirt do touch bread, or pottage
Mal. 1. 7 Ye offer polluted bread upon mine altar

2.*Bread, loaf (of wheat),* ἄρτος *artos.*
Matt. 4. 3 command that..stones be made bread
4. 4 Man shall not live by bread alone; 6. 11.
7. 9 son ask bread, will he give him a stone?
15. 2 wash not..hands when they eat bread
15. 26 not meet to take the children's bread
15. 33 Whence should we have so much bread
16. 5 his disciples..had forgotten to take bread
16. 7 (It is) because we have taken no bread
16. 8 because ye have brought no bread?
16. 11 I spake (it) not to you concerning bread
16. 12 he bade..not..of the leaven of [bread]
26. 26 Jesus took bread, and blessed (it), and
Mark 3. 20 that they could not so much as eat bread
6. 8 no scrip, no bread, no money in..purse
6. 36 the villages, and buy themselves [bread]
6. 37 buy two hundred pennyworth of bread
7. 2 saw some of his disciples eat bread with
7. 5 but eat bread with unwashen hands?
7. 27 not meet to take the children's bread
8. 4 with bread here in the wilderness?
8. 14 had forgotten to take bread
8. 16 saying, (It is) because we have no bread
8. 17 reason ye because ye have no bread
14. 22 Jesus took bread, and blessed, and brake
Luke 4. 3 command this stone that it be..bread
4. 4 man shall not live by bread alone, but
7. 33 John..came neither eating [bread] nor
9. 3 nor scrip, neither bread, neither money
11. 3 Give us day by day our daily bread
11. 11 If a son shall ask bread of any of you
14. 1 to eat bread on the sabbath day, that
14. 15 Blessed (is) he that shall eat [bread] in
15. 17 servants of my father's have bread
22. 19 he took bread, and gave thanks, and brake
24. 30 he took bread, and blessed (it), and brake
24. 35 known of them in breaking of bread
John 6. 5 Whence shall we buy bread, that these
6. 7 Two hundred penny worth of bread is
6. 23 the place where they did eat bread
6. 31 He gave them bread from heaven to eat
6. 32 Moses gave you not that bread from
6. 32 giveth you the true bread from heaven
6. 33 the bread of God is he which cometh down
6. 34 Lord, evermore give us this bread
6. 35 Jesus said unto them, I am the bread of
6. 41 I am the bread which came down from
6. 48 I am that bread of life
6. 50 This is the bread which cometh down
6. 51 I am the living bread..this bread
6. 51 the bread that I will give is my flesh
6. 58 This is that bread which came down
6. 58 he that eateth of this bread shall live for
13. 18 He that eateth bread with me hath
21. 9 they saw..fish laid thereon, and bread
21. 13 Jesus then cometh, and taketh bread
Acts 2. 42 in breaking of bread, and in prayers
2. 46 and breaking bread from house to house
20. 7 disciples came together to break bread
20. 11 When he..had broken bread, and eaten
27. 35 he took bread, and gave thanks to God
1 Co. 10. 16 The bread which we break, is it not the
10. 17 For we..many are one bread..one body
10. 17 we are all partakers of that one bread
11. 23 night in which..betrayed took bread
11. 26 as often as ye eat this bread, and drink
11. 27 whosoever shall eat this bread, and drink
11. 28 so let him eat of (that) bread, and drink
2 Co. 9. 10 the sower, both minister bread for..food
2 Th. 3. 8 Neither did we eat any man's bread
3. 12 with quietness they work, and eat..bread

BREAD, leavened —
1.*Any thing pungent, leavened,* חָמֵץ *chamets.*
Exod 12. 15 whosoever eateth leavened bread from
13. 3 there shall no leavened bread be eaten
13. 7 no leavened bread be seen with thee
23. 18 of my sacrifice with leavened bread
Deut 16. 3 Thou shalt eat no leavened bread with it
2.*Any thing leavened,* שְׂאֹר *seor.*
Deut 16. 4 there shall be no leavened bread seen

BREAD, shew —
1.*Bread set in array,* לֶחֶם מַעֲרֶכֶת *lechem maareketh.*
1 Ch. 9. 32 the shewbread, to prepare (it) every
23. 29 for the shewbread and for the fine flour
28. 16 gold for the tables of shewbread, for
2 Ch. 2. 4 for the continual shewbread, and for
13. 11 the shewbread also..upon the pure table
29. 18 vessels thereof, and the shewbread table
Neh. 10. 33 For the shewbread, and for the continual
2.*Bread set before (God),* לֶחֶם פָּנִים *lechem panim.*
Exod 25. 30 thou shalt set upon the table shewbread
35. 13 table..all his vessels, and the shewbread,
39. 36 the vessels thereof, and the shewbread
1 Sa. 21. 6 was no bread there but the shewbread
1 Ki. 7. 48 table of gold, whereupon the shewbread
2 Ch. 4. 19 and the tables whereon the shewbread
3.*Face, presence,* פָּנִים *panim.*
Num 4. 7 upon the table of shewbread they
4.*Loaves of setting out,* ἄρτοι τῆς προθέσεως.
Matt. 12. 4 entered..and did eat the shewbread
Mark 2. 26 went..and did eat the shewbread
Luke 6. 4 did take and eat the shewbread, and
5.*Setting forth of the loaves,* πρόθεσις τῶν ἄρτων.
Heb. 9. 2 wherein..the table, and the shewbread

BREAD, unleavened —
1.*Any thing squeezed together,* מַצָּה *matstsah.*
Gen. 19. 3 bake unleavened bread, and they did eat
Exod 12. 8 flesh in that night..and unleavened bread
12. 15 Seven days..eat unleavened bread
12. 17 ye shall observe..unleavened bread
12. 18 at even, ye shall eat unleavened bread
12. 20 habitations shall ye eat unleavened bread
13. 6 Seven days..eat unleavened bread
13. 7 Unleavened bread shall be eaten seven
23. 15 keep the feast of unleavened bread
23. 15 thou shalt eat unleavened bread seven
29. 23 unleavened bread that (is) before..LORD
34. 18 The feast of unleavened bread..keep
34. 18 seven days..eat unleavened bread
Lev. 6. 16 with unleavened bread shall it be eaten
8. 2 Take..a basket of unleavened bread
8. 26 out of the basket of unleavened bread
23. 6 feast of unleavened bread unto the LORD
23. 6 Seven days ye..eat unleavened bread
Num. 6. 15 a basket of unleavened bread, cakes
6. 15 wafers of unleavened bread anointed
6. 17 with the basket of unleavened bread
9. 11 eat it with unleavened bread and
28. 17 seven days shall unleavened bread be
Deut 16. 3 shalt thou eat unleavened bread
16. 8 Six days thou shalt eat unleavened bread
16. 16 in the feast of unleavened bread, and in
1 Sa. 28. 24 and did bake unleavened bread thereof
2 Ki. 23. 9 they did eat of the unleavened bread
2 Ch. 8. 13 in the feast of unleavened bread, and in
30. 13 to keep the feast of unleavened bread
30 21 kept the feast of unleavened bread seven
35. 17 the feast of unleavened bread seven days
Ezra 6. 22 kept the feast of unleavened bread seven
Eze. 45. 21 days; unleavened bread shall be eaten
2.*Any thing unleavened,* ἄζυμος *azumos.*
Matt 26. 17 Now the first..of the..unleavened bread
Mark 14. 1 two days was..of unleavened bread
14. 12 the first day of unleavened bread, when
Luke 22. 1 the feast of unleavened bread drew nigh
22. 7 Then came the day of unleavened bread
Acts 12. 3 Then were the days of unleavened bread
20. 6 after the days of unleavened bread
1 Co. 5. 8 with the unleavened (bread) of sincerity

BREAD, daily —
Necessary or sufficient food, ἄρτος ἐπιούσιος
Matt. 6. 11 Give us this day our daily bread

BREADTH —
1.*Breadth,* מֶרְחָב *merchab.*
Hab. 1. 6 march through the breadth of the land
2.*Openness,* פְּתִי *pethai.*
Ezra 6. 3 the breadth thereof threescore cubits
Dan. 3. 1 the breadth thereof six cubits: he set
3.*Breadth, broad place,* רַחַב *rachab.*
Job 38. 18 Hast thou perceived the breadth of the
4.*Width, breadth,* רֹחַב *rochab.*
Gen. 6. 15 the breadth of it fifty cubits, and the
13. 17 walk through the land..the breadth of it
Exod 25. 10, 17 a cubit and a half the breadth thereof
25. 23 a cubit the breadth thereof, and a cubit
26. 2, 8 the breadth of one curtain four cubits
26. 16 a cubit and a half..the breadth of one
27. 12 the breadth of the court on the west side
27. 13 the breadth of the court on the east side
27. 18 the breadth fifty everywhere, and the
28. 16 and a span..the breadth thereof
30. 2 a cubit the breadth thereof; foursquare
36. 9 the breadth of one curtain four cubits
36. 15 four cubits..the breadth of one curtain
36. 21 breadth of a board one cubit and a half
37. 1, 6 cubit and a half the breadth of it
37. 10 a cubit the breadth thereof, and a cubit
37. 25 the breadth of it a cubit..foursquare
38. 1 five cubits..breadth thereof..foursquare
38. 18 the height in the breadth..five cubits
39. 9 a span the breadth thereof..doubled
Deut. 3. 11 four cubits the breadth of it, after the
1 Ki. 6. 2 the breadth thereof twenty..and the
6. 3 according to the breadth of the house
6. 3 ten cubits..the breadth thereof before
6. 20 twenty cubits in breadth, and twenty
7. 2 the breadth thereof fifty cubits, and the
7. 6 the breadth thereof thirty cubits: and the
7. 27 four cubits the breadth thereof, and three
2 Ch. 3. 3 cubits, and the breadth twenty cubits
3. 4, 8 the breadth of the house, twenty cubits
3. 8 the breadth thereof twenty cubits; and
4. 1 twenty cubits the breadth thereof, and
Job 37. 10 the breadth of the waters is straitened
Isa. 8. 8 fill the breadth of thy land, O Immanuel
Eze. 40. 5, 11 he measured the breadth of the
40. 13 the breadth (was) five and twenty cubits
40. 19 he measured..breadth, from the forefront
40. 20 length thereof, and the breadth thereof

Eze. 40. 21, 25, 36 the breadth five and twenty cubits
40. 48 the breadth of the gate (was) three cubits
40. 49 and the breadth eleven cubits; and
41. 1 the breadth of the tabernacle
41. 2 the breadth of the door (was) ten cubits
41. 2 and he measured..the breadth, twenty
41. 3 the breadth of the door seven cubits
41. 4 and the breadth twenty cubits, before
41. 5 the breadth of (every) side chamber four
41. 7 the breadth of the house..upward
41. 11 the breadth of the place that was left
41. 14 the breadth of the face of the house, and
42. 2 and the breadth (was) fifty cubits
42. 4 a walk of ten cubits breadth inward
43. 13 the breadth a cubit, and the border thereof
43. 14 the breadth..the breadth (one) cubit
45. 1 an oblation..the breadth..ten thousand
45. 3 the breadth of ten thousand: and in it
45. 5 the ten thousand of breadth, shall also
48. 8 five and twenty thousand..breadth
48. 9 The oblation..ten thousand in breadth
48. 10 toward the west ten thousand in breadth
48. 10 toward the east ten thousand in breadth
48. 13 and ten thousand in breadth: all the
48. 13 and the breadth ten thousand
48. 15 thousand that are left in the breadth
Zech. 2. 2 to see what (is) the breadth thereof
5. 2 and the breadth thereof ten cubits

5. *Breadth, width,* πλάτος *platos.*
Eph. 3. 18 what (is) the breadth, and length, and
Rev. 20. 9 they went up on the breadth of the earth
21. 16 the length is as large as the breadth
21. 16 The length, and the breadth, and the

BREADTH, hand —

1. *Flat, spread out hand,* טֶפַח *tephach.*
1 Ki. 7. 26 it (was) an handbreadth thick, and the
2 Ch 4. 5 the thickness of it (was) an handbreadth
Psa. 39. 5 hast made my days (as) an handbreadth

2. *Flat, spread out hand,* טֹפַח *tophach.*
Exod 25. 25 make unto it a border of an handbreadth
37. 12 he made..a border of an handbreadth
Eze. 40. 5 by the cubit and an handbreadth: so he
43. 13 (is) a cubit and an handbreadth

BREADTH, foot —

Treading of the sole of the foot, מִדְרַךְ כַּף רֶגֶל [*midrak*].
Deut. 2. 5 no, not so much as a foot breadth

BREAK, to —

1. *To break the bone or substance,* גָּרַם *garam,* 3.
Num 24. 8 shall break their bones, and pierce
Eze. 23. 34 thou shalt break the sherds thereof, and

2. *To crush,* גָּרַס *garas.*
Psa. 119. 20 My soul breaketh for the longing (that)

3. *To crush,* גָּרַס *garas,* 5.
Lam. 3. 16 He hath also broken my teeth with gravel

4. *To dash by treading,* דּוּשׁ *dush.*
Job. 39. 15 that the wild beast may break them

5. *To beat thin,* דָּכָא *daka,* 3.
Psa. 89. 10 Thou hast broken Rahab in pieces

6. *To beat thin,* דָּכָה *dakah,* 3.
Psa. 51. 8 bones..thou hast broken may rejoice

7. *To be, happen,* הָיָה *hayah,* 2.
Dan. 2. 1 spirit was troubled, and his sleep brake

8. *To move tumultuously,* הָמַם *hamam.*
Isa. 28. 28 nor break (it with) the wheel of his cart

9. *To destroy, pull down,* הָרַס *haras.*
Psa. 58. 6 Break their teeth, O God, in their mouth

10. *To put down,* חָתַת *chathath,* 5.
Isa. 9. 4 thou hast broken the yoke of his burden

11. *To disallow,* נוּא *no,* 5.
Psa. 141. 5 shall not break my head: for yet my

12. *To dash,* נָפַץ *naphats.*
Judg. 7. 19 brake the pitchers that (were) in their

13. *To dash,* נָפַץ *naphats,* 3.
Jer. 48. 12 empty his vessels..break their bottles

14. *To draw asunder,* נָתַק *nathaq,* 3.
Judg 16. 9 And he brake the withs as a thread
16. 12 he brake them from off his arms like a
Psa. 2. 3 Let us break their bands asunder
Isa. 58. 6 and that ye break every yoke?

15. *To terrify,* עָרַץ *arats.*
Job 13. 25 Wilt thou break a leaf driven to and fro?

16. *To breathe, flow,* פּוּחַ *puach.*
Song 2. 17 Until the day break, and the shadows
4. 6 Until the day break, and the shadows

17. *To break, violate,* פּוּר *pur,* 5.
Eze. 17 19 my covenant that he hath broken, even

18. *To break in pieces,* פָּצַם *patsam.*
Psa. 60. 2 thou hast broken it: heal the breaches

19. *To break in pieces,* פָּצַח *patsach,* 3.
Mic. 3. 3 they break their bones, and chop them

20. *To break forth,* פָּרַץ *parats.*
2 Ch. 20. 37 the LORD hath broken thy works
Job 16. 14 He breaketh me with breach upon breach
Eccl. 10. 8 whoso breaketh an hedge, a serpent shall

21. *To break,* פָּרַק *paraq.*
Gen. 27. 40 thou shalt break his yoke from off thy

22. *To break off,* פָּרַר *parar,* 5.
Gen. 17. 14 that soul..hath broken my covenant
Lev. 26. 15 (but) that ye break my covenant
26. 44 to break my covenant with them: for
Num 15. 31 and hath broken his commandment
Deut 31. 16 break my covenant which I have made
31. 20 then will they..break my covenant
Judg. 2. 1 I will never break my covenant with you
1 Ki. 15. 19 break thy league with Baasha king of
2 Ch. 16. 3 break thy league with Baasha king of
Isa. 24. 5 have..broken the everlasting covenant
33. 8 he hath broken the covenant: he hath
Jer. 11. 10 house of Judah have broken my covenant
14. 21 remember, break not thy covenant with
31. 32 which my covenant they brake, although
33. 20 If ye can break my covenant of the day
Eze. 16. 59 despised the oath in breaking the coven.
17. 15 shall he break the covenant, and be
17. 16 whose covenant he brake, (even) with him
17. 18 despised the oath by breaking the coven.
44. 7 they have broken my covenant because
Zech 11. 10 I might break my covenant which I
11. 14 that I might break the brotherhood

23. *To spread out,* פָּרַשׂ *paras.*
Lam. 4. 4 no man breaketh (it) unto them

24. *To break,* רָעַע *raa.*
Psa. 2. 9 Thou shalt break them with a rod of iron
Jer. 15. 12 Shall iron break the northern iron; 2. 16

25. *To break,* רְעַע *rea,* 3.
Dan. 2. 40 as iron that breaketh all these, shall it

26. *To be broken in pieces,* רָצַץ *ratsats,* 2.
Eze. 29. 7 thou didst break, and rend all their

27. *To dash in pieces,* רָצַץ *ratsats,* 5.
Judg. 9. 53 millstone..and all to brake his skull

28. *To break, shiver,* שָׁבַר *shabar.*
Gen. 19. 9 and came near to break the door
Exod 12. 46 neither shall ye brake a bone thereof
Lev. 11. 33 shall be unclean; and ye shall break it
26. 13 I have broken the bands of your yoke
26. 19 I will brake the pride of your power
26. 26 I have broken the staff of your bread
Num. 9. 12 leave none..nor break any bone of it
Judg. 7. 20 blew the trumpets, and brake..pitchers
Psa. 10. 15 Break thou the arm of the wicked
29. 5 The voice of the LORD breaketh the cedars
69. 20 Reproach hath broken my heart
105. 16 he brake the whole staff of bread
Prov. 6. 15 suddenly shall he be broken without
25. 15 a soft tongue breaketh the bone
Isa. 14. 5 LORD hath broken the staff of the wicked
14. 25 That I will break the Assyrian
30. 14 he shall break it as the breaking
42. 3 A bruised reed shall he not break, and
Jer. 2. 20 I have broken thy yoke..burst thy bands
5. 5 these have altogether broken the yoke
19. 10 Then shalt thou break the bottle
19. 11 will I break..as (one) breaketh
28. 2 I have broken the yoke of the king of
28. 4 for I will break the yoke of the king of
28. 10 the prophet took the yoke..and brake it
28. 11 Even so will I break the yoke of N.
28. 12 the prophet had broken the yoke from off
28. 13 Thou hast broken the yokes of wood; but
30. 8 I will break his yoke from off thy neck
48. 38 I have broken Moab like a vessel
49. 35 I will break the bow of Elam, the chief
Eze. 4. 16 I will break the staff of bread in Jerusa.
5. 16 and will break your staff of bread
14. 13 will break the staff of the bread thereof
27. 26 the east wind hath broken thee in the
30. 18 I shall break there the yokes of Egypt
30. 21 I have broken the arm of Pharaoh king
30. 22 I..will break his arms, the strong
30. 24 I will break Pharaoh's arms, and he
34. 27 I have broken the bands of their yoke
Hos. 1. 5 I will break the bow of Israel in the valley
2. 18 I will break the bow and the sword
Amos 1. 5 I will break also the bar of Damascus
Nah. 1. 13 now will I break his yoke from off thee

29. *To be broken, shivered,* שָׁבַר *shabar,* 2.
Eze. 29. 7 thou brakest, and madest all their loins

30. *To break, shiver,* שָׁבַר *shabar,* 3.
Exod. 9. 25 and brake every tree of the field
32. 19 cast the tables..and brake them beneath
34. 1 the first tables, which thou brakest
34. 13 break their images, and cut down their
Deut. 9. 17 and brake them before your eyes
10. 2 in the first tables which thou brakest
12. 3 overthrow their altars, and break their
2 Ki. 18. 4 He removed the high places, and brake
Job 29. 17 I brake the jaws of the wicked, and
Psa. 3. 7 thou hast broken the teeth of the ungodly
29. 5 LORD breaketh the cedars of Lebanon
46 9 he breaketh the bow, and cutteth..spear
48. 7 Thou brakest the ships of Tarshish with an
74. 13 thou brakest the heads of the dragons in
76. 3 There brake he the arrows of the bow
105. 33 and brake the trees of their coasts
107. 16 For he hath broken the gates of brass
Isa. 21. 9 her gods he hath broken unto the ground
38. 13 so will he break all my bones
Jer. 43. 13 shall break also the images of Beth-shem.
52. 17 the Chaldeans brake, and carried all the

Lam. 2. 9 he hath destroyed and broken her bars
3. 4 made old; he hath broken my bones
Dan. 8. 7 smote the ram, and brake his two horns

31. *To bruise,* שׁוּף *shuph.*
Job 9. 17 For he breaketh me with a tempest

32. *To pierce, profane,* חָלַל *chalal,* 3.
Psa. 55. 20 he hath broken his covenant
89. 31 If they break my statutes, and keep not
89. 34 My covenant will I not break, nor

33. *To pierce, profane,* חָלַל *chalal,* 5.
Num 30. 2 he shall not break his word, he shall

34. *To break,* רָעַע *raa.*
Jer. 2. 16 children..have broken the crown of thy

35. *To break throughout,* διαρρήγνυμι *diarrhēgnumi.*
Luke 5. 6 multitude of fishes: and their net brake
8. 29 fetters; and he brake the bands, and

36. *To break down,* κατάγνυμι *katagnumi.*
Matt 12. 20 A bruised reed shall he not brake
John 19. 31 that their legs might be broken
19. 32 the soldiers..brake the legs of the first
19. 33 when they came to Jesus..they brake not

37. *To break down,* κατακλάω *kataklaō,* κλάζω *klazō.*
Mark 6. 41 blessed, and brake the loaves, and gave
Luke 9. 16 he blessed them, and brake, and gave to

38. *To break,* κλάω *klaō.*
Matt 14. 19 he blessed, and brake, and gave the
15. 36 gave thanks, and brake (them), and gave
26. 26 Jesus took bread..blessed (it), and brake
Mark 8. 6 seven loaves, and gave thanks, and brake
8. 19 when I brake the five loaves among
14. 22 Jesus took bread, and blessed, and brake
Luke 22. 19 took bread, and gave thanks, and brake
24. 30 took bread, and blessed (it), and brake
Acts 2. 46 breaking bread from house to house
20. 7 disciples came together to brake bread
20. 11 he..had broken bread, and eaten, and
27. 35 when he had broken (it), he began to eat
1 Co. 10. 16 The bread which we break, is it; 11. 24.

39. *To loose,* λύω *luō.*
Matt. 5. 19 Whosoever..shall break one of these
John. 5. 18; 7. 23; 10. 35; cts 27. 41; Eph. 2. 14.

40. *To break or burst,* ῥήγνυμι *rhēgnumi.*
Matt 9. 17 old bottles; else the bottles break

41. *To break together,* συνθρύπτω *sunthruptō.*
Acts 21. 13 What mean ye to weep and to break

42. *To rub together,* συντρίβω *suntribō.*
Mark 14. 3 she brake the box, and poured (it) on his

[*See also* Bones, covenant, neck, pieces, truce, wedlock.]

BREAK again, to —

To repeat to break, שׁוּב לְהָפֵר [*shub, parar,* 5].
Ezra 9. 14 Should we again break thy commandm.

BREAK asunder, to —

To break, violate, פָּרַר *parar,* 3.
Job 16. 12 ease, but he hath broken me asunder

BREAK away, to —

To break forth of, or for oneself, פָּרַץ *parats,* 7
1 Sa. 25. 10 many servants..that break away

BREAK clods, to —

To harrow, break up, שָׂדַד *sadad,* 3a.
Isa. 28. 24 doth he..break the clods of his ground?
Hos. 10. 11 Jacob shall break his clods

BREAK down, to —

1. *To beat, smite,* הָלַם *halam.*
Psa. 74. 6 now they break down the carved work
Isa. 16. 8 the heathen have broken down the

2. *To crush,* הָרַס *haras.*
Job 12. 14 he breaketh down, and it cannot be built
Jer. 45. 4 that which I..built..will I break down
Eze. 13. 14 So will I break down the wall
26. 4 they shall..break down her towers
26. 12 they shall break down thy walls, and

3. *To break down,* נָתַץ *nathats.*
Lev. 14. 45 he shall break down the house, the
Judg. 8. 9 he spake..I will break down this tower
2 Ki. 10. 27 they brake down the image of Baal
10. 27 brake down the house of Baal, and
11. 18 the house of Baal, and brake it down
23. 7 he brake down the houses of the
23. 8 brake down the high places of the gates
23. 15 altar and the high place he brake down
25. 10 brake down the walls of Jerusalem round
2 Ch. 23. 17 house of Baal, and brake it down
Isa. 22. 10 houses have ye broken down to fortify
Jer. 31. 28 to break down, and to throw down, and
39. 8 and brake down the walls of Jerusalem
52. 14 brake down all the walls of Jerusalem
Eze. 26. 9 with his axes he shall break down thy

4. *To break down,* נָתַץ *nathats,* 3.
2 Ch. 33. 3 his father had broken down
34. 4 they brake down the altars of Baalim in
34. 7 when he had broken down the altars and
36. 19 brake down the wall of Jerusalem, and
Eze. 16. 39 and shall break down thy high places

5. *To behead, cause to drop,* עָרַף *araph.*
Hos. 10. 2 he shall break down their altars, he shall

6. *To break forth or down,* פָּרַץ *parats.*
2 Ki. 14. 13 brake down the wall of Jerusalem from
2 Ch. 25. 23 brake down the wall of Jerusalem from
26. 6 brake down the wall of Gath, and the
Neh. 4. 3 he shall even break down their stone
Psa. 80. 12 Why hast thou (then) broken down her
89. 40 Thou hast broken down all his hedges
Eccl. 3. 3 a time to break down, and a time to
Isa. 5. 5 break down the wall thereof, and it shall

7. *To run, cause to run,* רוּץ *ruts.*
2 Ki. 23. 12 brake (them) down from thence, and

8. *To break, shiver,* שָׁבַר *shabar,* 3.
Exod 23. 24 thou shalt..quite break down their
Deut. 7. 5 their altars, and break down their
2 Ch. 14. 3 brake down the images, and cut down

BREAK forth, to —
1. *To be broken up, cleft, let go,* בָּקַע *baqa,* 2.
Isa. 58. 8 shall thy light break forth as the morning

2. *To come forth (with force),* גּוּחַ *guach.*
Job 38. 8 the sea with doors, when it brake forth

3. *To break forth,* פָּצַח *patsach.*
Isa. 14. 7 is quiet: they break forth into singing
44. 23 break forth into singing, ye mountains
49. 13 break forth into singing, O mountains
54. 1 break forth into singing, and cry aloud
55. 12 the hills shall break forth before you into

4. *To break forth, flourish,* פָּרַח *parach.*
Exod. 9. 9 a boil breaking forth (with) blains upon
9. 10 it became a boil breaking forth (with)

5. *To break forth in,* פָּרַץ *parats.*
Gen. 38. 29 she said, How hast thou broken forth?
Exod 19. 22 lest the LORD break forth upon them
19. 24 LORD, lest he break forth upon them
2 Sa. 5. 20 LORD hath broken forth upon mine
Isa. 54. 3 thou shalt break forth on the right hand

6. *To be opened up,* פָּתַח *pathach,* 2.
Jer. 1. 14 an evil shall break forth upon all the

7. *To break, burst,* ῥήγνυμι *rhēgnumi.*
Gal. 4. 27 break forth and cry, thou that

BREAK forth into joy —
To break forth, פָּצַח *patsach.*
Isa. 52. 9 Break forth into joy, sing together, ye

BREAK in, to —
To break forth, in, פָּרַץ *parats.*
1 Ch. 14. 11 God hath broken in upon mine enemies
Psa. 106. 29 the plague brake in upon them

BREAK in pieces, to —
1. *To bruise,* דָּכָא *daka,* 3.
Job 19. 2 and break me in pieces with words?
Psa. 72. 4 and shall break in pieces the oppressor
94. 5 They break in pieces thy people, O LORD

2. *To beat small,* דָּקַק *deqaq,* 5.
Dan. 2. 34 of iron and clay, and brake them to pieces
2. 40 iron breaketh in pieces and subdueth
2. 40 shall it break in pieces and bruise
2. 44 it shall break in pieces and consume
2. 45 that it brake in pieces the iron, the
6. 24 brake all their bones in pieces or ever
7. 7 it devoured and brake in pieces, and
7. 19 devoured, brake in pieces, and stamped
7. 23 shall tread it down, and break it in pieces

3. *To beat down or out,* כָּתַת *kathath,* 3.
2 Ki. 18. 4 brake in pieces the brasen serpent that

4. *To dash in pieces,* נָפַץ *naphats,* 3.
Jer. 51. 20 with thee will I break in pieces the nations
51. 21 with thee will I break in pieces the horse
51. 21 with thee will I break in pieces the chariot
51. 22 With thee also will I break in pieces man
51. 22 with thee will I break in pieces old and
51. 22 with thee will I break in pieces the young
51. 23 I will also break in pieces with thee the
51. 23 with thee will I break in pieces the husb.
51. 23 with thee will I break in pieces captains

5. *To break in pieces,* פּוּץ *puts,* 3a.
Jer. 23. 29 hammer (that) breaketh the rock in pieces

6. *To break, afflict,* רָעַע *raa.*
Job 34. 24 He shall break in pieces mighty men

7. *To break, shiver,* שָׁבַר *shabar,* 3.
1 Ki. 19. 11 brake in pieces the rocks, before the LORD
2 Ki. 11. 18 and his images brake they in pieces
23. 14 he brake in pieces the images, and cut
25. 13 Chaldees break in pieces, and carried the
2 Ch. 23. 17 brake his altars and his images in pieces
31. 1 and brake the images in pieces, and cut
34. 4 he brake in pieces, and made dust
Psa. 74. 14 Thou brakest the heads of leviathan in p.
Isa. 45. 2 I will break in pieces the gates of brass

8. *To rub together,* συντρίβω *suntribō.*
Mark 5. 4 the fetters broken in pieces: neither

BREAK into, to —
To cleave, בָּקַע *baqa.*
2 Ch. 21. 17 came up into Judah, and brake into

BREAK of day, at —
1. *To become light,* אוֹר *or,* 2.
2 Sa. 2. 32 they came to Hebron at break of day

2. *Shining,* αὐγή *augē.*
Acts 20. 11 a long while, even till break of day

BREAK off, to —
1. *To break off, rend,* פָּרַק *paraq,* 3.
Exod 32. 2 Break off the golden earrings which

2. *To break off of themselves,* פָּרַק *paraq,* 7.
Exod 32. 3 the people brake off the golden earrings
32. 24 hath any gold, let them break (it) off
Dan. 4. 27 break off thy sins by righteousness

3. *To break off from,* ἐκκλάω *ekklaō.*
Rom 11. 17 if some of the branches be broken off
11. 19 The branches were broken off, that I
11. 20 because of unbelief they were broken off

BREAK out, to —
1. *To be broken up,* בָּקַע *baqa,* 2.
Isa. 35. 6 in the wilderness shall waters break out
59. 5 that which is crushed breaketh out into

2. *To go forth,* יָצָא *yatsa.*
Exod 22. 6 If fire break out, and catch in thorns

3. *To break down or out,* נָתַץ *nathats.*
Psa. 58. 6 break out the great teeth of the young

4. *To break forth, flourish,* פָּרַח *parach.*
Lev. 13. 12 if a leprosy break out abroad in the skin
14. 43 if the plague come again, and break out

5. *To prosper,* צָלֵחַ *tsaleach.*
Amos 5. 6 lest he break out like fire in the house

BREAK ranks, to —
To break, embarrass, עָבַט *abat,* 3.
Joel 2. 7 and they shall not break their ranks

BREAK sore, to —
To bruise, דָּכָה *dakah,* 3.
Psa. 44. 19 Though thou hast sore broken us

BREAK (the day), to —
To go up, ascend, עָלָה *alah.*
Gen. 32. 26 said, Let me go, for the day breaketh

BREAK through, to —
1. *To cleave, rend,* בָּקַע *baqa.*
2 Sa. 23. 16 the three mighty men brake through the
1 Ch. 11. 18 the three brake through the host of the

2. *To cleave through,* בָּקַע *baqa,* 5.
2 Ki. 3. 26 break through..unto the king of Edom

3. *To break or throw down,* הָרַס *haras.*
Exod 19. 21 lest they break through unto the LORD
19. 24 the priests and the people break through

4. *To dig through,* διορύσσω *diorussō.*
Matt. 6. 19 where thieves break through and steal
6. 20 where thieves do not break through nor
Luke 12. 39 suffered his house to be broken through

BREAK to shivers, to —
To rub together, συντρίβω *suntribō.*
Rev. 2. 27 vessels..shall they be broken to shivers

BREAK up, to —
1. *To till, break up,* נִיר *nir.*
Jer. 4. 3 Break up your fallow ground, and sow
Hos. 10. 12 break up your fallow ground: for (it is)

2. *To break forth,* פָּרַץ *parats.*
2 Ch. 24. 7 that wicked woman, had broken up the
Mic. 2. 13 they have broken up, and have passed

3. *To break, shiver,* שָׁבַר *shabar.*
Job 38. 10 brake up for it my decreed (place), and

4. *To dig through,* διορύσσω *diorussō.*
Matt 24. 43 suffered his house to be broken up

5. *To dig out,* ἐξορύσσω *exorussō.*
Mark 2. 4 when they had broken (it) up, they let

6. *To loose,* λύω *luō.*
Acts 13. 43 when the congregation was broken up

BREAKER —
1. *To break forth,* פָּרַץ *parats.*
Mic. 2. 13 The breaker is come up before them

2. *Going beyond, trespasser,* παραβάτης *parabates.*
Rom. 2. 25 if thou be a breaker of the law, thy

BREAKER, covenant —
Not put together, faithless, ἀσύνθετος *asunthetos.*
Rom. 1. 31 Without understanding, covenant break.

BREAKER, truce —
Not offering libation, ἄσπονδος *aspondos.*
2 Ti. 3. 3 Without natural affection, truce breakers

BREAKING —
1. *To go up,* עָלָה *alah.*
Gen. 32. 24 a man with him until the breaking of the

2. *To break, violate,* פָּרַר *parar,* 5.
Eze. 16. 59 despised the oath in breaking the coven.
17. 18 despised the oath by breaking the coven.

3. *Breaking,* שֶׁבֶר *sheber.*
Job 41. 25 by reason of breakings they purify them.
Isa. 30. 13 whose breaking cometh suddenly at an
30. 14 as the breaking of the potter's vessel

4. *Breaking,* שִׁבָּרוֹן *shibbaron.*
Eze. 21. 6 Sigh..with the breaking of (thy) loins

5. *Breaking,* κλάσις *klasis.*
Luke 24. 35 was known of them in breaking of bread
Acts 2. 42 in breaking of bread, and in prayers

6. *Going beyond, trespass,* παράβασις *parabasis.*
Rom. 2. 23 through breaking the law dishonourest

BREAKING down —
To dig down, קוּר *qur,* 3a.
Isa. 22. 5 breaking down the walls, and of crying

BREAKING forth —
1. *Breaking forth,* מִשְׁבַּר *mashber.*
Hos. 13. 13 stay long in..the breaking forth of child.

2. *Breaking forth,* פֶּרֶץ *perets.*
1 Ch. 14. 11 like the breaking forth of waters

BREAKING in —
Breaking forth, פֶּרֶץ *perets.*
Job 30. 14 (upon me) as a wide breaking in
Psa. 144. 14 no breaking in, nor going out; that

BREAKING up —
Digging through, מַחְתֶּרֶת *machtereth.*
Exod 22. 2 If a thief be found breaking up,

BREAST —
1. *Breast,* דַּד *dad.*
Prov. 5. 19 let her breasts satisfy thee at all times
Eze 23. 8 they bruised the breasts of her virginity

2. *Breasts,* חֲדִין *chadin.*
Dan. 2. 32 his breast and his arms of silver

3. *Breast,* חָזֶה *chazeh.*
Exod 29. 26 thou shalt take the breast of the ram of
29. 27 thou shalt sanctify the breast of the wave
Lev. 7. 30 the fat with the breast, it shall he bring
7. 30 that the breast may be waved (for) a
7. 31 the breast shall be Aaron's and his
7. 34 the wave breast and the heave shoulder
8. 29 Moses took the breast, and waved it
9. 20 they put the fat upon the breasts, and he
9. 21 the breasts and the right shoulder
10. 14 the wave breast and heave shoulder shall
10. 15 The heave shoulder and the wave breast
Num. 6. 20 with the wave breast and heave shoulder
18. 18 as the wave breast and as the right

4. *Heart,* לֵבָב *lebab.*
Nah. 2. 7 doves, tabering upon their breasts

5. *Veins, sinews,* עֲטִין *atin.*
Job 21. 24 His breasts are full of milk, and his bones

6. *Breast,* שַׁד *shad.*
Gen. 49. 25 blessings of the breasts and of the womb
Job 3. 12 why the breasts that I should suck?
Psa. 22. 9 make me hope..upon my mother's breasts
Song 1. 13 he shall lie all night betwixt my breasts
4. 5 Thy two breasts (are) like two young roes
7. 3 Thy two breasts (are) like two young roes
7. 7 and thy breasts to clusters (of grapes)
7. 8 thy breasts shall be as clusters of the
8. 1 my brother, that sucked the breasts of
8. 8 We have a..sister, and she hath no breasts
8. 10 I (am) a wall, and my breasts like towers
Isa. 28. 9 from the milk..drawn from the breasts
Lam. 4. 3 Even the sea monsters draw out the b.
Eze. 16. 7 breasts are fashioned, and thine hair is
23. 3 there were their breasts pressed, and
23. 34 shalt..pluck off thine own breasts
Hos. 2. 2 her adulteries from between her breasts
9. 14 give..a miscarrying womb and dry breasts
Joel 2. 16 and those that suck the breasts: let the

7. *Breast,* שֹׁד *shod.*
Job 24. 9 They pluck the fatherless from the breast
Isa. 60. 16 thou..shalt suck the breast of kings
66. 11 satisfied with the breasts of her

8. *Breast, firm part,* στῆθος *stēthos.*
Luke 18. 13 smote upon his breast, saying, God be
23. 48 all..smote their breasts, and returned
John 13. 25 He then lying on Jesus' breast saith unto
21. 20 which also leaned on his breast at supper
Rev. 15. 6 having their breasts girded with golden

BREASTPLATE —
1. *Bag, covering on the breast,* חֹשֶׁן *choshen.*
Exod 25. 7 stones to be set..in the breastplate
28. 4 a breastplate, and an ephod, and a robe
28. 15 make the breastplate of judgment with
28. 22, 23 thou shalt make upon the breastplate
28. 23 rings on the two ends of the breastplate
28. 24 two rings..on the ends of the breastplate
28. 26 upon the two ends of the breastplate
28. 28 shall bind the breastplate by the rings
28. 28 breastplate be not loosed from the ephod
28. 29 breastplate of judgment upon his heart
28. 30 in the breastplate of judgment the Urim
29. 5 the ephod, and the breastplate, and gird
35. 9, 27 for the ephod, and for the breastplate
39. 8 he made the breastplate (of) cunning work
39. 9 they made the breastplate double
39. 15 they made upon the breastplate chains
39. 16 rings in the two ends of the breastplate
39. 17 two rings on the ends of the breastplate
39. 19 on the two ends of the breastplate
39. 21 they did bind the breastplate by his
39. 21 that the breastplate might not be loosed
Lev. 8. 8 he put the breastplate upon him
8. 8 he put in the breastplate the Urim and

2. *Coat of mail,* שִׁרְיָן *shiryan.*
Isa. 59. 17 put on righteousness as a breastplate

3. *Breastplate, cuirass,* θώραξ *thōrax.*
Eph. 6. 14 having on..breastplate of righteousness
1 Th. 5. 8 on the breastplate of faith and love
Rev. 9. 9 they had breastplates..breastplates of
9. 17 breastplates of fire, and of iacinth, and

BREATH —

1. *Breath, soul,* נֶפֶשׁ *nephesh.*
Job 41. 21 His breath kindleth coals, and a flame

2. *Breath,* נִשְׁמָא, נְשָׁמָה *neshamah, nishma.*
Gen. 2. 7 breathed into his nostrils the breath
7. 22 in whose nostrils..the breath [*See* No. 3.]
1 Ki. 17. 17 that there was no breath left in him
Job 27. 3 All the while my breath (is) in me
33. 4 breath of the Almighty hath given me life
34. 14 gather..his spirit and his breath
37. 10 By the breath of God frost is given
Isa. 2. 22 man, whose breath (is) in his nostrils
30. 33 the breath of the LORD..doth kindle it
42. 5 he that giveth breath unto the people
Dan. 5. 23 the God in whose hand thy breath (is)
10. 17 neither is there breath left in me

3. *Breath, air, wind, spirit,* רוּחַ *ruach.*
Gen. 6. 17 all flesh, wherein (is) the breath of life
7. 15 all flesh, wherein (is) the breath [*See* No. 2]
7. 22 in whose nostrils (was) the breath of life
2 Sa. 22. 16 the blast of the breath of his nostrils
Job 4. 9 by the breath of his nostrils are they
9. 18 He will not suffer me to take my breath
12. 10 In whose hand (is)..the breath of all
15. 30 by the breath of his mouth shall he go
17. 1 My breath is corrupt, my days are extinct
19. 17 My breath is strange to my wife, though
Psa. 18. 15 the blast of the breath of thy nostrils
33. 6 all the host of them by the breath of his
104. 29 thou takest away their breath, they die
135. 17 neither is there (any) breath in their
146. 4 His breath goeth forth, he returneth to
Eccl. 3. 19 they have all one breath: so that a man
Isa. 11. 4 with the breath of his lips shall he slay
30. 28 his breath, as an overflowing stream
33. 11 your breath, (as) fire shall devour you
Jer. 10. 14 falsehood, and (there is) no breath in
51. 17 falsehood..(there is) no breath in them
Lam. 4. 20 The breath of our nostrils, the anointed
Eze. 37. 5 I will cause breath to enter into you, and
37. 6 put breath in you, and ye shall live; and
37. 8 above: but (there was) no breath in them
37. 9 Come from the four winds, O breath
37. 10 the breath came into them, and they
Hab. 2. 19 no breath at all in the midst of it

4. *Wind, breath,* πνοή *pnoē.*
Acts 17. 25 he giveth to all life, and breath, and all

BREATH, that hath —
Breath, נְשָׁמָה *neshamah.*
Psa. 150. 6 Let every thing that hath breath praise

BREATHE, to —
1. *To breathe out,* נָפַח *naphach.*
Gen. 2. 7 breathed into his nostrils the breath of
Eze. 37. 9 Come..O breath, and breathe upon these
2. *Breath,* נְשָׁמָה *neshamah.*
Josh. 11. 11 there was not any left to breathe
11. 14 neither left they any to breathe

BREATHE on, to —
To breathe into, ἐμφυσάω *emphusaō.*
John 20. 22 when he had said this, he breathed on

BREATHE out, to —
To blow in or with, ἐμπνέω *empneō,* [ἐνπνέω.]
Acts 9. 1 breathing out threatenings and slaughter

BREATHE out, such as —
Breathing out, יָפֵחַ *yapheach.*
Psa. 27. 12 risen..and such as breathe out cruelty

BREATHED, that —
Breath, נְשָׁמָה *neshamah.*
Josh. 10. 40 utterly destroyed all that breathed, as
1 Ki. 15. 29 he left not..any that breathed, until

BREATHETH, that —
Breath, נְשָׁמָה *neshamah.*
Deut 20. 16 thou shalt save..nothing that breatheth

BREATHING —
Breathing, רְוָחָה *revachah.*
Lam. 3. 56 hide not thine ear at my breathing

BREECHES —
Breeches, trousers, מִכְנָסַיִם *miknesayim.*
Exod 28. 42 linen breeches to cover their nakedness
39. 28 linen breeches (of) fine twined linen
Lev. 6. 10 linen breeches shall he put upon his flesh
16. 4 he shall have the linen breeches upon
Eze. 44. 18 shall have linen breeches upon their loins

BREED —
Son, בֵּן *ben.*
Deut 32. 14 rams of the breed of Bashan, and goats

BREED worms, to —
To become high, grow up, רוּם *rum.*
Exod 16. 20 it bred worms, and stank: and Moses

BREED abundantly, to —
To swarm, creep, שָׁרַץ *sharats.*
Gen. 8. 17 that they may breed abundantly in the

BREEDING —
Overrunning, possession, מִמְשָׁק *mimshaq.*
Zeph. 2. 9 the breeding of nettles, and salt pits

BRETHREN —
1. *Brethren,* אַחִים *achim.*
Gen. 9. 22 and told his two brethren without
9. 25 servant..shall he be unto his brethren
13. 8 and thy herdmen; for we (be) brethren
16. 12 dwell in the presence of all his brethren
19. 7 I pray you, brethren, do not so wickedly
24. 27 me to the house of my master's brethren
25. 18 died in the presence of all his brethren
27. 29 bow down to thee: be lord over thy bre.
27. 37 all his brethren have I given to him for
29. 4 Jacob said..My brethren, whence (be) ye?
31. 23 he took his brethren with him, and
31. 25 his brethren pitched in the mount of
31. 32 let him not live: before our brethren
31. 37 before my brethren and thy brethren
31. 46 Jacob said unto his brethren, Gather
31. 54 and called his brethren to eat bread
34. 11 said unto her father and unto her breth.
34. 25 Dinah's brethren, took each man his
37. 2 was feeding the flock with his brethren
37. 4 his brethren saw that their father loved
37. 4 more than all his brethren, they hated
37. 5 and he told (it) his brethren: and they
37. 8 his brethren said..Shalt thou indeed reign
37. 9 another dream, and told it his brethren
37. 10 told (it) to his father, and to his brethren
37. 10 Shall I, and thy mother, and thy brethren
37. 11 And his brethren envied him; but his
37. 12 his brethren went to feed their father's
37. 13 Do not thy brethren feed (the flock) in
37. 14 see whether it be well with thy brethren
37. 16 he said, I seek my brethren: tell me
37. 17 Joseph went after his brethren, and found
37. 23 when Joseph was come unto his brethren
37. 26 Judah said unto his brethren, What
37. 27 our flesh. And his brethren were content
37. 30 he returned unto his brethren, and said
38. 1 Judah went down from his brethren, and
38. 11 Lest..he die also, as his brethren (did)
42. 3 Joseph's ten brethren went..to buy corn
42. 4 Jacob sent not with his brethren
42. 6 Joseph's brethren..bowed down
42. 7 Joseph saw his brethren, and he knew
42. 8 Joseph knew his brethren, but they knew
42. 13 they said, Thy servants (are) twelve bret.
42. 19 let one of your brethren be bound in the
42. 28 he said unto his brethren, My money is
42. 32 We (be) twelve brethren, sons of our father
42. 33 leave one of your brethren (here) with me
44. 14 Judah and his brethren came to Joseph's
44. 33 let the lad go up with his brethren
45. 1 made himself known unto his brethren
45. 3 Joseph said unto his brethren, I (am)
45. 3 his brethren could not answer him
45. 4 Joseph said unto his brethren, Come
45. 15 he kissed all his brethren, and wept
45. 15 after that his brethren talked with him
45. 16 Joseph's brethren are come: and it
45. 17 Say unto thy brethren, This do ye; lade
45. 24 So he sent his brethren away, and they
46. 31 Joseph said unto his brethren, and
46. 31 My brethren, and my father's house
47. 1 My father and my brethren, and their
47. 2 he took some of his brethren..five
47. 3 Pharaoh said unto his brethren, What
47. 5 Thy father and thy brethren are come
47. 6 make thy father and brethren to dwell
47. 11 Joseph placed his father and his brethren
47. 12 Joseph nourished his father, and his b.
48. 6 the name of their brethren in their
48. 22 given to..one portion above thy brethren
49. 5 Simeon and Levi (are) brethren
49. 8 thou (art he) whom thy brethren shall
49. 26 him that was separate from his brethren
50. 8 all the house of Joseph, and his brethren
50. 14 he, and his brethren, and all that went
50. 15 Joseph's brethren saw that their father
50. 17 the trespass of thy brethren, and their
50. 18 his brethren also went and fell down
50. 24 Joseph said unto his brethren, I die: and
Exod. 1. 6 Joseph died, and all his brethren, and
2. 11 he went out unto his brethren, and looked
2. 11 an Hebrew, one of his brethren
4. 18 Let me go..unto my brethren which
Lev. 10. 4 Come near, carry your brethren
10. 6 let your brethren..bewail the burning
21. 10 the high priest among his brethren, upon
25. 46 over your brethren the children of Israel
25. 48 one of his brethren may redeem him
Num. 8. 26 shall minister with their brethren, in
16. 10 all thy brethren the sons of Levi with
18. 2 thy brethren also of the tribe of Levi
18. 6 I have taken your brethren the Levites
20. 3 when our brethren died before the LORD!
25. 6 brought unto his brethren a..woman
27. 4 a possession among the brethren of our
27. 7 inheritance among their father's brethren
27. 9 give his inheritance unto his brethren
27. 10 his inheritance unto his father's brethren
27. 10 if he have no brethren, then ye shall
27. 11 if his father have no brethren, then ye
32. 6 Shall your brethren go to war
Deut. 1. 16 Hear (the causes) between your brethren
1. 28 our brethren have discouraged our heart
2. 4 to pass through the coast of your brethren
2. 8 when we passed by from our brethren
3. 18 pass over armed before your brethren
Deut. 3. 20 LORD have given rest unto your brethren
10. 9 Levi hath no part..with his brethren
15. 7 one of thy brethren within any of thy
17. 15 from among thy brethren shalt thou set
17. 20 be not lifted up above his brethren
18. 2 have no inheritance among their brethren
18. 7 as all his brethren the Levites (do)
18. 15 Prophet from the midst of..thy brethren
18. 18 a Prophet from among their brethren
20. 8 return unto his house, lest his brethren's
24. 7 be found stealing any of his brethren
24. 14 of thy brethren, or of thy strangers
25. 5 If brethren dwell together, and one of
33. 9 neither did he acknowledge his brethren
33. 16 him (that was) separated from his brethren
33. 24 let him be acceptable to his brethren
Josh. 1. 14 ye shall pass before your brethren armed
1. 15 Until the LORD have given your brethren
2. 13 father..my mother, and my brethren
2. 18 bring thy father..mother, and..brethren
6. 23 father, and..mother, and..brethren
14. 8 my brethren that went up with me
17. 4 an inheritance among our brethren
17. 4 an inheritance among the brethren
22. 3 Ye have not left your brethren these
22. 4 God hath given rest unto your brethren
22. 7 the (other) half..among their brethren
22. 8 the spoil of your enemies with..brethren
Judg. 8. 19 he said, They (were) my brethren..the
9. 1 his mother's brethren, and communed
9. 3 his mother's brethren spake of him in the
9. 5 he went..and slew his brethren the
9. 24 aided him in the killing of his brethren
9. 26 the son of Ebed came with his brethren
9. 31 the son of Ebed, and his brethren, be come
9. 41 Zebul thrust out Gaal and his brethren
9. 56 wickedness..in slaying his..brethren
11. 3 Jephthah fled from his brethren, and
14. 3 among the daughters of thy brethren
16. 31 his brethren and all the house..came
18. 8 they came unto their brethren to Zorah
18. 8 their brethren said unto them, What (say)
18. 14 the five men..said unto their brethren
19. 23 Nay, my brethren, (nay), I pray you
20. 13 hearken to the voice of their brethren
21. 22 their brethren come unto us to complain
Ruth 4. 10 dead be not cut off..among his brethren
1 Sa. 16. 13 anointed him in the midst of his brethren
17. 17 Take now for thy brethren an ephah of
17. 17 and run to the camp to thy brethren
17. 18 look how thy brethren fare, and take
17. 22 and came and saluted his brethren
20. 29 let me get away..and see my brethren
22. 1 his brethren and all his father's house
30. 23 Ye shall not do so, my brethren
2 Sa. 2. 26 return from following their brethren?
3. 8 to his brethren, and to his friends
15. 20 take back thy brethren: mercy and truth
19. 12 Ye (are) my brethren, ye (are) my bones
19. 41 Why have our brethren..stolen thee
1 Ki. 1. 9 called all his brethren the king's sons
12. 24 Ye shall not..fight against your brethren
2 Ki. 9. 2 make him..arise up from among his bret.
10. 13 Jehu met with the brethren of Ahaziah
10. 13 We (are) the brethren of Ahaziah
23. 9 eat of the..bread among their brethren
1 Ch. 4. 9 Jabez was more honourable..his brethren
4. 27 his brethren had not many children
5. 2 Judah prevailed above his brethren
5. 7 his brethren by their families, when
5. 13 their brethren, of the house of their
6. 44 their brethren the sons of Merari (stood)
6. 48 Their brethren also the Levites (were)
7. 5 their brethren among all the families of
7. 22 and his brethren came to comfort him
8. 32 these also dwelt with their brethren in
9. 6 their brethren, six hundred and ninety
9. 9 brethren, according to their generations
9. 13 their brethren, heads of the house of
9. 17 Talmon, and Ahiman, and their brethren
9. 19 the son of Korah, and his brethren, of
9. 25 their brethren (which were) in their
9. 32 of their brethren, of the sons of the
9. 38 they also dwelt with their brethren
9. 38 at Jerusalem, over against their brethren
12. 2 (even) of Saul's brethren of Benjamin
12. 32 all their brethren (were) at their
12. 39 their brethren had prepared for them
13. 2 let us send abroad unto our brethren
15. 5 his brethren an hundred and twenty
15. 6 his brethren two hundred and twenty
15. 7 his brethren an hundred and thirty
15. 8 and his brethren two hundred
15. 9 Eliel the chief, and his brethren foursc.
15. 10 the chief, and his brethren an hundred
15. 12 ye and your brethren, that ye may
15. 16 chief of the Levites to appoint their bre.
15. 17 of his brethren, Asaph the son of
15. 17 of the sons of Merari their brethren
15. 18 with them their brethren of the second
16. 7 into the hand of Asaph and his brethren
16. 37 he left there..Asaph and his brethren
16. 38 Obed-edom with their brethren, three
16. 39 the priest, and his brethren the priests
23. 22 their brethren the sons of Kish took
23. 32 charge of the sons of Aaron their brethren
24. 31 cast lots over against their brethren
24. 31 over against their younger brethren
25. 7 the number of them, with their brethren
25. 9 who with his brethren and sons (were)
So in v. 11, 12, 13, 14, 15, 16, 17, 18, 19, 20, 21, 22, 23, 24, 25, 26, 27, 28, 29, 30, 31.

1 Ch. 25. 10 his sons, and his brethren, (were) twelve
26. 7 Obed, Elzabad, whose brethren (were)
26. 8 they, and their sons, and their brethren
26. 9 Meshelemiah had sons and brethren
26. 11 the sons and brethren of Hosah (were)
26. 25 his brethren by Eliezer; Rehabiah
26. 26 Shelomith and his brethren (were) over all
26. 28 hand of Shelomith, and of his brethren
26. 30 Hashabiah and his brethren, men of
26. 32 his brethren, men of valour, (were) two
27. 18 Elihu, (one) of the brethren of David
28. 2 Hear me, my brethren, and my people
2 Ch. 5. 12 their brethren, (being) arrayed in white
11. 4 shall not..fight against your brethren
11. 22 the chief, (to be) ruler among his brethren
19. 10 to you of your brethren that dwell in
19. 10 upon you, and upon your brethren
21. 2 he had brethren the sons of Jehoshaphat
21. 4 slew all his brethren with the sword, and
21. 13 hast slain thy brethren of thy father's
22. 8 the sons of the brethren of Ahaziah
28. 8 carried away captive of their brethren
28. 11 ye have taken captive of your brethren
28. 15 their brethren: then they returned to
29. 15 they gathered their brethren, and sanct.
29. 34 their brethren the Levites did help them
30. 7 your brethren, which trespassed against
30. 9 your brethren..(shall find) compassion
31. 15 to give to their brethren by courses
35. 5 the fathers of your brethren the people
35. 6 sanctify yourselves..prepare your breth.
35. 9 Shemaiah and Nethaneel, his brethren
35. 15 their brethren the Levites prepared for
Ezra 3. 2 the son of Jozadak, and his brethren
3. 2 the son of Shealtiel, and his brethren
3. 8 the remnant of their brethren the priests
3. 9 Jeshua (with) his sons and his brethren
3. 9 their sons and their brethren the Levites
6. 20 for their brethren the priests, and for
8. 17 to his brethren the Nethinims, at the
8. 18 Sherebiah, with his sons and his brethren
8. 19 Merari, his brethren, and their sons
8. 24 ten of their brethren with them
10. 18 the son of Jozadak, and his brethren
Neh. 1. 2 Hanani, one of my brethren, came
3. 1 high priest rose up, with his brethren
3. 18 After him repaired their brethren
4. 2 he spake before his brethren and the
4. 14 fight for your brethren, your sons, and
4. 23 neither I, nor my brethren, nor my serv.
5. 1 a great cry..against their brethren the
5. 5 our flesh (is) as the flesh of our brethren
5. 8 We..have redeemed our brethren the
5. 8 will ye even sell your brethren?
5. 10 I likewise..my brethren, and my servants
5. 14 my brethren have not eaten the bread
10. 10 their brethren, Shebaniah, Hodijah
10. 29 They clave to their brethren, their nobles
11. 12 their brethren that did the work of the
11. 13 his brethren, chief of the fathers, two
11. 14 their brethren, mighty men of valour
11. 17 Bakbukiah..second among his brethren
11. 19 porters: Akkub, Talmon..their brethren
12. 7 of the priests and of their brethren
12. 8 Judah..Mattaniah..he and his brethren
12. 9 their brethren, (were) over against them
12. 24 with their brethren over against them
12. 36 his brethren, Shemaiah, and Azarael
13. 13 office (was) to distribute unto their bret.
Esth. 10. 3 accepted of the multitude of his brethren
Job 6. 15 My brethren have dealt deceitfully as a
19. 13 He hath put my brethren far from me
42. 11 Then came there..all his brethren
42. 15 them inheritance among their brethren
Psa. 22. 22 I will declare thy name unto my brethren
69. 8 become a stranger unto my brethren
122. 8 For my brethren..sakes, I will now say
133. 1 how pleasant (it is) for brethren to dwell
Prov. 6. 19 he that soweth discord among brethren
17. 2 shall have part..among the brethren
19. 7 the brethren of the poor do hate him
Isa. 66. 5 Your brethren that hated you..shall be
66. 20 they shall bring all your brethren (for)
Jer. 7. 15 I have cast out all your brethren
12. 6 thy brethren, and the house of thy father
29. 16 your brethren that are not gone forth
35. 3 I took Jaazaniah..and his brethren
41. 8 he..slew them not among their brethren
49. 10 his seed is spoiled, and his brethren
Eze. 11. 15 Son of man, thy brethren
11. 15 thy brethren, the men of thy kindred
Hos. 2. 1 Say ye unto your brethren, Ammi; and
13. 15 Though he be fruitful among (his) breth.
Mic. 5. 3 remnant of his brethren shall return

2. *Brethren,* אַחִין *achin.*

Ezra 7. 18 what..shall seem good..to thy brethren

3. *Brethren,* ἀδελφοί *adelphoi.*

Matt. 1. 2 Jacob begat Judas and his brethren
1. 11 Josias begat Jechonias and his brethren
4. 18 Jesus, walking by the sea..saw two bret.
4. 21 going..thence, he saw other two brethren
5. 47 if ye salute your brethren only
12. 46 mother and his brethren stood
12. 47 thy mother and thy brethren stand
12. 48 my mother? and who are my brethren?
12. 49 Behold my mother and my brethren!
13. 55 his brethren, James, and Joses, and Simon
19. 29 that hath forsaken houses, or brethren
20. 24 with indignation against the..brethren
22. 25 there were with us seven brethren
Matt 23. 8 Master..Christ; and all ye are brethren
25. 40 one of the least of these my brethren
28. 10 Be not afraid: go tell my brethren that
Mark 3. 31 There came then his brethren and his
3. 32 thy mother and thy brethren without
3. 33 Who is my mother, or my brethren?
3. 34 Behold my mother and my brethren!
10. 29 man that hath left house, or brethren
10. 30 houses, and brethren, and sisters, and
12. 20 Now there were seven brethren: and the
Luke 8. 19 Then came to him..his brethren
8. 20 Thy mother and thy brethren stand
8. 21 My mother and my brethren are these
14. 12 call not thy friends, nor thy brethren
14. 26 hate not his father..and brethren
16. 28 For I have five brethren; that he
18. 29 There is no man that hath left..brethren
20. 29 There were therefore seven brethren: and
21. 16 betrayed both by parents, and brethren
22. 32 thou art converted, strengthen thy breth.
John 2. 12 he, and his mother, and his brethren
7. 3 His brethren..said unto him, Depart
7. 5 neither did his brethren believe in him
7. 10 when his brethren were gone up, then
20. 17 Touch me not..but go to my brethren
21. 23 Then went this..abroad among the bret.
Acts 1. 14 Mary the mother of Jesus..with his bret.
1. 16 brethren, this scripture must needs have
2. 29 Men (and) brethren, let me freely speak
2. 37 Men (and) brethren, what shall we do?
3. 17 brethren, I wot that through ignorance
3. 22 A prophet..unto you of your brethren
6. 3 brethren, look ye out among you seven
7. 2 Men, brethren, and fathers, hearken
7. 13 Joseph was made known to his brethren
7. 23 came into his heart to visit his brethren
7. 25 he supposed his brethren would have
7. 26 Sirs, ye are brethren; why do ye wrong
7. 37 God raise up unto you of your brethren
9. 30 when the brethren knew, they brought
10. 23 certain brethren from Joppa accompanied
11. 1 brethren that were in Judea heard
11. 12 these six brethren accompanied me
11. 29 send..the brethren which dwelt in Judea
12. 17 show these things unto..the brethren
13. 15 brethren, if ye have any word..say on
13. 26 brethren, children..stock of Abraham
13. 38 Be it known unto you..brethren, that
14. 2 minds evil affected against the brethren
15. 1 certain men..taught the brethren
15. 3 caused great joy unto all the brethren
15. 7 Peter rose up, and said..Men..brethren
15. 13 Men (and) brethren, hearken unto me
15. 22 and Silas, chief men among the brethren
15. 23 The apostles and elders and brethren
15. 23 greeting unto the brethren which are of
15. 32 exhorted the brethren with many words
15. 33 were let go in peace from the brethren
15. 36 Let us go again and visit our brethren
15. 40 recommended by the brethren unto the
16. 2 was well reported of by the brethren
16. 40 when they had seen the brethren, they
17. 6 they drew..brethren unto the rulers
17. 10 the brethren immediately sent away Paul
17. 14 immediately the brethren sent away Paul
18. 18 Paul..then took his leave of the brethren
18. 27 the brethren wrote..the disciples to
20. 32 And now, brethren, I commend you to
21. 7 we..saluted the brethren, and abode with
21. 17 when we were come..brethren received
22. 1 Men, brethren, and fathers, hear ye my
22. 5 I received letters unto the brethren, and
23. 1 brethren, I have..in all good conscience
23. 5 I wist not, brethren, that he was the
23. 6 Men (and) brethren, I am a Pharisee, the
28. 14 we found brethren, and were desired to
28. 15 when the brethren heard of us, they
28. 17 brethren..I have committed nothing
28. 21 neither any of the brethren..spake any
Rom. 1. 13 I would not have you ignorant, brethren
7. 1 Know ye not, brethren, for I speak to
7. 4 my brethren, ye also are become dead to
8. 12 brethren, we are debtors, not to the flesh
8. 29 the firstborn among many brethren
9. 3 accursed from Christ for my brethren
10. 1 Brethren, my heart's desire and prayer to
11. 25 I would not, brethren, that ye should be
12. 1 I beseech..brethren, by the mercies of
15. 14 also am persuaded of you, my brethren
15. 15 brethren, I have written the more boldly
15. 30 I beseech you, brethren, for the Lord
16. 14 Salute..the brethren which are with
16. 17 I beseech you, brethren, mark them wh.
1 Co. 1. 10 I beseech you, brethren, by the name of
1. 11 hath been declared unto me of you, my b.
1. 26 For ye see your calling, brethren, how
2. 1 I, brethren, when I came to you, came
3. 1 I, brethren, could not speak unto you as
4. 6 brethren, I have in a figure transferred
6. 5 be able to judge between his brethren?
6. 8 wrong, and defraud, and that..brethren
7. 24 Brethren, let every man..therein abide
7. 29 this I say, brethren, the time (is) short
8. 12 when ye sin so against the brethren, and
9. 5 the brethren of the Lord, and Cephas?
10. 1 Moreover, brethren, I would not that ye
11. 2 Now I praise you, brethren, that ye
11. 33 brethren, when ye come together to eat
12. 1 brethren, I would not have you ignorant
14. 6 brethren, if I come unto you speaking
14. 20 Brethren, be not children in understand.
14. 26 brethren? when ye come together, every
1 Co. 14. 39 brethren..forbid not to speak with tong.
15. 1 brethren, I declare unto you the gospel
15. 6 was seen of above five hundred brethren
15. 50 brethren, that flesh and blood cannot
15. 58 my beloved brethren, be ye stedfast
16. 11 for I look for him with the brethren
16. 12 to come unto you with the brethren
16. 15 I beseech you, brethren, (ye know the)
16. 20 All the brethren greet you. Greet ye one
2 Co. 1. 8 we would not, brethren, have..ignorant
8. 1 brethren, we do you to wit of the grace
8. 23 Whether (any do enquire)..our brethren
9. 3 Yet have I sent the brethren, lest our
9. 5 thought it necessary to exhort..brethren
11. 9 brethren which came from Macedonia
13. 11 brethren, farewell. Be perfect, be of good
Gal. 1. 2 all the brethren which are with me, unto
1. 11 brethren, that the gospel which was
3. 15 Brethren, I speak after the manner of
4. 12 Brethren, I beseech you, be as I (am)
4. 28 we, brethren, as Isaac was, are the child.
4. 31 brethren, we are not children of the
5. 11 brethren..why do I yet suffer persecution
5. 13 brethren, ye have been called unto liberty
6. 1 Brethren, if a man be overtaken in a
6. 18 Brethren, the grace of our Lord Jesus
Eph. 6. 10 Finally, my brethren, be strong in..Lord
6. 23 Peace (be) to the brethren, and love
Phil. 1. 12 I would ye should understand, brethren
1. 14 many of the brethren in the Lord
3. 1 Finally, my brethren, rejoice in the Lord
3. 13 Brethren, I count not myself to have
3. 17 Brethren, be followers together of me
4. 1 Therefore, my brethren dearly beloved
4. 8 Finally, brethren, whatsoever things are
4. 21 brethren which are with me greet you
Col. 1. 2 To the..faithful brethren in Christ..at
4. 15 Salute the brethren which are in Laodicea
1 Th. 1. 4 Knowing, brethren beloved, your election
2. 1 yourselves, brethren, know our entrance
2. 9 ye remember, brethren, our labour and
2. 14 ye, brethren, became followers of the
2. 17 we, brethren, being taken from you for a
3. 7 brethren, we were comforted over you in
4. 1 we beseech you, brethren, and exhort (you)
4. 10 toward all the brethren which are in all
4. 10 we beseech you, brethren, that ye increase
4. 13 not have you to be ignorant, brethren
5. 1 of the time, and the seasons, brethren
5. 4 ye, brethren, are not in darkness, that
5. 12 brethren, to know them which labour
5. 14 brethren, warn them that are unruly
5. 25 Brethren, pray for us
5. 26 Greet all the brethren with an holy kiss
5. 27 epistle be read unto all the holy brethren
2 Th. 1. 3 to thank God always for you, brethren
2. 1 we beseech you, brethren, by the coming
2. 13 thanks alway to God for you, brethren
2. 15 brethren, stand fast, and hold the tradi.
3. 1 brethren, pray for us, that the word of
3. 6 we command you, brethren, in the name
3. 13 ye, brethren, be not weary in well doing
1 Ti. 4. 6 If thou put the brethren in remembrance
5. 1 entreat..the younger men as brethren
6. 2 not despise..because they are brethren
2 Ti. 4. 21 Linus, and Claudia, and all the brethren
Heb. 2. 11 he is not ashamed to call them brethren
2. 12 I..declare thy name unto my brethren
2. 17 behoved..to be made like..(his) brethren
3. 1 holy brethren, partakers of the heavenly
3. 12 Take heed, brethren, lest there be in any
7. 5 according..law, that is, of their brethren
10. 19 Having..brethren, boldness to enter into
13. 22 I beseech you, brethren, suffer the word
Jas. 1. 2 My brethren, count it all joy when ye fall
1. 16 Do not err, my beloved brethren
1. 19 my beloved brethren, let every man be
2. 1 My brethren, have not the faith of our
2. 5 Hearken, my beloved brethren, Hath not
2. 14 My brethren, though a man say he hath
3. 1 My brethren, be not many masters
3. 10 my brethren, these things ought not so
3. 12 Can the fig tree, my brethren, bear olive
4. 11 Speak not evil one of another, brethren
5. 7 Be patient..brethren, unto the coming
5. 9 Grudge not one against another, brethren
5. 10 Take, my brethren, the prophets, who
5. 12 above all things, my brethren, swear not
5. 19 Brethren, if any of you do err from the
2 Pe. 1. 10 brethren..make your calling and election
1 Jo. 2. 7 Brethren, I write no new commandment
3. 13 Marvel not, my brethren, if the world
3. 14 death..life because we love the brethren
3. 16 to lay down (our) lives for the brethren
3 Jo. 3 I rejoiced..when the brethren came
5 whatever thou doest to the brethren, and
10 neither doth he..receive the brethren
Rev. 6. 11; 12. 10; 19. 10; 22. 9.

4. *Brotherhood,* ἀδελφότης *adelphotēs.*

1 Pe. 5. 9 your brethren that are in the world

BRETHREN, false —

False or lying brother, ψευδάδελφος *pseudadelphos*

2 Co. 11. 26 perils in the sea..among false brethren
Gal. 2. 4 because of false brethren unawares

BRETHREN, love as —

Loving a brother, φιλάδελφος *philadelphos.*

1 Pe. 3. 8 love as brethren, (be) pitiful, (be)

BRETHREN, love of —
Love of brethren, φιλαδελφία *philadelphia.*
1 Pe. 1. 22 unto unfeigned love of the brethren

BRIBE —
1.*A covering*, כֹּפֶר *kopher.*
1 Sa. 12. 3 of whose hand have I received (any) bribe
Amos 5. 12 they afflict the just, they take a bribe
2.*Bribe, reward*, שֹׁחַד *shochad.*
1 Sa. 8. 3 took bribes, and perverted judgment
Psa. 26. 10 their right hand is full of bribes
Isa. 33. 15 shaketh his hands from holding of bribes

BRIBERY —
Bribe, שֹׁחַד *shochad.*
Job 15. 34 consume the tabernacles of bribery

BRICK —
Brick, (from its whiteness), לְבֵנָה *lebenah.*
Gen. 11. 3 Go to, let us make brick, and burn
11. 3 they had brick for stone, and slime had
Exod. 1. 14 with hard bondage, in mortar, and in br.
5. 7 Ye shall..give..straw to make brick
5. 8 the tale of the bricks, which they did
5. 16 and they say to us, Make brick: and
5. 18 yet shall ye deliver the tale of bricks
5. 19 Ye shall not minish..from your bricks
Isa. 9. 10 bricks are fallen down, but we will build

BRICK, altars of —
Anything made of brick, לְבֵנָה *lebenah.*
Isa. 65. 3 burneth incense upon altars of brick

BRICK, making —
To make bricks, לָבַן *laban.*
Exod. 5. 14 not fulfilled..task in making brick

BRICK KILN —
Place for making brick, מַלְבֵּן *malben.*
2 Sa. 12. 31 made them pass through the brick kiln
Jer. 43. 9 hide them in the clay in the brick kiln
Nah. 3. 14 tread the mortar, make strong the brick k.

BRIDE —
1.*The complete or perfect one*, כַּלָּה *kallah.*
Isa. 49. 18 bind them (on thee), as a bride (doeth)
61. 10 as a bride adorneth (herself) with her
62. 5 the bridegroom rejoiceth over the bride
Jer. 2. 32 Can a maid forget..(or) a bride her attire?
7. 34 the bridegroom, and the voice of the bride
16. 9 the bridegroom, and the voice of the bride
25. 10 the bridegroom, and the voice of the bride
33. 11 the bridegroom, and the voice of the bride
Joel 2. 16 go forth..and the bride out of her closet
2.*Bride*, νύμφη *numphē.*
John 3. 29 He that hath the bride is the bridegroom
Rev. 18. 23 the voice of the bridegroom and of the b.
21. 2 as a bride adorned for her husband
21. 9 I will show thee [the bride], the Lamb's
22. 17 And the Spirit and the bride say, Come

BRIDE CHAMBER —
Bride chamber, νυμφών *numphōn.*
Matt. 9. 15 the children of the bride chamber mourn
Mark 2. 19 the children of the bride chamber fast
Luke 5. 34 ye make the children of the bride cham.

BRIDEGROOM —
1.*One who contracts affinity*, חָתָן *chathan.*
Psa. 19. 5 bridegroom coming out of his chamber
Isa. 61. 10 as a bridegroom decketh (himself) with
62. 5 the bridegroom rejoiceth over the bride
Jer. 7. 34 the bridegroom, and the voice of the bride
16. 9 the bridegroom, and the voice of the bride
25. 10 the bridegroom, and the voice of the bride
33. 11 the bridegroom, and the voice of the bride
Joel 2. 16 let..bridegroom go forth..and the bride
2.*Bridegroom*, νυμφίος *numphios.*
Matt. 9. 15 as long as the bridegroom is with them?
9. 15 when the bridegroom shall be taken from
25. 1 and went forth to meet the bridegroom
25. 5 While the bridegroom tarried, they all
25. 6 Behold, the bridegroom cometh; go ye
25. 10 they went to buy, the bridegroom came
Mark 2. 19 [fast while the bridegroom is with them?]
2. 19 as long as they have the bridegroom with
2. 20 when the bridegroom shall be taken away
Luke 5. 34 fast while the bridegroom is with them?
5. 35 when the bridegroom shall be taken away
John 2. 9 the governor..called the bridegroom
3. 29 He that hath the bride is the bridegroom
3. 29 but the friend of the bridegroom, which
3. 29 rejoiceth..because of the bridegroom's
Rev. 18. 23 the voice of the bridegroom..shall be

BRIDLE —
1.*Muzzle*, מַחְסוֹם *machsom.*
Psa. 39. 1 I will keep my mouth with a bridle, while
2.*Bridle, bit*, מֶתֶג *metheg.*
2 Ki. 19. 28 I will put..my bridle in thy lips
Prov. 26. 3 for the horse, a bridle for the ass, and a
Isa. 37. 29 will I put..my bridle in thy lips
3.*Rein*, רֶסֶן *resen.*
Job 30. 11 they have also let loose the bridle
41. 13 come (to him) with his double bridle?
Psa. 32. 9 whose mouth must be held in with..brid.
Isa. 30. 28 and..a bridle in the jaws of the people
4.*Bit of a bridle*, χαλινός *chalinos.*
Rev. 14. 20 blood came out..unto the horse bridles

BRIDLE, to —
To lead with a bit, χαλιναγωγέω *chalinagōgeō.*
Jas. 1. 26 bridleth not his tongue, but deceiveth
3. 2 (and) able also to bridle the whole body

BRIEFLY —
Through a few (words), δι' ὀλίγων *di oligōn.*
1 Pe. 5. 12 I suppose, I have written briefly, exhorting

BRIEFLY comprehended, to be —
Be summed up, ἀνακεφαλαιόομαι *anakephalaioomai*
Rom 13. 9 it is briefly comprehended in this saying

BRIER —
1.*Brier*, חֵדֶק *chedeq.*
Mic. 7. 4 The best of them (is) as a brier; the most
2.*Brier, thorn*, סִלּוֹן *sillon.*
Eze. 28. 24 there shall be no more a pricking brier
3.*Thorn, nettle*, סִרְפַּד *sirpad.*
Isa. 55. 13 instead of the brier shall come up the
4.*Brier, diamond point, adamant*, שָׁמִיר *shamir.*
Isa. 5. 6 there shall come up briers and thorns
7. 23 it shall (even) be for briers and thorns
7. 24 the land shall become briers and thorns
7. 25 shall not come thither the fear of briers
9. 18 it shall devour the briers and thorns, and
10. 17 burn and devour his thorns and his briers
27. 4 who would set the briers..against me in
32. 13 Upon the land..shall come up..briers;
5.*A triple-pointed plant*, τρίβολος *tribolos.*
Heb. 6. 8 that which beareth thorns and briers

BRIERS —
1.*Threshing instruments*, בַּרְקָנִים *barqanim.*
Judg. 8. 7, 16 thorns of the wilderness and with briers
2.*Briers*, סָרָבִים *sarabim.*
Eze. 2. 6 though briers and thorns (be) with thee

BRIGANDINE —
Coat of mail, brigandine, סִרְיוֹן *siryon.*
Jer. 46. 4 furbish..(and) put on the brigandines
51. 3 lifteth himself up in his brigandine

BRIGHT —
1.*Light, bright*, אוֹר *or.*
Job 37. 11 he scattereth his bright cloud
2.*Bright*, בָּהִיר *bahir.*
Job 37. 21 see not the bright light which (is) in the
3.*Lightning, brightness*, בָּרָק *baraq.*
Eze. 21. 15 made bright, (it is) wrapped up for the
4.*Flame, blade*, לַהַב *lahab.*
Nah. 3. 3 The horseman lifteth up both the bright
5.*Light-giver, light-giving*, מָאוֹר *maor.*
Eze. 32. 8 All the bright lights of heaven will I make
6.*To polish*, מָרַט *marat*, 4.
1 Ki. 7. 45 and all these vessels..(were of) bright
7.*To scour, polish*, מָרַק *maraq.*
2 Ch. 4. 16 for the house of the LORD, of bright brass
8.*Shining*, נֹגַהּ *nogah.*
Eze. 1. 13 the fire was bright, and out of the fire
9.*Prepared, bright, shining*, עָשׁוֹת *ashoth.*
Eze. 27. 19 bright iron, cassia, and calamus, were in
10.*Prepared, shining*, עֶשֶׁת *esheth.*
Song 5. 14 his belly (is as) bright ivory overlaid (with)
11.*Bright, shining*, λαμπρός *lampros.*
Acts 10. 30 behold, a man stood before me in bright
Rev. 22. 16 (and) the bright and morning star
12.*Shining*, φωτεινός *phōteinos.*
Matt 17. 5 While he..spake, behold, a [bright] cloud

BRIGHT cloud —
Brightness, lightness, חָזִיז *chaziz.*
Zech. 10. 1 (so) the LORD shall make bright clouds

BRIGHT spot —
Freckled spot, בַּהֶרֶת *bahereth.*
Lev. 13. 2 a scab, or bright spot, and it be in the
13. 4 If the bright spot (be) white in the skin
13. 19 the place of the boil there be..a bright s.
13. 23, 28 if the bright spot stay in his place
13. 24 (flesh) that burneth have a white bright s.
13. 25 the hair in the bright spot be turned
13. 26 (there be) no white hair in the bright spot
13. 38 skin of their flesh bright spots..bright s.
13. 39 (if) the bright spots in the skin of their
14. 56 a rising, and for a scab, and for a bright s.

BRIGHT, to make —
1.*To cleanse*, בָּרַר *barar*, 5.
Jer. 51. 11 Make bright the arrows; gather the
2.*To make bright or sharp*, קָלַל *qalal*, 3 a.
Eze. 21. 21 he made (his) arrows bright, he consulted

BRIGHTNESS —
1.*Brightness, shining*, זֹהַר *zohar.*
Eze. 8. 2 as the appearance of brightness, as the
Dan. 12. 3 they..shall shine as the brightness of the
2.*Clearness, appearance*, זִיו *ziv.*
Dan. 2. 31 This great image, whose brightness (was)
4. 36 mine honour and brightness returned

3.*Shining (as of a city)*, יִפְעָה *yiphah.*
Eze. 28. 7 and they shall defile thy brightness
28. 17 thy wisdom by reason of thy brightness.
4.*Precious, rare*, יָקָר *yaqar.*
Job 31. 26 or the moon walking (in) brightness
5.*Shining (of fire, sun, moon, spear)*, נֹגַהּ *nogah.*
2 Sa. 22. 13 Through the brightness before him were
Psa. 18. 12 At the brightness..his thick clouds passed
Isa. 60. 3 and kings to the brightness of thy rising
60. 19 for brightness shall the moon give light
62. 1 righteousness..go forth as brightness
Eze. 1. 4 a brightness (was) about it, and out of the
1. 27 fire, and it had brightness round about
1. 28 so (was) the appearance of the brightness
10. 4 full of the brightness of the LORD'S glory
Amos 5. 20 even very dark, and no brightness in it?
Hab. 3. 4 And (his) brightness was as the light: he
6.*Shinings, brightnesses*, נְגֹהוֹת *negohoth.*
Isa. 59. 9 for brightness, (but) we walk in darkness
7.*Reflexion*, ἀπαύγασμα *apaugasma.*
Heb. 1. 3 Who being the brightness of (his) glory
8.*Manifestation*, ἐπιφάνεια *epiphaneia.*
2 Th. 2. 8 destroy with the brightness of his coming
9.*Shining, brilliancy*, λαμπρότης *lamprotēs.*
Acts 26. 13 light..above the brightness of the sun

BRIM —
1.*End, edge, border*, קָצֶה *qatseh.*
Josh. 3. 15 were dipped in the brim of the water
2.*Lip*, שָׂפָה *saphah.*
1 Ki. 7. 23 ten cubits from the one brim to the other
7. 24 And under the brim of it round about
7. 26 and the brim thereof was wrought
7. 26 like the brim of a cup, with flowers of
2 Ch. 4. 2 a molten sea of ten cubits from brim to b.
4. 5 (was) an handbreadth, and the brim of
4. 5 like the work of the brim of a cup, with

BRIM, up to the —
Up unto the upper part, ἕως ἄνω *heōs anō.*
John 2. 7 And they filled them up to the brim

BRIMSTONE —
1.*Bitumen, pitch*, גָּפְרִית *gophrith.*
Gen. 19. 24 Then the LORD rained..brimstone and
Deut 29. 23 (that) the whole land thereof (is) brimst.
Job 18. 15 brimstone shall be scattered upon his
Psa. 11. 6 Upon the wicked he shall rain..brimstone
Isa. 30. 33 breath of the LORD, like a stream of brim.
34. 9 and the dust thereof into brimstone
Eze. 38. 22 and great hailstones fire, and brimstone
2.*Divine fire, or sulphur*, θεῖον *theion.*
Luke 17. 29 it rained fire and brimstone from heaven
Rev. 9. 17 out of their mouths issued fire..and brim.
9. 18 by the smoke, and by the brimstone
14. 10 he shall be tormented with..brimstone
19. 20 into a lake..burning with brimstone
20. 10 cast into the lake of fire and brimstone
21. 8 which burneth with fire and brimstone

BRIMSTONE (of) —
Like as of sulphur, θειώδης *theiōdēs.*
Rev. 9. 17 having breastplates of fire..and brimstone

BRING, to —
1.*To add, gather*, אָסַף *asaph.*
Deut 22. 2 thou shalt bring it unto thine own house
Josh. 2. 18 thou shalt bring thy father, and thy
2.*To cause to come*, אֲתָא, אָתָה *atha, athah*, 5.
Isa. 21. 14 The inhabitants..brought water to him
Dan. 3. 13 Nebuchadnezzar..commanded to bring
3. 13 Then they brought these men before
5. 2 commanded to bring the golden..vessels
5. 3 Then they brought the golden vessels
5. 13 the king my father brought out of Jewry?
5. 23 they have brought the vessels of his
6. 16 the king commanded, and they brought
6. 24 brought those men which had accused
3.*To cause to come in*, בּוֹא *bo*, 5.
Gen. 2. 19 brought (them) unto Adam to see what
2. 22 made he a woman, and brought her unto
4. 3 Cain brought of the fruit of the ground
4. 4 he also brought of the firstlings of his
6. 17 I, do bring a flood of waters upon the earth
6. 19 of every living thing..shalt thou bring
18. 19 the LORD may bring upon Abraham that
20. 9 thou hast brought..and on my kingdom
24. 67 And Isaac brought her into his mother
26. 10 thou shouldest have brought guiltiness
27. 4 make me savoury meat..and bring (it)
27. 5 to hunt (for) venison, (and) to bring (it)
27. 7 Bring me venison, and make me..meat
27. 10 And thou shalt bring (it) to thy father
27. 12 I shall bring a curse upon me, and not a
27. 14 he went..and brought (them) to his
27. 25 and he brought him wine, and he drank
27. 31 and brought it unto his father, and said
27. 33 he that hath taken venison, and brought
29. 13 and kissed him, and brought him to his
29. 23 he took Leah his daughter, and brought
30. 14 and brought them unto his mother Leah
31. 39 was torn (of beasts) I brought not unto
37. 2 and Joseph brought unto his father their
37. 28 sold Joseph..and they brought Joseph
37. 32 they sent the coat..and..brought (it) to
39. 17 The Hebrew servant, which thou hast b.

Gen. 42. 20 But bring your youngest brother unto
42. 34 And bring your youngest brother unto
42. 37 Slay my two sons, if I bring him not to
43. 2 which they had brought out of Egypt
43. 9 if I bring him not unto thee, and set
43. 16 Bring (these) men home, and slay, and
43. 17 the man brought the men into Joseph's
43. 24 the man brought the men into Joseph's
43. 26 they brought him the present which (was)
44. 32 If I bring him not unto thee, then I shall
46. 7 and all his seed, brought he with him into
46. 32 and they have brought their flocks, and
47. 14 and Joseph brought the money into
47. 17 And they brought their cattle unto
Exod. 2. 10 and she brought him unto Pharaoh's
6. 8 And I will bring you in unto the land
10. 4 to-morrow will I bring the locusts into
11. 1 Yet will I bring one plague (more) upon
13. 5 when the LORD shall bring thee into the
13. 11 And it shall be, when the LORD shall
18. 19 that thou mayest bring the causes unto
18. 22 (that) every great matter they shall bring
18. 26 the hard causes they brought unto Moses
19. 4 (how) I bare you..and brought you unto
22. 13 (then) let him bring it (for) witness
23. 19 thou shalt bring into the house of..LORD
23. 20 to bring thee into the place which I have
32. 2 Break off the golden earrings..and bring
32. 3 brake off the golden earrings..and bro.
32. 21 thou hast brought so great a sin upon
34. 26 thou shalt bring unto the house of the
35. 5 whosoever (is) of a willing heart, let him
35. 25 and brought that which they had spun
35. 21 they brought the LORD'S offering to the
35. 22 brought bracelets, and earrings, and
35. 23 every man..whom was found..brought
35. 24 Every one that did offer..brought the
35. 24 every man with whom was..brought (it)
35. 27 And the rulers brought onyx stones, and
35. 29 The children..brought a willing offering
36. 3 the children..had brought for the work
36. 3 And they brought yet unto him free offer.
36. 5 The people bring much more than enough
36. 6 the people were restrained from bringing
39. 33 And they brought the tabernacle unto
40. 21 And he brought the ark into the tabernacle
Lev. 2. 2 And he shall bring it to Aaron's sons the
2. 8 And thou shalt bring the meat offering
4. 4 And he shall bring the bullock unto the
4. 5 and bring it to the tabernacle of the
4. 14 and bring him before the tabernacle of
4. 16 the priest..shall bring of the bullock's
4. 23 he shall bring his offering, a kid of the
4. 28 then he shall bring his offering, a kid of
4. 32 if he bring a lamb..he shall bring it
5. 6 he shall bring his trespass offering unto
5. 7 then he shall bring for his trespass, which
5. 8 And he shall bring them unto the priest
5. 11 But if he be not able to bring two turtle
5. 12 Then shall he bring it to the priest
5. 15 then he shall bring for his trespass unto
5. 18 And he shall bring a ram without blemish
6. 6 And he shall bring his trespass offering
7. 29 He..shall bring his oblation unto the
7. 30 His own hands shall bring the offerings
7. 30 the fat with the breast, it shall he bring
10. 15 shall they bring with the offerings made
12. 6 she shall bring a lamb of the first year
14. 23 And he shall bring them on the eighth
15. 29 and bring them unto the priest, to the
16. 12 sweet incense..and bring (it) within the
16. 15 shall he kill the goat..and bring his blood
17. 4 And bringeth it not unto the door of the
17. 5 may bring their sacrifices, which they offer
17. 5 even that they may bring them unto
17. 9 And bringeth it not unto the door of the
18. 3 whither I bring you, shall ye not do
19. 21 And he shall bring his trespass offering
20. 22 whither I bring you to dwell therein
23. 10 then ye shall bring a sheaf of the first
23. 14 that ye have brought an offering unto
23. 15 ye brought the sheaf of the wave offering
23. 17 Ye shall bring out of your habitations
24. 11 And they brought him unto Moses
26. 25 And I will bring a sword upon you, that
26. 41 and have brought them into the land of
Num. 5. 15 Then shall the man bring his wife unto
5. 15 and he shall bring her offering for her
6. 10 on the eighth day he shall bring two
6. 13 he shall be brought unto the door of the
6. 12 and shall bring a lamb of the first year
7. 3 brought their offering before the LORD
14. 3 hath the LORD brought us unto this land
14. 8 then he will bring us into this land, and
14. 16 the LORD was not able to bring this
14. 24 him will I bring into the land whereinto
15. 18 When ye come into the land whither I
15. 25 and they shall bring their offering, a sac.
16. 14 Moreover thou hast not brought us into
18. 13 which they shall bring unto the LORD
20. 4 have ye brought up the congregation
20. 5 to bring us in unto this evil place?
20. 12 ye shall not bring this congregation into
31. 12 And they brought the captives, and the
31. 54 and brought it into the tabernacle of the
32. 17 until we have brought them unto their
Deut. 6. 10 when the LORD..shall have brought thee
6. 23 that he might bring us in, to give us the
7. 1 thy God shall bring thee into the land
7. 26 Neither shalt thou bring an abomination
8. 7 the LORD thy God bringeth thee into a
9. 28 to bring them into the land which he
Deut. 12. 6 thither ye shall bring your burnt offerings
12. 11 thither shall ye bring all that I command
21. 12 Then thou shalt bring her home to thine
23. 18 Thou shalt not bring the hire of a whore
26. 2 which thou shalt bring of thy land that
26. 9 And he hath brought us into this place
26. 10 behold, I have brought the first fruits of
29. 27 to bring upon it all the curses that are
30. 5 And the LORD thy God will bring thee
31. 20 For when I shall have brought them
31. 21 before I have brought them into the land
31. 23 for thou shalt bring..Israel into the land
33. 7 and bring him unto his people: let his
Josh. 7. 23 they took them out..and brought them
18. 6 and bring..hither to me, that I may cast
23. 15 so shall the LORD bring upon you all evil
24. 7 brought the sea upon them, and covered
24. 8 I brought you into the land of the Amor.
Judg. 1. 7 And they brought him to Jerusalem
2. 1 and have brought you unto the land
7. 25 and brought the heads of Oreb and Zeeb
18. 3 and said unto him, Who brought thee
19. 3 and she brought him into her father's
19. 21 So he brought him into his house
21. 12 and they brought them unto the camp to
1 Sa. 1. 22 and (then) I will bring him, that he may
1. 24 brought him unto the house of the LORD
1. 25 they slew a bullock, and brought the
5. 1 brought it from Eben-ezer unto Ashdod
5. 2 they brought it into the house of Dagon
7. 1 brought it into the house of Abinadab
9. 7 behold, (if) we go, what shall we bring
9. 7 not a present to bring to the man of God
9. 22 and brought them into the parlour
10. 27 they despised him, and brought him no
15. 15 They have brought them from the Amal
15. 20 and have brought Agag the king of Ama
16. 17 Provide me now a man..and bring..to
17. 54 And David took the head..and brought
17. 57 brought him before Saul, with the head
18. 27 David brought their foreskins, and they
19. 7 And Jonathan brought David to Saul
20. 8 for thou hast brought thy servant into a
20. 8 for why shouldest thou bring me to thy
21. 14 wherefore (then) have ye brought him to
21. 15 that ye have brought this..to play the
25. 27 which thine handmaid hath brought unto
25. 35 David received..which she had brought
27. 11 David saved neither man..to bring
2 Sa. 1. 10 have brought them hither unto my lord
3. 13 except thou first bring Michal, Saul's
4. 8 And they brought the head of Ish-bosheth
7. 18 what (is) my house..thou hast brought
8. 7 took the shields..and brought them
14. 10 Whosoever saith (ought) unto thee, bring
14. 23 and brought Absalom to Jerusalem
17. 14 that the LORD might bring evil upon Ab.
23. 16 and took (it), and brought (it) to David
1 Ki. 1. 3 Abishag..and brought her to the king
2. 40 and Shimei went, and brought his
3. 1 and brought her into the city of David
3. 24 And the king said, Bring me a sword
4. 28 Barley also and straw..brought they unto
9. 9 The LORD brought upon them all this evil
9. 28 fetched..gold..and brought (it) to king
10. 25 And they brought every man his present
14. 10 I will bring evil upon the house of Jerob.
17. 6 the ravens brought him bread and flesh
20. 39 a man turned aside, and brought a man
21. 21 Behold, I will bring evil upon thee
21. 29 I will not bring the evil in his days
21. 29 in his son's days will I bring the evil
2 Ki. 4. 20 when he had taken him, and brought
4. 42 and brought the man of God bread of
5. 6 he brought the letter to the king of Israel
5. 20 receiving at his hands that which he
10. 8 They have brought the heads of the king's
10. 24 (If) any..whom I have brought into yours
11. 4 and brought them to him into the house
17. 24 the king..brought (men) from Babylon
19. 25 have I brought it to pass, that thou
20. 20 he made a pool..and brought water into
21. 12 I (am) bringing (such)..upon Jerusalem
22. 16 Behold, I will bring evil upon this place
22. 20 evil which I will bring upon this place
23. 8 he brought all the priests out of the
23. 30 his servants carried him..and brought
24. 16 even them the king of Babylon brought
1 Ch. 5. 26 and brought them unto Halah..Habor
10. 12 and brought them to Jabesh, and buried
11. 2 he that leddest out and broughtest in Is.
11. 18 and took (it), and brought (it) to David
11. 19 (the jeopardy of) their lives they brought
12. 40 Moreover they..brought bread on asses
13. 5 bring the ark of God from Kirjath-jearim
13. 12 How shall I bring the ark of God (home)
16. 1 they brought the ark of God, and set
17. 16 what (is) mine house, that thou hast b.
18. 7 David took the shields..and brought
21. 2 bring the number of them to me, that I
22. 4 they of Tyre, brought much cedar wood
22. 19 to bring the ark of the covenant of the
2 Ch. 2. 16 and we will bring it to thee in flotes by
7. 22 hath he brought all this evil upon them
8. 18 took..talents of gold, and brought (them)
9. 10 the servants of Solomon, which brought
9. 10 And the servants..brought algum trees
9. 12 beside (that) which she had brought
9. 14 Beside (that which) chapmen..brought
9. 14 all the kings of Arabia..brought gold and
9. 24 And they brought every man his present
15. 11 they offered..of the spoil (which) they b.
2 Ch. 15. 18 he brought into the house of God the
17. 11 (some) of the Philistines brought Jehosh
17. 11 and the Arabians brought him flocks
22. 9 they caught him..and brought him to
24. 11 the chest was brought unto the king's
24. 14 they brought the rest of the money before
25. 12 and brought them unto the top of the
25. 14 that he brought the gods of the children
25. 23 and brought him to Jerusalem, and brake
28. 5 a great multitude..and brought (them)
28. 8 and brought the spoil to Samaria
28. 13 Ye shall not bring in the captives hither
28. 15 brought them to Jericho, the city of
28. 27 but they brought him not into the
29. 21 they brought seven bullocks, and seven
29. 31 come near and bring sacrifices and
29. 32 number..which the congregation brought
31. 10 Since (the people) began to bring the
32. 23 And many brought gifts unto the LORD
33. 11 the LORD brought upon them the captains
34. 24 Behold I will bring evil upon this place
34. 28 all the evil that I will bring upon this
36. 10 Nebuchadnezzar..brought him to
36. 18 all (these) he brought to Babylon
Ezra 3. 7 to bring cedar trees from Lebanon to the
8. 17 that they should bring unto us ministers
8. 18 they brought us a man of understanding
8. 30 to bring (them) to Jerusalem unto the
Neh. 1. 9 bring them unto the place that I have
8. 1 to bring the book of the law of Moses
8. 2 And Ezra the priest brought the law
8. 16 the people went forth, and brought
9. 23 children also..broughtest them into the
10. 31 And (if) the people of the land bring
10. 34 to bring (it) into the house of our God
10. 35 And to bring the first fruits of our
10. 36 the firstborn of our sons..to bring to the
10. 37 we should bring the first fruits of our
10. 39 the children of Israel..shall bring the
11. 1 to bring one of ten to dwell in Jerusalem
12. 27 they sought the Levites..to bring them to
13. 12 Then brought all Judah the tithe of the
13. 15 which they brought into Jerusalem on
13. 16 which brought fish, and all manner of
13. 18 and did not our God bring all this evil
13. 19 there should no burden be brought in on
Esth. 1. 11 To bring Vashti the queen before the
3. 9 to bring (it) into the king's treasuries
6. 1 to bring the book of records of the Chron.
6. 14 to bring Haman unto the banquet that
Job 12. 6 whose hand God bringeth (abundantly)
14. 3 bringest me into judgment with thee?
42. 11 all the evil that the LORD had brought
Psa. 43. 3 let them bring me unto thy
66. 11 Thou broughtest us into the net
78. 54 And he brought them to the border of his
78. 71 he brought him to feed Jacob his people
105. 40 (The people) asked and he brought quails
Prov. 21. 27 (when) he bringeth it with a wicked mind?
31. 14 she bringeth her food from afar
Eccl. 3. 22 for who shall bring him to see what shall
11. 9 for all these (things) God will bring thee
12. 14 God shall bring every work into judgment
Song 1. 4 The King hath brought me into his
2. 4 He brought me to the banqueting house
3. 4 until I had brought him into my mother's
8. 2 (and) bring thee into my mother's house
8. 11 every..was to bring a thousand (pieces)
Isa. 1. 13 Bring no more vain oblations; incense is
7. 17 The LORD shall bring..upon thy people
14. 2 the people shall take them, and bring
31. 2 Yet he also (is) wise, and will bring evil
37. 26 have I brought it to pass..thou shouldest
43. 5 I will bring thy seed from the east, and
43. 6 bring my sons from far, and my daughters
43. 23 Thou hast not brought me the small
46. 11 I have spoken (it), I will also bring it to
48. 15 I have brought him, and he shall make
49. 22 they shall bring thy sons in (their) arms
56. 7 Even them will I bring to my holy
58. 7 that thou bring the poor that are cast
60. 9 the ships of Tarshish first, to bring thy
60. 11 (men) may bring unto thee the forces of
60. 17 For brass I will bring.. I will bring
66. 4 and will bring their fears upon them
66. 20 And they shall bring all your brethren
66. 20 as the children of Israel bring an offering
Jer. 2. 7 And I brought you into a plentiful
3. 14 and two of a family, and I will bring you
4. 6 I will bring evil from the north, and a
5. 15 Lo, I will bring a nation upon you from
6. 19 behold, I will bring evil upon this people
11. 8 I will bring upon them all the words of
11. 11 Behold, I will bring evil upon them
11. 23 for I will bring evil upon the men of
15. 8 I have brought upon them against the
17. 18 bring upon them the day of evil, and
17. 26 bringing burnt offerings, and sacrifices
17. 26 bringing sacrifices of praise, unto the
18. 22 thou shalt bring a troop suddenly upon
19. 3 Behold, I will bring evil upon this place
19. 15 Behold, I will bring upon this city..all
23. 12 for I will bring evil upon them, (even) the
24. 1 and had brought them to Babylon
25. 9 and will bring them against this land
25. 13 And I will bring upon that land all my
26. 23 and brought him unto Jehoiakim the
27. 11 the nations that bring their neck under
27. 12 Bring your necks under the yoke of the
31. 8 I will bring them from the north country
32. 42 Like as I have brought all this great evil
32. 42 so will I bring upon them all the good

Jer. 33. 11 (and) of them that shall bring the
35. 2 and bring them into the house of the
35. 17 Behold, I will bring upon Judah and upon
36. 31 I will bring upon them, and upon the
37. 14 so Irijah took Jeremiah, and brought him
39. 16 Behold, I will bring my words upon this
40. 3 Now the LORD hath brought (it), and
41. 5 to bring (them) to the house of the LORD
42. 17 from the evil that I will bring upon them
44 2 all the evil that I have brought upon Jer.
45. 5 for, behold, I will bring evil upon all
48. 44 for I will bring upon it, (even) upon
49. 5 Behold, I will bring a fear upon thee
49. 8 for I will bring the calamity of Esau upon
49. 32 I will bring their calamity from all sides
49. 36 And upon Elam will I bring the four
49. 37 I will bring evil upon them, (even) my
51. 64 from the evil that I will bring upon her
Lam. 1. 21 thou wilt bring the day (that) thou hast
Eze. 5. 17 and I will bring the sword upon thee
6. 3 I, (even) I, will bring a sword upon you
7. 24 I will bring the worst of the heathen
8. 3 and brought me in the visions of God to
8. 7 And he brought me to the door of the
8. 14 Then he brought me to the door of the
8. 16 And he brought me into the inner court
11. 1 the spirit lifted me up, and brought me
11. 8 I will bring a sword upon you, saith the
11. 24 the spirit took me up, and brought me
12. 13 I will bring him to Babylon (to) the land
14. 17 Or (if) I bring a sword upon that land
14. 22 concerning the evil that I have brought
14. 22 (even) concerning all that I have brought
17. 20 he shall be taken..and I will bring him
19. 4 they brought him with chains unto the
19. 9 and brought him to the king of Babylon
19. 9 they brought him into holds, that his
20. 10 I caused them to go forth..and brought
20. 15 that I would not bring them into the
20. 28 (For) when I had brought them into the
20. 35 I will bring you into the wilderness of the
20. 37 I will bring you into the bond of the
20. 42 when I shall bring you into the land of
23. 22 and I will bring them against thee on
26. 7 I will bring upon Tyrus Nebuchadrezzar
27. 26 Thy rowers have brought thee into great
28. 7 Behold..I will bring strangers upon thee
29. 8 Behold, I will bring a sword upon thee
32. 9 I shall bring thy destruction among the
33. 2 When I bring the sword upon a land
34. 13 and will bring them to their own land
36. 24 and will bring you into your own land
37. 12 and bring you into the land of Israel
37. 21 and bring them into their own land
38. 16 and I will bring thee against my land
38. 17 which prophesied..that I would bring
39. 2 and will bring thee upon the mountains of
40. 1 the hand..was upon me, and brought me
40. 2 In the visions of God brought he me into
40. 3 And he brought me thither, and, behold
40. 17 Then brought he me into the outward
40. 28 And he brought me to the inner court
40. 32 And he brought me into the inner court
40. 35 And he brought me to the north gate
40. 48 And he brought me to the porch of the
41. 1 he brought me to the temple, and
42. 1 he brought me forth into the outer court
43. 5 the spirit took me up, and brought me
44. 4 Then brought he me the way of the north
44. 7 In that ye..brought (into my sanctuary)
46 19 After he brought me through the entry
Dan. 1. 2 he brought the vessels into the treasure
1. 3 that he should bring (certain) of the
1. 18 then the prince of the eunuchs brought
9. 12 he hath confirmed his words..by bringing
9. 14 hath the LORD watched..and brought it
9. 24 and to bring in everlasting righteousness
11. 6 and they that brought her, and he that
Amos 4. 1 which say..Bring, and let us drink
4. 4 and bring your sacrifices every morning
Mic. 1. 15 Yet will I bring an heir unto thee, O
Zeph. 3. 20 At that time will I bring you (again)
Hag. 1. 8 Go up to the mountain, and bring wood
1. 9 when ye brought (it) home, I did blow
Zech. 8. 8 I will bring them, and they shall dwell
10. 10 and I will bring them into the land of
13. 9 I will bring the third part through the
Mal. 1. 13 and ye brought (that which was) torn, and
1. 13 thus ye brought an offering: should I
3. 10 Bring ye all the tithes into the storehouse

4. *To cut off, bring over,* גּוּז *guz.*
Num 11. 31 and brought quails from the sea, and let

5. *To carry away captive,* גָּלָה *galah,* 5.
2 Ki. 17. 27 Carry..one of the priests whom ye bro.

6. *To cause to flow or go,* יָבַל *yabal,* 5.
Psa. 60. 9 Who will bring me (into) the strong city?
68. 29 Because of thy temple..shall kings bring
76. 11 let all that be round about him bring
108. 10 Who will bring me into the strong city?
Zeph 3. 10 the daughter of my dispersed, shall bring

7. *To cause to flow or go,* יְבַל *yebal,* 5.
Ezra 5. 14 and brought them into the temple of
6. 5 and brought unto Babylon, be restored

8. *To give,* יְהַב *yehab.*
Ruth 3. 15 Bring me the veil that (thou hast) upon
Job 6. 22 Did I say, Bring unto me? or, Give a

9. *To cause to go,* יָלַךְ *yalak,* 5.
Deut 28. 36 The LORD shall bring thee, and thy king
1 Ki. 1. 38 and caused Solomon..and brought him

2 Ki. 6. 19 and I will bring you to the man whom
25. 20 and brought them to the king of Babylon
2 Ch. 35. 24 and they brought him to Jerusalem, and
Isa 42. 16 I will bring the blind by a way (that)
Jer 52. 26 and brought them to the king of Babylon
Lam. 3. 2 He hath led me, and brought (me into)
Eze. 40. 24 After that he brought me toward the
43. 1 Afterward he brought me to the gate
47. 6 Then he brought me, and caused me to
Hos. 2. 14 I will allure her, and bring her into the

10. *To take, receive,* לָקַח *laqach.*
Gen. 48. 9 Bring them, I pray thee, unto me, and I
Exod25. 2 that they may bring me an offering
27. 20 that they bring thee pure oil olive beaten
Lev 9. 5 brought (that) which Moses commanded
12. 8 then she shall bring two turtles, or two
24. 2 that they bring unto thee pure oil olive
Num 11. 16 and bring them unto the tabernacle
13. 20 be ye of good courage, and bring of the
19. 2 that they bring thee a red heifer without
23. 14 he brought him into the field of Zophim
23. 27 I pray thee, I will bring thee unto another
23. 28 And Balak brought Balaam unto the top
Deut 30 12 and bring it unto us, that we may hear it
30. 13 and bring it unto us, that we may hear it
Judg 14. 11 that they brought thirty companions to
1 Sa. 21. 8 for I have neither brought my sword nor
30. 11 they found an Egyptian..and brought
1 Ki. 3. 24 the king said, Bring me a sword. And
17. 11 Bring me, I pray thee, a morsel of bread
20. 33 Then he said, Go ye, bring him. Then
2 Ki. 2. 20 Bring me a new cruse..and they brought
3. 15 But now bring me a minstrel. And it
4. 41 But he said, Then bring meal: and he
1 Ch. 18. 8 Likewise from Tibhath..brought David

11. [*For the Hebrew see* Able *to bring under* Able.]
Lev. 5. 7 And if he be not able to bring a lamb
12. 8 And if she be not able to bring a lamb

12. *To touch, reach to,* נָגַע *naga,* 5.
Isa. 25. 12 lay low, (and) bring to the ground, (even)
26. 5 he bringeth it (even) to the dust

13. *To draw nigh,* נָגַשׁ *nagash,* 5.
Exod21. 6 Then his master shall bring him unto
21. 6 he shall also bring him to the door
Lev. 2. 8 he shall bring it unto the altar
8. 14 And he brought the bullock for the sin
1 Sa. 14. 34 And all the people brought every man
28. 25 And she brought (it) before Saul
2 Sa. 13. 11 when she had brought (them) unto him
17. 28 Brought beds, and basins, and earthen
1 Ki. 4. 21 they brought presents, and served Solo.
2 Ki. 4. 5 upon her sons, who brought (the vessels)
4. 6 she said unto her son, Bring me yet a
Isa. 45. 21 Tell ye, and bring (them) near; yea let

14. *To thrust,* נָדַח *nadach,* 5.
2 Sa 15. 14 bring evil upon us, and smite the city

15. *To lead on,* נָהַג *nahag,* 3.
Exod 10. 13 and the LORD brought an east wind
Psa. 78. 26 by his power he brought in the south

16. *To lead,* נָחָה *nachah,* 5.
Num 23. 7 Balak the king of Moab hath brought me
1 Sa. 22. 4 And he brought them before the king
Psa 107. 30 he bringeth them unto their desired
Prov. 18. 16 and bringeth him before great men

17. *To cause to journey,* נָסַע *nasa,* 5.
Exod 15. 22 So Moses brought Israel from the Red
1 Ki. 5. 17 and they brought great stones costly
Psa 80. 8 Thou hast brought a vine out of Egypt

18. *To lift up,* נָשָׂא *nasa.*
Gen. 45. 19 take you wagons..and bring your father
Exod 10. 13 when..the east wind brought the locusts
Deut 28. 49 The LORD shall bring a nation against
1 Sa. 4. 4 that they might bring from thence the
2 Sa. 6. 3 and brought it out of the house of Abin.
6. 4 they brought it out of the house of Abin.
8. 2 (so) the Moabites..brought gifts
8. 6 Syrians became servants..(and) brought
1 Ki. 10. 11 the navy..brought in from Ophir great
10. 22 bringing gold, and silver, ivory, and apes
2 Ki. 14. 20 And they brought him on horses; and he
1 Ch. 16. 29 bring an offering, and come before him
18. 2 Moabites..servants (and) brought gifts
18. 6 the Syrians..servants, (and) brought gifts
18. 11 that he brought from all (these) nations
2 Ch. 9. 21 the ships of Tarshish, bringing gold, and
25. 28 And they brought him upon horses, and
Job 40. 20 Surely the mountains bring him forth
Psa. 72. 3 The mountains shall bring peace to the
Psa. 96. 8 bring an offering, and come into his courts
126. 6 He..doubtless come again..bringing his
Isa. 60. 6 all they..shall come: they shall bring

19. *To cause to bear,* נָשָׂא *nasa,* 5.
2 Sa. 17. 13 then shall all Israel bring ropes to that

20. *To give,* נָתַן *nathan.*
1 Sa. 9. 23 Bring the portion which I gave thee
11. 12 bring the men, that we may put them to
1 Ki 8. 32 condemning the wicked, to bring his way
1 Ch. 14. 17 the LORD brought the fear of 2 Ch. 17. 5.
Job 14. 4 Who can bring a clean (thing) out of an
Psa. 1 3 that bringeth forth his fruit in his season
Prov. 29. 25 The fear of man bringeth a snare: but
Isa. 40. 23 That bringeth the princes to nothing
Jer. 23. 40 I will bring an everlasting reproach
26. 15 ye shall surely bring innocent blood
Eze. 21. 29 to bring thee upon the necks of (them)
28. 18 and I will bring thee to ashes upon the

Dan. 1. 9 Now God had brought Daniel into favour
Zeph. 3. 5 every morning doth..bring his judgment

21. *To cause to turn aside,* סוּר *sur,* 5.
1 Ch. 13 13 So David brought not the ark (home)

22. *To cause to pass over,* עָבַר *abar,* 5.
2 Sa. 19. 41 and have brought the king and Eze. 47. 3, 4

23. *To cause to go up,* עָלָה *alah,* 5.
Gen. 50. 24 and bring you out of this land unto the
Exod. 32. 7 thy people, which thou broughtest out of
Deut. 28. 61 them will the LORD bring upon thee
Josh. 7. 24 and they brought them unto the valley of
Judg 16. 18 the lords..came up unto her and brought
1 Sa. 2. 19 and brought (it) to him from year to
2 Ki. 17. 4 brought no present to the king of Assyria
2 Ch. 36. 17 Therefore he brought upon them the
Psa. 81. 10 the LORD thy God, which brought thee
Jer. 33. 6 I will bring it health and cure, and I will
Hos. 12 13 And by a prophet the LORD brought Israel

24. *To cause to step,* צָעַד *tsaad,* 5.
Job 18 14 and it shall bring him to the king of terrors

25. *To cause to draw near,* קָרַב *qarab,* 5.
Exod 29. 3 bring them in the basket, with the bullock
29. 4 thou shalt bring unto the door of the
29. 8 thou shalt bring his sons, and put coats
29. 10 thou shalt cause a bullock to be brought
40. 12 thou shalt bring Aaron and his sons
40. 14 thou shalt bring his sons, and clothe them
Lev 1 2 If any man of you bring an offering
1. 2 ye shall bring your offering of the cattle
1. 5 and the priests..shall bring the blood
1. 10 he shall bring it a male without blemish
1. 13 and the priests shall bring (it) all, and
1. 14 then he shall bring his offering of turtle
1. 15 the priest shall bring it unto the altar
2. 4 if thou bring an oblation of a meat offering
2. 11 No meat offering, which ye shall bring
4. 3 then let him bring for his sin..a young
8. 6 Moses brought Aaron and his sons
8. 13 Moses brought Aaron's sons, and put coats
8. 18 And he brought the ram for the burnt
8. 22 he brought the other ram, the ram of
8. 24 he brought Aaron's sons, and Moses put of
9. 9 And the sons of Aaron brought the blood
9. 15 And he brought the people's offering
9. 16 And he brought the burnt offering
9. 17 And he brought the meat offering, and
16. 9 And Aaron shall bring the goat
16. 11 Aaron shall bring the bullock of the sin
16. 20 when he hath made an end..he shall bring
27. 9 whereof men bring an offering unto the
Num. 5. 9 every offering..which they bring unto the
5. 16 And the priest shall bring her near
6. 16 the priest shall bring (them) before the
7. 3 they brought them before the tabernacle
8. 9 thou shalt bring the Levites before the
8. 10 And thou shalt bring the Levites before
9. 13 because he brought not the offering of the
15. 4 bring a meat offering of a tenth deal
15. 9 Then shall he bring with a bullock a meat
15. 27 then he shall bring a she goat of the first
15. 10 thou shalt bring for a drink offering half
15. 33 they..brought him unto Moses and Aaron
16. 17 and bring ye before the LORD every man
18. 2 bring thou with thee, that they may be
18. 15 Every thing..which they bring unto the
25. 6 and brought unto his..a Midianitish
27. 5 And Moses brought their cause before the
28. 26 when ye bring a new meat offering unto
31. 50 We have therefore brought an oblation
Deut. 1. 17 bring (it) unto me, and I will hear it
Josh. 7. 16 and brought Israel by their tribes
7. 17 And he brought..and he brought the
7. 18 And he brought his household man by man
8. 23 the king of Ai they took alive, and brought
Judg. 3. 17 And he brought the present unto Eglon
2 Ki. 16. 14 And he brought also the brasen altar

26. *To cause to meet,* קָרָה *qarah,* 5.
Gen. 27. 20 Because the LORD thy God brought (it) to

27. *To cause to ride,* רָכַב *rakab,* 5.
Esth. 6 9 bring him on horseback through the

28. *To put, place, set,* שׂוּם *sum.*
Exod 8. 12 frogs which he had brought against
15. 26 which I have brought upon the Egyptians
Deut 22. 8 that thou bring not blood upon thine
Psa. 89. 40 thou hast brought his s. to ruin Isa. 23. 13.

29. *To cause to turn back,* שׁוּב *shub,* 5.
Deut28. 60 he will bring upon thee all the diseases of
1 Sa. 6. 7 and bring their calves home from them
2 Ki. 20. 11 and he brought the shadow ten degrees
2 Ch. 34. 16 and brought the king word back again
Job 30. 23 For I know (that) thou wilt bring me (to)
Psa. 72. 10 The kings of Tarshish..shall bring pres.
94. 23 And he shall bring upon them their
Prov. 20. 26 and bringeth the wheel over them
Jon. 1. 13 the men rowed hard to bring (it) to land

30. *To put, place, set,* שִׁית *shith.*
Isa. 15. 9 for I will bring more upon Dimon, lions

31. *To send forth or away,* שָׁלַח *shalach,* 3.
Obad. 7 All the men..have brought thee..to the

32. *To put, place, set,* שָׁפַת *shaphath.*
Psa. 22. 15 and thou hast brought me into the dust

[*See also* Desolation, distress, evil, fruit, hastily, hither, horseback, low, more, near, nought, pass, remembrance, reproach, safe, salvation, straight, tidings.]

33. *To lead on,* ἄγω *agō.*
Matt 21. 2 loose (them), and bring (them) unto me
21. 7 And brought the ass, and the colt, and
Mark 11. 2 ye shall find a colt tied..[bring] (him)
11. 7 they [brought] the colt to Jesus, and cast
Luke 4. 9 he brought him to Jerusalem, and set
4. 40 all they that had..brought them unto
10. 34 brought him to an inn, and took care
19. 27 But those mine enemies..bring hither
19. 30 loose him, and bring (him hither)
19. 35 And they brought him to Jesus
John 1. 42 he brought him to Jesus. And when
7. 45 they said unto them, Why have ye not
8. 3 [the scribes..brought unto him a woman]
9. 13 They brought to the Pharisees him that
10. 16 them also I must bring, and they shall
19. 4 Behold, I bring him forth to you, that
19. 13 he brought Jesus forth, and sat down in
Acts 5. 26 Then went the captain..and brought
5. 27 when they had brought them, they set
6. 12 and caught him, and brought (him) to
9. 2 he might bring them bound unto Jerusa.
9. 21 he might bring them bound unto the
9. 27 Barnabas took him, and brought (him)
11. 26 when he had found him, he brought him
17. 5 and sought to [bring] them out to the
17. 15 they that conducted Paul brought him
17. 19 took him and brought him unto Areop.
18. 12 and brought him to the judgment seat
19. 37 For ye have brought hither these men
20. 12 And they brought the young man alive
21. 16 and brought with them one Mnason
22. 5 to bring them which were there bound
23. 10 to take him by force..and to bring (him)
23. 18 he took him, and brought (him) to the
23. 18 to bring this young man unto thee
23. 31 took Paul, and brought (him) by night
1 Th. 4. 14 even so them also..will God bring with
2 Ti. 4. 11 Take Mark, and bring him with thee
Heb. 2. 10 in bringing many sons unto glory, to

34. *To lead up,* ἀνάγω *anagō.*
Luke 2. 22 they brought..to Jerusalem, to present
Acts 9. 39 When he was come, they brought him
16. 34 And when he had brought them into his

35. *To lead away,* ἀπάγω *apagō.*
Acts 23. 17 Bring this young man unto the chief

36. *To bear away,* ἀποφέρω *apopherō.*
1 Co. 16. 3 to bring your liberality unto Jerusalem

37. *To bear upon or unto,* ἐπιφέρω *epipherō.*
Acts 19. 12 from his body [were brought] unto the
25. 18 they [brought] none accusation of such

38. *To lead or bring down,* κατάγω *katagō.*
Luke 5. 11 And when they had brought their ships

39. *To take care of, provide, bring,* κομίζω *komizō.*
Luke 7. 37 a woman..brought an alabaster box of

40. *To take, receive,* λαμβάνω *lambanō.*
Matt 16. 8 reason ye..because ye have [brought] no

41. *To hold near, afford,* παρέχω *parechō.*
Acts 16. 16 which brought her masters much gain
19. 24 brought no small gain unto the crafts.

42. *To lead toward,* προσάγω *prosagō.*
Luke 9. 41 and suffer you? Bring thy son hither
Acts 16. 20 And brought them to the magistrates
1 Pe. 3. 18 just for the unjust, that he might bring

43. *To bear toward,* προσφέρω *prospherō.*
Matt 25. 20 he..came and brought other five talents
Mark 10. 13 disciples rebuked those that brought

44. *To bear, carry,* φέρω *pherō.*
Matt 14. 11 And his head was brought in a charger
14. 11 and she brought (it) to her mother
14. 18 He said, Bring them hither to me
17. 17 how long shall I suffer you! Bring him
Mark 1. 32 they brought unto him all that were
2. 3 bringing one sick of the palsy, which
6. 27 and commanded his head to be brought
6. 28 And brought his head in a charger
7. 32 And they bring unto him one that was
8. 22 and they bring a blind man unto him
9. 17 Master, I have brought unto thee my
9. 19 how long shall I suffer you? Bring him
9. 20 And they brought him unto him: and
12. 15 Why tempt ye me? bring me a penny
12. 16 And they brought (it). And he saith
15. 22 And they bring him unto the place
Luke 5. 18 And, behold, men brought in a bed a
15. 23 bring hither the fatted calf, and kill (it)
24. 1 bringing the spices which they had
John 4. 33 Hath any man brought..(ought) to eat?
18. 29 What accusation bring ye against this
19. 39 Nicodemus..brought a mixture of myrrh
21. 10 Bring of the fish which ye have now caught
Acts 4. 34 as many as were possessors..brought
4. 37 Having..brought the money, and laid (it)
5. 2 his wife..brought a certain part, and laid
5. 16 There came also a multitude..bringing
14. 13 the priest..brought oxen and garlands
2 Ti. 4. 13 when thou comest, bring (with thee)..the
2 Pe. 2. 11; 2 Jo. 10; Rev. 21. 24; 21. 26.

45. *To do,* ποιέω *poieō.*
Acts 24. 17 I came to bring alms to my nation, and

BRING on horseback, to —
To cause to ride, רָכַב *rakab,* 5.
Esth. 6. 11 brought him on horseback through

BRING (a cloud), to —
To cloud, darken, עָנַן *anan,* 3.
Gen. 9. 14 it shall come to pass, when I bring a cloud

BRING about, to —
To bring round about, סָבַב *sabab,* 5.
1 Sa. 5. 10 They have brought about the ark of..God
2 Sa. 3. 12 to bring about all Israel unto thee

BRING again, to —
1. *To go,* הָלַךְ *halak.*
Ezra 6. 5 be restored, and brought again unto

2. *To bring round about,* סָבַב *sabab,* 5.
1 Ch. 13. 3 let us bring again the ark of our God

3. *To turn back,* שׁוּב *shub.*
Isa. 52. 8 when the LORD shall bring again Zion
Jer. 30. 3 I will bring again the captivity of my
30. 18 I will bring again the captivity of Jacob
31. 23 when I shall bring again their captivity
48. 47 Yet will I bring again the captivity
Eze. 16. 53 I shall bring again their captivity
29. 14 I will bring again the captivity of Egypt
Am. 9. 14 I will bring again the captivity of my

4. *To bring back,* שׁוּב *shub,* 3a.
Isa. 49. 5 his servant, to bring Jacob again to him
Jer. 50. 19 I will bring Israel again to his habitation
Eze. 39. 27 I have brought them again from the

5. *To bring back,* שׁוּב *shub,* 5.
Gen. 14. 16 brought again his brother Lot, and his
24. 5 I needs bring thy son again unto
24. 6 thou bring not my son thither again
24. 8 only bring not my son thither again
28. 15 I..will bring thee again into this land
37. 14 Go, I pray thee..and bring me word ag.
42. 37 I will bring him to thee again
43. 21 we have brought it again in our hand
44. 8 we brought again unto thee out of the
48. 21 God shall..bring you again unto the land
Exod 15. 19 the LORD brought again the waters
Num 17. 10 Bring Aaron's rod again before the testi.
22. 8 Lodge here..I will bring you word again
Deut 1. 22 bring us word again by what way we
1. 25 And they..brought us word again
22. 1 in any case bring them again unto
28. 68 shall bring thee into Egypt again
Josh 14. 7 I brought him word again as (it was)
22. 32 returned..and brought them word again
Judg 19. 3 to speak friendly..(and) to bring her again
1 Sa. 6. 21 The Philistines have brought again the
2 Sa. 3. 26 messengers..brought him again from
14. 21 bring the young man Absalom again
15. 8 the LORD shall bring me [V.L. *shub* 1.]
15. 25 he will bring me again, and show me..it
1 Ki 2. 30 Benaiah brought the king word again
8. 34 bring them again unto the land
12. 21 bring the kingdom again to Rehoboam
20. 9 departed and brought him word again
2 Ki 22. 9 the scribe..brought the king word again
22. 20 And they brought the king word again
1 Ch. 21. 12 I shall bring again to him that
2 Ch. 6. 25 bring them again unto the land which
11. 1 he might bring the kingdom again
12. 11 the guard..brought them again into the
24. 19 he sent prophets..to bring them again
33. 13 brought him again to Jerusalem into his
34. 28 So they brought the king word again
Neh 9. 29 thou mightest bring them again unto
13. 9 thither brought I again the vessels of the
Job 10. 9 and wilt thou bring me into dust again?
Psa 68. 22 I will bring again from Bashan; I will
Prov 19. 24 so much as bring it to his mouth again
26. 15 it grieveth him to bring it again to his
Isa 38. 8 I will bring again the shadow of the
46. 8 bring (it) again to mind, O ye transg.
49. 5 formed me..to bring Jacob again to him
Jer. 12. 15 and will bring them again every man
15. 19 return, then will I bring thee again
16. 15 I will bring them again into their land
23. 3 I..will bring them again to their folds
24. 6 I will bring them again to this land
28. 3 will I bring again into this place all
28. 4 I will bring again to this place..Jeconiah
28. 6 bring again the vessels of the LORD'S
29. 14 I will bring you again unto the place
32. 37 I will bring them again unto this
41. 16 the eunuchs..he had brought again
49. 6 will bring again the captivity of..Ammon
49. 39 I will bring again the cap.[V.L. *shub* 1.]
Eze. 34. 4 have ye brought again that which was
34. 16 I will..bring again that which was
39. 25 I bring again the captivity of Jacob
47. 1 he brought me again unto the door
Joel 3. 1 shall bring again the cap.[V.L. *shub* 1.]
Zech 10. 10 I will bring them again also out of the

6. *To lead up, back, or again,* ἀνάγω *anagō.*
Heb. 13. 20 that brought again from the dead our

7. *To turn away from,* ἀποστρέφω *apostrephō.*
Matt. 27. 3 brought [again] the thirty pieces of silver

BRING against, to —
To bring or bear upon, ἐπιφέρω *epipherō.*
Jude 9 he..durst not bring against him a railing

BRING away, to —
1. *To consume away,* בָּעַר *baar,* 3.
Deut 26. 13 I have brought away the hallowed things

2. *To lead away,* נָהַג *nahag.*
1 Sa. 23. 5 brought away their cattle, and smote them

BRING away captive, to —
To carry captive, שָׁבָה *shabah.*
2 Ki. 5. 2 Syrians..had brought away captive..a

BRING back, to —
1. *To turn back to,* שׁוּב *shub.*
Psa. 14. 7 the LORD bringeth back the captivity of
53. 6 When God bringeth back the captivity of
85. 1 thou hast brought back the captivity of

2. *To bring back,* שׁוּב *shub,* 5.
Gen. 14. 16 he brought back all the goods, and also
Exod 23. 4 thou shalt surely bring it back to him
Num 13. 26 and brought back word unto them
2 Sa. 17. 3 I will bring back all the people
19. 11 the last to bring the king back
19. 12 are ye the last to bring back the king?
1 Ki. 13. 18 Bring him back with thee into thine
13. 20 unto the prophet that brought him back
13. 23 the prophet whom he had brought back
13. 26 the prophet that brought him back from
13. 29 laid it upon the ass and brought it back
14. 28 the guard..brought them back into
2 Ch. 19. 4 brought them back unto the LORD God
Job 33. 30 To bring back his soul from the pit
Eze. 44. 1 he brought me back the way of the gate

BRING down, to —
1. *To bring down,* יָרַד *yarad,* 5.
Gen. 39. 1 Ishmeelites, which had brought him down
42. 38 ye bring down my grey hairs with sorrow
43. 7 he would say, Bring your brother down?
43. 22 other money have we brought down in
44. 21 Bring him down unto me, that I may set
44. 29 ye shall bring down my grey hairs with
44. 31 thy servants shall bring down the grey
45. 13 ye shall haste and bring down my father
Deut. 1. 25 and brought (it) down unto us, and
21. 4 bring down the heifer unto a rough
Judg. 7. 4 bring them down unto the water, and I
7. 5 he brought down the people unto the
16. 21 the Philistines..brought him down
1 Sa. 2. 6 he bringeth down to the grave, and
30. 15 Canst..bring me down to this company?
30. 15 I will bring thee down to this company
30. 16 when he had brought him down, behold
2 Sa. 22. 48 It (is) God..that bringeth down the people
1 Ki. 1. 33 ride upon mine..and bring him down
1. 53 they brought him down from the altar
2. 9 his hoar head bring thou down to the
5. 9 My servants shall bring (them) down
17. 23 Elijah..brought him down out of
18. 40 Elijah brought them down to the brook
2 Ki. 11. 19 they brought down the king from
2 Ch. 23. 20 he..brought down the king from
Psa. 55. 23 thou, O God, shalt bring them down
59. 11 scatter them by thy power; and bring..d.
Isa. 43. 14 I have..brought down all their nobles
63. 6 I will bring down their strength to the
Jer. 49. 16 I will bring thee down from thence
51. 40 I will bring them down like lambs
Eze. 26. 20 I shall bring thee down with them
28. 8 They shall bring thee down to the pit
Hos. 7. 12 I will bring them down as the fowls of
Amos 3. 11 he shall bring down thy strength from
9. 2 thence will I bring them down
Obad 3 Who shall bring me down to the ground?
4 will I bring thee down, saith the LORD

2. *To cause to bend,* כָּנַע *kana,* 5.
Deut. 9. 3 he shall bring them down before thy face
Psa. 107. 12 Therefore he brought down their heart
Isa. 25. 5 Thou shalt bring down the noise of

3. *To cause to touch,* נָגַע *naga,* 5.
Eze. 13. 14 bring it down to the ground, so that the

4. *To cause to bow,* שָׁחַח *shachach,* 5.
Isa. 25. 12 high fort of thy walls shall he bring down
26. 5 he bringeth down them that dwell on

5. *To humble,* שָׁפֵל *shaphel,* 5.
2 Sa. 22. 28 (that) thou mayest bring (them) down
Psa. 18. 27 For thou wilt..bring down high looks
Isa. 25. 11 and he shall bring down their pride
Eze. 17. 24 I the LORD have brought down the high

6. *To lead down,* κατάγω *katagō.*
Acts 9. 30 they brought him down to Cesarea, and
22. 30 the chief priests..brought Paul down
23. 15 that he bring him down unto you
23. 20 that thou wouldest bring down Paul
Rom 10. 6 that is, to bring Christ down (from above)

BRING forth, to —
1. *To cause to come in,* בּוֹא *bo,* 5.
Zech. 3. 8 will bring forth my servant The Branch

2. *To ripen, make ready,* בָּשַׁל *bashal,* 5.
Gen. 40. 10 the clusters..brought forth ripe grapes

3. *To cause to yield tender grass,* דָּשָׁא *dasha,* 5.
Gen. 1. 11 God said, Let the earth bring forth grass

4. *To be pained, travail in birth,* חָבַל *chabal,* 3.
Song 8. 5 there thy mother brought thee forth
8. 5 there she brought thee forth (that) bare

5. *To be pained, travail in birth,* חוּל *chul.*
Isa. 45. 10 What hast thou brought forth?

6. *To beget, bear,* יָלַד *yalad.*
Gen. 3. 16 in sorrow thou shalt bring forth children
30. 39 the flocks conceived..and brought forth
2 Ki. 19. 3 (there is) not strength to bring forth
Job 15. 35 They conceive mischief, and bring forth
39. 1 when the wild goats of the rock bring f.
39. 2 knowest thou the time when they bring f.
Psa. 7. 14 he..hath conceived..and brought forth
Prov 27. 1 thou knowest not what a day may bring f.
Isa. 26. 18 we have as it were brought forth wind
33. 11 Ye shall conceive chaff; ye shall bring
37. 3 (there is) not strength to bring forth
51. 18 all the sons (whom) she hath brought forth
65. 23 They shall not..bring forth for trouble
66. 7 Before she travailed, she brought forth
66. 8 she brought forth her children
Jer. 2. 27 Thou hast brought me forth: for they
Hos. 9. 16 shall bear no fruit; yea, though..bring f.
Mic. 5. 3 she which travaileth hath brought forth
Zeph. 2. 2 Before the decree bring forth, (before)

7. *To cause to bear or bring forth* יָלַד *yalad,* 5.
Isa. 59. 4 they conceive mischief, and bring forth

8. *To let go out,* יָצָא *yatsa.*
Deut 14. 22 the field bringeth forth year by year

9. *To cause to go out,* יָצָא *yatsa,* 5.
Gen. 1. 12 the earth brought forth grass, (and)
1. 24 Let the earth bring forth the living
8. 17 Bring forth with thee every living thing
14. 18 Melchizedek..brought forth bread and
15. 5 he brought him forth abroad, and said
19. 16 they brought him forth, and set him
19. 17 they had brought them forth abroad
24. 53 the servant brought forth jewels of
38. 24 Bring her forth, and let her be burnt
Exod. 3. 10 thou mayest bring forth my people
3. 11 I should bring forth the children of
3. 12 When thou hast brought forth..people
7. 4 bring forth mine armies, (and) my people
8. 18 to bring forth lice, but they could not
12. 39 dough which they brought forth out of
13. 16 the LORD brought us forth out of Egypt
16. 3 ye have brought us forth into this
16. 32 I brought you forth from the land of
19. 17 Moses brought forth the people out of
29. 46 I (am) the LORD..that brought them f.
32. 11 which thou hast brought forth out of the
Lev. 24. 14 Bring forth him that hath cursed
24. 23 they should bring forth him that had
25. 38 I (am) the LORD..which brought you f.
25. 42 they (are) my servants, which I brought f.
25. 55 they (are) my servants whom I brought f.
26. 10 bring forth the old because of the new
26. 13 I (am) the LORD..which brought you f.
26. 45 their ancestors, whom I brought forth
Num 17. 8 house of Levi was budded..brought forth
19. 3 bring her forth without the camp
20. 8 thou shalt bring forth to them water
20. 16 an angel..hath brought us forth out of
24. 8 God brought him forth out of Egypt
Deut. 1. 27 he hath brought us forth out of the land
4. 20 the LORD..brought you forth out of the
6. 12 the LORD, which brought thee forth out
9. 12 people..thou hast brought forth..have
9. 26 thou hast brought forth out of Egypt
14. 28 thou shalt bring forth all the tithe of
16. 1 thy God brought thee forth out of Egypt
17. 5 shalt thou bring forth that man or that
22. 15 bring forth (the tokens of) the damsel's
26. 8 the LORD brought us forth out of Egypt
29. 25 he brought them forth out of the land
Josh 10. 23 they..brought forth those five kings
Judg. 6. 8 brought you forth out of the house of
6. 18 I come unto thee, and bring forth my
19. 22 Bring forth the man that came into
19. 25 brought her forth unto them; and they
1 Sa. 12. 8 Moses and Aaron, which brought forth
2 Sa. 12. 30 he brought forth the spoil of the city
12. 31 he brought forth the people that (were)
22. 20 He brought me forth also into a large
22. 49 bringeth me forth from mine enemies
1 Ki. 8. 16 I brought forth my people..out of Egypt
8. 51 (be) thy people..which thou broughtest f.
9. 9 the LORD their God, who brought forth
2 Ki. 10. 22 Bring forth vestments for all the
10. 22 And he brought them forth vestments
10. 26 they brought forth the images out of the
11. 12 he brought forth the king's son, and put
23. 4 bring forth out of the temple..all the
2 Ch. 1. 17 And they..brought forth out of Egypt
6. 5 I brought forth my people out of the
7. 22 the LORD..which brought them forth
Ezra 1. 7 the king brought forth the vessels of the
1. 7 which Nebuchadnezzar had brought f.
1. 8 Even those did Cyrus..bring forth by
Neh. 9. 7 the LORD..who..broughtest him forth out
Job 10. 18 then hast thou brought me forth out of
28. 11 (the thing that is) hid bringeth he forth to
Psa. 18. 19 He brought me forth also into a large
37. 6 he shall bring forth thy righteousness
104. 14 he may bring forth food out of the earth
105. 37 He brought them forth also with silver
105. 43 And he brought forth his people with
Prov. 30. 33 Surely the churning of milk bringeth forth
30. 33 and the wringing of the nose bringeth f.
30. 33 so the forcing of wrath bringeth forth
Isa. 42. 1 he shall bring forth judgment to
Isa. 42. 3 he shall bring forth judgment unto truth
43. 8 Bring forth the blind people that have
43. 17 Which bringeth forth the chariot and
61. 11 as the earth bringeth forth her bud
65. 9 I will bring forth a seed out of Jacob
Jer. 10. 13 he..bringeth forth the wind out of
11. 4 I brought them forth out of the land
20. 3 Pashur brought forth Jeremiah out of
32. 21 And hast brought forth thy people Israel
34. 13 I brought them forth out of the land
50. 25 The LORD..hath brought forth the
51. 10 The LORD hath brought forth our right.
51. 16 he..bringeth forth the wind out of his
51. 44 I will bring forth out of his mouth
52. 31 Jehoiachin..brought him forth out
Eze. 11. 7 I will bring you forth out of the midst
12. 4 shalt thou bring forth thy stuff by day
12. 7 I brought forth my stuff by day
12. 7 I brought (it) forth in the twilight
20. 6 bring them forth of the land of Egypt
20. 9 made myself known..in bringing them f.
20. 22 in whose sight I brought them forth
28. 18 I bring forth a fire from the midst of thee
38. 4 I will bring thee forth, and all thine
42. 1 he brought me forth into the outer court
42. 15 he brought me forth toward the gate
46. 21 he brought me forth into the outer court
Dan. 9. 15 God..hast brought thy people forth out
Hos. 9. 13 Ephraim shall bring forth his children
Mic. 7. 9 he will bring me forth to the light
Hag. 1. 11 (that) which the ground bringeth forth
Zech. 4. 7 he shall bring forth the head stone
5. 4 I will bring it forth, saith the LORD of

10. *To cause to draw nigh,* נָגַשׁ *nagash,* 5.
2 Ch. 29. 23 they brought forth the he goats (for) the
Isa. 41. 21 bring forth your strong (reasons), saith
41. 22 Let them bring (them) forth, and show us

11. *To sprout, bring forth,* נוּב *nub.*
Prov 10. 31 The mouth of the just bringeth forth

12. *To lift up, bear,* נָשָׂא *nasa.*
Eze. 17. 23 it shall bring forth boughs, and bear fruit
Hag. 2. 19 and the olive tree, hath not brought forth

13 *To give,* נָתַן *nathan.*
Isa. 43. 9 let them bring forth their witnesses

14. *To do, make, yield,* עָשָׂה *asah.*
Gen. 41. 47 plenteous years the earth brought forth
Lev. 25. 21 it shall bring forth fruit for three years
Job 14. 9 it will bud, and bring forth boughs like
Isa. 5. 2 and it brought forth wild grapes
5. 4 brought it forth wild grapes?
Jer. 12. 2 they grow, yea, they bring forth fruit
Eze. 17. 6 it became a vine, and brought forth
17. 8 It was planted..that it might bring forth

15. *To cleave through,* פָּלַח *palach,* 3.
Job 39. 3 They bow themselves, they bring forth

16. *To bear fruit,* פָּרָה *parah.*
Isa. 45. 8 let them bring forth salvation, and let

17. *To spring up,* צָמַח *tsamach.*
Eccl. 2. 6 to water..the wood that bringeth forth

18. *To cause to spring up,* צָמַח *tsamach,* 5.
Gen. 3. 18 Thorns also and thistles shall it bring f.

19. *To cause to draw near,* קָרַב *qarab,* 5.
Judg. 5. 25 she brought forth butter in a lordly dish

20. *To set, make even,* שָׁוָה *shavah,* 3.
Hos. 10. 1 he bringeth forth fruit unto himself

21. *To lead, lead on,* ἄγω *agō.*
Acts 25. 17 commanded the man to be brought forth
25. 23 Festus' command. Paul was brought forth

22. *To lead up or again,* ἀνάγω *anagō.*
Acts 12. 4 intending after Easter to bring him forth

23. *To bear forth young,* ἀποκυέω *apokueō.*
Jas. 1. 15 when lust hath conceived, it bringeth f.

24. *To bud, sprout,* βλαστάνω *blastanō.*
Jas. 5. 18 the earth brought forth her fruit

25. *To give,* δίδωμι *didōmi.*
Matt 13. 8 into good ground, and brought forth fruit

26. *To cast forth,* ἐκβάλλω *ekballō.*
Matt 12. 35 good treasure of the heart, bringeth forth
12. 35 the evil treasure, bringeth forth evil
13. 52 bringeth forth..out of his treasure (things)

27. *To beget, bear,* γεννάω *gennaō.*
Luke 1. 57 should be delivered; and she brought f.

28. *To bear or bring forth,* ἐκφέρω *ekpherō.*
Luke 15. 22 Bring forth the best robe, and put (it) on
Acts 5. 15 they brought forth the sick into the streets

29. *To lead out,* ἐξάγω *exagō.*
Acts 5. 19 opened the prison doors, and brought f.

30. *To lead down,* κατάγω *katagō.*
Acts 23. 28 I brought him forth into their council

31. *To do, make,* ποιέω *poieō.*
Matt. 3. 8 Bring forth..fruits meet for repentance
3. 10 every tree which bringeth not forth good
7. 17 every good tree bringeth forth good fruit
7. 17 a corrupt tree bringeth forth evil fruit
7. 18 A good tree cannot bring forth evil fruit
7. 18 neither (can) a corrupt tree bring forth
Matt. 7. 19 Every tree that bringeth not forth good
13. 23 (it)..also beareth fruit and bringeth forth
13. 26 the blade was sprung up, and brought f.
21. 43 a nation bringing forth the fruits thereof
Luke 3. 8 Bring forth..fruits worthy of repentance
3. 9 every tree..which bringeth not forth
6. 43 a good tree bringeth not forth corrupt
6. 43 doth a corrupt tree bring forth good

32. *To lead forward,* προάγω *proagō.*
Acts 12. 6 Herod would have brought him forth
25. 26 I have brought him forth before you

33. *To bear forward,* προφέρω *propherō.*
Luke 6. 45 his heart bringeth forth that which is
6. 45 his heart bringeth forth that which is

34. *To bring forth,* τίκτω *tiktō.*
Matt. 1. 21 And she shall bring forth a son
1. 23 Behold, a virgin..shall bring forth a son
1. 25 And knew her not till she had brought f.
Luke 1. 31 behold, thou shalt..bring forth a son
2. 7 she brought forth her first born son
Heb. 6. 7 the earth..bringeth forth herbs meet for
Jas. 1. 15 sin, when it is finished, bringeth forth
Rev. 12. 5 And she brought forth a man child
12. 13 persecuted the woman which brought f.

35. *To bear,* φέρω *pherō.*
Mark 4. 8 And other fell..and brought forth
John 12. 24 if it die, it bringeth forth much fruit
15. 2 that it may bring forth more fruit
15. 5 the same bringeth forth much fruit
15. 16 I have chosen you..go and bring forth
[*See also* First child, fruit, new fruit, thousands.

BRING forth abundantly —
To swarm, שָׁרַץ *sharats.*
Gen. 1. 20 Let the waters bring forth abundantly
1. 21 the waters brought forth abundantly
9. 7 bring forth abundantly in the earth
Exod. 8. 3 the river shall bring forth frogs abund.

BRING forth children, to —
To beget, bear, יָלַד *yalad.*
Isa. 23. 4 I travail not, nor bring forth children

BRING forth fruit, to —
To burst forth, נוּב *nub.*
Psa. 92. 14 They shall still bring forth fruit in old

BRING forth in abundance, to —
To swarm, שָׁרַץ *sharats.*
Psa. 105. 30 Their land brought forth frogs in abund.

BRING forth plentifully, to —
To bear well, εὐφορέω *euphoreō.*
Luke 12. 16 of a rich man brought forth plentifully

BRING forth, to labour to —
To break forth, גּוּחַ *guach.*
Mic. 4. 10 Be in pain, and labour to bring forth

BRING forth, to be made to —
To be pained, or in travail, חוּל *chul,* 6.
Isa. 66. 8 Shall the earth be made to bring forth

BRING forth, to make to —
To cause to bear, יָלַד *yalad,* 5.
Isa. 55. 10 the rain..maketh it bring forth and bud

BRING forth, to cause to —
To cause to bear, יָלַד *yalad,* 5.
Isa. 66. 9 to the birth, and not cause to bring forth?
66. 9 shall I cause to bring forth, and shut

BRING forth young, to —
To beget, bear, יָלַד *yalad.*
Eze. 31. 6 all the beasts..bring forth their young

BRING hither, to —
To give, נָתַן *nathan.*
Psa. 81. 2 Take a psalm, and bring hither the timb.

BRING home (again), to —
To turn back, שׁוּב *shub,* 5.
Ruth 1. 21 Lord hath brought me home again empty
Judg 11. 9 If ye bring me home again to fight
Job 39. 12 Wilt thou believe..he will bring home

BRING forward on one's journey, to —
To send forward, προπέμπω *propempō.*
3 John 6 bring forward on their journey after a

BRING in, to —

1. *To cause to go or come in,* בּוֹא *bo,* 5.
Gen. 39. 14 he hath brought in an Hebrew unto us
47. 7 Joseph brought in Jacob his father
Exod 15. 17 Thou shalt bring them in, and plant
16. 5 shall prepare (that) which they bring in
23. 23 Angel shall go before thee, and bring in
26. 33 thou mayest bring in thither within the
40. 4 thou shalt bring in the table, and set in
40. 4 thou shalt bring in the candlestick
Lev. 6. 21 (when it is) baken, thou shalt bring it in
Num 14. 31 little ones..them will I bring in, and
27. 17 which may bring them in; that the
Deut. 4. 38 bring thee in, to give thee their land
9. 4 the LORD hath brought me in to possess
11. 29 the LORD thy God hath brought thee in to
1 Sa. 16. 12 he sent and brought him in. Now he
2 Sa. 3. 22 Joab came..and brought in a great spoil
5. 2 he that leddest out and broughtest in
6. 17 they brought in the ark of the LORD, and
9. 10 thou shalt bring in (the fruits), that thy

1 Ki. 7. 51 Solomon brought in the things..his father
8. 6 the priests brought in the ark of the
10. 11 the navy..brought in from Ophir..almug
15. 15 he brought in the things which his father
1 Ch. 9. 28 they should bring them in and out by
2 Ch. 5. 1 Solomon brought in (all) the things that
5. 7 priests brought in the ark of the covenant
15. 18 he brought into the house of God the
24. 6 hast thou not required..Lev. to bring in
24. 9 to bring in to the LORD the collection
24. 10 the people..brought in, and cast into
29. 4 he brought in the priests and the Levites
29. 31 the congregation brought in sacrifices and
30. 15 Levites..brought in the burnt offerings
31. 5 the children..brought in..the first fruits
31. 6 they also brought in the tithe of oxen
31. 12 brought in the offerings and the tithes
Neh. 13. 15 bringing in sheaves, and lading asses; as
13. 15 which they brought into Jerusalem on
Jer. 17. 21 bring (it) in by the gates of Jerusalem
17. 24 bring in no burden through the gates
35. 4 I brought them into the house of the
Dan. 1. 18 the king had said he should bring them in
9. 24 to bring in everlasting righteousness
Hag. 1. 6 Ye have sown much, and bring in little

2. *To cause to come up or in*, עָלַל *alal*, 5.
Dan. 2. 24 bring me in before the king, and I will
2. 25 Arioch brought in Daniel before the king
4. 6 to bring in all the wise (men) of Babylon
5. 7 The king cried aloud to bring in..astrolo.

3. *To lead to or into*, εἰσάγω *eisagō*.
Luke 2. 27 the parents brought in the child Jesus
14. 21 bring in hither..poor, and the maimed
John 18. 16 Then..that other disciple..brought in
Acts 7. 45 also our fathers..brought in with Jesus
Heb. 1. 6 again, when he bringeth in the first beg.

4. *To bear to or into*, εἰσφέρω *eispherō*.
Luke 5. 18 they sought (means) to bring him in
5. 19 find by what..they might bring him in

BRING in privily, to —
To lead in sideways, παρεισάγω *pareisagō*.
2 Pe. 2. 1 false teachers..privily shall bring in dam.

BRING in upon, to —
To lead upon, ἐπάγω *epagō*.
2 Pe. 2. 5 a preacher..bringing in the flood upon

BRING into, to —
1. *To lead in, toward*, εἰσάγω *eisagō*.
Luke 22. 54 they..brought him into the high priest's
Acts 9. 8 led..and brought (him) into Damascus
21. 28 and further brought Greeks also into
21. 29 that Paul had brought into the temple

2. *To bear in, toward*, εἰσφέρω *eispherō*.
1 Ti. 6. 7 For we brought nothing into (this) world
Heb. 13. 11 blood is brought into the sanctuary by
[*See also* Bondage, contempt, sware, subjection.]

BRING low, to —
1. *To cause to bend*, כָּנַע *kana*, 5.
2 Ch. 28. 19 For the LORD brought Judah low because
Job 40. 12 Look on every one..(and) bring him low

2. *To cause to bend or bow*, כָּרַע *kara*, 5.
Judg. 11. 35 Alas..thou hast brought me very low

3. *To make humble*, שָׁפֵל *shaphel*, 5.
1 Sa. 2. 7 The LORD..bringeth low and lifteth up
Prov. 29. 23 A man's pride shall bring him low: but

BRING near to —
1. *To bring near*, קָרַב *qarab*, 3.
Isa. 46. 13 I bring near my righteousness; it shall

2. *To cause to draw near*, קָרַב *qarab*, 5.
Num. 3. 6 Bring the tribe of Levi near, and
16. 9 bring you near to himself, to do the
16. 10 he hath brought thee near (to him), and

3. *To cause to draw near*, קָרַב *qereb*, 5.
Dan. 7. 13 and they brought him near before him

BRING on the way, to —
1. *To send on*, שָׁלַח *shalach*, 3.
Gen. 18. 16 Abraham went..to bring them on the way

2. *To send forward*, προπέμπω *propempō*.
Acts 15. 3 being brought on their way by the church
21. 5 they all brought us on our way, with
Rom. 15. 24 for I trust..to be brought on my way
2 Co. 1. 16 to be brought on my way toward Judea

BRING on the journey, to —
To send forward, προπέμπω *propempō*.
1 Co. 16. 6 that ye may bring me on my journey
Titus 3. 13 Bring Zenas the lawyer ..on their journey

BRING out, to —
1. *To cause to come forth*, יָצָא *yatsa*, 5.
Gen. 15. 7 I (am) the LORD that brought thee out
19. 5 bring them out unto us, that we may
19. 8 let me, I pray you, bring them out unto
19. 12 bring (them) out of this place
40. 14 make mention of me..and bring me out
43. 23 And he brought Simeon out unto them
48. 12 Joseph brought them out from between
Exod. 6. 6 I will bring you out from under the
6. 7 which bringeth you out from under the
6. 13 bring the children..out of the land
6. 27 to bring out the children..from Egypt
7. 5 bring out the children..from among
Exod. 12. 42 the LORD..bringing them out from the
12. 51 LORD did bring the children of Israel out
13. 3 the LORD brought you out from this
13. 9 the LORD brought thee out of Egypt
13. 14 the LORD brought us out from Egypt
16. 6 the LORD hath brought you out from the
18. 1 the LORD had brought Israel out of Egypt
20. 2 I (am) the LORD..which..brought thee out
32. 12 For mischief did he bring them out
Lev. 19. 36 I (am) the LORD..which brought you out
23. 43 I brought them out of the land of Egypt
Num. 15. 41 I (am) the LORD..which brought you out
17. 9 And Moses brought out all the rods
23. 22 God brought them out of Egypt; he hath
Deut. 4. 37 he..brought thee out in his sight
5. 6 I (am) the LORD..which brought thee out
5. 15 the LORD thy God brought thee out
6. 23 he brought us out from thence, that he
6. 21 and the LORD brought us out of Egypt
7. 8 the LORD brought you out with a mighty
7. 19 whereby the L. thy God brought thee out
9. 28 the land whence thou broughtest us out
9. 28 he hath brought them out to slay them
13. 5 the LORD..which brought you out of
13. 10 the LORD..which brought thee out of
21. 19 shall his father..bring him out to the
22. 21 Then they shall bring out the damsel
22. 24 bring them both out unto the gate
24. 11 the man..thou dost lend shall bring out
Josh. 6. 22 Go..and bring out thence the woman
6. 23 brought out Rahab, and her father, and
10. 22 bring out those five kings unto me out
10. 24 they brought out those kings unto Joshua
24. 5 them: and afterward I brought you out
24. 6 I brought your fathers out of Egypt
Judg. 2. 12 forsook the LORD..which brought them o
6. 19 and brought (it) out unto him under the
6. 30 Bring out thy son, that he may die
2 Sa. 10. 16 Hadarezer sent, and brought out the
13. 18 his servant brought her out, and bolted
1 Ki. 8. 21 he brought them out of the land of Egypt
8. 53 thou broughtest our fathers out of Egypt
10. 29 did they bring (them) out by their means
2 Ki. 23. 6 he brought out the grove from the house
1 Ch. 9. 28 they should bring them in and out
20. 2 he brought..much spoil out of the city
20. 3 he brought out the people that (were) in
2 Ch. 1. 17 so brought they out (horses) for all the
9. 28 they brought unto Solomon horses out
16. 2 Then Asa brought out silver and gold out
23. 11 Then they brought out the king's son, and
23. 14 the priest brought out the captains of
29. 16 priests..brought out all the uncleanness
34. 14 when they brought out the money that
Job 12. 22 He..bringeth out to light the shadow of
Psa. 25. 17 O bring thou me out of my distresses
66. 12 thou broughtest us out into a wealthy
68. 6 he bringeth out those which are bound
78. 16 He brought streams also out of the rock
107. 14 He brought them out of darkness and
107. 28 he bringeth them out of their distresses
135. 7 he bringeth the wind out of his treasuries
136. 11 brought out Israel from among them for
143. 11 Quicken me..bring my soul out of trouble
Isa. 40. 26 these (things), that bringeth out their host
42. 7 bring out the prisoners from the prison
Jer. 7. 22 I brought them out of the land of Egypt
8. 1 they shall bring out the bones of the
31. 32 to bring them out of the land of Egypt
38. 23 So they shall bring out all thy wives and
Eze. 11. 9 I will bring you out of the midst thereof
20. 14 in whose sight I brought them out
20. 34 I will bring you out from the people, and
20. 41 when I bring you out from the people
34. 13 I will bring them out from the people
47. 2 Then brought he me out of the way of the
Amos 6. 10 bring out the bones out of the house

2. *To lead out*, ἐξάγω *exagō*.
Acts 7. 36 He brought them out, after that he had
7. 40 Moses, which brought us out of the land
12. 17 the Lord had brought him out of
13. 17 with an high arm brought he them out
16. 39 they came..and brought (them) out, and

3. *To lead forward*, προάγω *proagō*.
Acts 16. 30 brought them out, and said, Sirs, what

BRING over, to —
1. *To carry into exile*, גָּלָה *gelah*, 5.
Ezra 4. 10 whom the great..Asnapper brought over
2. *To cause to pass over*, עָבַר *abar*, 5.
Num. 32. 5 bring us not over Jordan; Jos. 7. 7; 2 Sa. 2. 8.

BRING safe—
Save through, διασώζω *diasōzō*.
Acts 23. 24 and bring him safe unto Felix the governor

BRING through, to —
To cause to pass over, עָבַר *abar*, 5.
Eze. 47. 3, 4 he brought me through the waters; 47. 4

BRING to, to —
1. *To bear in to*, εἰσφέρω *eispherō*.
Acts 17. 20 thou bringest certain strange things to

2. *To bear toward*, προσφέρω *prospherō*.
Matt. 5. 23 if thou bring thy gift [to] the altar, and
9. 2 they brought to him a man sick of the
9. 32 brought to him a dumb man possessed
17. 16 I brought him to thy disciples, and they
Mark 10. 13 they brought young children to him, that
[*See also* Birth, honour, nothing, nought, shame.]

BRING to pass, to —
1. *To do*, עָשָׂה *asah*.
Gen. 41. 32, 50. 20; Psa. 37. 5, 7.

2. *To execute*, עָבַד *abad*.
Isa. 28. 21 and bring to pass his act, his strange act

BRING together, to —
1. *To gather*, קָבַץ *qabats*, 3.
Isa. 62. 9 they that have brought it together shall

2. *To bear together*, συμφέρω *sumpherō*.
Acts 19. 19 Many of them..brought their books tog.

BRING unto, to —
To bear toward, προσφέρω *prospherō*.
Matt. 4. 24 they brought unto him all sick people
8. 16 they brought unto him many that were
12. 22 Then was brought unto him one possessed
14. 35 brought unto him all that were
18. 24 one was [brought unto] him which owed
19. 13 then were there brought unto him little
22. 19 they brought unto him a penny
Luke 12. 11 when they [bring you] unto the synagogues
18. 15 they brought unto him also infants, that
23. 14 Ye have brought this man unto me, as

BRING up, to —
1. *To be faithful, steady, a nurse*, אָמַן *aman*.
2 Ki. 10. 1 them that brought up Ahab's (children)
Esth. 2. 7 he brought up Hadassah, that (is), Esther

2. *To make great, nourish*, גָּדַל *gadal*, 3.
2 Ki. 10. 6 the great men..which brought them up
Isa. 49. 21 who hath brought up these? Behold, I
51. 18 of all the sons (that) she hath brought up
Hos. 9. 12 Though they bring up their children

3. *To bear*, יָלַד *yalad*.
2 Sa. 21. 8 two sons..whom she brought up for

4. *To cause to come out*, יָצָא *yatsa*, 5.
Num. 13. 32 they brought up an evil report of the
14. 36 by bringing up a slander upon the land
14. 37 men that did bring up the evil report
Deut. 22. 14 bring up an evil name upon her, and
22. 19 he hath brought up an evil name upon a

5. *To go up*, עָלָה *alah*, (1), 5.
Gen. 46. 4 I will also surely bring thee up (again)

6. *To cause to go up*, עָלָה *alah*, 5.
Exod. 3. 8 I am come down..to bring them up
3. 17 I will bring you up out of the affliction
8. 7 brought up frogs upon the land of Egypt
17. 3 thou hast brought us up out of Egypt, to
32. 1 the man that brought us up out of the
32. 4 which brought thee up out of the land of
32. 8 These..have brought thee up out of the
32. 23 this Moses, the man that brought us up
33. 12 thou sayest unto me, Bring up this people
33. 1 the people which thou hast brought up
Num. 14. 13 thou broughtest up this people in thy
16. 13 thou hast brought us up out of a land
20. 25 Take Aaron..and bring them up unto
21. 5 Wherefore have ye brought us up out
22. 41 Balak..brought him up into the high
Deut. 20. 1 God (is) with thee, which brought thee up
Josh. 2. 6 she had brought them up to the roof of
24. 17 he (it is) that brought us up and our
24. 32 the children of Israel brought up out of
Judg. 6. 8 I brought you up from Egypt..out of the
6. 13 Did not the LORD bring us up from Egypt?
15. 13 they..brought him up from the rock
16. 8 the lords..brought up to her seven 16. 31
1 Sa. 2. 6 he bringeth down..and bringeth up
2. 14 all that the flesh hook brought up the
8. 8 I brought them up out of Egypt even
10. 18 I brought up Israel out of Egypt, and
12. 6 the LORD..that brought your fathers up
19. 15 Bring him up to me in the bed, that I
28. 8 bring me (him) up whom I shall name
28. 11 Whom shall I bring up unto thee?
28. 11 And he said, Bring me up Samuel
28. 15 Why hast thou disquieted..to bring me up
2 Sa. 2. 3 David bring up, every man with his
6. 2 to bring up from thence the ark of God
6. 12 So David..brought up the ark of God
6. 15 So David..brought up the ark of the
7. 6 I brought up the children of Israel out
21. 13 he brought up from thence the bones of
1 Ki. 8. 1 they might bring up the ark of the cove.
8. 4 they brought up the ark of the LORD
8. 4 even those did..the Levites bring up
12. 28 thy gods..brought thee up out of the
2 Ki. 17. 7 the LORD..had brought them up out of
17. 36 the LORD, who brought you up out of the
25. 6 took the king, and brought him up to
1 Ch. 13. 6 David went..to bring up thence the ark
15. 3 David gathered all Israel..to bring up
15. 12 ye may bring up the ark of the LORD
15. 14 the priests..bring up the ark of the LORD
15. 25 David..went to bring up the ark of the
15. 28 all Israel brought up the ark of the
17. 5 I brought up Israel unto this day
2 Ch. 1. 4 the ark..had David brought up
5. 2 bring up the ark of the covenant
5. 5 and they brought up the ark and the tab.
5. 5 these did the priests..bring up
8. 11 Solomon brought up the daughter of

Ezra 1. 11 bring up with (them of) the captivity
4. 2 king of Assur, which brought us up
Neh. 9. 18 This (is) thy god that brought thee up
10. 38 bring up the tithe of the tithes unto
12. 31 I brought up the princes of Judah upon
Psa. 30. 3 thou hast brought up my soul from
40. 2 He brought me up also out of an horrible
71. 20 bring me up again from the depths
Isa. 8. 7 the LORD bringeth up upon them the
63. 11 Where (is) he that brought them up
Jer. 2. 6 Where (is) the LORD that brought us up
11. 7 I brought them up out of the land
16. 14, 15 The LORD liveth, that brought up
23. 7 The LORD liveth, which brought up
23. 8 the LORD liveth, which brought up
27. 22 I bring them up, and restore them
39. 5 they brought him up to Nebuchadnezzar
Eze. 16. 40 They shall also bring up a company
19. 3 And she brought up one of her whelps
23. 46 I will bring up a company upon
26. 19 I shall bring up the deep upon thee
29. 4 I will bring thee up out of the midst
32. 3 they shall bring thee up in my net
37. 6 I will..bring up flesh upon you
37. 13 I have..brought you up out of your graves
Amos 2. 10 I brought you up from the land of Egypt
3. 1 I brought up from the land of Egypt
8. 10 I will bring up sackcloth upon all
9. 7 Have not I brought up Israel out
Jon. 2. 6 yet hast thou brought up my life
Mic. 6. 4 I brought thee up out of the land of Eg.

7. *To make great, nourish,* רָבָה *rabah*, 3.
Lam. 2. 22 brought up hath mine enemy consumed

8. *To make high,* רוּם *rum*, 3*a*.
Isa. 1. 2 I have nourished and brought up
23. 4 neither do I nourish..(nor) bring up

9. *To feed or nourish up,* ἀνατρέφω *anatrephō*.
Acts 22. 3 I am..brought up in this city

10. *To bear up,* ἀναφέρω *anapherō*.
Matt 17. 1 Jesus..bringeth them up into an high

11. *To nourish fully,* ἐκτρέφω *ektrephō*.
Eph. 6. 4 bring them up in the nurture and admo.

12. *To feed or nourish,* τρέφω *trephō*.
Luke 4. 16 Nazareth, where he had been brought up

BRING up again, to —
To lead up, back, again, ἀνάγω *anagō*.
Rom. 10. 7 Who..is, to bring up Christ again from

BRING up delicately, to —
To fondle, פָּנַק *panaq*, 3.
Prov. 29. 21 He that delicately bringeth up his serva.

BRING upon, to —
To lead upon, ἐπάγω *epagō*.
Acts 5. 28 intend to bring this man's blood upon us
2 Pe. 2. 1 the Lord..bring upon themselves swift

BRINGER up —
To be steady, faithful, a nurse, אָמַן *aman*.
2 Ki. 10. 5 the bringers up (of the children), sent to

BRINGING —
1. *To bear,* נָשָׂא *nasa*.
2 Ch. 9. 21 once came the ships..bringing gold, and
Psa. 126. 6 come again..bringing his sheaves

2. *To lead,* ἄγω *agō*.
Heb. 2. 10 it became him..in bringing many sons

3. *To bear, carry,* φέρω *pherō*.
Mark 2. 3 bringing one sick of the palsy, which was
Luke 24. 1 bringing the spices which they had
Acts 5. 16 There came also a multitude..bringing

BRINGING in —
A leading in upon, ἐπεισαγωγή *epeisagōgē*.
Heb. 7. 19 the bringing in of a better hope (did): by

[*See also* Birth, bondage, captivity, child, contempt, desolation, honour, light, low, nothing, nought, perfection, power, remembrance, safe, salvation, shame, snare, subjection, tidings, word.]

BRINK —
1. *End, border,* קָצָה *qatseh*.
Josh. 3. 8 ye are come to the brink of the water of

2. *Lip, edge,* שָׂפָה *saphah*.
Gen. 41. 3 and stood by..upon the brink of the
Exod. 2. 3 laid (it) in the flags by the river's brink
7. 15 thou shalt stand by the river's brink
Deut. 2. 36 by the brink of the river of Arnon, and
Eze. 47. 6 caused me to return to the brink of the

BROAD —
1. *Broad, wide,* רָחָב *rachab*.
Neh 3. 8 they fortified Jerusalem unto the broad
12. 38 tower of the furnaces even unto the broad
Job 11. 9 The measure..(is)..broader than the sea
Psa. 119. 96 thy commandment (is) exceeding broad
Jer. 51. 58 The broad walls of Babylon shall be

2. *Breadth, width,* רֹחַב *rochab*.
Exod 27. 1 five cubits long, and five cubits broad
1 Ki. 6. 6 five cubits broad..six cubits broad
6. 6 the third (was) seven cubits broad
2 Ch. 6. 13 of five cubits long, and five cubits broad
Eze. 40. 6 the gate, (which was) one reed broad, and
Eze. 40. 6 other..(gate, which was) one reed broad
40. 7 (every) little chamber..one reed broad
40. 29, 33 and five and twenty cubits broad
40. 30 arches round..(were)..five cubits broad
40. 42 a cubit and an half broad, and one cubit
40. 47 cubits long, and an hundred cubits broad
41. 1 the posts, six cubits broad on the one
41. 1 six cubits broad on the other side, (which)
41. 12 toward..west (was) seventy cubits broad
42. 11 as long as they, (and) as broad as they
42. 20 hundred (reeds) long..five hundred broad
43. 16 the altar (shall be) twelve (cubits)..broad
43. 17 fourteen (cubits) long and fourteen broad
45. 6 five thousand broad, and five and twenty
46. 22 joined of forty (cubits)..and thirty broad

3. *Beat out plates,* רִקֻּעִים *riqquim*.
Num 16. 38 let them make them broad plates (for) a

4. *Broad on both hands,* רַחֲבֵי יָדַיִם [*rachab yad*].
Isa. 33. 21 (will be) unto us a place of broad rivers

5. *Easy, wide,* εὐρύχωρος *euruchōros*.
Matt. 7. 13 broad (is) the way, that leadeth to

BROAD, to be made —
To beat out, expand, רָקַע *raqa*, 3.
Num 16. 39 they were made broad (plates for) a

BROAD, to make —
To make broad, wide, spacious, πλατύνω *platunō*.
Matt 23. 5 they make broad their phylacteries, and

BROAD place —
1. *Broad or wide place,* רַחַב *rachab*.
Job 36. 16 out of the strait (into) a broad place

2. *Broad or wide place,* רְחוֹב *rechob*.
Jer. 5. 1 seek in the broad places thereof, if ye

BROAD way —
Broad or wide place, רְחוֹב *rechob*.
Song 3. 2 in the streets, and in the broad ways I
Nah. 2. 4 they shall justle one..in the broad ways

BROIDERED —
1. *Variegated,* רִקְמָה *riqmah*.
Eze. 16. 18 tookest thy broidered garments, and
26. 16 put off their broidered garments: they

2. *Chequer work, tesselated stuff,* תַּשְׁבֵּץ *tashbets*.
Exod 28. 4 a broidered coat, a mitre, and a girdle

BROIDERED hair —
Twined or plaited work, πλέγμα *plegma*.
1 Ti. 2. 9 not with broidered hair, or gold, or

BROIDERED work —
Variegated work, רִקְמָה *riqmah*.
Eze. 16. 10 I clothed thee also with broidered work
16. 13 (of) fine linen, and silk, and broidered w.
27. 7 Fine linen with broidered work from Eg.
27. 16 with emeralds, purple, and broidered w.
27. 24 in blue clothes, and broidered work, and

BROILED —
Prepared by fire, ὀπτός *optos*.
Luke 24. 42 they gave him a piece of broiled fish

BROKEN —
1. *Brought down,* חַת *chath*.
1 Sa. 2. 4 The bows of the mighty men (are) broken

2. *To be weak, pained,* כָּאָה *kaah*, 2.
Psa. 109. 16 he might even slay the broken in heart

3. *Broken, bruised,* מָרוֹחַ *maroach*.
Lev. 21. 20 or scabbed, or hath his stones broken

4. *Smitten,* נָכֵא *nake*.
Prov 15. 13 sorrow of the heart the spirit is broken
17. 22 but a broken spirit drieth the bones

5. *To snap asunder,* נָפַץ *naphats*.
Jer. 22. 28 (Is) this man Coniah a despised broken

6. *To draw or pull asunder,* נָתַק *nathaq*.
Lev. 22. 24 Ye shall not offer..that which is..broken

7. *To break through,* פָּרַץ *parats*.
2 Ch. 32. 5 he..built up all the wall that was broken

8. *Breakage,* רֹעָה *roah*.
Prov 25. 19 in time of trouble (is like) a broken tooth

9. *To dash in pieces,* רָצַץ *ratsats*.
Isa. 36. 6 in the staff of this broken reed, on Egypt
Hos. 5. 11 Ephraim (is) oppressed (and) broken in

10. *To shiver, shatter,* שָׁבַר *shabar*.
Lev. 22. 22 Blind, or broken, or maimed, or having
Psa 147. 3 He healeth the broken in heart, and

11. *To be shivered, shattered,* שָׁבַר *shabar*, 2.
Psa. 34. 18 The LORD is nigh unto..a broken heart
51. 17 a broken spirit: a broken and a contrite
Jer. 2. 13 hewed them out cisterns, broken cisterns
Eze. 27. 34 In the time (when) thou shalt be broken
30. 22 the strong, and that which was broken
34. 4 have ye bound up (that which was) broken
34. 16 I..will bind up (that which was) broken
Dan. 8. 22 that being broken, whereas four stood
Zech 11. 16 nor heal that that is broken, nor feed

12. *To shiver, shatter,* תְּבַר *tebar*.
Dan. 2. 42 (so) the kingdom shall be partly..broken

BROKEN (meat) —
Fragment, κλάσμα *klasma*.
Matt 15. 37 and they took up of the broken (meat)
Mark 8. 8 they took up of the broken (meat)

BROKEN, to be —
1. *To be lost, destroyed,* אָבַד *abad*.
Psa. 31. 12 out of mind; I am like a broken vessel

2. *To be bruised,* דָּכָא *daka*, 4.
Job 22. 9 arms of the fatherless have been broken
Isa. 19. 10 they shall be broken in the purposes

3. *To smite, strike,* הָלַם *halam*.
Judg 5. 22 the horse hoofs broken by the means of

4. *To be brought down,* חָתַת *chathath*, 2.
Isa. 7. 8 five years shall Ephraim be broken

5. *To bring down,* חָתַת *chathath*, 3.
Jer. 51. 56 every one of their bows is broken

6. *To bring down,* נָחַת *nachath*, 3.
2 Sa. 22. 35 a bow of steel is broken by mine arms
Psa. 18. 34 a bow of steel is broken by mine arms

7. *To strike out,* נָתַע *natha*, 2.
Job 4. 10 the teeth of the young lions are broken

8. *To draw or pull asunder,* נָתַק *nathaq*, 2.
Judg 16. 9 as a thread of tow is broken
Eccl. 4. 12 a threefold cord is not quickly broken
Isa. 5. 27 nor the latchet of their shoes be broken
33. 20 neither shall any of the cords..be broken
Jer. 10. 20 and all my cords are broken: my children

9. *To become bare, exposed,* עָרַר *arar*, 7*a*.
Jer 51. 58 The broad walls..shall be..broken

10. *To break off,* פָּרַק *paraq*, 7.
Eze. 19. 12 her strong rods were broken and withered

11. *To be broken, violated,* פָּרַר *parar*, 6.
Jer. 33. 21 (Then) may also my covenant be broken
Zech 11. 11 And it was broken in that day

12. *To be excited,* רָגַע *raga*.
Job 7. 5 my skin is broken, and become loathsome

13. *To break, be broken,* רָעַע *raa*.
Jer. 11. 16 and the branches of it are broken

14. *To dash in pieces,* רָצַץ *ratsats*.
Eccl. 12. 6 or the golden bowl be broken

15. *To be dashed in pieces,* רָצַץ *ratsats*, 2.
Eccl. 12. 6 or the wheel broken at the cistern

16. *To be shivered, shattered,* שָׁבַר *shabar*, 2.
Lev. 6. 28 But the..vessel..shall be broken
15. 12 the vessel of earth..shall be broken
1 Sa. 4. 18 and his neck brake, and he died
1 Ki. 22. 48 for the ships were broken at Ezion-geber.
2 Ch. 20. 37 And the ships were broken, that they were
Job. 24. 20 wickedness shall be broken as a tree
31. 22 mine arm be broken from the bone
38. 15 and the high arm shall be broken
Psa. 34. 20 He keepeth all his bones: not one..broken
37. 15 and their bows shall be broken
37. 17 the arms of the wicked shall be broken
124. 7 the snare is broken, and we are escaped
Prov 6. 15 suddenly shall he be broken without
Eccl. 12. 6 or the pitcher be broken at the
Isa. 8. 15 many among them shall..be broken
14. 29 the rod of him that smote thee is broken
28. 13 and fall backward, and be broken
Jer. 14. 17 virgin daughter of my people is broken
23. 9 Mine heart within me is broken
48. 17 How is the strong staff broken
48. 25 and his arm is broken, saith the LORD
50. 23 How is the hammer..broken! how is B.
51. 30 her dwelling-places; her bars are broken
Eze. 6. 4 and your images shall be broken
6. 6 and your idols may be broken
6. 9; 26. 2; 31. 12; 32. 28; Dan. 8. 8; 8. 25; 11. 4; 11. 22; Jon. 1. 4.

17. *To be broken,* κλάομαι *klaomai*.
1 Co. 11. 24 this is my body which is broken for you

18. *To be wholly broken,* συντρίβομαι *suntribomai*.
John 19. 36 A bone of him shall not be broken

19. *To be rent,* σχίζομαι *schizomai*.
John 21. 11 for all..yet was not the net broken

20. *To be crushed together,* συνθλάομαι *sunthlaomai*.
Matt 21. 44 [shall fall on this stone shall be broken]
Luke 20. 18 shall fall upon that stone shall be broken

BROKEN down —
1. *A removing, keeping off,* מַסָּח *massach*.
2 Ki. 11. 6 of the house, that it be not broken down

2. *To break through,* פָּרַץ *parats*.
Neh. 2. 13 walls of Jerusalem..were broken down
Prov 25. 28 spirit (is like) a city (that is) broken down

BROKEN down, to be —
1. *To be broken or torn down,* הָרַס *haras*, 2.
Prov 24. 31 the stone wall thereof was broken down
Eze 30. 4 and her foundations shall be broken down
Joel 1. 17 the barns are broken down; for the corn

2. *To be brought down,* חָתַת *chathath*.
Jer. 48. 20 Moab is confounded; for it is broken down
48. 39 shall howl, (saying), How is it broken down

3. *To be torn down,* נָתַץ *nathats*, 2.
Jer. 4. 26 all the cities thereof were broken down

4. *To be torn down,* נָתַץ *nathats*, 6.
Lev 11. 35 And every (thing)..shall be broken down

5. *To be broken through,* פָּרַץ *parats,* 4.
Neh. 1. 3 the wall of Jerusalem also (is) broken d.

6. *To break oneself to pieces,* רָעַע *raa,* 7*a*.
Isa. 24. 19 The earth is utterly broken down, the

BROKEN in pieces —

1. *To be cleaved through,* בָּקַע *baqa,* 2.
2 Ch.25. 12 that they all were broken in pieces

2. *To be brought down,* חָתַת *chathath.*
Isa. 8. 9 O ye people, and ye shall be broken in p.
8. 9 yourselves, and ye shall be broken in p.
Jer. 50. 2 Merodach is broken in pieces; her idols
50. 2 her images are broken in pieces

3. *To be beaten down,* כָּתַת *kathath.*
Isa. 30 14 the potter's vessel that is broken in pieces

4. *Small fragments,* שְׁבָבִים *shebabim.*
Hos. 8. 6 the calf of Samaria shall be broken in p.

BROKEN off, to be —

1. *To be drawn asunder,* נָתַק *nathaq,* 2.
Job 17. 11 days are past, my purposes are broken off

2. *To be broken, shattered,* שָׁבַר *shabar,* 2.
Isa. 27. 11 boughs..withered..shall be broken off

BROKEN out, to be —

To break out, פָּרַח *parach.*
Lev. 13. 20 a plague of leprosy broken out of the
13. 25 it (is) a leprosy broken out of the burning

BROKEN, to be sore —

To be bruised, דָּכָה *dakah,* 2.
Psa 38. 8 I am feeble and sore broken: I have

BROKEN to pieces, to be —

1. *To be bruised small,* דּוּק *duq.*
Dan. 2. 35 the silver, and the gold, broken to pieces

2. *To be brought down,* חָתַת *chathath,* 2.
1 Sa. 2. 10 The adversaries..shall be broken to pieces

BROKEN up or through, to be —

1. *To be cleft through,* בָּקַע *baqa,* 2.
Gen. 7. 11 the fountains of the great deep broken up
2 Ki. 25. 4 the city was broken up, and all the men
Prov. 3. 20 his knowledge the depths are broken up
Jer. 52. 7 Then the city was broken up, and all the

2. *To be cleft through,* בָּקַע *baqa,* 6.
Jer 39. 2 the ninth (day)..the city was broken up

3. *To be gone up,* עָלָה *alah,* 2.
Jer 37. 11 the army of the Chaldeans was broken up

4. *To dig through,* διορύσσω *diorussō.*
Matt 24. 43 not..suffered his house to be broken up
Luke 12. 39 not..suffered his house to be broken thr.

BROKEN FOOTED or handed —

1. *A breach of the foot,* שֶׁבֶר רֶגֶל *sheber regel.*
Lev. 21. 19 Or a man that is broken footed

2. *A breach of the hand,* שֶׁבֶר יָד *sheber yad.*
Lev. 21. 19 Or a man that is..broken handed

BROKEN HEARTED —

1. *Broken of heart,* נִשְׁבַּר לֵב *nishbar leb* [*shabar*].
Isa. 61. 1 sent me to bind up the broken hearted

2. *Rubbed together as to the heart,* συντετριμμένος τὴν καρδίαν *suntetrimmenos tēn kardian.*
Luke 4. 18 [hath sent me to heal the broken hearted]

BROOD —

Nest, brood, νοσσιά *nossia.*
Luke 13. 34 as a hen..her [brood] under (her) wings

BROOK —

Brooks were abundant in Canaan The chief of those mentioned are: Arnon, Besor, Gaash, Cherith, Eshcol, Kidron Kishon, Zered, the Willows;—*which see.*

1. *A breaking forth,* אָפִיק *aphiq.*
Psa. 42. 1 the hart panteth after the water brooks

2. *A shining brook,* יְאֹר *yeor.*
Isa. 19. 6 the brooks of defence shall be emptied
19. 7 The paper reeds by..brooks..the brooks
19. 7 every thing sown by the brooks, shall
19. 8 they that cast angle into the brooks shall

3. *A small brook,* מִיכַל *mikal.*
2 Sa. 17. 20 They be gone over the brook of water

4. *A stream (in a valley),* נַחַל *nachal.*
Gen. 32. 23 he took them and sent them over..brook
Lev. 23. 40 of thick trees and willows of the brook
Num 13. 23 they came unto the brook of Eshcol and
13. 24 The place was called the brook Eshcol
21. 14 What he did..in the brooks of Arnon
21. 15 at the stream of the brooks that goeth
Deut. 2. 13 up, (said I), and get you over the brook
2. 13 and we went over the brook Zered
2. 14 until we were come over the brook Zered
8. 7 a good land; a land of brooks of water
9. 21 I cast the dust thereof into the brook
1 Sa. 17. 40 five smooth stones out of the brook, and
30. 9 So David went..and came to the brook B.
30. 10 they could not go over the brook Besor
30. 21 whom they had made..abide at the brook
2 Sa. 15. 23 the king..passed over the brook Kidron
23. 30 Benaiah..Hiddai of the brooks of Gaash
1 Ki. 2. 37 thou goest out, and passest over..brook
15. 13 her idol, and burnt (it) by the brook Kid.
17. 3 hide thyself by the brook Cherith, that
17. 4 be, (that) thou shalt drink of the brook
1 Ki. 17. 5 he went and dwelt by the brook Cherith
17. 6 bread and flesh..and he drank of the br.
17. 7 it came to pass..that the brook dried up
18 5 Go into the land..and unto all brooks
18. 40 Elijah brought them down to the brook
2 Ki. 23. 6 without Jerusalem, unto the brook Kid.
23. 6 burnt it at the brook Kidron..stamped
23. 12 cast the dust of them into the brook Ki.
1 Ch. 11. 32 Hurai of the brooks of Gaash, Abiel the
2 Ch. 15. 16 and burnt (it) at the brook Kidron
20. 16 shall find them at the end of the brook
29. 16 to carry (it) out abroad into the brook K.
30. 14 and cast (them) into the brook Kidron
32. 4 the brook that ran through the midst
Neh. 2. 15 Then went I up in the night by the brook
Job 6. 15 brethren..dealt deceitfully as a brook
6. 15 as the stream of brooks they pass away
20. 17 He shall not see..the brooks of honey
22. 24 (gold) of Ophir as..stones of the brooks
40. 22 the willows of the brook compass him
Psa. 83. 9 as (to) Sisera, as (to) Jabin, at the brook
110. 7 He shall drink of the brook in the way
Prov. 18. 4 well spring of wisdom (as) a flowing br.
Isa. 15. 7 shall they carry away to the brook of
Jer. 31. 40 all the fields unto the brook of Kidron

5. *Winter flowing,* χείμαρρος *cheimarrhos.*
John 18. 1 forth with his disciples over the brook

BROTH —

1. *Broth, soup,* מָרָק *maraq.*
Judg. 6. 19 he put the broth in a pot, and brought
6. 20 Take the flesh..and pour out the broth

2. *Broth, soup,* מָרָק *maraq* [V.L. פָּרָק *paraq*].
Isa. 65. 4 broth of abominable (things is in) their

BROTHER —

1. *Brother,* אָח *ach.*
Gen 4. 2 she again bare his brother Abel. And
4. 8 Cain talked with Abel his brother: and
4. 8 Cain rose up against Abel his brother
4. 9 LORD said..Where (is) Abel thy brother?
4. 9 I know not: (Am) I my brother's keeper?
4. 10 voice of thy brother's blood crieth unto
4. 11 to receive thy brother's blood from thy
4. 21 his brother's name (was) Jubal: he was
9. 5 at the hand of every man's brother will
10. 21 Unto Shem also..the brother of Japheth
10. 25 and his brother's name (was) Joktan
12. 5 Abram took..Lot his brother's son, and
14. 12 they took Lot, Abram's brother's son
14. 13 brother of Eshcol, and brother of Aner
14. 14 Abram heard that his brother was taken
14. 16 brought again his brother Lot, and his
20. 5 even she herself said, He (is) my brother
20. 13 that I said unto her..He (is) my brother
20. 16 I have given thy brother a thousand
22. 20 hath also born children unto thy brother
22. 21 Huz his first born, and Buz his brother
22. 23 Milcah did bear to Nahor, Abraham's br.
24. 15 Milcah, the wife of Nahor, Abraham's br.
24. 29 Rebekah had a brother, and his name
24. 48 to take my master's brother's daughter
24. 53 he gave also to her brother and to her
24. 55 her brother and her mother said, Let the
25. 26 after that came his brother out, and his
27. 6 thy father speak unto Esau thy brother
27 11 Behold, Esau my brother (is) a hairy man
27. 23 his hands were hairy, as his brother
27. 30 Esau his brother came in from his
27. 35 he said, Thy brother came with subtilty
27. 40 thy sword shalt thou..serve thy brother
27. 41 then will I slay my brother Jacob
27. 42 Behold, thy brother Esau, as touching
27. 43 flee thou to Laban my brother to Haran
27. 44 until thy brother's fury turn away
27. 45 Until thy brother's anger turn away from
28. 2 daughters of Laban thy mother's brother
28. 5 brother of Rebekah, Jacob's and Esau's
29. 10 Rachel..daughter..his mother's brother
29. 10 the sheep of Laban his mother's brother
29. 10 the flock of Laban his mother's brother
29. 12 Jacob told..he (was) her father's brother
29. 15 Laban said..Because..(art) my brother
32. 3 to Esau his brother, unto the land of Seir
32. 6 saying, We came to thy brother Esau
32. 11 Deliver me..from the hand of my brother
32 13 to his hand a present for Esau his brother
32. 17 When Esau my brother meeteth thee
33. 3 bowed..until he came near to his brother
33 9 Esau said, I have enough, my brother
35. 1 fleddest from the face of Esau thy brother
35. 7 when he fled from the face of his brother
36. 6 went..from the face of his brother Jacob
37. 26 What profit (is it) if we slay our brother
37. 27 for he (is) our brother (and) our flesh
38. 8 Go in unto thy brother's wife, and marry
38. 8 and raise up seed to thy brother
38. 9 when he went in unto his brother's wife
38. 9 that he should give seed to his brother
38 29 as he drew back his hand..his brother
38. 30 And afterward came out his brother
42. 4 But Benjamin, Joseph's brother, Jacob
42. 15 except your youngest brother come
42. 16 Send..and let him fetch your brother
42. 20 But bring your youngest brother unto me
42 21 We (are) verily guilty concerning our br.
42. 34 And bring your youngest brother unto me
42. 34 will I deliver you your brother, and ye
42. 38 son shall not go..for his brother is dead
43. 3, 5 except your brother (be) with you
43. 4 If thou wilt send our brother with us, we
Gen. 43. 6 tell..man whether ye had yet a brother?
43. 7 (Is) your father..have ye (anot.) brother?
43. 7 that he would say, Bring your brother
43. 13 Take also your brother, and arise, go again
43. 14 he may send away your other brother
43. 29 lifted up his eyes, and saw his brother B.
43. 29 and said, (Is) this your younger brother
43. 30 for his bowels did yearn upon his brother
44. 19 Have ye a father, or a brother?
44. 20 and his brother is dead, and he alone is
44. 23 Except your youngest brother come down
44. 26 if our youngest brother be with us
44. 26 except our youngest brother (be) with us
45. 4 And he said, I (am) Joseph your brother
45. 12 and the eyes of my brother Benjamin
45. 14 he fell upon his brother Benjamin's neck
48. 19 but truly his younger brother shall be
Exod. 4. 14 (Is) not Aaron the Levite thy brother?
7. 1 and Aaron thy brother shall be thy prophet
7. 2 and Aaron thy brother shall speak unto
28. 1 take thou unto thee Aaron thy brother
28. 2 make holy garments for Aaron thy brother
28. 4 make holy garments for Aaron thy brother
28. 41 thou shalt put them upon..thy brother
32. 27 in and out..and slay every man his bro.
32. 29 even every man upon..his brother; that
Lev. 16. 2 LORD said..Speak unto Aaron thy broth.
18. 14 shalt not uncover..thy father's brother
18. 16 Thou shalt not uncover..thy brother's wife
18. 16 it (is) thy brother's nakedness
19. 17 Thou shalt not hate thy brother in thine
20. 21 And if a man shall take his brother's wife
20. 21 hath uncovered his brother's nakedness
21. 2 But for his kin..and for his brother
25. 25 If thy brother be waxen poor, and hath
25. 25 shall he redeem that which his brother
25. 35 And if thy brother be waxen poor, and
25. 36 fear thy God, that thy brother may live
25. 39 And if thy brother (that dwelleth) by thee
25. 47 and thy brother (that dwelleth) by him
Num. 6. 7 He shall not make himself..for his bro.
20. 8 gather..together, thou and Aaron thy br.
20. 14 saith thy brother Israel, Thou knowest
27. 13 as Aaron thy brother was gathered
36. 2 of Zelophehad our brother unto his
Deut. 1. 16 judge righteously between..his brother
13. 6 If thy brother, the son of thy mother, or
15. 2 he shall not exact (it)..of his brother
15. 3 but (that) which is thine with thy brother
15. 7 nor shut thine hand from thy poor brother
15. 9 thine eye be evil against thy..brother
15. 11 open thine hand wide unto thy brother
15. 12 (And) if thy brother, an Hebrew man, or
17. 15 a stranger..which (is) not thy brother
19. 18 hath testified falsely against his brother
19. 19 had thought..have done unto his brother
22. 1 Thou shalt not see thy brother's ox..go
22. 1 thou shalt in any case bring..unto thy br.
22. 2 And if thy brother (be) not nigh unto thee
22. 2 it shall be with thee until thy brother
22. 3 and with all lost thing of thy brother's
22. 4 Thou shalt not see thy brother's ass or
23. 7 shalt not abhor..for he (is) thy brother
23. 19 shalt not lend upon usury to thy brother
23. 20 unto thy brother thou shalt not lend upon
25. 3 then thy brother should seem vile unto
25. 6 succeed in the name of his brother
25. 7 if the man like not to take his brother's
25. 9 Then shall his brother's wife come unto
28. 54 his eye shall be evil toward his brother
32. 50 as Aaron thy brother died in mount Hor
Josh. 15. 17 And Othniel..the brother of Caleb, took
Judg. 1. 3 And Judah said unto Simeon his brother
1. 13 And Othniel..Caleb's younger brother
1. 17 And Judah went with Simeon his brother
3. 9 (even) Othniel..Caleb's younger brother
9. 3 for they said He (is) our brother
9. 18 made A...king..because he (is) your brot.
9. 21 for fear of Abimelech his brother
9. 24 be laid upon Abimelech their brother
20. 23, 28 the children of Benjamin my brother?
21. 6 repented them for Benjamin their bro.
Ruth 4. 3 which (was) our brother Elimelech's
1 Sa. 14. 3 the son of Ahitub, I-chabod's brother
17. 28 Eliab his eldest brother heard when he
20. 29 my brother he hath commanded me (to)
26. 6 Abishai the son..Zeruiah brother to Joab
2 Sa. 1. 26 I am distressed for thee my brother Jon.
2. 22 I hold up my face to Joab thy brother
2. 27 every one from following his brother
3. 27 died for the blood of Asahel his brother
3. 30 So Joab..Abishai his brother slew Abner
3. 30 because he had slain their brother Asahel
4. 6 Rechab and Baanah his brother escaped
4. 9 David answered Rechab..his brother
10. 10 he delivered unto the hand of..his brother
13. 3, 32 the son of Shimeah, David's brother
13. 4 I love Tamar my brother Absalom's
13. 7 Go now to thy brother Amnon's house
13. 8 So Tamar went to her brother Amnon's
13. 10 brought (them)..to Amnon her brother
13. 12 Nay, my brother, do not force me; for no
13. 20 And Absalom her brother said unto her
13 20 Hath Amnon thy brother been with thee
13. 20 he (is) thy brother; regard not this thing
13. 20 Tamar remained..in her brother A.'s
13. 26 I pray thee let my brother Amnon go
14. 7 Deliver him that smote his brother
14. 7 for the life of his brother whom he slew
18. 2 Abishai the son of Zeruiah Joab's brother
20. 9 Joab said, (Art) thou in health, my bro.
20. 10 Joab and Abishai his brother pursued

2 Sa. 21. 21 Jonathan..the brother of David, slew
23. 18 And Abishai the brother of Joab, the son
23. 24 Asahel, the brother of Joab (was) one of
1 Ki. 1. 10 and Solomon his brother, he called not
2. 7 I fled because of Absalom thy brother
2. 15 the kingdom..is become my brother's: for
2. 21 Let Abishag..be given to Adonijah thy br
2. 22 for he (is) mine elder brother; even for
9. 13 What cities..thou hast given me, my br.
13. 30 they mourned..(saying), Alas, my brother!
20. 32 he said, (Is) he yet alive? he (is) my broth
20. 33 and they said, Thy brother Ben-hadad
1 Ch. 1. 19 Peleg..his brother's name (was) Joktan
2. 32 the sons of Jada the brother of Shammai
2. 42 the sons of Caleb the brother of Jerahmeel
4. 11 Chelub the brother of Shuah begat Mehir
6. 39 his brother Asaph, who stood on his right
7. 16 the name of his brother (was) Sheresh
7. 35 And the sons of his brother Helem; Zop.
8. 39 And the sons of Eshek his brother (were)
11. 20 And Abishai the brother of Joab, he was
11. 26 Asahel the brother of Joab, Elhanan the
11. 38 Joel the brother of Nathan, Mibhar the
11. 45 the son of Shimri, and Joha his brother
19. 11 unto the hand of Abishai his brother, and
19. 15 likewise fled before Abishai his brother
20. 5 Elhanan..slew Lahmi the brother of
20. 7 Jonathan the son of Shimea, David's bro.
24. 25 The brother of Michah (was) Isshiah: of
26. 22 of Jehieli; Zetham, and Joel his brother
27. 7 fourth (captain)..(was) Asahel the brother
2 Ch. 31. 12 and Shimei his brother (was) the next
31. 13 hand of Cononiah and Shimei his brother
36. 4 made Eliakim his brother king over Judah
36. 4 Necho took Jehoahaz his brother, and
36. 10 and made Zedekiah his brother king
Neh. 5. 7 Ye exact usury, every one of his brother
7. 2 That I gave my brother Hanani, and
Job 1. 13, 18 wine in their eldest brother's house
22. 6 For..hast taken a pledge from thy brother
30. 29 I am a brother to dragons, and a..to owls
Psa. 35. 14 behaved..as..(he had been) my..brother
49. 7 None..can by any means redeem his br.
50. 20 Thou sittest (and) speakest against thy br.
Prov. 17. 17 and a brother is born for adversity
18. 9 He..is brother to him that is a great
18. 19 A brother offended (is harder to be won)
18. 24 there is a friend..closer than a brother
27. 10 neither go into thy brother's house in the
27. 10 better (is) a neighbour..than a brother
Eccl 4. 8 yea, he hath neither child nor brother
Song 8. 1 Oh that thou (wert) as my brother, that
Isa. 3. 6 When a man shall take hold of his brother
9. 19 no man shall spare his brother
19. 2 fight every one against his brother
41. 6 and (every one) said to his brother, Be of
Jer. 9. 4 and trust ye not in any brother: for every
9. 4 brother will utterly supplant, and every
22. 18 Ah my brother! or, Ah my sister! they
23. 35 shall ye say..every one to his brother
31. 34 teach..every man his brother, saying
34. 9 none should serve himself of..his brother
34. 14 let ye go every man his brother an Heb.
34. 17 every one to his brother, and every man
Eze. 18. 18 spoiled his brother by violence, and did
33. 30 and speak..every one to his brother, saying
38. 21 every man's sword..against his brother
44. 25 for brother, or for sister that hath had
Hos. 12. 3 He took his brother by the heel in the
Amos 1. 11 because he did pursue his brother with
Obad. 10 For (thy) violence against thy brother
12 shouldest not have looked on..thy brother
Mic. 7. 2 they hunt every man his brother with a
Hag. 2. 22 every one by the sword of his brother
Zech. 7. 9 and show mercy..every man to his brother
7. 10 none of you imagine..against his brother
Mal. 1. 2 (Was) not Esau Jacob's brother? saith the
2. 10 why..every man against his brother

2. *Friend*, רֵעַ *rea.*
Deut 24. 10 When thou dost lend thy brother any

3. *Of the same womb, a brother, relative*, ἀδελφός.
Matt. 4. 18 Andrew his brother, casting a net into
4. 21 James..and John his brother, in a ship
5. 22 That whosoever is angry with his brother
5. 22 whosoever shall say to his brother, Raca
5. 23 that thy brother hath ought against thee
5. 24 first be reconciled to thy brother, and
7. 3 the mote that is in thy brother's eye, but
7. 4 Or how wilt thou say to thy brother, Let
7. 5 to cast out the mote out of thy brother's
10. 2 Peter, and Andrew his brother
10. 2 James..of Zebedee, and John his brother
10. 21 the brother shall deliver up the brother
12. 50 the same is my brother, and sister, and
14. 3 for Herodias sake, his brother Philip's
17. 1 Jesus taketh..James..John his brother
18. 15 Moreover, if thy brother shall trespass
18. 15 if he..hear..thou hast gained thy brother
18. 21 how oft shall my brother sin against me
18. 35 if ye..forgive not every one his brother
22. 24 If a man die..his brother shall marry his
22. 24 and raise up seed unto his brother
22. 25 having no issue, left..wife unto..brother
Mark 1. 16 he saw Simon, and Andrew his brother
1. 19 he saw James..and John his brother, who
3. 17 And James..and John the brother of Ja.
3. 35 the same is my brother, and my sister
5. 37 Peter, and James, and John the brother
6. 3 the brother of James, and Joses, and of
6. 17 for Herodias' sake, his brother Philip's
6. 18 lawful for thee to have thy brother's wife
Mark 12. 19 If a man's brother die, and leave (his)
12. 19 that his brother should take his wife
12. 19 and raise up seed unto his brother
13. 12 Now the brother shall betray the brother
Luke 3. 1 and his brother Philip tetrarch of Iturea
3. 19 being reproved..for Herodias his brother
6. 14 Simon..and Andrew his brother, James
6. 41 the mote that is in thy brother's eye
6. 42 how canst thou say to thy brother, Brot.
6. 42 pull out the mote..in thy brother's eye
12. 13 Master, speak to my brother, that he
15. 27 And he said unto him, Thy brother is
15. 32 for this thy brother was dead, and is
17. 3 If thy brother trespass against thee
20. 28 If any man's brother die, having a wife
20. 28 that his brother should take his wife
20. 28 and raise up seed unto his brother
John 1. 40 One..was Andrew, Simon Peter's brother
1. 41 He first findeth his own brother Simon
6. 8 Andrew, Simon Peter's brother, saith
11. 2 It was (that) Mary..whose brother Laz.
11. 19 to comfort them concerning their brother
11. 21, 32 Lord, if thou hadst been here, my br.
11. 23 Jesus saith unto her, Thy brother shall
Acts 9. 17 putting his hands on him, said, Brother
12. 2 he killed James the brother of John with
21. 20 Thou seest, brother, how many thousands
22. 13 said unto me, Brother Saul, receive thy
Rom 14. 10 But why dost thou judge thy brother?
14. 10 or why dost thou set at nought thy brother
14. 13 or an occasion to fall, in (his) brother's
14. 15 if thy brother be grieved with (thy) meat
14. 21 nor (any thing) whereby thy brother
16. 23 chamberlain..saluteth..Quartus a broth.
1 Co. 1. 1 Paul..an apostle..and Sosthenes..broth.
5. 11 if any man that is called a brother be a
6. 6 But brother goeth to law with brother
7. 12 If any brother hath a wife that believeth
7. 15 A brother or a sister is not under bondage
8. 11 shall the weak brother perish, for whom
8. 13 Wherefore, if meat make my brother to
8. 13 lest I make my brother to offend
16. 12 As touching (our) brother Apollos, I
2 Co. 1. 1 and Timothy (our) brother, unto the
2. 13 because I found not Titus my brother
8. 18 And we have sent with him the brother
8. 22 we have sent with them our brother
12. 18 I desired Titus..(him) I sent a brother
Gal. 1. 19 saw I none, save James the Lord's brother
Eph. 6. 21 a beloved brother and faithful minister
Phil. 2. 25 Epaphroditus, my brother, and companion
Col. 1. 1 Paul..and Timotheus (our) brother
4. 7 Tychicus..(who is) a beloved brother
4. 9 Onesimus, a faithful and beloved brother
1 Th. 3. 2 And sent Timotheus, our brother, and
4. 6 no(man) go beyond and defraud his brother
2 Th. 3. 6 withdraw yourselves from every brother
3. 15 but admonish (him) as a brother
Phm. 1 Paul..and Timothy (our) brother, unto
7 the bowels..refreshed by thee, brother
16 a brother beloved, specially to me, but
20 brother, let me have joy of thee in the
Heb. 8. 11 they shall not teach..man his brother
13. 23 Know ye that (our) brother Timothy is
Jas. 1. 9 Let the brother of low degree rejoice in
2. 15 If a brother or sister be naked, and
4. 11 He that speaketh evil of (his) brother
4. 11 and judgeth his brother, speaketh evil of
1 Pe. 5. 12 By Silvanus, a faithful brother unto you
2 Pe. 3. 15 even as our beloved brother Paul also
1 Jo. 2. 9 He that..hateth his brother, is in dark.
2. 10 He that loveth his brother abideth in the
2. 11 he that hateth his brother is in darkness
3. 10 neither he that loveth not his brother
3. 12 that wicked one, and slew his brother
3. 12 works were evil, and his brother's right.
3. 14 He that loveth not (his) [brother] abideth
3. 15 Whosoever hateth his brother is a murd.
3. 17 But whoso..seeth his brother have need
4. 20 say, I love God, and hateth his brother
4. 20 for he that loveth not his brother whom
4. 21 he who loveth God love his brother also
5. 16 If any man see his brother sin a sin
Jude 1 Jude, the servant..and brother of James
Rev. 1. 9 I John, who also am your brother, and
[*See also* Father's brother, husband's brother.]

BROTHER'S wife —
Deceased brother's widow, יְבֶמֶת *yebemeth.*
Deut 25. 7 man like not to take his brother's wife
25. 7 then let his brother's wife go up to the
25. 9 Then shall his brother's wife come unto

BROTHERHOOD —
1. *Unity*, אַחֲוָה *achavah.*
Zech 11. 14 that I might break the brotherhood

2. *Brotherly relation*, ἀδελφότης *adelphotēs.*
1 Pe. 2. 17 Honour all..Love the brotherhood

BROTHERLY —
Brother, אָח *ach.*
Amos 1. 9 remembered not the brotherly covenant

BROTHERLY kindness or love —
Brotherly love, φιλαδελφία *philadelphia.*
Rom 12. 10 kindly affectioned..with brotherly love
1 Th. 4. 9 as touching brotherly love ye need not
Heb. 13. 1 Let brotherly love continue
2 Pe. 1. 7 And to godliness brotherly kindness
1. 7 and to brotherly kindness charity

BROUGHT, to be — [*See* **BRING.**]
1. *To be gathered*, אָסַף *asaph*, 2.
Exod. 9. 19 shall not be brought home, the hail shall

2. *To be caused to come*, אֲתָא *atha*, 6.
Dan. 6. 17 a stone was brought, and laid upon the

3. *To come in*, בּוֹא *bo.*
Neh. 9. 33 thou (art) just in all that is brought upon

4. *To be caused to come in*, בּוֹא *bo*, 6.
Gen. 33. 11 Take..my blessing that is brought to
Lev. 6. 30 whereof (any) of the blood is brought
10. 18 the blood of it was not brought in within
13. 2 he shall be brought unto Aaron the
13. 9 then he shall be brought unto the priest
14. 2 He shall be brought unto the priest
Psa. 45. 14 that follow her shall be brought unto
Jer. 10. 9 Silver spread into plates is brought from
Eze. 23. 42 with the men..(were) brought Sabeans
30. 11 the nations, shall be brought to destroy
40. 4 show (them) unto thee (art) thou brought

5. *To be caused to flow or go*, יָבַל *yabal*, 6.
Job 21. 32 Yet shall he be brought to the grave, and
Psa. 45. 14; 45. 15; Isa. 18. 7; 53. 7; Jer. 11. 19.

6. *To be led*, ἄγομαι *agomai.*
Matt. 10. 18 ye shall be brought before governors and
Luke 18. 40; Acts 5. 21; 22. 24; 25. 6.

7. *To be taken, received*, לָקַח *laqach*, 2.
Esth. 2. 8 Esther was brought also unto the king's

8. *To lead on*, נָהַג *nahag.*
Isa. 60. 11 and (that) their kings (may be) brought

9. *To cause to go up or in*, עָלַל *alal*, 5.
Dan. 6. 18 neither were instruments..brought

10. *To be drawn near*, קָרַב *qarab*, 2.
Exod 22. 8 the master of the house shall be brought
Josh. 7. 14 therefore ye shall be brought according

11. *To become*, γίνομαι *ginomai.*
Acts 5. 36 and all..were scattered, and brought to

12. *To come*, ἔρχομαι *erchomai.*
Mark 4. 21 Is a candle brought to be put under a

13. *To set or place*, ἵστημι *histēmi.*
Mark 13. 9 ye shall be brought before rulers and
[*See also* Low, nought, secretly, silence.]

BROUGHT again or back, to be —
1. *To be caused to turn back*, שׁוּב *shub*, 6.
Gen. 43. 12 the money that was brought again in the
Exod 10. 8 Moses and Aaron were brought again
Jer. 27. 16 vessels..shall now shortly be brought aga.

2. *To be brought back*, שׁוּב *shub*, 3b.
Eze. 38. 8 the land (that is) brought back from the

BROUGHT, before it was —
A removing, מַסָּע *massa.*
1 Ki. 6. 7 made ready before it was brought thither

BROUGHT, to cause to be —
To cause to come near, קָרַב *qarab*, 5.
Exod 29. 10 thou shalt cause a bullock to be brought

BROUGHT down, to be —
1. *To be caused to come down*, יָרַד *yarad*, 6.
Gen. 39. 1 Joseph was brought down to Egypt; and
Isa. 14. 11 Thy pomp is brought down to the grave
14. 15 Yet thou shalt be brought down to hell
Eze. 31. 18 yet shalt thou be brought down with the
Zech 10. 11 pride of Assyria shall be brought down

2. *To be bent*, כָּרַע *kara.*
Psa. 20. 8 They are brought down and fallen; but

3. *To become low*, שָׁחַח *shachach*, 2.
Isa. 5. 15 the mean man shall be brought down

4. *To be humbled*, שָׁפֵל *shaphel.*
Isa. 29. 4 thou shalt be brought down, (and) shalt

5. *To cause to come down*, καταβιβάζω *katabibazō.*
Matt 11. 23 And thou..shalt be [brought down] to

BROUGHT before, to be —
To set or place alongside of, παρίστημι *paristēmi.*
Acts 27. 24 Paul; thou must be brought before Cæsar

BROUGHT unto, to be —
To bear, φέρω *pherō.*
1 Pe. 1. 13 for the grace that is to be brought unto

BROUGHT forth, to be —
1 *To be pained, be in travail*, חוּל *chul*, 4b.
Prov. 8. 24 When..no depths, I was brought forth
8. 25 before the hills was I brought forth

2. *To be caused to flow or go*, יָבַל *yabal*, 6.
Job 21. 30 they shall be brought forth to the day of

3. *To be begotten, born*, יָלַד *yalad*, 2.
Lev. 22. 27 a bullock, or a sheep..is brought forth

4. *To be begotten, born*, יָלַד *yalad*, 4.
Psa. 90. 2 Before the mountains were brought forth

5. *To be caused to come forth*, יָצָא *yatsa*, 6.
Gen. 38. 25 When she (was) brought forth, she sent
Jer. 38. 22 all the women..(shall be) brought forth
Eze. 14. 22 a remnant that shall be brought forth
38. 8 but it is brought forth out of the nations
47. 8 (which being) brought forth into the sea

6. *To give along or over*, παραδίδωμι *paradidōmi.*
Mark 4. 29 But when the fruit is brought forth

BROUGHT in, to be —
1. *To be gathered*, אָסַף *asaph*, 2.
Num12. 15 journeyed not till Miriam was brought in
2. *To be caused to come in*, בּוֹא *bo*, 6.
Gen 43. 18 at the first time are we brought in
Lev. 16. 27 whose blood was brought in to make
3. *To be caused to go up*, עֲלַל *alal*, 6.
Dan. 5. 13 Then was Daniel brought in before..king
5. 15 the astrologers, have been brought in

BROUGHT in unawares —
Led in sideways, παρείσακτος *pareisaktos.*
Gal. 2. 4 of false brethren unawares brought in

BROUGHT into, to be —
To be caused to come in, בּוֹא *bo*, 6.
Gen. 43 18 they were brought into Joseph's house
2 Ki. 12. 4 All the money..that is brought into the
12. 9 all the money (that was) brought into the
12. 13 the money (that was) brought into the
12. 16 money..was not brought into the house
22. 4 the silver which is brought into the house
2 Ch 34. 9 the money that was brought into the
34. 14 the money that was brought into the

BROUGHT into subjection, to be —
To be bent, כָּנַע *kana*, 2.
Psa 106. 42 they were brought into subjection under

BROUGHT low, to be —
1. *To be or become low*, עָנָה *anah.*
Isa. 25. 5 the branch..shall be brought low
2. *To be little, small*, צָעַר *tsaar.*
Job 14. 21 His sons come..and they are brought low
3. *To become low*, שָׁחַח *shachach*, 1, 2.
Psa 107. 39 they are minished and brought low
Eccl 12. 4 all the daughters..shall be brought low
4. *To be low, humble*, שָׁפֵל *shaphel.*
Isa. 2. 12 lifted up, and he shall be brought low
5. *To make low*, ταπεινόω *tapeinoō.*
Luke 3 5 mountain and hill shall be brought low

BROUGHT out —
Outgoing, produce, מוֹצָא *motsa.*
1 Ki 10 28 Solomon had horses brought out of Egypt
2 Ch 1 16 Solomon had horses brought out of Egypt

BROUGHT to pass, to be —
1. *To be, become*, הָיָה *hayah*, 2.
Eze 21. 7 it cometh, and shall be brought to pass
2. *To become*, γίνομαι *ginomai.*
1 Co 15 54 then shall be brought to pass the saying

BROUGHT to, to be —
Change of house, μετοικεσία *metoikesia.*
Matt 1 12 And after they were brought to Babylon

BROUGHT together, to be —
To be gathered, אָסַף *asaph*, 2.
Eze 29 5 thou shalt not be brought together, nor

BROUGHT under, to be —
To be bent, bowed down, כָּנַע *kana*, 2.
2 Ch 13 18 the children of Israel were brought under

BROUGHT up to be —
1. *Under care*, בְּאָמְנָה *be-omnah.*
Esth. 2. 20 as when she was brought up with him
1a. *Educate*, אָמַן *aman* (pass. part.).
Lam. 4. 5 they that were brought up in scarlet
2. *To be or become great*, גָּדַל *gadal.*
2 Ch. 10. 8, 10. 10; Job 31. 18.
3. *To be born*, יָלַד *yalad*, 4.
Gen 50 23 the children..were brought up upon
4 *To be brought up*, עָלָה *alah*, 2.
Ezra. 1. 11 that were brought up from Babylon
5. *To be brought up*, עָלָה *alah*, 6.
Nah. 2. 7 And Huzzab..shall be brought up

BROUGHT up, one —
Nourished, a workman, אָמוֹן *amon.*
Prov. 8 30 by him, (as) one brought up (with him)

BROUGHT up with —
Nourished with, σύντροφος *suntrophos.*
Acts 13. 1 which had been brought up with Herod

BROW —
1. *Forehead*, מֵצַח *metsach.*
Isa. 48. 4 an iron sinew, and thy brow brass
2. *Brow, eye brow*, ὀφρύς *ophrus.*
Luke 4. 29 and led him unto the brow of the hill

BROWN —
Brown, dusky, חוּם *chum.*
Gen. 30. 32 and all the brown cattle among the sheep
30. 33 every one that (is) not..brown among the
30. 35 and all the brown among the sheep
30. 40 and all the brown in the flock of Laban

BRUISE —
1. *Stripe*, (חַבּוּרָה), חַבּוּרָה *chabburah.*
Isa. 1. 6 (but) wounds, and bruises, and putrifying
2. *Breach*, שֶׁבֶר *sheber.*
Jer. 30. 12 Thy bruise (is) incurable, (and) thy wound
Nah. 3. 19 (There is) no healing of thy bruise

BRUISE, to —
1. *To bruise*, דָּכָא *daka*, 3.
Isa. 53. 10 Yet it pleased the LORD to bruise him
2. *To bruise small or thin*, דָּקַק *daqaq.*
Isa. 28. 28 nor bruise it (with) his horsemen
3. *To do, make*, עָשָׂה *asah*, 1, 3.
Eze. 23. 3 there they bruised the teats of their
23. 8 they bruised the breasts of her 23. 21.
4. *To break*, רָעַע *rea.*
Dan. 2. 40 shall it break in pieces and bruise
5. *To bruise*, שׁוּף *shuph.*
Gen. 3. 15 bruise thy head, and thou shalt bruise
6. *To break, break in pieces*, θραύω *thrauō.*
Luke 4. 18 to set at liberty them that are bruised
7. *To rub together*, συντρίβω *suntribō.*
Matt 12. 20 A bruised reed shall he not break, and
Luke 9. 39 and, bruising him, hardly departeth from
Rom. 16. 20 the God of peace shall bruise Satan

BRUISED —
1. *To press, squeeze, crush*, מָעַךְ *maak.*
Lev. 22. 24 Ye shall not offer..that which is bruised
2. *To crush*, רצץ *ratsats* (pass. partic.).
2 Ki. 18. 21 this bruised reed; Isa. 42. 3 a bruised reed

BRUISED, to be —
1. *To be bruised*, דָּכָא *daka*, 4.
Isa. 53 5 (he was) bruised for our iniquities: the
2. *To be made thin*, דָּקַק *daqaq*, 6.
Isa. 28. 28 Bread (corn) is bruised; because he will

BRUISING —
To do, make, עָשָׂה *asah.*
Eze. 23. 21 in bruising thy teats by the Egyptians

BRUIT —
1. *Hearing, report*, שְׁמוּעָה *shemuah.*
Jer. 10. 22 Behold, the noise of the bruit is come, and
2. *Report*, שֵׁמַע *shema.*
Nah. 3. 19 all that hear the bruit of thee shall clap

BRUTE —
Speechless, irrational, ἄλογος *alogos.*
2 Pe. 2. 12 But these, as natural brute beasts, made
Jude. 10 what they know naturally, as brute beasts

BRUTISH, to be, or become —
1. *To consume* (*or act like a brute*), בָּעַר *baar.*
Psa. 94 8 Understand, ye brutish among the people
Jer. 10. 8 they are altogether brutish and foolish
Eze 21. 31 deliver thee into the hand of brutish
2. *To become like a brute*, בָּעַר *baar*, 2.
Isa. 19 11 the wise counsellors..is become brutish
Jer. 10. 14 Every man is brutish in (his) knowledge
10. 21 For the pastors are become brutish, and
51 17 Every man is brutish by (his) knowledge

BRUTISH person —
To consume or act like a brute, בָּעַר *baar.*
Psa. 49. 10 likewise the fool and the brutish person
92. 6 A brutish man knoweth not; neither
Prov. 12. 1 but he that hateth reproof (is) brutish
30. 2 Surely I (am) more brutish than (any)

BUCKET —
Bucket, pail, דְּלִי דֳּלִי *deli, doli.*
Num 24. 7 He shall pour the water out of his buckets
Isa. 40 15 the nations (are) as a drop of a bucket

BUCKLER —
1. *Shield*, מָגֵן *magen.*
2 Sa 22. 31 he (is) a buckler to all them that trust
1 Ch. 5 18 men able to bear buckler and sword, and
2 Ch. 23. 9 bucklers, and shields, that (had been)
Job 15. 26 upon the thick bosses of his bucklers
Psa. 18. 2 my buckler, and the horn of my salvation
18. 30 he (is) a buckler to all those that trust in
Prov. 2. 7 (he is) a buckler to them that walk
Song 4. 4 whereon there hang a thousand bucklers
Jer. 46. 3 Order ye the buckler and shield, and
2. *Buckler, target*, סֹחֵרָה *socherah.*
Psa. 91. 4 his truth (shall be thy) shield and buckler
3. *Shield* (*of a larger size*), צִנָּה *tsinnah.*
Psa. 35. 2 Take hold of shield and buckler, and
Eze. 23. 24 (which) shall set against thee buckler and
26. 8 and lift up the buckler against thee
38. 4 (even) a great company (with) bucklers
39. 9 both the shields and the bucklers, the
4. *Javelin*, רֹמַח *romach.*
1 Ch. 12. 8 that could handle shield and buckler

BUD —
1. *Outgoing, outcome*, מוֹצָא *motsa.*
Job 38. 27 to cause the bud of the tender herb
2. *Blossom, flower*, פֶּרַח *perach.*
Num 17. 8 brought forth buds, and bloomed blossoms
Isa. 18. 5 For afore the harvest, when the bud is
3. *Sprout, shoot*, צֶמַח *tsemach.*
Isa. 61. 11 For as the earth bringeth forth her bud
Eze. 16. 7 I have caused thee to multiply as the bud
Hos. 8. 7 it hath no stalk; the bud shall yield no

BUD, to —
1. *To cause to shine, send out buds*, נוּץ *nuts*, 5.
Song 6. 11 to see whether..the pomegranates budded
2. *To break forth, sprout, blossom*, פָּרַח *parach.*
Gen. 40. 10 it (was) as though it budded, (and) her
Isa. 27. 6 Israel shall blossom and bud, and fill the
Eze. 7. 10 the rod..blossomed, pride hath budded
3. *To cause to sprout or break forth*, פָּרַח *parach*, 5.
Job 14. 9 through the scent of water it will bud
4. *To cause to sprout*, צָמַח *tsamach*, 5.
Isa. 55. 10 maketh it bring forth and bud, that it
5. *To bud, sprout*, βλαστάνω *blastanō.*
Heb. 9. 4 Aaron's rod that budded, and the tables

BUD forth, to —
To cause to shine, send out buds, נוּץ *nuts*, 5.
Song 7. 12 Let us see if..the pomegranates bud forth

BUD (forth), to cause or make to —
To cause to sprout, צָמַח *tsamach*, 5.
Eze. 29. 21 will I cause the horn..to bud forth, and
Psa. 132. 17 will I make the horn of David to bud

BUDDED, to be —
To break forth, sprout, or blossom, פָּרַח *parach.*
Num 17. 8 the rod of Aaron for..Levi was budded

BUFFET, to —
To buffet with the fist, κολαφίζω *kolaphizō.*
Matt 26. 67 they spit in his face, and buffeted him
Mark 14. 65 to cover his face, and to buffet him, and
1 Co. 4. 11 and are buffeted, and have no certain
2 Co. 12. 7 the messenger of Satan to buffet me, lest
1 Pe. 2. 20 if, when ye be buffeted for your faults, ye

BUILD, to —
1. *To build up*, בָּנָה *banah.*
Gen. 4. 17 he builded a city, and called the name of
8. 20 Noah builded an altar unto the LORD; and
10. 11 Out of that land went..and builded Nin.
11. 4 Go to, let us build us a city, and a tower
11. 5 tower, which the children of men builded
11. 8 and they left off to build the city
12. 7, 8 there builded he an altar unto the LORD
13. 18 and built there an altar unto the LORD
22. 9 Abraham built an altar there, and laid
26. 25 he builded an altar there and called
33 17 and built him an house, and made booths
35. 7 he built there an altar, and called the
Exod. 1. 11 they built for Pharaoh treasure cities
17. 15 Moses built an altar, and..the name of it
20. 25 thou shalt not build it of hewn stone
24. 4 builded an altar under the hill, and
32 5 when Aaron saw (it), he built an altar
Num 23. 1. 29 Balaam said..Build me here seven
23. 14 he brought him..and built seven altars
32. 16 We will build sheep folds here for our
32. 24 Build you cities for your little ones, and
32. 34 the children of Gad built Dibon, and At.
32. 37 the children of Reuben built Heshbon
32. 38 gave other names..which they builded
Deut 6. 10 to give thee..cities, which thou buildedst
8. 12 and hast built goodly houses, and dwelt
20. 5 What man (is there) that hath built a
20. 20 thou shalt build bulwarks against the
22. 8 When thou buildest a new house, then
25. 9 that will not build up his brother's house
27. 5 there shalt thou build an altar unto the
27. 6 Thou shalt build the altar of the LORD
28. 30 thou shalt build an house, and thou shalt
Josh. 6 26 that riseth up and buildeth this city
8. 30 Then Joshua built an altar unto the
19. 50 and he built the city and dwelt therein
22. 10 built there an altar by Jordan, a great
22. 11 have built an altar over against the land
22. 16 in that ye have builded you an altar, that
22. 19 in building you an altar beside the altar
22. 23 we have built us an altar to turn from
22. 26 Let us now prepare to build us an altar
22. 29 to build an altar for burnt offerings, for
24. 13 I have given you..cities which ye built
Judg. 1. 26 and built a city, and called the name
6. 24 Gideon built an altar there unto the
6. 26 build an altar unto the LORD thy God
18 28 And they built a city, and dwelt therein
21. 4 the people rose early, and built there an
Ruth 4. 11 which two did build the house of Israel
1 Sa. 2. 35 I will build him a sure house; and he
7. 17 and there he built an altar unto the LORD
14. 35 And Saul built an altar unto the LORD
14. 35 the same was the first altar that he built
2 Sa. 5. 9 David built round about from Millo and
5. 11 and they built David an house
7. 5 Shalt thou build me an house for me to
7. 7 Why build ye not me an house of cedar?
7. 13 He shall build an house for my name
7 27 I will build thee an house: therefore
24. 21 to build an altar unto the LORD, that
24. 25 David built there an altar unto the LORD
1 Ki. 2. 36 Build thee an house in Jerusalem, and
3. 1 he had made an end of building his own
5. 3 David..could not build an house unto
5. 5 I purpose to build an house unto the
5. 5 he shall build an house unto my name

1 Ki. 5. 18 they prepared timber..stones to build
6. 2 the house which king Solomon built for
6. 5 he built chambers round about, (against)
6. 9 So he built the house, and finished it
6. 10 (then) he built chambers against all the
6. 12 this house which thou art in building
6. 14 Solomon built the house, and finished it
6. 15 he built the walls of the house within
6. 16 he built twenty cubits on the sides of the
6. 16 he even built (them) for it within, (even)
6. 36 he built the inner court with three rows
6. 38 So was he seven years in building it
7. 1 But Solomon was building his own house
7. 2 He built also the house of the forest of
8. 13 I have surely built thee an house to
8. 16 I chose no city out of..Israel to build an
8. 17 David my father to build an house for
8. 18 it was in thine heart to build an house
8. 19 Nevertheless thou shalt not build the
8. 19 he shall build the house unto my name
8. 20 and have built an house for the name of
8. 27 much less this house that I have builded!
8. 43 this house, which I have builded, is
8. 44 the house that I have built for thy name
8. 48 the house which I have built for thy
9. 3 hallowed this house which thou hast built
9. 10 when Solomon had built the two houses
9. 15 for to build the house of the LORD, and
9. 17 Solomon built Gezer, and Beth-horon the
9. 19 that which Solomon desired to build in
9. 24 had built for her: then did he build M.
9. 25 upon the altar which he built unto the
10. 4 and the house that he had built
11. 7 Then did Solomon build an high place
11. 27 Solomon built Millo, (and) repaired the
11. 38 I will be with thee, and build thee a sure
11. 38 as I built for David, and will give Israel
12. 25 Jeroboam built Shechem..and built Pen.
14. 23 For they also built them high places
15. 17 And Baasha..went up..and built Ramah
15. 21 he left off building of Ramah, and dwelt
15. 22 timber..wherewith Baasha had builded
15. 22 and king Asa built with them Geba of
15. 23 and the cities which he built
16. 24 And he bought..and built on the hill
16. 24 called the name of the city which he built
16. 32 which he had built in Samaria
16. 34 In his days did Hiel..build Jericho
18. 32 And with the stones he built an altar
22. 39 and all the cities that he built
2 Ki. 14. 22 He built Elath, and restored it to Judah
15. 35 He built the higher gate of the house of
16. 11 And Urijah the priest built an altar
16. 18 covert for the sabbath that they had built
17. 9 they built them high places in all their
21. 3 For he built up again the high places
21. 4 he built altars in the house of the LORD
21. 5 he built altars for all the host of heaven
23. 13 which Solomon..had builded for Ashtor.
25. 1 they built forts against it round about
1 Ch. 6. 10 in the temple that Solomon built in Jer.
6. 32 until Solomon had built the house of the
7. 24 Sherah, who built Beth-horon the nether
8. 12 and Shamed, who built Ono and Lod
11. 8 And he built the city round about
14. 1 masons and carpenters, to build him
17. 4 Thou shalt not build me an house to dwell
17. 6 Why have ye not built me an house of
17. 10 I tell thee that the LORD will build thee
17. 12 He shall build me an house, and I will
17. 25 that thou wilt build him an house
21. 22 that I may build an altar therein unto
21. 26 David built there an altar unto the LORD
22. 2 he set masons..to build the house of God
22. 6 charged him to build an house for the
22. 7 it was in my mind to build an house unto
22. 8 thou shalt not build an house unto my
22. 10 He shall build an house for my name
22. 11 and build the house of the LORD thy God
22. 19 build ye the sanctuary of the LORD God
28. 2 I (had) in mine heart to build an house
28. 2 and had made ready for the building
28. 3 Thou shalt not build an house for my
28. 6 he shall build my house and my courts
28. 10 the LORD hath chosen thee to build an
29. 16 all this store..we have prepared to build
29. 19 and to do all..and to build the palace
2 Ch. 2. 1 Solomon determined to build an house
2. 3 and didst send him cedars to build
2. 4 I build an house to the name of the LORD
2. 5 And the house which I build (is) great
2. 6 But who is able to build him an house
2. 6 that I should build him an house
2. 12 that might build an house for the LORD
3. 1 Solomon began to build the house of the
3. 2 And he began to build in the second (day)
6. 2 I have built an house of habitation for
6. 5 I chose no city..of Israel to build an
6. 7 to build an house for the name of the
6. 8 as it was in thine heart to build an house
6. 9 thou shalt not build..he shall build
6. 10 and have built the house for the name of
6. 18 much less this house which I have built!
6. 33 this house, which I have built, is called
6. 34 the house which I have built for thy name
6. 38 toward the house which I have built
8. 1 wherein Solomon had built the house of
8. 2 the cities..Solomon built them, and
8. 4 And he built Tadmor..he built in Ham.
8. 5 Also he built Beth-horon the upper
8. 6 Solomon desired to build in Jerusalem
8. 11 unto the house that he had built for her
2 Ch. 8. 12 which he had built before the porch
9. 3 and the house that he had built
11. 5 Rehoboam..built cities for defence in J.
11. 6 He built even Beth-lehem, and Etam
14. 6 And he built fenced cities in Judah
14. 7 Let us build..So they built and prospered
16. 1 Baasha..came up..and built Ramah
16. 5 Baasha heard..he left off building of R.
16. 6 timber..wherewith Baasha was a-building
16. 6 he built therewith Geba and Mizpah
17. 12 he built in Judah castles, and cities of
20. 8 have built thee a sanctuary therein for
26. 2 He built Eloth, and restored it to Judah
26. 6 built cities about Ashod, and among the
26. 9 Uzziah built towers in Jerusalem at the
26. 10 Also he built towers in the desert, and
27. 3 He built the high gate of the house of
27. 3 and on the wall of Ophel he built much
27. 4 he built cities in the mountains of Judah
27. 4 in the forests he built castles and towers
32. 5 built up all the wall that was broken
33. 4 Also he built altars in the house of the
33. 5 he built altars for all the host of heaven
33. 14 after this he built a wall without the
33. 15 all the altars that he had built in the
33. 19 the places wherein he built high places
35. 3 the son of David king of Israel did build
36. 23 he hath charged me to build him
Ezra 1. 2 he hath charged me to build him an
1. 3 build the house of the LORD God of Israel
1. 5 to go up to build the house of the LORD
3. 2 his brethren..builded the altar of the
4. 1 the children..builded the temple unto
4. 2 Let us build with you: for we seek your
4. 3 Ye have nothing to do with us to build an
4. 3 but we ourselves together will build unto
4. 4 the people..troubled them in building
Neh. 2. 5 send me unto Judah..that I may build it
2. 17 let us build up the wall of Jerusalem
2. 18 And they said, Let us rise up and build
2. 20 we his servants will arise and build: but
3. 1 his brethren..builded the sheep gate
3. 2 next unto him builded the men
3. 2 next to them builded Zaccur the son of
3. 3 But the fish gate did the sons..build, who
3. 13 they built it, and set up the doors
3. 14 he built it, and set up the doors
3. 15 he built it, and covered it, and set up the
4. 1 Sanballat heard that we builded the wall
4. 3 Even that which they build, if a fox go up
4. 6 So built we the wall; and all the wall
4. 10 we are not able to build the wall
4. 17 They which builded on the wall
4. 18 sword girded by his side, and (so) builded
6. 1 our enemies, heard that I had builded
6. 6 for which cause thou buildest the wall
12. 29 for the singers had builded them villages
Job 3. 14 With kings..which built desolate places
20. 19 he hath..taken away..which he builded
27. 18 He buildeth his house as a moth
Psa. 28. 5 he shall destroy them, and not build them
51. 18 build thou the walls of Jerusalem
69. 35 For God will save Zion, and will build the
78. 69 And he built his sanctuary like high
89. 4 build up thy throne to all generations
102. 16 When the LORD shall build up Zion
127. 1 Except the LORD build the house
127. 1 they labour in vain that build it
147. 2 The LORD doth build up Jerusalem
Prov. 9. 1 Wisdom hath builded her house, she hath
14. 1 Every wise woman buildeth her house
24. 27 in the field; and afterwards build thine
Eccl. 2. 4 I builded me houses; I planted me vine.
3. 3 to break down, and a time to build up
9. 14 besieged it, and built great bulwarks
Song 8. 9 we will build upon her a palace of silver
Isa. 5. 2 and built a tower in the midst of it
9. 10 but we will build with hewn stones
45. 13 he shall build my city, and he shall let go
58. 12 (they that)..shall build the old waste
60. 10 And the sons..shall build up thy walls
61. 4 And they shall build the old wastes
65. 21 And they shall build houses, and inhabit
65. 22 They shall not build, and another inhabit
66. 1 where (is) the house that ye build unto
Jer. 1. 10 to throw down, to build, and to plant
7. 31 And they have built the high places
18. 9 a kingdom, to build and to plant (it)
19. 5 They have built also the high places of
22. 13 Woe unto him that buildeth his house
22. 14 I will build me a wide house
24. 6 I will build them, and not pull
29. 5, 28 Build ye houses, and dwell..and plant
31. 4 Again I will build thee, and thou shalt
31. 28 so will I watch over them, to build, and
32. 31 from the day that they built it even unto
32. 35 they built the high places of Baal
33. 7 and will build them, as at the first
35. 7 Neither shall ye build house, nor sow seed
35. 9 Nor to build houses for us to dwell in
42. 10 abide in this land, then will I build you
45. 4 (that) which I have built will I break
52. 4 and built forts against it round about
Lam. 3. 5 He hath builded against me, and
Eze. 4. 2 lay siege against it, and build a fort against
11. 3 (It is) not near; let us build houses: this
13. 10 one built up a wall, and, lo, others daubed
16. 24 thou hast also built unto thee an eminent
16. 25 Thou hast built thy high place at every
16. 31 thou buildest thine eminent place in the
17. 17 building forts, to cut off many persons
21. 22 to cast a mount, (and) to build a fort
Eze. 28. 26 they..shall build houses, and plant vine.
36. 36 I the LORD build the ruined (places)
Dan. 9. 25 the commandment to..build Jerusalem
Hos. 8. 14 Israel hath forgotten..and buildeth
Amos 5. 11 ye have built houses of hewn stone
9. 6 (It is) he that buildeth his stories in the
9. 11 I will build it as in the days of old
9. 14 and they shall build the waste cities
Mic. 3. 10 They build up Zion with blood
Hab. 2. 12 Woe to him that buildeth a town with
Zeph. 1. 13 they shall also build houses, but..inhabit
Hag. 1. 8 bring wood, and build the house; and
Zech. 5. 11 To build it an house in the land of Shinar
6. 12 he shall build the temple of the LORD
6. 13 Even he shall build the temple of the
6. 15 and build in the temple of the LORD
9. 3 Tyrus did build herself a stronghold
Mal. 1. 4 we will return and build the desolate
1. 4 They shall build, but I will throw down

2. *To build up,* בְּנָה *benah.*
Ezra 4. 12 building the rebellious and the bad city
5. 2 and began to build the house of God
5. 3 Who hath commanded you to build this
5. 9 Who commanded you to build this house
5. 11 which a great king of Israel builded and
5. 13 Cyrus made a decree to build this house
5. 17 of Cyrus the king to build this house of
6. 7 build this house of God in his place
6. 8 for the building of this house of God
6. 14 And the elders of the Jews builded, and
6. 14 and they builded, and finished (it)
Dan. 4. 30 that I have built for the house of the

3. *To thoroughly prepare or make ready,* κατασκευάζω *kata-skeuazō.*
Heb. 3. 3 inasmuch as he who hath builded the
3. 4 For every house is builded by some (man)
3. 4 but he that built all things (is) God

4. *To build a house,* οἰκοδομέω *oikodomeō.*
Matt. 7. 24 which built his house upon a rock
7. 26 which built his house upon the sand
16. 18 upon this rock I will build my church
21. 33 digged a winepress in it, and built a
23. 29 because ye build the tombs of the
26. 61 I am able to..build it in three days
27. 40 Thou that..buildest (it) in three days
Mark 12. 1 digged..the winefat, and built a tower
14. 58 within three days I will build another
15. 29 Ah! thou that..buildest (it) in three days
Luke 4. 29 of the hill whereon their city was built
6. 48 He is like a man which built an house
6. 49 built an house upon the earth; against
7. 5 and he hath built us a synagogue
11. 47 for ye build the sepulchres of the prophets
11. 48 they..killed..and ye build their sepulch.
12. 18 I will pull down my barns, and build
14. 28 For which of you, intending to build a
14. 30 Saying, This man began to build, and was
17. 28 they sold, they planted, they builded
Acts 7. 47 But Solomon built him an house
7. 49 what house will ye build me? saith the
Rom 15. 20 I should build upon another..foundation
Gal. 2. 18 For if I build again the things which I

BUILD or be built again, to —

1. *To return and build,* שׁוּב וּבָנָה *shub u-banah.*
2 Ch. 33. 3 For he built again the high places
Dan. 9. 25 the street shall be built again, and the

2. *To build again,* ἀνοικοδομέω *anoikodomeō.*
Acts 15. 16 will build again the tabernacle of David
15. 16 and I will build again the ruins thereof

BUILD, to begin to —

To build up, בָּנָה *banah.*
1 Ki. 6. 1 that he began to build the house of the

BUILD thereon or thereupon, to —

To build a house upon, ἐποικοδομέω *epoikodomeō.*
1 Co. 3. 10 I have laid..and another buildeth thereon
3. 10 take heed how he buildeth thereupon
3. 14 which he hath built thereupon

BUILD together, to —

To build a house together, συνοικοδομέω.
Eph. 2. 22 In whom ye also are builded together

BUILD up, to —

1. *To build upon,* ἐποικοδομέω *epoikodomeō.*
Acts 20. 32 which is able to [build you up]
Col. 2. 7 Rooted and built up in him

2. *To build a house,* οἰκοδομέω *oikodomeō.*
1 Pe. 2. 5 Ye also..are built up a spiritual house

BUILD up on or upon, to —

1. *To build upon,* ἐποικοδομέω *epoikodomeō.*
1 Co. 3. 12 Now if any man build upon..foundation
Eph. 2. 20 And are built upon the foundation of the

2. *To build upon,* ἐποικοδομέω *epoikodomeō.*
Jude 20 building up yourselves on your most

BUILD, to be about to —

To build up, בָּנָה *banah.*
2 Ch 2. 9 for the house which I am about to build

BUILDED, to be —

To be builded, בְּנָא *bena,* 2.
Ezra 4. 13 Be it known now..if this city be builded

Ezra 4. 16 We certify that, if this city be builded
4. 21 and that this city be not builded
5. 8 which is builded with great stones
5. 11 build the house that was builded these
5. 15 let the house of God be builded in his
6. 3 Let the house be builded, the place

BUILDED or built, to be —

1. *To build,* בָּנָה *banah.*
Judg 6. 28 was offered upon the altar (that was) b.
Neh. 7. 4 few therein, and the houses..not builded
Psa 122. 3 Jerusalem is builded as a city that is
Song 4. 4 the tower of David builded for an armoury

2. *To be built,* בָּנָה *banah,* 2.
Num 13. 22 Now Hebron was built seven years before
21. 27 let the city of Sihon be built and prepared
Deut 13. 16 it shall be an heap..it shall not be built
1 Ki. 3. 2 there was no house built unto the..LORD
6. 7 was built of stone made ready before it
1 Ch. 22. 19 [into the house that is to be built to the]
22. 5 the house (that is) to be builded for the
22. 19 that is to be built to the name of the LORD
Neh. 7. 1 Now it came to pass, when the wall was b.
Job 12. 14 he breaketh down, and it cannot be built
22. 23 If thou return..thou shalt be built up
Psa. 89. 2 Mercy shall be built up for ever: thy
Prov 24. 3 Through wisdom is an house builded
Isa. 25. 2 a palace..it shall never be built
44. 26 to the cities of Judah, Ye shall be built
44. 28 saying to Jerusalem, Thou shalt be built
Jer. 12. 16 then shall they be built in the midst of
30. 18 the city shall be builded upon her own
31. 4 and thou shalt be built, O virgin of Israel
31. 38 that the city shall be built to the LORD
Eze. 26. 14 thou shalt be built no more
36. 10 inhabited, and..wastes shall be builded
36. 33 the cities, and the wastes shall be builded
Hag. 1. 2 time that the Lord's house should be built
Zech. 1. 16 my house shall be built in it
8. 9 that the temple might be built

BUILDER —

1. *To build up,* בָּנָה *banah.*
1 Ki. 5. 18 Solomon's builders and Hiram's b.
2 Ki. 12. 11 and they laid it out to..the builders
22. 6 Unto carpenters, and builders, and
2 Ch. 34. 11 Even to the..builders gave they (it)
Ezra 3. 10 when the builders laid the foundation of
Neh. 4. 5 have provoked..to anger before the b.
4. 18 For the builders, every one had his sword
Psa. 118. 22 The stone..the builders refused is
Eze. 27. 4 thy builders have perfected thy beauty

2. *To build a house,* οἰκοδομέω *oikodomeō.*
Matt 21. 42 The stone which the builders rejected
Mark 12. 10 The stone which the builders rejected
Luke 20. 17 The stone which the builders rejected
Acts 4. 11 the stone..set at nought of you [builders]
1 Pe. 2. 7 the stone which the builders disallowed

3. *Artificer,* τεχνίτης *technitēs.*
Heb. 11. 10 whose builder and maker is God

BUILDING —

1. *Building,* בִּנְיָה *binyah.*
Eze. 41 13 and the building, with the walls thereof

2. *Building,* בִּנְיָן *binyan.*
Ezra 5. 4 names of the men that make this building
Eze 40. 5 he measured the breadth of the building
41. 12 the building that (was) before..separate
41. 12; 41. 15; 42. 1; 42. 5; 42. 10.

3. *Building,* οἰκοδομή *oikodomē.*
Matt. 24. 1. to show him the buildings of the temple
Mark 13. 1, 2; 1 Co. 3. 9; 2 Co. 5. 1; Eph. 2. 21.

4. *Beam work,* מְקָרֶה *meqareh.*
Eccl 10 18 By much slothfulness..building decayeth

5. *Thing built in,* ἐνδόμησις *endomēsis*
Rev. 21. 18 the building of the wall of it was (of)

6. *Making, creation,* κτίσις *ktisis.*
Heb 9. 11 that is to say not of this building

BUILDING, to be in —

1. *To be built,* בָּנָה *banah,* 2.
1 Ki. 6. 7 when it was in building. while it was in b.

2 *To build up,* בְּנָא *bena,* 7.
Ezra 5. 16 and since that..hath it been in building

3. *To build a house,* οἰκοδομέω *oikodomeō.*
John 2. 20 Forty and six years was..in building

BUK'-KI, בֻּקִּי *mouth of Jah.*
1. Son of Abishua and father of Uzzi, the fifth from Aaron in the line of the high priests, B.C. 1350.
1 Ch 6. 5 Abishua begat B., and B. begat Uzzi
6. 51 B. his son, Uzzi his son, Zerahiah his
Ezra 7. 4 the son of Uzzi the son of B.
2. A prince of Dan, and one of the ten chosen to apportion the land among the tribes, B.C. 1451.
Num 34. 22 the prince of the tribe of..Dan, B.

BUK-KI'-AH, בֻּקִּיָּהוּ *mouth of Jah.*
A Kohathite Levite, son of Heman and a musician in the temple, the leader of the sixth course in the service, B.C. 1015.
1 Ch. 25. 4 sons of Heman; B., Mattaniah, Uzziel
25. 13 The sixth to B., (he), his sons..brethren

BUL, בּוּל *rain-god.*
The month from the first new moon of November till the first one of December.
1 Ki. 6. 38 in the month B. ..was the house finished

BULL —

1. *Mighty one,* אַבִּיר *abbir.*
Psa. 50. 13 Will I eat the flesh of bulls, or drink the
68. 30 the multitude of the bulls, with the calves
Isa. 34. 7 and the bullocks with the bulls
Jer. 50. 11 ye are grown ... and bellow as bulls

2. *Son of the herd,* בֶּן־בָּקָר *ben baqar.*
Jer. 52. 20 twelve brasen bulls that (were) under the

3. *Bullock, bull,* פַּר, פָּר *par.*
Gen. 32. 15 ten bulls, twenty she asses, and ten foals,
Psa. 22. 12 Many bulls have compassed me

4. *Ox,* שׁוֹר *shor.*
Job 21. 10 Their bull gendereth, and faileth not

5. *Bull, beeve,* ταῦρος *tauros.*
Heb. 9. 13 if the blood of bulls and of goats
10. 4 the blood of bulls..should take away sins

BULL, wild —

Bull, gazelle, wild goat, תּוֹא *to.*
Isa. 51. 20 as a wild bull in a ne

BULLOCK —

1. *Steer, young bullock,* עֵגֶל *egel.*
Jer. 31. 18 and I was chastised, as a bullock
46. 21 in the midst of her like fatted bullocks

2. *Bullock, bull,* פַּר, פָּר *par.*
Exod 29. 3 with the bullock and the two rams
29. 10 thou shalt cause a bullock to be brought
29. 10 put their hands upon the..bullock
29. 11 kill the bullock before the LORD
29. 12 thou shalt take the blood of the bullock
29. 14 But the flesh of the bullock
29. 36 thou shalt offer every day a bullock
Lev 4. 4 he shall bring the bullock unto the door
4. 4 the bullock's head, and kill the bullock
4. 5 take of the bullock's blood
4. 7 pour all the blood of the bullock
4. 8 take off..the fat of the bullock
4. 11 And the skin of the bullock
4. 12 the whole bullock shall he carry forth
4. 15 lay their hands upon the head of the b.
4. 15 the bullock shall be killed before
4. 16 the priest shall bring of the b.'s
4. 20 he shall do with the bullock as he did
4. 20 with the bullock for a sin offering
4. 21 he shall carry forth the bullock
4. 21 burn him as he b. the first bullock
8. 2 and a bullock for the sin offering
8. 14 he brought the bullock for..sin offering
8. 14 hands upon the head of the bullock
8. 17 the bullock, his hide, and his flesh
16. 6 And Aaron shall offer his bullock
16. 11 And Aaron shall bring the bullock
16. 11 shall kill the bullock of the sin offering
16. 14 he shall take ... blood of the bullock
16. 15 he did with the blood of the bullock
16 18 of the blood of the bullock
16. 27 the bullock for the sin offering..was
Num. 7. 87 the burnt offering (were) twelve bullocks
7 88 the peace offerings..twenty and four bull
8. 12 lay their hands upon the..bullocks
23. 2 Balaam offered on (every) altar a bullock
23. 4 I have offered upon every altar a bullock
23 14 he..offered a bullock and a ram
23. 29 prepare me here seven bullocks
23. 30 Balak..offered a bullock and
28. 12 mingled with oil, for one bullock
28. 14 half an hin of wine unto a bullock
28. 20 three tenth deals..offer for a bullock
28. 28 three tenth deals unto one bullock
29. 3 three tenth deals for a bullock
29 9 three tenth deals to a bullock
29. 14 every bullock of the thirteen bullocks
29. 18, 21, 24, 27 30, 33 for the bullocks..and for
29. 20 eleven bullocks..fourteen lambs
29. 23 on the fourth day ten bullocks
29. 26 on the fifth day nine bullocks
29 29 on the sixth day eight bullocks
29. 32 on the seventh day seven bullocks
29. 36 one bullock, one ram, seven lambs
29. 37 for the bullock..and for the lambs
Judg. 6. 25 Take thy father's..the second bullock
6. 26 take the second bullock, and offer
6. 28 and the second bullock was offered
1 Sa. 1. 24 with three bullocks, and one ephah
1. 25 they slew a bullock, and brought
1 Ki. 18. 23 Let them therefore give us two bullocks
18 23 choose one bullock for themselves
18. 23 I will dress the other bullock
18. 25 Choose you one bullock for yourselves
18. 26 they took the bullock which was given
18. 33 he..cut the bullock in pieces
1 Ch. 15. 26 they offered seven bullocks and seven
29. 21 after that day, even a thousand bullocks
2 Ch. 29. 21 And they brought seven bullocks
30. 24 to the congregation a thousand bullocks
30. 24 to the congregation a thousand bullocks
Ezra 8. 35 twelve bullocks for all Israel, ninety
Job 42. 8 Take unto you now seven bullocks and
Psa. 50. 9 I will take no bullock out of thy house
51 19 then shall they offer bullocks upon thine
69. 31 better than an ox (or) bullock that hath
Isa. 1. 11 I delight not in the blood of bullocks
34. 7 the bullocks with the bulls..shall be
Jer. 50. 27 Slay all her bullocks; let them go down
Eze. 39. 18 Ye shall eat the flesh..goats, of bullocks
43. 21 take the bullock also of the sin offering
43. 22 they did cleanse (it) with the bullock
45. 22 shall (the) prince prepare for himself..a b
45. 23 seven bullocks and seven rams without
45. 24 he shall prepare..an ephah for a bullock
46. 7 he shall prepare..an ephah for a bullock
46. 11 the meat offering shall be..a bullock

3. *Ox,* שׁוֹר *shor.*
Lev. 4. 10 it was taken off from the bullock
9. 4 Also a bullock..for peace offerings
9. 18 He slew also the bullock and the ram
9. 19 the fat of the bullock and of the ram
22. 23 Either a bullock or a lamb that hath
22. 27 When a bullock, or a sheep..is brought
Num 15. 11 for one bullock, or for one ram
Deut 15. 19 no work with the firstling of thy bullock
17. 1 Thou shalt not sacrifice..(any) bullock
33. 17 His glory..the firstling of his bullock
Hos. 12. 11 they sacrifice bullocks in Gilgal

4. *Ox,* תּוֹר *tor.*
Ezra 6. 9 both young bullocks; 6. 17; 7. 17

5. *Son of the herd,* בֶּן־הַבָּקָר *ben hab-baqar.*
Lev. 1. 5 And he shall kill the bullock before the
Num. 15. 8, 9; 2 Ch. 29. 22, 32; 35. 7; Ps. 66. 15; Is. 65. 25

BULLOCK, young —

1. *Bullock, son of the herd,* פַּר בֶּן־בָּקָר *par ben baqar.*
Exod 29. 1 Take one young bullock and two rams
Lev. 4. 3 let him bring..a young bullock without
4. 14 congregation shall offer a young bullock
16. 3 shall Aaron come with a young bullock
23. 18 the first year..one young bullock and
Num. 7. 15, 21, 27, 33, 39, 45 One young bullock, one
7. 51, 57, 63, 69, 75, 81 One young bullock, one
8. 8 another young bullock shalt thou take
8. 8 let them take a young bullock with 15. 24
28. 11, 19, 27 two young bullocks, and one ram
29. 2, 8 one young bullock, one ram, and seven
29. 13 thirteen young bullocks..(and) fourteen
29. 17 twelve young bullocks..fourteen lambs
2 Ch. 13. 9 consecrate himself with a young bullock
Eze. 43. 19 give..a young bullock for a sin offering
43. 23 offer a young bullock; 43. 25; 45. 18; 46. 6

2. *Bullock of the ox,* פַּר הַשּׁוֹר *par hash-shor.*
Judg. 6. 25 Take thy father's young bullock

BULRUSH —

1. *Bulrush, rush,* אַגְמוֹן *agmon.*
Isa. 58. 5 (is it) to bow down his head as a bulrush

2. *Papyrus, rush,* גֹּמֶא *gome.*
Exod. 2. 3 she took for him an ark of bulrushes
Isa. 18. 2 even in vessels of bulrushes upon the

BULWARK —

1. *Strong object,* חֵל *chel.*
Isa. 26. 1 (God) appoint (for) walls and bulwarks

2. *Strong object,* חֵילָה *chelah.*
Psa. 48. 13 Mark ye well her bulwarks, consider her

3. *Fortress,* מָצוֹד *matsod.*
Eccl. 9. 14 and built great bulwarks against it

4. *Fortress,* מָצוֹר *matsor.*
Deut 20. 20 thou shalt build bulwarks against

5. *Corner,* פִּנָּה *pinnah.*
2 Ch. 26. 15 be on the towers and upon the bulwarks

BUNCH —

1. *Bundle,* אֲגֻדָּה *aguddah.*
Exod 12. 22 And ye shall take a bunch of hyssop

2. *Bunch,* דַּבֶּשֶׁת *dabbesheth.*
Isa. 30. 6 carry..their treasures upon the bunches

BUNCH — [See also RAISINS.]

1. *Thing compressed,* צְרוֹר *tseror.*
Gen. 42. 35 behold, every man's bundle of money
42. 35 and their father saw the bundles of
1 Sa. 25. 29 bound in the bundle of life
Song 1. 13 A bundle of myrrh (is) my well beloved

2. *Bundle,* δέσμη *desmē.*
Matt 13. 30 bind them in bundles to burn them

3. *Fulness, multitude,* πλῆθος *plēthos.*
Acts 28. 3 when Paul had gathered a bundle of

BU'-NAH, בּוּנָה *understanding.*
Son of Jerahmeel of the family of Pharez, B.C. 1540.
1 Ch. 2. 25 sons of Jerahmeel..were..B., and Oren

BUN'-NI, בֻּנִּי *my understanding.*
1. A Levite who helped Ezra in teaching the people the law of Moses, B.C. 536.
Neh. 9. 4 Then stood up..Shebaniah, B., Sherebiah
2. Another Levite, ancestor of Shemaiah, B.C. 445.
Neh. 11. 15 of the Levites..Hashabiah, the son of B.
3. A family of the Jews that, with Nehemiah, sealed the covenant, B.C. 445.
Neh. 10. 15 [The chief of the people]..B., Azgad

BURDEN —

1. *Bundle,* אֲגֻדָּה *aguddah.*
Isa. 58. 6 to undo the heavy burdens

2. *Burden, load, thing lifted up,* מַשָּׂא *massa.*
Exod 23. 5 the ass of him..lying under his burden

Num. 4. 15 These (things are) the burden of the sons
4. 19 every one to his service, and to his burden
4. 24 the service of the families..for burdens
4. 27 in all their burdens, and in all their
4. 27 appoint unto them in charge all..burdens
4. 31 And this (is) the charge of their burden
4. 32 instruments of the charge of their burden
4. 47 the service of the burden in the taber.
4. 49 his service, and according to his burden
11. 11 thou layest the burden of all this people
11. 17 they shall bear the burden of the people
Deut. 1. 12 can I myself alone bear your..burden
2 Sa. 15. 33 then thou shalt be a burden unto me
19. 35 thy servant be yet a burden unto my lord
2 Ki. 5. 17 be given to thy servant two mules' burden
8. 9 forty camels' burden..came and stood
9. 25 the LORD laid this burden upon him
2 Ch. 24. 27 the greatness of the burdens (laid) upon
35. 3 (it shall) not (be) a burden upon (your)
Neh. 13 15 and all (manner of) burdens
13. 19 there should no burden be brought in
Job 7. 20 so that I am a burden to myself?
Psa. 38. 4 an heavy burden they are too heavy for me
Isa. 13 1 The burden of Babylon which Isaiah the
14. 28 In the year..Ahaz died was this burden
15. 1 The burden of Moab
17. 1 The burden of Damascus
19. 1 The burden of Egypt
21. 1 The burden of the desert of the sea
21. 11 The burden of Dumah
21. 13 The burden upon Arabia
22. 1 The burden of the valley of vision
22. 25 the burden that (was) upon it shall be cut
23. 1 The burden of Tyre
30. 6 The burden of the beasts of the south
46. 1 (they are) a burden to the weary (beast)
46. 2 they could not deliver the burden
Jer. 17. 21 bear no burden on the sabbath day
17. 22 Neither carry forth a burden out
17. 24 bring in no burden through the gates
17. 27 the sabbath day, and not to bear a burden
23. 33 What is the burden of the LORD?
23. 33 What burden? I will even forsake you
23. 34 The burden of the LORD, I will even punish
23. 36 the burden of the LORD shall ye mention
23. 36 every man's word shall be his burden
23. 38 since ye say, The burden of the LORD
23. 38 The burden of the LORD..I have sent
23. 38 Ye shall not say, The burden of the LORD
Eze. 12. 10 This burden (concerneth) the prince
Hos. 8. 10 a little for the burden of the king of
Nah. 1. 1 The burden of Nineveh. The book of
Hab. 1. 1 The burden which Habakkuk..did see
Zech. 9. 1 The burden of the word of the LORD in
12. 1 The burden of the word of the LORD for
Mal. 1. 1 The burden of the word of the LORD

3. *Burden, lifting up*, מַשָּׂא *massaah.*
Isa. 30. 27 and the burden (thereof is) heavy

4. *Burden, lifting up*, מַשְׂאֵת *maseth.*
Lam. 2. 14 Thy prophets..have seen..false burdens
Amos 5. 11 ye take from him burdens of wheat
Zeph. 3 18 (to whom) the reproach of it (was) a burd.

5. *Burden bearer*, סֵבֶל, סַבָּל *sebel, sabbal.*
1 Ki. 5. 15 threescore and ten th that bare burdens
Neh. 4. 17 and they that bare burdens, with those
Psa 81. 6 I removed his shoulder from the burden

6. *Burden bearer*, סֹבֶל *sobel.*
Isa 9. 4 thou hast broken the yoke of his burden
10. 27 his burden shall be taken away from off
14 25 then shall..his burden depart from

7. *Burden*, סְבָלָה *sebalah.*
Exod 1. 11 to afflict them with their burdens
2. 11 his brethren, and looked on their burdens
5. 4 Wherefore..get you unto your burdens
5. 5 ye make them rest from their burdens
6. 6 I will bring you out..under the burdens
6. 7 bring you out from under the burdens

8. *To give*, יְהָב *yahab.*
Psa. 55 22 Cast thy burden upon the LORD

9. *Weight*, βάρος *baros.*
Matt 20. 12 to us, which have borne the burden and
Acts 15. 28 the Holy Ghost..lay..no greater burden
Gal. 6. 2 Bear ye one another's burdens, and so
Rev. 2 24 I will put upon you none other burden

10. *Freight (of a ship)*, γόμος *gomos.*
Acts 21. 3 there the ship was to unlade her burden

11. *Load (to be borne)*, φορτίον *phortion.*
Matt 11. 30 my yoke (is) easy, and my burden is light
23. 4 For they bind heavy burdens and griev.
Luke 11. 46 for ye lade men with burdens grievous
11. 46 and ye yourselves touch not the burdens
Gal. 6. 5 For every man shall bear his own burden

BURDEN, to —
To weigh down, καταβαρέω *katabareō.*
2 Co. 12. 16 be it so, I did not burden you: nevertheless

BURDEN, to be a —
To become a burden, סָבַל *sabal*, 7.
Eccl 12. 5 the grasshopper shall be a burden, and

BURDEN selves, to —
To burden, load, עָמַס *amas.*
Zech 12. 3 all that burden themselves with it shall

BURDENED —
Pressure, θλῖψις *thlipsis.*
2 Co. 8. 13 not that other men be eased, and ye b.

BURDENED, to be —
To be burdened, βαρέομαι *bareomai.*
2 Co. 5. 4 we..in (this) tabernacle..being burdened

BURDENS, two —
Double burdens, מִשְׁפְּתַיִם *mishpethayim.*
Gen. 49. 14 a strong ass crouching between two burd.

BURDENS, to bear —
Burden bearer, סַבָּל *sabbal.*
2 Ch. 2. 2 ten thousand men to bear burdens

BURDENS, bearer of —
Burden bearer, סַבָּל *sabbal.*
2 Ch. 2. 18 ten thousand..(to be) bearers of burdens
34. 13 (they were) over the bearers of burdens
Neh. 4. 10 The strength of the bearers of burdens

BURDENSOME —
A burden, weight, מַעֲמָסָה *maamasah.*
Zech 12. 3 I make Jerusalem a burdensome stone

BURDENSOME, to be —
1. *To become a burden*, ἐν βάρει εἶναι [*baros*].
1 Th. 2. 6 when we might have been burdensome

2. *To lie torpid against*, καταναρκέω *katanarkeō.*
2 Co. 12. 13 I myself was not burdensome to you?
12. 14 and I will not be burdensome to you

3. *Without weight*, ἀβαρής *abarēs.*
2 Co. 11. 9 kept myself from being burdensome

BURIAL —
1. *Burial, grave*, קְבוּרָה *qeburah.*
2 Ch. 26. 23 the burial which (belonged) to the kings
Eccl. 6. 3 and also (that) he have no burial
Isa. 14. 20 shalt not be joined with them in burial
Jer. 22. 19 He shall be buried with the burial of an

2. *To entomb*, τὸ ἐνταφιάσαι [*entaphiazō*].
Matt 26. 12 she did (it) for my burial

BURIED —
To bury, קָבַר *qabar.*
1 Ki. 13. 31 it came to pass, after he had buried him
Eccl. 8. 10 And so I saw the wicked buried

BURIED (with), to be —
1. *To be buried*, קָבַר *qabar*, 2.
Gen. 15. 15 thou shalt be buried in a good old age
35. 8 and she was buried beneath Beth-el under
35. 19 and was buried in the way to Ephrath
Num 20. 1 Miriam died there, and was buried there
Deut 10. 6 Aaron died, and there he was buried
Judg 8. 32 and was buried in the sepulchre
10. 2 and died, and was buried in Shamir
10. 5 Jair died, and was buried in Camon
12. 7 and was buried in (one of) the cities
12. 10 Then died Ibzan, and was buried at Beth.
12. 12 and was buried in Aijalon in..Zebulun
12. 15 And Abdon..died, and was buried
Ruth 1. 17 Where thou diest, will I die..be buried
2 Sa. 17. 23 was buried in the sepulchre of his father
1 Ki. 2. 10 and was buried in the city of David
2. 34 and he was buried in his own house
11. 43 was buried in the city of David his father
14. 31 and was buried with his fathers in the
15. 24 and was buried with his fathers in the
16. 6 So Baasha slept..and was buried in Tir.
16. 28 So Omri slept..and was buried in Samaria
22. 50 was buried with his fathers in the city
2 Ki. 8. 24 was buried with his fathers in the city
13. 13 and Joash was buried in Samaria
14. 16 was buried in Samaria with the kings of
14. 20 he was buried at Jerusalem with his
15. 38 was buried with his fathers in the city
16. 20 and was buried with his fathers in the
21. 18 and was buried in the garden of his own
2 Ch. 9 31 he was buried in the city of David
12 16 and was buried in the city of David
21. 1 and was buried with his fathers in the
35. 24 and was buried in (one of) the sepulchres
Job 27. 15 Those that remain..shall be buried in
Jer. 8. 2 they shall not be gathered, nor be buried
16. 4 they shall not..neither shall they be bur.
16. 6; 20. 6; 22. 19; 25. 33.

2. *To be entombed*, θάπτομαι *thaptomai.*
Acts 2. 29 David that he is both dead and buried

3. *To be buried*, קָבַר *qabar*, 4.
Gen. 25. 10 there was Abraham buried, and Sarah

4. *To bury*, קָבַר *qabar.*
2 Ki. 21. 26 he was buried in his sepulchre

5. *To be buried with*, συνθάπτομαι *sunthaptomai.*
Rom. 6. 4 we are buried with him by baptism into
Col. 2. 12 Buried with him in baptism, wherein

BURIER —
To bury, קָבַר *qabar*, 3.
Eze. 39. 15 till the buriers have buried it in the

BURN, to —
1. *To consume, be consumed*, בָּעַר *baar.*
Exod. 3. 2 and, behold, the bush burned with fire
Num 11. 1 the fire of the LORD burnt among them
11. 3 the fire of the LORD burnt among them
Deut. 4. 11 and the mountain burned with fire
5. 23 for the mountain did burn with fire
9. 15 and the mount burned with fire
Esth. 1. 12 Vashti refused..and his anger burned in
Job 1. 16 and hath burned up the sheep, and the
Psa. 39. 3 while I was musing the fire burned
79. 5 shall thy jealousy burn like fire?
83. 14 As the fire burneth a wood, and as the
89. 46 How long..shall thy wrath burn like
Isa. 1. 31 and they shall both burn together
9. 18 For wickedness burneth as the fire: it
10. 17 and it shall burn and devour his thorns
30 27 the name of the LORD..burning (with)
34. 9 the land..shall become burning pitch
42. 25 yet he knew not; and it burned him
62. 1 the salvation..as a lamp (that) burneth
Jer. 4. 4 and burn that none can quench (it)
7. 20 it shall burn, and shall not be
20. 9 as a burning fire shut up in my bones
21. 12 and burn that none can quench (it)
Lam. 2. 3 he burned against Jacob like a flaming
Eze. 1. 13 their appearance (was) like burning coals
Hos. 7. 6 in the morning it burneth as a flaming
Mal. 4. 1 the day..that shall burn as an oven

2. *To consume*, בָּעַר *baar*, 3.
Lev. 6. 12 the priest shall burn wood on it every
2 Ch. 4. 20 they should burn after the manner
13. 11 lamps thereof, to burn every evening
Neh. 10. 34 burn upon the altar of the LORD our God
Isa. 4. 4 of judgment, and ... spirit of burning
40. 16 Lebanon (is) not sufficient to burn
44. 15 Then shall it be for a man to burn
Eze. 39. 9 and they shall burn them with fire
39. 10 for they shall burn the weapons with fire

3. *To be consumed*, בָּעַר *baar*, 4.
Jer. 36. 22 (there was a fire) on the hearth burning

4. *To cause to consume*, בָּעַר *baar*, 5.
2 Ch. 28. 3 and burnt his children in the fire
Eze. 5. 2 Thou shalt burn with fire a third part
Nah. 2. 13 and I will burn her chariots in the smoke

5. *To be hot, heated*, חָרָה *charah.*
Gen. 44. 18 and let not thine anger burn against

6. *To be hot*, חָרַר *charar.*
Eze. 24. 11 that the brass of it may be hot..may burn

7. *To burn up*, יָצַת *yatsath*, 5.
Jer. 51. 30 they have burned her dwelling places

8. *To burn steadily*, יָקַד *yaqad.*
Deut 32. 22 and shall burn unto the lowest hell
Isa. 65. 5 in my nose, a fire that burneth all the

9. *To be made steadily to burn*, יָקַד *yaqad*, 6.
Lev. 6. 9 the fire of the altar shall be burning in
6. 12 the fire upon the altar shall be burning
6. 13 The fire shall ever be burning upon the
Jer. 15. 14 for a fire is kindled..(which) shall burn
17. 4 for ye have kindled a fire..shall burn for

10. *To set in flame, flame*, לָהַט *lahat*, 3.
Joel 1. 19 and the flame hath burnt all the trees
2. 3 and behind them a flame burneth

11. *To lift up*, נָשָׂא *nasa.*
2 Sa. 5. 21 and David and his men burnt them

12. *To set on fire*, נָשַׂק *nasaq*, 5.
Eze 39. 9 and shall set on fire and burn the

13. *To burn*, סָרַף *saraph*, 3.
Amos 6. 10 and he that burneth him, to bring out

14. *To set on fire*, צוּת *tsuth*, 5.
Isa. 27. 4 I would go through them, I would burn

15. *To be kindled*, קָדַח *qadach.*
Isa. 64. 2 As (when) the melting fire burneth, the

16. *To burn (as) incense*, קָטַר *qatar*, 3.
1 Sa. 2. 16 Let them not fail to burn the fat presently
Jer. 44 21 The incense that ye burnt in the cities

17. *To cause to burn (as) incense*, קָטַר *qatar*, 5.
Exod 29. 13 the fat that (is) upon them, and burn
29. 18 And thou shalt burn the whole ram
29. 25 burn (them) upon the altar for a burnt
30. 7 And Aaron shall burn thereon sweet
30. 20 to burn offering made by fire unto the
40. 27 And he burned sweet incense thereon
Lev. 1. 9 and the priest shall burn all on the altar
1. 13 the priest shall bring (it) all, and burn (it)
1. 15 and wring off his head, and burn (it)
1. 17 the priest shall burn it upon the altar
2. 2 the priest shall burn the memorial of it
2. 9 shall burn (it) upon the altar..an offering
2 11 for ye shall burn no leaven, nor any
2. 16 the priest shall burn the memorial of it
3. 5 Aaron's sons shall burn it on the altar
3. 11 the priest shall burn it upon the altar
3. 16 the priest shall burn them upon the altar
4. 10 the priest shall burn them upon the altar
4 19 he shall take all..and burn (it)
4. 26 he shall burn all his fat upon the altar
4. 31 the priest shall burn (it) upon the altar
4. 35 the priest shall burn them upon the altar
5. 12 a memorial..and burn (it) on the altar
6. 12 and he shall burn thereon the fat
6. 15 and shall burn (it) upon the altar
7. 5 the priest shall burn them upon the altar
7. 31 the priest shall burn the fat upon the
8. 16 and Moses burned (it) upon the altar
8. 20 and Moses burnt the head, and the pieces
8. 21 and Moses burnt the whole ram
8. 28 and burnt (them) on the altar upon the
9. 10 But the fat..he burnt upon the altar
9. 13 and he burnt (them) upon the altar
9. 14 and burnt (them) upon the burnt offering
9. 17 burnt (it) upon the altar, beside the burnt

Lev. 9. 20 and he burnt the fat upon the altar
16. 25 the fat..shall he burn upon the altar
17. 6 burn the fat for a sweet savour unto the
Num. 5. 26 (even) the memorial..and burn (it)
18. 17 and shalt burn their fat (for) an offering
1 Sa. 2. 15 before they burnt the fat, the priest's
2. 16 Let them not fail to burn the fat present.
2. 28 to burn incense, to wear an ephod before
2 Ki. 16. 13 he burnt his burnt offering and his
16. 15 Upon the great altar burn the morning
2 Ch. 2. 4 (and) to burn before him sweet incense
13. 11 And they burn unto the LORD every
29. 7 have not burnt incense nor offered

18. *To burn, heat,* שָׂרַף *saraph.*
Gen. 11. 3 let us make brick, and burn them throu.
Exod 12. 10 that which remaineth..ye shall burn with
29. 14 shalt thou burn with fire without the
29. 34 thou shalt burn the remainder with fire
32. 20 and burnt (it) in the fire, and ground (it)
Lev. 4. 12 and burn him on the wood with fire
4. 21 and burn him as he burned the first bull.
8. 17 he burnt with fire without the camp
8. 32 that which remaineth..shall ye burn with
9. 11 the flesh and the hide he burnt with fire
13. 52 He shall therefore burn that garment
13. 52 it shall be burnt in the fire
13. 55 thou shalt burn it in the fire; it (is) fret
16. 27 and they shall burn in the fire their skins
16. 28 he that burneth them shall wash his
Num 19. 5 (one) shall burn the heifer in his sight
19. 5 her dung, shall he burn
19. 8 he that burneth her shall wash his clothes
31. 10 they burnt all their cities wherein they
Deut. 7. 5 and burn their graven images with fire
7. 25 The graven images of their gods shall ye b.
9. 21 the calf which ye had made, and burnt it
12. 3 and burn their groves with fire; and ye
12. 31 they have burnt in the fire to their gods
13. 16 and shalt burn with fire the city
Josh. 6. 24 And they burnt the city with fire
7. 25 and burned them with fire, after they
8. 28 Joshua burnt Ai, and made it an heap for
11. 6 and burn their chariots with fire
11. 9 and burnt their chariots with fire
11. 11 and he burnt Hazor with fire
11. 13 Israel burnt none of them, save Hazor only
11. 13 save Hazor only; (that) did Joshua burn
Judg. 9. 52 and went hard unto the door..to burn it
12. 1 we will burn thine house upon thee with
14. 15 we burn thee and thy father's house with
15. 6 and burnt her and her father with fire
18. 27 smote them..and burnt the city with fire
1 Sa. 30. 1 the Amalekites..burnt it with fire
30. 14 and we burnt Ziklag with fire
31. 12 and came to Jabesh, and burnt them
1 Ki. 9. 16 and taken Gezer, and burnt it with fire
15. 13 idol, and burnt (it) by the brook Kidron
16. 18 and burnt the king's house over him with
2 Ki. 10. 26 the images..of Baal, and burned them
17. 31 and the Sepharvites burnt their children
23. 4 and he burned them without Jerusalem
23. 6 and burned it at the brook Kidron
23. 11 and burned the chariots of the sun with
23. 15 burned the high place, (and)..burned the
23. 16 and burned (them) upon the altar, and
23. 20 and burned men's bones upon them
25. 9 And he burnt the house of the LORD
25. 9 every great (man's) house burnt he with
2 Ch. 15. 16 and burnt (it) at the brook Kidron
34. 5 And he burnt the bones of the priests
36. 19 And they burnt the house of God, and
36. 19 and burnt all the palaces thereof with fire
Psa. 46. 9 he burneth the chariot in the fire
Isa. 44. 16 He burneth part thereof in the fire
44. 19 I have burnt part of it in the fire
47. 14 Behold..the fire shall burn them
Jer. 7. 31 to burn their sons and their daughters
19. 5 to burn their sons with fire (for) burnt
21. 10 and he shall burn it with fire
32. 29 and burn it with the houses upon whose
34. 2 Babylon, and he shall burn it with fire
34. 5 so shall they burn (odours) for thee; and
34. 22 and take it, and burn it with fire
36. 25 that he would not burn the roll; but he
36. 27 after that the king had burnt the roll
36. 28 which..the king of Judah hath burnt
36. 29 Thus saith the LORD; Thou hast burnt
36. 32 king of Judah had burnt in the fire
37. 8 and take it, and burn it with fire
37. 10 they rise up..and burn this city with fire
38. 18 and they shall burn it with fire, and thou
39. 8 And the Chaldeans burned the king's
43. 12 he shall burn them, and carry them away
43. 13 the houses of the gods..shall he burn
51. 32 the reeds they have burned with fire
52. 13 And burned the house of the LORD
52. 13 and all the houses..burned he with fire
Eze. 5. 4 and burn them in the fire..thereof
16. 41 they shall burn thine houses with fire
43. 21 and he shall burn it in the appointed
Amos 2. 1 because he burned the bones of the king

19. *To burn forth, flame up,* ἐκκαίομαι *ekkaiomai.*
Rom. 1. 27 woman, burned in their lust one

20. *To burn,* καίομαι *kaiomai.*
Luke 12. 35 your loins..and (your) lights burning
24. 32 Did not our heart burn within us, while
John 5. 35 He was a burning and a shining light
Heb. 12. 18 the mount..that burned with fire
Rev. 4. 5 (there were) seven lamps of fire burning
Rev. 8. 8 a great mountain burning with fire was
8. 10 a great star from heaven, burning as it
19. 20 both were cast..into a lake of fire burning
21. 8 part in the lake which burneth with fire

21. *To burn down,* κατακαίω *katakaiō.*
Matt 13. 30 bind them in bundles to burn them; but
13. 40 the tares are gathered and [burned]
Luke 3. 17 the chaff he will burn with fire
Acts 19. 19 brought their books together, and burned
1 Co. 3. 15 If any man's work..be burnt, he shall
Heb. 13. 11 those beasts..are burnt without the
Rev. 17. 16 and shall eat her flesh, and burn her

22. *To be on fire,* πυρόομαι *puroomai.*
1 Co. 7. 9 for it is better to marry than to burn
2 Co. 11. 29 who is offended, and I burn not?
Rev. 1. 15 fine brass, as if they burned in a furnace

BURN, to cause to —
To cause to go up, עָלָה *alah,* 5.
Exod 27. 20 to cause the lamp to burn always
Lev. 24. 2 to cause the lamps to burn continually

BURN incense (upon) to —
1. *To burn (as) incense,* קָטַר *qatar,* 3.
1 Ki. 22. 43 and burn incense yet in the high places
2 Ki. 12. 3 and burnt incense in the high places
14. 4 and burnt incense on the high places
15. 4 and burnt incense still on the high places
15. 35 and burnt incense still in the high places
16. 4 and burnt incense in the high places
17. 11 they burnt incense in all the high places
18. 4 the children of Israel did burn incense
22. 17 and have burned incense unto other gods
23. 5 to burn incense in the high places in the
23. 5 them also that burned incense unto Baal
23. 8 where the priests had burned incense
2 Ch. 25. 14 bowed down..and burned incense unto
28. 4 and burnt incense in the high places
28. 25 he made high places to burn incense unto
Isa. 65. 3 and burneth incense upon altars of brick
65. 7 which have burnt incense upon the
Jer. 1. 16 and have burned incense unto other gods
7. 9 and burnt incense unto Baal, and walk
11. 13 ye set up altars..to burn incense unto B
18. 15 they have burned incense to vanity
19. 4 and have burned incense in it unto other
19. 13 they have burned incense unto all the
44. 3 to anger, in that they went to burn incense
44. 5 to burn no incense unto other gods
44. 8 burning incense unto other gods in the
44. 15 their wives had burned incense unto
44. 17 burn incense unto the queen of heaven
44. 18 we left off to burn incense to the queen
44. 19 we burned incense to the queen of heaven
44. 21 The incense that ye burned in the cities
44. 23 Because ye have burned incense, and
44. 25 we have vowed, to burn incense to the
Hos. 4. 13 burn incense upon the hills, under oaks
11. 2 they went..and burned incense
Hab. 1. 16 they sacrifice..and burn incense

2. *To burn (as) incense,* קָטַר *qatar,* 5 (2 Ch. 34. 25, v. L. 3).
Exod 30. 7 Aaron shall burn thereon sweet incense
30. 8 at even, he shall burn incense upon it
1 Ki. 3. 3 he sacrificed and burnt incense
9. 25 he burnt incense upon the altar that
11. 8 all his strange wives, which burnt incense
12. 33 he offered upon the altar, and burnt inc.
13. 1 Jeroboam stood by the altar to burn inc.
13. 2 priests of the high places that burn inc.
1 Ch. 23. 13 he and his sons for ever, to burn incense
2 Ch. 26. 16 burn incense upon the altar of incense
26. 18 priests..are consecrated to burn incense
26. 18 Uzziah..burn incense unto the LORD
26. 19 and (had) a censer in his hand to burn in
28. 3 he burnt incense in the valley of the son
29. 11 that ye should minister..and burn inc.
32. 12 worship before one altar, and burn incense
34. 25 they have burned incense unto other gods
Jer. 48. 35 and him that burneth incense to his gods
Hos. 2. 13 visit upon her the days..she burned inc.

3. *To offer incense,* θυμιάω *thumiaō.*
Luke 1. 9 his lot was to burn incense when he

4. *To cause to remember,* זָכַר *zakar,* 5.
Isa. 66. 3 he that burneth incense, (as if) he blessed

BURN sacrifice, to —
To cause to burn (as) incense, קָטַר *qatar,* 5.
2 Ch. 2. 6 save only to burn sacrifice before him?

BURN up, to —
1. *To eat, consume,* אָכַל *akal.*
2 Ki. 1. 14 and burnt up the two captains of the

2. *To cause to flame,* לָהַט *lahat,* 3.
Psa. 97. 3 and burneth up his enemies round ab.
106. 18 the flame burned up the wicked
Mal. 4. 1 the day that cometh shall burn them up

3. *To burn,* שָׂרַף *saraph.*
Psa. 74. 8 burned up all the synagogues
Eze. 23. 47 and burn up their houses with fire

4. *To blow in, burn,* ἐμπρήθω *emprēthō.*
Matt 22. 7 the king heard..and burned up their city

5. *To burn down,* κατακαίω *katakaiō.*
Matt. 3. 12 but he will burn up the chaff with
2 Pe. 3. 10 works that are therein shall be burned up
Rev. 8. 7 the third part of trees was burnt up
8. 7 and all green grass was burnt up

BURN upon, to —
A place for burning incense on, מִקְטָר *miqtar.*
Exod 30. 1 make an altar to burn incense upon

BURN utterly, to —
To burn down, κατακαίω *katakaiō.*
Rev. 18. 8 she shall be utterly burned with fire

BURNED or burnt, to be —
1. *To be consumed,* בָּעַר *baar.*
Exod 3. 3 I will..see..why the bush is not burnt
Judg 15. 14 his arms became as flax that was burnt

2. *To be hot, heated,* חָרַר *charar.*
Job 30. 30 my bones are burned with heat.
Isa. 24. 6 the inhabitants of the earth are burned

3. *To become hot, heated,* חָרַר *charar,* 2.
Psa. 102. 3 my bones are burned as an hearth
Jer. 6. 29 The bellows are burnt, the lead
Eze. 15. 4 the ends..the midst of it is burnt
15. 5 fire hath devoured it, and it is burned?
24. 10 spice it well, and let the bones be burnt

4. *To burn,* יָצַת *yatsath.*
Isa. 33. 12 (as) thorns cut up shall they be burned
Jer. 49. 2 her daughters shall be burnt with fire
51. 58 her high gates shall be burnt with fire

5. *To be burnt,* יָצַת *yatsath,* 2.
Neh. 1. 3 and the gates..are burnt with fire
2. 17 and the gates..are burnt with fire
Jer. 2. 15 cities are burned without inhabitant

6. *To be marked,* כָּוָה *kavah,* 2.
Prov. 6. 28 hot coals, and his feet not be burnt?
Isa. 43. 2 when thou walkest..shalt not be burned

7. *To lift up,* נָשָׂא *nasa.*
Nah. 1. 5 and the earth is burned at his presence

8. *To go up,* עָלָה *alah.*
Lev. 2. 12 but they shall not be burnt on the altar

9. *To scorch,* צָרַב *tsarab,* 2.
Eze. 20. 47 all faces from the south..shall be burned

10. *To be made to burn (as) incense,* קָטַר *qatar,* 6.
Lev. 6. 22 a statute..it shall be wholly burnt

11. *To burn, be burned,* שָׂרַף *saraph.*
Lev. 20. 14 they shall be burnt with fire, both he and
1 Sa. 30. 3 came to the city, and, behold..burnt
1 Ki. 13. 2 and men's bones shall be burnt upon thee
Neh. 4. 2 the heaps of..rubbish which are burnt?
Psa. 80. 16 burnt with fire..cut down: they perish
Isa. 1. 7 desolate, your cities (are) burnt with

12. *To be burnt,* שָׂרַף *saraph,* 2.
Gen. 38. 24 Bring her forth, and let her be burnt
Lev. 4. 12 ashes are poured out shall he be burnt
6. 30 sin offering..it shall be burnt in the fire
7. 17 the remainder of the flesh..shall be burnt
7. 19 the flesh..it shall be burnt with fire
13. 52 leprosy; it shall be burnt in the fire
19. 6 if ought remain..it shall be burnt in the
21. 9 profaneth .she shall be burnt with fire
Josh. 7. 15 he..shall be burnt with fire, he and all
2 Sa. 23. 7 they shall be utterly burned with fire in
1 Ch. 14. 12 commandment, and they were burned
Prov. 6. 27 take fire..and his clothes not be burnt?
Jer. 38. 17 this city shall not be burnt with fire
Mic. 1. 7 all the hires thereof shall be burnt with

13. *To be burned,* שָׂרַף *saraph,* 4.
Lev. 10. 16 Moses..sought..and, behold, it was burnt

14. *To burn,* καίω *kaiō.*
John 15. 6 cast (them) into..fire..they are burned
1 Co 13. 3 and though I give my body to be burned

15. *A burning,* καῦσις *kausis.*
Heb. 6. 8 beareth thorns..whose end (is) to be burned

BURNED, to cause to be —
To burn, שָׂרַף *saraph.*
Jer. 38. 23 thou shalt cause this city to be burnt

BURNED up, to be —
1. *To be burned,* יָצַת *yatsath,* 2.
Jer. 9. 10 they are burnt up, so that none can
9. 12 the land perisheth (and) is burnt up

2. *A burning,* שְׂרֵפָה *serephah.*
Isa. 64. 11 Our holy..house..is burnt up with fire

BURNETH, that —
A marked place, מִכְוָה *mikvah.*
Lev. 13. 24 the quick (flesh) that burneth have a

BURNING —
1. *Fire,* אֵשׁ *esh.*
Gen. 15. 17 and a burning lamp that passed between

2. *To pursue, burn after,* דָּלַק *dalaq,* דְּלַק *delaq.*
Prov. 26. 23 Burning lips and a wicked heart (are)
Dan. 7. 9 his wheels (as) burning fire

3. *To burn steadily,* יְקַד *yeqad.*
Dan. 3. 6 cast into the midst of a burning fiery
3. 11 cast into the midst of a burning fiery
3. 15 cast..into the midst of a burning fiery
3. 17 God..is able to deliver us from..burning
3. 20 cast (them) into the burning fiery furn.
3. 21 cast into the midst of the burning fiery
3. 23 into the midst of the burning fiery furn.
3. 26 to the mouth of the burning fiery furnace

4. *Steadily burning,* יְקֵדָא *yeqeda.*
Dan. 7. 11 his body destroyed..given to..burning fl.

5. *A burning,* יְקוֹד *yeqod.*
Isa. 10. 16 shall kindle a burning like the burning

6. *Marking,* כְּוִיָּה *keviyyah.*
Exod21. 25 Burning for burning, wound for wound

7. *Mark, marking,* כִּי *ki.*
Isa. 3. 24 instead..well set hair baldness..burning

8. *Steadily burning,* מוֹקֵד *moqed.*
Isa. 33. 14 shall dwell with everlasting burnings?

9. *Steadily burning,* מוֹקְדָה *moqedah.*
Lev. 6. 9 because of the burning upon the altar all

10. *Mark,* מִכְוָה *mikvah.*
Lev. 13. 24 flesh, in the skin whereof..a hot burning
13. 25 it (is) a leprosy broken out of the burning
13. 28 burning..an inflammation of the burning

11. *Scorching,* צָרֶבֶת *tsarebeth.*
Lev. 13. 23 (and) spread not, it (is) a burning boil
Prov.16. 27 in his lips (there is) as a burning fire

12. *Burning,* שְׂרֵפָה *serephah.*
Lev. 10. 6 let your brethren..bewail the burning
Num 16. 37 take up the censers out of the burning
19. 6 cast (it) into the midst of the burning
Deut 29. 23 whole land..brimstone..(and) burning
2 Ch 16. 14 they made a very great burning for him
21. 19 made no burning for him
21. 19 like the burning of his fathers
Isa. 9. 5 shall be with burning (and) fuel of fire
Amos 4. 11 a firebrand plucked out of the burning

13. *Burning,* πύρωσις *purōsis.*
Rev. 18. 9 when..shall see the smoke of her burning
18. 18 cried when..saw..smoke of her burning

BURNING ague —
Burning ague or fever, קַדַּחַת *qaddachath.*
Lev. 26. 16 I will even appoint..the burning ague

BURNING coal —
1. *Burning coal,* גַּחֶלֶת *gacheleth.*
Prov.26. 21 (As) coals (are) to burning coals, and
2. *Flame, burning heat,* רֶשֶׁף *resheph.*
Hab. 3. 5 burning coals went forth at his feet

BURNING, extreme —
Extreme burning, חַרְחֻר *charchur.*
Deut 28. 22 LORD shall smite..an extreme burning

BURNING heat —
Flame, burning heat, רֶשֶׁף *resheph.*
Deut 32. 24 devoured with burning heat, and with

BURNING lamp —
Lamp, flame, לַפִּיד *lappid.*
Job 41. 19 Out of his mouth go burning lamps

BURNINGS —
Burnings, מִשְׂרָפוֹת *misraphoth.*
Isa. 33. 12 the people shall be (as) the burnings of
Jer. 34. 5 shalt die in peace: and with..burnings

BURNISHED —
Polished, קָלָל *qalal.*
Eze. 1. 7 they sparkled like the colour of burnished

BURNT —
1. *Emaciated, dried up,* מָזֶה *mazeh.*
Deut 32. 24 (They shall be) burnt with hunger
2. *Burning,* שְׂרֵפָה *serephah.*
Num 19. 17 they shall take of the ashes of the burnt
Jer. 51. 25 will make thee a burnt mountain

BURNT, that were —
To burn, שָׂרַף *saraph.*
Num 16. 39 wherewith they that were burnt had

BURNT OFFERING —
Burnt offerings as well as "meat offerings," and "peace offerings," were mere voluntary offerings (unlike "sin" and "trespass" offerings, which were compulsory), which, however, were to be presented in a uniform systematic manner, as laid down in Lev. i.-iii. The first *three* express generally the idea of "homage, self-dedication, and thanksgiving," the latter *two* that of "propitiation." The animals that might be used for burnt offerings might be from the flock or herd, or from the fowls, and were to be entirely burnt, their blood sprinkled on the altar, and their skins given to the priest for clothing. They were to be offered every morning and evening, every sabbath day, the first day of every month, the seven days of unleavened bread, and the day of Atonement. They were offered at the consecration of the priests, Levites, kings, sacred places, the purification of women, Nazarites, lepers, after-mercies, before war, and with sounding of trumpets at feasts.

1. *That which goes up,* עֹלָה, עוֹלָה *olah, alah.*
Gen. 8. 20 and offered burnt offerings on the altar
22. 2 and offer him there for a burnt offering
22. 3 and clave the wood for the burnt offering
22. 6 Abraham took the wood of the burnt off.
22. 7 but where (is) the lamb for a burnt offer.
22. 8 God will provide..a lamb for a burnt off.
22. 13 and offered him up for a burnt offering
Exod 10. 25 give us also sacrifices and burnt offerings
18. 12 Jethro..took a burnt offering..sacrifices
20. 24 and shalt sacrifice thereon thy burnt offer.
24. 5 sent young men..which offered burnt off.
29. 18 it (is) a burnt offering unto the LORD
29. 25 burn (them) upon the altar for a burnt off.
29. 42 a continual burnt offering throughout
30. 28 the altar of burnt offering with all his
31. 9 And the altar of burnt offering with all
32. 6 they rose..and offered burnt offerings
35. 16 The altar of burnt offering, with his
38. 1 he made the altar of burnt offering
40. 6 thou shalt set the altar of the burnt offer.
40. 10 anoint the altar of the burnt offering
40. 29 he put the altar of burnt offering
46. 29 and offered upon it the burnt offering
Lev. 1. 4 put..hand upon the head of the burnt off.
1. 6 And he shall flay the burnt offering
4. 7 at the bottom of the altar of..burnt off.
4. 10 burn them upon the altar of..burnt off.
4. 18 at the bottom of the altar of..burnt off.
4. 24 where they kill the burnt offering before
4. 25 upon the horns of the altar of burnt off.
4. 25 at the bottom of the altar of the burnt off.
4. 29 slay..sin offering..place of the burnt off.
4. 30 upon the horns of the altar of burnt off.
4. 33 in the place where they kill the burnt off.
4. 34 upon the horns of the altar of burnt off.
5. 7 and the other for a burnt offering
5. 10 shall offer the second (for) a burnt offering
6. 9 This (is) the law of the burnt offering
6. 9 It (is) the burnt offering, because of the
6. 10 the fire hath consumed with the burnt off.
6. 12 and lay the burnt offering in order upon
6. 25 In the place where the burnt offering is
7. 2 In the place where they kill the burnt off.
7. 8 the priest that offereth any..burnt offer.
7. 8 the priest shall have..skin of..burnt off.
7. 37 This (is) the law of the burnt offering
8. 18 he brought the ram for the burnt offering
8. 28 burnt..on the altar upon the burnt offer.
9. 2 Take thee..a ram for a burnt offering
9. 3 a lamb..without blemish, for a burnt off
9. 7 Go..and offer..thy burnt offering
9. 12 And he slew the burnt offering; and A.
9. 13 And they presented the burnt offering
9. 14 and burnt (them) upon the burnt offering
9. 16 he brought the burnt offering, and offered
9. 22 from offering of..the burnt offering
9. 24 consumed upon the altar the burnt offer.
10. 19 Behold..they offered..their burnt offer.
12. 6 she shall bring a lamb..for a burnt offer.
12. 8 the one for the burnt offering, and the
14. 13 where he shall kill the..burnt offering
14. 19 afterward he shall kill the burnt offering
14. 20 the priest shall offer the burnt offering
14. 22, 31 one..sin offering..other a burnt off.
15. 15, 30 one..sin offering..other..a burnt off.
16. 3 offering, and a ram for a burnt offering
16. 5 offering, and one ram for a burnt offering
16. 24 come forth, and offer his burnt offering
16. 24 and the burnt offering of the people
17. 8 that offereth a burnt offering or sacrifice
22. 18 which they will offer..for a burnt offer.
23. 12 for a burnt offering unto the LORD
23. 18 they shall be (for) a burnt offering unto
23. 37 a burnt offering, and a meat offering
Num. 6. 11 one..a sin offering..other..a burnt offer.
6. 14 one he lamb..for a burnt offering
6. 16 his sin offering, and his burnt offering
7. 15, 21 one lamb..for a burnt offering
[So in v. 27, 33, 39, 45, 51, 57, 63, 69, 75, 81.]
7. 87 All the oxen for the burnt offering (were)
8. 12 and the other (for) a burnt offering, unto
10. 10 with the trumpets over your burnt offer.
15. 3 will make an offering by fire..a burnt off.
15. 5 shalt thou prepare with the burnt offer.
15. 8 when thou preparest..(for) a burnt offer.
15. 24 the congregation shall offer..a burnt off.
23. 3 Stand by thy burnt offering, and I will
23. 15 Stand here by thy burnt offering, while
23. 17 he stood by his burnt offering, and the
28. 3 two lambs..(for) a continual burnt offer.
28. 6 a continual burnt offering, which was
28. 10 (This is) the burnt offering of every sabb.
28. 10 beside the continual burnt offering, and
28. 11 ye shall offer a burnt offering unto the
28. 13 (for) a burnt offering of a sweet savour
28. 14 this (is) the burnt offering of every month
28. 15 beside the continual burnt offering, and
28. 19 a sacrifice made by fire (for) a burnt offer.
28. 23 Ye shall offer these beside the burnt off.
28. 23 which (is) for a continual burnt offering
28. 24 it shall be offered beside the..burnt off.
28. 27 ye shall offer the burnt offering for a
28. 31 Ye shall offer (them) beside..burnt off.
29. 2 ye shall offer a burnt offering for a sweet
29. 6 Beside the burnt offering of the month
29. 6 and the daily burnt offering
29. 8 But ye shall offer a burnt offering unto
29. 11 and the continual burnt offering
29. 13 ye shall offer a burnt offering, a sacrifice
29. 16 beside the continual burnt offering, his
29. 19, 22, 25, 28 beside the continual burnt off.
29. 31, 34, 38 beside the continual burnt offering
29. 36 ye shall offer a burnt offering, a sacrifice
29. 39 for your burnt offerings, and for your
Deut 12. 6 thither ye shall bring your burnt offerings
12. 11 your burnt offerings, and your sacrifices
12. 13 Take heed..thou offer not thy burnt off.
12. 14 there thou shalt offer thy burnt offerings
Deut 12. 27 And thou shalt offer thy burnt offerings
27. 6 thou shalt offer burnt offerings thereon
Josh. 8. 31 and they offered thereon burnt offerings
22. 23 or if to offer thereon burnt offering or
22. 26 not for burnt offering, nor for sacrifice
22. 27 before him with our burnt offerings
22. 28 which our fathers made, not for burnt off.
22. 29 to build an altar for burnt offerings
Judg 11. 31 and I will offer it up for a burnt offering
13. 16 and if thou wilt offer a burnt offering
13. 23 he would not have received a burnt off.
20. 26 and offered burnt offerings..before the
21. 4 and offered burnt offerings and peace
1 Sa. 6. 14 and offered the kine a burnt offering
6. 15 and the men..offered burnt offerings
7. 9 and offered..a burnt offering wholly unto
7. 10 Samuel was offering up the burnt offering
10. 8 I will come..to offer burnt offerings
13. 9 Bring hither a burnt offering to me, and
13. 9 And he offered the burnt offering
13. 10 made an end of offering the burnt offering
13. 12 I forced myself..and offered a burnt offer
15. 22 Hath the LORD..delight in burnt offerings
2 Sa. 6. 17 and David offered burnt offerings and
6. 18 made an end of offering burnt offerings
24. 24 neither will I offer burnt offerings unto
24. 25 and offered burnt offerings and peace
1 Ki. 3. 4 a thousand burnt offerings did Solomon
3. 15 offered up burnt offerings, and offered
8. 64 for there he offered burnt offerings
8. 64 altar..(was) too little to receive the bt. off.
9. 25 in a year did Solomon offer burnt offering
2 Ki. 3. 27 and offered him..a burnt offering upon
5. 17 thy servant will..offer neither burnt off.
10. 24 when they went in to offer..burnt offer.
10. 25 made an end of offering the burnt offer.
16. 13 And he burnt his burnt offering and his
16. 15 burn the morning burnt offering, and the
16. 15 with the burnt offering of all the people
16. 15 upon it all the blood of the burnt offering
1 Ch. 6. 49 offered upon the altar of the burnt offer.
16. 2 made an end of offering..burnt offering
16. 40 To offer burnt offerings unto the LORD
16. 40 upon the altar of the burnt offering
21. 23 I give..the oxen..for burnt offerings
21. 24 nor offer burnt offerings without cost
21. 26 and offered burnt offerings and peace
21. 26 by fire upon the altar of burnt offering
21. 29 and the altar of the burnt offering
22. 1 this (is) the altar of the burnt offering
29. 21 offered burnt offerings unto the LORD
2 Ch. 1. 6 and offered a thousand burnt offerings
2. 4 and for the burnt offerings morning and
4. 6 things as they offered for the burnt offer.
7. 1 and consumed the burnt offering and the
7. 7 for there he offered burnt offerings
7. 7 was not able to receive the burnt offerings
8. 12 Then Solomon offered burnt offerings
23. 18 to offer the burnt offerings of the LORD
24. 14 they offered burnt offerings in the house
29. 7 not burned incense nor offered burnt off.
29. 18 We have cleansed..the altar of burnt off.
29. 24 the burnt offering and the sin offering
29. 27 to offer the burnt offering upon the altar
29. 27 And when the burnt offering began, the
29. 28 (this continued) until the burnt offering
29. 31 as many as were of a free heart, burnt off.
29. 32 And the number of the burnt offerings
29. 32 all these..for a burnt offering
29. 34 so that could not flay all the burnt offer.
29. 35 And also the burnt offerings (were) in
29. 35 the drink offerings for..burnt offerings
30. 15 brought in the burnt offerings into the
31. 2 priests and the Lev....for burnt offerings
31. 3 the king's portion..for the burnt offer.
31. 3 the morning and evening burnt offerings
31. 3 and the burnt offering for the sabbaths
35. 12 And they removed the burnt offerings
35. 14 priests..in offering of burnt offerings
35. 16 to offer burnt offerings upon the altar of
Ezra 3. 2 builded the altar..to offer burnt offerings
3. 3 they offered burnt offerings thereon unto
3. 3 (even) burnt offerings morning..evening
3. 4 and..the daily burnt offerings by number
3. 5 afterward..the continual burnt offering
3. 6 began they to offer burnt offerings unto
6. 9 for the burnt offerings of the God of
8. 35 the children..offered burnt offerings
8. 35 all (this was) a burnt offering unto the
Neh. 10. 33 for the continual burnt offering of the
Job 1. 5 offered burnt offerings..the number of
42. 8 offer up for yourselves a burnt offering
Psa. 40. 6 burnt offering and sin offering hast thou
50. 8 I will not reprove thee for..thy burnt off.
51. 16 thou delightest not in burnt offering
51. 19 burnt offering and whole burnt offering
66. 13 go into thy house with burnt offerings
Isa. 1. 11 I am full of the burnt offerings of rams
40. 16 the beasts thereof..for a burnt offering
43. 23 Thou hast not brought..thy burnt offering
56. 7 their burnt offerings and their sacrifices
61. 8 I hate robbery for burnt offering; and I
Jer. 6. 20 your burnt offerings (are) not acceptable
7. 21 Put your burnt offerings unto your sacri.
7. 22 I spake not..concerning burnt offerings
14. 12 and when they offer burnt offering and
17. 26 And they shall come..bringing burnt off.
19. 5 to burn their sons with fire (for) burnt off.
33. 18 want a man before me to offer burnt off.
Eze. 40. 38 where they washed the burnt offering
40. 39 to slay thereon the burnt offering and
40. 42 the four tables..for the burnt offering

Eze. 40. 42 wherewith they slew the burnt offering
43. 18 to offer burnt offerings thereon, and to
43. 24 they shall offer them up..a burnt offering
43. 27 priests shall make your burnt offerings
44. 11 they shall slay the burnt offering and
45. 15 for a meat offering, and for a burnt offer
45. 17 the prince's part (to give) burnt offerings
45. 17 he shall prepare..the burnt offering
45. 23 seven days..he shall prepare a burnt off.
45. 25 shall he do..according to the burnt offer.
46. 2 the priests shall prepare his burnt offer.
46. 4 And the burnt offering..six lambs
46. 12 the prince shall prepare a..burnt offering
46. 12 he shall prepare his burnt offering
46. 13 Thou shalt daily prepare a burnt offering
46. 15 every morning, (for) a continual burnt off.
Hos. 6. 6 the knowledge..more than burnt offer.
Amos 5. 22 Though ye offer me burnt offerings and
Mic. 6. 6 come before him with burnt offerings

2. *Whole burnt offering*, ὁλοκαύτωμα *holokautōma*.
Heb. 10. 6 In burnt offerings and (sacrifices) for sin
10. 8 Sacrifice and offering and burnt offerings

BURNT OFFERING, whole —

1. *Whole, complete*, כָּלִיל *kalil*.
Psa. 51. 19 with burnt offering, and whole burnt off

2. *Whole burnt offering*, ὁλοκαύτωμα *holokautōma*.
Mark12. 33 is more than all whole burnt offerings

BURNT SACRIFICE —

That which goes up, עֹלָה *'olah*.
Exod30. 9 Ye shall offer no strange..burnt sacrifice
Lev. 1. 3 If his offering (be) a burnt sacrifice of the
1. 9 on the altar, (to be) a burnt sacrifice, an
1. 10 if his offering (be)..for a burnt sacrifice
1. 13 it (is) a burnt sacrifice, an offering made
1. 14 if the burnt sacrifice for his offering
1. 17 it (is) a burnt sacrifice, an offering made
3. 5 upon the burnt sacrifice, which (is) upon
8. 21 a burnt sacrifice for a sweet savour
9. 17 beside the burnt sacrifice of the morning
Num 23. 6 lo, he stood by his burnt sacrifice, he
Judg. 6. 26 offer a burnt sacrifice with the wood of
2 Sa 24. 22 behold..oxen for burnt sacrifice, and
1 Ki 18. 33 with water, and pour (it) on..burnt sac.
18. 38 the fire..consumed the burnt sacrifice
2 Ki. 16. 15 the king's burnt sacrifice, and his meat
1 Ch. 16. 1 they offered burnt sacrifices..peace offer.
23. 31 to offer all burnt sacrifices unto the LORD
2 Ch. 13. 11 they burn..burnt sacrifices and sweet
Psa. 20. 3 Remember..and accept thy burnt sac.
66. 15 I will offer unto thee burnt sacrifices of

BURNT SACRIFICE, whole —

Whole, perfect, כָּלִיל *kalil*.
Deut 33. 10 whole burnt sacrifice upon thine altar

BURST, to —

1. *To draw asunder*, נָתַק *nathaq*, 3.
Jer. 2. 20 I have broken thy yoke..burst thy bands
5. 5 these have altogether..burst the bonds
30. 8 I will break..and will burst thy bonds
Nah. 1. 13 and will burst thy bonds in sunder

2. *To rend, burst*, ῥήγνυμι *rhēgnumi*.
Mark 2. 22 else the new wine doth burst the bottles
Luke 5. 37 else the new wine will burst the bottles

BURST asunder, to —

To sound, ring, break, λακέω *lakeō* (or λάσκω).
Acts 1. 18 falling headlong, he burst asunder in the

BURST out, to —

To burst through, פָּרַץ *parats*.
Prov. 3. 10 thy presses shall burst out with new wine

BURST, to be ready to —

To be cleft, rent, בָּקַע *baqa*, 2.
Job 32. 19 it is ready to burst like new bottles

BURSTING —

A breaking, מְכִתָּה *mekittah*.
Isa. 30. 14 there shall not be found in the bursting

BURY, to —

1. *To bury*, קָבַר *qabar*.
Gen. 23. 4 that I may bury my dead out of my sight
23. 6 in the choice of our sepulchres bury thy
23. 6 but that thou mayest bury thy dead
23. 8 that I should bury my dead out of my
23. 11 give I it thee: bury thy dead
23. 13 take (it) of me, and I will bury my dead
23. 15 what (is) that..bury therefore thy dead
23. 19 after this, Abraham buried Sarah his wife
25. 9 his sons Isaac and Ishmael buried him
35. 29 his sons Esau and Jacob buried him
47. 29 bury me not, I pray thee, in Egypt
47. 30 and bury me in their burying place
48. 7 and I buried her there in the way of
49. 29 bury me with my fathers in the cave
49. 31 There they buried Abraham and Sarah
49. 31 there they buried Isaac..there I buried
50. 5 in my grave..there shalt thou bury me
50. 5 let me go up, I pray t ee, and bury my
50. 6 Pharoah said, Go up and bury thy father
50. 7 And Joseph went up to bury his father
50. 13 buried him in the cave of the field of
50. 14 to bury his father, after he had buried
Num11 34 because there they buried the people
Deut21. 23 thou shalt in any wise bury him that
34. 6 he buried him in a valley in the land of
Josh 24. 30 they buried him in the border of his
24. 32 bones of Joseph..buried they in Shechem
24. 33 buried him in a hill (that pertained to)
Judg. 2. 9 they buried him in the border of his
16. 31 buried him between Zorah and Eshtaol
1 Sa. 25. 1 buried him in his house at Ramah
28. 3 Israel had lamented him, and buried him
31. 13 buried (them) under a tree at Jabesh
2 Sa. 2. 4 the men of Jabesh-gilead..buried Saul
2. 5 kindness..unto Saul, and have buried him
2. 32 buried him in the sepulchre of his father
3. 32 And they buried Abner in Hebron
4. 12 took the head of Ish-bosheth, and buried
21. 14 the bones..buried they in the country of
1 Ki. 2. 31 Do as he hath said..and bury him
13. 29 the old prophet came..to bury him
13. 31 it came to pass, after he had buried him
13. 31 bury me in the sepulchre wherein the
14. 13 Israel shall mourn for him, and bury him
14. 18 they buried him; and all Israel mourned
15. 8 they buried him in the city of David
22. 37 and they buried the king in Samaria
2 Ki. 9. 10 dogs shall eat J...and..none to bury (her)
9. 28 buried him in his sepulchre with his
9. 34 see now this cursed (woman), and bury
9. 35 they went to bury her; but they found
10. 35 and they buried him in Samaria
12. 21 they buried him with his fathers in the
13. 9 and they buried him in Samaria: and
13. 20 And Elisha died, and they buried him
13. 21 it came to pass, as they were burying a
15. 7 they buried him with his fathers in the
21. 26 he was buried in his sepulchre in the
23. 30 and buried him in his own sepulchre
1 Ch. 10. 12 buried their bones under the oak in Jabesh
2 Ch. 9. 31 he was buried in the city of David his
14. 1 and they buried him in the city of David
16. 14 they buried him in his own sepulchres
21. 20 they buried him in the city of David
22. 9 when they had slain him, they buried
24. 16, 25 they buried him in the city of David
24. 25 buried him not in the sepulchres of the
25. 28 buried him with his fathers in the city of
26. 23 they buried him with his fathers
27. 9 they buried him in the city of David
28. 27 buried him in the city..in Jerusalem
32. 33 they buried him in the chiefest of the
33. 20 and they buried him in his own house
Psa. 79. 3 and (there was) none to bury (them)
Jer. 7. 32 they shall bury in Tophet, till there be
19. 11 and they shall bury (them) in Tophet
19. 11 till (there be) no place to bury
Eze. 39. 11 there shall they bury Gog, and all his
39. 12 shall the house of Israel be burying of
39. 13 all the people of the land shall bury
39. 15 till the buriers have buried it in the

2. *To bury*, קָבַר *qabar*, 3.
Num33. 4 For the Egyptians buried all..first-born
1 Ki. 11. 15 Joab..was gone up to bury the slain
Jer. 14. 16 and they shall have none to bury them
Eze. 39. 14 passing through the land, to bury with
Hos. 9. 6 gather them up, Memphis shall bury

3. *To entomb*, ἐνταφιάζω *entaphiazō*.
John19. 40 as the manner of the Jews is to bury

4. *To bury*, θάπτω *thaptō*.
Matt. 8. 21 suffer me first to go and bury my father
8. 22 Follow me; and let the dead bury their
14. 12 disciples..took up the body, and buried
Luke 9. 59 suffer me first to go and bury my father
9. 60 Jesus said..Let the dead bury their dead
16. 22 the rich man also died, and was buried
Acts 5. 6 and carried (him) out, and buried 2. 29.
5. 9 the feet of them which have buried thy
5. 10 carrying..forth, buried (her) by her hus.
1 Co. 15. 4 that he was buried, and that he rose

BURY in, to —

Burial, ταφή *taphē*.
Matt27. 7 the potter's field, to bury strangers in

BURYING —

All nations that believe in the resurrection of the body have been careful to preserve the remains of the deceased as long as possible, as in the case of the ancient Egyptians and Jews, Christians and Mohammedans; while the Hindoos *burn* them, and the Parsees *expose* them to be devoured by birds of prey.

Entombment, ἐνταφιασμός *entaphiasmos*.
Mark14. 8 come. to anoint my body to the burying
John12 7 against the day of my burying hath she

BURYING place —

1. *Burial, grave*, קְבוּרָה *qeburah*.
Gen. 47. 30 and bury me in their burying place

2. *Burial place*, קֶבֶר *qeber*.
Gen. 23. 4 give me a possession of a burying place
23. 9, 20 for a possession of a burying place 49. 30.
50. 13 for a possession of a burying place of E.
Judg 16. 31 Zorah and Eshtaol, in the burying place

BUSH —

1. *Thorny bush*, סְנֶה *seneh*.
Exod. 3 2 flame of fire out of the midst of a bush
3. 2 the bush burned with fire, and the bush
3. 3 I will. see..why the bush is not burnt
3. 4 God called unto him out of the..bush
Deut 33. 16 good will of him that dwelt in the bush

2. *Plant, shrub*, שִׂיחַ *siach*.
Job 30. 4 Who cut up mallows by the bushes
30. 7 Among the bushes they brayed

3. *Commendable pastures*, נַהֲלֹלִים *nahalolim*.
Isa. 7. 19 and upon all thorns, and upon all bushes

4. *Bramble bush*, βάτος *batos*.
Mark12. 26 how in the bush God spake unto him
Luke20. 37 even Moses showed at the bush, when he
Acts 7. 30 of the Lord in a flame of fire in a bush
7. 35 Angel which appeared to him in the bush

BUSH, bramble —

Bramble bush, βάτος *batos*.
Luke 6. 44 nor of a bramble bush gather they grapes

BUSHEL —

A (dry) measure, μόδιος *modios*.
Matt. 5. 15 a candle, and put it under a bushel
Mark 4. 21 Is a candle brought..put under a bushel
Luke 11. 33 No man..putteth (it)..under a bushel

BUSHY —

Hanging, flowing, תַּלְתַּלִּים *taltallim*.
Song 5. 11 his locks (are) bushy, (and) black as a

BUSINESS —

1. *Word, matter*, דָּבָר *dabar*.
Deut 24. 5 neither..be charged with any business
Josh. 2. 14 Our life..if ye utter not this our business
2. 20 And if thou utter this our business, then
Judg18. 7, 28 had no business with (any) man
1 Sa. 21. 2 The king hath commanded me a business
21. 2 Let no man know..of the business
21. 8 because the king's business required haste

2. *Work*, מְלָאכָה *melakah*.
Gen. 39. 11 went into the house to do his business
1 Ch. 26. 30 on this side Jordan..in all the business
2 Ch. 13. 10 and the Levites..upon (their) business
17. 13 he had much business in the cities of Ju.
Neh. 11. 16 the oversight of the outward business of
11. 22 the singers..over the business of the
13. 30 the priests..every one in his business
Esth. 3. 9 those that have the charge of..business
Psa. 107. 23 that do business in great waters
Prov. 22. 29 Seest thou a man diligent in his business?
Dan. 8. 27 I rose up, and did the king's business

3. *Work, deed*, מַעֲשֶׂה *maaseh*.
1 Sa. 20. 19 when the business was..and shalt remain

4. *Travail*, עִנְיָן *inyan*.
Eccl. 5. 3 cometh through..multitude of business
8. 16 the business that is done upon the earth

5. *The things of*, τά *ta*.
Luke 2. 49 I must be about my Father's business?

6. *Deed, business*, πρᾶγμα *pragma*.
Rom 16. 2 assist her in whatsoever business she

7. *Speed*, σπουδή *spoudē*.
Rom. 12. 11 Not slothful in business; fervent in

8. *Use, need, necessity*, χρεία *chreia*.
Acts 6. 3 whom we may appoint over this business

BUSINESS, one's own —

One's own things, τὰ ἴδια *ta idia*.
1 Th. 4. 11 that ye study..to do your own business

BUSY, to be —

To do, עָשָׂה *asah*.
1 Ki 20. 40 as thy servant was busy here and there

BUSY body —

Working around, περίεργος *periergos*.
1 Ti. 5 13 not only idle, but tattlers..busy bodies

BUSY body, to be a —

To work all around, περιεργάζομαι *periergazomai*.
2 Th. 3 11 working not at all, but are busy bodies

BUSY body in other men's matters —

Overseer of another, ἀλλοτριοεπίσκοπος.
1 Pe. 4. 15 or (as) a busy body in other men's matters

BUT —

1. *But*, אֲבָל *abal*.
2 Ch. 1 4 But the ark of God had David brought
Ezra 10. 13 But the people (are) many, and (it is) a
Dan. 10. 7 but a great quaking fell upon them
10. 21 But I will shew thee that which is noted

2. *Yet, nevertheless*, אוּלָם *ulam*.
Gen 28. 19 but the name of that city (was)..Luz
1 Ki. 20. 23 but let us fight against them in the plain
Job 1. 11 But put forth thine hand now, and touch
2. 5 But put forth thine hand .touch his bone
11. 5 But oh that God would speak, and open
12. 7 But ask now the beasts, and they shall
13. 4 But ye (are) forgers of lies, ye (are) all

3. *Only*, אַךְ *ak*.
Gen 9. 4 But flesh with the life..the blood thereof
Judg. 7. 19 and they had but newly set the watch

4. *Surely*, אָכֵן *aken*.
Job. 32. 8 But (there is) a spirit in man: and the
Psa. 82. 7 But ye shall die like men, and fall like
Zeph 3. 7 but they rose early, (and) corrupted all

5. *Also*, אַף *aph*.
Psa. 44. 9 But thou hast cast off, and put us to

6. *Only*, אֶפֶס *ephes*.
Num23. 13 thou shalt see but the utmost part of

7. *Except, without*, בִּלְתִּי *bilti*.
Gen. 21. 26 neither yet heard I (of it), but to-day

8. *Nevertheless*, בְּרַם *beram.*
Ezra 5. 13 But in the first year of Cyrus the king
Dan. 2. 28 But there..God in heaven that revealeth

9. *Even, also*, גַּם *gam.*
Job. 12. 3 But I have understanding as well as you

10. *That which*, דִּי *di.*
Dan. 2. 9 But if ye will not make known unto me

11. *Except*, זוּלָה *zulah.*
1 Ki. 12. 20 there was none that followed..but the
Hos. 13. 4 and thou shalt know no god but me

12. *For*, כִּי *ki.*
Gen. 17. 15 but Sarah (shall) her name (be)

13. *Therefore*, לָהֵן *lahen.*
Ezra 5. 12 But after that our fathers had provoked
Dan. 2. 30 But for (their) sakes that shall

14. *Yet, still*, עוֹד *od.*
Gen. 35. 16 there was but a little way to come to Eph.

15. *Only*, רַק *raq.*
Exod 8. 29 but let not Pharaoh deal deceitfully any

16. *If not*, אִם־לֹא *im lo.*
Gen. 24. 38 But thou shalt go unto my father's house

17. *Now, but, further*, δέ *de.*
Matt. 1. 20 but while he thought on these things
2. 19 But when Herod was dead, behold, an
2. 22 But when he heard that Archelaus did
3. 7 but when he saw many of the Pharisees
[This particle occurs about 2700 times in N. T.]

18. *But*, ἀλλά *alla.*
Matt. 4. 4 but by every word that proceedeth
[This particle occurs about 630 times; Phil. 2. 7, etc.]

19. *For*, γάρ *gar.*
1 Pe. 4. 15 But let none of you suffer as a murderer
2 Pe. 1. 9 But he that lacketh these things is blind

20. *But, but now*, δέ *de.*
Matt. 5. 22 But I say unto you, That whosoever is an.
[*See also* 10. 17, 33; 12. 28, 36; 13. 16; 23. 5; 26. 56; etc.]

21. *If not*, ἐὰν μή *ean mē.*
Mark10. 30 But he shall receive an hundredfold now
John 5. 19 The Son can do nothing of himself, but
Gal. 2. 16 by the works of the law, but by the faith

22. *If not*, εἰ μή *ei mē.*
Matt. 5. 13 good for nothing, but to be cast out
11. 27 no man knoweth the Son, but the Father
12. 4 neither for them..but only for the priests?
12. 24 but by Beelzebub the prince of the devils
12. 39 but the sign of the prophet Jonas
14. 17 We have here but five loaves, and two
15. 24 I am not sent but unto the lost sheep
16. 4 there shall no sign be given..but the sign
17. 21 [this kind goeth not out but by prayer]
19. 17 [there is none good but one, (that is,) God]
21. 19 and found nothing thereon, but leaves
24. 36 angels of heaven, but my Father only
Mark 2. 7 who can forgive sins but God only?
2. 26 which is not lawful to eat but for the pr.
6. 4 A prophet is not without honour, but in
9. 29 This kind can come forth by nothing but
10. 18 (there is) none good but one, (that is) God
11. 13 when he came to it, he found nothing but
13. 32 Knoweth..neither the Son, but the Father
Luke 5. 21 Who can forgive sins but God alone?
6. 4 which it is not lawful to eat but for the
11. 29 there shall no sign be given it, but the
John 3. 13 but he that came down from heaven
10. 10 The thief cometh not, but for to steal
14. 6 no man cometh unto the Father, but by
17. 12 and none of them is lost, but the son of
19. 15 answered, We have no king but Cesar
Acts 11. 19 preaching the word to none but unto the
Rom. 7. 7 Nay, I had not known sin but by the law
11. 15 what (shall) the receiving..but life from
13. 1 For there is no power but of God: the
13. 8 Owe no man anything, but to love one
14. 14 but to him that esteemeth any thing to
1 Co. 1. 14 that I baptized none of you but Crispus
2. 11 the things of God knoweth no man, but
7. 17 But as God hath distributed to every man
8. 4 and that (there is) none other God but
10. 13 but such as is common to man
12. 3 no man can say..but by the Holy Ghost
2 Co. 2. 2 but the same which is made sorry by me?
12. 5 of myself I will not glory, but in mine
Gal. 1. 7 but there be some that trouble you, and
Eph. 4. 9 what is it but that he also descended first
Phil. 4. 15 no church communicated with me..but
Heb. 3. 18 they should not enter into his rest, but to
1 Jo. 2. 22 Who is a liar but he that denieth that
5. 5 but he that believeth that Jesus is the
Rev. 9. 4 but only those men which have not the
14. 3 no man could learn that song but the
19. 12 a name..no man knew but he himself
21. 27 but they which are written in the Lamb's

23. *Without, if not*, ἐκτὸς εἰ μή *ektos ei mē.*
1 Ti. 5. 19 but before two or three witnesses

24. *Than*, (ἀλλ') ἤ *(all') ē.*
1 Co. 3. 5 [but] ministers by whom ye bel.; Lu. 9. 13.

25. *And*, καί *kai.*
John 1. 20 but confessed, I am not the Christ
Acts 16. 7 but the Spirit suffered them not
1 Jo. 2. 27 But the anointing which ye have received

26. *Indeed, yet*, μέντοι *mentoi.*
John21. 4 but the disciples knew not that it was Je.

27. *Only*, μόνον *monon.*
Matt.9. 21 If I may but touch his garment, I shall

28. *Not*, μή *mē.*
Acts 4. 20 For we cannot but speak the things
20. 20 but have showed you, and have taught

29. *Then, therefore*, οὖν *oun.*
Luke21. 7 Master, but when shall these things be?
John 8. 5 [such should be stoned: but what sayest]
9. 18 But the Jews did not believe concerning
Acts 23. 21 But do not thou yield unto them; for
25. 4 But Festus answered, that Paul should

30. *But*, πλήν *plēn.*
Matt11. 22 But I say unto you, it shall be more
11. 24 But I say unto you, That it shall be more
18. 7 but woe to that man by whom the offence
Mark12. 32 and there is none other but he
Luke 6. 24 But woe unto you that are rich
6. 35 But love ye your enemies, and do good
10. 14 But it shall be more tolerable for Tyre
19. 27 But those mine enemies..bring hither
22. 21 But, behold, the hand of him that
22. 22 but woe unto that man by whom he is
23. 28 but weep for yourselves, and for your
John 8. 10 [and saw none but the woman, he said]
Acts 27. 22 shall be no loss of..life..but of the ship
Rev. 2. 25 But that which ye have..hold fast

BUT and if —

1. *Now or but if*, ἐὰν δέ *ean de.*
Matt.24 48 But and if that evil servant shall say
Luke12. 45 But and if that servant say in his heart
20. 6 But and if we say, Of men; all the people

2. *But even if*, ἀλλ' εἰ καί *all' ei kai.*
1 Pe. 3. 14 But and if ye suffer for righteousness' sake

BUT either —

Or, ἤ *ē.*
Acts 17. 21 but either to tell, or to hear some new

BUT if —

1. *If*, אִלּוּ *illu.*
Esth. 7. 4 But if we had been sold for bond men

2. *But even if*, ἀλλ' εἰ καί *all' ei kai.*
1 Co. 7. 21 but if thou mayest be made free, use (it)

3. *Now even if*, εἰ δὲ καί *ei de kai.*
2 Co. 4. 3 But if our gospel be hid, it is hid to them

BUT now —

Now, τανῦν *tanun.*
Acts 17. 30 but now commandeth all men every

BUT only —

Nevertheless, אֶפֶס *ephes.*
Num22. 35 but only the word that I shall speak unto

BUT rather —

1. *But rather*, ἀλλ' ἤ *all' ē.*
Luke12. 51 I tell you, Nay; but rather division

2. *But*, πλήν *plēn.*
Luke11. 41 But rather give alms of such things as ye
12. 31 But rather seek ye the kingdom of God

BUT that —

Not, μή *mē.*
Luke17. 1 It is impossible but that offences will

BUT, if —

Even if, κἄν *kan.*
Mark 5. 28 If I may touch but his clothes, I shall be
6. 56 they might touch if it were but the border

BUT, nay —

Indeed then, μενοῦνγε *menounge.*
Rom. 9. 20 [Nay but,] O man, who art thou that

BUT, no more —

No more than, οὐ πλεῖον ἤ *ou pleion ē.*
Luke 9. 13 We have no more but five loaves and two

BUT, though —

Yet, nevertheless, ὅμως *homōs.*
Gal. 3. 15 Though..but a man's covenant, yet

BUT, yet —

No more than, οὐ πλείους ἤ *ou pleious ē.*
Acts 24. 11 that there are yet but twelve days since I

BUTLER —

To give to drink, שָׁקָה *shaqah*, 5.
Gen. 40. 1 the butler..and (his) baker had offended
40. 2 wroth..against the chief of the butlers
40. 5 the butler and the baker of the king of
40. 9 the chief butler told his dream to Joseph
40. 13 the former manner when thou wast his b.
40. 20 he lifted up the head of the chief butler
40. 21 he restored the chief butler unto his
40. 23 Yet did not the chief butler remember
41. 9 Then spake the chief butler unto Pharaoh

BUTLERSHIP —

Butlership, מַשְׁקֶה *mashqeh.*
Gen. 40. 21 restored..chief butler unto his butlership

BUTTER —

1. *Curdled milk, cream, cheese*, חֶמְאָה *chemah.*
Gen. 18. 8 he took butter, and milk, and the calf
Deut32. 14 Butter of kine, and milk of sheep, with
Judg. 5. 25 she brought forth butter in a lordly dish
2 Sa. 17. 29 honey, and butter, and sheep, and cheese
Job 20. 17 He shall not see the..brooks of..butter
Prov.30. 33 the churning of milk bringeth forth butter
Isa. 7. 15 Butter and honey shall he eat, that he
7. 22 he shall eat butter: for butter and honey

2. *Curdled milk, cream, cheese*, חֵמָה *chemah.*
Job 29. 6 When I washed my steps with butter

3. *Buttered pieces*, מַחֲמָאֹת *machamaoth.*
Psa. 55. 21 of his mouth were smoother than butter

BUTTOCKS —

1. *Hip*, מִפְשָׂעָה *miphsaah.*
1 Ch.19. 4 cut off their garments..by their buttocks

2. *Seat, bottom*, שֵׁת *sheth.*
2 Sa. 10. 4 cut off their garments..to their buttocks
Isa. 20. 4 even with..buttocks uncovered, to the

BUY, to —

1. *To prepare, provide*, כָּרָה *karah.*
Deut. 2. 6 ye shall also buy water of them for money
Hos. 3. 2 So I bought her to me for fifteen..of silver

2. *To take, receive*, לָקַח *laqach.*
Neh. 5. 3 That we might buy corn, because of the
10. 31 (that) we would not buy it of them on
Prov.31. 16 She considereth a field, and buyeth it

3. *To obtain, acquire*, קְנָא *qena.*
Ezra 7. 17 That thou mayest buy speedily with this

4. *To acquire, obtain*, קָנָה *qanah.*
Gen. 33. 19 he bought a parcel of a field, where he
39. 1 Potiphar..bought him of the hands of
47. 19 buy us and our land for bread, and we
47. 20 Joseph bought all the land of Egypt for
47. 22 Only the land of the priests bought he
47. 23 I have bought you this day and your land
49. 30 which Abraham bought with the field of
50. 13 which Abraham bought with the field for
Exod21. 2 If thou buy an Hebrew servant, six years
Lev. 22. 11 But if the priest buy (any) soul with his
25. 14 or buyest..of thy neighbour's hand, ye
25. 15 According to..thou shalt buy of thy
25. 28 in the hand of him that hath bought it
25. 30 him that bought it, throughout his gener.
25. 44 of them shall ye buy bond men and bond
25. 45 of them shall ye buy, and of their families
25. 50 that bought him from the year that he
27. 24 field shall return..of whom it was bought
Deut28. 68 there ye shall be sold..no man shall buy
32. 6 (is) not he thy father (that) hath bought
Josh.24. 32 in a parcel of ground which Jacob bought
Ruth 4. 4 Buy (it) before the inhabitants, and
4. 5 What day thou buyest the field of the
4. 5 thou must buy (it) also of Ruth the Moab.
4. 8 the kinsman said unto Boaz Buy (it) for
4. 9 that I have bought all that (was) Elim.
2 Sa. 12. 3 which he had bought and nourished up
24. 21 David said, To buy the threshing floor of
24. 24 but I will surely buy (it) of thee at a price
24. 24 David bought the threshing floor and the
1 Ki. 16. 24 he bought the hill Samaria of Shemer
2 Ki. 12. 12 to buy timber and hewed stone to repair
22. 6 to buy timber and hewn stone to repair
1 Ch.21. 24 but I will verily buy it for the full price
2 Ch.34. 11 buy hewn stone, and timber for couplings
Neh. 5. 16 I continued in the work..neither bought
Prov 23. 23 Buy the truth, and sell (it) not
Isa. 43. 24 Thou hast bought me no sweet cane
Jer. 32. 7 Buy thee my field that (is) in Anathoth
32. 7 for the right of redemption..thine to buy
32. 8 Buy my field, I pray thee, that (is) in An.
32. 8 the redemption (is) thine; buy it for
32. 9 I bought the field of Hanameel my uncle's
32. 25 Buy thee the field for money, and take
32. 43 And fields shall be bought in this land
32. 44 Men shall buy fields for money, and
Amos 8. 6 That we may buy the poor for silver

5. *To break, buy corn*, שָׁבַר *shabar.*
Gen. 41. 57 all countries came into Egypt..to buy
42. 2 get you down thither, and buy for us
42. 3 Joseph's ten brethren went down to buy
42. 5 the sons of Israel came to buy..among
42. 7 From the land of Canaan to buy food
42. 10 Nay, my lord, but to buy food are thy
43. 2 Go again, buy us a little food
43. 4 we will go down and buy thee food
43. 20 came indeed down at the first time to buy
43. 22 other money have we brought..to buy
44. 25 our father said, Go again..buy us a little
47. 14 for the corn which they bought
Deut.2. 6 Ye shall buy meat of them for money
Isa. 55. 1 he that hath no money; come ye, buy
55. 1 come, buy wine and milk without money

6. *To use the market place*, ἀγοράζω *agorazō.*
Matt 13. 44 selleth all that he hath, and buyeth that
13. 46 went and sold all that he had, and bought
14. 15 go into the villages, and buy themselves
21. 12 cast out all them that..bought in the
25. 9 go ye rather to them that sell, and buy
25. 10 while they went to buy, the bridegroom
27. 7 bought with them the potter's field, to
Mark 6. 36 that they may go..and buy themselves
6. 37 Shall we go and buy two hundred penny
11. 15 to cast out them that sold and bought in
15. 46 he bought fine linen, and took him down
16. 1 Mary Magdalene..had bought sweet
Luke 9. 13 except we should go and buy meat for
14. 18 I have bought a piece of ground, and I
14. 19 another said, I have bought five yoke of

Luke 17. 28 they did eat, they drank, they bought
19. 45 [to cast out them that sold..and..bought]
22. 36 let him sell his garment, and buy one
John 4. 8 were gone away unto the city to buy meat
6. 5 Whence shall we buy bread, that these
13. 29 Buy..that we have need of against the
1 Co. 6. 20 ye are bought with a price: therefore
7. 23 bought with a price; be not ye the
7. 30 they that buy, as though they possessed
2 Pe. 2. 1 even denying the Lord that bought them
Rev. 3. 18 I counsel thee to buy of me gold tried in
13. 17 that no man might buy or sell, save he
18. 11 for no man buyeth their merchandise

7. *To buy, purchase,* ὠνέομαι *ōneomai.*
Acts 7. 16 the sepulchre that Abraham bought for

BUY and sell, to —
To go on in, ἐμπορεύομαι *emporeuomai.*
Jas. 4. 13 continue there a year, and buy and sell

BUYER —
To acquire, obtain, קָנָה *qanah.*
Prov 20. 14 (It is) naught, (it is) naught, saith the buyer
Isa. 24. 2 as with the buyer, so with the seller
Eze. 7. 12 let not the buyer rejoice, nor the seller

BUZ, בּוּז *contempt.*
1. Second son of Milcah and Nahor the brother of Abraham. His family probably settled in Arabia Petræa B.C. 1880.
Gen. 22. 21 Huz his first born, and B. his brother, and
2. A man of the tribe of Gad.
1 Ch. 5. 14 Jeshishai, the son of Jahdo, the son of B.

BU'-ZI, בּוּזִי *contemned of Jah.*
An Aaronite, father of Ezekiel the prophet, B.C. 595.
Eze. 1. 3 The word..came..unto Ezekiel..son of B.

BUZ'-ITE, הַבּוּזִי *the one belonging to Buz.*
An inhabitant of a region called Buz, Jer. 25. 23.
Job 32. 2 wrath of..the son of Barachel the B.
32. 6 Elihu the son of Barachel the B. answered

BY —
1. *Behind,* אַחַר *achar.*
Deut 11. 30 by the way where the sun goeth down

2. *Unto, to, at,* אֶל־ *el.*
Gen. 24. 11 to kneel down without the city by a well

3. *Near,* אֵצֶל *etsel.*
Gen. 39. 10 that he hearkened not unto her, to lie by
39. 16 And she laid up his garment by her
Judg 19. 14 by Gibeah, which (belongeth) to Benjamin
1 Sa. 5. 2 brought it into the house..and set it by
20. 19 and shalt remain by the stone Ezel
1 Ki. 1. 9 which (is) by En-rogel, and called all
2. 29 and, behold, (he is) by the altar. Then
4. 12 which (is) by Zartanah beneath Jezreel
13. 24 the ass stood by it, the lion also stood by
13. 25 the lion standing by the carcase: and they
13. 28 and the lion standing by the carcase
2 Ch. 9. 18 and two lions standing by the stays
Neh. 2. 6 king said unto me..queen also sitting by
3. 23 of Maaseiah the son of Ananiah by his
4. 3 Now Tobiah the Ammonite (was) by him
4. 12 when the Jews which dwelt by them came
4. 18 he that sounded the trumpet (was) by me
Prov. 8. 30 Then I was by him, (as) one brought up
Jer. 35. 4 which (was) by the chamber of the princes
41. 17 the habitation of Chimham, which is by
Eze. 1. 15 one wheel upon the earth by the living
1. 19 living creatures went, the wheels went by
10. 9 behold, the four wheels by the cherubim
10. 9 one wheel by one cherub, and another..by
10. 16 the cherubim went, the wheels went by
33. 30 children..still are talking against thee by
39. 15 then shall he set up a sign by it, till the
40. 7 by the porch of the gate within
43. 6 I heard (him) speaking..the man stood by
43. 8 their post by my posts, and the wall
Amos 2. 8 upon clothes laid to pledge by every

4. *With,* אֵת *eth.*
Gen. 49. 25 and by the Almighty, who shall bless thee

5. *Through, at,* בְּעַד *bead.*
1 Sa. 4. 18 he fell from off the seat backward by the

6. *From, out of,* מִן *min.*
Song 5. 4 My beloved put in his hand by the hole

7. *Over,* עֵבֶר *eber.*
1 Ki. 7. 20 over against the belly which (was) by the

8. *Unto,* עַד *ad.*
1 Sa. 25. 22 if I leave of all that (pertain) to him, by

9. *On, against,* עַל *al.*
Gen. 14. 6 unto El-paran, which (is) by the wilderness

10. *With,* עִם *im.*
Gen. 25. 11 and Isaac dwelt by the well Lahai-roi
Dan. 7. 2 Daniel..said, I saw in my vision by night

11. *From with,* מֵעִם *meim.*
Gen. 41. 32 because the thing (is) established by God

12. *With,* עִמָּד *immad.*
Deut. 5. 31 But as for thee, stand thou here by me

13. *Heel, consequence,* עֵקֶב *eqeb.*
Prov 22. 4 By humility, (and) the fear of the LORD

14. *By the hand of,* בְּיַד *be-yad.*
Exod 9. 35 as the LORD had spoken by Moses
Judg. 3 15 by him the children of Israel sent a present
1 Sa. 16. 20 and sent..by David his son unto Saul
28. 15 answered..neither by prophets, nor by
28. 17 the LORD hath done to him as he spake by
1 Ki. 12. 15 which the LORD spake by Ahijah the
15. 29 which he spake by his servant Ahijah
16. 12 which he spake against Baasha by Jehu
16. 34 which he spake by Joshua the son
17. 16 the word of the LORD, which he spake by
2 Ki. 9. 36 which he spake by his servant Elijah
10. 10 LORD hath done (that) which he spake by
17. 13 the LORD testified against Israel,..by all
17. 13 which I sent to you by my servants the
17. 23 as he had said by all his servants
21. 10 the LORD spake by his servants the pro.
24. 2 which he spake by his servants the pro.
1 Ch. 11. 3 according to the word of the LORD by
2 Ch. 23. 18 Jehoiada appointed the offices..by the
29. 25 the commandment of the LORD by his pro.
34. 14 the priest found a book..(given) by Moses
36. 15 the LORD God..sent to them by his
Ezra 9. 11 Which thou hast commanded by thy
Neh. 8. 14 which..LORD had commanded by Moses
10. 29 which was given by Moses the servant of
Esth. 1. 12 at the king's commandment by (his)
1. 15 the commandment..by the chamberlains?
3. 13 the letters were sent by posts into all the
8. 10 and sent letters by posts on horseback
Psa. 63. 10 They shall fall by the sword; they shall
Isa. 20. 2 At the same time spake the LORD by Isa.
37. 24 By thy servants hast thou reproached the
Jer. 37. 2 which he spake by the prophet Jeremiah
46. 6 fall toward the north by the river Euph.
50. 1 The word that the LORD spake..by Jere.
Eze. 38. 17 of whom I have spoken in old time by
Dan. 9. 10 which he set before us by his servants
Hag. 1. 3 came the word of the LORD by Haggai
2. 1, 10 came the word of the LORD by..prophet
Zech. 7. 7 the LORD hath cried by..former proph.
7. 12 the Lord..hath sent..by the former pro.
Mal. 1. 1 the word of the LORD to Israel by Malac.

15. *From,* ἀπό *apo.*
Matt. 7. 16 Ye shall know them by their fruits
7. 20 Wherefore [by] their fruits ye shall know
Acts 9. 13 Lord, I have heard by many of this man
12. 20 their country was nourished by the king's
2 Co. 3. 18 from glory to glory..as by the Spirit of
7. 13 because his spirit was refreshed by you
Heb. 5. 8 yet learned he obedience by the things
Jude 23 hating even the garment spotted by the
Rev. 18. 15 merchants..which were made rich by

16. *With a regard to,* εἰς *eis.*
Matt. 5. 35 neither by Jerusalem; for it is the city
Acts 7. 53 Who have received the law by the

17. *Out of,* ἐκ *ek.*
Matt 12. 33 for the tree is known by (his) fruit
12. 37 For by thy words thou shalt be justified
12. 37 by thy words thou shalt be condemned
15. 5 by whatsoever thou mightest be..by me
Mark 7. 11 by whatsoever thou mightest be..by me
Luke 6. 44 For every tree is known by his own fruit
John 3. 34 God giveth not the Spirit by measure
Acts 19. 25 Sirs, ye know that by this craft we have
Rom. 1. 4 according to the Spirit..by the resurrect.
1. 17 as it is written, The just shall live by
2. 27 shall not uncircumcision which is by
3. 20 by the deeds of the law there shall no
3. 30 which shall justify the circumcision by
4. 2 For if Abraham were justified by works
5. 1 being justified by faith, we have peace
5. 16 the judgment (was) by..to condemnation
9. 10 when Rebecca also had conceived by one
9. 32 Wherefore? Because (they sought it) not by
9. 32 but as it were by the works of the law
10. 17 So then faith (cometh) by hearing, and
2 Co. 2. 2 but the same which is made sorry by me?
7. 9 that ye might receive damage by us in
8. 14 by an equality..now at this time your
11. 26 perils of robbers, (in) perils by..country.
11. 26 perils by the heathen, (in) perils in the
13. 4 yet he liveth by the power of God
13. 4 we shall live with him by the power of
Gal. 2. 16 a man is not justified by the works of
2. 16 by the faith of Jesus Christ, even
2. 16 by the works of the law, for by the works
3. 2 by the works of the law, or by the hear.
3. 5 by the works of the law, or by the hearing
3. 11 The just shall live by faith
3. 21 verily righteousness should have been by
3. 22 that the promise by faith..might be
3. 24 that we might be justified by faith
4. 22 one by a bond maid, the other by a free
5. 5 through the Spirit wait for the hope..by
Titus 3. 5 Not by works of righteousness which we
Heb. 10. 38 Now the just shall live by faith: but if
Jas. 2. 18 I will show thee my faith by my works
2. 21 Was not Abraham our father justified by
2. 22 and by works was faith made perfect?
2. 24 by works a man is justified, and not by
2. 25 was not Rahab the harlot justified by
1 Pe. 2. 12 they may by..good works..glorify God
1 Jo. 3. 24 hereby we know..by the Spirit which he
Rev. 9. 18 [by] the fire, and [by] the smoke, and [by]

18. *In, by, with,* ἐν *en.*
Matt. 5. 34 Swear not at all: neither by heaven
5. 35 Nor by the earth; for it is his footstool
5. 36 Neither shalt thou swear by thy head
12. 24 This (fellow) doth not cast out devils..by
12. 27 If I by Beelzebub cast out devils, by
12. 28 But if I cast out devils by the Spirit of
14. 13 he departed thence by ship into a desert
17. 21 [this kind goeth not out but by prayer]
21. 23 By what authority doest..these things?
21. 24 I..will tell you by what authority I do
21. 27 Neither tell I you by what authority I
22. 1 Jesus answered..them again by parables
23. 16 swear by the temple..swear by the gold
23. 18 swear by the altar..sweareth by the gift
23. 20 swear by the altar, sweareth by it, and by
23. 21 swear by the temple, sweareth by..and by
23. 22 swear by heaven, sweareth by..and by
Mark 3. 22 by the prince of the devils casteth he out
4. 2 he taught them many things by parables
5. 21 when Jesus was passed over again by
8. 3 if I send them away..they will faint by
8. 27 by the way he asked his disciples, saying
9. 29 This kind can come forth by nothing but by
9. 33 What was it that ye disputed..by the way?
9. 34 [by] the way they had disputed among
11. 28 By what authority doest thou these
11. 29 I will tell you by what authority I do
11. 33 Neither do I tell you by what authority
12. 1 he began to speak unto them by parables
12. 36 David himself said by the Holy Ghost
14. 1 scribes sought how they might take..by
Luke 1. 77 To give knowledge of salvation..by the
2. 27 he came by the Spirit into the temple
4. 1 was led by the Spirit into the wilderness
11. 19 if I by Beelzebub cast out devils, by whom
20. 2 by what authority doest thou these things?
20. 8 Neither tell I you by what authority I do
24. 32 while he talked to us by the way, and
John 13. 35 By this shall all..know that ye are my
16. 30 by this we believe that thou camest forth
Acts 1. 3 after his passion by many infallible proofs
4. 7 By what power, or by what name, have
4. 10 by the name of Jesus Christ..(even) by
4. 30 By stretching forth thine hand to heal
7. 35 [by] the hand of the Angel which appeared
13. 39 by him all that believe are justified
13. 39 from which ye could not be justified by
17. 31 by (that) man whom he hath ordained
20. 19 which befell me by the lying in wait of
Rom. 1. 10 by the will of God to come unto you
5. 9 being now justified by his blood, we shall
5. 10 we shall be saved by his life
5. 15 more the grace of God, and the gift by
10. 5 which doeth those things shall live by
14. 14 I know, and am persuaded by the Lord
15. 16 the offering..being sanctified by the Holy
15. 19 by the power of the Spirit of God
1 Co. 1. 4 the grace of God which is given you by
1. 5 That in everything ye are enriched by him
3. 13 because it shall be revealed by fire
6. 2 if the world shall be judged by you, are
6. 11 ye are justified..by the Spirit of our God
7. 14 sanctified by the wife..sanctified by the
12. 3 no man speaking by the Spirit of God
12. 3 no man can say..Jesus is the Lord, but by
12. 9 faith by the same..healing by the same
12. 13 by one Spirit are we all baptized into one
14. 6 except I shall speak to you either by
14. 6 or by knowledge, or by prophesying, or by
16. 7 For I will not see you now by the way
2 Co. 1. 12 not with fleshly wisdom, but by the grace
6. 6 By pureness, by knowledge, by long-suff.
6. 6 by kindness, by the Holy Ghost, by love
6. 7 By the word of truth, by the power of
7. 6 God..comforted us by the coming of T.
7. 7 by the consolation wherewith he was
10. 12 they measuring themselves by themselves
10. 15 we shall be enlarged by you according to
Gal. 2. 17 while we seek to be justified by Christ
2. 20 I live by the faith of the Son of God
3. 11 But that no man is justified by the law
5. 4 whosoever of you are justified by the law
Eph. 2. 13 are made nigh by the blood of Christ
2. 18 we both have access by one Spirit
3. 5 as it is now revealed..by the Spirit
3. 21 Unto him (be) glory in the church by
4. 14 by the sleight of men, (and) cunning craft
4. 21 ye have heard him, and..been taught by
5. 26 with the washing of water by the word
Phil. 4. 19 according to his riches in glory by Christ
Col. 1. 16 For by him were all things created, that
1. 17 and by him all things consist
1. 21 and enemies in..mind by wicked works
2. 11 putting off..by the circumcision of Christ
1 Th. 3. 3 no man should be moved by these afflict.
4. 1 we beseech you..and exhort (you) by the
4. 15 this we say unto you by the word of the
2 Th. 3. 16 the Lord..give you peace always by all
1 Ti. 1. 18 that thou by them mightest war a good
Titus 1. 9 that he may be able by sound doctrine
Phm. 6 by the acknowledging of every good thing
Heb. 1. 1 spake in time past unto the fathers by the
1. 2 these last days spoken unto us by (his)
10. 10 By the which will we are sanctified
10. 19 to enter into the holiest by the blood of
11. 2 For by it the elders obtained a good
1 Pe. 1. 5 Who are kept by the power of God
3. 19 By which also he went and preached
5. 10 hath called us unto his eternal glory by
2 Pe. 1. 13 to stir you up by putting (you) in rememb.
1 Jo. 5. 2 By this we know that we love the children
5. 6 This is he that came by water and blood
5. 6 came by water..not by water only, but by
Jude 1 to them that are sanctified by God the
Rev. 5. 9 hast redeemed us to God by the blood
9. 20 the rest..which were not killed by these
10. 6 And sware by him that liveth for ever
18. 23 for by thy sorceries were all nations

19. *Upon,* ἐπί (*dat.*) *epi.*
Matt. 4. 4 Man shall not live by bread alone, but [by]
Luke 4. 4 man shall not live by bread alone, but [by]
John 5. 2 there is at Jerus., by the sheep (market)
Rom 10. 19 I will provoke you to jealousy by (them
10. 19 (and) by a foolish nation I will anger you
Phil. 3. 9 the righteousness which is of God by faith

20. *Through, by means of,* διά (*gen.*) *dia.*
Matt. 1. 22 which was spoken of the Lord by the
2. 5 for thus it is written by the prophet
2. 15 which was spoken of the Lord by the
2. 23 fulfilled which was spoken by..prophets
4. 14 which was spoken by Esaias the prophet
8. 17 which was spoken by Esaias the prophet
8. 28 so that no man might pass by that way
12. 17 which was spoken by Esaias the prophet
13. 35 fulfilled which was spoken by the prophet
18. 7 woe to that man by whom the offence
21. 4 fulfilled which was spoken by the prophet
24. 15 desolation, spoken of by Daniel the
26. 24 woe unto that man by whom the Son of
27. 9 which was spoken by Jeremy the prophet
Mark 6. 2; 10. [1]; 14. 21; Luke 1. 70; 5. [19]; 8. 4; 18.
31; 22. 22; John 1. 3, 10, 17, 17; 10. 1, 2, 9; 14. 6;
Acts 1. 16; 2. 16, 22, 23, 43; 3. 16, 18, 21; 4. 16, 25,
30; 5. 12, 19; 7. 25; 9. 25; 10. 36; 11. 28, 30; 12. [9];
14. 3; 15. 7, 12, 23, 27; 17. 10; 18. 9, 28; 19. 11; 21.
19; 23. 31; 24. 2, 2; 28. 25; Rom. 1. 2, 5, 12; 2. 12, 16,
27; 3. 20, 22, 27, 27; 5. 2, 5, 10, 11, 12, 12, 16, 17, 17,
18, 18, 19, 19, 21; 6. 4, 4; 7. 4, 5, 7, 8, 11, 11, 13, 13;
10. 17; 12. 1; 15. 18, 28, 32; 16. 18, 26; 1 Co. 1. 9, 10,
21, 21; 2. 10; 3. 5, 15; 6. 14; 8. 6, 6; 10. 1; 11. 12;
12. 8; 14. 9; 15. 2, 21, 21; 16. 3; 2 Co. 1. 1, 4, 5, 11,
16, 19, 19, 20; 2. 14; 4. [14]; 5. 7, 7, 18, 20; 6. 7, 8, 8;
8. 5; 9. 12, 13; 10. 1, 9, 11; 11. 33; 12. 17; Gal. 1. 1, 1,
12, 15; 2. 16, 21; 3. 18, 19, 26; 4. 23; 5. 6, 13; 6. [14];
Eph. 1. 1, 5; 2. 16; 3. 6, [9], 10, 12, 16, 17; 4. 16; 6. 18;
Phil. 1. 11, 20, 20, 26; Col. 1. 1, 16, 20, [20]; 2. 19; 3.
17; 1 Th. 3. 7; 4. 2; 5. 9; 2 Th. 2. 2, 2, 2, 14, 15; 3.
[12], 14; 1 Ti. 4. 5, 14; 2 Ti. 1. 1, 6, 10, 14; 4. 17;
Titus 3. 5; Phm. 7; Heb. 1. 2, [3]; 2. 2, 3, 10; 3. 16; 6.
18; 7. 11, 19, 21, 25; 9. 11, 12, 12, 26; 11. 4, 4, 7, 29;
13. 11, 15; Jas. 2. 12; 1 Pe. 1. 3, 12, 21, 23; 2. 5, 14;
3. 1, 20, 21; 5. 12; 2 Pe. 1. 4; 1 Jo. 5. 6; Rev. 1. 1.

21. *Through, on account of,* διά (*acc.*) *dia.*
Matt 15. 3 Why do ye also transgress..by your
15. 6 of God of none effect by your tradition
John 6. 57 I live by the Father..he shall live by me
Rom. 8. 11 by his Spirit that dwelleth in you
Heb. 6. 7 meet for them by whom it is dressed
Rev. 12. 11 overcame him by the blood..and by the
13. 14 And deceiveth them..by..those miracles

22. *Down through, over against,* κατά (*gen.*) *kata.*
Matt 26. 63 I adjure thee by the living God, that
Heb. 6. 13 he could swear by no greater, he sware by
6. 16 For men verily swear by the greater; and

23. *Down through, according to,* κατά (*acc.*) *kata.*
Luke 10. 4 and salute no man by the way
10. 31 by chance there came down a certain
John 10. 3 and he calleth his own sheep by name
19. 7 We have a law, and by our law he ought
Acts 27. 2 we launched, meaning to sail by the
28. 16 Paul was suffered to dwell by himself
Rom. 2. 7 To them who by patient continuance in
4. 16 (it is) of faith, that (it might be) by grace
11. 24 the olive tree, which is wild by nature
1 Co. 7. 6 by permission..not of commandment
12. 8 the word of knowledge by the same Spirit
14. 27 (let it be) by two, or at the most..three
14. 31 For ye may all prophesy one by one
2 Co. 8. 8 I speak not by commandment, but by
Gal. 2. 2 I went up by revelation..communicated
Eph 3. 3 by revelation he made known unto me
3. 7 given unto me by the effectual working
2 Th. 2. 3 Let no man deceive you by any means
1 Ti. 1. 1 an apostle of Jesus Christ by..command.
5. 21 without preferring..doing nothing by
Heb. 7. 22 By so much was Jesus made a surety of
9. 22 almost all things are by the law purged
10. 8 which are offered by the law
11. 7 heir of the righteousness which is by
3 John 14 Greet the friends by name

24. *Alongside of,* παρά (*dat.*) *para.*
Luke 9. 47 Jesus..took a child, and set him by
John 19. 25 there stood by the cross of Jesus his
1 Co. 16. 2 let every one of you lay by him in store

25. *Alongside of,* παρά (*acc.*) *para.*
Matt. 4. 18 Jesus, walking by the sea of Galilee, saw
Mark 1. 16 as he walked by the sea of Galilee
Luke 5. 1 it came to pass, that..he stood by the
5. 2 And saw two ships standing by the lake
Heb. 11. 12 as the sand which is by the sea shore

26. *Toward, to, at,* πρός (*acc.*) *pros.*
Mark 4. 1 multitude was by the sea on the land
11. 4 found the colt tied by the door without
Luke 22. 56 certain maid beheld him as he sat by
Acts 5. 10 carrying..forth, buried (her) by her

27. *Over, for the sake of,* ὑπέρ (*gen.*) *huper.*
2 Th. 2. 1 by the coming of our Lord Jesus Christ

28. *Under,* ὑπό (*gen.*) *hupo.*
Matt. 2. 17 Then was..that which was spoken [by]
3. 3 this is he that was spoken of [by] the
22. 31 that which was spoken unto you by God
27. 35 [that it might be..which was spoken by]
Mark 5. 4 the chains had been plucked asunder by
13. 14 [abomination of desolation, spoken of by]
Luke 2. 18 things which were told them by the
2. 26 it was revealed unto him by the Holy
3. 19 being reproved by him for Herodias his
5. 15 to be healed [by] him of their infirmities
9. 7 Herod..heard of all that was done [by]
13. 17 all the glorious things that were done by
16. 22 was carried by the angels into Abraham's
21. 16 ye shall be betrayed both by parents
23. 8 hoped to have seen some miracle done by
John 8. 9 [being convicted by..conscience]
Acts 4. 36 Joses, who by the apostles was surnamed
10. 22 was warned from God by an holy angel
13. 4 they, being sent forth by the Holy Ghost
13. 45 spake against those things..spoken by
15. 3 being brought on their way by the church
15. 40 being recommended by the brethren unto
16. 2 Which was well reported of by the bre.
24. 21 I am called in question [by] you this day
25. 14 There is a certain man left in bonds by
27. 11 those things which were spoken by Paul
Rom. 3. 21 being witnessed by the Law and the
15. 24 to be brought on my way thitherward [by]
1 Co. 1. 11 by them..of Chloe, that there are
2 Co. 3. 3 to be the epistle of Christ ministered by
8. 19 which is administered by us to the glory
8. 20 this abundance which is administered by
Eph. 2. 11 by that which is called the circumcision
5. 13 all..made manifest by the light
Phil. 1. 28 in nothing terrified by your adversaries
Col. 2. 18 vainly puffed up by his fleshly mind
2 Tim 2. 26 who are taken captive by him at his will
Heb. 2. 3 confirmed unto us by them that heard
3. 4 For every house is builded by some (man)
2 Pe. 1. 21 (as they were) moved by the Holy Ghost
3. 2 which were spoken before by the holy
Rev. 9. 18 [By] these three was the third part of

BY and by —
1. *At once,* ἐξαυτῆς *exautēs.*
Mark 6. 25 thou give me by and by..the head of
2. *Straightway,* εὐθέως *eutheōs.*
Luke 17 7 which of you..say unto him by and by
21. 9 but the end (is) not by and by
3. *Straightway,* εὐθύς *euthus.*
Matt 13. 21 when [illegible]ulation..ariseth..by and by he

BY selves —
1. *Separately,* לְבַד *le-baa.*
2 Sa. 10. 8 the Syrians..by themselves in the field
2. *Apart,* χωρίς *chōris.*
John 20. 7 wrapped together in a place by itself
3. *Alone,* μόνος *monos.*
Mark 9. 2 leadeth them up..apart by themselves
Luke 24. 12 beheld..linen clothes laid [by themselves]

BY...side —
Alongside of, παρά (*acc.*) *para.*
Matt 13. 1 Jesus out of the house, and sat by..sea si.
13. 4 when he sowed, some..fell by the way si.
13. 19 This is he which received seed by..way si.
20. 30 behold, two blind men sitting by..way si.
Mark 2. 13 he went forth again by the sea side
4. 1 he began again to teach by the sea side
4. 4 as he sowed, some fell by the way side
4. 15 And these are they by the way side
10. 46 blind Bartimeus..sat by the highway side
Luke 8. 5 as he sowed, some fell by the way side
8. 12 Those by the way side are they that hear
18. 35 a certain blind man sat by the way side
Acts. 10. 6 whose house is by the sea side
10. 32 in the house of (one) Simon..by the sea si.
16. 13 we went out of the city by a river side

BY reason of —
1. *Unto,* אֶל *el.*
Eze. 21. 12 terrors by reason of the sword shall be
2. *On, upon,* עַל *al.*
Eze. 28. 17 hast corrupted thy wisdom by reason of
3. *Through, on account of,* διά (*acc.*) *dia.*
John 12. 11 Because that by reason of him many of
Rom. 8. 20; Heb. 5. 14; 2 Pe. 2. 2.

BY this time, By that —
Already, ἤδη *ēdē.*
John 11. 39 Lord, by this time he stinketh
Till, during, עַד *ad.*
Exod 22. 26 thou shalt deliver it unto him by that

BY way of —
In, by, with, ἐν *en.*
2 Pe. 3. 1 I stir up your pure minds by way of

BY ways —
Crooked ways, אֳרָחוֹת עֲקַלְקַלּוֹת *orachoth aqalqalloth.*
Judg. 5. 6 the travellers walked through by ways

BY word —
1. *Word,* מִלָּה *millah.*
Job 30. 9 am I their song; yea, I am their by word
2. *Similitude,* מָשָׁל *mashal.*
Psa. 44. 14 Thou makest us a by word among the
3. *Similitude,* מְשֹׁל *meshol.*
Job 17. 6 He hath made me also a by word of the
4. *Sharp saying,* שְׁנִינָה *sheninah.*
Deut 28. 37 an astonishment..and a by word
1 Ki. 9. 7 Israel shall be a proverb and a by word
2 Ch. 7. 20 and will make it (to be)..a by word

[*See also* Called, charge, close, come, company, constraint, course, divide, fifties, force, fraud, go, hand, hard, heel, thereof, highway, hold, hundreds, inheritance, interpretation, know, lay, lest, means, one, order, pass, protest, reason, roots, sail, set, sevens, side, sit, soothsaying, space, stand, take, trade, way, year.]

C

CAB —
Measure containing above three pints, קַב *qab.*
2 Ki. 6. 25 the fourth part of a cab of dove's dung

CAB'-BON, כַּבּוֹן, Χαβρά, Χαββά *circle, hamlet, hilly.*
A town in the low country of Judah.
Josh. 15. 40 And C., and Lahmam, and Kithlish

CABIN —
Cell, dungeon, vault, חָנוּת *chanuth.*
Jer. 37. 16 Jeremiah was entered..into the cabins

CA'-BUL, כָּבוּל, Χαβώλ *dry, sandy.*
1. A border city of Asher, N.E. of Canaan. Its modern name is Kabûl, 9 miles E. of Akka, and 8 from Jefat. It is on the borders of Galilee.
Josh. 19. 27 and goeth out to C. on the left hand.
2. Name given by Hiram king of Tyre to the twenty cities in the land of Galilee which Solomon gave him, B.C. 1000.
1 Ki. 9. 13 And he called them the land of C.

CÆ'-SAR, Καῖσαρ.
Always in the New Testament, the Roman emperor. To him the Jews paid tribute, and to him those Jews that were "Roman citizens" had the right of appeal.
Matt. 22. 17 Is it lawful to give tribute unto C., or not?
22. 21 They say unto him C.'s. Then saith he
22. 21 Render..unto C. the things which are C.'s
Mark 12. 14 Is it lawful to give tribute to C., or not?
12. 16 And they said unto him, C.'s
12. 17 Render to C. the things that are C's., and
Luke 2. 1 there went out a decree from C. Augustus
3. 1 fifteenth year of the reign of Tiberius C.
20. 22 Is it lawful..to give tribute unto C., or
20. 24 Whose image..hath it? They answ...C.'s
20. 25 Render..unto C. the things which be C.'s
23. 2 found this..forbidding to give..to C.
John 19. 12 the Jews cried..thou art not C.'s friend
19. 12 maketh himself a..speaketh against C.
19. 15 priests answered, We have no king but C.
Acts 11. 28 great dearth..in the days of Claudius [C.]
17. 7 these all do contrary to the decrees of C.
25. 8 nor yet against C., have I offended any
25. 10 Then said Paul, I stand at C.'s judgment
25. 11 if there be none..I appeal unto C.
25. 12 Hast thou ap. unto C.? unto C. shalt
25. 21 to be kept till I..send him to C.
26. 32 if he had not appealed unto C.
27. 24 thou must be brought before C.: and, lo
28. 19 I was constrained to appeal unto C.
Phil. 4. 22 saints salute you..they..of C.'s household

CÆ-SAR-E'-A, Καισάρεια.
A seaport on the Mediterranean, 70 miles N.W. of Jerusalem, on the line of the great road from Tyre to Egypt, and midway between Joppa and Dora. Now entirely desolate. Cæsarea was founded by Herod the Great B.C. 10, and named in honour of Cæsar Augustus. Paul appeared before Felix, and was imprisoned at Cæsarea A.D. 58. It was made a metropolitan see at an early period. Councils were held here in 334 and 358. It must not, however, be confounded with Cæsarea Philippi, another town in Palestine.
Acts 8. 40 preached in all the cities, till he came to C.
9. 30 they brought him down to C., and sent him
10. 1 There was a certain man in C. called Cor.
10. 24 And the morrow after they entered into C.
11. 11 there were three men..sent from C.
12. 19 And he went down from Judea to C.
18. 22 And when he had landed at C., and
21. 8 company departed, and came unto C.
21. 16 There went..of the disciples of C.
23. 23 ready two hundred soldiers to go to C.
23. 33 they came to C., and..presented Paul
25. 1 after three days he ascended from C. to
25. 4 Paul should be kept at C., and that he
25. 6 tarried..ten days, he went. unto C.
25. 13 Bernice came unto C. to salute Festus

CÆ-SAR-E-A PHIL-IP'-PI, Καισάρεια ἡ Φιλίππου *Caesarea of Philip.*
A town near the source of the Jordan, in the extreme N. of Canaan, and the most northerly point of Christ's journeys. It stands at the easternmost and most important of the two main sources of the Jordan—the other being *Tell-el-Kadi.* It is now called *Banias,* from the medieval *Paneas,* and is about 30 miles from Tyre, 50 from Damascus, and 120 from Jerusalem.
Matt 16. 13 Jesus came into the coasts of C. P.
Mark 8. 27 Jesus went..into the towns of C. P.

CAGE —
1. *Cage, basket,* כְּלוּב *kelub.*
Jer. 5. 27 As a cage is full of birds, so (are) their
2. *Watch, guard, ward,* φυλακή *phulakē.*
Rev. 18. 2 a cage of every unclean and hateful bird

CAI-A'-PHAS, Καϊάφας *depression*.
The high priest of the Jews who presided at the trial of Jesus.
Matt26. 3 assembled..priests..unto the palace of C.
26. 57 they..led (him) away to C. the high priest
Luke 3. 2 Annas and C. being the high priests, the
John 11. 49 one of them..C..said unto them, Ye
18. 13 Annas..was father-in-law to C., which
18. 14 C. was he which gave counsel to the Jews
18. 24 Annas..sent him bound unto C. the high
18. 28 Then led they Jesus from C. unto the
Acts 4. 6 C., and John, and Alexander, and as

CA'-IN, קַיִן, Κάϊν *acquisition*.
1. Eldest son of Adam and Eve.
Gen. 4. 1 and she conceived, and bare C., and said
4. 2 but C. was a tiller of the ground
4. 3 C. brought..an offering unto the LORD
4. 5 unto C. and to his offering he had not
4. 5 C. was very wroth, and his countenance
4. 6 the LORD said unto C., Why art thou
4. 8 And C. talked with Abel his brother
4. 8 C. rose up against Abel his..and slew
4. 9 And the LORD said unto Cain, Where (is)
4. 13 C. said..My punishment (is) greater than
4. 15 whosoever slayeth C., vengeance shall be
4. 15 the LORD set a mark upon C., lest any
4. 16 C. went out from the presence of the LORD
4. 17 C. knew his wife; and she conceived, and
4. 24 If C. shall be avenged sevenfold, truly
4. 25 instead of Abel, whom C. slew
Heb. 11. 4 offered..a more..sacrifice than C. by
1 Jo. 3. 12 Not as C., (who)..slew his brother
Jude 11 they have gone in the way of C.
2. A town in the S. of Judah (properly "the Cain"), of which no one has traced the site.
Josh. 15. 57 C., Gibeah, and Timnah; ten cities with
3. The people mentioned in Balaam's prophecy as *Kenite* is in Hebrew called *Kain* (קַיִן), identical with *Cain*.
Num24. 22 Nevertheless the K. shall be wasted
Judg. 4. 11 Heber the K...severed himself from the

CAI'-NAN, KE'-NAN, קֵינָן *acquisition*, Καϊνάν.
1. A son of Enos, son of Seth, B.C. 3679.
Gen. 5. 9 And Enos lived ninety years, and begat C.
5. 10 Enos lived after he begat C. eight hundred
5. 12 And C. lived seventy years, and begat
5. 13 C. lived after he begat Mahalaleel eight
5. 14 the days of C. were nine hundred and
1 Ch. 1. 2 K., Mahalaleel, Jered
Luke 3. 37 Maleleel, which was (the son) of C.
2. A son of Arphaxad, B.C. 2000.
Luke 3. 36 Which was..of C., which was..of Arph.

CAKE —
1. *A perforated cake*, חַלָּה *challah*.
Exod29. 2 cakes unleavened tempered with oil, and
29. 23 one loaf of bread, and one cake of oiled
Lev. 2. 4 (it shall be) unleavened cakes of fine flour
7. 12 he shall offer..unleavened cakes mingled
7. 12 cakes mingled with oil, of fine flour, fried
7. 13 Besides the cakes, he shall offer (for) his
8. 26 he took one unleavened cake, and a cake
24. 5 take fine flour, and bake twelve cakes
24. 5 two tenth deals shall be in one cake
Num. 6. 15 cakes of fine flour mingled with oil, and
6. 19 one unleavened cake out of the basket
15. 20 Ye shall offer up a cake of the first of
2 Sa. 6. 19 to every one a cake of bread, and a good
2. *Cake baked on hot stones*, מָעוֹג *maog*.
1 Ki 17. 12 LORD thy God liveth, I have not a cake
3. *Cake baked on hot stones*, עֻגָה, עֻגָּה *ugah, uggah*.
Exod12. 39 they baked unleavened cakes of the
Num 11. 8 baked (it) in pans, and made cakes of it
1 Ki. 17. 13 but make me thereof a little cake first, and
19. 6 and, behold..a cake baken on the coals
Eze. 4. 12 thou shalt eat it (as) barley cakes, and
Hos. 7. 8 Ephraim is a cake not turned
4. *Round cake*, צְלִיל [V.L. צְלוּל *tselul*] *tselil*.
Judg. 7. 13 a cake of barley bread tumbled into the
5. *Thin cake*, רָקִיק *raqiq*.
1 Ch. 23. 29 for the unleavened cakes, and for (that)

CAKE of figs —
Lump of dry figs, דְּבֵלָה *debelah*.
1 Sa. 25. 18 two hundred cakes of figs, and laid (them)
30. 12 they gave him a piece of a cake of figs
1 Ch. 12. 40 (and) meat, meal, cakes of figs, and bun.

CAKE upon the hearth —
Cake baked on hot stones, עֻגָה *ugah*.
Gen. 18. 6 knead..and make cakes upon the hearth

CAKES —
1. *Cakes (with marks on them)*, כַּוָּנִים *kavvanim*.
Jer. 7. 18 the women knead..dough, to make cakes
44. 19 did we make her cakes to worship her
2. *Cakes (of the shape of a heart)*, לְבִבוֹת *lebiboth*.
2 Sa. 13. 6 make me a couple of cakes in my sight
13. 8 she took flour..and did bake the cakes
13. 10 Tamar took the cakes which she had

CAKES, to make —
To make cakes in the shape of a heart, לָבַב *labab*, 3.
2 Sa. 13. 8 and made cakes in his sight, and did bake

CAKES, unleavened —
Cake pressed out, מַצָּה *matstsah*.
Josh. 5. 11 unleavened cakes, and parched (corn) in
Judg. 6. 19 unleavened cakes of an ephah of flour
6. 20 Take the flesh and the unleavened cakes
6. 21 touched the flesh and the unleavened cakes
6. 21 consumed the flesh and the unleavened ca.

CA'-LAH, כֶּלַח *firm*.
One of the most ancient cities of Assyria. It was founded by Asshur. The site is marked by the *Nimrûd* ruins, which have furnished a large proportion of the Assyrian remains now in Britain. It was the capital of the Assyrian empire (B.C. 930–720), and was the residence of Sardanapalus and his successors down to the time of Sargon, who built a new capital, which he called by his own name, on the site of the modern *Khorsabad*.
Gen. 10. 11 Asshur..builded..the city..C.
10. 12 And Resen between Nineveh and C.

CALAMITY —
1. *Calamity, mist, vapour*, איד *ed*.
Deut.32. 35 for the day of their calamity (is) at hand
2 Sa. 22. 19 prevented me in the day of my calamity
Psa. 18. 18 They prevented me in..day of my calam.
Prov. 1. 26 I also will laugh at your calamity; I will
6. 15 Therefore shall his calamity come sud.
17. 5 he that is glad at calamities shall not
24. 22 For their calamity shall rise suddenly
27. 10 neither go..in the day of thy calamity
Jer. 18. 17 I will show them..day of their calamity
46. 21 the day of their calamity was come upon
48. 16 The calamity of Moab (is) near to come
49. 8 I will bring the calamity of Esau upon
49. 32 I will bring their calamity from all sides
Eze. 35. 5 shed (the blood)..in the time of their cal.
Obad.13,13, 13 Thou shouldest not..in..their calamity
2. *Accident, misfortune*, הַוָּה *havvah* [twice V.L. הַיָּה].
Job 6. 2 my calamity laid in the balances together
30. 13 They mar my path..set forward my cal.
Psa. 57. 1 make my refuge, until (these) calamities
Prov 19. 13 A foolish son (is) the calamity of his
3. *Evil, bad*, רַע *ra*.
Psa 141. 5 my prayer also..in their calamities

CALAMUS —
A reed, cane, קָנֶה *qaneh*.
Exod30. 23 sweet calamus two hundred and fifty
Song 4. 14 Spikenard and saffron; calamus and cin.
Eze. 27. 19 cassia, and calamus were in thy market

CAL'-COL, כַּלְכֹּל *sustaining*.
A son of Zerah, the son of Judah by his daughter-in-law Tamar, B.C 1680. See *Chalcol*, which in Hebrew is identical with *Calcol*.
1 Ch. 2. 6 sons of Zerah..Heman, and C., and Dara

CALDRON —
1. *Caldron*, אַגְמוֹן *agmon*.
Job 41. 20 (out) of a seething pot or caldron
2. *Kettle, basket*, דּוּד *dud*.
2 Ch. 35. 13 in caldrons, and in pans, and divided
3. *Pot*, סִיר *sir*.
Jer. 52. 18 The caldrons also, and the shovels, and
52. 19 fire pans, and the bowls, and the caldrons
Eze. 11. 3 this (city is) the caldron, and we (be) the
11. 7 they (are) the flesh..(city is) the caldron
11. 11 This (city) shall not be your caldron
4. *Caldron*, קַלַּחַת *qallachath*.
1 Sa. 2. 14 And he struck (it) into the..caldron
Mic. 3. 3 for the pot, and as flesh within the cald.

CA'-LEB, כָּלֵב *bold, impetuous*.
1. A son of Jephunneh, by which patronymic he is usually designated. He is mentioned among the chiefs sent to spy out Canaan, and with Joshua brought back a favourable report (B.C. 1490). He was a prince of Judah, as chief of the Hezronites, while Nahshon was Prince of the whole tribe. When 85 years of age he claimed possession of the land of the Anakims, Kirjath-arba or Hebron and the neighbouring hill-country, which was granted, and he courageously took possession of it, driving out the three sons of Anak, B.C. 1444.
Num 13. 6 Of the tribe of Judah, C. the son of Jeph.
13. 30 And C. stilled the people before Moses
14. 6 Joshua..and C...rent their clothes
14. 24 my servant C...him will I bring into the
14. 30 ye shall not come into the land..save C.
14. 38 and C. the son of Jephunneh..lived (still)
26. 65 there was not left a man..save C. the
32. 12 Save C. the son of Jephunneh the Kene.
34. 19 Of the tribe of Judah, C. the son of Jeph.
Deut. 1. 36 Save C. the son of Jephunneh; he shall
Josh.14. 6 C. the son of Jephunneh the Kenezite
14. 13 gave unto C. the son of Jephunneh Heb.
14. 14 Hebron..became the inheritance of C.
15. 13 unto C. the son of Jephunneh he gave a
15. 14 C. drove thence the three sons of Anak
15. 16 And C. said, He that smiteth Kirjath.
15. 17 the son of Kenaz, the brother of C., took
15. 18 and C. said unto her, What wouldest
21. 12 gave they to C. the son of Jephunneh
Judg. 1. 12 And C. said, He that smiteth Kirjath.
1. 13 Othniel the son of Kenaz, C.'s younger
1. 14 and C. said unto her, What wilt thou?
1. 15 C. gave her the upper springs and the
1. 20 they gave Hebron unto C., as Moses
3. 9 Othniel the son of Kenaz, C.'s younger
1 Sa 25. 3 (was) churlish..and he..of..house of C.
30. 14 made an invasion (upon)..the south of C.
1 Ch. 2. 46 Ephah, C.'s concubine, bare Haran, and
2. 48 Maachah, C.'s concubine, bare Sheber
1 Ch. 2. 49 and the daughter of C. (was) Achsa
4. 15 sons of C. the son of Jephunneh; Iru
6. 56 they gave to C. the son of Jephunneh
2. Son of Hezron son of Pharez son of Judah, and father of Hur by Ephrath or Ephratah, and so grandfather of Caleb the spy (No. 1.) There is some confusion about this Caleb. B.C. 1530–1430.
1 Ch. 2. 18 And C. the son of Hezron begat..of Azu.
2. 19 C. took unto him Ephrath, which bare
2. 42 the sons of C. the brother of Jerahmeel
3. Son of Hur son of Caleb (No. 2.) B.C. 1500.
1 Ch. 2. 50 These were the sons of C. the son of Hur

CA-LEB EPH-RA'-TAH, כָּלֵב אֶפְרָתָה.
A place near Bethlehem-Judah, supposed to have been named after Caleb and his wife Ephratah.
1 Ch. 2. 24 after that Hezron was dead in C.-e.

CALF —
Calf, the young of the herd, fed on milk and the branches of trees, fattened in stalls, offered in sacrifice when a year old, and considered a delicacy. It was worshipped in Egypt, which induced the impatient Israelites to demand that Aaron should make one that should go before them. This he did of the women's ornaments. It was molten in the fire, fashioned with a graving tool, an altar built to it, and worshipped with revelry. Jeroboam (B.C. 970) made two of gold, which he placed in Bethel and Dan, the extreme limits of his kingdom, appointed priests, built altars, and offered sacrifices. This, though denounced by a prophet, was carried on by every succeeding king of Israel, and became the great sin of Israel, for which they were punished, carried into Assyria, and finally perished in oblivion.
1. *Son of the herd*, בֶּן־בָּקָר *ben baqar*.
Gen. 18. 7 fetched a calf tender; 18. 8; 1 Sa. 14. 32.
1a. *Son*, בֵּן *ben*.
1 Sam. 6. 7 bring their calves home; 6. 10.
2. *Calf, heifer*, עֵגֶל *egel*.
Exod32. 4 after he had made it a molten calf
32. 8 they have made them a molten calf, and
32. 19 as soon as he came nigh..he saw the calf
32. 20 took the calf which they had made, and
32. 24 I cast it..and there came out this calf
32. 35 because they made the calf which Aaron
Lev. 9. 3 a calf and a lamb, (both) of the first year
9. 8 slew the calf of the sin-offering which
Deut. 9. 16 (and) had made you a molten calf
9. 21 I took your sin, the calf which ye had
1 Sa. 28. 24 the women had a fat calf in the house
1 Ki.12. 28 made two calves (of) gold, and said unto
12. 32 sacrificing unto the calves that he had
2 Ki.10. 29 (to wit), the golden calves that (were) in
17. 16 made them molten images..two calves
2 Ch.11. 15 and for the calves which he had made
13. 8 (there are) with you golden calves, which
Neh. 9. 18 when they had made them a molten calf
Psa. 29. 6 He maketh them also to skip like a calf
68. 30 the multitude of the bulls, with the calves
106. 19 They made a calf in Horeb..worshipped
Isa. 11. 6 the calf and the young lion and the
27. 10 there shall the calf feed, and there shall
Jer. 34. 18 when they cut the calf in twain, and
34. 19 which passed between..parts of the calf
Eze. 1. 7 their feet (was) like the sole of a calf's
Hos. 8. 5 Thy calf, O Samaria, hath cast (thee) off
8. 6 the calf of Samaria shall be broken in
13. 2 Let the men that sacrifice kiss the calves
Amos 6. 4 the calves out of the midst of the stall
Mic. 6. 6 shall I come before him..with calves of
Mal. 4. 2 and grow up as calves of the stall
3. *Calf*, עֶגְלָה *eglah*.
Hos. 10. 5 inhabitants..shall fear because of..calves
4. *A young bull, produce*, פַּר, פָּר *par*.
Hos. 14. 2 so will we render the calves of our lips
5. *A young calf*, μόσχος *moschos*.
Luke15. 23 bring hither the fatted calf, and kill (it)
15. 27 and thy father hath killed the fatted calf
15. 30 thou hast killed for him the fatted calf
Heb. 9. 12 Neither by the blood of goats and calves
9. 19 he took the blood of calves and of goats
Rev. 4. 7 and the second beast like a calf

CALF, to make a —
To make a calf, μοσχοποιέω *moschopoieō*.
Acts 7. 41 And they made a calf in those days

CALF, young —
A heifer, son of the herd, עֵגֶל בֶּן־בָּקָר *egel ben baqar*.
Lev. 9. 2 Take thee a young calf for a sin offering

CALKER —
Repairers of a breach, מַחֲזִיקֵי בֶדֶק [*chazaq* (5) *bedeq*].
Eze. 27. 9 wise (men) thereof were in thee..calkers
27. 27 calkers, and the occupiers of thy merch.

CALL, to —
1. *To say*, אָמַר *amar*.
Isa. 5. 20 Woe unto them that call evil good, and
Lam. 2. 15 that (men) call The perfection of beauty
2. *To cause to come in*, בּוֹא *bo*, 5.
Esth. 5. 10 he sent and called for his friends, and
3. *To cry (for help)*, זָעַק *zaaq*.
Judg 12. 2 when I called you, ye delivered me not
4. *To cause to cry (for help)*, זָעַק *zaaq*, 5.
Judg. 4. 10 Barak called Zebulun and Naphtali to

5. *To call, name,* קָרָא *qara.*

Gen. 1. 5 called the light Day..darkness he called
1. 8 And God called the firmament Heaven
1. 10 And God called the dry (land) Earth
1. 10 gathering..of the waters called he seas
2. 19 brought (them)..to see what he would call
2. 19 whatsoever Adam called every living
3. 9 the LORD God called unto Adam, and
3. 20 Adam called his wife's name Eve
4. 17 he builded a city, and called the name
4. 25 she bare a son, and called his name Seth
4. 26 and he called his name Enos
4. 26 then began men to call upon the name of
5. 2 and blessed them, and called their name
5. 3 begat (a son)..and called his name Seth
5. 29 called his name Noah, saying, This (same)
11. 9 Therefore is the name of it called Babel
12. 8 and called upon the name of the LORD
12. 18 Pharoah called Abram, and said, What
13. 4 there Abram called on the name of the
16. 11 bear a son..shalt call his name Ishmael
16. 13 she called the name of the LORD that
16. 15 and Abram called his son's name..Ish.
17. 15 thou shalt not call her name Sarai, but
17. 19 thou shalt call his name Isaac: and I will
19. 5 they called unto Lot, and said unto him
19. 37 bare a son, and called his name Moab
19. 38 bare a son, and called his name Ben-ammi
20. 8 called all his servants, and told all
20. 9 Abimelech called Abraham, and said
21. 3 Abraham called the name of his son..Is.
21. 17 the angel of God called to Hagar out of
21. 31 Wherefore he called that place Beer-sheba
21. 33 and called there on the name of the LORD
22. 11 the angel of the LORD called unto him
22. 14 Abraham called..that place Jehovah-ji.
22. 15 the angel of the LORD called unto Abra.
24. 57 they said, We will call the damsel, and
24. 58 they called Rebekah, and said unto her
25. 25 and they called his name Esau
26. 9 Abimelech called Isaac, and said, Behold
26. 18 and he called their names after the
26. 18 by which his father had called them
26. 20 and he called the name of the well Esek
26. 21 and he called the name of it Sitnah
26. 22 and he called the name of it Rehoboth
26. 25 and called upon the name of the LORD
26. 33 he called it Shebah..the name of the
27. 1 he called Esau his eldest son, and said
27. 42 and she..called Jacob her younger son
28. 1 Isaac called Jacob, and blessed him
28. 19 he called the name of that place Beth-el
29. 32 bare a son, and she called his name Reu.
29. 33 bare a son..and she called his name Sim.
29. 35 therefore she called his name Judah
30. 6 God..given me a son: therefore called
30. 8 and she called his name Naphtali
30. 11 A troop cometh: and she called his
30. 13 and she called his name Asher
30. 18 and she called his name Issachar
30. 20 and she called his name Zebulun
30. 21 she bare a daughter, and called her name
30. 24 she called his name Joseph; and said
31. 4 Jacob sent and called Rachel and Leah
31. 47 Laban called it Jegar-sahadutha
31. 47 but Jacob called it Galeed
31. 54 Then Jacob..called his brethren to eat
32. 2 and he called the name..Mahanaim
32. 30 Jacob called the name of the place Peniel
33. 20 an altar, and called it El-elohe-Israel
35. 7 he built there an altar, and called the
35. 10 and he called his name Israel
35. 15 Jacob called the name of the place
35. 18 as her soul was in departing..she called
35. 18 but his father called him Benjamin
38. 3 and he called his name Er
38. 4 and she called his name Onan
38. 5 bare a son; and called his name Shelah
39. 14 That she called unto the men of her house
41. 8 he sent and called for all the magicians
41. 14 Then Pharaoh sent and called Joseph
41. 45 And..called Joseph's name Zaphnath.
41. 51 And Joseph called the name of the first
41. 52 the name of the second called he Ephr.
46. 33 when Pharaoh shall call you, and shall
47. 29 he called his son Joseph, and said unto
49. 1 Jacob called unto his sons, and said
Exod. 1. 18 the king of Egypt called for..midwives
2. 7 Shall I go and call to thee a nurse of
2. 8 the maid went and called the child's
2. 10 she called his name Moses: and she
2. 20 call him, that he may eat bread
2. 22 she bare (him) a son, and he called his
3. 4 God called unto him out of the midst of
7. 11 Pharaoh also called the wise men and
8. 8 Pharaoh called for Moses and Aaron
8. 25 Pharaoh called for Moses and for Aaron
9. 27 Pharaoh sent, and called for Moses and
10. 16 Then Pharaoh called for Moses and Aaron
10. 24 Pharaoh called unto Moses, and said
12. 21 Moses called for all the elders of Israel
12. 31 he called for Moses and Aaron by night
16. 31 Israel called the name thereof Manna
17. 7 he called the name of the place Massah
17. 15 Moses built an altar, and called the
19. 3 the LORD called unto him out of the
19. 7 Moses came and called for the elders of
19. 20 the LORD called Moses (up) to the top of
24. 16 the seventh day he called unto Moses
31. 2 I have called by name Bezaleel the son of
33. 7 and called it the Tabernacle of the Con.
Exod 34. 15 and do sacrifice unto their gods, and..call
34. 31 Moses called unto them; and Aaron and
35. 30 the LORD hath called by name Bezaleel
36. 2 Moses called Bezaleel and Aholiab, and
Lev. 1. 1 the LORD called unto Moses, and spake
9. 1 (that) Moses called Aaron and his sons
10. 4 Moses called Mishael and Elzaphan, the
Num 11. 3 he called the name of the place Taberah
11. 34 he called..that place Kibroth-hattaavah
12. 5 called Aaron and Miriam..both came
13. 16 Moses called Oshea the son of Nun, Jeh.
16. 12 Moses sent to call Dathan and Abiram
21. 3 he called the name of the place Hormah
22. 5 He sent messengers..to call him
22. 20 If the men come to call thee, rise up
22. 37 Did I not earnestly send unto thee to call
24. 10 Balak said..I called thee to curse mine
25. 2 they called the people unto the sacrifices
32. 41 Jair..took..and called them Havoth-jair
32. 42 and called it Nobah, after his own name
Deut. 2. 11 but the Moabites call them Emims
2. 20 the Ammonites call them Zamzummims
3. 9 (Which) Hermon the Sidonians call Sirion
3. 9 and the Amorites call it Shenir
3. 14 and called them after his own name
4. 7 in all (things that) we call upon him (for)?
5. 1 Moses called all Israel, and said unto
25. 8 the elders of his city shall call him, and
29. 2 Moses called unto all Israel, and said
31. 7 Moses called unto Joshua, and said unto
31. 14 call Joshua, and present yourselves in
33. 19 They shall call the people unto the mount.
Josh. 4. 4 Joshua called the twelve men, whom he
6. 6 Joshua the son of Nun called the priests
9. 22 Joshua called for them, and he spake unto
10. 24 Joshua called for all the men of Israel
19. 47 and called Leshem, Dan, after the name
22. 1 Joshua called the Reubenites, and the
22. 34 the children of Reuben..called the altar
23. 2 Joshua called for all Israel, (and) for
24. 1 Joshua..called for the elders of Israel
24. 9 sent and called Balaam the son of Beor
Judg. 1. 26 and built a city, and called the name
2. 5 they called the name of that place Boch.
4. 6 she sent and called Barak the son of A.
6. 24 Gideon built an altar..and called it Jeh.
6. 32 on that day he called him Jerubbaal
8. 1 Why..served us thus, that thou calledst
9. 54 he called hastily unto the young man his
12. 1 and didst not call us to go with thee?
13. 24 the woman bare a son, and called his
14. 15 have ye called us to take that we have?
15. 17 and called that place Ramath-lehi
15. 18 he was sore athirst, and called on the
15. 19 wherefore he called..name..En-hakkore
16. 18 she sent and called for the lords of the
16. 19 she called for a man, and she caused him
16. 25 came to pass..they said, Call for Samson
16. 25 they called for Samson out of the prison
16. 28 Samson called unto the LORD, and said
18. 12 they called that place Mahaneh-dan unto
18. 29 they called the name of the city Dan
21. 13 and to call peaceably unto them
Ruth 1. 20 she said unto them, Call me not Naomi
1. 21 why (then) call ye me Naomi, seeing the
4. 17 There is a son born..and they called his
1 Sa. 1. 20 that she bare a son, and called his name
3. 4 the LORD called Samuel: and he answered
3. 5 and said, Here (am) I; for thou calledst
3. 5 And he said, I called not, lie down again
3. 6 Here (am) I; for thou didst call me
3. 6 he answered, I called not, my son; lie
3. 8 the LORD called Samuel again the third
3. 8 Eli perceived that the LORD had called
3. 9 if he call thee, that thou shalt say, Speak
3. 10 the LORD came..and called as at other
3. 16 Then Eli called Samuel, and said, Samuel
6. 2 the Philistines called for the priests and
7. 12 and called the name of it Eben-ezer, saying
9. 26 that Samuel called Saul to the top of the
12. 17 I will call unto the LORD, and he shall
12. 18 So Samuel called unto the LORD; and the
16. 3 call Jesse to the sacrifice, and I will
16. 5 he sanctified..and called them to the
16. 8 Jesse called Abinadab, and made him
19. 7 Jonathan called David, and Jonathan
22. 11 the king sent to call Ahimelech the priest
28. 15 I have called thee, that thou mayest
29. 6 Achish called David, and said unto him
2 Sa. 1. 7 he saw me, and called unto me: and I
1. 15 David called one of the young men, and
2. 26 Then Abner called to Joab, and said
5. 9 David dwelt in the fort, and called it, The
5. 20 Therefore he called the name of that
6. 8 and he called the name of the place Per.
9. 2 when they had called him unto David
9. 9 Then the king called to Ziba, Saul's
11. 13 when David had called him, he did eat
12. 24 she bare a son, and called his name
12. 25 he called his name Jedidiah, because
13. 17 he called his servant that ministered
14. 33 when he had called for Absalom, he came
15. 2 then Absalom called unto him, and said
17. 5 Then said Absalom, Call now Hushai
18. 18 he called the pillar after his own name
18. 26 the watchman called unto the porter
18. 28 Ahimaaz called, and said unto the king
21. 2 the king called the Gibeonites, and said
22. 4 I will call on the LORD, (who is)
22. 7 In my distress I called upon the LORD
1 Ki. 1. 9 called all his brethren the king's sons
1. 10 But Nathan the prophet..he called not
1 Ki. 1. 19 hath called all the sons of the king, and
1. 19 Solomon thy servant hath he not called
1. 25 hath called all the king's sons, and the
1. 26 But me, (even) me..hath he not called
1. 28 king David..said, Call me Bath-sheba
1. 32 Call me Zadok the priest, and Nathan
2. 36 the king sent and called for Shimei, and
2. 42 And the king sent and called for Shimei
7. 21 he set up the right pillar, and called the
7. 21 he set up the left pillar, and called the
8. 43 according to all that the stranger calleth
8. 52 to hearken unto them in all that they call
9. 13 he called them the land of Cabul unto
12. 3 That they sent and called him
12. 20 sent and called him unto the congregation
16. 24 and called the name of the city which he
17. 10 he called to her, and said, Fetch me, I
17. 11 as she was going to fetch (it), he called to
18. 3 And Ahab called Obadiah, which (was)
18. 24 call ye on the name of your gods
18. 24 and I will call on the name of the LORD
18. 25 call on the name of your gods, but put no
18. 26 called on the name of Baal from morning
20. 7 the king of Israel called all the elders
22. 9 Then the king of Israel called an officer
22. 13 the messenger that was gone to call Mic.
2 Ki. 3. 10 that the LORD hath called these three
3. 13 for the LORD hath called these three kings
4. 12 he said to Gehazi..Call this Shunammite
4. 12 when he had called her, she stood before
4. 15 said, Call her. And when he had called
4. 22 she called unto her husband, and said
4. 36 he called Gehazi, and said, Call this Shu.
4. 36 Call this Shunammite. So he called her
5. 11 and call on the name of the LORD his God
6. 11 he called his servants, and said unto
7. 10 So they came and called unto the porter
7. 11 he called the porters; and they told (it)
8. 1 for the LORD hath called for a famine
9. 1 Elisha the prophet called one of the
10. 19 therefore call unto me all the prophets
12. 7 Then king Jehoash called for Jehoiada
14. 7 and called the name of it Joktheel unto
18. 4 and he called it Nehushtan
18. 18 when they had called to the king, there
1 Ch. 4. 9 his mother called his name Jabez, saying
4. 10 Jabez called on the God of Israel, saying
7. 16 Maachah..bare a son, and she called his
7. 23 he called his name Beriah, because it
11. 7 therefore they called it the city of David
14. 11 called the name of that place Baal-pera.
15. 11 David called for Zadok and Abiathar the
16. 8 Give thanks unto the LORD, call upon his
21. 26 David built there an altar..and called
22. 6 he called for Solomon his son, and
2 Ch. 3. 17 called the name of that on the right hand
6. 33 all that the stranger calleth to thee for
10. 3 And they sent and called him
18. 8 the king of Israel called for one
18. 12 the messenger that went to call Micaiah
24. 6 the king called for Jehoiada the chief
Neh. 5. 12 I called the priests, and took an oath of
Esth. 4. 5 Then called Esther for Hatach, (one) of
9. 26 Wherefore they called these days Purim
Job 1. 4 sent and called for their three sisters, to
5. 1 Call now, if there be any that will answer
9. 16 If I had called, and he had answered me
12. 4 who calleth upon God, and he answereth
13. 22 Then call thou, and I will answer
14. 15 Thou shalt call, and I will answer thee
19. 16 I called my servant, and he gave (me) no
27. 10 will he always call upon God?
42. 14 he called the name of the first, Jemima
Psa. 4. 1 Hear me when I call, O God of my right.
4. 3 the LORD will hear when I call unto him
14. 4 and call not upon the LORD
17. 6 I have called upon thee, for thou wilt
18. 3 I will call upon the LORD, (who is) worthy
18. 6 In my distress I called upon the LORD
20. 9 let the King hear us when we call
31. 17 for I have called upon thee: let the
42. 7 Deep calleth unto deep at the noise of
49. 11 they call (their) lands after their own
50. 1 and called the earth, from the rising of
50. 4 He shall call to the heavens from above
50. 15 And call upon me in the day of trouble
53. 4 they have not called upon God
55. 16 As for me, I will call upon God; and
79. 6 that have not called upon thy name
80. 18 quicken us, and we will call upon thy
81. 7 Thou calledst in trouble, and I delivered
86. 5 plenteous in mercy unto all them that call
86. 7 In the day of my trouble I will call upon
88. 9 LORD, I have called daily upon thee
91. 15 He shall call upon me, and I will answer
99. 6 and Samuel among them that call upon
99. 6 they called upon the LORD, and he answ.
102. 2 in the day (when) I call answer me
105. 1 call upon his name: make known his
105. 16 he called for a famine upon the land
116. 2 will I call upon (him) as long as I live
116. 4 Then called I upon the name of the LORD
116. 13 and call upon the name of the LORD
116. 17 and will call upon the name of the LORD
118. 5 I called upon the LORD in distress
145. 18 The LORD (is) nigh unto all them that call
145. 18 to all that call upon him in truth
147. 4 he calleth them by all (their) names
Prov. 1. 24 Because I have called, and ye refused; I
1. 28 Then shall they call upon me, but I will
7. 4 and call understanding (thy) kinswoman
8. 4 Unto you, O men, I call; and my voice

Prov. 9. 15 To call passengers who go right on their
18. 6 and his mouth calleth for strokes
Song 5. 6 I called him, but he gave me no answer
Isa. 7. 14 bear a son, and shall call his name Im.
8. 3 Call his name Mahar-shalal-hash-baz.
12. 4 say, Praise the LORD, call upon his name
13. 3 I have also called my mighty ones for
21. 11 He calleth to me out of Seir, Watchman
22. 12 in that day did the Lord GOD of hosts call
22. 20 I will call my servant Eliakim the son
34. 12 They shall call the nobles..the kingdom
40. 26 he calleth them all by names by the
41. 2 called him to his foot, gave the nations
41. 4 calling the generations from the begin.
41. 9 and called thee from the chief men
41. 25 from the rising of the sun shall he call
42. 6 I..have called thee in righteousness
43. 1 I have called (thee) by thy name; thou
43. 22 But thou hast not called upon me, O Ja.
44. 5 another shall call (himself) by the name
44. 7 And who, as I, shall call, and shall
45. 3 I..which call (thee) by thy name, (am)
45. 4 I have even called thee by thy name
46. 11 Calling a ravenous bird from the east
48. 13 (when) I call unto them, they stand up
48. 15 I, (even) I, have spoken; yea, I have called
49. 1 The LORD hath called me from the
50. 2 when I called, (was there) none to
51. 2 for I called him alone, and blessed him
54. 6 the LORD hath called thee as a woman
55. 5 thou shalt call a nation..thou knowest
55. 6 call ye upon him while he is near
58. 5 wilt thou call this..an acceptable day
58. 9 shalt thou call, and the LORD shall answer
58. 13 and call the sabbath a delight, the holy
59. 4 None calleth for justice, nor (any) pleadeth
60. 14 they shall call thee, The city of the LORD
60. 18 but thou shalt call thy walls Salvation
61. 6 (men) shall call you the Ministers of our
62. 12 And they shall call them, The holy
64. 7 And (there is) none that calleth upon thy
65. 12 because when I called, ye did not answer
65. 15 and call his servants by another name
65. 24 that before they call, I will answer; and
66. 4 because when I called, none did answer
Jer. 1. 15 I will call all the families of the kingdoms
3. 17 they shall call Jerusalem the throne of
3. 19 and I said, Thou shalt call me, My father
6. 30 Reprobate silver shall (men) call them
7. 13 and I called you, but ye answered not
7. 27 thou shalt also call unto them; but they
9. 17 Consider ye, and call for the mourning
10. 25 upon the families that call not on thy
11. 16 The LORD called thy name, A green olive
12. 6 yea, they have called a multitude after
20. 3 LORD hath not called thy name Pashur
29. 12 Then shall ye call upon me, and ye shall
30. 17 because they called thee an Outcast
33. 3 Call unto me, and I will answer thee
35. 17 I have called..but they have..answered
36. 4 Then Jeremiah called Baruch the son of
42. 8 Then called he Johanan..son of Kareah
Lam. 1. 15 he hath called an assembly against me
1. 19 I called for my lovers, (but) they deceived
1. 21 wilt bring the day (that) thou hast called
2. 22 Thou hast called as in a solemn day my
3. 55 I called upon thy name, O LORD, out of
3. 57 I called upon thee: thou saidst, Fear
Eze. 9. 3 he called to the man clothed with linen
36. 29 I will call for the corn, and will increase
38. 21 I will call for a sword against him
39. 11 they shall call (it), The valley of Hamon.
Dan. 2. 2 the king commanded to call the magicians
8. 16 I heard a man's voice..which called, and
Hos. 1. 4 the LORD said..Call his name Jezreel
1. 6 (God) said..Call her name Lo-ruhamah
1. 9 Then said (God), Call his name Lo-ammi
2. 16 it shall be..(that) thou shalt call me Ishi
2. 16 and shalt call me no more Baali
7. 7 (there is) none among them that calleth
7. 11 they call to Egypt, they go to Assyria
11. 1 and called my son out of Egypt
11. 2 (As) they called them, so they went from
11. 7 though they called them to the Most
Joel 1. 14 Sanctify ye a fast, call a solemn assembly
2. 15 sanctify a fast, call a solemn assembly
2. 32 whosoever shall call on..name of the
2. 32 in the remnant whom the LORD shall call
Amos 5. 8 that calleth for the waters of the sea
5. 16 they shall call the husbandman
7. 4 behold, the Lord GOD called to contend
9. 6 he that calleth for the waters of the sea
Jon. 1. 6 O sleeper? arise, call upon thy God, if so
Zeph. 3. 9 that they may all call upon the name of
Hag. 1. 11 I called for a drought upon the land, and
Zech. 3. 10 shall ye call every man his neighbour
11. 7 I took unto me two staves..one I called
11. 7 the other I called Bands; and I fed the
13. 9 they shall call on my name, and I will
Mal. 1. 4 shall call them, The border of wickedness

6. *To say, speak,* εἶπον *eipon.*
John10. 35 If he called them gods unto whom the

7. *To call upon,* ἐπικαλέω *epikaleō.*
2 Co. 1. 23 Moreover I call God for a record upon

8. *To say, speak,* ἐρῶ *erō.*
John15. 15 but I have called you friends; for all

9. *To call, name,* καλέω *kaleō.*
Matt. 1. 21 thou shalt call his name Jesus; for he
1. 23 and they shall call his name Emmanuel
Matt. 1. 25 her first born son: and he called his
2. 7 when he had privily called the wise men
2. 15 Out of Egypt have I called my son
4. 21 he saw other two brethren..and he called
9. 13 for I am not come to call the righteous
10. 25 If they have called the master of the
20. 8 Call the labourers, and give them (their)
22. 3 sent forth his servants to call them that
22. 43 How then doth David in spirit call him
22. 45 If David then call him Lord, how is he
23. 9 call no (man) your father upon the earth
25. 14 (who) called his own servants, and
Mark 1. 20 straightway he called them: and they
2. 17 I came not to call the righteous, but
Luke 1. 13 and thou shalt call his name John
1. 31 bring forth a son, and shalt call his name
1. 59 they called him Zacharias, after..his
5. 32 I came not to call the righteous, but
6. 46 why call ye me, Lord, Lord, and do not
14. 13 call the poor, the maimed, the lame, the
19. 13 he called his ten servants, and delivered
20. 44 David therefore calleth him Lord, how is
John 10. 3 he calleth his own sheep by name, and
Acts 4. 18 they called them, and commanded them
14. 12 they called Barnabas, Jupiter; and Paul
Rom. 4. 17 who quickeneth the dead, and calleth
8. 30 whom he did..them he also called
8. 30 whom he called, them he also justified
9. 11 not of works, but of him that calleth
9. 24 Even us, whom he hath called, not of
9. 25 I will call them my people, which were
1 Co. 7. 15 but God hath called us to peace
7. 17 as the Lord hath called every one, so let
Gal. 1. 6 soon removed from him that called you
1. 15 it pleased God..and called (me) by his
5. 8 persuasion (cometh) not of him that calleth
1 Th. 2. 12 God, who hath called you unto his king.
4. 7 God hath not called us unto uncleanness
5. 24 Faithful (is) he that calleth you, who
2 Th. 2. 14 Whereunto he called you by our gospel
2 Ti. 1. 9 Who hath saved us, and called (us) with
Heb. 2. 11 he is not ashamed to call them brethren
1 Pe. 1. 15 he which hath called you is holy, so be
2. 9 of him who hath called you out of dark.
3. 6 as Sara obeyed Abraham, calling him
5. 10 who hath called us unto his eternal glory
2 Pe. 1. 3 him that hath called us to glory and

10. *To lay out in order, collect, say,* λέγω *legō.*
Matt19. 17 he said unto him, Why callest thou me
Mark10. 18 Jesus said..Why callest thou me good?
12. 37 David therefore himself calleth him Lord
15. 12 (unto him) whom ye call the King of the
Luke18. 19 Jesus said..Why callest thou me good?
20. 37 he calleth the Lord the God of Abraham
John15. 15 Henceforth I call you not servants
Acts 10. 28 that I should not call any man common
24. 14 after the way which they call heresy, so
Rev. 2. 20 Jezebel, which calleth herself a prophet.

11. *To call after to oneself,* μετακαλέω.
Acts 20. 17 and called the elders of the church

12. *To use a name,* ὀνομάζω *onomazō.*
Acts 19. 13 to call over them which had evil spirits

13. *To call toward,* προσκαλέω *proskaleō.*
Matt15. 10 he called the multitude, and said unto
18. 32 his lord, after that he had called him
Luke15. 26 he called one of the servants, and asked
Acts 2. 39 as many as the Lord our God shall call
5. 40 when they had called the apostles, and
16. 10 the Lord had called us for to preach the

14. *To sound, cry,* φωνέω *phōneō.*
Matt20. 32 Jesus stood still, and called them, and
Mark 3. 31 his brethren..sent unto him, [calling him]
9. 35 he sat down, and called the twelve, and
10. 49 they call the blind man..he calleth thee
15. 35 they heard (it), said, Behold, he calleth
Luke 8. 54 took her by the hand, and called, saying
14. 12 call not thy friends, nor thy brethren
16. 2 And he called him, and said..I hear this
John 1. 48 Before that Philip called thee..I saw
2. 9 the governor of the feast called the bride.
4. 16 Go, call thy husband, and come hither
9. 18 they called the parents of him that had
9. 24 Then again called they the man that was
11. 28 she went her way, and called Mary her
12. 17 when he called Lazarus out of his grave
13. 13 Ye call me Master and Lord: and ye say
18. 33 Then Pilate entered..and called Jesus
Acts 9. 41 when he had called the saints and
10. 7 he called two of his household servants
10. 18 And called and asked whether Simon

[*See also* Blessed, happy, record, remembrance, witness.]

CALL (a name), to—
To put, place, שׂוּם *sum.*
Judg. 8. 31 a son, whose name he called Abimelech

CALL back, to —
To cause to turn aside, סוּר *sur,* 5.
Isa. 31. 2 he..will not call back his words; but will

CALL for, to —
1. *To call, cry,* קָרָא *qara.*
1 Ki. 8. 52 in all that they call for unto thee

2. *To ask,* αἰτέω *aiteō.*
Acts 16. 29 Then he called for a light, and sprang in

3. *To call after to oneself,* μετακαλέω *metakaleō.*
Acts 24. 25 I have a convenient season I will call for

4. *To send after,* μεταπέμπω *metapempō.*
Acts 10. 5 call for (one) Simon, whose surname is P.
11. 13 Send men to Joppa, and call for Simon

5. *To call alongside,* παρακαλέω *parakaleō.*
Acts 28. 20 For this cause..have I called for you

6. *To call toward,* προσκαλέω *proskaleō.*
Acts 13. 7 a prudent man; who called for Barnabas
Jas. 5. 14 let him call for the elders of the church

7. *To sound, cry,* φωνέω *phōneō.*
Matt27. 47 Some..said, This (man) calleth for Elias
John11. 28 The Master is come, and calleth for thee

CALL hither, to —
To call after to oneself, μετακαλέω *metakaleō.*
Acts 10. 32 Send..to Joppa, and call hither Simon

CALL in, to —
To call in, εἰσκαλέω *eiskaleō.*
Acts 10. 23 Then called he them in, and lodged

CALL in question, to —
1. *To call in, accuse,* ἐγκαλέω *egkaleō.*
Acts 19. 40 we are in danger to be called in question

2. *To judge,* κρίνω *krinō.*
Acts 23. 6 I am a Pharisee..I am called in question
24. 21 I am called in question by you this day

CALL on, to —
To call upon, ἐπικαλέω *epikaleō.*
Acts 2. 21 whosoever shall call on the name of the
9. 14 to bind all that call on thy name
9. 21 which called on this name in Jerusalem
22. 16 wash away thy sins, calling on the name
Rom 10. 14 they call on him in whom they have not
2 Ti. 2. 22 peace, with them that call on the Lord
1 Pe. 1. 17 if ye call on the Father, who without

CALL selves, to —
To be called, קָרָא *qara,* 2.
Isa. 48. 2 For they call themselves of the holy city

CALL (to mind), to —
To cause to turn back, שׁוּב *shub,* 5.
Deut 30. 1 and thou shalt call (them) to mind among

CALL to, to —
1. *To receive, take,* λαμβάνω *lambanō.*
2 Ti. 1. 5 I call to remembrance the unfeigned faith

2. *To sound toward,* προσφωνέω *prosphōneō.*
Luke 7. 32 calling one to another..We have piped

CALL to (one), to —
1. *To call after to oneself,* μετακαλέω *metakaleō.*
Acts 7. 14 Joseph..called his father Jacob to (him)

2. *To call toward,* προσκαλέω *proskaleō.*
Mark10. 42 But Jesus called them (to him), and saith

3. *To sound toward,* προσφωνέω *prosphōneō.*
Luke13. 12 when Jesus saw her, he called (her to him)

CALL together, to —
1. *To cause to cry out,* צָעַק *tsaaq,* 5.
1 Sa. 10. 17 Samuel called the people together unto

2. *To make to hear,* שָׁמַע *shama,* 3.
1 Sa. 23. 8 Saul called all the people together to war

3. *To cause to hear,* שָׁמַע *shama,* 5.
Jer. 50. 29 Call together the archers against Babylon
51. 27 call together against her the kingdoms of

4. *To call together,* συγκαλέω *sugkaleō.*
Mark15. 16 and they call together the whole band
Luke 9. 1 he called his twelve disciples together
15. 6 when he cometh home, he calleth together
15. 9 when she hath found (it), she calleth
23. 13 he had called together the chief priests
Acts 5. 21 the high priest..called the council toget.
10. 24 Cornelius waited..and..called together
28. 17 Paul called the chief of the Jews together

5. *To crowd together,* συναθροίζω *sunathroizō.*
Acts 19. 25 Whom he called together with the work.

CALL unto, to —
To sound toward, προσφωνέω *prosphōneō.*
Matt11. 16 like unto children sitting..calling unto

CALL unto (one), to —
1. *To call toward,* προσκαλέω *proskaleō.*
Matt10. 1 when he had called unto (him) his twelve
15. 32 Then Jesus called his disciples (unto him)
18. 2 Jesus called a little child unto him
20. 25 But Jesus called them (unto him), and
Mark 3. 13 goeth..into a mountain, and calleth (unto)
3. 23 he called them (unto him), and said
6. 7 he called (unto him) the twelve, and
7. 14 when he had called all the people (unto)
8. 1 Jesus called his disciples (unto him)
8. 34 he had called the people (unto him), with
12. 43 he called (unto him) his disciples, and
15. 44 Pilate..calling (unto him) the centurion
Luke 7. 19 John calling (unto him) two..sent (them)
16. 5 called every one of..lord's debtors (unto)
18. 16 But Jesus called them (unto him), and
Acts 6. 2 the twelve called the multitude..(unto)
20. 1 Paul called unto (him) the disciples, and
23. 17 Paul called one of the centurions unto

Acts 23. 18 Paul the prisoner called me unto (him)
23. 23 he called unto (him) two centurions

2. *To sound toward*, προσφωνέω *prosphōneō*.
Luke 6. 13 when it was day, he called (unto him) his

CALL upon, to —

1. *To call*, קָרָא *qara*.
Psa. 31. 17 Let me not be ashamed..I have called up.
50. 15 call upon me in the day of trouble; I will
55. 16 As for me, I will call upon God; and the
86. 7 In the day of my trouble I will call upon
88. 9 LORD, I have called daily upon thee, I
91. 15 He shall call upon me, and I will answer
145. 18 LORD (is) nigh unto all them that call upon
Prov. 1. 28 Then shall they call upon me, but I will
Lam. 3. 57 Thou drewest near in the day..I called up.

2. *To call upon*, ἐπικαλέω *epikaleō*.
Acts 7. 59 they stoned Stephen, calling upon (God)
Rom 10. 12 the same Lord..unto all that call upon
10. 13 whosoever shall call upon the name of
1 Co. 1. 2 with all that in every place call upon the

CALL whereunto, to —

To call toward, προσκαλέω *proskaleō*.
Acts 13. 2 for the work whereunto I have called

CALLED —

1. *Called, invited*, κλητός *klētos*.
Matt 20. 16 [for many be called, but few chosen]
22. 14 For many are called, but few (are) chosen
Rom. 1. 1 Paul, a servant..called (to be) an apostle
1. 6 Among whom are ye also the called of
1. 7 To all that be in Rome..called (to be)
8. 28 to them who are the called according to
1 Co. 1. 1 Paul, [called] (to be) an apostle of Jesus
1. 2 that are sanctified..called (to be) saints
1. 24 But unto them which are called, both
Jude 1 to them that are sanctified..(and) called
Rev. 17. 14 they that are with him (are) called, and

2. *That is*, ὅ ἐστι *ho esti*.
Mark 15. 16 soldiers led him away into the hall called

3. *Name*, ὄνομα *onoma*.
Luke 24. 13 two of them went..to a village called
Acts 8. 9 there was a certain man called Simon
9. 11 enquire..for (one) called Saul, of Tarsus
10. 1 There was a certain man..called Cornelius

CALLED, to be —

1. *To be said*, אָמַר *amar*, 2.
Gen. 32. 28 Thy name shall be called no more Jacob
Isa. 4. 3 (he that) remaineth..shall be called holy
19. 18 one shall be called, The city of destruc.
Jer. 7. 32 that it shall no more be called Tophet

2. *To call*, קָרָא *qara*.
Gen. 16. 14 the well was called Beer-lahai-roi
19. 22 the name of the city was called Zoar
25. 26 and his name was called Jacob
25. 30 (am) faint: therefore was his name called
29. 34 therefore was his name called Levi
31. 48 Therefore was the name of it called Galeed
33. 17 the name of the place is called Succoth
35. 8 the name of it was called Allon-bachuth
38. 29 therefore his name was called Pharez
38. 30 and his name was called Zarah
50. 11 the name of it was called Abel-mizraim
Exod 15. 23 therefore the name of it was called
Num 13. 24 The place was called the brook Eshcol
Deut. 15. 2 because it is called the LORD'S release
Josh. 5. 9 the name of the place is called Gilgal
7. 26 the name of that place was called, The
Judg. 1. 17 the name of the city was called Hormah
10. 4 they had thirty cities, which are called
2 Sa. 15. 11 two hundred men..(that were) called
1 Ch. 13. 11 that place is called Perez-uzza to this
2 Ch. 20. 26 the same place was called, The valley of
Prov 24. 8 He that deviseth..evil shall be called
Isa. 47. 1 for thou shalt no more be called tender
47. 5 for thou shalt no more be called The
Jer. 23. 6 he shall be called, The LORD our Right.
33. 16 she shall be called, The LORD our Right.

3. *To be called*, קָרָא *qara*, 2.
Gen. 2. 23 she shall be called Woman, because she
17. 5 Neither shall thy name any more be called
21. 12 for in Isaac shall thy seed be called
35. 10 thy name shall not be called any more J.
48. 6 shall be called after the name of their
Deut. 3. 13 all Bashan, which was called the land
25. 10 And his name shall be called in Israel
28. 10 thou art called by the name of the LORD
1 Sa. 9. 9 a Prophet was beforetime called a Seer
2 Sa. 6. 2 whose name is called by the name of The
12. 28 I take the city, and it be called after my
18. 18 it is called unto this day, Absalom's
1 Ki. 8. 43 that this house..is called by thy name
1 Ch. 13. 6 (between) the cherubim, whose name is c.
2 Ch. 6. 33 this house, which I have built, is called
7. 14 If my people, which are called by my name
Ezra 2. 61 Barzillai..was called after their name
Neh. 7. 63 Barzillai..was called after their name
Esth. 2. 14 the king delighted..that she were called
3. 12 the king's scribes called on the thirteenth
4. 11 come unto the king..who is not called
4. 11 I have not been called to come in unto
8. 9 the king's scribes called at that time in
Prov 16. 21 The wise in heart shall be called prudent
Isa. 1. 26 thou shalt be called, The city of right.
4. 1 only let us be called by thy name, to take
32. 5 The vile person shall be no more called
35. 8 highway shall be..and it shall be called
43. 7 every one that is called by my name
48. 1 Hear ye this..which are called by the
54. 5 God of the whole earth shall he be called
56. 7 mine house shall be called an house
62. 4 but thou shalt be called Hephzi-bah
62. 12 thou shalt be called, Sought out, A city
63. 19 they were not called by thy name
Jer. 7. 10, 11, 14, 30 house, which is called by my
14. 9 we are called by thy name; leave us not
15. 16 for I am called by thy name, O LORD
19. 6 this place shall no more be called Tophet
25. 29 on the city which is called by my name
32. 34 in the house which is called by my name
34. 15 in the house which is called by my name
Eze. 20. 29 the name thereof is called Bamah unto
Dan. 9. 18 the city which is called by thy name
9. 19 and thy people are called by thy name
10. 1 unto Daniel, whose name was called
Amos 9. 12 all the heathen, which are called by my
Zech. 8. 3 Jerusalem shall be called, A city of truth

4. *To be called*, קָרָא *qara*, 4.
Isa. 48. 8 wast called a transgressor from the womb
48. 12 O Jacob and Israel, my called; I (am) he
58. 12 thou shalt be called, The repairer of the
61. 3 they might be called Trees of righteous.
62. 2 thou shalt be called by a new name
65. 1 Behold me..nation (that) was not called

5. *To be called*, קְרָא *qera*, 2.
Dan. 5. 12 now let Daniel be called, and he will

6. *To be called*, καλέομαι *kaleomai*.
Matt. 2. 23 He shall be called a Nazarene
5. 9 they shall be called the children of God
5. 19 he shall be called..least in the kingdom
5. 19 shall be called great in the kingdom of
21. 13 My house shall be called the house of
23. 7 and to be called of men, Rabbi, Rabbi
23. 8 But be not ye called Rabbi: for one is
23. 10 Neither be ye called masters: for one is
27. 8 that field was called, The field of blood
Mark 11. 17 My house shall be called of all nations
Luke 1. 32 shall be called the Son of the Highest
1. 35 that holy thing..shall be called the Son of
1. 36 sixth month with her, who was called
1. 60 said, Not (so); but he shall be called John
1. 61 none of thy kindred that is called by
1. 62 made signs..he would have him called
1. 76 thou, child, shalt be called the Prophet
2. 4 city of David, which is called Bethlehem
2. 21 his name was called Jesus, which was so
2. 23 Every male..shall be called holy to the
6. 15 (son) of Alpheus, and Simon called Zelotes
7. 11 that he went into a city called Nain; and
8. 2 Mary called Magdalene, out of whom
9. 10 belonging to the city called Bethsaida
10. 39 she had a sister called Mary, which
15. 19, 21 am no more worthy to be called thy
19. 29 the mount called (the mount) of Olives
21. 37 mount that is called (the mount) of Olives
22. 25 they that exercise..are called benefactors
23. 33 the place which is called Calvary
John 1. 42 thou shalt be called Cephas, which
2. 2 both Jesus was called, and his disciples
Acts 1. 12 from the mount called Olivet, which
1. 19 that field is called in their proper tongue
1. 23 Joseph called Barsabas, who was
3. 11 in the porch that is called Solomon's
9. 11 the street which is called Straight, and
10. 1 a centurion of the band called the Italian
13. 1 Simeon that was called Niger, and
14. 12 [they called Barnabas, Jupiter; and]
27. 8 a place which is called the Fair Havens
27. 14 a tempestuous wind, called Euroclydon
27. 16 a certain island which is called Clauda
28. 1 knew that the island was called Melita
Rom. 9. 7 but, In Isaac shall thy seed be called
9. 26 there shall they be called the children of
1 Co. 1. 9 by whom ye were called unto the fellow.
7. 18 Is any man called being circumcised?
7. 18 Is any called in uncircumcision? let
7. 20 the same calling wherein he was called
7. 21 Art thou called (being) a servant? care
7. 22 For he that is called in the Lord, (being)
7. 22 likewise also he that is called, (being)
7. 24 wherein he is called, therein abide
15. 9 that am not meet to be called an apostle
Gal. 5. 13 ye have been called unto liberty; only
Eph. 4. 1 of the vocation wherewith ye are called
4. 4 even as ye are called in one hope of your
Col. 3. 15 to the which also ye are called in one
1 Ti. 6. 12 whereunto thou art also called, and
Heb. 3. 13 exhort..while it is called To day; lest
5. 4 he that is called of God, as (was) Aaron
9. 15 they which are called might receive the
11. 8 Abraham, when he was called to go out
11. 18 That in Isaac shall thy seed be called
Jas 2. 23 and he was called the Friend of God
1 Pe. 2. 21 For..hereunto were ye called; because
3. 9 knowing that ye are thereunto called
1 Jo. 3. 1 we should be called the sons of God!
Rev. 1. 9 was in the isle that is called Patmos, for
11. 8 which spiritually is called Sodom and
12. 9 that old serpent, called the Devil, and
16. 16 a place called in the Hebrew tongue
19. 9 Blessed (are) they which are called unto
19. 11 he that sat upon him (was) called
19. 13 his name is called The Word of God

7. *To lay out, collect, say*, λέγω *legō*.
Matt. 1. 16 was born Jesus, who is called Christ
2. 23 came and dwelt in a city called Nazareth
4. 18 Simon called Peter, and Andrew his
10. 2 The first, Simon, who is called Peter
13. 55 is not his mother called Mary? and his
26. 3 the high priest, who was called Caiaphas
26. 14 one of the twelve, called Judas Iscariot
26. 36 unto a place called Gethsemane, and
27. 16 a notable prisoner, called Barabbas
27. 17 Barabbas, or Jesus which is called Christ
27. 22 I do then with Jesus which is called
27. 33 were come unto a place called Golgotha
Luke 22. 1 the feast..which is called the Passover
22. 47 he that was called Judas, one of the
John 4. 5 a city of Samaria, which is called Sychar
4. 25 Messias cometh, which is called Christ
9. 11 A man that is called Jesus made clay
11. 16 said Thomas, which is called Didymus
11. 54 into a city called Ephraim, and there
19. 13 in a place that is called the Pavement
19. 17 into a place called (the place) of a skull
19. 17 which is called in the Hebrew, Golgotha
21. 2 Thomas called Didymus, and Nathanael
Acts 3. 2 of the temple which is called Beautiful
6. 9 which is called (the synagogue) of the
9. 36 which by interpretation is called Dorcas
1 Co. 8. 5 For though there be that are called gods
Eph. 2. 11 who are called Uncircumcision by that
2. 11 which is called the Circumcision in
Col. 4. 11 Jesus, which is called Justus, who are of
2 Th. 2. 4 himself above all that is called God
Heb. 7. 11 not be called after the order of Aaron?
9. 2; 9. 3; 11. 24; Rev. 8. 11.

8. *To be laid out besides*, ἐπιλέγομαι *epilegomai*.
John 5. 2 which is called in the Hebrew tongue Be.

9. *To call upon*, ἐπικαλέω *epikaleō*.
Heb. 11. 16 God is not ashamed to be called their

10. *To use a name on*, ἐπονομάζω *eponomazō*.
Rom. 2. 17 Behold, thou art called a Jew, and restest

11. *To use a name*, ὀνομάζω *onomazō*.
1 Co. 5. 11 if any man that is called a brother be

12. *To address publicly*, προσαγορεύω *prosagoreuō*.
Heb. 5. 10 Called of God an High Priest after the

13. *To sound, cry*, φωνέω *phōneō*.
Mark 10. 49 and commanded him to be called
Luke 19. 15 he commanded these servants to be called

CALLED (a christian, an adulteress), to be —

To declare by an oracle, χρηματίζω *chrēmatizō*.
Acts 11. 26 the disciples were called Christians
Rom. 7. 3 she shall be called an adulteress

CALLED, falsely so —

Falsely named, ψευδώνυμος *pseudōnumos*.
1 Ti. 6. 20 oppositions of science falsely so called

CALLED by, to be —

To call upon, ἐπικαλέω *epikaleō*.
Jas. 2. 7 worthy name by the which ye are called?

CALLED upon, to be —

To call upon, ἐπικαλέω *epikaleō*.
Acts 15. 17 upon whom my name is called, saith the

CALLED forth, to be —

1. *To be called*, קָרָא *qara*, 2.
Isa. 31. 4 a multitude of shepherds is called forth

2. *To be called*, καλέομαι *kaleomai*.
Acts 24. 2 when he was called forth, Tertullus began

CALLED together, to be —

1. *To be cried to for help*, זָעַק *zaaq*, 2.
Josh. 8. 16 all the people..in Ai were called togeth.

2. *To be cried to for help*, צָעַק *tsaaq*, 2.
1 Sa. 13. 4 the people were called together after Saul

CALLING —

1. *Calling*, מִקְרָא *miqra*.
Num 10. 2 thou mayest use them for the calling of the

2. *To call*, קָרָא *qara*.
Isa. 1. 13 new moons and sabbaths, the calling of

3. *Calling*, κλῆσις *klēsis*.
Rom 11. 29 the gifts and calling of God (are) without
1 Cor. 1. 26 For ye see your calling, brethren
7. 20 Let every man abide in the same calling
Eph. 1. 18 know what is the hope of his calling
4. 4 are called in one hope of your calling
Phil. 3. 14 the high calling of God in Christ Jesus
2 Th. 1. 11 God would count..worthy of (this) calling
2 Ti. 1. 9 and called (us) with an holy calling, not
Heb. 3. 1 partakers of the heavenly calling
2 Pe. 1. 10 to make your calling and election sure

CALM —

1. *Dumbness, silence*, דְּמָמָה *demamah*.
Psa 107. 29 He maketh the storm a calm so that the

2. *Stillness*, γαλήνη *galēnē*.
Matt. 8. 26 he..rebuked..and there was a great calm
Mark 4. 39 Peace, be still..there was a great calm
Luke. 8. 24 they ceased, and there was a calm

CALM, to be —

To cease, be quiet, calm, שָׁתַק *shathaq*.
Jon. 1. 11 that the sea may be calm unto us? for
1. 12 so shall the sea be calm unto you: for I

CAL'-NEH, כַּלְנֵה כַּלְנֵה *fort of Ana or Anu.*
Ana or Anu was one of the chief objects of Babylonian worship. The site is probably the modern *Niffer,* which is in the Talmud *Nopher.* It is about 60 miles S.E. of Babylon, on the left bank of the Euphrates. The LXX. speak of Calneh or Calno as the place where the tower was built (Isa. 10. 9). In the 8th century it was taken by one of the Assyrian kings, and never recovered its prosperity.

Gen. 10. 10 the beginning of his kingdom was..C.
Amos 6. 2 Pass ye unto C. and see; and from thence

CAL'-NO, כַּלְנוֹ.
Perhaps identical with Calneh.

Isa. 10. 9 (Is) not C. as Carchemish? (is) not Ham.

CAL'-VA-RY, κρανίον *a skull.*
This name occurs only in Luke 23. 33, and is not a proper name, but arises from the translators having literally adopted the word *Calvaria* (*i.e.* "a bare skull"), the Latin word by which the Greek word is rendered in the Vulgate. This *Kranion* is simply the Greek translation of the Chaldee *Golgotha.* The place of crucifixion is by each of the four evangelists called *Kranion,* and is in every case translated by *Calvaria* in the Vulgate, and in every place but that in Luke the English version translates the word by "scull." There is no sanction for the expression "Mount Calvary," for it is only 18 feet high.

Luke 23. 33 they were come to the place..called C.

CALVE, to —
1. *To be in pain, travail,* חול *chul, 3a.*
Job 39. 1 canst thou mark when the hinds do calve?
2. *To yield, bring forth, bear,* יָלַד *yalad.*
Jer. 14. 5 Yea, the hind also calved in the field
3. *To let escape,* פָּלַט *palat,* 3.
Job 21 10 their cow calveth, and casteth not her calf

CALVE, to make to —
To pain, cause to travail, חול *chul, 3a.*
Psa. 29. 9 the LORD maketh the hinds to calve, and

CAME —
To come, arrive, אתא אֲתָא *atha.*
Dan. 7. 13 came to the Ancient of days, and they

CAME, by which —
Entrance, מָבוֹא *mabo.*
2 Ki. 11 16 by the way by the which the horses came

CAME out, that which —
Outlet, produce, מוֹצָא *motsa.*
Jer. 17. 16 that which came out of my lips was (right)

CAME, that —
To draw near, קְרַב *qareb.*
1 Ki. 4. 27 for all that came unto king Solomon's

CAME up in —
Son, בֵּן *ben.*
Jon. 4. 10 which came up in a night, and perished

CAMEL —
An unclean animal among the Jews, but very docile, with bunches on its back; abounding in the East, and used for riding, drawing chariots, carrying burdens, conveying messengers, and in war. It was often adorned with chains, treated with great care, esteemed a valuable prize, yet liable to plagues. A coarse cloth was made of its hair and used by the poor.
1. *Camel,* גָּמָל *gamal.*
Gen. 12. 16 maid servants, and she asses, and camels
24. 10 the servant took ten camels of the camels
24. 11 made his camels to kneel down without
24. 14 and I will give thy camels drink also
24. 19 I will draw (water) for thy camels also
24. 20 she hasted..and drew for all his camels
24. 22 it came to pass, as the camels had
24. 30 behold, he stood by the camels at the
24. 31 prepared..room for the camels
24. 32 man came..and he ungirded his camels
24. 32 gave straw and provender for the camels
24. 35 and maid servants, and camels, and
24. 44 and I will also draw for thy camels
24. 46 and I will give thy camels drink also
24. 46 and she made the camels drink also
24. 61 they rode upon the camels, and followed
24. 63 and, behold, the camels (were) coming
24. 64 when she saw..she lighted off the camel
30. 43 men servants, and camels, and asses
31. 17 and set his..wives upon camels
31. 34 Rachel..put them in the camel's furniture
32. 7 and the flocks, and herds, and the camels
32. 15 Thirty milch camels with their colts
37. 25 with their camels bearing spicery
Exod. 9. 3 horses, upon the asses, upon the camels
Lev. 11. 4 the camel, because he cheweth the cud
Deut 14. 7 the camel, and the hare, and the coney
Judg. 6. 5 they and their camels were without num.
7. 12 their camels (were) without number
8. 21 ornaments that (were) on their camel's
8. 26 chains that (were) about their camel's
1 Sa. 15. 3 suckling, ox and sheep, camel and ass
27. 9 took away the sheep..and the camels
30. 17 hundred young men, which rode..camels
1 Ki. 10. 2 camels that bare spices, and very much
2 Ki. 8. 9 forty camels' burden..stood before him
1 Ch 5. 21 they took away their..camels fifty thou.
12. 40 brought bread on asses, and on camels
27. 30 Over the camels also (was) Obil the Ish.
2 Ch. 9. 1 camels that bare spices, and gold in
14. 15 They..carried away sheep and camels
Ezra 2 67 Their camels, four hundred thirty and
Neh. 7. 69 camels, four hundred thirty and five
Job 1. 3 substance..was..three thousand camels
1. 17 The Chaldeans..fell upon the camels, and
42. 12 he had..sheep, and six thousand camels
Isa. 21. 7 chariot of asses, (and) a chariot of camels
30. 6 carry..their treasures upon..camels
60. 6 The multitude of camels shall cover thee
Jer. 49. 29 all their vessels, and their camels
49. 32 And their camels shall be a booty, and
Eze. 25. 5 I will make Rabbah a stable for camels
Zech 14. 15 the plague of the..camel..shall be in
2. *Camel,* κάμηλος *kamēlos.*
Matt. 3. 4 John had his raiment of camel's hair
19. 24 a camel to go through the eye of a needle
23. 24 strain at a gnat, and swallow a camel
Mark 1. 6 John was clothed with camel's hair, and
10. 25 a camel to go through the eye of a needle
Luke 18. 25 for a camel to go through a needle's eye

CAMELS —
Dromedary, אֲחַשְׁתְּרָנִים *achashteranim.*
Esth. 8. 10 on mules, camels..young dromedaries
8. 14 (So) the posts that rode upon..camels

CA'-MON, קָמוֹן *standing place.*
A town in Gilead.
Judg 10. 5 And Jair died, and was buried in C.

CAMP —
1. *Camp, encampment,* מַחֲנֶה *machaneh.*
Exod 14. 19 angel..which went before the camp
14. 20 camp of the Egyptians and the camp of
16. 13 the quails came up, and covered the camp
19. 16 all the people that (was) in the camp
19. 17 brought forth the people out of the camp
29. 14 shalt thou burn with fire without the camp
32. 17 (There is) a noise of war in the camp
32. 19 as soon as he came nigh unto the camp
32. 26 Then Moses stood in the gate of the camp
32. 27 go in and out..throughout the camp, and
33. 7 took..and pitched it without the camp
33. 7 off from the camp..without the camp
33. 11 And he turned again into the camp: but
36. 6 proclaimed throughout the camp, saying
Lev. 4. 12 shall he carry forth without the camp
4. 21 carry forth the bullock without the camp
6 11 carry forth the ashes without the camp
8. 17 he burnt with fire without the camp; as
9. 11 he burnt with fire without the camp
10. 4 from before the sanctuary out of..camp
10. 5 and carried them..out of the camp; as
13. 46 without the camp (shall) his habitation
14. 3 the priest shall go forth out of the camp
14. 8 after that he shall come into the camp
16. 26 and afterward come into the camp
16. 27 shall (one) carry forth without the camp
16. 28 afterward he shall come into the camp
17 3 in the camp..out of the camp
24. 10 and a man of Israel strove..in the camp
24. 14 him that hath cursed without the camp
24. 23 him that had cursed out of the camp
Num. 1. 52 their tents, every man by his own camp
2. 3 the camp of Judah pitch, throughout
2. 9 All..were numbered in the camp of Judah
2. 10 the south side..the standard of the camp
2. 16 All..were numbered in the camp of Reub.
2. 17 set forward with the camp
2. 17 the Levites in the midst of the camp: as
2. 18 the west side..the standard of the camp
2. 24 All..were numbered of the camp of Eph.
2. 25 The standard of the camp of Dan
2. 31 they that were numbered in the camp of
2. 32 those that were numbered of the camps
4. 5 when the camp setteth forward, Aaron
4. 15 as the camp is to set forward; after that
5. 2 that they put out of the camp every leper
5. 3 without the camp shall ye put them
5. 3 that they defile not their camps, in the
5. 4 and put them out without the camp: as
10. 2 trumpets..for the journeying of the camps
10. 5 the camps that lie on the east parts shall
10. 6 then the camps that lie on the south side
10. 14 the first..went the standard of the camp
10. 18 standard of the camp of Reuben set for.
10. 22 camp of the children of Ephraim set for.
10. 25 camp of the children of Dan set forward
10. 25 all the camps throughout their hosts
10. 34 when they went out of the camp
11. 1 in the uttermost parts of the camp
11. 9 dew fell upon the camp in the night
11. 26 there remained two..men in the camp
11. 26 and they prophesied in the camp
11. 27 Eldad and Medad do prophesy in the camp
11. 30 Moses gat him into the camp, he and the
11 31 and let (them) fall by the camp, as it
11. 31 the other side, round about the camp
11. 32 they spread (them) all..about the camp
12. 14 let her be shut out from the camp seven
12. 15 Miriam was shut out from the camp
14. 44 and Moses, departed not out of the camp
15. 35 stone him with stones without the camp
15. 36 congregation brought..without the camp
19. 3 he may bring her forth without the camp
19. 7 afterward he shall come into the camp
19. 9 lay (them) up without the camp in a
31. 12 unto the camp at the plains of Moab
31. 13 forth to meet them without the camp
31. 19 do ye abide without the camp seven days
31. 24 afterward ye shall come into the camp
Deut 23. 10 then shall he go abroad out of the camp
23. 10 he shall not come within the camp
23. 11 he shall come into the camp (again)
23. 12 Thou shalt have a place..without..camp
23. 14 God walketh in the midst of thy camp
23. 14 therefore shall thy camp be holy
29. 11 and thy stranger that (is) in thy camp
Josh. 5. 8 they abode in their places in the camp
6. 11 came into the camp, and lodged..camp
6. 14 returned into the camp: so they did six
6. 18 make the camp of Israel a curse, and
6. 23 and left them without the camp of Israel
9. 6 they went to Joshua unto the camp at
10. 6 the men..sent unto Joshua to the camp
10. 15, 43 Joshua returned..unto the camp to
10. 21 all the people returned to the camp to
Judg. 7. 17 when I come to the outside of the camp
7. 18 on every side of all the camp, and say
7. 19 came unto the outside of the camp in the
7. 21 every man in his place..about the camp
13. 25 began to move him at times in the camp
21. 8 behold, there came none to the camp from
21. 12 they brought them unto the camp to S.
1 Sa. 4. 3 when the people were come into the camp
4. 5 the ark..of the LORD came into the camp
4. 6 What (meaneth)..great shout in the camp
4. 6 ark of the LORD was come into the camp
4. 7 for they said, God is come into the camp
13. 17 the spoilers came out of the camp of the
14. 21 went up with them into the camp (from)
17. 4 there went out a champion out of..camp
17. 17 and run to the camp to thy brethren
26. 6 Who will go down with me..to the camp?
2 Sa. 1. 2 a man came out of the camp from Saul
1. 3 Out of the camp of Israel am I escaped
1 Ki. 16. 16 all..made Omri..king..in the camp
2 Ki. 3. 24 when they came to the camp of Israel
7. 5 they rose up..to go unto the camp of the
7. 5 come to the uttermost part of the camp
7. 7 left their tents, and..the camp as it (was)
7. 10 We came to the camp of the Syrians, and
7. 12 are they gone out of the camp to hide
19. 35 in the camp of the Assyrians an hundred
2 Ch. 22. 1 the Arabians to the camp had slain all
32. 21 in the camp of the king of Assyria
Psa. 78. 28 he let (it) fall in the midst of their camp
106. 16 They envied Moses also in the camp
Isa. 37. 36 angel of the LORD..smote in the camp
Eze. 4. 2 set the camp also against it, and set
Joel 2. 11 his camp (is) very great: for (he is) strong
Amos 4. 10 made the stink of your camps to come up
2. *Place of encampment,* תַּחֲנֹת *tachanoth.*
2 Ki. 6. 8 In such and such a place..my camp
3. *A camp, putting alongside,* παρεμβολή *parembolē.*
Heb. 13. 11 the bodies..are burnt without the camp
13. 13 go forth..unto him without the camp
Rev. 20. 9 compassed the camp of the saints about

CAMP, to —
To incline, recline, settle down, חָנָה *chanah.*
Exod 19. 2 there Israel camped before the mount
Isa. 29. 3 I will camp against thee round about
Jer. 50. 29 camp against it round about; let none
Nah. 3. 17 grasshoppers, which camp in the hedges

CAMPHIRE —
Camphire, a shrub like privet, כֹּפֶר *kopher.*
Song 1. 14 My beloved (is)..(as) a cluster of camphire
4. 13 pleasant fruits; camphire..spikenard

CAN, CANNOT —
1. *There is not that,* לָא אִיתַי דִּי *la ithai di.*
Dan. 4. 35 none can stay his hand, or say unto him
2. *(Not) to be able,* (לא)יָכֹל *lo)yakol.*
Gen. 13. 16 if a man can number the dust of the earth
19. 19 I cannot escape to the mountain, lest
19. 22 I cannot do any thing till thou be come
24. 50 we cannot speak unto thee bad or good
29. 8 We cannot, until all the flocks be gathered
31. 35 my lord..I cannot rise up before thee
34. 14 they said..We cannot do this thing, to
44. 1 food, as much as they can carry, and put
44. 22 The lad cannot leave his father: for
44. 26 And we said, We cannot go down: if our
Exod 10. 5 that one cannot be able to see the earth
19. 23 The people cannot come up..Sinai
33. 20 he said, Thou canst not see my face: for
Num 22. 18 I cannot go beyond the word of the LORD
24. 13 I cannot go beyond the commandment of
Deut. 7. 17 These nations..how can I dispossess them?
28. 27 the itch, whereof thou canst not be healed
28. 35 with a sore botch that cannot be healed
31. 2 I can no more go out and come in
Josh. 7. 13 thou canst not stand before thine enemies
24. 19 Joshua said..Ye cannot serve the LORD
Judg 11. 35 I have opened my mouth..and I cannot
14. 13 But if ye cannot declare (it) me, then
Ruth 4. 6 I cannot redeem (it) for myself, lest I
4. 6 redeem thou my right..for I cannot
1 Sa. 17. 39 David said unto Saul, I cannot go with
2 Sa. 12. 23 should I fast? can I bring him back again
Neh. 6. 3 so that I cannot come down: why should
Esth. 8. 6 how can I endure to see the evil that
8. 6 how can I endure to see the destruction
Job 4. 2 who can withhold himself from speaking?
33. 5 If thou canst answer me, set (thy words)
42 2 I know that thou canst do every (thing)
Psa. 78. 19 Can God furnish a table in the wilderness?
78. 20 can he give bread..for his people?
139. 6 it is high, I cannot (attain) unto it

Prov. 30. 21 and for four (which) it cannot bear
Eccl. 1. 8 things (are) full of labour, man cannot
1. 15 (which is) crooked cannot be made straight
1. 15 that which is wanting cannot be numbered
7. 13 who can make (that) straight which he
8. 17 a man cannot find out the work that is
Song 8. 7 Many waters cannot quench love, neither
Isa. 29. 11 and he saith, I cannot; for it (is) sealed
56. 10 they (are) all dumb dogs, they cannot
57. 20 like the troubled sea, when it cannot rest
59. 14 truth is fallen..and equity cannot enter
Jer. 6. 10 uncircumcised, and they cannot hearken
14. 9 as a mighty man (that) cannot save? yet
18. 6 cannot I do with you as this potter? saith
19. 11 a potter's vessel, that cannot be made
36. 5 I cannot go into the house of the LORD
38. 5 not (he that) can do (any) thing against
49. 23 sorrow on the sea; it cannot be quiet
Dan. 10. 17 how can the servant of this my lord talk
Hab. 1. 13 (Thou art) of purer eyes..and canst not

3. *To be able*, יְכִל *yekil.*
Dan. 2. 10 There is not a man..that can show the
2. 27 cannot the wise (men)..show unto the
3. 29 no other God..can deliver after this sort
5. 16 now if thou canst read the writing, and
5. 16 that thou canst make interpretations

4. *To learn to know*, γινώσκω *ginōskō.*
Matt 16. 3 ye can discern the face of the sky; but
Acts 21. 37 Who said, Canst thou speak Greek?

5. *To be able, have power*, δύναμαι *dunamai.*
Matt. 5. 14 A city that is set on an hill cannot be hid
5. 36 thou canst not make one hair white or
6. 24 No man can serve two masters: for either
6. 24 Ye cannot serve God and mammon
6. 27 Which of you, by taking thought, can add
7. 18 A good tree cannot bring forth evil fruit
8. 2 Lord, if thou wilt, thou canst make me
9. 15 Can the children of the bride chamber
12. 29 how can one enter into a strong man's
12. 34 how can ye, being evil, speak good things?
16. 3 can ye not (discern) the signs of the times?
17. 16 I brought him..and they could not cure
17. 19 and said, Why could not we cast him out?
19. 25 amazed, saying, Who then can be saved?
26. 53 that I cannot now pray to my Father, and
27. 42 He saved others; himself he cannot save
Mark 1. 40 If thou wilt, thou canst make me clean
1. 45 Jesus could no more openly enter into
2. 4 they could not come nigh unto him for
2. 7 who can forgive sins but God only?
2. 19 Can the children of the bride chamber
2. 19 [the bridegroom with them, they cannot]
3. 20 they could not so much as eat bread
3. 23 How can Satan cast out Satan?
3. 24 if a kingdom be divided..cannot stand
3. 25 if a house be divided..that house cannot
3. 26 if Satan..be divided, he cannot stand
3. 27 No man can enter into a strong man's
5. 3 no man could bind him, no, not with
6. 5 he could there do no mighty work, save
6. 19 would have killed him; but she could
7. 15 that entering into him can defile him
7. 18 entereth into the man, (it) cannot defile
7. 24 no man know (it): but he could not be
8. 4 whence can a man satisfy these (men)
9. 3 so as no fuller on earth can white them
9. 23 Jesus said unto him, If thou canst believe
9. 28 Why could not we cast him out?
9. 29 This kind can come forth by nothing but
9. 39 no man..can lightly speak evil of me
10. 26 saying among themselves, Who then can
10. 38 can ye drink of the cup that I drink of?
10. 39 they say unto him, We can. And Jesus
15. 31 He saved others; himself he cannot save
Luke 1. 22 when he came out, he could not speak
5. 12 if thou wilt, thou canst make me clean
5. 21 who can forgive sins but God alone?
5. 34 Can ye make the children..fast while the
6. 39 Can the blind lead the blind? shall they
6 42 how canst thou say to thy brother, Brother
8. 19 his brethren..could not come at him for
9. 40 to cast him out; and they could not
11. 7 in bed; I cannot rise and give thee
12. 25 which of you..can add to his stature
13. 11 and could in no wise lift up (herself)
14. 20 I have married a wife, and..cannot come
14. 26 his own life also, he cannot be my disciple
14. 27 whosoever doth..come after me, cannot
14. 33 all that he hath, he cannot be my disciple
16. 13 No servant can serve two masters: for
16. 13 Ye cannot serve God and mammon
16. 26 that they which would..to you cannot
18. 26 they..said, Who then can be saved?
19. 3 he sought to see Jesus..and could not
20. 36 Neither can they die any more: for they
John 1. 46 Can there any good thing come out of
3. 2 no man can do these miracles that thou
3. 3 Except a man be born again, he cannot
3. 4 How can a man be born..can he enter
3. 5 he cannot enter into the kingdom of God
3. 9 said unto him, How can these things be?
3. 27 A man can receive nothing, except it be
5. 19 The Son can do nothing of himself, but
5. 30 I can of mine own self do nothing: as I
5. 44 can ye believe, which receive honour one
6. 44 No man can come to me, except the
6. 52 How can this man give us (his) flesh to
6. 60 This is an hard saying; who can hear it?
6. 65 no man can come unto me, except it
7. 7 The world cannot hate you; but me it
John 7. 34, 36 where I am, (thither) ye cannot come
8. 21 I go..whither I go, ye cannot come
8. 22 because he saith, Whither I go, ye cannot
8. 43 (even) because ye cannot hear my word
9. 4 the night cometh, when no man can
9. 16 How can a man that is a sinner do such
9. 33 man were not of God, he could do nothing
10. 21 Can a devil open the eyes of the blind?
10. 35 and the Scripture cannot be broken
11. 37 Could not this man, which opened the
12. 39 they could not believe, because..Esaias
13. 33 Whither I go, ye cannot come; so now I
13. 36 Whither I go, thou canst not follow me
13. 37 Lord, why cannot I follow thee now?
14. 5 and how [can] we know the way?
14. 17 the world cannot receive, because it seeth
15. 4 the branch cannot bear fruit of itself
15. 5 for without me ye can do nothing
16. 12 but ye cannot bear them now
Acts 4. 16 dwell in Jerusalem; and we cannot deny
4. 20 we cannot but speak the things which we
5. 39 But if it be of God, ye cannot overthrow
8. 31 How can I, except some man should
10. 47 Can any man forbid water, that these
13. 39 from which ye could not be justified by
15. 1 Except ye be circumcised..ye cannot be
21. 34 when he could not know the certainty
24. 13 Neither can they prove..things whereof
27. 15 the ship..could not bear up into the
27. 31 Except these abide in the ship, ye cannot
27. 43 they which could swim should cast
Rom. 8. 7 to the law of God, neither indeed can be
8. 8 they that are in the flesh cannot please
1 Co. 2. 14 neither can he know (them), because they
3. 1 I..could not speak unto you as unto
3. 11 For other foundation can no man lay
10. 21 Ye cannot drink..ye cannot be partakers
12. 3 no man can say that Jesus is the Lord
12. 21 the eye cannot say unto the hand, I have
15. 50 flesh and blood cannot inherit the king.
2 Co. 3. 7 Israel could not stedfastly behold the
Gal. 3. 21 a law given which could have given life
1 Th. 3. 9 what thanks can we render to God
1 Ti. 5. 25 and they that are otherwise cannot be hid
6. 7 (it is) certain we can carry nothing out
6. 16 whom no man hath seen, nor can see
2 Ti. 2. 13 he abideth faithful: he cannot deny
Heb. 3. 19 So we see that they could not enter in
4. 15 an high priest which cannot be touched
5. 2 Who can have compassion on..ignorant
9. 9 that could not make him that did the
10. 1 can never with those sacrifices which
10. 11 sacrifices, which can never take away
Jas. 2. 14 and have not works? can faith save him?
3. 8 But the tongue can no man tame; (it is)
3. 12 Can the fig tree, my brethren, bear olive
4. 2 ye kill, and desire to have, and cannot
1 Jo. 3. 9 he cannot sin, because he is born of God
4. 20 how can he love God whom he hath not
Rev. 2. 2 thou canst not bear them which are evil
3. 8 an open door, and no man can shut it
7. 9 a great multitude, which no man could
9. 20 which neither can see, nor hear, nor
14. 3 no man could learn that song but the

6. *It is not*, οὐκ ἔστι *ouk esti.*
Heb. 9. 5 the mercy seat; of which we cannot now

7. *To have*, ἔχω *echō.*
Mark 14. 8 She hath done what she could: she is
Luke 14. 14 for they cannot recompense thee
Acts 4. 14 beholding..man..they could say nothing
Heb. 6. 13 because he could swear by no greater, he

8. *To have strength*, ἰσχύω *ischuō.*
Matt 26. 40 What! could ye not watch with me one
Mark 5. 4 neither could any (man) tame him
9. 18 should cast him out; and they could not
14. 37 Simon, sleepest thou? couldest not thou
Luke 6. 48 the stream beat..and could not shake it
8. 43 physicians, neither could be healed of any
14. 6 they could not answer him again to these
16. 3 I cannot dig; to beg I am ashamed
20. 26 they could not take hold of his words
Acts 25. 7 grievous complaints..they could not

9. *To know, see*, οἶδα *oida.*
Matt 27. 65 go your way, make (it) as sure as ye can
Luke 12. 56 ye can discern the face of the sky and of

CAN away with —
To be able, יָכֹל *yakol.*
Isa. 1. 13 I cannot away with; (it is) iniquity, even

CAN (NOT) be, it —
To receive in, admit, ἐνδέχομαι *endechomai.*
Luke 13. 33 it cannot be that a prophet perish out of

CAN do —
1. *To be able, have power*, δύναμαι *dunamai.*
Mark 9. 22 if thou canst do anything, have compas.
2 Co. 13. 8 For we can do nothing against the truth

2. *To have strength, be strong*, ἰσχύω *ischuō.*
Phil. 4. 13 I can do all things through Christ which

CAN (have) —
To know, be acquainted with, יָדַע *yada.*
Isa. 56. 11 greedy dogs (which) can never have
Jer. 1. 6 I cannot speak, for I am a child
[*See also under* **COULD.**]

CAN skill —
To know, be acquainted with, יָדַע *yada.*
1 Ki. 5. 6 not among us any that can skill to hew
2 Ch. 2. 7 that can skill to grave with the cunning
2. 8 that thy servants can skill to cut timber

CAN tell —
1. *To know, be acquainted with*, יָדַע *yada.*
Gen. 43. 22 we cannot tell who put our money in
1 Sa. 17. 55 thy soul liveth, O king, I cannot tell
2 Sa. 12. 22 can tell (whether) GOD will be gracious
Prov 30. 4 what (is) his son's name, if thou canst t.
Eccl. 10. 14 a man cannot tell what shall be
Jon. 3. 9 Who can tell (if) God will turn and re.

2. *To put before*, נָגַד *nagad*, 5.
Eccl. 6. 12 who can tell a man what shall be after
8. 7 for who can tell him when it 10. 14.

3. *To know, see*, οἶδα *oida.*
Matt 21. 27 they answered..and said, We cannot tell
Mark 11. 33 they answered and said..We cannot tell
Luke 20. 7 they answered, That they could not tell
John 3. 8 but canst not tell whence it cometh
8. 14 ye cannot tell whence I come, and whit.
16. 18 A little while? we cannot tell what he
2 Co. 12. 2 whether in the body, I cannot tell
12. 2 or whether out of the body, I cannot tell
12. 3 [whether..out of the body, I cannot tell]

[*See also* Approach, cease, condemn, contain, could, do, escape, find, forbear, Greek, have, lie, move, pass, receive, remove, see, speak, spoken, tempt, utter, wish.]

CA'-NA, Κανᾶ.
Cana of Galilee (once Cana *in* Galilee), a village memorable as the scene of Christ's first miracle, and of a subsequent one (John 4. 46, 54). It was also the native place of Nathanael. The name occurs in the Gospel of John only, and in these four instances no clue is furnished as to its situation. All we can make out is that it was not far from Capernaum, and on a more elevated situation. The traditional site is at *Kefr Kenna*, a small village 4½ miles N.E. of Nazareth. A rival site is further N., a village about 5 miles N. of *Suffurieh* (Sepphoris) and 9 from Nazareth, near the present *Jefat*, the *Jotapata* of the Jewish wars. This village still bears the name of *Kana-el-jelil*, which is the exact representative of the Hebrew original—as is *Kenna* widely different from it—and it is in this fact that the superiority of the northern *Kana* seems to rest.
John 2. 1 there was a marriage in C. of Galilee
2. 11 did Jesus in C. of Galilee, and manifested
4. 46 So Jesus came again into C. of Galilee
21. 2 Nathanael of C. in Galilee, and the (sons)

CA-NA'-AN, כְּנַעַן *low, flat*, Χαναάν.
1. A son of Ham and grandson of Noah, B.C. 2300.
Gen. 9. 18 Japheth: and Ham (is) the father of C.
9. 22 And Ham, the father of C., saw the nak.
9. 25 Cursed (be) C.; a servant of servants
9. 26 And he said..C. shall be his servant
9. 27 God shall enlarge Japheth..and C. shall
10. 6 sons of Ham; Cush, and Mizraim..and C.
10. 15 And C. begat Sidon his first born, and H.
1 Ch. 1. 8 The sons of Ham; Cush..Put, and C.
1. 13 And C. begat Zidon his first born, and H.

2. The name denotes both the people who sprang from Canaan and the country in which they dwelt, which lay chiefly in the low districts along the E. coast of the Mediterranean, N. of the Philistines.

Canaan, *lit.* the "low" country, was originally applied to that small stripe of flat land lying on the eastern shore of the Mediterranean Sea, extending from Egypt northward even to Sidon, but eventually it came to be applied to the possessions of the Hebrews on both sides of the Jordan, having Phoenicia, Lebanon, and Syria on the N.; Syria, Ammon, and Moab on the E.; Idumea and the Arabian desert on the S.; and the Mediterranean Sea on the W. Its extreme length was about 180 miles, and its breadth varied from 20 to 120 miles, containing in all about 11,000 square miles—a little less than Belgium, a little more than Wales, or one-third the size of Scotland. Its coast line, from Carmel to the S. of Gaza, is little more than 100 miles. Its population never exceeded 5,000,000.

The earliest inhabitants were a race of giants called *Anakim, Avim, Emim, Horim, Rephaim, Suzim* or *Zamzummim*, remnants of whom continued till at least the time of David, B.C. 1000. But they had much earlier been supplanted by the Amorites (between Hebron and the Salt Sea), the Arkites (at Arka, opposite the northern extremity of Lebanon), the Arvadites (around Arad), the Girgashites (near the sea of Tiberias), the Hamathites (around Hamath), the Hittites (around Hebron), the Hivites (around Hermon), the Jebusites (at Jebus or Jerusalem), the Perizzites (in Samaria), the Sinites (south of Arka), the Sidonians (at Sidon), and the Zerarites (south of Arad). These tribes were all confined to the W. of the Jordan, save the Amorites, who possessed two kingdoms on the E. of it—that of Sihon, between the Arnon and the Jabbok, and that of Og in Bashan, now called the Hauran.

The moral state of these tribes gradually became so bad that the land is represented as "spueing" them out. Under Joshua they were gradually subdued, but were never wholly exterminated, so that even at the present day there are relics of them to be found in the hill country. The land, being repeatedly promised to Abraham, received among his descendants such names as the Land of the Hebrews, of Israel, of Judah, of Canaan, of Promise, the Holy Land, and Palestine, which latter was derived from the Philistines who dwelt in the S.W. at the sea shore. Joshua divided it by lot to the twelve tribes, arranged in four divisions:

the *northern* part was assigned to Asher, Naphtali, Zebulun, and Issachar; the *middle* part to Ephraim and the half tribe of Manasseh; the *southern* part to Benjamin, Dan, Judah, and Simeon; and the *eastern* part, beyond the Jordan, to Reuben, Gad, and the half tribe of Manasseh. Solomon's division into twelve sections for governmental purposes may be seen in 1 Ki. 4. 7-19. After the secession of the ten tribes under Rehoboam, the territory of the tribes of Judah and Benjamin (with the intermixed cities of Dan and Simeon) were called "Judah," and the others "Israel," till the captivity of the latter, B.C. 728, after a separate existence of 250 years.

After the death of Alexander the Great, B.C. 330, Greek colonists settled in Ptolemais (Acre), Pella, and Gerasa, while the Nabataeans (an Arab tribe) settled at Petra, and gradually conquered Moab and Ammon in the north.

In New Testament times Canaan was divided into a variety of provinces. EAST of the Jordan were:—Iturea now *Jedur;* Gaulanitis, now *Jolan;* Trachonitis, now *Leja;* Batanaea, now *Nukra* (all in the north); Auranitis (now *Hauran,* on the east), and Peraea, now *Belka* (in the south). WEST of the Jordan were:—Galilee (Upper and Lower), on the north; Samaria, in the centre, and Judea, in the south.

In later times it was divided into four parts:—PALESTINA I., *Philistin* which included Judea and Samaria, with Cæsarea for its capital; PALESTINA II. *Urdun* (Jordan), including Galilee and Gilead, with Scythopolis for its capital; PALESTINA III., *Jibalod Sherat,* including the ancient Nabataea, and Aila eastward to the Arnon, with Petra for its capital; ARABIA, to the N.E. of Palestina III., including the Hauran, with Bostra for its capital.

Palestine successively fell under Persian, Greek, Roman and Turkish rule, under the last of which it still lies. It is now divided into two pachalics, that of *Sidon,* including the whole country on the W. of the Jordan, and that of *Damascus,* including the land on the E. The present population is only about 650,000.

Among its *wild* animals are the bear (in Lebanon), the wild boar, fallow deer, fox, gazelle, hyena, jackal, panther, wolf, &c., but no lions. The *domestic* animals are the ass, buffalo, (Arabian) camel, horse, mule, ox, broad tailed sheep, &c. Its *birds* are the crow, cuckoo, eagle, heron, jay, kingfisher, kite, nightingale, owl, partridge, raven, sparrow, stork, vulture, &c. Bats and lizards abound; fish swarm in the sea of Galilee, but none in the Salt Sea. On the sea-bound plain, and lower hill sides, the banana, orange, palm, and sugar cane grow. The maple, oak, pine, and willow flourish at from 1000 to 4000 feet above the sea; also the mulberry and olive. Barley, wheat, and the vine abound.

There are two great ranges of mountains, running parallel on both sides of the Jordan from north to south, the one terminating in the mountains of Sinai and the other on the shores of the Red Sea. The mountains of Samaria (the centre part of the range on the W. of the Jordan) average 2000 feet above the sea, and the highest summits of these are Ebal and Gerizim, about 2750 feet high. The mountains of Judea are highest near Hebron, which is 3030 feet above the *Great,* and 4342 above the *Salt* Sea. Jerusalem is 2550 feet above the former, and 3826 above the latter, Tabor is 1890, Little Hermon 1700, the Carmel range 1740, and the Promontory 600 feet high, while Lebanon rises even to 10,000, and Anti-Lebanon to 9000 feet above the Mediterranean.

The Jordan is the only great river in Palestine, and springs from the foot of Anti-Lebanon 1847 feet above the sea. Passing through the waters of Merom and the Sea of Galilee, it falls into the Salt Sea, where it is lost by evaporation. It is fed on the *east* side by the waters of the Jarmuk and the Jabbok. The Arnon falls into the Salt Sea, which is about 46 miles long, with an average breadth of 7 miles, and is thus nearly the size of the Lake of Geneva, or three times the size of Lough Neagh. For further particulars see the articles *Palestine, Judea, Galilee, Samaria, Perea,* &c.

Gen. 11. 31 they went forth..to go into the land of C.
12. 5 they went forth to go into the land of C.
12. 5 and into the land of C. they came
13. 12 Abram dwelt in the land of C., and
16. 3 Abram..dwelt ten years in the land of C.
17. 8 I will give unto thee..all the land of C.
23. 2 the same (is) Hebron in the land of C.
23. 19 the same (is) Hebron in the land of C.
28. 1 shalt not take a wife..daughters of C.
28. 6 shalt not take a wife of..daughters of C.
28. 8 Esau seeing that the daughters of C.
31. 18 to go to Isaac his father in the land of C.
33. 18 which (is) in the land of C., when he
35. 6 Jacob came to Luz, which (is) in..C.
36. 2 Esau took his wives of the daughters of C.
36. 5 which were born unto him in..land of C.
36. 6 which he had got in the land of C.; and
37. 1 And Jacob dwelt..in the land of C.
42. 5 for the famine was in the land of C.
42. 7 From the land of C. to buy food
42. 13 the sons of one man in the land of C.
42. 29 came unto Jacob..unto the land of C.
42. 32 the youngest (is) this day..in..land of C.
44. 8 we brought again unto thee..land of C.
45. 17 go, get you unto the land of C.
45. 25 and came into the land of C. unto
46. 6 which they had gotten in the land of C.
46. 12 Er and Onan died in the land of C.
46. 31 which (were) in the land of C., are come
47. 1 are come out of the land of C.; and,behold
47. 4 the famine (is) sore in the land of C.
Gen. 47. 13 the land of C.. fainted by reason of the
47. 14 the money..was found..in the land of C
47. 15 when money failed..in the land of C.
48. 3 appeared unto me at Luz in the land of C.
48. 7 Rachel died by me in the land of C.
49. 30 which (is) before Mamre, in the land of C
50. 5 I have digged for me in the land of C.
50. 13 his sons carried him into the land of C.
Exod. 6. 4 to give them the land of C. the land of
15. 15 all the inhabitants of C. shall melt away
16. 35 came unto the borders of the land of C.
Lev. 14. 34 When ye be come into the land of C.
18. 3 after the doings of the land of C., whither
25. 38 to give..the land of C., (and) to be your
Num 13. 2 that they may search the land of C., which
13. 17 Moses sent them to spy out the land of C.
26. 19 Er and Onan died in the land of C.
32. 30 have possessions among you in the..of C.
32. 32 We will pass over..into the land of C.
33. 40 which dwelt in the south in the land of C.
33. 51 ye are passed over Jordan into the..of C.
34. 2 When ye come into the land of C., this
34. 2 the land of C., with the coasts thereof
34. 29 unto the children of Israel in the..of C.
35. 10 ye be come over Jordan into the land of C.
35. 14 three cities shall ye give in the land of C.
Deut 32. 49 behold the land of C., which I give unto
Josh. 5. 12 they did eat of the fruit of the land of C.
14. 1 children of Israel inherited in the..of C.
21. 2 they spake unto them..in the land of C.
22. 9 which (is) in the land of C., to go unto
22. 10 that (are) in the land of C., the children
22. 11 built an altar over against the land of C.
22. 32 Phinehas..returned..unto the land of C.
24. 3 and led him throughout all the land of C.
Judg. 3. 1 as had not known all the wars of C.
4. 2 into the hand of Jabin king of C., that
4. 23 God subdued on that day..the king of C.
4. 24 prevailed against Jabin the king of C.
4. 24 they had destroyed Jabin king of C.
5. 19 then fought the kings of C. in Taanach
21. 12 to Shiloh, which (is) in the land of C.
1 Ch. 16. 18 Unto thee will I give the land of C., the
Psa 105. 11 Unto thee will I give the land of C., the
106. 38 whom they sacrificed unto the idols of C.
135. 11 Bashan, and all the kingdoms of C.
Isa. 19. 18 five cities..speak the language of C.
Eze. 16. 3 thy nativity (is) of the land of C.; thy
16. 29 thy fornication in the land of C. unto
Zeph. 2. 5 O C., the land of the Philistines, I will
Matt 15. 22 a woman of C. came out of..same coasts

CA-NA-AN-ITE, CA-NA-AN-IT-ISH, כְּנַעֲנִי *etc.*

Patronymic of the descendants of Canaan, afterwards restricted to the inhabitants of Canaan.

Gen. 10. 18 afterward were the families of..C. spread
10. 19 the border of the C. was from Sidon, as
12. 6 And the C. (was) then in the land
13. 7 And the C..dwelt then in the land
15. 21 the Amorites, and the C., and the
24. 3 thou shalt not take a wife..of the C.
24. 37 Thou shalt not take a wife..of the C.
34. 30 to make me to stink..among the C. and
38. 2 daughter of a certain C., whose name (was)
46. 10 and Shaul the son of a C. woman
50. 11 when..the C., saw the mourning in the
Exod. 3. 8 to bring them..unto the place of the C.
3. 17 I will bring you..unto the land of the C.
6. 15 and Shaul the son of a C. woman: these
13. 5 shall bring thee into the land of the C.
13. 11 shall bring thee into the land of the C.
23. 23 and bring thee in unto..the C., the Hivites
23. 28 which shall drive..the Hivite, the C.,and
33. 2 I will drive out the C., the Amorite, and
34. 11 I drive out before..the Amorite,and the C.
Num 13. 29 the C. dwell by the sea, and by the coast
14. 25 Now the..C. dwelt in the valley. To
14. 43 For the..C. (are) there before you, and
14. 45 and the C. which dwelt in that hill
21. 1 (when) king Arad the C., which dwelt in
21. 3 and delivered up the C.; and they utterly
33. 40 And king A. the C., which dwelt in
Deut. 1. 7 and go..to the land of the C., and unto
7. 1 and hath cast out..the C., and the
11. 30 (Are) they not..in the land of the C.
20. 17 But thou shalt utterly destroy..the C.
Josh. 3. 10 he will..drive out from before you the C.
5. 1 all the kings of the C., which (were) by the
7. 9 For the C...shall hear (of it), and shall
9. 1 when..Amorite, the C...heard (thereof)
11. 3 the C. on the east and on the west
12. 8 the Hittites, the Amorites, and the C.
13. 3 (which) is counted to the C.: five lords
13. 4 From the south, all the land of the C.
16. 10 they drave not out the C. that dwelt in
16. 10 but the C. dwell among the Ephraimites
17. 12 but the C. would dwell in that land
17. 13 they put the C. to tribute; but did not
17. 16 all the C. that dwell in the land of
17. 18 thou shalt drive out the C., though they
24. 11 the Amorites, and the Perizzites, and the
Judg. 1. 1 Who shall go up for us against the C. first
1. 3 that we may fight against the C.; and I
1. 4 the LORD delivered the C. and the Peri.
1. 5 they slew the C. and the Perizzites
1. 9 to fight against the C., that dwelt in the
1. 10 Judah went against the C. that dwelt
1. 17 they slew the C. that inhabited Zephath
1. 27 but the C. would dwell in that land
1. 28 they put the C. to tribute, and did not
1. 29 Neither did Ephraim drive out the C. that
1. 29 but the C. dwelt in Gezer among them
Judg. 1. 30 the C dwelt among them, and became
1. 32 the Asherites dwelt among the C., the
1. 33 but he dwelt among the C., the inhabitants
3. 3 all the C., and the Sidonians and the
3. 5 the children of Israel dwelt among the C.
2 Sa. 24. 7 to all the cities of the..C: and they went
1 Ki. 9. 16 and slain the C. that dwelt in the city
1 Ch. 2. 3 the daughter of Shua the C..tess, And Er
Ezra 9. 1 abominations, (even) of the C. the Hittites
Neh. 9. 8 to give the land of the C.. the Hittites
9. 24 and thou subduedst before them. the C.
Obad. 20 that of the C...unto Zarephath; and
Zech 14. 21 there shall be no more the C. in the house
Matt 10. 4 Simon the C., and Judas Iscariot, who
Mark 3. 18 and Thaddeus, and Simon the C.

CAN-DA'-CE, Κανδάκη.

A queen of Ethiopia. The name is not a proper name of an individual, but of a dynasty of Ethiopian queens.

Acts 8. 27 an eunuch of great authority under C.

CANDLE —

1. *A light,* נֵר *ner.*

Job 18. 6 his candle shall be put out with him
21. 17 How oft is the candle of the wicked put
29. 3 When his candle shined upon my head
Psa. 18. 28 For thou wilt light my candle: the LORD
Prov. 20. 27 The spirit of man (is) the candle of the
24. 20 the candle of the wicked shall be put out
31. 18 her candle goeth not out by night
Jer. 25. 10 take from them..the light of the candle
Zeph. 1. 12 I will search Jerusalem with candles

2. *A lamp,* λύχνος *luchnos.*

Matt 5. 15 Neither do men light a candle, and put
Mark 4. 21 Is a candle brought to be put under a
Luke 8. 16 No man, when he hath lighted a candle
11. 33 when he hath lighted a candle, putteth
11. 36 the bright shining of a candle doth give
15. 8 doth not light a candle, and sweep the
Rev. 18. 23 the light of a candle shall shine no more
22. 5 they need no candle, neither light of the

CANDLESTICK —

1. *Place of light, candlestick,* מְנוֹרָה *menorah.*

Exod. 25. 31 thou shalt make a candlestick (of) pure
25. 31 beaten work shall the candlestick be made
25. 32 three branches of the candlestick out of
25. 32 three branches of the candlestick out of
25. 33 the six branches..out of the candlestick
25. 34 in the candlestick..four bowls made like
25. 35 the six branches..out of the candlestick
26. 35 the candlestick over against the table
30. 27 and the candlestick and his vessels
31. 8 the pure candlestick with all his furniture
35. 14 The candlestick also for the light and
37. 17 he made the candlestick (of) pure gold
37. 17 beaten work made he the candlestick
37. 18, 18 three branches of the candlestick out
37. 19 six branches going out of the candlestick
37. 20 in the candlestick, (were) four bowls
39. 37 The pure candlestick, (with) the lamps
40. 4 thou shalt bring in the candlestick, and
40. 24 he put the candlestick in the tent of the
Lev. 24. 4 He shall order the..pure candlestick
Num. 3. 31 the candlestick, and the altars, and the
4. 9 take a cloth..and cover the candlestick
8. 2 seven lamps..over against the candlestick
8. 3 the lamps..over against the candlestick
8. 4 this work of the candlestick (was of)..gold
8. 4 so he made the candlestick
1 Ki. 7. 49 the candlesticks of pure gold, five on the
2 Ki. 4. 10 a table, and a stool, and a candlestick
1 Ch. 28. 15 the weight for the candlesticks of gold
28. 15 by weight for every candlestick, and for
28. 15 and for the candlesticks of silver by
28. 15 for the candlestick. of every candlestick
2 Ch. 4. 7 And he made ten candlesticks of gold
4. 20 the candlesticks with their lamps, that
13. 11 the candlestick of gold with the lamps
Jer. 52. 19 the caldrons, and the candlesticks, and
Zech. 4. 2 I have looked, and, behold, a candlestick
4. 11 upon the right (side) of the candlestick

2. *Candlestick,* נֶבְרַשְׁתָּא *nebrashta.*

Dan. 5. 5 wrote over against the candlestick upon

3. *Lamp stand,* λυχνία *luchnia.*

Matt 5. 15 a candle, and put it..on a candlestick
Mark 4. 21 Is a candle..not..set on a candlestick
Luke 8. 16 a candle..but setteth (it) on a candlestick
11. 33 a candle.. but on a candlestick
Heb. 9. 2 tabernacle..wherein..the candlestick
Rev. 1. 12 turned I saw seven golden candlesticks
1. 13 in the midst of the seven candlesticks
1. 20 and the seven golden candlesticks
1. 20 the seven candlesticks which thou sawest
2. 1 who walketh in the midst of..candlesticks
2. 5 will come..and..remove thy candlestick
11. 4 two olive trees, and the two candlesticks

CANE —

Cane, reed, קָנֶה *qaneh.*

Isa. 43. 24 Thou hast brought me no sweet cane
Jer. 6. 20 and the sweet cane from a far country?

CANKER —

A consumption, gangrene, γάγγραινα *gaggraina.*

2 Ti. 2. 17 their word will eat as doth a canker: of

CANKER WORM —

Hedge chafer, a kind of locust, יֶלֶק *yeleq.*

Joel 1. 4 locust hath left hath the canker worm
1. 4 that which the canker worm hath left

Joel 2. 25 the canker worm..the caterpillar, and
Nah. 3. 15 it shall eat thee up like the canker worm
3. 15 make thyself many as the canker worm
3. 16 the canker worm spoileth, and fleeth

CANKERED, to be —

To be rusted, κατιόομαι *katioomai*

Jas. 5. 3 Your gold and silver is cankered; and

CAN'-NEH, כַּנֵּה *set up, distinguished.*

In the S. coast of Arabia, now called *Canne.*

Eze. 27. 23 Haran, and C., and Eden, the merchants

CA-PER-NA'-UM, Καπερναούμ *village of Nahum.*

On the western shore of the Sea of Galilee, and near the northern end. It was in the land of Gennesaret, on the rich busy plain. The doom pronounced against it and the other cities has been singularly fulfilled, and in sacred topography there is no more difficult task than to discover the site. The spots in dispute are *Khan-Minyeh* and *Tell-Hûm;* the latter is 3 miles N. of the former, and about 3 miles from the entrance of the Jordan into the lake.

Matt. 4. 13 he came and dwelt in C., which is upon
8. 5 when Jesus was entered into C., there
11. 23 thou, C., which art exalted unto heaven
17. 24 when they were come to C., they that
Mark 1. 21 they went into C.; and straightway
2. 1 he entered into C. after (some) days
9. 33 he came to C.: and, being in the house
Luke 4. 23 whatsoever we have heard done in C.
4. 31 And came down to C., a city of Galilee
7. 1 when he had ended..he entered into C.
10. 15 thou, C., which art exalted to heaven
John 2. 12 After this he went down to C., he, and
4. 46 a certain nobleman..son was sick at C.
6. 17 and went over the sea toward C. And it
6. 24 and came to C., seeking for Jesus
6. 59 These things said he..as he taught in C.

CAPH'-TOR, כַּפְתּוֹר *cup.*

The principal seat of the Philistines, who are once called Caphtorim, as being of the same race as the Mizraite people of that name. The position of Caphtor may have been in Egypt, or near it. From Jer. 47. 4 some think it was an island, but "isle" means, in its wider application, a maritime land whether on the coast or an island.

Deut. 2. 23 Caphtorims, which came forth out of C.
Jer. 47. 4 Philistines..remnant of the country of C.
Amos 9. 7 and the Philistines from C., and the

CAPH-TO'-RIM, כַּפְתֹּרִים **(CAPHTHORIM).**

The people of Caphtor. The name seems to be preserved in that of the old Egyptian city *Coptus.*

Gen. 10. 14 of whom came Philistim, and C.
Deut. 2. 23 the C., which came forth out of C., destr.
1 Ch. 1. 12 of whom came the Philistines, and C.

CAP-PA-DO-CI'-A, Καππαδοκία.

An elevated table-land, intersected by mountain chains in the eastern part of Asia Minor, bounded on the N. by Pontus, W. by Lycaonia, S. by Cilicia, and E. by Syria and Armenia Minor. It was always deficient in wood. Its interest for students of scripture arises chiefly from the mention of its Jewish residents among the hearers of Peter's first sermon, and its Christian residents among the readers of his first epistle.

Acts 2. 9 dwellers in..C., in Pontus, and Asia
1 Pe. 1. 1 strangers scattered throughout..C., Asia

CAPTAIN —

1. *First, leader, chief,* אַלּוּף *alluph.*

Jer. 13. 21 for thou hast taught them (to be) captains

2. *Lord, owner, possessor,* בַּעַל *baal.*

Jer. 37. 13 a captain of the ward (was) there, whose

3. *Tiphsar, (a title of honour),* טִפְסַר *tiphsar.*

Jer. 51. 27 appoint a captain against her; cause the
Nah. 3. 17 and thy captains as..great grasshoppers

4. *A ram, leader,* כַּר *kar.*

Eze. 21. 22 appoint captains, to open the mouth in

5. *Leader, one before,* נָגִיד *nagid.*

1 Sa. 9. 16 thou shalt anoint him..captain over my
10. 1 the LORD hath anointed thee..captain
13. 14 LORD hath commanded him..captain
2 Sa. 5. 2 and thou shalt be a captain over Israel
2 Ki. 20. 5 tell Hezekiah the captain of my people
2 Ch. 11. 11 strong holds, and put captains in them

6. *Exalted, lifted up one,* נָשִׂיא *nasi.*

Num. 2. 3 the son of Amminadab..captain of the
2. 5 Zuar..captain of the children of Issachar
2. 7 Helon..captain of the children of Zebulun
2. 10 the captain of the children of Reuben
2. 12 the captain of the children of Simeon
2. 14 the captain of the sons of Gad..Eliasaph
2. 18 the captain of the sons of Ephraim
2. 20 the captain of the children of Manasseh
2. 22 the captain of the sons of Benjamin
2. 25 the captain of the children of Dan..Ahi.
2. 27 the captain of the children of Asher..P.
2. 29 the captain of the children of Naphtali

7. *Governor,* פֶּחָה *pechah.*

1 Ki. 20. 24 and put captains in their rooms
2 Ki. 18. 24 wilt thou turn..the face of one captain
Isa. 36. 9 wilt thou turn..the face of one captain
Jer. 51. 23 will I break in pieces captains and rulers
51. 28 the kings of the Medes, the captains
51. 57 her wise (men), her captains, and her
Eze. 23. 6 clothed with blue, captains and rulers
23. 12 captains and rulers clothed most gorge.
23. 23 desirable young men, captains and rulers
Dan. 3. 2,3,27 princes, the governors, and..captains
6. 7 princes, the counsellors, and the captains

8. *Ruler, judge,* קָצִין *qatsin.*

Josh. 10. 24 the captains of the men of war which
Judg. 11. 6 they said..Come, and be our captain
11. 11 the people made him head and captain

9. *Head,* רֹאשׁ *rosh.*

Num. 14. 4 Let us make a captain, and let us return
Deut. 29. 10 your captains of your tribes, your elders
1 Ch. 4. 42 having for their captains Pelatiah, and
11. 15 three of the thirty captains went down
11. 42 a captain of the Reubenites, and thirty
12. 14 the sons of Gad, captains of the host
12. 18 and made them captains of the band
12. 20 captains of the thousands that (were) of
27. 3 Perez (was) the chief of all the captains
2 Ch. 13. 12 God himself (is) with us for (our) captain

10. *Great one,* רַב *rab.*

2 Ki. 25. 8, 10, 11, 12, 15, 18, 20 Nebuzar-adan, captain
Jer. 39. 9, 10, 11, 13 Nebuzar-adan the captain
40. 1, 2, 5 the captain of the guard
41. 10 Nebuzar-adan the captain of the guard
43. 6 Nebuzar-adan the captain of the guard
52. 12 nineteenth..came Nebuzar-adan, captain
52. 14 all the army..with the captain of the
52. 15, 16, 19, 24, 26, 30 the captain of the guard
Dan. 2. 14 Arioch the captain of the king's guard

11. *Head,* שַׂר *sar.*

Gen. 37. 36 an officer of Pharaoh's..captain of..guard
39. 1 an officer of Pharoah, captain of..guard
40. 3 he put them..in the house of the captain
40. 4 the captain of the guard charged Joseph
41. 10 ward in the captain of the guard's house
41. 12 an Hebrew, servant to the captain of the
Num 31. 14 Moses was wroth with..the captains
31. 48 captains of thousands, and captains of
31. 52 captains of thousands, and of..captains
31. 54 the captains of thousands..of hundreds
Deut. 1. 15 captains over thousands, and captains
1. 15 captains over fifties, and captains over
20. 9 make captains of the armies to lead the
Josh. 5. 14 but (as) captain of the host of the LORD
5. 15 the captain of the LORD'S host said unto
Judg. 4. 2 the captain of whose host (was) Sisera
4. 7 I will draw unto thee..Sisera, the captain
1 Sa. 8. 12 he will appoint him captains over thous.
12 9 sold them into the hand..Sisera, captain
14. 50 name of the captain of his host..Abner
17. 18 carry these ten cheeses unto the captain
17. 55 Saul..said unto Abner, the captain of the
18. 13 Saul..made him his captain over a thous.
22. 2 and he became a captain over them
22. 7 will the son of Jesse..make..captains
26. 5 Abner the son of Ner, the captain of his
2 Sa. 2. 8 Abner the son of Ner, captain of Saul's
4. 2 Saul's son had two men..captains of ba.
10. 16 Shobach the captain of the host..(went)
10. 18 the Syrians..smote Shobach the captain
18. 1 set captains of thousands and captains
18. 5 the king gave all the captains charge
19. 13 if thou be not captain of the host
23. 19 he was their captain..he attained not
24. 2 Joab the captain of the host, which (was)
24. 4 and against the captains of the host
24. 4 Joab and the captains of the host went
1 Ki. 1. 19 hath called..Joab the captain of the host
1. 25 hath called all the..captains of the host
2. 5 to the two captains of the hosts of Israel
2. 32 Abner the son of Ner, captain of the host
2. 32 Amasa the son of Jether, captain of the
11. 15, 21 Joab the captain of the host was
11. 24 he gathered men..and became captain
15. 20 So Ben-hadad..sent the captains of the
16. 9 servant Zimri, captain of half..chariots
16. 16 all Israel made Omri, the captain of the
22. 32 captains of the chariots saw Jehoshaphat
22. 33 the captains of the chariots perceived
2 Ki. 1. 9 Then the king sent unto him a captain of
1. 10 and said to the captain of fifty, If I (be) a
1. 11 he sent unto him another captain of fifty
1. 13 he sent again a captain of the third fifty
1. 13 the third captain of fifty went up, and
1. 14 and burnt up the two captains of the
4. 13 be spoken for to..the captain of the host?
5. 1 Naaman, captain of the host of the king
8. 21 the captains..and the people fled into
9. 5 behold, the captains of the host..sitting
9. 5 I have an errand to thee, O captain
9. 5 And he said, To thee, O captain
11. 9 the captains over the hundreds did..all
11. 10 the captains over hundreds..that (were)
11. 15 the priest commanded the captains of
25. 23 the captains of the armies, they and their
25. 26 all the people..and the captains of the
1 Ch. 11. 6 Jebusites first shall be chief and captain
11. 21 Of the three..he was their captain
12. 21 they helped David..and were captains in
12. 28 of his father's..twenty and two captains
12. 34 of Naphtali a thousand captains, and
13. 1 And David consulted with the captains of
15. 25 the captains..went to bring up the ark of
19. 16, 18 Shophach the captain of the host
25. 1 the captains of the host separated to the
26. 26 the captains over thousands and hund.
26. 26 the captains of the host, had dedicated
27. 1 and captains of thousands and hundreds
1 Ch. 27. 3 of all the captains of the host for the first
27. 5 The third captain of the host for the third
28. 1 tribes, and the captains of the companies
28. 1 captains over the thousands and captains
29. 6 the captains of thousands..of hundreds
2 Ch. 1. 2 to the captains of thousands..hundreds
8. 9 chief of his captains, and captains of his
16. 4 Ben-hadad hearkened..sent the captains
17. 14 of Judah, the captains of thousands
17. 15 next to him..Jehohanan the captain
18. 30, 31, 32 the king of Syria..com. the capt.
21. 9 compassed him in, and the captains of
23. 1, 14, 20 took the captains of hundreds
23. 9 Jehoiada..delivered to the captains of
25. 5 captains over thousands, and cap. over
26. 11 under the hand..(one) of the king's capt.
32. 6 he set captains of war over the people
32. 21 the leaders and captains in the camp
33. 11 the LORD brought upon them the captains
33. 14 put captains of war in all the fenced cities
Job 39. 25 the thunder of the captains, and the
Isa. 3. 3 The captain of fifty, and the honourable
Jer. 40. 7, 13 the captains of the forces
41. 11, 13, 16 captains of the forces that (were)
42. 1, 8 all the captains of the forces..came
43. 4, 5 the captains of the forces, and all the

12. *Ruler, powerful one,* שַׁלִּיט *shallit.*

Dan. 2. 15 He answered..Arioch the king's captain

13. *Third, one of or over three,* שָׁלִישׁ *shalish.*

Exod 14. 7 he took..captains over every one of them
15. 4 his chosen captains also are drowned
2 Sa. 23. 8 The Tachmonite, chief among the cap.
1 Ki. 9. 22 servants, and his princes, and his captains
2 Ki. 9. 25 Then said (Jehu) to Bidkar his captain
10. 25 Jehu said to the guard and to the capta.
10. 25 the guard and the captains cast (them)
15. 25 the son of Remaliah, a captain of his
1 Ch. 11. 11 chief of the captains [V.L. *shalosh*].
12. 18 chief of the captains [V.L. *shalosh*].
2 Ch. 8. 9 and captains of his chariots and horsemen

14. *Chief leader,* ἀρχηγός *archēgos.*

Heb. 2. 10 make the captain of their salvation

15. *Leader of an army,* στρατηγός *stratēgos.*

Luke 22. 4 communed with the chief priest and cap.
22. 52 chief priests, and captains of the temple
Acts 4. 1 the captain of the temple..came upon
5. 24 the captain of the temple..heard these
5. 26 Then went the captain with the officers

16. *Leader of a thousand,* χιλίαρχος *chiliarchos.*

John 18. 12 and the captain and officers..took Jesus
Rev. 19. 18 ye may eat the flesh of..captains

CAPTAIN, chief (or high) —

1. *Head,* שַׂר *sar.*

Gen. 21. 22, 32 Phichol the chief captain of his host
26. 26 Phichol the chief captain of his army

2. *Leader of a thousand,* χιλίαρχος *chiliarchos.*

Mark 6. 21 his lords, high captains, and chief
Acts 21. 31 tidings came unto the chief captain
21. 32 they saw the chief captain and the soldiers
21. 33 the chief captain came near, and took him
21. 37 he said unto the chief captain, May I
22. 24 The chief captain commanded him to be
22. 26 he went and told the chief captain
22. 27 Then the chief captain came, and said
22. 28 the chief captain answered, With a great
22. 29 and the chief captain also was afraid
23. 10 the chief captain..commanded the sold.
23. 15 signify to the chief captain that he bring
23. 17 Bring this young man unto the chief cap.
23. 18 So he..brought (him) to the chief captain
23. 19 Then the chief captain took him by the h.
23. 22 the chief captain..let the young man dep.
24. 7 [the chief captain Lysias came (upon us)]
24. 22 Lysias the chief captain shall come down
25. 23 place of hearing, with the chief captains
Rev. 6. 15 the rich men, and the chief captains

CAPTAIN of the guard —

Chief of the camp, στρατοπεδάρχης *stratopedarchēs.*

Acts 28. 16 [delivered..to the captain of the guard]

CAPTAIN that had rule —

Head, שַׂר *sar.*

1 Ki. 22. 31 captains that had rule over his chariots

CAPTAINS —

1. *One ready, prepared,* כָּרִי *kari.*

2 Ki. 11. 4 rulers over hundreds, with the captains
11. 19 rulers over hundreds, and the captains

2. *Officers,* שָׁלִשִׁים *shalishim* [V.L. שְׁלוֹשִׁים].

1 Ch. 11. 11 Jashobeam..the chief of the captains
12. 18 came upon Amasai..chief of the captains

CAPTIVE —

1. *Exile, one removed or removing,* גּוֹלָה *golah.*

2 Ki. 24. 16 the king of Babylon brought captive to B.
Eze. 1. 1 I (was) among the captives by the river

2. *To remove into exile,* גָּלָה *galah.*

2 Ki 24. 14 men of valour..ten thousand captives
Isa. 49. 21 lost my children, and am..a captive

3. *Exile, removal,* גָּלוּת *galuth.*

Isa. 20. 4 lead..the Ethiopians captives, young
45. 13 and he shall let go my captives
Jer. 28. 4 with all the captives of Judah, that went

4. *Son of exile or removal,* בַּר־גָּלוּתָא *ben galutha.*

Dan. 2. 25 I have found a man of the captives of

5. *To take away captive,* שָׁבָה *shabah.*
Gen. 31. 26 carried away my daughters, as captives
Isa. 61. 1 to proclaim liberty to the captives, and

6. *One taken away captive,* שְׁבִי *shebi.*
Exod12. 29 the first born of the captive that (was)
Num31. 12 they brought the captives, and the prey
31. 19 purify (both) yourselves and your cap.
2 Ch.28. 17 the Edomites..carried away captives
Isa. 49. 24 Shall the prey..or the lawful captive
49. 25 Even the captives of the mighty shall
52. 2 bands of thy neck, O captive daughter
Jer. 48. 46 for thy sons are taken captives, and thy
Dan. 11. 8 shall also carry captives; Deut. 21. 10.

7. *Company of captives,* שִׁבְיָה *shibyah.*
Deut.21. 11 And seest among the captives a..woman
32. 42 the blood of the slain and of the captives
2 Ch. [28. 5 carried..a..multitude of them captives]
28. 11 hear me, therefore, and deliver the capt.
28. 13 Ye shall not bring in the captives hither
28. 14 So the armed men left the captives
28. 15 the men..rose up, and took the captives
Jer. 48. 46 sons are taken..thy daughters captives

8. *Captivity,* שְׁבִית *shebith.*
Eze. 16. 53 the captivity of thy captives in the midst

9. *One taken by the spear,* αἰχμάλωτος *aichmalōtos.*
Luke 4. 18 to preach deliverance to the captives, and
[*See also* Carried away, carry away, lead, led away.]

CAPTIVE, to go —
To remove into exile, גָּלָה *galah.*
Amos 6. 7 go captive with the first that go captive

CAPTIVE, to bring away —
To take away captive, שָׁבָה *shabah.*
2 Ki. 5. 2 Syrians..brought away captive..a little

CAPTIVE, to be carried —
To be taken away captive, שָׁבָה *shabah,* 2.
1 Ki. 8. 47 the land whither they were carried capt.
2 Ch. 6. 37 the land whither they were carried cap.
Eze. 6. 9 nations whither they shall be carried cap.

CAPTIVE, to be carried away —
1. *To be exiled,* גָּלָה *galah,* 6.
Jer. 40. 1 which were carried away captive unto
2. *To be taken away captive,* שָׁבָה *shabah,* 2.
Jer. 13. 17 the LORD'S flock is carried away captive

CAPTIVE, to carry —
1. *To take away captive,* שָׁבָה *shabah.*
1 Ki. 8. 47 land of them that carried them captives
8. 50 before them who carried them captive
2 Ch. 6. 38 whither they have carried them captives
Psa 106. 46 of all those that carried them captives
2. *To remove into exile,* גָּלָה *galah,* 5.
2 Ki.15. 29 and carried them captive to Assyria
16. 9 carried (the people of) it captive to Kir
Jer. 20. 4 he shall carry them captive into Babylon

CAPTIVE, to carry away —
1. *To take away captive,* שָׁבָה *shabah.*
Num24. 22 Asshur shall carry thee away captive
1 Ki. 8. 46 so that they carry them away captives
2 Ch. 6. 36 carry them away captives unto a land
25. 12 did the children..carry away captive
28. 5 carried away a great multitude of them
28. 8 carried away captive of their brethren
Psa 137. 3 they that carried us away captive
Jer. 41. 10 Ishmael carried away captive all the
41. 10 son of Nethaniah carried..away captive
41. 14 Ishmael had carried away captive from
43. 12 shall burn..and carry them away captives
Obad. 11. the strangers carried away captive his
2. *To remove into exile,* גָּלָה *galah,* 5.
Jer 24. 1 king of Babylon had carried away captive
27. 20 carried away captive Jeconiah the son
39. 9 carried away captive into Babylon the
43. 3 carry us away captives into Babylon
52. 15 guard carried away captive (certain) of
52. 28 Nebuchadrezzar carried away captive
52. 29 he carried away captive from Jerusalem
52. 30 the guard carried away captive of the Jews
Amos 1. 6 carried away captive the whole captivity

CAPTIVE, to cause to be carried away —
To remove into exile, גָּלָה *galah,* 5.
Jer. 29. 7 I have caused you to be carried away capt.
29. 14 I caused you to be carried away captive

CAPTIVE exile —
To be bent, bowed, צָעָה *tsaah.*
Isa. 51. 14 The captive exile hasteneth that he may

CAPTIVE, to lead —
1. *To take away captive,* שָׁבָה *shabah.*
Judg. 5. 12 lead thy captivity captive, thou son of
2 Ch 30. 9 before them that lead them captive, so
Psa. 68. 18 thou hast led captivity captive: thou
2. *To remove into exile,* גָּלָה *galah,* 5.
Jer. 22. 12 place whither they have led him captive
3. *To take by the spear,* αἰχμαλωτεύω *aichmalōteuō.*
Eph. 4. 8 he led captivity captive, and gave gifts
2 Ti. 3. 6 [lead captive] silly women laden with

CAPTIVE, to lead away —
1. *To take away captive,* שָׁבָה *shabah.*
1 Ki. 8. 48 their enemies which led them away cap.
2. *To be exiled,* גָּלָה *galah,* 4.
Nah. 2. 7 Huzzab shall be led away captive, she
3. *To take by the spear,* αἰχμαλωτίζω *aichmalōtizō.*
Luke21. 24 shall be led away captive into all nations

CAPTIVE, to take —
To take away captive, שָׁבָה *shabah.*
Gen. 34. 29 little ones..their wives took they captive
Num31. 9 Israel took..the women of Midian captives
[Deut21. 10 and thou hast taken them captive]
1 Sa. 30. 2 had taken the women captives that (were)
2 Ki. 6. 22 thou hast taken captive with thy sword
2 Ch.28. 11 captives..which ye have taken captive
Isa. 14. 2 and they shall take them captives, whose
Jer. 50. 33 all that took them captives held them

CAPTIVE, to be taken —
1. *To be taken away captive,* שָׁבָה *shabah,* 2.
Gen. 14. 14 heard that his brother was taken captive
1 Sa. 30. 3 and their daughters, were taken captives
30. 5 David's two wives were taken captives
2. *To catch alive,* ζωγρέω *zōgreō.*
2 Ti. 2. 26 who are taken captive by him at his will

CAPTIVITY —
1. *Exile, removal,* גּוֹלָה *golah.*
2 Ki.24. 15 (those) carried he into captivity from Jer.
1 Ch. 5. 22 dwelt in their steads until the captivity
Ezra 1. 11 bring up with..the captivity that were
2. 1 children..went up out of the captivity
4. 1 the children of the captivity builded the
6. 19 the children of the captivity kept the
6. 20 for all the children of the captivity
6. 21 which were come again out of captivity
10. 7 all the children of the captivity, that
10. 16 And the children of the captivity did so
Esth. 2. 6 Who..carried away..with the captivity
Jer. 29. 16 are not gone forth with you into captivity
29. 20 Hear..the word..all ye of the captivity
29. 31 Send to all them of the captivity, saying
46. 19 furnish thyself to go into captivity: for
48. 7 Chemosh shall go forth into captivity
48. 11 neither hath he gone into captivity
49. 3 for their king shall go into captivity
Eze. 3. 11 go, get thee to them of the captivity
3. 15 came to them of the captivity at Tel-abib
11. 24 in a vision..to them of the captivity
11. 25 Then I spake unto them of the captivity
12. 4 they that go forth into captivity
12. 7 I brought forth my stuff..for captivity
12. 11 they shall remove, (and) go into captivity
25. 3 Judah, when they went into captivity
Amos 1. 15 And their king shall go into captivity
Zech. 6. 10 Take of..the captivity..of Heldai
14. 2 half of..city shall go forth into captivity
2. *To remove into exile,* גָּלָה *galah.*
Judg18. 30 until the day of the captivity of the land
3. *Exile, removal,* גָּלוּת *galuth.*
2 Ki. 25. 27 seven and thirtieth year of the captivity
Ezra 6. 16 the children of the captivity, kept the
Jer. 29. 22 a curse by all the captivity of Judah
52. 31 in..seven and thirtieth year of..captivity
Eze. 1. 2 fifth year of king Jehoiachin's captivity
33. 21 in the twelfth year of our captivity
40. 1 the five..twentieth year of our captivity
Dan. 5. 13 (Art) thou..of the children of..captivity
6. 13 Daniel, which (is) of..children..captivity
Amos 1. 6 they carried..captive..whole captivity
1. 9 they delivered up the whole captivity
Obad. 20 And the captivity of this host of the
20 and the captivity of Jerusalem, which
4. *A casting away, or up and down,* טַלְטֵלָה *taltelah.*
Isa. 22. 17 will carry..away with a mighty captivity
5. *Captivity,* שְׁבוּת *shebuth.*
Deut30. 3 the LORD thy God will turn..captivity
Job 42. 10 the LORD turned the captivity of Job
Psa. 14. 7 the LORD bringeth back the captivity
53. 6 God bringeth back the captivity of his
85. 1 thou hast brought back the captivity of
126. 4 Turn again our captivity, O LORD
Jer. 29. 14 I will turn away your captivity
30. 3, 18 I will bring again the captivity of
31. 23 when I shall bring again their captivity
32. 44 I will cause their captivity to return
33. 7 I will cause the captivity of..Israel, to
33. 11 I will cause to return the captivity of
33. 26 I will cause their captivity to return
48. 47 Yet will I bring again the captivity of M.
49. 6 I will bring again the captivity of the
49. 39 I will bring again the captivity of Elam
Lam. 2. 14 iniquity, to turn away thy captivity
Eze. 29. 14 I will bring again the captivity of Egypt
Hos. 6. 11 when I returned the captivity of my
Joel 3. 1 I shall bring again the captivity of Judah
Amos 9. 14 I will bring again the captivity of my
Zeph. 2. 7 visit them, and turn away their captivity
3. 20 I turn back your captivity before your
6. *Captivity, captive,* שְׁבִי *shebi.*
Deut21. 13 put the raiment of her captivity from off
28. 41 for they shall go into captivity
Judg. 5. 12 lead thy captivity captive, thou son of A.
2 Ch. 6. 37 pray unto thee..land of their captivity
20. 9 our wives (are) in captivity for this
Ezra 2. 1 children..that went up out of..captivity
3. 8 they that were come out of the captivity
8. 35 children..were come out of the captivity
9. 7 to the sword, to captivity, and to a spoil
Neh. 1. 2 the Jews..which were left of the captivity
Neh. 1. 3 The remnant that are left of the captivity
7. 6 children..went up out of the captivity
8. 17 that were come again out of the captivity
Psa. 68. 18 thou hast led captivity captive: thou
78. 61 And delivered his strength into captivity
Isa. 46. 2 but themselves are gone into captivity
Jer. 15. 2 as (are) for the captivity, to the captivity
20. 6 all that dwell..shall go into captivity
22. 22 and thy lovers shall go into captivity
30. 10 I will save thee..land of their captivity
30. 16 every one of them, shall go into captivity
43. 11 such (as are) for captivity to captivity
46. 27 save thee..from the land of their capt.
Lam. 1. 5 her children are gone into captivity before
1. 18 and my young men are gone into captivity
Eze. 12. 11 they shall remove, (and) go into captivity
30. 17 and these (cities) shall go into captivity
30. 18 and her daughters shall go into captivity
Dan. 11. 33 by flame, by captivity, and by spoil
Amos 9. 4 they go into captivity before their enemies
Nah. 3. 10 she carried away, she went into captivity
Hab. 1. 9 they shall gather the captivity as the
7. *Captivity, (captive),* שִׁבְיָה *shibyah.*
Neh. 4. 4 for a prey in the land of captivity:
8. *Captivity,* שְׁבִית *shebith.*
Num21. 29 into captivity unto Sihon king of the
Job 42. 10 the LORD turned the captivity of Job
Psa. 85. 1 thou hast brought back the captivity of
126. 4 Turn again our captivity, O LORD, as the
Jer. 29. 14 I will turn away your captivity, and I
49. 39 I will bring again the captivity of Elam
Lam. 2. 14 not discovered..turn away thy captivity
Eze. 16. 53 When I shall bring again their captivity
16. 53 the captivity of Sodom and her daughters
16. 53 captivity of Samaria and her daughters
16. 53 then (will I bring again) the captivity of
Zeph. 2. 7 God shall..turn away their captivity
9. *Captivity, return,* שִׁיבָה *shibah.*
Psa. 126. 1 LORD turned again the captivity of Zion
10. *A taking by the spear,* αἰχμαλωσία *aichmalōsia.*
Eph. 4. 8 he led captivity captive, and Rev. 13. 10, 10

CAPTIVITY, to bring into —
To take by the spear, αἰχμαλωτίζω *aichmalōtizō.*
Rom. 7. 23 bringing me into captivity to the law of
2 Co. 10. 5 bringing into captivity every thought to

CAPTIVITY, to cause to go into —
To remove into exile, גָּלָה *galah,* 5.
Amos 5. 27 will I cause you to go into captivity

CAPTIVITY, to cause to be led into —
To remove into exile, גָּלָה *galah,* 5.
Eze. 39. 28 God..caused them to be led into captivity

CAPTIVITY, to carry away into —
To remove into exile, גָּלָה *galah,* 5.
Lam. 4. 22 no more carry thee away..into captivity

CAPTIVITY, to go into —
To remove into exile, גָּלָה *galah.*
Isa. 5. 13 my people are gone into captivity, because
Lam. 1. 3 Judah is gone into captivity because of
Eze. 39. 23 the house of Israel went into captivity
Amos 1. 5 Syria shall go into captivity unto Kir
5. 5 for Gilgal shall surely go into captivity
7. 17 Israel shall surely go into captivity forth
Mic. 1. 16 they are gone into captivity from thee

CARBUNCLE —
1. *Stone of brightness,* אֶבֶן אֶקְדָּח *eben eqdach.*
Isa. 54. 12 I will make..thy gates of carbuncles
2. *Glittering stone, emerald,* בָּרְקַת *bareqath.*
Eze. 28. 13 the sapphire, the emerald..the carbuncle
3. *Glittering stone,* בָּרֶקֶת *bareqeth.*
Exod28. 17 a sardius, a topaz, and a carbuncle
39. 10 a sardius, a topaz, and a carbuncle

CAR'-CAS, כַּרְכַּס *severe.*
The seventh chamberlain of Ahasuerus.
Esth. 1. 10 he commanded Mehuman..and C., the

CARCASE —
1. *Body,* גְּוִיָּה *geviyah.*
Judg14. 8 bees and honey in the carcase of the lion
14. 9 had taken the honey out of the carcase
2. *Fallen thing, carcase,* מַפֶּלֶת *mappeleth.*
Judg14. 8 turned aside to see the carcase of the lion
3. *Faded thing, carcase,* נְבֵלָה *nebelah.*
Lev. 5. 2 whether..a carcase of an unclean beast
5. 2 a carcase of unclean cattle, or the carcase
11. 8 their carcase shall ye not touch; they (are)
11. 11 ye shall have their carcases in abomina.
11. 24 whosoever toucheth the carcase of them
11. 25 whosoever beareth..the carcase of them
11. 27 whoso toucheth their carcase shall be
11. 28 he that beareth the carcase of them shall
11. 35 whereupon (any part) of their carcase
11. 36 that which toucheth their carcase shall
11. 37, 38 if (any part) of their carcase fall..it
11. 39 he that toucheth the carcase..shall be
11. 40 he that eateth of the carcase..shall wash
11. 40 he also that beareth the carcase..shall
Deut28. 26 thy carcase shall be meat unto all fowls
Josh. 8. 29 they should take his carcase down from
1 Ki.13. 22 thy carcase shall not come unto the sep.
13. 24 his carcase (was) cast in the way, and the

1 Ki. 13. 24 the lion also stood by the carcase
13. 25 men passed by, and saw the carcase
13. 25 and the lion standing by the carcase
13. 28 he went, and found his carcase cast in
13. 28 and the lion standing by the carcase
13. 28 the lion had not eaten the carcase, nor
13. 29 And the prophet took up the carcase of
13. 30 he laid his carcase in his own grave
2 Ki. 9. 37 the carcase of Jezebel shall be as dung
Isa. 5. 25 their carcases..torn in the midst of the
Jer. 7. 33 the carcases of this people shall be meat
9. 22 the carcases of men shall fall as dung
16. 4 their carcases shall be meat for the fowls
16. 18 filled mine inheritance with the carcase
19. 7 their carcases will I give to be meat for

4. *Carcase, faint, exhausted object,* פֶּגֶר *peger.*
Gen. 15. 11 the fowls came down upon the carcases
Lev. 26. 30 cast your carcases upon the carcases of
Num 14. 29 Your carcases shall fall in this wilderness
14. 32 your carcases, they shall fall in this wil.
14. 33 until your carcases be wasted in the wil.
1 Sa. 17. 46 I will give the carcases..unto the fowls of
Isa. 14. 19 as a carcase trodden under feet
34. 3 their stink shall come up out of their car.
66. 24 look upon the carcases of the men that
Eze. 43. 7 the carcases of their kings in their high
43. 9 let them put away..the carcases of their
Nah. 3. 3 and a great number of carcases; and

5. *Limb,* κῶλον *kōlon.*
Heb. 3. 17 whose carcases fell in the wilderness?

6. *Fallen thing,* πτῶμα *ptōma.*
Matt 24. 28 wheresoever the carcase is, there will the

CARCASE, dead —

1. *Carcase, faded object,* נְבֵלָה *nebelah.*
Deut 14. 8 ye shall not..touch their dead carcase

2. *Faint, exhausted,* פֶּגֶר *peger.*
Eze. 6. 5 I will lay the dead carcases of the child.

CAR-CHE'-MISH, כַּרְכְּמִישׁ *citadel of Chemosh.*
A city on the Euphrates occupying nearly the site of *Mabog* or *Hierapolis* in later times, but not to be confounded with the classical *Circesium,* which stood much further down the river.
2 Ch. 35. 20 Necho..came up to fight against Charch.
Isa. 10. 9 (Is) not Calno as C? (is) not Hamath
Jer. 46. 2 which was by the river Euphrates in C.

CARE —

1. *Anxious care,* דְּאָגָה *deagah.*
Eze. 4. 16 bread by weight, and with care

2. *Word, matter,* דָּבָר *dabar.*
1 Sa. 10. 2 thy father hath left the care of the asses

3. *Trembling, fear,* חֲרָדָה *charadah.*
2 Ki. 4. 13 been careful for us with all this care

4. *Division, distraction,* μέριμνα *merimna.*
Matt 13. 22 is he that heareth the word; and the care
Mark 4. 19 the cares of this..and the deceitfulness
Luke 8. 14 are choked with cares and riches
21. 34 your hearts be overcharged with..cares
2 Co. 11. 28 Besides those..care of all the churches
1 Pe. 5. 7 Casting all your care upon..for he careth

5. *Haste, speed,* σπουδή *spoudē.*
2 Co. 7. 12 our care for you in the sight of God might

6. *To be mindful,* φρονέω *phroneō.*
Phil. 4. 10 at..last your care for me hath flourished

CARE, earnest —
Haste, speed, σπουδή *spoudē.*
2 Co. 8. 16 put the same earnest care into the heart

CARE, to —

1. *To be an object of care,* μέλω *melō.*
Matt 22. 16 neither carest thou for any (man); for
Mark 4. 38 Master, carest thou not that we perish?
12. 14 Master, we know that thou..carest for
Luke 10. 40 dost thou not care that my sister hath
John 10. 13 he is an hireling, and careth not for the
12. 6 not that he cared for the poor; but because
Acts 18. 17 Gallio cared for none of those things
1 Co. 7. 21 Art thou called (being) a servant? care
1 Pe. 5. 7 all your care upon him; for he careth

2. *To become distracted, careful,* μεριμνάω *merimnaō.*
1 Co. 7. 32, 33 He that is unmarried careth for the
7. 34 The unmarried woman careth for the
7. 34 but she that is married careth for the
Phil. 2. 20 who will naturally care for your state

CARE, to have —
To become distracted, careful, μεριμνάω *merimnaō.*
1 Co. 12. 25 the members should have the same care

CARE, to take —
To be an object of care, μέλω *melō.*
1 Co. 9. 9 Doth God take care for oxen?

CARE for, to —

1. *To seek, search after,* דָּרַשׁ אַחֲרֵי *darash achare.*
Deut 11. 12 A land..the LORD thy God careth for
Psa. 142. 4 I looked..no man cared for my soul

2. *To set the heart to,* שׂוּם לֵב אֶל *sum leb el.*
2 Sa. 18. 3 if we flee away, they will not care for us
18. 3 neither if half of us die, will they care for

CARE of, to take —
To be careful about, ἐπιμελέομαι *epimeleomai.*
Luke 10. 34 brought him to an inn, and took care of
Luke 10. 35 Take care of him..I will repay thee
1 Ti. 3. 5 how..he take care of the church of God?

CARE, without —
Trustfully, confidently, לָבֶטַח *la-betach.*
Jer. 49. 31 wealthy nation, that dwelleth without care

CA-RE'-AH, קָרֵחַ *bald head.*
Father of Johanan, governor of Judah in the time of Gedaliah. Elsewhere in the English version it is spelt *Kareah.* B.C. 630.
2 Ki. 25. 23 came to Gedaliah..Johanan the son of C.

CAREFUL, to be —

1. *To be anxiously careful,* דָּאַג *daag.*
Jer. 17. 8 shall not be careful in the year of drought

2. *To tremble, fear,* חָרַד *charad.*
2 Ki. 4. 13 Behold, thou hast been careful for us

3. *To be or think necessary,* חָשַׁח *shashach.*
Dan. 3. 16 we (are) not careful to answer thee in

4. *To become distracted,* μεριμνάω *merimnaō.*
Luke 10. 41 thou art careful and troubled about
Phil. 4. 6 Be careful for nothing; but in every thing

5. *To be mindful,* φρονέω *phroneō.*
Phil. 4. 10 ye were also careful, but ye lacked

6. *To be thoughtful or mindful,* φροντίζω *phrontizō.*
Titus 3. 8 which..believed in God might be careful

CAREFULLY —
To hear, hearken, שָׁמַע *shama.*
Deut 15. 5 Only if thou carefully hearken unto the

CAREFULLY, the more —
More hastily, σπουδαιοτέρως *spoudaioterōs.*
Phil. 2. 28 I sent him therefore the more carefully

CAREFULNESS —

1. *Anxious care,* דְּאָגָה *deagah.*
Eze. 12. 18 drink thy water..with carefulness
12. 19 They shall eat their bread with careful.

2. *Haste,* σπουδή *spoudē.*
2 Co. 7. 11 what carefulness it wrought in you

CAREFULNESS, without —
Without distraction, ἀμέριμνος *amerimnos.*
1 Co. 7. 32 But I would have you without carefulness

CARELESS, Carelessly —
In confidence, בֶּטַח . לָבֶטַח [*betach*].
Judg 18. 7 the people..dwelt careless, after the
Isa. 47. 8 thou..that dwellest carelessly
Eze. 30. 9 to make the careless Ethiopians afraid
39. 6 them that dwell carelessly
Zeph 2. 15 city that dwelt carelessly

CARELESS one or woman —
To trust, be confident, בָּטַח *batach.*
Isa. 32. 9 careless daughters; 32. 10 careless women
32. 11 ye women..be troubled, ye careless ones

CAR'-MEL, כַּרְמֶל *fruitful place.*
1. It is nearly always with the article—"the park," the well-wooded place. A mountain which forms a striking and characteristic feature of Canaan. It projects into the Mediterranean, and stands as a wall between the maritime plain of Sharon on the S. and the more inland expanse of Esdraelon on the N. It is about 12 miles long from the sea till it terminates abruptly in the hills of *Janin* and Samaria, which form at that part the central mass of the country. Its highest point is about 4 miles from the E. end, at the village of *Es-fieh,* and measures in English feet 1728 above the sea level.
Josh 12. 22 the king of Jokneam of C., one
19. 26 reacheth to C. westward, and to Shihor.
1 Sa. 15. 12 Saul came to C., and, behold, he set him
1 Ki. 18. 19 gather to me all Israel unto mount C.
18. 20 gathered the prophets..unto mount C.
18. 42 Elijah went up to the top of C.; and he
2 Ki. 2. 25 he went from thence to mount C.
4. 25 came unto the man of God to mount C.
19. 23 I will enter into..the forest of his C.
2 Ch. 26. 10 vine dressers in the mountains, and in C.
Song 7. 5 Thine head upon thee (is) like C., and the
Isa. 33. 9 Bashan and C. shake off (their fruits)
35. 2 the excellency of C. and Sharon; they
37. 24 I will enter into..the forest of his C.
Jer. 46. 18 as C. by the sea, (so) shall he come
50. 19 he shall feed on C. and Bashan, and his
Amos 1. 2 The LORD will roar..and the top of C.
9. 3 though they hide themselves in..top of C.
Mic. 7. 14 which dwell solitarily..in the midst of C.
Nah. 1. 4 Bashan languisheth, and C., and
2. A town in the mountainous part of Judah, where Nabal resided with his wife Abigail. Here, no doubt, was the site of Uzziah's vineyards. The ruins of the town, now called *Kurmul,* still remain at 10 miles below Hebron in a slightly S. E. direction, close to those of *Main, Zif,* (Maon and Ziph), and other places named with Carmel in Josh. 15. 55.
Josh 15. 55 Maon, C., and Ziph, and Juttah
1 Sa. 25. 2 in Maon, whose possessions (were) in C.
25. 2 and he was shearing his sheep in C.
25. 5 Get you up to C., and go to Nabal
25. 7 all the while they were in C.
25. 40 the servants of David were come..to C.

CAR-MEL-ITE, CAR-MEL-IT-ESS כַּרְמְלִית ,כַּרְמְלִי.
An inhabitant of Carmel.
1 Sa. 27. 3 and Abigail the C., Nabal's wife
30. 5 and Abigail the wife of Nabal the C.
2 Sa. 2. 2 and Abigail, Nabal's wife, the C.
3. 3 Chileab, of Abigail the wife of Nabal..C.
23. 35 Hezrai the C., Paarai the Arbite
1 Ch. 3. 1 the second, Daniel, of Abigail the C.
11. 37 Hezro the C., Naarai the son of Ezbai

CAR'-MI, כַּרְמִי *fruitful, noble.*
1. Father of Achan "who troubled Israel." In 1 Ch. 4. 1 the name is given as a son of Judah, but the same person is probably intended, as no such son of Judah is elsewhere mentioned, and of the five names mentioned only one is really his son, Pharez, though the other four are called "sons." Hezron is of the 2d generation, Hur of the 4th, and Shobal of the 6th. B. C. 1480.
Josh. 7. 1 for Achan, the son of C., the son of Zabdi
7. 18 and Achan, the son of C...was taken
1 Ch. 2. 7 the sons of C.; Achar the troubler of Is.
4. 1 sons of Judah; Pharez, Hezron, and C.
2. One of the sons of Reuben, B.C. 1700.
Gen. 46. 9 sons of Reuben; Hanoch..Hezron, and C.
Exod. 6. 14 Hezron, and C.; these (be) the families of
Num 26. 6 of C., the family of the Carmites
1 Ch. 5. 3 sons..of Reuben..Pallu, Hezron, and C.

CARMITES, הַכַּרְמִי.
Family descended from the preceding, No. 2.
Num 26. 6 of Carmi, the family of the C.

CARNAL —

1. *Fleshly,* σαρκικός *sarkikos.*
Rom. 7. 14 but I am [carnal], sold under sin
1 Co. 3. 1 I..could not speak..but as unto [carnal]
3. 3 ye are yet [carnal]..are ye not carnal?
3. 4 I (am) of Apollos; are ye not [carnal]?
2 Co. 10. 4 weapons of our warfare (are) not carnal
Heb. 7. 16 not after the law of a [carnal] command.

2. *Flesh,* σάρξ *sarx.*
Rom. 8. 7 the carnal mind (is) enmity against God
Heb. 9. 10 drinks, and divers washings, and carnal

CARNAL things —
The fleshly (things), τὰ σαρκικά *ta sarkika.*
Rom 15. 27 to minister unto them in carnal things
1 Co. 9. 11 if we shall reap your carnal things?

CARNALLY —

1. *Lying of seed,* שִׁכְבַת זֶרַע [*shekabah*]; לְזֶרַע [*zera*].
Lev. 18. 20 Moreover thou shalt not lie carnally with
19. 20 whosoever lieth carnally with a woman
Num. 5. 13 a man lie with her carnally, and it be hid

2. *Flesh,* σάρξ *sarx.*
Rom. 8. 6 For to be carnally minded (is) death; but

CARPENTER —

1. *Artificer,* חָרָשׁ *charash.*
2 Ki. 22. 6 Unto carpenters, and builders, and mas.
2 Ch. 24. 12 hired masons and carpenters to repair
Ezra 3. 7 They gave money also unto..the carpen.
Isa. 41. 7 So the carpenter encouraged the goldsm.
Jer. 24. 1 the carpenters and smiths, from Jerusal.
29. 2 the carpenters, and the smiths, were de.
Zech 1. 20 the LORD showed me four carpenters

2. *Artificer in wood,* חָרָשׁ עֵץ *charash ets.*
2 Sa. 5. 11 cedar trees, and carpenters, and masons
2 Ki. 12. 11 they laid it out to the carpenters and
1 Ch. 14. 1 masons and carpenters, to build him
Isa. 44. 13 The carpenter stretcheth out (his) rule

3. *Artificer,* τέκτων *tektōn.*
Matt 13. 55 Is not this the carpenter's son? is not
Mark 6. 3 Is not this the carpenter, the son of Mary

CAR'-PUS, Κάρπος *fruit.*
A person at Troas in Mysia, with whom Paul left a cloak.
2 Ti. 4. 13 The cloak that I left at Troas with C.

CARRIAGE —

1. *Heaviness, weight,* כְּבוּדָּה *kebuddah.*
Judg 18. 21 and put..the carriage before them

2. *Vessel, instrument,* כְּלִי *keli.*
1 Sa. 17. 22 left his carriage..keeper of the carriage
Isa. 10. 28 at Michmash he hath laid up his carriages

3. *Thing lifted up or borne,* נְשׂוּאָה *nesuah.*
Isa. 46. 1 carriages (were) heavy loaden: (they)

CARRIAGE, to take up one's —
To pack baggage, ἀποσκευάζομαι *aposkeuazomai.*
Acts 21. 15 after those days we took up our carriages

CARRIED —
To lift up, bear, carry, נָשָׂא *nasa.*
Isa. 46. 3 (by me)..(which are) carried from the

CARRIED, to be —

1. *To be caused to go in,* בּוֹא *bo,* 6.
Jer. 27. 22 They shall be carried to Babylon, and

2. *To be caused to flow or go,* יָבַל *yabal,* 6.
Job 10. 19 I should have been carried from the
Hos. 10. 6 It shall be also carried unto Assyria (for)
12. 1 and oil is carried into Egypt

3. *To move, be moved,* מוּט *mot.*
Psa. 46. 2 though the mountains be carried into

4. *To be lifted up, borne, carried,* נָשָׂא *nasa,* 2.
2 Ki. 20. 17 all..in thine house..shall be carried into
Isa. 39. 6 all..in thine house..shall be carried to
49. 22 daughters shall be carried upon (their)

CARRIED about, to be —
To be carried round, סָבַב *sabab,* 2.
1 Sa. 5. 8 Let the ark..be carried about unto Gath

CARRIED away, to be —
1. *Exile*, גּוֹלָה *golah.*
Nah. 3. 10 Yet (was) she carried away, she went

2. *To remove into exile*, גָּלָה *galah.*
2 Ki. 17. 23 So was Israel carried away out of their
25. 21 So Judah was carried away out of their

3. *To be caused to go into exile*, גָּלָה *galah*, 6.
1 Ch. 9. 1 Israel and Judah..were carried away to
Esth. 2. 6 Who had been carried away from Jerus.
2. 6 captivity which had been carried away

4. *A change of dwelling*, μετοικεσία *metoikesia.*
Matt. 1. 11 the time they were carried away to Bab.

CARRIED away with, to be —
To lead away with, συναπάγω *sunapagō.*
Gal. 2. 13 Barnabas..was carried away with their

CARRIED away captive —
Exile, removed one, גּוֹלָה *golah.*
Jer. 28. 6 all that is carried away captive, from B.
29. 1 the elders which were carried away cap.
29. 4 all that are carried away captives, whom

CARRIED away captive, to be —
1. *To go into exile*, גָּלָה *galah.*
Jer. 52. 27 Thus Judah was carried away captive

2. *To be removed into exile*, גָּלָה *galah*, 6.
Jer. 13. 19 Judah shall be carried away captive all
40. 1 which were carried away captive unto B.
40. 7 the poor..were not carried away captive

CARRIED away captive, to be wholly —
To be caused to go into exile, גָּלָה *galah*, 6.
Jer. 13. 19 it shall be wholly carried away captive

CARRIED away captive, to cause to be —
To cause to go into exile, גָּלָה *galah*, 5.
Jer. 29. 7 caused you to be carried away captives
29. 14 I caused you to be carried away captive

CARRIED away captive, they that are —
Exile, state of exile, גָּלוּת *galuth.*
Jer. 24. 5 them that are carried away captive
40. 1 all that were carried away captive of J.

CARRIED away, those that had been —
An exile, removed one, גּוֹלָה *golah.*
Ezra 8. 35 children of those that had been carried a.
9. 4 of those that had been carried away
10. 6, 8 of those that had been carried away
Neh. 7. 6 captivity..those that had been carried a.

CARRIED headlong, to be —
To be hastened, מָהַר *mahar*, 2.
Job 5. 13 counsel of the froward is carried headlong

CARRY, to —
1. *To cause to come or go in*, בּוֹא *bo*, 5.
Gen. 42. 19 carry corn for the famine of your houses
1 Sa. 17. 18 carry these ten cheeses unto the captain
20. 40 said unto him, Go, carry (them) to the
2 Ki. 9. 2 make him arise..and carry him to an
25. 7 bound him with fetters..and carried him
2 Ch. 34. 16 Shaphan carried the book to the king
36. 4 Necho took Jehoahaz..and carried him
36. 7 Nebuchadnezzar..carried of the vessels
Jer. 20. 5 take them, and carry them to Babylon
28. 3 Nebuchadnezzar king of Babylon..carried
39. 7 bound him with chains, to carry him to
52. 11 bound him in chains, and carried him to
Eze. 17. 4 He cropped off the top..and carried it
Dan. 1. 2 the vessels..which he carried into the
11. 8 shall also carry captives into Egypt their
Joel 3. 5 ye..have carried into your temples my

2. *To cause to flow or go*, יָבַל *yabal*, 5.
Isa. 23. 7 her own feet shall carry her afar off to

3. *To cause to go or flow*, יְבַל *yebal*, 5.
Ezra 7. 15 to carry the silver and gold, which the

4. *To cause to go on*, הָלַךְ, *or* יָלַךְ *yalak* 5.
2 Ki. 17. 27 Carry thither one of the priests whom ye
24. 15 he carried away Jehoiachin to Babylon
2 Ch. 33. 11 bound him with fetters, and carried him
36. 6 bound him in fetters, to carry him to B.
Eccl. 10. 20 a bird of the air shall carry the voice, and

5. *To lead (as a flock)*, נָהַל *nahal*, 3.
2 Ch. 28. 15 anointed them, and carried all the feeble

6. *To cause to come down*, נְחַת *nechath*, 5.
Ezra 5. 15 carry them into the temple that (is) in

7. *To lift up, carry*, נָשָׂא *nasa.*
Gen. 44. 1 (with) food, as much as they can carry
45. 27 the wagons..Joseph had sent to carry
46. 5 the sons of Israel carried Jacob their
46. 5 which Pharaoh had sent to carry him
47. 30 thou shalt carry me out of Egypt, and
50. 13 For his sons carried him into the land
Lev. 10. 4 carry your brethren from before the
10. 5 So they went near, and carried them in
Num. 11. 12 Carry them in thy bosom, as a nursing
Deut. 14. 24 so that thou art not able to carry it
2 Ki. 4. 19 he said to a lad, Carry him to his mother
7. 8 these lepers came..and carried thence
7. 8 carried thence (also), and went and hid (it)
23. 4 carried the ashes of them unto Beth-el
25. 13 and carried the brass of them to Babylon
1 Ch. 15. 2 None ought to carry the ark of God but
15. 2 for them hath the LORD chosen to carry
Isa. 30. 6 carry their riches upon the shoulders of
40. 11 carry (them) in his bosom, (and) shall gen.
Jer. 52. 17 and carried all the brass of them to B.

8. *To lift up, carry*, נָשָׂא *nasa*, 3.
Isa. 63. 9 he bare..and carried them all the days

9. *To bear, support*, סָבַל *sabal.*
Isa. 46. 4 (even) to hoar hairs will I carry (you)
46. 4 even I will carry, and will deliver (you)
46. 7 they carry him, and set him in his place
53. 4 carried our sorrows yet we did esteem

10. *To cause to ride, put on horseback*, רָכַב *rakab*, 5.
2 Ki. 9. 28 his servants carried him in a chariot
1 Ch. 13. 7 they carried the ark of God in a new cart

11. *To throw or shoot (with a bow)*, רָמָה *ramah.*
Psa. 78. 9 The children..armed, (and) carrying bows

12. *To lead*, ἄγω *agō.*
Acts 21. 34 he commanded him to be carried into the

13. *To lift up, carry*, αἴρω *airō.*
John 5. 10 it is not lawful for thee to carry (thy) bed

14. *To bear off*, ἀποφέρω *apopherō.*
Luke 16. 22 the beggar..was carried by the angels

15. *To support, carry*, βαστάζω *bastazō.*
Luke 10. 4 Carry neither purse, nor scrip, nor shoes
Acts 3. 2 a certain man lame..was carried, whom
Rev. 17. 7 the mystery..of the beast that carrieth

16. *To drive, set in motion*, ἐλαύνω *elaunō*, ἐλάω.
2 Pe. 2. 17 These are..clouds that are carried with

17. *To bear together*, συγκομίζω *sugkomizō.*
Acts 8. 2 devout men carried Stephen..and made

18. *To bear, carry*, φέρω *pherō.*
John 21. 18 and another shall gird thee, and carry
[*See also* Captives, tales, tidings.]

CARRY about, to —
1. *To cause to go round*, סָבַב *sabab*, 5.
1 Sa. 5. 8 carried the ark of the God of Israel about
5. 9 it was..after they had carried it about

2. *To carry or bear round*, περιφέρω *peripherō.*
Mark 6. 55 and began to carry about in beds those
Eph. 4. 14 tossed to and fro, and carried about with
Heb. 13. 9 Be not carried about with divers and
Jude 12 without water, [carried about] of winds

CARRY again, to —
To cause to turn back, שׁוּב *shub*, 5.
Gen. 43. 12 the mouth of your sacks, carry (it) again
2 Ch. 24. 11 took it, and carried it to his place again

CARRY aside, to —
To cause to incline, נָטָה *natah*, 5.
2 Sam 6. 10 David carried it aside into the house of

CARRY away —
A burden, thing lifted up, מַשָּׂא *massa.*
2 Ch. 20. 25 jewels..more than they could carry away

CARRY away, to —
1. *To cause to go into exile*, גָּלָה *galah*, 5.
2 Ki. 17. 6 and carried Israel away into Assyria, and
17. 11 the heathen whom the LORD carried away
17. 28 the priests, whom they had carried away
17. 33 the nations whom they carried away from
18. 11 the king of Assyria did carry away Israel
24. 14 And he carried away all Jerusalem, and
24. 15 he carried away Jehoiachin to Babylon
25. 11 did Nebuzar-adan..captain..carry away
1 Ch. 5. 6 whom Tilgath-pilneser..carried away
5. 26 he carried them away..unto Halah, and
6. 15 when the LORD carried away Judah and
2 Ch. 36. 20 that had escaped..carried he away to B.
Ezra 2. 1 king of Babylon had carried away unto
Neh. 7. 6 the king of Babylon had carried away
Esth. 2. 6 the king of Babylon had carried away
Jer. 29. 1 Nebuchadnezzar had carried away captive

2. *To cause to go into exile*, גְּלָה *gelah*, 5.
Ezra 5. 12 and carried the people away into Babylon

3. *To steal*, גָּנַב *ganab.*
Job 21. 18 as chaff that the storm carrieth away

4. *To cast out or away*, טוּל *tul*, 3a.
Isa. 22. 17 will carry thee away with a mighty cap.

5. *To cause to go*, יָלַךְ *yalak*, 5.
Eccl. 5. 15 which he may carry away in his hand

6. *To receive, take*, לָקַח *laqach.*
1 Sa. 30. 18 all that the Amalekites had carried away
2 Ch. 12. 9 he carried away also the shields of gold
Job 1. 17 the camels, and have carried them away
15. 12 Why doth thine heart carry thee away?
Psa. 49. 17 when he dieth he shall carry nothing away

7. *To lead*, נָהַג *nahag.*
Gen. 31. 18 And he carried away all his cattle, and
1 Sa. 30. 2 carried (them) away, and went on their

8. *To lead*, נָהַג *nahag*, 3.
Gen. 31. 26 thou hast..carried away my daughters, as

9. *To lift up, bear, carry*, נָשָׂא *nasa.*
2 Ch. 14. 13 and they carried away very much spoil
16. 6 they carried away the stones of Ramah
Isa. 15. 7 they have laid up, shall they carry away
41. 16 and the wind shall carry them away
57. 13 the wind shall carry them all away

10. *To lift up, bear, carry*, נְשָׂא *nesa.*
Dan. 2. 35 and the wind carried them away, that no

11. *To lead away*, ἀπάγω *apagō.*
1 Co. 12. 2 Ye know that ye were Gentiles, carried a.

12. *To bear off*, ἀποφέρω *apopherō.*
Mark 15. 1 and bound Jesus, and carried (him) away
Rev. 17. 3 So he carried me away in the spirit
21. 10 And he carried me away in the spirit

13. *To cause a change of dwelling*, μετοικίζω.
Acts 7. 43 I will carry you away beyond Babylon

CARRY away as with a flood, to —
To inundate, זָרַם *zaram.*
Psa. 90. 5 Thou carriest them away as with a flood

CARRY away, to — [*See* CAPTIVE.]
To take away captive, שָׁבָה *shabah.*
[1 Ki. 8. 46 deliver them..carry them away captives]
[2 Ch. 6. 36 they carry them away captives unto]
14. 15 and carried away sheep and camels
21. 17 and carried away all the substance
28. 17 smitten Judah, and carried away captives

CARRY away safe, to —
To cause to escape, פָּלַט *palat*, 5.
Isa. 5. 29 and shall carry (it) away safe, and none

CARRY back, to —
To cause to turn back, שׁוּב *shub*, 5.
2 Sa. 15. 25 Carry back the ark of God into the city
1 Ki. 22. 26 carry him back unto Amon the governor
2 Ch. 18. 25 carry him back to Amon the governor

CARRY captive, to —
To cause to go into exile, גָּלָה *galah*, 5.
2 Ki. 15. 29 and carried them captive to Assyria
16. 9 and carried (the people of) it captive to
Jer. 20. 4 he shall carry them captive into Babylon

CARRY down, to —
To cause to go down, יָרַד *yarad*, 5.
Gen. 37. 25 Ishmaelites..going to carry (it) down to
43. 11 carry down the man a present, a little

CARRY forth, to —
1. *To cause to go forth*, יָצָא *yatsa*, 5.
Exod 12. 46 thou shalt not carry forth ought of the
14. 11 hast thou dealt thus..to carry us forth
Lev. 4. 21 he shall carry forth the bullock without
6. 11 And he shall..carry forth the ashes
14. 45 he shall carry..forth out of the city
16. 27 shall (one) carry forth without the camp
1 Ki. 21. 13 Then they carried..forth out of the city
2 Ch. 29. 5 carry forth the filthiness out of the holy
Jer. 17. 22 Neither carry forth a burden out of your

2. *To bear out*, ἐκφέρω *ekpherō.*
Acts 5. 10 and the young men..carrying (her) forth

CARRY out, to —
1. *To cause to go forth*, יָצָא *yatsa*, 5.
Deut 28. 38 Thou shalt carry much seed out into the
1 Ki. 21. 10 And then carry him out, and stone him
22. 34 Turn thine hand, and carry me out of the
2 Ki. 24. 13 he carried out thence all the treasures
Eze. 12. 5 Dig thou through the wall..and carry out
12. 12 they shall dig through the wall to carry out
37. 1 The hand..carried me out in the Spirit

2. *To carry out*, ἐκκομίζω *ekkomizō.*
Luke 7. 12 there was a dead man carried out, the

3. *To bear out*, ἐκφέρω *ekpherō.*
Acts 5. 6 And the young men..carried (him) out
5. 9 which have buried..shall carry thee out
1 Ti. 6. 7 (it is) certain we can carry nothing out

CARRY over, to —
1. *To cause to pass over*, עָבַר *abar*, 5.
Josh. 4. 3 ye shall carry them over with you
4. 8 carried them over with them unto the pl.
2 Sa. 19. 18 there went over a ferry boat to carry over

2. *To put in another place*, μετατίθημι *metatithēmi.*
Acts 7. 16 And were carried over into Sychem, and

CARRY through, to —
To bear through, διαφέρω *diapherō.*
Mark 11. 16 that any man should carry (any) vessel thr.

CARRY up, to —
1. *To cause to go up*, עָלָה *alah*, 5.
Gen. 50. 25 and ye shall carry up my bones from hence
Exod 13. 19 shall carry up my bones away hence with
33. 15 If thy presence go not..carry us not up

2. *To bear up*, ἀναφέρω *anapherō.*
Luke 24. 51 [he was parted from them, and carried up]

CARRYING —
To lift up, נָשָׂא *nasa.*
1 Sa. 10. 3 three men..one carrying three kids
10. 3 and another carrying three loaves of
10. 3 and another carrying a bottle of wine

CARRYING away into —
Change of dwelling, μετοικεσία *metoikesia.*
Matt. 1. 17 from David until the carrying away into
1. 17 from the carrying away into Babylon

CARRYING away captive —
To go into exile, גָּלָה *galah.*
Jer. 1. 3 the carrying away of Jerusalem captive

CAR-SHE'-NA, כַּרְשְׁנָא *lean, slender.*
One of the seven princes of Persia and Media in the time of Ahasuerus, B.C. 519.
Esth. 1. 14 And the next unto him (was) C., Shethar

CART —
Wagon (for threshing), עֲגָלָה *agalah.*
1 Sa. 6. 7 make a new cart..tie the kine to the cart
6. 8 take the ark..and lay it upon the cart
6. 10 tied them to the cart, and shut up their
6. 11 they laid the ark..upon the cart, and
6. 14 the cart came into the field of Joshua
6. 14 they clave the wood of the cart, and
2 Sa. 6. 3 they set the ark..upon a new cart, and
6. 3 Uzzah and Ahio..drave the new cart
1 Ch. 13. 7 they carried the ark..in a new cart
13. 7 Uzzah and Ahio drave the cart
Isa. 5. 18 and sin as it were with a cart rope
28. 27 neither is a cart wheel turned about
28. 28 break (it with) the wheel of his cart
Amos 2. 13 as a cart is pressed (that is) full of sheaves

CARVE, to —
To cut in, קָלַע *qala.*
1 Ki. 6. 29 And he carved all the walls of the house
6. 32 he carved upon them carvings of cheru.
6. 35 And he carved..cherubim and palm trees

CARVED (figure) —
1. *Hewn,* חֲטֻבוֹת *chatuboth.*
Prov. 7. 16 I have decked..bed..with carved (works)
2. *Cut in work, sculpture,* מִקְלַעַת *miqlaath.*
1 Ki. 6. 18 the cedar of the house within (was) carved
3. *Opened, an engraving,* פִּתּוּחַ *pittuach.*
1 Ki. 6. 29 carved figures of cherubim and palm

CARVED image —
1. *Graven object,* פֶּסֶל *pesel.*
Judg 18. 18 these went..and fetched the carved im.
2 Ch. 33. 7 he set a carved image, the idol which
2. *Graven objects,* פְּסִילִים *pesilim.*
2 Ch. 33. 22 Amon sacrificed unto all..carved images
34. 3 began to purge...and the carved images
34. 4 the groves, and the carved images, and

CARVED work —
1. *To engrave,* חָקָה *chaqah,* 4.
1 Ki. 6. 35 with gold fitted upon the carved work
2. *Engraving, opened thing,* פִּתּוּחַ *pittuach.*
Psa. 74. 6 now they break down the carved work

CARVING —
1. *Artificer work,* חֲרֹשֶׁת *charosheth.*
Exod 31. 5 in carving of timber, to work in all
35. 33 in carving of wood, to make any manner
2. *Sculptured work,* מִקְלַעַת *miqlaath.*
1 Ki. 6. 32 carved upon them carvings of cherubim

CASE —
1. *Word, matter,* דָּבָר *dabar.*
Deut. 19. 4 this (is) the case of the slayer which shall
2. *Cause, case,* αἰτία *aitia.*
Matt 19. 10 If the case of the man be so with (his)

CASE, in any —
To cause to turn back, שׁוּב *shub,* 5.
Deut. 22. 1 thou shalt in any case bring them again
24. 13 In any case thou shalt deliver him the

CASE, in such a —
Thus, as thus, כָּכָה *kakah.*
Psa 144. 15 people that is in such a case; (yea) happy

CASE, in no —
No not, οὐ μή *ou mē.*
Matt 5. 20 ye shall in no case enter into the kingdom

CASEMENT —
Lattice window, אֶשְׁנָב *eshnab.*
Prov. 7. 6 For..I looked through my casement

CA-SIPH'-IA, כָּסִפְיָא *white, shining.*
A place on the road between Babylon and Jerusalem. Neither the city of *Kaswin,* nor the *Caspiæ Pylæ,* which some writers have attempted to identify it with, are situated upon this route.
Ezra 8. 17 unto Iddo the chief at the place C.
8. 17 what they should say..at the place C.

CAS-LU'-HIM, כַּסְלֻחִים, Χασμωνιείμ.
A tribe descended from Mizraim, son of Ham. In both texts in which this word occurs it appears as if the Philistines came forth from the Casluhim, and not from the Caphtorim as is elsewhere expressly stated. Here, then, there would seem to be a transposition. The only clue we have to their position is their place among the sons of Mizraim between the Caphtorim and the Pathrusim. Probably their seat was in Upper Egypt. The LXX. seems to identify them with the *Hashmannim* (which see). In Psa. 68. 31 this word is rendered "princes," but some take it as a proper name.
Gen. 10. 14 And Pathrusim, and C...and Caphtorim
1 Ch. 1. 12 And Pathrusim, and C...and Caphtorim

CASSIA —
1. *Cassia, amber, or stacte,* קִדָּה *qiddah.*
Exod. 30 24 of cassia five hundred..after the shekel
Eze. 27 19 bright iron, cassia, and calamus, were
2. *Cassia (a bark like cinnamon),* קְצִיעוֹת *qetsioth.*
Psa. 45. 8 garments..of myrrh, and aloes..cassia

CAST —
A throwing, casting, βολή *bolē.*
Luke 22. 41 he was withdrawn..about a stone's cast

CAST —
1. *To pour out, cast (metal),* יָצַק *yatsaq.*
1 Ki. 7. 24 the knops (were) cast in two rows, when
2 Ch. 4. 3 two rows of oxen (were) cast, when it was
2. *To wrap up, cover,* לוּט *lut.*
Isa. 25. 7 he will destroy..the covering cast over
3. *To be caused to go out,* שָׁלַךְ *shalak,* 6.
1 Ki. 13. 24 and his carcase (was) cast in the way
13. 25 and saw the carcase cast in the way
13. 28 he went and found his carcase cast in the

CAST, to —
1. *To cast,* טוּל *tul,* 5.
1 Sa. 18. 11 Saul cast the javelin; for he said, I will
20. 33 Saul cast a javelin at him to smite him
2. *To throw or cast (lots),* יָדַד *yadad.*
Joel 3. 3 And they have cast lots for my people
Obad. 11 cast lots upon Jerusalem, even thou
Nah. 3. 10 they cast lots for her honourable men
3. *To cast, throw,* יָדָה *yadah,* 3.
Lam. 3. 53 They have..cast a stone upon me
4. *To pour out, cast (metal),* יָצַק *yatsaq.*
Exod 25. 12 And thou shalt cast four rings of gold
26. 37 thou shalt cast five sockets of brass for
36. 36 and he cast for them four sockets of silver
37. 3, 13 And he cast for it four rings of gold
38. 5 he cast four rings for the four ends
38. 27 of the hundred talents of silver were cast
1 Ki. 7. 46 In the plain..did the king cast them
2 Ch. 4. 17 plain of Jordan did the king cast them
5. *To cast, throw,* יָרָה *yarah.*
Gen. 31. 51 which I have cast betwixt me and thee
Exod 15. 4 and his host hath he cast into the sea
Josh. 18. 6 that I may cast lots for you here before
6. *To cause to cast or throw,* יָרָה *yarah,* 5.
Job 30. 19 He hath cast me into the mire, and I am
7. *To cause to move,* מוּט *mot,* 5.
Psa. 55. 3 they cast iniquity upon me, and in wrath
8. *To cause to be nigh,* נָגַע *naga,* 5.
Exod. 4. 25 cast (it) at his feet, and said, Surely a
9. *To cause to fall,* נָפַל *naphal,* 5.
Num 35. 23 and cast (it) upon him, that he die
Prov. 19. 15 Slothfulness casteth into a deep sleep
10. *To lift up,* נָשָׂא *nasa.*
Gen. 39. 7 his master's wife cast her eyes upon Jos.
11. *To draw off or out,* נָשַׁל *nashal.*
Deut 28. 40 not anoint..for thine olive shall cast
12. *To give,* נָתַן *nathan.*
Lev. 16. 8 Aaron shall cast lots upon the two goats
26. 30 I will..cast your carcases upon the car.
2 Ki. 19. 18 And have cast their gods into the fire
Isa. 37. 19 have cast their gods into the fire: for
13. *To scatter,* פּוּץ *puts,* 5.
Isa. 28. 25 doth he not cast abroad the fitches
14. *To form, frame,* צוּר *tsur.*
1 Ki. 7. 15 he cast two pillars of brass, of eighteen
15. *To melt, fuse,* צָרַף *tsaraph.*
Isa. 40. 19 the goldsmith spreadeth..and casteth
16. *To cast,* רְמָה *remah,* רְמָא *rema.*
Dan. 3. 20 to cast..into the burning fiery furnace
3. 24 Did not we cast three men bound into
6. 16 they brought Daniel, and cast (him) into
6. 24 they cast (them) into the den of lions
17. *To send,* שָׁלַח *shalach,* 3.
Job 20. 23 (God) shall cast the fury of his wrath upon
Psa. 74. 7 They have cast fire into thy sanctuary
78. 49 He cast upon them the fierceness of his
Eccl. 11. 1 Cast thy bread upon the waters: for thou
Jer. 28. 16 I will cast thee from off the face of the
18. *To cause to go,* שָׁלַךְ *shalak,* 5.
Gen. 21. 15 she cast the child under one of the shrubs
37. 20 Come now..and cast him into some pit
37. 22 Shed no blood..cast him into this pit that
37. 24 they took him, and cast him into a pit
Exod. 1. 22 Every son..ye shall cast into the river
4. 3 Cast it on the ground. And he cast it on
7. 9 Take thy rod, and cast (it) before Pharaoh
15. 25 (which) when he had cast into the waters
22. 31 torn of beasts..ye shall cast it to the dogs
32. 19 he cast the tables out of his hands, and
32. 24 then I cast it into the fire, and there came
Lev. 1. 16 and cast it beside the altar on the east part
14. 40 they shall cast them into an unclean place
Num 19. 6 And the priest shall..cast (it) into the
35. 22 But if he..have cast upon him anything
Deut. 9. 17 I took the two tables, and cast them out
9. 21 and I cast the dust thereof into the brook
29. 28 and cast them into another land, as
Josh. 8. 29 and cast it at the entering of the gate
10. 27 they..cast them into the cave wherein
18. 8 that I may here cast lots for you before
18. 10 And Joshua cast lots for them in Shiloh
Judg. 8. 25 And they..did cast therein every man
9. 53 And a certain woman cast a piece of mill.
2 Sa. 11. 21 did not a woman cast a piece of a millst.
18. 17 they took Absalom, and cast him into a
20. 12 he removed Amasa..and cast a cloth upon
2 Sa. 20. 22 they cut off the head..and cast (it) out to
1 Ki. 14. 9 and hast cast me behind thy back
19. 19 Elijah passed by him, and cast his mantle
2 Ki. 2. 16 the Spirit of the LORD hath..cast him
2. 21 he went forth..and cast the salt in there
3. 25 on every good piece of land cast every
4. 41 Then bring meal; and he cast (it) into
6. 6 he cut down a stick, and cast (it)
13. 21 they cast..into the sepulchre of Elisha
13. 23 neither cast he them from his presence
23. 6 cast the powder thereof upon the graves
23. 12 cast the dust of them into the brook Kid.
2 Ch. 24. 10 the princes..cast into the chest, until
30. 14 and cast (them) into the brook Kidron
33. 15 And he..cast (them) out of the city
Neh. 9. 26 they..cast thy law behind their backs
Job 27. 22 For (God) shall cast upon him, and not
Psa. 50. 17 Seeing thou..castest my words behind
55. 22 Cast thy burden upon the LORD, and he
60. 8 over Edom..cast out my shoe: Philistia
Isa. 2. 20 that day a man shall cast his idols of sil.
19. 8 all they that cast angle into the brooks
38. 17 thou hast cast all my sins behind thy ba.
Jer. 26. 23 who..cast his dead body into the graves
36. 23 he cut it..and cast (it) into the fire that
38. 6 Then took they Jeremiah, and cast him
38. 9 whom they have cast into the dungeon
41. 9 wherein Ishmael had cast all the dead
51. 63 shalt..cast it into the midst of Euphrates
Eze. 5. 4 take of them again, and cast them into
7. 19 They shall cast their silver in the streets
23. 35 thou hast forgotten me, and cast me
28. 17 I will cast thee to the ground, I will lay
43. 24 the priests shall cast salt upon them, and
Joel 1. 7 he hath made it clean bare, and cast (it)
Amos 4. 3 and ye shall cast (them) into the palace
Jon. 2. 3 For thou hadst cast me into the deep, in
Mic. 2. 5 thou shalt have none that shalt cast a
7. 19 thou wilt cast all their sins into the depths
Nah. 3. 6 I will cast abominable filth upon thee
Zech. 5. 8 And he cast it into the midst of the ephah
5. 8 he cast the weight of lead upon the mouth
11. 13 the LORD said unto me, Cast it unto the
11. 13 And I..cast them to the potter in the
19. *To shed, pour out,* שָׁפַךְ *shaphak.*
2 Sa. 20. 15 they cast up a bank against the city, and
2 Ki. 19. 32 He shall not..cast a bank against it
Isa. 37. 33 He shall not..cast a bank against it
Jer. 6. 6 Hew ye down trees, and cast a mount
Eze. 4. 2 build a fort..and cast a mount against
21. 22 to cast a mount, (and) to build a fort
26. 8 he shall..cast a mount against thee, and
Dan. 11. 15 the king..shall come, and cast up a mount
20. *To strike (down),* תָּקַע *taqa.*
Exod. 10. 19 And the LORD..cast them into the Red sea
21. *To cast,* βάλλω *ballō.*
Matt. 3. 10 therefore every tree..is..cast into the
4. 6 If thou be the Son of God, cast thyself
4. 18 Jesus..saw two brethren..casting a net
5. 13 it is thenceforth..to be cast out, and
5. 25 lest at any time..thou be cast into prison
5. 29 pluck it out, and cast (it) from thee: for
5. 29 thy whole body should be cast into hell
5. 30 cut it off, and cast (it) from thee: for it is
5. 30 thy whole body [should be cast] into hell
6. 30 and tomorrow is cast into the oven
7. 6 neither cast ye your pearls before swine
7. 19 Every tree..is..cast into the fire
13. 42 shall cast them into a furnace of fire
13. 47 a net, that was cast into the sea, and
13. 48 and gathered the good..but cast the bad
13. 50 shall cast them into the furnace of fire
15. 26 It is not meet..to cast (it) to dogs
17. 27 go thou to the sea, and cast an hook, and
18. 8 cut them off, and cast (them) from thee
18. 8 two feet to be cast into everlasting fire
18. 9 pluck it out, and cast (it) from thee: it
18. 9 rather than... be cast into hell fire
18. 30 but went and cast him into prison
21. 21 and be thou cast into the sea; it shall be
27. 35 and parted his garments, casting lots
27. 35 [and upon my vesture did they cast lots]
Mark 1. 16 saw Simon, and Andrew..[casting] a net
4. 26 if a man should cast seed into the ground
7. 27 it is not meet..to cast (it) unto the dogs
9. 22 And ofttimes it hath cast him into the
9. 42 and he were cast into the sea
9. 45 having two feet to be cast into hell
9. 47 than having two eyes to be cast into hell
11. 23 and be thou cast into the sea
12. 41 and beheld how the people cast money
12. 41 many that were rich cast in much
12. 43 this poor widow hath cast more in
12. 43 than all they which have cast into the
12. 44 (they) did cast in of their abundance
12. 44 of her want did cast in all that she had
15. 24 they parted his garments, casting lots
Luke 3. 9 every tree..is..cast into the fire
4. 9 If thou be the Son of God, cast thyself
12. 28 which..to morrow is cast into the oven
12. 58 and the officer cast thee into prison
13. 19 which a man took, and cast into his gar.
14. 35 nor yet for the dunghill; (but) men cast
21. 1 looked up, and saw the rich men casting
21. 2 he saw also a certain poor widow casting
21. 3 this poor widow hath cast in more than
21. 4 these have of their abundance cast in
21. 4 she of her penury hath cast in all the
23. 19 Who for..murder, was cast into prison
23. 25 released unto them him that..was cast

Luke23. 34 they parted his raiment, and cast lots
John 3. 24 For John was not yet cast into prison
8. 7 [let him first cast a stone at her]
8. 59 Then took they up stones to cast at him
15. 6 he is cast forth as a branch, and is
15. 6 and men gather them, and cast (them)
19. 24 for my vesture they did cast lots
21. 6 Cast the net on the right side of the ship
21. 6 They cast therefore, and now they were
21. 7 Peter..did cast himself into the sea
Acts 16. 23 they cast (them) into prison, charging
16. 37 and have cast (us) into prison; and now
Rev. 2. 10 the devil shall cast (some) of you into
2. 14 who taught Balac to cast a stumbling bl.
2. 22 Behold, I will cast her into a bed, and
4. 10 and cast their crowns before the throne
6. 13 even as a fig tree casteth her untimely
8. 5 And the angel..cast (it) into the earth
8. 7 and they were cast upon the earth: and
8. 8 a great mountain..was cast into the sea
12. 4 and did cast them to the earth: and the
12. 13 when the dragon saw that he was cast
12. 15 the serpent cast out of his mouth water
12. 16 which the dragon cast out of his mouth
14. 19 and cast (it) into the great wine press
18. 19 And they cast dust on their heads
18. 21 a mighty angel..cast (it) into the sea
19. 20 These both were cast alive into a lake of
20. 3 And cast him into the bottomless pit
20. 10 And the devil..was cast into the lake of
20. 14 death and hell were cast into the lake
20. 15 whosoever was not found..was cast into

22. *To cast out*, ἐκβάλλω *ekballō.*
Matt21. 39 caught him, and cast (him) out of the
22. 13; 25. 30; Mark 16. 9; Luke 20. 15.

23. *To hurl off*, ἀποῤῥίπτω *aporrhiptō.*
Acts 27. 43 should cast (themselves) first (into the s.)

24. *To hurl*, ῥίπτω *rhiptō.*
Luke 17. 2 and he cast into the sea, than that he
Acts 27. 29 they cast four anchors out of the stern

CAST, to be —

1. *To be cast away*, טוּל *tul*, 6.
Prov 16. 33 The lot is cast into the lap; but the

2. *To cause to fall*, נָפַל *naphal*, 5.
Psa.140. 10 let them be cast into the fire; into

3. *To be given*, נְתַן *nathan*, 2.
Eze. 15. 4 Behold, it is cast into the fire for fuel

4. *To cast*, רְמָא *rema*, רְמָה *remah.*
Dan. 3. 21 were cast into the midst of the..furnace

5. *To be cast*, רְמָא *rema*, רמה *remah*, 2.
Dan. 3. 6 shall the same hour be cast into the
3. 11 (that) he should be cast into the..furnace
3. 15 ye shall be cast the same hour into the
6. 7 he shall be cast into the den of lions
6. 12 shall be cast into the den of lions?

6. *To be sent*, שָׁלַח *shalach*, 4.
Job 18. 8 he is cast into a net by his own feet

7. *To be sent, cast away*, שָׁלַךְ *shalak*, 6.
Psa. 22. 10 I was cast upon thee from the womb
Isa. 14. 19 But thou art cast out of thy grave like
Jer. 22. 28 and are cast into a land which they

8. *To fall off*, ἐκπίπτω *ekpiptō.*
Acts 27. 26 we must be cast upon a certain island

CAST about, to —

1. *To go round*, סָבַב *sabab.*
Jer. 41. 14 So all the people..cast about and return.

2. *To cast around*, περιβάλλω *periballō.*
Luke19. 43 thine enemies shall cast a trench about
Acts 12. 8 Cast thy garment about thee, and follow

CAST about, to have —

To cast around, περιβάλλω *periballō.*
Mark14. 51 having a linen cloth cast about (his)

CAST abroad, to —

To scatter, פּוּץ *puts*, 5.
Job 40. 11 Cast abroad the rage of thy wrath

CAST away, to —

1. *To thrust away, expel*, הָדַף *hadaph.*
Prov 10. 3 casteth away the substance of the wicked

2. *To cast away, abandon*, זָנַח *zanach*, 5.
2 Ch. 29. 19 which king Ahaz..did cast away in his

3. *To scatter*, זָרָה *zarah.*
Isa. 30. 22 thou shalt cast them away as a..cloth

4. *To refuse, reject*, מָאַס *maas.*
Lev. 26. 44 I will not cast them away, neither will I
Job 8. 20 God will not cast away a perfect (man)
Isa. 31. 7 every man shall cast away his idols of
41. 9 have chosen thee, and not cast thee away
Jer. 33. 26 Then will I cast away the seed of Jacob
Hos. 9. 17 My God will cast them away, because

5. *To send away*, שָׁלַח *shalach*, 3.
Job 8. 4 and he have cast them away for their

6. *To send, cause to go*, שָׁלַךְ *shalak*, 5.
Judg15. 17 that he cast away the jawbone out of his
2 Ki. 7. 15 which the Syrians had cast away in their
Psa. 2. 3 Let us..cast away their cords from us
51. 11 Cast me not away from thy presence
Eccl. 3. 5 A time to cast away stones, and a time to
3. 6 a time to keep, and a time to cast away
Jer. 7. 29 Cut off thine hair..and cast (it) away
Eze 18. 31 Cast away from you all your transgressions
20. 7 Cast ye away every man the abominations
20. 8 they did not every man cast away the

7. *To cast off or away*, ἀποβάλλω *apoballō.*
Mark10. 50 And he, casting away his garment, rose
Heb 10 35 Cast not away therefore your confidence

8. *To thrust off from (one's self)*, ἀπωθέω *apōtheō.*
Rom 11. 1 I say then, Hath God cast away his
11 2 God hath not cast away his people which

CAST away, to be —

To cause to suffer loss, ζημιόω *zēmioō.*
Luke 9. 25 if he..lose himself, or be cast away?

CAST calf, to —

To bereave, lose their young, שָׁכַל *shakol*, 3.
Job 21. 10 their cow calveth, and casteth not her calf

CAST clouts —

Rags, tatters, סְחָבוֹת *sechaboth.*
Jer. 38. 11 took thence old cast clouts and old rotten
38. 12 Put now (these) old cast clouts and rotten

CAST down —

Low, humble, depressed, ταπεινός *tapeinos.*
2 Co. 7. 6 that comforteth those that are cast down

CAST down, to —

1. *To cause to go down, place*, נוּחַ *yanach*, 5.
Isa. 28. 2 which..shall cast down to the earth with

2. *To cause to go down*, יָרַד *yarad*, 5.
Prov21. 22 A wise (man)..casteth down the strength
Eze. 31. 16 when I cast him down to hell with them
32. 18 Son of man, wail..and cast them down

3. *To cause to bow down*, כָּרַע *kara*, 5.
Psa. 17. 13 O LORD, disappoint him, cast him down

4. *To cause to stumble*, כָּשַׁל *kashal*, 5.
2 Ch.25. 8 God hath power to help, and to cast down.

5. *To thrust down*, מָגַר *magar*, 3.
Psa. 89. 44 Thou hast..cast his throne down to the

6. *To separate, cast down*, נָדַח *nadach*, 5.
Psa. 62. 4 They only consult to cast (him) down

7. *To cause to fall*, נָפַל *naphal*, 5.
Job 29. 24 light of my countenance they cast not do.
Psa. 37. 14 The wicked have..cast down the poor
73. 18 thou castedst them down into destruction
Prov. 7. 26 For she hath cast down many wounded
Eze. 6. 4 I will cast down your slain (men) before
Dan. 8. 10 and it cast down (some) of the host
11. 12 he shall cast down (many) ten thousands

8. *To tear down*, נָתַץ *nathats.*
Judg. 6. 30 because he hath cast down the altar
6. 31 because (one) hath cast down his altar

9. *To send, cause to go*, שָׁלַךְ *shalak*, 5.
Exod. 7. 10 Aaron cast down his rod before Pha.
7. 12 For they cast down every man his rod
Josh 10. 11 the LORD cast down great stones from
2 Ch.25. 12 cast them down from the top of the
Job 18. 7 his own counsel shall cast him down
Psa 102. 10 thou hast lifted me up, and cast me down
Lam. 2. 1 cast down from heaven unto the earth
Dan. 8. 7 but he cast him down to the ground
8. 12 it cast down the truth to the ground

10. *To cause to be low*, שָׁפֵל *shaphel*, 5.
Psa.147. 6 he casteth the wicked down to the ground

11. *To put or lift down*, καθαιρέω *kathaireō.*
2 Co.10. 5 Casting down imaginations, and every

12. *To cast down*, καταβάλλω *kataballō.*
2 Co. 4. 9 cast down, but not destroyed
Rev. 12. 10 the accuser of our brethren is cast [down]

13. *To cast, hurl*, ῥίπτω *rhiptō.*
Matt15. 30 and cast them down at Jesus' feet
27. 5 And he cast down the pieces of silver

CAST down headlong, to —

To throw down a precipice, κατακρημνίζω.
Luke 4. 29. that they might cast him down headlong

CAST down, to be —

1. *To be thrust down*, דָּחָה *dachah*, 4.
Psa. 36. 12 they are cast down, and shall not be able

2. *To be cast down, out, forth*, טוּל *tul*, 6.
Job 41. 9 shall not (one) be cast down even at the

3. *To be stumbled*, כָּשַׁל *kashal*, 2.
Jer. 6. 15 they shall be cast down, saith the LORD
8. 12 they shall be cast down, saith the LORD

4. *To fall*, נָפַל *naphal.*
Neh. 6. 16 they were much cast down in their own

5. *To tear down*, נָתַץ *nathats*, 4.
Judg. 6. 28 the altar of Baal was cast down, and the

6. *To cast, throw down*, רְמָה *remah.*
Dan. 7. 9 I beheld till the thrones were cast down

7. *To bow oneself down*, שָׁחַח *shachach*, 7a.
Psa. 42. 5 Why art thou cast down, O my soul?
42. 6 my soul is cast down within me: therefo.
42. 11 Why art thou cast down, O my soul?
43. 5 Why art thou cast down, O my soul?

8. *To send*, שָׁלַךְ *shalak*, 6.
Eze. 19. 12 she was cast down to the ground, and the
Dan. 8. 11 the place of his sanctuary was cast down

9. *To cause to be low*, שָׁפֵל *shaphel*, 5.
Job 22. 29 When (men) are cast down, then thou

CAST down, to be utterly —

To be cast down, out, forth, טוּל *tul*, 6.
Psa. 37. 24 he shall not be utterly cast down; for the

CAST down to hell, to be —

To put in tartarus, ταρταρόω *tartaroō.*
2 Pe. 2. 4 but cast (them) down to hell, and delivered

CAST dust, to —

To dust, throw dust, עָפַר *aphar*, 3.
2 Sa.16 13 and threw stones at him, and cast dust

CAST far off, to be —

To be far off, הָלָא *hala*, 2.
Mic. 4. 7 her that was cast far off a strong nation

CAST forth, to —

1. *To shine, cast forth (glances)*, בָּרַק *baraq.*
Psa.144. 6 Cast forth lightning, and scatter them

2. *To cause to cast down, out, forth*, טוּל *tul*, 5.
Eze. 32. 4 I will cast thee forth upon the open field
Jon. 1. 5 cast forth the wares that (were) in the
1. 12 Take me up, and cast me forth into the
1. 15 So they..cast him forth into the sea

3. *To cause to strike deep*, נָכָה *nakah*, 5.
Hos. 14. 5 he shall..cast forth his roots as Lebanon

4. *To send*, שָׁלַךְ *shalak*, 5.
Neh. 13. 8 therefore I cast forth all the household
Psa.147. 17 He casteth forth his ice like morsels: who
Jer. 22. 19 drawn and cast forth beyond the gates
Amos 8. 3 they shall cast (them) forth with silence

5. *To cast out*, ἐκβάλλω *ekballō.*
Mark 7. 26 she besought him that he would cast forth

CAST fruit before the time, to —

To bereave, שָׁכַל *shakol*, 3.
Mal. 3. 11 your vine cast her fruit before the time

CAST in, to —

1. *To cause to fall*, נָפַל *naphal*, 5.
Prov. 1. 14 Cast in thy lot among us; let us all have

2. *To put, place*, שׂוּם *sum.*
Isa. 28. 25 and cast in the principal wheat, and the

CAST in one's mind, to —

To reason out, διαλογίζομαι *dialogizomai.*
Luke 1. 29 when she saw (him)..she cast in her mind

CAST in one's teeth, to —

To defame, rail at, ὀνειδίζω *oneidizō.*
Matt27. 44 The thieves..cast the same in his teeth

CAST into, to —

To cast into, ἐμβάλλω *emballō.*
Luke12. 5 Fear him, which..hath power to cast into

CAST into prison, to be —

To give up, over, betray, παραδίδωμι *paradidōmi.*
Matt. 4. 12 heard that John was cast into prison, he

CAST (lots), to —

To cause to fall, נָפַל *naphal*, 5.
1 Sa. 14. 42 Cast (lots) between me and Jonathan my
1 Ch.24. 31 These likewise cast lots over against
25. 8 And they cast lots, ward against (ward)
26. 13 they cast lots, as well the small as the
26. 14 they cast lots; and his lot came out
Neh. 10. 34 And we cast the lots among the priests
11. 1 the rest of the people also cast lots, to
Esth. 3. 7 they cast Pur, that (is), the lot before H.
9. 24 had cast Pur, that (is), the lot, to consume
Psa. 22. 18 and cast lots upon my vesture
Isa. 34. 17 And he hath cast the lot for them
Jon. 1. 7 let us cast lots: so they cast lots

CAST off, to —

1. *To cast off, abandon*, זָנַח *zanach.*
Psa. 43. 2 why dost thou cast me off? why go I
44. 9 thou hast cast off, and put us to shame
44. 23 arise, cast (us) not off for ever
60. 1 O God, thou hast cast us off, thou hast
60. 10 thou, O God, (which) hadst cast us off?
74. 1 O God, why hast thou cast (us) off for
77. 7 Will the Lord cast off for ever? and will
88. 14 LORD, why castest thou off my soul?
89. 38 But thou hast cast off and abhorred
108. 11 (Wilt) not (thou), O God (who) hast c. off
Lam. 2. 7 The Lord hath cast off his altar, he hath
3. 31 For the Lord will not cast off for ever
Hos. 8. 3 Israel hath cast off (the thing that is)
8. 5 Thy calf, O Samaria, hath cast (thee) off
Zech.10. 6 be as though I had not cast them off

2. *To cast off*, זָנַח *zanach*, 5.
1 Ch.28. 9 forsake him, he will cast thee off for
2 Ch.11. 14 Jeroboam and his sons had cast them off

8. *To refuse*, מָאַס *maas.*
2 Ki. 23. 27 will..cast off this city Jerusalem which
Jer. 31. 37 I will also cast off all the seed of Israel
33. 24 he hath even cast them off?

4. *To cast off, reject, leave*, נָטַשׁ *natash.*
Psa. 94. 14 For the LORD will not cast off his people

5. *To break off*, פָּרַר *parar*, 5.
Job 15. 4 Yea, thou castest off fear, and restrainest

6. *To corrupt, violate, mar*, שָׁחַת *shachath*, 3.
Amos 1. 11 because he..did cast off all pity

7. *To send off*, שָׁלַךְ *shalak*, 5.
Job 15. 33 and shall cast off his flower as the olive
Psa. 71. 9 Cast me not off in the time of old age

8. *To put aside, off, displace*, ἀθετέω *atheteō.*
1 Ti. 5. 12 because they have cast off their first

9. *To put off*, ἀποτίθεμαι *apotithemai.*
Rom. 13. 12 let us therefore cast off the works of

10. *To keep on throwing, hurl*, ῥιπτέω *rhipteō.*
Acts 22. 23 as they cried out, and cast off (their)

CAST on, to —
To cast upon, ἐπιβάλλω *epiballō.*
Mark 11. 7 And they..cast their garments on him

CAST out —
1. *Produce, what is cast forth*, מִגְרָשׁ *migrash.*
Eze. 36. 5 with despiteful minds, to cast it out for

2. *Expulsion*, מָרוּד *marud.*
Isa. 58. 7 that thou bring the poor that are cast out

3. *To be outcast*, נָדַח *nadach*, 2.
Neh. 1. 9 though there were of you cast out unto

4. *To be sent away*, שָׁלַח *shalach*, 4.
Isa. 16. 2 as a wandering bird cast out of the nest

CAST out, to —
1. *To cast out*, גָּרַשׁ *garash*, 3.
Gen. 21. 10 Cast out this bond woman and her son
2 Ch. 20. 11 to come to cast us out of thy possession
Psa. 78. 55 He cast out the heathen also before them
80. 8 thou hast cast out the heathen, and
Prov 22. 10 Cast out the scorner, and contention
Mic. 2. 9 The women of my people have ye cast out

2. *To force or drive out*, דּוּחַ *duach*, 5.
Jer. 51. 34 Nebuchadnezzar..hath cast me out

3. *To thrust away*, הָדַף *hadaph.*
Deut. 6. 19 To cast out all thine enemies from before
9. 4 after that the LORD..hath cast them out

4. *To cast away*, טוּל *tul*, 5.
Jer. 16. 13 Therefore will I cast you out of this land
22. 26 I will cast thee out, and thy mother

5. *To cast or throw*, יָדָה *yadah*, 3.
Zech. 1. 21 come to fray them, to cast out the horns

6. *To drive away*, יָרַשׁ *yarash*, 5.
Exod 34. 24 For I will cast out the nations before
Josh. 13. 12 these did Moses smite, and cast them out
1 Ki. 14. 24 which the LORD cast out before the chil.
21. 26 whom the LORD cast out before the chil.
2 Ki. 16. 3 whom the LORD cast out from before the
17. 8 whom the LORD cast out from before the
21. 2 whom the LORD cast out before the chil.
2 Ch. 28. 3 whom the LORD had cast out before the
33. 2 whom the LORD had cast out before the
Job 20. 15 God shall cast them out of his belly
Zech. 9. 4 Behold, the LORD will cast her out, and

7. *To separate, drive away (as filthy)*, נָדָה *nadah*, 3.
Isa. 66. 5 that cast you out for my name's sake

8. *To cause to drive out*, נָדַח *nadach*, 5.
2 Ch. 13. 9 Have ye not cast out the priests of the
Psa. 5. 10 cast them out in the multitude of their

9. *To cause to fall*, נָפַל *naphal*, 5.
Isa. 26. 19 and the earth shall cast out the dead

10. *To draw off*, נָשַׁל *nashal.*
Deut. 7. 1 hath cast out many nations before thee

11. *To face, turn the face*, פָּנָה *panah*, 3.
Zeph. 3. 15 he hath cast out thine enemy: the king

12. *To dig, make deep*, קוּר *qur*, 5.
Jer. 6. 7 As a fountain casteth out her waters
6. 7 so she casteth out her wickedness

13. *To empty, pour out*, רוּק *ruq*, 5.
Psa. 18. 42 I did cast them out as the dirt in the

14. *To send*, שָׁלַח *shalach*, 5.
Lev. 18. 24 the nations..which I cast out before you
20. 23 the nation which I cast out before you
1 Ki. 9. 7 this house..will I cast out of my sight
Job 39. 3 They bow..they cast out their sorrows
Psa. 44. 2 afflict the people, and cast them out
Jer. 15. 1 cast (them) out of my sight, and let them

15. *To cast, cause to go*, שָׁלַךְ *shalak*, 5.
2 Ki. 10. 25 the guard and the captains cast..out
17. 20 until he had cast them out of his sight
24. 20 until he had cast them out from his
2 Ch. 7. 20 this house..will I cast out of my sight
Psa. 60. 8 over Edom will I cast out my shoe
108. 9 over Edom will I cast out my shoe
Jer. 7. 15 I will cast you out..as I have cast out
9. 19 because our dwellings have cast (us) out
52. 3 till he had cast them out from his pres.

16. *To cast*, βάλλω *ballō.*
1 Jo. 4. 18 but perfect love casteth out fear: because
Rev. 12. 9 And the great dragon was cast out
12. 9 he was cast out..angels were cast out

17. *To cast out*, ἐκβάλλω *ekballō.*
Matt. 7. 5 first cast out the beam out of thine own
7. 5 then shalt thou see clearly to cast out
7. 22 and in thy name have cast out devils?
8. 12 the children..shall be cast out into outer
8. 16 and he cast out the spirits with (his) word
8. 31 If thou cast us out, suffer us to go away
9. 33 And when the devil was cast out, the
9. 34 He casteth out devils through the prince
10. 1 he gave them power..to cast them out
10. 8 raise the dead, cast out devils: freely ye
12. 24 This (fellow) doth not cast out devils
12. 26 And if Satan cast out Satan, he is
12. 27 And if I by Beelzebub cast out devils
12. 27 by whom do your children cast (them) out?
12. 28 if I cast out devils by the Spirit of God
15. 17 and is cast out into the draught?
17. 19 Why could not we cast him out?
21. 12 Jesus..cast out all them that sold and
Mark 1. 34 he healed many..and cast out many
1. 39 And he preached..and cast out devils
3. 15 And to have power..to cast out devils
3. 22 by the prince of the devils casteth he out
3. 23 How can Satan cast out Satan?
6. 13 And they cast out many devils, and
9. 18 that they should cast him out; and
9. 28 Why could not we cast him out?
9. 38 we saw one casting out devils in thy name
11. 15 Jesus..began to cast out them that sold
12. 8 and cast (him) out of the vineyard
16. 17 [In my name shall they cast out devils]
Luke 6. 22 and cast out your name as evil, for the
6. 42 cast out first the beam out of thine own
9. 40 I besought thy disciples to cast him out
9. 49 we saw one casting out devils in thy
11. 14 And he was casting out a devil, and it
11. 15 He casteth out devils through Beelzebub
11. 18 that I cast out devils through Beelzebub
11. 19 And if I by Beelzebub cast out devils
11. 19 by whom do your sons cast (them) out?
11. 20 I with the finger of God cast out devils
13. 32 tell that fox, Behold, I cast out devils
19. 45 and began to cast out them that sold
20. 12 wounded him also, and cast (him) out
John 6. 37 cometh to me I will in no wise cast out
9. 34 thou teach us? And they cast (him) out
9. 35 Jesus heard that they had cast him out
12. 31 shall the prince of this world be cast out
Acts 7. 58 And cast (him) out of the city, and stoned
27. 38 and cast out the wheat into the sea
Gal. 4. 30 Cast out the bondwoman and her son
3 Jo. 10 and casteth (them) out of the church

18. *To extend, send forth*, ἐκτείνω *ekteinō.*
Acts 27. 30 they would have cast anchors out of the

19. *To put out or forth*, ἐκτίθημι *ektithēmi.*
Acts 7. 21 And when he was cast out, Pharaoh's

20. *To make exposed*, ποιέω ἔκθετον *poieō ektheton.*
Acts 7. 19 so that they cast out their young children

21. *To hurl*, ῥίπτω *rhiptō.*
Acts 27. 19 we cast out with our own hands the tac.

CAST out, to be —
1. *To be cast out*, גָּרַשׁ *garash*, 2.
Amos 8. 8 and it shall be cast out and drowned
Jon. 2. 4 I am cast out of thy sight; yet I will

2. *To be cast down, out, forth*, טוּל *tul*, 6.
Jer. 22. 28 wherefore are they cast out, he and his

3. *To be sent, cast away*, שָׁלַךְ *shalak*, 6.
Isa. 34. 3 Their slain also shall be cast out
Jer. 14. 16 the people..shall be cast out in the
36. 30 his dead body shall be cast out in the
Eze. 16. 5 thou wast cast out in the open field

CAST self down, to —
1. *To kneel and bow down*, גָּהַר *gahar.*
1 Ki. 18. 42 he cast himself down upon the earth

2. *To cause oneself to fall*, נָפַל *naphal*, 7.
Ezra 10. 1 confessed, weeping and casting himself d.

CAST stones, to —
To stone, סָקַל *saqal*, 3.
2 Sa. 16. 6 he cast stones at David, and at all the

CAST up, to —
1. *To cast out, or forth*, גָּרַשׁ *garash.*
Isa. 57. 20 whose waters cast up mire and dirt

2. *To heap up*, סָלַל *salal.*
Isa. 57. 14 And shall say, Cast ye up, cast ye up
62. 10 cast up, cast up the highway; gather
Jer. 18. 15 to walk in paths, (in) a way not cast up
50. 26 cast her up as heaps, and destroy her

3. *To cause to go up*, עָלָה *alah*, 5.
Lam. 2. 10 they have cast up dust upon their heads
Eze. 27. 30 and shall cast up dust upon their heads

CAST, when —
A casting, שַׁלֶּכֶת *shalleketh.*
Isa. 6. 13 whose substance (is) in them, when they c.

CAST, when it was —
1. *A casting*, יְצֻקָה *yetsuqah.*
1 Ki. 7. 24 the knops..in two rows, when it was cast

2. *A casting, fusion*, מוּצֶקֶת *mutseqeth.*
2 Ch. 4. 3 Two rows of oxen (were)..when it was cast

CAST young, to —
To bereave, שָׁכֹל *shakol*, 3.
Gen. 31. 38 thy she goats have not cast their young
Exod 23. 26 There shall nothing cast their young

CAST upon, to —
1. *To cast upon*, ἐπιβάλλω *epiballō.*
1 Co. 7. 35 not that I may cast a snare upon you

2. *To hurl upon*, ἐπιῤῥίπτω *epirrhiptō.*
Luke 19. 35 they cast their garments upon the colt
1 Pe. 5. 7 Casting all your care upon him; for he

CASTAWAY —
Not approved, ἀδόκιμος *adokimos.*
1 Co. 9. 27 I myself should be a castaway

CASTING —
Something fused, מוּצָק *mutsaq.*
1 Ki. 7. 37 all of them had one casting, one measure

CASTING away —
A casting off, ἀποβολή *apobolē.*
Rom 11. 15 For if the casting away of them (be) the

CASTING down —
1. *A casting down*, חֲתַת *chathath.*
Job 6. 21 ye see (my) casting down, and are afraid

2. *Depression*, יֶשַׁח *yeshach.*
Mic. 6. 14 and thy casting down (shall be) in the

3. *To cause to lie down*, שָׁכַב *shakab*, 5.
2 Sa. 8. 2 casting them down to the ground; even

CASTING up —
To pour out, שָׁפַךְ *shaphak.*
Eze. 17. 17 by casting up mounts, and building forts

CASTLE —
1. *High place, palace*, אַרְמוֹן *armon.*
Prov 18. 19 contentions (are) like the bars of a castle

2. *Tower*, טִירָה *tirah.*
Gen. 25. 16 these (are) their names..by their castles
1 Ch. 6. 54 dwelling places throughout their castles

3. *Great or high tower*, מִגְדָּל *migdal.*
1 Ch. 27. 25 and in the villages, and in the castles

4. *Fortress*, מְצַד *metsad.*
1 Ch. 11. 7 And David dwelt in the castle; therefore

5. *Fortress*, מְצוּדָה *metsudah.*
1 Ch. 11. 5 Nevertheless David took..castle of Zion

6. *An interlining*, παρεμβολή *parembolē.*
Acts 21. 34 commanded him to be carried into the c.
21. 37 And as Paul was to be led into the castle
22. 24 to be brought into the castle, and bade
23. 10 to take..and to bring (him) into the cas.
23. 16 he went and entered into the castle, and
23. 32 On the morrow they..returned to the cas.

CASTLE, goodly —
A tower, טִירָה *tirah.*
Num 31. 10 they burnt..all their goodly castles, with

CASTLES —
Citadels, palaces, בִּירָנִיּוֹת *biraniyoth.*
2 Ch. 17. 12 he built in Judah castles, and cities of
27. 4 in the forests he built castles and towers

CASTOR and POLLUX, Διόσκουροι *sons of Jupiter.*
Instead of translating or retaining the term Διόσκουροι as it stands in the Greek text, the common version gives the two names "Castor and Pollux," who were reckoned sons of Jupiter by Leda, and regarded by sailors as their tutelary divinities, appearing in the heavens as the constellation of the Gemini or Twins. On shipboard they were recognised in the phosphoric lights which play about the masts and sails. Hence Roman poets so often allude to these divinities in relation to navigation.
Acts 28. 11 a ship..whose sign was C. and P.

CATCH, to —
1. *To lay or keep hold on*, אָחַז *achaz.*
Judg. 1. 6 they pursued after him, and caught him

2. *To take as spoil*, בָּזַז *bazaz.*
Num 31. 32 prey which the men of war had caught

3. *To take by violence*, גָּזַל *gazal.*
Judg 21. 23 took (them) wives..whom they caught

4. *To draw or sweep away*, גָּרַר *garar.*
Hab. 1. 15 they catch them in their net, and gather

5. *To make strong or hard*, חָזַק *chazaq*, 5.
Exod. 4. 4 he put forth his hand, and caught it
1 Sa. 17. 35 and when he arose..I caught
2 Sa. 2. 16 they caught every one his fellow by the
2 Ki. 4. 27 when she came..she caught him by the
Prov. 7. 13 So she caught him, and kissed him

6. *To snatch away*, חָטַף *chataph.*
Judg 21. 21 catch you every man his wife..daughters
Psa. 10. 9 he lieth in wait to catch the poor
10. 9 he doth catch the poor, when he draweth

7. *To draw out*, חָלַט *chalat*, 5.
1 Ki. 20. 33 Now the men..did hastily catch (it)

8. *To tear, rend,* טָרַף *taraph.*
Eze. 19. 3 it learned to catch the prey; it devoured
19. 6 learned to catch the prey, (and) devoured

9. *To capture, catch,* לָכַד *lakad.*
Judg. 8. 14 caught a young man of the men of Succoth
15. 4 Samson went and caught three hundred
2 Ch. 22. 9 he sought Ahaziah: and they caught him
Jer. 5. 26 they set a trap, they catch men

10. *To find,* מָצָא *matsa.*
Exod22. 6 If fire break out, and catch..thorns

11. *To extort, ensnare,* נָקַשׁ *naqash,* 3.
Psa.109. 11 Let the extortioner catch all that he hath

12. *Hunting,* צַיִד *tsayid.*
Lev. 17. 13 which hunteth and catcheth any beast or

13. *To lay hold of (by the hand),* תָּפַשׂ *taphas.*
Gen. 39. 12 And she caught him by his garment
1 Ki. 11. 30 And Abijah caught the new garment that
2 Ki. 7. 12 we shall catch them alive, and get into

14. *To catch, hunt (in the field),* ἀγρεύω *agreuō.*
Mark12. 13 they send..to catch him in (his) words

15. *To snatch at, or away,* ἁρπάζω *harpazō.*
John10. 12 the wolf catcheth them, and scattereth

16. *To take (hold) upon,* ἐπιλαμβάνω *epilambanō.*
Matt14. 31 Jesus stretched forth (his) hand..caught
Acts 16. 19 they caught Paul and Silas, and drew

17. *To hunt (a wild beast),* θηρεύω *thēreuō.*
Luke 11. 54 seeking to catch something out of his

18. *To take,* λαμβάνω *lambanō.*
Matt 21. 39 they caught him, and cast (him) out of
Mark12. 3 they caught (him), and beat him, and
2 Co. 12. 16 nevertheless, being crafty, I caught you

19. *To catch alive,* ζωγρέω *zōgreō.*
Luke 5. 10 from henceforth thou shalt catch men

20. *To seize,* πιάζω *piazō.*
John 21. 3 and that night they caught nothing
21. 10 Bring of the fish..ye have now caught

21. *To take together,* συλλαμβάνω *sullambanō.*
Acts 26. 21 For these causes the Jews caught me in

22. *To snatch away together,* συναρπάζω *sunarpazō.*
Luke 8. 29 For oftentimes it had caught him: and
Acts 6. 12 and came upon (him), and caught him
19. 29 and having caught Gaius and Aristarchus
27. 15 when the ship was caught, and could not

CATCH away —
To snatch away, ἁρπάζω *harpazō.*
Matt13. 19 catcheth away that which was sown
Acts 8. 39 Spirit of the Lord caught away Philip

CATCH hold, to —
1. *To lay or keep hold,* אָחַז *achaz.*
1 Ki. 1. 50,51 caught hold on the horns of the altar
2. 28 Joab..caught hold on the horns of the

2. *To become strong, or fast,* חָזַק *chazaq.*
2 Sa. 18. 9 and his head caught hold of the oak

CATCH self, to —
To capture, catch, לָכַד *lakad.*
Psa. 35. 8 let his net..he hath hid catch himself

CATCH up, to —
To snatch away, ἁρπάζω *harpazō.*
2 Co. 12. 2 such an one caught up to the third
12. 4 How that he was caught up into paradise
1 Th. 4. 17 Then we..shall be caught up together
Rev. 12. 5 and her child was caught up unto God

CATERPILLAR —
1. *A devourer (a kind of locust),* חָסִיל *chasil.*
1 Ki. 8. 37 If there be in the land..caterpillar
2 Ch. 6. 28 If there be dearth..or caterpillars
Psa. 78. 46 He gave..their increase unto the caterp.
Isa. 33. 4 shall be gathered (like)..the caterpillar
Joel. 1. 4 that which..hath left hath the caterpillar
2. 25 the cankerworm, and the caterpillar

2. *A cankerworm,* יֶלֶק *yeleq.*
Psa.105. 34 He spake..locusts came, and caterpillars
Jer. 51. 14 I will fill thee..as with caterpillars
51. 27 horses to come up as the rough cater.

CATTLE — [*See also* KEEP cattle.]
1. *Cattle, beast,* בְּהֵמָה *behemah.*
Gen. 1. 24 cattle, and creeping thing, and beast of
1. 25 God made the..cattle after their kind
1. 26 let them have dominion over..the cattle
2. 20 And Adam gave names to all cattle, and
3. 14 thou (art) cursed above all cattle, and
6. 20 cattle after their kind, of every creeping
7. 14 and all the cattle after their kind, and
7. 21 all flesh died..both of fowl, and of cattle
7. 23 both man, and cattle, and the creeping
8. 1 and all the cattle (that) was with him in
8. 17 and of cattle, and of every creeping thing
9. 10 of the fowl, of the cattle, and of every be.
47. 18 my lord also hath our herds of cattle
Exod12. 29 LORD smote..all the first born of cattle
20. 10 nor thy maid servant, nor thy cattle
Lev. 1. 2 shall bring your offering of the cattle
5. 2 whether (it be) a carcase..of unclean cat.
19. 19 Thou shalt not let thy cattle gender with
25. 7 And for thy cattle, and for the beast
Lev. 26. 22 shall rob you..and destroy your cattle
Num. 3. 41 and the cattle of the Levites instead of
3. 41 firstlings among the cattle of..Israel
3. 45 and the cattle of the Levites instead of
31. 9 and took the spoil of all their cattle
32. 26 our wives, our flocks, and all our cattle
35. 3 suburbs of them shall be for their cattle
Deut. 2. 35 Only the cattle we took for a prey
3. 7 all the cattle, and the spoil of the cities
5. 14 nor thine ass, nor any of thy cattle
7. 14 there shall not be..among your cattle
11. 15 And I will send grass..for thy cattle
13. 15 and the cattle thereof, with the edge of
20. 14 and the little ones, and the cattle, and
28. 4 and the fruit of thy cattle, the increase
28. 11 in the fruit of thy cattle, and in the
28. 51 And he shall eat the fruit of thy cattle
30. 9 in the fruit of thy cattle, and in the fruit
Josh. 8. 2 only the spoil thereof, and the cattle
8. 27 Only the cattle and the spoil of that city
11. 14 all the spoil of these cities, and the cattle
21. 2 with the suburbs thereof for our cattle
2 Ki. 3. 9 and for the cattle that followed them
Neh. 9. 37 over our bodies, and over our cattle
10. 36 the first born of our sons, and of our cattle
Psa. 50. 10 (and) the cattle upon a thousand hills
104. 14 causeth the grass to grow for the cattle
107. 38 suffereth not their cattle to decrease
148. 10 Beasts, and all cattle; creeping things
Isa. 46. 1 their idols were upon..the cattle
Jon. 4. 11 Nineveh..wherein are..(also) much cat.
Hag. 1. 11 upon men and upon cattle, and upon all
Zech. 2. 4 the multitude of men and cattle therein

2. *Beast,* בְּעִיר *beir.*
Num20. 4 that we and our cattle should die there?
Psa. 78. 48 He gave up their cattle also to the hail

3. *A possession, thing purchased,* מִקְנֶה *miqneh.*
Gen. 4. 20 he was the father..(of such as have) catt.
13. 2 And Abram (was) very rich in cattle
13. 7 between the herdmen of Abram's cattle
13. 7 and the herdmen of Lot's cattle: And
29. 7 neither (is it) time that the cattle should
30. 29 Thou knowest..how thy cattle was with
31. 9 Thus God hath taken away the cattle
31. 18 And he carried away all his cattle, and
31. 18 the cattle of his getting, which he had
33. 17 And Jacob..made booths for his cattle
34. 5 now his sons were with his cattle in the
34. 23 (Shall) not their cattle and their substan.
36. 6 and his cattle, and all his beasts
36. 7 could not..because of their cattle
46. 6 they took their cattle, and their goods
46. 32 their trade hath been to feed cattle
46. 34 Thy servants' trade hath been about catt.
47. 6 then make them rulers over my cattle
47. 16 And Joseph said, Give your cattle; and
47. 16 I will give you for your cattle, if money
47. 17 they brought their cattle unto Joseph
47. 17 for the cattle of the herds, and..the asses
47. 17 for all their cattle for that year
Exod. 9. 3 the hand of the LORD is upon thy cattle
9. 4 the LORD shall sever between the cattle
9. 4 and the cattle of Egypt; and there shall
9. 6 and all the cattle of Egypt died
9. 6 but of the cattle of the children of Is. died
9. 7 there was not one of the cattle of the Is.
9. 19 Send therefore now, (and) gather thy catt.
9. 20 made his servants and his cattle flee into
9. 21 left his servants and his cattle in the field
10. 26 Our cattle also shall go with us; there
12. 38 flocks and herds, (even) very much cattle
17. 3 thou hast brought us..to kill..our cattle
34. 19 and every firstling among thy cattle
Num20. 19 if I and my cattle drink of thy water
32. 1 had a very great multitude of cattle
32. 1 behold, the place (was) a place for cattle
32. 4 the country..(is) a land for cattle
32. 4 and thy servants have cattle
32. 16 We will build sheep folds..for our cattle
Deut. 3. 19 your little ones, and..cattle..shall abide
3. 19 (for) I know that ye have much cattle
Josh. 1. 14 Your wives, your little ones..your cattle
14. 4 with their suburbs for their cattle and
22. 8 Return..with very much cattle, with
Judg. 6. 5 they came up with their cattle, and their
18. 21 put the little ones and the cattle..before
1 Sa. 23. 5 brought away their cattle, and smote
30. 20 they drave before those (other) cattle
2 Ki. 3. 17 both ye, and your cattle, and your beasts
1 Ch. 5. 9 because their cattle were multiplied in
5. 21 they took away their cattle; of their
7. 21 they came down to take away their cattle
2 Ch. 14. 15 They smote also the tents of cattle, and
26. 10 he had much cattle, both in the low
Job 36. 33 the cattle also concerning the vapour
Isa. 30. 23 in that day shall thy cattle feed in large
Jer. 9. 10 can (men) hear the voice of the cattle
49. 32 and the multitude of their cattle a spoil
Eze. 38. 12 people..which have gotten cattle and
38. 13 to take away cattle and goods, to take

4. *Small cattle, sheep and goats,* צֹאן *tson.*
Gen. 30. 39 brought forth cattle ringstraked, speck.
30. 40 and put them not unto Laban's cattle
30. 41 whensoever the stronger cattle did con.
30. 41 Jacob laid the rods before..the cattle
30. 42 But when the cattle were feeble, he put
30. 43 and had much cattle, and maid servants
31. 8 then all the cattle bare speckled: and if
31. 8 then bare all the cattle ringstraked
31. 10 came to pass at the time that the cattle
Gen. 31. 10 the cattle (were) ringstraked, speckled
31. 12 all the rams which leap upon the cattle
31. 41 I served thee..six years for thy cattle
31. 43 and (these) cattle (are) my cattle, and all

5. *A sheep or goat,* שֶׂה *seh.*
Gen. 30. 32 removing..the speckled and spotted cat.
30. 32 all the brown cattle among the sheep
Eze. 34. 17 Behold, I judge between cattle and cattle
34. 20 I, (even) I..judge between the fat cattle
34. 20 and between the lean cattle
34. 22 I will judge between cattle and cattle

6. *Work,* מְלָאכָה *melakah.*
Gen. 33. 14 according as the cattle that goeth before

7. *What is fed or nourished,* θρέμμα *thremma.*
John 4. 12 drank thereof..his children, and his cat.

CATTLE, fat —
Fatlings, מְרִיא *meri.*
1 Ki. 1. 9 slew sheep and oxen and fat c.; 1. 19, 25.

CATTLE, great — [*See* **GREAT.**]

CATTLE, lesser —
Sheep or goats, שֶׂה *seh.*
Isa. 7. 25 and for the treading of lesser cattle

CATTLE, small —
1. *Small cattle, sheep and goats,* צֹאן *tson.*
Eccl. 2. 7 great possessions of great and small cattle

2. *Sheep or goat,* שֶׂה *seh.*
Isa. 43. 23 Thou hast not brought me the small cattle

CATTLE, to feed —
To shepherd, tend, ποιμαίνω *poimainō.*
Luke17. 7 a servant plowing or feeding cattle

CAUGHT, to be —
1. *To be laid hold of,* אָחַז *achaz,* 2.
Gen. 22. 13 a ram caught in a thicket by his horns

2. *To be laid hold of (by the hand),* תָּפַשׂ *taphas,* 2.
Jer. 50. 24 thou art found, and also caught, because

CAUL —
1. *Diaphragm or midriff,* יֹתֶרֶת *yothereth.*
Exod29. 13 thou shalt take..the caul (that is) above
29. 22 thou shalt take..the caul (above) the
Lev. 3. 4, 10, 15 the caul above the liver, with the
4. 9 the caul above the liver, with the kidneys
7. 4 the caul (that is) above the liver, with the
8. 16 the caul (above) the liver, and the two
8. 25 And he took..the caul (above) the liver
9. 10 the caul above the liver of the sin offering
9. 19 and the kidneys, and the caul (above) the

2. *Caul, pericardium,* סְגוֹר *segor.*
Hos. 13. 8 I..will rend the caul of their heart, and

3. *Cauls, netted caps,* שְׁבִיסִים *shebisim.*
Isa. 3. 18 the LORD will take away..(their) cauls

CAUSE —
1. *Causes, reasons,* אוֹדֹת *odoth.*
2 Sa. 13. 16 she said unto him, (There is) no cause
Jer. 3. 8 I saw, when for all the causes whereby

2. *Word, matter,* דָּבָר *dabar.*
Exod 18. 19 that thou mayest bring the causes unto
18. 26 the hard causes they brought unto Moses
22. 9 the cause of both parties shall come before
Deut. 1. 17 the cause that is too hard for you, bring
Josh. 5. 4 this (is) the cause why Joshua did cir.
20. 4 shall declare his cause in the ears of the
1 Sa. 17. 29 What have I..done? (Is there) not a cause
1 Ki. 11. 27 this (was) the cause that he lifted up (his)

3. *Word, matter,* דִּבְרָה *dibrah.*
Job 5. 8 and unto God would I commit my cause

4. *Plea, judgment,* דִּין *din.*
Psa. 9. 4 thou hast maintained..my cause; thou
140. 12 the LORD will maintain the cause of the
Prov 29. 7 The righteous considereth the cause of
31. 8 Open thy mouth..in the cause of all such
Jer. 5. 28 they judge not the cause, the cause of
22. 16 He judged the cause of the poor and
30. 13 (There is) none to plead thy cause, that

5. *Judgment,* מִשְׁפָּט *mishpat.*
2 Sa. 15. 4 every man which hath any..cause might
1 Ki. 8. 45, 49 hear thou..and maintain their cause
8. 59 the cause of his servant, and the cause of
2 Ch. 6. 35, 39 hear thou..and maintain their cause
Job 13. 18 Behold now, I have ordered (my) cause
23. 4 I would order (my) cause before him
31. 13 If I did despise the cause..man servant
Lam. 3. 59 LORD, thou hast seen..judge..my cause

6. *Turn (of events),* נְסִבָּה *nesibbah.*
2 Ch. 10. 15 the cause was of God, that the LORD might

7. *Turn (of events),* סִבָּה *sibbah.*
1 Ki. 12. 15 unto the people; for the cause was from

8. *Strife, controversy,* רִיב *rib*
Exod23. 2 neither shalt thou speak in a cause to
23. 3 countenance a poor man in his cause
23. 6 the judgment of thy poor in his cause
1 Sa. 24. 15 plead my cause, and deliver me out of
25. 39 hath pleaded the cause of my reproach
2 Ch. 19. 10 what cause soever shall come to you
Job 29. 16 the cause (which) I knew not I searched

Psa. 35. 23 (even) unto my cause..God and my Lord
43. 1 Judge me, O God, and plead my cause
74. 22 Arise, O God, plead thine own cause
119. 154 Plead my cause, and deliver me: quicken
Prov. 18. 17 (He that is) first in his own cause
22. 23 the LORD will plead their cause, and spoil
23. 11 he shall plead their cause with thee
25. 9 Debate thy cause with thy neighbour(him.)
Isa. 1. 23 neither doth the cause of the widow
41. 21 Produce your cause, saith the LORD 51.22
Jer. 11. 20 for unto thee have I revealed my cause
20. 12 for unto thee have I opened my cause
50. 34 he shall throughly plead their cause
51. 36 Behold, I will plead thy cause, and take
Lam. 3. 36 subvert a man in his cause, the Lord
3. 58 thou hast pleaded the causes of my soul
Mic. 7. 9 I have sinned..until he plead my cause

9. *Because of whom*, בְּשֶׁלְּמִי *be-shel-le-mi.*
Jon. 1. 7 for whose cause this evil (is) upon us

10. *Cause, accusation*, αἰτία *aitia.*
Matt 19. 3 a man to put away his wife for every cause?
Luke 8. 47 for what cause she had touched him, and
Acts 10. 21 what (is) the cause wherefore ye are come?
13. 28 though they found no cause of death
23. 28 And when I would have known the cause
28. 18 because there was no cause of death in
28. 20 For this cause therefore have I called for
2 Ti. 1. 12 For the which cause I also suffer these
Heb. 2. 11 for which cause he is not ashamed to call

11. *Causative of, causing, asking*, αἴτιον *aition.*
Luke 23. 22 I have found no cause of death in him
Acts 19. 40 there being no cause whereby we may

12. *Word, matter*, λόγος *logos.*
Matt. 5. 32 saving for..cause of fornication, causeth

CAUSE, for the same —
The same, τὸ αὐτό *to auto.*
Phil. 2. 18 For the same cause also do ye joy and

CAUSE, for this (or your) —
1. *Wholly over against this*, כָּל־קֳבֵל דְּנָה *kol qebel denah.*
Dan. 2. 12 For this cause the king was angry and

2. *Over against this*, ἀντὶ τούτου *anti toutou.*
Eph. 5. 31 For this cause shall a man leave his

3. *On account of this*, διὰ τοῦτο *dia touto.*
John 12. 18 For this cause the people also met him
12. 27 for this cause came I unto this hour
Rom. 1. 26 For this cause God gave them up unto vile
13. 6 For, for this cause pay ye tribute also
15. 9 For this cause I will confess to thee among
1 Co. 4. 17 For this cause have I sent unto you
11. 10 For this cause ought the woman to have
11. 30 For this cause many (are) weak and sickly
Col. 1. 9 For this cause we also..do not cease to
1 Th. 2. 13 For this cause also thank we God without
3. 5 For this cause, when I could no longer
2 Th. 2. 11 for this cause God shall send them strong
1 Ti. 1. 16 Howbeit for this cause I obtained mercy
Heb. 9. 15 And for this cause he is the Mediator of

4. *With a view to this*, εἰς τοῦτο *eis touto.*
John 18. 37 for this cause came I into the world, that
1 Pe. 4. 6 for this cause was the Gospel preached

5. *For the sake of this*, ἕνεκεν τούτου *heneken toutou.*
Matt. 19. 5 For this cause shall a man leave
Mark 10. 7; Acts 26. 21; 2 Co. 7. 12.

6. *To you*, ὑμῖν *humin.*
2 Co. 5. 13 whether we be sober..for your cause

CAUSE, for which —
1. *Therefore*, עַל־כֵּן *al ken.*
Neh. 6. 6 for which cause thou buildest the wall

2. *On account of which*, διό *dio.*
Rom 15. 22 For which cause also I have been much
2 Co. 4. 16 For which cause we faint not; but though

CAUSE, without (a) —
1. *Gratis, gratuitously*, חִנָּם *chinnam.*
1 Sa. 19. 5 wherefore..slay David without a cause?
Job 2. 3 movedst me..destroy him without cause
9. 17 and multiplieth..wounds without cause
Psa. 35. 7 For without cause have they hid for me
35. 7 without cause they have digged for my
35. 19 let..wink..that hate me without a cause
69. 4 They that hate me without a cause are
109. 3 they..fought against me without a cause
119. 161 have persecuted me without a cause
Prov. 1. 11 lurk privily for..innocent without cause
3. 30 Strive not with a man without cause
23. 29 who hath wounds without cause? who
24. 28 Be not a witness..without cause; and
Lam. 3. 52 chased me sore, like a bird, without cause
Eze. 14. 23 I have not done without cause all that I

2. *Vainly*, רֵיקָם *reqam.*
Psa. 7. 4 delivered him that without cause is
25. 3 ashamed which transgress without cause

3. *Falsehood*, שֶׁקֶר *sheqer.*
Psa. 119. 78 dealt perversely with me without a cause

4. *Gratuitously*, δωρεάν *dōrean.*
John 15. 25 They hated me without a cause

5. *Yieldingly, heedlessly*, εἰκῆ *eikē.*
Matt. 5. 22 angry with his brother without a cause

CAUSE, Paul's —
The things regarding (Paul), τὰ κατὰ *ta kata.*
Acts 25. 14 Festus declared Paul's cause unto the king

CAUSE (to be), to —
1. *To be to*, הָיָה לְ *hayah le.*
Num 31. 16 Behold, these caused the children of

2. *To give*, נָתַן *nathan.*
Lev. 24. 19 And if a man cause a blemish in his
24. 20 as he hath caused a blemish in a man
Deut 28. 7 the LORD shall cause thine enemies
28. 25 the LORD shall cause thee to be smitten
Prov 10. 10 He that winketh with the eye causeth
Jer. 15. 4 And I will cause them to be removed
Eze. 16. 7 I have caused thee to multiply as the
26. 17 which cause their terror (to be) on all
32. 23 which caused terror in the land of the
32. 24, 26 caused their terror in the land of the
32. 32 For I have caused my terror in the land

3. *To do, make*, ποιέω *poieō.*
Matt. 5. 32 for the cause of fornication, causeth her
John 11. 37 Could not this man..have caused that
Acts 15. 3 caused great joy unto all the brethren
Rom 16. 17 mark them which cause divisions and off.
Col. 4. 16 cause that it be read also in the church
Rev. 12. 15 that he might cause her to be carried
13. 12 causeth the earth and them which dwell
13. 15 cause that as many as would not worship
13. 16 And he causeth all, both small and great

4. *To work thoroughly*, κατεργάζομαι *katergazomai.*
2 Co. 9. 11 which causeth through us thanksgiving

CAUSED, to be —
To be given, נָתַן *nathan*, 2.
Eze. 32. 25 though their terror was caused in the land

CAUSELESS —
Gratuitously, חִנָּם *chinnam.*
1 Sa. 25. 31 either that thou hast shed blood causeless
Prov 26. 2 so the curse causeless shall not come

CAUSEWAY —
Way cast up, מְסִלָּה *mesillah.*
1 Ch. 26. 16 by the causeway of the going up, ward
26. 18 four at the causeway, (and) two at Parbar

CAVE —
1. *A hole*, חוֹר *chor.*
Job 30. 6 To dwell..(in) caves of the earth, and (in)

2. *Exposed place, open cave*, מְעָרָה *mearah.*
Gen. 19. 30 and he dwelt in a cave, he and his two
23. 9 That he may give me the cave of Machp.
23. 11 the field give I thee, and the cave that
23. 17 the field, and the cave which (was) therein
23. 19 buried Sarah his wife in the cave of the
23. 20 the field, and the cave that (is) therein
25. 9 his sons..buried him in the cave of Mac.
49. 29 bury me with my fathers in the cave
49. 30 In the cave that (is) in the field of Mach.
49. 32 The purchase of the field and of the cave
50. 13 buried him in the cave of the field of M.
Josh. 10. 16 hid themselves in a cave at Makkedah
10. 17 The five kings are found hid in a cave at
10. 18 Roll..stones upon the mouth of the cave
10. 22 said Joshua, Open the mouth of the cave
10. 22 bring out those five kings..out of the cave
10. 23 brought..those five kings..out of the cave
10. 27 and cast them into the cave, wherein
10. 27 and laid great stones in the cave's mouth
Judg. 6. 2 dens which (are) in the mountains..caves
1 Sa. 13. 6 the people did hide themselves in caves
22. 1 David..escaped to the cave Adullam
24. 3 came to the sheep cotes..where (was) a c.
24. 3 his men remained in the sides of the cave
24. 7 Saul rose up out of the cave, and went
24. 8 David also arose..went out of the cave
24. 10 had delivered thee to day..in the cave
2 Sa 23. 13 came to David..unto the cave of Adullam
1 Ki. 18. 4 hid them by fifty in a cave, and fed them
18. 13 I hid an hundred men..by fifty in a cave
19. 9 he came thither unto a cave, and lodged
19. 13 and stood in the entering in of the cave
1 Ch. 11. 15 went down..into the cave of Adullam
Psa. 57. *title.* when he fled from Saul in the cave
142. *title.* A Prayer when he was in the cave
Eze. 33. 27 they that (be) in the forts and in the caves

3. *Opening, hole*, ὀπή *opē.*
Heb. 11. 38 wandered..(in) dens and caves of the

4. *Cave, grotto*, σπήλαιον *spēlaion.*
John 11. 38 It was a cave, and a stone lay upon it

CAVES —
Holes, caves, מְחִלּוֹת *mechilloth.*
Isa. 2. 19 they shall go..into the caves of the earth

CEASE, to —
1. *To cease (from labour)*, בָּטֵל *batel.*
Eccl. 12. 3 the grinders cease, because they are few

2. *To cease*, בְּטֵל *betel.*
Ezra 4. 24 Then ceased the work of the house of

3. *To come to an end*, גָּמַר *gamar.*
Psa. 12. 1 Help, LORD; for the godly man ceaseth

4. *To be dumb, silent*, דָּמָה *damah.*
Jer. 14. 17 Let mine eyes run..let them not cease
Lam. 3. 49 Mine eye trickleth down, and ceaseth

5. *To be dumb, silent*, דָּמַם *damam.*
Psa. 35. 15 they did tear (me), and ceased not
Lam. 2. 18 let not the apple of thine eye cease

6. *To cease, leave off*, חָדַל *chadal.*
Gen. 18. 11 it ceased to be with Sarah after the
Exod. 9. 29 the thunder shall cease, neither shall
9. 33 the thunders and hail ceased, and the
9. 34 the hail and the thunders were ceased
Deut 15. 11 For the poor shall never cease out of the
Judg. 5. 7 the villages ceased, they ceased in Israel
15. 7 avenged of you, and after that I will cease
20. 28 Shall..go out to battle..or shall I cease?
1 Sa. 2. 5 and (they that were) hungry ceased: so
12. 23 I should sin..in ceasing to pray for you
Job 3. 17 There the wicked cease (from) troubling
10. 20 (Are) not my days few? cease (then, and)
14. 7 the tender branch thereof will not cease
Psa. 49. 8 redemption of their soul..ceaseth for
Prov. 19. 27 Cease, my son, to hear the instruction
23. 4 Labour not to be rich; cease from thine
Isa. 1. 16 put away the evil of your doings..cease
2. 22 Cease ye from man, whose breath (is) in
Amos 7. 5 Then said I, O Lord GOD, cease, I beseech

7. *To be silent*, חָרַשׁ *charesh*, 5.
1 Sa. 7. 8 Cease not to cry unto the LORD our God

8. *To add*, יָסַף *yasaph.*
Num 11. 25 they prophesied, and did not cease

9. *To be completed*, כָּלָה *kalah.*
Isa. 16. 4 the spoiler ceaseth, the oppressors are

10. *To remove*, מוּשׁ *mush*, 5.
Jer. 17. 8 neither shall cease from yielding fruit

11. *To rest*, נוּחַ *nuach.*
1 Sa. 25. 9 David's young men came, they..ceased

12. *To cause to fall*, נָפַל *naphal*, 5.
Judg. 2. 19 they ceased not from their own doings

13. *To stand*, עָמַד *amad.*
Jon. 1. 15 and the sea ceased from her raging

14. *To be languid*, פּוּג *pug.*
Psa. 77. 2 my sore ran in the night, and ceased not

15. *To let fall*, רָפָה *raphah*, 5.
Psa. 37. 8 Cease from anger, and forsake wrath: fret

16. *To cease, keep sabbath*, שָׁבַת *shabath.*
Gen. 8. 22 and summer and winter..shall not cease
Josh. 5. 12 And the manna ceased on the morrow
Neh. 6. 3 why should the work cease, whilst I
Job 32. 1 So these three men ceased to answer Job
Prov 22. 10 yea, strife and reproach shall cease
Isa. 14. 4 oppressor ceased! the golden city ceased
24. 8 The mirth of tabrets ceaseth, the noise
24. 8 the joy of the harp ceaseth
33. 8 the wayfaring man ceaseth: he hath
Jer. 31. 36 the seed of Israel also shall cease from
Lam. 5. 14 The elders have ceased from the gate
5. 15 The joy of our heart is ceased; our dance
Hos. 7. 4 ceaseth from raising after he hath

17. *To cease, keep sabbath*, שָׁבַת *shabath*, 2.
Isa. 17. 3 The fortress..shall cease from Ephraim
Eze. 6. 6 and your idols may be broken and cease
30. 18 and the pomp of her strength shall cease
33. 28 and the pomp of her strength shall cease

18. *Cessation*, שֶׁבֶת *shebeth.*
Prov. 20. 3 (It is) an honour for a man to cease from

19. *To turn back from*, שׁוּב מִן *shub min.*
Num. 8. 25 they shall cease waiting upon the service

20. *To cease, rest, be still*, שָׁתַק *shathaq.*
Prov. 26. 20 where (there is) no tale bearer, the strife c.

21. *To perfect, complete*, תָּמַם *tamam*, 5.
Isa. 33. 1 when thou shalt cease to spoil, thou shalt

22. *To leave throughout, intermit*, διαλείπω *dialeipō.*
Luke 7. 45 this woman..hath not ceased to kiss my

23. *To become still, quiet, silent*, ἡσυχάζω *hēsuchazō.*
Acts 21. 14 we ceased, saying, The will of the Lord

24. *To cease thoroughly*, καταπαύω *katapauō.*
Heb. 4. 10 he also hath ceased from his own works

25. *To make thoroughly idle*, καταργέω *katargeō.*
Gal. 5. 11 then is the offence of the cross ceased

26. *To cease, abate*, κοπάζω *kopazō.*
Matt 14. 32 when they were come..the wind ceased
Mark 4. 39 wind ceased, and there was a great calm
6. 51 the wind ceased: and they were sore

27. *To pause, cease*, παύομαι *pauomai.*
Luke 8. 24 and they ceased, and there was a calm
11. 1 when he ceased, one of his disciples said
Acts 5. 42 they ceased not to teach and preach
6. 13 This man ceaseth not to speak blasphem.
13. 10 wilt thou not cease to pervert the right
20. 1 after the uproar was ceased, Paul called
20. 31 I ceased not to warn every one night and
1 Co. 13. 8 whether..tongues, they shall cease
Eph. 1. 16 Cease not to give thanks for you, making
Col. 1. 9 For this cause we also..do not cease to
Heb. 10. 2 then would they not have ceased to be
1 Pe. 4. 1 he that hath suffered..hath ceased from

CEASE, that cannot —
Not ceasing thoroughly, ἀκατάπαυστος *akatapaustos.*
2 Pe. 2. 14 Having eyes..[that cannot cease] from

CEASE, to cause to —
1. *To cause to cease or leave off*, בְּטֵל *betel*, 3.
Ezra 4. 21 Give ye..to cause these men to cease
5. 5 that they could not cause them to cease

2. *To break asunder, disannul*, פָּרַר *parar*, 5.
Psa. 85. 4 and cause thine anger toward us to cease

3. *To cause to cease, keep sabbath,* שָׁבַת *shabath,* 5.
Neh. 4. 11 slay them, and cause the work to cease
Prov. 18. 18 The lot causeth contentions to cease, and
Isa. 13. 11 cause the arrogancy of the proud to cease
30. 11 cause the Holy One of Israel to cease:
Jer. 7. 34 Then will I cause to cease from the cities
16. 9 I will cause to cease out of this place in
36. 29 and shall cause to cease from thence
48. 35 I will cause to cease in Moab, saith the
Eze. 16. 41 I will cause thee to cease from playing
23. 48 Thus will I cause lewdness to cease out
26. 13 will cause the noise of thy songs to cease
30. 13 I will cause (their) images to cease out of
34. 10 cause them to cease from feeding the
34. 25 will cause the evil beasts to cease out of
Dan. 9. 27 cause the sacrifice and the oblation to cease
11. 18 a prince..shall cause the reproach..to ce.
Hos. 1. 4 will cause to cease the kingdom of the
2. 11 I will also cause all her mirth to cease

CEASE, to let —
To cause or let cease, שָׁבַת *shabath,* 5.
2 Ch. 16. 5 he left off building..and let his work ce.

CEASE, to make to —
1. *To cause to cease,* בְּטֵל *betel,* 3.
Ezra 4. 23 made them to cease by force and power
2. *To cause to cease, keep sabbath,* שָׁבַת *shabath* 5.
Deut 32. 26 make the remembrance of them to cease
Josh 22. 25 make our children cease from fearing the
Psa. 46. 9 He maketh wars to cease unto the end of
89. 44 Thou hast made his glory to cease
Isa. 16. 10 have made (their vintage) shouting to ce.
21. 2 the sighing thereof have I made to cease
Eze. 7. 24 make the pomp of the strong to cease
12. 23 I will make this proverb to cease, and
23. 27 Thus will I make thy lewdness to cease
30. 10 make the multitude of Egypt to cease
3. *To cause to settle down,* שָׁכַךְ *shakak,* 5.
Num 17. 5 I will make to cease from me the murm.

CEASED —
There was a cessation, הֲוָת בָּטְלָא [*betel*].
Ezra 4. 24 So it ceased unto the second year of

CEASING, without —
1. *Not thoroughly left, unintermitting,* ἀδιάλειπτος.
2 Ti. 1. 3 that without ceasing I have remembrance
2. *Unintermittingly,* ἀδιαλείπτως *adialeiptōs.*
Rom. 1. 9 that without ceasing I make mention of
1 Th. 1. 3 Remembering without ceasing your work
2. 13 cause also thank we God without ceasing
5. 17 Pray without ceasing
3. *Extended, outstretched,* ἐκτενής *ektenēs.*
Acts 12. 5 prayer was made [without ceasing] of the

CEDAR —
Cedar (so called from its firmness), אֶרֶז *erez.*
Lev. 14. 4 and cedar wood, and scarlet, and hyssop
14. 6 he shall take it, and the cedar wood
14. 49 he shall take..two birds, and cedar wood
14. 51 he shall take the cedar wood, and the
14. 52 shall cleanse the house..with the cedar
Num 19. 6 the priest shall take cedar wood, and
Judg. 9. 15 let fire come out..and devour the cedars
2 Sa. 5. 11 And Hiram king of Tyre sent..cedar trees
7. 2 See now, I dwell in an house of cedar
7. 7 Why build ye not me an house of cedar?
1 Ki 5. 8 I will do all thy desire concerning..cedar
5. 10 So Hiram gave Solomon cedar trees and
6. 9 covered the house with..boards of cedar
6. 10 rested on the house with timber of cedar
6. 15 he built the walls..with boards of cedar
6. 16 he built..the walls with boards of cedar
6. 18 And the cedar of the house within (was)
6. 18 all (was) cedar; there was no stone seen
6. 20 covered the altar (which was of) cedar
6. 36 the inner court with..cedar beams
7. 2 four rows of cedar pillars, with cedar
7. 3 covered with cedar above upon the beams
7. 7 covered with cedar from one side of the
7. 11 after the measures of hewed stones..ced.
7. 12 a row of cedar beams, both for the inner
9. 11 king..furnished Solomon with cedar tr.
10. 27 cedars made he (to be) as the sycamore tr.
2 Ki. 14. 9 The thistle..in Lebanon sent to the cedar
1 Ch. 14. 1 Hiram king of Tyre sent..timber of ced.
17. 1 Lo, I dwell in an house of cedars
17. 6 ye not built me an house of cedars?
22. 4 Also cedar trees in abundance; for the
22. 4 they of Tyre brought much cedar wood
2 Ch. 2. 3 and didst send him cedars to build him
2. 8 Send me also cedar trees, fir trees, and
25. 18 The thistle..in Lebanon sent to the cedar
Ezra 3. 7 to bring cedar trees from Lebanon to the
Job 40. 17 He moveth his tail like a cedar: the
Psa. 29. 5 The voice of the LORD breaketh the ce.
29. 5 yea, the LORD breaketh the cedars of
80. 10 boughs thereof (were like) the goodly ce.
92. 12 he shall grow like a cedar in Lebanon
104. 16 cedars of Lebanon, which he hath planted
148. 9 all hills; fruitful trees, and all cedars
Song 1. 17 The beams of our house (are) cedar, (and)
5. 15 his countenance (is)..excellent as the cedar
8. 9 we will enclose her with boards of cedar
Isa. 2. 13 And upon all the cedars of Lebanon
9. 10 but we will change (them into) cedars
14. 8 the fir trees rejoice at thee, (and) the ce.
37. 24 cut down the tall cedars thereof
41. 19 I will plant in the wilderness the cedar
44. 14 He heweth him down cedars, and taketh
Jer. 22. 7 they shall cut down thy choice cedars
22. 14 ceiled with cedar, and painted with ver.
22. 15 because thou closest (thyself) in cedar?
22. 23 that makest thy nest in the cedars
Eze. 17. 3 took the highest branch of the cedar
17. 22 of the highest branch of the high cedar
17. 23 bring forth boughs..and be a goodly ce.
27. 5 they have taken cedars from Lebanon to
31. 3 the Assyrian (was) a cedar in Lebanon
31. 8 The cedars in the garden of God could
Amos 2. 9 height (was) like the height of the cedars
Zech 11. 1 that the fire may devour thy cedars
11. 2 Howl, fir tree; for the cedar is fallen

CEDAR, made of —
Made of cedar, אֲרֻזִים *aruzim.*
Eze. 27. 24 bound with cords, and made of cedar

CEDAR tree —
A cedar tree, אֶרֶז *erez.*
Num 24. 6 (and) as cedar trees beside the waters
1 Ki. 4. 33 from the cedar tree that (is) in Lebanon
5. 6 that they hew me cedar trees out of Leb.
2 Ki. 19. 23 will cut down the tall cedar trees thereof
2 Ch. 1. 15 cedar trees made he as the sycamore
9. 27 cedar trees made he as the sycamore

CEDAR work —
Cedar work, אַרְזָה *arzah.*
Zeph. 2. 14 for he shall uncover the cedar work

CED'-RON, Κεδρών, Κέδρος *torrent.*
The name of the *Nahal Kidron* or "black torrent, which flows down the ravine below the E. wall of Jerusalem, and beyond it was the Garden of Gethsemane. It has no connection with "Cedar;" hence the τῶν κέδρων, *i.e.,* "brook of cedars," of some texts, as well as the LXX. in 2 Sa. 15. 23, is a gloss. Now *Wady Nar.*
John 18. 1 he went..with his disciples over..C.

CELEBRATE, to —
1. *To praise,* הָלַל *halal,* 3.
Isa. 38. 18 grave cannot..death can (not) celebrate
2. *To keep a festival,* חָגַג *chagag.*
Lev. 23. 41 ye shall celebrate it in the seventh month
3. *To keep a sabbath,* שָׁבַת *shabath.*
Lev. 23. 32 even, shall ye celebrate your sabbath

CELESTIAL —
Upon, over or above the heaven, ἐπουράνιος.
1 Co. 15. 40 also celestial bodies, and bodies terrestr.
15. 40 but the glory of the celestial (is) one

CELLAR —
Treasure, treasury, אוֹצָר *otsar.*
1 Ch. 27. 27 over the increase..for the wine cellars
27. 28 and over the cellars of oil (was) Joash

CEN-CHRE'-A, Κεγχρεαί.
It ought to be written *Cenchreæ;* the eastern harbour of Corinth (9 miles off) on the Saronic Gulf, and the emporium of its trade with Asia.
Acts 18. 18 having shorn (his) head in C.: for he had
Rom 16. 1 a servant of the church which is at C.

CENSER —
1. *A Censer,* מַחְתָּה *machtah.*
Lev. 10. 1 took either of them his censer, and put
16. 12 he shall take a censer full of burning
Num. 4. 14 they minister about it, (even) the censers
16. 6 Take you censers, Korah, and all his
16. 17 take every man his censer, and put
16. 17 and bring ye..every man his censer
16. 17 two hundred and fifty censers
16. 17 thou also, and Aaron, each..his censer
16. 18 they took every man his censer, and put
16. 37 that he take up the censers out of the
16. 38 The censers of these sinners against their
16. 39 Eleazar the priest took..brasen censers
16. 46 Take a censer, and put fire therein from
1 Ki. 7. 50 the spoons, and the censers (of) pure gold
2 Ch. 4. 22 the spoons, and the censers, (of) pure gold
2. *An incense censer,* מִקְטֶרֶת *miqtereth.*
2 Ch. 26. 19 a censer in his hand to burn incense
Eze. 8. 11 with every man his censer in his hand
3. *Incense censer,* θυμιατήριον *thumiatērion.*
Heb. 9. 4 Which had the golden censer
4. *Frankincense censer,* λιβανωτός *libanōtos.*
Rev. 8. 3 stood at the altar, having a golden censer
8. 5 the angel took the censer, and filled it

CENTURION —
1. *Leader of a hundred men,* ἑκατοντάρχης.
Acts 10. 1 a centurion of the band called the Italian
10. 22 Cornelius the centurion..was warned
24. 23 he commanded a centurion to keep Paul
27. 1 named Julius, a centurion of Augustus'
27. 31 Paul said to the centurion and to the
2. *Leader of a hundred men,* ἑκατόνταρχος.
Matt. 8. 5 there came unto him a centurion, beseech.
8. 8 The centurion answered and said, Lord
8. 13 Jesus said unto the [centurion], Go thy
27. 54 Now when the centurion..saw the earth.
Luke 7. 2 a certain centurion's servant..was sick
7. 6 the centurion sent friends to him, saying
23. 47 when the [centurion] saw what was done
Acts 21. 32 Who..took soldiers and [centurions]
22. 25 Paul said unto the centurion that stood
22. 26 When the [centurion] heard (that), he
23. 17 Paul called one of the centurions unto
23. 23 he called unto (him) two centurions
27. 6 the [centurion] found a ship of Alexandria
27. 11 Nevertheless the [centurion] believed the
27. 43 But the [centurion]..kept them from
28. 16 [the centurion delivered the prisoners to]
3. *Centurion; in Greek letters,* κεντυρίων *kenturiōn.*
Mark 15. 39 when the centurion..saw that he so cried
15. 44 calling (unto him) the centurion, he asked
15. 45 when he knew (it) of the centurion, he

CE-PHAS, Κηφᾶς *rock (man).*
A surname given to Simon Peter
John 1. 42 thou shalt be called C., which is..A stone
1 Co. 1. 12 I of Apollos; and I of C.; and I of Christ
3. 22 Whether Paul, or Apollos, or C...all are
9. 5 Have we not power to lead..as well as..C.?
15. 5 he was seen of C., then of the twelve
Gal. 2. 9 when James, [C.], and John..perceived

CEREMONIES —
Judgment, מִשְׁפָּט *mishpat.*
Num. 9. 3 according to all the ceremonies thereof

CERTAIN [men] —
1. *A man,* אֱנוֹשׁ *enosh.*
Num. 9. 6 there were certain men, who were defiled
16. 2 with certain of the children of Israel
Judg 19. 22 men of the city, certain sons of Belial
1 Ki. 11. 17 Hadad fled, he and certain Edomites
2 Ch. 28. 12 certain of the heads of the children
Ezra 10. 16 the priest, (with) certain chief of the
Neh. 13. 25 I..smote certain of them, and plucked
Jer. 26. 17 Then rose up certain of the elders of the
41. 5 there came certain from Shechem, from
Eze. 14. 1 Then came certain of the elders of Israel
20. 1 certain of the elders of Israel came to
2. *Mighty or strong man,* גְּבַר *gebar.*
Dan. 3. 8 certain Chaldeans came near, and accused
3. 12 certain Jews whom thou hast set over
3. *Set up, fixed,* יַצִּיב *yatstsib.*
Dan. 2. 45 the dream is certain, and..interpretation
4. *To be established, right,* כּוּן *kun,* 2.
Deut 13. 14 behold, (if it be) truth..the thing certain
17. 4 behold, (it be) true, (and) the thing certain
5. *Such a one,* פַּלְמוֹנִי *palmoni.*
Dan. 8. 13 another saint said unto that certain
6. *Times,* עִתִּים [*eth*].
Dan. 11. 13 come after certain years with a great
7. *Any one, any thing,* τις, τι, *tis, ti.*
Matt. 9. 3 behold, certain of the scribes said within
12. 38 certain of the scribes and of the Pharisees
Mark 2. 6 there were certain of the scribes sitting
7. 1 certain of the scribes, which came from
11. 5 certain of them that stood there said
12. 13 they send unto him certain of the Phar.
14. 57 there arose certain..bare false witness
Luke 6. 2 certain of the Pharisees said unto them
8. 2 certain women, which had been healed of
13. 31 same day there came certain of the Phar.
18. 9 he spake this parable unto certain which
20. 27 Then came to (him) certain of the Sadd.
20. 39 Then certain of the scribes answering
21. 2 he saw also a certain poor widow
24. 22 certain..of our company made us aston.
24. 24 certain of them which were with us went
John 12. 20 there were certain Greeks among them
Acts 6. 9 Then there arose certain of the synagogue
9. 19 Then was Paul certain days with the
10. 23 Peter went away with them, and certain
10. 48 Then prayed they him to tarry certain
12. 1 hands to vex certain of the church
13. 1 there were in..church..[certain] prophets
15. 1 certain men..came down from Judea
15. 2 Barnabas, and certain other of them
15. 5 there rose up certain of the sect of the
15. 24 certain which went out from us have
16. 12 we were in that city abiding certain days
17. 5 the Jews..took unto them certain lewd
17. 6 they drew Jason and certain brethren
17. 18 certain philosophers of the Epicureans
17. 20 thou bringest certain strange things to
17. 28 as certain also of your own poets have
17. 34 Howbeit certain men clave unto him
19. 1 Paul..came..and finding certain disciples
19. 13 Then certain of the vagabond Jews
19. 31 certain of the chief of Asia..sent unto
23. 12 when it was day, [certain] of the Jews
24. 18 Whereupon certain Jews from Asia found
24. 24 after certain days..he sent for Paul, and
25. 13 after certain days king Agrippa and B.
25. 19 certain questions against him of their
27. 1 they delivered Paul and certain other
Gal. 2. 12 For before that certain came from James
8. *Untripped up, certain,* ἀσφαλής *asphalēs.*
Acts 25. 26 Of whom I have no certain thing to write
9. *Evident,* δῆλος *dēlos.*
1 Ti. 6. 7 [certain] we can carry nothing out

CERTAIN, a —
1. *One,* אֶחָד *echad.*
Judg. 9. 53 a certain woman cast a piece of a mill.
13. 2 And there was a certain man of Zorah
1 Sa. 1. 1 was a certain man of Ramathaim-zophim
2 Sa. 18. 10 a certain man saw (it), and told Joab
1 Ki. 20. 35 a certain man of the sons of the prophets
2 Ki. 4. 1 there cried a certain woman of the wives

2 Ki. 8. 6 king appointed unto her a certain officer
Esth. 3. 8 There is a certain people scattered abroad
Dan. 10. 5 behold a certain man clothed in linen

2. *A man,* אִישׁ *ish.*
Gen. 38. 1 and turned in to a certain Adullamite
38. 2 Judah saw there a daughter of a certain
Judg 19. 1 there was a certain Levite sojourning on
Esth. 2. 5 there was a certain Jew, whose name (was)

3. *A man, human being,* ἄνθρωπος *anthrōpos.*
Matt 18. 23 likened unto a certain king, which would
21. 33 There was a certain householder, which
22. 2 The kingdom of heaven is like unto a cer.

4. *One,* εἷς *heis.*
Matt. 8. 19 a certain scribe came and said unto him
Mark 12. 42 there came a certain poor widow, and she
Luke 5. 12 came to pass, when he was in a certain
5. 17 it came to pass on a certain day, as he
8. 22 it came to pass on a certain day, that he

5. *Any one, any thing,* τις, τι, *tis, ti.*
Matt 21. 33 [There was a [certain] householder, which]
Mark 5. 25 [a certain] woman, which had an issue
14. 51 there followed him a certain young man
Luke 1. 5 a certain priest named Zacharias, of the
7. 2 a certain centurion's servant, who was
7. 41 There was a certain creditor which had
8. 27 there met him out of the city a certain
10. 25 a certain lawyer stood up, and tempted
10. 31 by chance there came down a certain
10. 33 a certain Samaritan..came where he was
10. 38 he entered into a certain village: and a c.
11. 1 as he was praying in a certain place
11. 27 a certain woman of the company lifted
11. 37 [a certain] Pharisee besought him to dine
12. 16 The ground of a certain rich man brought
14. 2 there was a certain man before him which
14. 16 A certain man made a great supper, and
15. 11 And he said, A certain man had two sons
16. 1, 19 There was a certain rich man which
16. 20 there was a certain beggar named Lazarus
17. 12 as he entered into a certain village
18. 18 And a certain ruler asked him, saying
18. 35 a certain blind man sat by the way side
19. 12 A certain nobleman went into a far co.
20. 9 [A certain] man planted a vineyard
21. 2 a certain poor widow casting in..mites
22. 56 a certain maid beheld him as he sat by
23. 19 Who for a certain sedition made in the
John 4. 46 there was a certain nobleman, whose son
5. 5 a certain man was there, which had an
Acts 3. 2 a certain man lame from his mother's
5. 1 a certain man named Ananias..sold a
5. 2 a certain part, and laid (it) at the apostles'
8. 9 there was a certain man called Simon
8. 36 they came unto a certain water: and the
9. 10 there was a certain disciple at Damascus
9. 33 found a certain man named Eneas, which
9. 36 there was at Joppa a certain disciple
10. 1 a certain man in Cesarea called Cornelius
10. 11 a certain vessel descending unto him
11. 5 I saw a vision, A certain vessel descend
13. 6 they found a certain sorcerer, a false pr.
14. 8 there sat a certain man at Lystra
16. 1 behold, a certain disciple was there
16 1 [a certain] woman, which was a Jewess
16. 14 And a certain woman named Lydia
16. 16 a certain damsel possessed with a spirit
18. 2 And found a certain Jew named Aquila
18. 24 a certain Jew named Apollos..came to E.
20. 9 there sat in a window a certain young
21. 10 there came down..a certain prophet
24. 1 a certain orator (named) Tertullus, who
25. 14 There is a certain man left in bonds by
27. 16 under a certain island which is called
27. 26 we must be cast upon a certain island
27. 39 they discovered a certain creek with a
Rom 15. 26 to make a certain contribution for the
Heb. 4. 7 Again, he limiteth a certain day, saying
10. 27 a certain fearful looking for of judgment

CERTAIN portion —
A stated thing, אֲמָנָה *amanah.*
Neh. 11. 23 certain portion should be for the singers

CERTAIN rate —
Matter (amount) of a day, דְּבַר יוֹם [*dabar*].
Exod 16. 4 the people shall..gather a certain rate
2 Ch. 8. 13 after a certain rate every day, offering

CERTAIN (man, other, thing, place,) a —
Any one, any thing, τις, τι, *tis, ti.*
Matt 20. 20 and desiring a certain thing of him
Luke 9. 57 as they went in the way, a certain (man)
10. 30 A certain (man) went down from Jer.
13. 6 A certain (man) had a fig tree planted
24. 1 [came unto the sepulchre..and certain o.]
John 11. 1 Now a certain (man) was sick, (named)
Acts 18. 7; 19. 24; 23. 17; Jude 4.

2. *Somewhere,* πού *pou.*
Heb. 2. 6 But one in a certain place testified; 4. 4.

CERTAINLY —
1. *But,* אַךְ *ak.*
Lam. 2. 16 certainly this (is) the day that we looked
2. *But, surely,* אָכֵן *aken.*
Jer. 8. 8 Lo, certainly in vain made he (it)
3. *To know,* יָדַע *yada.* [adv. infin.].
Gen. 43. 7 could we certainly know that he would
1 Sa. 20. 3 Thy father certainly knoweth that I have
20. 9 if I knew certainly that evil were deter.
Jer. 13. 12 Do we not certainly know that every
40. 14 And said..Dost thou certainly know
42. 19 know certainly that I have admonished
42. 22 know certainly that ye shall die by the
4. *That, because,* כִּי *ki.*
Exod. 3. 12 And he said, Certainly I will be with thee
5. *Being, actually, really,* ὄντως *ontōs.*
Luke 23. 47 glorified God, saying, Certainly this was

CERTAINTY, for (a) certain —
1. *To know, be acquainted with,* יָדַע *yada.*
Josh 23. 13 Know for a certainty that the LORD your
1 Ki. 2. 37 thou shalt know for certain that thou
2. 42 Know for a certain, on the day thou
Jer. 26. 15 But know ye for certain, that if ye put
2. *Set up, fixed,* יַצִּיב *yatstsib.*
Dan. 2. 8 I know of certainty that ye would gain
3. *To be established, right,* כּוּן *kun,* 2.
1 Sa. 23. 23 come ye again to me with the certainty
4. *Untripped up, certain,* ἀσφαλής *asphalēs.*
Acts 21. 34 when he could not know the certainty
22. 30 because he would have known the certainty
5. *Certainty,* ἀσφάλεια *asphaleia.*
Luke 1. 4 That thou mightest know the certainty

CERTIFY, to —
1. *To say,* אֲמַר *amar.*
Esth. 2. 22 Esther certified the king..in Mordecai's
2. *To cause to know,* יְדַע *yeda,* 5.
Ezra 4. 14 therefore have we sent and certified the
4. 16 We certify the king, that if this city be
5. 10 We asked their names also, to certify thee
7. 24 Also we certify you, that, touching any
3. *To put before,* נָגַד *nagad,* 5.
2 Sa. 15. 28 until there come word from you to certify
4. *To make known, cause to know,* γνωρίζω *gnōrizō.*
Gal. 1. 11 I certify you, brethren, that the gospel

CHAFED —
Bitter, מַר *mar.*
2 Sa. 17. 8 they (be) chafed in their minds, as a bear

CHAFF —
1. *Hay, dry grass,* חֲשַׁשׁ *chashash.*
Isa. 5. 24 and the flame consumeth the chaff
33. 11 Ye shall conceive chaff; ye shall bring
2. *Chaff,* מֹץ *mots.*
Job 21. 18 as chaff that the storm carrieth away
Psa. 1. 4 like the chaff which the wind driveth
35. 5 Let them be as chaff before the wind
Isa. 17. 13 chased as the chaff of the mountains
29. 5 and the multitude..as chaff that passeth
41. 15 and shalt make the hills as chaff
Hos. 13. 3 as the chaff (that) is driven with the
Zeph. 2. 2 (before) the day pass as the chaff, before
3. *Skin, chaff,* עוּר *ur.*
Dan. 2. 35 became like the chaff of the summer
4. *Straw,* תֶּבֶן *teben.*
Jer. 23. 28 What (is) the chaff to the wheat? saith
5. *Chaff, so called from its loose state,* ἄχυρον.
Matt. 3. 12 will burn up the chaff with unquenchable
Luke 3. 17 chaff he will burn with fire unquenchable

CHAIN —
1. *Bracelet, clasp (for the arm),* אֶצְעָדָה *etsadah.*
Num 31. 50 man hath gotten, of jewels of gold, chains
2. *Chain (for arm or neck),* הַמְנִיךְ *hamnik.*
Dan. 5. 7 and (have) a chain of gold about his neck
5. 16 and (have) a chain of gold about thy neck
5. 29 and (put) a chain of gold about his neck
3. *Hook, ring (in the nose),* חָח *chach.*
Eze. 19. 4 brought him with chains unto the land of
19. 9 they put him in ward in chains, and
4. *Brass,* נְחֹשֶׁת *nechosheth.*
Jer. 39. 7 bound him with chains, to carry him to
52. 11 the king of Babylon bound him in chains
Lam. 3. 7 he hath made my chain heavy
5. *Necklace,* עֲנָק *anaq.*
Judg. 8. 26 beside the chains that (were) about their
Prov. 1. 9 an ornament of grace..and chains about
Song 4. 9 with one of thine eyes, with one chain of
6. *Collar (for the neck),* רָבִיד *rabid.*
Gen. 41. 42 and put a gold chain about his neck
Eze. 16. 11 bracelets upon thy hands, and a chain on
7. *A chain,* רַתּוֹק *rattoq.*
Eze. 7. 23 Make a chain; for the land is full of blo.
8. *A chain,* רַתּוּקָה *rattuqah.*
1 Ki. 6. 21 he made a partition by the chains of gold
9. *A little chain or bracelet,* שַׁרְשָׁה *sharshah.*
Exod 28 22 make upon the breastplate chains at the
10. *A little chain or bracelet,* שַׁרְשְׁרָה *sharsherah.*
Exod 28. 14 two chains (of) pure gold at the ends
28. 14 fasten the wreathen chains to the
39. 15 they made upon the breastplate chains
1 Ki. 7. 17 wreaths of chain work, for the chapiters
2 Ch. 3. 5 and set thereon palm trees and chains
3. 16 And he made chains, (as) in the oracle
3. 16 pomegranates, and put..on the chains
11. *Bond, rope, chain,* ἅλυσις *halusis.*
Acts 28. 20 hope of Israel I am bound with this chain
2 Ti. 1. 16 he..was not ashamed of my chain
Rev. 20 1 I saw an angel..having..a great chain in

CHAINS —
1. *Manacles,* אֲזִקִּים *aziqqim.*
Jer. 40. 1 being bound in chains among all that were
40. 4 I loose thee this day from the chains
2. *Manacles,* זִקִּים *ziqqim.*
Psa. 149. 8 To bind their kings with chains, and
Isa. 45. 14 in chains they shall come over, and they
Nah. 3. 10 all her great men were bound in chains
3. *String of ornaments,* חֲרוּזִים *charuzim.*
Song 1. 10 thy neck with chains (of gold)
4. *Ear drops or pendants,* נְטִיפוֹת *netiphoth.*
Isa. 3. 19 The chains, and the bracelets, and the
5. *Chain,* רַתִּיקָה *rattiqah.*
1 Ki. 6. 21 by the chains of gold before the oracle
6. *Chain,* רְתֻקוֹת *rethuqoth.*
Isa. 40. 19 over with gold, and casteth silver chains
7. *Bonds, bands,* כּוֹשָׁרוֹת *kosharoth.*
Psa. 68. 6 he bringeth out those..bound with chains
8. *(Unloosed) chain,* ἅλυσις *halusis.*
Mark 5. 3 could bind him, no, not with chains
5. 4 been often bound with fetters and chains
5. 4 the chains had been plucked asunder
Luke 8. 29 and he was kept bound with chains
Acts 12. 6 between two soldiers, bound with..chains
12. 7 And his chains fell off from (his) hands
21. 33 commanded..to be bound with two chains
9. *Band, bond,* δεσμός *desmos.*
Jude 6 hath reserved in everlasting chains, under
10. *Cord, rope,* σειρά *seira.*
2 Pe. 2. 4 delivered (them) into [chains] of darkness
[*See* Compass about as a chain].

CHAINS, wreathen —
Thick bands, עֲבֹתוֹת [*aboth*].
Exod 39. 17 put the two wreathen chains of gold in
39. 18 the two ends of the two wreathen chains

CHALCEDONY —
A gem (like a cornelian), χαλκηδών *chalkēdōn.*
Rev. 21. 19 the third, [a chalcedony]; the fourth, an

CHAL'-COL, CAL'-COL, כַּלְכֹּל *sustaining.*
A son of Mahol whose offspring were noted for their wisdom, B.C. 1015.
1 Ki. 4. 31 he was wiser than..Heman, and C., and
1 Ch. 2. 6 the sons of Zerah..Heman, and C., and

CHAL-DE'-A, כַּשְׂדִּים, γῆ Χαλδαίων.
The southern portion of Babylonia. In the common version it is used, however, for the Hebrew *Kasdim* or Chaldeans, the term which designates the inhabitants of the entire country. The native term is *Kaldi* or *Kaldai,* not Casdim. Hence the name Chaldea has been connected with the city *Kaluadha,* the Chilmad of Eze. 27. 23.
Jer. 50. 10 And C. shall be a spoil..saith the LORD
51. 24 I will render..to all the inhabitants of C.
51. 35 My blood upon the inhabitants of C.
Eze. 11. 24 brought me in a vision..into C.
16. 29 hast..multiplied..fornication..unto C.
23. 15 after the manner of the Babylonians of C.
23. 16 she..sent messengers unto them into C.

CHAL-DE-ANS, CHAL'-DEES, כַּשְׂדִּים, Χαλδαῖοι.
In Scripture this people appears till the captivity as the inhabitants of the country which had Babylon for its capital, and is itself called Shinar. While this meaning is still found in the book of Daniel (5. 30 and 9. 1), a new acceptation shows itself. They are classed with astronomers and magicians, and form a class who have a peculiar "tongue" and "learning," and are consulted by the king on difficult subjects. Berosus, the native historian, himself a Chaldean in the narrower sense, uses the term in the wider one only; while Herodotus, Diodorus, Strabo and later writers almost universally employ it to signify a sect, regarding them chiefly as priests or philosophers. Hence the Chaldeans were regarded as the inhabitants of a particular part of Babylonia, the country bordering on the Persian Gulf and on Arabia. The *Kaldi* or *Kaldai* were merely one of the Cushite tribes that lived on the great alluvial plain known as Babylonia or Chaldæa. Their seat was most likely the southern portion of the country which has so late retained the name of Chaldea. Here was "Ur of the Chaldees," the modern *Mugheir,* which lies S. of the Euphrates, near its junction with the *Shal-el-hie.* That they were a Cushite race is proved by the remains of their language, which closely resembles the Galla- or ancient language of Ethiopia, the learned language for scientific and religious literature.
Gen. 11. 28 And Haran died..in Ur of the C.
11. 31 went forth with them from Ur of the C.
15. 7 I..brought thee out of Ur of the C.
2 Ki. 24. 2 the LORD sent against him bands of the C.
25. 4 the C. (were) against the city round
25. 5 the army of the C. pursued after the
25. 10 all the army of the C...brake down the
25. 13 and the brasen sea..did the C. break in
25. 24 Fear not to be the servants of the C.
25. 25 Ishmael..smote Gedaliah..and the C.
25. 26 Egypt; for they were afraid of the C.
2 Ch. 36. 17 brought upon them the king of the C.
Ezra 5. 12 Nebuchadnezzar..king of Babylon, the C.
Neh. 9. 7 broughtest him forth out of Ur of the C.
Job 1. 17 The C. made out three bands, and fell
Isa. 13. 19 And Babylon..the beauty of the C.
23. 13 Behold the land of the C.; this people
43. 14 I have sent..and..brought down..the C.
47. 1 no throne, O daughter of the C.: for

Isa. 47. 5 Sit thou silent..O daughter of the C.
48. 14 and his arm (shall be on) the C.
48. 20 Go ye forth..flee ye from the C.
Jer. 21. 4 weapons..wherewith ye fight against..C.
21. 9 he that goeth out, and falleth to the C.
22. 25 will give thee into the hand of..the C.
24. 5 whom I have sent..into the land of the C.
25. 12 I will punish..the land of the C.
32. 4 shall not escape out of the hand of the C.
32. 5 though ye fight with the C., ye shall not
32. 24, 25, 43 is given into the hand of the C.
32. 28 give this city into the hand of the C.
32. 29 the C...shall come and set fire on this
33. 5 They come to fight with the C., but (it is)
35. 11 let us go..for fear of the army of the C.
37. 5 when the C...heard tidings of them, they
37. 8 the C. shall come again, and fight against
37. 9 The C. shall surely depart from us
37. 10 had smitten the whole army of the C.
37. 11 when the army of the C. was broken up
37. 13 saying, Thou fallest away to the C.
37. 14 (It is) false ; I fall not away to the C.
38. 2 he that goeth forth to the C. shall live
38. 18 this city be given into the hand of the C.
38. 19 the Jews that are fallen to the C.
38. 23 they shall bring..thy children to the C.
39. 5 But the C.'s army pursued after them, and
39. 8 And the C. burned the king's house, and
40. 9 saying, Fear not to serve the C.
40. 10 I will dwell at Mizpah, to serve the C.
41. 3 Ishmael..slew..the C. that were found
41. 18 Because of the C.; for they were afraid
43. 3 to deliver us into the hand of the C.
50. 1 LORD spake..against the land of the C.
50. 8 go forth out of the land of the C.
50. 25 work of..God..in the land of the C.
50. 35 A sword (is) upon the C., saith the LORD
50. 45 purposed against the land of the C.
51. 4 slain shall fall in the land of the C.
51. 54 destruction from the land of the C.
52. 7 the C. (were) by the city round about
52. 8 the army of the C. pursued after the king
52. 14 the army of the C...brake down..walls
52. 17 and the brasen sea..the C. brake, and
Eze. 1. 3 in the land of the C., by the river Chebar
12. 13 will bring him to..the land of the C.
23. 14 images of the C. pourtrayed with vermil.
23. 23 The Babylonians, and all the C., Pekod
Dan. 1. 4 they might teach..the tongue of the C.
2. 2 the king commanded to call..the C., for
2. 4 Then spake the C. to the king in Syriac
2. 5 The king answered and said to the C.
2. 10 The C. answered before the king, and
2. 10 no king..asked such things at any..C.
3. 8 at that time certain C. came near, and
4. 7 Then came in the magicians..the C., and
5. 7 The king cried aloud to bring..the C.
5. 11 master of the magicians..C., (and) sooth.
5. 30 that night was..the king of the C. slain
9. 1 Darius..was made king over..the C.
Hab. 1. 6 For, lo, I raise up the C., (that) bitter and
Acts 7. 4 came he out of the land of the C.

CHALK STONE —

Lime stone, אֶבֶן גִּר *eben gir.*
Isa. 27. 9 all the stones of the altar as chalk-stones

CHALLENGE, to —

To say, אָמַר *amar.*
Exod 22. 9 which (another) challengeth to be his

CHAMBER —

1. *Inner chamber, enclosed place,* חֶדֶר *cheder.*
Gen. 43. 30 he entered into (his) chamber, and wept
Judg. 3. 24 covereth his feet in his summer chamber
15. 1 I will go in to my wife into the chamber
16. 9 abiding with her in the chamber
16. 12 liers in wait abiding in the chamber
2 Sa. 13. 10 Bring the meat into the chamber, that
13. 10 and brought (them) into the chamber
1 Ki. 1. 15 went in unto the king into the chamber
Job 9. 9 Which maketh..the chambers of the south
Psa. 105. 30 forth frogs..in the chambers..their kings
Prov. 7. 27 going down to the chambers of death
24. 4 by knowledge shall the chambers be filled
Song 1. 4 King hath brought me into his chambers
3. 4 the chamber of her that conceived me
Isa. 26. 20 Come..enter thou into thy chambers
Eze. 8. 12 every man in the chambers of his imagery
Joel 2. 16 the bridegroom go forth of his chamber

2. *A covering, bridal canopy,* חֻפָּה *chuppah.*
Psa. 19. 5 a bridegroom coming out of his chamber

3. *Chamber,* יָצוּעַ, יָצִיעַ *yatsua, yatsia.*
1 Ki. 6. 5 against the wall..he built chambers
6. 6 The nethermost chamber (was) five cubits
6. 10 he built chambers against all the house

4. *Lodging place,* לִשְׁכָּה *lishkah.*
2 Ki. 23. 11 by the chamber of Nathan-melech
1 Ch. 9. 26 these Levites...were over the chambers
9. 33 Levites, (who remaining) in the chambers
23. 28 in the courts, and in the chambers
28. 12 of all the chambers round about
2 Ch. 31. 11 Hezekiah commanded to prepare chamb.
Ezra 8. 29 the chambers of the house of the LORD
10. 6 Ezra rose..and went into the chamber
Neh. 10. 37 the chambers of the house of our God
10. 38 to the chambers, into the treasure house
10. 39 bring..the oil, unto the chambers, where
13. 4 the chamber of the house of our God
13. 5 he had prepared for him a great chamber
13. 8 I cast forth all..out of the chamber
Neh. 13. 9 they cleansed the chambers; and thither
Jer. 35. 2 bring them..into one of the chambers
35. 4 into the chamber of the sons of Hanan
35. 4 which (was) by the chamber of the princes
35. 4 which (was) above the chamb. of Maaseiah
36. 10 chamber of Gemariah the son of Shaphan
36. 12 Then he went..into the scribe's chamber
36. 20 they laid up the roll in the chamber of
36. 21 he took it out of..the scribe's chamber
Eze. 40. 17 lo, (there were) chambers, and a pavement
40. 17 thirty chambers (were) upon the pavement
40. 38 the chambers and the entries thereof
40. 44 without the inner gate (were) the chambers
40. 45 This chamber..(is) for the priests, the
40. 46 the chamber..toward the north (is) for
41. 10 between the chambers (was) the wideness
42. 1 he brought me into the chamber that
42. 4 before the chambers (was) a walk of ten
42. 5 Now the upper chambers (were) shorter
42. 7 the wall..over against the chambers
42. 7 toward the outer court..of the chambers
42. 8 the chambers that (were) in the outer
42. 9 under these chambers (was) the entry on
42. 10 The chambers (were) in the thickness of
42. 11 like the appearance of the chambers
42. 12 according to the doors of the chambers
42. 13 north chambers (and) the south chambers
42. 13 before the..place, they (be) holy chambers
44. 19 and lay them in the holy chambers, and
45. 5 for a possession for twenty chambers
46. 19 he brought me..into the holy chambers

5. *Lodging place,* נִשְׁכָּה *nishkah.*
Neh. 3. 30 son of Berechiah over against his chamber
12. 44 some appointed over the chambers for
13. 7 in preparing him a chamber in the courts

6. *Loft, upper room,* עֲלִיָּה *aliyyah.*
2 Sa. 18. 33 And the king..went up to the chamber
1 Ki. 17. 23 Elijah..brought him..out of the chamber
2 Ki. 4. 10 Let us make a little chamber, I pray thee
4. 11 and he turned into the chamber, and lay
Psa. 104. 3 Who layeth the beams of his chambers
104. 13 He watereth the hills from his chambers
Jer. 22. 13 Woe unto him that buildeth..chambers
22. 14 I will build me..large chambers, and

7. *Loft, upper room,* עִלִּית *illith.*
Dan. 6. 10 his windows being open in his chamber

8. *Side chamber, rib,* צֵלָע *tsela.*
1 Ki. 6. 5 And..he made chambers round about
6. 8 The door for the middle chamber (was)

9. *Marked off place,* תָּא *ta.*
1 Ki. 14. 28 brought them back into..guard chamber
2 Ch. 12. 11 brought them again into..guard chamber

CHAMBER, inner —

Chamber in a chamber, חֶדֶר בְּחֶדֶר [*cheder*].
1 Ki. 20. 30 Ben-hadad..came..into an inner chamber
22. 25 thou shalt go into an inner chamber to
2 Ki. 9. 2 Jehu..carry him to an inner chamber
2 Ch. 18. 24 thou shalt go into an inner chamber to

CHAMBER, little —

Place marked off, תָּא *ta.*
Eze. 40. 7 (every) little chamber (was) one reed
40. 7 between the little chambers (were) five
40. 10 the little chambers of the gate eastward
40. 12 the little chambers (was) one cubit
40. 12 the little chambers (were) six cubits on
40. 13 roof of (one) little chamber to the roof of
40. 16 narrow windows to the little chambers
40. 21 the little chambers..(were) three on this
verses 29, 33, 36 the little chambers..and the posts

CHAMBER, secret —

Place cut off, store room, ταμεῖον *tameion.*
Matt 24. 26 behold..(he is) in the secret chambers

CHAMBER, side —

Side chamber, rib, צֵלָע *tsela.*
Eze. 41. 5 the breadth of (every) side chamber four
41. 6 And the side chambers (were) three, one
41. 6 the house for the side chambers round
41. 7 a winding about..to the side chambers
41. 8 the foundations of the side chambers
41. 9 wall, which (was) for the side chamber
41. 9 the place of the side chambers that (were)
41. 11 the doors of the side chambers (were)
41. 26 (upon) the side chambers of the house

CHAMBER, upper —

1. *Loft, upper chamber,* עֲלִיָּה *aliyyah.*
2 Ki. 1. 2 through a lattice in his upper chamber
23. 12 altars..on the top of the upper chamber
1 Ch. 28. 11 and of the upper chambers thereof, and
2 Ch. 3. 9 he overlaid the upper chambers with

2. *Upper chamber,* ὑπερῷον *huperōon.*
Acts 9. 37 they laid (her) in an upper chamber
9. 39 they brought him into the upper chamber
20. 8 there were many lights..upper chamber

CHAMBERING —

Place for lying, couch, κοίτη *koitē.*
Rom 13. 13 Let us walk honestly..not in chambering

CHAMBERLAIN —

1. *Eunuch, officer,* סָרִיס *saris.*
2 Ki. 23. 11 by the chamber of..the chamberlain
Esth. 1. 10 the seven chamberlains that served in
1. 12 commandment by (his) chamberlains
1. 15 the king Ahasuerus by the chamberlains?
Esth. 2. 3 the custody of Hege the king's chamber.
2. 14 to the custody of..the king's chamber.
2. 15 what..the king's chamberlain..appointed
2. 21 two of the king's chamberlains, Bigthan
4. 4 Esther's maids and her chamberlains
4. 5 Hatach, (one) of the king's chamberlains
6. 2 Bigthana..two of the king's chamberlains
6. 14 came the king's chamberlains, and hasted
7. 9 Harbonah, one of the chamberlains, said

2. *One over the couch,* ἐπὶ τοῦ κοιτῶνος *epi tou koitōnos.*
Acts 12. 20 having made Blastus..king's chamberlain

3. *House ruler, steward,* οἰκονόμος *oikonomos.*
Rom 16. 23 Erastus the chamberlain of the city

CHAMELEON —

Chameleon, a kind of lizard, כֹּחַ *koach.*
Lev. 11. 30 the chameleon, and the lizard, and the

CHAMOIS —

Giraffe (the prunnea,) זֶמֶר *zemer.*
Deut 14. 5 pygarg, and the wild ox and the chamois

CHAMPAIGN —

Plain, waste, desert, עֲרָבָה *arabah.*
Deut 11. 30 dwell in the champaign over against

CHAMPION —

1. *Mighty one,* גִּבּוֹר *gibbor.*
1 Sa. 17. 51 when the Philistines saw their champion

2. *Man of intervention (?),* אִישׁ־הַבֵּנַיִם *ish hab-benayim.*
1 Sa. 17. 4 there went out a champion out of..camp
17. 23 there came up the champion..out of the

CHA-NA'-AN, Χαναάν, *See Canaan.*
Acts 7. 11 came a dearth over..the land of..C.
13. 19 he..destroyed seven nations in..C.

CHANCE —

1. *Chance, accident,* מִקְרֶה *miqreh.*
1 Sa. 6. 9 it (was) a chance (that) happened to us

2. *Occurrence,* פֶּגַע *pega.*
Eccl. 9. 11 but time and chance happeneth to them

3. *Concurrence,* συγκυρία *sugkuria.*
Luke 10. 31 by chance there came down a certain

CHANCE, to —

To meet, happen, קָרָא *qara,* 2.
Deut 22. 6 If a bird's nest chance to be before thee

CHANCE, by —

To meet, קָרָא *qara,* 2.
2 Sa. 1. 6 As I happened by chance upon mount

CHANCE, it may —

If it may be so, εἰ τύχοι *ei tuchoi.*
1 Co. 15. 37 it may chance of wheat, or of some other

CHANCELLOR —

Master of counsel, taste, reason, בְּעֵל טְעֵם *beel teem.*
Ezra 4. 8 Rehum the chancellor and Shimshai the
4. 9 Then (wrote) Rehum the chancellor, and
4. 17 sent..king..unto Rehum the chancellor

CHANGE —

1. *A change,* חֲלִיפָה *chaliphah.*
Gen. 45. 22 To all..he gave each..changes of raiment
45. 22 to Benjamin he gave..five changes of
Judg 14. 12 I will give you..thirty change of garment
14. 13 then shall ye give me..thirty change of
14. 19 took their spoil, and gave change of gar.
2 Ki. 5. 5 and took with him..ten changes of raim.
5. 22 a talent of silver, and two changes of
5. 23 two bags, with two changes of garments
Job 10. 17 changes and war (are) against me
14. 14 will I wait, till my change come
Psa. 55. 19 Because they have no changes, therefore

2. *Change, exchange,* תְּמוּרָה *temurah.*
Lev. 27. 33 it and the change thereof shall be holy

3. *A change, putting after,* μετάθεσις *metathesis.*
Heb. 7. 12 there is made of necessity a change also

CHANGE, to —

1. *To change, turn,* הָפַךְ *haphak.*
Jer. 13. 23 Can the Ethiopian change his skin, or

2. *To change,* חָלַף *chalaph.*
Isa. 24. 5 because they..changed the ordinance
Hab. 1. 11 Then shall (his) mind change, and he shall

3. *To change,* חָלַף *chalaph,* 3.
Gen. 41. 14 changed his raiment, and came in unto
2 Sa. 12. 20 changed his apparel, and came into the

4. *To change,* חָלַף *chalaph,* 5.
Gen. 31. 7 your father hath..changed my wages ten
31. 41 thou hast changed my wages ten times
35. 2 be clean, and change your garments
Psa. 102. 26 as a vesture shalt thou change them, and
Isa. 9. 10 but we will change (them into) cedars

5. *To change, exchange,* יָמַר *yamar,* 5.
Jer. 2. 11 hath a nation changed (their) gods, which

6. *To change,* מוּר *mur,* 5.
Lev. 27. 10 He shall not alter it, nor change it, a
27. 10 if he shall at all change beast for beast
27. 33 good or bad, neither shall he change it
27. 33 if he change it at all, then both it & the
Psa. 15. 4 (He that) sweareth..and changeth not
106. 20 changed their glory into the similitude
Jer. 2. 11 my people have changed their glory for
Hos. 4. 7 (therefore) will I change their glory into
Mic. 2. 4 he hath changed the portion of my people

7. *To change, rebel,* מָרָה *marah,* 5.
Eze. 5. 6 she hath changed my judgments into

8. *To put round,* סָבַב *sabab,* 5.
2 Ki. 24. 17 the king of Babylon..changed his name

9. *To put, place, set,* שׂוּם *sum.*
Job 17. 12 They change the night into day: the light

10. *To double, alter,* שְׁנָא *shana,* 3.
2 Ki. 25 29 And changed his prison garments

11. *To double, alter,* שְׁנָא *shena,* 5.
Dan. 2 21 he changeth the times and the seasons
7 25 and think to change times and laws

12. *To double, alter,* שְׁנָא *shena,* 3.
Dan. 3. 28 trusted in him, and have changed the

13. *To be changed,* שְׁנָא *shena,* 4.
Dan. 7. 28 and my countenance changed in me

14. *To change, alter,* שָׁנָה *shanah.*
Mal 3. 6 For I (am) the LORD, I change not

15. *To change, alter,* שָׁנָה *shanah,* 3.
1 Sa 21 13 he changed his behaviour before them
Job 14. 20 thou changest his countenance, and
Psa 34 1 *title.* David, when he changed his
Jer 2 36 Why gaddest..about so much to change
52 33 changed his prison garments: and he

16. *To make other, alter,* ἀλλάττω *allattō.*
Acts 6 14 and shall change the customs which Mo.
Rom 1 23 changed the glory of the uncorruptible
1 Co. 15 51 not all sleep, but we shall all be changed
15 52 In a moment..and we shall be changed
Gal. 4 20 I desire to be present..and to change my
Heb 1 12 And as a vesture..they shall be changed

17. *To alter afterward,* μεταλλάττω *metallattō.*
Rom. 1. 25 Who changed the truth of God into a lie
1. 26 for even their women did change the

18. *To make of another form,* μετασχηματίζω.
Phil. 3. 21 Who shall change our vile body, that it

19. *To put or place afterward,* μετατίθημι.
Heb. 7 12 the priesthood being changed, there is

CHANGE one's mind, to —

To cast over, turn about, μεταβάλλω *metaballō.*
Acts 28 6 they changed their minds, and said that

CHANGE, to be given to —

To alter, change, שָׁנָה *shanah.*
Prov 24. 21 meddle not with them..given to change

CHANGED, to be —

1. *To be turned,* הָפַךְ *haphak,* 2.
Lev. 13. 16 raw flesh turn again, and be changed

2. *To change, be changed,* חָלַף *chalaph.*
Psa 102. 26 change them, and they shall be changed

3. *To disguise oneself,* חָפַשׂ *chaphas,* 7.
Job 30. 18 By..(my disease) is my garment changed

4. *To be changed,* מוּר *mur,* 2.
Jer. 48. 11 his taste..and his scent is not changed

5. *To be caused to turn round,* סָבַב *sabab,* 6.
Num 32. 38 Baal-meon, their names being changed

6. *To be changed, altered,* שְׁנָא *shana.*
Lam. 4. 1 (how) is the most fine gold changed! the

7. *To be changed, altered,* שְׁנָא *shana,* 4.
Eccl. 8. 1 the boldness of his face shall be changed

8. *To be changed, altered,* שְׁנָא *shena.*
Dan. 3. 27 neither were their coats changed, nor the
5 6 the king's countenance was changed
5. 9 his countenance was changed in him
6. 17 that the purpose might not be changed

9. *To be changed, altered,* שְׁנָא *shena,* 3.
Dan. 4. 16 Let his heart be changed from man's

10. *To be changed, altered,* שְׁנָא *shena,* 4.
Dan 2. 9 before me, till the time be changed
3. 19 the form of his visage was changed
5. 10 nor let thy countenance be changed

11. *To change, alter,* שְׁנָא *shena,* 5.
Dan. 6. 8 sign the writing, that it be not changed
6. 15 no decree nor statute..may be changed

12. *To change one's form,* μεταμορφόομαι.
2 Co. 3. 18 changed into the same image from glory

CHANGER (of money), changing —

A small coin dealer, κολλυβιστής *kollubistēs.*
John 2. 15 poured out the changers' money, and over.
Money-changer, κερματιστής *kermatistēs,* Jo. 2. 14.
A change, exchange, תְּמוּרָה *temurah.*
Ruth 4. 7 concerning redeeming, and..changing

CHANNEL —

1. *Cavity,* אָפִיק *aphiq.*
2 Sa. 22. 16 And the channels of the sea appeared
Psa. 18. 15 Then the channels of waters were seen
Isa. 8. 7 he shall come up over all his channels

2. *Flood, stream,* שִׁבֹּלֶת *shibboleth.*
Isa. 27. 12 the LORD shall beat off from the channel

CHANT, to —

To part, separate, sing aloud, פָּרַט *parat.*
Amos 6. 5 That chant to the sound of the viol

CHAPEL —

Sanctuary, holy place, מִקְדָּשׁ *miqdash.*
Amos 7. 13 at Bethel: for it (is) the king's chapel

CHAPITER —

1. *Crown,* כֹּתֶרֶת *kothereth.*
1 Ki. 7. 16 he made two chapiters (of) molten brass
7. 16 the height of the one chapiter (was) five
7. 16 the height of the other chapiter (was) five
7. 17 the chapiters which (were) upon the top
7 17 the one chapiter..for the other chapiter
7. 18 one net work, to cover the chapiters that
7. 18 and so did he for the other chapiter
7. 19 the chapiters that (were) upon the top
7 20 And the chapiters upon the two pillars
7 20 rows round about upon the..chapiter
7. 31 the mouth of it within the chapiter
7. 41 and the two bowls of the chapiters
7. 41 to cover the (two) bowls of the chapiters
7. 42 to cover the two bowls of the chapiters
2 Ki. 25 17 and the chapiter upon it (was) brass
25 17 the height of the chapiter three cubits
25 17 pomegranates upon the chapiter
2 Ch. 4 12 the chapiters (which were) on the top of
4. 12 cover the two pommels of the chapiters
4. 13 cover the two pommels of the chapiters
Jer. 52 22 a chapiter of brass (was) upon it; and
52 22 the height of one chapiter (was) five cub.
52. 22 and pomegranates upon the chapiters

2. *Capital,* צֶפֶת *tsepheth.*
2 Ch. 3. 15 the chapiter that (was) on the top of each

3. *Head, top,* רֹאשׁ *rosh.*
Exod 36. 38 he overlaid their chapiters..with gold
38. 17 the overlaying of their chapiters (of) sil.
38. 19 the overlaying of their chapiters..(of) sil.
38. 28 overlaid their chapiters, and filleted

CHAPMAN —

A travelling merchant, אֱנוֹשׁ תָּר *enosh tar.*
2 Ch. 9. 14 Besides (that which) chapmen and merch.

CHAPT, to be —

To be brought down, חָתַת *chathath.*
Jer. 14. 4 the ground is chapt, for there was no rain

CHA-RA'-SHIM, חֲרָשִׁים *craftsmen.*
A place founded by Joab, a man of Judah and of the family of Othniel, and reinhabited by Benjamites after the exile. It was at the back of the plain of Sharon, E. of Jaffa.
1 Ch. 4. 14 Joab, the father of the valley of C.
Neh. 11. 35 Lod, and Ono, the valley of Craftsmen

CHARCHEMISH. *See* **CARCHEMISH.**

CHARGE —

1. *Hand,* יָד *yad.*
Num 31. 49 men of war which (are) under our charge

2. *Charge, thing to be watched,* מִשְׁמֶרֶת *mishmereth.*
Gen. 26. 5 obeyed my voice, and kept my charge
Lev. 8. 35 keep the charge of the LORD, that ye die
Num. 1. 53 keep the charge of the tabernacle of test.
3. 7 shall keep his charge, and the charge of
3. 8 they shall keep..the charge of the children
3. 25 the charge of the sons of Gershon in the
3. 28 keeping the charge of the sanctuary
3. 31 their charge (shall be) the ark, and the
3. 32 that keep the charge of the sanctuary
3. 36 (under) the custody and charge of the sons
3. 38 Aaron and his sons, keeping the charge
3. 38 for the charge of the children of Israel
4. 27 appoint unto them in charge all their
4. 28 their charge (shall be) under the hand of
4. 31 And this (is) the charge of their burden
4. 32 reckon the instruments of the charge of
8. 26 to keep the charge, and shall do no serv.
8. 26 do unto the Levites touching their charge
9. 19 the children of Israel kept the charge
9. 23 they kept the charge of the LORD, at the
18. 3 they shall keep thy charge, and the charge
18. 4 keep the charge of the tabernacle of the
18. 5 keep the charge of..and the charge of
18. 8 I also have given thee the charge of
31. 30 which keep the charge of the tabernacle
31. 47 which kept the charge of the tabernacle
Deut 11. 1 keep his charge, and his statutes, and
Josh. 22. 3 have kept..charge of the commandment
1 Ki. 2. 3 And keep the charge of the LORD thy God
1 Ch. 9. 27 because the charge (was) upon them, and
23. 32 And that they should keep the charge of
23. 32 and the charge of..and the charge of
2 Ch. 8. 14 he appointed..Levites to their charges
13. 11 for we keep the charge of the LORD our
31. 16 in their charges according to their courses
31. 17 in their charges by their courses
35. 2 And he set the priests in their charges
Eze. 40. 45 the keepers of the charge of the house
40. 46 the keepers of the charge of the altar
44. 8 ye have not kept the charge of mine holy
44. 8 ye have set keepers of my charge in
44. 14 I will make them keepers of the charge of
44. 15 kept the charge of my sanctuary when
44. 16 and they shall keep my charge
48. 11 which have kept my charge, which went
Zech. 3. 7 and if thou wilt keep my charge, then

3. *Judgment,* מִשְׁפָּט *mishpat.*
1 Ki. 4. 28 every man according to his charge

4. *Burden,* סֵבֶל *sebel.*
1 Ki. 11. 28 he made him ruler over all the charge of

5. *Oversight,* פְּקֻדָּה *pequddah.*
Eze. 44. 11 (having) charge at the gates of the house

6. *Provision, supplies,* ὀψώνιον *opsōnion.*
1 Cor. 9. 7 Who goeth a warfare..at his own charges

7. *Private or extra message,* παραγγελία *paraggelia*
Acts 16. 24 Who, having received such a charge
1 Ti. 1. 18 This charge I commit unto thee, son Tim.

CHARGE, to —

1. *To say,* אָמַר *amar.*
Neh. 13. 19 and charged that they should not be

2. *To give,* נָתַן *nathan.*
Neh. 10. 32 to charge ourselves yearly with the third
Job 1. 22 Job sinned not, nor charged God foolishly

3. *To give a testimony,* עוּד *ud,* 5.
Exod 19. 21 LORD said..Go down, charge the people
19. 23 thou chargedst us, saying, Set bounds

4. *To give an oversight,* פָּקַד *paqad.*
Gen. 40. 4 And the captain of the guard charged
2 Sa. 3. 8 that thou chargest me to-day with a fault
2 Ch. 36. 23 he hath charged me to build him an house
Ezra 1. 2 he hath charged me to build him an house

5. *To command, charge,* צָוָה *tsavah,* 3.
Gen. 26. 11 Abimelech charged all (his) people, saying
28. 1 blessed him, and charged him, and said
49. 29 he charged them, and said unto them
Exod 1. 22 Pharaoh charged all his people, saying
Deut. 1. 16 I charged your judges at that time, say.
3. 28 But charge Joshua, and encourage him
27. 11 Moses charged the people the same day
Josh 18. 8 Joshua charged them..went to describe
Ruth 2. 9 have I not charged the young men that
2 Sa. 11. 19 And charged the messenger, saying
18. 12 for in our hearing the king charged thee
1 Ki 2. 1 and he charged Solomon his son, saying
2. 43 the commandment that I have charged
13. 9 so was it charged me by the word of the
2 Ki. 17. 15 (concerning) whom the LORD had charged
1 Ch. 22. 6 charged him to build an house for the
22. 13 which the LORD charged Moses with
2 Ch. 19. 9 he charged them, saying, Thus shall ye
Esth. 2. 10 Mordecai had charged her that she should
2. 20 her kindred..as Mordecai had charged
4. 8 to charge her that she should go in unto
Jer. 32. 13 And I charged Baruch before them, say.
35. 8 all that he hath charged us, to drink no

6. *To put, place,* שׂוּם *sum.*
Job 4. 18 and his angels he charged with folly

7. *To cause to swear,* שָׁבַע *shaba,* 5.
Song 2. 7 I charge you, O ye daughters of Jerusa.
3. 5 I charge you, O ye daughters of Jerusa.
5. 8 I charge you, O daughters of Jerusalem
5. 9 thy beloved..that thou dost so charge us?
8. 4 I charge you, O daughters of Jerusalem

8. *To testify thoroughly,* διαμαρτύρομαι *diamarturo.*
1 Ti. 5. 21 I charge (thee) before God, and the Lord
2 Ti. 2. 14 charging (them) before the Lord that they
4. 1 I charge (thee)..before God, and the Lord

9. *To charge thoroughly,* διαστέλλομαι *diastellomai.*
Matt 16. 20 Then [charged] he his disciples that they
Mark 5. 43 he charged them straitly that no man
7. 36 he charged them that they should tell no
7. 36 the more he charged them, so much the
8. 15 he charged them, saying, Take heed
9. 9 he charged them that they should tell no

10. *To charge, arrange about,* ἐπιτάσσω *epitassō.*
Mark 9. 25 I charge thee, come out of him, and

11. *To put weight upon,* ἐπιτιμάω *epitimaō.*
Matt 12. 16 charged them that they should not make
Mark 3. 12 charged them that they should not make
8. 30 he charged them that they should tell no
10. 48 charged him that he should hold his

12. *To give in charge,* ἐντέλλομαι *entellomai.*
Matt 17. 9 Jesus charged them, saying, Tell the

13. *To testify,* μαρτυρέομαι *martureomai.*
1 Th. 2. 11 comforted and [charged] every one of you

14. *To adjure,* ὁρκίζω *horkizō.*
1 Th. 5. 27 I [charge]..by the Lord that this epistle

15. *To tell apart, beside,* παραγγέλλω *paraggellō.*
Luke 5. 14 he charged him to tell no man: but go
8. 56 charged them that they should tell no
Acts 16. 23 charging the jailor to keep them safely
23. 22 and charged..tell no man that thou hast
1 Ti. 1. 3 that thou mightest charge some that they
6. 17 Charge them that are rich in this world

CHARGE straitly, to —

1. *To charge strictly,* ἐμβριμάομαι *embrimaomai.*
Matt. 9. 30 and Jesus straitly charged them, saying
Mark 1. 43 he straitly charged him, and forthwith

2. *To put a weight upon,* ἐπιτιμάω *epitimaō.*
Luke 9. 21 straitly charged them, and commanded

CHARGE, without, to be at —

1. *Without expense,* ἀδάπανος *adapanos.*
1 Co. 9. 18 I may make the gospel..without charge

2. *To spend,* δαπανάω *dapanaō.*
Acts 21. 24 be at charges with them, that they may

CHARGE, to appoint to have the —

To give the oversight, פָּקַד *paqad,* 5.
2 Ki. 7. 17 appointed the lord..to have the charge of

CHARGE, to give (a) —

1. *To give an oversight,* פָּקַד *paqad.*
Job 34. 13 Who hath given him a charge over the

2. *To command,* צָוָה *tsavah,* 3.
Gen. 28. 6 as he blessed him, he gave him a charge
Exod. 6. 13 gave them a charge unto the children of
Num27. 19 and gave him a charge in their sight
27. 23 gave him a charge; as the LORD command.
Deut 31. 14 call Joshua..that I may give him a charge
31. 23 he gave Joshua the son of Nun a charge
1 Ch. 22. 12 and give thee charge concerning Israel
2 Sa. 14. 8 Go to thine house, and I will give charge
18. 5 when the king gave all the captains charge
Neh. 7. 2 gave my brother..charge over Jerusalem
Psa. 91. 11 For he shall give his angels charge over
Isa. 10. 6 against the people..I give him a charge
Jer. 39. 11 Nebuchadrezzar..gave charge concern.
47. 7 the LORD hath given it a charge against

3. *To give charge,* ἐντέλλομαι *entellomai.*
Matt. 4. 6 He shall give his angels charge concern.
Luke 4. 10 He shall give his angels charge over thee

4. *To tell apart, beside,* παραγγέλλω *paraggellō.*
1 Ti. 6. 13 I give thee charge in the sight of God

CHARGE, to give in —
To tell beside, announce, παραγγέλλω *paraggellō.*
1 Ti. 5 7 And these things give in charge, that

CHARGE of or over, to have the —
1. *To be over,* εἰμὶ ἐπί *eimi epi.*
Acts 8 27 who had the charge of all her treasure

2. *[Be] over,* עַל *al.*
1 Ch. 9. 28 And (certain) of them had the charge of

3. *Inspectors,* פְּקֻדּוֹת *pequddoth.*
Eze. 9 1 Cause them that have charge over the

4. *Inspector, overseer,* פָּקִיד *paqid.*
Jer 52. 25 which had the charge of the men of war

CHARGE, (to) lay to one's —
1. *To give in the heart of,* נָתַן בְּקֶרֶב *nathan be-qereb.*
Deut 21. 8 lay not..unto thy people of Israel's charge

2. *To ask, demand,* שָׁאַל *shaal.*
Psa. 35. 11 they laid to my charge..that I knew not

3. *To call in against,* ἐγκαλέω κατά *egkaleō kata.*
Rom 8. 33 Who shall lay any thing to the charge of

4. *A calling in (to court), charge,* ἔγκλημα *egklēma.*
Acts 23. 29 to have nothing laid to his charge worthy

5. *To set, place,* ἵστημι *histēmi.*
Acts 7. 60 Lord, lay not this sin to their charge

6. *To reckon,* λογίζομαι *logizomai.*
2 Ti. 4. 16 it may not be laid to their charge

CHARGE by or with an oath, to —
To cause to swear, שָׁבַע *shaba,* 5.
Num. 5. 19 the priest shall charge her by an oath
5. 21 priest shall charge the woman with an o.
1 Sa 14 27 father charged the people with the oath
14. 28 straitly charged the people with an oath

CHARGEABLE (to), to be —
1. *To be heavy,* כָּבֵד *kabed.*
2 Sa. 13. 25 lest we be chargeable unto thee

2. *To make heavy,* כָּבֵד *kabed,* 5.
Neh. 5 15 the former governors..were chargeable

3. *To put a burden upon,* ἐπιβαρέω *epibareō.*
2 Th. 3. 8 that we might not be chargeable to any

4. *To become torpid or heavy against,* καταναρκέω.
2 Co. 11 9 when I was present..I was chargeable to

CHARGEABLE unto, to be —
To put a burden or weight upon, ἐπιβαρέω.
1 Th. 2. 9 we would not be chargeable unto any of

CHARGED, to be —
1. *To command,* צָוָה *tsavah,* 3.
1 Ki. 13. 9 For so was it charged me by the word of
2. *To be weighed down, burdened,* βαρέομαι; 1 Ti. 5. 16.
3. *Pass upon,* עָבַר עַל *abar al;* Deut. 24. 5.

CHARGER —
1. *Dish,* קְעָרָה *qearah.*
Num. 7. 13 And his offering (was) one silver charger
So in v. 19 25, 31, 37, 43, 49, 55, 61, 67, 73, 79.
7. 84 twelve chargers of silver, twelve silver
7. 85 Each charger of silver (weighing) an

2. *Wooden trencher,* πίναξ *pinax.*
Matt 14. 8 Give..John Baptist's head in a charger
14. 11 his head was brought in a charger, and
Mark 6. 25 I will that thou give me..in a charger
6. 28 brought his head in a charger, and gave

CHARGERS —
Bason, bowl, אֲגַרְטָל *agartal.*
Ezra 1. 9 thirty chargers of gold, a thousand char.

CHARIOT —
1. *Couch, sofa,* אַפִּרְיוֹן *appiryon.*
Song 3. 9 King Solomon made himself a chariot of

2. *War chariot,* הֹצֶן *hotsen.*
Eze. 23. 24 shall come against thee with chariots

3. *Riding chariot,* מֶרְכָּב *merkab.*
1 Ki. 4. 26 thousand stalls of horses for his chariots

4. *Riding chariot,* מֶרְכָּבָה *merkabah.*
Gen. 41. 43 he made him to ride in the second chariot
46. 29 Joseph made ready his chariot, and went
Exod. 14. 25 took off their chariot wheels, that they
Exod 15 4 Pharaoh's chariots..hath he cast into the
Josh. 11. 6 thou shalt..burn their chariots with fire
11 9 and burnt their chariots with fire
Judg. 4. 15 Sisera lighted down off (his) chariot
5. 28 why tarry the wheels of his chariots?
1 Sa. 8 11 appoint (them) for himself, for..chariots
8. 11 and (some) shall run before his chariots
2 Sa. 15 1 Absalom prepared him chariots and
1 Ki. 7. 33 like the work of a chariot wheel
10. 29 a chariot came up and went out of Egypt
12. 18 made speed to get him up to his chariot
20. 33 he caused him to come up into..chariot
22. 35 the blood ran..into the midst of the chariot
2 Ki. 5. 21 he lighted down from the chariot to
5. 26 the man turned again from his chariot to
9. 27 Jehu..said, Smite him also in the chariot
10. 15 he took him up to him into the chariot
23. 11 burned the chariots of the sun with fire
1 Ch. 28 18 gold for the pattern of the chariot of the
2 Ch. 1. 17 brought forth out of Egypt a chariot
9. 25 thousand stalls for horses and chariots
10. 18 made speed to get him up to (his) chariot
14. 9 with an host of..three hundred chariots
18. 34 king..stayed (himself) up in (his) chariot
35. 24 servants..took him out of that chariot
Song 6. 12 my soul made me (like) the chariots of A.
Isa. 2. 7 neither (is there any)..of their chariots
22. 18 the chariots of thy glory (shall be) the
66. 15 and with his chariots like a whirlwind
Jer. 4. 13 his chariots (shall be) as a whirlwind
Joel 2. 5 Like the noise of chariots on the tops of
Mic. 1. 13 bind the chariot to the swift beast
5. 10 I will cut off..I will destroy thy chariots
Nah. 3. 2 prancing horses, and..jumping chariots
Hab. 3. 8 ride upon thine horses (and) thy chariots
Hag. 2. 22 I will overthrow the chariots, and those
Zech. 6. 1 there came four chariots out from between
6. 2 In the first chariot (were) red horses
6. 2 and in the second chariot black horses
6. 3 And in the third chariot white horses
6. 3 and in the fourth chariot grisled and bay

5. *Waggon, cart,* עֲגָלָה *agalah.*
Psa. 46. 9 he burneth the chariot in the fire

6. *Chariot,* רֶכֶב *rekeb.*
Gen. 50. 9 there went up with him both chariots
Exod. 14. 6 he made ready his chariot, and took his
14. 7 he took six hundred chosen chariots
14. 7 all the chariots of Egypt, and captains
14. 9 all the horses (and) chariots of Pharaoh
14. 17 upon all his host, upon his chariots, and
14. 18 upon his chariots, and upon his horsemen
14. 23 Pharaoh's horses, his chariots, and his
14. 26 their chariots, and upon their horsemen
14. 28 covered the chariots, and the horsemen
15. 19 horse of Pharaoh went in with his chariots
Deut 11. 4 unto their horses, and to their chariots
20. 1 and seest horses and chariots, (and) a
Josh. 11. 4 much people..with horses and chariots
17. 16 the Canaanites..have chariots of iron
17. 18 though they have iron chariots, (and)
24. 6 pursued after your fathers with chariots
Judg. 1. 19 because they had chariots of iron
4. 3 he had nine hundred chariots of iron
4. 7 with his chariots, and his multitude
4. 13 Sisera gathered together all his chariots
4. 13 nine hundred chariots of iron, and all
4. 15 discomfited Sisera, and all (his) chariots
4. 16 Barak pursued after the chariots, and
5. 28 Why is his chariot (so) long in coming?
1 Sa. 8. 12 to make..instruments of his chariots
13. 5 thirty thousand chariots, and six thous.
2 Sa. 1. 6 chariots and horsemen followed hard
8. 4 and David houghed all the chariot (horses)
8. 4 reserved of them (for) an hundred chariots
10. 18 slew (the men of) seven hundred chariots
1 Ki. 1. 5 he prepared him chariots and horsemen
9. 19 cities for his chariots, and cities for his
9. 22 his captains, and rulers of his chariots
10. 26 Solomon gathered together chariots
10. 26 a thousand and four hundred chariots
10. 26 he bestowed in the cities for chariots
16. 9 servant Zimri, captain of..(his) chariots
20. 1 and..with him..horses and chariots
20. 21 smote the horses and chariots, and slew
20. 25 horse for horse, and chariot for chariot
22. 31 captains, that had rule over his chariots
22. 32 captains of the chariot saw Jehoshaphat
22. 33 the captains of the chariots perceived
22. 35 and the king was stayed in his chariot
22. 38 washed the chariot in the pool of Samar.
2 Ki. 2. 11 a chariot of fire, and horses of fire, parted
2. 12 the chariot of Israel, and the horsemen
5. 9 Naaman came with..his chariot, and
6. 14 Therefore sent he..horses, and chariots
6. 15 host compassed the city..with..chariots
6. 17 mountain (was) full of horses and chariots
7. 6 a noise of chariots, and a noise of horses
7. 14 They took therefore two chariot horses
8. 21 Joram went over..and all the chariots
8. 21 compassed..the captains of the chariots
9. 21 And his chariot was made ready. And
9. 21 each in his chariot, and they went out
9. 24 Jehoram..and he sunk down in his chariot
10. 2 (there are) with you chariots and horses
10. 16 So they made him ride in his chariot
13. 7 ten chariots, and ten thousand footmen
13. 14 the chariot of Israel, and the horsemen
18. 24 put thy trust on Egypt for chariots and
19. 23 With the multitude of my chariots I am
1 Ch 18. 4 David took from him a thousand chariots
1 Ch. 18. 4 David also houghed all the chariot (horses)
18. 4 but reserved of them an hundred chariots
19. 6 to hire them chariots and horsemen out
19. 7 hired thirty and two thousand chariots
19. 18 seven thousand (men which fought in) cha.
2 Ch. 1. 14 Solomon gathered chariots and horsemen
1. 14 a thousand and four hundred chariots
1. 14 which he placed in the chariot cities, and
8. 6 all the chariot cities, and the cities of the
8. 9 captains of his chariots and horsemen
9. 25 he bestowed in the chariot cities, and
12. 3 With twelve hundred chariots, and three.
16. 8 a huge host, with very many chariots and
18. 30 commanded the captains of the chariots
18. 31 the captains of the chariot saw Jehosh.
18. 32 when the captains of the chariots per.
21. 9 Jehoram went forth..and all his chariots
21. 9 which compassed..captains of the chariots
35. 24 and put him in the second chariot that
Psa. 20. 7 Some (trust) in chariots, and some in ho.
68. 17 The chariots of God (are) twenty thousand
76. 6 the chariot and the horse are cast into
Song 1. 9 a company of horses in Pharaoh's chariots
Isa. 21. 7 saw a chariot (with) a couple of horsemen
21. 7 a chariot of asses, (and) a chariot of cam.
21. 9 behold, here cometh a chariot of men
22. 6 Elam bare the quiver with chariots of
22. 7 choicest valleys shall be full of chariots
31. 1 and stay on horses, and trust in chariots
36. 9 put thy trust on Egypt for chariots and
37. 24 By the multitude of my chariots am I
43. 17 bringeth forth the chariot and horse
66. 20 in chariots, and in litters, and upon
Jer. 17. 25 riding in chariots, and on horses, they
22. 4 kings..riding in chariots and on horses
46. 9 Come up, ye horses; and rage, ye chariots
47. 3 at the rushing of his chariots..the rumb.
50. 37 A sword (is) upon..their chariots, and
51. 21 will I break in pieces the chariot and his
Eze. 26. 7 with horses, and with chariots, and with
26. 10 and of the wheels, and of the chariots
39. 20 Thus ye shall be filled..with..chariots
Dan. 11. 40 like a whirlwind, with chariots, and
Nah. 2. 3 chariots (shall be) with flaming torches
2. 4 The chariots shall rage in the streets
2. 13 I will burn her chariots in the smoke
Zech. 9. 10 I will cut off the chariot from Ephraim

7. *Riding, driving,* רִכְבָּה *rikbah.*
Eze. 27. 20 Dedan (was) thy merchant..for chariots

8. *Chariot,* רְכוּב *rekub.*
Psa 104. 3 who maketh the clouds his chariot: who

9. *War chariot (with two wheels),* ἅρμα *harma.*
Acts 8. 28 sitting in his chariot read Esaias the pro.
8. 29 Go near, and join thyself to this chariot
8. 38 he commanded the chariot to stand still
Rev. 9. 9 the sound of chariots of many horses

10. *Travelling waggon (with four wheels),* ῥέδα *rheda.*
Rev. 18. 13 sheep, and horses, and chariots, and slaves

CHARIOT (man), driver of —
Rider, driver, רַכָּב *rakkab.*
1 Ki. 22. 34 he said unto the driver of his chariot
2 Ch. 18. 33 he said to the chariot man, Turn thine

CHARITABLY —
According to love, κατὰ ἀγάπην *kata agapēn.*
Rom 14. 15 now walkest thou not charitably

CHARITY —
Love, ἀγάπη *agapē.*
1 Co. 8. 1 Knowledge puffeth up, but charity edi.
13. 1 the tongues of men..and have not charity
13. 2 I have all faith..and have not charity
13. 3 though I give my body..and have not ch.
13. 4 Charity suffereth..(and is) kind; charity
13. 4 charity envieth not: charity vaunteth not
13. 8 Charity never faileth: but whether (there)
13. 13 now abideth faith, hope, charity
13. 13 but the greatest of these (is) charity
14. 1 Follow after charity, and desire spiritual
16. 14 Let all your things be done with charity
Col. 3. 14 above all these things (put on) charity
1 Th. 3. 6 good tidings of your faith and charity
2 Th. 1. 3 and the charity of every one of you all
1 Ti. 1. 5 the end of the commandment is charity
2. 15 if they continue in faith and charity and
4. 12 in word, in conversation, in charity, in
2 Ti. 2. 22 follow righteousness, faith, charity, peace
3. 10 purpose, faith, long-suffering, charity
Titus 2. 2 sound in faith, in charity, in patience
1 Pe. 4. 8 And above all things have fervent charity
4. 8 for charity shall cover the multitude of
5. 14 Greet ye one..with a kiss of charity
2 Pe. 1. 7 and to brotherly kindness charity
3 Jo. 6 Which have borne witness of thy charity
Rev. 2. 19 I know thy works, and charity, and serv.

CHARITY, feast of —
Love, ἀγάπη *agapē.*
Jude 12 These are spots in your feasts of charity

CHARMED —
A charm, לַחַשׁ *lachash.*
Jer. 8. 17 which (will) not (be) charmed, and they

CHARMER —
1. *Gentle ones, jugglers,* אִטִּים *ittim.*
Isa. 19. 3 seek to the idols, and to the charmers
2. *To join a joining, fascinate,* חָבַר חֶבֶר *chabar cheber.*
Deut 18. 11 Or a charmer, or a consulter with familiar

3. *To charm,* לָחַשׁ *lachash,* 3.
Psa. 58. 5 will not hearken to the voice of charmers

CHARMING —
To join a joining, חָבַר חֶבֶר *chabar cheber.*
Psa. 58. 5 the voice of charmers, charming never so

CHAR'-RAN, Χαῤῥάν. *See Haran.*
Acts 7. 2 unto..Abraham..before he dwelt in C.
7. 4 Then came he out..and dwelt in C

CHASE, to —
1. *To cause to flee,* בָּרַח *barach,* 5.
Neh. 13. 28 therefore I chased him from me
2. *To drive away,* דָּחָה *dachah.*
Psa. 35. 5 and let the angel of the LORD chase (them)
3. *To burn, pursue,* דָּלַק *dalaq.*
1 Sa. 17. 53 children of Israel returned from chasing
4. *To hunt,* צוּד *tsud.*
Lam. 3. 52 Mine enemies chased me sore, like a bird
5. *To pursue, follow after,* רָדַף *radaph.*
Lev 26. 7 ye shall chase your enemies, and they
26. 8 five of you shall chase an hundred, and
26. 36 sound of a shaken leaf shall chase them
Deut 1. 44 Amorites..came out against you..chased
32. 30 How should one chase a thousand, and
Josh. 7. 5 they chased them (from) before the gate
8. 24 in the wilderness wherein they chased
10. 10 chased them along the way that goeth up
11. 8 and chased them unto great Zidon, and
23. 10 One man of you shall chase a thousand
Judg 9. 40 Abimelech chased him, and he fled before
6. *To (cause to) pursue,* רָדַף *radaph,* 5.
Judg 20. 43 inclosed the Benjamites..chased them

CHASE away, to —
To cause to flee, בָּרַח *barach,* 5.
Prov 19. 26 wasteth (his) father, (and) chaseth away

CHASED —
To be forced away, נָדַח *nadach,* 6.
Isa. 13 14 it shall be as the chased roe, and as a sheep

CHASED, to be —
1. *To cause to move away,* נָדַד *nadad,* 5.
Job 18. 18 He shall be..chased out of the world
2. *To be pursued,* רָדַף *radaph,* 4.
Isa. 17. 13 shall be chased as the chaff of the moun.

CHASED away, to be —
To be caused to move away, נָדַד *nadad,* 6.
Job 20. 8 he shall be chased away as a vision of the

CHASTE —
Consecrated, ἁγνός *hagnos.*
2 Co. 11. 2 that I may present (you as) a chaste virgin
Titus 2. 5 discreet, chaste, keepers at home, good
1 Pe 3. 2 your chaste conversation (coupled) with

CHASTEN, to —
1. *To convict, make manifest,* יָכַח *yakach,* 5.
2 Sa. 7 14 I will chasten him with the rod of men
2. *To instruct,* יָסַר *yasar,* 3.
Deut. 8. 5 that, as a man chasteneth his son, (so) the
8. 5 (so) the LORD thy God chasteneth thee
21. 18 and (that), when they have chastened him
Psa 6. 1 neither chasten me in thy hot displeasure
38. 1 neither chasten me in thy hot displeasure
94. 12 Blessed..the man whom thou chastenest
118. 18 The LORD hath chastened me sore: but
Prov 19. 18 Chasten thy son while there is hope, and
3. *To instruct, train up,* παιδεύω *paideuō.*
1 Co. 11. 32 we are chastened of the Lord, that we
2 Co. 6. 9 we live; as chastened, and not killed
Heb. 12. 6 For whom the Lord loveth he chasteneth
12. 7 what son is he whom the father chasteneth
12. 10 they verily for a few days chastened (us)
Rev. 3. 19 As many as I love, I rebuke and chasten

CHASTEN self, to —
To humble oneself, עָנָה *anah,* 7.
Dan. 10. 12 and to chasten thyself before thy God

CHASTENED —
Reproof, conviction, תּוֹכַחַת *tokachath.*
Psa. 73. 14 have I been plagued, and chastened every

CHASTENED, to be —
To be convicted, יָכַח *yakach,* 6.
Job 33. 19 He is chastened also with pain upon his

CHASTENETH —
Instruction, מוּסָר *musar.*
Prov 13. 24 he that loveth him chasteneth him

CHASTENING —
1. *Instruction,* מוּסָר *musar.*
Job 5. 17 despise not thou the chastening of the
Prov. 3. 11 despise not the chastening of the LORD
Isa. 26. 16 (when) thy chastening (was) upon them
2. *Instruction, training,* παιδεία *paideia.*
Heb. 12. 5 despise not thou the chastening of the L.
12. 7 If ye endure chastening, God dealeth with
12. 11 no chastening for the present seemeth to

CHASTISE, to —
1. *To instruct, chastise,* יָסַר *yasar.*
Psa. 94. 10 He that chastiseth the heathen, shall not
Hos. 10. 10 (It is) in my desire that I should chastise
2. *To instruct, chastise,* יָסַר *yasar,* 3.
Lev. 26. 28 will chastise you seven times for your sins
Deut 22. 18 the elders..shall take..and chastise him
1 Ki. 12. 11 my father hath chastised you with whips
12. 11, 14 but I will chastise you with scorpions
12. 14 my father (also) chastised you with whips
2 Ch. 10. 11, 14 my father chastised you with whips
Jer. 31. 18 Thou hast chastised me, and I was
3. *To cause to instruct,* יָסַר *yasar,* 5.
Hos. 7. 12 I will chastise them, as their congregation
4. *To instruct, chastise,* παιδεύω *paideuō.*
Luke 23. 16 I will therefore chastise him, and release
23 22 I will therefore chastise him, and let..go

CHASTISED, to be —
To be instructed, chastised, יָסַר *yasar,* 2.
Jer. 31. 18 Thou hast chastised me, and I was chas.

CHASTISEMENT —
1. *Instruction, chastisement,* מוּסָר *musar.*
Deut 11. 2 which have not seen the chastisement of
Isa. 53. 5 the chastisement of our peace (was) upon
Jer. 30. 14 with the chastisement of a cruel one, for
2. *Instruction, chastisement,* παιδεία *paideia.*
Heb. 12. 8 But if ye be without chastisement, where.

CHATTER, to —
To chirp (as a bird), צָפַף *tsaphaph,* 3 *a.*
Isa. 38. 14 Like a.. swallow, so did I chatter

CHE'-BAR, כְּבָר *joining.*
A river rising near the Nisibis, an affluent of the Euphrates entering it at Carchemosh, the Aborras of Strabo, or Chaboras of Ptolemy, where Ezekiel saw his earlier visions. It is considered as identical with the Habor or River of Gozan to which a portion of Israel was removed by the Assyrians (2 Ki. 17. 6). But the *Nahr Malcha*, or Royal Canal of Nebuchadnezzar, the greatest of all the cuttings of Mesopotamia, best deserves acceptance as the *Chebar*.
Eze. 1. 1 among the captives by the river of C.
1. 3 the land of the Chaldeans, by the river C.
3. 15 came to them..dwelt by the river of C.
3. 23 the glory which I saw by the river of C.
10. 15 creature that I saw by the river of C.
10. 20 creature that I saw..by the river of C.
10. 22 faces which I saw by the river of C.
43. 3 vision that I saw by the river C.

CHECK —
Instruction, chastisement, מוּסָר *musar.*
Job 20. 3 I have heard the check of my reproach

CHECKER —
Lattice work, שְׂבָכָה *sebakah.*
1 Ki. 7. 17 nets of checker work, and wreaths of

CHE-DOR-LA-O'-MER, כְּדָרְלָעֹמֶר *sheaf band.*
A king of Elam in the time of Abram, B.C. 1917.
Gen. 14. 1 Arioch king of Ellasar, C. king of Elam
14. 4 Twelve years they served C., and in the
14. 5 And in the fourteenth year came C., and
14. 9 With C. the king of Elam, and with Tidal
14. 17 his return from the slaughter of C., and

CHEEK —
1. *Cheek, jaw,* לְחִי *lechi.*
1 Ki. 22. 24 went near, and smote Micaiah on the ch.
2 Ch. 18. 23 came near..smote Micaiah upon the ch.
Job 16. 10 they have smitten me upon the cheek
Song 1. 10 Thy cheeks are comely with rows (of jew.
5. 13 His cheeks (are) as a bed of spices, (as)
Isa. 50. 6 and my cheeks to them that plucked off
Lam. 1. 2 and her tears (are) on her cheeks: among
3. 30 He giveth (his) cheek to him that smiteth
Mic. 5. 1 shall smite..with a rod upon the cheek
2. *The cheek, jaw,* σιαγών *siagōn.*
Matt. 5. 39 shall smite thee on thy right cheek
Luke 6. 29 him that smiteth thee on the (one) cheek

CHEEK bone —
The cheek, jaw, לְחִי *lechi.*
Psa. 3. 7 smitten all mine enemies..the cheek b.

CHEEK teeth —
Great teeth, grinders, מְתַלְּעוֹת *methallaoth.*
Joel 1. 6 he hath the cheek teeth of a great lion

CHEEKS, two —
Two cheeks, לְחָיַיִם *[lechi].*
Deut 18. 3 the shoulder, and the two cheeks, and the

CHEER, to —
To do or make good or glad, טוֹב *tob,* 5.
Eccl. 11. 9 let thy heart cheer thee in the days of

CHEER (up), to —
To rejoice, שָׂמַח *sameach,* 3.
Deut 24. 5 and shall cheer up his wife which he
Judg. 9. 13 which cheereth God and man, and go to

CHEER, of good —
Well minded or disposed, εὔθυμος *euthumos.*
Acts 27. 36 Then were they all of good cheer, and

CHEER, to be of good —
1. *To be well minded, cheerful,* εὐθυμέω *euthumeō.*
Acts 27. 22 now I exhort you to be of good cheer: for
27. 25 Wherefore, sirs, be of good cheer: for I
2. *To take courage,* θαρσέω *tharseō.*
Matt. 9. 2 Son, be of good cheer; thy sins be forgiv.
14. 27 saying, Be of good cheer; it is I; be not
Mark 6. 50 saith unto them, Be of good cheer: it is
John 16. 33 but be of good cheer; I have overcome
Acts 23. 11 stood by him, and said, Be of good cheer

CHEERFUL —
1. *Good, glad,* טוֹב *tob.*
Zech. 8. 19 to the house of Judah..cheerful feasts
2. *Cheerful,* ἱλαρός *hilaros.*
2 Co. 9. 7 for God loveth a cheerful giver

CHEERFUL, to make —
1. *To make good or glad,* יָטַב *yatab,* 5.
Prov 15. 13 A merry heart maketh a cheerful counte.
2. *To grow, be fruitful (in words),* נוּב *nub,* 3 *a.*
Zech. 9. 17 Corn shall make the young men cheerful

CHEERFULLY, more —
More cheerfully, εὐθυμότερον *euthumoteron.*
Acts 24. 10 I do the [more cheerfully] answer for

CHEERFULNESS —
Hilarity, cheerfulness, ἱλαρότης *hilarotēs.*
Rom 12. 8 he that showeth mercy, with cheerfulness

CHEESE —
1. *Curdled milk,* גְּבִינָה *gebinah.*
Job 10 10 Hast thou not..curdled me like cheese?
2. *Cheese of kine,* שָׁפָה *shaphah.*
2 Sa. 17. 29 and sheep, and cheese of kine, for David
3. *Cuttings or slices of cheese,* חֲרִיצֵי הֶחָלָב *[charits].*
1 Sa. 17. 18 carry these ten cheeses unto the captain

CHE'-LAL, כְּלָל *completeness.*
One of the family of Pahath Moab that had a strange wife, B.C. 445.
Ezra 10. 30 sons of Pahath-moab; Adna, and C., B.

CHEL'-LUH, כְּלוּהִי *robust.*
One of the family of Bani that had married a strange wife, B.C. 445.
Ezra 10. 35 Benaiah, Bedeiah, C.

CHE'-LUB, כְּלוּב *boldness.*
1. A descendant of Caleb son of Hur, B.C. 1451.
1 Ch. 4. 11 And C. the brother of Shuah begat Mehir
2. Father of Ezri, superintendent of the tillers of the ground in the time of David, B.C. 1015.
1 Ch. 27. 26 over them..(was) Ezri the son of C.

CHE-LU'-BAI, כְּלוּבַי, Χαλέβ.
Son of Hezron, elsewhere called Caleb, B.C. 1451.
1 Ch. 2. 9 sons also of Hezron..Jerahmeel, and..C.

CHE-MA'-RIMS, כְּמָרִים *servants, priests.*
Zeph. 1. 4 I will cut off..the name of the C.

CHE'-MOSH, כְּמוֹשׁ *fire, hearth.*
The national idol of the Moabites and Ammonites, but not identical with Molech. By Jerome Chemosh is identified with Baal-peor; by others with Baal-zebub; others, Mars, and others Saturn, as the star of ill-omen. Dibon was the chief seat of its worship.
Num 21. 29 thou art undone, O people of C.
Judg 11. 24 Wilt not thou possess that which C.
1 Ki. 11. 7 Solomon build an high place for C.
11. 33 they..have worshipped..C. the god of
2 Ki. 23. 13 and for C. the abomination of the
Jer. 48. 7 C. shall go forth into captivity (with) his
48. 13 And Moab shall be ashamed of C.
48. 46 the people of C. perisheth: for thy sons

CHE-NA-A'-NAH, כְּנַעֲנָה *flat, low.*
1. Father of the false prophet Zedekiah that smote Micaiah when he foretold the fall of Ahab at Ramoth-Gilead, B.C. 930.
1 Ki. 22. 11 Zedekiah the son of C. made him horns
22. 24 Zedekiah the son of C. went near, and
2 Ch. 18. 10 Zedekiah the son of C. had made him
18. 23 Zedekiah the son of C. came near, and
2. Brother of Ehud, son of Bilhan a Benjamite, B.C. 1650.
1 Ch. 7. 10 the sons of Bilhan..Ehud, and C., and

CHE-NA'-NI, כְּנָנִי, Χωνενί *Jah, creator.*
A Levite that conducted the devotion of the people after Ezra had read to them the book of the law, B.C. 445.
Neh. 9. 4 Then stood up..of the Levites..Bani..C.

CHE-NAN'-IAH, כְּנַנְיָה, Χωνενίας, Χενενίας.
1. A chief Levite when David brought up the ark, B.C 1042.
1 Ch. 15. 22 And C., chief of the Levites..for song
15. 27 C. the master of the song with the sing.
2. An Izharite, an officer of David's, B.C. 1042.
1 Ch. 26. 29 Of the Izharites, C. and his sons..for

CHE-PHAR HA-AM-MO'-NAI, כְּפַר הָעַמּוֹנִי.
A town of Benjamin, once a "village of the Ammonites."
Josh. 18. 24 And C., and Ophni, and Gaba; twelve

CHE-PHI'-RAH, כְּפִירָה, *village, hamlet.*
Hivite village near Gibeon in Benjamin; now *Kefir.*
Josh. 9. 17 their cities (were) Gibeon, and C., and
18. 26 And Mizpeh, and C., and Mozah
Ezra 2. 25 The children of Kirjath-arim, C., and B.
Neh. 7. 29 The men of Kirjath-jearim, C., and Beeroth

CHE'-RAN, כְּרָן *union.*
Son of Dishon, son of Seir the Horite, B. C. 1700.
Gen. 36. 26 of Dishon..Eshban, and Ithran, and C.
1 Ch. 1. 41 of Dishon..Eshban, and Ithran, and C.

CHE-RE'-THITES, כְּרֵתִים *executioners* **(CHERETHIMS).**
1. A Philistine tribe in the S. of Canaan, emigrants from Crete.
1 Sa.30. 14 We made an invasion (upon)..the C., and
Eze 25. 16 I will cut off the C., and destroy the rem.
Zeph. 2. 5 Woe unto..the nation of the C.!
2. Officers who, along with the Pelethites, formed David's life-guards. B. C. 1050.
2 Sa. 8. 18 Benaiah..(was over) both the C. and the
15. 18 all the C...passed on before the king
20. 7 there went out after him..the C., and the
20. 23 Benaiah..(was) over the C. [V.L. *kari*].
1 Ki. 1. 38 Benaiah the son of Jehoiada, and the C.
1. 44 Benaiah the son of Jehoiada, and the C.
1 Ch. 18. 17 Benaiah..(was) over the C. and the Pel.

CHERISH, to —
1. *To be useful, profitable,* סָכַן *sakan.*
1 Ki. 1. 2 let her cherish him, and let her lie in thy
1. 4 (was) very fair, and cherished the king
2. *To heat, soften, cherish,* θάλπω *thalpō.*
Eph. 5. 29 nourisheth and cherisheth it, even as the
1 Th. 2. 7 as a nurse cherisheth her children

CHE'-RITH, כְּרִית *trench.*
A brook or wady E. of the Jordan in Gilead, near Jericho, now called *Wady Kelt.*
1 Ki 17. 3 Get thee hence..hide..by the brook C.
17. 5 he went and dwelt by the brook C.

CHERUB —
1. *One grasped, held fast,* כְּרוּב *kerub.*
Exod 25. 19 make one cherub on the one end
25. 19 and the other cherub on the other end
37. 8 One cherub on the end on this side, and
37. 8 another cherub on the (other) end on
2 Sa. 22. 11 he rode upon a cherub, and did fly
1 Ki. 6. 24 cubits (was) the one wing of the cherub
6. 24 five cubits the other wing of the cherub
6. 25 And the other cherub (was) ten cubits
6. 26 The height of the one cherub (was) ten
6. 26 and so (was it) of the other cherub
6. 27 the wing of the other cherub touched the
2 Ch. 3. 11 reaching to the wing of the other cherub
3. 12 And (one) wing of the other cherub (was)
3. 12 joining to the wing of the other cherub
Psa. 18. 10 he rode upon a cherub, and did fly
Eze. 9. 3 glory..was gone up from the cherub
10. 2 between..wheels, (even) under the cherub
10. 4 glory of the LORD went up from the cherub
10. 7 And (one) cherub stretched forth his hand
10. 9 one wheel by..cherub..by another cherub
10. 14 the first face (was) the face of a cherub
28. 14 Thou (art) the anointed cherub that cover.
28. 16 and I will destroy thee, O covering cherub
41. 18 tree (was) between a cherub and a cherub
41. 18 and (every) cherub had two faces
2. *An Israelite who returned with Zerubbabel.*
Ezra 2. 59 Tel-harsa, Ch., Addan, (and) Immer
Neh. 7. 61 Tel-haresha, Ch., Addon, and Immer

CHERUBIM —
1. *Those grasped, held fast,* כְּרוּבִים *kerubim.*
Gen. 3. 24 placed at the east..of Eden cherubims
Exod 25. 18 thou shalt make two cherubims (of) gold
25. 19 mercy seat shall ye make the cherubims
25. 20 the cherubims shall stretch forth (their)
25. 20 mercy seat shall the faces of the cherubims
25. 22 from between the two cherubims which
26. 1 cherubims of cunning work shalt thou
26. 31 with cherubims shall it be made
36. 8 cherubims of cunning work made he
36. 35 he made a veil..(with) cherubims made
37. 7 he made two cherubims (of) gold, beaten
37. 8 the mercy seat made he the cherubims on
37. 9 the cherubims spread out (their) wings on
37. 9 were the faces of the cherubims
Num. 7. 89 voice..from between the two cherubims
1 Sa. 4. 4 which dwelleth (between) the cherubims
2 Sa. 6. 2 that dwelleth (between) the cherubims
1 Ki. 6. 23 within the oracle he made two cherubims
6. 25 both the cherubims (were) of one measure
6. 27 he set the cherubims within the inner h.
6. 27 stretched forth the wings of the cherubims
6. 28 he overlaid the cherubims with gold
6. 29 carved figures of cherubims and palm
6. 32 carved upon them carvings of cherubims
6. 32 and spread gold upon the cherubims, and
6. 35 carved (thereon) cherubims and palm trees
7. 29 on the borders..lions, oxen, and cheru.
7. 36 he graved cherubims, lions, and..trees
8. 6 (even) under the wings of the cherubims
8. 7 For the cherubims spread forth (their)
8. 7 the cherubims covered the ark and the
2 Ki. 19. 15 God..which dwellest (between) the cher.
1 Ch. 13. 6 that dwelleth (between) the cherubims
28. 18 the pattern of the chariot of the cherubims
2 Ch. 3. 7 and graved cherubims on the walls
3. 10 he made two cherubims of image work
3. 11 wings of the cherubims (were) twenty c.
3. 13 the wings of these cherubims spread
3. 14 fine linen, and wrought cherubims thereon
5. 7 (even) under the wings of the cherubims
5. 8 the cherubims spread forth (their) wings
5. 8 and the cherubims covered the ark and
Psa. 80. 1 thou that dwellest (between) the cherubi.
99. 1 he sitteth (between) the cherubims let
Isa. 37. 16 that dwellest (between) the cherubims
Eze. 10. 1 that (was) above the head of the cherubims
10. 2 coals of fire from between the cherubims
10. 3 Now the cherubims stood on the right side
Eze. 10. 5 sound of the cherubim's wings was heard
10. 6 Take fire..from between the cherubims
10. 7 his hand from between the cherubims unto
10. 7 the fire that (was) between the cherubims
10. 8 there appeared in the cherubims the form
10. 9 behold the four wheels by the cherubims
10. 15 And the cherubims were lifted up
10. 16 And when the cherubims went, the wheels
10. 16 when the cherubims lifted up their wings
10. 18 and stood over the cherubims
10. 19 And the cherubims lifted up their wings
10. 20 and I knew that they (were) the cherubims
11. 22 Then did the cherubims lift up their wings
41. 18 And (it was) made with cherubims and p.
41. 20 above the door (were) cherubims and p.
41. 25 on the doors of the temple, cherubims and
2. *Those grasped or seized,* Χερουβίμ *cheroubim.*
Heb. 9. 5 And over it the cherubims of glory

CHE-SA'-LON, כְּסָלוֹן *fortress.*
A place on the W. part of the N. border of Judah, on the shoulder of Mount Jearim.
Josh 15. 10 the border..passed along unto..C., on

CHE'-SED, כֶּשֶׂד.
Fourth son of Nahor, and nephew of Abraham, B.C. 1870.
Gen. 22. 22 And C., and Hazo, and Pildash, and

CHE'-SIL, כְּסִיל *fleshy, fat.*
A town in the extreme S. of Canaan. This was an early variation of *Bethul,* now *Khelasa.*
Josh. 15. 30 And Eltolad, and C., and Hormah

CHESNUT tree —
Plane tree, עַרְמוֹן *armon.*
Gen. 30. 37 of the hazel and chesnut tree; and pilled
Eze. 31. 8 the chesnut trees were not like his bran.

CHEST —
1. *Ark, chest,* אָרוֹן *aron.*
2 Ki. 12. 9 But Jehoiada the priest took a chest, and
12. 10 saw that (there was) much money in the c.
2 Ch. 24. 8 they made a chest, and set it without at
24. 10 cast into the chest, until they had made
24. 11 that at what time the chest was brought
24. 11 priest's officer came..emptied the chest
2. *Coverings,* גְּנָזִים *genazim.*
Eze. 27. 24 in chests of rich apparel, bound with

CHE-SUL'-LOTH, כְּסֻלּוֹת *fatness, the loins.*
The word suggests that the town derived its name from its situation on the slope of a mountain (Josh. 19. 18). It seems to have been between Jezreel and Shunem (*Solam*). Now *Iksal.*
Josh 19. 18 their border was toward Jezreel, and C.

CHEW, to —
1. *To ruminate,* גָּרַר *garar,* 2.
Lev. 11. 7 yet he cheweth not the cud; he (is)
2. *To cause (the cud) to come up,* עָלָה *alah,* 5.
Lev. 11. 3 and is cloven footed, (and) cheweth the c.
11. 4 shall ye not eat of them that chew the c.
11. 4, 5, 6 because he cheweth the cud, but divi.
11. 26 (is) not cloven footed, nor cheweth the c.
Deut 14. 6 cheweth the cud among the beasts, that
14. 7 shall not eat of them that chew the cud
14. 7 for they chew the cud, but divide not the

CHEWED, to be —
To be cut off, כָּרַת *karath,* 2.
Num 11. 33 ere it was chewed, the wrath of the LORD

CHE'-ZIB, כְּזִיב *deceitful.*
Probably identical with *Achzib* or *Chozeba,* a town of the Canaanites, afterwards belonging to Judah. Now called *Achzib.*
Gen. 38. 5 and he was at C. when she bare him

CHICKEN —
A nestling, νοσσίον *nossion.*
Matt 23. 37 even as a hen gathereth her chickens

CHIDE, to —
To strive, contend, רִיב *rib.*
Gen. 31. 36 was wroth, and chode with Laban: and
Exod 17. 2 Wherefore the people did chide with Mo.
17. 2 Why chide ye with me? wherefore do ye
Num 20. 3 And the people chode with Moses, and
Judg. 8. 1 And they did chide with him sharply
Psa. 103. 9 He will not always chide; neither will

CHIDING —
Strife, contention, רִיב *rib.*
Exod 17. 7 because of the chiding of the children of

CHI'-DON, כִּידוֹן *destruction, a javelin.*
The scene where the accident to the ark and the death of Uzzah occurred. In 2 Sa. 6. 6, the name is *Nachon.*
1 Ch. 13. 9 came unto the threshing floor of C.

CHIEF —
1. *Father,* אָב *ab.*
Num 25. 14 a prince of a chief house among the Sim.
25. 15 he (was) head..of a chief house in Midian
Josh. 22. 14 of each chief house a prince throughout
2. *Mighty one,* גִּבּוֹר *gibbor.*
1 Ch. 9. 26 For these Levites, the four chief porters
3. *Leader, one in the front,* נָגִיד *nagid.*
1 Ch. 5. 2 and of him (came) the chief ruler; but
29. 22 the chief governor, and Zadok (to be)
Jer. 20. 1 who (was) also chief governor in the
4. *One lifted up, exalted,* נָשִׂיא *nasi.*
Num. 3. 24, 30, 35 the chief of the house of the father
3. 32 chief over the chief of the Levites
4. 34 And Moses and Aaron and the chief of
4. 46 Moses and Aaron and the chief of Israel
1 Ki. 8. 1 Solomon assembled..the chief of the
2 Ch. 5. 2 the chief of the fathers of the children of
5. *A corner (stone),* פִּנָּה *pinnah.*
Judg 20. 2 the chief of all the people, (even) of all
1 Sa. 14. 38 all the chief of the people; and know and
6. *Head,* רֹאשׁ *rosh.*
Num 31. 26 and the chief fathers of the congregation
32. 28 and the chief fathers of the tribes of the
36. 1 And the chief fathers of the families of
36. 1 the chief fathers of the children of Israel
Deut. 1. 15 So I took the chief of your tribes, wise
2 Ki. 25. 18 the captain..took Seraiah the chief priest
1 Ch. 5. 7 (were) the chief, Jeiel, and Zechariah
5. 12 Joel the chief, and Shapham the next
5. 15 chief of the house of their fathers
8. 28 These (were) heads of the fathers..chief
9. 17 Shallum (was) the chief
9. 33 singers, chief of the fathers of the Levites
9. 34 chief fathers of the Levites (were) chief
11. 6 smiteth the Jebusites first shall be chief
11. 6 So Joab..went first up, and was chief
11. 10 These also (are) the chief of the mighty men
11. 11 an Hachmonite, the chief of the captains
11. 20 brother of Joab, he was chief of the three
12. 3 The chief (was) Ahiezer, then Joash, the
12. 18 (who was) chief of the captains, (and he)
15. 12 Ye (are) the chief of the fathers of the
16. 5 Asaph the chief, and next to him Zechariah
23. 8 the chief (was) Jehiel, and Zetham, and
23. 9 These (were) the chief of the fathers of
23. 11 And Jahath was the chief, and Zizah
23. 16 Of the sons of..Shebuel (was) the chief
23. 17 sons of Eliezer (were) Rehabiah the chief
23. 18 Of the sons of Izhar; Shelomith the chief
23. 24 the chief of the fathers, as they were
24. 4 there were more chief men found of the
24. 6, 31 the chief of the fathers of the priests
26. 10 the chief..his father made him the chief
26. 12 among the chief men, (having) wards one
26. 21 chief fathers, (even) of Laadan the Gershon
26. 26 which..the chief fathers..had dedicated
26. 31 Jerijah the chief, (even) among the Hebr.
26. 32 two thousand and seven hundred chief
27. 1 chief fathers and captains of thousands
27. 5 The third captain..Benaiah..a chief pr.
2 Ch. 1. 2 to every governor in all Israel, the chief
11. 22 made Abijah the son of Maachah the chief
19. 8 of the chief of the fathers of Israel
19. 11 Amariah the chief priest (is) over you in
23. 2 the chief of the fathers of Israel, and they
24. 6 the king called for Jehoiada the chief
26. 12 The whole number of the chief of the
26. 20 Azariah the chief priest, and all the
31. 10 Azariah the chief priest of the house of
Ezra 1. 5 Then rose up the chief of the fathers
2. 68 And (some) of the chief of the fathers
3. 12 the priests..and chief of the fathers
4. 2, 3 to Zerubbabel, and to the chief of the
7. 5 Eleazar, the son of Aaron the chief priest
8. 1 These (are) now the chief of their fathers
8. 17 Iddo the chief at the place Casiphia
10. 16 Ezra the priest, (with) certain chief of the
Neh. 7. 70, 71 some of the chief of the fathers gave
8. 13 gathered together the chief of the fathers
10. 14 The chief of the people; Parosh, Pahath
11. 3 these (are) the chief of the province that
11. 13 And his brethren, chief of the fathers
11. 16 Shabbethai and Jozabad, of the chief of
12. 7 These (were) the chief of the priests and
12. 12 the chief of the fathers: of Seraiah
12. 22 The Levites..(were) recorded chief of the
12. 23 The sons of Levi, the chief of their fathers
12. 24 the chief of the Levites: Hashabiah
12. 46 in the days of David..(there were) chief
Job 12. 24 He taketh away the heart of the chief of
29. 25 I chose out their way, and sat chief
Psa. 137. 6 if I prefer not Jerusalem above my chief
Jer. 52. 24 the captain..took Seraiah the chief priest
Lam. 1. 5 Her adversaries are the chief, her enemies
Eze. 27. 22 they occupied in thy fairs with chief of all
38. 2 the chief prince of Meshech and Tubal
39. 1 the chief prince of Meshech and Tubal
7. *Head,* רֵאשׁ *resh.*
Ezra 5. 10 the names of the men that (were) the chief
8. *Beginning,* רֵאשִׁית *reshith.*
1 Sa. 15. 21 the chief of the things which should have
Job 40. 19 He (is) the chief of the ways of God
Psa. 78. 51 the chief of (their) strength in the
105. 36 the first born in their land, the chief of
Jer. 49. 35 the bow of Elam, the chief of their might
Dan. 11. 41 and the chief of the children of Ammon
Amos 6. 1 (which are) named chief of the nations
6. 6 and anoint themselves with the chief
9. *Great one,* רַב *rab.*
Dan. 2. 48 chief of the governors over all the wise
10. *Prince, head,* שַׂר *sar.*
Gen. 40. 2 was wroth..against the chief of the butlers
40. 2 and against the chief of the bakers
40. 9 the chief butler told his dream to Joseph
40. 16 the chief baker saw that the interpretation
40. 20 he lifted up the head of the chief butler
40. 20 and of the chief baker among his servants
40. 21 And he restored the chief butler unto his

Gen. 40. 22 But he hanged the chief baker
40. 23 Yet did not the chief butler remember
41. 9 Then spake the chief butler unto Pharaoh
41. 10 put me in ward..me and the chief baker
1 Ki. 5. 16 Beside the chief of Solomon's officers
9. 23 These (were) the chief of the officers
14. 27 committed..unto the hands of the chief
1 Ch. 15. 5 Of the sons of Kohath; Uriel the chief
15. 6 the sons of Merari; Asaiah the chief
15. 7 the sons of Gershom; Joel the chief
15. 8 the sons of Elizaphan; Shemaiah the chief
15. 9 the sons of Hebron; Eliel the chief
15. 10 the sons of Uzziel; Amminadab the chief
15. 16 David spake to the chief of the Levites
15. 22 And Chenaniah, chief of the Levites
2 Ch. 8. 9 chief of his captains, and captains of his
8. 10 these were the chief of king Solomon's
12. 10 committed them to the hands of the chief
17. 14 Adnah the chief, and with him mighty
35. 9 Jeiel and Jozabad, chief of the Levites
36. 14 Moreover all the chief of the priests, and
Ezra 8. 24 Then I separated twelve of the chief
8. 29 until ye weigh (them) before the chief of
8. 29 and chief of the fathers of Israel, at Jer.
10. 5 Then arose Ezra, and made the chief pr.

11. *Prince, the first, chief,* ἄρχων *archōn.*
Luke 11. 15 He casteth out devils through..the chief
14. 1 into the house of one of the chief Pharisees

12. *To lead, go before,* ἡγέομαι *hēgeomai.*
Acts 15. 22 Barsabas, and Silas, chief men, 14. 12.

13. *First, foremost,* πρῶτος *prōtos.*
Matt 20. 27 And whosoever will be chief among you
Luke 19. 47 and the chief of the people sought to
Acts 16. 12 which is the chief city of that part of
17. 4 and of the chief women not a few
25. 2 Then the high priest and the chief of the
28. 17 after three days Paul called the chief of
1 Ti. 1. 15 to save sinners; of whom I am chief

CHIEF (estate) —
First, foremost, πρῶτος *prōtos.*
Mark 6. 21 high captains..chief (estates) of Galilee

CHIEF friend—
First, chief, leader, familiar, אַלּוּף *alluph.*
Prov. 16. 28 a whisperer separateth chief friends

CHIEF man —
1. *Lord, owner, possessor,* בַּעַל *baal.*
Lev. 21. 4 (being) a chief man among his people, to
2. *Head,* רֹאשׁ *rosh.*
1 Ch. 7. 3 Joel, Ishiah, five: all of them chief men
24. 4 sixteen chief men of the house of (their)
Ezra 7. 28 gathered together out of Israel chief men
8. 16 Then sent I for Eliezer..chief men; also
3. *First, foremost,* πρῶτος *prōtos.*
Acts 13. 50 Jews stirred up..the chief men of the city
28. 7 were possessions of the chief man of the

CHIEF men —
Nobles, those near (the throne), אֲצִילִים *atsilim.*
Isa. 41. 9 called thee from the chief men thereof

CHIEF of Asia —
Asiarch (high official), Ἀσιάρχης *asiarchēs.*
Acts 19. 31 certain of the chief of Asia..sent unto

CHIEF one —
He goat, leader, עַתּוּד *attud.*
Isa. 14. 9 (even) all the chief ones of the earth; it

CHIEF ruler —
Priest, prince, כֹּהֵן *kohen.*
2 Sa. 8. 18 and David's sons were chief rulers
20. 26 Ira also the Jairite was a chief ruler about

CHIEF things —
Head, רֹאשׁ *rosh.*
Deut. 33. 15 And for the chief things of the ancient

CHIEF, to be —
To lead, go before, ἡγέομαι *hēgeomai.*
Luke 22. 26 and he that is chief, as he that doth serve

CHIEFEST —
1. *Mighty,* אַבִּיר *abbir.*
1 Sa. 21. 7 chiefest of the herdmen that (belonged)
2. *To be a standard bearer,* דָּגַל *dagal.*
Song 5. 10 My beloved (is)..the chiefest among ten
3. *Ascent,* מַעֲלֶה *maaleh.*
2 Ch. 32. 33 they buried him in the chiefest of the
4. *Beginning,* רֵאשִׁית *reshith.*
1 Sa. 2. 29 to make yourselves fat with the chiefest
5. *First, foremost,* πρῶτος *prōtos.*
Mark 10. 44 And whosoever of you will be the chiefest

CHIEFEST place —
Head, רֹאשׁ *rosh.*
1 Sa. 9. 22 made them sit in the chiefest place

CHIEFEST, very —
Very much, ὑπερλίαν *huperlian.*
2 Co. 11. 5 I was not a whit behind the very chiefest
12. 11 in nothing am I behind the very chiefest

CHIEFLY —
1. *Most of all,* μάλιστα *malista.*
Phil. 4. 22 chiefly they that are of Cesar's household
2 Pet. 2. 10 But chiefly them that walk after the flesh
2. *First, foremost,* πρῶτον *prōton.*
Rom. 3. 2 chiefly, because that unto them were

[*See also* Captain, corner, governor musician, priest, publican, room, ruler, seat, shepherd, speaker synagogue.]

CHILD —
1. *Son,* בֵּן *ben.*
2 Ki. 4. 14 Verily she hath no child, and her husband
2. *Him, (upon) him,* עָלָיו *al-av.*
2 Ki. 4. 34 and he stretched himself upon the child
3. *Child,* וָלָד *valad.*
Gen. 11. 30 But Sarai was barren; she (had) no child
4. *Child,* וֶלֶד *veled* [V. L. ולד].
2 Sa. 6. 23 Michal the daughter of Saul had no child
5. *Seed,* זֶרַע *zera.*
Lev. 22. 13 be a widow, or divorced, and have no child
1 Sa. 1. 11 wilt give unto thine handmaid a man child
6. *Child,* יֶלֶד *yeled.*
Gen. 21. 8 And the child grew, and was weaned: and
21. 14 and gave (it) unto Hagar..and the child
21. 15 she cast the child under one of the shrubs
21. 16 said, Let me not see the death of the child
37. 30 The child (is) not; and I, whither shall I
42. 22 saying, Do not sin against the child; and
44. 20 and a child of his old age, a little one; and
Exod 2. 3 daubed it..and put the child therein; and
2. 6 when she had opened (it), she saw the chi.
2. 7 that she may nurse the child for thee?
2. 8 the maid went and called the child's mo.
2. 9 Take this child away, and nurse it for me
2. 9 the woman took the child, and nursed it
2. 10 the child grew, and she brought him unto
Ruth 4. 16 Naomi took the child, and laid it in her
2 Sa. 12. 15 LORD struck the child that Uriah's wife
12. 18 And it came to pass..that the child died
12. 18 feared to tell him that the child was dead
12. 18 Behold, while the child was yet alive, we
12. 18 if we tell him that the child is dead?
12. 19 David perceived that the child was dead
12. 19 David said..Is the child dead? And
12. 21 Thou didst fast and weep for the child..but
12. 21 when the child was dead, thou didst rise
12. 22 While the child was yet alive, I fasted
12. 22 GOD will be gracious..the child may live
1 Ki. 3. 25 the king said, Divide the living child in
14. 12 when thy feet enter..the child shall die
17. 21 he stretched himself upon the child three
17. 21 let this child's soul come into him again
17. 22 the soul of the child came into him again
17. 23 Elijah took the child, and brought him
2 Ki. 4. 18 when the child was grown, it fell on a
4. 26 (is it) well with the child? And she an.
4. 34 And he went up, and lay upon the child
4. 34 and the flesh of the child waxed warm
Eccl. 4. 13 Better (is) a poor and a wise child than an
4. 15 with the second child that shall stand up
Isa. 9. 6 unto us a child is born, unto us a son is
Jer. 31. 20 Ephraim my dear son..a pleasant child?
7. *Lad,* נַעַר *naar.*
Judg 13. 5, 7 for the child shall be a Nazarite
13. 8 what we shall do unto the child that
13. 12 How shall we order the child, and (how)
13. 24 the child grew, and the LORD blessed him
1 Sa. 1. 22 (I will not go up) until the child be
1. 24 she took him up..and the child (was)
1. 25 they slew a bullock, and brought the child
1. 27 For this child I prayed; and the LORD
2. 11 child did minister unto the LORD before
2. 18 ministered..(being) a child, girded with a
2. 21 And the child Samuel grew before the
2. 26 the child Samuel grew on, and was in
3. 1 the child Samuel ministered unto the
3. 8 perceived..the LORD had called the child
4. 21 And she named the child I-chabod, saying
2 Sa. 12. 16 David..besought God for the child; and
1 Ki. 3. 7 I (am but) a little child: I know not (how)
11. 17 Hadad fled, he..(being) yet a little child
14. 3 tell thee what shall become of the child
14. 17 when she came to the threshold..the child
2 Ki. 4. 29 lay my staff upon the face of the child
4. 30 the mother of the child said, (As) the
4. 31 laid the staff upon the face of the child
4. 31 told him, saying, The child is not awaked
4. 32 behold, the child was dead, (and) laid
4. 35 the child sneezed..and the child opened
5. 14 his flesh came again like..a little child
Prov 20. 11 a child is known by his doings, whether
22. 6 Train up a child in the way he should go
22. 15 Foolishness (is) bound in the heart of a c.
23. 13 Withhold not correction from the child
29. 15 but a child left to (himself) bringeth his
Eccl. 10. 16 Woe to thee..when thy king (is) a child
Isa. 3. 5 the child shall behave himself proudly
7. 16 before the child shall know to refuse the
8. 4 before the child shall have knowledge to
10. 19 the rest..shall be few, that a child may
11. 6 and a little child shall lead them
65. 20 the child shall die an hundred years old
Jer. 1. 6 behold, I cannot speak, for I (am) a child
1. 7 the LORD said..Say not, I (am) a child: for
Hos. 11. 1 When Israel (was) a child, then I loved him
8. *Youth, lad,* נֹעַר *noar.*
Job 33. 25 His flesh shall be fresher than a child's
Prov 29. 21 bringeth up his servant from a child
9. *Suckling,* עוֹלֵל *olel.*
Jer. 44. 7 to cut off from you..child and suckling
10. *Babe (newly born or unborn),* βρέφος *brephos.*
2 Ti. 3. 15 that from a child thou hast known the
11. *Babe (without full power of speech),* νήπιος.
1 Co 13. 11 When I was a child, I spake as a child
13. 11 I understood as a child, I thought as a ch.
Gal. 4. 1 the heir, as long as he is a child, differeth
12. *A little or young lad,* παιδίον *paidion.*
Mark 9. 24 straightway the father of the child cried
9. 36 he took a child, and set him in the midst
Luke 1. 59 they came to circumcise the child; and
1. 66 What manner of child shall this be! And
1. 76 thou, child, shalt be called the Prophet
1. 80 the child grew, and waxed strong in spirit
2. 17 which was told them concerning this ch.
2. 21 days..for the circumcising of [the child]
2. 27 the parents brought in the child Jesus
2. 40 the child grew, and waxed strong in spirit
9. 47 And Jesus..took a child, and set him by
9. 48 Whosoever shall receive this child in my
John 4. 49 saith..Sir, come down ere my child die
16. 21 as soon as she is delivered of the child
Heb 11. 23 because they saw (he was) a proper child
13. *A lad, boy, child, servant,* παῖς *pais.*
Matt 17. 18 the child was cured from that very hour
Luke 2. 43 the child Jesus tarried behind in Jerus.
9. 42 healed the child, and delivered him again
Acts 4. 27 of a truth against thy holy child Jesus
4. 30 done by the name of thy holy child Jesus
14. *One born, a child,* τέκνον *teknon.*
Matt 10. 21 to death, and the father the child: and the
Luke 1. 7 they had no child, because that Elizabeth
Acts 7. 5 to his seed..when (as yet) he had no child
Rev. 12. 4 devour her child as soon as it was born
12. 5 her child was caught up unto God, and
15. *Son,* υἱός *huios.*
Matt 23. 15 make him twofold more the child of hell
Acts 13. 10 (thou) child of the devil, (thou) enemy of
Rev 12. 5 And she brought forth a man child, who

[*See also* Fatherless, first, maid, man child, suckling, weaned, young.]

CHILD, to be a —
To act as a speechless babe, νηπιάζω *nēpiazō.*
1 Co 14. 20 howbeit in malice be ye children, but in

CHILD bearing —
Bearing of children, τεκνογονία *teknogonia.*
1 Tim 2. 15 she shall be saved in child bearing, if

CHILD, to be delivered of a —
1. *To bear, bring forth,* יָלַד *yalad.*
1 Ki. 3. 17 I was delivered of a child with her in the
2. *To bear a child,* τίκτω *tiktō.*
Heb. 11. 11 [was delivered of a child] when she was

CHILD, great with —
Pregnant, holding in, conceiving, ἔγκυος *egkuos.*
Luke 2. 5 Mary his..wife, being great with child

CHILD, of a —
From boyhood, παιδιόθεν *paidiothen.*
Mark 9. 21 How long is it ago..And he said, Of a ch.

CHILD or children, little —
1. *Little one,* טַף *taph.*
Num 16. 27 and their sons, and their little children
Esth. 3. 13 both young and old, little children and
Eze. 9. 6 Slay..both maids, and little children
2. *Little or young child,* παιδίον *paidion.*
Matt. 18. 2 Jesus called a little child unto him, and
18. 3 Except ye be converted..as little children
18. 4 shall humble himself as this little child
18. 5 whoso shall receive one such little child
19. 13 Then were there brought..little children
19. 14 Suffer little children, and forbid them not
Mark 10. 14 Suffer the little children to come unto me
10. 15 receive the kingdom..as a little child
Luke 18. 16 Suffer little children to come unto me
18. 17 receive the kingdom..as a little child shall
1 Jo. 2. 13 I write unto you, little children, because
2. 18 Little children, it is the last time: and as
3. *Little or young child,* τεκνίον *teknion.*
John 13. 33 Little children, yet a little while I am
Gal 4. 19 My [little children], of whom I travail in
1 Jo. 2. 1 My little children, these things write I
2. 12 little children..your sins are forgiven you
2. 28 And now, little children, abide in him
3. 7 Little children, let no man deceive you
3. 18 My little children, let us not love in word
4. 4 Ye are of God, little children, and have
5. 21 Little children, keep yourselves from idols

CHILD, only —
1. *Only one,* יָחִיד *yachid.*
Judg 11. 34 daughter came..she (was his) only child
2. *Only born,* μονογενής *monogenēs.*
Luke 9. 38 I beseech thee..for he is mine only child

CHILD, sucking —
Suckling, עוּל *ul.*
Isa. 49. 15 Can a woman forget her sucking child

CHILD, young —
Little or young lad, παιδίον *paidion.*
Matt. 2. 8 Go and search..for the young child
2. 9 it..stood over where the young child was
2. 11 they saw the young child with Mary his
2. 13, 20 Arise, and take the young child and

Matt. 2. 13 Herod will seek the young child to destroy
2. 14 he took the young child and his mother
2. 20 they are dead which sought the young chi.
2. 21 he arose, and took the young child and

CHILD, she that is with —
Full, מְלֵאָה *meleah.*
Eccl. 11. 5 in the womb of her that is with child

CHILD, with —
To conceive, הָרָה *harah.*
Gen. 16. 11 Behold, thou (art) with child and shalt
38. 24 behold, she (is) with child by whoredom
38. 25 By the man whose these (are am) I with c.
Exod 21. 22 hurt a woman with child, so that her
2 Sa. 11. 5 and told David, and said, I (am) with chi.

CHILD, to be with —
1. *To conceive*, הָרָה *harah* (הָרִיָּה *hariyyah*).
Gen. 19. 36 Thus were both..with child by their father
Isa. 26. 18 We have been with child, we have been
2. *To have in the womb*, ἔχω ἐν γαστρί [*echō*].
Matt. 1. 18 she was found with child of the Holy Gho.
1. 23 Behold, a virgin shall be with child, and
24. 19 woe unto them that are with child, and
Mark 13. 17 But woe to them that are with child
Luke 21. 23 But woe unto them that are with child
1 Th. 5. 3 upon them, as..upon a woman with chi.
Rev. 12. 2 And she being with child cried, travailing

CHILD, to travail with —
1. *To be pained (in travail)*, חוּל *chul.*
Isa. 54. 1 thou (that) didst not travail with child
2. *To bring forth*, יָלַד *yalad.*
Jer. 30. 6 see whether a man doth travail with chi.
31. 8 her that travaileth with child together

CHILD, woman with —
To conceive, הָרָה *harah* (הָרִיָּה *hariyyah*).
2 Ki 8. 12 thou wilt..rip up their women with child
15. 16 women..that were with child he ripped
Isa. 26. 17 Like as a woman with child,(that) draweth
Jer. 31. 8 the woman with child and her that
Hos. 13 16 their women with child shall be ripped
Amos 1. 13 they have ripped up the women with chi.

CHILDHOOD —
1. *Youth*, יַלְדוּת *yalduth.*
Eccl. 11. 10 Therefore remove sorrow..for childhood
2. *Boyhood*, נְעוּרִים *neurim.*
1 Sa. 12. 2 I have walked..from my childhood unto

CHILDISH —
Babyish, νήπιος *nēpios.*
1 Co. 13. 11 when I became a man, I put away child.

CHILDLESS —
1. *Barren*, עֲרִירִי *ariri.*
Gen. 15. 2 wilt thou give me, seeing I go childless
Lev. 20. 20 bear their sin ; they shall die childless
20. 21 his brother's nakedness: they shall be ch.
Jer. 22. 30 Write ye this man childless, a man (that)
2. *Childless, without a child*, ἄτεκνος *ateknos.*
Luke 20. 30 the second took her..and he died ch.

CHILDLESS, to be —
To be bereaved, שָׁכֹל *shakol.*
1 Sa. 15. 33 so shall thy mother be childless among

CHILDLESS, to make —
To bereave, שָׁכֹל *shakol*, 3.
1 Sa. 15. 33 As thy sword hath made women childless

CHILDREN — [*See* **CHILD.**]
1. *Son (produce)*, בֵּן *ben.*
Gen. 3. 16 in sorrow thou shalt bring forth children
10. 21 also, the father of all the children of Eber
10. 22 The children of Shem ; Elam, and Asshur
10. 23 And the children of Aram ; Uz and Hul
11. 5 tower, which the children of men builded
18. 19 that he will command his children and
19. 38 the same (is) the father of the children of
21. 7 Sarah should have given children suck?
22. 20 she hath also born children unto thy bro.
23. 5 the children of Heth answered Abraham
23. 7 Abraham..bowed..to the children of Heth
23. 10 Ephron dwelt among the children of Heth
23. 10 in the audience of the children of Heth
23. 18 in the presence of the children of Heth
25. 4 All these (were) the children of Keturah
25. 22 the children struggled together within
30. 1 said..Give me children, or else I die
31. 16 that (is) our's, and our children's : now
31. 43 and (these) children (are) my children
31. 43 unto their children which they have born?
32. 11 smite me,(and) the mother with the child.
32. 32 Therefore the children of Israel eat not
33. 19 his tent, at the hand of the children of H.
36. 21 these (are) the dukes..the children of Seir
36. 22 children of Lotan were Hori and Heman
36. 23 the children of Shobal (were) these; Alvan
36. 24 these (are) the children of Zibeon; both
36. 25 the children of Anah (were) these ; Dishon
36. 26 these (are) the children of Dishon; Hem.
36. 27 The children of Ezer (are) these ; Bilhan
36. 28 the children of Dishan (are) these ; Uz
36. 31 there reigned any king over the children
37. 3 loved Joseph more than all his children
45. 10 thy children, and thy children's children
45. 21 the children of Israel did so : and Joseph
46. 8 these (are) the names of the children of Is.
49. 8 thy father's children shall bow down
49. 32 The purchase..(was) from the children of
Gen. 50. 23 And Joseph saw Ephraim's children of the
50. 23 the children also of Machir the son of
50. 25 And Joseph took an oath of the children
Exod. 1. 1 Now these (are) the names of the children
1. 7 the children..were fruitful, and increased
1. 9 the people of the children of Israel (are)
1. 12 were grieved because of the children of
1. 13 the Egyptians made the children of Israel
2. 23 the children of Israel sighed by reason
2. 25 God looked upon the children of Israel
3. 9 the cry of the children of Israel is come
3. 10 mayest bring forth my people the children
3. 11 should bring forth the children of Israel
3. 13 (when) I come unto the children of Israel
3. 14, 15 Thus shalt thou say unto the children
4. 29 Moses..gathered..elders of the children
4. 31 that the LORD had visited the children of
5. 14, 15, 19 the officers of the children of Israel
6. 5 also heard the groaning of the children
6. 6 say unto the children of Israel, I (am) the
6. 9 Moses spake so unto the children of Israel
6. 11 that he let the children of Israel go out
6. 12 the children of Israel have not hearkened
6. 13 gave them a charge unto the children of
6. 13 to bring the children of Israel out of the
6. 26 Bring out the children of Israel from the
6. 27 to bring out the children of Israel from
7. 2 that he send the children of Israel out of
7. 4 I may..bring forth..the children of Israel
7. 5 bring out the children of Israel from
9. 4 nothing die of all (that is) the children's
9. 6 but of the cattle of the children of Israel
9. 26 where the children of Israel (were) was
9. 35 neither would he let the children of Israel
10. 20 so that he would not let the children of
10. 23 but all the children of Israel had light
12. 26 it shall come to pass, when your children
12. 27 who passed over the houses of the children
12. 28 the children of Israel went away, and
12. 31 both ye and the children of Israel; and go
12. 35 the children of Israel did according to the
12. 37 the children of Israel journeyed from
12. 40 the sojourning of the children of Israel
12. 42 be observed of all the children of Israel
12. 50 Thus did all the children of Israel ; as the
12. 51 the LORD did bring the children of Israel
13. 2 openeth the womb among the children
13. 13 first born of man among thy children
13. 15 but all the first born of my children I
13. 18 the children of Israel went up harnessed
13. 19 for he had straitly sworn the children of
14. 2, 15 Speak unto the children of Israel, that
14. 3 Pharaoh will say of the children of Israel
14. 8 he pursued after the children of Israel
14. 8 and the children of Israel went out with
14. 10 when Pharaoh drew nigh, the children of
14. 10 the children of Israel cried out unto the
14. 16 and the children of Israel shall go on dry
14. 22 the children of Israel went into the
14. 29 the children of Israel walked upon dry
15. 1 Then sang Moses and the children of Is.
15. 19 but the children of Israel went on dry
16. 1, 2, 9, 10 congregation of the children of Is.
16. 3 And the children of Israel said unto
16. 12 have heard the murmurings of the children
16. 15 when the children of Israel saw (it), they
16. 17 the children of Israel did so, and gathered
16. 35 the children of Israel did eat manna forty
17. 1 congregation of the children of Israel
17. 3 to kill us and our children and our cattle
17. 7 because of the chiding of the children of
19. 1 when the children of Israel were gone
19. 3 Thus shalt thou..tell the children of Is.
19. 6 which thou shalt speak unto the children
20. 5 iniquity of the fathers upon the children
20. 22 Thus thou shalt say unto the children of
21. 5 I love my master, my wife, and my child.
22. 24 be widows, and your children fatherless
24. 5 he sent young men of the children of Isr.
24. 11 upon the nobles of the children of Israel
24. 17 sight..(was)..in the eyes of the children
25. 2 Speak unto the children of Israel, that
25. 22 commandment unto the children of Israel
27. 20 thou shalt command the children of Israel
27. 21 a statute..on the behalf of the children
28. 1 And take thou..from among the children
28. 9, 11, 21, 29 the names of the children of Isr.
28. 12 stones of memorial unto the children of
28. 21, 29, 30 of the children of Israel
28. 38 which the children of Israel shall hallow
29. 28 by a statute for ever from the children of
29. 28 heave offering from the children of Israel
29. 43 there I will meet with the children of Is.
29. 45 I will dwell among the children of Israel
30. 12 When thou takest the sum of the children
30. 16 take the atonement money of the children
30. 16 a memorial unto the children of Israel
30. 31 thou shalt speak unto the children of Isr.
31. 13 Speak thou also unto the children of Isr.
31. 16 children of Israel shall keep the sabbath
31. 17 It (is) a sign between me and the children
32. 20 and made the children of Israel drink
32. 28 And the children of Levi did according to
33. 5 Say unto the children of Israel, Ye (are) a
33. 6 the children of Israel stripped themselves
34. 7 and upon the children's children unto
34. 30 when Aaron and all the children of Israel
34. 32 afterward all the children of Israel came
34. 34 he came out and spake unto the children
34. 35 the children of Israel saw the face of Mos.
35. 1, 4, 20 the congregation of the children of Is.
35. 29 The children of Israel brought a willing
Exod. 35. 30 Moses said unto the children of Israel
36. 3 which the children of Israel had brought
39. 6, 14 the names of the children of Israel
39. 7 for a memorial to the children of Israel
39. 32 and the children of Israel did according
39. 42 so the children of Israel made all the
40. 36 the children of Israel went onward in all
Lev 1. 2 Speak unto the children of Israel, and
4. 2 Speak unto the children of Israel, saying
6. 18 All the males among the children of Aaron
7. 23, 29 Speak unto the children of Israel
7. 34 shoulder have I taken of the children of
7. 34 for ever from among the children of Israel
7. 36 to be given them of the children of Israel
7. 38 he commanded the children of Israel to
9. 3 And unto the children of Israel thou
10. 11 And that ye may teach the children of Is.
10. 14 out of the sacrifices..of the children of
11. 2 Speak unto the children of Israel, saying
12. 2 Speak unto the children of Israel, saying
15. 2 Speak unto the children of Israel, and say
15. 31 Thus shall ye separate the children of Is.
16. 5 the congregation of the children of Isr.
16. 19 from the uncleanness of the children of
16. 21 confess..all the iniquities of the children
16. 34 to make an atonement for the children
17. 2 Speak..unto all the children of Israel, and
17. 5 To the end that the children of Israel
17. 12, 14 Therefore I said unto the children of
17. 13 whatsoever man (there be) of the children
18. 2 Speak unto the children of Israel, and
19. 2 all the congregation of the children of
19. 18 nor bear any grudge against the children
20. 2 thou shalt say to the children of Israel
21. 24 to his sons, and unto all the children of
22. 2, 15 from the holy things of the children of
22. 3 which the children of Israel hallow unto
22. 18 to his sons, and unto all the children of
22. 32 I will be hallowed among the children of
23. 2, 10, 24, 34 Speak unto the children of Israel
23. 43 that I made the children of Israel to
23. 44 declared unto the children of Israel the
24. 2 Command the children of Israel, that they
24. 8 (being taken) from the children of Israel
24. 10 went out among the children of Israel
24. 15 And thou shalt speak unto the children
24. 23 And Moses spake to the children of Is.
24. 23 And the children of Israel did as the
25. 2 Speak unto the children of Israel, and
25. 33 their possession among the children of Is.
25. 41, 54 (both) he and his children with him
25. 45 Moreover of the children of the strangers
25. 46 as an inheritance for your children after
25. 46 but over your brethren the children of Is.
25. 55 unto me the children of Israel (are) serv.
26. 46 LORD made between him and the children
27. 2 Speak unto the children of Israel, and
27. 34 for the children of Israel in mount Sinai
Num. 1. 2, 53 congregation of the children of Israel
1. 10 Of the children of Joseph : of Ephraim
1. 20 And the children of Reuben, Israel's eldest
1. 22 Of the children of Simeon, by their genera.
1. 24 Of the children of Gad, by their genera.
1. 26 Of the children of Judah, by their genera.
1. 28 Of the children of Issachar, by their gen.
1. 30 Of the children of Zebulun, by their
1. 32 Of the children of Joseph..of the children
1. 34 Of the children of Manasseh, by their gen.
1. 36 Of the children of Benjamin, by their gen.
1. 38 Of the children of Dan, by their genera.
1. 40 Of the children of Asher, by their genera.
1. 42 Of the children of Naphtali, throughout
1. 45 were numbered of the children of Israel
1. 49 the sum of them among the children of
1. 52 the children of Israel shall pitch their
1. 54 the children of Israel did according to
2. 2 Every man of the children of Israel shall
2. 3 Nahshon..captain of the children of Judah
2. 5 Nathaneel..captain of the children of Iss.
2. 7 Eliab..captain of the children of Zebulun
2. 10, 12, 20, 25, 27, 29 captain of the children of
2. 32 numbered of the children of Israel
2. 33 were not numbered among the children
2. 34 And the children of Israel did according
3. 4 died..and they had no children : and E.
3. 8 and the charge of the children of Israel
3. 9 given unto him out of the children of Is.
3. 12 the Levites from among the children of
3. 12 openeth the matrix among the children
3. 15 Number the children of Levi after the
3. 38 for the charge of the children of Israel
3. 40 first born of the males of the children
3. 41, 42, 45 first born among the children of
3. 41 among the cattle of the children of Israel
3. 46, 50 of the first born of the children of Isr.
5. 2 Command the children of Israel, that
5. 4 And the children of Israel did so, and
5. 4 spake unto Moses, so did the children
5. 6, 12 Speak unto the children of Israel, and
5. 9 of all the holy things of the children
6. 2 Speak unto the children of Israel and
6. 23 On this wise ye shall bless the children
6. 27 shall put my name upon the children
7. 24 Eliab..prince of the children of Zebu.
7. 30 prince of the children of Reuben
7. 36 Shelumiel..prince of the children of S
7. 42 Eliasaph..prince of the children of G
7. 48 Elishama..prince of the children of
7. 54 Gamaliel..prince of the children of
7. 60 Abidan..prince of the children of B.
7. 66 Ahiezer..prince of the children of D.
7. 72 Pagiel..prince of the children of As.

Num. 7. 78 Ahira..prince of the children of N.
8. 6, 14 Take the Levites from among the chi.
8. 9 the whole assembly of the children of Is.
8. 10 the children of Israel shall put their
8. 11 an offering of the children of Israel
8. 16 given unto me from among the children
8. 16 the first born of all the children of Israel
8. 17, 18 all the first born of the children of Is.
8. 19 to his sons from among the children of I.
8. 19 to do the service of the children of Israel
8. 19 to make an atonement for the children
8. 19 there be no plague among the children
8. 19 when the children of Israel come nigh
8. 20 all the congregation of the children of
8. 20 so did the children of Israel unto them
9. 2 Let the children of Israel also keep the pa.
9. 4 And Moses spake unto the children of Isr.
9. 5 according to..so did the children of Isr.
9. 7 we may not offer..among the children
9. 10 Speak unto the children of Israel, saying
9. 17 then after that the children of Israel
9. 17 there the children of Israel pitched their
9. 18 At the commandment..the children of Isr.
9. 19 then the children of Israel kept the charge
9. 22 the children of Israel abode in their tents
10. 12 And the children of Israel took their
10. 14 the standard of the camp of the children
10. 15 the host of the tribe of the children of Iss.
10. 16, 19, 20 the host of the tribe of the child.
10. 22 the standard of the camp of the children
10. 23, 24 the host of the tribe of the children
10. 25 the standard of the camp of the children
10. 26, 27 the host of the tribe of the children
10. 28 (were) the journeyings of the children
11. 4 and the children of Israel also wept again
13. 2 which I give unto the children of Israel
13. 3 all those men (were) heads of the children
13. 24 which the children of Israel cut down
13. 26 to all the congregation of the children
13. 32 they had searched unto the children
14. 2 And all the children of Israel murmured
14. 5 of the congregation of the children of Is.
14. 7 unto all the company of the children
14. 10 appeared..before all the children of Israel
14. 18 visiting the iniquity..upon the children
14. 27 heard the murmurings of the children of
14. 33 your children shall wander in the wilder.
14. 39 told these sayings unto all the children
15. 2, 18, 38 Speak unto the children of Israel
15. 25, 26 all the congregation of the children
15. 29 him that is born among the children
15. 32 while the children of Israel were in the
16. 2 with certain of the children of Israel
16. 38 they shall be a sign unto the children
16. 40 a memorial unto the children of Israel
16. 41 all the congregation of the children
17. 2 Speak unto the children of Israel, and take
17. 5 the murmurings of the children of Israel
17. 6 And Moses spake unto the children of Is.
17. 9 before the LORD unto all the children
17. 12 And the children of Israel spake unto M.
18. 5 no wrath any more upon the children
18. 6 the Levites from among the children
18. 8 all the hallowed things of the children
18. 11 all the wave offerings of the children of
18. 19 which the children of Israel offer unto
18. 20 thine inheritance among the children of
18. 21 I have given the children of Levi all the
18. 22 Neither must the children of Israel
18. 23 among the children of Israel they have
18. 24 But the tithes of the children of Israel
18. 24 Among the children of Israel they shall
18. 26 When ye take of the children of Israel
18. 28 which ye receive of the children of Israel
18. 32 pollute the holy things of the children
19. 2 Speak unto the children of Israel, that
19. 9 for the congregation of the children of Is.
19. 10 and it shall be unto the children of Israel
20. 1 Then came the children of Israel, (even)
20. 12 to sanctify me in the eyes of the children
20. 13 because the children of Israel strove
20. 19 And the children of Israel said unto him
20. 22 And the children of Israel..journeyed
20. 24 which I have given unto the children of
21. 10 And the children of Israel set forward
21. 24 even unto the children of Ammon
21. 24 the border of the children of Ammon
22. 1 And the children of Israel set forward
22. 3 Moab was distressed because of the chil.
22. 5 the river..of the children of his people
24. 17 and destroy all the children of Sheth
25. 6 one of the children of Israel came and
25. 6 of all the congregation of the children of
25. 8 the plague was stayed from the children
25. 11 turned my wrath away from the children
25. 11 that I consumed not the children of
25. 13 made an atonement for the children
26. 2 of all the congregation of the children
26. 4 commanded Moses and the children
26. 5 the eldest son..the children of Reuben
26. 11 Notwithstanding the children of Korah
26. 15 The children of Gad after their families
26. 18 These (are) the families of the children
26. 44 (Of) the children of Asher after their
26. 51 These (were) the numbered of the child.
26. 62 not numbered among the children
26. 62 given them among the children of Israel
26. 63, 64 numbered the children of Israel in
27. 8 thou shalt speak unto the children of Is.
27. 11 it shall be unto the children of Israel
27. 12 which I have given unto the children
27. 20 all the congregation of the children

Num. 27. 21 and all the children of Israel with him
28. 2 Command the children of Israel, and say
29. 40 And Moses told the children of Israel
30. 1 Moses spake..concerning the children
31. 2 Avenge the children of Israel of the Mid.
31. 9 And the children of Israel took (all) the
31. 12 unto the congregation of the children
31. 16 Behold, these caused the children of Isr.
31. 30, 42, 47 of the children of Israel's half
31. 54 (for) a memorial for the children of Israel
32. 1 children of Reuben and the children of G.
32. 2, 25 The children of Gad and the children
32. 29, 31 the children of Gad and the children
32. 6 And Moses said unto the children of Gad
32. 6 And Moses said..to the children of Reu.
32. 7, 9 discourage ye..the children of Israel
32. 17 will go ready armed before the children
32. 18 until the children Israel have inherited
32. 28 fathers of the tribes of the children of Is.
32. 33 gave unto them, (even) to the children of
32. 33 and to the children of Reuben, and unto
32. 34 And the children of Gad built Dibon
32. 37 And the children of Reuben built Heshbon
32. 39 And the children of Machir..went to Gil.
33. 1 These (are) the journeys of the children
33. 3 on the morrow..the children of Israel
33. 5 And the children of Israel removed from
33. 38 after the children of Israel were come out
33. 40 heard of the coming of the children of Is.
33. 51 Speak unto the children of Israel, and
34. 2 Command the children of Israel, and say
34. 13 Moses commanded the children
34. 14 For the tribe of the children of Reuben
34. 14 and the tribe of the children of Gad
34. 20 And of the tribe of the children of Simeon
34. 22 the prince of the tribe of the children
34. 23 The prince of the children of Joseph
34. 23 for the tribe of the children of Manasseh
34. 24, 25, 26, 27, 28 of the tribe of the children
34. 29 divide the inheritance unto the children
35. 2 Command the children of Israel, that they
35. 8 the possession of the children of Israel
35. 10 Speak unto the children of Israel, and
35. 15 for the children of Israel, and for the
35. 34 for I the LORD dwell among the children
36. 1 of the families of the children of Gilead
36. 1 the chief fathers of the children of Israel
36. 2 for an inheritance by lot to the children
36. 3 of the (other) tribes of the children of Isr.
36. 4 when the jubilee of the children of Israel
36. 5 Moses commanded the children of Israel
36. 7 the inheritance of the children of Israel
36. 7 every one of the children of Israel shall
36. 8 in any tribe of the children of Israel
36. 8 that the children of Israel may enjoy
36. 9 every one of the tribes of the children
36. 13 Moses unto the children of Israel
Deut. 1. 3 Moses spake unto the children of Israel
1. 36 I give the land..and to his children
1. 39 and your children,..they shall go in
2. 4 coast of your brethren the children of E.
2. 8 from our brethren the children of Esau
2. 9, 19 I have given Ar unto the children of L.
2. 12 but the children of Esau succeeded them
2. 19 comest nigh over against the children
2. 19, 37 the land of the children of Ammon
2. 22 As he did to the children of Esau
2. 29 As the children of Esau which dwelt in S.
3. 11 (is) it not in Rabbath of the children of A.
3. 16 (which is) the border of the children of A.
3. 18 before your brethren the children of Isr.
4. 10 and (that) they may teach their children
4. 25 thou shalt beget children, and children's
4. 40 with thee, and with thy children after
4. 44 which Moses set before the children of I.
4. 45 which Moses spake unto the children of
4. 46 whom Moses and the children of Israel
5. 9 visiting the iniquity..upon the children
5. 29 with them, and with their children for
6. 7 thou shalt teach them..unto thy children
9. 2 A people great and tall, the children of
9. 2 Who can stand before the children of A.
10. 6 And the children of Israel took their
10. 6 from Beeroth of the children of Jaakan
11. 2 for (I speak) not with your children
11. 19 And ye shall teach them your children
11. 21 and the days of your children, in the
12. 25 with thee, and with thy children after
12. 28 and with thy children after thee for ever
13. 13 the children of Belial, are gone out from
14. 1 Ye (are) the children of the LORD your
17. 20 may prolong (his) days..and his children
21. 15 and they have born him children
23. 8 The children that are begotten of them
24. 7 stealing any of his brethren of the children
24. 16 for the children, neither shall the children
28. 54 and toward the remnant of his children
28. 55 to any..of the flesh of his children
28. 57 toward her children which she shall bear
29. 1 to make with the children of Israel in the
29. 22 of your children that shall rise up after
29. 29 unto us and to our children for ever
30. 2 thou and thy children, with all thine
31. 13 And (that) their children..may hear, and
31. 19 and teach it the children of Israel
31. 19 a witness for me against the children of
31. 22 and taught it the children of Israel
31. 23 for thou shalt bring the children of Isr.
32. 5 their spot (is) not (the spot) of his children
32. 8 according to the number of the children
32. 20 a very froward generation, children in
32. 46 which ye shall command your children

Deut. 32. 49 which I give unto the children of Israel
32. 51 against me among the children of Israel
32. 51 not in the midst of the children of
32. 52 unto the land which I give the children
33. 1 Moses the man of God blessed the child.
33. 9 nor knew his own children: for they have
33. 24 (Let) Asher (be) blessed with children
34. 8 And the children of Israel wept for Moses
34. 9 and the children of Israel hearkened unto
Josh. 1. 2 I do give to them..to the children of Isr.
2. 2 there came men..of the children of Israel
3. 1 to Jordan, he and all the children of Israel
3. 9 And Joshua said unto the children of Is.
4. 4 whom he had prepared of the children
4. 5, 8 according unto the number of the..ch.
4. 6 when your children ask (their fathers) in
4. 7 for a memorial unto the children of Isr.
4. 8 the children of Israel did so as Joshua
4. 12 the children of Reuben, and the children
4. 12 passed over armed before the children of
4. 21 And he spake unto the children of Israel
4. 21 When your children shall ask their
4. 22 Then ye shall let your children know
5. 1 dried up the waters..from before the ch.
5. 1 neither was there spirit..because of the ch.
5. 2 and circumcise again the children of Isr.
5. 3 and circumcised the children of Israel
5. 6 For the children of Israel walked forty
5. 7 And their children..them Joshua
5. 10 And the children of Israel encamped in
5. 12 neither had the children of Israel manna
6. 1 because of the children of Israel: none
7. 1 the children of Israel committed a
7. 1 anger of the LORD was kindled ag. the c.
7. 12 Therefore the children of Israel could not
7. 23 unto Joshua, and unto all the children of
8. 31 Moses..commanded the children of Israel
8. 32 in the presence of the children of Israel
9. 17 And the children of Israel journeyed
9. 18 And the children of Israel smote them
9. 26 out of the hand of the children of Israel
10. 4 with Joshua and with the children of Is.
10. 11 whom the children of Israel slew with
10. 12 up the Amorites before the children of I.
10. 20 Joshua and the children of Israel had
10. 21 his tongue against any of the children
11. 14 the children of Israel took for a prey
11. 19 that made peace with the children of Is.
11. 22 none..left in the land of the children of
12. 1 which the children of Israel smote
12. 2 (which is) the border of the children of A.
12. 6 Them did Moses..and the children of I.
12. 7 Joshua and the children of Israel smote
13. 6 drive out from before the children of Isra.
13. 10 unto the border of the children of Ammon
13. 13 Nevertheless the children of Israel expe.
13. 15 Moses gave unto..the children of Reuben
13. 22 Balaam..did the children of Israel slay
13. 23 the border of the children of Reuben
13. 23 This (was) the inheritance of the children
13. 24 unto the children of Gad according to
13. 25 half the land of the children of Ammon
13. 28 This (is) the inheritance of the children
13. 29 of the children of Manasseh by their
13. 31 (pertaining) unto the children of Machir
13. 31 to the one half of the children of Machir
14. 1 which the children of Israel inherited in
14. 1 the heads of the fathers of the..children
14. 4 For the children of Joseph were two tribes
14. 5 so the children of Israel did, and they
14. 6 Then the children of Judah came unto J.
14. 9 thine inheritance, and thy children's for
15. 1 of the children of Judah by their families
15. 12 This (is) the coast of the children of J.
15. 13 he gave a part among the children of J.
15. 20, 21 of the tribe of the children of Judah
15. 63 the children of Judah could not drive them
15. 63 the Jebusites dwell with the children of J.
16. 1 the lot of the children of Joseph fell from
16. 4 So the children of Joseph..took their
16. 5 the border of the children of Ephraim..
16. 8 This (is) the inheritance..of the children
16. 9 the separate cities for the children of E.
16. 9 among the inheritance of the children of
17. 2 for the rest of the children of Manasseh
17. 2 for the children of Abiezer..the children
17. 2 the children of Asriel..the children of S.
17. 2 the children of Hepher..the children of
17. 2 these were the male children of Manasseh
17. 8 Tappuah..(belonged) to the children of E.
17. 12 the children of Manasseh could not drive
17. 13 when the children of Israel were waxen
17. 14 And the children of Joseph spake unto J.
17. 16 And the children of Joseph said, The hill
18. 1 the whole congregation of the children
18. 2 remained among the children of Israel
18. 3 And Joshua said unto the children of I.
18. 10 Joshua divided the land unto the children
18. 11 the lot of the tribe of the children of B.
18. 11 children of Judah and the children of J.
18. 14 Kirjath-jearim, a city of the children of
18. 20 This (was) the inheritance of the children
18. 21 Now the cities..of the children of Benja.
18. 28 This (is) the inheritance of the children
19. 1, 8 the tribe of the children of Simeon
19. 1 within the inheritance of the children of
19. 9 Out of the portion of the children of Jud.
19. 9 the inheritance of the children of Simeon
19. 9 the part of the children of Judah was too
19. 9 therefore the children..had their inheri.
19. 10 the third lot came up for the children
19. 16 This (is) the inheritance of the children

Josh. 19. 17 for the children..according to their fam
19. 23 This (is) the inheritance..of the children
19. 24, 31 for the tribe of the children of Asher
19. 32 The sixth lot came out to the children of
19. 32 for the children of Naphtali according to
19. 39 This is the inheritance..of the children of
19. 40, 48 tribe of the children of Dan according
19. 47 And the coast of the children of Dan went
19. 47 therefore the children of Dan went up to
19. 49 the children of Israel gave an inheritance
19. 51 the heads of the fathers..of the children
20. 2 Speak to the children of Israel, saying
20. 9 appointed for all the children of Israel
21. 1 heads of the fathers..of the children of I.
21. 3 And the children of Israel gave unto the
21. 4 and the children of Aaron..had by lot
21. 5 And the rest of the children of Kohath
21. 6 the children of Gershon (had) by lot out
21. 7 The children of Merari by their families
21. 8 the children of Israel gave by lot unto
21. 9 they gave out of the tribe of the children
21. 9 and out of the tribe of the children of S.
21. 10 Which the children of Aaron..had
21. 10 of the Kohathites..of the children of L.
21. 13 Thus they gave to the children of Aaron
21. 19 All the cities of the children of Aaron
21. 20 the families of the children of Kohath
21. 20 Levites which remained of the children
21. 26 for the families of the children of Kohath
21. 27 unto the children of Gershon, of the fam.
21. 34 unto the families of the children of Merari
21. 40 So all the cities for the children of Merari
21. 41 within the possession of the children
22. 9 the children of Reuben, and the children
22. 9 and departed from the children of Israel
22. 10, 11, 21, 30, 34 children of Reuben, and the
22. 11 the children of Israel heard say, Behold
22. 11 at the passage of the children of Israel
22. 12 And when the children of Israel heard
22. 12 the whole congregation of the children
22. 13 children of Israel sent unto the children
22. 15 children of Reuben, and to the children
22. 24 your children might speak unto our chil.
22. 25 ye children of Reuben and children of G.
22. 25 your children make our children cease
22. 27 your children may not say to our children
22. 30 the children of Gad, and the children
22. 31 Phinehas..said unto the children of R.
22. 31 the children of Gad, and to the children
22. 32 Phinehas..returned from the children of
22. 32 from the children of Gad..to the children
22. 33 And the thing pleased the children of Is.
22. 33 and the children of Israel blessed God
22. 33 wherein the children of Reuben and Gad
24. 4 Jacob and his children went down into E.
24. 32 which the children of Israel brought up
24. 32 it became the inheritance of the children
Judg. 1. 1 that the children of Israel asked the LORD
1. 8 the children of Judah had fought against
1. 9 afterward the children of Judah went
1. 16 the children..Kenite, Moses' father-in-law
1. 16 with the children of Judah into the wilder.
1. 21 the children of Benjamin did not drive
1. 21 but the Jebusites dwell with the children
1. 34 the Amorites forced the children of Dan
2. 4 when the angel..spake..unto all the chil.
2. 6 the children of Israel went every man
2. 11 the children of Israel did evil in the sight
3. 2 generations of the children of Israel might
3. 5 the children of Israel dwelt among the C.
3. 7 the children of Israel did evil in the sight
3. 8, 14 the children of Israel served Chushan
3. 9, 15 the children of Israel cried unto the
3. 9 the LORD raised up a deliverer to the chi.
3. 12 the children of Israel did evil again
3. 13 he gathered unto him the children
3. 15 by him the children of Israel sent
3. 27 the children of Israel went down with him
4. 1 the children of Israel again did evil in
4. 3 the children of Israel cried unto the LORD
4. 3 he mightily oppressed the children of Is.
4. 5 the children of Israel came up to her for
4. 6 take..ten thousand men of the children
4. 11 Now Heber..of the children of Hobab
4. 23 God subdued..Jabin..before the children
4. 24 hand of the children of Israel prospered
6. 1 the children of Israel did evil in the sight
6. 2 the children of Israel made them the dens
6. 3, 33 the children of the east, even they
6. 6, 7 the children of Israel cried unto the
6. 8 the LORD sent a prophet unto the children
7. 12 all the children of the east lay along in the
8. 10 all the hosts of the children of the east
8. 18 each one resembled the children of a king
8. 28 Thus was Midian subdued before the chi.
8. 33 that the children of Israel turned again
8. 34 the children of Israel remembered not
10. 6 And the children of Israel did evil again
10. 6 the gods of Moab, and..of the children
10. 7 into the hands of the children of Ammon
10. 8 they vexed and oppressed the children
10. 8 eighteen years, all the children of Israel
10. 9 the children of Ammon passed over Jor.
10. 10 the children of Israel cried unto the LORD
10. 11 the LORD said unto the children of Israel
10. 11 (Did) not (I deliver you)..from the chil.
10. 15 the children of Israel said unto the LORD
10. 17 the children of Ammon were gathered
10. 17 the children of Israel assembled themse.
10. 18 will begin to fight against the children
11. 4, 5 the children of Ammon made war aga.
11. 6 that we may fight with the children of A.
11. 8, 9 fight against the children of Ammon and
11. 12, 13, 14, 28 the king of the children of A.
11. 15 nor the land of the children of Ammon
11. 27 the children of Israel and the children
11. 29, 30 he passed over (unto) the children of
11. 31 when I return in peace from the children
11. 32 Jephthah passed over unto the children
11. 33 the children..were subdued before the
11. 36 of thine enemies, (even) of the children of
12. 1 over to fight against the children of A.
12. 2 at great strife with the children of Amm.
12. 3 and passed over against the children
13. 1 the children of Israel did evil again in the
14. 16 thou hast put forth a riddle unto the chi.
14. 17 she told the riddle to the children of her
18. 2 the children of Dan sent of their family
18. 16 six hundred men..which (were) of the c.
18. 22 gathered together, and overtook the ch.
18. 23 And they cried unto the children of Dan
18. 25 And the children of Dan said unto him
18. 26 And the children of Dan went their way
18. 30 And the children of Dan set up the graven
19. 12 that (is) not of the children of Israel
19. 30 the day that the children of Israel came
20. 1 Then all the children of Israel went out
20. 3 Now the children of Benjamin heard that
20. 3 the children of Israel were gone up to M.
20. 7 Behold, ye (are) all children of Israel
20. 13 Now therefore deliver (us)..the children
20. 13 the children of Benjamin would not
20. 13 to the voice of their brethren the children
20. 14 the children of Benjamin gathered them.
20. 14 to go out to battle against the children
20. 15 And the children of Benjamin were num.
20. 18 the children of Israel arose, and went up
20. 18, 23, 28 against the children of Benjamin
20. 19 the children of Israel rose up in the
20. 21 the children of Benjamin came forth
20. 23 the children of Israel went up and wept
20. 24 the children of Israel came near against
20. 25 destroyed down to the ground of the chil.
20. 26 Then all the children of Israel..went up
20. 27 the children of Israel enquired of the LORD
20. 30 the children of Israel went up against
20. 31 the children of Benjamin went out
20. 32 the children of Benjamin said, They (are)
20. 32 the children Israel said, Let us flee
20. 35 the children of Israel destroyed of the
20. 36 the children of Benjamin saw that they
20. 48 turned again upon the children of Benja.
21. 5 the children of Israel said, Who (is there)
21. 6 the children of Israel repented them for
21. 13 sent (some) to speak to the children of B.
21. 18 for the children of Israel have sworn
21. 20 they commanded the children of Benja.
21. 23 And the children of Benjamin did so
21. 24 And the children of Israel departed thence
1 Sa. 2. 5 she that hath many children is waxed
2. 28 offerings made by fire of the children
7. 4 Then the children of Israel did put away
7. 6 Samuel judged the children of Israel in
7. 7 the children of Israel were gathered
7. 7 And when the children of Israel heard (it)
7. 8 And the children of Israel said to Samuel
9. 2 (there was) not among the children of Is.
10. 18 And said unto the children of Israel
10. 27 the children of Belial said, How shall this
11. 8 the children of Israel were three hundred
12. 12 the king of the children of Ammon came
14. 18 ark..was at that time with the children
14. 47 against the children of Ammon, and
15. 6 ye showed kindness to all the children
26. 19 if (they be) the children of men, cursed
30. 22 to every man his wife and his children
2 Sa. 1. 18 Also he bade them teach the children
7. 6 I brought up the children of Israel out of
7. 7 I have walked with all the children of Isr.
7. 10 neither shall the children of wickedness
7. 14 with the stripes of the children of men
8. 12 of the children of Ammon, and of the
10. 1 the king of the children of Ammon died
10. 2 came into the land of the children of A.
10. 3 the princes of the children of Ammon said
10. 6 And when the children of Ammon saw
10. 6 the children of Ammon sent and hired
10. 8 And the children of Ammon came out
10. 10 put (them) in array against the children
10. 11 if the children of Ammon be too strong
10. 14 And when the children of Ammon saw
10. 14 So Joab returned from the children of A.
10. 19 So the Syrians feared to help the children
11. 1 and they destroyed the children of Am.
12. 3 together with him and with his children
12. 9 slain him with the sword of the children
12. 26 against Rabbah of the children of Ammon
12. 31 unto all the cities of the children of Am.
17. 27 Nahash of Rabbah of the children of A.
21. 2 the Gibeonites (were) not of the children
21. 2 the children of Israel had sworn unto them
21. 2 in his zeal to the children of Israel and J.
1 Ki. 2. 4 If thy children take heed to their way
4. 30 excelled the wisdom of all the children
6. 1 after the children of Israel were come out
6. 13 I will dwell among the children of Israel
8. 1 chief of the fathers of the children of Is.
8. 9 the LORD made (a covenant) with the chil.
8. 25 so that thy children take heed to their
8. 39 thou..knowest the hearts of all the chil.
8. 63 all the children of Israel dedicated the
9. 6 from following me, ye or your children
9. 20 which (were) not of the children of Israel
9. 21 Their children that were left after them
1 Ki. 9. 21 whom the children of Israel also were not
9. 22 of the children of Israel did Solomon make
11. 2 the LORD said unto the children of Israel
11. 7 abomination of the children of Ammon
11. 33 Milcom the god of the children of Ammon
12. 17 But (as for) the children of Israel which
12. 24 against your brethren the children of Is.
12. 33 ordained a feast unto the children of Isr.
18. 20 So Ahab sent unto all the children of Isr.
19. 10, 14 the children of Israel have forsaken
20. 3 thy wives also and thy children, (even) the
20. 5 gold, and thy wives, and thy children
20. 7 he sent unto me..for my children
20. 15 all the children of Israel, (being) seven th.
20. 27 And the children of Israel were numbered
20. 29 and the children of Israel slew of the Syr.
21. 13 there came in two men, children of Belial
21. 26 whom the LORD cast out before the child.
2 Ki. 4. 7 and live thou and thy children of the rest
8. 12 that thou wilt do unto the children of Is.
8. 19 to give..alway a light, (and) to his children
9. 1 Elisha..called one of the children of
10. 13 we go down to salute the children of the
10. 30 thy children..shall sit on the throne of Is.
13. 5 the children of Israel dwelt in their tents
14. 6 the children of the murderers he slew not
14. 6 shall not be put to death for the children
16. 3 the LORD cast out from before the children
17. 7 that the children of Israel had sinned
17. 8 the LORD cast out from before the child.
17. 9 the children of Israel did secretly (those)
17. 22 the children of Israel walked in all the
17. 24 placed..instead of the children of Israel
17. 31 Sepharvites burnt their children
17. 34 the LORD commanded the children of J.
17. 41 children, and their children's children: as
18. 4 the children of Israel did burn incense to
19. 3 for the children are come to the birth, and
19. 12 children of Eden which (were) in T.?
21. 2, 9 before the children of Israel
23. 6 upon the graves of the children of the
23. 10 (is) in the valley of the children of H.
23. 13 Milcom the abomination of the children
24. 2 sent..bands of the children of Ammon
1 Ch. 1. 43 before (any) king reigned over the chil.
4. 27 but his brethren had not many children
4. 27 neither..multiply, like to the children of
5. 11 the children of Gad dwelt over against
5. 14 These (are) the children of Abihail the son
5. 23 the children of the half tribe of Manasseh
6. 3 And the children of Amram; Aaron, and
6. 33 they that waited with their children: of
6. 64 the children of Israel gave to the Levites
6. 65, 65 out of the tribe of the children of
6. 65 out of the tribe of the children of Benja.
7. 12 Shuppim also, and Huppim, the children
7. 29 by the borders of the children of Manas.
7. 29 In these dwelt the children of Joseph the
7. 33 These (are) the children of Japhlet
7. 40 All these (were) the children of Asher
9. 3 in Jerusalem dwelt of the children of J.
9. 3 children of Benjamin, and of the children
9. 4 the children of Pharez the son of Judah
9. 18 in the companies of the children of Levi
9. 23 they and their children (had) the oversight
11. 31 (that pertained) to the children of Benj.
12. 16 there came of the children of Benjamin
12. 24 the children of Judah that bare shield
12. 25 the children of Simeon, mighty men of
12. 26 Of the children of Levi, four thousand
12. 29 of the children of Benjamin, the kindred
12. 30 of the children of Ephraim twenty
12. 32 of the children of Issachar, (which were)
16. 13 ye children of Jacob, his chosen ones
17. 9 neither shall the children of wickedness
18. 11 from the children of Ammon, and from
19. 1 Nahash the king of the children of A.
19. 2 came into the land of the children of A.
19. 3 the princes of the children of Ammon said
19. 6 when the children of Ammon saw that
19. 6 Hanun and the children of Ammon sent
19. 7 the children of Ammon gathered them.
19. 9 the children of Ammon came out, and put
19. 11 they set..in array against the children of
19. 12 if the children of Ammon be too strong
19. 15 And when the children of Ammon saw
19. 19 neither would..help the children of Am.
20. 1 wasted the country of the children of A.
20. 3 with all the cities of the children of Am.
24. 2 Nadab and Abihu died..and had no chil.
27. 1 the children of Israel after their number
27. 3 Of the children of Perez (was) the chief
27. 10, 14, 20 of the children of Ephraim
28. 8 an inheritance for your children after you
2 Ch. 5. 2 the chief of the fathers of the children of
5. 10 LORD made (a covenant) with the child.
6. 11 that he made with the children of Israel
6. 16 yet so that thy children take heed to
6. 30 for thou only knowest..the children of
7. 3 when all the children of Israel saw how
8. 2 caused the children of Israel to dwell
8. 8 of their children..whom the children of
8. 9 of the children of Israel did Solomon
10. 17 (as for) the children of Israel that dwelt
10. 18 children of Israel stoned him with stones
11. 19 Which bare him children; Jeush, and
11. 23 dispersed of all his children throughout
13. 7 gathered unto him vain men, the children
13. 12 O children of Israel, fight ye not against
13. 16 the children of Israel fled before Judah
13. 18 the children of Israel were brought under
13. 18 the children of Judah prevailed, because

2 Ch. 20. 1 children of Moab, and the children of A.
20. 10, 23 the children of Ammon and Moab
20. 13 with their little ones..and their children
20. 19 children of the Kohathites, and of the ch.
20. 22 LORD set ambushments against the chil.
21. 14 thy children, and thy wives, and all thy
25. 4 he slew not their children, but (did) as (it
25. 4 The fathers shall not die for the children
25. 4 neither shall the children die for the
25. 7 (to wit, with) all the children of Ephraim
25. 11 smote of the children of Seir ten thous.
25. 12 did the children of Judah carry away
25. 14 that he brought the gods of the children
27. 5 the children of Ammon gave him the
27. 5 So much did the children of Ammon pay
28. 3 burnt his children in the fire, after the
28. 3 the LORD had cast out before the children
28. 8 the children of Israel carried away captive
28. 10 ye purpose to keep under the children of
28. 12 certain of the heads of the children of E.
30. 6 Ye children of Israel, turn again unto the
30. 9 your brethren and your children (shall)
30. 21 the children of Israel..kept the feast of
31. 1 Then all the children of Israel returned
31. 5 the children of Israel brought in
31. 6 (concerning) the children of Israel and J.
33. 2 whom the LORD had..before the children
33. 6 he caused his children to pass through the
33. 9 whom the LORD had..before the children
34. 33 that (pertained) to the children of Israel
35. 17 the children of Israel..kept the passover
Ezra 2. 1 these (are) the children of the province
2. 3 The children of Parosh, two thousand an
2. 4 The children of Shephatiah, three hundred
2. 5 The children of Arah, seven hundred
2. 6 children of Pahath-moab, of the children
2. 7 The children of Elam, a thousand two h.
2. 8 The children of Zattu, nine hundred forty
2. 9 The children of Zaccai, seven hundred and
2. 10 The children of Bani, six hundred forty
2. 11 The children of Bebai, six hundred twenty
2. 12 The children of Azgad, a thousand two
2. 13 The children of Adonikam, six hundred
2. 14 The children of Bigvai, two thousand fifty
2. 15 The children of Adin, four hundred fifty
2. 16 The children of Ater of Hezekiah, ninety
2. 17 The children of Bezai, three hundred
2. 18 The children of Jorah, an hundred and
2. 19 The children of Hashum, two hundred
2. 20 The children of Gibbar, ninety and five
2. 21 The children of Beth-lehem, an hundred
2. 24 The children of Azmaveth, forty and two
2. 25 The children of Kirjath-arim, Chephirah
2. 26 The children of Ramah and Gaba, six h.
2. 29 The children of Nebo, fifty and two
2. 30 The children of Magbish, an hundred fifty
2. 31 The children of..Elam, a thousand two
2. 32 The children of Harim, three hundred
2. 33 The children of Lod, Hadid, and Ono
2. 34 The children of Jericho, three hundred
2. 35 The children of Senaah, three thousand
2. 36 the children of Jedaiah, of the house of
2. 37 The children of Immer, a thousand fifty
2. 38 The children of Pashur, a thousand two
2. 39 The children of Harim, a thousand and
2. 40 the children of Jeshua, and Kadmiel
2. 40 of the children of Hodaviah, seventy and
2. 41 the children of Asaph, an hundred twenty
2. 42 The children of the porters: the children
2. 42 children of Talmon, the children of Ak.
2. 42 the children of Hatita, the children of
2. 43 The Nethinims: the children of Ziha
children of Hasupha, the ch. of Tabbaoth
2. 44 The children of Keros..children of Siaha
the children of Padon
2. 45 The children of Lebanah, the children of
Hagabah, the children of Akkub
2. 46 The children of Hagab, the children of
Shalmai, the children of Hanan
2. 47 The children of Giddel, the children of
Gahar, the children of Reaiah
2. 48 The children of Rezin, the children of
Nekoda, the children of Gazzam
2. 49 The children of Uzzah, the children of
Paseah, the children of Besai
2. 50 The children of Asnah, the children of
Mehunim, the children of Nephusim
2. 51 The children of Bakbuk, the children
of Hakupha, the children of Harhur
2. 52 The children of Bazluth, the children
of Mehida, the children of Harsha
2. 53 The children of Barkos, the children of
Sisera, the children of Thamah
2. 54 The children of Neziah..chil. of Hatipha
2. 55 The children of Solomon's servants
the children of Sotai, the children of
Sophereth, the children of Peruda
2. 56 The children of Jaalah, the children of
Darkon, the children of Giddel
2. 57 The ch. of Shephatiah, the ch. of Hattil
ch. of Pochereth of Zebaim, the ch. of Ami
2. 58 the children of Solomon's servants, (were)
2. 60 The children of Delaiah, the children of
2. 60 the children of Nekoda, six hundred fifty
2. 61 the children of the priests: the children
2. 61 the children of Koz, the children of
3. 1 and the children of Israel (were) in the
4. 1 the children of the captivity builded the
6. 16 the children of Israel, the priests, and the
6. 16 rest of the children of the captivity, kept
6. 19, 20 the children of the captivity
6. 21 the children of Israel..did eat
Ezra 7. 7 there went up (some) of the children
8. 35 the children of those that had been carried
9. 12 leave (it) for an inheritance to your chil.
10. 7 unto all the children of the captivity
10. 16 the children of the captivity did so
10. 44 had wives by whom they had children
Neh. 1. 6 for the children of Israel thy servants, and
1. 6 confess the sins of the children of Israel
2. 10 seek the welfare of the children of Israel
5. 5 our children as their children; and, lo, we
7. 6 These (are) the children of the province
7. 8 The children of Parosh, two thousand an
7. 9 The children of Shephatiah, three hun.
7. 10 The children of Arah, six hundred fifty
7. 11 of the children of Jeshua and Joab, two
7. 12 The children of Elam, a thousand two h.
7. 13 The children of Zattu, eight hundred
7. 14 The children of Zaccai, seven hundred
7. 15 The children of Binnui, six hundred forty
7. 16 The children of Bebai, six hundred
7. 17 The children of Azgad, two thousand
7. 18 The children of Adonikam, six hundred
7. 19 The children of Bigvai, two thousand
7. 20 The children of Adin, six hundred fifty
7. 21 The children of Ater of Hezekiah, ninety
7. 22 The children of Hashum, three hundred
7. 23 The children of Bezai, three hundred
7. 24 The children of Hariph, an hundred and
7. 25 The children of Gibeon, ninety and five
7. 34 The children of the other Elam, a thou.
7. 35, 42 The children of Harim, three hundred
7. 36 The children of Jericho, three hundred
7. 37 The children of Lod, Hadid, and Ono
7. 38 The children of Senaah, three thousand
7. 39 the children of Jedaiah, of the house of
7. 40 The children of Immer, a thousand fifty
7. 41 The children of Pashur, a thousand two
7. 43 the children of Jeshua..of the children of
7. 44 the children of Asaph, an hundred forty
7. 45 the children of Shallum, the children of
7. 45 the children of Talmon, the children of
7. 45 the children of Hatita, the children of
7. 46 The Nethinims: the children of Ziha
7. 46 the children of Hashupha, the children of
7. 47 The children of Keros, the children of Sia,
the children of Padon
7. 48 The children of Lebana, the children of
Hagaba, the children of Shalmai
7. 49 The children of Hanan, the children of
Giddel, the children of Gahar
7. 50 The children of Reaiah, the children of
Rezin, the children of Nekoda
7. 51 The children of Gazzam, the children of
Uzza, the children of Phaseah
7. 52 The children of Besai, the children of
Meunim, the children of Nephishesim
7. 53 The children of Bakbuk, the children of
Hakupha, the children of Harhur
7. 54 The children of Bazlith, the children of
Mehida, the children of Harsha
7. 55 The children of Barkos, the children of
Sisera, the children of Tamah
7. 56 The children of Neziah, the ch. of Hatipha
7. 57 The children of Solomon's servants
the children of Sotai, the children of
Sophereth, the children of Perida
7. 58 The children of Jaala, the children of
Darkon, the children of Giddel
7. 59 The children of Shephatiah, the ch. of H.
the children of Pochereth..the ch. of A.
7. 60 the children of Solomon's servants, (were)
7. 62 The children of Delaiah, the children of
Tobiah, the children of Nekoda
7. 63 And of the priests: the children of Hab.
7. 63 the children of Koz, the children of Bar.
7. 73 the children of Israel (were) in their cities
8. 14 that the children of Israel should dwell
8. 17 unto that day had not the children of Is.
9. 1 the children of Israel were assembled with
9. 23 Their children also multipliedst thou as
9. 24 So the children went in and possessed
10. 39 For the children of Israel and the chil.
11. 3 and the children of Solomon's servants
11. 4 at Jerusalem dwelt (certain) of the chil.
11. 4 dwelt (certain)..of the children of Benja.
11. 4 Of the children of Judah..of the children
11. 25 (some) of the children of Judah dwelt at
11. 31 The children also of Benjamin from Geba
12. 47 Levites sanctified (them) unto the children
13. 2 they met not the children of Israel with
13. 16 and sold..unto the children of Judah
13. 24 their children spake half in the speech of
Job 5. 4 His children are far from safety, and they
8. 4 If thy children have sinned against him
17. 5 even the eyes of his children shall fail
19. 17 I entreated for the children's (sake) of
20. 10 His children shall seek to please the poor
21. 19 God layeth up his iniquity for his children
27. 14 If his children be multiplied, (it is) for
30. 8 (They were) children of fools, yea, chil.
41. 34 he (is) a king over all the children of
Psa. 11. 4 behold, his eyelids try, the children of
12. 1 the faithful fail from among the children
14. 2 The LORD looked..upon the children of
17. 14 they are full of children, and leave the
21. 10 their seed from among the children of
34. 11 Come, ye children, hearken unto me
36. 7 therefore the children of men put their
45. 2 Thou art fairer than the children of men
45. 16 Instead of thy fathers shall be..children
53. 2 God looked down..upon the children of
66. 5 terrible (in his) doing toward the children
Psa. 69. 8 an alien unto my mother's children
72. 4 he shall save the children of the needy
73. 15 I should offend (against)..thy children
78. 4 We will not hide (them) from their chil.
78. 5 they should make..known to their chil.
78. 6 (even) the children (which) should
78. 6 (who) should..declare..to their children
78. 9 The children of Ephraim, (being) armed
82. 6 all of you (are) children of the Most High
83. 8 they have holpen the children of Lot
89. 30 If his children forsake my law, and walk
90. 3 and sayest, Return, ye children of men
90. 16 thy glory unto their children
102. 28 The children of thy servants shall
103. 7 He made known his ways..unto the chil.
103. 13 Like as a father pitieth (his) children, (so)
103. 17 his righteousness unto children's children
105. 6 O ye seed of Abraham..ye children of J.
107. 8, 15, 21, 31 his wonderful works to..chil.
109. 9 Let his children be fatherless, and his
109. 10 Let his children be continually vagabonds
113. 9 the barren woman..(be) a..mother of ch.
115. 14 The LORD shall increase..your children
115. 16 the earth hath he given to the children
127. 3 Lo, children (are) an heritage of the LORD
127. 4 As arrows..so (are) children of the youth
128. 3 thy children like olive plants round about
128. 6 Yea, thou shalt see thy children's chil.
132. 12 If thy children will keep my covenant
132. 12 their children shall also sit upon thy
137. 7 Remember..the children of Edom in the
144. 7, 11 deliver me..from..strange children
147. 13 he hath blessed thy children within thee
148. 14 He also exalteth the..children of Israel
149. 2 let the children of Zion be joyful in their
Prov. 4. 1 Hear, ye children, the instruction of a
5. 7 Hear me now therefore, O ye children
7. 24 Hearken unto me now..O ye children
8. 32 Now therefore hearken..O ye children
13. 22 an inheritance to his children's children
14. 26 his children shall have a place of refuge
15. 11 how much more..the hearts of the chil.
17. 6 Children's children (are) the crown of old
17. 6 the glory of children (are) their fathers
20. 7 his children (are) blessed after him
31. 28 Her children arise up, and call her
Song 1. 6 my mother's children were angry with
Isa. 1. 2 I have nourished and brought up children
1. 4 a seed of evil-doers, children that are
11. 14 the children of Ammon shall obey them
14. 21 Prepare slaughter for his children for the
17. 3 they shall be as the glory of the children
17. 9 which they left because of the children
21. 17 the mighty men of the children of Kedar
27. 12 shall be gathered one by one, O ye chil.
30. 1 Woe to the rebellious children, saith the
30. 9 lying children, children (that) will not
31. 6 (from) whom the children of Israel
37. 3 for the children are come to the birth
37. 12 and the children of Eden which (were) in
38. 19 the father to the children shall make
49. 17 Thy children shall make haste; thy
49. 20 The children which thou shalt have, after
49. 25 I will contend..I will save thy children
54. 1 for more (are) the children of the desolate
54. 1 than the children of the married wife
54. 13 all thy children (shall be) taught of the L.
54. 13 great (shall be) the peace of thy children
63. 8 (are) my people, children (that) will not lie
66. 8 Zion travailed, she brought forth..chil.
66. 20 as the children of Israel bring an offering
Jer. 2. 9 with your children's children will I plead
2. 16 the children of Noph and Tahapanes have
2. 30 In vain have I smitten your children; they
3. 14 Turn, O backsliding children, saith the L.
3. 19 How shall I put thee among the children
3. 21 weeping (and) supplications of the children
3. 22 Return, ye backsliding children, (and) I
4. 22 they (are) sottish children, and they have
5. 7 thy children have forsaken me, and sworn
6. 1 ye children of Benjamin, gather your.
7. 18 The children gather wood, and the fathers
7. 30 the children of Judah have done evil
9. 26 and Edom, and the children of Ammon
10. 20 my children are gone forth of me, and
16. 14, 15 LORD liveth, that brought up the chil.
17. 2 their children remember their altars
17. 19 stand in the gate of the children of the
18. 21 deliver up their children to the famine
23. 7 The LORD liveth, which brought up the chi.
25. 21 Edom, and Moab, and the children of A.
30. 20 Their children also shall be as aforetime
31. 15 Rachel weeping for her children
31. 15 refused to be comforted for her children
31. 17 (thy) children shall come again to their
31. 29 and the children's teeth are set on edge
32. 18 the iniquity..into..their children after
32. 30 the children of Israel and the children of
32. 30 the children of Israel have only provoked
32. 32 of the children of Israel, and of the child.
32. 39 for the good of..their children after them
38. 23 So they shall bring out all..thy children
47. 3 fathers shall not look..to (their) children
49. 6 bring again the captivity of the children
50. 4 the children of Israel shall come
50. 4 they and the children of Judah together
50. 33 The children of Israel and the children of
Eze. 2. 3 I send thee to the children of Israel, to a
2. 4 For (they are) impudent children, and
3. 11 go, get thee..unto the children of thy
4. 13 thus shall the children of Israel eat their
6. 5 I will lay the..carcases of the children

Eze. 16. 21 thou hast slain my children, and delivered
16. 36 the blood of thy children, which thou didst
16. 45 mother's daughter..loatheth her..childr.
16. 45 thy sisters, which loathed their..children
18. 2 and the children's teeth are set on edge?
20. 18 I said unto their children in the wilder.
20. 21 the children rebelled against me: they
23. 39 had slain their children to their idols
31. 14 in the midst of the children of men, with
33. 12 son of man, say unto the children of thy
33. 17 Yet the children of thy people say
33. 30 the children of thy people still are talking
35. 5 thou..hast shed (the blood of) the childr.
37. 16 For Judah, and for the children of Israel
37. 18 the children of thy people shall speak
37. 21 I will take the children of Israel from
37. 25 their children, and their children's chil.
43. 7 I will dwell in the midst of the children of
44. 9 of any stranger that (is) among the chil.
44. 15 when the children of Israel went astray
47. 22 the strangers..which shall beget children
47. 22 as born in the country among the children
48. 11 the children of Israel went astray, as the
Dan. 1. 3 he should bring (certain) of the children of
1. 6 Now among these were, of the children
2. 38 And wheresoever the children of men
5. 13 which (art) of the children of the captiv.
6. 13 which (is) of the children of the captivity
6. 24 they cast..their children, and their wives
11. 41 and the chief of the children of Ammon
12. 1 prince which standeth for the children of
Hos. 1. 10 the number of the children..shall be as
1. 11 the children of Judah and the children of
2. 4 I will not have mercy upon her children
2. 4 for they (be) the children of whoredoms
3. 1 love of the LORD toward the children of
3. 4 the children of Israel shall abide many
3. 5 Afterward shall the children of Israel
4. 1 Hear the word of the LORD, ye children of
4. 6 I will also forget thy children
5. 7 for they have begotten strange children
9. 12 Though they bring up their children, yet
9. 13 Ephraim shall bring forth his children to
10. 9 battle in Gibeah against the children of
10. 14 the mother was dashed..upon (her) chil.
11. 10 then the children shall tremble from the
13. 13 (the place of) the breaking forth of chil.
Joel 1. 3 Tell ye your children of it, and (let) your
1. 3 children (tell)their children, and their ch.
2. 23 Be glad then, ye children of Zion, and
3. 6 children also of Judah and the children of
3. 8 I will sell..into the hand of the children
3. 16 and the strength of the children of Israel
3. 19 for the violence (against) the children of
Amos 1. 13 For three transgressions of the children of
2. 11 O ye children of Israel? saith the LORD
3. 1 LORD hath spoken against you, O children
3. 12 so shall the children of Israel be taken
4. 5 O ye children of Israel, saith..Lord GOD
9. 7 (Are) ye not as children of the Ethiopians
9. 7 unto me, O children of Israel? saith the
Obad. 12 neither..have rejoiced over the children
20 captivity of this host of the children of
Mic. 1. 16 and poll thee for thy delicate children
5. 3 shall return unto the children of Israel
Zeph. 1. 8 I will punish..the king's children, and
2. 8 have heard..the revilings of the children
2. 9 and the children of Ammon as Gomorrah
Zech. 10. 7 their children shall see (it), and be glad
10. 9 and they shall live with their children
Mal. 4. 6 children, and the heart of the children to

2. *Little one,* טַף *taph.* [*See* **CHILD.**]
Exod 12. 37 six hundred..men, besides children
Num 14. 3 our wives and our children should be a
31. 18 all the women children, that have not
Deut. 3. 6 destroying the men, women, and children
31. 12 Gather the people together, men..and ch.
Judg 21. 10 with the women and the children
Jer. 40. 7 and had committed..women, and children
41. 16 the women, and the children, and the
43. 6 (Even) men, and women, and children

3. *To beget,* יָלַד *yalad.*
1 Ch. 14. 4 Now these (are) the names of (his) chil.

4. *Lad, boy,* יֶלֶד *yeled.*
Gen. 30. 26 Give (me) my wives and my children, for
33. 1 he divided the children unto Leah, and
33. 2 he put the handmaids and their children
33. 2 and Leah and her children after, and
33. 5 he lifted up his eyes, and saw..the chil.
33. 5 The children which God hath graciously
33. 6 the handmaidens..they and their chil.
33. 7 Leah also with her children came near
33. 13 My lord knoweth that the children (are)
33. 14 according as the cattle..and the child.
Exod 1. 17 the midwives..saved the men chil. alive
1. 18 Why have ye..saved the men chil alive?
2. 6 said, This (is one) of the Hebrew's chil.
21. 4 the wife and her children shall be her
1 Sa. 1. 2 had children, but Hannah had no children
2 Ki. 2. 24 and tare forty and two children of them
Ezra 10. 1 a very great congregation of..children
Neh. 12. 43 the wives also and the children rejoiced
Job 21. 11 like a flock, and their children dance
Isa. 2. 6 they please themselves in the children of
8. 18 the children whom the LORD hath given
29. 23 But when he seeth his children, the work
57. 4 (are) ye not children of transgression, a
57. 5 slaying the children in the valleys under
Lam. 4. 10 women have sodden their own children
Dan. 1. 4 Children in whom (was) no blemish but
Dan. 1. 10 worse liking than the children..(are) of
1. 13 the countenance of the children that eat
1. 15 and fatter in flesh than all the children
1. 17 As for these four children, God gave them
Hos. 1. 2 a wife of whoredoms and children of

5. *Lad, boy,* יָלִיד *yalid.*
Num 13. 22 Sheshai, and Talmai, the children of A.
13. 28 moreover we saw the children of Anak
1 Ch. 20. 4 Sippai, (that was) of the children of the

6. *Youth, young man,* נַעַר *naar.*
1 Sa. 16. 11 Samuel said..Are here all (thy) children?
2 Ki. 2. 23 there came forth little children out of the
Job 24. 5 wilderness (yieldeth) food for..children
29. 5 (when) my children (were) about me
Psa. 148. 12 Both young men and maidens..children
Isa. 3. 4 I will give children (to be) their princes
Lam. 5. 13 and the children fell under the wood

7. *To roll about, encircle,* עָלַל *alal,* 3 *a.*
Isa. 3. 12 my people, children (are) their oppres.

8. *Suckling,* עוֹלֵל *olel.*
1 Sa. 22. 19 both men and women, children and suck.
2 Ki. 8. 12 wilt dash their children, and rip up their
Isa. 13. 16 Their children also shall be dashed to
Jer. 6. 11 I will pour it out upon the children
9. 21 to cut off the children from without
Lam. 1. 5 her children are gone into captivity
2. 11 the children..swoon in the streets of the
2. 19 for the life of thy young children, that
2. 20 Shall..women eat..children of a span
Joel. 2. 16 assemble the elders, gather the children
Mic. 2. 9 from their children have ye taken away

9. *Babe, newly born or unborn,* βρέφος *brephos.*
Acts 7. 19 they cast out their young children

10. *Babe, without full power of speech,* νήπιος *nēpios.*
Gal. 4. 3 Even so we, when we were children, were
Eph. 4. 14 That we (henceforth) be no more children

11. *A little or young lad,* παιδίον. [*See* **CHILD.**]
Matt 14. 21 five thousand men, beside... children
15. 38 four thousand men, besides..children
Mark 7. 28 yet the dogs..eat of the children's crumbs
9. 37 receive one of such children in my name
10. 13 they brought young children to him, that
Luke 7. 32 They are like unto children sitting in the
11. 7 and my children are with me in bed
John 21. 5 Jesus saith..Children, have ye any meat?
1 Co. 14. 20 Brethren, be not children in understand.
Heb. 2. 13 I and the children which God hath given
2. 14 Forasmuch then as the children are part.

12. *A lad, boy, servant,* παῖς *pais.*
Matt. 2. 16 slew all the children that were in Beth.
21. 15 children crying in the temple, and saying

13. *One born, a child,* τέκνον *teknon.*
Matt. 2. 18 Rachel weeping (for) her children, and
3. 9 God is able..to raise up children unto A.
7. 11 how to give good gifts unto your children
10. 21 children shall rise up against..parents
11. 19 But Wisdom is justified of her children
15. 26 It is not meet to take the children's bread
18. 25 his wife and children, and all that he had
19. 29 every one that hath forsaken..children
22. 24 If a man die, having no children, his
23. 37 often would I have gathered thy children
27. 25 His blood (be) on us, and on our children
Mark 7. 27 Let the children first be filled: for it
7. 27 is not meet to take the children's bread
10. 24 Children, how hard is it for them that
10. 29 There is no man that hath left..children
10. 30 he shall receive..children, and lands
12. 19 If a man's brother..leave no children
13. 12 children shall rise up against(their)parents
Luke 1. 17 turn the hearts of the fathers to the ch.
3. 8 God is able..to raise up children unto A.
7. 35 But Wisdom is justified of all her children
11. 13 how to give good gifts unto your children
13. 34 often would I have gathered thy children
14. 26 hate not his father..and children, and
18. 29 There is no man that hath left..children
19. 44 shall lay..thy children within thee; and
20. 31 and they left no children, and died
23. 28 weep for yourselves, and for your children
John 8. 39 If ye were Abraham's children, ye would
11. 52 the children of God that were scattered
Acts 2. 39 promise is unto you, and to your children
13. 33 fulfilled the same unto us their children
21. 5 brought us on our way, with wives and c.
21. 21 ought not to circumcise (their) children
Rom. 8. 16 beareth witness..that we are the child.
8. 17 if children, then heirs; heirs of God, and
8. 21 into the glorious liberty of the children
9. 7 they are the seed..(are they) all children
9. 8 They which are the children of the flesh
9. 8 (are) not the children of God: but the ch.
1 Co. 7. 14 else were your children unclean; but
2 Co. 6. 13 I speak as unto (my) children, be ye also
12. 14 for the children ought not to lay up for
12. 14 but the parents for the children
Gal. 4. 25 which..is in bondage with her children
4. 27 the desolate hath many more children
4. 28 Now we..as Isaac was, are the children
4. 31 we are not children of the bond woman
Eph. 2. 3 were by nature the children of wrath
5. 1 Be..followers of God, as dear children
5. 8 but now..walk as children of light
6. 1 Children, obey your parents in the Lord
6. 4 ye fathers, provoke not your children to
Col. 3. 20 Children, obey (your) parents in all things
Col. 3. 21 Fathers, provoke not your children..lest
1 Th. 2. 7 even as a nurse cherisheth her children
2. 11 we exhorted..as a father (doth) his chil.
1 Tim. 3. 4 having his children in subjection with
3. 12 ruling their children and their own houses
5. 4 if any widow have children or nephews
Tit. 1. 6 having faithful children, not accused of
1 Pe. 1. 14 As obedient children, not fashioning
2 Pe. 2. 14 having eyes full of adultery..cursed chil.
1 Jo. 3. 10 In this the children of God are manifest
3. 10 and the children of the devil: whosoever
5. 2 By this we know that we love the children
2 Jo 1 unto the elect lady and her children
4 that I found of thy children walking in
13 The children of thy elect sister greet thee
3 Jo. 4 to hear that my children walk in truth
Rev. 2. 23 I will kill her children with death; and

14. *Son,* υἱός *huios.*
Matt. 5. 9 they shall be called the children of
5. 45 That ye may be the children of your
8. 12 children of the kingdom shall be cast
9. 15 Can the children of the bride chamber
12. 27 by whom do your children cast(them)out?
13. 38 the good seed are the children of the
13. 38 the tares are the children of the wicked
17. 25 of their own children, or of strangers?
17. 26 Jesus saith..Then are the children free
20. 20 Then came..the mother of Zebedee's chil
23. 31 children of them which killed the prophets
27. 9 whom they of the children of Israel did
27. 56 and the mother of Zebedee's children
Mark 2. 19 Can the children of the bride chamber
Luke 1. 16 many of the children of Israel shall be
5. 34 Can ye make the children of the bride.
6. 35 ye shall be the children of the Highest
16. 8 children of this world..wiser than the ch
20. 34 The children of this world marry, and are
20. 36 are the children of God, being the child.
John 4. 12 drank thereof himself, and his children
12. 36 that ye may be the children of light
Acts 3. 25 Ye are the children of the prophets, and
5. 21 all the senate of the children of Israel
7. 23 to visit his brethren the children of Israel
7. 37 which said unto the children of Israel
9. 15 and kings, and the children of Israel
10. 36 which (God) sent unto the children of Isr.
13. 26 children of the stock of Abraham, and
Rom. 9. 26 there shall they be called the children of
9. 27 Though the number of the children of
2 Co. 3. 7 so that the children of Israel could not
3. 13 children of Israel could not stedfastly
Gal. 3. 7 the same are the children of Abraham
3. 26 For ye are all the children of God by faith
Eph. 2. 2 worketh in the children of disobedience
5. 6 the wrath of God upon the children of
Col. 3. 6 cometh on the children of disobedience
1 Th. 5. 5 children of light, and the children of day
Heb. 11. 22 of the departing of the children of Israel
12. 5 which speaketh unto you as unto children
Rev. 2. 14 cast a stumblingblock before the children
7. 4 all the tribes of the children of Israel
21. 12 twelve tribes of the children of Israel

15. *A very little lad or boy,* παιδάριον *paidarion.*
Matt. 11. 16 It is like unto [children] sitting in the

CHILDREN, adoption of —
Placing as a son, υἱοθεσία *huiothesia.*
Eph. 1. 5 the adoption of children by Jesus Christ

CHILDREN, to bear —
To bear children, τεκνογονέω *teknogoneō.*
1 Ti. 5. 14 the younger women marry, bear children

CHILDREN, to bring up —
To nourish children, τεκνοτροφέω *teknotropheō.*
1 Ti. 5. 10 if she have brought up children, if she

CHILDREN, loving one's —
Loving children, φιλότεκνος *philoteknos.*
Titus 2. 4 teach the..women..to love their child.

CHILDREN, to obtain or have —
To be built up, בָּנָה *banah,* 2.
Gen. 16. 2 it may be that I may obtain children by
30. 3 that I may also have children by her

CHILDREN, without —
Childless, ἄτεκνος *ateknos.*
Luke 20. 28 having a wife, and he die without child
20. 29 took a wife, and died without children

CHILDREN or People of the East, בְּנֵי־קֶדֶם *bene qedem.*
People dwelling between Canaan and the Euphrates.
Gen. 29. 1 came into the land of the people of the e.
Judg. 6. 3 the children of the east, even they came
6. 33 and the children of the east were gathered
7. 12 the children of the east lay along in the

CHILDREN of Eden, בְּנֵי־עֶדֶן *bene eden.*
The inhabitants of Adiabene in Mesopotamia, near Gozan, Haren, and Reseph.
2 Ki. 19. 12 children of E. which (were) in Thelasar?
Isa. 37. 12 children of E. which (were) in Telassar?

CHIL'-EAB, כִּלְאָב, Δαλουΐα.
Second son of David, called Daniel in 1 Ch. 3. 1.
2 Sa. 3. 3 his second, C., of Abigail the wife of

CHIL'-ION, כִּלְיוֹן *pining.*
A son of Elimelech and Naomi, B.C. 1322.
Ruth 1. 2 name of his two sons Mahlon and C.
1. 5 Mahlon and C. died also both of them
4. 9 I have bought..all that (was) C.'s and M.'s

CHIL'-MAD, כִּלְמַד, Χαρμάν.
A region supposed to be between Assyria and Arabia, trading with Tyre.
Eze. 27. 23 the merchants of Sheba, Asshur, (and) C.

CHIM'-HAM, כִּמְהָם, *longing, pining.*
A man recommended to David by Barzillai, B.C. 1020.
2 Sa. 19. 37 but behold thy servant C.; let him go
19. 38 the king answered, C. shall go over with
19. 40 the king went..to Gilgal, and C. went
Jer. 41. 17 And they..dwelt in the habitation of C.

CHIMNEY —
Outlet of checquered work, אֲרֻבָּה *arubbah.*
Hos. 13. 3 shall be as the..smoke out of the chim.

CHIN-NER'-ETH, CHIN-NER'-OTH, CIN-NE'-ROTH, כִּנֶּרֶת (כִּנְּרוֹת) *circuit.*
A district, 30 stadia long and 20 broad, around the sea of Galilee.
Num 34. 11 border..shall reach unto..the sea of C.
Deut. 3. 17 from C., even unto the sea of the plain
Josh 11. 2 to the kings..of the plains south of C.
12. 3 from the plain to the sea of C. on the
13. 27 unto the edge of the sea of C. on the
19. 35 fenced cities..Hammath, Rakkath, and C.
1 Ki. 15. 20 Ben-hadad..the captains..against..C.

CHI'-OS, Χίος.
An island in the Grecian Archipelago, 12 miles west of Smyrna. Now *Scio.*
Acts 20. 15 we..came the next (day) over against C.

CHIS'-LEU, כִּסְלֵו *Orion, Mars, hunter.*
The 9th month of the Jews, which began with the new moon of December.
Neh. 1. 1 And it came to pass in the month C.
Zech. 7. 1 in the fourth..of the ninth month..C.

CHIS'-LON, כִּסְלוֹן *strong.*
Father of Elidad, the prince of Benjamin, who assisted in the division of the land W. of Jordan, B.C. 1490.
Num34. 21 of Benjamin, Elidad the son of C.

CHIS-LOTH TA'-BOR, כִּסְלֹת תָּבֹר. *loins of Tabor.*
A city of Zebulon at the foot of Tabor; perhaps the same as *Cessulloth* in Josh. 19. 18, or *Tabor* in 19. 22. Now *Iksal.*
Josh. 19. 12 turned from Sarid..unto the border of C.

CHIT'-TIM, כִּתִּים *terrible, giants; Citium, Cyprus.*
A family or race descended from Javan, closely related to the Dodanim. Chittim is often noticed in Scripture. Balaam predicted that a fleet should thence proceed for the destruction of Assyria. In Isa. 23. 12, it appears as the resort of the fleets of Tyre. In Jer. 2. 10, the Isles of Chittim are to the far W., as Kedar is to the E. of Canaan.
Num 24. 24 And ships..from the coast of C.
Isa. 23. 1 from the land of C. it is revealed to them
23. 12 O thou oppressed virgin..pass over to C.
Jer. 2. 10 For pass over the isles of C., and see
Eze. 27. 6 ivory, (brought) out of the isles of C.
Dan. 11. 30 For the ships of C. shall come

CHI'-UN, כִּיּוּן, Ῥαιφάν.
The god Saturn or Remphan. *See* Acts 7. 43.
Amos 5. 26 ye have borne the tabernacle..of C.

CHLO'-E, Χλόη.
A female disciple at the place whence Paul sent his first epistle to the Corinthians; perhaps Philippi.
1 Co. 1. 11 by them..of C., that there are contentions

CHOICE, choicest —
1. *To choose (after testing),* בָּחַר *bachar.*
2 Sa. 10. 9 he chose of all the choice (men) of Israel
1 Ch. 19. 10 he chose out of all the choice of Israel
2 Ch. 25. 5 found..three hundred thousand choice
2. *To be chosen (after testing),* בָּחַר *bachar,* 2.
Prov. 8. 10 Receive..knowledge rather than choice
8. 19 and my revenue than choice silver
10. 20 The tongue of the just (is as) choice sil.
3. *Pure,* בַּר *bar.*
Song 6. 9 she (is) the choice (one) of her that bare
4. *To purify,* בָּרַר *barar.*
1 Ch. 7. 40 these (were)..choice (and) mighty men of
Neh. 5. 18 prepared (for me) daily..six choice sheep
5. *Choice,* מִבְחוֹר *mibchor.*
2 Ki. 3. 19 ye shall smite every fenced..choice city
19. 23 I..will cut down the..choice fir trees
6. *Choice,* מִבְחָר *mibchar.*
Gen. 23. 6 in the choice of our sepulchres bury thy
Deut 12. 11 all your choice vows which ye vow unto
Isa. 22. 7 thy choicest valleys shall be full of char.
37. 24 I will cut down the..choice fir trees
Jer. 22. 7 they shall cut down thy choice cedars
Eze. 24. 4 Gather the pieces..fill (it) with the choice
24. 5 Take the choice of the flock, and burn also
31. 16 the trees..the choice and best of Lebanon

CHOICE young man —
Choice one, בָּחוּר *bachur.*
1 Sa. 9. 2 Saul, a choice young man, and a goodly

CHOICE, to make —
To lay out for oneself, ἐκλέγομαι *eklegomai.*
Acts 15. 7 a good while ago God made choice among

CHOKE, to —
1. *To choke off or utterly,* ἀποπνίγω *apopnigō.*
Matt 13. 7 the thorns sprung up and choked them
Luke 8. 7 thorns sprang up with it, and choked it
8. 33 herd ran..into the lake, and were choked
2. *To choke,* πνίγω *pnigō.*
Mark 5. 13 herd ran..into the sea..and were choked
3. *To choke together,* συμπνίγω *sumpnigō.*
Matt 13. 22 choke the word, and he becometh unfru.
Mark. 4. 7 and the thorns grew up, and choked it
4. 19 choke the word, and it becometh unfru.
Luke 8. 14 choked with cares and riches and pleas.

CHOLER, to be moved with —
To become or show oneself bitter, מָרַר *marar,* 7.
Dan 8. 7 and he was moved with choler against
11. 11 And the king..shall be moved with choler

CHOOSE —
1. *Choice one,* בָּחִיר *bachir.*
2 Sa. 21. 6 Let seven men..(whom) the LORD did cho.
2. *To choose (after testing),* בָּחַר *bachar.*
Gen. 6. 2 they took them wives..which they chose
13. 11 Then Lot chose him all the plain of Jor.
Exod 17. 9 Choose us out men, and go out, fight with
18. 25 And Moses chose able men out of all Is.
Num. 16. 5 (him) whom he hath chosen will he cause
16. 7 the man whom the LORD doth choose, he
17. 5 the man's rod, whom I shall choose, shall
Deut. 4. 37 he loved thy fathers, therefore he chose
7. 6 the LORD thy God hath chosen thee to be
7. 7 The LORD did not set his love..nor choose
10. 15 Only the LORD..chose their seed after
12. 5 the LORD..shall choose out of all your
12. 11 God shall choose to cause his name to
12. 14, 26 the place which the LORD shall choose
12. 18 in the place which the LORD..shall choose
12. 21 God hath chosen to put his name there
14. 2 the LORD hath chosen thee to be a pecu.
14. 23 in the place which he shall choose to place
14. 24 the LORD thy God shall choose to set his
14. 25 place which the LORD thy God shall cho.
15. 20 the LORD shall choose, thou and thy ho.
16. 2 the LORD shall choose to place his name
16. 6 thy God shall choose to place his name
16. 7 the place which the LORD thy God shall ch.
16. 11 thy God hath chosen to place his name
16. 15 in the place which the LORD shall choose
16. 16 in the place which he shall choose
17. 8 the place which the LORD..shall choose
17. 10 which the LORD shall choose shall show
17. 15 whom the LORD thy God shall choose
18. 5 God hath chosen him out of all thy tribes
18. 6 the place which the LORD shall choose
21. 5 the LORD thy God hath chosen to minister
23. 16 in that place which he shall choose in one
26. 2 God shall choose to place his name there
30. 19 therefore choose life, that both thou and
31. 11 in the place which he shall choose, thou
Josh. 8. 3 Joshua chose out thirty thousand mighty
9. 27 in the place which he should choose
24. 15 choose you this day whom ye will serve
24. 22 ye have chosen you the LORD, to serve him
Judg. 5. 8 They chose new gods; then (was) war in
10. 14 cry unto the gods which ye have chosen
1 Sa 2. 28 did I choose him out of all the tribes
8. 18 your king which ye shall have chosen you
10. 24 See ye him whom the LORD hath chosen
12. 13 behold the king whom ye have chosen
13. 2 Saul chose him three thousand (men) of
16. 8, 9 he said, Neither hath the LORD chosen
16. 10 said..The LORD hath not chosen these
17. 40 he..chose him five smooth stones out of
20. 30 I know that thou hast chosen the son of
2 Sa. 6. 21 the LORD, which chose me before thy
10. 9 he chose of all the choice (men) of Israel
16. 18 whom..all the men of Israel, choose, his
17. 1 Let me now choose out twelve thousand
24. 12 choose thee one of them, that I may (do it)
1 Ki. 3. 8 midst of thy people which thou hast chos.
8. 16 I chose no city..but I chose David
8. 44 toward the city which thou hast chosen
8. 48 the city which thou hast chosen, and the
11. 13 for Jerusalem's sake, which I have chosen
11. 32 I have chosen out of all the tribes of Isr.
11. 34 for David my servant's sake, whom I cho.
11. 36 I have chosen me to put my name there
14. 21 the LORD did choose out of all the tribes
18. 23 let them choose one bullock for themselv.
18. 25 Choose you one bullock for yourselves
2 Ki. 21. 7 I have chosen out of all tribes of Israel
23. 27 cast off this city..which I have chosen
1 Ch 15. 2 them hath the LORD chosen to carry the
19. 10 he chose out of all the choice of Israel
21. 10 choose thee one of them, that I may do (it)
28. 4 the LORD God of Israel chose me before
28. 4 for he hath chosen Judah (to be) the ruler
28. 5 he hath chosen Solomon my son to sit
28. 6 for I have chosen him (to be) my son, and
28. 10 the LORD hath chosen thee to build an h.
29. 1 Solomon..whom alone God hath chosen
2 Ch. 6. 5 I chose no city among all the tribes of
6. 5 neither chose I any man to be a ruler over
6. 6 But I have chosen Jerusalem, that my
6. 6 and have chosen David to be over my p.
6. 34 toward this city which thou hast chosen
6. 38 (toward) the city which thou hast chosen
7. 12 have chosen this place to myself for an
7. 16 now have I chosen and sanctified this h.
12. 13 the LORD had chosen out of all the tribes
2 Ch. 29. 11 the LORD hath chosen you to stand before
33. 7 I have chosen before all the tribes of Is.
Neh. 1. 9 the place that I have chosen to set my
9. 7 the LORD the God, who didst choose Ab.
Job 7. 15 So that my soul chooseth strangling
9. 14 choose out my words (to reason) with him?
15. 5 thou choosest the tongue of the crafty
29. 25 I chose out their way, and sat chief, and
34. 4 Let us choose to us judgment: let us
34. 33 whether thou refuse, or..thou choose
36. 21 this hast thou chosen rather than afflict.
Psa. 25. 12 he teach in the way (that) he shall choose
33. 12 the people (whom) he hath chosen for his
47. 4 He shall choose our inheritance for us
65. 4 Blessed (is the man whom) thou choosest
78. 67 and chose not the tribe of Ephraim
78. 68 But chose the tribe of Judah, the mount
78. 70 He chose David also his servant, and
105. 26 Moses his servant, (and) Aaron whom he
119. 30 I have chosen the way of truth; thy judg.
119. 173 Let thine hand help me: for I have chosen
132. 13 the LORD hath chosen Zion; he hath
135. 4 the LORD hath chosen Jacob unto himself
Prov. 1. 29 they..did not choose the fear of the LORD
3. 31 Envy thou not..choose none of his ways
Isa. 1. 29 for the gardens that ye have chosen
7. 15 to refuse the evil, and choose the good
7. 16 the child shall know to..choose the good
14. 1 For the LORD..will yet choose Israel, and
40. 20 He that..chooseth a tree (that) will not
41. 8 my servant, Jacob whom I have chosen
41. 9 I have chosen thee, and not cast thee
41. 24 an abomination (is he that) chooseth you
43. 10 and my servant whom I have chosen
44. 1 Yet now hear, O Jacob..whom I have cho.
44. 2 thou, Jesurun, whom I have chosen
48. 10 I have chosen thee in the furnace of
49. 7 the Holy One of Israel, and he shall cho.
56. 4 keep my sabbaths, and choose (the things)
58. 5 Is it such a fast that I have chosen? a day
58. 6 (Is) not this the fast that I have chosen?
65. 12 ye..did choose (that) wherein I delighted
66. 3 Yea, they have chosen their own ways
66. 4 I also will choose their delusions, and
66. 4 they..chose (that) in which I delighted
Jer. 33. 24 two families which the LORD hath chosen
Eze. 20. 5 In the day when I chose Israel, and
Hag. 2. 23 for I have chosen thee, saith the LORD
Zech. 1. 17 and the LORD..shall yet choose Jerusalem
2. 12 the LORD shall..choose Jerusalem again
3. 2 even the LORD that hath chosen Jeru.
3. *To appoint,* בָּרָא *bara,* 3.
Eze. 21. 19 choose thou a place, choose (it) at the
4. *To appoint,* בָּרָה *barah.*
1 Sa. 17. 8 choose you a man for you, and let him
5. *To receive,* קָבַל *qabal,* 3.
1 Ch. 21. 11 Thus saith the LORD, Choose thee
6. *To take, lift up for oneself,* αἱρέομαι *haireomai.*
Phil. 1. 22 Yet what I shall choose I wot not
2 Th. 2. 13 God hath from the beginning chosen you
Heb. 11. 25 Choosing rather to suffer affliction with
7. *To take, choose,* αἱρετίζω *hairetizō.*
Matt 12. 18 Behold my servant, whom I have chosen
8. *To lay out,* ἐκλέγω *eklegō.*
Mark 13. 20 for the elect's sake, whom he hath chosen
Luke 6. 13 of them he chose twelve, whom also he
10. 42 Mary hath chosen that good part, which
14. 7 he marked how they chose out the chief
John 6. 70 Have not I chosen you twelve, and one
13. 18 I know whom I have chosen: but, that
15. 16 Ye have not chosen me, but I have chosen
15. 19 but I have chosen you out of the world
Acts 1. 2 unto the apostles whom he had chosen
1. 24 show whether of these two thou hast cho.
6. 5 they chose Stephen, a man full of faith
13. 17 The God of this people..chose our fathers
1 Co. 1. 27 God hath chosen the foolish things of
1. 27 God hath chosen the weak things of the
1. 28 things which are despised, hath God cho.
Eph. 1. 4 According as he hath chosen us in him
Jas. 2. 5 Hath not God chosen the poor of this
9. *To lay upon,* ἐπιλέγω *epilegō.*
Acts 15. 40 Paul chose Silas, and departed, being
10. *To take in hand,* προχειρίζομαι *procheirizomai.*
Acts 22. 14 The God of our fathers hath chosen thee
11. *To extend the hand (in voting),* χειροτονέω.
2 Co. 8. 19 who was also chosen of the churches to

CHOOSE before, to —
To extend the hand (elect) before, προχειροτονέω.
Acts 10. 41 but unto witnesses chosen before of God

CHOOSE to be a soldier, to —
To levy an army, enlist, στρατολογέω *stratologeō.*
2 Ti. 2. 4 him who hath chosen him to be a soldier

CHOP in pieces, to —
To spread out, פָּרַשׂ *paras.*
Mic. 3. 3 chop them in pieces, as for the pot, and as

CHO-RA'-SHAN, כּוֹר עָשָׁן *smoking furnace.*
A town in Judah, perhaps the same as *Ashan* (Josh. 15. 42), which was given to Simeon.
1 Sa. 30. 30 and to them which (were) in C., and to

CHO-RAZ'-IN, Χοραζίν.
A city in which some of the mighty works of Christ were done. It was on the shore of the lake of Tiberias, 2 miles from Capernaum. Its modern name is likely *Tell Hum*, on the E. of the Jordan, or *Kerazah*.

Matt 11. 21 Woe unto thee, C.! woe unto thee, Beth.!
Luke10. 13 Woe unto thee C.! woe unto thee, Beth.!

CHOSEN —

1 *Choice, chosen, tried*, בָּחוּר *bachur*.

Psa. 78. 31 and smote down the chosen (men) of Isr.

2. *To choose (after testing)*, בָּחַר *bachar*.

Exod14. 7 he took six hundred chosen chariots, and
Judg. 20. 15, 16 seven hundred chosen men
20. 34 ten thousand chosen men out of all Israel
1 Sa. 24. 2 Saul took three thousand chosen men out
26. 2 having three thousand chosen men of Is.
2 Sa. 6. 1 David gathered together all (the) chosen
1 Ki.12. 21 four score thousand chosen men, which
2 Ch.11. 1 four score thousand chosen (men), which
13. 3 (even) four hundred thousand chosen men
13. 3 with eight hundred thousand chosen men
13. 17 there fell..five hundred thousand chosen
Psa. 89. 19 I have exalted (one) chosen out of the
Jer. 49. 19 who (is) a chosen (man, that) I may
50. 44 who (is) a chosen (man, that) I may

3. *To purify*, בָּרַר *barar*.

1 Ch. 9. 22 All these (which were) chosen to be
16. 41 the rest that were chosen, who were

4. *Choice*, מִבְחָר *mibchar*.

Exod 15. 4 his chosen captains were also drowned in
Jer. 48. 15 his chosen young men are gone down to
Eze. 23. 7 with all them (that were) the chosen men
Dan. 11. 15 neither his chosen people, neither

5. *To lay out for oneself*, ἐκλέγομαι *eklegomai*.

Acts 15. 22 to send chosen men of their own com.
15. 25 to send chosen men unto you with our

6. *Laid out, choice, chosen*, ἐκλεκτός *eklektos*.

Matt20. 16 [for many be called, but few chosen]
22. 14 For many are called, but few (are) chosen
Luke23. 35 save himself, if he be Christ, the chosen
Rom 16. 13 Salute Rufus chosen in the Lord, and his
1 Pe. 2. 4 disallowed..of men, but chosen of God
2. 9 But ye (are) a chosen generation, a royal
Rev. 17. 14 that are with him (are) called, and chosen

7. *A choice, selection*, ἐκλογή *eklogē*.

Acts 9. 15 for he is a chosen vessel unto me, to bear

CHOSEN (one) —

Choice, chosen, tried one, בָּחִיר *bachir*.

1 Ch.16. 13 ye children of Jacob, his chosen ones
Psa. 89. 3 I have made a covenant with my chosen
105. 6 ye children of Jacob his chosen
105. 43 brought forth..his chosen with gladness
106. 5 That I may see the good of thy chosen
106. 23 had not Moses his chosen stood before
Isa. 43. 20 to give drink to my people, my chosen
65. 15 leave your name for a curse unto my cho.

CHOSEN, to be —

To be chosen (after testing), בָּחַר *bachar*, 2.

Prov.16. 16 rather to be chosen than silver(22. 1, riches)
Jer. 8. 3 death shall be chosen rather than life by

CHO-ZE'-BA, כֹּזֵבָא *deceitful*.
A city of Judah, the same as Chezib (Gen. 38. 5), and Achzib (Josh. 15. 44).

1 Ch. 4. 22 And Jokim, and the men of C., and Joash

CHRIST, Χριστός *anointed*.
The official appellation of the long promised and long expected Saviour, denoting his kingly authority and mediatorial position as the "Servant of the Lord." JESUS was his common name among men during his lifetime, and he is generally so called in the Gospels, while the CHRIST or JESUS CHRIST is generally used in the Epistles.

Matt. 1. 17 from the carrying away..unto C. (are)
2. 4 he demanded of them where C. should be
11. 2 had heard in the prison the works of C.
16. 16 Thou art the C., the Son of the living God
16. 20 should tell no man..he was Jesus the C.
22. 42 Saying, What think ye of C.? whose son
23. 8, 10 for one is your Master, (even) C.
24. 5 shall come in my name, saying, I am C.
24. 23 if any man..say unto you, Lo, here (is) C.
26. 63 tell us whether thou be the C., the Son
26. 68 Prophesy unto us, thou C., Who is he that
27. 17 Barabbas, or Jesus which is called C.?
27. 22 What shall I do..with Jesus..called C.?
Mark 8. 29 And Peter saith unto him, Thou art the C.
9. 41 drink in my name, because ye belong to C.
12. 35 How say the scribes that C. is the son of
13. 21 if any man shall say to you, Lo, here (is) C.
14. 61 said..Art thou the C., the Son of the
15. 32 Let C. the King of Israel descend now
Luke 2. 11 in the city of David, a Saviour, which is C.
2. 26 not see death, before he had seen..C.
3. 15 all men mused..whether he were the C.
4. 41 Thou art C..for they knew that he was C.
9. 20 say ye..Peter answering said, The C.
20. 41 said..How say they that C. is David's son?
22. 67 Saying, Art thou the C.? tell us. And he
23. 2 We found..saying that he himself is C.
23. 35 let him save himself, if he be C., the
23. 39 saying, If thou be C., save thyself and us
24. 26 Ought not C. to have suffered these things
24. 46 thus it behoved C. to suffer, and to rise
John 1. 20 denied not; but confessed, I am not the C.
1. 25 if thou be not that C., nor Elias neither
1. 41 We have found the Messias, which is..C.
3. 28 me witness, that I said, I am not the C.
4. 25 know..Messias cometh, which is called C.
4. 29 Come, see a man..is not this the C.?
4. 42 know that this is indeed the C., the S.
6. 69 believe and are sure that thou art that C.
7. 26 rulers know indeed that this is the very C.?
7. 27 when C. cometh, no man knoweth whence
7. 31 When C. cometh, will he do more miracles
7. 41 This is the C..Shall C. come out of Galilee?
7. 42 That C. cometh of the seed of David, and
9. 22 if any man did confess that he was C.
10. 24 said unto him..If thou be the C., tell us
11. 27 Yea, Lord: I believe that thou art the C.
12. 34 heard out of the law that C. abideth for
20. 31 that ye might believe that Jesus is the C.
Acts 2. 30 God had sworn..he would raise up C. to
2. 31 He..spake of the resurrection of C., that
2. 36 made that same Jesus..both Lord and C.
3. 18 God before had shewed..that C. should
4. 26 rulers were gathered together against..C.
8. 5 Philip went down..and preached C. unto
9. 20 straightway he preached C. in the syna.
9. 22 conf. the Jews..proving that this is..C.
17. 3 alleging that C. must needs have suffered
17. 3 this Jesus, whom I preach unto you, is C.
18. 5 Paul..testified..(that) Jesus (was) C.
18. 28 showing by the Scriptures..Jesus (was) C.
24. 24 and heard him concerning the faith in C.
26. 23 That C. should suffer, (and) that he should
Rom. 1. 16 I am not ashamed of the gospel of C.: for
5. 6 For..in due time C. died for the ungodly
5. 8 in that, while we were yet sinners, C. died
6. 4 like as C. was raised up from the dead by
6. 8 Now if we be dead with C., we believe
6. 9 Knowing that C. being raised from the
7. 4 become dead to the law by the body of C.
8. 9 Now if any man have not the spirit of C.
8. 10 if C. (be) in you, the body (is) dead because
8. 11 he that raised up C. from the dead shall
8. 17 heirs of God, and joint heirs with C.; if so
8. 34 (It is) C. that died, yea rather, that is
8. 35 Who shall separate us from the love of C.?
9. 1 I say the truth in C., I lie not, my consci.
9. 3 I..wish that myself were accursed from C.
9. 5 C. (came), who is over all, God blessed for
10. 4 C. (is) the end of the law for righteousness
10. 6 Who shall ascend..to bring C. down (from)
10. 7 Who shall descend..to bring up C. again
12. 5 we, (being) many, are one body in C., and
14. 9 to this end C. both died, and rose, and
14. 10 we shall all stand before the..seat of C.
14. 15 Destroy not him..for whom C. died
14. 18 he that in these things serveth C. (is)
15. 3 even C. pleased not himself; but as it is
15. 7 as C. also received us, to the glory of God
15. 18 those things which C. hath not wrought
15. 19 I have fully preached the gospel of C.
15. 20 I strived to preach..not where C. was
15. 29 of the blessing of the gospel of C.
16. 5 who is the first fruits of Achaia unto C.
16. 7 among the apostles, who also were in C.
16. 9 Salute Urbane our helper in C., and Stac.
16. 10 Salute Apelles approved in C. Salute them
16. 16 The churches of C. salute you
1 Co. 1. 6 the testimony of C. was confirmed in you
1. 12 I of Apollos; and I of Cephas; and I of C.
1. 13 Is C. divided? was Paul crucified for you?
1. 17 C. sent me not to baptize, but to preach
1. 17 the cross of C. should be made of none
1. 23 we preach C. crucified, unto the Jews a
1. 24 C. the power of God, and the wisdom of G.
2. 16 But we have the mind of C.
3. 1 as unto carnal, (even) as unto babes in C.
3. 23 And ye are C.'s; and C. (is) God's
4. 1 the ministers of C. and stewards of the
4. 10 for C.'s sake, but ye (are) wise in C.
4. 15 ye have ten thousand instructors in C.
4. 17 remembrance..my ways which be in C.
5. 7 even C. our passover is sacrificed for us
6. 15 that your bodies are the members of C.?
6. 15 shall I then take the members of C., and
7. 22 also he that is called..is C.'s servant
8. 11 shall the weak..perish, for whom C. died?
8. 12 when ye sin so..ye sin against C.
9. 12 lest we should hinder the gospel of C.
9. 18 I may make the gospel of C. without
9. 21 without law to God, but under..law to C.
10. 4 drank of that..Rock..that Rock was C.
10. 9 Neither let us tempt C., as some of them
10. 16 is it not..communion of the blood of C.?
10. 16 is it not the communion of the body of C.
11. 1 Be ye followers of me, even as I..of C.
11. 3 know, that the head of every man is C.
11. 3 and the head of C. (is) God
12. 12 For as the body is one..so also (is) C.
12. 27 Now ye are the body of C., and members
15. 3 that C. died for our sins according
15. 12 if C. be preached that he rose from the d.
15. 13 no resurrection..then is C. not risen
15. 14 if C. be not risen, then (is) our preaching
15. 15 we have testified..that he raised up C.
15. 16 if the dead rise not, then is not C. raised
15. 17 if C. be not raised, your faith (is) vain; ye
15. 18 they also which are fallen asleep in C.
15. 19 If in this life only we have hope in C.
15. 20 now is C. risen from the dead, (and)
15. 22 even so in C. shall all be made alive
15. 23 every man in his own order: C. the first
15. 23 afterward they that are C.'s at his coming
2 Co. 1. 5 as the sufferings of C. abound in us
1. 5 so our consolation also aboundeth by C
1. 21 he which stablisheth us with you in C.
2. 10 (forgave I it) in the person of C.
2. 12 I came to Troas to (preach) C.'s gospel
2. 14 God, which..causeth us to triumph in C
2. 15 For we are unto God a sweet savour of C.
2. 17 in the sight of God speak we in C.
3. 3 (ye are)..declared to be the epistle of C.
3. 4 such trust have we through C. to God-wa.
3. 14 which (veil) is done away in C.
4. 4 the light of the glorious gospel of C., who
5. 10 we must all appear before the..seat of C.
5. 14 the love of C. constraineth us; because
5. 16 though we have known C. after the flesh
5. 17 if any man (be) in C., (he is) a new creature
5. 19 To wit, that God was in C., reconciling
5. 20 Now then we are ambassadors for C., as
5. 20 we pray (you) in C.'s stead, be ye reconcil.
6. 15 what concord hath C. with Belial? or what
8. 23 the churches, (and) the glory of C.
9. 13 your..subjection unto the gospel of C.
10. 1 by the meekness and gentleness of C., who
10. 5 every thought to the obedience of C.
10. 7 If any man trust to himself that he is C.'s
10. 7 that, as he (is) C.'s, even so (are) we C.'s
10. 14 to you also in (preaching) the gospel of C.
11. 2 may present (you as) a chaste virgin to C.
11. 3 corrupted from the simplicity..in C.
11. 10 As the truth of C. is in me, no man shall
11. 13 transforming..into the apostles of C.
11. 23 Are they ministers of C.?..I (am) more
12. 2 I knew a man in C. above fourteen years
12. 9 that the power of C. may rest upon me
12. 10 I take pleasure..in distresses, for C.'s sake
12. 19 we speak before God in C.: but (we do) all
13. 3 ye seek a proof of C. speaking in me
Gal 1. 6 him that called you into the grace of C.
1. 7 and would pervert the gospel of C.
1. 10 I should not be the servant of C.
1. 22 churches of Judea which were in C.
2. 16 we might be justified by the faith of C.
2. 17 if, while we seek to be justified by C., we
2. 17 (is) therefore C. the minister of sin? God
2. 20 I am crucified with C.: nevertheless I live
2. 20 yet not I, but C. liveth in me: and the
2. 21 if righteousness (come) by the law..C. is
3. 13 C. hath redeemed us from the curse of
3. 16 but as of one, And to thy seed, which is C
3. 17 covenant, that was confirmed..in C.
3. 24 law..schoolmaster (to bring us) unto C.
3. 27 as many..as have been baptized into C.
3. 29 if ye (be) C.'s, then are ye Abraham's seed
4. 7 if a son, then an heir of God through C.
4. 19 of whom I travail in birth again until C.
5. 1 Stand fast..in the liberty wherewith C.
5. 2 if ye be circumcised, C. shall profit you
5. 4 C. is become of no effect unto you, who.
5. 24 they that are C.'s have crucified the flesh
6. 2 Bear..burdens, and so fulfil the law of C
6. 12 lest they..suffer..for the cross of C.
Eph. 1. 3 who hath blessed us with..blessings..in C.
1. 10 he might gather..in one all things in C.
1. 12 praise of his glory, who..trusted in C.
1. 20 Which he wrought in C., when he raised
2. 5 hath quickened us together with C.
2. 12 at that time ye were without C., being
2. 13 ye..are made nigh by the blood of C.
3. 4 understand my knowledge..mystery of C.
3. 6 partakers of his promise in C. by the Gos.
3. 8 should preach..unsearchable riches of C.
3. 17 That C. may dwell in your hearts by faith
3. 19 to know the love of C., which passeth
4. 7 according to the measure of the gift of C.
4. 12 for the edifying of the body of C.
4. 13 unto the measure..of the fulness of C.
4. 15 grow up into him..which is the head ..C.
4. 20 But ye have not so learned C.
4. 32 as God for C.'s sake hath forgiven you
5. 2 walk in love, as C. also hath loved us, and
5. 5 hath any inheritance in the kingdom of C.
5. 14 arise from the dead, and C. shall give thee
5. 23 even as C. is the head of the church
5. 24 as the church is subject unto C., so (let)
5. 25 even as C. also loved the church, and gave
5. 32 but I speak concerning C. and the church
6. 5 in singleness of your heart, as unto C.
6. 6 but as the servants of C. doing the will of
Phil. 1. 10 that ye may be sincere..till the day of C.
1. 13 my bonds in C. are manifest in all the
1. 15 Some indeed preach C. even of envy and
1. 16 The one preach C. of contention, not
1. 18 notwithstanding, every way..C. is preach.
1. 20 now also C. shall be magnified in my body
1. 21 For to me to live (is) C., and to die (is) gain
1. 23 a desire to depart, and to be with C; which
1. 27 let your conversation be as..gospel of C.
1. 29 unto you it is given in the behalf of C.
2. 1 If (there be) therefore..consolation in C.
2. 16 that I may rejoice in the day of C., that
2. 30 Because for the work of C. he was nigh
3. 7 what..were gain..I counted loss for C.
3. 8 count them (but) dung, that I may win C.
3. 9 but that which is through the faith of C.
3. 18 (that they are)..enemies of the cross of C.
4. 13 I can do all things through C. which str
Col. 1. 2 To the saints and faithful brethren in C.
1. 7 who is for you a faithful minister of C.
1. 24 which is behind of the afflictions of C.
1. 27 which is C. in you, the hope of glory
2. 2 mystery of God..the Father, and of C.
2. 5 and the stedfastness of your faith in C.
2. 8 rudiments of the world, and not after C.
2. 11 sins of the flesh by the circumcision of C.

Col. 2. 17 are a shadow..but the body (is) of C.
2. 20 if ye be dead with C. from the rudiments
3. 1 If ye then be risen with C., seek those
3. 1 where C. sitteth on the right hand of God
3. 3 ye are dead, and your life is hid with C.
3. 4 When C., (who is) our life, shall appear
3. 11 bond (nor) free : but C. (is) all, and in all
3. 13 even as C. forgave you, so also (do) ye
3. 16 Let the word of C. dwell in you richly in
4. 3 to speak the mystery of C., for which I
4. 12 a servant of C., saluteth you, always lab.
1 Th. 2. 6 when..burdensome, as the apostles of C.
3. 2 our fellow labourer in the gospel of C.
4. 16 and the dead in C. shall rise first
2 Th. 2. 2 as that the day of C. is at hand
3. 5 and into the patient waiting for C.
1 Ti. 2. 7 I speak the truth in C., (and) lie not
5. 11 when they..wax wanton against C., they
2 Ti. 2. 19 let every one that nameth the name of C.
Phm. 8 though I might be much bold in C. to
Heb. 3. 6 But C. as a Son over his own house
3. 14 we are made partakers of C., if we hold
5. 5 So also C. glorified not himself to be made
6. 1 leaving..principles of the doctrine of C.
9. 11 C. being come an High Priest of good
9. 14 How much more shall the blood of C.
9. 24 C. is not entered into the holy places made
9. 28 C. was once offered to bear the sins of
11. 26 Esteeming the reproach of C. greater
1 Pe. 1. 11 the Spirit of C. which was in them did
1. 11 when it testified..the sufferings of C., and
1. 19 But with the precious blood of C., as of a
2. 21 because C. also suffered for us, leaving
3. 16 that..accuse your good conversation in C.
3. 18 For C. also hath once suffered for sins
4. 1 Forasmuch then as C. hath suffered for
4. 13 as ye are partakers of C.'s sufferings
4. 14 If ye be reproached for the name of C.
5. 1 and a witness of the sufferings of C.
1 Jo. 2. 22 but he that denieth that Jesus is the C.?
5. 1 Whosoever believeth that Jesus is the C.
2 Jo. 9 Whosoever..not in the doctrine of C.
9 He that abideth in the doctrine of C., he
Rev. 11. 15 (the kingdoms) of our Lord, and of his C.
12. 10 Now is come..the power of his C : for the
20. 4 they lived and reigned with C. a thousand
20. 6 but they shall be priests of God and of C.

CHRIST JESUS —

The Anointed Saviour, ὁ Χριστὸς Ἰησοῦς.

Acts 19. 4 that they should believe on him..C. Je.
Rom. 3. 24 through the redemption that is in C. Je.
8. 2 the law of the Spirit of life in C. J. 8-1.
8. 39 from the love of God, which is in C. Jesus
16. 3 Greet Priscilla..my helpers in C. Jesus
1 Co. 1. 2 to them that are sanctified in C. Jesus
2 Co. 4. 5 For we preach not ourselves, but C. Jesus
Gal. 2. 4 spy..our liberty which we have in C. Jesus
3. 26 the children of God by faith in C. Jesus
4. 14 received me as an angel..(even) as C. Je.
Eph. 2. 6 sit..in heavenly (places) in C. Jesus
2. 7 (his) kindness toward us through C. Jesus
2. 10 we are his workmanship, created in C. J.
2. 13 But now in C. Jesus ye who sometimes
3. 11 eternal purpose..he purposed in C. Je.
3. 21 Unto him (be) glory..by C. Jesus through.
Phil. 3. 3 which worship God..and rejoice in C. Je.
3. 8 excellency of the knowledge of C. Jesus
3. 12 for which..I am apprehended of C. Jesus
3. 14 of the high calling of God in C. Jesus
4. 7 shall keep your hearts..through C. Jesus
4. 19 according to..riches in glory by C. Jesus
4. 21 Salute every saint in C. Jesus
Col. 1. 4 Since we heard of your faith in C. Jesus
1. 28 may present every man perfect in C. Je.
2. 6 As ye have therefore received C. Jesus
1 Th. 2. 14 the churches of God which..are in C. J.
5. 18 for this is the will of God in C. Jesus
1 Ti. 1. 12 I thank C. Jesus our Lord, who hath
1. 14 with faith and love which is in C. Jesus
1. 15 that C. Jesus came into the world to save
2. 5 one mediator between God..the man C. J.
3. 13 boldness in the faith which is in C. Jesus
6. 13 I give thee charge..(before) C. Jesus, who
2 Ti. 1. 1 the promise of life which is in C. Jesus
1. 2 Grace, mercy, (and) peace, from..C. Je.
1. 9 which was given us in C. Jesus before the
1. 13 in faith and love which is in C. Jesus
2. 1 be strong in the grace that is in C. Jesus
2. 10 obtain the salvation which is in C. Jesus
3. 12 all that will live godly in C. Jesus shall
3. 15 through faith which is in C. Jesus
Phm. 6 every good..which is in you in C. Jesus
23 salute..my fellow prisoner in C. Jesus
Heb. 3. 1 consider the..High Priest..C. Jesus
1 Pe. 5. 10 called us unto..eternal glory by C. Jesus
5. 14 Peace (be) with you all that are in C. Je.

CHRISTS, false —

Lying Christs or anointed ones, ψευδόχριστοι.

Matt 24. 24 there shall arise false C.s, and false prop.
Mark 13. 22 For false C.s and false prophets shall rise

CHRISTIAN —

Belonging to Christ, Χριστιανός.

Acts 11. 26 the disciples were called C. first in Antioch
26. 28 Almost thou persuadest me to be a C.
1 Pe. 4. 16 yet if (any man suffer) as a C. let him not

CHRONICLES —

Matters of the days, דִּבְרֵי הַיָּמִים [dabar].

1 Ki. 14. 19 in the book of the Chronicles of the kings
So in chap. 15. 7, 23, 31; 16. 5, 14, 20, 27; 22. 39, 45; 2 Ki. 1. 18; 8. 23; 10. 34; 12. 19; 13. 8, 12; 14. 15, 18, 28; 15. 6, 11, 15, 21, 26, 31, 36; 16. 19; 20. 20; 21. 17, 25; 23. 28; 24. 5; Esth. 10. 2.
1 Ch. 27. 24 in the account of the Chronicles of king D
Esth. 2. 23 in the book of the Chronicles before the k.
6. 1 bring the book of records of the Chronic.

CHRYSOLITE —

A golden stone, a topaz, χρυσόλιθος *chrusolithos.*

Rev. 21. 20 the sixth, sardius; the seventh, chrysolite

CHRYSOPRASUS —

A golden leek, a beryl, χρυσόπρασος *chrusoprasos.*

Rev. 21. 20 the ninth, a topaz; the tenth a chrysopr.

CHUB, כּוּב.

Name of a people in alliance with Egypt in the time of Nebuchadnezzar. B.C. 610. Probably *Nub.*

Eze. 30. 5 and all the mingled people, and C.

CHUN, כּוּן *founding.*

A city in Aram-zobah on the highway to the Euphrates, and plundered by David.

1 Ch. 18. 8 Likewise from Tibhath, and from C.

CHURCH —

That which is called out, ἐκκλησία *ekklēsia.*

Matt 16. 18 upon this rock I will build my church; and
18. 17 if he..neglect..tell (it) unto the church
18. 17 but if he neglect to hear the church, let
Acts 2. 47 the Lord added [to the church] daily such
5. 11 And great fear came upon all the church
7. 38 that was in the church in the wilderness
8. 1 great persecution against the church
8. 3 As for Saul, he made havoc of the church
9. 31 Then had the churches rest throughout
11. 22 things came unto the ears of the church
11. 26 they assembled themselves with the ch.
12. 1 Herod..stretched forth..to vex..the ch.
12. 5 without ceasing of the church unto God
13. 1 in the church that was at Antioch certain
14. 23 had ordained them elders in every church
14. 27 they were come, and had gathered the ch.
15. 3 being brought on their way by the church
15. 4 they were received of the church, and
15. 22 apostles and elders, with the whole ch.
15. 41 went through Syria..confirming the chs.
16. 5 so were the churches established in the
18. 22 when he had..saluted the church, he
20. 17 sent..and called the elders of the church
20. 28 overseers, to feed the church of God,
Rom. 16. 1 which is a servant of the church which is
16. 4 but also all the churches of the Gentiles
16. 5 Likewise (greet) the church that is in their
16. 16 The churches of Christ salute you
16. 23 Gaius mine host, and of the whole church
1 Co. 1. 2 Unto the church of God which is at Cor.
4. 17 as I teach everywhere in every church
6. 4 who are least esteemed in the church
7. 17 And so ordain I in all churches
10. 32 Give none offence, neither..to the church
11. 16 have no such custom, neither the churches
11. 18 when ye come together in the church, I
11. 22 despise ye the church of God, and shame
12. 28 God hath set some in the church, first
14. 4 he that prophesieth edifieth the church
14. 5 that the church may receive edifying
14. 12 ye may excel to the edifying of the church
14. 19 Yet in the church I had rather speak five
14. 23 If therefore the whole church be come
14. 28 let him keep silence in the church; and
14. 33 but of peace, as in all churches of the
14. 34 Let your women keep silence in the chs.
14. 35 a shame for women to speak in the church
15. 9 because I persecuted the church of God
16. 1 as I have given order to the churches of
16. 19 The churches of Asia salute you. Aquila
16. 19 with the church that is in their house
2 Co. 1. 1 unto the church of God which is at Corinth
8. 1 the grace of God bestowed on the churches
8. 18 in the Gospel throughout all the churches
8. 19 who was also chosen of the churches to
8. 23 the messengers of the churches, (and) the
8. 24 show ye to them, and before the churches
11. 8 I robbed other churches, taking wages
11. 28 Besides..the care of all the churches
12. 13 wherein ye were inferior to other churches
Gal. 1. 2 all..with me, unto the churches of Galatia
1. 13 I persecuted the church of God, and
1. 22 And was unknown by face unto the chs.
Eph. 1. 22 the head over all (things) to the church
3. 10 by the church the manifold wisdom of God
3. 21 Unto him (be) glory in the church by C.
5. 23 even as Christ is the head of the church
5. 24 as the church is subject unto Christ, so
5. 25 even as Christ also loved the church, and
5. 27 a glorious church, not having spot, or
5. 29 but nourisheth..even as the Lord the ch.
5. 32 I speak concerning Christ and the church
Phil. 3. 6 Concerning zeal, persecuting the church
4. 15 no church communicated with me as con.
Col. 1. 18 he is the head of the body, the church
1. 24 for his body's sake, which is the church
4. 15 Salute..the church which is in his house
4. 16 cause that it be read also in the church
1 Th. 1. 1 the church of the Thessalonians (which is)
2. 14 became followers of the churches of God
2 Th. 1. 1 the church of the Thessalonians in God
1. 4 we ourselves glory in you in the churches
1 Ti. 3. 5 how shall he take care of the church of
3. 15 which is the church of the living God, the
5. 16 and let not the church be charged
Phm. 2 and to the church in thy house
Heb. 2. 12 in the midst of the church will I sing
12. 23 the general assembly and church
Jas. 5. 14 let him call for the elders of the church
3 Jo. 6 witness of thy charity before the church
9 I wrote unto the church
10 and casteth (them) out of the church
Rev. 1. 4 John to the seven churches which
1. 11 send (it) unto the seven churches
1. 20 seven stars are the angels of the..churches
1. 20 seven candlesticks..the seven churches
2. 1 Unto the angel of the church of Ephesus
2. 7 hear what the Spirit saith unto the chs.
2. 8 the angel of the church in Smyrna
2. 11 what the Spirit saith unto the churches
2. 12 to the angel of the church in Pergamos
2. 17, 29 hear what the Spirit saith unto the ch.
2. 18 unto the angel of the church in Thyatira
2. 23 all the churches shall know that v. 29.
3. 1 unto the angel of the church in Sardis
3. 6, 13, 22 hear what..spirit saith unto..ch.
3. 7 to the angel of the church in Philadelphia
3. 14 unto the angel of the church of the Laod.
22. 16 testify unto you these things in the chur.

CHURCHES, robber of —

A robber of temples, ἱερόσυλος *hierosulos.*

Acts 19. 37 which are neither robbers of churches

CHURL —

1. *Churl, avaricious,* כִּילַי *kilai.*

Isa. 32. 5 called liberal, nor the churl said (to be)

2. *Churl, avaricious,* כֵּלַי *kelai.*

Isa. 32. 7 The instruments also of the churl (are)

CHURLISH —

Hard, harsh, sharp, קָשֶׁה *qasheh.*

1 Sa. 25. 3 the man (was) churlish and evil in his

CHURNING —

Pressure, churning, מִיץ *mits.*

Prov. 30. 33 Surely the churning of milk bringeth

CHU-SHAN RISH-A-THA'-IM, כּוּשַׁן רִשְׁעָתַיִם.

A king of Mesopotamia, defeated by Othniel, B.C. 1394.

Judg. 3. 8 into the hand of C. king of Mesopotamia
3. 8 children of Israel served C. eight years
3. 10 the LORD delivered C...into his hand
3. 10 and his hand prevailed against C.

CHU'-ZA, Χουζᾶς.

Steward of Herod Antipas son of Herod the Great.

Luke 8. 3 Joanna the wife of C. Herod's steward

CIEL, to —

To cover, overlay, ciel, חָפָה *chaphah,* 3.

2 Ch. 3. 5 the greater house he cieled with fir tree

CIELED —

To cover over, ciel, סָפַן *saphan.*

Jer. 22. 14 (it is) cieled with cedar, and painted with
Hag. 1. 4 (Is it) time..to dwell in your cieled houses

CIELED with —

Thin board, שְׂחִיף *shechiph.*

Eze. 41. 16 cieled with wood round about, and from

CIELING —

A cieling, סִפֻּן *sippun.*

1 Ki. 6. 15 both the floor..and the walls of the cieling

CI-LI-CI'-A, Κιλικία.

A province of Asia Minor, bounded on the N. by Cappadocia, Lycaonia, and Isauria; S. by the Mediterranean; E. by Syria; and W. by Pamphylia.

Acts 6. 9 (the synagogue)..of them of C. and of Asia
15. 23 the Gentiles in Antioch and Syria and C.
15. 41 And he went through Syria and C.
21. 39 I am..a Jew of Tarsus, (a city) in C.
22. 3 I am..a Jew, born in Tarsus, (a city) in C.
23. 34 when he understood that (he was) of C.
27. 5 when we had sailed over the sea of C.
Gal. 1. 21 I came into the regions of Syria and C.

CINNAMON —

1. *Bark of the cinnamon tree,* קִנָּמוֹן *qinnamon.*

Exod 30. 23 Take thou also..of sweet cinnamon half
Prov. 7. 17 I have perfumed my bed with..cinnamon
Song 4. 14 calamus and cinnamon, with all trees of

2. *Cinnamon,* κινάμωμον *kinamōmon,* κιννάμωμον.

Rev. 18. 13 cinnamon, and odours, and ointments

CIN-NE'-ROTH, כִּנְּרוֹת *See Chinnereth.*

1 Ki. 15. 20 Ben-hadad..sent..against..all C.

CIRCLE —

Circle, arch, vault, compass, חוּג *chug.*

Isa. 40. 22 that sitteth upon the circle of the earth

CIRCUIT —

1. *Circle, arch, vault, compass,* חוּג *chug.*

Job 22. 14 and he walketh in the circuit of heaven

2. *Circuit, surrounding country,* סָבִיב *sabib.*

Eccl. 1. 6 the wind returneth again..to his circuits

3. *Revolution, circuit,* תְּקוּפָה *tequphah.*

Psa. 19. 6 and his circuit unto the ends of it: and

CIRCUIT, in —

To go round about, סָבַב *sabab.*

1 Sa. 7. 16 And he went from year to year in circuit

CIRCUMCISE, to —

1. *To cut off, away, around, circumcise,* מוּל *mul.*
Gen. 17. 23 circumcised the flesh of their foreskin in
21. 4 Abraham circumcised his son Isaac being
Exod 12. 44 when thou hast circumcised him, then
Deut 10. 16 Circumcise therefore the foreskin of your
30. 6 the LORD..will circumcise thine heart
Josh. 5. 2 circumcise again the children of Israel
5. 3 circumcised the children of Israel at the
5. 4 (is) the cause why Joshua did circumcise
5. 5 all the people..they had not circumcised
5. 7 their children..them Joshua circumcised
5. 7 because they had not circumcised them

2. *To be cut off, circumcised,* מָלַל *malal,* 2.
Gen. 17. 11 And ye shall circumcise the flesh of your

3. *To cut around, circumcise,* περιτέμνω *peritemnō.*
Luke 1. 59 on the eighth day they came to circumcise
John 7. 22 and ye on the sabbath day circumcise a
Acts 7. 8 so (Abraham) begat Isaac, and circumcised
15. 5 That it was needful to circumcise them
16. 3 took and circumcised him because of the J.
21. 21 they ought not to circumcise (their) chil.

CIRCUMCISE selves, to —

To be cut around, circumcised, מוּל *mul,* 2.
Jer. 4. 4 Circumcise yourselves to the LORD, and

CIRCUMCISED —

1. *Circumcision,* περιτομή *peritomē (dat.)*
Phil. 3. 5 Circumcised the eighth day, of the stock

2. *To cut around, circumcise,* מוּל *mul.*
Josh. 5. 5 all..that came out were circumcised
Jer. 9. 25 circumcised with the uncircumcised

CIRCUMCISED, to be or have —

1. *To be cut around, circumcised,* מוּל *mul,* 2.
Gen. 17. 10 Every man child..shall be circumcised
17. 12 he that is eight..shall be circumcised
17. 13 he that is bought..must..be circumcised
17. 14 the uncircumcised man child..is not cir.
17. 24, 25 when he was circumcised in the flesh
17. 26 the selfsame day was Abraham circum.
17. 27 all the men of his house..were circumcised
34. 15 that every male of you be circumcised
34. 17 ye will not hearken..to be circumcised
34. 22 be circumcised, as they (are) circumcised
34. 24 every male was circumcised, all that went
Exod 12. 48 let all his males be circumcised, and then
Lev. 12. 3 the flesh of his foreskin shall be circum.

2. *To circumcise,* περιτέμνω *peritemnō.*
Acts 15. 1 Except ye be circumcised after the man.
15. 24 [(Ye must) be circumcised, and keep the]
1 Co. 7. 18 Is any man called being circumcised?
7. 18 let him not be circumcised
Gal. 2. 3 was compelled to be circumcised
5. 2 if ye be circumcised, Christ shall profit
5. 3 testify..to every man that is circumcised
6. 12 they constrain you to be circumcised
6. 13 they themselves who are circumcised keep
6. 13 but desire to have you circumcised, that
Col. 2. 11 In whom also ye are circumcised with

CIRCUMCISED, though not —

Through uncircumcision, δι᾽ ἀκροβυστίας [*akrobustia*]
Rom. 4. 11 that believe, though they be not circum.

CIRCUMCISING —

1. *To be cut off, circumcised,* מוּל *mul,* 2.
Josh. 5 8 when they had done circumcising all

2. *To circumcise, cut around,* περιτέμνω *peritemnō.*
Luke 2. 21 were accomplished for the circumcising

CIRCUMCISION —

1. *Circumcision,* מוּלֹת *muloth.*
Exod 4. 26 A bloody husb...because of the circumci.

2. *A cutting round, circumcision,* περιτομή *peritomē.*
John 7. 22 Moses..gave unto you circumcision
7. 23 If a man..receive circumcision, that
Acts 7. 8 he gave him the covenant of circumcision
10. 45 they of the circumcision which believed
11. 2 they that were of the circumcision con.
Rom. 2. 25 circumcision verily profiteth, if thou keep
2. 25 thy circumcision is made uncircumcision
2. 26 uncircumcision be counted for circum.?
2. 27 by the letter and circumcision dost trans.
2. 28 neither (is that) circumcision which is out.
2. 29 and circumcision (is that) of the heart, in
3. 1 or what profit (is there) of circumcision?
3. 30 which shall justify the circumcision by fa.
4. 9 (Cometh) this blessedness..upon the cir.
4. 10 in circumcision, or in uncircumcision?
4. 10 Not in circumcision, but in uncircumcision
4. 11 And he received the sign of circumcision
4. 12 the father of circumcision to them who
4. 12 are not of the circumcision only, but
15. 8 Christ was a minister of the circumcision
1 Co. 7. 19 Circumcision is nothing, and uncircum.
Gal. 2. 7 as (the gospel) of the circumcision (was)
2. 8 to the apostleship of the circumcision, the
2. 9 that we (should go)..unto the circumci.
2. 12 fearing them which were of the circum.
5. 6 neither circumcision availeth anything
5. 11 I, brethren, if I yet preach circumcision
6. 15 neither circumcision availeth anything
Eph. 2. 11 by that which is called the Circumcision
Phil. 3. 3 For we are the circumcision, which wor.
Col. 2. 11 with the circumcision made without ha.
2. 11 in putting off the body..by the circum.
3. 11 circumcision nor uncircumcision
Col. 4. 11 And Jesus..who are of the circumcision
Titus 1. 10 many..specially they of the circumcision

CIRCUMSPECT, to be —

To be watchful, שָׁמַר *shamar,* 2.
Exod 23 13 I have said unto you be circumspect

CIRCUMSPECTLY —

Accurately, pointedly, ἀκριβῶς *akribōs.*
Eph. 5. 15 See then that ye walk circumspectly

CIS, Κίς.

Father of Saul, B.C. 1120. The Greek form of Kish.
Acts 13. 21 God gave them Saul, the son of Cis.

CISTERN —

1. *Cistern, well, pit,* בּאר *bor.*
Jer. 2. 13 (and) hewed..cisterns, broken cisterns

2. *Cistern, well, pit,* בּוֹר *bor.*
2 Ki. 18. 31 drink ye every one the waters of his cistern
Prov 5. 15 Drink waters out of thine own cistern
Eccl. 12. 6 or the wheel broken at the cistern
Isa. 36. 16 drink ye every one the waters of his .cis.

CITIES —

1. *A city (of busy concourse), enclosed place,* עִיר *ir.*
Gen. 13. 12 Lot dwelt in the cities of the plain, and
19. 25 he overthrew those cities, and all the p.
19. 25 all the inhabitants of the cities, and
19. 29 God destroyed the cities of the plain
19. 29 when he overthrew the cities in the
35. 5 the terror of God was upon the cities that
41. 35 and let them keep food in the cities
41. 48 and laid up the food in the cities
47. 21 he removed them to cities from (one) end
Exod. 1. 11 they built for Pharaoh treasure cities
Lev. 25. 32 Notwithstanding the cities of the Levites
25. 32 houses of the cities of their possession
25. 33 the houses of the cities of the Levites
25. 34 the field of the suburbs of their cities
26. 25 when ye are gathered..within your cities
26. 31 I will make your cities waste, and bring
26. 33 land shall be desolate, and..cities waste
Num. 13. 19 what cities (they be) that they dwell in
13. 28 and the cities (are) walled, and very great
21. 2 then I will utterly destroy their cities
21. 3 they..destroyed them and their cities
21. 25 Israel took all these cities: and Israel
21. 25 Israel dwelt in all the cities of the
31. 10 they burnt all their cities wherein they
32. 16 We will build..cities for our little ones
32. 17 our little ones shall dwell in the..cities
32. 24 Build you cities for your little ones, and
32. 26 little ones..shall be there in the cities
32. 33 the land, with the cities thereof in the
32. 33 (even) the cities of the country round
32. 36 Beth-nimrah, and Beth-haran, fenced c.
32. 38 gave other names unto the cities which
32. 38 that they gave unto the Levites..cities
35. 2 and ye shall give..suburbs for the cities
35. 3 the cities shall they have to dwell in
35. 4 the suburbs of the cities, which ye shall
35. 5 shall be to them..suburbs of the cities
35. 6 among the cities which ye shall give unto
35. 6 unto the Levites there shall be six cities
35. 6 to them ye shall add forty and two cities
35. 7 cities..(shall be) forty and eight cities
35. 8 the cities..shall be of the possession
35. 8 every one shall give of his cities unto
35. 11 ye shall appoint you cities to be cities
35. 12 they shall be unto you cities for refuge
35. 13 of these cities..six cities shall ye have
35. 14 Ye shall give three cities on this side
35. 14 three cities shall ye give in the land
35. 14 (which) shall be cities of refuge
35. 15 These six cities shall be a refuge (both)
Deut. 1. 22 and into what cities we shall come
1. 28 the cities (are) great and walled up to h.
2. 34 we took all his cities at that time, and
2. 35 and the spoil of the cities which we took
2. 37 (nor) unto any place..nor unto the cities
3. 4 we took all his cities at that time, there
3. 4 threescore cities, all the region of Argob
3. 5 All these cities (were) fenced with high w.
3. 7 the spoil of the cities, we took for a prey
3. 10 All the cities of the plain, and all Gilead
3. 10 cities of the kingdom of Og in Bashan
3. 12 half mount Gilead, and the cities thereof
3. 19 But your wives..shall abide in your cities
4. 41 Moses severed three cities on this side
4. 42 that fleeing unto one of these cities he
6. 10 to give thee great and goodly cities, which
9. 1 cities great, and fenced up to heaven
13. 12 If thou shalt hear..in one of thy cities
19. 1 dwellest in their cities, and in their
19. 2, 7 Thou shalt separate three cities for the
19. 5 he shall flee unto one of those cities
19. 9 then shalt thou add three cities more for
19. 11 and fleeth into one of these cities
20. 15 Thus shalt thou do unto all the cities
20. 15 which (are) not of the cities of these na.
20. 16 But of the cities of these people, which
21. 2 they shall measure unto the cities which
Josh. 9. 17 came unto their cities on the third day
9. 17 Now their cities (were) Gibeon, Chephirah
10. 2 Gibeon (was). as one of the royal cities
10. 19 suffer them not to enter into their cities
10. 20 that the rest..entered into fenced cities
10. 37, 39 king thereof, and all the cities thereof
11. 12 all the cities of those kings, and all the
11. 13 (as for) the cities that stood still in their
11. 14 And all the spoil of these cities, and the
Josh. 11. 21 Joshua destroyed them..with their cities
13. 10 all the cities of Sihon king of the Amorites
13. 17 Heshbon, and all her cities that (are) in
13. 21 all the cities of the plain, and all the
13. 23 the cities and the villages thereof
13. 25 their coast was Jazer, and all the cities
13. 28 This (is) the inheritance..the cities, and
13. 30 which (are) in Bashan, threescore cities
13. 31 cities of the kingdom of Og in Bashan
14. 4 they gave no part..save cities to dwell
14. 12 (that) the cities (were) great and fenced
15. 9 went out to the cities of mount Ephron
15. 21 the uttermost cities of the tribe of the
15. 32 all the cities (are) twenty and nine, with
15. 36 fourteen cities with their villages
15. 41 sixteen cities with their villages
15. 44, 54 nine cities with their villages
15. 51 eleven cities with their villages
15. 57 ten cities with their villages
15. 59, 62 six cities with their villages
15. 60 two cities with their villages
16. 9 the separate cities for the children of
16. 9 all the cities with their villages
17. 9 these cities of Ephraim (are) among the c.
17. 12 drive out (the inhabitants) of those cities
18. 9 described it by cities into seven parts
18. 21 now the cities of the tribe of the children
18. 24 twelve cities with their villages
18. 28 fourteen cities with their villages
19. 6 thirteen cities and their villages
19. 7 four cities and their villages
19. 8 the villages..round about these cities
19. 15 twelve cities with their villages
19. 16 these cities with their villages
19. 22 sixteen cities with their villages
19. 23, 39 This (is) the inheritance..the cities and
19. 30 twenty and two cities with their villages
19. 31, 48 This (is) the inheritance..these cities
19. 35 the fenced cities (are) Ziddim, Zer, and
19. 38 nineteen cities with their villages
20. 2 Appoint out for you cities of refuge
20. 4 that doth flee unto one of these cities
20. 9 These were the cities appointed for all
21. 2 to give us cities to dwell in, with the
21. 3 the children of Israel gave..these cities
21. 4 the tribe of Benjamin, thirteen cities
21. 5 of the half tribe of Manasseh, ten cities
21. 6 half tribe of Manasseh..thirteen cities
21. 7 out of the tribe of Zebulun, twelve cities
21. 8 the children of Israel gave..these cities
21. 9 these cities which are (here) mentioned
21. 16 nine cities out of those two tribes
21. 18 and Almon with her suburbs; four cities
21. 19 All the cities of the children of Aaron
21. 19 All the cities..were thirteen cities with
21. 20 even they had the cities of their lot ou
21. 22 Beth-horon with her suburbs; four cities
21. 24 Gath-rimmon with her suburbs; four c.
21. 25 Gath-rimmon with her suburbs; two c.
21. 26 All the cities (were) ten with their suburbs
21. 27 Beeshterah with her suburbs; two cities
21. 29 Engannim with her suburbs; four cities
21. 31 and Rehob with her suburbs; four cities
21. 32 and Kartan with her suburbs; three c.
21. 33 All the cities. were thirteen cities with
21. 35 Nahalal with her suburbs; four cities
21. 39 Jazer with her suburbs; four cities in all
21. 40 the cities..were (by)..lot twelve cities
21. 41 All the cities of the Levites within the
21. 41 the cities..(were) forty and eight cities
21. 42 These cities were every one with their
21. 42 thus (were) all these cities
24. 13 cities which ye built not, and ye dwell in
Judg. 10. 4 they had thirty cities, which are called
11. 26 in all the cities that (be) along by the
11. 33 smote them from Aroer..(even) twenty c.
12. 7 was buried in (one of) the cities of Gilead
20. 15 at that time out of the cities twenty and
20. 42 and them which (came) out of the cities
20. 48 also they set on fire all the cities that they
21. 23 and repaired the cities, and dwelt in them
1 Sa. 6. 18 (according to) the number of all the c.
6. 18 to the five lords, (both) of fenced cities
7. 14 And the cities..were restored to Israel
18. 6 that the women came out of all cities of I.
30. 29 to (them)..in the cities of the Jerahmeel.
30. 29 and to them..in the cities of the Kenites
31. 7 they forsook the cities, and fled; and
2 Sa. 2. 1 Shall I go up into any of the cities of
2. 3 and they dwelt in the cities of Hebron
8. 8 and from Betah, and from Berothai, c.
10. 12 let us play the men..for the cities of our
12. 31 thus did he unto all the cities of the chi.
20. 6 lest he get him fenced cities, and escape
24. 7 to all the cities of the Hivites, and of
1 Ki. 4. 13 threescore great cities with walls and
9. 11 king Solomon gave Hiram twenty cities
9. 12 Hiram came out from Tyre to see the c.
9. 13 What cities (are) these which thou hast
9. 19 all the cities of store that Solomon had
9. 19 cities for his chariots, and cities for
10. 26 whom he bestowed in the cities for
12. 17 the children..which dwelt in the cities
13. 32 places which (are) in the cities of Samar.
15. 20 which he had against the cities of Israel
15. 23 and the cities which he built, (are) they
20. 34 The cities which my father took from thy
22. 39 all that he did..and all the cities that he
2 Ki. 3. 25 And they beat down the cities, and on
13. 25 Jehoash the son of Jehoahaz took..the c.
13. 25 and recovered the cities of Israel
17. 6 and in the cities of the Medes

2 Ki. 17. 9 built..high places in all their cities
17. 24 and place (them) in the cities of Samaria
17. 24 they possessed..and dwelt in the cities
17. 26 and placed in the cities of Samaria
17. 29 every nation in their cities wherein they
18. 11 and put them..in the cities of the Medes
18. 13 against all the fenced cities of Judah
19. 25 shouldest be to lay waste fenced cities
23. 5 in the high places in the cities of Judah
23. 8 brought all the priests out of the cities
23. 19 the high places that (were) in the cities
1 Ch. 2. 22 who had three and twenty cities in the
2. 23 the towns thereof, (even) threescore cities
4. 31 These (were) their cities unto the reign of
4. 32 Rimmon, and Tochen, and Ashan, five c.
4. 33 villages that (were) round..the same c.
6. 57 to the sons of Aaron they gave the cities
6. 60 All their cities..(were) thirteen cities
6. 61 half (tribe) of Manasseh, by lot, ten cities
6. 62 out of..Manasseh in Bashan, thirteen c.
6. 63 Unto the sons of Merari..twelve cities
6. 64 Israel gave to the Levites (these) cities
6. 65 they gave by lot..these cities which are
6. 66 (the residue) of the families..had cities
6. 67 And they gave unto them, (of) the cities
9. 2 in their possessions in their cities
10. 7 then they forsook their cities, and fled
13. 2 the priests..(which are) in their cities
18. 8 Likewise from Tibhath..cities of Hader.
19. 7 gathered themselves..from their cities
19. 13 for our people, and for the cities of our
20. 3 Even so dealt David with all the cities
27. 25 storehouses in the fields, in the cities
2 Ch. 1. 14 which he placed in the chariot cities
8. 2 the cities which Huram had restored to
8. 4 all the store cities, which he built in
8. 5 fenced cities, with walls, gates, and bars
8. 6 all the store cities that Solomon had, and
8. 6 the chariot cities, and the cities of the
9. 25 whom he bestowed in the chariot cities
10. 17 that dwelt in the cities of Judah
11. 5 and built cities for defence in Judah
13. 19 Abijah pursued..and took cities from him
14. 5 he took away out of all the cities of
14. 7 Let us build these cities, and make about
14. 14 they smote all the cities round about
14. 14 they spoiled all the cities; for there was
15. 8 out of the cities which he had taken from
16. 4 sent the captains..against the cities of
16. 4 and all the store cities of Naphtali
17. 2 he placed forces in all the fenced cities
17. 2 in the cities of Ephraim, which Asa his
17. 7 to teach in the cities of Judah
17. 9 went about throughout all the cities of
17. 12 he built in Judah castles, and cities of
17. 13 he had much business in the cities of
17. 19 (those) whom the king put in the cities
19. 5 throughout all the fenced cities of Judah
19. 10 your brethren that dwell in their cities
23. 2 gathered the Levites out of all the cities
24. 5 said unto them, Go out unto the cities of
25. 13 soldiers of the army..fell upon the cities
26. 6 built cities about Ashdod, and among
27. 4 he built cities in the mountains of Judah
28. 18 Philistines also had invaded the cities
31. 1 all Israel..present went out to the cities
31. 1 every man..into their own cities
31. 6 that dwelt in the cities of Judah
31. 15 in the cities of the priests, in (their) set
31. 19 the fields of the suburbs of their cities
32. 1 encamped against the fenced cities, and
32. 29 Moreover he provided him cities
33. 14 put captains..in all the fenced cities
34. 6 (so did he) in the cities of Manasseh, and
Ezra 2. 70 the Nethinims, dwelt in their cities
2. 70 and all Israel in their cities
3. 1 the children of Israel (were) in the cities
10. 14 have taken strange wives in our cities
Neh. 7. 73 and all Israel, dwelt in their cities
7. 73 the children of Israel (were) in their cities
8. 15 publish and proclaim in all their cities
9. 25 they took strong cities, and a fat land
10. 37 might have the tithes in all the cities
11. 1 and nine parts (to dwell) in (other) cities
11. 3 but in the cities of Judah dwelt every
11. 3 in his possession in their cities, (to wit)
11. 20 residue of Israel..were in all the cities
12. 44 gather..out of the fields of the cities
Esth. 9. 2 Jews gathered..together in their cities
Job 15. 28 he dwelleth in desolate cities, and in
Psa. 69. 35 God will save Zion, and..build the cities
Isa. 1. 7 Your country (is) desolate, your cities (are)
6. 11 Until the cities be wasted without inhab.
14. 17 made the world..and destroyed the cities
17. 2 The cities of Aroer (are) forsaken; they
17. 9 shall his strong cities be as a forsaken
19. 18 In that day shall five cities in the land
33. 8 he hath despised the cities, he regardeth
36. 1 came up against all the defenced cities
37. 26 thou shouldest be to lay waste..cities
40. 9 say unto the cities of Judah, Behold your
42. 11 Let the wilderness and the cities thereof
44. 26 and to the cities of Judah, Ye shall be
54. 3 make the desolate cities to be inhabited
61. 4 they shall repair the waste cities, the
64. 10 thy holy cities are a wilderness, Zion is
Jer. 1. 15 and against all the cities of Judah
2. 15 his cities are burned without inhabitant
2. 28 (according) to the number of thy cities are
4. 5 and let us go into the defenced cities
4. 7 thy cities shall be laid waste, without
4. 16 give out their voice against the cities
Jer. 4. 26 all the cities thereof were broken down
5. 6 a leopard shall watch over their cities
5. 17 they shall impoverish thy fenced cities
7. 17 Seest thou not what they do in the cities
7. 34 Then will I cause to cease from the cities
8. 14 let us enter into the defenced cities
9. 11 I will make the cities of Judah desolate
10. 22 to make the cities of Judah desolate (and)
11. 6 Proclaim all these words in the cities
11. 12 Then shall the cities of Judah and inhab.
11. 13 (according to) the number of thy cities
13. 19 The cities of the south shall be shut up
17. 26 they shall come from the cities of Judah
20. 16 let that man be as the cities which the
22. 6 (and) cities (which) are not inhabited
25. 18 (To wit), Jerusalem, and the cities of Jud.
26. 2 and speak unto all the cities of Judah
31. 21 O virgin..turn again to these thy cities
31. 23 in the land of Judah, and in the cities
31. 24 and in all the cities thereof together
32. 44 in the cities of Judah, and in the cities
32. 44 and in the cities of the valley
32. 44 and in the cities of the south
33. 10 in the cities of Judah, and in the streets
33. 12 in all the cities thereof, shall be an
33. 13 In the cities of the mountains, in the cities
33. 13 in the cities of the south..the cities of J.
34. 1 and against all the cities thereof
34. 7 against all the cities of Judah that were
34. 7 defenced cities remained of the cities
34. 22 I will make the cities of Judah a desola.
36. 6 all Judah that come out of their cities
36. 9 that came from the cities of Judah unto
40. 5 king..hath made governor over the cities
40. 10 dwell in your cities that ye have taken
44. 2 I have brought..upon all the cities of
44. 6, 17, 21 in the cities of Judah, and in the
48. 9 for the cities thereof shall be desolate
48. 15 Moab is..gone up (out of) her cities, and
48. 24 upon all the cities of the land of Moab
48. 28 O ye that dwell in Moab, leave the cities
49. 1 and his people dwell in his cities
49. 13 all the cities thereof shall be perpetual
50. 32 I will kindle a fire in his cities, and it
51. 43 Her cities are a desolation, a dry land
Lam. 5. 11 They ravished..the maids in the cities
Eze. 6. 6 in all your dwelling places the cities
12. 20 the cities that (are) inhabited shall be
19. 7 he laid waste their cities; and the land
25. 9 from the cities, from his cities (which are
26. 19 like the cities that are not inhabited
29. 12 her cities among the cities (that are)
30. 7 cities shall be in the midst of the cities
35. 4 I will lay thy cities waste, and thou
35. 9 and thy cities shall not return
36. 4 to the desolate wastes, and to the cities
36. 10 the cities shall be inhabited, and the
36. 33 will also cause (you) to dwell in the cities
36. 35 ruined cities (are become) fenced, and
36. 38 so shall the waste cities be filled with
39. 9 they that dwell in the cities of Israel
Dan. 11. 15 king..shall..take the most fenced cities
Hos. 8. 14 and Judah hath multiplied fenced cities
8. 14 but I will send a fire upon his cities
11. 6 the sword shall abide on his cities, and
13. 10 where (is any other)..in all thy cities?
Amos 4. 6 have given you cleanness..in all your cities
4. 8 So two (or) three cities wandered unto one
9. 14 and they shall build the waste cities
Obad. 20 the captivity..shall possess the cities
Mic. 7. 12 he shall come..(from) the fortified cities
Zeph. 1. 16 A day of alarm against the fenced cities
3. 6 their cities are destroyed, so that there
Zech. 1. 12 on Jerusalem and on the cities of Judah
1. 17 My cities through prosperity shall yet be
7. 7 and the cities thereof round about her
8. 20 and the inhabitants of many cities

2. *A city (of busy concourse), enclosed place,* עָר *ar.*
Psa. 9. 6 and thou hast destroyed cities
Isa. 14. 21 fill the face of the world with cities
Mic. 5. 11 And I will cut off the cities of thy land
5. 14 so will I destroy thy cities

3. *A city (with walls),* קִרְיָה *qiryah.*
Ezra 4. 10 brought over, and set in the cities of Sam.

4. *A gate, (those assembling at it),* שַׁעַר *shaar.*
1 Ki. 8. 37 besiege them in the land of their cities
2 Ch. 6. 28 if their enemies besiege them in the cities

5. *City (walled),* πόλις *polis.*
Matt. 9. 35 Jesus went about all the cities and
10. 23 Ye shall not have gone over the cities
11. 1 departed thence, to teach..in their cities
11. 20 Then began he to upbraid the cities where.
14. 13 followed him on foot out of the cities
Mark 6. 33 ran afoot thither out of all cities, and
6. 56 into villages, or cities, or country, they
Luke 4. 43 I must preach..to other cities also
13. 22 he went through the cities and villages
19. 17 have thou authority over ten cities
19. 19 Be thou also over five cities
Acts 5. 16 came also a multitude (out) of the cities
8. 40 he preached in all the cities till he came
14. 6 fled unto Lystra and Derbe, cities of
16. 4 they went through the cities they
26. 11 persecuted (them) even unto strange cities
2 Pe. 2. 6 turning the cities of Sodom and Gomorrha
Jude 7 cities about them, in like manner giving
Rev. 16. 19 and the cities of the nations fell

CITIES, separate —
Separate places, מִבְדָּלוֹת *mibdaloth.*
Josh. 16. 9 And the separate cities for the children

CITIZEN —
Citizen, πολίτης *politēs.*
Luke 15. 15 he went and joined himself to a citizen
19. 14 his citizens hated him, and sent a message
Acts 21. 39 a Jew of Tarsus..a citizen of no mean c.

CITIZEN, fellow —
Joint citizen, συμπολίτης *sumpolitēs.*
Eph. 2. 19 but fellow citizens with the saints

CITY —
1. *A city (of busy concourse), enclosed place,* עִיר *ir.*
Gen. 4. 17 he builded a city..the name of the city
10. 11 builded Nineveh, and the city Rehoboth
10. 12 between Nineveh..the same (is) a great c.
11. 4 Go to, let us build us a city, and a tower
11. 5 the LORD came down to see the city
11. 8 and they left off to build the city
18. 24 Peradventure there be fifty..within the c.
18. 26 If I find in Sodom fifty..within the city
18. 28 wilt thou destroy all the city for (lack of)
19. 4 the men of the city..compassed the house
19. 12 and whatsoever thou hast in the city
19. 14 for the LORD will destroy this city
19. 15 be consumed in the iniquity of the city
19. 16 they brought him..without the city
19. 20 now, this city (is) near to flee unto
19. 21 I will not overthrow this city, for the
19. 22 the name of the city was called Zoar
23. 10, 18 that went in at the gate of his city
24. 10 and went..unto the city of Nahor
24. 11 to kneel down without the city by a well
24. 13 the daughters of the men of the city come
26. 33 therefore the name of the city (is) Beer-sh.
28. 19 but the name of that city (was called) Luz
33. 18 Jacob came to Shalem a city of Shechem
33. 18 and pitched his tent before the city
34. 20 his son came unto the gate of their city
34. 20 and communed with the men of their city
34. 24, 24 that went out of the gate of his city
34. 25 came upon the city boldly, and slew all
34. 27 spoiled the city, because they had defiled
34. 28 that which (was) in the city, and that
36. 32 and the name of his city (was) Dinhabah
36. 35 and the name of his city (was) Avith
36. 39 and the name of his city (was) Pau
41. 48 field, which (was) round about every city
44. 4 when they were gone out of the city, (and)
44. 13 laded every man..and returned to the c.
Exod. 9. 29 As soon as I am gone out of the city, I
9. 33 Moses went out of the city from Pharaoh
Lev. 14. 40 they shall cast them..without the city
14. 41 shall pour out the dust..without the city
14. 45 he shall carry (them) forth out of the city
14. 53 let go the living bird out of the city
25. 29 sell a dwelling house in a walled city
25. 30 the house that (is) in the walled city shall
25. 33 the house that was sold, and the city of
Num. 20. 16 a city in the uttermost of thy border
21. 26 Heshbon (was) the city of Sihon the king
21. 27 let the city of Sihon be built and prepared
22. 36 he went out to meet him unto a city of
24. 19 destroy him that remaineth of the city
35. 4 from the wall of the city and outward
35. 5 measure from without the city on the east
35. 5 and the city (shall be) in the midst
35. 25 congregation shall restore him to the city
35. 26 without the border of the city of his
35. 27 without the borders of the city of his
35. 28 he should have remained in the city of
35. 32 for him that is fled to the city of his
Deut. 2. 34 the little ones, of every city, we left none
2. 36 (from) the city that (is) by the river, even
3. 6 utterly destroying the men..of every city
13. 13 withdrawn the inhabitants of their city
13. 15 smite the inhabitants of that city with
13. 16 shalt burn with fire the city, and all the
19. 12 Then the elders of his city shall send
20. 10 When thou comest nigh unto a city to
20. 14 cattle, and all that is in the city, (even)
20. 19 When thou shalt besiege a city a long time
20. 20 shalt build bulwarks against the city
21. 3 the city (which is) next unto the slain
21. 3 even the elders of that city shall take
21. 4 the elders of that city shall bring down
21. 6 all the elders of that city..shall wash
21. 19 bring him out unto the elders of his city
21. 20 they shall say unto the elders of his city
21. 21 all the men of his city shall stone him
22. 15 bring..(tokens)..unto the elders of the c.
22. 17 spread..before the elders of the city
22. 18 the elders of that city shall take that
22. 21 the men of her city shall stone her with
22. 23 and a man find her in the city, and lie
22. 24 bring..both..unto the gate of that city
22. 24 because she cried not, (being) in the city
28. 3 Blessed (shalt) thou (be) in the city, and
28. 16 Cursed (shalt) thou (be) in the city, and
34. 3 Jericho, the city of palm trees, unto Zoar
Josh. 3. 16 upon an heap..far from the city Adam
6. 3 ye shall compass the city, all (ye) men of
6. 3 (and) go round about the city once
6. 4 the seventh day ye shall compass the city
6. 5 the wall of the city shall fall down flat
6. 7 Pass on, and compass the city, and let
6. 11 the ark of the LORD compassed the city
6. 14 the second day they compassed the city
6. 15 compassed the city after the same manner
6. 15 on that day they compassed the city seven
6. 16 for the LORD hath given you the city
6. 17 the city shall be accursed, (even) it, and
6. 20 went up into the city..and..took the c.

Josh. 6. 21 they utterly destroyed all..in the city
6. 24 they burned the city with fire, and all
6. 26 that riseth up and buildeth this city
8. 1 and his people, and his city, and his land
8. 2 lay thee an ambush for the city behind it
8. 4 against the city, (even) behind the city
8. 4 go not very far from the city, but be ye
8. 5 the people..will approach unto the city
8. 6 till we have drawn them from the city
8. 7 Then ye shall..seize upon the city
8. 8 taken the city, (that) ye shall set the city
8. 11 came before the city, and pitched on the
8. 12 set them..on the west side of the city
8. 13 all the host..on the north of the city
8. 13 liers in wait on the west of the city
8. 14 the men of the city went out against Isr
8. 14 that (there were) liers..behind the city
8. 16 and were drawn away from the city
8. 17 they left the city open, and pursued after
8. 18 that (he had) in his hand toward the city
8. 19 they entered into the city, and took it
8. 19 and hasted and set the city on fire
8. 20 the smoke of the city ascended up to
8. 21 saw that the ambush had taken the city
8. 21 that the smoke of the city ascended, then
8. 22 the other issued out of the city against
8. 27 Only the cattle, and the spoil of that city
8. 29 and cast it at the entering of the..city
10. 2 they feared..Gibeon (was) a great city
11. 19 There was not a city that made peace
13. 9, 16 the city that (is) in the midst of the
15. 62 Nibshan, and the c. of Salt, and En-gedi
18. 14 which (is) Kirjath-jearim, a city of the
19. 29 the coast turneth..to the strong city Tyre
19. 50 they gave him the city which he asked
19. 50 and he built the city, and dwelt therein
20. 4 gate of the city..the elders of that city
20. 4 they shall take him into the city unto them
20. 6 And he shall dwell in that city, until he
20. 6 come unto his own city..unto the city
21. 13, 21, 27, 32, 38 a city of refuge for the sla.
Judg. 1. 8 and smitten it..and set the city on
1. 16 the children..went up out of the city of
1. 17 the name of the city was called Hormah
1. 23 now the name of the city before (was) Luz
1. 24 spies saw a man come forth out of the c.
1. 24 Show us..the entrance into the city, and
1. 25 when he showed them..into the city, they
1. 25 smote the city with the edge of the sword
1. 26 built a city, and called the name..Luz
3. 13 and possessed the city of palm trees
6. 27 because he feared..the men of the city
6. 28 when the men of the city arose early in
6. 30 Then the men of the city said unto Joash
8. 16 he took the elders of the city, and thorns
8. 17 he beat down..and slew the men of the c.
8. 27 and put it in his city, (even) in Ophrah
9. 30 when Zebul the ruler of the city heard
9. 31 and, behold, they fortify the city against
9. 33 thou shalt rise early, and set upon the city
9. 35, 44 and stood in the entering..of the city
9. 43 the people (were) come forth out of the c.
9. 45 Abimelech fought against the city all that
9. 45 he took the city..and beat down the city
9. 51 there was a strong tower within the city
9. 51 men and women, and all they of the city
14. 18 And the men of the city said unto him on
16. 2 laid wait for him all night in..the city
16. 3 and took the doors of the gate of the city
17. 8 the man departed out of the city from
18. 27 they smote them..and burnt the city with
18. 28 And they built a city, and dwelt therein
18. 29 And they called the name of the city Dan
18. 29 howbeit the name of the city (was) Laish
19. 11 let us turn in into this city of the Jebu.
19. 12 We will not turn aside hither into the c.
19. 15 he sat him down in a street of the city
19. 17 a wayfaring man in the street of the city
19. 22 the men of the city..beset the house round
20. 11 So all the men..gathered against the city
20. 31 were drawn away from the city; and they
20. 32 draw them from the city unto the highw.
20. 37 smote all the city with the edge of the s.
20. 38 a great flame..to rise up out of the city
20. 40 flame began to arise up out of the city
20. 40 flame of the city ascended up to heaven
20. 48 as well the men of (every) city, as the b.
Ruth 1. 19 that all the city was moved about them
2. 18 she took (it) up, and went into the city
3. 15 laid (it) on her: and she went into the c.
4. 2 he took ten men of the elders of the city
1 Sa. 1. 3 this man went up out of his city yearly
4. 13 And when the man came into the city
4. 13 and told (it), all the city cried out
5. 9 the hand of the LORD was against the c.
5. 9 and he smote the men of the city, both
5. 11 was..destruction throughout all the city
5. 12 and the cry of the city went up to heaven
8. 22 Samuel said..Go ye every man unto his c.
9. 6 Behold now, (there is) in this city a man
9. 10 they went unto the city where the man
9. 11 as they went up the hill to the city, they
9. 12 haste now, for he came to day to the city
9. 13 As soon as ye be come into the city, ye
9. 14 And they went up into the city
9. 14 (and) when they were come into the city
9. 25 when they were come down..into the city
9. 27 were going down to the end of the city
10. 5 when thou art come thither to the city
15. 5 Saul came to a city of Amalek, and laid
20. 6 that he might run to Beth-lehem his city
20. 29 our family hath a sacrifice in the city
1 Sa. 20. 40 said unto him, Go, carry (them) to the c.
20. 42 he arose..and Jonathan went into the c.
22. 19 And Nob, the city of the priests, smote he
23. 10 that Saul seeketh..to destroy the city for
27. 5 should thy servant dwell in the royal city
28. 3 buried him in Ramah, even in his own c.
30. 3 So David and his men came to the city
2 Sa. 5. 7 of Zion: the same (is) the city of David
5. 9 the fort, and called it, The city of David
6. 10 would not remove the ark..into the city
6. 12 David..brought up the ark..into the city
6. 16 as the ark of the LORD came into the city
10. 3 to search the city, and to spy it out, and
10. 14 then fled they..and entered into the city
11. 16 came to pass, when Joab observed the c.
11. 17 the men of the city went out and fought
11. 20 approached ye so nigh unto the city when
11. 25 thy battle more strong against the city
12. 1 were two men in one city; the one rich
12. 26 And Joab fought..and took the royal city
12. 27 I have fought..and have taken the city
12. 28 encamp against the city..take the city
12. 30 he brought forth the spoil of the city in
15. 2 then Absalom..said, Of what city (art)
15. 12 Absalom sent for Ahithophel..from his c.
15. 14 smite the city with the edge of the sword
15. 24 people had done passing out of the city
15. 25 Carry back the ark of God into the city
15. 27 return into the city in peace, and your
15. 34 But if thou return to the city, and say
15. 37 Hushai, David's friend, came into the city
17. 13 Moreover if he be gotten into a city, then
17. 13 shall all Israel bring ropes to that city
17. 17 might not be seen to come into the city
17. 23 and gat him home to his house, to his city
18. 3 that thou succour us out of the city
19. 3 And the people gat them..into the city
19. 37 that I may die in mine own city, (and be
20. 15 they cast up a bank against the city, and
20. 16 Then cried a wise woman out of the city
20. 19 thou seekest to destroy a city and a mother
20. 21 deliver him..I will depart from the city
20. 22 they retired from the city, every man to
24. 5 on the right side of the city that (lieth)
1 Ki. 2. 10 and was buried in the city of David
3. 1 brought her into the city of David, until
8. 1 that they might bring up..out of the city
8. 16 I chose no city out of all the tribes of
8. 44 shall pray unto the LORD toward the city
8. 48 the city which thou hast chosen, and the
9. 16 the Canaanites that dwelt in the city
9. 24 Pharoah's daughter came up out of the c.
11. 27 repaired the breaches of the city of David
11. 32 the city which I have chosen out of all
11. 36 the city which I have chosen me to put
11. 43 was buried in the city of David his father
13. 25 they came and told (it) in the city where
13. 29 the old prophet came to the city, to mourn
14. 11 Him that dieth of Jeroboam in the city
14. 12 when thy feet enter into the city, the ch.
14. 21 the city which the LORD did choose out
14. 31 was buried with his fathers in the city
15. 8 and they buried him in the city of David
15. 24 was buried with his fathers in the city
16. 4 Him that dieth of Baasha in the city shall
16. 18 when Zimri saw that the city was taken
16. 24 called the name of the city which he built
17. 10 when he came to the gate of the city,
20. 2 he sent messengers to Ahab..into the c.
20. 12 set (themselves in array) against the city
20. 19 So these young men..came out of the city
20. 30 But the rest fled to Aphek, into the city
20. 30 Ben-hadad fled, and came into the city
21. 8 unto the elders..that (were) in his city
21. 11 the men of his city..in his city did as
21. 13 they carried him forth out of the city
21. 24 Him that dieth of Ahab in the city the
22. 26 carry him..unto..governor of the city
22. 36 Every man to his city, and every man to
22. 50 was buried with his fathers in the city
2 Ki. 2. 19 the men of the city said unto Elisha
2. 19 the situation of this city (is) pleasant, as
2. 23 came..little children out of the city
3. 19 every fenced city, and every choice city
6. 14 they came by night, and compassed the c.
6. 15 an host compassed the city both with
6. 19 not the way, neither (is) this the city
7. 4 If we say, We will enter into the city
7. 4 then the famine (is) in the city, and we
7. 10 they..called unto the porter of the city
7. 12 When they come out of the city
7. 12 we shall catch them..and get into the city
8. 24 was buried with his fathers in the city
9. 15 let none go forth..out of the city to go
9. 28 buried him in his sepulchre..in the city
10. 2 (there are) with you..a fenced city also
10. 5 he that (was) over the city, the elders also
10. 6 with the great men of the city, which
10. 25 went to the city of the house of Baal
11. 20 the people..rejoiced, and the city was in
12. 21 buried him with his fathers in the city
14. 20 he was buried..in the city of David
15. 7, 38 buried him with his fathers in the city
16. 20 was buried with his fathers in the city
17. 9 tower of the watchmen to the fenced city
18. 8 tower of the watchmen to the fenced city
18. 30 this city shall not be delivered into the
19. 13 the king of the city of Sepharvaim, of H.
19. 32 He shall not come into this city, nor shoot
19. 33 shall not come into this city, saith the
19. 34 I will defend this city, to save it, for
20. 6 I will deliver thee and this city out of
2 Ki. 20. 6 I will defend this city for mine own sake
20. 20 and brought water into the city
23. 8 gate of Joshua the governor of the city
23. 8 on a man's left hand at the gate of the c.
23. 17 the men of the city told him, (It is) the
23. 27 cast off this city..which I have chosen
24. 10 servants..came up..the city was besieged
24. 11 Nebuchadnezzar..came against the city
25. 2 the city was besieged unto the eleventh
25. 3 the famine prevailed in the city, and there
25. 4 the city was broken up, and all the men
25. 4 now the Chaldees (were) against the city
25. 11 the people (that were) left in the city, and
25. 19 out of the city he took an officer that
25. 19 five men..which were found in the city
25. 19 the people..(that were) found in the city
1 Ch. 1. 43 and the name of his city (was) Dinhabah
1. 46 and the name of his city (was) Avith
1. 50 and the name of his city (was) Pai
11. 5 castle of Zion, which (is) the city of David
11. 7 therefore they called it the city of David
11. 8 he built the city round about, even from
13. 13 David brought not the ark..to the city of
15. 1 (David) made him houses in the city of
15. 29 the ark of the covenant..came to the city
19. 9 battle in array before the gate of the city
19. 15 they likewise fled..and entered..the city
20. 2 he brought..much spoil out of the city
2 Ch. 5. 2 to bring up the ark..out of the city of
6. 5 I chose no city among all the tribes of
6. 34 they pray unto thee toward this city
6. 38 (toward) the city which thou hast chosen
8. 11 Solomon brought up..out of the city of
9. 31 he was buried in the city of David his
11. 23 all his children..unto every fenced city
12. 13 the city which the LORD had chosen out
12. 16 and was buried in the city of David
14. 1 and they buried him in the city of David
16. 14 which he had made for himself in the city
18. 25 carry him back to..governor of the city
19. 5 he set judges in the land..city by city
21. 1 was buried with his fathers in the city of
21. 20 they buried him in the city of David, but
23. 21 all the people..rejoiced: and the city was
24. 16, 25 they buried him in the city of David
25. 28 buried him with his fathers in the city
27. 9 and they buried him in the city of David
28. 15 the city of palm trees, to their brethren
28. 27 buried him in the city, (even) in Jerusalem
29. 20 gathered the rulers of the city, and went
30. 10 So the posts passed from city to city
32. 3 fountains which (were) without the city
32. 5 repaired Millo (in) the city of David, and
32. 6 in the street of the gate of the city
32. 18 that they might take the city
32. 30 brought it straight down to..the city
33. 14 after..he built a wall without the city
33. 15 took away..and cast (them) out of the c.
34. 8 and Maaseiah the governor of the city, and
Ezra 2. 1 and came again..every one unto his city
10. 14 with them the elders of every city, and
Neh. 2. 3 when the city..(lieth) waste, and the gates
2. 5 unto the city of my fathers' sepulchres
2 8 for the wall of the city, and for the house
3. 15 the stairs that go down from the city of
7. 4 the city (was) large and great; but the
7 6 and came again..every one unto his city
11. 1 to dwell in Jerusalem the holy city
11. 9 and Judah..(was) second over the city
11. 18 All the Levites in the holy city (were) two
12. 37 they went up by the stairs of the city
13. 18 did not our God bring all..upon this city?
Esth. 3. 15 but the city Shushan was perplexed
4. 1 went out into the midst of the city, and
4. 6 Hatach went..unto the street of the city
6. 9 bring him..through the street of the city
6. 11 brought him..through the street of..city
8. 11 granted the Jews which (were) in every c.
8. 15 the city of Shushan rejoiced and was glad
8. 17 And in every province, and in every city
9. 28 every family, every province..every city
Job 24. 12 Men groan from out of the city, and the
Psa. 31. 21 showed me..kindness in a strong city
46. 4 the streams..make glad the city of God
48. 1 greatly to be praised in the city of our
48. 8 so have we seen in the city..the city of
55. 9 for I have seen violence..in the city
59. 6, 14 make a noise..go round about the city
60. 9 Who will bring me (into) the strong city?
72. 16 (they) of the city shall flourish like grass
87. 3 Glorious things are spoken of thee, O city
101. 8 cut off all wicked doers from the city
107. 4 they found no city to dwell in
107. 7 that they might go to a city of habitation
107. 36 that they may prepare a city for habita.
108. 10 Who will bring me into the strong city?
122. 3 Jerusalem is builded as a city that is
127. 1 except the LORD keep the city, the watch.
Prov. 1. 21 in the city she uttereth her words, (saying)
16. 32 he that ruleth..he that taketh a city
21. 22 A wise (man) scaleth the city of the mighty
25. 28 He..(is like) a city (that is) broken down
Eccl. 7. 19 ten mighty (men) which are in the city
8. 10 they were forgotten in the city where they
9. 14 (There was) a little city, and few..within
9. 15 and he by his wisdom delivered the city
10. 15 he knoweth not how to go to the city
Song 3. 2 I will rise now, and go about the city in
3. 3 The watchmen that go about the city
5. 7 The watchmen that went about the city
Isa. 1. 8 as a lodge in a garden..as a besieged city
1. 26 shalt be called, The city of righteousness

Isa. 14. 31 Howl, O gate; cry, O city; thou, whole P.
17. 1 Damascus is taken away from (being) a c.
19. 2 city against city, (and) kingdom against
19. 18 one shall be called, The city of destruction
22. 2 that art full of stirs, a tumultuous city
22. 9 have seen also the breaches of the city
23. 16 Take an harp, go about the city, thou h.
24. 12 In the city is left desolation, and the gate
25. 2 thou hast made..(of) a defenced city a
25. 2 a palace of strangers to be no city; it
26. 1 We have a strong city; salvation will (G.)
27. 10 Yet the defenced city (shall be) desolate
32. 14 the multitude of the city shall be left
32. 19 and the city shall be low in a low place
36. 15 this city shall not be delivered into the
37. 13 the king of the city of Sepharvaim, Hena
37. 33 He shall not come into this city, nor
37. 34 shall not come into this city, saith the
37. 35 I will defend this city to save it, for
38. 6 I will deliver thee and this city out of
38. 6 and I will defend this city
45. 13 he shall build my city, and he shall let
48. 2 For they call themselves of the holy city
52. 1 put on..garments, O Jerusalem, the holy c.
60. 14 they shall call thee, The city of the LORD
62. 12 thou shalt be called, Sought out, A city
66. 6 A voice of noise from the city, a voice
Jer. 1. 18 I have made thee this day a defenced city
3. 14 I will take you one of a city, and two of
4. 29 The whole city shall flee for the noise
4. 29 every city (shall be) forsaken, and not a
6. 6 this (is) the city to be visited; she (is)
8. 16 the city, and those that dwell therein
14 18 if I enter into the city, then behold them
15 8 caused..to fall..terrors upon the city
17. 24 no burden through the gates of this city
17 25 shall..enter into the gates of this city
17 25 and this city shall remain for ever
19. 8 I will make this city desolate, and an
19. 11 so will I break this people, and this city
19. 12 and (even) make this city as Tophet
19. 15 upon this city and upon all her towns
20. 5 I will deliver..the strength of this city
21. 4 and I will assemble them into..this city
21. 6 will smite the inhabitants of this city
21. 7 and (such as are) left in this city from the
21. 9 He that abideth in this city shall die
21. 10 I have set my face against this city
22. 8 many nations shall pass by this city, and
22. 8 hath the LORD done thus unto this..city?
23. 39 the city that I gave you and your fathers
25. 29 I begin to bring evil on the city which
26. 6 will make this city a curse to all the
26. 9 this city shall be desolate without an
26. 11 he hath prophesied against this city, as
26 12 sent me to prophesy..against this city
26. 15 bring innocent blood..upon this city
26. 20 who prophesied against this city and
27. 17 wherefore should this city be laid waste?
27. 19 the residue..that remain in this city
29. 7 seek the peace of the city whither I have
29. 16 all the people that dwelleth in this city
30. 18 the city shall be builded upon her own
31. 38 the city shall be built to the LORD, from
32. 3 I will give this city into the hand of
32. 24 they are come unto the city to take it
32. 24, 25 the city is given into the hand of the
32. 28 I will give this city into the hand of
32 29 Chaldeans, that fight against this city
32. 29 Chaldeans..shall..set fire on this city
32. 31 this city hath been to me (as) a provoca.
32. 36 concerning this city, whereof ye say, It
33. 4 concerning the houses of this city and
33. 5 I have hid my face from this city
34. 2 I will give this city into the hand of
34. 22 and cause them to return to this city
37. 8 fight against this city, and take it, and
37. 10 (yet) should they rise, and burn this city
37. 21 until all the bread in the city were spent
38. 2 He that remaineth in this city shall die
38. 3 This city shall surely be given into the
38 4 hands of..men..that remain in this city
38. 9 for (there is) no more bread in the city
38 17 this city shall not be burnt with fire
38. 18 then shall this city be given into the
38. 23 thou shalt cause this city to be burnt
39. 2 the ninth (day)..the city was broken up
39 4 went forth out of the city by night, by
39. 9 the people that remained in the city, and
39. 16 I will bring my words upon this city for
41. 7 when they came into the midst of the c.
46. 8 I will destroy the city and the inhabitants
47. 2 the city, and them that dwell therein
48. 8 the spoiler shall come upon every city
49. 25 How is..not left, the city of my joy
51. 31 to show the king of Babylon that his city
52. 5 So the city was besieged unto the eleventh
52. 6 the famine was sore in the city, so that
52. 7 Then the city was broken up, and all the
52. 7 went forth out of the city by night, by
52. 7 now the Chaldeans (were) by the city
52. 15 residue of..people..remained in the city
52. 25 He took also out of the city an eunuch
52. 25 seven men..which were found in the city
52. 25 (that were) found in the midst of the c.
Lam. 1. 1 How doth the city sit solitary (that was)
1. 19 mine elders gave up the ghost in the city
2. 12 as the wounded in the streets of the city
2. 15 (Is) this the city that (men) call the Perf.
3. 51 because of all the daughters of my city
Eze. 4. 1 pourtray upon it the city, (even)
4 3 (for) a wall..between thee and the city

Eze. 5. 2 a third part in the midst of the city
7. 15 he that (is) in the city, famine..shall
7. 23 and the city is full of violence
9. 1 Cause them that have charge over the c.
9. 4 LORD said..Go through the midst of..c.
9. 5 Go ye after him through the city, and
9. 7 And they went forth, and slew in the city
9. 9 the land is full of blood, and the city full
10. 2 fill thine hand..scatter (them) over..city
11. 2 and give wicked counsel in this city
11. 6 have multiplied your slain in this city
11. 23 glory..went up from the midst of the city
11. 23 which (is) on the east side of the city
17. 4 he set it in a city of merchants
21. 19 choose (it) at the head of the way to..city
22. 2 wilt thou judge the bloody city? yea, thou
22. 3 The city sheddeth blood in the midst of
24. 6, 9 saith the LORD..Woe to..bloody city!
26. 10 as men enter into a city wherein is made
26. 17 the renowned city, which wast strong in
26. 19 When I shall make thee a desolate city
33. 21 (that) one..came..saying, The city is sm.
39. 16 the name of the city (shall be) Hamonah
40. 1 the fourteenth year after that the city
40. 2 which (was) as the frame of a city on the
43. 3 I saw when I came to destroy the city
45. 6 shall appoint the possession of the city
45. 7 and of the possession of the city, before the
45. 7 before the possession of the city from
48. 15 shall be a profane (place) for the city, for
48. 15 the city shall be in the midst thereof
48. 17 the suburbs of the city shall be toward
48. 18 for food unto them that serve the city
48. 19 they that serve the city shall serve it
48. 20 offer..with the possession of the city
48. 21 of the possession of the city, over against
48. 22 from the possession of the city, (being) in
48. 30 these (are) the goings out of the city on
48. 31 the gates of the city (shall be) after the
48. 35 the name of the city..The LORD (is) there
Dan. 9. 16 let thine anger..be turned..from thy city
9. 18 and the city which is called by thy name
9. 19 for thy city and thy people are called
9. 24 upon thy people, and upon thy holy city
9. 26 the people..shall destroy the city and
Hos. 11. 9 and I will not enter into the city
Joel 2. 9 They shall run to and fro in the city; they
Amos 3. 6 Shall a trumpet be blown in the city, and
3. 6 shall there be evil in a city, and the LORD
4. 7 I caused it to rain upon one city
4. 7 caused it not to rain upon another city
5. 3 The city that went out (by) a thousand
6. 8 will I deliver up the city, with all that
7. 17 Thy wife shall be an harlot in the city
Jon. 1. 2 Arise, go to Nineveh, that great city, and
3. 2 Arise, go unto Nineveh, that great city
3. 3 Now Nineveh was an exceeding great city
3. 4 Jonah began to enter into the city a day's
4. 5 So Jonah went out of the city
4. 5 and sat on the east side of the city
4. 5 might see what would become of the city
4 11 And should not I spare..that great city
Mic. 6. 9 The LORD'S voice crieth unto the city, and
Nah. 3. 1 Woe to the bloody city! it (is) all full
Zeph. 2. 15 This (is) the rejoicing city that dwelt
3. 1 Woe to her..to the oppressing city!
Zech. 8 3 Jerusalem shall be called, A city of truth
8. 5 the streets of the city shall be full of
14. 2 the city shall be taken, and the houses
14. 2 and half of the city shall go forth into
14. 2 people shall not be cut off from the city

2. *A city (with walls),* קִרְיָה *qiryah.*

Num 21 28 there is a flame from the city of Sihon
Deut. 2. 36 there was not one city too strong for us
3. 4 there was not a city which we took not
1 Ki. 1. 41 Wherefore (is this) noise of the city being
1. 45 are come up..rejoicing, so that the city
Job 39. 7 He scorneth the multitude of the city
Psa. 48. 2 (on) the sides of the north, the city of the
Prov. 10. 15 The rich man's wealth (is) his strong city
11. 10 When it goeth well..the city rejoiceth
18. 11 The rich man s wealth (is) his strong city
18. 19 (is harder to be won) than a strong city
29. 8 Scornful men bring a city into a snare
Isa. 1. 21 How is the faithful city become an harlot!
1. 26 thou shalt be called..The faithful city
22. 2 Thou that art full of stirs, joyous city
24. 10 The city of confusion is broken down
25. 2 For thou hast made of a city an heap; (of)
25. 3 the city of the terrible nations shall fear
26 5 the lofty city, he layeth it low; he layeth
29. 1 Woe to Ariel the city (where) David
32. 13 upon all the houses..(in) the joyous city
33 20 Look upon Zion, the city of our solemni.
Jer 49. 25 How is the city of praise not left, the
Lam. 2. 11 sucklings swoon in the streets of the city
Hos. 6. 8 Gilead (is) a city of them that work ini.
Mic. 4. 10 now shalt thou go forth out of the city
Hab. 2. 8, 17 of the city, and of all that dwell therein
2. 12 Woe to him that..stablisheth a city by

3. *A city (with walls),* קִרְיָא *qirya.*

Ezra 4. 12 building the rebellious and the bad city
4. 13 if this city be builded, and the walls set
4. 15 know, that this city (is) a rebellious city
4. 15 for which cause was this city destroyed
4. 16 if this city be builded (again), and the w.
4. 19 it is found that this city..hath made ins.
4. 21 that this city be not builded, until (ano.)

4. *A city (with walls),* קֶרֶת *qereth.*

Job 29. 7 I went out to the gate through the city

Prov. 8. 3 She crieth at the gates..of the city, at
9. 3 crieth upon the highest places of the city
9. 14 on a seat in the high places of the city
11. 11 By the blessing of the upright the city

5. *A gate, the people assembling there,* שַׁעַר *shaar.*

Ruth 3. 11 for all the city of my people doth know

6. *A city (with walls),* πόλις *polis.*

Matt. 2. 23 he came and dwelt in a city called Naz.
4. 5 the devil taketh him..into the holy city
5. 14 A city that is set on an hill cannot be
5. 35 for it is the city of the great King
8. 33 went their ways into the city, and told
8. 34 behold, the whole city came out to meet
9. 1 passed over, and came into his own city
10. 5 into (any) city of the Samaritans enter ye
10. 11 into whatsoever city or town ye shall
10 14 when ye depart out of that house or city
10. 15 be more tolerable..than for that city
10. 23 when they persecute you in this city, flee
12. 25 every city..divided against itself shall
21. 10 all the city was moved, saying, Who is
21. 17 he left them, and went out of the city
21. 18 Now..as he returned into the city, he
22. 7 he sent forth..and burned up their city
23. 34 and persecute (them) from city to city
26. 18 he said, Go into the city to such a man
27. 53 went into the holy city, and appeared
28. 11 some of the watch came into the city, and
Mark 1. 33 all the city was gathered together at
1. 45 Jesus could no more..enter into the city
5. 14 told (it) in the city, and in the country
6. 11 [be more tolerable..than for that city]
11. 19 when even was come, he went out of..c.
14. 13 and saith unto them, Go ye into the city
14. 16 his disciples..came into the city, and
Luke 1. 26 the angel..was sent from God unto a city
1. 39 Mary arose..and went..into a city of J.
2. 3 all went..every one into his own city
2. 4 Joseph also went up..out of the city of
2. 4 unto the city of David, which is called
2. 11 unto you is born this day, in the city of
2. 39 they returned into..their own city Naz.
4. 29 rose up, and thrust him out of the city
4. 29 of the hill whereon their city was built
4. 31 came down to Capernaum, a city of G.
5. 12 when he was in a certain city, behold a
7. 11 that he went into a city called Nain
7. 12 when he came nigh to the gate of the city
7. 12 and much people of the city was with
7. 37 a woman in the city..brought an alaba.
8. 27 there met him out of the city a certain
8. 34 went and told (it) in the city and in the
8. 39 published throughout the whole city how
9. 5 when ye go out of that city, shake off the
9. 10 into a desert place belonging to the city
10. 1 before his face into every city and place
10. 8, 10 into whatsoever city ye enter, and
10. 11 Even the very dust of your city, which
10. 12 be more tolerable..than for that city
14. 21 Go out quickly into..lanes of the city
18. 2 There was in a city a judge, which feared
18. 3 And there was a widow in that city; and
19. 41 he beheld the city, and wept over it
22. 10 Behold, when ye are entered into the c.
23. 19 Who for a certain sedition..in the city
23. 51 (he was) of Arimathea, a city of the Jews
24. 49 tarry ye in the city of Jerusalem, until ye
John 1. 44 Philip was of Bethsaida, the city of A.
4. 5 Then cometh he to a city of Samaria
4. 8 his disciples were gone away unto the c.
4. 28 went her way into the city, and saith to
4. 30 they went out of the city, and came
4. 39 many of the Samaritans of that city
11. 54 but went thence..into a city called E.
19 20 place where Jesus was..nigh to the city
Acts 7. 58 cast (him) out of the city, and stoned (him)
8. 5 Philip went down to the city of Samaria
8. 8 And there was great joy in that city
8. 9 which beforetime in the same city used
9. 6 Arise, and go into the city, and it shall
10. 9 they went..and drew nigh unto the city
11. 5 I was in the city of Joppa praying: and
12. 10 the iron gate that leadeth unto the city
13. 44 came almost the whole city together to
13 50 Jews stirred up..chief men of the city
14. 4 But the multitude of the city was divided
14. 13 the priest of J., which was before their c.
14. 19 having stoned Paul, drew (him) out of..c.
14. 20 he rose up, and came into the city
14. 21 they had preached the Gospel to that city
15. 36 Let us..visit our brethren in every city
16. 12 which is the chief city of that part of
16. 12 we were in that city abiding certain days
16. 13 on the sabbath we went out of the [city] by
16. 14 a certain woman named Lydia..of the c.
16. 20 These men..do exceedingly trouble our c.
16. 39 and desired (them) to depart out of the c.
17. 5 and set all the city on an uproar
17. 16 when he saw the city wholly given to
18. 10 for I have much people in this city
19. 29 the whole city was filled with confusion
19. 35 how that the city of the Ephesians is a
21. 5 brought us..till (we were) out of the city
21. 29 they had seen before with him in the city
21. 30 all the city was moved, and the people ran
21. 39 (which am) a Jew of Tarsus, (a city) in C.
21 39 a citizen of no mean city
22. 3 brought up in this city at the feet of
24. 12 neither in the synagogues, nor in the city

Acts 25. 23 with the..principal men of the city
27. 8 nigh whereunto was the city (of) Lasea
Rom 16. 23 the chamberlain of the city saluteth you
2 Co. 11. 26 (in) perils in the city, (in) perils in the
11. 32 the governor..kept the city of the Dam.
Titus 1. 5 ordain elders in every city, as I had
Heb. 11. 10 looked for a city which hath foundations
11. 16 for he hath prepared for them a city
12. 22 and unto the city of the living God, the
13. 14 For here have we no continuing city, but
Jas. 4. 13 To day..we will go into such a city, and
Rev. 3. 12 the name of the city of my God, (which is)
11. 2 the holy city shall they tread under foot
11. 8 (shall lie) in the street of the great city
11. 13 the tenth part of the city fell, and in
14. 8 Babylon is fallen..that great [city], 14.20.
14. 28 wine press was trodden without the city
16. 19 And the great city was divided into three
17. 18 woman which thou sawest is that..city
18 10 alas, that great city..that mighty city!
18. 16 alas, that great city, that was clothed in
18. 18 What (city is) like unto this great city!
18. 19 weeping..saying, Alas, alas, that great c.
18. 21 with violence shall that great city Baby.
20. 9 compassed the camp..and the beloved c.
21. 2 I John saw the holy city, new Jerusalem
21. 10 and showed me that great city, the holy
21. 14 wall of the city had twelve foundations
21. 15 had a golden reed to measure the city
21 16 the city lieth four square, and the length
21 16 he measured the city with the reed, tw.
21. 18 the city (was) pure gold, like unto clear
21. 19 the foundations of the wall of the city
21. 21 the street of the city (was) pure gold, as
21. 23 the city had no need of the sun, neither
22. 14 enter in through the gates into the city
22. 19 take away his part..out of the holy city

CITY of confusion, קִרְיַת־תֹּהוּ *qiryath-tohu.*
A symbolic name for Jerusalem.
Isa. 24. 10 The city of confusion is broken down

CITY of David, עִיר דָּוִד *ir David.*
That part of Jerusalem built on Mount Zion.
2 Sa. 5. 7 Zion: the same (is) the city of D.
5. 9 dwelt in the fort..called it The city of D.
6. 10 not remove the ark..into the city of D.
1 Ki. 2. 10 David..was buried in the city of D.
8. 1 might bring..ark..out of the city of D.
9. 24 Pharaoh's daughter..out of the city of D.
11. 43 Solomon..was buried in the city of D.
15. 8 and they buried him in the city of D.
2 Ki. 8. 24 buried with his fathers in the city of D.
12. 21 buried him..in the city of D.
1 Ch. 11. 7 therefore they called it the city of D.
13. 13 brought not the ark..to the city of D.
15. 1 (David) made him houses in the city of D.
15. 29 the ark..came to the city of D.
2 Ch. 5. 2 to bring up the ark..out of the city of D.
8. 11 out of the city of D. unto the house that
9. 31 Solomon..was buried in the city of D.
12. 16 Rehoboam..was buried in the city of D.
14. 1 and they buried him in the city of D.
16. 14 And they buried him..in the city of D.
21. 1 buried with his fathers in the city of D.
21. 20 howbeit they buried him in the city of D.
24. 16 And they buried him in the city of D.
24. 25 and they buried him in the city of D.
27. 9 and they buried him in the city of D.
32. 5 and repaired Millo (in) the city of D.
32. 30 brought it..the west side of the city of D.
Neh. 3. 15 stairs that go down from the city of D.
12. 37 they went up by..stairs of the city of D.
Isa. 22. 9 Ye have seen..breaches of the city of D.

CITY of destruction, עִיר הַהֶרֶס *city of the sun.*
A prophetic name given to one of the five cities of Egypt inhabited by Israelites.
Isa. 19. 18 one shall be called, The city of destruction

CITY, fenced —
Fenced, fortified place, מְצוּרָה *metsurah.*
2 Ch. 11. 10 which (are) in Judah..fenced cities
11. 23 and dispersed..unto every fenced city
12. 4 he took the fenced cities which (pertained)
14. 6 he built fenced cities in Judah: for the
21. 3 of precious things, with fenced cities in

CITY, golden —
Golden one, מַדְהֵבָה *madhebah.*
Isa. 14. 4 hath the oppressor ceased! the golden city

CITY of palm trees —
A name sometimes given to Jericho, עִיר הַתְּמָרִים.
Deut 34. 3 Jericho, the city of palm trees, unto Zoar
Judg. 3. 13 smote Israel..possessed the city of palm t.
2 Ch. 28. 15 brought them to Jericho, the city of palm t.

CITY, royal, עִיר הַמְּלוּכָה *city of the kingdom.*
Another name of Rabbah of the children of Ammon, and apparently the same as the "City of Waters."
2 Sa. 12. 26 Joab fought..and took the royal city

CITY, ruler of the —
Chief of the city, πολιτάρχης *politarchēs.*
Acts 17. 6 drew Jason..unto the rulers of the city
17. 8 they troubled..the rulers of the city, when

CITY of salt, עִיר הַמֶּלַח.
A city of Judah, near the Salt Sea.
Josh. 15. 62 And Nibshan, and the city of Salt, and

CITY, several —
City and city, עִיר וָעִיר *ir vair.*
2 Ch. 11. 12 in every several city (he put) shields and
28. 25 in every several city of Judah he made
31. 19 in every several city, the men that were

CITY of waters, עִיר הַמָּיִם *ir ham-mayim.*
The name given by Joab to part of Rabbah, the chief city of the Ammonites.
2 Sa. 12. 27 I have fought..and have taken the c. of w.

CLAD oneself, to —
To cover oneself, כָּסָה *kasah,* 7.
1 Ki. 11. 29 he had clad himself with a new garment

CLAD, to be —
To wrap oneself up, עָטָה *atah.*
Isa. 59. 17 and was clad with zeal as a cloak

CLAMOROUS —
To hum, make a noise, הָמָה *hamah.*
Prov. 9. 13 A foolish woman (is) clamorous; (she is)

CLAMOUR —
Cry, outcry, κραυγή *kraugē.*
Eph. 4. 31 and anger, and clamour, and evil speaking

CLAP, to —
1. *To smite (the) hands together,* מָחָא *macha.*
Psa. 98. 8 Let the floods clap (their) hands: let the
Isa. 55. 12 all the trees of the field shall clap (their)
2. *To smite (the) hands together,* מָחָא *macha,* 3.
Eze. 25. 6 Because thou hast clapped (thine) hands
3. *To (cause to) smite,* נָכָה *nakah,* 5.
2 Ki. 11. 12 they clapped their hands, and said, God save
4. *To clap (the hands) together,* סָפַק *saphaq.*
Job 34. 37 he clappeth (his hands) among us, and
Lam. 2. 15 All that pass by clap (their) hands at thee
5. *To clap (the hand) together,* שָׂפַק *saphaq.*
Job 27. 23 (Men) shall clap their hands at him, and
6. *To strike (the hands) together,* תָּקַע *taqa.*
Psa. 47. 1 O clap your hands, all ye people; shout
Nah. 3. 19 all that hear the bruit of thee shall clap

CLAU'-DA, Κλαύδη.
A small island S.W. of Crete. Mela and Pliny call it Gaudos, and Ptolemy calls it Klaudos. It is still called *Clauda-nesa* or *Guadonesi* by the Greeks, which the Italians have corrupted into *Gozzo.*
Acts 27. 16 a certain island which is called C.

CLAU-DI'-A, Κλαυδία.
A female disciple at Rome, supposed to be a British maiden and daughter of king Cogidubnus, who took the name of his imperial patron Tiberius Claudius. Her husband seems to have been Pudens, who is mentioned in the same verse.
2 Ti. 4. 21 Eubulus greeteth thee..and C., and all the

CLAU-DI'-US, Κλαύδιος.
1. The successor of Caligula as emperor, A.D. 41–54.
Acts 11. 28 which came to pass in the days of C.
18. 2 C. had commanded all Jews to depart
2. A Roman officer, chief captain in Jerusalem, A.D. 60.
Acts 23. 26 C. Lysias unto..Felix (sendeth) greeting

CLAW —
Cloven or parted hoof, פַּרְסָה *parsah.*
Deut. 14. 6 and cleaveth the cleft into two claws, (and)
Zech. 11. 16 but he shall..tear their claws in pieces

CLAY —
1. *Clay, (from its red colour), mortar,* חֹמֶר *chomer.*
Job 4. 19 less (in) them that dwell in houses of clay
10. 9 that thou hast made me as the clay
13. 12 your bodies to bodies of clay
27. 16 Though he..prepare raiment as the clay
33. 6 I also am formed out of the clay
38. 14 It is turned as clay (to) the seal; and they
Isa. 29. 16 shall be esteemed as the potter's clay
45. 9 Shall the clay say to him that fashioneth
64. 8 we (are) the clay, and thou our potter
Jer. 18. 4 the vessel that he made of clay was marred
18. 6 as the clay (is) in the potter's hand, so (are)
2. *Burnt clay of the potter,* חֲסַף *chasaph.*
Dan. 2. 33 his feet part of iron and part of clay
2. 34 his feet (that were) of iron and clay, and
2. 35 Then was the iron, the clay, the brass, the
2. 41 part of potter's clay, and part of iron
2. 41, 43 sawest the iron mixed with miry clay
2. 42 the toes..part of iron, and part of clay
2. 43 even as iron is not mixed with clay
2. 45 the iron, the brass, the clay, the silver
3. *Mire, mud,* טִיט *tit.*
Psa. 40. 2 He brought me up..out of the miry clay
Isa. 41. 25 and as the potter treadeth clay
Nah. 3. 14 go into clay, and tread the mortar, make
4. *Mortar, (from its softness),* מֶלֶט *melet.*
Jer. 43. 9 hide them in the clay in the brick kiln
5. *Thick clayey place,* מַעֲבֶה *maabeh.*
1 Ki. 7. 46 in the clay ground between Succoth and
6. *Thick clayey soil,* עָב *ab.*
2 Ch. 4. 17 in the clay ground between Succoth and

7. *Clay, mortar,* πηλός *pēlos.*
John 9. 6 he spat on the ground, and made clay of
9. 6 and he anointed the eyes..with the clay
9. 11 A man that is called Jesus made clay, and
9. 14 it was the sabbath..Jesus made the clay
9. 15 He put clay upon mine eyes, and I washed
Rom. 9. 21 Hath not the potter power over the clay

CLAY, thick —
Thick mire, heavy pledge, עַבְטִיט *abtit.*
Hab. 2. 6 him that ladeth himself with thick clay!

CLEAN —
1. *Clean, empty,* בַּר *bar.*
Job 11. 4 My doctrine (is) pure, and I am clean in
Psa. 73. 1 (even) to such as are of a clean heart
Prov. 14. 4 Where no oxen (are), the crib (is) clean
2. *Pure, pious,* זַךְ *zak.*
Job 33. 9 I am clean without transgression, I (am)
Prov. 16. 2 All the ways of a man (are) clean in
3. *Leavened,* חָמִיץ *chamits.*
Isa. 30. 24 The oxen likewise..shall eat clean prov.
4. *To make bare,* חָשַׂף *chasaph.*
Joel 1. 7 he hath made it clean bare, and cast (it)
5. *Pure, clean,* טָהוֹר *tahor.*
Gen. 7. 2 Of every clean beast thou shalt take to
7. 2 and of beasts that (are) not clean by two
7. 8 Of clean beasts and of beasts..not clean
8. 20 every clean beast, and of every clean fowl
Lev. 4. 12 without the camp unto a clean place
6. 11 carry forth the ashes..unto a clean place
7. 19 as for the flesh, all that be clean shall
10. 10 and between unclean and clean
10. 14 heave shoulder..eat in a clean place
11. 36 a fountain or pit..shall be clean
11. 37 And if (any part)..fall..it shall be clean
11. 47 between the unclean and the clean, and
13. 13 (if) the leprosy have covered..he (is) clean
13. 17 (if) the plague be turned..he (is) clean
13. 37 the scall is healed, he (is) clean
13. 39 it (is) a freckled spot..he (is) clean
13. 40 he (is) bald; (yet is) he clean
13. 41 he (is) forehead bald: (yet is) he clean
14. 4 take for him..two birds alive (and) clean
14. 57 when (it is) unclean, and when (it is) cl.
15. 8 And if he..spit upon him that is clean
20. 25 put difference between clean beasts and
20. 25 and between unclean fowls and clean
Num. 5. 28 if the woman be not defiled, but be clean
9. 13 the man that (is) clean, and is not in a
18. 11, 13 every one that is clean in thy house
19. 9 a man (that is) clean shall gather up the
19. 9 lay (them) up without the camp in a clean
19. 18 a clean person shall take hyssop, and dip
19. 19 the clean (person) shall sprinkle upon the
Deut 12. 15 the unclean and the clean may eat thereof
12. 22 the unclean and the clean, shall eat (of)
14. 11 (Of) all clean birds ye shall eat
14. 20 (But of) all clean fowls ye may eat
15. 22 the unclean and the clean (person shall)
23. 10 any man that is not clean, by reason of
1 Sa. 20. 26 he (is) not clean; surely he (is) not clean
2 Ch. 30. 17 passovers for..one (that was) not clean
Job 14. 4 Who can bring a clean (thing) out of an un.
Psa. 19. 9 The fear of the LORD (is) clean, enduring
51. 10 Create in me a clean heart, O God; and
Eccl. 9. 2 to the good and to the clean, and to the
Isa. 66. 20 bring an offering in a clean vessel into
Eze. 22. 26 between the unclean and the clean
36. 25 Then will I sprinkle clean water upon you
44. 23 discern between the unclean and the cl.
6. *Clean,* טְהֹר *tahor.*
Job 17. 9 he that hath clean hands shall be stronger
7. *To be or become dry,* יָבֵשׁ *yabesh.*
Zech. 11. 17 his arm shall be clean dried up, and his
8. *Innocent,* נָקִי *naqi.*
Psa. 24. 4 He that hath clean hands, and a pure h.
9. *To break,* פָּרַר *parar.*
Isa. 24. 19 the earth is clean dissolved, the earth is
10. *Clean, clear,* καθαρός *katharos.*
Matt 23. 26 that the outside of them may be clean
27. 59 he wrapped it in a clean linen cloth
Luke 11. 41 and, behold, all things are clean unto you
John 13. 10 He that is washed..is clean every whit
13. 10 and ye are clean, but not all
13. 11 therefore said he, Ye are not all clean
15. 3 Now ye are clean through the word which
Acts 18. 6 (be) upon your own heads; I (am) clean
Rev. 19. 8 arrayed in fine linen, clean and white
19. 14 clothed in fine linen, white and clean
11. *Actually, really,* ὄντως *ontōs.*
2 Pe. 2. 18 those that were [clean] escaped from them

CLEAN, to be —
1. *To be purified,* בָּרַר *barar,* 2.
Isa. 52. 11 be ye clean, that bear the vessels of the
2. *To be or become pure,* זָכָה *zakah.*
Job 15. 14 What (is) man, that he should be clean?
25. 4 how can he be clean (that is) born of a
3. *To be pure,* זָכַךְ *zakak.*
Job 15. 15 the heavens are not clean in his sight
4. *To be clean, cleansed,* טָהֵר *taher.*
Lev. 12. 8 atonement for her, and she shall be clean
13. 6, 34 he shall wash his clothes, and be clean

Lev. 13. 58 it shall be washed..and shall be clean
14. 8 and wash himself..that he may be clean
14. 9 he shall wash..and he shall be clean
14. 20 atonement for him, and he shall be clean
14. 53 for the house : and it shall be clean
15. 13 and wash his clothes..and shall be clean
15. 28 and after that she shall be clean
17. 15 he shall both wash..then shall he be clean
16. 30 (that) ye may be clean from all your sins
22. 4 he shall not eat..until he be clean
22. 7 when the sun is down, he shall be clean
Num 19. 12 and on the seventh day he shall be clean
19 12 then the seventh day he shall not be clean
19. 19 and bathe himself..and shall be clean
31. 23 ye shall make (it)..and it shall be clean
31. 24 and ye shall be clean, and afterward
2 Ki. 5. 10 Go and wash..and thou shalt be clean
5. 12 may I not wash in them, and be clean?
5. 13 when he saith to thee, Wash, and be clean?
5. 14 his flesh came again..and he was clean
Psa. 51. 7 Purge me with hyssop, and I shall be clean
Eze 36. 25 I sprinkle clean water..ye shall be clean

5. *To become or be made clean,* טָהֵר *taher,* 7.
Gen. 35. 2 and be clean, and change your garments

6. *To be made clean,* καθαρίζομαι [*katharizō*].
Matt. 8. 3 touched him, saying, I will ; be thou clean
Mark 1. 41 and saith unto him, I will ; be thou clean
Luke 5. 13 touched him, saying, I will : be thou clean

CLEAN gone, to be —
To be ended, ceased, אָפֵס *aphes.*
Psa. 77. 8 Is his mercy clean gone for ever?

CLEAN, to be made —
1. *To become clean,* טָהֵר *taher.*
Jer. 13. 27 O Jerusalem ! wilt thou not be made clean ?
2. *To be made pure,* טָהֵר *taher,* 7.
Lev. 14. 11 present the man that is to be made clean

CLEAN, to make —
1. *To make pure,* זָכָה *zakah,* 3.
Prov. 20. 9 Who can say, I have made my heart clean
2. *To show oneself pure,* זָכָה *zakah,* 7.
Isa. 1. 16 Wash you, make you clean ; put away the
3. *To make pure,* זָכַךְ *zakak,* 5.
Job 9. 30 and make my hands never so clean
4. *To make or declare clean,* טָהֵר *taher,* 3.
Lev. 14. 11 the priest that maketh (him) clean shall
Num 8. 7 and (so) make themselves clean
5. *To make clean, clear,* καθαρίζω *katharizō.*
Matt. 8. 2 if thou wilt, thou canst make me clean
23. 25 ye make clean the outside of the cup and
Mark 1. 40 If thou wilt, thou canst make me clean
Luke 5. 12 if thou wilt, thou canst make me clean
11. 39 Now do ye Pharisees make clean the out.

CLEAN passed, to be —
To be complete, finished, ended, תָּמַם *tamam.*
Josh. 3. 17 the people were passed clean over Jordan
4. 1 when all the people were clean passed over
4. 11 when all the people were clean passed over

CLEAN, to pronounce —
To declare clean, טָהֵר *taher,* 3.
Lev. 13. 6 the priest shall pronounce him clean
13. 13 he shall pronounce (him) clean (that hath)
13. 17, 23, 28, 34, 37 shall pronounce (him) clean
13. 59 to pronounce it clean, or to pronounce it
14. 7 shall pronounce him clean, and shall let
14. 48 priest shall pronounce the house clean

CLEANNESS —
1. *Cleanness, clearness, emptiness,* בֹּר *bor.*
2 Sa. 22. 21 according to the cleanness of my hands
22. 25 according to my cleanness in his eye
Psa. 18. 20 according to the cleanness of my hands
2. *Innocency, freedom, cleanness,* נִקָּיוֹן *niqqayon.*
Amos 4. 6 I also have given you cleanness of teeth

CLEANSE —
Cleansing, scouring [V.L. תַּמְרִיק] תַּמְרוּק *tamruq.*
Prov. 20. 30 blueness of a wound cleanseth away evil

CLEANSE, to —
1. *To make clear or clean,* בָּרַר *barar,* 5.
Jer. 4. 11 A dry wind..not to fan, nor to cleanse
2. *To purify,* זָכָה *zakah,* 3.
Psa. 73. 13 Verily I have cleansed my heart (in) vain
119. 9 Wherewithal shall a young man cleanse
3. *To remove sin or defect,* חָטָא *chata,* 3.
Exod 29. 36 thou shalt cleanse the altar, when thou
Lev. 14. 49 he shall take to cleanse the house two
14. 52 he shall cleanse the house with the blood
Eze. 43. 20 thus shalt thou cleanse and purge it
43. 22 cleanse the altar, as they did cleanse (it)
43. 23 When thou hast made an end of cleansing
45. 18 take a young bullock..cleanse the sanct.
4. *To cleanse, declare clean,* טָהֵר *taher,* 3.
Lev. 16. 19 and cleanse it, and hallow it from
16. 30 make an atonement for you, to cleanse you
Num. 8. 6 Take the Levites..and cleanse them
8. 7 thus shalt thou do..to cleanse them
8. 15 thou shalt cleanse them, and offer them
8. 21 made an atonement for them to cleanse
2 Ch. 29. 15 came..to cleanse the house of the LORD
29. 16 went into the inner part..to cleanse (it)
29. 18 We have cleansed all the house of..LORD
2 Ch. 34. 5 and cleansed Judah and Jerusalem
Neh. 13. 9 they cleansed the chambers ; and thither
13. 30 Thus cleansed I them from all strangers
Job 37. 21 the wind passeth, and cleanseth them
Psa. 51. 2 Wash me..and cleanse me from my sin
Jer. 33. 8 I will cleanse them from all their iniquity
Eze. 36. 25 and from all your idols, will I cleanse you
36. 33 that I shall have cleansed you from all
37. 23 wherein they have sinned, and will cleanse
39. 12 seven months..that they may cleanse the
39. 14 upon the face of the earth, to cleanse it
39. 16 Thus shall they cleanse the land
5. *To make or declare free, or innocent,* נָקָה *naqah,* 3.
Psa. 19 12 cleanse thou me from secret (faults)
Joel 3 21 I will cleanse..I have not cleansed
6. *To make clean, clear,* καθαρίζω *katharizō.*
Matt 8. 3 immediately his leprosy was cleansed
10. 8 Heal the sick, cleanse the lepers, raise
11. 5 the lame walk, the lepers are cleansed
23. 26 cleanse first that (which is) within the cup
Mark 1. 42 the leprosy departed..and he was cleansed
Luke 4. 27 none of them was cleansed, saving Naam
7. 22 the lame walk, the lepers are cleansed
17. 14 it came to pass, that..they were cleansed
17. 17 Were there not ten cleansed? but where
Acts 10. 15 What God hath cleansed, (that) call not
11. 9 What God hath cleansed, (that) call not
2 Co. 7. 1 let us cleanse ourselves from all filthiness
Eph. 5. 26 he might sanctify and cleanse it with
Jas. 4. 8 Cleanse (your) hands, (ye) sinners ; and
1 Jo. 1. 7 the blood of Jesus Christ..cleanseth us
1. 9 to cleanse us from all unrighteousness

CLEANSE selves, to —
To cleanse oneself, טָהֵר *taher,* 7.
2 Ch. 30. 18 a multitude..had not cleansed themselves
Neh. 13. 22 that they should cleanse themselves, and

CLEANSED, to be —
1. *To be clean, cleansed,* טָהֵר *taher.*
Lev. 11. 32 be put into water..so it shall be cleansed
12. 7 she shall be cleansed from the issue of
15. 13 when he that hath an issue is cleansed of
15. 28 But if she be cleansed of her issue, then
2. *To be clean, cleansed,* טָהֵר *taher,* 4.
Eze 22. 24 Thou (art) the land that is not cleansed
3. *To cleanse oneself, be cleansed,* טָהֵר *taher,* 7.
Lev. 14. 4 to take for him that is to be cleansed
14. 7 sprinkle upon him that is to be cleansed
14. 8 he that is to be cleansed shall wash his
14. 14, 17, 25, 28 ear of him that is to be clea.
14. 18, 29 upon the head of him that is to be clea.
14. 19, 31 atonement for him that is to be clea.
Josh 22. 17 from which we are not cleansed until this
4. *To be covered,* כָּפַר *kaphar,* 4.
Num 35. 33 the land cannot be cleansed of the blood
5. *To become, be counted righteous,* צָדַק *tsadaq,* 2.
Dan. 8. 14 then shall the sanctuary be cleansed

CLEANSED, is —
Cleansing, טָהֳרָה *tohorah.*
Eze 44 26 And after he is cleansed, they shall reckon

CLEANSING —
1. *Cleansing,* טָהֳרָה *tohorah.*
Lev. 13. 7 that he hath been seen..for his cleansing
13. 35 if the scall spread..after his cleansing
14. 2 the law..in the day of his cleansing
14. 23 he shall bring them..for his cleansing
14. 32 (that which pertaineth) to his cleansing
15. 13 then he shall number..for his cleansing
Num. 6. 9 his head in the day of his cleansing
2. *Cleansing,* καθαρισμός *katharismos.*
Mark 1. 44 offer for thy cleansing those things which
Luke 5. 14 but go..and offer for thy cleansing

CLEAR —
1. *Light,* אוֹר *or.*
Amos 8. 9 I will darken the earth in the clear day
2. *Clear,* בַּר *bar.*
Song 6. 10 fair as the moon, clear as the sun, (and)
3. *Rare, precious,* יָקָר *yaqar.*
Zech 14. 6 the light shall not be clear, (nor) dark
4. *Innocent,* נָקִי *naqi.*
Gen. 24 41 thou shalt be clear from
5. *Shining, white,* צַח *tsach.*
Isa. 18. 4 I will consider..like a clear heat upon
6. *Pure,* ἁγνός *agnos.*
2 Co. 7. 11 ye have approved yourselves to be clear
7. *Clean,* καθαρός *katharos.*
Rev. 21. 18 the city (was) pure gold, like unto clear
8. *Shining, bright,* λαμπρός *lampros.*
Rev. 22. 1 pure river of water of life, clear as cry.

CLEAR, to —
To declare innocent, free, נָקָה *naqah,* 3.
Exod. 34. 7 that will by no means clear (the guilty)

CLEAR, to be —
1. *To be pure,* זָכָה *zakah.*
Psa. 51. 4 (and) be clear when thou judgest
2. *To be innocent, free,* נָקָה *naqah,* 2.
Gen. 24. 8 then thou shalt be clear from this my
24. 41 Then shalt thou be clear from (this) my

CLEAR selves, to —
To justify oneself, צָדַק *tsadaq,* 7.
Gen 44 16 what..or how shall we clear ourselves ?

CLEARER, to be —
To rise up, קוּם *qum.*
Job 11. 17 (thine) age shall be clearer than the noon.

CLEARING —
To declare innocent, free, נָקָה *naqah,* 3.
Num 14. 18 and by no means clearing (the guilty)

CLEARING of one's self —
A speaking off (for oneself), ἀπολογία *apologia.*
2 Co. 7 11 yea, (what) clearing of yourselves, yea

CLEARLY —
1. *To be clear,* בָּרַר *barar.*
Job 33. 3 and my lips shall utter knowledge clearly
2. *Far shining, brilliantly,* τηλαυγῶς *tēlaugōs.*
Mark 8. 25 was restored, and saw every man clearly

CLEARNESS —
Clearness, טֹהַר *tohar.*
Exod 24 10 as..the body of heaven in (his) clearness

CLEAVE —
Cleaving, adhering to, דָּבֵק *dabeq.*
Deut. 4. 4 But ye that did cleave unto the LORD

CLEAVE, to —
1. *To cleave asunder,* בָּקַע *baqa.*
Judg 15. 19 But God clave an hollow place that (was)
Psa. 74. 15 Thou didst cleave the fountain and the
141. 7 as when one cutteth and cleaveth (wood)
Eccl. 10. 9 he that cleaveth wood shall be endangered
Isa. 48. 21 he clave the rock also, and the waters
2. *To be cleft asunder,* בָּקַע *baqa,* 2.
Zech. 14. 4 the mount of Olives shall cleave in the
3. *To cleave asunder,* בָּקַע *baqa,* 3.
Gen. 22. 3 clave the wood for the burnt offering
1 Sa. 6. 14 and they clave the wood of the cart, and
Psa. 78. 15 He clave the rocks in the wilderness, and
Hab. 3. 9 Thou didst cleave the earth with rivers
4. *To cleave, adhere to,* דָּבַק *dabaq.*
Gen. 2. 24 and shall cleave unto his wife : and they
34. 3 his soul clave unto Dinah the daughter of
Deut 10. 20 to him shalt thou cleave, and swear by
11. 22 to walk in all his ways, and to cleave unto
13. 4 ye shall serve him, and cleave unto him
13. 17 there shall cleave nought of the cursed
28. 60 and they shall cleave unto thee
30. 20 and that thou mayest cleave unto him
Josh 22. 5 to cleave unto him, and to serve him with
23. 8 But cleave unto the LORD your God, as ye
23. 12 cleave unto the remnant of these nations
Ruth 1. 14 Orpah kissed her mother..but Ruth clave
2 Sa. 20. 2 the men of Judah clave unto their king
23. 10 and his hand clave unto the sword
1 Ki. 11. 2 Solomon clave unto these in love
2 Ki. 3. 3 he cleaved unto the sins of Jeroboam the
5. 27 The leprosy therefore..shall cleave unto
18. 6 For he clave to the LORD, (and) departed
Job 19. 20 My bone cleaveth to my skin and to my
29 10 their tongue cleaved to the roof of their
31. 7 if any blot hath cleaved to mine hands
Psa. 44. 25 our belly cleaveth unto the earth
101. 3 hate the work of them..(it) shall not c.
102. 5 By reason..my bones cleave to my skin
119. 25 My soul cleaveth unto the dust : quicken
137. 6 let my tongue cleave to the roof of my
Jer. 13. 11 as the girdle cleaveth to the loins of a
Lam. 4. 4 The tongue..cleaveth to the roof of his
5. *To be made to adhere,* דָּבַק *dabaq,* 6.
Psa. 22. 15 and my tongue cleaveth to my jaws
6. *To cleave, adhere to,* דְּבַק *debaq.*
Dan. 2. 43 but they shall not cleave one to another
7. *To strengthen, hold fast to,* חָזַק *chazaq,* 5.
Neh. 10. 29 They clave to their brethren, their nobles
8. *To be joined to,* לָוָה *lavah,* 2.
Dan. 11. 34 many shall cleave to them with flatteries
9. *To adhere, stick on,* סָפַח *saphach,* 2.
Isa. 14. 1 they shall cleave to the house of Jacob
10. *To split, till,* פָּלַח *palach,* 3.
Job 16. 13 he cleaveth my reins asunder, and doth
11. *To stick fast,* צָפַד *tsaphad.*
Lam. 4. 8 their skin cleaveth to their bones ; it is
12. *To cleave, rend,* שָׁסַע *shasa.*
Deut 14. 6 cleaveth the cleft into two claws, (and)
13. *To cleave, rend,* שָׁסַע *shasa,* 3.
Lev. 1. 17 he shall cleave it with the wings thereof
14. *To be joined to,* (πρὸς) κολλάομαι (*pros*) *kollaomai.*
Matt 19. 5 For this cause shall a man..cleave to his
Mark 10. 7 For this cause shall a man..cleave to his
Luke 10. 11 Even the very dust..which cleaveth on
Acts 17. 34 Howbeit certain men clave unto him
Rom 12. 9 cleave to that which is good

CLEAVE unto, to —
To remain toward, προσμένω *prosmenō.*
Acts 11. 23 that..they would cleave unto the Lord

CLEAVE asunder, to —
To be cleft asunder, בָּקַע *baqa,* 2.
Num 16. 31 the ground clave asunder that (was) under

CLEAVE, to cause to —
To make to adhere, דָּבַק *dabaq.* 5.
Jer. 13. 11 so have I caused to cleave unto me the

CLEAVE fast, to —
To pour out (a metal), יָצַק *yatsaq.*
Psa. 41. 8 An evil disease, (say they), cleaveth fast

CLEAVE fast together, to —
To be firmly joined together, דָּבַק *dabaq,* 4.
Job 38. 38 and the clods cleave fast together

CLEAVE, to make —
To cause to adhere, דָּבַק *dabaq,* 5.
Deut28. 21 The LORD shall make the pestilence cleave
Eze. 3. 26 I will make thy tongue cleave to the roof

CLEFT —
1. *A cleft or rent,* בָּקִיעַ *baqia.*
Amos 6. 11 will smite..the little house with clefts
2. *A hollow place,* נְקָרָה *neqarah.*
Isa. 2. 21 To go into the clefts of the rocks, and
3. *A fissure,* שֶׁסַע *shesa.*
Deut 14. 6 cleaveth the cleft into two claws, (and)

CLEFT, to be —
To become cleft, בָּקַע *baqa,* 7.
Mic. 1. 4 the valleys shall be cleft, as wax before

CLEFTS —
Clefts, recesses, חֲגָוִים *chagavim.*
Song 2. 14 O my dove, (that art) in the clefts of the
Jer. 49. 16 O thou that dwellest in the clefts of the
Obad. 3 thou that dwellest in the clefts of the

CLEMENCY —
A yieldingness, pliability, ἐπιείκεια *epieikeia.*
Acts 24. 4 that thou wouldest hear us of thy clem.

CLE'-MENT, Κλήμης.
A fellow labourer with Paul at Philippi.
Phil. 4. 3 those women which laboured..with C.

CLE-O'-PAS, Κλεόπας.
One of the two disciples going to Emmaus when Jesus appeared to them.
Luke 24. 18 C. answering said unto him, Art thou only

CLEO'-PHAS, Κλωπᾶς.
Husband of one of the Marys; half-sister of the Virgin Mary.
John 19. 25 Mary the (wife) of C., and Mary Magdal.

CLERK, town —
Writer, scribe, γραμματεύς *grammateus.*
Acts 19. 35 when the town clerk had appeased the

CLIFF —
1. *Ascent,* מַעֲלֶה *maaleh.*
2 Ch.20. 16 behold, they come up by the cliff of Ziz
2. *Rugged, terrible,* עָרוּץ *aruts.*
Job 30. 6 To dwell in the cliffs of the valleys, (in)

CLIFT —
1. *Cleft, bored out place,* נְקָרָה *neqarah.*
Exod 33. 22 I will put thee in a clift of the rock
2. *A cleft, branch,* סְעִיף *saiph.*
Isa. 57. 5 children in the valleys under the clifts

CLIMB, to —
To go up, עָלָה *alah.*
Joel 2. 7 they shall climb the wall like men of war

CLIMB up, to —
1. *To go up,* עָלָה *alah.*
1 Sa. 14. 13 Jonathan climbed up upon his hands and
Jer. 4. 29 they shall..climb up upon the rocks
Joel 2. 9 they shall climb up upon the houses
Amos 9. 2 though they climb up to heaven, thence
2. *To go up,* ἀναβαίνω *anabainō.*
Luke 19. 4 climbed up into a sycamore tree to see
John 10. 1 but climbeth up some other way, the same

CLIP, to —
To diminish, גָּרַע *gara.*
Jer. 48. 37 every head..bald, and every beard clipped

CLOAK or CLOKE —
1. *An over covering,* ἐπικάλυμμα *epikalumma.*
1 Pe. 2. 16 not using (your) liberty for a cloak of
2. *Raiment, outer garment,* ἱμάτιον *himation.*
Matt. 5. 40 take away thy coat, let him have thy cloak
Luke 6. 29 him that taketh away thy cloak forbid
3. *Pretext,* πρόφασις *prophasis.*
John15. 22 but now they have no cloak for their
1 Th. 2. 5 neither..used we..cloak of covetousness
4. *A tunic, vest,* φαινόλης, φαιλόνης *phailonēs.*
2 Ti. 4. 13 The [cloak] that I left at Troas with Carp.

CLOD —
1. *A clod (of earth),* [V.L. גִּישׁ] גּוּשׁ *gush.*
Job 7. 5 My flesh is clothed with worms and clods
2. *Furrow,* מֶגְרָפָה *megraphah.*
Joel 1. 17 The seed is rotten under their clods, the
3. *Soft clod,* רֶגֶב *regeb.*
Job 21. 33 The clods of the valley shall be sweet
38. 38 and the clods cleave fast together?

CLOKE —
Robe (upper), מְעִיל *meil.*
Isa. 59. 17 and was clad with zeal as a cloke

CLOSE —
Strait, compressed, צַר *tsar.*
Job 41. 15 shut up together (as with) a close seal

CLOSE by —
Very near, nearer, ἆσσον *asson.*
Acts 27. 13 loosing (thence), they sailed close by
[*See also* Follow, keep, kept, round about, stick.]

CLOSE, to —
1. *To fret oneself,* חָרָה *charah,* 5a.
Jer. 22. 15 Shalt thou reign, because thou closest
2. *To cover,* כָּסָה *kasah,* 3.
Num 16. 33 and the earth closed upon them
3. *To shut,* סָגַר *sagar.*
Judg. 3. 22 The fat closed upon the blade, so that he
4. *To strengthen, harden,* עָצַם *atsam,* 3.
Isa. 29. 10 For the LORD..hath closed your eyes
5. *To move down, close, shut,* καμμύω *kammuō.*
Matt 13. 15 and their eyes they have closed
Acts 28. 27 and their eyes have they closed; lest they
6. *To fold up (a roll),* πτύσσω *ptussō.*
Luke 4. 20 he closed the book, and he gave (it) again

CLOSE, to keep —
To keep silent, still, σιγάω *sigaō.*
Luke 9. 36 they kept (it) close, and told no man in

CLOSE place —
Shut up place, מִסְגֶּרֶת *misgereth.*
2 Sa. 22. 46 they shall be afraid out of their close pl.
Psa. 18. 45 and be afraid out of their close places

CLOSE up, to —
1. *To hedge or wall up,* גָּדַר *gadar.*
Amos 9. 11 and close up the breaches thereof
2. *To shut up,* סָגַר *sagar.*
Gen. 2. 21 closed up the flesh instead thereof
3. *To restrain,* עָצַר *atsar.*
Gen. 20. 18 the LORD had fast closed up all the wombs

CLOSED, to be —
To close, be closed, זוּר *zur.*
Isa. 1. 6 they have not been closed, neither bound

CLOSED up —
To stop up, סָתַם *satham.*
Dan. 12. 9 the words (are) closed up and sealed till

CLOSET —
1. *Covert, chamber,* חֻפָּה *chuppah.*
Joel 2. 16 and the bride out of her closet
2. *Store or inner chamber,* ταμεῖον *tameion.*
Matt. 6. 6 when thou prayest, enter into thy closet
Luke12. 3 which ye have spoken in the ear in closets

CLOTH —
1. *Garment,* בֶּגֶד *beged.*
Exod31. 10 the cloths of service, and the holy garm.
35. 19 The cloths of service, to do service in the
39. 1 they made cloths of service, to do service
39. 41 The cloths of service to do service (in)
Num. 4. 6 shall spread over (it) a cloth wholly of
4. 7, 11 they shall spread a cloth of blue, and
4. 8 they shall spread upon them a cloth of
4. 9 they shall take a cloth of blue, and cover
4. 12 put (them) in a cloth of blue, and cover
4. 13 and spread a purple cloth thereon
1 Sa.19. 13 put a pillow..and covered (it) with a cloth
2 Sa.20. 12 he removed Amasa..and cast a cloth upon
2. *Raiment, a cloth,* שִׂמְלָה *simlah.*
Deut22. 17 they shall spread the cloth before the
1 Sa.21. 9 it (is here) wrapped in a cloth behind the
3. *Rags, tatter,* ῥάκος *rhakos.*
Matt. 9. 16 No man putteth a piece of new cloth unto
Mark 2. 21 No man also seweth a piece of new cloth

CLOTH or clothes, linen —
1. *A bandage,* ὀθόνιον *othonion.*
Luke24. 12 [he beheld the linen clothes laid by them]
John19. 40 wound it in linen clothes with the spices
20. 5 he stooping down..saw the linen clothes
20. 6 Peter following..seeth the linen clothes
20. 7 not lying with the linen clothes, but
2. *Fine linen cloth,* σινδών *sindōn.*
Matt27. 59 he wrapped it in a clean linen cloth
Mark14. 51 having a linen cloth cast about his naked
14. 52 he left the linen cloth, and fled from

CLOTH, thick —
A heavy or thick cloth, מַכְבֵּר *makber.*
2 Ki. 8. 15 he took a thick cloth, and dipped (it) in

CLOTHE, to —
1. *To clothe, put on (anything),* לָבַשׁ *labash.*
Isa. 49. 18 thou shalt surely clothe thee with them
Eze. 34. 3 Ye eat the fat, and ye clothe you with the
Hag. 1. 6 ye clothe you, but there is none warm
2. *To put on or give clothing,* לָבַשׁ *labash,* 5.
Gen. 3. 21 did the LORD God make coats..and clothe
Exod40. 14 thou shalt bring his sons, and clothe
Lev. 8. 7 clothed him with the robe, and put the
2 Sa. 1. 24 who clothed you in scarlet with (other)
2 Ch.28. 15 with the spoil clothed all that were naked
Esth. 4. 4 she sent raiment to clothe Mordecai, and
Job 10. 11 Thou hast clothed me with skin and flesh
39. 19 hast thou clothed his neck with thunder
Psa.132. 16 I will also clothe her priests with
132. 18 His enemies will I clothe with shame
Prov23. 21 drowsiness shall clothe a man with rags
Isa. 22. 21 I will clothe him with thy robe, and
50. 3 I clothe the heavens with blackness, and
61. 10 he hath clothed me with the garments of
Eze. 16. 10 I clothed thee also with broidered work
Zech. 3. 4 I will clothe thee with change of raiment
3. 5 and clothed him with garments
3. *To clothe,* לְבַשׁ *lebash,* 5.
Dan. 5. 29 they clothed Daniel with scarlet, and put
4. *To encircle, clothe round,* ἀμφιέννυμι *amphiennumi.*
Matt. 6. 30 if God so clothe the grass of the field
11. 8 A man clothed in soft raiment?
Luke 7. 25 A man clothed in soft raiment?
12. 28 If then God so clothe the grass, which is
5. *To use raiment, or a garment,* ἱματίζω *himatizō.*
Mark 5. 15 sitting, and clothed, and in his right mind
Luke 8. 35 sitting at the feet of Jesus, clothed, and
6. *To cast around,* περιβάλλω *periballō.*
Matt25. 36 Naked, and ye clothed me: I was sick
25. 38 When saw we thee..naked, and clothed
25. 43 naked, and ye clothed me not: sick, and

CLOTHE self, to —
To put on clothing, לָבַשׁ *labash.*
Psa.109. 18 As he clothed himself with cursing like
Jer. 4. 30 Though thou clothest thyself with crims.
Eze. 26. 16 they shall clothe themselves with tremb

CLOTHE with, to —
To go in, get into (clothes), ἐνδύω *enduō.*
Mark 15. 17 [clothed] him with purple, and platted

CLOTHED —
1. *To be girded,* כִּרְבֵּל *kirbel.*
1 Ch.15. 27 David (was) clothed with a robe of fine
2. *To be covered,* כָּסָה *kasah,* 4.
1 Ch.21. 16 the elders (of Israel, who were) clothed

CLOTHED, to be —
1. *To be clothed,* לָבַשׁ *labash.*
2 Ch. 6. 41 let thy priests..be clothed with salvation
Job 7. 5 My flesh is clothed with worms and clods
8. 22 They that hate thee shall be clothed with
29. 14 I put on righteousness, and it clothed me
Psa. 35. 26 let them be clothed with shame and
65. 13 The pastures are clothed with flocks
93. 1 The LORD reigneth; he is clothed with
93. 1 the LORD is clothed with strength, (where
104. 1 thou art clothed with honour and majesty
109. 29 Let mine adversaries be clothed with
132. 9 Let thy priests be clothed with righteous.
Prov31. 21 all her household (are) clothed with
Eze. 7. 27 the prince shall be clothed with desolation
9. 2 one man among them (was) clothed with
9. 3 he called to the man clothed with linen
9. 11 behold, the man clothed with linen
10. 2 he spake unto the man clothed with linen
10. 6 he had commanded the man clothed with
10. 7 hands of (him that was) clothed with linen
23. 6 (Which were) clothed with blue, captains
23. 12 captains and rulers clothed most gorgeous
38. 4 horses and horsemen, all of them clothed
44. 17 they shall be clothed with linen garments
Zeph. 1. 8 such as are clothed with strange apparel
Zech. 3. 3 Joshua was clothed with filthy garments
2. *To be clothed,* לָבַשׁ *labash,* 4.
2 Ch. 18. 9 clothed in their robes, and they sat in a
3. *To be clothed,* לְבַשׁ *lebash.*
Dan. 5. 7 shall be clothed with scarlet, and have a
5. 16 thou shalt be clothed with scarlet, and
10. 5 behold a certain man clothed in linen
12. 6 And (one) said to the man clothed in linen
12. 7 And I heard the man clothed in linen
4. *To go into,* ἐνδύω *enduō.*
2 Co. 5. 3 [being clothed]..shall not be found naked
5. *To cast around,* περιβάλλω *periballō.*
Rev. 3. 5 the same shall be clothed in white raiment
3. 18 white raiment that thou mayest be clothed
4. 4 twenty elders sitting, clothed in white

CLOTHED in, to be —
1. *To go into (clothes),* ἐνδιδύσκω *endiduskō.*
Luke16. 19 a certain rich man who was clothed in
2. *To go into (clothes),* ἐνδύω *enduō.*
Rev. 15. 6 clothed in pure and white linen, having
19. 14 followed him..clothed in fine linen, white
3. *To cast around,* περιβάλλω *periballō.*
Mark16. 5 sitting on the right side, clothed in a long
Rev. 11. 3 they shall prophesy..clothed in sackcloth
18. 16 that great city that was clothed in fine

CLOTHED with, to be —
1. *Clothing,* לְבוּשׁ *lebush.*
Esth. 4. 2 into the king's gate clothed w. sackcloth
2. *To bind on self,* ἐγκομβόομαι *egkomboomai.*
1 Pe. 5. 5 subject one to another, and be clothed w.
3. *To go into (clothes),* ἐνδύω *enduō.*
Mark 1. 6 John was clothed with camel's hair, and
Rev. 1. 13 the Son of man, clothed with a garment

4. *To cast around*, περιβάλλω *periballō.*
Rev. 7. 9 clothed with white robes, and palms in
10. 1 another mighty angel..clothed with a clo.
12. 1 a woman clothed with the sun, and the
19. 13 he (was) clothed with a vesture dipped in

CLOTHED upon, to be —
Put on over, ἐπενδύομαι *ependuomai.*
2 Co. 5. 2 earnestly desiring to be clothed upon with
5. 4 we would be unclothed, but clothed upon

CLOTHED wherewithal, to be —
To cast around, περιβάλλω *periballō.*
Matt. 6. 31 Wherewithal shall we be clothed?

CLOTHES —
1. *Garments*, בְּגָדִים *begadim.*
Gen. 37. 29 Reuben returned..and he rent his clothes
Lev. 10. 6 neither rend your clothes, lest ye die, and
11. 25, 28, 40, 40 shall wash his clothes, and be
13. 6, 34 he shall wash his clothes, and be clean
13. 45 his clothes shall be rent, and his head
14. 8 shall wash his clothes, and shave off all
14. 9 he shall wash his clothes, also he shall
14. 47 he that lieth..shall wash his clothes
14. 47 he that eateth..shall wash his clothes
15. 5, 6, 7, 8, 10, 11, 21, 22, 27 wash his clothes
16. 26, 28 shall wash his clothes, and bathe his
16. 32 put on the linen clothes, (even) the holy
17. 15 he shall both wash his clothes, and bathe
21. 10 not uncover his head, nor rend his clothes
Num. 8. 7 let them wash their clothes, and (so) make
8. 21 and they washed their clothes; and Aaron
14. 6 them that searched..rent their clothes
19. 7 the priest shall wash his clothes, and he
19. 8 he that burneth her shall wash his clothes
19. 10 shall wash his clothes; and be unclean
19. 19 wash his clothes, and bathe himself in
19. 21 he that sprinkleth..shall wash his clothes
31. 24 ye shall wash your clothes on the seventh
Judg 11. 35 he rent his clothes, and said, Alas, my
1 Sa. 19. 24 he stripped off his clothes also, and pro.
2 Sa. 1. 2 a man came out..with his clothes rent
1. 11 David took hold on his clothes, and rent
3. 31 Rend your clothes, and gird you with sack.
13. 31 his servants stood by with their clothes
19. 24 nor washed his clothes, from the day the
1 Ki. 1. 1 they covered him with clothes, but he gat
21. 27 rent his clothes, and put sackcloth upon
2 Ki. 5. 7 he rent his clothes, and said, (Am) I God
5. 8 the king of Israel had rent his clothes
5. 8 Wherefore hast thou rent thy clothes?
6. 30 he rent his clothes, and he passed by upon
11. 14 Athaliah rent her clothes, and cried
18. 37 with (their) clothes rent, and told him the
19. 1 he rent his clothes, and covered himself
22. 11 had heard the words..he rent his clothes
22. 19 hast rent thy clothes, and wept before
2 Ch. 23. 13 Athaliah rent her clothes, and said, Trea.
34. 19 had heard the words..he rent his clothes
34. 27 didst rend thy clothes, and weep before
Neh. 4. 23 none of us put off our clothes, (saving that)
Esth. 4. 1 Mordecai rent his clothes, and put on sac.
Prov. 6. 27 take fire..and his clothes not be burnt?
Isa. 36. 22 with (their) clothes rent, and told him the
37. 1 he rent his clothes, and covered himself
Jer. 41. 5 their beards shaven, and their clothes
Eze. 16. 39 they shall strip thee also of thy clothes
23. 26 shall also strip thee out of thy clothes
27. 20 Dedan (was) thy merchant in precious cl.
Amos 2. 8 they lay (themselves) down upon clothes

2. *Wrappings, clothes*, גְּלוֹם *gelom.*
Eze. 27. 24 in blue clothes, and broidered work, and

3. *Measure, long robe*, מַד *mad.*
1 Sa. 4. 12 with his clothes rent, and with earth upon

4. *Covering*, סוּת *suth.*
Gen. 49. 11 and his clothes in the blood of grapes

5. *Outer garment, raiment*, שַׂלְמָה *salmah.*
Deut 29. 5 your clothes are not waxen old upon you
Neh. 9. 21 their clothes waxed not old, and their feet
Job 9. 31 and mine own clothes shall abhor me

6. *Outer garment, raiment*, שִׂמְלָה *simlah.*
Gen. 37. 34 Jacob rent his clothes, and put sackcloth
44. 13 they rent their clothes, and laded every
Exod 12. 34 troughs being bound up in their clothes
19. 10 and let them wash their clothes
19. 14 and they washed their clothes
Josh. 7. 6 Joshua rent his clothes, and fell to the

7. *Raiment, garment*, ἱμάτιον *himation.*
Matt 21. 7 the ass..and put on them their clothes
24. 18 Neither let him..return..to take his [c.]
26. 65 Then the high priest rent his clothes
Mark 5. 28 If I may touch but his clothes, I shall be
5. 30 Jesus..said, Who touched my clothes?
15. 20 put his own clothes on him, and led him
Luke 8. 27 a certain man..ware no clothes, neither
19. 36 as he went, they spread their clothes in
Acts 7. 58 the witnesses laid down their clothes at
14. 14 they rent their clothes, and ran in among
16. 22 and the magistrates rent off their clothes
22. 23 they cried out, and cast off (their) clothes

8. *Coat*, χιτών *chitōn.*
Mark 14. 63 Then the high priest rent his clothes, and

CLOTHES, grave —
Bandages, κειρίαι *keiriai.*
John 11. 44 bound hand and foot with grave clothes

CLOTHING —
1. *Garment*, בֶּגֶד *beged.*
Job 22. 6 and stripped the naked of their clothing

2. *Clothing*, לְבוּשׁ *lebush.*
Job 24. 7 cause the naked to lodge without clothing
24. 10 cause (him) to go naked without clothing
31. 19 have seen any perish for want of clothing
Psa. 35. 13 when they were sick, my clothing (was)
45. 13 all glorious within; her clothing (is) of
Pro. 27. 26 The lambs (are) for thy clothing, and the
31. 22 coverings of tapestry; her clothing (is) silk
31. 25 strength and honour (are) her clothing
Jer. 10. 9 blue and purple (is) their clothing: they

3. *A covering*, מְכַסֶּה *mekasseh.*
Isa. 23. 18 eat sufficiently, and for durable clothing

4. *Raiment, a cloth*, שִׂמְלָה *simlah.*
Isa. 3. 6 Thou hast clothing, be thou our ruler, and
3. 7 in my house (is) neither bread nor clothing

5. *Clothing*, תִּלְבֹּשֶׁת *tilbosheth.*
Isa. 59. 17 the garments of vengeance (for) clothing

6. *Clothing*, ἔνδυμα *enduma.*
Matt. 7. 15 which come to you in sheep's clothing

7. *Robe*, ἐσθής *esthēs.*
Acts 10. 30 a man stood before me in bright clothing
Jas. 2. 3 to him that weareth the gay clothing, and

CLOTHING, long —
Robe, vestment, στολή *stolē.*
Mark 12. 38 the scribes..love to go in long clothing

CLOTHING, soft —
The soft things, τὰ μαλακά *ta malaka.*
Matt. 11. 8 they that wear soft (clothing) are in king's

CLOUD —
1. *Something lifted up and exalted*, נָשִׂיא *nasi.*
Prov. 25. 14 a false gift (is like) clouds and wind

1a. *Hand*, כַּף *kaph.*
Job 36. 32 With clouds he covereth the light

2. *A thickness, thick cloud*, עָב *ab.*
Judg. 5. 4; 2 Sa. 23. 4; 1 Ki. 18. 44; 18. 45
Job. 20. 6 and his head reach unto the clouds
30. 15 and my welfare passeth away as a cloud
36. 29 understand the spreading of the clouds
37. 16 know the balancings of the clouds, the
38. 34 Canst thou lift up thy voice to the clouds
Psa. 77. 17 The clouds poured out water, the skies
104. 3 who maketh the clouds his chariot; who
147. 8 Who covereth the heaven with clouds
Prov 16. 15 his favour (is) as a cloud of the latter
Eccl. 11. 3 If the clouds be full of rain, they empty
11. 4 he that regardeth the clouds shall not
12. 2 nor the clouds return after the rain
Isa. 5. 6 command the clouds that they rain no
14. 14 ascend above the heights of the clouds
18. 4 like a cloud of dew in the heat of harvest
19. 1 the LORD rideth upon a swift cloud
25. 5 (even) the heat with the shadow of a cloud
60. 8 Who (are) these (that) fly as a cloud, and

3. *A cloud*, עָנָן *anan.*
Gen. 9. 13 I do set my bow in the cloud, and it shall
9. 14 when I bring a cloud over the earth, that
9. 14 that the bow shall be seen in the cloud
9. 16 the bow shall be in the cloud; and I will
Exod 13. 21 by day in a pillar of a cloud to lead them
13. 22 He took not away the pillar of the cloud
14. 19 the pillar of the cloud went from before
14. 20 it was a cloud and darkness (to them), but
14. 24 through the pillar of fire and of the cloud
16. 10 the glory of the LORD appeared in the clo.
19. 9 I come unto thee in a thick cloud
19. 16 lightnings, and a thick cloud upon the
24. 15 Moses went up..and a cloud covered the
24. 16 and the cloud covered it six days
24. 16 he called unto Moses out of the..cloud
24. 18 Moses went unto the midst of the cloud
34. 5 the LORD descended in the cloud, and
40. 34 a cloud covered the tent of the congre.
40. 35 because the cloud abode thereon, and
40. 36 when the cloud was taken up from over
40. 37 if the cloud were not taken up, then they
40. 38 the cloud of the LORD (was) upon the
Lev. 16. 2 I will appear in the cloud upon the mercy
16. 13 the cloud of the incense may cover the
Num. 9. 15 the cloud covered the tabernacle
9. 16 the cloud covered it (by day), and the
9. 17 when the cloud was taken up from the
9. 17 and in the place where the cloud abode
9. 18 the cloud abode upon the tabernacle
9. 19 the cloud tarried long upon the taberna.
9. 20 the cloud was a few days upon the taber.
9. 21 the cloud abode from even unto the
9. 21 the cloud was taken up in the morning
9. 21 or by night that the cloud was taken up
9. 22 the cloud tarried upon the tabernacle
10. 11 the cloud was taken up from off the taber.
10. 12 the cloud rested in the wilderness of P.
10. 34 the cloud of the LORD (was) upon them
11. 25 LORD came down in a cloud, and spake
12. 5 came down in the pillar of the cloud
12. 10 the cloud departed from off the taber.
14. 14 (that) thy cloud standeth over them
14. 14 by day time in a pillar of a cloud, and in
16. 42 behold the cloud covered it, and the
Deut. 1. 33 went in the way before you..in a cloud
4. 11 with darkness, clouds and thick darkn.
Deut. 5. 22 out of the midst of the fire, of the cloud
31. 15 in the tabernacle in a pillar of a cloud
31. 15 the pillar of the cloud stood over the
1 Ki. 8. 10 the cloud filled the house of the LORD
8. 11 could not..minister because of the cloud
2 Ch. 5. 13 the house was filled with a cloud
5. 14 to minister by reason of the cloud
Neh. 9. 19 the pillar of the cloud departed not from
Job 7. 9 the cloud is consumed and vanisheth
26. 8 And the cloud is not rent under them
26. 9 He holdeth..(and) spreadeth his cloud
37. 11 he scattereth his bright cloud
37. 15 God..caused the light of his cloud to
38. 9 When I made the cloud the garment
Psa. 78. 14 he led them with a cloud, and all the
97. 2 Clouds and darkness (are) round about
105. 39 He spread a cloud for a covering, and fire
Isa. 4. 5 upon her assemblies, a cloud and smoke
44. 22 I have blotted out, as a..cloud thy sins
Jer. 4. 13 he shall come up as clouds, and his
Lam. 3. 44 Thou hast covered thyself with a cloud
Eze. 1. 4 a great cloud, and a fire infolding itself
1. 28 that is in the cloud in the day of rain
8. 11 and a thick cloud of incense went up
10. 3 and the cloud filled the inner court
10. 4 the house was filled with the cloud, and
30. 18 as for her, a cloud shall cover her, and
32. 7 I will cover the sun with a cloud, and the
38. 9 thou shalt be like a cloud to cover the
38. 16 thou shalt come..as a cloud to cover the
Hos. 6. 4 your goodness (is) as a morning cloud
13. 3 they shall be as the morning cloud, and
Joel 2. 2 a day of clouds and of thick darkness
Nah. 1. 3 the clouds are the dust of his feet
Zeph. 1. 15 a day of clouds and thick darkness

4. *A cloud*, עֲנָן *anan.*
Dan. 7. 13 Son of man came with the clouds

5. *A (heavy) cloud*, עֲנָנָה *ananah.*
Job 3. 5 let a cloud dwell upon it; let the black.

6. *A (thin) cloud*, שַׁחַק *shachaq.*
Job 35. 5 behold the clouds, (which) are higher
36. 28 Which the clouds do drop (and) distil
37. 21 bright light which (is) in the clouds
38. 37 Who can number the clouds in wisdom
Psa. 36. 5 thy faithfulness..unto the clouds
57. 10 heavens, and thy truth unto the clouds
68. 34 and his strength (is) in the clouds
78. 23 he had commanded the clouds from
108. 4 and thy truth reacheth unto the clouds
Prov. 3. 20 and the clouds drop down the dew
8. 28 When he established the clouds above

7. *A small or thin cloud*, νεφέλη *nephelē.*
Matt 17. 5 While he yet spake..a bright cloud
17. 5 behold a voice out of the cloud, which
24. 30 the Son of man coming in the clouds of
26. 64 and coming in the clouds of heaven
Mark 9. 7 there was a cloud that overshadowed
9. 7 a voice came out of the cloud, saying
13. 26 the Son of man coming in the clouds with
14. 62 and coming in the clouds of heaven
Luke 9. 34 there came a cloud, and overshadowed
9. 34 they feared as they entered into the cloud
9. 35 there came a voice out of the cloud, saying
12. 54 When ye see a cloud rise out of the west
21. 27 the Son of man coming in a cloud
Acts 1. 9 a cloud received him out of their sight
1 Co. 10. 1 all our fathers were under the cloud
10. 2 were all baptized unto Moses in the cloud
1 Th. 4. 17 caught up..with them in the clouds
2 Pe. 2. 17 [clouds] that are carried with a tempest
Jude 12 clouds (they are) without water, carried
Rev. 1. 7 Behold, he cometh with clouds; and
10. 1 another mighty angel..clothed with a cl.
11. 12 they ascended up to heaven in a cloud
14. 14 behold a white cloud, and upon the cloud
14. 15 crying..to him that sat on the cloud
14. 16 he that sat on the cloud thrust in his

8. *A cloud*, νέφος *nephos.*
Heb. 12. 1 with so great a cloud of witnesses

CLOUD, to cover with a —
To send a thickness, עוּב *ub*, 5.
Lam. 2. 1 covered the daughter of Sion with a cloud

CLOUD, dark —
Cloud (dark, thick or high), עֲרָפֶל *araphel.*
Job 22. 13 Can he judge through the dark cloud

CLOUD, thick —
Thick cloud, עָב *ab.*
2 Sa. 22. 12 dark waters, (and) thick clouds of the
Job 22. 14 Thick clouds (are) a covering to him, that
26. 8 bindeth up the waters in his thick cloud
37. 11 watering he wearieth the thick cloud
Psa. 18. 11 dark waters (and) thick clouds of the
18. 12 before him his thick clouds passed
Isa. 44. 22 I have blotted out, as a thick cloud, thy

CLOUDY —
A cloud, עָנָן *anan.*
Exod 33. 9 the cloudy pillar descended, and stood
33. 10 all the people saw the cloudy pillar stand
Neh. 9. 12 thou leddest them in the day by a cloudy
Psa. 99. 7 He spake unto them in the cloudy pillar
Eze. 30. 3 the day of the LORD is near, a cloudy day
34. 12 they have been scattered in the cloudy

CLOUTED —
To be spotted, patched, טָלָא *tala*, 4.
Josh. 9. 5 old shoes and clouted upon their feet, and

CLOVEN —
1. *To cleave or split,* שָׁסַע *shasa.*
Deut 14. 7 or of them that divide the cloven hoof
2. *To divide throughout,* διαμερίζω *diamerizō.*
Acts 2. 3 there appeared unto them cloven tongues

CLOVEN FOOTED —
1. *A cloven pointed hoof,* שֹׁסַע שֶׁסַע פַּרְסָה *[shasa].*
Lev. 11. 3 parteth the hoof, and is cloven footed
11. 7 divide the hoof, and be cloven footed
2. *A cloven cleft,* שֶׁסַע שֹׁסַע *[shasa].*
Lev 11 26 every beast which..(is) not cloven footed

CLUSTER —
1. *Stem, stalk, cluster,* אֶשְׁכּוֹל *eshkol.*
Gen. 40. 10 the clusters thereof brought forth ripe
Num 13. 23 cut..a branch with one cluster of grapes
Deut 32. 32 grapes of gall, their clusters (are) bitter
Song 1. 14 My beloved (is) unto me (as) a cluster of
7. 7 a palm tree, and thy breasts to clusters (of)
7. 8 thy breasts shall be as clusters of the v.
Isa. 65. 8 As the new wine is found in the cluster
Mic. 7. 1 of the vintage..(there is) no cluster to eat
2. *Cluster,* βότρυς *botrus.*
Rev. 14. 18 gather the clusters of the vine of the earth

CLUSTER of grapes —
Cluster, אֶשְׁכּוֹל *eshkol.*
Num 13 24 the cluster of grapes which the children

CLUSTERS of raisins —
Pressed cakes of raisins, צִמּוּקִים *tsimmuqim.*
1 Sa 25 18 and an hundred clusters of raisins, and
30. 12 a cake of figs, and two clusters of raisins

CNI'-DUS, Κνίδος.
A city on a promontory of Caria (or Doris), at the S.W. of Asia Minor.
Acts 27. 7 we..scarce were come over against C.

COAL —
1. *Burning coal,* גַּחֶלֶת *gacheleth.*
Lev 16 12 he shall take a censer full of burning coals
2 Sa 14. 7 they shall quench my coal which is left
22. 9 fire out of his mouth devoured: coals
22. 13 the brightness before him were coals of
Job 41. 21 His breath kindleth coals, and a flame
Psa 18. 8 fire out of his mouth devoured: coals
18 12, 13 clouds passed, hail (stones) and coals
120. 4 Sharp arrows of the mighty, with coals of
140 10 Let burning coals fall upon them: let them
Prov. 6. 28 Can one go upon hot coals and his feet
25. 22 thou shalt heap coals of fire upon his head
Isa. 44. 19 I have baked bread upon the coals thereof
47. 14 (there shall) not (be) a coal to warm at
Eze 1. 13 their appearance (was) like burning coals
10 2 fill thine hand with coals of fire from
24 11 Then set it empty upon the coals thereof
2. *Charcoal coal,* פֶּחָם *pecham.*
Prov 26 21 (As) coals (are) to burning coals, and wood
Isa. 44 12 The smith..both worketh in the coals
54. 16 the smith that bloweth the coals in the fire
3. *Hot or burning stone,* רֶשֶׁף *resheph.*
Song 8. 6 the coals thereof (are) coals of fire, which
Hab. 3. 5 and burning coals went forth at his feet
4. *Black, blackness,* שְׁחוֹר *shechor.*
Lam. 4. 8 Their visage is blacker than a coal; they
5. *A live coal,* ἄνθραξ *anthrax.*
Rom 12. 20 thou shalt heap coals of fire on his head

COALS, a fire of —
A heap of live coal, ἀνθρακιά *anthrakia.*
John 18. 18 the servants..who had made a fire of co.
21. 9 they saw a fire of coals there, and fish

COALS, baken on the —
Hot or burning stone, רֶצֶף *retseph.*
1 Ki. 19. 6 (there was) a cake baken on the coals, and

COALS, live —
Hot or burning stone, רִצְפָּה *ritspah.*
Isa 6. 6 Then flew one..having a live coal in his

COAST —
1. *Border,* גְּבוּל *gebul.*
Exod 10. 4 will I bring the locusts into thy coast
10. 14 and rested in all the coasts of Egypt
10. 19 remained not one locust in all the coasts
Num 20. 23 by the coast of the land of Edom, saying
21. 13 wilderness that cometh out of the coasts
22. 36 border of Arnon,..in the utmost coast
34. 11 the coast shall go down from Shepham to
Deut. 2. 4 Ye (are) to pass through the coast of your
2. 18 pass over through Ar, the coast of Moab
3. 14 the county of Argob unto the coasts of G.
3. 17 The plain also, and Jordan, and the coast
11. 24 unto the uttermost sea, shall your coast
16. 4 seen with thee in all thy coasts seven days
19. 3 and divide the coasts of thy land, which
19. 8 if the LORD thy God enlarge thy coast, as
28. 40 have olive trees throughout all thy coasts
Josh. 1. 4 going down of the sun, shall be your coast
12. 4 And the coast of Og king of Bashan
13. 16 their coast was from Aroer, that (is) on
13 25 their coast was Jazer, and all the cities
13. 30 And their coast was from Mahanaim, all
15. 4 the goings out of that coast were at the sea
15 4 this shall be your south coast
Josh. 15. 12 the great sea, and the coast (thereof)
15. 12 This (is) the coast of the children of J.
15. 21 toward the coast of Edom southward
16. 3 goeth down westward to the coast of J.
17. 7 the coast of Manasseh was from Asher to
17. 9 the coast descended unto the river Kanah
17. 9 the coast of Manasseh also (was) on the
18. 5 Judah shall abide in their coast on the
18. 5 Joseph shall abide in their coasts on the
18. 11 the coast of their lot came forth between
18. 19 end of Jordan: this (was) the south coast
19. 22 the coast reacheth to Tabor, and Shahaz.
19. 29 the coast turneth to Ramah, and to the
19. 29 and the coast turneth to Hosah
19. 33 their coast was from Heleph, from Allon
19. 34 the coast turneth westward to Aznoth-ta
19. 41 the coast of their inheritance was Zorah
19. 47 the coast of the children of Dan went
Judg. 1. 18 Judah took Gaza with the coast thereof
1. 18 and Askelon with the coast thereof
1. 18 and Ekron with the coast thereof
1. 36 the coast of the Amorites (was) from the
11. 20 trusted not Israel to pass..his coast
11. 22 possessed all the coasts of the Amorites
19. 29 and sent her into all the coasts of Israel
1 Sa. 5. 6 (even) Ashdod and the coasts thereof
6. 9 goeth up by the way of his own coast
7. 13 they came no more into the coast of Israel
7. 14 the coasts thereof did Israel deliver out
11. 3 may send messengers unto all the coasts
11. 7 (them) throughout all the coasts of Isr.
27. 1 to seek me any more in any coast of Isr.
2 Sa. 21. 5 from remaining in any of the coasts
1 Ki. 1. 3 they sought..throughout all the coasts
2 Ki. 10. 32 Hazael smote them in all the coasts of I.
14. 25 He restored the coast of Israel from the
15. 16 and the coasts thereof from Tirzah
1 Ch. 4. 10 bless me indeed, and enlarge my coast
6. 54 throughout their castles in their coasts
6. 66 sons of Kohath had cities of their coasts
21. 12 destroying throughout all the coasts of I.
2 Ch. 11. 13 resorted to him out of all their coasts
Psa. 105. 31 of flies, (and) lice in all their coasts
105. 33 He..brake the trees of their coasts
Eze. 47. 16 Hazar-hatticon, which (is) by the coast of
2. *Circuit,* גְּבוּלָה *gebulah.*
Num 32. 33 with the cities thereof in the coasts
34. 2 the land of Canaan, with the coasts
34. 12 with the coasts thereof round about
Josh 18. 20 by the coasts thereof round about, accor.
19. 49 the land for inheritance by their coasts
3. *Border,* גְּלִילָה *gelilah.*
Joel 3. 4 and Zidon, and all the coasts of Palestine
4. *Cord, rope,* חֶבֶל *chebel.*
Josh. 19. 29 at the sea from the coast to Achzib
Zeph. 2. 5 Woe unto the inhabitants of the sea coa.
2. 6 the sea coast shall be dwellings (and) cot.
2. 7 the coast shall be for the remnant of the
5. *Shore, haven,* חוֹף *choph.*
Josh 9. 1 in all the coasts of the great sea over
Eze. 25. 16 I will..destroy the remnant of the sea c.
6. *Hand,* יָד *yad.*
Num 13. 29 and by the coast of Jordan. 24. 24.
34. 3 south quarter shall be..along by the c.
Judg 11. 26 coasts of Arnon. Ezek. 48. 1. c. of Hethlon
7. *Thigh,* יַרְכָה *yarekah.* [..c. of Hamath
Jer. 25. 32 shall be raised up from the coasts of the
31. 8 gather them from the coasts of the earth
50. 41 kings shall be raised up from the coasts
8. *Elevated place,* נָפָה *naphah.*
Josh. 12. 23 The king of Dor in the coast of Dor, one
9. *End, extremity,* קָצָה *qatsah.*
Judg 18. 2 of their family five men from their coasts
Eze. 33. 2 the people..take a man of their coasts

COAST, (outmost) —
1. *End, extremity,* קָצֶה *qatseh.*
Num 34. 3 the outmost coast of the salt sea eastward
2. *Division, part,* μέρος *meros.*
Matt 15. 21 departed into the coasts of Tyre and S.
16. 13 came into the coasts of Cesarea Philippi
Acts 19. 1 having passed through the upper coasts
3. *Boundary,* ὅριον *horion.*
Matt. 2. 16 in Bethlehem, and in all the coasts
8. 34 that he would depart out of their coasts
15. 22 a woman..came out of the same coasts
15. 39 he..came into the coasts of Magdala
19. 1 came into the coasts of Judea beyond J.
Mark 5. 17 to pray him to depart out of their coasts
7. 31 departing from the coasts of Tyre and S.
7. 31 through the midst of the c. of Decapolis
10. 1 cometh into the coasts of Judea by the
Acts 13. 50 and expelled them out of their coasts
4. *Place, spot,* τόπος *topos.*
Acts 27. 2 meaning to sail by the coasts of Asia
5. *Space, region,* χώρα *chōra.*
Acts 26. 20 throughout all the coasts of Judea, and

COAST, sea —
Coast along the sea, παράλιος *paralios.*
Luke 6. 17 from the sea coast of Tyre and Sidon

COAT —
1. *A tunic, long coat,* כְּתֹנֶת ,כֻּתֹּנֶת *kethoneth.*
Gen. 3. 21 did the LORD God make coats of skins
Gen. 37. 3 he made him a coat of (many) colours
37. 23 out of his coat, (his) coat of (many) col.
37. 31 took Joseph's coat..and dipped the coat
37. 32 they sent the coat of (many) colours, and
37. 32 know now whether it (be) thy son's coat
37. 33 he knew it, and said, (It is) my son's coat
Exod 28. 4 a broidered coat, a mitre, and a girdle
28. 39 thou shalt embroider the coat of fine lin.
28. 40 for Aaron's sons thou shalt make coats
29. 5 put upon Aaron the coat, and the robe of
29. 8 thou shalt bring his sons, and put coats
39. 27 they made coats (of) fine linen, (of) woven
40. 14 bring his sons, and clothe them with coats
Lev. 8. 7 he put upon him the coat, and girded him
8. 13 Moses brought Aaron's sons, and put coats
10. 5 carried them in their coats out of the
16. 4 He shall put on the holy linen coat, and
2 Sa. 15. 32 came to meet him with his coat rent
Job 30. 18 bindeth me about as the collar of my c.
Song 5. 3 I have put off my coat; how shall I put
2. *Upper robe,* מְעִיל *meil.*
1 Sa. 2. 19 Moreover his mother made him a little c.
3. *Tunic, long robe,* χιτών *chitōn.*
Matt. 5. 40 if any man will..take away thy coat
10. 10 Nor scrip for..journey, neither two coats
Mark 6. 9 But (be) shod..and not put on two coats
Luke 3. 11 He that hath two coats, let him impart to
6. 29 forbid not (to take thy) coat also
9. 3 neither have two coats apiece
John 19. 23 and also (his) coat: now the coat was
Acts 9. 39 showing the coats and garments which

COAT, fisher's —
Upper clothing, ἐπενδύτης *ependutēs.*
John 21. 7 he girt (his) fisher's coat (unto him)

COAT (of mail) —
Coat of mail, breast plate, שִׁרְיוֹן *shiryon.*
1 Sa. 17. 5 And he was armed with a coat of mail
17. 5 the weight of the coat (was) five thousand
17. 38 also he armed him with a coat of mail

COATS —
Mantles, upper garments, סַרְבָּלִין *sarbalin.*
Dan. 3. 21 these men were bound in their coats
3. 27 neither were their coats changed, nor the

COCK —
House cock, ἀλέκτωρ *alektōr.*
Matt 26. 34, 75 before the cock crow, thou shall deny
26. 74 And immediately the cock crew
Mark 14. 30, 72 before the cock crow twice, thou shalt
14. 68 he went out into the porch; and [the cock]
14. 72 And the second time the cock crew
Luke 22. 34 the cock shall not crow this day, before
22. 60 immediately, while he yet spake, the cock
22. 61 Before the cock crow, thou shalt deny me
John 13. 38 The cock shall not crow, till thou hast
18. 27 and immediately the cock crew

COCK crowing —
Sounding of the cock, ἀλεκτοροφωνία *alektorophōnia.*
Mark 13. 35 or at the cock crowing, or in the morning

COCKATRICE —
1. *Cockatrice, basilisk, adder, viper,* צֶפַע *tsepha.*
Isa. 14. 29 serpent's..shall come forth a cockatrice
2. *Adder, cockatrice,* צִפְעֹנִי *tsiphoni.*
Isa. 11. 8 child..put his hand on the cockatrice' d.
59. 5 They hatch cockatrice' eggs, and weave
Jer. 8. 17 I will send serpents, cockatrices, among

COCKLE —
Useless weed, hemlock, darnel, בָּאְשָׁה *boshah.*
Job 31. 40 thistles grow instead of wheat, and cockle

COFFER —
Coffer, box, chest, אַרְגָּז *argaz.*
1 Sa. 6. 8 put the jewels..in a coffer by the side
6. 11 and the coffer with the mice of gold, and
6. 15 and the coffer that (was) with it, wherein

COFFIN —
Ark, coffin, chest, אָרוֹן *aron.*
Gen. 50. 26 and he was put in a coffin in Egypt

COGITATION —
Thought, sadness, רַעְיוֹן *rayon.*
Dan. 7. 28 As for me Daniel, my cogitations much

COLD —
1. *Cold, pot,* צִנָּה *tsinnah.*
Prov 25. 13 As the cold of snow in the time of harvest
2. *Cold, cool, excellent,* קַר *qar.*
Prov 25. 25 (As) cold waters to a thirsty soul, so (is)
Jer. 18. 14 shall the cold flowing waters..be forsak.
3. *Cold,* קֹר *qor.*
Gen. 8 22 cold and heat, and summer and winter
4. *Cold,* קָרָה *qarah.*
Job 24. 7 that (they have) no covering in the cold
37. 9 cometh the whirlwind; and cold out of the
Psa. 147. 17 who can stand before his cold?
Prov 25 20 that taketh away a garment in cold weat.
Nah. 3. 17 which camp in the hedges in the cold day
5. *Coldness,* ψῦχος *psuchos.*
John 18. 18 had made a fire of coals; for it was cold
Acts 28 2 the present rain, and because of the cold
2 Co. 11. 27 in fastings often, in cold and nakedness

6. *Cold, cool,* ψυχρός *psuchros.*
Matt 10. 42 whosoever shall give..a cup of cold (wat.)
Rev. 3. 15 that thou art neither cold nor hot
3. 15 I would thou wert cold or hot
3. 16 thou art luke warm, and neither cold nor

COLD, to wax —
To breathe, blow, cool, ψύχω *psuchō.*
Matt 24. 12 because..the love of many shall wax cold

COL-HO'-ZEH, כָּל־חֹזֶה *wholly a seer.*
1. One whose son helped to repair the wall, B.C. 470.
Neh. 3. 15 the fountain repaired Shallum..son of C.
2. One whom some think the same as No. 1. B.C. 470.
Neh. 11. 5 Maaseiah the son of Baruch, the son of C.

COLLAR —
Mouth, פֶּה *peh.*
Job 30. 18 bindeth me about as the collar of my coat

COLLARS —
Drops, droppings, נְטִיפוֹת *netiphoth.*
Judg. 8. 26 beside ornaments, and collars, and

COLLECTION —
1. *Burden, thing lifted up or borne,* מַשְׂאֵת *maseth.*
2 Ch. 24. 6 to bring in, out of Judah..the collection
24. 9 to bring in to the LORD the collection
2. *Collection, gathering,* λογία *logia.*
1 Co 16. 1 Now concerning the collection for the

COLLEGE —
Second part, place of repetition, college, מִשְׁנֶה.
2 Ki. 22. 14 now she dwelt in Jerusalem in the college
2 Ch 34 22 now she dwelt in Jerusalem in the college

COLLOPS —
Fat, fatness, פִּימָה *pimah.*
Job 15 27 and maketh collops of fat on (his) flanks

COLONY —
Colony (Roman), κολωνία *kolōnia (Lat.)* εια.
Acts 16. 12 which is the chief city..(and) a colony

CO-LOS'-SE, Κολοσσαί.
A city of Phrygia Pactiana, on the confines of Caria in Asia Minor, near the conflux of the Lycus and the Mæander.
Col. 1. 2 brethren in Christ which are at C.

COLOUR —
1. *Eye, aspect,* עַיִן *ayin.*
Lev 13. 55 (if) the plague have not changed his colour
Num 11. 7 the colour thereof as the colour of bdel.
Prov 23. 31 when it giveth his colour in the cup
Eze. 1. 4 out of the midst thereof as the colour of
1. 7 they sparkled like the colour of burnished
1. 16 The appearance..(was) like unto the col.
1. 22 the likeness..(was) as the colour of the
1. 27 And I saw as the colour of amber, as the
8. 2 appearance of brightness, as the colour
10. 9 the appearance..(was) as the colour of a
Dan. 10. 6 his arms and his feet like in colour to
2. *What is shown forth, pretence,* πρόφασις *prophasis.*
Acts 27. 30 under colour as though they would have

COLOURS, (divers or many) —
Pieces, ends (of anything), extremities, פַּסִּים *passim.*
Gen 37. 3 and he made him a coat of (many) colours
37. 23 (his) coat of (many) colours that (was) on
37. 32 And they sent the coat of (many) colours
2 Sa. 13. 18 (she had) a garment of divers colours
13. 19 and rent her garment of divers colours

COLOURS, fair —
Paint, פּוּךְ *puk.*
Isa. 54. 11 I will lay thy stones with fair colours

COLOURS, with divers —
To spot, patch, טָלָא *tala.*
Eze. 16. 16 deckedst thy..places with divers colours

COLT —
1. *Son, produce,* בֵּן *ben.*
Gen. 32. 15 Thirty milch camels with their colts
49. 11 and his ass's colt unto the choice vine
2. *Ass colt, (from its restiveness,)* עַיִר *ayir.*
Judg. 10. 4 thirty sons that rode on thirty ass colts
12. 14 rode on threescore and ten ass colts
Job 11. 12 man be born (like) a wild ass's colt
Zec. 9. 9 and upon a colt the foal of an ass
3. *Foal,* πῶλος *pōlos.*
Matt 21. 2 ye shall find an ass tied, and a colt with
21. 5 sitting upon an ass, and a colt the foal
21. 7 brought the ass, and the colt, and put on
Mark 11 2 ye shall find a colt tied, whereon never
11. 4 found the colt tied by the door without
11. 5 certain..said..What do ye, loosing the c.
11. 7 they brought the colt to Jesus, and cast
Luke 19. 30 ye shall find a colt tied, whereon yet
19. 33 as they were loosing the colt, the owners
19. 33 said unto them, Why loose ye the colt?
19. 35 they cast their garments upon the colt
John 12. 15 thy King cometh, sitting on an ass's colt

COME, to —
1. *The latter,* אַחֲרוֹן *acharon.*
Deut 29. 22 So that the generation to come of your
Psa. 78. 4 showing to the generation to come the
78. 6 That the generation to come might know
102. 18 be written for the generation to come
Prov 31. 25 and she shall rejoice in time to come
Eccl. 1. 11 remembrance of (things) that are to come
Isa. 30. 8 that it may be for the time to come for
2. *To come, arrive,* אָתָה *athah.*
Deut 33. 2 And he said, The LORD came from Sinai
33. 21 and he came with the heads of the people
Job 16. 22 When a few years are come, then I shall
30. 14 They came (upon me) as a wide breaking
37. 22 Fair weather cometh out of the north
Psa. 68. 31 Princes shall come out of Egypt; Ethiop.
Prov. 1. 27 your destruction cometh as a whirlwind
Isa. 21. 12 The morning cometh, and also the night
21. 12 if ye will enquire, enquire ye: return, co.
41. 5 the ends..were afraid, drew near, and ca.
41. 25 I have raised up (one)..and he shall come
56. 9 All ye beasts of the field, come to devour
56. 12 Come ye, (say they,) I will fetch wine
Jer. 3. 22 Behold, we come unto thee; for thou
Mic. 4. 8 unto thee shall it come, even the first
3. *To cause to come or arrive,* אָתָה *athah,* 5.
Jer. 12. 9 assemble all the beasts..come to devour
4. *To come, arrive,* אֲתָא *atha.*
Ezra 5. 3 At the same time came to them Tatnai
5. 16 Then came the same Sheshbazzar, (and)
Dan. 3. 2 to come to the dedication of the image
3. 26 and come (hither). Then Shadrach, Mes.
7. 13 (one) like the Son of man came with the
7. 22 Until the Ancient of days came and
5. *To come in,* בּוֹא *bo.*
Gen. 6. 18 and thou shalt come into the ark, thou
6. 20 two of every (sort) shall come unto thee
7. 1 Come thou and all thy house into the ark
10. 19 as thou comest to Gerar, unto Gaza; as
11. 31 and they came unto Haran, and dwelt
12. 5 and into the land of Canaan they came
13. 10 like the land of Egypt, as thou comest
13. 18 came and dwelt in the plain of Mamre
14. 5 in the fourteenth year came Chedorlao.
14. 7 they returned, and came to Enmishpat
14. 13 there came one that had escaped, and told
16. 8 whence camest thou? and whither wilt
18. 21 according to the cry of it, which is come
19. 1 there came two angels to Sodom at even
19. 8 therefore came they under the shadow of
20. 3 But God came to Abimelech in a dream
20. 13 at every place whither we shall come,
22. 9 they came to the place which God had
23. 2 Abraham came to mourn for Sarah
24. 30 that he came unto the man; and, behold
24. 32 And the man came into the house: and
24. 41 when thou comest to my kindred
24. 42 I came this day unto the well, and said
24. 62 Isaac came from the way of the well
24. 63 and, behold, the camels (were) coming
25. 29 Esau came from the field, and he (was)
26. 27 Wherefore come ye to me, seeing ye hate
26. 32 that Isaac's servants came, and told him
27. 18 he came unto his father, and said
27. 33 have eaten of all before thou camest, and
27. 35 he said, Thy brother came with subtilty
29. 6 Rachel his daughter cometh with the
29. 9 Rachel came with her father's sheep; for
30. 11 Leah said, A troop cometh: and she called
30. 16 Jacob came out of the field in the evening
30. 33 my righteousness answer..in time to c.
30. 33 when it shall come for my hire before thy
30. 38 they should conceive when they came
31. 24 God came to Laban the Syrian in a dream
32. 6 We came to thy brother Esau, and also he
32. 8 If Esau come to the one company, and
32. 11 I fear him, lest he will come and smite
32. 13 and took of that which came to his hand
33. 1 and looked, and, behold, Esau came, and
33. 14 until I come unto my lord unto Seir
33. 18 Jacob came to Shalem a city of Shechem
33. 18 when he came from Padan-aram; and
34. 7 the sons of Jacob came out of the field
34. 20 And Hamor..came unto the gate of their
34. 25 came upon the city boldly, and slew all
34. 27 The sons of Jacob came upon the slain
35. 6 Jacob came to Luz, which (is) in the land
35. 9 when he came out of Padan-aram, and
35. 16 and there was but a little way to come to
35. 27 Jacob came unto Isaac his father unto
37. 10 indeed come to bow down ourselves to
37. 14 he sent him out..and he came to Shechem
37. 19 they said..Behold, this dreamer cometh
37. 23 when Joseph was come unto his brethren
37. 25 a company of Ishmeelites came from Gil.
39. 16 laid up his garment..until his lord came
41. 29 there come seven years of great plenty
41. 35 all the food of those good years that come
41. 50 two sons before the years of famine came
41. 54 the seven years of dearth began to come
41. 57 all countries came into Egypt to Joseph
42. 5 came to buy (corn) among those that came
42. 6 and Joseph's brethren came, and bowed
42. 7 and he said unto them, Whence come ye?
42. 9 to see the nakedness of the land ye are c.
42. 10 but to buy food are thy servants come
42. 12 to see the nakedness of the land ye are c.
42. 15 except your youngest brother come hither
42. 21 therefore is this distress come upon us
42. 29 And they came unto Jacob their father
43. 21 it came to pass, when we came to the inn
43. 25 the present against Joseph came at noon
43. 26 when Joseph came home, they brought
44. 14 and his brethren came to Joseph's house
44. 30 when I come to thy servant my father
Gen. 45. 16 saying, Joseph's brethren are come
45. 18 take your father..and come unto me: and
45. 19 and bring your father, and come
45. 25 came into the land of Canaan unto Jacob
46. 1 came to Beersheba, and offered sacrifices
46. 6 they took their cattle..and came into
46. 8 the children of Israel which came into
46. 26 All the souls that came with Jacob into
46. 26 which came out of his loins, besides
46. 27 all the souls..which came into Egypt
46. 28 and they came into the land of Goshen
46. 31 My brethren..are come unto me
47. 1 Joseph came and told Pharaoh, and said
47. 1 My father and my brethren..are come
47. 4 to sojourn in the land are we come
47. 5 Thy father and thy brethren are come
47. 15 all the Egyptians came unto Joseph, and
47. 18 they came unto him the second year
48. 2 Behold, thy son Joseph cometh unto thee
48. 5 before I came unto thee into Egypt
48. 7 for me, when I came from Padan, Rachel
48. 7 but a little way to come unto Ephrath
49. 6 my soul, come not thou into their secret
49. 10 nor a lawgiver..until Shiloh come
50. 10 they came to the threshing floor of Atad
Exod. 1. 1 children of Israel, which came into Egypt
1. 1 every man and his household came with
2. 16 they came and drew (water), and filled
2. 17 the shepherds came and drove them aw.
2. 18 when they came to Reuel their father
2. 18 How (is it that) ye are come so soon to day
3. 1 came to the mountain of God..to Horeb
3. 9 the cry of the children of Israel is come
3. 13 (when) I come unto the children of Israel
3. 18 thou shalt come, thou and the elders of I.
5. 15 officers of the children of Israel came
5. 23 since I came to Pharaoh to speak in thy
8. 3 which shall go up and come into thine
8. 24 there came a grievous swarm (of flies) into
10. 26 we must serve the LORD until we come
12. 23 will not suffer the destroyer to come in
12. 25 when ye be come to the land which the
14. 20 it came between the camp of the Egypt.
14. 20 the one came not near the other all the
14. 28 all the host..that came into the sea after
15. 23 when they came to Marah, they could
15. 27 they came to Elim, where (were) twelve
16. 1 all the congregation..came unto the wild.
16. 22 all the rulers of the congregation came
16. 35 until they came to a land inhabited
16. 35 they came unto the borders of the land
17. 8 Then came Amalek, and fought with Is.
18. 5 Jethro..came with his sons and his wife
18. 6 I thy father in law Jethro am come unto
18. 7 Moses went out..and they came into
18. 12 Aaron came, and all the elders of Israel
18. 15 people come unto me to enquire of God
18. 16 When they have a matter, they come unto
19. 1 the same day came they (into) the wilder.
19. 2 and were come (to) the desert of Sinai
19. 7 Moses came and called for the elders of
19. 9 Lo, I come unto thee in a thick cloud
20. 20 Fear not: for God is come to prove you
20. 24 I will come unto thee, and I will bless
22. 9 the cause of both parties shall come before
22. 15 if it (be) an hired (thing), it came for his
23. 27 all the people to whom thou shalt come
24. 3 Moses came and told the people all the
29. 30 when he cometh into the tabernacle of
35. 10 every wise hearted among you shall come
35. 21 they came, every one whose heart stirred
35. 22 And they came both men and women
36. 4 And all the wise men..came every man
Lev. 11. 34 (that) on which (such) water cometh shall
12. 4 nor come into the sanctuary, until the
13. 16 he shall come unto the priest
14. 8 after that he shall come into the camp
14. 35 he that owneth the house shall come and
14. 44 priest shall come and look, and, behold
15. 14 come before the LORD unto the door of
16. 2 that he come not at all times into the
16. 3 Thus shall Aaron come into the holy (place)
16. 23 Aaron shall come into the tabernacle of
16. 26 and afterward come into the camp
16. 28 and afterward he shall come into the camp
19. 23 And when ye shall come into the land
25. 2 When ye come into the land which I give
25. 25 if any of his kin come to redeem it, then
Num. 4. 5 Aaron shall come, and his sons, and they
4. 15 the sons of Kohath shall come to bear (it)
4. 47 every one that came to do the service of
6. 6 All the days..he shall come at no dead
10. 21 set up the tabernacle against they came
13. 21 So they went up..as men come to Hamath
13. 22 they ascended by the south, and came
13. 23 they came unto the brook of Eshcol, and
13. 26 they went and came to Moses, and to A.
13. 27 We came unto the land whither thou
14. 30 Doubtless ye shall not come into the land
15. 18 When ye come into the land whither I
16. 43 Moses and Aaron came before the taber
19. 7 afterward he shall come into the camp
19. 14 all that come into the tent, and all that
20. 1 came the children of Israel, (even) the
20. 22 journeyed from Kadesh, and came unto
21. 1 that Israel came by the way of the spies
21. 7 the people came to Moses, and said, We
21. 23 came to Jahaz, and fought against Israel
21. 27 Come into Heshbon, let the city of Sihon
22. 7 they came unto Balaam, and spake unto
22. 9 God came unto Balaam, and said, What
22. 16 they came to Balaam, and said to him

Num 22. 20 And God came unto Balaam at night
22. 20 If the men come to call thee, rise up, (and)
22. 39 and they came unto Kirjath-huzoth
23. 17 when he came to him, behold, he stood by
25. 6 one of the children of Israel came and
31. 14 captains over hundreds, which came from
31. 24 afterward ye shall come into the camp
32. 2 the children of Reuben came and spake
33. 9 they removed from Marah, and came unto
33. 40 heard of the coming of the children of I
34. 2 When ye come into the land of Canaan
Deut. 1. 19 we departed from Horeb..and we came
1. 22 ye came near unto me every one of you
1. 22 and into what cities we shall come
1. 24 came unto the valley of Eshcol, and
1. 31 in all the way..until ye came into this
9. 7 from the day..until ye came unto this
11. 5 until ye came into this place
12. 5 (even) unto his habitation..thou shalt co.
12. 9 ye are not as yet come to the rest and to
14. 29 the fatherless, and the widow..shall come
17. 9 thou shalt come unto the priests the Lev.
18. 6 if a Levite come from any of thy gates
18. 6 come with all the desire of his mind unto
23. 10 he shall not come within the camp
23. 11 he shall come into the camp (again)
23. 24 when thou comest into thy neighbour's
23. 25 When thou comest into the standing
26. 1 when thou (art) come in unto the land
28. 2 And all these blessings shall come on
28. 15, 45 all these curses shall come upon thee
29. 7 when ye came unto this place, Sihon the
29. 22 So that the generation to come of your
29. 22 the stranger that shall come from a far
30. 1 when all these things are come upon thee
32. 44 Moses came and spake all the words of
33. 2 The LORD came from Sinai, and rose up
33. 2 and he came with ten thousands of saints
33. 16 let (the blessing) come upon the head of
Josh. 2. 1 they went, and came into an harlot's house
2. 4 There came men unto me, but I wist not
2. 18 (when) we come into the land, thou shalt
2. 22 they went, and came unto the mountain
2. 23 passed over, and came to Joshua the son
3. 1 they removed from Shittim, and came to J.
6. 11 they came into the camp, and lodged in
6. 19 they shall come into the treasury of the
8. 11 drew nigh, and came before the city, and
9. 8 Who (are) ye? and from whence come ye?
9. 17 came unto their cities on the third day
10. 9 Joshua therefore came unto them sud.
11 5 they came and pitched together at the
11. 7 So Joshua came and all the people of
11. 21 And at that time came Joshua, and cut
15. 18 she came (unto him), that she moved him
18. 4 and they shall come (again) to me
18. 9 came (again) to Joshua to the host at S.
20. 6 then shall the slayer return, and come
22. 10 when they came unto the borders of Jor.
22. 15 they came unto the children of Reuben
23. 7 That ye come not among these nations
24. 6 I brought your fathers..and ye came
24. 11 ye went over Jordan, and came unto Jer.
Judg. 1. 14 when she came (to him), that she moved
3. 20 Ehud came unto him; and he was sitting
3. 24 When he was gone out, his servants came
4. 20 when any man doth come and enquire of
4. 22 when he came into her (tent), behold, Sis.
5. 19 The kings came (and) fought, then fought
5. 23 they came not to the help of the LORD
5. 28 Why is his chariot (so) long in coming?
6. 4 till thou come unto Gaza, and left no
6. 5 they came as grasshoppers for multitude
6. 11 And there came an angel of the LORD
6. 18 Depart not hence..until I come unto thee
7. 13 came unto a tent, and smote it that it
7. 17 when I come to the outside of the camp
7. 19 came unto the outside of the camp in the
8. 4 Gideon came to Jordan, (and) passed over
8. 15 he came unto the men of Succoth, and
9. 15 (then) come (and) put your trust in my
9. 24 That the cruelty (done)..might come, and
9. 26 Gaal the son of Ebed came with his bre.
9. 31 Gaal..and his brethren, be come to Shech.
9. 37 See there come people down by the middle
9. 37 another company come along by the plain
9. 52 Abimelech come unto the tower, and
9. 57 upon them came the curse of Jotham
11. 16 unto the Red sea, and came to Kadesh
11. 18 came by the east side of the land of Moab
11. 18 but came not within the border of Moab
11. 33 from Aroer even till thou come to Minnith
11. 34 Jephthah came to Mizpeh unto his house
13. 6 the woman came and told her husband
13. 6 A man of God came unto me, and his
13. 8 let the man of God..come again unto us
13. 9 the angel of God came again unto the wo.
13. 10 Behold, the man..that came unto me the
13. 11 Manoah arose..and came to the man
14. 5 Samson..came to the vineyards of Tim.
15. 14 when he came unto Lehi, the Philistines
15. 14 the Spirit of the LORD came mightily
17. 8 the man departed..and he came to mount
17. 9 Micah said unto him, Whence comest thou?
18. 2 who when they came to mount E., to the
18. 7 the five men departed, and came to Laish
18. 8 they came unto their brethren to Zorah
18. 10 When ye go, ye shall come unto a people
18. 13 Ephraim, and came unto the house of
18. 15 they turned..and came to the house of
18. 27 they took (the things)..and came unto L.
19. 10 he rose up..and came over against Jebus
Judg 19. 16 there came an old man from his work out
19. 17 Whither goest thou? and whence comest
19. 22 Bring forth the man that came into thine
19. 26 Then came the woman in the dawning of
20. 4 I came into Gibeah that (belongeth) to
20. 10 when they come to Gibeah of Benjamin
20. 26 all the children of Israel..came unto the
20. 34 there came against Gibeah ten thousand
21. 2 the people came to the house of God, and
21. 8 behold, there came none to the camp from
21. 22 when their fathers or their brethren come
Ruth 1. 2 they came into the country of Moab, and
1. 19 two went until they came to Beth-lehem
1. 22 they came to Beth-lehem in the beginning
2. 3 she..came, and gleaned in the field after
2. 4 Boaz came from Bethlehem, and said unto
2. 7 she came, and hath continued even from
3. 7 she came softly, and uncovered his feet
3. 14 Let it not be known that a woman came
3. 16 when she came to her mother in law, she
1 Sa. 1. 19 they rose up..and came to their house to
2. 13 the priest's servant came, while the flesh
2. 14 unto all the Israelites that came thither
2. 15 they burnt the fat, the..servant came
2. 27 there came a man of God unto Eli, and
2. 31 the days come, that I will cut off thine
2. 34 this (shall be) a sign..that shall come
2. 36 that is left in thine house shall come
3. 10 the LORD came, and stood, and called as at
4. 3 Let us fetch the ark.. when it cometh
4. 5 covenant of the LORD came into the camp
4. 12 there ran a man..and came to Shiloh
4. 13 when the man came into the city, and told
4. 16 I (am) he that came out of the army, and
5. 5 nor any that come into Dagon's house
5. 10 it came to pass, as the ark of God came
6. 14 the cart came into the field of Joshua
7. 1 the men of Kirjath-jearim came, and
7. 13 the Philistines..came no more into the
8. 4 all the elders..came to Samuel unto R.
9. 12 haste now, for he came to day to the city
9. 13 for the people will not eat until he come
9. 15 LORD had told Samuel..before Saul came
10. 3 thou shalt come to the plain of Tabor
10. 5 thou shalt come to the hill of God, where
10. 5 when thou art come thither to the city
10. 8 till I come to thee, and show thee what
10. 10 when they came thither to the hill, behold
10. 13 he had made an end of prophesying, he
10. 14 that (they were) no where, we came to S.
10. 22 enquired..if the man should yet come
11. 4 Then came the messengers to Gibeah of
11. 5 Saul came after the herd out of the field
11. 9 they said unto the messengers that came
11. 9 the messengers came and showed (it) to
11. 11 they came into the midst of the host in
12. 12 the king of the children of Ammon came
13. 8 but Samuel came not to Gilgal; and the
13. 10 as soon as he had made..Samuel came
13. 11 thou camest not within the days appoint.
14. 20 Saul and all the people..came to the bat.
14. 25 all (they of) the land came to a wood
15. 5 Saul came to a city of Amalek, and laid
15. 7 (until) thou comest to Shur, that (is) over
15. 12 Saul came to Carmel, and..he set him
15. 13 Samuel came to Saul: and Saul said
16. 4 spake, and came to Beth-lehem
16. 4 the elders..said, Comest thou peaceably?
16. 5 and come with me to the sacrifice
16. 11 we will not sit down till he come hither
16. 21 David came to Saul, and stood before him
17. 20 he came to the trench, as the host was
17. 22 And David..came and saluted his breth.
17. 34 there came a lion..and took a lamb out of
17. 43 (Am) I a dog, that thou comest to me with
17. 45 Thou comest to me with a sword, and
17. 45 I come to thee in the name of the LORD
17. 52 until thou come to the valley, and to
18. 6 as they came..women came out of all
19. 18 So David..came to Samuel to Ramah
19. 22 and came to a great well that (is) in S.
19. 23 he..prophesied until he came to Naioth
20. 1 David..came and said before Jonathan
20. 9 evil were determined .. to come upon
20. 19 come to the place where thou didst hide
20. 21 come thou: for (there is) peace to thee
20. 27 cometh not the son of Jesse to meat
20. 29 he cometh not unto the king's table
20. 38 gathered up the arrows, and came to his
21. 1 Then came David to Nob to Ahimelech the
21. 15 shall this (fellow) come into my house?
22. 5 David departed, and came into the forest
22. 11 and they came all of them to the king
22. 9 I saw the son of Jesse coming to Nob, to
23. 10 come to Keilah, to destroy the city for
23. 27 there came a messenger unto Saul, saying
24. 3 he came to the sheep cotes by the way
25. 8 for we come in a good day: give, I pray
25. 8 whatsoever cometh to thine hand unto
25. 9 when David's young men came, they spake
25. 12 David's young men..came and told him all
25. 19 Go on before me; behold I come after
25. 26 the LORD hath withholden thee from com.
25. 33 which hast kept me this day from coming
25. 34 except thou hadst hasted and come to
25. 36 Abigail came to Nabal: and, behold, he
26. 1 the Ziphites came unto Saul to Gibeah
26. 3 he saw that Saul came after him into the
26. 5 David arose, and came to the place where
26. 7 So David and Abishai came to the people
26. 10 or his day shall come to die; or he shall
26. 15 for there came one of the people in to
1 Sa. 27. 9 David..returned, and came to Achish
28. 4 the Philistines..came and pitched in Sh.
28. 8 and they came to the woman by night
28. 21 the woman came unto Saul, and saw that
29. 6 I have not found..since the day of thy co.
30. 3 So David and his men came to the city
30. 9 So David..came to the brook Besor
30. 21 David came to the two hundred men
30. 23 the company that came against us into
30. 26 when David came to Ziklag, he sent of
31. 4 come and thrust me through, and abuse
31. 7 the Philistines came and dwelt in them
31. 8 when the Philistines came to strip the
31. 12 All the valiant men arose..and came to
2 Sa. 1. 2 behold a man came out of the camp
1. 2 (so) it was, when he came to David, that
1. 3 David said unto him..whence comest
2. 4 the men of Judah came, and there they
2. 23 as many as came to the place where Asa
2. 29 and they came to Mahanaim
3. 13 when thou comest to see my face
3. 20 Abner came to David to Hebron, and
3. 22 servants of David..came from (pursuing)
3. 23 Abner the son of Ner came to the king
3. 24 Then Joab came to the king, and said
3. 24 What hast thou done? behold, Abner came
3. 25 Abner the son of Ner..he came to deceive
3. 35 the people came to cause David to eat
4. 4 was five years old when the tidings came
4. 5 sons of Rimmon..came about the heat of
4. 6 they came thither into the midst of the
4. 7 when they came into the house, he lay on
5. 1 Then came all the tribes of Israel to David
5. 3 the elders of Israel came to the king to
5. 8 The blind and the lame shall not come
5. 18 The Philistines also came and spread
5. 20 David came to Baal-perazim, and David
5. 23 come upon them over against the mulb.
5. 25 from Geba until thou come to Gazer
6 6 when they came to Nachon's threshing
6. 9 How shall the ark of the LORD come to me?
6. 16 as the ark of the LORD came into the city
8. 5 the Syrians of Damascus came to succour
10. 2 And David's servants came into the land
10. 14 So Joab returned..and came to Jerusalem
10. 16 Syrians that (were) beyond..came to Hel.
10. 17 all Israel..passed over Jordan, and came
11. 10 Camest thou not from (thy) journey? why
11. 22 messenger went, and came and showed
12. 1 he came unto him, and said unto him
12. 4 there came a traveller unto the rich man
12. 20 David arose..and came into the house of
12. 20 then he came to his own house; and when
13. 5 when thy father cometh..let..Tamar come
13. 6 I pray thee, let Tamar my sister come
13. 11 said unto her, Come lie with me, my sister
13. 24 And Absalom came to the king, and said
13. 30 while they were in the way..tidings came
13. 35 Behold, the king's sons come: as thy
13. 36 as soon as he had..the king's sons came
14. 3 come to the king, and speak on this
14. 29 would not come..he would not come
14. 31 Then Joab arose, and came to Absalom
14. 32 Come hither, that I may send thee to the
14. 33 So Joab came to the king, and told him
14. 33 he came to the king, and bowed himself
15. 2 any man that had a controversy came
15. 4 every man which hath..cause might come
15. 6 to all Israel that came to the king for
15. 13 there came a messenger to David, saying
15. 18 six hundred men..came after him from G.
15. 20 Whereas thou camest (but) yesterday
15. 28 I will tarry..until there come word from
15. 37 Hushai, David's friend, came into the
15. 37 and Absalom came into Jerusalem
16. 5 when king David came to Bahurim
16. 14 and the people that (were) with him, came
16. 15 and all the people..came to Jerusalem
17. 2 I will come upon him while he (is) weary
17. 12 shall we come upon him in some place
17. 17 they might not be seen to come into the
17. 18 and came to a man's house in Buhurim
17. 20 Absalom's servants came to the woman to
17. 24 Then David came to Mahanaim. And Ab.
18. 27 a good man..cometh with good tidings
18. 31 And, behold, Cushi came; and Cushi said
19. 5 Joab came into the house to the king, and
19. 8 And all the people came before the king
19. 15 the king returned, and came to Jordan
19. 15 Judah came to Gilgal, to go to meet the
19. 24 until the day he came (again) in peace
19. 41 all the men of Israel came to the king
20. 3 David came to his house at Jerusalem
20. 12 every one that came by him stood still
20. 15 they came and besieged him in Abel of
23. 13 three of the thirty..came to David in
24. 6 they came to Gilead..they came to Dan-j.
24. 7 And came to the stronghold of Tyre, and
24. 8 they came to Jerusalem at the end of nine
24. 13 Gad came to David, and told him, and
24. 13 Shall seven years of famine come unto
24. 18 And Gad came that day to David, and
1 Ki. 1. 28 And she came into the king's presence
1. 32 And they came before the king
1. 35 that he may come and sit upon my throne
1. 42 the son of Abiathar the priest came
1. 47 the king's servants came to bless our
1. 53 he came and bowed himself to king Solo.
2. 13 And Adonijah the son of Haggith came
2. 13 And she said, Comest thou peaceably?
2. 28 Then tidings came to Joab, for Joab had
2. 30 Benaiah came to the tabernacle of the L.

1 Ki. 3. 15 he came to Jerusalem, and stood before
3. 16 Then came there two women..harlots
4. 34 there came of all people to hear the wisdom
7. 14 he came to king Solomon, and wrought
8. 3 all the elders of Israel came, and..took up
8. 31 the oath come before thine altar in this
8. 41 cometh out of a far country for thy name's
8. 42 he shall come and pray toward this house
9. 28 And they came to Ophir, and fetched..gold
10. 1 she came to prove him with hard questions
10. 2 she came to Jerusalem with a very great
10. 7 I believed not the words, until I came
10. 10 there came no more such abundance of
10. 12 there came no such almug trees, nor were
10. 14 the weight of gold that came to Solomon
10. 22 once in three years came the navy of Thar.
11. 18 they arose out of Midian, and came to P.
11. 18 they came to Egypt unto Pharaoh, king
12. 3 and all the congregation of Israel came
12. 12 the people came to Rehoboam the third
13 1 there came a man of God out of Judah
13 7 Come home with me, and refresh thyself
13. 10 he..returned not by the way that he came
13. 11 his sons came and told him all the works
13. 12 what way the man of God..which came
13. 14 the man of God that camest from Judah?
13. 21 unto the man of God that came from J.
13. 22 thy carcase shall not come unto the sep.
13. 25 they came and told (it) in the city where
13. 29 the old prophet came to the city, to mourn
14. 4 Jeroboam's wife..came to the house of
14. 5 the wife of Jeroboam cometh to ask a
14. 13 for he only..shall come to the grave
14. 17 Jeroboam's wife arose..and came to Tirz.
17. 10 when he came to the gate of the city
18. 12 when I come and tell Ahab, and he cannot
19. 3 he arose..and came to Beer-sheba, which
19. 4 he..came and sat down under a juniper
19. 9 he came thither unto a cave, and lodged
19. 15 when thou comest, anoint Hazael (to be)
20. 30 Ben-hadad fled, and came into the city
20. 32 So they..came to the king of Israel, and
20. 43 the king of Israel..came to Samaria
21. 4 Ahab came into his house heavy and
21. 5 Jezebel his wife came to him, and said
22. 15 So he came to the king. And the king
22. 27 with water of affliction, until I come in
2 Ki. 1. 13 came and fell on his knees before Elijah
2. 4 So they came to Jericho
2. 15 they came to meet him, and bowed them.
3. 20 behold, there came water by the way of
3. 24 when they came to the camp of Israel
4. 1 the creditor is come to take..my two sons
4. 7 Then she came and told the man of God
4. 10 it shall be, when he cometh to us, that he
4. 11 it fell on a day, that he came thither, and
4. 25 she went, and came unto the man of God
4. 27 she came to the man of God to the hill
4. 39 came and shred (them) into the pot of
4. 42 there came a man from Baal-shalisha
5. 8 let him come now to me, and he shall kno.
5. 9 Naaman came with his horses and with
5. 15 he and all his company..came and stood
5. 24 when he came to the tower, he took (them)
6. 4 when they came to Jordan, they cut
6. 14 they came by night, and compassed the
6. 23 So the bands of Syria came no more into
6. 32 ere the messenger came to him, he said
6. 32 when the messenger cometh, shut the
7. 6 the kings of the Egyptians..come upon
7. 8 these lepers came to the uttermost part
7. 8 came again, and entered into another
7. 10 they came and called unto the porter of
7. 10 We came to the camp of the Syrians, and
8. 1 it shall..come upon the land seven years
8. 7 Elisha came to Damascus; and Ben-hadad
8. 9 forty camels' burden, and came and stood
8. 14 he departed from Elisha, and came to his
9. 2 when thou comest thither, look out there
9. 5 when he came..the captains of the host
9. 17 spied the company of Jehu, as he came
9. 17 he came, and said, I see a company
9. 18 The messenger came to them, but he
9. 19 he sent out a second..which came to them
9. 20 came even unto them, and cometh not
10. 2 Now as soon as this letter cometh to you
10. 6 come to me..by to morrow this time
10. 7 it came to pass, when the letter came to
10. 8 there came a messenger, and told him
10. 17 when he came to Samaria, he slew all
10. 21 there was not a man left that came not
10. 21 all the worshippers of Baal came, so that
11. 8 he that cometh within the ranges, let him
11. 9 and came to Jehoiada the priest
11. 13 she came to the people into the temple of
11. 19 he..came by the way of the gate of the
12. 9 as one cometh into the house of the LORD
14. 13 came to Jerusalem, and brake down the
15. 14 Menahem..came to Samaria, and smote
15. 19 the king of Assyria came against the land
15. 29 In the days of Pekah..came Tiglath-pile.
16. 6 the Syrians came to Elath, and dwelt there
16. 11 against king Ahaz came from Damascus
17. 28 one of the priests..came and dwelt in
18. 17 and they went up, and came to Jerusalem
18. 17 they came and stood by the conduit of
18. 32 Until I come and take you away to a
18. 37 Then came Eliakim the son of Hilkiah
19. 5 servants of king Hezekiah came to Isaiah
19. 32 He shall not come into this city, nor
19. 32 nor come before it with shield, nor cast
19. 33 the way that he came, by the same shall
2 Ki. 19. 33 and shall not come into this city, saith
20. 1 Isaiah the son of Amoz came to him, and
20. 14 Then came Isaiah the prophet unto king
20. 14 and from whence came they unto thee?
20. 17 days come, that all that (is) in thine house
22. 9 Shaphan the scribe came to the king, and
23. 17 of the man of God, which came from Ju.
23. 18 the bones of the prophet that came out
23. 34 and he came to Egypt, and died there
24. 11 king of Babylon came against the city
25. 1 Nebuchadnezzar king of Babylon came
25. 8 in the fifth month..came Nebuzar-adan
25. 23 there came to Gedaliah to Mizpah
25. 25 came, and ten men with him, and smote
25. 26 all the people, both small and great..came
1 Ch. 2. 55 These (are) the Kenites that came of
4. 41 these written by name came in the days
7. 22 and his brethren came to comfort him
9. 25 their brethren..(were) to come after
10. 4 lest these uncircumcised come and abuse
10. 7 and the Philistines came and dwelt in
10. 8 when the Philistines came to strip the
11. 3 Therefore came all the elders of Israel to
11. 5 Thou shalt not come hither. Nevertheless
12. 1 Now these (are) they that came to David
12. 16 there came of the children of Benjamin
12. 19 when he came with the Philistines against
12. 22 day by day there came to David to help
12. 23 came to David to Hebron, to turn the
12. 31 which were expressed by name, to come
12. 38 All these men of war..came with a perfect
13. 9 when they came unto the threshing floor
14. 9 the Philistines came and spread them
14. 14 come upon them over against the mulberry
15. 29 (as) the ark..came to the city of David
16. 29 bring an offering, and come before him
16. 33 because he cometh to judge the earth
17. 16 David the king came and sat before the
18. 5 when the Syrians of Damascus came to
19. 2 so the servants of David came into the
19. 7 his people; who came and pitched before
19. 7 gathered themselves..and came to battle
19. 15 Then Joab came to Jerusalem
19. 17 he..passed over Jordan, and came upon
20. 1 and came and besieged Rabbah. But
21. 4 Joab departed..and came to Jerusalem
21. 11 So Gad came to David, and said unto him
21. 21 as David came to Ornan, Ornan looked
24. 19 to come into the house of the LORD
2 Ch. 1. 13 Solomon came (from his journey) to the
5. 4 the elders of Israel came; and the Levites
6. 22 the oath come before thine altar in this
6. 32 if they come and pray in this house
7. 11 and all that came into Solomon's heart
8. 11 the ark of the LORD hath come
9. 1 she came to prove Solomon with hard
9. 6 I believed not their words, until I came
9. 13 the weight of gold that came to Solomon
9. 21 every three years once came the ships of
10. 3 all Israel came and spake to Rehoboam
10. 12 Jeroboam and all the people came to R.
11. 16 all the tribes of Israel..came to Jerusalem
12. 3 without number that came with him out
12. 4 he took the fenced cities..and came to
12. 5 Then came Shemaiah the prophet to R.
12. 11 the guard came and fetched them, and
13. 9 whosoever cometh to consecrate himself
14. 9 Zerah the Ethiopian..came unto Maresh.
16. 7 the seer came to Asa king of Judah, and
19. 10 what..shall come to you of your brethren
20. 1 came against Jehoshaphat to battle
20. 2 there came some that told Jehoshaphat
20. 2 There cometh a great multitude against
20. 4 even out of all..cities of Judah they came
20. 9 (when) evil cometh upon us, (as) the
20. 10 when they came out of the land of Egypt
20. 11 to come to cast us out of thy possession
20. 12 this great company that cometh against
20. 24 Judah came toward the watch tower in
20. 25 his people came to take away the spoil
20. 28 they came to Jerusalem with psalteries
21. 12 there came a writing to him from Elijah
22. 1 the band of men that came with the Ar.
22. 7 the destruction..was of God, by coming
23. 2 they went about..and they came to Jeru.
23. 6 let none come into the house of the LORD
23. 12 she came to the people into the house of
23. 20 they came through the high gate into the
24. 11 the high priest's officer came and emptied
24. 17 after the death of Jehoiada came the pr.
24. 23 they came to Judah and Jerusalem, and
24. 24 the Syrians came with a small company
25. 7 But there came a man of God to him, say.
28. 9 he went out before the host that came to
28. 12 stood up against them that came from
28. 17 the Edomites had come and smitten Judah
28. 20 Tilgath-pilneser king of Assyria came
29. 15 they gathered their brethren..and came
29. 17 on the eighth day of the month came they
30. 1 they should come to the house of the L.
30. 5 they should come to keep the passover
30. 11 divers..humbled themselves, and came
30. 25 all the congregation that came out of Is.
30. 25 the strangers that came out of the land
30. 27 their prayer came (up) to his holy dwell.
31. 8 and the princes came and saw the heaps
32. 1 Sennacherib king of Assyria came, and
32. 4 Why should the kings of Assyria come
32. 26 the wrath of the LORD came not upon
34. 9 when they came to Hilkiah the high pri.
35. 22 and came to fight in the valley of Megiddo
Ezra 2. 2 Which came with Zerubbabel: Jeshua
Ezra 3. 8 the second year of their coming unto the
7. 8 he came to Jerusalem in the fifth month
7. 9 on the first (day) of the fifth month came
8. 32 we came to Jerusalem, and abode there
10. 8 whosoever would not come within three
10. 14 Let..our rulers..come at appointed
Neh. 1. 2 Hanani, one of my brethren, came, he
2. 7 convey me over till I come into Judah
2. 9 I came to the governors beyond the river
2. 11 I came to Jerusalem, and was there three
4. 8 to come (and) to fight against Jerusalem
4. 11 They shall not know..till we come in the
4. 12 when the Jews which dwelt by them came
5. 17 those that came unto us from among the
6. 10 I came unto the house of Shemaiah the
6. 10 for they will come to slay thee
6. 10 in the night will they come to slay thee
6. 17 and (the letters) of Tobiah came unto
7. 7 who came with Zerubbabel, Jeshua, N.
13. 1 the Moabite should not come into the
13. 6 came I unto the king, and after certain
13. 7 I came to Jerusalem, and understood of
13. 21 From that time forth came they no (more)
13. 22 I commanded..(that) they should come
Esth. 1. 12 queen Vashti refused to come at the king's
1. 17 to be brought in..but she came not
1. 19 That Vashti come no more before king A.
2. 13 Then thus came (every) maiden unto the
4. 2 And came even before the king's gate
4. 4 Esther's maids and her chamberlains came
4. 9 Hatach came and told Esther the words
4. 11 whosoever, whether man or woman, shall c.
5. 4 let the king and Haman come this day
5. 5 So the king and Haman came to the ban.
5. 8 let the king and Haman come to the ban.
5. 10 when he came home, he sent and called
7. 1 the king and Haman came to banquet
8. 1 and Mordecai came before the king
9. 25 But when (Esther) came before the king
Job 1. 6 there was a day..the sons of God came
1. 6 and Satan came also among them
1. 7 LORD said unto Satan, Whence comest
1. 14 there came a messenger unto Job, and
1. 16, 17, 18 While he (was)..speaking..came
1. 19 there came a great wind from the wilder.
2. 1 the sons of God came to present them.
2. 1 Satan came also among them, to present
2. 2 the LORD said..From whence comest thou?
2. 11 had made an appointment together to c.
3. 6 let it not come into the number of the
3. 7 let no joyful voice come therein
3. 24 For my sighing cometh before I eat, and
3. 26 neither was I quiet; yet trouble came
5. 21 be afraid of destruction when it cometh
5. 26 shalt come to (thy) grave in a full age
6. 20 they came thither and were ashamed
9. 32 (and) we should come together in judg.
13. 16 for an hypocrite shall not come before him
14. 14 will I wait, till my change come
17. 10 as for you all, do ye return, and come now
19. 12 His troops come together, and raise up
21. 17 (how oft) cometh their destruction upon
23. 3 (that) I might come (even) to his seat
27. 9 Will God hear..cry when trouble cometh
28. 20 Whence then cometh wisdom? and where
29. 13 The blessing of him..came upon me
30. 26 I looked for good, then evil came (unto me)
30. 26 when I waited for light, there came dark.
37. 9 out of the south cometh the whirlwind
38. 11 Hitherto shalt thou come, but no further
41. 13 (or) who can come (to him) with his
41. 16 that no air can come between them
42. 11 Then came there unto him all his brethren
Psa. 5. 7 I will come (into) thy house in the multi
18. 6 my cry came before him, (even) into his
22. 31 They shall come, and shall declare his
35. 8 Let destruction come upon him at una.
37. 13 for he seeth that his day is coming
40. 7 Then said I, Lo, I come: in the volume
41. 6 if he come to see (me), he speaketh vanity
42. 2 when shall I come and appear before God?
50. 3 Our God shall come, and shall not keep
51. *title.* when Nathan the prophet came unto
52. *title.* when Doeg the Edomite came and
54. *title.* when the Ziphims came and said to S.
65. 2 unto thee shall all flesh come
69. 27 let them not come into thy righteousness
71. 18 thy power to every one (that is) to come
79. 11 Let the sighing of the prisoner come
86. 9 nations whom thou hast made shall come
88. 2 Let my prayer come before thee: incline
95. 6 O come, let us worship and bow down; let
96. 8 bring an offering, and come into his courts
96. 13 for he cometh, for he cometh to judge the
98. 9 for he cometh to judge the earth: with
100. 2 come before his presence with singing
101. 2 O when wilt thou come unto me? I will
102. 1 O LORD..let my cry come unto thee
105. 19 Until the time that his word came: the
105. 23 Israel also came into Egypt; and Jacob
105. 31 He spake, and there came divers sorts of
105. 34 He spake, and the locusts came, and
109. 18 let it come into his bowels like water
118. 26 Blessed (be) he that cometh in the name
119. 170 Let my supplication come before thee
121. 1 unto the hills, from whence cometh my
132. 3 Surely I will not come into the tabernacle
Prov. 1. 26 I will mock when your fear cometh
1. 27 When your fear cometh as desolation, and
1. 27 your destruction cometh as a whirlwind
1. 27 when distress and anguish cometh upon
3. 25 Be not afraid of..fear..when it cometh

Prov. 6. 11 So shall thy poverty come as one that
6. 15 Therefore shall..calamity come suddenly
7. 20 He..will come home at the day appointed
11. 2 (When) pride cometh, then cometh shame
11. 8 and the wicked cometh in his stead
13. 12 (when) the desire cometh, (it is) a tree of
18. 3 When the wicked cometh, (then) cometh
18. 17 his neighbour cometh and searcheth him
24. 25 a good blessing shall come upon them
24. 34 So shall thy poverty come (as) one that
26. 2 so the curse causeless shall not come
Eccl. 1. 4 generation passeth away..(another)..c.
2. 12 what (can) the man (do) that cometh after
2. 16 the days to come shall all be forgotten
5. 3 a dream cometh through the multitude
5. 15 As he came forth of his mother's womb
5. 15 naked shall he return to go as he came
5. 16 in all points as he came, so shall he go
8. 10 who had come and gone from the place
9. 14 and there came a great king against it
11. 8 All that cometh (is) vanity
12. 1 while the evil days come not, nor the years
Song 2. 8 behold, he cometh, leaping upon the
4. 8 Come with me from Lebanon, (my) spouse
4. 16 come, thou south..Let my beloved come
Isa. 1. 12 When ye come to appear before me, who
1. 23 neither doth the cause of the widow come
5. 19 the Holy One of Israel draw nigh and c.
5. 26 behold, they shall come with speed
7. 17 shall bring..days that have not come
7. 19 they shall come, and shall rest all of them
7. 24 With arrows and with bows shall (men) c.
7. 25 there shall not come thither the fear of
10. 3 the desolation (which) shall come from far
13. 5 They come from a far country, from the
13. 6 it shall come as a destruction from the
13. 9 Behold, the day of the LORD cometh, cruel
13. 22 her time (is) near to come, and her days
14. 9 moved for thee to meet (thee) at thy com.
14. 31 there shall come from the north a smoke
16. 12 that he shall come to his sanctuary to pray
19. 1 the LORD rideth..shall come into Egypt
19. 23 the Assyrian shall come into Egypt, and
20. 1 In the year that Tartan came unto Ashdod
21. 1 it cometh from the desert, from a terrible
21. 9 And, behold, here cometh a chariot of
27. 6 cause them that come of Jacob to take
27. 11 the women come, (and) set them on fire
27. 13 they shall come which were ready to perish
30. 13 whose breaking cometh suddenly at an
30. 27 the name of the LORD cometh from far
30. 29 to come into the mountain of the LORD
32. 10 shall fail, the gathering shall not come
35. 4 behold, your God will come..he will come
35. 10 the ransomed..shall return, and come to
36. 17 Until I come and take you away to a land
36. 22 Then came Eliakim the son of Hilkiah
37. 5 the servants of king Hezekiah came to I.
37. 29 back by the way by which thou camest
37. 33 He shall not come into this city, nor shoot
37. 33 nor come before it with shields, nor cast
37. 34 By the way that he came, by the same
37. 34 and shall not come into this city, saith
38. 1 the son of Amoz, came unto him, and said
39. 3 Then came Isaiah the prophet unto king
39. 3 and from whence came they unto thee
39. 6 the days come, that all that (is) in thine
40. 10 the Lord GOD will come with a strong
41. 22 or declare us things for to come
41. 25 I have raised up..and he shall come
44. 7 and shall come, let them show unto them
45. 20 Assemble yourselves and come; draw
45. 24 (even) to him shall (men) come; and all
47. 9 these two (things) shall come to thee in
47. 9 they shall come upon thee in their perfe.
47. 11 Therefore shall evil come upon thee; thou
47. 11 desolation shall come upon thee suddenly
47. 13 (these things) that shall come upon thee
49. 12 Behold, these shall come from far; and
49. 18 all these gather themselves..(and) come
50. 2 Wherefore, when I came, (was there) no
51. 11 come with singing unto Zion; and ever.
52. 1 there shall no more come into thee the
56. 1 for my salvation (is) near to come, and
59. 20 And the Redeemer shall come to Zion
60. 4 they gather themselves together, they c.
60. 4 thy sons shall come from far, and thy
60. 5 forces of the Gentiles shall come unto thee
60. 6 all they from Sheba shall come: they
60. 13 The glory of Lebanon shall come unto thee
62. 11 Behold, thy salvation cometh; behold, his
63. 1 Who (is) this that cometh from Edom
66. 7 she brought forth; before her pain came
66. 15 behold, the LORD will come with fire, and
66. 18 it shall come, that I will gather all nations
66. 18 and they shall come, and see my glory
66. 23 shall all flesh come to worship before me
Jer. 1. 15 For, lo, I will call..and they shall come
2. 3 evil shall come upon them, saith the L.
2. 31 We are lords; we will come no more unto
3. 18 they shall come together out of the land
4. 12 a full wind..shall come unto me
4. 16 watchers come from a far country, and
5. 12 (It is) not he; neither shall evil come
6. 3 shepherds with their flocks shall come
6. 20 To what purpose cometh there to me
6. 22 Behold, a people cometh from the north
6. 26 the spoiler shall suddenly come upon us
7. 10 come and stand before me in this house
7. 32 behold, the days come, saith the LORD
8. 7 observe the time of their coming; but
9. 17 Consider ye..that they may come; and
Jer. 9. 17 send for..(women), that they may come
9. 25 Behold, the days come, saith the LORD
13. 20 and behold them that come from the north
14. 3 they came to the pits, (and) found no
16. 14 Therefore, behold, the days come, saith
16. 19 Gentiles shall come unto thee from the
17. 6 he..shall not see when good cometh
17. 8 he..shall not see when heat cometh, but
17. 15 the word of the LORD? let it come now
17. 26 they shall come from the cities of Judah
19. 6 behold, the days come, saith the LORD
19. 14 Then came Jeremiah from Tophet
20. 6 thou shalt come to Babylon, and there
22. 23 how..shalt thou be when pangs come
23. 5, 7 Behold, the days come, saith the LORD
23. 17 No evil shall come upon you
25. 31 A noise shall come (even) to the ends of
26. 2 speak unto all..which come to worship in
27. 3 the hand of the messengers which come
27. 7 until the very time of his land come
30. 3 For, lo, the days come, saith the LORD
31. 9 They shall come with weeping, and with
31. 12 they shall come and sing in the height of
31. 27, 31, 38 Behold, the days come, saith the
32. 7 Behold, Hanameel..shall come unto thee
32. 8 mine uncle's son, came to me in
32. 29 the Chaldeans..shall come and set fire
33. 5 They come to fight with the Chaldeans
33. 14 Behold, the days come, saith the LORD
35. 11 Come, and let us go to Jerusalem for fear
36. 6 of all Judah that come out of their cities
36. 9 to all the people that came from the cities
36. 14 took the roll in his hand, and came unto
36. 29 The king of Babylon shall certainly come
37. 19 The king of Babylon shall not come against
38. 25 if the princes hear..and they come unto
38. 27 Then came all the princes unto Jeremiah
39. 1 In the ninth year..came Nebuchadrezzar
40. 4 If it seem good unto thee to come with
40. 4 come, and I will look well unto thee; but
40. 4 if it seem ill unto thee to come with me
40. 8 Then they came to Gedaliah to Mizpah
40. 10 to serve the Chaldeans, which will come
40. 12 all the Jews..came to the land of Judah
40. 13 all the captains..came to Gedaliah to M.
41. 1 even ten men with him, came unto Geda.
41. 5 there came certain from Shechem, from
41. 6 Come to Gedaliah the son of Ahikam
41. 7 when they came into the midst of the city
43. 7 So they came into the land of Egypt: for
43. 7 Thus came they (even) to Tahpanhes
43. 11 when he cometh, he shall smite the land
46. 13 Nebuchadrezzar..should come (and) smite
46. 18 (As) I live, saith the King..shall he come
46. 20 Egypt (is like)..(but) destruction cometh
46. 20 it cometh out of the north
46. 22 come against her with axes, as hewers of
47. 4 the day that cometh to spoil all the Ph.
48. 8 the spoiler shall come upon every city
48. 12 behold, the days come, saith the LORD
48. 16 The calamity of Moab (is) near to come
49. 2 behold, the days come, saith the LORD
49. 4 (saying), Who shall come unto me?
49. 9 If grape-gatherers come to thee, would
49. 14 Gather ye together, and come against
49. 36 the outcasts of Elam shall not come
50. 4 the children of Israel shall come, they and
50. 5 Come, and let us join ourselves to the
50. 26 Come against her from the utmost border
50. 41 Behold, a people shall come from the
51. 10 come, and let us declare in Zion the work
51. 13 abundant in treasures, thine end is come
51. 33 and the time of her harvest shall come
51. 46 a rumour shall both come (one) year
51. 47 the days come, that I will do judgment
51. 48 the spoilers shall come unto her from
51. 52 behold, the days come, saith the LORD
51. 53 shall spoilers come unto her, saith the
51. 60 all the evil that should come upon Baby.
51. 61 When thou comest to Babylon..read all
52. 4 Nebuchadrezzar king of Babylon came
52. 12 in the tenth (day) of the month..came N.
Lam. 1. 4 because none come to the solemn feasts
1. 22 Let all their wickedness come before thee
Eze. 1. 4 behold, a whirlwind came out of the north
3. 15 I came to them of the captivity at Tel-a.
4. 14 neither came there abominable flesh into
7. 25 Destruction cometh; and they shall seek
7. 26 Mischief shall come upon mischief, and
9. 2 six men came from the way of the higher
11. 16 in the countries where they shall come
11. 18 they shall come thither, and they shall
12. 16 among the heathen whither they come
14. 1 Then came certain of the elders of Israel
14. 4, 7 his iniquity before his face, and cometh
14. 4, the LORD will answer him that cometh
16. 16 (the like things) shall not come, neither
16. 33 that they may come unto thee on every
17. 3 A great eagle..came unto Lebanon, and
20. 1 certain of the elders of Israel came to
21. 7 For the tidings, because it cometh: and
21. 7 behold, it cometh, and shall be brought
21. 19 sword of the king of Babylon may come
21. 20 Appoint a way, that the sword may come
21. 27 it shall be no (more), until he come whose
22. 3 in the midst of it, that her time may come
23. 17 the Babylonians came to her into the bed
23. 24 they shall come against thee with chariots
23. 39 they came the same day into my sanctuary
23. 40 that ye have sent for men to come from
23. 40 they came: for whom thou didst wash
24. 24 when this cometh, ye shall know that I
Eze. 24. 26 he that escapeth in that day shall come
30. 4 And the sword shall come upon Egypt
30. 9 as in the day of Egypt: for, lo, it cometh
33. 3 when he seeth the sword come upon the
33. 4 if the sword come and take him away, his
33. 6 But if the watchman see the sword come
33. 6 if the sword come and take (any) person
33. 21 one that had escaped out of Jerusalem c.
33. 22 afore he that was escaped came, and had
33. 22 until he came to me in the morning; and
33. 30 Come..and hear..the word that cometh
33. 31 they come unto thee as the people cometh
33. 33 lo it will come, then shall they know
36. 8 for they are at hand to come
37. 9 Come from the four winds, O breath, and
37. 10 and the breath came into them, and they
38. 8 in the latter years thou shalt come into
38. 9 Thou shalt ascend and come like a storm
38. 13 Art thou come to take a spoil? hast thou
38. 15 thou shalt come from thy place out of the
38. 18 Gog shall come against the land of Israel
39. 17 Assemble yourselves, and come; gather
40. 6 Then came he unto the gate which look.
43. 2 the glory of the God of Israel came from
43. 3 that I saw when I came to destroy the c.
43. 4 the glory of the LORD came into the house
44. 25 they shall come at no dead person to
46. 9 the people of the land shall come before
47. 9 whithersoever the rivers shall come, shall
47. 9 because these waters shall come thither
47. 9 shall live whither the river cometh
47. 20 till a man come over against Hamath
Dan. 1. 1 In the third year..came Nebuchadnezzar
2. 2 So they came and stood before the king
8. 5 behold, an he goat came from the west
8. 6 he came to the ram that had (two) horns
8. 17 So he came near..and when he came
9. 26 the people of the prince that shall come
10. 3 neither came flesh nor wine in my mouth
10. 13 one of the chief princes, came to help me
10. 20 Knowest thou wherefore I come unto thee?
10. 20 lo, the prince of Grecia shall come
11. 6 king's daughter of the south shall come
11. 7 which shall come with an army, and shall
11. 9 the king of the south shall come.
11. 10 (one) shall certainly come, and overflow
11. 13 shall certainly come after certain years
11. 15 So the king of the north shall come
11. 16 he that cometh..shall do according
11. 29 he shall return, and come toward the so.
11. 30 the ships of Chittim shall come against
11. 45 yet he shall come to his end, and none
Hos. 4. 15 come not ye unto Gilgal, neither go ye up
6. 3 he shall come unto us as the rain, as the
9. 4 their bread for their soul shall not come
10. 12 till he come and rain righteousness upon
13. 13 The sorrows of a..woman shall come
13. 15 an east wind shall come, the wind of the
Joel 1. 13 come, lie all night in sackcloth, ye minis.
1. 15 destruction from the Almighty shall..co.
2. 1 for the day of the LORD cometh, for (it is)
2. 31 before the great..day of the LORD come
3. 11 come, all ye heathen..gather yourselves
3. 11 cause thy mighty ones to come down, O
3. 13 come, get you down; for the press is full
Amos 4. 2 lo, the days shall come upon you, that
4. 4 Come to Beth-el, and transgress; at Gilgal
5. 9 the spoiled shall come against the fortress
6. 1 nations, to whom the house of Israel came!
8. 11 the days come, saith the Lord GOD, that
9. 13 Behold, the days come, saith the LORD
Obad. 5 If thieves came to thee, if robbers by
5 if the grape-gatherers came to thee
Jon. 1. 8 What..thine occupa.? and whence comest
Mic. 1. 15 he shall come unto Adullam the glory of
3. 11 none evil can come upon us
4. 8 unto thee shall it come, even the first do.
4. 8 the kingdom shall come to the daughter
5. 5 when the Assyrian shall come into our
5. 6 when he cometh into our land, and when
7. 4 the day of thy watchmen..cometh
7. 12 (In) that day (also) he shall come even to
Hab. 1. 8 and their horsemen shall come from far
1. 9 They shall come all for violence: their
2. 3 it will surely come, it will not tarry
3. 3 God came from Teman, and the Holy
Zeph. 2. 2 the fierce anger of the LORD come upon
2. 2 the day of the LORD'S anger come upon
Hag. 1. 14 they came and did work in the house
2. 7 and the desire of all nations shall come
2. 16 (one) came to an heap of twenty (measures)
2. 16 (one) came to the press fat for to draw
Zech. 1. 21 Then said I, What come these to do?
2. 10 I come, and I will dwell in the midst of
6. 10 come thou the same day, and go into the
6. 15 they (that are) far off shall come and build
8. 20 that there shall come people, and the
8. 22 strong nations shall come to seek the L.
9. 9 behold, thy King cometh unto thee
12. 9 all the nations that come against Jerusa
14. 1 Behold, the day of the LORD cometh, and
14. 5 the LORD my God shall come, (and) all the
14. 16 the nations which came against Jerusalem
14. 18 the family of Egypt go not up, and come
14. 18 the LORD will smite the heathen that come
14. 21 all they that sacrifice shall come and take
Mal. 3. 1 the LORD..ye seek, shall suddenly come
3. 1 behold, he shall come, saith the LORD of
3. 2 who may abide the day of his coming?
4. 1 the day cometh..the day that cometh
4. 5 the coming of the great and dreadful day
4. 6 I come and smite the earth with a curse

6. *To tread, proceed,* דָּרַךְ *darak.*
Num24. 17 there shall come a star out of Jacob, and

7. *To come,* הֲלַךְ *halak.*
Ezra 5. 5 to cease, till the matter came to Darius

8. *To be,* הָיָה *hayah.*
Gen. 15. 1 the word of the LORD came unto Abram

9. *To go, proceed, go on,* הָלַךְ *halak.*
Gen. 32. 6 also he cometh to meet thee, and four h.
Num22. 14 and said, Balaam refuseth to come with
22. 16 Let nothing..hinder thee from coming
22. 37 wherefore camest thou not unto me?
Deut. 2. 14 the space in which we came..(was) thirty
Josh. 6. 9 and the rereward came after the ark
6. 13 the rereward came after the ark of the
2 Sa. 13. 34 there came much people by the way of
1 Ki. 13. 9 by the same way that thou camest
13. 17 again to go by the way that thou camest
Job 20. 25 the glittering sword cometh out of his
Eccl. 1. 7 the place from whence the rivers come
Isa. 60. 3 the Gentiles shall come to thy light, and
60. 14 sons also of them..shall come bending
Mic. 4. 2 And many nations shall come, and say

10. *To be turned,* הָפַךְ *haphak,* 2.
1 Sa. 4. 19 she..travailed; for her pains came upon

11. *To be begotten, born,* יָלַד *yalad,* 2.
Deut 15. 19 All..that come of thy herd and of thy

12. *To go, proceed,* יָלַךְ *yalak.*
Gen. 19. 32 Come, let us make our father drink wine
29. 1 Then Jacob..came into the land of the
31. 44 come thou, let us make a covenant, I and
37. 13 come, and I will send thee unto them
37. 20 Come now therefore, and let us slay him
37. 27 Come, and let us sell him to the Ishmeel.
Exod. 3. 10 Come now..I will send thee unto Phara.
Num10. 29 come thou with us, and we will do thee
22. 6 Come now..I pray thee, curse me this
22. 11 come now curse me them; peradventure
22. 17 come therefore I pray thee, curse me
23. 7 Come, curse me Jacob, and come, defy I
23. 13 Come, I pray thee, with me unto another
23. 27 Come..I will bring thee unto another
24. 14 come (therefore, and) I will advertise
Judg. 4. 22 Come, and I will show thee the man whom
9. 10, 12, 14 Come thou (and) reign over us
11. 6 Come, and be our captain, that we may
19. 11 Come..let us turn in into this city of the
19. 13 Come and let us draw near to one of these
1 Sa. 9. 5 said Saul to his servant..Come, and let us
9. 9 Come, and let us go to the seer: for (he
9. 10 Saul said to his servant..come, let us go
11. 14 said Samuel to the people, Come, and let
14. 1 Come and let us go over to the Philistines'
14. 6 Come, and let us go over unto the garrison
17. 41 the Philistine came on and drew near unto
17. 44 Come to me, and I will give thy flesh unto
17. 48 the Philistine arose, and came and drew
20. 11 Come, and let us go out into the field
23. 3 how much more then if we come to Keilah
23. 27 Haste thee, and come; for the Philistines
1 Ki. 1. 12 come, let me, I pray thee, give thee
13 15 Come home with me, and eat bread
15. 19 come and break thy league with Baasha
2 Ki. 7. 4 come, and let us fall unto the host of the
7. 9 now therefore come, that we may go and
10. 16 Come with me and see my zeal for the L.
14. 8 Come, let us look one another in the face
2 Ch. 11. 14 left their suburbs..and came to Judah
25. 17 Come, let us see one another in the face
Ezra 10. 6 (when) he came thither, he did eat no br
Neh. 2. 17 come, and let us build up the wall of Jer.
6. 2 Come, let us meet together..in the plain
6. 7 Come now..and let us take counsel
Psa. 34. 11 Come, ye children, hearken unto me; I
46. 8 Come, behold the works of the LORD
66. 5 Come and see the works of God: (he is)
66. 16 Come (and) hear, all ye that fear God
80. 2 stir up thy strength, and come (and) save
83. 4 Come, and let us cut them off from (being)
95. 1 O Come, let us sing unto the LORD; let
Prov. 1. 11 Come with us, let us lay wait for blood
7. 18 Come, let us take our fill of love until the
9. 5 Come, eat of my bread, and drink of the
Song 7. 11 Come, my beloved, let us go forth into
Isa. 1. 18 Come now, and let us reason together
2. 3 Come ye, and let us go up to the mount.
2. 5 come ye, and let us walk in the light of
26. 20 Come, my people, enter..into thy chamb.
45. 14 they shall be thine: they shall come after
55. 1 come ye..come ye, buy and eat; yea, c.
55. 3 Incline your ear, and come unto me: hear
Jer. 12. 9 come ye, assemble all the beasts of the
18. 18 Then said they, Come, and let us devise
18. 18 come, and let us smite him with the
36. 14 Take in thine hand the roll..and come
48 2 come, and let us cut it off from (being) a
Hos. 6. 1 Come, and let us return unto the LORD
Jon. 1. 7 Come, and let us cast lots, that we may
Mic. 4. 2 Come, and let us go up to the mountain

13. *To go or come out,* יָצָא *yatsa.*
Gen. 10. 14 out of whom came Philistim and Caph.
24. 5 unto the land from whence thou camest
2 Ki. 24. 7 the king of Egypt came not again any
1 Ch. 1. 12 And Pathrusim..of whom came the P.
1 Ch. 2. 53 of them came the Zareathites, and the
Job 26. 4 and whose spirit came from thee?
Eccl. 4. 14 For out of prison he cometh to reign

14. *To arrive, reach,* מְטָא *meta,* מְטָה *metah.*
Dan. 4. 24 the decree of the Most High, which is c.
4. 28 All this came upon the king Nebuchad.
6. 24 or ever they came at the bottom of the
7. 13 and came to the Ancient of days, and
7. 22 the time came that the saints possessed

15. *To come upon, touch,* נָגַע *naga.*
Judg20. 41 for they saw that evil was come upon
Ezra 3. 1 when the seventh month was come, and
Neh. 7. 73 when the seventh month came, the chil.
Esth. 9. 26 and (of that)..which had come unto them
Isa. 16. 8 they are come (even) unto Jazer, they
Jon. 3. 6 For word came unto the king of Nineveh
Mic. 1. 9 her wound (is) incurable; for it is come

16. *To come upon, touch,* נָגַע *naga,* 5.
1 Sa. 14. 9 Tarry until we come to you; then we will
Esth. 2. 12 every maid's turn was come to go in to
2. 15 his daughter was come to go in unto the
4. 3 king's commandment and his decree came
4. 14 who knoweth whether thou art come to
6. 14 with him, came the king's chamberlains
8. 17 king's commandment and his decree came
Song. 2. 12 the time of the singing (of birds) is come
Dan. 8. 7 I saw him come close unto the ram, and
12. 12 Blessed (is) he that waiteth, and cometh

17. *To draw nigh,* נָגַשׁ *nagash.*
Exod19. 15 the third day: come not at your wives
24. 14 let him come unto them
Josh 14. 6 the children of Judah came unto Joshua
Ruth 2. 14 At meal time come thou hither, and eat
1 Ki. 18. 21 Elijah came unto all the people, and said
20. 22 the prophet came to the king of Israel
20. 28 there came a man of God, and spake unto
2 Ki. 2. 5 sons of the prophets..at Jericho came
Ezra 4. 2 they came to Zerubbabel, and to the chief

18. *To be drawn nigh,* נָגַשׁ *nagash,* 2.
Deut 25. 1 If there be a controversy..and they come
25. 9 shall his brother's wife come unto him
1 Ki. 20. 13 there came a prophet unto Ahab king of
Ezra 9. 1 these things were done, the princes came

19. *To give,* נָתַן *nathan.*
Prov 13. 10 Only by pride cometh contention: but

20. *To ascend, come up,* סְלֵק *seleq.*
Dan. 2. 29 thy thoughts came into thy mind upon

21. *To come over,* עֲבַר *abar.*
Gen. 18. 5 for therefore are ye come to your servant
Num. 5. 14, 14 the spirit of jealousy come upon him
5. 30 the spirit of jealousy cometh upon him
6. 5 there shall no razor come upon his head
Deut 29. 16 we came through the nations which ye.
Judg. 9 25 they robbed all that came along that way

22. *To go up,* עָלָה *alah.*
Lev. 19. 19 neither shall a garment..come upon thee
Num 19. 2 no blemish, (and) upon which never came
Judg13. 5 no razor shall come on his head: for
1 Sa. 1. 11 there shall no razor come upon his head
6. 7 on which there hath come no yoke, and
2 Ki. 12. 4 all the money that cometh into any
Job 5. 26 as a shock of corn cometh in
Song 3. 6 Who (is) this that cometh out of the wil.
Isa. 65. 17 former shall not be remembered, nor come
Jer. 7. 31 I commanded (them) not, neither came
19. 5 nor spake (it), neither came (it) into my
32. 35 I commanded them not, neither came it
51 50 and let Jerusalem come into your mind
Eze. 20. 32 that which cometh into your mind shall
38. 10 at the same time shall things come into
44. 17 no wool shall come upon them whiles

23. *To go up,* עֲלַל *alal.*
Dan. 5. 10 the queen, by reason..came into the ban.

24. *To come up or against,* פָּגַע *paga.*
Josh. 16. 7 And it went down..and came to Jericho

25. *To prosper, go on successfully,* צָלֵחַ *tsaleach.*
Judg 14. 19 the Spirit of the LORD came upon him
1 Sa. 10. 6 the Spirit of the LORD will come upon
10. 10 and the Spirit of God came upon him, and
11. 6 the Spirit of God came upon Saul when
16 13 And the Spirit of the LORD came upon
18. 10 that the evil spirit from God came upon

26. *To come near,* קָרַב *qarab.*
Exod36. 2 whose heart stirred him up to come unto
Num 9. 6 they came before Moses, and before A.
27. 1 Then came the daughters of Zelophehad
Deut 2. 37 Only unto the land..thou camest not
22. 14 when I came to her I found her not a m.
Josh 7. 14 tribe which the LORD taketh shall come
7 14. 14 which the LORD shall take shall come
1 Ki. 2. 7 for so they came to me when I fled
Psa. 27. 2 my foes came upon me to eat up my flesh
Jon. 1. 6 So the shipmaster came to him, and said

27. *To come near,* קְרֵב *qereb.*
Dan. 6. 20 when he came to the den, he cried

28. *To meet,* קָרָה *qarah,* 2.
Num23. 3 peradventure the LORD will come to meet

29. *To go up,* ἀναβαίνω *anabainō.*
Acts 7. 23 it came into his heart to visit his brethren
21. 31 tidings came unto the chief captain of the

30. *To come away,* ἀπέρχομαι *aperchomai.*
Mark 3. 13 calleth..whom he would: and they came
7. 30 when she was come to her house, she
Luke23. 33 they were [come] to the place..called
Rom 15. 28 I will come by you into Spain

31. *To go away,* ἀποβαίνω *apobainō.*
John21. 9 As soon then as they were come to land

32. *To become,* γίνομαι *ginomai.*
Matt. 8. 16 the even was come..and he cast out the
14. 23 when the evening was come, he was there
20. 8 So when even was come, the lord of the
26. 20 Now when the even was come, he sat
27. 1 When the morning was come, all the chief
27. 57 When the even was come, there came a
Mark 1. 11 And there came a voice from heaven
4. 35 the same day, when the even was come
6. 2 when the sabbath day was come, he began
6. 21 And when a convenient day was come
6. 47 when even was come, the ship was in the
9. 21 How long is it ago since this came unto
11. 19 when even was come, he went out of the
15. 33 when the sixth hour was come, there was
15. 42 when the even was come..before the sab.
Luke 1. 65 fear came on all that dwelt round about
3. 2 the word of God came unto John the son
3. 22 and a voice came from heaven, which said
9. 34 While he thus spake, there came a cloud
9. 35 there came a voice out of the cloud, saying
19. 9 This day is salvation come to this house
22. 14 when the hour was come, he sat down
John 1. 17 grace and truth came by Jesus Christ
5. 14 sin no more, lest a worse thing come unto
6. 16 when even was (now) come, his disciples
6. 25 said..Rabbi, when camest thou hither?
10. 35 unto whom the word of God came, and
12. 30 This voice came not because of me, but
13. 19 Now I tell you before it come, that, when
21. 4 when the morning was now come, Jesus
Acts 2. 2 suddenly there came a sound from heaven
2. 43 And fear came upon every soul: and
5. 5 great fear came on all them that heard
5. 11 great fear came upon all the church, and
7. 31 the voice of the Lord came unto him
9. 3 as he journeyed, he came near Damascus
10. 13 there came a voice to him, Rise, Peter
12. 11 when Peter was come to himself, he said
16. 29 came trembling, and fell down before Pa.
21. 17 when we were come to Jerusalem, the
21. 35 when he came upon the stairs; so it was
26. 22 Prophets and Moses did say should come
27. 7 we..scarce were come over against Cnidus
27. 16 we had much work to come by the boat
27. 27 when the fourteenth night was [come,] as
28. 6 after they had looked..saw no harm come
2 Co. 1. 8 of our trouble which came to us in Asia
Gal. 3. 14 That the blessing..might come on the
1 Th. 1. 5 our gospel came not unto you in word
1 Ti. 6. 4 whereof cometh envy, strife, railings, evil
2 Ti. 3. 11 Persecutions, afflictions, which came unto
Heb. 11. 24 Moses, when he was come to years, refused
Rev. 12. 10 Now is come salvation, and strength, and

33. *Hither, here, come!* δεῦρο *deuro.*
Matt19. 21 If thou wilt be perfect..come (and) follow
Mark10 21 come, take up the cross, and follow me
Luke18. 22 Yet lackest thou one thing..come, follow
John 11. 43 he cried with a loud voice, Lazarus, come
Acts 7. 3 come into the land which I shall show
7. 34 And now come I will send thee into Eg

34. *Hither, here, come!* δεῦτε *deute.*
Matt 11. 28 Come unto me, all (ye) that labour and
21. 38 This is the heir; come, let us kill him
22. 4 all things (are) ready: come unto the m.
25. 34 Come, ye blessed..inherit the kingdom
28. 6 Come, see the place where the Lord lay
Mark 1. 17 Jesus said unto them, Come ye after me
6. 31 Come ye yourselves apart into a desert
12. 7 This is the heir; come, let us kill him, and
Luke20. 14 This is the heir: [come,] let us kill him
John 4. 29 Come, see a man which told me all things
21. 12 Jesus saith unto them, Come (and) dine
Rev. 19. 17 Come and gather yourselves together unto

35. *To come through,* διέρχομαι *dierchomai.*
Acts 9. 38 that he would not delay to come to them

36. *To be,* εἰμί *eimi.*
Matt. 5. 37 whatsoever is more than these cometh of
Mark11. 11 and now the eventide was come, he went
John 1. 46 Can there any good thing come out of N.?
Acts 24. 25 temperance, and judgment to come
2 Ti. 4. 3 time will come when they will not endure

37. *To come in or into,* εἰσέρχομαι *eiserchomai.*
Matt 8. 8 that thou shouldest come under my roof
Luke17. 7 by and by, when he is come from the field

38. *To set in, arrive,* ἐνίστημι *enistēmi.*
2 Ti. 3. 1 in the last days perilous times shall come

39. *To come upon,* ἐπέρχομαι *eperchomai.*
Acts 14. 19 there came thither (certain) Jews from A
Eph. 2. 7 That in the ages to come he might show

40. *To go out of, forth,* ἐκπορεύομαι *ekporeuomai.*
Mark 7. 23 All these evil things come Mt. 15. 11.

41. *To come out of, forth,* ἐξέρχομαι *exerchomai.*
Matt 2. 6 for out of thee shall come a Governor, that
Mark11. 12 when they were come from Bethany, he
John 13. 3 he was come from God, and went to God
19. 5 Then came Jesus forth, wearing the crown
Acts 28. 15 they came to meet us as far as Appii For.

42. *To come,* ἔρχομαι *erchomai.*
Matt 2. 2 we have seen his star..and are come to

Matt. 2. 8 Go and search..that I may come and wo.
2. 9 it came and stood over where the young
2. 11 when they were come..they saw the
2. 21 he arose..and [came] into the land of Is.
2. 23 he came and dwelt in a city called Naza.
3. 7 Pharisees and Sadducees come to his ba.
3. 14 saying, I have need..and comest thou to
4. 13 leaving Nazareth, he came and dwelt in
5. 17 Think not that I am come to destroy the
5. 17 I am not come to destroy, but to fulfil
5. 24 first be reconciled..then come and offer
6. 10 Thy kingdom come. Thy will be done in
7. 15 Beware of false prophets, which come to
7. 25, 27 the rain descended, and the floods came
8. 2 there [came] a leper and worshipped him
8. 7 Jesus saith unto him, I will come and heal
8. 9 and to another, Come, and he cometh
8. 14 when Jesus was come into Peter's house
8. 28 when he was come to the other side
8. 29 art thou come hither to torment us before
9. 1 passed over, and came into his own city
9. 10 sinners came and sat down with him and
9. 13 for I am not come to call the righteous
9. 15 the days will come, when the bridegroom
9. 18 there [came] a certain ruler, and worship.
9. 18 come and lay thy hand upon her, and she
9. 23 when Jesus came into the ruler's house
9. 28 when he was come into the house, the bl.
10. 13 let your peace come upon it: but if it be
10. 23 have gone..till the Son of man be come
10. 34 that I am come to send peace on earth
10. 34 I came not to send peace, but a sword
10. 35 For I am come to set a man at variance
11. 14 this is Elias, which was for to come
11. 18 John came neither eating nor drinking
11. 19 The Son of man came eating and drinking
12. 42 she came from the uttermost parts of the
12. 44 and when he is come, he findeth (it) empty
13. 4 the fowls came and devoured them up
13. 19 then cometh the wicked (one), and catch.
13. 25 his enemy came and sowed tares among
13. 32 birds of the air come and lodge in the br.
13. 54 when he was come into his own country
14. 28 bid me come unto thee on the water
14. 29 And he said, Come. And when Peter was
14. 33 came and worshipped him, saying, Of a
14. 34 they came into the land of Gennesaret
15. 25 Then came she and worshipped him, say.
15. 29 Jesus departed..and came nigh unto the
15. 39 and came into the coasts of Magdala
16. 5 when his disciples were come to the other
16. 13 When Jesus came into the coasts of Ces.
16. 24 If any (man) will come after me, let him
16. 27 For the Son of man shall come in the
16. 28 see the Son of man coming in his kingdom
17. 10 Why then say..that Elias must first come
17. 11 Elias truly shall first come, and restore all
17. 12 I say unto you, That Elias is come already
17. 14 when they were come to the multitude
17. 24 when they were come to Capernaum, they
18. 7 for it must needs be that offences come
18. 7 woe to that man by whom the offence co.
18. 11 [For the Son of man is come to save that]
18. 31 came and told unto their lord all that was
19. 1 came into the coasts of Judea beyond J.
19. 14 Jesus said..forbid them not, to come
20. 9 when they came that (were hired) about
20. 10 the first came..and..received every man
20. 28 the Son of man came not to be ministered
21. 1 when they..were come to Bethphage
21. 5 Behold, thy King cometh unto thee, meek
21. 19 he came to it, and found nothing thereon
21. 23 when he was come into the temple, the
21. 32 came unto you in the way of righteousness
21. 40 When the lord..cometh, what will he
22. 3 them that were bidden..would not come
23. 35 upon you may come all the righteous blo.
24. 5 For many shall come in my name, saying
24. 30 they shall see the Son of man coming in
24. 39 knew not until the flood came, and took
24. 42 ye know not what hour your Lord doth c.
24. 43 known in what watch the thief would c.
24. 44 as ye think not the Son of man cometh
24. 46 his lord when he cometh shall find so
25. 6 Behold, the bridegroom [cometh]; go ye
25. 10 while they went to buy, the bridegroom c.
25. 11 Afterward came also the other virgins
25. 13 nor the hour wherein the Son of man [c.]
25. 19 After a long time the lord..cometh, and
25. 31 the Son of man shall come in his glory
25. 36 I was in prison, and ye came unto me
25. 39 when saw we thee..in prison, and came
26. 36 Then cometh Jesus with them unto a place
26. 40 he cometh unto the disciples, and findeth
26. 43 he came and found them asleep again: for
26. 45 Then cometh he to his disciples, and saith
26. 47 lo, Judas..came, and with him a great
26. 64 ye see the Son of man..coming in the cl.
27. 33 when they were come unto a place called
27. 49 let us see whether Elias will come to save
27. 57 When the even was..there came a rich m.
27. 64 lest his disciples come by night, and steal
28. 1 the first (day) of the week, came Mary M.
28. 11 some of the watch came into the city
28. 13 His disciples came by night, and stole
Mark 1. 7 There cometh one mightier than I after
1. 9 that Jesus came from Nazareth of Galilee
1. 14 Jesus came into Galilee, preaching the
1. 24 art thou come to destroy us? I know thee
1. 40 there came a leper to him, beseeching him
1. 45 and they came to him from every quarter
2. 3 they come unto him, bringing one sick of

Mark 2. 17 I came not to call the righteous, but sin.
2. 18 the Pharisees used to fast: and they come
2. 20 the days will come, when the bridegroom
3. 8 when they had heard..came unto him
3. 31 There came then his brethren and his m.
4. 4 the fowls of the air came and devoured it
4. 15 but, when they have heard, Satan cometh
4. 22 but that it should come abroad
5. 1 And they came over unto the other side
5. 15 they come to Jesus, and see him that was
5. 22 behold, there cometh one of the rulers of
5. 23 come and lay thy hands on her, that she
5. 27 came in the press behind, and touched his
5. 33 the woman..came and fell down before
5. 35 While he yet spake, there came from the
5. 38 he cometh to the house of the ruler of
6. 1 he went..and came into his own country
6. 29 they came and took up his corpse, and
6. 31 for there were many coming and going
6. 48 the fourth watch of the night he cometh
6. 53 they came into the land of Gennesaret
7. 1 and certain of the scribes, which came
7. 25 a (certain) woman..came and fell at his
7. 31 he came unto the sea of Galilee, through
8. 10 he..came into the parts of Dalmanutha
8. 22 he cometh to Bethsaida; and they bring
8. 34 Whosoever will [come] after me, let him
8. 38 when he cometh in the glory of his Father
9. 1 they have seen the kingdom of God come
9. 7 and a voice came out of the cloud, saying
9. 11 say the scribes that Elias must first co.
9. 12 he..told them, Elias verily cometh first
9. 13 I say unto you, That Elias is indeed come
9. 14 when he came to (his) disciples, he saw
9. 33 he came to Capernaum: and, being in
10. 1 he arose from thence, and cometh into
10. 14 Suffer the little children to come unto
10. 30 and in the world to come eternal life
10. 45 the Son of man came not to be ministered
10. 46 they came to Jericho: and as he went
10. 50 casting away his garment, rose, and came
11. 9 Blessed (is) he that cometh in the name
11. 10 Blessed (be) the kingdom..that cometh
11. 13 he came..and when he came to it, he fou.
11. 15 they come to Jerusalem: and Jesus went
11. 27 they come again to Jerusalem: and as he
11. 27 there come to him the chief priests, and
12. 9 He will come and destroy the husbandmen
12. 14 when they were come, they say unto him
12. 18 Then come unto him the Sadducees
12. 42 there came a certain poor widow, and
13. 6 For many shall come in my name, saying
13. 26 then shall they see the Son of man com.
13. 35 when the master of the house cometh
13. 36 Lest, coming suddenly, he find you sleep.
14. 3 there came a woman having an alabaster
14. 16 his disciples went forth, and came into
14. 17 in the evening he cometh with the twelve
14. 32 they came to a place which was named G.
14. 37 And he cometh, and findeth them sleep.
14. 41 he cometh the third time, and saith..Sleep
14. 41 it is enough, the hour is come; behold
14. 45 as soon as he was come, he..kissed him
14. 62 ye shall see the Son of man..coming in
14. 66 there cometh one of the maids of the
15. 21 Simon..who passed by, coming out of the
15. 36 let us see whether Elias will come to take
15. 43 Joseph of Arimathea..came, and went
16. 1 that they might come and anoint him
16. 2 they came unto the sepulchre at the
Luke 1. 43 the mother of my Lord should come to
1. 59 they came to circumcise the child; and
2. 16 they came with haste, and found Mary
2. 27 he came by the spirit into the temple
2. 51 he went down..and [came] to Nazareth
3. 3 he came into all the country about Jor.
3. 12 Then came also publicans to be baptized
3. 16 one mightier than I cometh, the latchet
4. 16 he came to Nazareth, where he had been
4. 34 art thou come to destroy us? I know thee
4. 42 the people sought him, and came unto
5. 7 they beckoned..that they should come
5. 7 they came, and filled both the ships, so
5. 17 which were [come] out..every town of G.
5. 32 I came not to call the righteous, but sin.
5. 35 days will come, when the bridegroom
6. 17 which came to hear him, and to be healed
6. 47 Whosoever cometh to me, and heareth
7. 3 beseeching him that he would come and
7. 7 neither thought I myself worthy to come
7. 8 and to another, Come, and he cometh
7. 33 John..came neither eating bread nor dr.
7. 34 The Son of man is come eating and drink.
8. 12 then cometh the devil, and taketh away
8. 17 that shall not be known and come abroad
8. 35 Then they went out..and came to Jesus
8. 41 there came a man named Jairus, and he
8. 47 she came trembling, and falling down
8. 49 While he yet spake, there cometh one
9. 23 If any (man) will come after me, let him
9. 26 he shall come in his own glory, and (in)
9. 56 the Son of man is not [come] to destroy
10. 1 every city..whither he himself would[co.]
10. 32 likewise a Levite..[came] and looked (on
10. 33 a certain Samaritan..came where he was
11. 2 Thy kingdom come. Thy will be done, as
11. 25 when he cometh, he findeth (it) swept
11. 31 she came from the utmost parts of the
12. 36 when he cometh and knocketh, they may
12. 37 the lord when he cometh shall find watch.
12. 38 shall [come] in the second watch, or come
12. 39 known what hour the thief would come

Luke 12. 40 the Son of man cometh at an hour when
12. 43 his lord when he cometh shall find so
12. 49 I am come to send fire on the earth; and
12. 54 There cometh a shower; and so it is
13. 6 he came and sought fruit thereon, and
13. 7 I come seeking fruit on this fig tree, and
13. 14 in them therefore come and be healed
13. 35 Blessed (is) he that cometh in the name
14. 9 he that bade thee and him come and say
14. 10 when he that bade thee cometh, he may
14. 17 Come; for all things are now ready
14. 20 I have married..therefore I cannot come
14. 26 any (man) come to me, and hate not his
14. 27 whosoever doth not bear..cross, and come
14. 31 with ten thousand to meet him that cometh
15. 6 when he cometh home, he calleth..(his)
15. 17 when he came to himself, he said, How
15. 20 he arose, and came to his father. But
15. 25 as he came and drew nigh to the house
15. 30 as soon as this thy son was come, which
16. 21 moreover the dogs came and licked his
16. 28 they also come into this place of torment
17. 1 is impossible but that offences will come
17. 1 woe (unto him) through whom they come!
17. 20 when the kingdom of God should come
17. 20 The kingdom of God cometh not with ob.
17. 22 The days will come, when ye shall desire
17. 27 the flood came, and destroyed them all
18. 3 was a widow in that city; and she came
18. 8 when the Son of man cometh, shall he find
18. 16 Suffer little children to come unto me
18. 30 and in the world to come life everlasting
19. 5 when Jesus came to the place, he looked
19. 10 For the Son of man is come to seek and
19. 13 and said unto them, Occupy till I come
19. 18 the second came, saying, Lord, thy pound
19. 20 another came, saying, Lord, behold, (here)
20. 16 He shall come and destroy these husband.
21. 6 (As for) these things..the days will come
21. 8 for many shall come in my name, saying
21. 27 shall they see the Son of man coming in a
22. 7 Then came the day of unleavened bread
22. 18 until the kingdom of God shall come
22. 45 when he..was come to his disciples, he
23. 26 a Cyrenian, coming out of the country
23. 42 remember me when thou comest into thy
24. 1 in the morning, they came unto the sep.
24. 23 they came, saying, that they had also
John 1. 7 The same came for a witness, to bear wit.
1. 9 every man that cometh into the world
1. 11 He came unto his own, and his own rece.
1. 29 next day John seeth Jesus coming unto
1. 30 After me cometh a man which is prefer.
1. 31 therefore am I come baptizing with wate.
1. 39 Come and see. They came and saw where
1. 46 Philip saith unto him, Come and see
1. 47 Jesus saw Nathanael coming to him, and
3. 2 The same came to Jesus by night, and said
3. 2 thou art a teacher come from God
3. 8 but canst not tell whence it cometh, and
3. 19 that light is come into the world
3. 20 neither cometh to the light, lest his deeds
3. 21 he that doeth truth cometh to the light
3. 22 After these things came Jesus and his
3. 26 they came unto John, and said..Rabbi
3. 26 the same baptizeth, and all (men) come
4. 5 Then cometh he to a city of Samaria
4. 7 There cometh a woman of Samaria to
4. 15 I thirst not, neither come hither to draw
4. 16 Go, call thy husband, and come hither
4. 21 Woman, believe me, the hour cometh
4. 23 But the hour cometh, and now is, when
4. 25 I know that Messias cometh, which is
4. 25 when he is come, he will tell us all things
4. 27 upon this came his disciples, and marv.
4. 30 they went out of the city, and came unto
4. 35 yet four months, and (then) cometh har.
4. 40 when the Samaritans were come unto him
4. 45 when he was come into Galilee, the Gal.
4. 46 So Jesus came again into Cana of Galilee
4. 54 when he was come out of Judea into G.
5. 24 hath everlasting life, and shall not come
5. 40 ye will not come to me, that ye might
5. 43 I am come in my Father's name, and ye
5. 43 another shall come in his own name, him
6. 5 Jesus..saw a great company come unto
6. 15 they would come and take him by force
6. 17 and Jesus was not come to them
6. 23 there came other boats from Tiberias
6. 24 his disciples..came to Capernaum, seeking
6. 35 he that cometh to me shall never hunger
6. 37 him that cometh to me I will in no wise
6. 44 No man can come to me, except the Fa.
6. 45 Every man therefore..cometh unto me
6. 65 no man can come unto me, except it were
7. 27 when Christ cometh, no man knoweth w.
7. 28 I am not come of myself, but he that sent
7. 30 because his hour was not yet come
7. 31 When Christ cometh, will he do more mi.
7. 34, 36 and where I am, (thither) ye cannot c.
7. 37 If any man thirst, let him come unto me
7. 41 Shall Christ come out of Galilee?
7. 42 Christ cometh of the seed of David, and
7. 45 Then came the officers to the chief priests
7. 50 he that came to Jesus by night, being one
8. 2 all the people [came] unto him; and he sat
8. 14 whence I came..ye cannot tell whence I c.
8. 20 for his hour was not yet come
8. 21, 22 whither I go, ye cannot come
8. 42 neither came I of myself, but he sent me
9. 4 the night cometh, when no man can work
9. 7 He went his way therefore..and came see.

John 9. 39 For judgment I am come into this world
10. 8 All that ever came before me are thieves
10 10 The thief cometh not..I am come that
10 12 But he that..seeth the wolf coming, and
11. 17 when Jesus came, he found that he had
11. 19 many of the Jews came to Martha and M.
11. 29 she arose quickly, and came unto him
11. 30 Jesus was not yet come into the town
11. 32 when Mary was come where Jesus was
11. 34 They said unto him, Lord, come and see
11. 38 Jesus therefore..cometh to the grave
11. 45 Then many of the Jews which came to M.
11. 48 the Romans shall come and take away
11. 56 that he will not come to the feast?
12. 1 Jesus..came to Bethany, where Lazarus
12. 9 they came not for Jesus' sake only, but
12. 12 much people that were come to the feast
12. 15 behold, thy King cometh, sitting on an
12. 22 Philip cometh and telleth Andrew
12. 23 The hour is come, that the Son of man
12. 27 but for this cause came I unto this hour
12. 28 Then came there a voice from heaven
12. 46 I am come a light into the world, that
12. 47 for I came not to judge the world, but to
13. 1 when Jesus knew that his hour was come
13. 6 Then cometh he to Simon Peter: and P.
13. 33 Whither I go, ye cannot come; so now
14. 3 I will come again, and receive you unto
14. 6 no man cometh unto the Father, but by
14. 18 not leave you comfortless: I will come
14. 23 we will come unto him, and make our
14 28 I go away, and come (again) unto you
14. 30 for the prince of this world cometh, and
15. 22 If I had not come and spoken unto them
15. 26 when the Comforter is come, whom I will
16. 2 the time cometh; that whosoever killeth
16. 4 when the time shall come, ye may remem.
16. 7 the Comforter will not come unto you
16. 8 when he is come, he will reprove the
16. 13 when he, the Spirit of truth, is come, he
16. 13 and he will show you things to come
16. 21 hath sorrow, because her hour is come
16. 25 the time cometh, when I shall no more
16. 28 and am come into the world: again, I
16. 32 the hour cometh, yea, is now come, that
17. 1 Father, the hour is come; glorify thy Son
17. 11 these are in the world, and I come to thee
17. 13 now come I to thee; and these things
18. 3 cometh thither with lanterns and torches
18. 4 knowing all things that should come upon
18 37 for this cause came I into the world, that
19 32 Then came the soldiers, and brake the
19. 33 But when they came to Jesus..he was dead
19. 38 He came..and took the body of Jesus
19. 39 And there came also Nicodemus, which
19. 39 at the first came to Jesus by night, and
20. 1 The first (day) of the week cometh Mary
20. 2 Then she runneth, and cometh to Simon
20. 3 Peter therefore..came to the sepulchre
20. 4 did outrun Peter, and came first to the
20. 6 Then cometh Simon Peter following him
20. 8 other disciple which came first to the
20. 18 Mary Magdalene came and told the dis.
20. 19 the same day at evening..came Jesus
20. 24 Thomas..was not with them,when Jesus c.
20 26 (Then) came Jesus, the doors being shut
21. 8 the other disciples came in a little ship
21. 13 Jesus then cometh, and taketh bread, and
21. 22 23 If I will that he tarry till I come
Acts 1. 11 this same Jesus..shall so come in like
2. 20 before that great..day of the Lord come
3. 19 when the times of refreshing shall come
7. 11 there came a dearth over all the land of
8. 27 the Ethiopians..had come to Jerusalem
8. 36 as they went on (their) way, they came
8. 40 in all the cities, till he came to Cesarea
9. 17 Jesus, that appeared..as thou camest
9. 21 in Jerusalem and came hither for that
10. 29 Therefore came I (unto you) without
11. 5 a great sheet..and it came even to me
12. 10 they came unto the iron gate that leadeth
12. 12 he came to the house of Mary the mother
13. 13 Now..they came to Perga in Pamphylia
13. 25 But, behold, there cometh one after me
13 51 they shook off the dust .and came unto
14. 24 after they had passed..they came to P
15. 30 when they were dismissed, they [came] to
16. 7 After they were come to Mysia, they
16. 37 let them come themselves and fetch us
16. 39 they came and besought them, and
17. 1 when they had passed..they came to Th.
17. 13 they came thither also, and stirred up
17. 15 a commandment..to come to him with
18. 1 after these things Paul departed..and ca.
18. 2 found a certain Jew..lately come from
18. 21 by all means keep this feast that [cometh]
19. 1 came to Ephesus: and finding certain
19. 6 the Holy Ghost came on them; and they
19. 18 many that believed came, and confessed
20. 2 when he had gone over..he came into G.
20. 6 we..came unto them to Troas in five days
20. 14 we took him in, and came to Mitylene
20. 15 and the next (day) we came to Miletus
21. 1 we came with a straight course unto C.
21. 8 And the next(day) we..came unto Cesarea
21. 11 when he was come unto us, he took Paul's
21. 22 for they will hear that thou art come
22. 11 when I could not see..I came unto Dam.
22. 13 Came unto me, and stood, and said unto
24. 8 Commanding his accusers to [come] unto
25. 23 on the morrow, when Agrippa was come
27. 8 came unto a place which is called the Fair

Acts 28. 13 and we came the next day to Puteoli
28. 16 when [we came] to Rome, the centurion
Rom. 1. 10 by the will of God to come unto you
1. 13 often times I purposed to come unto you
3. 8 say, Let us do evil, that good may come?
7. 9 when the commandment came, sin revived
9. 9 At this time will I come, and Sara shall
15. 23 having a .desire these many years to c.
15. 24 I will come to you: for I trust to see you
15. 29 I am sure that, when [I come] unto you
15 29 I shall come in the fulness of the blessing
15. 32 That I may come unto you with joy by
1 Co. 2. 1 I, brethren, when I came to you, came
4. 5 judge nothing..until the Lord come, who
4. 18 as though I would not come to you
4. 19 But I will come to you shortly, if the
4 21 shall I come unto you with a rod, or in
11. 26 ye do show the Lord s death till he come
11 34 the rest will I set in order when I come
13. 10 when that which is perfect is come, then
14. 6 if I come unto you speaking with tongues
15. 35 and with what body do they come?
16. 2 that there be no gatherings when I come
16. 5 I will come unto you, when I shall pass
16. 10 if Timotheus come, see that he may be
16. 11 conduct him..that he may come unto me
16. 12 I greatly desired him to come unto you
16. 12 will was not..to come..but he will come
2 Co. 1. 15 I was minded to come unto you before
1. 16 to come again out of Macedonia unto you
1. 23 to spare you I came as not yet unto Cor.
2. 1 I would not come again to you in ·eavi.
2. 3 lest, when I came, I should have sorrow
2. 12 when I came to Troas to (preach) Christ's
7. 5 when we were come into Macedonia, our
9. 4 if they of Macedonia come with me, and
11. 4 if he that cometh preacheth another Je.
11. 9 the brethren which came from Macedonia
12. 1 I will come to visions and revelations
12. 14 the third time I am ready to come to you
12. 20 lest, when I come, I shall not find you
12. 21 when I come again, my God will humble
13. 2 if I come again, I will not spare
Gal. 1. 21 Afterwards I came into the regions of S
2. 11 But when Peter was come to Antioch, I
2. 12 For before that certain came from James
2. 12 but when they were come, he withdrew
3. 19 the seed should come to whom the prom.
3. 23 before faith came, we were kept under
3. 25 after that faith is come, we are no longer
4. 4 when the fulness of the time was come
Eph. 2. 17 came and preached peace to you which
5. 6 because of these things cometh the wrath
Phil. 1. 27 whether I come and see you, or else be
2. 24 I trust in the Lord that I..shall come
Col. 3. 6 the wrath of God cometh on the children
4. 10 if he come unto you, receive him
1 Th. 1. 10 which delivered us from the wrath to come
2. 18 Wherefore we would have come unto you
3. 6 when Timotheus came from you unto us
5. 2 the day of the Lord so cometh as a thief
2 Th. 1. 10 When he shall come to be glorified in his
2. 3 except there come a falling away first
1 Ti. 1. 15 Jesus came into the world to save sinners
2. 4 to come unto the knowledge of the truth
3. 14 hoping to come unto thee shortly
4. 13 Till I come, give attendance to reading
2 Ti. 3. 7 never able to come to the knowledge of
4. 9 Do thy diligence to come shortly unto me
4. 13 The cloak..when thou comest, bring with
4. 21 Do thy diligence to come before winter
Titus 3. 12 be diligent to come unto me to Nicopolis
Heb. 6. 7 in the rain that cometh oft upon it
8. 8 Behold, the days come, saith the Lord
13. 23 with whom, if he come shortly, I will see
2 Pe 3. 3 there shall come in the last days scoffers
1 Jo. 2. 18 ye have heard that antichrist shall come
4. 2 3 that Jesus Christ is come in the flesh
4. 3 [ye have heard that it should come]
2 John 7 who confess not that Jesus Christ is come
10 If there come any unto you, and bring
12 but I trust [to come] unto you, and speak
3 John 3 I rejoiced greatly when the brethren came
10 if I come, I will remember his deeds which
Jude 14 the Lord cometh with ten thousand of his
Rev. 1. 7 Behold, he cometh with clouds; and every
2. 5. 16 or else I will come unto thee quickly
3 10 the hour of temptation, which shall come
3. 11 Behold, I come quickly: hold that fast
5. 7 he came and took the book out of the
6. 1 heard..one of the four beasts saying, Co.
6. 3 I heard the second beast say, Come and
6. 5 I heard the third beast say, Come and see
6. 7 the fourth beast say, Come and see
6. 17 For the great day of his wrath is come
7. 13 What are these..and whence came they?
7. 14 they which came out of great tribulation
8. 3 another angel came and stood at the altar
9. 12 behold, there come two woes more here
11. 14 (and), behold, the third woe cometh quic.
11. 18 nations were angry, and thy wrath is co.
14. 7 for the hour of his judgment is come: and
14. 15 for the time is come for thee to reap
16. 15 Behold, I come as a thief
17. 1 there came one of the seven angels which
17. 10 when he cometh, he must continue a short
17. 10 and one is, (and) the other is not yet come
18. 10 for in one hour is thy judgment come
19. 7 the marriage of the Lamb is come, and
21. 9 there came unto me one of the seven an.
22. 7 Behold, I come quickly: blessed (is) he
22. 12 behold, I come quickly; and my reward

Rev. 22. 17 And the Spirit and the bride say, Come
22. 17 And let him that heareth say, Come
22 17 And let him that is athirst come
22. 20 Surely I come quickly. Amen. Even so, c.

43. *To set on or against*, ἐφίστημι *ephistēmi.*
Acts 23. 27 then came I with an army, and rescued

44. *To have come, be here*, ἥκω *hēkō.*
Matt. 8. 11 many shall come from the east and west
23. 36 All these things shall come upon this
24. 14 and then shall the end come
24. 50 The lord of that servant shall come in a
Mark 8. 3 for divers of them [came] from far
Luke 12. 46 The lord of that servant will come in a
13. 29 they shall come from the east, and (from)
13. 35 until (the time) come when ye shall say
15. 27 he said unto him, Thy brother is come
19. 43 the days shall come upon thee, that thine
John 2. 4 Woman..mine hour is not yet come
4. 47 he heard that Jesus was come out of Ju.
6. 37 All that the Father giveth me shall come
8. 42 for I proceeded forth and came from
Acts 28. 23 there [came] many to him into (his) lodg.
Rom. 11. 26 There shall come out of Sion the Deliverer
Heb. 10. 7, 9 Lo, I come..to do thy will, O God
10. 37 he that shall come will come, and will
2 Pe. 3. 10 the day of the Lord will come as a thief
1 Jo. 5. 20 we know that the Son of God is come
Rev. 2. 25 that which ye have..hold fast till I come
3. 3 I will come on thee as a thief, and
3. 3 shalt not know what hour I will come
3. 9 I will make them to come and worship
15. 4 all nations shall come and worship before
18. 8 Therefore shall her plagues come in one

45. *To come down on or against*, καταντάω *katantaō.*
Acts 16. 1 Then came he to Derbe and Lystra
18. 19 he came to Ephesus, and left them there
18. 24 a certain Jew named Apollos..came to
20. 15 we..came..next (day) over against Chios
21. 7 when we had finished (our) course..we c.
25. 13 after certain days..Bernice came unto C.
26. 7 Unto which..twelve tribes..hope to come
28. 13 thence we fetched a compass, and came
1 Co. 10. 11 upon whom the ends of the world are co.
14. 36 or came it unto you only?
Eph. 4. 13 Till we all come in the unity of the faith

46. *To come down*, κατέρχομαι *katerchomai.*
Acts 11. 27 in these days came prophets from Jerusa.
18. 5 when Silas and Timotheus were come
27. 5 we came to Myra, (a city) of Lycia

47. *To be about to be*, μέλλω *mellō.*
Matt. 3. 7 who..warned you..from..wrath to come?
12. 32 in this world, neither in..(world) to come
Luke 3. 7 who..warned you..from..wrath to come?
Acts 24. 25 as he reasoned of..judgment to come
Heb. 2. 5 the world to come, whereof we speak
6. 5 and the powers of the world to come
9. 11 an High Priest of good things [to come]
10. 1 having a shadow of good things to come
13. 14 have we no..city, but we seek one to come

48. *To come alongside of*, παραγίνομαι *paraginomai.*
Matt. 2. 1 there came wise men from the east to J.
3. 1 In those days came John the Baptist
3. 13 Then cometh Jesus from Galilee to J.
Mark 14. 43 while he yet spake, cometh Judas, one of
Luke 7. 4 when they came to Jesus, they besought
7. 20 When the men were come unto him, they
8. 19 Then came to him (his) mother and his
11. 6 a friend of mine in his journey is come
12. 51 Suppose ye..I am come to give peace on
14. 21 that servant came, and showed his lord
19. 16 Then came the first, saying, Lord, thy
22. 52 and the elders, which were come to him
John 3. 23 and they came, and were baptized
8. 2 [in the morning he came again into the]
Acts 5. 21 But the high priest came, and they that
5. 22 the officers came, and found them not in
5. 25 Then came one and told them, saying
9. 26 when Saul was come to Jerusalem, he
9. 39 When he was come, they brought him
10. 32 [who, when he cometh, shall speak unto]
10. 33 thou hast well done that thou art come
11. 23 Who, when he came, and had seen the
13. 14 they came to Antioch in Pisidia, and
14. 27 when they were come, and had gathered
15. 4 when they were come to Jerusalem, they
17. 10 who coming (thither) went into the syna.
18. 27 who, when he was come, helped them
20. 18 when they were come to him, he said
23. 35 when thine accusers are also come
24. 17 after many years, I came to bring alms to
24. 24 after certain days when Felix came with
25. 7 when he was come, the Jews..stood
28. 21 neither any of the brethren that came
1 Co. 16. 3 when I come, whomsoever ye shall appr.
Heb. 9. 11 Christ being come an High Priest of good

49. *To be alongside of*, πάρειμι *pareimi.*
Matt 26. 50 Friend, wherefore art thou come?
John 7. 6 My time is not yet come: but your time
11. 28 The Master is come, and calleth for thee
Acts 10. 21 what (is) the cause wherefore ye are come?
12. 20 but they came with one accord to him
17. 6 These that have turned..are come hither
Col. 1. 6 Which is come unto you, as (it is) in all

50. *To come alongside of*, παρέρχομαι *parerchomai.*
Acts 24. 7 [the chief captain Lysias came (upon us)]

51. *To place alongside of*, παρίστημι *paristēmi.*
Mark 4. 29 putteth in the sickle..the harvest is come

52. *To come toward,* προσέρχομαι *proserchomai.*
Matt 4. 11 behold, angels came and ministered unto
8 19 a certain scribe came, and said unto him
9. 20 a woman, which was diseased..came beh.
13. 10 the disciples came, and said unto him
13. 27 the servants of the householder came
14. 12 his disciples came, and took up the body
15. 12 Then came his disciples, and said unto
15. 23 his disciples came and besought him, say.
16 1 Pharisees also with the Sadducees came
17. 7 Jesus came and touched them, and said
19. 16 one came and said unto him, Good Master
25. 20 he that had received five talents came
25 22 He also that..received two talents came
25. 24 he which..received the one talent came
26 50 Then came they, and laid hands on Jesus
26. 60 [yea, though many false witnesses came]
26 60 At the last came two false witnesses
28 2 the angel..came and rolled back the stone
28. 9 they came and held him by the feet, and
28 18 Jesus came and spake unto them, saying
Mark 1 31 he came and took her by the hand, and
12. 28 one of the scribes came, and hav. 14. 45.
Luke 7 14 And he came and touched the bier
8. 44 Came behind (him), and touched the..gar.
9. 12 then came the twelve, and said unto him
13. 31 The same day there came certain of the
John12. 21 The same came therefore to Philip, which
Acts 12. 13 a damsel came to hearken, named Rhoda
22. 27 the chief captain came, and said unto him
28. 9 others also, which had diseases..came
1 Pe. 2. 4 To whom coming, (as unto) a living stone

53. *To bear, be borne,* φέρω *pherō.*
2 Pe. 1. 17 when there came such a voice to him from
1. 18 this voice which came from heaven we
1. 21 the prophecy came not in old time by the

54. *To come or be beforehand,* φθάνω *phthanō.*
Matt 12 28 then the kingdom of God is come unto
Luke11. 20 the kingdom of God is come upon you
2 Co.10. 14 for we are come as far as to you also
1 Th. 2. 16 the wrath is come upon them to the

55. *To fill up together,* συμπληρόω *sumplēroō.*
Luke 9. 51 when the time was come that he should

56. *To come together,* συνέρχομαι *sunerchomai.*
Acts 5. 16 There came also a multitude (out) of the
25. 17 Therefore, when they were come hither

57. *To make or have space,* χωρέω *chōreō.*
2 Pe. 3. 9 but that all should come to repentance

58. *To go in upon,* ἐπιβαίνω *epibainō.*
Acts 20. 18 from the first day that I came into 25. 1.

59. *To come to,* ἐπιπορεύομαι *epiporeuomai.*
Luke 8. 4 and were come to him out of every city

[*See also* Come—again, against, another place, behind, ears, end, full, hither, morning, near, nearly, nigh, nought, pass, presumptuously, remembrance, round, round about, run, short, straight, tidings, time, time to, while, wrath.]

COME (in unto, or upon), to be —

1. *To come, arrive,* אָתָה *athah.*
Job 3. 25 thing which I greatly feared is come upon
16. 22 When a few years are come, then I shall

2. *To come, arrive,* אֲתָא *atha.*
Ezra 4. 12 the Jews..are come unto Jerusalem

3. *To go in,* בּוֹא *bo.*
Gen. 6. 13 The end of all flesh is come before me
12. 14 when Abram was come into Egypt, the
19. 22 for I cannot do anything till thou be come
34. 5 Jacob held his peace until they were come
Lev. 14 34 When ye be come into the land of Canaan
23. 10 When ye be come into the land which I
Num 15. 2 When ye be come into the land of your
22. 36 when Balak heard that Balaam was come
22. 38 Lo, I am come unto thee: have I now any
Deut. 1. 20 Ye are come unto the mountain of the A.
17. 14 When thou art come unto the land which
18. 9 When thou art come into the land which
26. 3 I am come unto the country which the L.
31. 11 When all Israel is come to appear before
Josh. 2. 3 Bring forth the men that are come to
2. 3 they be come to search out
3. 8 When ye are come to the brink of the
3. 15 as they that bare the ark were come unto
5. 14 but (as) captain of the host..am I..come
9. 6 We be come from a far country: now
9. 9 thy servants are come because of the name
23. 15 as all good things are come upon you
Judg 7. 13 when Gideon was come, behold, (there
11. 7 why are ye come unto me now when ye
11. 12 that thou art come against me to fight
16. 2 Samson is come hither. And they com.
19. 29 when he was come into his house, he took
Ruth 1. 19 when they were come to Beth-lehem..all
2. 12 under whose wings thou art come to
4. 11 The LORD make the woman that is come
1 Sa. 4. 3 when the people were come into the
4. 6 they understood that the ark..was come
4. 7 for they said, God is come into the camp
9. 5 when they were come to the land of Zuph
9. 13 As soon as ye be come into the city, ye
9. 14 when they were come into the city
9. 16 because their cry is come unto me
10. 5 when thou art come thither to the city
10. 7 when these signs are come unto thee
1 Sa. 12. 8 When Jacob was come into Egypt, and
14. 26 when the people were come into the wood
16. 2 and say, I am come to sacrifice to the L.
16. 5 I am come to sacrifice unto the LORD
19. 16 when the messengers were come in
20. 37 when the lad was come to the place of
23. 7 it was told Saul that David was come to
25. 40 when the servants of David were come to
26. 4 understood that Saul was come in very
29. 10 master's servants that are come with thee
30. 1 when David and his men were come to Zik.
2 Sa. 2. 24 the sun went down when they were come
3. 23 When Joab and all the host..were come
5. 13 David took..wives..after he was come
9. 6 when Mephibosheth..was come unto D.
11. 7 when Uriah was come unto him, David
12. 4 the wayfaring man that was come unto
12. 4 dressed it for the man that was come to
13. 6 and when the king was come to see him
14. 15 Now..that I am come to speak of this
14. 32 to say, Wherefore am I come from Geshur?
17. 27 when David was come to Mahanaim, that
19. 11 the speech of all Israel is come to the
19. 20 I am come the first this day of all the
19. 25 when he was come to Jerusalem to meet
19. 30 forasmuch as..the king is come again in
24. 21 Wherefore is my lord the king come to
1 Ki. 1. 23 when he was come in before the king, he
10. 2 when she was come to Solomon, she
12. 1 all Israel were come to Shechem to make
12. 21 when Rehoboam was come to Jerusalem
17. 18 art thou come unto me to call my sin to
2 Ki. 4. 4 when thou art come in, thou shalt shut
4. 32 when Elisha was come into the house
4. 36 when she was come in unto him, he said
5. 6 when this letter is come unto thee
5. 22 even now there be come to me from
7. 5 when they were come to the uttermost
8. 7 it was told him..The man of God is come
9. 30 when Jehu was come to Jezreel, Jezebel
9. 34 when he was come in, he did eat and
16. 12 when the king was come from Damascus
19. 3 for the children are come to the birth
20. 14 Hezekiah said, They are come from a far
1 Ch.12. 17 If ye be come peaceably unto me to help
19. 3 are not his servants come unto thee for
19. 9 the kings that were come (were) by them.
2 Ch. 6. 32 but is come from a far country for thy
9. 1 when she was come to Solomon, she
10. 1 for to Shechem were all Israel come to
11. 1 when Rehoboam was come to Jerusalem
18. 14 when he was come to the king, the king
20. 22 children of Ammon..which were come
22. 7 when he was come, he went out with J.
23. 15 when she was come to the entering of
25. 10 (to wit), the army that was come to him
32. 21 when he was come into the house of his
Ezra 3. 8 all they that were come out of the capti.
8. 35 which were come out of the captivity
9. 13 after all that is come upon us for our
Neh. 2. 10 there was come a man to seek the welfare
Esth. 6. 4 Now Haman was come into the outward
Job 2. 11 all this evil that was come upon him
3. 25 that which I was afraid of is come unto
4. 5 it is come upon thee, and thou faintest
Psa. 52. *title.* David is come to the house of Ahimel.
55. 5 Fearfulness and trembling are come upon
69. 1 for the waters are come in unto (my) soul
69. 2 I am come into deep waters, where the
79. 1 heathen are come into thine inheritance
102. 13 time to favour her..the set time, is come
Prov. 6. 3 when thou art come into the hand of
Song 5. 1 I am come into my garden, my sister
Isa. 10. 28 He is come to Aiath, he is passed to M.
37. 3 for the children are come to the birth
39. 3 They are come from a far country unto
44. 7 and the things that are coming, and shall
63. 4 and the year of my redeemed is come
Jer. 10. 22 the noise of the bruit is come, and a
12. 12 The spoilers are come upon all high
32. 24 they are come unto the city to take it
46. 21 the day of their calamity was come upon
47. 5 Baldness is come upon Gaza; Ashkelon
48. 21 judgment is come upon the plain country
50. 27 woe unto them! for their day is come
50. 31 for thy day is come, the time (that) I
51 51 strangers are come into the sanctuaries of
51. 56 Because the spoiler is come upon her
Lam. 4. 18 our days are fulfilled; for our end is come
Eze. 7. 2 the end is come upon the four corners of
7. 5 An evil, an only evil, behold, is come
7. 6 end is come, the end is come..it is come
7. 7 The morning is come..the time is come
7. 10 Behold the day, behold, it is come; the
7. 12 The time is come, the day draweth near
16. 7 and thou art come to excellent ornaments
17. 12 the king of Babylon is come to Jerusalem
20. 3 Are ye come to inquire of me? (As) I
21. 25, 29 whose day is come, when their iniquity
22. 4 art come (even) unto thy years; therefore
39. 8 Behold, it is come, and it is done, saith
Dan. 8. 23 when the transgressors are come to the
9. 13 all this evil is come upon us: yet made
10. 12 thy words were heard, and I am come
10. 14 I am come to make thee understand
Hos. 9. 7 The days..are come, the days..are come
Amos 8. 2 The end is come upon my people of Israel
Mic. 1. 9 incurable; for it is come unto Judah
Hag. 1. 2 This people say, The time is not come

4. *To meet,* קָרָא *qara.*
Isa. 51. 19 These two (things) are come unto thee

COME about —
A revolution, circuit, תְּקוּפָה *tequphah.*
1 Sa. 1. 20 when the time was come about after H.

COME about, to cause to —
To cause to go around, סָבַב *sabab,* 5.
2 Ch.13. 13 caused an ambushment to come about

COME abroad, to —
1. *To go forth,* יָצָא *yatsa.*
Esth. 1. 17 (this) deed of the queen shall come abroad

2. *To break forth,* פָּרַץ *parats.*
2 Ch.31. 5 as soon as the commandment came abroad

3. *To be come or arrived,* ἀφικνέομαι *aphikneomai.*
Rom.16 19 your obedience is come abroad unto all

COME aforehand, to —
To take beforehand, προλαμβάνω *prolambanō.*
Mark14. 8 she is come aforehand to anoint my body

COME after, to —
1. *Hinder, later,* אַחֲרוֹן *acharon.*
Job 18. 20 They that come after (him) shall be
Eccl. 4. 16 they also that come after shall not rejoice

2. *To receive in succession,* διαδέχομαι *diadechomai.*
Acts 7. 45 Which also our fathers that came after

COME again, to —
1. *To turn back,* שׁוּב *shub.*
Gen. 15. 16 they shall come hither again; for the
22. 5 and I and the lad will..come again to
28. 21 I come again to my father's house in
50. 5 let me go up..and I will come again
Exod14. 26 that the waters may come again upon the
24. 14 Tarry ye..until we come again unto you
Lev. 14. 39 the priest shall come again the seventh
14. 43 if the plague come again, and break out
Num 35. 32 that he should come again to dwell in
Josh. 18. 8 describe it, and come again to me, that I
Judg. 6. 18 I will tarry until thou come again
8. 9 When I come again in peace, I will break
15. 19 his spirit came again, and he revived
21. 14 And Benjamin came again at that time
Ruth 4. 3 Naomi, that is come again out of the
1 Sa. 23. 23 come ye again to me with the certainty
30. 12 when he had eaten, his spirit came again
1 Ki. 2. 41 that Shimei had gone. and was come a.
12. 5 Depart yet (for) three days, then come a.
12. 12 saying, Come to me again the third day
12. 20 Israel heard that Jeroboam was come a.
17 21 let this child's soul come into him again
17. 22 the soul of the child came into him again
19. 7 the angel of the LORD came again the
20. 5 the messengers came again, and said
2 Ki. 2. 18 when they came again to him..he said
4. 22 I may run to the man of God, and come a.
4. 38 Elisha came again to Gilgal: and (there
5. 10 thy flesh shall come again to thee, and
5. 14 his flesh came again like..a little child
7. 8 came again, and entered into another
9. 18 The messenger..cometh not again
9. 20 He came..unto them, and cometh not a.
9. 36 Wherefore they came again, and told him
2 Ch.10. 5 Come again unto me after three days
10. 12 Come again to me on the third day
30. 9 that they shall come again into this
Ezra 2. 1 came again unto Jerusalem and Judah
6. 21 which were come again out of captivity
Neh. 7. 6 came again to Jerusalem and to Judah
8. 17 that were come again out of the captivity
Esth. 6. 12 And Mordecai came again to the king's
Psa. 78. 39 that passeth away, and cometh not again
Prov. 3 28 Go, and come again, and to morrow I will
Jer. 31. 16 they shall come again from the land of
31. 17 (thy) children shall come again to their
37. 8 the Chaldeans shall come again
Zech. 4. 1 the angel that talked with me came again

2. *To come back upon,* ἐπανέρχομαι *epanerchomai.*
Luke10. 35 when I come again, I will repay thee

3. *To turn upon,* ἐπιστρέφω *epistrephō.*
Luke 8. 55 And her spirit came again, and she arose

4. *To turn back, or secretly,* ὑποστρέφω *hupostrephō.*
Acts 22. 17 when I was come again to Jerusalem

COME against, to —
To come in, בּוֹא *bo.*
Psa. 36. 11 Let not the foot of pride come against

COME at, to —
To meet with, συντυγχάνω *suntugchanō.*
Luke 8. 19 and could not come at him for the press

COME away, to —
To go or come on, יָלַךְ *yalak.*
Song 2. 10, 13 Rise up, my love .and come away

COME back, to —
To turn back, שׁוּב *shub.*
Ruth 2. 6 the Moabitish damsel that came back

COME before, to —
To come before, קָדַם *qadam,* 3.
2 Ki.19. 32 nor come before it with shield, nor cast
Psa. 95. 2 Let us come before his presence with
Isa. 37. 33 nor come before it with shields, nor cast
Mic. 6. 6 Wherewith shall I come before the LORD
6. 6 shall I come before him with burnt

COME betwixt, to —
To touch or strike upon, פָּגַע *paga,* 5.
Job 36. 32 (not to shine) by (the cloud)..cometh b.

COME by, to —
To become master of, περικρατὴς γίνομαι [*ginomai*].
Acts 27. 16 we had much work to come by the boat

COME, to cause to —
1. *To cause to come in,* בּוֹא *bo,* 5.
Job 34. 28 cause the cry of the poor to come unto
2. *To cause to find,* מָצָא *matsa,* 5.
Job 37. 13 He causeth it to come, whether for cor.
3. *To cause to meet,* קָרָא *qara,* 5.
Jer. 32. 23 thou hast caused all this evil to come

COME down —
Coming down, נָחֵת *nacheth.*
2 Ki. 6. 9 for thither the Syrians are come down

COME down, to —
1. *To come down,* יָרַד *yarad.*
Gen. 11. 5 the LORD came down to see the city and
15. 11 when the fowls came down upon the car.
43. 20 we came indeed down at the first time
44. 23 Except your youngest brother come down
45. 9 come down unto me, tarry not
Exod. 2. 5 the daughter of Pharaoh came down to
3. 8 And I am come down to deliver them out
9. 19 the hail shall come down upon them, and
11. 8 thy servants shall come down unto me
19. 11 the third day the LORD will come down
19. 20 the LORD came down upon mount Sinai
32. 1 saw that Moses delayed to come down
34. 29 when Moses came down from mount S.
34. 29 when he came down from the mount
Lev. 9. 22 came down from offering of the sin offer.
Num 11. 17 I will come down and talk with thee there
11. 25 the LORD came down in a cloud, and
12. 5 the LORD came down in the pillar of the
14. 45 the Amalekites came down, and the C.
20. 28 Moses and Eleazar came down from the
Deut. 9. 15 So I turned, and came down from the m.
10. 5 I turned myself, and came down from the
28. 24 from heaven shall it come down upon
28. 43 and thou shalt come down very low
28. 52 until thy high and fenced walls come d.
Josh. 3. 13 (from) the waters that come down from
3. 16 the waters which came down from above
3. 16 those that came down toward the sea of
18. 16 the border came down to the end of the
Judg. 1. 34 they would not suffer them to come down
5. 14 out of Machir came down governors, and
7. 24 Come down against the Midianites, and
9. 36 there come people down from the..moun.
9. 37 See there come people down by the
15. 12 We are come down to bind thee, that
16. 31 all the house of his father came down
1 Sa. 6. 21 come ye down (and) fetch it up to you
9. 25 when they were come down from the
10. 5 thou shalt meet a company..coming down
10. 8 I will come down unto thee, to offer
13. 12 The Philistines will come down now upon
17. 8 choose you a man..and let him come d.
17. 28 Why camest thou down hither? and with
17. 28 thou art come down that thou mightest
23. 6 he came down (with) an ephod in his
23. 11 will Saul come down, as thy servant hath
23. 11 and the LORD said, He will come down
23. 20 O king, come down, according to all
23. 20 the desire of thy soul to come down
23. 25 wherefore he came down into a rock
25. 20 she came down by the covert of the hill
25. 20 David and his men came down against
2 Sa 19. 16 and came down with the men of Judah to
19. 31 And Barzillai..came down from Rogelim
22. 10 He bowed the heavens also, and came do.
1 Ki. 2. 8 he came down to meet me at Jordan, and
22. 2 Jehoshaphat..came down to the king of
2 Ki. 1. 4, 6, 16 Thou shalt not come down from th.
1. 9 man of God, the king hath said, Come d.
1. 10, 12 let fire come down from heaven, and
1. 10 there came down fire from heaven, and
1. 11 thus hath the king said, Come down
1. 12 the fire of God came down from heaven
1. 14 there came fire down from heaven, and
6. 18 when they came down to him, Elisha
6. 33 behold, the messenger came down unto
7. 17 who spake when the king came down to
9. 16 And Ahaziah..was come down to see J.
13. 14 Joash the king of Israel came down unto
1 Ch. 7. 21 because they came down to take away
2 Ch. 7. 1 the fire came down from heaven, and
7. 3 Israel saw how the fire came down
Neh. 6. 3 a great work, so that I cannot come down
6. 3 whilst I leave it, and come down to you?
9. 13 Thou camest down also upon mount Sinai
Psa. 7. 16 his violent dealing shall come down upon
18. 9 He bowed the heavens also, and came d.
72. 6 He shall come down like rain upon the
144. 5 Bow thy heavens, O LORD, and come d.
Isa. 31. 4 so shall the LORD of hosts come down to
32. 19 When it shall hail, coming down on the
34. 5 it shall come down upon Idumea, and
34. 7 the unicorns shall come down with them
47. 1 Come down, and sit in the dust, O virgin
55. 10 as the rain cometh down..from heaven
64. 1 Oh..that thou wouldest come down
64. 3 when thou didst terrible..thou camest d.
Jer. 13. 18 for your principalities shall come down
Jer. 48. 18 Thou daughter..come down from thy
Lam. 1. 9 therefore she came down wonderfully
Eze. 26. 16 the princes..shall come down from their
27. 29 pilots..shall come down from their ships
30. 6 the pride of her power shall come down
47. 1 and the waters came down from under
Mic. 1. 3 and will come down, and tread upon the
1. 12 but evil came down from the LORD unto
Hag. 2. 22 horses and their riders shall come down
Zech. 11. 2 the forest of the vintage is come down
2. *To come down,* נָחַת *nachath.*
Jer. 21. 13 which say, Who shall come down against
3. *To come down,* נְחַת *nechath.*
Dan. 4. 13 an holy one came down from heaven
4. 23 an holy one coming down from heaven
4. *To come down,* καταβαίνω *katabainō.*
Matt. 8. 1 When he was come down from the mount
14. 29 when Peter was come down out of the
17. 9 as they came down from the mountain
24. 17 Let him..on the house top not come down
27. 40 If thou be the Son of God, come down
27. 42 let him now come down from the cross
Mark 3. 22 scribes which came down from Jerusal.
9. 9 as they came down from the mountain
15. 30 Save thyself, and come down from the
Luke 6. 17 he came down with them, and stood in
8. 23 there came down a storm of wind on the
9. 54 that we command fire to come down from
10. 31 there came down a certain priest that
17. 31 let him not come down to take it away
19. 5 Zaccheus, make haste, and come down
19. 6 he made haste, and came down, and
John 3. 13 he that came down from heaven, (even)
4. 47 besought him that he would come down
4. 49 Sir, come down ere my child die
6. 33 is he which cometh down from heaven
6. 38 I came down from heaven, not to do mine
6. 41 I am the bread which came down from
6. 42 is it then that he saith, I came down
6. 50 the bread which cometh down from hea.
6. 51 I am the living bread which came down
6. 58 that bread which came down from heaven
Acts 7. 34 and am come down to deliver them
8. 15 Who, when they were come down, prayed
14. 11 The gods are come down to us in the
16. 8 they passing by Mysia came down to T.
24. 22 When Lysias the..captain shall come d.
25. 7 the Jews which came down from Jeru.
Jas. 1. 17 and cometh down from the Father of
Rev. 3. 12 which cometh down out of heaven
10. 1 I saw another mighty angel come down
12. 12 the devil is come down unto you, having
13. 13 he maketh fire come down from heaven
18. 1 I saw another angel come down from heav.
20. 1 I saw an angel come down from heaven
20. 9 fire came down from God out of heaven
21. 2 coming down from God out of heaven
5. *To come down,* κατέρχομαι *katerchomai.*
Luke 4. 31 came down to Capernaum, a city of Gal.
9. 37 when they were come down from the
Acts 9. 32 he came down also to the saints which
15. 1 certain men which came down from J.
21. 10 there came down from Judea a certain

COME down, to cause to —
1. *To cause to come down,* יָרַד *yarad,* 5.
Eze. 34. 26 I will cause the shower to come down in
Joel 2. 23 he will cause to come down for you the
2. *To cause to come down,* נָחַת *nachath,* 5.
Joel. 3. 11 cause thy mighty ones to come down, O

COME forth, to—
1. *To come forth, burst forth,* גּוּחַ *guach.*
Eze. 32. 2 and thou camest forth with thy rivers
2. *To (cause to) come or burst forth,* גּוּחַ *guach,* 5.
Judg 20. 33 the liers in wait of Israel came forth out
3. *To go forth or out,* יָצָא *yatsa.*
Gen. 15. 4 he that shall come forth out of thine own
24. 43 that when the virgin cometh forth to draw
24. 45 Rebekah came forth with her pitcher on
Exod. 4. 14 behold, he cometh forth to meet thee
5. 20 met Moses and Aaron..as they came forth
8. 20 lo, he cometh forth to the water; and say
13. 8 did unto me when I came forth out of E.
16. 24 come forth, and offer his burnt offering
Num 11. 20 saying, Why came we forth out of Egypt
12. 5 called Aaron and M.: and..both came f.
Deut. 2. 23 which came forth out of Caphtor
4. 45 which Moses spake..after they came forth
4. 46 after they were come forth out of Egypt
16. 3, 3 thou camest forth out of the land of E.
16. 6 season that thou camest forth out of E.
21. 2 elders and thy judges shall come forth
23. 4 when ye came forth out of Egypt; and
24. 9 after that ye were come forth out of Egypt
25. 17 when ye were come forth out of Egypt
Josh. 5. 5 by the way as they came forth out of E.
9. 12 on the day we came forth to go unto you
18. 11 the coast of their lot came forth between
19. 1 And the second lot came forth to Simeon
Judg. 1. 24 spies saw a man come forth out of the c.
9. 43 the people (were) come forth out of the
11. 31 whatsoever cometh forth of the doors of
14. 14 Out of the eater came forth meat, and out
14. 14 of the strong came forth sweetness.
20. 21 children of Benjamin came forth out of G.
1 Sa. 11. 7 Whosoever cometh not forth after Saul
14. 11 the Hebrews come forth out of the holes
22. 3 Let my father and mother..come forth
2 Sa. 16. 5 he came forth, and cursed still as he
16 11 Behold, my son, which came forth of my
1 Ki. 2. 30 said unto him, Thus saith the king, Come f.
8. 19 that shall come forth out of thy loins, he
20. 33 Then Ben-hadad came forth to him; and
22. 21 there came forth a spirit, and stood before
2 Ki. 2. 3 sons of the prophets..came forth to E.
2. 23 there came forth little children out of the
2. 24 there came forth two she bears out of the
9. 11 Jehu came forth to the servants of his
10. 25 Go in (and) slay them; let none come forth
21. 15 since the day their fathers came forth out
1 Ch. 24. 7 the first lot came forth to Jehoiarib, the
25. 9 the first lot came forth for Asaph to Jos.
2 Ch. 6. 9 which shall come forth out of thy loins
Job 5. 6 although affliction cometh not forth of
14. 2 He cometh forth like a flower, and is cut
Psa. 17. 2 Let my sentence come forth from thy
88. 8 I (am) shut up, and I cannot come forth
Prov. 7. 15 Therefore came I forth to meet thee, dil.
25. 4 there shall come forth a vessel for the
Eccl. 5. 15 As he came forth of his mother's womb
7. 18 he that feareth God shall come forth of
Isa. 11. 1 there shall come forth a rod out of the
14. 29 out of the serpent's root shall come forth
28. 29 This also cometh forth from the LORD of
36. 3 Then came forth unto him Eliakim, Hil.
37. 9 He is come forth to make war with thee
48. 1 are come forth out of the waters of Judah
Jer. 1. 5 before thou camest forth out of the womb
4. 4 lest my fury come forth like fire, and burn
7. 25 Since the day that your fathers came forth
20. 18 Wherefore came I forth out of the womb
37. 5 Pharaoh's army was come forth out of
37. 7 Pharaoh's army, which is come forth to
46. 9 and let the mighty men come forth; the
48. 45 but a fire shall come forth out of Heshbon
Eze. 5. 4 thereof shall a fire come forth into all the
14. 22 behold, they shall come forth unto you
21. 19 both twain shall come forth out of one
33. 30 the word that cometh forth from the L.
Dan. 8. 9 out of one of them came forth a little horn
9. 22 I am now come forth to give thee skill and
9. 23 the commandment came forth, and I am
11. 11 and shall come forth and fight with him
Joel 3. 18 a fountain shall come forth of the house
Mic. 1. 3 the LORD cometh forth out of his place
1. 11 the inhabitant of Zaanan came not forth
5. 2 out of thee shall he come forth unto me
Zech. 10. 4 Out of him came forth the corner, out of
4. *Outcoming, offspring, issue,* יָצִיא *yatsi.*
2 Ch. 32. 21 they that came forth of his own bowels
5. *To come forth,* נְפַק *nephaq.*
Dan. 3. 26 servants of the most high God, come forth
3. 26 Then..came forth of the midst of the fire
5. 5 In the same hour came forth fingers of a
7. 10 A fiery stream issued and came forth
6. *To come out of, forth,* ἐκπορεύομαι *ekporeuomai.*
Luke 3. 7 to the multitude that came forth to be
John 5. 29 And shall come forth; they that have done
7. *To come out of, forth,* ἐξέρχομαι *exerchomai.*
Matt 13. 49 the angels shall come forth, and sever the
15. 18 things..out of the mouth come forth from
Mark 1. 38 Let us go..for therefore [came I forth]
8. 11 the Pharisees came forth, and began to
9. 29 This kind can come forth by nothing but
John 11. 44 And he that was dead came forth, bound
16. 28 I came forth from the Father, and am co.
16. 30 by this we believe that thou camest forth
Acts 7. 7 after that shall they come forth, and serve
8. *To come alongside of,* παρέρχομαι *parerchomai.*
Luke 12. 37 and will come forth and serve them

COME forth or out, that —
Outcoming, offspring, issue, צֶאֱצָאִים *tseetsaim.*
Isa. 34. 1 world, and all things that come forth of
42. 5 and that which cometh out of it; he that

COME hither—
Hither, here, come! δεῦρο *deuro.*
Rev. 17. 1 saying unto me, Come hither: I will show
21. 9 and talked with me, saying, Come hither

COME in, into, or unto, to —
1. *To come in,* בּוֹא *bo.*
Gen. 8. 11 the dove came in to him in the evening
19. 5 Where (are) the men which came in to
19. 9 This one (fellow) came in to sojourn, and
19. 31 not a man in the earth to come in unto
24. 31 he said, Come in, thou blessed of the L.
27. 30 Esau his brother came in from his hunt.
30. 16 Thou must come in unto me; for surely I
38. 16 Go to, I pray thee, let me come in unto
38. 16 What..that thou mayest come in unto me?
38. 18 he gave (it) her, and came in unto her
39. 14 he came in unto me to lie with me, and I
39. 17 The Hebrew servant..came in unto me
40. 6 Joseph came in unto them in the morn.
41. 14 changed his raiment, and came in unto
Exod. 1. 19 are delivered ere the midwives come in
10. 3 Moses and Aaron came in unto Pharoah
21. 3 If he came in by himself, he shall go out
28. 43 when they come in unto the tabernacle
Lev. 14. 48 if the priest shall come in, and look
25. 22 until her fruits come in ye shall eat (of)
Num 27. 21 at his word they shall come in, (both) he

Deut28. 6 Blessed (shalt) thou (be) when..comest in
28. 19 Cursed (shalt) thou (be) when..comest in
31. 2 I can no more go out and come in
Josh. 2. 2 Behold, there came men in hither to night
14. 11 for war, both to go out, and to come in
Judg18. 17 the five men..came in thither, (and) took
19. 22 Bring forth the man that came into thine
1 Sa. 4. 14 And the man came in hastily, and told E.
18. 13 he went out and came in before the peo.
29. 6 thy coming in with me in the host (is) good
2 Sa. 5. 6 thou shalt not come in hither: thinking
5. 6 David cannot come in hither
11. 4 she came in unto him, and he lay with
1 Ki. 1. 14 I also will come in after thee, and confirm
1. 22 Nathan the prophet also came in
1. 42 Come in; for thou (art) a valiant man, and
3. 7 I know not (how) to go out or come in
14. 5 it shall be, when she cometh in, that she
14. 6 as she came in at the door, that he said
14. 6 Come in, thou wife of Jeroboam; why
15. 17 might not suffer any to go out or come in
21. 13 there came in two men, children of Belial
2 Ki.11. 8 and be ye with the king..as he cometh in
11. 9 men that were to come in on the sabbath
13. 20 invaded the land at the coming in of the
19. 27 I know..thy going out, and thy coming in
1 Ch.27. 1 which came in and went out month by
2 Ch 1. 10 that I may go out and come in before
15. 5 that went out, nor to him that came in
16. 1 that he might let none go out or come in
23. 7 whosoever (else) cometh into the house
23. 7 be ye with the king when he cometh in
23. 8 men that were to come in on the sabbath
Esth 2. 14 she came in unto the king no more, except
4. 11 I have not been called to come in unto
6. 5 And the king said, Let him come in
6. 6 So Haman came in. And the king said
Job 22. 21 thereby good shall come unto thee
Psa. 24. 7 and the King of glory shall come in
109. 17 he loved cursing, so let it come unto him
119 41 Let thy mercies come also unto me, O L.
119. 77 Let thy tender mercies come unto me
121. 8 The LORD shall preserve..thy coming in
Prov 11. 27 that seeketh mischief, it shall come unto
Eccl. 6 4 he cometh in with vanity, and departeth
Isa 24. 10 every house is shut..no man may come in
28. 15 it shall not come unto us: for we have
37. 28 I know..thy going out and thy coming in
59. 19 When the enemy shall come in like a flood
Jer. 17. 19 whereby the kings of Judah come in, and
37. 4 Jeremiah came in and went out among the
39. 3 all the princes of the king..came in, and
Eze. 46. 9 shall not return by the way..he came in
Dan. 11. 21 he shall come in peaceably, and obtain
Hos. 7. 1 the thief cometh in, (and) the troop of
Jon. 2. 7 my prayer came in unto thee, into thine
Zech. 8. 10 to him that went out or came in because

2. *To come up or in,* עָלַל *alal.*
Dan. 4. 7 Then came in the magicians, the astrolo.
5. 8 Then came in all the king's wise (men)

3. *To come in or toward,* εἰσέρχομαι *eiserchomai.*
Matt 22. 11 when the king came in to see the guests
22. 12 Friend, how camest thou in hither not
Mark 5. 39 when he was come in, he saith unto them
6. 22 the daughter of the said Herodias came in
6. 25 And she came in straightway with haste
Luke 1. 28 And the angel came in unto her, and said
7. 45 but this woman since the time I came in
14. 23 and compel (them) to come in, that my
Acts 1. 13 when they were come in, they went up
5. 7 wife, not knowing what was done, came in
5. 10 the young men came in, and found her
9. 12 a man named Ananias coming in, and
10. 3 an angel of God coming in to him, and
10. 25 as Peter was coming in, Cornelius met
Rom 11. 25; 1 Co. 14. 23, 24; Heb. 10. 5; Jas. 2. 2;
Rev. 3. 20; Matt. 10. 12; 17. 25; 21. 10; Mark 9. 28;
Luke 8. 41, 51; Acts 11. 20; 23. 33; 14. 20; 16. 15.

4. *To go or come into,* ἐμβαίνω *embainō.*
Matt. 14. 32 when they were come into the; Mark 5. 18.

5. *To come in or toward,* εἰσπορεύομαι *eisporeuomai.*
Luke11. 33 that they which come in may see the light
Acts 9. 28 he was with them coming in and going out
28. 30 and received all that came in unto him

6. *To set oneself upon or over,* ἐφίστημι *ephistēmi.*
Luke 2 38 And she coming in that instant gave thanks

COME in, to let —
To cause to come in, בּוֹא *bo,* 5.
Esth. 5. 12 the queen did let no man come in with

COME in privily, to —
To come in alongside of, or privily, παρεισέρχομαι.
Gal. 2. 4 who came in privily to spy out our liberty

COME into one's room, to —
To receive a successor, λαμβάνω διάδοχον [*lambanō*].
Acts 24. 27 Porcius Festus came into Felix' room: and

COME like a whirlwind, to —
To show oneself tempestuous, שָׂעַר *saar,* 7.
Dan. 11. 40 the king..shall come..like a whirlwind

COME mightily, to —
To prosper, come successfully, צָלֵחַ *tsaleach.*
Judg 14. 6 the Spirit of the LORD came mightily upon
15. 14 the Spirit of the LORD came mightily upon

COME no more, to —
To add, יָסַף *yasaph.*
1 Sa. 15 35 And Samuel came no more to see Saul

COME near, to —
1. *To come nigh,* נָגַשׁ *nagash.*
Gen. 19. 9 and came near to break the door
27. 21 Come near, I pray thee, that I may feel
27. 26 Come near now, and kiss me, my son
27. 27 And he came near, and kissed him: and
33. 3 bowed himself..until he came near to his
33. 6 Then the handmaidens came near, they
33. 7 Leah also with her children came near
33. 7 after came Joseph near and Rachel, and
43. 19 they came near to the steward of Joseph's
44. 18 Then Judah came near unto him, and said
45. 4 Come near to me..And they came near
Exod28. 43 or when they come near unto the altar to
30. 20 or when they come near to the altar to
Num32. 16 And they came near unto him, and said
Josh.21. 1 Then came near the heads of the fathers
1 Sa. 30. 21 and when David came near to the people
1 Ki.18. 30 Elijah said unto all the people, Come near
18. 30 all the people came near unto him: and
18. 36 Elijah the prophet came near, and said
2 Ki. 4. 27 but Gehazi came near to thrust her away
5. 13 his servants came near, and spake unto
2 Ch.18. 23 Then Zedekiah..came near, and smote M.
29. 31 come near and bring sacrifices and thank
Isa. 41. 1 let them come near, then let them speak
50. 8 who (is) mine adversary? let him come near
65. 5 Stand by thyself, come not near to me
Jer. 42. 1 least even unto the greatest, came near
Eze. 9. 6 come not near any man upon whom
44. 13 they shall not come near unto me, to do
44. 13 to come near to any of my holy things, in

2. *To come nigh,* נָגַשׁ *nagash,* 2.
Exod19. 22 let the priests also, which come near to
Deut21. 5 priests the sons of Levi shall come near

3. *To come near,* קָרַב *qarab.*
Gen. 20. 4 But Abimelech had not come near her
37. 18 before he came near unto them, they
Exod12. 48 let him come near and keep it; and he
14. 20 the one came not near the other all the
16. 9 Come near before the LORD: for he hath
40. 32 when they came near unto the altar,
Lev. 10. 4 Come near, carry your brethren from
Num16. 40 come near to offer incense before the L.
31. 48 And the officers..came near unto Moses
36. 1 came near, and spake before Moses, and
Deut. 1. 22 ye came near unto me every one of you
4. 11 ye came near and stood under the moun.
5. 23 that ye came near unto me..(even) all the
Josh. 3. 4 come not near unto it, that ye may know
10. 24 Come near, put your feet upon the necks
10. 24 they came near, and put their feet upon
17. 4 they came near before Eleazar the priest
Judg20. 24 the children of Israel came near against
2 Sa. 20. 16 Come near hither, that I may speak with
20. 17 when he was come near unto her, the
Psa. 32. 9 lest they come near unto thee
119. 169 Let my cry come near before thee, O LORD
Isa. 34. 1 Come near, ye nations, to hear; and
41. 1 let us come near together to judgment
48. 16 Come ye near unto me, hear ye this; I
54. 14; Eze. 18. 6; 44. 15; 44. 16; Mal. 3. 5.

4. *To be or come nigh,* ἐγγίζω *eggizō.*
Luke 18. 40 when he was come near, he asked him
[*See also* 19. 41; Acts 9. 3; 21. 33; 23. 15.]

5. *To come near,* קְרֵב *qereb.*
Dan. 3. 8 at that time certain Chaldeans came near
3. 26 Nebuchadnezzar came near to the mouth
6. 12 they came near, and spake before the k.
7. 16 I came near unto one of them that stood

COME near, to be (or cause to) —
To bring or cause to come near, קָרַב *qarab,* 5.
Gen. 12. 11 when he was come near to enter into E.
Num16. 5 will cause (him) to come near unto him
16. 5 (him)..will he cause to come near unto
1 Sa. 10. 20 had caused all the tribes..to come near
10. 21 caused the tribe of Benjamin to come near

COME near, which —
Near, קָרֵב *qareb.*
Eze. 40. 46 which come near to the LORD to minister
45. 4 which shall come near to minister unto

COME nigh, to —
1. *To (cause to) touch,* נָגַע *naga,* 5.
Psa. 32. 6 in the floods..they shall not come nigh

2. *To come nigh,* נָגַשׁ *nagash.*
Exod24. 2 they shall not come nigh, neither shall
34. 30 and they were afraid to come nigh him
Lev. 21. 21 the priest shall come nigh to offer the
21. 21 he shall not come nigh to offer the bread
21. 23 nor come nigh unto the altar because he
Num. 8. 19 when the children of Israel come nigh
Psa. 91. 7 (but) it shall not come nigh thee

3. *To come near,* קָרַב *qarab.*
Exod 32. 19 as soon as he came nigh unto the camp
Num18. 3 they shall not come nigh the vessels of
18. 4 a stranger shall not come nigh unto you
18. 22 come nigh the tabernacle of the congre.
Deut. 2. 19 (when) thou comest nigh over against
20. 2 when ye are come nigh unto the battle
20. 10 When thou comest nigh unto a city to
2. Sa.15. 5 when any man came nigh (to him) to do
Psa. 91. 10 neither shall any plague come nigh thy
Pro. 5. 8 and come not nigh the door of her house

4. *Near,* קָרֵב *qareb.*
Num. 1. 51; 3. 10, 38 the stranger that cometh nigh
18. 7 the stranger that cometh nigh shall be

5. *To come nigh,* ἐγγίζω *eggizō.*
Mark 11. 1 When they came nigh to Jerusalem, unto
Luke 7. 12 when he came nigh to the gate of the city
10. 9, 11 The kingdom of God is come nigh unto
18. 35 as he was come nigh unto Jericho
19. 29 when he was come nigh to Bethphage
19. 37 when he was come nigh, even now at the
Acts 22. 6 was come nigh unto Damascus about

COME nigh, them that —
Near, קָרוֹב *qarob.*
Lev. 10. 3 be sanctified in them that come nigh me

COME nigh unto, to —
To come nigh toward, προσεγγίζω *proseggizō.*
Mark 2. 4 when they could not come nigh unto him

COME on —
To give (help or counsel), יָהַב *yahab.*
Exod. 1. 10 Come on, let us deal wisely with them

COME on (or upon), to —
1. *To find, meet,* מָצָא *matsa.*
Gen. 44. 34 lest..I see the evil that shall come on
Deut31. 17 Are not these evils come upon us, because
Neh. 9. 32 that hath come upon us, on our kings, on

2. *To face, turn the face,* פָּנָה *panah.*
Deut23. 11 when evening cometh on, he shall

3. *To come upon,* ἐπέρχομαι *eperchomai.*
Luke21. 35 as a snare [shall it come on] all them that

4. *To receive, take,* λαμβάνω *lambanō.*
Luke 7. 16 there came a fear on all: and they glori.

COME out, to —
1. *To come forth, out of,* יָצָא *yatsa.*
Gen. 15. 14 afterward shall they come out with great
17. 6 and kings shall come out of the
24. 13 daughters of the men of the city come out
24. 15 Rebekah came out, who was born to B.
25. 25 the first came out red, all over like an
25. 26 after that came his brother out, and his
35. 11 and kings shall come out of thy loins
38. 28 scarlet thread, saying, This came out first
38. 29 behold, his brother came out: and she
46. 26 All the souls..which came out of his loins
Exod. 1. 5 all the souls that came out of the loins
13. 3 Remember this day, in which ye came out
13. 4 This day came ye out, in the month Abib
17. 6 there shall come water out of it, that the
23. 15 for in it thou camest out from Egypt
25. 32 six branches shall come out of the sides
25. 33 branches that come out of the candlestick
28. 35 and when he cometh out, that he die not
32. 24 cast it into the fire, and there came out
34. 18 in the month Abib thou camest out from
34. 34 he took the veil off, until he came out
34. 34 he came out, and spake unto the children
Lev. 9. 23 and came out, and blessed the people
9. 24 there came a fire out from before the L.
16. 17 until he come out, and have made an
Num. 1. 1 the second year after they were come out
9. 1 the second year after they were come out
11. 20 until it come out at your nostrils, and
12. 4 Come out ye three..And..three came out
12. 12 when he cometh out of his mother's womb
16. 27 Dathan and Abiram came out, and stood in
16. 35 there came out a fire from the LORD, and
20. 11 the water came out abundantly, and the
20. 18 lest I come out against thee with the
20. 20 Edom came out against him with much
21. 13 the wilderness that cometh out of the
22. 5 there is a people come out from
22. 11 (there is) a people come out of Egypt
33. 38 the children of Israel were come out of
Deut. 1. 44 the Amorites..came out against you, and
2. 32 Sihon came out against us, he and all his
3. 1 Og the king of Bashan came out against
11. 10 the land of Egypt, from whence ye came o.
28. 7 they shall come out against thee one way
28. 57 her young one that cometh out from
29. 7 came out against us unto battle, and we
Josh. 2. 10 for you, when ye came out of Egypt
5. 4 All the people that came out of Egypt
5. 5 all the people that came out were circu.
5. 6 men of war, which came out of Egypt, were
8. 5 when they come out against us, as at the
8. 6 For they will come out after us, till we
19. 17 the fourth lot came out to Issachar, for
19. 24 the fifth lot came out for the tribe of
19. 32 The sixth lot came out to the children of
19. 40 the seventh lot came out for the tribe of
21. 4 the lot came out for the families of the
Judg. 3. 22 and the dirt came out
4. 22 Jael came out to meet him, and said unto
9. 15 let fire come out of the bramble, and
9. 20 let fire come out from Abimelech, and
9. 20 let fire come out from the men of Shech
9. 29 Increase thine army, and come out
9. 33 the people that (is) with him come out
11. 34 his daughter came out to meet him with
21. 21 if the daughters of Shiloh come out to
21. 21 come ye out of the vineyards, and catch
1 Sa. 2. 3 let (not) arrogancy come out of your
9. 14 Samuel came out against them, for to go
11. 3 and then..we will come out to thee
11. 7 and they came out with one consent
13. 17 the spoilers came out of the camp of the

1 Sa. 17. 8 Why are ye come out to set (your) battle
18. 6 the women came out of all cities of Israel
21. 5 about these three days, since I came out
23. 15 David saw that Saul was come out to
24. 14 After whom is the king of Israel come out
26. 20 the king of Israel is come out to seek a
2 Sa. 2. 23 that the spear came out behind him
3. 26 when Joab was come out from David, he
6. 20 Michal..came out to meet David, and
10. 8 the children of Ammon came out, and
11. 23 came out unto us into the field, and we
16. 5 thence came out a man of the family of
16. 7 Come out, come out, thou bloody man, and
18. 4 all the people came out by hundreds, and
1 Ki. 8. 9 when they came out of the land of Egypt
8. 10 when the priests were come out of the
9. 12 Hiram came out from Tyre to see the ci.
20. 17 saying, There are men come out of Samaria
20. 18 Whether they be come out for peace, take
20. 18 whether they be come out for war, take
20. 19 these young men..came out of the city
2 Ki. 5. 11 He will surely come out to me, and stand
7. 12 When they come out of the city, we shall
18. 18 there came out to them Eliakim the son
18. 31 Make (an agreement)..and come out to
19. 9 he is come out to fight against thee
1 Ch. 19. 9 the children of Ammon came out, and
26 14 they cast lots; and his lot came out north.
2 Ch. 5. 10 the children..when they came out of Eg.
5. 11 when the priests were come out of the
14 9 there came out against them Zerah the
18. 20 Then there came out a spirit, and stood
Job 1. 21 Naked came I out of my mother's womb
3. 11 give up the ghost when I came out of the
38. 29 Out of whose womb came the ice? and the
Psa. 19. 5 as a bridegroom coming out of his cham.
Prov. 12. 13 but the just shall come out of trouble
Isa. 26. 21 the LORD cometh out of his place to pun.
36. 16 Make (an agreement)..and come out to
Mic. 7. 15 According to the days of thy coming out
Nah. 1. 11 There is (one) come out of thee, that
Hag. 2. 5 I covenanted with you when ye came out
Zech. 5. 9 behold, there came out two women, and
6. 1 there came four chariots out from

2. *To come forth, out of,* ἐξέρχομαι *exerchomai.*
Matt. 5. 26 Thou shalt by no means come out thence
8. 28 coming out of the tombs, exceeding fierce
8. 32 And when they were come out, they went
8. 34 the whole city came out to meet Jesus
12. 44 into my house from whence I came out
15. 22 a woman of Canaan came out of the same
24. 27 as the lightning cometh out of the east
26. 55 Are ye come out as against a thief with
27. 32 as they came out, they found a man of
27. 53 came out of the graves after his resurrec.
Mark 6. 34 Jesus, when he came out, saw much peo.
9. 26 And..cried..and came out of him: and
Luke 1. 22 when he came out, he could not speak
4. 36 commandeth the..spirits, and they come o.
11. 24 return unto my house whence I came out
15. 28 therefore came his father out, and entre.
22. 39 he came out, and went, as he was wont
John 16 27 have believed that I came out from God
17 8 have known..that I came out from thee
Acts 16 18 to come out of her. And he came out the
1 Co. 14. 36 What! came the word of God out from
2 Co 6 17 come out from among them, and be ye
Heb. 11. 15 that (country) from whence they came out
Rev. 14. 18 another angel came out from the altar

COME over, to (be) —
1. *To come over,* עָבַר *abar.*
Num 35. 10 When ye be come over Jordan into the
Deut 2. 14 until we were come over the brook Zered
27. 12 when ye are come over Jordan
Josh 4 22 Israel came over this Jordan on dry land
2 Sa. 19. 18 before the king, as he was come over Jor.
19. 33 Come thou over with me, and I will feed
19. 39 when the king was come over, the king
Isa. 45. 14 Sabeans, men of stature, shall come over
2. *To come through,* διαβαίνω *diabainō.*
Acts 16. 9 Come over into Macedonia, and help us

COME round, to —
To encompass, κυκλόω *kukloō.*
John 10 24 Then came the Jews round about him

COME running together, to —
To run together to, ἐπισυντρέχω *episuntrechō.*
Mark 9. 25 saw that the people came running toget.

COME thereout, to —
1. *To come forth,* יָצָא *yatsa.*
Judg 15. 19 and there came water thereout
2. *To come forth, out of,* ἐξέρχομαι *exerchomai.*
John 19. 34 forthwith came thereout blood and water

COME thither, to —
To come upon, ἐπέρχομαι *eperchomai.*
Acts 14 19 there came thither (certain) Jews from A.

COME, things to —
1. *To come, arrive,* אָתָה *athah.*
Isa. 41. 23 Show the things that are to come hereafter
44. 7 things that are coming and shall come
45. 11 Ask me of things to come concerning my
2. *To come in,* בּוֹא *bo.*
Isa 41. 22 or declare us things for to come
3. *To be about to be.* μέλλω *mellō.*
Rom. 8. 38 nor things present; nor things to come
1 Co. 3. 22 or things present, or things to come
Col. 2. 17 Which are a shadow of things to come
Heb. 11. 20 Jacob and Esau concerning things to come

COME, things that —
A going up, מַעֲלָה *maalah.*
Eze. 11. 5 I know the things that come into your

COME, things that shall —
Ready, prepared, עָתִיד *athid.*
Deut. 32. 35 things that shall come upon them make

COME, time to —
1. *To morrow, hereafter,* מָחָר *machar.*
Gen. 30. 33 answer for me in time to come, when it
Exod 13. 14 when thy son asketh thee in time to come
Deut. 6. 20 when thy son asketh thee in time to come
Josh. 4. 6 ask (their fathers) in time to come, saying
4. 21 your children shall ask..in time to come
22. 24 In time to come your children might
22. 27 children may not say..in time to come
22. 28 say to..our generations in time to come
2. *To be about to be,* μέλλω *mellō.*
1 Ti. 6 19 good foundation against the time to come

COME to (or unto), to —
1. *To find,* מָצָא *matsa.*
1 Sa. 25. 8 whatsoever cometh to thine hand unto
Esth. 8. 6 the evil that shall come unto my people?
2. *To be found,* מָצָא *matsa,* 2.
Judg 20. 48 set on fire all the cities..they came to
3. *To come toward,* προσέρχομαι *proserchomai.*
Matt. 4 3 when the tempter came to him, he said
8. 25 his disciples came to (him), and awoke
9. 14 Then came to him the disciples of John
9. 28 the blind men came to him: and Jesus
14. 15 his disciples came to him, saying, This
15. 1 Then came to Jesus scribes and Pharisees
17. 14 there came to him a (certain) man, kneel.
17. 19 Then came the disciples to Jesus apart
17. 24 came to Peter, and said, Doth not your
18 21 Then came Peter to him and said, Lord
20. 20 Then came to him the mother of Zeb.
21. 14 the blind and the lame came to him in
21. 28 he came to the first, and said, Son, go
21. 30 he came to the second, and said likewise
22. 23 The same day came to him the Sadducees
24. 1 his disciples came to (him) for to show
26. 17 the disciples came to Jesus, saying unto
26. 49 forthwith he came to Jesus, and said
Mark 10. 2 the Pharisees came to him, and asked
Luke 8. 24 they came to him, and awoke him, saying
20. 27 Then came to (him) certain of the Sadd.
23. 36 coming to him, and offering him vinegar
Acts 23. 14 they came to the chief priests and elders
Heb. 11. 6 he that cometh to God must believe that
4. *To place upon, or before,* ἐφίστημι *ephistēmi.*
Luke 10. 40 came to him, and said, Lord, dost thou

COME to an end, to —
To perfect, fail, be complete, גָּמַר *gamar.*
Psa. 7. 9 wickedness of the wicked come to an end

COME to hand, to —
To be found, מָצָא *matsa,* 2.
Judg 20. 48 the beast, and all that came to hand

COME to nought, to —
To loose down, καταλύω *kataluō.*
Acts 5 38 this work be of men, it will come to nou.

COME to pass, to —
1. *To come in,* בּוֹא *bo.*
Deut 13. 2 the sign or the wonder come to pass
18. 22 if the thing follow not, nor come to pass
Josh 21. 45 There failed not ought..all came to pass
23. 14 all are come to pass unto you, (and) not
Judg 3. 27 it came to pass, when he was come, that
13. 12 said, Now let thy words come to pass
13. 17 when thy sayings come to pass we may do
1 Sa. 9. 6 all that he saith cometh surely to pass
10. 9 all those signs came to pass that day
16. 16 it came to pass, when they were come
2 Sa. 15. 32 it came to pass, that (when) David was
16. 16 it came to pass, when Hushai the Archite
2 Ki. 6. 20 it came to pass, when they were come into
Isa. 42. 9 the former things are come to pass, and
48. 3 did (them) suddenly, and they came to p.
48. 5 before it came to pass I showed (it) thee
Jer. 28. 9 when the word of..shall come to pass
Eze. 24. 14 it shall come to pass, and I will do (it)
33 33 when this cometh to pass, lo it will come
2. *To be,* הָיָה *hayah.*
Gen. 4. 14 it shall come to pass, (that) every one that
6. 1 it came to pass, when men began to multi
7. 10 it came to pass after seven days, that the
8. 6 it came to pass at the end of forty days
8. 13 it came to pass in the sixth hundredth
[This verb occurs many thousands of times]
3. *To be,* הֲוָא *hava.*
Dan. 2. 29 what should come to pass; 2. 29; 2. 45.
3a. *Be accomplished,* עֲשָׂה *asah,* 2; Eze. 12. 25.
4. *To meet,* קָרָה *qarah.*
Num 11. 23 whether my word shall come to pass unto
5. *To become, to come to be,* γίνομαι *ginomai.*
Matt. 7. 28 it came to pass, when Jesus had ended
Matt. 9. 10 it came to pass, as Jesus sat at meat in
11. 1 it came to pass, when Jesus had made
13. 53 it came to pass..when Jesus had finished
19. 1 it came to pass..when Jesus had finished
24. 6 for all..must come to pass, but the end
26. 1 it came to pass, when Jesus had finished
Mark 1. 9 it came to pass in those days, that Jesus
2. 15 it came to pass..as Jesus sat at meat in
2. 23 it came to pass..he went through the
4. 4 it came to pass, as he sowed, some fell by
11. 23 things which he saith shall come to pass
13. 29 ye shall see these things come to pass
Luke 1. 8 it came to pass, that, while he executed
1. 23 it came to pass, that, as soon as the days
1. 41 it came to pass, that, when Elisabeth
1. 59 it came to pass, that on the eighth day
2. 1 it came to pass in those days, that there
2. 15 it came to pass, as the angels were gone
2. 15 see this thing which is come to pass
2. 46 it came to pass, that after three days
3. 21 it came to pass, that Jesus also being bap.
5. 1 it came to pass, that, as the people pressed
5. 12 it came to pass, when he was in a certain
5. 17 it came to pass on a certain day, as he
6. 1 it came to pass, on the second sabbath
6. 6 it came to pass also on another sabbath
6. 12 it came to pass in those days, that he went
7. 11 it came to pass the day after, that he
8. 1 it came to pass afterward, that he went
8. 22 it came to pass on a certain day, that he
8. 40 it came to pass..when Jesus was retur.
9. 18 it came to pass, as he was alone praying
9. 28 it came to pass, about an eight days after
9. 33 it came to pass, as they departed from
9. 37 it came to pass, that on the next day
9. 51 it came to pass, when the time was come
9. 57 [it came to pass]..as they went in the way
10. 38 it came to pass, as they went, that he
11. 1 it came to pass..as he was praying in a
11. 14 it came to pass, when the devil was gone
11. 27 it came to pass, as he spake these things
12. 55 There will be heat; and it cometh to pass
14. 1 it came to pass, as he went into the house
16. 22 it came to pass, that the beggar died, and
17. 11 it came to pass, as he went to Jerusalem
17. 14 it came to pass, that, as they went, they
18. 35 it came to pass..as he was come nigh unto
19. 15 it came to pass, that, when he was returned
19. 29 it came to pass, when he was come nigh
20. 1 it came to pass, (that) on one of those days
21. 7 when these things shall come to pass?
21. 9 these things must first come to pass; but
21. 28 when these things begin to come to pass
21. 31 when ye see these things come to pass
21. 36 all these things that shall come to pass
24. 4 it came to pass, as they were much per.
24. 12 [wondering..at that which was come to p.]
24. 15 it came to pass, that, while they commun.
24. 18 the things which are come to pass there
24. 30 it came to pass, as he sat at meat with
24. 51 it came to pass, while he blessed them, he
John 13. 19 when it is come to pass, ye may believe
14. 29 I have told you before it come to pass
14. 29 when it is come to pass, ye might believe
Acts 4. 5 it came to pass on the morrow, that their
9. 32 it came to pass, as Peter passed through.
9. 37 it came to pass in those days, that she
9. 43 it came to pass, that he tarried many days
11. 26 it came to pass, that a whole year they
11. 28 which came to pass in the days of Claud.
14. 1 it came to pass in Iconium, that they went
16. 16 it came to pass, as we went to prayer, a
19. 1 it came to pass..while Apollos was at C.
21. 1 it came to pass, that after we were gotten
22. 6 it came to pass..as I made my journey
22. 17 it came to pass..when I was come again
27 44 it came to pass, that they escaped all safe
28. 8 it came to pass, that the father of Publius
28 17 it came to pass, that after three days
1 Th. 3. 4 even as it came to pass, and ye know
Rev 1. 1 things which must shortly come to pass
6. *To be, (it shall be),* εἰμί, (ἔσται), *eimi, (estai).*
Acts 2. 17 it shall come to pass in the last days
2. 21 it shall come to pass, (that) whosoever
3. 23 it shall come to pass, (that) every soul
Rom. 9. 26 it shall come to pass, (that) in the place

COME to (understanding), to —
To know understanding, יָדַע בִּינָה *yada binah.*
Isa. 29. 24 They also..shall come to understanding

COME together, to —
1. *To come near,* קָרַב *qarab.*
Eze. 37. 7 the bones came together, bone to his bone
2. *To come alongside together,* συμπαραγίνομαι
Luke 23. 48 all the people that came together to that
3. *To come together,* συνάγω *sunagō.*
Matt 27. 62 chief priests..came together unto Pilate
Mark 7. 1 Then came together unto him the Pharis.
Luke 22. 66 chief priests, and the scribes, came toget.
Acts 13. 44 And..came almost the whole city toget.
15. 6 the apostles and elders came together for
20. 7 when the disciples came together to break
4. *To come together,* συνέρχομαι *sunerchomai.*
Matt. 1. 18 before they came together, she was found
Mark 3. 20 the multitude cometh together again, so
6. 33 [many knew him..came together unto]
Luke 5. 15 great multitudes came together to hear
Acts 1. 6 When they therefore were come together
2. 6 the multitude came together, and were

Acts 10. 27 and found many that were come together
19. 32 knew not wherefore they were come tog.
21. 22 the multitude must needs come together
28. 17 when they were come together, he said
1 Co. 7. 5 give yourselves to..prayer; and [come to.]
11. 17 that ye come together not for the better
11. 18 when ye come together in the church
11. 20 When ye come together therefore into one
11. 33 my brethren, when ye come together to
11. 34 ye come not together unto condemnation
14. 23 If..the whole church [be come together]
14. 26 How is it then..when ye come together

COME unto, to —

1. *To place upon or over,* ἐφίστημι *ephistēmi.*
Acts 11. 11 there were three men already come unto

2. *To come toward,* προσέρχομαι *proserchomai.*
Matt. 5. 1 when he was set, his disciples came unto
8. 5 there came unto him a centurion, beseech.
13. 36 his disciples came unto him, saying
15. 30 great multitudes came unto him, having
18. 1 At the same time came the disciples unto
19. 3 The Pharisees also came unto him, tempt.
21. 23 the elders of the people came unto him
24. 3 the disciples came unto him privately
26. 7 There came unto him a woman having an
26. 69 a damsel came unto him, saying, Thou
26. 73 after a while came unto (him) they that
Mark 6. 35 his disciples came unto him, and said
Acts 10. 28 or come unto one of another nation
18. 2 a certain Jew..and came unto them
24. 23 forbid none..to minister or [come unto]
Heb. 4. 16 Let us therefore come boldly unto the
7. 25 to save them..that come unto God by
12. 18 ye are not come unto the mount that
12. 22 ye are come unto mount Sion, and unto

3. *To come toward,* προσπορεύομαι *prosporeuomai.*
Mark 10. 35 the sons of Zebedee, come unto him

COME up (or upon), to —

1. *To come in,* בּוֹא *bo.*
Deut 32. 17 to new (gods that) came newly up, whom
Job 15. 21 the destroyer shall come upon him
20. 22 every hand of the wicked shall come upon
Psa. 44. 17 All this is come upon us; yet have we not
Prov 10. 24 fear of the wicked, it shall come upon
28. 22 considereth not..poverty shall come upon
Eze 32. 11 The sword of the king..shall come upon

2. *To come up,* סְלֵק *seleq.*
Dan. 7. 3 four great beasts came up from the sea
7. 8 there came up among them another little
7. 20 and (of) the other which came up, and

3. *To come up,* סְלֵק *seleq.* 3a.
Ezra 4 12 the Jews which came up from thee to us

4. *To go up,* עָלָה *alah.*
Gen. 24. 16 and filled her pitcher, and came up
41. 2 there came up out of the river seven well
41. 3 seven other kine came up after them out
41. 5 seven ears of corn came up upon one
41. 18 there came up out of the river seven
41. 19 seven other kine came up after them
41. 22 seven ears came up in one stalk, full and
41. 27 the..kine that came up after them (are)
44. 24 when we came up unto thy servant my
Exod. 2. 23 their cry came up unto God by reason of
8. 4 the frogs shall come up both on thee, and
8. 6 the frogs came up, and covered the land
10. 12 that they may come up upon the land of
16. 13 at even the quails came up, and covered
19. 13 they shall come up to the mount
19. 23 The people cannot come up to mount Sin.
19. 24 thou shalt come up, thou, and Aaron
19. 24 break through to come up unto the LORD
24. 1 Come up unto the LORD, thou, and Aaron
24. 12 Come up to me into the mount, and be
33. 5 I will come up into the midst of thee in
34. 2 come up in the morning unto mount Sin.
34. 3 no man shall come up with thee neither
Num 16. 12 Dathan..which said, We will not come up
16. 14 wilt thou put out..we will not come up
32. 11 none of the men that came up out of E.
Deut. 10. 1 come up unto me into the mount, and
Josh. 2. 8 she came up unto them upon the roof
4. 16 Command..that they come up out of J.
4. 17 saying, Come ye up out of Jordan
4. 18 when the priests..were come up out of
4. 19 the people came up out of Jordan on the
10. 4 Come up unto me, and help me, that we
10. 6 come up to us quickly, and save us, and
10. 33 Horam king of Gezer came up to help L.
18. 11 the children of Benjamin came up accor.
19. 10 the third lot came up for the children of
Judg. 1. 3 Come up with me into my lot, that we
2. 1 an angel of the LORD came up from Gil.
4. 5 children of Israel came up..for judgment
6. 3 the Midianites came up, and the Amalek.
6. 3 even they came up against them
6. 5 they came up with their cattle and their
6. 35 and they came up to meet them
11. 13 Israel..when they came up out of Egypt
11. 16 when Israel came up from Egypt, and
12. 3 are ye come up unto me this day, to fight
14. 2 he came up, and told his father and his
15. 6 the Philistines came up, and burnt her
15. 10 Judah said, Why are ye come up against
15. 10 To bind Samson are we come up, to do to
16. 5 the lords of the Philistines came up unto

Judg 16. 18 Come up this once, for he hath showed
16. 18 Then the lords..came up unto her, and
19. 30 the children of Israel came up out of the
21. 5 all the tribes of Israel that came not up
21. 5 him that came not up to the LORD to M.
21. 8 the tribes of Israel that came not up to
1 Sa. 2. 19 when she came up with her husband to
11. 1 Then Nahash the Ammonite came up
13. 5 they came up, and pitched in Michmash
14. 10 if they say thus, Come up unto us
14. 12 Come up to us, and we will show you a
14. 12 said unto his armour bearer, Come up
15. 2 in the way, when he came up from Egypt
15. 6 when they came up out of Egypt
17. 23 there came up the champion the Philis.
17. 25 Have ye seen this man that is come up?
17. 25 surely to defy Israel is he come up
23. 19 Then came up the Ziphites to Saul to
28. 14 An old man cometh up; and he (is) covered
2 Sa. 5. 17 all the Philistines came up to seek David
5. 22 the Philistines came up yet again, and
17. 21 they came up out of the well, and went
1 Ki. 1. 35 ye shall come up after him, that he may
1. 40 all the people came up after him; and
1. 45 they are come up from thence rejoicing
9. 24 Pharaoh's daughter came up out of the
10. 29 a chariot came up and went out of Egypt
14. 25 Shishak king of Egypt came up against
20. 22 the king of Syria will come up against
2 Ki. 1. 6 There came a man up to meet us, and
1. 7 What..(was he) which came up to meet
3. 21 the kings were come up to fight against
12. 10 king's scribe and the high priest came up
16. 5 Pekah..came up to Jerusalem to war
16. 7 come up, and save me out of the hand of
17. 3 Against him came up Shalmaneser king
17. 5 the king of Assyria came up throughout
18. 9 came up against Samaria, and besieged it
18. 13 king of Assyria come up against all the
18. 17 And when they were come up, they
18. 25 Am I now come up without the LORD
19. 23 I am come up to the height of the moun.
19. 28 thy tumult is come up into mine ears
23. 9 the priests..came not up to the altar
24. 1 Nebuchadnezzar king of Babylon came up
24. 10 servants of Nebuchadnezzar..came up
1 Ch. 14. 11 So they came up to Baal-perazim
2 Ch. 12. 2 Shishak king of Egypt came up against
12. 9 So Shishak king of Egypt came up aga.
16. 1 Baasha king of Israel came up against
20. 16 behold, they come up by the cliff of Ziz
21. 17 they came up into Judah, and brake into
24. 23 the host of Syria came up against him
35. 20 Necho king of Egypt came up to fight a.
36. 6 Against him came up Nebuchadnezzar
Neh. 7. 5 them which came up at the first, and
Job 7. 9 goeth down to the grave shall come up
Psa. 78. 21 and anger also came up against Israel
Prov. 25. 7 that it be said unto thee, Come up hither
Song 4. 2 a flock..which came up from the washing
8. 5 Who (is) this that cometh up from the
Isa. 5. 6 but there shall come up briers and thorns
8. 7 he shall come up over all his channels
11. 16 that he came up out of the land of Egypt
14. 8 no feller is come up against us
24. 18 he that cometh up out of the midst of the
32. 13 Upon the land of my people shall come up
34. 3 their stink shall come up out of their
34. 13 thorns shall come up in her palaces
36. 1 Sennacherib..came up against all the
36. 10 am I now come up without the LORD aga.
37. 24 am I come up to the height of the moun.
37. 29 and thy tumult, is come up into mine ears
55. 13 Instead of the thorn shall come up the
55. 13 instead of the brier shall come up the
60. 7 they shall come up with acceptance on
Jer. 4. 7 The lion is come up from his thicket, and
4. 13 he shall come up as clouds, and his cha.
9. 21 death is come up into our windows, (and)
26. 10 they came up from the king's house unto
35. 11 when Nebuchadrezzar..came up into the
46. 7 Who (is) this (that) cometh up as a flood
46. 9 Come up, ye horses; and rage, ye chariots
49. 19 he shall come up like a lion from the
49. 22 he shall come up and fly as the eagle, and
50. 3 there cometh up a nation against her
50. 44 he shall come up like a lion from the
51. 42 The sea is come up upon Babylon: she is
Lam. 1. 14 they are wreathed, (and) come up upon
Eze. 37. 8 the sinews and the flesh came up upon
38. 16 thou shalt come up against my people
38. 18 my fury shall come up in my face
Dan 8. 3 one (was) higher..and the higher came up
8. 8 for it came up four notable ones, toward
11. 23 he shall come up, and shall become strong
Hos. 1. 11 and they shall come up out of the land
2. 15 when she came up out of the land of Eg.
10. 8 the thistle shall come up on their altars
13. 15 the wind of the LORD shall come up from
Joel 1. 6 a nation is come up upon my land, strong
2. 20 and his stink shall come up and
2. 20 his ill savour shall come up, because he
3. 9 let all the men of war..let them come up
3. 12 and come up to the valley of Jehoshaphat
Obad. 21 saviours shall come up on mount Zion to
Jon. 1. 2 for their wickedness is come up before
Mic. 2. 13 The breaker is come up before them
Nah. 2. 1 He that dasheth in pieces is come up be.
Hab. 3. 16 when he cometh up unto the people, he
Zech 14. 17 it shall be..whoso will not come up of
14. 18 the heathen that come not up to keep the
14. 19 all nations that come not up to keep the

5. *To come up,* ἀναβαίνω *anabainō.*
Matt 17. 27 and take up the fish that first cometh up
Mark 1. 10 straightway coming up out of the water
John 12. 20 them that came up to worship at the
Acts 8. 31 that he would come up and sit with him
8. 39 when they were come up out of the water
10. 4 Thy prayers and thine alms are come up
11. 2 when Peter was come up to Jerusalem
Rev. 4. 1 Come up hither, and I will show thee
11. 12 saying unto them, Come up hither
13. 11 I beheld another beast coming up out of

COME up again, to —

To come up, ἀναβαίνω *anabainō.*
Acts 20. 11 When he therefore was come up again

COME up with, to —

To come up together, συναναβαίνω *sunanabainō.*
Mark 15. 41 other women which came up with him
Acts 13. 31 which came up with him from Galilee to

COME up, to cause to —

To cause to go or come up, עָלָה *alah,* 5.
Exod. 8. 5 cause frogs to come up upon the land of
1 Ki. 20. 33 he caused him to come up into the char.
Jer. 50. 9 cause to come up against Babylon, an
Eze. 24. 8 That it might cause fury to come up to
26. 3 will cause many nations to come up ag.
26. 3 as the sea causeth his waves to come up
37. 12 cause you to come up out of your graves
39. 2 will cause thee to come up from the north

COME up, to make to —

To cause to go or come up, עָלָה *alah,* 5.
Num 20. 5 ye made us to come up out of Egypt
Amos 4. 10 made the stink of your camps to come up

COME upon, to —

1. *To lay hold,* אָחַז *achaz.*
2 Sa. 1. 9 slay me; for anguish is come upon me

2. *To come, arrive,* אָתָה *athah.*
Job 3. 25 the thing..I..feared is come upon me

3. *To go or come in,* בּוֹא *bo.*
Job 15. 21 the destroyer shall come upon him
20. 22 hand of the wicked shall come upon him
Psa. 35. 8 Let destruction come upon him at unaw.
44. 17 All this is come upon us; yet have we not
Prov 10. 24 fear of the wicked, it shall come upon
28. 22 that poverty shall come upon him
Eze. 32. 11 The sword of the king..shall come upon

4. *To clothe,* לָבֵשׁ *labesh.*
Judg. 6. 34 the Spirit of the LORD came upon Gideon
1 Ch. 12. 18 the spirit came upon Amasai, (who was)
2 Ch. 24. 20 the spirit of God came upon Zechariah the

5. *To find,* מָצָא *matsa.*
Exod 18. 8 all the travail that had come upon them
Deut. 4. 30 and all these things are come upon thee
2 Ki. 7. 9 some mischief will come upon us

6. *To meet,* קָרָא *qara.*
Job 4. 14 Fear came upon me, and trembling, which

7. *To come upon,* ἐπέρχομαι *eperchomai.*
Luke 1. 35 The Holy Ghost shall come upon thee
11. 22 a stronger than he shall come upon him
Acts 8. 24 that none of these things..come upon me
13. 40 Beware therefore, lest that come upon
Jas. 5. 1 for your miseries that shall come upon

8. *To place upon or over,* ἐφίστημι *ephistēmi.*
Luke 2. 9 the angel of the Lord came upon them
20. 1 chief priests and the scribes came upon
21. 34 and (so) that day come upon you unawares
Acts 4. 1 and the Sadducees, came upon them
6. 12 came upon (him), and caught him, and
12. 7 the angel of the Lord came upon (him)
1 Th. 5. 3 sudden destruction cometh upon them

9. *To take utterly,* καταλαμβάνω *katalambanō.*
John 12. 35 lest darkness come upon you: for he

COME with, to —

To come together, συνέρχομαι *sunerchomai.*
Luke 23. 55 the women also, which came with him
John 11. 33 the Jews also weeping which came with
Acts 10. 45 astonished, as many as came with Peter

COME without, to —

To come out, יָצָא *yatsa.*
Num 35. 26 if the slayer shall..come without the

COME, to be fully —

To fill up fully, συμπληρόω *sumplēroō.*
Acts 2. 1 when the day of Pentecost was fully come

COME, to be to —

To be about to be, μέλλω *mellō.*
Rom. 5. 14 who is the figure of him that was to come
Eph. 1. 21 but also in that which is to come
1 Ti. 4. 8 promise of the life..which is to come

COME, he that shall or should —

He who is coming, the Coming One, ὁ ἐρχόμενος.
Matt 11. 3 Art thou he that should come?
Luke 7. 19, 20 Art thou he that should come? or
John 6. 14 that prophet that should come into the
11. 27 Christ..which should come into the
Acts 19. 4 believe on him which should come after
Heb. 10. 37 he that shall come will come, and will

COME, he that is to —
He who is coming, the Coming One, ὁ ἐρχόμενος.
Rev. 1. 4 him..which was, and which is to come
1. 8 the Lord..which was, and which is to co.
4. 8 Almighty which was, and is, and is to co.
11. 17 which art and wast, and art to come

COME, he that was for to —
He who is about to come, ὁ μέλλων ἔρχεσθαι.
Matt 11 14 this is Elias, which was for to come

COMETH, he that —
He who is coming, the Coming One, ὁ ἐρχόμενος.
Matt 3. 11 he that cometh after me is mightier than
21. 9 Blessed (is) he that cometh in the name
23. 39 Blessed (is) he that cometh in the name
Luke19. 38 the King that cometh in the name of the
John 1. 15 He that cometh after me is preferred
3. 31 He that cometh from above is above all
3. 31 he that cometh from heaven is above all
12. 13 Blessed (is) the King of Israel that cometh

COMETH upon, that which —
The crowding, standing together upon, ἡ ἐπισύστασις *hē episustasis.*
2 Co.11. 28 that which [cometh upon] me daily, the

COMETH any thing near —
Near, קָרֵב *qareb.*
Num. 17 13 Whosoever cometh any thing near unto

COMETH, as —
Coming in, entrance, מָבוֹא *mabo.*
Eze. 33 31 they come unto thee as the people cometh

COMETH from or out, that which —
Excrement, צֵאָה *tseah.*
Deut23 13 and cover that which cometh from thee
Eze. 4. 12 bake it with dung that cometh out of man

COMETH nigh, that —
Near, קָרֵב *qareb.*
Num 1 51 the stranger that cometh nigh shall be
3 10 38 the stranger that cometh nigh shall be
18 7 the stranger that cometh nigh shall be

COMETH of, that —
Young one, offspring, שֶׁגֶר *sheger.*
Exod 13 12 every firstling that cometh of a beast

COMETH out, that which —
Offspring, צֶאֱצָאִים *tseetsaim.*
Isa. 42 5 the earth, and that which cometh out of

COMING —
1. *To meet,* קָרָא *qara.*
1 Sa. 16 4 elders of the town trembled at his coming
2. *Foot* רֶגֶל *regel*
Gen. 30. 30 LORD hath blessed thee since my coming
3. *Uncovering, revelation,* ἀποκάλυψις *apokalupsis.*
1 Co. 1 7 waiting for the coming of our Lord Jesus
4. *Way in, entrance,* εἴσοδος *eisodos.*
Acts 13 24 John had first preached before his coming
5. *A coming,* ἔλευσις *eleusis.*
Acts 7 52 which showed..the coming of the Just One
6. *To come,* ἔρχομαι *erchomai.*
Matt.24 48 shall say..My lord delayeth [his coming]
25 27 (then) at my coming I should have receiv.
Luke12. 45 My lord delayeth his coming; and shall
18. 5 lest by her continual coming she weary
19. 23 that at my coming I might have required
Rom.15. 22 I have been much hindered from coming
7. *A being alongside, presence,* παρουσία *parousia.*
Matt24. 3 what (shall be) the sign of thy coming
24. 27, 37, 39 so shall also the coming of the Son
1 Co 15. 23 they that are Christ's at his coming
16. 17 I am glad of the coming of Stephanas
2 Co 7. 6 comforted us by the coming of Titus
7. 7 not by his coming only, but by the conso.
Phil 1. 26 for me by my coming to you again
1 Th 2. 19 (Are) not even ye..at his coming?
3. 13 at the coming of our Lord Jesus Christ
4 15 (and) remain unto the coming of the Lord
5. 23 unto the coming of our Lord Jesus Christ
2 Th 2. 1 by the coming of our Lord Jesus Christ
2. 8 destroy with the brightness of his coming
2. 9 whose coming is after the working of Sa.
Jas 5. 7 Be patient..unto the coming of the Lord
5 8 for the coming of the Lord draweth nigh
2 Pe. 1. 16 power and coming of our Lord Jesus Ch.
3. 4 Where is the promise of his coming? for
3. 12 hasting unto the coming of the day of G.
1 Jo. 2. 28 not be ashamed before him at his coming

COMING down —
To come or go down, יָרַד *yarad.*
Isa. 32 19 When it shall hail, coming down on the

COMING in —
A coming in, entrance, מוֹבָא *moba.*
2 Sa. 3. 25 to know thy going out, and thy coming in
Eze. 43. 11 the goings out thereof, and the comings in

COMING on —
To come over, עָבַר *abar.*
2 Sa. 24. 20 saw the king and his servants coming on

COMING, to be —
To come, ἔρχομαι *erchomai.*
Luke23. 29 the days are coming, in the which they
John 5. 7 while I am coming, another steppeth
John 5. 25 The hour is coming, and now is, when the
5. 28 Marvel not at this: for the hour is coming
11. 20 as soon as she heard that Jesus was com.
12. 12 when they heard that Jesus was coming
2 Co.13. 1 This (is) the third (time) I am coming to

COMING, to be a —
To come toward, προσέρχομαι *proserchomai.*
Luke 9. 42 as he was yet a coming, the devil threw

COMING, who —
He who is coming, the Coming One, ὁ ἐρχόμενος.
John 1. 27 who coming after me, is preferred before

COMING on, to be —
To be about to be, μέλλω γίνεσθαι *mellō ginesthai.*
Acts 27. 33 while the day was coming on, Paul

COMING on, those things which are —
The things coming on, τὰ ἐπερχόμενα [*eperchomai*].
Luke21. 26 those things which are coming on the

COMELINESS —
1. *Honour,* הָדָר *hadar.*
Isa. 53. 2 he hath no form nor comeliness; and when
Eze. 16. 14 for it (was) perfect through my comeliness
27. 10 in thee; they set forth thy comeliness
2. *Beauty,* הוֹד *hod.*
Dan. 10. 8 for my comeliness was turned in me into
3. *Elegance,* εὐσχημοσύνη *euschēmosunē.*
1 Co. 12. 23 our uncomely (parts) have more..comeli.

COMELY —
1. *Grace, graceful,* חִין *chin.*
Job 41. 12 I will not conceal his..comely proportion
2. *Fair,* יָפֶה *yapheh.*
Eccl. 5. 18 (it is) good and comely..to eat and to
3. *Becoming,* נָאוֶה *naveh,* [fem. once נָוָה].
Psa. 33. 1 Rejoice..praise is comely for the upright
147. 1 for (it is) pleasant; (and) praise is comely
Song 1. 5 I (am) black, but comely, O ye daughters
2. 14 O my dove..thy countenance (is) comely
4. 3 thy speech (is) comely: thy temples (are)
6. 4 comely as Jerusalem, terrible as (an army)
Jer. 6. 2 likened the daughter of Zion to a comely
4. *Form,* תֹּאַר *toar.*
1 Sa. 16. 18 a comely person, and the LORD (is) with
5. *Beauty,* תִּפְאֶרֶת *tiphereth.*
Isa. 4. 2 the fruit of the earth (shall be)..comely
6. *Well fashioned,* εὐσχήμων *euschēmōn.*
1 Co.12 24 our comely (parts) have no need: but God

COMELY, to be —
1. *To do good, act well,* יָטַב *yatab,* 5.
Prov 30. 29 yea, four are comely in going
2. *To be becoming,* נָאָה *naah,* 3a.
Song 1. 10 Thy cheeks are comely with rows (of je.)
3. *To be becoming, befitting,* πρέπω *prepō.*
1 Co 11. 13 is it comely that a woman pray unto God

COMELY, that which is —
Well-fashioned, elegant, εὐσχήμων *euschēmōn.*
1 Co. 7 35 for that which is comely, and that ye may

COMER thereunto —
To come toward, προσέρχομαι *proserchomai.*
Heb 10. 1 make the comers thereunto perfect

COMFORT —
1. *To comfort, give forth sighs,* נָחַם *nacham,* 3.
Psa 119. 76 thy merciful kindness be for my comfort
2. *Comfort, consolation,* נֶחָמָה *nechamah.*
Job 6 10 Then should I yet have comfort; yea, I
Psa 119 50 This (is) my comfort in my affliction
3. *A calling alongside,* παράκλησις *paraklēsis.*
Acts 9. 31 in the comfort of the Holy Ghost, were
Rom 15. 4 comfort of the scriptures might have hope
2 Co. 1. 3 Father of mercies, and the God of all com.
1. 4 by the comfort wherewith we ourselves
7. 4 I am filled with comfort, I am exceeding
7. 13 we were comforted in your comfort: yea
4. *A consolation, a solace,* παραμυθία *paramuthia.*
1 Co. 14. 3 edification, and exhortation, and comfort
5. *Consolation, solace,* παραμύθιον *paramuthion.*
Phil. 2. 1 if any comfort of love, if any fellowship
6. *A soothing,* παρηγορία *parēgoria.*
Col. 4. 11 which have been a comfort unto me

COMFORT, to be a —
To comfort, give forth sighs, נָחַם *nacham,* 3.
Eze. 16. 54 in that thou art a comfort unto them

COMFORT, to be of good —
1. *To be refreshed, braced up,* εὐψυχέω *eupsucheō.*
Phil. 2. 19 that I also may be of good comfort when
2. *To be courageous, hearty,* θαρσέω *tharseō.*
Matt. 9. 22 Daughter, be of good comfort; thy faith
Mark10. 49 Be of good comfort rise; he calleth thee
Luke 8. 48 Daughter, [be of good comfort]: thy faith
3. *To call alongside of, help,* παρακαλέω *parakaleō.*
2 Co. 13. 11 Be perfect, [be of good comfort], be of one

COMFORT, to —
1. *To brighten up, encourage,* בָּלַג *balag,* 5.
Job 9. 27 I will leave off my heaviness, and comfort
2. *To comfort, give forth sighs,* נָחַם *nacham,* 3.
Gen. 5. 29 This (same) shall comfort us concerning
37. 35 all his sons..rose up to comfort him
50. 21 he comforted them, and spake kindly unto
Ruth 2. 13 for that thou hast comforted me, and for
2 Sa. 10. 2 David sent to comfort him by the hand
10. 3 [that he hath sent comforters unto thee?]
12. 24 David comforted Bath-sheba his wife, and
1 Ch. 7. 22 and his brethren came to comfort him
19. 2 David sent messengers to comfort him
19. 2 the servants of David came..to comfort
Job 2. 11 to mourn with him and to comfort him
7. 13 When I say, My bed shall comfort me, my
21. 34 How then comfort ye me in vain, seeing
29. 25 as one (that) comforteth the mourners
42. 11 they bemoaned him, and comforted him
Psa. 23. 4 thy rod and thy staff they comfort me
71. 21 Thou shalt..comfort me on every side
86. 17 thou, LORD, hast holpen me, and comfor.
119. 82 saying, When wilt thou comfort me?
Isa. 12. 1 I will praise thee..thou comfortedst me
22. 4 labour not to comfort me, because of the
40. 1 Comfort ye, comfort ye my people, saith
49. 13 the LORD hath comforted his people, and
51. 3 LORD shall comfort Zion: he will comfort
51. 12 I, (even) I, (am) he that comforteth you
51. 19 and the sword: by whom shall I comfort
52. 9 for the LORD hath comforted his people
61. 2 To proclaim..to comfort all that mourn
66. 13 mother comforteth, so will I comfort you
Jer. 16. 7 Neither shall (men)..comfort them for
31. 13 will comfort them, and make them rejoice
Lam. 1. 2 among all..she hath none to comfort (her)
1. 17 (there is) none to comfort her: the LORD
1. 21 (there is) none to comfort me: all mine
2. 13 that I may comfort thee, O virgin daugh.
Eze. 14. 23 they shall comfort you, when ye see their
Zech. 1. 17 the LORD shall yet comfort Zion, and
10. 2 have told false dreams; they comfort in
3. *To support, refresh,* סָעַד *saad.*
Gen. 18. 5 comfort ye your hearts; after that ye
Judg19. 5 Comfort thine heart with a morsel of
19. 8 Comfort thine heart, I pray thee
4. *To support,* רָפַד *raphad,* 3.
Song 2. 5 Stay me with flagons, comfort me with
5. *To call alongside, help,* παρακαλέω *parakaleō.*
Acts 16. 40 they comforted them, and departed
2 Co. 1. 4 Who comforteth us..that we may..comf.
2. 7 (ought) rather to forgive..and comfort
7. 6 that comforteth those that are cast
7 6 comforted us by the coming of Titus
Eph. 6 22 and (that) he might comfort your hearts
Col 4 8 that he might..comfort your hearts
1 Th. 2. 11 comforted and charged every one of you
3. 2 and to comfort you concerning your faith
4. 18 comfort one another with these words
5. 11 comfort yourselves together, and edify
2 Th. 2. 17 Comfort your hearts, and stablish you in
6. *Speak kindly to one,* παραμυθέομαι *paramutheomai.*
John 11. 19 to comfort them concerning their brother
11. 31 The Jews then which..comforted her
1 Th. 2. 11 As ye know how we exhorted and comf.
5. 14 comfort the feeble minded, support the

COMFORT, to receive —
To be sighed with, comforted, נָחַם *nacham,* 2.
Isa. 57. 6 Should I receive comfort in these?

COMFORT, to take —
To brighten up, בָּלַג *balag,* 5.
Job 10. 20 let me alone, that I may take comfort a

COMFORT self, to —
1. *My brightening up,* מַבְלִיגִית *mabligith.*
Jer. 8. 18 I would comfort myself against sorrow
2. *To comfort self, give vent to sighs,* נָחַם *nacham,* 7.
Gen. 27. 42 Esau..doth comfort himself. to kill thee
Psa. 119 52 I remembered..and have comforted my

COMFORTABLE —
1. *Rest, quietness,* מְנוּחָה *menuchah.*
2 Sa. 14. 17 The word..shall now be comfortable
2. *Comforts, sighs,* נִחוּמִים *nichumim.*
Zech. 1. 13 (with) good words (and) comfortable wor.

COMFORTABLY —
1. *Upon or unto the heart,* עַל־לֵב *al leb.*
2 Sa. 19. 7 go forth, and speak comfortably unto thy
2 Ch. 30. 22 Hezekiah spake comfortably unto all the
Isa. 40. 2 Speak ye comfortably to Jerusalem, and
Hos. 2. 14 I will..speak comfortably unto her
2. *Upon or unto the heart,* עַל־לֵבָב *al lebab.*
2 Ch. 32. 6 and spake comfortably to them, saying

COMFORTED, to be —
1. *To be sighed with, comforted,* נָחַם *nacham,* 2.
Gen. 24. 67 Isaac was comforted after his mother's
38. 12 Judah was comforted, and went up unto
2 Sa. 13. 39 he was comforted concerning Amnon
Psa. 77. 2 my soul refused to be comforted
Jer. 31. 15 refused to be comforted for her children
Eze. 14. 22 ye shall be comforted concerning the
31. 16 shall be comforted in the nether parts of
32. 31 shall be comforted over all his multitude

2. *To be sighed with, comforted,* נָחַם *nacham,* 4.
Isa. 54. 11 O thou afflicted..(and) not comforted !
66. 13 and ye shall be comforted in Jerusalem
3. *To give vent to one's sighs,* נָחַם *nacham,* 7.
Gen. 37. 35 but he refused to be comforted : and he
Eze. 5. 13 I will be comforted : and they shall know
4. *To call near, exhort,* παρακαλέω *parakaleō.*
Matt. 2. 18 Rachel..would not be comforted, because
5. 4 that mourn : for they shall be comforted
Luke16 25 now he is comforted, and thou art torme.
Acts 20. 12 and were not a little comforted
1 Co.14. 31 all may learn, and all may be comforted
2 Co. 1. 4 we ourselves are comforted of God
1. 6 whether we be comforted, (it is) for your
7. 7 consolation wherewith he was comforted
7. 13 we were comforted in your comfort
Col. 2. 2 That their hearts might be comforted
1 Th. 3. 7 we were comforted over you in all our

COMFORTED together, to be —
To comfort together, συμπαρακαλέω *sumparakaleō.*
Rom. 1. 12 that I may be comforted together with

COMFORTER —
1. *To comfort,* נָחַם *nacham,* 3.
2 Sa.10. 3 that he hath sent comforters unto thee ?
1 Ch.19. 3 that he hath sent comforters unto thee ?
Job 16. 2 miserable comforters (are) ye all
Psa 69. 20 I looked..for comforters, but I found none
Eccl. 4. 1 oppressed, and they had no comforter
Lam. 1. 9 she came down..she had no comforter
1. 16 because the comforter that should relie.
Nah. 3. 7 whence shall I seek comforters for thee ?
2. *One called alongside,* παράκλητος *paraklētos.*
John14. 16 he shall give you another Comforter, that
14. 26 But the Comforter..the Holy Ghost
15. 26 when the Comforter is come, whom I will
16. 7 the Comforter will not come unto you

COMFORTLESS —
An orphan, bereaved, ὀρφανός *orphanos.*
John14. 18 I will not leave you comfortless : I will

COMFORTS —
1. *Comforts,* נִחוּמִים *nichumim.*
Isa. 57. 18 restore comforts unto him, and to his
2. *Comforts,* תַּנְחוּמִים *tanchumim.*
Psa. 94. 19 within me thy comforts delight my soul

COMMAND —
The mouth, פֶּה *peh.*
Job 39. 27 Doth the eagle mount up at thy command

COMMAND, to —
1. *To say, lift up the voice,* אָמַר *amar.*
Exod. 8. 27 sacrifice to..God, as he shall command us
1 Sa. 16. 16 Let our lord now command thy servants
1 Ch.21. 17 (Is it) not I (that) commanded the people
21. 18 the angel of the LORD commanded Gad
21. 27 the LORD commanded the angel, and he
22. 2 David commanded to gather together the
2 Ch.14. 4 commanded Judah to seek the LORD God
29. 21 he commanded the priests the sons of A.
29. 24 the king commanded (that) the burnt
29. 27 Hezekiah commanded to offer the burnt
29 30 the king and the princes commanded the
31. 4 he commanded the people that dwelt in
31. 11 Hezekiah commanded to prepare cham.
32. 12 commanded Judah and Jerusalem, saying
33 16 commanded Judah to serve the LORD
35. 21 for God commanded me to make haste
Neh. 13. 9 I commanded, and they cleansed the
13. 19 I commanded that the gates should be
13. 22 I commanded the Levites that they
Esth. 1. 10 commanded Mehuman, Biztha, Harbona
1. 17 Ahasuerus commanded Vashti the queen
4. 13 Mordecai commanded to answer Esther
6. 1 commanded to bring the book of records
9. 14 the king commanded it so to be done
9. 25 he commanded by letters, that his wicked
Job 9. 7 Which commandeth the sun, and it
36 10 commandeth that they return from iniq.
Psa. 106. 34 concerning whom the LORD commanded
107. 25 he commandeth, and raiseth the stormy
Dan. 2. 2 the king commanded to call the magici.
2. 12 and commanded to destroy all the wise
2. 46 commanded that they should offer an
3. 13 Nebuchadnezzar..commanded to bring
3. 19 commanded that they should heat the
3. 20 he commanded the most mighty men
4. 26 they commanded to leave the stump of
5. 2 Belshazzar..commanded to bring the
5. 29 Then commanded Belshazzar, and they
6. 16 the king commanded, and they brought
6. 23 commanded that they should take Daniel
6. 24 the king commanded, and they brought
2. *To speak, lead forth words,* דָּבַר *dabar,* 3.
Num.16. 47 Aaron took as Moses commanded, and
27. 23 as the LORD commanded by the hand of
Job 42. 9 went and did according as the LORD com.
3. *To set up (a precept or command),* צָוָה *tsavah,* 3.
Gen. 2. 16 the LORD God commanded the man, say.
3. 11 I commanded thee that thou shouldest
3. 17 the tree, of which I commanded thee
6. 22 according to all that God commanded
7. 5 according unto all that the LORD com.
7. 9 went..into the ark..as God had comman.
7. 16 went in..as God had commanded him
12. 20 Pharaoh commanded (his) men concern.
Gen. 18. 19 he will command his children and his
21. 4 circumcised..as God had commanded .
27. 8 according to that which I command thee
32. 4 he commanded them, saying, Thus shall
32 17 he commanded the foremost, saying
32. 19 so commanded he the second, and the
42. 25 Joseph commanded to fill their sacks
44. 1 he commanded the steward of his house
47. 11 Joseph..gave..as Pharaoh had comman.
50. 2 Joseph commanded his servants the
50. 12 did..according as he commanded them
50. 16 Thy father did command before he died
Exod. 4. 28 told..the signs which he had commanded
5. 6 Pharaoh commanded the same day the
7. 2 Thou shalt speak all that I command thee
7. 6 Moses and Aaron did as the LORD comm.
7. 10 they did so as the LORD had commanded
7 20 and Aaron did so, as the LORD command.
12. 28 did as the LORD had commanded Moses
12. 50 as the LORD commanded Moses and
16. 16 thing which the LORD hath commanded
16. 32 This (is) the thing which the LORD comm.
16. 34 As the LORD commanded Moses, so Aaron
18. 23 If thou..do this thing, and God comm.
19. 7 these words which the LORD commanded
23. 15 shalt keep the feast..as I commanded
27. 20 thou shalt command the children of I.
29. 35 according to all..which I have command.
31. 6 they may make all that I have command.
31. 11 according to all that I have commanded
32. 8 out of the way which I commanded them
34. 4 went up..as the LORD had commanded
34. 11 Observe thou that which I command thee
34. 18 as I commanded thee, in the time of the
35. 1 the words which the LORD hath comm.
35. 4 This (is) the thing which the LORD comm.
35. 10 and make all that the LORD hath comm.
35. 29 which the LORD had commanded to be
36. 1 according to all that the LORD had com.
36. 5 for..the work which the LORD command.
38. 22 made all that the LORD commanded M.
39. 1, 5, 7, 21, 26, 29, 31 as the LORD command.
39. 32 42, according to all that the LORD com.
39. 43 they had done it as the LORD had comm.
40. 16 according to all that the LORD command.
40. 19, 21, 25, 27, 29, 32 as the LORD commanded
40. 23 he set..as the LORD had commanded M.
Lev. 6. 9 Command Aaron and his sons, saying
7. 36 Which the LORD commanded to be given
7. 38 Which the LORD commanded Moses in
7. 38 in the day that he commanded the chil.
8. 4 And Moses did as the LORD commanded
8. 5 This (is) the thing which the LORD comm.
8. 9, 13, 17, 21, 29 as the LORD commanded M.
8. 31 and there eat it..as I commanded, saying
8. 34 the LORD hath commanded to do, to make
8. 36 which the LORD commanded by the hand
9. 5 they brought (that) which Moses comm.
9. 6 This (is) the thing which the LORD comm.
9. 7 make an atonement..as the LORD comm.
9. 10 he burnt..as the LORD commanded M.
9. 21 wave offering..as Moses commanded
10. 1 fire..which he commanded them not
10. 15 shall be thine..as the LORD hath comm.
10. 18 should indeed have eaten..as I comman.
13. 54 the priest shall command that they wash
14. 4 Then shall the priest command to take
14. 5, 36, 40 the priest shall command that
16. 34 And he did as the LORD commanded M.
17. 2 the thing which the LORD hath comman.
24. 2 Command the children of Israel, that
24. 23 children of Israel did as the LORD com.
25. 21 I will command my blessing upon you in
27. 34 which the LORD commanded Moses for
Num. 1. 19 As the LORD commanded Moses, so he
1. 54 according to all that the LORD comman.
2. 33 not numbered..as the LORD commanded
2. 34 according to all that the LORD command.
3. 42 Moses numbered, as the LORD command.
3. 51 Moses gave..as the LORD commanded M
4. 49 were numbered..as the LORD commanded
5. 2 Command the children of Israel, that they
8. 3 Aaron did so..as the LORD commanded
8. 20 according unto all that the LORD com.
8. 22 as the LORD had commanded Moses con.
9. 5 according to all that the LORD command.
9. 8 I will hear what the LORD will command
15. 23 all that the LORD hath commanded you
15. 23 from the day that the LORD commanded
15. 36 stoned him..as the LORD commanded M.
17. 11 Moses did (so): as the LORD commanded
19. 2 ordinance..which the LORD hath com.
20. 9 Moses took the rod..as he commanded
20. 27 Moses did as the LORD commanded
26. 4 as the LORD commanded Moses and the
27. 11 a statute..as the LORD commanded Mo.
27. 22 Moses did as the LORD commanded him
28. 2 Command the children of Israel, and say
29. 40 according to all that the LORD command.
30. 1 the thing which the LORD hath command.
30. 16 statutes which the LORD commanded M.
31. 7, 31, 41, 47 as the LORD commanded Moses
31. 21 ordinance..which the LORD commanded
32. 25 Thy servants will do as my lord command
32. 28 concerning them Moses commanded Ele.
33. 38 went up..at the commandment of the L
34. 2 Command the children of Israel, and say
34. 13 Moses commanded the children of Isr.
34. 13 the land..which the LORD commanded
34. 29 These (are they) whom the LORD com.
35. 2 Command the children of Israel, that they
36. 2 The LORD commanded my lord to give the
Num 36. 5 Moses commanded the children of Israel
36. 6 the LORD doth command concerning the
36 10 as the LORD commanded Moses, so did the
36. 13 which the LORD commanded by the hand
Deut. 1. 18 I commanded you at that time all the
1. 19 we went..as the LORD our God command.
1. 41 to all that the LORD our God commanded
2. 4 command thou the people, saying, Ye
3. 18 I commanded you at that time, saying
3. 21 I commanded Joshua at that time, saying
4. 2 not add unto the word which I command
4. 2 the commandments..which I command
4. 5 even as the LORD my God commanded me
4. 13 his covenant, which he commanded you
4. 14 the LORD commanded me at that time to
4. 40 his commandments, which I command
5. 12, 16 as the LORD thy God hath commanded
5. 15 the LORD thy God commanded thee to
5. 32 as the LORD your God hath commanded
5. 33 which the LORD..hath commanded you
6. 1 which the LORD your God commanded to
6. 2 which I command thee, thou, and thy son
6. 6 these words, which I command thee this
6. 17 his statutes, which he hath commanded
6. 20 which the LORD our God hath commanded
6. 24 the LORD commanded us to do all these
6. 25 we observe to do..as he hath commanded
7. 11 which I command thee this day, to do
8. 1 the commandments which I command
8. 11 his statutes, which I command thee this
9. 12 out of the way which I commanded them
9. 16 the way which the LORD had commanded
10. 5 there they be, as the LORD commanded
10. 13 which I command thee this day for thy
11. 8 keep all the commandments which I com.
11. 13 which I command you this day, to love
11. 22 these commandments which I command
11. 27 A blessing..which I command you this
11. 28 out of the way which I command you this
12. 11 thither shall ye bring all that I command
12. 14 there thou shalt do all that I command
12. 21 thou shalt kill..as I have commanded
12. 28 hear all these words which I command
12. 32 What thing soever I command you, obse.
13. 5 which the LORD thy God commanded thee
13. 18 his commandments which I command
15. 5 these commandments which I command
15. 11 therefore I command thee, saying, Thou
15. 15 therefore I command thee this thing to.
17. 3 served..gods..which I have not com.
18. 18 he shall speak..all that I shall command
18. 20 which I have not commanded him to
19. 7 Wherefore I command thee, saying, Thou
19. 9 which I command thee this day, to love
20. 17 as the LORD thy God hath commanded
24. 8 as I commanded them, (so) ye shall
24. 18 22 therefore I command thee to do this
26. 13, 14 according to all..thou hast command.
26. 16 This day the LORD thy God hath com.
27. 1 Moses with the elders of Israel com.
27. 1 the commandments which I command
27. 4 which I command you this day, in mount
27. 10 his statutes, which I command thee this
28. 1 his commandments which I command
28. 8 The LORD shall command the blessing
28. 13 which I command thee this day, to obser.
28 14 from any of the words which I command
28. 15 his statutes, which I command thee this
28 45 and his statutes which he commanded
29. 1 which the LORD commanded Moses to
30. 2 according to all that I command thee this
30 8 his commandments, which I command
30. 11 For this commandment which I com
30 16 I command thee this day to love the LORD
31. 5 according unto all..I have commanded
31. 10 Moses commanded them, saying, At the
31. 25 Moses commanded the Levites, which
31. 29 from the way which I have commanded
32. 46 ye shall command your children to observe
33. 4 Moses commanded us a law, (even) the
34. 9 and did as the LORD commanded Moses
Josh. 1. 7 which Moses my servant commanded
1. 9 Have not I commanded thee? Be strong
1. 10 Then Joshua commanded the officers of
1. 11 Pass through the host, and command the
1. 13 Moses the servant of the LORD commanded
1. 16 All that thou commandest us we will do
1. 18 thy words in all that thou commandest
3. 3 they commanded the people, saying
3. 8 thou shalt command the priests that bear
4. 3 And command ye them, saying, Take you
4. 8 Israel did so as Joshua commanded, and
4. 10 every thing..that the LORD commanded
4. 10 according to all that Moses commanded
4. 16 Command the priests that bear the ark of
4. 17 Joshua therefore commanded the priests
6. 10 Joshua had commanded the people, saying
7. 11 my covenant which I commanded them
8. 4 he commanded them, saying, Behold, ye
8. 8 See, I have commanded you
8. 27 unto the word..which he commanded J.
8. 29 Joshua commanded that they should take
8. 31 As Moses the servant of the LORD com.
8. 33 the servant of the LORD had commanded
8. 35 not a word of all that Moses commanded
9. 24 how that the LORD thy God commanded
10. 27 Joshua commanded, and they took them
10. 40 as the LORD God of Israel commanded
11. 12 as Moses the servant of the LORD com.
11. 15 As the LORD commanded Moses his ser.
11. 15 so did Moses command Joshua, and so
11. 15 of all that the LORD commanded Moses

Josh. 11. 20 destroy them, as the LORD commanded
13. 6 for an inheritance, as I have commanded
14. 2 as the LORD commanded by the hand of
14. 5 As the LORD commanded Moses, so the
17. 4 The LORD commanded Moses to give us
21. 2, 8 The LORD commanded by the hand of
22. 2 Moses the servant of the LORD commanded
22. 2 obeyed my voice in all that I commanded
23. 16 which he commanded you, and have gone
Judg. 2. 20 covenant which I commanded their father
3. 4 which he commanded their fathers by the
4. 6 Hath not the LORD God of Israel com.
13. 14 all that I commanded her let her observe
21. 10 thousand men..commanded them, saying
21. 20 Therefore they commanded the children
Ruth 2. 15 Boaz commanded his young men, saying
1 Sa. 2. 29 which I have commanded (in my) habita.
13. 13 which he commanded thee: for now
13. 14 and the LORD hath commanded him (to
13. 14 kept (that) which the LORD commanded
17. 20 and went, as Jesse had commanded him
18. 22 Saul commanded his servants, (saying).
20. 29 and my brother, he hath commanded me
21. 2 The king hath commanded me a business
21. 2 and what I have commanded thee: and I
2 Sa. 4. 12 And David commanded his young men
5. 25 did so, as the LORD had commanded him
7. 7 whom I commanded to feed my people
7. 11 I commanded judges (to be) over my peo.
9. 11 my lord the king hath commanded his
13. 28 Now Absalom had commanded his serv.
13. 28 fear not: have not I commanded you? be
13. 29 did unto Amnon as Absalom had com.
18. 5 the king commanded Joab and Abishai
21. 14 they performed all that the king com.
24. 19 David..went up, as the LORD commanded
1 Ki. 2. 46 So the king commanded Benaiah the son
5. 6 Now therefore command thou that they
5. 17 the king commanded, and they brought
8. 58 judgments, which he commanded our fa.
9. 4 according to all that I have commanded
11. 10 had commanded him concerning this
11. 10 he kept not that which the LORD com.
11. 11 my statutes, which I have commanded
11. 38 hearken unto all that I command thee
13. 21 which the LORD thy God commanded thee
15. 5 from any (thing) that he commanded him
17. 4 I have commanded the ravens to feed thee
17. 9 I have commanded a widow woman there
22. 31 the king of Syria commanded his thirty
2 Ki 11. 5 he commanded them, saying, This (is)
11. 9 (things) that Jehoiada the priest com.
11. 15 Jehoiada the priest commanded the cap.
14. 6 the law of Moses, wherein the LORD com.
16. 15 king Ahaz commanded Urijah the priest
16. 16 according to all that king Ahaz command.
17. 13 according to all the law which I comman.
17. 27 Then the king of Assyria commanded
17. 34 which the LORD commanded the children
18. 6 which the LORD commanded Moses
18. 12 Moses the servant of the LORD command.
21. 8 according to all that I have commanded
21. 8 the law that my servant Moses command.
22. 12 the king commanded Hilkiah the priest
23. 4 the king commanded Hilkiah the high
23. 21 the king commanded all the people, saying
1 Ch. 6. 49 according to all that Moses..had com.
14. 16 David therefore did as God commanded
15. 15 as Moses commanded according to the
16. 15 the word (which) he commanded to a
16. 40 law of the LORD, which he commanded
17. 6 the judges of Israel, whom I commanded
17. 10 I commanded judges (to be) over my peo.
22. 17 David also commanded all the princes of
24. 19 as the LORD God of Israel had commanded
2 Ch. 7. 13 if I command the locusts to devour the
7. 17 according to all that I have commanded
18. 30 the king of Syria had commanded the
23. 8 all things that Jehoiada..had commanded
25. 4 book of Moses, where the LORD command.
33. 8 I have commanded them, according to
34. 20 the king commanded Hilkiah, and Ahik.
Ezra 4. 3 Cyrus the king of Persia hath command.
9. 11 thou hast commanded by thy servants
Neh. 1. 7 which thou commandedst thy servant Mo.
1. 8 the word that thou commandedst thy ser.
8. 1, 14 which the LORD had commanded to I.
9. 14 commandedst them precepts, statutes, and
Esth. 3. 2 the king had so commanded concerning
3. 12 according to all that Haman had com.
4. 17 according to all that Esther had com.
8. 9 according to all that Mordecai command.
Job 36. 32 he..commandeth it (not to shine) by (the)
37. 12 he commandeth them upon the face of
38. 12 Hast thou commanded the morning since
Psa. 7. 6 the judgment (that) thou hast command.
33. 9 he commanded, and it stood fast
42. 8 the LORD will command his loving kind.
44. 4 O God: command deliverances for Jacob
68. 28 Thy God hath commanded thy strength
78. 5 which he commanded our fathers, that
78. 23 Though he had commanded the clouds
105. 8 the word (which) he commanded to a
111. 9 he hath commanded his covenant for ever
119. 4 Thou hast commanded (us) to keep thy
119. 138 Thy testimonies (that) thou hast com.
133. 3 for there the LORD commanded the bless.
148. 5 for he commanded, and they were created
Isa. 5. 6 I will also command the clouds that they
13. 3 I have commanded my sanctified ones
34. 16 my mouth it hath commanded, and his
45. 11 concerning the work of my hands com.

Isa. 45. 12 and all their host have I commanded
48. 5 and my molten image, hath commanded
Jer. 1. 7 whatsoever I command thee thou shalt
1. 17 speak unto them all that I command thee
7. 22 nor commanded them in the day that I
7. 23 But this thing commanded I them, say.
7. 23 in all the ways that I have commanded
7. 31 I commanded (them) not, neither came
11. 4 Which I commanded your fathers in the
11. 4 according to all which I command you
11. 8 I commanded (them) to do, but they did
13. 5 So I went..as the LORD commanded me
13. 6 which I commanded thee to hide there
14. 14 neither have I commanded them, neither
17. 22 hallow ye the sabbath day, as I command.
19. 5 which I commanded not, nor spake (it)
23. 32 yet I sent them not, nor commanded
26. 2 all the words that I command thee to
26. 8 all that the LORD had commanded (him)
27. 4 command them to say unto their masters
29. 23 which I have not commanded them
32. 23 nothing of all that thou commandedst
32. 35 unto Molech; which I commanded them
34. 22 Behold, I will command, saith the LORD
35. 6 the son of Rechab our father commanded
35. 10 all that Jonadab our father commanded
35. 14 he commanded his sons not to drink wine
35. 16 which he commanded them; but this
35. 18 unto all that he hath commanded you
36. 5 Jeremiah commanded Baruch, saying, I
36. 8 all that Jeremiah the prophet command.
36. 26 the king commanded Jerahmeel the son
37. 21 Zedekiah the king commanded that they
38. 10 the king commanded Ebedmelech the E.
38. 27 these words that the king had command
50. 21 according to all that I have commanded
51. 59 which Jeremiah the prophet commanded
Lam. 1. 10 thou didst command (that) they should
1. 17 the LORD hath commanded concerning
2. 17 his word that he had commanded in the
3. 37 (when) the LORD commandeth (it) not?
Eze. 9. 11 I have done as thou hast commanded me
10. 6 he had commanded the man clothed with
37. 10 I prophesied, as he commanded me, and
Amos 2. 12 But ye..commanded the prophets, saying
6. 11 For, behold, the LORD commandeth, and
9. 3 I command the serpent, and he shall bite
9. 4 thence will I command the sword, and it
9. 9 I will command, and I will sift the house
Zech. 1. 6 I commanded my servants the prophets
Mal. 4. 4 which I commanded unto him in Horeb

4. *To arrange thoroughly,* διατάσσω *diatassō.*
Luke 8. 55 and he commanded to give her meat
17. 9 he did the things that were commanded
17. 10 all those things which are commanded
Acts 18. 2 Claudius had commanded all Jews to
23. 31 the soldiers, as it was commanded them
24. 23 he commanded a centurion to keep Paul

5. *To say, speak,* εἶπον *eipon.*
Matt. 4. 3 If thou be the Son of God, command that
Mark 5. 43 commanded that something should be
8. 7 commanded to set them also before (them)
10. 49 Jesus stood still, and commanded him to
Luke 4. 3 If thou be the Son of God, command
9. 54 wilt thou that we command fire to come
19. 15 he commanded these servants to be
2 Co. 4. 6 who commanded the light to shine out

6. *To give in charge,* ἐντέλλομαι *entellomai.*
Matt 15. 4 God [commanded,] saying, Honour thy
19. 7 Why did Moses then command to give a
28. 20 all things whatsoever I have commanded
Mark 10. 3 and said..What did Moses command you?
11. 6 they said..even as Jesus [had commanded]
13. 34 and commanded the porter to watch
John 8. 5 [Moses in the law commanded us, that]
15. 14 if ye do whatsoever I command you
15. 17 These things I command you, that ye
Acts 13. 47 For so hath the Lord commanded us

7. *To put upon, or over,* ἐπιτάσσω *epitassō.*
Mark 1. 27 with authority commandeth he even the
6. 27 and commanded his head to be brought
6. 39 he commanded them to make all sit down
Luke 4. 36 with authority..he commandeth the
8. 25 he commandeth even the winds and
8. 31 he would not command them to go out
14. 22 Lord, it is done as thou hast commanded
Acts 23. 2 the high priest Ananias commanded them

8. *To call to, urge on, command,* κελεύω *keleuō.*
Matt 14. 9 nevertheless..he commanded (it) to be
14. 19 he commanded the multitude to sit down
15. 35 [commanded] the multitude to sit down
18. 25 his lord commanded him to be sold, and
27. 58 Pilate commanded the body to be deliver.
27. 64 Command therefore that the sepulchre be
Luke 18. 40 and commanded him to be brought unto
Acts 4. 15 when they had commanded them to go
5. 34 commanded to put the apostles forth a
8. 38 he commanded the chariot to stand still
12. 19 commanded that (they) should be put to
16. 22 and the magistrates..commanded to beat
21. 33 commanded (him) to be bound with two
21. 34 he commanded him to be carried into the
22. 24 The chief captain commanded him to be
22. 30 commanded the chief priests and all their
23. 3 commandest me to be smitten contrary
23. 10 commanded the soldiers to go down, and
23. 35 he commanded him to be kept in Herod's
25. 6 and the next day..commanded Paul to
25. 17 and commanded the man to be brought

Acts 25. 21 I commanded him to be kept till I might
27. 43 commanded that they which could swim

9. *To announce alongside of,* παραγγέλλω *paraggellō.*
Matt 10. 5 Jesus sent forth, and commanded them
Mark 6. 8 commanded them that they should take
8. 6 he commanded the people to sit down on
Luke 8. 29 he had commanded the unclean spirit to
9. 21 commanded (them) to tell no man that
Acts 1. 4 commanded them that they should not
4. 18 commanded them not to speak at all nor
5. 28 Did not we straitly command you, that ye
5. 40 they commanded that they should not
10. 42 he commanded us to preach unto the
15. 5 to command (them) to keep the law of M.
16. 18 I command thee in the name of Jesus C.
17. 30 but now commandeth all men everywhere
1 Co. 7. 10 And unto the married I command, (yet)
1 Th. 4. 11 work with your own hands, as we com.
2 Th. 3. 4 and will do the things which we command
3. 6 we command you, brethren, in the name
3. 10 this we commanded you, that if any
3. 12 Now them that are such we command
1 Ti. 4. 11 These things command and teach

10. *To arrange, set in order,* προστάσσω *prostassō.*
Matt. 8. 4 offer the gift that Moses commanded, for
21. 6 the disciples went, and did as Jesus com.
Mark 1. 44 which Moses commanded, for a testimony
Luke 5. 14 according as Moses commanded, for a
Acts 10. 33 to hear all things that are commanded
10. 48 he commanded them to be baptized in

11. *To say, announce,* ῥέω *rheō.*
Rev. 9. 4 it was commanded them that they should

12. *To set or give a reason, or law,* שׂוּם טְעֵם *sum teem.*
Ezra 4. 19 I commanded, and search hath been made
5. 3 Who hath commanded you to build this
5. 9 Who commanded you to build this house

COMMANDED —
Precept, thing set up, מִצְוָה *mitsvah.*
2 Ch. 8. 14 so had David the man of God commanded

COMMANDED, to be —
1. *To say,* אֲמַר *amar.*
Dan. 3. 4 To you it is commanded, O people
2. *To be set up, receive a precept,* צָוָה *tsavah,* 4.
Gen. 45. 19 thou art commanded, this do ye; take
Exod 34. 34 and spake..(that) which he was comman.
Lev. 8. 35 that ye die not: for so I am commanded
10. 13 And ye shall eat..for so I am commanded
Num. 3. 16 the word of the LORD, as he was comman.
36. 2 my lord was commanded by the LORD to
Eze. 12. 7 I did so as I was commanded: I brought
24. 18 I did in the morning as I was commanded
37. 7 I prophesied as I was commanded: and
3. *Taste, reason, law,* טְעֵם *taam.*
Ezra 7. 23 Whatsoever is commanded by the God of
4. *To set throughout,* διαστέλλω *diastellō.*
Heb. 12. 20 could not endure that which was comman.

COMMANDED, which was —
Precept, thing set up, מִצְוָה *mitsvah.*
Neh. 13. 5 which was commanded (to be given) to

COMMANDER —
One who sets up, gives precepts, צָוָה *tsavah,* 3.
Isa. 55. 4 I have given him (for) a..commander to

COMMANDING —
1. *To set up, give precepts,* צָוָה *tsavah,* 3.
Gen. 49. 33 when Jacob had made an end of com.
2. *To arrange thoroughly,* διατάσσω *diatassō.*
Matt 11. 1 when Jesus had made an end of com.
3. *To call to, urge on,* κελεύω *keleuō.*
Acts 24. 8 Commanding his accusers to come unto.

COMMANDMENT —
1. *A saying,* אִמְרָה *imrah.*
Psa. 147. 15 He sendeth forth his commandment
2. *A word,* דָּבָר *dabar.*
Exod 34. 28 wrote upon the tables. the ten comman.
Deut. 4. 13 ten commandments; and he wrote them
10. 4 wrote on the tables..the ten command.
Josh. 8. 8 according to the commandment of the L.
1 Sa. 15. 11 for he..hath not performed my com.
15. 13 I have performed the commandment of
2 Sa. 12. 9 Wherefore hast thou despised the com.
1 Ch 28. 21 the people (will be) wholly at thy com.
2 Ch. 31. 5 as soon as the commandment came abr.
Esth. 1. 12 Vashti refused to come at the king's co.
1. 19 let there go a royal commandment from
2. 8 when the king's commandment and his
3. 15 being hastened by the king's command.
4. 3 whithersoever the king's commandment
8. 14 pressed on by the king's commandment
8. 17 whithersoever the king's commandment
9. 1 when the king's commandment and his
Psa. 103. 20 that do his commandments, hearkening
Dan. 9. 23 the commandment came forth, and I am
9. 25 from the going forth of the command.
3. *Thing given, a law, judgment,* דָּת *dath.*
Esth. 3. 14 for a commandment to be given in every
8. 13 The copy of the writing for a command.
4. *Statute,* חֹק *choq.*
Amos 2. 4 they have not kept his commandments

5. *Taste, reason, law,* טַעַם *taam.*
Ezra 4. 21 until (another) commandment shall be
6. 14 they builded..according to the comman.

6. *Taste, reason, law,* טְעֵם *teem.*
Ezra 4. 21 Give ye now commandment to cause
6. 14 according to the commandment of Cyrus

7. *Saying,* מַאֲמַר *maamar.*
Esth. 1. 15 she hath not performed the command.
2. 20 Esther did the commandment of Morde.

8. *Word,* מִלָּה *millah.*
Dan. 3. 22 because the king's commandment was

9. *Charge, command,* מִפְקָד *miphqad.*
2 Ch. 31. 13 at the commandment of Hezekiah the

10. *Precept,* מִצְוָה *mitsvah.*
Gen. 26. 5 Because that Abraham..kept..my com.
Exod15. 26 If thou wilt..give ear to his command.
16. 28 How long refuse ye to keep my comman.
20. 6 them that love me, and keep my comm.
24. 12 I will give thee..commandments which I
Lev. 4. 2, 13, 22, 27 the commandments of the LORD
5. 17 forbidden to be done by the command.
22. 31 Therefore shall ye keep my command.
26. 3 If ye..keep my commandments, and do
26. 14 if ye will not..do all these commandme.
26. 15 so that ye will not do all my command.
27. 34 These (are) the commandments, which the
Num 15. 22 and not observed all these command.
15 31 Because he hath..broken his command.
15. 39 that ye may..remember all the comma.
15. 40 That ye may..do all my commandments
36. 13 These (are) the commandments and the
Deut. 4. 2 that ye may keep the commandments of
4. 40 Thou shalt keep..his commandments
5. 10 them that love me, and keep my comma.
5. 29 that they would..keep all my command.
5. 31 I will speak unto thee all the command.
6. 1 these (are) the commandments, the stat.
6. 2 to keep all his statutes, and his comma.
6. 17 Ye shall diligently keep the command.
6. 25 if we observe to do all these command.
7. 9 that love him, and keep his command.
7. 11 Thou shalt therefore keep the command.
8. 1 All the commandments which I comma.
8. 2 whether thou wouldest keep his comma.
8. 6 Therefore thou shalt keep the command.
8. 11 in not keeping his commandments, and
10. 13 To keep the commandments of the LORD
11. 1 thou shalt..keep..his commandments
11. 8 Therefore shall ye keep all the command.
11. 13 ye shall hearken..unto my command.
11. 22 if ye shall..keep all these commandme.
11. 27, 28 obey the commandments of the LORD
13. 4 Ye shall..keep his commandments, and
13. 18 to keep all his commandments which I co.
15. 5 to observe to do all these commandments
17. 20 he turn not aside from the commandme.
19. 9 If thou shalt keep all these command.
26. 13 accordingto all thycommandments, which
26. 13 I have not transgressed thy command.
26. 17 to keep his statutes, and his command.
26. 18 that (thou) shouldest keep all his comma.
27 1 Keep all the commandments which I com.
27. 10 do his commandments and his statutes
28. 1 to observe (and) to do all his command.
28. 9 if thou shalt keep the commandments
28. 13 if that thou hearken unto the command.
28. 15 to observe to do all his commandments
28. 45 to keep his commandments and his statu.
30. 8 to do all his commandments which I com.
30. 10 If thou shalt..keep his commandments
30. 11 this commandment which I command
30. 16 to keep his commandments and his stat.
31. 5 do..according unto all the command.
Josh. 22. 3 have kept the charge of the command.
22. 5 take diligent heed to do the command.
22. 5 charged you..to keep his commandments
Judg. 2. 17 obeying the commandments of the LORD
3. 4 they would hearken unto the command.
1 Sa. 13. 13 thou hast not kept the commandment of
1 Ki. 2. 3 to keep his statutes, and his command.
2. 43 Why then hast thou not kept..the comm.
3. 14 to keep my statutes and my command.
6. 12 if thou wilt..keep all my commandments
8. 58 incline our hearts..to keep his command.
8. 61 to keep his commandments, as at this day
9. 6 if ye..will not keep my commandments
11. 34 because he kept my commandments and
11. 38 to keep my statutes and my command.
13. 21 thou hast..not kept the commandment
14. 8 my servant David, who kept my comman.
18. 18 ye have forsaken the commandments of
2 Ki. 17. 13 and keep my commandments (and) my
17. 16 they left all the commandments of the L.
17. 19 Judah kept not the commandments of
17. 34 or after the law and commandment which
17. 37 the law, and the commandment, which
18. 6 but kept his commandments, which the
18. 36 for the king's commandment was, saying
23. 3 made a covenant..to keep his command.
1 Ch. 28. 7 if he be constant to do my command.
28. 8 keep and seek for all the commandments
29. 19 to keep thy commandments, thy testi.
2 Ch. 7. 19 if ye..forsake..my commandments
8. 13 offering according to the commandment
8. 15 they departed not from the command.
14. 4 and to do the law and the commandment
17. 4 But..walked in his commandments, and
19. 10 between law and commandment, statutes
2 Ch. 24. 20 Why transgress ye the commandments of
24. 21 stoned him with stones at the command.
29. 15 came, according to the commandment of
29. 25 according to the commandment of David
29. 25 (so was) the commandment of the LORD
30. 6 according to the commandment of the
30. 12 one heart to do the commandment of the
31. 21 in the law, and in the commandments
34. 31 to keep his commandments and his testi.
35. 10 according to the king's commandment
35. 15 according to the commandment of David
35. 16 according to the commandment of king J.
Ezra 7. 11 a scribe of the words of the command.
9. 10 for we have forsaken thy commandments
9. 14 Should we again break thy commandme.
10. 3 of those that tremble at the command.
Neh. 1. 5 for them that..observe his command.
1. 7 We..have not kept the commandments
1. 9 (if) ye turn unto me, and keep my comm.
9. 13 gavest..good statutes and command.
9. 16 they..hearkened not to thy command.
9. 29 they..hearkened not unto thy command.
9. 34 nor hearkened unto thy commandments
10. 29 to observe and do all the commandments
11. 23 (it was) the king's commandment concern.
12. 24, 45 according to the commandment of D.
Esth. 3. 3 Why transgressest thou the king's com.
Job 23. 12 have I gone back from the command.
Psa. 19. 8 the commandment of the LORD (is) pure
78. 7 That they might..keep his command.
89. 31 If they break..and keep not my comman.
112. 1 delighteth greatly in his commandments
119. 6 when I have respect unto all thy com.
119. 10 let me not wander from thy command.
119. 19 hide not thy commandments from me
119. 21 which do err from thy commandments
119. 32 I will run the way of thy commandments
119. 35 to go in the path of thy commandments
119. 47 I will delight myself in thy command.
119. 48 will I lift up unto thy commandments
119. 60 I..delayed not to keep thy command.
119. 66 for I have believed thy commandments
119. 73 understanding, that I may learn thy com.
119. 86 All thy commandments (are) faithful
119. 96 (but) thy commandment (is) exceeding
119. 98 Thou through thy commandments hast
119. 115 I will keep the commandments of my G.
119. 127 I love thy commandments above gold
119. 131 for I longed for thy commandments
119. 143 (yet) thy commandments (are) my delig.
119. 151 and all thy commandments (are) truth
119. 166 I have hoped..and done thy command.
119. 172 all thy commandments (are) righteous.
119. 176 for I do not forget thy commandments
Prov. 2. 1 My son..hide my commandments with
3. 1 but let thine heart keep my command.
4. 4 Let thine heart..keep my commandment
6. 20 My son, keep thy father's commandment
6. 23 the commandment (is) a lamp; and the
7. 1 and lay up my commandments with thee
7. 2 Keep my commandments, and live; and
10. 8 The wise in heart will receive command.
13. 13 he that feareth the commandment shall
19. 16 He that keepeth the commandment
Eccl. 8. 5 Whoso keepeth the commandment shall
12. 13 Fear God, and keep his commandments
Isa. 36. 21 for the king's commandment was, saying
48. 18 O that thou hadst hearkened to my com.!
Jer. 35. 14 unto this day, but obey their father's co.
35. 16 the son's..have performed the command.
35. 18 Because ye have obeyed the command.
Dan. 9. 4 and to them that keep his command.
Mal. 2. 1 O ye priests, this commandment (is) for
2. 4 know that I have sent this command.

11. *The mouth,* פֶּה *peh.*
Gen. 45. 21 gave them wagons according to the com.
Exod17. 1 according to the commandment of the L.
38. 21 according to the commandment of Moses
Num. 3. 39 Aaron numbered at the commandment of
4. 37, 41, 49 did number, according to the com.
9. 18, 18, 23, 23 At the commandment of the
9. 20, 20 according to the commandment of the
10. 13 according to the commandment of the L.
13. 3 Moses by the commandment of the LORD
14. 41 do ye transgress the commandment of the
24. 13 I cannot go beyond the commandment
27. 14 ye rebelled against my commandment
33. 2 Moses wrote their goings..by the com.
33. 38 Aaron..went..at the commandment of
Deut. 1. 26, 43 rebelled against the commandment
9. 23 ye rebelled against the commandment of
Josh. 1. 18 that doth rebel against thy command.
15. 13 According to the commandment of the L.
17. 4 according to the commandment of the L.
21. 3 at the commandment of the LORD, these
1 Sa. 12. 14, 15 rebel against the commandment of
15. 24 I have transgressed the commandment
2 Ki. 23. 35 according to the commandment of Phar.
24. 3 Surely at the commandment of the LORD
1 Ch. 12. 32 their brethren (were) at their command.
Prov. 8. 29 the waters should not pass his command.
Eccl. 8. 2 (counsel thee) to keep the king's com.
Lam. 1. 18 I have rebelled against his command.

12. *Thing set up, precept,* צַו, צָו *tsav.*
Hos. 5. 11 he willingly walked after the command.

13. *Thing arranged,* διάταγμα *diatagma.*
Heb. 11. 23 were not afraid of the king's [command.]

14. *Thing given in charge,* ἔνταλμα *entalma.*
Matt 15. 9 teaching (for) doctrines the command.
Mark 7. 7 teaching (for) doctrines the command.
Col. 2. 22 after the commandments and doctrines

15. *Thing given in charge,* ἐντολή *entolē.*
Matt. 5. 19 shall break one of these least command.
15. 3 Why do ye also transgress the command.
15. 6 Thus have ye made [the commandment]
19. 17 enter into life, keep the commandments
22. 36 which (is) the great commandment in the
22. 38 This is the first and great commandment
22. 40 On these two commandments hang all
Mark 7. 8 laying aside the commandment of God
7. 9 Full well ye reject the commandment of
10. 19 Thou knowest the commandments, Do
12. 28 Which is the first commandment of all?
12. 29 [The first of all the commandments (is)]
12. 30 [This (is) the first commandment]
12. 31 There is none other commandment great.
Luke 1. 6 walking in all the commandments and
15. 29 neither transgressed I..thy command.
18. 20 Thou knowest the commandments
23. 56 and rested..according to the command.
John 10. 18 This commandment have I received of
11. 57 and the Pharisees had given a command.
12. 49 he gave me a commandment, what I
12. 50 I know that his commandment is life
13. 34 A new commandment I give unto you
14. 15 If ye love me, keep my commandments
14. 21 He that hath my commandments, and
15. 10 If ye keep my commandments, ye shall
15. 10 as I have kept my Father's command.
15. 12 This is my commandment, That ye love
Acts 17. 15 receiving a commandment unto Silas and
Rom. 7. 8 But sin, taking occasion by the command.
7. 9 when the commandment came, sin revived
7. 10 the commandment, which (was ordained)
7. 11 For sin, taking occasion by the command.
7. 12 and the commandment holy, and just
7. 13 that sin by the commandment might
13. 9 if (there be) any other commandment, it is
1 Co. 7. 19 but the keeping of the commandments of
14. 37 things that I write..are [the command.]
Eph. 2. 15 (even) the law of commandments (con.)
6. 2 which is the first commandment with
Col. 4. 10 touching whom ye received command.
1 Ti. 6. 14 That thou keep (this) commandment with.
Titus 1. 14 Not giving heed to..commandments of
Heb. 7. 5 verily they..have a commandment to
7. 16 not after the law of a carnal command.
7. 18 there is..a disannulling of the command.
2 Pe. 2. 21 to turn from the holy commandment
3. 2 be mindful..of the commandment of us
1 Jo. 2. 3 we do know..if we keep his command.
2. 4 and keepeth not his commandments, is a
2. 7 no new commandment..but an old com.
2. 7 The old commandment is the word which
2. 8 a new commandment I write unto you
3. 22 because we keep his commandments, and
3. 23 This is his commandment, That we should
3. 23 love one another, as he gave us command.
3. 24 he that keepeth his commandments
4. 21 this commandment have we from him
5. 2 when we love God, and keep his com.
5. 3 love of God, that we keep his command.
5. 3 and his commandments are not grievous
2 Jo. 4 as we have received a commandment from
5 as though I wrote a new commandment
6 that we walk after his commandments
6 This is the commandment, That, as ye
Rev. 12. 17 which keep the commandments of God
14. 12 here (are) they that keep the command.
22. 14 Blessed (are) they that do his command.

16. *Command, arrangement,* ἐπιταγή *epitagē.*
Rom. 16. 26 the commandment of the everlasting God
1 Co. 7. 6 by permission, (and) not of command.
7. 25 concerning virgins I have no command.
2 Co. 8. 8 I speak not by commandment, but by
1 Ti. 1. 1 an apostle..by the commandment of God
Titus 1. 3 according to the commandment of God

17. *Announcement (open),* παραγγελία *paraggelia.*
1 Th. 4. 2 ye know what commandments we gave
1 Ti. 1. 5 the end of the commandment is charity

COMMANDMENT, at the —

1. *To say,* אֲמַר *amar.*
2 Ch. 24. 8 at the king's commandment they made

2. *To urge on, command,* κελεύω *keleuō.*
Acts 25. 23 at Festus' commandment Paul was bro.

COMMANDMENT, to give (a) —

1. *To set up, give a precept,* צָוָה *tsavah,* 3.
Exod36. 6 Moses gave commandment, and they
Esth. 4. 5, 10 gave him a commandment to Mordecai
Psa. 71. 3 thou hast given commandment to save
Isa. 23. 11 the LORD hath given a commandment
Nah. 1. 14 the LORD hath given a commandment

2. *To set out thoroughly,* διαστέλλομαι *diastellomai.*
Acts 15. 24 to whom we gave no (such) commandment

3. *To give in charge,* ἐντέλλομαι *entellomai.*
John14. 31 as the Father [gave me commandment]
Acts 1. 2 he..had given commandments unto the
Heb. 11 22 and gave commandment concerning his

4. *To call to, urge on, command,* κελεύω *keleuō.*
Matt. 8 18 he gave commandment to depart unto

5. *To announce alongside,* παραγγέλλω *paraggellō.*
Acts 23. 30 I sent..to thee, and gave commandment

COMMANDMENT, to give in —
To set up, give a precept, צָוָה *tsavah,* 3.
Exod25. 22 which I will give thee in commandment
34. 32 he gave them in commandment all that
Deut 1. 3 the LORD had given him in command.

COMMANDMENT, to send with —
To cause to go forth, יָצָא *yatsa,* 5.
Ezra 8. 17 I sent them with commandment unto Id.

COMMANDMENTS —
Things committed to one's care, פִּקּוּדִים *piqqudim.*
Psa.103. 18 to those that remember his command.
111. 7 all his commandments (are) sure

COMMEND, to —
1. *To praise,* הָלַל *halal,* 3.
Gen. 12. 15 The princes also of Pharaoh..commend.
2. *To glorify,* שָׁבַח *shabach,* 3.
Eccl. 8. 15 I commended mirth, because a man hath
3. *To give praise to,* ἐπαινέω *epaineō.*
Luke16. 8 the lord commended the unjust steward
4. *To put along or over to,* παρατίθημι *paratithēmi.*
Luke23. 46 Father, into thy hands I commend my
Acts 14. 23 they commended them to the Lord, on
20. 32 I commend you to God, and to the word
5. *To set beside,* παρίστημι *paristēmi.*
1 Co. 8. 8 But meat commendeth us not to God
6. *To set together,* συνίστημι *sunistēmi.*
Rom. 3. 5 if our unrighteousness commend the
5. 8 But God commendeth his love toward us
16. 1 I commend unto you Phebe our sister
2 Co. 3. 1 Do we begin again to commend ourselves
4. 2 by manifestation of the truth commend.
5. 12 we commend not ourselves again unto
10. 12 compare ourselves with some that com.
10. 18 not he that commendeth himself is appr.
10. 18 but whom the Lord commendeth
12. 11 for I ought to have been commended of

COMMENDATION, of —
Setting together, συστατικός *sustatikos.*
2 Co. 3. 1 need we..epistles of commendation to
3. 1 or (letters) of commendation from you?

COMMENDED, to be —
To be praised, הָלַל *halal,* 4.
Prov 12. 8 A man shall be commended according to

COMMISSION —
1. *Law, judgment,* דָּת *dath.*
Ezra 8. 36 they delivered the king's commissions
2. *What is turned over upon one,* ἐπιτροπή *epitropē.*
Acts 26. 12 with authority and commission from the

COMMIT, to —
1. *To roll,* גָּלַל *galal.*
Psa. 37. 5 Commit thy way unto the LORD; trust
Prov.16. 3 Commit thy works unto the LORD and
2. *To be in,* הָיָה בְּ *hayah be.*
Deut 21. 22 if a man have committed a sin worthy of
3. *To deliver, give occasion,* מָסַר *masar.*
Num31 16 caused the children of Israel..to commit
4. *To give,* נָתַן *nathan.*
Gen. 39. 8 he hath committed all that he hath to
39. 22 the keeper of the prison committed to
Isa. 22. 21 I will commit thy government into his
Jer. 39. 14 committed him unto Gedaliah the son of
Eze. 23. 7 Thus she committed her whoredoms
5. *To do,* עָשָׂה *asah.*
Lev. 5. 17 if a soul sin, and commit any of these
18. 26 Ye shall..not commit (any) of these
18. 29 whosoever shall commit any of these
18. 29 the souls that commit (them) shall be cut
18. 30 commit not (any one) of these abomina.
20. 13 both of them have committed an abomi.
20. 23 for they committed all these things, and
Num. 5. 6 When a man or a woman shall commit
Deut17. 5 which have committed that wicked thing
19. 20 shall henceforth commit no more any such
Judg.20. 6 they have committed lewdness and folly
Prov 16. 12 abomination to kings to commit wicked.
Jer. 2. 13 For my people have committed two evils
6. 15 Were they ashamed when they had com.
8. 12 when they had committed abomination
29. 23 they have committed villany in Israel
44. 3 their wickedness which they have com.
44. 9 which they have committed in the land
44. 22 the abominations which ye have com.
44. 7 Wherefore commit ye (this) great evil
Eze. 3. 20 When a righteous (man) doth..commit
6. 9 for the evils which they have commit.
8. 6 abominations..house of Israel commit.
8. 17 the abominations which they commit
16. 43 thou shalt not commit this lewdness
16. 50 and committed abomination before me
18. 12 idols, hath committed abomination
18. 21 from all his sins that he hath committed
18. 22 his transgressions that he hath commit.
18. 24 committeth iniquity, (and) doeth accor.
18. 26 and committeth iniquity, and dieth in
18. 27 that he hath committed, and doeth that
18. 28 his transgressions that he hath committed
20. 43 for all your evils that ye have committed
22. 9 in the midst of thee they commit lewd.
22. 11 one hath committed abomination with
33. 13 trust to his own righteousness, and com.
Eze. 33. 13 but for his iniquity that he hath commit.
33. 15 walk in the statutes..without committing
33. 18 and committeth iniquity, he shall even
33. 29 abominations which they have commit.
43. 8 their abominations that they have com.
44. 13 their abominations which they have com.
Hos. 6. 9 by consent: for they commit lewdness
6. *To work,* פָּעַל *paal.*
Hos. 7. 1 they commit falsehood; and the thief
7. *To give in charge or trust,* פָּקַד *paqad,* 5.
1 Ki. 14. 27 committed (them) unto the hands of the
2 Ch 12. 10 committed (them) to the hands of the
Psa. 31. 5 Into thine hand I commit my spirit
Jer. 37. 21 that they should commit Jeremiah into
40. 7 had committed unto him men, and
41. 10 whom Nebuzar-adan..had committed to
8. *To put, place,* שִׂים *sim.*
Job 5. 8 and unto God would I commit my cause
9. *To give,* δίδωμι *didōmi.*
John 5. 22 hath committed all judgment unto the
10. *To let, let be,* ἐάω *eaō.*
Acts 27. 40 they committed (themselves) unto the
11. *To work, practise,* ἐργάζομαι *ergazomai.*
Jas. 2. 9 ye commit sin, and are convinced of the
12. *To give over,* παραδίδωμι *paradidōmi.*
Acts 8. 3 haling men and women, committed (them
1 Pe. 2. 23 but committed (himself) to him that judg.
13. *To put alongside of,* παρατίθημι *paratithēmi.*
Luke12. 48 to whom men have committed much of
1 Ti. 1. 18 This charge I commit unto thee, son T.
2 Ti. 2. 2 the same commit thou to faithful men
14. *To do,* ποιέω *poieō.*
Mark15. 7 who had committed murder in the insur.
Luke12. 48 he that knew not, and did commit things
John 8. 34 Whosoever committeth sin is the servant
Acts 28. 17 though I have committed nothing against
2 Co.11. 7 Have I committed an offence in abasing
Jas. 5. 15; 1 Jo. 3. 4; 3. 8; 3. 9.
15. *To commit fornication,* πορνεύω *porneuō.*
1 Co. 10. 8 as some of them committed, and fell in
16. *To practise, do,* πράσσω *prassō.*
Acts 25. 11 if I be an offender, or have committed
25. 25 when I found that he had committed
Rom. 1. 32 they which commit such things are
2. 2 against them which commit such things
2 Co 12. 21 lasciviousness, which they have commit.
17. *To place, put, set,* τίθημι *tithēmi.*
2 Co. 5. 19 hath committed unto us the word of rec.
[*See also* Abominable, adultery, fornication, iniquity, sacrilege, trust, ungodly, whoredom, wickedness.]

COMMIT self, to —
To leave, עָזַב *azab.*
Psa. 10. 14 the poor committeth himself unto thee

COMMIT (sin), to —
To sin, miss the mark, fall short, חָטָא *chata.*
Lev. 4. 35 for his sin that he hath committed, and
5. 7 which he hath committed, two turtle do.
1 Ki.14. 22 with their sins which they had commit.
Jer. 16. 10 what (is) our sin that we have committed
Eze. 16. 51 Neither hath Samaria committed half of
33. 16 None of his sins that he hath committed

COMMIT trespass or transgression, to —
To trespass, go beyond, מָעַל *maal.*
Lev. 5. 15 If a soul commit a trespass, and sin
6. 2 If a soul sin, and commit a trespass
Num. 5. 12 If any man's wife..commit a trespass
Josh. 7. 1 the children of Israel committed a tres.
22. 16 What trespass (is) this that ye have com.
22. 20 Did not Achan..commit a trespass in the
22. 31 because ye have not committed this tres.
1 Ch. 10. 13 for his transgression which he committed
Eze. 15. 8 because they have committed a trespass
20. 27 in that they have committed a trespass

COMMIT the keeping of —
To put alongside, παρατίθημι *paratithēmi.*
1 Pe. 4. 19 let them..commit the keeping of their

COMMIT to one's trust, to —
To trust, confide, πιστεύω *pisteuō.*
Luke 16. 11 who will commit to your trust the true
John 2. 24 Jesus did not commit himself..them

COMMIT unto, to —
To trust, confide, πιστεύω *pisteuō.*
Rom. 3. 2 unto them were committed the Jo. 2. 24.
1 Co. 9. 17 a dispensation (of the gospel) is com. un.
Gal. 2. 7 gospel of the uncircumcision was com. un.

COMMIT (whoredom), to —
To go a whoring, זָנָה *zanah.*
Eze. 23. 43 Will they now commit whoredoms with

COMMITTED, to be —
1. *To be, happen, come to pass,* הָיָה *hayah,* 2.
Jer. 5. 30 A wonderful and horrible thing is com.
2. *To be given,* נָתַן *nathan,* 2.
2 Ch. 34. 16 All that was committed to thy servants
3. *To be done,* עָשָׂה *asah,* 2.
Lev. 18. 30 abominable customs which were com.
Num. 15. 24 it shall be, if (ought) be committed by
Mal 2. 11 an abomination is committed in Israel
4. *To be trusted, entrusted with,* πιστεύομαι [*pisteuō*].
Titus 1. 3 which is committed unto me according

COMMITTED to or unto, that which is —
What is put down to, παρακαταθήκη *parakatathēkē.*
1 Ti. 6. 20 keep [that which is committed to] thy
2 Ti. 1. 14 [good thing which was committed unto]

COMMITTED unto him, that which is —
What is put alongside of, παραθήκη *parathēkē.*
2 Ti. 1. 12 that which I have committed unto him

COMMODIOUS, not —
Not well placed, ἀνεύθετος *aneuthetos.*
Acts 27. 12 because the haven was not commodious

COMMON —
1. *Profane, common,* חֹל *chol.*
1 Sa. 21. 4 no common bread under mine hand, but
21. 5 (the bread is) in a manner common, yea
2. *Of the land, earth,* אֶרֶץ *erets.*
Lev. 4. 27 if any one of the common people sin
3. *A son,* בֵּן *ben.*
Jer. 26. 23 cast..into the graves of the common
4. *Multitude of men,* רֹב אָדָם *rob adam.*
Eze. 23. 42 with the men of the common sort (were)
5. *Many, numerous,* רַב *rab.*
Eccl. 6. 1 There is an evil..and it (is) common
6. *Belonging to the public,* δημόσιος *dēmosios.*
Acts 5. 18 and put them in the common prison
7. *Common,* κοινός *koinos.*
Acts 2. 44 all that believed..had all things common
4. 32 but they had all things common
10. 14 I have never eaten anything that is com.
10. 28 that I should not call any man common
11. 8 nothing common or unclean hath..entered
Titus 1. 4 Titus, (mine) own son after the common
Jude 3 to write unto you of the common salva.
8. *Much, many, great,* πολύς *polus.*
Mark12. 37 And the common people heard him

COMMON, to call —
To make (or *regard as*) *common,* κοινόω *koinoō.*
Acts 10. 15 What God hath cleansed..call not thou c.
11. 9 What God hath cleansed..call not thou c.

COMMON death —
Death, מָוֶת *maveth.*
Num.16. 29 If these men die the common death of

COMMON things, to eat as —
To make common, חָלַל *chalal,* 3.
Jer. 31. 5 Thou shalt..eat (them) as common things

COMMON to man —
Human, ἀνθρώπινος *anthrōpinos*; 1 Co. 10. 13.

COMMONLY —
Wholly, fully, ὅλως *holōs.*
1 Co. 5. 1 It is reported commonly (that there is)

COMMONLY reported, to be —
To rumour throughout, διαφημίζω *diaphēmizō.*
Matt.28. 15 this saying is commonly reported among

COMMONWEALTH —
Polity, community, πολιτεία *politeia.*
Eph. 2. 12 being aliens from the commonwealth of

COMMOTION —
1. *Shaking, trembling,* רַעַשׁ *raash.*
Jer. 10. 22 a great commotion out of the north
2. *Instability,* ἀκαταστασία *akatastasia.*
Luke21. 9 when ye shall hear of wars and commo.

COMMUNE, to —
1. *To say,* אָמַר *amar.*
Psa. 4. 4 commune with your own heart upon your
2. *To speak,* דָּבַר *dabar.*
Zech. 1. 14 the angel that communed with me said
3. *To speak,* דָּבַר *dabar,* 3.
Gen. 18. 33 as soon as he had left communing with A.
23. 8 he communed with them, saying, If it
34. 6 Hamor..went out unto Jacob to com.
34. 8 Hamor communed with them, saying
34. 20 communed with the men of their city
42. 24 returned to them again, and communed
43. 19 they communed with him at the door of
Exod25. 22 I will commune with thee from above
31. 18 when he had made an end of communing
Judg. 9. 1 Abimelech..went..and communed with
1 Sa. 9. 25 (Samuel) communed with Saul upon the
18. 22 Commune with David secretly, and say
19. 3 and I will commune with my father of
25. 39 David sent and communed with Abigail
1 Ki.10. 2 when she was come to Solomon, she com.
2 Ki.22. 14 she dwelt in Jerusalem..and they com.
2 Ch. 9. 1 when she was come to Solomon, she com.
Eccl. 1. 16 I communed with mine own heart, saying
Dan. 1. 19 the king communed with them; and
4. *To count, rehearse,* סָפַר *saphar,* 3.
Psa. 64. 5 they commune of laying snares privily
5. *To meditate, talk,* שִׂיחַ *siach.*
Psa. 77. 6 I commune with mine own heart; and
6. *To talk thoroughly,* διαλαλέω *dialaleō.*
Luke 6. 11 communed one with another what they

7. *A word,* דָּבָר *dabar.*
Job 4. 2 (If) we assay to commune with thee

COMMUNE (together) or with, to —
1. *To be in a crowd together,* ὁμιλέω *homileō.*
Luke24. 15 while they communed (together) and
Acts 24. 26 he sent for him..and communed with
2. *To talk together,* συλλαλέω *sullaleō.*
Luke22. 4 he went his way, and communed with

COMMUNICATE, to —
1. *To place up again,* ἀνατίθεμαι *anatithemai.*
Gal. 2. 2 And I..communicated unto them that
2. *To make or use as common,* κοινωνέω *koinōneō.*
Gal. 6. 6 Let him that is taught in the word com.
Phil. 4. 15 no church communicated with me as
3. *The act of using as common,* κοινωνία *koinōnia.*
Heb. 13. 16 to do good and to communicate forget

COMMUNICATE, willing to —
Communicative, liberal, κοινωνικός *koinōnikos.*
1 Ti. 6. 18 that they be..willing to communicate

COMMUNICATE with, to —
To share with, συγκοινωνέω *sugkoinōneō.*
Phil. 4. 14 that ye did communicate with my afflic.

COMMUNICATION —
1. *A word,* דָּבָר *dabar.*
2 Sa. 3. 17 Abner had communication with the
2. *Meditation, talking,* שִׂיחַ *siach.*
2 Ki. 9. 11 Ye know the man, and his communication
3. *Act of using as common,* κοινωνία *koinōnia.*
Phm. 6 That the communication of thy faith
4. *A word,* λόγος *logos.*
Matt. 5. 37 let your communication be, Yea, yea
Luke 24. 17 What manner of communications (are)
Eph. 4. 29 Let no corrupt communication proceed
5. *A being crowded together,* ὁμιλία *homilia.*
1 Co. 15. 33 Be not deceived : evil communications

COMMUNION —
Act of using a thing in common, κοινωνία *koinōnia.*
1 Co. 10. 16 is it not the communion of the blood of
10. 16 is it not the communion of the body of
2 Co. 6. 14 what communion hath light with darknes.
13. 14 the love of God, and the communion of

COMPACT, to be —
To be joined, חָבַר *chabar,* 4.
Psa. 122. 3 Jerusalem is builded as a city that is com.

COMPACTED, to be —
To raise up together, συμβιβάζω *sumbibazō.*
Eph. 4. 16 From whom the whole body fitly..comp.

COMPANIES, by —
A drinking together, party, συμπόσιον *sumposion.*
Mark 6. 39 sit down by companies upon the green

COMPANION —
1. *Companion,* חָבֵר *chaber.*
Psa. 119 63 I (am) a companion of all (them) that
Prov.28. 24 the same (is) the companion of a destroy.
Song 1. 7 turneth aside by the flocks of thy com.
8. 13 the companions hearken to thy voice
Isa. 1. 23 Thy princes (are) rebellious, and com.
Eze. 37. 16 for the children of Israel his companions
37. 16 (for) all the house of Israel his compan.
2. *Companion,* חַבָּר *chabbar.*
Job 41. 6 Shall thy companions make a banquet
3. *Companion,* חֲבַר *chabar.*
Dan. 2. 17 Mishael, and Azariah, his companions
4. *Companion (female),* חֲבֶרֶת *chabereth.*
Mal. 2. 14 yet (is) she thy companion, and the wife
5. *An intimate,* כְּנָת *kenath.*
Ezra 4. 7 Tabeel, and the rest of their companions
4. 9 and the rest of their companions
4. 17 (to) the rest of their companions that
4. 23 Shimshai the scribe, and their compan.
5. 3 Shethar-boznai, and their companions
5. 6 his companions the Apharsachites, which
6. 6 your companions the Apharsachites
6. 13 their companions, according to that
6. *A friend,* מֵרֵעַ *merea.*
Judg14. 11 they brought thirty companions to be
14. 20 Samson's wife was (given) to his compan.
15. 2 therefore I gave her to thy companion
15 6 because he had..given her to his compan.
7. *A friend,* רֵעַ *rea.*
Exod.32 27 every man his companion, and every
1 Ch.27. 33 Hushai the Archite (was) the king's com.
Job 30. 29 I am a brother to dragons, and a compa.
35. 4 I will answer thee, and thy companions
Psa.122. 8 For my brethren and my companions'
8. *To feed, enjoy, have delight,* רָעָה *raah.*
Prov.13. 20 a companion of fools shall be destroyed
28. 7 he that is a companion of riotous (men)
9. *A friend,* רְעָה *reah.*
Judg.11. 38 she went with her companions, and
Psa. 45. 14 her companions that follow her shall be
10. *One who has something in common,* κοινωνός.
Heb. 10. 33 whilst ye became companions of them
11. *A joint companion,* συγκοινωνός *sugkoinōnos.*
Rev. 1. 9 who also am your brother, and [compan.]

COMPANION in labour —
Fellow worker, συνεργός *sunergos.*
Phil. 2. 25 companion in labour, and fellow soldier

COMPANION in travel —
Out from one's people with others, συνέκδημος.
Acts 19. 29 having caught..Paul's companions in tra.

COMPANY —
1. *To travel, be a wanderer, wayfarer,* אֹרַח *arach.*
Gen. 37. 25 a company of Ishmeelites came from G.
2. *Daughter,* בַּת *bath.*
Eze. 27. 6 the company of the Ashurites have made
3. *A troop,* גְּדוּד *gedud.*
1 Sa. 30. 15 Canst thou bring me down to this com.?
30. 15 I will bring thee down to this company
30. 23 the LORD..delivered the company that
2 Ki. 5. 2 the Syrians had gone out by companies
4. *A going, way, company,* הֲלִיכָה *halikah.*
Job 6. 19 the companies of Sheba waited for them
5. *A multitude,* הָמוֹן *hamon.*
2 Ch.20. 12 this great company that cometh against
6. *A cord, company,* חֶבֶל *chebel.*
1 Sa. 10. 5 thou shalt meet a company of prophets
10. 10 behold, a company of prophets met him
7. *A company,* חֶבֶר *cheber.*
Hos. 6. 9 the company of priests murder in the
8. *A company,* חֶבְרָה *chebrah.*
Job. 34. 8 Which goeth in company with the work.
9. *What is alive, living, active,* חַיָּה *chayyah.*
Psa. 68. 30 Rebuke the company of spearmen, the
10. *Strength, force,* חַיִל *chayil.*
2 Ch. 9. 1 a very great company, and camels that
11. *What is called together,* לַהֲקָה *lahaqah.*
1 Sa. 19. 20 when they saw the company of the prop.
12. *A chorus, dance,* מְחוֹלָה *mecholah.*
Song 6. 13 As it were the company of two armies
13. *A course, division, portion,* מַחֲלֹקֶת *machaloqeth.*
1 Ch.28. 1 the captains of the companies that
14. *A camp,* מַחֲנֶה *machaneh.*
Gen. 32. 8 If Esau come to the one company, and
32. 8 then the other company which is left
32. 21 himself lodged that night in the company
50. 9 horsemen: and it was a very great com.
2 Ki. 5. 15 he and all his company..came and stood
1 Ch. 9. 18 they (were) porters in the companies of
15. *A company met by appointment,* עֵדָה *edah.*
Num14. 7 they spake unto all the company of the
16. 5 spake unto Korah, and unto all his com.
16. 6 Take you censers, Korah, and all his c.
16. 11 For which cause (both) thou and..thy c.
16. 16 Be thou and all thy company before the
16. 40 be not as Korah, and as his company
26. 9 against Aaron in the company of Korah
26. 10 with Korah, when that company died
27. 3 he was not in the company of them that
27. 3 against the LORD in the company of Ko.
Job 16. 7 thou hast made desolate all my company
Psa.106. 17 and covered the company of Abiram
106. 18 And a fire was kindled in their company
16. *A host,* צָבָא *tsaba.*
Psa. 68. 11 great (was) the company of those that
17. *What is pressed or gathered together,* קִבּוּץ *qibbuts.*
Isa. 57. 13 When thou criest, let thy companies
18. *A congregation, what is called together,* קָהָל *qahal.*
Gen. 35. 11 a company of nations, shall be of thee
Num22. 4 Now shall this company lick up all (that)
Jer. 31. 8 a great company shall return thither
Eze. 16. 40 They shall also bring up a company aga.
17. 17 with (his) mighty army and great com.
23. 46 I will bring up a company upon them
23. 47 the company shall stone them with stones
26. 7 with horsemen, and companies, and
27. 27 all thy company which (is) in the midst
27. 34 all thy company in the midst of thee
32. 3 spread out my net over thee with a com.
32. 22 Asshur (is) there, and all her company
32. 23 her company is round about her grave
38. 4 a great company (with) bucklers and sh.
38. 7 all thy company that are assembled unto
38. 13 hast thou gathered thy company to take
38. 15 a great company, and a mighty army
19. *A head, detachment,* רֹאשׁ *rosh.*
Judg. 7. 16 he divided the..men (into) three com.
7. 20 the three companies blew the trumpets
9. 34 laid wait against Shechem in..companies
9. 37 another company come along by the pl.
9. 43 divided them into three companies, and
9. 44 the company that (was) with him, rushed
9. 44 the two (other) companies ran upon all
1 Sa. 11. 11 Saul put the people in three companies
13. 17 the spoilers came out..in three compan.
13. 17 one company turned unto the way (that
13. 18 another company turned the way (to) B.
13. 18 another company turned (to) the way of
20. *A tumultuous crowd,* רֶגֶשׁ *regesh.*
Psa. 55. 14 walked unto the house of God in com.
21. *Abundance, multitude,* שִׁפְעָה *shiphah.*
2 Ki. 9. 17 spied the company..and said, I see a com.
22. *A crowding together, a throng,* ὅμιλος *homilos.*
Rev. 18. 17 [every ship master, and all the company]
23. *A crowd,* ὄχλος *ochlos.*
Luke 5. 29 there was a great company of publicans
6. 17 he came down with..the company of his
9. 38 a man of the company cried out, saying
11. 27 a certain woman of the company lifted
12. 13 one of the company said unto him, Mas.
John 6. 5 Jesus..saw a great company come unto
Acts 6. 7 a great company of the priests were obed
24. *Fulness,* πλῆθος *plēthos.*
Luke23. 27 there followed him a great company of
25. *A journeying together,* συνοδία *sunodia.*
Luke 2. 44 supposing him to have been in the com

COMPANY, an innumerable —
A myriad, ten thousand, μυριάς *murias.*
Heb. 12. 22 and to an innumerable company of angels

COMPANY, travelling —
To travel, be a wanderer, אֹרַח *arach.*
Isa. 21. 13 O ye travelling companies of Dedanim

COMPANY, to gather a —
To make a crowd, ὀχλοποιέω *ochlopoieō.*
Acts17. 5 gathered a company, and set all the city

COMPANY, in a —
A company reclining at meals, κλισία *klisia.*
Luke 9. 14 Make them sit down by fifties in a com

COMPANY, one's own —
One's own, ἴδιος *idios.*
Acts 4. 23 they went to their own company, and

COMPANY, our —
Out of us, ἐξ ἡμῶν *ex hēmōn.*
Luke24. 22 certain women also of our company made

COMPANY, Paul and his —
Those around Paul, οἱ περὶ τὸν Παῦλον. [peri].
Acts13. 13 when Paul and his company loosed from

COMPANY, we that were of Paul's —
Those around Paul, οἱ περὶ τὸν Παῦλον. [peri].
Acts21. 8 [we that were of Paul's company departed

COMPANY, to come with such a —
To be called together, זָעַק *zaaq,* 2.
Judg.18. 23 that thou comest with such a company?

COMPANY with, to keep —
1. *To feed, enjoy, have delight,* רָעָה *raah.*
Prov.29. 3 but he that keepeth company with harlots
2. *To glue or cement together,* κολλάω *kollaō.*
Acts10. 28 for a man that is a Jew to keep company w
3. *To mix up together,* συναναμίγνυμι *sunanamign.*
1 Co. 5. 11 I have written..not to keep company w

COMPANY with, to (have) —
1. *To mix up together,* συναναμίγνυμι *sunanamignu.*
1 Co. 5. 9 I wrote..not to company with fornicators
2 Th. 3. 14 note that man, and have no company with
2. *To come or go with,* συνέρχομαι *sunerchomai.*
Acts 1. 21 these men which have companied with us

COMPARABLE —
To be weighed, סָלָא *sala,* 4.
Lam. 4. 2 precious sons of Zion, comparable to fine

COMPARE, to —
1. *To be like,* דָּמָה *damah,* 3.
Song 1. 9 I have compared thee, O my love, to a
2. *To compare, use a proverb,* מָשַׁל *mashal,* 5.
Isa. 46. 5 To whom will ye..compare me, that we
3. *To set in array, compare,* עָרַךְ *arak.*
Isa. 40. 18 or what likeness will ye compare unto
4. *To cast alongside,* παραβάλλω *paraballō.*
Mark 4. 30 with what comparison shall we [comp.]

COMPARE among or with, to —
To judge or sift together, συγκρίνω *sugkrinō.*
1 Co. 2. 13 comparing spiritual things with spiritual
2 Co. 10. 12 compare ourselves with some that com.
10. 12 comparing themselves among themselves

COMPARED, to be —
1. *To set in array, compare,* עָרַךְ *arak.*
Psa. 89. 6 who in the heaven can be compared unto
2. *To equal,* שָׁוָה *shavah.*
Prov. 3. 15 all the things..are not to be compared
8. 11 all the things..are not to be compared

COMPARISON —
A placing alongside, parable, παραβολή *parabolē.*
Mark 4. 30 with what comparison shall we compare

COMPARISON of, in —
As, even as, כְּ, כְּמוֹ *ke, kemo.*
Judg. 8. 2 What have I done now in comparison of
8. 3 what was I able to do in comparison of
Hag. 2. 3 in your eyes in compar. of it as nothing?

COMPASS —

1. *A circle, sphere,* חוּג *chug.*
Prov. 8. 27 set a compass upon the face of the depth

2. *Compass, circuit, margin,* כַּרְכֹּב *karkob.*
Exod27. 5 thou shalt put it under the compass of
38. 4 brazen grate of network under the com.

3. *A circuit, circle, compass,* מְחוּגָה *mechugah.*
Isa. 44. 13 he marketh it out with the compass, and

4. *What is round about,* סָבִיב *sabib.*
1 Ki. 7. 35 a round compass of half a cubit high

COMPASS, to —

1. *To encompass,* אָפַף *aphaph.*
2 Sa. 22. 5 When the waves of death compassed me
Psa 18. 4 The sorrows of death compassed me, and
40. 12 innumerable evils have compassed me
116. 3 The sorrows of death compassed me, and
Jon. 2. 5 The waters compassed me about,(even) to

2. *To surround,* זָרָה *zarah,* 3.
Psa 139. 3 Thou compassest my path and my lying

3. *To encircle,* חוּג *chug.*
Job. 26. 10 He hath compassed the waters with

4. *To go round, compass,* נָקַף *naqaph,* 5.
1 Ki.7.24 [round about (there were) knops compas.]
7.24 ten in a cubit, compassing the sea round
2 Ki.11.8 ye shall compass the king round about
2 Ch. 4.3 ten in a cubit, compassing the sea round
23. 7 the Levites shall compass the king round
Job 19. 6 God..hath compassed me with his net
Lam 3. 5 He hath..compassed (me) with gall and

5. *To be or go round about,* סָבַב *sabab.*
Gen 2. 11 which compasseth the whole land of Hav.
2. 13 the same (is) it that compasseth the
Num.21. 4 journeyed from mount Hor..to compass
Deut. 2. 1 and we compassed mount Seir many days
2. 3 Ye have compassed this mountain long
Josh. 6. 3 ye shall compass the city, all (ye) men of
6. 4 the seventh day ye shall compass the city
6. 7 said unto the people, Pass on, and com.
6. 14 the second day they compassed the city
6. 15 compassed..city after the same manner
6 15 that day they compassed the city seven
Judg11. 18 they went along..and compassed the
16. 2 they compassed (him) in, and laid wait
1 Ki. 7. 15 a line of twelve cubits did compass
7 23 a line of thirty cubits did compass it
7. 24 under the brim..(there were) knops com.
2 Ki. 6. 15 an host compassed the city both with
8. 21 smote the Edomites which compassed
2 Ch. 4. 2 a line of thirty cubits did compass it
4. 3 which did compass it round about; ten
18 31 they compassed about him to fight
21. 9 smote the Edomites which compassed
33. 14 compassed about Ophel, and raised it up
Psa. 17. 11 They have now compassed us in our steps
22. 12 Many bulls have compassed me: strong
22. 16 dogs have compassed me: the assembly
109. 3 They compassed me about also with
Jer. 52. 21 a fillet of twelve cubits did compass it

6. *To be or go round about,* סָבַב *sabab,* 2.
Josh.15. 10 the border compassed from Baalah west
18. 14 the border was drawn (thence), and com
19. 14 the border compasseth it on the north

7. *To go round about,* סָבַב *sabab,* 3a.
Psa. 26. 6 So will I compass thine altar, O LORD
Jer. 31. 22 a new thing. A woman shall compass a

8. *To go round about,* סָבַב *sabab,* 5.
Josh. 6 11 So the ark of the LORD compassed the c.

9. *To compass,* עָטַר *atar.*
1 Sa. 23. 26 Saul and his men compassed David and
Psa. 5. 12 with favour wilt thou compass him as

10. *To compass, encircle,* κυκλόω *kukloō.*
Luke21. 20 when ye shall see Jerusalem compassed

11. *To go round,* περιάγω *periagō.*
Matt 23 15 ye compass sea and land to make one

COMPASS about, to —

1. *To gird,* אָזַר *azar,* 3.
Isa. 50 11 that compass (yourselves) about with

2. *To compass,* כָּתַר *kathar,* 5.
Psa. 142. 7 the righteous shall compass me about
Hab. 1. 4 the wicked doth compass about the

3. *To set round,* נָקַף *naqaph.* 5.
2 Ki. 6. 14 by night, and compassed the city about
Psa. 17. 9 my..enemies, (who) compass me about
88. 17 They came..they compassed me about

4. *To be or go round about,* סָבַב *sabab.*
2 Sa. 18. 15 ten young men..compassed about and
22. 6 sorrows of hell compassed me about
Job 40. 22 willows of the brook compass him about
Psa. 18. 5 The sorrows of hell compassed me about
49. 5 iniquity of my heels shall compass me ab.
118. 10 All nations compassed me about: but
118. 11 They compassed me about, yea, they com.
118. 12 They compassed me about like bees
Hos. 11. 12 Ephraim compasseth me about with lies

5. *To be or go round about,* סָבַב *sabab,* 2.
Jer. 31. 39 the measuring line..shall compass about

6. *To go round about,* סָבַב *sabab,* 3a.
Psa. 7. 7 So shall the..people compass thee about
32. 7 thou shalt compass me about with songs
Psa. 32. 10 mercy shall compass him about
Jon. 2. 3 the floods compassed me about: all thy

7. *To compass, encircle,* κυκλόω *kukloō.*
Heb. 11. 30 after they were compassed about seven
Rev. 20. 9 [compassed] the camp of the saints about

COMPASS about as a chain, to —
To encircle as with a chain, עָנַק *anaq.*
Psa. 73. 6 pride compasseth them about as a chain

COMPASS about, that —
Set round about one, מֵסַב [partic. *sabab,* 5].
Psa 140. 9 the head of those that compass me about

COMPASS, to fetch a —

1. *To be or go round about,* סָבַב *sabab.*
2 Ki 3. 9 they fetched a compass of seven days'

2. *To be or go round about,* סָבַב *sabab,* 2.
Num34. 5 the border shall fetch a compass from A.
Josh 15. 3 went up to Adar, and fetched a compass

3. *To set or go round about,* סָבַב *sabab,* 5.
2 Sa 5. 23 Thou shalt not go up; (but) fetch a com.

4. *To come round about,* περιέρχομαι *perierchomai.*
Acts 28. 13 from thence we fetched a compass and ca.

COMPASS round, to —

1. *To go round about,* סָבַב *sabab.*
Job 16. 13 His archers compass me round about

2. *To be round about,* סָבַב *sabab,* 2.
Gen 19. 4 men of the city..compassed the house r.

3. *To circle round about,* περικυκλόω *perikukloō.*
Luke 19. 43 compass thee round, and keep thee in

COMPASSED (about) with, to be —
To be laid round about, περίκειμαι *perikeimai.*
Heb. 5. 2 he himself also is compassed with infir.
12. 1 seeing we also are compassed about with

COMPASSION —
Mercies, tender compassion, רַחֲמִים *rachamim.*
1 Ki. 8. 50 give them compassion before them who
2 Ch. 30. 9 your children (shall find) compassion
Lam. 3. 22 we are not consumed..because his comp.
Zech. 7. 9 show mercy and compassions every man

COMPASSION, full of —
Merciful, compassionate, רַחוּם *rachum.*
Psa 78 38 he, (being) full of compassion, forgave
86. 15 thou, O Lord, (art) a God full of compas.
111. 4 LORD (is) gracious, and full of compassion
112. 4 (he is) gracious, and full of compassion
145. 8 LORD (is) gracious, and full of compassion

COMPASSION, to be moved with —
To have the bowels yearning, σπλαγχνίζομαι *spla.*
Matt. 9. 36 he was moved with compassion on them
14. 14 and was moved with compassion toward
18. 27 the lord..was moved with compassion
Mark 1. 41 Jesus, moved with compassion, put forth
6. 34 and was moved with compassion toward

COMPASSION, to have —

1. *To pity, spare,* חָמַל *chamal.*
Exod. 2. 6 she had compassion on him, and said
1 Sa 23. 21 Blessed (be) ye..for ye have compassion
2 Ch. 36. 15 because he had compassion on his people
36. 17 had no compassion upon young man or
Eze 16. 5 None eye pitied..to have compassion upon

2. *To love, pity, be merciful,* רָחַם *racham,* 3.
Lam. 3. 32 yet will he have compassion according to
Mic 7. 19 will turn again he will have compassion

3. *To have the bowels yearning,* σπλαγχνίζομαι.
Matt 15. 32 I have compassion on the multitude
20. 34 Jesus had compassion on them, and
Mark 8. 2 I have compassion on the multitude
9. 22 any thing, have compassion on us, and
Luke 7. 13 when the Lord saw her, he had compas.
10. 33 when he saw him, he had compassion
15. 20 his father saw him, and had compassion

COMPASSION of, to have —

1. *To show mildness, kindness,* ἐλεέω *eleeō.*
Jude 22 [of some have compassion, making a di.]

2. *To suffer with (another),* συμπαθέω *sumpatheō.*
Heb. 10. 34 ye had compassion of me in my bonds

COMPASSION on, to have —

1. *To love, pity, be merciful,* רָחַם *racham,* 3.
1 Ki 8. 50 that they may have compassion on them
2 Ki. 13. 23 the LORD..had compassion on them, and
Isa 49. 15 that she should not have compassion on
Jer. 12. 15 I will return, and have compassion on

2. *To show mildness, kindness,* ἐλεέω *eleeō.*
Matt 18. 33 thou also have had compassion on thy
Mark 5. 19 the Lord..hath had compassion on thee

3. *Display moderation,* μετριοπαθέω *metriopatheō.*
Heb. 5. 2 Who can have compassion on the ignorant

4. *To have pity or mercy,* οἰκτείρω *oikteirō.*
Rom 9. 15 and I will have compassion on
9. 15 on whom I will have compassion

COMPASSION upon, to have —
To love, pity, be merciful, רָחַם *racham,* 3.
Deut 13. 17 show thee mercy, and have compassion u.
30. 3 the LORD..will..have compassion upon

COMPASSION one of another, having —
Suffering with (another), συμπαθής *sumpathēs.*
1 Pe. 3. 8 having compassion one of another, love as

COMPEL, to —

1. *To press, compel,* אָנַס *anas.*
Esth. 1. 8 none did compel: for so the king had

2. *To drive, force,* נָדַח *nadach,* 5.
2 Ch.21. 11 caused..and compelled Judah (thereto)

3. *To break forth upon, urge,* פָּרַץ *parats.*
1 Sa. 28. 23 But his servants..compelled him

4. *To impress (as on public service),* ἀγγαρεύω *agg.*
Matt 27. 32 Simon by name, him they compelled to
Mark15. 21 they compel one Simon a Cyrenian, who

5. *To necessitate, compel,* ἀναγκάζω *anagkazō.*
Luke14. 23 compel (them) to come in, that my house
Acts 26. 11 I punished them..and compelled (them)
2 Co.12. 11 I am become a fool..ye have compelled
Gal. 2. 3 a Greek, was compelled to be circumcised
2. 14 why compellest thou the Gentiles to live

COMPEL to serve —
Do work by means of, עָבַד בְּ *abad be*; Lev. 25. 39.

COMPEL to go, to —
To impress (as on public service), ἀγγαρεύω *agga.*
Matt. 5. 41 whosoever shall compel thee to go a mile

COMPLAIN, to —

1. *To sigh habitually,* אָנַן *anan,* 7a.
Num11. 1 (when)the people complained, it displeas.
Lam. 3. 39 Wherefore doth a living man complain

2. *To weep,* בָּכָה *bakah.*
Job 31. 38 the furrows likewise thereof complain

3. *To contend, strive,* רִיב *rib.*
Judg21. 22 their brethren come unto us to complain

4. *To meditate, talk,* שִׂיחַ *siach.*
Job 7. 11 I will complain in the bitterness of my
Psa. 77. 3 I complained, and my spirit was overwh.

COMPLAINER —
Finding fault with one's lot, μεμψίμοιρος *memps.*
Jude 16 These are murmurers, complainers, walk.

COMPLAINING —
Cry, outcry, צְוָחָה *tsevacha.*
Psa.144. 14 (there be) no complaining in our streets

COMPLAINT —

1. *Meditation, talk,* שִׂיחַ *siach.*
1 Sa. 1. 16 out of the abundance of my complaint
Job 7. 13 my couch shall ease my complaint
9. 27 I will forget my complaint, I will leave
10. 1 I will leave my complaint upon myself
21. 4 As for me, (is) my complaint to man? and
23. 2 Even to day (is) my complaint bitter: my
Psa. 55. 2 I mourn in my complaint, and make a
102. *title.* poureth out his complaint before the
142. 2 I poured out my complaint before him

2. *Cause of complaint,* αἰτίαμα *aitiama.*
Acts 25. 7 [laid many grievous complaints against]

COMPLETE —
Perfect, complete, תָּמִים *tamim.*
Lev. 23. 15 seven sabbaths shall be complete

COMPLETE, to —
To fill up, fill full, πληρόω *plēroō.*
Col. 2. 10 ye are complete in him, which is the head
4 12 that ye may stand perfect and [complete]

COMPOSITION —
Measure, proper quantity, מַתְכֹּנֶת *mathkōneth.*
Exod30. 32 neither shall ye make..after the comp.
30. 37 not make..according to the composition

COMPOUND —
Mixing, רֹקַח *roqach.*
Exod30. 25 an ointment compound after the art of

COMPOUND, to —
To perfume, season, spice, רָקַח *raqach.*
Exod.30. 33 Whosoever compoundeth (any) like it

COMPREHEND, to —

1. *To know, be acquainted with,* יָדַע *yada.*
Job 37. 5 great things..which we cannot compre.

2. *To contain, comprehend,* כּוּל *kul.*
Isa. 40. 12 comprehended the dust of the earth in a

3. *To receive fully,* καταλαμβάνω *katalambanō.*
John 1. 5 and the darkness comprehended it not
Eph. 3. 18 May be able to comprehend with all saints

COMPREHENDED, to be briefly —
To sum up under one head, ἀνακεφαλαιόω.
Rom.13. 9 if..any other..is briefly comprehended

CO-NAN'-IAH, כָּנַנְיָהוּ *Jah is founding.*
A chief Levite in the time of Josiah, B.C. 610.
2 Ch.35. 9 C. also, and Shemaiah and..his brethren

CONCEAL, to —

1. *To keep silence regarding anything,* חָרַשׁ *charash.*
Job 41. 12 I will not conceal his parts, nor his pow.

2. *To hide, cut off,* כָּחַד *kachad.*
Job 6. 10 I have not concealed the words of the
27. 11 (is) with the Almighty will I not conceal

Psa. 40. 10 I have not concealed thy loving kindness
Jer. 50. 2 Declare ye..publish, (and) conceal not

3. *To cover,* כָּסָה *kasah.*
Prov.12. 23 A prudent man concealeth knowledge

4. *To cover,* כָּסָה *kasah,* 3.
Gen. 37. 26 if we slay our brother, and conceal his
Deut.13. 8 spare, neither shalt thou conceal him
Prov.11. 13 he that is of a faithful spirit concealeth

5. *To hide,* סָתַר *sathar,* 5.
Prov.25. 2 (It is) the glory of God to conceal a

CONCEIT —

1. *Imagery, imagination,* מַשְׂכִּית *maskith.*
Prov 18. 11 and as an high wall in his own conceit

2. *Eye,* עַיִן *ayin.*
Prov 26. 5 lest he be wise in his own conceit
26. 12 Seest thou a man wise in his own conceit?
26. 16 The sluggard (is) wiser in his own conceit
28. 11 The rich man (is) wise in his own conceit

CONCEITS, in your own —

Beside, or alongside of yourselves, παρ' ἑαυτοῖς [*para*].
Rom.11. 25 lest ye should be wise [in] your own conc.
12. 16 Be not wise in your own conceits

CONCEIVE, to —

1. *Pregnant,* הָרָה *harah.*
Judg 13. 5 lo, thou shalt conceive, and bear a son
13. 7 Behold, thou shalt conceive, and bear a
Isa. 7. 14 a virgin shall conceive, and bear a son

2. *To conceive, become pregnant,* הָרָה *harah.*
Gen. 4. 1 she conceived..and said, I have gotten a
4. 17 and she conceived, and bare Enoch
16. 4 he went in unto Hagar, and she conceived
16. 4 when she saw that she had conceived, her
16. 5 when she saw that she had conceived
21. 2 Sarah conceived, and bare Abraham a son
25. 21 and Rebekah his wife conceived
29. 32 Leah conceived, and bare a son, and she
29. 33, 34, 35 she conceived again, and bare a son
30. 5 Bilhah conceived, and bare Jacob a son
30. 7 Bilhah, Rachel's maid, conceived again
30. 17 she conceived, and bare Jacob the fifth
30. 19 Leah conceived again, and bare Jacob
30. 23 she conceived, and bare a son; and said
38. 3, 4 she conceived, and bare a son; and he
38. 18 came in unto her; and she conceived by
Exod.2. 2 And the woman conceived, and bare a son
Num 11. 12 Have I conceived all this people? have I
Judg.13. 3 but thou shalt conceive, and bear a son
1 Sa. 1. 20 was come about after Hannah had con.
2. 21 she conceived, and bare three sons and
2 Sa. 11. 5 the woman conceived, and sent and told
2 Ki. 4. 17 the woman conceived, and bare a son at
1 Ch. 7. 23 she conceived and bare a son, and he
Job 15. 35 They conceive mischief, and bring forth
Psa. 7. 14 he travaileth..and hath conceived misc.
Isa 8. 3 went unto the prophetess; and she con.
33. 11 Ye shall conceive chaff; ye shall bring
59. 4 they conceive mischief, and bring forth
59. 13 conceiving and uttering from the heart
Hos. 1. 3 Gomer..which conceived, and bare him
1. 6 she conceived again, and bare a daughter
1. 8 when she had weaned Loruhamah, she co.

3. *To conceive, become pregnant,* הָרָה *harah.*
Song 3. 4 into the chamber of her that conceived
Hos. 2. 5 she that conceived them hath done shame.

4. *To be sown, receive seed,* זָרַע *zara,* 2.
Num. 5. 28 she shall be free, and shall conceive seed

5. *To think, devise, reckon,* חָשַׁב *chashab.*
Jer. 49. 30 Nebuchadrezzar..hath conceived a pur.

6. *To be or become warm, to conceive,* יָחַם *yacham.*
Gen. 30. 38 that they should conceive when they
30. 39 the flocks conceived before the rods, and

7. *To become warm, conceive,* יָחַם *yacham,* 3.
Gen. 30. 41 whensoever the stronger cattle did conce.
30. 41 that they might conceive among the rods
31. 10 at the time that the cattle conceived
Psa. 51. 5 and in sin did my mother conceive me

8. *To beget, conceive,* γεννάω *gennaō.*
Matt. 1 20 that which is conceived in her is of the

9. *For a casting down,* εἰς καταβολήν [*katabolē*].
Heb. 11. 11 Sara herself received strength to conceive

10. *To have a lying,* ἔχω κοίτην *echō koitēn.*
Rom. 9. 10 when Rebecca also had conceived by one

11. *To receive (seed),* συλλαμβάνω *sullambanō.*
Luke 1. 24 after those days..Elisabeth conceived
1. 31 thou shalt conceive in thy womb, and
1. 36 she hath also conceived a son in her old
2. 21 named of the angel before he was con.
Jas. 1. 15 when lust hath conceived, it bringeth

12. *To place, put, set,* τίθημι *tithēmi.*
Acts 5. 4 why hast thou conceived this thing in

CONCEIVE again, to —

To add, יָסַף *yasaph,* 5.
Gen. 38. 5 she yet again conceived, and bare a son

CONCEIVE seed, to —

To cause to sow, let sow, זָרַע *zara,* 5.
Lev. 12. 2 If a woman have conceived seed, and

CONCEIVED, to be —

To be conceived, הָרָה *harah,* 4.
Job 3. 3 There is a man child conceived

CONCEPTION —

1. *Conception,* הֵרוֹן *heron.*
Gen. 3. 16 I will greatly multiply thy..conception

2. *Conception,* הֵרָיוֹן *herayon.*
Ruth 4. 13 the LORD gave her conception, and she
Hos. 9. 11 from the womb, and from the conception

CONCERN, (those) things which —

The things about, τὰ (περὶ) *ta peri.*
Acts 28. 31 those things which concern the Lord J.
2 Co.11. 30 I will glory of the things which concern

CONCERNING —

1. *Unto, with reference to,* אֶל *el.*
1 Sa. 3. 12 all (things) which I have spoken concern.

1a. (*In reference*) *to,* לְ *le.*
Gen. 19. 21 concerning this thing also

2. *Concerning,* עַל *al.*
Gen. 24. 9 the servant..sware to him concerning
Ezra. 5. 5 they returned answer by letter concerning
5. 17 send his pleasure to us concerning this
7. 14 enquire concerning; Dan. 2. 18; 5. 29; 6. 12.

3. *Concerning, on account of,* עַל־אוֹדֹת *al odoth.*
Gen. 26. 32 servants came, and told him concerning
Josh 14. 6 said unto Moses the man of God concern.

4. *Concerning, on the side of,* צַד *tsad.*
Dan. 6. 4 against Daniel concerning the kingdom

5. *With a view or regard to,* εἰς *eis.*
Acts 2. 25 David speaketh concerning him, I fore.
Rom 16. 19 I would have you..simple concerning evil
2 Co. 8. 23 my partner and fellow helper concern.
Eph. 5. 32 speak [concerning] Christ and the church
1 Th. 5. 18 the will of God in Christ Jesus concern.

6. *Down or over against, as to,* κατά (acc.) *kata.*
Eph. 4. 22 concerning the former conversation, the
Phil. 3. 6 Concerning zeal, persecuting the church

7. *About, concerning, for,* περί (gen.) *peri.*
Matt. 4. 6 He shall give his angels charge concern.
11. 7 began to say unto the multitudes concer.
16. 11 I spake (it) not to you concerning bread
Mark. 5. 16 they..told them..concerning the swine
7. 17 disciples asked him [concerning] the
Luke 2. 17 the saying which was told them concern.
7. 24 began to speak unto the people concern.
24. 19 they said unto him, Concerning Jesus of
24. 44 written..(in) the Prophets..concerning
John 7. 12 there was much murmuring..concerning
7. 32 the people murmured such things concer.
9. 18 the Jews did not believe concerning him
11. 19 to comfort them concerning their brother
Acts 1. 16 the Holy Ghost..spake before concerning
19. 39 if ye enquire anything [concerning] other
21. 24 whereof they were informed concerning
22. 18 will not receive thy testimony concern.
23. 15 as though ye would enquire..concerning
24. 24 heard him concerning the faith in Christ
25. 16 licence to answer for himself concerning
28. 21 We neither received letters..concerning
28. 23 persuading them concerning Jesus, both
Rom. 1. 3 Concerning his Son Jesus Christ our Lord
1 Co. 7. 25 concerning virgins I have no command.
12. 1 concerning spiritual (gifts), brethren, I
16. 1 concerning the collection for the saints
1 Th. 3. 2 to comfort you [concerning] your faith
4. 13 concerning them which are asleep, that
Heb. 7. 14 of which tribe Moses spake nothing con.
11. 20 Isaac blessed Jacob and Esau concerning
11. 22 Joseph..gave commandment concerning
1 Jo. 2. 26 These..have I written unto you concern.

8. *About, concerning,* περί (acc.) *peri.*
1 Ti. 1. 19 which some having put away, concerning
6. 21 Which some professing have erred con.
2 Ti. 2. 18 Who concerning the truth have erred
3. 8 men of corrupt minds, reprobate concer.

9. *In behalf of,* ὑπέρ (gen.) *huper.*
Rom 9. 27 Esaias also crieth concerning Israel

10. *Concerning the matter(s) of,* עַל־דְּבַר *al dabar.*
2 Sa. 18. 5 when the king gave..charge concerning
Jer. 7. 22 I spake not..concerning burnt offerings
14. 1 The word..that came to Jeremiah con.

CONCERNING, as —

1. *With a view to the matter of,* εἰς λόγον *eis logon.*
Phil. 4. 15 no church communicated with me as con.

2. *Down through, as to,* κατά (acc.) *kata.*
Rom 9. 5 of whom as concerning the flesh Christ
11. 28 As concerning the Gospel, (they are)
2 Co.11. 21 I speak as concerning reproach, as though

3. *About, concerning, for,* περί (gen.) *peri.*
Acts 28. 22 as concerning this sect, we know that
1 Co. 8. 4 As concerning therefore the eating of

CONCERNING that, as —

Because that, ὅτι *hoti.*
Acts 13 34 as concerning that he raised him up from

CONCERNING, the things —

The things about or concerning, τὰ περὶ *ta peri.*
Luke22. 37 for the things concerning me have an end
24. 27 he expounded..the things concerning
Acts 8. 12 Philip preaching the things concerning
19. 8 disputing and persuading the things con.

CONCISION —

A cutting down, κατατομή *katatomē.*
Phil. 3. 2 beware of evil workers, beware of the co.

CONCLUDE, to —

1. *To reckon, account,* λογίζομαι *logizomai.*
Rom. 3. 28 we conclude that a man is justified by

2. *To judge, decide,* κρίνω *krinō.*
Acts 21. 25 we have written (and) concluded that

3. *To shut or close up together,* συγκλείω *sugkleiō.*
Rom 11. 32 God hath concluded them all in unbelief
Gal. 3. 22 the Scripture hath concluded all under

CONCLUSION —

End, סוֹף *suph.*
Eccl.12. 13 Let us hear the conclusion of the whole

CONCORD —

A sounding together, συμφώνησις *sumphōnēsis.*
2 Co. 6. 15 what concord hath Christ with Belial?

CONCOURSE —

1. *To hum, sound, make a noise,* הָמָה *hamah.*
Prov. 1. 21 She crieth in the chief place of concourse

2. *A turning together, gathering,* συστροφή *sustrophē.*
Acts 19. 40 we may give an account of this concourse

CONCUBINE —

1. *Concubine, singing damsel,* לְחֵנָה *lechenah.*
Dan. 5. 2 his wives, and his concubines, might
5. 3 his wives, and his concubines, drank in
5. 23 thy wives, and thy concubines, have drunk

2. *Concubine, a half wife,* פִּילֶגֶשׁ *pilegesh.*
Gen. 22. 24 his concubine, whose name (was) Reumah
25. 6 unto the sons of the concubines, which
35. 22 Reuben..lay with..his father's concubine
36. 12 Timna was concubine to Eliphaz, Esau's
Judg 8. 31 his concubine that (was) in Shechem, she
19. 1 who took to him a concubine out of Be.
19. 2 his concubine played the whore against
19. 9 when the man rose up..he, and his con.
19. 10 (there were) with him..his concubine
19. 24 my daughter, a maiden, and his concu.
19. 25 the man took his concubine, and brought
19. 27 the woman his concubine was fallen down
19. 29 laid hold on his concubine, and divided
20. 4 I came into Gibeah..I and my concubine
20. 5 my concubine have they forced, that she
20. 6 I took my concubine, and cut her in
2 Sa. 3. 7 Saul had a concubine, whose name (was)
3. 7 hast thou gone in unto my father's concu.?
5. 13 David took (him) more concubines and
15. 16 the king left ten women, which (were) con.
16. 21 Go in unto thy father's concubines, which
16. 22 Absalom went in unto his father's concu.
19. 5 the lives of thy wives, and..thy concu.
20. 3 the king took the ten women (his) concu.
21. 11 it was told David what..the concubine of
1 Ki.11. 3 And he had..three hundred concubines
1 Ch. 1. 32 the sons of Keturah, Abraham's concu.
2. 46 Ephah, Caleb's concubine, bare Haran
2. 48 Maachah, Caleb's concubine, bare Sheber
3. 9 besides the sons of the concubines, and
7. 14 his concubine the Aramitess bare Machir
2 Ch.11. 21 above all his wives and his concubines
11. 21 eighteen wives, and three score concu.
Esth 2. 14 chamberlain, which kept the concubines
Song 6. 8 three score queens, and four score concu.
6. 9 the queens and the concubines, and they

CONCUPISCENCE —

Over desire, ἐπιθυμία *epithumia.*
Rom 7. 8 wrought in me all manner of concupis.
Col. 3. 5 inordinate affection, evil concupiscence
1 Th. 4. 5 Not in the lust of concupiscence, even

CONDEMN, to —

1. *To make or declare wrong* (*in law*), רָשַׁע *rasha,* 5.
Exod22. 9 whom the judges shall condemn, he shall
Deut 25. 1 shall justify the righteous, and condemn
Job 9. 20 justify myself, mine own mouth shall con.
10. 2 I will say unto God, Do not condemn me
15. 6 Thine own mouth condemneth thee, and
32. 3 had found no answer, and (yet) had con.
34. 17 wilt thou condemn him that is most just?
40. 8 wilt thou condemn me, that thou mayest
Psa. 37. 33 The LORD will not..condemn him when
94. 21 They gather themselves..and condemn
Prov 12. 2 a man of wicked devices will he condemn
17. 15 he that condemneth the just, even they
Isa. 50. 9 who (is) he (that) shall condemn me?
54. 17 against thee in judgment thou shalt con.

2. *To fine, oppress,* עָנַשׁ *anash.*
2 Ch.36. 3 condemned the land in an hundred

3. *Know thing against,* καταγινώσκω *kataginōskō.*
1 Jo. 3. 20 if our heart condemn us, God is greater
3. 21 if our heart condemn us not, (then) have

4. *To judge against,* καταδικάζω *katadikazō.*
Matt 12. 7 would not have condemned the guiltless
12. 37 by thy words thou shalt be condemned
Luke 6. 37 condemn not, and ye shall not be con.
Jas. 5. 6 Ye have condemned (and) killed the just

5. *To judge down, condemn,* κατακρίνω *katakrinō.*
Matt 12. 41 with this generation, and shall condemn
12. 42 The queen of the south..shall condemn
20. 18 and they shall condemn him to death
27. 3 Judas..when he saw that he was con.

Mark10. 33 and they shall condemn him to death
14. 64 they all condemned him to be guilty of
Luke11. 32 The men of Nineve..shall condemn it
11. 31 The queen of the south shall..condemn
John 8. 10 [Woman..hath no man condemned thee?]
8. 11 [Neither do I condemn thee; go, and sin]
Rom. 2. 1 thou judgest another, thou condemnest
8. 3 and for sin, condemned sin in the flesh
8. 34 Who (is) he that condemneth? (It is) C.
1 Co.11. 32 we should not be condemned with the
Heb. 11. 7 by the which he condemned the world
Jas. 5. 9 Grudge not..brethren, lest ye be [cond.]
2 Pe. 2. 6 condemned (them) with an overthrow

6. *To judge, pronounce judgment,* κρίνω *krinō.*
John 3. 17 God sent not his Son..to condemn the
3. 18 He that believeth on him is not condem.
3. 18 he that believeth not is condem.Ac.13.27.
Rom 14. 22 Happy (is) he that condemneth not

7. *Toward a judging down,* πρὸς κατάκρισιν [*pros*].
2 Co. 7. 3 I speak not (this) to condemn (you): for

CONDEMN, that —
To judge or act as a magistrate, שָׁפַט *shaphat.*
Psa.109. 31 save (him) from those that condemn his

CONDEMNED —
To fine, oppress, עָנַשׁ *anash.*
Amos2. 8 they drink the wine of the condemned

CONDEMNED of one's self —
One judged down by himself, αὐτοκατάκριτος.
Titus 3. 11 and sinneth, being condemned of himself

CONDEMNED, to be —
1. *To go out (declared) wrong,* יָצָא רָשָׁע *yatsa rasha.*
Psa.109. 7 he shall be judged, let him be condemned
2. *With a view to a judgment,* εἰς κρίμα *eis krima.*
Luke24. 20 our rulers delivered him to be condemned

CONDEMNED, that cannot be —
One against whom nothing is known, ἀκατάγνωστος
Titus 2. 8 Sound speech, that cannot be condemned

CONDEMNATION —
1. *The judgment against,* κατάκριμα *katakrima.*
Rom. 5. 16 the judgment (was) by one to condemna.
5. 18 (come) upon all men to condemnation
8. 1 no condemnation to them which are in C.

2. *Condemning,* κατάκρισις *katakrisis.*
2 Co. 3. 9 if the ministration of condemnation
3. *The judgment (pronounced),* κρίμα *krima.*
Luke23. 40 seeing thou art in the same condemnation
1 Co.11. 34 ye come not together unto condemnation
1 Ti. 3. 6 lest..he fall into the condemnation of the
Jas. 3. 1 we shall receive the greater condemnation
Jude 4 who were..ordained to this condemnation

4. *The process of judgment,* κρίσις *krisis.*
John 3. 19 this is the condemnation, that light is
5. 24 He..shall not come into condemnation
Jas. 5. 12 swear not..lest ye fall into condemnation

CONDEMNING —
To make or declare wrong (in law) רָשַׁע *rasha,* 5.
1 Ki. 8. 32 judge thy servants, condemning the

CONDESCEND, to —
To be led away with, συναπάγομαι *sunapagomai.*
Rom 12. 16 but condescend to men of low estate

CONDITIONS of —
The things toward or touching, τὰ πρός *ta pros.*
Luke14. 32 he sendeth..and desireth conditions of

CONDUCT, to —
1. *To cause to go (or lead) over,* עָבַר *abar,* 5.
2 Sa. 19. 40 the people of Judah conducted the king
2. *To send away or forth,* שָׁלַח *shalach,* 3.
2 Sa. 19. 31 with the king, to conduct him over Jor.
3. *To set down,* καθίστημι *kathistēmi.*
Acts 17. 15 they that conducted Paul brought him

CONDUCT forth, to —
To send forward, προπέμπω *propempō.*
1 Co.16. 11 conduct him forth in peace, that he may

CONDUCT over, to —
To cause to go (or lead) over, עָבַר *abar,* 5.
2 Sa. 19. 15 to meet the king, to conduct the king o.

CONDUIT —
Aqueduct, תְּעָלָה *tealah.*
2 Ki. 18. 17 stood by the conduit of the upper pool
20. 20 made a pool and a conduit, and brought
Isa. 7. 3 at the end of the conduit of the upper
36. 2 he stood by the conduit of the upper

CONEY —
A hare, hedgehog, or rabbit, שָׁפָן *shaphan.*
Lev. 11. 5 the coney, because he cheweth the cud
Deut 14. 7 (as) the camel, and the hare, and the coney
Psa.104. 18 wild goats; (and) the rocks for the conies
Prov 30. 26 The conies (are but) a feeble folk, yet

CONFECTION —
Perfume, spice, רֹקַח *roqach.*
Exod30. 35 a confection after the art of the apothec.

CONFECTIONARY —
Perfumer, רַקָּחָה *raqqachah.*
1 Sa. 8. 13 take your daughters (to be) confectionar.

CONFEDERACY —
1. *A covenant, agreement,* בְּרִית *berith.*
Obad. 7 the men of thy confederacy have brought
2. *A conspiracy,* קֶשֶׁר *qesher.*
Isa. 8. 12 Say ye not, A confederacy, to all (them to
8. 12 this people shall say, A confederacy

CONFEDERATE —
Master of a covenant, an ally, בַּעַל בְּרִית [*baal*].
Gen. 14. 13 and these (were) confederate with Abram

CONFEDERATE, to be —
1. *To rest,* נוּחַ *nuach.*
Isa. 7. 2 saying, Syria is confederate with Ephraim
2. *To cut a covenant,* כָּרַת בְּרִית *karath berith.*
Psa. 83. 5 they are confederate against thee

CONFER, to —
1. *(His) word was,* דָּבָר הָיָה *dabar hayah.*
1 Ki. 1. 7 he conferred with Joab the son of Zeruiah
2. *To put (anything) up toward one,* προσανατίθημι.
Gal. 1. 16 immediately I conferred not with flesh
3. *To talk together,* συλλαλέω *sullaleō.*
Acts 25. 12 when he had conferred with the council
4. *To cast (words) together,* συμβάλλω *sumballō.*
Acts 4. 15 they conferred among themselves

CONFERENCE, add in —
To put (anything) up toward one, προσανατίθημι.
Gal. 2. 6 in conference added nothing to me

CONFESS, to —
1. *To confess (by throwing out the hand),* יָדָה *yadah,* 5.
1 Ki. 8. 33 shall turn again to thee, and confess thy
8. 35 confess thy name, and turn from their
2 Ch. 6. 24 shall return and confess thy name, and
6. 26 confess thy name, and turn from their
Job 40. 14 Then will I also confess unto thee that
Psa. 32. 5 I will confess my transgressions unto the
Prov.28. 13 whoso confesseth and forsaketh (them)
2. *To confess (for oneself),* יָדָה *yadah,* 7.
Lev. 5. 5 he shall confess that he hath sinned in
16. 21 confess over him all the iniquities of
26. 40 If they shall confess their iniquity, and
Num. 5. 7 they shall confess their sin which they
Ezra 10. 1 when he had confessed, weeping and
Neh. 1. 6 confess the sins of the children of Israel
9. 2 stood and confessed their sins, and the
9. 3 (another) fourth part they confessed, and
Dan. 9. 20 confessing my sin and the sin of my people
3. *To speak out the same,* ἐξομολογέω *exomologeō.*
Matt. 3. 6 were baptised of him in Jordan, confessing
Mark 1. 5 were all baptised of him..confessing their
Acts 19. 18 and confessed, and showed their deeds
Rom14. 11 and every tongue shall confess to God
15. 9 For this cause I will confess to thee
Phil. 2. 11 every tongue should confess that Jesus
James5. 16 Confess (your) faults one to another, and
Rev. 3. 5 will [confess] his name before my Father
4. *To speak the same thing,* ὁμολογέω *homologeō.*
Matt10. 32 Whosoever therefore shall confess me
10. 32 him will I confess also before my Father
Luke12. 8 Whosoever shall confess me before men
12. 8 him shall the Son of man also confess
John 1. 20 he confessed, and denied not; but con.
9. 22 if any man did confess that he was Christ
12. 42 because of the Pharisees they did not con.
Acts 23. 8 but the Pharisees confess both
24. 14 this I confess unto thee, that after the
Rom.10. 9 if thou shalt confess with thy mouth the
Heb. 11. 13 confessed that they were strangers and
1 Jo. 1. 9 If we confess our sins, he is faithful and
4. 2 that confesseth that Jesus Christ is come
4. 3 every spirit that confesseth not that J.
4. 15 Whosoever shall confess that Jesus is the
2 Jo. 7 who confess not that Jesus Christ is

CONFESSION, to make —
To confess (for oneself), יָדָה *yadah,* 7.
2 Ch. 30. 22 making confession to the LORD God of
Dan. 9. 4 made my confession, and said, O Lord

CONFESSION —
1. *Confession (by casting out the hand),* תּוֹדָה *todah.*
Jos. 7. 19 make confession unto him; and tell me
Ezra 10. 11 make confession unto the LORD God of
2. *Assent, profession,* ὁμολογία *homologia.*
1 Ti. 6. 13 who before..Pilate witnessed a good con.

CONFESSION is made —
To speak the same thing, ὁμολογέω *homologeō.*
Rom.10. 10 with the mouth confession is made unto

CONFIDENCE —
1. *Confidence, trust,* בֶּטַח *betach.*
Eze. 28. 26 they shall dwell with confidence, when I
2. *Confidence, trust,* בִּטְחָה *bitchah.*
Isa. 30. 15 in quietness and in confidence shall be
3. *Confidence, trust,* בִּטָּחוֹן *bittachon.*
2 Ki.18. 19 What confidence (is) this wherein thou
Isa. 36. 4 What confidence (is) this wherein thou
4. *Firmness, stoutness,* כֶּסֶל *kesel.*
Prov. 3. 26 the LORD shall be thy confidence, and
5. *Firmness, stoutness,* כִּסְלָה *kislah.*
Job 4. 6 (Is) not (this) thy fear, thy confidence
6. *Confidence, trust,* מִבְטָח *mibtach.*
Job 18. 14 His confidence shall be rooted out of his
31. 24 said to the..gold,(Thou art)my confidence
Psa. 65. 5 the confidence of all the ends of the earth
Prov 14. 26 In the fear of the LORD (is) strong confiden.
21. 22 casteth down the strength of the confid.
25. 19 Confidence in an unfaithful man..(is like)
Jer. 2. 37 the LORD hath rejected thy confidences
48. 13 house of Israel was ashamed of..their con.
Eze. 29. 16 it shall be no more the confidence of the
7. *Free-spokenness, boldness,* παῤῥησία *parrhēsia.*
Acts 28. 31 with all confidence, no man forbidding
Heb. 3. 6 if we hold fast the confidence and the
10. 35 Cast not away therefore your confidence
1 Jo. 2. 28 when he shall appear, we may have con.
3. 21 (then) have we confidence toward God
5. 14 this is the confidence that we have in him
8. *Confident persuasion,* πεποίθησις *pepoithēsis.*
2 Co. 1. 15 in this confidence I was minded to come
8. 22 upon the great confidence which (I have)
10. 2 when I am present with that confidence
Eph. 3. 12 In whom we have..access with confidence
Phil. 3. 4 Though I might also have confidence in
9. *What stands under one, substratum,* ὑπόστασις.
2 Co. 11. 17 as it were foolishly, in this confidence
Heb. 3. 14 if we hold the beginning of our confidence

CONFIDENCE, to have —
1. *To have good courage,* θαῤῥέω *tharrheō.*
2 Co. 7. 16 I rejoice therefore that I have confidence
2. *To persuade,* πείθω *peithō.*
2 Co. 2. 3 having confidence in you all, that my
Gal. 5. 10 I have confidence in you through the L.
Phil. 1. 25 having this confidence, I know that I
3. 3 and have no confidence in the flesh
2 Th. 3. 4 we have confidence in the Lord touching
Phm. 21 Having confidence in thy obedience I

CONFIDENCE, to put —
To be confident, have trust, בָּטַח *batach.*
Judg. 9. 26 the men of Shechem put their confidence
Psa.118. 8, 9 (It is) better..than to put confidence in
Mic. 7. 5 put ye not confidence in a guide

CONFIDENT —
1. *To have good courage,* θαῤῥέω *tharrheō.*
2 Co. 5. 6 (we are) always confident, knowing that
2. *What stands under one, substratum,* ὑπόστασις.
2 Co. 9. 4 ashamed in this same confident boasting

CONFIDENT, to be —
1. *To be confident, have trust,* בָּטַח *batach.*
Psa. 27. 3 against me, in this (will) I (be) confident
Prov 14. 16 but the fool rageth, and is confident
2. *To have good courage,* θαῤῥέω *tharrheō.*
2 Co. 5. 8 We are confident, (I say), and willing
3. *To persuade,* πείθω *peithō.*
Rom. 2. 19 And art confident that thou thyself art
Phil. 1. 6 Being confident of this very thing, that

CONFIDENT, to wax —
To persuade, πείθω *peithō.*
Phil. 1. 14 many of the brethren..waxing confident

CONFIRM, to —
1. *To harden,* אָמֵץ *amats,* 3.
Isa. 35. 3 Strengthen..and confirm the feeble knees
2. *To strengthen,* גָּבַר *gabar,* 5.
Dan. 9. 27 he shall confirm the covenant with many
3. *To keep hold on,* חָזַק *chazaq,* 5.
2 Ki. 15. 19 his hand might be with him to confirm
Dan. 11. 1 I, stood to confirm and to strengthen him
4. *To establish, make ready,* כּוּן *kun,* 3a.
2 Sa. 7. 24 thou hast confirmed to thyself thy people
Psa. 68. 9 whereby thou didst confirm thine inher.
5. *To establish,* כּוּן *kun,* 5.
1 Ch. 14. 2 that the LORD had confirmed him king
6. *To fill up or out,* מָלֵא *male,* 3.
1 Ki. 1. 14 I also will come in..and confirm thy
7. *To cause to stand, set up, settle,* עָמַד *amad,* 5.
1 Ch. 16. 17 hath confirmed the same to Jacob for a
Psa.105. 10 confirmed the same unto Jacob for a law
8. *To establish, confirm,* קוּם *qum,* 3.
Ruth 4. 7 concerning changing, for to confirm all
Esth. 9. 29 to confirm this second letter of Purim
9. 31 To confirm these days of Purim in their
9. 32 the decree of Esther confirmed these
Eze. 13. 6 to hope that they would confirm the word
9. *To establish, confirm,* קוּם *qum,* 5.
Num30. 14 he confirmeth them, because he held his
Deut27. 26 Cursed (be) he that confirmeth not (all)
Isa. 44. 26 That confirmeth the word of his servant
Dan. 9. 12 he hath confirmed his words, which he
10. *To make firm, strong or sure,* βεβαιόω *bebaioō.*
Mark16. 20 [confirming the word with signs follow.]
Rom 15. 8 to confirm the promises (made) unto the

1 Co. 1. 6 as the testimony of Christ was confirmed
1. 8 Who shall also confirm you unto the end
Heb. 2. 3 was confirmed unto us by them that

11. *To confirm fully,* ἐπιστηρίζω *epistērizō.*
Acts 14. 22 Confirming the souls of the disciples, (and)
15. 32 exhorted the brethren..and confirmed
15. 41 he went through Syria..confirming the

12. *To give power or validity,* κυρόω *kuroō.*
2 Co. 2. 8 that ye would confirm (your) love toward
Gal. 3. 15 (if it be) confirmed, no man disannulleth

13. *To be or act as a mediator,* μεσιτεύω *mesiteuō.*
Heb. 6. 17 Wherein God..confirmed (it) by an oath

CONFIRM before, to —
To give power or validity before, προκυρόω *prokuroō.*
Gal. 3. 17 that was confirmed before of God in Christ

CONFIRMATION —
Steadfast or firm establishment, βεβαίωσις *bebaiōsis.*
Phil. 1. 7 in the defence and confirmation of the
Heb. 6. 16 an oath for confirmation (is) to them an

CONFIRMED, to be —
To be strong, held fast, חָזַק *chazaq.*
2 Ki. 14. 5 as soon as the kingdom was confirmed in

CONFISCATION —
Fine, oppression, עֲנָשׁ *anash.*
Ezra 7. 26 to banishment, or to confiscation of goods

CONFLICT —
Contest, struggle, ἀγών *agōn.*
Phil. 1. 30 Having the same conflict which ye saw
Col. 2. 1 I would that ye knew what great conflict

CONFORMABLE unto, to make —
To make of the same form, συμμορφόω *summorphoō.*
Phil. 3. 10 being made conformable unto his death

CONFORMED to —
Having the same form, σύμμορφος *summorphos.*
Rom. 8. 29 did predestinate (to be) conformed to the

CONFORMED, to be —
To fashion in same way, συσχηματίζω *suschēmatizō.*
Rom 12. 2 be not conformed to this world; but be

CONFOUND, to —
1. *To mix, mingle,* בָּלַל *balal.*
Gen. 11. 7 let us go down, and there confound their
11. 9 the LORD did there confound the langu.

2. *To bring or put down,* חָתַת *chathath,* 5.
Jer. 1. 17 be not dismayed..lest I confound thee

3. *To put to shame utterly,* καταισχύνω *kataischunō.*
1 Co. 1. 27 foolish things of the world to confound
1. 27 the weak things of the world to confou.
1 Pe. 2. 6 he that believeth..shall not be confoun.

4. *To confuse, pour out together,* συγχύνω *sugchunō.*
Acts 2. 6 the multitude came..and were confoun.
9. 22 confounded the Jews which dwelt at D.

CONFOUNDED, to be —
1. *To be ashamed, become pale,* בּוֹשׁ *bosh.*
2 Ki. 19. 26 they were dismayed and confounded
Job 6. 20 They were confounded because they had
Psa. 22. 5 trusted in thee, and were not confounded
35. 4 Let them be confounded and put to shame
71. 13 Let them be confounded (and) consumed
71. 24 they are confounded, for they are brought
83. 17 Let them be confounded and troubled for
97. 7 Confounded be all they that serve graven
129. 5 Let them all be confounded and turned
Isa. 19. 9 that weave net works, shall be confoun.
37. 27 they were dismayed and confounded
Jer. 9. 19 we are greatly confounded, because we
17. 18 Let them be confounded that persecute
17 18 let not me be confounded; let them be
49. 23 Hamath is confounded, and Arpad; for
50. 12 Your mother shall be sore confounded
51. 47 her whole land shall be confounded, and
51. 51 We are confounded, because we have
Eze. 16. 52 be thou confounded also, and bear thy
16. 63 thou mayest remember, and be confoun.
Mic. 7. 16 The nations shall see, and be confound.

2. *To be ashamed, become red,* חָפֵר *chapher.*
Psa. 35 4 Let them be confounded and put to
40. 14 Let them be ashamed and confounded
70. 2 Let them be ashamed and confounded
Isa. 1. 29 ye shall be confounded for the gardens
24. 23 the moon shall be confounded, and the
Jer. 15. 9 she hath been ashamed and confounded
Mic. 3. 7 and the diviners confounded; yea, they

3. *To be ashamed, dried up,* יָבֵשׁ *yabash,* 5.
Psa. 35. 4 [Let them be confounded and put to]
40. 14 Let them be ashamed and confounded
48. 1 Kiriathaim is confounded (and) taken
48. 1 Misgab is confounded and dismayed
48. 20 Moab is confounded; for it is broken
50. 2 Bel is confounded, Merodach is broken
50. 2 her idols are confounded, her images are
51. 17 every founder is confounded by the gra.
Zech. 10. 5 the riders on horses shall be confounded

4. *To be put to shame, blush,* כָּלַם *kalam,* 2.
Psa. 69. 6 let not those that seek thee be confoun.
Isa. 41. 11 all they..shall be ashamed and confoun.
45. 16 They shall be ashamed, and also confou.
45. 17 ye shall not be ashamed nor confounded
50. 7 therefore shall I not be confounded
54. 4 not be ashamed: neither be thou confo.

Jer. 22. 22 then shalt thou be ashamed and confou.
31. 19 I was ashamed, yea, even confounded
Eze. 16. 54 and mayest be confounded in all that
36. 32 be ashamed and confounded for your

5. *To be made or caused to blush,* כָּלַם *kalam,* 6.
Jer. 14. 3 they were ashamed and confounded, and

CONFUSE, to —
To pour out together, confuse, συγχύνω *sugchunō.*
Acts 19. 32 for the assembly was confused; and the

CONFUSED noise —
Shaking, trembling, רַעַשׁ *raash.*
Isa. 9. 5 For every battle..(is) with confused noise

CONFUSION ;—
1. *Shame, paleness,* בֹּשֶׁת *bosheth.*
1 Sa. 20. 30 thou hast chosen..to thine own confusion
20. 30 and unto the confusion of thy mother's
Ezra 9. 7 to a spoil, and to confusion of face, as (it
Psa. 109. 29 cover themselves with their own confus.
Jer. 7. 19 not (provoke) themselves to the confusion
Dan. 9. 7 unto us confusion of faces, as at this day
9. 8 O Lord, to us (belongeth) confusion of

2. *Shame, blushing,* כְּלִמָּה *kelimmah.*
Psa. 44. 15 My confusion (is) continually before me
Isa. 30. 3 trust in the shadow..(your) confusion
45. 16 they shall go to confusion together (that)
61. 7 (for) confusion they shall rejoice in their
Jer. 3. 25 We lie down in our shame, and our conf.
20. 11 (their) everlasting confusion shall never

3. *Lightness, contempt,* קָלוֹן *qalon.*
Job 10. 15 (I am) full of confusion; therefore see

4. *Confusion,* תֶּבֶל *tebel.*
Lev. 18. 23 neither..stand before a beast..it (is) conf.
20. 12 they have wrought confusion: their blood

5. *Emptiness, wasteness,* תֹּהוּ *tohu.*
Isa. 24. 10 The city of confusion is broken down
34. 11 stretch out upon it the line of confusion
41. 29 their molten images (are) wind and conf.

6. *Instability,* ἀκαταστασία *akatastasia.*
1 Co. 14. 33 God is not (the author) of confusion, but
Jas. 3. 16 there (is) confusion and every evil work

7. *Confusion, a pouring out together,* σύγχυσις.
Acts 19. 29 the whole city was filled with confusion

CONFUSION, to be brought to —
To be ashamed, become red, חָפֵר *chapher.*
Psa. 35. 4, 26 Let them be..brought to confusion

CONFUSION, to be put to —
1. *To be ashamed, pale,* בּוֹשׁ *bosh.*
Psa. 71. 1 let me never be put to confusion

2. *To be made to blush,* כָּלַם *kalam,* 2.
Psa. 70. 2 Let them be..put to confusion, that des.

CONGEALED, to be —
To be congealed, hardened. קָפָא *qapha.*
Exod 15. 8 the depths were congealed in the heart

CONGRATULATE, to —
To declare blessed, בָּרַךְ *barak,* 3.
1 Ch. 18. 10 enquire of his welfare, and to congratu.

CONGREGATION —
1. *One dumb or bound,* אֵלֶם *elem.*
Psa. 58. 1 Do ye..speak righteousness, O congrega.

2. *Tribe,* חַיָּה *chaiyah.*
Psa. 68. 10 Thy congregation hath dwelt therein
74. 19 forget not the congregation of thy poor

3. *A meeting place; the meeting itself,* מוֹעֵד *moed.*
Exod 27. 21 the tabernacle of the congregation
So in 28. 43; 29. 4, 10, 11, 30, 32, 42, 44; 30. 16, 18, 20,
26, 36; 31. 7; 33. 7, 7; 35. 21; 38. 8, 30; 39. 32, 40; 40.
12; Lev. 1. 1, 3, 5; 3. 2, 8, 13; 4. 4, 5, 7, 7, 14, 16, 18, 18;
6. 16, 26, 30; 8. 3, 4, 31, 33, 35; 9. 5, 23; 10. 7, 9; 12. 6;
14. 11, 23; 15. 14, 29; 16. 7, 16, 17; 17. 4, 5, 6, 9; 19. 21;
24. 3; Num. 1. 1; 2. 2, 17; 3. 7, 8, 25, 25, 38; 4. 3, 4, 15,
23, 25, 25, 28, 30, 31, 33, 35, 37, 39, 41, 43, 47; 6. 10, 13,
18; 7. 5, 89; 8. 9, 15, 19, 22, 24, 26; 10. 3; 11. 16; 12. 4;
16. 18, 19, 42, 43, 50; 17. 4; 18. 4, 6, 21, 22, 23, 31; 19. 4;
20. 6; 25. 6; 27. 2; 31. 54; Deut. 31. 14, 14; Josh. 18. 1;
19. 51; 1 Sa. 2. 22; 1 Ki. 8. 4; 1 Ch. 6. 32; 9. 21; 23. 32;
2 Ch. 1. 3, 6, 13; 5. 5; Lev. 16. 20, 23, 33; Num. 14. 10.
Exod 40. 2 the tent of the congregation
[So in verses 6, 7, 22, 24, 26, 29, 30, 32, 34, 35.]
Num 14. 10 the congregation bade stone them with
16. 2 famous in the congregation, men of ren.
Psa. 74. 4 roar in the midst of thy congregations
75. 2 When I shall receive the congregation I
Isa. 14. 13 also upon the mount of the congregation

4. *An appointed meeting,* עֵדָה *edah.*
Exod 12. 3 Speak ye unto all the congregation of Is.
12. 6 the whole assembly of the congregation
12. 19 shall be cut off from the congregation
12. 47 the congregation of Israel shall keep it
16. 1 the congregation of the children of Israel
16. 2 the whole congregation of the children
16. 9 Say unto all the congregation of the chil.
16. 10 Aaron spake unto the whole congregation
16. 22 the rulers of the congregation came and
17. 1 all the congregation of the children of I.
34. 31 the rulers of the congregation returned
35. 1 gathered all the congregation of the chil.
35. 4, 20 the congregation of the children of I.
38. 25 that were numbered of the congregation

Lev. 4. 13 if the whole congregation of Israel sin
4. 15 the elders of the congregation shall lay
8. 3 gather thou all the congregation together
8. 5 Moses said unto the congregation, This
9. 5 all the congregation drew near and stood
10. 17 to bear the iniquity of the congregation
16. 5 he shall take of the congregation of the
19. 2 Speak unto all the congregation of the
24. 14 and let all the congregation stone him
24. 16 the congregation shall certainly stone him
Num. 1. 2 Take ye the sum of all the congregation
1. 16 These (were) the renowned of the congre.
1. 18 they assembled all the congregation tog.
1. 53 there be no wrath upon the congregation
3. 7 and the charge of the whole congregation
4. 34 the chief of the congregation numbered
8. 20 the congregation of the children of Israel
13. 26 the congregation..unto all the congrega.
14. 1 the congregation lifted up their voice
14. 2 and the whole congregation said unto
14. 5 all the assembly of the congregation
14. 10 all the congregation bade stone them
14. 27 (shall I bear with) this evil congregation
14. 35 do it unto all this evil congregation
14. 36 made all the congregation to murmur
15. 24 without the knowledge of the congrega.
15. 24 the congregation shall offer one young
15. 25 an atonement for all the congregation
15. 26 it shall be forgiven all the congregation
15. 33 brought him..unto all the congregation
15. 35 the congregation shall stone him with
15. 36 the congregation brought him without
16. 3 all the congregation (are) holy, every one
16. 9 hath separated you from the congregation
16. 9 to stand before the congregation to min.
16. 19 all the congregation .. unto all the c.
16. 21 Separate..from among this congrega.
16. 22 wilt thou be wroth with..the congrega.?
16. 24 Speak unto the congregation, saying, Get
16. 26 he spake unto the congregation, saying
16. 41 the congregation of the children of Israel
16. 42 when the congregation was gathered
16. 45 Get you up from among this congregation
16. 46 go quickly unto the congregation, and
19. 9 it shall be kept for the congregation of
20. 1 Then came..the whole congregation, into
20. 2 there was no water for the congregation
20. 8 thou shalt give the congregation and
20. 11 the congregation drank, and their beasts
20. 22 the whole congregation, journeyed from
20. 27 went up..in the sight of all the congrega.
20. 29 all the congregation saw that Aaron was
25. 6 in the sight of all the congregation of the
25. 7 rose up from among the congregation
26. 2 Take the sum of all the congregation of
26. 9 (which were) famous in the congregation
27. 2 before the princes and all the congrega.
27. 14 rebelled..in the strife of the congregation
27. 16 the LORD..set a man over the congrega.
27. 17 that the congregation of the LORD be not
27. 19 And he set him..before all the congrega.
27. 20 all the congregation of the children..may
27. 21 Israel with him, even all the congrega.
27. 22 and set him..before all the congregation
31. 12 unto the congregation of the children of
31. 13 all the princes of the congregation, went
31. 16 there was a plague among the congrega.
31. 26 and the chief fathers of the congregation
31. 27 between them..and..all the congregation
31. 43 half (that pertained unto) the congrega.
32. 2 unto the princes of the congregation
32. 4 the LORD smote before the congregation
35. 12 until he stand before the congregation
35. 24 the congregation shall judge between the
35. 25 the congregation shall deliver the slayer
35. 25 the congregation shall restore him to the
Josh. 9. 15 the princes of the congregation sware
9. 18 the princes of the congregation had
9. 18 the congregation murmured against the
9. 19 princes said unto all the congregation
9. 21 drawers of water unto all the congrega.
9. 27 and drawers of water for the congrega.
18. 1 the whole congregation..assembled toge.
20. 6 until he stand before the congregation for
20. 9 until he stood before the congregation
22. 12 the whole congregation..gathered them.
22. 16 Thus saith the whole congregation of the
22. 17 there was a plague in the congregation
22. 18 will be wroth with the whole congrega.
22. 20 wrath fell on all the congregation of Isr.
22. 30 the princes of the congregation, and heads
Judg. 20. 1 the congregation was gathered together
21. 10 the congregation sent thither twelve tho
21. 13 the whole congregation sent (some) to
21. 16 Then the elders of the congregation said
1 Ki. 8. 5 king Solomon, and all the congregation
12. 20 sent and called him unto the congrega.
2 Ch. 5. 6 king Solomon, and all the congregation
Job 15. 34 the congregation of hypocrites (shall be)
Psa. 1. 5 nor sinners in the congregation of the
7. 7 So shall the congregation..compass thee
74. 2 Remember thy congregation, (which)
82. 1 God standeth in the congregation of the
111. 1 in the assembly..and (in) the congrega.
Jer. 6. 18 hear, ye nations, and know, O congrega.
30. 20 their congregation shall be established
Hos. 7. 12 will chastise them, as their congregation

5. *An assembly called together,* קָהָל *qahal.*
Lev. 4. 14 then the congregation shall offer a young
4. 21 it (is) a sin offering for the congregation
16. 17 and for all the congregation of Israel

Lev. 16. 33 for all the people of the congregation
Num 10. 7 when the congregation is to be gathered
15. 15 One ordinance(shall be)..for..the congre.
16. 3 yourselves above the congregation of the
16. 33 they perished from among the congrega.
16. 47 ran into the midst of the congregation
19. 20 shall be cut off from..the congregation
20. 4 why have ye brought up the congregation
20. 10 Moses and Aaron gathered the congrega.
20. 12 ye shall not bring this congregation into
Deut.23. 1, 2, 2, 3, 3, 8 not enter into the congrega.
31. 30 spake in the ears of all the congregation
Josh. 8. 35 Joshua read not before all the congrega.
Judg.21. 5 that came not up with the congregation
1 Ki. 8. 14 blessed all the congregation of Israel
8. 14 and all the congregation of Israel stood
8. 22 in the presence of all the congregation
8. 55 he stood, and blessed all the congregation
8. 65 all Israel with him, a great congregation
12. 3 Jeroboam and all the congregation of Is.
1 Ch. 13. 2 David said unto all the congregation of
13. 4 all the congregation said that they would
28. 8 the sight of all Israel the congregation
29. 1 the king said unto all the congregation
29. 10 blessed the LORD before all the congrega.
29. 20 And David said to all the congregation
29. 20 the congregation blessed the LORD God
2 Ch. 1. 3 So Solomon, and all the congregation
1. 5 Solomon and the congregation sought
6. 3 blessed the whole congregation of Israel
6. 3 and all the congregation of Israel stood
6. 12 in the presence of all the congregation
6. 13 kneeled down..before all the congrega.
7. 8 Israel with him, a very great congrega.
20. 5 Jehoshaphat stood in the congregation of
20. 14 Spirit of the LORD in the..congregation
23. 3 all the congregation made a covenant
24. 6 servant of..the congregation of Israel
28. 14 before the princes and all the congrega.
29. 23 before the king and the congregation
29. 28 all the congregation worshipped, and the
29. 31 the congregation brought in sacrifices
29. 32 offerings, which the congregation brought
30. 2 all the congregation in Jerusalem, to keep
30. 4 the thing pleased..all the congregation
30. 13 there assembled..a very great congrega.
30. 17 For (there were) many in the congregation
30. 24 Hezekiah..did give to the congregation
30. 24 the princes gave to the congregation
30. 25 all the congregation of Judah, with the
30. 25 all the congregation that came out of Is.
31. 18 their daughters, through all the congre.
Ezra 2. 64 The whole congregation together (was)
10. 1 assembled unto him..a very great congre.
10. 8 and himself separated from the congre.
10. 12 all the congregation answered and said
10. 14 Let now our rulers of all the congregation
Neh. 5. 13 all the congregation said, Amen, and
7. 66 The whole congregation together (was)
8. 2 Ezra..brought the law before the congre.
8. 17 And all the congregation..made booths
13. 1 Moabite should not come into the congre.
Job 30. 28 I stood up, (and) I cried in the congrega.
Psa. 22. 22 in the midst of the congregation will I
22. 25 My praise..of thee in the great congrega.
26. 5 I have hated the congregation of evil
35. 18 I will give thee thanks in the great con.
40. 9 preached righteousness in the great con.
40. 10 thy truth from the great congregation
89. 5 thy faithfulness also in the congregation
107. 32 Let them exalt him also in the congrega.
149. 1 his praise in the congregation of saints
Prov. 5. 14 in all evil in the midst of the congrega.
21. 16 shall remain in the congregation of the
26. 26 shall be showed before the (whole) con.
Lam. 1. 10 they should not enter into thy congrega.
Joel 2. 16 Gather the people, sanctify the congrega.
Mic. 2. 5 cast a cord by lot in the congregation

6. *An assembly called together*, קְהִלָּה *qehillah*.
Deut 33. 4 the inheritance of the congregation of J.

7. *An assembly led together*, συναγωγή *sunagōgē*.
Acts 13. 43 when the congregation was broken up

CONGREGATIONS —

1. *Assemblies called together*, מַקְהֵלוֹת *maqheloth*.
Psa. 68. 26 Bless ye God in the congregations, (even)

2. *Assemblies called together*, מַקְהֵלִים *maqhelim*.
Psa. 26. 12 in the congregations will I bless the LORD

CON'-IAH, כָּנְיָהוּ *Jah is creating*.
A name given to Jehoiachin, king of Judah, who was carried captive by Nebuchadnezzar. B.C. 599.
Jer. 22. 24 C. the son of Jehoiakim king of Judah
22. 28 (Is) this man C. a despised broken idol?
37. 1 Josiah reigned instead of C. the son of J.

CO-NON'-IAH, כָּנַנְיָהוּ *Jah is creating*.
A Levite overseer in the days of Hezekiah, B.C. 726.
2 Ch. 31. 12 over which C. the Levite (was) ruler, and
31. 13 Mahath..Benaiah..under the hand of C.

CONQUER, to —
To have the victory, νικάω *nikaō*.
Rev. 6. 2 he went forth conquering, and to conquer

CONQUEROR, to be more than —
To have more than victory, ὑπερνικάω *hupernikaō*.
Rom. 8. 37 in all these..we are more than conquerors

CONSCIENCE —
A knowing with oneself, συνείδησις *suneidēsis*.
John 8. 9 being convicted by (their own) conscience
Acts 23. 1 I have lived in all good conscience before
24. 16 have always a conscience void of offence
Rom. 2. 15 their conscience also bearing witness, and
9. 1 my conscience also bearing me witness in
13. 5 not only for wrath, but also for conscience'
1 Co. 8. 7 for some with conscience of the idol unto
8. 7 their conscience being weak is defiled
8. 10 shall not the conscience of him which is
8. 12 when ye..wound their weak conscience
10. 25, 27 asking no question for conscience' sake
10. 28 not for his sake..and for conscience' sake
10. 29 Conscience, I say, not thine..another cons.
2 Co. 1. 12 is this, the testimony of our conscience
4. 2 commending ourselves to every..consci.
5. 11 also are made manifest in your consciences
1 Ti. 1. 5 a good conscience, and (of) faith unfeig.
1. 19 Holding faith, and a good conscience
3. 9 mystery of the faith in a pure conscience
4. 2 having their conscience seared with a hot
2 Ti. 1. 3 God, whom I serve..with pure conscience
Titus 1. 15 even their mind and conscience is defiled
Heb. 9. 9 perfect, as pertaining to the conscience
9. 14 purge your conscience from dead works
10. 2 should have had no more conscience of
10. 22 hearts sprinkled from an evil conscience
13. 18 we trust we have a good conscience, in all
1 Pe. 2. 19 if a man for conscience toward God endure
3. 16 Having a good conscience; that, whereas
3. 21 the answer of a good conscience toward

CONSECRATE, to —

1. *To devote*, חָרַם *charam*, 5.
Mic. 4. 13 I will consecrate their gain unto the LORD

2. *To separate*, נָזַר *nazar*, 5.
Num. 6. 12 he shall consecrate unto the LORD the days

3. *To set apart*, קָדַשׁ *qadesh*, 3.
Exod 28. 3 make Aaron's garments to consecrate him
30. 30 anoint Aaron and his sons, and consecrate

4. *To fill the hand*, מָלֵא יָד *male* (3) *yad* (1 in Exod. 32. 29).
Exod 28. 41 shalt anoint them, and consecrate them
29. 9 thou shalt consecrate Aaron and his sons
29. 29 to be anointed therein, and to be consec.
29. 33 made to consecrate (and) to sanctify them
29. 35 seven days shalt thou consecrate them
Lev. 32. 29 Consecrate yourselves to-day to the LORD
8. 33 for seven days shall he consecrate you
16. 32 whom he shall consecrate to minister in
21. 10 and that is consecrated to put on the
Num. 3. 3 whom he consecrated to minister in the
Judg 17. 5 consecrated one of his sons, who became
17. 12 And Micah consecrated the Levite; and
1 Ki. 13. 33 whosoever would, he consecrated him
1 Ch. 29. 5 who (then) is willing to consecrate his
2 Ch. 13. 9 whosoever cometh to consecrate himself
29. 31 ye have consecrated yourselves unto the
Eze. 43. 26 and they shall consecrate themselves

5. *To dedicate, make new*, ἐγκαινίζω *egkainizō*.
Heb. 10. 20 and living way, which he hath consecrated

6. *To make perfect*, τελειόω *teleioō*.
Heb. 7. 28 the Son, who is consecrated for evermore

CONSECRATED things —
Thing set apart, קֹדֶשׁ *qodesh*.
Josh. 6. 19 vessels of..iron,(are) consecrated things
2 Ch. 29. 33 the consecrated things (were) six hundred

CONSECRATED, to be —
To be set apart, קָדַשׁ *qadesh*, 4.
2 Ch. 26. 18 that are consecrated to burn incense
31. 6 of holy things which were consecrated
Ezra 3. 5 feasts of the LORD that were consecrated

CONSECRATION —

1. *Fillings in or up*, מִלֻּאִים *milluim*.
Exod 29. 22 for it (is) a ram of consecration
29. 26 breast of the ram of Aaron's consecration
29. 27 heaved up, of the ram of the consecration
29. 31 shalt take the ram of the consecration
29. 34 if ought of the flesh of the consecrations
Lev. 7. 37 trespass offering, and of the consecrations
8. 22 brought the other ram, the ram of conse.
8. 28 they (were) consecrations for a sweet sav.
8. 29 of the ram of consecration it was Moses'
8. 31 that (is) in the basket of consecrations
8. 33 until the days of your consecration be at

2. *Separation*, נֵזֶר *nezer*.
Num. 6. 7 the consecration of his God (is) upon his
6. 9 hath defiled the head of his consecration

CONSENT —

1. *Heart*, לֵב *leb*.
Psa. 83. 5 have consulted together with one consent

2. *A man*, אִישׁ *ish*.
1 Sa. 11. 7 and they came out with one consent

3. *Shoulder*, שְׁכֶם *shekem*.
Hos. 6. 9 priests murder in the way by consent
Zeph. 3. 9 to serve him with one consent

CONSENT, with —
From united voice, ἐκ συμφώνου *ek sumphōnou*.
1 Co. 7. 5 except (it be) with consent for a time

CONSENT, to —

1. *To be willing*, אָבָה *abah*.
Deut 13. 8 Thou shalt not consent unto him, nor
1 Ki. 20. 8 Hearken not (unto him), nor consent
Prov. 1. 10 My son, if sinners entice thee, consent

2. *To be inclined to*, אוּת *oth*, 2.
Gen. 34. 15 But in this will we consent unto you
34. 22 herein will the men consent unto us for
34. 23 let us consent unto them, and they will
2 Ki. 12. 8 the priests consented to receive no (more)

3. *To hearken*, שָׁמַע *shama*.
Dan. 1. 14 he consented to them in this matter, and

4. *To nod over (a thing), assent*, ἐπινεύω *epineuō*.
Acts 18. 20 When they desired..he consented not

CONSENT to, to —

1. *To come toward*, προσέρχομαι *proserchomai*.
1 Ti. 6. 3 If any man..consent not to wholesome

2. *To put down (a vote) with*, συγκατατίθημι.
Luke 23. 51 The same had not consented to the cou.

CONSENT unto, to —

1. *To say with*, σύμφημι *sumphēmi*.
Rom. 7. 16 I consent unto the law that (it is) good

2. *To think well (of) with*, συνευδοκέω *suneudokeō*.
Acts 8. 1 And Saul was consenting unto his death
22. 20 I..was standing by, and consenting unto

CONSENT with, to —
To be pleased with, רָצָה *ratsah*.
Psa. 50. 18 thou consentedst with him, and hast

CONSIDER, to —

1. *To say*, אָמַר *amar*.
Hos. 7. 2 they consider not in their hearts (that)

2. *To consider, understand*, בִּין *bin*.
Deut 32. 7 consider the years of many generations
32. 29 (that) they would consider their latter
Psa. 5. 1 O LORD; consider my meditation
50. 22 consider this, ye that forget God, lest I
Prov 23. 1 consider diligently what (is) before thee
24. 12 doth not he that pondereth..consider (it)

3. *To (cause to) consider, distinguish*, בִּין *bin*, 5.
Psa. 33. 15 He fashioneth their hearts..he consid.
Isa. 57. 1 none considering that the righteous is
Dan. 8. 5 as I was considering, behold, an he goat
9. 23 understand the matter, and consider the

4. *To consider (for oneself), distinguish*, בִּין *bin*, 7a.
1 Ki. 3. 21 when I had considered it in the morning
Job 11. 11 will he not then consider (it)?
23. 15 when I consider, I am afraid of him
37. 14 and consider the wondrous works of God
Psa. 119. 95 (but) I will consider thy testimonies
Isa. 1. 3 doth not know, my people doth not con.
14. 16 They that see thee shall..consider thee
43. 18 Remember ye not..neither consider the
52. 15 they had not heard shall they consider
Jer. 2. 10 send unto Kedar, and consider diligently
9. 17 Consider ye, and call for the mourning
23. 20 in the latter days ye shall consider it
30. 24 in the latter days ye shall consider it

5. *To devise, design, purpose*, זָמַם *zamam*.
Prov. 31. 16 She considereth a field, and buyeth it

6. *To think, devise, reckon*, חָשַׁב *chashab*, 3.
Psa. 77. 5 I have considered the days of old, the

7. *To know*, יָדַע *yada*.
Deut. 8. 5 Thou shalt also consider in thine heart
Judg. 18. 14 now therefore consider what ye have to
2 Ki. 5. 7 wherefore consider, I pray you, and see
Prov. 28. 22 considereth not that poverty shall come
29. 7 The righteous considereth the cause of
Eccl. 5. 1 for they consider not that they do evil

8. *To look, regard*, נָבַט *nabat*, 5.
Psa. 13. 3 Consider (and) hear me, O LORD my God
Isa. 18. 4 I will consider in my dwelling place like
Lam. 1. 11 see, O LORD, and consider; for I am bec.
2. 20 Behold, O LORD, and consider to whom
5. 1 O LORD..consider, and behold our repr.

9. *To give to*, נָתַן אֶל *nathan el*.
Eccl. 9. 1 all this I considered in my heart, even

10. *To cut up and divide, consider*, פָּסַג *pasag*, 3.
Psa. 48. 13 Mark ye well her bulwarks, consider her

11. *To see, behold*, רָאָה *raah*.
Exod 33. 13 consider that this nation (is) thy people
Lev. 13. 13 the priest shall consider: and, behold
1 Sa. 12. 24 consider how great (things) he hath done
25. 17 know and consider what thou wilt do
Psa. 8. 3 When I consider thy heavens, the work
9. 13 consider my trouble (which I suffer) of
25. 19 Consider mine enemies, for they are many
31. 7 thou hast considered my trouble; thou
45. 10 Hearken, O daughter, and consider, and
119. 153 Consider mine affliction, and deliver me
119. 159 Consider how I love thy precepts
Prov. 6. 6 Go..consider her ways, and be wise
Eccl. 4. 1 considered all the oppressions that are
4. 4 I considered all travail, and every right
4. 15 I considered all the living which walk
7. 13 Consider the work of God: for who can
7. 14 but in the day of adversity consider
Isa. 5. 12 neither consider the operation of his
Jer. 33. 24 Considerest thou not what this people

Eze. 12. 3 they will consider, though they (be) a
18. 14 seeth all his father's sins..and consider.
18. 28 Because he considereth, and turneth away
12. *To place, put, set,* שׂוּם *sum* [also with *leb* or *lebab*].
Judg19. 30 consider of it, take advice, and speak
Job 1. 8 Hast thou considered my servant Job
2. 3 Hast thou considered my servant Job
Isa. 41. 20 That they may see, and know, and consi.
41. 22 we may consider them, and know the
Hag. 1. 5, 7 thus saith the LORD..Consider your
2. 15 I pray you, consider from this day and
2. 18 Consider now from this day and upward
2. 18 day that the foundation..was laid, con.
13. *To consider or act wisely,* שָׂכַל *sakal,* 5.
Job 34. 27 they..would not consider any of his ways
Psa. 41. 1 Blessed (is) he that considereth the poor
64. 9 they shall wisely consider of his doing
Prov.21. 12 The righteous (man) wisely considereth
14. *To consider wisely,* שְׂכַל *sekal,* 2.
Dan. 7. 8 I considered the horns, and, behold, there
15. *To set my heart,* שִׁית לֵב *shith leb.*
Prov 24. 32 I saw, (and) considered (it) well; I looked
16. *To hearken,* שָׁמַע *shama.*
1 Ki. 5. 8 I have considered the things which thou
17. *To cause to turn back,* שׁוּב *shub,* 5.
Deut 4. 39 consider (it) in thine heart, that the LORD
Isa. 44. 19 none considereth in his heart, neither
8. *To view thoroughly, looking up to,* ἀναθεωρέω.
Heb. 13. 7 considering the end of (their) conversa.
19. *To reckon up,* ἀναλογίζομαι *analogizomai.*
Heb. 12. 3 consider him that endured such contra.
20. *To reckon thoroughly,* διαλογίζομαι *dialogizomai.*
John11. 50 consider that it is expedient for us, that
21. *To see,* εἶδον *eidon.*
Acts 15. 6 and elders came together for to consider
22. *To view, look,* θεωρέω *theōreō.*
Heb. 7. 4 consider how great this man (was), unto
23. *To learn thoroughly,* καταμανθάνω *katamanthanō.*
Matt 6. 28 Consider the lilies of the field, how they
24. *To perceive thoroughly (with the mind),* κατανοέω.
Matt 7. 3 but considerest not the beam that is in
Luke12. 24 Consider the ravens: for they neither sow
12. 27 Consider the lilies, how they grow: they
Acts 11. 6 I considered, and saw four footed beasts
Rom. 4. 19 he considered not his own body now dead
Heb. 3. 1 consider the Apostle and High Priest of
10. 24 let us consider one another to provoke
25. *To perceive (with the mind),* νοέω *noeō.*
2 Ti. 2. 7 Consider what I say; and the Lord give
26. *To look, watch,* σκοπέω *skopeō.*
Gal. 6. 1 considering thyself, lest thou also be
27. *To see or perceive with (self),* συνεῖδον *suneidon*
Acts 12. 12 when he had considered..he came to the
28. *To send or put together,* συνίημι *suniēmi.*
Mark 6. 52 they considered not (the miracle) of the

CONSIDER, to diligently —
To distinguish for oneself, בִּין *bin,* 7a.
Psa. 37. 10 thou shalt diligently consider his place

CONSIST, to —
1. *To be,* εἰμί *eimi.*
Luke12. 15 a man's life consisteth not in the abund.
2. *To set, put together,* συνίστημι *sunistēmi.*
Col. 1. 17 all things, and by him all things consist

CONSOLATION —
A calling alongside (for help), παράκλησις *paraklēsis.*
Luke 2. 25 waiting for the consolation of Israel
6. 24 for ye have received your consolation
Acts 4. 36 surnamed Barnabas..The son of consola.
15. 31 they rejoiced for the consolation
Rom15. 5 the God of patience and consolation
2 Co. 1. 5 our consolation also aboundeth by Christ
1. 6, 6 (it is) for your consolation and salva.
1. 7 so (shall ye be) also of the consolation
7. 7 the consolation wherewith he was comfo.
Phil. 2. 1 If (there be) therefore any consolation in
2 Th. 2. 16 hath given (us) everlasting consolation
Phm. 7 we have great joy and consolation in thy
Heb. 6. 18 That..we might have a strong consolation

CONSOLATIONS —
1. *Comforts,* תַּנְחוּמוֹת *tanchumoth.*
Job 15. 11 (Are) the consolations of God small with
21. 2 Hear..let this be your consolations
2. *Comforts,* תַּנְחוּמִים *tanchumim.*
Isa. 66. 11 with the breasts of her consolations
Jer. 16. 7 give them the cup of consolation to

CONSORT with, to —
To take a lot beside, προσκληρόω *prosklēroō.*
Acts 17. 4 some of them believed, and consorted w.

CONSPIRACY —
1. *Conspiracy, bond,* קֶשֶׁר *qesher.*
2 Sa. 15. 12 and the conspiracy was strong; for the
2 Ki. 17. 4 the king of Assyria found conspiracy in
Jer. 11. 9 A conspiracy is found among the men of
Eze. 22. 25 a conspiracy of her prophets in the midst
2. *A swearing together,* συνωμοσία *sunōmosia.*
Acts 23. 13 forty which had made this conspiracy

CONSPIRACY, to make a —
1. Same as No. 2.
2 Ki. 12. 20 his servants arose, and made a conspir.
2. *To bind a bond,* קָשַׁר קֶשֶׁר *qashar qesher.*
2 Ki.14. 19 they made a conspiracy against him in
15. 15 and his conspiracy which he made
15. 30 Hoshea the son of Elah made a conspir.
2 Ch.25. 27 they made a conspiracy against him in

CONSPIRATOR —
To bind, conspire, קָשַׁר *qashar.*
2 Sa. 15. 31 Ahithophel (is) among the conspirators

CONSPIRE, to —
1. *To show self deceitful, conspire,* נָכַל *nakal,* 7.
Gen. 37. 18 they conspired against him to slay him
2. *To bind, conspire together,* קָשַׁר *qashar.*
1 Sa. 22. 8 all of you have conspired against me
22. 13 Why have ye conspired against me, thou
1 Ki.15. 27 Baasha the son of Ahijah..conspired
16. 9 his servant Zimri..conspired against him
16. 16 Zimri hath conspired, and hath also
2 Ki.10. 9 I conspired against my master, and slew
15. 10 Shallum the son of Jabesh conspired
15. 25 a captain of his, conspired against him
21. 23 the servants of Amon conspired against
21. 24 slew all them that had conspired against
2 Ch.24. 21 they conspired against him, and stoned
33. 24 his servants conspired against him
33. 25 all them that had conspired against king
Neh. 4. 8 conspired all of them together to come
Amos7. 10 Amos hath conspired against thee in the
3. *To conspire together (for self),* קָשַׁר *qashar,* 7
2 Ki. 9. 14 So Jehu..conspired against Joram
2 Ch. 24. 25 his own servants conspired against him
24. 26 these are they that conspired against

CONSTANT, to be —
To be strong, take or keep hold of, חָזַק *chazaq.*
1 Ch.28. 7 if he be constant to do my commandments

CONSTANTLY —
Pre-eminently, perpetually, נֵצַח *netsach.*
Prov.21. 28 the man that heareth speaketh constantly

CONSTELLATION —
Firm, thick, stout one, Orion, כְּסִיל *kesil.*
Isa. 13. 10 the stars of heaven and the constellations

CONSTRAIN, to —
1. *To take or keep hold of,* חָזַק *chazaq,* 5.
2 Ki. 4. 8 and she constrained him to eat bread
2. *To press, straiten,* צוּק *tsuq,* 5.
Job 32. 18 the spirit within me constraineth me
3. *To necessitate,* ἀναγκάζω *anagkazō.*
Matt.14. 22 Jesus constrained his disciples to get
Mark 6. 45 he constrained his disciples to get into
Acts 28. 19 I was constrained to appeal unto Cesar
Gal. 6. 12 they constrain you to be circumcised
4. *To press beyond measure,* παραβιάζομαι *parabia.*
Luke24. 29 they constrained him, saying, Abide with
Acts 16. 15 she besought (us)..And she constrained
5. *To hold together,* συνέχω *sunechō.*
2 Co. 5. 14 the love of Christ constraineth us

CONSTRAINT, by —
Of necessity, ἀναγκαστῶς *anagkastōs.*
1 Pe. 5. 2 not by constraint, but willingly; not for

CONSULT, to —
1. *To give or take counsel,* יָעַץ *yaats.*
Psa. 62. 4 They only consult to cast (him) down
Mic. 6. 5 what Balak king of Moab consulted, and
Hab. 2. 10 Thou hast consulted shame to thy house
2. *To be consulted, take counsel,* יָעַץ *yaats,* 2.
1 Ki.12. 6 king Rehoboam consulted with old men
12. 8 consulted with the young men that were
1 Ch.13. 1 David consulted with the captains of
2 Ch.20. 21 when he had consulted with the people
Psa. 83. 5 they have consulted together with one
3. *To consult for oneself,* יָעַץ *yaats,* 7.
Psa. 83. 3 They have..consulted against thy hidden
4. *To be counselled, take counsel,* מָלַךְ *malak,* 2.
Neh. 5. 7 I consulted with myself, and I rebuked
5. *To ask, inquire,* שָׁאַל *shaal.*
Eze. 21. 21 he consulted with images, he looked in
6. *To take counsel,* βουλεύομαι *bouleuomai.*
Luke14. 31 consulteth whether he be able with ten
John12. 10 chief priests consulted that they might
7. *To take counsel with,* συμβουλεύω *sumbouleuō.*
Matt.26. 4 consulted that they might take Jesus by

CONSULT together, to —
To take counsel, יְעַט *yeat,* 2.
Dan. 6. 7 the captains, have consulted together to

CONSULTATION —
Counsel, συμβούλιον *sumboulion.*
Mark15. 1 the chief priests held a consultation with

CONSULTER —
To inquire, שָׁאַל *shaal.*
Deut18. 11 a charmer, or a consulter with familiar

CONSUME, to —
1. *To eat, devour,* אָכַל *akal.*
Gen. 31. 40 in the day the drought consumed me
Exod15. 7 thy wrath, (which) consumed them as
Lev. 6. 10 which the fire hath consumed with the
9. 24 there came a fire..and consumed upon
Num11. 1 fire..burnt among them, and consumed
16. 35 a fire..consumed the two hundred and
21. 28 a flame from the city..hath consumed Ar
Deut. 4. 24 the LORD thy God (is) a consuming fire
5. 25 Now therefore..for this great fire will con.
7. 16 thou shalt consume all the people which
9. 3 (as) a consuming fire he shall destroy
32. 22 a fire is kindled..and shall consume the
Judg 6. 21 consumed the flesh and the unleavened
1 Ki. 18. 38 fire of the LORD..consumed the burnt
2 Ki. 1. 10, 12 let fire come down from heaven, and c.
1. 10 there came down fire..and consumed
1. 12 fire..came down from heaven and consu.
2 Ch 7. 1 fire came down from heaven, and consu.
Job 1. 16 The fire..hath burnt..and consumed
15. 34 fire shall consume the tabernacles of
22. 20 the remnant of them the fire consumeth
31. 12 it (is) a fire (that) consumeth to destructi.
Psa. 78. 63 The fire consumed their young men; and
Jer. 49. 27 it shall consume the palaces of Ben-hadad
Eze. 19. 12 her strong rods..the fire consumed them
2. *To eat, devour,* אָכַל *akal,* 3.
Job 20. 26 a fire not blown shall consume him
3. *To cause to eat, feed,* אָכַל *akal,* 5.
Eze. 21. 28 the sword (is) drawn..to consume because
4. *Food, what is eaten,* אָכְלָה *oklah.*
Eze 35. 12 saying..they are given us to consume
5. *To fade, wear away,* בָּלָה *balah.*
Job 13. 28 he, as a rotten thing, consumeth, as a
6. *To fade, wear away,* בָּלָה *balah,* 3.
Psa. 49. 14 their beauty shall consume in the grave
7. *To take away by violence,* גָּזַל *gazal.*
Job 24. 19 Drought and heat consume the snow
8. *To trouble, crush,* הָמַם *hamam.*
Esth. 9. 24 to consume them, and to destroy them
9. *To consume, crop off,* חָסַל *chasal.*
Deut. 28. 38 little in; for the locust shall consume it
10. *To inherit, possess,* יָרַשׁ *yarash,* 3.
Deut. 28. 42 All thy trees..shall the locust consume
11. *To be completed, finished, consumed,* כָּלָה *kalah.*
Psa. 37. 20 they shall consume; into smoke shall
12. *To finish, consume,* כָּלָה *kalah,* 3.
Gen. 41. 30 and the famine shall consume the land
Exod32. 10 let me alone..that I may consume them
32. 12 to consume them from the face of the
33. 3 I will not go up..lest I consume thee in
33. 5 I will come up..and consume thee: there.
Lev. 26. 16 the burning ague, that shall consume the
Num16. 21, 45 that I may consume them in a mom.
25. 11 I consumed not the children of Israel
Deut 7. 22 thou mayest not consume them at once
28. 21 until he have consumed thee from off the
Jos. 24. 20 he will turn..and consume you..after that
1 Sa. 2. 33 the man of thine..(shall be) to consume
2 Sa. 21. 5 The man that consumed us, and that
22. 38 turned not again until I had consumed
22. 39 I have consumed them, and wounded
1 Ki.22. 11 push the Syrians, until thou have consu.
2 Ki.13. 17 thou shalt smite..till thou have consum.
13. 19 smitten Syria till thou hadst consumed (it)
2 Ch. 8. 8 whom the children of Israel consumed
Ezra 9. 14 angry with us till thou hadst consumed
Psa. 59. 13 Consume (them) in wrath, consume (them)
78. 33 their days did he consume in vanity, and
119 87 They had almost consumed me upon earth
Isa. 10. 18 And shall consume the glory of his forest
27. 10 there shall he lie down, and consume the
Jer. 5. 3 thou hast consumed them, (but) they have
9. 16 a sword after them, till I have consumed
10. 25 devoured him, and consumed him, and
14. 12 I will consume them by the sword, and
49. 37 sword after them, till I have consumed
Lam. 2. 22 brought up hath mine enemy consumed
Eze. 13. 13 to con. [Heb. *le-kalah, for destruction.*]
20. 13 would pour out my fury .. to consume
22. 31 I have consumed them with the fire of
43. 8 I have consumed them in mine anger
Hos. 11. 6 the sword..shall consume his branches
Zec. 5. 4 shall consume it with the timber thereof
13. *To melt, dissolve,* מוּג *mug.*
Isa. 64. 7 thou hast..consumed us, because of our
14. *To end, consume,* סוּף *suph,* 5.
Jer. 8. 13 I will surely consume them, saith the L.
Dan. 2. 44 break in pieces, and consume all these
Zeph. 1. 2 I will utterly consume all (things) from
1. 3 will consume man and beast; I will con.
15. *To end, consume,* סָפָה *saphah.*
Isa. 7. 20 a razor..shall also consume the beard
16. *To cut off, destroy,* צָמַת *tsamath,* 3.
Psa.119. 139 My zeal hath consumed me; because
17. *To be feeble,* רָפָה *raphah.*
Isa. 5. 24 the flame consumeth the chaff, (so) their
18. *To cut off, lay waste,* שָׁמַד *shemad,* 5.
Dan. 7. 26 to consume and to destroy (it) unto the

19. *To be perfect, finished, consumed,* תָּמַם *tamam.*
Jer. 27. 8 until I have consumed them by his hand

20. *To perfect, finish, consume,* תָּמַם *tamam,* 5.
Eze. 22. 15 will consume thy filthiness out of thee
24. 10 kindle the fire, consume the flesh, and

21. *To use up, consume,* ἀναλίσκω *analiskō.*
Luke 9. 54 and consume them, even as Elias did?
Gal. 5. 15 take heed that ye be not consumed one of
2 Th. 2. 8 whom the Lord[shall consume] with the

22. *To spend, be at charges,* δαπανάω *dapanaō.*
Jas. 4. 3 that ye may consume (it) upon your lusts

23. *To use up utterly, consume utterly,* καταναλίσκω.
Heb. 12 29 For our God (is) a consuming fire

CONSUME away, to —

1. *To be completed, finished, consumed,* כָּלָה *kalah.*
Psa. 37. 20 into smoke they shall consume away

2. *To become completed, wasted away,* מָקַק *maqaq,* 2.
Eze. 4. 17 and consume away for their iniquity
Zech. 14. 12 their eyes shall consume away in their
14. 12 their tongue shall consume away in their

3. *To waste or consume away,* מָקַק *maqaq,* 5.
Zech. 14. 12 Their flesh shall consume away in their

CONSUME away, to make to —

To melt, waste, מָסָה *masah,* 5.
Psa. 39. 11 thou makest his beauty to consume away

CONSUME, to utterly —

Make an ending, עָשָׂה כָּלָה *asah kalah.*
Neh. 9. 31 thou didst not utterly consume them, nor

CONSUMED, be —

To be completed, finished, consumed, כָּלָה *kalah.*
Dan. 11. 16 which by his hand shall be consumed

CONSUMED, to be —

1. *To be eaten, consumed,* אָכַל *akal,* 2.
Exod 22. 6 If..the field, be consumed (therewith); he
Num 12. 12 of whom the flesh is half consumed when

2. *To be eaten, consumed,* אָכַל *akal,* 4.
Exod. 3. 2 and the bush (was) not consumed
Neh. 2. 3 the gates thereof are consumed with fire?
2. 13 the gates thereof were consumed with fire

3. *To be extinguished, vanish,* דָּעַךְ *daak,* 2.
Job 6. 17 they are consumed out of their place

4. *To be completed, finished, consumed,* כָּלָה *kalah.*
Job 4. 9 by the breath of his nostrils are they con.
7. 9 (As) the cloud is consumed and vanisheth
19. 27 (though) my reins be consumed within me
Psa. 39. 10 I am consumed by the blow of thine hand
71. 13 Let them be confounded and consumed
90. 7 we are consumed by thine anger, and by
102. 3 my days are consumed like smoke, and
Prov. 5. 11 when thy flesh and thy body are con.
Isa. 1. 28 they that forsake the LORD shall be con.
29. 20 the scorner is consumed, and all that
Jer. 16. 4 they shall be consumed by the sword
20. 18 that my days should be consumed with
Eze. 5. 12 with famine shall they be consumed, in
13. 14 ye shall be consumed in the midst there.
Mal. 3. 6 therefore ye sons of Jacob are not con.

5. *To be ended, consumed,* סוּף *suph.*
Isa. 66. 17 abomination, and the mouse, shall be con.

6 *To end, consume,* סָפָה *saphah.*
Jer. 12. 4 the beasts are consumed, and the birds

7. *To be ended, consumed,* סָפָה *saphah,* 2.
Gen. 19. 15 lest thou be consumed in the iniquity of
19 17 escape to the mountain, lest thou be con.
Num 16. 26 lest ye be consumed in all their sins
1 Sa. 12. 25 ye shall be consumed, both ye and your

8. *To be old,* עָשֵׁשׁ *ashesh.*
Psa 6. 7 Mine eye is consumed because of grief
31. 9 mine eye is consumed with grief, (yea)
31. 10 strength faileth..my bones are consumed

9. *To be perfect, finished, consumed* תָּמַם *tamam.*
Num 17. 13 shall we be consumed with dying?
32. 13 until all the generation..was consumed
Deut. 2. 15 to destroy them..until they were consu.
2. 16 when all the men of war were consumed
Josh. 5. 6 men of war..were consumed, because
8. 24 were all fallen..until they were consumed
10. 20 slaying them.. till they were consumed
2 Ki. 7. 13 multitude of the Israelites that are con.
Psa. 73. 19 they are utterly consumed with terrors
Isa. 16. 4 the oppressors are consumed out of the
Jer. 6. 29 The bellows are burnt, the lead is con.
24. 10 among them, until they be consumed
36. 23 until all the wall was consumed in the
44. 12 they shall all be consumed, (and) fall in
44. 18 have been consumed by the sword and by
44. 27 all the men of Judah..shall be consumed
Lam. 3. 22 the LORD'S mercies that we are not con.
Eze. 24. 11 (that) the scum of it may be consumed
47. 12 neither shall the fruit thereof be con.

10. *To be finished, consumed,* תָּמַם *tamam,* 2.
Num 14. 35 in this wilderness they shall be consumed
Psa. 104. 35 Let the sinners be consumed out of the
Jer. 14. 15 By sword..shall those prophets be con.
44. 12 shall all be consumed..(even) be con.

CONSUMED —

To be gathered, אָסַף *asaph.*
Eze. 34. 29 they shall be no more consumed with

CONSUMMATION —

Completion, consumption, כָּלָה *kalah.*
Dan. 9. 27 even until the consummation, and that

CONSUMPTION —

1. *Completion, consumption,* כָּלָה *kalah.*
Isa. 10. 23 the LORD God of hosts shall make a con.
28. 22 from the LORD God of hosts a consumption

2. *Completion, consumption,* כִּלָּיוֹן *killayon.*
Isa. 10. 22 the consumption decreed shall overflow

3. *Consumption, wasting away,* שַׁחֶפֶת *shachepheth.*
Lev. 26. 16 I will even appoint over you terror, con.
Deut 28. 22 shall smite thee with a consumption, and

CONTAIN, to —

1. *To contain,* כּוּל *kul,* 3*a*.
1 Ki. 8. 27 the..heaven of heavens cannot contain
2 Ch. 2. 6 the..heaven of heavens cannot contain
6. 18 the heaven of heavens cannot contain

2. *To contain,* כּוּל *kul,* 5.
1 Ki. 7. 26 with flowers of lilies: it contained two
7. 38 one laver contained forty baths: (and)
Eze. 23. 32 thou shalt be..had in derision; it contain.

3. *To bear, contain,* נָשָׂא *nasa.*
Eze. 45. 11 that the bath may contain the tenth part

4. *To have space for,* χωρέω *chōreō.*
John 2. 6 containing two or three firkins apiece

CONTAIN, can —

1. *To have space for,* χωρέω *chōreō.*
John 21. 25 even the world itself could not contain

2. *To have inward power,* ἐγκρατεύομαι *egkrateuomai.*
1 Co. 7. 9 if they cannot contain, let them marry

CONTAINED, to be —

To hold around, περιέχω *periechō.*
1 Pe. 2. 6 also it is contained in the Scripture

CONTAINED in, the things —

The things, τά *ta.*
Rom. 2. 14 do by nature the things contained in the

CONTEMN, to —

1. *To loathe, despise, contemn,* בּוּז *buz.*
Song 8. 7 give all..it would utterly be contemned

2. *To refuse, reject,* מָאַס *maas.*
Eze. 21. 10 it contemneth the rod of my son, (as)
21. 13 what if (the sword) contemn even the rod?

3. *To despise,* נָאַץ *naats.*
Psa. 107. 11 contemned the counsel of the Most High

4. *To despise,* נָאַץ *naats,* 3.
Psa. 10. 13 Wherefore doth the wicked contemn God?

CONTEMNED, to be —

1. *To be loathed, despised, contemned,* בָּזָה *bazah,* 2.
Psa. 15. 4 In whose eyes a vile person is contemned

2. *To be lightly esteemed,* קָלָה *qalah,* 2.
Isa. 16. 14 and the glory of Moab shall be contemned

CONTEMPT —

1. *To loathe, despise, contemn,* בּוּז *buz.*
Job 12. 21 He poureth contempt upon princes, and
31. 34 or did the contempt of families terrify me
Psa. 107. 40 He poureth contempt upon princes, and
119. 22 Remove from me reproach and contempt
123. 3 we are exceedingly filled with contempt
123. 4 filled..with the contempt of the proud
Prov 18. 3 wicked cometh..cometh also contempt

2. *Loathing, despising, contempt,* בִּזָּיוֹן *biz-zayon.*
Esth. 1. 18 Thus..too much contempt and wrath

3. *Abhorrence, thrusting away,* דֵּרָאוֹן *deraon.*
Dan. 12. 2 some to shame..everlasting contempt

CONTEMPT, to bring into —

To make light of, קָלַל *qalal,* 5.
Isa. 23. 9 to bring into contempt all the honourable

CONTEMPTIBLE —

1. *To be loathed, despised, contemned,* בָּזָה *bazah,* 2.
Mal. 1. 7 The table of the LORD (is) contemptible
1. 12 and the fruit thereof..(is) contemptible
2. 9 have I also made you contemptible and

2. *To make, think nothing of,* ἐξουθενέω *exoutheneō.*
2 Co. 10. 10 presence (is) weak, and (his) speech con.

CONTEMPTUOUSLY —

In contempt, בְּבוּז *ba-buz.*
Psa. 31. 18 which speak grievous things..contempt.

CONTEND —

To contend, strive, רִיב *rib.*
Job 31. 13 If I did despise..when they contended

CONTEND, to —

1. *To stir up oneself, strive,* גָּרָה *garah,* 7.
Deut. 2. 9 Distress not the Moabites, neither contend
2. 24 begin to possess (it), and contend with
Prov 28. 4 but such as keep the law contend with

2. *To judge, enter into judgment,* דִּין *din.*
Eccl. 6. 10 neither may he contend with him that

3. *To fret oneself,* חָרָה *charah,* 5*a*.
Jer. 12. 5 then how canst thou contend with horses?

4. *To contend, strive,* רִיב *rib.*
Neh. 13. 11 Then contended I with the rulers, and
13. 17 I contended with the nobles of Judah, and
13. 25 I contended with them, and cursed them
Job 9. 3 If he will contend with him, he cannot
10. 2 show me wherefore thou contendest with
13. 8 accept his person? will ye contend for
40. 2 Shall he that contendeth with the Almig.
Isa. 49. 25 for I will contend with him that
50. 8 who will contend with me? let us stand
57. 16 I will not contend for ever, neither will
Amos 7. 4 the LORD God called to contend by fire
Mic. 6. 1 Arise, contend thou before the mountains

5. *To be taken into judgment,* שָׁפַט *shaphat,* 2.
Prov 29. 9 (If) a wise man contendeth with a foolish

6. *To judge diversely or differently,* διακρίνω *diakr.*
Acts 11. 2 that were of the circumcision contended
Jude 9 Michael, the archangel when contending

CONTEND earnestly for, to —

To contend about (anything), ἐπαγωνίζομαι *epagō.*
Jude 3 ye should earnestly contend for the faith

CONTENDED, that —

Debate, contention, מַצּוּת *matstsuth.*
Isa 41. 12 (even) them that contended with thee

CONTENDETH, that —

One that contends or strives, יָרִיב [*rib*].
Isa. 49. 25 with him that contendeth with thee
Jer. 18. 19 the voice of them that contend with me

CONTENT, to be —

1. *To be pleased, desirous,* יָאַל *yaal,* 5.
Exod. 2. 21 Moses was content to dwell with the man
Jos. 7. 7 would to God we had been content, and
Judg 17. 11 the Levite was content to dwell with the
19. 6 Be content, I pray thee, and tarry all
2 Ki. 5. 23 Naaman said, Be content, take two talents
6. 3 Be content, I pray thee, and go with thy
Job 6. 28 therefore be content; look upon me; for

2. *To hearken,* שָׁמַע *shama.*
Gen. 37. 27 sell him..And his brethren were content

3. *To ward off, help, suffice,* ἀρκέω *arkeō.*
Luke 3. 14 and be content with your wages
1 Ti. 6. 8 having food and raiment let us be..cont.
Heb. 13. 5 be content with such things as ye have
3 Jo. 10 prating against us..and not content there.

4. *Self sufficient,* αὐτάρκης *autarkēs.*
Phil. 4. 11 in whatsoever state I am..to be content

5. *To make sufficient, to satisfy,* ποιέω τὸ ἱκανόν.
Mark 15. 15 Pilate, willing to content the people

6. *To be good in the eyes of,* יָטַב בְּעֵינֵי *yatab be-ene.*
Lev. 10. 20 And when Moses heard (that), he was con.

CONTENTION —

1. *Strife, contention,* מָדוֹן *madon.*
Prov. 22. 10 Cast out the scorner, and contention
Jer. 15. 10 a man of strife and a man of contention
Hab. 1. 3 are (that) raise up strife and contention

2. *Debate,* מַצָּה *matstsah.*
Prov 13. 10 Only by pride cometh contention: but

3. *Contention, strife, pleading, cause,* רִיב *rib.*
Prov 17. 14 leave off contention, before it be meddled
18. 6 A fool's lips enter into contention, and

4. *Contest,* ἀγών *agōn.*
1 Th. 2. 2 to speak unto you..with much contention

5. *Strife, contention, wrangling,* ἐριθεία *eritheia.*
Phil. 1. 16 The one preach Christ of contention, not

6. *Strife, contention, wrangling,* ἔρις *eris.*
1 Co. 1. 11 that there are contentions among you
Tit. 3. 9 avoid foolish questions..and contentions

7. *Paroxysm, sharp dispute,* παροξυσμός *paroxusmos.*
Acts 15. 39 the contention was so sharp between

CONTENTIONS —

Strifes, contentions, מִדְיָנִים *midyanim* [V. L. מדונים twice].
Prov 18. 18 The lot causeth contentions to cease, and
18. 19 (their) contentions (are) like the bars of
19. 13 the contentions of a wife (are) a continual
23. 29 who hath sorrow? who hath contentions?

CONTENTIOUS —

1. *Strife, contention,* מִדְיָנִים *midyanim* [V. L. מָדוֹן *madon*].
Prov. 21. 19 than with a contentious and an angry
26. 21 so (is) a contentious man to kindle strife
27. 15 A continual dropping..and a contentious

2. *Loving strife,* φιλόνεικος *philoneikos.*
1 Co. 11. 16 if any man seem to be contentious, we

CONTENTIOUS, they that are —

Those of contention, οἱ ἐξ ἐριθείας *hoi ex eritheias.*
Rom. 2. 8 them that are contentious, and do not

CONTENTMENT —

Self sufficiency, αὐτάρκεια *autarkeia.*
1 Ti. 6. 6 godliness with contentment is great gain

CONTINUAL —

1. *To drive away, thrust on,* טָרַד *tarad.*
Prov. 19. 13 the contentions of a wife (are) a continual
27. 15 A continual dropping..and a contentious

2. *Continual,* תָּמִיד *tamid.*
Exod29. 42 a continual burnt offering throughout
Num. 4. 7 and the continual bread shall be thereon
28. 3 two lambs..(for) a continual burnt offer.
28. 6 a continual burnt offering, which was
28. 10, 15, 24 beside the continual burnt offer.
28. 23 which (is) for a continual burnt offering
28. 31 Ye shall offer (them) beside the continual
29. 11 the continual burnt offering, and the
29. 16, 19, 22, 25 beside the continual burnt offer.
29. 28, 31, 34, 38 beside the continual burnt offer.
2 Ki. 25. 30 his allowance (was) a continual allowance
2 Ch. 2. 4 for the continual showbread, and..burnt
Ezra 3. 5 afterward (offered) the continual burnt
Neh. 10. 33 the showbread, and for the continual
10. 33 for the continual burnt offering, of the
Prov 15. 15 a merry heart (hath) a continual feast
Jer. 52. 34 there was a continual diet given him of
Eze. 46. 15 the oil, every morning, (for) a continual

3. *Unintermitting, not left at all,* ἀδιάλειπτος *adia.*
Rom. 9. 2 I have great heaviness and continual

4. *To the end,* εἰς τέλος *eis telos.*
Luke18. 5 lest by her continual coming she weary

5. *Without turning aside,* בִּלְתִּי סָרָה *bilti sarah.*
Isa 14. 6 He who smote..with a continual stroke

CONTINUAL employment —
Continual, continuity, תָּמִיד *tamid.*
Eze. 39. 14 sever out men of continual employment

CONTINUALLY —
1. *With continuance,* בִּתְדִירָא *bi-tedira.*
Dan. 6. 16 Thy God, whom thou servest continually
6. 20 is thy God, whom thou servest continu.
2. *Continual,* תָּמִיד *tamid.*
Exod28. 29 for a memorial before the LORD continu.
28. 30 upon his heart before the LORD continu.
29. 38 of the first year day by day continually
Lev. 24. 2 to cause the lamps to burn continually
24. 3 shall Aaron order it..before the LORD con.
24. 4 order the lamps..before the LORD conti.
24. 8 in order before the LORD continually
2 Sa. 9. 7 shalt eat bread at my table continually
9. 13 So Mephibosheth..did eat continually
1 Ki. 10. 8 Happy (are) thy men..which stand conti.
2 Ki. 4. 9 an holy man..which passeth by us conti.
25. 29 he did eat bread continually before him
1 Ch. 16. 6 the priests with trumpets continually
16. 11 Seek the LORD..seek his face continually
16. 37 to minister before the ark continually
16. 40 upon the altar..continually morning and
23. 31 to offer all burnt sacrifices..continually b.
2 Ch. 9. 7 Happy (are) thy men..which stand con.
24. 14 they offered burnt offerings..continually
Psa. 34. 1 his praise (shall) continually (be) in my
35. 27 let them say continually, Let the LORD
38. 17 and my sorrow (is) continually before me
40. 11 let..thy truth continually preserve me
40. 16 let such as love thy salvation say contin.
50. 8 thy burnt offerings..continually before
69. 23 and make their loins continually to shake
70. 4 let such as love thy salvation say continu.
71. 3 whereunto I may continually resort
71. 6 my praise (shall be) continually of thee
71. 14 I will hope continually, and will yet
72. 15 prayer also shall be made for him contin.
73. 23 Nevertheless I (am) continually with thee
74. 23 the tumult..against thee increaseth con.
109. 15 Let them be before the LORD continually
109. 19 a girdle wherewith he is girded continu.
119. 44 So shall I keep thy law continually for
119. 109 My soul (is) continually in my hand: yet
119. 117 I will have respect unto thy statutes con.
Prov. 6. 21 Bind them continually upon thine heart
Isa. 21. 8 I stand continually upon the watch tower
49. 16 Behold..thy walls (are) continually before
51. 13 hast feared continually every day, because
52. 5 my name continually every day (is) blas.
58. 11 the LORD shall guide thee continually
60. 11 Therefore thy gates shall be open contin.
65. 3 that provoketh me to anger continually
Jer. 6. 7 before me continually (is) grief and
52. 33 he did continually eat bread before him
Eze. 46. 14 a meat-offering continually by a perpetual
Hos. 12. 6 judgment, and wait on thy God continu.
Obad. 16 (so) shall all the heathen drink continu.
Nah. 3. 19 thy wickedness passed continually?
Hab. 1. 17 not spare continually to slay the nations?
3. *All the day,* כָּל־הַיּוֹם *kol hay-yom.*
Gen. 6. 5 every imagination..only evil continually
1 Sa. 18. 29 and Saul became David's enemy continu.
2 Sa. 19. 13 if thou be not captain..continually
2 Ch. 12. 15 between Rehoboam and Jeroboam conti.
Job 1. 5 Job..offered..Thus did Job continually
Psa 42. 3 they continually say unto me, Where (is)
44. 15 My confusion (is) continualy before me
52. 1 the goodness of God (endureth) continu.
140. 2 continually are they gathered together
Jer. 33. 18 offerings, and to do sacrifice continually
4. *In all time,* בְּכָל־עֵת *be-kol eth*
Prov. 6. 14 he deviseth mischief continually
5. *Going and turning back,* הָלוֹךְ וָשׁוֹב [*halak va-shub*].
Gen. 8. 3 returned from off the earth continually
6. *Through all (time),* διαπαντός *diapantos.*
Luke24. 53 were continually in the temple, praising
Heb. 13. 15 the sacrifice of praise to God continually

7. *To the unbroken continuance,* εἰς τὸ διηνεκές, -ῆς.
Heb. 7. 3 Son of God; abideth a priest continually
10. 1 continually make the comers thereunto

CONTINUALLY upon, to attend —
To endure or persevere toward (anything), προσκαρτερέω *proskartereō.*
Rom. 13. 6 attending continually upon this very

CONTINUALLY to, to give one's self —
To endure or persevere toward (anything), προσκαρτερέω *proskartereō.*
Acts 6. 4 will give ourselves continually to prayer

CONTINUALLY, to wait on —
To endure or persevere toward (anything), προσκαρτερέω *proskartereō.*
Acts 10. 7 soldier..that waited on him continually

CONTINUANCE —
1. *Days,* יָמִים *yamim.*
Psa. 139. 16 (which) in continuance were fashioned
2. *Indefinite time,* עוֹלָם *olam.*
Isa. 64. 5 in those is continuance, and we shall be

CONTINUANCE, patient —
A remaining under (anything), ὑπομονή *hupomonē.*
Rom. 2. 7 who by patient continuance in well doing

CONTINUE —
To stand, קוּם *qum.*
1 Sa. 13. 14 thy kingdom shall not continue: the
Job 15. 29 neither shall his substance continue

CONTINUE, to —
1. *To tarry, delay,* אָחַר *achar,* 3.
Isa. 5. 11 that continue until night, (till) wine
2. *To keep hold,* חָזַק *chazaq,* 5.
Neh. 5. 16 also I continued in the work of this wall
3. *To add,* יָסַף *yasaph,* 5.
Job 27. 1 Job continued his parable, and said
29. 1 Job continued his parable, and said
4. *To sit,* יָשַׁב *yashab.*
Lev. 12. 4 she shall then continue in the blood of
12. 5 she shall continue in the blood of her
Judg 5. 17 Asher continued on the sea shore, and
2 Sa. 6. 11 the ark of the LORD continued in the
1 Ki. 22. 1 they continued three years without war
5. *To lodge (all night),* לִין *lun.*
Job 17. 2 mine eye continue in their provocation?
6. *To draw out,* מָשַׁךְ *mashak.*
Psa. 36. 10 O continue thy loving kindness unto them
7. *To stand,* עָמַד *amad.*
Exod21. 21 if he continue a day or two, he shall not
Ruth 2. 7 continued even from the morning until
Job 14. 2 he fleeth also as a shadow, and continueth
Jer. 32. 14 put them..that they may continue many
Dan. 11. 8 he shall continue (more) years than the
8. *To cause to arise, establish,* קוּם *qum,* 5.
1 Ki. 2. 4 That the LORD may continue his word
9. *To tabernacle, dwell,* שָׁכַן *shaken.*
Psa. 102. 28 The children of thy servants shall conti.
10. *To multiply, make many,* רָבָה *rabah,* 5.
1 Sa. 1. 12 as she continued praying before the Lo.
11. *To become, happen,* γίνομαι *ginomai.*
Acts 19. 10 this continued by the space of two years
12. *To remain throughout,* διαμένω *diamenō.*
Luke22. 28 Ye are they which have continued with
Gal. 2. 5 that the truth of the gospel might conti.
2 Pe. 3. 4 all things continue as..from the begin.
13. *To end fully,* διατελέω *diateleō.*
Acts 27. 33 ye have tarried and continued fasting
14. *To rub through, pass the time,* διατρίβω *diatri.*
John11. 54 and there continued with his disciples
Acts 15. 35 Barnabas continued in Antioch, teaching
15. *To remain on,* ἐπιμένω *epimenō.*
John 8. 7 when they continued asking him, he
Acts 12. 16 Peter continued knocking: and when they
16. *To set, place,* ἵστημι *histēmi.*
Acts 26. 22 I continue unto this day, witnessing both
17. *To sit down,* καθίζω *kathizō.*
Acts 18. 11 he continued..a year and six months
18. *To remain,* μένω *menō.*
John 2. 12 and they continued there not many days
8. 31 If ye continue in my word, (then) are ye
15. 9 so have I loved you: continue ye in my
1 Ti. 2. 15 if they continue in faith and charity and
2 Ti. 3. 14 continue thou in the things which thou
Heb. 7. 24 this (man), because he continueth ever
13. 1 Let brotherly love continue
13. 14 here have we no continuing city, but we
1 Jo. 2. 19 they would..have continued with us
2. 24 ye also shall continue in the Son, and in
Rev. 17. 10 he must continue a short space
19. *To remain on,* παραμένω *paramenō.*
Heb. 7. 23 they were not suffered to continue by
Jas. 1. 25 looketh into the perfect law..and contin.
20. *To extend on,* παρατείνω *parateinō.*
Acts 20. 7 and continued his speech until midnight

21. *To do,* ποιέω *poieō.*
Rev. 13. 5 power was given unto him to continue for

CONTINUE all night, to —
To spend the whole night, διανυκτερεύω.
Luke 6. 12 and continued all night in prayer to God

CONTINUE in, to —
1. *To remain in,* ἐμμένω *emmenō.*
Acts 14. 22 exhorting them to continue in the faith
Gal. 3. 10 Cursed (is) every one that continueth not in
Heb. 8. 9 they continued not in my covenant, and
2. *To remain on,* ἐπιμένω *epimenō.*
Acts 13. 43 persuaded them to continue in the grace
Rom. 6. 1 Shall we continue in sin, that grace may
11. 22 toward thee, goodness, if thou continue in
Col. 1. 23 If ye continue in the faith grounded and
1 Ti. 4. 16 Take heed unto thyself..continue in them
3. *To remain beside or further,* προσμένω *prosmenō.*
1 Ti. 5. 5 continueth in supplications and prayers
4. *To persevere toward (anything),* προσκαρτερέω.
Acts 1. 14 These all continued with one accord in
2. 46 continuing daily with one accord in the
Col. 4. 2 Continue in prayer, and watch in the

CONTINUE instant in, to —
To persevere toward (anything), προσκαρτερέω.
Rom 12. 12 Rejoicing in hope..continuing instant in

CONTINUE stedfastly, to —
To persevere toward a thing, προσκαρτερέω *prosk.*
Acts 2. 42 they continued stedfastly in the apostles'

CONTINUE with, to —
1. *To persevere toward (anything),* προσκαρτερέω.
Acts 8. 13 when he was baptized, he continued with
2. *To remain toward,* προσμένω *prosmenō.*
Matt15. 32 because they continue with me now three
3. *To remain alongside with,* συμπαραμένω *sumpa.*
Phil. 1. 25 I shall abide and continue with you all

CONTINUED, to be —
To continue, נוּן *nun,* 2, 5.
Psa. 72. 17 his name shall be continued as long as

CONTINUING —
To sojourn, גּוּר *gur,* 7a.
Jer. 30. 23 a continuing whirlwind: it shall fall with

CONTRADICT, to —
To speak against, ἀντιλέγω *antilegō.*
Acts 13. 45 things which were spoken by Paul, con.

CONTRADICTION —
A speaking against, ἀντιλογία *antilogia.*
Heb 7. 7 without all contradiction the less is bles.
12. 3 consider him that endured such contra.

CONTRARIWISE —
The opposite, on the contrary, τοὐναντίον *tounanti.*
2 Co. 2. 7 contrariwise ye (ought) rather to forgive
Gal. 2. 7 But contrariwise, when they saw that the
1 Pe. 3. 9 but contrariwise blessing; knowing that

CONTRARY —
1. *Contrariety, perversity, a turning,* הֶפֶךְ *hephek.*
Eze. 16. 34 the contrary is in thee from (other)
16. 34 no reward is given..thou art contrary
2. *Opposition,* קְרִי *qeri.*
Lev. 26. 21 if ye walk contrary unto me, and will
26. 23 these things, but will walk contrary unto
26. 24 Then will I also walk contrary unto you
26. 27 if ye will not..hearken..but walk contr.
26. 28 Then I will walk contrary unto you also
26. 40 that also they have walked contrary unto
26. 41 I also have walked contrary unto them
3. *Over against, opposite,* ἐναντίος *enantios.*
Matt14. 24 ship was..tossed..for the wind was con
Mark 6. 48 for the wind was contrary unto them
Acts 26. 9 I ought to do many things contrary to
27. 4 we sailed..because the winds were con.
1 Th. 2. 15 they please not God, and are contrary to
Titus 2. 8 he that is of the contrary part may be
4. *Set over against,* ὑπεναντίος *hupenantios.*
Col. 2. 14 which was contrary to us, and took it out

CONTRARY, to be —
To lie or be laid over against, ἀντίκειμαι *antikeimai.*
Gal. 5. 17 these are contrary the one to the other
1 Ti. 1. 10 if there be any other thing that is contrary

CONTRARY to —
1. *From over against,* ἀπέναντι *apenanti.*
Acts 17. 7 these all do contrary to the decrees of
2. *Contrary to,* παρά *para,* (acc.)
Acts 18. 13 persuadeth men to worship God contr. to
Rom. 11. 24 wert graffed contrary to nature into a
16. 17 which cause divisions..contrary to the

CONTRIBUTION —
Act of using a thing in common, κοινωνία *koinōnia.*
Rom. 15. 26 to make a certain contribution for the

CONTRITE —
1. *Bruised, contrite,* דַּכָּא *dakka.*
Psa. 34. 18 saveth such as be of a contrite spirit
Isa. 57. 15 with him also (that is) of a contrite..spirit

2. *To be bruised,* דָּכָה *dakah,* 2.
Psa. 51. 17 a broken and a contrite heart, O God

3. *Smitten,* נָכֶה *nakeh.*
Isa. 66. 2 (him that is) poor, and of a contrite spirit

CONTRITE one —
To be bruised, דַּכָּא *daka,* 2.
Isa. 57. 15 to revive the heart of the contrite ones

CONTROVERSY —
Strife, contention, pleading, cause, רִיב *rib.*
Deut 17. 8 matters of controversy, within thy gates
19. 17 both the men, between whom the contro.
21. 5 by their word shall every controversy and
25. 1 If there be a controversy between men
2 Sa. 15. 2 when any man that had a controversy
2 Ch. 19. 8 judgment of the LORD, and for controv.
Isa. 34. 8 the year of recompences for the controv.
Jer. 25. 31 for the LORD hath a controversy with the
Eze. 44. 24 in controversy they shall stand in judg.
Hos. 4. 1 for the LORD hath a controversy with the
12. 2 The LORD hath also a controversy with
Mic. 6. 2 Hear ye, O mountains, the LORD'S con.
6. 2 the LORD hath a controversy with his

CONTROVERSY, without —
Confessedly, said unanimously, ὁμολογουμένως.
1 Ti. 3. 16 without controversy great is the mystery

CONVENIENT —
1. *A statute, limited and apportioned thing,* חֹק *choq.*
Prov. 30. 8 feed me with food convenient for me

2. *Right, upright,* יָשָׁר *yashar.*
Jer. 40. 4 whither it seemeth good and convenient
40. 5 go wheresoever it seemeth convenient

3. *Well timed,* εὔκαιρος *eukairos.*
Mark 6. 21 when a convenient day was come, that

CONVENIENT, to be —
To have come up to, be becoming, ἀνήκω *anēkō.*
Eph. 5. 4 nor jesting, which are not convenient
Philemon 8 to enjoin thee that which is convenient

CONVENIENT, things not —
The things not seemly, τὰ μὴ καθήκοντα [*kathēkō*].
Rom. 1. 28 do these things which are not convenient

CONVENIENT season —
A season, time, καιρός *kairos.*
Acts 24. 25 when I have a convenient season I will

CONVENIENT time, to have —
To have good time or season, εὐκαιρέω *eukaireō.*
1 Co. 16. 12 come when he shall have convenient time

CONVENIENTLY —
In good time or season, εὐκαίρως *eukairōs.*
Mark 14. 11 he sought how he might conveniently

CONVERSANT, to be —
1. *To go on,* הָלַךְ *halak.*
Josh. 8. 35 the strangers that were conversant amo.

2. *To go on habitually,* הָלַךְ *halak,* 7.
1 Sa. 25. 15 as long as we were conversant with them

CONVERSATION —
1. *Way,* דֶּרֶךְ *derek.*
Psa. 37. 14 slay such as be of upright conversation
50. 23 to him that ordereth (his) conversation

2. *A turning up and down, behaviour,* ἀναστροφή.
Gal. 1. 13 ye have heard of my conversation in time
Eph. 4. 22 put off, concerning the former conversa.
1 Ti. 4. 12 an example of the believers..in convers
Heb. 13. 7 considering the end of (their) conversa.
Jas. 3. 13 let him show out of a good conversation
1 Pe. 1. 15 be ye holy in all manner of conversation
1. 18 vain conversation (received) by tradition
2. 12 Having your conversation honest among
3. 1 be won by the conversation of the wives
3. 2 While they behold your chaste conversa.
3. 16 that falsely accuse your good conversa.
2 Pe. 2. 7 vexed with the filthy conversation of the
3. 11 ought ye to be in (all) holy conversation

3. *Citizen state or life,* πολίτευμα *politeuma.*
Phil. 3. 20 our conversation is in heaven; from

4. *Turning, turn, manner,* τρόπος *tropos.*
Heb. 13. 5 conversation (be) without covetousness

CONVERSATION, to have one's —
To turn up and down, behave oneself, ἀναστρέφω.
2 Co. 1. 12 we have had our conversation in the
Eph. 2. 3 we all had our conversation in times past

CONVERSATION, let . be —
To act as a citizen, πολιτεύω *politeuō.*
Phil. 1. 27 let your conversation be as it becometh

CONVERSION —
A turning upon, ἐπιστροφή *epistrophē.*
Acts 15. 3 declaring the conversion of the Gentiles

CONVERT, to —
1. *To bring back, refresh,* שׁוּב *shub,* 5.
Psa. 19. 7 The law of the LORD (is) perfect, convert.

2. *To turn about or upon,* ἐπιστρέφω *epistrephō.*
Jas. 5. 19 do err from the truth, and one convert
5. 20 he which converteth the sinner from the

CONVERTED, to be —
1. *To be turned,* הָפַךְ *haphak,* 2.
Isa. 60. 5 abundance of the sea shall be converted

2. *To turn back,* שׁוּב *shub.*
Psa. 51. 13 and sinners shall be converted unto thee
Isa. 6. 10 understand with their heart, and convert

3. *To turn about or upon,* ἐπιστρέφω *epistrephō.*
Matt 13. 15 they..should be converted, and I should
Mark 4. 12 lest at any time they should be converted
Luke 22. 32 when thou art converted, strengthen thy
John 12. 40 and be converted, and I should heal them
Acts 3. 19 Repent ye therefore, and be converted
28. 27 should be converted, and I should heal

4. *To turn,* στρέφω *strephō.*
Matt 18. 3 Except ye be converted, and become as

CONVERTS —
To turn back, שׁוּב *shub.*
Isa. 1. 27 redeemed with judgment, and her con.

CONVEY, to —
To put, place, set, שׂוּם *sum.*
1 Ki. 5. 9 I will convey them by sea in floats unto

CONVEY over, to —
To cause to pass over, עָבַר *abar,* 5.
Neh. 2. 7 may convey me over, till I come into J.

CONVEY one's self away, to —
To move or glide out of (the way), ἐκνεύω *ekneuō.*
John 5. 13 for Jesus had conveyed himself away

CONVICT, to —
To convict, ἐλέγχω *elegchō.*
John 8. 9 being convicted by (their own) conscience

CONVINCE, to —
1. *To make manifest or prominent,* יָכַח *yakach,* 5.
Job 32. 12 (there was) none of you that convinced J.

2. *To convict,* ἐλέγχω *elegchō.*
John 8. 46 Which of you convinceth me of sin?
1 Co. 14. 24 he is convinced of all, he is judged of all
Titus 1. 9 to exhort and to convince the gainsayers
Jas. 2. 9 are convinced of the law as transgressors

3. *To convict utterly,* ἐξελέγχω *exelegchō.*
Jude 15 to convince all that are ungodly among

4. *To convict thoroughly,* διακατελέγχομαι.
Acts 18. 28 for he mightily convinced the Jews

CONVOCATION —
A calling (together), convocation, מִקְרָא *miqra.*
Exod 12. 16 (there shall be) an holy convocation, and
12. 16 there shall be an holy convocation to you
Lev. 23. 2 ye shall proclaim (to be) holy convocations
23. 3 the sabbath of rest, an holy convocation
23. 4 holy convocations, which ye shall procl.
23. 7 ye shall have an holy convocation
23. 8 in the seventh day (is) an holy convoca.
23. 21 it may be an holy convocation unto you
23. 24 blowing of trumpets, an holy convocation
23. 27 it shall be an holy convocation unto you
23. 35 the first day (shall be) an holy convoca.
23. 36 on the eighth day shall be an holy convo.
23. 37 which ye shall proclaim (to be) holy con.
Num 28. 18 In the first day (shall be) an holy convo.
28. 25, 26 ye shall have an holy convocation
29. 1, 12 ye shall have an holy convocation
29. 7 ye shall have..an holy convocation

COOK —
A slaughterer, cook, טַבָּח *tabbach.*
1 Sa. 9. 23 Samuel said unto the cook, Bring the
9. 24 the cook took up the shoulder, and (that)

COOKS —
Female cooks, טַבָּחוֹת *tabbachoth.*
1 Sa. 8. 13 he will take your daughters..(to be) cooks

COOL —
Wind, רוּחַ *ruach.*
Gen. 3. 8 in the garden in the cool of the day

COOL, to —
To cool down, καταψύχω *katapsuchō.*
Luke 16. 24 dip the tip of his finger..and cool my

COOS, Κῶς.
A small island on the coast of Caria, near Myndos and Cnidos; N.W. from Rhodes; now called *Stanchio* or *Stanko;* it was the birth place of Hippocrates, Apelles, and Simonides.
Acts 21. 1 we came with a straight course unto C.

COPING —
Open palm (of hand), projecting stone, טֶפַח *tephach.*
1 Ki. 7. 9 even from the foundation unto the coping

COPPER —
Copper, brass, נְחֹשֶׁת *nechosheth.*
Ezra 8. 27 vessels of fine copper, precious as gold

COPPERSMITH —
Brazier, coppersmith, χαλκεύς *chalkeus.*
2 Ti. 4. 14 Alexander the coppersmith did me much

COPULATION —
Effusion, שִׁכְבָה *shekabah.*
Lev. 15. 16 if any man's seed of copulation go out
15. 17 every skin, whereon is the seed of copula.
15. 18 whom man shall lie (with) seed of copu.

COPY —
1. *A second, double,* מִשְׁנֶה *mishneh.*
Deut 17. 18 he shall write him a copy of this law in
Josh. 8. 32 he wrote there upon the stones a copy of

2. *Copy, transcript,* פַּרְשֶׁגֶן *parshegen.*
Ezra 4. 11 This (is) the copy of the letter that they
4. 23 when the copy..(was) read before Rehum
5. 6 The copy of the letter that Tatnai, gov.
7. 11 Now this (is) the copy of the letter that

3. *Copy, transcript,* פַּתְשֶׁגֶן *pathshegen.*
Esth. 3. 14 The copy of the writing, for a command.
4. 8 gave him the copy of the writing of the
8. 13 The copy of the writing for a command.

COPY out, to —
To remove, transcribe, עָתַק *athaq,* 5.
Prov 25. 1 which the men of Hezekiah..copied out

COR —
Cor (a measure of dry and liquid things), כֹּר *kor.*
Eze. 45. 14 the tenth part of a bath out of the cor

CORAL —
Red coral, רָאמוֹת *ramoth.*
Job 28. 18 No mention shall be made of coral, or of
Eze. 27. 16 they occupied in thy fairs with..coral

CORBAN —
Anything brought near to God, κορβᾶν *korban, Heb.*
Mark 7. 11 If a man shall say..(It is) Corban, that

CORD —
1. *Rope, cord,* חֶבֶל *chebel.*
Josh. 2. 15 she let them down by a cord through the
Esth. 1. 6 fastened with cords of fine linen and
Job 36. 8 And..be holden in cords of affliction
41. 1 or his tongue with a cord..thou lettest
Psa. 140. 5 The proud have hid a snare..and cords
Prov. 5. 22 he shall be holden with the cords of his
Eccl. 12. 6 Or ever the silver cord be loosed, or the
Isa. 5. 18 that draw iniquity with cords of vanity
Jer. 38. 6 and they let down Jeremiah with cords
38. 11 let them down by cords into the dungeon
38. 12 under thine arm holes under the cords
38. 13 So they drew up Jeremiah with cords, and
Eze. 27. 24 in chests of rich apparel, bound with cords
Hos. 11. 4 I drew them with cords of a man, with
Mic. 2. 5 cast a cord by lot in the congregation of

2. *A thread, cord,* חוּט *chut.*
Eccl. 4. 12 and a threefold cord is not quickly broken

3. *A pin (of a tent),* יֶתֶר *yether.*
Job 30. 11 he hath loosed my cord, and afflicted me

4. *Cord, string,* מֵיתָר *methar.*
Exod 35. 18 and the pins of the court, and their cords
39. 40 the hanging for the court gate, his cords
Num. 3. 26 the cords of it, for all the service thereof
3. 37 the pillars of the court..and their cords
4. 26 their cords, and all the instruments of
4. 32 the pillars of the court..and their cords
Isa. 54. 2 lengthen thy cords, and strengthen thy
Jer. 10. 20 My tabernacle is spoiled, and all my cords

5. *Thick cord,* עֲבֹת *aboth.*
Judg 15. 13 they bound him with two new cords, and
15. 14 the cords that (were) upon his arms beca.
Psa. 2. 3 Let us..cast away their cords from us
118. 27 bind the sacrifice with cords, (even) unto
129. 4 he hath cut asunder the cords of the

CORDS, small —
A cord made of bulrushes, σχοινίον *schoinion.*
John 2. 15 when he had made a scourge of small co.

CO-RE, Κορέ.
The Greek form of *Korah.*
Jude 11 for they..perished in the gainsaying of C.

CORIANDER —
A round aromatic seed, גַּד *gad.*
Exod 16. 31 and it (was) like coriander seed, white
Num 11. 7 the manna (was) as coriander seed, and

CO-RINTH, Κόρινθος.
Capital of Achaia Proper, on the isthmus between the Peloponnesus and the mainland between the gulfs of Lepanto and Ægina. Here Paul dwelt eighteen months.
Acts 18. 1 After these things Paul..came to C
19. 1 while Apollos was at C., Paul having
1 Co. 1. 2 the church of God which is at C.
2 Co. 1. 1 the church of God which is at C.
1. 23 to spare you I came not as yet unto C.
2 Ti. 4. 20 Erastus abode at C.: but Trophimus have

CORINTHIAN, Κορίνθιος.
A native or inhabitant of Corinth.
Acts 18. 8 and many of the C. hearing believed, and
2 Co. 6. 11 O (ye) C., our mouth is open unto you

CORMORANT —
1. *Pelican,* קָאַת *qaath.*
Isa. 34. 11 the cormorant and the bittern shall pos.
Zeph. 2. 14 the cormorant and the bittern shall lodge

2. *Cormorant,* שָׁלָךְ *shalak.*
Lev. 11. 17 the little owl, and the cormorant, and the
Deut 14. 17 pelican, and the gier..and the cormorant

CORN —
1. *Mixed produce,* בְּלִיל *balil.*
Job 24. 6 They reap..his corn in the field: and

2. *Wheat, corn, grain,* בַּר,בָּר *bar.*
Gen. 41. 35 lay up corn under the hand of Pharaoh
41. 49 Joseph gathered corn as the sand of the
42. 3 ten brethren went down to buy corn in E.
42. 25 commanded to fill their sacks with corn
45. 23 ten she asses laden with corn and bread
Job 39. 4 Their young ones..they grow up with corn
Psa. 65. 13 valleys also are covered over with corn
72. 16 There shall be an handful of corn in the
Prov 11. 26 He that withholdeth corn, the people

3. *A threshing floor,* גֹּרֶן *goren.*
Deut 16. 13 after that thou hast gathered in thy corn

4. *Corn, grain,* דָּגָן *dagan.*
Gen. 27. 28 God give thee..plenty of corn and wine
27. 37 with corn and wine have I sustained him
Num 18. 27 as though..the corn of the threshing-flo.
Deut. 7. 13 he will also bless..thy corn, and thy wine
11. 14 that thou mayest gather in thy corn, and
12. 17 within thy gates the tithe of thy corn
14. 23 thou shalt eat..the tithe of thy corn
18. 4 The first fruit (also) of thy corn, of thy
28. 51 which (also) shall not leave thee..corn
33. 28 fountain of Jacob..upon a land of corn
2 Ki. 18. 32 Until I..take you away to..a land of corn
2 Ch. 31. 5 the first fruits of corn, wine, and oil, and
32. 28 Storehouses also for the increase of corn
Neh. 5. 2 we take up corn..that we may eat, and
5. 3 have mortgaged..that we might buy corn
5. 10 might exact of them money and corn: I
5. 11 also the hundredth (part) of the..corn
10. 39 Levi shall bring the offering of the corn
13. 5 the tithes of the corn, the new wine, and
13. 12 Then brought all..the tithe of the corn
Psa. 4. 7 more than in the time..their corn and
65. 9 thou preparest them corn, when thou
78. 24 and had given them of the corn of heaven
Isa. 36. 17 a land of corn and wine, a land of bread
62. 8 I will no more give thy corn (to be) meat
Lam. 2. 12 They say to their mothers, Where (is) corn
Eze. 36. 29 I will call for the corn, and will increase
Hos. 2. 8 she did not know that I gave her corn
2. 9 take away my corn in the time thereof
2. 22 the earth shall hear the corn, and the
7. 14 they assemble themselves for corn and
14. 7 they shall revive (as) the corn, and grow
Joel 1. 10 the land mourneth; for the corn is wasted
1. 17 the barns are broken down; for the corn
2. 19 I will send you corn, and wine, and oil
Hag. 1. 11 upon the corn, and upon the new wine
Zec. 9. 17 Corn shall make the young men cheer.

5. *Standing corn,* קָמָה *qamah.*
Deut 16. 9 beginnest (to put) the sickle to the corn
Isa. 17. 5 as when the harvest man gathereth the co.

6. *Grain, corn,* שֶׁבֶר *sheber.*
Gen. 42. 1 Jacob saw that there was corn in Egypt
42. 2 I have heard that there is corn in Egypt
42. 19 go ye, carry corn for the famine of your
42. 26 they laded their asses with the corn, and
43. 2 when they had eaten up the corn which
44. 2 put..in the sack's mouth..his corn money
47. 14 gathered up all the money..for the corn
Amos 8. 5 new moon be gone, that we may sell corn?

7. *Son, produce,* בֵּן *ben.*
Isa. 21. 10 O my threshing, and the corn of my floor

8. *A kernel, a grain, seed,* κόκκος *kokkos.*
John 12. 24 Except a corn of wheat fall into the grou.

9. *Wheat, corn, grain,* σῖτος *sitos.*
Mark 4. 28 then the ear, after that the full corn in
Acts 7. 12 when Jacob heard that there was corn in

10. *Sown fields of grain,* σπόριμα *sporima.*
Matt 12. 1 began to pluck the ears of corn, and to eat

CORN, beaten —
Corn beaten or bruised, גֶּרֶשׂ *geres.*
Lev. 2. 14 offer..(even) corn beaten out of full ears
2. 16 of the beaten corn thereof, and (part) of

CORN fields —
Sown fields of grain, σπόριμα *sporima.*
Mark 2. 23 he went through the corn fields on the
Luke 6. 1 that he went through the corn fields

CORN, ears of —
1. *An ear of grain,* שִׁבֹּלֶת *shibboleth.*
Gen. 41. 5 seven ears of corn came up upon one
Ruth 2. 2 glean ears of corn after (him) in whose
Job 24. 24 cut off as the tops of the ears of corn

2. *An ear of grain,* στάχυς *stachus.*
Matt 12. 1 began to pluck the ears of corn, and to
Mark 2. 23 disciples began..to pluck the ears of corn
Luke 6. 1 his disciples plucked the ears of corn

CORN, full ears of —
Garden land, grain, כַּרְמֶל *karmel.*
2 Ki. 4. 42 brought..full ears of corn in the husk

CORN, ground —
Pounded corn or grain, grits, רִפוֹת *riphoth.*
2 Sa. 17. 19 the woman..spread ground corn thereon

CORN, heap of —
A heap of grain, עֲרֵמָה *aremah.*
Ruth 3. 7 lie down at the end of the heap of corn

CORN, old —
Old corn or produce, עֲבוּר *abur.*
Josh. 5. 11 they did eat of the old corn of the land
5. 12 after they had eaten of the old corn of

CORN, parched —
Parched or roasted ears, קָלִי, קָלִיא *qali.*
Lev. 23. 14 shall eat neither bread, nor parched corn
Ruth 2. 14 he reached her parched (corn), and she
1 Sa. 17. 17 Take now..an ephah of this parched (corn)
25. 18 took..five measures of parched (corn)
2 Sa. 17. 28 Brought..flour, and parched (corn), and

CORN, standing —
What stands up, קָמָה *qamah.*
Exod 22. 6 so that..the standing corn, or the field
Deut 23. 25 When thou comest into the standing corn
23. 25 a sickle unto thy neighbour's standing co.
Judg 15. 5 he let (them) go into the standing corn of
15. 5 both the shocks, and also the standing co.

COR-NE'-LIUS, Κορνήλιος.
A converted Roman centurion at Cæsarea.
Acts 10. 1 There was a certain man..called C.
10. 3 an angel of God..saying unto him, C.
10. 7 when the angel which spake unto C. was
10. 17 the men which were sent from C. had
10. 21 men which were sent unto him from C.
10. 22 C...was warned from God by an holy angel
10. 24 C. waited for them, and..called together
10. 25 as Peter was coming in, C. met him, and
10. 30 C. said, Four days ago I was fasting
10. 31 C., thy prayer is heard, and thine alms

CORNER—
1. *Wing,* כָּנָף *kanaph.*
Isa. 11. 12 gather..from the four corners of the earth
Eze. 7. 2 the end is come upon the four corners of

2. *Shoulder,* כָּתֵף *katheph.*
2 Ki. 11. 11 about the king, from the right corner of
11. 11 to the left corner of the temple, (along)

3. *Angle,* מִקְצוֹעַ *miqtsoa.*
Exod 26. 24 both; they shall be for the two corners
36. 29 thus he did to both..in both the corners
Eze. 41. 22 the corners thereof, and the length there.
46. 21 caused me to pass by the four corners of
46. 21 in every corner of the court..(was) a court
46. 22 In the four corners of the court..courts

4. *Side, quarter,* פֵּאָה *peah.*
Exod 25. 26 put the rings in the four corners that
36. 25 the other side..toward the north corner
37. 13 put the rings upon the four corners that
Lev. 19. 9 thou shalt not wholly reap the corners of
19. 27 Ye shall not round the corners of your
19. 27 neither shalt thou mar the corners of thy
21. 5 neither shall they shave off the corner of
23. 22 the corners of thy field when thou reapest
Num 24. 17 shall smite the corners of Moab, and
Josh. 18. 14 compassed the corner of the sea southw.
Neh. 9. 22 didst divide them into corners: so they
Jer. 9. 26 Moab, and all..in the utmost corners
25. 23 Buz, and all..in the utmost corners
48. 45 shall devour the corner of Moab, and the
49. 32 them (that are) in the utmost corners
Amos 3. 12 that dwell in Samaria in the corner of a

5. *Corner,* פֵּן *pen.*
Prov. 7. 8 Passing through the street near her cor.
Zech. 14. 10 unto the corner gate, and (from) the

6. *Corner, front, a chief man,* פִּנָּה *pinnah.*
Exod 27. 2 make the horns..upon the four corners
38. 2 made the horns thereof on the four corn.
1 Ki. 7. 34 undersetters to the four corners of one
2 Ki. 14. 13 the gate of Ephraim unto the corner
2 Ch. 26. 9 Uzziah built towers..at the corner gate
28. 24 he made him altars in every corner of
Neh. 3. 24 from the house of Azariah..unto the cor.
3. 31 Miphkad, and to the going up of the cor.
3. 32 between the going up of the corner unto
Job 1. 19 a great wind..smote the four corners of
38. 6 or who laid the corner stone thereof
Psa. 118. 22 is become the head (stone) of the corner
Prov. 7. 12 without..and lieth in wait at every cor.
21. 9 better to dwell in a corner of the house
25. 24 better to dwell in a corner of the house
Isa. 28. 16 I lay in Zion..a precious corner (stone)
Jer. 31. 38 from the tower..unto the gate of the cor
31. 40 unto the corner of the horse gate toward
51. 26 shall not take of thee a stone for a corn.
Eze. 43. 20 put (it)..on the four corners of the settle
45. 19 upon the four corners of the settle of the
Zech. 10. 4 Out of him came forth the corner, out of

7. *Tread, foot,* פַּעַם *paam.*
Exod 25. 12 and put (them) in the four corners
37. 3 rings..(to be set) by the four corners of
1 Ki. 7. 30 the four corners thereof (had) undersetters

8. *Rib,* צֵלָע *tsela.*
Exod 30. 4 under the crown of it, by the two corners
37. 27 under the crown thereof, by the two cor.

9. *End, extremity,* קָצָה *qatsah.*
Exod 27. 4 four brasen rings in the four corners

10. *To be scraped, cornered,* קָצַע *qatsa,* 6.
Eze. 46. 22 these four corners (were) of one measure

11. *To turn the face, front,* פָּנָה *panah.*
2 Ch. 25. 23 from the gate of Ephraim to the corner

12. *A beginning,* ἀρχή *archē.*
Acts 10. 11 as..a great sheet knit at the four corners
11. 5 let down from heaven by four corners

13. *Angle, corner,* γωνία *gōnia.*
Matt. 6. 5 they love to pray standing..in the corners
21. 42 the same is become the head of the cor.
Mark 12. 10 stone..is become the head of the corner?
Luke 20. 17 the same is become the head of the cor.
Acts 4. 11 stone..is become the head of the corner
26. 26 for this thing was not done in a corner
1 Pe. 2. 7 the same is made the head of the corner
Rev. 7. 1 four angels standing on the four corners

CORNER, chief —
At the extreme angle, ἀκρογωνιαῖος *akrogōniaios.*
Eph. 2. 20 Jesus Christ himself being the chief cor.
1 Pe. 2. 6 I lay in Sion a chief corner stone, elect

CORNER stones —
Corner stones, זָוִיּוֹת *zaviyyoth.*
Psa. 144. 12 our daughters (may be) as corner stones

CORNERS —
1. *Corner stones,* זָוִיּוֹת *zaviyyoth.*
Zech. 9. 15 they shall be filled..as the corners of the

2. *Angles, corners,* מְקֻצְעֹת *mequtsoth.*
Exod 26. 23 two boards shalt thou make for the corn.
36. 28 two boards made he for the corners of

CORNET —
1. *Horn, cornet,* קֶרֶן *qeren.*
Dan. 3. 5, 15 what time ye hear the sound of the cor.
3. 7 the people heard the sound of the cornet
3. 10 man that shall hear the sound of the cor.

2. *Trumpet,* שׁוֹפָר *shophar.*
1 Ch. 15. 28 shouting, and with sound of the cornet
2 Ch. 15. 14 they sware unto the LORD..with cornets
Psa 98. 6 With trumpets and sound of cornet make
Hos. 5. 8 Blow ye the cornet in Gibeah..the trum.

CORNETS —
Cornets, sistra, מְנַעַנְעִים *menaanim.*
2 Sa. 6. 5 all the house of Israel played..on cornets

CORNFLOOR —
Cornfloor, גֹּרֶן דָּגָן *goren dagan.*
Hos. 9. 1 hast loved a reward upon every cornfloor

CORPSE —
1. *Body,* גְּוִיָּה *geviyyah.*
Nah. 3. 3 and (there is) none end of (their) corpses
3. 3 they stumble upon their corpses

2. *Carcase,* פֶּגֶר *peger.*
2 Ki. 19. 35 behold, they (were) all dead corpses
Isa. 37. 36 behold, they (were) all dead corpses

3. *A fallen object, carcase,* πτῶμα *ptōma.*
Mark 6. 29 they came and took up his corpse, and

CORRECT, to —
1. *To manifest, reason with, reprove,* יָכַח *yakach,* 5.
Job 5. 17 happy (is) the man whom God correcteth
Psa. 94. 10 He that chastiseth..shall not he correct
Prov. 3. 12 For whom the LORD loveth he correcteth

2. *To instruct, chastise,* יָסַר *yasar,* 3.
Psa. 39. 11 When thou with rebukes dost correct man
Prov 29. 17 Correct thy son, and he shall give thee rest
Jer. 2. 19 Thine own wickedness shall correct thee
10. 24 O LORD, correct me, but with judgment
30. 11 I will correct thee in measure, and will
46. 28 but correct thee in measure: yet will I not

CORRECTED, to be —
To be instructed, יָסַר *yasar,* 2.
Prov 29. 19 A servant will not be corrected by words

CORRECTED, which —
Instructor, παιδευτής *paideutēs.*
Heb 12. 9 had fathers of our flesh which corrected

CORRECTION —
1. *To manifest, reason with, reprove,* יָכַח *yakach,* 5.
Hab. 1. 12 thou hast established them for correction

2. *Instruction, correction,* מוּסָר *musar.*
Prov. 7. 22 as a fool to the correction of the stocks
15. 10 Correction (is) grievous unto him that
22. 15 the rod of correction shall drive it far
23. 13 Withhold not correction from the child
Jer. 2. 30 your children; they received no correc.
5. 3 they have refused to receive correction
7. 28 nor receiveth correction: truth is perish
Zeph. 3. 2 obeyed not..she received not correction

3. *Reproof, reasoning,* תּוֹכַחַת *tokachath.*
Prov. 3. 11 neither be weary of his correction

4. *A setting aright,* ἐπανόρθωσις *epanorthōsis.*
2 Ti. 3. 16 profitable for doctrine..for correction

5. *A rod,* שֵׁבֶט *shebet.*
Job 37. 13 whether for correction, or for his land

CORRUPT —
1. *To be corrupt,* שָׁחַת *shachath,* 2.
Eze. 20. 44 nor according to your corrupt doings, O

2. *To be corrupted,* שָׁחַת *shachath,* 6.
Prov 25. 26 a troubled fountain, and a corrupt spring

3. *To corrupt,* שְׁחַת *shechath.*
Dan. 2. 9 ye have prepared lying and corrupt words

4. *To corrupt thoroughly,* διαφθείρω *diaphtheirō.*
1 Ti. 6. 5 Perverse disputings of men of corrupt

5. *To corrupt utterly,* καταφθείρω *kataphtheirō.*
2 Ti. 3. 8 men of corrupt minds, reprobate concern.

6. *Bad, putrid, rotten,* σαπρός *sapros.*
Matt. 7. 17 a corrupt tree bringeth forth evil fruit

Matt. 7. 18 neither (can) a corrupt tree bring forth
12. 33 make the tree corrupt, and his fruit cor.
Luke 6. 43 a good tree bringeth not forth corrupt
6. 43 doth a corrupt tree bring forth good fruit
Eph. 4. 29 Let no corrupt communication proceed

CORRUPT, to —

1. *To rebuke,* גָּעַר *gaar.*
Mal. 2. 3 I will corrupt your seed, and spread dung

2. *To profane,* חָנֵף *chaneph,* 5.
Dan. 11. 32 And such..shall he corrupt by flatteries

3. *To corrupt,* שָׁחַת *shachath,* 3.
Exod32. 7 for thy people..have corrupted (them.)
Deut. 9. 12 for thy people..have corrupted (them.)
32. 5 They have corrupted themselves, their
Eze. 28. 17 thou hast corrupted thy wisdom by reason
Hos. 9. 9 They have deeply corrupted (themselves)
Mal. 2. 8 ye have corrupted the covenant of Levi

4. *To be or become corrupt,* שָׁחַת *shachath,* 5.
Gen. 6. 12 all flesh had corrupted his way upon the
Deut. 4. 16 Lest ye corrupt (yourselves), and make
4. 25 shall corrupt (yourselves), and make a
31. 29 after my death ye will utterly corrupt
Judg. 2. 19 corrupted (themselves) more than their
Zeph 3. 7 they rose early, (and) corrupted all their

5. *To cause to disappear,* ἀφανίζω *aphanizō.*
Matt 6. 19 where moth and rust doth corrupt, and
6. 20 where neither moth nor rust doth cor.

6. *To corrupt thoroughly,* διαφθείρω *diaphtheirō.*
Luke12. 33 no thief approacheth, neither moth cor.

7. *To act as a (corrupt) vintner,* καπηλεύω *kapēleuō.*
2 Co. 2. 17 we are not as many, which corrupt the

8. *To cause to become putrid,* σήπω *sēpō.*
Jas. 5. 2 Your riches are corrupted, and your gar.

9. *To corrupt,* φθείρω *phtheirō.*
1 Co.15. 33 evil communications corrupt good mann
2 Co. 7. 2 Receive us..we have corrupted no man
11. 3 your minds should be corrupted from the
Rev. 19. 2 which did corrupt the earth with her

CORRUPT, to be —

1. *To be corrupt,* חָבַל *chabal,* 4.
Job 17. 1 My breath is corrupt, my days are extinct

2. *To act corruptly,* מוּק *muq,* 5.
Psa. 73. 8 They are corrupt, and speak wickedly

3. *To become corrupt,* מָקַק *maqaq,* 2.
Psa. 38. 5 My wounds stink (and) are corrupt

4. *To become corrupt,* שָׁחַת *shachath,* 2.
Gen. 6. 11 The earth also was corrupt before God
6. 12 looked upon the earth, and..it was cor.

5. *To corrupt, make corrupt,* שָׁחַת *shachath,* 5.
Psa. 14. 1 They are corrupt; they have done abom.
53. 1 Corrupt are they, and have done abom.
Eze. 23. 11 she was more corrupt in her inordinate

6. *To corrupt,* φθείρω *phtheirō.*
Eph. 4. 22 which is corrupt according to the deceit.

CORRUPT thing —

To be corrupt, שָׁחַת *shachath,* 6.
Mal. 1. 14 sacrificeth unto the LORD a corrupt thing

CORRUPT one's self, to —

To corrupt, act corruptly, φθείρω *phtheirō.*
Jude 10 in those things they corrupt themselves

CORRUPTED, to be —

1. *To become corrupt,* שָׁחַת *shachath,* 2.
Exod 8. 24 the land was corrupted by reason of the

2. *To make corrupt, act corruptly,* שָׁחַת *shachath,* 5.
Eze. 16. 47 thou was corrupted more than they in

CORRUPTER —

To make corrupt, act corruptly שָׁחַת *shachath,* 5.
Isa. 1. 4 evil doers, children that are corrupters
Jer. 6. 28 brass and iron; they (are) all corrupters

CORRUPTIBLE —

Corruptible, φθαρτός *phthartos.*
Rom. 1. 23 an image made like to corruptible man
1 Co. 9. 25 Now they (do it) to obtain a corruptible
15. 53 For this corruptible must put on incor.
15. 54 So when this corruptible shall have put
1 Pe. 1. 23 Being born again, not of corruptible seed

CORRUPTIBLE things —

Corruptible, φθαρτός *phthartos.*
1 Pe. 1. 18 ye were not redeemed with corruptible th.

CORRUPTIBLE, not —

Incorruptible, ἄφθαρτος *aphthartos.*
1 Pe. 3. 4 heart, in that which is not corruptible

CORRUPTING —

To make corrupt, act corruptly, שָׁחַת *shachath,* 5.
Dan. 11. 17 give him the daughter of women, corru.

CORRUPTION —

1. *Wasting, fading away,* בְּלִי *beli.*
Isa. 38. 17 my soul (delivered it) from the pit of cor.

2. *Corruption,* מַשְׁחִית *mashchith.*
2 Ki 23. 13 on the right hand of the mount of Corru.
Dan. 10. 8 my comeliness was turned..into corrupt.

3. *Corrupt, corrupt thing,* מָשְׁחַת *moshchath.*
Lev. 22. 25 because their corruption (is) in them

4. *Corruption, place or state of,* שַׁחַת *shachath.*
Job 17. 14 I have said to corruption, Thou (art) my
Psa. 16. 10 wilt thou suffer thine Holy One to see cor.
49. 9 still live for ever, (and) not see corruption
Jona. 2. 6 hast thou brought up my life from cor.

5. *Thorough corruption,* διαφθορά *diaphthora.*
Acts 2. 27 wilt thou suffer thine Holy One to see cor.
2. 31 left in hell, neither his flesh did see cor.
13. 34 (now) no more to return to corruption
13. 35 not suffer thine Holy One to see corrup.
13. 36 laid unto his fathers, and saw corruption
13. 37 he, whom God raised again, saw no cor.

6. *Corruption,* φθορά, *phthora.*
Rom. 8. 21 delivered from the bondage of corruption
1 Co. 15. 42 It is sown in corruption; it is raised in
15. 50 neither doth corruption inherit incorrup.
Gal. 6. 8 he..shall of the flesh reap corruption
2 Pe. 1. 4 the corruption that is in the world
2. 12 utterly perish in their own corruption
2. 19 they..are the servants of corruption

CORRUPTLY, to deal —

To act wickedly, חָבַל *chabal.*
Neh. 1. 7 We have dealt very corruptly against thee

CORRUPTLY, to do —

To make corrupt, act corruptly, שָׁחַת *shachath,* 5.
2 Ch.27. 2 And the people did yet corruptly

CO-SAM, Κωσάμ.

A son of Elmodam, and the 5th before Zorobabel in the line of Joseph, husband of Mary.
Luke 3. 28 of C., which was (the son) of Elmodam

COST —

Expense, δαπάνη, *dapanē.*
Luke 14. 28 sitteth not down..and counteth the cost

COST nothing, to —

Gratis, gratuitous, חִנָּם *chinnam.*
2 Sa. 24. 24 of that which doth cost me nothing

COST, without —

Gratis, gratuitous, חִנָּם *chinnam.*
1 Ch.21. 24 nor offer burnt offerings without cost

COSTLINESS —

Preciousness, τιμιότης *timiotēs.*
Rev. 18. 19 made rich..by reason of her costliness!

COSTLY —

1. *Precious, rare,* יָקָר *yaqar.*
1 Ki. 5. 17 they brought great stones, costly stones
7. 9 these (were of) costly stones, according to
7. 10 the foundation (was of) costly stones, even
7. 11 above (were) costly stones, after the mea.

2. *High priced,* πολυτελής *polutelēs.*
1 Ti. 2. 9 not with..gold, or pearls, or costly array

COSTLY, very —

High priced, πολύτιμος, *polutimos.*
John12. 3 took..ointment of spikenard, very costly

COTES —

Cribs, stalls, אֻרוֹת *averoth.*
2 Ch.32. 28 all manner of beasts, and cotes for flocks

COTTAGE —

1. *A lodge,* מְלוּנָה *melunah.*
Isa. 24. 20 and shall be removed like a cottage

2. *A booth,* סֻכָּה *sukkah.*
Isa. 1. 8 daughter of Zion is left as a cottage in

COTTAGES —

Places cut out (of the rocks or earth), כָּרֹת *karoth.*
Zeph. 2. 6 sea coast shall be dwellings (and) cottages

COUCH —

1. *Anything spread out,* יָצוּעַ *yatsua.*
Gen. 49. 4 Unstable as water..he went up to my co.

2. *Place for lying down,* מִשְׁכָּב *mishkab.*
Job 7. 13 my couch shall ease my complaint

3. *Couch,* עֶרֶשׂ *eres.*
Psa. 6. 6 I water my couch with my tears
Amos 3. 12 that dwell..in Damascus (in) a couch
6. 4 stretch themselves upon their couches

4. *A small couch for reclining on,* κλινίδιον *klini.*
Luke 5. 19 with (his) couch into the midst before
5. 24 take up thy couch, and go unto thine

5. *A mattress,* κράββατος *krabbatos,* κράβαττος [Lat.]
Acts 5. 15 laid (them) on beds and couches, that at

COUCH, to —

1. *To bend down,* כָּרַע *kara.*
Num 24. 9 He couched, he lay down as a lion, and

2. *To crouch,* רָבַץ *rabats.*
Gen. 49. 9 he couched as a lion, and as an old lion
Deut 33. 13 and for the deep that coucheth beneath

3. *To bow down,* שָׁחַח *shachach.*
Job 38. 40 When they couch in (their) dens, (and)

COUCH down, to —

To crouch, רָבַץ *rabats.*
Gen. 49. 14 a strong ass couching down between two

COUCHING place —

Place for couching, מַרְבֵּץ *marbets.*
Eze. 25. 5 the Ammonites a couching place for flo.

COULD —

1. *To be able,* יָכֹל *yakol.*
Gen. 13. 6 so that they could not dwell together
36. 7 the land..could not bear them because
37. 4 and could not speak peaceably unto him
45. 1 Joseph could not refrain himself before
45. 3 his brethren could not answer him; for
Exod. 2. 3 when she could not longer hide him, she
7. 21, 24 could not drink of the water of the
8. 18 to bring forth lice, but they could not
9. 11 the magicians could not stand before M.
12. 39 they were thrust out of..and could not
15. 23 they could not drink of the waters of M.
Num. 9. 6 they could not keep the passover on that
Josh. 7. 12 the children of Israel could not stand
15. 63 the children of Judah could not drive
17. 12 the children of Manasseh could not drive
Judg. 2. 14 they could not any longer stand before
14. 14 they could not in three days expound the
1 Sa. 3. 2 eyes began to wax dim, (that) he could not
4. 15 eyes were dim, that he could not see
2 Sa. 3. 11 he could not answer Abner a word again
1 Ki. 5. 3 David my father could not build an house
8. 11 the priests could not stand to minister
13. 4 that he could could not pull it in again
14. 4 Ahijah could not see; for his eyes were
2 Ki. 3. 26 to break through..but they could not
4. 40 And they could not eat (thereof)
16. 5 they besieged Ahaz, but could not overc.
1 Ch. 21. 30 David could not go before it to enquire
2 Ch. 5. 14 the priests could not stand to minister
7. 2 the priests could not enter into the house
29. 34 they could not flay all the burnt offerings
30. 3 they could not keep it at that time, beca.
32. 14 that could deliver his people out of mine
Ezra 2. 59 they could not show their father's house
Neh. 7. 61 they could not show their father's house
Job 31. 23 by reason of his highness I could not
Isa. 7. 1 Jerusalem..but could not prevail against
46. 2 they could not deliver the burden, but
Jer. 3. 5 hast..done evil things as thou couldest
20. 9 weary with forbearing, and I could not
44. 22 the LORD could no longer bear, because
Lam. 4. 14 that men could not touch their garments
Eze. 47. 5 a river that I could not pass over: for the
Hos. 5. 13 yet could he not heal you, nor cure you
Jon. 1. 13 bring (it) to the land; but they could not

2. *To be able,* יְכִל *yekil.*
Dan. 6. 4 they could find none occasion nor fault

3. *To be able,* כְּהַל *kehal.*
Dan. 5. 8 they could not read the writing, nor
5. 15 they could not show the interpretation

4. *To know, distinguish,* נָכַר *nakar,* 5.
Neh. 13. 24 could not speak in the Jews' language

COULD not —

To move away, wander, נָדַד *nadad.*
Esth. 6. 1 that night could not the king sleep; and

COULD not do, what the law —

The impossible of the law, τὸ ἀδύνατον τοῦ νόμου.
Rom. 8. 3 what the law could not do, in that it was

COULD they —

To know, be acquainted with, יָדַע *yada.*
Jer. 6. 15 not at all ashamed, neither could 8. 12.

COULD, that I —

Able, δυνατός *dunatos.*
Acts 11. 17 what was I, that I could withstand God?

COULDEST —

To be able, יְכִל *yekil.*
Dan. 2. 47 seeing thou couldest reveal this secret.

COULD have—*Have,* ἔχω *echō;* John 19. 11.

COULTER —

An agricultural instrument, אֵת *eth.*
1 Sa. 13. 20 his coulter, and his ax, and his mattock
13. 21 for the coulters, and for the forks, and

COUNCIL —

1. *An assembly,* רִגְמָה *rigmah.*
Psa. 68. 27 the princes of Judah (and) their council

2. *A joint counsel, a council,* συμβούλιον *sumbouli.*
Matt12. 14 held a council against him, how they
Acts25. 12 when he had conferred with the council

3. *Sanhedrim, a sitting together,* συνέδριον *suned.*
Matt. 5. 22 shall be in danger of the council: but
10. 17 they will deliver you up to the councils
26. 59 priests, and elders, and all the council
Mark 13. 9 they shall deliver you up to councils
14. 55 the chief priests and all the council
15. 1 elders and scribes and the whole council
Luke22. 66 came..and led him into their council
John11. 47 Then gathered the chief priests..a council
Acts 4. 15 commanded them to go..out of the coun.
5. 21 called the council together, and all the
5. 27 they set (them) before the council: and
5. 34 Then stood there up one in the council
5. 41 departed from the presence of the council
6. 12 caught him, and brought (him) to the coun.
6. 15 all that sat in the council..saw his face
22. 30 the chief priests and all their council to
23. 1 Paul, earnestly beholding the council
23. 6 Paul..cried out in the council..I am a
23. 15 ye with the council signify to the chief
23. 20 bring down Paul tomorrow into the coun.
23. 28 I brought him forth into their council
24. 20 in me, while I stood before the council

COUNSEL —
1. *Word*, דָּבָר *dabar*.
Num 31. 16 Behold..through the counsel of Balaam
2. *To counsel*, יָעַץ *yaats*.
2 Ch 25. 16 Art thou made of the king's counsel?
3. *Counsel*, מְלַךְ *melak*.
Dan. 4. 27 O king, let my counsel be acceptable unto
4. *A sitting, session, assembly*, סוֹד *sod*.
Psa. 55 14 We took sweet counsel together, (and)
83. 3 They have taken crafty counsel against
Prov 15. 22 Without counsel purposes are disappoin
Jer. 23. 18 who hath stood in the counsel of the LORD
23. 22 But if they had stood in my counsel, and
5. *Counsel, advice*, עֵטָא *eta*.
Dan. 2. 14 Then Daniel answered with counsel and
6. *Counsel, advice*, עֵצָה *etsah*.
Deut 32. 28 they(are)a nation void of counsel, neither
Judg 20. 7 give here your advice and counsel
2 Sa. 15. 31 turn the counsel of Ahithophel into fool.
15. 34 for me defeat the counsel of Ahithophel
16. 20 Give counsel among you what we shall do
16. 23 the counsel of Ahithophel, which he coun.
16. 23 so (was) all the counsel of Ahithophel
17. 7 The counsel that Ahithophel hath given
17. 14 counsel of Hushai..better than the coun.
17. 14 to defeat the good counsel of Ahithophel
17. 23 when Ahithophel saw that his counsel
1 Ki. 1. 12 let me, I pray thee, give thee counsel, that
12. 8 he forsook the counsel of the old men
12. 13 the king..forsook the old men's counsel
12. 14 spake to them after the counsel of the
2 Ki 18. 20 Thou sayest..(I have) counsel and stren.
2 Ch. 10. 8 he forsook the counsel which the old men
10. 13 Rehoboam forsook the counsel of the old
22. 5 He walked also after their counsel, and
25. 16 and hast not hearkened unto my counsel
Ezra 10. 3 according to the counsel of my lord, and
10. 8 according to the counsel of the princes
Neh. 4. 15 God had brought their counsel to nought
Job 5 13 the counsel of the froward is carried
10. 3 and shine upon the counsel of the wicked?
12. 13 With him (is) wisdom..he hath counsel
18. 7 and his own counsel shall cast him down
21. 16 the counsel of the wicked is far from me
22. 18 the counsel of the wicked is far from me
29. 21 gave ear..and kept silence at my counsel
38. 2 Who (is) this that darkeneth counsel by
42. 3 Who (is) he that hideth counsel without
Psa. 1. 1 walketh not in the counsel of the ungodly
13. 2 How long shall I take counsel in my soul
14. 6 Ye have shamed the counsel of the poor
20. 4 Grant thee..and fulfil all thy counsel
33. 10 LORD bringeth the counsel of the heathen
33. 11 The counsel of the LORD standeth for
73. 24 Thou shalt guide me with thy counsel
106. 13 they waited not for his counsel
106. 43 they provoked (him) with their counsel
107. 11 contemned the counsel of the Most High
Prov. 1. 25 ye have set at nought all my counsel
1. 30 They would none of my counsel; they
8. 14 Counsel (is) mine, and sound wisdom
12. 15 he that hearkeneth unto counsel (is)
19. 20 Hear counsel, and receive instruction
19. 21 the counsel of the LORD, that shall stand
20. 5 Counsel in the heart of man (is like) deep
20. 18 (Every) purpose is established by counsel
21. 30 (There is) no wisdom..nor counsel against
27. 9 so (doth) the sweetness..by hearty coun.
Isa. 5. 19 let the counsel of the Holy One of Israel
[8. 10 Take counsel together, and it shall come]
11. 2 the spirit of counsel and might, the spirit
16. 3 Take counsel, execute judgment; make
19. 3 I will destroy the counsel thereof: and
19. 11 the counsel of the wise counsellors of
19. 17 because of the counsel of the LORD of
25. 1 (thy) counsels of old (are) faithfulness
28. 29 wonderful in counsel, (and) excellent in
29. 15 them that seek deep to hide their counsel
[30. 1 rebellious children..that take counsel]
36. 5 (I have) counsel and strength for war
44. 26 performeth the counsel of his messengers
46. 10 My counsel shall stand, and I will do all
46. 11 the man that executeth my counsel from
47. 13 wearied in the multitude of thy counsels
Jer. 18. 18 nor counsel from the wise, nor the word
18. 23 thou knowest all their counsel against me
19. 7 I will make void the counsel of Judah
32. 19 Great in counsel, and mighty in work
49. 7 is counsel perished from the prudent?
49. 20 hear the counsel of the LORD that he hath
49. 30 king of Babylon hath taken counsel
50. 45 hear ye the counsel of the LORD, that he
Eze. 7. 26 law shall perish..and counsel from the
11. 2 these (are) the men that..give wicked co.
Hos. 10. 6 Israel shall be ashamed of his own coun.
Mic. 4. 12 neither understand they his counsel
Zech. 6. 13 the counsel of peace shall be between
7. *Counsel, purpose, will*, βουλή *boulē*.
Luke 7. 30 Pharisees and lawyers rejected the counsel
23. 51 The same had not consented to the coun.
Acts 2. 23 delivered by the determinate counsel and
4. 28 to do whatsoever thy hand and thy coun.
5. 38 for if this counsel or this work be of men
20. 27 I have not shunned to declare..all the c.
27. 42 the soldiers' counsel was to kill the pris.
1 Co. 4. 5 make manifest the counsels of the heart
Eph. 1. 11 all things after the counsel of his own
Heb. 6. 17 the immutability of his counsel, confirmed
8. *A joint counsel*, συμβούλιον *sumboulion*.
Matt 22. 15 took counsel how they might entangle
27. 1 elders of the people took counsel against
27. 7 they took counsel, and bought with them
28. 12 when they..had taken counsel they gave
Mark 3. 6 the Pharisees went forth, and..took co

COUNSEL, to —
1. *To give counsel*, יָעַץ *yaats*.
2 Sa 16. 23 which he counselled in those days..as if
17. 11 I counsel that all Israel be..gathered
17. 15 Thus and thus did Ahithophel counsel
17. 15 thus and thus have I counselled
17. 21 thus hath Ahithophel counselled against
Job 26. 3 How hast thou counselled (him that hath)
2. *To give full counsel*, συμβουλεύω *sumbouleuō*.
Rev. 3. 18 I counsel thee to buy of me gold tried in

COUNSEL, to give —
1. *To give counsel*, יָעַץ *yaats*.
Exod 18 19 Hearken now..I will give thee counsel
Psa. 16. 7 bless the LORD, who hath given me coun.
Jer. 38. 15 if I give thee counsel, wilt thou not
2. *To be counselled*, יָעַץ *yaats*, 2.
1 Ki. 12. 9 What counsel give ye that we may answer
2 Ch. 10. 6 What counsel give ye (me) to return
3. *To counsel together or fully*, συμβουλεύω *sumbou.*
John 18. 14 Caiaphas was he which gave counsel to

COUNSEL, to take —
1. *To have a foundation laid*, יָסַד *yasad*, 2.
Psa. 2. 2 the rulers take counsel together
31. 13 they took counsel together against me
2. *To give counsel*, יָעַץ *yaats*.
Isa. 7. 5 have taken evil counsel against thee, say
23. 8 Who hath taken this counsel against Tyre
3. *To be counselled, receive counsel*, יָעַץ *yaats*, 2.
1 Ki. 12. 28 the king took counsel, and made two
2 Ki. 6. 8 the king of Syria..took counsel with his
2 Ch. 10. 6 king Rehoboam took counsel with the
10. 8 and took counsel with the young men
30. 2 the king had taken counsel, and the
30. 23 the whole assembly took counsel to keep
32. 3 He took counsel with his princes and his
Neh. 6. 7 Come now..let us take counsel together
Psa. 71. 10 they..take counsel; Isa. 40. 14; 45. 21.
3a. *Make counsel*, עָשָׂה עֵצָה *asah etsah*.
Isa. 30. 1 rebellious children..that take counsel
4. *To take counsel, consult*, βουλεύομαι *bouleuomai*.
Acts 5. 33 When they heard..[they took counsel] to
5. *Take counsel together*, συμβουλεύω *sumbouleuō*.
Acts 9. 23 And..the Jews took counsel to kill him

COUNSEL together, to take —
1. *Counsel together*, συμβουλεύω John 11. 53.
2. *Advise advice*, עוּץ עֵצָה [*uts*]; Isa. 8. 10.

COUNSELLOR —
1. *A lawyer, judge*, דְּתָבָר *dethabar*.
Dan. 3. 2 the counsellors, the sheriffs, and all the
3. 3 the counsellors, the sheriffs, and all the
2. *To give counsel*, יָעַץ *yaats*.
2 Sa. 15. 12 Absalom sent for..David's counsellor
1 Ch. 26. 14 for Zechariah his son, a wise counsellor
27. 32 Also Jonathan, David's uncle, was a coun.
27. 33 And Ahithophel (was) the king's counsel.
2 Ch. 22. 3 his mother was his counsellor to do
22. 4 they were his counsellors, after the
Ezra 4. 5 hired counsellors against them, to
7. 28 before the king, and his counsellors
8. 25 which the king, and his counsellors, and
Job 3. 14 With kings and counsellors of the earth
12. 17 He leadeth counsellors away spoiled, and
Prov 11. 14 but in the multitude of counsellors
12. 20 but to the counsellors of peace (is) joy
15. 22 but in the multitude of counsellors they
24. 6 in multitude of counsellors (there is)
Isa. 1. 26 will restore thy judges..and thy counsel.
3. 3 the honourable man, and the counsellor
9. 6 name shall be called, Wonderful, Coun.
19. 11 the counsel of the wise counsellors of
41. 28 For I beheld, and..no counsellor, that
Mic. 4. 9 (is there) no king in thee? is thy counsel.
Nah. 1. 11 evil against the LORD, a wicked counsellor
3. *Man of counsel*, אִישׁ עֵצָה *ish etsah*.
Psa. 119. 24 thy testimonies also (are) my..counsellors
Isa. 40. 13 or (being) his counsellor, hath taught
4. *Counsellor*, βουλευτής *bouleutēs*.
Mark 15. 43 Joseph of Arimathea, an honourable co.
Luke 23. 50 behold..a man named Joseph, a counsel.
5. *A joint counsellor*, σύμβουλος *sumboulos*.
Rom. 11. 34 or who hath been his counsellor?

COUNSELLORS —
1. *Viceroys, counsellors*, הַדָּבְרִין *haddaberin*.
Dan. 3. 24 Nebuchadnezzar..said unto his counsel.
3. 27 the king's counsellors, being gathered
4. 36 my counsellors and my lords sought unto
6. 7 the counsellors, and the captains, have
2. *To give counsel*, יְעַט *yeat*.
Ezra 7. 14 thou art sent..of his seven counsellors
7. 15 the king and his counsellors have freely

COUNSELS —
1. *Counsels*, מוֹעֵצוֹת *moetsoth*.
Psa. 5. 10 O God; let them fall by their own coun.
81. 12 (and) they walked in their own counsels
Prov 22. 20 Have not I written to thee..things in co.
Jer. 7. 24 but walked in the counsels (and) in the
Hos 11. 6 devour (them), because of their own co.
Mic. 6 16 ye walk in their counsels; that I should
2. *Combinations, plans*, תַּחְבֻּלוֹת *tachbuloth*.
Job 37. 12 it is turned round about by his counsels
Prov 11 14 Where no counsel (is), the people fall
12 5 (but) the counsels of the wicked (are)

COUNSELS, wise —
Combinations, plans, תַּחְבֻּלוֹת *tachbuloth*.
Prov. 1 5 and a (man)..shall attain unto wise coun.
24 6 by wise counsel thou shalt make thy war

COUNT, to —
1. *To think, devise, reckon*, חָשַׁב *chashab*.
Gen. 15. 6 he counted it to him for righteousness
Job 19. 11 he counteth me unto him as (one of) his
19. 15 and my maids count me for a stranger
33 10 Behold..he counteth me for his enemy
2. *To think, devise, reckon*, חָשַׁב *chashab*, 3.
Lev 25 27 let him count the years of the sale thereof
25. 52 unto the year of jubilee..he shall count
3. *To number*, מָנָה *manah*.
Num 23. 10 Who can count the dust of Jacob, and
4. *To give*, נָתַן *nathan*.
1 Sa. 1 16 Count not thine handmaid for a daughter
5. *To number*, סָפַר *saphar*.
Lev. 23. 15 ye shall count unto you from the morrow
Job 31. 4 Doth not he see my ways, and count all
Psa. 87 6 The LORD shall count, when he writeth
139. 18 (If) I should count them, they are more
Isa. 33. 18 where (is) he that counted the towers?
6. *To visit, inspect, number*, פָּקַד *paqad*.
1 Ch 21. 6 But Levi and Benjamin counted he not
7. *To have, hold*, ἔχω *echō*.
Matt 14. 5 because they counted him as a prophet
Mark 11. 32 all (men) counted John, that he was a
Acts 20. 24 neither [count I] my life dear unto myself
Phm. 17 If thou count me therefore a partner
8. *To lead out, account*, ἡγέομαι *hēgeomai*.
Phil. 3. 7 what things were gain..those I counted
3. 8 Yea doubtless, and I count all things
3. 8 do count them (but) dung, that I may
2 Th. 3. 15 Yet count (him) not as an enemy, but
1 Ti. 1. 12 he counted me faithful, putting me into
6. 1 Let as many servants..count their own
Heb. 10. 29 and hath counted the blood of the cove.
Jas. 1. 2 count it all joy when ye fall into divers
2 Pe. 2. 13 they that count it pleasure to riot in
3. 9 The Lord is not slack..as some men count
9. *To reckon, number, account*, λογίζομαι *logizomai*.
Rom. 2. 26 shall not his uncircumcision be counted
4. 3 it was counted unto him for righteousness
4. 5 his faith is counted for righteousness
9. 8 the children of the promise are counted
Phil. 3. 13 I count not myself to have apprehended
10. *To use pebbles together, calculate together*, συμψηφίζω *sumpsēphizō*.
Acts 19. 19 they counted the price of them, and found
11. *To use pebbles, calculate*, ψηφίζω *psēphizō*.
Luke 14. 28 sitteth not down first, and counteth the
Rev. 13. 18 Let him that hath understanding count
[*See also* Descent, happy, pure, uncircumcised, worthy.]

COUNT, to make —
To count, apportion, כָּסַס *kasas*.
Exod 12. 4 shall make your count for the lamb

COUNTED, to be —
1. *To be thought, reckoned*, חָשַׁב *chashab*, 2.
Gen. 31. 15 Are we not counted of him strangers?
Lev. 25. 31 the houses..shall be counted as the fields
Num 18. 30 it shall be counted unto the Levites as
Josh. 13. 3 Ekron northward, (which) is counted to
Neh. 13. 13 I made treasurers..for they were counted
Job 18. 3 are we counted as beasts..in your sight
41. 29 Darts are counted as stubble: he laugh.
Psa. 44. 22 we are counted as sheep for the slaughter
88. 4 I am counted with them that go down
106. 31 that was counted unto him for righteous.
Prov 17. 28 when he holdeth his peace, is counted wise
27. 14 it shall be counted a curse to him
Isa. 5. 28 horses' hoofs shall be counted like flint
32. 15 fruitful field be counted for a forest
40. 15 counted as the small dust of the balance
40. 17 All nations..are counted to him less than
Hos. 8. 12 (but) they were counted as a strange thing
2. *To visit, inspect, count*, פָּקַד *paqad*.
1 Ch. 23. 24 they were counted by number of names
3. *To be counted, numbered*, פָּקַד *paqad*, 4.
Exod 38. 21 tabernacle of testimony, as it was counted

COUNTENANCE —
1. *Face, anger*, אַף *aph*.
Psa. 10. 4 through the pride of his countenance
2. *Brightness, countenance*, זִיו *ziv*.
Dan. 5. 6 the king's countenance was changed, and
5. 9 his countenance was changed in him, and

Dan. 5. 10 nor let thy countenance be changed
7. 28 my countenance changed in me : but I

3. *Appearance*, מַרְאֶה *mareh*.
Judg13. 6 his countenance (was) like the counte.
1 Sa. 16. 7 Look not on his countenance, or on the
17. 42 a youth, and ruddy, and of a fair counte.
2 Sa. 14. 27 she was a woman of a fair countenance
Song 2. 14 let me see thy countenance, let me hear
2. 14 thy voice, and thy countenance (is) come.
5. 15 his countenance (is) as Lebanon, excellent
Dan. 1. 13 Then let our countenances be looked upon
1. 13 the countenance of the children that eat
1. 15 their countenances appeared fairer and

4. *Eyes*, עַיִן *ayin*.
1 Sa. 16. 12 Now he (was)..of a beautiful countenance

5. *Face, countenance*, פָּנִים *panim*.
Gen. 4. 5 Cain was very wroth, and his countenance
4. 6 and why is thy countenance fallen ?
31. 2 Jacob beheld the countenance of Laban
31. 5 I see your father's countenance, that it
Num 6. 26 The LORD lift up his countenance upon
1 Sa. 1. 18 and her countenance was no more (sad)
2 Ki. 8. 11 he settled his countenance stedfastly
Neh 2. 2 Why (is) thy countenance sad, seeing
2. 3 why should not my countenance be sad
Job 14. 20 thou changest his countenance, and send.
29 24 light of my countenance they cast not
Psa. 4. 6 lift thou up the light of thy countenance
11. 7 his countenance doth behold the upright
21. 6 exceeding glad with thy countenance
42. 5 praise him (for) the help of his counte.
42. 11 the health of my countenance, and my
43. 5 the health of my countenance, and my
44. 3 thine arm, and the light of thy counte.
80. 16 perish at the rebuke of thy countenance
89. 15 walk..in the light of thy countenance
90 8 secret (sins) in the light of thy counte.
Prov. 15 13 A merry heart maketh a cheerful counte.
16. 15 In the light of the king's countenance (is)
25. 23 so (doth) an angry countenance a back.
27. 17 so a man sharpeneth the countenance of
Eccl. 7. 3 for by the sadness of the countenance the
Isa. 3. 9 The show of their countenance doth
Eze 27 35 shall be troubled in (their) countenance
Dan. 8. 23 a king of fierce countenance..shall

6. *Form*, תֹּאַר *toar*.
1 Sa. 25. 3 (was) a woman of..beautiful countenance

7. *Aspect, appearance*, ἰδέα *idea*, εἰδέα *eidea*.
Matt28. 3 His countenance was like lightning, and

8. *Sight, appearance*, ὄψις *opsis*.
Rev. 1 16 his countenance (was) as the sun shineth

9. *Front, face*, πρόσωπον *prosōpon*.
Luke 9. 29 fashion of his countenance was altered
Acts 2. 28 make me full of joy with thy countenance
2 Co. 3. 7 for the glory of his countenance ; which

COUNTENANCE, of a sad —
Of a scowling face, σκυθρωπός *skuthrōpos*.
Matt 6. 16 not, as the hypocrites, of a sad counte.

COUNTENANCE, to —
To honour, הָדַר *hadar*.
Exod23. 3 Neither shalt thou countenance a poor

COUNTERVAIL, to —
To be equal, שָׁוָה *shavah*.
Esth 7. 4 enemy could not countervail the king's

COUNTRY —
1. *Ground, land*, אֲדָמָה *adamah*.
Jon. 4. 2 my saying when I was yet in my country

2. *Island*, אִי *i*.
Jer 47. 4 the remnant of the country of Caphtor

3. *Land, country*, אֶרֶץ *erets*.
Gen. 10. 20 in their countries, (and) in their nations
12. 1 Get thee out of thy country, and from
19. 28 the smoke of the country went up as the
20. 1 Abraham journeyed..toward the south c.
24. 4 thou shalt go unto my country, and to
24. 62 And Isaac..dwelt in the south country
25. 6 sent them away..unto the east country
26. 3 unto thy seed, I will give all these coun.
26. 4 give unto thy seed all these countries
30. 25 unto mine own place, and to my country
32 9 Return unto thy country, and to thy kin.
34. 2 when Shechem..prince of the country
36. 6 Esau..went into the country from the
41. 57 all countries came into Egypt to Joseph
42. 30 The man..took us for spies of the coun.
42. 33 the man, the lord of the country, said
Lev. 25 31 be counted as the fields of the country
Num 20. 17 Let us pass, I pray thee, through thy co.
32. 4 the country which the LORD smote before
32. 33 (even) the cities of the country round
Deut. 4. 43 in the wilderness, in the plain country
26. 3 I am come unto the country which the
Josh. 2. 2 there came men..to search out the coun.
2. 3 they be come to search out all the country
2. 24 even all the inhabitants of the country
6. 22 the two men that had spied out the coun.
6. 27 fame was (noised) throughout all the coun.
7. 2 Go up and view the country
9. 6 We be come from a far country : now
9. 9 From a very far country thy servants are
9. 11 the inhabitants of our country spake to
10. 40 So Joshua smote all the country of the
10. 41 all the country of Goshen, even unto G.
Josh. 12. 7 these (are) the kings of the country which
13. 21 dukes of Sihon, dwelling in the country
19. 51 they made an end of dividing the country
22. 9 to go unto the country of Gilead, to the
Judg. 8. 28 the country was in quietness forty years
11. 21 Amorites, the inhabitants of that country
12. 12 Elon..was buried in..the country of Zeb
16. 24 the destroyer of our country, which slew
18. 14 men that went to spy out the country of
2 Sa. 15. 23 all the country wept with a loud voice
21. 14 in the country of Benjamin in Zelah, in
1 Ki. 4. 19 the son of Uri (was) in the country of G.
4. 19 the country of Sihon king of the Amorites
8. 41 stranger, that..cometh out of a far coun.
10. 13 she turned, and went to her own country
10. 15 kings..and of the governors of the coun.
11. 21 that I may go to mine own country
11. 22 thou seekest to go to thine own country?
20. 27 kids; but the Syrians filled the country
22. 36 Every man to his city, and..his own coun.
2 Ki. 3. 20 and the country was filled with water
18. 35 gods of the countries..delivered their co.
20. 14 They are come from a far country..from
1 Ch. 20. 1 Joab..wasted the country of the children
22. 5 and of glory throughout all countries
29. 30 and over all the kingdoms of the countries
2 Ch. 6 32 but is come from a far country for thy
9. 14 governors of the country, brought gold
11. 23 dispersed..throughout all the countries
12. 8 service of the kingdoms of the countries
15. 5 upon all the inhabitants of the countries
20. 29 on all the kingdoms of (those) countries
30. 10 the posts passed..through the country of
34. 33 the abominations out of all the countries
Ezra 3. 3 because of the people of those countries
Psa. 110. 6 shall wound the heads over many coun.
Prov 25. 25 so (is) good news from a far country
Isa. 1. 7 Your country (is) desolate, your cities
8. 9 give ear, all ye of far countries : gird
13. 5 They come from a far country, from the
22. 18 toss thee (like) a ball into a large country
37. 18 all the nations, and their countries
39. 3 They are come from a far country unto
46. 11 executeth my counsel from a far country
Jer. 2. 7 I brought you into a plentiful country
4. 16 watchers come from a far country, and
6. 20 and the sweet cane from a far country?
6. 22 a people cometh from the north country
8. 19 because of them that dwell in a far coun.
10. 22 great commotion out of the north country
22. 10 return no more, nor see his native country
22. 26 will cast thee out..into another country
23. 3 will gather..my flock out of all countries
23. 8 the north country, and from all countries
28. 8 prophesied both against many countries
31. 8 I will bring them from the north country
32. 8 which (is) in the country of Benjamin
32. 37 I will gather them out of all countries
40. 11 the Jews..in all the countries, heard that
44. 1 at Noph, and in the country of Pathros
46. 10 hath a sacrifice in the north country by
48. 21 judgment is come upon the plain country
50. 9 of great nations from the north country
51. 9 let us go every one into his own country
Eze. 5. 5 and countries (that are) round about her
5. 6 my statutes more than the countries that
6. 8 shall be scattered through the countries
11. 16 have scattered them among the countries
11. 16 as a little sanctuary in the countries
11. 17 assemble you out of the countries where
12. 15 I shall..disperse them in the countries
20. 23 and disperse them through the countries
20. 32 We will be as..families of the countries
20. 34 I..will gather you out of the countries
20. 38 will bring them forth out of the country
20 41 the countries wherein ye have been
20. 42 the country (for) the which I lifted up mine
22. 4 I made thee..a mocking to all countries
22. 15 I will..disperse thee in the countries
25. 7 cause thee to perish out of the countries
25. 9 the glory of the country, Beth-jeshimoth
29. 12 desolate in the midst of the countries
29. 12 will disperse them through the countries
30. 7 desolate in the midst of the countries
30. 23 scatter..will disperse them through the c.
30. 26 and disperse them among the countries
32. 9 the countries which thou hast not known
32. 15 the country shall be destitute of that
34. 13 I will..gather them from the countries
34. 13 all the inhabited places of the country
35. 10 these two countries shall be mine, and we
36. 19 they were dispersed through the coun.
36. 24 I will..gather you out of all countries
Dan. 9. 7 through all the countries whither thou
11. 40 he shall enter into the countries, and
11. 42 stretch forth his hand..upon the countri
Jon. 1. 8 what (is) thy country ? and of what peo?
Zech. 6. 6 horses..go forth into the north country
6. 6 grisled go forth toward the south country
6. 8 these that go toward the north country
6. 8 quieted my spirit in the north country
8. 7 east country, and from the west country

4. *Circuit*, גְּלִילָה *gelilah*.
Eze. 47. 8 waters issue out toward the east country

5. *A cord, land measured off*, חֶבֶל *chebel*.
Deut. 3. 14 Jair..took all the country of Argob unto

6. *Place*, מָקוֹם *maqom*.
Gen. 29. 26 It must not be so done in our country, to

7. *Elevation, height*, נֶפֶת *nepheth*.
Josh. 17. 11 Megiddo and her towns, (even) three cou.

8. *An open village*, פְּרָזִי *perazi*.
1 Sa. 6. 18 (both) of fenced cities, and of country vil.

9. *A field, expanse, level place*, שָׂדֶה *sadeh*.
Gen. 14. 7 smote all the country of the Amalekites
32. 3 sent messengers..unto..the country of E.
Num21. 20 the valley that (is) in the country of M.
Judg20. 6 I..sent her throughout all the country
Ruth 1. 1 went to sojourn in the country of Moab
1. 2 they came into the country of Moab, and
1. 6 she might return from the country of M.
1. 6 she had heard in the country of Moab
1. 22 which returned out of the country of M.
2. 6 with Naomi out of the country of Moab
4. 3 that is come again out of the country of
1 Sa. 6. 1 the ark of the LORD was in the country of
27. 5 a place in some town in the country, that
27. 7 the time that David dwelt in the country
27. 11 all the while he dwelleth in the country
1 Ch. 8. 8 Shaharaim begat (children) in the count.
Hos. 12. 12 And Jacob fled into the country of Syria

10. *A (cultivated) field*, ἀγρός *agros*.
Mark 5. 14 told (it) in the city, and in the country
6. 36 they may go into the country round
6. 56 whithersoever..into villages, or..country
15. 21 Simon..passed by, coming out of the co.
16. 12 as they walked, and went into the [count.]
Luke 8. 34 told (it) in the city and in the country
9. 12 go into the towns and country round
23. 26 Simon, a Cyrenian, coming out of the co.

11. *Genus, race*, γένος *genos*.
Acts 4. 36 a Levite, (and) of the country of Cyprus

12. *Earth, land, country*, γῆ *gē*.
Matt. 9. 31 spead abroad his fame in all that country
Acts 7. 3 said unto him, Get thee out of thy count.

13. *Father-land*, πατρίς *patris*.
Luke 4. 23 heard done..do also here in thy country
John 4. 44 prophet hath no honour in his own cou.
Heb. 11. 14 declare plainly that they seek a country

14. *Space, place*, χώρα *chōra*.
Matt. 2. 12 they departed into their own country
8. 28 when he was come..into the country of
Mark 5. 1 they came..into the country of the Gada.
5. 10 would not send them away out of the c.
Luke 2. 8 there were in the same country shepherds
8. 26 they arrived at the country of the Gada.
15. 13 took his journey into a far country, and
15. 15 joined himself to a citizen of that coun.
19. 12 certain nobleman went into a far country
21. 21 let not them that are in the countries
John 11. 54 Jesus..went thence unto a country near
11. 55 many went out of the country up to Jer.
Acts 12. 20 their country was nourished by the king's
18. 23 went over (all) the country of Galatia
27. 27 deemed that they drew near to some c.
[*See also* Better, far, hill, king, low, south.]

15. *Country (round) about*, περίχωρος *perichōros*.
Matt 14. 35 sent out into all that country round abo.
Luke 3. 3 he came into all the country about Jor.
4. 37 the fame of him went out into..the coun.
8. 37 the country of the Gadarenes round about

COUNTRY, to go or travel into a far —
To be away from one's people, ἀποδημέω *apodēmeō*.
Matt 21. 33 let it out..and went into a far country
25. 14 as a man travelling into a far country
Mark 12. 1 let it out..and went into a far country
Luke 20. 9 went into a far country for a long time

COUNTRY, born in or of the —
Native, indigenous, אֶזְרָח *ezrach*.
Num 15. 13 All that are born of the country shall do
Eze. 47. 22 shall be unto you as born in the country

COUNTRY, one of your own —
Native, indigenous, אֶזְרָח *ezrach*.
Lev. 16. 29 one of your own country, or a stranger
17. 15 one of your own country, or a stranger
24. 22 one..law..for one of your own country

COUNTRY, one's own —
Fatherland, πατρίς *patris*.
Matt 13. 54 when he was come into his own country
13. 57 without honour, save in his own country
Mark 6. 1 went out..and came into his own count.
6. 4 not without honour, but in his own cou.
Luke 4. 24 No prophet is accepted in his own coun.

COUNTRYMAN —
1. *One of the same tribe*, συμφυλέτης *sumphuletēs*.
1 Th. 2. 14 suffered like things of your own country.

2. *Genus, race*, γένος *genos*.
2 Co. 11. 26 (in) perils by (mine own) countrymen

COUPLE —
1. *A pair, yoke*, צֶמֶד *tsemed*.
Judg 19. 3 having his servant with him, and a coup.
2 Sa. 16. 1 Ziba the servant..met him, with a couple
Isa. 21. 7 he saw a chariot (with) a couple of hors.
21. 9 here cometh a chariot of men, (with) a co.

2. *Two*, שְׁנַיִם *shenayim*.
2 Sa. 13. 6 make me a couple of cakes in my sight

COUPLE, to —
To couple or join together, חָבַר *chabar*, 3.
Exod26. 6 couple the curtains together with the
26. 9 shalt couple five curtains by themselves
26. 11 couple the tent together, that it may be
36. 10 he coupled the five curtains one unto
36. 10 five curtains he coupled one unto another
36. 13 coupled the curtains one unto another
36. 16 he coupled five curtains by themselves
36. 18 he made fifty taches..to couple the tent

COUPLE together, to —
To couple or join together, חָבַר *chabar.*
Exod39. 4 for it, to couple (it) together: by

COUPLED —
1. *To be or become twins,* תָּאַם *taam.*
Exod26. 24 they shall be coupled together beneath
36. 29 And they were coupled beneath, and
2. *To couple or join together,* חָבַר *chabar.*
Exod26. 3 five curtains (shall be) coupled one to

COUPLED together —
1. *To couple or join together,* חָבַר *chabar.*
Exod26. 3 five curtains shall be coupled together
2. *Twins,* תְּאֹמִים *tammim.*
Exod26. 24 they shall be coupled together above the
36. 29 coupled together at the head thereof, to

COUPLED together, to be —
To be coupled or joined together, חָבַר *chabar*, 4.
Exod39. 4 by the two edges was it coupled together

COUPLETH, which —
Coupling, joining, חֹבֶרֶת *chobereth.*
Exod26. 10 edge of the curtain which coupleth the
36. 17 edge of the curtain which coupleth the

COUPLING —
1. *Coupling, joining,* חֹבֶרֶת *chobereth.*
Exod26. 4 curtain, from the selvage in the coupling
26. 10 curtain (that is) outmost in the coupling
2. *A coupling, joining, junction,* מַחְבֶּרֶת *machbereth.*
Exod26. 4 curtain, in the coupling of the second
26. 5 that (is) in the coupling of the second
28. 27 over against the (other) coupling thereof
36. 11 edge..from the selvage in the coupling
36. 11 he made..(another) curtain..in the coup.
36. 12 of the curtain which was in the coupling
36. 17 uttermost edge of the curtain in the cou.
39. 20 over against the (other) coupling thereof

COUPLINGS —
Couplings, what joins together, מְחַבְּרוֹת *mechabberoth.*
2 Ch. 34. 11 buy hewn stone, and timber for couplings

COURAGE —
1. *Heart,* לֵבָב *lebab.*
Dan. 11. 25 shall stir up his power and his courage
2. *Spirit,* רוּחַ *ruach.*
Josh. 2. 11 neither did there remain any more cour.
3. *Courage, cheer,* θάρσος *tharsos.*
Acts 28. 15 whom when Paul saw, he..took courage

COURAGE, to be of good —
1. *To be sharp, strong, confirmed,* אָמֵץ *amats.*
Deut31. 6, 7, 23 Be strong, and of a good courage
Josh. 1. 6, 9, 18 Be strong and of a good courage
10. 25 be strong, and of good courage: for thus
1 Ch. 22. 13 be strong, and of good courage; dread
28. 20 Be strong and of good courage and do
2. *To be, or become strong,* חָזַק *chazaq.*
2 Sa. 10. 12 Be of good courage, and let us play the
1 Ch.19. 13 Be of good courage, and let us behave
Ezra 10. 4 we..(will be) with thee: be of good cour.
Psa. 27. 14 Wait on the LORD; be of good courage
31. 24 Be of good courage, and he shall streng.
Isa. 41. 6 said to his brother, Be of good courage
3. *To show oneself strong,* חָזַק *chazaq*, 7.
Num13. 20 be ye of good courage, and bring of the

COURAGE, to take —
To show oneself strong, חָזַק *chazaq*, 7.
2 Ch. 15. 8 he took courage, and put away the abom.

COURAGEOUS, COURAGEOUSLY —
1. *Confirmed of heart,* אַמִּיץ לֵב *ammits leb.*
Amos 2. 16 (he that is) courageous among the mighty
2. *To be or become confirmed,* אָמֵץ *amats.*
Josh. 1. 7 Only be thou strong and very courageous
2 Ch. 32. 7 Be strong and courageous, be not afraid
3. *To be or become strong,* חָזַק *chazaq.*
Josh 23. 6 Be ye..very courageous to keep and to do
2 Sa. 13. 28 have not I commanded you? be courage.
2 Ch. 19. 11 Deal courageously, and the LORD shall

COURSE —
1. *A passing on, change,* חֲלִיפָה *chaliphah.*
1 Ki. 5. 14 he sent..ten thousand a month by courses
2. *Course, portion, division,* מַחְלְקָא *machlega.*
Ezra 6. 18 they set..the Levites in their courses
3. *Portion, division, course,* מַחֲלֹקֶת *machaloqeth.*
1 Ch. 23. 6 David divided them into courses among
27. 1 that served..in any matter of the courses
27. 1 of every course (were) twenty and four th.
27. 2 Over the first course..(was) Jashobeam
27. 2 in his course (were) twenty and four thou.
1 Ch. 27. 4 over the course of the second month (was)
27. 4 of his course (was) Mikloth also the ruler
27. 4 in his course likewise (were) twenty and
27. 5, 7, 8, 9, 10, 11 in his course (were) twenty
27. 12, 13, 14, 15 in his course (were) twenty and
27. 6 and in his course (was) Ammizabad his son
28. 1 that ministered to the king by course
28. 13 for the courses of the priests and Levites
28. 21 the courses of the priests and the Levites
2 Ch. 5. 11 the priests..did not (then) wait by course
8. 14 the courses of the priests to their service
8. 14 porters also by their courses at every gate
23. 8 for Jehoiada..dismissed not the courses
31. 2 And Hezekiah appointed the courses of
31. 2 after their courses, every man according
31. 15 to give to their brethren by courses, as
31. 16 their charges according to their courses
31. 17 upward, in their charges by their courses
35. 4 houses of your fathers, after your courses
35. 10 and the Levites in their courses, accord.
4. *Highway,* מְסִלָּה *mesillah.*
Judg. 5. 20 the stars in their courses fought against
5. *Race, running,* מְרוּצָה *merutsah.*
Jer. 8. 6 every one turned to his course, as the
23. 10 and their course is evil, and their force
6. *Age, course of things,* αἰών *aiōn.*
Eph. 2. 2 ye walked according to the course of this
7. *Race, running,* δρόμος *dromos.*
Acts 13. 25 And as John fulfilled his course, he said
20. 24 so that I might finish my course with joy
2 Ti. 4. 7 fought a good fight, I have finished (my) c.
8. *Daily course,* ἐφημερία *ephēmeria.*
Luke 1. 5 a certain priest..of the course of Abia
1. 8 he executed..in the order of his course
9. *Sailing,* πλόος *ploos.*
Acts 21. 7 when we had finished (our) course from
10. *A runner, running course,* τροχός *trochos.*
Jas. 3. 6 and setteth on fire the course of nature

COURSE, by —
In part, by rotation, ἀνὰ μέρος *ana meros.*
1 Co. 14. 27 or at the most (by) three, and (that) by c.

COURSE, to be out of —
To be moved, מוֹט *mot*, 2.
Psa. 82. 5 all the foundations..are out of course

COURSE, to have —
To run, τρέχω *trechō.*
2 Th. 3. 1 that the word..may have (free) course

COURT —
1. *House,* בַּיִת *bayith.*
Amos 7. 13 the king's chapel, and it (is) the king's co.
2. *Enclosed place, court,* חָצִיר *chatsir.*
Isa. 34. 13 an habitation of dragons, (and) a court for
3. *Enclosed place, court,* חָצֵר *chatser.*
Exod27. 9 thou shalt make the court of the taberna.
27. 9 hangings for the court (of) fine twined
27. 12, 13 the breadth of the court on the
27. 16 for the gate of the court (shall be) an
27. 17 All the pillars round about the court
27. 18 The length of the court (shall be) an hun.
27. 19 all the pins of the court (shall be of) brass
35. 17 The hangings of the court, his pillars, and
35. 17 and the hanging for the door of the court
35. 18 and the pins of the court, and their cords
38. 9 And he made the court: on the south side
38. 9 hangings of the court (were of) fine twined
38. 15 for the other side of the court gate, on
38. 16 All the hangings of the court round about
38. 17 all the pillars of the court (were) filleted
38. 18 the hanging for the gate of the court (was)
38. 18 answerable to the hangings of the court
38. 20 pins..of the court round about, (were of)
38. 31 the sockets of the court round about, and
38. 31 the sockets of the court gate, and all the
38. 31 all the pins of the court round about
39. 40 hangings of the court..for the court gate
40. 8 shalt set up the court round about, and
40. 8 hang up the hanging at the court gate
40. 33 set up the hanging of the court gate
Lev. 6. 16, 26 in the court of the tabernacle of the
Num. 3. 26 And the hangings of the court, and the
3. 26 curtain for the door of the court, which
3. 37 the pillars of the court round about, and
4. 26 hangings of the court, and the hangings
4. 26 for the door of the gate of the court
4. 32 the pillars of the court round about, and
2 Sa. 17. 18 which had a well in his court, whither
1 Ki. 6. 36 he built the inner court with three rows
7. 8 his house..(had) another court within the
7. 9 (so) on the outside toward the great court
7. 12 the great court round about (was) with
7. 12 both for the inner court of the house of
8. 64 hallow the middle of the court that (was)
2 Ki.21. 5 he built altars..in the two courts of the
23. 12 Manasseh had made in the two courts of
1 Ch.23. 28 their office (was) to wait..in the courts
28. 6 he shall build my house and my courts
28. 12 the pattern..of the courts of the house of
2 Ch. 4. 9 Furthermore he made the court of the
7. 7 Solomon hallowed the middle of the co.
20. 5 stood..in the house..before the new co.
23. 5 all the people (shall be) in the courts of
24. 21 stoned him with stones..in the court of
29. 16 into the court of the house of the LORD
2 Ch. 33. 5 he built altars..in the two courts of the
Neh. 3. 25 king's high house, that (was) by the court
8. 16 in their courts, and in the courts of the
13. 7 in preparing him a chamber in the courts
Esth. 1. 5 in the court of the garden of the king's
2. 11 Mordecai walked..before the court of the
4. 11 come unto the king into the inner court
5. 1 Esther..stood in the inner court of the
5. 2 saw Esther the queen standing in the co.
6. 4 And the king said, Who (is) in the court?
6. 4 Haman was come into the outward court
6. 5 Behold, Haman standeth in the court
Psa. 65. 4 he may dwell in thy courts: we shall
84. 2 even fainteth for the courts of the LORD
84. 10 For a day in thy courts (is) better than a
92. 13 shall flourish in the courts of our God
96. 8 bring an offering, and come into his courts
100. 4 Enter..into his courts with praise: be
116. 19 In the courts of the LORD's house, in the
135. 2 Ye that stand..in the courts of the house
Isa. 1. 12 who hath required..to tread my courts?
62. 9 shall drink it in the courts of my holi.
Jer. 19. 14 he stood in the court of the LORD's house
26. 2 Stand in the court of the LORD's house
32. 2 Jeremiah..was shut up in the court of
32. 8 mine uncle's son, came to me in the court
32. 12 before all the Jews that sat in the court
33. 1 he was yet shut up in the court of the
36. 10 in the higher court, at the entry of the
36. 20 they went in to the king into the court
37. 21 they should commit Jeremiah into the c.
37. 21 Jeremiah remained in the court of the
38. 6 the dungeon..that (was) in the court of
38. 13 Jeremiah remained in the court of the
38. 28 Jeremiah abode in the court of the prison
39. 14 sent, and took Jeremiah out of the court
39. 15 he was shut up in the court of the prison
Eze. 8. 7 he brought me to the door of the court
8. 16 he brought me into the inner court of the
9. 7 Defile the house, and fill the courts with
10. 3 and the cloud filled the inner court
10. 4 the court was full of the brightness of
10. 5 sound..was heard (even) to the outer co.
40. 14 post of the court round about the gate
40. 17 Then brought he me into the outward c.
40. 17 a pavement made for the court round
40. 19 unto the forefront of the inner court
40. 20 the outward court that looked toward the
40. 23 the gate of the inner court (was) over
40. 27 a gate in the inner court toward the south
40. 28 he brought me to the inner court by the
40. 31, 34 the arches..(were) toward the outer c.
40. 32 he brought me into the inner court towa.
40. 37 posts thereof (were) toward the outer co.
40. 44 chambers of the singers in the inner co.
40. 47 he measured the court, an hundred cubits
41. 15 inner temple, and the porches of the co.
42. 1 he brought me forth into the outer court
42. 3 for the inner court..for the outer court
42. 6 not pillars as the pillars of the courts
42. 7 the outer court on the fore part of the
42. 8 the chambers that (were) in the outer co.
42. 9 as one goeth into them from the outer co.
42. 10 of the wall of the court toward the east
42. 14 shall they not go..into the outer court
43. 5 the spirit..brought me into the inner co.
44. 17, 17 the gates of the inner court
44. 19 outer court, (even) into the outer court
44. 21 when they enter into the inner court
44. 27 into the sanctuary, unto the inner court
45. 19 the posts of the gate of the inner court
46. 1 The gate of the inner court that looketh
46. 20 bear them not out into the outer court
46. 21 into the outer court..corners of the court
46. 21 every corner of the court (there was) a co.
46. 22 In..corners of the court (there were) co.
Zech. 3. 7 thou..shalt also keep my courts, and I
4. *Court, settle, border, edge,* עֲזָרָה *azarah.*
2 Ch. 4. 9 and the great court, and doors for the co.
6. 13 and had set it in the midst of the court
5. As No. 3 [V.L. עִיר].
2 Ki. 20. 4 Isaiah was gone out into the middle court
6. *Court, yard,* αὐλή *aulē.*
Rev. 11. 2 the court which is without the temple

COURTEOUS —
Friendly minded, φιλόφρων *philophrōn.*
1 Pe. 3. 8 as brethren, (be) pitiful, (be) [courteous]

COURTEOUSLY —
1. *As a friend of man,* φιλανθρώπως *philanthrōpōs.*
Acts 27. 3 Julius courteously entreated Paul, and
2. *In a friendly minded manner,* φιλοφρόνως *phil.*
Acts 28. 7 who received us, and lodged us..courte.

COUSIN —
One of the same race, συγγενής *suggenēs.*
Luke 1. 36 behold, thy [cousin] Elisabeth, she hath
1. 58 her neighbours and her cousin heard how

COVENANT —
1. *Covenant, league,* בְּרִית *berith.*
Gen. 6. 18 with thee will I establish my covenant
9. 9 I, behold, I establish my covenant with
9. 11 And I will establish my covenant with
9. 12, 17 This (is) the token of the covenant
9. 13 and it shall be for a token of a covenant
9. 15 And I will remember my covenant, which
9. 16 I may remember the everlasting covenant
15. 18 In that same day the LORD made a cove.

Gen. 17. 2 I will make my covenant between me
17. 4 As for me, behold, my covenant (is) with
17. 7 I will establish my covenant between me
17. 7 and thy seed..for an everlasting covenant
17. 9 Thou shalt keep my covenant therefore
17. 10 This (is) my covenant, which ye shall keep
17. 11 it shall be a token of the covenant
17. 13 covenant shall be..for an everlasting cov.
17. 14 he hath broken my covenant
17. 19 and I will establish my covenant with
17. 19 for an everlasting covenant, (and) with
17. 21 But my covenant will I establish with
21. 27 and both of them made a covenant
21. 32 Thus they made a covenant at Beer-sheba
26. 28 and let us make a covenant with thee
31. 44 Now..come thou, let us make a covenant
Exod. 2. 24 and God remembered his covenant with
6. 4 have also established my covenant with
6. 5 and I have remembered my covenant;
19. 5 if ye will obey..and keep my covenant
23. 32 Thou shalt make no covenant with them
24. 7 he took the book of the covenant, and
24. 8 and said, Behold the blood of the cove.
31. 16 keep the sabbath..(for) a perpetual cov.
34. 10 And he said, Behold, I make a covenant
34. 12, 15 lest thou make a covenant with the
34. 27 I have made a covenant with thee and
34. 28 He wrote..the words of the covenant
Lev. 2. 13 shalt thou suffer the salt of the covenant
24. 8 children..by an everlasting covenant
26. 9 and establish my covenant with you
26. 15 (but) that ye break my covenant
26. 25 shall avenge the quarrel of (my) covenant
26. 42 Then will I remember my covenant with
26. 42 and also my covenant with Isaac
26. 42 and also my covenant with Abraham will
26. 44 to break my covenant with them; for I
26. 45 will for their sakes remember the coven.
Num 10. 33 the ark of the covenant of the LORD went
14. 44 the ark of the covenant of the LORD, and
18. 19 it (is) a covenant of salt for ever before
25. 12 I give unto him my covenant of peace
25. 13 the covenant of an everlasting priesthood
Deut. 4. 13 he declared unto you his covenant, which
4. 23 lest ye forget the covenant of the LORD
4. 31 not forget the covenant of thy fathers
5. 2 The LORD our God made a covenant with
5. 3 The LORD made not this covenant with
7. 2 thou shalt make no covenant with them
7. 9 which keepeth covenant and mercy with
7. 12 thy God shall keep unto thee the covena.
8. 18 that he may establish his covenant which
9. 9 the tables of the covenant which the L.
9. 11 of stone, (even) the tables of the covenant
9. 15 tables of the covenant (were) in my two
10. 8 to bear the ark of the covenant of the L.
17. 2 wickedness..in transgressing his coven.
29. 1 These (are) the words of the covenant
29. 1 the covenant which he made with them
29. 9 Keep therefore the words of this covenant
29. 12 enter into covenant with the LORD thy G.
29. 14 with you only do I make this covenant
29. 21 the curses of the covenant that are writt.
29. 25 they have forsaken the covenant of the L.
31. 9 bare the ark of the covenant of the LORD
31. 16 break my covenant which I have made
31. 20 and provoke me, and break my covenant
31. 25 bare the ark of the covenant of the LORD
31. 26 of the ark of the covenant of the LORD
33. 9 observed thy word, and kept thy coven.
Josh. 3. 3 the ark of the covenant of the LORD your
3. 6 Take up the ark of the covenant, and pass
3. 6 they took up the ark of the covenant, and
3. 8 priests that bare the ark of the covenant
3. 11 the ark of the covenant of the LORD of
3. 14 the priests bearing the ark of the coven.
3. 17 priests that bear the ark of the covenant
4. 7 before the ark of the covenant of the L.
4. 9 priests which bare the ark of the coven.
4. 18 priests that bare the ark of the covenant
6. 6 Take up the ark of the covenant, and let
6. 8 ark of the covenant of the LORD followed
7. 11 transgressed my covenant which I comm.
7. 15 hath transgressed the covenant of the L.
8. 33 bare the ark of the covenant of the LORD
23. 16 When ye have transgressed the covenant
24. 25 Joshua made a covenant with the people
Judg. 2. 1 I will never break my covenant with you
2. 20 this people hath transgressed my coven.
20. 27 the ark of the covenant of God (was) there
1 Sa. 4. 3 fetch the ark of the covenant of the LORD
4. 4 bring from thence the ark of the covenant
4. 4 there with the ark of the covenant
4. 5 the ark of the covenant of the LORD came
11. 1 Make a covenant with us, and we will
18. 3 Then Jonathan and David made a cove.
20. 8 hast brought thy servant into a covenant
23. 18 they two made a covenant before the L.
2 Sa. 15. 24 bearing the ark of the covenant of God
23. 5 hath made with me an everlasting coven.
1 Ki. 3. 15 before the ark of the covenant of the L
6. 19 set there the ark of the covenant of the
8. 1 might bring up the ark of the covenant
8. 6 priests brought in the ark of the coven.
8. 21 the ark, wherein (is) the covenant of the
8. 23 who keepest covenant and mercy with
11. 11 hast not kept my covenant and my stat.
19. 10, 14 the children..have forsaken thy coven.
20. 34 I will send thee away with this covenant
20. 34 he made a covenant with him, and sent
2 Ki. 11. 4 made a covenant with them, and took an
11. 17 Jehoiada made a covenant between the L.
2 Ki. 13. 23 because of his covenant with Abraham
17. 15 his covenant that he made with their
17. 35 With whom the LORD had made a covena.
17. 38 the covenant that I have made with you
18. 12 obeyed not..but transgressed his coven.
23. 2 the book of the covenant (which was)
23. 3 made a covenant before the LORD, to
23. 3 to perform the words of this covenant
23. 3 and all the people stood to the covenant
23. 21 as..written in the book of this covenant
1 Ch. 11. 3 David made a covenant with them in H.
15. 25, 26, 28, 29 ark of the covenant of the LORD
16. 6 before the ark of the covenant of God
16. 15 Be ye mindful always of his covenant
16. 17 (and) to Israel (for) an everlasting coven.
16. 37 left there, before the ark of the covenant
17. 1 ark of the covenant of the LORD (remain.
22. 19 bring the ark of the covenant of the L.
28. 2 for the ark of the covenant of the LORD
2 Ch. 5. 2, 7 the ark of the covenant of the LORD
6. 11 the ark, wherein (is) the covenant of the
6. 14 which keepest covenant, and (showest)
13. 5 and to his sons by a covenant of salt
15. 12 they entered into a covenant to seek the
21. 7 because of the covenant that he had made
23. 1 took the captains..into covenant with him
23. 3 the congregation made a covenant with
23. 16 Jehoiada made a covenant between him
29. 10 (it is) in mine heart to make a covenant
34. 30 all the words of the book of the covenant
34. 31 the king..and made a covenant before
34. 31 to perform the words of the covenant
34. 32 inhabitants..did according to the cove.
Ezra 10. 3 let us make a covenant with our God to
Neh. 1. 5 that keepeth covenant and mercy for them
9. 8 madest a covenant with him, to give the
9. 32 the terrible God, who keepest covenant
13. 29 the covenant of the priesthood, and of
Job 31. 1 I made a covenant with mine eyes; why
41. 4 Will he make a covenant with thee? wilt
Psa. 25. 10 unto such as keep his covenant and his
25. 14 and he will show them his covenant
44. 17 have we dealt falsely in thy covenant
50. 5 those that have made a covenant with me
50. 16 shouldest take my covenant in thy mouth?
55. 20 his hands..he hath broken his covenant
74. 20 Have respect unto the covenant: for the
78. 10 They kept not the covenant of God, and
78. 37 neither were they stedfast in his covenant
89. 3 I have made a covenant with my chosen
89. 28 and my covenant shall stand fast with
89. 34 My covenant will I not break, nor alter
89. 39 Thou hast made void the covenant of thy
103. 18 To such as keep his covenant, and to
105. 8 He hath remembered his covenant for
105. 10 (and) to Israel (for) an everlasting cove.
106. 45 he remembered for them his covenant
111. 5 he will ever be mindful of his covenant
111. 9 he hath commanded his covenant for
132. 12 If thy children will keep my covenant
Prov. 2. 17 and forgetteth the covenant of her God
Isa. 24. 5 they have..broken the everlasting cove.
28. 15 We have made a covenant with death
28. 18 your covenant with death shall be disan.
33. 8 he hath broken the covenant, he hath
42. 6 give thee for a covenant of the people
49. 8 give thee for a covenant of the people
54. 10 neither shall the covenant of my peace be
55. 3 I will make an everlasting covenant with
56. 4 the eunuchs that..take hold of my cove.
56. 6 every one that..taketh hold of my cove.
59. 21 this (is) my covenant with them saith
61. 8 make an everlasting covenant with them
Jer. 3. 16 The ark of the covenant of the LORD
11. 2, 6 Hear ye the words of this covenant
11. 3 obeyeth not the words of this covenant
11. 8 upon them all the words of this covenant
11. 10 Israel and..Judah have broken my cove.
14. 21 remember, break not thy covenant with
22. 9 they have forsaken the covenant of the
31. 31 I will make a new covenant with the
31. 32 Not according to the covenant that I
31. 32 which my covenant they brake, although
31. 33 this (shall be) the covenant that I will
32. 40 I will make an everlasting covenant with
33. 20 my covenant of the day, and my covenant
33. 21 (Then) may also my covenant be broken
33. 25 If my covenant (be) not with day and
34. 8 the king Zedekiah had made a covenant
34. 10 people, which had entered into the cove.
34. 13 I made a covenant with your fathers in
34. 15 ye had made a covenant before me in the
34. 18 men that have transgressed my covenant
34. 18 not performed the words of the covenant
50. 5 in a perpetual covenant (that) shall not
Eze. 16. 8 I sware..and entered into a covenant
16. 59 despised the oath in breaking the cove.
16. 60 I will remember my covenant with thee
16. 60 establish unto thee an everlasting cove.
16. 61 I will give them..but not by thy cove.
16. 62 I will establish my covenant with thee
17. 13 made a covenant with him, and hath
17. 14 by keeping of his covenant it might stand
17. 15 shall he break the covenant, and be deli.?
17. 16 whose oath he despised, and whose cove.
17. 18 despised the oath by breaking the cove.
17. 19 my covenant that he hath broken, even
20. 37 bring you into the bond of the covenant
34. 25 will make with them a covenant of peace
37. 26 will make a covenant of peace with them
37. 26 shall be an everlasting covenant with them
44. 7 they have broken my covenant because of
Dan. 9. 4 keeping the covenant and mercy to them
9. 27 he shall confirm the covenant with many
11. 22 yea, also the prince of the covenant
11. 28 heart (shall be) against the holy covenant
11. 30 have indignation against the holy coven.
11. 30 with them that forsake the holy covenant
11. 32 such as do wickedly against the covenant
Hos. 2. 18 will I make a covenant for them with the
6. 7 But they..have transgressed the covenant
8. 1 they have transgressed my covenant, and
10. 4 swearing falsely in making a covenant
12. 1 they do make a covenant with the Assyr.
Amos 1. 9 and remembered not the brotherly cove.
Zech. 9. 11 by the blood of thy covenant I have sent
11. 10 might break my covenant which I had
Mal. 2. 4 that my covenant might be with Levi
2. 5 My covenant was with him of life and
2. 8 ye have corrupted the covenant of Levi
2. 10 by profaning the covenant of our fathers?
2. 14 yet (is) she..the wife of thy covenant
3. 1 even the messenger of the covenant

2. *Arrangement, covenant,* διαθήκη *diathēkē.*
Luke 1. 72 and to remember his holy covenant
Acts 3. 25 of the covenant which God made with
7. 8 he gave him the covenant of circumcis.
Rom. 9. 4 the covenants, and the giving of the law
11. 27 this (is) my covenant unto them, when I
Gal. 3. 15 Though (it be) but a man's covenant, yet
3. 17 the covenant that was confirmed before
4. 24 these are the two covenants; the one
Eph. 2. 12 strangers from the covenants of promise
Heb. 8. 6 he is the Mediator of a better covenant
8. 8 I will make a new covenant with the house
8. 9 Not according to the covenant that I made
8. 9 they continued not in my covenant, and
8. 10 this (is) the covenant that I will make
9. 4 the ark of the covenant overlaid round
9. 4 Aaron's rod..and the tables of the cove.
10. 16 This (is) the covenant that I will make
10. 29 hath counted the blood of the covenant
12. 24 to Jesus the mediator of the new coven.
13. 20 the blood of the everlasting covenant

COVENANT, to —

1. *To cut (make) a covenant,* כָּרַת בְּרִית *karath berith.*
2 Ch. 7. 18 according as I have covenanted with Da.
Hag. 2. 5 (According to) the word that I covenanted

2. *To set, put, arrange together,* συντίθημι *suntithēmi.*
Luke 22. 5 they were glad, and covenanted to give

COVENANT breaker —

Not bound by covenant, ἀσύνθετος *asunthetos.*
Rom. 1. 31 Without understanding, covenant brea.

COVENANT with for, to —

To set, establish, appoint, ἵστημι *histēmi.*
Matt 26. 15 they covenanted with him for thirty pieces

COVER —

1. *Cup, jug, can,* קַשְׂוָה, קְשָׂוָה, *qasvah* or *qasah,*
Exod 25. 29 spoons thereof, and covers thereof, and
37. 16 spoons, and his bowls, and his covers to
Num. 4. 7 and the bowls, and covers to cover withal

2. *To hedge in, enclose,* שָׂכַךְ *sakak.*
Exod 33. 22 will cover thee with my hand while I

COVER, to —

1. *To swallow up,* בָּלַע *bala,* 3.
Num. 4. 20 to see when the holy things are covered

2. *To cover,* חָפָה *chaphah.*
2 Sa. 15. 30 the people that (was) with him covered
Esth. 7. 8 As the word went out..they covered H.
Jer. 14. 3 they were ashamed..and covered their
14. 4 the plowmen..covered their heads

3. *To cover, overlay, protect,* חָפַף *chaphaph.*
Deut. 33. 12 (the) LORD shall cover him all the day long

4. *To shade, conceal, protect,* צָלַל *talal,* 3.
Neh. 3. 15 he built it, and covered it, and set up the

5. *To clothe, cover, wrap up in,* יָעַט *yaat.*
Isa. 61. 10 covered me with the robe of righteousness

6. *To cover, conceal,* כָּסָה *kasah.*
Prov 12. 16 but a prudent (man) covereth shame

7. *To cover, conceal,* כָּסָה *kasah,* 3.
Gen. 9. 23 and covered the nakedness of their father
38. 14 covered her with a veil, and wrapped
38. 15 an harlot; because she had covered her
Exod. 8. 6 frogs came up, and covered the land of E.
10. 5 they shall cover the face of the earth
10. 15 they covered the face of the whole earth
14. 28 waters returned and covered the chariots
15. 5 The depths have covered them: they
15. 10 Thou didst blow..the sea covered them
16. 13 the quails came up, and covered the
21. 33 if a man shall dig a pit, and not cover it
24. 15 Moses went up..and a cloud covered the
24. 16 and the cloud covered it six days
26. 13 on this side and on that side, to cover it
28. 42 shalt make them linen breeches to cover
29. 13 take all the fat that covereth the inwards
29. 22 the fat that covereth the inwards, and
40. 34 a cloud covered the tent of the congrega.
Lev. 3. 3, 9, 14 the fat that covereth the inwards
4. 8 the fat that covereth the inwards, and
7. 3 and the fat that covereth the inwards
13. 12 if..the leprosy cover all the skin of (him)
13. 13 (if) the leprosy have covered all his flesh
16. 13 the cloud of the incense may cover the

Lev. 17. 13 he shall even..cover it with dust
Num. 4. 5 and cover the ark of testimony with it
4. 8 cover the same with a covering of badg.
4. 9 cover the candlestick of the light, and
4. 11 cover it with a covering of badger's skins
4. 12 cover them with a covering of badger's
4. 15 have made an end of covering the sanc.
9. 15 the cloud covered the tabernacle,(namely)
9. 16 So it was alway: the cloud covered it
16. 42 the cloud covered it, and the glory of the
22. 5 they cover the face of the earth, and they
22. 11 which covereth the face of the earth
Deut 22. 12 vesture, wherewith thou coverest (thyse.)
23. 13 and cover that which cometh from thee
Josh. 24. 7 brought the sea upon them, and covered
Judg. 4. 18 when he had turned in..she covered him
4. 19 and gave him drink, and covered him
Sa. 19. 13 Michal took an image..and covered (it)
Ki. 1. 1 they covered him with clothes, but he
7. 18 to cover the chapiters that (were) upon
7. 41 to cover the two bowls of the chapiters
7. 42 to cover the two bowls of the chapiters
2 Ch. 4. 12 and the two wreaths to cover the two
4. 13 to cover the two pommels of the chapiters
5. 8 the cherubims covered the ark and the
Neh. 4. 5 cover not their iniquity, and let not their
Job 9. 24 he covereth the faces of the judges
15. 27 Because he covereth his face with his fat.
16. 18 cover not thou my blood, and let my cry
21. 26 They shall lie down..worms shall cover
22. 11 and abundance of waters cover thee
23. 17 (neither) hath he covered the darkness
31. 33 If I covered my transgressions as Adam
36. 30 Behold, he..covereth the bottom of the
36. 32 With clouds he covereth the light; and
38. 34 that abundance of waters may cover
Psa. 32. 1 Blessed (is he whose)..sin (is) covered
44. 15 and the shame of my face hath covered
44. 19 and covered us with the shadow of death
69. 7 I have borne reproach; shame hath cov.
85. 2 Thou hast forgiven..thou hast covered
104. 6 Thou coveredst it with the deep as (with)
104. 9 they turn not again to cover the earth
106. 11 the waters covered their enemies; there
106. 17 and covered the company of Abiram
140. 9 let the mischief of their own lips cover
147. 8 Who covereth the heaven with clouds
Prov. 10. 6, 11 violence covereth the mouth of the
10. 12 Hatred stirreth up..love covereth all sins
17. 9 He that covereth a transgression seeketh
24. 31 nettles had covered the face thereof, and
28. 13 He that covereth his sins shall not prosper
Isa. 6. 2 he covered his face, and with twain he co.
11. 9 shall be full..as the waters cover the
26. 21 the earth also..shall no more cover her
29. 10 and your rulers, the seers hath he cover.
51. 16 I..have covered thee in the shadow of
58. 7 thou seest the naked, that thou cover him
60. 2 For, behold, the darkness shall cover the
60. 6 The multitude of camels shall cover
Jer. 3. 25 We lie down..and our confusion cover.
46. 8 I will go up, (and) will cover the earth
51. 51 We are confounded..shame hath cover.
Eze. 1. 11 two..(were) joined..and two covered
1. 23 and every one had two, which covered
7. 18 and horror shall cover them; and shame
12. 6 thou shalt cover thy face, that thou see
12. 12 he shall cover his face that he see not
16. 8 I spread my skirt over thee, and covered
16. 10 I girded thee..and I covered thee with
16. 18 tookest thy..garments, and coveredst
18. 7, 16 and hath covered the naked with a
24. 7 she poured it not..to cover it with dust
26. 10 By reason of..horses their dust shall co.
26. 19 and great waters shall cover thee
30. 18 as for her, a cloud shall cover her, and
31. 15 I covered the deep for him, and I
32. 7 I will cover the heaven, and make the
32. 7 I will cover the sun with a cloud, and
38. 9 thou shalt be like a cloud to cover the
38. 16 thou shalt come up..as a cloud to cover
Hos. 2. 9 and my flax (given) to cover her nakedness
10. 8 Cover us; and to the hills, Fall on us
Obad. 10 For (thy) violence..shame shall cover
Jon. 3. 6 covered (him) with sackcloth, and sat in
Mic. 7. 10 shame shall cover her which said unto
Hab. 2. 14 earth shall be filled..as the waters cover
2. 17 the violence of Lebanon shall cover thee
3. 3 His glory covered the heavens, and the
Mal. 2. 13 covering the altar of the LORD with tears
2. 16 (one) covereth violence with his garment

8. *To press down*, כָּפַשׁ *kaphash*, 5.
Lam. 3. 16 he hath covered me with ashes

9. *To muffle up*, לָאַט *laat.*
2 Sa. 19. 4 the king covered his face, and the king

10. *A covering, coverlet*, מְכַסֶּה *mekasseh.*
Lev. 9. 19 the rump, and that which covereth (the
Isa. 14. 11 worm is spread..and the worms cover
Eze. 27. 7 blue and purple..was that which covered

11. *To pour out, cover, weave together*, נָסַךְ *nasak.*
Isa. 30. 1 that cover with a covering, but not of my

12. *To be poured out*, נָסַךְ *nasak*, 6.
Exod. 25. 29 and bowls thereof, to cover withal
37. 16 his bowls..to cover withal, (of) pure gold

13. *To cover, hedge in*, סָכַךְ *sakak.*
Exod 25. 20 covering the mercy seat with their wings
37. 9 covered with their wings over the mercy
40. 3 and cover the ark with the veil

1 Ki. 8. 7 the cherubims covered the ark and the
1 Ch. 28. 18 covered the ark of the covenant of the
Job 40. 22 The shady trees cover him (with) their
Psa. 139. 13 thou hast covered me in my mother's
140. 7 thou hast covered my head in the day
Lam. 3. 43 Thou hast covered with anger, and pers.
3. 44 Thou hast covered thyself with a cloud
Eze. 28. 14 Thou (art) the anointed cherub that cov.
28. 16 I will destroy thee, O covering cherub

14. *To cover, hedge in*, סָכַךְ *sakak*, 5.
Exod 40. 21 and covered the ark of the testimony
Judg 3. 24 Surely he covereth his feet in his sum.
1 Sa. 24. 3 Saul went in to cover his feet: and Da.
Psa. 91. 4 He shall cover thee with his feathers

15. *To cover, ceil, overlay*, סָפַן *saphan.*
1 Ki. 6. 9 covered the house with beams and boards

16. *To wrap up in, array, cover*, עָטָה *atah.*
Psa. 104. 2 Who coverest (thyself) with light as (with)
109. 19 Let it be..as the garment (which) cover.
Isa. 22. 17 the LORD will carry..and will surely cover
Eze. 24. 17 cover not (thy) lips, and eat not the bread
24. 22 ye shall not cover (your) lips, nor eat the
Mic. 3. 7 yea, they shall all cover their lips: for

17. *To wrap up in, array, cover*, עָטָה *atah*, 5.
Psa. 89. 45 thou hast covered him with shame

18. *To cover, clothe*, עָטַף *ataph.*
Psa. 73. 6 violence covereth them (as) a garment

19. *To overlay, cover, spread out*, צָפָה *tsaphah*, 3.
1 Ki. 6. 15 he covered (them) on the inside with
6. 15 covered the floor of the house with planks
6. 20 (so) covered the altar (which was of) cedar
6. 35 covered (them) with gold fitted upon the

20. *To cover, overlay*, קָרַם *qaram.*
Eze. 37. 6 cover you with skin, and put breath in
37. 8 the skin covered them above: but (there)

21. *To bruise, or cover*, שׁוּף *shuph.*
Psa. 139. 11 Surely the darkness shall cover me; even

22. *To cover over*, ἐπικαλύπτω *epikaluptō.*
Rom. 4. 7 Blessed (are) they..whose sins are covered

23. *To cover*, καλύπτω *kaluptō.*
Matt. 8. 24 insomuch that the ship was covered with
10. 26 nothing covered, that shall not
Luke 8. 16 No man..covereth it with a vessel, or
23. 30 Fall on us; and to the hills, Cover us
1 Pe. 4. 8 charity shall cover the multitude of sins

24. *To cover fully*, κατακαλύπτω *katakaluptō.*
1 Co. 11. 7 a man indeed ought not to cover (his)

25. *To cover round about*, περικαλύπτω *perikaluptō.*
Mark 14. 65 to cover his face, and to buffet him, and

26. *To cover together*, συγκαλύπτω *sugkaluptō.*
Luke 12. 2 nothing covered, that shall not be revealed

COVER self, to —

1. *To cover self*, כָּסָה *kasah*, 7.
Gen. 24. 65 she took a veil, and covered herself
2 Ki. 19. 1 covered himself with sackcloth, and went
Isa. 37. 1 he rent his clothes, and covered himself
59. 6 neither shall they cover themselves with

2. *To wrap self up*, עָטָה *atah.*
Psa. 109. 29 cover themselves with their own confus.

COVERED —

1. *To cover*, חָפָה *chaphah.*
2 Sa. 15. 30 he went up, and had his head covered
Esth. 6. 12 but Haman hasted..having his head cov.

2. *To be covered*, חָפָה *chaphah*, 2.
Psa. 68. 13 the wings of a dove covered with silver

3. *To cover, ceil, overlay*, סָפַן *saphan.*
1 Ki. 7. 3 covered with cedar above upon the beams
7. 7 covered with cedar from one side of the

4. *A roof, cover*, צַב *tsab.*
Num 7. 3 brought their offering..six covered wag.

5. *To spread out, cover, overlay*, צָפָה *tsaphah*, 4.
Prov 26. 23 (like) a potsherd covered with silver dross

COVERED, to be —

1. *To be covered, concealed*, כָּסָה *kasah*, 2.
Jer. 51. 42 she is covered with the multitude of the
Eze. 24. 8 that it should not be covered

2. *To be covered, concealed*, כָּסָה *kasah*, 4.
Gen. 7. 19 and all the high hills..were covered
7. 20 and the mountains were covered
Psa. 80. 10 The hills were covered with the shadow
Eccl. 6. 4 and his name shall be covered with dark.
Eze. 41. 16 and the windows (were) covered

3. *To cover self*, כָּסָה *kasah*, 7.
2 Ki. 19. 2 he sent Eliakim..covered with sackcloth
Prov 26. 26 (Whose) hatred is covered by deceit, his
Isa. 37. 2 he sent Eliakim..covered with sackcloth
Jon. 3. 8 let man and beast be covered with sack.

4. *To be thick, covered*, כָּשָׂה *kasah.*
Deut 32. 15 thou art grown thick, thou art covered

5. *To wrap up in, array*, עָטָה *atah.*
1 Sa. 28. 14 An old man..he (is) covered with a mantle
Psa. 71. 13 let them be covered (with) reproach and

6. *To cover fully*, κατακαλύπτω *katakaluptō.*
1 Co. 11. 6 woman be not covered, let her also be
11. 6 but if it be a shame..let her be covered

COVERED, to have one's head —

To have on the head, κατὰ κεφαλῆς ἔχω. [*echō*].
1 Co. 11. 4 Every man praying..having (his) head co.

COVERED over, to be —

To be or become covered, עָטַף *ataph.*
Psa. 65. 13 valleys also are covered over with corn

COVERING —

1. *A tent, (round bright thing,)* אֹהֶל *ohel.*
Exod 26. 7 (hair) to be a covering upon the tabernacle

2. *A covering*, כְּסוּי *kasui.*
Num. 4. 6 put thereon the covering of badger's sk.
4. 14 spread upon it a covering of badger's sk.

3. *A covering*, כְּסוּת *kesuth.*
Gen. 20. 16 behold, he (is) to thee a covering of the
Exod 22. 27 that (is) his covering only, it (is) his
Job 24. 7 that (they have) no covering in the cold
26. 6 and destruction hath no covering
31. 19 If I have seen..any poor without covering
Isa. 50. 3 and I make sackcloth their covering

4. *A veil*, לוֹט *lot.*
Isa. 25. 7 face of the covering cast over all people

5. *A covering*, מִכְסֶה *mikseh.*
Gen. 8. 13 Noah removed the covering of the ark, and
Exod 26. 14 thou shalt make a covering for the tent
26. 14 and a covering above (of) badgers' skins
35. 11 The tabernacle, his tent, and his covering
36. 19 he made a covering for the tent (of) ram's
36. 19 a covering (of) badgers' skin above (that)
39. 34 the covering of rams' skins dyed red, and
39. 34 the covering of badgers' skins, and the
40. 19 put the covering of the tent above upon
Num. 3. 25 the covering thereof, and the hanging
4. 8 cover the same with a covering of badgers'
4. 10 within a covering of badgers' skins, and
4. 11 cover it with a covering of badgers' skins
4. 12 cover them with a covering of badgers'
4. 25 his covering, and the covering of the bad.

6. *A covering, curtain*, מָסָךְ *masak.*
Exod 35. 12 mercy seat, and the veil of the covering
39. 34 and the veil of the covering
40. 21 set up the veil of the covering, and
Num. 4. 5 they shall take down the covering veil
2 Sa. 17. 19 the woman took and spread a covering
Psa. 105. 39 He spread a cloud for a covering, and
Isa. 22. 8 he discovered the covering of Judah, and

7. *A covering*, מַסֵּכָה *massekah.*
Isa. 28. 20 the covering narrower than that he can
30. 1 with a covering, but not of my Spirit, that

8. *A covering*, מְסֻכָּה *mesukkah.*
Eze. 28. 13 every precious stone (was) thy covering

9. *Riding seat*, מֶרְכָּב *merkab.*
Song 3. 10 the covering of it (of) purple, the midst

10. *A secret place*, סֵתֶר *sether.*
Job 22. 14 Thick clouds (are) a covering to him, that

11. *Coverlet, bracelet*, צָמִיד *tsamid.*
Num 19. 15 which hath no covering bound upon it.

12. *Overlaying, covering*, צִפּוּי *tsippui.*
Num 16. 38, 39 broad plates (for) a covering of the
Isa. 30. 22 Ye shall defile also the covering of thy

13. *Something cast around*, περιβόλαιον *peribolaion.*
1 Co. 11. 15 for (her) hair is given her for a covering

COVERING, to put a —

To wrap up in, array, עָטָה *atah.*
Lev. 13. 45 he shall put a covering upon his upper lip

COVERT —

1. *A covered walk*, מוּסָךְ, *musak* [V.L. מיסך].
2 Ki. 16. 18 the covert for the sabbath that they had

2. *A secret hiding place*, מִסְתּוֹר *mistor.*
Isa. 4. 6 and for a covert from storm and from rain

3. *Covert, booth*, סֹךְ *sok.*
Jer. 25. 38 He hath forsaken his covert, as the lion

4. *Covert, booth*, סֻכָּה *sukkah.*
Job 38. 40 (and) abide in the covert to lie in wait?

5. *Secret place*, סֵתֶר *sether.*
1 Sa. 25. 20 she came down by the covert of the hill
Job 40. 21 lieth under the shady trees..in the covert
Psa. 61. 4 I will trust in the covert of thy wings
Isa. 16. 4 a covert to them from the face of the
32. 2 from the wind, and a covert from the

COVET, to —

1. *To desire for oneself*, אָוָה *avah*, 7.
Deut. 5. 21 neither shalt thou covet thy neighbour's
Prov. 21. 26 He coveteth greedily all the day long: but

2. *To cut off, or gain (unlawfully)*, בָּצַע *batsa.*
Hab. 2. 9 him that coveteth an evil covetousness

3. *To desire*, חָמַד *chamad.*
Exod 20. 17 Thou shalt not covet thy neighbour's
20. 17 thou shalt not covet thy neighbour's wife
Josh. 7. 21 I coveted them, and took them; and
Mic. 2. 2 they covet fields, and take (them) by

4. *To fix the mind on*, ἐπιθυμέω *epithumeō.*
Acts 20. 33 I have coveted no man's silver, or gold
Rom. 7. 7 the law had said, Thou shalt not covet
13. 9 Thou shalt not covet; and if (there be) any

5. *To be zealous for*, ζηλόω *zēloō.*
1 Co. 14. 39 covet to prophesy, and forbid not to speak

COVET after, to —
To extend the arms for anything, ὀρέγομαι *oregomai.*
1 Ti. 6. 10 which while some coveted after, they have

COVET earnestly, to —
To be zealous for, ζηλόω *zēloō.*
1 Co. 12. 31 covet earnestly the best gifts: and yet

COVETOUS —
1. *To gain dishonestly*, בָּצַע *batsa.*
Psa. 10. 3 the covetous, (whom) the LORD abhorreth
2. *One who wishes more*, πλεονέκτης *pleonektēs.*
1 Co. 5. 10 with the covetous, or extortioners, or
5. 11 a fornicator, or covetous, or an idolator
6. 10 Nor thieves, nor covetous, nor drunkards
3. *A lover of silver*, φιλάργυρος *philarguros.*
Luke16. 14 the Pharisees also, who were covetous
2 Ti. 3. 2 lovers of their own selves, covetous

COVETOUS man —
One who wishes more, πλεονέκτης *pleonektēs.*
Eph. 5. 5 nor unclean person, nor covetous man

COVETOUS practices —
The wish to have more, πλεονεξία *pleonexia.*
2 Pe. 2. 14 have exercised with covetous practices

COVETOUSNESS —
1. *Dishonest gain*, בֶּצַע *betsa.*
Exod18. 21 provide..men of truth, hating covetous.
Psa.119. 36 Incline my heart..not to covetousness
Prov 28. 16 he that hateth covetousness shall prolong
Isa. 57. 17 For the iniquity of his covetousness was
Jer. 6. 13 every one (is) given to covetousness
8. 10 for every one..is given to covetousness
22. 17 eyes.. (are) not but for thy covetousness
51. 13 (and) the measure of thy covetousness
Eze. 33. 31 their heart goeth after their covetousness
Hab. 2. 9 to him that coveteth an evil covetousness
2. *The wish to have more*, πλεονεξία *pleonexia.*
Mark 7. 22 Thefts, covetousness, wickedness, deceit
Luke12. 15 Take heed, and beware of covetousness: for
Rom. 1. 29 fornication, wickedness, covetousness
2 Co. 9. 5 bounty, and not as (of) covetousness
Eph. 5. 3 all uncleanness, or covetousness, let it
Col. 3. 5 evil concupiscence, and covetousness
1 Th. 2. 5 neither..used we..a cloak of covetousness
2 Pe. 2. 3 through covetousness..make merchandise

COVETOUSNESS, without —
Not a lover of silver, ἀφιλάργυρος *aphilarguros.*
Heb. 13. 5 (Let your) conversation (be) without cov

COW —
1. *A heifer of the herd*, עֶגְלַת בָּקָר *eglath baqar.*
Isa 7. 21 a man shall nourish a young cow and
2. *A heifer, young cow*, פָּרָה *parah.*
Job 21. 10 their cow calveth, and casteth not her
Isa. 11. 7 And the cow and the bear shall feed
3. *A bullock, ox*, שׁוֹר *shor.*
Lev. 22. 28 (whether it be) cow or ewe, ye shall not
Num18. 17 the firstling of a cow..thou shalt not
4. *Cattle (for the plough), a herd*, בָּקָר *baqar.*
Eze. 4. 15 I have given thee cow's dung for man's

COZ, קוֹץ *nimble.*
A descendant of Caleb son of Hur, B.C. 1430.
1 Ch. 4. 8 And C. begat Anub, and Zobebah, and

COZ-BI, כָּזְבִּי *deceitful.*
A Midianitess slain with Zimri by Phinehas, B.C. 1452.
Num25. 15 Midianitish woman that was slain (was) C.
25. 18 they..beguiled you in the matter of..C.

CRACKLING —
A voice, קוֹל *qol.*
Eccl. 7. 6 as the crackling of thorns under a pot

CRACKNELS —
Small dry cakes, נִקֻּדִים *niqquddim.*
1 Ki.14. 3 take with thee ten loaves, and cracknels

CRAFT —
1. *Deceit*, מִרְמָה *mirmah.*
Dan. 8. 25 shall cause craft to prosper in his hand
2. *Guile, deceit, a bait*, δόλος *dolos.*
Mark14. 1 sought how they might take him by craft
3. *Work*, ἐργασία *ergasia.*
Acts 19. 25 ye know that by this craft we have our
4. *Part, portion*, μέρος *meros.*
Acts 19. 27 not only this our craft is in danger to
5. *Art, skill*, τέχνη *technē.*
Rev. 18. 22 no craftsman, of whatsoever craft (he be)

CRAFT, of the same —
One of the same art, ὁμότεχνος *homotechnos.*
Acts 18. 3 because he was of the same craft, he ab.

CRAFTINESS —
1. *Craftiness, cunning, subtilty*, עָרְם *orem.*
Job 5. 13 taketh the wise in their own craftiness
2. *Unscrupulousness*, πανουργία *panourgia.*
Luke20. 23 he perceived their craftiness, and said
1 Co. 3. 19 taketh the wise in their own craftiness
2 Co. 4. 2 not walking in craftiness, nor handling

CRAFTINESS, cunning —
Unscrupulousness, πανουργία *panourgia.*
Eph. 4. 14 the sleight of men, (and) cunning crafti.

CRAFTSMAN —
1. *One who plows, carves, engraves*, חָרָשׁ *charash.*
Deut 27. 15 the work of the hands of the craftsman
2 Ki. 24. 14 he carried away..all the craftsmen and
24. 16 craftsmen and smiths a thousand, all
Hos. 13. 2 all of it the work of the craftsmen
2. *Cutting, carving*, חֶרֶשׁ *cheresh.*
1 Ch. 4. 14 valley of Charashim; for they were craft.
Neh. 11. 35 Lod, and Ono, the valley of craftsmen
3. *Artificer, artisan*, τεχνίτης *technitēs.*
Acts 19. 24 brought no small gain unto the craftsmen
19. 38 and the craftsmen which are with him
Rev. 18. 22 no craftsman, of whatsoever craft (he be)

CRAFTY —
1. *Crafty, subtile*, עָרוּם *arum.*
Job 5. 12 disappointeth the devices of the crafty
15. 5 thou choosest the tongue of the crafty
2. *Working in every way*, πανοῦργος *panourgos.*
2 Co. 12. 16 nevertheless, being crafty, I caught you

CRAFTY counsel, to take —
To act craftily in counsel, עָרַם סוֹד *aram (5) sod.*
Psa. 83. 3 They have taken crafty counsel against

CRAG —
Tooth, שֵׁן *shen.*
Job 39. 28 upon the crag of the rock, and the strong

CRANE —
A swallow (from its alertness), [V.L. סִיס], סוּס *sus.*
Isa. 38. 14 Like a crane (or) a swallow, so did I chat.
Jer. 8. 7 the crane and the swallow observe the

CRASHING —
Breach, breaking, שֶׁבֶר *sheber.*
Zeph. 1. 10 and a great crashing from the hills

CRAVE, to —
1. *To cause to bend, or urge on*, אָכַף *akaph.*
Prov 16. 26 for his mouth craveth it of him
2. *To ask*, αἰτέω *aiteō.*
Mark15. 43 Joseph of Arimathea..and craved the

CREATE, to —
1. *To prepare, form, fashion, create*, בָּרָא *bara.*
Gen. 1. 1 God created the heaven and the earth
1. 21 God created great whales, and every
1. 27 So God created man in his (own) image
1. 27 in the image of God created he him
1. 27 male and female created he them
2. 3 rested from all his work which God cre.
5. 1 God created man, in the likeness of God
5. 2 Male and female created he them; and
6. 7 I will destroy man whom I have created
Deut. 4. 32 day that God created man upon the earth
Psa. 51. 10 Create in me a clean heart, O God; and
89. 12 The north and the south thou hast crea.
Isa. 4. 5 the LORD will create upon every dwelling
40. 26 and behold who hath created these (things)
41. 20 and the Holy One of Israel hath created
42. 5 he that created the heavens, and stretc.
43. 1 thus saith the LORD that created thee, O
43. 7 I have created him for my glory, I have
45. 7 I form the light, and create darkness
45. 7 I make peace, and create evil: I the L.
45. 8 spring up..I the LORD have created it
45. 12 I have made the earth, and created man
45. 18 saith the LORD that created the heavens
45. 18 he created it not in vain, he formed it to
54. 16 I have created the smith that bloweth
54. 16 and I have created the waster to destroy
57. 19 I create the fruit of the lips; Peace, peace
65. 17 I create new heavens, and a new earth
65. 18 rejoice for ever (in that) which I create
65. 18 behold, I create Jerusalem a rejoicing
Jer. 31. 22 for the LORD hath created a new thing in
Amos 4. 13 he that formeth the mountains, and cre.
Mal. 2. 10 hath not one God created us? why
2. *To make, produce*, κτίζω *ktizō.*
Mark13. 19 of the creation which God created unto
1 Co. 11. 9 Neither was the man created for the
Eph. 2. 10 created in Christ Jesus unto good works
3. 9 in God, who created all things by Jesus
4. 24 after God is created in righteousness and
Col. 1. 16 by him were all things created that are
1. 16 all things were created by him, and for
3. 10 after the image of him that created him
1 Ti. 4. 3 which God hath created to be received
Rev. 4. 11 for thou hast created all things, and for
4. 11 thy pleasure they are and were created
10. 6 who created heaven, and the things that

CREATED, to be —
To be prepared, formed, created, בָּרָא *bara*, 2.
Gen. 2. 4 and of the earth when they were created
5. 2 in the day when they were created
Psa.102. 18 people which shall be created shall praise
104. 30 sendest forth thy spirit, they are created
148. 5 he commanded, and they were created
Isa. 48. 7 created now, and not from the beginning
Eze. 21. 30 in the place where thou wast created, in
28. 13 in the day that thou wast created
28. 15 from the day that thou wast created

CREATION—
CREATION OF THE WORLD.—Dr Hales, in his work entitled, "A New Analysis of Chronology and Geography, History and Prophecy," (vol. i. p. 210), remarks: "In every system of historical chronology, sacred and profane, the two grand *æras*—of the *Creation of the World*, and of the *Nativity of Christ*—have been usually adopted as standards, by reference to which all subordinate epochs, æras, and periods have been adjusted." He gives a list of 120 dates, commencing B.C. 6984, and terminating B.C. 3616, to which this event has been assigned by different authorities, and he admits that it might be swelled to 300. He places it at B.C. 5411. The date commonly adopted is B.C. 4004; being that of Usher, Spanheim, Calmet, Blair, &c., and the one used in the English Bible. The following are some of the principal variations:—Alfonso X., according to (Muller), 6984, (Strauchius), 6484; Indian Chronology (Gentil), 6204, (Arab Records), 6174; Babylonian Chronology (Bailly), 6158; Chinese Chronology (Bailly), 6157; Diogenes Lærtius (Playfair), 6138; Egyptian Chronology (Bailly), 6081; Septuagint (Abulfaragi), 5586; Septuagint, Alexandrine (Scaliger), 5508; Persian Chronology (Bailly), 5507; Chronicle of Axum, Abyssinian (Bruce), 5500; Jackson, 5426; Josephus (Playfair), 5555, (Jackson), 5481, (Hales), 5402, (Univ. Hist.), 4698; Hales, 5411; Indian computation (Megasthenes), 5369; Talmudists (Petrus Alliacens), 5344; Septuagint, Vatican, 5270; Bede (Strauchius), 5199; Samaritan computation (Scaliger), 4427; Samaritan text (Univ. Hist.), 4305; Hebrew text, 4161; Playfair and Walker, 4008; Usher, English Bible, &c., 4004; Kepler (Playfair), 3993; Petavius, 3984; Melancthon (Playfair), 3964; Luther, 3961; Lightfoot, 3960; Cornelius a Lapide (Univ. Hist.), 3951; Scaliger, Isaacson, 3950; Strauchius, 3949; Vulgar Jewish computation (Strauchius), 3760; Rabbi Lipman (Univ. Hist.), 3616.

A making, thing made, κτίσις *ktisis.*
Mark10. 6 from the beginning of the creation God
13. 19 was not from the beginning of the crea.
Rom. 1. 20 invisible things of him from the creation
8. 22 we know that the whole creation groaneth
2 Pe. 3. 4 as (they were) from the beginning of the cr.
Rev. 3. 14 true Witness, the beginning of the crea.

CREATOR —
1. *To prepare, form, create*, בָּרָא *bara.*
Eccl. 12. 1 Remember now thy Creator in the days
Isa. 40. 28 the LORD, the Creator of the ends of the
43. 15 your Holy One, the Creator of Israel
2. *To make, produce*, κτίζω *ktizō.*
Rom. 1. 25 served the creature more than the Creator
3. *Maker*, κτίστης *ktistēs.*
1 Pe. 4. 19 in well doing, as unto a faithful Creator

CREATURE —
1. *Breathing creature*, נֶפֶשׁ *nephesh.*
Gen. 1. 21 and every living creature that moveth
1. 24 Let the earth bring forth the living crea.
2. 19 whatsoever Adam called every living cr.
9. 10, 12 every living creature that (is) with
9. 15 between me and you and every living c.
9. 16 between God and every living creature
Lev. 11. 46 of every living creature that moveth in
11. 46 of every creature that creepeth upon the
2. *A making, thing made*, κτίσις *ktisis.*
Mark16. 15 [preach the Gospel to every creature]
Rom. 1. 25 worshipped and served the creature
8. 19 the earnest expectation of the creature
8. 20 the creature was made subject to vanity
8. 21 the creature itself also shall be delivered
8. 39 Nor height, nor depth, nor any other cr.
2 Co. 5. 17 any man (be) in Christ, (he is) a new cre.
Gal. 6. 15 nor uncircumcision, but a new creature
Col. 1. 15 Who is..the first born of every creature
1. 23 (and) which was preached to every crea.
Heb. 4. 13 Neither is there any creature that is not
3. *Thing made*, κτίσμα *ktisma.*
1 Ti. 4. 4 every creature of God (is) good, and
Jas. 1. 18 a kind of first fruits of his creatures
Rev. 5. 13 every creature which is in heaven, and
8. 9 And the third part of the creatures which

CREATURE, living or moving —
1. *Living (thing)*, חַי *chai.*
Eze. 1. 5 (came) the likeness of four living creatures
1. 13 As for the likeness of the living creatures
1. 13 up and down among the living creatures
1. 14 the living creatures ran and returned as
1. 15 as I beheld the living creatures, behold
1. 15 upon the earth by the living creatures
1. 19 when the living creatures went, the
1. 19 the living creatures were lifted up from
1. 20, 21 the spirit of the living creature (was)
1. 22 upon the heads of the living creature
3. 13 noise of the wings of the living creatures
10. 15, 20 This (is) the living creature that I
10. 17 the spirit of the living creature (was) in
2. *A swarming creature*, שֶׁרֶץ *sherets.*
Gen. 1. 20 the moving creature that hath life, and

CREDITOR —
1. *To lend on usury*, נָשָׁה *nashah.*
2 Ki. 4. 1 the creditor is come to take unto him my
Isa. 50. 1 which of my creditors (is it) to whom I
2. *One who lends, a creditor*, δανειστής *daneistēs.*
Luke 7. 41 There was a certain creditor which had

3. *Master of the lending of the hand*, בַּעַל מַשֵּׁה יָד [*baal*].
Deut.15. 2 Every creditor that lendeth (ought) unto

CREEK —
Gulf, bay, κόλπος *kolpos*.
Acts 27. 39 they discovered a certain creek with a

CREEP —
1. *To creep, crawl*, רָמַשׂ *ramas*.
Gen. 1. 26 creeping thing that creepeth upon the
1. 30 every thing that creepeth upon the earth
7. 8 every thing that creepeth upon the earth
7. 14 creeping thing that creepeth upon the
8. 17 creeping thing that creepeth upon the
8. 19 (and) whatsoever creepeth upon the earth
Lev. 11. 44 creeping thing that creepeth upon the
20. 25 any manner of living thing that creepeth
Deut. 4. 18 The likeness of any thing that creepeth
Psa.104 20 the beasts of the forest do creep (forth)
Eze. 38. 20 all creeping things that creep upon the
2. *A swarming creature*, שֶׁרֶץ *sherets*.
Lev. 11. 20 All fowls that creep, going upon (all) four
11. 31 These (are) unclean . . among all that creep

CREEP, to —
To swarm, שָׁרַץ *sharats*.
Gen. 7. 21 every creeping thing that creepeth upon
Lev. 11. 29 creeping things that creep upon the
11. 41 every creeping thing that creepeth upon
11. 42 creeping things that creep upon the earth
11. 43 with any creeping thing that creepeth
11. 46 of every creature that creepeth upon the

CREEP in unawares, to —
To come in sideways, παρεισδύνω *pareisdunō*.
Jude 4 there are certain men crept in unawares

CREEP into, to —
To go in to, ἐνδύνω εἰς *endunō eis*.
2 Ti. 3. 6 this sort are they which creep into houses

CREEPETH, that —
A creeping creature, רֶמֶשׂ *remes*.
Gen. 1. 25 every thing that creepeth upon the earth
8. 17 every creeping thing that creepeth upon

CREEPING thing —
1. *A creeping creature*, רֶמֶשׂ *remes*.
Gen. 1. 24 cattle, and creeping thing, and beast of
1. 26 every creeping thing that creepeth upon
6. 7 creeping thing, and the fowls of the air
6. 20 every creeping thing of the earth after
7. 14 every creeping thing that creepeth upon
7. 23 the creeping things, and the fowl of the
8. 19 every creeping thing, and every fowl
1 Ki. 4. 33 of creeping things, and of fishes
Psa.104. 25 wherein (are) things creeping innumer.
148. 10 Beasts, and all cattle; creeping things, and
Eze. 8. 10 every form of creeping things, and abom.
38. 20 all creeping things that creep upon the
Hos. 2. 18 (with) the creeping things of the ground
Hab. 1. 14 the creeping things, (that have) no ruler
2. *A swarming creature*, שֶׁרֶץ *sherets*.
Gen. 7. 21 of beast, and of every creeping thing that
Lev. 5. 2 the carcase of unclean creeping things
11. 21 every flying creeping thing that goeth
11. 23 all (other) flying creeping things, which
11. 29 the creeping things that creep upon the
11. 41 every creeping thing that creepeth upon
11. 42 all creeping things that creep upon the
11. 43 with any creeping thing that creepeth
11. 44 with any manner of creeping thing that
22. 5 Or whosoever toucheth any creeping thi.
Deut14. 19 every creeping thing that flieth (is) uncl.
3. *A creeping thing*, ἑρπετόν *herpeton*.
Acts 10. 12 and creeping things, and fowls of the air
11. 6 and creeping things, and fowls of the air
Rom. 1. 23 four footed beasts, and creeping things

CRES'-CENS, Κρήσκης.
A disciple with Paul at Rome.
2 Ti. 4. 10 C. to Galatia, Titus unto Dalmatia

CRETE, Κρήτη.
A large island midway between Syria and Malta, now called *Candia*.
Acts 27. 7 we sailed under C., over against Salmone
27. 12 (which is) an haven of C., and lieth
27. 13 loosing (thence), they sailed close by C.
27. 21 ye should . . not have loosed from C.
Titus 1. 5 For this cause left I thee in C.

CRETES, CRETIANS, Κρῆτες.
The inhabitants of Crete.
Acts 2. 11 C. and Arabians, we do hear them speak
Titus 1. 12 The C. (are) alway liars, evil beasts, slow

CRIB —
Crib, feeding place, אֵבוּס *ebus*.
Job 39. 9 willing to serve thee, or abide by thy crib?
Prov.14. 4 Where no oxen (are), the crib (is) clean
Isa. 1. 3 and the ass his master's crib

CRIED, to be —
To be called, קָרָא *qara*, 2.
Jer. 4. 20 Destruction upon destruction is cried
Eze. 10. 13 it was cried unto them in my hearing

CRIME —
Cause, case, αἰτία *aitia*.
Acts 25. 27 to signify the crimes (laid) against him

CRIME laid against —
Indictment, charge, ἔγκλημα *egklēma*.
Acts 25. 16 concerning the crime laid against him

CRIMES —
Judgment, מִשְׁפָּט *mishpat*.
Eze. 7. 23 the land is full of bloody crimes, and the

CRIMSON —
1. *Carmine colour*, כַּרְמִיל *karmil*.
2 Ch. 2. 7 in purple, and crimson, and blue, and
2. 14 in blue, and in fine linen, and in crimson
3. 14 the veil (of) blue, and purple, and crimson
2. *Scarlet colour*, שָׁנִי *shani*.
Jer. 4. 30 Though thou clothest thyself with crim.
3. *Crimson colour*, תּוֹלָע *tola*.
Isa. 1. 18 though they be red like crimson, they

CRIPPLE, being a —
Lame, cripple, halt, χωλός *chōlos*.
Acts 14. 8 being a cripple from his mother's womb

CRISPING pin —
Pockets, bags, חֲרִיטִים *charitim*.
Isa. 3. 22 and the wimples, and the crisping pins

CRIS-PUS, Κρίσπος.
A convert at Corinth, baptised by Paul.
Acts 18. 8 C. . . chief ruler of the synagogue, believed
1 Co. 1. 14 I baptized none of you but C. and Gaius

CROOK BACKT —
Hump backed, גִּבֵּן *gibben*.
Lev. 21. 20 Or crook-backt, or a dwarf, or that hath a

CROOKED —
1. *Fleeing, shooting*, בָּרִיחַ *bariach*.
Job 26. 13 his hand hath formed the crooked serpent
2. *To be perverse or perverted*, עָוַת *avath*, 4.
Eccl. 1. 15 (That which is) crooked cannot be made
3. *Deceitful, inscrutable*, עָקֹב *aqob*.
Isa. 40. 4 the crooked shall be made straight, and
4. *Twisted, crooked*, עֲקַלָּתוֹן *aqallathon*.
Isa. 27. 1 even leviathan that crooked serpent
5. *Froward, perverse*, עִקֵּשׁ *iqqesh*.
Prov. 2. 15 Whose ways (are) crooked, and (they) fro.
6. *Wrestling*, פְּתַלְתֹּל *pethaltol*.
Deut32. 5 (they are) a perverse and crooked gener.
7. *Crooked, perverse*, σκολιός *skolios*.
Luke 3. 5 the crooked shall be made straight, and
Phil. 2. 15 midst of a crooked and perverse nation

CROOKED, to make —
1. *To overturn, pervert*, עָוָה *avah*, 3.
Lam. 3. 9 he hath made my paths crooked
2. *To pervert*, עָוַת *avath*, 3.
Eccl. 7. 13 make (that) straight which he . . made cr.
3. *To make froward, perverse*, עָקַשׁ *aqash*, 3.
Isa. 59. 8 they have made them crooked paths

CROOKED place, thing, way —
1. *To be high, elevated*, הָדַר *hadar*.
Isa. 45. 2 I will . . make the crooked places straight
2. *Froward, perverse*, מַעֲקַשִּׁים *maaqashshim*.
Isa. 42. 16 I will make . . crooked things straight
3. *Twisted, crooked*, עֲקַלְקַל *aqalqal*.
Psa.125. 5 such as turn aside unto their crooked w.

CROP —
Crop (of a bird), מֻרְאָה *murah*.
Lev. 1. 16 he shall pluck away his crop with his

CROP off, to —
To crop off, pluck, קָטַף *qataph*.
Eze. 17. 4 He cropped off the top of his young twigs
17. 22 I will crop off from the top of his young

CROSS —
Stake, σταυρός *stauros*.
Matt 10. 38 And he that taketh not his cross, and
16. 24 let him . . take up his cross, and follow me
27. 32 him they compelled to bear his cross
27. 40 thou be the Son . . come down from the c.
27. 42 let him now come down from the cross
Mark 8. 34 let him . . [take up his cross, and] follow
10. 21 and come, take up the cross, and follow
15. 21 they compel one Simon . . to bear his cross
15. 30 Save thyself, and come down from the c.
15. 32 Let Christ . . descend now from the cross
Luke 9. 23 [and take up his cross daily, and follow]
14. 27 whosoever doth not bear his cross, and
23. 26 on him they laid the cross, that he might
John 19. 17 he bearing his cross went forth into a
19. 19 wrote a title, and put (it) on the cross
19. 25 there stood by the cross of Jesus his
19. 31 bodies should not remain upon the cross
1 Co. 1. 17 lest the cross of Christ should be made
1. 18 preaching of the cross is to them that
Gal. 5. 11 then is the offence of the cross ceased
6. 12 suffer persecution for the cross of Christ
6. 14 save in the cross of our Lord Jesus Christ
Eph. 2. 16 both unto God in one body by the cross
Phil. 2. 8 unto death, even the death of the cross
3. 18 (they are) the enemies of the cross of Ch.
Col. 1. 20 made peace through the blood of its cr.
2. 14 out of the way, nailing it to his cross
Heb. 12. 2 endured the cross, despising the shame

CROSSWAY —
Crossway, פֶּרֶק *pereq*.
Obad. 14 shouldest thou have stood in the cross

CROUCH, to —
1. *To be cast down, bruise self*, דָּכָה *dakah*.
Psa. 10. 10 He croucheth, (and) humbleth himself
2. *To bow self down*, שָׁחָה *shachah*, 7.
1 Sa. 2. 36 crouch to him for a piece of silver and

CROW, to —
To give forth the voice, sound, crow, φωνέω *phōneō*.
Matt 26. 34 before the cock crow, thou shalt deny me
26. 74 And immediately the cock crew
26. 75 Before the cock crow, thou shalt deny me
Mark14. 30 before the cock crow twice, thou shalt
14. 68 went out into the porch; [and the cock c.]
14. 72 the second time the cock crew. And Pe.
14. 72 Before the cock crow twice, thou shalt
Luke22. 34 the cock shall not crow this day, before
22. 60 while he yet spake, the cock crew
22. 61 Before the cock crow, thou shalt deny me
John 13. 38 The cock shall not crow, till thou hast
18. 27 and immediately the cock crew

CROWN —
1. *Crown, border, ring, edge, ledge*, זֵר *zer*.
Exod25. 11 make upon it a crown of gold round
25. 24 make thereto a crown of gold round
25. 25 thou shalt make a golden crown to the
30. 3 make unto it a crown of gold round
30. 4 shalt thou make to it under the crown
37. 2 made a crown of gold to it round about
37. 11 made thereunto a crown of gold round
37. 12 he . . made a crown of gold for the border
37. 26 made unto it a crown of gold round
37. 27 two rings of gold for it under the crown
2. *Crown, diadem*, כֶּתֶר *kether*.
Esth. 1. 11 To bring Vashti . . with the crown royal
2. 17 that he set the royal crown upon her
6. 8 the crown royal which is set upon his
3. *Chaplet*, נֵזֶר *nezer*.
Exod29. 6 and put the holy crown upon the mitre
39. 30 the plate of the holy crown (of) pure
Lev. 8. 9 he put the golden plate, the holy crown
21. 12 the crown of the anointing oil of his God
2 Sa. 1. 10 I took the crown that (was) upon his head
2 Ki.11. 12 put the crown upon him, and (gave him)
2 Ch.23. 11 put upon him the crown, and (gave him)
Psa. 89. 39 thou hast profaned his crown (by casting)
132. 18 but upon himself shall his crown flourish
Prov.27. 24 doth the crown (endure) to every genera.?
Zech. 9. 16 (they shall be as) the stones of a crown
4. *Crown*, עֲטָרָה *atarah*.
2 Sa. 12. 30 took their king's crown from off his head
1 Ch.20. 2 took the crown of their king from off his
Esth. 8. 15 Mordecai went out . . with a great crown of
Job 19. 9 He hath . . taken the crown (from) my
31. 36 Surely I would . . bind it (as) a crown to
Psa. 21. 3 settest a crown of pure gold on his head
Prov. 4. 9 a crown of glory shall she deliver to thee
12. 4 A virtuous woman (is) a crown to her
14. 24 The crown of the wise (is) their riches
16. 31 The hoary head (is) a crown of glory, (if)
17. 6 Children's children (are) the crown of old
Song 3. 11 behold king Solomon with the crown
Isa. 28. 1 Woe to the crown of pride, to the drunk.
28. 3 The crown of pride, the drunkards of E.
28. 5 shall the LORD of hosts be for a crown
62. 3 Thou shalt also be a crown of glory in
Jer. 13. 18 shall come down, (even) the crown of
Lam. 5. 16 The crown is fallen (from) our head: woe
Eze. 16. 12 I put . . a beautiful crown upon thine head
21. 26 Remove the diadem, and take off the cro.
23. 42 and beautiful crowns upon their heads
Zech. 6. 11 take silver and gold, and make crowns
6. 14 the crowns shall be to Helem, and to Tob.
5. *Crown or top of the head*, קָדְקֹד *qodqod*.
Job 2. 7 from the sole of his foot unto his crown
6. *Diadem*, διάδημα *diadēma*.
Rev. 12. 3 ten horns, and seven crowns upon his
13. 1 upon his horns ten crowns, and upon
19. 12 and on his head (were) many crowns
7. *Crown*, στέφανος *stephanos*.
Matt 27. 29 when they had platted a crown of thorns
Mark15. 17 platted a crown of thorns, and put it
John 19. 2 the soldiers platted a crown of thorns
19. 5 Then came Jesus forth, wearing the cro.
1 Co. 9. 25 they (do it) to obtain a corruptible crown
Phil. 4. 1 beloved and longed for, my joy and crown
1 Th. 2. 19 what (is) our hope . . or crown of rejoicing?
2 Ti. 4. 8 laid up for me a crown of righteousness
Jas. 1. 12 he shall receive the crown of life, which
1 Pe. 5. 4 ye shall receive a crown of glory that
Rev. 2. 10 and I will give thee a crown of life
3. 11 hold . . fast . . that no man take thy crown
4. 4 they had on their heads crowns of gold
4. 10 and cast their crowns before the throne
6. 2 a crown was given unto him: and he
9. 7 on their heads (were) as it were crowns
12. 1 and upon her head a crown of twelve
14. 14 having on his head a golden crown, and

CROWN, to —
1. *To compass, crown*, עָטַר *atar*, 3.
Psa. 8. 5 hast crowned him with glory and honour
65. 11 Thou crownest the year with thy goodness

Psa.103. 4 who crowneth thee with loving kindness
Song 3. 11 his mother crowned him in the day of

2. *To crown*, στεφανόω *stephanoō*.
2 Ti. 2. 5 (yet) is he not crowned, except he strive
Heb. 2. 7 thou crownedst him with glory and hon.
2. 9 we see Jesus..crowned with glory and hon.

CROWN of the head —
Crown or top of the head, קָדְקֹד *qodqod*.
Gen. 49. 26 on the crown of the head of him that
Deut 33. 20 teareth the arm with the crown of the he.
2 Sa. 14. 25 his foot even to the crown of his head
Isa. 3. 17 smite with a scab the crown of the head
Jer. 2. 16 have broken the crown of thy head
48. 45 the crown of the head of the tumultuous

CROWNED —
Crowned ones, מִנְּזָרִים *minnezarim*.
Nah. 3. 17 Thy crowned (are) as the locusts, and

CROWNED, to be —
To compass about, crown, כָּתַר *kathar*, 5.
Prov 14. 18 the prudent are crowned with knowledge

CROWNING —
To compass, crown, עָטַר *atar*, 5.
Isa. 23. 8 the crowning (city), whose merchants (are)

CRUCIFY, to —
1. *To fix to, crucify*, προσπήγνυμι *prospēgnumi*.
Acts 2. 23 by wicked hands have crucified and slain

2. *To crucify*, σταυρόω *stauroō*.
Matt 20. 19 mock, and to scourge, and to crucify (him)
23. 34 (some) of them ye shall kill and crucify
26. 2 Son of man is betrayed to be crucified
27. 22 all say unto him, Let him be crucified
27. 23 But they cried out..Let him be crucified
27. 26 he delivered (him) to be crucified
27. 31 and led him away to crucify (him)
27. 35 they crucified him, and parted his gar.
27. 38 Then were there two thieves crucified
28. 5 that ye seek Jesus, which was crucified
Mark 15. 13 And they cried out again, Crucify him
15. 14 cried out the more exceedingly, Crucify
15. 15 and delivered Jesus..to be crucified
15. 20 and led him out to crucify him
15. 24 when they had crucified him, they parted
15. 25 the third hour, and they crucified him
15. 27 And with him they crucify two thieves
16. 6 Ye seek Jesus..which was crucified
Luke 23. 21 they cried, saying, Crucify (him), crucify
23. 23 requiring that he might be crucified
23. 33 called Calvary, there they crucified him
24. 7 be crucified, and the third day rise again
24. 20 condemned to death, and have crucified
John 19. 6 cried out, saying, Crucify (him), crucify
19. 6 Take ye him, and crucify (him): for I
19. 10 knowest thou..I have power to crucify
19. 15 Away with (him), away with (him), crucify
19. 15 Pilate saith..shall I crucify your King?
19. 16 Then delivered he him..to be crucified
19. 18 they crucified him, and two other with
19. 20 the place where Jesus was crucified was
19. 23 the soldiers, when they had crucified Jesus
19. 41 in the place where he was crucified there
Acts 2. 36 that same Jesus, whom ye have crucified
4. 10 Jesus Christ of Nazareth, whom ye cruci.
1 Co. 1. 13 Is Christ divided? was Paul crucified for
1. 23 we preach Christ crucified, unto the Jews
2. 2 save Jesus Christ, and him crucified
2. 8 they would not have crucified the Lord
2 Co. 13. 4 he was crucified through weakness, yet
Gal. 3. 1 Jesus Christ hath been..crucified among
5. 24 they that are Christ's have crucified the
6. 14 by whom the world is crucified unto me
Rev. 11. 8 Egypt, where also our Lord was crucified

CRUCIFY afresh, to —
To crucify anew, ἀνασταυρόω *anastauroō*.
Heb. 6. 6 crucify to themselves the Son of God afr.

CRUCIFY with, to —
To crucify together, συσταυρόω *sustauroō*.
Matt 27 44 The thieves also, which were crucified with
Mark 15. 32 they that were crucified with him reviled
John 19. 32 the other which was crucified with him
Rom. 6. 6 that our old man is crucified with (him)
Gal. 2. 20 I am crucified with Christ: nevertheless

CRUEL —
1. *Fierce*, אַכְזָר *akzar*.
Deut 32. 33 Their wine (is)..the cruel venom of asps
Job 30. 21 Thou art become cruel to me; with thy
Lam. 4. 3 the daughter of my people (is become) cr.

2. *Fierce*, אַכְזָרִי *akzari*.
Prov 5. 9 Lest thou give..thy years unto the cruel
11. 17 (he that is) cruel troubleth his own flesh
12. 10 tender mercies of the wicked (are) cruel
17. 11 a cruel messenger shall be sent against
Isa. 13. 9 cruel both with wrath and fierce anger
Jer. 6. 23 they (are) cruel, and have no mercy
50. 42 they (are) cruel, and will not show mercy

3. *Fierceness*, אַכְזְרִיּוּת *akzeriyyuth*.
Prov 27. 4 Wrath (is) cruel, and anger (is) outrageous

4. *Violence*, חָמָס *chamas*.
Psa. 25. 19 and they hate me with cruel hatred

5. *Sharp, hard*, קָשֶׁה *qasheh*.
Exod. 6. 9 anguish of spirit, and for cruel bondage
Isa. 19. 4 give over into the hand of a cruel lord

CRUEL, to be —
To be sharp, hard, קָשָׁה *qashah*.
Gen. 49. 7 Cursed (be)..their wrath, for it was cruel

CRUEL man —
Violent, חָמֵץ *chomets*.
Psa. 71. 4 the hand of the unrighteous and cruel m.

CRUEL one —
Fierce, אַכְזָרִי *akzari*.
Jer. 30. 14 with the chastisement of a cruel one

CRUELLY —
Oppression, עֹשֶׁק *osheq*.
Eze. 18. 18 because he cruelly oppressed, spoiled his

CRUELTY —
1. *Violence*, חָמָס *chamas*.
Gen. 49. 5 instruments of cruelty (are in) their habi.
Judg. 9. 24 the cruelty (done) to the three score and
Psa. 27. 12 and such as breathe out cruelty
74. 20 are full of the habitations of cruelty

2. *Breach, burglary*, פֶּרֶךְ *perek*.
Eze. 34. 4 and with cruelty have ye ruled them

CRUMB —
A little bit or crumb, ψιχίον *psichion*.
Matt 15. 27 the crumbs which fall from their master's
Mark 7. 28 yet the dogs..eat of the children's crumbs
Luke 16. 21 desiring to be fed with [the crumbs] which

CRUSE —
1. *Bottle, guglet*, בַּקְבּוּק *baqbuq*.
1 Ki. 14. 3 take with thee..a cruse of honey, and go

2. *Dish, pan, cruse*, צְלֹחִית *tselochith*.
2 Ki. 2. 20 Bring me a new cruse, and put salt there.

3. *Dish, cruse, flask*, צַפַּחַת *tsappachath*.
1 Sa. 26. 11 take thou now..the cruse of water, and
26. 12 David took the spear and the cruse of
26. 16 cruse of water that (was) at his bolster
1 Ki. 17. 12 and a little oil in a cruse: and, behold
17. 14 neither shall the cruse of oil fail, until
17. 16 neither did the cruse of oil fail, accord.
19. 6 and a cruse of water at his head: and he

CRUSH, to —
1. *To bruise*, דָּכָא *daka*, 3.
Lam. 3. 34 crush under his feet all the prisoners of

2. *To trouble, crush, destroy*, הָמַם *hamam*.
Jer. 51. 34 he hath crushed me, he hath made me

3. *To press*, זוּר *zur*.
Job 39. 15 forgetteth that the foot may crush them

4. *To oppress, press, crush*, לָחַץ *lachats*.
Num. 22. 25 and crushed Balaam's foot against the

5. *To break, oppress, bruise*, רָצַץ *ratsats*.
Amos 4. 1 oppress the poor, which crush the needy

6. *To break in pieces, destroy*, שָׁבַר *shabar*.
Lam. 1. 15 called an assembly..to crush my young

CRUSHED —
1. *To beat down or out*, כָּתַת *kathath*.
Lev. 22. 24 that which is bruised, or crushed, or

2. *To break, oppress, bruise*, רָצַץ *ratsats*.
Deut 28. 33 thou shalt be only oppressed and crushed

CRUSHED, to be —
1. *To bruise*, דָּכָא *daka*, 3.
Job 4. 19 them..(which) are crushed before the moth

2. *To bruise self*, דָּכָא *daka*, 7.
Job 5. 4 they are crushed in the gate, neither (is

CRUSHED, that which is —
What is pressed, זוּרֶה *zureh*.
Isa. 59. 5 that which is crushed breaketh out into

CRY —
1. *To cry out, call*, זָעַק *zaaq*.
Isa. 30. 19 very gracious..at the voice of thy cry

2. *Cry, crying out*, זְעָקָה *zeaqah*.
Gen. 18. 20 the cry of Sodom and Gomorrah is great
Neh. 5. 6 I was very angry when I heard their cry
9. 9 and heardest their cry by the Red sea
Esth. 4. 1 and cried with a loud and a bitter cry
9. 31 the matters of the fastings and their cry
Job 16. 18 and let my cry have no place
Prov 21. 13 Whoso stoppeth his ears at the cry of the
Eccl. 9. 17 more than the cry of him that ruleth
Isa. 15. 5 they shall raise up a cry of destruction
15. 8 the cry is gone round about the borders
Jer. 18. 22 Let a cry be heard from their houses
20. 16 let him hear the cry in the morning, and
48. 4 little ones have caused a cry to be heard
48. 34 From the cry of Heshbon (even) unto E.
50. 46 and the cry is heard among the nations
51. 54 A sound of a cry (cometh) from Babylon
Eze. 27. 28 shall shake at the sound of the cry of

3. *Cry, crying*, צְוָחָה *tsevachah*.
Jer. 14. 2 and the cry of Jerusalem is gone up
46. 12 thy cry hath filled the land: for the

4. *Cry, crying out*, צְעָקָה *tseaqah*.
Gen. 18. 21 according to the cry of it, which is come
19. 13 the cry of them is waxen great before the
27. 34 with a great and exceeding bitter cry
Exod. 3. 7 have heard their cry by reason of their
3. 9 the cry of the children of Israel is come
11. 6 there shall be a great cry throughout all
Exod 12. 30 there was a great cry in Egypt; for (there
22. 23 I will surely hear their cry
1 Sa. 9. 16 because their cry is come unto me
Neh. 5. 1 there was a great cry of the people, and
Job 27. 9 Will God hear his cry when trouble com.
34. 28 they cause the cry of the poor to come
34. 28 and he heareth the cry of the afflicted
Psa. 9. 12 he forgetteth not the cry of the humble
Isa. 5. 7 for righteousness, but behold a cry
Jer. 25. 36 A voice of the cry of the shepherds, and
48. 5 the enemies have heard a cry of destruc.
49. 21 at the cry, the noise thereof was heard
Zeph. 1. 10 the noise of a cry from the fish gate

5. *Voice*, קוֹל *qol*.
Num 16. 34 And all Israel..fled at the cry of them

6. *Loud cry, proclamation*, רִנָּה *rinnah*.
1 Ki. 8. 28 to hearken unto the cry and to the prayer
2 Ch. 6. 19 to hearken unto the cry and the prayer
Psa. 17. 1 O LORD, attend unto my cry, give ear
61. 1 Hear my cry, O God; attend unto my pra
88. 2 incline thine ear unto my cry
106. 44 their affliction, when he heard their cry
119. 169 Let my cry come near before thee, O L.
142. 6 Attend unto my cry; for I am brought
Isa. 43. 14 the Chaldeans, whose cry (is) in the ships
Jer. 7. 16 neither lift up cry nor prayer for them
11. 14 neither lift up cry nor prayer for them
14. 12 When they fast, I will not hear their cry

7. *Crying aloud*, שֶׁוַע *sheva*.
Psa. 5. 2 Hearken unto the voice of my cry, my K.

8. *Loud cry, crying*, שַׁוְעָה *shavah*.
Exod. 2. 23 their cry came up unto God by reason of
1 Sa. 5. 12 the cry of the city went up to heaven
2 Sa. 22. 7 and my cry (did enter) into his ears
Psa. 18. 6 my cry came before him, (even) into his
34. 15 and his ears (are open) unto their cry
39. 12 Hear..O LORD, and give ear unto my cry
40. 1 and he inclined unto me, and heard my c.
102. 1 Hear..O LORD, and let my cry come unto
145. 19 he also will hear their cry, and will save
Jer. 8. 19 of the cry of the daughter of my people
Lam. 3. 56 hide not thine ear..at my cry

9. *A cry*, βοή *boē*.
Jas. 5. 4 the cries of them which have reaped are

10. *A crying, cry*, κραυγή *kraugē*.
Matt 25. 6 at midnight there was a cry made, Behold
Acts 23. 9 there arose a great cry: and the scribes
Rev. 14. 18 with a loud cry to him that had the sharp

CRY, to —
1. *To groan*, אָנַק *anaq*.
Eze. 26. 15 when the wounded cry, when the slaug.

2. *To groan together*, אָנַק *anaq*, 2.
Eze. 9. 4 that cry for all the abominations that
24. 17 Forbear to cry, make no mourning for

3. *To cry out*, זָעַק *zaaq*.
Exod. 2. 23 and the children of Israel..cried; and
Judg. 3. 9, 15 the children of Israel cried unto the
6. 6, 7 children of Israel cried unto the LORD
10. 10 children of Israel cried unto the LORD
10. 14 Go and cry unto the gods which ye have
1 Sa. 7. 8 Cease not to cry unto the LORD our God
7. 9 and Samuel cried unto the LORD for Israel
12. 8 your fathers cried unto the LORD, then
12. 10 they cried unto the LORD, and said, We
15. 11 it grieved Samuel; and he cried unto the
28. 12 she cried with a loud voice: and the
2 Sa. 13. 19 her hand on her head, and went on crying
19. 4 the king cried with a loud voice, O my son
19. 28 what right therefore have I yet to cry
1 Ch. 5. 20 they cried to God in the battle, and he
2 Ch. 20. 9 cry unto thee in our affliction, then thou
32. 20 the prophet Isaiah..prayed and cried to
Neh. 9. 4 cried with a loud voice unto the LORD
9. 28 when they returned, and cried unto thee
Esth. 4. 1 and cried with a loud and a bitter cry
Job 31. 38 If my land cry against me, or that the
Psa. 22. 5 They cried unto thee, and were delivered
107. 13 they cried unto the LORD in their trouble
107. 19 they cry unto the LORD in their trouble
142. 1 I cried unto the LORD with my voice
142. 5 I cried unto thee, O LORD: I said, Thou
Isa. 14. 31 cry, O city; thou, whole Palestina, (art)
15. 4 Heshbon shall cry, and Elealeh: their
57. 13 When thou criest, let thy companies
Jer. 11. 11 though they shall cry unto me, I will not
11. 12 cry unto the gods unto whom they offer
25. 34 Howl, ye shepherds, and cry; and wallow
30. 15 Why criest thou for thine affliction?
47. 2 the men shall cry, and all the inhabitants
48. 20 howl and cry; tell ye it in Arnon, that
Lam. 3. 8 when I cry and shout, he shutteth
Eze. 9. 8 I fell upon my face, and cried, and said
11. 13 cried with a loud voice, and said, Ah
21. 12 Cry and howl, son of man; for it shall be
27. 30 shall cry bitterly, and shall cast up dust
Hos. 7. 14 they have not cried unto me with their
8. 2 Israel shall cry unto me, My God, we
Joel 1. 14 Sanctify ye a fast..and cry unto the LORD
Jon. 1. 5 mariners..cried every man unto his god
Mic. 3. 4 shall they cry unto the LORD, but he will

4. *To cry out*, זָעַק *zaaq*, 5.
Zech. 6. 8 Then cried he upon me, and spake unto

5. *To cry out*, זְעִק *zeiq*.
Dan. 6. 20 cried with a lamentable voice unto Daniel

6. *To cry out (painfully),* יָבַב *yabab,* 3.
Judg. 5. 28 The mother of Sisera..cried through the

7. *To answer, respond,* עָנָה *anah.*
Exod32. 18 neither (is it) the voice of (them that) cry
Isa. 13. 22 the wild beasts of the islands shall cry

8. *To pant, long for,* עָרַג *arag.*
Joel 1. 20 The beasts of the field cry also unto thee

9. *To cry, scream,* פָּעָה *paah.*
Isa. 42. 14 (now) will I cry like a travailing woman

10. *To cry out,* צָעַק *tsaaq.*
Gen. 4. 10 the voice of thy brother's blood crieth
27. 34 when Esau heard the words..he cried
41. 55 the people cried to Pharaoh for bread
Exod. 5. 8 they cry, saying, Let us go (and) sacrifice
5. 15 the officers..came and cried unto Phara.
8. 12 Moses cried unto the LORD because of the
14. 15 the LORD said..Wherefore criest thou un.?
15. 25 he cried unto the LORD; and the LORD
17. 4 Moses cried unto the LORD, saying, What
22. 23 If thou afflict them..and they cry at all
22. 27 it shall come to pass, when he crieth unto
Num11. 2 the people cried unto Moses; and when
12. 13 Moses cried unto the LORD, saying, Heal
20. 16 when we cried unto the LORD he heard
Deut 22. 24 the damsel, because she cried not, (being)
22. 27 the betrothed damsel cried, and (there
26. 7 we cried unto the LORD God of our fathers
Josh.24. 7 when they cried unto the LORD, he put
Judg. 4. 3 the children of Israel cried unto the L.
10. 12 ye cried to me, and I delivered you out
1 Ki.20. 39 as the king passed by, he cried unto the
2 Ki. 4. 1 there cried a certain woman of the wives
6. 5 he cried, and said, Alas, master! for it
6. 26 there cried a woman unto him, saying
8. 3 she went forth to cry unto the king for
8. 5 the woman..cried to the king for her
2 Ch.13. 14 they cried unto the LORD, and the priests
Neh. 9. 27 they cried unto thee, thou heardest
Job 19. 7 I cry out of wrong, but I am
35. 12 they cry, but none giveth answer, because
Psa. 34. 17 (The righteous) cry, and the LORD heareth
77. 1 I cried unto God with my voice, (even)
88. 1 I have cried day (and) night before thee
107. 6 they cried unto the LORD in their trouble
107. 28 they cry unto the LORD in their trouble
Isa. 19. 20 they shall cry unto the LORD because of
33. 7 Behold, their valiant ones shall cry with.
42. 2 He shall not cry..nor cause his voice to
46. 7 shall cry unto him, yet can he not answer
65. 14 but ye shall cry for sorrow of heart, and
Jer. 22. 20 Go up to Lebanon, and cry; and lift up
22. 20 cry from the passages: for all thy lovers
49. 3 cry, ye daughters of Rabbah, gird you
Lam. 2. 18 Their heart cried unto the Lord, O wall

11. *To cry out,* צָעַק *tsaaq,* 3.
2 Ki. 2. 12 And Elisha saw (it), and he cried, My fa.

12. *To shriek, roar,* צָרַח *tsarach.*
Zeph. 1. 14 the mighty man shall cry there bitterly

13. *To call,* קָרָא *qara.*
Gen. 39. 14 he came in..and I cried with a loud voice
39. 15, 18 I lifted up my voice and cried, that
41. 43 and they cried before him, Bow the knee
45. 1 he cried, Cause every man to go out from
Lev. 13. 45 covering upon his upper lip, and shall cry
Deut 15. 9 and he cry unto the LORD against thee
24. 15 lest he cry against thee unto the LORD
Judg. 7. 20 and they cried, The sword of the LORD
9. 7 lifted up his voice and cried, and said
18. 23 And they cried unto the children of Dan
1 Sa. 17. 8 he stood and cried unto the armies of Is.
20. 37 Jonathan cried after the lad, and said
20. 38 Jonathan cried after the lad, Make speed
24. 8 cried after Saul, saying, My lord the king
26. 14 David cried to the people, and to Abner
26. 14 Who (art) thou (that) criest to the king?
2 Sa. 18. 25 And the watchman cried, and told the
20. 16 Then cried a wise woman out of the city
22. 7 I called upon the LORD, and cried to my
1 Ki. 13. 2 he cried against the altar in the word of
13. 4 the man of God, which had cried against
13. 21 he cried unto the man of God that came
13. 32 which he cried by the word of the LORD
17. 20, 21 cried unto the LORD, and said, O LORD
18. 27 Elijah mocked them, and said, Cry aloud
18. 28 And they cried aloud, and cut themselves
2 Ki. 11. 14 Athaliah rent her clothes, and cried
18. 28 Rab-shakeh stood, and cried with a loud
20. 11 Isaiah the prophet cried unto the LORD
2 Ch. 14. 11 Asa cried unto the LORD his God, and said
32. 18 they cried with a loud voice in the Jew's
Psa. 3. 4 I cried unto the LORD with my voice, and
22. 2 I cry in the day time, but thou hearest not
27. 7 Hear, O LORD, (when) I cry with my voice
28. 1 Unto thee will I cry, O LORD my rock
30. 8 I cried to thee, O LORD; and unto the L.
34. 6 This poor man cried, and the LORD heard
56. 9 When I cry (unto thee), then shall mine
57. 2 I will cry unto God most high; unto God
61. 2 From the end of the earth will I cry unto
66. 17 I cried unto him with my mouth, and he
86. 3 Be merciful..O LORD: for I cry unto thee
119. 145 I cried with (my) whole heart; hear me
120. 1 I cried unto the LORD, and he heard me
138. 3 In the day when I cried thou answeredst
141. 1 I cry unto thee: make haste unto me
147. 9 (and) to the young ravens which cry
Prov. 1. 21 She crieth in the chief place of concourse
2. 3 Yea, if thou criest after knowledge
8. 1 Doth not wisdom cry? and understanding
9. 3 she crieth upon the highest places of the
21. 13 he also shall cry himself, but shall not
Isa. 6. 3 And one cried unto another, and said
6. 4 moved at the voice of him that cried, and
8. 4 the child shall have knowledge to cry
21. 8 he cried, A lion: My lord, I stand conti.
30. 7 therefore have I cried concerning this
34. 14 and the satyr shall cry to his fellow
36. 13 Rabshakeh stood, and cried with a loud
40. 2 cry unto her, that her warfare is accom.
40. 3 voice of him that crieth in the wilderness
40. 6 The voice said, Cry, And he said
40. 6 What shall I cry? All flesh (is) grass, and
58. 1 Cry aloud, spare not, lift up thy voice
Jer. 2. 2 Go and cry in the ears of Jerusalem
3. 4 Wilt thou not from this time cry unto
4. 5 cry, gather together . . Assemble yoursel.
4. 20 Destruction upon destruction is cried
11. 14 neither lift up a cry or prayer for them
11. 14 not hear (them) in the time that they cry
20. 8 I cried violence and spoil; because the w.
31. 6 the watchmen upon the mount..shall cry
46. 17 They did cry there, Pharaoh king of Eg.
49. 29 shall cry unto them, Fear (is) on every
Lam. 4. 15 They cried unto them, Depart ye; (it is)
Eze. 8. 18 though they cry in mine ears with a loud
9. 1 He cried also in mine ears with a loud
Joel 1. 19 O LORD, to thee will I cry: for the fire
Jon. 1. 2 go to Nineveh, that great city, and cry
1. 14 they cried unto the LORD, and said, We
2. 2 I cried by reason of mine affliction unto
3. 4 Jonah..cried, and said, Yet forty days
3. 8 But let man..cry mightily unto God; yea
Mic. 3. 5 that bite with their teeth, and cry, Peace
6. 9 The LORD'S voice crieth unto the city, and
Zech. 1. 4 unto whom the former prophets have cri.
1. 14 the angel..said unto me, Cry thou, saying
1. 17 Cry yet, saying, Thus saith the LORD of
7. 7 which the LORD hath cried by the former
7. 13 (that) as he cried, and they would not
7. 13 So they cried, and I would not hear, saith

14. *To call,* קְרָא *qera.*
Dan. 3. 4 an herald cried aloud, To you it is com.
4. 14 He cried aloud, and said thus, Hew down
5. 7 The king cried aloud to bring in the astro.

15. *To shout,* רוּעַ *rua,* 5.
Judg. 7. 21 and all the host ran, and cried, and fled
Job 30. 5 they cried after them as (after) a thief
Isa. 42. 13 he shall cry, yea, roar; he shall prevail

16. *To cry aloud,* שָׁוַע *shava,* 3.
Job 29. 12 I delivered the poor that cried, and the
30. 20 I cry unto thee, and thou dost not hear
30. 28 I stood up, (and) I cried in the congrega.
36. 13 they cry not when he bindeth them
38. 41 his young ones cry unto God, they wander
Psa. 18. 6 I called upon the LORD, and cried unto
18. 41 They cried, but (there was) none to save
22. 24 but when he cried unto him, he heard
28. 2 when I cry unto thee, when I lift up my
30. 2 I cried unto thee, and thou hast healed
31. 22 thou heardest the voice..when I cried
72. 12 shall deliver the needy when he crieth
88. 13 But unto thee have I cried, O LORD
119. 147 I prevented the dawning..and cried
Isa. 58. 9 thou shalt cry, and he shall say, Here I
Jon. 2. 2 out..of hell cried I, (and) thou
Hab. 1. 2 how long shall I cry, and thou wilt not

17. *To cry out, play, delight,* שָׁעַע *shaa.*
Isa. 29. 9 Stay yourselves, and wonder..and cry

18. *Cry, crying out,* שׁוּעַ *shua.*
Job 30. 24 though they cry in his destruction

19. *To give forth the voice,* נָתַן קוֹל *nathan qol.*
Num.14. 1 congregation lifted up their voice, and cr.
Amos 3. 4 will a young lion cry out of his den if

20. *To cry out,* ἀναβοάω *anaboaō.*
Matt27. 46 about the ninth hour Jesus [cried] with a

21. *To let go, send away,* ἀφίημι *aphiēmi.*
Mark15. 37 Jesus cried with a loud voice, and gave

22. *To cry, shout,* βοάω *boaō.*
Matt. 3. 3 The voice of one crying in the wilderness
Mark 1. 3 The voice of one crying in the wilderness
15. 34 at the ninth hour Jesus cried with a loud
Luke 3. 4 The voice of one crying in the wilderness
18. 7 which cry day and night unto him, though
18. 38 he cried, saying, Jesus, (thou) son of Da.
John 1. 23 the voice of one crying in the wilderness
Acts 8. 7 unclean spirits, crying with loud voice
17. 6 they drew Jason..unto the rulers..crying
21. 34 some [cried] one thing, some another
Gal. 4. 27 break forth and cry, thou that travailest

23. *To cry about (anything),* ἐπιβοάω *epiboaō.*
Acts 25. 24 [crying] that he ought not to live any lo.

24. *To give forth the voice upon (anything),* ἐπιφωνέω.
Luke 23. 21 they cried, saying, Crucify (him), crucify

25. *To cry out,* κράζω *krazō.*
Matt. 9. 27 two blind men followed him, crying, and
14. 30 beginning to sink, he cried, saying, Lord
15. 23 Send her away; for she crieth after us
20. 31 they cried the more, saying, Have mercy
21. 9 the multitudes..cried, saying, Hosanna
Matt 21. 15 the children crying in the temple, and
27. 50 when he had cried again with a loud voice
Mark 1. 26 [cried] with a loud voice, he came out of
3. 11 and cried, saying, Thou art the Son of God
5. 5 in the mountains, and in the tombs, cry.
5. 7 cried with a loud voice, and said, What
9. 26 (the spirit) cried, and rent him sore, and
10. 48 he cried..a great deal, (Thou) son of Da.
11. 9 they that followed, cried..Hosanna!
Luke18. 39 he cried so much the more, (thou) son
John 1. 15 John bare witness of him, and cried
7. 28 Then cried Jesus in the temple as he
7. 37 Jesus stood and cried, saying, If any man
12. 13 went forth to meet him, and [cried,] Hos.
12. 44 Jesus cried and said, He that believeth
Acts 7. 60 he kneeled down, and cried with a loud
16. 17 The same followed Paul and us, and cried
19. 32 Some..cried one thing, and some another
21. 36 the people followed after, crying, Away
24. 21 I [cried] standing among them, Touching
Rom. 8. 15 the Spirit of adoption, whereby we cry
9. 27 Esaias also crieth concerning Israel
Gal. 4. 6 Spirit of his Son into your hearts, crying
Jas. 5. 4 Behold, the hire of the labourers..crieth
Rev. 6. 10 they cried with a loud voice, saying, How
7. 2 he cried with a loud voice to the four
7. 10 cried with a loud voice, saying, Salvation
10. 3 cried with a loud voice, as (when) a lion
10. 3 when he had cried, seven thunders
12. 2 she being with child cried, travailing in
14. 15 crying with a loud voice to him that sat
18. 2 he cried mightily with a strong voice
18. 18 cried when they saw the smoke of her
18. 19 they cast dust on their heads, and cried
19. 17 he cried with a loud voice, saying to all

26. *To make a cry or clamour,* κραυγάζω *kraugazō.*
Matt 12. 19 He shall not strive, nor cry; neither shall
15. 22 woman of Canaan came..and [cried] unto
John11. 43 he cried with a loud voice, Lazarus, come
18. 40 Then cried they all again, saying, Not

27. *To give forth the voice, sound,* φωνέω *phōneō.*
Luke 8. 8 he cried, He that hath ears to hear, let
16. 24 he cried and said, Father Abraham, have
23. 46 when Jesus had cried with a loud voice
Acts 16. 28 But Paul cried with a loud voice, saying
Rev. 14. 18 cried with a loud cry to him that had the

CRY alarm, to —
To shout, רוּעַ *rua,* 5.
2 Ch.13. 12 with sounding trumpets to cry alarm

CRY against, to —
To give forth the voice upon (a thing), ἐπιφωνέω.
Acts 22. 24 might know wherefore they cried so ag.

CRY aloud, to —
1. *To make a noise,* הָמָה *hamah.*
Psa. 55. 17 and at noon, will I pray, and cry aloud
2. *To cry aloud, rejoice,* צָהַל *tsahal.*
Isa. 24. 14 they shall cry aloud from the sea
3. *To cry aloud, rejoice,* צָהַל *tsahal,* 3.
Isa. 54. 1 break forth into singing, and cry aloud
4. *To shout,* רוּעַ *rua,* 5.
Hos. 5. 8 cry aloud (at) Beth-aven, after thee, O
5. *To cry out,* שָׁוַע *shava,* 3.
Job 19. 7 I cry aloud, but (there is) no judgment
6. *To cry out,* ἀναβοάω *anaboaō.*
Mark15. 8 the multitude, [crying aloud,] began to

CRY, to make to —
To cause to cry out, זָעַק *zaaq,* 5.
Job 35. 9 they make (the oppressed) to cry

CRY out, to —
1. *To cry aloud, rejoice,* צָהַל *tsahal,* 3.
Isa. 12. 6 Cry out and shout, thou inhabitant of Z.
2. *To cry out,* זָעַק *zaaq.*
1 Sa. 4. 13 came..and told (it)..all the city cried out
5. 10 the Ekronites cried out, saying, They have
8. 18 cry out in that day because of your king
1 Ki. 22. 32 they turned..and Jehoshaphat cried out
2 Ch.18. 31 Jehoshaphat cried out, and the LORD
Isa. 15. 5 My heart shall cry out for Moab
26. 17 as a woman with child..crieth out in her
Jer. 20. 8 For since I spake, I cried out, I
48. 31 will I howl for Moab, and I will cry out
Hab. 1. 2 cry out unto thee (of) violence, and thou
2. 11 the stone shall cry out of the wall
3. *To cry out,* צָעַק *tsaaq.*
Exod14. 10 children of Israel cried out unto the L.
2 Ki. 4. 40 it came to pass..that they cried out, and
Job 19. 7 I cry out of wrong, but I am not heard
4. *To shout,* רוּעַ *rua,* 5.
Isa. 15. 4 the armed soldiers of Moab shall cry out
Mic. 4. 9 why dost thou cry out aloud? (is there) no
5. *To sing, cry aloud,* רָנַן *ranan.*
Lam. 2. 19 cry out in the night; in the beginning of
6. *To sing, cry aloud,* רָנַן *ranan,* 3.
Psa. 84. 2 my flesh crieth out for the living God
7. *To cry aloud,* שָׁוַע *shava,* 3.
Job 24. 12 the soul of the wounded crieth out: yet
35. 9 cry out by reason of the arm of the
8. *To cry out for self, play, delight,* שָׁעַע *shaa,* 7a.
Isa. 29. 9 Stay yourselves, and wonder; cry ye out

9. *To cry out,* ἀναβοάω *anaboaō.*
Luke 9. 38 a man of the company [cried out,] saying
10. *To cry out,* ἀνακράζω *anakrazō.*
Mark 1. 23 a man with an unclean spirit..cried out
6. 49 they supposed it..a spirit, and cried out
Luke 4. 33 there was a man..and cried out with a
8. 28 When he saw Jesus, he cried out, and fell
23. 18 they cried out all at once, saying, Away
11. *To cry,* κράζω *krazō.*
Matt. 8. 29 they cried out, saying, What have we to
14. 26 It is a spirit: and they cried out for
20. 30 two blind men sitting..cried out
27. 23 they cried out the more, saying, Let him
Mark 9. 24 the father of the child cried out,
10. 47 he began to cry out, and say, Jesus, (thou)
15. 13 And they cried out again, Crucify him
15. 14 they cried out the more exceedingly
15. 39 the centurion..saw that he so [cried out]
Luke 4. 41 devils also came out of many, [crying out]
9. 39 a spirit taketh him, and he..crieth out
19. 40 I tell you..the stones would..cry out
John 19. 12 the Jews [cried out,] saying, If thou let
Acts 7. 57 they cried out with a loud voice, and
14. 14 and ran in among the people, crying out
19. 28 they were full of wrath, and cried out
19. 34 all with one voice..cried out, Great (is)
21. 28 Crying out, Men of Israel, help: This is
23. 6 he cried out in the council, Men (and)
12. *To make an outcry,* κραυγάζω *kraugazō.*
John 19. 6 they cried out, saying, Crucify (him)
19. 15 they cried out, Away with (him), away
Acts 22. 23 as they cried out, and cast off (their)
13. *To give forth the voice,* נָתַן קוֹל *nathan qol.*
Jer. 12. 8 it crieth out against me: therefore have

CRY unto, to —
To call, קָרָא *qara.*
Psa 89 26 He shall cry unto me, Thou (art) my
119. 146 I cried unto thee, save me, and I shall
130. 1 Out of the depths have I cried unto thee
141. 1 give ear unto my voice, when I cry unto

CRYING —
1. *Cry, crying out,* זְעָקָה *zeaqah.*
Isa 65. 19 be no more heard..the voice of crying
2. *Cry, crying,* צְוָחָה *tsevachah.*
Isa. 24. 11 (There is) a crying for wine in the streets
3. *Cry, crying out,* צְעָקָה *tseaqah.*
1 Sa. 4. 14 when Eli heard the noise of the crying
Jer. 48. 3 A voice of crying (shall be) from Horon.
4. *To call,* קָרָא *qara.*
Psa. 69. 3 I am weary of my crying; my throat is
5. *Crying,* שׁוֹעַ *shoa.*
Isa. 22. 5 (it is) a day..of crying to the mountains
6. *Cry, crying, noise,* תְּשֻׁאוֹת *teshuoth.*
Job 39. 7 neither regardeth he the crying of the
7. *To put to death,* מוּת *muth,* 5.
Prov 19. 18 and let not thy soul spare for his crying
8. *A crying out,* κραυγή *kraugē.*
Heb. 5. 7 offered up prayers..with strong crying
Rev 21 4 there shall be no more death..nor crying

CRYING out—
Groan, groaning, אֲנָקָה *anaqah.*
Mal 2 13 with weeping and with crying out

CRYSTAL —
1. *Glass, crystal,* זְכוּכִית *zekukith.*
Job 28. 17 The gold and the crystal cannot equal
2. *Ice,* קֶרַח *qerach.*
Eze. 1. 22 (was) as the colour of the terrible crystal
3. *Crystal,* κρύσταλλος *krustallos.*
Rev. 4. 6 (there was) a sea of glass like unto cryst.
22. 1 river of water of life, clear as crystal

CRYSTAL, clear as —
To be as crystal, κρυσταλλίζω *krustallizō.*
Rev. 21. 11 even like a jasper stone, clear as crystal

CUBIT —
1. *Cubit,* אַמָּה *ammah.*
Gen. 6. 15 length of the ark..three hundred cubits
6. 15 the breadth of it fifty cubits
6. 15 and the height of it thirty cubits
6. 16 and in a cubit shall thou finish it above
7. 20 Fifteen cubits upward did the waters
Exod 25. 10 two cubits and a half (shall be) the length
25. 10, 17 a cubit and a half the breadth thereof
25. 10 and a cubit and a half the height thereof
25. 17 two cubits and a half (shall be) the length
25. 23 two cubits (shall be) the length thereof
25. 23 a cubit the breadth thereof, and a cubit
26. 2 curtain (shall be) eight and twenty cubits
26. 2, 8 the breadth of one curtain four cubits
26. 8 The length of one curtain..thirty cubits
26. 13 a cubit on the one side, and a cubit on
26. 16 Ten cubits (shall be) the length of a boa.
26. 16 a cubit and a half (shall be) the breadth
27. 1 five cubits long, and five cubits broad
27. 1 the height thereof (shall be) three cubits
27. 9 of an hundred cubits long for one side
27. 12 (shall be) hangings of fifty cubits
27. 13 the breadth of the court..fifty cubits
27. 14 The hangings..(shall be) fifteen cubits
27. 16 (shall be) an hanging of twenty cubits
Exod 27. 18 The length of the court..an hundred cu.
27. 18 the height five cubits (of) fine twined
30. 2 A cubit (shall be) the length..and a cubit
30. 2 two cubits (shall be) the height thereof
36. 9 The length..(was) twenty and eight cubits
36. 9 the breadth of one curtain four cubits
36. 15 length of one curtain (was) thirty cubits
36. 15 four cubits (was) the breadth of one cur.
36. 21 The length of a board (was) ten cubits
36. 21 the breadth of a board one cubit and a
37. 1 two cubits and a half (was) the length of
37. 1 and a cubit and a half the breadth of it
37. 1 and a cubit and a half the height of it
37. 6 two cubits and a half (was) the length
37. 6 one cubit and a half the breadth thereof
37. 10 two cubits (was) the length thereof, and
37. 10 a cubit the breadth thereof, and a cubit
37. 25 altar..the length of it (was) a cubit
37. 25 and the breadth of it a cubit
37. 25 (it was) four square; and two cubits (was)
38. 1 five cubits (was) the length thereof, and
38. 1 five cubits the breadth..and three cubits
38. 9 hangings of the court..an hundred cubits
38. 11 (the hangings were) an hundred cubits
38. 12 west side (were) hangings of fifty cubits
38. 13 for the east side eastward fifty cubits
38. 14 hangings of the one side..fifteen cubits
38. 15 on this hand..hangings of fifteen cubits
38. 18 and twenty cubits (was) the length, and
38. 18 the height in the breadth (was) five cub.
Num 11. 31 two cubits (high) upon the face of the
35. 4 (shall reach)..outward a thousand cubits
35. 5 and on the south side two thousand cubits
35. 5 and on the west side two thousand cubits
35. 5 and on the north side two thousand cub.
Deut. 3. 11 nine cubits (was) the length thereof, and
3. 11 four cubits the breadth..after the cubit
Josh. 3. 4 about two thousand cubits by measure
1 Sa. 17. 4 Goliath..whose height (was) six cubits and
1 Ki. 6. 2 the length thereof (was) threescore cubits
6. 2 and the height thereof thirty cubits
6. 3 twenty cubits (was) the length thereof
6. 3 ten cubits (was) the breadth thereof
6. 6 The nethermost chamber (was) five cubits
6. 6 and the middle (was) six cubits broad
6. 6 and the third (was) seven cubits broad
6. 10 (then) he built chambers..five cubits high
6. 16 he built twenty cubits on the sides of
6. 17 the temple before it, was forty cubits (long)
6. 20 oracle in the fore part (was) twenty cubits
6. 20 twenty cubits in breadth, and twenty cu.
6. 23 two cherubims (of) olive tree..ten cubits
6. 24 five cubits (was) the one wing of the cher.
6. 24 five cubits the other wing of the cherub
6. 24 from the uttermost part..(were) ten cub.
6. 25 the other cherub (was) ten cubits
6. 26 height of the one cherub (was) ten cubits
7. 2 the length thereof (was) an hundred cub.
7. 2 and the breadth thereof fifty cubits
7. 2 and the height thereof thirty cubits
7. 6 the length thereof (was) fifty cubits
7. 6 and the breadth thereof thirty cubits
7. 10 stones of ten cubits, and..of eight cubits
7. 15 two pillars of brass, of eighteen cubits
7. 15 a line of twelve cubits did compass either
7. 16 height of the one chapiter (was) five cub.
7. 16 height of the other chapiter..five cubits
7. 19 the chapiters..in the porch, four cubits
7. 23 ten cubits from the one brim to the other
7. 23 and his height (was) five cubits
7. 23 a line of thirty cubits did compass it
7. 24 ten in a cubit, compassing the sea round
7. 27 four cubits (was) the length of one base
7. 27 four cubits the breadth..and three cub.
7. 31 within the chapiter and above (was) a c.
7. 31 the mouth thereof..a cubit and an half
7. 32 the height. (was) a cubit and half a cu.
7. 35 a round compass of half a cubit high
7. 38 (and) every laver was four cubits
2 Ki. 14. 13 unto the corner gate, four hundred cubits
25. 17 height of the one..(was) eighteen cubits
25. 17 the height of the chapiter three cubits
1 Ch. 11. 23 And he slew an Egyptian..five cubits hi
2 Ch. 3. 3 length by cubits..(was) threescore cubits
3. 3 and the breadth twenty cubits
3. 8 according to the breadth..twenty cubits
3. 8 and the breadth thereof twenty cubits
3. 11 the wings..(were) twenty cubits
3. 11 wing (of the one cherub was) five cubits
3. 11 the other wing (was likewise) five cubits
3. 12 (one) wing of the other cherub (was) f. c.
3. 12 and the other wing (was) five cubits (also)
3. 13 The wings..spread..forth twenty cubits
3. 15 two pillars of thirty and five cubits high
3. 15 the chapiter..on the top..(was) five cub.
4. 1 altar..twenty cubits the length thereof
4. 1 twenty cubits the breadth..and ten cub.
4. 2 he made a molten sea of ten cubits from
4. 2 and five cubits the height thereof
4. 2 a line of thirty cubits did compass it
4. 3 ten in a cubit, compassing the sea round
6. 13 a brasen scaffold, of five cubits long
6. 13 five cubits broad, and three cubits high
25. 23 to the corner gate, four hundred cubits
Neh. 3. 13 a thousand cubits on the wall unto the
Esth. 5. 14 Let a gallows be made of fifty cubits high
7. 9 the gallows fifty cubits high, which Ha.
Jer. 52. 21 height of one pillar (was) eighteen cubits
52. 21 a fillet of twelve cubits did compass it
52. 22 height of one chapiter (was) five cubits
Eze. 40. 5 reed of six cubits (long) by the cubit and
40. 7 between the..chambers (were) five cubits
Eze. 40. 9 Then measured he the porch..eight cub.
40. 9 and the posts thereof, two cubits
40. 11 the breadth of the entry..ten cubits
40. 11 the length of the gate, thirteen cubits
40. 12 one cubit (on this side)..one cubit on that
40. 12 six cubits on this side, and six cubits
40. 13 the breadth (was) five and twenty cubits
40. 14 He made also posts of threescore cubits
40. 15 from the face of the gate..fifty cubits
40. 19 an hundred cubits eastward and northw
40. 21 the length thereof (was) fifty cubits
40. 21 and the breadth five and twenty cubits
40. 23 from gate to gate an hundred cubits
40. 25, 36 the length (was) fifty cubits
40. 25 and the breadth five and twenty cubits
40. 27 toward the south an hundred cubits
40. 29, 33 fifty cubits long..five and twenty cu.
40. 30 twenty cubits long, and five cubits broad
40. 36 and the breadth five and twenty cubits
40. 42 four tables (were)..a cubit and an half
40. 42 a cubit and an half broad, and one cubit
40. 47 he measured the court, an hundred cub.
40. 47 and an hundred cubits broad, four square
40. 48 five cubits on this side, and five cubits
40. 48 three cubits on this side, and three cub.
40. 49 The length of the porch (was) twenty cu.
40. 49 and the breadth eleven cubits
41. 1 six cubits..on the one side, and six cub.
41. 2 the breadth of the door (was) ten cubits
41. 2 the sides of the doors (were) five cubits
41. 2 and five cubits on the other side
41. 2 forty cubits, and the breadth, twenty cu.
41. 3 post..two cubits, and the door six cubits
41. 3 and the breadth of the door seven cubits
41. 4 he measured the length thereof, twenty c.
41. 4 twenty cubits, and the breadth, twenty c.
41. 5 measured the wall of the house, six cub.
41. 5 breadth of (every) side chamber four cub.
41. 8 a full reed of six great cubits
41. 9 thickness of the wall..(was) five cubits
41. 10 between the chambers (was)..twenty cu.
41. 11 the breadth of the place..(was) five cub.
41. 12 the building..(was) seventy cubits broad
41. 12 the wall of the building (was) five cubits
41. 12 and the length thereof ninety cubits
41. 13 measured the house, an hundred cubits
41. 14 place toward the east, an hundred cubits
41. 15 the galleries thereof..an hundred cubits
41. 22 three cubits high, and the length..two c.
42. 2 Before the length of an hundred cubits
42. 2 and the breadth (was) fifty cubits
42. 4 ten cubits breadth..a way of one cubit
42. 7 the length thereof (was) fifty cubits
42. 8 the length of the chambers..fifty cubits
43. 13 the measures of the altar after the cubits
43. 13 The cubit (is) a cubit and an handbreadth
43. 13 (shall be) a cubit, and the breadth a cubit
43. 14 two cubits, and the breadth one cubit
43. 14 four cubits, and the breadth (one) cubit
43. 15 So the altar (shall be) four cubits
43. 17 the border about it (shall be) half a cubit
43. 17 the bottom thereof (shall be) a cubit about
45. 2 fifty cubits round about for the suburbs
47. 3 he measured a thousand cubits, and he
Zech. 5. 2 the length thereof (is) twenty cubits
5. 2 and the breadth thereof ten cubits
2. *Span,* גֹּמֶד *gomed.*
Judg 3. 16 Ehud made him a dagger..of a cubit len.
3. *The fore arm, a cubit,* πῆχυς *pēchus.*
Matt 6. 27 Which of you..can add one cubit unto
Luke 12. 25 can add to his stature one cubit?
John 21. 8 but as it were two hundred cubits
Rev. 21. 17 an hundred (and) forty (and) four cubits

CUBITS —
Cubits, אַמִּין *ammin.*
Ezra 6. 3 the height thereof threescore cubits
6. 3 (and) the breadth thereof threescore cub.
Dan. 3. 1 whose height (was) threescore cubits
3. 1 (and) the breadth thereof six cubits

CUCKOO —
Sea maw, sea gull, שַׁחַף *shachaph.*
Lev. 11. 16 the cuckoo, and the hawk after his kind
Deut 14 15 the cuckoo, and the hawk after his kind

CUCUMBER —
Place of water melon, מִקְשָׁה *miqshah.*
Isa. 1. 8 as a lodge in a garden of cucumbers, as a

CUCUMBERS —
Water melons, cucumbers, gourd, קִשֻּׁאִים *qishshuim.*
Num 11. 5 the cucumbers, and the melons, and the

CUD —
Chewed food, גֵּרָה *gerah.*
Lev. 11. 3 Whatsoever..cheweth the cud, among the
11. 4 these shall ye not eat..that chew the cud
11. 4 the camel, because he cheweth the cud
11. 5 the coney, because he cheweth the cud
11. 6 the hare, because he cheweth the cud
11. 7 the swine..yet he cheweth not the cud
11. 26 (is) not cloven footed, nor cheweth the cud
Deut 14. 6 (and) cheweth the cud among the beasts
14. 7 shall not eat of them that chew the cud
14. 7 they chew the cud, but divide not the
14. 8 the swine..cheweth not the cud, it (is)

CUMBER —
1. *To make useless, work against.* καταργέω *katargeō.*
Luke 13. 7 cut it down; why cumbereth it the ground

2. *To draw around, distract,* περισπάω *perispaō.*
Luke10. 40 Martha was cumbered about much serv.
CUMBRANCE —
Burden, pressure, טֹרַח *torach.*
Deut. 1. 12 can I myself alone bear your cumbrance
CUMI —
Arise, (the imperative of the Hebrew word קוּם *qum),* κοῦμι *koumi.*
Mark 5. 41 Talitha [cumi], which is..Damsel..arise
CUMMIN —
1. *Cummin, (from the sharp smell),* כַּמֹּן *kammon.*
Isa. 28. 25 doth he not..scatter the cummin, and
28. 27 cart wheel turned about upon the cummin
28. 27 with a staff, and the cummin with a rod
2. *Cummin,* κύμινον *kuminon.*
Matt23. 23 pay tithe of mint and anise and cummin
CUNNING —
1. *Knowledge,* דַּעַת *daath.*
1 Ki. 7. 14 and cunning to work all works in brass
2. *Wise, skilful,* חָכָם *chakam.*
2 Ch. 2. 7 Send me..a man cunning to work in gold
2. 13 I have sent a cunning man, endued with
Isa. 3. 3 the cunning artificer, and the eloquent
40. 20 he seeketh unto him a cunning workman
Jer. 9. 17 send for cunning (women), that they may
10. 9 they (are) all the work of cunning (men)
3. *To think, devise, design,* חָשַׁב *chashab.*
Exod26. 1 (with) cherubim of cunning work shalt
26. 31 and fine twined linen, of cunning work
28. 6 and fine twined linen, with cunning work
28. 15 make the breastplate..with cunning work
36. 8, 35 (with) cherubims of cunning work
39. 3 and in the fine linen, (with) cunning work
39. 8 he made the breastplate (of) cunning w.
4. *To know, be acquainted with,* יָדַע *yada.*
Dan. 1. 4 cunning in knowledge and understanding
5. *Thought, device, design,* מַחֲשֶׁבֶת *machashebeth.*
Exod35. 33 to make any manner of cunning work
CUNNING, to be —
To be intelligent, give understanding, בִּין *bin,* **5.**
1 Ch.25. 7 number of them..all that were cunning
CUNNING man —
1. *Wise, skilful,* חָכָם *chakam.*
1 Ch. 22. 15 all manner of cunning men for every
2 Ch. 2. 7 can skill to grave with the cunning men
2. 14 thy cunning men, and with the cunning m.
2. *To think, devise, design,* חָשַׁב *chashab.*
2 Ch.26. 15 he made..engines, invented by cunning m.
CUNNING work —
1. *Work of a designer,* מַעֲשֵׂה חֹשֵׁב *[maaseh].*
Exod36. 8 (with) cherubim of cunning work made
2. *Thought, device, design,* מַחֲשֶׁבֶת *machashebeth.*
Exod31. 4 To devise cunning works, to work in gold
35. 35 and of those that devise cunning work
CUNNING workman —
1. *Artificer,* אָמָּן *aman.*
Song 7. 1 work of the hands of a cunning workman
2. *To think, devise, design,* חָשַׁב *chashab.*
Exod35 35 the engraver, and of the cunning workman
38. 23 an engraver, and a cunning workman, and
CUP —
1. *Basin, bason,* אַגָּן *aggan.*
Isa. 22. 24 from the vessels of cups, even to all the
2. *Goblet, cup, calyx,* גָּבִיעַ *gabia.*
Gen. 44. 2 put my cup, the silver cup, in the sack's
44. 12 and the cup was found in Benjamin's sack
44. 16 and (he) also with whom the cup is found
44. 17 the man in whose hand the cup is found
3. *Cup,* כּוֹס *kos.*
Gen. 40. 11 Pharaoh's cup (was) in my hand : and I
40. 11 into Pharaoh's cup, and I gave the cup
40. 13 thou shalt deliver Pharaoh's cup into his
40. 21 and he gave the cup into Pharaoh's hand
2 Sa. 12. 3 drank of his own cup, and lay in his bosom
1 Ki. 7. 26 brim..was wrought like the brim of a cup
2 Ch. 4. 5 brim..like the work of the brim of a cup
Psa. 11. 6 (this shall be) the portion of their cup
16. 5 portion of mine inheritance and of my cup
23. 5 thou anointest my head..my cup runneth
75. 8 in the hand of the LORD (there is) a cup
116. 13 I will take the cup of salvation, and call
Isa. 51. 17 which hast drunk..the cup of his fury
51. 17 thou hast drunken the dregs of the cup
51. 22 I have taken out of thine hand the cup
51. 22 (even) the dregs of the cup of my fury
Jer. 16. 7 neither shall (men) give them the cup of
25. 15 Take the wine cup of this fury at my
25. 17 Then took I the cup at the LORD'S hand
25. 28 if they refuse to take the cup at thine
35. 5 I set..pots full of wine, and cups, and I
49. 12 whose judgment (was) not to drink of the c.
51. 7 Babylon (hath been) a golden cup in the
Lam. 4. 21 the cup also shall pass through unto thee
Eze. 23. 31 will I give her cup into thine hand
23. 32 Thou shalt drink of thy sister's cup deep
23. 33 the cup of astonishment and desolation
23. 33 with the cup of thy sister Samaria
Hab. 2. 16 the cup of the LORD'S right hand shall be

4. *Cup,* כּוֹס *kos* [V.L. כִּיס].
Prov.23. 31 when it giveth his colour in the cup
5. *Basin, cup,* סַף *saph.*
Zech.12. 2 I will make Jerusalem a cup of trembling
6. *Cup, dish, bowl,* קַשְׂוָה ,קְשָׂוָה *qasah* or *qasvah.*
1 Ch.28. 17 pure gold for the flesh hooks..and the c.
7. *Drinking vessel,* ποτήριον *potērion.*
Matt10. 42 a cup of cold (water) only in the name of
20. 22 Are ye able to drink of the cup that
20. 23 Ye shall drink indeed of my cup, and be
23. 25 ye make clean the outside of the cup and
23. 26 cleanse..that (which is) within the cup
26. 27 he took the cup, and gave thanks, and
26. 39 if it be possible, let this cup pass from
26. 42 if this [cup] may not pass away from me
Mark 7. 4 [the washing of cups, and pots, brazen]
7. 8 (as) the washing of pots and cups
9. 41 whosoever shall give you a cup of water
10. 38 can ye drink of the cup that I drink of?
10. 39 Ye shall indeed drink of the cup that I
14. 23 he took the cup, and when he had given
14. 36 all things (are) possible..take away this c.
Luke11. 39 make clean the outside of the cup and
22. 17 he took the cup, and gave thanks, and
22. 20 Likewise also the cup after supper
22. 20 This cup (is) the new testament in my
22. 42 if thou be willing, remove this cup from
John18. 11 the cup which my Father hath given me
1 Co. 10. 16 The cup of blessing which we bless, is it
10. 21 Ye cannot drink the cup of the LORD...cup
11. 25 After the same manner..(he took) the cup
11. 25 This cup is the new testament in my
11. 26 For as often as ye..drink this cup, ye do
11. 27 shall eat this bread, and drink (this) cup
11. 28 eat of (that) bread, and drink of (that) c.
Rev. 14. 10 poured out without mixture into the cup
16. 19 to give unto her the cup of the wine of
17. 4 having a golden cup in her hand full of
18. 6 in the cup which she hath filled fill to
CUP bearer —
To give to drink, שָׁקָה *shaqah,* **5.**
1 Ki.10. 5 the attendance..his cup bearers, and
2 Ch. 9. 4 his cup bearers also, and their apparel
Neh. 1. 11 For I was the king's cup bearer
CURDLE, to —
To congeal, harden, curdle, קָפָא *qapha,* **5.**
Job 10. 10 Hast thou not..curdled me like cheese?
CURE —
1. *Healing, cure,* מַרְפֵּא *marpe.*
Jer. 33. 6 I will bring it health and cure, and I will
2. *Healing, cure,* ἴασις *iasis.*
Luke13. 32 I do cures to day and to morrow, and the
CURE, to —
1. *To remove, cure,* גָּהָה *gahah.*
Hos. 5. 13 yet could he not heal you, nor cure you
2. *To heal,* רָפָא *raphah.*
Jer. 33. 6 I will cure them, and will reveal unto
3. *To cherish, cure, attend,* θεραπεύω *therapeuō.*
Matt17. 16 I brought him..and they could not cure
17. 18 the child was cured from that very hour
Luke 7. 21 he cured many of (their) infirmities and
9. 1 and gave them power..to cure diseases
John 5. 10 The Jews..said unto him that was cured
CURED, be —
There is (no) bandage for, אֵין תְּעָלָה לְ *tealah en le.*
Je . 46. [illegible] ou shalt not be cured
CURIOUS arts, used —
Working round about, περίεργος *periergos.*
Acts 19. 19 Many of them also which used curious a.
CURIOUS works —
Thought, device, design, מַחֲשֶׁבֶת *machashebeth.*
Exod 35. 32 to devise curious works, to work in gold
CURIOUSLY wrought —
To be embroidered, רָקַם *raqam,* **4.**
Psa. 139. 15 curiously wrought in the lowest parts
CURRENT —
To pass over, עָבַר *abar.*
Gen. 23. 16 silver, current (money) with the merchant
CURSE —
1. *Oath, execration, imprecation,* אָלָה *alah.*
Num. 5. 21 The LORD make thee a curse and an oath
5. 23 the priest shall write these curses in a
5. 27 the woman shall be a curse among her
Deut29. 19 when he heareth the words of this curse
29. 20 all the curses that are written in this
29. 21 according to all the curses of the covenant
30. 7 LORD thy God will put all these curses
2 Ch.34. 24 all the curses that are written in the
Neh. 10. 29 entered into a curse, and into an oath
Job 31. 30 Neither..by wishing a curse to his soul
Isa. 24. 6 Therefore hath the curse devoured the
Jer. 29. 18 to be a curse, and an astonishment, and
Dan. 9. 11 the curse is poured upon us, and the
Zech. 5. 3 This (is) the curse that goeth forth over
2. *A devoted thing,* חֵרֶם *cherem.*
Josh. 6. 18 make the camp of Israel a curse, and
Isa. 34. 5 come down..upon the people of my curse
43. 28 have given Jacob to the curse, and Israel
Mal. 4. 6 I come and smite the earth with a curse

3. *Curse, execration,* מְאֵרָה *meerah.*
Prov. 3. 33 The curse of the LORD (is) in the house
28. 27 hideth his eyes shall have many a curse
Mal. 2. 2 I will even send a curse upon you, and
3. 9 Ye (are) cursed with a curse : for ye
4. *A reviling, thing lightly esteemed,* קְלָלָה *qelalah.*
Gen. 27. 12 bring a curse upon me, and not a blessing
27. 13 Upon me (be) thy curse, my son : only ob.
Deut 11. 26 I set..this day a blessing and a curse
11. 28 a curse, if ye will not obey the command.
11. 29 thou shalt put..the curse upon mount E.
23. 5 the LORD thy God turned the curse into
27. 13 these shall stand upon mount Ebal to cur.
28. 15, 45 all these curses shall come upon thee
29. 27 to bring upon it all the curses that are
30. 1 the curse, which I have set before thee
Judg. 9. 57 upon them came the curse of Jotham
1 Ki. 2. 8 with a grievous curse in the day when
2 Ki. 22. 19 should become a desolation and a curse
Neh. 13. 2 our God turned the curse into a blessing
Prov.26. 2 so the curse causeless shall not come
27. 14 it shall be counted a curse to him
Jer. 24. 9 reproach and a proverb, a taunt and a cu.
25. 18 to make them a desolation..and a curse
26. 6 will make this city a curse to all the
29. 22 of them shall be taken up a curse by all
42. 18 ye shall be an execration..and a curse
44. 8 that ye might be a curse and a reproach
44. 12 they shall be an execration..and a curse
44. 22 therefore is your land..a curse, without
49. 13 shall become a desolation..and a curse
Zech. 8. 13 as ye were a curse among the heathen, O
5. *Swearing, oath,* שְׁבוּעָה *shebuah.*
Isa. 65. 15 ye shall leave your name for a curse unto
6. *Oath, imprecation, execration,* תַּאֲלָה *taalah.*
Lam. 3. 65 Give them sorrow of heart, thy curse
7. *A thing put up for execration,* κατανάθεμα.
Rev. 22. 3 there shall be no more [curse] : but the
8. *A thorough curse,* κατάρα *katara.*
Gal. 3. 10 the works of the law are under the curse
3. 13 Christ hath redeemed us from the curse of
3. 13 being made a curse for us : for it is writ.
CURSE, to bind under a —
To place under an anathema, ἀναθεματίζω.
Acts 23. 12 bound themselves under a curse, saying
CURSE, to bind under a great —
To place under anathema, ἀναθέματι ἀναθεματίζω.
Acts 23. 14 have bound ourselves under a great curse
CURSE, to —
1. *To swear, take oath, execrate,* אָלָה *alah.*
Judg17. 2 about which thou cursedst, and spakest
2. *To curse,* אָרַר *arar.*
Gen. 12. 3 bless them that bless thee, and curse him
27. 29 cursed (be) every one that curseth thee
Exod22. 28 nor curse the ruler of thy people
Num22. 6 Come..I pray thee, curse me this people
22. 6 for I wot that..he whom thou cursest
22. 12 thou shalt not curse the people : for they
23. 7 Come, curse me Jacob, and come, defy I
24. 9 and cursed (is) he that curseth thee
Judg. 5. 23 Curse ye Meroz..curse ye bitterly the
Job 3. 8 Let them..that curse the day, who are
Mal. 2. 2 and I will curse your blessings ; yea
2. 2 I have cursed them already, because ye
3. *To curse,* אָרַר *arar,* **3.**
Gen. 5. 29 the ground which the LORD hath cursed
4. *To bless, (bid farewell to ?),* בָּרַךְ *barak,* **3.**
Job 1. 5 sinned, and cursed God in their hearts
1. 11 and he will curse thee to thy face
2. 5 and he will curse thee to thy face
2. 9 retain thine integrity ? curse God, and
5. *To pierce, execrate,* נָקַב *naqab.*
Num23. 8 How shall I curse, whom God hath not
23. 25 Neither curse them at all, nor bless them
Job 3. 8 Let them curse it..who are ready to raise
5. 3 but suddenly I cursed his habitation
Prov. 11. 26 He that withholdeth..people shall curse
24. 24 him shall the people curse, nations shall
6. *To pierce, execrate,* קָבַב *qabab.*
Num22. 11 (there is) a people come out..curse me
22. 17 come..I pray thee, curse me this people
23. 8 How shall I..whom God hath not cursed ?
23. 11 I took thee to curse mine enemies, and
23. 13 and curse me them from thence
23. 27 that thou mayest curse me them from
24. 10 I called thee to curse mine enemies, and
7. *To lightly esteem, vilify, revile,* קָלַל *qalal,* **3.**
Gen. 8. 21 I will not again curse the ground any
12. 3 him that curseth thee : and in thee shall
Exod21. 17 he that curseth his father or his mother
Lev. 19. 14 Thou shalt not curse the deaf, nor put a
20. 9 every one that curseth his father or his
20. 9 he hath cursed his father or his mother
24. 11 the..woman's son blasphemed..and cur.
24. 14 Bring forth him that hath cursed without
24. 15 Whosoever curseth his God shall bear his
24. 23 should bring forth him that had cursed
Deut 23. 4 hired against thee Balaam..to curse thee
Josh.24. 9 called Balaam the son of Beor to curse you
Judg 9. 27 did eat and drink, and cursed Abimelech
1 Sa. 17. 43 the Philistine cursed David by his gods
2 Sa. 16. 5 he came forth, and cursed still as he ca.

2 Sa. 16. 7 thus said Shimei when he cursed, Come
16. 9 Why should this dead dog curse my lord
16. 10 What have I to do with you..let him cu.
16. 10 the LORD hath said unto him, curse Da.
16. 11 let him curse; for the LORD hath bidden
16. 13 Shimei went along..and cursed as he
19. 21 because he cursed the LORD'S anointed?
1 Ki. 2. 8 Shimei the son of Gera..which cursed me
2 Ki. 2. 24 and cursed them in the name of the LORD
Neh. 13. 2 hired Balaam..that he should curse them
13. 25 I contended with them, and cursed them
Job 3. 1 After this opened Job his mouth, and cu.
Psa. 37. 22 (they that be) cursed off him shall be cut
62. 4 they bless with their mouth, but they cur.
109. 28 Let them curse, but bless thou: when
Prov 20. 20 Whoso curseth his father or his mother
30. 10 lest he curse thee, and thou be found
30. 11 (There is) a generation (that) curseth
Eccl. 7. 21 lest thou hear thy servant curse thee
7. 22 thou thyself likewise hast cursed others
10. 20 Curse not the king..and curse not the
Isa. 8. 21 they shall..curse their king and their G.
Jer. 15. 10 (yet) every one of them doth curse me

8. *To anathematize*, ἀναθεματίζω *anathematizō*.
Mark 14. 71 he began to curse and to swear, (saying)

9. *To speak evil of*, κακολογέω *kakologeō*.
Matt 15. 4 He that curseth father or mother, let him
Mark 7. 10 Whoso curseth father or mother, let him

10. *To anathematize thoroughly*, καταναθεματίζω.
Matt 26. 74 Then began he [to curse] and to swear

11. *To wish a curse against (one)*, καταράομαι.
Matt. 5. 44 [Love your enemies, bless them that curse]
Mark 11. 21 the fig tree which thou cursedst is withe.
Luke 6. 28 Bless them that curse you, and pray for
Rom 12. 14 Bless them which persecute you..curse
Jas. 3. 9 therewith curse we men, which are made

CURSE, to cause the —
To curse, אָרַר *arar*, 3.
Num. 5. 18, 19, 24 bitter water that causeth the curse
5. 22, 24, 27 water that causeth the curse shall

CURSED —
1. *To curse*, אָרַר *arar*.
Gen. 3. 14 thou (art) cursed above all cattle, and
3. 17 cursed (is) the ground for thy sake
4. 11 now (art) thou cursed from the earth, which
9. 25 Cursed (be) Canaan; a servant of servants
27. 29 cursed (be) every one that curseth thee
49. 7 Cursed (be) their anger, for it (was) fierce
Num 24. 9 Blessed (is) he that blesseth..and cursed
Deut 27. 15 Cursed (be) the man that maketh (any)
27. 16 Cursed (be) he that setteth light by his
27. 17 Cursed (be) he that removeth his neighb.
27. 18 Cursed (be) he that maketh the blind to
27. 19 Cursed (be) he that perverteth the judg.
27. 20, 21, 22, 23 Cursed (be) he that lieth with
27. 24 Cursed (be) he that smiteth his neighbour
27. 25 Cursed (be) he that taketh reward to slay
27. 26 Cursed (be) he that confirmeth not (all)
28. 16 Cursed (shalt) thou (be) in the city, and cu.
28. 17 Cursed (shall be) thy basket and thy store
28. 18 Cursed (shall be) the fruit of thy body, and
28. 19 Cursed (shalt) thou (be) when thou comest
28. 19 cursed (shalt) thou (be) when thou goest
Josh. 6. 26 Cursed (be) the man before the LORD that
9. 23 therefore ye (are) cursed; and there shall
Judg 21. 18 Cursed (be) he that giveth a wife to Benja.
1 Sa. 14. 24, 28 Cursed (be) the man that eateth (any)
26. 19 if (they be) the children of men, cursed
2 Ki. 9. 34 Go, see now this cursed (woman), and
Psa. 119. 21 hast rebuked the proud (that are) cursed
Jer. 11. 3 Cursed (be) the man that obeyeth not
17. 5 Cursed (be) the man that trusteth in man
20. 14 Cursed (be) the day wherein I was born
20. 15 Cursed (be) the man who brought tidings
48. 10 Cursed (be) he that doeth the work of the
48. 10 cursed (be) he that keepeth back his sword
Mal. 1. 14 cursed (be) the deceiver, which hath in

2. *One upon whom a curse lies*, ἐπικατάρατος.
John 7. 49 people who knoweth not the law [are cur.]
Gal. 3. 10 Cursed (is) every one that continueth not
3. 13 Cursed is every one that hangeth on a

3. *A curse*, κατάρα *katara*.
2 Pe. 2. 14 beguiling unstable souls..cursed children

CURSED, to be —
1. *To be cursed*, אָרַר *arar*, 2.
Mal. 3. 9 Ye (are) cursed with a curse: for ye have

2. *To be made cursed*, אָרַר *arar*, 6.
Num 22. 6 and he whom thou cursest is cursed

3. *To be lightly esteemed, vilified*, קָלַל *qalal*, 4.
Job 24. 18 their portion is cursed in the earth

4. *To wish a curse against one*, καταράομαι *katara.*
Matt 25. 41 Depart from me, ye cursed, into ever.

CURSED thing —
A devoted thing, חֵרֶם *cherem*.
Deut. 7. 26 lest thou be a cursed thing like it
7. 26 utterly abhor it; for it (is) a cursed thing
13. 17 shall cleave nought of the cursed thing

CURSING —
1. *Oath, execration, imprecation*, אָלָה *alah*.
Num. 5. 21 charge the woman with an oath of cursing
Psa. 10. 7 His mouth is full of cursing and deceit
59. 12 for cursing and lying (which) they speak
Prov 29. 24 he heareth cursing, and bewrayeth (it)

2. *A curse*, מְאֵרָה *meerah*.
Deut 28. 20 The LORD shall send upon thee cursing

3. *Reviling, thing lightly esteemed*, קְלָלָה *qelalah*.
Deut 30. 19 have set before you..blessing and cursing
Josh. 8. 34 he read all the..blessings and cursings
2 Sa. 16. 12 the LORD will requite me good for his cu.
Psa. 109. 17 As he loved cursing, so let it come unto
109. 18 he clothed himself with cursing like as

4. *A curse, cursing*, ἀρά *ara*.
Rom. 3. 14 Whose mouth (is) full of cursing..bitter.

5. *Full cursing*, κατάρα *katara*.
Heb. 6. 8 which beareth thorns..(is) nigh unto curs.
Jas. 3. 10 Out of the same mouth proceedeth..cur.

CURTAIN —
1. *Thin veil*, דֹּק *doq*.
Isa 40. 22 stretcheth out the heavens as a curtain

2. *Curtain, veil*, יְרִיעָה *yeriah*.
Exod 26. 1 make the tabernacle (with) ten curtains
26. 2, 8 The length of one curtain (shall be)
26. 2, 8 the breadth of one curtain four cubits
26. 2 every one of the curtains shall have one
26. 3 The five curtains shall be coupled togeth.
26. 3 (other) five curtains (shall be) coupled one
26. 4 of blue upon the edge of the one curtain
26. 4 in the uttermost edge of (another) curtain
26. 5 Fifty loops..make in the one curtain, and
26. 5 shalt thou make in the edge of the curtain
26. 6 couple the curtains together with the
26. 7 thou shalt make curtains (of) goats' (hair)
26. 7 eleven curtains shalt thou make
26. 8 the eleven curtains (shall be all) of one
26. 9 shalt couple five curtains..and six cur. by
26. 9 shalt double the sixth curtain in the fore
26. 10 fifty loops on the edge of the one curtain
26. 10 fifty loops in the edge of the curtain
26. 12 the remnant that remaineth of the curtai.
26. 13 remaineth in the length of the curtains
36. 8 made ten curtains (of) fine twined linen
36. 9 The length of one curtain (was) twenty
36. 9 the breadth of one curtain four cubits
36. 9 the curtains (were) all of one size
36. 10 he coupled the five curtains one unto
36. 10 (the other) five curtains he coupled one
36. 11 loops of blue on the edge of one curtain
36. 11 in the uttermost side of (another) curtain
36. 12 Fifty loops made he in one curtain, and
36. 12 loops made he in the edge of the curtain
36. 13 coupled the curtains one unto another
36. 14 he made curtains (of) goats' (hair) for the
36. 14 eleven curtains he made them
36. 15 The length of one curtain (was) thirty cu.
36. 15 four cubits (was) the breadth of one curtain
36. 16 he coupled five curtains..and six curtains
36. 17 fifty loops upon the..edge of the curtain
36. 17 fifty loops..upon the edge of the curtain
Num 4. 25 shall bear the curtains of the tabernacle
2 Sa. 7. 2 the ark of God dwelleth within curtains
1 Ch. 17. 1 ark..of the LORD (remaineth) under cur.
Psa. 104. 2 who stretchest out the heavens like a cu.
Song 1. 5 the tents of Kedar, as the curtains of So.
Isa. 54. 2 and let them stretch forth the curtains of
Jer. 4. 20 suddenly are my tents spoiled, (and) my c.
10. 20 (there is) none..to set up my curtains
49. 29 they shall take to themselves their cur.
Hab. 3. 7 (and) the curtains of the land of Midian

3. *Veil, hanging*, מָסָךְ *masak*.
Num 3. 26 and the curtain for the door..which (is) by

CUSH, כּוּשׁ *black*.
1. Eldest son of Ham and grandson of Noah, B.C. 2250.
Gen. 10. 6 sons of Ham; C., and Mizraim, and Phut
10. 7 sons of C.; Seba, and Havilah, and Sabtah
10. 8 And C. begat Nimrod: he began to be a
1 Ch. 1. 8 The sons of Ham; C., and Mizraim, Put
1. 9 sons of C.; Seba, and Havilah, and Sabta
1. 10 C. begat Nimrod: he began to be mighty

2. This title was of great antiquity. It is applied in the Hebrew original to the people that sprang from Cush; but in the common version is translated "Ethiopian."

3. It is also used to denote the land in which the descendants of Cush dwelt, Ethiopia or Abyssinia.
Isa. 11. 11 from Pathros, and from C., and from E.

4. A Benjamite, and enemy of David.
Psa. 7. *title*. concerning the words of C. the Benjamite

5. The land S. of Ethiopia adduced with Phut and Lud.
Isa. 18. 1 Woe to the land..beyond the rivers of E.

6. Meroe enclosed by the Nile and the Atbar.
Psa. 68. 31 Ethiopia shall..stretch out her hands

7. A district in Susiana and Media.
Gen. 2. 13 compasseth the whole land of Ethiopia

CU-SHAN, כּוּשָׁן
Perhaps the same as Chushan-rishathaim (Judg. 3. 8, 10), king of Mesopotamia. This seems favoured by the order of events alluded to by Habakkuk. Others think the land of Midian as far as Sinai, between Elath and Moab, is meant.
Hab. 3. 7 I saw the tents of C. in affliction

CU-SHI, כּוּשִׁי *black*, Αἰθίοπες.
1. Joab's messenger to David concerning the battle in which Absalom fell, B.C. 1023.
2 Sa. 18. 21 C., Go tell the king what thou hast seen
18. 21 And C. bowed himself unto Joab, and
18. 22 let me, I pray thee..run after C.
2 Sa. 18. 23 Then Ahimaaz ran..and overran C.
18. 31 And, behold, C. came; and C. said
18. 32 And the king said unto C., (Is)..Absalom
18. 32 C. answered, The enemies of my lord..be

2. Ancestor of Jehudi, who was about Jehoiakim, B.C. 690.
Jer. 36. 14 Nathaniah..son of Shelemiah..son of C.

3. Father of Zephaniah the prophet, who lived in the time of Josiah king of Judah, B.C. 640.
Zeph. 1. 1 which came unto Zephaniah the son of C.

CUSTODY —
1. *Hand*, יָד *yad*.
Esth. 2. 3 the custody of Hege the king's chamber.
2. 8 maidens were gathered..to the custody
2. 8 to the custody of Hegai, keeper of the
2. 14 the custody of Shaashgaz, the king's cha.

2. *Inspection*, פְּקֻדָּה *pequddah*.
Num. 3. 36 the custody and charge of the sons of M.

CUSTOM —
1. *Way*, דֶּרֶךְ *derek*.
Gen. 31. 35 for the custom of women (is) upon me

2. *Road tax, toll*, הֲלָךְ *halak*.
Ezra 4. 13 will they not pay toll, tribute, and custom
4. 20 tribute, and custom, was paid unto them
7. 24 impose toll, tribute, or custom, upon them

3. *Statute*, חֹק *choq*.
Judg 11. 39 And it was a custom in Israel
Jer. 32. 11 sealed (according) to the law and custom

4. *Statute*, חֻקָּה *chuqqah*.
Lev. 18. 30 not (any one) of these abominable customs
Jer. 10. 3 For the customs of the people (are) vain

5. *Judgment*, מִשְׁפָּט *mishpat*.
1 Sa. 2. 13 the priest's custom with the people (was)
Ezra 3. 4 according to the custom, as the duty of

6. *To accustom*, ἐθίζω *ethizō*.
Luke 2. 27 to do for him after the custom of the law

7. *Custom*, ἔθος *ethos*.
Luke 1. 9 According to the custom of the priest's
2. 42 they went up to Jerusalem after the cus.
Acts 6. 14 shall change the customs which Moses
16. 21 And teach customs, which are not lawful
21. 21 they ought not..to walk after the customs
26. 3 to be expert in all customs and questions
28. 17 committed nothing against the people or c.

8. *A common usage*, συνήθεια *sunētheia*.
John 18. 39 ye have a custom, that I should release
1 Co. 11. 16 we have no such custom, neither the

9. *Custom, toll*, τέλος *telos*.
Matt 17. 25 of whom do the kings..take custom or
Rom. 13. 7 custom to whom custom; fear to whom

CUSTOM, receipt of —
Custom house, toll house, τελώνιον *telōnion*.
Matt. 9. 9 a man..sitting at the receipt of custom
Mark 2. 14 Levi..sitting at the receipt of custom
Luke 5. 27 a publican..sitting at the receipt of cus.

CUSTOM was, as his —
According to his custom, κατὰ τὸ εἰωθὸς αὐτῷ.
Luke 4. 16 as his custom was, he went into the syna.

CUT, to —
1. *To cut (off)*, בָּצַע *batsa*.
Amos 9. 1 and cut them in the head, all of them

2. *To hew (down)*, חָצַב *chatsab*, 5.
Isa. 51. 9 (Art) thou not it that hath cut Rahab

3. *To cut (down, out, off)*, כָּרַת *karath*.
Exod 34. 13 break their images, and cut down their
Lev. 22. 24 Ye shall not offer..that which is..cut
Deut 23. 1 He that..hath his privy member cut off
1 Sa. 5. 4 both the palms of his hands (were) cut off
2 Ch. 2. 8 I know that thy servants can skill to cut
2. 10 I will give to..the hewers that cut timber
2. 16 And we will cut wood out of Lebanon, as
Prov 10. 31 but the froward tongue shall be cut out
Jer. 10. 3 for (one) cutteth a tree out of the forest
34. 18 when they cut the calf in twain, and pas.

4. *To cut in pieces*, נָתַח *nathach*, 3.
Exod 29. 17 thou shalt cut the ram in pieces, and wash
Lev. 1. 6 he shall flay..and cut it into his pieces
1. 12 he shall cut it into his pieces with his
8. 20 he cut the ram into pieces; and Moses burnt

5. *To split*, פָּלַח *palach*.
Psa. 141. 7 as when one cutteth and cleaveth (wood)

6. *To cut asunder or off*, קָצַץ *qatsats*, 3.
Exod 39. 3 cut (it into) wires [to work (it) in the blue

7. *To cut out or away*, קָרַע *qara*.
Jer. 36. 23 he cut it with the penknife, and cast (it)

8. *To saw*, שׂוּר *sur*.
1 Ch. 20. 3 he brought out the people..and cut (them)

9. *To cut against or greatly*, κατακόπτω *katakoptō*.
Mark 5. 5 crying, and cutting himself with stones

CUT, to be —
1. *To be cut*, כָּרַת *karath*, 4.
Eze. 16. 4 day thou wast born thy navel was not cut

2. *To saw through*, διαπρίω *diapriō*.
Acts 7. 54 they were cut to the heart, and..gnashed

3. *To be made,* עֲבַד *abad,* 4.
Dan. 2. 5 ye shall be cut in pieces, and your houses
3. 29 That every people..shall be cut in pieces

CUT (to the heart), to be —
To saw through, διαπρίω *diapriō.*
Acts 5. 33 they were cut (to the heart), and took

CUT asunder, to —
1. *To cut down, off, asunder,* גָּדַע *gada.*
Zech 11. 10 I took my staff..and cut it asunder
11. 14 I cut asunder mine other staff, (even) Ba.
2. *To cut asunder or off,* קָצַץ *qatsats,* 3.
Psa. 129. 4 hath cut asunder the cords of the wicked
3. *To cut in two,* διχοτομέω *dichotomeō.*
Mat. 24. 51 shall cut him asunder, and appoint (him)

CUT asunder, to be —
To be cut down, off, asunder, גָּדַע *gada,* 2.
Jer. 50. 23 How is the hammer..cut asunder and

CUT down, to —
1. *To prepare, form, make, cut down,* בָּרָא *bara,* 3.
Josh. 17. 15 to the wood (country), and cut down for
17. 18 it (is) a wood, and thou shalt cut it down
2. *To cut down, off, asunder,* גָּדַע *gada,* 3.
Deut. 7. 5 break down their images, and cut down
2 Ch. 14. 3 brake down the images, and cut down the
31. 1 brake the images in pieces, and cut down
34. 4 the images that (were) on high..he cut d.
34. 7 cut down all the idols throughout all the
3. *To cut down or off,* גָּזַר *gazar.*
2 Ki. 6. 4 when they came to Jordan, they cut down
4. *To cut, hew,* חָטַב *chatab.*
Eze. 39. 10 neither cut down (any) out of the forests
5. *To cut off or down,* כָּרַת *karath.*
Num 13. 23 and cut down from thence a branch with
13. 24 which the children of Israel cut down
Deut 19. 5 his hand fetcheth a stroke..to cut down
20. 19 and thou shalt not cut them down..to
20. 20 thou shalt destroy and cut them down
Judg. 6. 25 and cut down the grove that (is) by it
6. 26 with the wood..which thou shalt cut do.
6. 30 he hath cut down the grove that (was) by
9. 48 Abimelech..cut down a bough from the
9. 49 the people..cut down every man his bou.
2 Ki. 18. 4 brake the images, and cut down the groves
19. 23 will cut down the tall cedar trees thereof
23. 14 brake in pieces the images, and cut down
2 Ch 15. 16 Asa cut down her idol, and stamped (it)
Isa 37. 24 I will cut down the tall cedars thereof
Jer. 22. 7 they shall cut down thy choice cedars
46. 23 They shall cut down her forest, saith the
6. *To (cause to) cut down,* כָּרַת *karath,* 5.
Lev. 26. 30 cut down your images, and cast your car.
7. *To go round, compass,* נָקַף *naqaph,* 3.
Isa. 10. 34 he shall cut down the thickets of the
8. *To cut, shear,* קָצַב *qatsab.*
2 Ki. 6. 6 he cut down a stick, and cast (it) in
9. *To shorten, reap,* קָצַר *qatsar.*
Deut 24. 19 When thou cuttest down thine harvest in
10. *To (cause to) cut down,* תָּזַז *tazaz,* 5.
Isa. 18. 5 and take away (and) cut down the branch.
11. *To cut off or out,* ἐκκόπτω *ekkoptō.*
Luke 13. 7 cut it down; why cumbereth it the gr.?
13. 9 (then) after that thou shalt cut it down
12. *To cut,* κόπτω *koptō.*
Matt 21. 8 others cut down branches from the trees
Mark 11. 8 others cut down branches off the trees

CUT down, to be —
1. *To be cut down, off, asunder,* גָּדַע *gada,* 2.
Isa. 14. 12 (how) art thou cut down to the ground
22. 25 In that day..shall the nail..be cut down
Eze. 6. 6 your images may be cut down, and your
2. *To be cut down, off, asunder,* גָּדַע *gada,* 4.
Isa. 9. 10 the sycamores are cut down, but we will
3. *To be cut off, shaven, shorn,* גָּזַז *gazaz,* 2.
Nah 1. 12 yet thus shall they be cut down, when he
4. *To be cut off, silent, cease,* דָּמָה *damah,* 2.
Zeph. 1. 11 for all the merchant people are cut down
5. *To be silent, cease,* דָּמַם *damam,* 2.
Jer. 25. 37 the peaceable habitations are cut down
48. 2 Also thou shalt be cut down, O Madmen
6. *To be hid, cut off,* כָּחַד *kachad,* 2.
Job 22. 20 our substance is not cut down, but the
7. *To cut down,* כָּסַח *kasach.*
Psa. 80. 16 (It is) burnt with fire; (it is) cut down
8. *To be cut down,* כָּרַת *karath,* 2.
Job 14. 7 there is hope of a tree if it be cut down
9. *To be cut down,* כָּרַת *karath,* 4.
Judg. 6. 28 the grove was cut down that (was) by it
10. *To cut off,* מוּל *mul,* 3*a.*
Psa. 90. 6 in the evening it is cut down, and wither.
11. *To be cut off,* מָלַל *malal.*
Job 14. 2 cometh forth like a flower, and is cut do.
Psa. 37. 2 they shall soon be cut down like the grass
12. *To be cropt, plucked,* קָטַף *qataph,* 2.
Job 8. 12 (is) yet in his greenness, (and) not cut d.

13. *To be laid hold on,* קָמַט *qamat,* 4.
Job 22. 16 Which were cut down out of time, whose

CUT in pieces, to —
1. *To cut in pieces,* נָתַח *nathach,* 3.
Judg 20. 6 I took my concubine, and cut her in pie.
1 Ki. 18. 23 choose one bullock..and cut it in pieces
18. 33 cut the bullock in pieces, and laid (him)
2. *To cut off, asunder,* קָצַץ *qatsats,* 3.
2 Ki. 24. 13 cut in pieces all the vessels of gold
2 Ch. 28. 24 cut in pieces the vessels of the house of

CUT in pieces, to be —
1. *To be cut off,* מוּל *mul,* 7*a.*
Psa. 58. 7 let them be as cut in pieces
2. *To be cut,* שָׂרַט *sarat,* 2.
Zech 12. 3 burden themselves..shall be cut in pieces

CUT in sunder, to —
1. *To cut down, off, asunder,* גָּדַע *gada,* 3.
Isa. 45. 2 I will..cut in sunder the bars of iron
2. *To cut off, asunder,* קָצַץ *qatsats,* 3.
Psa. 46. 9 breaketh the bow, and cutteth..in sunder
3. *To cut in two,* διχοτομέω *dichotomeō.*
Luke 12. 46 will come..will cut him in sunder

CUT off —
To be cut off, asunder, קָצַץ *qatsats,* 4.
Judg. 1. 7 their thumbs and their great toes cut off

CUT off, to — [*See also* **NECK.**]
1. *To cut off (dishonestly),* בָּצַע *batsa,* 3.
Job 6. 9 would let loose his hand, and cut me off
Isa. 38. 12 he will cut me off with pining sickness
2. *To gather, cut off,* בָּצַר *batsar.*
Psa. 76. 12 He shall cut off the spirit of princes
3. *To cut off, down, asunder,* גָּדַע *gada.*
1 Sa. 2. 31 the days come, that I will cut off thine
Psa. 75. 10 horns of the wicked also will I cut off
Lam. 2. 3 He hath cut off in (his) fierce anger all
Isa. 15. 2 (shall be) baldness..every beard cut off
4. *To cut off, shave, shear,* גָּזַז *gazaz.*
Jer. 7. 29 Cut off thine hair, (O Jerusalem,) and
5. *To pass on,* חָלַף *chalaph.*
Job 11. 10 If he cut off, and shut up, or gather
6. *To hide, cut off,* כָּחַד *kachad,* 5.
Exod 23. 23 and the Jebusites; and I will cut them o.
1 Ki. 13. 34 this thing became sin..even to cut (it) off
2 Ch. 32. 21 the LORD sent an angel, which cut off all
Psa. 83. 4 let us cut them off from (being) a nation
Zech 11. 8 Three shepherds also I cut off in one
7. *To cut down, off,* כָּרַת *karath.*
Exod. 4. 25 Zipporah..cut off the foreskin of her
1 Sa. 17. 51 slew him, and cut off his head therewith
24. 4 David arose, and cut off the skirt of
24. 5 because he had cut off Saul's skirt
24. 11 for in that I cut off the skirt of thy robe
31. 9 they cut off his head, and stripped off
2 Sa. 10. 4 Hanun..cut off their garments in the
20. 22 they cut off the head of Sheba the son of
1 Ch. 19. 4 Hanun..cut off their garments in the
Isa. 18. 5 he shall both cut off the sprigs with
Jer. 11. 19 let us cut him off from the land of
50. 16 Cut off the sower from Babylon, and
Eze. 31. 12 terrible of the nations, have cut him off
8. *To (cause to) cut down, off,* כָּרַת *karath,* 5.
Lev. 17. 10 I will..cut him off from among his people
20. 3 I will..cut him off from among his people
20. 5 I will..cut him off, and all that go
20. 6 I will..cut him off from among his people
Num. 4. 18 Cut ye not off the tribe of the families
Deut 12. 29 When the LORD thy God shall cut off the
19. 1 When the LORD thy God hath cut off the
Josh. 7. 9 shall environ us round, and cut off our
11. 21 at that time came Joshua, and cut off the
23. 4 with all the nations that I have cut off
1 Sa. 2. 33 man of thine, (whom) I shall not cut off
20. 15 thou shalt not cut off thy kindness from
20. 15 not when the LORD hath cut off the
24. 21 that thou wilt not cut off my seed after
28. 9 he hath cut off those that have familiar
2 Sa. 7. 9 have cut off all thine enemies out of thy
1 Ki. 9. 7 Then will I cut off Israel out of the land
11. 16 until he had cut off every male in Edom
14. 10 I will..cut off from Jereboam him that
14. 14 who shall cut off the house of Jeroboam
18. 4 when Jezebel cut off the prophets of the
21. 21 I..will cut off from Ahab him that
2 Ki. 9. 8 I will cut off from Ahab him that pisseth
1 Ch. 17. 8 I have..cut off all thine enemies from
2 Ch. 22. 7 whom the LORD had anointed to cut off
Psa. 12. 3 The LORD shall cut off all flattering lips
34. 16 to cut off the remembrance of them from
101. 8 that I may cut off all wicked doers from
109. 13 Let his posterity be cut off; (and) in the
109. 15 that he may cut off the memory of them
Isa. 9. 14 the LORD will cut off from Israel head
10. 7 to destroy and cut off nations not a few
14. 22 cut off from Babylon the name, and
48. 9 refrain for thee, that I cut thee not off
Jer. 9. 21 to cut off the children from without
44. 7 to cut off from you man and woman
44. 8 that ye might cut yourselves off, and
44. 11 I will set my face..to cut off all Judah
47. 4 the day that cometh..to cut off from
48. 2 and let us cut it off from (being) a nation

Jer. 51. 62 spoken against this place, to cut it off
Eze. 14. 8 I will cut him off from the midst of my
14. 13 and will cut off man and beast from it
14. 17 so that I cut off man and beast from it
14. 19, 21 to cut off from it man and beast
17. 17 building forts, to cut off many persons
21. 3, 4 will cut off from thee the righteous and
25. 7 I will cut thee off from the people, and
25. 13 and will cut off man and beast from it
25. 16 I will cut off the Cherethims, and destroy
29. 8 and cut off man and beast out of thee
30. 15 and I will cut off the multitude of No
35. 7 cut off from it him that passeth out and
Amos 1. 5 I will..cut off the inhabitant from the
1. 8 I will cut off the inhabitant from Ashdod
2. 3 I will cut off the judge from the midst
Mic. 5. 10 that I will cut off thy horses out of the
5. 11 I will cut off the cities of thy land, and
5. 12 I will cut off witchcrafts out of thine
5. 13 Thy graven images also will I cut off
Nah. 1. 14 will I cut off the graven image and the
2. 13 I will cut off thy prey from the earth
3. 15 the sword shall cut thee off, it shall eat
Obad. 14 to cut off those of his that did escape
Zeph. 1. 3 I will cut off man from off the land
1. 4 I will cut off the remnant of Baal from
3. 6 I have cut off the nations: their towers
Zech. 9. 6 I will cut off the pride of the Philistines
9. 10 I will cut off the chariot from Ephraim
13. 2 (that) I will cut off the names of the idols
Mal. 2. 12 The LORD will cut off the man that doeth
9. *To cut off, destroy, silence,* צָמַת *tsamath.*
Lam. 3. 53 They have cut off my life in the dungeon
10. *To cut off, destroy, silence,* צָמַת *tsamath,* 3*a.*
Psa. 88. 16 over me; thy terrors have cut me off
11. *To (cause to) cut off, destroy,* צָמַת *tsamath,* 5.
Psa. 54. 5 He shall reward evil..cut them off in thy
94. 23 shall cut them off in their own wickedness
94. 23 the LORD our God shall cut them off
101. 5 slandereth his neighb., him will I cut off
143. 12 of thy mercy cut off mine enemies, and
12. *To cut or pluck off,* קָסַס *qasas,* 3*a.*
Eze. 17. 9 cut off the fruit thereof, that it wither?
13. *To cut off, draw together,* קָפַד *qaphad,* 3.
Isa. 38. 12 I have cut off like a weaver my life
14. *To cut off, end,* קָצָה *qatsah,* 3.
Prov 26. 6 He that sendeth a message..cutteth off
15. *To cut off or asunder,* קָצַץ *qatsats.*
Deut 25. 12 thou shalt cut off her hand, thine eye
16. *To cut off, asunder,* קָצַץ *qatsats,* 3.
Judg. 1. 6 and cut off his thumbs and his great toes
2 Sa. 4. 12 cut off their hands and their feet, and
2 Ki. 16. 17 king Ahaz cut off the borders of the bases
18. 16 that time did Hezekiah cut off (the gold)
17. *To cut off, asunder,* קְצַץ *qetsats,* 3.
Dan. 4. 14 Hew down the tree, and cut off his bran.
18. *To take away,* ἀφαιρέω *aphaireō.*
Mark 14. 47 and smote a servant..and cut off his ear
Luke 22. 50 And one of them..cut off his right ear
19. *To cut away,* ἀποκόπτω *apokoptō.*
Mark 9. 43 And if thy hand offend thee, cut it off
9. 45 And if thy foot offend thee, cut it off
John 18. 10 smote the..servant, and cut off his right
18. 26 (his) kinsman whose ear Peter cut off
Acts 27. 32 the soldiers cut off the ropes of the
Gal. 5. 12 I would they were even cut off which
20. *To cut off or out,* ἐκκόπτω *ekkoptō.*
Matt. 5. 30 if thy right hand offend thee, cut it off
18. 8 hand or thy foot offend thee, cut them off
Rom 11. 22 otherwise thou also shalt be cut off
2 Co. 11. 12 that I may cut off occasion from them

CUT off, to be —
1. *To be cut down, off, asunder,* גָּדַע *gada,* 2.
Judg 21. 6 There is one tribe cut off from Israel
Jer. 48. 25 The horn of Moab is cut off, and his arm
Amos 3. 14 the horns of the altar shall be cut off
2. *To cut off,* גּוּז *guz.*
Hab. 3. 17 the flock shall be cut off from the fold
3. *To cut down, off,* גָּזַר *gazar.*
2 Ch. 26. 21 he was cut off from the house of the LORD
Psa. 88. 5 and they are cut off from thy hand
4. *To be cut down, off,* גָּזַר *gazar,* 2.
Psa. 90. 10 for it is soon cut off, and we fly away
Isa. 53. 8 he was cut off out of the land of the living
Lam. 3. 54 flowed over mine head..I am cut off
Eze. 37. 11 hope is lost: we are cut off for our parts
5. *To be cut off,* גָּרַז *garaz,* 2.
Psa. 31. 22 I am cut off from before thine eyes
6. *To be silent, cut off,* דָּמָה *damah,* 2.
Jer. 47. 5 Ashkelon is cut off (with) the remnant of
Hos. 10. 7 her king is cut off as the foam upon the
10. 15 in a morning shall the king..be cut off
Obad. 5 if robbers by night, how art thou cut off
7. *To be silent, cut off,* דָּמַם *damam,* 2.
Jer. 49. 26 the men of war shall be cut off in that
50. 30 her men of war shall be cut off in that
51. 6 be not cut off in her iniquity; for this (is)
8. *To be hid,* כָּחַד *kachad,* 2.
Exod. 9. 15 and thou shalt be cut off from the earth
Job 4. 7 or where were the righteous cut off?

Zech 11. 9 that is to be cut off, let it be cut off
11. 16 shall not visit those that be cut off

9. *To be cut down, off, asunder,* כָּרַת *karath,* 2.
Gen. 9. 11 neither shall all flesh be cut off any
17. 14 that soul shall be cut off from his people
Exod12. 15 that soul shall be cut off from Israel
12. 19 even that soul shall be cut off from the
30. 33, 38 Whosoever compoundeth..be cut off
31. 14 that soul shall be cut off from among
Lev. 7. 20, 21, 27 even that soul shall be cut off from
7. 25 the soul that eateth (it) shall be cut off
17. 4, 9 that man shall be cut off from among
17. 14 whosoever eateth it shall be cut off
18. 29 souls that commit (them) shall be cut off
19. 8 that soul shall be cut off from among his
20. 17 they shall be cut off in the sight of their
20. 18 both of them shall be cut off from among
22. 3 that soul shall be cut off from my pres.
23. 29 he shall be cut off from among his people
Num. 9. 13 the same soul shall be cut off from among
15. 30 that soul shall be cut off from among his
15. 31 that soul shall utterly be cut off
19. 13 that soul shall be cut off from Israel
19. 20 that soul shall be cut off from among the
Josh. 3. 13 the waters of Jordan shall be cut off
3. 16 those that came down..were cut off
4. 7 That the waters of Jordan were cut off
4. 7 the waters of Jordan were cut off
Ruth 4. 10 that the name of the dead be not cut off
Psa. 37. 9 evil doers shall be cut off: but those that
37. 22 (that be) cursed of him shall be cut off
37. 28 the seed of the wicked shall be cut off
37. 34 when the wicked are cut off, thou shalt
37. 38 the end of the wicked shall be cut off
Prov. 2. 22 the wicked shall be cut off from the earth
23. 18 and thine expectation shall not be cut off
24. 14 and thy expectation shall not be cut off
Isa 11. 13 the adversaries of Judah shall be cut off
22. 25 burden that (was) upon it shall be cut off
29. 20 all that watch for iniquity are cut off
48. 19 his name should not have been cut off nor
55. 13 everlasting sign (that) shall not be cut off
56. 5 everlasting name, that shall not be cut off
Jer. 7. 28 truth is..cut off from their mouth
Dan. 9. 26 shall Messiah be cut off, but not for
Hos. 8. 4 made them idols, that they may be cut off
Joel. 1. 5 for it is cut off from your mouth
1. 16 Is not the meat cut off before our eyes
Obad. 9 every one..may be cut off by slaughter
10 and thou shalt be cut off for ever
Mic. 5. 9 and all thine enemies shall be cut off
Nah. 1. 15 wicked shall no more pass..he is..cut off
Zeph. 1. 11 all they that bear silver are cut off
3. 7 so their dwelling should not be cut off
Zech. 9. 10 and the battle bow shall be cut off
13. 8 two parts therein shall be cut off (and)
14. 2 residue of the people shall not be cut off

10. *To be cut down, off, asunder,* כָּרַת *karath,* 6.
Joel 1. 9 the drink offering is cut off from

11. *To be cut off,* מָלַל *malal,* 2.
Job 18. 16 and above shall his branch be cut off
24 24 cut off as the tops of the ears of corn

12. *To be free, acquitted,* נָקָה *naqah,* 2.
Zech. 5. 3 every one that stealeth shall be cut off
5. 3 every one that sweareth shall be cut off

13. *To go up,* עָלָה *alah.*
Job 36. 20 when people are cut off in their place

14. *To be cut off, destroyed, silenced,* צָמַת *tsamath,* 2.
Job 23. 17 I was not cut off before the darkness

15. *To be cut off,* קוֹט *qot.*
Job 8. 14 Whose hope shall be cut off, and whose

CUT out, to —

1. *To cleave, rend, rip up,* בָּקַע *baqa,* 3.
Job 28. 10 He cutteth out rivers among the rocks

2. *To rend away, cut out,* קָרַע *qara.*
Jer. 22. 14 will build..and cutteth him out windows

3. *To cut off, or out,* ἐκκόπτω *ekkoptō.*
Rom 11. 24 thou wert cut out of the olive tree

CUT out, to be —

To be cut off, גָּזַר *gezar,* 2.
Dan. 2. 34 Thou sawest till that a stone was cut out
2. 45 the stone was cut out of the mountain

CUT selves, to —

To cut self, גָּדַד *gadad,* 7a.
Deut14. 1 Ye shall not cut yourselves, nor make any
1 Ki. 18 28 they cried aloud, and cut themselves
Jer. 16. 6 nor cut themselves, nor make themselves
41. 5 clothes rent, and having cut themselves
47. 5 how long wilt thou cut thyself?

CUT short, to —

1. *To end,* קָצָה *qatsah,* 3.
2 Ki. 10. 32 the LORD began to cut Israel short

2. *To cut together,* συντέμνω *suntemnō.*
Rom. 9. 28 [he will finish the work, and cut (it) short]

CUT up, to —

To crop, pluck, קָטַף *qataph.*
Job 30. 4 Who cut up mallows by the bushes, and

CUT up, to be —

To cut down, כָּסַח *kasach.*
Isa. 33. 12 (as) thorns cut up shall they be burned in

CU-THAH, or CUTH, כּוּתָה, כּוּת.
Josephus fixes the residence of the Cutheans in the interior of Media and Persia. There was a district and town between the Tigris and the Euphrates, after which the 4th canal of Xenophon was named. The site of the town has been identified with the ruins of *Towibah*, adjacent to Babylon; the canal may be the river to which Josephus refers. The other locality corresponds with the statement that the Cutheans came from the interior of Persia and Media. They have been identified with the *Cossæi*, a warlike and lawless tribe that occupied the mountain ranges dividing those two countries. Alexander the Great subdued them wholly.
2 Ki. 17. 24 king of Assyria brought (men)..from C.
17. 30 and the men of C. made Nergal, and the

CUTTING —

1. *A cutting, furrow,* גְּדוּד *gedud.*
Jer. 48. 37 upon all the hands (shall be) cuttings, and

2. *Engraving, carving,* חֲרֹשֶׁת *charosheth.*
Exod31. 5 in cutting of stones, to set (them), and in
35. 33 in the cutting of stones, to set (them)

CUTTING off —

1. *Silence, cutting off,* דְּמִי *demi.*
Isa. 38. 10 I said in the cutting off of my days, I

2. *To cut off, end,* קָצָה *qatsah.*
Hab. 2. 10 Thou hast consulted shame..by cutting o.

CUTTINGS —

1. *A cutting, incision,* שֶׂרֶט *seret.*
Lev. 19. 28 Ye shall not make any cuttings in your

2. *A cutting, incision,* שָׂרֶטֶת *sareteth.*
Lev. 21. 5 They shall not..make any cuttings in

CYMBAL —

1. *Pair of cymbals,* מְצִלְתַּיִם *metsiltayim.*
1 Ch. 13. 8 with timbrels, and with cymbals, and with
15. 16 psalteries and harps and cymbals, soun.
15. 19 (appointed) to sound with cymbals of
15. 28 with trumpets, and with cymbals, making
16. 5 but Asaph made a sound with cymbals
16. 42 with trumpets and cymbals for those
25. 1 with psalteries, and with cymbals
25. 6 with cymbals, psalteries, and harps, for
2 Ch. 5. 12 arrayed in white linen, having cymbals
5. 13 lifted up (their) voice with the..cymbals
29. 25 he set the Levites..with cymbals
Ezra 3. 10 Levites..with cymbals, to praise the LORD
Neh. 12. 27 with singing, (with) cymbals, psalteries

2. *Cymbals,* צֶלְצְלִים *tseltselim.*
2 Sa. 6. 5 timbrels, and on cornets, and on cymbals
Psa. 150. 5 Praise him upon the loud cymbals
150. 5 praise him upon the high sounding cym.

3. *Cymbal,* κύμβαλον *kumbalon.*
1 Co. 13. 1 I am become (as)..a tinkling cymbal

CYPRESS, —

Cypress, holm, oak, ilex, תִּרְזָה *tirzah.*
Isa. 44. 14 He..taketh the cypress and the oak, which

CY'-PRUS, Κύπρος, Κύπριος.
An island of the E. coast of Cilicia in the Mediterranean. It was closely connected with Phœnicia, and seems to be referred to in Eze. 27. 6. It was colonised by the Phœnicians at a very early period, and passed under the supremacy of the Syrians, the Greeks, the Egyptians, and the Persians. On the death of Alexander the Great it was incorporated with Egypt. It was made a Roman province, B.C. 58. Cæsar gave it to Arsinoë and Ptolemy, the sister and brother of Cleopatra, B.C. 47. It was made an imperial province B.C. 27, but was given up to the senate B.C. 22. Paul and Barnabas visited the island A.D. 44.
Acts 4. 36 Barnabas..a Levite..of the country of C.
11. 19 Stephen travelled as far as Phenice, and C.
11. 20 some of them were men of C. and Cyrene
13. 4 and from thence they sailed to C.
15. 39 Barnabas took Mark, and sailed unto C.
21. 3 Now when we had discovered C., we left
21. 16 and brought with them one Mnason of C.
27. 4 from thence, we sailed under C.

CY-RE'-NE, Κυρήνη.
A city of Libya in Cyrenaica, N. Africa. It was the chief of the five cities called Pentapolitana. The projecting portion of the coast called *Tripoli* corresponds to the Cyrenaica of classical writers; though on the African coast Cyrene was a Greek city, in which Jews settled in large numbers. Under the Romans it was connected with Crete. The Greek colonisation began B.C 631.
Matt 27. 32 as they came out, they found a man of C.
Acts 2. 10 and in the parts of Libya about C., and
11. 20 some of them were men of Cyprus and C.
13. 1 Niger, and Lucius of C., and Manaen

CY-RE-NI-AN, Κυρηναῖος.
A native or inhabitant of Cyrene.
Mark15. 21 And they compel one Simon a C.
Luke23. 26 they laid hold upon one Simon, a C.
Acts 6. 9 which is called (the synagogue) of the..C.

CY-RE-NI-US, Κυρήνιος.
Governor of Syria A.D. 6. His full name was Publius Sulpicius *Quirinus*. B.C. 12 he was made consul. His special mission to Syria was to make the census, both there and in Judæa. Luke apparently makes the census at the birth of Christ, when Syria was under the governorship of Sentius Saturninus; but perhaps the reference is to the conclusion of the census, not its beginning.
Luke 2. 2 this taxing was..made when C. was gov.

CY'-RUS, כּוֹרֶשׁ *sun, throne.*
The founder of the Persian empire, who conquered Babylon, and assisted the Jews, B.C. 536.
2 Ch. 36. 22 in the first year of C...the spirit of
36. 23 Thus saith C. king of Persia, All the
Ezra 1. 1 in the first year of C. king of Persia
1. 1 the LORD stirred up the spirit of C. king
1. 2 Thus saith C. king of Persia, The LORD
1. 7 C. the king brought forth the vessels
1. 8 Even those did C. king of Persia bring
3. 7 the grant..they had of C. king of Persia
4. 3 C. the king of Persia hath commanded us
4. 5 all the days of C. king of Persia, even
5. 13 in the first year of C. the king of Babylon
5. 13 king C. made a decree to build
5. 14 those did C. the king take out of the
5. 17 a decree was made of C. the king to build
6. 3 In the first year of C. the king
6. 3 C...made a decree (concerning) the house
6. 14 according to the commandment of C.
Isa. 44. 28 That saith of C., (He is) my shepherd
45. 1 Thus saith the LORD to his anointed, to C.
Dan. 1. 21 continued..unto the first year of king C.
6. 28 Daniel prospered..reign of C. the Persian
10. 1 In the third year of C. king of Persia a

D

DA-BA'-REH, דָּבְרַת *pasture.*
A Levitical city of Issachar, on the border Now *Duburieh*. [*See* Daberath.]
Josh 21. 28 of the tribe of Issachar..D. with her sub.

DAB-BA'-SHETH, דַּבֶּשֶׁת *height.*
A border city of Zebulon and Issachar.
Josh 19. 11 And their border..reached to D, and

DA-BE'-RATH, דָּבְרַת *pasture.*
See *Dabareh*, which is erroneously given for Daberath.
Josh 19. 12 and then goeth out to D., and goeth up
1 Ch. 6. 72 of the tribe of Issachar..D with her sub.

DAGGER —

Destroying weapon, חֶרֶב *chereb.*
Judg. 3. 16 Ehud made him a dagger which had two
3. 21 took the dagger from his right thigh, and
3. 22 he could not draw the dagger out of his

DA'-GON, דָּגוֹן *fish.*
The national god of the Philistines, whose most famous temples were at Gaza and Ashdod. Its form had the face and hands of a man, and the tail of a fish.
Judg16. 23 to offer a great sacrifice unto D. their god
1 Sa. 5. 2 into the house of D., and set it by D.
5. 3 D. (was) fallen upon his face to the earth
5. 3 they took D., and set him in his place
5. 4 D. (was) fallen upon his face to the ground
5. 4 head of D. and both..his hands (were) cut
5. 4 only (the stump of) D. was left to him
5. 5 Therefore neither the priests of D.
5. 5 nor any that come into D.'s house
5. 5 tread on the threshold of D...unto this
5. 7 for his hand is sore..upon D. our god
1 Ch. 10. 10 fastened his head in the temple of D

DAILY —

1. *Day by day,* יוֹם בְּיוֹם *yom be-yom.*
Exod. 5. 13 Fulfil your works, (your) daily tasks, as
5. 19 (ought) from your bricks of your daily task
16. 5 be twice as much as they gather daily
Num28. 24 After this manner ye shall offer daily
Judg16. 16 when she pressed him daily with her
2 Ki. 25. 30 a daily rate for every day, all the days
2 Ch. 31. 16 unto every one..his daily portion for
Ezra 3. 4 (offered) the daily burnt offerings by num.
Esth. 3. 4 when they spake daily unto him, and he
Psa. 42. 10 they say daily unto me, Where (is) thy God?
56. 1 he fighting daily oppresseth me
56. 2 Mine enemies would daily swallow (me) up
61. 8 that I may daily perform my vows
68. 19 (who) daily loadeth us (with benefits)
72. 15 he shall live..daily shall he be praised
74. 22 the foolish man reproacheth thee daily
86. 3 Be merciful..for I cry unto thee daily
88. 9 I have called daily upon thee, I have
88. 17 They came round about me daily like
Prov. 8. 30 I was daily (his) delight, rejoicing always
8. 34 the man that heareth me, watching daily
Isa. 58. 2 they seek me daily, and delight to know
Jer. 7. 25 daily rising up early and sending (them)
20. 7 I am in derision daily, every one mocketh
20. 8 a reproach unto me, and a derision, daily
Eze. 45. 23 seven rams without blemish daily the
45. 23 a kid of the goats daily (for) a sin offering
46. 13 Thou shalt daily prepare a burnt offering
Dan. 1. 5 the king appointed them a daily provision
Hos. 12. 1 he daily increaseth lies and desolation

2. *Daily, by day,* יוֹמָם *yomam.*
Psa. 13. 2 (having) sorrow in my heart daily
Eze. 30. 16 and Noph (shall have) distresses daily

3. *Continual,* תָּמִיד *tamid.*
Num. 4. 16 the daily meat offering, and the anoint
29. 6 the daily burnt offering, and his meat

Dan. 8. 11 by him the daily (sacrifice) was taken
8. 12 was given (him) against the daily (sacrifice)
8. 13 the vision (concerning) the daily (sacri.)
11. 31 shall take away the daily (sacrifice), and
12. 11 from the time (that) the daily (sacrifice)

4. *For one day*, לְיוֹם אֶחָד *le-yom echad.*
Neh. 5. 18 (that) which was prepared (for me) daily

5. *Sufficient, appointed*, ἐπιούσιος *epiousios.*
Matt. 6. 11 Give us this day our daily bread
Luke 11. 3 Give us day by day our daily bread

6. *Daily, for the day*, ἐφήμερος *ephēmeros.*
Jas. 2. 15 If a brother..be..destitute of daily food

7. *Every day, daily*, καθημερινός *kathēmerinos.*
Acts 6. 1 were neglected in the daily ministration

8. *According to each day*, καθ' ἑκάστην ἡμέραν.
Heb. 3. 13 exhort one another daily, while it is

9. *According to the day, each day*, καθ' ἡμέραν
Matt 26. 55 I sat daily with you teaching in the
Mark 14. 49 I was daily with you in the temple teac.
Luke 9. 23 [let him..take up his cross daily, and fol.]
19. 47 And he taught daily in the temple
22. 53 When I was daily with you in the temple
Acts 2. 46 continuing daily with one accord in the
2. 47 the Lord added to the church daily such
3. 2 whom they laid daily at the gate of the
16. 5 the churches..increased in number daily
17. 11 These..searched the Scriptures daily
19. 9 disputing daily in the school of one
1 Co. 15. 31 I protest by your rejoicing..I die daily
2 Co. 11. 28 that which cometh upon me daily, the
Heb. 7. 27 Who needeth not daily, as those high pr.
10. 11 every priest standeth daily ministering

10. *Through every day*, κατὰ πᾶσαν ἡμέραν.
Acts 17. 17 in the market daily with them that met

11. *Every day*, πᾶσαν ἡμέραν, *pasan hēmeran.*
Acts 5. 42 daily in the temple, and in every house

DAINTIES, dainty (meats) —

1. *Things full of taste*, מַטְעַמּוֹת *matammoth.*
Prov. 23. 3 Be not desirous of his dainties; for they
23. 6 neither desire thou his dainty meats

2. *Pleasant things*, מַנְעַמִּים *manammim.*
Psa. 141. 4 and let me not eat of their dainties

3. *Dainty, delight*, מַעֲדָן *maadan.*
Gen. 49. 20 and he shall yield royal dainties

4. *Object of desire*, תַּאֲוָה *taavah.*
Job 33. 20 abhorreth bread, and his soul dainty meat

5. *Fat, shining*, λιπαρός *liparos.*
Rev. 18. 14 all things which were dainty and goodly

DA-LA'-IAH, דְּלָיָה *Jah is deliverer.*
A descendant of Shechaniah.
In the original this name is the same as that of several persons who are called *Delaiah* in the common version.
1 Ch. 3. 24 Johanan, and D., and Anani, seven

DALE —
Deep place, valley, עֵמֶק *emeq.*
Gen. 14. 17 valley of Shaveh, which (is) the king's dale
2 Sa. 18. 18 a pillar, which (is) in the king's dale

DAL-MA-NU'-THA, Δαλμανουθά.
A village or small town on the W. side of the sea of Galilee, near Magdala, close to the shore, at the south end of the plain of Gennesaret. It is now called *Ain-el-Bârideh.*
Mark 8. 10 he..came into the parts of D.

DAL-MA'-TIA, Δαλματία.
A province on the E. coast of the Adriatic Sea, extending from the Naro in the S. to the Savus in the N. It became a part of (or another name for) the Roman province of Illyricum after the expedition of Tiberius (A.D. 9).
2 Ti. 4. 10 Crescens to Galatia, Titus unto D.

DAL'-PHON, דַּלְפוֹן Persian word; otherwise *dropping.*
The second of the ten sons of Haman, B.C. 510.
Esth. 9. 7 And Parshandatha, and D., and Aspatha

DAM —
Mother, אֵם *em.*
Exod 22. 30 seven days it shall be with his dam
Lev. 22. 27 then it shall be seven days under the dam
Deut 22. 6 the dam sitting upon the young, or upon
22. 6 thou shalt not take the dam with the
22. 7 (But) thou shalt in any wise let the dam

DAMAGE —

1. *Violence, hurt*, חֲבָל *chabal.*
Ezra 4. 22 why should damage grow to the hurt of

2. *Violence*, חָמָס *chamas.*
Prov 26. 6 cutteth off the feet, (and) drinketh damage

3. *Loss*, נֶזֶק *nezeq.*
Esth. 7. 4 could not countervail the king's damage

4. *Damage*, ζημία *zēmia.*
Acts 27. 10 voyage will be with hurt and much dam.

DAMAGE, to have —
To suffer loss, נְזַק *nezaq.*
Dan. 6. 2 and the king should have no damage

DAMAGE, to receive —
To cause loss, ζημιόω *zēmioō.*
2 Co. 7. 9 ye might receive damage by us in nothing

DA-MA'-RIS, Δάμαρις.
A woman in Athens converted by Paul, A.D. 54.
Acts 17. 34 a woman named D., and others with them

DA-MAS-CENES, Δαμασκηνοί, *belonging to Damasc.*
The people of Damascus.
2 Co. 11. 32 the king kept the city of the D. with a gar.

DAM-AS'-CUS, דַּמֶּשֶׂק, דַּרְמֶשֶׂק, דּוּמֶּשֶׂק, Δαμασκός.
The most ancient and important city in Syria. It stands in a plain of great fertility E. of the great chain of Antilibanus, on the edge of the desert. The modern *Barada* (the *Amana* of Scripture) waters this plain, which is 30 miles in diameter and nearly circular. According to Josephus Damascus was founded by Uz, son of Aram and grandson of Shem. It is apparently first mentioned in the time of Abraham, B.C. 1912. It was taken by David B.C. 1040 and was the capital of Syria during the reign of Ben-hadad, B.C. 930. Jeroboam restored it to Israel B.C. 822, but Tiglath-Pileser, king of Assyria, took it B.C. 740, and carried its inhabitants captive to Kir. It afterwards remained subject to the Assyrians and Persians till B.C. 333, when it was taken by Parmenio, the general of Alexander the Great. Pompey effected its capture B.C. 64. Paul commenced his ministry at Damascus A.D. 33.
Gen. 14. 15 Hobah, which (is) on the left hand of D.
15. 2 steward of my house (is) this Eliezer of D.?
2 Sa. 8. 5 And when the Syrians of D. came to suc.
8. 6 Then David put garrisons in Syria of D.
1 Ki. 11. 24 he gathered men..and they went to D.
11. 24 dwelt therein, and reigned in D.
15. 18 Hezion, king of Syria, that dwelt at D.
19. 15 return on thy way to the wilderness of D.
20. 34 thou shalt make streets for thee in D.
2 Ki. 5. 12 (Are) not Abana and Pharpar, rivers of D.
8. 7 And Elisha came to D.; and..the king
8. 9 even of every good thing of D., forty ca.
14. 28 how he warred, and how he recovered D.
16. 9 the king of Assyria went up against D.
16. 10 And king Ahaz went to D. to meet
16. 10 and saw an altar that (was) at D.
16. 11 all that king Ahaz had sent from D.
16. 11 made (it) against king Ahaz came from D.
16. 12 when the king was come from D.
1 Ch. 18. 5 Syrians of D. came to help Hadarezer
18. 6 David put (garrisons) in Syria-d.
2 Ch. 16. 2 Ben-hadad king of Syria, that dwelt at D.
24. 23 and sent all the spoil..unto the king of D.
28. 5 and they..brought them to D.
28. 23 For he sacrificed unto the gods of D.
Song 7. 4 the tower..which looketh toward D.
Isa. 7. 8 For the head of Syria (is) D.
7. 8 and the head of D. (is) Rezin
8. 4 the riches of D...shall be taken away
10. 9 (is) not Samaria as D.?
17. 1 The burden of D. Behold D. is taken away
17. 3 Ephraim, and the kingdom from D., and
Jer. 49. 23 Concerning D. Hamath is confounded
49. 24 D. is waxed feeble, (and) turneth..to flee
49. 27 I will kindle a fire in the wall of D.
Eze. 27. 18 D. (was) thy merchant in the..wares of
47. 16 between the border of D. and the border
47. 17 the border..shall be..the border of D.
47. 18 the east side ye shall measure from..D.
48. 1 the border of D. northward, to the coast
Amos 1. 3 For three transgressions of D., and for four
1. 5 I will break also the bar of D., and cut off
3. 12 corner of a bed, and in D. (in) a couch
5. 27 to go into captivity beyond D., saith the
Zech. 9. 1 and D. (shall be) the rest thereof
Acts 9. 2 And desired of him letters to D.
9. 3 as he journeyed, he came near D.
9. 8 led him..and brought (him) into D.
9. 10 there was a certain disciple at D.
9. 19 Then was Saul certain days..at D.
9. 22 confounded the Jews which dwelt at D.
9. 27 and how he had preached boldly at D.
22. 5 whom..I received letters..and went to D.
22. 6 and was come nigh unto D. about noon
22. 10 the Lord said..Arise, and go into D.
22. 11 led by the hand..I came into D.
26. 12 Whereupon, as I went to D. with author.
26. 20 showed first unto them of D., and at Jer.
2 Co. 11. 32 In D. the governor under Aretas..kept
Gal. 1. 17 I went..and returned again unto D.

DAMNABLE —
Destruction, loosing away, ἀπώλεια *apōleia.*
2 Pe. 2. 1 privily shall bring in damnable heresies

DAMNATION —

1. *Destruction, loosing away*, ἀπώλεια *apōleia.*
2 Pe. 2. 3 and their damnation slumbereth not

2. *Judgment, condemnation*, κρίμα *krima.*
Matt. 23. 14 ye shall receive the greater damnation
Mark 12. 40 these shall receive greater damnation
Luke 20. 47 the same shall receive greater damnation
Rom. 3. 8 Let us do evil..whose damnation is just
13. 2 shall receive to themselves damnation
1 Co. 11. 29 eateth and drinketh damnation to him.
1 Ti. 5. 12 Having damnation, because they have

3. *Judgment*, κρίσις *krisis.*
Matt. 23. 33 how can ye escape the damnation of
Mark 3. 29 but is in danger of eternal [damnation]
John 5. 29 unto the resurrection of damnation

DAMNED, to be —

1. *To judge one down*, κατακρίνω *katakrinō.*
Mark 16. 16 [but he that believeth not shall be dam.]
Rom. 14. 23 he that doubteth is damned if he eat

2. *To judge*, κρίνω *krinō.*
2 Th. 2. 12 That they all might be damned who beli.

DAMSEL —

1. *Lass, girl*, יַלְדָּה *yaldah.*
Gen. 34. 4 saying, Get me this damsel to wife

2. *Damsel, young woman*, נַעֲרָה *naarah.*
Gen. 24. 14 that the damsel to whom I shall say, Let
24. 16 the damsel (was) very fair to look upon
24. 28 the damsel ran, and told (them of) her
24. 55 Let the damsel abide with us (a few) days
24. 57 We will call the damsel, and enquire at
24. 61 Rebekah arose, and her damsels, and
34. 3 his soul clave..and he loved the damsel
34. 3 and spake kindly unto the damsel
34. 12 but give me the damsel to wife
Deut 22. 15 Then shall the father of the damsel, and
22. 15 take..(the tokens of) the damsel's virgini.
22. 16 the damsel's father shall say unto the
22. 19 give (them) unto the father of the dam.
22. 20 virginity be not found for the damsel
22. 21 they shall bring out the damsel to the
22. 23 If a damsel (that is) a virgin be betrothed
22. 24 the damsel, because she cried not, (being
22. 25 if a man find a betrothed damsel in the
22. 26 But unto the damsel thou shalt do noth.
22. 26 (there is) in the damsel no sin (worthy) of
22. 27 the betrothed damsel cried, and (there
22. 28 If a man find a damsel (that is) a virgin
22. 29 shall give unto the damsel's father fifty
Judg. 19. 3 when the father of the damsel saw him
19. 4 the damsel's father, retained him
19. 5 damsel's father said unto his son in law
19. 6 the damsel's father had said unto the man
19. 8 the damsel's father said, Comfort thine
19. 9 the damsel's father, said unto him, Behold
Ruth 2. 5 Then said Boaz..Whose damsel (is) this?
2. 6 It (is) the Moabitish damsel that came
1 Sa. 25. 42 with five damsels of hers that went after
1 Ki. 1. 3 they sought for a fair damsel throughout
1. 4 the damsel (was) very fair, and cherished

3. *Young woman, virgin*, עַלְמָה *almah.*
Psa. 68. 25 among (them were) the damsels playing

4. *Womb*, רַחַם *racham.*
Judg. 5. 30 to every man a damsel (or) two; to Sisera

5. *A little girl*, κοράσιον *korasion.*
Matt 14. 11 his head was..given to the damsel
Mark 5. 41 and said..Damsel, I say unto thee, arise
5. 42 straightway the damsel arose, and
6. 22 the king said unto the damsel, Ask of
6. 28 brought his head..and gave it to the dam.
6. 28 and the damsel gave it to her mother

6. *A young or little child*, παιδίον *paidion.*
Mark 5. 39 the damsel is not dead, but sleepeth
5. 40 the father and the mother of the damsel
5. 40 entereth in where the damsel was lying
5. 41 he took the damsel by the hand, and

7. *A young damsel*, παιδίσκη *paidiskē.*
Matt 26. 69 a damsel came unto him, saying, Thou
John 18. 17 Then saith the damsel that kept the door
Acts 12. 13 a damsel came to hearken, named Rhoda
16. 16 a certain damsel possessed with a spirit

DAN, דָּן *judge.*

1. Fifth son of Jacob, and first of Bilhah, Rachel's maid. Dan was the own brother of Naphtali. B.C. 1747.
Gen. 30. 6 a son: therefore called she his name D.
35. 25 sons of Bilhah, Rachel's handmaid; D.
46. 23 And the sons of D.; Hushim
49. 16 D. shall judge his people, as one of the
49. 17 D. shall be a serpent by the way
Exod. 1. 4 D., and Naphtali, Gad, and Asher
Num 26. 42 These (are) the sons of D. after their fami.
26. 42 These (are) the families of D. after their
Josh. 19. 47 children of D. went up to fight against L.
1 Ch. 2. 2 D., Joseph, and Benjamin, Naphtali

2. The most northern city of Canaan, as seen in the common expression "from Dan even to Beersheba." The name was originally *Laish* or *Leshem* (Josh. 19. 47). The inhabitants lived like the Zidonians, engaged in commerce, and without defence. Hence the Danites easily conquered the place, and named it *Dan*. *Tell-el-Kadi*, its modern name, is the western and smaller of the two sources of the Jordan, 4 miles from Paneas, on the road to Tyre. The long level top of the *Tell* is strewed with ruins, and is probably the site of the town and citadel of Dan. The spring is called *El-Leddân*, and the stream from it *Nahr-ed-dhân.*
Gen. 14. 14 armed his..(servts.) and pursued..unto D.
Deut. 34. 1 LORD showed him..land of Gilead, unto D.
Josh. 19. 47 called Leshem, D., after the name of Dan
Judg 18. 29 called the name..D., after the name of D.
20. 1 the congregation was gathered..from D.
1 Sa. 3. 20 all Israel, from D. even to Beer-sheba
2 Sa. 3. 10 to set up the throne of David..from D.
17. 11 all Israel be..gathered..from D. even to
24. 2 through all the tribes of Israel, from D.
24. 15 there died..from D...to Beer-sheba sev.
1 Ki. 4. 25 from D...to Beer-sheba, all the days of S.
12. 29 set..one in Bethel, and the other..in D.
12. 30 people went (to worship)..(even) unto D.
15. 20 Ben-hadad..sent..and smote Ijon, and D.

2 Ki. 10. 29 departed not from..golden calves..in D.
1 Ch 21. 2 number Israel from Beer-sheba even to D.
2 Ch. 16. 4 and they smote Ijon, and D., and Abel-m.
30. 5 established a decree..Beer-sheba..to D.
Jer. 4. 15 For a voice declareth from D., and publi.
8. 16 snorting of his horses was heard from D.
Eze 27. 19 D ..going to and fro occupied in thy fairs
Amos 8. 14 They that swear..and say, Thy God, O D.

3. The name is used to denote the tribe that sprang from Dan, as well as their territory.

Exod 31. 6 I have given..Aholiab..of the tribe of D.
35. 34 may teach..Aholiab..of the tribe of D.
38. 23 with him (was) Aholiab..of the tribe of D.
Lev 24. 11 daughter of Dibri, of the tribe of D.
Num. 1. 12 Of D ; Ahiezer the son of Ammi-shaddai
1. 38 Of the children of D., by their generations
1. 39 that were numbered..of the tribe of D.
2. 25 The standard of the camp of D. (shall be)
2. 25 the captain of the children of D. (shall be)
2. 31 they that were numbered in..camp of D.
7. 66 Ahiezer..prince of the children of D.
10. 25 the standard of the camp..of D. set for.
13. 12 Of the tribe of D., Ammiel the son of G.
26. 42 These (are) the sons of D. after their fa.
26. 42 These (are) the families of D. after their
34. 22 prince of the tribe of the children of D.
Deut 27. 13 Reuben, Gad, and Asher, Zebulun, D.
33. 22 of D. he said, D. (is) a lion's whelp
Josh. 19. 40 the seventh lot came..for the tribe..of D.
19. 47 the children of D. went..to fight against
19. 47 called Leshem, D., after..Dan their fath.
19. 48 inheritance of..the children of D.
21. 5 and out of the tribe of D., and out of the
21. 23 And out of the tribe of D., Eltekeh
Judg. 1. 34 the Amorites forced the children of D.
5. 17 and why did D. remain in ships?
13. 25 in the camp of D. between Zorah and Esh.
18. 2 the children of D. sent of their family five
18. 16 six hundred men..of the children of D.
18. 22 the men..overtook the children of D.
18. 23 And they cried unto the children of D.
18. 25 And the children of D. said unto him
18. 26 And the children of D. went their way
18. 30 the children of D. set up the graven image
18. 30 his sons were priests to the tribe of D.
1 Ch. 27. 22 Of D.; Azareel the son of Jeroham
2 Ch. 2. 14 son of a woman of the daughters of D.
Eze. 48. 1 sides east (and) west; a (portion for) D.
48. 2 And by the border of D., from the east
48. 32 one gate of Benjamin, one gate of D.

The following localities were in the territory of Dan:—Ajalon, Baalath, Bene-barak, Dan, Elon, Eltekeh, Eshtaol, Gath-rimmon, Gibbethon, Ir-shemesh, Japho, Jethlah, Laish, Leshem, Me-jarkon, Rakkon, Shaalabin, Timnah, Zorah, &c.

DANCE —

Dance, dancing, chorus, מָחוֹל *machol.*

Psa. 149. 3 Let them praise his name in the dance
150. 4 Praise him with the timbrel and dance
Jer. 31. 4 in the dances of them that make merry
31. 13 shall the virgin rejoice in the dance
Lam. 5. 15 our dance is turned into mourning

DANCE, to —

1. *To keep festival,* חָגַג *chagag.*
1 Sa. 30. 16 (they were)..drinking, and dancing

2. *To dance, turn, twist,* חוּל *chul.*
Judg 21. 21 daughters of Shiloh come out to dance

3. *To dance, turn, twist,* חוּל *chul, 3a.*
Judg 21. 23 of them that danced, whom they caught

4. *To dance, move round,* כָּרַר *karar, 3a.*
2 Sa. 6. 14 David danced before the LORD with all (his)

5. *To dance, skip,* רָקַד *raqad.*
Eccl. 3. 4 a time to mourn, and a time to dance

6. *To dance, skip,* רָקַד *raqad,* 3.
1 Ch. 15. 29 saw king David dancing and playing
Job 21. 11 They send forth..and their children dance
Isa 13. 21 dwell there, and satyrs shall dance there

7. *To lift up (the feet), dance,* ὀρχέομαι *orcheomai.*
Matt 11. 17 piped unto you, and ye have not danced
14. 6 the daughter of Herodias danced before
Mark 6. 22 when the daughter of..Herodias..danced
Luke 7. 32 piped unto you, and ye have not danced

DANCES —

Dance, dancing, chorus, מְחוֹלָה *mecholah.*

Exod 15. 20 after her with timbrels and with dances
Judg 11. 34 to meet him with timbrels and..dances
21. 21 the daughters..come out to dance in dan.
1 Sa 21. 11 sing one to another of him in dances
29. 5 they sang one to another in dances, saying

DANCING —

1. *To dance, move round,* כָּרַר *karar, 3a.*
2 Sa 6. 16 saw king David leaping and dancing bef.

2. *Dance, dancing, chorus,* מָחוֹל *machol.*
Psa. 30. 11 turned for me my mourning into dancing

3. *Dance, dancing, chorus,* מְחוֹלָה *mecholah.*
Exod 32. 19 that he saw the calf, and the dancing
1 Sa. 18. 6 singing and dancing, to meet king Saul

4. *A chorus, company of dancers,* χορός *choros.*
Luke 15. 25 as he came..he heard music and dancing

DANDLED, to be —

To play with, delight in, dandle, שָׁעַע *shaa, 4b.*

Isa. 66. 12 be borne upon (her) sides, and be dandled

DANGER, to be in —

To incur danger, κινδυνεύω *kinduneuō.*

Acts 19. 27 craft is in danger to be set at nought
19. 40 we are in danger to be called in question

DANGER of, in —

Held in, liable to, ἔνοχος *enochos.*

Matt. 5. 21, 22 shall be in danger of the judgment
5. 22 shall be in danger of the council
5. 22 shall say, Thou fool! shall be in danger of
Mark 3. 29 but is in danger of eternal damnation

DANGEROUS —

Insecure, perilous, ἐπισφαλής *episphalēs.*

Acts 27. 9 when sailing was now dangerous, because

DA-NI'-EL, דָּנִיֵּאל, Δανιήλ *God is judge.*

1. Second son of David, called also Chileol, B.C. 1050.
1 Ch. 3. 1 the second, D., of Abigail the Carmelitess

2. A descendant of Ithamar who came up with Ezra, and sealed the covenant, B.C. 457.
Ezra 8. 2 of the sons of Ithamar; D.: of the sons of
Neh. 10. 6 D., Ginnethon, Baruch

3. The fourth of the so-called *greater* prophets. He appears to have been of royal or noble descent, and was taken to Babylon in the third year of Jehoiakim (B.C. 604), and trained with three companions for the king's service. The parallel between his character and that of Joseph is striking. At the accession of Darius he was made the first of three presidents, and in the third year of Cyrus he saw his last recorded vision on the banks of the Tigris (B.C. 530).

Eze. 14. 14 these three men, Noah, D., and Job, were
14. 20 Though Noah, D., and Job, (were) in it
28. 3 Behold, thou (art) wiser than D.
Dan. 1. 6 these were, of the children of Judah, D.
1. 7 he gave unto D. (the name) of Belteshazzar
1. 8 D. purposed..that he would not defile
1. 9 Now God had brought D. into favour
1. 10 And the prince of the eunuchs said unto D.
1. 11 Then said D. to Melzar, whom
1. 11 the prince of the eunuchs had set over D.
1. 17 and D. had understanding in all visions
1. 19 among them all was found none like D.
1. 21 D. continued (even) unto the first year of
2. 13 they sought D. and his fellows to be slain
2. 14 Then D. answered with counsel and wis.
2. 15 Then Arioch made the thing known to D
2. 16 Then D. went in, and desired of the king
2. 17 Daniel went to his house, and made the
2. 18 that D. and his fellows should not perish
2. 19 unto D. in a night vision. Then D.
2. 20 D. answered.. Blessed be the name of G.
2. 24 D. went in unto Arioch, whom the king
2. 25 Then Arioch brought in D. before the
2. 26 The king answered and said to D.
2. 27 D. answered in the presence of the king
2. 46 fell upon his face, and worshipped D.
2. 47 The king answered unto D., and said
2. 48 Then the king made D. a great man
2. 49 Then D. requested of the king, and he set
2. 49 but D (sat) in the gate of the king
4. 8 But at the last D. came in before me
4. 19 Then D...was astonied for one hour
5. 12 spirit, and knowledge..were found in..D.
5. 12 let D be called, and he will show the int.
5. 13 Then was D. brought in before the king
5. 13 the king..said unto D, (Art) thou that D.
5. 17 Then D. answered and said before the ki.
5. 29 and they clothed D. with scarlet
6. 2 over these three presidents, of whom D.
6. 3 D. was preferred above the presidents and
6. 4 princes sought to find occasion against D.
6. 5 shall not find any occasion against this D.
6. 10 when D knew that the writing was sign.
6. 11 these men assembled, and found D pray.
6. 13 That D..regardeth not thee, O king
6. 14 the king..set (his) heart on D. to deliver
6. 16 the king commanded, and they brought D.
6. 16 the king..said unto D., Thy God..will
6. 17 purpose might not be changed concern. D.
6. 20 he cried with a lamentable voice unto D
6. 20 the king spake and said to D., O D., ser.
6. 21 said D unto the king, O king, live for ever
6. 23 commanded that they should take D up
6. 23 So D was taken up out of the den
6. 24 brought those men which had accused D.
6. 26 tremble and fear before the God of D.
6. 27 who hath delivered D from the power of
6. 28 this D. prospered in the reign of Darius
7. 1 In the first year of Belshazzar..D. had a
7. 2 D ..said, I saw in my vision by night
7. 15 I D. was grieved in my spirit
7. 28 As for me D, my cogitations much
8. 1 a vision appeared unto me..me D.
8. 15 when I, (even) I D, had seen the vision
8. 27 And I D. fainted, and was sick (certain)
9. 2 I D. understood by books the number of
9. 22 O D., I am..come forth to give thee skill
10. 1 a thing was revealed unto D.
10. 2 I D. was mourning three full weeks
10. 7 And I D. alone saw the vision
10. 11 O D...understand the words..I speak
10. 12 Then said he unto me, Fear not, D.
12. 4 But thou, O D., shut up the words
Dan. 12. 5 I D. looked, and..there stood other two
12. 9 And he said, Go thy way, D.: for the
Matt 24. 15 shall see the..desolation, spoken of by D.
Mark 13. 14 [shall see the..desolation, spoken of by D.]

DANITES, הַדָּנִי *had-dani, the Danite.*

Patronymic of the tribe of Dan.
Judg 13. 2 man of Zorah, of the family of the D.
18. 1 the tribe of the D. sought them an inher.
18. 11 there went..of the family of the D.
1 Ch. 12. 35 of the D...twenty..eight thousand..six

DAN JA'-AN, דָּן יַעַן *Dan playing the pipe.*

A place between Gilead and Zidon, somewhere near Dan (Laish) at the sources of the Jordan. It may mean "Dan in the wood," which accords with *Tel-el Kadi*, and the surrounding country.
2 Sa 24. 6 they came to D., and about to Zidon

DAN'-NAH, דַּנָּה *low.*

A city of Judah near Kirjath-Sannah.
Josh 15. 49 And D., and Kirjath-sannah, which (is)

DA'-RA, דָּרַע *bearer, holder.*

Son of Zerah son of Judah by Tamar. Some identify him with Darda(?).
1 Ch. 2. 6 of Zerah; Zimri, and Ethan..and D.

DAR'-DA, דַּרְדַּע.

A wise man not later than Solomon, and considered by some identical with *Dara*.
1 Ki. 4. 31 wiser than all men; than Ethan..and D.

DARE, (durst), to—

To dare, have daring, τολμάω *tolmaō.*

Matt 22. 46 neither durst any (man) from that day fo.
Mark 12. 34 no man after that durst ask him (any ques.)
Luke 20. 40 they durst not ask him any (question at
John 21. 12 none of the disciples durst ask him, Who
Acts 5. 13 of the rest durst no man join himself to
7. 32 Then Moses trembled, and durst not beh.
Rom. 5. 7 for a good man some even would dare to
15. 18 I will not dare to speak of any of those
1 Co. 6. 1 Dare any of you, having a matter against
2 Co. 10. 12 we dare not make ourselves of the num
Jude 9 durst not bring against him a railing

DA-RI'-US, דָּרְיָוֶשׁ *(etymology uncertain).*

1. A king of Persia, *i.e.*, Darius Hystaspes, B.C. 521.
Ezra 4. 5 until the reign of D. king of Persia
4. 24 it ceased unto the second year..of D.
5. 5 to cease, till the matter came to D.
5. 6 The copy of the letter..sent unto D.
5. 7 Unto D. the king, all peace
6. 1 Then D. the king made a decree
6. 12 I D. have made a decree; let it be done
6. 13 according to that which D..had sent
6. 14 they builded..according to the com.of..D.
6. 15 this house was finished..sixth year..of D.
Hag. 1. 1 In the second year of D. the king
1. 15 in the second year of D. the king
2. 10 in the second year of D., came the word
Zech. 1. 1 in the second year of D., came the word
1. 7 in the second year of D, came the word
7. 1 it came to pass in the fourth year of..D.

2. Another king, *i.e.*, Darius Nothus, B.C. 423.
Neh. 12. 22 also the priests, to the reign of D.

3. Darius the Mede, "the son of Ahasuerus of the seed of the Medes," who succeeded to the kingdom of Babylon on the death of Belshazzar, and was then 62 years of age. He was Cyaxares, and son and successor of Astyages the king of Media, B.C. 538.
Dan. 5. 31 And D. the Median took the kingdom
6. 1 It pleased D. to set over the kingdom
6. 6 said thus unto him, King D..live for ever
6. 9 king D. signed the writing and the decree
6. 25 Then king D. wrote unto all people
6. 28 So this Daniel prospered in the reign of D.
9. 1 In the first year of D. the son of Ahasuerus
11. 1 Also I, in the first year of D the Mede

DARK —

1. *Thick darkness, gloominess,* אֲפֵלָה *aphelah.*
Prov. 7. 9 the evening, in the black and dark night

2. *Darkness (of night),* חֹשֶׁךְ *choshek.*
Josh. 2. 5 when it was dark, that the men went out
Job 12. 25 They grope in the dark without light, and
24. 16 In the dark they dig through houses
Psa. 35. 6 Let their way be dark and slippery: and
88. 12 Shall thy wonders be known in the dark?
Isa. 45. 19 in secret, in a dark place of the earth
Eze. 8. 12 the house of Israel do in the dark

3. *Darkness,* חֶשְׁכָה *cheshkah.*
Psa. 18. 11 pavilion round about him (were) dark

4. *Darkness,* חֲשֵׁכָה *choshkah.*
Mic. 3. 6 it shall be dark unto you, that ye shall

5. *Darkness, collection, binding,* חַשְׁרָה *chashrah.*
2 Sa. 22. 12 dark waters, (and) thick clouds of the

6. *Dark place,* מַחְשָׁךְ *machshak.*
Isa. 29. 15 their works are in the dark, and they say

7. *Twilight,* נֶשֶׁף *nesheph.*
Jer. 13. 16 before your feet stumble upon the dark m.

8. *Darkness,* עֲלָטָה *alatah.*
Gen. 15. 17 when the sun went down, and it was dark

9. *Thick darkness, secret or high place,* עֲרָפֶל *araphel.*
Job. 22. 13 can he judge through the dark cloud?
Eze. 34. 12 been scattered in the cloudy and dark day

10. *Dense darkness, congelation,* קִפָּאוֹן *qippaon.*
Zech. 14. 6 the light shall not be clear, (nor) dark

11. *Dry, squalid,* αὐχμηρός *auchmēros.*
2 Pe. 1. 19 unto a light that shineth in a dark place

12. *Dark,* σκοτεινός *skoteinos.*
Luke 11. 36 (be) full of light, having no part dark, the

13. *Darkness,* σκοτία *skotia.*
John 6. 17 it was now dark, and Jesus was not come
20. 1 cometh Mary Magdalene..it was yet dark

DARK, to be —

1. *To be or become dark,* חָשַׁךְ *chashak.*
Job 3. 9 the stars of the twilight thereof be dark
18. 6 The light shall be dark in his tabernacle
Mic. 3. 6 and the day shall be dark over them

2. *To be enfolded, black,* קָדַר *qadar.*
Joel 2. 10 the sun and the moon shall be dark, and
Mic. 3. 6 and it shall be dark unto you, that ye

DARK, to begin to be —
To be or become dark, צָלַל *tsalal.*
Neh. 13. 19 the gates of Jerusalem began to be dark

DARK, to make —

1. *To darken, send darkness, hide,* חָשַׁךְ *chashak,* 5.
Psa. 105. 28 He sent darkness, and made it dark; and
Amos 5. 8 and maketh the day dark with night: that

2. *To enfold, blacken, mourn,* קָדַר *qadar,* 5.
Eze. 32. 7 I will..make the stars thereof dark; I
32. 8 bright lights of heaven will I make dark

DARK place —
Dark place, מַחְשָׁךְ *machshak.*
Psa. 74. 20 for the dark places of the earth are full
Lam. 3. 6 He hath set me in dark places, as..dead

DARK saying or sentence, speech —
A knot, acute hidden saying or thing, חִידָה *chidah.*
Num 12. 8 will I speak..not in dark speeches
Psa. 49. 4 I will open my dark saying upon the harp
78. 2 I will utter dark sayings of old
Prov. 1. 6 words of the wise, and their dark sayings
Dan. 8. 23 a king..understanding dark sentences

DARK, darkish, somewhat —
Weak, dim, כֵּהָה *kehah.*
Lev. 13. 6 behold, (if) the plague (be) somewhat dark
13. 21 lower than the skin, but (be) somewhat d.
13. 26 the (other) skin, but (be) somewhat dark
13. 28 spread not..but it (be) somewhat dark
13. 39 (if) the bright spots..(be) darkish white
13. 56 the plague (be) somewhat dark after the

DARK, very —
Very dark, אָפֵל *aphel.*
Amos. 5. 20 even very dark, and no brightness in it?

DARKEN, be darkened, to — V.L. [חשך].

1. *To be or become dark,* חָשַׁךְ *chashak* [Eze. 30. 18,
Exod 10. 15 so that the land was darkened; and they
Psa. 69. 23 Let their eyes be darkened, that they see
Eccl. 12. 2 While..the stars, be not darkened, nor
12. 3 and those that look out..be darkened
Isa. 5. 30 the light is darkened in the heavens
13. 10 the sun shall be darkened in his going
Eze. 30. 18 also the day shall be darkened, when I

2. *To cause darkness, darken, hide,* חָשַׁךְ *chashak,* 5.
Job 38. 2 Who (is) this that darkeneth counsel by
Amos 8. 9 I will darken the earth in the clear day

3. *To be or become weak or dim,* כָּהָה *kahah.*
Zech 11. 17 his right eye shall be utterly darkened

4. *To be or become dark,* עָרַב *arab.*
Isa. 24. 11 all joy is darkened, the mirth of the land

5. *To be consumed,* עָתַם *atham,* 2.
Isa. 9. 19 Through the wrath..is the land darkened

6. *To be enfolded, black,* קָדַר *qadar.*
Joel 3. 15 The sun and the moon shall be darkened

7. *To be darkened, made dark,* σκοτίζομαι *skotizo.*
Matt 24. 29 after..those days shall the sun be dark.
Mark 13. 24 in those days..the sun shall be darkened
Luke 23. 45 the sun was darkened, and the veil of the
Rom. 1. 21 and their foolish heart was darkened
11. 10 Let their eyes be darkened that they may
Eph. 4. 18 Having the understanding [darkened]
Rev. 8. 12 so as the third part of them was darkened
9. 2 the sun and the air [were darkened] by

DARKLY —
In an enigma, ἐν αἰνίγματι *en ainigmati.*
1 Co. 13. 12 For now we see through a glass, darkly

DARKNESS —

1. *Thick darkness,* אֹפֶל *ophel.*
Job 3. 6 (As for) that night, let darkness seize upon
10. 22 darkness..and (where) the light (is) as da.
23. 17 hath he covered the darkness from my
28. 3 the stones of darkness, and the shadow
30. 26 when I waited for light, there came dark.
Psa. 91. 6 for the pestilence (that) walketh in dark.

2. *Thick darkness, gloominess,* אֲפֵלָה *aphelah.*
Deut 28. 29 as the blind gropeth in darkness, and
Prov. 4. 19 The way of the wicked (is) as darkness
Isa. 8. 22 and (they shall be) driven to darkness
Isa. 58. 10 and thy darkness (be) as the noon day
59. 9 for brightness, (but) we walk in darkness
Jer. 23. 12 their way shall be..as..in the darkness

3. *Darkness,* חָשׁוֹךְ *chashok.*
Dan. 2. 22 he knoweth what (is) in the darkness, and

4. *Darkness,* חֲשֵׁכָה, חֲשֵׁיכָה *chashekah.*
Gen. 15. 12 an horror of great darkness fell upon him
Psa. 82. 5 They know not..they walk on in darkness
139. 12 the darkness and the light (are) both alike
Isa. 8. 22 trouble and darkness, dimness of anguish
50. 10 Who (is) among you..that walketh in da.

5. *Darkness,* חֹשֶׁךְ *choshek.*
Gen. 1. 2 and darkness (was) upon the face of the
1. 4 God divided the light from the darkness
1. 5 and the darkness he called Night. And
1. 18 and to divide the light from the darkness
Exod 10. 21 that there may be darkness over the land
10. 21 of Egypt, even darkness (which) may be
10. 22 there was a thick darkness in all the land
14. 20 it was a cloud and darkness (to them)
Deut 4. 11 and the mountain burned with..darkness
5. 23 the voice out of the midst of the darkness
1 Sa. 2. 9 and the wicked shall be silent in darkness
2 Sa. 22. 12 he made darkness pavilions round about
22. 29 and the LORD will lighten my darkness
Job 3. 4 Let that day be darkness; let not God
3. 5 Let darkness and the shadow of death
5. 14 They meet with darkness in the day time
10. 21 to the land of darkness, and the shadow
12. 22 He discovereth deep things out of dark.
15. 22 that he shall return out of darkness, and
15. 23 he knoweth that the day of darkness is
15. 30 He shall not depart out of darkness; the
17. 12 the light (is) short because of darkness
17. 13 I have made my bed in the darkness
18. 18 shall be driven from light into darkness
19. 8 and he hath set darkness in my paths
20. 26 All darkness (shall be) hid in his secret
22. 11 Or darkness, (that) thou canst not see
23. 17 I was not cut off before the darkness
28. 3 He setteth an end to darkness, and
29. 3 by his light I walked (through) darkness
34. 22 (There is) no darkness, nor shadow of de.
37. 19 we cannot order..by reason of darkness
38. 19 (as for) darkness where (is) the place
Psa. 18. 11 He made darkness his secret place; his
18. 28 LORD my God will enlighten my darkness
104. 20 Thou makest darkness, and it is night
105. 28 He sent darkness, and made it dark
107. 10 Such as sit in darkness, and in the
107. 14 He brought them out of darkness and
112. 4 there ariseth light in the darkness: (he is)
139. 11 If I say, Surely the darkness shall cover
139. 12 Yea, the darkness hideth not from thee
Prov. 2. 13 Who leave..to walk in the ways of dark.
20. 20 his lamp shall be put out in..darkness
Eccl. 2. 13 as far as light excelleth darkness
2. 14 the fool walketh in darkness: and I myself
5. 17 All his days also he eateth in darkness
6. 4 cometh in..and departeth in darkness
6. 4 his name shall be covered with darkness
11. 8 let him remember the days of darkness
Isa. 5. 20 darkness for light, and light for darkness
5. 30 behold darkness (and) sorrow, and the
9. 2 The people that walked in darkness have
29. 18 eyes of the blind shall see out of..dark.
42. 7 to bring..them that sit in darkness out of
45. 3 I will give thee the treasures of darkness
45. 7 I form the light, and create darkness; I
45. 19 Sit thou silent and get thee into darkness
49. 9 mayest say..to them that (are) in darkness
60. 2 the darkness shall cover the earth, and
Lam. 3. 2 brought (me into) darkness, but not (into)
Eze. 32. 8 set darkness upon thy land, saith the L.
Joel 2. 2 A day of darkness and of gloominess, a
2. 31 The sun shall be turned into darkness
Amos 5. 18 the day of the LORD (is) darkness, and
5. 20 (Shall) not the day of the LORD (be) dark.
Mic. 7. 8 when I sit in darkness, the LORD (shall be)
Nah. 1. 8 and darkness shall pursue his enemies
Zeph. 1. 15 a day of darkness and gloominess, a day

6. *Thick darkness,* מַאְפֵל *maaphel.*
Josh. 24. 7 he put darkness between you and the E.

7. *Thick darkness of Jah,* מַאְפֵלְיָה *mapelyah.*
Jer. 2. 31 Have I been..a land of darkness?

8. *Dark place,* מַחְשָׁךְ *machshak.*
Psa. 88. 6 laid me in the lowest pit, in darkness
88. 18 (and) mine acquaintance into darkness
143. 3 he hath made me to dwell in darkness
Isa. 42. 16 I will make darkness light before them

9. *Obscurity,* עֵיפָה *ephah.*
Job 10. 22 A land of darkness..(and) of the shadow
Amos 4. 13 that maketh the morning darkness, and

10. *Thick darkness, secret or high place,* עֲרָפֶל *araphel.*
2 Sa. 22. 10 and darkness (was) under his feet
Psa. 18. 9 and darkness (was) under his feet
97. 2 Clouds and darkness (are) round about

11. *Gloom, blackness,* ζόφος *zophos.*
2 Pe. 2. 4 delivered (them) into chains of darkness
Jude 6 in everlasting chains, under darkness

12. *Darkness,* σκοτία *skotia.*
Matt 10. 27 What I tell you in darkness, (that) speak
Luke 12. 3 whatsoever ye have spoken in darkness
John 1. 5 light shineth in darkness; and the dark.
8. 12 followeth me shall not walk in darkness
12. 35 Walk while ye have the light, lest dark.
John 12. 35 he that walketh in darkness, knoweth
12. 46 believeth on me should not abide in dark.
1 Jo. 1. 5 God is light, and in him is no darkness
2. 8 the darkness is past, and the true light
2. 9 He that..hateth his brother, is in dark
2. 11 is in darkness, and walketh in darkness
2. 11 because that darkness hath blinded his

13. *Darkness,* σκότος *skotos.*
Matt 4. 16 The people which sat in [darkness] saw
6. 23 be darkness, how great (is) that darkness!
8. 12 shall be cast out into outer darkness
22. 13 take..and cast (him) into outer darkness
25. 30 cast ye the..servant into outer darkness
27. 45 from the sixth hour there was darkness
Mark 15 33 there was darkness over the whole land
Luke 1. 79 To give light to them that sit in darkness
11. 35 light which is in thee be not darkness
22. 53 your hour, and the power of darkness
23. 44 there was a darkness over all the earth
John 3. 19 and men loved darkness rather than light
Acts 2. 20 The sun shall be turned into darkness
13. 11 there fell on him a mist and a darkness
26. 18 to turn (them) from darkness to light
Rom. 2. 19 a light of them which are in darkness
13. 12 let us..cast off the works of darkness
1 Co. 4. 5 to light the hidden things of darkness
2 Co. 4. 6 commanded the light to shine out of da.
6. 14 what communion hath light with dark.
Eph. 5. 8 ye were sometimes darkness, but now
5. 11 with the unfruitful works of darkness
6. 12 the rulers of the darkness of this world
Col. 1. 13 delivered us from the power of darkness
1 Th. 5. 4 But ye, brethren are not in darkness, that
5. 5 we are not of the night, nor of darkness
Heb. 12. 18 nor unto blackness, and [darkness,] and
1 Pe. 2. 9 him who hath called you out of darkness
2 Pe. 2. 17 to whom the mist of darkness is reserved
1 Jo. 1. 6 fellowship with him, and walk in dark.
Jude 13 is reserved the blackness of darkness for

DARKNESS, full of —
Dark, σκοτεινός *skoteinos.*
Matt. 6. 23 thy whole body shall be full of darkness
Luke 11. 34 thy body also (is) full of darkness

DARKNESS, to be full of —
To be darkened, σκοτόομαι *skotoomai.*
Rev. 16. 10 and his kingdom was full of darkness

DARKNESS, to cause —
To cause darkness, חָשַׁךְ *chashak,* 5.
Jer. 13. 16 Give glory..before he cause darkness

DARKNESS, gross or thick —
Thick darkness, secret or high place, עֲרָפֶל *araphel.*
Exod 20. 21 Moses drew near unto the thick darkness
Deut. 4. 11 the midst of heaven, with..thick dark.
5. 22 of the cloud, and of the thick darkness
1 Ki. 8. 12 that he would dwell in the thick darkness
2 Ch. 6. 1 that he would dwell in the thick darkness
Job 38. 9 thick darkness a swaddling band for it
Isa. 60. 2 shall cover the earth, and gross darkness
Jer. 13. 16 (and) make (it) gross darkness
Joel 2. 2 A day of clouds and of thick darkness
Zeph. 1. 15 a day of clouds and thick darkness

DAR'-KON, דַּרְקוֹן *bearer.*
A servant of Solomon, whose descendants came up from the exile with Zerubbabel, B.C. 536.
Ezra 2. 56 The children of Jaalah, the children of D.
Neh. 7. 58 The children of Jaala, the children of D

DARLING —
Only, lonely, singly, יָחִיד *yachid.*
Psa. 22. 20 my darling from the power of the dog
35. 17 rescue..my darling from the lions

DART —

1. *Arrow,* חֵץ *chets.*
Prov. 7. 23 Till a dart strike through his liver

2. *Dart, missile,* מַסָּע *massa*
Job 41. 26 the spear, the dart, nor the habergeon

3. *Rod, reed,* שֵׁבֶט *shebet.*
2 Sa. 18. 14 he took three darts in his hand, and

4. *Missile, dart, spear,* שֶׁלַח *shelach.*
2 Ch. 32. 5 and made darts and shields in abundance

5. *Club,* תּוֹתָח *tothach.*
Job 41. 29 Darts are counted as stubble: he laugheth

6. *A missile, dart, arrow,* βέλος *belos.*
Eph. 6. 16 quench all the fiery darts of the wicked

7. *A missile, dart, arrow,* βολίς *bolis.*
Heb 12. 20 [be stoned, or thrust through with a dart]

DASH, to —

1. *To smite, plague,* נָגַף *nagaph.*
Psa. 91. 12 lest thou dash thy foot against a stone

2. *To dash, beat,* נָפַץ *naphats,* 3.
Psa. 137. 9 dasheth thy little ones against the stones
Jer. 13. 14 I will dash them one against another

3. *To dash in pieces,* רָטַשׁ *ratash,* 3.
2 Ki. 8 12 wilt dash their children, and rip up their

4. *To strike toward or against,* προσκόπτω *proskoptō.*
Matt. 4. 6 lest at any time thou dash thy Lu. 4. 11.

DASH in pieces, to —

1. *To dash, beat,* נָפַץ *naphats,* 3.
Psa. 2. 9 thou shalt dash them in pieces like a

2. *To crush*, רָצַץ *raats.*
Exod15. 6 right hand, O LORD, hath dashed in pieces

DASH to pieces —
To dash in pieces, רָטַשׁ *ratash*, 3.
Isa. 13. 18 also shall dash the young men to pieces

DASHED in or to pieces, to be —
To be dashed in pieces or to the ground, רָטַשׁ *ratash*, 4.
Isa. 13. 16 children also shall be dashed to pieces
Hos. 10. 14 the mother was dashed in pieces upon
13. 16 their infants shall be dashed in pieces
Nah. 3. 10 young children also were dashed in pieces

DASHETH in pieces, that —
To scatter, break in pieces, פּוּץ *puts*, 5.
Nah. 2. 1 He that dasheth in pieces is come up bef.

DA'-THAN, דָּתָן *fount.*
A son of Eliab the Reubenite, who with Korah a Levite, and Abiram and On, other two Reubenites, conspired against Moses and Aaron in the wilderness, and perished there. B.C. 1471.
Num16. 1 Now Korah..and D. and Abiram..took
16. 12 And Moses sent to call D. and Abiram
16. 24 Get you up from..the tabernacle of..D.
16. 25 And Moses rose up, and went unto D.
16. 27 they gat up from the tabernacle of..D.
16. 27 and D. and Abiram came out, and stood
26. 9 And the sons of Eliab; Nemuel, and D.
26. 9 This (is that) D. and Abiram (which were)
Deut11. 6 And what he did unto D. and Abiram
Psa.106. 17 The earth opened and swallowed up D.

DAUB, to —
1. *To daub*, חָמַר *chamar.*
Exod. 2. 3 daubed it with slime and with pitch, and
2. *To plaister, overlay*, טוּחַ *tuach.*
Eze. 13. 10 others daubed it with untempered (mor.
13. 11 Say unto them which daub (it) with unte.
13. 12 the daubing wherewith ye have daubed
13. 14 break down the wall that ye have daubed
13. 15 upon them that have daubed it with
13. 15 no (more), neither they that daubed it
22. 28 prophets have daubed them with untem.

DAUBING —
Plaistering, daubing, טִיחַ *tiach.*
Eze. 13. 12 Where (is) the daubing wherewith ye

DAUGHTER—
1. As No. 3 [V.L. בַּיִת *house*].
Isa. 10. 32 (against) the mount of the daughter of Z.
2. As No. 3 [V.L. בֵּן *son*].
2 Ch. 11. 18 Mahalath the daughter of Jerimoth
3. *Daughter, child, descendant*, בַּת *bath.*
Gen. 11. 29 Nahor's wife, Milcah, the daughter of
20. 12 indeed..she (is) the daughter of my fath.
20. 12 but not the daughter of my mother; and
24. 23 Whose daughter (art) thou? tell me, I
24. 24 I (am) the daughter of Bethuel the son of
24. 47 I asked her, and said, Whose daughter
24. 47 The daughter of Bethuel, Nahor's son
24. 48 to take my master's brother's daughter
25. 20 the daughter of Bethuel the Syrian of
26. 34 Judith the daughter of Beeri the Hittite
26. 34 Bashemath the daughter of Elon the
28. 9 Mahalath the daughter of Ishmael, A.
29. 6 Rachel his daughter cometh with the s.
29. 10 when Jacob saw Rachel the daughter of L.
29. 18 serve thee seven years for..thy..daughter
29. 23 he took Leah his daughter, and brought
29. 24 Laban gave unto his daughter Leah
29. 28 he gave him Rachel his daughter to wife
29. 29 Laban gave to Rachel his daughter Bilhah
30. 21 afterwards she bare a daughter, and
34. 1 Dinah the daughter of Leah, which she
34. 3 clave unto Dinah the daughter of Jacob
34. 5 that he had defiled Dinah his daughter
34. 7 folly..in lying with Jacob's daughter
34. 8 my son Shechem longeth for your daugh.
34. 17 then will we take our daughter, and we
34. 19 because he had delight in Jacob's daugh.
36. 2 Adah the daughter of Elon the Hittite
36. 2 Aholibamah the daughter of Anah
36. 2 the daughter of Zibeon the Hivite
36. 3 Bashemath Ishmael's daughter, sister of
36. 14 the daughter of Anah, the daughter of Z.
36. 18 Aholibamah the daughter of Anah, Esau's
36. 25 and Aholibamah the daughter of Anah
36. 39 the daughter of Matred, the daughter of
38. 2 Judah saw there a daughter of a certain
38. 12 the daughter of Shuah, Judah's wife, died
41. 45, 50 Asenath the daughter of Poti-pherah
46. 15 the sons of..Jacob..with his daughter
46 18 whom Laban gave to Leah his daughter
46. 20 Asenath the daughter of Poti-pherah priest
46. 25 which Laban gave unto Rachel his daug.
Exod. 1. 16 if it (be) a daughter, then shall she live
1. 22 and every daughter ye shall save alive
2. 1 a man..took (to wife) a daughter of Levi
2. 5 the daughter of Pharaoh came down to
2. 7 Then said his sister to Pharaoh's daugh.
2. 8 And Pharaoh's daughter said to her, Go
2. 9 Pharaoh's daughter said unto her, Take
2. 10 she brought him unto Pharaoh's daugh.
2. 21 and he gave Moses Zipporah his daugh.
6. 23 took him Elisheba, daughter of Ammina.
20. 10 thou, nor thy son, nor thy daughter, thy
21. 7 if a man sell his daughter to be a maid
21. 31 have gored a son, or have gored a daugh.

Lev. 12. 6 for a son, or for a daughter, she shall
18. 9 the daughter of thy father, or daughter
18. 10 son's daughter, or of thy daughter's dau.
18. 11 nakedness of thy father's wife's daughter
18. 17 the nakedness of a woman and her daug.
18. 17 son's daughter, or her daughter's daugh.
19. 29 Do not prostitute thy daughter, to cause
20. 17 father's daughter, or his mother's daugh.
21. 2 for his son, and for his daughter, and for
21. 9 the daughter of any priest, if she profane
22. 12 If the priest's daughter also be (married)
22. 13 if the priest's daughter be a widow, or
24. 11 name (was) Shelomith, the daughter of D.
Num25. 15 Cozbi, the daughter of Zur: he (was)
25. 18 Cozbi, the daughter of a prince of Midian
26. 46 name of the daughter of Asher (was) Sa.
26. 59 Jochebed, the daughter of Levi, whom
27. 8 inheritance to pass unto his daughter
27. 9 if he have no daughter, then ye shall
30. 16 between the father and his daughter
36. 8 every daughter, that possesseth an inherit.
Deut. 5. 14 thou, nor thy son, nor thy daughter, nor
7. 3 thy daughter thou shalt not give unto his
7. 3 his daughter shalt thou take unto thy son
12. 18 thou, and thy son, and thy daughter, and
13. 6 thy mother, or thy son, or thy daughter
16. 11, 14 thou, and thy son, and thy daughter
18. 10 that maketh his son or his daughter to
22. 16 I gave my daughter unto this man to wife
22. 17 saying, I found not thy daughter a maid
22. 17 (are the tokens of) my daughter's virgin.
27. 22 daughter of his father, or the daughter
28. 56 toward her son, and toward her daughter
Josh.15. 16 to him will I give Achsah my daughter to
15. 17 he gave him Achsah his daughter to wife
Judg. 1. 12 to him will I give Achsah my daughter
1. 13 he gave him Achsah his daughter to wife
11. 34 his daughter came out to meet him with
11. 34 beside her he had neither son nor daugh.
11. 35 Alas, my daughter! thou hast brought
11. 40 to lament the daughter of Jephthah the
19. 24 (here is) my daughter, a maiden, and his
21. 1 There shall not any of us give his daug.
Ruth 2. 2 And she said unto her, Go, my daughter
2. 8 Hearest thou not, my daughter? Go not to
2. 22 (It is) good, my daughter that thou go
3. 1 My daughter, shall I not seek rest for
3. 10 Blessed (be) thou of the LORD, my daug.
3. 11 now, my daughter, fear not; I will do to
3. 16 Who (art) thou, my daughter? And she
3. 18 Sit still, my daughter, until thou know
1 Sa. 1. 16 Count not thine handmaid for a daughter
14. 50 Saul's wife (was) Ahinoam, the daughter
17. 25 will give him his daughter, and make his
18. 17 Behold my elder daughter Merab, her
18. 19 at the time when Merab, Saul's daughter
18. 20 Saul's daughter, loved David: and they
18. 27 Saul gave him Michal his daughter
18. 28 and (that) Michal, Saul's daughter, loved
25. 44 Saul had given Michal his daughter, D.'s
2 Sa. 3. 3 the son of Maacah the daughter of Tal.
3. 7 whose name (was) Rizpah, the daughter
3. 13 thou first bring Michal Saul's daughter
6. 16 Michal, Saul's daughter, looked through
6. 20 Michal the daughter of Saul came out to
6. 23 Michal the daughter of Saul had no child
11. 3 Bath-sheba, the daughter of Eliam
12. 3 and was unto him as a daughter
14. 27 and one daughter, whose name (was) T.
17. 25 went in to Abigail the daughter of Na.
21. 8 took the two sons of..the daughter of A.
21. 8 five sons of Michal the daughter of Saul
21. 10 Rizpah the daughter of Aiah took sackc.
21. 11 Rizpah the daughter of Aiah the concu.
1 Ki. 3. 1 took Pharaoh's daughter, and brought her
4. 11 which had Taphath the daughter of Sol.
4. 15 took Basmath the daughter of Solomon to
7. 8 made also an house for Pharaoh's daugh.
9. 16 given it (for) a present unto his daughter
9. 24 Pharaoh's daughter came up out of the
11. 1 together with the daughter of Pharaoh
15. 2, 10 name (was) Maachah, the daughter of
16. 31 to wife Jezebel, the daughter of Ethbaal
22. 42 Azubah, the daughter of Shilhi
2 Ki. 8. 18 for the daughter of Ahab was his wife
8. 26 Athaliah, the daughter of Omri king of I.
9. 34 and bury her; for she (is) a king's daugh.
11. 2 Jehosheba, the daughter of king Joram
14. 9 Give thy daughter to my son to wife
15. 33 name (was) Jerusha, the daughter of Zad.
18. 2 Abi, the daughter of Zachariah
19. 21 the daughter of Zion hath despised thee
19. 21 the daughter of Jerusalem hath shaken
21. 19 Meshullemeth, the daughter of Haruz
22. 1 name (was) Jedidah, the daughter of Ad.
23. 10 no man might make his son or his daug.
23. 31 name (was) Hamutal, the daughter of J
23. 36 name (was) Zebudah, the daughter of P
24. 8 name (was) Nehusta, the daughter of E.
24. 18 Hamutal, the daughter of Jeremiah of L.
1 Ch. 1. 50 the daughter of Matred, the daughter of
2. 3 the daughter of Shua the Canaanitess
2. 21 Hezron went in to the daughter
2. 35 Sheshan gave his daughter to Jarha
2. 49 the daughter of Caleb (was) Achsa
3. 2 the daughter of Talmai king of Geshur
3. 5 four, of Bath-shua the daughter of Amm.
4. 18 the daughter of Pharaoh, which Mered
7. 24 his daughter (was) Sherah, who built
15. 29 Michal the daughter of Saul, looking
2 Ch. 8. 11 Solomon brought up the daughter of
11. 18 the daughter..Abihail the daughter

2 Ch. 11. 20 he took Maachah the daughter of Absal.
11. 21 loved Maachah the daughter of Absalom
13. 2 Michaiah the daughter of Uriel of Gibe.
20. 31 name (was) Azubah the daughter of Shi.
21. 6 for he had the daughter of Ahab to wife
22. 2 (was) Athaliah the daughter of Omri
22. 11 Jehoshabeath, the daughter of the king
25. 18 Give thy daughter to my son to wife
27. 1 (was) Jerushah, the daughter of Zadok
29. 1 name (was) Abijah, the daughter of Zech.
Neh. 6. 18 Johanan had taken the daughter of
Esth. 2. 7 Hadassah, that (is), Esther, his uncle's da.
2. 7 whom Mordecai..took for his own daug.
2. 15 Esther, the daughter of Abihail the
2. 15 Mordecai, who had taken her for his dau.
9. 29 Esther the queen, the daughter of Abih.
Psa. 9. 14 in the gates of the daughter of Zion
45. 10 Hearken, O daughter, and consider
45. 12 the daughter of Tyre (shall be there)
45. 13 The King's daughter (is) all glorious
137. 8 O daughter of Babylon, who art to be
Song 7. 1 How beautiful are thy feet..O..daughter!
Isa. 1. 8 the daughter of Zion is left as a cottage
10. 30 Lift up thy voice, O daughter of Gallim
10. 32 the mount of the daughter of Zion
16. 1 unto the mount of the daughter of Zion
22. 4 the spoiling of the daughter of my people
23. 10 Pass through thy land..O daughter of T.
23. 12 O thou oppressed virgin, daughter of Zi.
37. 22 the daughter of Zion..the daughter of J.
47. 1 sit in the dust, O virgin daughter of B.
47. 1 (there is) no throne, O daughter of the
47. 5 get thee into darkness, O daughter of the
52. 2 loose thyself..O captive daughter of Zi.
62. 11 Say ye to the daughter of Zion, Behold
Jer. 4. 11 wilderness toward the daughter of my
4. 31 the voice of the daughter of Zion, (that)
6. 2 I have likened the daughter of Zion to
6. 23 for war, against thee, O daughter of Zion
6. 26 O daughter of my people, gird (thee) with
8. 11 healed the hurt of the daughter of my
8. 19 the voice of the cry of the daughter of
8. 21 For the hurt of the daughter of my peo.
8. 22 is not the health of the daughter of my
9. 1 the slain of the daughter of my people?
9. 7 how shall I do for the daughter of my
14. 17 the virgin daughter of my people is
31. 22 How long wilt thou go about, O..daugh.?
46. 11 take balm, O virgin, the daughter of Eg.
46. 19 O thou daughter dwelling in Egypt
46. 24 The daughter of Egypt shall be confoun.
48. 18 Thou daughter that dost inhabit Dibon
49. 4 Wherefore gloriest thou..backsliding d.
50. 42 against thee, O daughter of Babylon
51. 33 The daughter of Babylon (is) like a thresh.
52. 1 name (was) Hamutal, the daughter of
Lam. 1. 6 from the daughter of Zion all her beauty
1. 15 trodden the virgin, the daughter of Jud.
2. 1 the Lord covered the daughter of Zion
2. 2 the strongholds of the daughter of Judah
2. 4 the tabernacle of the daughter of Zion
2. 5 hath increased in the daughter of Judah
2. 8 destroy the wall of the daughter of Zion
2. 10 The elders of the daughter of Zion sit
2. 11 destruction of the daughter of my people
2. 13 I liken to thee, O daughter of Jerusalem?
2. 13 comfort thee, O virgin daughter of Zion?
2. 15 wag their head at the daughter of Jerus.
2. 18 O wall of the daughter of Zion, let tears
3. 48 destruction of the daughter of my people
4. 3 the daughter of my people (is become)
4. 6 the iniquity of the daughter of my people
4. 10 destruction of the daughter of my people
4. 21 Rejoice and be glad, O daughter of Edom
4. 22 The punishment..is accomplished, O dau.
4. 22 visit thine iniquity, O daughter of Edom
Eze. 14. 20 shall deliver neither son nor daughter
16. 44 saying, As (is) the mother, (so is) her da.
16. 45 Thou (art) thy mother's daughter, that
22. 11 humbled his sister, his father's daughter
44. 25 or for mother, or for son, or for daughter
Dan. 11. 6 the king's daughter of the south shall
11. 17 he shall give him the daughter of women
Hos. 1. 3 and took Gomer the daughter of
1. 6 she conceived again, and bare a daughter
Mic. 1. 13 the beginning of the sin to the daughter
4. 8 the stronghold of the daughter of Zion
4. 8 shall come to the daughter of Jerusalem
4. 10 labour to bring forth, O daughter of Zion
4. 13 Arise and thresh, O daughter of Zion
5. 1 Now gather thyself..O daughter of troops
7. 6 the daughter riseth up against her moth.
Zeph. 3. 10 (even) the daughter of my dispersed, shall
3. 14 Sing, O daughter of Zion; shout, O Israel
3. 14 Be glad and rejoice..O daughter of Jer.
Zech. 2. 7 dwellest (with) the daughter of Babylon
2. 10 Sing and rejoice, O daughter of Zion
9. 9 Rejoice, daughter of Zion; shout, O daug
Mal. 2. 11 hath married the daughter of a strange

Daughter, θυγάτηρ *thugatēr.*
Matt 9. 18 My daughter is even now dead: but come
9. 22 Daughter, be of good comfort; thy faith
10. 35 the daughter against her mother, and the
10. 37 he that loveth son or daughter more than
14. 6 the daughter of Herodias danced before
15. 22 my daughter is grievously vexed with a
15. 28 her daughter was made whole from that
21. 5 Tell ye the daughter of Zion, Behold, thy
Mark 5. 34 Daughter, thy faith hath made thee whole
5. 35 Thy daughter is dead: why troublest
6. 22 when the daughter of the said Herodias

Mark 7. 26 cast forth the devil out of her daughter
7. 29 the devil is gone out of thy daughter
7. 30 and her [daughter] laid upon the bed
Luke 1. 5 his wife (was) of the daughters of Aaron
2. 36 Anna, a prophetess, the daughter of Pha.
8. 42 he had one only daughter, about twelve
8. 48 Daughter, be of good comfort: thy faith
8. 49 Thy daughter is dead; trouble not the
12. 53 against the daughter, and the daughter
13. 16 this woman, being a daughter of Abraham
John 12. 15 Fear not, daughter of Sion: behold, thy
Acts 7. 21 Pharaoh's daughter took him up, and
Heb. 11. 24 to be called the son of Pharaoh's daughter

DAUGHTER, little or young —

Little or young daughter, θυγάτριον *thugatrion.*
Mark 5. 23 My little daughter lieth at the point of d.
7. 25 a (certain) woman, whose young daughter

DAUGHTER IN LAW —

1. *Bride, spouse, son's wife*, כַּלָּה *kallah.*
Gen. 11. 31 Sarai his daughter in law, his son Abram's
38. 11 said Judah to Tamar his daughter in law
38. 16 knew not that she (was) his daughter in la.
38. 24 Tamar thy daughter in law hath played
Lev. 18. 15 the nakedness of thy daughter in law
20. 12 if a man lie with his daughter in law
Ruth 1. 6 Then she arose with her daughters in law
1. 7 her two daughters in law with her; and
1. 8 Naomi said unto her two daughters in law
1. 22 Ruth the Moabitess, her daughter in law
2. 20 And Naomi said unto her daughter in law
2. 22 Naomi said unto Ruth her daughter in la.
4. 15 for thy daughter in law, which loveth thee
1 Sa. 4. 19 his daughter-in-law, Phinehas' wife
1 Ch. 2. 4 Tamar his daughter in law bare him P.
Eze. 22. 11 hath lewdly defiled his daughter in law
Mic. 7. 6 the daughter in law against her mother

2. *Veiled one, bride, spouse*, νύμφη *numphē.*
Matt 10. 35 the daughter in law against her mother
Luke 12. 53 mother in law against her daughter in la.
12. 53 the daughter in law against her mother

DAUGHTERS —

1. *Daughters, descendants*, בָּנוֹת *banoth.*
Gen. 5. 4, 7, 10, 13, 16, 19 begat sons and daughters
5. 22, 26, 30 and begat sons and daughters
6. 1 and daughters were born unto them
6. 2 the sons of God saw the daughters of men
6. 4 sons of God came in unto the daughters
11. 11, 13, 15, 17, 19, 21 begat sons and daughters
11. 23, 25 and begat sons and daughters
19. 8 I have two daughters which have not
19. 12 son in law, and thy sons, and thy daughters
19. 14 sons in law, which married his daughters
19. 15 take thy wife, and thy two daughters
19. 16 upon the hand of his two daughters
19. 30 dwelt in the mountain, and his two dau.
19. 30 dwelt in a cave, he and his two daughters
19. 36 Thus were both the daughters of Lot with
24. 3 thou shalt not take..of the daughters
24. 13 the daughters of the men of the city come
24. 37 take a wife to my son of the daughters
27. 46 weary of my life because of the daughters
27. 46 if Jacob take a wife of the daughters of
27. 46 such as these (which are) of the daughters
28. 1, 6 Thou shalt not take a wife of the daug.
28. 2 a wife from thence of the daughters of
28. 8 Esau seeing that the daughters of Canaan
29. 16 Laban had two daughters: the name of
30. 13 for the daughters will call me blessed
31. 26 carried away my daughters, as captives
31. 28 to kiss my sons and my daughters
31. 31 thou wouldest take by force thy daughters
31. 41 fourteen years for thy two daughters
31. 43 (These) daughters (are) my daughters
31. 43 what can I do this day unto these my dau.
31. 50 If thou shalt afflict my daughters, or if
31. 50 take (other) wives besides my daughters
31. 55 kissed his sons and his daughters, and
34. 1 went out to see the daughters of the land
34. 9 (and) give your daughters unto us
34. 9 and take our daughters unto you
34. 16 Then will we give our daughters unto
34. 16 we will take your daughters to us, and
34. 21 let us take their daughters to us for wives
34. 21 and let us give them our daughters
36. 2 Esau took his wives of the daughters of
36. 6 his wives and his sons, and his daught.
37. 35 all his sons and all his daughters rose up
46. 7 his daughters, and his sons' daughters
46. 15 all the souls of his sons and his daughters
Exod. 2. 16 the priest of Midian had seven daughters
2. 20 he said unto his daughters, And where
3. 22 upon your sons, and upon your daughters
6. 25 took him (one) of the daughters of Putiel
10. 9 with our sons and with our daughters
21. 4 and she have born him sons or daughters
21. 9 with her after the manner of daughters
32. 2 of your sons, and of your daughters, and
34. 16 thou take of their daughters unto thy
34. 16 their daughters go a whoring after their
Lev. 10. 14 and thy sons, and thy daughters with thee
26. 29 the flesh of your daughters shall ye eat
Num 18. 11 to thy sons and to thy daughters with
18. 19 and thy sons and thy daughters with thee
21. 29 his daughters, into captivity unto Sihon
25. 1 to commit whoredom with the daughters
26. 33 the son of Hepher had no sons, but daug.
26. 33 the names of the daughters of Zelophehad
27. 1 Then came the daughters of Zelophehad
Num 27. 1 these (are) the names of his daughters
27. 7 The daughters of Zelophehad speak right
36. 2 give the inheritance..unto his daughters
36. 6 concerning the daughters of Zelophehad
36. 10 so did the daughters of Zelophehad
36. 11 daughters of Zelophehad, were married
Deut 12. 12 ye, and your sons, and your daughters
12. 31 their sons and their daughters they have
23. 17 There shall be no whore of the daughters
28. 32 Thy sons and thy daughters (shall be) given
28. 41 Thou shalt beget sons and daughters
28. 53 flesh of thy sons and of thy daughters
32. 19 provoking of his sons and of his daught.
Josh. 7. 24 his sons, and his daughters, and his oxen
17. 3 But Zelophehad..had no sons, but daugh.
17. 3 these (are) the names of his daughters
17. 6 the daughters of Manasseh had an inher.
Judg. 3. 6 they took their daughters to be their
11. 40 the daughters of Israel went yearly to
12. 9 and thirty daughters, (whom) he sent
12. 9 took in thirty daughters from abroad for
14. 1, 2 a woman in Timnath of the daughters
14. 3 (Is there) never a woman among the da.
21. 7 we will not give them of our daughters
21. 18 may not give them wives of our daught.
21. 21 if the daughters of Shiloh come out to
21. 21 catch..every man his wife of the daughters
Ruth 1. 11 Turn again, my daughters; why will ye
1. 12 Turn again, my daughters, go (your way)
1. 13 nay, my daughters; for it grieveth me
1 Sa. 1. 4 to all her sons and her daughters
2. 21 and bare three sons and two daughters
8. 13 he will take your daughters (to be) con.
14. 49 the names of his two daughters (were
30. 3 wives, and their sons, and their daughters
30. 6 every man for his sons and for his daugh.
30. 19 neither sons nor daughters, neither spoil
2 Sa. 1. 20 lest the daughters of the Philistines
1. 20 lest the daughters of the uncircumcised
1. 24 Ye daughters of Israel, weep over Saul
5. 13 there were yet sons and daughters born
13. 18 with such robes were the king's daughters
19. 5 lives of thy sons and of thy daughters
2 Ki. 17. 17 they caused their sons and their daught.
1 Ch. 2. 34 Now Sheshan had no sons, but daughters
4. 27 Shimei had sixteen sons and six daught.
7. 15 Zelophehad: and Zelophehad had daugh.
14 3 and David begat more sons and daughters
23. 22 Eleazar died, and had no sons, but daug.
25. 5 to Heman fourteen sons and three daug.
2 Ch. 2. 14 son of a woman of the daughters of Dan
11. 21 eight sons, and threescore daughters
13. 21 twenty and two sons, and sixteen daugh.
24. 3 and he begat sons and daughters
28. 8 hundred thousand, women, sons, and da.
29. 9 our sons and our daughters and our wives
31. 18 wives, and their sons, and their daught.
Ezra 2. 61 which took a wife of the daughters of B.
9. 2 they have taken of their daughters for
9. 12 give not your daughters unto their sons
9. 12 neither take their daughters unto your
Neh. 3. 12 repaired Shallum..he and his daughters
4. 14 your sons, and your daughters, your
5. 2 We, our sons, and our daughters, (are)
5. 5 into bondage our sons and our daughters
5. 5 (some) of our daughters are brought unto
7. 63 took (one) of the daughters of Barzillai
10. 28 their wives, their sons, and their daught.
10. 30 that we would not give our daughters
10. 30 nor take their daughters for our sons
13. 25 Ye shall not give your daughters unto
13. 25 nor take their daughters unto your sons
Job 1. 2 unto him seven sons and three daughters
1. 13 a day when his sons and his daughters
1. 18 Thy sons and thy daughters (were) eating
42. 13 had also seven sons and three daughters
42. 15 no women found (so) fair as the daughters
Psa. 45. 9 Kings' daughters (were) among thy
48. 11 let the daughters of Judah be glad
97. 8 the daughters of Judah rejoiced because
106. 37 sacrificed their sons and their daughters
106. 38 blood of their sons and of their daughters
144. 12 (that) our daughters (may be) as corner
Prov 30. 15 The horse leach hath two daughters
31. 29 Many daughters have done virtuously
Eccl. 12. 4 the daughters of music shall be brought
Song 1. 5 I (am) black, but comely, O ye daughters
2. 2 so (is) my love among the daughters
2. 7 I charge you, O ye daughters of Jerusa.
3. 5 I charge you, O ye daughters of Jerusa.
3. 10 the midst..(with) love, for the daughters
3. 11 Go forth, O ye daughters of Zion, and
5. 8 I charge you, O daughters of Jerusalem
5. 16 This (is) my friend, O daughters of Jerus.
6. 9 The daughters saw her, and blessed her
8. 4 I charge you, O daughters of Jerusalem
Isa. 3. 16 Because the daughters of Zion are haugh.
3. 17 crown of the head of the daughters of Z.
4. 4 the LORD..away the filth of the daughters
16. 2 (so) the daughters of Moab shall be at
32. 9 hear my voice, ye careless daughters
43. 6 bring my sons from far, and my daughters
49. 22 thy daughters shall be carried upon
56. 5 name better than of sons and of daugh.
60. 4 thy daughters shall be nursed at (thy)
Jer. 3. 24 their flocks..their sons and their daugh.
5. 17 (which) thy sons and thy daughters should
7. 31 to burn their sons and their daughters in
9. 20 teach your daughters wailing, and every
11. 22 their sons and their daughters shall die
14. 16 wives, nor their sons, nor their daughters
16. 2 neither shalt thou have sons or daughters
Jer. 16. 3 concerning the daughters that are born
19. 9 the flesh of their daughters, and they
29. 6 Take ye wives, and beget sons and daugh.
29. 6 give your daughters to husbands
29. 6 that they may bear sons and daughters
32. 35 to cause their sons and their daughters
35. 8 we, our wives, our sons, nor our daugh.
41. 10 (even) the king's daughters, and all the
43. 6 women, and children, and the king's da.
48. 46 sons are taken captives, and thy daugh.
49. 2 her daughters shall be burnt with fire
49. 3 cry, ye daughters of Rabbah, gird you
Lam. 3. 51 because of all the daughters of my city
Eze. 13. 17 set thy face against the daughters of thy
14. 16, 18 shall deliver neither sons nor daugh.
14. 22 be brought forth, (both) sons and daugh.
16. 20 thou hast taken thy sons and thy daugh.
16. 27 the daughters of the Philistines, which
16. 46 she and her daughters that dwell at thy
16. 46 younger sister..Sodom and her daughters
16. 48 Sodom..hath not..nor her daughters
16. 48 as thou hast done, thou and thy daughters
16. 49 abundance of idleness was..in her daugh.
16. 53 the captivity of Sodom and her daughters
16. 53 the captivity of Samaria and her daugh.
16. 55 Sodom and her daughters, shall return to
16. 55 and Samaria and her daughters
16. 55 then thou and thy daughters shall return
16. 57 (thy) reproach of the daughters of Syria
16. 57 the daughters of the Philistines, which
16. 61 I will give them unto thee for daughters
23. 2 two women, the daughters of one mother
23. 4 and they bare sons and daughters
23. 10 they took her sons and her daughters, and
23. 25 they shall take thy sons and thy daugh.
23. 47 shall slay their sons and their daughters
24. 21 your sons and your daughters whom ye
24. 25 they set..their sons and their daughters
26. 6 her daughters which (are) in the field
26. 8 shall slay with the sword thy daughters
30. 18 and her daughters shall go into captivity
32. 16 the daughters of the nations shall lament
32. 18 (even) her, and the daughters of the
Hos. 4. 13 your daughters shall commit whoredom
4. 14 I will not punish your daughters when
Joel 2. 28 sons and your daughters shall prophesy
3. 8 I will sell your sons and your daughters
Amos 7. 17 thy sons and thy daughters shall fall by

2. *Daughter, descendant*, θυγάτηρ *thugatēr.*
Luke 23. 28 Daughters of Jerusalem, weep not for me
Acts 2. 17 sons and your daughters shall prophesy
21. 9 the same man had four daughters, virgins
2 Co. 6. 18 ye shall be my sons and daughters, saith

3. *Child*, τέκνον *teknon.*
1 Pe. 3. 6 whose daughters ye are as long as ye do

DA-VID, דָּוִיד, דָּוִד, Δαβίδ, Δαυείδ *beloved.*

Youngest son of one Jesse of Bethlehem-Ephratah in the land of Judah, born B.C. 1086. He had seven older brothers and two sisters, Zeruiah and Abigail (who is however called in 2 Sa. 17. 25 the daughter of *Nahash*). His mother's name is not mentioned; perhaps she was the daughter, sister, or concubine of Nahash king of Ammon, whom Jesse married in his advanced years (1 Sa. 17. 12). This would account for the kindness David received from Nahash and his son Shobi (2 Sa. 10. 2; 17. 27; Psa. 51. 5). We can only give a brief summary of his eventful life. He was tending his father's sheep when sent for and anointed by Samuel, after which he received the Spirit, was sent for by Saul and made his armour bearer and musician (1 Sa. xvi.); he engages to conquer Goliath, and succeeds (ch. xvii.); Jonathan loves him, but Saul envies him, and to entrap him gives him Michal his daughter for a wife (ch. xviii.); while Jonathan befriends him, Saul assaults him, and he escapes to Naioth (ch. xix.); he and Jonathan make a covenant, but Saul remains perverse, and David and Jonathan separate (ch. xx.); David resides at Nob and at Gath, (ch. xxi.); and then in the cave of Adullam, at Mizpah, and at the forest of Hareth, when Saul and Doeg slay the priests, &c. (ch. xxii.); David resides at Keilah, in the wilderness of Ziph, at the hill of Hachilah, and in the wilderness of Maon (ch. xxiii.); and at En-gedi he spares Saul's life (ch. xxiv.); Samuel dies; Nabal is churlish, but Abigail prudent, so that when Nabal dies David marries her (ch. xxv.); at Hachilah David spares Saul's life (ch. xxvi.); and a second time at Gath, where he is trusted by Achish (ch. xxvii.); but being suspected by the Philistines he is dismissed by him (ch. xxix.); David overtakes the Amalekites and defeats them (ch. xxx.); receives tidings of the death of Saul and Jonathan, and eulogises them (2 Sa. i.); is made king over Judah at Hebron, when a contest takes place between the men of Joab and those of Abner (ch. ii.); the latter having come over to David, is slain by the former, but lamented by David (ch. iii.); he also punishes the murderers of Ishbosheth (ch. iv.), and becomes king of all Israel, takes Zion from the Jebusites, is helped by Hiram, and twice defeats the Philistines (ch. v.); bringing the ark to Zion he is despised by Michal (ch. vi.); designing to build the temple, he is praised, yet restrained, and blessed (ch. vii.); he conquers successively the Philistines, Moabites, Syrians, and Edomites (ch. viii); is kind to Mephibosheth (ch. ix.); overcomes the Ammonites and Syrians (ch. x.); but offends against Uriah, and at last marries Bath-sheba (ch. xi.); Nathan puts a parable before him, his child dies, Solomon is born, and Rabbah captured (ch. xii.); conduct of Amnon, Tamar, and Absalom (ch. xiv.); Absalom's artifice, conspiracy, and David's flight (ch.

xv.); Ziba's deceit, and Shimei's cursing (2 Sa. 16. 1–14); Hushai and Ahithophel (2 Sam 16. 15–17. 14); David's secret information, Ahithophel's death, Absalom's conduct; and kindness shown to David at Mahanaim (2 Sa. 17. 15–29.); battle, with death of Absalom, and grief of David (ch. xviii.); Joab's appeal, and conduct of Shimei, Mephibosheth, Barzillai, and Israel (ch. xix.); revolt and death of Sheba (ch. xx.); the Gibeonites' complaint, and war with the Philistines (ch. xxi.); David's thanksgiving (Psa. xx.); his last words, and list of his mighty men (ch. xxiii.); he numbers the people, and chooses the pestilence; conduct of Araunah (ch. xxiv.); Adonijah presumes, but Solomon is anointed king; his promise to Adonijah (1 Ki. i.); David dies, B.C. 1016, aged 70, after reigning 7 years in Hebron and 33 in Jerusalem. Seventy-five of the Psalms have his name prefixed to them, and remain imperishable monuments of his poetic genius, and his unfeigned piety, repentance, and hope in God, though marred by grievous follies and crimes against both God and man.

Ruth 4. 17 the father of Jesse, the father of D.
4. 22 And Obed begat Jesse, and Jesse begat D.
1 Sa. 16. 13 the Spirit of the LORD came upon D.
16. 19 Send me D. thy son, which (is) with the
16. 20 Jesse..sent (them) by D. his son unto S.
16. 21 D. came to Saul, and stood before him
16. 22 Let D., I pray thee, stand before me
16. 23 D. took an harp, and played with his hand
17. 12 D. (was) the son of that Ephrathite of B.
17. 14 D. (was) the youngest: and the three eldest
17. 15 D.. returned from Saul to feed his fath.
17. 17 And Jesse said unto D. his son
17. 20 And D. rose up early in the morning
17. 22 D. left his carriage in the hand of the
17. 23 Goliath..spake..the same words: and D.
17. 26 D. spake to the men that stood by him
17. 28 Eliab's anger was kindled against D., and
17. 29 And D. said, What have I now done?
17. 31 when the words were heard which D.
17. 32 D. said to Saul, Let no man's heart fail
17. 33 Saul said to D., Thou art not able
17. 34 D. said..Thy servant kept his father's
17. 37 D. said moreover, The LORD..will deliver
17. 37 Saul said unto D., Go, and the LORD be
17. 38 And Saul armed D. with his armour
17. 39 And D. girded his sword upon his armour
17. 39 And D. said..I cannot go with these
17. 39 And D. put them off him
17. 41 the Philistine came on and drew..unto D.
17. 42 when the Philistine..saw D., he disdained
17. 43 the Philistine said unto D., (Am) I a dog
17. 43 And the Philistine cursed D. by his gods
17. 44 the Philistine said to D., Come to me
17. 45 said D..Thou comest to me with a sword
17. 48 drew nigh to meet D., that D. hasted
17. 49 And D. put his hand in his bag
17. 50 D. prevailed over the Philistine with a
17. 50 (there was) no sword in the hand of D.
17. 51 Therefore D. ran, and stood upon the P.
17. 54 And D. took the head of the Philistine
17. 55 Saul saw D. go forth against the Philis.
17. 57 D. returned from the slaughter of the P.
17. 58 D. answered, (I am) the son of thy servt. J.
18. 1 soul of Jona. was knit with the soul of D.
18. 3 Then Jonathan and D. made a covenant
18. 4 himself of the robe..and gave it to D.
18. 5 and D. went out whithersoever Saul sent
18. 6 when D. was returned from the slaughter
18. 7 Saul hath slain his thousands, and D. his
18. 8 They have ascribed unto D. ten thousands
18. 9 Saul eyed D. from that day and forward
18. 10 D. played with his hand, as at other times
18. 11 I will smite D. even to the wall
18. 11 And D. avoided out of his presence twice
18. 12 Saul was afraid of D., because the LORD
18. 14 D. behaved himself wisely in all his ways
18. 16 But all Israel and Judah loved D.
18. 17 Saul said to D., Behold my..daughter M.
18. 18 And D. said unto Saul, Who (am) I?
18. 19 Merab..should have been given to D.
18. 20 And Michal, Saul's daughter, loved D.
18. 21 Saul said to D., Thou shalt..be my son-in-l.
18. 22 Commune with D. secretly, and say, Be.
18. 23 spake those words in the ears of D.
18. 24 told him..On this manner spake D.
18. 25 And Saul said, Thus shall ye say to D.
18. 25 But Saul thought to make D. fall
18. 26 And when his servant's told D. these
18. 26 it pleased D. well to be the king's son-in-l.
18. 27 D. arose and went, he and his men
18. 27 D. brought their foreskins, and they gave
18. 28 Saul..knew that the LORD (was) with D.
18. 29 Saul was yet the more afraid of D.
18. 29 and Saul became D.'s enemy continually
18. 30 D. behaved himself more wisely than all
19. 1 to..his servants, that they should kill D.
19. 2 Jonathan, Saul's son, delighted much in D.
19. 2 Jonathan told D..my father seeketh to
19. 4 Jonathan spake good of D. unto Saul his
19. 4 Let not the king sin..against D.
19. 5 wherefore..wilt thou..slay D. without a
19. 7 Jonathan called D., and..showed him
19. 7 And Jonathan brought D. to Saul
19. 8 D. went out and fought with the Philis.
19. 9 he sat..with his javelin..and D. played
19. 10 Saul sought to smite D. even to the wall
19. 10 and D. fled, and escaped that night
19. 11 Saul also sent messengers unto D.'s house
19. 11 and Michal, D.'s wife, told him, saying
19. 12 So Michal let D. down through a window
19. 14 And when Saul sent messengers to take D.
1 Sa. 19. 15 Saul sent the messengers (again) to see D.
19. 18 D. fled, and escaped, and came to Samuel
19. 19 Behold, D. (is) at Naioth in Ramah
19. 20 And Saul sent messengers to take D.
19. 22 he asked and said, Where (are) S. and D.?
20. 1 and D. fled from Naioth in Ramah
20. 3 D. sware..and said, Thy father certainly
20. 4 said Jonathan unto D., Whatsoever thy
20. 5 D. said unto Jonathan..to morrow (is)
20. 6 D...asked..that he might run to Beth-le.
20. 10 said D. to Jonathan, Who shall tell me?
20. 11 Jonathan said unto D...let us go out into
20. 12 Jonathan said unto D., O LORD God of Is.
20. 12 and, behold, (if there be) good toward D.
20. 15 the LORD hath cut off the enemies of D.
20. 16 J. made (a covenant) with the house of D.
20. 16 Let the LORD..require..at the hand of D.'s
20. 17 And Jonathan caused D. to swear again
20. 18 Jonathan said to D., To morrow (is) the
20. 24 So D. hid himself in the field
20. 25 Abner sat by Saul's side, and D.'s place
20. 27 on the morrow..D.'s place was empty
20. 28 D...asked (leave) of me (to go) to Beth-le.
20. 33 it was determined of his father to slay D.
20. 34 he was grieved for D., because his father
20. 35 went out..at the time appointed with D.
20. 39 only Jonathan and D. knew the matter
20. 41 D. arose out of (a place) toward the south
20. 41 wept one with another, until D. exceeded
20. 42 And Jonathan said to D., Go in peace
21. 1 Then came D. to Nob to Ahimelech the
21. 1 Ahimelech was afraid at the meeting of D.
21. 2 D. said..The king hath commanded me a
21. 4 And the priest answered D., and said
21. 5 D. answered the priest, and said unto him
21. 8 D. said unto Ahimelech..is there not..sp.
21. 9 D. said, (There is) none like that; give it
21. 10 D. arose, and fled..for fear of Saul
21. 11 (Is) not this D. the king of the land?
21. 11 Saul hath slain his thousands..D. his ten
21. 12 D. laid up these words in his heart
22. 1 D...departed thence, and escaped to..A.
22. 3 And D. went thence to Mizpeh of Moab
22. 4 all the while that D. was in the hold
22. 5 Gad said unto D., Abide not in the hold
22. 5 D. departed, and came into the forest of
22. 6 When Saul heard that D. was discovered
22. 14 (is so) faithful among..thy servants as D.
22. 17 because their hand also (is) with D.
22. 20 one of the sons of Ahimelech..fled after D.
22. 21 Abiathar showed D. that Saul had slain
22. 22 D. said unto Abiathar, I knew (it) that d.
23. 1 they told D...the Philistines fight against
23. 2 Therefore D. enquired of the LORD, say.
23. 2 And the LORD said unto D., Go
23. 3 D.'s men said unto him..we be afraid
23. 4 Then D. enquired of the LORD yet again
23. 5 So D. and his men went to Keilah
23. 5 So D. saved the inhabitants of Keilah
23. 6 when Abiathar..fled to D. to Keilah
23. 7 it was told Saul that D. was come
23. 8 Saul called all the people..to besiege D.
23. 9 D. knew that Saul..practised mischief
23. 10 Then said D., O LORD God of Israel
23. 12 Then said D., Will the men of Keilah
23. 13 D. and his men..departed out of Keilah
23. 13 it was told Saul that D. was escaped
23. 14 D. abode in the wilderness in strong holds
23. 15 And D. saw that Saul was come out
23. 15 and D. (was) in the wilderness of Ziph
23. 16 Jonathan..arose, and went to D. into the
23. 18 And D. abode in the wood, and Jonathan
23. 19 Doth not D. hide himself..in the wood
23. 24 D. and his men (were) in the wilderness
23. 25 they told D.: wherefore he came down
23. 25 he pursued after D. in the wilderness of
23. 26 and D. and his men on that side
23. 26 D. made haste to get away for fear of
23. 26 for Saul and his men compassed D.
23. 28 Saul returned from pursuing after D.
23. 29 D. went up from thence, and dwelt in
24. 1 Behold, D. (is) in the wilderness of En-g.
24. 2 Then Saul..went to seek D. and his men
24. 3 D...remained in the sides of the cave
24. 4 And the men of D. said unto him
24. 4 D...cut off the skirt of Saul's robe
24. 5 D.'s heart smote him, because he..cut
24. 7 So D. stayed his servants with these words
24. 8 D. also arose..and went out of the cave
24. 8 D. stooped with his face to the earth
24. 9 D. said to Saul, Wherefore hearest thou
24. 9 saying, Behold, D. seeketh thy hurt?
24. 16 when D...made an end of speaking these
24. 16 Saul said, (Is) this thy voice, my son D.?
24. 17 he said to D., Thou (art) more righteous
24. 22 D. sware unto Saul. And Saul went
24. 22 D. and his men gat them up unto the hold
25. 1 D...went down to the wilderness of Paran
25. 4 D. heard..that Nabal did shear his sheep
25. 5 And D. sent out ten young men
25. 5 and D. said unto the young men
25. 8 cometh to thine hand..to thy son D.
25. 9 And when D.'s young men came, they
25. 9 spake..those words in the name of D.
25. 10 And Nabal answered D.'s servants, and
25. 10 Who (is) D.? and who (is) the son of Jesse?
25. 12 So D.'s young men turned their way
25. 13 And D. said unto his men, Gird ye on
25. 13 and D. also girded on his sword
25. 13 there went up after D. about four hundred
25. 14 D. sent messengers out of the wilderness
25. 20 D. and his men came down against her
1 Sa. 25. 21 Now D. had said, Surely in vain have I
25. 22 more also do God unto the enemies of D.
25. 23 And when Abigail saw D., she hasted
25. 23 and fell before D. on her face, and
25. 32 D. said to Abigail, Blessed (be) the LORD
25. 35 D. received..(that) which she had brought
25. 39 And when D. heard that Nabal was dead
25. 39 And D. sent and communed with Abigail
25. 40 when the servants of D. were come to A.
25. 40 D. sent us unto thee, to take thee to
25. 42 she went after the messengers of D.
25. 43 D. also took Ahinoam of Jezreel
25. 44 Saul had given..D.'s wife, to Phalti
26. 1 Doth not D. hide himself in the hill
26. 2 Saul arose..to seek D. in the wilderness
26. 3 But D. abode in the wilderness; and he
26. 4 D. therefore sent out spies, and under.
26. 5 And D. arose, and came to the place
26. 5 and D. beheld the place where Saul lay
26. 6 Then answered D., and said to Ahimelech
26. 7 So D. and Abishai came to the people
26. 8 Then said Abishai to D., God hath deliv.
26. 9 And D. said to Abishai, Destroy him not
26. 10 D. said furthermore, (As) the LORD liveth
26. 12 D. took the spear and the cruse of water
26. 13 Then D. went over to the other side
26. 14 And D. cried to the people, and to Abner
26. 15 And D. said to Abner, (Art) not thou
26. 17 And Saul knew D.'s voice, and said
26. 17 (Is) this thy voice, my son D.?
26. 17 And D. said, (It is) my voice, my lord
26. 21 I have sinned: return, my son D.
26. 22 D. answered and said, Behold the king's
26. 25 Then Saul said to D.
26. 25 Blessed (be) thou, my son D.
26. 25 So D. went on his way, and Saul returned
27. 1 And D. said in his heart, I shall now
27. 2 And D. arose, and he passed over with
27. 3 And D. dwelt with Achish at Gath
27. 3 D. with his two wives, Ahinoam..and A.
27. 4 it was told Saul that D. was fled
27. 5 And D. said unto Achish, If I have
27. 7 the time that D. dwelt in the country
27. 8 And D. and his men went up, and
27. 9 And D. smote the land, and left neither
27. 10 And D. said, Against the south of Judah
27. 11 D. saved neither man nor woman alive
27. 11 So did D., and so (will be) his manner all
27. 12 And Achish believed D., saying, He hath
28. 1 Achish said unto D., Know thou assuredly
28. 2 D. said to Achish, Surely thou shalt know
28. 2 Achish said to D., Therefore will I make
28. 17 and given it to thy neighbour, (even) to D.
29. 2 D. and his men passed on..with Achish
29. 3 (Is) not this D., the servant of Saul the king
29. 5 (Is) not this D., of whom they sang one
29. 5 Saul slew his thousands, and D. his ten
29. 6 Then Achish called D., and said unto him
29. 8 And D. said unto Achish, But what have
29. 9 And Achish answered and said to D.
29. 11 So D. and his men rose up early to depart
30. 1 when D. and his men were come to Zik.
30. 3 So D. and his men came to the city
30. 4 D. and the people..lifted up their voice
30. 5 And D.'s two wives were taken captives
30. 6 And D. was greatly distressed
30. 6 but D. encouraged himself in the LORD
30. 7 And D. said to Abiathar the priest
30. 7 Abiathar brought thither the ephod to D.
30. 8 And D. enquired at the LORD, saying
30. 9 So D. went, he and the..men that (were)
30. 10 But D. pursued, he and four hundred
30. 11 And they..brought him to D., and gave
30. 13 D. said..To whom (belongest) thou?
30. 15 And D. said to him, Canst thou bring me
30. 17 And D. smote them from the twilight
30. 18 D. recovered all that the Amalekites
30. 18 and D. rescued his two wives
30. 19 they had taken to them: D. recovered
30. 20 D. took all the flocks and the herds
30. 20 and said, This is D.'s spoil
30. 21 And D. came to the two hundred men
30. 21 so faint that they could not follow D.
30. 21 and they went forth to meet D.
30. 21 when D. came near..he saluted them
30. 22 Then answered..those that went with D.
30. 23 Then said D., Ye shall not do so
30. 26 And when D. came to Ziklag, he sent of
30. 31 where D. himself and his men were wont
2 Sa. 1. 1 when D. was returned from the slaughter
1. 1 and D. had abode two days in Ziklag
1. 2 and (so) it was, when he came to D.
1. 3 D. said unto him, From whence comest
1. 4 D. said unto him, How went the matter?
1. 5 D. said unto the young man that told him
1. 11 Then D. took hold on his clothes, and
1. 13 D. said unto the young man that told him
1. 14 And D. said unto him, How wast thou
1. 15 And D. called one of the young men
1. 16 D. said unto him, Thy blood (be) upon
1. 17 D. lamented..over Saul and over Jonath
2. 1 D. said, Whither shall I go up?
2. 1 D. enquired of the LORD, saying, Shall I
2. 2 D. went up thither, and his two wives
2. 3 his men that (were) with him did D. bring
2. 4 and there they anointed D. king over the
2. 4 And they told D., saying, (That) the men
2. 5 D. sent messengers unto the men of J.
2. 10 But the house of Judah followed D.
2. 11 the time that D. was king in Hebron..was
2. 13 and the servants of D., went out, and met
2. 15 Then there arose..twelve of the se. of D.

2 Sa. 2. 17 A. was beaten..before the servants of D.
2. 30 there lacked of D.'s servants nineteen men
2. 31 servants of D. had smitten of Benjamin
3. 1 the house of Saul and the house of D.
3. 2 And unto D. were sons born in Hebron
3. 5 And the sixth, Ithream, by Eglah, D.'s
3. 5 These were born to D. in Hebron
3. 6 the house of Saul and the house of D.
3. 8 have not delivered thee into the hand of D.
3. 9 as the LORD hath sworn to D.
3. 10 to set up the throne of D. over Israel, and
3. 12 Abner sent messengers to D. on his behalf
3. 14 D. sent messengers to Ish-bosheth, Saul's
3. 17 Ye sought for D. in times past (to be) king
3. 18 the LORD hath spoken of D., saying
3. 18 By the hand of my servant D. I will save
3. 19 Abner went also to speak in the ears of D.
3. 20 So Abner came to D. to Hebron
3. 20 and D. made Abner, and the men..a feast
3. 21 Abner said unto D., I will arise and go
3. 21 D. sent Abner away; and he went in peace
3. 22 behold, the servants of D. and Joab came
3. 22 but Abner (was) not with D. in Hebron
3. 26 And when Joab was come out from D.
3. 26 he sent messengers after Abner..but D.
3. 28 And afterward when D. heard (it) he said
3. 31 And D. said to Joab..King D. followed
3. 35 all the people came to cause D. to eat
3. 35 D. sware, saying, So do God to me, and
4. 8 brought the head of Ish-bosheth unto D.
4. 9 D. answered Rechab and Baanah his
4. 12 D. commanded his young men, and they
5. 1 Then came all the tribes..to D. unto H.
5. 3 king D. made a league with them in Heb.
5. 3 and they anointed D. king over Israel
5. 4 D. (was) thirty years old when he began
5. 6 which spake unto D., saying, Except thou
5. 6 thinking, D. cannot come in hither
5. 7 D. took the stronghold of Zion
5. 7 the same (is) the city of D.
5. 8 and D. said on that day, Whosoever gette.
5. 8 lame and the blind, (that are) hated of D.'s
5. 9 D. dwelt in the fort, & called it the city of D
5. 9 and D. built round about from Millo
5. 10 And D. went on, and grew great
5. 11 Hiram king of Tyre sent messengers to D.
5. 11 and they built D. an house
5. 12 D. perceived that the LORD had establish.
5. 13 D. took (him) more concubines and wives
5. 13 there were yet sons and daugh. born to D.
5. 17 they had anointed D. king over Israel
5. 17 came up to seek D.; and D. heard
5. 19 And D. enquired of the LORD, saying
5. 19 And the LORD said unto D., Go up
5. 20 And D. came to Baal-perazim
5. 20 and D. smote them there, and said
5. 21 and D. and his men burnt them
5. 23 And when D. enquired of the LORD, he
5. 25 D. did so, as the LORD had commanded
6. 1 D. gathered together all (the) chosen (men)
6. 2 D. arose, and went with all the people
6. 5 and all the house of Israel played
6. 8 D. was displeased, because the LORD had
6. 9 D. was afraid of the LORD that day
6. 10 D. would not remove the ark of the LORD
6. 10 into the city of D.; but D. carried it
6. 12 And it was told king D., saying
6. 12 So D. went and brought up the ark of God
6. 12 into the city of D. with gladness
6. 14 D. danced before the LORD with all (his)
6. 14 D. (was) girded with a linen ephod
6. 15 D. and all the house of Israel brought up
6. 16 the ark of the LORD came into the city of D.
6. 16 and saw king D. leaping and dancing
6. 17 the tabernacle that D. had pitched for it
6. 17 D. offered burnt offerings..before the L.
6. 18 D. had made an end of offering burnt
6. 20 Then D. returned to bless his household.
6. 20 the daughter of Saul came out to meet D.
6. 21 D. said unto Michael, (It was) before the
7. 5 Go and tell my servant D., thus saith the
7. 8 so shalt thou say unto my servant D.
7. 17 so did Nathan speak unto D.
7. 18 Then went king David in, and sat before
7. 20 And what can D. say more unto thee?
7. 26 let the house of thy servant D. be estab.
8. 1 it came to pass, that D. smote the Philis.
8. 1 D. took Methag-ammah out of the hand
8. 2 and (so) the Moabites became D.'s servants
8. 3 D. smote also Hadadezer, the son of Reh.
8. 4 And D. took from him a thousand (char.
8. 4 and D. houghed all the chariot (horses)
8. 5 slew of the Syrians two and twenty thou.
8. 6 Then D. put garrisons in Syria of Damas.
8. 6 and the Syrians became servants to D.
8. 6 the LORD preserved D. whithersoever he
8. 7 And D. took the shields of gold that were
8. 8 king D. took exceeding much brass
8. 9 D. had smitten all the host of Hadadezer
8. 10 Toi sent Joram his son unto king D.
8. 11 Which also king D. did dedicate unto the
8. 13 And D. gat (him) a name when he return.
8. 14 D.'s servants. And the LORD preserved D.
8. 15 And D. reigned over all Israel
8. 15 and D. executed..justice unto all his pe.
8. 18 and D.'s sons were chief rulers
9. 1 D. said, Is there yet any..of the house of
9. 2 and when they had called him unto D.
9. 5 Then king D. sent, and fetched him
9. 6 Now when Mephibosheth was come unto D.
9. 6 D. said, Mephibosheth. And he answer.
9. 7 And D. said unto him, Fear not: for I

2 Sa. 10. 2 Then said D., I will show kindness unto
10. 2 And D. sent to comfort him..for his fath.
10. 2 D.'s servants came into the land of..Am.
10. 3 Thinkest thou that D. doth honour thy
10. 3 hath not D. (rather) sent his servants unto
10. 4 Wherefore Hanun took D.'s servants, and
10. 5 When they told (it) unto D., he sent to
10. 6 the children of Ammon..stank before D.
10. 7 and when D. heard of (it), he sent Joab
10. 17 when it was told D., he gathered all Isr.
10. 17 Syrians set themselves in array against D.
10. 18 D. slew (the men of) seven hundred char.
11. 1 And it came to pass..that D. sent Joab
11. 1 But D. tarried still at Jerusalem
11. 2 in an evening tide..D. arose from off his
11. 3 And D. sent and enquired after the wom.
11. 4 And D. sent messengers and took her
11. 5 and told D., and said, I (am) with child
11. 6 D. sent to Joab, (saying), Send me Uriah
11. 6 And Joab sent Uriah to D.
11. 7 when Uriah was come..D. demanded (of)
11. 8 D. said to Uriah, Go down to thy house
11. 10 And when they had told D. saying
11. 10 D. said unto Uriah, Camest thou not from
11. 11 And Uriah said unto D., The ark, and Is.
11. 12 D. said to Uriah, Tarry here to-day also
11. 13 when D. had called him, he did eat and
11. 14 it came to pass..that D. wrote a letter
11. 17 and there fell (some)..of the servants of D.
11. 18 Then Joab sent and told D. all the things
11. 22 the messenger..showed D. all that Joab
11. 23 And the messenger said unto D., Surely
11. 25 Then D. said unto the messenger, Thus
11. 27 D. sent and fetched her to his house
11. 27 the thing that D. had done displeased the
12. 1 And the LORD sent Nathan unto D.
12. 5 D.'s anger was greatly kindled against
12. 7 Nathan said to D., Thou (art) the man
12. 13 And D. said unto Nathan, I have sinned
12. 13 And Nathan said unto D...thou shalt not
12. 15 the child that Uriah's wife bare unto D.
12. 16 D. therefore besought God for the child
12. 16 and D. fasted, and went in, and lay
12. 18 And the servants of D. feared to tell him
12. 19 when D. saw that his servants whispered
12. 19 D. perceived that the child was dead
12. 19 D. said unto his servants, Is the child d.?
12. 20 Then D. arose from the earth, and washed
12. 24 And D. comforted Bath-sheba his wife
12. 27 And Joab sent messengers to D., and said
12. 29 And D. gathered all the people together
12. 30 and it was (set) on D.'s head
12. 31 So D. and all the people returned unto
13. 1 Absalom the son of D. had a fair sister
13. 1 and Ammon the son of D. loved her
13. 3 Jonadab, the son of Shimeah, D.'s brother
13. 7 Then D. sent home to Tamar, saying
13. 21 But when king D. heard of all these things
13. 30 it came to pass..that tidings came to D.
13. 32 And Jonadab, the son of Shimeah, D.'s b.
13. 39 king D. longed to go forth unto Absalom
15. 12 Absalom sent for Ahithophel..D's coun.
15. 13 And there came a messenger to D
15. 14 And D. said unto all his servants that
15. 22 D. said to Ittai, Go and pass over
15. 30 D. went up by the ascent of (mount) Oli.
15. 31 And (one) told D., saying, Ahithophel (is)
15. 31 And D. said, O LORD, I pray thee, turn
15. 32 (when) D. was come to the top (of the
15. 33 D. said, If thou passest on with me, then
15. 37 So Hushai, D.'s friend, came into the city
16. 1 when D. was a little past the top (of the
16. 5 And when king D. came to Bahurim
16. 6 And he cast stones at D.
16. 6 and at all the servants of king D.
16. 10 the LORD hath said unto him, Curse D.
16. 11 D. said to Abishai, and to all his servants
16. 13 And as D. and his men went by the way
16. 16 when Hushai the Archite, D.'s friend, was
16. 23 so (was) all the counsel of Ahi..with D.
17. 1 I will arise and pursue after D. this night
17. 16 Now therefore send quickly and tell D.
17. 17 and they went and told king D.
17. 21 came up out of the well..and told king D.
17. 21 and said unto D., Arise, and pass quickly
17. 22 D. arose, and all the people that (were)
17. 24 Then D. came to Mahanaim. And Absalom
17. 27 it came to pass, when D. was come to M.
17. 29 sheep, and cheese of kine, for D..to eat
18. 1 D. numbered the people that (were) with
18. 2 D. sent forth a third part of the people
18. 7 were slain before the servants of D.
18. 9 And Absalom met the servants of D.
18. 24 And D. sat between the two gates
19. 11 D. sent to Zadok and to Abiathar the pries.
19. 16 and came down..to meet king D.
19. 22 And D. said, What have I to do with you
19. 41 and have brought the king..and all D.'s
19. 43 we have also more (right) in D. than ye
20. 1 and said, We have no part in D., neither
20. 2 every man of Israel went up from..D.
20. 3 And D. came to his house at Jerusalem
20. 6 D. said to Abishai, Now shall Sheba the
20. 11 he that (is) for D., (let him go) after Joab
20. 21 hath lifted up his hand..(even) against D.
20. 26 And Ira also..was a chief ruler about D.
21. 1 there was a famine in the days of D.
21. 1 and D. enquired of the LORD. And the
21. 3 Wherefore D. said unto the Gibeonites
21. 7 the LORD'S oath that (was) between..D.
21. 11 And it was told D. what Rizpah, the
21. 12 And D. went and took the bones of Saul

2 Sa. 21. 15 and D. went down, and his servants with
21. 15 and fought against the Philistines: and D.
21. 16 And Ishbi-benob..thought to have slain D.
21. 17 Then the men of D. sware unto him, say.
21. 21 the son of Shimeah, the brother of D.
21. 22 These four..fell by the hand of D., and
22. 1 D. spake unto the LORD the words of this
22. 51 showeth mercy to his anointed, unto D.
23. 1 Now these (be) the last words of D.
23. 8 the names of the mighty men whom D.
23. 9 (one) of the three mighty men with D.
23. 13 and came to D. in the harvest time unto
23. 14 And D. (was) then in an hold, and the
23. 15 And D. longed, and said, Oh that one
23. 16 and took (it), and brought (it) to D.
23. 23 and D. set him over his guard
24. 1 and he moved D. against them to say
24. 10 And D.'s heart smote him after that he
24. 10 D. said unto the LORD, I have sinned
24. 11 For when D. was up in the morning
24. 11 word..came unto the prophet Gad, D's
24. 12 Go and say unto D., Thus saith the LORD
24. 13 So Gad came to D., and told him
24. 14 D. said unto Gad, I am in a great strait
24. 17 And D. spake unto the LORD, when he saw
24. 18 And Gad came that day to D., and said
24. 19 And D...went up, as the LORD commanded
24. 21 D. said, To buy the threshing floor of
24. 22 And Araunah said unto D., Let my lord
24. 24 So D. bought the threshing floor and the
24. 25 D. built there an altar unto the LORD
1 Ki. 1. 1 Now king D. was old (and) stricken in
1. 8 the mighty men which (belonged) to D.
1. 11 and D. our lord knoweth (it) not?
1. 13 Go and get thee in unto king D., and say
1. 28 D. answered and said, Call me Bath-sheba
1. 31 Let my lord king D. live for ever
1. 32 And king D. said, Call me Zadok the
1. 37 greater than the throne of my lord..D.
1. 38 caused Solomon to ride upon king D.'s
1. 43 our lord king D. hath made Solomon king
1. 47 the king's servants came to bless..king D.
2. 1 the days of D. drew nigh that he should
2. 10 So D. slept with his fathers, and was
2. 10 and was buried in the city of D.
2. 11 days that D. reigned..(were) forty years
2. 12 Then sat Solomon upon the throne of D.
2. 24 the LORD..set me on the throne of D. my
2. 26 barest the ark of the LORD God before D
2. 32 and slew them with the sword..D. not
2. 33 but upon D...shall there be peace for
2. 44 the wickedness..that thou didst to D
2. 45 the throne of D. shall be established
3. 1 and brought her into the city of D.
3. 3 walking in the statutes of D. his father
3. 6 Thou hast showed unto..D. my father
3. 7 hast made thy servant king instead of D.
3. 14 keep my statutes..as thy father D. did
5. 1 for Hiram was ever a lover of D.
5. 3 D. my father could not build an house
5. 5 as the LORD spake unto D. my father
5. 7 the LORD..hath given unto D. a wise son
6. 12 my word..which I spake unto D. thy
7. 51 the things which D. his father had dedi.
8. 1 bring up the ark..out of the city of D.
8. 15 which spake with his mouth unto D. my
8. 16 but I chose D. to be over my people Isr.
8. 17 it was in the heart of D. my father to
8. 18 And the LORD said unto D. my father
8. 20 I am risen up in the room of D. my father
8. 24 Who hast kept with thy servant D. my
8. 25 keep with thy servant D. my father that
8. 26 which thou spakest unto thy servant D.
8. 66 goodness that the LORD had done for D.
9. 4 if thou wilt walk before me, as D. thy
9. 5 as I promised to D. thy father, saying
9. 24 Pharaoh's daughter..out of the city of D.
11. 4 was not perfect..as (was) the heart of D.
11. 6 went not fully after the LORD, as (did) D.
11. 12 I will not do it for D. thy father's sake
11. 13 I...give one tribe to thy son for D. v. 34.
11. 15 it came to pass, when D. was in Edom
11. 21 when Hadad heard..that D. slept with
11. 24 he gathered men unto him..when D. slew
11. 27 (and) repaired the breaches of the city of D.
11. 32 he shall have one tribe for..D.'s sake
11. 33 (to keep) my statutes..as (did) D. his fath.
11. 36 I give one tribe that D...may have a
11. 38 to keep my statutes..as D. my servant
11. 38 build thee a sure house, as I built for D.
11. 39 I will for this afflict the seed of D.
11. 43 and was buried in the city of D. his fath.
12. 16 saying, What portion have we in D.?
12. 16 now see to thine own house, D.
12. 19 Israel rebelled against the house of D.
12. 20 was none that followed the house of D.
12. 26 Now shall the kingdom return to..D.
13. 2 a child shall be born unto the house of D.
14. 8 the kingdom away from the house of D.
14. 8 thou hast not been as my servant D.
14. 31 Rehoboam..was buried..in the city of D.
15. 3 heart was not perfect..as the heart of D.
15. 4 for D.'s sake did the LORD..give him a
15. 5 D. did..right in the eyes of the LORD
15. 8 and they buried him in the city of D.
15. 11 Asa did..right..as (did) D. his father
15. 24 Asa..was buried..in the city of D.
22. 50 buried with his fathers in the city of D.
2 Ki. 8. 19 the LORD would not destroy Judah for D.
8. 24 buried with his fathers in the city of D.
9. 28 buried him..with his fa. in the city of D.
11. 10 to the captains..did the priest give..D.'s

2 Ki. 12. 21 buried him with his fathers in the city of D.
14. 3 he did..right..yet not like D. his father
14. 20 buried..with his fathers in the city of D.
15. 7 and they buried him..in the city of D.
15. 38 and was buried..in the city of D.
16. 2 Ahaz..did not..right..like D. his father
16. 20 Ahaz slept..was buried..in the city of D.
17. 21 he rent Israel from the house of D.
18. 3 according to all that D. his father did
19. 34 I will defend this city..for my servant D.'s
20. 5 Thus saith the LORD, the God of D. thy
20. 6 I will defend this city..for my servant D.'s
21. 7 of which the LORD said to D., and
22. 2 and walked in all the way of D. his father
1 Ch. 2. 15 Ozem the sixth, D. the seventh
3. 1 Now these were the sons of D., which
3. 9 (These were) all the sons of D., beside
4. 31 These(were)their cities unto the reign of D.
6. 31 these (are they) whom D. set over the
7. 2 whose number (was) in the days of D.
9. 22 whom D. and Samuel the seer did ordain
10. 14 and turned the kingdom unto D.
11. 1 all Israel gathered themselves to D. unto
11. 3 D. made a covenant...they anointed D.
11. 4 D. and all Israel went to Jerusalem
11. 5 the inhabitants of Jebus said to D
11 5 Nevertheless D. took the castle of Zion
11. 5 which (is) the city of D.
11. 6 D. said, Whosoever smiteth the Jebusites
11. 7 And D. dwelt in the castle
11. 7 therefore they called it the city of D
11. 9 So D. waxed greater and greater: for
11. 10 chief of the mighty men whom D v. 11.
11 13 He was with D. at Pas-dammim, and
11. 15 thirty captains went down to the rock to D.
11 16 And D. (was) then in the hold, and the
11 17 And D. longed, and said, Oh that
11. 18 and took (it), and brought (it) to D.
11. 18 but D. would not drink (of) it, but poured
11. 25 and D. set him over his guard
12. 1 these (are) they that came to D. to Ziklag
12 8 there separated themselves unto D...men
12. 16 came of the children of Benjamin..unto D.
12. 17 D. went out to meet them, and answered
12. 18 Thine (are we), D., and on thy side
12. 18 Then D. received them, and made them
12. 19 And there fell (some) of Manasseh to D.
12. 21 they helped D. against the band (of the
12. 22 day by day there came to D. to help him
12. 23 the bands (that)..came to D. to Hebron
12. 31 to come and make D. king
12. 38 All these men..came..to make D. king
12. 38 the rest..(were) of one heart to make D.
12. 39 And there they were with D. three days
13. 1 D. consulted with the captains of thous.
13. 2 D. said unto all the congregation of Israel
13. 5 So D. gathered all Israel together, from
13. 6 D. went up, and all Israel, to Baalah
13. 8 And D. and all Israel played before God
13. 11 D. was displeased, because the LORD had
13. 12 And D. was afraid of God that day
13. 13 So D. brought not the ark (home)
13. 13 to himself to the city of D.
14. 1 Hiram king of Tyre sent messengers to D.
14. 2 D. perceived that the LORD had confirmed
14. 3 And D. took more wives at Jerusalem
14. 3 and D. begat more sons and daughters
14. 8 when the Philistines heard that D. was
14. 8 all the Philistines went up to seek D.
14. 8 D. heard (of it), and went out against
14. 10 D. enquired of God..Shall I go up
14. 11 they came..to Baal-perazim..D smote
14. 11 D. said, God hath broken in upon mine
14. 12 D. gave a commandment, and they were
14. 14 Therefore D. enquired again of God
14. 16 D. therefore did as God commanded him
14. 17 the fame of D went out into all lands
15 1 city of D., and prepared a place for the
15. 2 D. said, None ought to carry the ark..but
15. 3 And D. gathered all Israel together to J.
15. 4 And D. assembled the children of Aaron
15. 11 D. called for Zadok and Abiathar the
15. 16 D. spake to the chief of the Levites to
15. 25 So D...went to bring up the ark of the
15. 27 D. (was) clothed with a robe of fine linen
15. 27 D. also (had) upon him an ephod of linen
15. 29 (as) the ark..came to the city of D
15. 29 Michal..saw king D dancing and playing
16. 1 the tent that D. had pitched for it
16. 2 when D. had made an end of offering
16. 7 D. delivered first (this psalm), to thank
16. 43 and D. returned to bless his house
17. 1 it came to pass, as D. sat in his house
17. 2 Nathan said unto D., Do all that (is) in
17. 4 Go and tell D. my servant, Thus saith
17. 7 thus shalt thou say unto my servant D.
17. 15 so did Nathan speak unto D.
17. 16 D. the king came and sat before the L.
17 18 What can D. (speak) more to thee
17. 24 (let) the house of D...(be) established
18. 1 D. smote the Philistines, and subdued
18. 2 the Moabites became D.'s servants, (and)
18. 3 D. smote Hadarezer king of Zobah unto
18. 4 And D. took from him a thousand chariots
18. 4 D. also houghed all the chariot (horses)
18. 5 D. slew of the Syrians two and twenty
18. 6 Then D. put (garrisons) in Syria-damascus
18. 6 the Syrians became D.'s servants, (and)
18. 6 Thus the LORD preserved D. whithersoever
18 7 D. took the shields..and brought them
18. 8 cities of Hadarezer, brought D. very much
18. 9 when Tou..heard how D. had smitten all
1 Ch. 18. 10 He sent Hadoram his son to king D.
18. 11 Them also king D. dedicated unto the L.
18. 13 all the Edomites became D.'s servants
18. 13 Thus the LORD preserved D. whithersoever
18. 14 D. reigned over all Israel, and executed
18. 17 the sons of D. (were) chief about the king
19. 2 D. said, I will show kindness unto Hanun
19. 2 D. sent messengers to comfort him conc.
19. 2 So the servants of D. came..to Hanun
19. 3 Thinkest thou that D. doth honour thy
19. 4 Wherefore Hanun took D.'s servants
19. 5 Then there went (certain), and told D.
19. 6 they had made themselves odious to D.
19. 8 when D. heard (of it), he sent Joab
19. 17 it was told D.; and he gathered all Israel
19. 17 when D. had put the battle in array
19. 18 D. slew of the Syrians seven thous v. 19.
20. 1 D. tarried at Jerusalem. And Joab smote
20. 2 And D. took the crown of their king
20. 2 and it was set upon D.'s head
20. 3 Even so dealt D. with all the cities
20. 3 D. and all the people returned to Jerusa.
20. 7 when he defied Israel, Jonathan..D.'s
20. 8 and they fell by the hand of D.
21. 1 Satan stood up against Israel, and pro. D.
21. 2 D. said to Joab, and to the rulers
21. 5 Joab gave the sum of the number..unto D.
21. 8 D. said unto God, I have sinned greatly
21. 9 And the LORD spake unto Gad, D.'s seer
21. 10 Go and tell D., saying, Thus saith the L.
21. 11 So Gad came to D., and said unto him
21. 13 D. said unto Gad, I am in a great strait
21. 16 D. lifted up his eyes, and saw the angel
21. 16 D. and the elders..fell upon their faces
21. 17 And D. said unto God, (Is it) not I (that)
21. 18 commanded Gad to say to D., that D.
21. 19 And D. went up at the saying of Gad
21. 21 And as D. came to Ornan
21. 21 Ornan looked, and saw D.
21. 21 and bowed himself to D. with (his) face
21. 22 Then D. said to Ornan, Grant me the
21. 23 And Ornan said unto D., Take (it) to
21. 24 And king D. said to Ornan, Nay
21. 25 So D. gave to Ornan..six hundred shekels
21. 26 D. built there an altar unto the LORD
21. 28 D. saw that the LORD had answered him
21. 30 But D. could not go before it to enquire
22. 1 D. said, This (is) the house of the LORD
22. 2 D. commanded to gather together the
22. 3 D. prepared iron in abundance for the
22. 4 they of T., brought much cedar wood to D.
22. 5 D. said, Solomon my son (is) young and
22. 5 So D. prepared abundantly before his
22. 7 And D. said to Solomon, My son, as for
22. 17 D. also commanded all the princes of Is.
23. 1 So when D. was old and full of days
23. 6 And D. divided them into courses among
23. 25 D. said, The LORD..hath given rest unto
23. 27 by the last words of D. the Levites (were)
24. 3 And D. distributed them, both Zadok of
24. 31 likewise cast lots..in the presence of D.
25. 1 Moreover D and the captains of the host
26. 26 the dedicated things, which D. the king
26. 31 In the fortieth year of the reign of D.
26. 32 king D. made rulers over the Reubenites
27. 18 Elihu, (one) of the brethren of D.
27. 23 But D. took not the number of them
27. 24 the account of the Chronicles of king D.
27. 31 of the substance which (was) king D.'s
27. 32 Jonathan, D.'s uncle, was a counsellor
28. 1 D. assembled all the princes of Israel
28. 2 D. the king stood up upon his feet
28. 11 D. gave to Solomon his son the pattern
28. 20 And D. said to Solomon his son, Be
29. 1 D. the king said unto all the congrega.
29. 9 D. the king also rejoiced with great joy
29. 10 Wherefore D. blessed the LORD before
29. 10 D. said, Blessed (be) thou, LORD God of
29. 20 D. said to all the congregation, Now bless
29. 22 they made Solomon the son of D. king
29. 23 Solomon sat..as king instead of D. his
29. 24 the sons likewise of king D., submitted
29. 26 D. the son of Jesse reigned over all Israel
29. 29 the acts of D...(are) written in the book
2 Ch. 1. 1 the son of D. was strengthened in his
1. 4 But the ark of God had D. brought up
1. 4 to (the place which) D. had prepared for
1. 8 Thou hast showed great mercy unto D.
1. 9 let thy promise unto D...be established
2. 3 As thou didst deal with D. my father
2. 7 a man..whom D. my father did provide
2. 12 who hath given to D. the king a wise son
2. 14 with the cunning men of my lord D. thy
2. 17 the numbering wherewith D...had num.
3. 1 where (the LORD) appeared unto D. his
3. 1 in the place that D. had prepared in
5. 1 the things that D. his father had dedica.
5. 2 to bring up the ark..out of the city of D.
6. 4 he spake with his mouth to my father D.
6. 6 and have chosen D. to be over my people
6. 7 it was in the heart of D...to build an ho.
6. 8 But the LORD said to D. my father
6. 10 I am risen up in the room of D.
6. 15 which hast kept with thy servant D.
6. 16 keep with thy servant D...that which
6. 17 thou hast spoken unto thy servant D.
6. 42 remember the mercies of D. thy servant
7. 6 which D. had made to praise the LORD
7. 6 when D praised by their ministry
7. 10 good. that the LORD had showed unto D.
7. 17 if thou wilt walk before me, as D. thy
7. 18 according as I have covenanted with D.
2 Ch. 8. 11 out of the city of D. unto the house
8. 11 My wife shall not dwell in the house of D.
8. 14 according to the order of D. his father
8. 14 for so had D. the man of God commanded
9. 31 Solomon..was buried in the city of D.
10. 16 saying, What portion have we in D.?
10. 16 (and) now, D., see to thine own house
10. 19 Israel rebelled against the house of D.
11. 17 they walked in the way of D. and Solom.
11. 18 the daughter of Jerimoth the son of D.
12. 16 Rehoboam..was buried in the city of D.
13. 5 God..gave the kingdom over..to D. for
13. 6 the servant of Solomon the son of D., is
13. 8 of the LORD in the hand of the sons of D.
14. 1 they buried him in the city of D.
16. 14 they buried him..in the city of D.
17. 3 he walked in the first ways of his father D.
21. 1 Jehoshaphat..was buried..in the city of D.
21. 7 LORD would not destroy the house of D.
21. 7 the covenant that he had made with D.
21. 12 Thus saith the LORD God of D. thy father
21. 20 they buried him in the city of D., but not
23. 3 as the LORD hath said of the sons of D.
23. 9 and shields, that (had been) king D.'s
23. 18 whom D. had distributed in the house of
23. 18 with singing, (as it was ordained) by D.
24. 16 they buried him in the city of D. among
24. 25 and they buried him in the city of D.
27. 9 and they buried him in the city of D.
28. 1 he did not..right..like D. his father
29. 2 all that D. his father had done
29. 25 with harps, according to the com. of D.
29. 26 Levites stood with the instruments of D.
29. 27 instruments (ordained) by D. king of Isr.
29. 30 praise unto the LORD with the words of D.
30. 26 since the time of Solomon the son of D.
32. 5 and repaired Millo (in) the city of D.
32. 30 to the west side of the city of D.
32. 33 chiefest of the sepulchres of the sons of D.
33. 7 of which God had said to D. and to Solo.
33. 14 he built a wall without the city of D.
34. 2 and walked in the ways of D. his father
34. 3 to seek after the God of D. his father
35. 3 which Solomon the son of D...did build
35. 4 according to the writing of D. king of Isr.
35. 15 according to the commandment of D., and
Ezra 3. 10 after the ordinance of D. king of Israel
8. 2 of the sons of D.; Hattush
8. 20 Nethinims, whom D...had appointed for
Neh. 3. 15 the stairs that go down from the city of D.
3. 16 place) over against the sepulchres of D.
12. 24 according to the commandment of D. the
12. 36 with the musical instruments of D. the
12. 37 they went up..the stairs of the city of D.
12. 37 going up of the wall, above the house of D.
12. 45 according to the commandment of D.
12. 46 in the days of D...(there were) chief of
Psa. 3. *title.* A Psalm of D., when he fled from Abs.
4. „ To the chief Musician..A Psalm of D.
5. „ To the chief Musician..A Psalm of D.
6. „ To the chief Musician..A Psalm of D.
7. „ Shiggaion of D., which he sang unto
8. „ To the chief Musician..A Psalm of D.
9. „ To the chief Musician..A Psalm of D.
11. „ To the chief Musician, (A Psalm) of D.
12. „ To the chief Musician..A Psalm of D.
13. „ To the chief Musician, A Psalm of D.
14. „ To the chief Musician, (A Psalm) of D.
15. „ A Psalm of D. LORD, who shall abide
16. „ Michtam of D. Preserve me, O God
17. „ A Prayer of D. Hear the right, O LORD
18. „ To the chief Musician, (A Psalm) of D.
18. 50 and showeth mercy to his anointed, to D.
19. *title.* To the chief Musician, A Psalm of D.
20. „ To the chief Musician, A Psalm of D.
21. „ To the chief Musician, A Psalm of D.
22. „ A Psalm of D. My God, my God
23 „ A Psalm of D. The LORD (is) my shep.
24. „ A Psalm of D. The earth (is) the LORD'S
25. „ (A Psalm) of D. Unto thee, O LORD
26. „ (A Psalm) of D. Judge me, O LORD
27. „ (A Psalm) of D. The LORD (is) my light
28. „ (A Psalm) of D. Unto thee will I cry
29. „ A Psalm of D. Give unto the LORD
30. „ (at) the dedication of the house of D.
32. „ (A Psalm) of D. Maschil. Blessed (is he
34. „ (A Psalm) of D., when he changed his
35. „ (A Psalm) of D. Plead (my cause), O L.
36. „ To the chief Musician, (A Psalm) of D.
37. „ (A Psalm) of D. Fret not thyself
38. „ A Psalm of D., to bring to remembran.
39. „ To the chief Musician..A Psalm of D.
40. „ To the chief Musician, A Psalm of D.
41. „ To the chief Musician, A Psalm of D.
51. „ To the chief Musician, A Psalm of D.
52. „ To the chief Musician..(A Psalm) of D.
52. „ D. is come to the house of Ahimelech
53. „ To the chief Musician..(A Psalm) of D.
54. „ To the chief Musician..(A Psalm) of D.
54. „ Doth not D. hide himself with us?
55. „ To the chief Musician..(A Psalm) of D.
56. „ Michtam of D., when the Philistines!
57. „ To the chief Musician..Michtam of D.
58. „ To the chief Musician..Michtam of D.
59. „ To the chief Musician..Michtam of D.
60. „ To the chief Musician..Michtam of D.
61. „ To the chief Musician..(A Psalm) of D.
62. „ To the chief Musician..A Psalm of D.
63. „ A Psalm of D., when he was in the wil
64. „ To the chief Musician, A Psalm of D
65. „ To the chief Mus. A Psalm..of D.
68. „ To the chief Mus. A Psalm..of D.

Psa. 69. *title.* To the chief Musician..(A Psalm) of D.
70. ,, (A Psalm) of D., to bring to remembra.
72. 20 The prayers of D...are ended
78. 70 He chose D. also his servant, and took
86. *title.* A Prayer of D. Bow down thine ear
89. 3 I have sworn unto D. my servant
89. 20 I have found D. my servant
89. 35 have I sworn..I will not lie unto D.
89. 49 (which) thou swarest unto D. in thy truth?
101. *title.* A Psalm of D. I will sing of mercy
103. ,, (A Psalm) of D. Bless the LORD, O my
108. ,, A Song (or) Psalm of D.
109. ,, To the chief Musician, A Psalm of D.
110. ,, A Psalm of D. The LORD said unto
122. ,, A Song of degrees of D. I was glad
122. 5 the thrones of the house of D.
124. *title.* A Song of degrees of D. If (it had not
131. ,, A Song of degrees of D.
132. 1 LORD, remember D., (and) all his afflictions
132. 10 For thy servant D.'s sake turn not away
132. 11 The LORD hath sworn (in) truth unto D..
132. 17 There will I make the horn of D. to bud
133. *title.* A Song of degrees of D. Behold, how
138. ,, (A Psalm) of D. I will praise thee
139. ,, To the chief Musician, A Psalm of D.
140. ,, To the chief Musician, A Psalm of D.
141. ,, A Psalm of D. LORD, I cry unto thee
142. ,, Maschil of D.; A Prayer when he was
143. ,, A Psalm of D. Hear my prayer, O L.
144 ,, (A Psalm) of D. Blessed (be) the LORD
144. 10 who delivereth D. his servant from the
145. *title.* D.'s (Psalm) of praise. I will extol
Prov. 1. 1 The Proverbs of Solomon the son of D.
Eccl. 1. 1 The words of the Preacher, the son of D.
Song 4. 4 Thy neck (is) like the tower of D.
Isa. 7. 2 And it was told the house of D., saying
7. 13 Hear ye now, O house of D.
9. 7 no end, upon the throne of D., and upon
16. 5 he shall sit upon it..in the taberna. of D.
22. 9 have seen..the breaches of the city of D.
22. 22 And the key of the house of D. will I lay
29. 1 Woe to Ariel..the city (where) D. dwelt!
37. 35 I will defend this city..for..D.'s sake
38. 5 Thus saith the LORD, the God of D.
55. 3 (even) the sure mercies of D.
Jer. 13. 13 even the kings that sit upon D.'s throne
17. 25 kings and princes sitting upon the th. of D.
21. 12 O house of D., thus saith the LORD
22. 2 k. of Judah, that sittest upon the th. of D.
22. 4 kings sitting upon the throne of D.
22. 30 sitting upon the throne of D., and ruling
23. 5 I will raise unto D. a righteous Branch
29. 16 the king that sitteth upon the th. of D.
30. 9 But they shall serve..D. their king
33. 15 Branch of righteous. to grow up unto D.
33. 17 D. shall never want a man to sit upon the
33. 21 may..my covenant be broken with D.
33. 22 so will I multiply the seed of D.
33. 26 Then will I cast away the seed of..D. my
36. 30 none to sit upon the throne of D.
Eze. 34. 23 he shall feed them, (even) my servant D.
34. 24 my servant D. a prince among them
37. 24 And D. my servant (shall be) king over
37. 25 my servant D. (shall be) their prince for
Hos. 3. 5 the LORD their God, and D. their king
Amos 6. 5 invent..instruments of music, like D.
9. 11 I raise up the tabernacle of D. that is
Zech 12. 7 that the glory of the house of D. and the
12. 8 and he that is feeble..shall be as D.
12. 8 and the house of D. (shall be) as God
12. 10 And I will pour upon the house of D.
12. 12 the family of the house of D. apart
13. 1 shall be a fountain opened to the ho. of D.
Matt. 1. 1 Jesus Christ, the son of D., the son of A.
1. 6 And Jesse begat D. the king; and D. the k.
1. 17 from Abraham to D. (are) fourteen gene.
1. 17 from D. until the carrying away into Ba.
1. 20 Joseph, thou son of D., fear not to take
9. 27 (Thou) son of D., have mercy on us
12. 3 Have ye not read what D. did, when
12. 23 the people..said, Is not this the son of D.?
15. 22 Have mer. on me, O Lord, (thou) son of D.
20. 30 Have mer. on us, O Lord, (thou) son of D.!
20. 31 Have mercy on us O Lord, thou son of D.!
21. 9 multi...cried..Hosanna to the son of D.!
21. 15 children crying..Hosanna to the son of D.
22. 42 They say unto him, (The son) of D.
22. 43 How then doth D. in spirit call him Lord
22. 45 If D. then call him Lord, how is he his
Mark 2. 25 Have ye never read what D. did, when
10. 47 Jesus, (thou) son of D., have mercy on me
10. 48 Thou son of D., have mercy on me
11. 10 Blessed (be) the kingdom of our father D.
12. 35 How say the scribes that C. is the son of D.
12. 36 For D. himself said by the Holy Ghost
12. 37 D. therefore himself calleth him Lord
Luke 1. 27 man whose name was J., of the ho. of D.
1. 32 give unto him the throne of his father D.
1. 69 salvation for us in the house of his ser. D.
2. 4 Joseph also went..unto the city of D.
2. 4 he was of the house and lineage of D.
2. 11 unto you is born this day, in the city of D.
3. 31 Nathan, which was (the son) of D.
6. 3 Have ye not read so much..what D. did
18. 38 Jesus, (thou) son of D., have mercy on me!
18. 39 (Thou) son of D., have mercy on me!
20. 41 How say they that Christ is D.'s son?
20. 42 D. himself saith in the book of Psalms
20. 44 D. therefore calleth him Lord, how is he
John 7. 42 That Christ cometh of the seed of D.
7. 42 out of the town of Bethlehem, where D.
Acts 1. 16 the Holy Ghost, by the mouth of D., spake
Acts 2. 25 D. speaketh concerning him, I foresaw
2. 29 freely speak unto you of the patriarch D.
2. 34 For D. is not ascended into the heavens
4. 25 Who by the mouth of thy servant D. hast
7. 45 whom God drave out..unto the days of D.
13. 22 he raised up unto them D. to be their
13. 22 and said, I have found D. the (son) of J.
13. 34 I will give you the sure mercies of D.
13. 36 For D..fell on sleep..and saw corruption
15. 16 and I will build again the tabernacle of D.
Rom. 1. 3 Jesus Christ..made of the seed of D.
4. 6 D. also describeth the blessedness of the
11. 9 D. saith, Let their table be made a snare
2 Ti. 2. 8 Jesus Christ of the seed of D. was raised
Heb. 4. 7 he limiteth a certain day, saying in D.
11. 32 D. also, and Samuel, and (of) the proph.
Rev. 3. 7 he that hath the key of D., he that openeth
5. 5 Lion of the tribe of Juda, the Root of D.
22. 16 I am the root and the offspring of D., (and)

DAWN, to —
To shine through, διαυγάζω *diaugazō.*
2 Pe. 1. 19 until the day dawn, and the day star arise

DAWN, to begin to —
To begin to dawn upon, ἐπιφώσκω *epiphōskō.*
Matt 28. 1 as it began to dawn toward the first (day)

DAWNING —
1. *To go up, ascend,* עָלָה *alah.*
Josh. 6. 15 that they rose early about the dawning
2. *Eye lids,* עַפְעַפַּיִם *aphappim.*
Job 3. 9 neither let it see the dawning of the day
3. *To face, front, turn about, look,* פָּנָה *panah.*
Judg 19. 26 Then came the woman in the dawning of

DAWNING of the day or morning —
Twilight, נֶשֶׁף *nesheph.*
Job 7. 4 to and fro unto the dawning of the day
Psa. 119. 147 I prevented the dawning of the morning

DAY —
1. *Morning,* בֹּקֶר *boqer.*
Judg 19. 26 came the woman in the dawning of the d.
2 Sa. 13. 4 Why (art) thou..lean from day to day?
2. *Day,* יוֹם *yom.*
Gen. 1. 5 God called the light Day, and the dark.
1. 5 evening and..morning were the first day
1. 8 evening and..morning were the second d.
1. 13 evening and..morning were the third day
1. 14 Let there be lights..to divide the day
1. 16 the greater light to rule the day, and the
1. 18 to rule over the day and over the night
1. 19 evening and..morning were the fourth d.
1. 23 evening and the morning were the fifth d.
1. 31 evening and the morning were the sixth d.
2. 2 And on the seventh day God ended his
2. 2 he rested on the seventh day from all his
2. 3 blessed the seventh day, and sanctified it
2. 4 in the day that the LORD God made the
2. 17 in the day that thou eatest thereof thou
3. 5 God doth know that in the day ye eat
3. 8 in the garden in the cool of the day: and
4. 14 thou hast driven me out this day from
5. 1 In the day that God created man, in the
5. 2 blessed them..in the day when they were
7. 11 the seventeenth day..the same day were
7. 13 In the self same day entered Noah, and S.
8. 4 on the seventeenth day of the month
8. 14 on the seven and twentieth day of the
8. 22 summer and winter, and day and night
15. 18 In that same day the LORD made a cove.
17. 23 circumcised the flesh..the self same day
17. 26 the self same day was Abraham circum.
18. 1 in the tent door in the heat of the day
19. 37 the father of the Moabites unto this day
19. 38 the father of the children..unto this day
21. 8 Abraham made a great feast the (same) d.
22. 4 Then on the third day Abraham lifted up
22. 14 as it is said (to) this day, In the mount of
24. 12 I pray thee, send me good speed this day
24. 42 And I came this day unto the well, and
25. 31 Jacob said, Sell me this day thy birthright
25. 33 Jacob said, Swear to me this day; and he
26. 32 it came to pass the same day, that Isaac's
26. 33 of the city (is) Beer-sheba unto this day
27. 2 I am old, I know not the day of my death
27. 45 I be deprived also of you both in one day?
29. 7 (it is) yet high day, neither (is it) time
30. 35 he removed that day the he goats that
31. 22 it was told Laban on the third day that
31. 39 (whether) stolen by day, or stolen by night
31. 40 (Thus) I was; in the day the drought con.
31. 43 and what can I do this day unto these
31. 48 a witness between me and thee this day
32. 32 the hollow of the thigh, unto this day
33. 13 if men should over drive them one day
33. 16 Esau returned that day on his way unto
34. 25 And it came to pass on the third day
35. 3 who answered me in the day of my dis.
35. 20 the pillar of Rachel's grave unto this day
40. 20 third day, (which was) Pharaoh's birthday
41. 9 saying, I do remember my faults this day
42. 13 the youngest (is) this day with our father
42. 18 Joseph said unto them the third day
42. 32 the youngest (is) this day with our father
47. 23 I have bought you this day and your
47. 26 And Joseph made it a law..unto this day
Gen. 48. 15 fed me all my life long unto this day
48. 20 he blessed them that day, saying, In thee
50. 20 as (it is) this day, to save much people
Exod. 2. 13 And when he went out the second day
5. 6 commanded the same day the taskmasters
6. 28 it came to pass, on the day (when) the L.
8. 22 I will sever in that day the land of Gos.
10. 6 have seen, since the day..unto this day
10. 13 an east wind upon the land all that day
10. 28 for in (that) day thou seest my face thou
12. 6 keep it up until the fourteenth day of
12. 14 this day shall be unto you for a memorial
12. 15 even the first day ye shall put away leav.
12. 15 from the first day until the seventh day
12. 16 And in the first day (there shall be) an
12. 16 in the seventh day there shall be an holy
12. 17 in this self same day have I brought your
12. 17 therefore shall ye observe this day in
12. 18 on the fourteenth day of the month at
12. 18 the one and twentieth day of the month
12. 41 even the self same day it came to pass
12. 51 And it came to pass the self same day
13. 3 Remember this day, in which ye came
13. 4 This day came ye out, in the month Abib
13. 6 the seventh day (shall be) a feast to the
13. 8 thou shalt show thy son in that day, say.
14. 30 Thus the LORD saved Israel that day out
16. 1 on the fifteenth day of the second month
16. 5 on the sixth day they shall prepare (that)
16. 22 on the sixth day they gathered twice as
16. 26 but on the seventh day..in it there shall
16. 27 there went out..on the seventh day for
16. 29 therefore he giveth you on the sixth day
16. 29 let no man go out..on the seventh day
16. 30 So the people rested on the seventh day
19. 1 the same day came they (into) the wilder.
19. 11 And be ready against the third day: for
19. 11 the third day the LORD will come down
19. 15 he said..Be ready against the third day
19. 16 And it came to pass on the third day, in
20. 8 Remember the sabbath day, to keep it
20. 10 the seventh day (is) the sabbath of the L.
20. 11 rested the seventh day: wherefore the
20. 11 LORD blessed the sabbath d. and hallowed
22. 30 on the eighth day thou shalt give it me
23. 12 and on the seventh day thou shalt rest
24. 16 and the seventh day he called unto M.
31. 15 doeth (any) work in the sabbath day, he
31. 17 seventh day he rested, and was refreshed
32. 28 there fell of the people that day about
32. 29 he may bestow upon you a blessing this day
32. 34 in the day when I visit I will visit their
34. 11 that which I command thee this day
34. 21 but on the seventh day thou shalt rest
35. 2 the seventh day there shall be..an h. d.
35. 3 shall kindle no fire..upon the sabbath d.
40. 2 On the first day..shall thou set up the
40. 37 they journeyed not till the day that it
Lev. 6. 5 give it..in the day of his trespass offering
6. 20 unto the LORD in the day when he is
7. 15 the flesh..shall be eaten the same day
7. 16 it shall be eaten the same day that he
7. 17 on the third day shall be burnt with fire
7. 18 if (any)..be eaten at all on the third day
7. 35 the day (when) he presented them to
7. 36 in the day that he anointed them, (by) a
7. 38 in the day that he commanded the child.
8. 34 As he hath done this day, (so) the LORD
9. 1 came to pass on the eighth day, (that) M.
10. 19 this day have they offered their sin offer.
12. 3 in the eighth day the flesh of his foreskin
13. 5 priest shall look on him the seventh day
13. 6 shall look on him again the seventh day
13. 27 priest shall look upon him the seventh d.
13. 32, 34 in the seventh day the priest shall look
13. 51 look on the plague on the seventh day
14. 2 be the law..in the day of his cleansing
14. 9 it shall be on the seventh day, that he
14. 10 the eighth day he shall take two he lambs
14. 23 he shall bring them on the eighth day
14. 39 priest shall come again the seventh day
15. 14 on the eighth day he shall take to him
15. 29 on the eighth day she shall take unto
16. 30 For on that day shall..make an atone.
19. 6 It shall be eaten the same day ye offer it
19. 6 if ought remain until the third day, it
19. 7 if it be eaten at all on the third day
22. 27 and from the eighth day and thenceforth
22. 28 cow or ewe, ye shall not kill..in one day
22. 30 On the same day it shall be eaten up; ye
23. 3 but the seventh day (is) the sabbath of
23. 6 on the fifteenth day of the same month
23. 7 In the first day ye shall have an holy
23. 8 in the seventh day (is) an holy convocation
23. 12 ye shall offer that day when ye wave the
23. 14 until the self same day that ye have broug.
23. 15 from the day that ye brought the sheaf
23. 21 ye shall proclaim on the self same day
23. 27 a day of atonement: it shall be an holy
23. 28 And ye shall do no work in that same day
23. 28 for it (is) a day of atonement, to make an
23. 29 shall not be afflicted in that same day
23. 30 that doeth any work in that same day
23. 34 The fifteenth day of this seventh month
23. 35 the first day (shall be) an holy convocation
23. 36 eighth day shall be an holy convocation
23. 37 drink offerings, every thing upon his day
23. 39 Also in the fifteenth day of the seventh
23. 39 on the first day (shall be) a sabbath
23. 39 on the eighth day (shall be) a sabbath
23. 40 ye shall take you on the first day the
25. 9 in the day of atonement shall ye make

Lev. 27. 23 shall give thine estimation in that day
Num. 3. 1 in the day (that) the LORD spake with M.
3. 13 on the day that I smote all the first born
6. 9 shave his head in the day of his cleansing
6. 9 on the seventh day shall he shave it
6. 10 the eighth day he shall bring two turtles
6. 11 and shall hallow his head that same day
7. 1 it came to pass on the day that Moses had
7. 10 for dedicating of the altar in the day
7. 11 They shall offer..each prince on his day
7. 12 he that offered his offering the first day
7. 18 On the second day Nethaneel the son of Z.
7. 24 On the third day Eliab the son of Helon
7. 30 On the fourth day Elizur the son of S.
7. 36 On the fifth day Shelumiel the son of Zur.
7. 42 On the sixth day Eliasaph the son of De.
7. 48 On the seventh day Elishama the son of A.
7. 54 On the eighth day (offered) Gamaliel the
7. 60 On the ninth day Abidan the son of Gid.
7. 66 On the tenth day Ahiezer the son of Am.
7. 72 On the eleventh day Pagiel the son of O.
7. 78 On the twelth day Ahira the son of Enan
7. 84 in the day when it was anointed, by the
8. 17 on the day that I smote every first born
9. 3 In the fourteenth day of this month, at
9. 5 kept the passover on the fourteenth day
9. 6 could not keep the passover on that day
9. 6 and they came before Moses..on that day
9. 11 The fourteenth day of the second month
9. 15 on the day that the tabernacle was reared
10. 10 Also in the day of your gladness, and in
11. 19 Ye shall not eat one day, nor two
11. 31, 31 as it were a day's journey on
11. 32 stood up all that day..all the next day
15. 23 from the day that the LORD commanded
15. 32 gathered sticks upon the sabbath day
19. 12 He shall purify himself..on the third day
19. 12 and on the seventh day he shall be clean
19. 12 but if he purify not himself the third day
19. 12 then the seventh day he shall not be clean
19. 19 on the third day, and on the seventh day
19. 19 on the seventh day he shall purify him.
22. 30 ever since (I was) thine unto this day?
25. 18 in the day of the plague for Peor's sake
28. 9 on the sabbath day two lambs of the
28. 16 the fourteenth day of the first month
28. 17 in the fifteenth day of this month (is) the
28. 18 the first day (shall be) an holy convocation
28. 25 on the seventh day ye shall have an holy
28. 26 Also in the day of the first fruits, when
29. 1 it is a day of blowing the trumpets unto
29. 12 on the fifteenth day of the seventh month
29. 17 the second day (ye shall offer) twelve
29. 20 on the third day eleven bullocks, two
29. 23 on the fourth day ten bullocks, two rams
29. 26 on the fifth day nine bullocks, two rams
29. 29 on the sixth day eight bullocks, two rams
29. 32 on the seventh day seven bullocks, two
29. 35 eighth day ye shall have a solemn assem.
30. 5 if her father disallow her in the day that
30. 7 held his peace at her in the day that he
30. 8 if her husband disallowed her on the day
30. 12 her husband..made them void on the day
30. 14 hold his peace at her from day to day
30. 14 held his peace..in the day that he heard
31. 19 on the third day, and on the seventh day
31. 24 wash your clothes on the seventh day
33. 3 on the fifteenth day of the first month
Deut. 1. 10 ye (are) this day as the stars of heaven
1. 39 which in that day had no knowledge
2. 18 to pass over..the coast of Moab, this day
2. 22 dwelt in their stead even unto this day
2. 25 This day will I begin to put the dread of
2. 30 deliver him into thy hand, as..this day
3. 14 name, Bashan-havoth-jair, unto this day
4. 4 ye..(are) alive every one of you this day
4. 8 this law, which I set before you this day
4. 10 the day that thou stoodest before the L.
4. 15 the day (that) the LORD spake unto you
4. 20 people of inheritance, as (ye are) this day
4. 26 I call heaven..against you this day, that
4. 32 since the day that God created man upon
4. 38 to give thee their land..as (it is) this day
4. 39 Know therefore this day, and consider
4. 40 I command thee this day, that it may go
5. 1 I speak in your ears this day, that ye may
5. 3 who (are) all of us here alive this day
5. 12 Keep the sabbath day to sanctify it, as
5. 14 the seventh day (is) the sabbath of the L.
5. 15 commanded thee to keep the sabbath day
5. 24 we have seen this day that God doth talk
6. 6 these words..I command thee this day
6. 24 preserve us alive, as (it is) at this day
7. 11 statutes..which I command thee this day
8. 1 which I command thee this day shall ye
8. 11 statutes, which I command thee this day
8. 18 sware unto thy fathers, as (it is) this day
8. 19 I testify against you this day, that ye
9. 1 Thou (art) to pass over Jordan this day
9. 3 Understand..this day, that the LORD thy
9. 7 the day that thou didst depart out of the
9. 10 out of the midst of the fire, in the day of
9. 24 Ye have been rebellious..from the day
10. 4 out of the midst of the fire, in the day
10. 8 and to bless in his name, unto this day
10. 13 I command thee this day for thy good?
10. 15 you above all people, as (it is) this day
11. 2 know ye this day: for (I speak) not with
11. 4 LORD hath destroyed them unto this day
11. 8 I command you this day, that ye may be
11. 13 I command you this day, to love the L.
11. 26 Behold, I set before you this day

Deut. 11. 27 commandments..I command you this day
11. 28 I command you this day, to go after other
11. 32 judgments..I set before you this day
12. 8 all (the things) that we do here this day
13. 18 which I command thee this day, to do
15. 5 command. which I command thee this day
16. 3 that thou mayest remember the day when
16. 4 which thou sacrificedst the first day at
16. 8 and on the seventh day (shall be) a
18. 16 in the day of the assembly, saying, Let
19. 9 I command thee this day, to love the LORD
20. 3 ye approach this day unto battle against
21. 23 thou shalt in any wise bury him that day
24. 15 At his day thou shalt give (him) his hire
26. 3 I profess this day unto the LORD thy God
26. 16 This day the LORD thy God hath com
26. 17 Thou hast avouched the LORD this day to
26. 18 the LORD hath avouched thee this day to
27. 1 commandments..I command you this day
27. 2 the day when ye shall pass over Jordan
27. 4 ye shall set up these stones..this day, in
27. 9 this day thou art become the people of
27. 10 statutes, which I command thee this day
27. 11 Moses charged the people the same day
28. 1 commandments..I command thee this d.
28. 13 I command thee this day, to observe and
28. 14 words which I command thee this day
28. 15 his statutes, which I command thee this d.
28. 32 (with longing) for them all the day long
29. 4 eyes to see, and ears to hear, unto this day
29. 10 Ye stand this day all of you before the L.
29. 12 which..LORD..maketh with thee this day
29. 15 with us this day before the LORD our God
29. 15 (him) that (is) not here with us this day
29. 18 whose heart turneth away this day from
29. 28 into another land, as (it is) this day
30. 2 I command thee this day, thou and
30. 8 and do all..I command thee this day
30. 11 commandment..I command thee this d
30. 15 See, I have set before thee this day life
30. 16 I command thee this day to love the Lo.
30. 18 I denounce unto you this day, that ye
30. 19 I call heaven..to record this day against
31. 2 an hundred and twenty years old this day
31. 17 my anger shall be kindled..in that day
31. 17 so that they will say in that day, Are not
31. 18 I will surely hide my face in that day for
31. 22 therefore wrote this song the same day
31. 27 while I am yet alive with you this day
32. 35 for the day of their calamity (is) at hand
32. 46 words which I testify among you this day
32. 48 spake unto Moses that selfsame day
33. 12 shall cover him all the day long, and
34. 6 knoweth of his sepulchre unto this day
Josh. 3. 7 This day will I begin to magnify thee in
4. 9 twelve stones..they are there unto this d.
4. 14 On that day the LORD magnified Joshua
5. 9 This day have I rolled away the reproach
5. 9 the place is called Gilgal unto this day
5. 10 kept the passover on the fourteenth day
5. 11 unleavened cakes..in the self same day
6. 4 the seventh day ye shall compass the city
6. 10 until the day I bid you shout; then shall
6. 14 the second day they compassed the city
6. 15 it came to pass on the seventh day, that
6. 15 on that day they compassed the city sev.
6. 25 she dwelleth in Israel (even) unto this
7. 25 the LORD shall trouble thee this day
7. 26 a great heap of stones unto this day
7. 26 called, The valley of Achor, unto this day
8. 25 (so) it was, (that) all that fell that day
8. 28 made it an heap for ever..unto this day
8. 29 heap of stones, (that remain,) unto this day
9. 12 on the day we came forth to go unto you
9. 17 came unto their cities on the third day
9. 27 Joshua made them that day hewers of
9. 27 even unto this day, in the place which he
10. 12 in the day when the LORD delivered up
10. 13 hasted not to go down about a whole day
10. 14 there was no day like that before it or
10. 27 stones..until this very day
10. 28 that day Joshua took Makkedah, and
10. 32 Israel, which took it on the second day
10. 35 And they took it on that day, and smote
10. 35 he utterly destroyed that day, according
13. 13 dwell among the Israelites until this day
14. 9 Moses sware on that day, saying, Surely
14. 10 I (am) this day fourscore and five years old
14. 11 strong this day as (I was) in the day that
14. 12 whereof the LORD spake in that day; for
14. 12 heardest in that day how the Anakims
14. 14 became the inheritance..unto this day
15. 63 dwell with the children..unto this day
16. 10 the Canaanites dwell..unto this day, and
22. 3 have not left your brethren..unto this d.
22. 16 turn away this day from following the L.
22. 16 ye might rebel this day against the LORD?
22. 17 we are not cleansed until this day, alth.
22. 18 ye must turn away this day from follow.
22. 22 if in transgression..save us not this day
22. 29 God forbid that we should..turn this day
22. 31 This day we perceive that the LORD (is)
23. 8 But cleave..as ye have done unto this d.
23. 9 able to stand before you unto this day
23. 14 this day I (am) going the way of all the
24. 15 choose you this day whom ye will serve
24. 25 So Joshua made a covenant..that day
Judg. 1. 21 dwell with the children..unto this day
1. 26 which (is) the name thereof unto this day
3. 30 So Moab was subdued that day under the
4. 14 the day in which the LORD hath delivered
4. 23 So God subdued on that day Jabin the

Judg. 5. 1 Then sang Deborah..on that day, saying
6. 24 unto this day it (is) yet in Ophrah of the
6. 32 Therefore on that day he called him Jer.
9. 18 ye are risen up..this day, and have
9. 19 with Jerubbaal and with his house this d.
9. 45 fought against the city all that day; and
10. 4 which are called Havoth-jair unto this d.
10. 15 deliver us only, we pray thee, this day
11. 27 be judge this day between the children
12. 3 are ye come up unto me this day, to fight
13. 7 from the womb to the day of his death
13. 10 man..that came unto me the (other) day
14. 15, 17 it came to pass on the seventh day
14. 18 on the seventh day before the sun went
15. 19 En-hakkore, which (is) in Lehi unto this d.
18. 1 for unto that day (all their) inheritance
18. 12 that place Mahaneh-dan unto this day
18. 30 his sons were priests..until the day
19. 5 it came to pass on the fourth day, when
19. 8 he arose early..on the fifth day to depart
19. 9 Behold, now the day draweth toward
19. 9 behold, the day groweth to an end; lodge
19. 11 when they (were) by Jebus, the day was
19. 30 the day that the children of Israel came
19. 30 out of the land of Egypt unto this day
20. 21 and destroyed..of the Israelites that day
20. 22 they put themselves in array the first day
20. 24 children of Israel came..the second day
20. 25 Benjamin went forth..the second day
20. 26 there before the LORD, and fasted that d.
20. 30 children of Israel went up..the third d.
20. 35 destroyed of the Benjamites that day
20. 46 all which fell that day of Benjamin were
21. 6 is one tribe cut off from Israel this day
Ruth 3. 18 until he have finished the thing this day
4. 5 What day thou buyest the field of the
4. 9, 10 Ye (are) witnesses this day
4. 14 not left thee this day without a kinsman
1 Sa. 2. 34 in one day they shall die both of them
3. 12 In that day I will perform against Eli
4. 12 came to Shiloh the same day, with his
5. 5 tread on the threshold..unto this day
6. 15 sacrificed sacrifices the same day unto
6. 16 they returned to Ekron the same day
6. 18 (which stone remaineth) unto this day in
7. 6 fasted on that day, and said there, We
7. 10 thundered with a great thunder on that d.
8. 8 since the day that I brought them up out
8. 8 even unto this day, wherewith they have
8. 18 ye shall cry out in that day because of
8. 18 the LORD will not hear you in that day
9. 15 told Samuel in his ear a day before Saul
9. 24 So Saul did eat with Samuel that day
10. 9 and all those signs came to pass that day
10. 19 ye have this day rejected your God, who
11. 11 and slew..until the heat of the day: and
11. 13 shall not a man be put to death this day
12. 2 I have walked before you..unto this day
12. 5 his anointed (is) witness this day, that ye
12. 18 the LORD sent thunder and rain that day
13. 22 So it came to pass, in the day of battle
14. 1 it came to pass upon a day, that Jonath.
14. 23 So the LORD saved Israel that day: and
14. 24 the men of Israel were distressed that d.
14. 28 Cursed (be) the man that eateth..this d.
14. 31 they smote the Philistines that day from
14. 33 said..roll a great stone unto me this day
14. 37 But he answered him not that day
14. 38 see wherein this sin hath been this day
14. 45 for he hath wrought with God this day
15. 28 hath rent the kingdom..from thee this d.
15. 35 Samuel came no more..until the day of
16. 13 came upon David from that day forward
17. 10 said, I defy the armies of Israel this day
17. 46 This day will the LORD deliver thee into
17. 46 I will give the carcases..this day unto
18. 2 Saul took him that day, and would let
18. 9 Saul eyed David from that day and forw.
18. 21 Thou shalt this day be my son in law in
19. 24 lay down naked all that day and all that
20. 26 Saul spake not any thing that day: for
20. 34 Jonathan..did eat no meat the second d.
21. 5 though it were sanctified this day in the
21. 6 to put hot bread in the day when it was
21. 7 a certain man..(was) there that day
21. 10 David arose, and fled that day for fear
22. 8 hath stirred up my servant..at this day?
22. 13 he should rise against me..as at this day?
22. 18 slew on that day fourscore and five per.
22. 22 David said..I knew (it) that day, when
23. 14 And Saul sought him every day; but
24. 4 men of David said unto him, Behold the d.
24. 10 Behold, this day thine eyes have seen
24. 18 thou hast showed this day how that thou
24. 19 for that thou hast done unto me this da.
25. 8 for we come in a good day: give, I pray
25. 32 which sent thee this day to meet me
25. 33 which hast kept me this day from coming
26. 8 God hath delivered thine enemy..this d.
26. 10 the LORD shall smite him; or his day
26. 19 for they have driven me out this day
26. 21 because my soul was precious..this day
26. 24 thy life was much set by this day in
27. 1 I shall now perish one day by the hand
27. 6 Then Achish gave him Ziklag that day
27. 6 wherefore Ziklag pertaineth..unto this d.
28. 18 hath the LORD done this thing..this day
28. 20 he had eaten no bread all the day, nor all
29. 3 since he fell (unto me) unto this day
29. 6 since the day of thy coming..unto this d.
29. 8 as I have been with thee unto this day
30. 1 men were come to Ziglag on the third d.

1 Sa. 30. 25 And it was (so) from that day forward
30. 25 he made it a statute..unto this day
31. 6 Saul died..and all his men, that same d.
2 Sa. 1. 2 It came even to pass on the third day
2. 17 there was a very sore battle that day: and
3. 8 show kindness this day unto the house
3. 35 David to eat meat while it was yet day
3. 37 For..all Israel, understood that day
3. 38 and a great man fallen this day in Israel?
3. 39 I (am) this day weak, though anointed
4. 3 and were sojourners there until this day
4. 5 and came about the heat of the day to
4. 8 the LORD hath avenged my lord..this d
5. 8 said on that day, Whosoever getteth
6. 8 name of the place Perez-uzzah to this d.
6. 9 David was afraid of the LORD that day
6. 23 had no child unto the day of her death
7. 6 Whereas I have not dwelt..to this day
11. 12 So Uriah abode in Jerusalem that day
12. 18 it came to pass on the seventh day, that
13. 32 this hath been determined from the day
13. 37 And (David) mourned for his son every d.
15. 20 should I this day make thee go up and
16. 12 requite me good for his cursing this day
18. 7 there was there a great slaughter that day
18. 8 the wood devoured more people that day
18. 18 it is called unto this day, Absalom's place
18. 20 Thou shalt not bear tidings this day
18. 20 but thou shalt bear tidings another day
18. 20 this day thou shalt bear no tidings, bec.
18. 31 the LORD hath avenged thee this day of
19. 2 the victory that day was (turned) into
19. 2 the people heard say that day how the
19. 3 the people gat them by stealth that day
19. 5 Thou hast shamed this day the faces of
19. 5 which this day have saved thy life, and
19. 6 for thou hast declared this day, that thou
19. 6 for this day I perceive, that if Absalom
19. 6 and all we had died this day, then it had
19. 19 the day that my lord the king went out
19. 20 I am come the first this day of all the
19. 22 that ye should this day be adversaries
19. 22 shall..any man be put to death this day
19. 22 do not I know that I (am) this day king
19. 24 the day the king departed until the day
19. 35 I (am) this day fourscore years old: (and)
20. 3 they were shut up unto the day of their
22. 1 in the day (that) the LORD had delivered
22. 19 They prevented me in the day of my cal.
23. 10 the LORD wrought a great victory that d.
24. 18 Gad came that day to David, and said
1 Ki. 1. 25 he is gone down this day, and hath slain
1. 30 even so will I certainly do this day
1. 48 given (one) to sit on my throne this day
2. 8 cursed me with a grievous curse in the d.
2. 24 Adonijah shall be put to death this day
2. 37 it shall be, (that) on the day thou goest
2. 42 on the day thou goest out, and walkest
3. 6 to sit on his throne, as (it is) this day
3. 18 the third day after that I was delivered
4. 22 Solomon's provision for one day was thir.
5. 7 Blessed (be) the LORD this day, which
8. 8 and there they are unto this day
8. 16 Since the day that I brought forth my peo.
8. 24 and hast fulfilled (it)..as (it is) this day
8. 29 be open toward this house night and day
8. 61 to keep his commandments, as at this d
8. 64 The same day did the king hallow the
8. 66 On the eighth day he sent the people aw.
9. 13 called..the land of Cabul unto this day
9. 21 a tribute of bond service unto this day
10. 12 came no such almug trees..unto this day
12. 7 be a servant unto this people this day
12. 12 people came to Rehoboam the third day
12. 12 saying, Come to me again the third day
12. 19 against the house of David unto this day
12. 32 a feast..on the fifteenth day of the month
12. 33 the fifteenth day of the eighth month
13. 3 he gave a sign the same day, saying, This
13. 11 that the man of God had done that day
14. 14 cut off the house of Jeroboam that day
16. 16 king over Israel that day in the camp
17. 14 until the day (that) the LORD sendeth rain
18. 36 let it be known this day that thou (art)
19. 4 he himself went a day's journey into the
20. 13 will deliver it into thine hand this day
20. 29 in the seventh day the battle was joined
20. 29 an hundred thousand footmen in one day
22. 25 thou shalt see in that day, when thou
22. 35 the battle increased that day: and the
2 Ki. 2. 22 So the waters were healed unto this day
4. 8 it fell on a day, that Elisha passed to
4. 11 it fell on a day, that he came thither
4. 18 it fell on a day, that he went out to his
6. 29 I said unto her on the next day, Give thy
6. 31 if the head..shall stand on him this day
7. 9 this day (is) a day of good tidings, and we
8. 6 since the day that she left the land, even
8. 22 under the hand of Judah unto this day
10. 27 and made it a draught house unto this day
14. 7 called the name..Joktheel unto this day
15. 5 he was a leper unto the day of his death
16. 6 the Syrians..dwelt there unto this day
17. 23 their own land to Assyria unto this day
17. 34 Unto this day they do after the former
17. 41 did their fathers, so do they..this day
19. 3 This day (is) a day of trouble, and of reb.
20. 5 on the third day thou shalt go up unto
20. 8 into the house of the LORD the third day?
20. 17 have laid up in store unto this day, shall
21. 15 the day their fathers came..unto this day
1 Ch. 4. 41 destroyed them utterly unto this day
1 Ch. 4. 43 and dwelt there unto this day
5. 26 brought them unto Halah..unto this day
11. 22 and slew a lion in a pit in a snowy day
13. 11 place is called Perez-uzza to this day
13. 12 David was afraid of God that day, saying
16. 7 on that day David delivered first (this
16. 23 show forth from day to day his salvation
17. 5 day that I brought up Israel unto this d.
26. 17 northward four a day, southward four a d.
28. 7 if he be constant to do..as at this day
29. 5 willing to consecrate his service this day
29. 21 on the morrow after that day, (even) a
29. 22 eat and drink before the LORD on that d.
2 Ch. 5. 9 And there it is unto this day
6. 5 Since the day that I brought forth my
6. 15 and hast fulfilled (it)..as (it is) this day
7. 9 in the eighth day they made a solemn
7. 10 on the three and twentieth day of the
8. 8 make to pay tribute until this day
8. 16 the day of the foundation of the house
10. 12 people came to Rehoboam on the third d.
10. 12 saying, Come again to me on the third day
10. 19 against the house of David unto this day
18. 24 thou shalt see on that day when thou
18. 34 the battle increased that day: howbeit
20. 26 on the fourth day they assembled
20. 26 The valley of Berachah, unto this day
21. 10 from under the hand of Judah unto this d.
26. 21 king was a leper unto the day of his death
28. 6 hundred and twenty thousand in one day
29. 17 on the eighth day of the month came
29. 17 in the sixteenth day of the first month
35. 21 I (come) not against thee this day, but
35. 25 spake..in their lamentations to this day
Ezra 3. 6 From the first day of the seventh month
6. 15 this house was finished on the third day
8. 33 on the fourth day was the silver and the
9. 7 (been) in a great trespass unto this day
9. 7 to confusion of face, as (it is) this day
9. 15 we remain yet escaped, as (it is) this day
10. 13 neither (is this) a work of one day or two
10. 16 sat down in the first day of the tenth
10. 17 by the first day of the first month
Neh. 1. 11 prosper, I pray thee, thy servant, this d.
4. 2 will they make an end in a day? will
4. 22 be a guard to us, and labour on the day
5. 11 Restore, I pray you, to them, even this d.
8. 2 upon the first day of the seventh month
8. 9 This day (is) holy unto the LORD your God
8. 10 for (this) day (is) holy unto our LORD
8. 11 Hold your peace, for the day (is) holy
8. 13 on the second day were gathered together
8. 17 unto that day had not the children of
8. 18 from the first day unto the last day he
8. 18 on the eighth day (was) a solemn assem.
9. 1 the twenty and fourth day of this month
9. 3 they..read..(one) fourth part of the day
9. 10 didst thou get..a name, as (it is) this day
9. 32 of the kings of Assyria unto this day
9. 36 we (are) servants this day; and (for) the
10. 31 bring..any victuals on the sabbath day
10. 31 would not buy it of them..on the holy d.
12. 43 that day they offered great sacrifices
13. 1 On that day they read in the book of M.
13. 15 in the day wherein they sold victuals
13. 15 brought into Jerusalem on the sabbath d.
13. 17 What..(is) this that ye do..the sabbath d.?
13. 19 burden be brought in on the sabbath day
13. 22 keep the gates, to sanctify the sabbath d.
Esth. 1. 10 On the seventh day, when the heart of
1. 18 ladies of Persia and Media say this day
2. 11 Mordecai walked every day before the
3. 7 from day to day, and from month to
3. 12 called on the thirteenth day of the first
3. 13 little children and women, in one day
3. 14 they should be ready against that day
4. 16 and neither eat nor drink..night or day
5. 1 it came to pass on the third day, that
5. 4 let the king and Haman come this day
5. 9 Then went Haman forth that day joyful
7. 2 said again unto Esther on the second day
8. 1 On that day did the king Ahasuerus give
8. 12 Upon one day, in all the provinces of
8. 13 the Jews should be ready against that d.
8. 17 joy and gladness, a feast and a good day
9. 1 the month Adar, on the thirteenth day
9. 1 in the day that the enemies of the Jews
9. 11 On that day the number of those that
9. 13 also according unto this day's decree
9. 15 on the fourteenth day also of the month
9. 17 On the thirteenth day of the month Adar
9. 17 on the fourteenth day of the same rested
9. 17, 18 made it a day of feasting and gladness
9. 19 made the fourteenth day of the month
9. 19 a good day, and of sending portions one
9. 21 that they should keep the fourteenth day
9. 21 and the fifteenth day of the same, yearly
9. 22 to joy, and from mourning into a good d.
Job 1. 4 feasted (in their) houses, every one his
1. 6 there was a day when the sons of God
1. 13 there was a day when his sons and his
2. 1 there was a day when the sons of God ca.
3. 1 opened Job his mouth, and cursed his day
3. 3 Let the day perish wherein I was born
3. 4 Let that day be darkness; let not God
3. 5 let the blackness of the day terrify it
3. 8 Let them curse it that curse the day
14. 6 shall accomplish, as an hireling, his day
15. 23 he knoweth that the day of darkness is
17. 12 They change the night into day: the
18. 20 They that come..be astonied at his day
20. 28 shall flow away in the day of his wrath
Job 21. 30 is reserved to the day of destruction?
21. 30 shall be brought forth to the day of wrath
38. 23 against the day of battle and war?
Psa. 2. 7 Thou (art) my Son; this day have I bego.
7. 11 God is angry (with the wicked) every day
18. *title* in the day (that) the LORD delivered
18. 18 prevented me in the day of my calamity
19. 2 Day unto day uttereth speech, and night
20. 1 The LORD hear thee in the day of trouble
25. 5 on thee do I wait all the day
32. 3 waxed old through my roaring all the day
35. 28 shall speak..of thy praise all the day
37. 13 for he seeth that his day is coming
38. 6 I am troubled..I go mourning all the day
38. 12 They..imagine deceits all the day long
44. 8 In God we boast all the day long, and
44. 22 for thy sake are we killed all the day
50. 15 And call upon me in the day of trouble
56. 5 Every day they wrest my words: all their
59. 16 been my defence and refuge in the day
71. 8 Let my mouth be filled..all the day
71. 15 show forth..thy salvation all the day
71. 24 talk of thy righteousness all the day long
73. 14 all the day long have I been plagued, and
74. 16 The day (is) thine, the night also (is) thine
77. 2 In the day of my trouble, I sought the L.
78. 9 carrying bows, turned back in the day of
78. 42 (nor) the day when he delivered them
81. 3 time appointed, on our solemn feast day
84. 10 For a day in thy courts (is) better than a
86. 7 In the day of my trouble I will call upon
88. 1 I have cried day (and) night before thee
89. 16 In thy name..they rejoice all the day
92. *title.* A Psalm (or) Song for the sabbath day
95. 8 the day of temptation in the wilderness
96. 2 show forth his salvation from day to day
102. 2 Hide not thy face from me in the day
102. 2 in the day (when) I call answer me
102. 8 Mine enemies reproach me all the day
110. 3 Thy people (shall be) willing in the day
110. 5 shall strike through kings in the day of
118. 24 This (is) the day (which) the LORD hath
119. 91 They continue this day according to thine
119. 97 thy law! it (is) my meditation all the day
119. 164 Seven times a day do I praise thee
137. 7 the children of Edom in the day of Jeru.
138. 3 In the day when I cried thou answeredst
139. 12 but the night shineth as the day
140. 7 hast covered my head in the day of battle
145. 2 Every day will I bless thee; and I will
146. 4 in that very day his thoughts perish
Prov. 4. 18 shineth more and more unto the perf. day
6. 34 will not spare in the day of vengeance
7. 14 (I have) peace..this day have I
7. 20 (and) will come home at the day appoin.
11. 4 Riches profit not in the day of wrath
16. 4 yea, even the wicked for the day of evil
21. 26 He coveteth greedily all the day long
21. 31 horse (is) prepared against the day of
22. 19 I have made known to thee this day, even
23. 17 in the fear of the LORD all the day long
24. 10 (If) thou faint in the day of adversity, thy
27. 1 knowest not what a day may bring forth
27. 10 into thy brother's house in the day of thy
27. 15 A continual dropping in a very rainy day
Eccl. 7. 1 day of death than the day of one's birth
7. 14 In the day of prosperity be joyful
7. 14 but in the day of adversity consider
8. 8 neither (hath he) power in the day of
8. 16 neither day nor night seeth sleep with his
12. 3 In the day when the keepers of the house
Song 2. 17 Until the day break, and the shadows flee
3. 11 in the day of his espousals, and in the day
4. 6 Until the day break, and the shadows flee
8. 8 in the day when she shall be spoken for?
Isa 2. 11, 17 LORD alone shall be exalted in that d.
2. 12 the day of the LORD of hosts (shall be)
2. 20 In that day a man shall cast his idols
3. 7 In that day shall he swear, saying, I will
3. 18 In that day the LORD will take away the
4. 1 in that day seven women shall take hold
4. 2 In that day shall the branch of the LORD
5. 30 in that day they shall roar against them
7. 17 from the day that Ephraim departed from
7. 18, 21, 23 it shall come to pass in that day
7. 20 In the same day shall the LORD shave
9. 4 of his oppressor, as in the day of Midian
9. 14 head and tail, branch and rush, in one day
10. 3 what will ye do in the day of visitation
10. 17 devour his thorns and..briers in one day
10. 20, 27 it shall come to pass in that day
10. 32 As yet shall he remain at Nob that day
11. 10 in that day there shall be a root of Jesse
11. 11 it shall come to pass in that day, (that)
11. 16 in the day that he came up out of the
12. 1 in that day thou shalt say, O LORD, I will
12. 4 in that day shall ye say, Praise the LORD
13. 6 Howl ye; for the day of the LORD (is) at
13. 9 the day of the LORD cometh, cruel both
13. 13 and in the day of his fierce anger
14. 3 it shall come to pass in the day that the
17. 4 in that day it shall come to pass, (that)
17. 7 At that day shall a man look to his Maker
17. 9 In that day shall his strong cities be as a
17. 11 In the day shalt thou make thy plant to
17. 11 the day of grief and of desperate sorrow
19. 16 In that day shall Egypt be like unto
19. 18 In that day shall five cities in the land of
19. 19 In that day there shall be an altar to
19. 21 Egyptians shall know the LORD in that d.
19. 23 In that day shall there be a highway out
19. 24 In that day shall Israel be the third

Isa. 20. 6 the inhabitant..shall say in that day
22. 5 (it is) a day of trouble, and of treading
22. 8 thou didst look in that day to the armour
22. 12 in that day did the Lord GOD of hosts
22. 20 it shall come to pass in that day, that
22. 25 In that day, saith the LORD of hosts
23. 15 it shall come to pass in that day, that
24. 21 it shall come to pass in that day, (that)
25. 9 it shall be said in that day, Lo, this (is)
26. 1 In that day shall this song be sung in
27. 1 In that day the LORD..shall punish levi.
27. 2 In that day sing ye unto her, A vineyard
27. 3 lest (any) hurt it..keep it night and day
27. 8 he stayeth his rough wind in the day of
27. 12, 13 it shall come to pass in that day (that)
28. 5 In that day shall the LORD of hosts be
28. 24 Doth the plowman plow all day to sow?
29. 18 in that day shall the deaf hear the words
30. 23 in that day shall thy cattle feed in large
30. 25 rivers (and) streams of waters in the day
30. 26 in the day that the LORD bindeth up the
31. 7 in that day every man shall cast away his
34. 8 (it is) the day of the LORD's vengeance
37. 3 This day (is) a day of trouble, and of reb.
38. 12 from day even to night wilt thou make
38. 13 from day (even) to night wilt thou make
38. 19 he shall praise thee, as I (do) this day
39. 6 have laid up in store until this day
43. 13 Yea, before the day (was) I (am) he; and
47. 9 shall come to thee in a moment in one d.
48. 7 before the day when thou heardest them
49. 8 in a day of salvation have I helped thee
51. 13 hast feared continually every day, because
52. 5 my name continually every day (is) blas.
52. 6 (they shall know) in that day that I (am)
56. 12 to morrow shall be as this day, (and) much
58. 3 in the day of your fast ye find pleasure
58. 4 ye shall not fast as (ye do this) day, to
58. 5 a day for a man to afflict his soul?
58. 5 and an acceptable day to the LORD?
58. 13 (from) doing thy pleasure on my holy day
61. 2 To proclaim..the day of vengence of our
62. 6 shall never hold their peace day nor night
63. 4 the day of vengeance (is) in mine heart
65. 2 I have spread out my hands all the day
65. 5 a fire that burneth all the day
66. 8 earth be made to bring forth in one day?
Jer. 1. 10 I have this day set thee over the nations
1. 18 I have made thee this day a defenced city
3. 25 from our youth even unto this day
4. 9 it shall come to pass at that day, saith
6. 4 Woe unto us! for the day goeth away, for
7. 22 in the day that I brought them out of
7. 25 Since the day that your fathers came forth
7. 25 unto this day I have even sent unto you
11. 4 In the day (that) I brought them forth out
11. 5 with milk and honey as (it is) this day
11. 7 in the day (that) I brought them up out
11. 7 of the land of Egypt, (even) unto this day
12. 3 and prepare them for the day of slaughter
16. 19 and my refuge in the day of affliction
17. 16 neither have I desired the woeful day
17. 17 thou (art) my hope in the day of evil
17. 18 bring upon them the day of evil, and
17. 21 bear no burden on the sabbath day, nor
17. 22 out of your houses on the sabbath day
17. 22 hallow ye the sabbath day, as I comman.
17. 24 the gates of the city on the sabbath day
17. 24 but hallow the sabbath day, to do no
17. 27 to hallow the sabbath day, and not to
17. 27 at the gates of Jerusalem on the sabbath d.
18. 17 I will show them the back..in the day of
20. 14 Cursed be the day wherein I was born
20. 14 let not the day wherein my mother bare
25. 3 From the thirteenth year..unto this day
25. 18 an hissing, and a curse, as (it is) this day
25. 33 slain of the LORD shall be at that day
27. 22 there shall they be until the day that I
30. 7 that day (is) great, so that none (is) like it
30. 8 it shall come to pass in that day, saith
31. 6 there shall be a day (that) the watchmen
31. 32 in the day (that) I took them by the hand
32. 20 in the land of Egypt, (even) unto this day
32. 20 and hast made thee a name, as at this day
32. 31 day that they built it even unto this day
33. 20 If ye can break my covenant of the day
34. 13 in the day that I brought them forth out
35. 14 for unto this day they drink none, but
36. 2 from the day I spake unto thee, from the
36. 30 dead body shall be cast out in the day
38. 28 until the day that Jerusalem was taken
39. 16 they shall be (accomplished) in that day
39. 17 I will deliver thee in that day, saith
40. 4 I loose thee this day from the chains
41. 4 it came to pass, the second day after he
42. 19 know..that I have admonished you this d.
42. 21 I have this day declared (it) to you; but
44. 2 this day they (are) a desolation, and no
44. 6 are wasted (and) desolate, as at this day
44. 10 They are not humbled (even) unto this day
44. 22 without an inhabitant, as at this day
44. 23 evil is happened unto you, as at this day
46. 10 the day of the Lord GOD of hosts, a day
46. 21 the day of their calamity was come upon
47. 4 Because of the day that cometh to spoil
48. 41 at that day shall be as the heart of a
49. 22 at that day shall the heart of the mighty
49. 26 all the men of war..be cut off in that day
50. 27 for their day is come, the time
50. 30 men of war shall be cut off in that day
50. 31 thy day is come, the time (that) I will visit
51. 2 in the day of trouble they shall be against
Jer. 52. 11 put him in prison till the day of his death
Lam 1. 12 afflicted (me) in the day of his fierce anger
1. 13 made me desolate (and) faint all the day
1. 21 thou wilt bring the day (that) thou hast
2. 1 remembered not his footstool in the day
2. 7 a noise..as in the day of a solemn feast
2. 16 this (is) the day that we looked for
2. 21 hast slain (them) in the day of thine anger
2. 22 Thou hast called as in a solemn day my
2. 22 so that in the day of the LORD's anger
3. 3 turneth his hand (against me) all the day
3. 14 a derision..(and) their song all the day
3. 57 Thou drewest near in the day (that) I
3. 62 and their device against me all the day
Eze. 1. 28 that is in the cloud in the day of rain
7. 7 time is come, the day of trouble (is) near
7. 10 Behold the day, behold, it is come
7. 12 The time is come, the day draweth near
7. 19 not be able to deliver them in the day of
13. 5 stand in the battle in the day of the LORD
16. 4 in the day thou wast born thy navel was
16. 5 to the loathing of thy person, in the day
16. 56 by thy mouth in the day of thy pride
20. 5 In the day when I chose Israel, and
20. 6 In the day (that) I lifted up mine hand
20. 29 name..is called Bamah unto this day
20. 31 with all your idols, even unto this day
21. 25 wicked prince of Israel, whose day is come
21. 29 whose day is come, when their iniquity
22. 24 nor rained upon in the day of indignation
23. 38 defiled my sanctuary in the same day
23. 39 they came the same day into my sanctu.
24. 2 name of the day, (even) of this same day
24. 2 set himself against Jerusalem this day
24. 25 in the day when I take from them their
24. 26 he that escapeth in that day shall come
24. 27 In that day shall thy mouth be opened
26. 18 the isles tremble in the day of thy fall
27. 27 midst of the seas in the day of thy ruin
28. 13 in thee in the day that thou wast created
28. 15 from the day that thou wast created, till
29. 21 In that day will I cause the horn of the
30. 2 Thus..Howl ye, Woe worth the day!
30. 3 the day (is) near, even the day of the LORD
30. 3 a cloudy day; it shall be the time of the
30. 9 In that day shall messengers go forth
30. 9 come upon them, as in the day of Egypt
30. 18 At Tehaphnehes also the day shall be
31. 15 In the day when he went down to the
32. 10 every man for his own life, in the day of
33. 12 deliver him in the day of..transgression
33. 12 day that he turneth from his wickedness
33. 12 for his (righteousness) in the day that he
34. 12 in the day that he is among his sheep
34. 12 been scattered in the cloudy and dark day
36. 33 In the day that I shall have cleansed you
38. 14 In that day when my people of Israel
38. 19 in that day there shall be a great shaking
39. 8 this (is) the day whereof I have spoken
39. 11 it shall come to pass in that day, (that)
39. 13 renown, the day that I shall be glorified
39. 22 I (am) the LORD their God from that day
40. 1 in the selfsame day the hand of the LORD
43. 18 in the day when they shall make it, to
43. 22 the second day thou shalt offer a kid
43. 27 it shall be, (that) upon the eighth day
44. 27 in the day that he goeth into the sanctuary
45. 21 in the fourteenth day of the month, ye
45. 22 upon that day shall the prince prepare
45. 25 in the fifteenth day of the month, shall
46. 1 in the day of the new moon it shall be
46. 4 offer unto the LORD in the sabbath day
46. 6 in the day of the new moon
46. 12 prepare..as he did on the sabbath day
48. 35 name of the city from (that) day (shall be)
Dan. 6. 10 kneeled upon his knees three times a d.
6. 13 but maketh his petition three times a d.
9. 7 unto us confusion of faces as at this day
9. 15 hast gotten thee renown, as at this day
10. 4 in the four and twentieth day of the first
10. 12 from the first day that thou didst set
Hos. 1. 5 it shall come to pass at that day, that I
1. 11 for great (shall be) the day of Jezreel
2. 3 set her as in the day that she was
2. 15 as in the day when she came up out of
2. 16 it shall be at that day, saith the LORD
2. 18 in that day will I make a covenant for
2. 21 it shall come to pass in that day, I will
4. 5 Therefore shalt thou fall in the day, and
5. 9 Ephraim shall be desolate in the day of
6. 2 in the third day he will raise us up
7. 5 In the day of our king the princes have
9. 5 in the solemn day, and in the day of the
10. 14 spoiled Beth-arbel in the day of battle
Joel 1. 15 Alas for the day! for the day of the LORD
2. 1 the day of the LORD cometh, for (it is)
2. 2 A day of darkness..a day of clouds and
2. 11 the day of the LORD (is) great and very
2. 31 before the great and the terrible day of
3. 14 the day of the LORD (is) near in the valley
3. 18 it shall come to pass in that day, (that)
Amos 1. 14 with shouting in the day of battle, with
1. 14 a tempest in the day of the whirlwind
2. 16 mighty shall flee away naked in that day
3. 14 That in the day that I shall visit the
5. 8 and maketh the day dark with night
5. 18 Woe unto you that desire the day of the
5. 18 the day of the LORD (is) darkness, and
5. 20 (Shall) not the day of the LORD (be) dark.
6. 3 Ye that put far away the evil day, and
8. 3 the songs..shall be howlings in that day
8. 9 it shall come to pass in that day, saith
Amos 8. 9 I will darken the earth in the clear day
8. 10 and the end thereof as a bitter day
8. 13 In that day shall the fair virgins and
9. 11 In that day will I raise up the tabernacle
Obad. 8. Shall I not in that day, saith the LORD
11 In the day that thou stoodest on the
11 in the day that the strangers carried away
12 shouldest not have looked on the day
12 thy brother in the day that he became
13. 13, 13 in the day of their calamity
14 that did remain in the day of distress
15 the day of the LORD (is) near upon all the
Jon. 3. 4 Jonah..to enter into the city a day's jour.
Mic. 2. 4 In that day shall (one) take up a parable
3. 6 and the day shall be dark over them
4. 6 In that day, saith the LORD, will I assem.
5. 10 it shall come to pass in that day, saith
7. 4 the day of thy watchmen (and) thy visit.
7. 11 (In) the day that thy walls are to be
7. 11 (in) that day shall the decree be far
7. 12 (In) that day (also) he shall come even to
Nah. 1. 7 The LORD (is)..a stronghold in the day of
2. 3 torches in the day of his preparation
3. 17 which camp in the hedges in the cold d.
Hab. 3. 16 that I might rest in the day of trouble
Zeph 1. 7 for the day of the LORD (is) at hand
1. 8 it shall come to pass in the day of the
1. 9 In the same day also will I punish all
1. 10 it shall come to pass in that day, saith
1. 14 The great day of the LORD (is) near, (it is)
1. 14 (even) the voice of the day of the LORD
1. 15 That day (is) a day of wrath, a day of
1. 15 a day of wasteness, a day of darkness
1. 15 a day of clouds and thick darkness
1. 16 A day of the trumpet and alarm against
1. 18 deliver them in the day of the LORD'S
2. 2 (before) the day pass as the chaff, before
2. 2 before the day of the LORD'S anger come
2. 3 be hid in the day of the LORD'S anger
3. 8 until the day that I rise up to the prey
3. 11 In that day shalt thou not be ashamed for
3. 16 In that day it shall be said to Jerusalem
Hag. 1. 1 in the sixth month, in the first day of
1. 15 In the four and twentieth day of the
2. 15 I pray you, consider from this day and
2. 18 Consider now from this day and upward
2. 18 from the four and twentieth day of the
2. 18 from the day that the foundation of the
2. 19 from this day will I bless (you)
2. 23 In that day, saith the LORD of hosts
Zech. 1. 7 Upon the four and twentieth day of the
2. 11 shall be joined to the LORD in that day
3. 9 remove the iniquity of that land in..day
3. 10 In that day, saith the LORD of hosts
4. 10 who hath despised the day of small
6. 10 come thou the same day, and go into the
8. 9 in the day (that) the foundation of the
9. 16 their God shall save them in that day
11. 11 it was broken in that day: and so the
12. 3 in that day will I make Jerusalem a bur.
12. 4 In that day, saith the LORD, I will smite
12. 6 In that day will I make the governors of
12. 8 In that day shall the LORD defend the
12. 8 he that is feeble among them at that day
12. 9 it shall come to pass in that day, (that)
12. 11 In that day shall there be a great mour.
13. 1 In that day there shall be a fountain
13. 2, 4 And it shall come to pass in that day
14. 1 the day of the LORD cometh, and thy
14. 3 as when he fought in the day of battle
14. 4 his feet shall stand in that day upon the
14. 6, 13 it shall come to pass in that day
14. 7 shall be one day which shall..not day
14. 8 shall be in that day, (that) living waters
14. 9 in that day shall there be one LORD
14. 20 In that day shall there be upon the bells of
14. 21 in that day there shall be no more the
Mal. 3. 2 who may abide the day of his coming?
3. 17 in that day when I make up my jewels
4. 1 the day cometh, that shall burn as an
4. 1 the day that cometh shall burn them up
4. 3 in the day that I shall do (this), saith
4. 5 the coming of the great and dreadful day

3. *Daily, by day,* יוֹמָם *yomam.*

Lev. 8. 35 shall ye abide (at) the door..day and ni.
Deut 28. 66 thou shalt fear day and night, and shalt
Josh. 1. 8 thou shalt meditate therein day and ni.
1 Sa. 25. 16 a wall unto us, both by night and day
1 Ki. 8. 59 nigh unto the LORD our God day and ni.
1 Ch. 9. 33 were employed in (that) work day and
2 Ch. 6. 20 may be open upon this house day and ni.
Neh. 1. 6 which I pray before thee now, day and ni.
4. 9 set a watch against them day and night
9. 12 thou leddest them in the day by a cloudy
Psa. 1. 2 in his law doth he meditate day and nig.
32. 4 day and night thy hand was heavy upon
42. 3 My tears have been my meat day and ni.
55. 10 Day and night they go about it upon the
Isa. 34. 10 It shall not be quenched night nor day
60. 11 they shall not be shut day nor night
Jer. 9. 1 that I might weep day and night for the
14. 17 eyes run down with tears night and day
15. 9 her sun is gone down while (it was) yet d.
16. 13 shall ye serve other gods day and night
33. 20 If ye can break my covenant of the day
33. 25 If my covenant (be) not with day and ni.
Lam. 2. 18 tears run down like a river day and night

4. *Dawn,* שַׁחַר *shachar.*

Gen. 32. 24 with him until the breaking of the day
32. 26 And he said, Let me go, for the day brea.

Josh. 6. 15 rose early, about the dawning of the day
Judg 19. 25 when the day began to spring, they let
1 Sa. 9. 26 came to pass, about the spring of the day
Job 3. 9 neither let it see the dawning of the day

5. *Light*, אוֹר *or*.
Judg 16. 2 In the morning, when it is day, we shall
Job 26. 10 until the day and night come to an end

6. *Evening and morning*, עֶרֶב בֹּקֶר *ereb boqer*.
Dan. 8. 14 Unto two thousand and three hundred d.

7. *Day*, ἡμέρα *hēmera*.
Matt. 6. 34 Sufficient unto the day (is) the evil
7. 22 Many will say to me in that day, Lord
11. 22 It shall be more tolerable..at the day of
11. 24 it shall be more tolerable..in the day of
12. 36 shall give account thereof in the day of
13. 1 The same day went Jesus out of the house
16. 21 killed, and be raised again the third day
17. 23 the third day he shall be raised again
20. 2 when he had agreed..for a penny a day
20. 6 saith..Why stand ye here all the day idle?
20. 12 have borne the burden and heat of the d.
20. 19 crucify (him): and the third day he shall
22. 23 The same day came to him the Sadducees
22. 46 neither durst any (man) from that day
24. 36 But of that day and hour knoweth no
24. 38 until the day that Noe entered into the
24. 50 shall come in a day when he looketh not
25. 13 for ye know neither the day nor the hour
26. 29 until that day when I drink it new with
27. 64 sepulchre be made sure until the third d.
Mark 4. 35 the same day when the even was come
5. 5 And always night and day, he was in the
6. 11 It shall be more tolerable..in the day of
6. 21 when a convenient day was come, that H.
9. 31 after that he is killed..rise the third day
10. 34 and the third day he shall rise again
13. 32 But of that day and (that) hour knoweth
14. 12 the first day of unleavened bread, when
14. 25 until that day that I drink it new in the
Luke 1. 20 until the day that these things shall be
1. 59 on the eighth day they came to circum.
1. 80 was in the deserts till the day of his
2. 37 served (God) with fastings..night and day
2. 44 But they..went a day's journey; and
4. 16 into the synagogue on the sabbath day
4. 42 when it was day, he departed and went
6. 13 when it was day, he called (unto him)
6. 23 Rejoice ye in that day, and leap for joy
9. 12 And when the day began to wear away
9. 22 and be slain, and be raised the third day
9. 37 it came to pass, that on the next day when
10. 12 it shall be more tolerable in that day
12. 46 will come in a day when he looketh not
13. 14 therefore come..not on the sabbath day
13. 16 loosed from this bond on the sabbath day
13. 31 The same [day] there came certain of the
14. 5 will not..pull him out on the sabbath d.
17. 4 if he trespass..seven times in a day, and
17. 4 seven times [in a day] turn again to thee
17. 24 [so shall also the Son of man be in his d.]
17. 27 until the day that Noe entered into the
17. 29 the same day that Lot went out of Sodom
17. 30 thus shall it be in the day when the Son
17. 31 In that day, he which shall be upon the
18. 7 which cry day and night unto him
18. 33 and the third day he shall rise again
19. 42 even thou, at least in this thy day, the
21. 34 and (so) that day come upon you unawa.
22. 7 Then came the day of unleavened bread
22. 66 as soon as it was day, the elders of the
23. 12 the same day Pilate and Herod were
23. 54 that day was the preparation, and the
24. 7 be crucified, and the third day rise again
24. 13 two of them went that same day to a vil.
24. 21 to day is the third day since these things
24. 29 it is toward evening, and the day is far
24. 46 and to rise from the dead the third day
John 1. 39 abode with him that day: for it was about
2. 1 the third day there was a marriage in
5. 9 and on the same day was the sabbath
6. 39 should raise it up again at the last day
6. 40, 44, 54 I will raise him up at the last day
7. 37 In the last day, that great (day) of the
8. 56 Your father Abraham rejoiced to see my d.
9. 4 I must work..while it is day: the night
11. 9 Are there not twelve hours in the day?
11. 9 If any man walk in the day, he stumbleth
11. 24 that he shall rise again..at the last day
11. 53 Then from that day forth they took cou.
12. 7 Let her alone: against the day of my bu.
12. 48 the same shall judge him in the last day
14. 20 At that day ye shall know that I (am) in
16. 23 And in that day ye shall ask me nothing
16. 26 At that day ye shall ask in my name
19. 31 remain upon the cross on the sabbath d.
20. 19 Then the same day at evening, being the
Acts 1. 2 Until the day in which he was taken up
1. 22 unto that same day that he was taken up
2. 1 when the day of Pentecost was fully co.
2. 15 seeing it is (but) the third hour of the d.
2. 20 before that great and notable day of the
2. 29 and his sepulchre is with us unto this d.
2. 41 the same day there were added (unto
7. 8 and circumcised him the eighth day; and
7. 26 the next day he showed himself unto
9. 24 they watched the gates day and night to
10. 3 about the ninth hour of the day, an angel
10. 40 Him God raised up the third day, and
12. 18 Now as soon as it was day, there was no
Acts 12. 21 upon a set day Herod, arrayed in royal
13. 14 into the synagogue on the sabbath day
16. 35 when it was day, the magistrates sent the
17. 31 Because he hath appointed a day, in the
20. 16 to be at Jerusalem the day of Pentecost
20. 18 Ye know, from the first day that I came
20. 31 I ceased not to warn..night and day with
21. 7 we came..and abode with them one day
21. 26 the next day purifying himself with them
23. 12 when it was day, certain of the Jews
26. 7 instantly serving (God) day and night
26. 22 I continue unto this day, witnessing both
27. 29 cast four anchors..and wished for the d.
27. 33 while the day was coming on, Paul beso.
27. 33 This..is the fourteenth day that ye have
27. 39 when it was day, they knew not the land
28. 13 and after one day the south wind blew
28. 23 when they had appointed him a day
Rom. 2. 5 against the day of wrath and revelation
2. 16 In the day when God shall judge the
8. 36 For thy sake we are killed all the day long
10. 21 All day long I have stretched forth my
11. 8 they should not hear; unto this day
13. 12 The night is far spent, the day is at hand
13. 13 Let us walk honestly, as in the day; not
14. 5 One man esteemeth one day above another
14. 5 another esteemeth every day (alike). Let
14. 6 He that regardeth the day, regardeth (it)
14. 6 and he that regardeth not [the day,] to the
1 Co. 1. 8 blameless in the day of our Lord Jesus C.
3. 13 for the day shall declare it, because it
5. 5 that the spirit may be saved in the day
10. 8 fell in one day three and twenty thousand
15. 4 he rose again the third day according to
2 Co. 1. 14 even as ye also (are) ours in the day of
6. 2 in the day of salvation have I succoured
6. 2 behold, now (is) the day of salvation
Eph. 4. 30 ye are sealed unto the day of redemption
6. 13 may be able to withstand in the evil day
Phil. 1. 5 your fellowship..from the first day until
1. 6 will perform (it) until the day of Jesus C.
1. 10 without offence till the day of Christ
2. 16 that I may rejoice in the day of Christ
Col. 1. 6 since the day ye heard (of it), and knew
1. 9 since the day we heard (it), do not cease
1 Th. 2. 9 for labouring night and day, because we
3. 10 Night and day praying exceedingly that
5. 2 the day of the Lord so cometh as a thief
5. 4 that day should overtake you as a thief
5. 5 Ye are all the children..of the day: we
5. 8 But let us, who are of the day, be sober
2 Th. 1. 10 in all them that believe..in that day
2. 2 as that the day of Christ is at hand
3. 8 with labour and travail night and day
1 Ti. 5. 5 supplications and prayers night and day
2 Ti. 1. 3 remembrance of thee..night and day
1. 12 committed unto him against that day
1. 18 he may find mercy of the Lord in that d.
4. 8 which the Lord..shall give me at that d.
Heb. 3. 8 in the day of temptation in the wilderness
4. 4 God did rest the seventh day from all his
4. 7 he limiteth a certain day, saying in David
4. 8 not afterward have spoken of another d.
8. 9 covenant that I made..in the day when
10. 25 the more as ye see the day approaching
Jas. 5. 5 have nourished your hearts, as in a day of
1 Pe. 2. 12 glorify God in the day of visitation
2 Pe. 1. 19 in a dark place, until the day dawn
2. 8 vexed (his) righteous soul from day to d.
2. 9 to reserve the unjust unto the day of
2. 13 count it pleasure to riot in the day time
3. 7 reserved unto fire against the day of
3. 8 one day (is) with the Lord as a thousand
3. 8 years, and a thousand years as one day
3. 10 the day of the Lord will come as a thief
3. 12 hasting unto the coming of the day of
1 Jo. 4. 17 that we may have boldness in the day of
Jude 6 unto the judgment of the great day
Rev. 4. 8 they rest not day and night, saying, Holy
6. 17 For the great day of his wrath is come
7. 15 serve him day and night in his temple
8. 12 the day shone not for a third part of it
9. 15 were prepared for an hour, and a day
12. 10 accused them before our God day and
14. 11 and they have no rest day nor night, who
16. 14 battle of that great day of God Almighty
18. 8 shall her plagues come in one day, death
20. 10 shall be tormented day and night for ever
21. 25 shall not be shut at all by day: for there

DAY, by —
By day, daily, יוֹמָם *yomam*.
Exod 13. 21 went before them by day in a
13. 21 to give them light; to go by day and night
13. 22 He took not away the pillar..by day, nor
40. 38 the cloud..(was) upon the tabernacle by d.
Num. 9. 21 whether (it was) by day or by night that
10. 34 cloud of the LORD (was) upon them by d.
Deut. 1. 33 in fire by night..and in a cloud by day
Judg. 6. 27 that he could not do (it) by day, that he
2 Sa. 21. 10 birds of the air to rest on them by day
Neh. 9. 19 the pillar..departed not from them by d.
Psa. 91. 5 (nor) for the arrow (that) flieth by day
121. 6 The sun shall not smite thee by day nor
136. 8 The sun to rule by day: for his mercy
Isa. 4. 5 upon her assemblies, a cloud..by day
28. 19 shall it pass over, by day and by night
60. 19 The sun shall be no more thy light by d.
Jer. 31. 35 which giveth the sun for a light by day
Eze. 12. 3 prepare..and remove by day in their
12. 4 shalt thou bring forth thy stuff by day
12. 7 I brought forth my stuff by day, as stuff

DAY, each —
Day day, יוֹם יוֹם *yom yom*.
Num 14. 34 each day for a year, shall ye bear your
Eze. 4. 6 have appointed thee each day for a year

DAY by day —
1. *Day day*, יוֹם יוֹם *yom yom*.
Gen. 39. 10 as she spake to Joseph day by day, that
Exod 29. 38 two lambs of the first year day by day
Num 28. 3 two lambs of the first year..day by day
1 Ch. 12. 22 day by day there came to David to help
2 Ch. 21. 15 out by reason of the sickness day by day
24. 11 Thus they did day by day, and gathered
30. 21 the priests praised the LORD day by day
Ezra 6. 9 let it be given them day by day without
Neh. 8. 18 Also day by day..he read in the book of
2. *Day and day*, ἡμέρᾳ καὶ ἡμέρᾳ *hēm. kai hēmera*.
2 Co. 4. 16 yet the inward (man) is renewed day by d.
3. *According to the day*, καθ' ἡμέραν *kath hēmeran*.
Luke 11. 3 Give us day by day our daily bread

DAY, a certain —
One of the days, μιᾷ τῶν ἡμερῶν *mia tōn hēmerōn*.
Luke 5. 17 it came to pass on a certain day, as he
8. 22 it came to pass on a certain day, that he

DAY, before —
In the night, ἔννυχον *ennuchon*.
Mark 1. 35 rising up a great while [before day,] he

DAY, break of —
Light, brightness, dawn, αὐγή *augē*.
Acts 20. 11 talked a long while, even till break of day

DAY, the Lord's —
The day to the Lord, ἡ κυριακὴ ἡμέρα *hē kuriakē h.*
Rev. 1. 10 I was in the Spirit on the Lord's day, and

DAY, this —
1. *Now, just now*, ἄρτι *arti*.
1 Co. 4. 13 off scouring of all things unto this day
2. *To day*, σήμερον *sēmeron*.
Matt. 6. 11 Give us this day our daily bread
11. 23 it would have remained until this day
27. 8 called, The field of blood, unto this day
27. 19 I have suffered many things this day in
28. 15 reported among the Jews until this day
Mark 14. 30 That this day, (even) in this night, before
Luke 2. 11 unto you is born this day, in the city
4. 21 This day is this scripture fulfilled in
19. 9 This day is salvation come to this house
22. 34 the cock shall not crow this day, before
Acts 4. 9 If we this day be examined of the good
13. 33 Thou art my Son, this day have I begotten
19. 40 called in question for this day's uproar
20. 26 take you to record this day, that I (am)
22. 3 zealous toward God, as ye all are this day
24. 21 I am called in question by you this day
26. 2 I shall answer for myself this day
26. 29 but also all that hear me this day, were
27. 33 This day is the fourteenth..that ye have
Rom. 11. 8 [and the rest were blinded]..unto this d.
2 Co. 3. 14 until this day remaineth the same veil
3. 15 even unto this day, when Moses is read
Heb. 1. 5 Thou art my Son, this day have I begotten

DAY was far spent, when the —
Many hours having been, ὥρας πολλῆς γενομένης.
Mark 6. 35 when the day was now far spent, his disc.

DAY, every —
1. *Day day*, יוֹם יוֹם *yom yom*.
Exod 16. 4 and gather a certain rate every day
29. 36 thou shalt offer every day a bullock (for)
2 Ki. 25. 30 a daily rate for every day, all the days
1 Ch. 16. 37 continually, as every day's work required
2 Ch. 8. 13 after a certain rate every day, offering
8. 14 as the duty of every day required
Ezra 3. 4 custom, as the duty of every day required
Neh. 11. 23 a certain portion..due for every day
12. 47 and the porters, every day his portion
Jer. 52. 34 every day a portion until the day of his
Eze. 43. 25 shalt thou prepare every day a goat (for)
2. *According to the day*, καθ' ἡμέραν *kath hēmeran*.
Luke 16. 19 and fared sumptuously every day

DAYS, two —
Two days, יוֹמַיִם *yomayim*.
Num. 9. 22 (whether it were) two days, or a month
Hos. 6. 2 After two days will he revive us

DAY following —
Upon the morrow, ἐπαύριον *epaurion*.
John 1. 43 The day following Jesus would go forth
6. 22 The day following, when the people

DAY (after), the next —
Upon the morrow, ἐπαύριον *epaurion*.
Matt 27. 62 the next day, that followed the day of
John 1. 29 The next day John seeth Jesus coming
1. 35 the next day after, John stood, and two
12. 12 On the next day much people that were
Acts 14. 20 the next day he departed with Barnabas
25. 6 the next day, sitting on the judgment seat

DAY, at mid —
At mid day, ἡμέρας μέσης *hēmeras mesēs*.
Acts 26. 13 At mid day, O king, I saw in the way a

DAY spring —

1. *Dawn*, שַׁחַר *shachar*.
Job 38. 12 caused the day spring to know his place

2. *Uprising*, ἀνατολή *anatolē*.
Luke 1. 78 dayspring from on high hath visited us

DAY star —

Light bearer, φωσφόρος *phōsphoros*.
2 Pe. 1. 19 and the day star arise in your hearts

DAY time —

1. *Daily, by day*, יוֹמָם *yomam*.
Num14. 14 by day time in a pillar of cloud, and
Job 5. 14 They meet with darkness in the day time
24. 16 marked for themselves in the day time
Psa. 22. 2 I cry in the day time, but thou hearest
42. 8 his loving kindness in the day time
78. 14 In the day time also he led them with a
Isa. 4. 6 tabernacle for a shadow in the day time
21. 8 upon the watchtower in the day time, and

2. *The days*, τὰς ἡμέρας *tas hēmeras*.
Luke21. 37 in the day time he was teaching in the

DAYS —

1. *Days*, יָמִים *yamim*.
Gen. 1. 14 for seasons, and for days, and years
3. 14 dust shalt thou eat all the days of thy
3. 17 shalt thou eat (of) it all the days of thy
5. 4 days of Adam . . were eight hundred years
5. 5 all the days . . were nine hundred and
5. 8 all the days of Seth were nine hundred
5. 11 all the days of Enos were nine hundred
5. 14 the days of Cainan were nine hundred
5. 17 the days of Mahalaleel were eight hund.
5. 20 the days of Jared were nine hundred
5. 23 the days of Enoch were three hundred
5. 27 the days of Methuselah were nine hund.
5. 31 all the days of Lamech were seven hund.
6. 3 his days shall be an hundred and twenty
6. 4 were giants in the earth in those days
7. 4 For yet seven days, and I will cause it
7. 4 to rain upon the earth forty days and
7. 10 it came to pass after seven days, that
7. 12 the rain was upon the earth forty days
7. 17 the flood was forty days upon the earth
7. 24 upon the earth an hundred and fifty days
8. 3 the end of the hundred and fifty days
8. 6 it came to pass at the end of forty days
8. 10, 12 he stayed yet other seven days; and
9. 29 all the days of Noah were nine hundred
10. 25 for in his days was the earth divided
11. 32 the days of Terah were two hundred and
14. 1 it came to pass in the days of Amraphel
17. 12 he that is eight days old shall be circum.
21. 4 circumcised . . Isaac being eight days old
21. 34 sojourned in the Philistines' land many d.
24. 55 Let the damsel abide with us (a few) days
25. 7 the days of the years of Abraham's life
25. 24 her days to be delivered were fulfilled
26. 1 the first famine that was in the days of
26. 15, 18 had digged in the days of Abraham his
27. 41 The days of mourning for my father are
27. 44 And tarry with him a few days, until thy
29. 20 they seemed unto him (but) a few days
29. 21 Give (me) my wife, for my days are fulfil.
30. 14 Reuben went in the days of wheat harv.
30. 36 he set three days' journey betwixt him.
31. 23 and pursued after him seven days' journ.
35. 28 the days of Isaac were an hundred and
35. 29 Isaac . . died . . (being) old and full of days
37. 34 Jacob . . mourned for his son many days
40. 12 The three branches (are) three days
40. 13, 19 within three days shall Pharaoh lift up
40. 18 answered . . three baskets (are) three days
42. 17 put them altogether into ward three da.
47. 9 The days of the years of my pilgrimage
47. 9 few and evil have the days of the years
47. 9 have not attained unto the days of the
47. 9 fathers in the days of their pilgrimage
49. 1 which shall befall you in the last days
50. 3 And forty days were fulfilled for him
50. 3 so are fulfilled the days of those which
50. 3 mourned for him three score and ten da.
50. 4 when the days of his mourning were past
50. 10 made a mourning for his father seven d.
Exod. 2. 11 it came to pass in those days, when Moses
3. 18 let us go . . three days' journey into the w.
5. 3 three days' journey into the desert
7. 25 seven days were fulfilled, after that the
8. 27 We will go three days' journey into the
10. 22 darkness in all the land . . three days
10. 23 neither rose any . . for three days
12. 15 Seven days shall ye eat unleavened bread
12. 19 Seven days shall there be no leaven
13. 6 Seven days thou shalt eat unleavened
13. 7 Unleavened bread shall be eaten seven d.
15. 22 they went three days in the wilderness
16. 26 Six days ye shall gather it; but on the
16. 29 on the sixth day the bread of two days
20. 9 Six days shalt thou labour and do all
20 11 (in) six days the LORD made heaven and
20. 12 that thy days may be long upon the land
22. 30 seven days it shall be with his dam
23. 12 Six days thou shalt do thy work, and on
23 15 shalt eat unleavened bread seven days
23. 26 the number of thy days I will fulfil
24. 16 Sinai, and the cloud covered it six days
24 18 Moses was in the mount forty days and
29. 30 that son . . shall put them on seven days
29. 35 seven days shalt thou consecrate them
Exod29. 37 Seven days thou shalt make an atonem.
31. 15 Six days may work be done; but in the
31. 17 (in) six days the LORD made heaven and
34. 18 Seven days thou shalt eat unleavened
34. 21 Six days thou shalt work; but on the
34. 28 he was there with the LORD forty days
35. 2 Six days shall work be done, but on the
Lev. 8. 33 And ye shall not go out . . (in) seven days
8. 33 until the days of your consecration be
8. 35 shall ye abide (at) the door . . seven days
12. 2 then she shall be unclean seven days
12. 2 according to the days of the separation
12. 4 of her purifying three and thirty days
12. 4 until the days of her purifying be fulfilled
12. 5 of her purifying threescore and six days
12. 6 when the days of her purifying are fulfi.
13. 4, 31, 33 priests shall shut . . (him) . . seven d.
13. 21, 26 priest shall shut him up seven days
13. 46 All the days wherein the plague (shall be)
13. 50 shut up (it that hath) the plague seven d.
13. 54 and he shall shut it up seven days more
14. 8 tarry abroad out of his tent seven days
14. 38 priest shall . . shut up the house seven d.
15. 13 he shall number to himself seven days
15. 19 she shall be put apart seven days
15. 24 he shall be unclean seven days
15. 25 if a woman have an issue . . many days
15. 25 the days of the issue of her uncleanness
15. 25 shall be as the days of her separation
15. 26 whereon she lieth all the days of her iss.
15. 28 then she shall number to herself seven d.
22. 27 then it shall be seven days under the
23. 3 Six days shall work be done: but the
23. 6 seven days ye must eat unleavened bread
23. 8 offer an offering made by fire . . seven da.
23. 16 unto the morrow after . . number fifty days
23. 34 the feast of tabernacles (for) seven days
23. 36 Seven days ye shall offer an offering
23. 39 keep a feast unto the LORD seven days
23. 40 rejoice before the LORD your God seven d.
23. 41 keep it a feast unto the LORD seven days
23. 42 Ye shall dwell in booths seven days
Num. 6. 4 All the days of his separation shall he
6. 5 the days of the vow of his separation
6. 5 until the days be fulfilled, in the which
6. 6 All the days that he separateth (himself)
6. 8 All the days of his separation he (is) holy
6. 12 consecrate . . the days of his separation
6. 12 the days that were before shall be lost
6. 13 the days of his separation are fulfilled
9. 19 tarried long upon the tabernacle many d.
9. 20 cloud was a few days upon the tabernacle
10. 33 departed from the mount . . three days
10. 33 before them in the three days' journey
11. 19 Ye shall not eat one day, nor two days
11. 19 five days, neither ten days, nor twenty d.
12. 14 should she not be ashamed seven days?
12. 14 be shut out from the camp seven days
12. 15 was shut out from the camp seven days
13. 25 searching of the land after forty days
14. 34 the number of the days . . (even) forty d.
19. 11 He that toucheth . . be unclean seven days
19. 14 all that (is) in . . be unclean seven days
19. 16 whosoever toucheth . . be unclean seven d.
20. 29 they mourned for Aaron thirty days
24. 14 shall do to thy people in the latter days
28. 17 seven days shall unleavened bread be
28. 24 offer daily, throughout the seven days
29. 12 keep a feast unto the LORD seven days
31. 19 do ye abide without the camp seven days
33. 8 went three days' journey in the wilder.
Deut. 1. 2 (There are) eleven days' (journey) from
1. 46 ye abode in Kadesh many days
1. 46 according unto the days that ye abode
2. 1 and we compassed mount Seir many days
4. 9 from thy heart all the days of thy life
4. 10 all the days that they shall live upon
4. 26 ye shall not prolong (your) days upon it
4. 30 (even) in the latter days, if thou turn to
4. 32 ask now of the days that are past, which
4. 40 that thou mayest prolong (thy) days upon
5. 13 Six days thou shalt labour, and do all thy
5. 16 that thy days may be prolonged, and
5. 33 (that) ye may prolong (your) days in the
6. 2 the days of thy life, and that thy days
9. 9 I abode in the mount forty days and forty
9. 11 it came to pass, at the end of forty days
9. 18 I fell down before the LORD . . forty days
9. 25 I fell down before the LORD forty days
10. 10 I stayed in the mount . . forty days and
11. 9 that ye may prolong (your) days in the
11. 21 your days may be multiplied, and the d.
11. 21 as the days of heaven upon the earth
12. 1 all the days that ye live upon the earth
16. 3 seven days shalt thou eat unleavened
16. 3 mayest remember . . all the days of thy life
16. 4 with thee in all thy coasts seven days
16. 8 Six days thou shalt eat unleavened bread
16. 13 observe the feast of tabernacles seven d.
16. 15 Seven days shalt thou keep a solemn feast
17. 9 unto the judge that shall be in those days
17. 19 he shall read therein all the days of his
17. 20 to the end that he may prolong (his) days
19. 17 the judges which shall be in those days
22. 7 and (that) thou mayest prolong (thy) days
22. 19 he may not put her away all his days
22. 29 he may not put her away all his days
23. 6 shalt not seek their peace . . all thy days
25. 15 that thy days may be lengthened in the
26. 3 the priest that shall be in those days
30. 18 ye shall not prolong (your) days upon
30. 20 thy life, and the length of thy days
Deut31. 14 thy days approach that thou must die
31. 29 evil will befall you in the latter days
32. 7 Remember the days of old, consider the
32. 47 through this . . ye shall prolong (your) d.
33. 25 and as thy days, (so shall) thy strength
34. 8 the children of Israel wept . . thirty days
34. 8 the days of weeping (and) mourning for
Josh. 1. 5 stand before thee all the days of thy life
1. 11 within three days ye shall pass over this
2. 16 hide yourselves there three days, until
2. 22 they went . . and abode there three days
3. 2 it came to pass after three days, that the
4. 14 they feared Moses, all the days of his life
6. 3 Thus shalt thou do six days
6. 14 compassed the city . . so they did six days
9. 16 it came to pass, at the end of three days
20. 6 high priest that shall be in those days
22. 3 not left your brethren these many days
24. 31 all the days of Joshua, and all the days
Judg. 2. 7 all the days of Joshua, and all the days
2. 18 delivered them . . all the days of the judge
5. 6 In the days of Shamgar the son of Anath
5. 6 in the days of Jael, the highways were
8. 28 country was in quietness . . in the days of
11. 40 to lament the daughter . . four days in
14. 12 if ye . . declare it me within the seven d.
14. 14 they could not in three days expound
14. 17 she wept before him the seven days
15. 20 judged Israel in the days of the Philist.
17. 6 In those days (there was) no king in Israel
18. 1 In those days (there was) no king in Israel
18. 1 in those days the tribe of the Danites
19. 1 in those days, when (there was) no king
19. 4 he abode with him three days: so they
20. 27 ark of the covenant . . there in those days
20. 28 Phinehas . . stood before it in those days
21. 25 In those days (there was) no king in Israel
Ruth 1. 1 in the days when the judges ruled
1 Sa. 1. 11 will give him unto the LORD all the days
2. 31 the days come, that I will cut off thine
3. 1 the word . . was precious in those days
7. 13 against the Philistines all the days of
7. 15 judged Israel all the days of his life
10. 8 seven days shalt thou tarry, till I come
11. 3 Give us seven days' respite, that we may
13. 8 he tarried seven days, according to the
13. 11 thou camest not within the days appointed
14. 52 there was sore war . . all the days of Saul
17. 12 went among men (for) an old man in the d.
17. 16 Philistine . . presented himself forty days
18. 26 and the days were not expired
25. 28 hath not been found in thee (all) thy days
25. 38 it came to pass about ten days (after)
28. 1 And it came to pass in those days, that
29. 3 which hath been with me these days, or
30. 12 no bread, nor drunk (any) water, three d.
31. 13 under a tree . . and fasted seven days
2 Sa. 7. 12 when thy days be fulfilled, and thou shalt
16. 23 which he counselled in those days, (was)
20. 4 Assemble me the men of . . within three d.
21. 1 there was a famine in the days of David
21. 9 were put to death in the days of harvest
24. 8 at the end of nine months and twenty d.
24. 13 there be three days' pestilence in thy land
1 Ki. 2. 1 the days of David drew nigh that he
2. 11 the days that David reigned over Israel
2. 38 And Shimei dwelt in Jerusalem many d.
3. 2 was no house built . . until those days
3. 13 not be any . . like unto thee all thy days
3. 14 then I will lengthen thy days
4. 21 and served Solomon all the days of his
4. 25 dwelt safely . . all the days of Solomon
8. 40 That they may fear thee all the days that
8. 65 seven days and seven days . . fourteen days
10. 21 it was nothing accounted of in the days of
11. 12 in thy days I will not do it for David
11. 25 an adversary to Israel all the days
11. 34 make him prince all the days of his life
12. 5 Depart yet (for) three days, then come
14. 20 the days which Jeroboam reigned (were)
14. 30 was war betw. Rehoboam . . all (their) d.
15. 5 turned not aside . . all the days of his life
15. 6 there was war . . all the days of his life
15. 14 was perfect with the LORD all his days
15. 16, 32 there was war . . all their days
16. 15 did Zimri reign seven days in Tirzah
16. 34 In his days did Hiel the Bethelite build
17. 15 and he, and her house, did eat (many) days
18. 1 it came to pass, (after) many days, that
19. 8 in the strength of that meat forty days
20. 29 one over against the other seven days
21. 29 the evil in his days . . in his son's days
22. 46 remained in the days of his father Asa
2 Ki. 2. 17 they sought three days, but found him
3. 9 fetched a compass of seven days' journey
8. 20 In his days Edom revolted from under
10. 32 In those days the LORD began to cut Israel
12. 2 did (that which was) right . . all his days
13. 3 into the hand of Ben-hadad . . all (their) d.
13. 22 oppressed Israel all the days of Jehoahaz
15. 18 he departed not all his days from the sins
15. 29 In the days of Pekah king of Israel came
15. 37 In those days the LORD began to send
18. 4 unto those days the children of Israel did
20. 1 In those days was Hezekiah sick unto
20. 6 I will add unto thy days fifteen years
20. 17 the days come, that all that (is) in thine
20. 19 peace and truth be in my days?
23. 22 from the days of the judges that judged
23. 22 nor in all the days of the kings of Israel
23. 29 In his days Pharaoh-nechoh king of Egypt
24. 1 In his days Nebuchadnezzar king of B.

2 Ki. 25. 29 before him all the days of his life
25. 30 a daily rate..all the days of his life
1 Ch. 1. 19 because in his days the earth was divided
4. 41 came in the days of Hezekiah king of J.
5. 10 in the days of Saul they made war with
5. 17 by genealogies in the days of Jotham
5. 17 in the days of Jeroboam king of Israel
7. 2 whose number (was) in the days of David
7. 22 Ephraim their father mourned many days
9. 25 (were) to come after seven days from
10. 12 buried their bones..and fasted seven days
12. 39 there they were with David three days
13. 3 enquired not at it in the days of Saul
17. 11 when thy days be expired that thou must
21. 12 or else three days the sword of the LORD
22. 9 quietness unto Israel in his days
23. 1 when David was old and full of days he
29. 15 our days on the earth (are) as a shadow
29. 28 he died in a good old age, full of days
2 Ch. 7. 8 Solomon kept the feast seven days, and
7. 9 seven days, and the feast seven days
9. 20 (not)..accounted of in the days of Solomon
10. 5 Come again unto me after three days
13. 20 strength again in the days of Abijah
14. 1 In his days the land was quiet ten years
15. 17 the heart of Asa was perfect all his days
20. 25 they were three days in gathering of the
21. 8 In his days the Edomites revolted from
24. 2 Joash did..right..all the days of Jehoiada
24. 14 continually all the days of Jehoiada
24. 15 Jehoiada waxed old, and was full of days
26. 5 he sought God in the days of Zechariah
29. 17 they sanctified the house..in eight days
30. 21 the feast of unleavened bread seven days
30. 22 did eat throughout the feast seven days
30. 23 took counsel to keep other seven days
30. 23 they kept (other) seven days with glad.
32. 24 In those days Hezekiah was sick to the
32. 26 came not upon them in the days of Heze.
34. 33 all his days they departed not from
35. 17 the feast of unleavened bread seven days
35. 18 from the days of Samuel the prophet
36. 9 he reigned three months and ten days in
Ezra 4. 2 we do sacrifice unto him since the days
4. 5 all the days of Cyrus king of Persia, even
4. 7 in the days of Artaxerxes wrote Bishlam
6. 22 the feast of unleavened bread seven days
8. 15 and there abode we in tents three days
8. 32 to Jerusalem, and abode there three days
9. 7 Since the days of our fathers (have) we
10. 8 whosoever would not come within three d.
10. 9 together unto Jerusalem within three d.
Neh. 1. 4 mourned (certain) days, and fasted, and
2. 11 to Jerusalem, and was there three days
5. 18 once in ten days store of all sorts of
6. 15 wall was finished..in fifty and two days
6. 17 in those days the nobles of Judah sent
8. 17 since the days of Jeshua the son of Nun
8. 18 And they kept the feast seven days
12. 7 These (were) the chief..in the days of J.
12. 12 And in the days of Joiakim were priests
12. 22 The Levites, in the days of Eliashib, Jo.
12. 23 until the days of Johanan the son of
12. 26 These (were) in the days of Joiakim the
12. 26 in the days of Nehemiah the governor
12. 46 in the days of David and Asaph of old
12. 47 the days of Zerubbabel, and in the days
13. 6 after certain days obtained I leave of
13. 15 In those days saw I in Judah (some)
13. 23 In those days also saw I Jews (that) had
Esth. 1. 1 it came to pass, in the days of Ahasuerus
1. 2 in those days, when the king Ahasuerus
1. 4 honour of his excellent majesty, many d.
1. 4 (even) an hundred and four score days
1. 5 when these days were expired..seven days
2. 12 so were the days of their purifications
2. 21 In those days, while Mordecai sat in the
4. 11 come in unto the king these thirty days
4. 16 neither eat nor drink three days, night
9. 22 As the days wherein the Jews rested from
9. 22 they should make them days of feasting
9. 26 they called these days Purim, after the
9. 27 that they would keep these two days
9. 28 (that) these days (should be) remembered
9. 28 and (that) these days of Purim should not
9. 31 To confirm these days of Purim in their
Job 1. 5 when the days of (their) feasting were
2. 13 sat..with him upon the ground seven days
3. 6 let it not be joined unto the days of the
7. 1 (are not) his days also like the days of
7. 6 My days are swifter than a weaver's
7. 16 let me alone; for my days (are) vanity
8. 9 because our days upon earth (are) a sha.
9. 25 Now my days are swifter than a post
10. 5 (Are) thy days as the days of man?
10. 5 (are) thy years as man's days
10. 20 (Are) not my days few? cease (then, and)
12. 12 and in length of days understanding
14. 1 born of a woman (is) of few days
14. 5 Seeing his days (are) determined, the
14. 14 All the days of my appointed time will I
15. 20 man travaileth with pain all (his) days
17. 1 My breath is corrupt, my days are extinct
17. 11 My days are past, my purposes are broken
21. 13 They spend their days in wealth, and in
24. 1 do they that know him not see his days?
29. 2 the days (when) God preserved me
29. 4 As I was in the days of my youth, when
29. 18 and I shall multiply (my) days as the sand
30. 16 the days of affliction have taken hold
30. 27 the days of affliction prevented me
32. 7 Days should speak, and multitude of

Job 33. 25 he shall return to the days of his youth
36. 11 they shall spend their days in prosperity
38. 12 commanded the morning since thy days
38. 21 (because) the number of thy days (is)
42. 17 So Job died, (being) old, and full of days
Psa. 21. 4 (even) length of days for ever and ever
23. 6 shall follow me all the days of my life
27. 4 that..in the house of the LORD all the days
34. 12 (and) loveth (many) days, that he may
37. 18 The LORD knoweth the days of the upri.
37. 19 in the days of famine they shall be satis.
39. 4 mine end, and the measure of my days
39. 5 thou hast made my days (as) an handbr.
44. 1 (what) work thou didst in their days, in
49. 5 Wherefore should I fear in the days of
55. 23 men shall not live out half their days
72. 7 In his days shall the righteous flourish
77. 5 I have considered the days of old, the
78. 33 their days did he consume in vanity, and
89. 29 and his throne as the days of heaven
89. 45 The days of his youth hast thou shortened
90. 9 all our days are passed away in thy wrath
90. 10 The days of our years (are) three score
90. 12 teach (us) to number our days, that we
90. 14 we may rejoice and be glad all our days
90. 15 Make us glad according to the days
94. 13 give him rest from the days of adversity
102. 3 my days are consumed like smoke, and
102. 11 My days (are) like a shadow that declin.
102. 23 He weakened..he shortened my days
102. 24 take me not away in the midst of my d.
103. 15 (As for) man, his days (are) as grass; as a
109. 8 Let his days be few; (and) let another
119. 84 How many (are) the days of thy servant?
128. 5 see the good of Jerusalem all the days
143. 5 I remember the days of old; I meditate
144. 4 days (are) as a shadow that passeth away
Prov. 3. 2 For length of days, and long life, and
3. 16 Length of days (is) in her right hand; (and)
9. 11 by me thy days shall be multiplied, and
10. 27 The fear of the LORD prolongeth days
15. 15 All the days of the afflicted (are) evil
28. 16 hateth covetousness shall prolong (his) d.
31. 12 will do him good..all the days of her life
Eccl. 2. 3 which they should do..all the days of
2. 16 in the days to come shall all be forgotten
2. 23 all his days (are) sorrows, and his travail
5. 17 All his days also he eateth in darkness
5. 18 to enjoy the good..all the days of his life
5. 20 not much remember the days of his life
6. 3 so that the days of his years be many
6. 12 all the days of his vain life which he
7. 10 the former days were better than these?
7. 15 All (things) have I seen in the days of my
8. 13 neither shall he prolong (his) days
8. 15 shall abide with him..the days of his life
9. 9 whom thou lovest all the days of the life
9. 9 which he hath given thee..all the days
11. 1 for thou shalt find it after many days
11. 8 yet let him remember the days of dark.
11. 9 let thy heart cheer thee in the days of
12. 1 Remember now thy Creator in the days
12. 1 while the evil days come not, nor the
Isa. 1. 1 concerning Judah..in the days of Uzziah
2. 2 it shall come to pass in the last days
7. 1 it came to pass, in the days of Ahaz the
7. 17 LORD shall bring..days that have not
13. 22 and her days shall not be prolonged
23. 7 (city), whose antiquity (is) of ancient da.!
23. 15 according to the days of one king
24. 22 and after many days shall they be visited
30. 26 sevenfold, as the light of seven days
32. 10 Many days and years shall ye be troubled
38. 1 In those days was Hezekiah sick unto
38. 5 I will add unto thy days fifteen years
38. 10 I said in the cutting off of my days, I
38. 20 sing my songs..all the days of our life
39. 6 the days come, that all that (is) in thine
39. 8 there shall be peace and truth in my days
51. 9 awake! as in the ancient days, in the
53. 10 see (his) seed, he shall prolong (his) days
60. 20 the days of thy mourning shall be ended
63. 9 and carried them all the days of old
63. 11 he remembered the days of old, Moses
65. 20 shall be no more thence an infant of days
65. 20 an old man that hath not filled his days
65. 22 as the days of a tree (are) the days of my
Jer. 1. 2 word of the LORD came in the days of J.
1. 3 It came also in the days of Jehoiakim
2. 32 my people have forgotten me days with.
3. 6 said also unto me in the days of Josiah
3. 16 in those days, saith the LORD, they shall
3. 18 In those days the house of Judah shall
5. 18 in those days, saith the LORD, I will not
6. 11 the aged with (him that is) full of days
7. 32 behold, the days come, saith the LORD
9. 25 the days come, saith the LORD, that I
13. 6 it came to pass after many days, that the
16. 9 and in your days, the voice of mirth, and
16. 14 the days come, saith the LORD, that I
17. 11 shall leave them in the midst of his days
19. 6 the days come, saith the LORD, that this
20. 18 that my days should be consumed with
22. 30 a man (that) shall not prosper in his days
23. 5 the days come, saith the LORD, that I
23. 6 In his days Judah shall be saved, and Is.
23. 7 the days come, saith the LORD, that they
23. 20 in the latter days ye shall consider it
25. 34 the days of your slaughter and of your
26. 18 prophesied in the days of Hezekiah king
30. 3 the days come, saith the LORD, that I
30. 24 in the latter days ye shall consider it

Jer. 31. 27 the days come, saith the LORD
31. 29 In those days they shall say no more
31. 31 the days come, saith the LORD
31. 33 After those days, saith the LORD, I will
31. 38 the days come, saith the LORD, that the
32. 14 that they may continue many days
33. 14 the days come, saith the LORD, that I
33. 15 In those days, and at that time, will I
33. 16 In those days shall Judah be saved, and
35. 1 in the days of Jehoiakim the son of Josiah
35. 7 but all your days ye shall dwell in tents
35. 7 that ye may live many days in the land
35. 8 charged us, to drink no wine all our days
36. 2 from the days of Josiah, even unto this d.
37. 16 Jeremiah had remained there many days
42. 7 it came to pass after ten days, that the
46. 26 shall be inhabited, as in the days of old
48. 12 the days come, saith the LORD, that I
48. 47 the captivity of Moab in the latter days
49. 2 the days come, saith the LORD, that I
49. 39 it shall come to pass in the latter days
50. 4, 20 In those days, and in that time, saith
51. 47 the days come, that I will do judgment
51. 52 the days come, saith the LORD, that I will
52. 33 eat bread before him all the days of his
52. 34 a continual diet..all the days of his life
Lam. 1. 7 Jerusalem remembered in the days of her
1. 7 things that she had in the days of old
2. 17 that he..commanded in the days of old
4. 18 our end is near, our days are fulfilled
5. 21 Turn thou us..renew our days as of old
Eze. 3. 15 remained there..astonished..seven days
3. 16 it came to pass at the end of seven days
4. 4 (according) to the number of the days
4. 5 the days, three hundred and ninety days
4. 6 bear the iniquity..of Judah forty days
4. 8 till thou hast ended the days of thy siege
4. 9 (according) to the number of the days that
4. 9 three hundred and ninety days shalt thou
5. 2 when the days of the siege are fulfilled
12. 22 The days are prolonged, and every vision
12. 23 The days are at hand, and the effect of
12. 25 in your days, O rebellious house, will I
12. 27 vision..he seeth (is) for many days (to c.)
16. 22, 43 hast not remembered the days of thy
16. 60 covenant with thee in the days of thy
22. 4 thou hast caused thy days to draw near
22. 14 in the days that I shall deal with thee?
23. 19 to remembrance the days of her youth
38. 8 After many days thou shalt be visited
38. 16 it shall be in the latter days, and I will
38. 17 which prophesied in those days (many)
43. 25 Seven days shalt thou prepare every day
43. 26 Seven days shall they purge the altar
43. 27 when these days are expired, it shall be
44. 26 they shall reckon unto him seven days
45. 21 have the passover, a feast of seven days
45. 23 seven days of the feast he shall prepare
45. 23 rams without blemish daily the seven day.
45. 25 the like in the feast of the seven days
46. 1 gate..shall be shut the six working days
Dan. 1. 12 Prove thy servants, I beseech thee, ten d.
1. 14 he consented..and proved them ten days
1. 15 at the end of ten days their countenances
1. 18 at the end of the days that the king had
2. 28 what shall be in the latter days
2. 44 in the days of these kings shall the God
4. 34 at the end of the days I Nebuchadnezzar
5. 11 in the days of thy father, light and under.
6. 7 petition of any god or man for thirty days
6. 12 of any god or man within thirty days
7. 9 the Ancient of days did sit, whose garmen.
7. 13 came to the Ancient of days, and they
7. 22 Until the Ancient of days came, and judg.
8. 26 the vision; for it (shall be) for many days
8. 27 Daniel fainted, and was sick (certain) days
10. 2 In those days I Daniel was mourning three
10. 13 prince..withstood me one and twenty d.
10. 14 befall thy people in the latter days
10. 14 for yet the vision (is) for (many) days
11. 20 but within few days he shall be destroyed
11. 33 they shall fall by the sword..(many) days
12. 11 thousand two hundred and ninety days
12. 12 three hundred and five and thirty days
12. 13 stand in thy lot at the end of the days
Hos. 1. 1 in the days of Uzziah, Jotham, Ahaz
1. 1 in the days of Jeroboam the son of Joash
2. 13 I will visit upon her the days of Baalim
2. 15 sing there, as in the days of her youth
3. 3 Thou shalt abide for me many days; thou
3. 4 children of Israel shall abide many days
3. 5 shall fear the LORD..in the latter days
9. 7 The days of visitation are come, the days
9. 9 corrupted (themselves), as in the days of
10. 9 thou hast sinned from the days of Gibeah
12. 9 as in the days of the solemn feast
Joel 1. 2 been in your days, or even in the days of
2. 29 in those days will I pour out my Spirit
3. 1 in those days, and in that time, when I
Amos 1. 1 concerning Israel in the days of Uzziah
1. 1 in the days of Jeroboam the son of Joash
4. 2 the days shall come upon you, that he will
8. 11 the days come, saith the Lord GOD, that I
9. 11 I will build it as in the days of old
9. 13 the days come, saith the LORD, that the
Jon. 1. 17 was in the belly of the fish three days
3. 3 exceeding great city of three days' jour
3. 4 Yet forty days, and Nineveh shall be over.
Mic. 1. 1 in the days of Jotham, Ahaz, (and) Hez.
4. 1 in the last days it shall come to pass
7. 14 let them feed (in) Bashan..as in the days
7. 15 According to the days of thy coming out

Mic. 7. 20 thou hast sworn..from the days of old
Hab. 1. 5 (I) will work a work in your days, (which)
Zeph. 1. 1 in the days of Josiah the son of Amon
Zech. 8. 6 the remnant of this people in these days
8. 9 ye that hear in these days these words
8. 10 before these days there was no hire for
8. 11 now I (will) not (be)..as in the former d.
8. 15 have I thought in these days to do well
8. 23 In those days (it shall come to pass), that
14. 5 the earthquake in the days of Uzziah
Mal. 3. 4 as in the days of old, and as in former
3. 7 Even from the days of your fathers ye are

2. *Days*, ἡμέραι *hēmerai*.
Matt. 2. 1 in the days of Herod the king, behold
3. 1 In those days came John the Baptist
4. 2 when he had fasted forty days and forty
9. 15 the days will come, when the bridegroom
11. 12 from the days of John the Baptist until
12. 40 as Jonas was three days and three nights
12. 40 so shall the Son of man be three days and
15. 32 continue with me now three days, and
17. 1 after six days Jesus taketh Peter, James
23. 30 If we had been in the days of our fathers
24. 19 woe..to them that give suck, in those d.
24. 22 except those days should be shortened
24. 22 but for the elect's sake those days shall
24. 29 after the tribulation of those days shall
24. 37 But as the days of Noe (were), so shall
24. 38 For as in the days that were before the
26. 2 know that after two days is (the feast of)
26. 61 said, I am able..to build it in three days
27. 40 Thou that..buildest (it) in three days
27. 63 said..After three days I will rise again
Mark 1. 9 it came to pass in those days, that Jesus
1. 13 he was there in the wilderness forty days
2. 1 he entered into Capernaum after (some) d.
2. 20 the days will come, when the bridegroom
2. 20 and then shall they fast in those days
8. 1 In those days the multitude being very
8. 2 they have now been with me three days
8. 31 be killed, and after three days rise again
9. 2 after six days Jesus taketh (with him) P.
13. 17 woe..to them that give suck, in those d.!
13. 19 For (in) those days shall be affliction, such
13. 20 the Lord had shortened those days, no
13. 20 for the elect's sake..shortened the days
13. 24 in those days, after that tribulation, the
14. 1 After two days was (the feast of) the pas.
14. 58 and within three days I will build another
15. 29 Ah! thou that..buildest (it) in three da.
Luke 1. 5 There was, in the days of Herod the king
1. 23 as soon as the days of his ministration
1. 24 after those days his wife Elisabeth conc.
1. 25 hath the Lord dealt with me in the days
1. 39 Mary arose in those days, and went into
1. 75 In holiness and righteousness..all the d.
2. 1 it came to pass in those days, that there
2. 6 the days were accomplished that she
2. 21 when eight days were accomplished for
2. 22 And when the days of her purification
2. 43 when they had fulfilled the days, as they
2. 46 after three days they found him in the
4. 2 Being forty days tempted of the devil
4. 2 in those days he did eat nothing: and
4. 25 many widows were in Israel in the days
5. 35 the days will come, when the bridegroom
5. 35 and then shall they fast in those days
6. 12 it came to pass in those days, that he
9. 28 about an eight days after these sayings
9. 36 told no man in those days any of those
13. 14 There are six days in which men ought to
15. 13 not many days after, the younger son
17. 22 The days will come, when ye shall desire
17. 22 to see one of the days of the Son of man
17. 26 as it was in the days of Noe, so shall it
17. 26 be also in the days of the Son of man
17. 28 Likewise also as it was in the days of Lot
19. 43 For the days shall come upon thee, that
20. 1 on one of those days, as he taught the
21. 6 the days will come, in the which there
21. 22 For these be the days of vengeance, that
21. 23 woe..to them that give suck, in those d.!
23. 29 For, behold, the days are coming, in the
24. 18 which are come to pass there in these d.?
John 2. 12 and they continued there not many days
2. 19 Destroy this temple, and in three days I
2. 20 and wilt thou rear it up in three days?
4. 40 besought him..and he abode there two d.
4. 43 Now after two days he departed thence
11. 6 he abode two days still in the same place
11. 17 he had (lain) in the grave four days already
12. 1 Jesus, six days before the passover, came
20. 26 after eight days, again his disciples were
Acts 1. 3 being seen of them forty days, and speak.
1. 5 ye shall be baptized..not many days hence
2. 17 it shall come to pass in the last days
2. 18 I will pour out in those days of my Spirit
3. 24 have likewise foretold of these days
5. 36 For before these days rose up Theudas
5. 37 rose up Judas of Galilee in the days of
6. 1 in those days, when the number of the
7. 41 they made a calf in those days, and offer.
7. 45 brought in with Jesus..unto the days of D.
9. 9 he was three days without sight, and
9. 19 Then was Saul certain days with the dis.
9. 23 after that many days were fulfilled, the
9. 37 it came to pass in those days, that she
9. 43 he tarried many days in Joppa with one
10. 30 Four days ago I was fasting until this hour
10. 48 Then prayed they him to tarry certain d.
11. 27 in these days came prophets from Jeru.
Acts 12. 3 Then were the days of unleavened bread
13. 31 he was seen many days of them which
13. 41 for I work a work in your days, a work
15. 36 some days after, Paul said unto Barnabas
16. 12 we were in that city abiding certain days
16. 18 And this did she many days. But Paul
20. 6 sailed away from Philippi after the days
20. 6 in five days; where we abode seven days
21. 4 finding disciples, we tarried there seven d.
21. 5 when we had accomplished those days,
21. 10 as we tarried (there) many days, there
21. 15 after those days we took up our carriages
21. 26 to signify the accomplishment of the days
21. 27 when the seven days were almost ended
21. 38 before these days madest an uproar, and
24. 1 after five days Ananias the high priest
24. 11 there are yet but twelve days since I went
24. 24 after certain days, when Felix came with
25. 1 after three days he ascended from Cesarea
25. 6 tarried among them more than ten days
25. 13 after certain days king Agrippa and
25. 14 when they had been there many days, F.
27. 7 when we had sailed slowly many days, and
27. 20 when neither sun nor stars in many days
28. 7 received us, and lodged us three days
28. 12 at Syracuse, we tarried (there) three days
28. 14 desired to tarry with them seven days:
28. 17 after three days Paul called the chief of
Gal. 1. 18 I went up..and abode with him fifteen d.
4. 10 Ye observe days, and months, and times
Eph. 5. 16 Redeeming the time, because the days are
2 Ti. 3. 1 in the last days perilous times shall come
Heb. 1. 2 Hath in these last days spoken unto us
5. 7 Who in the days of his flesh, when he had
7. 3 having neither beginning of days, nor end
8. 8 Behold, the days come, saith the Lord
8. 10 covenant that I will make..after those d.
10. 16 covenant that I will make..after those d.
10. 32 call to remembrance the former days, in
11. 30 after they were compassed about seven d.
12. 10 For they verily for a few days chastened
Jas. 5. 3 heaped treasure together for the last da.
1 Pe. 3. 10 he that will love life, and see good days
3. 20 waited in the days of Noah, while the ark
2 Pe. 3. 3 there shall come in the last days scoffers
Rev. 2. 10 and ye shall have tribulation ten days
2. 13 even in those days wherein Antipas (was)
9. 6 in those days shall men seek death, and
10. 7 But in the days of the voice of the seven.
11. 3 two hundred (and) three score days
11. 6 that it rain not in the days of their
11. 9 shall see their dead bodies three days
11. 11 after three days and an half the Spirit of
12. 6 her..two hundred (and) three score days

DAYS, now a —
To-day, הַיּוֹם *hay-yom*.
1 Sa. 25. 10 There be many servants now a days that

DAYS, these —
Yesterday, תְּמוֹל *temol*.
1 Sa. 21. 5 (been) kept from us about these three days

DAYS, four —
The fourth day, τεταρταῖος *tetartaios*.
John 11. 39 stinketh: for he hath been (dead) four d.

DAYS of, in the —
Upon, at the time of, ἐπί (*gen.*) *epi*.
Mark 2. 26 in the days of Abiathar the high priest
Acts 11. 28 came to pass in the days of Claudius Ces.
[*See also* After, eighth, feast, first, holy, night, noon, sabbath, third, to day.]

DAYSMAN —
To reason, reprove, decide, יָכַח *yakach*, 5.
Job 9. 33 Neither is there any daysman betwixt us

DEACON —
Ministrant, διάκονος *diakonos*.
Phil. 1. 1 the saints..with the bishops and deacons
1 Ti. 3. 8 Likewise (must) the deacons (be) grave
3. 12 Let the deacons be the husbands of one

DEACON, to use the office of a —
To act as a ministrant, διακονέω *diakoneō*.
1 Ti. 3. 10 then let them use the office of a deacon
3. 13 they that have used the office of a deacon

DEAD —
1. *To die*, מוּת *muth*.
Gen. 23. 3 Abraham stood up from before his dead
23. 4 that I may bury my dead out of my sight
23. 6 in the choice of our sepulchres bury thy d.
23. 6 but that thou mayest bury thy dead
23. 8 that I should bury my dead out of my
23. 11 the field give I thee..bury thy dead
23. 13 take (it) of me, and I will bury my dead
23. 15 me and thee? bury therefore thy dead
Exod. 12. 33 for they said, We (be) all dead (men)
14. 30 Israel saw the Egyptians dead upon the
21. 34 give money..and the dead (beast) shall
21. 35 and the dead (ox) also they shall divide
21. 36 pay ox for ox; and the dead shall be his
Lev. 21. 11 Neither shall he go in to any dead body
Num. 6. 6 All the days..he shall come at no dead
12. 12 Let her not be as one dead, of whom the
16. 48 he stood between the dead and the living
Deut. 14. 1 baldness between your eyes for the dead
25. 5 wife of the dead shall not marry
25. 6 in the name of his brother (which is) de.
26. 14 nor given (ought) thereof for the dead
Judg. 3. 25 their lord (was) fallen down dead on the
Judg. 4. 22 Sisera lay dead, and the nail (was) in his
16. 30 the dead..were more than (they) which
Ruth 1. 8 as ye have dealt with the dead, and with
2. 20 hath not left off his kindness..to the de.
4. 5 the wife of the dead..the name of the d.
4. 10 to raise up the name of the dead upon
4. 10 that the name of the dead be not cut off
1 Sa. 24. 14 after whom dost thou pursue? after a d.
2 Sa. 9. 8 look upon such a dead dog as I (am)?
14. 2 had a long time mourned for the dead
16. 9 Why should this dead dog curse my lord
1 Ki. 3. 20 and laid her dead child in my bosom
3. 22 the living (is) my son, and the dead (is)
3. 22 the dead (is) thy son, and the living (is)
3. 23 This (is) my son..and thy son (is) the d.
3. 23 thy son (is) the dead, and my son (is) the
2 Ki. 4. 32 the child was dead, (and) laid upon his
19. 35 in the morning, behold, they (were) all d.
23. 30 his servants carried him in a chariot de.
Psa. 88. 5 Free among the dead, like the slain that
88. 10 Wilt thou show wonders to the dead?
106. 28 and ate the sacrifices of the dead
115. 17 The dead praise not the LORD, neither
143. 3 as those that have been long dead
Eccl. 4. 2 I praised the dead which are already de.
9. 3 and after that (they go) to the dead
9. 4 for a living dog is better than a dead lion
9. 5 but the dead know not anything, neither
Isa. 8. 19 unto their God? for the living to the de.?
22. 2 not slain with the sword, nor dead in
26. 14 (They are) dead, they shall not live; (they
26. 19 Thy dead (men) shall live, (together with)
37. 36 in the morning, behold, they (were) all d.
59. 10 (we are) in desolate places as dead (men)
Jer. 16. 7 in mourning, to comfort them for the d.
22. 10 Weep ye not for the dead, neither bemoan
Lam. 3. 6 in dark places, as (they that be) dead of
Eze. 24. 17 make no mourning for the dead, bind
44. 25 they shall come at no dead person to

2. *Death*, מָוֶת *maveth*.
2 Sa. 19. 28 all (of) my father's house were but dead
Eccl. 10. 1 Dead flies cause the ointment of the apo.

3. *Soul*, נֶפֶשׁ *nephesh*.
Lev. 19. 28 cuttings in your flesh for the dead, nor
21. 1 There shall none be defiled for the dead
22. 4 any thing (that is) unclean (by) the dead
Num. 5. 2 and whosoever is defiled by the dead
6. 11 for him, for that he sinned by the dead

4. *The shades* (*of the dead*), רְפָאִים *rephaim*.
Job 26. 5 Dead (things) are formed from under
Psa. 88. 10 shall the dead arise (and) praise thee?
Prov. 2. 18 unto death, and her paths unto the dead
9. 18 But he knoweth not that the dead (are)
21. 16 remain in the congregation of the dead
Isa. 14. 9 it stirreth up the dead for thee, (even)
26. 19 and the earth shall cast out the dead

5. *To destroy*, שָׁדַד *shadad*.
Judg. 5. 27 where he bowed, there he fell down de.

6. *Dead*, νεκρός *nekros*.
Matt. 8. 22 Follow me; and let the dead bury their d.
10. 8 cleanse the lepers, [raise the dead,] cast
11. 5 the deaf hear, the dead are raised up
14. 2 he is risen from the dead; and therefore
17. 9 Son of man be risen again from the dead
22. 31 as touching the resurrection of the dead
22. 32 God is not the God of the dead, but of the
27. 64 unto the people, He is risen [from the d.]
28. 7 tell..that he is risen from the dead; and
Mark 6. 14 John the Baptist was risen from the dead
6. 16 It is John..he is risen from the dead
9. 9 the Son of man were risen from the dead
9. 10 what the rising from the dead should
12. 25 For when they shall rise from the dead
12. 26 And as touching the dead, that they rise
12. 27 He is not the God of the dead, but the G.
Luke 7. 22 the deaf hear, the dead are raised, to the
9. 7 it was said..John was risen from the dead
9. 60 Jesus said..Let the dead bury their dead
16. 30 if one went unto them from the dead
16. 31 be persuaded though one rose from the d.
20. 35 and the resurrection from the dead
20. 37 the dead are raised, even Moses showed
20. 38 not a God of the dead, but of the living
24. 5 Why seek ye the living among the dead?
24. 46 and to rise from the dead the third day
John 2. 22 When therefore he was risen from the d.
5. 21 For as the Father raiseth up the dead
5. 25 when the dead shall hear the voice of the
12. 1 Lazarus..whom he raised from the dead
12. 9 Lazarus..whom he had raised from the d.
12. 17 called Lazarus..and raised him from the d.
20. 9 that he must rise again from the dead
21. 14 after that he was risen from the dead
Acts 3. 15 whom God hath raised from the dead
4. 2 preached..the resurrection from the dead
4. 10 whom God raised from the dead, (even) by
10. 41 drink with him after he rose from the d.
10. 42 was ordained..the Judge of quick and d.
13. 30 But God raised him from the dead
13. 34 as..that he raised him up from the dead
17. 3 suffered, and risen again from the dead
17. 31 in that he hath raised him from the dead
17. 32 they heard of the resurrection of the dead
23. 6 of the hope and resurrection of the dead
24. 15 there shall be a resurrection [of the dead]
24. 21 Touching the resurrection of the dead
26. 8 incredible..that God should raise the d.?
26. 23 the first that should rise from the dead
Rom. 1. 4 declared..by the resurrection from the d.

Rom. 4. 17 (even) God, who quickeneth the dead
4. 24 that raised up Jesus our Lord from the d.
6. 4 like as Christ was raised up from the dead
6. 9 Christ being raised from the dead dieth
6. 13 as those that are alive from the dead
7. 4 to him who is raised from the dead, that
8. 11 him that raised up Jesus from the dead
8. 11 he that raised up Christ from the dead
10. 7 to bring up Christ again from the dead
10. 9 that God hath raised him from the dead
11. 15 receiving (of them be), but life from the d.?
14. 9 that he might be Lord both of the dead
1 Co. 15. 12 be preached that he rose from the dead
15. 12 that there is no resurrection of the dead?
15. 13 if there be no resurrection of the dead
15. 15 raised not up, if so be that the dead rise
15. 16 if the dead rise not, then is not Christ
15. 20 But now is Christ risen from the dead
15. 21 (came) also the resurrection of the dead
15. 29 for the dead, if [the dead] rise not at all?
15. 29 why are they then baptised for the dead?
15. 32 what advantageth it me, if the dead rise
15. 35 some..say, How are the dead raised up?
15. 42 So also (is) the resurrection of the dead
15. 52 the dead shall be raised incorruptible
2 Co. 1. 9 but in God which raiseth the dead
Gal. 1. 1 the Father, who raised him from the dead
Eph. 1. 20 when he raised him from the dead, and
5. 14 arise from the dead, and Christ shall give
Phil. 3. 11 attain unto the resurrection of the dead
Col. 1. 18 who is..the first born from the dead
2. 12 God, who hath raised him from the dead
1 Th. 1. 10 his Son..whom he raised from the dead
4. 16 and the dead in Christ shall rise first
2 Ti. 2. 8 Jesus Christ..was raised from the dead
4. 1 who shall judge the quick and the dead
Heb. 6. 2 of hands, and of resurrection of the dead
11. 19 able to raise (him) up, even from the dead
11. 35 Women received their dead raised to life
13. 20 that brought again from the dead our Lord
1 Pe. 1. 3 the resurrection of Jesus..from the dead
1. 21 in God, that raised him up from the dead
4. 5 is ready to judge the quick and the dead
Rev. 1. 5 (and) the first begotten of the dead, and
11. 18 wrath is come, and the time of the dead
14. 13 Blessed (are) the dead which die in the L.
20. 5 But the rest of the dead lived not again
20. 12 I saw the dead, small and great, stand
20. 12 the dead were judged out of those things
20. 13 the sea gave up the dead which were in it
20. 13 death and hell delivered up the dead which

DEAD —
Dead, νεκρός *nekros, (adj.)*
Luke 15. 24 this my son was dead, and is alive again
15. 32 thy brother was dead, and is alive again
Acts 5. 10 the young men came in, and found her d.
20. 9 and fell down..and was taken up dead
28. 6 swollen, or fallen down dead suddenly
Rom. 6. 11 reckon ye also yourselves to be dead
7. 8 For without the law sin (was) dead
8. 10 And if Christ (be) in you, the body (is) d.
Eph. 2. 1 who were dead in trespasses and sins
2. 5 Even when we were dead in sins, hath
Col. 2. 13 you, being dead in your sins, and the
Heb. 6. 1 not laying again..from dead works, and
9. 14 purge your conscience from dead works to
Jas. 2. 17 Even so faith, if it hath not works, is [d.]
2. 20 wilt thou know..faith without works is d.
2. 26 For as the body without the spirit is dead
2. 26 so faith without works is dead also
Rev. 1. 17 when I saw him, I fell at his feet as dead
1. 18 I (am) he that liveth, and was dead; and
2. 8 the First and the Last, which was dead
3. 1 that thou hast a name..and art dead

DEAD, be —
Death, מָוֶת *maveth.*
Lev. 11. 31 doth touch them, when they be dead
11. 32 (any) of them, when they are dead
Judg. 2. 19 it came to pass, when the judge was dead
2 Ki. 3. 5 it came to pass, when Ahab was dead
1 Ch. 2. 24 after that Hezron was dead in Caleb-eph.
Esth. 2. 7 when her father and mother were dead

DEAD, to be —
1. *To expire,* גָּוַע *gava.*
Num 20. 29 congregation saw that Aaron was dead
2. *To die,* מוּת *muth.*
Gen. 42. 38 for his brother is dead, and he is left
44. 20 and his brother is dead, and he alone is
50. 15 brethren saw that their father was dead
Exod. 4. 19 all the men are dead which sought thy
9. 7 there was not one of the cattle..dead
Deut. 2. 16 the men of war were consumed and dead
Josh. 1. 2 Moses my servant is dead; now therefore
Judg. 4. 1 children..did evil..when Ehud was dead
8. 33 it came to pass, as soon as Gideon was d.
9. 55 men of Israel saw that Abimelech was d.
20. 5 concubine have they forced, that she is d.
1 Sa. 4. 17 Hophni and Phinehas are dead, and the
4. 19 her father in law and her husband were d.
17. 51 Philistines saw their champion was dead
25. 39 when David heard that Nabal was dead
28. 3 Samuel was dead, and all Israel had lamen.
31. 5 his armour bearer saw that Saul was dead
31. 7 and that Saul and his sons were dead, they
2 Sa. 1. 4 and many of the people also are..dead
1. 4 Saul and Jonathan his son are dead also
1. 5 How knowest thou that Saul..be dead?
2. 7 ye valiant: for your master Saul is dead

2 Sa. 4. 1 Saul's son heard that Abner was dead in
4. 10 one told me, saying, Behold, Saul is dead
11. 21 Thy servant Uriah the Hittite is dead also
11. 24 and (some) of the king's servants be dead
11. 24 thy servant Uriah the Hittite is dead
11. 26 heard that Uriah her husband was dead
12. 18 feared to tell him that the child was dead
12. 18 if we tell him that the child is dead?
12. 19 David perceived that the child was dead
12. 19 Is the child dead? And they said, He is d.
12. 21 when the child was dead, thou didst rise
12. 23 now he is dead, wherefore should I fast?
13. 32 Amnon only is dead: for by the appoint.
13. 33 king's sons are dead..Amnon only is d.
13. 39 concerning Amnon, seeing he was dead
14. 5 a widow woman, and mine husband is d.
18. 20 no tidings, because the king's son is dead
19. 10 Absalom, whom we anointed over us, is d.
1 Ki. 3. 21 to give my child suck, behold, it was dead
11. 21 Joab the captain of the host was dead
13. 31 When I am dead, then bury me in the
21. 14 saying, Naboth is stoned, and is dead
21. 15 heard that Naboth was stoned, and was d.
2 Ki. 4. 1 Thy servant my husband is dead; and
11. 1 when Athaliah..saw that her son was d.
1 Ch. 1. 44 when Bela was dead, Jobab..reigned in
1. 45 when Jobab was dead, Husham..reigned
1. 46 when Husham was dead, Hadad..reigned
1. 47 when Hadad was dead, Samlah..reigned
1. 48 when Samlah was dead, Shaul..reigned
1. 49 when Shaul was dead, Baal-hanan..reign.
1. 50 when Baal-hanan was dead, Hadad reigned
2. 19 when Azubah was dead, Caleb took unto
10. 5 his armour bearer saw that Saul was dead
10. 7 and that Saul and his sons were dead
2 Ch. 22. 10 when Athaliah..saw that her son was dead
Job 1. 19 fell upon the young men, and they are d.
Eccl. 4. 2 which are already dead, more than the
3. *To be come off from,* ἀπογίνομαι *apoginomai.*
1 Pe. 2. 24 that we, being dead to sins, should live
4. *To die away,* ἀποθνήσκω *apothnēskō.*
Matt. 9. 24 for the maid is not dead, but sleepeth
Mark 5. 35 Thy daughter is dead: why troublest
5. 39 the damsel is not dead, but sleepeth
9. 26 insomuch that many said, He is dead
15. 44 asked..whether he had been any while d.
Luke 8. 52 Weep not; she is not dead, but sleepeth
8. 53 they laughed..knowing that she was dead
John 6. 49 Your fathers did eat manna..and are dead
6. 58 as your fathers did eat manna, and are d.
8. 52 Abraham is dead, and the prophets
8. 53 which is dead? and the prophets are dead
11. 14 said Jesus unto them..Lazarus is dead
11. 25 though he were dead, yet shall he live
Acts 7. 4 when his father was dead, he removed
Rom. 5. 15 if through the offence of one, many be d.
6. 2 How shall we, that are dead to sin, live
6. 7 For he that is dead is freed from sin
6. 8 Now if we be dead with Christ, we believe
7. 2 but if the husband be dead, she is loosed
7. 3 but if her husband be dead, she is free
7. 6 [that being dead] wherein we were held
2 Co. 5. 14 if one died for all, then were all dead
Gal. 2. 19 For I through the law am dead to the
2. 21 by the law, then Christ is dead in vain
Col. 2. 20 Wherefore, if ye be dead with Christ
3. 3 ye are dead, and your life is hid with Ch.
Heb. 11. 4 and by it he, being dead, yet speaketh
Jude 12 without fruit, twice dead, plucked up by
5. *To die,* θνήσκω *thnēskō.*
Matt. 2. 20 they are dead which sought the young
Mark 15. 44 Pilate marvelled if he were already dead
Luke 8. 49 Thy daughter is dead; trouble not v. 12.
John 11. 39 Martha, the sister of him that was dead
11. 41 [(from the place) where the dead was]
11. 44 And he that was dead came forth, bound
12. 1 where Lazarus was [which had been dead]
19. 33 saw that he was dead already, they brake
Acts 14. 19 drew (him) out..supposing he had been d.
25. 19 and of one Jesus, which was dead, whom
1 Ti. 5. 6 she that liveth in pleasure is dead while
6. *To put to sleep,* κοιμάω *koimaō.*
1 Co. 7. 39 if her husband be dead, she is at liberty
7. *To put to death,* νεκρόω *nekroō.*
Rom. 4. 19 he considered not his own body now dead
Heb. 11. 12 even of one, and him as good as dead
8. *To end (life),* τελευτάω *teleutaō.*
Matt. 2. 19 But when Herod was dead, behold, an
9. 18 saying, My daughter is even now dead
Acts 2. 29 that he is both dead and buried, and

DEAD with, to be —
To die off with, συναποθνήσκω *sunapothnēskō.*
2 Ti. 2. 11 For if we be dead with (him), we shall

DEAD, after men are —
Over the dead, ἐπὶ νεκροῖς *epi nekrois.*
Heb. 9. 17 a testament (is) of force after men are d.

DEAD, to become —
To put to death, θανατόω *thanatoō.*
Rom. 7. 4 ye also are become dead to the law by the

DEAD body or carcase —
1. *Carcase, corpse,* גְּוִיָּה *geviyyah.*
Psa. 110. 6 fill (the places) with the dead bodies; he
2. *To die,* מוּת *muth.*
Num. 19. 11 that toucheth the dead body of any man

Num 19. 13 Whosoever toucheth the dead body of any
19. 16 or a dead body, or a bone of a man, or a
2 Ki. 8. 5 how he had restored a dead body to life
3. *Carcase,* פֶּגֶר *peger.*
2 Ch. 20. 24 they (were) dead bodies fallen to the earth
20. 25 they found..riches with the dead bodies
Jer. 31. 40 And the whole valley of the dead bodies
33. 5 (it is) to fill them with the dead bodies of
41. 9 Ishmael had cast all the dead bodies of
Amos 8. 3 many dead bodies in every place; they
4. *Fallen thing,* נְבֵלָה *nebelah.*
Deut 14. 8 ye shall not..touch their dead carcase
Psa. 79. 2 The dead bodies of thy servants have they
Isa. 26. 19 (together with) my dead body shall they
Jer. 26. 23 cast his dead body into the graves of the
34. 20 their dead bodies shall be for meat unto
36. 30 his dead body shall be cast out in the
5. *Soul,* נֶפֶשׁ *nephesh.*
Num. 9. 6 who were defiled by the dead body of a
9. 7 We (are) defiled by the dead body of a
9. 10 shall be unclean by reason of a dead body
6. *A fallen thing,* πτῶμα *ptōma.*
Rev. 11. 8 their dead bodies (shall lie) in the street
11. 9 shall see their dead bodies three days
11. 9 shall not suffer their dead bodies to be

DEAD (man) —
1. *To die,* מוּת *muth.*
Gen. 20. 3 Behold, thou (art but) a dead man, for
Psa. 31. 12 I am forgotten as a dead man out of mind
2. *To die,* θνήσκω *thnēskō.*
Luke 7. 12 there was a dead man carried out, the
3. *Dead,* νεκρός *nekros.*
Matt 23. 27 but are within full of dead (men's) bones
28. 4 keepers did shake, and became as dead (m.)
Rev. 16. 3 it became as the blood of a dead (man)

DEAD, half —
Half dead, ἡμιθανής *hēmithanēs.*
Luke 10. 30 and departed, leaving (him) half dead

DEAD of itself —
Fallen thing, carcase, dead body, נְבֵלָה *nebelah.*
Eze. 44. 31 any thing that is dead of itself, or torn

DEAD, he that is —
Dead, νεκρός *nekros.*
Luke 7. 15 he that was dead sat up, and began to
1 Pe. 4 6 preached also to them that are dead

DEAD, one —
1. *To die,* מוּת *muth.*
Exod 12. 30 not a house where (there was) not one d.
Num 19. 18 or one slain, or one dead, or a grave
2. *Dead,* νεκρός *nekros.*
Mark 9. 26 out of him: and he was as one dead

DEADLY —
1. *Soul,* נֶפֶשׁ *nephesh.*
Psa. 17. 9 (from) my deadly enemies, (who) compass
2. *Death,* מָוֶת *maveth.*
1 Sa. 5. 11 there was a deadly destruction throughout
3. *Death bearing,* θανατηφόρος *thanatēphoros.*
Jas. 3. 8 an unruly evil, full of deadly poison
4. *Death,* θάνατος *thanatos.*
Rev. 13. 3 and his deadly wound was healed: and
13. 12 first beast, whose deadly wound was heal.

DEADLY thing —
Belonging to death, θανάσιμος *thanasimos.*
Mark 16. 18 [if they drink any deadly thing, it shall]

DEADNESS —
A deadening, putting to death, νέκρωσις *nekrōsis.*
Rom. 4. 19 neither yet the deadness of Sarah's wo.

DEAF —
1. *Deaf, silent,* חֵרֵשׁ *cheresh.*
Exod. 4. 11 or who maketh the dumb, or deaf, or the
Lev. 19. 14 Thou shalt not curse the deaf, nor put a
Psa. 38. 13 But I, as a deaf (man), heard not
58. 4 like the deaf adder (that) stoppeth her ear
Isa. 29. 18 in that day shall the deaf hear the words
35. 5 ears of the deaf shall be unstopped
42. 18 Hear, ye deaf; and look, ye blind, that
42. 19 or deaf, as my messenger (that) I sent?
43. 8 have eyes, and the deaf that have ears
2. *Blunted, dull, dumb,* κωφός *kōphos.*
Matt 11. 5 the lepers are cleansed, and the deaf
Mark 7. 32 they bring unto him one that was deaf
7. 37 he maketh both the deaf to hear, and the
9. 25 (Thou) dumb and deaf spirit..come out
Luke 7. 22 lame walk, the lepers are cleansed, the d.

DEAF, to be —
To be silent, deaf, חָרַשׁ *charash.*
Mic. 7. 16 they shall lay..their ears shall be deaf

DEAL, to —
1. *To apportion,* חָלַק *chalaq,* 3.
2 Sa. 6. 19 he dealt among all the people, (even)
1 Ch. 16. 3 he dealt to every one of Israel, both man
2. *To do,* עָשָׂה *asah.*
Gen. 24. 49 if ye will deal kindly and truly with my
47. 29 deal kindly and truly with me; bury me
Exod. 5. 15 Wherefore dealest thou thus with thy
14. 11 wherefore hast thou dealt thus with us

Exod 21. 9 he shall deal with her after the manner
23. 11 In like manner thou shalt deal with thy
Numb 11. 15 if thou deal thus with me, kill me, I pray
Deut. 7. 5 But thus shall ye deal with them ; ye
Josh. 2. 14 that we will deal kindly and truly with
Judg. 9. 16 and if ye have dealt well with Jerubbaal
9. 19 If ye then have dealt truly and sincerely
18. 4 Thus and thus dealeth Micah with me
Ruth 1. 8 deal kindly with you, as ye have dealt
1 Sa. 20. 8 Therefore thou shalt deal kindly with
24. 18 how that thou hast dealt well with me
2 Ki. 12. 15 on workmen ; for they dealt faithfully
22. 7 because they dealt faithfully
1 Ch. 20. 3 Even so dealt David with all the cities of
2 Ch. 2. 3 As thou didst deal with David my father
19. 11 Deal courageously, and the LORD shall
Job 42. 8 lest I deal with you (after your) folly, in
Psa. 103. 10 He hath not dealt with us after our sins
119. 65 Thou hast dealt well with thy servant, O
119. 124 Deal with thy servant according unto
147. 20 He hath not dealt so with any nation
Prov 10. 4 He becometh poor that dealeth (with) a
12. 22 but they that deal truly (are) his delight
13. 16 Every prudent (man) dealeth with know.
14. 17 (He that is) soon angry dealeth foolishly
21. 24 his name who dealeth in proud wrath
Jer. 6. 13 from the prophet..every one dealeth
8. 10 unto the priest every one dealeth falsely
18. 23 deal (thus) with them in the time of
21. 2 if so be that the LORD will deal with us
Eze. 8. 18 Therefore will I also deal in fury: mine
16. 59 I will even deal with thee as thou hast
18. 9 and hath kept my judgments, to deal
22. 7 they dealt by oppression with the stran
22. 14 in the days that I shall deal with thee?
23. 25 and they shall deal furiously with thee
23. 29 And they shall deal with thee hatefully
25. 12 that Edom hath dealt against the house
25. 15 Because the Philistines have dealt by rev.
31. 11 he shall surely deal with him: I have
Dan. 1. 13 and as thou seest, deal with thy servants
11. 7 shall deal against them, and shall prev.
Zech. 1. 6 according to our doings, so hath he dealt

3. *To deal out, divide, break asunder,* פָּרַס *paras.*
Isa. 58. 7 (Is it) not to deal thy bread to the hungry

4. *To part, portion out,* μερίζω *merizō.*
Rom 12 3 according as God hath dealt to every man

[*See also* Bitterly corruptly. deceitfully, falsely, foolishly. ill, perversely, proudly, subtilely, tenth, treacherously. unfaithfully, unjustly, well, wickedly wisely, worse]

DEAL bountifully, to —
To do, confer benefit, גָּמַל *gamal.*
Psa. 13. 6 because he hath dealt bountifully with
116. 7 for the LORD hath dealt bountifully with
119 17 Deal bountifully with thy servant, (that)
142. 7 for thou shalt deal bountifully with me

DEAL hardly with —
To humble, afflict, עָנָה *anah,* 3.
Gen. 16. 6 when Sarai dealt hardly with her, she

DEAL subtilly, to —
1. *To show self deceitful,* נָכַל *nakal,* 7.
Psa. 105. 25 He turned their heart..to deal subtilly
2. *To act wisely against,* κατασοφίζομαι *katasophi.*
Acts 7. 19 The same dealt subtilly with our kindred

DEAL with, to —
1. *To do,* עָשָׂה *asah.*
Gen. 34. 31 Should he deal with our sister as with an
2 Ki. 21. 6 and dealt with familiar spirits and wiza.
2 Ch. 33. 6 used witchcraft, and dealt with a familiar
2. *To fall in with,* ἐντυγχάνω *entugchanō.*
Acts 25. 24 multitude of the Jews have dealt with
3. *To do,* ποιέω *poieō.*
Luke 1. 25 Thus hath the Lord dealt with me in the
2. 48 Son, why hast thou thus dealt with us?
4. *To bear toward,* προσφέρω *prospherō.*
Heb. 12. 7 God dealeth with you as with sons; for

DEALINGS with, to have —
To use together, or in common, συγχράομαι *sugch.*
John 4. 9 the Jews have no dealings with the Sam.

DEAR —
1. *Precious,* יַקִּיר *yaqqir*
Jer. 31. 20 (Is) Ephraim my dear son? (is he) a plea.
2. *Love,* ἀγάπη *agapē.*
Col. 1. 13 translated (us) into the kingdom of his d.
3. *Loved, beloved,* ἀγαπητός *agapētos.*
Eph. 5. 1 Be ye..followers of God, as dear children
Col. 1. 7 As ye also learned of..our dear fellow ser.
1 Th. 2. 8 we were willing..because ye were dear
4. *Much prized,* ἔντιμος *entimos.*
Luke 7. 2 a certain centurion's servant, who was de.
5. *Prized,* τίμιος *timios.*
Acts 20. 24 neither count I my life dear unto myself

DEARTH —
1. *Restraint, dearth,* בַּצֹּרֶת *batstsoreth.*
Jer. 14. 1 came to Jeremiah concerning the dearth
2. *Hunger, famine,* רָעָב *raab.*
Gen. 41. 54 the seven years of dearth began to come
41. 54 the dearth was in all lands; but in all
2 Ki. 4. 38 and (there was) a dearth in the land ; and
2 Ch. 6. 28 If there be dearth in the land, if there be
Neh. 5. 3 we might buy corn, because of the dearth
3. *Hunger, want,* λιμός *limos.*
Acts 7. 11 Now there came a dearth over all the land
11. 28 there should be great dearth throughout

DEATH —
1. *To die,* מוּת *muth.*
Num 35. 31 of a murderer, which (is) guilty of death
Judg. 5. 18 jeoparded their lives unto the death in
16. 16 (so) that his soul was vexed unto death
1 Sa. 4. 20 about the time of her death the women
2 Sa. 20. 3 shut up unto the day of their death
2 Ki. 20. 1 In those days was Hezekiah sick unto de.
2 Ch. 32. 24 those days Hezekiah was sick to the death
Isa. 38. 1 In those days was Hezekiah sick unto d.
2. *Death,* מָוֶת *maveth.*
Gen. 21. 16 for she said, Let me not see the death of
25. 11 it came to pass after the death of Abrah.
26. 18 had stopped them after the death
27. 2 I am old, I know not the day of my death
27. 7 bless thee before the LORD before my de.
27 10 that he may bless thee before his death
Exod 10. 17 he may take away from me this death
Lev. 16 1 after the death of the two sons of Aaron
Num 16 29 If these men die the common death of
23 10 Let me die the death of the righteous
35 25 he shall abide in it unto the death of the
35 28 remained..until the death of the high
35 28 after the death of the high priest the
35 32 come again..until the death of the priest
Deut 22 26 in the damsel no sin (worthy) of death
30. 15 I have set..life and good, and death and
30. 19 (that) I have set before you life and death
31. 27 and how much more after my death!
31. 29 For I know that after my death ye will
33. 1 blessed the children of Israel before his d.
Josh. 1. 1 after the death of Moses..it came to pass
2. 13 save alive..deliver our lives from death
20. 6 until the death of the high priest that
Judg. 1. 1 after the death of Joshua it came to pass
13. 7 from the womb to the day of his death
16. 30 the dead which he slew at his death were
Ruth 1. 17 (if ought) but death part thee and me
2. 11 all that thou hast done..since the death
1 Sa. 15. 32 Surely the bitterness of death is past
15. 35 came no more..until the day of his death
20. 3 but a step between me and death
2 Sa. 1. 1 it came to pass after the death of Saul
1. 23 and in their death they were not divided
6. 23 had no child unto the day of her death
15. 21 whether in death or life, even there also
22. 5 When the waves of death compassed me
22. 6 the snares of death prevented me
1 Ki. 11. 40 was in Egypt until the death of Solomon
2 Ki. 1. 1 Moab rebelled..after the death of Ahab
2. 21 shall not be from thence any more death
4. 40 (thou) man of God, (there is) death in the
14. 17 lived after the death of Jehoash, son of
15. 5 he was a leper unto the day of his death
1 Ch. 22. 5 David prepared abundantly before his d.
2 Ch. 22. 4 after the death of his father, to his destr.
24. 17 Now after the death of Jehoiada came the
25. 25 Amaziah..lived after the death of Joash
26. 21 was a leper unto the day of his death
32. 33 inhabitants..did him honour at his death
Job 3. 21 Which long for death, but it (cometh) not
5. 20 In famine he shall redeem thee from de.
7. 15 my soul chooseth strangling, (and) death
18. 13 (even) the first born of death shall devour
27. 15 Those that remain..be buried in death
28. 22 Destruction and death say, We have heard
30. 23 I know (that) thou wilt bring me (to) d.
38. 17 Have the gates of death been opened un.
Psa. 6. 5 For in death (there is) no remembrance
7. 13 prepared for him the instruments of de.
9. 13 that liftest me up from the gates of dea.
13. 3 lighten..lest I sleep the (sleep of) death
18. 4 The sorrows of death compassed me, and
18. 5 the snares of death prevented me
22. 15 hast brought me into the dust of death
33. 19 To deliver their soul from death, and to
49. 14 death shall feed on them ; and the uprig.
55. 4 the terrors of death are fallen upon me
55. 15 Let death seize upon them, (and) let them
56. 13 thou hast delivered my soul from death
68. 20 unto GOD..(belong) the issues from death
73. 4 For (there are) no bands in their death
78. 50 he spared not their soul from death
89. 48 liveth, and shall not see death? shall he
107. 18 they draw near unto the gates of death
116. 3 The sorrows of death compassed me, and
116. 8 thou hast delivered my soul from death
116. 15 Precious..(is) the death of his saints
118. 18 but he hath not given me over unto dea.
Prov. 2. 18 her house inclineth unto death, and her
5. 5 Her feet go down to death ; her steps
7. 27 going down to the chambers of death
8. 36 all they that hate me love death
10. 2 but righteousness delivereth from death
11. 4 but righteousness delivereth from death
11. 19 so he..(pursueth it) to his own death
12. 28 (in) the pathway (thereof there is) no de.
13. 14 to depart from the snares of death
14. 12 but the end thereof (are) the ways of de.
14. 27 to depart from the snares of death
14. 32 but the righteous hath hope in his death
16. 14 wrath of a king (is as) messengers of de.
16. 25 but the end thereof (are) the ways of de.
18. 21 Death and life (are) in the power of the
Prov 21. 6 tossed to and fro of them that seek death
24. 11 to deliver (them that are) drawn unto d.
26. 18 who casteth fire brands, arrows, and de.
Eccl. 7. 1 the day of death than the day of one's
7. 26 I find more bitter than death the woman
8. 8 neither (hath he) power in the day of de.
Song 8. 6 love (is) strong as death ; jealousy (is)
Isa. 25. 8 He will swallow up death in victory; and
28. 15 We have made a covenant with death
28. 18 your covenant with death shall be
38. 18 the grave cannot praise thee, death can
53. 9 made his grave..with the rich in his de.
53. 12 he hath poured out his soul unto death
Jer. 8. 3 death shall be chosen rather than life
9. 21 death is come up into our windows
15. 2 Such as (are) for death, to death ; and
18. 21 let their men be put to death ; (let) their
21. 8 the way of life, and the way of death
43. 11 (and deliver) such (as are) for death to d.
52. 11 put him in prison till the day of his dea.
52. 34 a portion until the day of his death
Lam. 1. 20 abroad the sword bereaveth, at home..d.
Eze. 18. 32 I have no pleasure in the death of him
28. 10 shalt die the deaths of the uncircumcised
31. 14 they are all delivered unto death, to the
33. 11 I have no pleasure in the death of the
Hos. 13. 14 I will redeem them from death : O death
Jon. 4. 9 I do well to be angry, (even) unto death
Hab. 2. 5 who enlargeth his desire..and (is) as de.
3. *Death,* מוֹת *moth.*
Ezra 7. 26 whether (it be) unto death, or to banish.
4. *Dying, death,* מוּת *muth.*
Psa. 48. 14 he will be our guide (even) unto death
5. *Death,* תְּמוּתָה *temuthah.*
Psa. 102. 20 loose those that are appointed to death
6. *A lifting or taking up,* ἀναίρεσις *anairesis.*
Acts 8. 1 And Saul was consenting unto his death
22. 20 standing by, and consenting unto [his de.]
7. *Death,* θάνατος *thanatos.*
Matt. 4. 16 which sat in the region and shadow of d.
10. 21 shall deliver up the brother to death
15. 4 He that curseth..let him die the death
16. 28 some..which shall not taste of death
20. 18 and they shall condemn him to death
26. 38 My soul is..sorrowful, even unto death
26. 66 answered and said, He is guilty of death
Mark 7. 10 Whoso curseth..let him die the death
9. 1 some..which shall not taste of death
10. 33 they shall condemn him to death, and
13. 12 brother shall betray the brother to death
14. 34 My soul is exceeding sorrowful unto de.
14. 64 all condemned him to be guilty of death
Luke 1. 79 sit in darkness and (in) the shadow of d.
2. 26 that he should not see death, before he
9. 27 some..which shall not taste of death
22. 33 with thee, both into prison, and to death
23. 15 nothing worthy of death is done unto
23. 22 I have found no cause of death in him
24. 20 delivered him to be condemned to death
John 5. 24 but is passed from death unto life
8. 51 keep my saying, he shall never see death
8. 52 my saying, he shall never taste of death
11. 4 This sickness is not unto death, but for
11. 13 Jesus spake of his death : but they
12. 33 signifying what death he should die
18. 32 signifying what death he should die
21. 19 signifying by what death he should glor.
Acts 2. 24 Whom God..having loosed the pains of [d.]
13. 28 though they found no cause of death
22. 4 And I persecuted this way unto the dea.
23. 29 nothing laid to his charge worthy of de.
25. 11 have committed anything worthy of dea.
25. 25 he had committed nothing worthy of d.
26. 31 This man doeth nothing worthy of death
28. 18 because there was no cause of death in
Rom. 1. 32 commit such things are worthy of death
5. 10 reconciled to God by the death of his Son
5. 12 death by sin; and so [death] passed upon
5. 14 death reigned from Adam to Moses, even
5. 17 if by one man's offence death reigned by
5. 21 as sin hath reigned unto death, even so
6. 3 many of . . were baptized into his death?
6. 4 are buried with him by baptism into de.
6. 5 together in the likeness of his death
6. 9 death hath no more dominion over him
6. 16 whether of sin [unto death,] or of obedi.
6. 21 for the end of those things (is) death
6. 23 the wages of sin (is) death ; but the gift
7. 5 did work..to bring forth fruit unto death
7. 10 (was ordained) to life, I found..unto d.
7. 13 Was then that which is good made death
7. 13 working death in me by that which is
7. 24 deliver me from the body of this death?
8. 2 made me free from the law of sin and d.
8. 6 to be carnally minded (is) death; but to
8. 38 neither death, nor life, nor angels, nor
1 Co. 3. 22 or life, or death, or things present, or
11. 26 ye do show the Lord's death till he come
15. 21 since by man (came) death, by man
15. 26 last enemy..shall be destroyed (is) death
15. 54 Death is swallowed up in victory
15. 55 O death, where (is) thy sting? O grave
15. 56 The sting of death (is) sin ; and the stren.
2 Co. 1. 9 we had the sentence of death in ourselves
1. 10 Who delivered us from so great a death
2. 16 the savour of death unto death
3. 7 if the ministration of death, written (and)
4. 11 we..are alway delivered unto death for
4. 12 So then death worketh in us, but life in

2 Co. 7. 10 but the sorrow of the world worketh d.
11. 23 in prisons more frequent, in deaths oft
Phil. 1. 20 whether (it be) by life, or by death
2. 8 became obedient unto death, even the d.
2. 27 For indeed he was sick nigh unto death
2. 30 he was nigh unto death, not regarding
3. 10 being made comformable unto his death
Col 1. 22 In the body of his flesh through death
2 Ti. 1. 10 Jesus Christ, who hath abolished death
Heb. 2. 9 Jesus..for the suffering of death, crowned
2. 9 by the grace of God should taste death
2. 14 that through death he might destroy him
2. 14 him that had the power of death, that is
2. 15 who through fear of death were all their
5. 7 him that was able to save him from death
7. 23 suffered to continue by reason of death
9 15 that by means of death, for the redemp.
9. 16 there must also of necessity be the death
11. 5 translated that he should not see death
Jas. 1. 15 when it is finished, bringeth forth death
5. 20 shall save a soul from death, and shall
1 Jo. 3. 14 We know that we have passed from death
3. 14 loveth not..abideth in death
5. 16 brother sin a sin (which is) not unto death
5. 16 not unto death. There is a sin unto death
5. 17 and there is a sin not unto death
Rev. 1. 18 and have the keys of hell and of death
2. 10 be thou faithful unto death, and I will
2. 11 He..shall not be hurt of the second death
2. 23 And I will kill her children with death
6. 8 his name that sat on him was Death, and
6. 8 with sword, and with hunger, and with d.
9. 6 in those days shall men seek death, and
9. 6 shall desire to die, and death shall flee
12. 11 they loved not their lives unto the death
13. 3 one of his heads as it were wounded to d.
18. 8 shall her plagues come in one day, death
20. 6 on such the second death hath no power
20. 13 death and hell delivered up the dead w.
20. 14 And death and hell were cast into the lake
20. 14 This is the second death
21. 4 there shall be no more death, neither
21. 8 with fire..which is the second death

8. *End*, τελευτή *teleutē*.
Matt. 2. 15 And was there until the death of Herod

DEATH, appointed to —
Condemned to death, ἐπιθανάτιος *epithanatios*.
1 Co. 4. 9 as it were appointed to death: for we are

DEATH, to be at the point of —
To be about to die off, μέλλω ἀποθνήσκειν [*mellō*].
John 4. 47 his son: for he was at the point of death

DEATH, to lie at the point of —
To hold extremely (ill), be dying, ἐσχάτως ἔχω.
Mark 5. 23 My..daughter lieth at the point of death

DEATH, to put to —
1. *To put to death, cause to die*, מוּת *muth*, 5.
Deut 13 9 be first upon him to put him to death
17. 7 shall be first upon him to put him to d.
Judg 20. 13 that we may put them to death, and put
1 Sa. 11. 12 bring the men, that we may put them to d.
2 Sa. 8. 2 two lines measured he to put to death
1 Ki. 2. 8 will not put thee to death with the sword
2. 26 will not at this time put thee to death
Esth. 4. 11 one law of his to put (him) to death
Jer. 26. 15 if ye put me to death, ye shall surely
26. 19 Hezekiah king of J...put him at all to d.?
26. 21 the king sought to put him to death: but
26. 24 hand of the people to put him to death
38 15 wilt thou not surely put me to death? and
38. 16 I will not put thee to death, neither will
38. 25 and we will not put thee to death
43. 3 that they might put us to death, and
52. 27 put them to death in Riblah in the land

2. *To lift or take up or away*, ἀναιρέω *anaireō*.
Luke 23. 32 led with him to be put to death
Acts 26. 10 when they were put to death, I gave my

3. *To go or lead away*, ἀπάγω *apagō*.
Acts 12. 19 commanded that (they) should be put to d.

4. *To kill off hand*, ἀποκτείνω *apokteinō*.
Mark 14. 1 take him by craft, and put (him) to death
Luke 18. 33 shall scourge (him), and put him to death
John 11. 53 took counsel together for to put him to d.
12. 10 that they might put Lazarus also to death
18. 31 It is not lawful..to put any man to death

5. *To put to death*, θανατόω *thanatoō*.
Matt 26. 59 sought false witness..to put him to death
27. 1 counsel against Jesus to put him to death
Mark 14. 55 sought for witness..to put him to death
1 Pe. 3. 18 being put to death in the flesh, but quick.

DEATH, would have put to —
To wish to kill, θέλω ἀποκτεῖναι *thelō apokteinai*.
Matt 14. 5 when he would have put him to death

DEATH, to be put to —
1. *To die*, מוּת *muth*, 6 [V.L. 1].
2 Ki. 14. 6 every man shall be put to death for his

2. *To be caused to die, put to death*, מוּת *muth*, 6.
Gen. 26. 11 shall surely be put to death
Exod 19. 12 toucheth the mount shall be..put to death
21. 12 smiteth a man..shall be..put to death
21. 15 smiteth his father..shall be..put to death
21. 16 he that stealeth..shall..be put to death
21. 17 he that curseth..shall..be put to death
21. 29 and his owner also shall be put to death
Exod 22. 19 lieth with a beast shall..be put to death
31. 14 defileth it shall..be put to death
31. 15 he shall surely be put to death
35. 2 doeth work..shall be put to death
Lev. 19. 20 they shall not be put to death, because
20. 2, 15 he shall surely be put to death
20. 9 shall be surely put to death
20. 10 adulteress shall surely be put to death
20. 11, 12 both of them shall surely be put to d.
20. 13, 16 they shall surely be put to death
20. 27 a wizard, shall surely be put to death
24. 16 he shall surely be put to death, (and) all
24. 16 the stranger..shall be put to death
24. 17 killeth any man shall..be put to death
24. 21 killeth a man, he shall be put to death
27. 29 (but) shall surely be put to death
Num. 1. 51 that cometh nigh shall be put to death
3. 10, 38 that cometh nigh shall be put to dea.
15. 35 The man shall be surely put to death
18. 7 that cometh nigh shall be put to death
35. 16, 17, 18 murderer shall surely be put to d.
35. 21 he that smote (him) shall..be put to d.
35. 31 but he shall be surely put to death
Deut 13. 5 dreamer of dreams, shall be put to death
17. 6 put to death..he shall not be put to death
21. 22 and he be to be put to death, and thou
24. 16 The fathers shall not be put to death for
24. 16 neither shall the children be put to death
24. 16 every man shall be put to death for his
Josh. 1. 18 will not hearken..he shall be put to d.
Judg. 6. 31 let him be put to death whilst (it is yet)
21. 5 saying, He shall surely be put to death
1 Sa. 11. 13 There shall not a man be put to death
2 Sa. 19. 21 Shall not Shimei be put to death for this
19. 22 shall there any man be put to death this
21. 9 were put to death in the days of harvest
1 Ki. 2. 24 Adonijah shall be put to death this day
2 Ki. 14. 6 The fathers shall not be put to death for
14. 6 nor the children be put to death for the
2 Ch. 15. 13 should be put to death, whether small or
23. 7 he shall be put to death: but be ye
Jer. 38. 4 let this man be put to death: for thus he

3. *To murder, slay, crush*, רָצַח *ratsach*.
Num 35. 30 the murderer shall be put to death by the

DEATH, to cause to be put to —
To put to death, θανατόω *thanatoō*.
Matt 10. 21 and cause them to be put to death
Mark 13. 12 and shall cause them to be put to death
Luke 21. 16 shall they cause to be put to death

DEATH seize, let —
Desolations, יְשִׁימוֹת *yeshimoth*.
Psa. 55. 15 Let death seize upon them, (and) let them

DEATH, worthy of —
1. *To die*, מוּת *muth*.
Deut 17. 6 shall he that is worthy of death be put to

2. *A man of death*, אִישׁ מָוֶת *ish maveth*.
1 Ki. 2. 26 for thou (art) worthy of death

3. *Judgment of death*, מִשְׁפַּט מָוֶת *mishpat maveth*.
Deut 19. 6 he (was) not worthy of death, inasmuch
21. 22 a man have committed a sin worthy of d.

DEATHS —
Death, the dead, מְמוֹת *mamoth*.
Jer. 16. 4 They shall die of grievous deaths
Eze. 28. 8 thou shalt die the deaths of (them that

DEBASE, to —
To make low or humble, שָׁפֵל *shaphel*, 5.
Isa. 57. 9 and didst debase (thyself even) unto hell

DEBATE —
1. *Debate*, מַצָּה *matstsah*.
Isa. 58. 4 ye fast for strife and debate, and to smite

2. *Strife*, ἔρις *eris*.
Rom. 1. 29 full of envy, murder, debate, deceit
2 Co. 12. 20 lest (there be) debates, envyings, wraths

DEBATE, to —
To strive, plead, רִיב *rib*.
Prov 25. 9 Debate thy cause with thy neighbour
Isa. 27. 8 when it shooteth forth, thou wilt debate

DE'-BIR, דְּבִיר *speaker*.
1. An Amorite king of Eglon, slain by Joshua, B.C. 1450.
Josh. 10. 3 and unto D. king of Eglon, saying

2. A city in the S. of Judah near Hebron, and the same as Kirjath-sepher, and Kirjath-sannah.
Josh. 10. 38 Joshua returned..Israel with him, to D.
10. 39 as he had done to Hebron, so he did to D.
11. 21 Joshua..cut off the A.'s..from H., from D.
12. 13 The king of D., one; the king of Geder
15. 7 And the border went up toward D. from
15. 15 he went up thence to the inhabitants of D.
15. 15 name of D. before (was) Kirjath-sepher
15. 49 Dannah..Kirjath-sannah, which (is) D.
21. 15 Holon with her suburbs, and D. with her
Judg. 1. 11 thence he went against..inhabitants of D.
1. 11 the name of D. before (was) Kirjath-seph.
1 Ch. 6. 58 Hilen with her suburbs, D. with her sub.

3. The "border of Debir" is mentioned as part of the boundary of Gad, and as not far from Mahanaim.
Josh. 13. 26 and from Mahanaim unto the border of D.

DE-BO'-RAH, דְּבוֹרָה *bee, wasp*.
1. Rebekah's nurse, B.C. 1732.
Gen. 35. 8 But D. Rebekah's nurse died, and she

2. A prophetess who judged Israel. Her name was an Egyptian symbol of regal power; and among the Greeks it was applied not only to the poets and those peculiarly chaste, but especially to the priestesses of Delphi, Cybele and Artemis. She was probably of Ephraim, though some suppose her to have belonged to Issachar from the expression in Judg. 5. 15. The common version calls her "wife of Lapidoth;" but another rendering of the phrase is Tennyson's "the great dame of Lapidoth;" or, *mulier splendorum*, that is, one divinely illuminated, since "*lapidoth*" is="lightnings". The rabbis however say that she was one who tended the tabernacle lamps.
Judg. 4. 4 And D., a prophetess..judged Israel at
4. 5 And she dwelt under the palm tree of D.
4. 9 And D. arose, and went with Barak to K.
4. 10 and D. went up with him
4. 14 And D. said unto Barak, Up; for this (is)
5. 1 Then sang D. and Barak the son of Abin.
5. 7 I D. arose, that I arose a mother in Israel
5. 12 Awake, awake, D.; awake, awake, utter
5. 15 And the princes of Issachar (were) with D.

DEBT —
1. *Hand*, יָד *yad*.
Neh. 10. 31 seventh year, and the exaction of every d.

2. *Loan, debt, biting interest*, מַשָּׁאָה *mashshaah*.
Prov 22. 26 (or) of them that are sureties for debts

3. *Debt, biting interest*, נְשִׁי *neshi*.
2 Ki. 4. 7 he said, Go, sell the oil, and pay thy de.

4. *To bite, be a usurer*, נָשָׁא *nasha*.
1 Sa. 22. 2 every one that (was) in debt, and every

5. *A loan, what is lent*, δάνειον *daneion*.
Matt. 18. 27 and loosed him, and forgave him the d.

6. *What is owing, indebtedness*, ὀφειλή *opheilē*.
Matt. 18. 32 I forgave thee all that debt, because

7. *What is owing, indebtedness*, ὀφείλημα *opheilēma*.
Matt. 6. 12 forgive us our debts, as we forgive our
Rom. 4. 4 reward not reckoned of grace, but of de.

8. *To owe, be indebted*, ὀφείλω *opheilō*.
Matt. 18. 30 into prison, till he should pay the debt

DEBTOR —
1. *Debtor, one bound, indebted; debt*, חוֹב *chob*.
Eze. 18. 7 hath restored to the debtor his pledge

2. *Debtor, one owing anything*, ὀφειλέτης *opheiletēs*.
Matt. 6. 12 forgive us our debts, as we forgive our d.
Rom. 1. 14 I am debtor both to the Greeks, and to
8. 12 we are debtors, not to the flesh, to live
15. 27 pleased them..and their debtors they
Gal. 5. 3 that he is a debtor to do the whole law

3. *One owing a debt*, χρεωφειλέτης, χρεοφειλέτης.
Luke 7. 41 a certain creditor which had two debtors
16. 5 he called every one of his lord's debtors

DEBTOR, to be a —
To owe, be indebted, ὀφείλω *opheilō*.
Matt. 23. 16 by the gold of the temple, he is a debtor!

DE-CA'-PO-LIS, Δεκάπολις, *Ten cities (collectively)*.
A district named from its containing ten cities, which were mostly on the E. of the Jordan, extending from near Damascus to near the N. end of the Salt Sea.
Matt. 4. 25 followed him..multitudes..(from)..D.
Mark 5. 20 he departed, and began to publish in D.
7. 31 through the midst of the coasts of D.

DECAY, to —
1. *To be dried up*, חָרֵב *chareb*.
Job 14. 11 and the flood decayeth and drieth up

2. *To be brought low*, מָכַךְ *makak*, 2.
Eccl. 10. 18 By much slothfulness the building decay.

3. *To make old*, παλαιόω *palaioō*.
Heb. 8. 13 Now that which decayeth and waxeth

DECAY, to be fallen in —
To move, slip, fail, מוֹט *mot*.
Lev. 25. 35 fallen in decay with thee; then thou shalt

DECAYED, to be —
To be feeble, stumble, כָּשַׁל *kashal*.
Neh. 4. 10 The strength of the bearers..is decayed

DECAYED place —
A waste, dried up place, חָרְבָּה *chorbah*.
Isa. 44. 26 I will raise up the decayed places thereof

DECEASE —
Outgoing, ἔξοδος *exodos*.
Luke 9. 31 his decease which he should accomplish
2 Pe. 1. 15 ye may be able after my decease to have

DECEASE, to —
To end (life), τελευτάω *teleutaō*.
Matt. 22. 25 when he had married a wife, deceased

DECEASED —
Shades, fearful ones, רְפָאִים *rephaim*.
Isa. 26. 14 (they are) deceased, they shall not rise

DECEIT —
1. *Deceit*, מִרְמָה *mirmah*.
Job 15. 35 vanity, and their belly prepareth deceit
31. 5 or if my foot hath hasted to deceit
Psa. 10. 7 His mouth is full of cursing and deceit
36. 3 words of his mouth (are) iniquity and d
38. 12 and imagine deceits all the day long

Psa. 50. 19 mouth to evil, and thy tongue frameth d.
Prov.12. 5 (but) the counsels of the wicked (are) de.
12. 17 but a false witness deceit
12. 20 Deceit is in the heart of them that
14. 8 his way: but the folly of fools (is) deceit
26. 24 he that hateth..layeth up deceit within
Isa. 53. 9 neither (was any) deceit in his mouth
Jer. 5. 27 so (are) their houses full of deceit
9. 6 Thine habitation (is) in the midst of dec
9. 6 through deceit they refuse to know me
9. 8 it speaketh deceit: (one) speaketh
Hos. 11. 12 and the house of Israel with deceit: but
12. 7 the balances of deceit (are) in his hand
Amos 8. 5 and falsifying the balances by deceit?
Zeph. 1. 9 fill their masters' houses with..deceit

2. *Deceit, deception,* מַשָּׁאוֹן *mashshaon.*
Prov.26. 26 (Whose) hatred is covered by deceit, his

3. *Deceit, fraud,* רְמִיָּה *remiyyah.*
Job 27. 4 wickedness, nor my tongue utter deceit
Psa.101. 7 He that worketh deceit shall not dwell

4. *Falsehood,* שֶׁקֶר *sheqer.*
Prov.20. 17 Bread of deceit (is) sweet to a man; but

5. *Fraud, oppression,* תֹּךְ *tok.*
Psa. 55. 11 deceit and guile depart not from her
72. 14 He shall redeem their soul from deceit

6. *Deceit,* תַּרְמִית, [V.L. תרמות], *tarmith.*
Jer. 14. 14 a thing of nought, and the deceit of their

7. *Deceit,* תַּרְמִית *tarmith.*
Psa.119. 118 Thou hast trodden down..for their dec.
Jer. 8. 5 they hold fast deceit, they refuse to retu.
23. 26 prophets of the deceit of their own heart

8. *Deceit,* ἀπάτη *apatē.*
Col. 2. 8 through philosophy and vain deceit, after

9. *Bait, guile,* δόλος *dolos.*
Mark 7. 22 Thefts, covetousness, wickedness, deceit
Rom. 1. 29 full of envy, murder, debate, deceit

10. *Wandering, leading astray, error,* πλάνη *planē.*
1 Th. 2. 3 For our exhortation (was) not of deceit

DECEIT, to use —
To use a bait, guile, δολιόω *dolioō.*
Rom. 3. 13 with their tongues they have used deceit

DECEITFUL —
1. *A lie, lying,* כָּזָב *kazab.*
Prov.23. 3 Be not desirous..for they (are) deceitful

2. *Deceit,* מִרְמָה *mirmah.*
Psa. 5. 6 will abhor the bloody and deceitful man
35. 20 but they devise deceitful matters against
43. 1 deliver me from the deceitful and unjust
52. 4 lovest all devouring words, O (thou) decei.
55. 23 and deceitful men shall not live out half
109. 2 and the mouth of the deceitful are opened
Prov.14. 25 but a deceitful (witness) speaketh lies
Mic. 6. 11 and with the bag of deceitful weights?

3. *Crooked, slippery,* עָקֹב *aqob.*
Jer. 17. 9 The heart (is) deceitful above all (things)

4. *To be abundant,* עָתַר *athar,* 2.
Prov 27. 6 but the kisses of an enemy (are) deceitful

5. *Deceit, remissness,* רְמִיָּה *remiyyah.*
Psa. 78. 57 turned aside like a deceitful bow
120. 2 lying lips, (and) from a deceitful tongue
Hos. 7. 16 they are like a deceitful bow: their prin.
Mic. 6. 12 their tongue (is) deceitful in their mouth

6. *Falsehood,* שֶׁקֶר *sheqer.*
Prov 11. 18 The wicked worketh a deceitful work
31. 30 Favour (is) deceitful, and beauty (is) vain

7. *Frauds, oppressions,* תְּכָכִים *tekakim.*
Prov 29. 13 The poor and the deceitful man meet tog.

8. *Deceit,* תַּרְמִית *tarmith.*
Zeph. 3. 13 neither shall a deceitful tongue be found

9. *Deceit,* ἀπάτη *apatē.*
Eph. 4. 22 corrupt according to the deceitful lusts

10. *Guileful,* δόλιος *dolios.*
2 Co 11. 13 For such (are) false apostles, deceitful

DECEITFULLY —
1. *With deceit,* בְּמִרְמָה *be-mirmah,* לְמִרְמָה *le-mirmah.*
Gen. 34. 13 the sons of Jacob answered..deceitfully
Psa. 24. 4 who hath not lifted up..nor sworn deceit.
Dan 11. 23 after the league..he shall work deceit.

2. *Deceit,* רְמִיָּה *remiyyah.*
Job 13. 7 Will ye speak..and talk deceitfully for
Psa. 52. 2 like a sharp razor, working deceitfully
Jer. 48. 10 doeth the work of the LORD deceitfully

DECEITFULLY, to deal —
1. *To deal treacherously, deceive,* בָּגַד *bagad.*
Exod 21. 8 seeing he hath dealt deceitfully with her
Job 6. 15 My brethren have dealt deceitfully as a

2. *To deceive, mock,* הָתַל *hathal,* 3; *or* תָּלַל *talal,* 5.
Exod. 8. 29 let not Pharaoh deal deceitfully any more

DECEITFULLY, to get —
To get by oppression, עָשַׁק *ashaq.*
Lev. 6. 4 the thing which he hath deceitfully got.

DECEITFULLY, to handle —
To use guilefully, δολόω *doloō.*
2 Co. 4. 2 nor handling the word of God deceitfully

DECEITFULNESS —
Deceit, ἀπάτη *apatē.*
Matt 13 22 the deceitfulness of riches choke the w.
Mark 4. 19 the deceitfulness of riches..choke the w.
Heb 3. 13 hardened through the deceitfulness of sin

DECEITS —
Deceits, deceitful things, מַהֲתַלּוֹת *mahathalloth.*
Isa. 30. 10 speak unto us smooth things, prophesy d.

DECEIVABLENESS —
Deceit, ἀπάτη *apatē.*
2 Th. 2. 10 with all deceivableness of unrighteous.

DECEIVE, to —
1. *To deceive, mock, play upon one,* הָתַל *hathal,* 3.
Gen. 31. 7 And your father hath deceived me, and
Jer. 9. 5 they will deceive every man his neigh.

2. *To lie, feign,* כָּחַשׁ *kachash,* 3.
Zech 13. 4 shall they wear a rough garment to dece.

3. *To lead astray,* נָשָׁא *nasha,* 5.
2 Ki. 18. 29 Let not Hezekiah deceive you; for he
19. 10 thy God in whom thou trustest deceive
2 Ch. 32. 15 therefore let not Hezekiah deceive you
Isa. 36. 14 Let not Hezekiah deceive you; for he
37. 10 thy God in whom thou trustest deceive
Jer. 4. 10 surely thou hast greatly deceived this pe.
29. 8 Let not your prophets..deceive you
37. 9 Thus saith the LORD, Deceive not your.
49. 16 Thy terribleness hath deceived thee, (and)
Obad. 3 The pride of thine heart hath deceived
7 men that were at peace..have deceived

4. *To oppress,* עָשַׁק *ashaq.*
Lev 6. 2 or hath deceived his neighbour

5. *To entice, persuade, deceive,* פָּתָה *pathah,* 3.
2 Sa. 3. 25 Thou knowest..that he came to deceive
Prov 24. 28 Be not a witness..and deceive (not) with
Jer. 20. 7 LORD, thou hast deceived me, and I was
Eze. 14. 9 I the LORD have deceived that prophet

6. *To throw down, deceive,* רָמָה *ramah,* 3.
1 Sa. 19. 17 Why hast thou deceived me so, and sent
28. 12 Why hast thou deceived me? for thou
2 Sa. 19. 26 My Lord, O king, my servant deceived
Prov 26. 19 the man (that) deceiveth his neighbour
Lam. 1. 19 I called for my lovers, (but) they deceiv.

7. *To deceive, lead astray,* שָׁלָה *shalah,* 5.
2 Ki. 4. 28 did I not say, Do not deceive me?

8. *To deceive,* ἀπατάω *apataō.*
Eph. 5. 6 Let no man deceive you with vain words
1 Ti. 2. 14 And Adam was not deceived, but the w.
2. 14 [being deceived] was in the transgression
Jas. 1. 26 bridleth not his tongue, but deceiveth

9. *To deceive greatly,* ἐξαπατάω *exapataō.*
Rom. 7. 11 For sin..deceived me, and by it slew (me)
16. 18 by good words..deceive the hearts of the
1 Co. 3. 18 Let no man deceive himself. If any man
2 Th. 2. 3 Let no man deceive you by any means

10. *To reason amiss,* παραλογίζομαι *paralogizomai.*
Jas. 1. 22 not hearers only, deceiving your own sel.

11. *To lead astray,* πλανάω *planaō.*
Matt 24. 4 Take heed that no man deceive you
24. 5 saying, I am Christ; and shall deceive
24. 11 many false prophets..shall deceive many
24. 24 if (it were) possible, they shall deceive
Mark 13. 5 Take heed lest any (man) deceive you
13. 6 saying, I am (Christ); and shall deceive
Luke 21. 8 Take heed that ye be not deceived
John 7. 12 others said, Nay; but he deceiveth the
7. 47 answered..Pharisees, Are ye also deceiv.?
1 Co. 6. 9 Be not deceived: neither fornicators, nor
15. 33 Be not deceived: evil communications
Gal. 6. 7 Be not deceived; God is not mocked
2 Ti. 3. 13 wax worse..deceiving, and being deceived
Titus 3. 3 sometimes foolish, disobedient, deceived
1 Jo. 1. 8 that we have no sin, we deceive ourselves
3. 7 Little children, let no man deceive you
Rev. 12. 9 and Satan, which deceiveth the whole
13. 14 deceiveth them that dwell on the earth
18. 23 by thy sorceries were all nations deceived
19. 20 with which he deceived them that had
20. 3 that he should deceive the nations no
20. 8 shall go out to deceive the nations which
20. 10 the devil, that deceived them, was cast

12. *Wandering, leading astray,* πλάνη *planē.*
Eph. 4. 14 whereby they lie in wait to deceive

13. *To deceive the mind,* φρεναπατάω *phrenapataō.*
Gal. 6. 3 when he is nothing, he deceiveth himself

DECEIVED —
1. *To be deceived,* הָתַל *hathal,* 4; *or* תָּלַל *talal,* 6.
Isa. 44. 20 a deceived heart hath turned him aside

2. *To err, go astray,* שָׁגַג *shagag.*
Job 12. 16 the deceived and the deceiver (are) his

DECEIVED, to be —
1. *To be led astray,* נָשָׁא *nasha,* 2.
Isa. 19. 13 the princes of Noph are deceived

2. *To be enticed, persuaded, deceived,* פָּתָה *pathah.*
Deut. 11. 16 Take heed..your heart be not deceived

3. *To be enticed, persuaded, deceived,* פָּתָה *pathah,* 2.
Job 31. 9 If mine heart have been deceived by a
Jer. 20. 7 I was deceived; thou art stronger than I

4. *To be enticed, persuaded, deceived,* פָּתָה *pathah,* 4.
Eze. 14. 9 if the prophet be deceived when he hath

5. *To err, go astray,* שָׁגָה *shagah.*
Prov 20. 1 whosoever is deceived thereby is not wise

6. *To err, wander, go astray,* תָּעָה *taah,* 2.
Job 15. 31 Let not him that is deceived trust in

DECEIVER —
1. *To show self deceitful,* נָכַל *nakal.*
Mal. 1. 14 cursed (be) the deceiver, which hath in

2. *To cause to err, go astray,* שָׁגָה *shagah,* 5.
Job 12. 16 the deceived and the deceiver (are) his

3. *To err, go astray,* תָּעַע *taa,* 3a.
Gen. 27. 12 and I shall seem to him as a deceiver

4. *Leader astray, deceiver,* πλάνος *planos.*
Matt 27. 63 Sir, we remember that that deceiver said
2 Co. 6. 8 By honour and dishonour..as deceivers
2 Jo. 7 many deceivers are entered into the world
7 This is a deceiver and an antichrist

5. *One who deceives the mind,* φρεναπάτης *phrena.*
Titus 1. 10 many unruly..vain talkers and deceiv.

DECEIVING —
Deceit, ἀπάτη *apatē.*
2 Pe. 2. 13 sporting themselves with their own [dece.]

DECENTLY —
Becomingly, εὐσχημόνως *euschēmonōs.*
1 Co. 14. 40 all things be done decently and in order

DECIDE, to —
To determine, חָרַץ *charats.*
1 Ki. 20. 40 thy judgment be; thyself hast decided

DECISION —
Decision, determination, חָרוּץ *charuts.*
Joel 3. 14 multitudes in the valley of decision
3. 14 the day..(is) near in the valley of decision

DECK, to —
1. *To make fair, beautify,* יָפָה *yaphah,* 3.
Jer. 10. 4 They deck it with silver and with gold

2. *To prepare,* כָּהַן *kahan,* 3.
Isa. 61. 10 as a bridegroom decketh (himself) with

3. *To adorn,* עָדָה *adah.*
Eze. 16. 11 I decked thee also with ornaments, and

4. *To do, make,* עָשָׂה *asah.*
Eze. 16. 16 deckedst thy high places with divers

5. *To deck, spread out,* רָבַד *rabad.*
Prov. 7. 16 I have decked my bed with coverings of

6. *To make golden,* χρυσόω *chrusoō.*
Rev. 17. 4 decked with gold, and precious stones
18. 16 decked with gold, and precious stones

DECK (self) —
To adorn (self), עָדָה *adah.*
Job 40. 10 Deck thyself now (with) majesty and ex
Jer. 4. 30 though thou deckest thee with ornaments
Eze. 23. 40 and deckedst thyself with ornaments
Hos. 2. 13 she decked herself with her earrings and

DECKED to be —
To adorn (self), עָדָה *adah.*
Eze. 16. 13 Thus wast thou decked with gold and

DECLARATION —
1. *Showing, declaration,* אַחֲוָה *achvah.*
Job 13. 17 Hear diligently..my declaration with

2. *Explanation, exposition,* פָּרָשָׁה *parashah.*
Esth. 10. 2 declaration of the greatness of Mordecai

3. *A leading through, full declaration,* διήγησις.
Luke 1. 1 to set forth in order a declaration of

DECLARE (to), to —
1. *To say,* אָמַר *amar.*
Psa. 40. 10 I have declared thy faithfulness and thy
Dan. 4. 18 declare the interpretation thereof

2. *To explain,* בָּאַר *baar,* 3.
Deut. 1. 5 began Moses to declare this law, saying

3. *To explain,* בּוּר *bur.*
Eccl. 9. 1 I considered in my heart, even to declare

4. *To speak,* דָּבַר *dabar,* 3.
Lev. 23. 44 Moses declared unto the children of Isr.
Josh 20. 4 shall declare his cause in the ears of

5. *To make known,* יָדַע *yada,* 5.
Neh. 8. 12 the words that were declared unto them
Job 26. 3 (how) hast thou plentifully declared the
40. 7 demand of thee, and declare thou unto
42. 4 demand of thee, and declare thou unto
Psa. 77. 14 thou hast declared thy strength among
Isa. 12. 4 declare his doings among the people, make

6. *To put before (one),* נָגַד *nagad,* 5.
Gen. 41. 24 (there was) none that could declare (it)
Deut. 4. 13 he declared unto you his covenant, which
Judg 14. 12 if ye can certainly declare it me within
14. 13 if ye cannot declare (it) me, then shall ye
14. 15 that he may declare unto us the riddle
2 Sa. 19. 6 thou hast declared this day, that thou
Esth. 4. 8 to declare (it) unto her, and to charge
Job 21. 31 Who shall declare his way to his face?
31. 37 I would declare unto him the number of
38. 4 declare, if thou hast understanding
38. 18 declare if thou knowest it all

Psa. 9. 11 declare among the people his doings
22. 31 shall declare his righteousness unto a
30. 9 praise thee? shall it declare thy truth?
38. 18 I will declare mine iniquity; I will be
40. 5 I would declare and speak (of them)
50. 6 the heavens shall declare his righteousne.
64. 9 fear, and shall declare the work of God
71. 17 hitherto have I declared thy wondrous
75. 9 I will declare for ever; I will sing praises
97. 6 The heavens declare his righteousness
145. 4 and shall declare thy mighty acts
Isa. 3. 9 they declare their sin as Sodom, they hide
21. 6 set a watchman, let him declare what he
21. 10 that which I have heard..have I declared
41. 26 Who hath declared from the beginning
42. 9 come to pass, and new things do I declare
42. 12 and declare his praise in the islands
43. 9 who among them can declare this, and
43. 12 I have declared, and have saved, and I
44. 7 who, as I, shall call, and shall declare it
44. 8 have not I told thee..and have declared
45. 19 I the LORD..declare things that are right
46. 10 Declaring the end from the beginning
48. 3 I have declared the former things from
48. 5 I have even from the beginning declared
48. 6 see all this; and will not ye declare (it)?
48. 14 which among them hath declared these
48. 20 with a voice of singing declare ye, tell
57. 12 I will declare thy righteousness, and thy
66. 19 they shall declare my glory among the
Jer. 4. 5 Declare ye in Judah, and publish in Jeru.
4. 15 a voice declareth from Dan, and publish.
5. 20 Declare this in the house of Jacob, and
9. 12 and (who is he)..that he may declare it
31. 10 declare (it) in the isles afar off, and say
36. 13 Michaiah declared unto them all the wor.
38. 15 If I declare (it) unto thee, wilt thou not
38. 25 Declare unto us now what thou hast said
42. 4 I will declare (it) unto you; I will keep
42. 20 so declare unto us, and we will do (it)
42. 21 I have this day declared (it) to you
46. 14 Declare ye in Egypt, and publish in Mig.
50. 2 Declare ye among the nations, and publish
50. 28 to declare in Zion the vengeance of the
Eze. 23. 36 yea, declare unto them their abomination
40. 4 declare all that thou seest to the house
Hos. 4. 12 their staff declareth unto them: for the
Amos 4. 13 he..declareth unto man what (is) his
Mic. 1. 10 Declare ye (it) not at Gath, weep ye not
3. 8 declare unto Jacob his transgression
Zech. 9. 12 to day do I declare (that) I will render

7. *To recount, declare,* סָפַר *saphar,* 3.
1 Ch. 16. 24 Declare his glory among the heathen
Job 12. 8 fishes of the sea shall declare unto thee
15. 17 and that (which) I have seen I will decl.
28. 27 Then did he see it, and declare it
Psa. 2. 7 I will declare the decree: the LORD hath
19. 1 The heavens declare the glory of God
22. 22 I will declare thy name unto my brethren
50. 16 What hast thou to do to declare my stat.
66. 16 I will declare what he hath done for my
73. 28 that I may declare all thy works
75. 1 (that) thy name (is) near thy..works dec.
78. 6 arise and declare (them) to their children
96. 3 Declare his glory among the heathen
102. 21 To declare the name of the LORD in Zion
107. 22 and declare his works with rejoicing
118. 17 and declare the works of the LORD
119. 13 With my lips have I declared all the judg.
119. 26 I have declared my ways, and thou heard.
145. 6 and I will declare thy greatness
Isa. 43. 26 declare thou, that thou mayest be justi.
Jer. 51. 10 let us declare in Zion the work of
Eze. 12. 16 that they may declare all their abomina.

8. *To meditate, declare,* שִׂיחַ *siach,* 3a.
Isa. 53. 8 and who shall declare his generation?

9. *To cause to hear,* שָׁמַע *shama,* 5.
Isa. 41. 22 or declare us things for to come
41. 26 yea, (there is) none that declareth
45. 21 who hath declared this from ancient

10. *To tell again,* ἀναγγέλλω *anaggellō.*
Acts 15. 4 they declared all things that God had
20. 27 I have not shunned to declare unto you
1 Jo. 1. 5 which we have heard of him, and declare

11. *To put or place up,* ἀνατίθεμαι *anatithemai.*
Acts 25. 14 Festus declared Paul's cause unto the k.

12. *To tell off,* ἀπαγγέλλω *apaggellō.*
Luke 8. 47 she declared unto him before all the peo.
Heb. 2. 12 I will declare thy name unto my brethren
1 Jo. 1. 3 That which we have seen and heard dec.

13. *To make known,* γνωρίζω *gnōrizō.*
John 17. 26 I have declared..and will declare (it)
1 Co. 15. 1 I declare unto you the gospel which I
Col. 4. 7 All my state shall Tychicus declare unto

14. *To manifest,* δηλόω *dēloō.*
1 Co. 1. 11 it hath been declared unto me of you
3. 13 for the day shall declare it, because it
Col. 1. 8 Who also declared unto us your love in

15. *To tell fully,* διαγγέλλω *diaggellō.*
Rom. 9. 17 my name might be declared throughout

16. *To lead through,* διηγέομαι *diēgeomai.*
Acts 8. 33 who shall declare his generation? for
9. 27 declared unto them how he had seen the
12. 17 he..declared unto them how the Lord had

17. *To lead throughout,* ἐκδιηγέομαι *ekdiēgeomai.*
Acts 13. 41 in no wise believe, though a man declare
15. 3 they passed through..declaring the conv.

18. *A shewing,* ἔνδειξις *endeixis.*
Rom. 3. 25 declare his righteousness for the remis.
3. 26 declare, (I say), at this time his righteo.

19. *To lead out,* ἐξηγέομαι *exēgeomai.*
John 1. 18 the only begotten Son..hath declared
Acts 10. 8 when he had declared all (these) things
15. 12 declaring what miracles and wonders God
15. 14 Simeon hath declared how God..did visit
21. 19 he declared particularly what things God

20. *To tell fully,* καταγγέλλω *kataggellō.*
Acts 17. 23 ye ignorantly worship, him declare I unto
1 Co. 2. 1 declaring unto you the testimony of God

21. *To mark out,* ὁρίζω *horizō.*
Rom. 1. 4 declared (to be) the Son of God with

22. *To tell near,* παραγγέλλω *paraggellō.*
1 Co. 11. 17 I declare (unto you) I praise (you) not

23. *To explain.* φράζω *phrazō.*
Matt 13. 36 [Declare] unto us the parable of the tares
15. 15 said unto him, Declare unto us this par.

24. *To tell good news,* εὐαγγελίζω *euaggelizō.*
Rev. 10. 7 he hath declared to his servants the pro.

DECLARE glad tidings unto, to —
To tell good news, εὐαγγελίζω *euaggelizō.*
Acts 13. 32 we declare unto you glad tidings, how

DECLARE manifestly, to —
To manifest, φανερόω *phaneroō.*
2 Co. 3. 3 manifestly declared to be the epistle of

DECLARE plainly, to —
To manifest, ἐμφανίζω *emphanizō.*
Heb. 11. 14 declare plainly that they seek a country

DECLARED, to be —
1. *To be put before,* נָגַד *nagad,* 6.
Isa. 21. 2 A grievous vision is declared unto me; the

2. *To number,* סָפַר *saphar,* 3.
Exod. 9. 16 that my name may be declared throughout

3. *To be numbered,* סָפַר *saphar,* 4.
Psa. 88. 11 Shall thy loving kindness be declared in

4. *To be spread out, explained,* פָּרַשׁ *parash,* 4.
Num 15. 34 it was not declared what should be done

DECLINE, to —
1. *To incline, stretch down or out,* נָטָה *natah.*
Exod 23. 2 shalt thou speak in a cause to decline
Psa. 44. 18 neither have our steps declined from thy
102. 11 My days (are) like a shadow that declin.
109. 23 gone like the shadow when it declineth
119. 51 (yet) have I not declined from thy law
119. 157 (yet) do I not decline from thy testimo.
Prov. 4. 5 neither decline from the words of my

2. *To (cause to) incline,* נָטָה *natah,* 5.
Job 23. 11 his way have I kept, and not declined

3. *To turn aside,* סוּר *sur.*
Deut 17. 11 thou shalt not decline from the sentence
2 Ch. 34. 2 declined (neither) to the right hand nor

4. *To turn aside,* שָׂטָה *satah.*
Prov. 7. 25 Let not thine heart decline to her ways

DECREASE, to —
1. *To be or become lacking,* חָסֵר *chaser.*
Gen. 8. 5 the waters decreased continually until

2. *To lessen,* ἐλαττόω *elattoō.*
John 3. 30 He must increase, but I (must) decrease

DECREASE, to suffer to —
To cause or let be few, מָעַט *maat,* 5.
Psa. 107. 38 He..suffereth not their cattle to decrease

DECREE —
1. *A bond,* אֱסָר *esar.*
Dan. 6. 7 have consulted..to make a firm decree
6. 8 O king, establish the decree, and sign the
6. 9 Darius signed the writing and the decree
6. 12 and spake..concerning the king's decree
6. 12 Hast thou not signed a decree, that every
6. 13 nor the decree that thou hast signed, but
6. 15 no decree nor statute which the king

2. *A thing cut out or decided,* גְּזֵרָה *gezerah.*
Dan. 4. 17 This matter (is) by the decree of the
4. 24 O king, and this (is) the decree of the

3. *A word, matter, thing,* דָּבָר *dabar.*
2 Ch. 30. 5 So they established a decree to make

4. *Law, a thing given forth,* דָּת *dath.*
Esth. 2. 8 when the king's..decree was heard, and
3. 15 and the decree was given in Shushan the
4. 3 the king's commandment and his decree
4. 8 the writing of the decree that was given
8. 14 decree was given at Shushan the palace
8. 17 the king's commandment and his decree
9. 1 the king's commandment and his decree
9. 13 according unto this day's decree, and let
9. 14 the decree was given at Shushan; and
Dan. 2. 9 (there is but) one decree for you; for ye
2. 13 the decree went forth that the wise (men)
2. 15 Why (is) the decree (so) hasty from the

5. *Statute, thing decreed, or marked out,* חֹק *choq.*
Job 28. 26 When he made a decree for the rain, and
Psa. 2. 7 I will declare the decree: the LORD hath
148. 6 he hath made a decree which shall not
Prov. 8. 29 When he gave to the sea his decree, that
Jer. 5. 22 bound of the sea by a perpetual decree
Mic. 7. 11 that day shall the decree be far removed
Zeph. 2. 2 Before the decree bring forth, (before) the

6. *Statute, thing decreed or marked out,* חֵקֶק *cheqeq.*
Isa. 10. 1 unrighteous decrees, and that write

7. *Taste, discretion,* טַעַם *taam.*
Jon. 3. 7 by the decree of the king and his nobles

8. *Taste, discretion,* טְעֵם *teem.*
Ezra 5. 13 Cyrus made a decree to build this house
5. 17 that a decree was made of Cyrus the king
6. 1 the king made a decree, and search was
6. 3 the king made a decree (concerning) the
6. 8 I make a decree what ye shall do to the
6. 11 I have made a decree, that whosoever
6. 12 I Darius have made a decree; let it be
7. 13 I make a decree, that all they of the
7. 21 I..do make a decree to all the treasurers
Dan. 3. 10 Thou, O king, hast made a decree, that
3. 29 I make a decree, That every people, nation
4. 6 Therefore made I a decree to bring in all
6. 26 I make a decree, That in every dominion

9. *Saying,* מַאֲמַר *maamar.*
Esth. 9. 32 the decree of Esther confirmed these

10. *Matter, thing,* פִּתְגָם *pithgam.*
Esth. 1. 20 when the king's decree which he shall

[11. *Anything set up or established,* קְיָם *qeyam.*
Dan. 6. 7 to make a firm decree, that whosoever]

12. *Dogma, decree,* δόγμα *dogma.*
Luke 2. 1 there went out a decree from Cesar Aug.
Acts 16. 4 they delivered them the decrees for to
17. 7 all do contrary to the decrees of Cesar

DECREE, to —
1. *To cut out, separate, polish,* גָּזַר *gazar.*
Job 22. 28 Thou shalt also decree a thing, and it

2. *To cut out, mark out,* חָקַק *chaqaq.*
Isa. 10. 1 Woe unto them that decree unrighteous

3. *To cut out, mark out,* חָקַק *chaqaq,* 3a.
Prov. 8. 15 kings reign, and princes decree justice

4. *To raise up, confirm, establish,* קוּם *qum,* 3.
Esth. 9. 31 as they had decreed for themselves, and

5. *To judge,* κρίνω *krinō.*
1 Co. 7. 37 hath so decreed in his heart that he will

DECREED (place) —
1. *Statute,* חֹק *choq.*
Job 38. 10 And brake up for it my decreed (place)

2. *To determine,* חָרַץ *charats.*
Isa. 10. 22 the consumption decreed shall overflow

DECREED, to be —
To be cut out, separated, גָּזַר *gazar,* 2.
Esth. 2. 1 remembered..what was decreed against

DE'-DAN, דְּדָן *low.*
1. A grandson of Cush son of Ham, B.C. 2200.
Gen. 10. 7 the sons of Raamah; Sheba, and D.
1 Ch. 1. 9 the sons of Raamah; Sheba, and D.
2. A son of Abraham by Keturah, B.C. 1810.
Gen. 25. 3 And Jokshan begat Sheba and D.
25. 3 the sons of D. were Asshurim, and Let.
1 Ch. 1. 32 And the sons of Jokshan; Sheba, and D.
3. A district near Edom between Sela and the Salt Sea, not far from Edom.
Jer. 25. 23 D., and Tema, and Buz, and all (that are)
49. 8 turn back, dwell deep, O inhabitants of D.
Eze. 25. 13 and they of D. shall fall by the sword
27. 15 The men of D. (were) thy merchants
27. 20 D. (was) thy merchant in precious clothes
38. 13 Sheba, and D., and the merchants of Tar.

DE-DA'-NIM, דְּדָנִים.
Descendants of Raamah, grandson of Ham, B.C. 2200.
Isa. 21. 13 O ye travelling companies of D.

DEDICATE, to —
1. *To press in or on, dedicate,* חָנַךְ *chanak.*
Deut 20. 5 What man..hath not dedicated it? let
20. 5 lest he die..and another man dedicate it
1 Ki. 8. 63 children of Israel dedicated the house
2 Ch. 7. 5 all the people dedicated the house of God

2. *To cause a separation, hallow,* קָדַשׁ *qadesh,* 5.
Judg 17. 3 I had wholly dedicated the silver unto
2 Sa. 8. 11 Which also king David did dedicate unto
8. 11 the silver and gold that he had dedicated
2 Ki. 12. 18 his fathers, kings of Judah, had dedicat.
1 Ch. 18. 11 Them also king David dedicated unto the
26. 26 the captains of the host, had dedicated
26. 27 the spoils won in battles did they dedicate
26. 28 Joab the son of Zeruiah, had dedicated
26. 28 whosoever had dedicated (any thing), (it
2 Ch. 2. 4 to dedicate (it) to him, (and) to burn

3. *To make anew,* ἐγκαινίζω *egkainizō.*
Heb. 9. 18 neither the first (testament) was dedica.

DEDICATED thing —
1. *A thing devoted to God,* חֵרֶם *cherem.*
Eze. 44. 29 every dedicated thing in Israel shall be

2. *A thing separated, hallowed,* קֹדֶשׁ *qodesh.*
1 Ki. 7. 51 the things which David..had dedicated

1 Ki. 15. 15 the things which his father had dedicated
15. 15 the things which himself had dedicated
2 Ki. 12. 4 All the money of the dedicated things
1 Ch.26. 20 the treasures of the dedicated things
26. 26 all the treasures of the dedicated things
28. 12 of the treasuries of the dedicated things
2 Ch. 5. 1 things that David his father had dedica.
15. 18 the things that his father had dedicated
15. 18 the things..that he himself had dedicated
24. 7 the dedicated things of the house of the
31. 12 tithes and the dedicated (things) faithful.

DEDICATING, DEDICATION —
A pressing in, dedication, חֲנֻכָּה *chanukkah.*
Num. 7. 10 the princes offered for dedicating of the
7. 11 offering..for the dedicating of the altar
7. 84, 88 This (was) the dedication of the altar
2 Ch. 7. 9 they kept the dedication of the altar
Ezra 6. 16 kept the dedication of this house of God
6. 17 offered at the dedication of this house
Neh. 12. 27 at the dedication of the wall of Jerusal.
12. 27 bring them..to keep the dedication with
Psa. 30. *title.* (at) the dedication of the house of D.
Dan. 3. 2 to come to the dedication of the image
3. 3 provinces, were gathered..unto the dedi.

DEDICATION, feast of the —
The renewals, τὰ ἐγκαίνια *ta egkainia.*
John 10. 22 at Jerusalem the feast of the dedication

DEED —
1. *Deed, recompense,* גְּמוּלָה *gemulah.*
Isa. 59. 18 According to (their) deeds, accordingly
2. *Word, thing, matter,* דָּבָר *dabar.*
2 Ch.35. 27 his deeds, first and last, behold, they (are)
Esth. 1. 17 (this) deed of the queen shall come abro.
1. 18 which have heard of the deed of the que.
Jer. 5. 28 they overpass the deeds of the wicked
3. *Work, deed,* מַעֲשֶׂה *maaseh.*
Gen. 20. 9 thou hast done deeds unto me that ought
44. 15 What deed (is) this that ye have done?
Ezra 9. 13 that is come upon us for our evil deeds
4. *Doing, deed,* עֲלִילָה *alilah.*
1 Ch.16. 8 make known his deeds among the people
Psa.105. 1 make known his deeds among the people
5. *Act, action,* פֹּעַל *poal.*
Psa. 28. 4 Give them according to their deeds, and
Jer. 25. 14 recompense them according to their deeds
6. *Work,* ἔργον *ergon.*
Luke 11. 48 that ye allow the deeds of your fathers
24. 19 which was a prophet mighty in deed and
John 3. 19 loved darkness..because their deeds were
3. 20 neither cometh..lest his deeds should be
3. 21 that his deeds may be made manifest
8. 41 Ye do the deeds of your father
Acts 7. 22 and was mighty in words and in deeds
Rom. 2. 6 render to every man according to his de.
3. 20 by the deeds of the law there shall no
3. 28 by faith without the deeds of the law
15. 18 the Gentiles obedient, by word and deed
1 Co. 5. 2 that he that hath done this deed might
2 Co. 10. 11 such (will we be) also in deed when we
Col. 3. 17 whatsoever ye do in word or deed, (do) all
2 Pe. 2. 8 from day to day with (their) unlawful d.
1 Jo. 3. 18 neither in tongue; but in deed, and in
2 Jo. 11 For he..is partaker of his evil deeds
3 Jo. 10 I will remember his deeds which he do.
Jude 15 all their ungodly deeds which they have
Rev. 2. 6 hatest the deeds of the Nicolaitanes
2. 22 except they repent of their deeds
16. 11 and repented not of their deeds
7. *A doing,* ποίησις *poiēsis.*
Jas. 1. 25 this man shall be blessed in his deed
8. *A doing,* πρᾶξις *praxis.*
Luke23. 51 consented to the counsel and deed of them
Acts 19. 18 came, and confessed, and showed their d.
Rom. 8. 13 if ye..do mortify the deeds of the body
Col. 3. 9 have put off the old man with his deeds

DEED, to do this —
To work this, κατεργάζομαι τοῦτο *katergazomai*
1 Co. 5. 3 (concerning) him that hath so done this d.

DEED done to, good —
Well doing, εὐεργεσία *euergesia.*
Acts 4. 9 be examined of the good deed done to the

DEEDS, our —
What we practised, ἃ ἐπράξαμεν *ha epraxamen.*
Luke 23. 41 for we receive the due reward of our de.
[*See also* Done, good, mighty, such, this, very, worthy.]

DEEM, to —
To suspect, ὑπονοέω *huponoeō.*
Acts 27. 27 the shipmen deemed that they drew near

DEEP —
1. *Deep places or things,* מַעֲמַקִּים *maamaqqim.*
Psa. 69. 2 I am come into deep waters, where the
69. 14 be delivered..out of the deep waters
2. *Shady place,* מְצוֹלָה *metsolah.*
Neh. 9. 11 persecutors thou threwest into the deeps
Psa. 88. 6 the lowest pit, in darkness, in the deeps
3. *Shady place,* מְצוּלָה *metsulah.*
Job 41. 31 He maketh the deep to boil like a pot
Psa. 69. 15 neither let the deep swallow me up
107. 24 the works of..his wonders in the deep
Jon. 2. 3 thou hadst cast me into the deep
Zech 10. 11 all the deeps of the river shall dry
4. *A sunk down place,* מִשְׁקָע *mishqa.*
Eze. 34. 18 to have drunk of the deep waters
5. *Deep,* עָמִיק *amiq.*
Dan. 2. 22 He revealeth the deep and secret things
6. *To make deep, deepen, go deep,* עָמַק *amaq,* 5.
Jer. 49. 8 turn back, dwell deep, O inhabitants
49. 30 get you far off, dwell deep, O ye inhab.
7. *Deep,* עָמֹק *amoq.*
Lev. 13. 3 the plague in sight (be) deeper than the
13. 4 and in sight (be) not deeper than the skin
13. 25, 30 it (be in) sight deeper than the skin
13. 31 it (be) not in sight deeper than the skin
13. 32 scall (be) not in sight deeper than the
13. 34 nor (be) in sight deeper than the skin
Job 11. 8 deeper than hell; what canst thou know?
Psa. 64. 6 the inward(thought)..and the heart,(is)d.
Prov 18. 4 words of a man's mouth (are as) deep wa.
20. 5 Counsel in the heart..(is like)deep water
22. 14 The mouth of strange women (is) a deep
23. 27 For a whore (is) a deep ditch; and a
Eze. 23. 32 drink of thy sister's cup deep and large
8. *Shady place,* צוּלָה *tsulah.*
Isa. 44. 27 That saith to the deep, Be dry, and I will
9. *Deep place, the deep (sea),* תְּהוֹם *tehom.*
Gen. 1. 2 darkness (was) upon the face of the deep
7. 11 the fountains of the great deep
8. 2 The fountains also of the deep and the
49. 25 blessings of the deep that lieth under
Deut 33. 13 and for the deep that coucheth beneath
Job 38. 30 and the face of the deep is frozen
41. 32 (one) would think the deep (to be) hoary
Psa. 36. 6 thy judgments (are) a great deep
42. 7 Deep calleth unto deep at the noise of
104. 6 Thou coveredst it with the deep as
148. 7 Praise the LORD..dragons, and all deeps
Prov. 8. 28 strengthened the fountains of the deep
Isa. 51. 10 the sea, the waters of the great deep
63. 13 That led them through the deep, as an
Eze. 26. 19 when I shall bring up the deep upon thee
31. 4 the deep set him up on high with her
31. 15 I covered the deep for him, and I restrain
Amos 7. 4 it devoured the great deep, and did eat
Hab. 3. 10 the deep uttered his voice, (and) lifted
10. *Very deep place,* ἄβυσσος *abussos.*
Luke 8. 31 not command them to go out into the d.
Rom 10. 7 Who shall descend into the deep? that
11. *The deep,* βάθος *bathos.*
Luke 5. 4 Launch out into the deep, and let down
2 Co. 8. 2 their deep poverty abounded unto the
12. *Deep,* βαθύς *bathus.*
John 4. 11 nothing to draw with, and the well is d.
Acts 20. 9 Eutychus, being fallen into a deep sleep
13. *Depth,* βυθός *buthos.*
2 Co. 11. 25 night and a day I have been in the deep
14. *A root,* שֹׁרֶשׁ *shoresh.*
Psa. 80. 9 didst cause it to take deep root, and it

DEEP things —
1. *Deep,* עָמֹק *amoq.*
Job 12. 22 He discovereth deep things out of dark.
2. *The depth,* βάθος *bathos.*
1 Co. 2. 10 all things, yea, the deep things of God

DEEP, to be —
To be deep, עָמַק *amaq.*
Psa. 92. 5 O LORD..thy thoughts are very deep

DEEP, to dig —
To dig and deepen, σκάπτω καὶ βαθύνω [*bathunō*].
Luke 6. 48 man which built an house, and digged d.

DEEP, exceeding —
Deep deep, עָמֹק עָמֹק *amoq amoq.*
Eccl. 7. 24 That which is far off, and exceeding deep

DEEP, to make —
1. *To make deep,* עָמַק *amaq,* 5.
Isa. 30. 33 he hath made (it) deep (and) large
2. *To cause to sink,* שָׁקַע *shaqa,* 5.
Eze. 32. 14 Then will I make their waters deep, and

DEEP pits —
Nets, pits, floods, מַהֲמֹרוֹת *mahamoroth.*
Psa.140. 10 into deep pits, that they rise not up again

DEEP place —
1. *Deep, concealed, innermost place,* מֶחְקָר *mechqar.*
Psa. 95. 4 In his hand (are) the deep places of the
2. *A deep place,* תְּהוֹם *tehom.*
Psa.135. 6 in earth, in the seas, and all deep places

DEEP, to seek —
To make deep, עָמַק *amaq,* 5.
Isa. 29. 15 Woe unto them that seek deep to hide

DEEP sleep —
Deep sleep, תַּרְדֵּמָה *tardemah.*
Gen 2. 21 the LORD God caused a deep sleep to fall
15. 12 a deep sleep fell upon Abram; and, lo
1 Sa 26. 12 a deep sleep from the LORD was fallen
Job 4. 13 the night, when deep sleep falleth on men
33. 15 the night, when deep sleep falleth upon
Prov 19. 15 Slothfulness casteth into a deep sleep
Isa. 29. 10 out upon you the spirit of deep sleep

DEEPER —
Deep, עָמֵק *ameq.*
Isa. 33. 19 people of a deeper speech than thou canst

DEEPLY, to have —
To make deep, go deep, עָמַק *amaq,* 5.
Isa. 31. 6 children of Israel have deeply revolted
Hos. 9. 9 They have deeply corrupted (themselves)

DEEPNESS —
Depth, βάθος *bathos.*
Matt 13. 5 because they had no deepness of earth

DEFAME, to —
To speak injuriously, βλασφημέω *blasphēmeō.*
1 Co. 4. 13 [Being defamed,] we entreat: we are made

DEFAMING —
Slander, evil report, דִּבָּה *dibbah.*
Jer. 20. 10 I heard the defaming of many, fear on

DEFEAT, to —
To break, frustrate, make void, פָּרַר *parar,* 5.
2 Sa. 15. 34 then mayest thou for me defeat the cou.
17. 14 the LORD had appointed to defeat the

DEFENCE, (place of) —
1. *A defence, defence,* בֶּצֶר *betser.*
Job 22. 25 the Almighty shall be thy defence, and
2. *Covering, overlaying,* חֻפָּה *chuppah.*
Isa. 4. 5 for upon all the glory (shall be) a defence
3. *Shield,* מָגֵן *magen.*
Psa. 7. 10 My defence (is) of God, which saveth the
89. 18 the LORD (is) our defence; and the Holy
4. *Fortress, stronghold, defence,* מְצוּדָה *metsudah.*
Psa. 31. 2 for an house of defence to save me
5. *Fortress,* מָצוֹר *matsor.*
2 Ch. 11. 5 and built cities for defence in Judah
Isa. 19. 6 the brooks of defence shall be emptied
6. *High tower, place of defence,* מִשְׂגָּב *misgab.*
Psa. 59. 9 I wait upon thee: for God (is) my defence
59. 16 thou hast been my defence and refuge in
59. 17 God (is) my defence, (and) the God of my
62. 2, 6 rock and my salvation; (he is) my def.
94. 22 the LORD is my defence; and my God (is)
Isa. 33. 16 his place of defence (shall be) the muni.
7. *To cover, defend, hedge in,* סָכַךְ *sakak.*
Nah. 2. 5 and the defence shall be prepared
8. *Shade, shadow, defence,* צֵל *tsel.*
Num 14. 9 their defence is departed from them, and
Eccl. 7. 12 wisdom (is) a defence..money (is) a def.
9. *Apology,* ἀπολογία *apologia.*
Acts 22. 1 hear ye my defence (which I make) now
Phil. 1. 7 in the defence and confirmation of the
1. 17 I am set for the defence of the Gospel

DEFENCE, to make —
To apologize, speak off, ἀπολογέομαι *apologeomai.*
Acts 19. 33 would have made his defence unto the

DEFENCED —
1. *To be fenced off,* בָּצַר *batsar.*
Isa. 25. 2 thou hast made..(of) a defenced city a
27. 10 the defenced city (shall be) desolate, (and)
36. 1 came up against all the defenced cities
37. 26 to lay waste defenced cities (into) ruinous
Eze. 21. 20 and to Judah in Jerusalem the defenced
2. *Place fenced off,* מִבְצָר *mibtsar.*
Jer. 1. 18 have made thee this day a defenced city
4. 5 and let us go into the defenced cities
8. 14 let us enter into the defenced cities, and
34. 7 these defenced cities remained of the cit.

DEFEND, to —
1. *To defend, hedge about,* גָּנַן *ganan.*
2 Ki. 19. 34 I will defend this city, to save it, for
20. 6 I will defend this city for mine own sake
Isa. 31. 5 defending also he will deliver (it)
37. 35 I will defend this city to save it, for
38. 6 deliver thee..and I will defend this city
2. *To defend,* גָּנַן *ganan,* 5.
Isa. 31. 5 will the LORD of hosts defend Jerusalem
Zech. 9. 15 The LORD of hosts shall defend them
12. 8 In that day shall the LORD defend the
3. *To save, give width, freedom,* יָשַׁע *yasha,* 5.
Judg 10. 1 there arose, to defend Israel, Tola the son
4. *To deliver, snatch away,* נָצַל *natsal,* 5.
2 Sa. 23. 12 the midst of the ground, and defended it
5. *To cover, defend, hedge in,* סָכַךְ *sakak,* 5.
Psa. 5. 11 shout for joy, because thou defendest
6. *To exalt, make high,* שָׂגַב *sagab,* 3.
Psa. 20. 1 the God of Jacob defend thee
59. 1 defend me from them that rise up against
7. *To judge,* שָׁפַט *shaphat.*
Psa. 82. 3 Defend the poor and fatherless; do jus.
8. *To avert, repel,* ἀμύνομαι *amunomai.*
Acts 7. 24 he defended (him), and avenged him that

DEFER, to —
1. *To be behind, tarry, defer,* אָחַר *achar,* 3.
Gen. 34. 19 the young man deferred not to do the

Eccl. 5. 4 vowest a vow unto God, defer not to pay
Dan. 9. 19 defer not, for thine own sake, O my God

2. *To make long, prolong,* אָרַךְ *arak,* 5.
Prov. 19. 11 The discretion of a man deferreth his
Isa. 48. 9 For my name's sake will I defer mine

3. *To cast back,* ἀναβάλλομαι *anaballomai.*
Acts 24. 22 heard these things..he deferred them

DEFERRED —
To be drawn out, מָשַׁךְ *mashak,* 4.
Prov 13. 12 Hope deferred maketh the heart sick

DEFILE, to —
1. *Defilement, pollution,* גֹּאֵל *goel.*
Neh. 13. 29 they have defiled the priesthood, and the

2. *To pierce, pollute,* חָלַל *chalal,* 3.
Gen. 49. 4 thy father's bed; then defiledst thou (it)
Exod 31. 14 every one that defileth it shall surely
1 Ch. 5. 1 forasmuch as he defiled his father's bed
Psa. 74. 7 they have defiled (by casting down) the
Jer. 16. 18 they have defiled my land, they have
Eze. 7. 22 robbers shall enter into it, and defile it
28. 7 and they shall defile thy brightness
28. 18 Thou hast defiled thy sanctuaries by

3. *To profane,* חָנֵף *chaneph.*
Jer. 3. 9 that she defiled the land, and committed

4. *To make profane,* חָנֵף *chaneph,* 5.
Num 35. 33 for blood it defileth the land

5. *To render unclean,* טָמֵא *tame,* 3.
Gen. 34. 5 Jacob heard that he had defiled Dinah his
34. 13 because he had defiled Dinah their sister
34. 27 because they had defiled their sister
Lev. 11. 44 neither shall ye defile yourselves with
15. 31 when they defile my tabernacle that (is)
18. 28 spue not you out also, when ye defile it
20. 3 to defile my sanctuary, and to profane
Num. 5. 3 defile not their camps, in the midst
6. 9 hath defiled the head of his consecration
19. 13 defileth the tabernacle of the LORD; and
19. 20 he hath defiled the sanctuary of the LORD
35. 34 Defile not therefore the land which ye
2 Ki. 23. 8 defiled the high places where the priests
23. 10 he defiled Topheth, which (is) in the va.
23. 13 And the high places..did the king defile
Psa. 79. 1 thy holy temple have they defiled; they
Isa. 30. 22 defile also the covering of thy graven
Jer. 2. 7 but when ye entered, ye defiled my land
32. 34 But they set their abominations..to def.
Eze. 5. 11 thou hast defiled my sanctuary with all
9. 7 Defile the house, and fill the courts with
18. 6 neither hath defiled his neighbour's wife
18. 11 but even hath..defiled his neighbour's
18. 15 hath not defiled his neighbour's wife
22. 11 hath lewdly defiled his daughter in law
23. 17 they defiled her with their whoredom, and
23. 38 they have defiled my sanctuary
33. 26 ye defile every one his neighbour's wife
36. 17 they defiled it by their own way and by
43. 7 shall the house of Israel no more defile
43. 8 they have even defiled my holy name

6. *To defile, or wind about,* טָנַף *tanaph,* 3.
Song 5. 3 washed my feet; how shall I defile them?

7. *To roll,* עָלַל *alal,* 3a.
Job 16. 15 I have..defiled my horn in the dust

8. *To humble,* עָנָה *anah,* 3.
Gen. 34. 2 took her, and lay with her, and defiled

9. *To make common or unclean,* κοινόω *koinoō.*
Matt. 15. 11 that which goeth into the mouth defileth
15. 11 that which cometh out..defileth a man
15. 18 from the heart; and they defile the man
15. 20 These are (the things) which defile a man
15. 20 to eat with unwashen hands defileth not
Mark 7. 15 that entering into him can defile him
7. 15 those are they that defile the man
7. 18 entereth into the man, (it) cannot defile
7. 20 That which cometh out..defileth the
7. 23 come from within, and defile the man
Rev. 21. 27 enter into it anything that [defileth]

10. *To stain, tinge, colour, defile,* μιαίνω *miainō.*
John 18. 28 lest they should be defiled, but that
Titus 1. 15 unto them that are defiled and unbeliev.
1. 15 even their mind and conscience is defiled
Heb. 12. 15 trouble (you), and thereby many be defil.
Jude 8 these (filthy) dreamers defile the flesh

11. *To defile, make filthy,* μολύνω *molunō.*
1 Co. 8. 7 their conscience being weak is defiled
Rev. 3. 4 which have not defiled their garments
14. 4 they which were not defiled with women

12. *To spot, defile, stain,* σπιλόω *spiloō.*
Jas. 3. 6 it defileth the whole body, and setteth

13. *To corrupt, deprave,* φθείρω *phtheirō.*
1 Co. 3. 17 If any man defile the temple of God

DEFILE oneself with mankind —
Lying with a male, ἀρσενοκοίτης *arsenokoitēs.*
1 Ti. 1. 10 them that defile themselves with manki.

DEFILE self, to —
1. *To make self free or defiled,* גָּאַל *gaal,* 7.
Dan. 1. 8 he would not defile himself with
1. 8 requested..that he might not defile him,

2. *To be or become unclean,* טָמֵא *tame.*
Lev. 18. 20 neighbour's wife, to defile thyself with
18. 23 thou lie with any beast to defile thyself
Lev. 22. 8 shall not eat to defile himself therewith
Eze. 22. 3 idols against herself to defile herself
22. 4 hast defiled thyself in thine idols which
44. 25 for father..they may defile themselves

3. *To be or become unclean,* טָמֵא *tame,* 2.
Eze. 23. 7 with all their idols she defiled herself

4. *To make self unclean,* טָמֵא *tame,* 7.
Lev. 18. 24 Defile not ye yourselves in any of these
18. 30 that ye defile not yourselves therein
21. 4 he shall not defile himself, (being) a chief
21. 11 nor defile himself for his father, or for
Eze. 20. 7 defile not yourselves with the idols of
20. 18 nor defile yourselves with their idols
37. 23 Neither shall they defile themselves any
44. 25 come at no dead person to defile themsel.

DEFILED —
Unclean, טָמֵא *tame.*
Num. 5. 2 and whosoever is defiled by the dead
9. 6 there were certain men, who were defiled
9. 7 We (are) defiled by the dead body of a man
Jer. 19. 13 shall be defiled as the place of Tophet
Eze. 4. 13 eat their defiled bread among the Genti.

DEFILED, to be —
1. *To become defiled,* גָּאַל *gaal,* 2.
Isa. 59. 3 your hands are defiled with blood, and

2. *To be pierced, profaned,* חָלַל *chalal,* 2.
Eze. 7. 24 and their holy places shall be defiled

3. *To be or become profane,* חָנֵף *chaneph.*
Isa. 24. 5 The earth also is defiled under the

4. *To be or become unclean,* טָמֵא *tame.*
Lev. 5. 3 that a man shall be defiled withal
13. 46 he shall be defiled; he (is) unclean
15. 32 whose seed goeth from him, and is defil.
18. 25 the land is defiled: therefore I do visit
18. 27 before you, and the land is defiled
19. 31 neither seek after wizards, to be defiled
Psa. 106. 39 Thus were they defiled with their own

5. *To be or become unclean,* טָמֵא *tame,* 2.
Lev. 18. 24 for in all these the nations are defiled
Num. 5. 13 she be defiled, and (there be) no witness
5. 14 jealous of his wife, and she be defiled
5. 14 jealous of his wife, and she be not defil.
5. 20 if thou be defiled, and some man have
5. 27 if she be defiled, and have done trespass
5. 28 if the woman be not defiled, but be clean
5. 29 when a wife goeth aside..and is defiled
Eze. 20. 43 your doings, wherein ye have been defiled
23. 13 I saw that she was defiled, (that) they
Hos. 5. 3 committest whoredom, (and) Israel is d.
6. 10 the whoredom of Ephraim, Israel is de.

6. *To defile,* טָמֵא *tame,* 3.
Deut 21. 23 that thy land be not defiled, which the

7. *To make self unclean,* טָמֵא *tame,* 7.
Lev. 21. 1 There shall none be defiled for the dead
21. 3 for his sister a virgin..may he be defiled

8. *To be made unclean,* טָמֵא *tame,* 7a.
Deut 24. 4 to be his wife, after that she is defiled

9. *To be or become unclean,* טָמָה *tamah,* 2.
Lev. 11. 43 that ye should be defiled thereby

10. *To be separated, hallowed,* קָדַשׁ *qadesh.*
Deut 22. 9 and the fruit of thy vineyard, be defiled

11. *To become polluted,* חָלַל *chalal,* 2.
Eze. 7. 24 and their holy places shall be defiled

DEFILED —
Common, κοινός *koinos.*
Mark 7. 2 disciples eat bread with defiled..hands

DEFRAUD, to —
1. *To oppress,* עָשַׁק *ashaq.*
1 Sa. 12. 3 whom have I defrauded? whom have I
12. 4 Thou hast not defrauded us, nor oppres.
Lev. 19. 13 Thou shalt not defraud thy neighbour

2. *To deprive of,* ἀποστερέω *apostereō.*
Mark 10. 19 Defraud not, Honour thy father and mo.
1 Co. 6. 7 Why do ye not rather..be defrauded?
6. 8 ye do wrong, and defraud, and that (your)
7. 5 Defraud ye not one the other, except

3. *To have or claim more,* πλεονεκτέω *pleonekteō.*
2 Co. 7. 2 corrupted no man, we have defrauded
1 Th. 4. 6 no (man) go beyond and defraud his

DEFY, to —
1. *To be indignant, defy,* זָעַם *zaam.*
Num 23. 7 Come, curse me Jacob, and come, defy I.
23. 8 shall I defy, (whom) the LORD hath not d.

2. *To reproach,* חָרַף *charaph,* 3.
1 Sa. 17. 10 said, I defy the armies of Israel this day
17. 25 surely to defy Israel is he come up: and
17. 26 that he should defy the armies of the
17. 36 seeing he hath defied the armies of the
17. 45 God of the armies..whom thou hast defie.
2 Sa. 21. 21 when he defied Israel, Jonathan the son
23. 9 when they defied the Philistines (that)
1 Ch. 20. 7 when he defied Israel, Jonathan the son

DEGENERATE —
Turned aside, סוּר *sur.*
Jer. 2. 21 art thou turned into the degenerate plant

DEGREE —
1. *A going up, ascent,* מַעֲלָה *maalah.*
2 Ki. 20. 9 forward ten degrees or go back ten deg.
2 Ki. 20. 10 for the shadow to go down ten degrees
20. 10 the shadow return backward ten degrees
20. 11 brought the shadow ten degrees backw.
Psa. 120. *title.* A Song of degrees. In my distress I c.
121. „ A Song of degrees. I will lift up mine
122. „ A Song of degrees of David. I was
123. „ A Song of degrees. Unto thee lift I up
124. „ A Song of degrees of David. If (it had
125. „ A Song of degrees. They that trust in
126. „ A Song of degrees. When the LORD
127. „ A Song of degrees for Solomon. Exce.
128. „ A Song of degrees. Blessed (is) every
129. „ A Song of degrees. Many a time have
130. „ A Song of degrees. Out of the depths
131. „ A Song of degrees of David. LORD, my
132. „ A Song of degrees. LORD, remember D.
133. „ A Song of decrees of David. Behold
134. „ A Song of degrees. Behold, bless ye
Isa. 38. 8 bring again the shadow of the degrees
38. 8 the sun dial of Ahaz, ten degrees back.
38. 8 sun returned ten degrees, by which degre.

2. *A step, ascent,* βαθμός *bathmos.*
1 Ti. 3. 13 well purchase to themselves a good degr.

DEGREE, high —
A going up, ascent, מַעֲלָה *maalah.*
1 Ch. 17. 17 to the estate of a man of high degree

DEGREE, low —
Low, ταπεινός *tapeinos.*
Luke 1. 52 He hath..exalted them of low degree
Jas. 1. 9 Let the brother of low degree rejoice in

DE-HA-VITES, דֶּהָוֵא, דֶּהָיֵא, *dehave, dehaye.*
The inhabitants of modern *Dehistan* or *Daikh,* E. of the Caspian Sea, who were transferred to Samaria by Shalmaneser.
Ezra 4. 9 the Susanchites, the D.s, (and)..Elamites

DE'-KAR, דֶּקֶר *lance bearer.*
Father of one of Solomon's officers at Makaz, B.C. 1015.
1 Ki. 4. 9 The son of D., in Makaz, and in Shaalbim

DE-LA'-IAH, דְּלָיָה, דְּלָיָהוּ *Jah is deliverer.*
1. One of David's priests, B.C. 1015.
1 Ch. 24. 18 The three and twentieth to D., the four

2. Founder of a family whose genealogy was lost, B.C. 536.
Ezra 2. 60 The children of D., the children of Tobiah
Neh. 7. 62 The children of D., the children of Tobiah

3. One who tried to dishearten Nehemiah, B.C. 480.
Neh. 6. 10 unto the house of Shemaiah the son of D.

4. A prince in Judah under Jehoiakim, B.C. 610.
Jer. 36. 12 princes sat there, (even) Elishama..and D.
36. 25 D...had made intercession to the king

DELAY —
Casting back, ἀναβολή *anabolē.*
Acts 25. 17 without any delay on the morrow I sat

DELAY, to —
1. *To keep behind,* אָחַר *achar,* 3.
Exod 22. 29 Thou shalt not delay (to offer) the first of

2. *To delay, be long,* בּוֹשׁ *bosh,* 3a.
Exod 32. 1 when the people saw that Moses delayed

3. *To tarry, linger, delay or stay self,* מָהַהּ *mahah,* 7a.
Psa. 119. 60 and delayed not to keep thy command.

4. *To hesitate, be tardy,* ὀκνέω *okneō.*
Acts 9. 38 that he would not delay to come to them

5. *To use time,* χρονίζω *chronizō.*
Matt 24. 48 shall say..My lord delayeth his coming
Luke 12. 45 if that servant say..My lord delayeth his

DELECTABLE thing —
To desire, חָמַד *chamad.*
Isa. 44. 9 their delectable things shall not profit

DELICACY —
Hardness, wantonness, στρῆνος *strēnos.*
Rev. 18. 3 through the abundance of her delicacies

DELICATE —
1. *Dainty,* עֵדֶן *eden.*
Jer. 51. 34 hath filled his belly with my delicates

2. *To be delicate, luxurious,* עָנַג *anag,* 4.
Jer. 6. 2 likened the daughter..to a..delicate

3. *Delicate, luxurious,* עָנֹג *anog.*
Deut 28. 54 the man (that is) tender..and very deli.
28. 56 The tender and delicate woman among
Isa. 47. 1 no more be called tender and delicate

4. *Delicate, luxurious,* תַּעֲנוּג *taanug.*
Mic. 1. 16 and poll thee for thy delicate children

DELICATELY —
1. *Dainty, daintily,* מַעֲדָן *maadan.*
1 Sa. 15. 32 And Agag came unto him delicately
Lam. 4. 5 They that did feed delicately are desolate

2. *In pleasure,* ἐν τρυφῇ *en truphē.*
Luke 7. 25 gorgeously apparelled, and live delicately

DELICATENESS —
To show self delicate, עָנַג *anag,* 7.
Deut 28. 56 her foot upon the ground for delicateness

DELICIOUSLY, to live —

To live hard or wantonly, στρηνιάω *strēniaō.*

Rev. 18. 7 glorified herself, and lived deliciously
18. 9 committed fornication and lived delicio.

DELIGHT –

1. *Delight, pleasure, desire,* חֵפֶץ *chephets.*

1 Sa. 15. 22 Hath the LORD (as great) delight in burnt
Psa. 1. 2 But his delight (is) in the law of the LORD
16. 3 the excellent, in whom (is) all my delight

2. *Dainty, daintily,* מַעֲדָן *maadan.*

Prov 29. 17 yea, he shall give delight unto thy soul

3. *Dainty thing,* עֵדֶן *eden.*

2 Sa. 1. 24 clothed you in scarlet, with (other) deli.

4. *Delicate, luxurious,* עֹנֶג *oneg.*

Isa. 58. 13 call the sabbath a delight, the holy of

5. *Acceptable, good pleasure,* רָצוֹן *ratson.*

Prov 11. 1 but a just weight (is) his delight
11. 20 (are) upright in (their) way (are) his deli.
12. 22 but they that deal truly (are) his delight
15. 8 the prayer of the upright (is) his delight
16. 13 Righteous lips (are) the delight of kings

6. *Delights,* שַׁעֲשֻׁעִים *shaashuim.*

Psa. 119. 24 Thy testimonies also (are) my delight
119. 77 that I may live: for thy law (is) my del.
119. 92 Unless thy law (had been) my delights, I
119. 143 (yet) thy commandments (are) my deli.
119. 174 and thy law (is) my delight
Prov. 8. 30 I was daily (his) delight, rejoicing always
8. 31 and my delights (were) with the sons of

7. *Delicate, luxurious,* תַּעֲנוּג *taanug.*

Prov 19. 10 Delight is not seemly for a fool; much
Eccl. 2. 8 the delights of the sons of men, (as)
Song 7. 6 how pleasant art thou, O love, for delights

DELIGHT, to —

1. *To desire,* חָמַד *chamad.*

Prov. 1. 22 the scorners delight in their scorning

2. *To have delight,* חָפֵץ *chaphets.*

Num 14. 8 If the LORD delight in us, then he will
1 Sa. 19. 2 Jonathan, Saul's son, delighted much in
2 Sa. 22. 20 delivered me, because he delighted in me
24. 3 why doth my lord the king delight in
1 Ki. 10. 9 the LORD thy God, which delighted in thee
2 Ch. 9. 8 the LORD thy God, which delighted in
Esth. 2. 14 except the king delighted in her, and
6. 6, 7, 9, 9, 11 the king delighteth to honour
6. 6 whom would the king delight to do hon.
Psa. 18. 19 delivered me, because he delighted in
22. 8 deliver him, seeing he delighted in him
37. 23 and he delighteth in his way
40. 8 I delight to do thy will, O my God: yea
68. 30 scatter thou the people (that) delight in
109. 17 he delighted not in blessing, so let it
112. 1 delighteth greatly in his commandments
119. 35 Make me to go..for therein do I delight
147. 10 He delighteth not in the strength of the
Isa. 1. 11 I delight not in the blood of bullocks
13. 17 (as for) gold, they shall not delight in it
58. 2 seek me daily, and delight to know my
62. 4 the LORD delighteth in thee, and thy
65. 12 did choose (that) wherein I delighted not
66. 3 their soul delighteth in their abominat.
66. 4 and chose (that) in which I delighted
Jer. 9. 24 these (things,) I delight, saith the LORD
Mic. 7. 18 for ever, because he delighteth (in) mercy
Mal. 2. 17 the LORD, and he delighteth in them

3. *To accept, be pleased,* רָצָה *ratsah.*

Psa. 51. 16 thou delightest not in burnt offering
62. 4 they delight in lies: they bless with
Prov. 3. 12 as a father the son (in whom) he delight.
Isa. 42. 1 mine elect, (in whom) my soul delighteth

4. *To delight self,* שָׁעַע *shaa, 3a.*

Psa. 94. 19 thy comforts delight my soul
119. 70 as fat as grease; (but) I delight in thy law

DELIGHT, to be —

To be pleasant, נָעֵם *naem.*

Prov. 24. 25 to them that rebuke (him) shall be deli.

DELIGHT, great —

To desire, חָמַד *chamad, 3.*

Song 2. 3 down under his shadow with great delig.

DELIGHT to have —

1. *To have delight,* חָפֵץ *chaphets.*

Gen. 34. 19 because he had delight in Jacob's daug.
Deut. 21. 14 if thou have no delight in her, then
1 Sa. 18. 22 the king hath delight in thee, and all
2 Sa. 15. 26 if he thus say, I have no delight in thee
Prov. 18 2 A fool hath no delight in understanding
Jer. 6. 10 they have no delight in it

2. *To cleave to, delight in,* חָשַׁק *chashaq.*

Deut. 10. 15 the LORD had a delight in thy fathers to

3. *To delight self,* עָנַג *anag, 7.*

Job 22. 26 shalt thou have thy delight in the Almi.

DELIGHT in, to —

1. *To have delight, pleasure,* חָפֵץ *chaphets*

Mal. 3. 1 even the messenger..whom ye delight in

2. *To have pleasure with,* συνήδομαι *sunēdomai.*

Rom. 7. 22 For I delight in the law of God after the

DELIGHT self —

1. *To delight self,* עָדַן *adan, 7.*

Neh. 9. 25 delighted themselves in thy great good.

2. *To delight self,* עָנַג *anag, 7.*

Job 27. 10 Will he delight himself in the Almighty?
Psa. 37. 4 Delight thyself also in the LORD; and he
37. 11 shall delight themselves in the abundan.
Isa. 55. 2 let your soul delight itself in fatness
58. 14 shalt thou delight thyself in the LORD

3. *To show self pleasing,* רָצָה *ratsah.*

Job 34. 9 that he should delight himself with God

4. *To delight self,* שָׁעַע *shaa, 7a.*

Psa. 119. 16 I will delight myself in thy statutes
119. 47 I will delight myself in thy command.

DELIGHT, to take —

To have delight, חָפֵץ *chaphets.*

Isa. 58. 2 they take delight in approaching to God

DELIGHTED, to be —

To delight self, עָנַג *anag, 7.*

Isa. 66. 11 and be delighted with the abundance of

DELIGHTSOME —

Delight, pleasure, חֵפֶץ *chephets.*

Mal. 3. 12 ye shall be a delightsome land, saith the

DE-LI'-LAH, דְּלִילָה *languishing.*

A Philistine woman in the vale of Sorek, who inveigled and betrayed Samson, B.C. 1120.

Judg 16. 4 he loved a woman..whose name (was) D.
16. 6 D. said to Samson, Tell me, I pray thee
16. 10 D. said unto Samson..thou hast mocked
16. 12 D. therefore took new ropes, and bound
16. 13 D. said unto Samson..thou hast mocked
16. 18 D. saw that he had told her all his heart

DELIVER, to —

1. *To cause to come or happen,* אָנָה *anah, 3.*

Exod 21. 13 but God deliver (him) into his hand

2. *To free,* גָּאַל *gaal.*

Psa. 119. 154 Plead my cause, and deliver me: quicken

3. *To draw out, away, deliver,* חָלַץ *chalats, 3.*

2 Sa. 22. 20 he delivered me, because he delighted in
Job 36. 15 He delivereth the poor in his affliction
Psa. 6. 4 Return, O LORD, deliver my soul: oh save
7. 4 I have delivered him that without cause
18. 19 he delivered me, because he delighted in
34. 7 encampeth round about..and delivereth
50. 15 I will deliver thee, and thou shalt glorify
81. 7 calledst in trouble, and I delivered thee
91. 15 I will deliver him, and honour him
116. 8 thou hast delivered my soul from death
119. 153 Consider mine affliction, and deliver me
140. 1 Deliver me, O LORD, from the evil man

4. *To give,* יְהַב *yehab.*

Ezra 5. 14 they were delivered unto (one), whose

5. *To save,* יָשַׁע *yasha, 5.*

Judg. 2. 16, 18 delivered them out of the hand of
3. 9 raised up a deliverer..who delivered
3. 31 Shamgar..he also delivered Israel
8. 22 thou hast delivered us from the hand of
10. 12 and I delivered you out of their hand
10. 13 wherefore I will deliver you no more
10. 14 let them deliver you in the time of your
12. 2 ye delivered me not out of their hands
12. 3 when I saw that ye delivered (me) not, I
13. 5 he shall begin to deliver Israel out of

6. *To cover, give freely, deliver up,* מָגַן *magan, 3.*

Gen. 14. 20 which hath delivered thine enemies into
Prov. 4. 9 a crown of glory shall she deliver to thee
Hos. 11. 8 (how) shall I deliver thee, Israel? how

7. *To let or cause to escape,* מָלַט *malat, 3.*

2 Sa. 19. 9 he delivered us out of the hand of the
Job 6. 23 Deliver me from the enemy's hand? or
22. 30 He shall deliver the island of the inno.
29. 12 I delivered the poor that cried, and the
Psa. 33. 17 neither shall he deliver (any) by his great
41. 1 the LORD will deliver him in time of tro.
89. 48 shall he deliver his soul from the hand
107. 20 and delivered (them) from their destruct.
116. 4 O LORD, I beseech thee, deliver my soul
Eccl. 8. 8 neither shall wickedness deliver those
9. 15 and he by his wisdom delivered the city
Isa. 46. 2 they could not deliver the burden, but
46. 4 even I will carry, and will deliver (you)
Jer. 39. 18 I will surely deliver thee, and thou shalt
51. 6 Flee out..and deliver every man his soul
51. 45 deliver ye every man his soul from the
Eze. 33. 5 taketh warning shall deliver his soul
Amos 2. 14 neither shall the mighty deliver himself
2. 15 (he that is) swift of foot shall not deliver
2. 15 he that rideth the horse deliver himself

8. *To cause to find,* מָצָא *matsa, 5.*

2 Sa. 3. 8 have not delivered thee into the hand of
Zech 11. 6 I will deliver the men every one into his

9. *To turn aside,* נָטָה *natah, 5.*

Job 36. 18 then a great ransom cannot deliver thee

10. *To make known, give over,* נָכַר *nakar, 3.*

1 Sa. 23. 7 God hath delivered him into mine hand

11. *To snatch or take away,* נְצַל *natsal; 3.*

Eze. 14. 14 they should deliver (but) their own souls

12. *To snatch or take away,* נָצַל *natsal, 5.*

Gen. 32. 11 Deliver me, I pray thee, from the hand
37. 21 and he delivered him out of their hands
Exod. 2. 19 An Egyptian delivered us out of the hand
3. 8 I am come down to deliver them out of
5. 23 neither hast thou delivered thy people
Exod 12. 27 smote the Egyptians, and delivered our
18. 4 delivered me from the sword of Pharaoh
18. 8 and (how) the LORD delivered them
18. 9 whom he had delivered out of the hand
18. 10 who hath delivered you out of the hand
18. 10 who hath delivered the people from under
Num 35. 25 the congregation shall deliver the slayer
Deut 23. 14 to deliver thee, and to give up thine
25. 11 draweth near for to deliver her husband
32. 39 neither (is there) any that can deliver out
Josh. 2. 13 and deliver our lives from death
9. 26 delivered them out of the hand of the
22. 31 ye have delivered the children of Israel
24. 10 so I delivered you out of his hand
Judg. 6. 9 I delivered you out of the hand of the
8. 34 who had delivered them out of the hands
9. 17 delivered you out of the hand of Midian
10. 15 deliver us only, we pray thee, this day
1 Sa. 4. 8 who shall deliver us out of the hand of
7. 3 he will deliver you out of the hand of
7. 14 the coasts thereof did Israel deliver out
10. 18 and delivered you out of the hand of the
12. 10 deliver us out of the hand of our enemies
12. 11 delivered you out of the hand of your
12. 21 (things), which cannot profit nor deliver
14. 48 delivered Israel out of the hands of them
17. 35 and delivered (it) out of his mouth
17. 37 The LORD that delivered me out of the
17. 37 he will deliver me out of the hand of this
26. 24 let him deliver me out of all tribulation
2 Sa. 12. 7 I delivered thee out of the hand of Saul
14. 16 to deliver his handmaid out of the hand
22. 1 the day (that) the LORD had delivered
22. 18 He delivered me from my strong enemy
22. 49 hast delivered me from the violent man
2 Ki. 17. 39 he shall deliver you out of the hand of
18. 29 he shall not be able to deliver you out
18. 30 The LORD will surely deliver us, and this
18. 32 saying, The LORD will deliver us
18. 33 any of the gods of the nations delivered
18. 35 that have delivered their country out of
18. 35 that the LORD should deliver Jerusalem
19. 12 Have the gods of the nations delivered
20. 6 I will deliver thee and this city out of
1 Ch. 11. 14 and delivered it, and slew the Philistines
16. 35 deliver us from the heathen, that we may
2 Ch. 25. 15 which could not deliver their own people
32. 11 The LORD our God shall deliver us out
32. 13 to deliver their lands out of mine hand
32. 14 that could deliver his people out of mine
32. 14 be able to deliver you out of mine hand
32. 15 was able to deliver his people out of
32. 15 God deliver you out of mine hand
32. 17 have not delivered their people out of
32. 17 deliver his people out of mine hand
Ezra 8. 31 delivered us from the hand of the enemy
Neh. 9. 28 and many times didst thou deliver them
Job 5. 4 neither (is there) any to deliver (them)
5. 19 He shall deliver thee in six troubles
10. 7 none that can deliver out of thine hand
Psa. 7. 1 all them that persecute me, and deliver
7. 2 rending..while (there is) none to deliver
18. *title.* in the day (that) the LORD delivered
18. 17 He delivered me from my strong enemy
18. 48 hast delivered me from the violent man
22. 8 let him deliver him, seeing he delighted
22. 20 Deliver my soul from the sword; my
25. 20 O keep my soul, and deliver me: let me
31. 2 deliver me speedily: be thou my strong
31. 15 deliver me from the hand of my enemies
33. 19 To deliver their soul from death, and to
34. 4 and delivered me from all my fears
34. 17 delivereth them out of all their troubles
34. 19 the LORD delivereth him out of them all
35. 10 which deliverest the poor from him that
39. 8 Deliver me from all my transgressions
40. 13 Be pleased, O LORD, to deliver me: O L.
50. 22 lest I tear..(there be) none to deliver
51. 14 Deliver me from blood guiltiness, O God
54. 7 he hath delivered me out of all trouble
56. 13 thou hast delivered my soul from death
59. 1 Deliver me from mine enemies, O my
59. 2 Deliver me from the workers of iniquity
69. 14 Deliver me out of the mire, and let me
70. 1 (Make haste,) O God, to deliver me; make
71. 2 Deliver me in thy righteousness, and
71. 11 take him; (for there) is none to deliver
72. 12 he shall deliver the needy when he crieth
79. 9 deliver us, and purge away our sins, for
86. 13 thou hast delivered my soul from the
91. 3 he shall deliver thee from the snare of
97. 10 he delivereth them out of the hand of the
106. 43 Many times did he deliver them; but
107. 6 delivered them out of their distresses
109. 21 because thy mercy (is) good, deliver thou
119. 170 deliver me according to thy word
120. 2 Deliver my soul, O LORD, from lying lips
142. 6 deliver me from my persecutors; for
143. 9 Deliver me, O LORD, from mine enemies
144. 7 deliver me out of great waters, from the
144. 11 deliver me from the hand of strange chil.
Prov. 2. 12 To deliver thee from the way of the evil
2. 16 To deliver thee from the strange woman
10. 2 but righteousness delivereth from death
11. 4 but righteousness delivereth from death
11. 6 righteousness of the upright shall deliver
12. 6 mouth of the upright shall deliver them
14. 25 A true witness delivereth souls: but a
19. 19 if thou deliver (him), yet thou must do it
23. 14 and shalt deliver his soul from hell
24. 11 If thou forbear to deliver (them that are)
Isa. 5. 29 carry (it) away safe, and none shall deli.

Isa. 19. 20 a great one, and he shall deliver them
31. 5 defending also he will deliver (it; and)
36. 14 for he shall not be able to deliver you
36. 15 The LORD will surely deliver us: this
36. 18 saying, The LORD will deliver us
36. 18 any of the gods of the nations delivered
36. 19 have they delivered Samaria out of my
36. 20 that have delivered their land out of my
36. 20 that the LORD should deliver Jerusalem
37. 12 Have the gods of the nations delivered
38. 6 I will deliver thee and this city out of
42. 22 they are for a prey, and none delivereth
43. 13 (there is) none that can deliver out of
44. 17 Deliver me; for thou (art) my god
44. 20 that he cannot deliver his soul, nor say
47. 14 they shall not deliver themselves from
50. 2 have I no power to deliver? behold
57. 13 criest, let thy companies deliver thee
Jer. 1. 8 I (am) with thee to deliver thee, saith
1. 19 I (am) with thee, saith the LORD, to deli.
15. 20 to save thee, and to deliver thee, saith
15. 21 I will deliver thee out of the hand of
20. 13 he hath delivered the soul of the poor
21. 12 deliver (him that is) spoiled out of the
22. 3 deliver the spoiled out of the hand of
39. 17 I will deliver thee that day, saith
42. 11 save you, and to deliver you from his
Eze. 3. 19 but thou hast delivered thy soul
3. 21 also thou hast delivered thy soul
7. 19 gold shall not be able to deliver them
13. 21 and deliver my people out of your hand
13. 23 I will deliver my people out of your hand
14. 16, 18 shall deliver neither sons nor daught.
14. 20 shall deliver neither son nor daughter
14. 20 they shall (but) deliver their own souls
33. 9 but thou hast delivered thy soul
33. 12 shall not deliver him in the day of his
34. 10 I will deliver my flock from their mouth
34. 12 will deliver them out of all places where
34. 27 delivered them out of the hand of those
Hos. 2. 10 none shall deliver her out of mine hand
Jon. 4. 6 a shadow..to deliver him from his grief
Mic. 5. 6 thus shall he deliver (us) from the Assyri.
5. 8 teareth in pieces, and none can deliver
Zeph. 1. 18 shall be able to deliver them in the day
Zech 11. 6 I will deliver the men every one into
11. 6 out of their hand I will not deliver (them)

13. *To snatch away, deliver,* נָצַל *netsal,* 5.
Dan. 3. 29 no other God that can deliver after this
6. 14 till the going down of the sun to deliver
8. 4 neither (was there any) that could deliver
8. 7 there was none that could deliver the

14. *To give,* נָתַן *nathan.*
Gen. 32. 16 he delivered (them) into the hand of his
40. 13 shalt deliver Pharaoh's cup into his hand
42. 34 (so) will I deliver you your brother, and
42. 37 deliver him into my hand, and I will
Exod. 5. 18 yet shall ye deliver the tale of bricks
22. 7, 10 If a man shall deliver unto his neigh.
23. 31 I will deliver the inhabitants of the
Num 21. 2 If thou wilt indeed deliver this people
21. 3 and delivered up the Canaanites
21. 34 I have delivered him into thy hand, and
Deut. 1. 27 to deliver us into the hand of the Amor.
2. 30 that he might deliver him into thy hand
2. 33 the LORD our God delivered him before
2. 36 the LORD our God delivered all unto us
3. 2 I will deliver him, and all his people
3. 3 the LORD our God delivered into our
5. 22 tables of stone, and delivered them unto
7. 2 when the LORD thy God shall deliver
7. 16 which the LORD thy God shall deliver
7. 23 LORD thy God shall deliver them unto
7. 24 he shall deliver their kings into thine
9. 10 the LORD delivered unto me two tables of
19. 12 deliver him into the hand of the avenger
20. 13 when the LORD thy God hath delivered it
21. 10 the LORD thy God hath delivered them
31. 9 Moses wrote this law, and delivered it
Josh. 2. 24 the LORD hath delivered into our hands
7. 7 to deliver us into the hand of the Amor.
8. 7 the LORD your God will deliver it into
10. 8 for I have delivered them into thine
10. 12 when the LORD delivered up the Amorites
10. 19 the LORD your God hath delivered them
10. 30 the LORD delivered it also, and the king
10. 32 the LORD delivered Lachish into the
11. 6 will I deliver them up all slain before
11. 8 the LORD delivered them into the hand
21. 44 the LORD delivered all their enemies into
24. 11 and I delivered them into your hand
Judg. 1. 2 I have delivered the land into his hand
1. 4 the LORD delivered the Canaanites and
2. 14 he delivered them into the hands of
2. 23 neither delivered he them into the hand
3. 10 the LORD delivered Chushan-rishathaim
3. 28 the LORD hath delivered your enemies
4. 7 and I will deliver him into thine hand
4. 14 hath delivered Sisera into thine hand
6. 1 the LORD delivered them into the hand of
6. 13 delivered us into the hands of the Mid.
7. 7 deliver the Midianites into thine hand
7. 9 for I have delivered it into thine hand
7. 14 into his hand hath God delivered Midian
7. 15 the LORD hath delivered into your hand
8. 3 God hath delivered into your hands the
8. 7 when the LORD hath delivered Zebah
11. 9 and the LORD deliver them before me
11. 21 the LORD God of Israel delivered Sihon
11. 30 If thou shalt without fail deliver the
Judg 11. 32 the LORD delivered them into his hands
12. 3 and the LORD delivered them into my
13. 1 the LORD delivered them into the hand of
15. 12 that we may deliver thee into the hand
15. 13 bind thee fast, and deliver thee into their
16. 23 Our god hath delivered Samson our enemy
16. 24 Our god hath delivered into our hands
20. 13 deliver (us) the men, the children of Bel.
20. 28 tomorrow I will deliver them into thine
1 Sa. 14. 10 the LORD hath delivered them into our
14. 12 the LORD hath delivered them into the
14. 37 wilt thou deliver them into the hand of
23. 4 I will deliver the Philistines into thine
23. 14 but God delivered him not into his hand
24. 4 I will deliver thine enemy into thine
24. 10 how that the LORD had delivered thee
26. 23 the LORD delivered thee into (my) hand to
28. 19 the LORD will also deliver Israel with
28. 19 the LORD also shall deliver the host of
30. 23 delivered the company that came against
2 Sa. 3. 14 Deliver (me) my wife Michal, which I
5. 19 wilt thou deliver them into mine hand?
5. 19 I will doubtless deliver the Philistines
10. 10 the rest of the people he delivered into
14. 7 Deliver him that smote his brother, that
16. 8 the LORD hath delivered the kingdom
20. 21 deliver him only, and I will depart from
21. 9 he delivered them into the hands of the
1 Ki. 8. 46 deliver them to the enemy, so that they
13. 26 the LORD hath delivered him unto the lion
15. 18 delivered them into the hand of his ser.
17. 23 and delivered him unto his mother
18. 9 that thou wouldest deliver thy servant
20. 5 Thou shalt deliver me thy silver, and thy
20. 13 I will deliver it into thine hand this
20. 28 will I deliver all this great
22. 6, 15 the LORD shall deliver (it) into the
22. 12 the LORD shall deliver (it) into the king's
2 Ki. 3. 10, 13 to deliver them into the hand of Mo.
3. 18 he will deliver the Moabites also into
12. 7 deliver it for the breaches of the house
12. 15 into whose hand they delivered the money
13. 3 he delivered them into the hand of Haz.
17. 20 delivered them into the hand of spoilers
18. 23 I will deliver thee two thousand horses
18. 30 saying, The LORD will surely deliver us
18. 30 this city shall not be delivered into
21. 14 deliver them into the hand of their ene.
22. 5 let them deliver it into the hand of the
22. 9 have delivered it into the hand of them
22. 10 Hilkiah the priest hath delivered me a
1 Ch. 14. 10 and wilt thou deliver them into mine
14. 10 for I will deliver them into thine hand
16. 7 on that day David delivered first (this)
22. 18 the rest of the people he delivered unto
2 Ch. 6. 36 deliver them over before (their) enemies
13. 16 and God delivered them into their hand
16. 8 he delivered them into thine hand
18. 5 God will deliver (it) into the king's hand
18. 11 the LORD shall deliver (it) into the hand
23. 9 Jehoiada the priest delivered to the
24. 24 the LORD delivered a very great host into
25. 20 that he might deliver them into the hand
28. 5 Wherefore the LORD his God delivered
28. 9 he hath delivered them into your hand
29. 8 he hath delivered them to trouble, to
34. 9 they delivered the money that was brou.
34. 15 Hilkiah delivered the book to Shaphan
34. 17 have delivered it into the hand of the
Ezra 8. 36 they delivered the king's commissions
Neh. 9. 27 thou deliveredst them into the hand of
Esth. 6. 9 let this apparel and horse be delivered
Psa. 27. 12 Deliver me not over unto the will of mine
41. 2 thou wilt not deliver him unto the will
74. 19 O deliver not the soul of thy turtle dove
78. 61 delivered his strength into captivity
Prov. 31. 24 and delivereth girdles unto the merchant
Isa. 29. 11 deliver to one that is learned
34. 2 he hath delivered them to the slaughter
Jer. 15. 9 the residue of them will I deliver to
18. 21 Therefore deliver up their children to the
20. 5 I will deliver all the strength of this
21. 7 I will deliver Zedekiah king of Judah
24. 9 I will deliver them to be removed into
29. 18 will deliver them to be removed to all
29. 21 I will deliver them into the hand of
38. 19 lest they deliver me into their hand, and
38. 20 Jeremiah said, They shall not deliver
43. 3 to deliver us into the hand of the Chalde.
46. 26 I will deliver them into the hand of
Lam. 1. 14 the LORD hath delivered me into (their)
Eze. 11. 9 deliver you into the hands of strangers
16. 21 delivered them to cause them to pass
16. 27 delivered thee unto the will of them that
21. 31 deliver thee into the hand of brutish men
23. 9 I have delivered her into the hand of her
23. 28 I will deliver thee into the hand (of them)
25. 4 I will deliver thee to the men of the
25. 7 will deliver thee for a spoil to the heath.
31. 11 I have therefore delivered him into the

15. *To shut up or in,* סָגַר *sagar,* 3.
1 Sa. 17. 46 This day will the LORD deliver thee into
24. 18 when the LORD had delivered me into
26. 8 God hath delivered thine enemy into
2 Sa. 18. 28 which hath delivered up the men that

16. *To shut up,* סָגַר *sagar,* 5.
Deut 23. 15 Thou shalt not deliver unto his master
Josh 20. 5 they shall not deliver the slayer up into
1 Sa. 23. 12 Will the men of Keilah deliver me and
23. 20 to deliver him into the king's hand
30. 15 nor deliver me into the hands of my mast.
Job 16. 11 God hath delivered me to the ungodly

17. *To free, redeem,* פָּדָה *padah.*
Job 33. 28 He will deliver his soul from going into
Psa. 55. 18 He hath delivered my soul in peace from
69. 18 deliver me, because of mine enemies
78. 42 (nor) the day when he delivered them
119. 134 Deliver me from the oppression of man

18. *To free, redeem,* פָּרַע *pada.*
Job 33. 24 Deliver him from going down to the pit

19. *To let escape,* פָּלַט *palat,* 3.
2 Sa. 22. 44 Thou also hast delivered me from the
Job 23. 7 so should I be delivered for ever from
Psa. 17. 13 deliver my soul from the wicked, (which
18. 43 Thou hast delivered me from the strivings
18. 48 He delivereth me from mine enemies; yea
22. 4 they trusted, and thou didst deliver them
22. 8 trusted on the LORD (that) he would deli.
31. 1 deliver me in thy righteousness
37. 40 the LORD shall help them, and deliver
37. 40 he shall deliver them from the wicked
43. 1 O deliver me from the deceitful and
71. 4 Deliver me, O my God, out of the hand
82. 4 Deliver the poor and needy: rid (them)
91. 14 therefore will I deliver him: I will set
Mic. 6. 14 (that) which thou deliverest will I give

20. *To cause to (or let) escape,* פָּלַט *palat,* 5.
Mic. 6. 14 thou shalt take hold, but shalt not deliver

21. *To open, free,* פָּצָה *patsah.*
Psa. 144. 10 who delivereth David his servant from

22. *To break off, rend,* פָּרַק *paraq.*
Lam. 5. 8 (there is) none that doth deliver (us) out

23. *To cause to turn back,* שׁוּב *shub,* 5.
Exod 22. 26 thou shalt deliver it unto him by that

24. *To deliver, set free,* שֵׁיזֵב *shezab,* 3.
Dan. 3. 15 who (is) that God that shall deliver you
3. 17 God whom we serve is able to deliver us
3. 17 he will deliver (us) out of thine hand
3. 28 delivered his servants that trusted in
6. 14 set (his) heart on Daniel to deliver him
6. 16 God, whom thou servest..will deliver
6. 20 is thy God..able to deliver thee from the
6. 27 He delivereth and rescueth, and he work.
6. 27 who hath delivered Daniel from the

25. *To finish, restore,* שְׁלַם *shelam,* 5.
Ezra 7. 19 (those) deliver thou before the God of

26. *To judge,* שָׁפַט *shaphat.*
1 Sa. 24. 15 and deliver me out of thine hand

27. *To give up,* ἀναδίδωμι *anadidōmi.*
Acts 23. 33 delivered the epistle to the governor

28. *To set free, change from,* ἀπαλλάσσω *apallassō.*
Luke 12. 58 that thou mayest be delivered from him
Heb. 2. 15 deliver them who through fear of death

29. *To give away,* ἀποδίδωμι *apodidōmi.*
Matt 27. 58 Pilate commanded the body to be delive.

30. *To give,* δίδωμι *didōmi.*
Luke 7. 15 And he [delivered] him to his mother
19. 13 delivered them ten pounds, and said unto

31. *To give safety or salvation,* δίδωμι σωτηρίαν.
Acts 7. 25 that God by his hand would deliver them

32. *To free,* ἐλευθερόω *eleutheroō.*
Rom. 8. 21 creature itself also shall be delivered

33. *To give over, or upon,* ἐπιδίδωμι *epididōmi.*
Luke 4. 17 there was delivered unto him the book of
Acts 15. 30 when they had gathered..they delivered

34. *To take up out of,* ἐξαιρέω *exaireō.*
Acts 7. 10 delivered him out of all his afflictions
7. 34 and am come down to deliver them
12. 11 hath delivered me out of the hand of H.
26. 17 Delivering thee from the people, and
Gal. 1. 4 that he might deliver us from this present

35. *To make useless, or without effect,* καταργέω.
Rom. 7. 6 now we are delivered from the law, that

36. *To give over to or alongside of,* παραδίδωμι.
Matt. 5. 25 the adversary deliver thee to the judge
5. 25 and the judge [deliver thee] to the officer
11. 27 All things are delivered unto me of my
18. 34 delivered him to the tormentors, till he
20. 19 shall deliver him to the Gentiles to mock
25. 14 and delivered unto them his goods
25. 20 thou deliveredst unto me five talents
25. 22 thou deliveredst unto me two talents
26. 15 and I will deliver him unto you
27. 2 delivered him to Pontius Pilate the gover.
27. 18 knew that for envy they had delivered
27. 26 he delivered (him) to be crucified
Mark 7. 13 your tradition, which ye have delivered
9. 31 The Son of man is delivered into the hands
10. 33 the Son of man shall be delivered unto
10. 33 and shall deliver him to the Gentiles
15. 1 carried (him) away, and delivered (him)
15. 10 chief priests had delivered him for envy
15. 15 delivered Jesus, when he had scourged
Luke 1. 2 as they delivered them unto us, which
4. 6 for that is delivered unto me; and to
9. 44 Son of man shall be delivered into the
10. 22 All things are delivered to me of my
12. 58 and the judge deliver thee to the officer

Luke 18. 32 he shall be delivered unto the Gentiles
20. 20 they might deliver him unto the power
21. 12 delivering (you) up to the synagogues
23. 25 but he delivered Jesus to their will
24. 7 The Son of man must be delivered into
24. 20 rulers delivered him to be condemned to
John 18. 30 we would not have delivered him up unto
18. 35 the chief priests have delivered thee
18. 36 I should not be delivered to the Jews
19. 11 he that delivered me unto thee hath the
19. 16 Then delivered he him..to be crucified
Acts 6. 14 change the customs which Moses deliver.
12. 4 delivered (him) to four quaternions of
16. 4 they delivered them the decrees for to
21. 11 deliver (him) into the hands of the Gen.
22. 4 binding and delivering into prisons both
27. 1 they delivered Paul and certain other
28. 16 [the centurion delivered the prisoners to]
28. 17 yet was I delivered prisoner from Jeru.
Rom. 4. 25 Who was delivered for our offences, and
6. 17 that form of doctrine which was deliver.
1 Co. 5. 5 To deliver such an one unto Satan for
11. 2 keep the ordinances, as I delivered (them)
11. 23 that which also I delivered unto you
15. 3 For I delivered unto you first of all that
2 Co. 4. 11 we which live are alway delivered unto
1 Ti. 1. 20 whom I have delivered unto Satan, that
2 Pe. 2. 4 delivered (them) into chains of darkness
2. 21 the holy commandment delivered unto
Jude 3 faith which was once delivered unto the

37. *To rescue*, ῥύομαι *rhuomai.*
Matt. 6. 13 lead us not into temptation, but deliver.
27. 43 let him deliver him now, if he will have
Luke 11. 4 lead us not into temptation: but deliver
Rom. 7. 24 who shall deliver me from the body of
2 Co. 1. 10 Who delivered us from so great a death
1. 10 doth deliver..we trust that he will yet d.
Col. 1. 13 Who hath delivered us from the power
1 Th. 1. 10 Jesus, which delivered us from the wrath
2 Ti. 3. 11 but out of (them) all the Lord delivered
4. 18 the Lord shall deliver me from every evil
2 Pe. 2. 7 And delivered just Lot, vexed with the
2. 9 The Lord knoweth how to deliver the god.

38. *To grant (as a matter of favour)*, χαρίζομαι.
Acts 25. 11 no man may deliver me unto them
25. 16 It is not the manner..to deliver any man

DELIVER again, to —
1. *To cause to turn back*, שׁוּב *shub*, 5.
Gen. 37. 22 to deliver him to his father again
Lev. 26. 26 they shall deliver (you) your bread again
Deut 24. 13 thou shalt deliver him the pledge again

2. *To give away*, ἀποδίδωμι *apodidōmi.*
Luke 9. 42 and delivered him again to his father

DELIVER self, to —
1. *To be escaped, escape*, מָלַט *malat*, 2.
Zech. 2. 7 Deliver thyself, O Zion, that dwellest

2. *To snatch away*, נָצַל *natsal*, 2.
Prov. 6. 3 deliver thyself, when thou art come
6. 5 Deliver thyself as a roe from the hand

DELIVER up, to —
1. *To give*, נָתַן *nathan.*
Num 21. 3 the LORD..delivered up the Canaanites
Josh 10. 12 when the LORD delivered up the Amorites

2. *To (cause to) shut up*, סָגַר *sagar*, 5.
1 Sa. 23. 11 Will the men..deliver me up into his
23. 12 the Lord said, They will deliver (thee) up
Amos 1. 6 they carried away..deliver (them) up
1. 9 they delivered up the whole captivity
6. 8 I deliver up the city, with all that is
Obad. 14 neither shouldest thou have delivered up

3. *To give*, δίδωμι *didōmi.*
Rev. 20. 13 death and hell delivered up the dead

4. *To give over to*, παραδίδωμι *paradidōmi.*
Matt 10. 17 they will deliver you up to the councils
10. 19 when they deliver you up, take no thou.
10. 21 the brother shall deliver up the brother
24. 9 Then shall they deliver you up to be
Mark 13. 9 for they shall deliver you up to councils
13. 11 they shall lead (you), and deliver you up
Acts 3. 13 ye delivered up, and denied him in the
Rom. 8. 32 He ..delivered him up for us all, how
1 Co. 15. 24 he shall have delivered up the kingdom

DELIVERANCE —
1. *A snatching away*, הַצָּלָה *hatstsalah.*
Esth. 4. 14 deliverance arise to the Jews from

2. *Safety*, יְשׁוּעָה *yeshuah.*
Psa. 18. 50 Great deliverance giveth he to his king
44. 4 O God: command deliverances for Jacob
Isa. 26. 18 not wrought any deliverance in the earth

3. *Escape*, פַּלֵּט *pallet.*
Psa. 32. 7 compass me about with songs of deliver.

4. *Escape*, פְּלֵיטָה *peletah.*
Gen. 45. 7 to save your lives by a great deliverance
2 Ch. 12. 7 I will grant them some deliverance
Ezra 9. 13 thou..hast given us (such) deliverance
Joel 2. 32 in Jerusalem shall be deliverance
Obad. 17 upon mount Zion shall be deliverance

5. *Safety*, תְּשׁוּעָה *teshuah.*
Judg 15. 18 Thou hast given this great deliverance
2 Ki. 5. 1 the LORD hath given deliverance unto
13. 17 The arrow of the LORD'S deliverance
2 Ki. 13. 17 and the arrow of deliverance from
1 Ch. 11. 14 the LORD saved..by a great deliverance

6. *A loosing away*, ἀπολύτρωσις *apolutrōsis.*
Heb. 11. 35 and others were tortured, not accepting d.

7. *A sending away*, ἄφεσις *aphesis.*
Luke 4. 18 preach deliverance to the captives

DELIVERED, to be —
1. *To be drawn out*, חָלַץ *chalats*, 2.
Psa. 60. 5 That thy beloved may be delivered
108. 6 That thy beloved may be delivered
Prov. 11. 8 The righteous is delivered out
11. 9 knowledge shall the just be delivered

2. *To bring forth*, יָלַד *yalad.*
Gen. 25. 24 when her days to be delivered were fulfi.
Exod. 1. 19 are delivered ere the midwives come in
1 Sa. 4. 19 was with child, (near) to be delivered
1 Ki. 3. 17 I was delivered of a child with her in the
3. 18 the third day after that I was delivered
3. 18 that this woman was delivered also: and

3. *To be escaped, escape*, מָלַט *malat*, 2.
Job 22. 30 and it is delivered by the pureness of
Psa. 22. 5 They cried unto thee, and were delivered
Prov 11. 21 the seed of the righteous shall be deliver.
28. 26 whoso walketh wisely, he shall be delive.
Isa. 49. 24 the mighty, or the lawful captive deliv.?
49. 25 the prey of the terrible shall be delivered
Eze. 17. 15 shall he break the covenant, and be del.?
Dan. 12. 1 at that time thy people shall be delivered
Joel 2. 32 whosoever shall call..shall be delivered
Amos 9. 1 he that escapeth..shall not be delivered
Mal. 3. 15 (they that) tempt God are even delivered

4. *To cause or let escape*, מָלַט *malat*, 5.
Isa. 66. 7 before her pain came, she was delivered

5. *To give, give over*, מָסַר *masar*, 2.
Num 31. 5 there were delivered out of the thousands

6. *To be snatched away*, נָצַל *natsal*, 2.
Psa. 33. 16 a mighty man is not delivered by much
Isa. 20. 6 whither we flee for help to be delivered
37. 11 thou hast heard..and shalt thou be deli.?
Jer. 7. 10 We are delivered to do all these abomin.?
Mic. 4. 10 there shalt thou be delivered; there the
Hab. 2. 9 he may be delivered from the power of

7. *To be given*, נָתַן *nathan*, 2.
Gen. 9. 2 into your hand are they delivered
Lev. 26. 25 ye shall be delivered into the hand of
2 Ki. 18. 30 this city shall not be delivered into the
19. 10 Jerusalem shall not be delivered into the
22. 7 money that was delivered into their hand
1 Ch. 5. 20 the Hagarites were delivered into their
2 Ch. 18. 14 they shall be delivered into your hand
28. 5 he was also delivered into the hand
Isa. 29. 12 the book is delivered to him that is not
Jer. 32. 4, 32. 36, 34. 3, 37. 17, 46. 24; Eze. 31. 14, 32. 20.

8. *To be given*, נָתַן *nathan*, 6.
2 Sa. 21. 6 Let seven men of his sons be delivered

9. *To pass over*, עָבַר *abar.*
Psa. 81. 6 his hands were delivered from the pots

10. *Be entrusted, deposited*, פָּקַד *paqad*, 7.
Lev. 6. 4 that which was delivered him to keep

11. *To rescue*, ῥύομαι *rhuomai.*
Luke 1. 74 we, being delivered out of the hand of our
Rom 15. 31 I may be delivered from them that do
2 Th. 3. 2 we may be delivered from..wicked men
2 Ti. 4. 17 I was delivered out of the mouth of the

12. *To bring forth a child*, τίκτω *tiktō.*
Luke 1. 57 full time came, that she should be deliv.
2. 6 accomplished that she should be deliver.
Rev. 12. 2 travailing in birth, and pained to be deli.
12. 4 the woman which was ready to be deliv.

DELIVERED him to keep, that which was —
A deposit, פִּקָּדוֹן *piqqadon.*
Lev. 6. 2 in that which was delivered him to keep

DELIVERED of, to be —
1. *To bear, bring forth*, γεννάω *gennaō.*
John 16. 21 as soon as she is delivered of the child

2. *To bring forth a child*, τίκτω *tiktō.*
Heb. 11. 11 Through faith also Sara..[was deliv. of]

DELIVERED, being —
Given out or forth, ἔκδοτος *ekdotos.*
Acts 2. 23 being delivered by the determinate

DELIVERER —
1. *To save*, יָשַׁע *yasha*, 5.
Judg. 3. 9 the LORD raised up a deliverer
3. 15 the LORD raised them up a deliverer

2. *To snatch away*, נָצַל *natsal.*
Judg 18. 28 (there was) no deliverer, because it (was)

3. *To let escape*, פָּלַט *palat*, 3.
2 Sa. 22. 2 The LORD (is) my rock..and my deliverer
Psa. 18. 2 The LORD (is) my rock..and my deliverer
40. 17 thou (art) my help and my deliverer
70. 5 thou (art) my help and my deliverer; O
144. 2 my high tower, and my deliverer; my

4. *A looser, deliverer*, λυτρωτής *lutrōtēs.*
Acts 7. 35 the same did God send (to be) a..deliverer

5. *The rescuer*, ὁ ῥυόμενος *ho rhuomenos.*
Rom 11. 26 There shall come out of Sion the Deliverer

DELIVERY, time of —
To bring forth, יָלַד *yalad.*
Isa. 26. 17 draweth near the time of her delivery, is

DELUSION —
1. *Vexations*, תַּעֲלוּלִים *taalulim.*
Isa. 66. 4 I also will choose their delusions, and

2. *Wandering, error*, πλάνη *planē.*
2 Th. 2. 11 this cause God shall send them strong d.

DEMAND —
Request, requirement, שְׁאֵלָא *sheelah.*
Dan. 4. 17 the demand by the word of the holy ones

DEMAND, to —
1. *To say*, אֲמַר *amar.*
Exod. 5. 14 officers..set over them..(and) demanded

2. *To ask, beg*, שָׁאַל *shaal.*
2 Sa. 11. 7 David demanded (of him) how Joab did
Job 38. 3 I will demand of thee, and answer thou
40. 7 I will demand of thee, and declare thou
42. 4 I will demand of thee, and declare thou

3. *To ask*, שְׁאֵל *sheel.*
Dan. 2. 27 The secret which the king hath demanded

4. *To ask of or at any one, question*, ἐπερωτάω.
Luke 17. 20 when he was demanded of the Pharisees

5. *To ask, enquire*, πυνθάνομαι *punthanomai.*
Matt. 2. 4 he demanded of them where Christ should
Acts 21. 33 demanded who he was, and what he had

DEMAND of, to —
To ask of or at, (any one), ἐπερωτάω *eperōtaō.*
Luke 3. 14 the soldiers likewise demanded of him

DE'-MAS, Δημᾶς.
A fellow disciple of Paul at Rome.
Col. 4. 14 Luke, the beloved physician, and D., greet
Phm. 24 Marcus, Aristarchus, D., Lucus, my
2 Ti. 4. 10 For D. hath forsaken me, having loved

DE-ME'-TRI-US, Δημήτριος.
1. A silversmith of Ephesus who opposed Paul.
Acts 19. 24 For a certain (man) named D., a silver
19. 38 D., and the craftsmen which are with him

2. A convert well spoken of,
3 Jo. 12 D. hath good report of all (men), and of

DEMONSTRATION —
A showing or pointing out, ἀπόδειξις *apodeixis.*
1 Co. 2. 4 demonstration of the Spirit and of power

DEN —
1. *Lying in wait, covert, den*, אֶרֶב *ereb.*
Job 37. 8 the beasts go into dens, and remain in

2. *Den, pit*, גֹּב *gob.*
Dan. 6. 7 he shall be cast into the den of lions
6. 12 shall be cast into the den of lions?
6. 16 and cast (him) into the den of lions
6. 17 and laid upon the mouth of the den
6. 19 and went in haste unto the den of lions
6. 20 when he came to the den, he cried with
6. 23 they should take Daniel up out of the den
6. 23 Daniel was taken up out of the den
6. 24 they cast (them) into the den of lions
6. 24 ever they came at the bottom of the den

3. *Den, place of light, opening, hole*, מְאוּרָה *meurah.*
Isa. 11. 8 shall put his hand on the cockatrice' den

4. *Habitation, den*, מָעוֹן *maon.*
Jer. 9. 11 make Jerusalem heaps, (and) a den of
10. 22 Judah desolate, (and) a den of dragons

5. *Habitation, den*, מְעוֹנָה *meonah.*
Job 38. 40 When they couch in (their) dens, (and)
Psa. 104. 22 and lay them down in their dens
Song 4. 8 from the lions' dens, from the mountains
Amos 3. 4 will a young lion cry out of his den if
Nah. 2. 12 filled his holes with prey, and his dens

6. *Den, cave*, מְעָרָה *mearah.*
Isa. 32. 14 and towers shall be for dens for ever
Jer. 7. 11 become a den of robbers in your eyes?

7. *Covert, covering*, סֹךְ *sok.*
Psa. 10. 9 He lieth..secretly as a lion in his den

8. *Cave, den, (Lat. spelaeum,)* σπήλαιον *spēlaion.*
Matt 21. 13 but ye have made it a den of thieves
Mark 11. 17 but ye have made it a den of thieves
Luke 19. 46 but ye have made it a den of thieves
Heb. 11. 38 and (in) dens and caves of the earth
Rev. 6. 15 in the dens and in the rocks of the moun.

DENOUNCE, to —
To put before, נָגַד *nagad*, 5.
Deut 30. 18 I denounce unto you this day, that ye

DENS —
Dens, hollows, light holes, מִנְהָרוֹת *minharoth.*
Judg. 6. 2 children of Israel made them the dens

DENY, to —
1. *To lie, feign*, כָּחַשׁ *kachash*, 3.
Gen. 18. 15 Sarah denied, saying, I laughed not; for
Josh 24. 27 a witness unto you, lest ye deny your G.
Job 8. 18 (it) shall deny him, (saying), I have not
31. 28 should have denied the God (that is)
Prov 30. 9 Lest I be full, and deny (thee,) and say

2. *To withhold, keep back*, מָנַע *mana.*
1 Ki. 20. 7 and for my gold; and I denied him not
Prov. 30. 7 deny me (them) not before I die

3. *Turn back face of*, שׁוּב פָּנִים *shub* (5) *panim*.
1 Ki. 2. 16 I ask one petition of thee, deny me not
4. *To speak against*, ἀντιλέγω *antilegō*.
Luke 20. 27 which [deny] that there is any resurrection
5. *To deny utterly*, ἀπαρνέομαι *aparneomai*.
Matt 16. 24 let him deny himself, and take up his
26. 35 die with thee, yet will I not deny thee
26. 75 Before the cock crow, thou shalt d. v. 34.
Mark 8. 34 let him deny himself, and take up his c.
14. 30 before the cock crow..thou shalt deny me
14. 31 I will not deny thee in any wise
14. 72 Before the cock crow..thou shalt deny
Luke 9. 23 let him [deny himself,] and take up his
12. 9 shall be denied before the angels of God
22. 34 shalt thrice deny that thou knowest me
22. 61 Before the cock crow, thou shalt deny me
John 13. 38 till [thou hast denied] me thrice
6. *To deny, disown*, ἀρνέομαι *arneomai*.
Matt 10. 33 But whosoever shall deny me before men
10. 33 him will I also deny before my Father
26. 70 he denied before (them) all, saying, I
26. 72 he denied with an oath, I do not know
Mark 14. 68 But he denied, saying, I know not
14. 70 he denied it again. And a little after
Luke 8. 45 When all denied, Peter and they that were
12. 9 he that denieth me before men shall be
22. 57 he denied him..I know him not
John 1. 20 he confessed, and denied not; but confe.
18. 25 He denied (it), and said, I am not
18. 27 Peter then denied again: and immediately
Acts 3. 13 denied him in the presence of Pilate
3. 14 ye denied the Holy One and the Just, and
4. 16 miracle hath been done..we cannot deny
1 Ti. 5. 8 he hath denied the faith, and is worse
2 Ti. 2. 12 if we deny (him), he also will deny us
2. 13 abideth faithful..he cannot deny himself
3. 5 but denying the power thereof
Titus 1. 16 in works they deny (him), being abomina.
2. 12 denying ungodliness and worldly lusts
2 Pe. 2. 1 denying the Lord that bought them, and
1 Jo. 2. 22 he that denieth that Jesus..denieth the
2. 23 Whosoever denieth the Son, the same
Jude 4 denying the only Lord God, and our Lord
Rev. 2. 13 hast not denied my faith, even in those
3. 8 kept my word, and hast not denied my

DEPART, to —

1. *To go in*, בּוֹא *bo*.
2 Ki. 10. 12 arose and departed, and came to Samar.
2. *To remove*, גָּלָה *galah*.
Job 20. 28 The increase of his house shall depart
3. *To go on*, הָלַךְ *halak*.
Judg. 6. 21 the angel of the LORD departed out of
1 Ki. 20. 36 as soon as thou art departed from me
Jer. 37. 9 The Chaldeans shall surely depart from
50. 3 they shall depart, both man and beast
4. *To go on for oneself, to and fro*, הָלַךְ *halak*, 7.
Judg 21. 24 the children of Israel departed thence
5. *To go on*, יָלַךְ *yalak*.
Gen. 12. 4 Abram departed, as the LORD had spoken
14. 12 they took Lot..and his goods, and depa.
21. 14 departed, and wandered in the wilderness
24. 10 the servant took ten camels..and depar.
26. 17 Isaac departed thence, and pitched his
26. 31 and they departed from him in peace
31. 55 Laban departed, and returned unto his
42. 26 laded their asses..and departed thence
45. 24 sent his brethren away, and they depar.
Exod 33. 1 Depart, (and) go up thence, thou and
Num 10. 30 I will depart to mine own land, and to
12. 9 was kindled against them; and he depa.
22. 7 elders of Midian departed with the
Josh. 2. 21 And she sent them away, and they depa.
22. 9 departed from the children of Israel out
Judg. 9. 55 they departed every man unto his place
17. 8 the man departed out of the city from
18 7 the five men departed, and came to Laish
18. 21 they turned and departed, and put the
19. 5 in the morning, that he rose up to depart
19. 7 when the man rose up to depart, his
19. 8 arose early..on the fifth day to depart
19. 9 when the man rose up to depart, he
19. 10 he rose up and departed, and came over
1 Sa. 6. 6 let the people go, and they departed?
10. 2 When thou art departed from me to day
20. 42 he arose and departed: and Jonathan
22. 1 David therefore departed thence, and
22. 5 depart, and get thee into the land of
22. 5 David departed, and came into the forest
29. 10 and as soon as ye be up early. depart
29. 11 David and his men rose up early to dep.
30. 22 that they may lead (them) away, and de.
2 Sa. 6. 19 people departed every one to his house
12. 15 And Nathan departed unto his house
15. 14 make speed to depart, lest he overtake
17. 21 it came to pass, after they were departed
19. 24 from the day the king departed until the
20. 21 deliver him only, and I will depart from
1 Ki. 12. 5 Depart yet (for) three days, then come
12. 5 And the people departed
12. 16 So Israel departed unto their tents
12. 24 returned to depart, according to the
14. 17 Jeroboam's wife arose, and departed, and
19. 19 he departed thence, and found Elisha
20. 9 the messengers departed, and brought
20. 36 as soon as he was departed from him
20. 38 the prophet departed, and waited for the
2 Ki. 1. 4 but shalt surely die. And Elijah depar.
5. 5 he departed, and took with him ten
5. 19 So he departed from him a little way
5. 24 and he let the men go, and they depart.
8. 14 he departed from Elisha, and came to
10. 15 when he was departed thence, he lighted
1 Ch. 16. 43 all the people departed every man to his
2 Ch. 10. 5 And the people departed
21. 20 and departed without being desired
24. 25 when they were departed from him
Job 27. 21 wind carrieth him away, and he depart.
Psa. 34. *title* who drove him away, and he departed
Eccl. 6. 4 cometh in with vanity, and departeth in
Jer. 41. 10 and departed to go over to the Ammon.
41. 17 they departed, and dwelt in the habitat.
Mic. 2. 10 Arise ye, and depart; for this (is) not
6. *To go out*, יָצָא *yatsa*.
Gen. 12. 4 when he departed out of Haran
Exod 21. 22 so that her fruit depart (from her), and
35. 20 the children of Israel departed from the
Lev. 25. 41 (then) shall he depart from thee, (both) he
Deut. 9. 7 the day that thou didst depart out of the
24. 2 when she is departed out of his house
1 Sa. 23. 13 arose and departed out of Keilah, and
2 Sa. 11. 8 Uriah departed out of the king's house
1 Ch. 21. 4 Joab departed, and went throughout all
Psa. 105. 38 Egypt was glad when they departed
Jer. 29. 2 After..smiths, were departed from Jeru.
Lam. 1. 6 daughter of Zion all her beauty is depar.
Eze. 10. 18 the glory of the LORD departed from off
7. *To sink down, be disjointed*, יָקַע *yaqa*.
Jer. 6. 8 Be thou instructed..lest my soul depart
8. *To turn aside*, לוּז *luz*.
Prov. 3. 21 son, let not them depart from thine eyes
9. *To turn aside*, לוּז *luz*, 5.
Prov. 4. 21 Let them not depart from thine eyes
10. *To move, depart*, מוּשׁ *mush*.
Num 14. 44 and Moses, departed not out of the camp
Josh. 1. 8 This book of the law shall not depart out
Judg. 6. 18 Depart not hence, I pray thee, until I
Prov 17. 13 evil shall not depart from his house
Isa. 54. 10 For the mountains shall depart, and the
54. 10 but my kindness shall not depart from
59 21 my words. .shall not depart out of thy
Jer. 31. 36 If those ordinances depart from before me
11. *To move*, מוּשׁ *mush*, 5.
Exod 33. 11 a young man, departed not out of the
Psa. 55. 11 deceit and guile depart not from her streets
Nah. 3. 1 full of lies (and) robbery; the prey depa.
12. *To flee, move, wander away*, נָדַד *nadad*.
Gen. 31. 40 and my sleep departed from mine eyes
13. *To journey, move*, נָסַע *nasa*.
Gen. 37. 17 They are departed hence; for I heard
Exod 19. 2 For they were departed from Rephidim
Num 10. 33 they departed from the mount of the L.
33. 3 they departed from Rameses in the first
33. 6 they departed from Succoth, and pitched
33. 8 And they departed from before Pihahiroth
33. 13 they departed from Dophkah, and enca.
33. 15 they departed from Rephidim, and pitc.
33. 17 they departed from Kibroth hattaavah
33. 18 they departed from Hazeroth, and pitched
33. 19 they departed from Rithmah, and pitch.
33. 20 they departed from Rimmon parez, and
33 27 they departed from Tahath, and pitched
33 30 they departed from Hashmonah, and enc.
33 31 they departed from Moseroth, and pitc.
33. 35 they departed from Ebronah, and enca.
33. 41 they departed from mount Hor, and pit.
33. 42 they departed from Zalmonah, and pitc.
33. 43 they departed from Punon, and pitched
33. 44 they departed from Oboth, and pitched
33. 45 they departed from Iim, and pitched in
33 48 they departed from the mountains of A.
Deut. 1 19 when we departed from Horeb, we went
2 Ki. 3. 27 and they departed from him and returned
19. 8 he had heard that he was departed from L.
19. 36 So Sennacherib king of Assyria departed
Ezra 8. 31 Then we departed from the river of Ah.
Isa. 37. 8 for he had heard that he was departed
37. 37 So Sennacherib king of Assyria departed
14. *To turn aside*, סוּר *sur*.
Gen. 49. 10 The sceptre shall not depart from Judah
Exod. 8. 11 the frogs shall depart from thee, and
8. 29 the swarms (of flies) may depart from P.
Lev. 13. 58 if the plague be departed from them, then
Num 12. 10 cloud departed from off the tabernacle
14. 9 their defence is departed from them, and
16. 26 Depart, I pray you, from the tents of these
Deut. 4. 9 lest they depart from thy heart all the
Judg 16. 20 he wist not that the LORD was departed
1 Sa. 15. 6 Go, depart, get you down from among
15. 6 the Kenites departed from among the A.
16. 14 the Spirit of the LORD departed from Saul
16. 23 and the evil spirit departed from him
18. 12 the LORD was with him, and was departed
28. 15 God is departed from me, and answereth
28. 16 seeing the LORD is departed from thee
2 Sa. 7. 15 my mercy shall not depart away from
12. 10 the sword shall never depart from thine
22. 23 his statutes, I did not depart from them
2 Ki. 3. 3 sins of Jeroboam. he departed not there
10. 29 Jehu departed not from after them, (to
10. 31 he departed not from the sins of Jerob.
13. 2 sins of Jeroboam. he departed not there.
13. 6 they departed not from the sins of the
2 Ki. 13. 11 he departed not from all the sins of Jer.
14. 24 he departed not from all the sins of Jer.
15. 9, 24, 28 he departed not from the sins of J.
15. 18 he departed not all his days from the sins
17. 22 the children of Israel..departed not from
18. 6 he..departed not from following him, but
2 Ch. 8. 15 they departed not from the commandm.
20. 32 he walked in the way..and departed not
34. 33 they departed not from following the L.
35. 15 they might not depart from their
Neh. 9. 19 the pillar of the cloud departed not from
Job 15. 30 He shall not depart out of darkness
21. 14 Depart from us; for we desire not the
22. 17 Which said unto God, Depart from us
28. 28 and to depart from evil (is) understanding
Psa. 6. 8 Depart from me, all ye workers of iniqu.
34. 14 Depart from evil, and do good; seek peace
37. 27 Depart from evil, and do good; and dwell
101. 4 A froward heart shall depart from me: I
119. 102 I have not departed from thy judgments
119. 115 Depart from me, ye evil doers: for I will
139. 19 depart from me therefore, ye bloody men
Prov. 3. 7 fear the LORD, and depart from evil
5. 7 and depart not from the words of my mo.
13. 14 to depart from the snares of death
13. 19 abomination to fools to depart from evil
14. 16 A wise (man) feareth, and departeth from
14. 27 to depart from the snares of death
15. 24 that he may depart from hell beneath
16. 6 by the fear of the LORD (men) depart
16. 17 The highway of the upright (is) to depart
22. 6 when he is old, he will not depart from
27. 22 will not his foolishness depart from him
Isa. 7. 17 the day that Ephraim departed from Ju.
11. 13 The envy also of Ephraim shall depart
14. 25 then shall his yoke depart from off them
14. 25 and his burden depart from off their
52. 11 Depart ye, depart ye, go ye out from
59. 15 he (that) departeth from evil maketh
Jer. 17. 5 and whose heart departeth from the Lo.
32. 40 that they shall not depart from me
Lam. 4. 15 Depart ye; (it is) unclean; depart, depart
Eze. 6. 9 which hath departed from me, and with
16. 42 and my jealousy shall depart
Zech 10. 11 the sceptre of Egypt shall depart away
Mal. 2. 8 But ye are departed out of the way; ye
15. *To pass on*, עָדָה *adah*.
Dan. 4. 31 The kingdom is departed from thee
16. *To go up*, עָלָה *alah*.
1 Ki. 15. 19 break thy league..that he may depart
2 Ch. 16. 3 break thy league..that he may depart
17. *To be gone up*, עָלָה *alah*, 2.
Jer. 37. 5 the Chaldeans..heard tidings..they depa.
18. *To turn aside*, שׂוּר *sur*.
Hos. 9. 12 woe also to them when I depart from them
19. *To look*, שָׁעָה *shaah*.
Job 7. 19 How long wilt thou not depart from me
20. *To lead up, put to sea*, ἀνάγω *anagō*.
Acts 27. 12 the more part advised to depart thence
28. 10 when we departed, they laded (us) with
28. 11 after three months we departed in a ship
21. *To loose up (an anchor)*, ἀναλύω *analuō*.
Phil. 1. 23 having a desire to depart, and to be with
22. *To withdraw*, ἀναχωρέω *anachōreō*.
Matt. 2. 12 they departed into their own country
2. 13 when they were departed, behold, the
2. 14 took the young child..and departed into
4. 12 when Jesus had heard..he departed into
14. 13 he departed thence by ship into a desert
15. 21 Then Jesus went thence, and departed
27. 5 and departed, and went and hanged him.
John 6. 15 he departed again into a mountain him.
23. *To change from, let go*, ἀπαλλάσσω *apallassō*.
Acts 19. 12 the diseases departed from them, and the
24. *To come or go away*, ἀπέρχομαι *aperchomai*.
Matt. 8. 18 he gave commandment to depart unto
9. 7 And he arose, and departed to his house
14. 16 They need not depart; give ye them to
16. 4 And he left them, and departed
27. 60 and he rolled a great stone..and departed
Mark 1. 35 departed into a solitary place, and there
1. 42 immediately the leprosy departed from
5. 17 they began to pray him to depart out of
5. 20 he departed, and began to publish in Dec.
6. 32 they departed into a desert place by ship
6. 46 when he had sent them away, he depart.
8. 13 he..entering into the ship again, departed
Luke 1. 23 it came to pass..he departed to his own
1. 38 And the angel departed from her
5. 13 immediately the leprosy departed from
5. 25 departed to his own house, glorifying God
7. 24 when the messengers of John were depa.
8. 37 the whole multitude..besought him to d.
10. 30 thieves, which..wounded (him), and dep.
24. 12 Peter..[departed,] wondering in himself
John 4. 3 He left Judea, and departed again into
4. 43 after two days he departed thence, and
5. 15 The man departed, and told the Jews
12. 36 These things spake Jesus, and departed
Acts 10. 7 angel which spake unto Cornelius was d.
28. 29 the Jews [departed,] and had great reason.
Rev. 18. 14 the fruits..are departed from thee, and
18. 14 things which were dainty..[are departed]
25. *To loose off or away*, ἀπολύω *apoluō*.
Acts 28. 25 when they agreed not..they departed

26. *To withdraw away,* ἀποχωρέω *apochōreō.*
Matt. 7. 23 depart from me, ye that work iniquity
Luke 9. 39 bruising him, hardly departeth from him
Acts 13. 13 John departing from them returned to J.

27. *To be withdrawn,* ἀποχωρίζομαι *apochōrizomai.*
Rev. 6. 14 the heaven departed as a scroll when it

28. *To be thoroughly withdrawn,* διαχωρίζομαι.
Luke 9. 33 as they departed from him, Peter said

29. *To come or go through,* διέρχομαι *dierchomai.*
Acts 13. 14 when they departed from Perga, they ca.

30. *To go or come out or forth,* ἐκπορεύομαι *ekpor.*
Matt20. 29 as they departed from Jericho, a great
Mark 6. 11 when ye depart thence, shake off the dust
Acts 25. 4 and that he himself would depart shortly

31. *To go out or forth,* ἔξειμι *exeimi.*
Acts 17. 15 and receiving a commandment..they de.
20. 7 Paul preached..ready to depart on the

32. *To come or go out or forth,* ἐξέρχομαι *exercho.*
Matt. 9. 31 when they were departed, spread abroad
28. 8 they [departed] quickly from the sepulchre
Mark 6. 10 there abide till ye depart from that place
7. 31 departing from the coasts of Tyre and Si.
9. 30 they departed thence, and passed through
Luke 4. 42 when it was day, he departed and went
5. 8 Depart from me; for I am a sinful man
8. 35, 38 out of whom the devils were departed
9. 4 whatsoever house..abide, and thence de.
9. 6 they departed, and went through the
10. 35 on the morrow, when [he departed,] he
12. 59 I tell thee, thou shalt not depart thence
John 4. 43 after two days he departed thence, and
Acts 11. 25 Then departed Barnabas to Tarsus, for to
12. 17 he departed, and went into another place
14. 20 next day he departed with Barnabas to
15. 40 Paul chose Silas, and departed, being
16. 36 now therefore depart, and go in peace
16. 40 when they had seen the brethren, they..d.
17. 33 So Paul departed from among them
18. 23 after he had spent some time..he depar.
20. 1 Paul..departed for to go into Macedonia
20. 11 even till break of day, so he departed
21. 5 we departed and went our way; and they
21. 8 we that were of Paul's company departed
Phil. 4. 15 when I departed from Macedonia, no

33. *To come or go down,* κατέρχομαι *katerchomai.*
Acts 13. 4 So they..departed unto Seleucia; and

34. *To go after, away or back,* μεταβαίνω *metabainō.*
Matt. 8. 34 that he would depart out of their coasts
11. 1 he departed thence, to teach and to
12. 9 when he was departed thence, he went
15. 29 Jesus departed from thence, and came
John 7. 3 Depart hence, and go into Judea, that
13. 1 his hour was come that he should depart
Acts 18. 7 he departed thence, and entered into a

35. *To lift up and remove,* μεταίρω *metairō.*
Matt13. 53 when Jesus had finished..he departed
19. 1 he departed from Galilee, and came into

36. *To go on beyond,* παράγω *paragō.*
Matt. 9. 27 when Jesus departed thence, two blind

37. *To go on,* πορεύομαι *poreuomai.*
Matt. 2. 9 when they had heard the king, they dep.
11. 7 as they departed, Jesus began to say unto
19. 15 he laid (his) hands on them, and departed
24. 1 Jesus went out, and departed from the
25. 41 Depart from me, ye cursed, into everlast.
Luke 4. 42 that he should not depart from them
13. 31 Get thee out, and depart hence: for Her.
John16. 7 but if I depart, I will send him unto you
Acts 5. 41 they departed from the presence of the
22. 21 Depart: for I will send thee far hence
2 Ti. 4. 10 Demas..having loved..is departed unto

38. *To go secretly or quietly,* ὑπάγω *hupagō.*
Mark 6. 33 the people saw them departing, and
Jas. 2. 16 Depart in peace, be (ye) warmed and fill

39. *To put apart,* χωρίζω *chōrizō.*
Acts 1. 4 they should not depart from Jerusalem
18. 1 After these things Paul departed from A.
18. 2 had commanded all Jews to depart from
1 Co. 7. 10 Let not the wife depart from (her) husb.
7. 11 if she depart, let her remain unmarried
7. 15 if the unbelieving depart, let him depart
Phm. 15 perhaps he therefore departed for a sea.

DEPART asunder, to —
To be withdrawn, ἀποχωρίζομαι *apochōrizomai.*
Acts 15. 39 they departed asunder one from the other

DEPART early, to —
To turn about, round, צָפַר *tsaphar.*
Judg. 7. 3 let him..depart early from mount Gilead

DEPART from, to —
To place off from, ἀφίστημι *aphistēmi.*
Luke 2. 37 a widow..which departed not from the
4. 13 he departed from him for a season
13. 27 depart from me, all (ye) workers of ini.
Acts 12. 10 and forthwith the angel departed from
15. 38 who departed from them from Pamphy.
19. 9 he departed from them, and separated
22. 29 straightway they departed from him
2 Co 12. 8 I besought..that it might depart from
1 Ti. 4. 1 in the latter times some shall depart from
2 Ti. 2. 19 And, let every one..depart from iniquity
Heb. 3. 12 Take heed..in departing from the living

DEPART out, to —
To withdraw out, ἐκχωρέω *ekchōreō.*
Luke21. 21 which are in the midst of it depart out

DEPART out of, to —
To come out or forth, ἐξέρχομαι *exerchomai.*
Matt10. 14 when ye depart out of that house or city
17. 18 he departed out of him; and the child
Acts 16. 39 they..desired (them) to [depart out of]

DEPART, to let —
1. *To send on,* שָׁלַח *shalach,* 3.
Exod18. 27 Moses let his father in law depart; and
Josh 24. 28 let the people depart, every man unto his
2 Sa. 11. 12 and to morrow I will let thee depart
1 Ki. 11. 21 Let me depart, that I may go to mine

2. *To loose away,* ἀπολύω *apoluō.*
Luke 2. 29 lettest thou thy servant depart in peace
Acts 23. 22 let the young man depart, and charged

DEPART, they that —
One that turns aside, יָסוּר *yasur.*
Jer. 17. 13 they that depart from me shall be written

DEPARTED, to be —
1. *To remove,* גָּלָה *galah.*
1 Sa. 4. 21, 22 The glory is departed from Israel
Hos. 10. 5 for the glory thereof..is departed from

2. *To be removed,* נָסַע *nasa,* 2.
Isa. 38. 12 Mine age is departed, and is removed from

DEPARTING —
1. *To go out,* יָצָא *yatsa.*
Gen. 35. 18 came to pass, as her soul was in depart.
Exod16. 1 the second month after their departing

2. *To turn aside,* סוּר *sur.*
Dan. 9. 5 by departing from thy precepts and from
9. 11 transgressed thy law, even by departing

3. *A going away,* ἄφιξις *aphixis.*
Acts 20. 29 after my departing shall grievous wolves

4. *Outgoing,* ἔξοδος *exodos.*
Heb. 11. 22 of the departing of the children of Israel

DEPARTING away —
Separate self, fall away, נָסוֹג [*sug,* 2].
Isa. 59. 13 and departing away from our God, speak.

DEPARTURE —
1. *To go out,* יָצָא *yatsa.*
Eze. 26. 18 isles..shall be troubled at thy departure

2. *A loosing up or off,* ἀνάλυσις *analusis.*
2 Ti. 4. 6 and the time of my departure is at hand

DEPOSED, to be —
To be put down, נָחַת *nechath,* 6.
Dan. 5. 20 he was deposed from his kingly throne

DEPRIVE, to —
To cause to forget, נָשָׁה *nashah,* 5.
Job 39. 17 God hath deprived her of wisdom, neither

DEPRIVED, to be —
1. *To be lacking, numbered,* פָּקַד *paqad,* 4.
Isa. 38. 10 I am deprived of the residue of my years

2. *To be bereaved,* שָׁכֹל *shakol.*
Gen. 27. 45 why should I be deprived also of you both

DEPTH —
1. *Depth, the deep,* מְצוּלָה *metsulah.*
Psa. 68. 22 bring (my people) again from the depths
Mic. 7. 19 all their sins into the depths of the sea

2. *To make deep,* עָמַק *amaq,* 5.
Isa. 7. 11 ask it either in the depth, or in the height

3. *Deep place, depth,* עֵמֶק *emeq.*
Prov. 9. 18 her guests (are) in the depths of hell

4. *Depth, deep,* עֹמֶק *omeq.*
Prov 25. 3 heaven for height, and the earth for depth

5. *Deep, the deep,* תְּהוֹם *tehom.*
Exod15. 5 The depths have covered them: they sank
15. 8 the depths were congealed in the heart
Deut. 8. 7 depths that spring out of valleys and
Job 28. 14 The depth saith, It (is) not in me; and
38. 16 thou walked in the search of the depth?
Psa. 33. 7 he layeth up the depth in storehouses
71. 20 bring me up again from the depths of
77. 16 were afraid: the depths also were troubled
78. 15 gave (them) drink as (out of) the great d.
106. 9 he led them through the depths, as thro.
107. 26 they go down again to the depths
Prov. 3. 20 By his knowledge the depths are broken
8. 24 When (there were) no depths, I was
8. 27 set a compass upon the face of the depth
Jon. 2. 5 the depth closed me round about, the

6. *Depth, the depth, deep things,* βάθος *bathos.*
Mark 4. 5 because it had no depth of earth
Rom. 8. 39 Nor height, nor depth, nor any other
11. 33 O the depth of the riches both of the
Eph. 3. 18 what (is) the breadth..length, and depth
Rev. 2. 24 which have not known [the depths] of S.

7. *The high or open sea,* πέλαγος *pelagos.*
Matt18. 6 he were drowned in the depth of the sea

DEPTHS —
Deep places, מַעֲמַקִּים *maamaqqim.*
Psa.130. 1 Out of the depths have I cried unto thee
Isa. 51. 10 that hath made the depths of the sea
Eze. 27. 34 by the seas in the depths of the water

DEPUTY —
1. *To be set up,* נָצַב *natsab,* 2.
1 Ki. 22. 47 then no king in Edom: a deputy (was)

2. *Governor, stadholder,* פֶּחָה *pechah.*
Esth. 8. 9 the deputies and rulers of the provinces
9. 3 the deputies, and officers of the king

3. *A pro-consul,* ἀνθύπατος *anthupatos.*
Acts 13. 7 Which was with the deputy of the country
13. 8 seeking to turn away the deputy from the
13. 12 the deputy, when he saw what was done
19. 38 the law is open, and there are deputies

DEPUTY, to be —
To be or act as a pro-consul, ἀνθυπατεύω *anthupa.*
Acts 18. 12 when Gallio [was the deputy] of Achaia

DER-BE, Δέρβη.
A city of Lycaonia, not far from Pisidia; but its exact position is not known. It was in the eastern part of the great upland plain of Lycaonia, which stretches from Iconium eastwards along the north side of the Taurus chain, near the pass called the Galician gates, which opened a way from the low plain of Cilicia to the interior tableland. By Col. Leake it is supposed to be at *Bin-bir Kilisseh,* at the foot of the *Kara-dagh;* but this is the site of Lystra. Kiepert's map puts it further east, at a spot where there are ruins, in the line of the Roman road. Hamilton and Texier place it at *Diolé,* a little south west of the last position and nearer to the roots of Taurus.
Acts 14. 6 They..fled unto Lystra and D., cities of
14. 20 next day he departed with Barnabas to D.
16. 1 Then came he to D. and Lystra
20. 4 there accompanied him..Gaius of D., and

DERIDE, to —
1. *To laugh at, deride,* שָׂחַק *sachaq.*
Hab. 1. 10 they shall deride every stronghold; for

2. *To turn up the nose at,* ἐκμυκτηρίζω *ekmuktērizō.*
Luke16. 14 And the Pharisees also..they derided him
23. 35 the rulers also with them derided (him)

DERISION —
1. *Scorn, scorning,* לַעַג *laag.*
Eze. 36. 4 which became a prey and derision to the
Hos. 7. 16 This (shall be) their derision in the land

2. *Derision, scoffing,* קֶלֶס *qeles.*
Psa. 44. 13 a scorn and a derision to them that are
79. 4 a scorn and derision to them that are
Jer. 20. 8 made a reproach unto me, and a derision

3. *Laughter, derision,* שְׂחוֹק *sechoq.*
Jer. 20. 7 I am in derision daily, every one mocketh
48. 26 Moab..he also shall be in derision
48. 27 For was not Israel a derision unto thee?
48. 39 so shall Moab be a derision and a dismay.
Lam. 3. 14 I was a derision to all my people

DERISION to have in —
1. *To scorn,* לוּץ *luts,* 5.
Psa.119. 51 The proud have had me greatly in derision

2. *To scorn,* לָעַג *laag.*
Psa. 2. 4 the LORD shall have them in derision
59 8 shalt have all the heathen in derision
Eze. 23. 32 be laughed to scorn and had in derision

3. *To laugh at, deride,* שָׂחַק *sachaq.*
Job 30. 1 younger than I have me in derision

DESCEND, to —
1. *To go or come down,* יָרַד *yarad.*
Gen. 28. 12 angels of God ascending and descending
Exod19. 18 because the LORD descended upon it in
33. 9 the cloudy pillar descended, and stood
34. 5 the LORD descended in the cloud, and
Num34. 11 the border shall descend, and shall reach
Deut. 9. 21 the brook that descended out of the
Josh. 2. 23 descended from the mountain, and passed
17. 9 the coast descended unto the river Kanah
18. 13 the border descended to Ataroth-adar
18. 16 and descended to the valley of Hinnom
18. 16 on the south, and descended to En-rogel
18. 17 descended to the stone of Bohan the son
1 Sa. 26. 10 he shall descend into battle, and perish
Psa. 49. 17 his glory shall not descend after him
133. 3 (the dew) that descended upon the moun.
Prov 30. 4 hath ascended up into heaven, or descen.
Isa. 5. 14 he that rejoiceth, shall descend into it
Eze. 26. 20 down with them that descend into the
31. 16 down..with them that descend into the

2. *To go or come down,* καταβαίνω *katabainō.*
Matt. 3. 16 he saw the Spirit of God descending like
7. 25, 27 the rain descended, and the floods
28. 2 angel of the LORD descended from heaven
Mark 1. 10 Spirit like a dove descending upon him
15. 32 Let Christ the King of Israel descend now
Luke 3. 22 the Holy Ghost descended in a bodily
John 1. 32 the Spirit descending from heaven like
1. 33 thou shalt see the Spirit descending, and
1. 51 angels of God ascending and descending
Acts 10. 11 a certain vessel descending unto him, as
11. 5 A certain vessel descend, as it had been
24. 1 Ananias the high priest descended with
Rom 10. 7 Who shall descend into the deep? that is
Eph. 4. 9 what is it but that he also descended
4. 10 He that descended is the same also that
1 Th. 4. 16 the LORD himself shall descend from
Rev. 21. 10 Jerusalem, descending out of heaven

3. *To come down,* κατέρχομαι *katerchomai.*
Jas. 3. 15 This wisdom descendeth not from above

DESCENT —
A coming down, κατάβασις *katabasis.*
Luke19. 37 at the descent of the mount of Olives

DESCENT counted, to have one's —
To have one's genealogy reckoned, γενεαλογέομαι.
Heb. 7. 6 he whose descent is not counted from

DESCENT, without —
Without a genealogy, ἀγενεαλόγητος *agenealogētos.*
Heb. 7. 3 without descent, having neither beginning

DESCRIBE, to —
1. *To write,* כָּתַב *kathab.*
Josh 18. 4 describe it according to the inheritance
18. 6 describe the land (into) seven parts
18. 8 them that went to describe the land
18. 8 walk through the land, and describe it
18. 9 described it by cities into seven parts
Judg. 8. 14 he described unto him the princes of
2. *To write,* γράφω *graphō.*
Rom 10. 5 Moses describeth the righteousness which
3. *To lay out, say,* λέγω *legō.*
Rom. 4. 6 David also describeth the blessedness

DESCRY, to send to —
To go about, search, spy out, תּוּר *tur.*
Judg. 1. 23 the house of Joseph sent to descry Beth-el

DESERT —
1. *Deed, recompense,* גְּמוּל *gemul.*
Psa. 28. 4 Give them..render to them their desert
2. *Judgment,* מִשְׁפָּט *mishpat.*
Eze 7. 27 according to their deserts will I judge

DESERT —
1. *Dry or waste place,* חָרְבָּה *chorbah.*
Psa.102. 6 I am like an owl of the desert
Isa. 48. 21 led them through the deserts: he caused
Eze. 13. 4 prophets are like the foxes in the deserts
2. *Desolation,* יְשִׁימוֹן *yeshimon.*
Psa. 78. 40 oft did they..grieve him in the desert
106. 14 and tempted God in the desert
Isa. 43. 19 I will even make..rivers in the desert
43. 20 rivers in the desert, to give drink to my
3. *Plain, wilderness, desert,* מִדְבָּר *midbar.*
Exod. 3. 1 the flock to the back side of the desert!
5. 3 three days' journey into the desert
19. 2 were come (to) the desert of Sinai, and
23. 31 and from the desert unto the river
Num20. 1 whole congregation, into the desert of
27. 14 against my commandment in the desert
33. 16 they removed from the desert of Sinai
Deut32. 10 He found him in a desert land, and in the
2 Ch.26. 10 he built towers in the desert, and digged
Job 24. 5 (as) wild asses in the desert, go they forth
Isa. 21. 1 from the desert, from a terrible land
Jer. 25. 24 mingled people that dwell in the desert
4. *Plain, wilderness, Arabah,* עֲרָבָה *arabah.*
Isa. 35. 1 the desert shall rejoice, and blossom as
35. 6 waters break out, and streams in the des.
40. 3 make straight in the desert a highway
41. 19 I will set in the desert the fir tree
51. 3 her desert like the garden of the LORD
Jer. 2. 6 through a land of deserts and of pits
17. 6 he shall be like the heath in the desert
50. 12 be) a wilderness, a dry land, and a desert
Eze. 47. 8 down into the desert, and go into the sea
5. *A desert, solitude,* ἐρημία *erēmia.*
Heb. 11. 38 they wandered in deserts, and (in) mou
6. *A desert, solitary place,* ἔρημος *erēmos.*
Matt24. 26 Behold, he is in the desert; go not forth
Luke 1. 80 was in the deserts till the day of his
John 6 31 Our fathers did eat manna in the desert

DESERT —
Desert, solitary, ἔρημος *erēmos.*
Matt 14. 13 departed thence by a ship into a desert
14. 15 This is a desert place, and the time is
Mark 1. 45 but was without in desert places
6. 31 Come ye yourselves..into a desert place
6 32 they departed into a desert place by ship
6. 35 This is a desert place, and now the time
Luke 4. 42 he departed and went into a desert place
9. 10 [went aside privately into a desert place]
9. 12 for we are here in a desert place
Acts 8. 26 from Jerusalem unto Gaza, which is des.

DESERT, wild beasts of the —
Inhabitants of the desert, צִיִּים *tsiyyim.*
Isa. 13. 21 wild beasts of the desert shall lie there
34. 14 The wild beasts of the desert shall also
Jer. 50. 39 the wild beasts of the desert with the

DESERT OF THE SEA, מִדְבַּר יָם *midbar yam.*
An unknown portion of Arabia.
Isa. 21. 1 The burden of the desert of the sea.

DESERVING —
Deed, recompense, גְּמוּל *gemul.*
Judg. 9. 16 according to the deserving of his hands

DESIRABLE —
Desire, חֶמֶד *chemed.*
Eze. 23. 6, 12, 23 all of them desirable young men

DESIRE —
1. *Desire, or father,* אָב *ab.*
Job 34. 36 My desire (is, that) Job may be tried
2. *Desire, the caper-berry,* אֲבִיּוֹנָה *abiyonah.*
Eccl.12. 5 shall be a burden, and desire shall fail
3. *Desire, longing,* אַוָּה *avvah.*
Deut 18. 6 come with all the desire of his mind
1 Sa. 23. 20 according to all the desire of thy soul
Hos. 10. 10 (It is) in my desire that I should chastise
4. *Desire, desirableness,* חֶמְדָּה *chemdah.*
1 Sa. 9. 20 And on whom (is) all the desire of Israel?
Dan. 11. 37 nor the desire of women, nor regard any
Hag. 2. 7 and the Desire of all nations shall come
5. *Delight, pleasure,* חֵפֶץ *chephets.*
2 Sa. 23. 5 (this is) all my salvation, and all (my) d.
1 Ki. 5. 8 I will do all thy desire concerning timber
5. 9 thou shalt accomplish my desire, in
5. 10 and fir trees, (according to) all his desire
9. 11 and with gold, according to all his desire
10. 13 unto the queen of Sheba all her desire
2 Ch. 9. 12 gave to the queen of Sheba all her desire
Job 31. 16 have withheld the poor from (their) desi.
6. *Desire, delight,* חֵשֶׁק *chesheq.*
1 Ki. 9. 1 all Solomon's desire which he was pleased
7. *Desired or desirable thing,* מַחְמָד *machmad.*
Eze. 24. 16 take away from thee the desire of thine
24. 21 the desire of your eyes, and that which
24. 25 joy of their glory, the desire of their eyes
8. *Asking, request,* מִשְׁאָלָה *mishalah.*
Psa. 37. 4 shall give thee the desires of thine heart
9. *Soul,* נֶפֶשׁ *nephesh.*
Eccl. 6. 9 Better..than the wandering of the desire
Mic. 7. 3 he uttereth his mischievous desire
Hab. 2. 5 who enlargeth his desire as hell, and (is)
10. *Acceptance, good pleasure,* רָצוֹן *ratson.*
2 Ch.15. 15 and sought him with their whole desire
Psa.145. 16 satisfiest the desire of every living thing
145. 19 fulfil the desire of them that fear him
11. *Desire, longing,* תַּאֲוָה *taavah.*
Psa. 10. 3 the wicked boasteth of his heart's desire
10. 17 thou hast heard the desire of the humble
21. 2 Thou hast given him his heart's desire
38. 9 Lord, all my desire (is) before thee; and
78. 29 for he gave them their own desire
112. 10 the desire of the wicked shall perish
Prov.10. 24 desire of the righteous shall be granted
11. 23 The desire of the righteous (is) only good
13. 12 (when) the desire cometh, (it is) a tree of
13. 19 The desire accomplished is sweet to the
18. 1 Through desire a man, having separated
19. 22 The desire of a man (is) his kindness
21. 25 The desire of the slothful killeth him
Isa. 26. 8 the desire of (our) soul (is) to thy name
12. *Desire, mark,* תָּו *tav.*
Job 31. 35 my desire (is, that) the Almighty would
13. *Desire, longing,* תְּשׁוּקָה *teshuqah.*
Gen. 3. 16 thy desire (shall be) to thy husband
4. 7 unto thee (shall be) his desire, and thou
Song 7. 10 I (am) my beloved's, and his desire (is)
14. *Great or over desire,* ἐπιθυμία *epithumia.*
Luke22. 15 With desire I have desired to
Phil. 1. 23 having a desire to depart, and to be
1 Th. 2. 17 to see your face with great desire
15. *Good pleasure,* εὐδοκία *eudokia.*
Rom.10. 1 my heart's desire and prayer to God for
16. *Wish, will, willing,* θέλημα *thelēma.*
Eph. 2. 3 fulfilling the desires of the flesh

DESIRE, earnest —
Great desire, longing after, ἐπιπόθησις *epipothēsis.*
2 Co. 7. 7 when he told us your earnest desire

DESIRE, great —
Great desire, longing after, ἐπιποθία *epipothia.*
Rom 15. 23 having a great desire these many years

DESIRE, vehement —
Great desire, ἐπιπόθησις *epipothēsis.*
2 Co. 7. 11 yea, (what) vehement desire, yea, (what)

DESIRE, to —
1. *To desire, incline to,* אָוָה *avah,* 3.
1 Sa. 2. 16 and (then) take (as much) as thy soul de.
2 Sa. 3. 21 reign over all that thine heart desireth
1 Ki.11. 37 according to all that thy soul desireth
Job 23. 13 (what) his soul desireth, even (that) he
Psa.132. 13 he hath desired (it) for his habitation
132. 14 here will I dwell; for I have desired it
Prov 21. 10 The soul of the wicked desireth evil: his
Isa. 26. 9 With my soul have I desired thee in the
Mic. 7. 1 my soul desired the first ripe fruit
2. *To desire for oneself,* אָוָה *avah,* 7.
Prov 13. 4 The soul of the sluggard desireth, and
23. 6 neither desire thou his dainty meats
24. 1 Be not thou envious..neither desire to be
Eccl. 6. 2 wanteth nothing..of all that he desireth
Jer. 17. 16 neither have I desired the woeful day
Amos 5. 18 Woe unto you that desire the day of the
3. *To say,* אָמַר *amar.*
1 Sa.20. 4 Whatsoever thy soul desireth, I will even
Esth. 2. 13 whatsoever she desired was given her to

4. *To enquire after,* בְּעָא, בָּעָה *beah, bea.*
Dan. 2. 16 desired of the king that he would give
2. 18 That they would desire mercies of the G.
2. 23 made known unto me now what we desi.
5. *To seek, require,* בָּקַשׁ *baqash,* 3.
Exod10. 11 serve the LORD; for that ye did desire
6. *To desire, have delight,* חָמַד *chamad.*
Exod34. 24 neither shall any man desire thy land
Deut. 5. 21 Neither shalt thou desire thy neighbour's
7. 25 thou shalt not desire the silver or gold
Job 20. 20 shall not save of that which he desired
Psa. 68. 16 (this is) the hill (which) God desireth to
Prov 12. 12 The wicked desireth the net of evil (men)
Isa. 1. 29 ashamed of the oaks which ye..desired
53. 2 (there is) no beauty that we should desire
7. *To desire, have pleasure,* חָפֵץ *chaphets.*
Job 13. 3 Surely I would speak..and I desire to
21. 14 we desire not the knowledge of thy ways
33. 32 If thou hast..speak, for I desire to justify
Psa. 40. 6 Sacrifice and offering thou didst not des.
51. 6 Behold, thou desirest truth in the inward
51. 16 For thou desirest not sacrifice, else would
73. 25 none upon earth (that) I desire beside
Jer. 42. 22 in the place whither ye desire to go
Hos. 6. 6 For I desired mercy, and not sacrifice
8. *Desiring,* חָפֵץ *chaphets.*
Neh. 1. 11 thy servants, who desire to fear thy name
Psa. 34. 12 What man (is he that) desireth life, (and)
70. 2 let them be..put to confusion, that desire
9. *Desire,* חֵפֶץ *chephets.*
1 Sa. 18. 25 The king desireth not any dowry, but an
10. *To cleave to, delight in,* חָשַׁק *chashaq.*
1 Ki. 9. 19 which Solomon desired to build in Jeru.
2 Ch. 8. 6 all that Solomon desired to build in Jeru.
11. *To ask,* שָׁאַל *shaal.*
Deut14. 26 or for whatsoever thy soul desireth: and
18. 16 According to all that thou desirest of the
Judg. 8. 24 Gideon said..I would desire a request of
1 Sa. 12. 13 king whom ye have chosen, (and)..de.!
1 Ki. 2. 20 said, I desire one small petition of thee
2 Ki. 4. 28 she said, Did I desire a son of my lord?
2 Ch. 11. 23 And he desired many wives
Psa. 27 4 One (thing) have I desired of the LORD
Eccl. 2. 10 whatsoever mine eyes desired I kept not
12. *To swallow up, pant after,* שָׁאַף *shaaph.*
Job 36. 20 Desire not the night, when people are
13. *To lift up the soul,* נָשָׂא נֶפֶשׁ 3, *nasa nephesh.*
Jer. 22. 27 to the land whereunto they desire to
14. *To ask,* αἰτέω *aiteō.*
Matt20. 20 worshipping (him), and desiring a certain
Mark10. 35 do for us whatsoever we shall desire
11. 24 What things soever ye desire, when ye
15. 6 released..prisoner, whomsoever they de.
15. 8 began to desire (him to do) as he had
Luke23. 25 he released unto them..whom they..de
Acts 3. 14 desired a murderer to be granted unto
7. 46 desired to find a tabernacle for the God
9. 2 desired of him letters to Damascus to the
12. 20 desired peace; because their country was
13. 21 And afterward they desired a king: and
13. 28 yet desired they Pilate that he should be
25. 3 desired favour against him, that he would
25. 15 desiring (to have) judgment against him
Eph. 3. 13 I desire that ye faint not at my tribula.
Col. 1. 9 to desire that ye might be filled with the
1 Jo. 5. 15 have the petitions that we desired of him
15. *To think worthy,* ἀξιόω *axioō.*
Acts 28. 22 desire to hear of thee what thou thinkest
16. *To ask excessively,* ἐξαιτέω *exaiteō.*
Luke22. 31 Simon, behold, Satan hath desired..you
17. *To ask at or of,* ἐπερωτάω *eperōtaō.*
Matt 16. 1 desired him that he would show them a
18. *To seek after,* ἐπιζητέω *epizēteō.*
Acts 13. 7 and desired to hear the word of God
Phil. 4. 17 Not because I desire a gift: but I desire
19. *To desire greatly,* ἐπιθυμέω *epithumeō.*
Matt13. 17 have desired to see (those things) which
Luke16. 21 desiring to be fed with the crumbs which
17. 22 ye shall desire to see one of the days of
22. 15 I have desired to eat this passover with
1 Ti. 3. 1 he desireth a good work
Heb. 6. 11 we desire that every one of you do show
1 Pe. 1. 12 which things the angels desire to look
Rev. 9. 6 shall desire to die, and death shall flee
20. *To desire greatly,* ἐπιποθέω *epipotheō.*
1 Pe. 2. 2 As new born babes, desire the sincere
21. *To ask, desire,* ἐρωτάω *erōtaō.*
Luke 7. 36 one of the Pharisees desired him that he
14. 32 he sendeth an ambassage, and desireth
John12. 21 desired him, saying, Sir, we would see J
Acts 16. 39 and desired (them) to depart out of the
18. 20 they desired (him) to tarry longer time
23. 20 The Jews have agreed to desire thee that
22. *To be zealous of,* ζηλόω *zēloō.*
1 Co. 14. 1 Follow after charity, and desire spiritual
23. *To seek,* ζητέω *zēteō.*
Matt 12. 46 his brethren stood without, desiring to
12. 47 thy brethren stand without, desiring to
Luke 9. 9 who is this..And he desired to see him
24. *To wish, will,* θέλω *thelō.*
Mark 9. 35 If any man desire to be first, (the same)

Luke 5. 39 having drunk old (wine) straightway de.
8. 20 thy brethren stand without, desiring to
10. 24 many prophets..have desired to see those
20. 46 scribes, which desire to walk in long rob.
2 Co. 11. 12 cut off occasion from them which desire
12. 6 For though I would desire to glory, I
Gal. 4. 9 whereunto ye desire again to be in bon.?
4. 20 I desire to be present with you now, and
4. 21 Tell me, ye that desire to be under the
6. 12 As many as desire to make a fair show in
6. 13 but desire to have you circumcised, that
1 Ti. 1. 7 Desiring to be teachers of the law: und.

25. *To stretch the arms for*, ὀρέγομαι *oregomai.*
1 Ti. 3. 1 If a man desire the office of a bishop, he
Heb. 11. 16 But now they desire a better (country)

26. *To call alongside of*, παρακαλέω *parakaleō.*
Matt 18. 32 I forgave thee all..because thou desiredst
Acts 8. 31 he desired Philip that he would come up
9. 38 desiring (him) that he would not delay to
19. 31 desiring (him) that he would not advent.
28. 14 were desired to tarry with them seven d.
1 Co. 16. 12 I greatly desired him to come unto you
2 Co. 8. 6 Insomuch that we desired Titus, that as
12. 18 I desired Titus, and with (him) I sent

DESIRE earnestly or greatly, to —

1. *To desire for oneself*, אָוָה *avah*, 7.
Psa. 45. 11 shall the King greatly desire thy beauty

2. *To swallow up, pant after*, שָׁאַף *shaaph.*
Job 7. 2 a servant earnestly desireth the shadow

3. *To desire greatly*, ἐπιποθέω *epipotheō.*
2 Co. 5. 2 earnestly desiring to be clothed upon
1 Th. 3. 6 desiring greatly to see us, as we also (to
2 Ti. 1. 4 Greatly desiring to see thee, being mind.

DESIRE to have, to —

To be zealous of or for, ζηλόω *zēloō.*
Jas. 4. 2 kill, and desire to have, and cannot obtain

DESIRE, to have a —

1. *To cleave to, delight in*, חָשַׁק *chashaq.*
Deut 21. 11 and hast a desire unto her, that thou

2. *To have desire*, כָּסַף *kasaph.*
Job 14. 15 thou wilt have a desire to the work of

3. *To lift up the soul*, נָשָׂא נֶפֶשׁ 3, *nasa nephesh.*
Jer. 44. 14 they have a desire to return to dwell

DESIRED —

1. *To be desired*, כָּסַף *kasaph*, 2.
Zeph. 2. 1 yea, gather together, O nation not desired

2. *Desire, pleasure*, חֵפֶץ *chephets.*
Psa. 107. 30 bringeth them unto their desired haven

DESIRED, to be —

1. *To be desired*, חָמַד *chamad*, 2.
Gen. 3. 6 and a tree to be desired to make (one)
Psa. 19. 10 More to be desired (are they) than gold
Prov 21. 20 (There is) treasure to be desired and oil

2. *Desire, desirableness*, חֶמְדָּה *chemdah.*
2 Ch. 21. 20 departed without being desired: howbeit

3. *Delight, pleasure*, חֵפֶץ *chephets.*
Prov. 8. 11 all the things that may be desired are

DESIRED, things —

Desire, pleasure, חֵפֶץ *chephets.*
Prov. 3. 15 all the things thou canst desire are not
8. 11 all the things that may be desired are not

DESIRES —

Desires, longings, מַאֲוַיִּים *maavayyim.*
Psa. 140. 8 Grant not, O LORD, the desires of the wic.

DESIROUS, to be —

1. *To show self desirous*, אָוָה *avah*, 7.
Prov 23. 3 Be not desirous of his dainties: for they

2. *To wish*, θέλω *thelō.*
Luke 23. 8 for he was desirous to see him of a long
John 16. 19 Jesus knew that they were desirous to ask
2 Co. 11. 32 the governor..kept the city..desirous to

DESIROUS of, to be affectionately —

To send one's love after, ἱμείρομαι *himeiromai.*
1 Th. 2. 8 So [being affectionately desirous of] you

DESIROUS of vain glory —

Vain glorious, κενόδοξος *kenodoxos.*
Gal. 5. 26 Let us not be desirous of vain glory, prov.

DESOLATE, most —

A waste and a waste, שְׁמָמָה וּמְשַׁמָּה [*shimamah*].
Eze. 35. 7 Thus will I make mount Seir most des.

DESOLATE —

1. *Alone, separate*, בָּדָד *badad.*
Isa. 27. 10 Yet the defenced city (shall be) desolate

2. *Desolations*, בַּתּוֹת *battoth.*
Isa. 7. 19 shall rest all of them in the desolate

3. *Silent, gloomy*, גַּלְמוּד *galmud.*
Job 15. 34 For the congregation..(shall be) desolate
Isa. 49. 21 I have lost my children, and am desolate

4. *To be dry, waste*, חָרֵב *chareb*, 2.
Eze. 26. 19 When I shall make thee a desolate city
[30. 7 midst of the countries (that are) desolate]

5. *Dry, waste*, חָרֵב *chareb.*
Jer. 33. 10 which ye say (shall be) desolate without
33. 12 which is desolate without man and with.

6. *Dryness, waste*, חָרְבָּה *chorbah.*
Jer. 7. 34 Then..for the land shall be desolate
Eze. 25. 13 and I will make it desolate from Teman

7. *Only, lonely, singly*, יָחִיד *yachid.*
Psa. 25. 16 have mercy upon me; for I (am) desolate

8. *To be cut off, hidden*, כָּחַד *kachad*, 2.
Job 15. 28 he dwelleth in desolate cities, (and) in

9. *Desolation, astonishment, waste*, מְשַׁמָּה *meshammah.*
Isa. 15. 6 the waters of Nimrim shall be desolate
Jer. 48. 34 waters also of Nimrim shall be desolate
Eze. 6. 14 more desolate than the wilderness toward

10. *Wasting, desolation*, שׁוֹאָה *shoah.*
Job 30. 3 the wilderness in former time desolate
38. 27 To satisfy the desolate and waste (ground)

11. *Desolation, astonishment, waste*, שַׁמָּה *shammah.*
Isa. 5. 9 many houses shall be desolate, (even)
13. 9 and fierce anger, to lay the land desolate
Jer. 4. 7 from his place to make thy land desolate
18. 16 make their land desolate, (and) a perpet.
19. 8 make this city desolate, and an hissing
25. 38 their land is desolate because of the
48. 9 for the cities thereof shall be desolate
50. 3 which shall make her land desolate, and
Hos. 5. 9 Ephraim shall be desolate in the day of
Zech. 7. 14 for they laid the pleasant land desolate

12. *To be desolate*, שָׁמֵם *shamem.*
2 Sa. 13. 20 Tamar remained desolate in her brother
Isa. 49. 8 cause to inherit the desolate heritages
54. 1 more (are) the children of the desolate
Lam. 1. 4 her gates are desolate: her priests sigh
1. 13 he hath made me desolate (and) faint all
1. 16 my children are desolate, because the
3. 11 He hath turned..he hath made me desol.
Eze. 36. 4 to the desolate wastes, and to the cities
Dan. 9. 27 that..shall be poured upon the desolate

13. *To be or become desolate*, שָׁמֵם *shamem*, 2.
Psa. 69. 25 Let their habitation be desolate; (and) let
Isa. 54. 3 make the desolate cities to be inhabited
Jer. 33. 10 streets of Jerusalem, that are desolate
Eze. 29. 12 midst of the countries (that are) desolate
30. 7 the midst of the countries (that are) des.
36. 34 the desolate land shall be tilled, whereas
36. 35 This land that was desolate is become
36. 35 the waste and desolate and ruined cities

14. *Desolate*, שָׁמֵם *shamem.*
Jer. 12. 11 (and being) desolate it mourneth unto
Dan. 9. 17 shine upon thy sanctuary that is desolate

15. *Desolation*, שְׁמָמָה *shemamah.*
Exod 23. 29 lest the land become desolate, and the
Lev. 26. 33 your land shall be desolate, and your
Isa. 1. 7 Your country (is) desolate, your
1. 7 (it is) desolate, as overthrown by strangers
6. 11 and the land be utterly desolate 62. 4.
Jer. 4. 27 The whole land shall be desolate; yet
6. 8 lest I make thee desolate, a land not
9. 11 I will make the cities of Judah desolate
10. 22 to make the cities of Judah desolate, (and)
12. 10 my pleasant portion a desolate wilderness
12. 11 They have made it desolate, (and being) d.
32. 43 (It is) desolate without man or beast
44. 6 they are wasted (and) desolate, as at this
49. 2 and it shall be a desolate heap, and her
50. 13 but it shall be wholly desolate; every one
51. 26 thou shalt be desolate for ever, saith the
51. 62 but that it shall be desolate for ever
Eze. 6. 14 and make the land desolate; yea, more
12. 20 laid waste, and the land shall be desolate
14. 15 they spoil it, so that it be desolate, that
14. 16 but the land shall be desolate
15. 8 I will make the land desolate, because
29. 9 land of Egypt shall be desolate and waste
29. 10 make the land of Egypt..waste (and) des.
29. 12 I will make the land of Egypt desolate
29. 12 the cities..laid waste shall be desolate
32. 15 I shall make the land of Egypt desolate
33. 28 I will lay the land most desolate, and the
33. 29 when I have laid the land most desolate
35. 3 I will make thee most desolate
35. 4 lay thy cities waste, and thou shalt be d.
35. 7 Thus will I make mount Seir most des.
35. 14 saith the Lord..I will make thee desolate
35. 15 thou shalt be desolate, O mount Seir
36. 34 whereas it lay desolate in the sight of all
Joel 2. 3 behind them a desolate wilderness
2. 20 will drive him into a land..desolate
3. 19 Edom shall be a desolate wilderness
Mic. 1. 7 all the idols thereof will I lay desolate
7. 13 Notwithstanding the land shall be des.

16. *Deserted*, ἔρημος *erēmos.*
Matt 23. 38 your house is left unto you [desolate]
Luke 13. 35 your house is left unto you [desolate]
Acts 1. 20 Let his habitation be desolate, and let no
Gal. 4. 27 the desolate hath many more children

17. *To make a desert*, ἐρημόω *erēmoō.*
Rev. 17. 16 shall make her desolate and naked

18. *To leave alone*, μονόω *monoō.*
1 Ti. 5. 5 Now she that is a widow..and desolate

DESOLATE, to be —

1. *To be or become desolate*, אָשֵׁם *ashem.*
Psa. 34. 21 that hate the righteous shall be desolate
34. 22 none..that trust in him shall be desolate
Isa. 24. 6 they that dwell therein are desolate: ther.

2. *To be or become dried up, wasted*, חָרֵב *chareb.*
Jer. 2. 12 and be horribly afraid, be ye very deso.
26. 9 city shall be desolate without an inhabit.?

3. *To be burned*, יָצַת *yatsath*, 2.
Jer. 46. 19 Noph shall be waste and desolate witho

4. *To be desolate*, יָשַׁם *yasham.*
Gen. 47. 19 give (us) seed..that the land be not des.
Eze. 6. 6 the high places shall be desolate
12. 19 her land may be desolate from all
19. 7 the land was desolate, and the fulness

5. *To be empty, free, acquitted*, נָקָה *naqah*, 2.
Isa. 3. 26 and she, (being) desolate, shall sit upon

6. *To be wasted, desolate*, שָׁאָה *shaah*, 2.
Isa. 6. 11 and the land be utterly desolate

7. *To be desolate*, שָׁמֵם *shamem.*
Psa. 40. 15 Let them be desolate for a reward
Lam. 5. 18 the mountain of Zion, which is desolate
Eze. 33. 28 the mountains..shall be desolate
35. 15 Israel, because it was desolate

8. *To be or become desolate*, שָׁמֵם *shamem*, 2.
Lev. 26. 22 your (high) ways shall be desolate
Lam. 4. 5 They that did feed..are desolate in the
Eze. 6. 4 And your altars shall be desolate
25. 3 the land of Israel, when it was desolate
30. 7 they shall be desolate in the midst
36. 36 (and) plant that that was desolate
Amos 7. 9 And the high places..shall be desolate
Zeph. 3. 6 I have cut..their towers are desolate
Zech. 7. 14 the land was desolate after them

9. *To feel self desolate*, שָׁמֵם *shamem*, 7a.
Psa. 143. 4 my heart within me is desolate

DESOLATE, to become —

To be or become desolate, אָשֵׁם *ashem.*
Hos. 13. 16 Samaria shall become desolate; for she

DESOLATE houses —

Forsaken habitations, אַלְמָנוֹת *almanoth.*
Isa. 13. 22 shall cry in their desolate houses

DESOLATE, to be laid—

1. *Be desolate*, [V.L. שְׁמָמָה], שָׁמֵם *shamem.*
Eze. 35. 12 They are laid desolate, they are given

2. *To be or become desolate*, שָׁמֵם *shamem*, 2.
Joel 1. 17 The seed..the garners are laid desolate

DESOLATE, to lie —

To be made desolate, שָׁמֵם *shamem*, 6.
Lev. 26. 34 as long as it lieth desolate, and ye (be) in
26. 35 As long as it lieth desolate it shall
26. 43 while she lieth desolate without them
2 Ch. 36. 21 as long as she lay desolate she kept sab.

DESOLATE, to be made —

1. *To be desolate*, אָשֵׁם *ashem.*
Eze. 6. 6 that your altars may be..made desolate

2. *To be or become desolate*, אָשֵׁם *ashem*, 2.
Joel 1. 18 the flocks of sheep are made desolate

3. *To be or become desolate*, שָׁמֵם *shamem*, 2.
Jer. 12. 11 the whole land is made desolate

DESOLATE to make —

1. *To desolate*, שָׁמֵם *shamem.*
Eze. 36. 3 Because they have made (you) desolate
Dan. 12. 11 abomination that maketh desolate

2. *To desolate*, שָׁמֵם *shamem*, 3a.
Dan. 9. 27 he shall make (it) desolate, even until
11. 31 they shall place..that maketh desolate

3. *To make desolate*, שָׁמֵם *shamem*, 5.
Job 16. 7 thou hast made desolate all my company
Jer. 10. 25 and have made his habitation desolate.
49. 20 he shall make their habitations desolate
50. 45 he shall make (their) habitation desolate
Eze. 20. 26 that I might make them desolate
30. 14 And I will make Pathros desolate

4. *To leave desolate*, ἐρημόω *erēmoō.*
Rev. 18. 19 for in one hour is she made desolate

DESOLATE, making —

To make desolate, שָׁמֵם *shamem*, 5.
Mic. 6. 13 in making (thee) desolate because of thy

DESOLATE palaces —

Forsaken habitations, אַלְמָנוֹת *almanoth.*
Eze 19. 7 And he knew their desolate palaces

DESOLATE place —

1. *Desolate places*, אַשְׁמַנִּים *ashmannim.*
Isa. 59. 10 (we are) in desolate places as dead (men)

2. *Dry or waste place*, חָרְבָּה *chorbah.*
Job 3. 14 which built desolate places for themselves
Psa. 109. 10 bread) also out of their desolate places
Eze. 26. 20 in places desolate of old, with them that
38. 12 turn thine hand upon the desolate places
Mal. 1. 4 will return and build the desolate places

3. *To be desolate*, שָׁמֵם *shamem.*
Isa. 49. 19 thy waste and thy desolate places, and

DESOLATION —

1. *Drought, dry, waste place*, חֹרֶב *choreb.*
Zeph. 2. 14 desolation (shall be) in the thresholds

2. *Drought, dry or waste place*, חָרְבָּה *chorbah.*
Ezra 9. 9 to repair the desolations thereof, and to
Jer. 22. 5 that this house shall become a desolation
25. 9 and an hissing, and perpetual desolations

Jer. 25. 11 this whole land shall be a desolation
25. 18 (To wit)..to make them a desolation, an
44. 2 this day they (are) a desolation, and
44. 22 therefore is your land a desolation, and
Dan. 9. 2 seventy years in the desolations of

3. *Desolation, waste,* מְשׁוֹאָה *meshoah.*
Zeph. 1. 15 a day of wasteness and desolation, a day

4. *Desolations, wastes,* מַשּׁוּאוֹת *mashshuoth.*
Psa. 74. 3 thy feet unto the perpetual desolations

5. As No. 8 [V.L. שַׁאֲוָה *shaavah*].
Prov. 1. 27 When your fear cometh as desolation

6 *Desolation, wasting,* שֵׁאת *sheth.*
Lam. 3. 47 Fear..is come upon us, desolation and

7. *Destruction, spoiling,* שֹׁד *shod.*
Isa. 51. 19 These two (things) are come..desolation
Hos. 12. 1 he daily increaseth lies and desolation

8. *Desolation, wasting,* שׁוֹאָה *shoah.*
Job 30. 14 in the desolation they rolled themselves
Prov. 3. 25 neither of the desolation of the wicked
Isa. 10. 3 the desolation (which) shall come from
47. 11 desolation shall come upon thee suddenly

9. *Desolation,* שַׁמָּה *shammah.*
2 Ki. 22. 19 that they should become a desolation
2 Ch. 30. 7 therefore gave them up to desolation
Psa. 46. 8 what desolations he hath made in the
73. 19 How are they (brought) into desolation
Isa. 24. 12 In the city is left desolation, and the
Jer. 49. 13 Bozrah shall become a desolation
49. 17 Edom shall be a desolation : every one
50. 23 how is Babylon become a desolation
51. 29 to make the land of Babylon a desolation
51. 43 Her cities are a desolation, a dry land
Mic. 6. 16 that I should make thee a desolation
Zeph. 2. 15 how is she become a desolation, a place

10. *To be desolate,* שָׁמֵם *shamem.*
Isa. 61. 4 they shall raise up the former desolations
61. 4 the desolations of many generations
Dan. 8. 13 and the transgression of desolation
9. 18 behold our desolations, and the city
9. 26 end of the war desolations are determined

11. *Desolation,* שְׁמָמָה *shemamah.*
Josh. 8. 28 made it an heap..(even) a desolation
Isa. 17. 9 and there shall be desolation
64. 10 is a wilderness, Jerusalem a desolation
Jer. 25. 12 and will make it perpetual desolations
34. 22 make the cities of Judah a desolation
49. 33 a dwelling for dragons, (and) a desolation
Eze. 7. 27 prince shall be clothed with desolation
23. 33 the cup of astonishment and desolation
Joel 3. 19 Egypt shall be a desolation, and Edom
Zeph. 1. 13 and their houses a desolation : they shall
2. 4 be forsaken, and Ashkelon a desolation
2. 9 and saltpits, and a perpetual desolation
2. 13 will make Nineveh a desolation, (and) dry

12. *Desolation,* שִׁמָמָה *shimamah.*
Eze. 35. 9 I will make thee a perpetual desolation

13. *A making desolate or desert,* ἐρήμωσις *erēmōsis.*
Matt. 24. 15 shall see the abomination of desolation
Mark 13. 14 shall see the abomination of desolation
Luke 21. 20 know that the desolation thereof is nigh

DESOLATION, to bring into —

1. *To make desolate,* שָׁמֵם *shamem,* 5.
Lev. 26. 31 bring your sanctuaries unto desolation
26. 32 And I will bring the land into desolation

2. *To make a desert,* ἐρημόω *erēmoō.*
Matt. 12. 25 against itself is brought to desolation
Luke 11. 17 against itself is brought to desolation

DESPAIR, to —

1. *To despair,* יָאַשׁ *yaash,* 2.
1 Sa. 27. 1 Saul shall despair of me, to seek me any

2. *To have no outlet whatever,* ἐξαπορέομαι *exapor.*
2 Co. 1. 8 insomuch that we despaired even of life

DESPAIR, to be in —

To have no outlet whatever, ἐξαπορέομαι *exaporeo,*
2 Co. 4. 8 (we are) perplexed, but not in despair

DESPAIR, to cause to —

To cause to despair, יָאַשׁ *yaash,* 3.
Eccl. 2. 20 went about to cause my heart to despair

DESPERATE —

To be or become sickly, אָנַשׁ *anash.*
Isa. 17. 11 the day of grief and of desperate sorrow

DESPERATE, one that is —

To be despairing, יָאַשׁ *yaash,* 2.
Job 6. 26 and the speeches of one that is desperate

DESPERATELY wicked —

To be sick, אָנַשׁ *anash.*
Jer. 17. 9 above all (things), and desperately wicked

DESPISE, to —

1. *To despise, contemn, tread on,* בּוּז *buz.*
Prov. 1. 7 (but) fools despise wisdom and instruction
6. 30 (Men) do not despise a thief, if he steal
11. 12 He that is void of wisdom despiseth his
13. 13 Whoso despiseth the word shall be dest.
14. 21 He that despiseth his neighbour sinneth
23. 9 he will despise the wisdom of thy words
23. 22 despise not thy mother when she is old
30. 17 and despiseth to obey (his) mother
Song 8. 1 yea, I should not be despised
Zech. 4. 10 who hath despised the day of small

2. *To despise, contemn,* בָּזָה *bazah.*
Gen. 25. 34 thus Esau despised (his) birthright
Num. 15. 31 he hath despised the word of the LORD
1 Sa. 2. 30 they that despise me shall be lightly
10. 27 they despised him, and brought
2 Sa. 6. 16 and she despised him in her heart
12. 9 Wherefore hast thou despised the com.
12. 10 thou hast despised me, and hast taken
2 Ki. 19. 21 the daughter of Zion, hath despised thee
1 Ch. 15. 29 and she despised him in her heart
2 Ch. 36. 16 despised his words, and misused his
Neh. 2. 19 they laughed us to scorn, and despised
Psa. 22. 24 he hath not despised nor abhorred the
51. 17 contrite heart, O God, thou wilt not des.
69. 33 and despiseth not his prisoners
73. 20 when thou awakest, thou shalt despise
102. 17 He will regard..and not despise their
Prov. 14. 2 (he that is) perverse in his ways despiseth
15. 20 but a foolish man despiseth his mother
19. 16 (but) he that despiseth his ways shall die
Isa. 37. 22 the daughter of Zion, hath despised thee
Eze. 16. 59 which hast despised the oath in breaking
17. 16 whose oath he despised, and whose cov.
17. 18 he despised the oath by breaking the
17. 19 surely mine oath that he hath despised
22. 8 Thou hast despised mine holy things, and
Mal. 1. 6 unto you, O priests, that despise my name
1. 6 Wherein have we despised thy name?

3. *To despise, render contemptible,* בָּזָה *bazah,* 5.
Esth. 1. 17 they shall despise their husbands in their

4. *Despised one,* בָּזֹה *bazoh.*
Isa. 49. 7 to him whom man despiseth, to him

5. *To lightly esteem,* זוּל *zul,* 5.
Lam. 1. 8 all that honoured her despise her, because

6. *To loathe, despise, reject,* מָאַס *maas.*
Lev. 26. 15 if ye shall despise my statutes, or if
26. 43 even because they despised my judgments
Num. 11. 20 ye have despised the LORD which (is)
14. 31 shall know the land which ye have desp.
Judg. 9. 38 this the people that thou hast despised?
Job 5. 17 despise not thou the chastening of the
9. 21 (Though) I (were) perfect..I would despise
10. 3 that thou shouldest despise the work of
19. 18 young children despised me ; I arose
31. 13 If I did despise the cause of my man serv.
36. 5 Behold, God (is) mighty, and despiseth not
Psa. 53. 5 to shame, because God hath despised
106. 24 Yea, they despised the pleasant land
Prov. 3. 11 despise not the chastening of the LORD
15. 32 He that refuseth instruction despiseth
Isa. 30. 12 Because ye despise this word, and trust
33. 8 he hath despised the cities, he regardeth
33. 15 he that despiseth the gain of oppressions
Jer. 4. 30 (thy) lovers will despise thee, they will
Eze. 20. 13 they despised my judgments, which (if)
20. 16 they despised my judgments, and walked
20. 24 despised my statutes, and had polluted
Amos 2. 4 they have despised the law of the LORD
5. 21 I despise your feast days, and I will not

7. *To despise,* נָאַץ *naats.*
Prov. 1. 30 they despised all my reproof
5. 12 and my heart despised reproof
15. 5 A fool despiseth his father's instruction
Jer. 33. 24 they have despised my people, that they
Lam. 2. 6 hath despised in the indignation of his

8. *To despise,* נָאַץ *naats,* 3.
Isa. 5. 24 despised the word of the Holy One of Is.
60. 14 they that despised thee shall bow thems.

9. *To lightly esteem,* קָלַל *qalal,* 5.
2 Sa. 19. 43 why then did ye despise us, that our

10. *To despise, tread, push away,* שׁוּט *shut.*
Eze. 16. 57 daughters of the Philistines, which desp.
28. 24 all (that are) round about..that despised
28. 26 those that despise them round about

11. *To put aside,* ἀθετέω *atheteō.*
Luke 10. 16 and he that despiseth you despiseth me
10. 16 he that despiseth me despiseth him that
1 Th. 4. 8 He therefore that despiseth, despiseth
Heb. 10. 28 He that despised Moses' law died without
Jude 8 despise dominion, and speak evil of

12. *To dishonour,* ἀτιμάζω *atimazō.*
Jas. 2. 6 But ye have despised the poor

13. *To think nothing of, set at nought,* ἐξουθενέω.
Luke 18. 9 they were righteous, and despised others
Rom. 14. 3 Let not him that eateth despise him that
1 Co. 1. 28 things which are despised, hath God
16. 11 Let no man therefore despise him
Gal. 4. 14 temptation..in my flesh ye despised not
1 Th. 5. 20 Despise not prophesyings

14. *To think down upon,* καταφρονέω *kataphroneō.*
Matt. 6. 24 hold to the one, and despise the other
18. 10 Take heed that ye despise not one of these
Luke 16. 13 hold to the one, and despise the other
Rom. 2. 4 despisest thou the riches of his goodness
1 Co. 11. 22 despise ye the church of God, and shame
1 Ti. 4. 12 Let no man despise thy youth; but be
6. 2 let them not despise (them), because they
Heb. 12. 2 endured the cross, despising the shame
2 Pe. 2. 10 walk after the flesh..and despise govern.

15. *To be reckoned for nothing,* λογίζομαι εἰς οὐδέν.
Acts 19. 27 the temple of..Diana should be despised

16. *To care little for,* ὀλιγωρέω *oligōreō.*
Heb. 12. 5 despise not thou the chastening of the Lo.

17. *To think around, despise,* περιφρονέω *periphro.*
Titus 2. 15 Let no man despise thee

DESPISED —

1. *Despised thing,* בּוּז *buz.*
Job 12. 5 (is as) a lamp despised in the thought
Prov. 12. 8 he..a perverse heart shall be despised

2. *Despised thing,* בּוּזָה *buzah.*
Neh. 4. 4 Hear, O our God; for we are despised: and

3. *Dishonoured, lacking honour,* ἄτιμος *atimos.*
1 Co. 4. 10 ye (are) honourable, but we (are) despised

DESPISED, to be —

1. *To be despised,* בָּזָה *bazah,* 2.
*Psa. 22. 6 reproach of men, and despised of the
119. 141 I (am) small and despised; (yet) do not I
*Eccl. 9. 16 the poor man's wisdom (is) despised, and
Isa. 53. 3 He is despised and rejected of men; a
53. 3 he was despised, and we esteemed him
Jer. 22. 28 (Is) this man Coniah a despised broken
*49. 15 lo, I will make thee..despised among
*Obad. 2 thou art greatly despised
* Pass. part. of *bazah* 1.

2. *To be or become light,* קָלָה *qalah,* 2.
Prov. 12. 9 (He that is) despised, and hath a servant

3. *To be or become light,* קָלַל *qalal.*
Gen. 16. 4 her mistress was despised in her eyes
16. 5 when..she had conceived, I was despised

DESPISER —

One who thinks down upon (another), καταφρονητής.
Acts 13. 41 Behold, ye despisers, and wonder, and

DESPISER of those that are good —

Not friendly to the good, ἀφιλάγαθος *aphilagathos.*
2 Ti. 3. 3 fierce, despisers of those that are good

DESPITE —

Despite, שְׁאָט *sheat.*
Eze. 25. 6 rejoiced in heart with all thy despite

DESPITE unto, to do —

To use despitefully, ἐνυβρίζω *enubrizō.*
Heb. 10. 29 done despite unto the Spirit of grace?

DESPITEFUL —

1. *Despite,* שְׁאָט *sheat.*
Eze. 25. 15 taken vengeance with a despiteful heart
36. 5 with despiteful minds, to cast it out for

2. *Despiteful,* ὑβριστής *hubristēs.*
Rom. 1. 30 despiteful, proud, boasters, inventors of

DESPITEFULLY, to use —

1. *To use spitefully,* ἐπηρεάζω *epēreazō.*
Matt. 5. 44 [pray for them which despitefully use]
Luke 6. 28 pray for them which despitefully use you

2. *To use despitefully,* ὑβρίζω *hubrizō.*
Acts 14. 5 to use (them) despitefully, and to stone

DESTITUTE —

1. *Lacking,* חָסֵר *chaser.*
Prov. 15. 21 joy to (him that is) destitute of wisdom

2. *Naked, destitute,* עַרְעָר *arar.*
Psa. 102. 17 will regard the prayer of the destitute

3. *To deprive of,* ἀποστερέω *apostereō.*
1 Ti. 6. 5 corrupt minds, and destitute of the truth

4. *To leave, lack,* λείπω *leipō.*
Jas. 2. 15 be naked, and destitute of daily food

DESTITUTE, to be —

1. *To be or become desolate,* שָׁמֵם *shamem,* 2.
Eze. 32. 15 the country shall be destitute of that

2. *To be last, behind,* ὑστερέω *hustereō.*
Heb. 11. 37 being destitute, afflicted, tormented

DESTITUTE, to leave —

1. *To forsake, leave,* עָזַב *azab.*
Gen. 24. 27 who hath not left destitute my master

2. *To make naked, expose,* עָרָה *arah,* 3.
Psa. 141. 8 leave not my soul destitute

DESTROY, to —

1. *To destroy,* אָבַד *abad,* 3.
Deut. 11. 4 (how) the LORD had destroyed them
12. 2 Ye shall utterly destroy all the places
12. 3 destroy the names of them out of that
Num. 33. 52 destroy all their pictures, and destroy
2 Ki. 11. 1 arose and destroyed all the seed royal
13. 7 for the king of Syria had destroyed them
19. 18 therefore they have destroyed them
21. 3 which Hezekiah his father had destroyed
Esth. 4. 7 the money..for the Jews, to destroy them
8. 5 which he wrote to destroy the Jews
9. 6 Jews slew and destroyed five hundred
9. 12 have slain and destroyed five hundred
9. 24 devised against the Jews to destroy
9. 24 to consume them, and to destroy them
Job 12. 23 increaseth the nations, and destroyeth
Psa. 5. 6 Thou shalt destroy them that speak
9. 5 thou hast destroyed the wicked, thou
21. 10 Their fruit shalt thou destroy from the
119. 95 wicked have waited for me to destroy me
Prov. 1. 32 prosperity of fools shall destroy them
Eccl. 7. 7 and a gift destroyeth the heart
9. 18 but one sinner destroyeth much good
Isa. 37. 19 therefore they have destroyed them
Jer. 12. 17 utterly pluck up and destroy that nation
15. 7 I will bereave..I will destroy my people

Jer. 23. 1 Woe be unto the pastors that destroy
51. 55 and destroyed out of her the great voice
Lam. 2. 9 he hath destroyed and broken her bars
Eze. 6. 3 and I will destroy your high places
22. 27 to shed blood, (and) to destroy souls
28. 16 I will destroy thee, O covering cherub
Zeph. 2. 13 stretch out his hand..and destroy Assyr.

2. *To destroy*, אָבַד *abad*, 5.
Lev. 23. 30 the same soul will I destroy from among
Num 24. 19 destroy him that remaineth of the city
Deut. 7. 10 repayeth them that hate..to destroy
7. 24 shalt destroy their name from under
9. 3 drive them out, and destroy them quickly
28. 51 until he have destroyed thee
28. 63 LORD will rejoice over you to destroy you
Josh. 7. 7 the hand of the Amorites, to destroy us?
2 Ki. 10. 19 he might destroy the worshippers of B.
24. 2 sent them against Judah to destroy it
Job 14. 19 and thou destroyest the hope of man
Psa. 143. 12 and destroy all them that afflict my soul
Jer. 1. 10 root out, and to pull down, and to destroy
18. 7 and to pull down, and to destroy (it)
31. 28 to throw down, and to destroy, and to
46. 8 will destroy the city and the inhabitants
49. 38 will destroy from thence the king and
Eze. 25. 16 and destroy the remnant of the sea coast
30. 13 I will also destroy the idols, and I will
32. 13 I will destroy also all the beasts thereof
Obad. 8 destroy the wise (men) out of Edom, and
Mic. 5. 10 and I will destroy thy chariots
Zeph. 2. 5 I will even destroy thee, that there shall

3. *To destroy*, אֲבַד *abad*, 5.
Dan. 2. 12 commanded to destroy all the wise (men)
2. 24 ordained to destroy the wise (men) of B.
2. 24 Destroy not the wise (men) of Babylon
7. 26 consume and to destroy (it) unto the end

4. *To gather*, אָסַף *asaph*.
1 Sa. 15. 6 Go, depart..lest I destroy you with them

5. *To make or declare guilty or desolate*, אָשַׁם *ashem* 5.
Psa. 5. 10 Destroy thou them, O God; let them fall

6. *To swallow up*, בָּלַע *bala*, 3.
Job 2. 3 movedst me..to destroy him without
8. 18 If he destroy him from his place, then (it)
10. 8 have made me..yet thou dost destroy me
Psa. 55. 9 Destroy, O LORD, (and) divide their tongu.
Isa. 3. 12 and destroy the way of thy paths
19. 3 and I will destroy the counsel thereof
25. 7 will destroy in this mountain the face
Lam. 2. 8 not withdrawn his hand from destroying

7. *To catch, draw, drag*, גָּרַר *garar*.
Prov 21. 7 robbery of the wicked shall destroy them

8. *To speak*, דָּבַר *dabar*, 3 (error in Heb. text).
2 Ch. 22. 10 arose and destroyed all the seed royal of

9. *To bruise*, דָּכָא *daka*, 3.
Job 6. 9 that it would please God to destroy me

10. *To cut off*, דָּמָה *damah*.
Hos. 4. 5 and I will destroy thy mother

11. *To move, destroy*, הוּם *hum*.
Deut. 7. 23 shall destroy them with a mighty destru.

12. *To move, trouble, crush*, הָמַם *hamam*.
Exod 23. 27 will destroy all the people to whom thou
Deut 2. 15 to destroy them from among the host
Psa. 144. 6 shoot out thine arrows, and destroy them

13. *To kill*, הָרַג *harag*.
Psa. 78. 47 He destroyed their vines with hail, and

14. *To break or throw down*, הָרַס *haras*.
1 Ch. 20. 1 And Joab smote Rabbah, and destroyed
Psa. 28. 5 shall destroy them, and not build them
Isa. 14. 17 and destroyed the cities thereof

15. *To destroy, act wickedly, corrupt*, חָבַל *chabal*, 3.
Eccl. 5. 6 and destroy the work of thine hands
Isa. 13. 5 They come..to destroy the whole land
32. 7 he deviseth wicked devices to destroy the
54. 16 and I have created the waster to destroy
Mic. 2. 10 it shall destroy (you), even with a sore

16. *To destroy, act wickedly, corrupt*, חֲבַל *chabal*, 3.
Ezra 6. 12 to destroy this house of God which (is) at
Dan. 4. 23 saying, Hew the tree down, and destroy

17. *To make dry, or waste*, חָרֵב *chareb*, 5.
2 Ki. 19. 17 the kings of Assyria have destroyed the

18. *To oppress, break, thrust out*, יָנָה *yanah*.
Psa. 74. 8 They said..Let us destroy them together

19. *To dispossess, take as possession*, יָרַשׁ *yarash*, 5.
Exod 15. 9 draw my sword, my hand shall destroy

20. *To finish, consume*, כָּלָה *kalah*, 3.
Job 9. 22 He destroyeth the perfect and the wicked

21. *To cut off or down*, כָּרַת *karath*.
1 Ki. 15. 13 Asa destroyed her idol, and burnt (it) by

22. *To cut off or down*, כָּרַת *karath*, 5.
Exod 8. 9 to destroy the frogs from thee and thy
Lev. 26. 22 destroy your cattle, and make you few in
Judg. 4. 24 they had destroyed Jabin king of Canaan

23. *To beat down or out*, כָּתַת *kathath*, 5.
Deut. 1. 44 destroyed you in Seir, (even) unto Hor.

24. *To cast down*, מְגַר *megar*, 3.
Ezra 6. 12 destroy all kings and people that shall

25. *To cut off*, מוּל *mul*, 5.
Psa. 118. 10, 11, 12 the name of the LORD I will destroy

26. *To put to death*, מוּת *muth*, 5.
2 Sa. 20. 19 thou seekest to destroy a city and a mot.

27. *To blot out, wipe away*, מָחָה *machah*.
Gen. 6. 7 I will destroy man whom I have created
7. 4 will I destroy from off the face of the

28. *To (cause to) blot out or wipe away*, מָחָה *machah*.
Prov 31. 3 thy ways to that which destroyeth kings

29. *Destroying, corrupting*, מַשְׁחִית *mashchith*.
Exod 12. 13 plague shall not be upon you to destroy
2 Ch. 20. 23 every one helped to destroy another
Eze. 21. 31 hand of brutish men, (and) skilful to de.
25. 15 to destroy (it) for the old hatred

30. *To pull down or away*, נָסַח *nasach*.
Prov 15. 25 LORD will destroy the house of the proud

31. *To go or set round, compass*, נָקַף *naqaph*, 3.
Job 19. 26 after my skin (worms) destroy this (body)

32. *To blow, destroy, make desolate*, נָשַׁם *nasham*.
Isa. 42. 14 I will destroy and devour at once

33. *To break down*, נָתַץ *nathats*.
Exod 34. 13 ye shall destroy their altars, break their
Deut. 7. 5 ye shall destroy their altars, and break
Job 19. 10 He hath destroyed me on every side, and
Psa. 52. 5 God shall likewise destroy thee for ever
Eze. 26. 12 and they shall destroy thy pleasant houses

34. *To pluck up*, נָתַשׁ *nathash*.
Psa. 9. 6 and thou hast destroyed cities

35. *To end, consume*, סָפָה *saphah*.
Gen. 18. 23 Wilt thou also destroy the righteous with
18. 24 wilt thou also destroy and not spare the
Psa. 40. 14 that seek after my soul to destroy it

36. *To hide, destroy*, סְתַר *sethar*.
Ezra 5. 12 who destroyed this house, and carried the

37. *To cut off, destroy*, צָמַת *tsamath*, 5.
2 Sa. 22. 41 that I might destroy them that hate me
Psa. 18. 40 that I might destroy them that hate me
69. 4 they that would destroy me, (being)
73. 27 thou hast destroyed all them that go a
101. 8 early destroy all the wicked of the land

38. *To dig, dig down, destroy*, קוּר *qur*, 3a.
Num 24. 17 and destroy all the children of Sheth

39. *To break, shiver, destroy*, שָׁבַר *shabar*.
Jer. 17. 18 and destroy them with double destruction
Dan. 11. 26 they that feed..shall destroy him

40. *To destroy, spoil*, שָׁדַד *shadad*.
Prov 11. 3 perverseness of transgressors shall dest.

41. *Wasting, desolation*, שׁוֹאָה *shoah*.
Psa. 63. 9 But those (that) seek my soul, to destroy

42. *To mar, corrupt, destroy*, שָׁחַת *shachath*, 3.
Gen. 6. 17 to destroy all flesh, wherein (is) the brea.
9. 11 shall there any more be a flood to destroy
9. 15 shall no more become a flood to destroy
13. 10 before the LORD destroyed Sodom and
19. 13 and the LORD hath sent us to destroy it
19. 29 God destroyed the cities of the plain
Num 32. 15 and ye shall destroy all this people
Josh 22. 33 to destroy the land wherein the children
Judg. 6. 5 they entered into the land to destroy it
1 Sa. 23. 10 to come to Keilah, to destroy the city
2 Sa. 1. 14 thine hand to destroy the LORD'S anoin.
14. 11 revengers of blood to destroy any more
24. 16 his hand upon Jerusalem to destroy it
2 Ki. 19. 12 them which my fathers have destroyed
Isa. 14. 20 thou hast destroyed thy land, (and) slain
Jer. 5. 10 Go ye up upon her walls, and destroy
12. 10 Many pastors have destroyed my vineya.
48. 18 he shall destroy thy strong holds
Lam. 2. 5 he hath destroyed his strong holds, and
2. 6 hath destroyed his places of the assembly
Eze. 5. 16 (and) which I will send to destroy you
20. 17 mine eye spared them from destroying
22. 30 for the land, that I should not destroy it
26. 4 they shall destroy the walls of Tyrus
30. 11 shall be brought to destroy the land
43. 3 that I saw when I came to destroy the c
Hos. 11. 9 I will not return to destroy Ephraim

43. *To mar, corrupt, destroy*, שָׁחַת *shachath*, 5.
Gen. 6. 13 behold, I will destroy them with the earth
18. 28 wilt thou destroy all the city for (lack of)
18. 28 I find..forty and five, I will not destroy
18. 31 I will not destroy (it) for twenty's sake
18. 32 I will not destroy (it) for ten's sake
19. 13 For we will destroy this place
19. 14 for the LORD will destroy this city
Exod 12. 23 will not suffer the destroyer to come in
Deut. 4. 31 will not forsake thee, neither destroy
9. 26 destroy not thy people and thine inher.
10. 10 the LORD would not destroy thee
20. 19 thou shalt not destroy the trees thereof
20. 20 thou shalt destroy and cut them down
Judg. 6. 4 destroyed the increase of the earth, till
20. 21, 25 and destroyed down to the ground of
20. 35 the children of Israel destroyed of the
20. 42 they destroyed in the midst of them
1 Sa. 26. 9 Destroy him not: for who can stretch
26. 15 there came one of the people in to destroy
2 Sa. 11. 1 they destroyed the children of Ammon
20. 20 that I should swallow up or destroy
24. 16 said to the angel that destroyed the
2 Ki. 8. 19 the LORD would not destroy Judah for D.
13. 23 and would not destroy them, neither
18. 25 Am I now come up..to destroy it?
18. 25 Go up against this land, and destroy it
1 Ch. 21. 12 angel of the LORD destroying throughout
21. 15 said to the angel that destroyed, It is
2 Ch. 12. 7 I will not destroy them, but I will grant
12. 12 that he would not destroy (him) altogether
21. 7 the LORD would not destroy the house of
24. 23 destroyed all the princes of the people
25. 16 that God hath determined to destroy thee
34. 11 which the kings of Judah had destroyed
35. 21 forbear thee..that he destroy thee not
36. 19 destroyed all the goodly vessels thereof
Psa. 78. 38 forgave (their) iniquity, and destroyed
78. 45 He sent..frogs, which destroyed them
106. 23 turn away his wrath, lest he..destroy
Prov. 6. 32 he (that) doeth it destroyeth his own soul
11. 9 with (his) mouth destroyeth his neighbour
Isa. 11. 9 hurt nor destroy in all my holy mountain
36. 10 am I now come up..to destroy it?
36. 10 Go up against this land, and destroy it
37. 12 them which my fathers have destroyed
51. 13 as if he were ready to destroy?
65. 8 Destroy it not; for a blessing (is) in it
65. 8 that I may not destroy them all
65. 25 hurt nor destroy in all my holy mountain
Jer. 2. 30 hath devoured..like a destroying lion
6. 5 by night, and let us destroy her palaces
11. 19 Let us destroy the tree with the fruit
13. 14 nor spare, nor have mercy, but destroy
15. 3 beasts of the earth, to devour and destroy
15. 6 my hand against thee, and destroy thee
36. 29 shall certainly come and destroy this
49. 9 they will destroy till they have enough
51. 1 Behold, I will raise up..a destroying wind
51. 11 device (is) against Babylon, to destroy it
51. 20 and with thee will I destroy kingdoms
51. 25 which destroyest all the earth
Lam. 2. 8 The LORD hath purposed to destroy the
Eze. 9. 8 wilt thou destroy all the residue of
Dan. 8. 24 he shall destroy wonderfully, and shall
8. 24 destroy the mighty and the holy people
8. 25 and by peace shall destroy many
9. 26 shall destroy the city and the sanctuary
Mal. 3. 11 he shall not destroy the fruits of your

44. *To bereave*, שָׁכֹל *shakol*, 3.
Deut 32. 25 shall destroy both the young man and the

45. *To destroy, cut off, waste*, שָׁמַד *shamad*, 5.
Lev. 26. 30 I will destroy your high places, and cut
Deut. 1. 27 to deliver us..to destroy us
2. 12 they had destroyed them from before
2. 21 but the LORD destroyed them before them
2. 22 he destroyed the Horims from before
2. 23 destroyed them, and dwelt in their stead
4. 3 God hath destroyed them from among
6. 15 destroy thee from off the face of the earth
7. 4 be kindled against you, and destroy thee
7. 24 until thou have destroyed them
9. 3 (as) a consuming fire he shall destroy
9. 8 was angry with you, to have destroyed
9. 14 Let me alone, that I may destroy them
9. 19 LORD was wroth against you to destroy
9. 20 angry with Aaron to have destroyed him
9. 25 the LORD had said he would destroy you
28. 48 put a yoke..until he have destroyed thee
31. 3 he will destroy these nations from before
31. 4 unto the land of them, whom he destroyed
33. 27 and shall say, Destroy (them)
Josh. 7. 12 except ye destroy the accursed from
9. 24 to destroy all the inhabitants of the land
11. 14 until they had destroyed them, neither
11. 20 that he might destroy them, as the LORD
23. 15 until he have destroyed you from off this
24. 8 and I destroyed them from before you
1 Sa. 24. 21 thou wilt not destroy my name out of my
2 Sa. 14. 7 we will destroy the heir also: and so they
14. 11 lest they destroy my son
14. 16 the hand of the man (that would) destroy
22. 38 pursued mine enemies, and destroyed
1 Ki. 13. 34 destroy (it) from off the face of the earth
15. 29 until he had destroyed him, according
16. 12 Thus did Zimri destroy all the house of
2 Ki. 10. 17 till he had destroyed him, according to
10. 28 Thus Jehu destroyed Baal out of Israel
21. 9 nations whom the LORD destroyed before
1 Ch. 5. 25 whom God destroyed before them
2 Ch. 20. 10 turned from them, and destroyed them
20. 23 utterly to slay and destroy (them)
33. 9 whom the LORD had destroyed before the
Esth. 3. 6 Haman sought to destroy all the Jews
3. 13 to destroy, to kill, and to cause to perish
4. 8 decree that was given at Shushan to des.
8. 11 to stand for their life, to destroy, to slay
Psa. 106. 23 he said that he would destroy them, had
106. 34 They did not destroy the nations, con.
145. 20 but all the wicked will he destroy
Isa. 10. 7 (it is) in his heart to destroy and cut off
13. 9 destroy the sinners thereof out of it
23. 11 to destroy the strongholds thereof
26. 14 therefore hast thou visited and destroyed
Lam. 3. 66 and destroy them in anger from under
Eze. 14. 9 will destroy him from the midst of my
25. 7 I will destroy thee; and thou shalt know
34. 16 but I will destroy the fat and the strong
Dan. 11. 44 shall go forth with great fury to destroy
Amos 2. 9 Yet destroyed I the Amorite before them
2. 9 yet I destroyed his fruit from above, and
9. 8 I will destroy it from off the face of the
9. 8 not utterly destroy the house of Jacob

Mic. 5. 14 so will I destroy thy cities
Hag. 2. 22 will destroy the strength of the kingdoms
Zech 12. 9 I will seek to destroy all the nations

46. *To make desolate*, שָׁמֵם *shamem*. 5.
1 Sa. 5. 6 he destroyed them, and smote them with
Hos. 2. 12 I will destroy her vines, and her fig trees

47. *To desolate*, שָׁמֵם *shamem*.
Isa. 42. 14 I will destroy and devour at once

48. *To lose off or away, destroy*, ἀπόλλυμι *apollu*.
Matt. 2. 13 will seek the young child to destroy him
10. 28 fear him which is able to destroy both
12. 14 against him, how they might destroy him
21. 41 He will miserably destroy those wicked
22. 7 destroyed those murderers, and burned
27. 20 they should ask Barabbas, and destroy J.
Mark 1. 24 art thou come to destroy us? I know thee
3. 6 took counsel..how they might destroy
9. 22 the fire, and into the waters, to destroy
11. 18 and sought how they might destroy him
12. 9 He will come and destroy the husbandm.
Luke 4. 34 art thou come to destroy us? I know thee
6. 9 Is it lawful..to save life or to [destroy]
9. 56 Son of man is not come to [destroy] men's
17. 27 and the flood came, and destroyed them
17. 29 brimstone from heaven, and destroyed
19. 47 chief of the people sought to destroy him
20. 16 shall come and destroy these husbandmen
John 10. 10 for to steal, and to kill, and to destroy
Rom 14. 15 Destroy not him with thy meat for whom
1 Co. 1. 19 I will destroy the wisdom of the wise, and
Jas. 4. 12 who is able to save and to destroy
Jude 5 afterward destroyed them that believed

49. *To mar or corrupt thoroughly*, διαφθείρω *diaph.*
Rev. 8. 9 third part of the ships were destroyed
11. 18 destroy them which destroy the earth

50. *To destroy utterly*, ἐξολοθρεύω *exolothreuō*.
Acts 3. 23 every soul..shall be destroyed from amo.

51. *To take down*, καθαιρέω *kathaireō*.
Acts 13. 19 when he had destroyed seven nations in
19. 27 her magnificence should be destroyed

52. *To loose down*, καταλύω *kataluō*.
Matt. 5. 17 Think not that I am come to destroy the
5. 17 I am not come to destroy, but to fulfil
26. 61 I am able to destroy the temple of God
27. 40 Thou that destroyest the temple, and
Mark 14. 58 I will destroy this temple that is made
15. 29 Thou that destroyest the temple, and
Acts 6. 14 Jesus of Nazareth shall destroy this place
Rom. 14. 20 For meat destroy not the work of God
Gal. 2. 18 build again the things which I destroyed

53. *To make of none effect*, καταργέω *katargeō*.
Rom. 6. 6 that the body of sin might be destroyed
1 Co. 6. 13 but God shall destroy both it and them
15. 26 enemy (that) shall be destroyed
2 Th. 2. 8 shall destroy with the brightness of his
Heb. 2. 14 through death he might destroy him that

54. *To loose*, λύω *luō*.
John 2. 19 Destroy this temple, and in three days I
1 Jo. 3. 8 he might destroy the works of the devil

55. *To destroy*, ὀλοθρεύω *olothreuō*, ὀλεθρεύω.
Heb. 11. 28 lest he that destroyed the first born

56. *To lay waste*, πορθέω *portheō*.
Acts 9. 21 Is not this he that destroyed them
Gal. 1. 23 preacheth the faith which once he destr.

57. *To mar, corrupt*, φθείρω *phtheirō*.
1 Co. 3. 17 defile the temple..him shall God destroy

DESTROY self, to —

1. *To mar, corrupt, destroy (self)*, שָׁחַת *shachath*, 3.
Hos. 13. 9 O Israel, thou hast destroyed thyself

2. *To desolate (self)*, שָׁמֵם *shamem*, 7a.
Eccl. 7. 16 why shouldest thou destroy thyself?

DESTROY, to utterly —

1. *To devote (to God or destruction)*, חָרַם *charam*, 5.
Num 21. 2 then I will utterly destroy their cities
21. 3 utterly destroyed them and their cities
Deut. 2. 34 utterly destroyed the men, and the women
3. 6 we utterly destroyed them, as we did
3. 6 utterly destroying the men, women, and
7. 2 shalt smite them, (and) utterly destroy
13. 15 destroying it utterly, and all that (is)
20. 17 thou shalt utterly destroy them; (namely)
Josh. 2. 10 Sihon and Og, whom ye utterly destroyed
6. 21 they utterly destroyed all that (was) in
8. 26 until he had utterly destroyed all the
10. 1 had taken Ai, and had utterly destroyed
10. 28 the king thereof he utterly destroyed
10. 35 that (were) therein he utterly destroyed
10. 37 destroyed it utterly, and all the souls
10. 39 utterly destroyed all the souls that (were)
10. 40 utterly destroyed all that breathed, as
11. 11 they smote all..utterly destroying (them)
11. 12 he utterly destroyed them, as Moses the
11. 20 that he might destroy them utterly, (and)
11. 21 Joshua destroyed them utterly with their
Judg. 1. 17 that inhabited..and utterly destroyed it
21. 11 ye shall utterly destroy every male, and
1 Sa. 15. 3 utterly destroy all that they have, and
15. 8 utterly destroyed all the people with the
15. 9 and refuse, that they destroyed utterly
15. 9 would not utterly destroy them: but
15. 15 and the rest we have utterly destroyed
15. 18 utterly destroy the sinners the Amalekites
15. 20 have utterly destroyed the Amalekites
1 Ki. 9. 21 Israel also were not able utterly to destroy
2 Ki. 19. 11 to all lands, by destroying them utterly
1 Ch. 4. 41 destroyed them utterly unto this day, and
2 Ch. 32. 14 nations that my father utterly destroyed
Isa. 11. 15 the LORD shall utterly destroy the tongue
34. 2 he hath utterly destroyed them
37. 11 to all lands by destroying them utterly
Jer. 25. 9 will utterly destroy them, and make
50. 21 waste and utterly destroy after them
50. 26 cast her up as heaps..destroy her utterly
51. 3 destroy ye utterly all her host

2. *To finish, consume*, כָּלָה *kalah*, 3.
Lev. 26. 44 will I abhor them, to destroy them utterly
2 Ch. 31. 1 until they had utterly destroyed them all

DESTROYED —

One cut off, דּוּמָה *dummah*.
Eze. 27. 32 like the destroyed in the midst of

DESTROYED, to be —

1. *To be lost*, אָבַד *abad*.
Exod 10. 7 knowest thou not..that Egypt is destro.
Deut. 7. 20 be destroyed; Esth. 4. 14; Eze. 26. 17.

1a. *To destroy*, אבר *abad*, 3. Esth. 3. 9.

2. *To be destroyed*, אָבַד *abad*, 6.
Dan. 7. 11 beast was slain, and his body destroyed

3. *To be swallowed up*, בָּלַע *bala*, 4.
Isa. 9. 16 (they that are) led of them (are) destroyed

4. *To be bruised, bruise self*, דָּכָא *daka*, 7.
Job 34. 25 in the night, so that they are destroyed

5. *To be cut off*, דָּמָה *damah*, 2.
Hos. 4. 6 My people are destroyed for lack of

6. *To be or become marred or corrupted*, חָבַל *chabal*, 2.
Prov 13. 13 despiseth the word shall be destroyed

7. *To be marred or corrupted*, חָבַל *chabal*, 4.
Isa. 10. 27 the yoke shall be destroyed because of

8. *To be marred or corrupted*, חָבַל *chabal*, 4.
Dan. 2. 44 a kingdom, which shall never be destroy.
6. 26 kingdom (that) which shall not be destr.
7. 14 kingdom (that) which shall not destroyed

9. *To be dried up or wasted*, חָרַב *charab*, 6.
Ezra 4. 15 for which cause was this city destroyed

10. *To be beaten down*, כָּתַת *kathath*, 4.
2 Ch. 15. 6 nation was destroyed of nation, and city

11. *To be beaten down*, כָּתַת *kathath*, 6.
Job 4. 20 are destroyed from morning to evening

12. *To be blotted out or wiped away*, מָחָה *machah*, 2.
Gen. 7. 23 every living substance was destroyed
7. 23 and they were destroyed from the earth
Judg 21. 17 a tribe be not destroyed out of Israel

13. *To be ended, consumed*, סָפָה *saphah*, 2.
1 Ch. 21. 12 three months to be destroyed before thy
Prov 13. 23 (that is) destroyed for want of judgment

14. *To be hunted, destroyed*, צָדָה *tsadah*, 2.
Zeph. 3. 6 none passeth by; their cities are destroy.

15. *Be broken*, רעע *raa*, 2.
Prov 13. 20 a companion of fools shall be destroyed

16. *To be broken, shivered*, שָׁבַר *shabar*, 2.
2 Ch. 14. 13 they were destroyed before the LORD, and
Prov 29. 1 shall suddenly be destroyed, and that
Jer. 22. 20 for all thy lovers are destroyed
48. 4 Moab is destroyed; her little ones have
51. 8 Babylon is suddenly fallen and destroyed
Eze. 30. 8 (when) all her helpers shall be destroyed
Dan. 11. 20 but within few days he shall be destroyed

17. *To be spoiled, destroyed*, שָׁדַד *shadad*.
Psa. 137. 8 daughter of Babylon, who art to be dest.

18. *To be cut off, laid waste, destroyed*, שָׁמַד *shamad*, 2.
Gen. 34. 30 and I shall be destroyed, I and my house
Deut. 4. 26 but shall utterly be destroyed
7. 23 until they be destroyed
12. 30 that they be destroyed from before thee
28. 20 until thou be destroyed, and until thou
28. 24 down upon thee, until thou be destroyed
28. 51 eat..the fruit..until thou be destroyed
28. 45 and overtake thee, till thou be destroyed
28. 61 bring upon thee, until thou be destroyed
Judg 21. 16 seeing the women are destroyed out
2 Sa. 21. 5 we should be destroyed from remaining
Psa. 37. 38 transgressors shall be destroyed together
92. 7 that they shall be destroyed for ever
Isa. 48. 19 his name should not have been..destroy.
Jer. 48. 8 the plain shall be destroyed, as the LORD
48. 42 Moab shall be destroyed from (being) a
Eze. 32. 12 the multitude thereof shall be destroyed
Hos. 10. 8 the sin of Israel, shall be destroyed: the

19. *To destroy*, שָׁמַד *shamad*, 5.
Esth. 7. 4 are sold, I and my people, to be destroy.

20. *To loose off or away, destroy*, ἀπόλλυμι.
1 Co. 10. 9 as some of them..were destroyed of serp.
10. 10 as some..were destroyed of the destroyer
2 Co. 4. 9 Persecuted..cast down, but not destroyed

21. *For marring or corruption*, εἰς φθορὰν *eis phthoran*
2 Pe. 2. 12 But these..made to be taken and destro.

DESTROYED, thing utterly —

Thing devoted (to God or destruction), חֵרֶם *cherem*.
1 Sa. 15. 21 things which should have been utterly de.

DESTROYED, to be utterly —

To be devoted, compressed, חָרַם *charam*, 6.
Exod 22. 20 He that sacrificeth..shall be utterly des.

DESTROYER —

1. *To break, throw down*, הָרַס *haras*, 3.
Isa. 49. 17 thy destroyers and they that made thee

2. *To dry up, waste*, חָרֵב *chareb*, 5.
Judg 16. 24 the destroyer of our country, which slew

3. *To put to death*, מוּת *muth*, 5.
Job 33. 22 soul draweth..and his life to the destroy.

4. *Burglar, one who breaks in or forth*, פָּרִיץ *parits*.
Psa. 17. 4 kept (me from) the paths of the destroyer

5. *To destroy, spoil*, שָׁדַד *shadad*.
Job 15. 21 in prosperity the destroyer shall come

6. *To mar, corrupt, destroy*, שָׁחַת *shachath*, 5.
Exod 12. 23 the LORD..will not suffer the destroyer
*Prov 28. 24 the same (is) the companion of a destroyer
Jer. 4. 7 the destroyer of the Gentiles; Jer. 22. 7.
* Hebrew, *ish mashchith*.

7. *To spoil, take spoil*, שָׁסָה *shasah*.
Jer. 50. 11 ye rejoiced, O ye destroyers of mine heri.

8. *A destroyer*, ὀλοθρευτής *olothreutēs*.
1 Co. 10. 10 some of them..were destroyed of the des.

DESTROYING —

1. *Marring, destroying*, מַשְׁחִית *mashchith*.
Jer. 51. 25 I (am) against thee, O destroying moun.

2. *Marring, destroying*, מַשְׁחֵת *mashcheth*.
Eze. 9. 1 every man (with) his destroying weapon

3. *Destruction*, קֶטֶב *qeteb*.
Isa. 28. 2 a destroying storm, as a flood of mighty

DESTRUCTION —

1. *To be lost*, אָבַד *abad*.
Obad. 12 children..in the day of their destruction

2. *Destruction*, אֲבַדּוֹן [V.L. אֲבַדֹּה] *abaddon*.
Prov 27. 20 Hell and destruction are never full; so

3. *Destruction*, אֲבַדּוֹן *abaddon*.
Job 26. 6 Hell (is) naked..and destruction hath no
28. 22 Destruction and death say, We have heard
31. 12 it (is) a fire (that) consumeth to destruc.
Psa. 88. 11 (or) thy faithfulness in destruction?
Prov 15. 11 Hell and destruction (are) before the L.

4. *Destruction*, אָבְדָן, אָבְדַן *abdan*.
Esth. 8. 6 how can I endure to see the destruction
9. 5 Jews smote all their enemies with..des.

5. *Vapour, calamity*, אֵיד *ed*.
Job 18. 12 destruction (shall be) ready at his side
21. 17 (how, oft) cometh their destruction upon
21. 30 wicked is reserved to the day of destruc.
30. 12 they raise up..the ways of their destruc.
31. 3 (Is) not destruction to the wicked? and a
31. 23 For destruction (from) God (was) a terror
Prov. 1. 27 your destruction cometh as a whirlwind

6. *Destruction, contrition*, דַּכָּא *dakka*.
Psa. 90. 3 Thou turnest man to destruction; and

7. *Ruin, breaking or throwing down*, הֲרִיסוּת *harisuth*.
Isa. 49. 19 the land of thy destruction, shall even now

8. *Breaking or throwing down, ruin*, הֶרֶס *heres*.
Isa. 19. 18 one shall be called, The city of destruction

9. *Destruction*, חֶבֶל *chebel*.
Mic. 2. 10 destroy (you), even with a sore destruction

10. *Waste, drought*, חָרְבָּה *chorbah*.
Psa. 9. 6 destructions are come to a perpetual end

11. *Destruction, misfortune*, כִּיד *kid*.
Job 21. 20 His eyes shall see his destruction, and he

12. *Trouble, destruction*, מְהוּמָה *mehumah*.
Deut. 7. 23 destroy them with a mighty destruction
1 Sa. 5. 9 with a very great destruction: and he
5. 11 there was a deadly destruction throughout

13. *Downfall, ruin*, מְחִתָּה *mechittah*.
Prov 10. 14 mouth of the foolish (is) near destruction
10. 15 the destruction of the poor (is) their
10. 29 but destruction (shall be) to the workers
13. 3 he that openeth wide..shall have destru.
14. 28 in the want of people (is) the destruction
18. 7 A fool's mouth (is) his destruction, and
21. 15 but destruction (shall be) to the workers

14. *Wastes, desolations*, מַשּׁוּאוֹת *mashshuoth*.
Psa. 73. 18 thou castedst them down into destruction

15. *Marring, destruction*, מַשְׁחִית *mashchith*.
2 Ch. 22. 4 the death of his father to his destruction
Eze. 5. 16 shall be for (their) destruction, (and)

16. *Ruin, calamity*, פִּיד *pid*.
Job 30. 24 though they cry in his destruction
31. 29 I rejoiced at the destruction of him that

17. *Destruction*, קֶטֶב *qeteb*.
Deut 32. 24 burning heat, and with bitter destruction
Psa. 91. 6 destruction (that) wasteth at noon-day

18. *Destruction*, קֹטֶב *qoteb*.
Hos. 13. 14 O grave, I will be thy destruction. repe.

19. *Cutting off, destruction*, קְפָדָה *qephadah*.
Eze. 7. 25 Destruction cometh; and they shall seek

20. *Destruction, rapid moving,* קֶרֶץ *qerets.*
Jer. 46. 20 destruction cometh; it cometh out of
21. *Wasting, desolation,* שְׁאִיָּה *sheiyyah.*
Isa. 24. 12 and the gate is smitten with destruction
22. *Breaking, breach,* שֶׁבֶר *sheber.*
Prov 16. 18 Pride (goeth) before destruction, and an
17. 19 that exalteth his gate seeketh destruction
18. 12 Before destruction the heart of man is
Isa. 1. 28 the destruction of the transgressors and
15. 5 they shall raise up a cry of destruction
51. 19 destruction, and the famine, and the
59. 7 wasting and destruction (are) in their
60. 18 wasting nor destruction within thy bor.
Jer. 4. 6 for I will bring evil..a great destruction
4. 20 Destruction upon destruction is cried
6. 1 for evil appeareth..and great destruction
48. 3 spoiling and great destruction
48. 5 enemies have heard a cry of destruction
50. 22 A sound of battle..and of great destruct.
51. 54 destruction from the land of the Chald.
Lam. 2. 11 destruction of the daughter of my people
3. 47 come upon us, desolation and destruct.
3. 48 destruction of the daughter of my people
4. 10 destruction of the daughter of my people
Eze. 32. 9 when I shall bring thy destruction among
23. *Breaking,* שִׁבָּרוֹן *shibbaron.*
Jer. 17. 18 and destroy them with double destruction
24. *Destruction, spoiling,* שֹׁד *shod.*
Job 5. 21 neither shalt thou be afraid of destruct.
5. 22 At destruction and famine thou shalt
Prov 24. 2 their heart studieth destruction, and
Isa. 13. 6 it shall come as a destruction from the
Hos. 7. 13 destruction unto them! because they
9. 6 they are gone because of destruction
Joel 1. 15 as a destruction from the Almighty shall
25. *Vanity, falsehood,* שׁוֹא *sho.*
Psa. 35. 17 rescue my soul from their destructions
26. *Wasting, desolation,* שׁוֹאָה *shoah.*
Psa. 35. 8 Let destruction come upon him at unawa.
35. 8 into that very destruction let him fall
27. *Corruption, destruction, pit,* שְׁחִית *shechith.*
Psa. 107. 20 He..delivered (them) from their destruc.
28. *To mar, corrupt, destroy,* שָׁחַת *shachath,* 5.
2 Ch. 26. 16 heart was lifted up to (his) destruction
29. *Corruption, destruction,* שַׁחַת *shachath.*
Psa. 55. 23 them down into the pit of destruction
103. 4 Who redeemeth thy life from destruction
30. *To cut off, lay waste,* שָׁמַד *shamad,* 5.
Isa. 14. 23 sweep it with the besom of destruction
31. *A treading down,* תְּבוּסָה *tebusah.*
2 Ch. 22. 7 the destruction of Ahaziah was of
32. *A wearying out,* תַּבְלִית *tablith.*
Isa. 10. 25 and mine anger, in their destruction
33. *Passing on, change,* חֲלוֹף *chaloph.*
Prov 31. 8 all such as are appointed to destruction
34. *Loss,* ἀπώλεια *apōleia.*
Matt. 7. 13 (is) the way, that leadeth to destruction
Rom. 9. 22 vessels of wrath fitted to destruction
Phil. 3. 19 Whose end (is) destruction, whose god (is
2 Pe. 2. 1 bring upon themselves swift destruction
3. 16 as (they do)..unto their own destruction
35. *A taking down,* καθαίρεσις *kathairesis.*
2 Co 10. 8 edification, and not for your destruction
13. 10 to edification, and not to destruction
36. *Destruction,* ὄλεθρος *olethros.*
1 Co. 5. 5 unto Satan for the destruction of the flesh
1 Th. 5. 3 sudden destruction cometh upon them
2 Th. 1. 9 be punished with everlasting [destruction]
1 Ti. 6. 9 which drown men in destruction and
37. *A breaking together,* σύντριμμα *suntrimma.*
Rom. 3. 16 Destruction and misery (are) in their ways

DESTRUCTION, utter — [Zech. 14. 11.]
Devotion (to God or destruction), חֵרֶם *cherem.*
1 Ki. 20. 42 whom I appointed to utter destruction

DETAIN, to —
To keep in, restrain, detain, עָצַר *atsar.*
Judg 13. 15 let us detain thee, until we shall have
13. 16 Though thou detain me, I will not eat of

DETAINED —
To be kept in, restrained, detained, עָצַר *atsar,* 2.
1 Sa. 21. 7 there that day, detained before the LORD

DETERMINATE —
To mark out, ὁρίζω *horizō.*
Acts 2. 23 delivered by the determinate counsel and

DETERMINATION —
Judgment, מִשְׁפָּט *mishpat.*
Zeph. 3. 8 my determination (is) to gather the nations

DETERMINE, to —
1. *To say,* אָמַר *amar.*
2 Ch. 2. 1 Solomon determined to build an house
2. *To be determined,* חָתַךְ *chathak,* 2.
Dan. 9. 24 Seventy weeks are determined upon thy
3. *To give counsel,* יָעַץ *yaats.*
2 Ch. 25. 16 that God hath determined to destroy
Isa. 19. 17 which he hath determined against it
4. *To take counsel,* βουλεύομαι *bouleuomai.*
Acts 15. 37 Barnabas [determined] to take with them
5. *To loose thereupon, decide,* ἐπιλύω *epiluō.*
Acts 19. 39 shall be determined in a lawful assembly
6. *To judge, decide,* κρίνω *krinō.*
Acts 3. 13 when he was determined to let (him) go
20. 16 Paul had determined to sail by Ephesus
25. 25 to Augustus, I have determined to send
27. 1 when it was determined that we should
1 Co. 2. 2 I determined not to know any thing
2 Co. 2. 1 I determined this with myself, that I
Titus 3. 12 for I have determined there to winter
7. *To mark out,* ὁρίζω *horizō.*
Luke 22. 22 the Son of man goeth, as it was determ.
Acts 11. 29 determined to send relief unto the breth.
17. 26 and hath determined the times before
8. *To arrange,* τάσσω *tassō.*
Acts 15. 2 they determined that Paul and Barnabas

DETERMINE before, to —
To mark out beforehand, προορίζω *proorizō.*
Acts 4. 28 thy counsel determined before to be done

DETERMINED —
1. *To determine, move sharply, be cut off,* חָרַץ *charats.*
Job 14. 5 Seeing his days (are) determined, the
2. *To place, set, put,* שִׂים, שׂוּם *sum, sim.*
2 Sa. 13. 32 this hath been determined from the day

DETERMINED, to be —
1. *To be determined,* חָרַץ *charats,* 2.
Isa. 10. 23 shall make a consumption, even determin.
28. 22 even determined upon the whole earth
Dan. 9. 26 end of the war desolations are determined
9. 27 that determined shall be poured upon the
11. 36 for that that is determined shall be done
2. *To complete, finish, determine,* כָּלָה *kalah.*
1 Sa. 20. 7 be sure that evil is determined by him
20. 9 knew certainly that evil were determined
20. 33 was determined of his father to slay David
25. 17 for evil is determined against our master
Esth. 7. 7 there was evil determined against him by

DETEST, to —
To have in abomination, שָׁקַץ *shaqats,* 3.
Deut. 7. 26 thou shalt utterly detest it, and thou

DETESTABLE —
Abominable thing, שִׁקּוּץ *shiqquts.*
Jer. 16. 18 with the carcases of their detestable and
Eze. 5. 11 with all thy detestable things, and with
7. 20 (and) of their detestable things therein
11. 18 shall take away all the detestable things
11. 21 after the heart of their detestable things
37. 23 nor with their detestable things, nor with

DE-U'-EL, דְּעוּאֵל *God is knowing.*
Father of Eliasaph, prince of Gad, B.C. 1510.
Num. 1. 14 Of Gad; Eliasaph, the son of D.
2. 14 of Gad..Eliasaph the son of D. [or Reuel]
7. 42 D. prince of the children of Gad, (offered)
7. 47 the offering of Eliasaph the son of D.
Deut 10. 20 children of Gad..Eliasaph the son of D.

DEVICE —
1. *Meditation,* הִגָּיוֹן *higgayon.*
Lam. 3. 62 and their device against me all the day
2. *Reason, device, reckoning,* חֶשְׁבּוֹן *cheshbon.*
Eccl. 9. 10 (there is) no work, nor device, nor know.
3. *Wicked device,* מְזִמָּה *mezimmah.*
Job 21. 27 the devices (which) ye wrongfully imagine
Psa. 10. 2 in the devices that they have imagined
Jer. 51. 11 his device (is) against Babylon, to destroy
4. *Thought, device,* מַחֲשָׁבָה *machashabah.*
Jer. 18 11 I frame..and devise a device against you
5. *Thought, device,* מַחֲשֶׁבֶת *machashebeth.*
2 Ch. 2. 14 to find out every device which shall be
Esth. 8 3 device that he had devised against the
9. 25 his wicked device, which he devised
Job 5. 12 disappointeth the devices of the crafty
Psa. 33. 10 maketh the devices of the people of none
Prov 19 21 (There are) many devices in a man's heart
Jer. 11. 19 that they had devised devices against me
18. 12 we will walk after our own devices, and
18. 18 let us devise devices against Jeremiah
Dan. 11. 24 he shall forecast his devices against the
11. 25 they shall forecast devices against him
6. *Inward or inner thought,* ἐνθύμησις *enthumēsis.*
Acts 17. 29 or stone, graven by art and man's device
7. *Thought, plan,* νόημα *noēma.*
2 Co. 2. 11 for we are not ignorant of his devices

DEVICES —
Counsels, מוֹעֵצוֹת *moetsoth.*
Prov. 1. 31 and be filled with their own devices

DEVIL —
1. *Hairy one, kid, goat,* שָׂעִיר *sair.*
Lev. 17. 7 no more offer their sacrifices unto devils
2 Ch. 11. 15 for the high places, and for the devils
2. *Spoiler, destroyer,* שֵׁד *shed.*
Deut 32. 17 They sacrificed unto devils, not to God
Psa. 106. 37 their sons and their daughters unto devils
3. *Daimon, demon, shade,* δαιμόνιον *daimonion.*
Matt. 7. 22 in thy name have cast out devils? and in
9. 33 when the devil was cast out, the dumb
9. 34 devils through the prince of the devils
10. 8 the lepers, raise the dead, cast out devils
11. 18 nor drinking, and they say, He hath a devil
12. 24 This (fellow) doth not cast out devils
12. 24 but by Beelzebub the prince of the devils
12. 27 if I by Beelzebub cast out devils, by whom
12. 28 if I cast out devils by the Spirit of God
17. 18 Jesus rebuked the devil; and he departed
Mark 1. 34 divers diseases, and cast out many devils
1. 34 suffered not the devils to speak, because
1. 39 throughout all Galilee, and cast out devils
3. 15 to heal sicknesses, and to cast out devils
3. 22 prince of the devils casteth he out devils
6. 13 they cast out many devils, and anointed
7. 26 cast forth the devil out of her daughter
7. 29 the devil is gone out of thy daughter
7. 30 she found the devil gone out, and her
9. 38 saw one casting out devils in thy name
16. 9 [out of whom he had cast seven devils]
16. 17 [In my name shall they cast out devils]
Luke 4. 33 which had a spirit of an unclean devil
4. 35 when the devil had thrown him in the
4. 41 devils also came out of many, crying out
7. 33 nor drinking wine, and ye say, He hath a d.
8. 2 Magdalene, out of whom went seven dev.
8. 27 a certain man, which had devils
8. 30 because many devils were entered into
8. 33 Then went the devils out of the man, and
8. 35, 38 man, out of whom the devils were de.
9. 1 them power and authority over all devils
9. 42 the devil threw him down, and tare (him)
9. 49 saw one casting out devils in thy name
10. 17 the devils are subject unto us through
11. 14 he was casting out a devil, and it was
11. 14 when the devil was gone out, the dumb
11. 15 some of them said, He casteth out devils
11. 15 through Beelzebub the chief of the devils
11. 18 that I cast out devils through Beelzebub
11. 19 if I by Beelzebub cast out devils, by
11. 20 if I with the finger of God cast out devils
13. 32 I cast out devils, and I do cures to day
John 7 20 Thou hast a devil: who goeth about to
8. 48 thou art a Samaritan, and hast a devil?
8. 49 I have not a devil; but I honour my
8. 52 Now we know that thou hast a devil
10. 20 He hath a devil, and is mad; why hear
10. 21 Can a devil open the eyes of the blind?
1 Co. 10. 20 they sacrifice to devils, and not to God
10. 20 ye should have fellowship with devils
10. 21 the cup of the Lord, and the cup of devils
10. 21 the Lord's table, and of the table of devils
1 Ti. 4. 1 seducing spirits, and doctrines of devils
Jas. 2. 19 the devils also believe, and tremble
Rev. 9. 20 they should not worship devils, and idols
4. *A deified spirit,* δαίμων *daimōn.*
Matt. 8. 31 the devils besought him, saying, If thou
Mark 5. 12 [the devils] besought him, saying, Send us
Luke 8. 29 driven [of the devil] into the wilderness
Rev. 16. 14 they are the spirits of [devils,] working
18. 2 is become the habitation of [devils,] and
5. *Accuser, calumniator,* διάβολος *diabolos.*
Matt. 4. 1 the wilderness to be tempted of the dev
4. 5 devil taketh him up into the holy city
4. 8 the devil taketh him up into an exceed.
4. 11 the devil leaveth him! and, behold, angels
13. 39 The enemy that sowed them is the devil
25. 41 prepared for the devil and his angels
Luke 4. 2 Being forty days tempted of the devil
4. 3 the devil said unto him, If thou be the
4. 5 [the devil,] taking him up into an high
4. 6 the devil said unto him, All this power
4. 13 the devil had ended all the temptation
8. 12 then cometh the devil, and taketh away
John 6. 70 you twelve, and one of you is a devil?
8. 44 Ye are of (your) father the devil, and the
13. 2 the devil having now put into the heart
Acts 10. 38 all that were oppressed of the devil
13. 10 (thou) child of the devil, (thou) enemy of
Eph. 4. 27 Neither give place to the devil
6. 11 to stand against the wiles of the devil
1 Ti. 3. 6 fall into the condemnation of the devil
3. 7 into reproach and the snare of the devil
2 Ti. 2. 26 themselves out of the snare of the devil
Heb. 2. 14 had the power of death, that is, the devil
Jas. 4. 7 Resist the devil, and he will flee from you
1 Pe. 5. 8 your adversary the devil, as a roaring lion
1 Jo. 3. 8 He that committeth sin is of the devil
3. 8 for the devil sinneth from the beginning
3. 8 he might destroy the works of the devil
3. 10 and the children of the devil; whosoever
Jude 9 when contending with the devil, he dis.
Rev. 2. 10 devil shall cast (some) of you into prison
12. 9 that old serpent, called the Devil, and
12. 12 the devil is come down unto you, having
20. 2 that old serpent, which is the Devil, and
20. 10 the devil that deceived them was cast

DEVIL, to be possessed with a —
To be demonized, δαιμονίζομαι *daimonizomai.*
Matt. 9. 32 to him a dumb man possessed with a dev.
12. 22 unto him one possessed with a devil
Mark 5. 15 see him that was possessed with the devil
5. 16 to him that was possessed with the devil
5. 18 he that had been possessed with the devil

DEVIL, to have or be vexed with a —
To be demonized, δαιμονίζομαι *daimonizomai.*
Matt 15. 22 daughter is grievously vexed with a devil
John 10. 21 not the words of him that hath a devil

DEVILISH —
Demoniacal, δαιμονιώδης *daimoniōdēs.*
Jas. 3. 15 but (is) earthly, sensual, devilish

DEVILS, to be possessed with or of the —
To be demonized, δαιμονίζομαι *daimonizomai.*
Matt. 4. 24 those which were possessed with devils
8. 16 many that were possessed with devils
8. 28 there met him two possessed with devils
8. 33 befallen to the possessed of the devils
Mark 1. 32 and them that were possessed with devils
Luke 8. 36 he that was possessed of the devils was

DEVISE, to —
1. *To devise, feign*, בָּדָא *bada.*
1 Ki. 12. 33 which he had devised of his own heart
2. *To think, devise*, דָּמָה *damah*, 3.
2 Sa. 21. 5 that deviseth against us (that) we should
3. *To devise, design, purpose*, זָמַם *zamam.*
Psa. 31. 13 they devised to take away my life
Jer. 51. 12 the LORD hath both devised and done that
Lam. 2. 17 LORD hath done (that) which he had devis.
4. *To plow, grave, devise*, חָרַשׁ *charash.*
Prov. 3. 29 Devise not evil against thy neighbour
6. 14 he deviseth mischief continually
6. 18 heart that deviseth wicked imaginations
14. 22 Do they not err that devise evil? but
14. 22 truth (shall be) to them that devise good
5. *To think, devise, reckon*, חָשַׁב *chashab.*
Exod31. 4 To devise cunning works, to work in gold
35. 32 to devise curious works, to work in gold
35. 35 and of those that devise cunning work
2 Sa. 14. 14 yet doth he devise means, that his banis.
Esth. 8. 3 that he had devised against the Jews
9. 24 had devised against the Jews to destroy
9. 25 which he devised against the Jews, should
Psa. 35. 4 let them be..brought to confusion that d.
35. 20 they devise deceitful matters against
36. 4 He deviseth mischief upon his bed; he
41. 7 against me do they devise my hurt
52. 2 Thy tongue deviseth mischiefs; like a
Prov 16. 30 shutteth his eyes to devise froward things
Jer. 11. 19 and I knew not that they had devised
18. 11 I frame evil against you, and devise a
18. 18 Then said they, Come, and let us devise
48. 2 Heshbon they have devised evil against it
Eze. 11. 2 these (are) the men that devise mischief
Mic. 2. 1 Woe to them that devise iniquity, and
2. 3 against this family do I devise an evil
6. *To think, devise, reckon*, חָשַׁב *chashab*, 3.
Prov 16. 9 A man's heart deviseth his way: but the
24. 8 He that deviseth to do evil shall be called
7. *To give counsel*, יָעַץ *yaats.*
Isa. 32. 7 he deviseth wicked devices to destroy the
32. 8 But the liberal deviseth liberal things

DEVISE, to cunningly —
To make wise, σοφίζω *sophizō.*
2 Pe. 1. 16 not followed cunningly devised fables

DEVISED —
Thought, device, מַחֲשֶׁבֶת *machashebeth.*
Esth. 8. 5 the letters devised by Haman the son of

DEVOTE, to —
To devote (to God or destruction), חָרַם *charam*, 5.
Lev. 27. 28 that a man shall devote unto the LORD of

DEVOTED —
A thing devoted (to God or destruction), חֵרֶם *cherem.*
Lev. 27. 21 be holy unto the LORD, as a field devoted
27. 29 None devoted..shall be redeemed; (but)

DEVOTED, to be —
To be devoted, חָרַם *charam*, 6.
Lev. 27. 29 which shall be devoted of men, shall be

DEVOTED thing —
A thing devoted, חֵרֶם *cherem.*
Lev. 27. 28 Notwithstanding no devoted thing that a
27. 28 every devoted thing (is) most holy unto
Num 18. 14 Every thing devoted in Israel shall be

DEVOTION —
Object of worship or devotion, σέβασμα *sebasma.*
Acts 17. 23 I passed by, and beheld your devotions

DEVOUR, to —
1. *To eat, consume, devour*, אָכַל *akal.*
Gen. 31. 15 and hath quite devoured also our money
37. 20 Some evil beast hath devoured him: and
37. 33 an evil beast hath devoured him
49. 27 in the morning he shall devour the prey
Exod 24. 17 glory of the LORD (was) like devouring fire
Lev. 10. 2 out fire from the LORD, and devoured them
Num26. 10 fire devoured two hundred and fifty men
Deut31. 17 they shall be devoured, and many evils
32. 42 and my sword shall devour flesh
Judg. 9. 15 let fire..devour the cedars of Lebanon
9. 20 devour the men of Shechem, and the house
9. 20 the house of Millo, and devour Abimelech
2 Sa. 2. 26 Shall the sword devour for ever? knowest
11. 25 sword devoureth one as well as another
18. 8 devoured more..than the sword devoured
22. 9 and fire out of his mouth devoured
2 Ch. 7. 13 I command the locusts to devour the land
Job 18. 13 It shall devour the strength of his skin
18. 13 first born of death shall devour his stren.
Psa. 18. 8 and fire out of his mouth devoured
21. 9 his wrath, and the fire shall devour them
Psa. 50. 3 a fire shall devour before him, and it
78. 45 flies among them, which devoured them
79. 7 they have devoured Jacob, and laid waste
105. 35 and devoured the fruit of their ground
Prov.30. 14 to devour the poor from off the earth
Isa. 1. 7 land, strangers devour it in your presence
5. 24 as the fire devoureth the stubble, and the
9. 12 they shall devour Israel with open mouth
9. 18 it shall devour the briers and thorns, and
10. 17 devour his thorns and his briers in one
24. 6 Therefore hath the curse devoured the
26. 11 fire of thine enemies shall devour them
31. 8 sword, not of a mean man, shall devour
33. 11 your breath, (as) fire, shall devour you
56. 9 All ye beasts of the field, come to devour
Jer. 2. 3 all that devour him shall offend
2. 30 your own sword hath devoured your pro.
3. 24 shame hath devoured the labour of our
5. 14 thy mouth fire..and it shall devour them
8. 16 have devoured the land, and all that is
10. 25 they have eaten up Jacob, and devoured
12. 12 sword of the LORD shall devour from the
15. 3 the beasts of the earth, to devour and de.
17. 27 it shall devour the palaces of Jerusalem
21. 14 shall devour all things round about it
30. 16 they that devour thee shall be devoured
46. 10 the sword shall devour, and it shall be
46. 14 the sword shall devour round about thee
48. 45 shall devour the corner of Moab, and the
50. 7 All that found them have devoured them
50. 17 the king of Assyria hath devoured him
50. 32 and it shall devour all round about him
51. 34 the king of Babylon hath devoured me
Lam. 2. 3 flaming fire, (which) devoureth round
4. 11 it hath devoured the foundations thereof
Eze. 7. 15 famine and pestilence shall devour him
15. 4 the fire devoureth both the ends of it
15. 5 when the fire hath devoured it, and it is
15. 7 and (another) fire shall devour them
16. 20 thou sacrificed unto them to be devoured
19. 3 learned to catch the prey; it devoured m.
19. 6 learned to catch the prey, (and) devoured
19. 14 hath devoured her fruit, so that she
20. 47 it shall devour every green tree in thee
22. 25 they have devoured souls; they have taken
28. 18 it shall devour thee, and I will bring thee
33. 27 will I give to the beasts to be devoured
34. 28 shall the beast of the land devour them
36. 14 thou shalt devour men no more, neither
Hos. 5. 7 now shall a month devour them with their
7. 7 and have devoured their judges
7. 9 Strangers have devoured his strength
8. 14 and it shall devour the palaces thereof
11. 6 devour (them), because of their own cou.
13. 8 and there will I devour them like a lion
Joel 1. 19, 20 the fire hath devoured the pastures
2. 3 A fire devoureth before them, and behind
2. 5 flame of fire that devoureth the stubble
Amos 1. 4 shall devour the palaces of Ben-hadad
1. 7, 10 which shall devour the palaces thereof
1. 12 which shall devour the palaces of Bozrah
1. 14 it shall devour the palaces thereof, with
2. 2 it shall devour the palaces of Kirioth
2. 5 it shall devour the palaces of Jerusalem
4. 9 the palmer worm devoured (them)
5. 6 fire in the house of Joseph, and devour (it)
7. 4 it devoured the great deep, and did eat
Obad. 18 they shall kindle in them, and devour
Nah. 2. 13 the sword shall devour thy young lions
3. 13 the fire shall devour thy bars
3. 15 There shall the fire devour thee; the
Hab. 3. 14 rejoicing (was) as to devour the poor sec.
Zech. 9. 15 they shall devour, and subdue with sling
11. 1 that the fire may devour thy cedars
12. 6 they shall devour all the people round
2. *To eat, consume, devour*, אֲכַל *akal.*
Dan. 7. 5 said thus unto it, Arise, devour much fl.
7. 7 it devoured and brake in pieces, and
7. 19 (which) devoured, brake in pieces, and
7. 23 shall devour the whole earth, and shall
3. *Eating, food*, אָכְלָה *oklah.*
Jer. 12. 9 the beasts of the field, come to devour
Eze. 23. 37 for them through (the fire), to devour
39. 4 the beasts of the field to be devoured
4. *To swallow up*, בָּלַע *bala.*
Gen. 41. 7 the seven thin ears devoured the seven
41. 24 thin ears devoured the seven good ears
5. *To swallow up*, בָּלַע *bala*, 3.
Prov 19. 28 mouth of the wicked devoureth iniquity
Hab. 1. 13 when the wicked devoureth (the man that)
6. *To swallow, devour, retain*, יָלַע *yala.*
Prov 20. 25 the man (who) devoureth (that which is)
7. *To eat, consume*, לָחַם *lacham.*
Deut32. 24 devoured with burning heat, and with bi.
8. *To feed, consume*, רָעָה *raah.*
Psa. 80. 13 wild beast of the field doth devour it
9. *To pant after, swallow up*, שָׁאַף *shaaph.*
Isa. 42. 14 I will destroy and devour at once
10. *To eat, eat up*, ἐσθίω *esthiō.*
Heb. 10. 27 which shall devour the adversaries
11. *To drink down, swallow up*, καταπίνω *katapinō.*
1 Pe. 5. 8 walketh about, seeking whom he may d.
12. *To eat down*, καταφάγω *kataphagō.*
Matt23. 14 ye devour widows' houses, and for a pre.
Mark12. 40 Which devour widows' houses, and for a
Luke 8. 5 and the fowls of the air devoured it
Luke15. 30 which hath devoured thy living with har.
20. 47 Which devour widows' houses, and for a
2 Co. 11. 20 if a man devour (you), if a man take (of
Gal. 5. 15 if ye bite and devour one another, take
Rev. 11. 5 fire proceedeth..and devoureth their
12. 4 to devour her child as soon as it was born
20. 9 from God out of heaven, and devoured

DEVOUR up, to —
1. *To eat, consume, devour*, אָכַל *akal.*
Eze. 36. 13 Thou (land) devourest up men, and hast
2. *To eat down*, καταφάγω *kataphagō.*
Matt 13. 4 and the fowls came and devoured them up
Mark 4. 4 fowls of the air came and devoured it up

DEVOURED, to be —
1. *To be eaten up, consumed*, אָכַל *akal*, 2.
Jer. 30. 16 Therefore all they..shall be devoured
Eze. 23. 25 thy residue shall be devoured by the fire
Zeph. 1. 18 the whole land shall be devoured by the
3. 8 the earth shall be devoured with the fire
Zech 9. 4 and she shall be devoured with fire
2. *To be eaten up, consumed*, אָכַל *akal*, 4.
Isa. 1. 20 ye shall be devoured with the sword
Nah. 1. 10 shall be devoured as stubble fully dry

DEVOURER —
To eat, consume, devour, אָכַל *akal.*
Mal. 3. 11 I will rebuke the devourer for your sakes

DEVOURING —
1. *To eat, consume, devour*, אָכַל *akal.*
Isa. 29. 6 tempest, and the flame of devouring fire
30. 27 and his tongue as a devouring fire
30. 30 the flame of a devouring fire..scattering
33. 14 shall dwell with the devouring fire? who
2. *Swallowing up*, בֶּלַע *bela.*
Psa. 52. 4 Thou lovest all devouring words, O (thou)

DEVOUT (persons) —
1. *Taking or receiving well, devout*, εὐλαβής *eulabēs.*
Luke 2. 25 the same man (was) just and devout
Acts 2. 5 devout men, out of every nation under
8. 2 devout men carried Stephen (to his burial)
2. *Reverential*, εὐσεβής *eusebēs.*
Acts 10. 2 (A) devout (man), and one that feared God
10. 7 a devout soldier of them that waited on
22. 12 Ananias, a devout man according to the
3. *To worship, be devout, reverential*, σέβομαι.
Acts 13. 50 Jews stirred up the devout and honour.
17. 4 and of the devout Greeks a great multit.
17. 17 with the Jews, and with the devout persons

DEW —
Dew, טַל *tal.*
Gen. 27. 28 God give thee of the dew of heaven, and
27. 39 and of the dew of heaven from above
Exod16. 13 in the morning the dew lay round about
16. 14 when the dew that lay was gone up
Num 11. 9 dew fell upon the camp in the night
Deut 32. 2 my speech shall distil as the dew, as the
33. 13 the precious things of heaven, for the d.
33. 28 also his heavens shall drop down dew
Judg. 6. 37 if the dew be on the fleece only, and
6. 38 wringed the dew out of the fleece, a bowl
6. 39 upon all the ground let there be dew
6. 40 and there was dew on all the ground
2 Sa. 1. 21 (let there be) no dew, neither (let there
17. 12 we will light upon him as the dew falleth
1 Ki. 17. 1 there shall not be dew nor rain these
Job 29. 19 the dew lay all night upon my branch
38. 28 or who hath begotten the drops of dew?
Psa. 110. 3 morning: thou hast the dew of thy youth
133. 3 As the dew of Hermon..that descended
Prov. 3. 20 and the clouds drop down the dew
19. 12 but his favour (is) as dew upon the grass
Song 5. 2 for my head is filled with dew, (and) my
Isa. 18. 4 like a cloud of dew in the heat of harvest
26. 19 for thy dew (is as) the dew of herbs, and
Dan. 4. 15, 23 let it be wet with the dew of heaven
4. 25 shall wet thee with the dew of heaven
4. 33 his body was wet with the dew of heaven
5. 21 his body was wet with the dew of heaven
Hos. 6. 4 for your goodness (is) as..the early dew
13. 3 and as the early dew that passeth away
14. 5 I will be as the dew unto Israel: he shall
Mic. 5. 7 in the midst of many people as a dew
Hag. 1. 10 the heaven over you is stayed from dew
Zech. 8. 12 the heavens shall give their dew; and I

DIADEM —
1. *Mitre*, מִצְנֶפֶת *mitsnepheth.*
Eze. 21. 26 Remove the diadem, and take off the cr.
2. *Diadem*, צָנִיף, [V.L. צָנוּף] *tsaniph.*
Isa. 62. 3 Thou shalt also be..a royal diadem in
3. *Diadem, hood*, צָנִיף *tsaniph.*
Job 29. 14 my judgment (was) as a robe and a diad.
4. *Diadem, tiara*, צְפִירָה *tsephirah.*
Isa. 28. 5 for a diadem of beauty, unto the residue

DIAL —
Going up, ascent, step, מַעֲלָה *maalah.*
2 Ki. 20. 11 by which it had gone down in the dial of
Isa. 38. 8 is gone down in the sun-dial of Ahaz, ten

DIAMOND —
1. *Diamond, adamant, emerald*, יַהֲלֹם *yahalom.*
Exod28. 18 the second row (shall be)..a diamond
39. 11 an emerald, a sapphire, and a diamond
Eze. 28. 13 the sardius, topaz, and the diamond, the

2. *Brier, diamond, point*, שָׁמִיר *shamir*.
Jer. 17. 1 The sin..(is) written..the point of a dia.

DI-A'-NA, Ἄρτεμις, *Artemis*.
One of the principal goddesses of the Greeks and Romans. Artemis is her Greek name.
Acts 19. 24 a silversmith..made silver shrines for D.
19. 27 the temple of the great goddess D. should
19. 28 saying, Great (is) D. of the Ephesians
19. 34 cried out, Great (is) D. of the Ephesians
19. 35 city of..Ephesians is a worshipper of..D.

DIB-LA'-IM, דִּבְלַיִם *double embrace*.
Father of Gomer wife of Hosea the prophet, B.C. 800.
Hos. 1. 3 went and took Gomer the daughter of D.

DIB'-LATH, דִּבְלָה *circle*.
A place in the N. of Canaan, which should be spelled Diblah, or rather Riblah.
Eze. 6. 14 desolate than the wilderness toward D.

DI'-BON, דִּיבֹן, דִּבֹן *river course*.
1. A city N. of the Arnon, S.W. of Heshbon, rebuilt by Gad, given to Reuben, and retaken by Moab.
Num 21. 30 Heshbon is perished even unto D., and
32. 3 Ataroth, and D., and Jazer, and Nimrah
32. 34 And the children of Gad built D., and A.
Isa. 15. 2 He is gone up to Bajith, and to D.
2. A city, perhaps the same as No. 1.
Josh. 13. 9 and all the plain of Medeba unto D.
13. 17 D., and Bamoth-baal, and Beth-baal-meon
Jer. 48. 18 Thou daughter that dost inhabit D.
48. 22 And upon D., and upon Nebo, and upon
3. A town in Judah; perhaps the same as (Dimonah) Dibon.
Neh. 11. 25 and at D., and (in) the villages thereof

DI'-BON GAD, דִּיבֹן גָּד.
A halting place of the Israelites after leaving Egypt, and was in Moab between *Ije-Abarim* and *Almon-diblathaim*, and is no doubt the same place called Dibon.
Num 33. 45 departed from Iim and pitched in D.-g.
33. 46 they removed from D.-g., and encamped

DIB'-RI, דִּבְרִי *on the pasture born*.
A Danite, whose daughter had married an Egyptian and whose son was stoned for blasphemy, B.C. 1490.
Lev. 24. 11 Shelomith, the daughter of D., of the tribe

DID, he —
Vaheb, (a place in Suph,) וָהֵב *vaheb*.
Num 21. 14 What he did in the Red sea, and in the

DI-DY'-MUS, Δίδυμος *a twin*.
The surname of the apostle Thomas.
John 11. 16 Then said Thomas, which is called D.
20. 24 Thomas, one of the twelve, called D.
21. 2 together Simon Peter, and T. called D.

DIE —
1. *Death*, מָוֶת *maveth*.
Num. 6. 7 not make himself unclean..when they d.
1 Sa. 20. 31 fetch him unto me, for he shall surely die
26. 16 (As) the LORD liveth, ye (are) worthy to d.
2 Sa. 3. 33 the king lamented..and said..as a fool d.
12. 5 the LORD liveth, the man..shall surely die
Psa. 49. 17 For when he dieth he shall carry nothing
Prov 11. 7 When a wicked man dieth, (his) expecta.
Eccl. 3. 19 as the one dieth, so dieth the other; yea
Jer. 26. 11 saying, This man (is) worthy to die; for
26. 16 This man (is) not worthy to die: for he
Eze. 18. 23 pleasure at all that the wicked should d.?
Jon. 4. 3,8 (It is) better for me to die than to live
2. *Death, dying*, תְּמוּתָה *temuthah*.
Psa. 79. 11 preserve..those that are appointed to die

DIE, to —
1. *To expire, gasp, breathe out*, גָּוַע *gava*.
Gen. 6. 17 everything that (is) in the earth shall die
7. 21 all flesh died that moved upon the earth
Num 17. 12 Behold, we die, we perish, we all perish
17. 13 shall we be consumed with dying?
20. 3 spake, saying, Would God that we had d.
20. 3 when our brethren died before the LORD
Job 27. 5 till I die I will not remove mine integrity
29. 18 I shall die in my nest, and I shall multi.
36. 12 and they shall die without knowledge
Psa. 88. 15 afflicted and ready to die from (my) youth
104. 29 they die, and return to their dust
Zech 13. 8 parts therein shall be cut off (and) die
2. *To die*, מוּת *muth*.
Gen. 2. 17 thou eatest thereof thou shalt surely die
3. 3 neither shall ye touch it, lest ye die
3. 4 unto the woman, Ye shall not surely die
5. 5 nine hundred and thirty years: and he d.
5. 8 nine hundred and twelve years: and he d.
5. 11 nine hundred and five years: and he died
5. 14 nine hundred and ten years: and he died
5. 17 hundred ninety and five years: and he d.
5. 20 hundred sixty and two years: and he died
5. 27 hundred sixty and nine years: and he died
5. 31 seventy and seven years: and he died
7. 22 of all that (was) in the dry (land,) died
9. 29 nine hundred and fifty years: and he died
11. 28 Haran died before his father Terah in the
11. 32 two hundred and five years: and Terah d.
19. 19 lest some evil take me, and I die
20. 7 know thou that thou shalt surely die, thou
23. 2 Sarah died in Kirjath-arba; the same (is)
25. 8 Abraham gave up the ghost, and died in
Gen. 25. 17 he gave up the ghost and died, and was
25. 32 I (am) at the point to die; and what profit
26. 9 Because I said, Lest I die for her
27. 4 that my soul may bless thee before I die
30. 1 unto Jacob, Give me children, or else I die
33. 13 overdrive them one day..flock will die
35. 8 Rebekah's nurse, died, and she was buried
35. 18 her soul was in departing, for she died
35. 19 Rachel died, and was buried in the way
35. 29 Isaac gave up the ghost, and died, and
36. 33 Bela died, and Jobab the son of..reigned
36. 34 And Jobab died, and Husham of the land
36. 35 Husham died, and Hadad the son of B.
36. 36 Hadad died, and Samlah of Masrekah reig.
36. 37 Samlah died, and Saul of Rehoboth (by)
36. 38 Saul died, and Baal-hanan the son of A.
36. 39 Baal-hanan the son of Achbor died, and
38. 11 peradventure he die also, as his brethren
38. 12 the daughter of Shuah, Judah's wife, died
42. 2 buy for us..that we may live, and not die
42. 20 words be verified, and ye shall not die
43. 8 that we may live, and not die, both we
44. 9 both let him die, and we also will be my
44. 22 leave his father..(his father) would die
44. 31 the lad (is) not (with us), that he will die
45. 28 I will go and see him before I die
46. 12 Er and Onan died in the land of Canaan
46. 30 Now let me die, since I have seen thy face
47. 15 why should we die in thy presence? for the
47. 19 Wherefore shall we die before thine eyes
47. 19 give (us) seed, that we may live, and not d.
47. 29 the time drew nigh that Israel must die
48. 7 Rachel died by me in the land of Canaan
48. 21 I die; but God shall be with you, and
50. 5 Lo, I die: in my grave which I have dig.
50. 24 I die: and God will surely visit you, and
50. 26 Joseph died, (being) an hundred and ten
Exod. 1. 6 Joseph died, and all his brethren, and
2. 23 it came to pass..the king of Egypt died
7. 18 the fish that (is) in the river shall die
7. 21 fish that (was) in the river died
8. 13 the frogs died out of the houses, out of
9. 4 there shall nothing die of all (that is)
9. 6 and all the cattle of Egypt died
9. 6 but of the cattle of..Israel died not
9. 19 come down upon them, and they shall die
10. 28 day thou seest my face thou shalt die
11. 5 first born in the land of Egypt shall die
14. 11 taken us away to die in the wilderness
14. 12 than that we should die in the wilderness
16. 3 Would to God we had died by the
20. 19 but let not God speak with us, lest we die
21. 12 He that smiteth a man so that he die
21. 14 take him from mine altar, that he may die
21. 18 and he die not, but keepeth (his) bed
21. 20 if a man smite his servant..and he die
21. 28 ox gore a man or a woman, that they die
21. 35 if one man's ox hurt another's, that he die
22. 2 If a thief..be smitten that he die
22. 10 it die, or be hurt, or driven away, no man
22. 14 it be hurt, or die, the owner (thereof)
28. 35 and when he cometh out, that he die not
28. 43 that they bear not iniquity, and die
30. 20 shall wash with water, that they die not
30. 21 shall wash their hands..that they die not
Lev. 8. 35 keep the charge of the LORD, that ye die
10. 2 devoured them; and they died before the
10. 6 neither rend your clothes, lest ye die, and
10. 7 ye shall not go out..lest ye die
10. 9 Do not drink wine..lest ye die
11. 39 And if any beast of which ye may eat die
15. 31 that they die not in their uncleanness
16. 1 when they offered before the Lord, and d.
16. 2 he come not at all times..that he die not
16. 13 he shall put the incense..that he die not
20. 20 bear their sin; they shall die childless
22. 9 lest they bear sin for it, and die therefore
Num. 3. 4 Nadab and Abihu died before the LORD
4. 15 not touch (any) holy thing, lest they die
4. 19 that they may live, and not die, when they
4. 20 they shall not go in..lest they die
6. 9 if any man die very suddenly by him, and
14. 2 Would God that we had died in the land
14. 2 or would God we had died in this
14. 35 in this wilderness..there they shall die
14. 37 died by the plague before the Lord
15. 36 and stoned him with stones, and he died
16. 29 these men die the common death of..men
16. 49 they that died in the plague were fourteen
16. 49 them that died about the matter of Korah
17. 10 their murmurings from me, that they die
17. 13 unto the tabernacle of the LORD shall die
18. 3 that neither they, nor ye also, die
18. 22 lest they bear sin, and die
18. 32 neither shall ye pollute..lest ye die
19. 14 This (is) the law, when a man dieth in a
20. 1 Miriam died there, and was buried there
20. 4 that we and our cattle should die there?
20. 26 gathered (unto his people,) and shall die
20. 28 Aaron died there in the top of the mount
21. 5 up out of Egypt to die in the wilderness
21. 6 and much people of Israel died
23. 10 Let me die the death of the righteous
25. 9 those that died in the plague were twenty
26. 11 the children of Korah died not
26. 19 Er and Onan died in the land of Canaan
26. 61 Nadab and Abihu died, when they offered
26. 65 They shall surely die in the wilderness
27. 3 Our father died in the wilderness, and he
27. 3 but died in his own sin, and had no sons
27. 8 If a man die, and have no son, then ye
33. 38 Aaron the priest went up..and died there
Num 35. 12 that the manslayer die not, until he stand
35. 16 with an instrument of iron, so that he die
35. 17, 18 wherewith he may die, and he die, he
35. 20 hurl at him by laying of wait, that he die
35. 21 smite him with his hand, that he die
35. 23 with any stone, wherewith a man may die
35. 23 cast (it) upon him, that he die, and (was)
35. 30 against any person (to cause him) to die
Deut. 5. 25 why should we die? for this great fire
5. 25 if we hear the voice..then we shall die
10. 6 there Aaron died, and there he was buried
13. 10 shalt stone him with stones, that he die
17. 5 stone them with stones, till they die
17. 12 the man that will..not hearken..shall d.
18. 16 neither let me see this..that I die not
18. 20 prophet which shall presume..shall die
19. 5 lighteth upon his neighbour, that he die
19. 11 smite him mortally that he die, and fleeth
19. 12 and fetch him thence..that he may die
20. 5, 6, 7 lest he die in the battle, and another
21. 21 shall stone him with stones, that he die
22. 21 shall stone her with stones that she die
22. 22 they shall both of them die, (both) the m.
22. 24 stone them with stones that they die
22. 25 the man only that lay with her shall die
24. 3 if the latter husband die, which took her
24. 7 that thief shall die; and thou shalt put
25. 5 one of them die, and have no child, the
32. 50 die in the mount whither thou goest up
32. 50 as Aaron thy brother died in mount Hor
33. 6 Let Reuben live, and not die; and let
34. 5 So Moses..died there in the land of Moab
Josh. 5. 4 the men of war, died in the wilderness by
10. 11 LORD cast down great stones..and they d.
10. 11 (they were) more which died with hailst.
20. 9 not die by the hand of the avenger of
24. 29 it came to pass..that Joshua..died
24. 33 Eleazar the son of Aaron died; and they
Judg. 1. 7 brought him to Jerusalem, and there he d.
2. 8 Joshua..the servant of the LORD, died
2. 21 nations which Joshua left when he died
3. 11 And Othniel the son of Kenaz died
4. 21 he was fast asleep and weary: so he died
6. 23 Peace (be) unto thee..thou shalt not die
6. 30 Bring out thy son, that he may die
8. 32 Gideon the son of Joash died in a good
9. 49 the men of the tower of Shechem died
9. 54 young man thrust him through, and he d.
10. 2 he judged Israel..and died, and was
10. 5 And Jair died, and was buried in Camon
12. 7 Then died Jephthah the Gileadite, and
12. 10 Then died Ibzan, and was buried at Beth.
12. 15 Abdon the son of Hillel the Pirathonite d.
13. 22 We shall surely die, because we have
15. 18 now shall I die for thirst, and fall into
16. 30 Samson said, Let me die with the Philis.
Ruth. 1. 3 Elimelech, Naomi's husband, died; and
1. 5 Mahlon and Chilion died also both of them
1. 17 Where thou diest, will I die, and there
1 Sa. 2. 33 all the increase of thine house shall die
2. 34 in one day they shall die both of them
4. 18 he died; for he was an old man, and
5. 12 men that died not were smitten with the
12. 19 Pray for thy servants..that we die not
14. 39 be in Jonathan my son, he shall surely d.
14. 44 answered..thou shalt surely die, Jonat.
14. 45 Shall Jonathan die, who hath wrought
14. 45 the people rescued Jonathan, that he died
20. 2 God forbid; thou shalt not die: behold
20. 14 show me the kindness..that I die not
22. 16 Thou shalt surely die, Ahimelech, thou
25. 1 Samuel died; and all the Israelites were
25. 37 his heart died within him, and he became
25. 38 that the LORD smote Nabal, that he died
26. 10 smite him; or his day shall come to die
31. 5 he fell likewise upon his sword, and died
31. 6 So Saul died, and his three sons, and his
2 Sa. 1. 15 And he smote him that he died
2. 23 fell down there, and died in the same
2. 23 place where Asahel fell down and died
2. 31 three hundred and threescore men died
3. 27 smote him there..that he died, for the
3. 33 the king lamented..and said, Died Abner
6. 7 God smote him..and there he died by the
10. 1 the king of the children of Ammon died
10. 18 and smote Shobach the captain..who died
11. 15 that he may be smitten, and die
11. 17 and Uriah the Hittite died also
11. 21 cast a piece of a millstone..that he died
12. 13 hath put away thy sin; thou shalt not die
12. 14 child also (that is) born..shall surely die
12. 18 And it came to pass..that the child died
14. 14 we must needs die, and (are) as water
17. 23 and hanged himself, and died, and was
18. 3 neither if half of us die, will they care
18. 33 would God I had died for thee, O Absalom
19. 6 if Absalom had lived, and all we had died
19. 23 king said unto Shimei, Thou shalt not die
19. 37 that I may die in mine own city, (and be)
20. 10 and struck him not again; and he died
24. 15 there died of the people from Dan even
1 Ki. 1. 52 if wickedness..be found..he shall die
2. 1 days of David drew nigh..he should die
2. 25 and he fell upon him that he died
2. 30 And he said, Nay; but I will die here
2. 37 for certain that thou shalt surely die
2. 42 day thou goest out..thou shalt surely die
2. 46 went out, and fell upon him, that he died
3. 19 And this woman's child died in the night
12. 18 all Israel stoned him..that he died
14. 11 Him that dieth of Jeroboam in the city
14. 11 him that dieth in the field shall the

1 Ki. 14. 12 enter into the city, the child shall die
14. 17 came to the threshold..the child died
16. 4 Him that dieth of Baasha in the city
16. 4 him that dieth of his in the fields shall
16. 18 burnt the king's house over him..and died
16. 22 so Tibni died, and Omri reigned
17. 12 and my son, that we may eat it, and die
19. 4 requested for himself that he might die
21. 10 carry him out, and stone him, that he..d.
21. 13 and stoned him with stones, that he died
21. 24 Him that dieth of Ahab in the city the
21. 24 him that dieth in the field shall the fowls
22. 35 was stayed up in his chariot..and died
22. 37 the king died, and was brought to Sama.
2 Ki. 1. 4, 6, 16 Thou shalt not come..but shalt..die
1. 17 he died according to the word of the LORD
4. 20 he sat on her knees till noon, and..died
7. 3 they said..Why sit we here until we die?
7. 4 famine (is) in the city, and we shall die
7. 4 and if we sit still here, we die also
7. 4 and if they kill us, we shall but die
7. 20 trode upon him in the gate, and he died
8. 10 hath showed me that he shall surely die
8. 15 and spread (it) on his face, so that he died
9. 27 And he fled to Megiddo, and died there
12. 21 his servants, smote him, and he died
13. 14 sick of his sickness whereof he died
13. 20 And Elisha died, and they buried him
13. 24 Hazael king of Syria died; and Ben-hadad
18. 32 take you away..ye may live, and not die
20. 1 for thou shalt die, and not live
23. 34 and he came to Egypt, and died there
25. 25 smote Gedaliah, that he died, and the
1 Ch. 1. 51 Hadad died also. And the dukes of Ed.
2. 30 but Seled died without children
2. 32 and Jether died without children
10. 5 he fell likewise on the sword, and died
10. 6 So Saul died, and his three sons
10. 6 and all his house died together
10. 13 Saul died for his transgression which he
13. 10 smote him..and there he died before God
19. 1 the king of the children of Ammon died
23. 22 And Eleazar died, and had no sons, but
24. 2 Nadab and Abihu died before their father
29. 28 he died in a good old age, full of days
2 Ch. 10. 18 and..stoned him with stones, that he died
13. 20 and the LORD struck him, and he died
16. 13 died in the one and fortieth year of his
18. 34 the time of the sun going down he died
21. 19 bowels fell out...so he died of sore diseases
24. 15 and was full of days when he died
24. 25 slew him on his bed, and he died: and
25. 4 The fathers shall not die for the children
25. 4 neither shall the children die for the fath.
25. 4 but every man shall die for his own sin
32. 11 persuade you to give over yourselves to d.
35. 24 they brought him to Jerusalem, and he d.
Job 2. 9 Then said his wife..curse God, and die
3. 11 Why died I not from the womb? (why)
4. 21 go away? they die, even without wisdom
12. 2 No doubt..and wisdom shall die with you
14. 8 and the stock thereof die in the ground
14. 10 But man dieth, and wasteth away; yea
14. 14 If a man die, shall he live (again)? all
21. 23 One dieth in his full strength, being
21. 25 another dieth in the bitterness of his soul
34. 20 In a moment shall they die, and the peo.
36. 14 They die in youth, and their life (is)
42. 17 So Job died, (being) old and full of days
Psa. 41. 5 When shall he die, and his name perish?
49. 10 For he seeth (that) wise men die, likewise
82. 7 ye shall die like men, and fall like one of
118. 17 I shall not die, but live, and declare the
Prov. 5. 23 He shall die without instruction; and in
10. 21 feed many: but fools die for want of wisd.
15. 10 (and) he that hateth reproof shall die
19. 16 (but) he that despiseth his ways shall die
23. 13 for (if) thou beatest..he shall not die
30. 7 Two (things)..deny me..not before I die
Eccl. 2. 16 And how dieth the wise (man)? as the fool
3. 2 A time to be born, and a time to die
7. 17 why shouldest thou die before thy time?
9. 5 For the living know that they shall die:
Isa. 22. 13 eat and drink, for to morrow we shall die
22. 14 shall not be purged from you till ye die
22. 18 there shalt thou die, and there the char.
38. 1 Set..in order: for thou shalt die, and not
50. 2 their fish stinketh..and dieth for thirst
51. 6 they that dwell therein shall die in like
51. 12 be afraid of a man (that) shall die, and
51. 14 that he should not die in the pit, nor that
59. 5 he that eateth of their eggs dieth, and
65. 20 the child shall die an hundred years old
66. 24 for their worm shall not die, neither shall
Jer. 11. 21 Prophesy not..that thou die not by our
11. 22 the young men shall die by the sword
11. 22 their sons and their daughters shall die
16. 4 They shall die of grievous deaths; they
16. 6 Both the great and the small shall die in
20. 6 there thou shalt die, and shalt be buried
21. 6 both man and beast: they shall die of a
21. 9 He that abideth in this city shall die by
22. 12 But he shall die in the place whither they
22. 26 into another country..and there shall ye d.
26. 8 took him, saying, Thou shalt surely die
27. 13 Why will ye die, thou and thy people by
28. 16 this year thou shalt die, because thou hast
28. 17 Hananiah the prophet died the same year
31. 30 every one shall die for his own iniquity
34. 4 Thus saith the LORD..Thou shalt not die
34. 5 (But) thou shalt die in peace: and with
37. 20 cause me not to return..lest I die there
Jer. 38. 2 He that remaineth in this city shall die
38. 10 take up Jeremiah the prophet..before he d.
38. 24 Let no man know..and thou shalt not die
38. 26 he would not cause me to return..to die
42. 16 famine..shall follow..and there ye shall d.
42. 17 they shall die by the sword, by the famine
42. 22 know certainly that ye shall die by the
44. 12 shall die, from the least..unto the great.
Eze. 3. 18 Thou shalt surely die; and thou givest
3. 18 the same wicked (man) shall die in his
3. 19 he shall die in his iniquity; but thou hast
3. 20 a stumbling block before him, he shall d.
3. 20 he shall die in his sin, and his righteous.
5. 12 A third part of thee shall die with the
6. 12 He that is far off shall die of the pestilence
6. 12 he that..is besieged shall die by the
7. 15 he that (is) in the field shall die with the
11. 13 that Palatiah the son of Benaiah died
12. 13 shall not see it, though he shall die there
13. 19 to slay the souls that should not die, and
17. 16 (even) with him in the midst..he shall die
18. 4, 20 the soul that sinneth, it shall die
18. 13 he shall surely die; his blood shall be
18. 17 he shall not die for the iniquity of his
18. 18 lo, even he shall die in his iniquity
18. 21, 28 he shall surely live, he shall not die
18. 24 in his sin..he hath sinned..shall he die
18. 26 committeth iniquity, and dieth in them
18. 26 iniquity that he hath done shall he die
18. 31 for why will ye die, O house of Israel?
18. 32 no pleasure in the death of him that die.
24. 18 at even my wife died; and I did in the
28. 8 thou shalt die the deaths of (them that
28. 10 Thou shalt die the deaths of the
33. 8 O wicked (man), thou shalt surely die
33. 8 that wicked (man) shall die in his iniquity
33. 9 if he do not turn..he shall die in his
33. 11 for why will ye die, O house of Israel?
33. 13 but for his iniquity..he shall die for it
33. 14 I say unto the wicked, Thou shalt surely d.
33. 15 he shall surely live, he shall not die
33. 18 committeth iniquity, he shall even die
33. 27 they..in the caves shall die of the
Hos. 13. 1 but when he offended in Baal, he died
Amos 2. 2 Moab shall die with tumult, with
6. 9 if there remain ten men..they shall die
7. 11 Jeroboam shall die by the sword, and
7. 17 and thou shalt die in a polluted land
9. 10 the sinners of my people shall die by the
Jon. 4. 8 he fainted, and wished in himself to die
Hab. 1. 12 my God, mine Holy One? we shall not d.
Zech. 11. 9 that that dieth, let it die; and that that

3. *To be put to death*, מוּת *muth*, 6.
Eze. 18. 13 he shall surely die; his blood shall be

4. *To fall*, נָפַל *naphal.*
Gen. 25. 18 he died in the presence of all his breth.

5. *To die off or away*, ἀποθνήσκω *apothnēskō.*
Matt. 22. 24 Moses said, If a man die, having no
22. 27 And last of all the woman died also
26. 35 Though I should die with thee, yet
Mark 12. 19 If a man's brother die, and leave (his)
12. 20 first took a wife, and dying left no seed
12. 21 the second took her, and died, neither
12. 22 last of all the woman died also
Luke 16. 22 the beggar died, and was carried by
16. 22 the rich man also died, and was buried
20. 28 If any man's brother die, having a wife
20. 28 he die without children, that his brother
20. 29 took a wife, and died without children
20. 30 the second took her to wife, and he died
20. 31 and they left no children, and died
20. 32 Last of all the woman died also
20. 36 Neither can they die any more: for
John 4. 49 Sir, come down ere my child die
6. 50 that a man may eat thereof, and not die
8. 21 ye shall seek me, and shall die in your
8. 24, 24 ye shall die in your sins
11. 16 Let us also go, that we may die with him
11. 26 And whosoever liveth..shall never die
11. 32 hadst been here, my brother had not died
11. 37 that even this man should not have died?
11. 50 that one man should die for the people
11. 51 that Jesus should die for that nation
12. 24 Except a corn of wheat fall..and die
12. 24 but if it die, it bringeth forth much fruit
12. 33 signifying what death he should die
18. 32 signifying what death he should die
19. 7 We have a law..by our law he ought to d.
21. 23 that that disciple should not die
21. 23 Jesus said not unto him, He shall not d.
Acts 9. 37 it came to pass..that she was sick, and d.
21. 13 but also to die at Jerusalem for the
25. 11 thing worthy of death, I refuse not to d.
Rom. 5. 6 in due time Christ died for the ungodly
5. 7 scarcely for a righteous man will one die
5. 7 a good man some would even dare to die
5. 8 while we were yet sinners, Christ died for
6. 9 Christ being raised from the dead dieth
6. 10 in that he died, he died unto sin once
7. 9 when the commandment came..I died
8. 13 For if ye live after the flesh, ye shall die
8. 34 (It is) Christ that died, yea rather
14. 7 For none..and no man dieth to himself
14. 8 whether we die, we die unto the Lord
14. 8 whether we live..or die, we are the Lord's
14. 9 For to this end Christ both died, and rose
14. 15 Destroy not him..for whom Christ died
1 Co. 8. 11 weak brother perish, for whom Christ d.?
9. 15 for (it were) better for me to die
15. 3 how that Christ died for our sins accord.
1 Co. 15. 22 For as in Adam all die, even so in Christ
15. 31 which I have in Christ Jesus..I die daily
15. 32 eat and drink; for to morrow we die
15. 36 that..is not quickened, except it die
2 Co. 5. 14 that if one died for all, then were all dead
5. 15 (that) he died for all, that they which live
5. 15 him which died for them, and rose again
6. 9 as dying, and, behold, we live; as chast.
Phil. 1. 21 to live (is) Christ, and to die (is) gain
1 Th. 4. 14 if we believe that Jesus died and rose
5. 10 Who died for us, that, whether we wake
Heb. 7. 8 And here men that die receive tithes
9. 27 And as it is appointed unto men once to d.
10. 28 He that despised Moses' law died without
11. 13 These all died in faith, not having receiv.
Rev. 3. 2 things which remain, that are ready to d.
8. 9 which were in the sea, and had life, died
8. 11 and many men died of the waters
9. 6 and shall desire to die; and death shall
14. 13 Blessed (are) the dead which die in the
16. 3 and every living soul died in the sea

6. *To lose off, destroy*, ἀπόλλυμι *apollumi.*
John 18. 14 that one man should [die] for the people

7. *To die, be dying*, θνήσκω *thnēskō.*
John 11. 21 hadst been here, my brother had not died

8. *To end (life)*, τελευτάω *teleutaō.*
Matt 15. 4 curseth father or mother, let him die the
Mark 7. 10 curseth father or mother, let him die the
9. 44 Where their worm dieth not, and the fire
9. 46, 48 Where their worm dieth not, and the
Luke 7. 2 servant, who..was sick, and ready to die
Acts 7. 15 Jacob went down into Egypt, and died
Heb. 11. 22 Joseph, when he died, made mention of

9. *To destruction*, εἰς ἀπώλειαν *eis apōleian.*
Acts 25. 16 to deliver any man to die, before that he

DIE, to cause to —
To put to death, cause to die, מוּת *muth*, 5.
1 Sa. 28. 9 snare for my life, to cause me to die?

DIE, to be like to, or must —
To die, מוּת *muth.*
Deut. 4. 22 I must die in this land, I must not go
31. 14 thy days approach that thou must die
1 Sa. 14. 43 that (was) in mine hand..lo, I must die
Jer. 38. 9 he is like to die for hunger in the place

DIE with, to —
To die off with, συναποθνήσκω *sunapothnēskō.*
Mark 14. 31 If I should die with thee, I will not deny
2 Co. 7. 3 ye are in our hearts to die and live with

DIED —
Death, מָוֶת *maveth.*
Gen. 50. 16 Thy father did command before he died
Num 26. 10 with Korah, when that company died
33. 39 hundred and twenty three..when he died
Deut 34. 7 hundred and twenty years old when he d.
2 Ch. 24. 15 hundred and thirty years..when he died
24. 22 when he died, he said, The LORD look
Isa. 6. 1 the year that king Uzziah died I saw
14. 28 In the year that king Ahaz died was this

DIED, which —
Fallen thing, carcase, נְבֵלָה *nebelah.*
Lev. 17. 15 that eateth that which died (of itself)

DIET —
Usual or customary diet or allowance, אֲרֻחָה *aruchah.*
Jer. 52. 34 (for) his diet, there was a continual diet

DIETH of itself, (beast that) —
Fallen thing, carcase, נְבֵלָה *nebelah.*
Lev. 7. 24 the fat of the beast that dieth of itself
22. 8 That which dieth of itself, or is torn
Deut 14. 21 not eat (of) any thing that dieth of itself
Eze. 4. 14 not eaten of that which dieth of itself

DIFFER from, to —
To bear or carry diversely, διαφέρω *diapherō.*
1 Co. 15. 41 (one) star differeth from (another) star
Gal. 4. 1 differeth nothing from a servant, though

DIFFER, to make to —
To judge diversely, διακρίνω *diakrinō.*
1 Co. 4. 7 who maketh thee to differ (from another)?

DIFFERENCE —
1. *Division, act of dividing*, διαίρεσις *diairesis.*
1 Co. 12. 5 there are differences of administrations

2. *A sending apart, distinction*, διαστολή *diastolē.*
Rom. 3. 22 and upon all them..there is no difference
10. 12 there is no difference between the Jew

DIFFERENCE between —
To divide into parts, μερίζω *merizō.*
1 Co. 7. 34 There is difference (also) between a wife

DIFFERENCE, to make a —
1. *To separate*, בָּדַל *badal*, 5.
Lev. 11. 47 To make a difference between the unclean

2. *To judge diversely*, διακρίνω *diakrinō.*
Jude 22 of some have compassion, making a diff.

DIFFERENCE, to put (a) —
1. *To separate*, בָּדַל *badal*, 5.
Lev. 10. 10 that ye may put difference between holy
20. 25 therefore put difference between clean
Eze. 22. 26 they have put no difference between the

2. *To make a separation,* פָּלָה *palah,* 5.
Exod11. 7 the LORD doth put a difference between

3. *To judge diversely,* διακρίνω *diakrinō.*
Acts 15. 9 put no difference between us and them

DIFFERING —
Bearing diversely, different, διάφορος *diaphoros.*
Rom 12. 6 Having then gifts differing according to

DIG, to —
1. *To seek, dig, search,* חָפַר *chaphar.*
Gen. 21. 30 witness unto me, that I have digged this
26. 15 which his father's servants had digged
26. 18 Isaac digged again the wells of water
26. 18 which they had digged in the days of
26. 19 Isaac's servants digged in the valley, and
26. 21 they digged another well, and strove for
26. 22 removed from thence, and digged another
26. 32 concerning the well which they had dig.
Exod. 7. 24 the Egyptians digged round about the
Num21. 18 The princes digged the well, the nobles of
Deut23. 13 thou shalt dig therewith, and shalt turn
Job 3. 21 and dig for it more than for hid treasures
11. 18 yea, thou shalt dig (about thee, and) thou
Psa. 7. 15 He made a pit, and digged it, and is fallen
35. 7 (which) without cause they have digged
Eccl.10. 8 He that diggeth a pit shall fall into it
Jer. 13. 7 I went to Euphrates, and digged, and

2. *To hew, dig,* חָצַב *chatsab.*
Deut. 6. 11 and wells digged, which thou diggedst
8. 9 out of whose hills thou mayest dig brass
2 Ch.26. 10 he built towers.. and digged many wells
Neh. 9. 25 houses full of all goods, wells digged

3. *To dig through,* חָתַר *chathar.*
Eze. 8. 8 dig now in the wall : and when I had digged
12. 5 Dig thou through the wall in their sight
12. 7 I digged through the wall with mine hand
12. 12 they shall dig through the wall to carry
Amos 9. 2 Though they dig into hell, thence shall

4. *To dig, prepare,* כָּרָה *karah.*
Gen. 26. 25 and there Isaac's servants digged a well
50. 5 in my grave which I have digged for me
Exod21. 33 if a man shall dig a pit, and not cover
Num21. 18 the nobles of the people digged it, by (the)
Job 6. 27 ye overwhelm the fatherless, and ye dig·
Psa. 57. 6 they have digged a pit before me, into the
119. 85 The proud have digged pits for me, which
Prov 16. 27 An ungodly man diggeth up evil
26. 27 Whoso diggeth a pit shall fall therein
Jer. 18. 20 for they have digged a pit for my soul
18. 22 for they have digged a pit to take me

5. *To dig,* קוּר *qur.*
2 Ki. 19. 24 I have digged and drunk strange waters
Isa. 37. 25 I have digged, and drunk water; and with

6. *To dig,* ὀρύσσω *orussō,* ὀρύττω.
Matt21. 33 digged a wine press in it, and built a
25. 18 digged in the earth, and hid his lord's
Mark12. 1 digged (a place for) the winefat, and built

7. *To delve, scoop, hollow out,* σκάπτω *skaptō.*
Luke 6. 48 man which built an house, and digged
13. 8 till I shall dig about it, and dung (it)
16. 3 I cannot dig; to beg I am ashamed

DIG down, to —
1. *To root out,* עָקַר *aqar,* 3.
Gen. 49. 6 in their self will they digged down a wall

2. *To delve beneath, undermine,* κατασκάπτω *kata.*
Rom 11. 3 killed thy prophets, and digged down

DIG through, to —
To dig through, חָתַר *chathar.*
Job 24. 16 they dig through houses (which) they

DIGGED, to be —
1. *To be prepared, digged,* כָּרָה *karah,* 2.
Psa. 94. 13 until the pit be digged for the wicked

2. *To be picked out,* נָקַר *naqar,* 4.
Isa. 51. 1 the hole of the pit (whence) ye are digged

3. *To be set in order, arranged,* עָדַר *adar,* 2
Isa. 5. 6 it shall not be pruned nor digged
7. 25 (on) all hills that shall be digged

DIGNITY —
1. *Greatness,* גְּדוּלָּה *gedulah.*
Esth. 6. 3 What honour and dignity hath been done

2. *High place,* מָרוֹם *marom.*
Eccl.10. 6 Folly is set in great dignity, and the

3. *A lifting up, exaltation,* שְׂאֵת *seeth.*
Gen. 49. 3 excellency of dignity, and the excellency
Hab. 1. 7 their dignity shall proceed of themselves

4. *Glory, esteem, reputation,* δόξα *doxa.*
2 Pe. 2. 10 not afraid to speak evil of dignities
Jude 8 despise dominion.. speak evil of dignities

DIK'-LAH, דִּקְלָה *palm grove.*
A son of Joktan of the family of Shem, whose offspring inhabited a district in Arabia, B.C. 2240.
Gen. 10. 27 And Hadoram, and Uzal, and D.
1 Ch. 1. 21 Hadoram also, and Uzal, and D.

DIL'-EAN, דִּלְעָן *gourd.*
A city in the plains of Judah.
Josh 15. 38 And D., and Mizpeh, and Joktheel

DILIGENCE —
1. *Guard, charge,* מִשְׁמָר *mishmar.*
Prov. 4. 23 Keep thy heart with all diligence; for out

2. *Work,* ἐργασία *ergasia.*
Luke12. 58 give diligence that thou mayest be deliv.

3. *Haste, speed,* σπουδή *spoudē.*
Rom.12. 8 he that ruleth, with diligence; he that
2 Co. 8. 7 (in) all diligence, and (in) your love to us
Heb. 6. 11 do show the same diligence to the full
2 Pe. 1. 5 giving all diligence, add to your faith
Jude 3 when I gave all diligence to write unto

DILIGENCE, to do or give —
To use haste or speed, σπουδάζω *spoudazō.*
2 Ti. 4. 9 Do thy diligence to come shortly unto me
4. 21 Do thy diligence to come before winter
2 Pe. 1. 10 give diligence to make your calling and

DILIGENT —
1. *To be searched out,* חָפַשׂ *chaphas,* 4.
Psa. 64. 6 they accomplish a diligent search

2. *Diligent, sharp pointed, determined,* חָרוּץ *charuts.*
Prov 10. 4 the hand of the diligent maketh rich
12. 24 The hand of the diligent shall bear rule
12. 27 substance of a diligent man (is) precious
13. 4 soul of the diligent shall be made fat
21. 5 The thoughts of the diligent (tend) only

3. *To do good or well,* יָטַב *yatab,* 5.
Deut 13. 14 enquire, and make search, and ask dilig.
17. 4 hast heard (of it,) and enquired diligently
19. 18 judges shall make diligent inquisition

4. *Might,* מְאֹד *meod.*
Deut 4. 9 keep thy soul diligently, lest thou forget
24. 8 that thou observe diligently, and do
Josh.22. 5 take diligent heed to do the commandm.
Psa.119. 4 commanded (us) to keep.. precepts dilige.
Jer. 2. 10 send unto Kedar, and consider diligently

5. *Hasty, hasting,* מָהִיר *mahir.*
Prov 22. 29 Seest thou a man diligent in his business?

6. *Hasting, speedy,* σπουδαῖος *spoudaios.*
2 Co. 8. 22 we have oftentimes proved diligent in
8. 22 but now much more diligent, upon the

DILIGENT, to be —
1. *To know, be acquainted with,* יָדַע *yada.*
Prov 27. 23 Be thou diligent to know the state of

2. *To use haste or speed,* σπουδάζω *spoudazō.*
Tit. 3. 12 be diligent to come unto me to Nicopolis
2 Pet 3. 14 be diligent that ye may be found of him

DILIGENTLY — [*See* DILIGENT.]
1. *Honourably, diligently,* אַדְרַזְדָּא *adrazda.*
Ezra 7. 23 let it be diligently done for the house

2. *Attention,* קֶשֶׁב *qesheb.*
Isa. 21. 7 he hearkened diligently with much heed

3. *Accurately, exactly,* ἀκριβῶς *akribōs.*
Matt. 2. 8 search diligently for the young child
Acts 18. 25 he spake and taught diligently the things

4. *Carefully, with anxiety,* ἐπιμελῶς *epimelōs.*
Luke 15. 8 and seek diligently till she find (it)?

5. *Hastily, speedily,* σπουδαίως *spondaiōs.*
Titus 3. 13 Bring Zenas ..and Apollos.. diligently

DILIGENTLY, very —
More speedily or hastily, σπουδαιότερον *spoudaiot.*
2 Ti. 1. 17 he sought me out very diligently, and
[*See also* Consider, observe, seek, teach.]

DIM, to be —
1. *To be or become dark or dim,* חָשַׁךְ *chashak.*
Lam. 5 17 for these (things) our eyes are dim

2. *To be or become weak,* כָּהָה *kahah.*
Gen. 27. 1 when Isaac was old, and his eyes were d.
Deut34 7 his eye was not dim, nor his natural force
Job 17. 7 Mine eye also is dim by reason of sorrow

3. *To look, be dazzled,* שָׁעָה *shaah.*
Isa. 32. 3 eyes of them that see shall not be dim

4. *To be heavy, weighty,* כָּבֵד *kabed.*
Gen. 48. 10 Now the eyes of Israel were dim for age

5. *To stand, stand still,* קוּם *qum.*
1 Sam4. 15 his eyes were dim, that he could not see

DIM, to become —
To become concealed, darkened, עָמַם *amam,* 6.
Lam. 4. 1 How is the gold become dim! (how) is the

DIM, to wax —
Becoming weak, dim, כֵּהָה *kehah.*
1 Sa. 3. 2 and his eyes began to wax dim, (that) he

DIMINISH, to —
1. *To diminish, withdraw,* גָּרַע *gara.*
Exod 5. 8 ye shall not diminish (ought) thereof
21. 10 her duty of marriage, shall he not dimin.
Deut 4. 2 neither shall ye diminish (ought) from it
12. 32 not add thereto, nor diminish from it
Jer. 26. 2 to speak unto them; diminish not a word
Eze. 5. 11 therefore will I also diminish (thee)
16. 27 I.. have diminished thine ordinary (food)

2. *To make few or small,* מָעַט *maat,* 5.
Lev. 25. 16 thou shalt diminish the price of it
Eze. 29. 15 I will diminish them, that they shall no

DIMINISHED, to be —
1. *To be diminished, withdrawn,* גָּרַע *gara,* 2.
Exod 5. 11 not ought of your work shall be dimin.

2. *To be or become few or little,* מָעַט *maat.*
Pro. 13. 11 Wealth (gotten) by vanity shall be dim.
Isa. 21. 17 the mighty men.. shall be diminished
Jer. 29. 6 may be increased there, and not dimin.

DIMINISHING —
A being less, smaller, worse, ἥττημα *hēttēma.*
Rom 11. 12 the diminishing of them the riches of the

DIM'-NAH, דִּמְנָה *dung.*
A Levitical city of Zebulun. In 1 Ch. 6. 77 occurs Rimmon (more accurately Rimmono), which may be a variation of Dimnah, yet Rimmon is probably the real name.
Josh.21. 35 D. with her suburbs, Nahalal with her

DIMNESS —
1. *Dimness, weariness,* מוּעָף *muaph.*
Isa. 9. 1 the dimness (shall) not (be) such as (was)

2. *Dimness, weariness,* מָעוּף *mauph.*
Isa. 8. 22 trouble and darkness, dimness of anguish

DI'-MON, דִּימוֹן *river bed.*
A city of Moab, the same as Dibon, (No 1.)
Isa. 15. 9 For the waters of D. shall be full of blood
15. 9 for I will bring more upon D., lions upon

DI-MO'-NAH, דִּימוֹנָה.
A city in the S. of Judah, probably the same as Dibon (See Dibon No 3.)
Josh 15. 22 And Kinah, and D., and Adadah

DI'-NAH, דִּינָה *judged or avenged.*
Daughter of Jacob by Leah; she was violated by Shechem son of Hamor when about 14 or 15 years of age, B.C. 1740.
Gen. 30. 21 bare a daughter, and called her name D.
34. 1 D. the daughter of Leah, which she bare
34. 3 And his soul clave unto D. the daughter
34. 5 Jacob heard that he had defiled D. his
34. 13 and said, because he had defiled D. their
34. 25 Simeon and Levi, D.'s brethren, took each
34. 26 and took D. out of Shechem's house, and
46. 15 she bare unto Jacob.. with his daughter D.

DI-NA-ITES, דִּינָיֵא.
Assyrian tribe carried to Samaria by Shalmaneser. B.C. 721-678.
Ezra 4. 9 Then (wrote).. the D., the Apharsathchites

DINE, to —
1. *To eat,* אָכַל *akal.*
Gen. 43. 16 for (these) men shall dine with me at noon

2. *To breakfast,* ἀριστάω *aristaō.*
Luke 11. 37 Pharisee besought him to dine with him
John21. 12 Jesus saith unto them, Come (and) dine
21. 15 when they had dined, Jesus saith to Sim.

DIN-HA'-BAH, דִּנְהָבָה.
The capital and probably birthplace of Bela son of Beor, king of Edom, a Horite.
Gen. 36. 32 and the name of his city (was) D.
1 Ch. 1. 43 and the name of his city (was) D.

DINNER —
1. *Usual or customary dish,* אֲרֻחָה *aruchah.*
Prov.15. 17 Better (is) a dinner of herbs where love

2. *Breakfast,* ἄριστον *ariston.*
Matt22. 4 I have prepared my dinner: my oxen and
Luke11. 38 that he had not first washed before dinner
14. 12 When thou makest a dinner or a supper

DIO-NY-SI'-US, Διονύσιος.
A convert, a member of the supreme court at Athens.
Acts 17. 34 among the which (was) D. the Areopagite

DI-O-TRE'-PHES, Διοτρεφής.
A disciple that loved pre-eminence.
3 John 9 I wrote unto the church: but D... receiv.

DIP, to —
1. *To moisten, besprinkle,* טָבַל *tabal.*
Gen. 37. 31 and dipped the coat in the blood
Exod12. 22 dip (it) in the blood that (is) in the basin
Lev. 4. 6 the priest shall dip his finger in the blood
4. 17 the priest shall dip his finger (in some) of
9. 9 he dipped his finger in the blood, and put
14. 6 shall dip them and the living bird in the
14. 16 the priest shall dip his right finger in
14. 51 dip them in the blood of the slain bird
Num19. 18 dip (it) in the water, and sprinkle (it)
Deut33. 24 and let him dip his foot in oil
Ruth 2. 14 and dip thy morsel in the vinegar
1 Sa. 14. 27 dipped it in an honeycomb, and put his
2 Ki. 5. 14 and dipped himself seven times in Jorda.
8. 15 dipped (it) in water, and spread (it) on

2. *To dip,* βάπτω *baptō.*
Luke16. 24 may dip the tip of his finger in water
John13. 26 I shall give a sop, when I have dipped (it)
Rev. 19. 13 clothed with a vesture dipped in blood

3. *To dip in,* ἐμβάπτω *embaptō.*
Matt26. 23 He that dippeth (his) hand with me in
Mark14. 20 one of the twelve, that dippeth with me
John 13. 26 when he had dipped the sop, he gave (it)

DIPPED, to be —
1. *To be moistened,* טָבַל *tabal,* 2.
Josh. 3. 15 were dipped in the brim of the water

2. *To smite, dash,* מָחַץ *machats.*
Psa. 68. 23 That thy foot may be dipped in the blood
DIRECT, to —
1. *To understand,* בִּין *bin.* [V.L. as No. 4.]
Prov.21. 29 (as for) the upright, he directeth his way
2. *To shoot, show, direct,* יָרָה *yarah,* 5.
Gen. 46. 28 to direct his face unto Goshen
3. *To keep straight, direct,* יָשַׁר *yashar,* 3.
Prov. 3. 6 acknowledge him, and he shall direct thy
11. 5 righteousness of the perfect shall direct
Isa. 45. 13 and I will direct all his ways
4. *To prepare, establish,* כּוּן *kun,* 5.
Prov16. 9 but the LORD directeth his steps
Jer. 10. 23 not in man that walketh to direct his
5. *To make right,* כָּשֵׁר *kasher,* 5.
Eccl.10. 10 but wisdom (is) profitable to direct
6. *To give,* נָתַן *nathan.*
Isa. 61. 8 I will direct their work in truth, and I
7. *To arrange, set in array,* עָרַךְ *arak.*
Job 32. 14 hath not directed (his) words against me
Psa. 5. 3 in the morning will I direct (my prayer)
8. *To direct, let loose,* שָׁרָה *sharah.*
Job 37. 3 He directeth it under the whole heaven
9. *To weigh, ponder, mete out,* תָּכַן *takan,* 3.
Isa. 40. 13 Who hath directed the Spirit of the LORD
10. *To make thoroughly straight,* κατευθύνω.
1 Th. 3. 11 Lord Jesus Christ, direct our way unto
2 Th. 3. 5 the Lord direct your hearts into the love
DIRECTED, to be —
To be prepared, established, כּוּן *kun,* 2.
Psa.119. 5 O that my ways were directed to keep
DIRECTLY —
1. *Bending to, direct,* הָגִין *hagin.*
Eze. 42. 12 the way directly before the wall toward
2. *Over against, straight forward,* נֹכַח *nokach.*
Num 19. 4 sprinkle of her blood directly before the
DIRT —
1. *Mire, mud,* טִיט *tit.*
Psa. 18. 42 cast them out as the dirt in the streets
Isa. 57. 20 whose waters cast up mire and dirt
2. *Dung, fundament, porch,* פַּרְשְׁדֹנָה *parshedonah.*
Judg. 3. 22 out of his belly; and the dirt came out
DISALLOW, to —
1. *To discourage, break, disallow,* נוּא *no,* 5.
Num30. 5 if her father disallow her in the day that
30. 5 because her father disallowed her
30. 8 if her husband disallowed her on the day
30. 11 held his peace at her, (and) disallowed
2. *To disapprove off,* ἀποδοκιμάζω *apodokimazō.*
1 Pe. 2. 4 disallowed indeed of men, but chosen of
2. 7 the stone which the builders disallowed
DISANNUL, to —
1. *To break, make void,* פָּרַר *parar,* 5.
Job 40. 8 Wilt thou also disannul my judgment?
Isa. 14. 27 hath purposed, and who shall disannul
2. *To put aside,* ἀθετέω *atheteō.*
Gal. 3. 15 no man disannulleth, or addeth thereto
3. *To deprive of lordship,* ἀκυρόω *akuroō.*
Gal. 3. 17 the covenant..cannot disannul, that it
DISANNULLED, to be —
To be covered, weakened, כָּפַר *kaphar,* 4.
Isa. 28. 18 covenant with death shall be disannulled
DISANNULLING —
A putting aside, ἀθέτησις *athetēsis.*
Heb. 7. 18 there is verily a disannulling of the com.
DISAPPOINT, to —
1. *To break, make void,* פָּרַר *parar,* 5.
Job 5. 12 disappointeth the devices of the crafty
2. *To go or come before,* קָדַם *qadam,* 3.
Psa. 17. 13 Arise, O LORD, disappoint him, cast him
DISAPPOINTED, to be —
To break, make void, פָּרַר *parar,* 5.
Prov.15. 22 Without counsel purposes are disappoint.
DISCERN, to —
1. *To understand, consider, discern,* בִּין *bin.*
Prov. 7. 7 I discerned among the youths, a young
2. *To cause to understand, instruct,* בִּין *bin,* 5.
1 Ki. 3. 9 that I may discern between good and bad
3. *To know, be acquainted with,* יָדַע *yada.*
Eccl. 8. 5 and a wise man's heart discerneth both
4. *To discern, acknowledge,* נָכַר *nakar,* 5.
Gen. 27. 23 he discerned him not, because his hands
31. 32 before our brethren discern thou what (is)
38. 25 Discern, I pray thee, whose (are) these
1 Ki.20. 41 the king of Israel discerned him that he
5. *To see,* רָאָה *raah.*
Mal. 3. 18 discern between the righteous and the
6. *To hear,* שָׁמַע *shama.*
2 Sa. 14. 17 so (is) my lord the king, to discern good
1 Ki. 3. 11 asked..understanding to discern
7. *To judge closely, examine,* ἀνακρίνω *anakrinō.*
1 Co. 2. 14 because they are spiritually discerned
8. *To judge thoroughly,* διακρίνω *diakrinō.*
Matt 16. 3 ye can discern the face of the sky
1 Co.11. 29 drinketh..not discerning the Lord's body
9. *To make proof,* δοκιμάζω *dokimazō.*
Luke12. 56 ye can discern the face of the sky and
12. 56 how is it that ye do not discern this time?
10. *Toward a thorough judging,* πρὸς διάκρισιν.
Heb. 5. 14 exercised to discern both good and evil
DISCERN, can —
1. *To know, be acquainted with,* יָדַע *yada.*
2 Sa. 19. 35 (and) can I discern between good and evil?
Jon. 4. 11 that cannot discern between their right
2. *To understand, consider, discern,* בִּין *bin.*
Job 6. 30 cannot my taste discern perverse things?
3. *To discern, acknowledge,* נָכַר *nakar,* 5.
Ezra 3. 13 the people could not discern the noise
Job 4. 16 It stood still, but I could not discern the
DISCERN, to cause —
To cause to know or discern, יָדַע *yada,* 5.
Eze. 44. 23 and cause them to discern between the
DISCERNER —
Critic, judge, κριτικός *kritikos.*
Heb. 4. 12 and (is) a discerner of the thoughts and
DISCERNING —
A thorough judging, διάκρισις *diakrisis.*
1 Co. 12. 10 prophecy; to another discerning of spirits
DISCHARGE —
A sending away, מִשְׁלַחַת *mishlachath.*
Eccl. 8. 8 and (there is) no discharge in (that) war
DISCHARGED, to cause to be —
To spread out, נָפַץ *naphats,* 3.
1 Ki. 5. 9 and will cause them to be discharged
DISCIPLE —
1. *Taught or trained one,* לִמּוּד *limmud.*
Isa. 8. 16 Bind up..seal the law among my discip.
2. *Taught or trained one,* μαθητής *mathētēs.*
Matt. 5. 1 when he was set, his disciples came unto
8. 21 another of his disciples said unto him
8. 23 when he was entered..his disciples
8. 25 [his disciples] came to (him), and awoke
9. 10 and sat down with him and his disciples
9. 11 they said unto his disciples, Why eateth
9. 14 Then came to him the disciples of John
9. 14 Pharisees fast oft, but thy disciples fast
9. 19 and followed him, and (so did) his disci.
9. 37 Then saith he unto his disciples, The
10. 1 he had called unto (him) his twelve disc.
10. 24 The disciple is not above (his) master
10. 25 It is enough for the disciple that he be as
10. 42 shall give..only in the name of a disciple
11. 1 an end of commanding his twelve discip.
11. 2 when John had heard..he sent two..di.
12. 1 his disciples were an hungered, and
12. 2 thy disciples do that which is not lawful
12. 49 stretched forth his hand toward his disc.
13. 10 the disciples came, and said unto him
13. 36 his disciples came unto him, saying
14. 12 his disciples came, and took up the body
14. 15 when it was evening, his disciples came
14. 19 loaves to (his) disciples, and the disciples
14. 22 straightway Jesus constrained his discip.
14. 26 when the disciples saw him walking
15. 2 Why do thy disciples transgress the
15. 12 Then came his disciples, and said unto
15. 23 his disciples came and besought him
15. 32 Then Jesus called his disciples (unto him)
15. 33 his disciples say unto him, Whence
15. 36 gave to his disciples, and the disciples to
16. 5 when his disciples were come to the
16. 13 he asked his disciples, saying, Whom do
16. 20 Then charged he his disciples that they
16. 21 began Jesus to show unto his disciples
16. 24 Then said Jesus unto his disciples, If
17. 6 when the disciples heard (it), they fell
17. 10 his disciples asked him, saying, Why
17. 13 Then the disciples understood that he
17. 16 I brought him to thy disciples, and they
17. 19 Then came the disciples to Jesus apart
18. 1 At the same time came the disciples unto
19. 10 His disciples say unto him, If the case
19. 13 little children..and the disciples rebuked
19. 23 Then said Jesus unto his disciples, Verily
19. 25 When his disciples heard (it), they were
20. 17 took the twelve [disciples] apart in the
21. 1 drew nigh..then sent Jesus two disciples
21. 6 disciples went, and did as Jesus com.
21. 20 when the disciples saw (it), they marvel.
22. 16 they sent out unto him their disciples
23. 1 to the multitude, and to his disciples
24. 1 his disciples came to (him), for to show
24. 3 the disciples came unto him privately
26. 1 it came to pass..he said unto his discip.
26. 8 when his disciples saw (it), they had indi.
26. 17 disciples came to Jesus, saying unto him
26. 18 I will keep the passover..with my disci.
26. 19 disciples did as Jesus had appointed them
26. 26 gave (it) to the disciples, and said, Take
26. 35 Likewise also said all the disciples
26. 36 saith unto the disciples, Sit ye here
26. 40 he cometh unto the disciples, and findeth
26. 45 Then cometh he to his disciples, and
26. 56 Then all the disciples forsook him, and
27. 64 his disciples come by night, and steal
Matt 28. 7 [go quickly, and tell his disciples]
28. 8 [and did run to bring his disciples word]
28. 9 [as they went to tell his disciples, behold]
28. 13 Say ye, His disciples came by night, and
28. 16 the eleven disciples went away into
Mark 2. 15 sat also together with Jesus and his disc.
2. 16 said unto his disciples, How is it that he
2. 18 the disciples of John and of the Pharisees
2. 18 the disciples of John..but thy disciples
2. 23 his disciples began, as they went, to pluck
3. 7 Jesus withdrew himself with his discipl.
3. 9 he spake to his disciples, that a small
4. 34 he expounded all things to his disciples
5. 31 his disciples said unto him, Thou seest
6. 1 And he went out..and his disciples
6. 29 when his disciples heard (of it), they
6. 35 his disciples came unto him, and said
6. 41 gave (them) to his disciples to set before
6. 45 straightway he constrained his disciples
7. 2 when they saw some of his disciples eat
7. 5 Why walk not thy disciples according
7. 17 his disciples asked him concerning the
8. 1 Jesus called his disciples (unto him), and
8. 4 his disciples answered him, From whence
8. 6 gave to his disciples to set before (them)
8. 10 he entered into a ship with his disciples
8. 27 Jesus went out, and his disciples
8. 27 he asked his disciples, saying unto them
8. 33 But when he had..looked on his disciples
8. 34 when he had called..his disciples also, he
9. 14 when he came to (his) disciples, he saw a
9. 18 I spake to thy disciples that they should
9. 28 his disciples asked him privately, Why
9. 31 he taught his disciples, and said unto
10. 10 in the house his disciples asked him again
10. 13 disciples rebuked those that brought
10. 23 Jesus looked..and saith unto his discip.
10. 24 the disciples were astonished at his words
10. 46 he went out of Jericho with his disciples
11. 1 he sendeth forth two of his disciples
11. 14 No man eat fruit..And his disciples heard
12. 43 he called (unto him) his disciples, and
13. 1 one of his disciples saith unto him, Mas.
14. 12 killed the passover, his disciples said
14. 13 And he sendeth forth two of his disciples
14. 14 I shall eat the passover with my disciples
14. 16 his disciples went forth, and came into
14. 32 he saith to his disciples, Sit ye here, while
16. 7 go your way, tell his disciples and Peter
Luke 5. 30 Pharisees murmured against his disciples
5. 33 Why do the disciples of John fast often
6. 1 his disciples plucked the ears of corn, and
6. 13 he called (unto him) his disciples: and of
6. 17 and the company of his disciples, and a
6. 20 he lifted up his eyes on his disciples, and
6. 40 The disciple is not above his master: but
7. 11 many of his disciples went with him, and
7. 18 the disciples of John showed him of all
7. 19 John calling (unto him) two of his disci.
8. 9 his disciples asked him, saying, What
8. 22 he went into a ship with his disciples
9. 1 Then he called his twelve [disciples] toge.
9. 14 he said to his disciples, Make them sit
9. 16 gave to the disciples to set before the
9. 18 his disciples were with him: and he
9. 40 I besought thy disciples to cast him out
9. 43 while they wondered..he said unto his d.
9. 54 when his disciples James and John saw
10. 23 he turned him unto (his) disciples, and
11. 1 one of his disciples said unto him, Lord
11. 1 to pray, as John also taught his disciples
12. 1 he began to say unto his disciples first of
12. 22 he said unto his disciples, Therefore I
14. 26 hate not his father..he cannot be my di.
14. 27 whosoever doth not bear..cannot be my d.
14. 33 that forsaketh not all..cannot be my d.
16. 1 he said also unto his disciples, There was
17. 1 Then said he unto the disciples, It is im.
17. 22 he said unto the disciples, The days will
18. 15 when (his) disciples saw (it), they rebuked
19. 29 came to pass..he sent two of his disciples
19. 37 the whole multitude of the disciples began
19. 39 said unto him, Master, rebuke thy disci.
20. 45 [in the audience..he said unto his disci.]
22. 11 I shall eat the passover with my disciples
22. 39 came out..and his disciples also followed
22. 45 when he..was come to his disciples
John 1. 35 Again..John stood, and two of his disci.
1. 37 the two disciples heard him speak, and
2. 2 both Jesus was called, and his disciples
2. 11 manifested forth his glory; and his disc.
2. 12 his mother, and his brethren, and his d.
2. 17 his disciples remembered that it was writ.
2. 22 his disciples remembered that he had said
3. 22 After these things came Jesus and his d.
3. 25 a question between (some) of John's dis.
4. 1 Jesus made and baptized more disciples
4. 2 Jesus himself baptized not, but his dis.
4. 8 For his disciples were gone away unto
4. 27 upon this came his disciples, and marv.
4. 31 In the meanwhile his disciples prayed him
4. 33 Therefore said the disciples one to another
6. 3 went..and there he sat with his disciples
6. 8 One of his disciples, Andrew, Simon P.'s
6. 11 [to the disciples, and the discip. to them]
6. 12 he said unto his disciples, Gather up the
6. 16 when even was (now) come, his disciples
6. 22 [save that one whereinto his disciples]
6. 22 Jesus went not with his disciples into the
6. 22 but (that) his disciples were gone away
6. 24 that Jesus was not there, neither his dis.
6. 60 Many therefore of his disciples, when

John 6. 61 When Jesus knew in himself that his di.
6. 66 From that (time) many of his disciples
7. 3 that thy disciples also may see the works
8. 31 If ye continue..(then) are ye my discip.
9. 2 his disciples asked him, saying, Master
9. 27 He answered them..will ye also be his d.
9. 28 art his disciple; but we are Moses' dis.
11. 7 after that saith he to (his) disciples, Let
11. 8 (His) disciples say unto him, Master, the
11. 12 Then said his disciples, Lord, if he sleep
11. 54 and there continued with his disciples
12. 4 Then saith one of his disciples, Judas Is.
12. 16 These things understood not his disciples
13. 5 began to wash the disciples' feet, and to
13. 22 Then the disciples looked one on another
13. 23 there was leaning..one of his disciples
13. 35 know that ye are my disciples, if ye have
15. 8 bear much fruit; so shall ye be my dis.
16. 17 Then said (some) of his disciples among
16. 29 His disciples said unto him, Lo, now
18. 1 he went forth with his disciples over the
18. 1 into the which he entered, and his dis.
18. 2 oftimes resorted thither with his disci.
18. 15 Peter followed Jesus, and..another disci.
18. 16 Then went out that other disciple, which
18. 17, 25 Art not thou..(one) of this man's dis.
18. 19 high priest..asked Jesus of his disciples
19. 26 the disciple standing by whom he loved
19. 27 Then saith he to the disciple, Behold thy
19. 27 from that hour that disciple took her
19. 38 Joseph of Arimathea, being a disciple of
20. 2 to the other disciple whom Jesus loved
20. 3 Peter..went forth, and that other disci
20. 4 the other disciple did outrun Peter, and
20. 8 Then went in also that other disciple
20. 10 the disciples went away again unto their
20. 18 Magdalene came and told the disciples
20. 19 where the disciples were assembled for
20. 20 Then were the disciples glad when they
20. 25 The other disciples therefore said unto
20. 26 again his disciples were within, and Th.
20. 30 did Jesus in the presence of his disciples
21. 1 showed himself again to the disciples
21. 2 of Zebedee, and two other of his disciples
21. 4 the disciples knew not that it was Jesus
21. 7 that disciple whom Jesus loved saith
21. 8 the other disciples came in a little ship
21. 12 none of the disciples durst ask him
21. 14 that Jesus showed himself to his disciples
21. 20 seeth the disciple whom Jesus loved
21. 23 that that disciple should not die: yet
21. 24 This is the disciple which testifieth of
Acts 1. 15 stood up in the midst of the [disciples]
6. 1 when the number of the disciples was
6. 2 called the multitude of the disciples
6. 7 the number of the disciples multiplied
9. 1 slaughter against the disciples of the
9. 10 there was a certain disciple at Damascus
9. 19 was Saul certain days with the disciples
9. 25 the disciples took him by night, and let
9. 26 assayed to join himself to the disciples
9. 26 and believed not that he was a disciple
9. 38 the disciples had heard that Peter was
11. 26 the disciples were called Christians first
11. 29 the disciples, every man according to his
13. 52 the disciples were filled with joy, and
14. 20 as the disciples stood round about him
14. 22 Confirming the souls of the disciples
14. 28 they abode long time with the disciples
15. 10 put a yoke upon the neck of the disciples
16. 1 certain disciple was there, named Timot.
18. 23 in order, strengthening all the disciples
18. 27 exhorting the disciples to receive him
19. 1 Paul..to Ephesus: and finding certain di.
19. 9 separated the disciples, disputing daily
19. 30 the disciples suffered him not
20. 1 Paul called unto (him) the disciples, and
20. 7 when [the disciples] came together to
20. 30 to draw away disciples after them
21. 4 finding disciples, we tarried there seven
21. 16 also (certain) of the disciples of Cesarea
21. 16 an old disciple, with whom we should

3. *A female pupil or disciple*, μαθήτρια *mathētria.*
Acts 9. 36 at Joppa a certain disciple named Tabit.

DISCIPLE, to be a —
To make or be a disciple, μαθητεύω *mathēteuō.*
Matt 27. 57 who also himself [was Jesus' disciple]

DISCIPLE, fellow —
A fellow pupil, συμμαθητής *summathētēs.*
John 11. 16 said Thomas..unto his fellow disciples

DISCIPLINE —
Chastisement, instruction, מוּסָר *musar.*
Job 36. 10 He openeth also their ear to discipline

DISCLOSE, to —
To remove, uncover, reveal, גָּלָה *galah*, 3.
Isa. 26. 21 the earth also shall disclose her blood

DISCOMFIT, to —
1. *To trouble, crush, destroy*, הָמַם *hamam.*
Josh. 10. 10 the LORD discomfited them before Israel
Judg. 4. 15 the LORD discomfited Sisera, and all (his)
1 Sa. 7. 10 upon the Philistines, and discomfited
2 Sa. 22. 15 sent out..lightning, and discomfited
Psa. 18. 14 shot out lightnings, and discomfited them
2. *To weaken*, חָלַשׁ *chalash.*
Exod 17. 13 Joshua discomfited Amalek and his peo.
3. *To cause to tremble or trouble*, חָרַד *charad*, 5.
Judg. 8. 12 he pursued..and discomfited all the host
4. *To beat down*, כָּתַת *kathath*, 5.
Num 14. 45 and smote them, and discomfited them

DISCOMFITED —
Tribute, tributary, מַס *mas.*
Isa. 31. 8 and his young men shall be discomfited

DISCOMFITURE —
Trouble, destruction, מְהוּמָה *mehumah.*
1 Sa. 14. 20 (and there was) a very great discomfiture

DISCONTENTED —
Bitter of soul, מַר נֶפֶשׁ *mar nephesh.*
1 Sa. 22. 2 every one (that was) discontented, gath.

DISCONTINUE, to —
To let go, release, שָׁמַט *shamat.*
Jer. 17. 4 shalt discontinue from thine heritage

DISCORD —
1. *Strife, contention*, מָדוֹן *madon.*
Prov. 6. 14 he deviseth mischief..he soweth discord
2. *Strifes, contentions*, מְדָנִים *medanim.*
Prov. 6. 19 and he that soweth discord among breth.

DISCOURAGE, to —
1. *To melt*, מָסַס *masas*, 5.
Deut. 1. 28 our brethren have discouraged our heart
2. *To break*, נוּא *no*, 5 [V.L. 1].
Num 32. 7 wherefore discourage ye the heart of the
3. *To break*, נוּא *no*, 5.
Num 32. 9 they discouraged the heart of the children

DISCOURAGED, to be —
1. *To be cast or broken down*, חָתַת *chathath*, 2.
Deut. 1. 21 possess..fear not, neither be discouraged
2. *To be broken*, רָצַץ *ratsats.*
Isa. 42. 4 He shall not fail nor be discouraged, till
3. *To be disheartened, lose heart*, ἀθυμέω *athumeō.*
Col. 3. 21 Fathers, provoke not..lest they be disc.

DISCOURAGED, to be much —
To be or become shortened, קָצַר *qatsar.*
Num 21. 4 soul of the people was much discouraged

DISCOVER, to —
1. *To remove, uncover, reveal*, גָּלָה *galah*, 3.
Deut 22. 30 A man shall not..discover his father's
Job 12. 22 He discovereth deep things out of dark.
41. 13 Who can discover the face of his garment?
Prov 25. 9 and discover not a secret to another
Isa. 22. 8 And he discovered the covering of Judah
57. 8 for thou hast discovered (thyself to)
Lam. 2. 14 they have not discovered thine iniquity
4. 22 O daughter of Edom; he will discover thy
Eze. 16. 37 and will discover thy nakedness unto
22. 10 In thee have they discovered their fath.
23. 10 These discovered her nakedness: they
23. 18 discovered her whoredoms, and discovered
Hos. 2. 10 now will I discover her lewdness in the
Mic. 1. 6 I will discover the foundations thereof
Nah. 3. 5 I will discover thy skirts upon thy face
2. *To make bare*, חָשַׂף *chasaph.*
Psa. 29. 9 The voice of the LORD..discovereth the
Jer. 13. 26 Therefore will I discover thy skirts upon
3. *To make bare or naked*, עָרָה *arah*, 3.
Isa. 3. 17 the LORD will discover their secret parts
4. *To make bare or naked*, עָרָה *arah*, 5.
Lev. 20. 18 he hath discovered her fountain, and she
5. *To be shown up*, ἀναφαίνομαι *anaphainomai.*
Acts 21. 3 Now when we had discovered Cyprus, we
6. *To perceive thoroughly*, κατανοέω *katanoeō.*
Acts 27. 39 they discovered a certain creek with a

DISCOVER self, to —
1. *To be removed, uncovered, revealed*, גָּלָה *galah*, 2.
1 Sa. 14. 8 and we will discover ourselves unto them
14. 11 both of them discovered themselves unto
2. *To show self uncovered, revealed*, גָּלָה *galah*, 7.
Prov 18. 2 but that his heart may discover itself

DISCOVERED, to be —
1. *To be removed, uncovered, revealed*, גָּלָה *galah*, 2.
Exod 20. 26 that thy nakedness be not discovered
2 Sa. 22. 16 foundations of the world were discovered
Psa. 18. 15 foundations of the world were discovered
Jer. 13. 22 For the greatness..are thy skirts discov.
Eze. 13. 14 the foundation thereof shall be discovered
16. 36 and thy nakedness discovered through
16. 57 Before thy wickedness was discovered, as
21. 24 in that your transgressions are discovered
23. 29 nakedness of thy whoredoms shall be dis.
Hos. 7. 1 the iniquity of Ephraim was discovered
2. *To be or become known*, יָדַע *yada*, 2.
1 Sa. 22. 6 Saul heard that David was discovered

DISCOVERING —
To make naked, עָרָה *arah*, 3.
Hab. 3. 13 by discovering the foundation unto the

DISCREET —
1. *To be intelligent, have understanding*, בִּין *bin*, 2.
Gen. 41. 33 let Pharaoh look out a man discreet and
Gen. 41. 39 none so discreet and wise as thou (art)
2. *Of sound mind*, σώφρων *sōphrōn.*
Titus 2. 5 discreet, chaste, keepers at home, good

DISCREETLY —
With understanding, νουνεχῶς *nounechōs.*
Mark 12. 34 Jesus saw that he answered discreetly, he

DISCRETION —
1. *Taste, discretion, sense*, טַעַם *taam.*
Prov 11. 22 a fair woman which is without discretion
2. *Device, discretion, thoughtfulness*, מְזִמָּה *mezimmah*
Prov. 1. 4 to the young man knowledge and discre.
2. 11 Discretion shall preserve thee, understa.
3. 21 My son..keep sound wisdom and discre.
5. 2 That thou mayest regard discretion, and
3. *Judgment*, מִשְׁפָּט *mishpat.*
Psa. 112. 5 he will guide his affairs with discretion
Isa. 28. 26 For his God doth instruct him to discre.
4. *Understanding, wisdom, meaning*, שֶׂכֶל *sekel.*
Prov 19. 11 The discretion of a man deferreth his
5. *Understanding, skilfulness*, תְּבוּנָה *tebunah.*
Jer. 10. 12 stretched out the heavens by his discretion

DISDAIN, to —
1. *To despise, contemn*, בָּזָה *bazah.*
1 Sa. 17. 42 when the Philistine..saw David, he dis
2. *To loathe, despise, reject*, מָאַס *maas.*
Job 30. 1 whose fathers I would have disdained to

DISEASE —
1. *Sickness, weakness*, חֳלִי *choli.*
2 Ki. 1. 2 whether I shall recover of this disease
8. 8, 9 saying, Shall I recover of this disease?
2 Ch. 16. 12 until his disease (was) exceeding (great)
16. 12 in his disease he sought not to the LORD
21. 18 the LORD smote him..with an incurable d.
Eccl. 6. 2 this (is) vanity, and it (is) an evil disease
2. *Disease, sickness*, מַדְוֶה *madveh.*
Deut. 7. 15 will put none of the evil diseases of Egypt
28. 60 he will bring upon thee all the diseases
3. *Sickness, disease*, מַחֲלֶה *machaleh.*
2 Ch. 21. 15 thou (shalt have) great sickness by disease
4. *Sickness, disease*, מַחֲלָה *machalah.*
Exod 15. 26 I will put none of these diseases upon
5. *Thing, matter*, דָּבָר *dabar.*
Psa. 41. 8 An evil disease, (say they), cleaveth fast
6. *Want of strength, weakness*, ἀσθένεια *astheneia.*
Acts 28. 9 which had diseases in the island, came
7. *Softness*, μαλακία *malakia.*
Matt. 4. 23 and all manner of disease among the peo.
9. 35 healing every sickness and every disease
10. 1 to heal..all manner of disease
8. *Sickness, unsoundness*, νόσημα *nosēma.*
John 5. 4 [made whole..whatsoever disease he had]
9. *Sickness, unsoundness*, νόσος *nosos.*
Matt. 4. 24 people that were taken with divers disea.
Mark 1. 34 healed many that were sick of divers dis.
Luke 4. 40 they that had any sick with divers disea.
6. 17 which came..to be healed of their diseas.
9. 1 authority over all devils, and to cure dis.
Acts 19. 12 the diseases departed from them, and the

DISEASED, (to be) —
1. *To be diseased, sick*, חָלָא *chala.*
Eze. 34. 4 The diseased have ye not strengthened
34. 21 pushed all the diseased with your horns
2. *To be or become sick, or diseased*, חָלָה *chalah.*
2 Ch. 16. 12 Asa..was diseased in his feet, until his
3. *To be or become sick or diseased*, חָלָה *chalah*, 2.
1 Ki. 15. 23 in the time of his old age he was diseased
4. *To lack strength*, ἀσθενέω *astheneō.*
John 6. 2 which he did on them that were diseased
5. *To have badly, be ill*, ἔχω κακῶς *echō kakōs.*
Matt 14. 35 brought unto him all that were diseased
Mark 1. 32 brought unto him all that were diseased

DISEASES —
1. *Sicknesses, diseases*, מַחֲלֻיִים *machaluyim.*
2 Ch. 24. 25 for they left him in great diseases, his
2. *Sicknesses, diseases*, תַּחֲלֻאִים *tachaluim.*
2 Ch. 21. 19 bowels fell out..so he died of sore diseases
Psa. 103. 3 Who forgiveth..who healeth all thy dis.

DISFIGURE, to —
To cause to disappear, hide, ἀφανίζω *aphanizō.*
Matt. 6. 16 for they disfigure their faces, that they

DISGRACE, to —
To dishonour, cause to fade, נָבֵל *nabel*, 3.
Jer. 14. 21 do not disgrace the throne of thy glory

DISGUISE, to —
1. *To change or disguise self*, שָׁנָה *shanah*, 7.
1 Ki. 14. 2 Arise, I pray thee, and disguise thyself
2. *To put in secret*, שׂוּם סֵתֶר *sum sether.*
Job 24. 15 No eye shall see me; and disguiseth (his)

DISGUISE self, to —
To hide or disguise self, חָפַשׂ *chaphas*, 7.
1 Sa. 28. 8 Saul disguised himself, and put on other
1 Ki. 20. 38 disguised himself with ashes upon his face

1 Ki.22. 30 I will disguise myself, and enter into the
22. 30 and the king of Israel disguised himself
2 Ch.18. 29 I will disguise myself, and will go to the
18. 29 So the king of Israel disguised himself
35. 22 Josiah would not turn..but disguised h.

DISH —
1. *Dish, cup, little bowl,* סֵפֶל *sephel.*
Judg. 5. 25 she brought forth butter in a lordly dish
2. *Dish, pan, cruise,* צַלַּחַת *tsallachath.*
2 Ki.21. 13 wipe Jerusalem as (a man) wipeth a dish
3. *Dish, saucer,* קְעָרָה *qearah.*
Exod25. 29 And thou shalt make the dishes thereof
37. 16 his dishes, and his spoons, and his bowls
Num. 4. 7 put thereon the dishes and the spoons
4. *A dish, tureen,* τρύβλιον *trublion.*
Matt26. 23 He that dippeth..with me in the dish
Mark14. 20 twelve, that dippeth with me in the dish

DI'-SHAN, דִּישָׁן *leaping.*
The youngest son of Seir the Horite. B.C. 1780.
Gen. 36. 21 And Dishon, and Ezer, and D.: these are
36. 28 The children of D. (are) these; Uz, and A.
36. 30 Duke Dishon, duke Ezer, duke D.
1 Ch. 1. 38 the sons of Seir..Dishon, and Ezer, and D.
1. 42 The sons of D.; Uz, and Aran

DI'-SHON (Gen.36.26, Heb. **DISHAN**), דִּשֹׁן, דִּשׁוֹן, דִּישֹׁן, דִּישׁוֹן.
1. Fifth son of Seir the Horite. B.C. 1780.
Gen. 36. 21 And D., and Ezer, and Dishan
36. 26 And these (are) the children of D.
36. 30 Duke D., duke Ezer, duke Dishan
1 Ch. 1. 38 the sons of Seir..D., and Ezer, and Dish.
2. Son of Anah and grandson of Seir.
Gen. 36. 25 And the children of Anah (were) these; D.
1 Ch. 1. 38 the sons of Seir..D., and Ezer, and Dish.
1. 41 The sons of Anah; D. And the sons of D.
1. 41 And the sons of D.; Amram, and Eshban

DISHONEST gain —
Dishonest gain, a cutting off, בֶּצַע *betsa.*
Eze. 22. 13 thy dishonest gain which thou hast made
22. 27 (and) to destroy souls, to get dishonest g.

DISHONESTY —
Shame, αἰσχύνη *aischunē.*
2 Co. 4. 2 renounced the hidden things of dishonesty

DISHONOUR —
1. *Blushing, shame,* כְּלִמָּה *kelimmah.*
Psa. 35. 26 let them be clothed with..dishonour that
69. 19 Thou hast known..my shame, and my dis.
71. 13 let them be covered (with)..dishonour
2. *Bareness, nakedness,* עֶרְוָה *arvah.*
Ezra 4. 14 not meet for us to see the king's dishonour
3. *Lightness, shame, confusion,* קָלוֹן *qalon.*
Prov. 6. 33 A wound and dishonour shall he get
4. *Dishonour, without honour,* ἀτιμία *atimia.*
Rom. 9. 21 unto honour..another unto dishonour?
1 Co.15. 43 It is sown in dishonour; it is raised in
2 Co. 6. 8 By honour and dishonour, by evil report
2 Ti. 2. 20 and some to honour, and some to dishonour

DISHONOUR, to —
1. *To dishonour, make foolish,* נָבֵל *nabel,* 3.
Mic. 7. 6 For the son dishonoureth the father, the
2. *To dishonour,* ἀτιμάζω *atimazō.*
John 8. 49 I honour my Father, and ye do dishonour
Rom. 1. 24 to dishonour their own bodies between
2. 23 through breaking the law dishonourest
3. *To put thoroughly to shame,* καταισχύνω *katais.*
1 Co. 11. 4 having (his) head covered, dishonoureth
11. 5 But every woman that prayeth..dishon.

DISINHERIT, to —
To take possession, יָרַשׁ *yarash,* 5.
Num14. 12 disinherit them, and will make of thee

DISMAYED —
Broken down thing, חַת *chath.*
Jer. 46. 5 Wherefore have I seen them dismayed

DISMAYED, to be —
1. *To be troubled, hastened,* בָּהַל *bahel,* 2.
Isa. 21. 3 I was dismayed at the seeing (of it)
2. *To be broken or cast down, affrighted,* חָתַת *chathath.*
2 Ki. 19. 26 they were dismayed and confounded
Isa. 37. 27 they were dismayed and confounded: they
Jer. 8. 9 wise (men) are ashamed, they are dismay.
48. 1 Misgab is confounded and dismayed
50. 36 mighty men; and they shall be dismayed
Obad. 9 thy mighty (men)..shall be dismayed, to
3. *To be, become broken, cast down,* חָתַת *chathath,* 2.
Deut31. 8 fear not, neither be dismayed
Josh. 1. 9 be not afraid, neither be thou dismayed
8. 1 Fear not, neither be thou dismayed: take
10. 25 Fear not, nor be dismayed; be strong
1 Sa. 17. 11 they were dismayed, and greatly afraid
1 Ch.22. 13 be strong..dread not, nor be dismayed
28. 20 fear not, nor be dismayed; for the LORD
2 Ch.20. 15 Be not afraid nor dismayed by reason of
20. 17 fear not, nor be dismayed; to morrow go
32. 7 Be strong..be not afraid nor dismayed for
Jer. 1. 17 be not dismayed at their faces, lest I con.
10. 2 be not dismayed at the signs of heaven
10. 2 for the heathen are dismayed at them
17. 18 them be dismayed, but let not me be dis.
Jer. 23. 4 they shall fear no more, nor be dismayed
30. 10 neither be dismayed, O Israel: for, lo, I
46. 27 be not dismayed, O Israel: for, behold, I
Eze. 2. 6 nor be dismayed at their looks, though
3. 9 fear them not, neither be dismayed at
4. *To look out for oneself, be dazzled,* שָׁעָה *shaah,* 7.
Isa. 41. 10 be not dismayed; for I (am) thy God: I
41. 23 do evil, that we may be dismayed, and

DISMAYED, to cause to be —
To break or cast down, חָתַת *chathath,* 5.
Jer. 49. 37 For I will cause Elam to be dismayed

DISMAYING —
A casting down, terror, מְחִתָּה *mechittah.*
Jer. 48. 39 so shall Moab be..a dismaying to all them

DISMISS, be dismissed, to —
1. *To free, open, let away,* פָּטַר *patar.*
2 Ch. 23. 8 for Jehoiada the priest dismissed not the
2. *To loose away,* ἀπολύω *apoluō.*
Acts 15. 30 when they were dismissed, they came to
19. 41 when he had thus spoken, he dismissed

DISOBEDIENCE —
1. *Disobedience,* ἀπείθεια *apeitheia.*
Eph. 2. 2 now worketh in the children of disobed.
5. 6 wrath of God upon the children of disob.
Col. 3. 6 cometh on the children of disobedience
2. *A hearing amiss, lack of attention,* παρακοή.
Rom. 5. 19 by one man's disobedience many were
2 Co.10. 6 a readiness to revenge all disobedience
Heb. 2. 2 disobedience received a just recompense

DISOBEDIENT —
1. *Insubordinate,* ἀνυπότακτος *anupotaktos.*
1 Ti. 1. 9 but for the lawless and disobedient, for
2. *Disobedient, not persuaded,* ἀπειθής *apeithēs.*
Luke 1. 17 the disobedient to the wisdom of the just
Acts 26. 19 Whereupon..I was not disobedient unto
Rom. 1. 30 inventors of evil things, disobedient to
2 Ti. 3. 2 blasphemers, disobedient to parents
Titus 1. 16 deny (him), being abominable, and disob.
3. 3 we ourselves also were sometimes..dis.
3. *To be unpersuaded,* ἀπειθέω *apeitheō.*
Rom10. 21 I have stretched forth..unto a disobedient

DISOBEDIENT, to be —
1. *To be or become bitter, rebel,* מָרָה *marah.*
1 Ki.13. 26 the man of God, who was disobedient unto
Neh. 9. 26 were disobedient, and rebelled against
2. *To be unpersuaded,* ἀπειθέω *apeitheō.*
1 Pe. 2. 7 but unto them which be disobedient, the
2. 8 which stumble at the word, being disob.
3. 20 Which sometimes were disobedient, when

DISOBEY, to —
To be or become bitter, rebel, מָרָה *marah.*
1 Ki.13. 21 thou hast disobeyed the mouth of the L.

DISORDERLY —
Disorderly, not in order, ἀτάκτως *ataktōs.*
2 Th. 3. 6 from every brother that walketh disorder.
3. 11 are some which walk among you disorde.

DISORDERLY, to behave oneself —
To be disorderly, out of order, ἀτακτέω *atakteō.*
2 Th. 3. 7 for we behaved not ourselves disorderly

DISPATCH, to —
To cut off or down, בָּרָא *bara,* 3.
Eze. 23. 47 the company shall..dispatch them with

DISPENSATION —
Law or arrangement of a house, οἰκονομία *oikonomia.*
1 Co. 9. 17 if against my will, a dispensation..is com.
Eph. 1. 10 That in the dispensation of the fulness of
3. 2 If ye have heard of the dispensation of
Col. 1. 25 according to the dispensation of God which

DISPERSE, to —
1. *To scatter, spread, winnow,* זָרָה *zarah,* 3.
Prov 15. 7 The lips of the wise disperse knowledge
Eze. 12. 15 when I shall..disperse them in the coun.
20. 23 I would scatter them..and disperse them
22. 15 disperse thee in the countries, and will
29. 12 I will scatter..and will disperse them
30. 23 I will scatter..and will disperse them
30. 26 I will scatter..and disperse them among
2. *To scatter,* פָּזַר *pazar,* 3.
Psa.112. 9 He hath dispersed, he hath given to the
3. *To break, spread, or burst forth,* פָּרַץ *parats.*
2 Ch. 11. 23 he dealt wisely, and dispersed of all his

DISPERSE abroad, to —
To scatter, σκορπίζω *skorpizō.*
2 Co. 9. 9 As it is written, He hath dispersed abroad

DISPERSE selves, to —
To be or become scattered, פּוּץ *puts.*
1 Sa. 14. 34 Disperse yourselves among the people, and

DISPERSED —
1. *To spread out, scatter,* נָפַץ *naphats.*
Isa. 11. 12 gather together the dispersed of Judah
2. *To be or become scattered,* פּוּץ *puts.*
Prov. 5. 16 Let thy fountains be dispersed abroad
Zeph. 3. 10 the daughter of my dispersed, shall bring
3. *What is sown or scattered throughout,* διασπορά.
John 7. 35 will he go unto the dispersed among the

DISPERSED, to be —
1. *To be scattered, spread,* זָרָה *zarah,* 2.
Eze. 36. 19 they were dispersed through the countr..
2. *To be separated,* פָּרַד *parad,* 4.
Esth. 3. 8 dispersed among the people in all the
3. *To scatter thoroughly,* διασκορπίζω *diaskorpizō.*
Acts 5. 37 (even) as many as obeyed him, were disp.

DISPERSION —
Scattering, תְּפוֹצָה *tephotsah.*
Jer. 25. 34 days of your..dispersions are accomplis.

DISPLAYED, to be —
To show self fleeing, be displayed, נוּס *nus,* 7a.
Psa. 60. 4 it may be displayed because of the truth

DISPLEASE, to —
1. *To grieve,* עָצַב *atsab.*
1 Ki. 1. 6 his father had not displeased him at any
2. *To be evil in the ears,* רָעַע בְּאָזְנַיִם *raa be-oznayim.*
Num11. 1 (when) the people complained, it displeas.
3. *To be evil in the eyes,* יֵרַע בְּעֵינַיִם *yera be-enayim.*
Gen. 38. 10 thing which he did displeased the LORD
48. 17 it displeased him; and he held up his
1 Sa. 8. 6 the thing displeased Samuel, when they
18. 8 very wroth, and the saying displeased him
2 Sa. 11. 25 Let not this thing displease thee, for the
11. 27 thing that David had done displeased the
Isa. 59. 15 displeased him that (there was) no judg.
[Num. 22. 34; Prov. 24. 18; *raa be-enayim*].
4. *To do evil in the eye,* עָשָׂה רַע בְּעַיִן *asah ra be-ayin*
1 Sa. 29. 7 that thou displease not the lords of the

DISPLEASED —
Wroth, sad, morose, זָעֵף *zaeph.*
1 Ki. 20. 43 went to his house heavy and displeased
21. 4 came into his house heavy and displeased

DISPLEASED, to be —
1. *To be angry,* אָנַף *anaph.*
Psa. 60. 1 scattered us, thou hast been displeased
2. *To be or become stinking,* בָּאַשׁ *beesh.*
Dan. 6. 14 the king..was sore displeased with him.
3. *To burn, be wroth, displeasing,* חָרָה *charah.*
2 Sa. 6. 8 David was displeased, because the LORD
1 Ch. 13. 11 David was displeased, because the LORD
Hab. 3. 8 Was the LORD displeased against the ri?
4. *To be evil in the eyes,* רָעַע בְּעֵינַיִם *raa be-enayim.*
1 Ch. 21. 7 And God was displeased with; Num.11.10.
5. *To be wroth,* קָצַף *qatsaph.*
Zech. 1. 2 The LORD hath been sore displeased with
1. 15 I am very sore displeased with the heath.
1. 15 I was but a little displeased, and they
6. *It was evil unto,* יֵרַע אֶל *yera el.*
Jon. 4. 1 it displeased Jonah exceedingly, and he

DISPLEASED, to be much or sore —
To be much weighed down, ἀγανακτέω *aganakteō.*
Matt21. 15 saying, Hosanna..they were sore displ.
Mark10. 14 when Jesus saw (it), he was much displ.
10. 41 they began to be much displeased with J.

DISPLEASED with, to be highly —
To fight with or in the mind, θυμομαχέω *thumoma.*
Acts 12. 20 Herod was highly displeased with them

DISPLEASURE, (hot or sore) —
1. *Heat, fury, poison,* חֵמָה *chemah.*
Deut. 9. 19 afraid of the anger and hot displeasure
Psa. 6. 1 neither chasten me in thy hot displeasure
38. 1 neither chasten me in thy hot displeasure
2. *Fierceness, heat, wrath,* חָרוֹן *charon.*
Psa. 2. 5 and vex them in his sore displeasure
3. *Evil,* רַע *ra.*
Judg15. 3 blameless..though I do them a displeas.

DISPOSE, to —
To put, place, set, שׂוּם *sum.*
Job 34. 13 or who hath disposed the whole world?
37. 15 Dost thou know when God disposed them

DISPOSED, to be —
1. *To wish, desire,* βούλομαι *boulomai.*
Acts 18. 27 when he was disposed to pass unto Acha
2. *To wish,* θέλω *thelō.*
1 Co. 10. 27 bid you (to a feast), and ye be disposed

DISPOSING —
Judgment, מִשְׁפָּט *mishpat.*
Prov 16. 33 whole disposing thereof (is) of the LORD

DISPOSITION —
Arrangement, διαταγή *diatagē.*
Acts 7. 53 received the law by the disposition o.

DISPOSSESS, to —
To take possession, יָרַשׁ *yarash,* 5.
Num32. 39 dispossessed the Amorite which (was) in..
33. 53 ye shall dispossess (the inhabitants of)
Deut. 7. 17 (are) more than I; how can I dispossess
Judg11. 23 the LORD God of Israel hath dispossessed

DISPUTATION —
1. *Reasoning,* διαλογισμός *dialogismos.*
Rom 14. 1 (but) not to doubtful disputations
2. *Joint seeking,* συζήτησις *suzētēsis.*
Acts 15. 2 had no small dissension and [disputation]
DISPUTE, to —
1. *To reason with one another,* יָכַח *yakach,* 2.
Job 23. 7 There the righteous might dispute with
2. *To speak diversely,* διαλέγομαι *dialegomai.*
Mark 9. 34 for by the way they had disputed among
Acts 17. 17 Therefore disputed he in the synagogue
19. 8 for the space of three months, disputing
19. 9 disputing daily in the school of one
24. 12 neither found me..disputing with any
Jude 9 when contending with the devil, he dis.
3. *To reckon diversely,* διαλογίζομαι *dialogizomai.*
Mark 9. 33 What was it that ye disputed among
4. *To seek together or jointly,* συζητέω *suzēteō.*
Acts 9. 29 spoke boldly..and disputed against the
DISPUTE with, to —
To seek together or jointly, συζητέω *suzēteō.*
Acts 6. 9 Then there arose certain..disputing with
DISPUTER —
A joint-seeker, disputer, συζητητής *suzētētēs.*
1 Co. 1. 20 where (is) the disputer of this world?
DISPUTING —
1. *A joint seeking,* συζήτησις *suzētēsis.*
Acts 15. 7 when there had been much disputing
2. *Diverse reckoning,* διαλογισμός *dialogismos.*
Phil. 2. 14 Do all things without..disputings
DISPUTINGS, perverse —
Misplaced contentions, παραδιατριβαί *paradiatrib.*
1 Ti. 6. 5 [Perverse disputings] of men of corrupt
DISQUIET, to —
To give trouble, cause to be angry, רָגַז *ragaz,* 5.
1 Sa. 28. 15 Why hast thou disquieted me, to bring
Jer. 50. 34 may give rest to the land, and disquiet
DISQUIETED, to be —
1. *To roar, move, sound, make a noise,* הָמָה *hamah.*
Psa. 39. 6 surely they are disquieted in vain: he heap.
42. 5 and (why) art thou disquieted in me? hope
42. 11 why art thou disquieted within me? hope
43. 5 why art thou disquieted within me? hope
2. *To be troubled,* רָגַז *ragaz.*
Prov 30. 21 For three (things) the earth is disquieted
DISQUIETNESS —
Howling, disquietude, נְהָמָה *nehamah.*
Psa. 38. 8 I have roared by reason of the disquiet.
DISSEMBLE, to —
1. *To lie, deny, feign,* כָּחַשׁ *kachash,* 3.
Jos. 7. 11 dissembled also, and they have put (it)
2. *To dissemble; be known,* נָכַר *nakar,* 2.
Prov 26. 24 He that hateth dissembleth with his lips
3. *To cause to err, wander,* תָּעָה *taah,* 5.
Jer. 42. 20 For ye dissembled in your hearts, when
DISSEMBLE with, to —
To act hypocritically with, συνυποκρίνομαι *sunup.*
Gal. 2. 13 other Jews dissembled likewise with him
DISSEMBLER —
To be hidden, concealed, עָלַם *alam,* 2.
Psa. 26. 4 neither will I go in with dissemblers
DISSENSION —
A standing up, στάσις *stasis.*
Acts 15. 2 Paul and Barnabas had no small dissen.
23. 7 there arose a dissension between the
23. 10 when there arose a great dissension, the
DISSIMULATION —
Hypocrisy, ὑπόκρισις *hupokrisis.*
Gal. 2. 13 was carried away with their dissimulation
DISSIMULATION, without —
Not hypocritical, ἀνυπόκριτος *anupokritos.*
Rom 12. 9 (Let) love be without dissimulation
DISSOLVE, to —
1. *To melt, dissolve, soften,* מוּג *mug,* 3b.
Job 30. 22 Thou liftest me up..and dissolvest my
2. *To solve, loose,* שְׁרָא *shere.*
Dan. 5. 16 canst make interpretations, and dissolve
3. *To solve, loose,* שְׁרָא *shere,* 3.
Dan. 5. 12 dissolving of doubts, were found in the
DISSOLVED, to be —
1. *To be melted,* מוּג *mug,* 2.
Psa. 75. 3 all the inhabitants thereof are dissolved
Isa. 14. 31 thou, whole Palestina, (art) dissolved: for
Nah. 2. 6 and the palace shall be dissolved
2. *To become corrupted, wasted,* מָקַק *maqaq,* 2.
Isa. 34. 4 all the host of heaven shall be dissolved
3. *To break self, be broken,* פָּרַר *parar,* 7a.
Isa. 24. 19 the earth is clean dissolved, the earth is
4. *To loose down,* καταλύω *kataluō.*
2 Co. 5. 1 that if our earthly house..were dissolved
5. *To loose,* λύω *luō.*
2 Pe. 3. 11 (that) all these things shall be dissolved
3. 12 the heavens being on fire shall be dissol.
DISTAFF —
Circuit, staff, distaff, פֶּלֶךְ *pelek.*
Prov 31. 19 the spindle, and her hands hold the distaff
DISTANT, equally —
To be joined, שָׁלַב *shalab,* 4.
Exod 36. 22 two tenons, equally distant one from
DISTIL, to —
1. *To flow,* נָזַל *nazal.*
Deut 32. 2 my speech shall distil as the dew, as the
2. *To drop, distil,* רָעַף *raaph.*
Job 36. 28 Which the clouds do drop (and) distil
DISTINCTION —
Distinction, a sending forth diversely, διαστολή.
1 Co. 14. 7 except they give a distinction in the sou.
DISTINCTLY —
To be explained, פָּרַשׁ *parash,* 4.
Neh. 8. 8 So they read in the book..distinctly, and
DISTRACTED, to be —
To be distracted, cold, numb, wearied, פּוּן *pun.*
Psa. 88. 15 I suffer thy terrors I am distracted
DISTRACTION, without —
Not drawn around about, ἀπερισπάστως *aperispas.*
1 Co. 7. 35 attend upon the Lord without distraction
DISTRESS —
1. *Straitness, distress,* מָצוֹק *matsoq.*
1 Sa. 22. 2 every one (that was) in distress..gathered
2. *Straitness, distress,* מְצוּקָה *metsuqah.*
Psa. 25. 17 O bring thou me out of my distresses
107. 6 he delivered them out of their distresses
107. 13 cried..(and) he saved them out of their d.
107. 19 cry..(and) he saveth them out of their d.
107. 28 cry..and he bringeth them out of their d.
Zeph. 1. 15 a day of wrath, a day of trouble and dis.
3. *Straitness, distress,* מֵצַר *metsar.*
Psa. 118. 5 I called upon the LORD in distress: the
4. *Strait, distress,* צַר, צָר *tsar.*
2 Sa. 22. 7 In my distress I called upon the LORD
Psa. 4. 1 hast enlarged me (when I was) in distress
18. 6 In my distress I called upon the LORD
Isa. 25. 4 a strength to the needy in his distress
Eze. 30. 16 and Noph (shall have) distresses daily
5. *Straitness, distress,* צָרָה *tsarah.*
Gen. 35. 3 answered me in the day of my distress
42. 21 would not hear; therefore is this distress
1 Ki. 1. 29 hath redeemed my soul out of all distress
Neh. 9. 37 have dominion..and we (are) in great dis.
Psa. 120. 1 In my distress I cried unto the LORD
Prov. 1. 27 when distress and anguish cometh upon
Obad. 12 have spoken proudly in the day of distr.
14 that did remain in the day of distress
6. *To straiten, send distress,* צָרַר *tsarar,* 5.
2 Ch. 28. 22 in the time of his distress did he trespass
7. *Evil,* רַע *ra.*
Neh. 2. 17 Ye see the distress that we (are) in
8. *Necessity, constraint,* ἀνάγκη *anagkē.*
Luke 21. 23 for there shall be great distress in the
1 Co. 7. 26 that this is good for the present distress
1 Th. 3. 7 we were comforted..in all our..distress
9. *Strait place or state,* στενοχωρία *stenochōria.*
Rom. 8. 35 (shall) tribulation, or distress, or persecu.
2 Co. 6. 4 in much patience, in afflictions..in distr.
12. 10 Therefore I take pleasure in..distresses
10. *A holding fast together,* συνοχή *sunochē.*
Luke 21. 25 upon the earth distress of nations, with
DISTRESS, to —
1. *To distress, oppress, straiten,* צוּק *tsuq,* 5.
Deut 28. 53, 55, 57 wherewith thine enemies shall dis.
Isa. 29. 2 Yet I will distress Ariel, and there shall
29. 7 even all that..distress her, shall be as a
2. *To bind, distress, besiege,* צוּר *tsur.*
Deut. 2. 9 the LORD said unto me, Distress not the
2. 19 distress them not, nor meddle with them
2 Ch. 28. 20 king of Assyria came..and distressed him
3. *To straiten, send distress,* צָרַר *tsarar,* 5.
Jer. 10. 18 will distress them, that they may find (it)
DISTRESS, to bring —
To straiten, send distress, צָרַר *tsarar,* 5.
Zeph. 1. 17 I will bring distress upon men, that they
DISTRESS, to be in —
To be distressed, צָרַר *tsarar.*
Judg. 11. 7 why are ye come..when ye are in distress?
Lam. 1. 20 Behold, O LORD, for I (am) in distress
DISTRESSED, to be —
1. *To be distressed, straitened,* יָצַר *yatsar.*
Gen. 32. 7 Then Jacob was greatly afraid and distr.
Judg. 2. 15 had sworn..and they were greatly distr.
10. 9 to fight..so that Israel was sore distres.
1 Sa. 30. 6 David was greatly distressed; for the
2. *To be exacted, urged on,* נָגַשׂ *nagas,* 2.
1 Sa. 13. 6 for the people were distressed, then the
14. 24 the men of Israel were distressed that day
3. *To be distressed,* צָרַר *tsarar.*
1 Sa. 28. 15 Saul answered, I am sore distressed; for
2 Sa. 1. 26 I am distressed for thee, my brother Jon.
4. *To be vexed, weary,* קוּץ *quts.*
Num 22. 3 Moab was distressed because of the chil.
5. *To put in a strait space,* στενοχωρέω *stenochōreō.*
2 Co. 4. 8 troubled on every side, yet not distressed
DISTRIBUTE, to —
1. *To apportion, distribute, share,* חָלַק *chalaq.*
2 Ch. 23. 18 David had distributed in the house of the
Neh. 13. 13 their office (was) to distribute unto their
2. *To be apportioned, distributed,* חָלַק *chalaq,* 2.
1 Ch. 24. 3 David distributed them, both Zadok of
3. *To apportion, distribute, share,* חָלַק *chalaq,* 3.
Job 21. 17 (God) distributeth sorrows in his anger
4. *To give,* נָתַן *nathan.*
2 Ch. 31. 14 to distribute the oblations of the LORD
5. *To deal throughout, give out,* διαδίδωμι *diadidōmi.*
Luke 18. 22 sell all that thou hast, and [distribute]
John 6. 11 when he had given thanks, he distributed
6. *To make common,* κοινωνέω *koinōneō.*
Rom 12. 13 Distributing to the necessity of saints
7. *To divide into parts,* μερίζω *merizō.*
1 Co. 7. 17 But as God hath distributed to every man
2 Co. 10. 13 the rule which God hath distributed to us
DISTRIBUTE, ready to —
Willing to impart or give away, εὐμετάδοτος.
1 Ti. 6. 18 be rich in good works, ready to distribute
DISTRIBUTION —
A sharing, participation, κοινωνία *koinōnia.*
2 Co. 9. 13 and for (your) liberal distribution unto
DISTRIBUTION, to make —
To deal out, give throughout, διαδίδωμι *diadidōmi.*
Acts 4. 35 and distribution was made unto every
DITCH —
1. *Ditch,* גֵּב *geb.*
2 Ki. 3. 16 saith the LORD, Make this valley full of d.
2. *Ditch, collection of water,* מִקְוָה *miqvah.*
Isa. 22. 11 Ye made also a ditch between the two
3. *Pit, ditch,* שׁוּחָה *shuchah.*
Prov. 23. 27 For a whore (is) a deep ditch; and a
4. *Corruption, pit, ditch,* שַׁחַת *shachath.*
Job 9. 31 Yet shalt thou plunge me in the ditch, and
Psa. 7. 15 He..is fallen into the ditch (which) he
5. *Deep place, pit,* βόθυνος *bothunos.*
Matt 15. 14 both shall fall into the ditch
Luke 6. 39 shall they not both fall into the ditch
DIVERS —
1. *Man; some, certain,* אֱנוֹשׁ *enosh.*
2 Ch. 30. 11 Nevertheless divers of Asher and Man.
2. *Differing,* διάφορος *diaphoros.*
Heb. 9. 10 in meats and drinks, and divers washings
3. *Variegated, spotted, various, different,* ποικίλος.
Matt. 4. 24 sick people that were taken with divers
Mark 1. 34 he healed many that were sick of divers
Luke 4. 40 all they that had any sick with divers dis.
2 Ti. 3. 6 silly women..led away with divers lusts
Titus 3. 3 disobedient, deceived, serving divers lusts
Heb. 2. 4 signs and wonders, and with divers mir.
13. 9 Be not carried about with divers and
Jas. 1. 2 joy when ye fall into divers temptations
4. *A certain one, some one,* τις *tis.*
Mark 8. 3 will faint by the way: for divers of them
Acts 19. 9 when divers were hardened, and believed
DIVERS colours —
1. *Finger or painted work,* צֶבַע *tseba.*
Judg. 5. 30 of divers colours, a prey of divers colours
5. 30 of divers colours of needlework on both
2. *Embroidery,* רִקְמָה *riqmah.*
1 Ch. 29. 2 divers colours, and all manner of precious
Eze. 17. 3 full of feathers, which had divers colours
DIVERS manners, in —
In many ways or turns, πολυτρόπως *polutropōs.*
Heb. 1. 1 at sundry times and in divers manners
DIVERS measures —
An ephah and an ephah, אֵיפָה וְאֵיפָה *ephah ve-ephah.*
Deut 25. 14 Thou shalt not have..divers measures, a
Prov 20. 10 (and) divers measures, both of them (are)
DIVERS places, in —
Down through (divers) places, κατὰ τόπους *kata.*
Matt 24. 7 there shall be..earthquakes, in divers pl.
Mark 13. 8 shall be earthquakes in divers places
Luke 21. 11 earthquakes shall be in divers places
DIVERS seeds —
Two different kinds, כִּלְאַיִם *kilayim.*
Deut 22. 9 Thou shalt not sow thy vineyard with d.s.
DIVERS weights —
A stone and a stone, אֶבֶן וָאֶבֶן *eben va-eben.*
Deut 25. 13 Thou shalt not have..divers weights, a
Prov 20. 10 Divers weights..both of them (are) alike
20. 23 Divers weights (are) an abomination unto

DIVERSE —
1. *To be changed, different,* שָׁנָה *shanah.*
Esth. 3. 8 and their laws (are) diverse from all peo.
2. *To be changed, different,* שְׁנָא *shena.*
Dan. 7. 3 four great beasts..diverse one from
7. 19 the fourth beast which was diverse from
3. *To change, be different,* שְׁנָא *shena,* 3.
Dan. 7. 7 it (was) diverse from all the beasts that

DIVERSE, to be —
1. *To be changed, different,* שְׁנָא *shena.*
Dan. 7. 23 fourth kingdom upon earth..shall be di.
7. 24 he shall be diverse from the first, and he
2. *To be changed, different,* שָׁנָה *shanah.*
Esth. 1. 7 the vessels being diverse one from another

DIVERSE kind —
Two different kinds, כִּלְאַיִם *kilayim.*
Lev. 19. 19 not let thy cattle gender with a diverse k.

DIVERSITY —
1. *Genus, race, sort,* γένος *genos.*
1 Co. 12. 28 helps, governments, diversities of ton.
2. *Diverse parting, distribution,* διαίρεσις *diairesis.*
1 Co. 12. 4 there are diversities of gifts, but the same
12. 6 there are diversities of operations, but

DIVIDE, to —
1. *To separate,* בָּדַל *badal,* 5.
Gen. 1. 4 (it was) good: and God divided the light
1. 6 let it divide the waters from the waters
1. 7 God..divided the waters which (were)
1. 14 divide the day from the night; and let
1. 18 and to divide the light from the darkness
Exod 26. 33 the veil shall divide unto you between the
2. *To cleave, rend,* בָּקַע *baqa.*
Exod 14. 16 stretch out thine hand..and divide it; and
Neh. 9. 11 thou didst divide the sea before them
Psa. 78. 13 He divided the sea, and caused them to
Isa. 63. 12 led (them) by the right hand..dividing
3. *To dissect, part, separate,* בָּתַר *bathar.*
Gen. 15. 10 against another: but the birds divided he
4. *To dissect, part, separate,* בָּתַר *bathar,* 3.
Gen. 15. 10 he took unto him all these, and divided
5. *To cut down,* גָּזַר *gazar.*
1 Ki. 3. 25 Divide the living child in two, and give
3. 26 Let it be neither mine nor thine, (but) div.
Psa. 136. 13 To him which divided the Red sea into
6. *To apportion,* חָלַק *chalaq.*
Deut. 4. 19 which the LORD thy God hath divided
Josh. 14. 5 children of Israel did, and they divided
22. 8 divide the spoil of your enemies with your
2 Sa. 19. 29 I have said, Thou and Ziba divide the
Neh. 9. 22 nations, and didst divide them into cor.
Job 27. 17 and the innocent shall divide the silver
7. *To be apportioned,* חָלַק *chalaq,* 2.
1 Ch. 23. 6 David divided them into courses among
8. *To apportion,* חָלַק *chalaq,* 3.
Gen. 49. 7 I will divide them in Jacob, and scatter
49. 27 and at night he shall divide the spoil
Exod 15. 9 I will overtake, I will divide the spoil
Josh 13. 7 divide this land for an inheritance unto
18. 10 Joshua divided the land unto the children
19. 51 divided for an inheritance by lot in Shi.
19. 51 they made an end of dividing the country
Judg. 5. 30 Have they not sped? have they (not) divi.
1 Ki. 18. 6 they divided the land between them, to
Psa. 60. 6 I will divide Shechem, and mete out the
68. 12 she that tarried at home divided the spoil
108. 7 I will divide Shechem, and mete out the
Prov 16. 19 than to divide the spoil with the proud
Isa. 9. 3 as (men) rejoice when they divide the
34. 17 his hand hath divided it unto them by
53. 12 Therefore will I divide him (a portion)
53. 12 he shall divide the spoil with the strong
Lam. 4. 16 The anger of the LORD hath divided them
Eze. 5. 1 balances to weigh, and divide the (hair)
47. 21 So shall ye divide this land unto you
Dan. 11. 39 and shall divide the land for gain
Mic. 2. 4 turning away he hath divided our fields
9. *To apportion for self,* חָלַק *chalaq,* 7.
Josh. 18. 5 And they shall divide it into seven parts
10. *To hew, dig through,* חָצַב *chatseb.*
Psa. 29. 7 voice of the LORD divideth the flames
11. *To halve, divide,* חָצָה *chatsah.*
Gen. 32. 7 he divided the people that (was) with him
33. 1 he divided the children unto Leah, and
Exod 21. 35 sell the live ox, and divide the money
21. 35 and the dead (ox) also they shall divide
Num 31. 27 divide the prey into two parts, between
31. 42 Moses divided from the men that warred
Judg. 7. 16 he divided the three hundred men (into)
9. 43 divided them into three companies, and
12. *To give for inheritance,* נָחַל *nachal.*
Num 34. 17 the men which shall divide the land unto
13. *To cause to fall,* נָפַל *naphal,* 5.
Psa. 78. 55 He..divided them an inheritance by line
14. *To cut in pieces,* נָתַח *nathach,* 3.
Judg 19. 29 laid hold on his concubine, and divided
15. *To divide,* פָּלַג *palag,* 3.
Job 38. 25 Who hath divided a water course for the
Psa. 55. 9 Destroy, O LORD, (and) divide their tong.
16. *To divide, cleave,* פָּרַס *paras,* 5.
Lev. 11. 4 not eat..of them that divide the hoof
11. 4, 5 cheweth the cud, but divideth not the
11. 7 the swine, though he divide the hoof, and
11. 26 every beast which divideth the hoof
Deut 14. 7 or of them that divide the cloven hoof
14. 7 chew the cud, but divide not the hoof
14. 8 the swine, because it divideth the hoof
17. *To break, divide,* פָּרַר *parar,* 3a.
Psa. 74. 13 Thou didst divide the sea by thy strength
18. *To quiet,* רָגַע *raga.*
Job 26. 12 He divideth the sea with his power, and
Isa. 51. 15 I (am) the LORD thy God, that divided
Jer. 31. 35 which divideth the sea when the waves
19. *To mark off,* ἀφορίζω *aphorizō.*
Matt 25. 32 shepherd divideth (his) sheep from the
20. *To give through, deal out,* διαδίδωμι *diadidōmi.*
Luke 11. 22 taketh..his armour..and divideth his
21. *To take diversely or apart,* διαιρέω *diaireō.*
Luke 15. 12 And he divided unto them (his) living
1 Co. 12. 11 dividing to every man severally as he

DIVIDE by lot, to —
1. *To cause to fall, apportion,* נָפַל *naphal,* 5.
Josh. 13. 6 divide thou it by lot unto the Israelites
23. 4 have divided unto you by lot these
Eze. 45. 1 when ye shall divide by lot the land for
47. 22 shall divide it by lot for an inheritance
48. 29 the land which ye shall divide by lot unto
2. *To give by lot thoroughly,* κατακληροδοτέω *kata.*
Acts 13. 19 [he divided their land to them by lot]

DIVIDE asunder, to —
To separate, בָּדַל *badal,* 5.
Lev. 1. 17 (but) shall not divide (it) asunder: and
5. 8 wring off..but shall not divide (it) asun.

DIVIDE self —
To apportion, divide, distribute, חָלַק *chalaq,* 2.
Gen. 14. 15 he divided himself against them, he and

DIVIDE speedily, to —
To cause to run, רוּץ *ruts,* 5.
2 Ch. 35. 13 divided (them) speedily among all the

DIVIDE rightly, to —
To cut straight or right, ὀρθοτομέω *orthotomeō.*
2 Ti. 2. 15 a workman..rightly dividing the word of

DIVIDED —
To be divided, פְּלַג *pelag.*
Dan. 2. 41 the kingdom shall be divided; but there

DIVIDED, to be —
1. *To be cleft,* בָּקַע *baqa,* 2.
Exod 14. 21 dry (land), and the waters were divided
2. *To be apportioned, divided,* חָלַק *chalaq.*
1 Ch. 24. 4 more chief men..and (thus) were they d.
Hos. 10. 2 Their heart is divided; now shall they be
3. *To be or become apportioned, divided,* חָלַק *chalaq,* 2.
Num 26. 53 Unto these the land shall be divided for
26. 55 Notwithstanding the land shall be divi.
26. 56 the possession thereof be divided
1 Ki. 16. 21 Then were the people of Israel divided
4. *To be or become apportioned,* חָלַק *chalaq,* 4.
Isa. 33. 23 then is the prey of a great spoil divided
Amos 7. 17 thy land shall be divided by line; and
Zech. 14. 1 thy spoil shall be divided in the midst
5. *To be halved,* חָצָה *chatsah,* 2.
2 Ki. 2. 8 and they were divided hither and
Eze. 37. 22 neither shall they be divided into two
Dan. 11. 4 shall be broken, and shall be divided
6. *To be divided, cleaved, separated,* פָּלַג *palag,* 2.
Gen. 10. 25 for in his days was the earth divided
1 Ch. 1. 19 because in his days the earth was divided
7. *To be separated,* פָּרַד *parad,* 2.
Gen. 10. 5 By these were the isles..divided in their
10. 32 by these were the nations divided in the
2 Sa. 1. 23 in their death they were not divided
8. *To be dealt out, divided,* פְּרַס *peras.*
Dan. 5. 28 Thy kingdom is divided, and given to
9. *To become,* γίνομαι *ginomai.*
Rev. 16. 19 the great city was divided into three parts
10. *To divide into parts throughout,* διαμερίζω.
Luke 11. 17 Every kingdom divided against itself is
11. 18 If Satan also be divided against himself
12. 52 there shall be five in one house divided
12. 53 The father shall be divided against the
22. 17 Take this, and divide (it) among yoursel.
11. *To divide into parts,* μερίζω *merizō.*
Matt 12. 25 Every kingdom divided against itself is
12. 25 every city or house divided against itself
12. 26 if Satan cast out Satan, he is divided ag.
Mark 3. 24 if a kingdom be divided against itself
3. 25 if a house be divided against itself, that
3. 26 rise up against himself, and be divided
6. 41 the two fishes divided he among them all
Luke 12. 13 that he divide the inheritance with me
1 Co. 1. 13 Is Christ divided? was Paul crucified for
12. *To rend,* σχίζω *schizō.*
Acts 14. 4 But the multitude of the city was divided
23. 7 and the multitude was divided

DIVIDER —
One who divides into parts, μεριστής *meristēs.*
Luke 12. 14 made me a judge or a divider over you?

DIVIDING —
To divide, cleave, separate, פְּלַג *pelag.*
Dan. 7. 25 a time and times and the dividing of

DIVIDING asunder —
Division into parts, μερισμός *merismos.*
Heb. 4. 12 even to the dividing asunder of soul and

DIVINATION —
1. *Divination,* מִקְסָם *miqsam.*
Eze. 12. 24 nor flattering divination within the
13. 7 have ye not spoken a lying divination
2. *To divine,* קָסַם *qasam.*
Eze. 21. 23 shall be unto them as a false divination
3. *Divination,* קֶסֶם *qesem.*
Num 23. 23 neither (is there) any divination against
Deut 18. 10 that useth divination, (or) an observer of
2 Ki. 17. 17 and used divination and enchantments
Jer. 14. 14 they prophesy..a false vision and divina.
Eze. 13. 6 They have seen vanity and lying divinat.
13. 23 see no more vanity, nor divine divinations
21. 21 head of the two ways, to use divination
21. 22 At his right hand was the divination for
4. *Python,* πύθων *puthōn.*
Acts 16. 16 possessed with a spirit of divination met

DIVINATION, reward of —
Divination, קֶסֶם *qesem.*
Num. 22. 7 departed with the rewards of divination

DIVINE —
Divine, godly, god-like, θεῖος *theios.*
2 Pe. 1. 3 as his divine power hath given unto us
1. 4 might be partakers of the divine nature

DIVINE sentence —
Divination, קֶסֶם *qesem.*
Prov. 16. 10 A divine sentence (is) in the lips of the

DIVINE service —
Public worship, λατρεία *latreia.*
Heb. 9. 1 had also ordinances of divine service

DIVINE, to —
1. *To divine, use enchantment,* נָחַשׁ *nachash,* 3.
Gen. 44. 5 and whereby indeed he divineth? Ye
44. 15 that such a man as I can certainly divine
2. *To cut off, divine, use divinations,* קָסַם *qasam.*
1 Sa. 28. 8 I pray thee, divine unto me by the
Eze. 13. 9 that see vanity, and that divine lies
13. 23 see no more vanity, nor divine divinations
21. 29 whiles they divine a lie unto thee, to
Mic. 3. 6 it shall be dark..that ye shall not divine
3. 11 the prophets thereof divine for money

DIVINER —
To cut off, divine, קָסַם *qasam.*
Deut 18. 14 hearkened unto observers..and unto div
1 Sa. 6. 2 Philistines called for the..diviners
Isa. 44. 25 That frustrateth..and maketh diviners
Jer. 27. 9 hearken not..to your diviners..dreamers
29. 8 Let not..your diviners..deceive you
Mic. 3. 7 seers be ashamed, and the diviners
Zech 10. 2 diviners have seen a lie, and have told

DIVINING —
To cut off, divine, קָסַם *qasam.*
Eze. 22. 28 divining lies unto them, saying, Thus

DIVISION —
1. *Apportioning, division,* חֲלֻקָּה *chaluqqah.*
2 Ch. 35. 5 division of the families of the Levites
2. *Course, division,* מַחֲלֹקֶת *machaloqeth.*
Josh 11. 23 according to their divisions by their
12. 7 possession according to their divisions
18. 10 the children..according to their divisions
1 Ch. 24. 1 (these are) the divisions of the sons of
26. 1 Concerning the divisions of the porters
26. 12 these (were) the divisions of the porters
26. 19 These (are) the divisions of the porters
Neh. 11. 36 of the Levites (were) divisions (in) Judah
3. *Separation,* פְּדוּת *peduth.*
Exod. 8. 23 I will put a division between my people
4. *Division,* פְּלַגָּה *pelaggah.*
Judg. 5. 15, 16 the divisions of Reuben (there were)
5. *Division,* פְּלֻגָּה *peluggah.*
2 Ch. 35. 5 according to the divisions of the families
Ezra 6. 18 they set the priests in their divisions
6. *A division into parts throughout,* διαμερισμός.
Luke 12. 51 I tell you, Nay; but rather division
7. *A twofold upstanding,* διχοστασία *dichostasia.*
Rom 16. 17 mark them which cause divisions and
1 Co. 3. 3 (there is) among you envying..and [divis.]
8. *A rent, cleft, schism,* σχίσμα *schisma.*
John 7. 43 there was a division among the people
9. 16 And there was a division among them
10. 19 There was a division therefore again

1 Co. 1. 10 and (that) there be no divisions among
11. 18 I hear that there be divisions among you

DIVISIONS —
Divisions, מִפְלַגּוֹת *miphlaggoth.*
2 Ch.35. 12 might give according to the divisions

DIVORCE —
A cutting off, כְּרִיתוּת *kerithuth.*
Jer. 3. 8 put her away, and given..a bill of divorce

DIVORCED, to be —
To loose off or away, ἀπολύω *apoluō.*
Matt. 5. 32 whosoever shall marry her that is divorced

DIVORCED, woman —
To cast out, divorce, גָּרַשׁ *garash.*
Lev. 21. 14 a divor. woman, or profane, (or) an harlot
22. 13 priest's daughter be a widow, or divorced
Num30. 9 of a widow, and of her that is divorced

DIVORCEMENT, (writing of) —
1. *A cutting off,* כְּרִיתוּת *kerithuth.*
Deut24. 1 let him write her a bill of divorcement
24. 3 and write her a bill of divorcement, and
Isa. 50. 1 the bill of your mother's divorcement
2. *A setting or standing off or away,* ἀποστάσιον.
Matt 5. 31 let him give her a writing of divorcement
19. 7 command to give a writing of divorce.
Mark10. 4 suffered to write a bill of divorcement

DI-ZA'-HAB, דִּי זָהָב *golden, lord of gold.*
A place in the wilderness of Sinai, not far from the Red Sea, over against Suph, the modern *Dahab,* a cape on the W. shore of the *Gulf of Akabah,* about two thirds down its length. Gold was most likely found here.
Deut. 1. 1 Tophel, and Laban, and Hazeroth, and D.

DO—
1. *Work,* מַעֲשֶׂה *maaseh.*
Judg13. 12 How shall we order..(how) shall we do
2. *Peace, completeness,* שָׁלוֹם *shalom.*
2 Sa. 11. 7 how Joab did, and how the people did
Esth. 2. 11 to know how Esther did, and what should

DO (earnestly, a deed), to —
1. *To do,* הָיָה *hayah.*
1 Sa. 2. 11 the child did minister unto the LORD
2. *To serve,* עָבַד *abad.*
Num. 3. 7, 8 to do the service of the tabernacle
4. 23, 30 to do the work in the tabernacle of
4. 41 that might do service in the tabernacle
4. 47 came to do the service of the ministry
7. 5 that they may be to do the service of the
8. 15 to do the service of the tabernacle of
8. 19 to do the service of the children of Israel
8. 22 to do their service in the tabernacle of
8. 26 to keep the charge. and shall do no ser.
16. 9 to do the service of the tabernacle of
18. 6 to do the service of the tabernacle of
Josh22. 27 that we might do the service of the LORD
Isa. 19. 21 and shall do sacrifice and oblation
3. *To do, serve,* עֲבַד *abad.*
Ezra 4. 22 Take heed now that ye fail not to do this
7. 18 to do with the rest of the silver and the
7. 18 that do after the will of your God
7. 26 whosoever will not do the law of thy God
Dan. 4. 35 he doeth according to his will in the
4. 35 or say unto him, What doest thou?
6. 10 and gave thanks before his God, as he did
6. 22 before thee, O king have I done no hurt
Ezra 6. 8 I make a decree what ye shall do to the
4. *To do, act,* עֲלַל *alal,* 3a.
Lam. 1 22 do unto them as thou hast done unto me
2. 20 and consider to whom thou hast done
5. *To do,* עָשָׂה *asah.*
Gen. 3. 13 What (is) this (that) thou hast done?
3. 14 Because thou hast done this, thou (art)
4. 10 What hast thou done? the voice of thy
6. 22 Thus did Noah; according to all..so did
7. 5 Noah did according unto all that the
8. 21 neither will I again smite..as I have done
9. 24 what his younger son had done unto him
11. 6 this they begin to do: and now nothing
11. 6 which they have imagined to do
12. 18 What (is) this (that) thou hast done unto
16. 6 Behold, thy maid. do to her as it pleaseth
18. 5 and they said, So do, as thou hast said
18. 17 Shall I hide..that thing which I do
18. 19 keep the way of the LORD, to do justice
18. 21 see whether they have done altogether
18. 25 be far from thee to do after this manner
18. 25 Shall not the Judge of all the earth do ri.
18. 29 he said, I will not do (it) for forty's sake
18. 30 I will not do (it) if I find thirty there
19. 8 do ye to them as (is) good in your eyes
19. 8 unto these men do nothing; for therefore
19. 22 I cannot do any thing till thou be come
20. 5 in..innocency of my hands, have I done
20. 6 didst this in the integrity of thy heart
20. 9 What hast thou done unto us? and what
20. 9 thou hast done deeds unto me that ought
20. 10 What sawest thou, that thou hast done
21. 1 the LORD did unto Sarah as he had spoken
21. 22 God (is) with thee in all that thou doest
21. 23 have done unto thee, thou shalt do unto
21. 26 said, I wot not who hath done this
22. 12 neither do thou anything unto him

Gen.22. 16 because thou hast done this thing, and
24. 66 told Isaac all things that he had done
26. 10 What (is) this thou hast done unto us?
26. 29 thou wilt do us no hurt, as we have not
26. 29 as we have done unto thee nothing but
27. 19 I have done according as thou badest
27. 37 and what shall I do now unto thee
27. 45 forget (that) which thou hast done to him
28. 15 until I have done (that) which I have
29. 25 What (is) this thou hast done unto me
29. 28 And Jacob did so, and fulfilled her week
30. 31 If thou wilt do this thing for me, I will
31. 12 have seen all that Laban doeth unto thee
31. 16 whatsoever God hath said unto thee, do
31. 26 What hast thou done, that thou hast
31. 28 Thou hast now done foolishly in (so) doing
31. 29 It is in the power of my hand to do you
31. 43 what can I do this day unto these my
34. 14 We cannot do this thing, to give our
34. 19 young man deferred not to do the thing
38. 10 thing which he did displeased the LORD
39. 3 all that he did to prosper in his hand
39. 9 how then can I do this great wickedness
39. 11 went into the house to do his business
39. 19 After this manner did thy servant to me
39. 22 and whatsoever they did there, he was
39. 23 which he did, the LORD made (it) to prosp.
40. 15 here also have I done nothing that they
41. 25 showed Pharaoh what he (is) about to do
41. 28 What God (is) about to do he showeth
41 34 Let Pharaoh do (this), and let him appoint
41 55 Go unto Joseph; what he saith to you, do
42. 18 said unto them the third day, This do
42 20 bring your youngest brother..they did so
42. 25 and thus did he unto them
42. 28 What (is) this (that) God hath done unto
43. 11 If (it must be) so now, do this; take
43. 17 the man did as Joseph bade; and the
44. 2 he did according to the word that Joseph
44. 5 Ye have done evil in so doing
44. 7 God forbid that thy servants should do
44. 15 What deed (is) this that ye have done?
44. 17 God forbid that I should do so: (but) the
45. 17 This do ye; lade your beasts, and go, get
45. 19 thou art commanded, this do ye; take you
45. 21 the children of Israel did so: and Joseph
47. 30 And he said, I will do as thou hast said
50. 12 his sons did unto him according as he
Exod. 1. 17 did not as the king of Egypt commanded
1. 18 Why have ye done this thing, and have
3. 20 all my wonders which I will do in the
4. 15 and will teach you what ye shall do
4. 17 this rod..wherewith thou shalt do signs
4. 21 see that thou do all those wonders before
4. 30 did the signs in the sight of the people
6. 1 Now shalt thou see what I will do to P.
7. 6 did as the LORD commanded them, so did
7. 10 and they did so as the LORD had comma.
7. 11 they also did in like manner with their
7. 20 and Aaron did so, as the LORD command.
7. 22 the magicians of Egypt did so with their
8. 7 magicians did so with their enchantments
8. 13, 31 LORD did according to the word of M.
8. 17 they did so: for Aaron stretched out his
8. 18 magicians did so with their enchantmen.
8. 24 the LORD did so: and there came a griev.
8. 26 It is not meet so to do; for we shall
9. 5 the LORD shall do this thing in the land
9. 6 LORD did that thing on the morrow
11. 10 Moses and Aaron did all these wonders
12. 28 did as the LORD had commanded..so did
12. 35 the children of Israel did according to
12. 50 Thus did all the children..so did they
13. 8 because of that (which) the LORD did unto
14. 4 know that I (am) the LORD. And they did
14. 5 Why have we done this, that we have let
14. 31 saw that great work which the LORD did
15. 11 holiness, fearful (in) praises, doing wond.
15. 26 wilt do that which is right in his sight
16. 17 children of Israel did so, and gathered
17. 4 What shall I do unto this people?
17. 6 Moses did so in the sight of the elders
17. 10 Joshua did as Moses had said to him
18. 1 heard of all that God had done for Moses
18. 8 all that the LORD had done unto Pharaoh
18. 9 the goodness which the LORD had done
18. 14 Moses' father in law saw all that he did
18. 14 What (is) this thing that thou doest to
18. 17 The thing that thou doest (is) not good
18. 20 must walk, and the work..they must do
18. 23 If thou shalt do this thing, and God com.
18. 24 So Moses..did all that he had said
19. 4 have seen what I did unto the Egyptians
19. 8 All that the LORD hath spoken we will do
20. 9 Six days shalt thou labour and do all
20. 10 thou shalt not do any work, thou, nor thy
21. 11 if he do not these three unto her, then
22. 30 Likewise shalt thou do with thine oxen
23. 12 Six days thou shalt do thy work, and on
23. 22 obey his voice, and do all that I speak
23. 24 nor serve them, nor do after their works
24. 3 words..the LORD hath said will we do
24. 7 All that the LORD hath said will we do
29. 1 this (is) the thing that thou shalt do unto
29. 35 thus shalt thou do unto Aaron, and to
29. 41 shalt do thereto according to the meat
31. 11 all that I have commanded..shall they do
31. 14 whosoever doeth (any) work therein, that
31. 15 Six days may work be done; but in the
31. 15 whosoever doeth (any) work in the sab.
32. 14 which he thought to do unto his people
32. 21 What did this people unto thee, that thou

Exod32. 28 the children of Levi did according to
33. 5 that I may know what to do unto thee
33. 17 do this thing also that thou hast spoken
34. 10 before all thy people I will do marvels
34. 10 terrible thing that I will do with thee
35. 1 LORD hath command., that (ye) should do
35. 2 Six days shall work be done, but on the
35. 2 whosoever doeth work therein shall be
35. 35 of them that do any work, and of those
36. 2 stirred him up..unto the work to do it
36. 29 he did to both of them in both the cor.
39. 32 the children of Israel did according to
39. 32 that the LORD commanded Moses, so did
39. 43 they had done it as the LORD had com.
39. 43 even so had they done it
40. 16 Thus did Moses: according to all..did
Lev. 4. 2 which ought not to be done, and shall do
4. 13 they have done (somewhat against) any of
4. 13, 22 (things) which should not be done
4. 20 he shall do with the bullock as he did
4. 20 a sin offering, so shall he do with this
4. 22 done (somewhat) through ignorance
4. 27 he doeth (somewhat against) any of the
4. 27 (things) which ought not to done
6. 3 in any of all these that a man doeth
6. 7 that he hath done in trespassing therein
8. 4 And Moses did as the LORD commanded
8. 5 thing which the LORD commanded to be d.
8. 34 As he hath done this day, (so) the LORD
8. 34 hath commanded to do, to make an ato.
8. 36 Aaron and his sons did all things which
9. 6 the LORD commanded that ye should do
10. 7 they did according to the word of Moses
16. 15 do with that blood as he did with the
16. 16 so shall he do for the tabernacle of
16. 29 shall afflict your souls, and do no work
16. 34 And he did as the LORD commanded M.
18. 3, 3 After the doings..shall ye not do
18. 4 Ye shall do my judgments, and keep
18. 5 which if a man do, he shall live in them
18. 27 abomin. have the men of the land done
19. 15 Ye shall do no unrighteousness in judgm.
19. 35 shall do no unrighteousness in judgment
19. 37 statutes, and all my judgments, and do
20. 8 And ye shall keep my statutes, and do
20. 22 statutes, and all my judgments, and do
22. 31 keep my commandments, and do them
23. 3 Six days shall work be done: but the
23. 3 ye shall do no work (therein): it (is) the
23. 7, 8, 21, 25, 36 ye shall do no servile work
23. 28 And ye shall do no work in that same d.
23. 30 that doeth any work in that same day
23. 31 Ye shall do no manner of work: (it shall)
24. 19 as he hath done, so shall it be done to
24. 23 the children of Israel did as the LORD
25. 18 do my statutes..keep my judgm. and do
26. 3 and keep my commandments, and do
26. 14 and will not do all these commandments
26. 15 that ye will not do all my commandments
26. 16 I also will do this unto you; I will even
Num. 1. 54 the children of Israel did according to
1. 54 that the LORD commanded Moses, so did
2. 34 the children of Israel did according to all
4. 3 to do the work in the tabernacle of the
4. 19 But thus do unto them, that they may
5. 4 the children..did so, and put them out
5. 4 as the LORD spake..so did the children
5. 7 confess their sin which they have done
6. 21 must do after the law of his separation
8. 3 Aaron did so; he lighted the lamps
8. 7 thus shalt thou do unto them, to cleanse
8. 20 and Aaron..did to the Levites according
8. 20 so did the children of Israel unto them
8. 22 to do their service in the tabernacle of
8. 22 as the LORD had..so did they unto them
8. 26 Thus shalt thou do unto the Levites
9. 5 according to. so did the children of Isr.
9. 14 according to the manner..so shall he do
14. 22 and my miracles which I did in Egypt
14 28 as ye have spoken..so will I do to you
14 35 I will surely do it unto all this evil
15. 12 so shall ye do to every one according to
15. 13 All..shall do these things after this
15. 14 as ye do, so he shall do
15. 30 But the soul that doeth..presumptuously
15 39 remember all the commandments..and do
15. 40 may remember, and do all my command.
16. 6 This do: Take you censers, Korah, and
16. 28 LORD hath sent me to do all these works
17. 11 And Moses did (so)..so did he
20. 27 And Moses did as the LORD commanded
21. 34 thou shalt do to him as thou didst unto
22. 2 Balak..saw all that Israel had done to
22. 17 I will do whatsoever thou sayest unto
22. 18 I cannot go beyond..to do less or more
22. 20 which I shall say..that shalt thou do
22. 28 and she said..What have I done unto
22. 30 was I ever wont to do so unto thee? And
23. 2 And Balak did as Balaam had spoken
23. 11 Balak said..What hast thou done unto
23. 19 hath he said, and shall he not do (it)
23. 26 All that the LORD speaketh, that I must
23. 30 And Balak did as Baalam had said, and
24. 13 to do (either) good or bad of mine own
24. 14 advertise thee what this people shall do
24. 18 shall be a possession..and Israel shall do
27. 22 Moses did as the LORD commanded him
28. 18 ye shall do no manner of servile work
28. 25, 26 ye shall do no servile work
29. 1, 12, 35 ye shall do no servile work
29. 7 ye shall not do any work (therein)
29. 39 These (things) ye shall do unto the LORD

Num. 30. 2 he shall do according to all that proceed.
31. 31 and Eleazar..did as the LORD comman.
32. 8 Thus did your fathers, when I sent them
32. 13 that had done evil in the sight of the
32. 20 If ye will do this thing, if ye will
32. 23 if ye will not do so, behold, ye have
32. 24 do that which hath proceedeth out of
32. 25 servants will do as my lord commandeth
32. 31 As the LORD hath said..so will we do
33. 56 I shall do unto you, as I thought to do
36. 10 so did the daughters of Zelophehad
Deut. 1. 14 which thou hast spoken (is) good..to do
1. 18 commanded..all the things..ye should do
1. 30 according to all that he did for you
1. 44 out against..and chased you, as bees do
2. 12 Israel did unto the land of his possession
2. 22 As he did to the children of Esau, which
2. 29 As the children of Esau..did unto me
3. 2 thou shalt do unto him as thou didst
3. 6 as we did unto Sihon king of Heshbon
3. 21 all that the LORD your God hath done
3. 21 so shall the LORD do unto all the kingd.
3. 24 that can do according to thy works, and
4. 1 for to do (them), that ye may live, and
4. 3 Your eyes have seen what the LORD did
4. 5 that ye should do so in the land whither
4. 6 Keep therefore and do (them): for this
4. 14 that ye might do them in the land
4. 25 shall do evil in the sight of the LORD
4. 34 all that the LORD your God did for
5. 1 ye may learn them, and keep and do
5. 13 Six days thou shalt labour, and do all
5. 14 (in it) thou shalt not do any work, thou
5. 27 speak thou..and we will hear (it), and do
5. 31 that they may do (them) in the land
5. 32 Ye shall observe to do therefore as the
6. 1 that ye might do (them) in the land
6. 3 Hear therefore..and observe to do (it)
6. 18 thou shalt do (that which is) right and
6. 24 the LORD commanded us to do all these
6. 25 if we observe to do all these command.
7. 11 which I command thee this day, to do
7. 12 if ye hearken to..and keep and do them
7. 18 what the LORD thy God did unto Pharaoh
7. 19 so shall the LORD thy God do unto all the
8. 1 All the command...shall ye observe to do
9. 18 I did neither eat bread, nor drink water
9. 18 in doing wickedly in the sight of the
10. 21 that hath done for thee these..things
11. 3 which he did in the midst of Egypt
11. 4 what he did unto the army of Egypt
11. 5 what he did unto you in the wilderness
11. 6 what he did unto Dathan and Abiram
11. 7 the great acts of the LORD which he did
11. 22 which I command you, to do them, to
11. 32 ye shall observe to do all the statutes
12. 1 judgments which ye shall observe to do
12. 4 shall not do so unto the LORD your God
12. 8 not do after all (the things) that we do
12. 14 thou shalt do all that I command thee
12. 25 when thou shalt do (that which is) right
12. 28 when thou doest (that which is) good
12. 30 even so will I do likewise
12. 31 Thou shalt not do so unto the LORD thy
12. 31 every abomination..have they done unto
12. 32 What thing..I command..observe to do
13. 11 shall do no more any such wickedness as
13. 18 to do (that which is) right in the eyes of
14. 29 the work of thine hand which thou doest
15. 5 to observe to do all these commandmen.
15. 17 unto thy maid servant thou shalt do
15. 18 shall bless thee in all that thou doest
16. 8 thou shalt do no work (therein)
16. 12 thou shalt observe and do these statutes
17. 10 thou shalt do according to the sentence
17. 10 thou shalt observe to do according to
17. 11 which they shall tell thee, thou shalt do
17. 12 the man that will do presumptuously, and
17. 13 and fear, and do no more presumptuously
17. 19 this law and these statutes, to do them
18. 9 thou shalt not learn to do after the
18. 12 all that do these things (are) an abomina.
19. 9 keep all these commandments to do them
19. 19 do unto him as...thought to have done
20. 15 Thus shalt thou do unto all the cities
20. 18 not to do after all their abominations
20. 18 which they have done unto their gods
21. 9 when thou shalt do (that which is) right
22. 3 In like manner shalt thou do with his ass
22. 3 and so shalt thou do with his raiment
22. 3 with all lost thing..shalt thou do likewise
22. 5 all that do so (are) abomination unto the
22. 26 But unto the damsel thou shalt do
24. 8 do according to all that the priests the
24. 8 as I commanded..ye shall observe to do
24. 9 what the LORD thy God did unto Miriam
24. 18, 22 therefore I command thee to do this
25. 16 all that do such things, (and) all that do
25. 17 what Amalek did unto thee by the way
26. 14 have done according to all that thou hast
26. 16 to do these statutes and judgments
26. 16 keep and do them with all thine heart
27. 10 and do his commandments and his statu.
27. 26 confirmeth not..words to do them
28. 1 to do all his commandments which I com.
28. 13 hearken unto the commandments..to do
28. 15 to do all his commandments and his
28. 20 thou settest thine hand unto for to do
28. 20 because of the wickedness of thy doings
28. 58 If thou wilt not observe to do all the
29. 2 Ye have seen all that the LORD did before
29. 9 Keep..words of this covenant, and do
Deut. 29. 9 that ye may prosper in all that ye do
29. 24 Wherefore hath the LORD done thus unto
29. 29 that (we) may do all the words of this law
30. 8 do all his commandments which I comm.
30. 12, 13 bring it..that we may hear it, and do
30. 14 and in thy heart that thou mayest do
31. 4 the LORD shall do unto them as he did to
31. 5 that ye may do unto them according
31. 12 observe to do all the words of this law
31. 29 ye will do evil in the sight of the LORD
32. 46 command your children to observe to do;
34. 9 and did as the LORD commanded Moses
34. 11 wonders which the LORD sent him to do
Josh. 1. 8 that thou mayest observe to do according
1. 16 All that thou commandest us we will do
2. 10 what ye did unto the two kings of
3. 5 to morrow the LORD will do wonders
4. 8 the children of Israel did so as Joshua
4. 23 as the LORD your God did to the Red sea
5. 15 Loose thy shoe..And Joshua did so
6. 3 Thus shalt thou do six days
6. 14 compassed the city..so they did six days
7. 9 and what wilt thou do unto thy great
7. 19 tell me now what thou hast done; hide
7. 20 I have sinned..thus and thus have I done
8. 2 shalt do to Ai and her king as thou didst
8. 8 accor. to the commandment..shall ye do
9. 3 what Joshua had done unto Jericho and
9. 9 heard the fame of him, and all that he d.
9. 10 all that he did to the two kings of the
9. 20 This we will do to them; we will even let
9. 24 we were sore afraid..and have done
9. 25 good and right unto thee to do unto us d.
9. 26 so did he unto them, and delivered them
10. 1 as he had done to Jericho and her king
10. 1 so he had done to Ai and her king
10. 23 they did so, and brought forth those five
10. 25 thus shall the LORD do to all your enem.
10. 28 he did to the king of Makkedah as he d.
10. 30 did unto the king thereof as he did unto
10. 32, 35, 37 according to all that he had done
10. 39 left none remaining: as he had done to
10. 39 so he did to Debir..as he had done
11. 9 Joshua did unto them as the LORD bade
11. 15 so did Moses command Joshua, and so d.
14. 5 As the LORD commanded..so..Israel did
22. 5 take diligent heed to do the command.
22. 24 And if we have not..done it for fear of
23. 3 ye have seen all that the LORD..hath done
23. 6 and to do all that is written in the book
23. 8 But cleave..as ye have done unto this
24. 5 according to that which I did among them
24. 7 your eyes have seen what I have done in
24. 17 which did those great signs in our sight
24. 31 the works of the LORD, that he hath done
Judg. 1. 7 as I have done, so God hath requited me
2. 2 ye have not obeyed..why have ye done
2. 7 the great works of the LORD that he did
2. 10 nor yet the works which he had done for
2. 11 the children of Israel did evil in the sight
2. 17 obeying the commandments..(but) they d.
3. 7 the children of Israel did evil in the sight
3. 12 And the children of Israel did evil again
3. 12 they had done evil in the sight of the L.
4. 1 the children of Israel again did evil
6. 1 the children of Israel did evil in the sight
6. 20 pour out the broth. And he did so
6. 27 and did as the LORD had said unto him,
6. 27 he could not do (it) by day, that he did
6. 29 they said..Who hath done this thing?
6. 29 Gideon the son of Joash hath done this
6. 40 And God did so that night: for it was dry
7. 17 he said..Look on me, and do likewise
7. 17 it shall be, (that) as I do, so shall ye do
8. 2 What have I done now in comparison of
8. 3 what was I able to do in comparison of
9. 16 if ye have done truly and sincerely
9. 16 and have done unto him according to the
9. 33 then mayest thou do to them as thou
9. 48 What ye have seen me do..haste..do
9. 56 rendered the wickedness..which he did
10. 6 the children of Israel did evil again in
10. 15 do thou unto us whatsoever seemeth good
11. 10 if we do not so according to thy words
11. 27 thou doest me wrong to war against me
11. 36 do to me according to that which hath
11. 39 who did with her (according) to his vow
13. 1 And the children of Israel did evil again
13. 8 teach us what we shall do unto the
13. 19 and (the angel) did wondrously; and M.
14. 6 but he told not..what he had done
14. 10 for so used the young men to do
15. 3 though I do them a displeasure
15. 6 the Philistines said, Who hath done
15. 7 Though ye have done this, yet will I be
15. 10 to do to him as he hath done to us
15. 11 what (is) this..thou hast done unto us?
15. 11 As they did unto me, so have I done unto
17. 6 every man did (that which was) right in
18. 14 therefore consider what ye have to do
18. 18 Then said the priest unto them, What do
19. 23 seeing that this man is come..do not
19. 24 do with them what seemeth good unto
19. 24 but unto this man do not so vile a thing
20. 9 the thing which we will do to Gibeah
20. 10 that they may do, when they come to G.
21. 7, 16 How shall we do for wives for them
21. 11 And this (is) the thing that ye shall do
21. 23 And the children of Benjamin did so, and
21. 25 every man did (that which was) right in
Ruth 1. 17 the LORD do so to me, and more also
2. 11 all that thou hast done unto thy mother
Ruth 3. 4 he will tell thee what thou shalt do
3. 5 All that thou sayest unto me I will do
3. 6 she went down..and did according to
3. 11 I will do to thee all that thou requirest
3. 16 she told her all that the man had done to
4. 11 do thou worthily in Ephratah, and be
1 Sa. 1. 7 And (as) he did so year by year, when she
1. 23 her husband said..Do what seemeth thee
2. 14 So they did in Shiloh unto all the Israelit.
2. 22 heard all that his sons did unto all Israel
2. 23 said unto them, Why do ye such things?
2. 35 shall do according to (that) which (is) in
3. 11 Behold, I will do a thing in Israel, at
3. 17 God do so to thee, and more also, if thou
3. 18 let him do what seemeth him good
5. 8 What shall we do with the ark of the God
6. 2 What shall we do to the ark of the LORD?
6. 9 (then) he hath done us this great evil
6. 10 the men did so; and took two milch kine
8. 8 which they have done since the day that
8. 8 served other gods, so do they also unto
10. 2 saying, What shall I do for my son?
10. 7 (that) thou do as occasion serve thee; for
10. 8 till I..shew thee what thou shalt do
11. 10 ye shall do with us all that seemeth good
12. 7 which he did to you and to your fathers
12. 16 which the LORD will do before your eyes
12. 17 which ye have done in the sight of the L.
12. 20 Fear not: ye have done all this wickedn.
13. 11 And Samuel said, What hast thou done?
14. 7 Do all that (is) in thine heart: turn thee
14. 36 they said, Do whatsoever seemeth good
14. 40 the people said..Do what seemeth good
14. 43 Saul said..Tell me what thou hast done?
14. 44 Saul answered, God do so and more
15. 2 I remember (that) which Amalek did to
15. 19 and didst evil in the sight of the LORD?
16. 3 I will shew thee what thou shalt do
16. 4 Samuel did that which the LORD spake
17. 29 David said, What have I now done?
19. 18 told him all that Saul had done to him
20. 1 What have I done? what (is) mine iniq.?
20. 2 my father will do nothing either great or
20. 4 Whatsoever thy soul desireth, I will ..do
20. 13 The LORD do so and much more to Jona.
20. 32 shall he be slain? what hath he done?
22. 3 till I know what God will do for me
24. 4 that thou mayest do to him as it shall
24. 6 The LORD forbid that I should do this
24. 19 for that thou hast done unto me this day
25. 17 know and consider what thou wilt do
25. 22 So and more also do God unto the enemies
25. 30 when the LORD shall have done to my
26. 16 This..(is) not good that thou hast done
26. 18 for what have I done? or what evil
26. 25 thou shalt both do great (things), and
27. 11 So did David, and so (will be) his manner
28. 2 thou shalt know what thy servant can do
28. 9 Behold, thou knowest what Saul hath d.
28. 15 thou mayest make known..what I shall do
28. 17 the LORD hath done to him, as he spake
28. 18 therefore hath the LORD done this thing
29. 8 And David said..But what have I done?
30. 23 Then said David, Ye shall not do so, my
31. 11 of that which the Philistines had done to
2 Sa. 2. 6 because ye have done this thing
3. 9 So do God to Abner, and more also, except
3. 9 as the LORD hath sworn..even so I do to
3. 18 Now then do (it): for the LORD hath spok.
3. 24 What hast thou done? behold, Abner ca.
3. 25 Abner..came..to know all that thou do.
3. 35 So do God to me, and more also, if I
3. 36 as whatsoever the king did pleased all
3. 39 the LORD shall reward the doer of evil
5. 25 David did so, as the LORD had commanded
7. 3 Go, do all that (is) in thine heart; for the
7. 21 For thy word's sake..hast thou done all
7. 23 to do for you great things and terrible
7. 25 establish (it) for ever, and do as thou
9. 11 According to all..so shall thy servant do
10. 12 the LORD do that which seemeth him
11. 11 thy soul liveth, I will not do this thing
11. 27 the thing that David had done displeased
12. 5 the man that hath done this (thing) shall
12. 6 he did this thing, and because he had no
12. 9 to do evil in his sight? thou hast killed
12. 12 thou didst (it) secretly: but I will do this
12. 21 What thing (is) this that thou hast done?
12. 31 thus did he unto all the cities of the chil.
13. 2 hard for him to do any thing to her
13. 12 my brother..do not thou this folly
13. 16 greater than the other that thou didst
13. 29 the servants..did..as Absalom had com.
14. 20 hath thy servant Joab done this thing
14. 21 Behold now, I have done this thing: go
15. 6 on this manner did Absalom to all Israel
15. 26 let him do to me as seemeth good unto
16. 10 Wherefore hast thou done so?
16. 20 Give counsel among you what we shall do
17. 6 shall we do (after) his saying? if not
18. 4 What seemeth you best I will do
19. 13 God do so to me, and more also, if thou
19. 18 and to do what he thought good
19. 27 do therefore (what is) good in thine eyes
19. 37 do to him what shall seem good unto thee
19. 38 I will do to him that which shall seem
19. 38 and whatsoever..(that) will I do for thee
21. 3 David said..What shall I do for you?
21. 4 What ye shall say, (that) will I do for you
21. 11 it was told David what Rizpah..had done
23. 17 Be it far from me..that I should do this
23. 17 These things did these three mighty men

2 Sa. 23. 22 These (things) did Benaiah the son of
24. 10 I have sinned greatly in that I have done
24. 17 I have sinned, and I have done wickedly
24. 17 but these sheep, what have they done?
1 Ki. 1. 6 saying, Why hast thou done so? and he
1. 30 even so will I certainly do this day
2. 3 mayest prosper in all that thou doest
2. 5 thou knowest also what Joab..did to me
2. 5 what he did to the two captains of the
2. 6 Do therefore according to thy wisdom
2. 9 and knowest what thou oughtest to do
2. 23 saying, God do so to me, and more also
2. 31 Do as he hath said, and fall upon him
2. 38 my lord..hath said, so will thy servant do
2. 44 that thou didst to David my father
3. 12 I have done according to thy words
3. 28 the wisdom of God (was) in him to do ju.
5. 8 I will do all thy desire concerning timber
7. 18 and so did he for the other chapiter
7. 40 Hiram made an end of doing all the work
8. 32 Then hear thou in heaven, and do, and
8. 39 and forgive, and do, and give to every
8. 43 do according to all that the stranger
8. 66 all the goodness that the LORD had done
9. 1 Solomon's desire..he was pleased to do
9. 4 to do according to all that I have comma.
9. 8 Why hath the LORD done thus unto this
10. 9 therefore made he thee king, to do judg
11. 6 Solomon did evil in the sight of the LORD
11. 8 likewise did he for all his strange wives
11. 12 I will not do it for David thy father's
11. 33 to do (that which is) right in mine eyes
11. 38 and wilt walk in my ways, and do (that is)
11. 38 keep my statutes..as David..did
11. 41 and all that he did, and his wisdom
12. 27 If this people go up to do sacrifice in
12. 32 So did he in Beth-el, sacrificing unto
13. 11 that the man of God had done that day
14. 4 And Jeroboam's wife did so, and arose
14. 8 to do (that) only (which was) right in
14. 9 But hast done evil above all that were
14. 22 And Judah did evil in the sight of the L.
14. 22 above all that their fathers had done
14. 24 they did according to all the abominations
14. 29 rest of the acts..and all that he did
15. 3 all the sins..which he had done before
15. 5, 11 did (that which was) right in the
15. 7, 31 rest of the acts..all that he did
15. 23 and all his might, and all that he did
15. 26, 34 And he did evil in the sight of the L.
16. 5 and what he did, and his might
16. 7 all the evil that he did in the sight of the
16. 14 rest of the acts..and all that he did
16. 19 in doing evil in the sight of the LORD
16. 19 in his sin which he did, to make Israel to
16. 27 the rest of the acts of Omri which he did
16. 30 Ahab..did evil in the sight of the LORD
16. 33 Ahab did more to provoke the LORD
17. 5 did according unto the word of the LORD
17. 13 Fear not; go (and) do as thou hast said
17. 15 she went, and did according to the saying
18. 13 what I did when Jezebel slew the proph.
18. 36 I have done all these things at thy word
19. 1 Ahab told Jezebel all that Elijah had done
19. 2 So let the gods do (to me), and more also
19. 20 Go back again: for what have I done to
20. 9 All..I will do: but this..I may not do
20. 10 The gods do so unto me, and more also
20. 22 and mark, and see what thou doest
20. 24 And do this thing; Take the kings away
20. 25 he hearkened unto their voice, and did so
21. 11 the men..did as Jezebel had sent unto
21. 26 he did..according to all (things) as did
22. 22 Thou shalt persuade..go forth, and do so
22. 39 rest of the acts..and all that he did
22. 43 doing (that which was) right in the eyes
22. 52 And he did evil in the sight of the LORD
22. 53 according to all that his father had done
2 Ki. 1. 18 rest of the acts of Ahaziah which he did
2. 9 Ask what I shall do for thee, before I
4. 2 Elisha said unto her, What shall I do
4. 13 what (is) to be done for thee? wouldest
5. 13 wouldest thou not have done (it)?
6. 15 Alas, my master! how shall we do?
6. 31 he said, God do so and more also to me
7. 9 they said one to another, We do not well
7. 12 what the Syrians have done to us
8. 2 did after the saying of the man of God
8. 4 the great things that Elisha hath done
8. 12 Because I know the evil that thou wilt do
8. 13 that he should do this great thing?
8. 18 And he walked..as did the house of Ahab
8. 18, 27 did evil in the sight of the LORD
8. 23 rest of the acts..and all that he did
10. 5 and will do all that thou shalt bid us
10. 5 do thou (that which is) good in thine eyes
10. 10 the LORD hath done (that) which he spake
10. 19 But Jehu did (it) in subtilty, to the intent
10. 30 Because thou hast done well in executing
10. 30 hast done unto the house of Ahab accor.
10. 34 rest of the acts of Jehu, and all..he did
11. 5 This (is) the thing that ye shall do
11. 9 the captains over the hundreds did accor.
12. 2 And Jehoash did (that which was) right
12. 11 into the hands of them that did the work
12. 19 rest of the acts..all that he did
13. 2, 11 he did (that which was) evil in the
13. 8, 12 rest of the acts..all that he did
14. 3 he did (that which was) right in the sight
14. 3 he did..as Joash his father did
14. 15 rest of the acts of Jehoash which he did
14. 24 And he did (that which was) evil in

2 Ki. 14. 28 all that he did, and his might, how
15. 3, 34 And he did (that which was) right in
15. 3, 34 according to all..his father..had done
15. 6 rest of the acts..all that he did
15. 9, 18, 24, 28 he did (that which was) evil in
15. 9 as his fathers had done: he departed not
15. 21, 26, 31, 36 rest of the acts..all that he did
15. 34 did according to all that..Uzziah had done
16. 2 and did not (that which was) right in
16. 16 Thus did Urijah the priest, according to
16. 19 rest of the acts of Ahaz which he did
17. 2 And he did (that which was) evil in the
17. 12 LORD had said..Ye shall not do this
17. 15 that they should not do like them
17. 17 and sold themselves to do evil in the
17. 22 in all the sins of Jeroboam which he did
17. 34 Unto this day they do after the former
17. 34 neither do they after their statutes
17. 37 ye shall observe to do for evermore
17. 40 but they did after their former manner
17. 41 as did their fathers, so do they unto this
18. 3 did..according to all that David..did
18. 12 and would not hear (them), nor do (them)
19. 11 what the kings of Assyria have done to
19. 25 Hast thou not heard..(how) I have done
19. 31 the zeal of the LORD (of hosts) shall do
20. 3 and have done (that which is) good in
20. 9 the LORD will do the thing that he hath
21. 2 And he did (that which was) evil in the
21. 3 and made a grove, as did Ahab king of I.
21. 8 only if they will observe to do according
21. 9 seduced them to do more evil than did
21. 11 hath done these..hath done wickedly
21. 15 they have done (that which was) evil in
21. 16 in doing (that which was) evil in the sight
21. 17 rest of the acts..all that he did
21. 20 And he did..as his father Manasseh did
21. 25 rest of the acts of Amon which he did
22. 2 And he did (that which was) right in
22. 9 into the hand of them that do the work
22. 13 to do according unto all that which is
23. 17 proclaimed these things that thou hast d.
23. 19 Josiah took away, and did to them acco.
23. 19 to all the acts that he had done in Beth.
23. 28 rest of the acts..all that he did
23. 32, 37 did..according to all..his fathers had d.
24. 3 Manasseh, according to all that he did
24. 5 rest of the acts..all that he did
24. 9 did..according to all..his father had d.
24. 19 did..according to all..Jehoiakim had do.
1 Ch. 10. 11 heard all that the Philistines had done
11. 19 God forbid it me, that I should do this
11. 19 These things did these three mightiest
11. 24 These (things) did Benaiah the son of Je.
12. 32 to know what Israel ought to do
13. 4 the congregation said that they would do
14. 16 David therefore did as God commanded
16. 12 his marvellous works that he hath done
17. 2 Do all that (is) in thine heart; for God
17. 19 according to thine own heart, hast thou d.
17. 23 be established..and do as thou hast said
19. 13 let the LORD do (that which is) good in
21. 8 I have sinned..because I have done this
21. 10 choose thee one of them, that I may do
21. 17 (as for) these sheep, what have they done?
21. 23 let my lord the king do (that which is)
22. 16 be doing, and the LORD be with thee
23. 24 that did the work for the service of the
27. 26 over them that did the work of the field
28. 7 be constant to do my commandments
28. 10 Take heed now..be strong, and do (it)
28. 20 Be strong and of good courage and do
29. 19 to do all (these things), and to build the
2 Ch. 6. 23 and do, and judge thy servants, by
6. 33 do according to all that the stranger
7. 17 do according to all that I have command.
7. 21 Why hath the LORD done thus unto this
9. 8 made he thee king..to do judgment and
12. 14 he did evil, because he prepared not his
14. 2 Asa did (that which was) good and right
14. 4 to do the law and the commandment
18. 21 thou shalt also prevail: go out, and do
19. 6 said to the judges, Take heed what ye do
19. 7 take heed, and do (it): for (there is) no
19. 9 Thus shall ye do in the fear of the LORD
19. 10 this do, and ye shall not trespass
20. 12 neither know we what to do: but our
20. 32 doing (that which was) right in the sight
20. 35 king of Israel, who did very wickedly
21. 6 he walked..like as did the house of Ahab
22. 4 Wherefore he did evil in the sight of the
23. 4 This (is) the thing that ye shall do
23. 8 So the Levites and all Judah did accord.
24. 2 And Joash did (that which was) right
24. 11 Thus they did day by day, and gathered
24. 12 to such as did the work of the service
24. 16 because he had done good in Israel, both
24. 22 which Jehoiada his father had done to
25. 2 And he did (that which was) right in
25. 8 if thou wilt go, do (it), be strong for the
25. 9 what shall we do for the hundred talents
25. 16 to destroy thee, because thou hast done
26. 4 did..according to all that..Amaziah did
27. 2 he did..according to all that..Uzziah did
28. 1 he did not (that which was) right in the
29. 2 did..according to all..David..had done
29. 6 done (that which was) evil in the eyes of
30. 5 they had done (it) of a long (time in)
30. 12 to do the commandment of the king and
31. 20 thus did Hezekiah throughout all Judah
31. 21 did (it) with all his heart, and prospered
32. 13 Know ye..what I and my fathers have d.

2 Ch. 32. 33 inhabitants of Jerusalem did him honour
33. 2 did (that which was) evil in the sight of
33. 8 to do all that I have commanded them
33. 9 to do worse than the heathen, whom the
33. 22 did (that which was) evil..as did Manasseh
34. 2 he did (that which was) right in the sight
34. 12 And the men did the work faithfully
34. 16 All..committed to thy servants, they do
34. 21 to do after all that is written in this
34. 32 the inhabitants of Jerusalem did accor.
35. 6 that (they) may do according to the word
36. 5, 9, 12 he did (that which was) evil in the
36. 8 his abominations which he did, and tha.
Ezra 7. 10 to seek the law of the LORD, and to do
10. 4 be of good courage, and do (it)
10. 5 they should do according to this word
10. 11 make confession..and do his pleasure
10. 12 As thou hast said, so must we do
10. 16 And the children of the captivity did so
Neh. 1. 9 keep my commandments, and do them
2. 12 had put in my heart to do at Jerusalem
2. 16 knew not whither I went, or what I did
2. 16 nor to the rulers, nor to the rest that did
2. 19 What (is) this thing that ye do? will ye
4. 2 What do these feeble Jews? will they
5. 9 It (is) not good that ye do: ought ye not
5. 12 so will we do as thou sayest
5. 12 they should do according to this promise
5. 13 the people did according to this promise
5. 15 so did not I, because of the fear of God
5. 19 (according) to all that I have done for
6. 2 But they thought to do me mischief
6. 3 I (am) doing a great work, so that I can.
6. 13 that I should be afraid, and do so, and
8. 17 had not the children of Israel done so
9. 17 thy wonders that thou didst among them
9. 24 they might do with them as they would
9. 28 did evil again..and many times didst
9. 29 which if a man do, he shall live in them
9. 33 hast done right, but we have done wick.
10. 29 to observe and do all the commandments
11. 12 their brethren that did the work of the
13. 7 the evil that Eliashib did for Tobiah
13. 10 Levites and the singers, that did the work
13. 14 my good deeds that I have done for the
13. 17 What evil thing (is) this that ye do, and
13. 18 Did not your fathers thus, and
13. 27 then hearken unto you to do all this
Esth. 1. 8 should do according to every man's plea.
1. 15 What shall we do unto the queen Vashti
1. 21 king did according to the word of Mem.
2. 1 remembered Vashti, and what she had d.
2. 4 the thing pleased the king; and he did so
2. 20 Esther did the commandment of Morde.
3. 11 do with them as it seemeth good to thee
4. 17 and did according to all that Esther had
5. 5 haste, that he may do as Esther hath
5. 8 will do to morrow as the king hath said
6. 6 What shall be done unto the man whom
6. 6 delight to do honour more than to myself
6. 10 and do even so to Mordecai the Jew, that
7. 5 that durst presume in his heart to do so?
9. 5 did what they would unto those that ha.
9. 12 what have they done in the rest of the
9. 12 what (is) thy request..and it shall be do.
9. 13 to do to morrow also according unto this
9. 23 Jews undertook to do as they had begun
Job 1. 5 Thus did Job continually
1. 9 and said, Doth Job fear God for nought?
5. 9 Which doeth great things and unsearch.
9. 10 Which doeth great things past finding
9. 12 who will say unto him, What doest thou?
13. 20 do not two (things) unto me; then will
21. 31 who shall repay him (what) he hath done
23. 13 (what) his soul desireth, even (that) he d.
31. 14 What then shall I do when God riseth
35. 6 transgressions be multiplied, what doest
37. 5 great things doeth he, which we cannot
42. 9 did according as the LORD commanded
Psa. 1. 3 and whatsoever he doeth shall prosper
7. 3 O LORD my God, if I have done this
14. 1, 3 (there is) none that doeth good
15. 3 nor doeth evil to his neighbour, nor
15. 5 He that doeth these..shall never be
22. 31 shall declare..that he hath done (this)
31. 23 and plentifully rewardeth the proud doer
34. 14 Depart from evil, and do good; seek
34. 16 the LORD (is) against them that do evil
37. 3 Trust in the LORD, and do good; (so)
37. 27 Depart from evil, and do good; and dwell
39. 9 opened not my mouth; because thou di.
40. 5 thy wonderful works (which) thou hast d
40. 8 I delight to do thy will, O my God
50. 21 These..hast thou done, and I kept silen.
51. 4 and done (this) evil in thy sight; that
52. 9 I will praise thee..because thou hast do
53. 1, 3 (there is) none that doeth good
56. 4 I will not fear what flesh can do unto
56. 11 I will not be afraid what man can do
60. 12 Through God we shall do valiantly
66. 16 I will declare what he hath done for my
71. 19 O God..who hast done great things: O
72. 18 the God of Israel, who only doeth
77. 14 Thou (art) the God that doest wonders
78. 4 his wonderful works that he hath done
78. 12 Marvellous things did he in the sight of
83. 9 Do unto them as (unto) the Midianites
86. 10 For thou (art) great, and doest wondrous
98. 1 for he hath done marvellous things
103. 18 that remember his commandments to do
103. 20 that excel in strength, that do his com.
103. 21 (ye) ministers of his, that do his pleasure

Psa 105. 5 his marvellous works that he hath done
106. 3 he that doeth righteousness at all times
106. 6 We have sinned..we have done wickedly
106. 21 which had done great things in Egypt
107. 23 that do business in great waters
108. 13 Through God we shall do valiantly
109. 21 But do thou for me, O GOD the Lord
109. 27 may know that..thou, LORD, hast done
111. 10 good understanding have all they that do
115. 3 he hath done whatsoever he hath
118. 6 I will not fear: what can man do unto
118. 15, 16 the right hand of the LORD doeth
119. 121 I have done judgment and justice
119. 166 LORD, I have..done thy commandments
126. 2, 3 The LORD hath done great things for
135. 6 Whatsoever the LORD pleased, (that) did
136. 4 To him who alone doeth great wonders
143. 10 Teach me to do thy will; for thou (art)
Prov. 2. 14 Who rejoice to do evil, (and) delight in
3. 27 when..in the power of thine hand to do
6 3 Do this now, my son, and deliver thyself
6. 32 he (that) doeth it destroyeth his own
10. 23 (It is) as sport to a fool to do mischief
21. 3 To do justice and judgment (is) more
21. 7 because they refuse to do judgment
21. 15 (It is) joy to the just to do judgment
24. 29 I will do so to him as he hath done to me
25. 8 lest (thou know not) what to do in the
31. 29 Many daughters have done virtuously
Eccl. 2. 2 I said..of mirth, What doeth it?
2. 3 which they should do under the heaven
2. 11 the labour that I had laboured to do
3. 12 for (a man) to rejoice, and to do good in
3. 14 whatsoever God doeth, it shall be for
3. 14 God doeth (it), that (men) should fear
5. 1 for they consider not that they do evil
7. 20 not a just man upon the earth, that do.
8. 3 for he doeth whatsoever pleaseth
8. 4 who may say unto him, What doest thou?
8. 10 were forgotten..where they had so done
8. 11 the heart..is fully set in them to do evil
8. 12 Though a sinner do evil an hundred
9. 10 Whatsoever thy hand findeth to do, do
Song 8. 8 what shall we do for our sister in the
Isa. 5. 4 What..more..that I have not done in it?
5. 5 I will tell you what I will do to my vine.
10. 3 what will ye do in the day of visitation
10. 11 as I have done unto Samaria and her
10. 11 Shall I not..so do to Jerusalem and her
10. 13 By the strength of my hand I have done
12. 5 for he hath done excellent things: this
19. 15 which the head or tail..may do
20. 2 And he did so, walking naked and
25. 1 for thou hast done wonderful (things)
28. 21 that he may do his work, his strange
33. 13 Hear, ye (that are) far off, what I have d.
37. 11 what the kings of Assyria have done to
37. 26 Hast thou not heard..(how) I have done
37. 32 the zeal of the LORD of hosts shall do
38. 3 and have done..good in thy sight
38. 7 the LORD will do this thing that he hath
38. 15 he hath both spoken..and..hath done
41. 4 Who hath wrought and done (it), calling
41. 20 that the hand of the LORD hath done
42. 16 These things will I do unto them, and
43. 19 I will do a new thing; now it shall
44. 23 Sing, O ye heavens; for the LORD hath d.
45. 7 create evil: I the LORD do all these
46. 10 Declaring..(the things) that are not (yet) d.
46. 10 My counsel shall stand, and I will do all
46. 11 I have purposed (it), I will also do it
48. 3 I did (them) suddenly, and they came
48. 5 thou shouldest say, Mine idol hath done
48. 11 for mine own sake, will I do (it): for
48. 14 he will do his pleasure on Babylon, and
53. 9 because he hath done no violence
56. 1 Keep ye judgment, and do justice
56. 2 Blessed (is) the man (that) doeth this
56. 2 and keepeth his hand from doing any
58. 2 as a nation that did righteousness, and
58. 13 (from) doing thy pleasure on my holy day
58. 13 and shalt honour him, not doing thine
64. 3 When thou didst terrible things
65. 8 so will I do for my servant's sakes, that
65. 12 did evil before mine eyes, and did choose
66. 4 they did evil before mine eyes, and chose
Jer. 2. 23 See thy way..know what thou hast done
3. 5 thou hast spoken and done evil things
3. 6 Hast thou seen (that)..Israel hath done?
3. 7 And I said after she had done all these
4. 30 thou (art) spoiled, what wilt thou do?
5. 19 Wherefore doeth the LORD our God all
5. 31 and what will ye do in the end thereof?
7. 10 We are delivered to do all these abomin.
7. 12 see what I did to it for the wickedness of
7. 13 now, because ye have done all these
7. 14 Therefore will I do unto (this) house
7. 14 and to your fathers, as I have done to S.
7. 17 Seest thou not what they do in the cities
7. 30 the children of Judah have done evil in
8. 6 What have I done? every one turned to
9. 7 how shall I do for the daughter of my
11. 4 Obey my voice, and do them, according
11. 6 Hear ye the words of this covenant, and do
11. 8 which I commanded..to do..but they did
11. 17 the evil..which they have done against
12. 5 how wilt thou do in the swelling of Jor.?
14. 7 O LORD..do thou (it) for thy name's sake
15. 4 for (that) which he did in Jerusalem
16. 12 ye have done worse than your fathers
17. 22 neither do ye any work; but hallow ye
17. 24 hallow the sabbath day, to do no work

Jer. 18. 6 cannot I do with you as this potter!
18. 8 will repent of the evil that I thought to do
18. 10 If it do evil in my sight, that it obey not
18. 12 we will every one do the imagination of
18. 13 the virgin of Israel hath done a very
19. 12 Thus will I do unto this place, saith
22. 4 For if ye do this thing indeed, then
22. 8 Wherefore hath the LORD done thus unto
22. 15 Did not thy father..do judgment and
22. 17 for oppression, and for violence, to do (it)
26. 3 to do..because of the evil of their doings
26. 14 do with me as seemeth good..unto you
28. 6 the LORD do so: the LORD perform thy
29. 32 shall he behold the good that I will do for
30. 15 I have done these things unto thee
30. 24 shall not return, until he have done (it)
31. 37 for all that they have done, saith the L.
32. 23 they have done nothing of all that thou
32. 23 that thou commandest them to do: ther.
32. 30 the children of Judah have only done
32. 32 which they have done to provoke me to
32. 35 that they should do this abomination
33. 9 which shall hear all the good that I do
33. 18 meat offerings, and to do sacrifice cont.
34. 15 ye were now turned, and had done right
35. 10 But we have..done according to all that
35. 18 kept all his precepts, and done according
36. 3 all the evil which I purpose to do unto
36. 8 Baruch the son of Neriah did according
38. 9 in all that they have done to Jeremiah
38. 12 under the cords. And Jeremiah did so
39. 12 look well to him, and do him no harm
39. 12 but do unto him even as he shall say
40. 3 the LORD hath..done according as he
40. 16 Thou shalt not do this thing; for thou
41. 11 all the evil that Ishmael..had done
42. 3 God may show..the thing that we may do
42. 5 if we do not even according to all things
42. 10 I repent me of the evil that I have done
42. 20 so declare unto us, and we will do (it)
44. 4 Oh, do not this abominable thing that
44. 17 we will certainly do whatsoever thing
48. 10 Cursed (be) he that doeth the work of the
50. 15 Shout..as she hath done, do unto her
50. 21 do according to all that I have comman.
50. 29 according to all that she hath done, do
51. 12 the LORD hath both devised and done
51. 24 all their evil that they have done in Zion
52. 2 he did (that which was) evil in the eyes
52. 2 according to all that Jehoiakim had done
Lam. 1. 21 they are glad that thou hast done (it)
2. 17 The LORD hath done (that) which he had
Eze. 3. 20 his righteousness which he hath done
5. 7 neither have done according to the judg.
5. 9 I will do..that which I have not done
5. 9 whereunto I will not do any more the
6. 10 not said in vain that I would do this evil
7. 27 I will do unto them after their way, and
8. 6 Son of man, seest thou what they do?
8. 9 behold the..abominations that they do
8. 12 the ancients of the house of Israel do in
8. 13 see greater abominations that they do
9. 11 I have done as thou hast commanded
11. 12 but have done after the manner, of the
11. 20 keep mine ordinances, and do them
12. 7 And I did so as I was commanded
12. 9 the rebellious house, said..What doest
12. 11 like as I have done, so it shall be done
14. 23 and ye shall know that I have not done
14. 23 all that I have done in it, saith the LORD
15. 3 Shall wood be taken thereof to do
16. 5 None eye pitied thee, to do any of these
16. 30 seeing thou doest all these (things)
16. 47 not walked after their ways, nor done
16. 48 sister hath not done..as thou hast done
16. 51 all thine abominations which thou hast d.
16. 54 be confounded in all that thou hast done
16. 59 will even deal with thee as thou hast done
16. 63 pacified..for all that thou hast done, saith
17. 15 shall he escape that doeth such (things)?
17. 18 when, lo, he..hath done all these (things)
17. 24 I the LORD have spoken and have done
18. 5 if a man be just, and do that which is
18. 10 (that) doeth the like to (any) one of these
18. 11 that doeth not any of those (duties), but
18. 13 he shall not live: he hath done all these
18. 14 all his father's sins which he hath done
18. 14 and considereth, and doeth not such like
18. 18 did (that) which (is) not good among his
18. 19 the son hath done that which is lawful
18. 19 and hath done them, he shall surely live
18. 21 the wicked will turn..and do that which
18. 22 in his righteousness that he hath done he
18. 24 doeth according to all the abominations
18. 24 that the wicked (man) doeth, shall he live?
18. 24 All his righteousness that he hath done
18. 26 for his iniquity that he hath done shall
18. 27 and doeth that which is lawful and right
20. 11 which (if) a man do, he shall even live in
20. 13 which (if) a man do, he shall even live in
20. 19 and keep my judgments, and do them
20. 21 neither kept my judgments to do them
20. 21 which (if) a man do, he shall even live in
22. 14 I the LORD have spoken (it), and will do
23. 30 I will do these (things) unto thee, because
23. 38 Moreover this they have done unto me
23. 39 lo, thus have they done in the midst of
23. 48 all women may be taught not to do after
24. 14 it shall come to pass, and I will do (it); I
24. 18 I did in the morning as I was com.
24. 19 Wilt thou not tell us..that thou doest
24. 22 ye shall do as I have done: ye shall not

Eze. 24. 24 all that he hath done shall ye do; and
25. 14 they shall do in Edom according to mine
33. 14, 19 do that which is lawful and right
33. 16 he hath done that which is lawful and
33. 31 hear thy words, but they will not do them
33. 32 they hear thy words, but they do them not
35. 11 I will even do according to thine
35. 15 so will I do unto thee: thou shalt be
36. 22 I do not (this) for your sakes, O house of
36. 27 ye shall keep my judgments, and do
36. 32 Not for your sakes do I (this), saith the
36. 36 I the LORD have spoken (it), and I will do
36. 37 to do (it) for them; I will increase them
37. 24 and observe my statutes, and do them
39. 24 have I done unto them, and hid
43. 11 be ashamed of all that they have done
43. 11 all the ordinances thereof, and do them
45. 20 so thou shalt do the seventh (day) of the
45. 25 shall he do the like in the feast of the
46. 12 prepare..as he did on the sabbath day
Dan. 8. 4 he did according to his will, and became
8. 27 I rose up, and did the king's business
9. 14 righteous in all his works which he doeth
9. 19 O Lord, forgive; O Lord, hearken and do
11. 3 that shall rule..and do according to his
11. 16 he that cometh against him shall do
11. 17 thus shall he do: and he shall give him
11. 24 He shall enter..and he shall do (that)
11. 24 which his fathers have not done, nor his
11. 28 he shall do (exploits), and return to his
11. 30 so shall he do; he shall even return, and
11. 32 people..shall be strong, and do (exploits)
11. 36 the king shall do according to his will
11. 39 Thus shall he do in the most strong holds
Hos. 6. 4 O Ephraim, what shall I do unto thee?
6. 4 O Judah, what shall I do unto thee?
9. 5 What will ye do in the solemn day, and
10. 3 what then should a king do to us?
10. 15 So shall Beth-el do unto you because of
Joel 2. 20 come up, because he hath done great
2. 21 be glad..for the LORD will do great things
Amos 3. 6 and the LORD hath not done (it?)
3. 7 Surely the Lord GOD will do nothing, but
3. 10 For they know not to do right, saith the
4. 12 Therefore thus will I do unto thee, O
4. 12 because I will do this unto thee, prepare
9. 12 saith the LORD that doeth this
Obad. 15 as thou hast done, it shall be done unto
Jon. 1. 10 said unto him, Why hast thou done this?
1. 11 What shall we do unto thee, that the sea
1. 14 for thou, O LORD, hast done as it pleased
3. 10 that he would do unto them; and he did
Mic. 6. 3 O my people, what have I done unto thee?
6. 8 to do justly, and to love mercy, and to
Zeph. 3. 5 he will not do iniquity: every morning d
3. 13 remnant of Israel shall not do iniquity
Hag. 1. 14 they came and did work in the house of
Zech. 1. 6 did they not take hold of your fathers?
1. 6 Like as the LORD of hosts thought to do
1. 21 Then said I, What come these to do? And
7. 3 as I have done these so many years?
8. 16 These (are) the things that ye shall do
Mal. 2. 12 The LORD will cut off the man that doeth
2. 13 this have ye done again, covering the
2. 17 Every one that doeth evil (is) good in the
4. 1 all the proud, yea, and all that do
4. 3 that I shall do (this), saith the LORD of

6. *To act, work, do, make,* פָּעַל *paal.*
Deut 32. 27 and the LORD hath not done all this
Job 7. 20 what shall I do unto thee, O thou
11. 8 as high as heaven; what canst thou do?
22. 17 and what can the Almighty do for them?
34. 32 if I have done iniquity, I will do no more
35. 6 If thou sinnest, what doest thou against
Psa. 11. 3 be destroyed, what can the righteous do?
44. 1 fathers have told us, (what) work thou d.
119. 3 They also do no iniquity: they walk in
Prov 30. 20 and saith, I have done no wickedness

7. *Act, work, deed, doing,* פֹּעַל *poal.*
Job 37. 12 that they may do whatsoever he command.

8. *To set, put, place,* שׂוּם *sum.*
Exod 10. 2 my signs which I have done among them

9. *To do, recompense,* גָּמַל *gamal.*
Gen. 50. 15 requite us all the evil which we did unto
50. 17 forgive..their sin; for they did unto thee
Prov. 3. 30 Strive not..if he have done thee no harm
31. 12 She will do him good and not evil all the

10. *To work in,* ἐνεργέω *energeō.*
Phil. 2. 13 both to will and to do of (his) good

11. *To end thoroughly,* ἐπιτελέω *epiteleō.*
Luke 13. 32 I cast out devils, and I [do] cures to day

12. *To work, labour, perform,* ἐργάζομαι *ergazomai.*
Gal. 6. 10 let us do good unto all (men), especially
Col. 3. 23 do (it) heartily as unto the Lord, and not
3 John 5 whatsoever thou doest to the brethren

13. *To have, hold,* ἔχω *echō.*
Acts 15. 36 Let us go again and..(see) how they do

14. *To put or lay down,* κατατίθημι *katatithēmi.*
Acts 25. 9 Festus, willing to do the Jews a pleasure

15. *To work out thoroughly,* κατεργάζομαι *katergaz.*
Rom. 2. 9 upon every soul of man that doeth evil
7. 15 For that which I do I allow not: for
7. 17; 7. 20; 1 Co. 5. 3; Eph. 6. 13.

16. *To shew,* ἐνδείκνυμι *endeiknumi.*
2 Ti. 4. 14 Alexander the coppersmith did me much

17. *To do,* ποιέω *poieō.*

Matt. 1. 24 being raised from sleep, did as the angel
5. 19 but whosoever shall do and teach (them)
5. 44 do good to them that hate you, and pray
5. 46 do not even the publicans the same?
5. 47 what do ye more..do not even the
6. 1 Take heed that ye do not your alms
6. 2 thou doest..alms..as the hypocrites do
6. 3 But when thou doest alms, let not thy
6. 3 know what thy right hand doeth
7. 12 men should do to you, do ye even so to
7. 21 but he that doeth the will of my Father
7. 22 in thy name done many wonderful works?
7. 24 whosoever..doeth them, I will liken him
7. 26 doeth them not, shall be likened unto a
8. 9 to my servant, Do this, and he doeth (it)
9. 28 Believe ye that I am able to do this?
12. 2 do that which is not lawful to do upon
12. 3 Have ye not read what David did
12. 12 it is lawful to do well on the sabbath days
12. 50 whosoever shall do the will of my Father
13. 28 He said..An enemy hath done this
13. 41 all things that offend, and them which do
13. 58 he did not many mighty works there
17. 12 they..have done unto him whatsoever
18. 35 So likewise shall my heavenly Father do
19. 16 Master, what good thing shall I do,
20. 5 went out about the sixth..hour, and did
20. 15 Is it not lawful for me to do what I will
20. 32 What will ye that I shall do unto you?
21. 6 the disciples went, and did as Jesus
21. 15 saw the wonderful things that he did
21. 21 ye shall not only do this..to the fig-tree
21. 23 By what authority doest thou these
21. 24, 27 by what authority I do these things
21. 31 Whether of them twain did the will of
21. 36 Again..they did unto them likewise
21. 40 what will he do unto those husbandmen
23. 3 whatsoever they bid you observe..do
23. 3 do not ye after their works: for they..do
23. 5 all their works they do for to be seen of
23. 23 these ought ye to have done, and not
24. 46 whom his lord..shall find so doing
25. 40 as ye have done (it)..ye have done (it)
25. 45 ye did (it) not..ye did (it) not to me
26. 12 in that..she did (it) for my burial
26. 13 also this, that this woman hath done
26. 19 the disciples did as Jesus had appointed
27. 22 What shall I do then with Jesus which
27. 23 governor said, Why, what evil hath he d.
28. 15 So they took the money, and did as they
Mark 2. 24 why do they on the sabbath day that
2. 25 Have ye never read what David did
3. 8 had heard what great things he did
3. 35 For whosoever shall do the will of God
5. 19 how great things the Lord hath done for
5. 20 how great things Jesus had done for
5. 32 looked..about to see her that had done
6. 5 And he could there do no mighty work
6. 20 when he heard him, he did many things
6. 30 what they had done, and what they had
7. 8 [and many other such like things ye do]
7. 12 ye suffer him no more to do ought for
7. 13 and many such like things do ye
7. 37 saying, He hath done all things well
9. 13 they have done unto him whatsoever they
9. 39 there is no man which shall do a miracle
10. 17 what shall I do that I may inherit eternal
10. 35 we would that thou shouldest do for us
10. 36 What would ye that I should do for you?
10. 51 What wilt thou that I should do unto
11. 3 [if any man say unto you, Why do ye this?]
11. 5 certain..said..What do ye, loosing the
11. 28 By what authority doest thou these things?
11. 28 who gave thee this authority to do these
11. 29 I will tell you by what authority I do
11. 33 do I tell you by what authority I do these
12. 9 What shall..the lord of the vineyard do?
14. 7 whensoever ye will ye may do them good
14. 8 She hath done what she could: she is
14. 9 (this) also that she hath done shall be
15. 8 to (desire him to do) as he had ever done
15. 12 What will ye then that I shall do (unto)
15. 14 Pilate said..Why, what evil hath he done?
Luke 1. 49 For he that is mighty hath done to me
2. 27 to do for him after the custom of the law
3. 10 the people asked..What shall we do then?
3. 11 he that hath meat, let him do likewise.
3. 12 publicans..said..what shall we do?
3. 14 soldiers likewise..And what shall we do?
3. 19 for all the evils which Herod had done
4. 23 whatsoever we have heard..do also here
5. 6 they had this done, they inclosed a great
6. 2 Why do ye that which is not lawful [to do]
6. 3 Have ye not read..what David did, when
6. 10 And [he did] so: and his hand was restor.
6. 11 communed..what they might do to Jesus
6. 23 for in the like manner did their fathers
6. 26 so did their fathers to the false prophets
6. 27 Love your enemies, do good to them
6. 31 that men should do to you, do ye also
6. 33 for sinners also do even the same
6. 46 why call ye me, Lord..and do not the
6. 47 heareth my sayings, and doeth them
6. 49 But he that heareth, and doeth not, is
7. 8 to my servant, Do this, and he doeth (it)
8. 21 these which hear the word..and do it
8. 39 show how great things God hath done
8. 39 how great things Jesus had done unto
9. 10 told him all that they had done
9. 15 they did so, and made them all sit down
9. 43 every one at all things which Jesus did
Luke 9. 54 [and consume them, even as Elias did?]
10. 25 what shall I do to inherit eternal life?
10. 28 he said..this do, and thou shalt live
10. 37 then said Jesus..Go, and do thou likewise
11. 42 these ought ye to have done, and not to
12. 4 after that have no more that they can do
12. 17 What shall I do, because I have no room
12. 18 This will I do: I will pull down my barns
12. 43 whom his lord..shall find so doing
12. 47 prepared not (himself), neither did acco.
16. 3 the steward said..What shall I do?
16. 4 I am resolved what to do, that, when I am
16. 8 because he had done wisely: for the
17. 9 because he did the things that were com.
17. 10 when ye shall have done all those things
17. 10 have done that which was our duty to do
18. 18 what shall I do to inherit eternal life?
18. 41 What wilt thou that I shall do unto thee?
19. 48 could not find what they might do
20. 2 Tell us, by what authority doest thou these
20. 8 Neither tell I..by what authority I do
20. 13 Then said the lord..What shall I do?
20. 15 What..shall the lord of the vineyard do
22. 19 for you: this do in remembrance of me
23. 22 he said..Why, what evil hath he done?
23. 31 if they do these things in a green tree
23. 34 forgive..for they know not what [they do]
John 2. 5 Whatsoever he saith unto you, do (it)
2. 11 This beginning of miracles did Jesus in
2. 18 seeing that thou doest these things?
2. 23 when they saw the miracles which he did
3. 2 can do these miracles that thou doest
3. 21 he that doeth truth cometh to the light
4. 29 which told me all things that ever I did
4. 34 My meat is to do the will of him
4. 39 He told me all that ever I did
4. 45 having seen all the things that he did
4. 54 This (is)..the second miracle..Jesus did
5. 16 because he had done these things on
5. 19 The Son can do nothing of himself
5. 19 but what he seeth the Father do
5. 19 what..he doeth, then also doeth the Son
5. 20 showeth him all things that himself doeth
5. 29 shall come forth; they that have done g.
5. 30 I can of mine own self do nothing
5. 36 the same works that I do, bear witness
6. 2 they saw his miracles which he did on
6. 6 for he himself knew what he would do
6. 14 they had seen the miracle that Jesus did
6. 28 What shall we do, that we might work
6. 38 I came down from heaven, not to do
7. 3 also may see the works that thou doest
7. 4 doeth any thing in secret, and he himself
7. 4 If thou do these things, show thyself to
7. 17 If any man will do his will, he shall know
7. 21 I have done one work, and ye all marvel
7. 31 When Christ cometh, will he do more
7. 51 before it hear him and know..he doeth
8. 28 I am (he), and (that) I do nothing of myself
8. 29 for I do always those things that please
8. 38 ye do that which ye have seen with
8. 39 ye would do the works of Abraham
8. 40 which I have heard of God: this did
8. 41 Ye do the deeds of your father
8. 44 and the lusts of your father ye will do
9. 16 How can a man that is a sinner do such
9. 26 What did he to thee? how opened he
9. 31 be a worshipper of God, and doeth his
9. 33 If this man were not of God, he could do
10. 25 the works that I do in my Father's name
10. 37 If I do not the works of my Father
10. 38 But if I do, though ye believe not me
10. 41 many resorted..and said, John did
11. 45 had seen the things which Jesus did
11. 46 told them what things Jesus had done
11. 47 What do we? for this man doeth many
12. 16 they had done these things unto him
12. 18 they heard that he had done this miracle
12. 37 though he had done so many miracles
13. 7 What I do thou knowest not now; but
13. 12 Know ye what I have done to you?
13. 15 that ye should do as I have done to you
13. 17 If ye know..happy are ye if ye do them
13. 27 Then said Jesus..That thou doest, do
14. 10 the Father, that dwelleth in me, he doeth
14. 12 the works that I do shall he do also
14. 12 greater (works) than these shall he do
14. 13 whatsoever ye shall ask..that will I do
14. 14 If ye shall ask anything..I will do (it)
14. 31 gave me commandment, even so I do
15. 5 for without me ye can do nothing
15. 14 Ye are my friends, if ye do whatsoever
15. 15 servant knoweth not what his lord doeth
15. 21 all these things will they do unto you
15. 24 If I had not done among them
15. 24 the works which none other man did
16. 3 These things will they do unto you
17. 4 work which thou gavest me to do
18. 35 Am I a Jew?..what hast thou done?
19. 24 these things therefore the soldiers did
20. 30 And many other signs truly did Jesus
21. 25 also many other things which Jesus did
Acts 1. 1 of all that Jesus began both to do and
2. 22 wonders and signs, which God did by
2. 37 Men (and) brethren, what shall we do?
4. 7 By what power..have ye done this?
4. 16 What shall we do to these men? for that
4. 28 to do whatsoever thy hand and thy coun.
6. 8 Stephen, full of faith and power, did
8. 6 hearing and seeing the miracles..he did
9. 6 [Lord, what wilt thou have me to do?]
9. 6 it shall be told thee what thou must do
Acts 9. 13 how much evil he hath done to thy saints
9. 36 was full of good works..which she did
10. 6 [shall tell thee what thou oughtest to do]
10. 33 thou hast well done that thou art come
10. 39 we are witnesses of all things which he d.
11. 30 Which also they did, and sent it to the
12. 8 bind on thy sandals. And so he did
14. 11 when the people saw what Paul had done
14. 15 saying, Sirs, why do ye these things?
14. 27 they rehearsed all that God had done
15. 4 they declared all things that God had d.
15. 17 saith the Lord, who doeth all these things
16. 18 And this did she many days
16. 30 Sirs, what must I do to be saved?
19. 14 chief of the priests, which did so
21. 23 Do therefore this that we say to thee
21. 33 who he was, and what he had done
22. 10 And I said, What shall I do, Lord?
22. 10 things which are appointed for thee to do
22. 26 Take heed what thou doest: for this man
26. 10 Which thing I also did in Jerusalem
Rom. 1. 28 to do those things which are not conven
1. 32 not only do the same, but have pleasure
2. 3 and doest the same, that thou shalt
2. 14 do by nature the things contained in the
3. 8 Let us do evil, that good may come?
3. 12 there is none that doeth good, no, not
7. 15 but what I hate, that do I
7. 16 If then I do that which I would not
7. 19 For the good that I would I do not
7. 20 if I do that I would not, it is no more
7. 21 when I would do good, evil is present
10. 5 That the man which doeth these things
12. 20 in so doing thou shalt heap coals of fire
13. 3 Do that which is good, and thou shalt
13. 4 if thou do that which is evil, be afraid
1 Co. 5. 2 [he that hath done] this deed might
6. 18 Every sin that a man doeth is without
7. 36 let him do what he will, he sinneth not
7. 37 that he will keep his virgin, doeth well
7. 38 that giveth (her) in marriage doeth well
7. 38 giveth (her) not in marriage doeth better
9. 23 And this I do for the gospel's sake
10. 31 whatsoever ye do, do all to the glory of
11. 24 Take, eat..this do in remembrance of me
11. 25 this do ye, as oft as ye drink (it), in rem.
15. 29 Else what shall they do which are bap.
16. 1 as I have given order..even so do ye
2 Co. 8. 10 not only to do, but also to be forward
11. 12 what I do, that I will do, that I may
13. 7 that ye do no evil..that ye should do
Gal. 2. 10 the same which I also was forward to do
3. 10 continueth not in all things..to do them
3. 12 The man that doeth them shall live in
5. 3 that he is a debtor to do the whole law
Eph. 3. 20 Now unto him that is able to do
6. 6 doing the will of God from the heart
6. 8 whatsoever good thing any man doeth
6. 9 And, ye masters, do the same things unto
Phil. 2. 14 Do all things without murmurings and
4. 14 ye have well done that ye did commun.
Col. 3. 17 And whatsoever ye do in word or deed
3. 23 And whatsoever ye do..as to the Lord
1 Th. 4. 10 And indeed ye do it toward all the bre.
5. 11 edify one another, even as also ye do
5. 24 Faithful (is) he..who also will do (it)
2 Th. 3. 4 ye both do and will do the things which
1 Ti. 1. 13 obtained mercy, because I did (it) ignor.
5. 21 preferring one before another, doing
2 Ti. 4. 5 endure afflictions, do the work of an
Titus 3. 5 Not by works..which we have done, but
Phm. 14 But without thy mind would I do nothing
21 knowing that thou wilt also do more than
Heb. 6. 3 And this will we do, if God permit
7. 27 this he did once, when he offered up him.
10. 7 Then said I, Lo, I come..to do thy will
10. 9 Then said he, Lo, I come to do thy will, O
10. 36 after ye have done the will of God, ye
13. 6 I will not fear what man shall do unto
13. 17 that they may do it with joy, and not
13. 19 But I beseech (you) the rather to do this
13. 21 perfect in every good work to do his will
Jas. 2. 8 If ye fulfil the royal law..ye do well
2. 12 so do, as they that shall be judged by the
2. 19 Thou believest..thou doest well: the dev.
4. 15 If the Lord will, we shall live, and do
4. 17 to him that knoweth to do good, and do.
1 Pe. 2. 22 Who did no sin, neither was guile found
3. 11 Let him eschew evil, and do good; let
3. 12 face of the Lord (is) against them that do
2 Pe. 1. 10 if ye do these things, ye shall never
1. 19 whereunto ye do well that ye take heed
1 Jo. 1. 6 If we say..we lie, and do not the truth
2. 17 he that doeth the will of God abideth for
2. 29 every one that doeth righteousness is born
3. 7 he that doeth righteousness is righteous
3. 10 [whosoever doeth not righteousness is not]
3. 22 do those things that are pleasing in his
3 Jo. 5 doest faithfully whatsoever thou doest
6 if thou bring forward..thou shalt do well
10 I will remember his deeds which he doeth
Rev. 2. 5 do the first works; or else I will come
13. 13 he doeth great wonders, so that he maketh
13. 14 which he had power to do in the sight of
22. 14 Blessed (are) they that [do] his command.

18. *To practice, do,* πράσσω *prassō.*

Luke 22. 23 which of them it was that should do
23. 15 nothing worthy of death is done unto
23. 41 but this man hath done nothing amiss
John 3. 20 every one that doeth evil hateth the
5. 29 and they that have done evil, unto the

Acts 3. 17 through ignorance ye did (it), as (did) also
5. 35 what ye intend to do as touching these
15. 29 if ye keep yourselves, ye shall do well
16. 28 Do thyself no harm; for we are all here
17. 7 these all do contrary to the decrees
19. 36 ye ought to be quiet, and to do nothing
26. 9 I ought to do many things contrary to
26. 20 they should..do works meet for repent.
26. 26 for this thing was not done in a corner
26. 31 This man doeth nothing worthy of death
Rom. 1. 32 but have pleasure in them that do them
2. 1 for thou that judgest doest the same
2. 3 judgest them which do such things
7. 15 what I would, that do I not; but what I
7. 19 the evil which I would not, that I do
9. 11 neither having done any good or evil
13. 4 to (execute) wrath upon him that doeth
1 Co. 9. 17 if I do this thing willingly, I have a
2 Co. 5. 10 according to that he hath done, whether
Gal. 5. 21 they which do such things shall not
Eph. 6. 21 also may know my affairs, (and) how I do
Phil. 4. 9 Those things..do: and the God of peace
1 Th. 4. 11 to be quiet, and to do your own business

19. *To bear toward*, προσφέρω *prospherō*.
John16. 2 will think that he doeth God service

[*See also* Abominable, abominably, again, better, can, corruptly, despite, diligence, done, evil, foolishly, good, great, harm, have, honour, hurt, judgment, marvellous, mischief, more, murder, office of a priest, perversely, reverence, sacrifice, second time, secretly, service, shame, shamefully, third time, violence, well, what, wickedly, wit, worse, wrong.]

DO away, to —
To cause to pass over, עָבַר *abar*, 5.
1 Ch.21. 8 I beseech thee, do away the iniquity of

DO, can —
1. *To be strong, have strength*, ἰσχύω *ischuō*.
Phil. 4. 13 I can do all things through Christ which
2. *To do*, ποιέω *poieō*.
Gal. 5. 17 ye cannot do the things that ye would

DO for, to —
To hold alongside of, offer, παρέχω *parechō*.
Luke 7. 4 was worthy for whom he should do this

DO, with whom we have to —
Of whom we are speaking, πρὸς ὃν ἡμῖν ὁ λόγος.
Heb. 4. 13 the eyes of him with whom we have to do

DO, have any matters to —
Owner of matters, בַּעַל דְּבָרִים *baal debarim*.
Exod24. 14 if any man have any matters to do, let

DO good, to —
1. *To do, recompense*, גָּמַל *gamal*.
Prov 11. 17 The merciful man doeth good to his own
2. *To do good*, טוֹב *tob*, 5.
Num10. 29 come thou with us, and we will do thee g.
Jer. 32. 41 I will rejoice over them to do them good
Psa.119. 68 Thou (art) good, and doest good: teach
125. 4 Do good, O LORD, unto (those that be) g.

DO (goodness), to —
To do good, יָטַב *yatab*, 5.
Num. 10. 32 shall do unto us.. will we do unto thee

DO (a trespass), to —
To trespass, מָעַל *maal*.
Num. 5. 6 to do a trespass against the LORD, and

DOCTOR —
Teacher, διδάσκαλος *didaskalos*.
Luke 2. 46 sitting in the midst of the doctors, both

DOCTOR of the law —
Teacher of law, νομοδιδάσκαλος *nomodidaskalos*.
Luke 5. 17 Pharisees and doctors of the law sitting
Acts 5. 34 named Gamaliel, a doctor of the law

DOCTRINE —
1. *The receiving, what is (to be) received*, לֶקַח *leqach*.
Deut32. 2 My doctrine shall drop as the rain
Job 11. 4 My doctrine (is) pure, and I am clean in
Prov. 4. 2 I give you good doctrine, forsake ye not
Isa. 29. 24 they that murmured shall learn doctrine
2. *Chastisement, instruction*, מוּסָר *musar*.
Jer. 10. 8 But..the stock (is) a doctrine of vanities
3. *What is heard*, שְׁמוּעָה *shemuah*.
Isa. 28. 9 whom shall he make to understand doct.
4. *Teaching, (the substance)*, διδασκαλία *didaskalia*.
Matt15. 9 teaching (for) doctrines the command.
Mark 7. 7 teaching (for) doctrines the command.
Eph. 4. 14 carried about with every wind of doctr.
Col. 2. 22 after the commandments and doctrines
1 Ti. 1. 10 thing that is contrary to sound doctrine
4. 1 giving heed to seducing spirits, and doc.
4. 6 in the words of faith and of good doctrine
4. 13 Till I come, give attendance..to doctrine
4. 16 Take heed unto thyself, and unto the do.
5. 17 they who labour in the word and doctri.
6. 1 that the name of God and (his) doctrine
6. 3 the doctrine which is according to godli.
2 Ti. 3. 10 But thou hast fully known my doctrine
2 Ti. 3. 16 All scripture..(is) profitable for doctrine
4. 3 when they will not endure sound doctr.
Titus 1. 9 that he may be able by sound doctrine
2. 1 things which become sound doctrine
2. 7 in doctrine (showing) uncorruptness
2. 10 that they may adorn the doctrine of God
5. *Teaching, (the act)*, διδαχή *didachē*.
Matt. 7. 28 the people were astonished at his doctr.
16. 12 but of the doctrine of the Pharisees and
22. 33 they were astonished at his doctrine
Mark 1. 22 And they were astonished at his doctri.
1. 27 What thing is this? what new doctrine
4. 2 and said unto them in his doctrine
11. 18 all the people was astonished at his doc.
12. 38 And he said unto them in his doctrine
Luke 4. 32 And they were astonished at his doctri.
John 7. 16 My doctrine is not mine, but his that
7. 17 he shall know of the doctrine, whether
18. 19 The high priest then asked..his doctrine
Acts 2. 42 continued stedfastly in the apostles' do.
5. 28 ye have filled Jerusalem with your doct.
13. 12 being astonished at the doctrine of the
17. 19 May we know what this new doctrine
Rom. 6. 17 obeyed from the heart that form of doc.
16. 17 contrary to the doctrine which ye have
1 Co. 14. 6 except I shall speak to you..by doctrine
14. 26 every one of you hath a psalm, hath a d.
2 Ti. 4. 2 exhort, with all long suffering and doctr.
Heb. 6. 2 Of the doctrine of baptisms, and of
13. 9 Be not carried about with divers..doctr.
2 Jo. 9 abideth not in the doctrine of Christ
9 He that abideth in the doctrine of Christ
10 If there come..and bring not this doctr.
Rev. 2. 14 thou hast there them that hold the doct.
2. 15 So hast thou also them that hold the do.
2. 24 But..as many as have not this doctrine
6. *Word*, λόγος *logos*.
Heb. 6. 1 leaving the principles of the doctrine of

DO'-DAI, דּוֹדַי *beloved of Jah*.
An Ahohite, one of David's captains.
1 Ch. 27. 4 over..course of the second month (was) D.

DO-DA'-NIM, or RO-DA'-NIM, דֹּדָנִים, רוֹדָנִים.
A race descended from Javan son of Japheth. Authorities vary as to the form of the name: the Hebrew text has both; but the weight of authority is in favour of Dodanim, which is regarded as identical with Dardani.
Gen. 10. 4 the sons of Javan..Tarshish, Kittim..D.
1 Ch. 1. 7 the sons of Javan..Tarshish, Kittim..D.

DO-DA'-VAH, דֹּדָוָהוּ *Jah is loving*.
Father of one who prophesied to Jehoshaphat. B.C. 960.
2 Ch. 20. 37 Then Eliezer the son of D. of Mareshah

DO'-DO, דּוֹדוֹ.
1. Grandfather of the judge Tola of the tribe of Issachar. B.C. 1206.
Judg10. 1 Tola the son of Puah, the son of D.
2. Father of the second of David's thirty valiant men. B.C. 1070.
2 Sa. 23. 9 And after him (was) Eleazar the son of D.
1 Ch.11. 12 And after him (was) Eleazar the son of D.
3. Father of one of David's thirty mighty men. B.C. 1070.
2 Sa. 23. 24 Elhanan the son of D. of Beth-lehem
1 Ch. 11. 26 Elhanan the son of D. of Beth-lehem

DO'-EG, דֹּאֵג, דּוֹאֵג, [V.L. דּוֹיֵג thrice], *fearful*.
Chief of Saul's herdsmen, an Edomite who informed Saul of Ahimelech's having assisted David. B.C. 1062.
1 Sa. 21. 7 and his name (was) D., an Edomite, the
22. 9 Then answered D. the Edomite, which was
22. 18 And the king said to D., Turn thou, and
22. 18 D. the Edomite turned, and he fell upon
22. 22 I knew (it)..when D. the Edomite (was)
Psa. 52. *title*. Doeg the Edomite came and told Saul

DOER —
1. *To do*, עָשָׂה *asah*.
Gen. 39. 22 whatsoever they did there, he was the d.
2 Ki.22. 5 the doers of the work..doers of the work
2. *To act, work, do, make*, פָּעַל *paal*.
Psa.101. 8 that I may cut off all wicked doers
3. *A maker, performer*, ποιητής *poiētēs*.
Rom. 2. 13 but the doers of the law shall be justifi.
Jas. 1. 22 be ye doers of the word, and not hearers
1. 23 a hearer of the word, and not a doer
1. 25 not a forgetful hearer, but a doer of the
4. 11 thou art not a doer of the law, but a

DOG —
1. *Dog*, כֶּלֶב *keleb*.
Exod11. 7 shall not a dog move his tongue, against
22. 31 torn of beasts..ye shall cast it to the dogs
Deut23. 18 Thou shalt not bring..the price of a dog
Judg. 7. 5 Every one that lappeth..as a dog lappe.
1 Sa. 17. 43 (Am) I a dog, that thou comest to me
24. 14 after whom dost thou pursue?..a dead d.
2 Sa. 3. 8 (Am) I a dog's head, which against
9. 8 shouldest look upon such a dead dog
16. 9 Why should this dead dog curse my lord
1 Ki. 14. 11 of Jeroboam in the city shall the dogs
16. 4 of Baasha in the city shall the dogs eat
21. 19 where the dogs licked..shall dogs lick
21. 23 The dogs shall eat Jezebel by the wall
21. 24 dieth of Ahab in the city the dogs shall
22. 38 and the dogs licked up his blood; and
2 Ki. 8. 13 But what! (is) thy servant a dog, that he
9. 10 the dogs shall eat Jezebel in the portion
9. 36 In the portion of Jezreel shall dogs eat
Job 30. 1 disdained to have set with the dogs of my
Psa. 22. 16 For dogs have compassed me; the assem.
22. 20 my darling from the power of the dog
59. 6 they make a noise like a dog, and go
59. 14 let them make a noise like a dog, and go
68. 23 (and) the tongue of thy dogs in the same
Prov 26. 11 As a dog returneth to his vomit, (so) a
26. 17 (is like) one that taketh a dog by the ears
Eccl. 9. 4 for a living dog is better than a dead lion
Isa. 56. 10 they (are) all dumb dogs, they cannot
56. 11 (they are) greedy dogs (which) can never
66. 3 sacrificeth a lamb, (as if) he cut off a dog's
Jer. 15. 3 the dogs to tear, and the fowls of the
2. *A little dog*, κυνάριον *kunarion*.
Matt15. 26 It is not meet..to cast (it) to dogs
15. 27 Truth, Lord: yet the dogs eat of the
Mark 7. 27 it is not meet..to cast (it) unto the dogs
7. 28 the dogs under the table eat of the chil.
3. *A dog, hound*, κύων *kuōn*.
Matt. 7. 6 Give not that which is holy unto the dogs
Luke16. 21 moreover the dogs came and licked his
Phil. 3. 2 Beware of dogs, beware of evil workers
2 Pe. 2. 22 The dog (is) turned to his own vomit
Rev. 22. 15 For without (are) dogs, and sorcerers, and

DOING —
1. *Doing*, מַעֲלָל *maalal* [V.L. מעליל].
Zech. 1. 4 Turn ye now from your evil..doings: but
2. *Doing*, מַעֲלָל *maalal*.
Deut 28. 20 because of the wickedness of thy doings
Judg. 2. 19 they ceased not from their own doings
1 Sa. 25. 3 man (was) churlish, and evil in his doings
Prov 20. 11 Even a child is known by his doings
Isa. 1. 16 put away the evil of your doings from
3. 8 their tongue and their doings (are) against
3. 10 for they shall eat the fruit of their doings
Jer. 4. 4 because of the evil of your doings
4. 18 thy doings have procured these (things)
7. 3 Amend your ways and your doings, and
7. 5 if ye throughly amend..your doings
11. 18 then thou showedst me their doings
17. 10 to give..according to the fruit of his do
18. 11 make your ways and your doings good
21. 12 because of the evil of your doings
21. 14 according to the fruit of your doings
23. 2 visit upon you the evil of your doings
23. 22 have turned..from the evil of their do.
25. 5 Turn ye..from the evil of your doings
26. 3 because of the evil of their doings
26. 13 now amend your ways and your doings
32. 19 to give..according to the fruit of his do.
35. 15 Return ye now..and amend your doings
44. 22 because of the evil of your doings
Eze. 36. 31 Then shall ye remember your..doings
Hos. 4. 9 I will punish..and reward them their do.
5. 4 They will not frame their doings to turn
7. 2 now their own doings have beset them
9. 15 for the wickedness of their doings I will
12. 2 according to his doings will he recompe.
Mic. 2. 7 (are) these his doings? do not my words
3. 4 have behaved themselves ill in their do.
7. 13 be desolate..for the fruit of their doings
Zech. 1. 6 according to our doings, so hath he
3. *Work, occupation*, מַעֲשֶׂה *maaseh*.
Lev. 18. 3 After the doings of the land of Egypt
18. 3 and after the doings of the land of Can.
2 Ch.17. 4 and walked..not after the doings of Isr.
Psa. 64. 9 for they shall wisely consider of his do.
4. *Doing*, עֲלִילָה *alilah*.
Psa. 9. 11 declare among the people his doings
66. 5 terrible (in his) doing toward the child.
77. 12 I will meditate..and talk of thy doings
Isa. 12. 4 call upon his name, declare his doings
Eze. 14. 22 ye shall see their way and their doings
14. 23 when ye see their ways and their doings
20. 43 there shall ye remember..all your doings
20. 44 nor according to your corrupt doings, O
21. 24 in all your doings your sins do appear
24. 14 according to thy doings, shall they judge
36. 17 by their own way and by their doings
36. 19 according to their doings I judged them
Zeph. 3. 7 rose early, (and) corrupted all their doings
3. 11 thou not be ashamed for all thy doings
5. *To do*, עָשָׂה *asah*.
Exod15. 11 glorious in holiness, fearful..praises, do.
1 Ch.22. 16 Arise..and be doing, and the LORD be
Isa. 58. 13 If thou turn..(from) doing thy pleasure
58. 13 honour him, not doing thine own ways
6. *Work*, ἔργον *ergon*.
Rom. 2. 7 who by patient continuance in well doing
7. *To do*, ποιέω *poieō*.
2 Co. 8. 11 Now therefore perform the doing (of it)

DOING, in —
To do, ποιέω *poieō*.
Gal. 6. 9 let us not be weary in well doing: for in
1 Ti. 4. 16 for in doing this thou shalt..save thyself

DOING, to be one's —
To become, γίνομαι *ginomai*.
Matt21. 42 this is the Lord's doing, and it is marvel.
Mark12. 11 the Lord's doing, and it is marvellous

DOLEFUL, doleful creatures —
1. *Wailing*, נְהִיָה *nihyah*. [uncertain if from *hayah*, 2].
Mic. 2. 4 and lament with a doleful lamentation
2. *Howlings*, אֹחִים *ochim*.
Isa. 13. 21 houses shall be full of doleful creatures
DOMINION —
1. *Hand*, יָד *yad*.
1 Ch. 18. 3 his d. by the river; 2 Ch. 21. 8 the d. of Judah
2. *Rule, dominion*, מִמְשָׁל *mimshal*.
Dan. 11. 3 a mighty king..with great dominion
11. 5 his..(shall be) a great dominion
3. *Rule, dominion*, מֶמְשָׁלָה *memshalah*.
1 Ki. 9. 19 and in all the land of his dominion
2 Ki. 20. 13 there was nothing..in all his dominion
2 Ch. 8. 6 throughout all the land of his dominion
Psa. 103. 22 all his works in all places of his domin.
114. 2 Judah was his sanctuary..Israel his do.
145. 13 thy dominion..throughout all generati.
Isa. 39. 2 there was nothing..in all his dominion
Jer. 34. 1 kingdoms of the earth of his d. [with *yad*]
51. 28 Prepare..all the land of his dominion
Dan. 11. 5 and his dominion (shall be) a great
Mic. 4. 8 unto thee shall it come, even the first d.
4. *Dominion, authority*, מִשְׁטָר *mishtar*.
Job 38. 33 canst thou set the dominion thereof in
5. *To cause to rule*, מָשַׁל *mashal*, 5.
Job 25. 2 Dominion and fear (are) with him; he
6. *Rule*, מֹשֶׁל *moshel*.
Dan. 11. 4 nor according to his dominion which he
Zech. 9. 10 his dominion (shall be) from sea (even)
7. *Rule, dominion*, שָׁלְטָן *sholtan*.
Dan. 4. 3 his dominion (is) from generation to gen.
4. 22 and thy dominion to the end of the earth
4. 34 whose dominion is an everlasting domin.
6. 26 That in every dominion of my kingdom
6. 26 his dominion (shall be even) unto the end
7. 6 the beast..dominion was given to it
7. 12 they had their dominion taken away
7. 14 there was given him dominion and glory
7. 14 his dominion (is) an everlasting dominion
7. 26 and they shall take away his dominion
7. 27 the kingdom and dominion, and the
7. 27 all dominions shall serve and obey him
8. *Strength, power*, κράτος *kratos*.
1 Pe. 4. 11 to whom be praise and dominion for ever
5. 11 To him (be) glory and dominion for ever
Jude 25 dominion and power, both now and ever
Rev. 1. 6 to him (be) glory and dominion for ever
9. *Lordship*, κυριότης *kuriotēs*.
Eph. 1. 21 might, and dominion, and every name
Col. 1. 16 thrones, or dominions, or principalities
Jude 8 despise dominion, and speak evil of dig.
DOMINION, to come to have —
To rule, tread down, רָדָה *radah*.
Num 24. 19 shall come he that shall have dominion
DOMINION, to have —
1. *To rule, possess, have, marry*, בָּעַל *baal*.
1 Ch. 4. 22 who had the dominion in Moab, and Jas.
Isa. 26. 13 lords besides thee have had dominion
2. *To rule*, מָשַׁל *mashal*.
Gen. 37. 8 shalt thou indeed have dominion over us?
Judg 14. 4 the Philistines had dominion over Israel
Neh. 9. 37 also they have dominion over our bodies
Psa. 19. 13 let them not have dominion over me
Dan. 11. 5 shall be strong above him, and have do.
3. *To rule, tread down*, רָדָה *radah*.
Gen. 1. 26 let them have dominion over the fish
1. 28 have dominion over the fish of the sea
1 Ki. 4. 24 For he had dominion over all (the region)
Neh. 9. 28 that they had the dominion over them
Psa. 49. 14 the upright shall have dominion 72. 8.
4. *To rule*, רוּד *rud*, 5.
Gen. 27. 40 when thou shalt have the dominion, that
5. *To be sultan*, שְׁלַט *shalat*, 5.
Psa. 119. 133 let not any iniquity have dominion over
DOMINION, to make to have —
1. *To cause to rule*, מָשַׁל *mashal*, 5.
Psa. 8. 6 Thou madest him to have dominion over
2. *To rule, tread down*, רָדָה *radah*, 3.
Judg. 5. 13 he made him that remaineth have domi.
5. 13 the LORD made me have dominion over
DOMINION over, to have —
To have or exercise lordship, κυριεύω *kurieuō*.
Rom. 6. 9 death hath no more domin.; 6. 14, 7. 1.
2 Co. 1. 24 Not for that we have dominion over your
DOMINION over, to exercise —
To have or exercise lordship against, κατακυριεύω.
Matt 20. 25 princes of the Gentiles exercise dom. over
DONE —
The affair, דָּבָר *dabar*.
1 Sam. 4. 16 What is there done my son?
DONE, to be —
1. *To be prepared, done*, בָּרָא *bara*, 2.
Exod 34. 10 as have not been done in all the earth
2. *To be*, הָיָה *hayah*, 2.
Judg 20. 12 What wickedness (is) this that is done
1 Ki. 1. 27 Is this thing done; 2 Ch. 11. 4; Neh. 6. 8.
Jer. 48. 19 O inhabitant of Aroer..say, What is done?
Eze. 39. 8 Behold, it is come, and it is done, saith
3. *To be completed, finished*, כָּלָה *kalah*.
Isa. 24. 13 gleaning grapes when the vintage is done
4. *To be given*, נָתַן *nathan*, 2.
Lev. 24. 20 as he hath caused..so shall it be done
5. *To be done*, עֲבַד *abad*, 4.
Ezra 6. 12 have made a decree; let it be done with
7. 21 shall require of you, it be done speedily
7. 23 let it be diligently done for the house of
6. *To be rolled, done*, עָלַל *alal*, 4a.
Lam. 1. 12 unto my sorrow, which is done unto me
7. *To do, make*, עָשָׂה *asah*.
Exod 3. 16 I have..(seen) that which is done to you
8. *To be done, made*, עָשָׂה *asah*, 2.
Gen. 20. 9 deeds unto me that ought not to be done
29. 26 It must not be so done in our country, to
34. 7 folly..which thing ought not to be done
Exod. 2. 4 stood afar off, to wit what would be done
12. 16 no manner of work shall be done in them
12. 16 man must eat, that only may be done of
21. 31 according to this judgment shall it be d.
31. 15 Six days may work be done; but in the
35. 2 Six days shall work be done, but on the
Lev. 4. 2, 27 (c. things) which ought not to be done
4. 13, 22 (c. things) which should not be done
5. 17 which are forbidden to be done by the
11. 32 wherein (any) work is done, it must be
23. 3 Six days shall work be done: but the
24. 19 cause a blemish..so shall it be done
Num 15. 11 Thus shall it be done for one bullock, or
15. 34 was not declared what should be done
Deut 25. 9 So shall it be done unto that man
Judg 11. 37 Let this thing be done for me: let me
1 Sa. 11. 7 so shall it be done unto his oxen. And
17. 26 What shall be done to the man that
17. 27 So shall it be done to the man that
2 Sa. 13. 12 no such thing ought to be done in Israel
Ezra 10. 3 and let it be done according to the law
Neh. 6. 9 shall be weakened..that it be not done
Esth. 6. 9, 11 Thus shall it be done to the man whom
9. 12 what (is) thy request..it shall be done
Eccl. 1. 9 which is done (is) that which shall be d.
1. 13 concerning all (things) that are done
1. 14 I have seen all the works that are done
4. 1 all the oppressions that are done under
4. 3 hath not seen the evil work that is done
8. 9 unto every work that is done under the
8. 14 There is a vanity which is done upon the
8. 16 to see the business that is done upon the
8. 17 cannot find out the work that is done un.
9. 3 evil among all (things) that are done under
9. 6 in any (thing) that is done under the sun
Isa. 46. 10 Declaring..(the things) that are not..d.
Jer. 3. 16 neither shall (that) be done any more
5. 13 thus shall it be done unto them
Eze. 9. 4 for all the abominations that be done in
12. 11 so shall it be done unto them: they shall
12. 28 word which I have spoken shall be done
44. 14 and for all that shall be done therein
Dan. 9. 12 hath not been done as hath been done
11. 36 for that that is determined shall be done
Obad. 15 it shall be done unto thee: thy reward
9. *To become*, γίνομαι *ginomai*.
Matt. 1. 22 Now all this was done, that it might be
6. 10 Thy kingdom come; thy will be done in
8. 13 as thou hast believed, (so) be it done
11. 20 wherein most of his..works were done
11. 21 which were done in you had been done in
11. 23 which have been done in thee, had been d.
18. 19 it shall be done for them of my Father
18. 31 when his fellow servants saw what was d.
18. 31 told unto their lord all that was done
21. 4 All this was done, that it might be ful.
21. 21 be thou cast into the sea; it shall be done
26. 42 if..except I drink it, thy will be done
26. 56 But all this was done, that the scriptures
27. 54 centurion..saw..those things that were d.
28. 11 and showed..all the things that were d.
Mark 4. 11 all (these) things are done in parables
5. 14 went out to see what it was that was d.
5. 33 knowing what was done in her, came
13. 30 shall not pass, till all these things be d.
Luke 4. 23 whatsoever we have heard done in
8. 34 they that fed (them) saw what was done
8. 35 Then they went out to see what was done
8. 56 they should tell no man what was done
9. 7 the tetrarch heard of all that was done
10. 13 if the mighty works had been done in
10. 13 which have been done in you, they had
11. 2 Thy will be done, as in heaven, so in
13. 17 for all the glorious things that were done
14. 22 Lord, it is done as thou hast commanded
22. 42 nevertheless not my will, but thine, be d.
23. 8 hoped to have seen some miracle done by
23. 31 if..in a green..what shall be done in
23. 47 when the centurion saw what was done
23. 48 beholding the things which were done
24. 21 third day since these things were done
John 1. 28 These things were done in Bethabara
15. 7 ask what ye will, and it shall be done unto
19. 36 these things were done, that the scripture
Acts 2. 43 many wonders and signs were done by
4. 16 that..a notable miracle hath been done
4. 21 glorified God for that which was done
4. 28 thy counsel determined before to be done
4. 30 wonders may be done by the name of
5. 7 his wife, not knowing what was done
Acts 8. 13 the miracles and signs which were done
10. 16 This was done thrice: and the vessel was
11. 10 this was done three times: and all were
12. 9 wist not that it was true which was done
13. 12 the deputy, when he saw what was done
14. 3 granted signs and wonders to be done
21. 14 saying, The will of the Lord be done
24. 2 worthy deeds are done unto this nation
28. 9 So when this was done, others also
DONE away, to be —
1. *To be withdrawn*, גָּרַע *gara*, 2.
Num 27. 4 the name of our father be done away from
2. *To make useless*, καταργέω *katargeō*.
1 Co. 13. 10 that which is in part shall be done away
2 Co. 3. 7 which (glory) was to be done away
3. 11 For if that..is done away (was) glorious
3. 14 which (veil) is done away in Christ
DONE, deed to be —
To be, happen, come to pass, befall, הָיָה *hayah*, 2.
Judg 19. 30 There was no such deed done nor seen
DONE, to have —
1. *To finish*, כָּלָה *kalah*, 3.
Gen. 24. 15 it came to pass, before he had done spea.
24. 19 when she had done giving him drink
24. 19 camels also, until they have done drink.
24. 22 it came to pass, as the camels had done
24. 45 before I had done speaking in mine heart
Exod 34. 33 And (till) Moses had done speaking with
Ruth 3. 3 until he shall have done eating and dri.
2. *To perfect, finish*, תָּמַם *tamam*.
Josh. 5. 8 when they had done circumcising all the
2 Sa. 15. 24 until all the people had done passing out
DONE, when...were —
To finish, כָּלָה *kalah*, 3.
Ezra 9. 1 when these things were done, the princes
DOOR —
1. *House*, בַּיִת *bayith*.
1 Ki. 14. 17 when she came to the threshold of the d.
2. *Door*, דַּל *dal*.
Psa. 141. 3 Set a watch..keep the door of my lips
3. *Door*, דָּלָה *dalah*. [v. L. דלת].
Isa. 26. 20 Come, my people..shut thy doors about
4. *Door*, דֶּלֶת *deleth*.
Gen. 19. 6 Lot went out..and shut the door after
19. 9 they..came near to break the door
19. 10 pulled Lot into..and shut to the door
Exod 21. 6 he shall also bring him to the door
Deut 15. 17 thrust (it) through his ear unto the door
Josh. 2. 19 whosoever shall go out of the doors of
Judg. 3. 23 Ehud..shut the doors of the parlour upon
3. 24 the doors of the parlour (were) locked
3. 25 he opened not the doors of the parlour
11. 31 whatsoever cometh forth of the doors
16. 3 Samson..took the doors of the gate of
19. 22 certain sons of Belial..beat at the door
19. 27 her lord..opened the doors of the house
1 Sa. 3. 15 Samuel..opened the doors of the house
21. 13 and scrabbled on the doors of the gate
2 Sa. 13. 17 Put..out..and bolt the door after her
13. 18 brought her out, and bolted the door after
1 Ki. 6. 31 And for the entering..he made doors
6. 32 The two doors also (were of) olive tree
6. 34 And the two doors (were of) fir tree
6. 34 leaves of the one door..of the other door
7. 50 for the doors of..for the doors of the
2 Ki. 4. 4 thou shalt shut the door upon thee
4. 5 she went from him, and shut the door
4. 33 He went in therefore, and shut the door
6. 32 when the messenger cometh, shut the d.
6. 32 and hold him fast at the door: (is) not
9. 3 open the door, and flee, and tarry not
9. 10 And he opened the door, and fled
18. 16 Hezekiah cut off (the gold from) the doors
1 Ch. 22. 3 for the nails for the doors of the gates
2 Ch. 3. 7 He overlaid also the..doors thereof, with
4. 9 he made..the great court, and doors for
4. 9 overlaid the doors of them with brass
4. 22 the inner doors thereof for the most holy
4. 22 the doors of the house of the temple
28. 24 shut up the doors of the house of the L.
29. 3 opened the doors of the house of the
29. 7 they have shut up the doors of the porch
Neh. 3. 1 they sanctified it, and set up the doors of
3. 3, 6, 13, 14, 15 set up the doors thereof, the
6. 1 I had not set up the doors upon the gates
6. 10 and let us shut the doors of the temple
7. 1 I had set up the doors, and the porters
7. 3 let them shut the doors, and bar (them)
Job 3. 10 Because it shut not up the doors of my
31. 32 (but) I opened my doors to the traveller
38. 8 Or (who) shut up the sea with doors
38. 10 brake up for it..and set bars and doors
41. 14 Who can open the doors of his face?
Psa. 78. 23 Though he had..opened the doors of hea.
Prov 26. 14 the door turneth upon his hinges, so
Eccl. 12. 4 the doors shall be shut in the streets
Song 8. 9 if she (be) a door, we will inclose her
Isa. 26. 20 Come, my people..shut thy doors about
57. 8 Behind the doors also and the posts hast
Eze. 41. 23 temple and the sanctuary had two doors
41. 24 And the doors had two leaves (apiece)
41. 24 two (leaves) for the one door, and two
41. 25 on the doors of the temple, cherubim

Zech 11. 1 Open thy doors, O Lebanon, that the fire
Mal. 1. 10 even among you that would shut the d.

5. *Threshold, lintel,* סַף *saph.*
2 Ki. 12. 9 the priests that kept the door put therein
22. 4 the keepers of the door have gathered of
23. 4 the keepers of the door, to bring forth
25. 18 took..the three keepers of the door
2 Ch. 23. 4 third part..(shall be) porters of the doors
34. 9 which the Levites that kept the doors
Esth. 2. 21 two..of those which kept the door, were
6. 2 chamberlains, the keepers of the door
Isa. 6. 4 the posts of the door moved at the voice
Jer. 35. 4 Maaseiah..the keeper of the door
52. 24 took..the three keepers of the door
Eze. 41. 16 over against the door, cieled with wood

6. *Opening, entrance of a door,* פֶּתַח *pethach.*
Gen. 4. 7 if thou doest not well, sin lieth at the d.
6. 16 the door of the ark shalt thou set in the
18. 1 he sat in the tent door in the heat of the
18. 2 he ran to meet them from the tent door
18. 10 Sarah heard (it) in the tent door, which
19. 6 Lot went out at the door unto them
19. 11 they smote the men that (were) at the door
19. 11 they wearied themselves to find the door
43. 19 they communed with him at the door of
Exod 12. 22 none of you shall go out at the door of
12. 23 the LORD will pass over the door, and
26. 36 thou shalt make an hanging for the door
29. 4, 32 the door of the tabernacle of the
29. 11 kill the bullock..(by) the door
33. 8 and stood every man (at) his tent door
33. 9 the cloudy pillar..stood (at) the door of
33. 10 the cloudy pillar stand (at) the..door
33. 10 worshipped, every man (in) his tent door
35. 15 incense, and the hanging for the door at
36. 37 made an hanging for the tabernacle door
38. 8, 30 the door of the tabernacle of the con.
39. 38 the hanging for the tabernacle door
40. 5 put the hanging of the door to the taber.
40. 6 altar of the burnt offering before the door
40. 12 thou shalt bring Aaron..unto the door
40. 28 he set up the hanging (at) the door of
40. 29 put the altar of burnt offering (by) the d.
Lev. 1. 3 offer it of his own voluntary will at the d.
1. 5 upon the altar that (is by) the door of the
3. 2 shall..kill it (at) the door of the taberna.
4. 4 he shall bring the bullock unto the door
4. 7, 18 the door of the tabernacle of the con.
8. 3 the congregation together unto the door
8. 4 the assembly was gathered..unto the d.
8. 31 Boil the flesh (at) the door of the tabern.
8. 33 ye shall not go out of the door of the
8. 35 Therefore shall ye abide (at) the door of
10. 7 ye shall not go out from the door of the
12. 6 unto the door of the tabernacle of the c.
14. 11, 23 the door of the tabernacle of the con.
14. 38 shall go out of the house to the door
15. 14 come before the LORD unto the door of
15. 29 bring them..to the door of the taberna.
16. 7 present them before the LORD (at) the d.
17. 4, 9 bringeth it not unto the door of the ta.
17. 5 unto the door of the tabernacle of the
17. 6 altar of the LORD (at) the door of the ta.
19. 21 bring his trespass offering..unto the do.
Num. 3. 25 the hanging for the door of the taberna.
3. 26 the curtain for the door of the court
4. 25, 26 the hanging for the door of the
6 10 to the door of the tabernacle of the con.
6. 13 he shall be brought unto the door of
6. 18 the head of his separation (at) the door
10. 3 assemble themselves to thee at the door
11. 10 every man in the door of his tent
12. 5 the LORD..stood (in) the door of the tab.
16. 18 every man..stood in the door of the tab.
16. 19 Korah gathered all..unto the door of
16. 27 Dathan and Abiram..stood in the door
16 50 Aaron returned unto Moses unto the d.
20. 6 Moses and Aaron went from..unto the d.
25. 6 weeping (before) the door of the taberna.
27. 2 they stood..(by) the door of the taberna.
Deut 22. 21 shall bring out the damsel to the door
31. 15 pillar of the cloud stood over the door
Josh. 19. 51 divided..at the door of the tabernacle of
Judg. 4. 20 Stand in the door of the tent; and it
9. 52 Abimelech..went hard unto the door
19. 26 the woman..fell down at the door of
19. 27 was fallen down (at) the door of the
1 Sa. 2. 22 the women that assembled (at) the door
2 Sa. 11. 9 Uriah slept at the door of the king's
1 Ki. 6. 8 The door for the middle chamber (was)
6. 33 So also made he for the door of the tem.
7. 5 And all the doors and posts (were) square
14. 6 as she came in at the door, that he said
14. 27 chief of the guard, which kept the door
2 Ki. 4. 15 he had called her, she stood in the door
5. 9 Naaman..stood at the door of the house
1 Ch. 9. 21 Zechariah..(was) porter of the door of
Neh. 3. 20 the turning (of the wall) unto the door
3. 21 another piece, from the door of the house
Job 31. 9 I have laid wait at my neighbour's door
31. 34 kept silence, (and) went not out of the d.
Psa. 24. 7 be ye lift up, ye everlasting doors
24. 9 lift (them) up, ye everlasting doors, and
Prov. 5. 8 come not nigh the door of her house
8. 3 She crieth..at the coming in at the doo.
8. 34 waiting at the posts of my doors
9. 14 she sitteth at the door of her house
Eze. 8. 3 to the door of the inner gate that looketh
8. 7 he brought me to the door of the court
8. 8 I had digged in the wall, behold, a door
Eze. 8. 14 Then he brought me to the door of the
8. 16 at the door of the temple of the LORD
10. 19 stood at the door of the east gate of the
11. 1 at the door of the gate five and twenty
33. 30 by the walls, and in the doors of the
40. 13 five and twenty cubits, door against door
41. 2 the breadth of the door (was) ten cubits
41. 2 the sides of the door (were) five cubits
41. 3 and measured the post of the door
41. 3 the door..the breadth of the door seven
41. 11 And the doors of the side chambers
41. 11 one door toward..and another door tow.
41. 17 To that above the door, even unto the
41. 20 From the ground unto above the door
42. 2 Before the length..(was) the north door
42. 4 and their doors toward the north
42. 11 their fashions, and according to their d.
42. 12 according to the doors of the chambers
42. 12 toward the south (was) a door in the
46. 3 shall worship at the door of this gate
47. 1 he brought me again unto the door of
Hos. 2. 15 the valley of Achor for a door of hope
Mic. 7. 5 keep the doors of thy mouth from her

7. *A gate,* שַׁעַר *shaar.*
Exod 35. 17 the hanging for the door of the court
Job 38. 17 hast thou seen the doors of the shadow

8. *Door,* θύρα *thura.*
Matt. 6. 6 when thou hast shut thy door, pray to thy
24. 33 know that it is near, (even) at the doors
25. 10 while they went to buy..the door was sh.
27. 60 he rolled a great stone to the door of the
28. 2 [and rolled back the stone from the door]
Mark 1. 33 all the city was gathered..at the door
2. 2 no room..not so much as about the door
11. 4 they..found the colt tied by the door
13. 29 know that it is nigh, (even) at the doors
15. 46 and rolled a stone unto the door of the
16. 3 shall roll us away the stone from the door
Luke 11. 7 Trouble me not: the door is now shut
13. 25 hath shut to the door..knock at the door
John 10. 1 He that entereth not by the door into
10. 2 he that entereth in by the door is the
10. 7 I say unto you, I am the door of the sheep
10. 9 I am the door: by me if any man enter
18. 16 But Peter stood at the door without
20. 19 doors were shut where the disciples were
20. 26 (Then) came Jesus, the doors being shut
Acts 5. 9 (are) at the door, and shall carry thee
5. 19 opened the prison doors, and brought
5. 23 standing without before the doors: but
12. 6 the keepers before the door kept the
12. 13 as Peter knocked at the door of the gate
14. 27 how he had opened the door of faith unto
16. 26 immediately all the doors were opened
16. 27 seeing the prison doors open, he drew out
21. 30 drew him out..forthwith the doors were
1 Co. 16. 9 a great door and effectual is opened unto
2 Co. 2. 12 a door was opened unto me of the Lord
Col. 4. 3 God would open unto us a door of utter.
Jas. 5. 9 behold, the judge standeth before the door
Rev. 3. 8 I have set before thee an open door, and
3. 20 Behold, I stand at the door and knock
3. 20 open the door, I will come into him, and
4. 1 behold, a door (was) opened in heaven

DOOR keeper, or keeper of the door —
1. *Gate keeper,* שׁוֹעֵר *shoer.*
1 Ch. 15. 23 Berechiah and Elkanah (were) door kee.
15. 24 Obed-edom and Jehiah (were) door keep.

2. *A door keeper,* θυρωρός *thurōros.*
John 18. 16 spake unto her that kept the door, and
18. 17 Then saith the damsel that kept the door

DOOR keeper, to be a —
To keep self at the threshold, סָפַף *saphaph, 7a.*
Psa. 84. 10 I had rather be a door keeper in the house

DOOR post —
Threshold, lintel, door, סַף *saph.*
Eze. 41. 16 The door posts, and the narrow windows

DOOR post, upper —
Lintel, upper door post, מַשְׁקוֹף *mashqoph.*
Exod 12. 7 and on the upper door post of the houses

DOPH'-KAH, דָּפְקָה *cattle driving.*
Eighth station of Israel, between Sin and Sinai.
Num 33. 12 took their journey..and encamped in D.
33. 13 And they departed from D., and encamped

DOR, דֹּאר, דּוֹר *circle.*
An ancient royal city of the Canaanites, whose ruler was an ally of Jabin king of Hazor against Joshua. It was the most southern settlement of the Phoenicians on the coast of Syria, and a maritime city on the W. border of Manasseh and the N. border of Dan.
Josh 11. 2 and in the borders of D. on the west
12. 23 The king of D. in the coast of D., one
17. 11 and the inhabitants of D. and her towns
Judg. 1. 27 nor the inhabitants of D. and her towns
1 Ki. 4. 11 The son of Abinadab, in all..region of D.
1 Ch. 7. 29 Megiddo and her towns, D. and her towns

DOR'-CAS, Δορκάς, *doe, gazelle.*
A female disciple restored to life at Joppa.
Acts 9. 36 Tabitha..by interpretation is called D.
9. 39 showing the coats and garments which D.

DOTE, to —
1. *To become foolish,* יָאַל *yaal,* 2.
Jer. 50. 36 upon the liars; and they shall dote: a
2. *To dote on, love,* עָגַב *agab.*
Eze. 23. 5 she doted on her lovers, on the Assyrians
23. 7 with all on whom she doted: with all
23. 9 hand of the Assyrians, upon whom she do.
23. 12 She doted upon the Assyrians (her) neigh.
23. 16 she doted upon them, and sent messen.
23. 20 For she doted upon their paramours
3. *To be sick,* νοσέω *noseō.*
1 Ti. 6. 4 doting about questions and strifes of

DO'-THAN, דֹּתָן, דֹּתַיִן, *double feast.*
A city of Manasseh, W. of the Jordan, near Mount Gilboa, N.E. of Samaria, and still called *Dothan.*
Gen. 37. 17 I heard them say, Let us go to D.
37. 17 And Joseph went..and found them in D.
2 Ki. 6. 13 was told him, saying, Behold, (he is) in D.

DOUBLE —
1. *Double, fold,* כֶּפֶל *kephel.*
Job 11. 6 that (they are) double to that which is!
41. 13 who can come (to him) with his double
Isa. 40. 2 she hath received..double for all her sins
2. *To double,* כָּפַל *kaphal.*
Exod 39. 9 they made the breastplate double: a span
3. *A second, repetition,* מִשְׁנֶה *mishneh.*
Gen. 43. 12 take double money in your hand: and the
43. 15 they took double money in their hand
Deut 15. 18 he hath been worth a double hired serva.
Isa. 61. 7 For your shame (ye shall have) double
61. 7 in their land they shall possess the double
Jer. 16. 18 I will recompense..their sin double
17. 18 destroy them with double destruction
Zech. 9. 12 I will render double unto thee
4. *Two, twofold,* שְׁנַיִם *shenayim.*
Exod 22. 4 whether it be ox, or ass..shall restore d.
22. 7 if the thief be found, let him pay doubl.
22. 9 he shall pay double unto his neighbour
Deut 21. 17 by giving him a double portion of all that
2 Ki. 2. 9 let a double portion of thy spirit be upon
5. *Double, twofold,* διπλοῦς *diplous.*
1 Ti. 5. 17 Let the elders..be counted worthy of do.
Rev. 18. 6 unto her double according to her works
18. 6 cup which she hath filled fill to her dou.

DOUBLE, to —
1. *To double,* כָּפַל *kaphal.*
Exod 26. 9 thou shalt..double the sixth curtain in
2. *To double,* διπλόω *diploō.*
Rev. 18. 6 even as she rewarded you, and double

DOUBLE heart —
Heart and heart, לֵב וָלֵב *leb va-leb.*
1 Ch. 12. 33 such as went forth..not of double heart
Psa. 12. 2 (and) with a double heart, do they speak

DOUBLE minded —
Two souled, δίψυχος *dipsuchos.*
Jas. 1. 8 A double minded man (is) unstable in all
4. 8 purify (your) hearts, (ye) double minded

DOUBLE tongued —
Double worded, δίλογος *dilogos.*
1 Ti. 3. 8 not double tongued, not given to much

DOUBLED, to be —
1. *To be doubled,* כָּפַל *kaphal,* 2.
Eze. 21. 14 let the sword be doubled the third time
2. *To be repeated, done a second time,* שָׁנָה *shanah,* 2.
Gen. 41. 32 the dream was doubled unto Pharaoh

DOUBLED —
To double, כָּפַל *kaphal.*
Exod 28. 16 Four square it shall be, (being) doubled
39. 9 a span the breadth thereof, (being) doub.

DOUBT —
A knot, doubt, joint, קְטַר *qetar.*
Dan. 5. 12 Forasmuch as..dissolving of doubts, were
5. 16 that thou canst..dissolve doubts: now if

DOUBT, to —
1. *To be without resource,* ἀπορέομαι *aporeomai.*
John 13. 22 the disciples looked..doubting of whom
Acts 25. 20 because I doubted of such manner of
2. *To judge diversely,* διακρίνω *diakrinō.*
Matt 21. 21 If ye have faith, and doubt not, ye shall
Mark 11. 23 shall not doubt in his heart, but shall
Acts 10. 20 go with them, doubting nothing: for I
11. 12 bade me go with them, nothing [doubt.]
Rom 14. 23 he that doubteth is damned if he eat
3. *To be without any resource,* διαπορέω *diaporeō.*
Acts. 5. 24 doubted of them whereunto this would
10. 17 while Peter doubted in himself what this
4. *To stand divided,* διστάζω *distazō.*
Matt 14. 31 O thou..wherefore didst thou doubt?
28. 17 they worshipped him: but some doubted

DOUBT, to be in —
To be without any resource, διαπορέω *diaporeō.*
Acts. 2. 12 they were all amazed, and were in doubt

DOUBT, to make to —
To lift up the soul, αἴρω ψυχὴν *airō psuchēn.*
John 10. 24 How long dost thou make us to doubt? If

DOUBT, to stand in —
To be without resource, ἀπορέομαι *aporeomai.*
Gal. 4. 20 change my voice, for I stand in doubt of

DOUBT, no —
1. *Truly, indeed,* אָמְנָם *omnam.*
Job 12. 2 No doubt but ye (are) the people, and wis.
2. *Then, therefore,* ἄρα *ara.*
Luke 11. 20 no doubt the kingdom of God is come
3. *Verily then, for,* γάρ *gar.*
1 Co. 9. 10 For our sakes, no doubt, (this) is written
4. *Altogether, by all means,* πάντως *pantōs.*
Acts 28. 4 No doubt this man is a murderer, whom

DOUBT, without —
To tear, טָרַף *taraph.*
Gen. 37. 33 Joseph is without doubt rent in pieces

DOUBTFUL —
Diverse judging, διάκρισις *diakrisis.*
Rom 14. 1 receive ye, (but) not to doubtful disput.

DOUBTFUL mind, to be of —
To lift up on high, μετεωρίζω *meteōrizō.*
Luke 12. 29 neither be ye of doubtful mi

DOUBTING —
Reasoning, διαλογισμός *dialogismos.*
1 Ti. 2. 8 lifting up holy hands, without..doubting

DOUBTLESS —
1. *That, because,* כִּי *ki.*
Isa. 63. 16 Doubtless thou (art) our Father, though
2. *At least,* γέ *ge.*
1 Co. 9. 2 If I be not..yet doubtless I am to you
3. *Doubtless, truly, certainly,* δή *dē.*
2 Co. 12. 1 [not expedient for me doubtless to glory]

DOUBTLESS, again —
To come in, בּוֹא *bo.*
Psa. 126 6 shall doubtless come again with rejoicing

DOUBTLESS, not —
If, אִם *im.*
Num 14 30 Doubtless ye shall not come into the land

DOUGH —
1. *Dough, swelled,* בָּצֵק *batseq.*
Exod 12. 34 took their dough before it was leavened
12. 39 they baked unleavened cakes of the dough
Jer. 7. 18 the women knead (their) dough, to make
Hos. 7. 4 raising after he hath kneaded the dough
2. *Dough, mixed dough,* עֲרִיסָה *arisah.*
Num 15. 20 offer up a cake of the first of your dough
15. 21 Of the first of your dough ye shall give
Neh. 10. 37 should bring the first fruits of our dough
Eze. 44. 30 unto the priest the first of your dough

DOVE —
1. *Dove,* יוֹנָה *yonah.*
Gen. 8. 8 he sent forth a dove from him, to see if
8. 9 the dove found no rest for the sole of
8. 10 he sent forth the dove out of the ark
8. 11 the dove came in to him in the evening
8. 12 sent forth the dove; which returned not
Psa. 55. 6 Oh that I had wings like a dove
68. 13 the wings of a dove covered with silver
Song 1. 15 behold, thou (art) fair; thou (hast) doves'
2. 14 O my dove, (that art) in the clefts of the
4. 1 thou (hast) doves' eyes within thy locks
5. 2 Open to me, my sister, my love, my dove
5. 12 (the eyes) of doves by the rivers of waters
6. 9 My dove, my undefiled is (but) one; she
Isa. 38. 14 I did mourn as a dove: mine eyes fail
59. 11 We roar all..and mourn sore like doves
60. 8 and as the doves to their windows
Jer. 48. 28 be like the dove (that) maketh her nest
Eze. 7. 16 shall be on the mountains like doves of
Hos. 7. 11 Ephraim also is like a silly dove without
11 11 and as a dove out of the land of Assyria
Nah. 2 7 shall lead (her) as with the voice of doves
2. *Dove, pigeon,* περιστερά *peristera.*
Matt. 3. 16 the spirit of God descending like a dove
10. 16 wise as serpents, and harmless as doves
21. 12 and the seats of them that sold doves
Mark 1. 10 Spirit like a dove descending upon him
11. 15 and the seats of them that sold doves
Luke 3. 22 descended in a bodily shape like a dove
John 1. 32 Spirit descending from heaven like a dove
2. 14 those that sold oxen and sheep and doves
2. 16 said unto them that sold doves, Take

DOVE'S dung —
Roasted chick pea, דִּבְיוֹנִים *dibyonim.*
2 Ki. 6. 25 fourth part of a cab of dove's dung for

DOWN —
1. *Beneath, low,* מַטָּה *mattah.*
2 Ch. 32. 30 brought it straight down to the west side
2. *Down, down from,* κατά *kata (gen.)*
Matt 8. 32 whole herd of swine ran violently down
Mark 5. 13 the herd ran violently down a steep place
Luke 8. 33 the herd ran violently down a steep place
3. *Downward,* κάτω *katō.*
Matt 4. 6 thou be the Son of God, cast thyself down
Luke 4. 9 If thou be the Son of God, cast thyself d.
John 8. 6 [Jesus stooped down and with (his) finger]
John 8. 8 [again he stooped down, and wrote on the]
Acts 20. 9 fell down from the third loft

[*See also* Beat, beaten, bow, bowed, bowing, break, breaking, bring, broken, brought, carry, cast, cast self, casting, come, coming, couch, cut, dig, drive, drop, fall, falling, flow, get, go, go up, going, hang, hew, hewn, kneel, laid, lay, let, lie, light, lighting, look, lying, make go, pluck, pour, poured, press, pull, pulled, pulling, push, put, ran, reap, roll, run, set, sink, sit, sitting, smite, smitten, step, stoop, swallow, take, taken, throw, thrown, thrust, tossed, tread, treading, trickle, trodden, turn upside, turning upside, walk up, wander.]

DOWN sitting —
To sit down, יָשַׁב *yashab.*
Psa. 139. 2 Thou knowest my down sitting and mine

DOWNWARD —
Beneath, low, מַטָּה *mattah.*
2 Ki. 19. 30 Judah shall yet again take root downwa.
Eccl. 3. 21 the beast that goeth downward to the
Isa. 37. 31 of Judah shall again take root downward
Eze. 1. 27 the appearance of his loins even downwa.
8. 2 the appearance of his loins even downw.

DOWRY —
1. *Dowry,* זֶבֶד *zebed.*
Gen. 30. 20 God hath endued me (with) a good dowry
2. *Dowry, purchase money,* מֹהַר *mohar.*
Gen. 34. 12 Ask me never so much dowry and gift
Exod 22. 17 shall pay money according to the dowry
1 Sa. 18. 25 The king desireth not any dowry, but an

DRAG —
Net, drag, מִכְמֶרֶת *mikmereth.*
Hab. 1. 15 they..gather them in their drag
1 16 they..burn incense unto their drag

DRAG, to —
To draw, drag, σύρω *surō.*
John 21. 8 came..dragging the net with fishes

DRAGON —
1. *Howlers, jackals,* תַּנּוֹת *tannoth.*
Mal. 1. 3 waste for the dragons of the wilderness
2. *Howlers, jackals* תַּנִּים *tannim.*
Job 30. 29 I am a brother to dragons, and a compa
Psa. 44. 19 hast sore broken us in the place of dragons
Isa. 13. 22 cry in their desolate houses, and dragons
34. 13 it shall be an inhabitation of dragons
35. 7 in the habitation of dragons, where each
43. 20 The beast..shall honour me, the dragons
Jer. 9 11 I will make Jerusalem..a den of dragons
10 22 to make the cities..a den of dragons
14. 6 they snuffed up the wind like dragons
49. 33 And Hazor shall be a dwelling for dragons
51. 37 And Babylon..a dwelling place for drago.
Eze. 29. 3 Pharaoh king of Egypt, the great dragon
Mic. 1. 8 I will make a wailing like the dragons
3. *Sea-serpent,* תַּנִּין *tannin.*
Deut 32 33 Their wine (is) the poison of dragons
Psa. 74. 13 thou brakest the heads of the dragons in
91 13 the young lion and the dragon shalt thou
148. 7 Praise the LORD..ye dragons, and all
Isa. 27. 1 he shall slay the dragon that (is) in the
51. 9 (Art) thou not it that..wounded the drago.
Jer. 51. 34 he hath swallowed me up like a dragon
4. *A dragon,* δράκων *drakōn.*
Rev. 12. 3 a great red dragon, having seven heads
12. 4 the dragon stood before the woman which
12. 7 against the dragon; and the dragon fought
12. 9 And the great dragon was cast out, that
12. 13 when the dragon saw that he was cast
12. 16 the flood which the dragon cast out of his
12. 17 the dragon was wroth with the woman
13. 2 the dragon gave him his power, and his
13. 4 they worshipped the dragon which gave
13. 11 like a lamb, and he spake as a dragon
16. 13 frogs (come) out of the mouth of the dra.
20. 2 he laid hold on the dragon, that old serp.

DRAGON WELL, עֵין הַתַּנִּין *fountain of jackals.*
A fountain near the S. walls of Jerusalem.
Neh. 2. 13 I went out..even before the dragon well

DRAMS —
1. *Darics, (Persian coin),* אֲדַרְכֹנִים *adarkonim.*
1 Ch. 29. 7 five thousand talents and ten thousand d.
Ezra 8. 27 twenty basins of gold of a thousand dra.
2. *Darics (Persian coin),* דַּרְכְּמֹנִים *darkemonim.*
Ezra 2. 69 threescore and one thousand drams of
Neh. 7. 70 gave to the treasure a thousand drams of
7. 71 treasure of the work twenty thousand dr.
7. 72 the people gave (was) twenty thousand d.

DRANK —
Drinking, banquet, מִשְׁתֶּה *mishteh.*
Dan. 1. 5 provision..of the wine which he drank
1. 8 nor with the wine which he drank

DRAUGHT —
1. *A catch, draught,* ἄγρα *agra.*
Luke 5. 4 and let down your nets for a draught
5. 9 he was astonished..at the draught of the
2. *A privy, seat without,* ἀφεδρών *aphedrōn.*
Matt 15. 17 whatsoever..is cast out into the draught
Mark 7. 19 goeth out into the draught, purging all

DRAUGHT house —
Goings out, מוֹצָאוֹת *motsaoth* [V.L. מַחֲרָאוֹת *macharaoth*]
2 Ki. 10. 27 made it a draught house unto this day

DRAW with strength. *See* **STRENGTH.**

DRAW, to —
1. *To draw up,* דָּלָה *dalah.*
Exod. 2. 16 they came and drew (water), and filled
2. 19 also drew (water) enough for us, and
2. *To tread (the bow),* דָּרַךְ *darak.*
2 Ch. 14. 8 had an army (of men) that..drew bows
3. *To draw out,* מָשָׁה *mashah.*
Exod. 2. 10 Because I drew him out of the water
4. *To draw out,* מָשַׁךְ *mashak.*
Gen. 37. 28 they drew and lifted up Joseph out of the
Deut. 21. 3 heifer..which hath not drawn in the yoke
Judg. 4. 6 Go and draw toward mount Tabor, and
4. 7 I will draw unto thee, to the river Kishon
20. 37 the liers in wait drew (themselves) along
1 Ki. 22. 34 a (certain) man drew a bow at a venture
2 Ch. 18. 33 a (certain) man drew a bow at a venture
Job 21. 33 and every man shall draw after him
24. 22 He draweth also the mighty with his
Psa. 10. 9 when he draweth him into his net
28. 3 Draw me not away with the wicked
Song 1. 4 Draw me, we will run after thee. The
Isa. 5. 18 Woe unto them that draw iniquity with
66. 19 Pul, and Lud, that draw the bow, (to)
Jer. 31. 3 with loving kindness have I drawn thee
38. 13 So they drew up Jeremiah with cords
Eze. 32. 20 draw her and all her multitudes
Hos. 11. 4 I drew them with cords of a man, with
5. *To draw away or off,* נָתַק *nathaq.*
Judg 20. 32 Let us flee, and draw them from the city
6. *To draw away or out,* נָתַק *nathaq,* 5.
Josh. 8. 6 till we have drawn them from the city
7. *To draw about or along,* סָחַב *sachab.*
2 Sa. 17. 13 and we will draw it into the river, until
8. *To draw out, empty,* רוּק *ruq,* 5.
Exod 15. 9 I will draw my sword, my hand shall
Eze. 28. 7 they shall draw their swords against
30. 11 they shall draw their swords against
9. *To draw out or off,* שָׁלַף *shalaph.*
Judg. 3. 22 he could not draw the dagger out of his
8. 10 and twenty thousand men that drew
8. 20 but the youth drew not his sword; for
9. 54 Draw thy sword, and slay me, that men
20. 2 hundred thousand footmen that drew
20. 15 twenty and six thousand men that drew
20. 17 four hundred thousand men that drew
20. 25 eighteen thousand men; all these drew
20. 35 and an hundred men: all these drew the
20. 46 twenty and five thousand men that drew
1 Sa. 17. 51 and drew it out of the sheath thereof
31. 4 Draw thy sword, and thrust me through
2 Sa. 24. 9 valiant men that drew the sword
2 Ki. 3 26 with him seven hundred men that drew
1 Ch. 10. 4 Draw thy sword, and thrust me through
21. 5 an hundred thousand men that drew
21. 5 ten thousand men that drew sword
10. *To cause to go up (or land),* ἀναβιβάζω *anabibazō.*
Matt 13. 48 Which, when it was full, they drew to
11. *To draw or bale out,* ἀντλέω *antleō.*
John 2. 9 the servants which drew the water knew
4. 7 There cometh a woman..to draw water
4. 15 I thirst not, neither come hither to draw
12. *To draw away or out,* ἀποσπάω *apospaō.*
Matt. 26. 51 stretched out (his) hand, and drew his
13. *To become, begin to be,* γίνομαι *ginomai.*
John 6. 19 see Jesus walking on the sea, and drawing
14. *To draw, draw out or towards,* ἑλκύω *helkuō.*
John 6. 44 the Father which..sent me draw him
12. 32 And I..will draw all (men) unto me
18. 10 Then Simon Peter having a sword drew
21. 6 now they were not able to draw it for
21. 11 Simon Peter went up, and drew the net
Acts 16. 19 drew (them) into the market place unto
15. *To draw out or towards,* ἕλκω *helkō.*
Acts 21. 30 they took Paul, and drew him out of the
Jas. 2. 6 and draw you before the judgment seats?
16. *To draw, draw out,* σπάω *spaō.*
Mark 14. 47 one of them that stood by drew a sword
17. *To draw, drag,* σύρω *surō.*
Acts 14. 19 having stoned Paul, drew (him) out of
17 6 they drew Jason and certain brethren
Rev. 12. 4 his tail drew the third part of the stars
18. *To cause to advance,* προβιβάζω *probibazō.*
Acts 19. 33 [they drew Alexander out of the multit.]

DRAW away, to —
1. *To draw off or away,* ἀποσπάω *apospaō.*
Acts 20. 30 speaking perverse things, to draw away
2. *To set off or away,* ἀφίστημι *aphistēmi.*
Acts 5. 37 and drew away much people after him

DRAW back, to —
1. *To turn or draw back,* שׁוּב *shub,* 5.
Gen. 38. 29 it came to pass, as he drew back his hand
Josh. 8. 26 For Joshua drew not his hand back
Lam. 2. 3 he hath drawn back; [Heb. *shub* (5) *achor*].

2. *To send back,* ὑποστέλλω *hupostellō.*
Heb.10. 38 if (any man) draw back, my soul shall

DRAW back, of them who —
A sending (self) back, ὑποστολή *hupostolē.*
Heb. 10. 39 we are not of them who draw back

DRAW forth, to —
To cause to go or come forth, יָצָא *yatsa,* 5.
1 Ch.19. 16 drew forth the Syrians that (were) beyond
Eze. 21. 3 draw forth my sword out of his sheath
21. 5 I the LORD have drawn forth my sword

DRAW near, to —
1. *To come on,* נָגַע *naga,* 5.
Esth. 9. 1 his decree drew near to be put in execution
Psa.107. 18 they draw near unto the gates of death
Eze. 7. 12 The time is come, the day draweth near
2. *To come near,* קָרַב *qarab.*
Lev. 9. 5 all the congregation drew near and stood
Deut.25. 11 the wife of the one draweth near for to
Judg.19. 13 Come, and let us draw near to one of these
1 Sa. 14. 36 Let us draw near hither unto God
Esth. 5. 2 Esther drew near, and touched the top of
Job 33. 22 his soul draweth near unto the grave, and
Isa. 41. 5 ends of the earth were afraid, drew near
57. 3 draw near hither, ye sons of the sorceress
Lam. 3. 57 Thou drewest near in the day (that) I ca.
Zeph. 3. 2 she trusted not..she drew not near to her
3. *To cause to come near,* קָרַב *qarab,* 5.
Isa. 26. 17 (that) draweth near the time of her deli.
4. *Coming near,* קְרָבָה *qerabah.*
Psa. 73. 28 But (it is) good for me to draw near to G.
5. *To draw nigh,* ἐγγίζω *eggizō.*
Matt 21. 34 when the time of the fruit drew near, he
Luke15. 1 Then drew near unto him all the publi.
21. 8 and the time draweth near: go ye not
22. 47 went before them, and drew near unto
24. 15 Jesus himself drew near, and went with
6. *To lead toward,* προσάγω *prosagō.*
Acts 27. 27 that they drew near to some country
7. *To come toward,* προσέρχομαι *proserchomai.*
Acts 7. 31 as he drew near to behold (it), the voice
Heb. 10. 22 Let us draw near with a true heart, in

DRAW near, to cause to —
To cause to come near, קָרַב *qarab,* 5.
Jer. 30. 21 I will cause him to draw near, and he
Eze. 9. 1 Cause them that have charge..to draw n.
22. 4 thou hast caused thy days to draw near

DRAW nigh, to —
1. *To come on,* נָגַע *naga,* 5.
Psa. 88. 3 and my life draweth nigh unto the grave
Eccl.12. 1 nor the years draw nigh, when thou shalt
2. *To come near,* קָרַב *qarab.*
Gen. 47. 29 the time drew nigh that Israel must die
Exod. 3. 5 Draw not nigh hither: put off thy shoes
1 Sa. 17. 48 came and drew nigh to meet David, that
1 Ki. 2. 1 days of David drew nigh that he should
Psa. 69. 18 Draw nigh unto my soul, (and) redeem it
119. 150 They draw nigh that follow after misch.
Isa. 5. 19 the counsel of the Holy One..draw nigh
3. *To (cause to) come near,* קָרַב *qarab,* 5.
Exod14. 10 when Pharaoh drew nigh, the children of
4. *To become,* γίνομαι *ginomai.*
John 6. 19 Jesus walking on the sea, and drawing n.
5. *To draw nigh,* ἐγγίζω *eggizō.*
Matt 15. 8 This people draweth nigh unto me with
21. 1 when they drew nigh unto Jerusalem
Luke 15. 25 as he came and drew nigh to the house
21. 28 look..for your redemption draweth n.
22. 1 the feast of unleavened bread drew nigh
24. 28 they drew nigh unto the village whither
Acts 7. 17 when the time of the promise drew nigh
10. 9 went on their journey, and drew nigh
Heb. 7. 19 by the which we draw nigh unto God
Jas. 4. 8 Draw nigh to God, and he will draw nigh
5. 8 for the coming of the Lord draweth nigh

DRAW off, to —
To draw off, שָׁלַף *shalaph.*
Ruth 4. 8 Buy (it) for thee. So he drew off his shoe

DRAW out, to —
1. *To make long, lengthen,* אָרַךְ *arak,* 5.
1 Ki. 8. 8 they drew out the staves, that the ends
2 Ch. 5. 9 And they drew out the staves (of the ark)
Isa. 57. 4 make ye a wide mouth, (and) draw out
2. *To draw up,* דָּלָה *dalah.*
Prov 20. 5 a man of understanding will draw it out
3. *To draw out,* חָלַץ *chalats.*
Lam. 4. 3 Even the sea monsters draw out the
4. *To draw up or out,* חָשַׂף *chasaph.*
Hag. 2. 16 (one) came to the press fat for to draw o.
5. *To draw out,* מָשָׁה *mashah,* 5.
2 Sa. 22. 17 he took me; he drew me out of many
Psa. 18. 16 he took me, he drew me out of many
6. *To draw out,* מָשַׁךְ *mashak.*
Exod 12. 21 Draw out and take you a lamb according
Job 41. 1 Canst thou draw out leviathan with an
Psa. 85. 5 draw out thine anger to all generations?
7. *To draw about or along,* סָחַב *sachab.*
Jer. 49. 20 least of the flock shall draw them out
50. 45 the least of the flock shall draw them out

8. *To cause to go out or forth,* פּוּק *puq,* 5.
Isa. 58. 10 (if) thou draw out thy soul to the hungry
9. *To open,* פָּתַח *pathach.*
Psa. 37. 14 The wicked have drawn out the sword
10. *To draw out,* רוּק *ruq,* 5.
Lev. 26. 33 and will draw out a sword after you
Psa. 35. 3 Draw out also the spear, and stop (the)
Eze. 5. 2, 12 and I will draw out a sword after them
12. 14 and I will draw out the sword after them
11. *To draw out,* ἀντλέω *antleō.*
John 2. 8 Draw out now, and bear unto the gover.
12. *To draw, draw out or forth,* σπάω *spaō.*
Acts 16. 27 he drew out his sword, and would have

DRAW on, to —
To shine or dawn upon, ἐπιφώσκω *epiphōskō.*
Luke23. 54 the preparation, and the sabbath drew on

DRAW to the shore, to —
To anchor near, προσορμίζω *prosormizō.*
Mark 6. 53 they came..and drew to the shore

DRAW (toward evening), to —
To be feeble, fall, רָפָה *raphah.*
Judg19. 9 the day draweth toward evening, I pray

DRAW up, to —
1. *To draw up,* גּוּחַ, גִּיחַ *giach, guach.*
Job 40. 23 that he can draw up Jordan into his
2. *To draw up,* ἀνασπάω *anaspaō.*
Acts 11. 10 and all were drawn up again into heaven

DRAW (water), to —
To draw (water), שָׁאַב *shaab.*
Gen. 24. 13 men of the city come out to draw water
24. 19 I will draw (water) for thy camels also
24. 20 unto the well to draw (water), and drew
24. 43 the virgin cometh forth to draw (water)
24. 44 and I will also draw for thy camels
24. 45 went down unto the well, and drew (wa.)
Ruth 2. 9 of (that) which the young men have dra.
1 Sa. 7. 6 gathered together to Mizpeh,..drew (w.)
9. 11 young maidens going out to draw water
2 Sa. 23. 16 drew water out of the well of Beth-lehem
1 Ch. 11. 18 drew water out of the well of Beth-lehem
Isa. 12. 3 draw water out of the wells of salvation
Nah. 3. 14 Draw thee waters for the siege, fortify

DRAW with, to —
Bucket, something to draw with, ἄντλημα *antlēma.*
John 4. 11 thou hast nothing to draw with, and the

DRAW, woman to —
To draw (water), שָׁאַב *shaab.*
Gen. 24. 11 the time that women go out to draw

DRAWER—
To draw up (water), שָׁאַב *shaab.*
Deut29. 11 the hewer of thy wood unto the drawer of
Josh. 9. 21, 23, be hewers of wood and drawers of w.
9. 27 hewers of wood and drawers of water for

DRAWING water, places of —
Places for drawing water, מַשְׁאַבִּים *mashabbim.*
Judg. 5. 11 noise of archers in..places of drawing w.

DRAWN —
1. *To take,* לָקַח *laqach.*
Prov.24. 11 If thou forbear to deliver..drawn unto d.
2. *To spread out,* נָטַשׁ *natash.*
Isa. 21. 15 For they fled..from the drawn sword
3. *To draw, tear,* סָחַב *sachab.*
Jer. 22. 19 drawn and cast forth beyond the gates of
4. *Removed,* עַתִּיק *attiq.*
Isa. 28. 9 weaned from the milk, (and) drawn from
5. *To open,* פָּתַח *pathach.*
Eze. 21. 28 say thou, The sword, the sword (is) drawn
6. *To draw out,* שָׁלַף *shalaph.*
Num22. 23 ass saw the angel..and his sword drawn
22. 31 saw the angel..and his sword drawn in
Josh. 5. 13 there stood a man..with his sword drawn
1 Ch. 21. 16 the angel..having a drawn sword in his

DRAWN, to be —
1. *To draw out,* שָׁלַף *shalaph.*
Job 20. 25 It is drawn, and cometh out of the body
2. *To be marked out,* תָּאַר *taar.*
Josh.15. 9 the border was drawn from the top
15. 9 and the border was drawn to Baalah
15. 11 and the border was drawn to Shicron
18. 14 the border was drawn (thence), and
18. 17 And was drawn from the north, and

DRAWN away, to be —
1. *To be driven or forced away,* נָדַח *nadach,* 2.
Deut.30. 17 but shalt be drawn away, and worship
2. *To be drawn away or out,* נָתַק *nathaq,* 2.
Josh. 8. 16 all the people..were drawn away from
3. *To be drawn away,* נָתַק *nathaq,* 6.
Judg20. 31 the children of Benjamin..were drawn a.
4. *To be drawn out or forth,* ἐξέλκομαι *exelkomai.*
Jas. 1. 14 he is drawn away of his own lust, and

DREAD —
1. *Terror,* אֵימָה *emah.*
Job 13. 21 and let not thy dread make me afraid

2. *Terror, fright,* חַת *chath.*
Gen. 9. 2 the dread of you shall be upon every
3. *Fear, reverence,* מוֹרָא *mora.*
Deut 11. 25 the dread of you upon all the land that
4. *Fear, dread,* פַּחַד *pachad.*
Exod.15.16 Fear and dread shall fall upon them
Deut. 2. 25 This day will I begin to put the dread
Job 13. 11 Shall not..his dread fall upon you?

DREAD, to —
1. *To fear, be afraid,* יָרֵא *yare.*
1 Ch.22. 13 be strong, and of good courage; dread not
2. *To fear, be afraid, terrified,* עָרַץ *arats.*
Deut. 1. 29 Dread not, neither be afraid of them

DREAD, to be —
To declare or hold as fearful, עָרַץ *arats,* 5.
Isa. 8. 13 Sanctify the LORD..(let) him (be) your dr.

DREADFUL —
1. *To be afraid, terrible,* דְּחַל *dechal.*
Dan. 7. 7 behold, a fourth beast, dreadful and terr.
7. 19 of the fourth beast, which was..dreadful
2. *To be feared, reverenced,* יָרֵא *yare,* 2.
Gen. 28. 17 And he..said, How dreadful (is) this
Dan. 9. 4 O Lord, the great and dreadful God
Hab. 1. 7 They (are) terrible and dreadful: their
Mal. 1. 14 and my name (is) dreadful among the h.
4. 5 the coming of the great and dreadful day
3. *Fear, terror,* פַּחַד *pachad.*
Job 15. 21 A dreadful sound (is) in his ears
4. *Fear, reverence,* יִרְאָה *yirah.*
Eze. 1. 18 they were so high that they were dreadf.

DREAM —
1. *Dream,* חֲלוֹם *chalom.*
Gen. 20. 3 God came to Abimelech in a dream by
20. 6 God said unto him in a dream, Yea, I kn.
31. 10 I lifted up mine eyes, and saw in a dream
31. 11 angel of God spake unto me in a dream
31. 24 God came to Laban the Syrian in a dream
37. 5 Joseph dreamed a dream, and he told (it)
37. 6 Hear..this dream which I have dreamed
37. 8 And they hated him yet..for his dreams
37. 9 And he dreamed yet another dream
37. 9 Behold, I have dreamed a dream more
37. 10 What (is) this dream that thou hast dre.?
37. 20 we shall see what will become of his drea.
40. 5 they dreamed a dream both of them
40. 5 each man his dream in one night
40. 5 according to the interpretation of his dre.
40. 8 they said unto him, We have dreamed a d.
40. 9 And the chief butler told his dream to
40. 9 In my dream, behold, a vine (was) before
40. 16 chief baker..said..I also (was) in my d.
41. 7 Pharaoh awoke, and, behold..a dream
41. 8 and Pharaoh told them his dream; but
41. 11 we dreamed a dream in one night, I and
41. 11 according to the interpretation of his d.
41. 12 and he interpreted to us our dreams
41. 12 to each man according to his dream he
41. 15 Pharaoh said..I have dreamed a dream
41. 15 thou canst understand a dream to inter.
41. 17 In my dream, behold, I stood upon the
41. 22 I saw in my dream, and, behold, seven
41. 25 Joseph said..The dream of Pharaoh (is)
41. 26 seven good ears..the dream (is) one
41. 32 the dream was doubled unto Pharaoh twi.
42. 9 Joseph remembered the dreams which
Num 12. 6 (and) will speak unto him in a dream
Deut 13. 1 a prophet, or a dreamer of dreams, and
13. 3 that prophet, or that dreamer of dreams
13. 5 dreamer of dreams, shall be put to death
Judg. 7. 13 a man that told a dream unto his fellow
7. 13 I dreamed a dream, and, lo, a cake of
7. 15 Gideon heard the telling of the dream
1 Sa. 28. 6 LORD answered him not, neither by dre.
28. 15 neither by prophets, nor by dreams
1 Ki. 3. 5 the LORD appeared to Solomon in a dream
3. 15 Solomon awoke; and, behold, (it was) a d.
Job 7. 14 thou scarest me with dreams, and terri.
20. 8 He shall fly away as a dream, and shall
33. 15 In a dream, in a vision of the night, when
Psa. 73. 20 As a dream when (one) awaketh; (so), O
Eccl. 5. 3 a dream cometh through the multitude
5. 7 in the multitude of dreams and many
Isa. 29. 7 shall be as a dream of a night vision
Jer. 23. 27 people to forget my name by their dreams
23. 28 that hath a dream, let him tell a dream
23. 32 against them that prophesy false dreams
29. 8 neither hearken to your dreams which ye
Dan. 1. 17 understanding in all visions and dreams
2. 1 Nebuchadnezzar dreamed dreams, where.
2. 2 for to show the king his dreams
2. 3 said unto them, I have dreamed a dream
2. 3 my spirit was troubled to know the dre.
Joel 2. 28 your old men shall dream dreams, your
Zech.10. 2 seen a lie, and have told false dreams
2. *Dream,* חֵלֶם *chelem.*
Dan. 2. 4 tell thy servants the dream, and we will
2. 5 ye will not make known unto me the dr.
2. 6 ye show the dream, and the interpretation
2. 6 show me the dream, and the interpretat.
2. 7 Let the king tell his servants the dream
2. 9 ye will not make known unto me the dr.
2. 9 tell me the dream, and I shall know that
2. 26 able to make known unto me the dream

Dan. 2. 28 Thy dream, and the visions of thy head
2. 36 This (is) the dream; and we will tell the
2. 45 dream (is) certain, and the interpretation
4. 5 I saw a dream which made me afraid, and
4. 6 unto me the interpretation of the dream
4. 7 I told the dream before them; but they
4. 8 and before him I told the dream, (saying)
4. 9 tell me the visions of my dream that I
4. 18 This dream I king Nebuchadnezzar have
4. 19 let not the dream, or the interpretation
4. 19 the dream (be) to them that hate thee
5. 12 interpreting of dreams, and showing of
7. 1 Daniel had a dream and vision of his
7. 1 he wrote the dream, (and) told the sum

3. *What happens in sleep, a dream*, ἐνύπνιον.
Acts. 2. 17 and your old men shall dream dreams

4. *A dream*, ὄναρ *onar*.
Matt. 1. 20 the angel..appeared unto him in a dream
2. 12 being warned of God in a dream that
2. 13 the angel..appeareth to Joseph in a dr.
2. 19 angel of the Lord appeareth in a dream
2. 22 being warned of God in a dream, he tur.
27. 19 suffered many things this day in a dream

DREAM, to —
1. *To dream*, חָלַם *chălam*.
Gen. 28. 12 he dreamed, and behold a ladder set up
37. 5 Joseph dreamed a dream, and he told (it)
37. 6 Hear..this dream which I have dreamed
37. 9 he dreamed yet another dream, and told
37. 9 I have dreamed a dream more; and
37. 10 What (is) this dream that thou hast dre?
40. 5 they dreamed a dream both of them, each
40. 8 We have dreamed a dream, and (there is)
41. 1 Pharaoh dreamed: and, behold, he stood
41. 5 And he slept and dreamed the second
41. 11 we dreamed a dream in one night, I and
41. 11 we dreamed each man according to the
41. 15 I have dreamed a dream, and (there is)
42. 9 remembered the dreams which he drea.
Judg. 7. 13 I dreamed a dream, and, lo, a cake of
Psa. 126. 1 LORD turned..we were like them that d.
Isa. 29. 8 even be as when a hungry (man) dream.
29. 8 when a thirsty (man) dreameth, and, be.
Jer. 23. 25 saying, I have dreamed, I have dreamed
Dan. 2. 1 Nebuchadnezzar dreamed dreams, where.
2. 3 I have dreamed a dream, and my spirit
Joel 2. 28 your old men shall dream dreams, your

2. *To dream (frequently)*, ἐνυπνιάζομαι *enupniazō*.
Acts 2. 17 and your old men shall dream dreams

DREAMED, to cause to be —
To cause to be dreamed, חָלַם *chalam*, 5
Jer. 29. 8 your dreams which ye caused to be drea.

DREAMER —
1. *To dream*, חָלַם *chalam*.
Deut 13. 1 arise among you a prophet, or a dreamer
13. 3 the words of that prophet, or that drea.
13. 5 dreamer of dreams, shall be put to death
Jer. 27. 9 nor to your diviners, nor to your dream.

2. *Master of dreams*, בַּעַל חֲלוֹם *baal chalom*.
Gen. 37. 19 to another, Behold, this dreamer cometh

3. *To dream (frequently)*, ἐνυπνιάζομαι *enupniazomai*.
Jude 8 these (filthy) dreamers defile the flesh

DREGS —
1. *Goblet, bowl, large cup*, קֻבַּעַת *qubbaath*.
Isa. 51. 17 thou hast drunken the dregs of the cup
51. 22 (even) the dregs of the cup of my fury

2. *Preserves, dregs, lees*, שְׁמָרִים *shemarim*.
Psa. 75. 8 but the dregs..all the wicked of the earth

DRESS, to —
1. *To do good, make right*, יָטַב *yatab*, 5.
Exod 30. 7 when he dresseth the lamps, he shall

2. *To serve, till*, עָבַד *abad*.
Gen. 2. 15 put him into the garden..to dress it
Deut 28. 39 Thou shalt plant vineyards, and dress

3. *To do, make*, עָשָׂה *asah*.
Gen. 18. 7 gave (it) unto a young man..to dress it
18. 8 he took..the calf which he had dressed
2 Sa. 12. 4 to take of his own..to dress for the
12. 4 took the poor man's lamb, and dressed
13. 5 let..Tamar..dress the meat in my sight
13. 7 saying, Go now..and dress him meat
19. 24 had neither dressed his feet, nor trimmed
1 Ki. 17. 12 that I may go in and dress it for me and
18. 23 and I will dress the other bullock, and
18. 25 Choose you one bullock..and dress (it)
18. 26 they took the bullock..and they dressed

DRESSED, to be —
1. *To be done, made*, עָשָׂה *asah*, 2.
Lev. 7. 9 and all that is dressed in the frying pan

2. *To be a husbandman*, γεωργέομαι *geōrgeomai*.
Heb. 6. 7 herbs meet for them by whom it is dress.

DRESSED, ready —
To do, make, עָשָׂה *asah*.
1 Sa. 25. 18 Abigail..took..five sheep ready dressed

DREW near —
To come near, קָרַב *qarab*.
1 Sa. 17. 41 the Philistine came on and drew near
2 Sa. 18. 25 And he came apace, and drew near

DRIED —
1. *To be dry, or dried up*, יָבֵשׁ *yabesh*.
Num. 6. 3 neither shall he..eat moist grapes, or dr.

2. *To roast*, קָלָה *qalah*.
Lev. 2. 14 thy first fruits green ears of corn dried by

DRIED, to be —
1. *To be dried*, חָרֵב *chareb*, 4.
Judg 16. 7 seven green withs that were never dried
16. 8 green withs which had not been dried

2. *To be burnt, scorched*, חָרַר *charar*, 2.
Psa. 69. 3 weary of my crying; my throat is dried

3. *To be dry or dried up*, יָבֵשׁ *yabesh*.
Gen. 8. 14 in the second month..was the earth dried
Eze. 37. 11 Our bones are dried, and our hope is lost

DRIED away —
1. *To be dry or dried up*, יָבֵשׁ *yabesh*.
Num 11. 6 But now our soul (is) dried away

DRIED up —
Dried up, צִחֶה *tsicheh*.
Isa. 5. 13 their multitude dried up with thirst

DRIED up, to be —
1. *To be or become lean, poor, low, weak*, דָּלַל *dalal*.
Job 28. 4 they are dried up, they are gone away

2. *To be dried up*, חָרֵב *chareb*.
Gen. 8. 13 the waters were dried up from off the
Psa. 106. 9 the Red sea also, and it was dried up
Isa. 19. 6 the brooks of defence shall be..dried up
Hos. 13. 15 his fountain shall be dried up: he shall

3. *To be dry or dried up*, יָבֵשׁ *yabesh*.
Gen. 8. 7 until the waters were dried up from off
1 Ki. 13. 4 his hand..dried up, so that he could not
17. 7 the brook dried up, because there had
Job 18. 16 His roots shall be dried up beneath, and
Psa. 22. 15 My strength is dried up like a potsherd
Isa. 19. 5 the river shall be wasted and dried up
Jer. 23. 10 the pleasant places..are dried up, and
50. 38 they shall be dried up: for it (is) the land
Hos. 9. 16 their root is dried up, they shall bear no
Joel 1. 20 for the rivers of waters are dried up, and
Zech. 11. 17 his arm shall be clean dried up, and his

4. *To make or become dry*, יָבֵשׁ *yabesh*, 5.
Joel 1. 10 new wine is dried up, the oil languisheth
1. 12 The vine is dried up, and the fig tree

DRINK —
1. *Drink, juice*, מַשְׁקֶה *mashqeh*.
Lev. 11. 34 all drink that may be drunk in every (such)
Isa. 32. 6 he will cause the drink of the thirsty to

2. *Banquet, drinking*, מִשְׁתֶּה *mishteh*.
Ezra 3. 7 They gave..meat, and drink, and oil, unto
Dan. 1. 10 hath appointed your meat and your drink

3. *Anything sucked up*, סֹבֶא *sobe*.
Hos. 4. 18 Their drink is sour: they have committed

4. *Juice, marrow, refreshment*, שִׁקּוּ *shiqquv*.
Psa. 102. 9 I have..mingled my drink with weeping

5. *Juice, marrow, refreshment*, שִׁקּוּי *shiqqui*.
Hos. 2. 5 that give..my flax, mine oil and my dri.

6. *Anything drunk*, πόμα *poma*.
1 Co. 10. 4 did all drink the same spiritual drink
Heb. 9. 10 (Which stood) only in meats and drinks

7. *A drinking*, πόσις *posis*.
John 6. 55 For my..blood is drink indeed
Rom 14. 17 the kingdom of God is not meat and dri.
Col. 2. 16 Let no man therefore judge you..in drink

DRINK, to —
1. *A banquet, drinking*, מִשְׁתֶּה *mishteh*.
Dan. 1. 16 took away..the wine that they should dr.

2. *To drink, banquet*, שָׁתָה *shathah*.
Gen. 9. 21 And he drank of the wine, and was drun.
24. 14 Let down thy pitcher..that I may drink
24. 14 Drink, and I will give thy camels..also
24. 18 Drink, my lord: and she hasted, and let
24. 44 Both drink thou, and I will also draw for
24. 46 Drink, and I will give..so I drank, and
24. 54 And they did eat and drink, he and the
25. 34 he did eat and drink, and rose up, and
26. 30 made..a feast, and they did eat and dri.
27. 25 and he brought him wine, and he drank
30. 38 when the flocks came to drink, that they
30. 38 should conceive when they came to drink
43. 34 And they drank, and were merry with him
44. 5 (Is) not this (it) in which my lord drink.
Exod. 7. 18 the Egyptians shall loathe to drink of
7. 21 Egyptians could not drink of the water
7. 24 the Egyptians digged..for water to drink
7. 24 could not drink of the water of the river
15. 23 they could not drink of the waters of M.
15. 24 murmured..saying, What shall we drink?
17. 1 (there was) no water for the people to d.
17. 2 and said, Give us water that we may dr.
17. 6 shall come water..that the people may d.
24. 11 also they saw God, and did eat and drink
32. 6 the people sat down to eat and to drink
34. 28 he did neither eat bread, nor drink water
Lev. 10. 9 Do not drink wine nor strong drink, thou
Num. 6. 3 He shall..drink no vinegar of wine, or
6. 3 neither shall he drink any liquor of
6. 20 after that the Nazarite may drink wine
20. 5 neither (is) there any water to drink
20. 11 the congregation drank, and their beasts
20. 17 neither will we drink (of) the water of the
20. 19 and if I and my cattle drink of thy water
Num 21. 22 we will not drink (of) the waters of the
23. 24 until he eat (of) the prey, and drink the
33. 14 was no water for the people to drink
Deut. 2. 6 buy water of them..that ye may drink
2. 28 give me water..that I may drink: only
9. 9 I neither did eat bread nor drink water
9. 18 I did neither eat bread, nor drink water
11. 11 and drinketh water of the rain of heaven
28. 39 but shalt neither drink (of) the wine, nor
29. 6 neither have ye drunk wine or strong dr.
32. 14 thou didst drink the pure blood of the
32. 38 Which..drank the wine of their drink off.
Judg. 7. 5 that boweth down upon his knees to d.
7. 6 bowed down upon their knees to drink
9. 27 did eat and drink, and cursed Abimelech
13. 4 beware, I pray thee, and drink not wine
13. 7 bear a son; and now drink no wine nor
13. 14 neither let her drink wine..nor eat any
15. 19 when he had drunk, his spirit came again
19. 4 they did eat and drink, and lodged there
19. 6 they sat down, and did eat and drink
19. 21 washed their feet, and did eat and drink
Ruth 2. 9 drink of (that) which the young men have
3. 7 when Boaz had eaten and drunk, and his
1 Sa. 1. 9 So Hannah rose up..after they had drunk
1. 15 I have drunk neither wine nor strong dr.
30. 12 had eaten no bread, nor drunk (any) water
2 Sa. 11. 11 shall I then go into mine house..to drink
11. 13 he did eat and drink before him; and he
12. 3 and drank of his own cup, and lay in his
16. 2 the wine, that such as be faint..may dr.
19. 35 taste what I eat or what I drink? can I
23. 16 he would not drink thereof, but poured
23. 17 the blood..therefore he would not drink it
1 Ki. 1. 25 behold, they eat and drink before him
13. 8, 16 neither will I eat bread nor drink wat.
13. 9 Eat no bread, nor drink water, nor turn
13. 17 Thou shalt eat no bread nor drink water
13. 18 that he may eat bread and drink water
13. 19 did eat bread in his house, and drank w.
13. 22 and hast eaten bread and drunk water
13. 22 Eat no bread, and drink no water; thy
13. 23 it came to pass..after he had drunk, that
17. 4 it shall be, (that) thou shalt drink of the
17. 6 ravens brought him bread..and he drank
17. 10 a little water in a vessel, that I may dr.
18. 41 Get thee up, eat and drink; for (there is)
18. 42 So Ahab went up to eat and to drink
19. 6 he did eat and drink, and laid him down
19. 8 he arose, and did eat and drink, and went
2 Ki. 3. 17 ye may drink, both ye, and your cattle
6. 22 they may eat and drink, and go to their
6. 23 when they had eaten and drunk, he sent
7. 8 went into one tent, and did eat and drink
9. 34 when he was come in, he did eat and dr.
18. 27 may eat their own dung, and drink their
18. 31 drink ye every one the waters of his cist.
19. 24 I have digged and drunk strange waters
1 Ch. 11. 18 David would not drink (of) it, but poured
11. 19 shall I drink the blood of these men that
11. 19 Therefore he would not drink it. These
29. 22 did eat and drink before the LORD on that
Ezra 10. 6 he did eat no bread, nor drink water: for
Neh. 8. 10 eat the fat, and drink the sweet, and send
8. 12 went their way to eat, and to drink, and
Esth. 3. 15 And the king and Haman sat down to dr.
4. 16 and neither eat nor drink three days
Job 1. 4 called for their three sisters..to drink
6. 4 the poison whereof drinketh up my spirit
15. 16 man, which drinketh iniquity like water?
21. 20 he shall drink of the wrath of the Almi.
34. 7 What man (is) like Job, (who) drinketh
Psa. 50. 13 Will I eat..or drink the blood of goats?
75. 8 all the wicked of the earth shall..drink
78. 44 turned their rivers..they could not dri.
110. 7 He shall drink of the brook in the way
Prov. 4. 17 For they..drink the wine of violence
5. 15 Drink waters out of thine own cistern
9. 5 drink of the wine (which) I have mingled
23. 7 Eat and drink, saith he to thee; but his
26. 6 cutteth off the feet, (and) drinketh dam.
31. 4 (It is) not for kings to drink wine; nor
31. 5 Lest they drink, and forget the law, and
31. 7 Let him drink, and forget his poverty
Eccl. 2. 24 that he should eat and drink, and..enjoy
3. 13 also that every man should eat and dri.
5. 18 good and comely..to eat and to drink
8. 15 a man hath no better..than..to..drink
9. 7 Go..drink thy wine with a merry heart
Song 5. 1 I have drunk my wine..O friends; drink
Isa. 5. 22 mighty to drink wine, and men of stren.
21. 5 Prepare the table..eat, drink: arise, ye
22. 13 let us eat and drink; for to morrow we
24. 9 They shall not drink wine with a song
24. 9 shall be bitter to them that drink it
29. 8 a thirsty man dreameth..he drinketh
36. 12 they may..drink their own piss with you.
36. 16 drink ye every one the waters of his own
37. 25 I have digged, and drunk water; and
44. 12 he drinketh no water, and is faint
51. 17 which hast drunk..thou hast drunken
51. 22 dregs..thou shalt no more drink it again
62. 8 the sons of the stranger shall not drink
62. 9 they that have brought it..shall drink
65. 13 behold, my servants shall drink, but ye
Jer. 2. 18 what hast thou to do..to drink the waters
2. 18 to drink the waters of the river?
16. 8 Thou shalt not..sit with them..to drink
22. 15 did not thy father eat and drink, and do
25. 16 they shall drink, and be moved, and be
25. 26 the king of Sheshach shall drink after
25. 27 Drink ye, and be drunken, and spue, and

Jer. 25. 28 to take the cup at thine hand to drink
25. 28 Thus saith the LORD..Ye shall..drink
35. 5 and I said unto them, Drink ye wine
35. 6 But they said, We will drink no wine
35. 6 Ye shall drink no wine, (neither) ye, nor
35. 8 to drink no wine all our days, we, our
35. 14 he commanded his sons not to drink
35. 14 for unto this day they drink none, but
49. 12 not to drink..have assuredly drunken
49. 12 but thou shalt surely drink (of it)
51. 7 the nations have drunken of her wine
Lam. 5. 4 We have drunken our water for money
Eze. 4. 11 Thou shalt drink also water by measure
4. 11 from time to time shalt thou drink
4. 16 and they shall drink water by measure
12. 18 drink thy water with trembling and with
12. 19 and drink their water with astonishment
23. 32 Thou shalt drink of thy sister's cup
23. 34 Thou shalt even drink it and suck (it) out
25. 4 and they shall drink thy milk
31. 14 their trees stand..all that drink water
31. 16 all that drink water, shall be comforted
34. 18 and to have drunk of the deep waters
34. 19 they drink that which ye have fouled
39. 17 that ye may eat flesh, and drink blood
39. 18 Ye shall..drink the blood of the princes
39. 19 and shall..drink blood till ye be drunken
44. 21 Neither shall any priest drink wine
Dan. 1. 12 give us pulse to eat, and water to drink
Joel 3. 3 sold a girl for wine, that they might dri.
Amos 2. 8 they drink the wine of the condemned
4. 1 which say..Bring, and let us drink
4. 8 So..three cities wandered..to drink wa.
5. 11 but ye shall not drink wine of them
6. 6 That drink wine in bowls, and anoint
9. 14 they shall plant..and drink the wine
Obad. 16 as ye have drunk upon my holy mountain
16 shall all the heathen drink..they shall d.
Jon. 3. 7 let them not feed, nor drink water
Mic. 6. 15 and sweet wine, but shalt not drink wine
Hab. 2. 16 drink thou also, and let thy foreskin be
Zeph. 1. 13 they shall plant vineyards, but not drink
Hag. 1. 6 ye drink, but ye are not filled with drink
Zech. 7. 6 when ye did drink..did not ye..drink
9. 15 they shall drink, (and) make a noise as

To drink, banquet, שָׁתָה *shethah.*
Dan. 5. 1 Belshazzar the king..drank wine before
5. 2 that..his concubines, might drink therein
5. 3 wives, and his concubines, drank in them
5. 4 They drank wine, and praised the gods
5. 23 thy concubines, have drunk wine in them

To drink, πίνω *pinō.*
Matt. 6. 25 what ye shall eat, [or what ye shall drink]
6. 31 What shall we eat?..What shall we d.?
11. 18 John came neither eating nor drinking
11. 19 The Son of man came eating and drinking
24. 38 they were eating and drinking, marrying
24. 49 and to eat and drink with the drunken
26. 27 gave (it) to them, saying, Drink ye all of
26. 29 I will not drink henceforth of this fruit
26. 29 when I drink it new with you in my Fa.
26. 42 pass..except I drink it, thy will be done
27. 34 gave him vinegar to drink mingled with
27 34 when he had tasted..he would not drink
Mark 2. 16 [and drinketh] with publicans and sinners
14. 23 he gave (it) to them: and they all drank
14. 25 I will drink no more of the fruit of the
14. 25 that I drink it new in the kingdom of
15. 23 gave him [to drink] wine mingled with
16. 18 [if they drink any deadly thing, it shall]
Luke 1. 15 and shall drink neither wine nor strong
5. 30 eat and drink with publicans and sinners?
5. 33 they said unto him..but thine eat and d.?
5. 39 No man also having drunk old (wine)
7. 33 neither eating bread nor drinking wine
7. 34 Son of man is come eating and drinking
10. 7 and drinking such things as they give
12. 19 take thine ease, eat, drink, (and) be merry
12. 29 what ye shall eat, or what ye shall drink
12. 45 and to eat and drink, and to be drunken
13. 26 We have eaten and drunk in thy presen.
17. 8 serve me, till I have eaten and drunken
17. 8 and afterward thou shalt eat and drink
17. 27 They did eat, they drank, they married
17. 28 they did eat, they drank, they bought
22. 18 I will not drink of the fruit of the vine
22. 30 That ye may eat and drink at my table
John 4. 7 Jesus saith unto her, Give me to drink
4. 9 that thou, being a Jew, askest drink of
4. 10 it is that saith to thee, Give me to drink
4. 12 gave us the well, and drank thereof him.
4. 13 Whosoever drinketh of this water shall
4. 14 whosoever drinketh of the water that I
6. 53 drink his blood, ye have no life in you
6. 54 Whoso eateth my flesh, and drinketh my
6. 56 He that eateth my flesh, and drinketh my
7. 37 thirst, let him come unto me, and drink
18. 11 the cup..given me, shall I not drink it?
Acts 9. 9 three days..neither did eat nor drink
23. 12 eat nor drink till they had killed Paul
23. 21 eat nor drink till they have killed him
Rom 14. 21 neither to eat flesh, nor to drink wine
1 Co. 9. 4 Have we not power to eat and to drink?
10. 4 did all drink the same spiritual drink
10. 4 they drank of that spiritual Rock that
10. 7 The people sat down to eat and drink
10. 21 Ye cannot drink the cup of the Lord
10. 31 Whether therefore ye eat, or drink, or
11. 22 have ye not houses to eat and to drink in?
11. 25 as oft as ye drink (it), in remembrance
1 Co. 11. 26 as often as ye eat this bread, and drink
11. 27 whosoever shall eat this bread, and drink
11. 28 so let him eat of (that) bread, and drink
11. 29 drinketh unworthily, eateth and drinketh
15. 32 let us eat and drink; for to morrow we d.
Heb. 6. 7 the earth which drinketh in the rain that
Rev. 14. 10 The same shall drink of the wine of the
16. 6 and thou hast given them blood to drink
18. 3 all nations have drunk of the wine of

DRINK abundantly, to —
To drink to satiety, שָׁכַר *shakar.*
Song 5. 1 yea, drink abundantly, O beloved

DRINK, to cause to —
To cause or give to drink, to water, שָׁקָה *shaqah*, 5.
Num. 5. 24 he shall cause the woman to drink the
5. 26 shall cause the woman to drink the water
Song 8. 2 I would cause thee to drink of spiced wi.
Jer. 25. 15 and cause all the nations..to drink it

DRINK, to be filled with —
To drink to satiety, שָׁכַר *shakar.*
Hag. 1. 6 ye drink, but ye are not filled with drink

DRINK, to give, to give to —
1. *To cause or give to drink, to water*, שָׁקָה *shaqah*, 5.
Gen. 21. 19 bottle with water, and gave the lad drink
24. 14, 46 and I will give thy camels drink also
24. 18 pitcher upon her hand, and gave him dr.
24. 43 Give me, I pray..a little water..to drink
Num 20. 8 give the congregation and..beasts drink
Judg. 4. 19 Give me, I pray..a little water to drink
4. 19 opened a bottle of milk, and gave him d.
2 Sa. 23. 15 Oh that one would give me drink of the
1 Ch. 11. 17 Oh that one would give me drink of the
Esth. 1. 7 they gave (them) drink in vessels of gold
Job 22. 7 not given water to the weary to drink
Psa. 69. 21 in my thirst they gave me vinegar to dr.
78. 15 gave (them) drink as (out of) the great
80. 5 givest them tears to drink in great mea.
104. 11 give drink to every beast of the field
Prov 25. 21 if he be thirsty, give him water to drink
Isa. 43. 20 to give drink to my people, my chosen
Jer. 8. 14 given us water of gall to drink, because
9. 15 and give them water of gall to drink
16. 7 give them the cup of consolation to drink
35. 2 bring them..and give them wine to drink
2 Ch. 28. 15; Amos 2. 12; Hab. 2. 15
2. *To give to drink*, ποτίζω *potizō.*
Matt 25. 35 I was thirsty, and ye gave me drink: I
25. 37 when saw we thee..thirsty, and gave..d.
25. 42 I was thirsty, and ye gave me no drink
Rom 12. 20 if he thirst, give him drink: for in so

DRINK, to give to —
To give to drink, ποτίζω *potizō.*
Matt 10. 42 whosoever shall give to drink unto one
27. 48 put (it) on a reed, and gave him to drink
Mark 9. 41 give you a cup of water to drink in my
15. 36 put (it) on a reed, and gave him to drink

DRINK, giving —
To give to drink, שָׁקָה *shaqah*, 5.
Gen. 24. 19 when she had done giving him drink

DRINK, to let —
1. *To suffer to suck up or swallow*, גָּמָא *gama*, 5.
Gen. 24. 17 Let me, I pray thee, drink a little water
2. *To cause or give to drink*, שָׁקָה *shaqah*, 5.
Gen. 24. 45 I said unto her, Let me drink, I pray thee

DRINK, to make —
1. *To cause or give to drink*, שָׁקָה *shaqah*, 5.
Gen. 19. 32 Come, let us make our father drink wine
19. 33, 35 they made their father drink wine
19. 34 let us make him drink wine this night
24. 46 and she made the camels drink also
Exod 32. 20 and made the children of Israel drink
1 Sa. 30. 11 he did eat; and they made him drink
Psa. 36. 8 thou shalt make them drink of the river
2. *To give to drink*, ποτίζω *potizō.*
Rev. 14. 8 she made all nations drink of the wine of

DRINK, to make to —
1. *To cause or give to drink*, שָׁקָה *shaqah*, 5.
Num. 5. 27 when he hath made her to drink the
Psa. 60. 3 thou hast made us to drink the wine of
Jer. 25. 17 I..made all the nations to drink, unto
2. *To give to drink*, ποτίζω *potizō.*
1 Co. 12. 13 have been all made to drink into one spi.

DRINK offering —
1. *Mixed or spiced drink*, מִמְסָךְ *mimsak.*
Isa. 65. 11 that furnish the drink offering unto that
2. *Anything poured out*, נָסִיךְ *nasik.*
Deut 32. 38 drank the wine of their drink offerings?
3. *Anything poured out*, נֶסֶךְ *nesek.*
Gen. 35. 14 and he poured a drink offering thereon
Exod 29. 40 fourth part of an hin of wine..a drink off.
29. 41 according to the drink offering thereof
30. 9 neither shall ye pour drink offering there.
Lev. 23. 13 the drink offering thereof (shall be) of
23. 18 their meat offering and their drink offe.
23. 37 drink offerings, everything upon his day
Num. 6. 15, 17 meat offering, and their drink offer.
15. 5 fourth..of an hin of wine for a drink off.
15. 7 for a drink offering thou shalt offer the
Num 15. 10 bring for a drink offering half an hin of
15. 24 his meat offering, and his drink offering
28. 7 the drink offering thereof (shall be) the
28. 7 the strong wine..(for) a drink offering
28. 8 as the drink offering thereof, thou shalt
28. 9 mingled with oil, and the drink offering
28. 10, 15, 24 burnt offering, and his drink offer.
28. 14 their drink offerings shall be half an hin
28. 31 his meat offering..and their drink offer.
29. 6 meat offering, and their drink offerings
[So in v. 11, 16, 18, 19, 21, 22, 24, 25, 27, 28, 30, 31, 33, 34, 37, 38, 39.]
2 Ki. 16. 13 and poured his drink offering..upon the
16. 15 meat offering, and their drink offerings
1 Ch. 29. 21 a thousand lambs, with their drink offer.
2 Ch. 29. 35 peace offerings, and the drink offerings
Psa. 16. 4 their drink offerings of blood will I not
Isa. 57. 6 to them hast thou poured a drink offer.
Jer. 7. 18 to pour out drink offerings unto other g.
19. 13 have poured out drink offerings unto
32. 29 poured out drink offerings unto other
44. 17 But we will..pour out drink offerings
44. 18 to pour out drink offerings unto her, we
44. 19 and poured out drink offerings unto her
44. 19 and pour out drink offerings unto her
44. 25 to pour out drink offerings unto her
Eze. 20. 28 poured out there their drink offerings
45. 17 meat offerings, and drink offerings
Joel 1. 9 the drink offering is cut off from the hou
1. 13 the drink offering is withholden from the
2. 14 a meat offering and a drink offering un
4. *Anything poured out*, נְסַךְ *nesak.*
Ezra 7. 17 meat offerings and their drink offerings

DRINK, strong —
1. *Sweet drink (what satiates or intoxicates)*, שֵׁכָר *shekar.*
Lev. 10. 9 Do not drink wine nor strong drink, thou
Num. 6. 3 shall separate (himself) from..strong dr.
6. 3 shall drink no..vinegar of strong drink
Deut 14. 26 shalt bestow that money..for strong dri.
29. 6 neither have ye drunk..strong drink
Judg 13. 4 and drink not wine nor strong drink
13. 7 now drink no wine nor strong drink
13. 14 neither let her drink wine or strong drink
1 Sa. 1. 15 have drunk neither wine nor strong drink
Prov 20. 1 Wine (is) a mocker, strong drink (is) rag.
31. 4 to drink wine, nor for princes strong dri.
31. 6 Give strong drink unto him that is ready
Isa. 5. 11 (that) they may follow strong drink; that
5. 22 men of strength to mingle strong drink
24. 9 strong drink shall be bitter to them that
28. 7 through strong drink are out of the way
28. 7 prophet have erred through strong drink
28. 7 are out of the way through strong drink
29. 9 they stagger, but not with strong drink
56. 12 we will fill ourselves with strong drink
Mic. 2. 11 prophesy..of wine and of strong drink
2. *Sweet drink, (often fermented)*, σίκερα, שֵׁכָר *Heb.*
Luke 1. 15 shall drink neither wine nor strong drink

DRINK of, to —
To drink, πίνω *pinō.*
Matt 20. 22 to drink of the cup that I shall drink of
20. 23 Ye shall drink indeed of my cup, and be
Mark 10. 38 can ye drink of the cup that I drink of?
10. 39 indeed drink of the cup that I drink of

DRINK up, to —
To press upon, עָשַׁק *ashaq.*
Job 40. 23 he drinketh up a river, (and) hasteth not

DRINK with, to —
To drink with, συμπίνω *sumpinō.*
Acts 10. 41 did eat and drink with him after he rose

DRINKER —
To drink, banquet, שָׁתָה *shathah.*
Joel 1. 5 howl, all ye drinkers of wine, because of

DRINKING —
1. *Drink, juice*, מַשְׁקֶה *mashqeh.*
1 Ki. 10. 21 Solomon's drinking vessels (were of) gold
2 Ch. 9. 20 drinking vessels of king Solomon (were of)
2. *To drink*, שָׁתָה *shathah.*
Gen. 24. 19 camels also, until they have done drink.
24 22 as the camels had done drinking, that the
Ruth 3. 3 he shall have done eating and drinking
1 Sa. 30. 16 eating and drinking, and dancing, because
1 Ki. 4. 20 eating and drinking, and making merry
16. 9 drinking himself drunk in the house of
20. 12 heard this message, as he (was) drinking
20. 16 Ben-hadad (was) drinking himself drunk
1 Ch. 12. 39 with David three days, eating and drink.
Job 1. 13, 18 (were) eating and drinking wine in
Isa. 22. 13 And behold..eating flesh and drinking w
3. *Drinking*, שְׁתִיָּה *shethiyyah.*
Esth. 1. 8 the drinking (was) according to the law

DRIVE, to —
1. *To thrust away or out*, הָדַף *hadaph.*
Isa. 22. 19 I will drive thee from thy station, and
Jer. 46. 15 stood not, because the LORD did drive
2. *To drive away*, טְרַד *terad.*
Dan. 4. 25, 32 they shall drive thee from men, and
3. *To drive away*, [V.L. נָדָא, 5] נָדַח *nadach*, 5.
2 Ki. 17. 21 Jeroboam drave Israel from following the
4. *To drive or force away*, נָדַח *nadach*, 5.
Deut 30. 1 whither the LORD thy God hath driven

Jer. 8. 3 the places whither I have driven them
16. 15 all the lands whither he had driven them
23. 3 all countries whither I have driven them
23. 8 all countries whither I had driven them
24. 9 in all places whither I shall drive them
29. 14 all the places whither I have driven you
29. 18 the nations whither I have driven them
32. 37 all countries whither I have driven them
46. 28 the nations whither I have driven thee
Eze. 4. 13 among the Gentiles, whither I will drive
Dan. 9. 7 countries whither thou hast driven them
Joel 2. 20 will drive him into a land barren and

5. *To lead, drive,* נָהַג *nahag.*
1 Sa. 30. 20 (which) they drave before those (other)
2 Sa. 6. 3 the sons of Abinadab, drave the new cart
2 Ki. 4. 24 Drive, and go forward; slack not (thy)
9. 20 Jehu the son of Nimshi; for he driveth
1 Ch. 13. 7 and Uzza and Ahio drave the cart

6. *To lead, drive,* נָהַג *nahag,* 3.
Exod. 14. 25 took off their..wheels, that they drave

7. *To cast out,* נָשַׁל *nashal,* 3.
2 Ki. 16. 6 king of Syria..drave the Jews from Elath

8. *To scatter,* פּוּץ *puts,* 5.
Job 18. 11 Terrors..shall drive him to his feet

9. *To drive away,* ἀπελαύνω *apelaunō.*
Acts 18. 16 And he drave them from the judgment

10. *To cast out,* ἐκβάλλω *ekballō.*
Mark 1. 12 Spirit driveth him into the wilderness
John 2. 15 he drove them all out of the temple, and

DRIVE asunder, to —
To shake off, cause to move, נָתַר *nathar,* 5.
Hab. 3. 6 he beheld, and drove asunder the nations

DRIVE away, to —
1. *To cause to flee,* בָּרַח *barach,* 5.
1 Ch. 8. 13 who drove away the inhabitants of Gath

2. *To cast out, drive away,* גָּרַשׁ *garash,* 3.
Exod. 2. 17 the shepherd came and drove them away
Psa. 34. title. who drove him away, and he departed

3. *To bring forth,* חִיל, חוּל *chil, chul,* 3a.
Prov 25. 23 The north wind driveth away rain; so

4. *To drive or force away,* נָדַח *nadach,* 5.
Jer. 23. 2 scattered my flock, and driven them away
50. 17 the lions have driven (him) away; first

5. *To drive or thrust away,* נָדַף *nadaph.*
Psa. 1. 4 the chaff which the wind driveth away
68. 2 As smoke is driven..so drive them away

6. *To lead away,* נָהַג *nahag.*
Job 24. 3 They drive away the ass of the fatherless

7. *To blow or drive away,* נָשַׁב *nashab,* 5.
Gen. 15. 11 the fowls came..Abram drove them away

DRIVE far, to —
To put far off, רָחַק *rachaq,* 5.
Prov 22. 15 rod of correction shall drive it far from

DRIVE out, to —
1. *To cast out, drive away,* גָּרַשׁ *garash.*
Exod 34. 11 I drive out before thee the Amorite, and

2. *To cast out, drive away,* גָּרַשׁ *garash,* 3.
Gen. 3. 24 he drove out the man; and he placed at
4. 14 thou hast driven me out from the face of
Exod. 6. 1 a strong hand shall he drive them out of
10. 11 were driven out from Pharaoh's presence
23. 28 hornets..which shall drive out the Hivite
23. 29 I will not drive them out from before
23. 30 I will drive them out from before thee
23. 31 and thou shalt drive them out before
33. 2 I will drive out the Canaanite, the
Num 22. 6 and (that) I may drive them out of the
22. 11 to overcome them, and drive them out
Josh 24. 12 which drave them out from before you
24. 18 the LORD drave out from before us all
Judg. 2. 3 I will not drive them out from before
6. 9 drave them out from before you, and
1 Sa 26. 19 they have driven me out this day from
1 Ch. 17. 21 by driving out nations from before thy
Eze. 31. 11 I have driven him out for his wickedness
Hos. 9. 15 I will drive them out of mine house
Zeph. 2. 4 they shall drive out Ashdod at the noon d.

3. *To possess, occupy, succeed,* יָרַשׁ *yarash.*
Num 21. 32 drove out the Amorites that (were) there

4. *To (cause to) possess, dispossess,* יָרַשׁ *yarash,* 5.
Num 32. 21 driven out his enemies from before him
33. 52 ye shall drive out all the inhabitants
33. 55 if ye will not drive out the inhabitants
Josh. 3. 10 he will without fail drive out from
13. 6 them will I drive out from before the
14. 12 I shall be able to drive them out, as the
15. 63 children of Judah..not drive them out
16. 10 they drave not out the Canaanites that
17. 12 children of Manasseh could not drive out
17. 13 but did not utterly drive them out
17. 18 for thou shalt drive out the Canaanites
23. 5 and drive them from out of your sight
23. 9 the LORD hath driven out from before
23. 13 the LORD your God will no more drive out
Judg. 1. 19 drave out (the inhabitants of) the moun.
1. 19 could not drive out the inhabitants of
1. 21 children of Benjamin did not drive out
1. 27 Neither did Manasseh drive out (the in.
1. 28 and did not utterly drive them out
1. 29 Neither did Ephraim drive out the Cana.
Judg. 1. 30 Neither did Zebulun drive out the inha.
1. 31 Neither did Asher drive out the inhabit.
1. 32 for they did not drive them out
1. 33 Neither did Naphtali drive out the inha.
2. 21 I also will not henceforth drive out any
2. 23 without driving them out hastily; neither
11. 24 the LORD our God shall drive out from
2 Ch. 20. 7 (who) didst drive out the inhabitants of
Psa. 44. 2 (How) thou didst drive out the heathen

5. *To drive or force away,* נָדַח *nadach,* 5.
Jer. 27. 10 that I should drive you out, and ye
27. 15 that I might drive you out, and that ye

6. *To drive or thrust out,* ἐξωθέω *exōtheō.*
Acts 7. 45 whom God drave out before the face of

DRIVE up and down, to —
To bear diversely, in different directions, διαφέρω.
Acts 27. 27 we were driven up and down in Adria

DRIVE, to let —
To give over to be driven, ἐπιδίδωμι φέρειν.
Acts 27. 15 bear up into the wind, we let (her) drive

DRIVEN —
1. *To be driven or forced away,* נָדַח *nadach,* 4.
Isa. 8. 22 and (they shall be) driven to darkness

2. *To be driven or thrust away,* נָדַף *nadaph,* 2.
Isa. 41. 2 gave (them)..as driven stubble to his bow

DRIVEN, to be —
1. *To thrust out or away,* הָדַף *hadaph.*
Job 18. 18 He shall be driven from light into dark.

2. *To drive away,* טְרַד *terad.*
Dan. 4. 33 he was driven from men, and did eat
5. 21 he was driven from the sons of men

3. *To be driven or forced away,* נָדַח *nadach,* 2.
Deut. 4. 19 shouldest be driven to worship them
Jer. 40. 12 out of all places whither they were driv.
43. 5 nations whither they had been driven
Eze. 34. 4 brought again that which was driven
34. 16 bring again that which was driven away

4. *To be turned round about,* סָבַב *sabab,* 2.
Psa. 114. 3 sea saw (it), and fled: Jordan was driven
114. 5 thou Jordan, (that) thou wast driven

5. *To be turned back,* סוּג *sug,* 2.
Psa. 40. 14 let them be driven backward and put to

6. *To drive,* ἐλαύνω *elaunō,* ἐλάω *elaō.*
Luke 8. 29 and was driven of the devil into the wil.
Jas. 3. 4 Behold also the ships..driven of fierce

7. *To be borne or carried,* φέρομαι *pheromai.*
Acts 27. 17 fearing..strake sail, and so were driven

DRIVEN away, to be —
1. *To be thrust or driven away or down,* דָּחָה *dachah,* 2.
Prov 14. 32 The wicked is driven away in his wicked.

2. *To be driven or thrust away,* נָדַף *nadaph,* 2.
Psa. 68. 2 As smoke is driven away..as wax melteth
Isa. 19. 7 shall wither, be driven away, and be no

3. *To be taken captive,* שָׁבָה *shabah,* 2.
Exod 22. 10 be hurt, or driven away, no man seeing

DRIVEN forth, to be —
To be cast out or driven away, גָּרַשׁ *garash,* 4.
Job 30. 5 They were driven forth from among

DRIVEN on, to be —
To be thrust or driven away or down, דָּחָה *dachah,* 2.
Jer. 23. 12 they shall be driven on, and fall therein

DRIVEN out, to be —
To be driven or forced away, נָדַח *nadach,* 2.
Deut 30. 4 If (any) of thine be driven out unto the
Jer. 49. 5 shall be driven out every man right forth
Mic. 4. 6 I will gather her that is driven out
Zeph. 3. 19 I will..gather her that was driven out

DRIVEN quite, to be —
To be driven or forced away, נָדַח *nadach,* 2.
Job 6. 13 and is wisdom driven quite from me?

DRIVEN to and fro —
To be driven or thrust away, נָדַף *nadaph,* 2.
Job 13. 25 Wilt thou break a leaf driven and fro?

DRIVER —
To exact, נָגַשׂ *nagas.*
Job 39. 7 neither regardeth he the crying of the d.

DRIVER of a chariot —
Rider, charioteer, רַכָּב *rakkab.*
1 Ki. 22. 34 he said unto the driver of his chariot

DRIVING —
Leading on, מִנְהָג *minhag.*
2 Ki. 9. 20 the driving is like the driving of Jehu

DRIVING out —
To (cause to) possess, dispossess, יָרַשׁ *yarash,* 5.
Judg. 2. 23 left those nations, without driving..out

DROMEDARY —
1. *A young camel, dromedary,* בִּכְרָה, בֶּכֶר *beker, bikrah.*
Isa. 60. 6 the dromedaries of Midian and Ephah
Jer. 2. 23 (thou art) a swift dromedary traversing

2. *Swift beast, courser,* רֶכֶשׁ *rekesh.*
1 Ki. 4. 28 straw for the horses and dromedaries

3. *Mare, mule,* רַמָּךְ *rammak.*
Esth. 8. 10 riders on mules, camels, (and) young dro.

DROP —
A drop, מַר *mar.*
Isa. 40. 15 Behold the nations (are) as a drop of a

DROP, to —
1. *To flow,* נָזַל *nazal.*
Job 36. 28 Which the clouds do drop (and) distil

2. *To drop,* נָטַף *nataph.*
Judg. 5. 4 the heavens dropped, the clouds also dr.
Job 29. 22 they spake not again, and my speech dr.
Psa. 68. 8 the heavens also dropped at the presence
Prov. 5. 3 the lips of a strange woman drop (as) an
Song 4. 11 Thy lips, O (my) spouse, drop (as) the hon.
5. 5 I rose up..and my hands dropped (with)

3. *To (cause to) drop,* נָטַף *nataph,* 5.
Eze. 20. 46 set thy face toward the south, and drop
21. 2 set thy face toward Jerusalem, and drop
Amos 7. 16 drop not (thy word) against the house of
9. 13 the mountains shall drop sweet wine, and

4. *To be poured out,* נָתַךְ *nathak,* 2.
2 Sa. 21. 10 beginning of harvest until water dropped

5. *To drop, be abundant,* עָרַף *araph.*
Deut. 32. 2 My doctrine shall drop as the rain, my

6. *To drop, distil,* רָעַף *raaph..*
Psa. 65. 11 Thou crownest..and thy paths drop fat.
65. 12 They drop (upon) the pastures of the wil.

DROP down, to —
1. *To drop,* נָטַף *nataph.*
Joel 3. 18 the mountains shall drop down new wine

2. *To drop, be abundant,* עָרַף *araph.*
Deut 33. 28 also his heavens shall drop down dew

3. *To drop, distil,* רָעַף *raaph.*
Prov. 3. 20 and the clouds drop down the dew

4. *To (cause to) drop, distil,* רָעַף *raaph,* 5.
Isa. 45. 8 Drop down, ye heavens, from above, and

DROP through, to —
To drop, דָּלַף *dalaph.*
Eccl. 10. 18 through idleness..the house droppeth th.

DROPPED —
Flow, stream, הֵלֶךְ *helek.*
1 Sa. 14. 26 when the people were come..honey drop.

DROPPING —
1. *Dropping,* דֶּלֶף *deleph.*
Prov 19. 13 contentions of a wife (are) a continual dr.
27. 15 A continual dropping in a very rainy day

2. *To drop,* נָטַף *nataph.*
Song 5. 13 his lips..dropping sweet smelling myrrh

DROPS —
1. *Drops,* אֶגְלִים *agalim.*
Job 38. 28 or who hath begotten the drops of dew?

2. *Drop,* נָטַף *nataph.*
Job 36. 27 For he maketh small the drops of water

3. *Dropping,* רְסִיסִים *resisim.*
Song 5. 2 (and) my locks with the drops of the night

DROPS, great —
A clot, drop, θρόμβος *thrombos.*
Luke 22. 44 [great drops of blood falling down to the]

DROPSY, having the —
Dropsical, full of water, ὑδρωπικός *hudrōpikos.*
Luke 14. 2 a certain man..which had the dropsy

DROSS —
1. *Dross,* סוּג *sug.*
Eze. 22. 18 the house of Israel is to me become dross

2. *Dross,* סִיג *sig.*
Psa. 119. 119 Thou puttest away all the wicked..dross
Prov. 25. 4 Take away the dross from the silver, and
26. 23 a potsherd covered with silver dross
Isa. 1. 22 Thy silver is become dross, thy wine mix.
1. 25 I will..purely purge away thy dross, and
Eze. 22. 18 all they (are) brass..the dross of silver
22. 19 Because ye are all become dross, behold

DROUGHT —
1. *Restraint, dearth,* בַּצֹּרֶת *bitstsoreth.*
Jer. 17. 8 and shall not be careful in the year of d.

2. *Drought, waste,* חֹרֶב *choreb.*
Gen. 31. 40 in the day the drought consumed me
Jer. 50. 38 A drought (is) upon her waters, and they
Hag. 1. 11 And I called for a drought upon the land

3. *Drought,* חֲרָבוֹן *charabon.*
Psa. 32. 4 is turned into the drought of summer

4. *Drought,* צַחְצָחוֹת *tsachtsachoth.*
Isa. 58. 11 the LORD shall..satisfy thy soul in drought

5. *Drought,* צִיָּה *tsiyyah.*
Job 24. 19 Drought and heat consume the snow w.
Jer. 2. 6 through a land of drought, and of the

6. *Thirst,* צִמָּאוֹן *tsimmaon.*
Deut. 8. 15 fiery serpents, and scorpions, and drought

DROUGHT, great —
Droughts, תַּלְאוּבוֹת *taluboth.*
Hos. 13. 5 know thee..in the land of great drought

DROVE —
1. *Camp,* מַחֲנֶה *machaneh.*
Gen. 33. 8 What (meanest) thou by all this drove

2. *Drove, flock, herd, order,* עֵדֶר *eder.*
Gen. 32. 16 he delivered..every drove by themselves
32. 16 and put a space betwixt drove and drove
32. 19 and all that followed the droves

DROWN, to —
1. *To overflow, wash away,* שָׁטַף *shataph.*
Song 8. 7 neither can the floods drown it
2. *To make to sink,* βυθίζω *buthizō.*
1 Ti. 6 9 drown men in destruction and perdition
3. *To drink down, swallow up,* καταπίνω *katapinō.*
Heb. 11. 29 Egyptians assaying to do were drowned

DROWNED, to be —
1. *To be sunk,* טָבַע *taba,* 4.
Exod 15. 4 captains also are drowned in the Red sea
2. *To be watered, to sink,* שָׁקַע *shaqa,* 2 [V.L. שָׁקְעָה].
Amos 8. 8 it shall be cast out and drowned, as (by)
3. *To sink, water,* שָׁקַע *shaqa.*
Amos 9. 5 shall be drowned, as (by) the flood of E.
4. *To be made to sink down,* καταποντίζομαι.
Matt 18. 6 he were drowned in the depth of the sea

DROWSINESS —
Slumber, drowsiness, נוּמָה *numah.*
Prov. 23. 21 drowsiness shall clothe (a man) with rags

DRUNK —
Satiated, merry, שִׁכּוֹר *shikkur.*
1 Ki. 16. 9 drinking himself drunk in the house of
20. 16 drinking himself drunk in the pavilions

DRUNK, to be —
1. *To be drunk,* שָׁתָה *shathah,* 2.
Lev. 11. 34 and all drink that may be drunk in every
2. *To begin to be softened,* μεθύσκω *methuskō.*
Eph. 5. 18 be not drunk with wine, wherein is excess

DRUNK, to be made —
1. *To be filled, satisfied,* רָוָה *ravah.*
Jer. 46. 10 be satiate and made drunk with their
2. *To be softened (with drink),* μεθύω *methuō.*
Rev. 17. 2 have been made drunk with the wine of

DRUNK, to make —
1. *To satiate, make merry,* שָׁכַר *shakar,* 3.
2 Sa. 11. 13 he made him drunk: and at even he
Isa. 63. 6 make them drunk in my fury, and I will
2. *To satiate, make merry,* שָׁכַר *shakar,* 5.
Deut 32. 42 I will make mine arrows drunk with bl.
Jer. 51. 57 I will make drunk her princes, and her

DRUNK, to have well —
To be softened with drink, μεθύω *methuō.*
John 2. 10 when men have well drunk, then that

DRUNKARD —
1. *To suck up, be satiated,* סָבָא *saba.*
Deut 21. 20 This our son (is)..a glutton and a drun.
Prov. 23. 21 drunkard and the glutton shall come to
Nah. 1. 10 while they are drunken (as) drunkards
2. *Satiated, merry,* שִׁכּוֹר *shikkur.*
Prov. 26. 9 thorn goeth up into the hand of a drunk.
Isa. 24. 20 earth shall reel to and fro like a drunkard
28. 1 Woe to the crown..to the drunkards of E.
28. 3 the drunkards of Ephraim, shall be trod.
Joel. 1. 5 Awake, ye drunkards, and weep; and
3. *To drink sweet drink,* שָׁתָה שֵׁכָר *shathah shekar.*
Psa 69. 12 and I (was) the song of the drunkards
4. *Softened with drink,* μέθυσος *methusos.*
1 Co. 5. 11 or an idolater, or a railer, or a drunkard
6. 10 Nor thieves, nor covetous, nor drunkards

DRUNKEN —
1. *To drink,* סָבָא *saba* (or סֹבֶא).
Nah. 1. 10 while they are drunken (as) drunkards
2. *Satiated, merry,* שִׁכּוֹר *shikkur.*
1 Sa. 1. 13 therefore Eli thought she had been drun.
25. 36 merry within him, for he (was) very drun.
Job 12. 25 maketh them to stagger like (a) drunken
Isa. 19. 14 err..as a drunken (man) staggereth in his
Jer. 23. 9 I am like a drunken man, and like a man
3. *To be satiated, merry,* שָׁכַר *shakar.*
Isa. 51. 21 hear now this, thou afflicted, and drunken
4. *To be softened, soaked with drink,* μεθύω *methuō.*
Matt 24. 49 and to eat and drink with the drunken
Acts 2. 15 For these are not drunken as ye suppose
1 Co. 11. 21 and one is hungry, and another is drunken
1 Th. 5. 7 and they that..are drunken in the night
Rev. 17. 6 I saw the woman drunken with the blood

DRUNKEN, be —
Satiety, merriment, שִׁכָּרוֹן *shikkaron.*
Eze. 39. 19 and drink blood till ye be drunken, of

DRUNKEN, to be —
1. *To be satiated, merry,* שָׁכַר *shakar.*
Gen. 9. 21 And he drank of the wine, and was dru.
Isa. 29. 9 they are drunken, but not with wine; they
49. 26 they shall be drunken with their own bl.
Jer. 25. 27 be drunken, and spue, and fall, and rise
Lam. 4. 21 shalt be drunken, and shalt make thyself
Nah. 3. 11 Thou also shalt be drunken; thou shalt
2. *To be (show self) drunken, merry,* שָׁכַר *shakar,* 7.
1 Sa. 1. 14 How long wilt thou be drunken? put
3. *To begin to be softened,* μεθύσκω *methuskō.*
Luke 12. 45 and to eat and drink, and to be drunken
1 Th. 5. 7 and they that be drunken..in the night

DRUNKEN, to make —
1. *To be filled, satisfied,* רָוָה *ravah,* 5.
Lam. 3. 15 he hath made me drunken with wormw.
2. *To satiate, make merry,* שָׁכַר *shakar,* 3.
Jer. 51. 7 cup..that made all the earth drunken
Hab. 2. 15 and makest (him) drunken also, that thou
3. *To satiate, make merry,* שָׁכַר *shakar,* 5.
Jer. 48. 26 Make ye him drunken; for he magnified
51. 39 I will make them drunken, that they may

DRUNKEN man —
Satiated, merry, שִׁכּוֹר *shikkur.*
Psa. 107. 27 They reel..and stagger like a drunken m.

DRUNKENNESS —
1. *Fulness, satiety,* רָוֶה *raveh.*
Deut 29. 19 though I walk..to add drunkenness to
2. *Satiety, merriment,* שִׁכָּרוֹן *shikkaron.*
Jer. 13. 13 I will fill all..Jerusalem, with drunken.
Eze 23. 33 Thou shalt be filled with drunkenness
3. *Drinking, carousing,* שְׁתִי *shethi.*
Eccl. 10. 17 eat..for strength, and not..drunkenness!
4. *Drink, mulled drink,* μέθη *methē.*
Luke 21. 34 overcharged with surfeiting, and drunk.
Rom 13. 13 Let us walk..not in rioting and drunken.
Gal. 5. 21 drunkenness, revellings, and such like

DRU-SIL'-LA, Δρούσιλλα.
A daughter of Herod Agrippa I. She became wife of Felix governor of Judea.
Acts 24. 24 when Felix came with his wife D.

DRY —
1. *Dry,* חָרֵב *chareb.*
Lev. 7. 10 meat offering mingled with oil, and dry
Prov. 17. 1 Better (is) a dry morsel, and quietness
2. *Dry, drought,* חֹרֶב *choreb.*
Judg. 6. 37 and (it be) dry upon all the earth (beside)
6. 39 let it now be dry only upon the fleece
6. 40 for it was dry upon the fleece only
3. *A dry place,* חָרָבָה *charabah.*
Eze. 30. 12 I will make the rivers dry, and sell the
4. *Dry, dried up, withered,* יָבֵשׁ *yabesh.*
Job 13. 25 and wilt thou pursue the dry stubble?
Isa. 56. 3 neither let the eunuch say..I (am) a dry
Eze. 17. 24 and have made the dry tree to flourish
20. 47 and it shall devour every..dry tree
37. 2 very many..and, lo, (they were) very dry
37. 4 O ye dry bones, hear the word of the L.
Nah. 1. 10 shall be devoured as stubble fully dry
5. *A dry place,* יַבָּשָׁה *yabbashah.*
Gen. 1. 9 let the dry (land) appear: and it was so
1. 10 And God called the dry (land) Earth
Exod. 4. 9 it upon the dry (land)..blood upon the
14. 16 the children of Israel shall go on dry
14. 22 children of Israel went..upon the dry
14. 29 the children of Israel walked upon dry
15. 19 but the children of Israel went on dry
Psa. 66. 6 He turned the sea into dry (land)
Jon. 1. 9 which hath made the sea and the dry
2. 10 and it vomited out Jonah upon the dry
6. *A dry place,* יַבֶּשֶׁת *yabbesheth.*
Exod. 4. 9 shall become blood upon the dry (land)
Psa. 95. 5 and his hands formed the dry (land)
7. *Clear, shining,* צַח *tsach.*
Jer. 4. 11 A dry wind of the high places in the wil.
8. *A dry place, glowing, burning,* צִיָּה *tsiyyah.*
Psa. 63. 1 my flesh longeth for thee in a dry and
107. 35 He turneth..dry ground..water-springs
Isa. 41. 18 I will make..the dry land springs of
53. 2 grow up..as a root out of a dry ground
Jer. 51. 43 Her cities are a desolation, a dry land
Eze. 19. 13 planted..in a dry and thirsty ground
Hos. 2. 3 Lest I..set her like a dry land, and slay
Zeph. 2. 13 will make Nineveh..dry like a wilderness
9. *To be dry, dried up, pressed,* צָמַק *tsamaq.*
Hos. 9. 14 give them a miscarrying womb and dry
10. *Waterless, without water,* ἄνυδρος *anudros.*
Matt 12. 43 he walketh through dry places, seeking
Luke 11. 24 he walketh through dry places, seeking
11. *Dry, withered,* ξηρός *xēros.*
Luke 23. 31 in a green..what shall be done in the dry?

DRY, to —
To dry up, wither, יָבֵשׁ *yabesh,* 3.
Prov 17. 22 but a broken spirit drieth the bones

DRY, to be —
1. *To be dry,* חָרֵב *chareb.*
Gen. 8. 13 behold, the face of the ground was dry
Isa. 44. 27 That saith to the deep, Be dry, and I will
2. *To be or become dry, withered,* יָבֵשׁ *yabesh.*
Josh. 9. 5 all the bread of their provision was dry
9. 12 now, behold, it is dry, and it is mouldy

DRY, to become —
To be dried up, ashamed, בּוֹשׁ *bosh.*
Hos. 13. 15 and his spring shall become dry, and his

DRY, ground —
1. *A dry place,* חָרָבָה *charabah.*
Josh. 3. 17 the priests..stood firm on dry ground in
3. 17 the Israelites passed over on dry ground
2 Ki. 2. 8 so that they two went over on dry ground
2. *A dry place,* יַבָּשָׁה *yabbashah.*
Isa. 44. 3 I will pour..floods upon the dry ground
3. *A thirsty place,* צִמָּאוֹן *tsimmaon.*
Psa 107. 33 He turneth..water-springs into dry gro.

DRY land —
1. *A dry place,* חָרָבָה *charabah.*
Gen. 7. 22 of all that (was) in the dry (land), died
Exod 14. 21 and made the sea dry (land), and the
Josh. 4. 18 priests' feet were lifted up unto the dry l.
Hag. 2. 6 I will shake the heavens..and the dry (l.)
2. *A dry place,* יַבָּשָׁה *yabbashah.*
Josh. 4. 22 Israel came over this Jordan on dry land
Neh. 9. 11 went through..the sea on the dry land
3. *A clear, shining place,* צְחִיחָה *tsechichah.*
Psa. 68. 6 but the rebellious dwell in a dry (land)
4. *A dry place, glowing, burning,* צִיָּה *tsiyyah.*
Jer. 50. 12 nations (shall be) a wilderness, a dry land
5. *Dry, withered,* ξηρός *xēros.*
Heb. 11. 29 passed through the Red sea as by dry (l.)

DRY, to make —
1. *To dry up, wither,* יָבֵשׁ *yabesh,* 3.
Nah. 1. 4 He rebuketh the sea, and maketh it dry
2. *To cause to dry up,* יָבֵשׁ *yabesh,* 5.
Jer. 51. 36 dry up her sea, and make her springs dry

DRY place —
1. *A dry place, glowing, burning,* צִיּוֹן *tsayon.*
Isa. 25. 5 as the heat in a dry place; (even) the
32. 2 as rivers of water in a dry place; as the
2. *A dry place, glowing, burning,* צִיָּה *tsiyyah.*
Psa. 105. 41 they ran in the dry places (like) a river

DRY scall —
Scall, scurf, scab, mange, נֶתֶק *netheq.*
Lev 13. 30 it (is) a dry scall, (even) a leprosy upon

DRY up, to —
1. *To dry up,* חָרֵב *charab,* 5.
2 Ki. 19. 24 with the sole of my feet have I dried up
Isa. 37. 25 with the sole of my feet have I dried up
50. 2 at my rebuke I dry up the sea, I make
Jer. 51. 36 will dry up her sea, and make her springs
Nah. 1. 4 rebuketh the sea..drieth up all the rivers
2. *To be or become dry, withered,* יָבֵשׁ *yabesh.*
1 Ki. 13. 4 his hand, which he put forth..dried up
17. 7 after a while, that the brook dried up
Job 12. 15 withholdeth the waters, and they dry up
14. 11 and the flood decayeth and drieth up
3. *To dry up, wither,* יָבֵשׁ *yabesh,* 3.
Job 15. 30 the flame shall dry up his branches; and
4. *To (cause to) dry up,* יָבֵשׁ *yabesh,* 5.
Josh. 2. 10 how the LORD dried up the water of the
4. 23 the LORD your God dried up the waters
4. 23 which he dried up from before us, until
5. 1 that the LORD had dried up the waters of
Psa. 74. 15 thou driedst up mighty rivers
Isa. 42. 15 I will..dry up all their herbs
42. 15 make the rivers islands, and I will dry up
44. 27 That saith..I will dry up thy rivers
Eze. 17. 24 have dried up the green tree, and have
19. 12 and the east wind dried up her fruit
Zech 10. 11 all the deeps of the river shall dry up
5. *To dry up,* ξηραίνω *xērainō.*
Mark 5. 29 the fountain of her blood was dried up
11. 20 saw the fig tree dried up from the roots
Rev. 16. 12 the water thereof was dried up, that the

DRY shod —
With shoes, sandals, בַּנְּעָלִים *ban-nealim.*
Isa. 11. 15 and shall..make (men) go over dry-shod

DUE —
1. *Thing, matter,* דָּבָר *dabar.*
Neh. 11. 23 a certain portion..due for every day
2. *Statute, portion, limit,* חֹק *choq.*
Lev. 10. 13 it (is) thy due, and thy sons' due, of the
10. 14 (they be) thy due, and thy sons' due
3. *Judgment,* מִשְׁפָּט *mishpat.*
Deut 18. 3 shall be the priest's due from the people
4. *What is due, a debt,* ὀφειλή *opheilē.*
Rom 13. 7 Render therefore to all their dues
5. *Own, proper,* ἴδιος *idios.*
Gal. 6. 9 in due season we shall reap, if we faint
1 Ti. 2. 6 ransom for all, to be testified in due time
Titus 1. 3 hath in due times manifested his word
6. *To owe, be due,* ὀφείλω *opheilō.*
1 Co. 7. 3 render unto the wife [due benevolence]

DUE, to be —
To owe, be due, ὀφείλω *opheilō.*
Matt 18. 34 he should pay all that was due unto him

DUE season — [**DUE time,** *see* **BORN**]
Time, season, עֵת *eth.*
Lev. 26. 4 I will give you rain in due season, and
Deut 11. 14 the rain of your land in his due season

Psa. 104. 27 mayest give (them) their meat in due se.
145. 15 thou givest them their meat in due season
Prov 15. 23 word (spoken) in due season, Eccl. 10. 17.

DUE (reward), those to whom it is —

1. *Worthy, meet things*, ἄξια *axia*.
Luke 23. 41 we receive the due reward of our deeds

Its owners, בְּעָלָיו [*baal*].
Prov. 3. 27 Withhold not good from..whom it is due

DUKE —

1. *Leader, head of a thousand*, אַלּוּף, אַלֻּף *alluph*.
Gen. 36. 15 These (were) dukes of the sons of Esau
36. 15 duke Teman, duke Omar, duke Zepho, d.
36. 16 Duke Korah, duke Gatam, (and) duke A.
36. 16 these (are) the dukes (that came) of Elip.
36. 17 duke Nahath, duke Zerah, d. Shammah, d.
36. 17 these (are) the dukes (that came) of Reuel
36. 18 duke Jeush, duke Jaalam, duke Korah
36. 18 (were) the dukes (that came) of Aholiba.
36. 19 These (are) the sons..these (are) their d.
36. 21 these (are) the dukes of the Horites, the
36. 29 (are) the dukes (that came) of the Horites
36. 29 duke Lotan, duke Shobal, duke Zibeon, d.
36. 30 Duke Dishon, duke Ezer, duke Disdan
36. 30 these (are) the dukes (that came) of Hori
36. 30 among their dukes in the land of Seir
36. 40 these (are) the names of the dukes (that
36. 40 duke Timnah, duke Alvah, duke Jetheth
36. 41 Duke Aholibamah, duke Elah, duke Pinon
36. 42 Duke Kenaz, duke Teman, duke Mibzar
36. 43 D. Magdiel, duke Iram: these (be) the d.
Exod 15. 15 Then the dukes of Edom shall be amazed
1 Ch. 1. 51 dukes..were; duke Timnah, d. Aliah, d.
1. 52 Duke Aholibamah, duke Elah, duke Pin.
1. 53 Duke Kenaz, duke Teman, duke Mibzar
1. 54 Duke Magdiel, duke Iram..dukes of Ed.

2. *Prince, one anointed, ruler*, נָסִיךְ *nasik*.
Josh 13. 21 dukes of Sihon, dwelling in the country

DULCIMER —

1. *Bagpipe, symphony*, סוּמְפֹּנְיָה *sumponeyah*.
Dan. 3. 5, 15 at what time ye hear the..dulcimer

2. *Bagpipe*, סִיפֹּנְיָה [V.L. סיפניה], *supponeyah*.
Dan. 3. 10 that every man that shall hear the..dulc.

DULL —

Slothful, νωθρός *nōthros*.
Heb. 5. 11 hard to be uttered, seeing ye are dull of

DU'-MAH, דּוּמָה *silence*.

1. Son of Ishmael son of Abraham by Hagar. B.C. 1840.
Gen. 25. 14 And Mishma, and D., and Massa
1 Ch. 1. 30 Mishma, and D., Massa, Hadad, and T.

2. A city of the tribe of Judah.
Josh 15. 52 Arab, and D., and Eshean

3. A city whose site is doubtful.
Isa. 21. 11 The burden of D. He calleth to me out of

DUMB —

1. *Dumb, bound, tied*, אִלֵּם *illem*.
Exod 4. 11 man's mouth? or who maketh the dumb
Prov 31. 8 Open thy mouth for the dumb in the ca.
Isa. 35. 6 Then shall..the tongue of the dumb sing
56. 10 they (are) all dumb dogs, they cannot bark
Hab. 2. 18 the maker..trusteth therein, to make d.

2. *Silent, still*, דּוּמָם *dumam*.
Hab. 2. 19 to the dumb stone, Arise, it shall teach!

3. *Speechless*, ἄλαλος *alalos*.
Mark 7. 37 he maketh..the deaf to hear, and the d.
9. 17 brought..my son, which hath a dumb
9. 25 dumb and deaf spirit, I charge thee, come

4. *Voiceless*, ἄφωνος *aphōnos*.
Acts 8. 32 like a lamb dumb before his shearer, so
1 Co. 12. 2 carried away unto these dumb idols, even
2 Pe. 2. 16 the dumb ass speaking with man's voice

5. *Blunted, dumb*, κωφός *kōphos*.
Matt 9. 32 behold, they brought to him a dumb man
9. 33 when the devil was cast out, the dumb s.
12. 22 Then was brought unto him one..dumb
12. 22 insomuch that the blind and dumb both
15. 30 having with them..dumb, maimed, and
15. 31 when they saw the dumb to speak, the
Luke 11. 14 he was casting out a devil, and it was d.
11. 14 when the devil was gone out, the dumb

6. *To be silent*, σιωπάω *siōpaō*.
Luke 1. 20 thou shalt be dumb, and not able to speak

DUMB, to be or become —

To be dumb, bound, tied, אָלַם *alam*, 2.
Psa. 39. 2 I was dumb with silence, I held my peace
39. 9 I was dumb, I opened not my mouth
Isa. 53. 7 as a sheep before her shearers is dumb
Eze. 3. 26 that thou shalt be dumb, and shalt not
24. 27 thou shalt speak, and be no more dumb
33. 22 mouth was opened, and I was no more d.
Dan. 10. 15 face toward the ground, and I became d.

DUMB man —

Dumb, bound, tied, אִלֵּם *illem*.
Psa. 38. 13 as a dumb man (that) openeth not his m.

DUNG —

1. *Dung, dirt, rubbish*, אַשְׁפֹּת, אַשְׁפּוֹת *ashpoth*.
Neh. 2. 13 before the dragon well, and to the dung
3. 13 the wall unto the dung gate; 3. 14, 12. 31.

2. *Dung*, גֵּלֶל *gelel*.
Job 20. 7 he shall perish for ever like his own dung
Eze. 4. 12 thou shalt bake it with dung that cometh
4. 15 I have given thee cow's..for man's dung
Zeph. 1. 17 out as dust, and their flesh as the dung

3. *Dung, dunghill*, גָּלָל *galal*.
1 Ki. 14. 10 as a man taketh away dung, till it be all

4. *Dung, dung heap, dunghill*, דֹּמֶן *domen*.
2 Ki. 9. 37 And the carcase of Jezebel shall be as du.
Psa. 83. 10 they became (as) dung for the earth
Jer. 8. 2 they shall be for dung upon the face of
9. 22 the carcases of men shall fall as dung up.
16. 4 they shall be as dung upon the face of
25. 33 they shall be dung upon the ground

5. *Dung, offscourings*, חֲרִים *charim*.
2 Ki. 6. 25 the fourth part of a cab of dove's dung

6. *Dung, excrement*, פֶּרֶשׁ *peresh*.
Exod 29. 14 the flesh of the bullock..and his dung
Lev. 4. 11 the skin of the bullock..and his dung
8. 17 the bullock, and his hide..and his dung
16. 27 they shall burn in the fire their..dung
Num 19. 5 her blood, with her dung, shall he burn
Mal. 2. 3 I will..spread dung..the dung of your

7. *Outcome* [V.L. חֲרִים *charim*, חֲרָאִים *charaim*] צוֹאָה *tsoah*
2 Ki. 18. 27 they may eat their own dung, and drink
Isa. 36. 12 they may eat their own dung, and drink

8. *Dung, what is blown out*, צְפִיעַ *tsaphua*.
Eze. 4. 15 I have given thee cow's dung for man's

9. *Dung, what is blown out*, צְפִיעַ *tsaphia*.
Eze. 4. 15 I have given thee cow's dung for man's

10. *Dregs, refuse*, σκύβαλον *skubalon*.
Phil. 3. 8 and do count them..dung, that I may

DUNG, to —

To cast dung, βάλλω κοπρίαν *ballō koprian*.
Luke 13. 8 till I shall dig about it, and [dung] (it)

DUNGEON —

1. *Pit, dungeon*, בּוֹר *bor*.
Gen. 40. 15 that they should put me into the dungeon
41. 14 they brought him hastily out of the dung.
Jer. 38. 6 cast him into the dungeon of Malchiah
38. 6 And in the dungeon..no water, but mire
38. 7 they had put Jeremiah in the dungeon
38. 9 whom they have cast into the dungeon
38. 10 take up Jeremiah..out of the dungeon
38. 11 let them down by cords into the dungeon
38. 13 and took him up out of the dungeon: and
Lam. 3. 53 They have cut off my life in the dungeon
3. 55 I called..O LORD, out of the low dungeon

2. *House of the pit*, בֵּית הַבּוֹר *beth hab-bor*.
Exod 12. 29 of the captive that (was) in the dungeon
Jer. 37. 16 Jeremiah was entered into the dungeon

DUNGHILL —

1. *Dung, dirt*, אַשְׁפֹּת, אַשְׁפָּה *ashpoth, ashpath*.
1 Sa. 2. 8 lifteth up the beggar from the dunghill
Psa. 113. 7 (and) lifteth the needy out of the dungh.
Lam. 4. 5 that were brought up..embrace dungh.

2. *Dunghill, dung heap*, מַדְמֵנָה *madmenah*.
Isa. 25. 10 as straw is trodden down for the dunghill

3. *Dunghill or heap*, נְוָלוּ *nevalu*.
Ezra 6. 11 let his house be made a dunghill for this

4. *Dunghill, heap*, נְוָלִי *nevali*.
Dan. 2. 5 and your houses shall be made a dungh.
3. 29 and their houses shall be made a dungh.

5. *Dunghill*, κοπρία *kopria*.
Luke 14. 35 fit for the land, nor yet for the dunghill

DUNG GATE or PORT, שַׁעַר הָאַשְׁפֹּת, *shaar ashpoth*.

A gate at the S.W. of Jerusalem.
Neh. 2. 13 before the dragon well, and to the dung p.
3. 14 the dung gate repaired Malchiah the son
12. 31 right hand upon the wall toward the d. g.

DU'-RA, דּוּרָא *circle*.

A plain in the province of Babylon where Nebuchadnezzar set up a golden image.
Dan. 3. 1 he set it up in the plain of D., in the pro.

DURABLE, dureth —

1. *Lasting*, עָתִיק *athiq*.
Isa. 23. 18 eat sufficiently, and for durable clothing

2. *Lasting*, עָתֵק *atheq*.
Prov. 8. 18 (yea), durable riches and righteousness

3. *It is*, ἐστί *esti*, Matt. 13. 21.

DURST —

To fear, be afraid, יָרֵא *yare*.
Job 32. 6 and durst not show you mine opinion

DUST —

1. *Dust (pounded small)*, אָבָק *abaq*.
Isa. 5. 24 their blossom shall go up as dust: because
29. 5 the multitude..shall be like small dust
Eze. 26. 10 By reason..their dust shall cover thee
Nah. 1. 3 and the clouds (are) the dust of his feet

2. *Ashes, clay, dust*, עָפָר *aphar*.
Gen. 2. 7 the LORD God formed man (of) the dust
3. 14 dust shalt thou eat all the days of thy
3. 19 for dust thou (art), and unto dust shalt
13. 16 I will make thy seed as the dust of the
13. 16 so that if a man can number the dust of
18. 27 taken upon me..which (am but) dust and
28. 14 thy seed shall be as the dust of the earth
Exod 8. 16 Stretch out thy rod, and smite the dust
8. 17 smote the dust of the earth, and it became
8. 17 all the dust of the land became lice
Lev. 14. 41 they shall pour out the dust that they
17. 13 pour out the blood..and cover it with d.
Num. 5. 17 and of the dust that is in the floor of the
23. 10 Who can count the dust of Jacob, and
Deut. 9. 21 was as small as dust: and I cast the d.
28. 24 the rain of thy land powder and dust
32. 24 with the poison of serpents of the dust
Josh. 7. 6 and the elders..put dust upon their heads
1 Sa. 2. 8 He raiseth up the poor out of the dust
2 Sa. 16. 13 and threw stones at him, and cast dust
22. 43 Then did I beat them as small as the du.
1 Ki. 16. 2 as I exalted thee out of the dust, and
18. 38 fire..fell, and consumed..the dust, and
20. 10 if the dust of Samaria shall suffice for
2 Ki. 13. 7 had made them like the dust by threshing
23. 12 cast the dust of them unto the brook
2 Ch. 1. 9 king over a people like the dust of the
Job 2. 12 they..sprinkled dust upon their heads
4. 19 whose foundation (is) in the dust, (which)
5. 6 affliction cometh not forth of the dust
7. 5 is clothed with worms and clods of dust
7. 21 for now shall I sleep in the dust; and
10. 9 and wilt thou bring me into dust again?
14. 19 things which grow (out) of the dust of
16. 15 I have..defiled my horn in the dust
17. 16 when (our) rest together (is) in the dust
20. 11 His bones..shall lie down..in the dust
21. 26 They shall lie down alike in the dust
22. 24 Then shalt thou lay up gold as dust
27. 16 Though he heap up silver as the dust
28. 6 The stones of it..hath dust of gold
30. 19 and I am become like dust and ashes
34. 15 and man shall turn again unto dust
38. 38 When the dust groweth into hardness
39. 14 her eggs..and warmeth them in dust
40. 13 Hide them in the dust together; (and)
42. 6 I abhor (myself), and repent in dust and
Psa. 7. 5 Let the enemy..lay mine honour in the d.
18. 42 Then did I beat them small as the dust
22. 15 thou hast brought me into the dust of
22. 29 all they that go down to the dust shall
30. 9 Shall the dust praise thee? shall it declare
44. 25 For our soul is bowed down to the dust
72. 9 and his enemies shall lick the dust
78. 27 He rained flesh also upon them as dust
102. 14 For thy servants..favour the dust thereof
103. 14 For he..remembereth that we (are) dust
104. 29 they die, and return to their dust
113. 7 He raiseth up the poor out of the dust
119. 25 My soul cleaveth unto the dust: quicken
Prov. 8. 26 nor the highest part of the dust of the
Eccl. 3. 20 all are of the dust, and all turn to dust
12. 7 shall the dust return to the earth as it
Isa. 2. 10 hide thee in the dust, for fear of the LORD
25. 12 (and) bring to the ground, (even) to the d.
26. 5 ground; he bringeth it (even) to the du.
26. 19 Awake and sing, ye that dwell in dust
29. 4 thy speech shall be low out of the dust
29. 4 thy speech shall whisper out of the dust
34. 7 and their dust made fat with fatness
34. 9 the dust thereof into brimstone, and the
40. 12 comprehended the dust of the earth in
41. 2 he gave (them) as the dust to his sword
47. 1 Come down, and sit in the dust, O virgin
49. 23 they shall..lick up the dust of thy feet
52. 2 Shake thyself from the dust; arise, (and)
65. 25 and dust (shall be) the serpent's meat
Lam. 2. 10 they have cast up dust upon their heads
3. 29 He putteth his mouth in the dust; if so
Eze. 24. 7 she poured it not..to cover it with dust
26. 4 I will also scrape her dust from her, and
26. 12 they shall lay..thy dust in the midst of
27. 30 and shall cast up dust upon their heads
Dan. 12. 2 many of them that sleep in the dust of
Amos 2. 7 That pant after the dust of the earth on
Mic. 1. 10 in the house of Aphrah roll..in the dust
7. 17 They shall lick the dust like a serpent
Hab. 1. 10 for they shall heap dust, and take it
Zeph. 1. 17 their blood shall be poured out as dust
Zech. 9. 3 Tyrus..heaped up silver as the dust

3. *Dust*, κονιορτός *koniortos*.
Matt 10. 14 when ye depart..shake off the dust of
Luke 9. 5 shake off the very dust from your feet
10. 11 Even the very dust of your city, which
Acts 13. 51 they shook off the dust of their feet
22. 23 And as they cried out..and threw dust

4. *Clay, earth*, χόος *choos*.
Mark 6. 11 shake off the dust under your feet for a
Rev. 18. 19 they cast dust on their heads, and cried

DUST, to make —

To beat small, thin, דָּקַק *daqaq*, 5.
2 Ch. 34. 4 he brake in pieces, and made dust (of

DUST, small —

1. *Dust (pounded small)*, אָבָק *abaq*.
Exod. 9. 9 it shall become small dust in all the land

2. *Small, thin, or fine dust*, שַׁחַק *shachaq*.
Isa. 40. 15 are counted as the small dust of the bal.

DUTY —

Matter, דָּבָר *dabar*.
2 Ch. 8. 14 to praise..as the duty of every day requ.
Ezra 3. 4 according..as the duty of every day req.

DUTY, to be one's —
To owe, be due, ὀφείλω *opheilō.*
Luke 17. 10 we have done that which was our duty
Rom 15. 27 their duty is also to minister unto them

DUTY of marriage —
Habitation, עוֹנָה *onah.*
Exod 21. 10 her duty of marriage, shall he not dimin.

DWARF —
Lean, thin, small, דַּק *daq.*
Lev. 21. 20 Or crook backt, or a dwarf, or that hath

DWELL, to —
1. *To sojourn, inhabit, draw together,* גּוּר *gur.*
Lev. 19. 34 the stranger that dwelleth with you shall
Job 19. 15 They that dwell in mine house, and my
Psa. 5. 4 For..neither shall evil dwell with thee
Isa. 11. 6 The wolf also shall dwell with the lamb
16. 4 Let mine outcasts dwell with thee, Moab
33. 14 who among us shall dwell with the dev.
33. 14 who among us shall dwell with everlast.
Jer. 43. 5 returned..to dwell in the land of Judah
44. 8 whither ye be gone to dwell, that ye
49. 18 neither shall a son of man dwell in it
49. 33 nor (any) son of man dwell in it
50. 40 neither shall any son of man dwell there.

2. *To dwell,* דּוּר *dur.*
Psa. 84. 10 than to dwell in the tents of wickedness

3. *To dwell,* דּוּר *dur.*
Dan. 2. 38 And wheresoever the children of men d.
4. 1 unto all people,..that dwell in all the
4. 12 the fowls of the heaven dwelt in the
4. 21 under which the beasts of the field dwelt
6. 25 all people..that dwell in all the earth

4. *To camp,* חָנָה *chanah.*
Isa. 29. 1 to Ariel, the city (where) David dwelt!

5. *To sit down or still,* יָשַׁב *yashab.*
Gen. 4. 16 Cain went out..and dwelt in the land of
4. 20 the father of such as dwell in tents
11. 2 they found a plain..and they dwelt there
11. 31 they came unto Haran, and dwelt there
13. 6 that they might dwell together
13. 6 so that they could not dwell together
13. 7 the Canaanite and the Perezzite dwelt
13. 12 Abram dwelt in the land of Canaan
13. 12 Lot dwelt in the cities of the plain
13. 18 came and dwelt in the plain of Mamre
14. 7 also the Amorites, that dwelt in Hazezon.
14. 12 And they took Lot..who dwelt in Sodom
16. 3 after Abram had dwelt ten years in the
19. 29 overthrew the cities in the which Lot d.
19. 30 Lot went up out of Zoar, and dwelt in the
19. 30 feared to dwell in Zoar: and he dwelt
20. 1 and dwelled between Kadesh and Shur
20. 15 Abimelech said..dwell where it pleaseth
21. 20 and he grew, and dwelt in the wilderness
21. 21 And he dwelt in the wilderness of Paran
22. 19 and Abraham dwelt at Beer-sheba
23. 10 Ephron dwelt among the children of H.
24. 3 of the Canaanites, among whom I dwell
24. 37 of the Canaanites, in whose land I dwell
24. 62 And Isaac..dwelt in the south country
25. 11 and Isaac dwelt by the well Lahai-roi
26. 6 And Isaac dwelt in Gerar
26. 17 in the valley of Gerar, and dwelt there
34. 10 ye shall dwell with us..dwell and trade
34. 16 we will dwell with you, and we will
34. 21 let them dwell in the land, and trade
34. 22 men consent unto us for to dwell with us
34. 23 consent unto them, and they will dwell
35. 1 Arise, go up to Beth-el, and dwell there
36. 7 more than that they might dwell togeth.
36. 8 Thus dwelt Esau in mount Seir: Esau
37. 1 Jacob dwelt in the land wherein his
38. 11 Tamar went and dwelt in her father's
45. 10 thou shalt dwell in the land of Goshen
46. 34 that ye may dwell in the land of Goshen
47. 4 thy servants dwell in the land of Goshen
47. 6 make thy father and brethren to dwell
47. 6 in the land of Goshen let them dwell
47. 27 Israel dwelt in the land of Egypt, in the
50. 22 dwelt in Egypt, he and his father's house
Exod. 2. 15 Moses fled..and dwelt in the land of M.
2. 21 Moses was content to dwell with the
12. 40 the children of Israel, who dwelt in Eg.
15. 17 thou hast made for thee to dwell in
23. 33 They shall not dwell in thy land, lest
Lev. 13. 46 he (is) unclean: he shall dwell alone
18. 3 the land of Egypt, wherein ye dwelt
20. 22 land, whither I bring you to dwell
23. 42 Ye shall dwell in booths seven days
23. 42 Israelites born shall dwell in booths
25. 18 and ye shall dwell in the land in safety
25. 19 eat your fill, and dwell therein in safety
26. 5 and ye shall..dwell in your land safely
26. 32 your enemies which dwell therein shall
26. 35 it did not rest..when ye dwelt upon it
Num 13. 18 and the people that dwelleth therein
13. 19 And what the land (is) that they dwell
13. 19 what cities (they be) that they dwell in
13. 28 people (be) strong that dwell in the land
13. 29 Amalekites dwell in the land of the
13. 29 and the Amorites, dwell in the mountains
13. 29 the Canaanites dwell by the sea, and by
14. 25 and the Canaanites dwelt in the valley
14. 45 the Canaanites which dwelt in that hill
20. 15 and we have dwelt in Egypt a long time
21. 1 the Canaanite, which dwelt in the south
Num 21. 25 dwelt in all the cities of the Amorites
21. 31 Israel dwelt in the land of the Amorites
21. 34 king of the Amorites, which dwelt at H.
32. 17 our little ones shall dwell in the fenced
32. 40 gave Gilead unto Machir..he dwelt
33. 40 Arad the Canaanite, which dwelt in the
33. 53 dispossess..the land, and dwell therein
33. 55 vex you in the land wherein ye dwell
35. 2 give unto the Levites..cities to dwell in
35. 3 the cities shall they have to dwell in
35. 32 should come again to dwell in the land
Deut. 1. 4 king of the Amorites, which dwelt in
1. 4 the king of Bashan, which dwelt at Ast.
1. 6 Ye have dwelt long enough in this mount
1. 44 the Amorites, which dwelt in that moun.
2. 4 the children of Esau, which dwell in Se.
2. 8, 22 children of Esau, which dwelt in Seir
2. 10 The Emims dwelt therein in times past
2. 12 The Horims also dwelt in Seir beforetime
2. 12 succeeded them..and dwelt in their
2. 20 giants dwelt therein in old time
2. 21, 22 succeeded them, and dwelt in their
2. 23 the Avims which dwelt in Hazerim
2. 23 destroyed them, and dwelt in their stead
2. 29 dwell in Seir, and the Moabites which d.
3. 2 king of the Amorites, which dwelt at H.
4. 46 king of the Amorites, who dwelt at Hes.
8. 12 built goodly houses, and dwelt (therein)
11. 30 which dwell in the champaign over
11. 31 and ye shall possess it, and dwell therein
12. 10 dwell in the land which the LORD your
12. 10 giveth you rest..that ye dwell in safety
12. 29 succeedest them, and dwellest in their
13. 12 thy God hath given thee to dwell there
17. 14 shalt possess it, and shalt dwell therein
19. 1 dwellest in their cities, and in their
23. 16 He shall dwell with thee, (even) among
25. 5 If brethren dwell together, and one of
26. 1 and possessest it, and dwellest therein
28. 30 and thou shalt not dwell therein
29. 16 how we have dwelt in the land of Egypt
30. 20 that thou mayest dwell in the land
Josh. 2. 15 and she dwelt upon the wall
6. 25 she dwelleth in Israel (even) unto this
7. 7 been content and dwelt on the other side
9. 7 Peradventure ye dwell among us; and
9. 16 they heard..(that) they dwelt among
9. 22 very far from you; when ye dwell among
10. 6 kings of the Amorites that dwell in the
12. 2 king of the Amorites, who dwelt in Hes.
12. 4 that dwelt at Ashtaroth and at Edrei
13. 13 Maachathites dwell among the Israelites
13. 21 dukes of Sihon, dwelling in the country
14. 4 save cities to dwell (in), with their subu.
15. 63 the Jebusites dwell with the children
16. 10 the Canaanites that dwelt in Gezer
16. 10 Canaanites dwell among the Ephraimites
17. 12 the Canaanites would dwell in that land
17. 16 the Canaanites that dwell in the land of
19. 47 possessed it, and dwelt therein, and
19. 50 and he built the city, and dwelt therein
20. 4 give him a place, that he may dwell
20. 6 he shall dwell in that city, until he stand
21. 2 to give us cities to dwell in, with the
21. 43 and they possessed it, and dwelt therein
22. 33 the land wherein the children of..Gad d.
24. 2 Your fathers dwelt on the other side of
24. 7 and ye dwelt in the wilderness a long
24. 8 which dwelt on the other side Jordan
24. 13 cities which ye built not, and ye dwell
24. 15 of the Amorites, in whose land ye dwell
24. 18 the Amorites which dwelt in the land
Judg. 1. 9 to fight against the Canaanites, that dwelt
1. 10 against the Canaanites that dwelt in Heb.
1. 16 and they went and dwelt among the peo.
1. 21 the Jebusites dwell with the children of
1. 27 the Canaanites would dwell in that land
1. 29 the Canaanites dwelt in Gezer among
1. 30 the Canaanites dwelt among them, and
1. 32 the Asherites dwelt among the Canaanites
1. 33 but he dwelt among the Canaanites
1. 35 the Amorites would dwell in mount Heres
3. 3 the Hivites that dwelt in mount Lebanon
3. 5 the children of Israel dwelt among the C.
4. 2 which dwelt in Harosheth of the Gentiles
4. 5 she dwelt under the palm tree of Deborah
6. 10 gods of the Amorites, in whose land ye d.
8. 29 the son of Joash..dwelt in his own house
9. 21 Jotham..went to Beer, and dwelt there
9. 41 And Abimelech dwelt at Arumah
9. 41 that they should not dwell in Shechem
10. 1 he dwelt in Shamir in mount Ephraim
11. 3 Then Jephthah fled..and dwelt in the
11. 26 While Israel dwelt in Heshbon and her
15. 8 he went down and dwelt in the top of the
17. 10 Dwell with me, and be unto me a father
17. 11 the Levite was content to dwell with the
18. 1 Danites sought them an inheritance to d.
18. 7 the five men..saw..how they dwelt care.
18. 28 And they built a city, and dwelt therein
21. 23 they..repaired the cities..and dwelt in
Ruth 1. 4 they dwelt there about ten years
2. 23 So she..dwelt with her mother-in-law
1 Sa. 4. 4 of the LORD of hosts, which dwelleth
12. 11 enemies on every side, and ye dwelled
19. 18 And he and Samuel went and dwelt in
22. 4 and they dwelt with him all the while
23. 29 And David..dwelt in strong holds at En.
27. 3 And David dwelt with Achish at Gath
27. 5 some town in the country, that I may dw.
27. 5 why should thy servant dwell in the royal
27. 7 the time that David dwelt in the country
1 Sa. 27. 11 all the while he dwelleth in the country
31. 7 the Philistines came and dwelt in them
2 Sa. 2. 3 and they dwelt in the cities of Hebron
5. 9 David dwelt in the fort, and called it, The
6. 2 name of The LORD of hosts, that dwelleth
7. 2 See now, I dwell in an house of cedar, but
7. 2 the ark of God dwelleth within curtains
7. 5 Shalt thou build me an house..to dwell
7. 6 I have not dwelt in (any) house since the
9. 13 So Mephibosheth dwelt in Jerusalem; for
14. 28 So Absalom dwelt two full years in Jeru.
1 Ki. 2. 36 Build thee an house..and dwell there
2. 38 And Shimei dwelt in Jerusalem many da.
3. 17 I and this woman dwell in one house
4. 25 And Judah and Israel dwelt safely, every
7. 8 And his house where he dwelt (had) ano.
8. 27 But will God indeed dwell on the earth?
9. 16 Pharaoh..had..slain the C.'s that dwelt
11. 24 they went to Damascus, and dwelt therein
12. 2 fled..and Jeroboam dwelt in Egypt
12. 17 the children of Israel which dwelt in the
12. 25 Jeroboam built Shechem..and dwelt
13. 11 Now there dwelt an old prophet in Beth.
13. 25 in the city where the old prophet dwelt
15. 18 the son of Hezion..that dwelt at Damas.
15. 21 he left off building..and dwelt in Tirzah
17. 5 he went and dwelt by the brook Cherith
17. 9 get thee to Zarephath..and dwell there
2 Ki. 4. 13 she answered, I dwell among mine own
6. 1 the place where we dwell with thee is too
6. 2 make us a place there, where we may dw.
13. 5 the children of Israel dwelt in their tents
15. 5 so that he was a leper..and dwelt in a
16. 6 the Syrians..dwelt there unto this day
17. 24 they possessed Samaria, and dwelt in the
17. 27 let them go and dwell there, and let him
17. 28 one of the priests..came and dwelt in B.
17. 29 every nation in..cities..wherein they d.
19. 15 O LORD God of Israel, which dwellest
19. 36 So Sennacherib king of Assyria..dwelt at
22. 14 she dwelt in Jerusalem in the college
25. 24 dwell in the land, and serve the king of B.
1 Ch. 2. 55 the families of the scribes which dwelt at
4. 23 those that dwelt among plants and hedges
4. 23 there they dwelt with the king for his
4. 28 And they dwelt at Beer-sheba, and Mol.
4. 40 for (they) of Ham had dwelt there of old
4. 41 these written by name..dwelt in their
4. 43 they smote the rest..and dwelt there unto
5. 8 the son of Joel, who dwelt in Aroer
5. 10 they dwelt in their tents throughout all
5. 11 And the children of Gad dwelt over aga.
5. 16 And they dwelt in Gilead in Bashan
5. 22 And they dwelt in their steads until the
5. 23 the children of the half tribe..dwelt in
7. 29 In these dwelt the children of Joseph the
8. 28 These (were) heads..These dwelt in Jeru.
8. 29 And at Gibeon dwelt the father of Gibeon
8. 32 And these also dwelt with their brethren
9. 3 in Jerusalem dwelt of the children of Ju.
9. 16 the son of Elkanah, that dwelt in the vil.
9. 34 These chief fathers of the Levites..dwelt
9. 35 And in Gibeon dwelt the father of Gibeon
9. 38 they also dwelt with their brethren at J.
10. 7 the Philistines came and dwelt in them
11. 7 David dwelt in the castle; therefore they
13. 6 the ark of God the LORD, that dwelleth
17. 1 I dwell in an house of cedars, but the ark
17. 4 Thou shalt not build me an house to dw.
17. 5 I have not dwelt in an house since the day
2 Ch. 2. 3 to build him an house to dwell therein
6. 18 will God in very deed dwell with men
8. 11 My wife shall not dwell in the house of
10. 17 the children of Israel that dwelt in the
11. 5 Rehoboam dwelt in Jerusalem, and
16. 2 to Benhadad king of Syria, that dwelt at
19. 4 Jehoshaphat dwelt at Jerusalem; and he
19. 10 of your brethren that dwell in their cities
20. 8 they dwelt therein, and have built thee
26. 7 against the Arabians that dwelt in Gur
26. 21 the king was a leper..and dwelt in a
28. 18 had invaded the cities..and they dwelt
30. 25 the strangers..that dwelt in Judah
31. 4 he commanded the people that dwelt in
31. 6 the children of Israel..that dwelt in the
34. 22 she dwelt in Jerusalem in the college
Ezra 2. 70 and the Nethinims, dwelt in their cities
Neh. 3. 26 Moreover the Nethinims dwelt in Ophel
4. 12 when the Jews which dwelt by them came
7. 73 the Nethinims, and all Israel, dwelt in
8. 14 the children of Israel should dwell in
11. 1 And the rulers of the people dwelt at J.
11. 1 to bring one of ten to dwell in Jerusalem
11. 2 willingly offered themselves to dwell at
11. 3 the chief of the province that dwelt in J.
11. 3 in the cities of Judah dwelt every one in
11. 4 at Jerusalem dwelt (certain) of the child.
11. 6 All the sons of Perez that dwelt at Jeru.
11. 21 But the Nethinims dwelt in Ophel
11. 25 the children of Judah dwelt at Kirjath.
13. 16 There dwelt men of Tyre also therein
Esth. 9. 19 the Jews..that dwelt in the unwalled
Job 22. 8 and the honourable man dwelt in it
Psa. 9. 11 Sing praises to the LORD, which dwelleth
23. 6 I will dwell in the house of the LORD for
24. 1 the world, and they that dwell therein
27. 4 that I may dwell in the house of the L.
65. 8 They also that dwell in the uttermost
68. 10 Thy congregation hath dwelt therein
68. 16 the hill (which) God desireth to dwell in
69. 25 (and) let none dwell in their tents
69. 35 that they may dwell there, and have it

Psa. 80. 1 thou that dwellest (between) the cherub.
84. 4 Blessed (are) they that dwell in thy house
91. 1 He that dwelleth in the secret place of
98. 7 the world, and they that dwell therein
101. 6 the faithful..that they may dwell with
101 7 He that worketh deceit shall not dwell
107. 34 for the wickedness of them that dwell
113. 5 the LORD our God, who dwelleth on high
123. 1 O thou that dwellest in the heavens
132. 14 here will I dwell; for I have desired it
133. 1 how pleasant (it is) for brethren to dwell
140. 13 the upright shall dwell in thy presence
Prov. 3. 29 seeing he dwelleth securely by thee
21. 9 (It is) better to dwell in a corner of the
21. 19 (It is) better to dwell in the wilderness
25. 24 (It is) better to dwell in the corner of the
Song 8. 13 Thou that dwellest in the gardens, the
Isa. 6. 5 I dwell in the midst of a people of
9. 2 they that dwell in the land of the shadow
10. 24 O my people that dwellest in Zion, be
23. 18 merchandise shall be for them that dwell
24. 6 they that dwell therein are desolate
26. 5 he bringeth down them that dwell on
30. 19 the people shall dwell in Zion at Jerusa.
32. 18 And my people shall dwell in a peaceable
33. 24 the people that dwell therein (shall be)
37. 16 O LORD of hosts..that dwellest (between)
37. 37 So Sennacherib king of Assyria..dwelt at
40. 22 spreadeth them out as a tent to dwell in
47. 8 Therefore hear now this..that dwellest
49. 20 give place to me that I may dwell
51. 6 they that dwell therein shall die in like
58. 12 The restorer of paths to dwell in
Jer. 2. 6 through a land..where no man dwelt?
4. 29 every city..forsaken, and not a man dwell
8. 16 the city, and those that dwell therein
9. 26 and all..that dwell in the wilderness
12. 4 for the wickedness of them that dwell
20. 6 all that dwell in thine house, shall go
23. 8 and they shall dwell in their own land
24. 8 and them that dwell in the land of Egypt
25. 5 dwell in the land that the LORD hath
27. 11 and they shall till it, and dwell therein
29. 5, 28 Build ye houses, and dwell (in them)
29. 16 of all the people that dwelleth in this city
29. 32 he shall not have a man to dwell among
31. 24 there shall dwell in Judah itself, and in
35. 7 but all your days ye shall dwell in tents
35. 9 we have dwelt in tents, and have obeyed
35. 10 Nor to build houses for us to dwell in
35. 11 for fear of the army..so we dwell at Jer.
35. 15 ye shall dwell in the land which I have
39. 14 Even they sent..so he dwelt among the
40. 5 dwell with him among the people, or go
40. 6 dwelt with him among the people that
40. 9 dwell in the land, and serve the king of
40. 10 As for me, behold, I will dwell at Mizpah
40. 10 dwell in your cities that ye have taken
41. 17 and dwelt in the habitation of Chimham
42. 13 But if ye say, We will not dwell in this
42. 14 but we will go..and there will we dwell
43. 4 obeyed not the voice..to dwell in the l.
44. 1 all the Jews which dwell in the land of
44. 1 which dwell at Migdol, and
44. 2 desolation, and no man dwelleth therein
44. 13 I will punish them that dwell in the land
44. 14 they have a desire to return to dwell
44. 15 even all the people that dwelt in the land
44. 26 all Judah that dwell in the land of Egypt
47. 2 the city, and them that dwell therein
48. 9 shall be desolate, without any to dwell
48. 28 O ye that dwell in Moab, leave the cities
49. 1 why (then) doth..his people dwell in his
49. 8 turn back, dwell deep, O inhabitants of
49. 30 dwell deep, O ye inhabitants of Hazor
49. 31 the wealthy nation, that dwelleth without
50. 3 none shall dwell therein: they shall
50. 39 the wild beasts of the islands shall dwell
50. 39 the owls shall dwell therein: and it shall
51. 1 against them that dwell in the midst of
51. 43 a land wherein no man dwelleth, neither
Lam. 1. 3 she dwelleth among the heathen, she
4. 21 O daughter of Edom, that dwellest in the
Eze. 2. 6 and thou dost dwell among scorpions: be
3. 15 that dwelt by the river of Chebar, and
7. 7 O thou that dwellest in the land: the
12. 2 thou dwellest in the midst of a rebellious
12. 19 violence of all them that dwell therein
16. 46 she and her daughters that dwell at thy
16. 46 thy younger sister, that dwelleth at thy
28. 25 then shall they dwell in their land that
28. 26 they shall dwell safely therein, and shall
28. 26 yea, they shall dwell with confidence
31. 6 under his shadow dwelt all great nations
31. 17 dwelt under his shadow in the midst of
32. 15 when I shall smite all them that dwell
34. 25 they shall dwell safely in the wilderness
34. 28 they shall dwell safely, and none shall
36. 17 when the house of Israel dwelt in their
36. 28 ye shall dwell in the land that I gave to
37. 25 they shall dwell in the land that I have
37. 25 fathers have dwelt: and they shall dwell
38. 8 and they shall dwell safely all of them
38. 11 that dwell safely, all of them dwelling
38. 12 that dwelt in the midst of the land
38. 14 when my people of Israel dwelleth safely
39. 6 among them that dwell carelessly in the
39. 9 they that dwell in the cities of Israel
39. 26 when they dwelt safely in their land, and
Hos. 4. 3 every one that dwelleth therein shall
9. 3 They shall not dwell in the LORD'S land
14. 7 They that dwell under his shadow shall
Joel 3. 20 Judah shall dwell for ever, and Jerusalem
Amos 3. 12 that dwell in Samaria in the corner of
5. 11 ye have built houses..ye shall not dwell
8. 8 and every one mourn that dwelleth
9. 5 and all that dwell therein shall mourn
Mic. 7. 13 because of them that dwell therein, for
Nah. 1. 5 yea, the world, and all that dwell therein
Hab. 2. 8, 17 of the city, and of all that dwell ther.
Zeph. 1. 18 a speedy riddance of all them that dwell
2. 15 This (is) the rejoicing city that dwelt
Hag. 1. 4 (Is it) time..to dwell in your cieled hou.
Zech. 2. 7 that dwellest (with) the daughter of B.
8. 4 old women dwell in the streets of Jerus.
9. 6 And a bastard shall dwell in Ashdod, and
14. 11 (men) shall dwell in it, and there shall be

6. *To sit down or still,* יְתִב *yethib.*
Ezra 4. 17 and (to) the rest..that dwell in Samaria

7. *To lodge, pass the night,* לִין, לוּן *lun, lin.*
Psa. 25. 13 His soul shall dwell at ease; and his seed

8. *To stand up or still,* עֲמַד *amad.*
Exod. 8. 22 land of Goshen, in which my people dw.

9. *To tabernacle,* שָׁכַן *shaken.*
Gen. 9. 27 he shall dwell in the tents of Shem; and
14. 13 for he dwelt in the plain of Mamre the
16. 12 he shall dwell in the presence of all his
25. 18 And they dwelt from Havilah unto Shur
26. 2 dwell in the land which I shall tell thee
35. 22 it came to pass, when Israel dwelt in that
49. 13 Zebulun shall dwell at the haven of the
Exod25. 8 make me a sanctuary; that I may dwell am.
29. 45 I will dwell among the children of Israel
29. 46 that I may dwell among them
Num. 5. 3 their camps, in the midst whereof I dwell
23. 9 the people shall dwell alone, and shall
35. 34 land..ye shall inhabit, wherein I dwell
35. 34 I the LORD dwell among the children
Deut33. 12 The beloved of the LORD shall dwell in
33. 12 and he shall dwell between his shoulders
33. 16 goodwill of him that dwelt in the bush
33. 20 he dwelleth as a lion, and teareth the arm
33. 28 Israel then shall dwell in safety alone
Josh 22. 19 wherein the LORD'S tabernacle dwelleth
2 Sa. 7. 10 they may dwell in a place of their own
1 Ki. 6. 13 I will dwell among the children of Israel
8. 12 The LORD said that he would dwell in
1 Ch. 17. 9 they shall dwell in their place, and shall
23. 25 that they may dwell in Jerusalem for
2 Ch. 6. 1 that he would dwell in the thick darkness
Job 3. 5 let a cloud dwell upon it; let the black.
4. 19 much less (in) them that dwell in houses
15. 28 he dwelleth in desolate cities, (and) in
18. 15 It shall dwell in his tabernacle, because
29. 25 sat chief, and dwelt as a king in the army
30 6 To dwell in the cliffs of the valleys
38. 19 Where (is) the way (where) light dwelleth?
39. 28 She dwelleth and abideth on the rock
Psa. 15. 1 who shall dwell in thy holy hill?
37. 3 (so) shalt thou dwell in the land, and
37. 27 and do good; and dwell for evermore
37. 29 inherit the land, and dwell therein for
65. 4 (that) he may dwell in thy courts
68. 6 but the rebellious dwell in a dry (land)
68. 16 yea, the LORD will dwell (in it) for ever
68. 18 that the LORD God might dwell (among
69. 36 they that love his name shall dwell
74. 2 this mount Zion, wherein thou hast dwelt
85. 9 that glory may dwell in our land
94. 17 my soul had almost dwelt in silence
120. 5 Woe..(that) I dwell in the tents of Kedar!
120. 6 My soul hath long dwelt with him that
135. 21 Blessed be the LORD..which dwelleth at
139. 9 dwell in the uttermost parts of the sea
Prov. 1. 33 hearkeneth unto me shall dwell safely
2. 21 the upright shall dwell in the land, and
8. 12 I wisdom dwell with prudence, and find
Isa. 8. 18 LORD of hosts, which dwelleth in mount Z.
13. 20 neither shall it be dwelt in from genera.
13. 21 owls shall dwell there, and satyrs shall
26. 19 Awake and sing, ye that dwell in dust
32. 16 judgment shall dwell in the wilderness
33. 5 The LORD is exalted; for he dwelleth on
33. 16 He shall dwell on high: his place of
34. 11 the owl also and the raven shall dwell
34. 17 generation to generation shall they dwell
57. 15 I dwell in the high and holy (place), with
65. 9 and my servants shall dwell there
Jer. 23. 6 In his days..Israel shall dwell safely
25. 24 mingled people that dwell in the desert
33. 16 those days..Jerusalem shall dwell safely
48. 28 leave the cities, and dwell in the rock
49. 16 that dwellest in the clefts of the rock
49. 31 neither gates nor bars, (which) dwell
51. 13 O thou that dwellest upon many waters
Eze. 17. 23 under it shall dwell all fowl of every
17. 23 shadow of the branches..shall they dwell
43. 7 where I will dwell in the midst of the
43. 9 will dwell in the midst of them for ever
Joel 3. 17 I (am) the LORD your God dwelling in
3. 21 for the LORD dwelleth in Zion
Obad. 3 that dwellest in the clefts of the rock
Mic. 4. 10 thou shalt dwell in the field, and thou
7. 14 which dwell solitarily (in) the wood
Nah. 3. 18 thy nobles shall dwell (in the dust): thy
Zech. 2. 10 I will dwell in the midst of thee, saith
2. 11 I will dwell in the midst of thee
8. 3 and will dwell in the midst of Jerusalem
8. 8 shall dwell in the midst of Jerusalem

10. *To cause to tabernacle,* שָׁכַן *shaken,* 5.
Judg. 8. 11 by the way of them that dwelt in tents
Job 11. 14 let not wickedness dwell in thy tabernacle

11. *To dwell,* שְׁרָא *shere.*
Dan. 2. 22 and the light dwelleth with him

12. *To sit down,* κάθημαι *kathēmai.*
Luke 21. 35 that dwell on the face of the whole earth

13. *To settle down,* κατοικέω *katoikeō.*
Matt. 2. 23 came and dwelt in a city called Nazareth
4. 13 he came and dwelt in Capernaum, which
12. 45 and they enter in and dwell there
Luke 11. 26 and they enter in, and dwell there
13. 4 above all men that dwelt in Jerusalem?
Acts 1. 20 be desolate, and let no man dwell there.
2. 5 there were dwelling at Jerusalem Jews
7. 2 Mesopotamia, before he dwelt in Charran
7. 4 Then came he out..and dwelt in Charran
7. 4 into this land, wherein ye now dwell
7. 48 the Most High dwelleth not in temples
9. 22 confounded the Jews which dwelt at D.
11. 29 unto the brethren which dwelt in Judæa
13. 27 they that dwell at Jerusalem, and their
17. 24 God..dwelleth not in temples made with
17. 26 for to dwell on all the face of the earth
22. 12 good report of all the Jews which dwelt
Eph. 3. 17 Christ may dwell in your hearts by faith
Col. 1. 19 that in him should all fulness dwell
2. 9 For in him dwelleth all the fulness of
Heb. 11. 9 dwelling in tabernacles with Isaac and J.
Jas. 4. 5 The spirit that [dwelleth] in us 2 Pe. 3. 13.
Rev. 2. 13 where thou dwellest..where Satan dwel.
3. 10 to try them that dwell upon the earth
6. 10 avenge our blood on them that dwell on
11. 10 they that dwell upon the earth shall rej.
11. 10 two prophets tormented them that dwelt
13. 8 all that dwell upon the earth shall
13. 12 the earth and them that dwell therein
13. 14, 14 them that dwell on the earth
14. 6 to preach unto [them that dwell] on the
17. 8 they that dwell on the earth shall wonder

14. *To remain,* μένω *menō.*
John 1. 38 They said unto him..Where dwellest th.?
1. 39 They came and saw where he dwelt
6. 56 He that eateth my flesh..dwelleth in me
14. 10 the Father that dwelleth in me, he doeth
14. 17 he dwelleth with you, and shall be in
Acts 28. 16 Paul was suffered to dwell by himself
28. 30 Paul dwelt two whole years in his own
1 Jo. 3. 17 how dwelleth the love of God in him?
3. 24 And he that keepeth..dwelleth in him
4. 12 God dwelleth in us, and his love is perf.
4. 13 Hereby know we that we dwell in him
4. 15 God dwelleth in him, and he in God
4. 16 he that dwelleth in love dwelleth in God
2 Jo. 2 For the truth's sake, which dwelleth in

15. *To use or have a house,* οἰκέω *oikeō.*
Rom. 7. 17, 20 no more I..but sin that dwelleth in
7. 18 I know that in me..dwelleth no good
8. 9 if so be that the Spirit of God dwell in
8. 11 But if the Spirit of him..dwell in you
1 Co. 3. 16 (that) the Spirit of God dwelleth in you?
7. 12 and she be pleased to dwell with him
7. 13 and if he be pleased to dwell with her
1 Ti. 6. 16 dwelling in the light which no man can

16. *To tent, tabernacle,* σκηνόω *skēnoō.*
John 1. 14 the Word was made flesh, and dwelt
Rev. 7. 15 he that sitteth on the throne shall dwell
12. 12 rejoice, (ye) heavens, and ye that dwell
13. 6 to blaspheme..them that dwell in heaven
21. 3 he will dwell with them, and they shall

DWELL, to cause to —

1. *To cause to sit down or still,* יָשַׁב *yashab,* 5.
2 Ch. 8. 2 caused the children of Israel to dwell
Jer. 32. 37 and I will cause them to dwell safely
Eze. 36. 33 I will also cause (you) to dwell in the

2. *To make to tabernacle,* שָׁכַן *shaken,* 3.
Deut 12. 11 choose to cause his name to dwell there
Jer. 7. 3 and I will cause you to dwell in this
7. 7 Then will I cause you to dwell in this

3. *To make to tabernacle,* שְׁכַן *shekan,* 3.
Ezra 6. 12 that hath caused his name to dwell there

DWELL among, to —

To settle down among, ἐγκατοικέω *egkatoikeō.*
2 Pe. 2. 8 For that righteous man dwelling among

DWELL at, to —

To settle down, κατοικέω *katoikeō.*
Acts 2. 14 all (ye) that dwell at Jerusalem, be this
9. 32 also to the saints which dwelt at Lydda
19. 17 the Jews and Greeks also dwelling at E.

DWELL in, to —

1. *A habitation,* זְבֻל, זְבוּל *zebul.*
1 Ki. 8. 13 I have surely built..an house to dw. in

2. *A seat,* מוֹשָׁב *moshab.*
Psa. 107. 4 wandered..they found no city to dwell in

3. *To be in a house,* ἐνοικέω *enoikeō.*
Rom. 8. 11 by his spirit that dwelleth in you
2 Co. 6. 16 God hath said, I will dwell in them, and
Col. 3. 16 Let the word of Christ dwell in you
2 Ti. 1. 5 which dwelt first in thy grandmother Lois
1. 14 keep by the Holy Ghost that dwelleth in

4. *To settle down,* κατοικέω *katoikeō.*
Matt 23. 21 sweareth..by him that dwelleth therein
Acts 4. 16 manifest to all them that dwell in Jerus.
9. 35 all that dwelt at Lydda and Saron saw
19. 10 all they which dwelt in Asia heard the

DWELL, to make (to) —
1. *To cause to sit down or still,* יָשַׁב *yashab,* 5.
Gen. 47. 6 make thy father and brethren to dwell
Lev. 23. 43 that I made..Israel to dwell in booths
1 Sa. 12. 8 and made them dwell in this place
Psa. 4. 8 thou, LORD, only makest me dwell in
107. 36 there he maketh the hungry to dwell
143. 3 he hath made me to dwell in darkness
Hos. 12. 9 I..will yet make thee to dwell in tabern.
2. *To make to tabernacle,* שָׁכַן *shaken,* 3.
Num14. 30 which I sware to make you dwell therein
3. *To cause to tabernacle,* שָׁכַן *shaken,* 5.
Psa. 78. 55 and made the tribes..to dwell in their

DWELL round about, to —
To dwell round about, περιοικέω *perioikeō.*
Luke 1. 65 fear came on all that dwelt round about

DWELL with, to —
1. *To dwell,* זָבַל *zabal.*
Gen. 30. 20 now will my husband dwell with me
2. *To dwell along with,* συνοικέω *sunoikeō.*
1 Pe. 3. 7 Likewise, ye husbands, dwell with (them)

DWELLERS —
1. *To tabernacle,* שָׁכַן *shaken.*
Isa. 18. 3 All ye..dwellers on the earth, see ye
2. *To settle down,* κατοικέω *katoikeō.*
Acts 1. 19 it was known unto all the dwellers at
2. 9 Elamites, and the dwellers in Mesopo.

DWELLETH — [*See* **DWELL.**]
Tabernacle, dwelling, מִשְׁכָּן *mishkan.*
Psa. 26. 8 the place where thine honour dwelleth

DWELLING —
1. *Tent,* אֹהֶל *ohel.*
Psa. 91. 10 shall any plague come nigh thy dwelling
2. *Habitation, dwelling,* זְבֻל ,זְבוּל *zebul.*
Psa. 49. 14 consume in the grave from their dwelling
3. *To sit down or still,* יָשַׁב *yashab.*
Gen. 25. 27 Jacob (was) a plain man, dwelling in tents
Num. 21. 15 that goeth down to the dwelling of Ar
1 Ki. 8. 30, 39, 43, 49 hear thou in heaven thy dwell.
21. 8 the nobles that (were) in his city, dwelling
2 Ki. 17. 25 it was at the beginning of their dwelling
2 Ch. 6. 2 and a place for thy dwelling for ever
6. 21 hear thou from thy dwelling place
6. 30 hear thou from heaven thy dwelling place
6. 33, 39 hear thou from..thy dwelling place
Jer. 46. 19 O thou daughter dwelling in Egypt
4. *Place of sojourn,* מָגוּר *magur.*
Job 18. 19 nor any remaining in his dwellings
Psa. 55. 15 for wickedness (is) in their dwellings
5. *Place of dwelling,* מְדוֹר *medor.*
Dan. 4. 25, 32 thy dwelling shall be with the beasts
5. 21 his dwelling (was) with the wild asses
6. *Dwelling-place,* מְדָר *medar.*
Dan. 2. 11 except the gods, whose dwelling is not
7. *A seat, sitting, dwelling,* מוֹשָׁב *moshab.*
Gen. 10. 30 And their dwelling was from Mesha
27. 39 thy dwelling shall be the fatness of the
Exod 10. 23 children of Israel had light in their d.
Lev. 3. 17 a perpetual statute..throughout..your d.
7. 26 of fowl, or of beast, in any of your dwell.
23. 3 sabbath of the LORD in all your dwellings
23. 14, 21, 31 a statute for ever..in all your d.
25. 29 if a man sell a dwelling house in a walled
Num35. 29 shall be for a statute..in all your dwell.
Eze. 48. 15 be a profane (place) for the city, for dwel.
8. *Habitation,* מָעוֹן *maon.*
Jer 49. 33 Hazor shall be a dwelling for dragons
Nah 2. 11 Where (is) the dwelling of the lions
Zeph 3. 7 so their dwelling should not be cut off
9. *Tabernacle,* מִשְׁכָּן *mishkan.*
Job 18. 21 Surely such (are) the dwellings of the
21. 28 where (are) the dwelling places of the
39. 6 I have made..the barren land his dwell.
Psa. 87. 2 more than all the dwellings of Jacob
Isa. 32. 18 my people shall dwell..in sure dwellings
Jer 9. 19 because our dwellings have cast (us) out
Eze. 25. 4 they shall..make their dwellings in thee
10. *Home, habitation, fold,* נָוֶה *naveh.*
Prov 21. 20 and oil in the dwelling of the wise
24. 15 against the dwelling of the righteous
Zeph. 2. 6 And the sea coast shall be dwellings
11. *A settled house or dwelling,* κατοίκησις *katoikēsis.*
Mark 5. 3 Who had (his) dwelling among the tombs

DWELLING place —
1. *Tent,* אֹהֶל *ohel.*
Job 8. 22 the dwelling place of the wicked shall
Psa. 52. 5 pluck thee out of (thy) dwelling place
2. *A seat,* מוֹשָׁב *moshab.*
Num. 24. 21 Strong is thy dwelling place, and thou
1 Ch. 6. 54 Now these (are) their dwelling places
Eze. 6. 6 In all your dwelling places the cities
37. 23 will save them out of all their dwelling p.
3. *Fixed place,* מָכוֹן *makon.*
Isa. 4. 5 LORD will create upon every dwelling p.
18. 4 I will consider in my dwelling place like
4. *Habitation,* מָעוֹן *maon.*
2 Ch. 30. 27 prayer came (up) to his holy dwelling p.
36. 15 he had compassion..on his dwelling place
Psa. 90. 1 LORD, thou hast been our dwelling place
Jer. 51. 37 Babylon shall become..a dwelling place
5. *Habitation,* מְעוֹנָה *meonah.*
Psa. 76. 2 tabernacle, and his dwelling place in Zion
6. *Tabernacle,* מִשְׁכָּן *mishkan.*
1 Ch. 6. 32 they ministered before the dwelling place
Psa. 49. 11 (and) their dwelling places to all genera.
74. 7 they have defiled..the dwelling place
Jer. 30. 18 I will..have mercy on his dwelling places
51. 30 they have burned her dwelling places
Hab. 1. 6 march..to possess the dwelling places
7. *Home, habitation, fold,* נָוֶה *naveh.*
Psa. 79. 7 they have..laid waste his dwelling place

DWELLING place, to have no certain —
To be unsettled, ἀστατέω *astateō.*
1 Co. 4. 11 buffeted, and have no certain dwelling p.

DWELT in, to be —
To tabernacle, שָׁכַן *shaken.*
Jer. 50. 39 neither shall it be dwelt in from genera.

DWELT in (that); or wherein they dwelt —
Sitting, seat, sitter, מוֹשָׁב *moshab.*
Num31. 10 burnt all their cities wherein they dwelt
2 Sa. 9. 12 all that dwelt in the house of Ziba (were)

DYED —
Leavened, brightened, חָמֵץ *chamets.*
Isa. 63. 1 Who is this that cometh..with dyed gar.

DYED attire —
Turbans, dyed attire, טְבוּלִים *tebulim.*
Eze. 23. 15 exceeding in dyed attire upon their heads

DYED red, to be —
To be made red, אָדַם *adam,* 4.
Exod25. 5 rams' skins dyed red, and badgers' skins
26. 14 cov. for the tent (of) rams' skins dyed red
35. 7 rams' skins dyed red, and badgers' skins
36. 19 cov. for the tent (of) rams' skins dyed red
39. 34 And the covering of rams' skins dyed red

DYING —
A putting to death, νέκρωσις *nekrōsis.*
2 Co. 4. 10 bearing about in the body the dying of

DYING, to be or lie a —
To die off, ἀποθνήσκω *apothnēskō.*
Luke 8. 42 one only daughter..and she lay a dying
Heb. 11. 21 Jacob, when he was a dying, blessed both

E

EACH —
1. *One,* אֶחָד *echad.*
Num. 7. 11 They shall offer their offering, each prince
7. 85 Each charger of silver..each bowl seventy
29. 14 two tenth deals to each ram of the two
29. 15 a several tenth deal to each lamb of the
Josh 22. 14 with him ten princes, of each chief house
2 Ki. 15. 20 of each man fifty shekels of silver, to give
2 Ch. 4. 13 two rows of pomegranates on each wreath
2. *A man, each one,* אִישׁ *ish.*
Gen. 15. 10 and laid each piece one against another
Num. 1. 44 each one was for the house of his fathers
16. 17 thou also, and Aaron, each..his censer
1 Ki. 22. 10 sat each on his throne, having put on
2 Ki. 9. 21 each in his chariot, and they went out
3. *A woman, each one,* אִשָּׁה *ishshah.*
Ruth 1. 8 Go, return each to her mother's house
1. 9 LORD grant you that ye may find rest, each
4. *One by one, apiece,* ἓν καθ' ἑαυτό *hen kath heauto.*
Rev. 4. 8 [the four beasts had each of them six]
5. *Each, each one,* ἕνα ἕκαστον *hena hekaston.*
Acts 2. 3 cloven tongues..sat upon each of them

EACH, a like of —
Part by part, בַּד בְּבַד *bad be-bad.*
Exod30. 34 sweet spices..of each shall there be a like

EACH man —
1. *One, each one,* אֶחָד *echad.*
1 Ki. 4. 7 each man his month in a year made pro.
2. *A man, each one,* אִישׁ *ish.*
Gen. 34. 25 Dinah's brethren, took each man his sword
40. 5 each man his dream..each man according
41. 11 we dreamed each man according to the
41. 12 to each man according to his dream he
45. 22 he gave each man changes of raiment
Judg21. 22 we reserved not to each man his wife in

EACH one —
1. *One, each one,* אֶחָד *echad.*
Num. 7. 3 for two of the princes, and for each one
Isa. 6. 2 Above it stood the seraphims: each one
2. *Each, each one,* ἕκαστος *hekastos.*
Luke13. 15 doth not each one of you on the sabbath

EAGLE —
1. *An eagle,* נֶשֶׁר *nesher.*
Exod19. 4 I bare you on eagles' wings, and brought
Lev. 11. 13 the eagle, and the ossifrage, and the osp.
Deut 14. 12 the eagle, and the ossifrage, and the osp.
28. 49 from the end of the earth..as the eagle
32. 11 As an eagle stirreth up her nest, fluttereth
2 Sa. 1. 23 swifter than eagles, they were stronger
Job 9. 26 as the eagle (that) hasteth to the prey
39. 27 Doth the eagle mount up at thy command
Psa. 103. 5 thy youth is renewed like the eagle's
Prov 23. 5 they fly away as an eagle toward heaven
30. 17 shall pick it out, and the young eagles
30. 19 The way of an eagle in the air; the way
Isa. 40. 31 they shall mount up with wings as eagles
Jer. 4. 13 Behold..his horses are swifter than eagles
48. 40 he shall fly as an eagle, and shall spread
49. 16 shouldest make thy nest as high as the e.
49. 22 he shall come up and fly as the eagle
Lam. 4. 19 Our persecutors are swifter than the eag.
Eze. 1. 10 they four also had the face of an eagle
10. 14 and the fourth the face of an eagle
17. 3 A great eagle with great wings, long
17. 7 There was also another great eagle with
Hos. 8. 1 as an eagle against the house of the LORD
Obad. 4 Though thou exalt (thyself) as the eagle
Mic. 1. 16 enlarge thy baldness as the eagle; for
Hab. 1. 8 they shall fly as the eagle (that) hasteth
2. *An eagle,* נְשַׁר *neshar.*
Dan. 4. 33 till his hairs were grown like eagle's
7. 4 The first (was) like a lion, and had eagle's
3. *An eagle,* ἀετός *aetos.*
Matt 24. 28 there will the eagles be gathered together
Luke17. 37 thither will the eagles be gathered toget.
Rev. 4. 7 the fourth beast (was) like a flying eagle
12. 14 woman were given two wings of a great e.

EAR —
1. *Ear,* אֹזֶן *ozen.*
Gen. 20. 8 and told all these things in their ears
35. 4 the..ear rings which (were) in their ears
44. 18 let..speak a word in my lord's ears
50. 4 speak, I pray you, in the ears of Pharaoh
Exod 10. 2 thou mayest tell in the ears of thy son
11. 2 Speak now in the ears of the people
17. 14 and rehearse (it) in the ears of Joshua
21. 6 his master shall bore his ear through with
29. 20 put (it) upon the tip of the right ear of
29. 20 upon the tip of the right ear of his sons
32. 2 golden ear rings, which (are) in the ears
32. 3 golden ear rings, which (were) in their ears
Lev. 8. 23 put (it) upon the tip of Aaron's right ear
8. 24 put of the blood upon..their right ear
14. 14, 17, 25, 28 upon the tip of the right ear
Num 11. 18 for ye have wept in the ears of the LORD
14. 28 as ye have spoken in mine ears, so will I
Deut. 5. 1 judgments which I speak in your ears
15. 17 and thrust (it) through his ear unto the
29. 4 the LORD hath not given you..ears to
31. 28 I may speak these words in their ears
31. 30 spake in the ears of all the congregation
32. 44 Moses..spake all the words..in the ears
Josh. 20. 4 declare his cause in the ears of the elders
Judg. 7. 3 go to, proclaim in the ears of the people
9. 2 Speak, I pray you, in the ears of all the
9. 3 brethren spake of him in the ears of all
17. 2 which thou..spakest of also in mine ears
1 Sa. 3. 11 both the ears of every one that heareth
8. 21 he rehearsed them in the ears of the LORD
9. 15 the LORD had told Samuel in his ear a day
11. 4 told the tidings in the ears of the people
15. 14 What (meaneth) then this..in mine ears
18. 23 servants spake those words in the ears of
2 Sa 3. 19 Abner also spake in the ears of Benjamin
3. 19 Abner went also to speak in the ears of D.
7. 22 to all that we have heard with our ears
22. 7 hear..and my cry (did enter) into his ears
2 Ki. 18. 26 in the ears of the people that (are) on the
19. 16 LORD, bow down thine ear, and hear
19. 28 and thy tumult is come up into mine ears
21. 12 whosoever heareth of it, both his ears
23. 2 he read in their ears all the words of the
1 Ch. 17. 20 to all that we have heard with our ears
2 Ch. 6. 40 (let) thine ears (be) attent unto the prayer
7. 15 and mine ears attent unto the prayer
34. 30 he read in their ears all the words of the
Neh. 1. 6 Let thine ear now be attentive, and thine
1. 11 let now thine ear be attentive to the
8. 3 ears of all the people (were attentive) unto
Job 4. 12 and mine ear received a little thereof
12. 11 Doth not the ear try words? and the
13. 1 mine ear hath heard and understood it
13. 17 Hear..my declaration with your ears
15. 21 A dreadful sound (is) in his ears: in pros.
28. 22 have heard the fame thereof with our ears
29. 11 When the ear heard (me), then it blessed
33. 16 he openeth the ears of men, and sealeth
34. 3 the ear trieth words, as the mouth tasteth
36. 10 He openeth also their ear to discipline
36. 15 and openeth their ears in oppression
42. 5 heard of thee by the hearing of the ear
Psa. 10. 17 thou wilt cause thine ear to hear
17. 6 incline thine ear unto me, (and hear) my
18. 6 cry came before him, (even) into his ears
31. 2 Bow down thine ear to me; deliver me
34. 15 and his ears (are open) unto their cry
40. 6 mine ears hast thou opened: burnt offer.
44. 1 We have heard with our ears, O God, our
45. 10 consider, incline thine ear; forget also
49. 4 I will incline mine ear to a parable: I will
58. 4 like the deaf adder (that) stoppeth her ear
71. 2 incline thine ear unto me, and save me
78. 1 incline your ears to the words of my
86. 1 Bow down thine ear, O LORD, hear me

Psa. 88. 2 incline thine ear unto my cry
92. 11 mine ears shall hear (my desire) of the
94. 9 He that planted the ear, shall he not h.?
102. 2 I am in trouble; incline thine ear unto
115. 6 They have ears, but they hear not: noses
116. 2 Because he hath inclined his ear unto
130. 2 let thine ears be attentive to the voice of
135. 17 They have ears, but they hear not; neit.
Prov. 2. 2 So that thou incline thine ear unto wis.
4. 20 My son..incline thine ear unto my sayings
5. 1 bow thine ear to my understanding
5. 13 nor inclined mine ear to them that inst.
15. 31 The ear that heareth the reproof of life
18. 15 and the ear of the wise seeketh knowledge
20. 12 The hearing ear, and the seeing eye, the
21. 13 Whoso stoppeth his ears at the cry of the
22. 17 Bow down thine ear, and hear the words
23. 9 Speak not in the ears of a fool; for he
23. 12 Apply..thine ears to the words of know.
25. 12 a wise reprover upon an obedient ear
26. 17 (is like) one that taketh a dog by the ears
28. 9 turneth away his ear from hearing the
Eccl. 1. 8 the eye is not satisfied..nor the ear filled
Isa. 5. 9 In mine ears (said) the LORD of hosts, Of
6. 10 make their ears heavy, and shut their eyes
6. 10 hear with their ears, and understand with
11. 3 reprove after the hearing of his ears
22. 14 it was revealed in mine ears by the LORD
30. 21 thine ears shall hear a word behind thee
32. 3 the ears of them that hear shall hearken
33. 15 he that..stoppeth his ears from hearing
35. 5 the ears of the deaf shall be unstopped
36. 11 in the ears of the people that (are) on the
37. 17 Incline thine ear, O LORD, and hear
37. 29 thy tumult, is come up into mine ears
42. 20 opening the ears, but he heareth not
43. 8 Bring forth..the deaf that have ears
48. 8 that time (that) thine ear was not opened
49. 20 children..shall say again in thine ears
50. 4 he wakeneth mine ear to hear as the
50. 5 The Lord GOD hath opened mine ear, and
55. 3 Incline your ear, and come unto me: hear
59. 1 neither his ear heavy, that it cannot hear
Jer. 2. 2 Go and cry in the ears of Jerusalem
5. 21 O foolish people..which have ears, and
6. 10 their ear (is) uncircumcised, and they
7. 24 hearkened not, nor inclined their ear
7. 26 hearkened not..nor inclined their ear
9. 20 let your ear receive the word of his
11. 8 they obeyed not, nor inclined their ear
17. 23 obeyed not, neither inclined their ear
19. 3 the which whosoever heareth, his ears
25. 4 have not hearkened, nor inclined your e.
26. 11 as ye have heard with your ears
26. 15 to speak all these words in your ears
28. 7 in thine ears, and in the ears of all the
29. 29 the priest read this letter in the ears of
34. 14 hearkened not..neither inclined their ear
35. 15 ye have not inclined your ear, nor heark.
36. 6 read..in the ears of the people, in the L.
36. 6 thou shalt read them in the ears of all
36. 10 at the entry..in the ears of all the people
36. 13 Baruch read the book in the ears of the
36. 14 wherein thou hast read in the ears of the
36. 15 Sit down now, and read it in our ears
36. 15 So Baruch read (it) in their ears
36. 20 told all the words in the ears of the king
36. 21 in the ears of the king, and in the ears of
44. 5 hearkened not, nor inclined their ear
Lam. 3. 56 hide not thine ear at my breathing, at my
Eze. 3. 10 all my words..hear with thine ears
8. 18 they cry in mine ears with a loud voice
9. 1 He cried also in mine ears with a loud
12. 2 they have ears to hear, and hear not
16. 12 And I put..ear rings in thine ears
23. 25 shall take away thy nose and thine ears
24. 26 to cause (thee) to hear (it) with (thine) e?
40. 4 with thine eyes, and hear with thine ears
44. 5 with thine eyes, and hear with thine ears
Dan. 9. 18 O my God, incline thine ear, and hear
Amos 3. 12 As the shepherd taketh..a piece of an ear
Mic. 7. 16 (their) hand upon (their) mouth, their ears
Zech. 7. 11 they..stopped their ears, that they should

2. *Hearing*, ἀκοή *akoē*.
Mark 7. 35 And straightway his ears were opened
Acts 17. 20 thou bringest..strange things to our ears
2 Ti. 4. 3 heap to themselves..having itching ears
4. 4 they shall turn away (their) ears from the

3. *The ear*, οὖς *ous*.
Matt 10. 27 what ye hear in the ear. (that) preach ye
11. 15 He that hath ears to hear, let him hear
13. 9 Who hath ears to hear, let him hear
13. 15 and (their) ears are dull of hearing
13. 15 lest..they should..hear with (their) ears
13. 16 But blessed (are) your..ears, for they hear
13. 43 Who hath ears to hear, let him hear
Mark 4. 9 He that hath ears to hear, let him hear
4. 23 If any man have ears to hear, let him
7. 16 If any man have ears..let him hear
7. 33 put his fingers into his ears, and he spit
8. 18 having ears, hear ye not? and do ye not
Luke 1. 44 of thy salutation sounded in mine ears
4. 21 day is this scripture fulfilled in your ears
8. 8 He that hath ears to hear, let him hear
9. 44 Let these sayings sink down into your e.
12. 3 that which ye have spoken in the ear
14. 35 He that hath ears to hear, let him hear
22. 50 And one of them..cut off his right ear
Acts 7. 51 Ye..uncircumcised in heart and ears
7. 57 they cried out..and stopped their ears
Acts 11. 22 tidings of these things came unto the ears
28. 27 their ears are dull..hear with..ears
Rom 11. 8 God hath given them..ears that they
1 Co. 2. 9 written, Eye hath not seen, nor ear heard
12. 16 if the ear shall say, Because I am not the
Jas. 5. 4 cries of them..are entered into the ears
1 Pe. 3. 12 his ears (are open) unto their prayers
Rev. 2. 7, 11, 17, 29 He that hath an ear, let him
3. 6, 13, 22 He that hath an ear, let him hear
13. 9 If any man have an ear, let him hear

4. *The ear, its external lobe*, ὠτίον, *ōtion*.
Matt26. 51 drew..and struck..and smote off his ear
Mark14. 47 And one of them..cut off his [ear]
Luke22. 51 And he touched his ear, and healed him
John18. 10 Then Simon Peter..cut off his right [ear]
18. 26 being (his) kinsman..whose ear Peter cut

5. *Budding, sprout, ear*, אָבִיב *abib*.
Exod. 9. 31 the barley (was) in the ear, and the flax

6. *An ear of grain or corn*, στάχυς *stachus*.
Mark 4. 28 the ear, after that the full corn in the e.

EAR of corn —
An ear of grain or corn, στάχυς *stachus*.
Matt12. 1 disciples..began to pluck the ears of c.
Mark 2. 23 disciples began..to pluck the ears of c.
Luke 6. 1 his disciples plucked the ears of corn

EAR, to —
1. *To plough*, חָרַשׁ *charash*.
1 Sa. 8. 12 he will..(set them) to ear his ground
2. *To serve*, עָבַד *abad*.
Isa. 30. 24 the young asses that ear the ground

EAR, to give —
1. *To give ear*, אָזַן *azan*, 5.
Exod15. 26 and wilt give ear to his commandments
Deut. 1. 45 hearken to your voice, nor give ear unto
32. 1 Give ear, O ye heavens, and I will speak
Judg. 5. 3 give ear, O ye princes; I, (even) I, will
2 Ch.24. 19 testified..they would not give ear
Neh. 9. 30 many years..yet would they not give ear
Job 32. 11 I gave ear to your reasons, whilst ye
34. 2 give ear unto me, ye that have knowledge
Psa. 5. 1 Give ear to my words, O LORD; consider
17. 1 give ear unto my prayer,(that goeth) not
39. 12 Hear my prayer, O LORD, and give ear
49. 1 give ear, all (ye) inhabitants of the world
54. 2 O God; give ear to the words of my mouth
55. 1 Give ear to my prayer, O God; and hide
77. 1 I cried unto God..and he gave ear unto
78. 1 Give ear, O my people, (to) my law: incl
80. 1 Give ear, O Shepherd of Israel, thou that
84. 8 hear my prayer: give ear, O God of Jacob
86. 6 Give ear, O LORD, unto my prayer; and
141. 1 give ear unto my voice, when I cry unto
143. 1 O LORD, give ear to my supplications
Prov 17. 4 (and) a liar giveth ear to a naughty tongue
Isa. 1. 2 Hear, O heavens, and give ear, O earth
1. 10 give ear unto the law of our God, ye pe.
8. 9 and give ear, all ye of far countries
28. 23 Give ye ear, and hear my voice; hearken
32. 9 careless daughters; give ear unto my sp.
42. 23 Who among you will give ear to this?
51. 4 give ear unto me, O my nation: for a law
Jer. 13. 15 Hear ye, and give ear; be not proud: for
Hos. 5. 1 and give ye ear, O house of the king
Joel 1. 2 give ear, all ye inhabitants of the land
2. *To hear, hearken*, שָׁמַע *shama*.
Job 29. 21 Unto me (men) gave ear, and waited, and

EAR, to perceive by the —
To give ear, אָזַן *azan*, 5.
Isa. 64. 4 have not heard, nor perceived by the ear

EARED, to be —
To be served, עָבַד *abad*, 2.
Deut21. 4 a rough valley, which is neither eared

EARING (time) —
Ploughing, cutting, חָרִישׁ *charish*.
Gen. 45. 6 (there shall) neither (be) earing nor harv.
Exod34. 21 in earing time and in harvest thou shalt

EARLY —
1. *Morning*, בֹּקֶר *boqer*.
Psa. 46. 5 God shall help her, (and that) right early
90. 14 satisfy us early with thy mercy; that we
101. 8 will early destroy all the wicked of the
2. *Dawn*, שַׁחַר *shachar*.
Psa. 57. 8 Awake up..I (myself) will awake early
108. 2 Awake, psaltery..I (myself) will awake e.
3. *To rise or go early*, שָׁכַם *shakam*, 5.
Psa.127. 2 (It is) vain for you to rise up early
Hos. 6. 4 and as the early dew it goeth away
13. 3 and as the early dew that passeth away
4. *At early dawn*, ὄρθριος *orthrios*.
Luke24. 22 women..which were [early] at the sepul.
5. *Early, before*, πρωΐ *prōi*.
Mark16. 9 [when (Jesus) was risen early the first (d.)]
John20. 1 first day of the week cometh Mary..ear.
6. *Early (rain)*, πρώϊμος *prōimos*, πρόϊμος.
Jas. 5. 7 he receive the early and latter rain
7. *Early*, πρωΐα *prōia*.
John 18. 28 it was early; and they themselves went
[*See also* Arise, depart, inquire, morning, rise, rise up, rising, rising up, seek.]

EARLY, to be up —
To rise or go early, שָׁכַם *shakam*, 5.
1 Sa. 29. 10 as soon as ye be up early in the morning

EARLY, to get (oneself) —
To rise or go early, שָׁכַם *shakam*, 5.
Judg19. 9 to morrow get you early on your way, that

EARLY, to get up —
To rise or go early, שָׁכַם *shakam*, 5.
Gen. 19. 27 Abraham gat up early in the morning to
Song 7. 12 Let us get up early to the vineyards

EARLY in the morning, very —
Early, שְׁפַרְפָּרָא *shepharpara*.
Dan. 6. 19 the king arose very early in the morning

EARN wages, to —
To hire self out, שָׂכַר *sakar*, 7.
Hag. 1. 6 he that earneth wages, earneth wages (to)

EARNEST —
Surety, pledge, earnest, ἀρραβών *arrhabōn*. [Heb.]
2 Co. 1. 22 the earnest of the spirit in our hearts
5. 5 given unto us the earnest of the spirit
Eph. 1. 14 Which is the earnest of our inheritance

EARNESTLY —
With prayer, προσευχῇ *proseuchē*.
Jas. 5. 17 prayed earnestly that it might not rain

EARNESTLY, to behold —
To look stedfastly, ἀτενίζω *atenizō*.
Acts 23. 1 And Paul, earnestly beholding the coun.

EARNESTLY on or upon, to look —
To look stedfastly, ἀτενίζω *atenizō*.
Luke22. 56 and earnestly looked upon him, and said
Acts 3. 12 why look ye so earnestly on us, as though

EARNESTLY, more —
More fervently, stretched out, ἐκτενέστερον *ektene.*
Luke22. 44 being in an agony, he prayed more earn.

EAR RING —
1. *Charm, whisper, amulet*, לַחַשׁ *lachash*.
Isa. 3. 20 head bands, and the tablets, and the ear r.
2. *Ring for ear or nose*, נֶזֶם *nezem*.
Gen. 24. 22 the man took a golden ear ring of half
24. 30 when he saw the ear ring, and bracelets
24. 47 and I put the ear ring upon her face
35. 4 And they gave unto Jacob all the..ear r.
Exod32. 2 Break off the golden ear rings which
32. 3 all the people brake off the golden ear r.
35. 22 many as were willing..brought..ear rings
Judg. 8. 24 ye would give me every man the ear rings
8. 24 they had golden ear rings, because they
8. 25 did cast therein every man the ear rings
8. 26 the weight of the golden ear rings that
Job 42. 11 every man also gave him..an ear ring of
Prov 25. 12 an ear ring of gold, and an ornament of
Hos. 2. 13 she decked herself with her ear rings and
3. *A ring*, עָגִיל *agil*.
Num31. 50 what every man hath gotten, of..ear rings
Eze. 16. 12 And I put..ear rings in thine ears, and

EARS —
1. *Ear of corn, sprout*, מְלִילָה *melilah*.
Deut23. 25 thou mayest pluck the ears with thine
2. *Ear of corn, branch, sprout*, שִׁבֹּלֶת *shibboleth*.
Gen. 41. 5 seven ears of corn came up upon one
41. 6 seven thin ears..sprung up after them
41. 7 seven thin ears devoured the..full ears
41. 22 seven ears came up in one stalk, full and
41. 23 seven ears..sprung up after them
41. 24 thin ears devoured the seven good ears
41. 26 and the seven good ears (are) seven years
41. 27 the seven empty ears, blasted with the
Ruth 2. 2 Let me now go..and glean ears of corn
Job 24. 24 cut off as the tops of the ears of corn
Isa. 17. 5 the harvest man..reapeth the ears with
17. 5 as he that gathereth ears in the valley of

EARS (of corn), **full or green** —
1. *Grain, (for garden land)*, כַּרְמֶל *karmel*.
Lev. 2. 14 green ears of corn dried by the fire
2. 14 (even) corn beaten out of full ears
2 Ki. 4. 42 full ears of corn in the husk thereof
2. *Budding, sprout, ear*, אָבִיב *abib*.
Lev. 23. 14 ye shall eat neither bread..nor green ears

EARS, to come to one's —
To hear about, ἀκούω ἐπί *akouō epi*.
Matt 28. 14 And if this come [to] the governor's ears

EARTH —
1. *Ground, soil, land*, אֲדָמָה *adamah*.
Gen. 1. 25 every thing that creepeth upon the earth
4. 11 now (art) thou cursed from the earth
4. 14 driven me out..from the face of the earth
6. 1 began to multiply on the face of the earth
6. 7 destroy man..from the face of the earth
6. 20 of every creeping thing of the earth after
7. 4 I destroy from off the face of the earth
7. 8 of every thing that creepeth upon the ea.
9. 2 upon all that moveth (upon) the earth
12. 3 in thee shall all families of the earth be
28. 14 shall all the families of the earth

Exod 10. 6 the day that they were upon the earth
20. 24 An altar of earth thou shalt make unto
32. 12 consume them from the face of the earth?
33. 16 from all the people..upon..the earth
Num 12. 3 all the men which (were) upon..the earth
16. 30 But if..the earth open her mouth, and
Deut. 4. 10 the days..they shall live upon the earth
4. 40 mayest prolong (thy) days upon the earth
6. 15 destroy thee from off the face of the earth
7. 6 all people that (are) upon..the earth
12. 1 all the days that ye live upon the earth
12. 19 as long as thou livest upon the earth
14. 2 all the nations that (are) upon the earth
26. 2 of the first of all the fruit of the earth
1 Sa. 4. 12 ran a man..with earth upon his head
20. 15 every one from the face of the earth
2 Sa. 1. 2 clothes rent, and earth upon his head
14. 7 name nor remainder upon the earth
15. 32 his coat rent, and earth upon his head
1 Ki. 13. 34 destroy (it) from off the face of the earth
17. 14 the LORD sendeth rain upon the earth
18. 1 Go..I will send rain upon the earth
2 Ki. 5. 17 thy servant two mules' burden of earth?
Neh. 9. 1 with sackclothes, and earth upon them
Psa. 83. 10 they became (as) dung for the earth
104. 30 thou renewest the face of the earth
146. 4 His breath..he returneth to his earth
Isa. 23. 17 all the kingdoms..upon..the earth
24. 21 the kings of the earth upon the earth
30. 23 give..bread of the increase of the earth
45. 9 potsherd..with the potsherds of the earth
Jer. 16. 4 they shall be as dung upon..the earth
25. 26 and all the kingdoms..upon..the earth
Eze. 38. 20 creeping things that creep upon the earth
38. 20 all the men that (are) upon..the earth
Dan. 12. 2 them that sleep in the dust of the earth
Amos 3. 2 You only have I known of all..the earth
3. 5 shall (one) take up a snare from the earth
9. 8 I will destroy it from off..the earth

2. *Earth, land,* אֲרַע *ara.*
Ezra 5. 11 servants of the God of heaven and earth
Jer. 10. 11 they shall perish from the earth, and
Dan. 2. 35 became a..mountain, and filled the..ea.
2. 39 which shall bear rule over all the earth
4. 1 all people..that dwell in all the earth
4. 10 behold a tree in the midst of the earth
4. 11 sight thereof to the end of all the earth
4. 15 leave the stump of his roots in the earth
4. 15 with the beasts in the grass of the earth
4. 20 and the sight thereof to all the earth
4. 22 and thy dominion to the end of the earth
4. 23 leave the stump of the roots..in the ear.
4. 35 inhabitants of the earth (are) reputed as
4. 35 and (among) the inhabitants of the earth
6. 25 all people..that dwell in all the earth
6. 27 signs and wonders in heaven and in earth
7. 4 it was lifted up from the earth, and made
7. 17 kings, (which) shall arise out of the earth
7. 23 shall be the fourth kingdom upon earth
7. 23 shall devour the whole earth, and shall

3. *Earth, land,* אֶרֶץ *erets.*
Gen. 1. 1 God created the heaven and the earth
1. 2 And the earth was without form and
1. 10 And God called the dry (land) Earth
1. 11 God said, Let the earth bring forth
1. 11 whose seed (is) in itself, upon the earth
1. 12 the earth brought forth grass, (and) herb
1. 15 for lights..to give light upon the earth
1. 17 set them..to give light upon the earth
1. 20 fowl (that) may fly above the earth in the
1. 22 and let fowl multiply in the earth
1. 24 Let the earth bring forth the living crea.
1. 24 and beast of the earth after his kind
1. 25 God made the beast of the earth after
1. 26 over the cattle, and over all the earth
1. 26 creeping thing that creepeth upon..earth
1. 28 and multiply, and replenish the earth
1. 28 living thing that moveth upon the earth
1. 29 which (is) upon the face of all the earth
1. 30 to every beast of the earth, and to every
1. 30 every thing that creepeth upon the earth
2. 1 the heavens and the earth were finished
2. 4 generations of the heavens and of the earth
2. 4 LORD God made the earth and the heavens
2. 5 every plant..before it was in the earth
2. 5 had not caused it to rain upon the earth
2. 6 there went up a mist from the earth, and
4. 12 and a vagabond shalt thou be in the earth
4. 14 a fugitive and a vagabond in the earth
6. 4 There were giants in the earth in those
6. 5 wickedness of man (was) great in the ea.
6. 6 that he had made man on the earth
6. 11 The earth also was corrupt before God
6. 11 and the earth was filled with violence
6. 12 God looked upon the earth, and, behold
6. 12 all flesh..corrupted his way upon the ea.
6. 13 the earth is filled with violence through
6. 13 behold, I will destroy them with the ea.
6. 17 do bring a flood of waters upon the earth
6. 17 every thing that (is) in the earth shall die
7. 3 seed alive upon the face of all the earth
7. 4 I will cause it to rain upon the earth
7. 6 the flood of waters was upon the earth
7. 10 waters of the flood were upon the earth
7. 12 the rain was upon the earth forty days
7. 14, 21 thing that creepeth upon the earth
7. 17 the flood was forty days upon the earth
7. 17 and it was lift up above the earth
7. 18 and were increased greatly upon the ea.
7. 19 waters prevailed..upon the earth
Gen 7. 21 all flesh died that moved upon the earth
7. 23 and they were destroyed from the earth
7. 24 the waters prevailed upon the earth an
8. 1 God made a wind to pass over the earth
8. 3 returned from off the earth continually
8. 7 waters were dried up from off the earth
8. 9 waters (were) on the face of the whole e.
8. 11 the waters were abated from off the earth
8. 13 waters were dried up from off the earth
8. 14 in the second month..was the earth dri.
8. 17 creeping thing that creepeth upon the e.
8. 17 they may breed abundantly in the earth
8. 17 be fruitful, and multiply upon the earth
8. 19 whatsoever creepeth upon the earth, after
8. 22 While the earth remaineth, seedtime
9. 1 and multiply, and replenish the earth
9. 2 shall be upon every beast of the earth
9. 7 bring forth abundantly in the earth, and
9. 10 and of every beast of the earth with you
9. 10 all that go..to every beast of the earth
9. 11 any more be a flood to destroy the earth
9. 13 of a covenant between me and the earth
9. 14 when I bring a cloud over the earth
9. 16 of all flesh that (is) upon the earth
9. 17 and all flesh that (is) upon the earth
9. 19 of them was the whole earth overspread
10. 8 he began to be a mighty one in the earth
10. 25 for in his days was the earth divided
10. 32 were the nations divided in the earth
11. 1 the whole earth was of one language, and
11. 4 abroad upon the face of the whole earth
11. 8 thence upon the face of all the earth
11. 9 confound the language of all the earth
11. 9 abroad upon the face of all the earth
13. 16 make thy seed as the dust of the earth
13. 16 a man can number the dust of the earth
14. 19 high God, possessor of heaven and earth
14. 22 God, the possessor of heaven and earth
18. 18 all the nations of the earth shall be bless.
18. 25 Shall not the Judge of all the earth do
19. 23 The sun was risen upon the earth when
19. 31 and (there is) not a man in the earth
19. 31 to come..after the manner of all the earth
22. 18 shall all the nations of the earth be bles.
24. 3 swear by..the God of the earth, that
24. 52 worshipped the LORD..to the earth
26. 4 shall all the nations of the earth be bles
27. 28 give thee of..the fatness of the earth, and
27. 39 dwelling shall be the fatness of the earth
28. 12 and behold a ladder set up on the earth
28. 14 thy seed shall be as the dust of the earth
37. 10 to bow down ourselves to thee to the ea.?
41. 56 famine was over all the face of the earth
42. 6 Joseph's brethren..bowed down..to the e.
43. 26 and bowed themselves to him to the ear.
45. 7 to preserve you a posterity in the earth
48. 12 he bowed himself with his face to the ea.
48. 16 into a multitude in the midst of the ear.
Exod. 9. 14 (there is) none like me in all the earth
9. 15 thou shalt be cut off from the earth
9. 16 may be declared throughout all the earth
9. 29 mayest know how that the earth (is) the
9. 33 the rain was not poured upon the earth
10. 5 they shall cover the face of the earth
10. 5 one cannot be able to see the earth
10. 15 they covered the face of the whole earth
15. 12 Thou stretchedst out..earth swallowed
19. 5 above all people: for all the earth (is)
20. 4 above, or that (is) in the earth beneath
20. 4 or that (is) in the water under the earth
20. 11 six days the LORD made heaven and earth
34. 8 and bowed his head toward the earth
34. 10 as have not been done in all the earth
Lev. 11. 2 among all the beasts that (are) on the e.
11. 21 legs..to leap withal upon the earth
11. 29, 42 creeping things that creep upon the e.
11. 41, 44 thing that creepeth upon the earth
11. 46 creature that creepeth upon the earth
26. 19 and I will make your..earth as brass
Num 14. 21 all the earth shall be filled with the glory
16. 32 the earth opened her mouth, and swall.
16. 33 the earth closed upon them; and they
16. 34 for they said, Lest the earth swallow us
22. 5 behold, they cover the face of the earth
22. 11 which covereth the face of the earth
26. 10 the earth opened her mouth, and swall.
Deut. 3. 24 what God (is there) in heaven or in earth
4. 17 of any beast that (is) on the earth
4. 18 that (is) in the waters beneath the earth
4. 26 I call heaven and earth to witness against
4. 32 that God created man upon the earth
4. 36 upon earth he shewed thee his great fire
4. 39 he (is) God..upon the earth beneath
5. 8 above, or that (is) in the earth beneath
5. 8 or that (is) in the waters beneath the earth
10. 14 the earth (also), with all that therein (is)
11. 6 how the earth opened her mouth, and
11. 21 as the days of heaven upon the earth
12. 16, 24 shall pour it upon the earth as water
13. 7 end of the earth..(other) end of the earth
28. 1 on high above all nations of the earth
28. 10 all people of the earth shall see that
28. 23 the earth that (is) under thee (shall be)
28. 25 removed..into all the kingdoms of the e.
28. 26 shall be meat..unto the beasts of the ea.
28. 49 bring a nation..from the end of the earth
28. 64 from the one end of the earth even unto
30. 19 I call heaven and earth to record this day
31. 28 I may..call heaven and earth to record
32. 1 hear, O earth, the words of my mouth
32. 13 ride on the high places of the earth
32. 22 shall consume the earth with her increase
Deut 33. 16 for the precious things of the earth and
33. 17 push the people..to the ends of the earth
Josh. 2. 11 he (is) God in heaven above, and in earth
3. 11, 13 the ark..of the LORD of all the earth
4. 24 That all the people of the earth might
7. 6 Joshua..fell to the earth upon his face
7. 9 and cut off our name from the earth
7. 21 they (are) hid in the earth in the midst of
23. 14 I (am) going the way of all the earth
Judg. 5. 4 the earth trembled, and the heavens dr.
6. 4 and destroyed the increase of the earth
6. 37 and (it be) dry upon all the earth (beside)
1 Sa. 2. 10 the LORD shall judge the ends of the ear.
4. 5 great shout, so that the earth rang again
5. 3 Dagon..fallen upon his face to the earth
14. 15 the earth quaked: so it was a very great
17. 46 will give..to the wild beasts of the earth
17. 46 that all the earth may know that there
17. 49 and he fell upon his face to the earth
24. 8 David stooped with his face to the earth
25. 41 bowed herself on (her) face to the earth
26. 8 with the spear even to the earth at once
26. 20 let not my blood fall to the earth before
28. 13 I saw gods ascending out of the earth
28. 20 Saul fell straightway all along on the ea.
28. 23 So he arose from the earth, and sat upon
30. 16 spread abroad upon all the earth, eating
2 Sa 1. 2 he fell to the earth, and did obeisance
4. 11 shall I not..take you away from the earth
7. 9 of the great (men) that (are) in the earth
7. 23 what one nation in the earth (is) like thy
12. 16 went in, and lay all night upon the earth
12. 17 to raise him up from the earth: but he
12. 20 Then David arose from the earth, and
13. 31 the king arose..and lay on the earth
14. 11 there shall not one hair..fall to the earth
14. 20 to know all (things) that (are) in the earth
18. 9 taken up between the heaven and the e.
18. 28 he fell down to the earth upon his face
22. 8 Then the earth shook and trembled; the
22. 43 beat..as small as the dust of the earth
23. 4 the tender grass (springing) out of the ear.
1 Ki. 1. 31 bowed with (her) face to the earth
1. 40 the earth rent with the sound of them
1. 52 shall not an hair of him fall to the earth
2. 2 I go the way of all the earth: be thou
4. 34 there came..from all kings of the earth
8. 23 in heaven above, or on earth beneath
8. 27 But will God indeed dwell on the earth?
8. 43 that all people of the earth may know
8. 53 from among all the people of the earth
8. 60 all the people of the earth may know that
10. 24 all the earth sought to Solomon, to hear
18. 42 he cast himself down upon the earth and
2 Ki. 5. 15 no God in all the earth, but in Israel
10. 10 there shall fall unto the earth nothing of
19. 15 God..of all the kingdoms of the earth
19. 15 thou hast made heaven and earth
19. 19 all the kingdoms of the earth may know
1 Ch. 1. 10 he began to be mighty upon the earth
1. 19 because in his days the earth was divided
16. 14 his judgments (are) in all the earth
16. 23 Sing unto the LORD, all the earth; shew
16. 30 Fear before him, all the earth: the world
16. 31 heavens be glad, and let the earth rejoice
16. 33 because he cometh to judge the earth
17. 8 of the great men that (are) in the earth
17. 21 one nation in the earth (is) like thy people
21. 16 stand between the earth and the heaven
22. 8 hast shed much blood upon the earth
29. 11 for all (that is) in..the earth (is thine)
29. 15 our days on the earth (are) as a shadow
2 Ch. 1. 9 like the dust of the earth in multitude
2. 12 that made heaven and earth, who hath
6. 14 (there is) no god like thee..in the earth
6. 18 But will God..dwell with men on the ear.
6. 33 all people of the earth may know thy
9. 22 passed all the kings of the earth in riches
9. 23 kings of the earth sought the presence of
16. 9 run to and fro throughout the whole ear.
20. 24 they (were) dead bodies fallen to the earth
32. 19 against the gods of the people of the earth
36. 23 All the kingdoms of the earth hath the
Ezra 1. 2 given me all the kingdoms of the earth
Neh. 9. 6 thou hast made heaven..the earth, and
Job 1. 7 From going to and fro in the earth, and
1. 8 that (there is) none like him in the earth
2. 2 From going to and fro in the earth, and
2. 3 (there is) none like him in the earth, a
3. 14 With kings and counsellors of the earth
5. 10 Who giveth rain upon the earth, and
5. 22 thou be afraid of the beasts of the earth
5. 25 thine offspring as the grass of the earth
7. 1 not an appointed time to man upon earth?
8. 9 because our days upon earth (are) a sha.
9. 6 Which shaketh the earth out of her place
9. 24 earth is given into the hand of the wicked
11. 9 measure thereof (is) longer than the earth
12. 8 Or speak to the earth, and it shall teach
12. 15 them out, and they overturn the earth
12. 24 of the chief of the people of the earth
14. 8 the root wax old in the earth, and the
14. 19 which grow (out) of the dust of the earth
15. 19 Unto whom alone the earth was given
15. 29 prolong the perfection..upon the earth
16. 18 O earth, cover not thou my blood, and let
18. 4 shall the earth be forsaken for thee? and
18. 17 remembrance shall perish from the earth
20. 4 since man was placed upon earth
20. 27 and the earth shall rise up against him
22. 8 (as for) the mighty man, he had the earth
24. 4 the poor of the earth hide themselves

[Judg. 3. 25 fallen down dead on the earth; 18. 10 no want of any thing..in the earth; 1 Sam. 2. 8 pillars of the earth (are) the LORD'S]

Job 24. 18 their portion is cursed in the earth: he
26. 7 He stretcheth out..and hangeth the earth
28. 5 (As for) the earth, out of it cometh bread
28. 24 For he looketh to the ends of the earth
30. 8 base men: they were viler than the ear.
34. 13 hath given him a charge over the earth?
35. 11 more than the beasts of the earth, and
37. 3 He directeth..unto the ends of the earth
37. 6 he saith to the snow, Be thou (on) the ear.
37. 12 upon the face of the world in the earth
37. 17 when he quieteth the earth by the south
38. 4 when I laid the foundations of the earth?
38. 13 might take hold of the ends of the earth
38. 18 thou perceived the breadth of the earth?
38. 24 scattereth the east wind upon the earth?
38. 26 To cause it to rain on the earth, (where)
38. 33 set the dominion thereof in the earth?
39. 14 Which leaveth her eggs in the earth, and
2. 2 The kings of the earth set themselves, and
2. 8 the uttermost parts of the earth (for) thy
2. 10 be instructed, ye judges of the earth
7. 5 tread down my life upon the earth, and
8. 1, 9 how excellent (is) thy name in all the e.
10. 18 man of the earth may no more oppress
12. 6 silver tried in a furnace of earth, purified
16. 3 to the saints that (are) in the earth, and
17. 11 set their eyes bowing down to the earth
18. 7 Then the earth shook and trembled
19. 4 Their line is gone..through all the earth
21. 10 Their fruit shalt thou destroy from..ea.
22. 29 All..fat upon earth shall eat and worship
24. 1 The earth (is) the LORD'S, and the fulness
25. 13 and his seed shall inherit the earth
33. 5 the earth is full of the goodness of the L.
33. 8 Let all the earth fear the LORD: let
33. 14 looketh upon all the inhabitants of the ear.
34. 16 the remembrance of them from the earth
37. 9 those that wait..shall inherit the earth
37. 11 But the meek shall inherit the earth
37. 22 blessed of him shall inherit the earth
41. 2 he shall be blessed upon the earth
44. 25 For..our belly cleaveth unto the earth
45. 16 thou mayest make princes in all the earth
46. 2 will not we fear, though the earth be
46. 6 he uttered his voice, the earth melted
46. 8 desolations he hath made in the earth
46. 9 wars to cease unto the end of the earth
46. 10 Be still..I will be exalted in the earth
47. 2 (he is) a great King over all the earth
47. 7 For God (is) the King of all the earth
47. 9 for the shields of the earth (belong) unto
48. 2 the joy of the whole earth, (is) mount Zion
48. 10 thy praise unto the ends of the earth
50. 1 God..hath spoken, and called the earth
50. 4 He shall call to..the earth, that he may
57. 5, 11 (let) thy glory (be) above all the earth
58. 2 weigh..violence of..hands in the earth
58. 11 he is a God that judgeth in the earth
59. 13 God ruleth..unto the ends of the earth
60. 2 Thou hast made the earth to tremble
61. 2 From the end of the earth will I cry unto
63. 9 shall go into the lower parts of the earth
65. 5 the confidence of all the ends of the earth
65. 9 Thou visitest the earth, and waterest it
66. 4 All the earth shall worship thee, and
67. 2 That thy way may be known upon earth
67. 4 thou shalt..govern the nations upon ear
67. 6 (Then) shall the earth yield her increase
67. 7 all the ends of the earth shall fear him
68. 8 The earth shook, the heavens also dropped
68. 32 Sing unto God, ye kingdoms of the earth
69. 34 Let the heaven and earth praise him
71. 20 up again from the depths of the earth
72. 6 come down..showers (that) water the e.
72. 8 from the river unto the ends of the earth
72. 16 shall be an handful of corn in the earth
72. 16 shall flourish like grass of the earth
72. 19 let the whole earth be filled (with) his
73. 9 their tongue walketh through the earth
73. 25 none upon earth..I desire beside thee
74. 12 working salvation in the midst of the e.
74. 17 Thou hast set all the borders of the earth
74. 20 the dark places of the earth are full of
75. 3 The earth and all the inhabitants thereof
75. 8 all the wicked of the earth shall wring
76. 8 the earth feared, and was still
76. 9 God arose..to save all the meek of the e.
76. 12 (he is) terrible to the kings of the earth
77. 18 thunder (was) in the heaven..the earth
78. 69 like the earth which he hath established
79. 2 of thy saints unto the beasts of the earth
82. 5 all the foundations of the earth are out
82. 8 Arise, O God, judge the earth: for thou
83. 18 thou..(art) the Most High over all the e.
85. 11 Truth shall spring out of the earth; and
89. 11 The heavens (are) thine, the earth also
89. 27 make him..higher than the kings of the e.
90. 2 or ever thou hadst formed the earth and
94. 2 Lift up thyself, thou judge of the earth
95. 4 In his hand..the deep places of the earth
96. 1 sing unto the LORD, all the earth
96. 9 fear before him, all the earth
96. 11 Let the heavens rejoice..let the earth
96. 13 he cometh..he cometh to judge the earth
97. 1 The LORD reigneth; let the earth rejoice
97. 4 His lightnings..the earth saw, and trem.
97. 5 presence of the Lord of the whole arth
97. 9 thou, LORD (art) high above all the earth
98. 3 all the ends of the earth have seen the
98. 4 Make a joyful noise..all the earth
98. 9 LORD; for he cometh to judge the earth
99. 1 let the people tremble..let the earth be

Psa. 102. 15 and all the kings of the earth thy glory
102. 19 from heaven did the LORD behold the e.
102. 25 hast thou laid the foundation of the earth
103. 11 as the heaven is high above the earth
104. 5 (Who) laid the foundations of the earth
104. 9 that they turn not again to cover the e.
104. 13 the earth is satisfied with the fruit of thy
104. 14 he may bring forth food out of the earth
104. 24 O LORD..the earth is full of thy riches
104. 32 He looketh on the earth, and it trembleth
104. 35 Let..sinners be consumed out of the ear.
105. 7 his judgments (are) in all the earth
106. 17 The earth opened and swallowed up D.
108. 5 Be thou exalted..above all the earth
109. 15 cut off the memory of them from the e.
112. 2 His seed shall be mighty upon earth
113. 6 things that are) in heaven and in the ear.
115. 15 of the LORD, which made heaven and ea.
115. 16 the earth hath he given to the children
119. 19 I (am) a stranger in the earth: hide not
119. 64 The earth O LORD, is full of thy mercy
119. 87 They had almost consumed me upon ea.
119. 90 hast established the earth, and it abide.
119. 119 puttest away all the wicked of the eart.
121. 2 the LORD, which made heaven and earth
124. 8 the LORD, who made heaven and earth
134. 3 The LORD that made heaven and earth
135. 6 (that) did he in heaven, and in earth, in
135. 7 to ascend from the ends of the earth
136. 6 him that stretched out the earth above
138. 4 the kings of the earth shall praise thee
139. 15 wrought in the lowest parts of the earth
140. 11 evil speaker be established in the earth
141. 7 cutteth and cleaveth (wood) upon the ea.
146. 6 Which made heaven, and earth, the sea
147. 8 who prepareth rain for the earth, who
147. 15 sendeth forth his commandment (upon) e.
148. 7 Praise the LORD from the earth, ye dra.
148. 11 Kings of the earth, and all people
148. 11 princes, and all judges of the earth
148. 13 his glory (is) above the earth and heaven
Prov. 2. 22 wicked shall be cut off from the earth
3. 19 The LORD by wisdom hath founded the e.
8. 16 nobles, (even) all the judges of the earth
8. 23 from the beginning, or ever the earth
8. 26 While as yet he had not made the earth
8. 29 appointed the foundations of the earth
8. 31 Rejoicing in..habitable part of his earth
10. 30 the wicked shall not inhabit the earth
11. 31 righteous..be recompensed in the earth
17. 24 eyes of a fool (are) in..ends of the earth
25. 3 heaven for height, and the earth for dep.
30. 4 established all the ends of the earth?
30. 14 to devour the poor from off the earth
30. 16 the earth (that) is not filled with water
30. 21 For three (things) the earth is disquieted
30. 24 (things which are) little upon the earth
Eccl. 1. 4 but the earth abideth for ever
3. 21 beast that goeth downward to the earth?
5. 2 for God (is) in heaven, and thou upon e.
5. 9 Moreover the profit of the earth is for
7. 20 (there is) not a just man upon earth
8. 14 a vanity which is done upon the earth
8. 16 the business that is done upon the earth
10. 7 princes walking as servants upon the ea.
11. 2 knowest not..evil shall be upon the ear.
11. 3 they empty (themselves) upon the earth
12. 7 the dust return to the earth as it was
Song 2. 12 The flowers appear on the earth; the
Isa. 1. 2 Hear, O heavens, and give ear, O earth
2. 19, 21 he ariseth to shake terribly the earth
4. 2 the fruit of the earth (shall be) excellent
5. 8 placed alone in the midst of the earth
5. 26 hiss unto them from the end of the earth
6. 3 the whole earth (is) full of his glory
8. 22 they shall look unto the earth; and be.
10. 14 have I gathered all the earth; and then
11. 4 with equity for the meek of the earth
11. 4 he shall smite the earth with the rod of
11. 9 the earth shall be full of the knowledge
11. 12 Judah from the four corners of the earth
12. 5 this (is) known in all the earth
13. 13 the earth shall remove out of her place
14. 7 The whole earth is at rest, (and) is quiet
14. 9 (even) all the chief ones of the earth
14. 16 the man that made the earth to tremble
14. 26 that is purposed upon the whole earth
18. 3 and dwellers on the earth, see ye, when
18. 6 and to the beasts of the earth
18. 6 beasts of the earth shall winter upon
23. 8 traffickers (are) the honourable of the ea.
23. 9 into contempt..the honourable of the e.
24. 1 the LORD maketh the earth empty, and
24. 4 The earth mourneth (and) fadeth away
24. 4 haughty people of the earth do languish
24. 5 The earth also is defiled under the
24. 6 hath the curse devoured the earth
24. 6 the inhabitants of the earth are burned
24. 16 From the uttermost part of the earth
24. 17 (are) upon thee, O inhabitant of the ear.
24. 18 and the foundations of the earth do
24. 19 earth is utterly broken down, the earth
24. 19 the earth is moved exceedingly
24. 20 The earth shall reel to and fro like a
25. 8 shall he take away from off all the earth
26. 9 when thy judgments (are) in the earth
26. 15 far (unto) all the ends of the earth
26. 18 not wrought any deliverance in the earth
26. 19 and the earth shall cast out the dead
26. 21 to punish the inhabitants of the earth
26. 21 the earth also shall disclose her blood
28. 2 shall cast down to the earth with the ha.

Isa. 28. 22 even determined upon the whole earth
33. 9 The earth mourneth (and) languisheth
34. 1 let the earth hear, and all that is therein
37. 16 alone, of all the kingdoms of the earth
37. 16 thou hast made heaven and earth
37. 20 that all the kingdoms of the earth may
40. 12 comprehended the dust of the earth in a
40. 21 understood from..foundations of the ea.
40. 22 that sitteth upon the circle of the earth
40. 23 maketh the judges of the earth as vanity
40. 24 stock shall not take root in the earth
40. 28 the Creator of the ends of the earth
41. 5 the ends of the earth were afraid, drew
41. 9 I have taken from the ends of the earth
42. 4 till he have set judgment in the earth
42. 5 God..he that spread forth the earth
42. 10 Sing..his praise from the end of the earth
43. 6 my daughters from the ends of the earth
44. 23 shout, ye lower parts of the earth: break
44. 24 that spreadeth abroad the earth by myself
45. 8 let the earth open, and let them bring
45. 12 I have made the earth, and created man
45. 18 God himself that formed the earth and
45. 19 not spoken..in a dark place of the earth
45. 22 be ye saved, all the ends of the earth
48. 13 also hath laid the foundation of the earth
48. 20 utter it (even) to the end of the earth
49. 6 be my salvation unto the end of the earth
49. 8 to establish the earth, to cause to inherit
49. 13 Sing, O heavens; and be joyful, O earth
49. 23 they shall bow down..toward the earth
51. 6 Lift up your eyes..look upon the earth
51. 6 the earth shall wax old like a garment
51. 13 and laid the foundations of the earth
51. 16 and lay the foundations of the earth
52. 10 all the ends of the earth shall see the
54. 5 God of the whole earth shall he be called
54. 9 waters..should no more go over the earth
55. 9 the heavens are higher than the earth
55. 10 but watereth the earth, and maketh it
58. 14 to ride upon the high places of the earth
60. 2 darkness shall cover the earth, and gross
61. 11 For as the earth bringeth forth her bud
62. 7 till he made Jerusa. a praise in the earth
63. 6 will bring down their strength to the e.
65. 16 he who blesseth himself in the earth
65. 16 and he that sweareth in the earth shall
65. 17 I create new heavens and a new earth
66. 1 heaven (is) my throne, and the earth (is)
66. 8 Shall the earth be made to bring forth
66. 22 For as the new heavens and the new earth
Jer. 6. 19 Hear, O earth: behold, I will bring evil
6. 22 shall be raised from the sides of the earth
7. 33 shall be meat..for the beasts of the earth
9. 3 not valiant for the truth upon the earth
9. 24 judgment, and righteousness, in the earth
10. 10 at his wrath the earth shall tremble
10. 12 He hath made the earth by his power
10. 13 to ascend from the ends of the earth
14. 4 for there was no rain in the earth
15. 3 the beasts of the earth, to devour and
15. 4 removed into all kingdoms of the earth
15. 10 a man of contention to the whole earth
16. 4 shall be meat for....beasts of the earth
16. 19 come unto thee from the ends of the earth
17. 13 depart from me shall be written in the e.
19. 7 to be meat for..the beasts of the earth
22. 29 O earth, earth, earth, hear the word of
23. 5 execute judgment and justice in the earth
23. 24 Do not I fill heaven and earth? saith the
24. 9 into all the kingdoms of the earth for
25. 29 upon all the inhabitants of the earth
25. 30 against all the inhabitants of the earth
25. 31 shall come (even) to the ends of the earth
25. 32 be raised up from the coasts of the earth
25. 33 end of the earth..unto..end of the earth
26. 6 a curse to all the nations of the earth
27. 5 I have made the earth, the man, and the
29. 18 removed to all the kingdoms of the earth
31. 22 hath created a new thing in the earth
31. 37 the foundations of the earth searched out
32. 17 thou hast made the heaven and the earth
33. 9 honour before all the nations of the earth
33. 25 the ordinances of heaven and earth
34. 1 all the kingdoms of the earth of his dom.
34. 17 removed into all the kingdoms of the ea.
34. 20 for meat..to the beasts of the earth
46. 8 I will go up, (and) will cover the earth
49. 21 The earth is moved at the noise of their
50. 23 How is the hammer of the whole earth
50. 41 be raised up from the coasts of the earth
50. 46 the earth is moved, and the cry is heard
51. 7 a golden cup..that made all the earth
51. 15 He hath made the earth by his power
51. 16 to ascend from the ends of the earth
51. 25 mountain..which destroyest all the earth
51. 41 how is the praise of the whole earth sur.!
51. 48 Then the heaven and the earth, and all
51. 49 so..shall fall the slain of all the earth
Lam. 2. 1 cast down from heaven unto the earth the
2. 11 my liver is poured upon the earth
2. 15 (Is) this..the joy of the whole earth?
3. 34 To crush..all the prisoners of the earth
4. 12 The kings of the earth, and all the
Eze. 1. 15 one wheel upon the earth by the living
1. 19 creatures were lifted up from the earth
1. 21 when those were lifted up from the earth
7. 21 to the wicked of the earth for a spoil
8. 3 the spirit lifted me up between the earth
8. 12 say..the LORD hath forsaken the earth
9. 9 The LORD hath forsaken the earth
10. 16 their wings to mount up from the earth

Eze. 10. 19 cherubims..mounted, up from the earth
26. 20 shall set thee in the low parts of the earth
27. 33 thou didst enrich the kings of the earth
28. 18 I will bring thee to ashes upon the earth
31. 14 death, to the nether parts of the earth
31. 16 comforted in the nether parts of the earth
31. 18 unto the nether parts of the earth
32. 4 I will fill the beasts of the whole earth
32. 18 cast..unto the nether parts of the earth
32. 24 gone..into the nether parts of the earth
34. 6 was scattered upon all the face of the e.
34. 27 and the earth shall yield her increase
35. 14 When the whole earth rejoiceth, I will
39. 14 that remain upon the face of the earth
39. 18 drink the blood of the princes of the earth
Dan. 8. 5 from the west on the face of the whole e.
Hos. 2. 21 the heavens, and they shall hear the earth
2. 22 the earth shall hear the corn, and the
2. 23 I will sow her unto me in the earth
6. 3 the latter (and) former rain unto the ea.
Joel 2. 30 wonders in the heavens and in the earth
3. 16 the heavens and the earth shall shake
Amos 2. 7 That pant after the dust of the earth on
3. 5 Can a bird fall in a snare upon the earth
4. 13 treadeth upon the high places of the ea.
5. 7 and leave off righteousness in the earth
5. 8 and poureth them out upon..the earth
8. 9 I will darken the earth in the clear day
9. 6 and hath founded his troop in the earth
9. 6 and poureth them out upon..the earth
9. 9 shall not the least grain fall upon the ea.
Jon. 2. 6 the earth with her bars (was) about me
Mic. 4. 13 substance unto the Lord of the..earth
5. 4 he be great unto the ends of the earth
6. 2 Hear ye..strong foundations of the earth
7. 2 The good..is perished out of the earth
7. 17 out of their holes like worms of the earth
Nah. 1. 5 and the earth is burned at his presence
2. 13 I will cut off thy prey from the earth
Hab. 2. 14 the earth shall be filled with the know.
2. 20 let all the earth keep silence before him
3. 3 and the earth was full of his praise
3. 6 He stood, and measured the earth
3. 9 Thou didst cleave the earth with rivers
Zeph. 2. 3 Seek ye the LORD, all ye meek of the earth
2. 11 he will famish all the gods of the earth
3. 8 all the earth shall be devoured with the
3. 20 a praise among all people of the earth
Hag. 1. 10 and the earth is stayed (from) her fruit
2. 6, 21 I will shake the heavens, and the earth
Zech. 1. 10 sent to walk to and fro through the earth
1. 11 have walked to and fro through the earth
1. 11 all the earth sitteth still, and is at rest
4. 10 run to and fro through the whole earth
4. 14 that stand by the Lord of the whole earth
5. 3 the curse that goeth forth over the..earth
5. 6 their resemblance through all the earth
5. 9 lifted up the ephah between the earth
6. 5 standing before the Lord of all the earth
6. 7 might walk to and fro through the earth
6. 7 walk to and fro through the earth
6. 7 they walked to and fro through the earth
9. 10 from the river..to the ends of the earth
12. 1 and layeth the foundation of the earth
12. 3 though all the people of the earth be
14. 9 the LORD shall be king over all the earth
14. 17 come up of (all) the families of the earth
Mal. 4. 6 I come and smite the earth with a curse

4. *Earth, land,* אַרְקָא *arqa.*
Jer. 10. 11 The gods that have not made the..earth

5. *Earthen ware,* חֶרֶשׂ *cheres.*
Lev. 15. 12 the vessel of earth, that he toucheth

6. *Dry land,* יַבָּשֶׁת *yabbesheth.*
Dan. 2. 10 There is not a man upon the earth that

7. *Dust,* עָפָר *aphar.*
Gen. 26. 15 Philistines had..filled them with earth
Job 8. 19 and out of the earth shall others grow
19. 25 stand at the latter (day) upon the earth
28. 2 Iron is taken out of the earth, and brass
30. 6 To dwell..(in) caves of the earth, and (in)
41. 33 Upon earth there is not his like, who is
Isa. 2. 19 they shall go into..caves of the earth
Dan. 12. 2 them that sleep in the dust of the earth

8. *Earth, land,* γῆ *gē.*
Matt. 5. 5 the meek: for they shall inherit the earth
5. 13 Ye are the salt of the earth: but if the
5. 18 Till heaven and earth pass, one jot or
5. 35 Nor by the earth; for it is his footstool
6. 10 thy will be done in earth, as (it is) in hea.
6. 19 Lay not up..treasures upon earth, where
9. 6 that the Son of man hath power on earth
10. 34 that I am come to send peace on earth
11. 25 Father, Lord of heaven and earth, because
12. 40 and three nights in the heart of the earth
12. 42 from the uttermost parts of the earth
13. 5 fell..where they had not much earth
13. 5 because they had no deepness of earth
16. 19 whatsoever thou shalt bind on earth
16. 19 whatsoever thou shalt loose on earth
17. 25 of whom do the kings of the earth take
18. 18 Whatsoever ye shall bind on earth shall
18. 18 whatsoever ye shall loose on earth shall
18. 19 That if two of you shall agree on earth
23. 9 call no (man) your father upon the earth
23. 35 the righteous blood shed upon the earth
24. 30 then shall all the tribes of the earth mo.
24. 35 Heaven and earth shall pass away, but
25. 18 he..went and digged in the earth, and
Matt 25. 25 I..went and hid thy talent in the earth
27. 51 the earth did quake, and the rocks rent
28. 18 All power is given unto me in..earth
Mark 2. 10 the Son of man hath power on earth to
4. 5 fell..where it had not much earth
4. 5 because it had no depth of earth
4. 28 the earth bringeth forth fruit of herself
4. 31 when it is sown in the earth, is less
4. 31 than all the seeds that be in the earth
9. 3 so as no fuller on earth can white them
13. 27 from the uttermost part of the earth to
13. 31 Heaven and earth shall pass away: but
Luke 2. 14 and on earth peace, good will toward
5. 24 hath power upon earth to forgive sins
6. 49 man that..built an house upon the earth
10. 21 O Father, Lord of heaven and earth
11. 2 Thy will be done, as in heaven, so in earth
11. 31 came from the uttermost parts of the e.
12. 49 I am come to send fire on the earth
12. 51 that I am come to give peace on earth?
12. 56 the face of the sky and of the earth
16. 17 it is easier for heaven and earth to pass
18. 8 shall he find faith on the earth?
21. 25 upon the earth distress of nations, with
21. 33 Heaven and earth shall pass away: but
21. 35 that dwell on the face of the whole earth
23. 44 there was a darkness over all the earth
24. 5 and bowed down (their) faces to the earth
John 3. 31 he that is of the earth is earthly
3. 31 and speaketh of the earth
12. 32 I, if I be lifted up from the earth, will
17. 4 I have glorified thee on the earth: I have
Acts 1. 8 and unto the uttermost part of the earth
2. 19 I will show..signs in the earth beneath
3. 25 all the kindreds of the earth be blessed
4. 24 which hast made heaven and earth, and
4. 26 The kings of the earth stood up, and the
7. 49 Heaven (is) my throne, and earth..my foot.
8. 33 for his life is taken from the earth
9. 4 he fell to the earth, and heard a voice
9. 8 Saul arose from the earth; and when his
10. 11 a great sheet..let down to the earth
10. 12 all manner of four footed beasts of..ea.
11. 6 I..saw four footed beasts of the earth
13. 47 for salvation unto the ends of the earth
14. 15 which made heaven, and earth, and the
17. 24 seeing that he is Lord of heaven and earth
17. 26 for to dwell on all the face of the earth
22. 22 Away with such a (fellow) from the earth
26. 14 when we were all fallen to the earth, I
Rom. 9. 17 might be declared throughout all the e.
9. 28 will the Lord make upon the earth
10. 18 their sound went into all the earth, and
1 Co. 8. 5 called gods, whether in heaven or in earth
10. 26, 28 The earth (is) the Lord's, and the ful.
15. 47 The first man (is) of the earth, earthy
Eph. 1. 10 are in heaven, and which are on earth
3. 15 whole family in heaven and earth is
4. 9 first into the lower parts of the earth
6. 3 and thou mayest live long on the earth
Col. 1. 16 that are in heaven, and that are in earth
1. 20 whether (they be) things in earth, or
3. 2 things above, not on things on the earth
3. 5 your members which are upon the earth
Heb. 1. 10 hast laid the foundation of the earth
6. 7 the earth which drinketh in the rain
8. 4 For if he were on earth he should not be
11. 13 were strangers and pilgrims on the earth
11. 38 and (in) dens and caves of the earth
12. 25 who refused him that spake on earth
12. 26 Whose voice then shook the earth: but
12. 26 shake not the earth only, but also heaven
Jas. 5. 5 Ye have lived in pleasure on the earth
5. 7 for the precious fruit of the earth
5. 12 neither by heaven, neither by the earth
5. 17 it rained not on the earth by the space
5. 18 and the earth brought forth her fruit
2 Pe. 3. 5 the earth standing out of the water and
3. 7 the heavens and the earth which are now
3. 10 the earth also and the works that are
3. 13 look for new heavens and a new earth
1 Jo. 5. 8 there are three that bear witness in earth
Rev. 1. 5 and the prince of the kings of the earth
1. 7 kindreds of the earth shall wail because
3. 10 to try them that dwell upon the earth
5. 3 nor in earth, neither under the earth
5. 6 spirits of God sent..into all the earth
5. 10 and we shall reign on the earth
5. 13 on the earth, and under the earth, and
6. 4 sat thereon to take peace from the earth
6. 8 power..over the fourth part of the earth
6. 8 death, and with the beasts of the earth
6. 10 our blood on them that dwell on the earth
6. 13 stars of heaven fell unto the earth
6. 15 the kings of the earth, and the great men
7. 1 standing on the four corners of the earth
7. 1 holding the four winds of the earth, that
7. 1 the wind should not blow on the earth
7. 2 was given to hurt the earth and the sea
7. 3 Hurt, not the earth, neither the sea, nor
8. 5 the censer..and cast (it) into the earth
8. 7 and they were cast upon the earth
8. 13 woe, woe to the inhabiters of the earth
9. 1 a star fall from heaven unto the earth
9. 3 there came out..locusts upon the earth
9. 3 as the scorpions of the earth have power
9. 4 should not hurt the grass of the earth
10. 2 and he set..(his) left (foot) on the earth
10. 5 stand upon the sea and upon the earth
10. 6 the earth, and the things that therein are
10. 8 standeth upon the sea and upon the earth
11. 4 standing before the God of the earth
Rev. 11. 6 to smite the earth with all plagues, as
11. 10 they that dwell upon the earth shall rejo.
11. 10 tormented them that dwelt on the earth
11. 18 destroy them which destroy the earth
12. 4 his tail..did cast them to the earth
12. 9 he was cast out into the earth, and his
12. 12 Woe to the inhabiters of the earth and
12. 13 dragon saw that he was cast unto the ea.
12. 16 the earth helped the woman, and the ea.
13. 8 all that dwell upon the earth shall wor.
13. 11 another beast coming up out of the earth
13. 12 and causeth the earth and them which
13. 13 maketh fire come down..on the earth
13. 14, 14 deceive. them that dwell on the earth
14. 3 which were redeemed from the earth
14. 6 preach unto them that dwell on the ear.
14. 7 worship him that made heaven, and earth
14. 15 for the harvest of the earth is ripe
14. 16 on the earth; and the earth was reaped
14. 18 gather the clusters of the vine of the ea.
14. 19 angel thrust in his sickle into the earth
14. 19 and gathered the vine of the earth, and
16. 1 vials of the wrath of God upon the earth
16. 2 and poured out his vial upon the earth
16. 14 go forth unto the kings of the earth and
16. 18 as was not since men were upon the earth
17. 2 With whom the kings of the earth have
17. 2 and the inhabitants of the earth have
17. 5 of harlots and abominations of the earth
17. 8 they that dwell on the earth shall won.
17. 18 which reigneth over the kings of the ear
18. 1 and the earth was lightened with his
18. 3 the kings of the earth have committed
18. 3 the merchants of the earth are waxed
18. 9 And the kings of the earth, who have
18. 11 And the merchants of the earth shall
18. 23 merchants were the great men of the ea.
18. 24 and of all that were slain upon the earth
19. 2 which did corrupt the earth with her
19. 19 I saw the beast, and the kings of the ea.
20. 8 are in the four quarters of the earth
20. 9 they went up on the breadth of the earth
20. 11 from whose face the earth and the heaven
21. 1 I saw a new heaven and a new earth
21. 1 for the first heaven and the first earth
21. 24 the kings of the earth do bring their

9. *Inhabited earth or land,* οἰκουμένη *oikoumenē*
Luke 21. 26 things which are coming on the earth

EARTH, in —
On earth, terrestrial, ἐπίγειος *epigeios.*
Phil. 2. 10 of (things) in heaven, and (things) in earth

EARTH, of —
Made of earthenware, ὀστράκινος *ostrakinos.*
2 Ti. 2. 20 but also of wood and of earth; and some

EARTH, under the —
Under ground, καταχθόνιος *katachthonios.*
Phil. 2. 10 in heaven..and (things) under the earth

EARTHEN —
1. *Earthen ware,* חֶרֶשׂ *cheres.*
Lev. 6. 28 the earthen vessel wherein it is sodden
11. 33 every earthen vessel, whereinto (any) of
14. 5 the birds be killed in an earthen vessel
14. 50 shall kill the one of the birds in an earth.
Num. 5. 17 shall take holy water in an earthen vessel
Jer. 19. 1 Go and get a potter's earthen bottle
32. 14 put them in an earthen vessel that they
Lam. 4. 2 how are they esteemed as earthen pitch.

2. *Made of earthen ware,* ὀστράκινος *ostrakinos.*
2 Co. 4. 7 we have this treasure in earthen vessels

3. *To form, fashion, frame,* יָצַר *yatsar.*
2 Sa. 17. 28 Brought beds, and basons, and earthen

EARTHLY —
1. *Out of the earth,* ἐκ τῆς γῆς *ek tēs gēs.*
John 3. 31 he that is of the earth is earthly, and

2. *Upon earth,* ἐπίγειος *epigeios.*
2 Co. 5. 1 For we know that if our earthly house
Jas. 3. 15 descendeth not from above, but (is) ear.

EARTHLY things —
Upon earth, ἐπίγειος *epigeios.*
John 3. 12 If I have told you earthly things, and ye
Phil. 3. 19 in their shame, who mind earthly things

EARTHQUAKE —
1. *Shaking, trembling,* רַעַשׁ *raash.*
1 Ki. 19. 11 and after the wind an earthquake
19. 11 the LORD (was) not in the earthquake
19. 12 And after the earthquake a fire
Isa. 29 6. with earthquake, and great noise, with
Amos 1. 1 he saw..two years before the earthquake
Zech. 14. 5 as ye fled from before the earthquake in

2. *A shaking,* σεισμός *seismos.*
Matt 24. 7 there shall be famines..and earthquakes
27. 54 when the centurion..saw the earthquake
28. 2 behold, there was a great earthquake
Mark 13. 8 there shall be earthquakes in divers pla.
Luke 21. 11 great earthquakes shall be in divers
Acts 16. 26 suddenly there was a great earthquake
Rev. 6. 12 and, lo, there was a great earthquake
8. 5 voices..and lightnings, and an earthqu.
11. 13 the same hour was there a great earthqu
11. 13 and in the earthquake were slain of men
11. 19 voices, and thunderings, and an earthqu.
16. 18 there was a great earthquake, such as
16. 18 so mighty an earthquake (and) so great

EARTHY —
Made of earth or clay, χοϊκός *choikos.*
1 Co. 15. 47 The first man (is) of the earth, earthy
15. 48 the earthy, such (are) they also that are e.
15. 49 as we have borne the image of the earthy

EASE —
Place of rest, ease, מְנוּחָה *menuchah.*
Judg 20. 43 trode them down with ease over against

EASE, to —
1. *To lift up,* נָשָׂא *nasa.*
Job 7. 13 bed shall comfort me, my couch shall ease
2. *To make light,* קָלַל *qalal,* 5.
2 Ch. 10. 4 ease thou somewhat the grievous servi.
10. 9 Ease somewhat the yoke that thy father

EASE, at —
1. *Good,* טוֹב *tob.*
Psa. 25. 13 His soul shall dwell at ease; and his seed
2. *Rest, quiet, safe, secure,* שָׁלֵו, שְׁלֵיו *shalev.*
Job 16. 12 I was at ease, but he hath broken me

EASE, to be at —
To be quiet, at ease, secure, שָׁאַן *shaan,* 3a.
Jer. 46. 27 be in rest and at ease, and none shall
48. 11 Moab hath been at ease from his youth

EASE, being at —
1. *Safe, at ease,* שָׁלֵו *shalev.*
Eze. 23. 42 voice of a multitude being at ease (was)
2. *Quick, at ease, secure,* שַׁלְאֲנָן *shalanan.*
Job 21. 23 in his full strength, being wholly at ease

EASE, to find —
To cause, give, or let rest, רָגַע *raga,* 5.
Deut 28. 65 among these nations..thou find no ease

EASE, to take —
To cause to cease, ἀναπαύω *anapauō.*
Luke 12. 19 take thine ease, eat, drink, (and) be merry

EASE (one's self), to —
To be comforted, get breath again, נָחַם *nacham,* 2.
Isa. 1. 24 I will ease me of mine adversaries, and

EASE self, to —
To sit down, יָשַׁב *yashab.*
Deut 23. 13 when thou wilt ease thyself abroad, thou

EASE, (that is) at —
Ease, quiet, at rest, שַׁאֲנָן *shaanan.*
Job 12. 5 in the thought of him that is at ease
Psa. 123. 4 the scorning of those that are at ease
Isa. 32. 9 Rise up, ye women that are at ease; hear
32. 11 Tremble, ye women that are at ease
Amos 6. 1 Woe to them (that are) at ease in Zion
Zech. 1. 15 displeased with..heathen (that are) at e.

EASED, to be —
1. *To go from,* הָלַךְ מִן *halak min.*
Job 16. 6 and (though) I forbear, what am I eased?
2. *A sending back, release,* ἄνεσις *anesis.*
2 Co. 8. 13 that other men be eased, and ye burdened

EASIER —
Less wearisome or laborious, εὐκοπώτερος *eukopō.*
Matt. 9. 5 For whether is easier to say, (Thy) sins be
19. 24 It is easier for a camel to go through
Mark 2. 9 Whether is it easier to say to the sick
10. 25 It is easier for a camel to go through
Luke 5. 23 Whether is easier, to say, Thy sins be
16. 17 it is easier for heaven and earth to pass
18. 25 it is easier for a camel to go through a

EASIER, to be —
To make light, קָלַל *qalal,* 5.
Exod 18. 22 so shall it be easier for thyself, and they

EAST —
1. *Pottery,* חַרְסִית, [V.L. הַרְסוּת], *charsith.*
Jer. 19. 2 which (is) by the entry of the east gate
2. *Outgoing (of the sun),* מוֹצָא *motsa.*
Psa. 75. 6 promotion (cometh) neither from the east
3. *Rising (of the sun),* מִזְרָח *mizrach.*
Josh. 4. 19 in Gilgal; in the east border of Jericho
11. 3 the Canaanite on the east and on the w.
12. 1 Hermon, and all the plain on the east
12. 3 to the sea of Chinneroth on the east
12. 3 (even) the salt sea on the east, the way
16. 1 unto the water of Jericho on the east, to
[16. 5 of their inheritance on the east side]
16. 6 and passed by it on the east to Janohah
17. 10 on the north, and in Issachar on the east
18. 7 inheritance beyond Jordan on the east
19. 13 on along on the east to Gittah-hepher
1 Ki. 7. 25 and three looking toward the east
1 Ch. 5. 10 throughout all the east (land) of Gilead
9. 24 toward the east, west, north, and south
12. 15 toward the east, and toward the west
2 Ch. 4. 4 and three looking toward the east
5. 12 stood at the east end of the altar, and
29. 4 gathered them together into the east
31. 14 porter toward the east, (was) over the
Neh. 3. 26 against the water gate toward the east
3. 29 of Shechaniah, the keeper of the east gate
Psa. 103. 12 As far as the east is from the west, (so) far
107. 3 from the east, and from the west, from
Isa. 41. 2 raised up the righteous (man) from the e.
43. 5 I will bring thy seed from the east, and
46. 11 Calling a ravenous bird from the east
Jer. 31. 40 corner of the horse gate toward the east
Dan. 8. 9 toward the east, and toward the pleasant
11. 44 But tidings out of the east and out of the
Amos 8. 12 from the north even to the east, they shall
Zech. 8. 7 will save my people from the east country
14. 4 in the midst thereof toward the east
4. *East, what is before,* קָדִים *qadim.*
Exod 10. 13 brought an east wind..the east wind
14. 21 caused the sea to go (back) by a strong e.
Psa. 48. 7 Thou breakest the ships..with an east
Jer. 18. 17 I will scatter them as with an east wind
Eze. 17. 10 wither, when the east wind toucheth it?
19. 12 the east wind dried up her fruit; her
27. 26 east wind hath broken thee in the midst
40. 6 the gate which looketh toward the east
40. 22 of the gate that looketh toward the east
40. 23 over against the gate..toward the east
40. 32 into the inner court toward the east: and
40. 44 one at the side of the east gate (having)
41. 14 and of the separate place toward the east
42. 10 of the wall of the court toward the east
42. 12 directly before the wall toward the east
42. 15 the gate whose prospect (is) toward the e.
42. 16 He measured the east side with the me.
43. 1 (even) the gate that looketh toward the e.
43. 2 the glory..came from the way of the east
43. 4 the gate whose prospect (is) toward the e.
43. 17 and his stairs shall look toward the east
44. 1 sanctuary which looketh toward the east
45. 7 from the west border unto the east bor.
46. 1 inner court that looketh toward the east
46. 12 the gate that looketh toward the east
47. 1 front of the house (stood toward) the east
47. 18 the east side ye shall measure from Hau.
47. 18 from the border..And (this is) the east
48. 1 for these are his sides east (and) west
48. 2, 4, 5, 7, 8, 8, 23, 24, 25, 26, 27 from the east
48. 3, 6 from the east side even unto the west
48. 10 toward the east ten thousand in breadth
48. 16, 32 on the east side four thousand and five
48. 17 toward the east two hundred and fifty
48. 21 of the oblation toward the east border
Hos. 13. 15 an east wind shall come, the wind of the
Jon. 4. 8 that God prepared a vehement east wind
5. *East,* קֶדֶם *qedem.*
Gen. 3. 24 he placed at the east of the garden of E.
10. 30 goest unto Sephar a mount of the east
11. 2 as they journeyed from the east, that
12. 8 from thence unto a mountain on the east
12. 8 Beth-el on the west; and Hai on the east
13. 11 Lot journeyed east: and they separated
25. 6 and sent them away..unto the east coun.
29. 1 into the land of the people of the east
Num 23. 7 out of the mountains of the east, (saying)
Judg. 6. 3 the children of the east, even they came
6. 33 children of the east were gathered togeth.
7. 12 all the children of the east lay along in
8. 10 all the hosts of the children of the east
8. 11 them that dwelt in tents on the east of
1 Ki. 4. 30 the wisdom of all the children of the east
Job 1. 3 was the greatest of all the men of the ea.
Isa. 2. 6 because they be replenished from the ea.
11. 14 they shall spoil them of the east togeth.
Jer. 49. 28 Arise ye, go..and spoil the men of the e
Eze. 25. 4 I will deliver thee to the men of the east
25. 10 Unto the men of the east with the Amm
Zech 14. 4 which (is) before Jerusalem on the east
6. *East,* קֵדְמָה *qedem.*
Gen. 28. 14 and thou shalt spread abroad..to the east
Exod 27. 13 the breadth of the court on the east side
38. 13 And for the east side eastward fifty cubi.
Num. 3 38 encamp before the tabernacle toward the e.
34. 10 ye shall point out your east border from
35. 5 from without the city on the east side two
Josh. 15. 5 the east border (was) the salt sea, (even)
18. 20 Jordan was the border of it on the east
19. 13 from thence passeth on along on the east
Eze. 8. 16 the temple..and their faces toward the e.
8. 16 they worshipped the sun toward the east
45. 7 from the west..and from the east side
7. *East, eastward,* קִדְמָה *qidmah.*
Gen. 2. 14 that (is) it which goeth toward the east of
4. 16 dwelt in the land of Nod, on the east of E.
Eze. 39. 11 valley of the passengers on the east of the
8. *East, eastern,* קַדְמוֹן *qadmon.*
Eze. 47. 8 waters issue out toward the east country
9. *East, eastern,* קַדְמוֹנִי *qadmoni.*
Eze. 10. 19 stood at the door of the east gate of the
11. 1 brought me unto the east gate of the L.
47. 18 from the border unto the east sea
Joel 2. 20 with his face toward the east sea, and
10. *East, uprising (of the sun),* ἀνατολή *anatolē.*
Matt 2. 1 came wise men from the east to Jerus.
2. 2 we have seen his star in the east, and
2. 9 the star, which they saw in the east, went
8. 11 many shall come from the east and west
24. 27 as the lightening cometh out of the east
Luke 13. 29 they shall come from the east, and (from)
Rev. 7. 2 I saw another angel ascending from the e.
16. 12 the way of the kings of the east might
21. 13 On the east, three gates; on the north

EAST end or part —
The east, קֶדֶם *qedem.*
Lev. 1. 16 cast it beside the altar on the east part
Num 10. 5 camps that lie on the east parts shall
2 Ch. 4. 10 the sea on the right side of the east end

EAST side —
1. *Rising (of the sun),* (מִזְרַח־(שֶׁמֶשׁ *mizrach-(shemesh.)*
Judg 11. 18 came by the east side of the land of Moab
21. 19 on the east side of the highway; Josh. 16. 5.
1 Ch. 4. 39 unto the east side of the valley, to seek
6. 78 by Jericho, on the east side of Jordan
2. *East, what is before,* קָדִים *qadim.*
Eze. 42. 9 the entry on the east side, as one goeth
3. *East,* קֶדֶם *qedem.*
Num 34. 11 Shepham to Riblah, on the east side of
Josh. 7. 2 Beth-aven, on the east side of Beth-el
Eze. 11. 23 which (is) on the east side of the city
Jon. 4. 5 and sat on the east side of the city
4. *East,* קֶדֶם *qedem.*
Num. 2. 3 on the east side toward the rising of

EAST wind —
East (wind), קָדִים *qadim.*
Gen. 41. 6 thin ears and blasted with the east wind
41. 23 thin, (and) blasted with the east wind
41. 27 empty ears, blasted with the east wind
Job 15. 2 and fill his belly with the east wind?
27. 21 The east wind carrieth him away, and he
38. 24 scattereth the east wind upon the earth?
Psa. 78. 26 caused an east wind to blow in the heaven
Isa. 27. 8 rough wind in the day of the east wind
Hos. 12. 1 Ephraim..followeth after the east wind
Hab. 1. 9 their faces shall sup up (as) the east wind

EASTER —
Passover (from Heb. פֶּסַח *a passing over);* πάσχα.
Acts 12. 4 intending after Easter to bring him forth

EASTWARD —
1. *Rising (of the sun),* מִזְרָח *mizrach.*
Exod 27. 13 the court on the east side eastward
38. 13 for the east side eastward fifty cubits
Num. 3. 38 tabernacle of the congregation eastward
32. 19 fallen to us on this side Jordan eastward
Deut. 3. 17 the salt sea, under Ashdoth-pisgah eastw.
3. 27 northward, and southward, and eastward
4. 49 the plain on this side Jordan eastward
Josh. 11. 8 and unto the valley of Mizpeh eastward
13. 8 Moses gave them, beyond Jordan eastw.
13. 27 on the other side Jordan eastward
13. 32 the other side Jordan, by Jericho, eastw.
16. 6 went about eastward unto Taanath-shiloh
20. 8 the other side Jordan by Jericho eastw.
2 Ki. 10. 33 Jordan eastward [Heb. *mizrach shemesh*].
1 Ch. 5. 9 eastward he inhabited unto the entering
7. 28 eastward Naaran, and westward Gezer
9. 18 hitherto (waited) in the king's gate eastw.
26. 14 And the lot eastward fell to Shelemiah
26. 17 Eastward (were) six Levites, northward
Neh. 12. 37 even unto the water gate eastward
2. *East, eastward,* קָדִים *qadim.*
Eze. 11. 1 the east gate..which looketh eastward
40. 19 an hundred cubits eastward and north.
45. 7 westward, and from the east side eastw.
47. 1 under the threshold of the house eastw.
47. 2 gate by the way that looketh eastward
47. 3 the line in his hand went forth eastward
48. 18 (portion shall be) ten thousand eastward
3. *East, eastward,* קֶדֶם *qedem.*
Gen. 2. 8 God planted a garden eastward in Eden
4. *East, eastward,* קֵדְמָה *qedem.*
Gen. 13. 14 art northward, and southward, and eastw.
25. 6 sent them away from Isaac..eastward
Lev. 16. 14 his finger upon the mercy seat eastward
Num 34. 3 outmost coast of the salt sea eastward
34. 11 side of the sea of Chinnereth eastward
34. 15 on this side Jordan (near) Jericho eastw.
Josh. 19. 12; 1 Ki. 7. 39, 17. 3; 2 Ki. 13. 17.
5. *The east,* קִדְמָה *qidmah.*
1 Sa. 13. 5 in Michmash, eastward from Beth-aven
6. *The way of the east,* דֶּרֶךְ הַקָּדִים *derek haq-qadim.*
Eze. 40. 10 the little chambers of the gate eastward

EASY —
Useful, good, kind, χρηστός *chrēstos.*
Matt 11. 30 my yoke (is) easy, and my burden is light

EASY, to be —
To be light, קָלַל *qalal,* 2.
Prov. 14. 6 knowledge (is) easy unto him that under

EAT, to —
1. *To eat,* אָכַל *akal.*
Gen. 2. 16 Of every tree..thou mayest freely eat
2. 17 But of the tree..thou shalt not eat of it
2. 17 in the day that thou eatest thereof thou
3. 1 shall not eat of every tree of the garden?
3. 2 We may eat of the fruit of the trees of
3. 3 Ye shall not eat of it, neither shall ye
3. 5 God doth know that in the day ye eat
3. 6 she took of the fruit thereof, and did eat
3. 6 gave..unto her husband..and he did eat
3. 11 Hast thou eaten of the tree, whereof
3. 11 commanded..that thou shouldest not e.?
3. 12 she gave me of the tree, and I did eat
3. 13 The serpent beguiled me, and I did eat
3. 14 dust shalt thou eat all the days of thy
3. 17 Because thou hast..eaten of the tree, of
3. 17 Thou shalt not eat of it: cursed (is) the
3. 17 shalt thou eat (of) it all the days of thy
3. 18 and thou shalt eat the herb of the field
3. 19 In the sweat of thy face shalt thou eat
3. 22 take also..and eat, and live for ever
9. 4 flesh with the life..shall ye not eat

Gen. 14. 24 only that which the young men have ea.
18. 8 stood..under the tree, and they did eat
19. 3 bake unleavened bread, and they did eat
24. 33 And there was set (meat) before him to eat
24. 33 I will not eat, until I have told mine
24. 54 they did eat and drink, he and the men
25. 34 he did eat and drink, and rose up, and
26. 30 he made them a feast, and they did eat
27. 4 and bring (it) to me, that I may eat
27. 7 make me savoury meat, that I may eat
27. 10 bring (it) to thy father, that he may eat
27. 19 arise, I pray thee, sit and eat of my veni.
27. 25 Bring (it) near to me, and I will eat of
27. 25 he brought (it) near to him, and he did e.
27. 31 Let my father arise, and eat of his son's
27. 33 I have eaten of all before thou camest
28. 20 and will give me bread to eat, and raim.
31. 38 the rams of thy flock have I not eaten
31. 46 and they did eat there upon the heap
31. 54 Jacob..called his brethren to eat bread
31. 54 they did eat bread, and tarried all night
32. 32 the children of Israel eat not (of) the
37. 25 And they sat down to eat bread: and
39. 6 ought..save the bread which he did eat
40. 17 the birds did eat them out of the basket
40. 19 the birds shall eat thy flesh from off thee
43. 2 when they had eaten up the corn which
43. 25 they heard that they should eat bread
43. 32 for the Egyptians which did eat with
43. 32 because the Egyptians might not eat br.
45. 18 and ye shall eat the fat of the land
47. 22 for the priests..did eat their portion
Exod. 2. 20 he said..call him, that he may eat bread
10. 5 they shall eat..and shall eat every tree
10. 12 and eat every herb of the land, (even) all
10. 15 and they did eat every herb of the land
12. 4 every man according to his eating shall
12. 7 the houses, wherein they shall eat it
12. 8 they shall eat the flesh in that night
12. 8 (and) with bitter (herbs) they shall eat
12. 9 Eat not of it raw, nor sodden at all with
12. 11 thus shall ye eat it; (with) your loins
12. 11 eat it in haste: it (is) the LORD's passov
12. 15 Seven days shall ye eat unleavened bread
12. 15 whosoever eateth leavened bread from
12. 18 ye shall eat unleavened bread, until the
12. 19 whosoever eateth that which is leavened
12. 20 Ye shall eat nothing leavened
12. 20 in all your habitations shall ye eat unle.
12. 43 There shall no stranger eat thereof
12. 44 hast circumcised him, then shall he eat
12. 45 an hired servant shall not eat thereof
12. 48 no uncircumcised person shall eat thereof
13. 6 Seven days thou shalt eat unleavened b
16. 3 when we did eat bread to the full! for ye
16. 8 shall give you in the evening flesh to eat
16. 12 At even ye shall eat flesh, and in the mo
16. 25 Eat that to day; for to day (is) a sabbath
16. 35 the children of Israel did eat manna forty
16. 35 they did eat manna, until they came unto
18. 12 Aaron came..to eat bread with Moses'
22. 31 neither shall ye eat (any) flesh (that is)
23. 11 that the poor of thy people may eat
23. 11 and what they leave the beasts..shall e.
23. 15 thou shalt eat unleavened bread seven d.
24. 11 also they saw God, and did eat and dri.
29. 32 Aaron and his sons shall eat the flesh of
29. 33 they shall eat those things wherewith
29. 33 a stranger shall not eat..because
32. 6 the people sat down to eat and to drink
34. 15 call thee, and thou eat of his sacrifice
34. 18 Seven days thou shalt eat unleavened
34. 28 he did neither eat bread, nor drink water
Lev. 3. 17 statute..that ye eat neither fat nor blood
6. 16 remainder..shall Aaron and his sons eat
6. 16 in the..congregation they shall eat it
6. 18 males among the children..shall eat of it
6. 26 The priest that offereth it..shall eat it
6. 29 All the males among the priests shall e.
7. 6 Every male among the priests shall eat
7. 18 the soul that eateth of it shall bear his
7. 19 as for the flesh, all that be clean shall e.
7. 20 the soul that eateth (of) the flesh of the
7. 21 eat of the flesh of the sacrifice of peace
7. 23 Ye shall eat no manner of fat, of ox, or
7. 24 be used..but ye shall in no wise eat of it
7. 25 For whosoever eateth the fat of the beast
7. 25 the soul that eateth (it) shall be cut off
7. 26 Moreover ye shall eat no manner of blood
7. 27 Whatsoever soul (it be) that eateth any
8. 31 there eat it with the bread that (is) in
8. 31 saying, Aaron and his sons shall eat it
10. 12 and eat it without leaven beside the
10. 13 And ye shall eat it in the holy place
10. 14 wave breast..shall ye eat in a clean place
10. 17 Wherefore have ye not eaten the sin off.
10. 18 ye should indeed have eaten it in the holy
10. 19 (if) I had eaten the sin offering to day
11. 2 These (are) the beasts which ye shall eat
11. 3 Whatsoever parteth the hoof..shall ye eat
11. 4 Nevertheless these shall ye not eat of them
11. 8 Of their flesh shall ye not eat, and their
11. 9 These shall ye eat of all that (are) in the
11. 9 whatsoever hath fins..them shall ye eat
11. 11 ye shall not eat of their flesh, but ye shall
11. 21 Yet these may ye eat of every flying cree.
11. 22 these of them ye may eat; the locust
11. 40 he that eateth of the carcase of it shall
11. 42 them ye shall not eat; for they (are) an
14. 47 he that eateth in the house shall wash his
17. 10 that eateth any manner of blood
17. 10 set my face against that soul that eateth

Lev. 17. 12 I said..No soul of you shall eat blood
17. 12 neither shall any stranger..eat blood
17. 14 Ye shall eat the blood of no manner of
17. 14 whosoever eateth it shall be cut off
17. 15 every soul that eateth that which died
19. 8 that eateth it shall bear his iniquity
19. 25 in the fifth year shall ye eat of the fruit
19. 26 Ye shall not eat (any thing) with the
21. 22 He shall eat the bread of his God
22. 4 he shall not eat of the holy things, until
22. 6 shall not eat of the holy things, unless
22. 7 he shall..afterward eat of the holy things
22. 8 he shall not eat to defile himself therewith
22. 10 There shall no stranger eat (of) the holy
22. 10 an hired servant, shall not eat (of) the
22. 11 if the priest buy..he shall eat of it
22. 11 he that is born in his house..shall eat of
22. 12 she may not eat of an offering of the holy
22. 13 she shall eat of her father's meat
22. 13 but there shall no stranger eat thereof
22. 14 if a man eat (of) the holy thing unwitt.
22. 16 when they eat their holy things: for I
23. 6 seven days ye must eat unleavened bread
23. 14 ye shall eat neither bread, nor parched
24. 9 and they shall eat it in the holy place
25. 12 ye shall eat the increase thereof out of
25. 19 ye shall eat your fill, and dwell therein
25. 20 What shall we eat the seventh year?
25. 22 eat (yet) of old fruit until the ninth year
25. 22 until her fruits come in ye shall eat (of)
26. 5 and ye shall eat your bread to the full
26. 10 ye shall eat old store, and bring forth the
26. 16 sow..in vain, for your enemies shall eat
26. 26 and ye shall eat, and not be satisfied
26. 29 And ye shall eat the flesh of your sons
26. 29 the flesh of your daughters shall ye eat
26. 38 the land of your enemies shall eat you up
Num. 6. 3 neither shall he..eat moist grapes, or
6. 4 shall he eat nothing that is made of the
9. 11 at even they shall keep it, (and) eat it with
11. 5 We remember the fish which we did eat
11. 13 saying, Give us flesh, that we may eat
11. 18 Sanctify yourselves..ye shall eat flesh
11. 18 LORD will give you flesh, and ye shall eat
11. 19 Ye shall not eat one day, nor two days
11. 21 I will give them flesh, that they may eat a
13. 32 a land that eateth up the inhabitants
15. 19 when ye eat of the bread of the land
18. 10 In the most holy..shalt thou eat it
18. 10 every male shall eat it: it shall be holy
18. 11, 13 that is clean in thy house shall eat
18. 31 And ye shall eat it in every place
23. 24 he shall not lie down until he eat (of) the
25. 2 the people did eat, and bowed down to
Deut. 2. 6 shall buy meat of them..that ye may eat
2. 28 sell me meat for money, that I may eat
4. 28 ye shall serve gods..which neither..eat
6. 11 when thou shalt have eaten, and be full
8. 9 A land wherein thou shalt eat bread
8. 10, 12 When thou hast eaten and art full
9. 9, 18 neither did eat bread nor drink water
11. 15 And I will send..that thou mayest eat
12. 7 there ye shall eat before the LORD your
12. 15 thou mayest kill and eat flesh in all thy
12. 15, 22 the unclean and the clean may eat
12. 16 Only ye shall not eat the blood; ye shall
12. 17 Thou mayest not eat within thy gates the
12. 18 thou must eat them before the LORD thy
12. 20 and thou shalt say, I will eat flesh
12. 20 because thy soul longeth to eat flesh
12. 20 thou mayest eat flesh, whatsoever thy
12. 21 thou shalt eat in thy gates whatsoever
12. 22 shalt eat them..the clean shall eat
12. 23 Only be sure that thou eat not the blood
12. 23 thou mayest not eat the life with the flesh
12. 24 Thou shalt not eat it; thou shalt pour it
12. 25 Thou shalt not eat it, that it may go
12. 27 thou shalt offer..and thou shalt eat the
14. 3 Thou shalt not eat any abominable thing
14. 4 These (are) the beasts which ye shall eat
14. 6 among the beasts, that ye shall eat
14. 7 shall not eat of them that chew the cud
14. 8 ye shall not eat of their flesh, nor touch
14. 9 shall eat of all that (are) in the waters
14. 9 that have fins and scales shall ye eat
14. 10 hath not fins and scales ye may not eat
14. 11 (Of) all clean birds ye shall eat
14. 12 these (are they) of which ye shall not eat
14. 20 (But of) all clean fowls ye may eat
14. 21 not eat (of) anything that dieth of itself
14. 21 unto the stranger..that he may eat it
14. 23 thou shalt eat before the LORD thy God
14. 26 shalt eat there before the LORD thy God
14. 29 shall come, and shall eat and be satisfied
15. 20 Thou shalt eat (it) before the LORD thy
15. 22 Thou shalt eat it within thy gates
15. 23 Only thou shalt not eat the blood thereof
16. 3 Thou shalt eat no leavened bread with
16. 3 seven days shalt thou eat unleavened
16. 7 thou shalt roast and eat (it) in the place
16. 8 Six days thou shalt eat unleavened bread
18. 1 they shall eat the offerings of the LORD
18. 8 They shall have like portions to eat
20. 14 thou shalt eat the spoil of thine enemies
20. 19 thou mayest eat of them, and thou shalt
23. 24 thou mayest eat grapes thy fill at
26. 12 may eat within thy gates, and be filled
26. 14 I have not eaten thereof in my mourning
27. 7 offer peace offerings, and shalt eat there
28. 31 Thine ox..thou shalt not eat thereof
28. 39 (the grapes); for the worms shall eat them
28. 51 he shall eat the fruit of thy cattle, and

Deut. 28. 53 thou shalt eat the fruit of thine own body
28. 55 flesh of his children whom he shall eat
28. 57 she shall eat them for want of all (things)
29. 6 Ye have not eaten bread, neither have ye
31. 20 shall have eaten and filled themselves
32. 13 he might eat the increase of the fields
32. 38 Which did eat the fat of their sacrifices
Josh. 5. 11 they did eat of the old corn of the land
5. 12 had eaten of the old corn of the land
5. 12 they did eat of the fruit of the land of
24. 13 oliveyards which ye planted not do ye eat
Judg. 9. 27 did eat and drink, and cursed Abimelech
13. 4 drink not wine..and eat not any unclean
13. 7 drink no wine..neither eat any unclean
13. 14 eat of any (thing) that cometh of the vine
13. 14 neither let her..eat any unclean (thing)
13. 16 Though thou detain me, I will not eat of
14. 9 took thereof in his hands..went on eating
14. 9 and he gave them, and they did eat
19. 4 they did eat and drink, and lodged there
19. 6 did eat and drink both of them together
19. 8 tarried until afternoon, and they did eat
19. 21 washed their feet, and did eat and drink
Ruth 2. 14 eat of the bread, and dip thy morsel in
2. 14 and she did eat, and was sufficed, and
3. 3 he shall have done eating and drinking
3. 7 when Boaz had eaten and drunk, and his
1 Sa. 1. 7 therefore she wept, and did not eat
1. 8 why weepest thou? and why eatest thou
1. 9 Hannah rose up after they had eaten in
1. 18 the woman went her way, and did eat
2. 36 that I may eat a piece of bread
9. 13 before he go up to the high place to eat
9. 13 for the people will not eat until he come
9. 13 (and) afterwards they eat that be bidden
9. 19 ye shall eat with me to day; and to morrow
9. 24 which is left! set (it) before thee, (and) eat
9. 24 So Saul did eat with Samuel that day
14. 24, 28 Cursed (be) the man that eateth (any)
14. 30 if haply the people had eaten freely
14. 32 the people did eat (them) with the blood
14. 33 in that they eat with the blood
14. 34 his sheep, and slay (them) here, and eat
14. 34 sin not against the LORD in eating with
20. 24 the king sat him down to eat meat
20. 34 did eat no meat the second day of the
28. 20 eaten no bread all the day, nor all the
28. 22 eat, that thou mayest have strength when
28. 23 But he refused, and said, I will not eat
28. 25 She brought (it)..and they did eat
30. 11 and gave him bread, and he did eat
30. 12 when he had eaten, his spirit came again
30. 12 he had eaten no bread, nor drunk (any)
30. 16 eating and drinking, and dancing, beca.
2 Sa. 9. 7 shalt eat bread at my table continually
9. 10 that thy master's son may have food to eat
9. 10 master's son shall eat bread alway at my
9. 11 eat at my table, as one of the king's sons
9. 13 he did eat continually at the king's table
11. 11 go into mine house, to eat and to drink
11. 13 when David had called him, he did eat
12. 3 it did eat of his own meat, and drank of
12. 20 they set bread before him, and he did eat
12. 21 child was dead, thou didst rise and eat
13. 5 that I may see (it), and eat (it) at her hand
13. 9 poured (them) out..but he refused to eat
13. 11 when she had brought..unto him to eat
16. 2 summer fruit for the young men to eat
17. 29 for the people that (were) with him, to eat
19. 28 them that did eat at thine own table
19. 35 can thy servant taste what I eat or what
19. 42 have we eaten at all of the king's (cost)?
1 Ki. 1. 25 they eat and drink before him, and say
1. 41 heard (it) as they had made an end of eat.
2. 7 let them be of those that eat at thy table
4. 20 eating and drinking, and making merry
13. 8, 16 neither will I eat bread nor drink
13. 9 Eat no bread, nor drink water, nor turn
13. 15 Come home with me, and eat bread
13. 17 Thou shalt eat no bread nor drink water
13. 18 Bring him back..that he may eat bread
13. 19 So he went back with him, and did eat
13. 22 But camest back, and hast eaten bread
13. 22 Eat no bread, and drink no water
13. 23 it came to pass, after he had eaten bread
13. 28 the lion had not eaten the carcase, nor
14. 11 dieth..in the city shall the dogs eat
14. 11 dieth in the field shall the fowls..eat
16. 4 dieth..in the city shall the dogs eat
16. 4 dieth..in the fields shall the fowls..eat
17. 12 of meal..that we may eat it, and die
17. 15 and she, and he, and her house, did eat
18. 19 the prophets..which eat at Jezebel's table
18. 41 Elijah said..Get thee up, eat and drink
18. 42 So Ahab went up to eat and to drink
19. 5 angel touched him, and said..Arise..eat
19. 6 he did eat and drink, and laid him down
19. 8 And he arose, and did eat and drink
19. 21 he..gave unto the people, and they did e.
21. 4 he..turned away..and would eat no bre.
21. 5 Why is thy spirit so sad, that thou eatest
21. 7 Arise..eat bread, and let thine heart be
21. 23 The dogs shall eat Jezebel by the wall of
21. 24 dieth..in the city the dogs shall eat
21. 24 dieth in the field shall the fowls..eat
2 Ki. 4. 8 and she constrained him to eat bread
4. 8 as he passed by, he turned in..to eat
4. 40 So they poured out for the men to eat
4. 40 as they were eating of the pottage, that
4. 40 And they could not eat (thereof)
4. 41 he said, Pour out..that they may eat
4. 42 Give unto the people, that they may eat

2 Ki. 4. 43 Give the people, that they may eat
4. 43 They shall eat, and shall leave (thereof)
4. 44 he set (it) before them, and they did eat
6. 22 set bread and water..that they may eat
6. 23 and when they had eaten and drunk
6. 28, 29 Give thy son, that we may eat him
6. 28 and we will eat my son to morrow
6. 29 So we boiled my son, and did eat him
7. 2, 19 thou shalt see..but shalt not eat
7. 8 they went into one tent, and did eat
9. 10 the dogs shall eat Jezebel in the portion
9. 34 he was come in, he did eat and drink
9. 36 In the portion of Jezreel shall dogs eat
18. 27 that they may eat their own dung, and
18. 31 eat ye every man of his own vine
19. 29 Ye shall eat this year such things as grow
19. 29 plant vineyards, and eat the fruits there.
23. 9 they did eat of the unleavened bread
25. 29 he did eat bread continually before him
1 Ch. 12. 39 they were with David..eating and drink.
29. 22 And did eat and drink before the LORD
2 Ch. 30. 18 yet did they eat the passover otherwise
30. 22 they did eat throughout the feast seven
31. 10 we have had enough to eat, and have
Ezra 2. 63 the Tirshatha said..they should not eat
6. 21 all..as had separated themselves..did e.
9. 12 that ye may be strong, and eat the good
10. 6 he did eat no bread, nor drink water
Neh 5. 2 we take up corn..that we may eat, and
5. 14 I and my brethren have not eaten the
7. 65 the Tirshatha said..they should not eat
8. 10 Go your way, eat the fat, and drink the
8. 12 all the people went their way to eat
9. 25 so they did eat, and were filled, and
9. 36 thou gavest unto our fathers to eat the
Esth. 4. 16 neither eat nor drink three days, night
Job 1. 4 called for their three sisters to eat
1. 13 his sons and his daughters (were) eating
1. 18 Thy sons and thy daughters (were) eating
21. 25 And another..never eateth with pleasure
31. 8 let me sow, and let another eat; yea
31. 17 Or have eaten my morsel myself alone
31. 17 and the fatherless hath not eaten thereof
31. 39 If I have eaten the fruits thereof without
40. 15 Behold now behemoth..he eateth grass
42. 11 they..did eat bread with him in his hou.
Psa 14. 4 who eat up my people.. they eat bread
22. 26 The meek shall eat and be satisfied
22. 29 All..fat upon earth shall eat and worship
27. 2 When..my foes, came upon me to eat up
41. 9 mine own..friend..which did eat of my
50. 13 Will I eat the flesh of bulls, or drink the
53. 4 who eat up my people..they eat bread
78. 24 had rained down manna upon them to e.
78. 25 Man did eat angels' food: he sent them
78. 29 So they did eat, and were well filled
102. 4 heart is smitten..so that I forget to eat
102. 9 For I have eaten ashes like bread, and
105. 35 And did eat up all the herbs in their
106. 20 the similitude of an ox that eateth grass
106. 28 They joined..and ate the sacrifices of the
127. 2 vain for you..to eat the bread of sorrows
128. 2 thou shalt eat the labour of thine hands
Prov. 1. 31 Therefore shall they eat of the fruit of
13. 2 A man shall eat good by the fruit of (his)
13. 25 righteous eateth to the satisfying of his
18. 21 they that love it shall eat the fruit
23. 7 Eat and drink, saith he to thee; but his
23. 8 morsel (which) thou hast eaten shalt thou
24. 13 My son, eat thou honey, because (it is)
25. 16 eat so much as is sufficient for thee
25. 27 (It is) not good to eat much honey; so
27. 18 Whoso keepeth the fig tree shall eat the
30. 17 and the young eagles shall eat it
30. 20 she eateth, and wipeth her mouth, and
31. 27 and eateth not the bread of idleness
Eccl. 2. 24 that he should eat and drink, and (that)
2. 25 For who can eat, or who else can hasten
3. 13 also that every man should eat and drink
4. 5 The fool..eateth his own flesh
5. 11 increase, they are increased that eat them
5. 12 (is) sweet, whether he eat little or much
5. 17 All his days also he eateth in darkness
5. 18 (it is) good and comely (for one) to eat
5. 19 hath given him power to eat thereof, and
6. 2 to eat thereof, but a stranger eateth it
8. 15 no better thing under the sun, than to e.
9. 7 eat thy bread with joy, and drink thy
10. 16 and thy princes eat in the morning!
10. 17 thy princes eat in due season, for strength
Song 4. 16 his garden, and eat his pleasant fruits
5. 1 I have eaten my honey comb with my h.
5. 1 eat, O friends; drink, yea, drink abun.
Isa. 1. 19 obedient, ye shall eat the good of the
3. 10 they shall eat the fruit of their doings
4. 1 We will eat our own bread, and wear our
5. 17 and the waste places..shall strangers eat
7. 15 Butter and honey shall he eat, that he
7. 22 for the abundance of milk..he shall eat
7. 22 butter and honey shall every one eat
9. 20 he shall eat on the left hand, and they
9. 20 eat every man the flesh of his own arm
11. 7 and the lion shall eat straw like the ox
21. 5 watch in the watch tower, eat, drink
22. 13 killing sheep, eating flesh, and drinking
22. 13 eat and drink; for to morrow we shall die
23. 18 eat sufficiently, and for durable clothing
29. 8 hungry (man) dreameth, and, behold, he e.
30. 24 young asses..shall eat clean provender
36. 12 they may eat their own dung, and drink
36. 16 eat ye every one of his vine, and every
37. 30 eat (this) year such as groweth of itself

Isa. 37. 30 plant vineyards, and eat the fruit thereof
44. 16 with part thereof he eateth flesh
44. 19 I have roasted flesh, and eaten (it)
51. 8 and the worm shall eat them like wool
55. 1 come ye, buy, and eat; yea, come, buy wine
55. 2 eat ye (that which is) good, and let your
59. 5 he that eateth of their eggs dieth, and
61. 6 ye shall eat the riches of the Gentiles
62. 9 they that have gathered it shall eat it
65. 4 eat swine's flesh, and broth of abominable
65. 13 servants shall eat, but ye shall be hungry
65. 21 plant vineyards, and eat the fruit of them
65. 22 they shall not plant, and another eat
65. 25 the lion shall eat straw like the bullock
66. 17 eating swine's flesh, and the abomination
Jer. 2. 7 to eat the fruit thereof, and the goodness
5. 17 thy sons and thy daughters should eat
7. 21 put..offerings unto..sacrifices, and eat
15. 16 Thy words were found, and I did eat them
16. 8 to sit with them to eat and to drink
19. 9 shall eat every one the flesh of his friend
22. 15 Did not thy father eat and drink, and do
29. 5, 28 plant gardens, and eat the fruit of
31. 29 The fathers have eaten a sour grape, and
31. 30 every man that eateth the sour grape
41. 1 they did eat bread together in Mizpah
52. 33 he did continually eat bread before him
Lam. 2. 20 Shall the women eat their fruit, (and)
Eze. 2. 8 open thy mouth, and eat that I give thee
3. 1 Son of man, eat that thou findest; eat
3. 3 Then did I eat (it); and it was in my mo.
4. 9 hundred and ninety days shalt thou eat
4. 10 meat which thou shalt eat (shall be) by
4. 10 from time to time shalt thou eat it
4. 12 thou shalt eat it (as) barley cakes, and
4. 13 the children of Israel eat their defiled
4. 14 have I not eaten of that which dieth of
4. 16 they shall eat bread by weight, and with
5. 10 fathers shall eat the sons in the midst
5. 10 and the sons shall eat their fathers
12. 18 eat thy bread with quaking, and drink
12. 19 shall eat their bread with carefulness
16. 13 didst eat fine flour, and honey, and oil
18. 2 The fathers have eaten sour grapes, and
18. 6 hath not eaten upon the mountains
18. 11 hath eaten upon the mountains, and de.
18. 15 (That) hath not eaten upon the mount.
22. 9 and in thee they eat upon the mountains
24. 17 cover not (thy) lips, and eat not the bread
24. 22 cover your lips, nor eat the bread of men
25. 4 they shall eat thy fruit, and they shall
33. 25 Ye eat with the blood, and lift up your
34. 3 Ye eat the fat, and ye clothe you with
39. 17 that ye may eat flesh, and drink blood
39. 18 Ye shall eat the flesh of the mighty, and
39. 19 ye shall eat fat till ye be full, and drink
42. 13 priests..shall eat the most holy things
44. 3 he shall sit in it to eat bread before the
44. 29 They shall eat the meat offering, and the
44. 31 The priests shall not eat of any thing
Dan. 1. 12 let them give us pulse to eat, and water
1. 13 the countenance of the children that eat
1. 15 than all the children which did eat the
10. 3 I ate no pleasant bread, neither came
Hos. 2. 12 and the beasts of the field shall eat them
4. 10 For they shall eat, and not have enough
8. 13 They sacrifice flesh..offerings..and eat
9. 3 they shall eat unclean (things) in Assyria
9. 4 all that eat thereof shall be polluted
10. 13 ye have eaten the fruit of lies: because
Joel 1. 4 locust eaten, cankerworm eaten..eaten
2. 25 the years that the locust hath eaten
2. 26 ye shall eat in plenty, and be satisfied
Amos 6. 4 That..eat the lambs out of the flock, and
7. 2 when they had made an end of eating the
7. 12 there eat bread, and prophesy there
9. 14 they shall also make gardens, and eat
Mic. 3. 3 Who also eat the flesh of my people
6. 14 Thou shalt eat, but not be satisfied
7. 1 no cluster to eat; my soul desired the
Nah. 3. 15 it shall eat thee up like the cankerworm
Hab. 1. 8 shall fly as the eagle (that) hasteth to eat
Hag. 1. 6 ye eat, but ye have not enough
Zech. 7. 6 when ye did eat, and when ye did drink
7. 6 did ye not eat..and drink (for yourselves)
11. 9 let the rest eat every one the flesh of
11. 16 but he shall eat the flesh of the fat

2. *To be eaten,* אֲכַל *akal,* 2.
Exod 12. 16 save (that) which every man must eat

3. *To eat,* אֲכַל *akal.*
Dan. 4. 33 did eat grass as oxen, and his body was

4. *Eating, food,* אָכְלָה *oklah.*
Exod 16. 15 which the LORD hath given you to eat
Lev. 11. 39 And if any beast, of which ye may eat

5. *To eat, nourish, fill,* בָּרָה *barah.*
2 Sa. 12. 17 neither did he eat bread with them
13. 6 in my sight, that I may eat at her hand
13. 10 Bring the meat..that I may eat of thine

6. *To eat (bread),* לָחַם *lacham.*
Psa. 141. 4 and let me not eat of their dainties
Prov. 4. 17 For they eat the bread of wickedness
9. 5 Come, eat of my bread, and drink of the
23. 1 When thou sittest to eat with a ruler
23. 6 Eat thou not the bread of..an evil eye

7. *To feed, enjoy, consume,* רָעָה *raah.*
Eze. 34. 19 they eat that which ye have trodden with

8. *To eat,* βιβρώσκω *bibrōskō.*
John 6. 13 over and above unto them that had eaten

9. *To taste,* γεύομαι *geuomai.*
Acts 10. 10 became very hungry, and would have ea.
20. 11 he..was come up again and..had..eaten
23. 14 we will eat nothing until we have slain

10. *To eat,* ἐσθίω *esthiō.*
Matt. 9. 11 Why eateth your Master with..sinners?
11. 18 John came neither eating nor drinking
11. 19 The Son of man came eating and drinking
12. 1 began to pluck the ears of corn, and to e.
14. 21 they that had eaten were about five tho.
15. 2 wash not their hands when they eat
15. 27 yet the dogs eat of the crumbs which
15. 38 they that did eat were four thousand
24. 49 And shall begin..to eat and drink with
26. 21 as they did eat, he said, Verily I say
Mark 1. 6 and he did eat locusts and wild honey
2. 16 the scribes..saw him eat with publicans
2. 16 How is it that he eateth and drinketh
7. 2 they saw some of his disciples eat bread
7. 3 the Jews..eat not, holding the tradition
7. 4 the market..except..they wash..eat not
7. 5 thy disciples..eat bread with unwashen
7. 28 yet the dogs under the table eat of the
14. 18 as they sat and did eat, Jesus said
14. 18 One of you which eateth with me, shall
14. 22 as they did eat, Jesus took bread, and
Luke 5. 30 Why do ye eat and drink with publicans
5. 33 the disciples of John fast..but thine eat
6. 1 his disciples plucked..and did eat
7. 33 John the Baptist came neither eating
7. 34 The Son of man is come eating and drin.
10. 7 in the same house remain, eating and d.
10. 8 eat such things as are set before you
12. 45 to eat and drink, and to be drunken
15. 16 with the husks that the swine did eat
17. 27 They did eat, they drank, they married
17. 28 they did eat, they drank, they bought
22. 30 That ye may eat and drink at my table
Acts 27. 35 when he had broken (it), he began to eat
Rom 14. 2 another, who is weak, eateth herbs
14. 3 that eateth despise him that eateth not
14. 3 which eateth not judge him that eateth
14. 6 He that eateth, eateth to the Lord, for
14. 6 he that eateth not, to the Lord he eateth
14. 20 evil for that man who eateth with offence
1 Co. 8. 7 eat (it) as a thing offered unto an idol
8. 10 to eat those things which are offered to
9. 7 who planteth a vineyard, and eateth not
9. 7 who feedeth a flock, and eateth not of
10. 18 are not they which eat of the sacrifices
10. 25 eat, asking no questions for conscience
10. 27 whatsoever is set before you, eat, asking
10. 28 This is offered in sacrifice..eat not for
10. 31 Whether therefore ye eat, or drink, or
11. 22 have ye not houses to eat and to drink in
11. 26 as often as ye eat this bread, and drink
11. 27 whosoever shall eat this bread, and drink
11. 28 so let him eat of (that) bread, and drink
11. 29 For he that eateth and drinketh unworth.
11. 29 eateth and drinketh damnation to himself
11. 34 if any man hunger, let him eat at home
2 Th. 3. 10 would not work, neither should he eat
3. 12 that with quietness they work, and eat

11. *To take or receive over,* μεταλαμβάνω *metalam.*
Acts 2. 46 they..did eat their meat with gladness

12. *To have pasture,* ἔχω νομήν *echō nomēn.*
2 Ti. 2. 17 And their word will eat as doth a canker

13. *To eat, gnaw, chew, devour,* τρώγω *trōgō.*
Matt 24. 38 they were eating and drinking, marrying
John 6. 54, 56 eateth my flesh, and drinketh my blood
6. 57 so he that eateth me, even he shall live
6. 58 he that eateth of this bread shall live for
13. 18 He that eateth bread with me hath lifted

14. *To eat,* φάγω *phagō.*
Matt 6. 25 Take no thought..what ye shall eat
6. 31 take no thought..What shall we eat?
12. 4 entered into the house of God, and did eat
12. 4 which was not lawful for him to eat
14. 16 They need not depart; give ye them to eat
14. 20 And they did all eat, and were filled
15. 20 to eat with unwashen hands defileth not
15. 32 now three days, and have nothing to eat
15. 37 And they did all eat, and were filled
26. 17 wilt thou that we prepare for thee to eat
26. 26 and said, Take, eat; this is my body
Mark 2. 26 How he went..and did eat the shewbread
2. 26 which is not lawful to eat but for the
3. 20 that they could not so much as eat bread
5. 43 that something should be given her to e.
6. 31 they had no leisure so much as to eat
6. 36 buy..bread: for they having nothing to e.
6. 37 He answered..Give ye them to eat
6. 37 Shall we..buy..and give them to eat?
6. 42 And they did all eat, and were filled
6. 44 they that did eat of the loaves were
8. 1 the multitude..having nothing to eat
8. 2 three days, and have nothing to eat
8. 8 So they did eat, and were filled
8. 9 they that had eaten were about four
11. 14 No man eat fruit of thee hereafter for
14. 12 that thou mayest eat the passover?
14. 14 where I shall eat the passover with my
14. 22 and said, Take, eat: this is my body
Luke 4. 2 And in those days he did eat nothing
6. 4 and did take and eat the shewbread, and
6. 4 which it is not lawful to eat but for the
7. 36 desired him that he would eat with him
9. 13 he said unto them, Give ye them to eat
9. 17 And they did eat, and were all filled

Luke 12. 19 take thine ease, eat, drink, (and) be
12. 22 Take no thought..what ye shall eat
12. 29 And seek not ye what ye shall eat
13. 26 We have eaten and drunk in thy presence
14. 1 he went into the house..to eat bread on
14. 15 Blessed (is) he that shall eat bread in the
15. 23 and kill (it); and let us eat, and be merry
17. 8 and serve me, till I have eaten and drunk.
17. 8 afterward thou shalt eat and drink?
22. 8 prepare..the passover, that we may eat
22. 11 where I shall eat the passover with my
22. 15 With desire I have desired to eat this
22. 16 I will not any more eat thereof, until it
24. 43 And he took (it), and did eat before them
John 4. 31 disciples prayed him, saying, Master, eat
4. 32 he said unto them, I have meat to eat
4. 33 Hath any man brought him (ought) to e.?
6. 5 Whence shall we buy..that these may eat?
6. 23 unto the place where they did eat bread
6. 26 because ye did eat of the loaves, and
6. 31 Our fathers did eat manna in the desert
6. 31 He gave them bread from heaven to eat
6. 49 Your fathers did eat manna in the wild.
6. 50 that a man may eat thereof, and not die
6. 51 If any man eat of this bread, he shall live
6. 52 How can this man give us..flesh to eat?
6. 53 Except ye eat the flesh of the Son of man
6. 58 not as your fathers did eat manna
18. 28 but that they might eat the passover
Acts 9. 9 three days..and neither did eat nor drink
10. 13 there came a voice..Peter; kill, and eat
10. 14 for I have never eaten any thing that is
11. 7 a voice saying..Arise, Peter; slay, and e.
23. 12, 21 neither eat nor drink till they had
Rom 14. 2 one believeth that he may eat all things
14. 21 good neither to eat flesh, nor to drink
14. 23 he that doubteth is damned if he eat
1 Co. 8. 8 for neither, if we eat, are we the better
8. 8 neither, if we eat not, are we the worse
8. 13 I will eat no flesh while the world stand.
9. 4 Have we not power to eat and to drink?
10. 3 And did all eat the same spiritual meat
10. 7 The people sat down to eat and drink
11. 20 (this) is not to eat the Lord's supper
11. 24 he brake (it), and said, Take, eat: this is
11. 33 when ye come together to eat, tarry one
15. 32 let us eat and drink; for to morrow we
2 Th. 3. 8 Neither did we eat any man's bread for
Heb. 13. 10 whereof they have no right to eat which
Jas. 5. 3 and shall eat your flesh as it were fire
Rev. 2. 7, 17 him that overcometh will I give to e.
2. 14 to eat things sacrificed unto idols, and to
2. 20 to eat things sacrificed unto idols
10. 10 soon as I had eaten it, my belly was bitter
17. 16 shall eat her flesh, and burn her with fire
19. 18 That ye may eat the flesh of kings, and

15. *My food,* לַחְמִי [*lechem*].
Job 3. 24 For my sighing cometh before I eat

16. *In his mouth was,* בְּפִיו [*peh*].
Gen. 25. 28 Isaac loved Esau, because he did eat of

17. *To make common,* חָלַל *chalal,* 3.
Deut 20. 6 and hath not (yet) eaten of it? let him
20. 6 lest he die..and another man eat of it

18. *To go in unto the heart,* בּוֹא אֶל־קֶרֶב *bo el qereb.*
Gen. 41. 21 it could not be known that they had eaten

EAT, to cause or make to —

1. *To cause or give to eat,* אָכַל *akal,* 5.
Jer. 19. 9 I will cause them to eat the flesh of
Eze. 3. 2 and he caused me to eat that roll
3. 3 Son of man, cause thy belly to eat, and

2. *To cause to eat,* בָּרָה *barah,* 5.
2 Sa. 3. 35 people came to cause David to eat meat

3. *To (cause to) taste,* טְעַם *team.*
Dan. 4. 25, 32 they shall make thee to eat grass as

EAT enough —

To satiate, satisfy, fill, κορέννυμι *korennumi.*
Acts 27. 38 when they had eaten enough, they light.

EAT up, to —

1. *To eat,* אָכַל *akal.*
Gen. 41. 4, 20 And the ill favoured..kine did eat up
Num 24. 8 he shall eat up the nations his enemies
Deut 28. 33 shall a nation..thou knowest not eat up
Job 5. 5 Whose harvest the hungry eateth up, and
Psa. 69. 9 the zeal of thine house hath eaten me up
Isa. 50. 9 wax old..the moth shall eat them up
51. 8 moth shall eat them up like a garment
Jer. 5. 17 And they shall eat up thine harvest
5. 17 they shall eat up thy flocks and thine h.
10. 25 they have eaten up Jacob, and devoured
Hos. 4. 8 They eat up the sin of my people, and
Amos 7. 4 devoured the great deep, and did eat up

2. *To swallow up,* בָּלַע *bala.*
Isa. 28. 4 while it is yet in his hand he eateth it up

3. *To consume,* בָּעַר *baar,* 3.
Isa. 3. 14 ye have eaten up the vineyard; the spoil
5. 5 take away the hedge..it shall be eaten up

4. *To feed, enjoy, consume,* רָעָה *raah.*
Eze. 34. 18 a small thing unto you to have eaten up

5. *To go in unto the heart,* בּוֹא אֶל־קֶרֶב *bo el-qereb.*
Gen. 41. 21 And when they had eaten them up

6. *To eat down or fully,* καταφάγω *kataphagō.*
John 2. 17 The zeal of thine house hath eaten me up

Rev. 10. 9 he said unto me, Take (it), and eat it up
10. 10 I took the little book..and ate it up

EAT with, to —

To eat with, συνεσθίω *sunesthiō.*
Luke 15. 2 This..receiveth sinners, and eateth with
Acts 10. 41 who did eat and drink with him after he
11. 3 Thou wentest in..and didst eat with
1 Co. 5. 11 written..with such an one no not to eat
Gal. 2. 12 he did eat with the Gentiles: but when

EATEN, to be —

1. *To be eaten,* אָכַל *akal,* 2.
Gen. 6. 21 take thou unto thee of all food that is e.
Exod 12. 46 In one house shall it be eaten: thou
13. 3 there shall no leavened bread be eaten
13. 7 Unleavened bread shall be eaten seven
21. 28 and his flesh shall not be eaten; but the
29. 34 it shall not be eaten, because it (is) holy
Lev. 6. 16 with unleavened bread shall it be eaten
6. 23 every meat offering..shall not be eaten
6. 26 in the holy place shall it be eaten
6. 30 And no sin offering..shall be eaten; it
7. 6 it shall be eaten in the holy place: it (is)
7. 15 the flesh..shall be eaten the same day
7. 16 it shall be eaten the same day that he
7. 16 also the remainder of it shall be eaten
7. 18 And if (any) of the flesh..be eaten at all
7. 19 And the flesh..unclean..shall not be eat.
11. 13 they shall not be eaten, they (are) an ab.
11. 34 Of all meat which may be eaten, (that) on
11. 41 every creeping thing..shall not be eaten
11. 47 between the beast that may be eaten
11. 47 and the beast that may not be eaten
17. 13 any beast or fowl that may be eaten
19. 6 It shall be eaten the same day ye offer it
19. 7 if it be eaten at all on the third day
19. 23 three years..it shall not be eaten of
22. 30 On the same day it shall be eaten up
Num 28. 17 seven days shall unleavened bread be ea.
Deut 12. 22 as the roebuck and the hart is eaten
14. 19 every creeping thing..shall not be eaten
Job 6. 6 Can that which is unsavoury be eaten
Jer. 24. 2 which could not be eaten, they were so
24. 3 that cannot be eaten, they are so evil
24. 8 which cannot be eaten, they are so evil
29. 17 like vile figs, that cannot be eaten
Eze. 45. 21 unleavened bread shall be eaten

2. *To cause to burn, consume,* בָּעַר *baar,* 3.
Isa. 6. 13 and (it) shall return, and shall be eaten

EATEN, to cause to be —

To cause to eat up, consume, בָּעַר *baar,* 5.
Exod 22. 5 If a man shall cause a field..to be eaten

EATER —

To eat, אָכַל *akal.*
Judg 14. 14 Out of the eater came forth meat, and
Isa. 55. 10 seed to the sower, and bread to the eater
Nah. 3. 12 even fall into the mouth of the eater

EATING —

1. *Eating, food,* אֹכֶל *okel.*
Exod 12. 4 every man according to his eating shall
16. 16, 18, 21 every man according to his eating

2. *Eating, (the act),* βρῶσις *brōsis.*
1 Co. 8. 4 concerning therefore the eating of those

3. *To eat,* φάγω *phagō.*
1 Co. 11. 21 in eating every one taketh before (other)

EATING, to be —

To eat, ἐσθίω *esthiō.*
Matt 26. 26 as they were eating, Jesus took bread

EATING, while...is —

Food, לְחוּם *lechum.*
Job 20. 23 shall rain (it) upon him while he is eating

E'-BAL, עֵיבָל *bare.*

1. Son of Shobal, son of Seir the Horite. B.C. 1797.
Gen. 36. 23 children of Shobal (were) these..E.
1 Ch. 1. 40 The sons of Shobal..E., Shephi, and On.

2. A rocky mountain in Ephraim.
Deut 11. 29 and the curse upon mount E.
27. 4 I command you this day, in mount E.
27. 13 these shall stand upon mount E. to curse
Josh. 8. 30 Then Joshua built an altar..in mount E.
8. 33 and half of them over against mount E.

3. A son of Joktan, son of Eber grandson of Shem, B.C. 2200.
1 Ch. 1. 22 And E., and Abimael, and Sheba

E'-BED, עֶבֶד *servant, slave.*

1. An Ephriamite, father of Gaal who rebelled against Abimelech when he was reigning in Shechem, B.C. 1209.
Judg. 9. 26 Gaal the son of E. came with his brethren
9. 28 Gaal the son of E. said, Who (is) Abimel.
9. 30 heard the words of Gaal the son of E.
9. 31 Gaal the son of E., and his brethren, be
9. 35 Gaal the son of E. went out, and stood

2. One of the Bene-Adin that came up with Ezra, B.C. 457.
Ezra 8. 6 E. the son of Jonathan, and with him

EBED ME'-LECH, עֶבֶד מֶלֶךְ *servant of the king.*

An Ethiopian eunuch in the service of Zedekiah, through whose aid Jeremiah was released from prison, B.C. 589.
Jer. 38. 7 Now, when E. the Ethiopian..heard that
38. 8 E. went forth out of the king's house
38. 10 Then the king commanded E. the Ethio.

Jer. 38. 11 So E. took the men with him, and went
38. 12 And E. the Ethiopian said unto Jeremiah
39. 16 Go and speak to E. the Ethiopian, saying

E'-BER, HE'-BER, עֵבֶר *a shoot.*

1. A great grandson of Shem, B.C. 2255.
Gen. 10. 21 the father of all the children of E.
10. 24 Arphaxad begat Salah; and S. begat E.
10. 25 unto E. were born two sons: the name
11. 14 Salah lived thirty years, and begat E.
11. 15 Salah lived after he begat E. four hundred
11. 16 E. lived four and thirty years, and begat
11. 17 E. lived after he begat Peleg four hundred
1 Ch. 1. 18 Arphaxad begat Shelah, and S. begat E.
1. 19 unto E. were born two sons: the name
1. 25 E., Peleg, Reu

2. The head of a family in Gad, B.C. 800.
1 Ch. 5. 13 Jorai, and Jachan, and Zia, and H.

3. A son of Elpaal, a Benjamite, B.C. 1100.
1 Ch. 8. 12 sons of Elpaal; E., and Misham, and

4. A son of Shashak, a Benjamite, B.C. 1340.
1 Ch. 8. 22 And Ishpan, and H., and Eliel

5. A priest of the family of Amok, B.C. 447.
Neh. 12. 20 Of Sallai, Kallai; of Amok, E.

6. This name seems used as a patronymic denoting the descendants of Eber; but it may also be understood as referring to those "beyond the river."
Num 24. 24 And ships..shall afflict E., and he also

E-BEN E'-ZER, אֶבֶן הָעֵזֶר *stone of the help.*

A stone set up by Samuel after a defeat of the Philistines as a memorial of the help received, B.C. 1141. It stood between Mizpeh ("the watch-tower," a few miles N. of Jerusalem) and Shen ("the tooth or crag").
1 Sa. 4. 1 Israel went out..and pitched beside E.
5. 1 Philistines..brought it from E. unto Ash.
7. 12 Then Samuel..called the name of it E.

EB-IA'-SAPH, אֶבְיָסָף *the father of gathering.*

A great-grandson of Korah, B.C. 1470. (See *Abiasaph.*)
1 Ch. 6. 23 Elkanah his son, and E. his son, and
6. 37 Assir, the son of E., the son of Korah
9. 19 Kore, the son of E., the son of Korah, and

EBONY —

Ebony, הָבְנִים *hobnim.*
Eze. 27. 15 (for) a present horns of ivory and ebony

EB-RO'-NAH, עַבְרֹנָה *bank, beach, coast.*

The thirtieth station of the Israelites in the Wilderness, and the nineteenth from Sinai, near Ezion-geber on the Red Sea.
Num 33. 34 they removed..and encamped at E.; 33. 35.

EDAR. *See* **EDER.**

E'-DEN, עֵדֶן *delight.*

1. The place of man's creation and first abode; the situation of which is uncertain.
Gen. 2. 8 And the LORD planted a garden..in E.
2. 10 a river went out of E. to water the garden
2. 15 put him into the garden of E. to dress it
3. 23 sent him forth from the garden of E.
3. 24 he placed at the east of the garden of E.
4. 16 in the land of Nod, on the east of E.
Isa. 51. 3 he will make her wilderness like E., and
Eze. 28. 13 Thou hast been in E. the garden of God
31. 9 so that all the trees of E...envied him
31. 16 all the trees of E...shall be comforted
31. 18 whom art thou..among the trees of E.?
31. 18 be brought down with the trees of E.
36. 35 This land..is..like the garden of E.
Joel 2. 3 the land (is) as the garden of E. before

2. A Gershomite, son of Joah, B.C. 726.
2 Ch. 29. 12 Joah the son of Zimmah, and E. the son

3. A Levite in the time of Hezekiah appointed to distribute the oblations, B.C. 726.
2 Ch. 31. 15 next him (were) E., and Miniamin, and

4. A mart that supplied Tyre with richly embroidered stuffs. It is associated with Haran, Sheba, and Asshur. The sons of Eden are mentioned with Gozan, Haran, and Rezeph as victims of Assyrian conquest. It probably lay to the N.W. of Mesopotamia, or near Damascus.
2 Ki. 19. 12 children of E. which (were) in Thelasar?
Isa. 37. 12 children of E. which (were) in Telassar?
Eze. 27. 23 Haran, and Canneh, and E., the mercha.
Amos 1. 5 holdeth the sceptre from the house of E.

E'-DER, E'-DAR, עֵדֶר *flock.*

1. A place near Ephrath in Bethlehem.
Gen. 35. 21 spread his tent beyond the tower of E.

2. A border city in the S. of Judah towards Edom. See also *Adar* and *Arad.*
Jos. 15. 21 uttermost cities..of Judah..were..E.

3. A grandson of Merari son of Levi, B.C. 1015.
1 Ch. 23. 23 sons of Mushi; Mahli, and E., and Jer.
24. 30 sons also of Mushi; Mahli, and E., and

EDGE —

1. *Mouth,* פֶּה *peh.*
Gen. 34. 26 slew Hamor..with the edge of the sword
Exod 17. 13 discomfited Amalek..with the edge of
Num 21. 24 smote him with the edge of the sword
Deut 13. 15 surely smite..with the edge of the sword
13. 15 cattle thereof, with the edge of the sword
20. 13 shalt smite..with the edge of the sword
Josh. 6. 21 destroyed all..with the edge of the swo.
8. 24 were all fallen on the edge of the sword
8. 24 and smote it with the edge of the sword

Josh 10. 28, 30 smote it with the edge of the sword
10. 32, 35, 37 smote it with the edge of the
10. 39 smote them with the edge of the sword
11. 11 smote all..with the edge of the sword
11. 12 smote them with the edge of the sword
11. 14 they smote with the edge of the sword
19. 47 smote it with the edge of the sword, and
Judg. 1. 8 and smitten it with the edge of the swo.
1. 25 smote the city with the edge of the swo.
4. 15 discomfited Sisera..with the edge of the
4. 16 the host..fell upon the edge of the sword
18. 27 smote them with the edge of the sword
20. 37 smote..the city with the edge of the sword
20. 48 smote them with the edge of the sword
21. 10 smite the inhabitants..with the edge of
1 Sa. 15. 8 destroyed all the people with the edge of
22. 19 smote he with the edge of the sword
22. 19 and sheep, with the edge of the sword
2 Sa. 15. 14 smite the city with the edge of the sword
2 Ki. 10. 25 smote them with the edge of the sword
Job 1. 15, 17 slain the servants with the edge of
Jer. 21. 7 smite them with the edge of the sword

2. *Mouth*, פֶּה *peyah.*
Judg. 3. 16 made him a dagger which had two edges

3. *Faces, face*, פָּנִים *panim.*
Eccl. 10. 10 iron be blunt, and he do not whet the e.

4. *Sharpness*, צוּר *tsur.*
Psa. 89. 43 hast also turned the edge of his sword

5. *End, extremity*, קָצָה *qatsah.*
Exod. 28. 7 shoulder pieces..joined at the two edges

6. *End, extremity*, קָצֶה *qatseh.*
Exod. 13. 20 in Etham, in the edge of the wilderness
26. 5 fifty loops shalt thou make in the edge
36. 12 fifty loops made he in the edge of the
Num 33. 6 which (is) in the edge of the wilderness
33. 37 mount Hor, in the edge of the land of
Josh. 13. 27 unto the edge of the sea of Chinnereth

7. *End, extremity*, קְצָוָה *qitsvah.*
Exod. 39. 4 by the two edges was it coupled together

8. *Lip*, שָׂפָה *saphah.*
Exod 26. 4 loops of blue upon the edge of the one
26. 4 in the uttermost edge of (another) curta.
26. 10 loops on the edge of the one curtain
26. 10 fifty loops in the edge of the curtain
36. 11 loops of blue on the edge of one curtain
36. 17 upon the uttermost edge of the curtain
36. 17 fifty loops made he upon the edge of the
Eze. 43. 13 the border thereof by the edge thereof

9. *Mouth*, στόμα *stoma.*
Luke 21. 24 they shall fall by the edge of the sword
Heb. 11. 34 escaped the edge of the sword, out of

EDGE, to be set on —
To be blunt, קָהָה *qahah.*
Jer. 31. 29 and the children's teeth are set on edge
31. 30 sour grape, his teeth shall be set on ed.
Eze. 18. 2 and the children's teeth are set on edge?

EDGES, with two —
Two mouthed, δίστομος *distomos.*
Rev. 2. 12 which hath the sharp sword with two ed.

EDIFICATION —
Building up, οἰκοδομή *oikodomē.*
Rom 15. 2 please (his) neighbour..to edification
1 Co. 14. 3 speaketh unto men (to) edification
2 Co. 10. 8 the Lord hath given us for edification
13. 10 the Lord hath given me to edification

EDIFY, to —
To build up, οἰκοδομέω *oikodomeō.*
Acts 9. 31 had the churches rest..and were edified
1 Co. 8. 1 Knowledge puffeth up, but charity edifi.
10. 23 lawful for me, but all things edify not
14. 4 speaketh in an (unknown) tongue edifieth
14. 4 he that prophesieth edifieth the church
14. 17 but the other is not edified
1 Th. 5. 11 and edify one another, even as also ye do

EDIFY, things wherewith one may —
The things of the building up, τὰ τῆς οἰκοδομῆς.
Rom. 14. 19 things wherewith one may edify another

EDIFYING —
1. *Building up*, οἰκοδομή *oikodomē.*
1 Co. 14. 5 that the church may receive edifying
14. 12 may excel to the edifying of the church
14. 26 Let all things be done unto edifying
2 Co. 12. 19 but (we do) all things..for your edifying
Eph. 4. 12 for the edifying of the body of Christ
4. 16 increase of the body unto the edifying
4. 29 that which is good to the use of edifying

2. *Building up*, οἰκοδομία *oikodomia.*
1 Ti. 1. 4 rather than godly edifying which is in faith

E'-DOM, אֱדֹם *red.*
1. Elder son of Isaac, and so named from the colour of the lentile pottage for which he sold his birthright to his twin brother Jacob, B.C. 1809.
Gen. 25. 30 therefore was his name called E.
36. 1 these..the generations of Esau, who (is) E.
36. 8 Thus dwelt Esau in..Seir : Esau (is) E.
36. 19 These (are) the sons of Esau, who (is) E.

2. This name is also employed to designate both the people that sprang from Esau and the country in which they lived. (In Mark 3. 8 only is the country called *Idumea*). Previously the country was called Mount Seir, from the progenitor of the Horites, who had their name from Hori grandson of Seir, because it was descriptive of their habits as dwellers in caves.
Gen. 32. 3 unto the land of Seir, the country of E.
36. 16 the dukes..of Eliphaz in the land of E.
36. 17 the dukes..of Reuel in the land of E.
36. 21 the children of Seir in the land of E.
36. 31 the kings that reigned in the land of E.
36. 32 Bela the son of Beor reigned in E.
36. 43 duke Magdiel..these (be) the dukes of E.
Exod 15. 15 Then the dukes of E. shall be amazed
Num 20. 14 sent messengers..unto the king of E.
20. 18 E. said unto him, Thou shalt not pass by
20. 20 E. came out against him with much pe.
20. 21 E. refused to give Israel passage through
20. 23 by the coast of the land of E., saying
21. 4 journeyed..to compass the land of E.
24. 18 E. shall be a possession, Seir also shall
33. 37 Hor, in the edge of the land of E.
34. 3 the wilderness..along by the coast of E.
Josh. 15. 1 to the border of E. the wilderness of
15. 21 cities of..Judah toward the coast of E.
Judg. 5. 4 thou marchedst out of the field of E.
11. 17 sent messengers unto the king of E.
11. 17 but the king of E. would not hearken
11. 18 Then they..compassed the land of E.
1 Sa. 14. 47 Saul..fought..against E., and against
2 Sa. 8. 14 he put garrisons in E.; throughout all E.
1 Ki. 9. 26 the shore of the Red sea, in the land of E.
11. 14 he (was) of the king's seed in E.
11. 15 it came to pass, when David was in E.
11. 15 after he had smitten every male in E.
11. 16 until he had cut off every male in E.
22. 47 then no king in E. ; a deputy (was) king
2 Ki. 3. 8 The way through the wilderness of E.
3. 9 the king of Judah, and the king of E.
3. 12 Jehoshaphat and the king of E. went
3. 20 behold, there came water by the way of E.
3. 26 to break through..unto the king of E.
8. 20, 22 E. revolted from under the hand of
14. 7 He slew of E. in the valley of Salt ten
14. 10 Thou hast indeed smitten E., and thine
1 Ch. 1. 43 the kings that reigned in the land of E.
1. 51 the dukes of E. were ; duke Timnah, d.
1. 54 duke Iram. These (are) the dukes of E.
18. 11 from E., and from Moab, and from the
18. 13 he put garrisons in E. ; and all the Edo.
2 Ch. 8. 17 to Eloth, at the sea side in the land of E.
25. 20 because they sought after the gods of E.
Psa. 60. *title.* and smote of E. in the valley of Salt
60. 8 over E. will I cast out my shoe : Philistia
60. 9 the strong city? who will lead me into E.?
83. 6 The tabernacles of E., and the Ishmael.
108. 9 over E. will I cast out my shoe; over P.
108. 10 the strong city? who will lead me into E.?
137. 7 Remember, O LORD, the children of E. in
Isa. 11. 14 they shall lay their hand upon E. and M.
63. 1 Who (is) this that cometh from E., with
Jer. 9. 26 Egypt, and Judah, and E., and the chil.
25. 21 E., and Moab, and the children of Amm.
27. 3 send them to the king of E., and to the
40. 11 Likewise..all the Jews that (were) in..E.
49. 7 Concerning E., thus saith the LORD of
49. 17 Also E. shall be a desolation : every one
49. 20 of the LORD, that he hath taken against E.
49. 22 shall the heart of the mighty men of E.
Lam. 4. 21 Rejoice and be glad, O daughter of E.
4. 22 he will visit thine iniquity, O daughter of E.
Eze. 25. 12 Because that E. hath dealt against the
25. 13 I will..stretch out mine hand upon E
25. 14 And I will lay my vengeance upon E.
25. 14 they shall do in E. according to mine
32. 29 There (is) E., her kings, and all her prin.
Dan. 11. 41 these shall escape out of his hand..E.
Joel 3. 19 E. shall be a desolate wilderness, for the
Amos 1. 6 the whole captivity, to deliver..up to E.
1. 9 delivered up the whole captivity to E.
1. 11 For three transgressions of E...I will not
2. 1 he burned the bones of the king of E. into
9. 12 That they may possess the remnant of E.
Obad. 1 Thus saith the Lord GOD concerning E.
8 Shall I not..destroy the wise..out of E.
Mal. 1. 4 Whereas E. saith, We are impoverished

E-DOM-ITES, אֲדוֹמִים, אֱדוֹם *adomim, edom.*
The patronymic of the descendants of Edom or Esau. Their first form of government resembled that of the modern Bedawin, each tribe having a petty chief or Sheikh.
Gen. 36. 9 Esau the father of the E. in mount Seir
36. 43 he (is) Esau the father of the E.
Deut 23. 7 Thou shalt not abhor an E. ; for he (is)
1 Sa. 21. 7 his name (was) Doeg, an E., the chiefest of
22. 9 Then answered Doeg the E., which was
22. 18 Doeg the E. turned, and he fell upon the
1 Ki. 11. 1 Solomon loved..women of the..E., Zidon.
11. 14 And the LORD stirred up..Hadad the E.
2 Ki. 8. 21 he rose by night, and smote the E. which
1 Ch. 18. 12 the son of Zeruiah slew of the E. in the
18. 13 and all the E. became David's servants
2 Ch. 21. 8 In his days the E. revolted from under
21. 9 he rose up by night, and smote the E.
21. 10 So the E. revolted from under the hand
25. 14 was come from the slaughter of the E.
25. 19 Thou sayest, Lo, thou hast smitten the E.
28. 17 For again the E. had come and smitten
Psa. 52. *title.* when Doeg the E. came and told Saul

ED-RE'-I, אֶדְרֶעִי *sown land.*
1. A city of Og, in the S. of Bashan, and N. of the river Jabbok, given to Manasseh. It is 25 miles from Bozrah and 9 from Abila (now *Draa*), which is itself 24 from Damascus.
Num 21. 33 he, and all his people, to the battle at E.
Deut 1. 4 and Og..which dwelt at Astaroth in E.
3. 1 he and all his people, to the battle at E.
3. 10 Salchah and E., cities of the kingdom of
Josh. 12. 4 Og..that dwelt at Ashtaroth and at E.
13. 12 Og..which reigned in Ashtaroth and in E.
13. 31 Ashtaroth, and E., cities of the kingdom

2. A city of the tribe of Naphtali.
Josh. 19. 37 And Kedesh, and E., and En-hazor

EFFECT —
1. *Matter*, דָּבָר *dabar.*
Eze 12. 23 The days are at hand, and the effect of

2. *Service*, עֲבוֹדָה *abodah.*
Isa. 32. 17 the effect of righteousness quietness and

EFFECT, to become of no —
To be made useless, καταργέομαι *katargeomai.*
Gal. 5. 4 Christ is become of no effect unto you

EFFECT, to make of none —
1. *To break, discourage, disallow*, נוּא *no*, 5.
Psa. 33. 10 he maketh the devices..of none effect

2. *To break, make void*, פָּרַר *parar*, 5.
Num 30. 8 he shall make her vow..of none effect

3. *To make powerless, lordless*, ἀκυρόω *akuroō.*
Matt. 15. 6 Thus have ye made..of none effect by
Mark 7. 13 making the word of God of none effect

4. *To make useless*, καταργέω *katargeō.*
Rom. 4. 14 and the promise made of none effect
Gal. 3. 17 it should make the promise of none effect

5. *To make vain, empty*, κενόω *kenoō.*
1 Co. 1. 17 the cross..should be made of none effect

EFFECT, to make without —
To make useless, καταργέω *katargeō.*
Rom. 3. 3 make the faith of God without effect?

EFFECT, to take none —
To fall out of, ἐκπίπτω *ekpiptō.*
Rom. 9. 6 the word of God hath taken none effect

EFFECT, to (prosperously) —
1. *To do*, עָשָׂה *asah.*
Jer. 48. 30 saith the LORD..his lies shall not so effect

2. *To cause to prosper*, צָלַח *tsaleach*, 5.
2 Ch. 7. 11 all that came..he prosperously effected

EFFECTUAL —
In working, ἐνεργής *energēs.*
1 Co. 16. 9 For a great door and effectual is opened
Phm. 6 That the communication..may become e.

EFFECTUAL, to be —
To work in, ἐνεργέω *energeō.*
2 Co. 1. 6 which is effectual in the enduring of the

EFFECTUAL fervent —
To work in, ἐνεργέω *energeō.*
Jas. 5. 16 The effectual fervent prayer of a righteous

EFFECTUAL working —
Inworking, ἐνέργεια *energeia.*
Eph. 3. 7 given unto me by the effectual working
4. 16 according to the effectual working in the

EFFECTUALLY in, to work —
To work in, ἐνεργέω *energeō.*
Gal. 2. 8 For he that wrought effectually in Peter
1 Th. 2. 13 which effectually worketh also in you that

EFFEMINATE —
Soft, μαλακός *malakos.*
1 Co. 6. 9 nor effeminate, nor abusers of themselves

EGG —
1. *Egg, yolk, curdled milk*, חַלָּמוּת *challamuth.*
Job 6. 6 is there (any) taste in the white of an egg?

2. *Eggs*, בֵּיצִים *betsim.*
Deut 22. 6 young ones, or eggs, and the dam
22. 6 and the dam sitting upon..the eggs
Job 39. 14 Which leaveth her eggs in the earth, and
Isa. 10. 14 and as one gathereth eggs (that are) left
59. 5 They hatch cockatrice' eggs, and weave
59. 5 he that eateth of their eggs dieth, and that

3. *Egg*, ᾠόν *ōon.*
Luke 11. 12 Or if he shall ask an egg, will he offer

EG'-LAH, עֶגְלָה *calf.*
One of David's wives, and mother of his 6th son, B.C. 1050.
2 Sa. 3. 5 And the sixth, Ithream, by E., David's
1 Ch. 3. 3 the sixth, Ithream by E., his wife

EG-LA'-IM, אֶגְלַיִם *double spring.*
A city of Moab, eight miles S. of Areopolis.
Isa. 15. 8 the howling thereof unto E., and..Beer.

EG'-LON, עֶגְלוֹן *circle.*
1. An Amorite city in N.W. of Judah (now *Ajlan*), in the *Shefelah* or "low country." King Debir was its ruler when Joshua conquered it and its four confederate cities.
Josh. 10. 3 sent..unto Debir king of E., saying
10. 5 king of Lachish, the king of E., gathered
10. 23 the king of Lachish, (and) the king of E.
10. 34 from Lachish Joshua passed unto E.
10. 36 Joshua went up from E., and all Israel
10. 37 according to all that he had done to E.
12. 12 The king of E., one ; the king of Gezer
15. 39 Lachish, and Bozkath and E.

2. A king of the Moabites who, aided by the Ammonites and Amalekites, crossed the Jordan and took "the city of Palm-trees," or Jericho, where he built a palace and continued for eighteen years to oppress the Israelites. He was slain by Ehud, son of Gera, a Benjamite, B.C. 1336.

Judg. 3. 12 the LORD strengthened E. the king of
3. 14 So the children of Israel served E. the
3. 15 Israel sent a present unto E. the king of
3. 17 E. king of Moab : and E. (was) a very fat

E'-GYPT, מִצְרַיִם, Αἴγυπτος, Μεσραΐν.

A country at the N.E. angle of Africa, and lying between 31° 37' and 24° 1' N.; and 27° 13' and 34° 12' E. Its limits appear to have been almost always the same. In Eze. 29. 10 and 30. 6 the whole country is spoken of as extending from Migdol to Syene, which indicates the same limits to the E. and S. as at present. The tract irrigated by the Nile was, in ancient times, the real extent of Egypt. In modern times alone has the name been used in a more extended sense. In the Bible the common name is "*Mitsraim*" or "the land of Mitsraim." It was colonised by the descendants of Ham. The word Mitsraim is dual, and indicates the natural division of the country into an upper and lower region—the plain of the Delta, and the narrow valley above, as it has been commonly called at all times. When the singular form *Matsor* occurs, some suppose it points out Lower Egypt only. *Matsor* means "red mud." The "land of Ham," is also poetically used in the Bible for Egypt.

The following table has been compiled from the works of the best authorities:—In B.C. 2717 Menes, the first king of Egypt, and founder of the Thinite dynasty, begins to reign; 2280 Thebes founded; 2188 Memphis founded; 2126 Egypt divided into Egypt proper, Lower Egypt, This, and Memphis; 2122 Hieroglyphics invented by Athotes; 2120 Suphis and his brother Sensuphis build pyramids to the north of Memphis, which still exist; 2100 Osymandyas extends his conquests into Asia; the worship of Osiris, Isis, Phtha, and Ammon introduced; 2080 Memphis taken by the shepherd kings of Phœnicia, who establish their dynasty; 1938 lake Mœris constructed; 1920 arrival of Abraham, and expulsion of the shepherd kings; 1891 Syphoas introduces common letters; 1828 the Phœnicians expelled from Lower Egypt; 1822 Memnon invents the Egyptian alphabet; 1821 Amenophis I. becomes king of all Egypt; 1728 Joseph sold into Egypt; 1706 settlement of Jacob and his family in Goshen; 1635 death of Joseph; 1618 accession of Sesostris; 1615 the Ethiopians obtain a footing in Egypt; 1491 the ten plagues are suffered by the Egyptians, and the exodus of the Israelites is accomplished; 1485 reign of Egyptus, from whom the country is named Egypt instead of Mizraim; 1322 commencement of first Sothic cycle; 1308 reign of Sethos, who builds the temple of Vulcan at Memphis, and other works; 1214 reign of Thuoris, or Proteus; 1183 Menelaus arrives in Egypt after the Trojan war, and receives Helen from Thuoris; 1082 reign of Cheops; 1004 alliance between Shishak, king of Egypt, and Solomon; 972 Shishak invades Judea, and takes Jerusalem; 825 accession of Peterbastes, founder of the Tanaite dynasty; 786 Egypt establishes her supremacy over the Mediterranean; 781 commencement of the Saite dynasty; 769 So, the Ethiopian, deposes Anysis; 722 alliance with Hoshea king of Israel; 719 So abdicates and returns to Ethiopia; 711 invaded by Sennacherib king of Assyria; 685 Egypt divided between twelve kings; 660 Psammetichus I. obtains the sovereignty of the whole of Egypt; 630 siege of Azotus, or Ashdod, by Psammetichus—it lasts twenty years; 610 Pharaoh Necho attempts to connect the Mediterranean and Red Seas by a canal; but, after losing 120,000 men, compelled to relinquish the undertaking; 605 Pharaoh Necho defeated by Nebuchadnezzar; 600 Psammis, king of Egypt, invades Ethiopia; 581 Nebuchadnezzar deposes Pharaoh Hophra, or Apries; 572 he ravages Egypt; 569 makes Amasis king, during whose reign Egypt contains 20,000 cities; 554 Solon visits it; 536 Pythagoras visits it; 535 Cyrus renders Egypt tributary; 525 Cambyses invades Egypt, and abolishes the empire of the Pharaohs; 484 Xerxes suppresses an insurrection of the Egyptians; 460 Inarus rebels against the Persians; 418 Herodotus visits Egypt; 413 Amyrtæus restores it to independence; 350 it is again subjected to Persia by Ochus; 332 Alexandria founded by Alexander the Great; 322 Ptolemy I. (Soter) restores the independence of Egypt, and transfers the seat of government to Alexandria; 320 revolt of Phœnicia, and immigration of about 100,000 Jews; 314 Phœnicia is wrested from Egypt by Antigonus, king of Phrygia; 301 battle of Ipsus, which secures the independence of Egypt, and final restoration of Phœnicia; 273 an Egyptian embassy arrives at Rome; 272 Memphis is made capital; 246 Ptolemy III. invades Syria; 217 battle of Raphia, which subjects Coele-Syria and Palestine to the Egyptian yoke; 203 alliance concluded with Rome—Judea is lost; 198 Syria regains its independence; 183 an insurrection quelled by Polycrates; 171 Antiochus Epiphanes defeats Eulæus, regent of Egypt, and makes him prisoner; 164 kingdom divided between Ptolemy VI. and his brother Physcon; 146 Ptolemy falls in battle, and Physcon usurps the throne; 131 Physcon (Ptolemy VII.) puts away his wife Cleopatra and marries her daughter by his own brother; 129 is compelled to flee to Cyprus; 128 a pestilence, caused by swarms of locusts, carries off 800,000 of the population; 107 Cleopatra compels Ptolemy VIII. to retire to Cyprus, and governs Egypt; 88 civil war between Ptolemy VIII. and Alexander I.; 82 capture and destruction of Thebes; 80 abdication of Alexander III., and election of Ptolemy X., who renders his country tributary to the Romans; 58 the Egyptians expel Ptolemy X., and establish Berenice and Tryphæna; 51 death of Ptolemy, who leaves his kingdom to Ptolemy XI. and Cleopatra; 49 Ptolemy expels Cleopatra, and civil war ensues.

Gen. 12. 10 Abram went down into E. to sojourn there
12. 11 when he was come near to enter into E.
12. 14 it came to pass..Abram was come into E.
13. 1 Abram went up out of E., he, and his
13. 10 like the land of E., as thou comest unto
15. 18 from the river of E. unto the great river
21. 21 took him a wife out of the land of E.
25. 18 from Havilah unto Shur, that (is) before E.
26. 2 And the LORD..said, Go not down into E.
37. 25 bearing..myrrh..to carry (it) down to E.
37. 28 and they brought Joseph into E.
37. 36 the Midianites sold him into E. unto P.
39. 1 And Joseph was brought down to E.
40. 1 the butler of the king of E. and (his) ba.
40. 1 had offended their lord the king of E.
40. 5 the butler and the baker of the king of E.
41. 8 sent and called for all the magicians of E.
41. 19 such as I never saw in all the land of E.
41. 29 great plenty throughout all the land of E.
41. 30 plenty shall be forgotten in the land of E.
41. 33 man..wise, and set him over the land of E.
41. 34 take up the fifth part of the land of E.
41. 36 of famine, which shall be in the land of E.
41. 41 I have set thee over all the land of E.
41. 43 made him (ruler) over all the land of E.
41. 44 shall no man lift up his hand..in..E.
41. 45 Joseph went out over..the land of E.
41. 46 when he stood before Pharaoh king of E.
41. 46 Jos...went throughout all the land of E.
41. 48 seven years, which were in the land of E.
41. 53 seven years of plenteousness..in..E., were
41. 54 in all the land of E. there was bread
41. 55 And when all the land of E. was famished
41. 56 the famine waxed sore in the land of E.
41. 57 all countries came into E..to buy (corn)
42. 1 Jacob saw that there was corn in E.
42. 2 I have heard that there is corn in E.
42. 3 ten brethren went down to buy corn in E.
43. 2 corn which they had brought out of E.
43. 15 rose up, and went down to E., and stood
45. 4 Jos. your brother, whom ye sold into E.
45. 8 and a ruler throughout all the land of E.
45. 9 God hath made me lord of all E.
45. 13 shall tell my father of all my glory in E.
45. 18 will give you the good of the land of E.
45. 19 take you wagons out of the land of E.
45. 20 for the good of all the land of E. (is)
45. 23 asses laden with the good things of E.
45. 25 they went up out of E., and came into
45. 26 he (is) governor over all the land of E.
46. 3 fear not to go down into E.; for I will there
46. 4 I will go down with thee into E.
46. 6 they took their cattle..and came into E.
46. 7 all his seed, brought he with him into E.
46. 8 the children of Israel which came into E.
46. 20 unto Joseph in the land of E. were born
46. 26 the souls that came with Jacob into E.
46. 27 sons of Joseph, which were born him in E.
46. 27 souls of the house of Jacob..came into E.
47. 6 The land of E. (is) before thee: in the
47. 11 gave them a possession in the land of E.
47. 13 the land of E...fainted by reason of the
47. 14 the money that was found in the land of E.
47. 15 And when money failed in the land of E.
47. 20 Joseph bought all the land of E. for Ph.
47. 21 removed them..from (one) end of..E.
47. 26 Joseph made it a law over the land of E.
47. 27 And Israel dwelt in the land of E.
47. 28 Jacob lived in the land of E. seventeen
47. 29 bury me not, I pray thee, in E.
47. 30 thou shalt carry me out of E., and bury
48. 5 Ephr. and Manasseh..were born..in..E.
48. 5 before I came unto thee into E., (are)
50. 7 and all the elders of the land of E.
50. 14 Joseph returned into E., he, and his
50. 22 Joseph dwelt in E., he and his father's
50. 26 and he was put in a coffin in E.

Exod. 1. 1 children of Israel, which came into E.
1. 5 for Joseph was in E. (already)
1. 8 Now there arose up a new king over E.
1. 15 And the king of E spake to the Hebrew
1. 17 midwives..did not as the king of E. co.
1. 18 And the king of E called for the midwives
2. 23 in process of time..the king of E. died
3. 7 affliction of my people which (are) in E.
3. 10 mayest bring forth my people..out of E.
3. 11 I should bring forth..Israel out of E.?
3. 12 hast brought forth the people out of E.
3. 16 have..(seen) that which is done to you in E.
3. 17 will bring you up out of the affliction of E.
3. 18 and thou shalt come..unto the king of E.
3. 19 the king of E. will not let you go, no
3. 20 I will stretch out my hand, and smite E.
4. 18 return unto my brethren which (are) in E.
4. 19 And the LORD said..Go, return into E.
4. 20 and he returned to the land of E.
4. 21 When thou goest to return into E., see
5. 4 the king of E. said unto them, Wherefore
5. 12 scattered..throughout all the land of E.
6. 11 Go in, speak unto Pharaoh king of E.
6. 13 them a charge unto..Pharaoh king of E.
6. 13 to bring the children of Israel out of..E.
6. 26 Bring out the children of Israel from..E.
6. 27 they which spake to Paraoh king of E.
6. 27 to bring out the children of Israel from E.
6. 28 LORD spake unto Moses in the land of E.
6. 29 speak thou unto Pharaoh king of E. all

Exod. 7. 3 multiply..my wonders in the land of E.
7. 4 that I may lay my hand upon E.
7. 4 out of the land of E. by great judgments
7. 5 when I stretch forth mine hand upon E.
7. 11 the magicians of E., they also did in like
7. 19 stretch..thine hand upon the waters of E.
7. 19 may be blood throughout all the land of E.
7. 22 the magicians of E. did so with their v.21
8. 5 cause frogs to come up upon the land of E.
8. 6 stretched..his hand over the waters of E.
8. 6 frogs came up, and covered the land of E.
8. 7 and brought up frogs upon the land of E.
8. 16 become lice throughout all the land of E.
8. 17 became lice throughout all the land of E.
8. 24 there came..(flies) into..all the land of E.
9. 4 the cattle of Israel and the cattle of E.
9. 6 and all the cattle of E. died: but of
9. 9 become small dust in all the land of E.
9. 9 upon beast, throughout all the land of E.
9. 18 such as hath not been in E. since the fou.
9. 22 there may be hail in all the land of E.
9. 22 every herb..throughout the land of E.
9. 23 the LORD rained hail upon the land of E.
9. 24 there was none like it in all the land of E.
9. 25 hail smote throughout all the land of E.
10. 2 what things I have wrought in E., and my
10. 7 knowest thou not yet that E. is destroyed?
10. 12 Stretch out thine hand over the land of E.
10. 12 they may come up upon the land of E.
10. 13 stretched forth his rod over the land of E.
10. 14 the locusts went up over all the land of E.
10. 14 and rested in all the coasts of E.
10. 15 not any green thing..through..E.
10. 19 not one locust in all the coasts of E.
10. 21 there may be darkness over the land of E.
10. 22 there was..darkness in all the land of E.
11. 1 will I bring one plague (more) upon..E.
11. 3 Moses (was) very great in the land of E.
11. 4 midnight will I go out into the midst of E.
11. 5 all the first born in the land of E. shall
11. 6 shall be a great cry throughout all..E.
11. 9 wonders may be multip. in the land of E.
12. 1 LORD spake unto Moses..in the land of E.
12. 12 I will pass through the land of E. this
12. 12 will smite all the first born in the land of E.
12. 12 against all the gods of E. I will execute
12. 13 when I smite the land of E.
12. 17 I brought your armies out of the land of E.
12. 27 passed over the houses of..Israel in E.
12. 29 smote all the first born in the land of E.
12. 30 and there was a great cry in E.; for
12. 39 dough which they brought forth out of E.
12. 39 because they were thrust out of E., and
12. 40 of the children of Israel, who dwelt in E.
12. 41 all the hosts of the LORD went out..of E.
12. 42 for bringing them out from the land of E.
12. 51 the LORD did bring..Israel out of..E.
13. 3 this day, in which ye came out from E.
13. 8 unto me when I came forth out of E.
13. 9 hath the LORD brought thee out of E.
13. 14 the LORD brought us out from E., from
13. 15 slew all the first born in the land of E.
13. 16 strength..LORD brought..us out of E.
13. 17 the people repent..and..return to E.
13. 18 went up harnessed out of the land of E.
14. 5 it was told the king of E. that the people
14. 7 And he took..all the chariots of E., and
14. 8 the LORD hardened..Pharaoh king of E.
14. 11 Because (there were) no graves in E., hast
14. 11 dealt thus..to carry us forth out of E.?
14. 12 (Is) not this..that we did tell thee in E.
16. 1 month after their departing out of..E.
16. 3 had died by the hand of the LORD in..E
16. 6 hath brought you out from the land of E.
16. 32 I brought you forth from the land of E.
17. 3 thou hast brought us up out of E., to kill
18. 1 the LORD had brought Israel out of E.
19. 1 when..Israel were gone forth out of..E.
20. 2 which have brought thee out of..E.
22. 21 for ye were strangers in the land of E.
23. 9 seeing ye were strangers in the land of E.
23. 15 for in it thou camest out from E.
29. 46 brought them forth out of the land of E.
32. 1 that brought us up out of the land of E.
32. 4 brought thee up out of the land of E.
32. 7 which thou broughtest out of the land of E.
32. 8 brought thee up out of the land of E.
32. 11 hast brought forth out of the land of E.
32. 23 that brought us up out of the land of E.
33. 1 hast brought up out of the land of E.
34. 18 the month Abib thou camest out from E.

Lev. 11. 45 the LORD that bringeth you up out of..E.
18. 3 After the doings of the land of E.
19. 34 for ye were strangers in the land of E.
19. 36 which brought you out of the land of E.
22. 33 That brought you out of the land of E.
23. 43 when I brought them out of the land of E.
25. 38 brought you forth out of the land of E.
25. 42 servants, which I brought forth out of..E.
25. 55 servants whom I brought forth out of..E.
26. 13 God, which brought you forth out of..E.
26. 45 ancestors, whom I brought forth out of..E.

Num. 1. 1 after they were come out of the land of E.
3. 13 I smote all the first born in the land of E.
8. 17 I smote every first born in the land of E.
9. 1 after they were come out of the land of E.
11. 5 We remember the fish..we did eat in E.
11. 18 flesh to eat? for (it was) well with us in E.
11. 20 saying, Why came we forth out of E.?
13. 22 Hebron was built..before Zoan in E.
14. 2 Would God that we had died in..E.!
14. 3 Were it not better for us to return into E.

Num 14. 4 make a captain, and let us return into E.
14. 19 forgiven this people, from E. even until
14. 22 my miracles, which I did in E. and in
15. 41 which brought you out of the land of E.
20. 5 have ye made us to come up out of E., to
20. 15 How our fathers went down into E.
20. 15 and we have dwelt in E. a long time
20 16 and hath brought us forth out of E.
21. 5 have ye brought us up out of E. to die
22. 5, 11 Behold..a people come out from E.
23. 22 God brought them out of E.; he hath
24. 8 God brought him forth out of E.; he hath
26. 4 which went forth out of the land of E.
26. 59 whom (her mother) bare to Levi in E.
32. 11 none of the men that came up out of E.
33. 1 which went forth out of the land of E.
33. 38 Israel were come out of the land of E.
34. 5 compass from Azmon unto the river of E.
Deut. 1. 27 hath brought us forth out of the land of E.
1. 30 according to all that he did for you in E.
4. 20 the LORD hath taken you..out of E.
4. 34 according to all..God did for you in E.
4. 37 thee..with his mighty power out of E.
4. 45 spake..after they came forth out of E.
4. 46 after they were come forth out of E.
5. 6 which brought thee out of the land of E.
5. 15 thou wast a servant in the land of E.
6. 12 brought thee forth out of the land of E.
6. 21 We were Pharaoh's bondmen in E.
6. 21 LORD brought us out of E. with a mighty
6. 22 LORD showed signs and wonders..upon E.
7. 8 from the hand of Pharaoh king of E.
7. 15 will put none of the evil diseases of E.
7. 18 remember what..God did..unto all E.
8. 14 brought thee forth out of the land of E.
9. 7 thou didst depart out of the land of E.
9. 12, 26 which thou hast brought forth out of E.
10. 19 for ye were strangers in the land of E.
10. 22 Thy fathers went down into E. with three.
11. 3 miracles..which he did in the midst of E.
11. 3 unto Pharaoh the king of E., and unto
11. 4 what he did unto the army of E., unto
11. 10 land..(is) not as the land of E., from
13. 5, 10 which brought you out of the land of E.
15. 15 thou wast a bondman in the land of E.
16. 1 God brought thee forth out of E. by night
16. 3, 3 thou camest forth out of the land of E.
16. 6 season that thou camest forth out of E.
16. 12 remember that thou wast a bondman in E.
17. 16 shall not .cause the people to return to E.
20. 1 brought thee up out of the land of E.
23. 4 met you not..when ye came fo. out of E.
24. 9 after that ye were come forth out of E.
24. 18, 22 remember..thou wast a bondman in E.
25 17 when ye were come forth out of E.
26. 5 he went down into E., and sojourned
26 8 And the LORD brought us forth out of E.
28. 27 LORD will smite thee with the botch of E.
28. 60 bring upon thee all the diseases of E.
28. 68 the LORD shall bring thee into E. again
29. 2 all that the LORD did..in the land of E.
29. 16 know how we have dwelt in the land of E.
29. 25 brought them forth out of the land of E.
34 11 which the LORD sent him to do in..E.
Josh. 2. 10 dried up the..sea..when ye came out of E.
5. 4 All the people that came out of E.
5. 4 of war, died..after they came out of E.
5. 5 by the way as they came forth out of E.
5. 6 men of war, which came out of E., were
5. 9 I rolled away the reproach of E. from off
9. 9 we have heard..all that he did in E.
13. 3 From Sihor, which (is) before E., even
15. 4 Azmon, and went out unto the river of E.
15. 47 unto the river of E., and the great sea
24. 4 Jacob and his children went down into E.
24. 5 I sent Moses also..and I plagued E.
24. 6 And I brought your fathers out of E.
24. 7 eyes have seen what I have done in E.
24. 14 gods which your fathers served..in E.
24. 17 brought..our fathers out of the land of E.
24. 32 children of Israel brought up out of E.
Judg. 2. 1 and said, I made you to go up out of E.
2. 12 which brought them out of the land of E.
6. 8 saith the LORD..I brought you up from E.
6. 13 Did not the LORD bring us up from E.?
11. 13 my land, when they came up out of E.
11. 16 But when Israel came up from E.
19. 30 that..Israel came up out of the land of E.
1 Sa. 2. 27 when they were in E. in Pharaoh's house?
8. 8 day that I brought them up out of E.
10. 18 saith the LORD..I brought up..out of E.
12. 6 LORD..brought your fathers up out of..E.
12. 8 When Jacob was come into E., and your
12. 8 which brought forth your fathers out of E.
15. 2 I remember..when he came up from E.
15. 6 kindness..when they came up out of E.
15. 7 comest to Shur, that (is) over against E.
27. 8 goest to Shur, even unto the land of E.
30. 13 he said, I (am) a young man of E., servant
2 Sa. 7. 6 since the time..I brought..Isr. out of E.
7. 23 which thou redeemedst to thee from E.
1 Ki. 3. 1 made affinity with Pharaoh king of E.
4. 21 Solomon reigned..unto the border of E.
4. 30 Solomon's wisdom excelled..wisdom of E.
6. 1 children of Israel were come out of..E.
8. 9 when they came out of the land of E.
8. 16 I brought forth my people..out of E.
8. 21 he brought them out of the land of E.
8. 51 which thou broughtest forth out of E.
8. 53 thou broughtest our fathers out of E.
8. 65 from..Hamath unto the river of E.
9. 9 brought forth their fathers out of..E.

1 Ki. 9. 16 (For) Pharaoh king of E. had gone up and
10. 28 Solomon had horses brought out of E.
10. 29 a chariot came up and went out of E. for
11. 17 That Hadad fled..to go into E.
11. 18 came to E., unto Pharaoh king of E.
11. 21 Hadad heard in E. that David slept with
11. 40 fled into E., unto Shishak king of E.
11. 40 and was in E. until the death of Solomon
12. 2 when Jeroboam..who was yet in E.
12. 2 was fled from..Solomon, and..dwelt in E.
12. 28 which brought thee..out of the land of E.
14. 25 Shishak king of E. came up against Jer.
2 Ki. 17. 4 he had sent messengers to So king of E.
17. 7 brought them up out of the land of E.
17. 7 from under the hand of Pharaoh king of E.
17. 36 the LORD, who brought you up out of..E.
18. 21 the staff of this bruised reed..upon E.
18. 21 so (is) Pharaoh king of E. unto all that
18. 24 put thy trust on E. for chariots and for
21. 15 the day their fathers came forth out of E.
23. 29 In his days Pharaoh-nechoh king of E.
23. 34 and he came to E., and died there
24. 7 And the king of E. came not again any
24. 7 king..had taken from the river of E. unto
24. 7 all that pertained to the king of E.
25. 26 the captains of the armies..came to E.
1 Ch. 13. 5 from Shihor of E. even unto the entering
17. 21 people..thou hast redeemed out of E.?
2 Ch. 1. 16 Solomon had horses brought out of E.
1. 17 And they..brought forth out of E. a cha.
5. 10 children of Israel, when they ca. out of E.
6. 5 I brought forth my people out of..E.
7. 8 from..Hamath unto the river of E.
7. 22 brought them forth out of the land of E.
9. 26 reigned over all..to the border of E.
9. 28 brought unto Solomon horses out of E.
10. 2 Jeroboam..in E...returned out of E.
12. 2 Shishak king of E. came up against Jer.
12. 3 without number that came..out of E.
12. 9 So Shishak king of E. came up against
20. 10 when they came out of the land of E.
26. 8 name spread..to the entering in of E.
35. 20 Necho king of E. came up to fight against
36. 3 the king of E. put him down at Jerusalem
36. 4 the king of E. made Eliakim his brother
36. 4 Necho took Jehoahaz..and carried..to E.
Neh 9. 9 didst see the affliction of our fathers in E.
9. 18 God that brought thee up out of E.
Psa. 68. 31 Princes shall come out of E.; Ethiopia
78. 12 Marvellous things did he..in the land of E.
78. 43 How he had wrought his signs in E.
78. 51 And smote all the first born in E.
80. 8 Thou hast brought a vine out of E.
81. 5 when he went out through the land of E.
81. 10 which brought thee out of the land of E.
105. 23 Israel also came into E.; and Jacob
105. 38 E. was glad when they departed: for the
106. 7 fathers understood not thy wonders in E.
106. 21 saviour, which had done great things in E.
114. 1 When Israel went out of E., the house of
135. 8 Who smote the first born of E., both of
135. 9 sent..wonders into the midst of thee, O E.
136. 10 To him that smote E. in their first born
Prov. 7. 16 have decked my bed..with fine linen of E.
Isa. 7. 18 in the uttermost part of the rivers of E.
10. 24 lift up his staff..after the manner of E.
10. 26 shall he lift it up after the manner of E.
11. 11 recover the remnant of his peo...from E.
11. 16 day that he came up out of the land of E.
19. 1 The burden of E..Behold, the LORD rideth
19. 1 Behold, the LORD..shall come into E.
19. 1 the idols of E. shall be moved at his pre.
19. 1 the heart of E. shall melt in the midst of
19. 3 the spirit of E. shall fail in the midst
19. 12 what the LORD of hosts..purposed upon E.
19. 13 they have also seduced E., (even they
19. 14 they have caused E. to err in every work
19. 15 Neither shall there be (any) work for E.
19. 16 that day shall E. be like unto women
19. 17 land of Judah shall be a terror unto E.
19. 18 In that day..five cities in the land of E.
19. 19 an altar to the LORD in the midst of..E.
19. 20 witness unto the LORD..in the land of E.
19. 21 And the LORD shall be known to E.
19. 22 the LORD shall smite E.: he shall smite
19. 23 In that day shall..be a highway out of E.
19. 23 and the Assyrian shall come into E.
19. 24 In that day shall Israel be..with E. and
19. 25 Blessed (be) E. my people, and Assyria
20. 3 a sign and wonder upon E. and upon Eth.
20. 4 buttocks uncovered, to the shame of E.
20. 5 they shall be..ashamed of..E. their
23. 5 As at the report concerning E., (so) shall
27. 12 from the channel..unto the stream of E.
27. 13 and the outcasts in the land of E...shall
30. 2 That walk to go down into E., and have
30. 2 and to trust in the shadow of E.!
30. 3 the trust in the shadow of E. (your) con.
31. 1 Woe to them that go down to E. for help
36. 6 thou trustest in..this broken reed, on E.
36. 6 so (is) Pharaoh king of E. to all that trust
36. 9 put thy trust on E. for chariots and for
43. 3 I gave E. (for) thy ransom, Ethiopia and
45. 14 The labour of E...shall come over unto
52. 4 My people went down aforetime into E.
Jer 2. 6 LORD..brought us up out of the land of E.
2. 18 what hast thou to do in the way of E.
2. 36 thou also shalt be ashamed of E., as thou
7. 22 the day that I brought them out of..E.
7. 25 day..your fathers came forth out of..E.
9. 26 E., and Judah, and Edom, and the chil.
11. 4 I brought them forth out of the land of E.

Jer. 11. 7 I brought them up out of the land of E
16. 14 brought up the child. of Israel out of..E.
23. 7 brought up the children of Is. out of..E.
24. 8 and them that dwell in the land of E.
25. 19 Pharaoh king of E...and all his people
26. 21 he was afraid, and fled, and went into E.
26. 22 Jehoiakim the king sent men into E.
26. 22 and (certain) men with him into E.
26. 23 And they fetched forth Urijah out of E.
31. 32 to bring them out of the land of E.
32. 20 Which hast set signs..in the land of E.
32. 21 hast brought forth thy people..out of..E.
34. 13 I brought them forth out of the land of E.
37. 5 Pharaoh's army was come forth out of E.
37. 7 Pharaoh's army..shall return to E. into
41. 17 And they departed..to go to enter into E.
42. 14 No; but we will go into the land of E.
42. 15 ye wholly set your faces to enter into E.
42. 16 sword..shall overtake you there in..E.
42. 16 shall follow close after you there in E.
42. 17 the men that set their faces to go into E.
42. 18 upon you, when ye shall enter into E.
42. 19 ye remnant of Judah; Go ye not into E.
43. 2 to say, Go not into E. to sojourn there
43. 7 So they came into the land of E.; for they
43. 11 he cometh, he shall smite the land of E.
43. 12 kindle a fire in..houses of the gods of E.
43. 12 shall array himself with the land of E.
43. 13 Beth-shemesh, that (is) in the land of E.
44. 1 the Jews which dwell in the land of E.
44. 8 incense unto other gods in the land of E.
44. 12 set their faces to go into the land of E.
44. 12 they shall all..fall in the land of E.
44. 13 punish them that dwell in the land of E.
44. 14 which are gone into the land of E., to
44. 15 the people that dwelt in the land of E.
44. 24 all Judah that (are) in the land of E.
44. 26 all Judah that dwell in the land of E.
44. 26 any man of Judah in all the land of E.
44. 27 men of Judah that (are) in the land of E.
44. 28 number..shall return out of the la. of E.
44. 28 that are gone into the land of E.
44. 30 I will give Pharaoh-hophra king of E.
46. 2 Against E., against the army of..E.
46. 8 E. riseth up like a flood, and (his) waters
46. 11 take balm, O virgin, the daughter of E.
46. 13 Nebuchadrezzar..come (and) smite..E.
46. 14 Declare ye in E., and publish in Migdol
46. 17 Pharaoh king of E. (is but) a noise
46. 19 O thou daughter dwelling in E., furnish
46. 20 E. (is like) a very fair heifer, (but) destr.
46. 24 The daughter of E. shall be confounded
46. 25 I will punish..Pharaoh, and E., with
Eze 17. 15 rebelled against him in sending..into E.
19. 4 brought..with chains unto the land of E.
20. 5 made myself known unto them in..E.
20. 6 to bring them forth of the land of E.
20. 7 defile not yourselves with the idols of E.
20. 8 neither did they forsake the idols of E.
20. 8 accomplish my anger..in the midst of..E.
20. 9 bringing them forth out of the land of E.
20. 10 I caused them to go..out of the land of E.
20. 36 as..with your fathers in the..land of E.
23. 3 And they committed whoredoms in E.
23. 8 Neither left she her whoredoms..from E.
23. 19 she had played the harlot in the land of E.
23. 27 and thy whoredom..from the land of E.
23. 27 thou shalt not..remember E. any more
27. 7 Fine linen with broidered work from E.
29. 2 set thy face against Pharaoh king of E.
29. 2 prophesy against him, and against all E.
29. 3 I (am) against thee, Pharaoh king of E.
29. 6 inhabitants of E. shall know that I (am)
29. 9 the land of E. shall be desolate and waste
29. 10 I will make the land of E. utterly waste
29. 12 And I will make the land of E. desolate
29. 14 And I will bring again the captivity of E.
29. 19 I will give the land of E. unto Nebucha.
29. 20 I have given him the land of E. (for) his
30. 4 And the sword shall come upon E., and
30. 4 when the slain shall fall in E., and they
30. 6 They also that uphold E. shall fall
30. 8 when I have set a fire in E., and (when)
30. 9 great pain shall come..as in the day of E.
30. 10 I will also make the multitude of E. to
30. 11 they shall draw their swords against E.
30. 13 there shall be no more a prince of..E.
30. 13 and I will put a fear in the land of E.
30. 15 pour my fury upon..the strength of E.
30. 16 And I will set fire in E.: Sin shall have
30. 18 when I shall break there the yokes of E
30. 19 Thus will I execute judgments in E.
30. 21 I have broken the arm of Pha. king of E.
30. 22 Behold, I (am) against Pharaoh king of E.
30. 25 shall stretch it out upon the land of E.
31. 2 speak unto Pharaoh king of E., and to
32. 2 take up a lamentation for Pharaoh..of E.
32. 12 and they shall spoil the pomp of E., and
32. 15 When I shall make the land of E. deso.
32. 16 they shall lament for her..for E., and
32. 18 Son of man, wail for the multitude of E
Dan. 9. 15 hast brought thy people forth out of..E.
11. 8 And shall also carry captives into E. their
11. 42 and the land of E. shall not escape
11. 43 power..over all the precious things of E
Hos. 2. 15 when she came up out of the land of E.
7. 11 they call to E., they go to Assyria
7. 16 (shall be) their derision in the land of E.
8. 13 and visit their sins: they shall return to E
9. 3 Ephraim shall return to E., and they
9. 6 E. shall gather them up, Memphis shall
11. 1 I loved him, and called my son out of E

Hos. 11. 5 He shall not return into the land of E.
11. 11 They shall tremble as a bird out of E.
12. 1 and oil is carried into E.
12. 9 I..the LORD thy God from the land of E.
12. 13 by a prophet the LORD brought..out of E.
13. 4 I..the LORD thy God from the land of E.
Joel 3. 19 E. shall be a desolation, and Edom shall
Amos 2. 10 I brought you up from the land of E.
3. 1 which I brought up from the land of E.
3. 9 Publish..in the palaces in the land of E.
4. 10 have sent among you the pestilence..of E.
8. 8 and drowned, as (by) the flood of E.
9. 5 shall be drowned, as (by) the flood of E.
9. 7 I brought up Israel out of the land of E.?
Mic. 6. 4 I brought thee up out of the land of E.?
7. 15 days of thy coming out of the land of E.
Nah. 3. 9 Ethiopia and E. (were) her strength, and
Hag. 2. 5 I covenanted with you..ye came out of E.
Zech 10. 10 I will bring them..out of the land of E.
10. 11 and the sceptre of E. shall depart away
14. 18 if the family of E. go not up, and come
14. 19 This shall be the punishment of E., and
Matt. 2. 13 and take the young child..and flee into E.
2. 14 When he arose..and departed into E.
2. 15 Out of E. have I called my son
2. 19 LORD appeareth in a dream to Joseph in E.
Acts 2. 10 Phrygia, and Pamphilia, in E., and in
7. 9 And the patriarchs..sold Joseph into E.
7. 10 favour..in the sight of Pha. king of E.
7. 10 he made him governor over E. and all his
7. 11 came a dearth over all the land of E.
7. 12 Jacob heard that there was corn in E.
7. 15 So Jacob went down into E., and died
7. 17 the people grew and multiplied in E.
7. 34 I have seen the affliction..which is in E.
7. 34 And now come, I will send thee into E.
7. 36 he had showed wonders..in the land of E.
7. 39 their hearts turned back again into E.
7. 40 which brought us out of the land of E.
13. 17 they dwelt as strangers in the land of E.
Heb. 3. 16 howbeit not all that came out of E. by Mo.
8. 9 hand to lead them out of the land of E.
11. 26 greater riches than the treasures in E.
11. 27 By faith he forsook E., not fearing the
Jude 5 saved the people out of the land of E.
Rev. 11. 8 which spiritually is called Sodom and E.

EGYPTIAN, EGYPTIANS, מִצְרַיִם, מִצְרִים, Αἰγύπτιος.
1 The inhabitants of Egypt—descendants of Mitsraim the son of Ham.
Gen. 12. 12 when the E. shall see thee, that they shall
12. 14 the E. beheld the woman that she (was)
16. 1 she had an handmaid, an E., whose name
16. 3 And Sarai..took Hagar her maid, the E.
21. 9 And Sarah saw the son of Hagar the E.
25. 12 Ishmael..whom Hagar the E...bare unto
39. 1 an E., bought him of the hands of the Is.
39. 2 he was in the house of his master the E.
39. 5 the LORD blessed the E.'s house for Jose.
41. 55 Pharaoh said unto all the E., Go unto J.
41. 56 Joseph..sold unto the E.; and the famine
43. 32 and for the E. which did eat with him
43. 32 because the E. might not eat bread with
43. 32 that (is) an abomination unto the E.
45. 2 the E. and the house of Pharaoh heard
46. 34 shepherd (is) an abomination unto the E.
47. 15 all the E. came unto Joseph, and said
47. 20 for the E. sold every man his field, beca.
50. 3 the E. mourned for him threescore and
50. 11 This (is) a grievous mourning to the E.
Exod. 1. 13 the E. made the children of Israel to
1. 19 the Hebrew women (are) not as the E.
2. 11 and he spied an E. smiting an Hebrew
2. 12 he slew the E., and hid him in the sand
2. 14 thou to kill me, as thou killedst the E.?
2. 19 An E. delivered us out of the hand of the
3. 8 to deliver them out of the hand of the E.
3. 9 the oppression wherewith the E. oppress
3. 21 I will give..favour in the sight of the E.
3. 22 and ye shall spoil the E.
6. 5 the children of Israel, whom the E. keep
6. 6, 7 out from under the burdens of the E
7. 5 the E. shall know that I (am) the LORD
7. 18 the E. shall loathe to drink of the water
7. 21 the E. could not drink of the water of the
7. 24 all the E. digged round about the river
8. 21 the houses of the E. shall be full..(of flies)
8. 26 shall sacrifice the abomination of the E.
8. 26 shall we sacrifice the abomination of the E.
9. 11 for the boil was upon..all the E.
10. 6 they shall fill..the houses of all the E.
11. 3 the people favour in the sight of the E.
11. 7 LORD doth put a difference between the E.
12. 23 the LORD will pass through to smite the E.
12. 27 when he smote the E., and delivered our
12. 30 he, and all his servants, and all the E.
12. 33 And the E. were urgent upon the people
12. 35 they borrowed of the E. jewels of silver
12. 36 sight of the E...and they spoiled the E.
14. 4 that the E. may know that I (am) the L.
14. 9 But the E. pursued after them, all the
14. 10 and, behold, the E. marched after them
14. 12 Let us alone, that we may serve the E.?
14. 12 (it had been) better for us to serve the E.
14. 13 for the E. whom ye have seen to day, ye
14. 17 I will harden the hearts of the E.
14. 18 the E. shall know that I (am) the LORD
14. 20 it came between the camp of the E. and
14. 23 And the E. pursued, and went in after
14. 24 the LORD looked unto the host of the E.
14. 24 and troubled the host of the E.
14. 25 the E. said, Let us flee from the face of
Exod 14. 25 the LORD fighteth for them against the E.
14. 26 the waters may come again upon the E.
14. 27 and the E. fled against it
14. 27 the LORD overthrew the E. in the midst
14. 30 saved Israel..out of the hand of the E.
14. 30 Israel saw the E. dead upon the sea shore
14. 31 work which the LORD did upon the E.
15. 26 diseases..I have brought upon the E.
18. 8 all that the LORD had done unto..the E.
18. 9 had delivered out of the hand of the E.
18. 10 delivered you out of the hand of the E.
18. 10 delivered the people from under the..E.
19. 4 Ye have seen what I did unto the E.
32. 12 Wherefore should the E. speak, and say
Lev. 24. 10 Israelitish woman, whose father (was) an E.
Num 14. 13 Then the E. shall hear (it), for thou bro.
20. 15 and the E. vexed us and our fathers
33. 3 Israel went out..in the sight of all the E.
33. 4 For the E. buried all..first born, which
Deut 23. 7 thou shalt not abhor an E., because thou
26. 6 And the E. evil entreated us, and afflicted
Josh 24. 6 the E. pursued after your fathers with
24. 7 he put darkness between you and the E.
Judg. 6. 9 I delivered you out of the hand of the E.
10. 11 (Did) not (I deliver you) from the E.
1 Sa. 4. 8 these (are) the Gods that smote the E.
6. 6 as the E. and Pharaoh hardened their h.?
10. 18 delivered you out of the hand of the E.
30. 11 And they found an E. in the field, and
2 Sa. 23. 21 And he slew an E., a goodly man
23. 21 and the E. had a spear in his hand
23. 21 and plucked the spear out of the E.'s
2 Ki. 7. 6 the kings of the E., to come upon us
1 Ch. 2. 34 And Sheshan had a servant, an E., whose
11. 23 he slew an E., a man of (great) stature
11. 23 in the E.'s hand (was) a spear like a wea.
11. 23 and plucked the spear out of the E.'s hand
Ezra 9. 1 the Moabites, the E., and the Amorites
Isa. 19. 2 I will set the E. against the E. 11. 15.
19. 4 the E. will I give over into the hand of
19. 21 the E. shall know the LORD in that day
19. 23 and the E. into Assyria; and the E. shall
20. 4 So shall the king..lead away the E. pris.
30. 7 the E. shall help in vain, and to no purp.
31. 3 Now the E. (are) men, and not God
Jer. 43. 13 the houses of the gods of the E. shall he
Lam. 5. 6 We have given the hand (to) the E., (and to)
Eze. 16. 26 hast..committed fornication with the E.
23. 21 in bruising thy teats by the E. for the
29. 12 and I will scatter the E. among the nati.
29. 13 I gather the E. from the people whither
30. 23, 26 I will scatter the E. among the nations
Acts 7. 22 was learned in all the wisdom of the E.
7. 24 him that was oppressed, and smote the E.
7. 28 kill me, as thou diddest the E. yesterday?
21. 38 Art not thou that E., which..madest an
Heb 11. 29 which the E. assaying to do were drow.
2. As an adjective, an epithet applied to the whole or only the northern part of the Red Sea.
Isa. 11. 15 LORD shall..destroy the tongue of the E.

E'-HI, אֵחִי *unity.*
Son of Benjamin, same as Ehud in 1 Ch. 8. 6. B.C. 1690.
Gen. 46. 21 sons of Benjamin (were)..Naaman, E.

E'-HUD, אֵהוּד *strong.*
1. Ehud the great-grandson of Benjamin. B.C. 1690.
1 Ch. 7. 10 sons of Bilhan..Benjamin, and E., and
8. 6 these (are) the sons of E.: these are the
2. The son of Gera, the second judge (or deliverer) of the Israelites, B.C. 1336. He slew Eglon, who had established himself in Jericho, which was within the boundaries of Benjamin.
Judg 3. 15 E. the son of Gera, a Benjamite, a man
3. 16 E. made him a dagger which had two ed.
3. 20 E. came unto him; and he was sitting in
3. 20 E. said, I have a message from God unto
3. 21 E. put forth his left hand, and took the
3. 23 E. went forth through the porch, and
3. 26 E. escaped while they tarried, and passed
4. 1 Israel again did evil..when E. was dead

EIGHT —
1. *Eight*, שְׁמֹנֶה, שְׁמֹנָה *shemoneh, shemonah.*
Gen. 5. 4 the days of Adam..were eight hundred
5. 7 Seth lived..eight hundred and seven
5. 10 Enos lived..eight hundred and fifteen
5. 13 Cainan lived..eight hundred and forty
5. 16 Mahalaleel lived..eight hundred and th.
5. 17 all the days of Mahalaleel were eight
5. 19 Jared lived..eight hundred years, and
17. 12 he that is eight days old shall be circum.
21. 4 circumcised his son Isaac being eight
22. 23 these eight Milcah did bear to Nahor
Exod 26. 2 The length of one curtain..eight and
26. 25 they shall be eight boards, and their soc.
36. 9 The length of one..(was) twenty and eig.
36. 30 there were eight boards; and their sock.
Num. 2. 24 an hundred thousand and eight thousand
3. 28 eight thousand and six hundred, keeping
4. 48 eight thousand and five hundred and
7. 8 four wagons and eight oxen he gave unto
29. 29 on the sixth day eight bullocks, two rams
35. 7 give to the Levites..forty and eight cities
Deut. 2. 14 the space..(was) thirty and eight years
Josh 21. 41 All the cities..(were) forty and eight cities
Judg. 3. 8 the children of Israel served..eight years
12. 14 and he judged Israel eight years
1 Sa. 4. 15 Now Eli was ninety and eight years old
17. 12 he had eight sons: and the man went
2 Sa. 23. 8 (he lift up his spear) against eight hund.
2 Sa. 24. 9 there were in Israel eight hundred thou
1 Ki. 7. 10 of ten cubits, and stones of eight cubits
2 Ki. 8. 17 he reigned eight years in Jerusalem
10. 36 And the time..(was) twenty and eight
22. 1 Josiah (was) eight years old when he
1 Ch. 12. 24 six thousand and eight hundred, ready
12. 30 twenty thousand and eight hundred
12. 35 of the Danites..twenty and eight thous.
16. 38 with their brethren, threescore and eight
23. 3 man by man, was thirty and eight thou.
24. 4 and eight among the sons of Ithamar
25. 7 was two hundred fourscore and eight
2 Ch. 11. 21 Rehoboam..begat twenty and eight sons
13. 3 with eight hundred thousand chosen m.
21. 5, 20 he reigned eight years in Jerusalem
29. 17 sanctified the house of the LORD in eight
34. 1 Josiah (was) eight years old when he
36. 9 Jehoiachin (was) eight years old when he
Ezra 2. 6 two thousand eight hundred and twelve
2. 16 The children of Ater..ninety and eight
2. 23 of Anathoth, an hundred twenty and eig.
2. 41 of Asaph, an hundred twenty and eight
8. 11 and with him twenty and eight males
Neh. 7. 11 two thousand and eight hundred (and) e.
7. 13 of Zattu, eight hundred forty and five
7. 15 of Binnui, six hundred forty and eight
7. 16 of Bebai, six hundred twenty and eight
7. 21 of Ater of Hezekiah, ninety and eight
7. 22 of Hashum, three hundred twenty and e.
7. 26 of Bethlehem..hundred fourscore and e.
7. 27 of Anathoth, an hundred twenty and ei.
7. 44 of Asaph, an hundred forty and eight
7. 45 The porters..hundred thirty and eight
11. 6 of Perez..four hundred threescore and e.
11. 8 Sallai, nine hundred twenty and eight
11. 12 their brethren..eight hundred twenty
11. 14 their brethren..hundred twenty and ei.
Eccl. 11. 2 Give a portion to seven, and also to eight
Jer. 41. 15 escaped from Johanan with eight men
52. 29 he carried away captive..eight hundred
Eze. 40. 9 the porch of the gate, eight cubits
40. 31, 34, 37 the going up to it (had) eight steps
40. 41 eight tables, whereupon they slew (their
Mic. 5. 5 shall we raise against him..eight..men
2. *Eight*, ὀκτώ *oktō.*
Luke 2. 21 when eight days were accomplished for
9. 28 it came to pass, about an eight days after
John 5. 5 had an infirmity thirty and eight years
20. 26 after eight days, again his disciples were
Acts 9. 33 which had kept his bed eight years
1 Pe. 3. 20 few, that is, eight souls, were saved by

EIGHTEEN —
1. *Eight (and) ten*, שְׁמֹנָה עָשָׂר *shemonah asar.*
Gen. 14. 14 own house, three hundred and eighteen
Judg. 3. 14 the children of Israel served..eighteen
10. 8 they vexed..the children..eighteen years
20. 25 eighteen thousand men; all these drew
20. 44 there fell of Benjamin eighteen thousand
2 Sa. 8. 13 smiting of the Syrians..eighteen thousa.
1 Ki. 7. 15 he cast two pillars..eighteen cubits high
2 Ki. 24. 8 Jehoiachin (was) eighteen years old
25. 17 The height of the one pillar (was) eight.
1 Ch. 12. 31 half tribe of Manasseh eighteen thousand
18. 12 slew..in the valley of salt eighteen tho.
26. 9 Meshelemiah had..strong men, eighteen
2 Ch. 11. 21 he took eighteen wives, and threescore
Ezra 8. 9 with him two hundred and eighteen
8. 18 with his sons and his brethren, eighteen
Neh. 7. 11 thousand and eight hundred (and) eight.
Jer. 52. 21 the height of one pillar (was) eighteen
Eze. 48. 35 (It was) round about eighteen thousand
2. *Ten and eight*, δέκα καὶ ὀκτώ *deka kai oktō.*
Luke 13. 4 Or those eighteen, upon whom the tower
13. 11 which had a spirit of infirmity eighteen
13. 16 whom Satan hath bound, lo, these eight.

EIGHTEEN thousand—
A myriad and 8,000, רִבּוֹ וּשְׁמֹנַת אֲלָפִים [*ribbo*].
1 Ch. 29. 7 and of brass eighteen thousand talents

EIGHTEENTH —
Eight (and) ten, שְׁמֹנָה עָשָׂר *shemonah asar.*
1 Ki. 15. 1 in the eighteenth year of king Jeroboam
2 Ki. 3. 1 the eighteenth year of Jehoshaphat king
22. 3 in the eighteenth year of king Josiah
23. 23 in the eighteenth year of king Josiah
1 Ch. 24. 15 seventeenth to Hezir, the eighteenth to
25. 25 The eighteenth to Hanani, (he), his sons
2 Ch. 13. 1 in the eighteenth year of king Jeroboam
34. 8 in the eighteenth year of his reign, when
35. 19 In the eighteenth year of the reign of J.
Jer. 32. 1 the eighteenth year of Nebuchadrezzar
52. 29 the eighteenth year of Nebuchadrezzar

EIGHTH —
1. *Eighth*, שְׁמִינִי *shemini.*
Exod 22. 30 on the eighth day thou shalt give it me
Lev. 9. 1 it came to pass on the eighth day, (that)
12. 3 the eighth day the flesh of his foreskin
14. 10 on the eighth day he shall take two he
14. 23 he shall bring them on the eighth day for
15. 14 on the eighth day he shall take to him
15. 29 on the eighth day she shall take unto her
22. 27 from the eighth day and thenceforth it
23. 36 on the eighth day shall be an holy
23. 39 and on the eighth day (shall be) a sabbath
25. 22 ye shall sow the eighth year, and eat (yet)
Num. 6. 10 on the eighth day he shall bring two
7. 54 On the eighth day (offered) Gamaliel the
29. 35 On the eighth day ye shall have a solemn

1 Ki. 6. 38 the month Bul, which (is) the eighth mon.
8. 66 On the eighth day he sent the people away
12. 32 ordained a feast in the eighth month, on
12. 33 the fifteenth day of the eighth month
1 Ch. 12. 12 Johanan the eighth, Elzabad the ninth
24. 10 seventh to Hakkoz, the eighth to Abijah
25. 15 The eighth to Jeshaiah, (he), his sons, and
26. 5 Issachar the seventh, Peulthai the eighth
27. 11 The eighth (captain) for the eighth month
2 Ch. 7. 9 eighth day they made a solemn assembly
Neh. 8. 18 on the eighth day (was) a solemn assembly
Eze. 43. 27 upon the eighth day, and (so) forward, the
Zech. 1. 1 In the eighth month, in the second year

2. *Eight*, שְׁמֹנָה, שְׁמֹנֶה *shemonah, shemoneh.*
1 Ki. 16. 29 in the thirty and eighth year of Asa king
2 Ki. 15. 8 In the thirty and eighth year of Azariah
24. 12 took him in the eighth year of his reign
2 Ch. 29. 17 on the eighth day of the month, came they
34. 3 in the eighth year of his reign, while he

3. *Eighth*, ὄγδοος *ogdoos.*
Luke 1. 59 on the eighth day they came to circumcise
Acts 7. 8 (Abraham)..circumcised him the eighth d.
2 Pe. 2. 5 saved Noah, the eighth (person), a prea.
Rev. 17. 11 he, is the eighth, and is of the seven, and
21. 20 the eighth, beryl; the ninth, a topaz

EIGHTH day, the —
Eighth day, ὀκταήμερος *oktaēmeros.*
Phil. 3. 5 Circumcised the eighth day, of the stock

EIGHTIETH —
Eighty, שְׁמֹנִים *shemonim.*
1 Ki. 6. 1 in the four hundred and eightieth year

EIGHTY —
Eighty, שְׁמֹנִים *shemonim.*
Gen. 5. 25 Methuselah lived an hundred eighty and
5. 26 seven hundred eighty and two years
5. 28 Lamech lived an hundred eighty and two

EITHER —
1. *Or*, אוֹ *o.*
Lev 13. 49, 53 either in the warp, or in the woof, or

2. *If*, אִם *im.*
1 Ch. 21. 12 Either three years' famine; or three mo.

3. *And*, וְ *ve.*
Deut 17. 3 either the sun, or moon, or any of the

4. *That*, כִּי *ki.*
1 Ki. 18. 27 either he is talking, or he is pursuing

5. *Either*, ἤ *ē.*
Matt. 6. 24 either he will hate the one, and love the
12. 33 Either make the tree good, and his fruit
Luke 6. 42 Either how canst thou say to thy brother
15. 8 Either what woman, having ten pieces of
16. 13 either he will hate the one, and love the
Acts 17. 21 either to tell, or to hear some new thing
1 Co. 14. 6 shall speak to you either by revelation
Phil 3. 12 as though I had already attained, either
Jas. 3. 12 Can the fig tree..bear..berries? either

EITHER side, on —
Hence and hence, ἐντεῦθεν καὶ ἐντεῦθεν [*enteuthen*].
John 19. 18 and two other with him, on either side
Rev. 22. 2 on either side of the river, (was there) the

EITHER of them —
1. *A man*, אִישׁ *ish.*
Lev. 10. 1 took either of them his censer; 2 Ch. 18. 9.

2. *The second pillar*, הָעַמּוּד הַשֵּׁנִי [*ammud*].
1 Ki. 7. 15 a line..did compass either of them about

EITHER...or —
Even...even, גַּם...גַּם *gam.. gam.*
Eccl. 9. 1 no man knoweth either love or hatred (by)

E'-KER, עֵקֶר *root.*
Descendant of Judah through Hezron and Jerahmeel. B.C. 1421.
1 Ch. 2. 27 of Ram..were Maaz, and Jamin, and E.

EK'-RON, עֶקְרוֹן *naturalisation.*
The most northerly of the five cities belonging to the Philistines. It was in the low country or *Shefelah*, as well as the other four, and fell to the lot of Judah, and then to Dan. It is now called *Akir* and lies five miles S.W. of Ramleh, and three due E. of Jabneh (*Yebna*), on the N. side of the *Wady Surar.*
Josh 13. 3 From Sihor..unto the borders of E. nort.
15. 11 the border went out unto the side of E.
15. 45 E., with her towns and her villages
15. 46 From E. even unto the sea, all that (lay)
19. 43 And Elon, and Thimnathah, and E.
Judg. 1. 18 Askelon..and E. with the coast thereof
1 Sa. 5. 10 Therefore they sent the ark of God to E.
5. 10 as the ark of God came to E.
6. 16 they returned to E. the same day
6. 17 for Askelon one, for Gath one, for E. one
7. 14 cities..were restored..from E. even unto
17. 52 until thou come..to the gates of E.
17. 52 Philistines fell down by the way..unto E.
2 Ki. 1. 2 Go, enquire of Baal-zebub the god of E.
1. 3, 6, 16 enquire of Baal-zebub the god of E.?
Jer. 25. 20 all the kings of the land of..E., and
Amos 1. 8 and I will turn mine hand against E.
Zeph. 2. 4 at the noon day, and E. shall be rooted
Zech. 9. 5 Gaza also..and be very sorrowful, and E.
9. 7 as a governor in Judah, and E. as a Jeb.

EK-RON-ITE and EK-RON-ITES, עֶקְרוֹנִי.
The inhabitants of Ekron.
Josh 13. 3 Eshkalonites, the Gittites, and the E.
1 Sa. 5. 10 the E. cried..They have brought about

EL-A'-DAH, אֶלְעָדָה *God is ornament.*
Descendant of Ephraim in the fourth degree. B.C. 1570.
1 Ch. 7. 20 and E. his son, and Tahath his son

E'-LAH, אֵלָה, אֵלָא *oak.*
1. A duke, chief, or prince of Edom. B.C. 1470.
Gen. 36. 41 Duke Aholibamah, duke E., duke Pinon
1 Ch. 1. 52 Duke Aholibamah, duke E., duke Pinon

2. A valley in Judah where David slew Goliath. Now called *Wady Sumt.*
1 Sa. 17. 2 And Saul..pitched by the valley of E.
17. 19 Saul, and they..(were) in the valley of E.
21. 9 whom thou slewest in the valley of E.

3. Father of a Benjamite commissariat officer under Solomon. B.C. 1015.
1 Ki. 4. 18 Shimei the son of E. in Benjamin

4. Son and successor of Baasha king of Israel. He reigned little more than a year, being killed (while drunk) by Zimri while his army was absent at the siege of Gibbethon. B.C. 930.
1 Ki. 16. 6 and E. his son reigned in his stead
16. 8 began E. the son of Baasha to reign over
16. 13 For all the sins of Baasha, and..of E. his
16. 14 Now the rest of the acts of E., and all

5. Father of Hoshea, last king of Israel. B.C. 739.
2 Ki. 15. 30 Hoshea the son of E. made a conspiracy
17. 1 began Hoshea the son of E. to reign in
18. 1 in the third year of Hoshea son of E.
18. 9 the seventh year of Hoshea son of E. king

6. A son of Caleb son of Jephunneh. B.C. 1450.
1 Ch. 4. 15 Iru, E., and Naam: and the sons of E.

7. One of the tribe of Benjamin. B.C. 445.
1 Ch. 9. 8 E. the son of Uzzi, the son of Michri, and

E'-LAM, עֵילָם, עוֹלָם *youth.*
1. A son of Shem, whose family gave his name to a district which lay S. of Assyria and E. of Persia Proper. B.C. 2300.
Gen. 10. 22 children of Shem; E., and Asshur, and
1 Ch. 1. 17 sons of Shem; E., and Asshur, and Arp.

2. Country inhabited by the descendants of Elam, *i.e.*, Persia.
Gen. 14. 1 Chedorlaomer king of E., and Tidal king
14. 9 With Chedorlaomer the king of E., and
Isa. 11. 11 from E., and from Shinar, and from H.
21. 2 Go up, O E.: besiege, O Media: all the
22. 6 E. bare the quiver with chariots of men
Jer. 25. 25 all the kings of E., and all the kings of
49. 34 came to Jeremiah the prophet against E.
49. 35 I will break the bow of E., the chief of
49. 36 upon E. will I bring the four winds from
49. 36 no nation whither the outcasts of E. shall
49. 37 I will cause E. to be dismayed before
49. 38 I will set my throne in E., and will dest.
49. 39 I will bring again the captivity of E.
Eze. 32. 24 There (is) E. and all her multitude round
Dan. 8. 2 Shusham..which (is) in the province of E

3. Son of Shashak, a Benjamite. B.C. 1340.
1 Ch. 8. 24 And Hananiah, and E., and Antothijah

4. A son of Meshelemiah, a Kohathite. B.C. 1015.
1 Ch. 26. 3 E. the fifth, Jehohanan the sixth, Elioe.

5. Progenitor of a family that came up from exile. B.C. 536.
Ezra 2. 7 children of E., a thousand two hundred
Neh. 7. 12 children of E., a thousand two hundred

6. Another whose posterity returned from exile. B.C. 536.
Ezra 2. 31 children of the other E., a thousand two
Neh. 7. 34 children of the other E., a thousand two

7. One whose descendants came up with Ezra. B.C. 457.
Ezra 8. 7 of the sons of E.; Jeshaiah the son of

8. An ancestor of Shechaniah, who made confession of the people having trespassed in taking strange wives. B.C. 457.
Ezra 10. 2 Jehiel..of the sons of E., answered and
10. 26 of the sons of E.; Mattaniah, Zechariah

9. A Chief that, with Nehemiah, sealed the covenant, B.C. 457.
Neh. 10. 14 chief of the people..E., Zatthu, Bani

10. A priest who took part in the ceremonial of purifying the wall of Jerusalem after it had been rebuilt. B.C. 445.
Neh. 12. 42 and Malchijah, and E., and Ezer

E-LAM-ITES, עֵלְמָיֵא, Ἐλαμῖται.
The inhabitants of Elam carried to Samaria. B.C. 721.
Ezra 4. 9 Susanchites, the Dehavites, (and) the E.
Acts 2. 9 Parthians, and Medes, and E., and the

E-LA'-SAH, E-LEA'-SAH, אֶלְעָשָׂה *God is doer.*
1. A priest who had married a strange wife. B.C. 445.
Ezra 10. 22 of the sons of Pashur..Jozabad, and E.

2. An ambassador whom Zedekiah sent to Nebuchadnezzar. B.C. 599.
Jer. 29. 3 By the hand of E. the son of Shaphan

E'-LATH, E'-LOTH, אֵילַת, אֵילוֹת *palm grove.*
An Elamite port now called *Eyleh*, on the E. or Elanitic gulf of the Red Sea, near Eziongeber, and now called *Gelana.*
Deut. 2. 8 through the way of the plain from E.
2 Ki. 14. 22 He built E., and restored it to Judah
16. 6 recovered E...and drave the Jews from E.
16. 6 and the Syrians came to E., and dwelt

EL BETH'-EL, אֵל בֵּית־אֵל *god of the house of God.*
The name given to the place where God appeared to Jacob when flying from his brother Esau. B.C. 1739.
Gen. 35. 7 built..an altar, and called the place E.

EL-DA'-AH, אֶלְדָּעָה *whom God called.*
The last in order of the sons of Midian. B.C. 1800.
Gen. 25. 4 the sons of Midian..Abidah, and E.
1 Ch. 1. 33 the sons of Midian..Abida, and E.

EL'-DAD, אֶלְדָּד *God is a friend.*
One of two elders to whom was given the prophetic power of Moses. B.C. 1492.
Num 11. 26 name of the one (was) E., and the name
11. 27 E. and Medad do prophesy in the camp

ELDER, (woman) —
1. *Great*, גָּדוֹל *gadol.*
Gen. 10. 21 Eber, the brother of Japheth the elder
27. 42 these words of Esau her elder son were
29. 16 the name of the elder (was) Leah, and the
1 Sa. 18. 17 Behold my elder daughter Merab, her
1 Ki. 2. 22 kingdom also; for he (is) mine elder broth.
Eze. 16. 46 thine elder sister (is) Samaria, she and
16. 61 thy sisters, thine elder and thy younger
23. 4 Aholah the elder, and Aholibah her sister

2. *Old, aged, bearded*, זָקֵן *zaqen.*
Gen. 50. 7 elders of his house, and all the elders
Exod. 3. 16 gather the elders of Israel together, and
3. 18 shalt come, thou and the elders of Israel
4. 29 gathered together all the elders of the
12. 21 Moses called for all the elders of Israel
17. 5 and take with thee of the elders of Israel
17. 6 did so in the sight of the elders of Israel
18. 12 Aaron came, and all the elders of Israel
19. 7 and called for the elders of the people
24. 1, 9 Abihu, and seventy of the elders of Is.
24. 14 he said unto the elders, Tarry ye here for
Lev. 4. 15 the elders of the congregation shall lay
9. 1 Aaron and his sons, and the elders of
Num 11. 16 seventy men of the elders of Israel
11. 16 knowest to be the elders of the people
11. 24 seventy men of the elders of the people
11. 25 and gave (it) unto the seventy elders
11. 30 gat him into the camp, he and the elders
16. 25 the elders of Israel followed him
22. 4 And Moab said unto the elders of Midian
22. 7 elders of Moab and the elders of Midian
Deut. 5. 23 the heads of your tribes, and your elders
19. 12 the elders of his city shall send and
21. 2 thy elders and thy judges shall come
21. 3 elders of that city shall take an heifer
21. 4 the elders of that city shall bring down
21. 6 the elders of that city, (that are) next
21. 19 bring him out unto the elders of his city
21. 20 shall say unto the elders of his city
22. 15 unto the elders of the city in the gate
22. 16 damsel's father shall say unto the elders
22. 17 the cloth before the elders of the city
22. 18 the elders of that city shall take that
25. 7 wife go up to the gate unto the elders
25. 8 the elders of his city shall call him
25. 9 unto him in the presence of the elders
27. 1 Moses with the elders of Israel comman.
29. 10 your captains of your tribes, your elders
31. 9 and unto all the elders of Israel
31. 28 Gather unto me all the elders of your
32. 7 thy elders, and they will tell thee
Josh. 7. 6 he and the elders of Israel, and put dust
8. 10 and went up, he and the elders of Israel
8. 33 all Israel, and their elders, and officers
9. 11 our elders, and all the inhabitants of
20. 4 in the ears of the elders of that city
23. 2 called for all Israel, (and) for their elders
24. 1 called for the elders of Israel, and for
24. 31 days of the elders that overlived Joshua
Judg. 2. 7 days of the elders that outlived Joshua
8. 14 princes of Succoth, and the elders
8. 16 he took the elders of the city, and thorns
11. 5 elders of Gilead went to fetch Jephthah
11. 7, 9 Jephthah said unto the elders of Gil.
11. 8, 10 elders of Gilead said unto Jephthah
11. 11 Jephthah went with the elders of Gilead
21. 16 Then the elders of the congregation said
Ruth 4. 2 he took ten men of the elders of the city
4. 4 Buy (it)..before the elders of my people
4. 9 Boaz said unto the elders, and (unto) all
4. 11 and the elders, said, (We are) witnesses
1 Sa. 4. 3 people were come..elders of Israel said
8. 4 the elders of Israel gathered themselves
11. 3 the elders of Jabesh said unto him; Give
15. 30 before the elders of my people, and
16. 4 the elders of the town trembled at his
30. 26 he sent of the spoil unto the elders of J.
2 Sa. 3. 17 communication with the elders of Israel
5. 3 the elders of Israel came to the king to
12. 17 the elders of his house arose, (and went)
17. 4 pleased Absalom well, and all the elders
17. 15 counsel Absalom and the elders of Israel
19. 11 Speak unto the elders of Judah, saying
1 Ki. 8. 1 Solomon assembled the elders of Israel

1 Ki. 8. 3 the elders of Israel came, and the priests
20. 7 king..called all the elders of the land
20. 8 the elders, and all the people, said unto
21. 8 sent the letters unto the elders and to
21. 11 the elders and the nobles who were the
2 Ki. 6. 32 in his house, and the elders sat with him
6. 32 he said to the elders, See ye how this
10. 1 unto the rulers of Jezreel, to the elders
10. 5 he that (was) over the city, the elders
19. 2 the scribe, and the elders of the priests
23. 1 they gathered unto him all the elders of
1 Ch. 11. 3 Therefore came all the elders of Israel
15. 25 David, and the elders of Israel, and
21. 16 David and the elders..fell upon their
2 Ch. 5. 2 Solomon assembled the elders of Israel
5. 4 the elders of Israel came; and the Lev.
34. 29 gathered together all the elders of Judah
Ezra 10. 8 the counsel of the princes and the elders
10. 14 with them the elders of every city, and
Psa. 107. 32 praise him in the assembly of the elders
Prov. 31. 23 he sitteth among the elders of the land
Isa. 37. 2 the scribe, and the elders of the priests
Jer. 26. 17 rose up certain of the elders of the land
29. 1 unto the residue of the elders which
Lam. 1. 19 my priests and mine elders gave up the
2. 10 The elders of the daughter of Zion sit
4. 16 the priests, they favoured not the elders
5. 12 the faces of elders were not honoured
5. 14 The elders have ceased from the gate
Eze. 8. 1 and the elders of Judah sat before me
14. 1 Then came certain of the elders of Israel
20. 1 certain of the elders of Israel came to
20. 3 speak unto the elders of Israel, and say
Joel 1. 14 gather the elders (and) all the inhabitants
2. 16 assemble the elders, gather the children

3. *Great*, רַב *rab*.
Gen. 25 23 and the elder shall serve the younger

4. *Grey headed*, שָׂב *sab*.
Ezra 5. 5 eye of their God was upon the elders of
5. 9 Then asked we those elders, (and) said
6. 7 the governor of the Jews, and the elders
6. 8 ye shall do to the elders of these Jews
6. 14 the elders of the Jews builded, and they

5. *Aged as to days*, זְקֵנִים לְיָמִים *zeqenim le-yamim*.
Job 32. 4 because they (were) elder than he

6. *Greater*, μείζων *meizōn*.
Rom. 9. 12 The elder shall serve the younger

7. *Elder, aged person*, πρεσβύτερος *presbuteros*.
Matt 15. 2 transgress the tradition of the elders?
16. 21 and suffer many things of the elders and
21. 23 chief priests and the elders of the people
26. 3 the scribes, and the elders of the people
26. 47 chief priests and elders of the people
26. 57 the scribes and the elders were assembled
26. 59 the chief priests, and elders, and all the
27. 1 chief priests and elders of the people
27. 3 silver to the chief priests and elders
27. 12 accused of the chief priests and elders
27. 20 the chief priests and elders persuaded
27. 41 mocking (him), with the scribes and elders
28. 12 when they were assembled with the elders
Mark 7. 3 holding the tradition of the elders
7. 5 according to the tradition of the elders
8. 31 and be rejected of the elders, and (of) the
11. 27 priests, and the scribes, and the elders
14. 43 priests and the scribes and the elders
14. 53 all the chief priests and the elders and
15. 1 held a consultation with the elders and
Luke 7. 3 he sent unto him the elders of the Jews
9. 22 and be rejected of the elders and 15. 25.
20. 1 the scribes came upon (him) with the eld.
22. 52 and captains of the temple, and the elders
Acts. 4. 5 that their rulers, and elders, and scribes
4. 8 rulers of the people, and elders of Israel
4. 23 all that the chief priests and elders had
6. 12 they stirred up the people, and the elders
11. 30 sent it to the elders by the hands of
14. 23 had ordained them elders in every church
15. 2 to Jerusalem unto the apostles and elders
15. 4 church, and (of) the apostles and elders
15. 6 the apostles and elders came together
15. 22 Then pleased it the apostles and elders
15. 23 The apostles and elders and brethren
16. 4 were ordained of the apostles and elders
20. 17 and called the elders of the church
21. 18 and all the elders were present
23. 14 they came to the chief priests and elders
24. 1 the high priest descended with the elders
25. 15 the chief priests and the elders of the
1 Ti 5. 1 Rebuke not an elder, but entreat (him) as
5. 17 Let the elders that rule well be counted
5. 19 Against an elder receive not an accusation
Titus 1. 5 and ordain elders in every city, as I had
Heb. 11. 2 by it the elders obtained a good report
Jas. 5. 14 let him call for the elders of the church
1 Pe. 5. 1 The elders which are among you
2 Jo. 1 The elder unto the elect lady and her
3 Jo. 1 The elder unto the well beloved Gaius
Rev. 4. 4 I saw four and twenty elders sitting
4. 10 The four and twenty elders fall down
5. 5 one of the elders saith unto me, Weep not
5. 6 in the midst of the elders, stood a Lamb
5. 8 four (and) twenty elders fell down before
5. 11 the throne and the beasts and the elders
5. 14 the four (and) twenty elders fell down and
7. 11 about the throne, and (about) the elders
7. 13 one of the elders answered, saying unto
11. 16 the four and twenty elders which sat
Rev. 14. 3 and before the four beasts, and the elders
19. 4 the four and twenty elders, and the four

ELDER, also an —
A fellow elder, συμπρεσβύτερος *sumpresbuteros*.
1 Pe. 5. 1 who am also an elder, and a witness of

ELDERS, (estate of) the —
1. *Eldership, presbytery*, πρεσβυτέριον *presbuterion*.
Luke 22. 66 the elders of the people, and the chief
Acts 22. 5 and all the estate of the elders

2. *Elder, aged person*, πρεσβύτερος *presbuteros*.
Luke 15. 25 his elder son was in the field: and as he
1 Ti. 5. 2 The elder women as mothers; the younger
1 Pe. 5. 5 younger, submit yourselves unto the eld.

ELDEST (son) —
1. *First born*, בְּכוֹר *bekor*.
Num. 1. 20 the children of Reuben, Israel's eldest s.
26. 5 Reuben, the eldest son of Israel
2 Ki. 3. 27 he took his eldest son, that should have
Job 1. 13 drinking..in their eldest brother's house
1. 18 drinking..in their eldest brother's house

2. *Great*, גָּדוֹל *gadol*.
Gen. 27. 1 he called Esau his eldest son, and said
27. 15 goodly raiment of her eldest son Esau
44. 12 began at the eldest, and left at the young.
1 Sa. 17. 13 the three eldest sons of Jesse went (and)
17. 14 and the three eldest followed Saul
17. 28 Eliab his eldest brother heard when he

3. *Aged*, זָקֵן *zaqen*.
Gen. 24. 2 Abraham said unto his eldest servant of

4. *First*, רִאשׁוֹן *rishon*.
2 Ch. 22. 1 the band of men..had slain all the eldest

5. *Elder*, πρεσβύτερος *presbuteros*.
John 8. 9 beginning at the eldest, (even) unto the

EL'-EAD, אֶלְעָד *God is witness*.
A descendant of Ephraim, slain by invaders. B.C. 1680.
1 Ch. 7. 21 Ezer, and E., whom the men of Gath

EL-EA'-LEH, אֶלְעָלֵא אֶלְעָלֵה *God is exalted*.
A place on the E. of the Jordan in the pastoral country taken possession of by Reuben. The modern name is *El-A'al* ("the high"), a mile N. of Heshbon. Extensive ruins are still seen.
Num 32. 3 Heshbon, and E., Shebam, and Nebo
32. 37 children of Reuben built Heshbon, and E.
Isa. 15. 4 Heshbon shall cry, and E.: their voice
16. 9 I will water thee with..tears, O..E.
Jer. 48. 34 From the cry of Heshbon (even) unto E.

EL-EA'-SAH, EL-A'-SAH, אֶלְעָשָׂה *God is doer*.
1. A son of Helez of the family of Hezron. B.C. 1305.
1 Ch. 2. 39 Azariah begat Helez, and Helez begat E.
2. 40 E. begat Sisamai, and Sisamai begat Sha.
2. A son of Rapha or Raphaiah, a descendant of Saul. B.C. 960.
1 Ch. 8. 37 Rapha..his son, E. his son, Azel his son
9. 43 Rephaiah his son, E. his son, Azel his

EL-EA'-ZAR, אֶלְעָזָר, Ἐλεάζαρ *God is helper*.
1. Third son of Aaron by Elisheba, daughter of Amminadab, a descendant of Judah through Pharez. B.C. 1452.
Exod. 6. 23 she bare him Nadab, and Abihu, E., and
6. 25 E., Aaron's son, took..of the daughters of
28. 1 Nadab and Abihu, E. and Ithamar
Lev. 10. 6 Moses said unto Aaron, and unto E.
10. 12 Moses spake unto Aaron, and unto E.
10. 16 he was angry with E. and Ithamar, the
Num 3. 2 Nadab the first born, and Abihu, E., and
3. 4 E. and Ithamar ministered in the priest's
3. 32 E...(shall be) chief over the chief of the
4. 16 And to the office of E...the oil for the
16. 37 Speak unto E. the son of Aaron the pri.
16. 39 E. the priest took the brasen censers
19. 3 ye shall give her unto E. the priest, that
19. 4 E. the priest shall take of her blood with
20. 25 Take Aaron and E. his son, and bring
20. 26, 28 and put them upon E. his son
25. 7 when Phinehas, the son of E... saw (it)
25. 11 Phinehas, the son of E...hath turned my
26. 1 LORD spake unto Moses and unto E. the
26. 3 Moses and E. the priest spake with them
26. 60 unto Aaron was born Nadab, and Abihu, E.
26. 63 that were numbered by Moses and E.
27. 2 they stood before Moses, and before E.
27. 19 set him before E. the priest, and before
27. 21 he shall stand before E. the priest, who
27. 22 he took Joshua, and set him before E. the
31. 6 them and Phinehas the son of E. the pr.
31. 12 they brought the captives..unto..E. the
31. 13 Moses, and E. the priest..went forth to
31. 21 E. the priest said unto the men of war
31. 26 Take the sum of the prey..thou, and E.
31. 29 Take (it) of their half, and give (it) unto E.
31. 31 Moses and E. the priest did as the LORD
31. 41 Moses gave the tribute..unto E. the pri.
31. 51, 54 And Moses and E. the priest took the
32. 2 the children of Reuben..spake unto..E.
32. 28 So concerning them Moses commanded E.
34. 17 E. the priest, and Joshua the son of Nun
Deut 10. 6 E. his son ministered in the priest's office
Josh 14. 1 which E. the priest..distributed for inh.
17. 4 they came near before E. the priest, and
19. 51 These (are) the inheritances, which E.
21. 1 Then came..the Levites unto E. the
22. 13 Phinehas the son of E. the priest
Josh. 22. 31 Phinehas the son of E. the priest said
22. 32 Phinehas the son of E. the priest..retu.
24. 33 E. the son of Aaron died; and they bur.
Judg 20. 28 Phinehas, the son of E...stood before it
1 Ch. 6. 3 The sons also of Aaron..E., and Ithamar
6. 4 E. begat Phinehas, Phinehas begat Abish.
6. 50 E. his son, Phinehas his son, Abishua
9. 20 Phinehas the son of E. was the ruler over
24. 1 sons of Aaron..Abihu, E., and Ithamar
24. 2 E. and Ithamar executed the priest's office
24. 3 both Zadok of the sons of E., and Ahim.
24. 4 more chief men found of the sons of E.
24. 4 Among the sons of E...sixteen chief men
24. 5 governors..were of the sons of E., and
24. 6 principal household being taken for E.
Ezra 7. 5 Abishua..son of Phinehas..son of E.
2. Son of Abinadab of Kirjath-jearim, set apart to take care of the ark after it was sent back by the Philistines. B.C. 1120.
1 Sa. 7. 1 sanctified E. his son to keep the ark of
3. A son of Dodo, the Ahohite, one of the three chief captains of David's army. B.C. 1048.
2 Sa. 23. 9 after him (was) E. the son of Dodo the A.
1 Ch. 11. 12 after him (was) E. the son of Dodo, the A.
4. A Merarite and son of Mahli. He had daughters only, who were married to their cousins. B.C. 1015.
1 Ch. 23. 21 The sons of Mahli; E. and Kish
23. 22 E. died, and had no sons, but daughters
24. 28 Of Mahli (came) E., who had no sons
5. A priest who participated in the feast of the dedication of the wall under Nehemiah. B.C. 445.
Neh. 12. 42 Maaseiah, and Shemaiah, and E., and U.
6. A son of Phinehas, a Levite. B.C. 457.
Ezra 8. 33 and with him..E. the son of Phinehas
7. Son of Eliud, three generations above Joseph the husband of Mary.
Matt. 1. 15 Eliud begat E.; and E. begat Matthan

ELECT —
1. *Chosen, choice*, בָּחִיר *bachir*.
Isa. 42. 1 my servant, whom I uphold; mine elect
45. 4 For..Israel mine elect, I have even called
65. 9 mine elect shall inherit it, and my ser.
65. 22 mine elect shall long enjoy the work of

2. *Laid out, chosen, choice*, ἐκλεκτός *eklektos*.
Matt 24. 22 for the elect's sake those days shall be
24. 24 if..possible, they shall deceive the very e.
24. 31 and they shall gather together his elect
Mark 13. 20 no flesh should be saved: but for the el.
13. 22 to seduce, if (it were) possible, even the e.
13. 27 and shall gather together his elect from
Luke 18. 7 And shall not God avenge his own elect
Rom. 8. 33 lay anything to the charge of God's elect?
Col. 3. 12 Put on therefore, as the elect of God, holy
1 Ti. 5. 21 I charge..before God..and the elect
2 Ti. 2. 10 I endure all things for the elect's sake
Titus 1. 1 according to the faith of God's elect, and
1 Pe. 1. 2 Elect according to the foreknowledge of
2. 6 I lay in Sion a chief corner stone, elect
2 Jo. 1 The elder unto the elect lady and her
13 The children of thy elect sister greet thee

ELECTED together with —
Chosen along with, συνεκλεκτός *suneklektos*.
1 Pe. 5. 13 at Babylon, elected together with

ELECTION —
Choice, a laying out, ἐκλογή *eklogē*.
Rom. 9. 11 according to election might stand, not
11. 5 there is a remnant according to the ele.
11. 7 the election hath obtained it, and the
11. 28 but as touching the election, (they are)
1 Th. 1. 4 Knowing, brethren beloved, your elec.
2 Pe. 1. 10 to make your calling and election sure

EL ELO-HE IS-RA'-EL, אֵל אֱלֹהֵי יִשְׂרָאֵל *God, the God of Israel*.
The name given by Jacob to the altar he erected near Shechem, where he pitched his tent and afterwards purchased from the sons of Hamor. B.C. 1732.
Gen. 33. 20 he erected..an altar, and called it E.

ELEMENTS —
Elements, rudiments, first step, στοιχεῖον *stoicheion*.
Gal. 4. 3 were in bondage under the elements of
4. 9 to the weak and beggarly elements
2 Pe. 3. 10, 12 the elements shall melt with fervent

E'-LEPH, אֶלֶף *union, ox*.
A town of Benjamin, and named next to Jerusalem.
Josh. 18. 28 Zelah, E., and Jebusi, which (is) Jerusa.

ELEVEN —
1. *Eleven, one (and) ten*, אַחַד עָשָׂר *achad asar*.
Gen. 32. 22 his two women, servants, and his eleven
37. 9 the eleven stars, made obeisance to me
2 Ki. 23. 36 Jehoiakim..reigned eleven years in Jer.
24. 18 Zedekiah..reigned eleven years in Jeru.
2 Ch. 36. 5 Jehoiakim..reigned eleven years in Jer
36. 11 Zedekiah..reigned eleven years in Jeru.
Jer. 52. 1 Zedekiah..reigned eleven years in Jeru.

2. *Eleven*, (עֶשְׂרֵה) עַשְׁתֵּי עָשָׂר *ashte asar*.
Exod 26. 7 upon the tabernacle: eleven curtains
26. 8 the eleven curtains (shall be all) of one
36. 14 over the tabernacle: eleven curtains he
36. 15 the eleven curtains (were) of one size
Num 29. 20 on the third day eleven bullocks, two
Eze. 40. 49 and the breadth eleven cubits; and

3. *Eleven, one (and) ten*, ἕνδεκα *hendeka*.
Matt 28. 16 Then the eleven disciples went away

ELEVEN—(*achad asar*). Deut. 1. 2 (There are) eleven days' (journey) from Horeb.

Mark16. 14 he appeared unto the eleven as they sat
Luke24. 9 and told all these things unto the eleven
24. 33 they rose up..and found the eleven
Acts 1. 26 he was numbered with the eleven apost.
2. 14 Peter, standing up with the eleven

ELEVENTH —

1. *Eleven*, (עֶשְׂרֵה) עַשְׁתֵּי עָשָׂר *ashte asar.*
Num. 7. 72 On the eleventh day Pagiel..(offered)
Deut. 1. 3 in the eleventh month, on the first (day)
1 Ki. 6. 38 in the eleventh year, in the month Bul
2 Ki. 9. 29 in the eleventh year of Joram the son of
25. 2 the city was besieged unto the eleventh
1 Ch. 12. 13 Jeremiah the tenth, Machbanai the elev.
24. 12 The eleventh to Eliashib, the twelfth to
25. 18 The eleventh to Azareel, (he), his sons
27. 14 The eleventh (captain) for the eleventh
Jer. 1. 3 unto the end of the eleventh year of Zed.
39. 2 (And) in the eleventh year of Zedekiah
52. 5 the city was besieged unto the eleventh
Eze. 26. 1 And it came to pass in the eleventh year
30. 20 it came to pass in the eleventh year, in
31. 1 it came to pass in the eleventh year, in
Zech. 1. 7 and twentieth day of the eleventh month

2. *Eleventh*, ἑνδέκατος *hendekatos.*
Matt20. 6 And about the eleventh hour he went
20. 9 they came that (were hired) about the el.
Rev. 21 20 the eleventh, a jacinth; the twelfth, an

EL-HA'-NAN, אֶלְחָנָן *God is gracious.*
1. Son of Jair, who slew Lahmi the brother of Goliath the Gittite. B.C. 1048.
1 Ch. 20. 5 E. the son of Jair slew Lahmi the brother
2 Sa. 21. 19 E. the son of Jaare-oregim..slew (the br.)
2. A son of Dodo the Bethlehemite, and one of the thirty of David's chief men. B.C. 1048.
2 Sa. 23. 24 E. the son of Dodo of Beth-lehem
1 Ch. 11. 26 E. the son of Dodo of Beth-lehem

E'-LI, עֵלִי *Jah is high.*
High priest and judge of Israel, who immediately preceded Samuel. His descent was through Ithamar the younger of Aaron's two surviving sons.
1 Sa. 1. 3 And the two sons of E...(were) there
1. 9 E. the priest sat upon a seat by a post of
1. 12 it came to pass..that E. marked her mo.
1. 13 therefore E. thought she had been drunk.
1. 14 E. said unto her, How long wilt thou be
1. 17 E. answered and said, Go in peace: and
1. 25 slew a bullock, and brought the child to E.
2. 11 child did minister unto the LORD before E
2. 12 Now the sons of E. (were) sons of Belial
2. 20 E. blessed Elkanah and his wife, and said
2. 22 E. was very old, and heard all that his
2. 27 And there came a man of God unto E.
3. 1 Samuel ministered unto the L. before E.
3. 2 when E. (was) laid down in his place, and
3. 5 And he ran unto E., and said, Here (am)
3. 6 Samuel arose and went to E. and said
3. 8 he arose and went to E., and said, Here
3. 8 E. perceived that the LORD had called
3. 9 E. said unto Samuel, Go, lie down: and
3. 12 I will perform against E. all..which I
3. 14 I have sworn unto the house of E., that
3. 14 the iniquity of E.'s house shall not be
3. 15 And Samuel feared to show E. the vision
3. 16 E. called Samuel, and said, Samuel, my
4. 4 the two sons of E...(were) there with the
4. 11 the two sons of E., Hophni and Phinehas
4. 13 E. sat upon a seat by the wayside watch
4. 14 when E heard the noise of the crying, he
4. 14 And the man came in hastily, and told E.
4. 15 Now E. was ninety and eight years old
4. 16 the man said unto E. I (am) he that came
14. 3 Phinehas, the son of E., the LORD'S priest
1 Ki. 2. 27 he spake concerning the house of E. in

E-LI, Ἠλί; *in Heb.* אֵלִי *eli, my God.*
Matt 27. 46 cried with a loud voice, saying, Eli! Eli!

E-LI'-AB, אֱלִיאָב *God is father.*
1. A son of Helon, and leader of the tribe of Zebulun at the time of the census in the wilderness. B.C. 1490.
Num. 1. 9 Of Zebulun; E the son of Helon
2. 7 E. the son of Helon..captain of the chil.
7. 24 On the third day E. the son of Helon
7. 29 this (was) the offering of E. the son of H.
10. 16 over the host..of Zebulun..E. the son of
2. A Reubenite, son of Pallu or Phallu, and father of Dathan and Abiram. B.C. 1490.
Num16. 1 Dathan and Abiram the sons of E...took
16. 12 to call Dathan and Abiram, the sons of E.
26. 8 And the sons of Pallu; E.
26. 9 the sons of E.; Nemuel, and Dathan, and
Deut 11. 6 did unto Dathan and Abiram..sons of E
3. The eldest son of Jesse and brother of David. He is called Elihu in 1 Ch 27. 18 B.C. 1065.
1 Sa. 16. 6 it came to pass. that he looked on E.
17. 13 three sons that went to the battle (were) E.
17. 28 E. his eldest brother heard when he spake
17. 28 E.'s anger was kindled against D., and he
1 Ch. 2. 13 Jesse begat his first born E., and Abina.
2 Ch. 11. 18 Abihail the daughter of E. the son of Je.
4. A Levite in the time of David, and was both a porter and a musician on the psaltery. B.C. 1015.
1 Ch. 15. 18 Jehiel, and Unni, E., and Benaiah, and
15. 20 Jehiel, and Unni, and E., and Maaseiah
16. 5 Jehiel, and Mattithiah, and E., and Ben.
5. A Gadite warlike leader who with others came over to David in the wilderness. B.C. 1058.
1 Ch. 12. 9 Ezer the first, Obadiah the second, E. the

6. An ancestor of Samuel the prophet; a Kohathite Levite, son of Nahath. In other statements of the genealogy he is called Elihu (1 Sa. 1. 1); and Eliel (1 Ch. 6. 34).
1 Ch. 6. 27 E. his son, Jeroham his son, Elkanah his

EL-IA'-DA, אֶלְיָדָע *God is knowing.*
1. One of the sons of David. B.C. 1030.
2 Sa. 5. 16 And Elishama, and E., and Eliphalet
1 Ch. 3. 8 And Elishama, and E., and Eliphalet
2. A Benjamite mighty warrior who led 200,000 of his tribe to the army of Jehoshaphat. B.C. 941.
2 Ch. 17. 17 of Benjamin; E. a mighty man of valour

EL-IA'-DAH, אֶלְיָדָע *God is knowing.*
An Aramite of Zobah, father of Rezon, the captain of a marauding band that annoyed Solomon. B.C. 1025.
1 Ki. 11. 23 Rezon the son of E., which fled from his

E-LI'-AH, אֵלִיָּה *God is Jah.*
1. A son of Jeroham the Benjamite, and head of his tribe. B.C. 1300.
1 Ch. 8. 27 Jaresiah, and E., and Zichri, the sons of
2. One of the Bene-Elam that married a strange wife. B.C. 456.
Ezra 10. 26 Jehiel, and Abdi, and Jeremoth, and E.

EL-IAH'-BA, אֶלְיַחְבָּא *God hides.*
A Shaalbonite, one of David's famous guard of thirty. B.C. 1048.
2 Sa. 23. 32 E. the Shaalbonite, of the sons of Jashen
1 Ch. 11. 33 Azmaveth the Baharumite, E. the Shaal.

EL-IA'-KIM, אֶלְיָקִים, Ἐλιακείμ *God is setting up.*
1. A son of Hilkiah, successor of Shebna as master of Hezekiah's household. B.C. 710.
2 Ki. 18. 18 there came out to them E. the son of H.
18. 26 Then said E. the son of Hilkiah, and Sh.
18. 37 Then came E. the son of Hilkiah, which
19. 2 And he sent E., which (was) over the ho
Isa. 22. 20 I will call my servant E. the son of Hilk.
36. 3 Then came forth unto him E., Hilkiah's
36. 11 Then said E. and Shebna and Joah unto
36. 22 Then came E...that (was) over the house.
37. 2 And he sent E., who (was) over the house.
2. Original name of king Jehoiakim. B.C. 599.
2 Ki. 23. 34 Pharaoh-nechoh made E. the son of Josiah
2 Ch. 36. 4 the king of Egypt made E. his brother
3. A priest that assisted at the dedication of the wall in the time of Nehemiah. B.C. 445.
Neh. 12. 41 the priests; E., Maaseiah, Miniamin, Mi.
4. Eldest son of Abiud or Judah; brother of Joseph, and father of Azor in the genealogy of Christ.
Matt. 1. 13 Abiud begat E.; and E. begat Azor
Luke 3. 30 (son) of Jonan, which was (the son) of E.

E-LI'-AM, אֱלִיעָם *God is founder of the people.*
1. Father of Bath-sheba, wife of David, B.C. 1060. Called also *Ammiel.*
2 Sa. 11. 3 not this Bath-sheba, the daughter of E.
2. One of David's thirty mighty men. B.C. 1048.
2 Sa. 23. 34 E. the son of Ahithophel the Gilonite

E-LI'-AS, Ἠλίας, *the Greek form of Elijah.*
Matt11. 14 if ye will receive (it), this is E., which
16 14 Some..John the Baptist; some, E.
17. 3 there appeared unto them Moses and E.
17. 4 thee, and one for Moses, and one for E.
17. 10 Why then say the scribes that E. must
17. 11 E. truly shall first come, and restore all
17. 12 E. is come already, and they knew him
27. 47 Some..said, This (man) calleth for E.
27. 49 let us see whether E. will come to save
Mark 6. 15 Others said, That it is E And others said
8. 28 but some..E.; and others, One of the pr
9. 4 there appeared unto them E. with Moses
9. 5 thee, and one for Moses, and one for E.
9. 11 Why say the scribes that E. must first c.?
9. 12 E. verily cometh first, and restoreth all
9. 13 E. is indeed come, and they have done
15. 35 some of them..said, Behold, he calleth E.
15. 36 let us see whether E. will come to take
Luke 1. 17 shall go before him in the spirit..of E.
4. 25 many widows..in Israel in the days of E.
4. 26 unto none of them was E. sent, save unto
9. 8 And of some, that E. had appeared; and
9. 19 They answering said..but some (say), E.
9. 30 talked with him two men..Moses and E.
9. 33 thee, and one for Moses, and one for E.
9. 54 and consume them, even as E. did?
John 1. 21 they asked him, What then? Art thou E.?
1. 25 Why baptizest thou..if thou be not..E.
Rom 11. 2 Wot ye not what the Scripture saith of E.?
Jas. 5 17 E. was a man subject to like passions as

EL-IA'-SAPH, אֶלְיָסָף *God is gatherer.*
1. Son of Deuel and head of the tribe of Gad at the census in the wilderness. B.C. 1490.
Num. 1. 14 Of Gad; E. the son of Deuel
2. 14 the captain of the sons of Gad..E.
7. 42 On the sixth day E. the son of Deuel
7. 47 this..the offering of E. the son of Deuel
10. 20 over..the children of Gad..E. the son of
2. Son of Lael a chief of the house of the father of the Gershonites at the census in the wilderness. B.C. 1490.
Num. 3. 24 the chief..of the Gershonites..E. the son

EL-IA'-SHIB, אֶלְיָשִׁיב *God is requiter.*
1. A priest in the time of David. B.C. 1015.
1 Ch. 24. 12 The eleventh to E., the twelfth to Jakim

2. A descendant of the royal family of Judah. B.C. 445
1 Ch. 3. 24 the sons of Elioenai..Hodaiah, and E.
3. The high priest at the time of the rebuilding of the wall under Nehemiah. B.C. 445.
Neh. 3. 1 E. the high priest rose up, with his breth.
3. 20 unto the door of the house of E. the high
3. 21 house of E...to the end of the house of E.
13. 4 E. the priest..(was) allied unto Tobiah
13. 7 I..understood..the evil that E. did for
13. 28 Joiada, the son of E. the high priest
4. A singer who married a strange wife in the exile. B.C. 445.
Ezra 10. 24 Of the singers also; E.: and of the
5. A son of Zattu, whose wife was a stranger. B.C. 445.
Ezra 10. 27 of the sons of Zattu; Elioenai, E., Matt.
6. A son of Bani, who married a strange wife. B.C. 445.
Ezra 10. 36 Vaniah, Meremoth, E.
7. An ancestor of Johanan who assisted Ezra in the assembly about strange wives. B.C. 445.
Ezra 10. 6 into the chamber of Johanan the son of E.
Neh. 12. 10 J. begat Joiakim, Joiakim also begat E.
12. 22 The Levites, in the days of E...(were)
12. 23 until the days of Johanan the son of E.

E-LI-A'-THAH, אֱלִיאָתָה *God is come.*
A son of Heman appointed by lot for the service of song in the sanctuary. B.C. 1015.
1 Ch. 25. 4 Hem.: the sons of Heman; Bukkiah..E.
25. 27 The twentieth to E., (he), his sons, and

E-LI'-DAD, אֱלִידָד *God is a friend.*
A chief of Benjamin chosen to represent his tribe in the allotment of Canaan. B.C. 1452.
Num. 34. 21 Of the tribe of Benjamin, E. the son of

E-LI'-EL, אֱלִיאֵל *God is God.*
1. Great-grandfather of Samuel the prophet: in 1 Ch. 6. 27 it is *Eliab.*
1 Ch. 6. 34 Jeroham, the son of E., the son of Toah
2. Head of the house of Manasseh in Bashan. B.C. 800.
1 Ch. 5. 24 E...heads of the house of their fathers
3. A son of Shimhi the Benjamite. B.C. 1340
1 Ch. 8. 20 And Elienai, and Zilthai, and E.
4. A son of Shashak, a Benjamite. B.C. 1340.
1 Ch. 8. 22 And Ishpan, and Heber, and E.
5. A captain of David's army. B.C. 1048.
1 Ch. 11. 46 E. the Mahavite, and Jeribai and Josh.
6. Another of David's valiant men. B.C. 1048.
1 Ch 11 47 E., and Obed, and Jasiel the Mesobaite
7. A Gadite that joined David at Ziklag; perhaps the same as No. 5. or 6.
1 Ch 12. 11 Attai the sixth, E. the seventh
8. A chief of Judah in David's time; perhaps the same as No. 5
1 Ch. 15. 9 Of the sons of Hebron; E. the chief
9. A chief Levite whom David called on to assist in bringing up the Ark from the house of Obed-edom. B.C. 1042
1 Ch. 15. 11 David called for..the priests, and..E.
10. A Levite, overseer of the dedicated things in the time of Hezekiah. B.C. 726
2 Ch. 31. 13 E., and Ismachiah, and Mahath..overs.

E-LI-E'-NAI, אֱלִיעֵינַי *unto God are mine eyes.*
A son of Shimhi, a Benjamite. B.C. 1340.
1 Ch. 8. 20 And E., and Zilthai, and Eliel

E-LI-E'-ZER, אֱלִיעֶזֶר, Ἐλιέζερ *God is help.*
1. Abraham's chief servant, called by him "Eliezer of Damascus," (or rather *Damascus Eliezer*). The common version makes him born in Abraham's house; but the original is simply "son of my house" (Gen 15. 3), which imports no more than that he was one of the household. B.C. 1913.
Gen. 15. 2 the steward of my house (is) this E. of D.
2. Second son of Moses and Zipporah, to whom his father gave this name as a memento of his gratitude to God. B.C. 1500.
Exod. 18. 4 the name of the other (was) E.; for the
1 Ch. 23. 15 The sons of Moses (were) Gershom and E.
23. 17 the sons of E. (were) Rehabiah the chief
23. 17 And E. had none other sons
26. 25 And his brethren by E.; Rehabiah his
3. A grandson of Benjamin. B.C. 1650.
1 Ch. 7. 8 And the sons of Becher; Zemira, and..E.
4. A priest who assisted in bringing up the ark from the house of Obed-edom. B.C. 1042.
1 Ch. 15. 24 Benaiah, and E., the priests, did blow
5. A ruler of Reuben in the time of David. B.C. 1015.
1 Ch. 27. 16 the ruler of the Reubenites (was) E.
6. A prophet that rebuked Jehoshaphat for joining with Ahaziah king of Israel in an expedition to Ophir. B.C. 896.
2 Ch. 20. 37 E. the son of Dodavah..prophesied agai.
7. A chief sent with others to induce some Levites and others to accompany Ezra to Jerusalem. B.C. 457.
Ezra 8. 16 Then sent I for E., for Ariel, for Shemai.
8. A priest who had taken a strange wife. B.C. 456.
Ezra 10. 18 Maaseiah, and E., and Jarib, and Gedaliah
9. A Levite who had trespassed like No. 8.
Ezra 10. 23 Levites; Jozabad, and Shimei..and E.

10. One of the sons of Harim who had done likewise.
Ezra 10. 31 And (of) the sons of Harim; E., Ishijah
11. An ancestor of Joseph husband of Mary in the line traced by Luke. Luke 3. 29.

ELIHOENAI. *See* **ELIOENAI.**

E-LI-HO'-REPH, אֱלִיחֹרֶף *God of harvest rain.*
A scribe or secretary of Solomon. B.C. 1015.
1 Ki. 4. 3 E. and Ahiah, the sons of Shisha, scribes

E-LI'-HU, אֱלִיהוּ *God himself.*
1. Great-grandfather of Samuel the prophet, and son of Tohu. Both *Eliel* and *Eliab* are used of this man in 1 Ch. vi. B.C. 1230.
1 Sa. 1. 1 the son of Jeroham, the son of E.
2. Manassehite who joined David at Ziglag. B.C. 1058.
1 Ch. 12. 20 E., and Zilthai, captains of the thousands
3. A Kohathite of the family of Korah, and a porter at the tabernacle in the time of David. B.C. 1022.
1 Ch. 26. 7 whose brethren (were) strong men, E.
4. A brother of David (same as Eliab), made ruler over Judah. B.C. 1060.
1 Ch. 27. 18 Of Judah; E., (one) of the brethren of D.
5. Youngest of Job's four friends. B.C. 1520.
Job 32. 2 Then was kindled the wrath of E. the son
32. 4 Now E. had waited till Job had spoken
32. 5 When E. saw that (there was) no answer
32. 6 E...said, I (am) young, and ye (are) very
34. 1 Furthermore, E. answered and said, Hear
35. 1 E. spake moreover, and said, Thinkest
36. 1 E. also proceeded, and said, Suffer me

E-LI'-JAH, אֵלִיָּהוּ *my God is Jah, or God himself.*
1. The grandest and most romantic character that Israel ever produced. "Elijah the Tishbite of the inhabitants of Gilead," is literally all we know of his parentage. B.C. 897.
1 Ki. 17. 1 And E. the Tishbite..said unto Ahab
17. 13 And E. said unto her, Fear not; go!
17. 15 she..did according to the saying of E.
17. 16 word of the LORD, which he spake by E.
17. 18 she said unto E., What have I to do with
17. 22 the LORD heard the voice of E.; and the
17. 23 E. took the child, and brought him down
17. 23 and E. said, See, thy son liveth
17. 24 the woman said to E., Now by this I know
18. 1 the word of the LORD came to E. in the
18. 2 And E. went to show himself unto Ahab
18. 7 as Obadiah was in the way, behold, E.
18. 7 and said, (Art) thou that my lord E.?
18. 8, 11, 14 go, tell thy lord, Behold, E. (is here)
18. 15 E. said, (As) the LORD of hosts liveth
18. 16 and Ahab went to meet E.
18. 17 it came to pass, when Ahab saw E., that
18. 21 E. came unto all the people, and said
18. 22 Then said E. unto the people, I..I only
18. 25 And E. said unto the prophets of Baal
18. 27 E. mocked them, and said, Cry aloud
18. 30 E. said unto all the people, Come near
18. 31 E. took twelve stones, according to the
18. 36 E. came near, and said, LORD God of Ab.
18. 40 E. said unto them, Take the prophets of
18. 40 E. brought them down to the brook K.
18. 41 E. said unto Ahab, Get thee up, eat and
18. 42 and E. went up to the top of Carmel
18. 46 And the hand of the LORD was on E.
19. 1 Ahab told Jezebel all that E. had done
19. 2 Jezebel sent a messenger unto E., saying
19. 9 said unto him, What doest thou here, E.?
19. 13 E. heard (it)..what dost thou here, E.?
19. 19 E. passed by him, and cast his mantle
19. 20 And he left the oxen, and ran after E.
19. 21 he arose, and went after E., and ministe.
21. 17 the word of the LORD came to E. the T.
21. 20 Ahab said to E., Hast thou found me, O
21. 28 the word of the LORD came to E., the T.
2 Ki. 1. 3 the angel of the LORD said to E. the Ti.
1. 4 Thou..shalt surely die. And E. departed
1. 8 And he said, It (is) E. the Tishbite
1. 10 E. answered and said to the captain of
1. 12 E. answered and said unto them, If I (be)
1. 13 third captain..fell on his knees before E.
1. 15 the angel of the LORD said unto E., Go
1. 17 died according to the word..which E. had
2. 1 the LORD would take up E. into heaven
2. 1 that E. went with Elisha from Gilgal
2. 2 E. said unto Elisha, Tarry here, I pray
2. 4 E. said unto him, Elisha, Tarry here
2. 6 E. said unto him, Tarry, I pray thee
2. 8 E. took his mantle, and wrapped (it)
2. 9 E. said unto Elisha, Ask what I shall do
2. 11 E. went up by a whirlwind into heaven
2. 13 He took up also the mantle of E. that
2. 14 he took the mantle of E...and smote the
2. 14 and said, Where (is) the LORD God of E.?
2. 15 The spirit of E. doth rest on Elisha
3. 11 Elisha..poured water on the hands of E.
9. 36 which he spake by his servant E. the
10. 10 LORD hath done..which he spake by..E.
10. 17 saying of the LORD, which he spake to E.
2 Ch. 21. 12 there came a writing to him from E.
Mal. 4. 5 Behold, I will send you E. the prophet
2. One who took a strange wife during the exile. B.C. 456.
Ezra 10. 21 of the sons of Harim; Maaseiah, and E.

E-LI'-KA, אֱלִיקָא *God is rejector.*
A Harodite, one of David's guard. The name is omitted in 1 Ch. xi. B.C. 1048.
2 Sa. 23. 25 Shammah the Harodite, E. the Harodite

E'-LIM, אֵילִם *palm trees.*
Second encampment of Israel after they crossed the Red Sea. It had twelve fountains of water, and seventy palm trees; hence its name.
Exod 15. 27 they came to E., where (were) twelve
16. 1 they took their journey from E., and all
16. 1 wilderness of Sin, which (is) between E.
Num 33. 9 from M. and came unto E.: and in E.
33. 10 they removed from E., and encamped by

E-LI-ME'-LECH, אֱלִימֶלֶךְ *God is king.*
A man of Judah, and of the Hezronite family dwelling in Bethlehem Ephratah in the days of the Judges. He became husband of Naomi and father in law of Ruth. B.C. 1322.
Ruth 1. 2 the name of the man (was) E., and the
1. 3 E., Naomi's husband, died; and she was
2. 1 a kinsman..of the family of E.; and his
2. 3 unto Boaz, who (was) of the kindred of E.
4. 3 parcel of land..(was) our brother E.'s
4. 9 I have bought all that (was) E.'s and all

EL-IO-E'-NAI, אֶלְיוֹעֵינַי, אֶלְיְהוֹעֵינַי *to Jah are mine eyes.*
1. A son of Neariah of the family of David. B.C. 460.
1 Ch. 3. 23 the sons of Neariah; E., and Hezekiah
3. 24 the sons of E...Hodaiah, and Eliashib
2. Head of a family of Simeon. B.C. 800.
1 Ch. 4. 36 E., and Jaakobah, and Jeshohaiah, and
3. Head of one of the families of the sons of Becher son of Benjamin. B.C. 1650.
1 Ch. 7. 8 the sons of Becher; Zemira..and E., and
4. A priest in Ezra's time who put away his strange wife. Perhaps the same as the one in Neh. 12. 41. B.C. 457.
Ezra 10. 22 of the sons of Pashur; E., Maaseiah
5. A son of Zattu who married a strange wife. B.C. 457.
Ezra 10. 27 of the sons of Zattu; E., Eliashib, Mat.
6. Probably the same as No. 4.
Neh. 12. 41 the priests; Eliakim, Maaseiah..E., Zec.
7. Better *Elihoenai*; the seventh son of Meshelemiah the son of Kore, of the sons of Asaph, and one of the doorkeepers of the temple. B.C. 1015.
1 Ch. 26. 3 Elam the fifth, Jehohanan the sixth, E.
8. A descendant of Pahath Moab, who came up with Ezra in Artaxerxes' time. B.C. 457.
Ezra 8. 4 E...son of Zerahiah, and with him two

E-LI'-PHAL, אֱלִיפַל *God is judge.*
A captain in David's army. B.C. 1048.
1 Ch. 11. 35 Ahiham..son of Sacar..E. the son of Ur

E-LI-PHA'-LET, E-LI-PHE'-LET אֱלִיפֶלֶט, *God is escape.*
1. The last of David's thirteen sons by his wives. The names Elphalet and Phaltiel are=Eliphalet.
2 Sa. 5. 16 And Elishama, and Eliada, and E.
1 Ch. 3. 8 And Elishama, and Eliada, and E., nine
14. 7 And Elishama, and Beeliada, and E.
2. Another of David's sons, born after his establishment in Jerusalem. Called *Elphalet* in 1 Ch. 14. 5. B.C. 1040.
1 Ch. 3. 6 Ibhar also, and Elishama, and E.
3. One of David's thirty valiant men. B.C. 1048.
2 Sa. 23. 34 E. the son of Ahasbai, the son of the
4. A Benjamite, a son of Eshek and descendant of Saul through Jonathan. B.C. 830.
1 Ch. 8. 39 the sons of Eshek his brother (were)..E.
5. A leader of the sons of Adonikam who came up with Ezra from the exile.
Ezra 8. 13 the last sons of Adonikam..E., Jeiel, and
6. One who took a strange wife; the same as No. 5.
Ezra 10. 33 sons of Hashum; Mattenai..Zabad, E.

E-LI'-PHAZ, אֱלִיפַז *God is dispenser.*
1. Son of Esau by the daughter of Elon. B.C. 1790.
Gen 36. 4 Adah bare to Esau E.; and Bashemath
36. 10 These (are) the names of Esau's sons; E.
36. 11 the sons of E. were Teman, Omar, Zepho
36. 12 Timna was concubine to E., Esau's son
36. 12 she bare to E. Amalek: these (were) the
36. 15 the sons of E. the first born (son) of Esau
36. 16 these (are) the dukes (that came) of E. in
1 Ch. 1. 35 The sons of Esau; E., Reuel, and Jeush
1. 36 The sons of E.; Teman, and Omar, Zephi
2. The chief of Job's three friends, a descendant of Teman son of Eliphaz, from whom a portion of Arabia took its name, and whose name is used in Jer. 49. 20 as a poetical parallel to Edom. B.C. 1530.
Job 2. 11 E. the Temanite, and Bildad the Shuhite
4. 1 Then E. the Temanite answered and said
15. 1 Then answered E. the Temanite, and said
22. 1 Then E. the Temanite answered and said
42. 7 the LORD said to E. the Temanite, My
42. 9 E...did according as the LORD comman.

E-LI-PHE'-LEH, אֱלִיפְלֵהוּ *Jah is distinction.*
A Levite set over the choral service when the ark was brought up from the house of Obed-edom. B.C. 1042.
1 Ch. 15. 18 their brethren of the second..E., and
15. 21 Mattithiah, and E., and Mikneiah, and

E-LI-SA'-BETH, Ἐλισάβετ (*from the Heb.*) *God is swearer.*
Wife of Zacharias and mother of John the Baptist. She was of a priestly family and a relation of the Virgin Mary whom she was the first to greet as the mother of her "Lord."
Luke 1. 5 of the daughters of Aaron..her name..E.
1. 7 they had no child, because..E. was barren
1. 13 thy wife E. shall bear thee a son
1. 24 after those days his wife E. conceived
1. 36 E...hath also conceived a son in her old
1. 40 the house of Zacharias, and saluted E.
1. 41 when E. heard the salutation of Mary
1. 41 and E. was filled with the Holy Ghost
1. 57 E.'s full time came that she should be

E-LIS-E'-US, Ἐλισσαῖος.
The form in which the name of *Elisha* appears in the Common Version of the New Testament and Apocrypha.
Luke 4. 27 were in Israel in the time of E. the prophet

E-LI'-SHA, אֱלִישָׁע *God is saviour.*
Son of Shaphat of Abel-meholah; the attendant and disciple of Elijah, and his successor as prophet in Israel. His call by Elijah was (B.C. 901), four years before the death of Ahab (B.C. 897), and he held the office of prophet in Israel for 55 years. The thrilling incidents of his life are related in the 1 and 2 Books of Kings.
1 Ki. 19. 16 E...shalt thou anoint (to be) prophet in
19. 17 that escapeth from the sword..shall E.
19. 19 So he departed thence, and found E. the
2 Ki. 2. 1 Elijah went with E. from Gilgal
2. 2 Elijah said unto E., Tarry here, I pray
2. 2 E. said..I will not leave thee. So they
2. 3 the sons of the prophets..came forth to E.
2. 4 Elijah said unto him, E., tarry here, I pray
2. 5 the sons of the prophets..came to E., and
2. 9 Elijah said unto E...And E. said, I pray
2. 12 E. saw (it), and he cried, My father, my
2. 14 they parted hither and thither: and E.
2. 15 said, The spirit of Elijah doth rest on E.
2. 19 the men of the city said unto E., Behold
2. 22 according to the saying of E. which he
3. 11 Here (is) E. the son of Shaphat, which
3. 13 E. said unto the king of Israel, What
3. 14 E. said, (As) the LORD of hosts liveth
4. 1 there cried a certain woman..unto E.
4. 2 E. said unto her, What shall I do
4. 8 E. passed to Shunem, where (was) a great
4. 17 at that season that E. had said unto her
4. 32 when E. was come into the house, behold
4. 38 And E. came again to Gilgal: and
5. 8 E...heard that the king..rent his clothes
5. 9 Na...stood at the door of the house of E.
5. 10 E. sent a messenger unto him, saying
5. 20 Gehazi, the servant of E. the man of G.
5. 25 And E. said unto him, Whence..Gehazi?
6. 1 the sons of the prophets said unto E.
6. 12 E., the prophet..telleth the king of Israel
6. 17 E. prayed..LORD..open his eyes, that he
6. 17 horses and chariots of fire round about E.
6. 18 E. prayed unto the LORD, and said, Smite
6. 18 blindness according to the word of E.
6. 19 E. said unto them, This (is) not the way
6. 20 E. said, LORD, open the eyes of these
6. 21 the king of Israel said unto E., when he
6. 31 if the head of E...stand on him this day
6. 32 E. sat in his house, and the elders sat
7. 1 E. said, Hear ye the word of the LORD
8. 1 Then spake E. unto the woman, whose
8. 4 Tell me..the great things that E. hath
8. 5 this (is) her son, whom E. restored to
8. 7 E. came to Damascus; and Ben-hadad
8. 10 E. said unto him, Go, say unto him, Thou
8. 13 E. answered, The LORD hath showed me
8. 14 he departed from E., and came to his
8. 14 who said to him, What said E. to thee?
9. 1 E. the prophet called one of the children
13. 14 E. was fallen sick of his sickness whereof
13. 15 E. said unto him, Take bow and arrows
13. 16 E. put his hands upon the king's hands
13. 17 E. said, Shoot: and he shot. And he
13. 20 And E. died, and they buried him
13. 21 cast the man into the sepulchre of E.
13. 21 when the man..touched the bones of E.

E-LI'-SHAH, אֱלִישָׁה.
Eldest son of Javan grandson of Noah, and ancestor of the Æolians, a leading Hellenic tribe. The designation of a race rather than of a locality. Javan represents the Ionians, and Elishah the Æolians. B.C. 2250.
Gen. 10. 4 sons of Javan; E., 1 Ch. 1. 7; Eze. 27. 7.

E-LI-SHA'-MA, אֱלִישָׁמָע *God is hearer.*
1. Grandfather of Joshua, and son of Ammihud a chief of Ephraim in the wilderness. B.C. 1490.
Num. 1. 10 of Ephraim; E. the son of Ammihud
2. 18 the captain of the sons of Ephraim..E.
7. 48 On the seventh day E...(offered)
7. 53 this..the offering of E. the son of Amm.
10. 22 over his host (was) E. the son of Ammihud
1 Ch. 7. 26 Laadan his son, Ammihud his son, E. his
2. A son of king David: one of the thirteen sons born to him in Jerusalem. B.C. 1030.
2 Sa. 5. 16 And E., and Eliada, and Eliphalet
1 Ch. 3. 8 And E., and Eliada, and Eliphelet
14. 7 And E., and Beeliada, and Eliphalet
3. Another son, who is also called *Elishua*. B.C. 1050.
1 Ch. 3. 6 Ibhar also, and E., and Eliphelet
4. A descendant of Judah. B.C. 1280.
1 Ch. 2. 41 Shallum begat Jekam...Jekam. begat E.
5. The same, according to Jerome, as No. 4.: father of Nethaniah and grandfather of Ishmael "of the seed royal," who lived at the time of the exile. B.C. 635.

2 Ki. 25. 25 Ishmael..son of Nethaniah, the son of E.
Jer. 41. 1 Ishmael the son of Nethaniah..son of E.

6. A scribe or secretary to Jehoiakim. B.C. 606.

Jer. 36. 12 all the princes sat there..E. the scribe
36. 20 laid up the roll in the chamber of E.
36. 21 he took it out of E. the scribe's chamber

7. A priest sent by Jehoshaphat to teach the law. B.C. 912.

2 Ch.17. 8 and with them E. and Jehoram, priests

E-LI-SHA'-PHAT, אֱלִישָׁפָט *God is judge.*

One of the "captains of hundreds" whom Jehoiada the priest employed to collect the Levites and other leaders to Jerusalem before bringing forward Joash as king. B.C. 878.

2 Ch.23. 1 Jehoiada..took..E...into covenant with

E-LI-SHE'-BA, אֱלִישֶׁבַע *God is swearer.*

Daughter of Amminadab, sister of Naashon. B.C. 1490.

Exod. 6. 23 And Aaron took him E...to wife; and she

E-LI'-SHUA, אֱלִישׁוּעַ *God is rich.*

A son of David, B.C. 1030. He is called *Elishama* in 1 Ch. 3. 6.

2 Sa. 5. 15 Ibhar also, and E., and Nepheg, and Ja.
1 Ch.14. 5 And Ibhar, and E., and Elpalet

E-LI'-UD, Ἐλιούδ *(from the Heb.)*

Son of Achim in the genealogy of Jesus four generations before Joseph.

Matt 1. 14 Sadoc begat Achim; and Achim begat E.
1. 15 E. begat Eleazar; and Eleazar begat M.

E-LI-ZA'-PHAN, אֱלִיצָפָן *God is protector.*

1. Son of Uzziel, a Levite, chief of the Kohathites at the taking of the census at Sinai. B.C. 1490.

Num. 3. 30 the chief..(shall be) E. the son of Uzziel
1 Ch.15. 8 Of the sons of E.; Shemaiah the chief

2. Son of Parnach, "prince" of Zebulun, and appointed to assist in apportioning the land. B.C. 1490.

Num34 25 the prince of the tribe..of Zebulun, E.

3. Ancestor of certain Levites that assisted in cleansing the temple in the time of Hezekiah. B.C. 724.

2 Ch.29 13 of the sons of E.; Shimri, and Jeiel

E-LI'-ZUR, אֱלִיצוּר *God is a rock.*

A chief Reubenite who assisted in taking the census under Moses. B.C. 1490.

Num. 1. 5 of (the tribe of) Reuben; E. the son of S
2. 10 the captain of the children of Reuben..E.
7 30 On the fourth day E. the son of Shedeur
7 35 this (was) the offering of E. the son of S.
10 18 over his host (was) E. the son of Shedeur

EL-KA'-NAH, אֶלְקָנָה *God is possessing.*

1 A grandson of Korah grandson of Kohath. B.C. 1490.

Exod. 6 24 the sons of Korah; Assir, and E., and A.
1 Ch. 6 23 E his son, and Ebiasaph his son

2. Father of the prophet Samuel, and a descendant of No. 1. in the fifth generation. B.C. 1171.

1 Sa. 1. 1 his name (was) E., the son of Jeroham
1. 4 when the time was that E. offered, he
1. 8 Then said E...to her, Hannah, why weep.
1. 19 E. knew Hannah..and the LORD remem.
1. 21 E...went up to offer unto the LORD the
1. 23 E...said unto her, Do what seemeth thee
2. 11 And E. went to Ramah to his house
2. 20 Eli blessed E. and his wife, and said, The
1 Ch 6. 27 Eliab his son, Jeroham his son, E. his son
6. 34 The son of E., the son of Jeroham, the

3. A descendant of Levi through Kohath. B.C. 1490.

1 Ch. 6. 25 the sons of E.; Amasai, and Ahimoth
6. 36 The son of E., the son of Joel, the son of

4. A descendant of Kohath, (the same as No. 3?)

1 Ch 6 26 (As for) E.: the sons of E.; Zophai his
6 35 The son of Zuph, the son of E., the son

5. An ancestor of Netophathite villagers. B.C. 500.

1 Ch. 9 16 Berechiah, the son of Asa, the son of E.

6. A Korhite who joined David at Ziklag. B.C. 1058.

1 Ch. 12. 6 E, and Jesiah, and Azareel, and Joezer

7 A Levite doorkeeeper of the ark; (the same as No. 6?)

1 Ch.15 23 Berechiah and E...doorkeepers for the

8. An officer in the household of king Ahaz, slain when Pekah invaded Judah. B.C. 741.

2 Ch.28. 7 and E. (that was) next to the king

EL-KO-SHITE, אֶלְקֹשִׁי.

A native of Elkosh, the birthplace of the prophet Nahum, which in Jerome's time was considered to be in Galilee. B.C. 713.

Nah. 1. 1 The book of the vision of Nahum the E.

EL-LA'-SAR, אֶלָּסָר.

A Chaldean town, the city of Arioch. In the native dialect it was called *Larsa* or *Larancha,* and was known to the Greeks as Larissa or Larachôn. This suits the connection with Elam and Shinar. Larsa was in Lower Babylonia or Chaldea, midway between Ur and Erech (now called *Mugheir* and *Warka*) on the left of the Euphrates. It is now called *Senkereh.*

Gen. 14. 1 in the days of..Arioch king of E.
14. 9 Arioch king of E.; four kings with five

ELM —

Oak, terebinth, אֵלָה *elah.*

Hos. 4. 13 upon the hills, under oaks..and elms

EL-MO'-DAM, Ἐλμωδάμ, Ἐλμαδάμ.

Son of Er, six generations earlier than Zerubbabel in the genealogy of Joseph the husband of Mary.

Luke 3. 28 which was (the son) of E., which was

EL-NA'-AM, אֶלְנַעַם *God is pleasant.*

Father of David's guard, Jeribai and Joshaviah. B.C. 1050.

1 Ch.11. 46 Jeribai, and Joshaviah, the sons of E.

EL-NA'-THAN, אֶלְנָתָן *God is giving.*

1. Father of Nehushta, Jehoiakim's queen. B.C. 640.

2 Ki.24. 8 Nehushta, the daughter of E. of Jerusalem
Jer. 26. 22 E. the son of Achbor, and..men with
36. 12 the princes sat there..Elishama..and E.
36. 25 Nevertheless E...had made intercession

2. Name of three Levites in the time of Ezra. B.C. 457

Ezra 8. 16 Then sent I for E...and for E...and for E.

ELOI, Ἐλωΐ; *in Heb.* אֱלֹהַי *elohai, my God.*

Mark15. 34 a loud voice, saying, Eloi, Eloi, lama saba.

E'-LON, אֵילוֹן *oak, strong.*

1. Father of the wife of Esau. B.C. 1796.

Gen. 26. 34 Bashemath the daughter of E. the Hittite
36. 2 Adah the daughter of E. the Hittite

2. The second of Zebulun's three sons. B.C. 1700.

Gen. 46. 14 the sons of Zebulun; Sered, and E., and
Num 26. 26 of E., the family of the Elonites: of

3. A town in the border of Dan, between Ajalon and Ekron.

Josh.19. 43 And E., and Thimnathah, and Ekron

4. The Zebulonite who judged Israel for ten years and was buried in Aijalon. *Elon* and *Aijalon* are (in Hebrew) composed of precisely the same letters; hence "Aijalon" may have had its name from Elon being buried there.

Judg.12. 11 after him E., a Zebulonite, judged Israel
12. 12 E. the Zebulonite died, and was buried

E-LON BETH HA'-NAN, אֵילוֹן בֵּית־חָנָן *oak of the house of grace.*

One of the three Danite towns that formed one of Solomon's commissariat districts, (the same as the Elon of Joshua 19. 43?)

1 Ki. 4. 9 in Shaalbim, and Beth-shemesh, and E.

E-LO-NITES, אֵלֹנִי *belonging to Elon.*

Descendants of Elon, son of Zebulon.

Num 26. 26 of Zebulon..of Elon, the family of the E.

ELOQUENT —

1. *To be intelligent,* בִּין *bin,* 2.

Isa. 3. 3 the cunning artificer, and the eloquent

2. *A man of words,* אִישׁ דְּבָרִים *ish debarim.*

Exod. 4. 10 I (am) not eloquent, neither heretofore

3. *Eloquent, full of words,* λόγιος *logios.*

Acts 18. 24 an eloquent man, (and) mighty in the s.

E'-LOTH, אֵילוֹת *oak or terebinth grove.*

Another orthography of *Elath,* which see.

1 Ki. 9. 26 beside E., on the shore of the Red sea
2 Ch. 8. 17 went Solomon to Ezion-geber, and to E.
26. 2 He built E., and restored it to Judah

EL-PA'-AL, אֶלְפַּעַל *God is working.*

Son of Shaharaim, a Benjamite. B.C. 1400.

1 Ch. 8. 11 And of Hushim he begat Abitub, and E.
8. 12 sons of E.; Eber, and Misham, and Sha.
8. 18 and Jezliah, and Jobab, the sons of E.

EL-PA'-LET, אֶלְפָּלֶט *God is escape.*

A son of David, called Eliphalet in 1 Ch. 3. 6, but omitted in 2 Sa. 5. B.C. 1040.

1 Ch. 14. 5 And Ibhar, and Elishua, and E.

EL PA'-RAN, אֵיל פָּארָן *oak of Paran.*

A place in the S. of Canaan and W. of Edom, where the Horites dwelt in Seir.

Gen. 14. 6 the Horites in their mount Seir, unto E.

ELSE —

1. *If not,* אִם אַיִן *im ayin.*

Gen. 30. 1 unto Jacob, Give me children, or else I die

2. *Because, for, but, surely,* כִּי *ki.*

Exod 10. 4 Else, if thou refuse to let my people go

3. *Again, yet, any more,* עוֹד *od.*

Deut. 4. 35 he (is) God: (there is) none else beside

4. *But (or now) if not,* εἰ δὲ μή *ei de mē.*

Mark 2. 21 else the new piece that filled it up taketh
2. 22 else the new wine doth burst the bottles

5. *But if not indeed,* εἰ δὲ μήγε *ei de mēge.*

Matt 9. 17 else the bottles break, and the wine run.
Luke 5. 37 else the new wine will burst the bottles

6. *Since if so, if otherwise,* ἐπεὶ *epei.*

1 Co. 14. 16 Else when thou shalt bless with the spirit
15. 29 Else what shall they do which are bapti.

7. *Since otherwise indeed,* ἐπεὶ ἄρα *epei ara.*

1 Co. 7. 14 else were your children unclean; but now

8. *The other,* ἕτερος *heteros.*

Acts 17. 21 spent their time in nothing else but

9. *And, even,* καί *kai.*

Rom 2. 15 accusing or else excusing one another

ELSE, or —

And if not, וְאִם־לֹא *ve-im-lo.*

Gen. 42. 16 or else by the life of Pharaoh surely ye

EL-TE'-KEH, אֶלְתְּקֵא, אֶלְתְּקֵה *God is Teqe.*

A city in Dan given to the Kohathites.

Josh.19. 44 And E., and Gibbethon, and Baalath
21. 23 out of the tribe of Dan, E. with her sub.

EL-TE'-KON, אֶלְתְּקֹן *God is firm.*

A city in the mountains of Judah, three or four miles N. of Hebron.

Josh.15. 59 And Maarath, and Beth-anoth, and E.

EL-TO'-LAD, אֶלְתּוֹלַד *God is begetter.*

A city in the S. of Judah given to Simeon, and in possession of the tribe until the time of David. In 1 Ch. 4. 29 it is *Tolad,* now *El-Toula.*

Josh.15. 30 And E., and Chesil, and Hormah
19. 4 And E., and Bethul, and Hormah

EL'-UL, אֱלוּל *the gleaning month.*

The sixth month of the sacred year of the Jews, beginning with the last new moon of September and ending with the first one of November.

Neh. 6. 15 in the twenty and fifth (day) of..E.

EL-U'-ZAI, אֶלְעוּזַי *God is strong.*

A Benjamite who joined David at Ziklag. B.C. 1048.

1 Ch 12. 5 E., and Jerimoth, and Bealiah, and Shem.

EL-Y'-MAS, Ἐλύμας *a sorcerer.*

A false prophet who withstood Saul and Barnabas at Paphos in Cyprus.

Acts 13. 8 E. the sorcerer..withstood them, seeking

EL-ZA'-BAD, אֶלְזָבָד *God is endowing.*

1 A Gadite who joined David at Ziklag. He was the ninth of the eleven heroes of his tribe that crossed the Jordan to assist David. B.C. 1058.

1 Ch.12. 12 Johanan the eighth, E. the ninth

2. A Korhite Levite, son of Shemaiah. B.C. 1000.

1 Ch.26. 7 E., whose brethren (were) strong men

EL-ZA'-PHAN, אֶלְצָפָן *God is protecting.*

1. Second son of Uzziel and grandson of Levi. He was thus cousin to Miriam Aaron, and Moses. Called also *Elizaphan.* B.C. 1490

Exod. 6. 22 And the sons of Uzziel; Mishael, and E.
Lev. 10. 4 Moses called Mishael and E...and said

2. A prince of Zebulun, who was one of those appointed to divide the land B.C. 1490.

Num34. 25 the prince of the tribe..of Zebulun, E.

EMBALM, to —

To embalm, חָנַט *chanat.*

Gen. 50. 2 commanded the physicians to embalm his
50. 2 and the physicians embalmed Israel
50. 3 the days of those which are embalmed
50. 26 they embalmed him, and he was put in

EMBOLDEN, to —

To make powerful, embolden, מָרַץ *marats,* 5.

Job 16. 3 what emboldeneth thee that thou answe.

EMBOLDENED, to be —

To build up, οἰκοδομέω *oikodomeō.*

1 Co. 8. 10 him which is weak be emboldened to eat

EMBRACE, to —

1. *To embrace, clasp,* חָבַק *chabaq.*

2 Ki. 4. 16 About this season..thou shalt embrace
Eccl. 3. 5 a time to embrace..to refrain from embr.

2. *To embrace, clasp, cleave to,* חָבַק *chabaq,* 3.

Gen. 29. 13 embraced him, and kissed him, and bro.
33. 4 Esau ran to meet him, and embraced
48. 10 and he kissed them, and embraced them
Job 24. 8 embrace the rock for want of a shelter
Prov 4. 8 to honour, when thou dost embrace her
5. 20 and embrace the bosom of a stranger?
Song 2. 6 and his right hand doth embrace me
8. 3 and his right hand should embrace me
Lam. 4. 5 that were brought up in scarlet embrace

3. *To draw to oneself, salute,* ἀσπάζομαι *aspazomai.*

Acts 20. 1 called unto (him) the disciples, and emb.
Heb. 11. 13 were persuaded of (them), and embraced

4. *To take round about,* συμπεριλαμβάνω *sumperi.*

Acts 20. 10 and fell on him, and embracing (him)

EMBROIDER, to —

To interweave, שָׁבַץ *shabats,* 3.

Exod28. 39 shalt embroider the coat of fine linen

EMBROIDERER —

To embroider, רָקַם *raqam.*

Exod35. 35 of the embroiderer, in blue, and in purple
38. 23 an embroiderer in blue, and in purple

EMERALD —

1. *Carbuncle, ruby, emerald,* נֹפֶךְ *nophek.*

Exod28. 18 And the second row (shall be) an emerald
39. 11 the second row, an emerald, a sapphire
Eze. 27. 16 they occupied in thy fairs with emeralds
28. 13 the jasper, the sapphire, the emerald, and

2. *Of emerald, light green,* σμαράγδινος *smaragdin.*

Rev. 4. 3 a rainbow..in sight like unto an emerald

3. *Emerald, light green stone,* σμάραγδος *smaragdos.*

Rev. 21. 19 third, a chalcedony; the fourth, an emera.

EMERODS —

1.*Emerods, tumors,* טְחוֹרִים *techorim.*
1 Sa. 6. 11 of gold, and the images of their emerods
6. 17 these (are) the golden emerods which the

2.*Boil, emerod,* עֹפֶל *ophel.*
Deut28. 27 The LORD will smite thee..with the em.
1 Sa. 5. 6 destroyed them, and smote them with e.
5. 9 they had emerods in their secret parts
5. 12 men that died not..with the emerods
6. 4 Five golden emerods, and five golden mice
6. 5 ye shall make images of your emerods

E'-MIMS, אֵימִים *the terrible.*
A race of gigantic stature originally dwelling on the E. of the Salt Sea. Anciently the whole country was held by a race of giants—the Rephaim on the N.; next, the Zuzim; and next the Emim; then the Horim on the S. Afterwards the kingdom of Bashan embraced the territories of the Rephaim; the Ammonites that of the Zuzim; the Moabites that of the Emim; while Edom embraced the mountains of the Horim. The Emim were related to the Anakim, and generally called by the same name; but their conquerors, the Moabites, called them Emim—"The Terrible."
Gen. 14. 5 and the E. in Shaveh Kiriathaim
Deut. 2. 10 The E. dwelt therein in times past
2. 11 but the Moabites call them E.

EMINENT (place) —

1.*An arched place,* גַּב *gab.*
Eze. 16. 24 also built unto thee an eminent place
16. 31 In that thou buildest thine eminent pla.
16. 39 they shall throw down thine eminent pl.

2. *To be lofty,* תָּלַל *talal.*
Eze. 17. 22 plant (it) upon an high mountain and em.

EM-MA-NU'-EL, Ἐμμανουήλ. See IMMANUEL.
Matt. 1. 23 they shall call his name E., which, being

EM-MA'-US, Ἐμμαούς.
A village about 7½ miles from Jerusalem to which two of the disciples of Christ were going when He appeared to them on the day of his resurrection.
Luke24. 13 two of them went that same day to..E.

EM'-MOR, Ἐμμόρ, Ἐμμώρ.
The father of Sychem. See HAMOR.
Acts 7. 16 sepulchre that Abraham bought..of E.

EMPIRE —
Kingdom, מַלְכוּת *malekuth.*
Esth. 1. 20 shall be published throughout all his em.

EMPLOY, to —
To go in from before, בּוֹא מִפָּנִים *bo mip-panim.*
Deut20. 19 not cut them..to employ (them) in the

EMPLOYED, to be —
To stand, stand still, עָמַד *amad.*
Ezra 10. 15 Jonathan..and Jahaziah..were employed

EMPTIED —
Empty, vain, רֵיק, רֵק *req.*
Neh. 5. 13 even thus be he shaken out, and emptied

EMPTIED, to be —

1. *To be emptied,* בָּקַק *baqaq,* 2.
Isa. 24. 3 The land shall be utterly emptied, and

2.*To be or become lean, poor, low, weak,* דָּלַל *dalal.*
Isa. 19. 6 the brooks of defence shall be emptied

3.*To be drawn out, emptied,* רוּק *ruq,* 6.
Jer. 48. 11 Moab..hath not been emptied from ves.

EMPTIER —
To empty, make void, בָּקַק *baqaq.*
Nah. 2. 2 for the emptiers have emptied them out

EMPTINESS —
Emptiness, בֹּהוּ *bohu.*
Isa. 34. 11 line of confusion, and the stones of empt.

EMPTY —

1.*To (be) empty,* בָּקַק *baqaq.*
Hos. 10. 1 Israel (is) an empty vine, he bringeth fo.

2.*Emptiness, voidness,* בּוּקָה *buqah.*
Nah. 2. 10 She is empty, and void, and waste

3.*Empty, vain,* רֵיק, רֵק *req.*
Gen. 37. 24 the pit (was) empty, (there was) no water
41. 27 the seven empty ears, blasted with the e.
Judg. 7. 16 with empty pitchers, and lamps within
2 Ki. 4. 3 borrow..empty vessels; borrow not a few
Isa. 29. 8 but he awaketh, and his soul is empty
Eze. 24. 11 Then set it empty upon the coals thereof

4.*Empty, vain,* רִיק *riq.*
Jer. 51. 34 he hath made me an empty vessel, he

5.*Empty, in vain,* רֵיקָם *reqam.*
Gen. 31. 42 surely thou hadst sent me away now em.
Exod. 3. 21 when ye go, ye shall not go empty
23. 15 and none shall appear before me empty
34. 20 And none shall appear before me empty
Deut15. 13 thou shalt not let him go away empty
16. 16 shall not appear before the LORD empty
Ruth 1. 21 LORD hath brought me home again empty
3. 17 Go not empty unto thy mother in law
1 Sa. 6. 3 If ye send away..send it not empty
2 Sa. 1. 22 and the sword of Saul returned not empty
Job 22. 9 Thou hast sent widows away empty
Jer. 14. 3 they returned with their vessels empty

6.*Empty,* κενός *kenos.*
Mark12. 3 they..beat him, and sent (him) away em
Luke 1. 53 and the rich he hath sent empty away
20. 10 but..beat him, and sent (him) away emp.
20. 11 beat him also..and sent (him) away emp.

7.*To be free, at leisure, unoccupied,* σχολάζω.
Matt12. 44 when he is come, he findeth (it) empty

EMPTY, to —

1. *To empty,* בָּקַק *baqaq,* 3*a*.
Jer. 51. 2 fanners, that..shall empty her land: for

2. *To expose, make naked, empty out,* עָרָה *arah,* 3.
Gen. 24. 20 and emptied her pitcher into the trough
2 Ch.24. 11 the high priest's officer came and emptied

3.*To prepare,* פָּנָה *panah,* 3.
Lev. 14. 36 that they empty the house, before the

4. *To draw out, empty out,* רוּק *ruq,* 5.
Gen. 42. 35 as they emptied their sacks, that, behold
Eccl.11. 3 If the clouds be full of rain, they empty
Jer. 48. 12 and shall empty his vessels, and break
Hab. 1. 17 Shall they therefore empty their net, and
Zech. 4. 12 which through the two golden pipes emp.

EMPTY, to be —
To be inspected, looked after, פָּקַד *paqad,* 2.
1 Sa. 20. 18 shalt be missed, bec. thy seat will be em.
20. 25 Abner sat..and David's place was empty
20. 27 the second (day) ..David's place was em.

EMPTY, to make —

1.*To empty, make void,* בָּקַק *baqaq.*
Isa. 24. 1 Behold, the LORD maketh the earth empty

2.*To draw out, empty out,* רוּק *ruq,* 5.
Isa. 32. 6 to make empty the soul of the hungry

EMPTY out, to —
To empty, make void, בָּקַק *baqaq.*
Nah. 2. 2 for the emptiers have emptied them out

EMPTY place —
Emptiness, תֹּהוּ *tohu.*
Job 26. 7 stretcheth out the north over the empty p.

EMULATION —
Zeal, ζῆλος *zēlos.*
Gal. 5. 20 Idolatry, witchcraft, hatred, variance, e.

EMULATION, to provoke to —
To make one zealous, παραζηλόω *parazēloō.*
Rom 11. 14 If by any means I may provoke to emu.

ENABLE, to —
To put strength in, ἐνδυναμόω *endunamoō.*
1 Ti. 1. 12 I thank Christ..who hath enabled me

E'-NAM, עֵינָם *double fountains.*
A city in the lowlands of Judah.
Josh 15. 34 Zanoah, and En-gannim, Tappuah, and E.

E'-NAN, עֵינָן *fountain.*
Father of Ahira, of the tribe of Naphtali, appointed to assist Moses in taking the census at Sinai.
Num. 1. 15 Of Naphtali; Ahira the son of E.
2. 29 captain..of Naphtali..Ahira the son of E.
7. 78 On the twelfth day Ahira the son of E.
7. 83 this..the offering of Ahira the son of E.
10. 27 And over the host..Ahira the son of E.

ENCAMP, to —
To encamp, settle down, חָנָה *chanah.*
Exod13. 20 they took their journey..and encamped
14. 2 Speak unto..Israel, that they turn and e.
14. 2 before it shall ye encamp by the sea
14. 9 overtook them encamping by the sea
15. 27 and they encamped there by the waters
18. 5 where he encamped at the mount of God
Num. 1. 50 and shall encamp round about the taber.
2. 17 as they encamp, so shall they set forward
2. 27 And those that encamp by him (shall be)
3. 38 those that encamp before the tabernacle
10. 31 thou knowest how we are to encamp in
33. 10 they removed from Elim, and encamped
33. 11 removed from the Red Sea, and encamp.
33. 12 they took their journey..and encamped
33. 13 they departed..and encamped in Alush
33. 14 they removed from Alush, and encamped
33. 17 they departed..and encamped at Hazero.
33. 24 they removed..and encamped in Harad.
33. 26 they removed..and encamped at Tahath
33. 30 they departed..and encamped at Mosero.
33. 32 they removed..and encamped at Hor-ha.
33. 34 they removed..and encamped at Ebronah
33. 35 departed..and encamped at Ezion-gaber
33. 46 removed..and encamped in Almon-dib.
Josh. 4. 19 the people came..and encamped in Gil.
5. 10 the children of Israel encamped in Gilgal
10. 5 they and all their hosts, encamped before
10. 31, 34 encamped against it, and fought
Judg. 6. 4 they encamped against them, and destr.
9. 50 Then went Abimelech..and encamped
10. 17 encamped in Gilead..encamped in Miz.
20. 19 the children of Israel..encamped against
1 Sa. 11. 1 Nahash..came up, and encamped against
13. 16 but the Philistines encamped in Michmash
2 Sa. 11. 11 servants..are encamped in the open fields
12. 28 therefore gather the rest..and encamp
1 Ki. 16. 15 the people (were) encamped against Gibb.
16. 16 the people (that were) encamped heard
1 Ch. 11. 15 the host of the Philistines encamped in
2 Ch. 32. 1 and encamped against the fenced cities
Job 19. 12 and encamp round about my tabernacle
Psa. 27. 3 Though an host should encamp against
34. 7 The angel of the LORD encampeth round
53. 5 scattered the bones of him that encamp.
Zech. 9. 8 And I will encamp about mine house

ENCHANTER —

1. *To whisper, use enchantment,* נָחַשׁ *nachash,* 3.
Deut18. 10 an observer of times, or an enchanter or

2.*To observe the clouds,* עָנַן *anan,* 3*a*.
Jer. 27. 9 hearken not ye..to your enchanters, nor

ENCHANTMENT —

1.*Joining, charm,* חֶבֶר *cheber.*
Isa. 47. 9 for the great abundance of thine enchant.
47. 12 Stand now with thine enchantments, and

2.*A whisper, charm, amulet,* לַחַשׁ *lachash.*
Eccl. 10. 11 Surely the serpent will bite without en.

3.*Secret, enchantment, gentleness,* לָט *lat.*
Exod. 7. 22 magicians did so with their enchantments
8. 7, 18 magicians did so with their enchant.

4. *Whisper, enchantment,* נַחַשׁ *nachash.*
Num 23. 23 Surely (there is) no enchantment against
24. 1 went not, as at other times, to seek for e.

5.*To whisper, use enchantment,* נָחַשׁ *nachash,* 3.
2 Ki.17. 17 pass through the fire, and used..enchan.

ENCHANTMENT, to use —
To whisper, use enchantment, נָחַשׁ *nachash,* 3.
Lev. 19. 26 neither shall ye use enchantment, nor
2 Ki.21. 6 observed times, and used enchantments
2 Ch.33. 6 he observed times, and used enchantme.

ENCHANTMENTS —
Flashings, לְהָטִים *lehatim.*
Exod. 7. 11 did in like manner with their enchantm.

ENCOUNTER, to —
To throw (selves) together, συμβάλλω *sumballō.*
Acts 17. 18 Then certain philosophers..encountered

ENCOURAGE, to —
To strengthen, harden, fix, חָזַק *chazaq,* 3.
Deut. 1. 38 encourage him; for he shall cause Israel
3. 28 encourage him, and strengthen him: for
2 Sa. 11. 25 overthrow it; and encourage thou him
2 Ch.35. 2 he..encouraged them to the service of
Psa. 64. 5 They encourage themselves (in) an evil
Isa. 41. 7 So the carpenter encouraged the goldsm.

ENCOURAGE self, to —
To strengthen self, חָזַק *chazaq,* 7.
Judg20. 22 the men of Israel, encouraged themselves
1 Sa. 30. 6 David encouraged himself in the LORD

ENCOURAGED, to be —
To be or become strong, חָזַק *chazaq.*
2 Ch.31. 4 that they might be encouraged in the law

END —

1. *Latter end, hinder part,* אַחֲרִית *acharith.*
Deut11. 12 from the beginning..unto the end of the
32. 20 he said..I will see what their end (shall
Psa. 37. 37 Mark..behold..for the end of (that) man
37. 38 the end of the wicked shall be cut off
73. 17 Until I went..(then) understood I their e.
Prov. 5. 4 her end is bitter as wormwood, sharp as
14. 12 the end thereof (are) the ways of death
14. 13 and the end of that mirth (is) heaviness
16. 25 the end thereof (are) the ways of death
20. 21 but the end thereof shall not be blessed
23. 18 For surely there is an end; and thine
25. 8 lest (thou know not) what to do in the end
Eccl. 7. 8 Better (is) the end of a thing than the
10. 13 end of his talk (is) mischievous madness
Isa. 46. 10 Declaring the end from the beginning
Jer. 5. 31 and what will ye do in the end thereof?
17. 11 not by right..at his end shall be a fool
29. 11 not of evil, to give you an expected end
31. 17 there is hope in thine end, saith the LORD
Dan. 12. 8 what (shall be) the end of these (things)?
Amos 8. 10 I will make..the end thereof as a bitter

2.*End, cessation, ancle,* אֶפֶס *ephes.*
Deut 33. 17 he shall push the people..to the ends of
1 Sa. 2. 10 the LORD shall judge the ends of the
Psa. 22. 27 All the ends of the world shall remember
59. 13 God ruleth..unto the ends of the earth
67. 7 and all the ends of the earth shall fear
72. 8 from the river unto the ends of the earth
98. 3 all the ends of the earth have seen the
Prov 30. 4 who hath established all the ends of the
Isa. 45. 22 be ye saved, all the ends of the earth
52. 10 all the ends of the earth shall see the
Jer. 16. 19 Gentiles shall come..from the ends of
Mic. 5. 4 he be great unto the ends of the earth
Zech. 9. 10 from the river..to the ends of the earth

3.*Border,* גַּבְלוּת *gabluth.*
Exod28. 22 make upon the breastplate chains at the e.
39. 15 made upon the breastplate chains at the e.

4.*Intent,* דִּבְרָה *dibrah.*
Eccl. 7. 14 to the end that man should find nothing

5. *To be completed, finished, consumed,* כָּלָה *kalah.*
Ruth 2. 23 to glean unto the end of barley harvest

6.*Completion, consumption, end,* כָּלָה *kalah.*
Eze. 20. 17 neither did I make an end of them in the

7. *Wing*, כָּנָף *kanaph.*
Job 37. 3 his lightning unto the ends of the earth
38. 13 That it might take hold of the ends of

8. *Pre-eminence, perpetuity*, נֵצַח, נֶצַח *netsach.*
Job 34. 36 Job may be tried unto the end, because
Jer. 3. 5 will he keep (it) to the end? Behold, thou

9. *End, rear, last*, סוֹף *soph.*
2 Ch. 20. 16 ye shall find them at the end of the brook
Eccl. 3. 11 maketh from the beginning to the end
7. 2 that (is) the end of all men; and the living
Dan. 4. 11 the sight thereof to the end of all the ea.
4. 22 and thy dominion to the end of the earth
6. 26 his dominion (shall be even) unto the end
7. 26 consume and to destroy (it) unto the end
7. 28 Hitherto (is) the end of the matter. As

10. *Heel, rear*, עֵקֶב *eqeb.*
Psa. 119. 33 the way..and I shall keep it (unto) the e.
119. 112 perform thy statutes..even (unto) the e.

11. *Corner, side*, פֵּאָה *peah.*
Eze. 41. 12 before the separate place at the end

12. *Mouth*, פֶּה *peh.*
2 Ki. 10. 21 the house of Baal was full from one end
21. 16 till he had filled Jerusalem from one end
Ezra 9. 11 have filled it from one end to another

13. *End, extremity*, קֵץ *qets.*
Gen. 6. 13 The end of all flesh is come before me; for
8. 6 it came to pass at the end of forty days
41. 1 it came to pass at the end of two full ye.
Exod 12. 41 it came to pass at the end of the four
Deut. 9. 11 it came to pass, at the end of forty days
15. 1 At the end of (every) seven years thou
31. 10 At the end of every seven years, in the
Judg 11. 39 it came to pass, at the end of two months
2 Sa. 14. 26 it was at every year's end that he polled
1 Ki. 2. 39 it came to pass at the end of three years
2 Ch. 8. 1 And it came to pass at the end of twenty
21. 19 after the end of two years, his bowels
Job 6. 11 what (is) mine end, that I should prolong
16. 3 Shall vain words have an end? or what
18. 2 How long (will it be ere) ye make an end
28. 3 He setteth an end to darkness, and sear.
Psa. 39. 4 LORD, make me to know mine end, and
119. 96 I have seen an end of all perfection
Eccl. 4. 8 yet (is there) no end of all his labour
4. 16 no end of all the people..of all that have
12. 12 of making many books (there is) no end
Isa. 9. 7 no end, upon the throne of David, and
23. 15 after the end of seventy years shall Tyre
23. 17 it shall come to pass, after the end of
Jer. 34. 14 At the end of seven years let ye go every
51. 13 thine end is come..the measure of thy
Lam. 4. 18 our end is near..for our end is come
Eze. 7. 2 An end, the end is come upon the four
7. 3 Now (is) the end (come) upon thee, and
7. 6 An end is come, the end is come: it wat.
21. 25 is come, when iniquity (shall have) an end
21. 29 when their iniquity (shall have) an end
29. 13 At the end of forty years will I gather
35. 5 the time (that their) iniquity (had) an end
Dan. 8. 17 at the time of the end (shall be) the vision
8. 19 at the time appointed the end (shall be)
9. 26 and the end thereof (shall be) with a flood
9. 26 unto the end of the war desolations are
11. 6 in the end of years they shall join them.
11. 27 yet the end (shall be) at the time appoin.
11. 35 make..white..to the time of the end
11. 40 at the time of the end shall the king of
11. 45 he shall come to his end, and none shall
12. 4 seal the book..to the time of the end
12. 6 How long (shall it be) to the end of these
12. 9 closed up and sealed till the time of the e.
12. 13 But go thou thy way till the end (be)
12. 13 and stand in thy lot at the end of the
Amos 8. 2 The end is come upon my people of Isra.
Hab. 2. 3 but at the end it shall speak, and not lie

14. *End, extremity*, קָצָה *qatsah.*
Exod 25. 18 make..in the two ends of the mercy-seat
25. 19 on the one end, and..on the other end
25. 19 make the cherubim on the two ends
28. 23 shalt put the two rings on the two ends
28. 24 two rings..on the ends of the breastplate
28. 25 (the other) two ends of the two wreathen
28. 26 thou shalt put them upon the two ends
37. 7 made..on the two ends of the mercy
37. 8 One cherub on the end on this side
37. 8 another cherub on the..end on that side
37. 8 made he the cherubim on the two ends
39. 16 put the two rings in the two ends of the
39. 17 in the two rings on the ends of the breast.
39. 18 And the two ends of the two wreathen
39. 19 put (them) on the two ends of the breast.
Job 28. 24 For he looketh to the ends of the earth
Psa. 19. 6 and his circuit unto the ends of it
Isa. 40. 28 the Creator of the ends of the earth
41. 5 the ends of the earth were afraid, drew
41. 9 (Thou) whom I have taken from the ends
Eze. 15. 4 the fire devoureth both the ends of it

15. *End, extremity*, קָצֶה *qatseh.*
Gen. 8. 3 after the end of the hundred and fifty
23. 9 the cave..which (is) in the end of his field
47. 21 he removed them to cities from (one) end
47. 21 the borders of Egypt even to the (other) e.
Exod 26. 28 the boards shall reach from end to end
36. 33 through the boards from the one end
Deut 13. 7 from thee, from the (one) end of the earth
13. 7 even unto the (other) end of the earth
14. 28 At the end of three years thou shalt bring
Deut 28. 49 bring a nation..from the end of the earth
28. 64 the one end of the earth even unto the
Josh. 9. 16 it came to pass, at the end of three days
15. 5 (was) the salt sea, (even) unto the end
15. 8 at the end of the valley of the giants
18. 15 And the south quarter (was) from the end
18. 16 the border came down to the end of the
18. 19 the salt sea at the south end of Jordan
Judg. 6. 21 the angel of the LORD put forth the end
Ruth 3. 7 he went to lie down at the end of the heap
1 Sa 9. 27 they were going down to the end of the
14. 27 wherefore he put forth the end of the rod
14. 43 taste a little honey with the end of the rod
2 Sa. 24. 8 they came to Jerusalem at the end of nine
1 Ki. 9. 10 it came to pass at the end of twenty years
2 Ki. 8. 3 it came to pass at the seven years' end
18. 10 at the end of three years they took it
Psa. 19. 4 Their line is gone..their words to the end
19. 6 His going forth (is) from the end of the
46. 9 He maketh wars to cease unto the end
61. 2 From the end of the earth will I cry unto
135. 7 to ascend from the ends of the earth
Prov 17. 24 the eyes of a fool (are) in the ends of the e.
Isa. 5. 26 he will..hiss..from the end of the earth
7. 3 at the end of the conduit of the upper
13. 5 from a far country, from the end of hea.
42. 10 Sing..his praise from the end of the earth
43. 6 bring my..daughters from the ends of
48. 20 utter it (even) to the end of the earth
49. 6 be my salvation unto the end of the earth
62. 11 the LORD hath proclaimed unto the end
Jer. 10. 13 causeth the vapours to ascend from the e.
12. 12 the sword..shall devour from the (one) e.
12. 12 even to the (other) end of the land
25. 31 A noise shall come (even) to the ends
25. 33 at that day from (one) end of the earth
25. 33 even unto the (other) end of the earth
51. 16 the vapours to ascend from the ends
51. 31 show the king..his city is taken at (one) e.
Eze. 3. 16 it came to pass at the end of seven days
39. 14 after the end of seven months shall they
48. 1 From the north end to the coast of the

16. *End, extremity*, קְצָה *qetseh.*
Isa. 2. 7 neither (is there any) end of their treasures
2. 7 neither (is there any) end of their chariots
Nah. 2. 9 (there is) none end of the store (and) glory
3. 3 and (there is) none end of (their) corpses

17. *End, extremity*, קֶצֶו *qetsev.*
Psa. 48. 10 so (is) thy praise unto the ends of the ea.
65. 5 the confidence of all the ends of the earth
Isa. 26. 15 thou hast removed (it) far (unto) all the e.

18. *End, extremity*, קִצְוָה *qitsvah.*
Exod 37. 8 made..cherubim on the two ends thereof
38. 5 he cast four rings for the four ends of the

19. *End, extremity*, קְצָת *qetsath.*
Dan. 1. 5 at the end thereof they might stand be.
1. 15 at the end of ten days their countenances
1. 18 at the end of the days..he should bring
4. 29 At the end of twelve months he walked
4. 34 at the end of the days I..lifted up mine

20. *Head*, רֹאשׁ *rosh.*
1 Ki. 8. 8 the ends of the staves were seen out in
2 Ch. 5. 9 the ends of the staves were seen from the

21. *Perfection, end*, תַּכְלִית *taklith.*
Neh. 3. 21 even to the end of the house of Eliashib
Job 26. 10 until the day and night come to an end

22. *To be perfect, finished, complete*, תָּמַם *tamam.*
Jer. 1. 3 unto the end of the eleventh year of Zed.

23. *Revolution, circuit, end*, תְּקוּפָה *tequphah.*
Exod 34. 22 the feast of ingathering at the year's end
2 Ch. 24. 23 it came to pass at the end of the year

24. *Outgoing*, ἔκβασις *ekbasis.*
Heb. 13. 7 whose faith follow, considering the end

25. *Extremity*, πέρας *peras.*
Rom 10. 18 and their words unto the ends of the wo.
Heb. 6. 16 an oath for confirmation (is) to them an e.

26. *Full end*, συντέλεια *sunteleia.*
Matt 13. 39 the harvest is the end of the world
13. 40 so shall it be in the end of this world
13. 49 So shall it be at the end of the world
24. 3 what (shall be) the sign..of the end
28. 20 I am with you alway, (even) unto the end
Heb. 9. 26 once in the end of the world hath he ap.

27. *End*, τέλος *telos.*
Matt 10. 22 he that endureth to the end shall be
24. 6 all these things must come..but the end
24. 13 he that shall endure unto the end..shall
24. 14 in all the world..and then shall the end
26. 58 Peter..sat with the servants, to see the e.
Mark 3. 26 he cannot stand, but hath an end
13. 7 needs be; but the end (shall) not (be) yet
13. 13 he that shall endure unto the end
Luke 1. 33 of his kingdom there shall be no end
21. 9 these things must come first..the end (is)
22. 37 for the things concerning me have an end
John 13. 1 his own..he loved them unto the end
Rom. 6. 21 for the end of those things (is) death
6. 22 unto holiness, and the end everlasting
10. 4 Christ (is) the end of the law for righteo.
1 Co. 1. 8 Who shall also confirm you unto the end
10. 11 upon whom the ends of the world are co.
15. 24 the end, when he shall have delivered
2 Co. 1. 13 ye shall acknowledge even to the end
3. 13 to the end of that which is abolished
11. 15 whose end shall be according to their
Phil. 3. 19 Whose end (is) destruction, whose god
1 Ti. 1. 5 Now the end of the commandment is ch.
Heb. 3. 6 rejoicing of the hope firm unto the end
3. 14 of our confidence stedfast unto the end
6. 8 nigh unto cursing; whose end (is) to be
6. 11 to the full assurance of hope unto the e.
7. 3 neither beginning of days, nor end of life
Jas. 5. 11 Ye..have seen the end of the Lord; that
1 Pe. 1. 9 Receiving the end of your faith..the sal.
4. 7 But the end of all things is at hand: be
4. 17 what shall the end (be) of them that
Rev. 2. 26 he that..keepeth my works unto the end
21. 6 I am Alpha..the beginning and the end
22. 13 I am..the beginning and the end, the first

[*See also* cast, Come to, grow to, hinder, what, world.]

END, to —

1. *To cease, leave off, forbear*, חָדַל *chadal.*
Isa. 24. 8 the noise of them that rejoice endeth

2. *To be complete, finished*, כָּלָה *kalah*, 3.
Gen. 2. 2 on the seventh day God ended his work
Ruth 2. 21 until they have ended all my harvest
Eze. 4. 8 till thou hast ended the days of thy siege

3. *To perfect, finish*, תָּמַם *tamam*, 5.
2 Sa. 20. 18 surely ask..at Abel: and so they ended

4. *To fill up or out*, πληρόω *plēroō.*
Luke 7. 1 when he had ended all his sayings in the
Acts 19. 21 After these things were ended, Paul pur.

5. *To end together or fully*, συντελέω *sunteleō.*
Matt. 7. 28 it came to pass, when Jesus had ended
Luke 4. 2 when they were ended, he afterward hu.
4. 13 when the devil had ended all the tempt.
Acts 21. 27 when the seven days were almost ended

END, to be at an —

1. *To cease, fail, have an end*, אָפֵס *aphes.*
Isa. 16. 4 the extortioner is at an end, the spoiler

2. *To be swallowed up*, בָּלַע *bala*, 7.
Psa. 107. 27 They..stagger..and are at their wit's end

3. *To fill in, complete, be full*, מָלֵא *male.*
Lev. 8. 33 until..your consecration be at an end

END, to come to an —

To be perfected, finished, תָּמַם *tamam.*
Psa. 9. 6 destructions are come to a perpetual end

END, full —

Completion, consumption, כָּלָה *kalah.*
Jer. 4. 27 desolate; yet will I not make a full end
5. 10 make not a full end; take away her bat.
5. 18 I will not make a full end with you
30. 11 though I make a full end of all nations
30. 11 yet will I not make a full end of thee
46. 28 I will make a full end of all the nations
46. 28 but I will not make a full end of thee
Eze. 11. 13 wilt thou make a full end of the remnant

END, to have an —

1. *To be ended, consumed*, סוּף *suph.*
Amos 3. 15 and the great houses shall have an end

2. *To be perfected*, תָּמַם *tamam*, 2.
Psa. 102. 27 But thou..thy years shall have no end

END, to make an —

1. *To finish, seal up*, חָתַם *chatham.* [V.L. of No. 5.]
Dan. 9. 24 transgression, and to make an end of sins

2. *To finish, consume, determine*, כָּלָה *kalah*, 3.
Gen. 27. 30 as soon as Isaac had made an end of
49. 33 when Jacob had made an end of comma.
Exod 31. 18 when he had made an end of communing
Lev. 16. 20 when he hath made an end of reconciling
Num. 4. 15 Aaron and his sons have made an end of
16. 31 as he had made an end of speaking all
Deut. 20. 9 when the officers have made an end of
26. 12 When thou hast made an end of tithing
31. 24 when Moses had made an end of writing
32. 45 And Moses made an end of speaking all
Josh. 8. 24 when Israel had made an end of slaying
10. 20 when..Israel had made an end of slaying
19. 49 When they had made an end of dividing
19. 51 So they made an end of dividing the
Judg. 3. 18 when he had made an end to offer the
15. 17 when he had made an end of speaking
1 Sa. 3. 12 when I begin, I will also make an end
10. 13 when he had made an end of prophesying
13. 10 as soon as he had made an end of offering
18. 1 when he had made an end of speaking
24. 16 when David had made an end of speaking
2 Sa. 6. 18 as soon as David had made an end of
11. 19 When thou hast made an end of telling
13. 36 as soon as he had made an end of speak.
1 Ki. 1. 41 as they had made an end of eating
3. 1 until he had made an end of building his
7. 40 So Hiram made an end of doing all the
8. 54 when Solomon had made an end of pray.
2 Ki. 10. 25 as soon as he had made an end of offering
1 Ch. 16. 2 when David had made an end of offering
2 Ch. 7. 1 when Solomon had made an end of pray.
20. 23 when they had made an end of the inha.
24. 10 brought in..until they had made an end
29. 17 in the sixteenth day..they made an end
29. 29 when they had made an end of offering
Ezra 10. 17 And they made an end with all the men
Neh. 4. 2 will they make an end in a day? will
Jer. 26. 8 when Jeremiah had made an end of spea.
43. 1 when Jeremiah had made an end of spe.
51. 63 when thou hast made an end of reading

Eze. 42. 15 when he had made an end of measuring
43. 23 When thou hast made an end of cleans.
Amos 7. 2 when they had made an end of eating

3. *To make an end, complete,* נָלָה *nalah,* 5.
Isa. 33. 1 when thou shalt make an end to deal

4. *To finish,* שָׁלַם *shalam,* 5.
Isa. 38. 12, 13 to night wilt thou make an end of me

5. *To perfect, finish,* תָּמַם *tamam,* 5. [See No. 1.]
Dan. 9. 24 to finish..and to make an end of sins

6. *To end,* τελέω *teleō.*
Matt 11. 1 when Jesus had made an end of comman.

END of, to be an —
To be completed, finished, consumed, כָּלָה *kalah.*
Jer. 44. 27 be consumed..until there be an end of

END of, in the —
To go out or forth, יָצָא *yatsa.*
Exod 23. 16 in the end of the year, when thou hast

END, in the —
Late in the evening, ὀψέ *opse.*
Matt 28. 1 In the end of the sabbath, as it began to

END, to the —
1. *To the intent,* לְמַעַן *lemaan.*
Exod. 8. 22 to the end thou mayest know that I (am)

2. *With a view to,* εἰς τό *eis to.*
Acts 7. 19 cast out..to the end they might not live
Rom. 1. 11 gift, to the end ye may be established
4. 16 to the end the promise might be sure
1 Th. 3. 13 To the end he may stablish your hearts

3. *Perfectly, completely,* τελείως *teleiōs.*
1 Pe. 1. 13 hope to the end for the grace that is to

END, to this —
With a view to this, εἰς τοῦτο *eis touto.*
John 18. 37 To this end was I born, and for this cause
Rom 14. 9 For to this end Christ both died, and rose
2 Co. 2. 9 For to this end also did I write, that I

END that, to this —
Toward this, πρὸς τό *pros to.*
Luke 18. 1 spake a parable unto them (to this e.) that

END, the latter —
The last things, τὰ ἔσχατα *ta eschata.*
2 Pe. 2. 20 the latter end is worse with them than

END, utter —
Completion, consumption, end, כָּלָה *kalah.*
Nah. 1. 8 he will make an utter end of the place
1. 9 he will make an utter end: affliction shall

END to the other, from one —
From point unto point, ἀπ' ἄκρων ἕως ἄκρων.
Matt 24. 31 from one end of heaven to the other

END, world without —
Unto ages of duration, עַד עוֹלְמֵי עַד *ad oleme ad.*
Isa. 45. 17 shall not be ashamed..world without end

ENDAMAGE, to —
To cause loss, נְזַק *nezaq,* 5.
Ezra 4. 13 thou shalt endamage the revenue of the

ENDANGER, to make —
To endanger, forfeit, cause to owe, חוּב *chub,* 3.
Dan. 1. 10 then shall ye make (me) endanger my

ENDANGERED, to be —
To be endangered, סָכַן *sakan,* 2.
Eccl. 10. 9 he that cleaveth wood shall be endang.

ENDEAVOUR, to —
1. *To seek,* ζητέω *zēteō.*
Acts 16. 10 immediately we endeavoured to go into

2. *To make speed or haste,* σπουδάζω *spoudazō.*
Eph. 4. 3 Endeavouring to keep the unity of the
1 Th. 2. 17 we..endeavoured the more..to see your
2 Pe. 1. 15 I will endeavour that ye may be able

ENDEAVOURS —
Doing, acting, מַעֲלָל *maalal.*
Psa. 28. 4 according to the wickedness of their en.

ENDED, to be —
1. *To be completed, finished,* כָּלָה *kalah.*
Gen. 41. 53 seven years of plenteousness..were ended
2 Ch. 29. 34 Levites did help..till the work was ended
Jer. 8. 20 The harvest is past, the summer is ended

2. *To be completed, finished,* כָּלָה *kalah,* 4.
Psa. 72. 20 The prayers of..the son of Jesse are ended

3. *To be finished, complete,* שָׁלַם *shalam.*
1 Ki. 7. 51 So was ended all the work that king Sol.
Isa. 60. 20 the days of thy mourning shall be ended

4. *To be perfected, finished,* תָּמַם *tamam.*
Gen. 47. 18 When that year was ended, they came
Deut 31. 30 words of this song, until they were ended
34. 8 days of weeping..for Moses were ended
Job 31. 40 The words of Job are ended

5. *To become,* γίνομαι *ginomai.*
John 13. 2 And supper being ended, the devil having

ENDING —
End, τέλος *telos.*
Rev. 1. 8 beginning and the ending, saith the LORD

ENDLESS —
1. *Not loosed down,* ἀκατάλυτος *akatalutos.*
Heb. 7. 16 made..after the power of an endless life

2. *Endless, unpierced through,* ἀπέραντος *aperantos.*
1 Ti. 1. 4 Neither give heed to fables and endless

EN'-DOR, עֵין דּאֹר or דּוֹר *fountain of Dor.*
A city of Manasseh, four miles S. of Tabor, or at the S. of the sea of Galilee in Issachar. It is now called *Endur,* and the rock on which it stands is hollowed into caves. From the slopes of Gilboa to Endor is seven or eight miles over rugged ground.
Josh 17. 11 the inhabitants of E. and her towns
1 Sa. 28. 7 a woman that hath a familiar spirit at E.
Psa. 83. 10 perished at E.: they became (as) dung

ENDOW, to —
To endow, purchase, מָהַר *mahar.*
Exod 22. 16 he shall surely endow her to be his wife

ENDS —
1. *Borders,* מִגְבָּלֹת *migbaloth.*
Exod 28. 14 And two chains (of) pure gold at the ends

2. *Last or extreme point,* ἔσχατος *eschatos.*
Acts 13. 47 shouldest be for salvation unto the ends

ENDUE, to —
To endow, endue, זָבַד *zabad.*
Gen. 30. 20 God hath endued me (with) a good dowry

ENDUED with —
1. *To know, be acquainted with,* יָדַע *yada.*
2 Ch. 2. 12 endued with prudence and understanding
2. 13 a cunning man, endued with understand.

2. *To go in, be clothed with,* ἐνδύω *enduō.*
Luke 24. 49 until ye be endued with power from on

ENDURE, to (can) —
1. *To be,* הָיָה *hayah.*
Psa. 72. 17 His name shall endure for ever: his name
81. 15 their time should have endured for ever
89. 36 His seed shall endure for ever, and his
104. 31 The glory of the LORD shall endure for

2. *To be able, endure,* יָכֹל *yakol.*
Esth. 8. 6 how can I endure..how can I endure to
Job 31. 23 by reason of his highness I could not en.

3. *To sit down or still,* יָשַׁב *yashab.*
Psa. 9. 7 the LORD shall endure for ever: he hath
102. 12 thou, O LORD, shalt endure for ever, and

4. *To lodge, pass the night,* לוּן *lun.*
Psa. 30. 5 weeping may endure for a night, but joy

5. *Until not,* עַד בְּלִי *ad beli.*
Psa. 72. 7 peace so long as the moon endureth

6. *With...and before,* עִם...וְלִפְנֵי *im...ve-li-phene.*
Psa. 72. 5 as long as the sun and moon endure

7. *To stand, stand still,* עָמַד *amad.*
Exod 18. 23 thou shalt be able to endure, and all this
Psa. 19. 9 fear of the LORD (is) clean, enduring for
102. 26 They shall perish, but thou shalt endure
111. 3 and his righteousness endureth for ever
111. 10 of the LORD..his praise endureth for ever
112. 3, 9 his righteousness endureth for ever
Eze. 22. 14 Can thine heart endure, or can thine

8. *To rise up, stand still,* קוּם *qum.*
Job 8. 15 shall hold it fast, but it shall not endure

9. *To hold up,* ἀνέχομαι *anechomai.*
2 Th. 1. 4 in all your..tribulations that ye endure
2 Ti. 4. 3 when they will not endure sound doctr.

10. *To be strong, firm,* καρτερέω *kartereō.*
Heb. 11. 27 he endured, as seeing him who is invisi.

11. *To remain,* μένω *menō.*
John 6. 27 meat which endureth unto everlasting
Heb. 10. 34 a better and an enduring substance
1 Pe. 1. 25 the word of the Lord endureth for ever

12. *To bear, carry,* φέρω *pherō.*
Rom. 9. 22 endured with much long suffering the
Heb. 12. 20 could not endure that which was com.

13. *To remain under,* ὑπομένω *hupomenō.*
Matt 10. 22 that endureth to the end shall be saved
24. 13 he that shall endure unto the end, the
Mark 13. 13 he that shall endure unto the end, the
1 Co. 13. 7 hopeth all things, endureth all things
2 Ti. 2. 10 I endure all things for the elect's sakes
Heb. 10. 32 ye endured a great fight of afflictions
12. 2 endured the cross, despising the shame
12. 3; 12. 7; Jas. 1. 12; 5. 11.

14. *It is,* ἐστί *esti.*
Mark 4. 17 have no root...and so endure but for

15. *To bear up under,* ὑποφέρω *hupopherō.*
2 Ti. 3. 11 at... what persecutions I endured
1 Pe. 2. 19 for conscience toward God endure grief

ENDURE hardness, to —
To suffer evil, κακοπαθέω *kakopatheō.*
2 Ti. 2. 3 therefore endure hardness, as a good sol.

ENDURE patiently, to —
To be long or patient minded, μακροθυμέω *makro.*
Heb. 6. 15 after he had patiently endured, he obtain.

ENDURING —
Remaining up under, ὑπομονή *hupomonē.*
2 Co. 1. 6 which is effectual in the enduring of the

E-NE'-AS, Αἰνέας *(from Hebrew, praise of Jah.)*
A man of Lydda healed by Peter.
Acts 9. 33 there he found a certain man named Æ.
9. 34 Æ., Jesus Christ maketh thee whole

EN EG-LA'-IM, עֵין עֶגְלַיִם *fountain of two calves.*
A place near the Salt Sea; but not the same as *Eglaim.* See BETH-HOGLAH.
Eze. 47. 10 shall stand upon it from Engedi..unto E.

ENEMY —
1. *Enemy,* אֹיֵב *oyeb.*
Gen. 22. 17 shall possess the gate of his enemies
49. 8 (shall be) in the neck of thine enemies
Exod 15. 6 hand..hath dashed in pieces the enemy
15. 9 enemy said, I will pursue, I will overtake
23. 4 If thou meet thine enemy's ox or his ass
23. 22 I will be an enemy unto thine enemies
23. 27 I will make all thine enemies turn their
Lev. 26. 7 ye shall chase your enemies, and they
26. 8 your enemies shall fall before you by the
26. 16 your seed..for your enemies shall eat it
26. 17 and ye shall be slain before your enemies
26. 25 be delivered into the hand of the enemy
26. 32 your enemies which dwell therein shall
26. 34 as long as..ye (be) in your enemies' land
26. 36 faintness..in the land of their enemies
26. 37 no power to stand before your enemies
26. 38 the land of your enemies shall eat you up
26. 39 in their iniquity in your enemies' lands
26. 41 brought them into..land of their enem.
26. 44 when they be in the land of their enem.
Num 10. 9 go to war in your land against the enemy
10. 35 Rise..and let thine enemies be scattered
14. 42 ye be not smitten before your enemies
23. 11 I took thee to curse mine enemies, and
24. 10 I called thee to curse mine enemies, and
24. 18 shall be a possession for his enemies
32. 21 until he hath driven out his enemies
35. 23 (was) not his enemy, neither sought his
Deut. 1. 42 lest ye be smitten before your enemies
6. 19 To cast out all thine enemies from befo.
12. 10 rest from all your enemies round about
20. 1 goest out to battle against thine enemies
20. 3 this day unto battle against your enem.
20. 4 to fight for you against your enemies
20. 14 thou shalt eat the spoil of thine enemies
21. 10 goest forth to war against thine enemies
23. 9 host goeth forth against thine enemies
23. 14 and to give up thine enemies before thee
25. 19 given thee rest from all thine enemies
28. 7 The LORD shall cause thine enemies that
28. 25 to be smitten before thine enemies
28. 31 thy sheep (shall be) given unto thine ene.
28. 48 Therefore shalt thou serve thine enemies
28. 53, 55, 57 wherewith thine enemies shall
28. 68 there ye shall be sold unto your enemies
30. 7 will put all these curses upon thine ene.
32. 27 it not that I feared the wrath of the ene.
32. 31 even our enemies themselves (being)
32. 42 the beginning of revenges upon the ene.
33. 27 he shall thrust out the enemy from
33. 29 thine enemies shall be found liars unto
Josh. 7. 8 Israel turneth their backs before their en.
7. 12 Israel could not stand before their enem.
7. 12 turned (their) backs before their enemies
7. 13 thou canst not stand before thine enem.
10. 13 had avenged themselves upon their ene.
10. 19 stay ye not..pursue after your enemies
10. 25 to all your enemies against whom ye fight
21. 44 there stood not a man of all their enem.
21. 44 the LORD delivered all their enemies into
22. 8 divide the spoil of your enemies with
23. 1 rest unto Israel from all their enemies
Judg. 2. 14 he sold them into the hands of their ene.
2. 14 they could not..stand before their ene.
2. 18 delivered..out of the hand of their ene.
3. 28 the LORD hath delivered your enemies
5. 31 So let all thine enemies perish, O LORD
8. 34 out of the hands of all their enemies
11. 36 taken vengeance for thee of thine enemies
16. 23 Our god hath delivered Samson our ene.
16. 24 hath delivered into our hands our enemy
1 Sa. 2. 1 my mouth is enlarged over mine enemies
4. 3 it may save us out of the hand of our ene.
12. 10 deliver us out of the hand of our ene.
12. 11 delivered you out of the hand of..ene.
14. 24 that I may be avenged on mine enemies
14. 30 spoil of their enemies which they found?
14. 47 Saul..fought against all his enemies on
18. 25 to be avenged of the king's enemies
18. 29 Saul became David's enemy continually
19. 17 Why hast thou..sent away mine enemy
20. 15 when the LORD hath cut off the enemies
20. 16 even require (it) at the hand of David's en.
24. 4 I will deliver thine enemy into thine hand
24. 19 if a man find his enemy, will he let him
25. 22 So and more also do God unto the ene.
25. 26 now let thine enemies..be as Nabal
25. 29 thine enemies, them shall he sling out
26. 8 God hath delivered thine enemy into
29. 8 that I may not go fight against the enem.
30. 26 of the spoil of the enemies of the LORD
2 Sa. 3. 18 and out of the hand of all their enemies
4. 8 Saul thine enemy, which sought thy life
5. 20 LORD hath broken forth upon mine ene.
7. 1 had given him rest..from all his enemies

2 Sa. 7. 9 and have cut off all thine enemies out of
7. 11 I..caused thee to rest from all thine ene.
12. 14 thou hast given great occasion to the ene.
18. 19 the LORD hath avenged him of his ene.
18. 32 And Cushi answered, The enemies of my
19. 9 king saved us out of the hand of our ene.
22. 1 him out of the hand of all his enemies
22. 4 so shall I be saved from mine enemies
22. 18 He delivered me from my strong enemy
22. 38 I have pursued mine enemies, and destr.
22. 41 hast also given me the necks of mine ene.
22. 49 that bringeth me forth from mine ene.
1 Ki. 3. 11 nor hast asked the life of thine enemies
8. 33 Israel be smitten down before the ene.
8. 37 if their enemy besiege them in the land
8. 44 If thy people go out..against their ene.
8. 46 and deliver them to the enemy, so that
8. 46 carry them..unto the land of the enemy
8. 48 in the land of their enemies which led
21. 20 Hast thou found me, O mine enemy?
2 Ki. 17. 39 he shall deliver you out of..all your en.
21. 14 deliver them into the hand of their ene.
21. 14 they shall become..a spoil to all their ene.
1 Ch. 14. 11 God hath broken in upon mine enemies
17. 8 and have cut off all thine enemies from
17. 10 Moreover I will subdue all thine enemies
21. 12 while that the sword of thine enemies
22. 9 I will give him rest from all his enemies
2 Ch. 6. 24 Israel be put to the worse before the ene.
6. 28 if their enemies besiege them in the cities
6. 34 If thy people go out..against their ene.
6. 36 and deliver them over before (their) en.
20. 27 had made them to rejoice over their ene.
20. 29 the LORD fought against the enemies of
25. 8 God shall make thee fall before the enemy
26. 13 army..to help the king against the ene.
Ezra 8. 22 to help us against the enemy in the way
8. 31 he delivered us from the hand of the ene.
Neh. 4. 15 when our enemies heard that it was
5. 9 the reproach of the heathen our enemies?
6. 1 the rest of our enemies, heard that I had
6. 16 it came to pass, that when all our ene.
9. 28 leftest thou them in the hand of their e.
Esth. 7. 6 The adversary and enemy (is) this wicked
8. 13 ready..to avenge themselves on their e.
9. 1 in the day that the enemies of the Jews
9. 5 Thus the Jews smote all their enemies
9. 16 had rest from their enemies, and slew
9. 22 wherein the Jews rested from their ene.
Job 13. 24 Wherefore..holdest me for thine enemy?
27. 7 Let mine enemy be as the wicked, and he
33. 10 Behold..he counteth me for his enemy
Psa 3. 7 for thou hast smitten all mine enemies
6. 10 Let all mine enemies be ashamed and
7. 5 Let the enemy persecute my soul, and
8. 2 thou mightest still the enemy and the
9. 3 When mine enemies are turned back, they
9. 6 O thou enemy, destructions are come to
13. 2 how long shall mine enemy be exalted
13. 4 Lest mine enemy say, I have prevailed
17. 9 my deadly enemies, (who) compass me ab.
18. *title* from the hand of all his enemies, and
18. 3 so shall I be saved from mine enemies
18. 17 He delivered me from my strong enemy
18. 37 I have pursued mine enemies, and over.
18. 40 hast..given me the necks of mine enemies
18. 48 He delivereth me from mine enemies
21. 8 Thine hand shall find out all thine ene.
25. 2 let not mine enemies triumph over me
25. 19 Consider mine enemies, for they are many
27. 6 mine head be lifted up above mine ene.
31. 8 not shut me up into the hand of the ene.
31. 15 deliver me from the hand of mine enemies
35. 19 Let not them that are mine enemies
37. 20 the enemies of the LORD..as the fat of la.
38. 19 mine enemies (are) lively..they are strong
41. 2 not deliver him unto the will of his ene.
41. 5 Mine enemies speak evil of me, When sh.
41. 11 mine enemy doth not triumph over me
42. 9 because of the oppression of the enemy
44. 16 by reason of the enemy and avenger
45. 5 sharp in the heart of the..enemies
54. 7 and mine eye hath seen..upon mine ene.
55. 3 Because of the voice of the enemy
55. 12 For..not an enemy (that) reproached me
56. 9 then shall mine enemies turn back: this
59. 1 Deliver me from mine enemies, O my God
61. 3 hast been..a strong tower from the enemy
64. 1 preserve my life from fear of the enemy
66. 3 shall thine enemies submit themselves
68. 1 Let God arise, let his enemies be scattered
68. 21 God shall wound the head of his enemies
68. 23 foot may be dipped in the blood of..ene.
69. 4 mine enemies wrongfully, are mighty
69. 18 deliver me, because of mine enemies
71. 10 For mine enemies speak against me; and
72. 9 and his enemies shall lick the dust
74. 3 all (that) the enemy hath done wickedly
74. 10 shall the enemy blaspheme thy name for
74. 18 Remember this, (that) the enemy hath
78. 53 but the sea overwhelmed their enemies
80. 6 and our enemies laugh among themselves
81. 14 I should soon have subdued their enemies
83. 2 For, lo, thine enemies make a tumult
89. 10 thou hast scattered thine enemies with
89. 22 The enemy shall not exact upon him
89. 42 thou hast made all his enemies to rejoice
89. 51 Wherewith thine enemies have reproach.
92. 9 thine enemies, O LORD..thine enemies
102. 8 Mine enemies reproach me all the day
106. 10 redeemed them from the hand of the e.
106. 42 Their enemies also oppressed them, and
Psa. 110. 1 until I make thine enemies thy footstool
110. 2 rule thou in the midst of thine enemies
119. 98 Thou..hast made me wiser than mine e.
127. 5 they shall speak with the enemies in the
132. 18 His enemies will I clothe with shame
138. 7 stretch forth..against the wrath of mine e.
139. 22 I hate them..I count them mine enemies
143. 3 For the enemy hath persecuted my soul
143. 9 Deliver me, O LORD, from mine enemies
143. 12 And of thy mercy cut off mine enemies
Prov16. 7 he maketh even his enemies to be at peace
24. 17 Rejoice not when thine enemy falleth
Isa. 1. 24 Ah, I will..avenge me of mine enemies
9. 11 the LORD shall..join his enemies together
42. 13 The LORD..shall prevail against his ene.
59. 18 he will repay..recompence to his enemies
62. 8 I will no more give..meat for thine ene.
63. 10 therefore he was turned to be their ene.
66. 6 LORD that rendereth recompence to his e.
66. 14 and (his) indignation toward his enemies
Jer. 6. 25 the sword of the enemy..(is) on every side
12. 7 beloved of my soul into the hand of her e.
15. 9 I deliver to the sword before their enemies
15. 11 I will cause the enemy to entreat thee
15. 14 I will make (thee) to pass with thine en.
17. 4 I will cause thee to serve thine enemies
18. 17 I will scatter them..before the enemy
19. 7 I will cause them to fall..before their e.
19. 9 wherewith their enemies..shall straiten
20. 4 they shall fall by the sword of their ene.
20. 5 will I give into the hand of their enemies
21. 7 and into the hand of their enemies
30. 14 wounded thee with the wound of an ene.
31. 16 shall come again from the land of the en.
34. 20 will..give them into the hand of their e.
34. 21 will I give into the hand of their enemies
44. 30 I will give..into the hand of his enemies
44. 30 Nebuchadnezzar king of B., his enemy
49. 37 before thine enemies, and before them
Lam. 1. 2 all her friends..are become her enemies
1. 5 Her adversaries are the chief, her enemies
1. 9 O LORD, behold my affliction; for the e.
1. 16 my children are desolate, because the e.
1. 21 all mine enemies have heard of my tro.
2. 3 he hath drawn back..from before the e.
2. 4 He hath bent his bow like an enemy
2. 5 The LORD was an enemy: he hath swall.
2. 7 hath given up into the hand of the enemy
2. 16 thine enemies have opened their mouth
2. 17 caused (thine) enemy to rejoice over thee
2. 22 those that I..swaddled..enemy consum.
3. 46 our enemies have opened their mouths
3. 52 Mine enemies chased me sore, like a bird
4. 12 that the adversary and the enemy should
Eze. 36. 2 the enemy hath said against you, Aha!
39. 27 gathered them out of their enemies' lands
Hos. 8. 3 Israel..the enemy shall pursue him
Amos 9. 4 go into captivity before their enemies
Mic. 2. 8 of late my people is risen up as an enemy
4. 10 redeem thee from the hand of thine enem.
5. 9 and all thine enemies shall be cut off
7. 6 man's enemies (are) the men of his own
7. 8 Rejoice not against me, O mine enemy
7. 10 (she that is) mine enemy shall see (it)
Nah. 1. 2 and he reserveth (wrath) for his enemies
1. 8 and darkness shall pursue his enemies
3. 11 shalt seek strength because of the enemy
3. 13 shall be set wide open unto thine enemies
Zeph. 3. 15 he hath cast out thine enemy

2. *Enemy, one awake,* עָר *ar.*
1 Sa. 28. 16 seeing the LORD..is become thine enemy
Psa. 139. 20 (and) thine enemies take (thy name) in
Dan. 4. 19 interpretation thereof to thine enemies

3. *Adversary, a distresser, straitener,* צַר, צָר *tsar.*
Gen. 14. 20 delivered thine enemies into thy hand
Num 10. 9 against the enemy that oppresseth you
24. 8 he shall eat up the nations his enemies
Deut 32. 41 I will render vengeance to mine enemies
33. 7 be thou an help (to him) from his enemies
1 Sa. 2. 32 thou shalt see an enemy (in my) habita.
2 Sa. 24. 13 flee three months before thine enemies
1 Ch. 12. 17 (ye be come) to betray me to mine enem.
Neh. 9. 27 into the hand of their enemies, who vex.
9. 27 them out of the hand of their enemies
Esth. 7. 4 enemy could not countervail the king's
Job 6. 23 Deliver me from the enemy's hand? or
16 9 mine enemy sharpeneth his eyes upon
19. 11 counteth me..as (one of) his enemies
Psa. 27. 2 When the wicked..mine enemies and my
27. 12 Deliver me not..unto the will of mine e.
44. 5 Through thee will we push down our en.
44. 7 But thou hast saved us from our enemies
44. 10 Thou makest us to turn back from the e.
60. 12 for he..shall tread down our enemies
78. 42 day when he delivered them from the en.
78. 61 delivered..his glory into the enemy's ha.
78. 66 he smote his enemies in the hinder part
97. 3 A fire..burneth up his enemies round
105. 24 he..made them stronger than their ene.
106. 11 And the waters covered their enemies
107. 2 whom he hath redeemed from..the ene.
108. 13 he..shall tread down our enemies
112. 8 until he see (his desire) upon his enemies
119. 139 because mine enemies have forgotten
119. 157 Many (are) my persecutors and mine e.
136. 24 And hath redeemed us from our enemies
Isa. 26. 11 the fire of thine enemies shall devour
59. 19 When the enemy shall come in like a
Jer. 48. 5 the enemies have heard a cry of destruc.
Lam. 1. 5 are gone into captivity before the enemy
Lam. 1. 7 her people fell into the hand of the ene.
Eze. 39. 23 I..gave them into the hand of their ene.

4. *To straiten, distress,* צָרַר *tsarar.*
Esth. 3. 10 the son of Hammedatha..the Jews' ene.
8. 1 give the house of Haman, the Jews' enemy
9. 10 The ten sons of Haman..the enemy of the
9. 24 Haman..the enemy of all the Jews, had
Psa. 6. 7 it waxeth old because of all mine enemies
7. 4 I have delivered him that..is my enemy
7. 6 because of the rage of mine enemies
8. 2 thou ordained strength because of thine e.
10. 5 (as for) all his enemies, he puffeth at them
23. 5 before me in the presence of mine enem.
31. 11 I was a reproach among all mine enemies
42. 10 with a sword in my bones, mine enemies
74. 4 Thine enemies roar in the midst of thy c.
74. 23 Forget not the voice of thine enemies

5. *To stand up, withstand,* קוּם *qum.*
Exod32. 25 had made them naked..among their en.

6. *To hate,* שָׂנֵא *sane.*
Exod. 1. 10 they join also unto our enemies, and fight
2 Sa. 19. 6 In that thou lovest thine enemies, and
2 Ch. 1. 11 hast not asked..the life of thine enemies
Prov 25. 21 If thine enemy be hungry, give him bread
27. 6 but the kisses of an enemy (are) deceitful

7. *To behold, look, watch,* שׁוּר *shur.*
Psa. 92. 11 Mine eye also shall see..mine enemies

8. *To behold, observe, watch,* שָׁרַר *sharar.*
Psa. 5. 8 Lead me, O LORD..because of mine ene.
27. 11 Teach me thy way..because of mine ene.
54. 5 He shall reward evil unto mine enemies
56. 2 Mine enemies would daily swallow (me)
59. 10 God shall let me see..mine enemies

9. *Enemy, opponent,* ἐχθρός *echthros.*
Matt. 5. 43 love thy neighbour, and hate thine enemy
5. 44 Love your enemies, bless them that curse
13. 25 But while men slept, his enemy v. 28.
13. 39 The enemy that sowed them is the devil
22. 44 till I make thine enemies thy footstool?
Mark12. 36 till I make thine enemies thy footstool
Luke 1. 71 That we should be saved from our ene.
1. 74 being delivered out of the hand of our e.
6. 27 Love your enemies, do good to them which
6. 35 But love ye your enemies, and do good
10. 19 power..over all the power of the enemy
19. 27 But those mine enemies, which would
19. 43 thine enemies shall cast a trench about
20. 43 Till I make thine enemies thy footstool
Acts 13. 10 child of the devil..enemy of all righteo.
Rom. 5. 10 For if, when we were enemies, we were
11. 28 As concerning the Gospel..enemies for
12. 20 Therefore if thine enemy hunger, feed
1 Co. 15. 25 till he hath put all enemies under his
15. 26 The last enemy (that) shall be destroyed
Gal. 4. 16 Am I therefore become your enemy, be.
Phil. 3. 18 (they are) the enemies of the cross of
Col. 1. 21 you, that were sometime alienated, and e.
2 Th. 3. 15 Yet count..not as an enemy, but admonish
Heb. 1. 13 until I make thine enemies thy footstool
10. 13 expecting till his enemies be made his
Jas. 4. 4 a friend of the world is the enemy of
Rev. 11. 5 fire proceedeth..and devoureth their e.
11. 12 they ascended up..and their enemies

10. *Man, enemy,* ἐχθρὸς ἄνθρωπος *echthros anthr.*
Matt 13. 28 He said unto them, An enemy hath done

ENEMY, to be an —

To be at enmity, אָיַב *ayab.*
Exod23. 22 then I will be an enemy unto thine ene.

ENFLAME selves, to —

To become warm, enflamed, חָמַם *chamam,* 2.
Isa. 57. 5 Enflaming yourselves with idols under

ENGAGE, to —

To pledge, עָרַב *arab.*
Jer. 30. 21 for who (is) this that engaged his heart

EN GAN'-NIM, עֵין גַּנִּים *fountain of gardens.*

1. A city in the lowlands of Judah between Zanoah and Tappuah. Now called *Genin.*
Josh. 15. 34 Zanoah, and E., Tappuah, and Enam

2. A city on the border of Issachar allotted to the Gershonites, now called *Jenin,* and surrounded with orchards or gardens; the spring is still the characteristic of the place. In 1 Ch. 6. 73, *Anem* is put for *Engannim.*
Josh 19. 21 Remeth, and E.-g., and En-haddah, and
21. 29 E.-g. with her suburbs; four cities

EN GE'-DI, עֵין גֶּדִי *fountain of Gad, or Kid.*

A town on the W. shore of the Salt Sea, in the wilderness of Judah. Its original name was *Hazazon-Tamar* ("pruning of the palm,") from the palm-groves around it. Now called *Ain Jidy.*
Josh. 15. 62 Nibshan, and the city of Salt, and E.
1 Sa. 23. 29 David..dwelt in strongholds at E
24. 1 Behold, David (is) in the wilderness of E
2 Ch. 20. 2 they (be) in Hazazon-tamar, which (is) E.
Song 1. 14 cluster of camphire in..vineyards of E.
Eze. 47. 10 the fishers shall stand upon it from E.

ENGINES —

1. *Inventions, thoughtful works,* חִשְּׁבֹנוֹת *chishshebonoth.*
2 Ch. 26. 15 he made in Jerusalem engines, invented

2. *Battering ram,* מְחִי *mechi.*
Eze. 26. 9 he shall set engines of war against thy

ENGRAFTED —
Implanted, ἔμφυτος *emphutos.*
Jas. 1. 21 receive with meekness the engrafted

ENGRAVE, to —
1. *To open up,* פָּתַח *pathach,* 3.
Exod28. 11 shalt thou engrave the two stones with
Zech. 3. 9 behold, I will engrave the graving there.
2. *To strike, carve, or cut in,* ἐντυπόω *entupoō.*
2 Co. 3. 7 if the ministration of death..engraven

ENGRAVER —
Opener up, engraver, carver, חָרָשׁ *charash.*
Exod28. 11 With the work of an engraver in stone
35. 35 to work all manner of work of the eng.
38. 23 Aholiab..an engraver, and a cunning wo.

ENGRAVING —
A graving, carving, פִּתּוּחַ *pittuach.*
Exod28. 11, 21, 36 (like) the engravings of a signet
39. 14, 30 (like) the engravings of a signet

EN HAD'-DAH, עֵין חַדָּה *swift fountain.*
A city on the border of Issachar, near Engannim. Van de Velde identifies it with *Ain-haud* on the W. side of Carmel and about two miles from the sea.
Josh.19. 21 Remeth, and En-gannim, and E., and B.

EN HAK-KO'-RE, עֵין הַקּוֹרֵא *fountain of the crier.*
The spring that burst forth in answer to the "cry" of Samson. The name is a pun on the word YIKRA ("he called") in verse 18. *Lechi,* "jaw," is the name of a place as well as Maktesh, the "hollow place."
Judg15. 19 wherefore he called the name thereof E.

EN HA'-ZOR, עֵין חָצוֹר *fountain of the village.*
A fenced city in Naphtali, distinct from *Hazor,* and near Kedesh.
Josh 19. 37 And Kedesh, and Edrei, and E.

ENJOIN, to —
1. *To charge, look after,* פָּקַד *paqad.*
Job. 36. 23 Who hath enjoined him his way? or who
2. *To raise up, cause to stand,* קוּם *qum,* 3.
Esth. 9. 31 and Esther the queen had enjoined them
3. *To enjoin on,* ἐντέλλομαι *entellomai.*
Heb. 9. 20 the testament which God hath enjoined
4. *To arrange over or about,* ἐπιτάσσω *epitassō.*
Phm. 8 bold..to enjoin thee that which is conv.

ENJOY, ENJOY pleasures —
1. *To become (belong) to,* הָיָה לְ *hayah le.*
Deut28. 41 thou shalt not enjoy them; for they
2. *To possess,* יָרַשׁ *yarash.*
Num36. 8 that the children of Israel may enjoy
Josh. 1. 15 ye shall return unto the land..and enjoy
3. *To see,* רָאָה *raah.*
Eccl. 2. 1 I will prove thee with mirth; therefore e.
3. 13 that every man should..enjoy the good
5. 18 and to enjoy the good of all his labour
4. *To be pleased with, enjoy,* רָצָה *ratsah.*
Lev. 26. 34 Then shall the land enjoy her sabbaths
26. 43 The land also..shall enjoy her sabbaths
2 Ch.36. 21 until the land had enjoyed her sabbaths
5. *To be pleased with, enjoy,* רָצָה *ratsah,* 5.
Lev. 26. 34 then shall the land rest, and enjoy her
6. *With a view to full enjoyment,* εἰς ἀπόλαυσιν.
1 Ti. 6. 17 God, who giveth us richly all things to e.
7. *To happen upon,* τυγχάνω *tugchanō.*
Acts 24. 2 Seeing that by thee we enjoy great quie.
8. *To have full enjoyment,* ἔχω ἀπόλαυσιν [*echō*].
Heb.11. 25 than to enjoy the pleasures of sin for a

ENJOY long, to —
To wear out, בָּלָה *balah,* 3.
Isa. 65. 22 mine elect shall long enjoy the work of

ENJOY, to make —
To cause to see or enjoy, רָאָה *raah,* 5.
Eccl. 2. 24 he should make his soul enjoy good in

ENLARGE, to —
1. *To open, extend, entice, persuade,* פָּתָה *pathah,* 5.
Gen. 9. 27 God shall enlarge Japheth, and he shall
2. *To make large, great,* רָבָה *rabah,* 5.
1 Ch. 4. 10 Oh that thou wouldest..enlarge my coast
3. *To make broad, wide,* רָחַב *rachab,* 5.
Exod34. 24 For I will..enlarge thy borders: neither
Deut12. 20 When the LORD thy God shall enlarge
19. 8 if the LORD thy God enlarge thy coast
33. 20 he said, Blessed (be) he that enlargeth
2 Sa. 22. 37 Thou hast enlarged my steps under me
Psa. 4. 1 thou hast enlarged me..in distress
18. 36 Thou hast enlarged my steps under me
119. 32 I will run..when thou shalt enlarge my
Isa. 5. 14 Therefore hell hath enlarged herself
54. 2 Enlarge the place of thy tent, and let
57. 8 thou hast enlarged thy bed, and made
Amos 1. 13 ripped up..that they might enlarge their
Mic. 1. 16 enlarge thy baldness as the eagle; for
Hab. 2. 5 a proud man..who enlargeth his desire
4. *To spread out,* שָׁטַח *shatach.*
Job 12. 23 he enlargeth the nations, and straiteneth
5. *To make great,* μεγαλύνω *megalunō.*
Matt23. 5 they..enlarge the borders of their gar.
2 Co. 10. 15 that we shall be enlarged by you accord.
6. *To make broad, wide,* πλατύνω *platunō.*
2 Co. 6. 11 our mouth is open..our heart is enlarged
6. 13 for a recompence..be ye also enlarged

ENLARGED, to be —
To be enlarged, broad, wide, רָחַב *rachab.*
1 Sa. 2. 1 my mouth is enlarged over mine enemies
Isa 60. 5 thine heart shall fear, and be enlarged

ENLARGEMENT —
Space, respite, רֶוַח *revach.*
Esth. 4. 14 (then) shall there enlargement and deliv.

ENLARGING, (to be) an —
To be enlarged, broad, wide, רָחַב *rachab.*
Eze. 41. 7 And (there was) an enlarging and a wind.

ENLIGHTEN, to —
1. *To cause (to give) light, shine,* אוֹר *or,* 5.
Psa. 19. 8 commandment..(is) pure, enlightening
97. 4 His lightnings enlightened the world
2. *To cause to shine, enlighten,* נָגַהּ *nagah,* 5.
Psa. 18. 28 LORD my God will enlighten my darkne.
3. *To give light,* φωτίζω *phōtizō.*
Eph. 1. 18 The eyes of your understanding being en.
Heb. 6. 4 impossible for those who were once en.

ENLIGHTENED, to be —
1. *To be or become light, shining,* אוֹר *or.*
1 Sa. 14. 27 hand to his mouth; and his eyes were en.
14. 29 see..how mine eyes have been enlighten.
2. *To become light, shining,* אוֹר *or,* 2.
Job 33. 30 to be enlightened with the light of the

EN MISH'-PAT עֵין מִשְׁפָּט *fountain of judgment.*
A place called Kadesh in the wilderness of Paran (not in *Zin*).
Gen. 14. 7 they returned, and came to E., which(is)

ENMITY —
1. *Enmity,* אֵיבָה *ebah.*
Gen. 3. 15 I will put enmity between thee and the
Num35. 21 Or in enmity smite him with his hand
35. 22 if he thrust him suddenly without enmity
2. *Enmity,* ἔχθρα *echthra.*
Luke23. 12 for before they were at enmity between
Rom. 8. 7 Because the carnal mind (is) enmity
Eph. 2. 15 Having abolished in his flesh the enmity
2. 16 the cross, having slain the enmity thereby
Jas. 4. 4 friendship of the world is enmity with G.

E'-NOCH, HE'-NOCH, חֲנוֹךְ, Ἑνώχ *tuition, teacher.*
1. Eldest son of Cain. B.C. 3875.
Gen. 4. 17 she conceived, and bare E.: and he buil.
4. 18 unto E. was born Irad: and Irad begat
2. A city built by Cain and called after his son's name.
Gen. 4. 17 builded a city, and called the name..E.
3. A son of Jared a descendant of Seth. B.C. 3382–3017
Gen. 5. 18 hundred sixty and two..and he begat E.
5. 19 Jared lived after he begat E. eight hund.
5. 21 And E. lived sixty and five years
5. 22 E. walked with God..three hundredv.24.
5. 23 the days of E. were three hundred sixty
1 Ch. 1. 3 Henoch, Methuselah, Lamech
Luke 3. 37 Mathusala, which was (the son) of E.
Heb. 11. 5 By faith E. was translated that he should
Jude 14 And E. also, the seventh from Adam, pro.

ENOS, אֱנוֹשׁ, Ἐνώς *mortal.*
Son of Seth and grandson of Adam. B.C. 3769–2864.
Gen. 4. 26 And to Seth..and he called his name E.
5. 6 an hundred and five years, and begat E.
5. 7 And Seth lived after he begat E. eight
5. 9 E. lived ninety years, and begat Cainan
5. 10 E. lived after he begat Cainan eight hun.
5. 11 the days of E. were nine hundred and
1 Ch. 1. 1 Adam, Sheth, Enosh.
Luke 3. 38 Which was (the son) of E...(the son) of S.

ENOUGH —
1. *Sufficiency,* דַּי *dai.*
Prov27. 27 And..goats' milk enough for thy food, for
Nah. 2. 12 The lion did tear in pieces enough for his
Mal. 3. 10 that (there shall) not (be room) enough
2. *To draw (up) water,* דָּלָה *dalah.*
Exod. 2. 19 An Egyptian..drew..enough for us, and
3. *Wealth, substance, sufficiency,* הוֹן *hon.*
Prov30. 15 (yea), four (things) say not, (It is) enough
30. 16 and the fire (that) saith not, (It is) enough
4. *All,* כֹּל *kol.*
Gen. 33. 11 God hath dealt graciously..and..I have e.
5. *Abundant, much,* רַב *rab.*
Gen. 24. 25 We have both straw and provender eno.
33. 9 I have enough, my brother; keep that
45. 28 (It is) enough; Joseph my son (is) yet
Exod.9. 28 Entreat the LORD for (it is) enough
2 Sa. 24. 16 It is enough; stay now thine hand
1 Ki.19. 4 It is enough; now, O LORD, take away my
1 Ch.21. 15 said to the angel..It is enough, stay now
6. *Satiety, fulness,* שָׂבְעָה *sobah.*
Isa. 56. 11 greedy dogs (which) can never have eno.
7. *On two hands,* יָד *yad.*
Gen. 34. 21 behold, (it is) large enough for them
8. *Sufficient, enough,* ἀρκετός *arketos.*
Matt10. 25 It is enough for the disciple that he be
9. *Enough, sufficient,* ἱκανός *hikanos.*
Luke22. 38 And he said unto them, It is enough

ENOUGH, to be —
1. *To be found, met, come upon,* מָצָא *matsa,* 2.
Josh. 17. 16 The hill is not enough for us: and all the
2. *To be enough,* ἀρκέω *arkeō.*
Matt25. 9 lest there be not enough for us and you

ENOUGH, to have —
1. *Sufficiency,* דַּי *dai.*
Jer. 49. 9 they will destroy till they have enough
Obad. 5 would they not have..till they had eno.
2. *To be satisfied, satiated,* שָׂבַע *saba.*
2 Ch.31. 10 we have had enough to eat, and have left
Prov 28. 19 he that followeth..shall have poverty en.
Hos. 4. 10 For they shall eat, and not have enough
3. *Satiety, fulness,* שָׂבְעָה *sobah.*
Hag. 1. 6 ye eat, but ye have not enough; ye drink

ENOUGH and to spare, have —
Abound, περισσεύω *perisseuō.*
Luke15. 17 How many..have bread enough and to

ENOUGH, it is —
To hold off, ἀπέχω *apechō.*
Mark14. 41 take..rest: it is enough, the hour is come

ENOUGH, more than —
Sufficiency, דַּי *dai.*
Exod36. 5 The people bring much more than enough

ENQUIRE, (for), to —
1. *To enquire,* בָּעָה *baah.*
Isa. 21. 12 if ye will enquire, enquire ye: return
2. *To seek, enquire,* בָּקַר *baqar,* 3.
2 Ki. 16. 15 the brasen altar shall be for me to enqui.
Psa. 27. 4 behold the beauty of the LORD, and to e.
3. *To seek, enquire,* בְּקַר *beqar,* 3.
Ezra 7. 14 of his seven counsellors, to enquire conc.
4. *To seek, enquire, require, request,* בָּקַשׁ *baqash,* 3.
2 Sa. 21. 1 year after year; and David enquired of
Job 10. 6 That thou enquirest after mine iniquity
Dan. 1. 20 that the king enquired of them, he found
5. *To seek, enquire, require,* דָּרַשׁ *darash.*
Gen. 25. 22 And she went to enquire of the LORD
Exod18. 15 Because the people come unto me to en.
Deut12. 30 Take heed..that thou enquire not after
13. 14 Then shalt thou enquire, and make search
17. 4 thou hast heard (of it), and enquired dil.
17. 9 thou shalt come unto the priest..and en.
Judg. 6. 29 when they enquired and asked, they said
1 Sa. 9. 9 when a man went to enquire of God
28. 7 that I may go to her, and enquire of her
2 Sa. 11. 3 David sent and enquired after the wom.
1 Ki. 22. 5 Enquire, I pray thee, at the word of the
22. 7 not here a prophet..that we might enqu.
22. 8 by whom we may enquire of the LORD
2 Ki. 1. 2, 3, 6, 16 enquire of Baal-zebub the god of
1. 16 no God in Israel to enquire of his word
3. 11 not here a prophet..that we may enquire
8. 8 meet the man of God, and enquire of
22. 13 Go ye, enquire of the LORD for me, and
22. 18 the king of Judah, which sent you to en.
1 Ch.10. 13 of (one that had) a familiar spirit, to enq.
10. 14 And enquired not of the LORD: therefore
13. 3 we enquired not at it in the days of Saul
21. 30 David could not go before it to enquire
2 Ch.18. 4 Enquire, I pray thee, at the word of the
18. 6 not here a prophet..that we might enqu.
18. 7 by whom we may enquire of the LORD
32. 31 who sent unto him to enquire of the wo.
34. 21 Go, enquire of the LORD for me, and
34. 26 who sent you to enquire of the LORD
Jer. 21. 2 Enquire, I pray thee, of the LORD for us
37. 7; Eze. 14. 7, 20. 1, 20. 3; Zeph. 1. 6.
6. *To ask, demand, beg, desire,* שָׁאַל *shaal.*
Gen. 24. 57 We will call the damsel, and enquire at
Judg. 4. 20 when any man doth come and enquire
8. 14 And caught a young man..and enquired
20. 27 the children of Israel enquired of the
1 Sa. 10. 22 Therefore they enquired of the LORD
17. 56 Enquire thou whose son the stripling (is)
22. 10 And he enquired of the LORD for him
22. 13 that thou hast..enquired of God for him
22. 15 Did I then begin to enquire of God for
23. 2 David enquired of the LORD, saying, Shall
23. 4 David enquired of the LORD yet again
28. 6 when Saul enquired of the LORD, the
30. 8 David enquired at the LORD, saying
2 Sa. 2. 1 that David enquired of the LORD, saying
5. 19 David enquired of the LORD, saying, Shall
5. 23 when David enquired of the LORD, he
16. 23 as if a man had enquired at the oracle of
1 Ch.14. 10 David enquired of God, saying, Shall I go
14. 14 Therefore David enquired again of God
18. 10 to enquire of his welfare, and to congra.
Job 8. 8 For enquire, I pray thee, of the former
Eccl. 7. 10 thou dost not enquire wisely concerning
7. *To know thoroughly,* διαγινώσκω *diaginōskō.*
Acts 23. 15 as though ye would enquire something
8. *To seek after,* ἐπιζητέω *epizēteō.*
Acts 19. 39 But if ye enquire any thing concerning
9. *To search out,* ἐξετάζω *exetazō.*
Matt.10. 11 enquire who in it is worthy; and there

10. *To seek,* ζητέω *zēteō.*
John16. 19 Do ye enquire among yourselves of that
Acts 9. 11 enquire in the house of Judas for (one)

11. *To ask, enquire,* πυνθάνομαι *punthanomai.*
John 4. 52 Then enquired he of them the hour when
Acts 23. 20 as though they would enquire somewhat

12. *To seek together,* συζητέω *suzēteō.*
Luke22. 23 they began to enquire among themselves

ENQUIRE or search diligently, to —

1. *To enquire exactly,* ἀκριβόω *akriboō.*
Matt. 2. 7 Then Herod..enquired of them diligently
2. 16 which he had diligently enquired of the

2. *To seek out,* ἐκζητέω *ekzēteō.*
1 Pe. 1. 10 prophets have enquired and searched di.

ENQUIRE early, to —

To seek early, שָׁחַר *shachar,* 3.
Psa. 78. 34 they returned and enquired early after

ENQUIRED of, to be —

To be sought, דָּרַשׁ *darash,* 2.
Eze. 14. 3 should I be enquired of at all by them ?
20 3 (As) I live..I will not be enquired of by
20. 31 shall I be enquired of by you, O house of
36. 37 I will yet (for) this be enquired of by the

ENQUIRY (for), to make —

1. *To seek, enquire,* בָּקַר *baqar,* 3.
Prov 20. 25 holy, and after vows to make enquiry

2. *To ask or enquire thoroughly,* διερωτάω *dierōtaō.*
Acts 10. 17 the men which were sent..made enq. for

ENRICH, to —

1. *To enrich,* עָשַׁר *ashar,* 5.
1 Sa. 17. 25 the king will enrich him with great riches
Psa. 65. 9 thou greatly enrichest it with the river
Eze. 27. 33 thou didst enrich the kings of the earth

2. *To make rich,* πλουτίζω *ploutizō.*
1 Co. 1. 5 That in every thing ye are enriched by
2 Co. 9. 11 Being enriched in everything to all

EN RIM'-MON, עֵין רִמּוֹן *fountain of Rimmon.*
A city of Judah, the same as Ain and Rimmon (Josh. 15. 32), Ain, Remmon (19. 7: and see 1 Ch 4, 32).
Neh. 11. 29 at E., and at Zareah, and at Jarmuth

EN RO'-GEL, עֵין רֹגֵל *the fullers's fountain.*
A fountain near Jerusalem on the boundary line between Judah and Benjamin. It was the point next to Jerusalem and at a lower level. Its modern name is *Ain-Ummed-Daraj,* "fountain of the virgin."
Josh 15. 7 and the goings out thereof were at E.-r.
18. 16 And the border..descended to E.-r.
2 Sa. 17. 17 Jonathan and Ahimaaz stayed by E.-r.
1Ki. 1. 9 the stone of Zoheleth, which (is) by E.-r

ENSAMPLE —

1. *A type,* τύπος *tupos.*
1 Co. 10. 11 things happened unto them [for ensam.]
Phil. 3. 17 which walk so as ye have us for an ensa.
1 Th. 1. 7 So that ye were ensamples to all that
2 Th. 3. 9 to make ourselves an ensample unto you
1 Pe. 5. 3 Neither as being lords..but being ensam.

2. *A wider or secret sign,* ὑπόδειγμα *hupodeigma.*
2 Pe. 2. 6 an ensample unto those that after should

EN SHE'-MESH, עֵין שֶׁמֶשׁ *fountain of the sun.*
A spring forming one of the landmarks between the tribe of Judah and Benjamin, at the E. of Jerusalem and the Mount of Olives. Now called *Ain Haud,* about a mile from Bethany, the first halting-place on the road to Jericho.
Josh. 15. 7 border passed toward the waters of E.
18. 17 drawn from the north, and went forth to E.

ENSIGN —

1. *Sign, ensign, token, signal,* אוֹת *oth.*
Num. 2. 2 with the ensign of their father's house
Psa. 74. 4 Thine enemies..set up their ensigns (for)

2. *Sign, ensign, banner, sail,* נֵס *nes.*
Isa. 5. 26 he will lift up an ensign to the nations
11. 10 which shall stand for an ensign of the
11. 12 he shall set up an ensign for the nations
18. 3 see ye, when he lifteth up an ensign on the
30. 17 till ye be left..as an ensign on an hill
31. 9 his princes shall be afraid of the ensign

ENSIGN, to lift up as an —

To lift self up, display self, נָסַס *nasas,* 7a.
Zech. 9. 16 lifted up as an ensign upon his land

ENSNARED, to be —

Snare, מוֹקֵשׁ *moqesh.*
Job 34. 30 reign not, lest the people be ensnared

ENSUE, to —

To cause to flee, pursue, διώκω *diōkō.*
1 Pe. 3. 11 let him seek peace, and ensue it

ENTANGLE, to —

To entrap, ensnare, παγιδεύω *pagideuō.*
Matt 22. 15 took counsel how they might entangle

ENTANGLE in, to —

To entangle (self) in, ἐμπλέκω *emplekō.*
2 Pe. 2. 20 For if..they are again entangled therein

ENTANGLE one's self with, to —

To entangle (self) in, ἐμπλέκω *emplekō.*
2 Ti. 2. 4 No man that warreth entangleth himself

ENTANGLED with, to be —

1. *To be perplexed, entangled,* בּוּךְ *buk,* 2.
Exod14. 3 They (are) entangled in the land, the wild.

2. *To hold in,* ἐνέχω *enechō.*
Gal. 5. 1 be not entangled again with the yoke of

EN TAP-PU'-AH, עֵין תַּפּוּחַ *fountain of Tappuah.*
The boundary of Manasseh went from facing Shechem "to the inhabitants of En-tappuah." Probably identical with Tappuah, but not to be confounded with *Beth-tappuah* in the mountains of Judah.
Josh. 17. 7 the right hand unto the inhabitants of E.

ENTER, to —

1. *To go in, enter,* בּוֹא *bo.*
Gen. 7. 13 In the selfsame day entered Noah, and
19. 3 and they turned in unto him, and entered
19. 23 The sun was risen..when Lot entered
31. 33 Then went he out..and entered into R.
43. 30 he entered into (his) chamber, and wept
Exod33. 9 as Moses entered into the tabernacle
40. 35 Moses was not able to enter into the tent
Num 4. 3 all that enter into the host, to do the
4. 30, 35, 39, 43 every one that entereth into
5. 24, 27 the water that causeth the curse s. e.
20. 24 he shall not enter into the land which
Deut23. 1, 2, 3 shall not enter into the congregation
23. 2 to his tenth generation shall he not enter
23. 3 their tenth generation shall they not en.
23. 8 children that are begotten of them shall e.
Josh. 2. 3 Bring forth the men..which are entered
8. 19 they entered into the city, and took it
10. 19 suffer them not to enter into their cities
10. 20 the rest (which) remained of them enter.
Judg. 6. 5 they entered into the land to destroy it
9. 46 they entered into an hold of the house
18. 9 be not slothful to go..to enter to possess
2 Sa. 10. 14 the children of Ammon..entered into the
1 Ki. 14. 12 when thy feet enter into the city, the
22. 30 I will disguise myself, and enter into the
2 Ki. 7. 4 If we say, We will enter into the city
7. 8 they..came again and entered
19. 23 I will enter into the lodgings of his bord.
1 Ch. 19. 15 they likewise fled..and entered into the
2 Ch. 7. 2 the priests could not enter into the house
12. 11 when the king entered into the house of
15. 12 they entered into a covenant to seek the
27. 2 he entered not into the temple of the L.
30. 8 enter into his sanctuary, which he hath
31. 16 unto every one that entereth into the
32. 1 Sennacherib..entered into Judah, and
Neh. 2. 8 and for the house that I shall enter into
2. 15 Then went I up..and entered by the gate
10. 29 They clave to their brethren..and entered
Esth. 4. 2 none (might) enter into the king's gate
Job 22. 4 will he enter with thee into judgment?
38. 16 Hast thou entered into the springs of the
38. 22 Hast thou entered into the treasures of
Psa. 37. 15 Their sword shall enter into their own
45. 15 they shall enter into the king's palace
95. 11 that they should not enter into my rest
100. 4 Enter into his gates with thanksgiving
118. 20 gate..into which the righteous shall enter
143. 2 enter not into judgment with thy servant
Prov. 2. 10 When wisdom entereth into thine heart
4. 14 Enter not into the path of the wicked
18. 6 A fool's lips enter into contention, and
23. 10 enter not into the fields of the fatherless
Isa. 2. 10 Enter into the rock, and hide thee in the
3. 14 The LORD will enter into judgment with
26. 20 Come, my people, enter thou into thy
37. 24 I will enter into the height of his border
57. 2 He shall enter into peace: they shall rest
59. 14 truth is fallen..and equity cannot enter
Jer. 2. 7 but when ye entered, ye defiled my land
7. 2 that enter in at these gates to worship
8. 14 and let us enter into the defenced cities
9. 21 For death..is entered into our palaces
14. 18 if I enter into the city, then behold them
16. 5 Enter not into the house of mourning
17. 25 Then shall there enter into the gates of
21. 13 or who shall enter into our habitations?
34. 10 which had entered into the covenant
37. 16 When Jeremiah was entered into the du.
41. 17 they departed..to go to enter into Egypt
Lam. 1. 10 she hath seen..the heathen entered into
1. 10 they should not enter into thy congrega.
4. 12 the enemy should have entered into the
Eze. 2. 2 the spirit entered into me when he spake
3. 24 the spirit entered into me, and set me
7. 22 the robbers shall enter into it, and defile
13. 9 neither shall they enter into the land of
16. 8 I sware unto thee, and entered into a cov.
20. 38 they shall not enter into the land of Isr.
26. 10 when he shall enter into thy gates, as
36. 20 when they entered unto the heathen
41. 6 they entered into the wall which (was) of
44. 3 he shall enter by the way of the porch
44. 9 No stranger..shall enter into my sanctua.
44. 16 They shall enter into my sanctuary
44. 21 when they enter into the inner court
46. 2 the prince shall enter by the way of the
46. 8 And when the prince shall enter, he shall
46. 9 he that entereth by the way of the south
Dan. 11. 7 and shall enter into the fortress of the
11. 17 He shall also set his face to enter with
11. 24 He shall enter peaceably even upon the
11. 40 and he shall enter into the countries
11. 41 He shall enter also into the glorious land
Hos. 11. 9 I (am) God..I will not enter into the city
Amos 5 5 But seek not Beth-el, nor enter into Gilgal
Obad. 13 Thou shouldest not have entered into the
Jon. 3. 4 Jonah began to enter into the city a day's
Hab. 3. 16 rottenness entered into my bones, and
Zech. 5. 4 it shall enter into the house of the thief

2. *To go on, proceed,* הָלַךְ *halak.*
Job 34. 23 he should enter into judgment with God

3. *To come down,* נָחַת *nachath.*
Prov. 17. 10 A reproof entereth more into a wise man

4. *To go or pass over,* עָבַר *abar.*
Deut29. 12 That thou shouldest enter into covenant

5. *To go up into,* ἀναβαίνω *anabainō.*
John21. 3 They went forth, and [entered] into a ship
1 Co. 2. 9 neither have entered into the heart of m.

6. *To come or go into,* εἰσέρχομαι *eiserchomai.*
Matt. 5. 20 ye shall in no case enter into the kingdom
6. 6 when thou prayest, enter into thy closet
7. 21 Not every one..shall enter into the king.
8. 5 when Jesus was entered into Capernaum
10. 5 into (any) city of the Samaritans enter ye
10. 11 into whatsoever city or town ye shall en.
12. 4 How he entered into the house of God
12. 29 how can one enter into a strong man's
18. 3 ye shall not enter into the kingdom of
18. 8, 9 it is better for thee to enter into life
19. 17 if thou wilt enter into life keep the com.
19. 23 a rich man shall hardly enter into the
19. 24 than for a rich man [to enter] into the
23. 13 neither suffer ye them that are entering
24. 38 until the day that Noe entered into the
25. 21, 23 enter thou into the joy of thy lord
26. 41 pray, that ye enter not into temptation
Mark 1. 21 [entered] into the synagogue, and taught
1. 45 Jesus could no more openly enter into
2. 1 again he entered into Capernaum after
3. 1 And he entered again into the synagogue
3. 27 No man can enter into a strong man's
5. 12 Send us into the swine, that we may enter
5. 13 the unclean spirits went out, and entered
6. 10 In what place soever ye enter into an ho.
7. 17 when he was entered into the house from
7. 24 from thence he arose..and entered into
9. 25 come out of him, and enter no more into
9. 43, 45, 47 it is better for thee to enter..into
10. 15 as a little child, he shall not enter therein
10. 23 hardly shall they that have riches enter
10. 24 for them that trust in riches to enter into
10. 25 than for a rich man to enter into the kin.
11. 11 Jesus entered into Jerusalem, and into
13. 15 neither enter..to take anything out of
14. 38 pray, lest ye [enter] into temptation
16. 5 and [entering] into the sepulchre, they saw
Luke 1. 40 And entered into the house of Zacharias
4. 38 he arose out of the synagogue, and entered
6. 6 he entered into the synagogue and taught
7. 1 when he had ended..he entered into Cap.
7. 6 I am not worthy that thou shouldest enter
7. 44 I entered into thine house, thou gavest me
8. 30 because many devils were entered into
8. 32 that he would suffer them to enter into
8. 33 Then went the devils out..and entered
9. 4 whatsoever house ye enter into, there ab.
9. 34 they feared as they entered into the cloud
9. 52 and entered into a village of the Samar.
10. 5 into whatsoever house ye enter, first
10. 8, 10 into whatsoever city ye enter, and they
10. 38 that he entered into a certain village
17. 12 as he entered into a certain village, there
17. 27 until the day that Noe entered into the
18. 17 as a little child shall in no wise enter
18. 24 hardly shall they that have riches [enter]
18. 25 than for a rich man to enter into the kin.
19. 1 And (Jesus) entered and passed through
21. 21 let not them..in the countries enter the.
22. 3 Then entered Satan into Judas surnamed
22. 10 when ye are entered into the city
22. 40 Pray that ye enter not into temptation
22. 46 rise and pray, lest ye enter into temptat.
24. 26 Ought not Christ..to enter into his glory?
John 3. 4 can he enter the second time into his mo.
3. 5 he cannot enter into the kingdom of God
4. 38 other men laboured, and ye are entered
10. 1 He that entereth not by the door into the
13. 27 And after the sop Satan entered into him
18. 1 a garden, into the which he entered, and
18. 33 Then Pilate entered into the judgment
Acts 3. 8 And he..entered with them into the tem.
5. 21 when they heard (that), they entered into
9. 17 Ananias went his way, and entered into
10. 24 the morrow after they entered into
11. 8 nothing..unclean hath at any time enter.
11. 12 and we entered into the man's house
14. 22 we must through much tribulation enter
16. 40 they went out of the prison, and entered
18. 19 but he himself entered into the synagogue
21. 8 we entered into the house of Philip the
23. 16 he went and entered into the castle, and
25. 23 and was entered into the place of hearing
Rom. 5. 12 as by one man sin entered into the world
Heb. 3. 11 I sware..They shall not enter into my rest
3. 18 that they should not enter into his rest
4. 1 a promise being left (us) of entering into
4. 3 For we which have believed do enter into
4. 3, 5 if they shall enter into my rest
4. 6 Seeing..remaineth that some must ent.
4. 10 For he that is entered into his rest
4. 11 Let us labour therefore to enter into that
6. 19 which entereth into that within the veil
6. 20 Whither the forerunner is for us entered
9. 24 For Christ is not entered into the 10. 19

Heb. 9. 25 as the high priest entereth into the holy
Jas. 5. 4 cries of them which have reaped are en.
2 Jo. 7 many deceivers [are entered] into the wo.
Rev. 11. 11 the Spirit of life from God entered into
15. 8 no man was able to enter into the temple
21. 27 there shall in no wise enter into it any

7. *To pass over into,* εἰσπορεύομαι *eisporeuomai.*
Mark 6. 56 whithersoever he entered..they laid the
7. 15 There is nothing..entering into v. 18. 19.
11. 2 as soon as ye be entered into it, ye shall
Luke 19. 30 at your entering ye shall find a colt tied
Acts 3. 2 to ask alms of them that entered into the

8. *To go into,* ἐμβαίνω *embainō.*
Matt 8. 23 when he was entered into a ship, his dis.
9. 1 And he entered into a ship, and passed
Mark 4. 1 he entered into a ship, and sat in the sea
8. 10 he entered into a ship with his disciples
8. 13 and, entering into the ship again, departed
Luke 5. 3 And he entered into one of the ships
John 6. 17 And entered into a ship, and went over
6. 22 [that one whereinto his disciples were en.]

9. *To go into,* εἴσειμι *eiseimi.*
Acts 21. 26 Paul..the next day..entered into the

10. *Way in,* εἴσοδος *eisodos.*
Heb. 10. 19 Having..boldness to enter into the hol.

11. *To go or come,* ἔρχομαι *erchomai.*
Mark 1. 29 they entered into the house of Simon and
Acts 18. 7 he departed thence, and [entered] into a

12. *To come into sideways,* παρεισέρχομαι *pareis.*
Rom. 5. 20 the law entered, that the offence might

ENTER, to cause to —
To cause to go or come in, בּוֹא *bo,* 5.
Eze. 37. 5 I will cause breath to enter into you
Lam. 3. 13 He hath caused the arrows..to enter into

ENTER in, to —
1. *To go or come in,* בּוֹא *bo.*
Num. 4. 23 all that enter in to perform the service
2 Ki. 9. 31 as Jehu entered in at the gate, she said
11. 5 A third part of you that enter in on the
2 Ch. 23. 19 none..unclean in any thing should en. in
Jer. 17. 20 all the inhabitants..that enter in by
22. 2 and thy people that enter in by these
22. 4 then shall there enter in by the gates of
Eze. 44. 2 This gate..no man shall enter in by it
44. 17 when they enter in at the gates of the
46. 9 he that entereth in by the way of the
Joel 2. 9 they shall enter in at the windows like a

2. *To go or come into,* εἰσέρχομαι *eiserchomai.*
Matt. 7. 13 Enter ye in at the strait gate: for wide
12. 45 they enter in and dwell there: and the
Luke 11 26 [they enter in,] and dwell there: and the
11. 52 lawyers..ye enter not in yourselves
11. 52 them that were entering in ye hindered
13. 24 Strive to enter in at the strait gate
13. 24 will seek to enter in, and shall not be
24. 3 they entered in, and found not the body
John 10. 2 But he that entereth in by the door is
10. 9 I am the door: by me if any man enter in
Acts 19. 30 when Paul would have entered in unto
20. 29 shall grievous wolves enter in among you
28. 8 to whom Paul entered in, and prayed
Heb. 3. 19 So we see that they could not enter in
4. 6 they..entered not in because of unbelief
9. 12 he entered in once into the holy place
Rev. 22. 14 and may enter in through the gates into

3. *To pass over into,* εἰσπορεύομαι *eisporeuomai.*
Matt 15. 17 whatsoever entereth in at the mouth
Mark 4. 19 the lusts of other things entering in
5. 40 and entereth in where the damsel was
Luke 8. 16 that they which enter in may see the light
22. 10 into the house where he entereth in

ENTER into or therein, to —
1. *To go or come in,* בּוֹא *bo.*
Gen. 12. 11 when he was come near to enter into E.
Jer. 42. 15 If ye wholly set your faces to enter into
42. 18 when ye shall enter into Egypt..ye shall
Eze. 42. 12 toward the east, as one entereth into
42. 14 When the priests enter therein, then shall
Obad. 11 foreigners entered into his gates, and

2. *To go up on,* ἐπιβαίνω *epibainō.*
Acts 27. 2 entering into a ship of Adramyttium

3. *To pass over into,* εἰσπορεύομαι *eisporeuomai.*
Acts 8 3 made havoc of the church, entering into

ENTER into, as men —
Going in, entrance, מָבוֹא *mabo.*
Eze 26. 10 as men enter into a city wherein is made

ENTERING —
1. *Going in, entrance,* מָבוֹא *mabo.*
2 Ch 23. 15 when she was come to the entering of

2. *Opening,* פֶּתַח *pethach.*
Josh. 8. 29 cast it at the entering of the gate of the
20. 4 shall stand at the entering of the gate
Judg. 9. 35 Gaal..stood in the entering of the gate
9. 40 chased him..unto the entering of the
9. 44 stood in the entering of the gate of the
18. 16 of the children of Dan, stood by the ent.
18. 17 the priest stood in the entering of the
2 Sa. 11. 23 we were upon them even unto the enter.
1 Ki. 6. 31 for the entering of the oracle he made
Jer. 1. 15 the entering of the gates of Jerusalem

ENTERING in —
1. *To go or come in,* בּוֹא *bo.*
Judg. 3. 3 from..Baal-hermon unto the entering in
1 Ki. 8. 65 from the entering in of Hamath unto the
2 Ki. 23. 11 at the entering in of the house of the L.
1 Ch. 5. 9 he inhabited unto the entering in of the
2 Ch. 7. 8 from the entering in of Hamath unto the
26. 8 his name spread..to the entering in of
33. 14 even to the entering in at the fish gate
Isa. 23. 1 so that there is no house, no entering in
Jer. 17. 27 even entering in at the gates of Jerusa.
Amos 6. 14 they shall afflict you from the entering in

2. *Entrance,* מָבוֹא *mabo.*
2 Ch. 23. 13 stood at his pillar at the entering in
Eze. 44. 5 mark well the entering in of the house

3. *Opening,* פֶּתַח *pethach.*
Exod 35. 15 door at the entering in of the tabernacle
2 Sa. 10. 8 in array at the entering in of the gate
1 Ki. 19. 13 and stood in the entering in of the cave
2 Ki. 7. 3 were four leprous men at the entering in
10. 8 Lay ye..in two heaps at the entering in
23. 8 the gates that (were) in the entering in
2 Ch. 18. 9 at the entering in of the gate of Samaria

4. *Way in,* εἴσοδος *eisodos.*
1 Th. 1. 9 what manner of entering in we had unto

ENTERING into —
To go or come in, בּוֹא *bo.*
Josh. 13. 5 mount Hermon unto the entering into

ENTERPRISE —
Substance, wisdom, תּוּשִׁיָּה *tushiyyah.*
Job 5. 12 their hands cannot perform (their) enter.

ENTERTAIN, to —
To receive strangers, ξενίζω *xenizō.*
Heb. 13. 2 thereby some have entertained angels

ENTICE, to —
1. *To move, persuade,* סוּת *suth,* 5.
Deut 13. 6 If thy brother..entice thee secretly, say.

2. *To entice, persuade,* פָּתָה *pathah,* 3.
Exod 22. 16 if a man entice a maid that is not betro.
Judg 14 15 Entice thy husband, that he may declare
16. 5 Entice him, and see wherein his great
2 Ch. 18. 19 Who shall entice Ahab king of Israel
18. 20 a spirit..stood..and said, I will entice
18. 21 Thou shalt entice (him), and thou shalt
Prov. 1. 10 My son, if sinners entice thee, consent
16. 29 A violent man enticeth his neighbour

3. *To bait or entice,* δελεάζω *deleazō.*
Jas. 1. 14 is drawn away of his own lust, and entic.

ENTICED, to be —
1. *To be enticed, persuaded,* פָּתָה *pathah.*
Job 31. 27 And my heart hath been secretly enticed

2. *To be enticed,* פָּתָה *pathah,* 4.
Jer. 20. 10 he will be enticed, and we shall prevail

ENTICING —
Persuasive, πειθός *peithos.*
1 Co. 2. 4 not with enticing words of man's wisdom

ENTICING words —
Persuasive speech, πιθανολογία *pithanologia.*
Col. 2. 4 man should beguile you with enticing wor.

ENTIRE —
Whole in every part, ὁλόκληρος *holoklēros.*
Jas. 1. 4 that ye may be perfect and entire want.

ENTRANCE —
1. *Entrance, strength,* אִיתוֹן *ithon.*
Eze. 40. 15 from the face of the gate of the entrance

2. *To go in,* בּוֹא *bo.*
Num 34. 8 point out..unto the entrance of Hamath
1 Ki. 18. 46 ran before Ahab to the entrance of Jezr.

3. *Entrance,* מָבוֹא *mabo.*
1 Ch. 4. 39 they went to the entrance of Gedor, (even)

4. *Opening,* פֶּתַח *pethach.*
1 Ki. 22. 10 in a void place in the entrance of the gate
2 Ch. 12. 10 the guard, that kept the entrance of the
Mic. 5. 6 the land of Nimrod in the entrances

5. *Opening,* פֵּתַח *pethach.*
Psa. 119. 130 The entrance of thy words giveth light

6. *Way in,* εἴσοδος *eisodos.*
2 Pe. 1. 11 For so an entrance shall be ministered

ENTRANCE in —
Way in, εἴσοδος *eisodos.*
1 Th. 2. 1 For yourselves..know our entrance in

ENTRANCE into —
Going in, entrance, מָבוֹא *mabo.*
Judg. 1. 24 Show us, we pray thee, the entrance into
1. 25 when he showed them the entrance into

ENTREAT, to —
1. *To meet, come upon,* פָּגַע *paga.*
Gen. 23. 8 entreat for me to Ephron the son of Zohar

2. *To ask, desire,* ἐρωτάω *erōtaō.*
Phil. 4. 3 And I entreat thee also, true yokefellow

3. *To ask (a thing) away,* παραιτέομαι *paraiteomai.*
Heb. 12. 19 they that heard entreated that the word

4. *To call alongside of one,* παρακαλέω *parakaleō.*
Luke 15. 28 therefore came his father out, and entre.
1 Co. 4. 13 Being defamed, we entreat: we are made
1 Ti. 5. 1 Rebuke not an elder, but entreat (him)

5. *To use,* χράομαι *chraomai.*
Acts 27. 3 And Julius courteously entreated Paul

ENTREAT, to cause to —
To cause to meet, פָּגַע *paga,* 5.
Jer. 15. 11 I will cause the enemy to entreat thee

ENTREAT, shamefully —
Luke 20. 11 (ἀτιμάζω *dishonour*).
1 Thes. 2. 2 (ὑβρίζω *act insolently towards*).

ENTREATED, easy to be —
Easily persuaded, εὐπειθής *eupeithēs.*
Jas. 3. 17 then peaceable, gentle, (and) easy to be e.

ENTREATY —
A calling alongside for help, παράκλησις *paraklē.*
2 Co. 8. 4 Praying us with much entreaty that we

ENTRY —
1. *Going in, entrance,* בִּאָה *biah.*
Eze. 8. 5 behold..this image of jealousy in the en

2. *Entrance,* מָבוֹא *mabo* [v.L. בּוֹא *bo,* 5, partic.].
Eze. 42. 9 from under these chambers (was) the en.

3. *Going in, entrance,* מָבוֹא *mabo.*
2 Ki. 16. 18 the king's entry without, turned he from
1 Ch. 9. 19 their fathers..(were) keepers of the entry
Jer. 38. 14 the third entry that (is) in the house of
Eze. 27. 3 O thou that art situate at the entry of the
46. 19 After he brought me through the entry

4. *Mouth,* פֶּה *peh.*
Prov. 8. 3 She crieth at the gates, at the entry of

5. *Opening,* פֶּתַח *pethach.*
2 Ch. 4. 22 the entry of the house, the inner doors
Jer. 19. 2 which (is) by the entry of the east gate
26. 10 sat down in the entry of the new gate of
36. 10, 43. 9; Eze. 40. 11, 40. 38, 40. 40.

ENVIED —
Zeal, envy, קִנְאָה *qinah.*
Eccl. 4. 4 that for this a man is envied of his neigh.

ENVIOUS, to be —
To be zealous, jealous, envious, קָנָא *qana,* 3.
Psa. 37. 1 neither be thou envious against the wor.
73. 3 For I was envious at the foolish, (when) I
Prov 24. 1 Be not thou envious against evil men
24. 19 neither be thou envious at the wicked

ENVIRON, to —
To be, go, turn round about, סָבַב *sabab,* 2.
Josh. 7. 9 shall hear (of it), and shall environ us

ENVY —
1. *Zeal, jealousy, envy,* קִנְאָה *qinah.*
Job 5. 2 wrath killeth the foolish man, and envy
Prov 14. 30 but envy the rottenness of the bones
27. 4 but who (is) able to stand before envy?
Eccl. 9. 6 their hatred, and their envy, is now peris.
Isa. 11. 13 The envy also of Ephraim shall depart
26. 11 shall see, and be ashamed for (their) en.
Eze. 35. 11 according to thine envy, which thou hast

2. *Zeal, envy, jealousy,* ζῆλος *zēlos.*
Acts 13. 45 they were filled with envy, and spake

3. *Envy, jealousy,* φθόνος *phthonos.*
Matt 27. 18 he knew that for envy they had delivered
Mark 15. 10 the chief priests had delivered him for e.
Rom. 1. 29 full of envy, murder, debate, deceit
Phil. 1. 15 Some indeed preach Christ even of envy
1 Ti. 6. 4 whereof cometh envy, strife, railings, evil
Titus 3. 3 living in malice and envy, hateful
Jas. 4. 5 spirit that dwelleth in us lusteth to envy?
1 Pe. 2. 1 Wherefore, laying aside all..envies, and

ENVY, to —
1. *To be zealous, jealous, envious,* קָנָא *qana,* 3.
Gen. 26. 14 servants: and the Philistines envied him
30. 1 she bare Jacob no children, Rachel envied
37. 11 his brethren envied him; but his father
Num 11. 29 Moses said..Enviest thou for my sake?
Psa. 106. 16 They envied Moses also in the camp, (and)
Prov. 3. 31 Envy thou not the oppressor, and choose
23. 17 Let not thine heart envy sinners: but
Isa. 11. 13 Ephraim shall not envy Judah, and Judah
Eze. 31. 9 the trees..in the garden of God, envied

2. *To be zealous,* ζηλόω *zēloō.*
1 Co. 13. 4 charity envieth not; charity vaunteth not

3. *To be envious,* φθονέω *phthoneō.*
Gal. 5. 26 provoking one another, envying one ano.

ENVY, to be moved with —
To be zealous, ζηλόω *zēloō.*
Acts 7. 9 the patriarchs, moved with envy, sold J.
17. 5 [moved with envy,] took unto them certain

ENVYING —
1. *Zeal, envy, jealousy,* ζῆλος *zēlos.*
Rom. 13. 13 Let us walk..not in strife and envying
1 Co. 3. 3 for whereas (there is) among you envying
2 Co. 12. 20 lest (there be) debates, envyings, wraths
Jas. 3. 14 if ye have bitter envying and strife in
3. 16 where envying and strife (is,) there (is) c.

2. *Envy, jealousy,* φθόνος *phthonos.*
Gal. 5. 21 Envyings, murders, drunkenness, revel

EP-A'-PHRAS, Ἐπαφρᾶς.
A fellow-labourer of the apostle Paul.
Col. 1. 7 As ye also learned of E. our dear fellow.
4. 12 E., who is (one) of you, a servant of Christ
Phm. 23 There salute thee E., my fellow prisoner

EP-A-PHRO-DI'-TUS, Ἐπαφρόδιτος.
A messenger between Paul and the churches.
Phil. 2. 25 I supposed it necessary to send to you E.
4. 18 having received of E. the things..from

EP-Æ'-NE'-TUS, Ἐπαίνετος.
A native of Asia or Achaia.
Rom. 16. 5 Salute my well beloved E., who is the first

E'-PHAH, עֵיפָה *obscurity*.
1. A concubine of Caleb in the line of Judah. B.C. 1500.
1 Ch. 2. 46 E., Caleb's concubine, bare Haran, and
2. A son of Jahdai, also in the line of Judah. B.C. 1455.
1 Ch. 2. 47 And the sons of Jahdai; Regem..and E.
3. A son of Midian son of Abraham by Keturah. The name is also used of his posterity and their land. B.C. 1800.
Gen. 25. 4 And the sons of Midian; E., and Epher
1 Ch. 1. 33 And the sons of Midian; E., and Epher
Isa. 60. 6 the dromedaries of Midian and E.

EPHAH —
Ephah, a measure, three seah, אֵיפָה *ephah*.
Exod. 16. 36 an omer (is) the tenth (part) of an ephah
Lev. 5. 11 the tenth part of an ephah of fine flour
6. 20 the tenth part of an ephah of fine flour
19. 36 Just balances, just weights, a just ephah
Num. 5. 15 the tenth (part) of an ephah of barley
28. 5 And a tenth (part) of an ephah of flour
Judg. 6. 19 unleavened cakes of an ephah of flour
Ruth 2. 17 and it was about an ephah of barley
1 Sa. 1. 24 one ephah of flour, and a bottle of wine
17. 17 Take now for thy brethren an ephah of
Isa. 5. 10 the seed of an homer shall yield an ephah
Eze. 45. 10 just balances, and a just ephah, and a
45. 11 The ephah and the bath shall be of one
45. 11 and the ephah the tenth part of an homer
45. 13, 13 the sixth part of an ephah of an homer
45. 24 shall prepare a meat offering of an ephah
45. 24 an ephah for a ram..of oil for an ephah
46. 5 an ephah for a ram..oil to an ephah
46. 7 an ephah for..an ephah for..an ephah
46. 11 an ephah to..an ephah to..to an ephah
46. 14 an ephah, and the third part of an hin
Amos 8. 5 making the ephah small, and the shekel
Zech. 5. 6 said, This (is) an ephah that goeth forth
5. 7 woman that sitteth in the midst of the e.
5. 8 And he cast it into the midst of the ephah
5. 9 they lifted up the ephah between the ea.
5. 10 said I..Whither do these bear the ephah?

E'-PHAI, עֵיפַי *obscuring*.
One whose sons were among "the captains of the forces" left in Judah after the carrying away to Babylon. They submitted themselves to Gedaliah the governor, and seem to have been murdered with him by Ishmael (Jer. 41. 3, compare 40. 13). B.C. 620.
Jer. 40. 8 the sons of E. the Netophathite, and Jez.

E'-PHER, עֵפֶר *young deer or calf*.
1. Second son of Midian son of Abraham. B.C. 1800.
Gen. 25. 4 And the sons of Midian; Ephah, and E.
1 Ch. 1. 33 And the sons of Midian; Ephah, and E.
2. One of the descendants of Judah, and possibly of the family of Caleb son of Jephunneh. B.C. 1400.
1 Ch. 4. 17 the sons of Ezra (were) Jether..and E.
3. A chief of Manasseh E. of the Jordan. B.C. 800.
1 Ch. 5. 24 heads of the house of their fathers, even E.

E-PHES DAM'-MIM, אֶפֶס דַּמִּים *extension of brooks*.
A place between Shochoh and Azekah, now called *Damim*.
1 Sa. 17. 1 pitched betw. Shochoh and Azekah, in E.

E-PHE-SI-AN, Ἐφέσιος *belonging to Ephesus*.
Acts 19. 28 cried..saying, Great (is) Diana of the E.s
19. 34 cried out, Great (is) Diana of the E.s
19. 35 the city of the E.s is a worshipper of..D.
21. 29 For they had seen before with him..an E.

E-PHE'-SUS, Ἔφεσος.
A famous city in Ionia nearly opposite the island of Samos, and about the middle of the W. coast of Asia Minor. The "Asia" of the New Testament was the western province of the peninsula, with Ephesus as its capital.
Acts 18. 19 And he came to E., and left them there
18. 21 if God will. And he sailed from E.
18. 24 a certain Jew named Apollos..came to E.
19. 1 through the upper coasts came to E.
19. 17 known to..the Jews and Greeks..at E.
19. 26 ye see and hear, that not alone at E.
19. 35 men of E., what man is there that know.
20. 16 For Paul had determined to sail by E.
20. 17 from Miletus he sent to E., and called
1 Co. 15. 32 If..I have fought with beasts at E.
16. 8 But I will tarry at E. until Pentecost
Eph. 1. 1 Paul..to the saints which are [at E.]
1 Ti. 1. 3 As I besought thee to abide still at E.
2 Ti. 1. 18 many things he ministered unto me at E.
4. 12 And Tychicus have I sent to E.
Rev. 1. 11 send (it) unto the seven churches..unto E.
2. 1 Unto the angel of the church [of E.] write

EPH'-LAL, אֶפְלָל *judging*.
Descendant of Pharez through Jerahmeel
1 Ch. 2. 37 And Zabad begat E., and E. begat Obed

E'-PHOD, אֵפֹד *oracular*.
Father of Hanniel, prince of Manasseh, one of Joshua's assistants in dividing the land.
Num. 34. 23 tribe..of Manasseh, Hanniel the son of E.

EPHOD —
1. *Ephod, a priestly garment*, אֵפֹד, אֵפוֹד *ephod*.
Exod. 25. 7 stones, and stones to be set in the ephod
28. 4 a breastplate, and an ephod, and a robe
28. 6 they shall make the ephod (of) gold, (of)
28. 12 stones upon the shoulders of the ephod
28. 15 after the work of the ephod thou shalt
28. 25 on the shoulder pieces of the ephod
28. 26 in the side of the ephod inward
28. 27 on the two sides of the ephod underneath
28. 27, 28 above the curious girdle of the ephod
28. 28 bind..unto the rings of the ephod
28. 28 the breastplate be not loosed from the e.
28. 31 thou shalt make the robe of the ephod
29. 5 take..the robe of the ephod, and the ep.
29. 5 gird..with the curious girdle of the ephod
35. 9, 27 stones to be set, for the ephod, and for
39. 2 he made the ephod (of) gold, blue, and
39. 7 he put them on the shoulders of the ep.
39. 8 cunning work, like the work of the ephod
39. 18 put..on the shoulder pieces of the ephod
39. 19 which (was) on the side of the ephod inw.
39. 20 put them on the two sides of the ephod
39. 20, 21 above the curious girdle of the ephod
39. 21 by his rings unto the rings of the ephod
39. 21 might not be loosed from the ephod
39. 22 he made the robe of the ephod (of) woven
Lev. 8. 7 clothed him..and put the ephod upon
8. 7 with the curious girdle of the ephod
Judg. 8. 27 Gideon made an ephod thereof, and put
17. 5 and made an ephod, and teraphim, and
18. 14 know that there is in these houses an ep.
18. 17 took the graven image, and the ephod
18. 18 fetched the carved image, the ephod
18. 20 priest's heart was glad; and he took the e.
1 Sa. 2. 18 Samuel..a child, girded with a linen ephod
2. 28 I choose him..to wear an ephod before
14. 3 LORD'S priest in Shiloh, wearing an ephod
21. 9 wrapped in a cloth behind the ephod
22. 18 slew..persons that did wear a linen ephod
23. 6 he came down (with) an ephod in his
23. 9 said to..the priest, Bring hither the eph.
30. 7 I pray thee, bring me hither the ephod
30. 7 And Abiathar brought thither the ephod
2 Sa. 6. 14 David (was) girded with a linen ephod
1 Ch. 15. 27 David also (had) upon him an ephod of
Hos. 3. 4 and without an ephod, and..teraphim
2. *Ephod, garment*, אֲפֻדָּה *aphuddah*.
Exod. 28. 8 the curious girdle of the ephod, which
39. 5 the curious girdle of his ephod, that (was)

EPHPHATHA. *See* page 305, col. 1.

EPH-RA'-IM, אֶפְרַיִם, Ἐφραίμ *doubly fruitful*.
1. Second son of Joseph by Asenath. B.C. 1711.
Gen. 41. 52 the name of the second called he E.: For
46. 20 in the land..were born Manasseh and E.
48. 1 with him his two sons, Manasseh and E.
48. 5 thy two sons, E. and Manasseh..(are)
48. 13 Joseph took them both, E...and Manasseh
48. 14 his right hand, and laid (it) upon E.'s
48. 17 laid his right hand upon the head of E.
48. 17 to remove it from E.'s head unto Mana.
48. 20 God make thee as E., and as Manasseh
48. 20 and he set E. before Manasseh
50. 23 Joseph saw E.'s children of the third
Num. 26. 28 sons of Joseph..(were) Manasseh and E.
1 Ch. 7. 20 the sons of E.; Shuthelah, and Bered
7. 22 And E. their father mourned many days
2. The tribe that sprang from Ephraim or their territory.
Num. 1. 10 of E.; Elishama the son of Ammihud
1. 32 of the children of E., by their generations
1. 33 the tribe of E...forty thousand and five
2. 18 (shall be) the standard of the camp of E.
2. 18 the captain of the sons of E...Elishama
2. 24 that were numbered of the camp of E.
7. 48 Elishama..prince of the children of E.
10. 22 the standard..of the children of E. set
13. 8 Of the tribe of E., Oshea the son of Nun
26. 35 These (are) the sons of E. after their fa.
26. 37 These (are) the families of the sons of E.
34. 24 prince of the tribe of the children of E.
Deut. 33. 17 and they (are) the ten thousands of E.
34. 2 And all Naphtali, and the land of E.
Josh. 14. 4 the children of Joseph..Manasseh and E.
16. 4 the children of Joseph, Manasseh and E.
16. 5 the border of the children of E...was (thus)
16. 8 the inheritance..of the children of E.
16. 9 the separate cities for the children of E.
17. 8 Tappuah..(belonged) to the children of E.
17. 9 these cities of E. (are) among the cities
17. 10 Southward (it was) E.'s, and northward
17. 17 Joshua spake..(even) to E. and to Mana.
21. 5 by lot out of the families of the tribe of E.
21. 20 the cities of their lot out of the tribe of E.
Judg. 1. 29 Neither did E. drive out the Canaanites
5. 14 Out of E. (was there) a root of them aga.
7. 24 all the men of E. gathered themselves
8. 1 And the men of E. said unto him, Why
8. 2 (Is) not the gleaning of the grapes of E.
10. 9 to fight also..against the house of E.
12. 1 the men of E. gathered themselves toget.
Judg. 12. 4 gathered..men of Gil. and fought with E.
12. 4 and the men of Gilead smote E., because
12. 4 said, Ye Gileadites (are) fugitives of E.
12. 15 Abdon..was buried..in the land of E.
2 Sa. 2. 9 made him king over Gilead..and over E.
1 Ch. 6. 66 had cities..out of the tribe of E.
9. 3 and of the children of E., and Manasseh
12. 30 the children of E. twenty thousand and
27. 10 Helez the Pelonite, of the children of E.
27. 14 Benaiah the Pirathonite, of the chil. of E.
27. 20 Of the children of E., Hoshea the son of.
2 Ch. 15. 9 and the strangers with them out of E.
17. 2 set garrisons..in the cities of E., which
25. 7 LORD (is) not..(with) all the children of E.
25. 10 the army that was come to him out of E.
28. 7 Zichri, a mighty man of E., slew Maaseiah
28. 12 certain of the heads of the children of E.
30. 1 Hezekiah..wrote letters also to E. and
30. 10 posts passed..through the country of E.
30. 18 many of E...had not cleansed themselves
31. 1 threw down the high places..altars..in E.
34. 6 (did)..in the cities of Manasseh and E.
34. 9 Levites had gathered of the hand of..E.
Psa. 60. 7 E. also (is) the strength of mine head
78. 9 The children of E...armed..turned back
78. 67 and chose not the tribe of E.
80. 2 Before E. and Benjamin..stir up thy str.
108. 8 E. also (is) the strength of mine head
Isa. 7. 2 saying, Syria is confederate with E.
7. 5 Syria, E...have taken evil counsel against
7. 8 within threescore and five years shall E.
7. 9 And the head of E. (is) Samaria
7. 17 from the day that E. departed from Jud.
9. 9 And all the people shall know..E., and
9. 21 Manasseh, E.; and E., Manasseh..they
11. 13 The envy..of E. shall depart..E. shall
11. 13 and Judah shall not vex E.
17. 3 The fortress also shall cease from E.
28. 1 Woe to the crown..to the drunkards of E.
28. 3 the drunkards of E., shall be trodden
Jer. 7. 15 as I have cast out..the whole seed of E.
31. 9 I am a father to Israel, and E. (is) my
31. 18 I have surely heard E. bemoaning hims.
31. 20 (Is) E. my dear son? (is he) a pleasant ch.?
Eze. 37. 16 write upon it, For Joseph, the stick of E.
37. 19 which (is) in the hand of E., and the tribes
48. 5 unto the west side, a (portion for) E.
48. 6 by the border of E...a (portion for) Reu.
Hos. 4. 17 E. (is) joined to idols: let him alone
5. 3 I know E., and Israel is not hid from me
5. 3 O E., thou committest whoredom, (and)
5. 5 therefore shall Israel and E. fall in their
5. 9 E. shall be desolate in the day of rebuke
5. 11 E. (is) oppressed..broken in judgment
5. 12 Therefore (will) I (be) unto E. as a moth
5. 13 When E. saw his sickness, and Judah
5. 13 then went E. to the Assyrian, and sent
5. 14 For I (will be) unto E. as a lion, and as
6. 4 O E., what shall I do unto thee?
6. 10 there (is) the whoredom of E., Israel is
7. 1 then the iniquity of E. was discovered
7. 8 E., he hath mixed himself..E. is a cake
7. 11 E. also is like a silly dove without heart
8. 9 alone by himself: E. hath hired lovers
8. 11 Because E. hath made many altars to sin
9. 3 but E. shall return to Egypt, and they
9. 8 The watchman of E. (was) with my God
9. 11 E., their glory shall fly away like a bird
9. 13 E...(is) planted in a pleasant place
9. 13 E. shall bring forth his children to the
9. 16 E. is smitten, their root is dried up
10. 6 E. shall receive shame..Israel shall be
10. 11 And E. (is as) an heifer (that is) taught
10. 11 I will make E. to ride; Judah shall plow
11. 3 I taught E. also to go, taking them by
11. 8 How shall I give thee up, E.?..shall I
11. 9 I will not return to destroy E.: for I (am)
11. 12 E. compasseth me about with lies, and
12. 1 E. feedeth on wind, and followeth after
12. 8 And E. said, Yet I am become rich, I have
12. 14 E. provoked..to anger most bitterly
13. 1 When E. spake trembling, he exalted h.
13. 12 The iniquity of E. (is) bound up; his sin
14. 8 E. (shall say,) What have I to do any more
Obad. 19 and they shall possess the fields of E.
Zech. 9. 10 And I will cut off the chariot from E.
9. 13 When I have..filled the bow with E.
10. 7 (they of) E. shall be like a mighty (man)

The following localities were in the territory of Ephraim:—Abel-meholah, Ajalon, Arumah, Ataroth Adar, Baal-hazor, Baal-shalisha, Beth-horon the Upper, Ebal, Gaash, Gazer, Gerizim, Janoah, Jeshanah, Jokmeam, Kibzain, Lebonah, Michmethah, Maarah, Ramah, Samaria, Shalisha, Shamir, Shechem, Taanath, Shiloh, Tabbath, Thebez, Timnath-heres, Tiphsah, Tirzah, Uzzen-sherah, Zuph, &c.

3. A town which was "by" or "beside" Absalom's sheep-farm.
2 Sa. 13. 23 sheep shearers in Baal-hazor..beside E.

4. A city in the wilderness, to which Christ retired with his disciples from the violence of the priests. By the "wilderness" is probably meant the hill-country N.E. of Jerusalem, lying between the central towns and the Jordan valley. Hence Ophrah and Ephraim are identical, and now called *et Tanjibeh*, a village on a conical hill, overlooking the valley of the Jordan and the Salt Sea. It stands five miles E. of Bethel, and sixteen from Jerusalem.
John 11. 54 but went thence..into a city called E., and

EPH-RA'-IM, Gate of, שַׁעַר אֶפְרַיִם *shaar ephrayim.*
A gate of Jerusalem at the north, nearly at the position of the modern "Damascus Gate."
2 Ki.14. 13 from the gate of E. unto the corner gate
2 Ch. 25. 23 from the gate of E. to the corner gate
Neh. 8. 16 and in the street of the gate of E.
12. 39 from above the gate of E., and above the

EPH-RA'-IM, Wood of, יַעַר אֶפְרַיִם *yaar ephrayim.*
A forest in which a battle was fought between the armies of David and Absalom, on the E. side of the Jordan. Perhaps it was so named from the tribe of Ephraim being the chief sufferers in this battle. *See also* Jud. 12. 4.
2 Sa. 18. 6 and the battle was in the wood of E.

EPHRAIMITES, אֶפְרָתִי, אֶפְרַיִם.
The descendants of Ephraim, son of Joseph.
Josh.16. 10 Canaanites dwell among the E. unto this
Judg12. 4 (are) fugitives of Ephraim among the E.
12. 5 took the passages of Jordan before the E.
12. 5 when those E...said, Let me go over
12. 5 the men of Gilead said..(Art) thou an E.?
12. 6 there fell..of the E. forty and two thous.

EPH-RA'-IN, עֶפְרַיִן [V.L. עפרון] *hamlet.*
A city in Benjamin eight miles from Jerusalem, and near Bethel in the wilderness of Judah.
2 Ch. 13. 19 and E. with the towns thereof

EPH-RA'-TAH, אֶפְרָתָה *fertility.*
1. The ancient name of Bethlehem-Judah.
Ruth 4. 11 do thou worthily in E., and be famous in
Psa.132. 6 Lo, we heard of it at E.; we found it in
Mic. 5. 2 But thou, Beth-lehem E., (though) thou
2. Second wife of Caleb son of Hezron. She was the mother of Hur, and grandmother of Caleb son of Jephunneh. B.C. 1540.
1 Ch. 2. 50 the son of Hur, the first born of E.
4. 4 the sons of Hur, the first born of E.

EPH'-RATH, אֶפְרָת (אפרתה).
1. A city of Judah; the same as *Ephratah.*
Gen. 35. 16 there was but a little way to come to E.
35. 19 R. died, and was buried in the way to E.
48. 7 (there was)..a little way to come unto E.
48. 7 and I buried her there in the way of E.
2. Caleb's second wife. See *Ephratah* (No 2.)
1 Ch. 2. 19 Caleb took unto him E., which bare him

EPH-RA-THITE, אֶפְרָתִי.
1. An inhabitant of Bethlehem-Judah.
Ruth 1. 2 his two sons Mahlon and Chilion, E.s of
1 Sa. 17. 12 David (was) the son of that E. of Beth.
2. A certain Ephraimite, twice so designated.
1 Sa. 1. 1 the son of Tohu, the son of Zuph, an E.
1 Ki. 11. 26 Jeroboam the son of Nebat, an E. of Ze.

EPH'-RON, עֶפְרוֹן *strong.*
1. Son of Zohar a Hittite, from whom Abraham purchased a field (opposite Mamre or Hebron), containing a cave, and buried Sarah therein. B.C. 1860.
Gen. 23. 8 hear me, and entreat for me to E. the son
23. 10 E. dwelt among the children of Heth
23. 10 E. the Hittite answered Abraham in the
23. 13 he spake unto E. in the audience of the
23. 14 E. answered Abraham, saying unto him
23. 16 And Abraham hearkened unto E.
23. 16 Abraham weighed to E. the silver
23. 17 the field of E., which (was) in Machpelah
25. 9 in the field of E. the son of Zohar the H.
49. 29 in the cave that (is) in the field of E. the
49. 30 Abraham bought with the field of E.
50. 13 which Abraham bought..of E. the Hit.
2. A mountain between Judah and Benjamin, between the water of Nephtoah and Kirjath-jearim.
Josh.15. 9 and went out to the cities of mount E.

EPH-PHA'-THA —
Be opened, ἐφφαθά *from Chald.* פְּתַח *to open.*
Mark 7. 34 and saith..Ephphatha, that is, Be opened

E-PI-CU-RE'-AN, Ἐπικούρειος.
A sect of philosophers that derived its name from *Epicurus* (B.C. 342-271), a philosopher of Attic descent, whose garden at Athens replaced the "Porch" and the "Academy." His aim was to discover a practical guide to happiness; his search was for pleasure, not absolute truth; and he relied on experience as the test, not on reason.
Acts 17 18 Then certain philosophers of the E.

EPISTLE —
Epistle, letter, ἐπιστολή *epistolē.*
Acts 15. 30 multitude together, they delivered the e.
23. 33 and delivered the epistle to the governor
Rom 16. 22 I Tertius, who wrote (this) epistle, salute
1 Co. 5. 9 I wrote unto you in an epistle not to
2 Co. 3. 1 need we..epistles of commendation to
3. 2 Ye are our epistle written in our hearts
3. 3 manifestly declared to be the epistle of C.
7. 8 I perceive that the same epistle hath
Col. 4. 16 And when this epistle is read among you
1 Th. 5. 27 I charge you by the Lord that this epistle
2 Th. 2. 15 been taught, whether by word, or our ep.
3. 14 if any man obey not our word by this ep.
3. 17 which is the token in every epistle
2 Pe. 3. 1 This second epistle, beloved, I now write
3. 16 As also in all (his) epistles, speaking in

EQUAL —
1. *Valuation, arrangement,* עֵרֶךְ *erek.*
Psa. 55. 13 But (it was) thou, a man mine equal, my
2. *One of the same age,* συνηλικιώτης *sunēlikiōtēs.*
Gal. 1. 14 above many my equals in mine own
3. *Equal to, the same as,* ἴσος, ἴσος *isos.*
Matt 20. 12 and thou hast made them equal unto us
John 5. 18 God was his Father, making himself equal
Phil. 2. 6 thought it not robbery to be equal with
Rev. 21. 16 breadth and the height of it are equal

EQUAL, to —
1. *To be set in array, arrange,* עָרַךְ *arak.*
Job 28. 17 The gold and the crystal cannot equal it
28. 19 The topas of Ethiopia shall not equal it
2. *To make equal,* שָׁוָה *shavah,* 5.
Lam. 2. 13 what shall I equal to thee that I may

EQUAL, to make —
To make equal, שָׁוָה *shavah,* 5.
Isa. 46. 5 will ye liken me, and make (me) equal

EQUAL, to be —
To be weighed, pondered, תָּכַן *takan,* 2.
Eze. 18. 25 ye say, The way of the LORD is not equal
18. 25 O house of Israel; Is not my way equal?
18. 29 The way of the LORD is not equal
18. 29 O house of Israel, are not my ways equal?
33. 17 The way of the LORD is not equal
33. 17 but, as for them, their way is not equal
33. 20 ye say, The way of the LORD is not equal

EQUAL, to be not —
To be thin, lean, poor, weak, דָּלַל *dalal.*
Prov 26. 7 The legs of the lame are not equal; so

EQUAL, that are —
Uprightness, upright things, מֵישָׁרִים *mesharim.*
Psa. 17. 2 thine eyes behold the things that are eq.

EQUAL, that which is —
The equality, ἡ ἰσότης *hē isotēs.*
Col. 4. 1 give unto..servants that which is..equal

EQUALITY —
Equality, ἰσότης *isotēs.*
2 Co. 8. 14 an equality..that there may be equality

EQUITY —
1. *Right, uprightness,* יָשָׁר *yashar.*
Mic. 3. 9 abhor judgment, and pervert all equity
2. *Uprightness,* יֹשֶׁר *yosher.*
Prov 17. 26 not good..to strike princes for equity
3. *What is right, equity, benefit,* כִּשְׁרוֹן *kishron.*
Eccl. 2. 21 in wisdom, and in knowledge, and in eq.
4. *Uprightness,* מִישׁוֹר *mishor.*
Isa. 11. 4 reprove with equity for the meek of the
Mal. 2. 6 he walked with me in peace and equity
5. *Uprightness, upright things,* מֵישָׁרִים *mesharim.*
Psa. 98. 9 judge the world, and the people with eq.
99. 4 thou dost establish equity, thou executest
Prov. 1. 3 To receive the instruction of..equity
2. 9 Then shalt thou understand..equity
6. *Straightforwardness,* נְכֹחַ *nakoach.*
Isa. 59. 14 truth is fallen in the street, and equity

ER, עֵר, Ἤρ *watcher.*
1. Eldest son of Judah by the daughter of Shua the Canaanite. B.C. 1720.
Gen. 38. 3 bare a son; and he called his name E.
38. 6 Judah took a wife for E. his first born
38. 7 E...was wicked in the sight of the LORD
46. 12 the sons of Judah; E., and Onan, and
46. 12 E. and Onan died in the land of Canaan
Num 26. 19 sons of Judah..E. and Onan: and Er
1 Ch. 2. 3 sons of Judah; E., and Onan, and Shelah
2. 3 E...was evil in the sight of the LORD
2. A son of Shelah, youngest son of Judah by the daughter of Shua the Canaanite. B.C. 1660.
1 Ch. 4. 21 sons of Shelah..(were) E...and Laadah
3. An ancestor of Jesus.
Luke 3. 28 Elmodam, which was (the son) of E.

E'-RAN, עֵרָן *watcher.*
A son of Ephraim's eldest son Shuthelah. B.C. 1452.
Num26. 36 of E., the family of the Eranites

ERANITES, עֵרָנִי *belonging to Eran.*
Descendants of Eran, grandson of Ephraim.
Num 26. 36 of Eran, the family of the E.

E-RAST'-US, Ἔραστος.
1. A Christian sent by Paul into Macedonia.
Acts 19. 22 So he sent..two..Timotheus and E.; but
2 Ti. 4. 20 E. abode at Corinth: but Trophimus have
2. Chamberlain of Corinth, a convert of Paul's; perhaps the same as No. 1.
Rom 16. 23 E. the chamberlain of the city saluteth

ERE —
1. *Before, (not) yet,* טֶרֶם *terem.*
Num 11. 33 ere it was chewed, the wrath of the LORD
Exod. 1. 19 are delivered ere the midwives come in
2. *Not,* לֹא *lo.*
Jer. 47. 6 how long..ere thou be quiet? Put up
Hos. 8. 5 how long..ere they attain to innocency?
3. *Before, ere,* πρίν *prin.*
John 4. 49 The nobleman saith..Sir, come down ere

E'-RECH, אֶרֶךְ *length, size.*
One of the cities of Nimrod's kingdom in the land of Shinar. It is the same as *Orchoë,* eighty-two miles S. and forty-three E. of Babylon, and is now *Warka, Irka,* and *Irak.* It was the necropolis of the Assyrian kings, the whole neighbourhood being covered with mounds, and strewed with bricks and coffins.
Gen. 10. 10 the beginning of his kingdom was..E.

ERECT, to —
To set up, נָצַב *natsab,* 5.
Gen. 33. 20 he erected there an altar, and called it

E'-RI, עֵרִי *my watcher.*
A son of Gad. B.C. 1700.
Gen. 46. 16 And the sons of Gad; Ziphion, and..E.
Num26. 16 of E., the family of the Erites

E'-RITES, עֵרִי *belonging to Er.*
The descendants of Eri son of Gad.
Num26. 16 of Eri, the family of the E.

ERR, to —
1. *To err, go astray,* שָׁגַג *shagag.*
Lev. 5. 18 concerning his ignorance wherein he erred
2. *To err, go astray,* שָׁגָה *shagah.*
Num15. 22 if ye have erred, and not observed all
1 Sa. 26. 21 I have played the fool, and have erred ex.
Job 6. 24 me to understand wherein I have erred
19. 4 And be it indeed (that) I have erred
Psa.119. 21 which do err from thy commandments
119. 118 Thou hast trodden..all them that err
Prov 19. 27 hear the instruction (that causeth) to err
Isa. 28. 7 But they also have erred through wine
28. 7 the priest and the prophet have erred
28. 7 they err in vision, they stumble (in) judg.
Eze. 45. 20 thou shalt do..for every one that erreth
3. *To err, wander, go astray,* תָּעָה *taah.*
Psa. 95. 10 It (is) a people that do err in their heart
119. 110 yet I erred not from thy precepts
Prov.14. 22 Do they not err that devise evil? but
Isa. 29. 24 They also that erred in spirit shall come
35. 8 wayfaring men, though fools, shall not err
4. *To cause to err, wander, go astray,* תָּעָה *taah,* 5.
Prov 10. 17 but he that refuseth reproof erreth
5. *To wander off,* ἀποπλανάομαι *apoplanaomai.*
1 Ti. 6. 10 while some coveted after, they have erred
6. *To miss the mark, swerve,* ἀστοχέω *astocheō.*
1 Ti. 6. 21 Which some professing have erred concer.
2 Ti. 2. 18 Who concerning the truth have erred
7. *To wander,* πλανάομαι *planaomai.*
Matt22. 29 Ye do err, not knowing the Scriptures
Mark12. 24 Do ye not therefore err, because ye know
12. 27 God of the living: ye therefore do..err
Heb. 3. 10 They do alway err in (their) heart; and
Jas. 1. 16 Do not err, my beloved brethren
5. 19 if any of you do err from the truth

ERR, to cause to —
To cause to err, wander, go astray, תָּעָה *taah,* 5.
Isa. 3. 12 they which lead thee cause (thee) to err
9. 16 leaders of the people cause (them) to err
19. 14 they have caused Egypt to err in every
30. 28 in the jaws of the people, causing..to err
Jer 23. 13 prophesied..and caused my people..to err
23. 32 and cause my people to err by their lies
Hos. 4. 12 spirit of whoredoms have caused..to err
Amos 2. 4 their lies caused them to err, after the

ERR, to make (to) —
To cause to err, wander, go astray, תָּעָה *taah,* 5.
2 Ch.33. 9 So Manasseh made Judah..to err
Isa. 63. 17 O LORD, why hast thou made us to err
Mic. 3. 5 the prophets that make my people err

ERRAND —
Word, matter, דָּבָר *dabar.*
Gen.24. 33 I will not eat, until I have told mine err.
Judg.3. 19 I have a secret errand unto thee, O king
2 Ki. 9. 5 said, I have an errand to thee, O captain

ERROR —
1. *Error, oversight, wandering,* מְשׁוּגָה *meshugah.*
Job 19. 4 I have erred; mine error remaineth with
2. *Error, wandering,* שְׁגָגָה *shegagah.*
Eccl. 5. 6 neither say thou..that it (was) an error
10. 5 as an error (which) proceedeth from the
3. *Error, rashness,* שַׁל *shal.*
2 Sa. 6. 7 and God smote him there for (his) error
4. *Error, rashness, mistake,* שָׁלוּ *shalu.*
Dan. 6. 4 neither was there any error or fault found
5. *Error, injury,* תּוֹעָה *toah.*
Isa. 32. 6 iniquity..to utter error against the LORD
6. *Ignorance,* ἀγνόημα *agnoēma.*
Heb. 9. 7 he offered for himself, and (for) the errors
7. *Wandering,* πλάνη *planē.*
Matt 27. 64 so the last error shall be worse than the
Rom. 1. 27 that recompence of their error which was
Jas. 5. 20 which converteth the sinner from the e.
2 Pe. 2. 18 clean escaped from them who live in e.
3. 17 being led away with the error of the wi.
1 Jo. 4. 6 the spirit of truth, and the spirit of error
Jude 11 and ran greedily after the error of Balaam

ERRORS —

1. *Errors,* שְׁגִיאוֹת *shegioth.*
Psa. 19. 12 Who can understand (his) errors? cleanse

2. *Errors,* תַּעְתֻּעִים *tatuim.*
Jer. 10. 15 They (are) vanity, (and) the work of errors
51. 18 They (are) vanity, the work of errors

E-SA-I'-AS, Ἡσαΐας, Ἡσαΐας *the Greek form of Isaiah.*
Matt. 3. 3 For this is he that was spoken of by..E.
4. 14 be fulfilled which was spoken by E. the
8. 17 be fulfilled which was spoken by E. the
12. 17 be fulfilled which was spoken by E. the
13. 14 in them is fulfilled the prophecy of E.
15. 7 hypocrites, well did E. prophesy of you
Mark 7. 6 Well hath E. prophesied of you hypocrit.
Luke 3. 4 is written in the book of the words of E.
4. 17 was delivered unto him the book of..E.
John 1. 23 Make straight the way..as said..E.
12. 38 the saying of E. the prophet might be
12. 39 they could not believe, because that E.
12. 41 These things said E., when he saw his
Acts 8. 28 sitting in his chariot read E. the prophet
8. 30 and heard him read the prophet E.
28. 25 Well spake the Holy Ghost by E. the
Rom. 9. 27 E. also crieth concerning Israel, Though
9. 29 as E. said before, Except the Lord of S.
10. 16 E. saith, Lord, who hath believed our
10. 20 E. is very bold, and saith, I was found of
15. 12 E. saith, There shall be a root of Jesse

E-SAR-HAD'-DON, אֵסַר־חַדּוֹן *victorious, conqueror.*
One of the greatest of the kings of Assyria. He was son of Sennacherib and grandson of Sargon, who succeeded Shalmaneser. B.C. 698.
2 Ki. 19. 37 And E. his son reigned in his stead
Ezra 4. 2 do sacrifice unto him since the days of E.
Isa. 37. 38 And E. his son reigned in his stead

E'-SAU, עֵשָׂו Ἡσαῦ *hirsute, hairy.*
1. Eldest son of Isaac and twin brother of Jacob by Rebekah. B.C. 1837.
Gen. 25. 25 first came..and they called his name E.
25. 26 and his hand took hold on E.'s heel
25. 27 E. was a cunning hunter, a man of the
25. 28 Isaac loved E., because he did eat of (his)
25. 29 E. came from the field, and he (was) faint
25. 30 E. said to Jacob, Feed me, I pray thee
25. 32 E. said, Behold, I (am) at the point to die
25. 34 Jacob gave E. bread and pottage of lenti.
25. 34 thus E. despised (his) birthright
26. 34 E. was forty years old when he took to
27. 1 when Isaac was old..he called E. his
27. 5 Rebekah heard when Isaac spake to E.
27. 5 E. went to the field to hunt (for) venison
27. 6 I heard thy father speak unto E. thy
27. 11 Behold, E. my brother (is) a hairy man
27. 15 Re. took goodly raiment of her..son E.
27. 19 Jacob said unto his father, I (am) E.
27. 21 whether thou (be) my very son E. or not
27. 22 the hands (are) the hands of E.
27. 23 his hands were hairy, as his brother E.'s
27. 24 he said, (Art) thou my very son E.?
27. 30 E. his brother came in from his hunting
27. 32 he said, I (am) thy son, thy first born E.
27. 34 when E. heard the words of his father, he
27. 37 Isaac answered and said unto E., Behold
27. 38 E. said unto his father, Hast thou but one
27. 38 And E. lifted up his voice, and wept
27. 41 E. hated Jacob because of the blessing w.
27. 41 E. said in his heart, The days of mourn.
27. 42 these words of E...were told to Rebekah
27. 42 Behold, thy brother E...doth comfort
28. 5 the brother of Rebekah, Jacob's and E.'s
28. 6 When E. saw that Isaac had blessed Jac.
28. 8 E. seeing that the daughters of Canaan
28. 9 Then went E. unto Ishmael, and took
32. 3 Jacob sent messengers before him to E.
32. 4 Thus shall ye speak unto my lord E.
32. 6 We came to thy brother E., and also he
32. 8 If E. come to the one company, and
32. 11 Deliver..I pray thee, from the hand of E.
32. 13 and took..a present for E. his brother
32. 17 When E. my brother meeteth thee, and
32. 18 it (is) a present sent unto my lord E.
32. 19 On this manner shall ye speak unto E.
33. 1 E. came, and with him four hundred
33. 4 E. ran to meet him, and embraced him
33. 9 And E. said, I have enough, my brother
33. 15 E. said, Let me now leave with thee
33. 16 So E. returned that day on his way unto
35. 1 thou fleddest from the face of E. thy
35. 29 and his sons E. and Jacob buried him
36. 1 Now these..the generations of E., who
36. 2 E. took his wives of the daughters of C.
36. 4 Adah bare to E. Eliphaz; and Bashem.
36. 5 these..the sons of E., which were born
36. 6 E. took his wives, and his sons, and his
36. 8 Thus dwelt E. in mount Seir: E. (is) Ed.
36. 9 these..the generations of E. the father
36. 10 of E.'s sons..of Adah the wife of E.
36. 10 Reuel the son of Bashemath the wife of E.
36. 12 Eliphaz, E.'s son..the sons of Adah, E.'s
36. 13 these were the sons of Bashemath, E.'s
36. 14 daughter of Zibeon, E.'s wife..bare to E.
36. 15 sons of E...Eliphaz the first born..of E.
36. 17 of Reuel E.'s son..of Bashemath, E.'s wife
36. 18 of Aholibamah, E.'s wife..Anah, E.'s wife
36. 19 These (are) the sons of E., who (is) Edom
36. 40 these..the names of the dukes..of E.
36. 43 he (is) E. the father of the Edomites
Josh. 24. 4 And I gave unto Isaac Jacob and E.
24. 4 I gave unto E. mount Seir, to possess
1 Ch. 1. 34 The sons of Isaac; E. and Israel
1. 35 sons of E.; Eliphaz, Reuel, and Jeush
Mal. 1. 2 (Was) not E. Jacob's brother? saith the
1. 3 I hated E., and laid his mountains

2. The name Esau is sometimes (not often) used as a patronymic to denote the descendants of Esau or the country they dwelt in.
Deut. 2. 5 I have given mount Seir unto E...a poss.
Jer. 49. 8 I will bring the calamity of E. upon him
49. 10 I have made E. bare, I have uncovered
Obad. 6 How are (the things) of E. searched out!

So also in such elliptical expressions as these:—
Deut. 2. 4 Ye (are) to pass through the coast of..E.
2. 8 our brethren the children of E., which
2. 12 but the children of E. succeeded them
2. 22 As he did to the children of E., which
2. 29 As the children of E. which dwell in Seir
Obad. 8 and understanding out of the mount of E.?
9 every one of the mount of E. may be cut
18 and the house of E. for stubble, and
18 there shall not be..of the house of E.
19 the south shall possess the mount of E.
21; Rom. 9. 13; Heb. 11. 20; 12. 16.

ESCAPE —

1. *Place of escape,* מִפְלָט *miphlat.*
Psa. 55. 8 I would hasten my escape from the windy

2. *Escaped one,* פָּלֵט *palet.*
Jer. 44. 14 none shall return but such as shall escape
50. 28 The voice of them that flee and escape out
51. 50 Ye that have escaped the sword, go away

3. *Escape,* פַּלֵּט *pallet.*
Psa. 56. 7 Shall they escape by iniquity? in (thine)

4. *One escaped,* פָּלִיט *palit.*
Josh. 8. 22 that they let none of them remain or es.
2 Ki. 9. 15 let none go forth (nor) escape out of the
Jer. 42. 17 none of them shall remain or escape from
44. 14 none of the remnant..shall escape or re.

5. *Escape,* פְּלֵיטָה *peletah.*
Gen. 32. 8 the other company which is left shall es.
2 Sa. 15. 14 for we shall not (else) escape from Absal.
Jer. 50. 29 that bend the bow..let none thereof es.
Dan. 11. 42 and the land of Egypt shall not escape
Joel 2. 3 yea, and nothing shall escape them

ESCAPE, to —

1. *To go out or forth,* יָצָא *yatsa.*
1 Sa. 14. 41 Jonathan were taken: but the people es.
Jer. 11. 11 which they shall not be able to escape

2. *To escape, slip away,* מָלַט *malat,* 2.
Gen. 19. 17 Escape for thy life; look not behind thee
19. 17 escape to the mountain, lest thou be con.
19. 19 I cannot escape to the mountain, lest
19. 20 let me escape thither, (is) it not a little
19. 22 escape thither; for I cannot do any thing
Judg. 3. 26 And Ehud escaped while they tarried, and
3. 26 and passed beyond the quarries, and esc.
3. 29 men of valour; and there escaped not a
1 Sa. 19. 10 and David fled, and escaped that night
19. 12 and he went, and fled, and escaped
19. 18 So David fled, and escaped, and came to
22. 1 David..escaped to the cave Adullam: and
22. 20 Abiathar, escaped, and fled after David
27. 1 escape into the land of the Philistines
27. 1 so shall I escape out of his hand
30. 17 there escaped not a man of them, save
2 Sa. 4. 6 Rechab and Baanah his brother escaped
1 Ki. 18. 40 Elijah said..let not one of them escape
19. 17 him that escapeth the sword of Hazael
19. 17 him that escapeth from the sword of Jehu
20. 20 king of Syria escaped on an horse with
2 Ki. 10. 24 any..men..whom I have brought..escape
19. 37 and they escaped into the land of Arm.
2 Ch. 16. 7 king of Syria escaped out of thine hand
Esth. 4. 13 that thou shalt escape in the king's house
Prov 19. 5 (he that) speaketh lies shall not escape
Eccl. 7. 26 whoso pleaseth God shall escape from
Isa. 20. 6 we flee for help..and how shall we esc.?
37. 38 they escaped into the land of Armenia
Jer. 32. 4 Zedekiah king of Judah shall not escape
34. 3 thou shalt not escape out of his hand
38. 18, 23 thou shalt not escape out of their hand
41. 15 the son of Nethaniah escaped from Johan.
46. 6 Let not..the mighty man escape
48. 8 upon every city, and no city shall escape
48. 19 ask him that fleeth, and her that escapeth
Eze. 17. 15 shall he escape that doeth such (things)?
17. 18 done all these (things), she shall not esc.
Dan. 11. 41 these shall escape out of his hand, (even)

3. *To pass over,* עָבַר *abar.*
Psa. 141. 10 whilst that I withal escape

4. *To escape, slip away,* פָּלַט *palat.*
Eze. 7. 16 they that escape of them shall escape

5. *To deliver oneself,* נָצַל *natsal,* 5.
2 Sa. 20. 6 he get him fenced cities, and escape us

6. *To flee away,* ἀποφεύγω *apopheugō.*
2 Pe. 1. 4 having escaped the corruption that is in
2. 18 those that were clean escaped from them
2. 20 after they have escaped the pollutions

7. *To save thoroughly,* διασώζω *diasōzō.*
Acts 28. 1 when they were escaped, then they knew
28. 4 though he hath escaped the sea, yet

8. *To flee different ways,* διαφεύγω *diapheugō.*
Acts 27. 42 lest any of them should swim out and es.

9. *To flee out or forth,* ἐκφεύγω *ekpheugō.*
Luke 21. 36 ye may be accounted worthy to escape
Rom. 2. 3 thou shalt escape the judgment of God?
2 Co. 11. 33 in a basket was I let down..and escaped
1 Th. 5. 3 destruction cometh..they shall not escape
Heb. 2. 3 How shall we escape, if we neglect so

10. *To come out or forth,* ἐξέρχομαι *exerchomai.*
John 10. 39 to take him: but he escaped out of their

11. *To flee,* φεύγω *pheugō.*
Heb. 11. 34 escaped the edge of the sword, out of
12. 25 if they [escaped] not who refused him that

ESCAPE, can —
To flee from, φεύγω ἀπό *pheugō apo.*
Matt 23. 33 how can ye escape the damnation of hell?

ESCAPE, to cause to —
To let to escape, פָּלַט *palat,* 3.
Psa. 71. 2 cause me to escape: incline thine ear

ESCAPE, not —
Refuge has perished, אָבַד מָנוֹס *abad manos.*
Job 11. 20 wicked shall fail, and they shall not esc.

ESCAPE, that —
One that escapes or slips away, פָּלִיט *palet.*
Isa. 66. 19 I will send those that escape of them
Jer. 44. 28 escape the sword; Eze. 6. 8, 6. 9, 7. 16.

ESCAPE safe, to —
To save thoroughly, διασώζω *diasōzō.*
Acts 27 44 came to pass, that they escaped all safe

ESCAPE, way to —
A going up out of, ἔκβασις *ekbasis.*
1 Co 10. 13 but will..also make a way to escape

ESCAPED —
An escaped party, פְּלֵיטָה *peletah.*
2 Ch. 20. 24 fallen to the earth, and none escaped

ESCAPED, to be —

1. *To be slipped away,* מָלַט *malat,* 2.
1 Sa. 19. 17 sent away mine enemy, that he is escaped
23. 13 it was told Saul that David was escaped
2 Sa. 1. 3 Out of the camp of Israel am I escaped
Job 1. 15, 16, 17, 19 I only am escaped alone to tell
Psa. 124. 7 Our soul is escaped..and we are escaped

2. *To slip away for oneself,* מָלַט *malat,* 7.
Job 19. 20 I am escaped with the skin of my teeth

3. *To be snatched or slipt away,* נָצַל *natsal,* 2.
Deut 23. 15 the servant which is escaped from his

ESCAPED, that —

1. *One that escapes or slips away,* פָּלִיט *palet.*
Num 21. 29 Moab..he hath given his sons that escap.

2. *One that escapes or slips away,* פָּלִיט *palit.*
Gen. 14. 13 And there came one that had escaped
Judg 12. 5 those Ephraimites which were escaped
Isa. 45. 20 draw near together, ye (that are) escaped
Eze. 33. 21 one that had escaped out of Jerusalem
33. 22 evening, afore he that was escaped came

ESCAPED, that had —
Remnant, residue, שְׁאֵרִית *sheerith.*
2 Ch. 36. 20 And them that had escaped from the swo.

ESCAPED, that have —
One that slips away or escapes, פָּלֵט *palet.*
Jer. 51. 50 Ye that have escaped the sword, go away

ESCAPED, that is —
Escape, escaped party, פְּלֵיטָה *peletah.*
Exod 10. 5 eat the residue of that which is escaped
Judg 21. 17 an inheritance for them that be escaped
2 Ki. 19. 30 the remnant that is escaped of the house
1 Ch. 4. 43 the rest of the Amalekites that were esc.
2 Ch. 30. 6 that are escaped out of the hand of the
Neh. 1. 2 asked..concerning the Jews that had es.
Isa. 4. 2 comely for them that are escaped of Israel
10. 20 such as are escaped of the house of Jacob

ESCAPETH, that —
One that escapes or slips away, פָּלִיט *palit.*
Eze. 24. 26 he that escapeth in that day shall come
Amos 9. 1 he that escapeth of them shall not be

ESCAPING —
Escape, escaped party, פְּלֵיטָה *peletah.*
Ezra 9. 14 (there should be) no remnant nor escaping?

ESCHEW, to —

1. *To turn aside,* סוּר *sur.*
Job 1. 1 one that feared God, and eschewed evil
1. 8 one that feareth God, and escheweth evil?
2. 3 one that feareth God, and escheweth evil?

2. *To incline or bend out of,* ἐκκλίνω *ekklinō.*
1 Pe. 3. 11 Let him eschew evil, and do good; let

E'-SEK, עֵשֶׂק *contention.*
A well in the valley of Gerar, dug by the servants of Isaac, and striven for by the servants of Abimelech.
Gen. 26. 20 and he called the name of the well E.

ESH-BA'-AL, אֶשְׁבַּעַל *a man of Baal.*
Fourth son of Saul according to 1 Ch. 8. 33 and 9. 39. He is no doubt identical with *Ishbosheth* ("man of shame.")
1 Ch. 8. 33 and Malchi-shua, and Abinadab, and E.
9. 39 and Malchi-shua, and Abinadab, and E.

ESH'-BAN, אֶשְׁבָּן *man of understanding.*
A son of Dishon or Dishan, son of Seir.
Gen. 36. 26 Hemdan, and E., and Ithran, and Cheran
1 Ch. 1. 41 Amram, and E., and Ithran, and Cheran

ESH'-COL, אֶשְׁכֹּל, אֶשְׁכּוֹל *cluster of grapes.*
1. Brother of Mamre and Aner the Amorites, allies of Abraham in pursuing the four kings who had carried off Lot. B.C. 1918.
Gen. 14. 13 of Mamre the Amorite, brother of E.
14. 24 the men which went with me, Aner, E.

2. Valley or brook of Eshcol in the neighbourhood of Hebron, and explored by the spies sent out by Moses. In the valley that crosses the vale of Hebron N.E. and S.W. and about two miles N. of the town there is a fine spring now called *Ain-Eshkali.*
Num13. 23 they came unto the brook of E., and cut
13. 24 The place was called the brook E.
32. 9 they went up unto the valley of E., and
Deut. 1. 24 And they..came unto the valley of E.

ESH-E'-AN, אֶשְׁעָן *slope.*
A city in the mountains of Judah.
Josh.15. 52 Arab, and Dumah, and E.

E'-SHEK, עֵשֶׁק *strife.*
A descendant of Saul through Jonathan.
1 Ch. 8. 39 the sons of E. his brother..Ulam his

ESH-KA-LO-NITES, אֶשְׁקְלוֹנִי *belonging to Ashkelon.*
The inhabitants of Ashkelon.
Josh.13. 3 Ashdothites, the E., the Gittites, and

ESH-TA'-OL, אֶשְׁתָּאוֹל *hollow way.*
A town in the country of Judah, grouped with Zorah. It is now called *Stual* and is west of Zorah, which is now called *Surah.*
Josh.15. 33 in the valley, E., and Zoreah, and Ashnah
19. 41 coast of their inheritance was..E., and
Judg13. 25 the camp of Dan between Zorah and E.
16. 31 buried him between Zorah and E., in the
18. 2 men of valour, from Zorah, and from E.
18. 8 came unto their brethren to Zorah and E.
18. 11 there went from thence..out of E., six

ESH-TA-UL-ITES, אֶשְׁתָּאֻלִי *belonging to Eshtaol.*
The inhabitants of Eshtaol, descendants of Shobal son of Caleb son of Hur.
1 Ch. 2. 53 of them came the Zareathites..the E.

ESH-TE-MO'-A, ESH-TE'-MOH, אֶשְׁתְּמוֹעַ אֶשְׁתְּמֹה.
1. A Levitical town in the mountains of Judah. It is now called *Semua,* a village seven miles S of Hebron.
Josh.15. 50 And Anab, and E., and Anim
21. 14 Jattir..and E. with her suburbs
1 Sa. 30. 28 and to (them) which (were) in E.
1 Ch. 6. 57 to the sons of Aaron they gave..E. with

2. A Maachathite, a descendant of Ezra.
1 Ch. 4. 17 she bare..Ishbah the father of E.
4. 19 Keilah the Garmite, and E. the Maacha.

ESH'-TON, אֶשְׁתּוֹן *rest.*
Grandson of Chelub, through Caleb.
1 Ch. 4. 11 Mehir, which (was) the father of E.
4. 12 E. begat Beth-rapha, and Paseah, and

ES'-LI, Ἐσλί, Ἐσλεί.
This was probably *Azaliah* in the genealogy of Christ; the name occurs in the line of the ancestors of Joseph husband of Mary.
Luke 3. 25 Naum, which was (the son) of E., which

ESPECIALLY —
1. *Might,* מְאֹד *meod.*
Psa. 31. 11 I was a reproach..especially among my

2. *Most of all,* μάλιστα *malista.*
Acts 26. 3 Especially (because I know) thee to be
Gal. 6. 10 especially unto them who are of the hou.
1 Ti. 5. 17 especially they who labour in the word
2 Ti. 4. 13 the books, (but) especially the parchments

ESPOUSAL —
1. *Espousal, marriage,* חֲתֻנָּה *chathunnah.*
Song 3. 11 crowned him in the day of his espousals

2. *Espousals,* כְּלוּלוֹת *keluloth.*
Jer. 2. 2 the love of thine espousals, when thou

ESPOUSE, to —
1. *To betrothe, espouse,* אָרַשׂ *aras,* 3.
2 Sa. 3. 14 Deliver (me) my wife..which I espoused

2. *To be fitted together,* ἁρμόζομαι *harmozomai.*
2 Co.11. 2 for I have espoused you to one husband

ESPOUSED, to be —
To ask in marriage, μνηστεύω *mnēsteuō.*
Matt. 1. 18 When as his mother Mary was espoused
Luke 1. 27 To a virgin espoused to a man whose
2. 5 To be taxed with Mary his espoused wife

ESPY, to —
1. *To watch, look out,* צָפָה *tsaphah,* 3.
Jer. 48. 19 O inhabitant..stand by the way, and espy

2. *To see,* רָאָה *raah.*
Gen. 42. 27 as one of them opened his sack..he espied

3. *To search, spy out,* תּוּר *tur.*
Eze. 20. 6 into a land that I had espied for them

ESPY out, to —
To traverse, spy out, רָגַל *ragal,* 3.
Josh.14. 7 Moses..sent me..to espy out the land

ES'-ROM, Ἐσρώμ.
Son of Phares in the genealogy of Jesus.
Matt. 1. 3 Phares begat E.; and E. begat Aram
Luke 3. 33 Aram, which was (the son) of E., which

ESTABLISH, to —
1. *To strengthen, harden,* אָמַץ *amats,* 3.
Prov 8. 28 When he established the clouds above

2. *To found, lay a foundation,* יָסַד *yasad.*
Psa. 78. 69 like the earth which he hath established
Hab. 1. 12 thou hast established them for correction

3. *To set up, place, stay,* יָצַג *yatsag,* 5.
Amos 5. 15 love the good, and establish judgment

4. *To cause to dwell or sit, settle,* יָשַׁב *yashab,* 5.
Job 36. 7 he doth establish them for ever, and they

5. *To form, prepare, establish,* כּוּן *kun,* 3a.
Exod15. 17 the sanctuary..thy hands have establis.
Deut32. 6 hath he not made thee, and established
Psa. 24. 2 and established it upon the floods
40. 2 He brought me up..(and) established my
48. 8 God will establish it for ever. Selah
87. 5 the Highest himself shall establish her
90. 17 establish thou the work of our hands
90. 17 the work of our hands establish thou it
99. 4 thou dost establish equity, thou executest
119. 90 thou hast established the earth, and it
Prov 3. 19 by understanding hath he established the
Isa. 45. 18 he hath established it, he created it not
62. 7 And give him no rest, till he establish

6. *To prepare, establish,* כּוּן *kun,* 5.
1 Sa. 13. 13 now would the LORD have established
2 Sa. 5. 12 the LORD had established him king over
7. 12 will set up..and I will establish his kin.
1 Ki. 2. 24 the LORD liveth, which hath established
1 Ch.17. 11 raise up..and I will establish his kingd.
22. 10 I will establish the throne of his kingdom
28. 7 I will establish his kingdom for ever
2 Ch.12. 1 when Rehoboam had established the kin.
Psa. 89. 2 thy faithfulness shalt thou establish in
89. 4 Thy seed will I establish for ever, and
Jer. 10. 12 he hath established the world by his wis.
33. 2 the LORD that formed it, to establish it
51. 15 he hath established the world by his wis.

7. *To set up,* נָצַב *natsab,* 5.
Prov.15. 25 he will establish the border of the widow

8. *To support, stay,* סָעַד *saad.*
Isa. 9. 7 to establish it with judgment and with

9. *To cause to stand, set up, establish,* עָמַד *amad,* 5.
1 Ki.15. 4 set up his son after him; and to establish
2 Ch. 9. 8 loved Israel, to establish them for ever
30. 5 So they established a decree to make
Prov.29. 4 king by judgment establisheth the land
Dan. 11. 14 exalt themselves to establish the vision

10. *To raise up, establish, confirm,* קוּם *qum,* 5.
Gen. 6. 18 with thee will I establish my covenant
9. 9 I establish my covenant with you, and
9. 11 And I will establish my covenant with
9. 17 which I have established between me and
17. 7 I will establish my covenant between me
17. 19 I will establish my covenant with him
17 21 my covenant will I establish with Isaac
Exod. 6. 4 I have also established my covenant with
Lev. 26. 9 and establish my covenant with you
Num30. 13 Every vow..her husband may establish it
30. 14 he establisheth all her vows, or all her
Deut. 8. 18 he may establish his covenant which he
28. 9 The LORD shall establish thee an holy
29. 13 That he may establish thee to day for a
1 Sa. 1. 23 only the LORD establish his word
2 Sa. 7. 25 establish (it) for ever, and do as thou hast
1 Ki. 9. 5 I will establish the throne of thy kingdom
Psa. 78. 5 he established a testimony in Jacob, and
Prov 30. 4 established all the ends of the earth
Isa. 49. 8 to establish the earth, to cause to inherit
Eze. 16. 60 I will establish unto thee an everlasting
16. 62 I will establish my covenant with thee

11. *To establish,* קוּם *qum,* 3.
Dan. 6. 7 consulted together to establish a royal

12. *To raise up, establish,* קוּם *qum,* 5.
Dan. 6. 8 establish the decree, and sign the writing
6. 15 nor statute which the king establisheth

13. *To make firm, establish,* βεβαιόω *bebaioō.*
Heb. 13. 9 that the heart be established with grace

14. *To place, set, cause to stand,* ἵστημι *histēmi.*
Rom. 3. 31 God forbid: yea, we establish the law
10. 3 to establish their own righteousness
Heb. 10. 9 that he may establish the second

15. *To appoint a law,* νομοθετέω *nomotheteō.*
Heb. 8. 6 which was established upon better pro.

16. *To make stable, or strong,* στερεόω *stereoō.*
Acts 16. 5 so were the churches established in the

17. *To set or make fast, fix,* στηρίζω *stērizō.*
Rom. 1. 11 to the end ye may be established
1 Th. 3. 2 to establish you, and to comfort you
2 Pe. 1. 12 and be established in the present truth

ESTABLISHED —
To sustain, support, סָמַךְ *samak.*
Psa.112. 8 His heart (is) established, he shall not be

ESTABLISHED, to be —
1. *To be or become steady or firm,* אָמַן *aman,* 2.
1 Sa. 3. 20 established (to be) a prophet of the LORD
1 Ch.17. 23 concerning his house, be established for
17. 24 Let it even be established, that thy name
2 Ch. 1. 9 let thy promise unto David..be establish.
20. 20 Believe..so shall ye be established
Isa. 7. 9 surely ye shall not be established

2. *To be or become strong,* חָזַק *chazaq.*
2 Ch.25. 3 when the kingdom was established to him

3. *To be formed, prepared, established,* כּוּן *kun,* 2.
Gen. 41. 32 because the thing (is) established by God
1 Sa. 20. 31 shalt not be established, nor thy kingdom
2 Sa. 7. 16 shall be established for ever before thee
7. 26 house of thy servant David be established
1 Ki. 2. 12 and his kingdom was established greatly
2. 45 the throne of David shall be established
2. 46 kingdom was established in the hand of
1 Ch.17. 14 throne shall be established for evermore
17. 24 house of David thy servant be established
Job 21. 8 Their seed is established in their sight
Psa. 89. 21 With whom my hand shall be established
89. 37 It shall be established for ever as the
93. 2 Thy throne (is) established of old: thou
96. 10 world also shall be established that it
102. 28 seed shall be established before thee
140. 11 Let not an evil speaker be established in
Prov. 4. 26 and let all thy ways be established
12. 3 man shall not be established by wicked.
12. 19 lip of truth shall be established for
16. 3 and thy thoughts shall be established
16. 12 throne is established by righteousness
20. 18 (Every) purpose is established by counsel
25. 5 throne shall be established in righteous.
29. 14 his throne shall be established for ever
Isa. 2. 2 the mountain..shall be established in the
Jer. 30. 20 congregation shall be established before
Mic. 4. 1 the mountain..shall be established in the

4. *To be prepared, established,* כּוּן *kun,* 6.
Isa. 16. 5 in mercy shall the throne be established
Zech. 5. 11 it shall be established, and set there

5. *To establish self,* כּוּן *kun,* 7a.
Prov 24. 3 and by understanding it is established
Isa. 54. 14 In righteousness shalt thou be established

6. *To rise up, stand up, be established,* קוּם *qum.*
Lev. 25. 30 the house..shall be established for ever
1 Sa. 24. 20 kingdom of Israel shall be established
Job 22. 28 and it shall be established unto thee
Prov 15. 22 in the multitude..they are established

7. *To be made straight or right,* תְּקַן *teqan,* 6.
Dan. 4. 36 and I was established in my kingdom, and

8. *To cause to stand,* ἵστημι *histēmi.*
Matt18. 16 that..every word may be established
2 Co.13. 1 In the mouth..every word be established

ESTABLISHMENT —
Truth, faithfulness, steadfastness, אֱמֶת *emeth.*
2 Ch.32. 1 After these things, and the establishment

ESTATE —
1. *Order, condition,* דִּבְרָה *dibrah.*
Eccl. 3. 18 concerning the estate of the sons of men

2. *Station,* כֵּן *ken.*
Dan. 11. 7 shall (one) stand up in his estate, which
11. 20 Then shall stand up in his estate a
11. 21 in his estate shall stand up a vile person
11. 38 in his estate shall he honour the God of

3. *Form, turn,* תּוֹר *tor.*
1 Ch.17. 17 according to the estate of a man of high

ESTATE, your —
The things concerning you, τὰ περὶ ὑμῶν *ta peri.*
Col. 4. 8 that he might know [your] estate, and

ESTEEM, to —
1. *To think, reckon,* חָשַׁב *chashab.*
Job 41. 27 He esteemeth iron as straw, (and) brass
Isa. 53. 3 he was despised, and we esteemed him
53. 4 we did esteem him stricken, smitten of

2. *To set in array, value,* עָרַךְ *arak.*
Job 36. 19 Will he esteem thy riches? (no), not gold

3. *To lay up, hide, conceal,* צָפַן *tsaphan.*
Job 23. 12 I have esteemed the words of his mouth

4. *To lead, lead out,* ἡγέομαι *hēgeomai.*
Phil. 2. 3 each esteem other better than themselves
1 Th. 5. 13 to esteem them very highly in love for
Heb. 11. 26 Esteeming the reproach of Christ greater

5. *To judge,* κρίνω *krinō.*
Rom 14. 5 One man esteemeth one day above another
14. 5 another esteemeth every day (alike)

6 *To reckon,* λογίζομαι *logizomai.*
Rom 14. 14 that esteemeth any thing to be unclean

ESTEEMED, highly —
High, exalted, ὑψηλός *hupsēlos.*
Luke16. 15 that which is highly esteemed among men

ESTEEMED, to be —
To be reckoned, thought, esteemed, חָשַׁב *chashab,* 2.
Isa. 29. 16 shall be esteemed as the potter's clay
29 17 fruitful field shall be esteemed as a
Lam. 4. 2 are they esteemed as earthen pitchers

ESTEEMED, to be least —
To think nothing of, ἐξουθενέω *exoutheneō.*
1 Co. 6. 4 who are least esteemed in the church

ESTEEMED, to be lightly —

1. *To be lightly esteemed,* קָלָה *qalah,* 2.
1 Sa. 18. 23 I (am) a poor man, and lightly esteemed

2. *To be or become lightly esteemed,* קָלַל *qalal.*
1 Sa. 2. 30 that despise me shall be lightly esteemed

ES'-THER, אֶסְתֵּר *the planet Venus.*
The Persian name of *Hadassah,* daughter of Abihail son of Shimei son of Kish, a Benjamite (Mordecai), and cousin of Mordecai. She was an orphan captive, and was selected by Ahasuerus (Xerxes son of Darius Hystaspis) as his queen instead of Vashti. B.C. 479.

Esth. 2. 7 he brought up Hadassah, that (is), E.
2. 8 E. was brought also unto the king's house
2. 10 E. had not showed her people nor her
2. 11 Mordecai walked..to know how E. did
2. 15 when the turn of E...was come to go in
2. 15 E. obtained favour in the sight of all them
2. 16 E. was taken unto king Ahasuerus into
2. 17 the king loved E. above all the women
2. 18 the king made a great feast..E.'s feast
2. 20 E. had not..showed her kindred nor her
2. 20 E. did the commandment of Mordecai
2. 22 to Mordecai, who told (it) unto E. the
2. 22 E. certified the king..in Mordecai's name
4. 4 E.'s maids and her chamberlains came
4. 5 Then called E. for Hatach, (one) of the
4. 8 to show (it) unto E., and to declare (it)
4. 9 Hatach came and told E. the words of
4. 10 Again E. spake unto Hatach, and gave
4. 12 And they told to Mordecai E.'s words
4. 13 Then Mordecai commanded to answer E.
4. 15 Then E. bade..return Mordecai (this an.)
4. 17 did according to all that E. had comma.
5. 1 on the third day..E. put on..royal (app.)
5. 2 the king saw E. the queen standing in the
5. 2 the king held out to E. the golden sceptre
5. 2 E. drew near, and touched the top of the
5. 3 What wilt thou, queen E.? and what (is)
5. 4 E. answered, If..good unto the king, let
5. 5 that he may do as E. hath said
5. 5 came to the banquet that E had prepared
5. 6 the king said unto E. at the banquet of
5. 7 answered E., and said, My petition and my
5. 12 E. the queen did let no man come in
6. 14 bring Haman unto the banquet that E.
7. 1 Haman came to banquet with E. the qu.
7. 2 the king said again unto E. on the second
7. 2 What (is) thy petition, queen E.? and it
7. 3 Then E. the queen answered and said, If
7. 5 Ahasuerus answered and said unto E. the
7. 6 E. said, The adversary..(is) this wicked
7. 7 Haman stood up to make request..to E.
7. 8 Ha. was fallen upon the bed whereon E.
8. 1 did..give the house of Haman..unto E.
8. 1 for E. had told what he (was) unto her
8. 2 E. set Mordecai over the house of Haman
8. 3 And E. spake yet again before the king
8. 4 held out the golden sceptre toward E.
8. 4 So E. arose, and stood before the king
8. 7 king Ahasuerus said unto E. the queen
8. 7 Behold, I have given E. the house of Ha.
9. 12 And the king said unto E. the queen
9. 13 Then said E., If it please the king, let it
9. 29 Then E. the queen..wrote with all auth.
9. 31 according as..E. the queen had enjoined
9. 32 the decree of E. confirmed these matters

ESTIMATE, to —

To set in array, value, עָרַךְ *arak,* 5.
Lev. 27. 14 the priest shall estimate it, whether it
27. 14 as the priest shall estimate it, so shall

ESTIMATION —

Array, order, valuation, עֵרֶךְ *erek.*
Lev. 5. 15 with thy estimation by shekels of silver
5. 18 with thy estimation, for a trespass offering
6. 6 thy estimation, for a trespass offering
27. 2 (shall be) for the LORD by thy estimation
27. 3 thy estimation shall be of the male from
27. 3 thy estimation shall be fifty shekels of
27. 4 thy estimation shall be thirty shekels
27. 5 thy estimation shall be of the male twenty
27. 6 thy estimation shall be of the male five
27. 6 thy estimation shall be three shekels of
27. 7 thy estimation shall be fifteen shekels
27. 8 if he be poorer than thy estimation, then
27. 13 a fifth (part) thereof unto thy estimation
27. 15, 19 (part) of the money of thy estimation
27. 16 thy estimation shall be according to the
27. 17 according to thy estimation it shall stand
27. 18 it shall be abated from thy estimation
27. 23 shall reckon..the worth of thy estimation
27. 23 he shall give thine estimation in that
27. 25 thy estimations shall be according to the
27. 27 redeem (it) according to thine estimation
27 27 shall be sold according to thy estimation
Num 18. 16 thou redeem according to thine estima.

ESTRANGE, to —

To make unknown, נָכַר *nakar,* 3.
Jer. 19. 4 forsaken me, and have estranged this pla.

ESTRANGED, to be —

1. *To be strange, estranged,* זוּר *zur.*
Job 19. 13 mine acquaintance are verily estranged
Psa. 58. 3 The wicked are estranged from the womb
78. 30 They were not estranged from their lust

2. *To become strange, estranged,* זוּר *zur,* 2.
Eze. 14. 5 they are all estranged from me through

E'-TAM, עֵיטָם *wild beasts' lair.*

1. A village of the tribe of Simeon, now called *Urtas.*
1 Ch. 4. 32 their villages..E., and Ain, Rimmon, and

2. A place in Judah rebuilt by Rehoboam.
2 Ch. 11. 6 He built even Beth-lehem, and E., and

3. A name occurring in the list of Judah's descendants, but probably referring to the place named in No. 2.
1 Ch. 4. 3 And these (were of) the father of E.

4. A rocky district in the W. of Judah.
Judg 15. 8 went..and dwelt in the top of the rock E.
15. 11 Judah went to the top of the rock E.

ETERNAL —

1. *Age lasting,* עוֹלָם *olam.*
Isa. 60. 15 I will make thee an eternal excellency

2. *What is before in time or place,* קֶדֶם *qedem.*
Deut 33. 27 eternal God (is thy) refuge, and under.

3. *Perpetual,* ἀΐδιος *aidios.*
Rom. 1. 20 (even) his eternal power and Godhead

4. *Age,* αἰών *aiōn, (pl).*
Eph. 3. 11 According to the eternal purpose which
1 Ti. 1. 17 unto the King eternal, immortal, invisi.

5. *Age lasting,* αἰώνιος *aiōnios.*
Matt 19. 16 shall I do, that I may have eternal life
25. 46 but the righteous into life eternal
Mark 3. 29 but is in danger of eternal damnation
10. 17 what shall I do that I..inherit eternal
10. 30 and in the world to come eternal life
Luke 10. 25 what shall I do to inherit eternal life?
18. 18 what shall I do to inherit eternal life?
John 3. 15 should not perish, but have eternal life
4. 36 and gathereth fruit unto life eternal
5. 39 for in them ye think ye have eternal life
6. 54 Whoso eateth my flesh..hath eternal life
6. 68 thou hast the words of eternal life
10. 28 And I give unto them eternal life
12. 25 and he..shall keep it unto life eternal
17. 2 that he should give eternal life to as
17. 3 this is life eternal, that they might know
Acts 13. 48 as many as were ordained to eternal life
Rom. 2. 7 To them who..seek for glory..eternal life
5. 21 through righteousness unto eternal life
6. 23 the gift of God (is) eternal life through
2 Co. 4. 17 more exceeding (and) eternal weight of
4. 18 things which are not seen (are) eternal
5. 1 not made with hands, eternal in the
1 Ti. 6. 12 lay hold on eternal life, whereunto thou
6. 19 that they may lay hold on [eternal] life
2 Ti. 2. 10 obtain the salvation..with eternal glory
Titus 1. 2 In hope of eternal life, which God, that
3. 7 according to the hope of eternal life
Heb. 5. 9 he became the author of eternal salvation
6. 2 of resurrection..and of eternal judgment
9. 12 having obtained eternal redemption (for
9. 14 who through the eternal Spirit offered
9. 15 receive the promise of eternal inheritan.
1 Pe. 5. 10 who hath called us unto his eternal glory
1 Jo. 1. 2 show unto you that eternal life which
2. 25 he hath promised us, (even) eternal life
3. 15 no murderer hath eternal life abiding in
5. 11 God hath given to us eternal life, and
5. 13 ye may know that ye have eternal life
5. 20 This is the true God, and eternal life
Jude 7 suffering the vengeance of eternal fire
21 the mercy of our Lord..unto eternal life

ETERNITY —

Duration, continuity, עַד *ad.*
Isa. 57. 15 and lofty One that inhabiteth eternity

E'-THAM, אֵתָם.
The second station of Israel after leaving Egypt. It is said to be in the edge of the wilderness near the present *Seba Biar,* or "seven wells," about three miles from the western side of the ancient head of the gulf.
Exod 13. 20 took their journey..and encamped in E.
Num 33. 6 they departed..and pitched in E., which
33. 7 they removed from E., and turned again
33. 8 went three days' journey in the w. of E.

E'-THAN, אֵיתָן *ancient.*

1. A sage renowned in the time of Solomon.
1 Ki. 4. 31 he was wiser than all men; than E. the
Psa. 89. *title.* Maschil of E. the Ezrahite

2. A son of Zerah son of Judah.
1 Ch. 2. 6 Zimri, and E., and Heman, an Calcol
2. 8 And the sons of E.; Azariah

3. A descendant of Gershon son of Levi.
1 Ch. 6. 42 The son of E., the son of Zimmah, the son

4. A descendant of Merari the son of Levi.
1 Ch. 6. 44 E. the son of Kishi, the son of Abdi
15. 17 their brethren, E. the son of Kushaiah
15. 19 Asaph, and E...to sound with cymbals of

E-THA'-NIM, הָאֵתָנִים *the perennial.*
The seventh month of the sacred year of the Hebrews, from the last new moon of October till the first one of November.
1 Ki. 8. 2 the month E., which (is) the seventh

ETH-BA'-AL, אֶתְבַּעַל *with Baal or Baal's man.*
A king of Sidon, father of Jezebel wife of Ahab. He was king of the Tyrians as well, and is the same as *Eithobalus* (a priest of Astarte), who, after having murdered Pheles, held the throne of Tyre for thirty-two years.
1 Ki. 16. 31 took to wife Jezebel, the daughter of E.

E'-THER, עֶתֶר *riches, fulness.*
A city in the lowlands of Judah, afterwards allotted to Simeon, now *Athar.* In 1 Ch. 4. 32 *Tochen* is substituted for *Ether.*
Josh. 15. 42 Libnah, and E., and Ashan
19. 7 Ain, Remmon, and E., and Ashan; four

E-THI-O-PI-A, כּוּשׁ, Αἰθίοψ.
1. This is the word used by the Greeks and Romans for the Hebrew name *Cush.* Cush was the son of Ham, and his descendants occupied the country to the S. of Egypt, and comprehended, in its widest sense, the modern Nubia, Sennar, Kordofan, and northern Abyssinia, but in its more limited sense, only the kingdom of Meroe, from the junction of the White and Blue branches of the Nile to the S. border of Egypt. *Syene* was the division between both countries.
Gen. 2. 13 it that compasseth the whole land of E.
Esth. 1. 1 Ahasu...reigned from India even unto E.
8. 9 rulers of..provinces..from India unto E.
Job 28. 19 The topaz of E. shall not equal it
Psa. 87. 4 Tyre, with E.; this (man) was born there
Isa. 18. 1 land..which (is) beyond the rivers of E.
Eze. 29. 10 tower of Syene even unto the border of E.
Zeph. 3. 10 From beyond the rivers of E. my suppli.
Acts 8. 27 and, behold, a man of E., an eunuch

2. This name is also used to denote the people who occupied the land of *Cush.*
2 Ki. 19. 9 when he heard say of Tirhakah king of E.
Psa. 68. 31 E. shall soon stretch out her hands unto
Isa. 20. 3 sign and wonder upon Egypt and upon E.
20. 5 they shall be afraid and ashamed of E.
37. 9 heard say concerning Tirhakah king of E.
43. 3 Egypt (for) thy ransom, E. and Seba for
45. 14 labour of Egypt, and merchandise of E.
Eze. 30. 4 upon Egypt, and great pain shall be in E.
30. 5 E...and Lydia, and all the mingled peo.
38. 5 Persia, E., and Libya with them
Nah. 3. 9 E. and Egypt..her strength, and (it was)

E-THI-O-PI-AN, and E-THI-O-PI-ANS, כּוּשִׁי, כּוּשׁ, Αἰθίοψ.
The name generally given in the English Bible to the descendants of Cush son of Ham. It is used both as a noun and an adjective.
Num 12. 1 because of the E. woman whom he had
12. 1 for he had married an E. woman
2 Ch. 12. 3 the Lubims, the Sukkiims, and the E s.
14. 9 there came out against them Zerah the E.
14. 12 the LORD smote the E...and the E. fled
14. 13 the E. were overthrown, that they could
16. 8 Were not the E. and the Lubims a huge
21. 16 of the Arabians, that (were) near the E.
Isa. 20. 4 and the E. captives, young and old
Jer. 13. 23 Can the E. change his skin, or the leop.
38. 7 Ebed-melech the E., one of the eunuchs
38. 10 the king commanded Ebed-melech the E.
38. 12 Ebed-melech the E. said unto Jeremiah
39. 16 Go and speak to Ebed-melech the E., say
46. 9 the E. and the Libyans, that handle the
Eze. 30. 9 in ships to make the careless E. afraid
Dan. 11. 43 and the E. (shall be) at his steps
Amos 9. 7 (Are) ye not as children of the E unto me
Zeph. 2. 12 Ye E. also, ye (shall be) slain by my sword
Acts 8. 27 authority under Candace queen of the E.

ETH'-NAN, אֶתְנָן *gift.*
Grandson of Ashur through Caleb son of Hur. B C. 1500.
1 Ch. 4. 7 the sons of Helah..Zereth..and E.

ETH'-NI, אֶתְנִי *my gift.*
Ancestor of Asaph whom David set over the service of song. B.C. 1020.
1 Ch. 6. 41 The son of E., the son of Zerah

EU-BU'-LUS, Εὔβουλος.
A disciple at Rome who saluted Timothy.
2 Ti. 4. 21 E. greeteth thee, and Pudens, and Linus

EU-NI'-CE, Εὐνίκη.
Timothy's mother; in Acts 16. 1 she is spoken of as a "Jewess that believed."
2 Ti. 1. 5 grandmother Lois, and thy mother E.

EUNUCH —

1. *Eunuch, officer,* סָרִיס *saris.*
2 Ki. 9. 32 looked out to him two (or) three eunuchs
20. 18 they shall be eunuchs in the palace of
Isa. 39. 7 they shall be eunuchs in the palace of
56. 3 neither let the eunuch say, Behold, I (am)
56. 4 unto the eunuchs that keep my sabbaths
Jer. 29. 2 the king, and the queen, and the eunuchs
34. 19 the princes of Jerusalem, the eunuchs
38. 7 one of the eunuchs which was in the
41. 16 women, and the children, and the eunu.
52. 25 He took also out of the city an eunuch
Dan. 1. 3 Ashpenaz the master of his eunuchs
1. 7 whom the prince of the eunuchs gave
1. 8 he requested of the prince of the eunuch
1. 9 love with the prince of the eunuchs
1. 10 prince of the eunuchs said unto Daniel
1. 11 whom the prince of the eunuchs had set
1. 18 prince of the eunuchs brought them in

2. *Eunuch,* εὐνοῦχος *eunouchos.*
Matt. 19. 12 there are some eunuchs..are some eun.
19. 12 there be eunuchs, which have made
Acts 8. 27 an eunuch of great authority under
8. 34 the eunuch answered Philip, and said
8. 36 the eunuch said, See, (here is) water
8. 38 into the water, both Philip and the eunuch
8. 39 that the eunuch saw him no more

EUNUCH, to make —

To make a eunuch, εὐνουχίζω *eunouchizō.*

Matt 19. 12 which were made eunuchs of men
19. 12 which have made themselves eunuchs

EU-O-DI'-AS, Εὐωδία, Εὐοδία.

This name is more accurately *Euodia;* a Christian woman at Philippi. The two persons here mentioned by Paul are both women.

Phil. 4. 2 I beseech E., and beseech Syntyche, that

EU-PHRA'-TES, פְּרָת, Εὐφράτης *bursting, sweet.*

The River (*Ha-na-har* in Heb. often), as pre-eminently the river of Asia in contrast to the short-lived torrents of Canaan. Its modern name is *Frat,* which is nearly the Hebrew spelling. It rises in Armenia, flows S. like the Tigris, and falls into the Persian Gulf.

Gen. 2. 14 And the fourth river (is) E.
15. 18 from the river of Egypt unto..the river E.
Deut. 1. 7 Lebanon, unto the..river, the river E.
11. 24 from..the river E., even unto the utter.
Josh. 1. 4 From the wilderness..unto the..river E.
2 Sa. 8. 3 to recover his border at the river E.
2 Ki. 23. 29 against the king of Assyria to the..E.
24. 7 from the river of Egypt unto the river E.
1 Ch. 5. 9 of the wilderness from the river E.
18. 3 to stablish his dominion by the river E.
2 Ch. 35. 20 up to fight against Carchemish by E.
Jer. 13. 4 arise, go to E., and hide it there in a hole
13. 5 So I went, and hid it by E., as the LORD
13. 6 Arise, go to E., and take the girdle from
13. 7 Then I went to E., and digged, and took
46. 2 against the army..which was by the..E.
46. 6 and fall toward the north by the river E.
46. 10 a sacrifice in the north..by the river E.
51. 63 and cast it into the midst of E.
Rev. 9. 14 angels which are bound in the great..E.
16. 12 poured out his vial upon the..river E.

EU-RO-CLY'-DON, Εὐροκλύδων, Εὐρυκλύδων, Εὐρακύλων.

A tempestuous wind often experienced by navigators in the Levant; it blows from N.E. or E.N.E. The name really means the united winds *Eurus* and *Aquilo.*

Acts 27. 14 there arose..a tempestuous wind, called E.

EU-TY'-CHUS, Εὔτυχος.

A young man of Troas restored to life.

Acts 20. 9 in a window a certain young man named E.

EVANGELIST —

One who announces good tidings, εὐαγγελιστής.

Acts 21. 8 into the house of Philip the evangelist
Eph. 4. 11 and some, prophets; and some, evangel.
2 Ti. 4. 5 do the work of an evangelist, make full

EVE, חַוָּה, Εὔα *life, life-giving.*

The name of the first woman.

Gen. 3. 20 And Adam called his wife's name E.
4. 1 Adam knew E. his wife; and she concei.
2 Co. 11. 3 as the serpent beguiled E. through his
1 Ti. 2. 13 For Adam was first formed, then E.

EVEN —

1. *Only,* אַךְ *ak.*

Exod. 12. 15 even the first day ye shall put away

2. *Also,* אַף *aph.*

Lev. 26. 28 I, even I, will chastise you seven times

3. *Even, also,* גַּם *gam.*

Gen. 20. 5 even she herself said, He (is) my brother

4. *Lo, lo as,* הָא *he.*

Dan. 2. 43 even as iron is not mixed with clay

5. *That, when, because,* כִּי *ki.*

Exod. 32. 29 even every man upon his son, and upon

6. *Till, unto, during, which,* עַד *ad.*

Lev. 23. 16 Even unto the morrow after the seventh

7. *Only, surely, nevertheless,* רַק *raq.*

2 Ch. 28. 10 (are there) not with you, even with you

8. *For, verily then,* γάρ *gar.*

Jas. 4. 14 It is [even] a vapour, that appeareth for a

9. *But, moreover,* δέ *de.*

Rom. 3. 22 Even the righteousness of God (which is)
9. 30 even the righteousness which is of faith
Phil. 2. 8 unto death, even the death of the cross

10. *Any more, any longer, yet, still,* ἔτι *eti.*

Luke 1. 15 the Holy Ghost, even from his mother's

11. *Unto, up to,* ἕως *heōs.*

Mark 14. 54 even into the palace of the high priest

12 *And, even,* καί *kai.*

Matt. 5. 46 do not even the publicans the same?
5. 47 do not even the publicans so?
7. 12 should do to you, do ye even so to them
8. 27 that even the winds and the sea obey
12. 8 Son of man is Lord even of the sabbath
13. 12 shall be taken away even that he hath
18. 33 compassion..[even] as I had pity on thee?
20. 14 give unto this last even as unto thee
25. 29 be taken away even that which he hath
Mark 1. 27 commandeth he even the unclean spirits
4. 25 shall be taken even that which he hath
4. 41 that even the wind and the sea obey him?
6. 2 even such mighty works are wrought by
13. 22 seduce, if (it were) possible, even the
Luke 8. 18 taken even that which he seemeth to
8. 25 he commandeth even the winds and
9. 54 and consume them, even as Elias did
10. 11 Even the very dust of your city, which
12. 41 this parable unto us, or even to all
12. 57 why even of yourselves judge ye not
18. 11 unjust, adulterers, or even as this publi.
19. 26 even that he hath shall be taken away
19. 42 known, even thou, at least in this thy day
20. 37 even Moses showed at the bush, when he
24. 24 found (it)[even] so as the women had said
John 5. 21 even so the Son quickeneth whom he will
8. 25 Even (the same) that I said unto you from
11. 22 even now, whatsoever thou wilt ask of
11. 37 that even this man should not have died
Acts 15. 8 the Holy Ghost, even as (he did) unto us
26. 11 persecuted (them) even unto strange cit.
Rom. 1. 13 you also, even as among other Gentiles
5. 14 even over them that had not sinned after
5. 18 even so by the righteousness of one (the)
5. 21 even so might grace reign through
8. 23 even we ourselves groan within ourselves
8. 34 who is [even] at the right hand of God
9. 24 Even us, whom he hath called, not of the
11. 5 Even so then at this present time also
15. 3 even Christ pleased not himself; but, as
15. 6 even the Father of our Lord Jesus Christ
1 Co. 2. 11 even so the things of God knoweth no
3. 5 even as the Lord gave to every man?
7. 7 would that all men were even as I myself
9. 14 Even so hath the Lord ordained that
14. 12 Even so ye, forasmuch as ye are zealous
15. 22 even so in Christ shall all be made alive
15. 24 the kingdom to God, even the Father
16. 1 as I have given order..even so do ye
2 Co. 1. 3 even the Father of our Lord Jesus Christ
1. 8 insomuch that we despaired even of life
1. 13 ye shall acknowledge [even] to the end
7. 14 even so our boasting, which (I made) be.
10. 7 as he (is) Christ's, even so (are) we Christ's
10. 13 a measure to reach even unto you
11. 12 wherein they glory they may be..even as
Gal. 2. 16 even we have believed in Jesus Christ
4. 3 Even so we, when we were children, were
4. 29 (born) after the Spirit, even so (it is) now
5. 12 would they were even cut off which tro.
Eph. 2. 3 the children of wrath, even as others
4. 4 even as ye are called in one hope of your
4. 32 even as God for Christ's sake hath forgi.
5. 12 For it is a shame even to speak of those
5. 23 even as Christ is the head of the church
5. 29 cherisheth it, even as the Lord the church
Phil. 1. 15 preach Christ even of envy and strife
3. 15 God shall reveal even this unto you
3. 18 and now tell you even weeping, (that they)
4. 16 even in Thessalonica ye sent once and
Col. 3. 13 even as Christ forgave you, so also (do)
1 Th. 2. 14 suffered..even as they (have) of the Jews
2. 19 (Are) not even ye in the presence of our
3. 4 even as it came to pass, and ye know
3. 12 toward all (men), even as we (do) toward
3. 13 in holiness before God, even our Father
4. 5 even as the Gentiles which know not God
4. 13 even as others which have no hope
2 Th. 2. 16 [even] our Father, which hath loved us
3. 1 and be glorified, even as (it is) with you
Phm. 19 owest unto me even thine own self besides
Heb. 7. 4 [even] the patriarch Abraham gave the
11. 12 sprang there even of one and him as good
11. 19 able to raise (him) up, even from the de.
Jas. 2. 17 Even so faith, if it hath not works, is
3. 5 Even so the tongue is a little member
2 Pe. 1. 14 even as our Lord Jesus Christ hath show.
2. 1 even denying the Lord that bought them
Jude 23 hating even the garment spotted by the
Rev. 2. 13 [even] in those days wherein Antipas
17. 11 even he is the eighth, and is of the seven
18. 6 Reward her even as she rewarded you

13. *Indeed, truly,* μέν *men.*

1 Th. 2. 18 come unto you, even I Paul, once and

14. *Thus, so,* οὕτω, οὕτως *houtō, houtōs.*

Acts 27. 25 that it shall be even as it was told me

15. *And, also,* τε *te.*

Rom. 1. 26 even their women did change the natural

16. *Right, righteousness, just,* צֶדֶק *tsedeq.*

Job 31. 6 Let me be weighed in an even balance

EVEN —

1. *Evening,* עֶרֶב *ereb.*

*Exod 16. 12 At even ye shall eat flesh, and in the
18. 14 stand by thee from morning unto even
*29. 39, 41 other lamb thou shalt offer at even
*30. 8 when Aaron lighteth the lamps at even
Lev. 11. 24, 27, 31, 32, 39 be unclean until the even
11. 25, 28, 40, 40 and be unclean until the even
14. 46 shall be unclean until the even
15. 5, 6, 7, 8, 10, 11, 16, 17 unclean until the e.
15. 10, 18, 19, 21, 22, 23, 27 unclean until the e.
17. 15 bathe..and be unclean until the even
22. 6 any such shall be unclean until even
*23. 5 fourteenth (day) of the first month at even
*Num. 9. 3 at even, ye shall keep it in his appointed
*9. 5 fourteenth day of the first month at even
*9. 11 fourteenth day of the second month at e.
9. 21 cloud abode from even unto the morning
19. 7 priest shall be unclean until the even
19. 8, 10 be unclean until the even; 19. 21, 22.
*28. 4, 8 the other lamb shalt thou offer at even
Deut 28. 67 thou shalt say Would God it were even!

*Heb., *between the two evening times.*

Judg 20. 23 and wept before the LORD until even, and
20. 26 fasted that day until even, and offered
21. 2 and abode there till even before God
Ruth 2. 17 she gleaned in the field until even, and
2 Sa. 1. 12 and fasted until even, for Saul, and for
2 Ch. 18. 34 stayed (himself) up..until the even
Eze. 12. 7 in the even I digged through the wall

2. *Late (in the evening),* ὀψέ *opse.*

Mark 11. 19 when even was come, he went out of the

3. *Evening,* ὀψία *opsia.*

Matt. 8. 16 When the even was come, they brought
20. 8 So when even was come, the lord of the
26. 20 when the even was come, he sat down
27. 57 When the even was come, there came a
Mark 4. 35 when the even was come, he saith unto
6. 47 when even was come, the ship was in the
15. 42 when the even was come, because it was
John 6. 16 when even was (now) come, his disciples

EVEN, at —

1. *Evening,* עֶרֶב *ereb.*

Gen. 19. 1 there came two angels to Sodom at even
Exod 12. 18 the fourteenth day of the month at even
12. 18 and twentieth day of the month at even
16. 6 At even, then ye shall know that the LORD
16. 13 at even the quails came up, and covered
Lev. 23. 32 in the ninth (day) of the month at even
Num. 9. 15 at even there was upon the tabernacle as
19. 19 bathe himself..and shall be clean at even
Deut 16. 4 thou sacrificedst the first day at even
16. 6 thou shalt sacrifice the passover at even
28. 67 at even thou shalt say, Would God it
Josh. 5. 10 the fourteenth day of the month at even
Judg 19. 16 from his work out of the field at even
1 Sa. 20. 5 in the field unto the third (day) at even
2 Sa. 11. 13; 1 Ki. 22. 35; 1 Ch. 23. 30; Eze. 12. 4.

2. *Evening having come,* ὀψίας γενομένης.

Mark 1. 32 And at even, when the sun did set

3. *Late (in the evening),* ὀψέ *opse.*

Mark 13. 35 at even, or at midnight, or at the cock

EVEN as —

1. *Even as,* καθάπερ *kathaper.*

Rom. 4. 6 Even as David also describeth the bless.
2 Co. 1. 14 even as ye also (are) ours in the day of

2. *According as,* καθώς *kathōs.*

Mark 11. 6 said unto them even as Jesus had comm.
Luke 1. 2 Even as they delivered them unto us
19. 32 and found even as he had said unto them
John 5. 23 the Son, even as they honour the Father
12. 50 even as the Father said unto me, so I
15. 10 even as I have kept my Father's comman.
17. 14, 16 even as I am not of the world
17. 22 that they may be one, even as we are one
Rom. 1. 28 even as they did not like to retain God
1 Co. 1. 6 Even as the testimony of Christ was
11. 1 followers of me, even as I also (am) of Chr.
13. 12 then shall I know even as also I am
Gal. 3. 6 Even as Abraham believed God, and it
Phil. 1. 7 Even as it is meet for me to think this
1 Th. 5. 11 and edify one another, even as also ye do
1 Jo. 2. 6 ought..also so to walk, even as he walked
2. 27 even as it hath taught you, ye shall abide
3. 3 purifieth himself, even as he is pure
3. 7 is righteous, even as he is righteous
3 Jo. 2 be in health, even as thy soul prospereth
3 even as thou walkest in the truth

3. *In what turn or manner,* ὃν τρόπον *hon tropon.*

Matt. 23. 37 even as a hen gathereth her chickens

4. *So, according to what manner,* (οὕτως) καθ' ὃν τρόπον. (*houtōs*) *kath' hon tropon.*

Acts 15. 11 believe..we shall be saved, even as they
27. 25 that it shall be even as it was told me

5. *As,* ὡς *hōs.*

Matt 15. 28 be it unto thee even as thou wilt
Mark 4. 36 they took him even as he was in the ship
1 Co. 12. 2 Gentiles, carried away..even as ye were
Eph. 5. 33 every one..love his wife even as himself
1 Pe. 3. 6 Even as Sara obeyed Abraham, calling
Jude 7 Even as Sodom and Gomorrha, and the

6. *Even as,* ὥσπερ *hōsper.*

Matt. 5. 48 [even as] your Father which is in heaven
20. 28 Even as the Son of man came not to be

EVEN like —

As, according as, ὡς *hōs.*

Rev. 21. 11 even like a jasper stone, clear as crystal

EVEN ..not —

Not even, οὐδέ *oude.*

John 21. 25 even the world itself could not contain

EVEN now —

1. *To day,* הַיּוֹם *hay-yom.*

Deut. 31. 21 even now, before I have brought them

2. *Now,* ἄρτι *arti.*

Matt. 9. 18 My daughter is even now dead: but

3. *Now, already,* ἤδη *ēdē.*

Luke 19. 37 even now at the descent of the mount of

EVEN place —

Uprightness, a plain, מִישׁוֹר *mishor.*

Psa. 26. 12 My foot standeth in an even place : in

EVEN so —

1. *As thus,* כָּכָה *kakah.*

Jer. 19. 11 Even so will I break this people, and this

2. *So, thus,* כֵּן *ken.*
Exod39. 43 LORD..commanded, even so had they

3. *Yes, yea,* ναί *nai.*
Matt11. 26 Even so, Father; for so it seemed good in
Luke10. 21 even so, Father; for so it seemed good
Rev. 1. 7 shall wail because of him. Even so. A.
16. 7 Even so, Lord God Almighty, true and
22. 20 come quickly. Amen. [Even so], come

4. *Thus, so,* οὕτω, οὕτως *houtō, houtōs.*
Matt. 7. 17 Even so every good tree bringeth forth
12. 45 Even so shall it be also unto this wicked
18. 14 Even so it is not the will of your Father
23. 28 Even so ye also outwardly appear right.
John 3. 14 even so must the Son of man be lifted
14. 31 Father gave me commandment, even so
Acts 12. 15 constantly affirmed that it was even so
Rom. 6. 4 even so we also should walk in newness
6. 19 even so now yield your members servants
11. 31 Even so have these also now not believed
1 Co. 11. 12 even so (is) the man also by the woman
1 Th. 2. 4 But as we were allowed..even so we
4. 14 even so them also which sleep in Jesus

5. *Even so,* ὡσαύτως *hōsautōs.*
1 Ti. 3. 11 Even so (must their) wives (be) grave

EVEN to, unto, until —

1. *Unto,* עַד *ad.*
Exod27. 5 may be even to the midst of the altar

2. *Unto, up to,* ἕως *heōs.*
Matt26 38 is exceeding sorrowful, even unto death
2 Co. 3. 15 even unto this day, when; 1 Jo. 2. 9.

3. *Until, as far as,* ἄχρι ἄχρις *achri achris.*
Acts 11. 5 a great sheet..and it came; Heb. 4. 12.
1 Co. 4 11 even unto this present hour

EVEN thus —
According to these things, κατὰ ταῦτα *kata tauta.*
Luke17. 30 Even thus shall it be in the day when the

EVEN...very —
And, καί *kai.*
Luke12. 7 even the very hairs of your head are all

EVEN, also —
And, καί *kai.*
Luke 6. 33 have ye? for sinners also do even the same

EVEN, and —

1. *And,* καί *kai.*
1 Jo. 4. 3 and even now already is it in the world

2. *Yet even, at the same time,* ὅμως *homōs.*
1 Co. 14. 7 even things without life giving sound

EVENING —

1. *To do (it) in the evening,* עָרַב *arab,* 5.
1 Sa. 17. 16 Philistine drew near morning and evening

2. *Evening,* עֶרֶב *ereb.*
Gen. 1. 5, 8, 13, 19, 23, 31 evening and the morning
*8. 11 the dove came in to him in the evening
24. 11 at the time of the evening, (even) the time
29. 23 it came to pass in the evening, that he
30. 16 Jacob came out of the field in the even.
†Exod12. 6 Israel shall kill it in the evening
16. 8 shall give you in the evening flesh to eat
18. 13 stood..from the morning unto the even.
27. 21 shall order it from evening to morning
Lev. 24. 3 order it from the evening unto the morn.
Deut23. 11 when evening cometh on, he shall wash
Josh10. 26 hanging upon the trees until the evening
1 Sa. 14. 24 man that eateth (any) food until evening
30. 17 even unto the evening of the next day
1 Ki.17. 6 and bread and flesh in the evening
2 Ki.16. 15 the evening meat offering, and the king's
1 Ch.16. 40 offering continually morning and evening
2 Ch. 2. 4 the burnt offerings morning and evening
13. 11 every morning and every evening burnt
13. 11 the lamps thereof, to burn every evening
31. 3 the morning and evening burnt offerings
Ezra 3. 3 (even) burnt offerings morning and even.
9. 4 sat astonied until the evening sacrifice
9. 5 at the evening sacrifice I arose up from
Esth. 2. 14 In the evening she went, and on the mor.
Job 4. 20 They are destroyed from morning to ev.
Psa. 55. 17 Evening, and morning, and at noon, will
59. 6 They return at evening; they make a
59. 14 at evening let them return; (and)
65. 8 outgoings of the morning and evening
90. 6 in the evening it is cut down, and with.
104. 23 and to his labour until the evening
141. 2 lifting up of my hands (as) the evening
‡Prov. 7. 9 in the evening, in the black and dark
Eccl.11. 6 in the evening withhold not thine hand
Jer. 6. 4 shadows of the evening are stretched out
Eze. 33. 22 hand of the LORD..upon me in the even.
46. 2 gate shall not be shut until the evening
Dan. 8. 26 the vision of the evening and the morn.
9. 21 about the time of the evening oblation
Hab. 1. 8 are more fierce than the evening wolves
Zeph. 2. 7 shall they lie down in the evening
3. 3 her judges (are) evening wolves; they
Zech 14. 7 (that) at evening time it shall be light

3. *A plain, wilderness, Arabah,* עֲרָבָה *arabah.*
Jer. 5. 6 a wolf of the evenings shall spoil them,

4. *Evening, eventide,* ἑσπέρα *hespera.*
Luke24. 29 it is toward evening, and; Acts 28. 23.

*Hebrew, *eth ereb.* †Hebrew, *between the two evening times.* ‡Hebrew, *ereb yom.*

5. *Evening,* ὀψία *opsia.*
Matt14. 15 when it was evening, his disciples came
16. 2 When it is evening, ye say, (It will be)

EVENING, at —
It being late, οὔσης ὀψίας *ousēs opsias.*
John20. 19 the same day at evening, being the first

EVENING, in the —
Evening having come, ὀψίας γενομένης *opsias gen.*
Mark14. 17 in the evening he cometh with the twelve

EVENING, toward —
To be late, לַעֲרוֹב *la-arob.*
Judg19. 9 the day draweth toward evening, I pray

EVENING tide, or eventide —

1. *Time of evening,* עֵת עֶרֶב *eth ereb.*
2 Sa. 11. 2 it came to pass in an evening tide, that
Isa. 17. 14 behold at evening tide trouble; (and)

2. *Evening,* ἑσπέρα *hespera.*
Acts 4. 3 unto the next day: for it was now even.

3. *The hour being late,* ὀψίας τῆς ὥρας. [*hōra*].
Mark11. 11 the eventide was come, he went out unto

EVENT —
Chance, occurrence, event, מִקְרֶה *miqreh.*
Eccl. 2. 14 also that one event happeneth to them all
9. 2 (there is) one event to the righteous, and
9. 3 that (there is) one event unto all

EVENTIDE —

1. *Evening,* עֶרֶב *ereb.*
Josh. 7. 6 and fell to the earth..until the eventide

2. *Time of evening,* עֵת עֶרֶב *eth ereb.*
Josh. 8. 29 of Ai he hanged on a tree until eventide

3. *Approach of evening,* פְּנוֹת עֶרֶב *penoth ereb.*
Gen. 24. 63 to meditate in the field at the eventide

EVER —

1. *To pre-eminence, perpetuity,* לָנֶצַח *la-netsach.*
Isa. 28. 28 he will not ever be threshing it, 33. 20.

2. *Age, age-lasting,* עוֹלָם *olam.*
Gen. 13. 15 will I give it, and to thy seed for ever
Exod12. 24 ordinance to thee and..thy sons for ever
27. 21 (It shall be) a statute for ever unto their
28. 43 (It shall be) a statute for ever unto him
29. 28 a statute for ever from the children of
30. 21 it shall be a statute for ever to them
Lev. 6. 18 (It shall be) a statute for ever in your
6. 22 (it is) a statute for ever unto the LORD
7. 34 by a statute for ever from among the
7. 36 (by) a statute for ever throughout their
10. 9 (it shall be) a statute for ever throughout
10. 15 it shall be thine..by a statute for ever
16. 29 (this) shall be a statute for ever unto you
16. 31 afflict your souls, by a statute for ever
17. 7 This shall be a statute for ever unto them
23. 14, 21, 31, 41 (it shall be) a statute for ever
24. 3 (it shall be) a statute for ever in your
Num10. 8 shall be to you for an ordinance for ever
15. 15 an ordinance for ever in your generations
18. 8 and to thy sons, by an ordinance for ever
18. 11, 19, daughters with thee, by a statute for e.
18. 23 (It shall be) a statute for ever through.
19. 10 unto the stranger..for a statute for ever
Deut12. 28 and with thy children after thee for ever
13. 16 it shall be an heap for ever; it shall not
15. 17 and he shall be thy servant for ever
23. 3 not enter into the congregation..for ever
28. 46 be upon thee..and upon thy seed for ever
29. 29 unto us and to our children for ever
Josh. 4. 7 unto the children of Israel for ever
8. 28 made it an heap for ever, (even) a desola.
14. 9 inheritance, and thy children's for ever
1 Sa. 1. 22 before the LORD, and there abide for ever
2. 30 thy house..should walk before me for e.
3. 13 that I will judge his house for ever for
3. 14 not be purged with sacrifice..for ever
13. 13 established..kingdom upon Israel for ev.
20. 15 cut..thy kindness from my house for ev.
20. 23 the LORD (be) between thee and me for e.
20. 42 and between my seed and thy seed for ev.
27. 12 therefore he shall be my servant for ever
2 Sa. 3. 28 (are) guiltless before the LORD for ever
7. 13 establish..throne of his kingdom for ever
7. 16 shall be established for ever before thee
7. 16 thy throne shall be established for ever
7. 24 Israel (to be) a people unto thee for ever
7. 25 concerning his house, establish (it) for ev.
7. 26 let thy name be magnified for ever
1 Ki. 2. 33 there be peace for ever from the LORD
2. 45 be established before the LORD for ever
8. 13 settled place for..to abide in for ever
9. 3 this house..to put my name there for ever
1 Ch.15. 2 chosen..to minister unto him for ever
16. 36 Blessed (be) the LORD God..for ever and e.
17. 12 and I will establish his throne for ever
17. 14 in mine house and in my kingdom for ever
17. 22 didst thou make thine own people for ev.
17. 23 let the thing..be established for ever
17. 24 that thy name may be magnified for ever
22. 10 and I will establish the throne..for ever
23. 13 he and his sons for ever, to burn incense
23. 13 and to bless in his name for ever
28. 8 for your children after you for ever
2 Ch. 6. 2 and a place for thy dwelling for ever
7. 16 house, that my name may be there for e.
Ezra 9. 12 nor seek their peace or their wealth for e.
9. 12 an inheritance to your children for ever
Neh. 9. 5 bless the LORD your God for ever and ever
Neh. 13. 1 not come into the congregation..for ever
Job 41. 4 wilt thou take him for a servant for ever?
Psa. 5. 11 let them ever shout for joy, because thou
10. 16 The LORD (is) King for ever and
21. 4 (even) length of days for ever and
28. 9 feed them also, and lift them up for ever
45. 6 Thy throne, O God, (is) for ever and
48. 8 God will establish it for ever
48. 14 For this God (is) our God for ever and
52. 8 I trust in the mercy of God for ever and
61. 4 I will abide in thy tabernacle for ever
61. 7 He shall abide before God for ever
66. 7 He ruleth by his power for ever; his
89. 1 sing of the mercies of the LORD for ever
89. 2 said, Mercy shall be built up for ever
89. 4 Thy seed will I establish for ever, and
89. 37 It shall be established for ever as the
104. 5 (that) it should not be removed for ever
111. 5 he will ever be mindful of his covenant
111. 8 They stand fast for..ever, (and are)
119. 98 mine enemies; for they (are) ever with
125. 2 his people from henceforth, even for ever
131. 3 in the LORD from henceforth and for ever
148. 6 also established them for..ever
Isa. 9. 7 justice from henceforth even for ever
30. 8 for the time to come for..ever
32. 14 and towers shall be for dens for ever
32. 17 quietness and assurance for ever
34. 17 they shall possess it for ever, from gener.
59. 21 saith the LORD..henceforth and for ever
Jer. 7. 7 I gave to your fathers, for ever and ever
17. 4 kindled a fire..(which) shall burn for ever
25. 5 you and to your fathers for ever and ever
35. 6 drink no wine..ye, nor your sons for ever
49. 33 And Hazor shall be..a desolation for ever
51. 26 thou shalt be desolate for ever, saith the
51. 62 but that it shall be desolate for ever
Eze. 37. 25 and their children's children, for ever
Dan. 12. 7 sware by him that liveth for ever, that
Joel 2. 2 there hath not been ever the like, neither
Mic. 4. 7 the LORD shall reign over them..for ever
Mal. 1. 4 whom the LORD hath indignation for ever

3. *To strive,* רִיב *rib.*
Judg11. 25 did he ever strive against Israel, or did

4. *Continually,* תָּמִיד *tamid.*
Psa. 25. 15 Mine eyes (are) ever toward the LORD; for
51. 3 and my sin (is) ever before me

5. *What is before (in time or place),* קֶדֶם *qedem.*
Prov. 8. 23 from the beginning, or ever the earth was

6. *Always, aye,* ἀεί *aei.*
Mark15. 8 (him to do) as he had ever done unto

7. *To the age,* εἰς τὸν αἰῶνα *eis ton aiōna.*
Heb. 7. 24 this (man), because he continueth ever

8. *To all the ages,* εἰς πάντας τοὺς αἰῶνας *eis pantas.*
Jude 25 dominion and power, both now and ever

9. *Alway, at all time,* πάντοτε *pantote.*
Luke15. 31 Son, thou art ever with me, and all that
John18. 20 I ever taught in the synagogue, and in
1 Th. 4. 17 so shall we ever be with the Lord
5. 15 ever follow that which is good, both
2 Ti. 3. 7 Ever learning, and never able to come to
Heb. 7. 25 he ever liveth to make intercession for

EVER, for —

1. *To pre-eminence, perpetuity,* לָנֶצַח *la-netsach,* נֶצַח *netsach.*
2 Sa. 2. 26 Shall the sword devour for ever? knowest
Job 4. 20 perish for ever without any regarding
14. 20 Thou prevailest for ever against him, and
20. 7 shall perish for ever like his own dung
23. 7 should I be delivered for ever from my
36. 7 he doth establish them for ever, and they
Psa. 13. 1 How long wilt thou forget..O LORD? for e.?
44. 23 O LORD? arise, cast (us) not off for ever
49. 9 he should still live for ever, (and) not see
52. 5 God shall likewise destroy thee for ever
68. 16 yea, the LORD will dwell (in it) for ever
74. 1 O God, why hast thou cast (us) off for e.?
74. 10 the enemy blaspheme thy name for ever?
74 19 forget not the congregation..for ever
77. 8 Is his mercy clean gone for ever? doth
79. 5 wilt thou be angry for ever? shall thy
89. 46 wilt thou hide thyself for ever? shall thy
Jer. 50. 39 it shall be no more inhabited for ever
Lam. 5. 20 Wherefore dost thou forget us for ever
Amos 1. 11 and he kept his wrath for ever

2. *Duration, continuity,* עַד *ad.*
Num24. 20 end (shall be) that he perish for ever
24. 24 Eber, and he also shall perish for ever
1 Ch.28. 9 forsake him, he will cast thee off for ever
Job 19. 24 they were graven..in the rock for ever
Psa. 9. 18 expectation..shall (not) perish for ever
19. 9 The fear of the LORD..enduring for ever
21. 6 thou hast made him most blessed for ever
22. 26 your heart shall live for ever
37. 29 righteous shall..dwell therein for ever
61. 8 will I sing praise unto thy name for ever
83. 17 them be confounded and troubled for ever
89. 29 seed also will I make (to endure) for ever
92. 7 that they shall be destroyed for ever
111. 3 and his righteousness endureth for ever
111. 8 They stand fast for ever and
111. 10 his praise endureth for ever
112. 3, 9 his righteousness endureth for ever
132. 14 This (is) my rest for ever: here will I
148. 6 also stablished them for ever and ever
Prov 12. 19 lip of truth shall be established for ever

Prov 29. 14 his throne shall be established for ever
Isa. 26. 4 Trust ye in the LORD for ever: for in the
64. 9 LORD, neither remember iniquity for ever
65. 18 rejoice for ever (in that) which I create
Mic. 7. 18 he retaineth not his anger for ever, because

3. *Age-lasting*, לְעוֹלָם, עַד־עוֹלָם. (*le* or *ad*) *olam.*
Gen. 3. 22 take also of the tree..and live for ever
Exod 3. 15 this (is) my name for ever, and this (is)
12. 14 keep it a feast by an ordinance for ever
12. 17 ye observe..by an ordinance for ever
14. 13 ye shall see them again no more for ever
19. 9 people may hear..and believe thee for ev.
21. 6 and he shall serve him for ever
31. 17 a sign between me and..Israel for ever
32. 13 seed, and they shall inherit (it) for ever
Lev. 25. 46 they shall be your bondmen for ever: but
Num18. 19 it (is) a covenant of salt for ever before
Deut. 5. 29 with them, and with their children for e.
23. 6 nor their prosperity all thy days for ever
32. 40 lift up my hand..and say, I live for ever
2 Sa. 7. 29 that it may continue for ever before thee
7. 29 house of thy servant be blessed for ever
1 Ki. 1. 31 said, Let my lord king David live for ever
2. 33 and upon the head of his seed for ever
2. 33 shall there be peace for ever from the
9. 5 Then I will establish the throne..for ever
10. 9 because the LORD loved Israel for ever
2 Ki. 5. 27 unto thee, and unto thy seed for ever
21. 7 In this house..will I put my name for ever
1 Ch. 16. 34 (he is) good..his mercy (endureth) for ever
16. 41 because his mercy (endureth) for ever
17. 27 that it may be before thee for ever
23. 25 that they may dwell in Jerusalem for ever
28. 4 chose me..to be king over Israel for ever
28. 7 I will establish his kingdom for ever, if
29. 18 keep this for ever in the imagination of
2 Ch. 2. 4 This (is an ordinance) for ever to Israel
5. 13 (he is) good..his mercy (endureth) for e.
7. 3 (he is) good..his mercy (endureth) for ever
7. 6 because his mercy (endureth) for ever
9. 8 loved Israel, to establish them for ever
13. 5 gave the kingdom..to David for ever
20. 7 gavest it to the seed of Abraham..for ever
20. 21 Praise the LORD..mercy (endureth) for e.
30. 8 which he hath sanctified for ever
33. 4 In Jerusalem shall my name be for ever
Ezra 3. 11 his mercy (endureth) for ever toward Is.
Neh. 2. 3 Let the king live for ever: why should
Psa. 9. 7 the LORD shall endure for ever: he hath
12. 7 preserve..from this generation for ever
29. 10 yea, the LORD sitteth King for ever
30. 12 God, I will give thanks unto thee for ever
33. 11 The counsel of the LORD standeth for e.
37. 18 and their inheritance shall be for ever
37. 28 they are preserved for ever: but the seed
41. 12 and settest me before thy face for ever
44. 8 we boast..and praise thy name for ever
45. 2 therefore God hath blessed thee for ever
49. 8 For the redemption..ceaseth for ever
49. 11 (that) their houses (shall continue) for e.
52. 9 I will praise thee for ever, because thou
72. 17 His name shall endure for ever: his name
72. 19 And blessed (be) his glorious name for e.
73. 26 of my heart, and my portion for ever
75. 9 I will declare for ever; I will sing praises
77. 7 Will the Lord cast off for ever? and will
78. 69 earth which he hath established for ever
79. 13 So we..will give thee thanks for ever
81. 15 their time should have endured for ever
85. 5 Wilt thou be angry with us for ever? wilt
89. 36 His seed shall endure for ever, and his
102. 12 thou, O LORD, shalt endure for ever, and
103. 9 neither will he keep (his anger) for ever
104. 31 glory of the LORD shall endure for ever
105. 8 He hath remembered his covenant for e.
106. 1 (he is) good..his mercy (endureth) for e.
107. 1 (he is) good..his mercy (endureth) for e.
110. 4 Thou (art) a priest for ever after the order
111. 9 he hath commanded his covenant for e.
112. 6 Surely he shall not be moved for ever
117. 2 the truth of the LORD (endureth) for ever
118. 1, 2, 3, 4, 29 his mercy (endureth) for ever
119. 89 For ever, O LORD, thy word is settled in
119. 111 testimonies..taken as an heritage for ever
119. 152 that thou hast founded them for ever
119. 160 thy righteous judgments (endureth) for e.
125. 1 cannot be removed, (but) abideth for e.
135. 13 Thy name, O LORD, (endureth) for ever
136. 1, 2, 3, 4, 5 for his mercy (endureth) for ev.
[So in v. 6, 7, 8, 9, 10, 11, 12, 13, 14, 15, 16, 17, 18, 19, 20, 21, 22, 23, 24, 25, 26.]
138. 8 thy mercy, O LORD, (endureth) for ever
146. 6 which keepeth truth for ever
146. 10 The LORD shall reign for ever, (even) thy
Prov 27. 24 riches (are) not for ever: and doth the
Eccl. 1. 4 but the earth abideth for ever
2. 16 no remembrance of the wise..for ever
3. 14 whatsoever God doeth, it shall be for ev.
9. 6 neither have they..more a portion for e.
Isa. 34. 10 the smoke thereof shall go up for ever
40. 8 the word of our God shall stand for ever
47. 7 thou saidst, I shall be a lady for ever
51. 6 but my salvation shall be for ever, and
51. 8 my righteousness shall be for ever, and
57. 16 I will not contend for ever, neither will
60. 21 they shall inherit the land for ever, the
Jer. 3. 5 Will he reserve (his anger) for ever? will
3. 12 (and) I will not keep (anger) for ever
17. 25 and this city shall remain for ever
31. 40 nor thrown down any more for ever
33. 11 good; for his mercy (endureth) for ever
Lam. 3. 31 For the Lord will not cast off for ever
5. 19 Thou, O LORD, remainest for ever; thy
Eze. 37. 25 and their children's children for ever
37. 25 David (shall be) their prince for ever
43. 7 midst of the children of Israel for ever
43. 9 will dwell in the midst of them for ever
Hos. 2. 19 And I will betroth thee unto me for ever
Joel 3. 20 Judah shall dwell for ever, and Jerusa.
Obad. 10 and thou shalt be cut off for ever
Jon. 2. 6 earth with her bars (was) about me for e.
Mic. 2. 9 have ye taken away my glory for ever
Zech. 1. 5 and the prophets, do they live for ever?

4. *To the age*, לְעֵילוֹם *le-elom.*
2 Ch. 33. 7 In this house..will I put my name for e.

5. *Hidden time*, עָלַם *alam.*
Dan. 2. 4 O king, live for ever: tell thy servants the
2. 44 and the kingdom..shall stand for ever
3. 9 They spake and said..O king, live for ever
4. 34 honoured him that liveth for ever, whose
5. 10 O king, live for ever: let not thy thoughts
6. 6 and said thus..King Darius, live for ever
6. 21 Then said Daniel..O king, live for ever
6. 26 (is) the living God, and stedfast for ever

6. *A cutting off, extinction*, צְמִיתֻת *tsemithuth.*
Lev. 25. 23 The land shall not be sold for ever: for
25. 30 walled city shall be established for ever

7. *For length of days*, לְאֹרֶךְ יָמִים *le-orek yamim.*
Psa. 23. 6 dwell in the house of the LORD for ever
93. 5 holiness becometh thine house..for ever

8. *Age-lasting*, αἰώνιος *aiōnios.*
Phm. 15 that thou shouldest receive him for ever

9. *To the age*, εἰς αἰῶνα *eis aiōna.*
Matt. 6. 13 and the power, and the glory for ever
21. 19 no fruit grow on thee henceforward for ev.
Mark 11. 14 No man eat fruit of thee..for ever
Luke 1. 33 reign over the house of Jacob for ever
1. 55 to Abraham, and to his seed [for ever]
John 6. 51 eat of this bread, he shall live for ever
6. 58 eateth of this bread shall live for ever
8. 35 servant abideth not in the house for ever
8. 35 (but) the Son abideth ever
12. 34 We have heard..Christ abideth for ever
14. 16 that he may abide with you for ever
Rom. 1. 25 than the Creator, who is blessed for ever
9. 5 who is over all, God blessed for ever
11. 36 (are) all things: to whom (be) glory for e.
16. 27 (be) glory, through Jesus Christ for ever
2 Co. 9. 9 his righteousness remaineth for ever
Heb. 5. 6 Thou (art) a priest for ever after the
6. 20 (even) Jesus, made an high priest for ever
7. 17, 21 Thou (art) a priest for ever, after the
13. 8 same yesterday, and to day, and for ever
1 Pe. 1. 23 word..which liveth and abideth [for ever]
1. 25 the word of the Lord endureth for ever
2 Pe. 2. 17 the mist of darkness is reserved [for ever]
1 Jo. 2. 17 doeth the will of God abideth for ever
2 Jo. 2 dwelleth in us..shall be with us for ever
Jude 13 reserved..blackness of darkness for ever

10. *To the day of the age*, εἰς ἡμέραν αἰῶνος.
2 Pe. 3. 18 To him (be) glory both now and for ever

11. *Continuously*, εἰς τὸ διηνεκές *eis to diēnekes.*
Heb. 10. 12 had offered one sacrifice for sins for ever
10. 14 perfected for ever them that are sancti.

EVER (and ever), for —

1. *To perpetuity*, לְנֵצַח נְצָחִים *le-netsach netsachim.*
Isa. 34. 10 none shall pass through it for ever and ev.

2. *To the age and onward*, לְעוֹלָם וָעֶד *le-olam va-ed.*
Exod 15 18 The LORD shall reign for ever and ever
Psa. 9. 5 hast put out their name for ever and ever
10. 16 The LORD (is) king for ever and ever
21. 4 (even) length of days for ever and ever
45. 6 Thy throne, O God, (is) for ever and ever
45. 17 the people praise thee for ever and ever
48. 14 For this God (is) our God for ever and ever
52. 8 I trust in the mercy of God for ever and e.
104. 5 (that) it should not be removed for ever
111. 8 They stand fast for ever and ever, (and are)
119. 44 keep thy law continually for ever and ev.
145. 1 I will bless thy name for ever and ever
145. 2 I will praise thy name for ever and ever
145. 21 bless his holy name for ever and ever
Isa. 30. 8 be for the time to come for ever and ever
Dan. 12. 3 shine..as the stars for ever and ever
Mic. 4. 5 name of the LORD..God for ever and ev.

3. *From eternity to eternity*, מִן הָעוֹלָם וְעַד הָעוֹלָם [*olam*].
1 Ch. 16. 36 Blessed (be) the LORD..for ever and ever
29. 10 Blessed (be) thou, LORD.. for ever and e.
Neh. 9. 5 bless the LORD your God for ever and e.

4. *From age even unto age*, מִן־עָלְמָא וְעַד עָלְמָא [*alema*].
Dan. 2. 20 Blessed be the name..for ever and ever
7. 18 kingdom for ever, even for ever and ever

5. *To ages of ages*, εἰς αἰῶνας αἰώνων [*aiōn*].
Rev. 14 11 smoke..ascendeth up for ever and ever

6. *To the age of the age*, εἰς τὸν αἰῶνα τοῦ αἰῶνος.
Heb. 1. 8 Thy throne, O God, (is) for ever and ever

7. *To the ages of the ages*, εἰς τοὺς αἰῶνας τῶν αἰώνων [*aiōn*].
Gal. 1. 5 To whom (be) glory for ever and ever. A.
Phil. 4. 20 Now unto God..(be) glory for ever and e.
1 Ti. 1. 17 (be) honour and glory for ever and ever
2 Ti. 4. 18 to whom (be) glory for ever and ever. A.
Heb. 13. 21 to whom (be) glory for ever [and ever]. A.
1 Pe. 4. 11 be praise and dominion for ever and ever
5. 11 (be) glory and dominion for ever [and ev.]
Rev. 1. 6 (be) glory and dominion for ever [and ev.]
4. 9 to him..who liveth for ever and ever
4. 10 worship him that liveth for ever and ever
5. 13 and unto the Lamb for ever and ever
5. 14 worshipped him..[liveth for ever and ev.]
7. 12 (be) unto our God for ever and ever, Am.
10. 6 sware by him that liveth for ever and ever
11. 15 and he shall reign for ever and ever
15. 7 wrath of God, who liveth for ever and e.
19. 3 And her smoke rose up for ever and ever
20. 10 tormented day and night for ever and e.
22. 5 and they shall reign for ever and ever

EVER yet —

Once, at any time, ποτέ *pote.*
Eph. 5. 29 no man ever yet hated his own flesh; but

EVER, or —

Before, πρό *pro.*
Acts 23. 15 we, or ever he come near, are ready to

EVER of old —

Age, age-lasting, עוֹלָם *olam.*
Psa. 25. 6 mercies..for they (have been) ever of old

EVERLASTING —

1. *Duration, continuity*, עַד *ad.*
Isa. 9. 6 everlasting Father, The Prince of Peace
Hab. 3. 6 the everlasting mountains were scattered

2. *Age, age-lasting*, עוֹלָם *olam.*
Gen. 9. 16 I may remember the everlasting coven.
17. 7 for an everlasting covenant, to be a God
17. 8 Canaan, for an everlasting possession
17. 13 my covenant..for an everlasting covenant
17. 19 with him for an everlasting covenant
21. 33 the name of the LORD, the everlasting G.
48. 4 this land..(for) an everlasting possession
49. 26 the utmost bound of the everlasting hills
Exod 40. 15 shall surely be an everlasting priesthood
Lev. 16. 34 shall be an everlasting statute unto you
24. 8 (being taken)..by an everlasting covenant
Num 25. 13 the covenant of an everlasting priesthood
Deut 33. 27 and underneath (are) the everlasting arms
2 Sa. 23. 5 hath made with me an everlasting cove.
1 Ch. 16. 17 (and) to Israel (for) an everlasting cove.
Psa. 24. 7 and be ye lift up, ye everlasting doors
24. 9 even lift (them) up, ye everlasting doors
41. 13 God..from everlasting, and to everlasting
90. 2 from everlasting to everlasting, thou (art)
93. 2 of old; thou (art) from everlasting
100. 5 the LORD is good; his mercy (is) everlast.
103. 17 LORD (is) from everlasting to everlasting
105. 10 (and) to Israel (for) an everlasting cove.
106. 48 Blessed..from everlasting to everlasting
112. 6 righteous shall be in everlasting remem.
119. 142 righteousness (is)..everlasting right.
119. 144 Thy righteousness..(is) an everlasting
139. 24 and lead me in the way everlasting
145. 13 Thy kingdom (is) an everlasting kingdom
Prov. 8. 23 I was set up from everlasting, from the
10. 25 righteous (is) an everlasting foundation
Isa. 24. 5 have..broken the everlasting covenant
26. 4 the LORD JEHOVAH (is) everlasting stre
33. 14 shall dwell with everlasting burnings?
35. 10 and everlasting joy upon their heads
40. 28 thou not heard, (that) the everlasting God
45. 17 be saved..with an everlasting salvation
51. 11 everlasting joy (shall be) upon their head
54. 8 with everlasting kindness will I have
55. 3 I will make an everlasting covenant with
55. 13 for an everlasting sign (that) shall not be
56. 5 I will give them an everlasting name
60. 19 shall be unto thee an everlasting light
60. 20 the LORD shall be thine everlasting light
61. 7 everlasting joy shall be unto them
61. 8 make an everlasting covenant with them
63. 12 to make himself an everlasting name
63. 16 our Redeemer; thy name (is) from ever.
Jer. 10. 10 the living God, and an everlasting king
20. 11 (their) everlasting confusion shall never
23. 40 bring an everlasting reproach upon you
31. 3 have loved thee with an everlasting love
32. 40 make an everlasting covenant with them
Eze. 16. 60 establish unto thee an everlasting coven.
37. 26 be an everlasting covenant with them
Dan. 9. 24 to bring in everlasting righteousness, and
12. 2 some to everlasting life, and some to..ev.
Mic. 5. 2 (have been) from of old, from everlasting
Hab. 3. 6 hills did bow: his ways (are) everlasting

3. *Age, age-lasting*, עָלַם *alam.*
Dan. 4. 3 his kingdom (is) an everlasting kingdom
4. 34 whose dominion (is) an everlasting dom.
7. 14 his dominion (is) an everlasting dominion
7. 27 whose kingdom (is) an everlasting king.

4. *What is before (in time or place)*, קֶדֶם *qedem.*
Hab. 1. 12 (Art) thou not from everlasting, O LORD

5. *Perpetual*, ἀΐδιος *aidios.*
Jude 6 he hath reserved in everlasting chains

6. *Age-lasting*, αἰώνιος *aiōnios.*
Matt 18. 8 or two feet to be cast into everlasting fire
19. 29 and shall inherit everlasting life
25. 41 Depart..ye cursed, into everlasting fire
25. 46 shall go away into everlasting punishment
Luke 16. 9 receive you into everlasting habitations
18. 30 and in the world to come life everlasting
John 3. 16 not perish, but have everlasting life
3. 36 believeth on the Son hath everlasting

John 4. 14 water springing up into everlasting life
5. 24 hath everlasting life, and shall not come
6. 27 meat which endureth unto everlasting
6. 40 believeth on him, may have everlasting
6. 47 believeth on me hath everlasting life
12. 50 that his commandment is life everlasting
Acts 13. 46 yourselves unworthy of everlasting life
Rom. 6. 22 holiness, and the end everlasting life
16. 26 the commandment of the everlasting God
Gal. 6. 8 shall of the Spirit reap life everlasting
2 Th. 1. 9 be punished with everlasting destruction
2. 16 hath given (us) everlasting c nsolation
1 Ti. 1. 16 believe on him to life everlasting
6. 16 to whom (be) honour and power everlas.
Heb. 13. 20 the blood of the everlasting covenant
2 Pe. 1. 11 abundantly into the everlasting kingdom
Rev. 14. 6 having the everlasting gospel to preach

EVER MORE —

1. *Pre-eminence, perpetuity,* נֵצַח *netsach.*
Psa. 16. 11 (there are) pleasures for evermore

2. *Age, age-lasting,* עוֹלָם *olam.*
2 Sa. 22. 51 unto David, and to his seed for evermore
1 Ch. 17. 14 throne shall be established for evermore
Psa. 18. 50 to David, and to his seed for evermore
106. 31 for righteousness unto all..for evermore
113. 2 from this time forth and for evermore
115. 18 from this time forth and for evermore
121. 8 from this time forth, and even for ever.
133. 3 the blessing, (even) life for evermore

3. *Continual, continually,* תָּמִיד *tamid.*
Psa. 105. 4 Seek the LORD..seek his face evermore

4. *To the age,* εἰς τὸν αἰῶνα. [*aiōn*].
2 Co. 11. 31 Jesus Christ, which is blessed for ever.
Heb. 7. 28 the Son, who is consecrated for evermore

5. *To the ages of the ages,* εἰς τοὺς αἰῶνας τῶν αἰώνων.
Rev. 1. 18 I am alive for evermore, Amen; and

6. *Alway, at all time,* πάντοτε *pantote.*
John 6. 34 Lord, evermore give us this bread
1 Th. 5. 16 Rejoice evermore

7. *To generation and generation,* לְדֹר וָדֹר *le-dor va-dor.*
Psa. 77. 8 doth (his) promise fail for evermore?

8. *All the days,* כָּל־הַיָּמִים *kol hay-yamim.*
Deut. 28 29 be only oppressed and spoiled evermore

EVER MORE, for —

1. *Durations of duration,* עֲדֵי־עַד *ade ad.*
Psa. 132. 12 also sit upon thy throne for evermore

2. *To the age,* לְעוֹלָם *le-olam.*
Psa. 37. 27 and do good; and dwell for evermore
86. 12 and I will glorify thy name for evermore
89. 28 My mercy will I keep for him for everm.
89. 52 Blessed (be) the LORD for evermore Am.
92. 8 But thou, LORD, (art most) high for ever.
Eze. 37. 26 my sanctuary in the midst..for evermore
37. 28 be in the midst of them for evermore

EVERY (in, out of, throughout, which) —

1. *One,* אֶחָד *echad.*
Exod 36. 30 of silver, under every board two sockets
Num 29. 14 three tenth deals unto every bullock
Josh. 3. 12 twelve men..out of every tribe of man
1 Ki. 7. 38 (and) every laver was four cubits: (and)

2. *A man,* אִישׁ *ish.*
1 Ki. 7. 30 undersetters..at the side of every addition

3. *A woman,* אִשָּׁה *ishshah.*
Amos 4. 3 every (cow at that which is) before her

4. *A man which,* אִישׁ אֲשֶׁר *ish asher.*
Gen. 49. 28 every one according to his blessing he

5. *All, every,* כָּל־ *kol.*
Gen. 7. 4 every living substance that I have made
Psa. 39. 5 every man at his best state (is) altogether
Dan. 3. 10 every man that shall hear the sound
3. 29 every people, nation, and language
6. 12 every man that shall ask (a petition) of
6. 26 in every dominion of my kingdom men

6. *Each one,* εἷς ἕκαστος *heis hekastos.*
Eph. 4. 16 working in the measure of every part

7. *Each,* ἕκαστος *hekastos.*
Luke 4. 40 he laid his hands on every one of them
6. 44 For every tree is known by his own fruit
16. 5 he called every one of his lord's debtors
John 19. 23 made four parts, to every soldier a part
Acts 17. 27 though he be not far from every one of
20. 31 I ceased not to warn every one night and
21. 26 should be offered for every one of them
1 Co. 12. 18 the members every one of them in the
15. 38 God giveth..to every seed his own body
Eph. 4. 7 But unto every one of us is given grace
1 Th. 2. 11 comforted and charged every one of you
2 Th. 1. 3 charity of every one of you all toward

8. *Down along or during,* κατά *kata,* (acc.)
Luke 2. 41 his parents went to Jerusalem every year
16. 19 and fared sumptuously every day
Heb. 9. 25 entereth into the holy place every year
10. 3; Luke 8. 1, 4; Acts 14. 23; 15. 21; 20. 23.

9. *Down through each one,* κατὰ ἕνα ἕκαστον.
Rev. 22. 2 (and) yielded her fruit [every] month

10. *All, every,* πᾶς *pas.*
Matt. 3. 10 every tree which bringeth not forth good
Matt. 4. 4 by every word that proceedeth out of
7. 17 every good tree bringeth forth good
7. 19 Every tree that bringeth not forth good
9. 35 healing every sickness and every disease
12. 25 Every kingdom divided against itself is
12. 25 every city or house divided against itself
12. 36 every idle word that men shall speak
13. 47 into the sea, and gathered of every kind
13. 52 every scribe (which is) instructed unto
15. 13 Every plant, which my heavenly Father
18. 16 that..every word may be established
19. 3 man to put away his wife for every cause?
Mark 9. 49 [every sacrifice shall be salted with salt]
16 15 [and preach the Gospel to every creature]
Luke 2. 23 Every male that openeth the womb shall
3. 5 Every valley shall be filled, and every
3. 9 every tree therefore which bringeth not
4. 4 [by bread alone, but by every word of]
4. 37 every place of the country round about
5. 17 were come out of every town of Galilee
10. 1 before his face into every city and place
11. 17 Every kingdom divided against itself is
John 1. 9 which lighteth every man that cometh
2. 10 Every man at the beginning doth set
15. 2 Every branch in me that beareth not fr.
15. 2 every (branch) that beareth fruit he pur.
Acts 2. 5 men, out of every nation under heaven
2. 43 fear came upon every soul: and many
3. 23 (that) every soul, which will not hear
10. 35 in every nation he that feareth him, and
13. 27 Prophets which are read every sabbath
15. 21 read in the synagogues every sabbath day
15. 36 visit our brethren in every city where
18. 4 reasoned in the synagogue every sabbath
20. 31 warn every one night and day with tears
26. 11 I punished them oft in every synagogue
Rom. 2. 9 upon every soul of man that doeth evil
3. 2 Much every way: chiefly, because that
3. 4 yea, let God be true, but every man a liar
3. 19 every mouth may be stopped, and all the
13. 1 every soul be subject unto the higher
14. 5 another esteemeth every day (alike)
14. 11 every knee shall bow to me, and every
1 Co. 1. 2 all that in every place call upon the
4. 17 as I teach every where in every church
6. 18 Every sin that a man doeth is without the
11. 3 know, that the head of every man is Chr.
11. 4 Every man praying or prophesying, havi.
11. 5 every woman that prayeth or prophesieth
15. 30 And why stand we in jeopardy every h.?
2 Co. 2. 14 of his knowledge by us in every place
4. 2 to every man's conscience in the sight of
7. 5 but we were troubled on every side
9. 8 that ye..may abound to every good work
10. 5 and every high thing that exalteth itself
10. 5 every thought to the obedience of Christ
13. 1 shall every word be established
Gal. 5. 3 I testify again to every man that is
Eph. 1. 21 every name that is named, not only in this
4. 14 carried about with every wind of doctrine
4. 16 by that which every joint supplieth
Phil. 1. 3 thank my God upon every remembrance
1. 4 in every prayer of mine for you all making
1. 18 every way, whether in pretence, or in tru.
2. 9 him a name which is above every name
2. 10 the name of Jesus every knee should bow
2. 11 every tongue should confess that Jesus
4. 21 Salute every saint in Christ Jesus
Col. 1. 10 being fruitful in every good work, and
1. 15 the first born of every creature
1. 23 (and) which was preached to every creat.
1. 28 warning every man, and teaching every
1. 28 we may present every man perfect in C.
1 Th. 1. 8 in every place your faith to Godward is
2 Th. 2. 17 stablish you in every good word and work
3. 6 withdraw yourselves from every brother
3. 17 hand, which is the token in every epistle
1 Ti. 4. 4 every creature of God (is) good, and noth.
5. 10 have diligently followed every good work
2 Ti. 2. 21 (and) prepared unto every good work
4. 18 shall deliver me from every evil work
Titus 1. 16 and unto every good work reprobate
3. 1 in mind..to be ready to every good work
Phm. 6 by the acknowledging of every good thing
Heb. 2. 2 and every transgression and disobedience
3. 4 every house is builded by some (man)
5. 1 every high priest taken from among men
8. 3 every high priest is ordained to offer
9. 19 when Moses had spoken every precept to
10. 11 every priest standeth daily ministering
12. 1 let us lay aside every weight, and the sin
12. 6 and scourgeth every son whom he receive.
13. 21 Make you perfect in every good work to
Jas. 1. 17 Every good gift and every perfect gift
1. 19 let every man be swift to hear, slow to
3. 7 every kind of beasts, and of birds, and of
3. 16 there (is) confusion and every evil work
1 Pe. 2. 13 Submit yourselves to every ordinance of
1 Jo. 4. 1 believe not every spirit, but try the
4. 2 Every spirit that confesseth that Jesus
4. 3 every spirit that confesseth not that
Rev. 1. 7 every eye shall see him, and they (also)
5. 9 to God by thy blood out of every kindred
5. 13 every creature which is in heaven, and
6. 14 every mountain and island were moved out
6. 15 and every bondman, and [every] free man
14. 6 to every nation, and kindred, and tongue
16. 3 and every living soul died in the sea
16 20 every island fled away, and the mount.
18. 2 is become..the hold of every foul spirit
18. 2 a cage of every unclean and hateful bird
18. 17 every ship master, and all the company

EVERY (man) —
Head, רֹאשׁ *rosh.*
Judg. 5. 30 to every man a damsel (or) two; to Sisera

EVERY man (woman) —
1. *A man,* אִישׁ *ish.*
Gen. 9. 5 at the hand of every man's brother will
42. 25 restore every man's money into his sack
45. 1 Cause every man to go out from me
47. 20 the Egyptians sold every man his field
Exod. 1. 1 every man and his household came with
7. 12 they cast down every man his rod, and
12. 3 they shall take to them every man a lamb
16. 16 Gather of it every man according to his
16. 16 take ye every man for (them) which (are)
16. 18 gathered every man according to his eat.
16. 21 gathered..every man according to his e.
16. 29 abide ye every man in his place; let no
25. 2 of every man that giveth it willingly
30. 12 they give every man a ransom for his
32. 27 Put every man his sword by his side
32. 27 (and) go in..and slay every man his bro.
32. 27 every man his companion, and every man
32. 29 even every man upon his son, and upon
33. 8 and stood every man (at) his tent door
33. 10 and worshipped, every man (in) his tent
36. 4 every man from his work; Heb. *ish ish.*
Lev. 19. 3 fear every man his mother and his father
25. 10, 13 return every man unto his possession
25. 10 shall return every man unto his fam.
Num. 1. 52 every man by his own camp, and every m.
2. 2 Every man of the children of Israel shall
2. 17 every man in his place by their standards
5. 10 every man's hallowed things shall be his
7. 5 to every man according to his service
11. 10 every man in the door of his tent
16. 17 take every man his censer, and put inse.
16. 17 before the LORD every man his censer
16. 18 they took every man his censer, and put
17. 2 write thou every man's name upon his
17. 9 they looked, and took every man his rod
31. 50 what every man hath gotten, of jewels of
31. 53 had taken spoil, every man for himself
36. 8 every man the inheritance of his fathers
Deut. 1. 41 girded on every man his weapons of war
3. 20 ye return every man unto his possession
12. 8 every man whatsoever (is) right in his own
16. 17 Every man (shall give) as he is able
24. 16 every man shall be put to death for his
Josh 6. 5 ascend up every man straight before him
6. 20 every man straight before him, and they
24. 28 depart, every man unto his inheritance
Judg. 2. 6 Israel went every man unto his inheri.
7. 7 (other) people go every man unto his pl.
7. 21 they stood every man in his place round
7. 22 set every man's sword against his fellow
8. 24, 25 every man the earrings of his prey
9. 49 likewise cut down every man his bough
9. 55 they departed every man unto his place
17. 6 every man did (that which was) right
21. 21 catch you every man his wife of the dau.
21. 24 every man to his tribe and to his family
21. 24 from thence every man to his inheritance
1 Sa. 4. 10 and they fled every man into his tent
8. 22 Go ye every man unto his city
10. 25 the people away, every man to his house
13. 2 the rest..he sent every man to his tent
13. 20 to sharpen every man his share, and his
14. 20 every man's sword was against his fellow
14. 34 hither every man his ox, and every man
14. 34 brought every man his ox with him that
25. 10 that break away every man from his
25. 13 Gird ye on every man his sword
25. 13 And they girded on every man his sword
26. 23 render to every man his righteousness
27. 3 every man with his household, (even) D.
30. 6 every man for his sons and for his daugh.
30. 22 to every man his wife and his children
2 Sa. 2. 3 bring up, every man with his household
13. 9 And they went out every man from him
13. 29 every man gat him up upon his mule, and
15. 4 every man which hath any suit or cause
15. 30 the people..covered every man his head
19. 8 for Israel had fled every man to his tent
20. 1 every man to his tents, O Israel
20. 2 every man of Israel went up from after
20. 22 from the city, every man to his tent
1 Ki. 4. 25 every man under his vine and under his
4. 27 all that came..every man in his month
4. 28 every man according to his charge
8. 39 give to every man according to his ways
10. 25 they brought every man his present, ves.
12. 24 return every man to his house; for this
20. 24 Take..away, every man out of his place
22. 17 return every man to his house in peace
22. 36 Every man to his city, and every man to
2 Ki. 3. 25 piece of land cast every man his stone
9. 13 took every man his garment, and put
11. 8, 11 every man with his weapons in his
11. 9 they took every man his men that were
12. 4 the money that every man is set at, (and)
12. 5 to them, every man of his acquaintance
14. 6 every man shall be put to death for his
14. 12 and they fled every man to their tents
18. 31 (then) eat ye every man of his own vine
1 Ch. 16. 43 people departed every man to his house
2 Ch. 6. 30 render unto every man according unto all
9. 24 they brought every man his present, ves.
10. 16 every man to your tents, O Israel: (and)
11. 4 return every man to his house; for this
18. 16 return (therefore) every man to his house

2 Ch.23. 7 every man with his weapons in his hand
23. 8 took every man his men that were to co.
23. 10 every man having his weapon in his hand
25. 4 but every man shall die for his own sin
25. 22 they fled every man to his tent
31. 1 every man to his possession, into their
31. 2 every man according to his service, the
Neh. 5. 13 God shake out every man from his house
Esth. 1. 8 according to every man's [Heb *ish ish.*]
1. 22 every man should bear rule in his own
Job 34. 11 every man to find according to (his) ways
42. 11 every man also gave him a piece
Psa. 39. 6 Surely every man walketh in a vain show
62. 12 renderest to every man according to his
Isa. 9. 20 eat every man the flesh of his own arm
31. 7 every man shall cast away his idols of
Jer. 12. 15 every man to his heritage, and every man
17. 10 to give every man according to his ways
22. 8 they shall say every man to his neighbour
23. 27 they tell every man to his neighbour
23. 36 for every man's word shall be his burden
26. 3 turn every man from his evil way, that I
29. 26 every man (that is) mad, and maketh him.
31. 34 every man his neighbour, and every man
34. 9 every man should let his man servant
34. 9 every man his maid servant..go free
34. 14 let ye go every man his brother an Hebr.
34. 15, 17 proclaiming .every man to his neigh
34. 16 caused every man his servant, and every m.
35. 15 Return ye now every man from his evil
36. 3 may return every man from his evil way
37. 10 should they rise up every man in his tent
49. 5 shall be driven out every man right forth
51. 6 Flee out..and deliver every man his soul
51. 45 deliver ye every man his soul from the
Eze. 8. 11 with every man his censer in his hand
8. 12 every man in the chambers of his imagery
9. 1 every man (with) his destroying weapon
9. 2 every man a slaughter weapon in his hand
14. 4 Every man of the house of [Heb. *ish ish.*]
20. 7 Cast ye away every man the abominations
20. 8 they did not every man cast away the
32. 10 every man for his own life, in the day of
38. 21 every man's sword shall be against his
46. 18 scattered every man from his possession
Jon. 1. 5 cried every man unto his god, and cast
Mic. 4. 4 they shall sit every man under his vine
7. 2 hunt every man his brother with a net
Hag. 1. 9 and ye run every man unto his own house
Zech. 3. 10 call every man his neighbour under the
7. 9 show mercy and compassions every man
8. 4 every man with his staff in his hand for
8. 16 Speak ye every man the truth to his
Mal. 2. 10 deal treacherously every man against his

2. *Any one*, ἄν τις *an tis*.
Acts 2. 45 parted them to all..as every man had

3. *Up to, up by, apiece*, ἀνά *ana*.
Matt20. 9 they received every man a penny
20. 10 they likewise received every man a penny

4. *All together, all at once*, ἅπας *hapas*.
Mark 8. 25 he was restored, and saw every man

5. *Each one*, εἷς ἕκαστος *heis hekastos*.
Acts 2. 6 every man heard them speak in his own
Col. 4. 6 may know how ye ought to answer every

6. *Each*, ἕκαστος *hekastos*
Matt16. 27 reward every man according to his works
25. 15 every man according to his several ability
Mark13. 34 gave..to every man his work, and comm
John 7. 53 [And every man went unto his own house]
16. 32 shall be scattered, every man to his own
Acts 2. 8 how hear we every man in our own tongue
4. 35 unto every man according as he had need
11. 29 every man according to his ability
Rom. 2. 6 render to every man according to his
12. 3 dealt to every man the measure of faith
14. 5 Let every man be fully persuaded in his
1 Co. 3. 5 even as the Lord gave to every man
3. 8 every man shall receive his own reward
3. 10 let every man take heed how he buildeth
3. 13 Every man's work shall be made manifest
3. 13 try every man's work of what sort it is
4. 5 then shall every man have praise of God
7. 2 every man have his own wife..every wom.
7. 7 every man hath his proper gift of God
7. 17 But as God hath distributed to every man
7. 20 Let every man abide in the same calling
7. 24 let every man, wherein he is called
10. 24 seek his own, but [every man] another's
12. 7 is given to every man to profit withal
12. 11 dividing to every man severally as he will
15. 23 every man in his own order: Christ the
2 Co. 9. 7 Every man according as he purposeth in
Gal. 6. 4 let every man prove his own work
6. 5 For every man shall bear his own burden
Eph. 4. 25 speak every man truth with his neighbour
Phil. 2. 4 every man on his own things, but every m.
Heb. 8. 11 every man his neighbour, and every man
Jas. 1. 14 But every man is tempted, when he is
1 Pe. 1. 17 judgeth according to every man's work
4. 10 As every man hath received the gift,(even)
Rev. 20. 13 judged every man according to their
22. 12 every man according as his work shall be

7. *All, every one*, πᾶς *pas*.
Luke 6. 30 Give to every man that asketh of thee
16. 16 the kingdom..every man presseth into it
John 6. 45 Every man therefore that hath heard
Rom. 2. 10 and peace, to every man that worketh
12. 3 to every man that is among you, not to

1 Co. 8. 7 (there is) not in every man that knowledge
9. 25 every man that striveth for the mastery
2 Co. 8. 7 as ye abound in every thing, (in) faith
Heb. 2. 9 that he..should taste death for every man
1 Pe. 3. 15 always to (give) an answer to every man
1 Jo. 3. 3 And every man that hath this hope in him
Rev. 22. 18 I testify unto every man that heareth

8. *Who—what?* τίς τί *tis ti*.
Mark15. 24 lots upon them, what every man should

EVERY man, how much —
Who—what? τίς τί *tis ti*.
Luke19. 15 how much [every] man had gained by tra

EVERY one —
1. *A man*, אִישׁ *ish*.
Gen. 10. 5 every one after his tongue, after their
49. 28 every one according to his blessing he
Exod28. 21 every one with his name shall they be
39. 14 every one with his name, according to the
Lev. 20. 9 every one that curseth his [Heb *ish ish.*]
Num. 2. 34 set forward, every one after their families
4. 19 appoint them every one to [Heb. *ish ish.*]
4. 49 every one according to his [Heb. *ish ish.*]
25. 5 Slay ye every one his men that were joined
26. 54 to every one shall his inheritance be given
35. 8 every one shall give of his cities unto
36. 7 every one of the children of Israel shall
36. 9 every one of the tribes of the children
Judg16. 5 we will give thee, every one of us, eleven
1 Sa. 20. 15 every one from the face of the earth
2 Sa. 2. 16 caught every one his fellow by the head
6. 19 to every one a cake of bread, and a good
6. 19 people departed every one to his house
18. 17 and all Israel fled every one to his tent
1 Ki. 20. 20 And they slew every one his man: and
2 Ki. 18. 31 and every one of his fig-tree
18. 31 and drink ye every one the waters of his
23. 35 of every one according to his taxation
1 Ch. 16. 3 he dealt to every one of Israel, both man
16. 3 to every one a loaf of bread, and a good
Ezra 2. 1 and came again..every one unto his city
Neh. 3. 28 priests, every one over against his house
4. 15 we returned..every one unto his work
4. 18 every one had his sword girded by his
4. 22 Let every one with his servant lodge
4. 23 (that) every one put them off for washing
5. 7 Ye exact usury, every one of his brother
7. 3 every one in his watch, and every one
7. 6 and came again every one unto his city
8. 16 every one upon the roof of his house, and
11. 3 dwelt every one in his possession in their
11. 20 of Judah, every one in his inheritance
13. 10 Levites .were fled every one to his field
13. 30 the Levites, every one in his business
Job 1. 4 feasted (in their) houses, every one his
2. 11 they came every one from his own place
2. 12 and they rent every one his mantle, and
42. 11 and every one an ear ring of gold
Psa. 12. 2 speak vanity every one with his neighb.
64. 6 the inward (thought) of every one (of th.)
Prov 20. 6 will proclaim every one his own goodness
Song 8. 11 every one for the fruit thereof was to
Isa. 3. 5 every one by another, and every one by
14. 18 lie in glory, every one in his own house
19. 2 every one against his brother .every one
36. 16 every one of his vine, and every one of
36. 16 drink ye every one the waters of his own
41. 6 They helped every one his neighbour
47. 15 shall wander every one to his quarter
53. 6 we have turned every one to his own way
56. 11 every one for his gain, from his quarter
Jer 1. 15 they shall set every one his throne at
5. 8 every one neighed after his neighbour's
6. 3 they shall feed every one in his place
9. 4 Take ye heed every one of his neighbour
9. 5 they will deceive every one his neighbour
11. 8 every one in the imagination of their
16. 12 every one after the imagination of his
18. 11 return ye now every one from his evil
18. 12 every one do the imagination of his evil
19. 9 eat every one the flesh of his friend
22. 7 against thee, every one with his weapons
23. 30 that steal my words every one from his
23. 35 every one to his neighbour, and every one
25. 5 Turn ye..now every one from his evil
31. 30 every one shall die for his own iniquity
32. 19 to give every one according to his ways
34. 10 that every one should let his man serva.
34. 10 every one his maid servant, go free, that
34. 17 in proclaiming every one to his brother
50. 16 they shall turn every one to his people
50. 16 they shall flee every one to his own land
51. 9 let us go every one into his own country
Eze. 1. 9, 12 they went every one straight forward
1. 11 two (wings) of every one (were) joined
1. 23, 23 every one had two, which covered on
7. 16 all..mourning, every one for his iniquity
10. 22 they went every one straight forward
14. 7 every one of the house of [Heb. *ish ish.*]
18. 30 judge..every one according to his ways
20. 39 serve ye every one his idols, and hereafter
22. 6 every one were in thee to their power to
33. 20 will judge you every one after his ways
33. 26 ye defile every one his neighbour's wife
33. 30 speak..every one to his brother, saying
45. 20 thou shalt do..for every one that erreth
Joel 2. 7 they shall march every one on his ways
Obad. 9 to the end that every one of the mount
Jon. 1. 7 they said every one to his fellow, Come
3. 8 let them turn every one from his evil way

Mic. 4. 5 walk every one in the name of his god
Zeph. 2. 11 every one from his place, (even) all the
Hag. 2. 22 every one by the sword of his brother
Zech. 8. 10 all men every one against his neighbour
10. 1 of rain, to every one grass in the field
11. 6 men every one into his neighbour's hand
13. 4 shall be ashamed every one of his vision
14. 13 every one on the hand of his neighbour

2. *A man*, גֶּבֶר *geber*.
Joel 2. 8 they shall walk every one in his path

3. *All, every*, כָּל־, כֹּל *kol*.
Gen. 30. 33 every one that (is) not speckled and
Isa. 43. 7 (Even) every one that is called by my na.

4. *All together*, ἅπας *hapas*.
Acts 5. 16 and they were healed every one

5. *Each*, ἕκαστος *hekastos*.
Matt 18. 35 from your hearts forgive not every one
26. 22 began every one of them to say unto him
Luke 2. 3 to be taxed, every one into his own city
John 6. 7 that every one of them may take a little
Acts 2. 38 be baptized every one of you in the name
3. 26 in turning away every one of you from
Rom. 14. 12 every one of us shall give account of
15. 2 Let every one of us please (his) neighbour
1 Co. 1. 12 that every one of you saith, I am of Paul
7. 17 as the Lord hath called every one, so let
11. 21 every one taketh before (other) his own
14. 26 every one of you hath a psalm, hath a
16. 2 let every one of you lay by him in store
2 Co. 5. 10 every one may receive the things (done)
1 Th. 4. 4 That every one of you should know how
Heb. 6. 11 we desire that every one of you do show
Rev. 2. 23 will give unto every one of you according
5. 8 having every one of them harps, and
6. 11 robes were given unto [every one of] them

6. *One by one*, καθ' ἕν *kath hen*.
John21. 25 which, if they should be written every one
Rom. 12. 5 and every one members one of another

7. *All, every*, πᾶς *pas*.
Matt. 7. 8 every one that asketh receiveth; and he
7. 21 Not every one that saith unto me, Lord
7. 26 every one that heareth these sayings of
19. 29 every one that hath forsaken houses, or
25. 29 unto every one that hath shall be given
Mark 7. 14 Hearken unto me every one (of you), and
9. 49 [every one shall be salted with fire, and]
Luke 6. 40 every one that is perfect shall be as his
9. 43 they wondered every one at all things
11. 4 forgive every one that is indebted to us
11. 10 every one that asketh receiveth; and he
18. 14 every one that exalteth himself shall be
19. 26 unto every one which hath shall be given
John 3. 8 is every one that is born of the Spirit
3. 20 For every one that doeth evil hateth the
6. 40 that every one which seeth the Son, and
18. 37 Every one that is of the truth heareth
Acts 16. 26 opened, and every one's bands were loosed
28. 2 received us every one, because of the
Rom. 1. 16 unto salvation to every one that believeth
10. 4 righteousness to every one that believeth
1 Co. 16. 16 and to every one that helpeth with (us)
Gal. 3. 10 Cursed (is) every one that continueth not
3. 13 Cursed (is) every one that hangeth on a
2 Ti. 2. 19 let every one that nameth the name of
Heb. 5. 13 every one that useth milk (is) unskilful
1 Jo. 2. 29 every one that doeth righteousness is
4. 7 every one that loveth is born of God, and
5. 1 every one that loveth him that begat

EVERY one in particular —
Each one by one, καθ' ἕνα ἕκαστος.
Eph. 5. 33 let every one of you in particular so love

EVERY place —
All, whole, every, any, כֹּל *kol*.
Isa. 30. 32 (in) every place where the grounded staff

EVERY several —
Each one separately, ἀνὰ εἷς ἕκαστος.
Rev. 21. 21 every several gate was of one pearl: and

EVERY side, on —
1. *To be round about*, סָבַב *sabab*.
Psa. 71. 21 Thou shalt..comfort me on every side

2. *In every*, ἐν παντί *en panti*.
2 Co. 4. 8 (We are) troubled on every side, yet not

3. *From every*, πάντοθεν *pantothen*.
Luke19. 43 compass..and keep thee in on every side

EVERY thing —
1. *All, whole, every, any*, כֹּל *kol*.
Gen. 6. 17 every thing that (is) in the earth shall

2. *All, every*, πᾶς *pas*.
Matt. 8. 33 told every thing, and what was befallen to
1 Co. 1. 5 in every thing ye are enriched by him
2 Co. 9. 11 enriched in every thing to all
Eph. 5. 24 so (let) the wives (be)..in every thing
Phil. 4. 6 in every thing by prayer and supplication
1 Th. 5. 18 In every thing give thanks: for this is

EVERY where —
1. *In every*, ἐν παντί *en panti*.
Phil. 4. 12 every where and in all things I am

2. *In every place*, ἐν παντὶ τόπῳ *en panti topō*.
1 Ti. 2. 8 will therefore that men pray every where

3. *Every where*, πανταχοῦ *pantachou*.
Mark16. 20 [they went forth, and preached every wh.]

Luke 9. 6 preaching..and healing every where
Acts 17. 30 commandeth all men every where to rep.
21. 28 teacheth all (men) [every where] against
28. 22 that every where it is spoken against
1 Co. 4. 17 as I teach every where in every church

EVERY whit —

1. *Complete, completely,* כָּלִיל *kalil.*
Deut 13. 16 all the spoil thereof every whit, for the

2. *Whole,* ὅλος *holos.*
John 7. 23 I have made a man every whit whole on
13. 10 He that is washed..is clean every whit

EVERY, in or into —

Down along, κατά *(acc.) kata.*
Acts 5. 42 in every house, they ceased not to teach
8. 3 entering into every house, and haling
14. 23 had ordained them elders in every church
15. 21 Moses of old time hath in every city them
20. 23 the Holy Ghost witnesseth in every city
22. 19 imprisoned and beat in every synagogue
Titus 1. 5 and ordain elders in every city, as I had

EVERY, out of or throughout —

Down, along, κατά *(acc.) kata.*
Luke 8. 1 he went throughout every city and villa.
8. 4 and were come to him out of every city

EVERY quarter, from —

From every where, πανταχόθεν *pantachothen.*
Mark 1. 45 and they came to him [from every quarter]

E'-VI, אֱוִי *desire.*

A prince of Midian, slain in the plains of Moab, whose lands were afterwards given to Reuben. B.C. 1452.
Num31. 8 E., and Rekem, and Zur, and Hur, and
Josh 13. 21 princes of Midian, E., and Rekem, and

EVIDENCE —

1. *Book, letter,* סֵפֶר *sepher.*
Jer. 32. 10 I subscribed the evidence, and sealed (it)
32. 11 So I took the evidence of the purchase
32. 12 I gave the evidence of the purchase unto
32. 14 Take these evidences, this evidence of the
32. 14 both which is sealed, and this evidence
32. 16 Now when I had delivered the evidence
32. 44 and subscribe evidences, and seal (them)

2. *Conviction,* ἔλεγχος *elegchos.*
Heb. 11. 1 Now faith is..the evidence of things not

EVIDENT, more evident —

1. *On the face,* עַל־פְּנֵים *al panim.*
Job 6. 28 look upon me: for (it is) evident unto

2. *Manifest,* δῆλος *dēlos.*
Gal. 3. 11 that no man is justified..(it is) evident

3. *Very manifest,* κατάδηλος *katadēlos.*
Heb. 7. 15 it is yet far more evident: for that after

4. *Manifest beforehand,* πρόδηλος *prodēlos.*
Heb. 7. 14 (it is) evident that our Lord sprang out

EVIDENTLY —

Openly, manifestly, φανερῶς *phanerōs.*
Acts 10. 3 He saw in a vision evidently..an angel

EVIL —

1. *Vanity, iniquity,* אָוֶן *aven.*
Prov 12. 21 There shall no evil happen to the just

2. *Worthlessness,* בְּלִיַּעַל *beliyyaal.*
Psa. 41. 8 An evil disease..cleaveth fast unto him

3. *Evil, bad,* רַע *ra.*
Gen. 2. 9 the tree of knowledge of good and evil
2. 17 the tree of the knowledge of good and e.
3. 5 shall be as gods, knowing good and evil
3. 22 as one of us, to know good and evil
6. 5 every imagination..(was) only evil conti.
8. 21 for the imagination of man's heart (is) e.
19. 19 lest some evil take me, and I die
37. 2 brought unto his father their evil report
37. 20 Some evil beast hath devoured him: and
37. 33 an evil beast hath devoured him: Joseph
44. 4 Wherefore have ye rewarded evil for good?
44. 34 see the evil that shall come on my father
47. 9 few and evil have the days of the years
48. 16 Angel which redeemed me from all evil
50. 15 and will certainly requite us all the evil
50. 17 for they did unto thee evil: and now
50. 20 as for you, ye thought evil against me
Exod. 5. 19 did see (that) they (were) in evil (case)
10. 10 he said..look (to it); for evil (is) before
23. 2 shalt not follow a multitude to (do) evil
32. 12 and repent of this evil against thy people
32. 14 the LORD repented of the evil which he
33. 4 when the people heard these evil tidings
Lev. 26. 6 I will rid evil beasts out of the land
Num 14. 27 How long (shall I bear with) this evil
14. 35 I will surely do it unto all this evil cong.
14. 37 those men that did bring up the evil rep.
20. 5 to bring us in unto this evil place?
32. 13 that had done evil in the sight of the L.
Deut. 1. 35 not one of these men of this evil genera.
1. 39 had no knowledge between good and evil
4. 25 shall do evil in the sight of the LORD thy
7. 15 will put none of the evil diseases of Egypt
13. 5 so shalt thou put the evil away from the
17. 7 So thou shalt put the evil away from
17. 12 thou shalt put away the evil from Israel
19. 19 so shalt thou put the evil away from
19. 20 no more any such evil [Heb. *dabar ra.*]
21. 21 so shalt thou put evil away from among
Deut 22. 14 bring up an evil name upon her, and say
22. 19 he hath brought up an evil name upon a
22. 21 shalt thou put evil away from among you
22. 22 so shalt thou put away evil from Israel
22. 24 so thou shalt put away evil from among
24. 7 thou shalt put evil away from among you
29. 21 the LORD shall separate him unto evil
30. 15 I have set before thee..death and evil
31. 17 many evils and troubles shall befall them
31. 17 Are not these evils come upon us, because
31. 18 for all the evils which they shall have
31. 21 when many evils and troubles are befal.
31. 29 and evil will befall you in the latter days
31. 29 ye will do evil in the sight of the LORD
Josh 23. 15 shall the LORD bring upon you all evil
Judg. 2. 11 children of Israel did evil in the sight of
2. 15 hand of the LORD was against them for e.
3. 7 children of Israel did evil in the sight
3. 12 children of Israel did evil again in the
3. 12 they had done evil in the sight of the L.
4. 1 children of Israel again did evil in the
6. 1 children of Israel did evil in the sight
9. 23 God sent an evil spirit between Abimele.
9. 57 all the evil..did God render upon their
10. 6 children of Israel did evil again in the
13. 1 the children of Israel did evil again in
20. 13 that we may..put away evil from Israel
20. 34 but they knew not that evil (was) near
20. 41 they saw that evil was come upon them
1 Sa. 2. 23 I hear of your evil dealings by all this
6. 9 (then) he hath done us this great evil
12. 19 we have added unto all our sins (this) ev.
15. 19 and didst evil in the sight of the LORD?
16. 14 an evil spirit from the LORD troubled
16. 15 an evil spirit from God troubleth thee
16. 16 when the evil spirit from God is upon
16. 23 and the evil spirit departed from him
18. 10 the evil spirit from God came upon Saul
19. 9 evil spirit from the LORD was upon Saul
20. 7 be sure that evil is determined by him
20. 9 if I knew certainly that evil were deter.
20. 13 but if it please my father (to do) thee ev.
24. 11 and see that (there is) neither evil nor
24. 17 whereas I have rewarded thee evil
25. 3 the man (was) churlish and evil in his
25. 17 for evil is determined against our master
25. 21 and he hath requited me evil for good
25. 26 they that seek evil to my lord, be as Na.
25. 28 evil hath not been found in thee (all) thy
25. 39 and hath kept his servant from evil: for
26. 18 what have I done? or what evil (is) in
29. 6 for I have not found evil in thee since the
2 Sa. 3. 39 LORD shall reward the doer of evil acco.
12. 9 Wherefore hast thou despised..to do ev.
12. 11 Behold, I will raise up evil against thee
13. 16 this evil in sending me away (is) greater
15. 14 overtake us suddenly, and bring evil
17. 14 that the LORD might bring evil upon Ab.
19. 7 than all the evil that befell thee from
19. 35 (and) can I discern between good and ev.?
24. 16 the LORD repented him of the evil
1 Ki. 5. 4 (there is) neither adversary nor evil occu.
9. 9 the LORD brought upon them all this ev.
11. 6 Solomon did evil in the sight of the LORD
13. 33 Jeroboam returned not from his evil way
14. 10 I will bring evil upon the house of Jero.
14. 22 Judah did evil in the sight of the LORD
15. 26, 34 he did evil in the sight of the LORD
16. 7 even for all the evil that he did in the
16. 19 in doing evil in the sight of the LORD
16. 25 Omri wrought evil in the eyes of the LORD
16. 30 Ahab..did evil in the sight of the LORD
21. 20 to work evil in the sight of the LORD
21. 21 Behold, I will bring evil upon thee, and
21. 29 I will not bring the evil in his days
21. 29 (but) in his son's days will I bring the e.
22. 8 for he doth not prophesy good..but evil
22. 18 he would prophesy no good..but evil?
22. 23 the LORD hath spoken evil concerning
22. 52 he did evil in the sight of the LORD, and
2 Ki. 3. 2 he wrought evil in the sight of the LORD
6. 33 Behold, this evil (is) of the LORD; what
8. 12 Because I know the evil that thou wilt do
8. 18, 27 did evil in the sight of the LORD
13. 2, 11 (that which was) evil in the sight of
14. 24 (that which was) evil in the sight of the
15. 9, 18, 24, 28 (that which was) evil in the sight
17. 2 (that which was) evil in the sight of the
17. 13 saying, Turn ye from your evil ways, and
17. 17 sold themselves to do evil in the sight of
21. 2, 16, 20 (that which was) evil in the sight of
21. 9 Manasseh seduced them to do more evil
21. 12 I (am) bringing (such) evil upon Jerusalem
21. 15 they have done (that which was) evil in
22. 16 Behold, I will bring evil upon this place
22. 20 and thine eyes shall not see all the evil
23. 32, 37 (that which was) evil in the sight of
24. 9, 19 (that which was) evil in the sight of
1 Ch. 2. 3 E...was evil in the sight of the LORD
4. 10 that thou wouldest keep (me) from evil
7. 23 because it went evil with his house
21. 15 he repented him of the evil, and said to
2 Ch. 7. 22 therefore hath he brought all this evil
12. 14 he did evil, because he prepared not his
18. 7 he never prophesied good ..but always e.
18. 17 would not prophesy good unto me, but e.?
18. 22 the LORD hath spoken evil against thee
20. 9 If, (when) evil cometh upon us, (as) the
21. 6 (that which was) evil in the eyes of the
22. 4 Wherefore he did evil in the sight of the
29. 6 (that which was) evil in the eyes of the
33. 2, 22 (that which was) evil in the sight of
2 Ch. 33. 6 he wrought much evil in the sight of the
34. 24 Behold, I will bring evil upon this place
34. 28 neither shall thine eyes see all the evil
36. 5, 9, 12 (that which was) evil in the sight of
Ezra 9. 13 that is come upon us for our evil deeds
Neh. 6. 13 they might have (matter) for an evil rep.
9. 28 But after..they did evil again before
13. 7 and understood of the evil that E. did
13. 17 What evil thing (is) this that ye do, and
13. 18 did not our God bring all this evil upon
13. 27 hearken unto you to do all this great evil
Esth. 7. 7 he saw that there was evil determined
8. 6 how can I endure to see the evil that shall
Job 1. 1 and one that feared God, and eschewed e.
1. 8 one that feareth God, and escheweth evil?
2. 3 one that feareth God, and escheweth ev.?
2. 10 and shall we not receive evil? In all
2. 11 heard of all this evil that was come upon
5. 19 in seven there shall no evil touch thee
28. 28 and to depart from evil (is) understand.
30. 26 When I looked for good, then evil came
31. 29 or lifted up myself when evil found him
42. 11 over all the evil that the LORD had brou.
Psa. 5. 4 neither shall evil dwell with thee
7. 4 If I have rewarded evil unto him that
10. 15 Break thou the arm of..the evil (man)
15. 3 nor doeth evil to his neighbour, nor tak.
21. 11 For they intended evil against thee; they
23. 4 Yea, though I walk..I will fear no evil
34. 13 Keep thy tongue from evil, and thy lips
34. 14 Depart from evil, and do good; seek pe.
34. 16 the LORD (is) against them that do evil, to
34. 21 Evil shall slay the wicked; and they that
35. 12 They rewarded me evil for good, (to) the
36. 4 He deviseth mischief..he abhorreth not e.
37. 19 They shall not be ashamed in the evil time
37. 27 Depart from evil, and do good; and dwell
38. 20 They also that render evil for good are
40. 12 innumerable evils have compassed me
40. 14 them be..put to shame that wish me evil
41. 5 Mine enemies speak evil of me, When
49. 5 Wherefore should I fear in the days of e.
50. 19 Thou givest thy mouth to evil, and thy
51. 4 and done (this) evil in thy sight; that
52. 3 Thou lovest evil more than good; (and)
54. 5 He shall reward evil unto mine enemies
56. 5 all their thoughts (are) against me for e.
64. 5 They encourage themselves (in) an evil
78. 49 by sending evil angels (among them)
90. 15 (and) the years (wherein) we have seen e.
91. 10 There shall no evil befall thee, neither
97. 10 Ye that love the LORD, hate evil: he
109. 5 And they have rewarded me evil for good
109. 20 of them that speak evil against my soul
112. 7 He shall not be afraid of evil tidings: his
119. 101 I have refrained my feet from every e.
121. 7 The LORD shall preserve thee from all evil
140. 1 Deliver me, O LORD, from the evil man
140. 11 evil shall hunt the violent man to overth.
141. 4 Incline not my heart to (any) evil thing
Prov. 1. 16 For their feet run to evil, and make haste
1. 33 and shall be quiet from fear of evil
2. 12 To deliver thee from the way of the evil
2. 14 Who rejoice to do evil, (and) delight in
3. 7 fear the LORD, and depart from evil
3. 29 Devise not evil against thy neighbour
4. 14 and go not in the way of evil (men)
4. 27 Turn not..remove thy foot from evil
5. 14 I was almost in all evil in the midst of
6. 24 To keep thee from the evil woman, from
8. 13 The fear of the LORD (is) to hate evil
8. 13 and arrogancy, and the evil way, and the
11. 19 he that pursueth evil (pursueth it) to his
12. 12 The wicked desireth the net of evil (men)
12. 20 (is) in the heart of them that imagine evil
13. 19 abomination to fools to depart from evil
13. 21 Evil pursueth sinners: but to the righte.
14. 16 wise (man) feareth, and departeth from e.
14. 19 The evil bow before the good; and the w.
14. 22 Do they not err that devise evil? but me.
15. 3 in every place, beholding the evil and the
15. 15 All the days of the afflicted (are) evil?
16. 4 yea, even the wicked for the day of evil
16. 6 by the fear of the LORD..depart from evil
16. 17 The highway..(is) to depart from evil: he
16. 27 An ungodly man diggeth up evil; and in
16. 30 moving his lips he bringeth evil to pass
17. 11 evil (man) seeketh only rebellion; there.
17. 13 Whoso rewardeth evil for good, evil shall
19. 23 he shall not be visited with evil
20. 8 A king..scattereth away all evil with his
20. 22 Say not thou, I will recompense evil
20. 30 blueness of a wound cleanseth away evil
21. 10 The soul of the wicked desireth evil: his
22. 3 A prudent (man) forseeth the evil, and
23. 6 the bread of (him that hath) an evil eye
24. 1 Be not thou envious against evil men
24. 20 For there shall be no reward to the evil
27. 12 A prudent (man) forseeth the evil, (and)
28. 5 Evil men understand not judgment: but
28. 10 causeth..to go astray in an evil way, he
28. 22 He that hasteth to be rich (hath) an evi
29. 6 In the transgression of an evil man
31. 12 She will do him good and not evil all the
Eccl. 2. 21 This also (is) vanity and a great evil
4. 3 who hath not seen the evil work that is
5. 1 for they consider not that they do evil
5. 13 There is a sore evil (which) I have seen
5. 14 But those riches perish by evil travail
5. 16 And this also (is) a sore evil, (that) in all
6. 1 There is an evil which I have seen under
6. 2 this (is) vanity, and it (is) an evil disease

Eccl. 8. 3 stand not in an evil thing; for he doeth
8. 5 Whoso keepeth..shall feel no evil thing
8. 11 sentence against an evil work is not exe.
8. 11 the heart..is fully set in them to do evil
8. 12 Though a sinner do evil an hundred times
9. 3 This (is) an evil among all (things) that
9. 3 heart of the sons of men is full of evil
9. 12 as the fishes that are taken in an evil net
9. 12 so (are) the sons of men snared in an evil
10. 5 There is an evil (which) I have seen under
11. 2 thou knowest not what evil shall be upon
11. 10 and put away evil from thy flesh: for
12. 1 while the evil days come not, nor the ye.
12. 14 whether (it be) good, or whether (it be) e.
Isa. 3. 9 they have rewarded evil unto themselves
5. 20 unto them that call evil good, and good e.
7. 5 Syria, Ephraim..have taken evil counsel
7. 15 that he may know to refuse the evil, and
7. 16 the child shall know to refuse the evil
13. 11 And I will punish the world for (their) e.
31. 2 Yet he also (is) wise, and will bring evil
32. 7 The instruments also of the churl (are) e.
33. 15 and shutteth his eyes from seeing evil
45. 7 I make peace, and create evil: I the Lo.
47. 11 Therefore shall evil come upon thee
56. 2 and keepeth his hand from doing any evil
57. 1 the righteous is taken away from the evil
59. 7 Their feet run to evil, and they make
59. 15 he (that) departeth from evil maketh
65. 12 ye did not hear; but did evil before mine
66. 4 they did evil before mine eyes, and chose
Jer. 1. 14 Out of the north an evil shall break forth
2. 3 evil shall come upon them, saith the LORD
2. 13 For my people have committed two evils
2. 19 and see that (it is) an evil (thing) and
3. 5 Behold, thou hast spoken and done evil
3. 17 after the imagination of their evil heart
4. 6 for I will bring evil from the north, and
5. 12 neither shall evil come upon us; neither
6. 1 for evil appeareth out of the north, and
6. 19 behold, I will bring evil upon this people
7. 24 in the imagination of their evil heart
7. 30 children of Judah have done evil in my
8. 3 of them that remain of this evil family
9. 3 for they proceed from evil to evil, and
11. 8 in the imagination of their evil heart
11. 11 Behold, I will bring evil upon them, which
11. 17 pronounced evil against thee, for the evil
11. 23 I will bring evil upon the men of Anath.
12. 14 saith the LORD against all mine evil
13. 10 This evil people..shall even be as this
15. 11 in the time of evil and in the time of affl.
16. 10 pronounced all this great evil against us?
16. 12 after the imagination of his evil heart
17. 17 thou (art) my hope in the day of evil
17. 18 bring upon them the day of evil, and
18. 8 If that nation..turn from their evil, I
18. 8 will repent of the evil that I thought to
18. 10 If it do evil in my sight, that it obey not
18. 11 I frame evil against you, and devise a
18. 11 return ye now every one from his evil
18. 12 every one do the imagination of his evil
18. 20 Shall evil be recompensed for good? for
19. 3 Behold, I will bring evil upon this place
19. 15 I will bring upon this city..all the evil
21. 10 have set my face against this city for evil
23. 10 their course is evil, and their force (is)
23. 12 for I will bring evil upon them, (even)
23. 17 they say..No evil shall come upon you
23. 22 turned them from their evil way, and
24. 3 the evil, very evil, that cannot be eaten
24. 8 And as the evil figs, which cannot be
25. 5 Turn ye..now every one from his evil way
25. 32 evil shall go forth from nation to nation
26. 3 and turn every man from his evil way
26. 3 that I may repent me of the evil which
26. 13 the LORD will repent him of the evil that
26. 19 the LORD repented him of the evil which
26. 19 Thus might we procure great evil against
28. 8 of war, and of evil, and of pestilence
29. 11 thoughts of peace, and not of evil, to give
32. 23 therefore thou hast caused all this evil to
32. 30 the children of Judah have only done e.
32. 32 Because of all the evil of the children of
32. 42 Like as I have brought all this great evil
35. 15 Return ye now every man from his evil
35. 17 I will bring..all the evil that I have
36. 3 all the evil which I purpose to do unto
36. 3 they may return every man from his evil
36. 7 will return every one from his evil way
36. 31 I will bring upon them..all the evil that
39. 16 will bring my words upon this city for e.
40. 2 LORD thy God hath pronounced this evil
41. 11 But when Johanan..heard of all the evil
42. 6 Whether (it be) good, or whether (it be) e.
42. 10 I repent me of the evil that I have done
42. 17 or escape from the evil that I will bring
44. 2 have seen all the evil that I have brought
44. 7 Wherefore commit ye (this) great evil
44. 11 I will set my face against you for evil
44. 17 (then) had we plenty..and saw no evil
44. 23 therefore this evil is happened unto you
44. 27 Behold, I will watch over them for evil
44. 29 shall surely stand against you for evil
45. 5 behold, I will bring evil upon all flesh
48. 2 in Heshbon they have devised evil against
49. 23 for they have heard evil tidings: they are
49. 37 I will bring evil upon them, (even) my
51. 24 all their evil that they have done in Zion
51. 60 Jeremiah wrote..all the evil that should
51. 64 shall not rise from the evil that I will
52. 2 (that which was) evil in the eyes of the

Lam. 3. 38 Out of the mouth..proceedeth not evil
Eze. 5. 16 When I shall send upon them the evil
5. 17 So will I send upon you..evil beasts, and
6. 9 for the evils which they have committed
6. 10 that I would do this evil unto them
6. 11 Alas for all the evil abominations of the
7. 5 An evil, an only evil, behold, is come
14. 22 concerning the evil that I have brought
20. 43 for all your evils that ye have committed
33. 11 turn ye, turn ye from your evil ways; for
34. 25 will cause the evil beasts to cease out of
36. 31 Then shall ye remember your own evil
38. 10 and thou shalt think an evil thought
Dan. 9. 12 by bringing upon us a great evil: for
9. 13 As (it is) written..all this evil is come
9. 14 hath the LORD watched upon the evil
Joel 2. 13 kindness, and repenteth him of the evil
Amos 3. 6 shall there be evil in a city, and the LORD
5. 13 silence in that time; for it (is) an evil time
5. 14 Seek good, and not evil, that ye may live
5. 15 Hate the evil, and love the good, and
6. 3 Ye that put far away the evil day, and
9. 4 I will set mine eyes upon them for evil
9. 10 The evil shall not overtake nor prevent
Jon. 1. 7 we may know for whose cause this evil
1. 8 for whose cause this evil (is) upon us?
3. 8 let them turn every one from his evil way
3. 10 that they turned from their evil way
3. 10 God repented of the evil that he had said
4. 2 kindness, and repentest thee of the evil
Mic. 1. 12 evil came down from the LORD unto the
2. 1 Woe to them that..work evil upon their
2. 3 against this family do I devise an evil
2. 3 neither shall ye go..for this time (is) evil
3. 2 Who hate the good, and love the evil
3. 11 (Is) not the LORD among us? none evil
7. 3 That they may do evil with both hands
Nah. 1. 11 that imagineth evil against the LORD
Hab. 1. 13 (Thou art) of purer eyes than to behold e.
2. 9 Woe to him that coveteth an evil covetous.
2. 9 may be delivered from the power of evil!
Zeph. 3. 15 thou shalt not see evil any more
Zech. 1. 4 Turn ye now from your evil ways
1. 4 and (from) your evil doings: but they
7. 10 let none of you imagine evil against his
8. 17 let none of you imagine evil in your hea.
Mal. 1. 8 if ye offer the blind..(is it) not evil? and
1. 8 and if ye offer the lame..(is it) not evil?
2. 17 Every one that doeth evil (is) good in the

4. *Evil, badness,* רֹעַ *roa.*
Isa. 1. 16 put away the evil of your doings from
Jer. 4. 4 because of the evil of your doings
21. 12 because of the evil of your doings
23. 2 I will visit upon you the evil of your
23. 22 and from the evil of their doings
25. 5 from the evil of your doings, and dwell
26. 3 because of the evil of their doings
44. 22 could no longer bear, because of the evil

5. *To be evil,* רָעַע *raa.*
Josh. 24. 15 if it seem evil unto you to serve the LORD

6. *To do evil,* רָעַע *raa,* 5.
Prov 24. 19 Fret not thyself because of evil (men)

7. *Evil,* κακία *kakia.*
Matt. 6. 34 Sufficient unto the day (is) the evil thereof

8. *Evil,* κακός, κακόν *kakos, kakon.*
Matt 24. 48 if that evil servant shall say in his heart
27. 23 Why, what evil hath he done? But they
Mark 7. 21 For from within..proceed evil thoughts
15. 14 Why, what evil hath he done? And they
Luke 23. 22 Why, what evil hath he done? I have
John 18. 23 If I have spoken..bear witness of the evil
Acts 9. 13 how much evil he hath done to thy saints
23. 9 saying, We find no evil in this man: but
Rom. 2. 9 upon every soul of man that doeth evil
3. 8 Let us do evil, that good may come?
7. 19 but the evil which I would not, that I do
7. 21 when I would do good, evil is present
9. 11 neither having done any good or evil
12. 17 Recompense to no man evil for evil
12. 21 Be not overcome of evil, but overcome e.
13. 3 not a terror to good works, but to the evil
13. 4 to (execute) wrath upon him that doeth e.
14. 20 (it is) evil for that man who eateth with
16. 19 which is good, and simple concerning evil
1 Co. 13. 5 is not easily provoked, thinketh no evil
15. 33 evil communications corrupt good mann.
2 Co 13. 7 Now I pray to God that ye do no evil
Phil. 3. 2 Beware of dogs, beware of evil workers
Col. 3. 5 evil concupiscence, and covetousness,
1 Th. 5. 15 See that none render evil for evil unto
1 Ti. 6. 10 love of money is the root of all evil
2 Ti. 4. 14 the coppersmith did me much evil: the
Titus 1. 12 The Cretians (are) alway liars, evil beasts
Heb. 5. 14 exercised to discern both good and evil
Jas. 1. 13 for God cannot be tempted with evil
3. 8 (it is) an unruly evil, full of deadly poison
1 Pe. 3. 9 Not rendering evil for evil, or railing for
3. 10 let him refrain his tongue from evil
3. 11 Let him eschew evil, and do good; let
3. 12 but the face..(is) against them that do e.

9. *Evilly,* κακῶς *kakōs.*
John 18. 23 If I have spoken evil, bear witness of the
Acts 23. 5 Thou shalt not speak evil of the ruler of

10. *The evil,* (ὁ) πονηρός *(ho) ponēros.*
Matt. 5. 37 for whatsoever is more..cometh of evil
5. 39 I say unto you, That ye resist not evil
5. 45 he maketh his sun to rise on the evil and
6. 13 lead us not..but deliver us from evil

Matt. 6. 23 But if thine eye be evil, thy whole body
7. 11 If ye then, being evil, know how to give
7. 17 but a corrupt tree bringeth forth evil
7. 18 A good tree cannot bring forth evil frui.
9. 4 Wherefore think ye evil in your hearts?
12. 34 how can ye, being evil, speak good thin.
12. 35 and an evil man, out of the evil treasure
12. 39 An evil and adulterous generation seek.
15. 19 For out of the heart proceed evil thoughts
20. 15 Is thine eye evil, because I am good?
Mark 7. 22 an evil eye, blasphemy, pride, foolishne.
Luke 3. 19 for all the evils which Herod had done
6. 22 and cast out your name as evil, for the
6. 35 kind unto the unthankful and (to) the e.
6. 45 an evil man out of the evil treasure of
7. 21 infirmities and plagues, and of evil spirits
8. 2 which had been healed of evil spirits and
11. 4 lead us not..but deliver us from evil
11. 13 If ye then, being evil, know how to give
11. 29 he began to say, This is an evil generat.
11. 34 when (thine eye) is evil, thy body also (is)
John 3. 19 men loved..because their deeds were evil
7. 7 I testify..that the works thereof are evil
Acts 19. 12 and the evil spirits went out of them
19. 13 to call over them which had evil spirits
19. 15 the evil spirit answered and said, Jesus
19. 16 the man in whom the evil spirit was le.
Gal. 1. 4 deliver us from this present evil world
Eph. 5. 16 Redeeming the time..the days are evil
6. 13 may be able to withstand in the evil day
1 Th. 5. 22 Abstain from all appearance of evil
2 Th. 3. 3 stablish you, and keep (you) from evil
1 Ti. 6. 4 whereof cometh envy..evil surmisings
2 Ti. 3. 13 evil men and seducers shall wax worse
4. 18 the Lord shall deliver me from every evil
Heb. 3. 12 lest there be in any of you an evil heart
10. 22 having our hearts sprinkled from an evil
Jas. 2. 4 and are become judges of evil thoughts?
4. 16 now ye rejoice..all such rejoicing is evil
1 Jo. 3. 12 because his own works were evil, and

11. *Evil word,* πονηρὸν ῥῆμα *ponēron rhēma.*
Matt. 5. 11 shall say all manner of evil against you

12. *Worthless,* φαῦλος *phaulos.*
John 3. 20 every one that doeth evil hateth the light
5. 29 that have done evil, unto the resurrect.
Jas. 3. 16 there (is) confusion and every evil work

EVIL, to be —

1. *To be evil,* יָרַע *yera.*
Deut 28. 54 his eye shall be evil toward his brother
28. 56 her eye shall be evil toward the husband

2. *To be evil,* רָעַע *raa.*
Deut. 15. 9 thine eye be evil against thy poor brother

EVIL, to be so —

From badness, מֵרֹעַ *meroa.*
Jer. 24. 3, 8 cannot be eaten, they are so evil
29. 17 that cannot be eaten, they are so evil

EVIL, to bring —

To do evil, treat ill, רָעַע *raa,* 5.
1 Ki. 17. 20 hast thou also brought evil upon the wi.
Jer. 25. 29 lo, I begin to bring evil on the city which

EVIL, to do —

1. *Evil,* רַע *ra.*
Jer. 11. 15 when thou doest evil, then thou rejoicest

2. *To do evil, treat ill,* רָעַע *raa,* 5.
Gen. 44. 5 Ye have done evil in so doing
Exod. 5. 23 since I came..he hath done evil to this
Lev. 5. 4 pronouncing with (his) lips to do evil
1 Ki. 14. 9 hast done evil above all that were before
1 Ch. 21. 17 that have sinned, and done evil indeed
Psa. 37. 8 fret not thyself in anywise to do evil
Prov 24. 8 He that deviseth to do evil shall be
Isa. 1. 16 Wash you, make you clean..cease to do e.
41. 23 or do evil, that we may be dismayed
Jer. 4. 22 they (are) wise to do evil, but to do good
10. 5 for they cannot do evil, neither also (is
13. 23 do good, that are accustomed to do evil
38. 9 these men have done evil in all that they
Zeph. 1. 12 will not do good, neither will he do evil

3. *To do evil,* κακοποιέω *kakopoieō.*
Mark 3. 4 Is it lawful to do good..or to do evil?
Luke 6. 9 Is it lawful..to do good, or to do evil?
3 Jo. 11 but he that doeth evil hath not seen God

EVIL entreat, to —

1. *To evil entreat,* רָעָה *raah.*
Job 24. 21 He evil entreateth the barren (that) bear

2. *To do evil, treat ill,* רָעַע *raa,* 5.
Exod. 5. 22 wherefore hast thou (so) evil entreated
Deut 26. 6 Egyptians evil entreated us, and afflicted

3. *To do evil to,* κακόω *kakoō.*
Acts 7. 6 and entreat (them) evil four hundred
7. 19 dealt subtilly..and evil entreated our

EVIL man —

Evil, bad, רַע *ra.*
Job 35. 12 answer, because of the pride of evil men

EVIL report —

Evil account or report, דִּבָּה *dibbah.*
Gen. 37. 2 brought unto his father their evil report
Num 13. 32 they brought up an evil report of the
14. 37 that did bring up the evil report upon

EVIL speaker —
A man of tongue, אִישׁ לָשׁוֹן *ish lashon.*
Psa.140. 11 Let not an evil speaker be established in

EVIL things —
1. *Evil,* רַע *ra.*
Prov 15. 28 mouth of the wicked poureth out evil th.
2. *Evil, bad,* κακός *kakos.*
Luke16. 25 and likewise Lazarus evil things : but
Rom. 1. 30 proud, boasters, inventors of evil things
1 Co. 10. 6 we should not lust after evil things, as
3. *Evil,* πονηρός *ponēros.*
Matt12. 35 and an evil man..bringeth forth evil thi.
Mark 7. 23 All these evil things cometh from within
2 Jo. 11 that biddeth..is partaker of his evil deeds
4. *Worthless,* φαῦλος *phaulos.*
Titus 2. 8 ashamed, having no evil thing to say of

EVIL doing —
1. *Injustice,* ἀδίκημα *adikēma.*
Acts 24. 20 if they have found any evil doing in me
2. *To do evil,* κακοποιέω *kakopoieō.*
1 Pe. 3. 17 suffer for well doing, than for evil doing

EVIL doer —
1. As No. 2.
Isa. 31. 2 arise against the house of the evil doers
2. *To do evil, treat ill,* רָעַע *raa,* 5.
Job 8. 20 neither will he help the evil doers
Psa. 26. 5 have hated the congregation of evil doers
37. 1 Fret not thyself because of evil doers
37. 9 For evil doers shall be cut off : but those
94. 16 Who will rise up for me against the evil d.?
119. 115 Depart from me, ye evil doers : for I will
Isa. 1. 4 a seed of evil doers, children that are cor.
9. 17 every one (is) an hypocrite and an evil d.
14. 20 seed of evil doers shall never be renowned
Jer. 20. 13 hath delivered..from the hand of evil d.
23. 14 they strengthen also the hands of evil d.
3. *Evil doer,* κακοποιός *kakopoios.*
1 Pe. 2. 12 they speak against you as evil doers, they
2. 14 by him for the punishment of evil doers
3. 16 [whereas they speak..of you, as of evil d.]
4. 15 (as) a thief, or (as) an evil doer, or (as) a
4. *Evil worker,* κακοῦργος *kakourgos.*
2 Ti. 2. 9 Wherein I suffer trouble, as an evil doer

EVIL favouredness —
Evil thing, דָּבָר רַע *dabar ra.*
Deut17. 1 wherein is blemish, (or) any evil favour.

EVIL, that which is —
1. *That which is evil or bad,* ὁ κακός *ho kakos.*
Rom13. 4 if thou do that which is evil, be afraid
3 Jo. 11 Beloved, follow not that which is evil, but
2. *That which is evil,* ὁ πονηρός *ho ponēros.*
Luke 6. 45 bringeth forth that which is evil : for of
Rom 12. 9 Abhor that which is evil; cleave to that

EVIL, the —
That which is evil, ὁ πονηρός *ho ponēros.*
John 17. 15 thou shouldest keep them from the evil

EVIL, they which are —
Evil, bad, κακός *kakos.*
Rev. 2. 2 thou canst not bear them which are evil

EVIL affected, to make —
To make bad, κακόω *kakoō.*
Acts 14. 2 made their minds evil affected against

E-VIL ME-RO'-DACH, אֱוִיל מְרֹדַךְ.
Son and successor of Nebuchadnezzar. He released Jehoiakin whom his father had kept in prison for thirty-seven years. His reign was short, from 561-559. B.C.
2 Ki.25. 27 E...did lift up the head of Jehoiachin
Jer. 52. 31 E..lifted up the head of Jehoiachin king

EWE —
1. *Ewe, lamb,* רָחֵל *rachel.*
Gen. 31. 38 thy ewes..have not cast their young, and
32. 14 he goats, two hundred ewes, and twenty
2. *Young lamb, kid, sheep,* שֶׂה *seh.*
Lev. 22. 28 (whether it be) cow or ewe, ye shall not

EWE LAMB —
Ewe lamb, כַּבְשָׂה, כִּבְשָׂה *kabsah, kibsah.*
Gen. 21. 28 Abraham set seven ewe lambs of the flock
21. 29 What (mean) these seven ewe lambs which
21. 30 For (these) seven ewe lambs shalt thou
Lev. 14. 10 one ewe lamb of the first year without
Num. 6. 14 one ewe lamb of the first year without
2 Sa. 12. 3 had nothing, save one little ewe lamb

EWES great with young —
Suckling, one giving milk, עוּל *ul.*
Psa. 78. 71 From following the ewes great with young

EXACT, to —
1. *To cause to come out, bring forth,* יָצָא *yatsa,* 5.
2 Ki.15. 20 And Menahem exacted the money of Israel
2. *To exact,* נָגַשׂ *nagas.*
Deut15. 2 he shall not exact (it) of his neighbour
15. 3 Of a foreigner thou mayest exact (it again)
2 Ki.23. 35 he exacted the silver and the gold of the
Isa. 58. 3 ye find pleasure, and exact all your lab.
3. *To exact, lift up,* נָשָׁא *nasha.*
Neh. 5. 7 Ye exact usury every one of his brother
4. *To (cause to) exact,* נָשָׁא *nasha,* 5.
Psa. 89. 22 The enemy shall not exact upon him ; nor
5. *To exact,* נָשָׁה *nashah.*
Neh. 5. 10 I likewise..might exact of them money
5. 11 Restore..to them..that ye exact of them
6. *To (cause to) exact,* נָשָׁה *nashah,* 5.
Job 11. 6 Know therefore that God exacteth of thee
7. *To do, practise, produce,* πράσσω *prassō.*
Luke 3. 13 Exact no more than that which is appoin.

EXACTION —
1. *Expulsion, exaction,* גְּרֻשָׁה *gerushah.*
Eze. 45. 9 take away your exactions from my people
2. *An exaction, lifting up,* מַשָּׁא *mashsha.*
Neh.10. 31 would leave..and the exaction of every

EXACTOR —
To exact, נָגַשׂ *nagas.*
Isa. 60. 17 also make..thine exactors righteousness

EXALT, to —
1. *To make high,* גָּבַהּ *gabah,* 5.
Prov 17. 19 he that exalteth his gate seeketh destruc.
Eze. 17. 24 know that I the LORD..have exalted the
21. 26 exalt (him that is) low, and abase (him
Obad. 4 Though thou exalt (thyself) as the eagle
2. *To lift up (self),* נָשָׂא *nasa.*
Hos. 13. 1 he exalted himself in Israel ; but when
3. *To lift up,* נָשָׂא *nasa,* 3.
2 Sa. 5. 12 he had exalted his kingdom for his people
4. *To raise up, exalt,* סָלַל *salal,* 3a.
Prov. 4. 8 Exalt her, and she shall promote thee
5. *To lift up, exalt,* רוּם *rum,* 3a.
Exod 15. 2 The LORD (is) my strength..and I will e.
Job 17. 4 therefore shalt thou not exalt (them)
Psa. 34. 3 and let us exalt his name together
37. 34 and he shall exalt thee to inherit the land
99. 5 Exalt ye the LORD our God, and worship
99. 9 Exalt the LORD our God, and worship at his
107. 32 Let them exalt him also in the congreg.
118. 28 praise thee · (thou art) my God, I will e.
Prov 14. 34 Righteousness exalteth a nation : but
Isa. 25. 1 O LORD..I will exalt thee, I will praise
Hos. 11. 7 though they called..none at all would e.
6. *To lift up, exalt,* רוּם *rum,* 5.
1 Sa. 2. 10 and exalt the horn of his anointed
1 Ki. 14. 7 as I exalted thee from among the people
16. 2 Forasmuch as I exalted thee out of the
2 Ki. 19. 22 against whom hast thou exalted (thy) voi.
Psa. 89. 19 I have exalted (one) chosen out of the
92. 10 my horn shalt thou exalt like (the horn of)
148. 14 He also exalteth the horn of his people
Prov 14. 29 (he that is) hasty of spirit exalteth folly
Isa. 13. 2 exalt the voice unto them, shake the hand
14. 13 I will exalt my throne above the stars of
37. 23 against whom hast thou exalted (thy) voi.
7. *To set on high,* שָׂגַב *sagab,* 5.
Job. 36. 22 Behold, God exalteth by his power : who
8. *To raise high, elevate,* ὑψόω *hupsoō.*
Matt11. 23 And thou..which art exalted unto heaven
23. 12 whosoever shall exalt himself shall be
23. 12 that shall humble himself shall be exal.
Luke 1. 52 put down the mighty..and exalted them
10. 15 And thou..which art exalted to heaven
14. 11 whosoever exalteth himself shall be aba.
14. 11 he that humbleth himself shall be exalted
18. 14 every one that exalteth himself shall be
18. 14 he that humbleth himself shall be exalted
Acts 2. 33 being by the right hand of God exalted
5. 31 Him hath God exalted with his right
13. 17 exalted the people when they dwelt as
2 Co.11. 7 in abasing myself that ye might be exalted
1 Pe. 5. 6 that he may exalt you in due time

EXALT self, to —
1. *To be or become high,* גָּבַהּ *gabah.*
Eze. 31. 14 To the end that none..exalt themselves
2. *To lift up self,* נָשָׂא *nasa,* 7.
1 Ki. 1. 5 the son of Haggith exalted himself, saying
Eze. 29. 15 neither shall it exalt itself any more
Dan. 11. 14 also the robbers..shall exalt themselves
3. *To raise up self,* סָלַל *salal,* 7a.
Exod. 9. 17 As yet exaltest thou thyself against my
4. *To be high, lifted up,* רוּם *rum.*
Psa. 66. 7 let not the rebellious exalt themselves
140. 8 further not..(lest) they exalt themselves
5. *To lift up self,* רוּם *rum,* 7a.
Dan. 11. 36 he shall exalt himself, and magnify
6. *To lift up upon or against,* ἐπαίρω *epairō.*
2 Co.10. 5 and every high thing that exalteth itself
11. 20 if a man exalt himself, if a man smite
7. *To lift up above,* ὑπεραίρω *huperairō.*
2 Th. 2. 4 Who opposeth and exalteth himself

EXALT highly, to —
To lift up above, ὑπερυψόω *huperupsoō.*
Phil. 2. 9 God also hath highly exalted him, and

EXALTED, to be —
1. *To be or become high or haughty,* גָּבַהּ *gabah.*
Job 36. 7 doth establish them..and they are exalt.
Isa. 5. 16 LORD of hosts shall be exalted in judg.
Eze. 19. 11 her stature was exalted among the thick
31. 5 his height was exalted above all the trees
2. *To be lifted up,* נָשָׂא *nasa,* 2.
Isa. 2. 2 shall be exalted above the hills ; and all
40. 4 Every valley shall be exalted, and every
Mic. 4. 1 it shall be exalted above the hills ; and
3. *To lift up self,* נָשָׂא *nasa,* 7.
Num24. 7 higher..and his kingdom shall be exalted
1 Ch. 29. 11 and thou art exalted as head above all
4. *To be gone up,* עָלָה *alah,* 2.
Psa. 47. 9 (belong) unto God : he is greatly exalted
97. 9 For thou, LORD..art exalted far above
5. *To be high, lifted up,* רוּם *rum.*
1 Sa. 2. 1 mine horn is exalted in the LORD ; my
2 Sa. 22. 47 exalted be the God of the rock of my salv.
Psa. 12. 8 wicked walk..when the vilest men are e.
13. 2 how long shall mine enemy be exalted
18. 46 and let the God of my salvation be exal.
21. 13 Be thou exalted, LORD, in thine own
46. 10 I will be exalted..I will be exalted in
57. 5, 11 Be thou exalted, O God, above the
89. 16 in thy righteousness shall they be exalt.
89. 24 and in my name shall his horn be exalted
108. 5 Be thou exalted, O God, above the heavens
112. 9 his horn shall be exalted with honour
Prov 11. 11 By the blessing..the city is exalted
Isa. 30. 18 therefore will he be exalted, that he
49. 11 and my highways shall be exalted
52. 13 he shall be exalted and extolled, and be
Hos. 13. 6 were filled, and their heart was exalted
6. *To be lifted up, exalted,* רוּם *rum,* 3b.
Neh. 9. 5 which is exalted above all blessing and
Psa. 75. 10 the horns of the righteous shall be exal.
7. *Be lifted up, exalted,* רוּם *rum,* 1 [V.L. 5].
Psa. 89. 17 in thy favour our horn shall be exalted
8. *To be high,* רָמַם *ramam.*
Job 24. 24 They are exalted for a little while, but
Psa.118. 16 The right hand of the LORD is exalted
9. *To be or become high,* רוּם *rum,* 7a.
Isa. 33. 10 Now will I rise..now will I be exalted
10. *To be high or strong,* שָׂגַב *sagab.*
Job 5. 11 those which mourn may be exalted to saf.
11. *To be or become high or strong,* שָׂגַב *sagab,* 2.
Isa. 2. 11, 17 the LORD alone shall be exalted in
12. 4 make mention that his name is exalted
33. 5 The LORD is exalted ; for he dwelleth

EXALTED above measure, to be —
To lift up above, ὑπεραίρω *huperairō.*
2 Co.12. 7, 7 lest I should be exalted above measure

EXALTED, in that he is —
In his lifting up, ἐν τῷ ὕψει αὐτοῦ. [*hupsos*].
Jas 1. 9 Let the brother..rejoice in that he is ex.

EXAMINATION —
A judging up, examination, investigation, ἀνάκρισις *anakrisis.*
Acts 25. 26 after examination had, I might have so.

EXAMINE, be examined, to —
1. *To try, prove, test,* בָּחַן *bachan.*
Psa. 26. 2 Examine me, O LORD, and prove me ; try
2. *To examine, seek, enquire,* דָּרַשׁ *darash.*
Ezra 10. 16 and sat down..to examine the matter
3. *To examine, investigate,* ἀνακρίνω *anakrinō.*
Luke23. 14 I, having examined (him) before you, have
Acts 4. 9 If we this day be examined of the good
12. 19 he examined the keepers, and commanded
24. 8 by examining of whom thyself mayest
28. 18 Who, when they had examined me, would
1 Co. 9. 3 Mine answer to them that do examine
4. *To examine fully,* ἀνετάζω *anetazō.*
Acts 22. 24 bade that he should be examined by sc.
22. 29 from him which should have examined
5. *To prove,* δοκιμάζω *dokimazō.*
1 Co. 11. 28 let a man examine himself, and so let him
6. *To try,* πειράζω *peirazō.*
2 Co. 13. 5 Examine yourselves, whether ye be in the

EXAMPLE —
1. *Sample, exhibition,* δεῖγμα *deigma.*
Jude 7 the cities..are set forth for an example
2. *A type, model,* τύπος *tupos.*
1 Co.10. 6 Now these things were our examples, to
1 Ti. 4. 12 but be thou an example of the believers
3. *Copy, an under-writing,* ὑπογραμμός *hupogra.*
1 Pe. 2. 21 leaving us an example, that ye should
4. *A sample, exhibition,* ὑπόδειγμα *hupodeigma.*
John 13. 15 I have given you an example, that ye
Heb. 4. 11 lest any man fall after the same example
8. 5 Who serve unto the example and shadow
Jas. 5. 10 for an example of suffering affliction, and

EXAMPLE, to make a public —
To exhibit publicly, παραδειγματίζω *paradeigmati.*
Matt. 1. 19 not willing [to make her a public example]

EXCEED, to —
1. *To show self mighty,* גָּבַר *gabar,* 7.
Job 36. 9 their transgressions that they have exce.

2. *To be or become great*, גָּדַל *gadal*.
1 Ki. 10. 23 So king Solomon exceeded all the kings of

3. *To make or become great*, גָּדַל *gadal*, 5.
1 Sa. 20. 41 wept one with another, until David exc.

4. *To add*, יָסַף *yasaph*.
2 Ch. 9. 6 (for) thou exceedest the fame that I heard

5. *To add*, יָסַף *yasaph*, 5.
Deut 25. 3 not exceed: lest, (if) he should exceed
1 Ki. 10. 7 thy wisdom and prosperity exceedeth the

6. *To be over and above, abound, exceed*, περισσεύω.
Matt. 5. 20 except your righteousness shall exceed
2 Co. 3. 9 much more doth the ministration..exceed

EXCEEDING —

1. *Excellent, abundant*, יַתִּיר *yattir*.
Dan. 3. 22 the furnace exceeding hot, the flame of
7. 19 exceeding dreadful, whose teeth (were of)

2. *Superabundance, excellency*, יֶתֶר *yether*.
Dan. 8. 9 a little horn, which waxed exceeding gr.

3. *Might*, מְאֹד *meod*.
Gen. 15. 1 I (am) thy shield, (and) thy exceeding g.
17. 6 And I will make thee exceeding fruitful
27. 34 he cried with a great and exceeding bitter
Exod. 1. 7 multiplied, and waxed exceeding mighty
19. 16 the voice of the trumpet exceeding loud
Num 14. 7 The land..(is) an exceeding good land
2 Sa. 8. 8 from Betah..king David took exceeding
12. 2 The rich (man) had exceeding many floc.
1 Ki. 4. 29 God gave Solomon wisdom..exceeding
7. 47 because they were exceeding many
1 Ch 20. 2 he brought also exceeding much spoil out
2 Ch. 32. 27 Hezekiah had exceeding much riches and
Psa. 119. 96 (but) thy commandment (is) exceeding
Jer. 48. 29 the pride of Moab, he is exceeding proud
Eze. 9. 9 The iniquity of the house .(is) exceeding
16. 13 thou wast exceeding beautiful, and thou
37. 10 and stood up..an exceeding great army
47. 10 as the fish of the great sea, exceeding

4. *Above, upward, onward*, לְמַעְלָה *le-malah*.
1 Ch. 22. 5 the house..(must be) exceeding magnifical
2 Ch. 16. 12 until his disease (was) exceeding (great)

5. *To spread out*, סָרַח *sarach*.
Eze. 23. 15 exceeding in dyed attire upon their heads

6. *Many, much, enough, abundant*, רַב *rab*.
2 Ch. 14. 14 for there was exceeding much spoil in

7. *To make great or abundant*, רָבָה מְאֹד *rabah meod*, 5
2 Ch. 11. 12 (he put) shields..and made them exceed

8. *Great*, שַׂגִּיא *saggi*.
Dan. 6. 23 Then was the king exceeding glad for

9. *Beyond surpassing*, καθ' ὑπερβολήν *kath huper*.
Rom. 7. 13 that sin..might become exceeding sinful

10. *Very, greatly*, λίαν *lian*.
Matt. 2. 16 Then Herod..was exceeding wroth, and
4. 8 taketh him up into an exceeding high
8. 28 two possessed with devils..exceeding
Mark 9. 3 became shining, exceeding white as snow
Luke 23. 8 when Herod saw Jesus, he was exceeding

11. *To God*, τῷ θεῷ *tō theō*.
Acts 7. 20 Moses was born, and was exceeding fair

12. *Greatly, vehemently*, σφόδρα *sphodra*.
Matt 2. 10 they rejoiced with exceeding great joy
17. 23 And they were exceeding sorry
26. 22 they were exceeding sorrowful, and began
Rev. 16. 21 for the plague thereof was exceeding

13. *Over, above*, ὑπέρ *huper*.
Eph. 3. 20 Now unto him that is able to do exceed.

14. *To cast beyond, surpass*, ὑπερβάλλω *huperballō*.
2 Co. 9. 14 which long after you for the exceeding
Eph. 1. 19 the exceeding greatness of his power to
2. 7 he might show the exceeding riches of his

15. *To be over and above*, ὑπερπερισσεύω *huperper*.
2 Co. 7. 4 am exceeding joyful in all our tribulation

16. *To God*, לֵאלֹהִים *l-elohim*.
Jon. 3. 3 Now Nineveh was an exceeding great city

17. *To be made wise*, חָכַם *chakam*, 4.
Prov 30. 24 little upon the earth, but they (are) exceed.

18. *With joy, gladness, mirth*, בְּשִׂמְחָה *be-simchah*.
Psa. 21. 6 thou hast made him exceeding glad with
43. 4 Then will I go..unto God my exceeding

19. *With great joy*, שִׂמְחָה גְדֹלָה *simchah gedolah*.
Jon. 4. 6 So Jonah was exceeding glad of the gourd

EXCEEDING, far more —

Beyond measure surpassing, καθ' ὑπερβολὴν εἰς ὑπερβολήν.
2 Co. 4. 17 a far more exceeding (and) eternal weight

EXCEEDING proudly —

High, haughty, גָּבֹהַּ *gaboah*.
1 Sa. 2. 3 Talk no more so exceeding proudly; let

EXCEEDINGLY —

1. *Abundant, excellent*, יַתִּיר *yattir*.
Dan. 7. 7 dreadful and terrible, and strong exceed.

2. *Might*, (כְּאֹר) מְאֹד *meod (meod)*.
Gen. 7. 19 the waters prevailed exceedingly upon
13. 13 and sinners before the LORD exceedingly
17. 2 and will multiply thee exceedingly
17. 20 and will multiply him exceedingly; twelve
30. 43 the man increased exceedingly, and had
47. 27 and grew, and multiplied exceedingly
2 Ki. 10. 4 But they were exceedingly afraid, and
Esth. 4. 4 Then was the queen exceedingly grieved
Psa. 119. 167 thy testimonies; and I love them exce.

3. *Above, upward, onward*, לְמַעְלָה *le-malah*.
1 Ch. 29. 25 the LORD magnified Solomon exceedingly
2 Ch. 1. 1 God (was) with him, and magnified him e.
17. 12 And Jehoshaphat waxed great exceedin.
26. 8 for he strengthened (himself) exceedingly

4. *Many, much, enough, abundant*, רַב *rab*.
Psa. 123. 3 for we are exceedingly filled with conte.
123. 4 Our soul is exceedingly filled with the

5. *To make many or abundant*, רָבָה מְאֹד *rabah meod*, 5.
Gen. 16. 10 I will multiply thy seed exceedingly, that
1 Sa. 26. 21 have played the fool, and have erred ex.

6. *To joy, rejoicing*, אֱלֵי־גִיל *ele gil*.
Job 3. 22 Which rejoice exceedingly, (and) are glad

7. *A trembling*, חֲרָדָה *charadah*.
Gen. 27 33 Isaac trembled very exceedingly and

8. *With rejoicing, gladness, mirth*, בְּשִׂמְחָה *be-simchah*.
Psa. 68. 3 rejoice before God; yea, let them exceed.

9. *Desire, lust*, תַּאֲוָה *taavah*.
Psa. 106. 14 But lusted exceedingly in the wilderness

10. *Great displeasure or fear*, רַע or יִרְאָה נ׳ [*ra, yirah*].
Neh. 2. 10 it grieved them exceedingly that there
Jon. 1. 10 Then were the men exceedingly afraid
1. 16 the men feared the LORD exceedingly, and
4 1 But it displeased Jonah exceedingly, and

11. *With very great hatred*, שִׂנְאָה גְּדוֹלָה מְאֹד [*sinah*].
2 Sa. 13. 15 Then Amnon hated her exceedingly; so

12. *More abundantly*, περισσοτέρως *perissoterōs*.
2 Co. 7. 13 and exceedingly the more joyed we for

13. *Exceedingly*, περισσῶς *perissōs*.
Acts 26. 11 and, being exceedingly mad against them

14. *Greatly, vehemently*, σφόδρα *sphodra*.
Matt 19. 25 they were exceedingly amazed, saying

15. *Greatly, vehemently*, σφοδρῶς *sphodrōs*.
Acts 27. 18 we being exceedingly tossed with a temp.

16. *Above out of measure*, ὑπὲρ ἐκ περισσοῦ.
1 Th. 3 10 Night and day praying exceedingly that

17. *A great fear*, φόβον μέγαν *phobon megan*.
Mark 4. 41 they feared exceedingly, and said one to

EXCEEDINGLY, the more —

More abundantly, περισσοτέρως *perissoterōs*.
Mark 15. 14 they cried out [the more exceedingly]
Gal. 1. 14 being [more exceedingly] zealous of the

EXCEL, to —

1. *Mighty*, גִּבּוֹר *gibbor*.
Psa. 103. 20 ye his angels, that excel in strength, that

2. *To make abundant*, יָתַר *yathar*, 5.
Gen. 49. 4 Unstable as water thou shalt not excel

3. *To be pre-eminent, excel*, נָצַח *natsach*, 3.
1 Ch. 15. 21 with harps on the Sheminith to excel

4. *To go up*, עָלָה *alah*.
Prov. 31. 29 done virtuously, but thou excellest them

5. *To be abundant*, רָבָה *rabah*.
1 Ki. 4. 30 Solomon's wisdom excelled the wisdom

6. *To be over and above*, περισσεύω *perisseuō*.
1 Co. 14. 12 seek that ye may excel to the edifying

7. *To cast beyond, surpass*, ὑπερβάλλω *huperballō*.
2 Co. 3. 10 by reason of the glory that excelleth

EXCELLENCY —

1. *Rising, excellency*, גַּאֲוָה *gaavah*.
Deut 33. 26 (who) rideth..in his excellency on the sky
33. 29 and who (is) the sword of thy excellency!
Psa. 68. 34 his excellency (is) over Israel, and his

2. *Rising, excellency*, גָּאוֹן *gaon*.
Exod 15. 7 in the greatness of thine excellency thou
Job 37 4 thundereth with..voice of his excellency
Psa. 47. 4 the excellency of Jacob, whom he loved
Isa. 13. 19 the beauty of the Chaldees' excellency
60. 15 I will make thee an eternal excellency, a
Eze. 24. 21 excellency of your strength, the desire
Amos 6. 8 I abhor the excellency of Jacob, and hate
8. 7 LORD hath sworn by the excellency of Jac.
Nah. 2. 2 excellency of Jacob, as the excellency of

3. *Height, loftiness*, גֹּבַהּ *gobah*.
Job 40. 10 Deck thyself..(with) majesty and excell.

4. *Honour, beauty, majesty*, הָדָר *hadar*.
Isa. 35. 2 the excellency of Carmel and Sharon
35. 2 shall see..the excellency of our God

5. *Superabundance, excellency*, יֶתֶר *yether*.
Gen. 49. 3 excellency of dignity, and the excellency
Job 4. 21 Doth not their excellency (which is) in

6. *Advantage*, יִתְרוֹן *yithron*.
Eccl. 7. 12 excellency of knowledge (is, that) wisdom

7. *Excellence, rising*, שְׂאֵת *seeth*.
Job 13. 11 Shall not his excellency make you afraid?
Psa. 62. 4 to cast (him) down from his excellency

8. *Excellency*, שִׂיא *si*.
Job 20. 6 his excellency mount up to the heavens

9. *A casting beyond, surpassing*, ὑπερβολή *huperb.*
2 Co. 4. 7 the excellency of the power may be of God

10. *The pre-eminence*, τὸ ὑπερέχον *to huperechon*.
Phil. 3. 8 the excellency of the knowledge of Christ

11. *A holding over or beyond*, ὑπεροχή *huperochē*.
1 Co. 2. 1 with excellency of speech or of wisdom

EXCELLENT —

1. *Honourable*, אַדִּיר *addir*.
Psa. 8. 1, 9 how excellent (is) thy name in all the ea.
16. 3 the excellent, in whom (is) all my delight
76. 4 Thou (art) more glorious (and) excellent

2. *To choose, try, fix on*, בָּחַר *bachar*.
Song 5. 15 (is) as Lebanon, excellent as the cedars

3. *Rising, excellency, pride*, גָּאוֹן *gaon*.
Isa. 4. 2 the fruit of the earth (shall be) excellent

4. *To make or become great*, גָּדַל *gadal*, 5.
Isa. 28. 29 wonderful in counsel..excellent in wor.

5. *Precious*, יָקָר *yaqar*.
Psa. 36. 7 How excellent (is) thy loving kindness, O

6. *Excellent, abundant*, יַתִּיר *yattir*.
Dan. 2. 31 great image, whose brightness (was) ex.
4. 36 and excellent majesty was added unto me
5. 12 as an excellent spirit, and knowledge, and
5. 14 and excellent wisdom is found in thee
6. 3 because an excellent spirit (was) in him

7. *Superabundance, excellency*, יֶתֶר *yether*.
Prov 17. 7 Excellent speech becometh not a fool

8. *Excellent*, יָקָר *yaqar* [V.L. קַר *qar*].
Prov 17. 27 man of understanding is..excellent spirit

9. *Abundance*, רֹב *rob*.
Psa 150. 2 praise him..to his excellent greatness

10. *Great*, שַׂגִּיא *saggi*.
Job 37. 23 (he is) excellent in power, and in judgment

11. *Ornaments*, עֲדִי *adi*.
Eze. 16. 7 and thou art come to excellent ornaments

12. *Beauty*, תִּפְאֶרֶת *tiphereth*.
Esth. 1. 4 and the honour of his excellent majesty

13. *Proper or becoming to the great*, μεγαλοπρεπής.
2 Pe. 1. 17 a voice to him from the excellent glory

EXCELLENT, more —

1. *Greater, better, widely different*, διαφορώτερος.
Heb. 1. 4 obtained a more excellent name than
8. 6 he obtained a more excellent ministry

2. *Very surpassing*, καθ' ὑπερβολήν. [*huperbolē*].
1 Co. 12. 31 yet show I unto you a more excellent way

3. *More, greater, fuller*, πλείων *pleiōn*.
Heb. 11. 4 a more excellent sacrifice than Cain

EXCELLENT, most —

A host, powerful, noble, κράτιστος *kratistos*.
Luke 1. 3 write unto thee..most excellent Theoph.
Acts 23. 26 Claudius Lysias unto the most excellent

EXCELLENT, things that are (more) —

Things that differ, are pre-eminent, τὰ διαφέροντα.
Rom. 2. 18 approvest..things that are more excellent
Phil. 1. 10 ye may approve things that are excellent

EXCELLENT, to be —

1. *To become set on high*, שָׂגַב *sagab*, 2.
Psa. 148. 13 his name alone is excellent; his glory

2. *To cause to go about or spy out*, תּוּר *tur*, 5.
Prov. 12. 26 The righteous (is) more excellent than his

EXCELLENT thing —

1. *Rising, excellency*, גֵּאוּת *geuth*.
Isa. 12. 5 he hath done excellent things: this (is)

2. *Foremost, leading*, נָגִיד *nagid*.
Prov. 8. 6 Hear; for I will speak of excellent things

3. *Threefold, excellent, weighty*, שָׁלִישׁ *shalish*.
Prov 22. 20 Have not I written..thee excellent things

EXCELLENT (oil) —

Head, top, רֹאשׁ *rosh*.
Psa. 141. 5 (it shall be) an excellent oil, (which) shall

EXCELLETH —

Advantage, יִתְרוֹן *yithron*.
Eccl. 2. 13 excelleth folly, as far as light excelleth

EXCEPT —

1. *When not*, וְאַיִן *ve-ayin*.
Gen. 44 26 except our youngest brother (be) with us

2. *To the separation of*, לְבַד *le-bad*.
Esth. 4. 11 except such to whom the king shall hold

3. *Without*, בִּלְתִּי *bilti*.
Gen. 43. 3 shall not see my face except your brot.
Amos 3. 3 two walk together, except they be agreed?

4. *That, because, when*, כִּי *ki*.
Num. 16. 13 except thou make thyself altogether

5. *Therefore, except, but*, לָהֵן *lahen*.
Dan. 2. 11 except the gods, whose dwelling is not
6. 5 except we find (it) against him concerning

6. *If not*, לוּלֵא *lule*.
Gen. 43. 10 except we had lingered surely now we

7. *If not*, לוּלֵי *lule*.
1 Sa. 25. 34 except thou hadst hasted and come to
Isa. 1. 9 Except the LORD of hosts had left unto

8. *Only, surely, nevertheless*, רַק *raq*.
Gen. 47. 26 except the land of..priests only, (which)

9. *If...not*, ἐὰν...μή *ean...mē*.
Matt. 5. 20 except your righteousness shall exceed
12. 29 except he first bind the strong man :
18. 3 Except ye be converted, and become as
26. 42 not pass away from me, except I drink
Mark 3. 27 except he will first bind the strong man
7. 3 except they wash (their) hands oft, eat
7. 4 except they wash, they eat not Lu.13. 3. 5
John 3. 2 do these miracles..except God be with
3. 3 Except a man be born again, he cannot
3. 5 Except a man be born of water and (of)
3. 27 except it be given him from heaven
4. 48 Except ye see signs and wonders, ye will
6. 44 except the Father which hath sent me
6. 53 Except ye eat the flesh of the Son of man
6. 65 except it were given unto him of my
12. 24 Except a corn of wheat fall into the
15. 4 bear fruit..except it abide in the vine
15. 4 no more can ye, except ye abide 20. 25.
Acts 8. 31 How can I, except some man should
15. 1 Except ye be circumcised after the
27. 31 Except these abide in the ship, ye cannot
Rom. 10. 15 how shall they preach except they be
1 Co. 14. 6 except I shall speak to you either by
14. 7 except they give a distinction in the
14. 9 except ye utter by the tongue words easy
15. 36 that..is not quickened, except it die
2 Th. 2. 3 except there come a falling away first
2 Ti. 2. 5 not crowned, except he strive lawfully
Rev. 2. 5 remove thy candlestick..except thou re.
2. 22 except they repent of their deeds

10. *If not*, εἰ μή *ei mē*.
Matt 19. 9 [except (it be) for fornication, and shall]
24. 22 And except those days should be shorte.
John 19. 11 except it were given thee from above
Rom. 7. 7 except the law had said, Thou shalt not
9. 29 Except the Lord of Sabaoth had left us
2 Co. 12. 13 except (it be) that I..was not burdenso.

11. *If not*, εἰ μή τι *ei mē ti*.
Luke 9. 13 except we should go and buy meat for
1 Co. 7. 5 except (it be) with consent for a time
2 Co. 13. 5 Christ is in you, except ye be reprobates

12. *If not, except*, ἐκτὸς εἰ μή *ektos ei mē*.
1 Co. 14. 5 except he interpret, that the church

13. *Near by, without, outside of*, παρεκτός *parektos*.
Acts 26. 29 altogether such as I am, except these

14. *More than, except*, πλήν *plēn*.
Acts 8. 1 were all scattered..except the apostles

15. *But if, except*, כִּי אִם *ki im*.
Gen. 32. 26 will not let thee go, except thou bless me

16. *If not*, אִם לֹא *im lo*.
Gen. 44. 23 Except your youngest brother come down
Deut 32. 30 except their Rock had sold them and
Josh. 7. 12 except ye destroy the accursed from

EXCEPT it be —
Either, or, ἤ *ē*.
Acts 24. 21 Except it be for this one voice, that I

EXCEPT that —
If not, εἰ μή *ei mē*.
Mark 13. 20 except that the Lord had shortened those

EXCEPTED, to be —
Without, outside, ἐκτός *ektos*.
1 Co. 15. 27 he is excepted which did put all things

EXCESS —
1. *Incontinence*, ἀκρασία *akrasia*.
Matt 23. 25 they are full of extortion and [excess]

2. *A pouring out upon*, ἀνάχυσις *anachusis*.
1 Pe. 4. 4 not with (them) to the same excess of

3. *Prodigality*, ἀσωτία *asōtia*.
Eph. 5. 18 be not drunk with wine, wherein is exc.

EXCESS of wine —
Overflowing of wine, οἰνοφλυγία *oinophlugia*.
1 Pe. 4. 3 in lasciviousness, lusts, excess of wine

EXCHANGE —
Change, exchange, תְּמוּרָה *temurah*.
Lev. 27. 10 it and the exchange thereof shall be holy
Job 28. 17 exchange of it (shall not be for) jewels of

EXCHANGE, in —
An equivalent, fair exchange, ἀντάλλαγμα *antall.*
Matt 16. 26 what shall a man give in exchange for
Mark 8. 37 what shall a man give in exchange for

EXCHANGE, to —
To change, exchange, מוּר *mur*, 5.
Eze. 48. 14 neither exchange, nor alienate the first

EXCHANGER —
One who sits at a table, exchanger, τραπεζίτης.
Matt 25. 27 to have put my money to the exchangers

EXCLUDE, to —
To shut out, ἐκκλείω *ekkleiō*.
Rom. 3. 27 Where (is) boasting then? It is excluded
Gal. 4. 17 they would exclude you, that ye might

EXCUSE, to make —
To ask off from, or away, παραιτέομαι *paraiteomai*.
Luke 14. 18 all with one (consent) began to make ex.

EXCUSE, without —
Without apology, ἀναπολόγητος *anapologētos*.
Rom. 1. 20 so that they are without excuse

EXCUSE (one's) self, to —
To speak self off, apologise, ἀπολογέομαι *apologeo.*
Rom. 2. 15 accusing or else excusing one another
2 Co. 12. 19 think ye that we excuse ourselves unto

EXCUSED, to be —
To ask off from, παραιτέομαι *paraiteomai*.
Luke 14. 18 go and see it : I pray thee have me exc.
14. 19 to prove them : I pray thee have me ex.

EXECRATION —
Execration, oath, curse, אָלָה *alah*.
Jer. 42. 18 shall be an execration, and an astonish.
44. 12 shall be an execration, (and) an astonish.

EXECUTE, to —
1. *To do*, עָבַד *abad*.
Num. 8. 11 they may execute the service of the LORD

2. *To do*, עָשָׂה *asah*.
Exod 12. 12 the gods of Egypt I will execute judgment
Num. 5. 30 priest shall execute upon her all this
33. 4 gods also the LORD executed judgments
Deut 10. 18 execute the judgment of the fatherless
33. 21 he executed the justice of the LORD, and
1 Sa. 28. 18 executedst his fierce wrath upon Amalek
2 Sa. 8. 15 David executed judgment and justice
1 Ki. 6. 12 and execute my judgments, and keep all
1 Ch. 18. 14 executed judgment and justice among all
2 Ch. 24. 24 So they executed judgment against Joash
Psa. 9. 16 known (by) the judgment (which) he exe
99. 4 thou executest judgment and righteous.
103. 6 LORD executeth righteousness and judg.
119. 84 execute judgment on them that persecute
146. 7 Which executeth judgment for the oppr.
149. 7 To execute vengeance upon the heathen
149. 9 To execute upon them the judgment
Isa. 16. 3 execute judgment ; make thy shadow as
Jer. 5. 1 if there be (any) that executeth judgment
7. 5 if ye throughly execute judgment betw.
22. 3 Execute ye judgment and righteousness
23. 5 execute judgment and justice in the earth
23. 20 until he have executed, and till he have
33. 15 shall execute judgment and righteousness
Eze. 5. 8 will execute judgments in the midst of
5. 10 I will execute judgments in thee, and the
5. 15 I shall execute judgments in thee in anger
11. 9 and will execute judgments among you
11. 12 neither executed my judgments, but have
16. 41 execute judgments upon thee in the sight
18. 8 executed true judgment between man and
18. 17 hath executed my judgments, hath walked
20. 24 they had not executed my judgments, but
23. 10 for they had executed judgment upon her
25. 11 I will execute judgments upon Moab
25. 17 I will execute great vengeance upon them
28. 22 I shall have executed judgments in her
28. 26 I have executed judgments upon all those
30. 14 and will execute judgments in No
30. 19 Thus will I execute judgments in Egypt
39. 21 see my judgment that I have executed
45. 9 execute judgment and justice, take away
Hos. 11. 9 not execute the fierceness of mine anger
Joel 2. 11 for (he is) strong that executeth his word
Mic. 5. 15 will execute vengeance in anger and fury
7. 9 plead my cause..execute judgment for

3. *To judge, act as magistrate*, שָׁפַט *shaphat*.
Zech. 7. 9 Execute true judgment, and show mercy
8. 16 execute the judgment of truth and peace

4. *To do*, ποιέω *poieō*.
John 5. 27 given him authority to execute judgment
Jude 15 To execute judgment upon all, and to

EXECUTE (judgment), to —
To judge, decide, דִּין *din*.
Jer. 21. 12 Execute judgment in the morning, and

EXECUTED, to be —
1. *To be done, performed*, עָבַד *abad*, 4.
Ezra 7. 26 let judgment be executed speedily upon

2. *To be done, performed*, עָשָׂה *asah*, 2.
Eccl. 8 11 an evil work is not executed speedily

EXECUTING —
To do, עָשָׂה *asah*.
2 Ki. 10. 30 executing (that which is) right in mine

EXECUTION, to be put in —
To be done, עָשָׂה *asah*, 2.
Esth. 9. 1 decree drew near to be put in execution

EXECUTIONER —
A spearman (from Lat. speculator), σπεκουλάτωρ.
Mark 6. 27 king sent an executioner, and commanded

EXEMPTED —
Free, acquitted, exempt, נָקִי *naqi*.
1 Ki. 15. 22 throughout all Judah; none (was) exem.

EXERCISE —
Gymnastic exercise, γυμνασία *gumnasia*.
1 Ti. 4. 8 For bodily exercise profiteth little ; but

EXERCISE, to —
1. *To do*, עָשָׂה *asah*.
Jer. 9. 24 the LORD which exercise loving kindness

2. *To work up*, ἀσκέω *askeō*.
Acts 24. 16 herein do I exercise myself, to have alw.

3. *To use exercise, train up*, γυμνάζω *gumnazō*.
1 Ti. 4. 7 exercise thyself (rather) unto godliness
Heb. 5. 14 exercised to discern both good and evil
12. 11 unto them which are exercised thereby
2 Pe. 2. 14 have exercised with covetous practices

4. *To do*, ποιέω *poieō*.
Rev. 13. 12 he exerciseth all the power of the first

EXERCISE (robbery), to —
To take away violently, גָּזַל *gazal*.
Eze. 22. 29 exercised robbery, and have vexed the

EXERCISE self, to —
To go, walk, proceed, הָלַךְ *halak*, 3.
Psa. 131. 1 neither do I exercise myself in great

EXERCISED, to be —
To be afflicted, humbled, עָנָה *anah*.
Eccl. 1. 13 hath God given..to be exercised therew.
3. 10 to the sons of men to be exercised in it

EXHORT, to —
1. *To exhort, recommend*, παραινέω *paraineō*.
Acts 27. 22 I exhort you to be of good cheer : for

2. *To call near, or for*, παρακαλέω *parakaleō*.
Acts 2. 40 other words did he testify and exhort
11. 23 exhorted them all, that with purpose
14. 22 exhorting them to continue in the faith
15. 32 exhorted the brethren with many words
Rom 12. 8 he that exhorteth, on exhortation : he
2 Co. 9. 5 thought..necessary to exhort the breth.
1 Th. 2. 11 As ye know how we exhorted and comfo.
4. 1 exhort (you) by the Lord Jesus, that as ye
5. 14 we exhort you, brethren, warn them that
2 Th. 3. 12 exhort by our Lord Jesus Christ, that with
1 Ti. 2. 1 I exhort therefore, that, first of all
6. 2 These things teach and exhort
2 Ti. 4. 2 exhort, with..long suffering and doctri.
Titus 1. 9 to exhort and to convince the gainsayers
2. 6 Young men likewise exhort to be sober
2. 15 and exhort, and rebuke with all author.
Heb. 3. 13 But exhort one another daily, while it is
1 Pe. 5. 1 The elders which are among you I exh.
5. 12 exhorting, and testifying that this is the
Jude 3 and exhort (you) that ye should earnestly

3. *To turn forward, propel*, προτρέπω *protrepō*.
Acts 18. 27 exhorting the disciples to receive him

EXHORT (one another), to —
To call near or for, παρακαλέω *parakaleō*.
Heb. 10. 25 exhorting (one another) : and so much

EXHORTATION —
A calling near or for, παράκλησις *paraklēsis*.
Acts 13. 15 if ye have any word of exhortation for
Rom 12. 8 he that exhorteth, on exhortation : he
1 Co. 14. 3 edification, and exhortation, and comfort
2 Co. 8. 17 he accepted the exhortation ; but being
1 Th. 2. 3 our exhortation (was) not of deceit, nor
1 Ti. 4. 13 to reading, to exhortation, to doctrine
Heb. 12. 5 ye have forgotten the exhortation which
13. 22 brethren, suffer the word of exhortation

EXHORTATION, to give much —
To call near with much discourse, παρακαλέω λόγῳ πολλῷ. *parakaleō logō pollō*.
Acts 20. 2 had given them much exhortation, he

EXHORTATION, in one's —
To call near or for, παρακαλέω *parakaleō*.
Luke 3. 18 And many other things in his exhortation

EXILE —
To remove, גָּלָה *galah*.
2 Sa. 15. 19 for thou (art) a stranger, and also an ex.

EXILE, captive —
Wanderer, צֹעֶה *tsoeh*.
Isa. 51. 14 The captive exile hasteneth that he may

EXORCIST —
One who adjures out demons, ἐξορκιστής *exorkistēs*.
Acts 19. 13 certain of the vagabond Jews, exorcists

EXPECT, to —
1. *To receive from, expect, wait for*, ἐκδέχομαι.
Heb. 10. 13 expecting till his enemies be made his

2. *To think toward, look for*, προσδοκάω *prosdokaō*.
Acts 3. 5 expecting to receive something of them

EXPECTATION —
1. *Expectation*, מַבָּט *mabbat*.
Isa. 20. 5 and ashamed of Ethiopia their expecta.
20. 6 such (is) our expectation, whither we flee

2. *Expectation*, מֶבָּט *mebbat*.
Zech. 9. 5 Ekron, for her expectation, shall be asha.

3. *Hope, expectation*, תִּקְוָה *tiqvah*.
Psa. 9. 18 expectation of the poor shall (not) perish
62. 5 for my expectation (is) from him
Prov 10. 28 expectation of the wicked shall perish
11. 7 man dieth, (his) expectation shall perish
11. 23 the expectation of the wicked (is) wrath
23. 18 thine expectation shall not be cut off
24. 14 and thy expectation shall not be cut off

4. *Thinking toward, looking for*, προσδοκία *prosdokia*.
Acts 12. 11 (from) all the expectation of the people of

EXPECTATION, to be in —
To think toward, look for, προσδοκάω *prosdokaō*.
Luke 3. 15 as the people were in expectation, and all

EXPECTATION, earnest —
A thinking or looking away to, ἀποκαραδοκία.
Rom. 8. 19 the earnest expectation of the creature
Phil. 1. 20 According to my earnest expectation and

EXPECTED —
Hope, expectation, תִּקְוָה *tiqvah.*
Jer. 29. 11 not of evil, to give you an expected end

EXPEDIENT, to be —
To bear together, συμφέρω *sumpherō.*
John 11. 50 it is expedient for us, that one man should
16. 7 It is expedient for you that I go away
18. 14 that it was expedient that one man should
1 Co. 6. 12 lawful..but all things are not expedient
10. 23 lawful..but all things are not expedient
2 Co. 8. 10 this is expedient for you, who have begun
12. 1 It is not expedient for me doubtless to

EXPEL, to —
1. *To cast out,* גָּרַשׁ *garash,* 3.
Judg 11. 7 expel me out of my father's house? and
2. *To thrust out,* הָדַף *hadaph.*
Josh. 23. 5 he shall expel them from before you, and
3. *To take possession of, dispossess,* יָרַשׁ *yarash,* 5.
Josh. 13. 13 Israel expelled not the Geshurites, nor
Judg. 1. 20 expelled thence the three sons of Anak
4. *To cast out,* ἐκβάλλω *ekballō.*
Acts 13. 50 and expelled them out of their coasts

EXPELLED, to be —
To drive or force away, נָדַח *nadach.*
2 Sa. 14. 14 his banished be not expelled from him

EXPENSES —
Outgoing, expenditure, נִפְקָא *niphqa.*
Ezra 6. 4 let the expenses be given out of the king's
6. 8 expenses be given unto these men, that

EXPERIENCE —
Proof, testing, δοκιμή *dokimē.*
Rom 5. 4 patience, experience; and experience

EXPERIENCE, to have —
To see, רָאָה *raah.*
Eccl. 1. 16 had great experience of wisdom and kno.

EXPERIENCE, to learn by —
To observe diligently, נָחַשׁ *nachash,* 3.
Gen. 30. 27 I have learned by experience that the

EXPERIMENT —
Proof, trying, δοκιμή *dokimē.*
2 Co. 9. 13 by the experiment of this ministration

EXPERT —
1. *To be taught, accustomed,* לָמַד *lamad,* 4.
Song 3. 8 They all hold swords, (being) expert in
2. *To cause to act wisely,* שָׂכַל *sakal,* 5.
Jer. 50. 9 arrows (shall be) as of a mighty expert
3. *One that knows,* γνώστης *gnōstēs.*
Acts 26. 3 I know) thee to be expert in all customs

EXPERT in —
To set in array, עָרַךְ *arak.*
1 Ch. 12. 33 expert in war, with all instruments of
12. 35 of the Danites expert in war twenty and
12. 36 went forth to battle, expert in war, forty

EXPIRE, to —
1. *To fill out,* πληρόω *plēroō.*
Acts 7. 30 And when forty years were expired, there
2. *To end,* τελέω *teleō.*
Rev. 20. 7 [when the thousand years are expired]

EXPIRED, be —
Return, revolution, תְּשׁוּבָה *teshubah.*
2 Sa. 11. 1 after the year was expired, at the time
1 Ch. 20. 1 after the year was expired, at the time
2 Ch. 36. 10 the year was expired, king Nebuchadne.

EXPIRED, to be —
1. *To finish, consume,* כָּלָה *kalah,* 3.
Eze. 43. 27 when these days are expired, it shall be
2. *To be full,* מָלֵא *male.*
1 Sa. 18. 26 and the days were not expired
1 Ch. 17. 11 when thy days be expired that thou must
Esth. 1. 5 when these days were expired, the king

EXPOUND, to —
1. *To put or bring before,* נָגַד *nagad,* 5.
Judg 14. 14 could not in three days expound the rid.
14. 19 unto them which expounded the riddle
2. *To interpret thoroughly,* διερμηνεύω *diermēneuō.*
Luke 24. 27 expounded unto them in all the Scriptures
3. *To put forth,* ἐκτίθημι *ektithēmi.*
Acts 11. 4 expounded (it) by order unto them, saying
18. 26 expounded unto him the way of God more
28. 23 to whom he expounded and testified the
4. *To loose further, solve,* ἐπιλύω *epiluō.*
Mark 4. 34 he expounded all things to his disciples

EXPRESSED, to be —
To be pierced, defined, marked out, נָקַב *naqab,* 2.
Num 1. 17 men which are expressed by (their) names
1 Ch. 12. 31 half tribe..which were expressed by na.
16. 41 were chosen, who were expressed by name
2 Ch. 28. 15 men which were expressed by name rose
31. 19 the men that were expressed by name, to
Ezra 8. 20 all of them were expressed by name

EXPRESSLY — [*See also* Eze. 1. 3.]
1. *To say,* אָמַר *amar.*
1 Sa. 20. 21 If I expressly say unto the lad, Behold
2. *In express words,* ῥητῶς *rhētōs.*
1 Ti. 4. 1 the Spirit speaketh expressly, that in the

EXTEND, to —
1. *To draw out,* מָשַׁךְ *mashak.*
Psa. 109. 12 there be none to extend mercy unto him
2. *To stretch out,* נָטָה *natah.*
Isa. 66. 12 I will extend peace to her like a river
3. *To stretch out,* נָטָה *natah,* 5.
Ezra 7. 28 hath extended mercy unto me before the
9. 9 hath extended mercy unto us in the sight

EXTINCT, to be —
1. *To be extinguished,* דָּעַךְ *daak.*
Isa. 43. 17 they are extinct, they are quenched as
2. *To become extinguished,* זָעַךְ *zaak,* 2.
Job 17. 1 my days are extinct; the graves (are ready)

EXTOL, to —
1. *To exalt, raise up,* סָלַל *salal.*
Psa. 68. 4 extol him that rideth upon the heavens
2. *To lift up, exalt,* רוּם *rum,* 3a.
Psa. 30. 1 I will extol thee, O LORD; for thou hast
145. 1 I will extol thee, my God, O king; and I
3. *To lift up, exalt,* רוּם *rum,* 3a.
Dan. 4. 37 and extol and honour the King of heaven

EXTOLLED, to be —
1. *To be lifted up,* נָשָׂא *nasa,* 2.
Isa. 52. 13 he shall be exalted and extolled, and be
2. *Be lifted up,* רוּם *rum,* 4a [or רוֹמָם *romam*].
Psa. 66. 17 and he was extolled with my tongue

EXTORTION —
1. *Oppression, strife,* עֹשֶׁק *osheq.*
Eze. 22. 12 thou hast greedily gained..by extortion
2. *Snatching away,* ἁρπαγή *harpagē.*
Matt 23. 25 within they are full of extortion and ex.

EXTORTIONER —
1. *To wring out, extol,* מוּץ *muts.*
Isa. 16. 4 the extortioner is at an end, the spoiler
2. *To bite, lend on usury,* נָשָׁה *nashah.*
Psa. 109. 11 Let the extortioner catch all that he
3. *One that snatches away,* ἅρπαξ *harpax.*
Luke 18. 11 I am not as other men (are), extortioners
1 Co. 5. 10 with the covetous, or extortioners, or
5. 11 or a railer, or a drunkard, or an extortion.
6. 10 nor extortioners, shall inherit the kingd.

EXTREMITY —
Extremity, פַּשׁ *pash.*
Job 35. 15 yet he knoweth (it) not in great extrem.

EYE —
1. *Eye,* עַיִן *ayin.*
Gen. 3. 5 then your eyes shall be opened, and ye
3. 6 and that it (was) pleasant to the eyes
3. 7 And the eyes of them both were opened
6. 8 Noah found grace in the eyes of the LORD
13. 10 Lot lifted up his eyes, and beheld all the
13. 14 Lift up now thine eyes, and look from
16. 4 her mistress was despised in her eyes
16. 5 when she saw..I was despised in her eyes
18. 2 And he lift up his eyes and looked
19. 8 and do ye to them as (is) good in your ey.
20. 16 behold he (is) to thee a covering of the ey.
21. 19 God opened her eyes, and she saw a well
22. 4 the third day Abraham lifted up his eyes
22. 13 Abraham lifted up his eyes, and looked
24. 63 he lifted up his eyes, and saw, and, beh.
24. 64 And Rebekah lifted up her eyes, and
27. 1 his eyes were dim, so that he could not
30. 27 if I have found favour in thine eyes, (tarry)
30. 41 Jacob laid the rods before the eyes of
31. 10 I lifted up mine eyes, and saw in a dream
31. 12 he said, Lift up now thine eyes and see
31. 40 and my sleep departed from mine eyes
33. 1 Jacob lifted up his eyes, and looked, and
33. 5 he lifted up his eyes, and saw the women
34. 11 Let me find grace in your eyes, and what
37. 25 and they lifted up their eyes and looked
39. 7 his master's wife cast her eyes upon Jos.
41. 37 in the eyes of Pharaoh, and in the eyes of
42. 24 Simeon, and bound him before their eyes
43. 29 he lifted up his eyes, and saw his brother
44. 21 that I may set mine eyes upon him
45. 12 your eyes see, and the eyes of my brother
46. 4 Joseph shall put his hand upon thine ey.
47. 19 Wherefore shall we die before thine eyes
48. 10 Now the eyes of Israel were dim for age
49. 12 His eyes..red with wine, and his teeth
50. 4 If now I have found grace in your eyes
Exod. 5. 21 in the eyes of Pharaoh, and in the eyes
8. 26 shall we sacrifice..before their eyes, and
13. 9 and for a memorial between thine eyes
13. 16 and for frontlets between thine eyes
14. 10 the children of Israel lifted up their eyes
21. 24 Eye for eye, tooth for tooth, hand for
21. 26 if a man smite the eye of his servant
21. 26 or the eye of his maid, that it perish
Exod 21. 26 he shall let him go free for his eye's sake
24. 17 fire..in the eyes of the children of Israel
Lev. 4. 13 the thing be hid from the eyes of the
20. 4 if the people..hide their eyes from the
21. 20 or that hath a blemish in his eye, or be
24. 20 Breach for breach, eye for eye, tooth for
26. 16 burning ague, that shall consume the ey.
Num. 5. 13 and it be hid from the eyes of her husba.
10. 31 and thou mayest be to us instead of eyes
11. 6 (there is) nothing at all..(before) our eyes
15. 39 after your own heart and your own eyes
16. 14 wilt thou put out the eyes of these men?
20. 8 speak ye unto the rock before their eyes
20. 12 to sanctify me in the eyes of the children
22. 31 Then the LORD opened the eyes of Balaam
24. 2 Balaam lifted up his eyes, and he saw
24. 3, 15 the man whose eyes are open hath
24. 4, 16 falling..but having his eyes open
27. 14 sanctify me at the water before their ey.
33. 55 that those..(shall be) pricks in your eyes
Deut. 1. 30 according to all..he did..before your ey.
3. 21 Thine eyes have seen all that the LORD
3. 27 and behold (it) with thine eyes: for thou
4. 3 Your eyes have seen what the LORD did
4. 9 forget the things..thine eyes have seen
4. 19 lest thou lift up thine eyes unto heaven
4. 34 to all that the LORD..did..before your e.?
6. 8 shall be as frontlets between thine eyes
6. 22 the LORD showed signs..before our eyes
7. 16 thine eye shall have no pity upon them
7. 19 The great temptations which thine eyes
9. 17 I took..and brake them before your eyes
10. 21 terrible things which thine eyes have
11. 7 But your eyes have seen all the great acts
11. 12 the eyes of the LORD thy God (are) always
11. 18 they may be as frontlets between your e.
12. 8 every man whatso. (is) right in his own ey.
13. 8 neither shall thine eye pity him, neither
13. 18 to do..right in the eyes of the LORD
14. 1 nor make any baldness between your eyes
15. 9 and thine eye be evil against thy poor br.
16. 19 for a gift doth blind the eyes of the wise
19. 13 Thine eye shall not pity him: but thou
19. 21 And thine eye shall not pity
19. 21 life..for life, eye for eye, tooth for
21. 7 and say..neither have our eyes seen
24. 1 that she find no favour in his eyes
25. 12 Then..thine eye shall not pity (her)
28. 31 Thine ox..slain before thine eyes, and
28. 32 thine eyes shall look, and fail..for them
28. 34 shalt be mad for the sight of thine eyes
28. 54 his eye shall be evil toward his brother
28. 56 her eye shall be evil toward the husband
28. 65 and failing of eyes, and sorrow of mind
28. 67 for the sight of thine eyes which thou
29. 2 all that the LORD did before your eyes
29. 3 The great temptations which thine eyes
29. 4 and eyes to see, and ears to hear, unto
32. 10 he kept him as the apple of his eye
34. 4 I have caused thee to see..with thine ey.
34. 7 his eye was not dim, nor his natural force
Josh. 5. 13 he lifted up his eyes and looked, and
23. 13 but they shall be..thorns in your eyes
24. 7 your eyes have seen what I have done in
Judg 16. 21 Philistines took him, and put out his eyes
16. 28 I may be at once avenged..for my two e.
17. 6 every man did..right in his own eyes
19. 17 when he had lifted up his eyes, he saw
21. 25 every man did..right in his own eyes
Ruth 2. 9 (Let) thine eyes (be) on the field that they
2. 10 Why have I found grace in thine eyes
1 Sa. 2. 33 the man..(shall be) to consume thine eyes
3. 2 his eyes began to wax dim, (that) he could
4. 15 his eyes were dim, that he could not see
6. 13 they lifted up their eyes, and saw the ark
11. 2 that I may thrust out all your right eyes
12. 3 (any) bribe to blind mine eyes therewith?
12. 16 which the LORD will do before your eyes
14. 27 and his eyes were enlightened
14. 29 how mine eyes have been enlightened
20. 3 that I have found grace in thine eyes
20. 29 now, if I have found favour in thine eyes
24. 10 Behold, this day thine eyes have seen how
25. 8 let the young men find favour in thine ey
26. 21 my soul was precious in thine eyes this
26. 24 thy life was much set by..in mine eyes
26. 24 let my life be much set by in the eyes of
27. 5 If I have now found grace in thine eyes
2 Sa. 6. 20 who uncovered himself to day in the eyes
12. 11 and I will take thy wives before thine e.
13. 34 And the young man..lifted up his eyes
15. 25 if I shall find favour in the eyes of the
18. 24 lifted up his eyes, and looked, and behold
22. 28 but thine eyes (are) upon the haughty
24. 3 that the eyes of my lord the king may see
1 Ki. 1. 20 And thou..the eyes of all Israel (are) upon
1. 48 to sit on my throne this day, mine eyes
8. 29 That thine eyes may be open toward this
8. 52 That thine eyes may be open unto the
9. 3 mine eyes and mine heart shall be there
10. 7 until I came, and mine eyes had seen (it)
11. 33 not walked..to do..right in mine eyes
14. 4 for his eyes were set by reason of his age
14. 8 who followed..to do..right in mine eyes
15. 5, 11 did..right in the eyes of the LORD
16. 25 Omri wrought evil in the eyes of the LORD
20. 6 whatsoever is pleasant in thine eyes
22. 43 doing..right in the eyes of the LORD
2 Ki. 4. 34 his eyes upon his eyes, and his hands
4. 35 seven times, and the child opened his ey.
6. 17 I pray thee, open his eyes, that he may see

2 Ki. 6. 17 And the LORD opened the eyes of the
6. 20 open the eyes of these..that they may
6. 20 the LORD opened their eyes, and they
7. 2, 19 Behold, thou shalt see..with thine ey.
10. 5 do thou (that which is) good in thine eyes
10. 30 in executing..right in mine eyes
19. 16 and hear; open, LORD, thine eyes, and see
19. 22 against whom hast thou..lifted up thine e.
22. 20 thine eyes shall not see all the evil
25. 7 slew the sons of Zedekiah before his eyes
25. 7 put out the eyes of Zedekiah, and bound
1 Ch. 13. 4 the thing was right in the eyes of all the
17. 17 this was a small thing in thine eyes, O G.
21. 16 David lifted up his eyes, and saw the an.
21. 23 let my lord..do..good in his eyes
2 Ch. 6. 20 That thine eyes may be open upon this
6. 40 let, I beseech thee, thine eyes be open
7. 15 Now mine eyes shall be open, and mine
7. 16 mine eyes and mine heart shall be there
9. 6 until I came, and mine eyes had seen (it)
14. 2 Asa did..good and right in the eyes of the
16. 9 For the eyes of the LORD run to and fro
20. 12 our God..our eyes (are) upon thee
21. 6 he wrought..evil in the eyes of the LORD
29. 6 and done..evil in the eyes of the LORD
29. 8 and to hissing, as ye see with your eyes
Ezra 3. 12 the foundation..was laid before their ey.
5. 5 But the eye of their God was upon the
9. 8 that our God may lighten our eyes, and
Neh 1. 6 Let thine ear..be attentive, and thine e.
6. 16 were much cast down in their own eyes
Esth. 1. 17 shall despise their husbands in their eyes
Job 2. 12 when they lifted up their eyes afar off
3. 10 not shut..nor hid sorrow from mine eyes
4. 16 an image (was) before mine eyes..silence
7. 7 mine eye shall no more see good
7. 8 The eye of him that hath seen me shall
7. 8 thine eyes (are) upon me, and I (am) not
10. 4 Hast thou eyes of flesh? or seest thou as
10. 18 I had given up the ghost, and no eye had
11. 4 thou hast said..I am clean in thine eyes
11. 20 But the eyes of the wicked shall fail
13. 1 Lo, mine eye hath seen all..mine ear
14. 3 dost thou open thine eyes upon such an
15. 12 carry thee away? and what do thy eyes
16. 9 mine enemy sharpeneth his eyes upon me
16. 20 mine eye poureth out (tears) unto God
17. 2 doth not mine eye continue in their pro.
17. 5 even the eyes of his children shall fail
17. 7 Mine eye also is dim by reason of sorrow
19. 27 Whom I shall see..and mine eyes shall
20. 9 The eye also (which) saw him shall (see
21. 8 and their offspring before their eyes
21. 20 His eyes shall see his destruction, and
24. 15 The eye also of the adulterer waiteth for
24. 15 No eye shall see me; and disguiseth (his)
24. 23 safety..yet his eyes (are) upon their ways
27. 19 The rich..openeth his eyes, and he (is)
28. 7 and which the vulture's eye hath not seen
28. 10 and his eye seeth every precious thing
28. 21 Seeing it is hid from the eyes of all living
29. 11 when the eye saw (me), it gave witness to
29. 15 I was eyes to the blind, and feet (was) I
31. 1 I made a covenant with mine eyes; why
31. 7 and mine heart walked after mine eyes
31. 16 have caused the eyes of the widow to fail
32. 1 because he (was) righteous in his own e.
34. 21 For his eyes (are) upon the ways of man
36. 7 He withdraweth not his eyes from the
39. 29 From thence..her eyes behold afar off
40. 24 He taketh it with his eyes; (his) nose
41. 18 his eyes (are) like the eyelids of the
42. 5 I have heard..but now mine eye seeth
Psa. 6. 7 Mine eye is consumed because of grief
10. 8 his eyes are privily set against the poor
11. 4 his eyes behold, his eyelids try, the chil.
13. 3 lighten mine eyes, lest I sleep the..death
15. 4 In whose eyes a vile person is contemned
17. 2 let thine eyes behold the things that are
17. 8 Keep me as the apple of the eye; hide
17. 11 they have set their eyes bowing down to
19. 8 rejoicing the heart..enlightening the e.
25. 15 Mine eyes (are) ever toward the LORD
26. 3 thy loving kindness (is) before mine eyes
31. 9 mine eye is consumed with grief..my
31. 22 I am cut off from before thine eyes
32. 8 I will guide thee with mine eye
33. 18 the eye of the LORD (is) upon them that
34. 15 The eyes of the LORD (are) upon the righ.
35. 19 let them wink with the eye that hate me
35. 21 (and) said, Aha, aha! our eye hath seen
36. 1 (there is) no fear of God before his eyes
36. 2 For he flattereth himself in his own eyes
38. 10 as for the light of mine eyes, it also is gone
50. 21 and set..in order before thine eyes
54. 7 mine eye hath seen (his desire) upon mine
66. 7 his eyes behold the nations: let not the
69. 3 mine eyes fail while I wait for my God
69. 23 Let their eyes be darkened, that they see
73. 7 Their eyes stand out with fatness
77. 4 Thou holdest mine eyes waking: I am so
88. 9 Mine eye mourneth by reason of affliction
91. 8 Only with thine eyes shalt thou behold
92. 11 Mine eye also shall see (my desire) on
94. 9 he that formed the eye, shall he not see?
101. 3 I will set no wicked thing before mine e.
101. 6 Mine eyes (shall be) upon the faithful of
115. 5 they speak not; eyes have they, but they
116. 8 mine eyes from tears..my feet from
118. 23 LORD's doing; it (is) marvellous in our e.
119. 18 Open thou mine eyes, that I may behold
119. 37 Turn away mine eyes from beholding va.
Psa. 119. 82 Mine eyes fail for thy word, saying
119. 123 Mine eyes fail for thy salvation, and
119. 136 Rivers of waters run down mine eyes
119. 148 Mine eyes prevent the (night) watches
121. 1 I will lift up mine eyes unto the hills
123. 1 Unto thee lift I up mine eyes, O thou
123. 2 as the eyes of servants..unto the hand
123. 2 as the eyes of a maiden unto the hand
123. 2 so our eyes..upon the LORD our God
131. 1 my heart is not haughty, nor mine eyes
132. 4 I will not give sleep to mine eyes, (or)
135. 16 they speak not; eyes have they, but they
139. 16 Thine eyes did see my substance, yet
141. 8 mine eyes (are) unto thee, O GOD the
145. 15 The eyes of all wait upon thee; and thou
Prov. 3. 7 Be not wise in thine own eyes: fear the
3. 21 son, let not them depart from thine eyes
4. 21 Let them not depart from thine eyes
4. 25 Let thine eyes look right on, and let
5. 21 the ways of man (are) before the eyes of
6. 4 Give not sleep to thine eyes, nor slumber
6. 13 He winketh with his eyes, he speaketh
7. 2 Keep..my law as the apple of thine eye
10. 10 He that winketh with the eye causeth
10. 26 as smoke to the eyes, so (is) the sluggard
12. 15 The way of a fool (is) right in his own eyes
15. 3 The eyes of the LORD (are) in every place
15. 30 The light of the eyes rejoiceth the heart
16. 2 the ways of a man (are) clean in his own e.
16. 30 He shutteth his eyes to devise froward
17. 8 A gift (is as) a precious stone in the eyes
17. 24 but the eyes of a fool (are) in the ends of
20. 8 A king..scattereth away all evil with his e.
20. 12 The hearing ear, and the seeing eye, the
20. 13 open thine eyes..thou shalt be satisfied
21. 2 way of a man (is) right in his own eyes
21. 10 his neighbour findeth no favour in his e.
22. 9 He that hath a bountiful eye shall be
22. 12 The eyes of the LORD preserve knowledge
23. 5 Wilt thou set thine eyes upon that which
23. 6 Eat thou not the bread of..an evil eye
23. 26 My son..let thine eyes observe my ways
23. 29 without cause? who hath redness of eyes?
23. 33 Thine eyes shall behold strange women
25. 7 presence of the prince whom thine eyes
27. 20 so the eyes of man are never satisfied
28. 22 that hasteth to be rich (hath) an evil eye
28. 27 he that hideth his eyes shall have many
29. 13 the LORD lighteneth both their eyes
30. 12 a generation..pure in their own eyes
30. 13 a generation, O how lofty are their eyes!
30. 17 The eye (that) mocketh at (his) father
Eccl. 1. 8 the eye is not satisfied with seeing, nor
2. 10 whatsoever mine eyes desired I kept not
2. 14 The wise man's eyes (are) in his head
4. 8 neither is his eye satisfied with riches
5. 11 saving the beholding..with their eyes?
6. 9 Better (is) the sight of the eyes than the
8. 16 neither day nor night seeth..with his e.
11. 7 pleasant..for the eyes to behold the sun
11. 9 of thine heart, and in the sight of thine e.
Song 1. 15 thou (art) fair; thou (hast) doves' eyes
4. 1 thou (hast) doves' eyes within thy locks
4. 9 ravished my heart with one of thine eyes
5. 12 His eyes (are) as..of doves by the rivers
6. 5 Turn away thine eyes from me, for they
7. 4 thine eyes..the fishpools in Heshbon, by
8. 10 then was I in his eyes as one that found
Isa. 1. 15 spread..your hands, I will hide mine eyes
1. 16 the evil of your doings from before mine e.
3. 8 against the LORD, to provoke the eyes of
3. 16 with stretched forth necks, and wanton e.
5. 15 and the eyes of the lofty shall be humbled
5. 21 Woe unto..wise in their own eyes, and
6. 5 mine eyes have seen the King, the LORD
6. 10 make their ears heavy, and shut their e.
6. 10 lest they see with their eyes, and hear
11. 3 he shall not judge after the sight of his e.
13. 16 shall be dashed to pieces before their e.
13. 18 no pity..their eye shall not spare children
17. 7 his eyes shall have respect to the Holy
29. 10 of deep sleep, and hath closed your eyes
29. 18 the eyes of the blind shall see out of ob.
30. 20 but thine eyes shall see thy teachers
32. 3 the eyes of them that see shall not be
33. 15 and shutteth his eyes from seeing evil
33. 17 Thine eyes shall see the King in his beauty
33. 20 thine eyes shall see Jerusalem a quiet
35. 5 Then the eyes of the blind shall be opened
37. 17 Incline thine ear..open thine eyes, O
37. 23 against whom hast thou..lifted up thine e.
38. 14 mine eyes fail (with looking) upward
40. 26 Lift up your eyes on high, and behold
42. 7 To open the blind eyes, to bring out the
43. 8 Bring forth the blind..that have eyes
44. 18 he hath shut their eyes, that they cannot
49. 5 yet shall I be glorious in the eyes of the
49. 18 Lift up thine eyes round about, and beh.
51. 6 Lift up your eyes to the heavens, and look
52. 8 they shall see eye to eye, when the LORD
52. 10 made bare his holy arm in the eyes of all
59. 10 and we grope as if..no eyes: we stumble
60. 4 Lift up thine eyes round about, and see
64. 4 perceived by the ear, neither hath the eye
65. 12 did not hear; but did evil before mine e.
65. 16 and because they are hid from mine eyes
66. 4 not hear: but they did evil before mine e.
Jer. 3. 2 Lift up thine eyes unto the high places
5. 3 O LORD, (are) not thine eyes upon the
5. 21 which have eyes, and see not; which
7. 11 become a den of robbers in your eyes?
9. 1 and mine eyes a fountain of tears, that I
Jer. 9. 18 that our eyes may run down with tears
13. 17 mine eye shall weep sore, and run down
13. 20 Lift up your eyes, and behold them that
14. 6 their eyes did fail, because..no grass
14. 17 Let mine eyes run down with tears night
16. 9 to cease out of this place in your eyes
16. 17 For mine eyes (are) upon all their ways
16. 17 neither is..iniquity hid from mine eyes
20. 4 they shall fall..and thine eyes shall be.
22. 17 But thine eyes and thine heart (are) not
24. 6 For I will set mine eyes upon them for
29. 21 and he shall slay them before your eyes
31. 16 Refrain..thine eyes from tears: for thy
32. 4 and his eyes shall behold his eyes
32. 19 thine eyes (are) open upon all the ways
34. 3 thine eyes shall behold the eyes of the
39. 6 slew the sons of Zedekiah..before his ey.
39. 7 Moreover he put out Zedekiah's eyes
42. 2 a few of many, as thine eyes do behold
52. 2 he did..evil in the eyes of the LORD
52. 10 slew the sons of Zedekiah before his eyes
52. 11 Then he put out the eyes of Zedekiah
Lam. 1. 16 mine eye, mine eye runneth down with
2. 4 and slew all..pleasant to the eye in the
2. 11 Mine eyes do fail with tears, my bowels
2. 18 let not the apple of thine eye cease
3. 48 Mine eye runneth down with rivers of w.
3. 49 Mine eye trickleth down, and ceaseth not
3. 51 Mine eye affecteth mine heart because of
4. 17 our eyes as yet failed for our vain help
5. 17 heart is faint; for these..our eyes are dim
Eze. 1. 18 their rings..full of eyes round about them
5. 11 neither shall mine eye spare, neither will
6. 9 with their eyes, which go a whoring after
7. 4, 9 mine eye shall not spare..neither will
8. 5 lift up thine eyes now the way toward
8. 5 I lifted up mine eyes the way toward the
8. 18 mine eye shall not spare, neither will I
9. 5 let not your eye spare, neither have ye
9. 10 as for me also, mine eye shall not spare
10. 12 and the wheels..full of eyes round about
12. 2 which have eyes to see, and see not
12. 12 that he see not the ground with (his) eyes
16. 5 None eye pitied thee, to do any of these
18. 6, 12, 15 hath lifted up his eyes to the idols
20. 7 every man the abominations of his eyes
20. 8 cast away the abominations of their eyes
20. 17 mine eye spared them from destroying
20. 24 their eyes were after their fathers' idols
21. 6 and with bitterness sigh before their eyes
22. 26 and have hid their eyes from my sabbaths
23. 16 as soon as she saw them with her eyes
23. 27 so that thou shalt not lift up thine eyes
23. 40 thou didst wash thyself, paintedst thine e.
24. 16 I take away..the desire of thine eyes with
24. 21 the excellency..the desire of your eyes
24. 25 joy of their glory, the desire of their eyes
33. 25 and lift up your eyes toward your idols
36. 23 I shall be sanctified..before their eyes
37. 20 the sticks..in thine hand before their e.
38. 16 I shall be sanctified..before their eyes
38. 23 I will be known in the eyes of many nat.
40. 4 behold with thine eyes, and hear with
44. 5 behold with thine eyes, and hear with
Dan. 4. 34 I Nebuchadnezzar lifted up mine eyes
7. 8 in this horn (were) eyes like the eyes of
7. 20 even (of) that horn that had eyes, and a
8. 3 I lifted up mine eyes, and saw, and, beh.
8. 5 goat (had) a notable horn between his e.
8. 21 the great horn that (is) between his eyes
9. 18 open thine eyes, and behold our desola.
10. 5 I lifted up mine eyes, and looked, and
10. 6 his eyes as lamps of fire, and his arms
Hos. 13. 14 repentance shall be hid from mine eyes
Joel 1. 16 Is not the meat cut off before our eyes
Amos 9. 4 I will set mine eyes upon them for evil
9. 8 the eyes of the Lord GOD (are) upon the
Mic. 4. 11 Let her be defiled, and let our eye look
7. 10 mine eyes shall behold her: now shall
Hab. 1. 13 of purer eyes than to behold evil, and
Zeph. 3. 20 turn back your captivity before your eyes
Hag. 2. 3 in your eyes in comparison of it as nothing?
Zech. 1. 18 Then lifted I up mine eyes, and saw
2. 1 I lifted up mine eyes again, and looked
2. 8 toucheth you toucheth the apple of his e.
3. 9 For..upon one stone (shall be) seven eyes!
4. 10 they (are) the eyes of the LORD, which
5. 1 Then I turned, and lifted up mine eyes
5. 5 said unto me, Lift up now thine eyes
5. 9 Then lifted I up mine eyes, and looked
6. 1 I turned, and lifted up mine eyes, and
8. 6 If it be marvellous in the eyes of the
8. 6 should it also be marvellous in mine eyes?
9. 1 when the eyes of man, as of all the tribes
9. 8 for now have I seen with mine eyes
11. 17 sword..upon his arm, and upon his right e.
11. 17 his right eye shall be utterly darkened
12. 4 I will open mine eyes upon the house of
14. 12 their eyes shall consume away in their
Mal. 1. 5 And your eyes shall see, and ye shall say

2. *The eye; sight,* ὄμμα *omma.*

Mark 8. 23 when he had spit on his eyes..he asked

3. *The eye,* ὀφθαλμός *ophthalmos.*

Matt. 5. 29 if thy right eye offend thee, pluck it out
5. 38 An eye for an eye, and a tooth for a tooth
6. 22 The light of the body is the eye
6. 22 if therefore thine eye be single, thy whole
6. 23 But if thine eye be evil, thy whole body
7. 3 beholdest..the mote..in thy brother's eye
7. 3 considerest not the beam..in thine own e.
7. 4 Let me pull..the mote out of thine eye

Matt. 7. 4 and, behold, a beam (is) in thine own eye?
7. 5 first cast..the beam out of thine own eye
7. 5 to cast..the mote out of thy brother's eye
9. 29 Then touched he their eyes, saying, Acc.
9. 30 their eyes were opened: and Jesus straitly
13. 15 and their eyes they have closed; lest
13. 15 any time they should see with (their) eyes
13. 16 But blessed (are) your eyes, for they see
17. 8 And when they had lifted up their eyes
18. 9 if thine eye offend thee, pluck it out
18. 9 rather than having two eyes to be cast
20. 15 Is thine eye evil, because I am good?
20. 33 Lord, that our eyes may be opened
20. 34 had compassion..and touched their eyes
20. 34 immediately [their eyes] received sight
21. 42 doing, and it is marvellous in our eyes?
26. 43 asleep again: for their eyes were heavy
Mark 7. 22 an evil eye, blasphemy, pride, foolishness
8. 18 Having eyes, see ye not? and having ears
8. 25 he put (his) hands again upon his eyes
9. 47 if thine eye offend thee, pluck it out
9. 47 than having two eyes to be cast into
12. 11 doing, and it is marvellous in our eyes?
14. 40 asleep again, for their eyes were heavy
Luke 2. 30 For mine eyes have seen thy salvation
4. 20 And the eyes of all..were fastened on
6. 20 And he lifted up his eyes on his disciples
6. 41 beholdest..the mote..in thy brother's eye
6. 41 perceivest not the beam..in thine own e.?
6. 42 let me pull out the mote..in thine eye
6. 42 beholdest not the beam..in thine own eye?
6. 42 out of thine own eye..in thy brother's eye
10. 23 Blessed (are) the eyes which see the things
11. 34 The light of the body is the eye
11. 34 therefore when thine eye is single, thy
16. 23 in hell he lift up his eyes, being in tor.
18. 13 would not lift up so much as (his) eyes
19. 42 but now they are hid from thine eyes
24. 16 their eyes were holden that they should
24. 31 their eyes were opened, and they knew
John 4. 35 Lift up your eyes, and look on the fields
6. 5 When Jesus then lifted up (his) eyes, and
9. 6 he anointed the eyes of the blind man
9. 10 said they..How were thine eyes opened?
9. 11 Jesus made clay, and anointed mine eyes
9. 14 Jesus made the clay, and opened his eyes
9. 15 He put clay upon mine eyes, and I washed
9. 17 thou of him, that he hath opened thine e.?
9. 21 or who hath opened his eyes, we know
9. 26 What did he..how opened he thine eyes?
9. 30 he is, and (yet) he hath opened mine eyes
9. 32 that any man opened the eyes of one that
10. 21 Can a devil open the eyes of the blind?
11. 37 man, which opened the eyes of the blind
11. 41 Jesus lifted up (his) eyes, and said, Father
12. 40 He hath blinded their eyes, and hardened
12. 40 that they should not see with (their) eyes
17. 1 and lifted up his eyes to heaven, and
Acts 9. 8 when his eyes were opened, he saw no
9. 18 there fell from his eyes as it had been
9. 40 she opened her eyes: and when she saw
26. 18 To open their eyes..to turn..from dark.
28. 27 their ears are dull..their eyes have they
28. 27 lest they should see with (their) eyes
Rom. 3. 18 There is no fear of God before their eyes
11. 8 God hath given them..eyes that they
11. 10 Let their eyes be darkened, that they
1 Co. 2. 9 as it is written, Eye hath not seen, nor
12. 16 Because I am not the eye, I am not of
12. 17 If the whole body (were) an eye, where
12. 21 And the eye cannot say unto the hand
15. 52 In a moment, in the twinkling of an eye
Gal. 3. 1 before whose eyes Jesus Christ hath been
4. 15 ye would have plucked out your own eyes
Eph. 1. 18 The eyes of your understanding being
Heb. 4. 13 unto the eyes of him with whom we have
1 Pe. 3. 12 For the eyes of the Lord (are) over the
2 Pe. 2. 14 Having eyes full of adultery, and that
1 Jo. 1. 1 That..which we have seen with our eyes
2. 11 because that darkness hath blinded his e.
2. 16 the lust of the eyes..is not of the Father
Rev. 1. 7 and every eye shall see him, and they
1. 14 and his eyes (were) as a flame of fire
2. 18 who hath his eyes like unto a flame of
3. 18 anoint thine eyes with eyesalve, that
4. 6 four beasts, full of eyes before and behind
4. 8 full of eyes within: and they rest not
5. 6 having seven horns and seven eyes
7. 17 shall wipe away all tears from their eyes
19. 12 His eyes (were) as a flame of fire, and
21. 4 shall wipe away all tears from their eyes

4. *Hole, a boring*, τρυμαλιά *trumalia.*
Mark 10. 25 It is easier..to go through the eye of a n.
Luke 18. 25 it is easier..to go through a needle's [e.]

5. *Hole, a boring*, τρύπημα *trupēma.*
Matt. 19. 24 It is easier..to go through the eye of a

EYE, with one —
One-eyed, μονόφθαλμος *monophthalmos.*
Matt. 18. 9 better..to enter into life with one eye
Mark 9. 47 to enter into the kingdom..with one eye

EYE, to —
To eye, עָוַן, עַיִן *avan, ayan.* [V.L. [עָיַן], *ayan.*
1 Sa. 18. 9 Saul eyed David from that day and for.

EYE brows —
The arches of the eyes, גַּבֹּת עֵינַיִם *gabboth enayim* [*gab*].
Lev. 14. 9 shall shave all his hair off his..eyebrows

EYE lids —
Eyelids, עַפְעַפַּיִם *aphappim.*
Job 16. 16 and on my eyelids (is) the shadow of death
41. 18 his eyes (are) like the eyelids of the morn.
Psa. 11. 4 his eyes behold, his eyelids try, the child.
132. 4 sleep to mine eyes..slumber to mine eye.
Prov. 4. 25 let thine eyelids look straight before
6. 4 thine eyes, nor slumber to thine eyelids
6. 25 neither let her take thee with her eyelids
30. 13 how lofty are their eyes! and their eyelids
Jer. 9. 18 and our eyelids gush out with waters

EYE salve —
Collyrium, a small cake, κολλούριον, κολλύριον.
Rev. 3. 18 anoint thine eyes with eye salve, that

EYE service —
Eye service, ὀφθαλμοδουλεία *ophthalmodouleia.*
Eph. 6. 6 Not with eye-service, as men pleasers; but
Col. 3. 22 not with eye-service, as men pleasers; but

EYE sight —
Eye, עַיִן *ayin.*
2 Sa. 22. 25 according to my cleanness in his eyesight
Psa. 18. 24 according to the cleanness..in his eyesi.

EYE witness —
1. *One who beholds for himself*, αὐτόπτης *autoptēs.*
Luke 1. 2 which from the beginning were eyewitn.

2. *A looker on*, ἐπόπτης *epoptēs.*
2 Pe 1. 16 but were eyewitnesses of his majesty

EZAR, 1 Ch. 1. 38. *See* **EZER.**

EZ'-BAI, אֶזְבַּי *shining, beautiful.*
The father of one of David's thirty mighty men. In 2 Sa. 23. 35, the words are "Paarai the Arbite." B.C. 1048.
1 Ch. 11. 37 Hezro the Carmelite, Naarai the son of E.

EZ'-BON, אֶצְבּוֹן *splendour.*
1. Son of Gad and founder of a Gadite family. In Nu. 26. 16, the name is written "Ozni." B.C 1700.
Gen. 46. 16 Shuni, and E., Eri, and Arodi, and Areli

2. Son of Bela son of Benjamin. It is strange that while Ezbon is not elsewhere mentioned among the children of Bela or of Benjamin he appears here with Iri, which was *not* a Benjamite family, but which is found with Ezbon (Ozni) among *Gadite* families, both in Gen. 46. 16, ("Eri") and Num. 26. 16. B.C. 1670.
1 Ch. 7. 7 the sons of Bela; E., and Uzzi, and Uzz.

E-ZE-KI'-AS, Ἐζεκίας, *the Greek form of Hezekiah.*
Matt. 1. 9 Joatham begat Achaz; and Achaz begat E.
1. 10 E. begat Manasses; and Manasses begat

E-ZE-KI'-EL, יְחֶזְקֵאל *God is strong.*
A priest who prophesied to the exiles in Mesopotamia, by the river Chebar, (the *Nahr Malcha*) and wrote the book in the Old Testament which bears his name. He is one of the four so called "greater prophets," but he rarely alludes to himself. He prophesied from the fifth year (B.C. 595) of Jehoiachin.
Eze. 1. 3 word of the LORD came expressly unto E.
24. 24 Thus E. is unto you a sign: according to

E'-ZEL, אֶזֶל *division, separation.*
A memorial stone near Saul's residence, the scene of the final parting of David and Jonathan. The place or "Heap of Stones" was between Rama and Nob.
1 Sa. 20. 19 thou..shalt remain by the stone E.

E'-ZEM, עֶצֶם *strength.*
A city of Simeon. The name appears in Joshua (15. 29. and 19. 3) as Azem.
1 Ch. 4. 29 And at Bilhah, and at E., and at Tolad

E'-ZER, עֵזֶר, עֶזֶר, עֵזֶר *help.*
1. A son of Ephraim slain by the inhabitants of Gath while carrying off their cattle. B.C. 1680.
1 Ch. 7. 21 and Shuthelah his son, and E., and Elead

2. A priest noticed in the book of Nehemiah. B.C. 445.
Neh. 12. 42 Jeh., and Malchijah, and Elam, and E.

3. A descendant of Judah through Caleb son of Hur. Perhaps the same as Ezra in 1 Ch. 4. 17.
1 Ch. 4. 4 Penuel the father of Gedor, and E. the

4. A valiant Gadite who joined David at Ziklag. B.C. 1048.
1 Ch. 12. 9 E. the first, Obadiah the second, Eliab

5. A Levite who assisted in repairing the wall of Jerusalem in the time of Nehemiah. B.C. 445.
Neh. 3. 19 next to him repaired E. the son of Jeshua

E'-ZER, אֵצֶר *union.*
A son of Seir the Horite. B.C. 1780.
Gen. 36. 21 Dishon, and E., and Dishan: these (are)
36. 27 children of E...these; Bilhan, and Za.
36. 30 Duke Dishon, duke E., duke Dishan
1 Ch. 1. 38 Anah, and Dishon, and E., and Dishan
1. 42 sons of E.; Bilhan, and Zavan, (and) J.

EZ-ION GA'-BER, עֶצְיוֹן גֶּבֶר *backbone of a mighty one.* [**EZION GEBER.**]
The last station of the Israelites before coming to the "wilderness of Zin, which is Kadesh." It was subsequently the station of Solomon's navy; that at which Jehoshaphat's ships were broken. This port is at the Modern *Ain-el Ghudyan* about ten miles up the dry bed of the Arabah, and near Elath or Berenice.
Num 33. 35 And they departed..and encamped at E.
33. 36 And they removed from E., and pitched
Deut. 2. 8 the plain from Elath, and from E.

1 Ki. 9. 26 king Solomon made a navy of ships in E.
22. 48 went not; for the ships were brok. at E.
2 Ch. 8. 17 Then went Solomon to E., and to Eloth
20. 36 and they made the ships in E.

EZ'-NITE, הָעֶצְנִי *the one belonging to Etsen.*
Patronymic of Adino one of David's worthies.
2 Sa. 23. 8 the same (was) Adino the E.: (he lift up

EZ'-RA, עֶזְרָא, עֶזְרָה *help.*
1. The head of one of the twenty-two courses of priests that came up from exile with Zerubbabel and Jeshua Nehemiah (10. 2–8) has the name *Azariah* as is probably the case in Ezra 7. 1.
Neh. 12. 1 Seraiah, Jeremiah, E.

2. A descendant of Judah through Caleb.
1 Ch. 4. 17 the sons of E...Jether, and Mered, and

3. A famous scribe and priest descended from Hilkiah the high priest.
Ezra 7. 1 E. the son of Seraiah, the son of Azariah
7. 6 This E. went up from Babylon; and he
7. 10 E. had prepared his heart to seek the
7. 11 the king Artaxerxes gave unto E. the
7. 12 Artaxerxes, king of kings, unto E. the
7. 21 whatsoever E...shall require of you, it
7. 25 thou, E...set magistrates and judges
10. 1 when E. had prayed, and when he had
10. 2 Shechaniah..answered and said unto E.
10. 5 Then arose E., and made the chief prie.
10. 6 E. rose up from before the house of God
10. 10 E. the priest stood up, and said unto them
10. 16 E. the priest, (with) certain chief of the
Neh. 8. 1 they spake unto E. the scribe to bring
8. 2 E. the priest brought the law before the
8. 4 E. the scribe stood upon a pulpit of wood
8. 5 E. opened the book in the sight of all
8. 6 And E. blessed the LORD, the great G.
8. 9 E. the priest..said unto all the people
8. 13 were gathered together..unto E...to
12. 13 Of E., Meshullam; of Amariah, Jehoha.
12. 26 in the days of..E. the priest, the scribe
12. 33 And Azariah, E., and Meshullam
12. 36 of David the man of God, and E. the

EZ-RA-HITE, אֶזְרָחִי *belonging to Ezrach.*
Patronymic of Ethan and Heman. The word is derivable from *Ezrah* or *Zerach*; and Ethan and Heman are both given as sons of Zerah, son of Judah. Another Ethan and Heman are named as Levite musicians in 1 Ch. vi.
1 Ki. 4. 31 he was wiser than..Ethan the E.
Psa. 88. *title.* Maschil of Heman the E.
89. *title.* Maschil of Ethan the E.

EZ'-RI, עֶזְרִי *my help.*
One of the superintendents of David. B.C. 1015.
1 Ch. 27. 26 And over them..E. the son of Chelub

F

FABLE —
Talk, tale, legend, myth, μῦθος *muthos.*
1 Ti. 1. 4 Neither give heed to fables and endless
4. 7 But refuse profane and old wives' fables
2 Ti. 4. 4 turn away..and shall be turned unto fa.
Titus 1. 14 Not giving heed to Jewish fables, and
2 Pe. 1. 16 have not followed cunningly devised fa.

FACE —
1. *Face*, אַנְפִּין *anpin.*
Dan. 2. 46 the king Nebuchadnezzar fell upon h

2. *Face, nose*, אַף *aph.*
Gen. 3. 19 In the sweat of thy face shalt thou eat
19. 1 bowed himself with his face toward the
24. 47 and I put the ear ring upon her face, and
42. 6 and bowed down..(with) their faces to
48. 12 he bowed himself with his face to the
Num 22. 31 he bowed down..and fell flat on his face
1 Sa. 20. 41 fell on his face to the ground, and bowed
24. 8 David stooped with his face to the earth
25. 41 and bowed herself on (her) face to the e.
28. 14 and he stooped with (his) face to the gr.
2 Sa. 14. 4 she fell on her face to the ground, and
14. 33 and bowed himself on his face to the gr.
18. 28 he fell down to the earth upon his face
24. 20 bowed himself before the king on his face
1 Ki. 1. 23 he bowed himself..with his face to the g.
1. 31 Then Bath-sheba bowed with (her) face
1 Ch. 21. 21 and bowed himself..with (his) face to
2 Ch. 7. 3 they bowed themselves with their faces
20. 18 Jehoshaphat bowed his head with (his) f.
Neh. 8. 6 worshipped the LORD with (their) faces
Eze. 38. 18 (that) my fury shall come up in my face

3. *Eye, aspect*, עַיִן *ayin.*
Exod 10. 5 And they shall cover the face of the earth
10. 15 they covered the face of the whole earth
Num 14. 14 that thou, LORD, art seen face to face
22. 5 behold, they cover the face of the earth
22. 11 (there is) a people..which covereth the f.
1 Ki. 20. 38 disguised himself with ashes upon his face
20. 41 and took the ashes away from his face
2 Ki. 9. 30 she painted her face, and tired her head

4. *Face*, פָּנִים *panim.*
Gen. 1. 2 and darkness (was) upon the face of the
1. 2 the Spirit of God moved upon the face of
1. 29 which (is) upon the face of all the earth
2. 6 and watered the whole face of the ground

Gen. 4. 14 thou hast driven me out..from the face
4. 14 and from thy face shall I be hid; and I
6. 1 when men began to multiply upon the f.
6. 7 I will destroy man..from the face of the
7. 3 to keep seed alive upon the face of all
7. 4 will I destroy from off the face of the
7. 18 and the ark went upon the face of the
7. 23 which was upon the face of the ground
8. 8 the waters were abated from off the face
8. 9 for the waters (were) on the face of the
8. 13 and, behold, the face of the ground was
9. 23 their faces (were) backward, and they saw
11. 4 scattered abroad upon the face of the..e.
11. 8 the LORD scattered them..upon the face
11. 9 scatter them abroad upon the face of all
16. 6 Sarai dealt hardly..she fled from her face
16. 8 I flee from the face of my mistress Sarai
17. 3 Abram fell on his face: and God talked
17. 17 Then Abraham fell upon his face, and la.
19. 13 cry of them is waxen great before the fa.
30. 33 it shall come for my hire before thy face
30. 40 set the faces of the flocks toward the ri.
31. 21 and set his face (toward) the mount Gilead
32. 20 afterward I will see his face; peradven.
32. 30 I have seen God face to face, and my
33. 10 seen thy face, as though I had seen the f.
35. 1 when thou fleddest from the face of Esau
35. 7 when he fled from the face of his brother
36. 6 went into the country from the face of
38. 15 an harlot; because she had covered her f.
41. 56 the famine was over all the face of the
43. 3, 5 Ye shall not see my face, except your
43. 31 And he washed his face, and went out
44. 23 Except..ye shall see my face no more
44. 26 for we may not see the man's face, except
46. 28 he sent Judah..to direct his face unto
46. 30 Now let me die, since I have seen thy f.
48. 11 I had not thought to see thy face; and, lo
50. 1 And Joseph fell upon his father's face, and
50. 18 also went and fell down before his face
Exod. 2. 15 But Moses fled from the face of Pharaoh
3. 6 Moses hid his face; for he was afraid to
10. 28 Get thee from me..see my face no more
10. 28 for in (that) day thou seest my face thou
10. 29 Thou hast spoken well, I will see thy face
14. 25 Let us flee from the face of Israel; for
16. 14 behold, upon the face of the wilderness
19. 7 and laid before their faces all these words
20. 20 that his fear may be before your faces
25. 20 and their faces (shall look) one to another
25. 20 toward the mercy seat shall the faces of
32. 12 consume them from the face of the earth?
33. 11 the LORD spake unto Moses face to face
33. 16 all the people that (are) upon the face of
33. 20 And he said, Thou canst not see my face
33. 23 back parts; but my face shall not be seen
34. 29 the skin of his face shone while he talked
34. 30 skin of his face shone; and they were
34. 33 Moses had done..he put a veil on his face
34. 35 the children of Israel saw the face of M.
34. 35 that the skin of Moses' face shone: and
34. 35 Moses put the veil upon his face again
37. 9 cherubim..with their faces one to anot.
37. 9 to the mercy seatward were the faces of
Lev. 9. 24 they shouted, and fell on their faces
13. 41 from the part of his head toward his face
17. 10 I will even set my face against that soul
20. 3, 5 I will set my face against that man, and
20. 6 I will even set my face against that soul
26. 17 I will set my face against you, and ye
Num. 6. 25 The LORD make his face shine upon thee
11. 31 two cubits (high) upon the face of the
12. 3 all the men which (were) upon the face
12. 14 If her father had but spit in her face
14. 5 Moses and Aaron fell on their faces before
16. 4 when Moses heard (it), he fell upon his f.
16. 22 they fell upon their faces, and said, O God
16. 45 Get you up..And they fell upon their fa.
20. 6 they fell upon their faces: and the glory
24. 1 but he set his face toward the wilderness
Deut. 1. 17 shall not be afraid of the face of man
5. 4 The LORD talked with you face to face in
6. 15 destroy thee from off the face of the earth
7. 6 above all people that (are) upon the face
7. 10 repayeth them that hate him to their face
7. 10 not be slack..he will repay him to his face
8. 20 which the LORD destroyeth before your f.
25. 2 to be beaten before his face, according to
25. 9 spit in his face, and shall answer and say
28. 7 thine enemies..to be smitten before thy f.
28. 31 violently taken away from before thy face
31. 5 LORD shall give them up before your face
31. 17 I will hide my face from them, and they
31. 18 And I will surely hide my face in that day
32. 20 And he said, I will hide my face from
34. 10 Moses, whom the LORD knew face to face
Josh. 5. 14 Joshua fell on his face to the earth, and
7. 6 fell to the earth upon his face before the
Judg. 6. 22 have seen an angel of the LORD face to f.
13. 20 Manoah and his wife..fell on their faces
18. 23 they turned their faces, and said unto
Ruth 2. 10 Then she fell on her face, and bowed
1 Sa. 5. 3, 4, Dagon (was) fallen upon his face to the
17. 49 and he fell upon his face to the earth
20. 15 cut off..every one from the face of the
25. 23 fell before David on her face, and bowed
26. 20 let not my blood fall..before the face of
2 Sa. 2. 22 how then should I hold up my face to J.
3. 13 Thou shalt not see my face, except thou
3. 13 Michal..when thou comest to see my face
9. 6 he fell on his face, and did reverence
14. 24 And the king said..let him not see my f.

2 Sa. 14. 24, 28 So Absalom..saw not the king's face
14. 32 now therefore let me see the king's face
18. 8 battle was there scattered over the face
19. 4 the king covered his face, and the king
19. 5 Thou hast shamed this day the faces of
1 Ki. 2. 15 set their faces on me, that I should reign
8. 14 the king turned his face about, and blessed
13. 6 Entreat now the face of the LORD thy
13. 34 to destroy (it) from off the face of the
18. 7 he knew him, and fell on his face, and
18. 39 they fell on their faces; and they said
18. 42 and put his face between his knees
19. 13 when Elijah heard (it)..he wrapped his f.
20. 2 he turned his face to the wall, and prayed
21. 4 he laid him down..and turned away his f.
2 Ki. 4. 29 and lay my staff upon the face of the ch.
4. 31 and laid the staff upon the face of the
8. 15 and spread (it) on his face, so that he
9. 32 he lifted up his face to the window, and
9. 37 the carcase..shall be as dung upon the f.
12. 17 Hazael set his face to go up to Jerusalem
13. 14 Joash..came down..and wept over his f.
14. 8 Come, let us look one another in the face
14. 11 looked one another in the face at Beth-s.
20. 2 he turned his face to the wall, and prayed
1 Ch. 12. 8 whose faces (were like) the faces of lions
16. 11 Seek the LORD..seek his face continually
21. 16 David and the elders..fell upon their faces
2 Ch. 3. 13 they stood on their feet, and their faces
6. 3 king turned his face, and blessed..Israel
6. 42 turn not away the face of thine anointed
25. 17 Come, let us see one another in the face
25. 21 they saw one another in the face, (both)
29. 6 turned away their faces from the habita.
30. 9 will not turn away (his) face from you, if
32. 21 So he returned with shame of face to his
35. 22 Josiah would not turn his face from him
Ezra 9. 6 I am ashamed and blush to lift up my f.
9. 7 and to confusion of face, as (it is) this day
Esth. 7. 8 the word went..they covered Haman's f.
Job 1. 11 put forth..and he will curse thee to thy f.
2. 5 put forth..and he will curse thee to thy f.
4. 15 Then a spirit passed before my face; the
9. 24 he covereth the faces of the judges there.
11. 15 For then shalt thou lift up thy face
13. 24 Wherefore hidest thou thy face, and
16. 8 my leanness..beareth witness to my face
16. 16 My face is foul with weeping, and on my
21. 31 Who shall declare his way to his face?
22. 26 For then shalt thou..lift up thy face
24. 15 shall see me; and disguiseth (his) face
26. 9 He holdeth back the face of his throne
30. 10 abhor..and spare not to spit in my face
33. 26 he shall see his face with joy: for he will
34. 29 when he hideth (his) face, who then can
37. 12 commanded them upon the face of the
38. 30 The waters are hid..and the face of the
40. 13 them in the dust..(and) bind their faces
41. 13 Who can discover the face of his garment?
41. 14 Who can open the doors of his face? his
Psa. 5. 8 make thy way straight before my face
10. 11 he hideth his face; he will never see (it)
13. 1 how long wilt thou hide thy face from me?
17. 15 I will behold thy face in righteousness
21. 12 upon thy strings against the face of them
22. 24 neither hath he hid his face from him
24. 6 This (is) the generation..that seek thy f.
27. 8 Seek ye my face..Thy face, LORD, will I
27. 9 Hide not thy face (far) from me; put not
30. 7 thou didst hide thy face, (and) I was
31. 16 Make thy face to shine upon thy servant
34. 5 They looked..and their faces were not
34. 16 The face of the LORD (is) against them
41. 12 upholdest..and settest me before thy fa.
44. 15 and the shame of my face hath covered
44. 24 Wherefore hidest thou thy face, (and)
51. 9 Hide thy face from my sins, and blot out
67. 1 bless us; (and) cause his face to shine
69. 7 for thy sake..shame hath covered my face
69. 17 hide not thy face from thy servant; for
80. 3, 7, 19 cause thy face to shine; and we
83. 16 Fill their faces with shame; that they
84. 9 and look upon the face of thine anointed
88. 14 LORD..(why) hidest thou thy face from
89. 14 mercy and truth shall go before thy face
89. 23 I will beat down his foes before his face
102. 2 Hide not thy face from me in the day
104. 15 oil to make (his) face to shine, and bread
104. 29 Thou hidest thy face, they are troubled
104. 30 and thou renewest the face of the earth
105. 4 Seek the LORD..seek his face evermore
119. 135 Make thy face to shine upon thy servant
132. 10 turn not away the face of thine anointed
143. 7 hide not thy face from me, lest I be like
Prov. 7. 15 came I..diligently to seek thy face
8. 27 when he set a compass upon the face of
21. 29 A wicked man hardeneth his face: but (as)
24. 31 (and) nettles had covered the face thereof
27. 19 As in water face (answereth) to face, so
Eccl. 8. 1 man's wisdom maketh his face to shine
8. 1 the boldness of his face shall be changed
Isa. 3. 15 What mean ye (that) ye..grind the faces
6. 2 with twain he covered his face, and with
8. 17 that hideth his face from the house of
13. 8 be amazed one at another; their faces
14. 21 nor fill the face of the world with cities
16. 4 be thou a covert to them from the face
23. 17 of the world upon the face of the earth
25. 7 face of the covering cast over all people
25. 8 GOD will wipe away tears from off all fa.
27. 6 and fill the face of the world with fruit
29. 22 neither shall his face now wax pale
36. 9 How then wilt thou turn away the face of

Isa. 38. 2 Hezekiah turned his face toward the wall
50. 6 I hid not my face from shame and spitting
50. 7 therefore have I set my face like a flint
53. 3 and we hid as it were (our) faces from
54. 8 I hid my face from thee for a moment
59. 2 your sins have hid (his) face from you
64. 7 for thou hast hid thy face from us, and
65. 3 A people that provoketh me..to my face
Jer. 1. 8 Be not afraid of their faces: for I (am)
1. 13 and the face thereof (is) toward the north
1. 17 be not dismayed at their faces, lest I con.
2. 27 (their) back unto me, and not (their) face
5. 3 they have made their faces harder than a
7. 19 to the confusion of their own faces?
8. 2 they shall be for dung upon the face of
13. 26 will I discover thy skirts upon thy face
16. 4 they shall be as dung upon the face of
16. 17 they are not hid from my face, neither is
18. 17 I will shew them the back, and not the f.
21. 10 I have set my face against this city for
22. 25 the hand of (them) whose face thou
25. 26 which (are) upon the face of the earth
28. 16 I will cast thee from off the face of the
30. 6 and all faces are turned into paleness?
32. 31 I should remove it from before my face
32. 33 turned unto me the back, and not the fa.
33. 5 I have hid my face from this city
42. 15 If ye wholly set your faces to enter into
42. 17 be with all the men that set their faces
44. 11 I will set my face against you for evil
44. 12 that have set their faces to go into the
50. 5 shall ask the way to Zion, with their faces
51. 51 shame hath covered our faces; for
Lam. 2. 19 pour out..like water before the face of
3. 35 To turn aside..before the face of the
5. 12 the faces of elders were not honoured
Eze. 1. 6 every one had four faces, and every one
1. 8 they four had their faces and their wings
1. 10 As for the likeness of their faces, they
1. 10 had the face of a man, and the face of
1. 10 they four had the face of an ox on the
1. 10 they four also had the face of an eagle
1. 11 Thus (were) their faces: and their wings
1. 15 behold one wheel..with his four faces
1. 28 I fell upon my face, and I heard a voice
3. 8 made thy face strong against their faces
3. 23 arose, and went forth..and I fell on my f.
4. 3 set thy face against it, and it shall be
4. 7 Therefore thou shalt set thy face toward
6. 2 set thy face toward the mountains of Isr.
7. 18 and shame (shall be) upon all faces, and
7. 22 My face will I turn also from them, and
8. 16 their faces toward the east; and they
9. 8 I fell upon my face, and cried, and said
10. 14 every one had four faces: the first face
10. 14 the face of a cherub, and the second face
10. 14 face of a man, and the third the face of
10. 14 and the fourth the face of an eagle
10. 21 Every one had four faces apiece, and
10. 22 likeness of their faces (was) the same fa.
11. 13 Then fell I down upon my face, and cried
12. 6 thou shalt cover thy face, that thou see
12. 12 he shall cover his face, that he see not
13. 17 set thy face against the daughters of thy
14. 3 the stumblingblock..before their face
14. 4, 7 the stumblingblock..before his face
14. 6 turn away your faces from all your abo.
14. 8 And I will set my face against that man
15. 7 I will set my face against them; they
15. 7 ye shall know..when I set my face
20. 35 there will I plead with you face to face
20. 46 Son of man, set thy face toward the south
20. 47 all faces from the south to the north
21. 2 Son of man, set thy face toward Jerusal.
21. 16 Go thee..whithersoever thy face (is) set
25. 2 Son of man, set thy face against the Am.
28. 21 Son of man, set thy face against Zidon
29. 2 Son of man, set thy face against Pharaoh
34. 6 my flock was scattered upon all the face
35. 2 Son of man, set thy face against mount
38. 2 Son of man, set thy face against Gog, the
38. 20 all the men that (are) upon the face of
39. 14 those that remain upon the face of the
39. 23 therefore hid I my face from them, and
39. 24 According..have I done..and hid my fa.
39. 29 Neither will I hide my face any more
40. 15 from the face of the gate of the entrance
40. 15 unto the face of the porch of the inner
41. 19 So that the face of a man (was) toward the
41. 19 face of a young lion toward the palm tree
41. 21 (and) the face of the sanctuary; the
41. 25 thick planks upon the face of the porch
43. 3 like the vision..and I fell upon my face
44. 4 and I looked..and I fell upon my face
Dan. 1. 10 for why should he see your faces worse
8. 5 an he goat came from the west, on the f.
8. 17 I was afraid, and fell upon my face: but
8. 18 I was in a deep sleep on my face toward
9. 3 I set my face unto the Lord God, to seek
9. 7 but unto us confusion of faces, as at this
9. 8 to us (belongeth) confusion of face, to
10. 6 his face as the appearance of lightning
10. 9 in a deep sleep on my face, and my face
10. 15 I set my face toward the ground, and I
11. 17 He shall also set his face to enter with
11. 18 After this shall he turn his face unto the
11. 19 Then he shall turn his face toward the
Hos. 5. 5 the pride of Israel doth testify to his face
5. 15 till they acknowledge..and seek my face
7. 10 And the pride of Israel testifieth to his f.
Joel 2. 6 Before their face the people shall be
2. 20 with his face toward the east sea, and

Amos 5. 8 poureth them out upon the face of the
9. 6 poureth them out upon the face of the
9. 8 I will destroy it from off the face of the
Mic. 3. 4 he will even hide his face from them at
Nah. 2. 1 He that dasheth..is come up before thy f.
2. 10 the faces of them all gather blackness
3. 5 I will discover thy skirts upon thy face
Hab. 1. 9 their faces shall sup up (as) the east wind
Zech. 5. 3 curse that goeth forth over the face of
Mal. 2. 3 and spread dung upon your faces, (even)

5. *Face*, ὄψις *opsis.*
John 11. 44 and his face was bound about with a nap.

6. *Face*, πρόσωπον *prosōpon.*
Matt. 6. 16 for they disfigure their faces, that they
6. 17 anoint thine head, and wash thy face
11. 10 I send my messenger before thy face
16. 3 ye can discern the face of the sky ; but
17. 2 and his face did shine as the sun, and
17. 6 they fell on their face, and were sore
18. 10 their angels do always behold the face
26. 39 fell on his face, and prayed, saying, O my
26. 67 Then did they spit in his face, and buffeted
Mark 1. 2 I send my messenger before thy face
14. 65 to cover his face, and to buffet him, and to
Luke 1. 76 for thou shalt go before the face of the
2. 31 Which thou hast prepared before the face
5. 12 seeing Jesus, fell on (his) face, and besou.
7. 27 I send my messenger before thy face
9. 51 he stedfastly set his face to go to Jerusa.
9. 52 sent messengers before his face : and
9. 53 his face was as though he would go to J.
10. 1 sent them two and two before his face
12. 56 ye can discern the face of the sky and of
17. 16 fell down on (his) face at his feet, giving
21. 35 all them that dwell on the face of the
22. 64 they struck him on the face, and asked
24. 5 bowed down (their) faces to the earth
Acts 6. 15 saw his face as it had been the face of an
7. 45 whom God drave out before the face of our
17. 26 for to dwell on all the face of the earth
20. 25 I know that ye all..shall see my face no
20. 38 that they should see his face no more
1 Co. 13. 12 For now we see..but then face to face
14. 25 falling down on (his) face he will worship
2 Co. 3. 7 could not stedfastly behold the face of M.
3. 13 as Moses, (which) put a veil over his face
3. 18 we all, with open face beholding as in a
4. 6 to (give) the light..in the face of Jesus
11. 20 ye suffer..if a man smite you on the face
Gal. 1. 22 was unknown by face unto the churches
2. 11 I withstood him to the face, because he
Col. 2. 1 and (for) as many as have not seen my f.
1 Th. 2. 17 endeavoured..to see your face with great
3. 10 praying..that we might see your face
Jas. 1. 23 a man beholding his natural face in a
1 Pe. 3. 12 the face of the Lord (is) against them
Rev. 4. 7 and the third beast had a face as a man
6. 16 hide us from the face of him that sitteth
7. 11 and fell before the throne on their faces
9. 7 and their faces (were) as the faces of men
10. 1 and his face (was) as it were the sun, and
11. 16 fell upon their faces, and worshipped
12. 14 half a time, from the face of the serpent
20. 11 from whose face the earth and the heaven
22. 4 And they shall see his face ; and his name

FACE to face —

1. *Face to face*, κατὰ πρόσωπον *kata prosōpon.*
Acts 25. 16 he which..have the accusers face to face

2. *Mouth to mouth*, στόμα πρὸς στόμα. [*stoma*].
2 John 12 but I trust to come..and speak face to f.
3 John 14 and we shall speak face to face. Peace

FADE (away), to —

1. *To fade*, בָּלַל *balal*, 5.
Isa. 64. 6 all do fade as a leaf ; and our iniquities

2. *To fade or wear away*, נָבֵל *nabel.*
2 Sa. 22. 46 Strangers shall fade away, and they shall
Psa. 18. 45 The strangers shall fade away, and be
Isa. 1. 30 ye shall be as an oak whose leaf fadeth
24. 4 The earth mourneth (and) fadeth away
24. 4 the world languisheth (and) fadeth away
28. 1 whose glorious beauty (is) a fading flower
28. 4 the glorious beauty..shall be a fading
40. 7, 8 The grass withereth, the flower fadeth
Jer. 8. 13 the leaf shall fade ; and (the things that)
Eze. 47. 12 whose leaf shall not fade, neither shall

3. *To cause to fade*, μαραίνω *marainō.*
Jas. 1. 11 so also shall the rich man fade away in

FADETH not away, that —

1. *Unfading*, ἀμαράντινος *amarantinos.*
1 Pe. 5. 4 a crown of glory that fadeth not away

2. *Unfading*, ἀμάραντος *amarantos.*
1 Pe. 1. 4 To an inheritance..that fadeth not away

FAIL —

1. *Is not*, אַיִן *ayin.*
Isa. 44. 12 yea, he is hungry, and his strength faileth

2. *To sit*, יָשַׁב *yashab.*
1 Sa. 20. 5 I should not fail to sit with the king at

3. *Failing, consumption*, כָּלֶה *kaleh.*
Deut 28. 32 and fail (with longing) for them all the

4. *To perish, be lost*, אָבַד *abad.*
Psa. 142. 4 refuge failed me ; no man cared for my
Eze. 12. 22 days are prolonged, and every vision fail.

5. *To go away*, אָזַל *azal.*
Job 14. 11 (As) the waters fail from the sea, and the

6. *To cease, fail, have an end*, אָפֵס *aphes.*
Gen. 47. 15 why should we die..for the money faileth
47. 16 will give you for your cattle, if money fail

7. *To be emptied, made void*, בָּקַק *baqaq*, 2.
Isa. 19. 3 the spirit of Egypt shall fail in the midst

8. *To fail*, גָּמַר *gamar.*
Psa. 77. 8 doth (his) promise fail for evermore?

9. *To loathe, cast away*, גָּעַל *gaal*, 5.
Job 21. 10 Their bull gendereth, and faileth not

10. *To be lean, poor, low, weak*, דָּלַל *dalal.*
Isa. 38. 14 mine eyes fail (with looking) upward : O

11. *To cease, leave off, forbear*, חָדַל *chadal.*
Job 19. 14 My kinsfolk have failed, and my familiar

12. *To lack, abate*, חָסֵר *chaser.*
1 Ki. 17. 14 neither shall the cruise of oil fail, until
Isa. 51. 14 not die..nor that his bread should fail

13. *Lacking*, חָסֵר *chaser.*
1 Ki. 17. 16 neither did the cruise of oil fail, accord.
Eccl. 10. 3 a fool walketh by the way, his wisdom f.

14. *To go out or forth*, יָצָא *yatsa.*
Gen. 42. 28 their heart failed..and they were afraid
Song 5. 6 my soul failed when he spake : I sought

15. *To be or become weak, dim*, כָּהָה *kahah.*
Isa. 42. 4 He shall not fail nor be discouraged, till

16. *To lie, deceive*, כָּזַב *kazab*, 3.
Isa. 58. 11 like a spring of water, whose waters fail

17. *To fail*, כָּחַשׁ *kachash.*
Psa. 109. 24 are weak..and my flesh faileth of fatness

18. *To fail, lie, deceive*, כָּחַשׁ *kachash*, 3.
Hos. 9. 2 not feed..the new wine shall fail in her
Hab. 3. 17 the labour of the olive shall fail, and the

19. *To be completed, consumed, ended*, כָּלָה *kalah.*
Job 11. 20 the eyes of the wicked shall fail, and
17. 5 even the eyes of his children shall fail
Psa. 69. 3 mine eyes fail while I wait for my God
71. 9 forsake me not when my strength faileth
73. 26 My flesh and my heart faileth..God
119. 82 Mine eyes fail for thy word, saying
119. 123 Mine eyes fail for thy salvation, and for
143. 7 my spirit faileth : hide not thy face from
Prov 22. 8 and the rod of his anger shall fail
Isa. 15. 6 the grass faileth, there is no green thing
21. 16 and all the glory of Kedar shall fail
31. 3 fall down, and they all shall fail together
32. 10 for the vintage shall fail, the gathering
Jer. 14. 6 their eyes did fail because..no grass
Lam. 2. 11 Mine eyes do fail with tears, my bowels
3. 22 consumed, because his compassions fail
4. 17 our eyes as yet failed for our vain help

20. *To be cut off*, כָּרַת *karath*, 2.
2 Sa. 3. 29 let there not fail from the house of Joab
1 Ki. 2. 4 there shall not fail thee..a man on the
8. 25 There shall not fail thee a man in my
9. 5 There shall not fail thee a man upon the
2 Ch. 6. 16 There shall not fail thee a man, in my
7. 18 There shall not fail thee a man (to be)

21. *To stumble, be feeble*, כָּשַׁל *kashal.*
Psa. 31. 10 strength faileth, because of mine iniquity

22. *To fall*, נָפַל *naphal.*
Josh 21. 45 There failed not ought of any good thing
23. 14 not one thing hath failed of all the good
23. 14 (and) not one thing hath failed thereof
1 Sa. 17. 32 Let no man's heart fail because of him
1 Ki. 8. 56 there hath not failed one word of all his

23. *To be dried up*, נָשַׁת *nashath.*
Isa. 41. 17 their tongue faileth for thirst, I the LORD
Jer. 51. 30 in (their) holds ; their might hath failed

24. *To become dried up*, נָשַׁת *nashath*, 2.
Isa. 19. 5 the waters shall fail from the sea, and

25. *To pass over, away, by*, עָבַר *abar.*
Esth. 9. 27 so as it should not fail, that they would
9. 28 these days of Purim should not fail from

26. *To be lacking*, עָדַר *adar*, 2.
Isa. 34. 16 no one of these shall fail, none shall want
40. 26 for that (he is) strong in power ; not one f.
59. 15 Yea, truth faileth..the LORD saw (it), and
Zeph. 3. 5 he faileth not ; but the unjust knoweth

27. *To leave, forsake, abandon*, עָזַב *azab.*
Psa. 38. 10 My heart panteth, my strength faileth
40. 12 they are more..therefore my heart faileth

28. *To be feeble, covered*, עָטַף *ataph.*
Isa. 57. 16 for the spirit should fail before me, and

29. *To pass away, come to an end*, פָּסַס *pasas.*
Psa. 12. 1 for the faithful fail from among..men

30. *To break, make void, fail*, פָּרַר *parar*, 5.
Eccl. 12. 5 they shall be afraid..desire shall fail

31. *To make feeble, let be feeble*, רָפָה *raphah*, 5.
Deut. 31. 6 he will not fail thee, nor forsake thee
31. 8 he will not fail thee, neither forsake thee
Josh. 1. 5 I will not fail thee, nor forsake thee
1 Ch. 28. 20 he will not fail thee, nor forsake thee

32. *Error, mistake*, שָׁלוּ *shalu.*
Ezra. 4. 22 Take heed now that ye fail not to do this
6. 9 it be given them day by day without fail

33. *To lie, deceive*, שָׁקַר *shaqar*, 3.
Psa 89. 33 from him, nor suffer my faithfulness to f.

34. *To be finished, consumed*, תָּמַם *tamam.*
Gen. 47. 15 when money failed in the land of Egypt
Josh. 3. 16 those that came down toward the sea..f.

35. *Not to be steadfast*, לֹא אָמַן *lo aman*, 2.
Jer. 15. 18 be..as a liar, (and as) waters (that) fail?

36. *To leave out, cease*, ἐκλείπω *ekleipō.*
Luke 16. 9 when ye fail, they may receive you into
22. 32 But I have prayed..that thy faith fail not
Heb. 1. 12 thou art the same..thy years shall not fa.

37. *To fall off or away*, ἐκπίπτω *ekpiptō.*
1 Co. 13. 8 Charity never [faileth]: but whether (there

38. *To leave upon or besides*, ἐπιλείπω *epileipō.*
Heb. 11. 32 for the time would fail me to tell of G.

39. *To make useless*, καταργέω *katargeō.*
1 Co. 13. 8 prophecies, they shall fail ; whether (there

40. *To fall*, πίπτω *piptō.*
Luke 16. 17 to pass, than one tittle of the law to fail

41. *To be behind, lack*, ὑστερέω *hustereō.*
Heb. 12. 15 lest any man [fail] of the grace of God

FAIL, to cause to —

1. *To cause to be lacking*, חָסֵר *chaser*, 5.
Isa. 32. 6 will cause the drink of the thirsty to fail

2. *To finish, consume*, כָּלָה *kalah*, 3.
Job 31. 16 have caused the eyes of the widow to fail

3. *To cause to cease*, שָׁבַת *shabath*, 5.
Jer. 48. 33 I have caused wine to fail from the wine.

FAIL, to let —

To cause or let fall, נָפַל *naphal*, 5.
Esth. 6. 10 let nothing fail of all that thou hast spo.

FAIL, to make to —

To cause to cease, שָׁבַת *shabath*, 5.
Amos 8. 4 even to make the poor of the land to fail

FAILETH not, that —

Not leaving off, unfailing, ἀνέκλειπτος *anekleiptos.*
Luke 12. 33 a treasure in the heavens that faileth not

FAILING —

Consumption, failing, כִּלָּיוֹן *killayon.*
Deut 28. 65 and failing of eyes, and sorrow of mind

FAILING, hearts —

To swoon away, ἀποψύχω *apopsuchō.*
Luke 21. 26 Men's hearts failing them for fear, and

FAIN, would —

1. *To flee*, בָּרַח *barach.*
Job 27. 22 he would fain flee out of his hand

2. *To fix the mind or desire on*, ἐπιθυμέω *epithum.*
Luke 15. 16 he would fain have filled his belly with

FAINT —

1. *Sick*, דָּוֶה *daveh.*
Lam. 1. 13 he hath made me desolate..faint all the
5. 17 For this our heart is faint ; for these

2. *Sick*, דַּוָּי *davvai.*
Isa. 1. 5 The whole head is sick..the..heart faint
Jer. 8. 18 I would comfort myself..my heart (is) f.
Lam. 1. 22 my sighs (are) many, and my heart (is) f.

3. *Weary*, יָעֵף *yaeph.*
2 Sa. 16. 2 that such as be faint in the wilderness
Isa. 40. 29 He giveth power to the faint ; and to

4. *Wearied*, עָיֵף *ayeph.*
Gen. 25. 29 Esau came from the field, and he (was) f.
25. 30 Feed me, I pray thee..for I (am) faint
Deut 25. 18 smote..when thou (wast) faint and weary
Judg. 8. 4 Gideon..passed over..faint, yet pursuing
8. 5 Give, I pray you, loaves..for they (be) f.
Isa. 29. 8 (he is) faint, and his soul hath appetite

FAINT, to —

1. *To become, happen*, הָיָה *hayah*, 2.
Dan. 8. 27 And I Daniel fainted, and was sick

2. *To labour, be weary*, יָגַע *yaga.*
Jer. 45. 3 I fainted in my sighing, and I find no rest

3. *To be weary*, יָעַף *yaaph.*
Isa. 40. 28 the Creator..fainteth not, neither is wea.?
40. 30 Even the youths shall faint and be weary
40. 31 (and) they shall walk, and not faint
44. 12 he drinketh no water, and is faint

4. *To become weak, restrain*, כָּהָה *kahah*, 3.
Eze. 21. 7 shall be feeble, and every spirit shall fa.

5. *To be complete, finished, consumed*, כָּלָה *kalah.*
Psa. 84. 2 My soul longeth, yea, even fainteth for
119. 81 My soul fainteth for thy salvation

6. *To be feeble, weary*, לָאָה *laah.*
Job 4. 5 it is come upon thee, and thou faintest

7. *To faint, be feeble*, לָהָה *lahah.*
Gen. 47. 13 Canaan, fainted by reason of the famine

8. *To melt, dissolve*, מוּג *mug.*
Eze. 21. 15 that (their) heart may faint, and (their)

9. *To be melted*, מוּג *mug*, 2.
Josh. 2. 24 the inhabitants of the country do faint

10. *To faint, be melted*, מָסַס *masas.*
Isa. 10. 18 as when a standard bearer fainteth

11. *To be melted*, מָסַס *masas*, 2.
Deut 20. 8 lest his brethren's heart faint as well as

12. *To show self feeble,* עָטַף *ataph,* 7.
Psa. 107. 5 Hungry and thirsty, their soul fainted
Jon. 2. 7 When my soul fainted within me I re.

13. *To be covered, wrapped up, faint,* עָלַף *alaph,* 4.
Isa. 51. 20 Thy sons have fainted, they lie at the head

14. *To cover or wrap self up, faint,* עָלַף *alaph,* 7.
Amos 8. 13 In that day shall the fair virgins..faint
Jon. 4. 8 he fainted, and wished in himself to die

15. *To be feeble, cease, faint,* פּוּג *pug.*
Gen. 45. 26 Jacob's heart fainted, for he believed

16. *To be tender, soft, timid,* רָכַךְ *rakak,* 2.
Deut 20. 3 let not your hearts faint, fear not, and do
Isa. 7. 4 fear not, neither be faint hearted for the
Jer. 51. 46 lest your heart faint, and ye fear for the

17. *To show self feeble,* רָפָה *raphah,* 7.
Prov 24. 10 (If) thou faint in the day of adversity

18. *To turn out badly, cave in,* ἐκκακέω *ekkakeō.*
Luke 18. 1 ought always to pray, and not to faint
2 Co. 4. 1 as we have received mercy, we faint not
4. 16 For which cause we faint not; but though
Eph. 3. 13 Wherefore I desire that ye faint not at

19. *To loose out, relax,* ἐκλύω *ekluō.*
Matt. 9. 36 because [they fainted], and were scattered
15. 32 I will not send them..lest they faint in
Mark 8. 3 if I send them away..they will faint by
Gal. 6. 9 in due season we shall reap, if we faint
Heb. 12. 3 lest ye be wearied and faint in your
12. 5 nor faint when thou art rebuked of him

20. *To toil, work out, weary,* κάμνω *kamnō.*
Rev. 2. 3 And hast borne..and hast not fainted

FAINT, to be —

1. *To be weary,* עוּף *uph.*
1 Sa. 14. 28 And the people were faint
14. 31 and the people were very faint

2. *To be or become faint,* פָּגַר *pagar,* 3.
1 Sa. 30. 10 two hundred..which were so faint that
30. 21 two hundred men, which were so faint

3. *To be feeble,* רָפָה *raphah.*
Isa. 13. 7 Therefore shall all hands be faint, and

FAINT, that —

To be feeble, עָטַף *ataph.*
Lam. 2. 19 thy young children, that faint for hunger

FAINT, to wax —

To be weary, עוּף *uph.*
2 Sa. 21. 15 David went down..and David waxed faint

FAINT hearted —

Tender of heart, רַךְ לֵבָב *rak lebab.*
Deut 20. 8 What man..fearful and faint hearted?

FAINT hearted, to be —

To be melted, מוּג *mug,* 2.
Jer. 49. 23 they are faint hearted..sorrow on the sea

FAINTED —

Faintness, עֻלְפֶּה *ulpeh.*
Eze. 31. 15 all the trees of the field fainted for him

FAINTNESS —

Faintness, מֹרֶךְ *morek.*
Lev. 26. 36 I will send a faintness into their hearts

FAIR, fairer —

1. *Clean, pure,* טָהוֹר *tahor.*
Zech. 3. 5 Let them set a fair mitre upon his head
3. 5 So they set a fair mitre upon his head

2. *Good, fair,* טוֹב *tob.*
Gen. 6. 2 the daughters of men that they (were) fair
24. 16 And the damsel (was) very fair to look
26. 7 because she (was) fair to look upon
Judg 15. 2 (is) not her..sister fairer than she?
Esth. 1. 11 the queen..for she (was) fair to look on
Isa. 5. 9 many houses..great and fair, without in.
Dan. 1. 15 their countenances appeared fairer and

3. *Goodness,* טוּב *tub.*
Hos. 10. 11 but I passed over upon her fair neck

4. *Fair, beautiful,* יָפֶה *yapheh.*
Gen. 12. 11 I know that thou (art) a fair woman to
12. 14 beheld the woman, that she (was) very fair
1 Sa. 17. 42 a youth, and ruddy, and of a fair counte.
2 Sa 13. 1 Absalom the son of David, had a fair sis.
14. 27 she was a woman of a fair countenance
1 Ki. 1. 3 they sought for a fair damsel throughout
1. 4 the damsel (was) very fair, and cherished
Job 42. 15 no women found (so) fair as the daughters
Prov 11. 22 a fair women which is without discretion
Song 1. 15 thou (art) fair, my love..thou art fair
1. 16 thou (art) fair, my beloved, yea, pleasant
4. 1 thou art fair, my love..thou art fair
4. 7 Thou (art) all fair, my love..no spot in
6. 10 fair as the moon, clear as the sun
Jer. 11. 16 A green olive tree, fair..of goodly fruit
Eze. 31. 3 a cedar in Lebanon with fair branches
31. 9 I have made him fair by the multitude of
Amos 8. 13 In that day shall the fair virgins..faint

5. *Good in appearance,* טוֹב מַרְאֶה *tob mareh.*
Esth. 2. 2 Let there be fair young virgins sought
2. 3 gather together all the fair young virgins

6. *Fair, beautiful,* שַׁפִּיר *shappir.*
Dan. 4. 12 The leaves thereof (were) fair, and the
4. 21 Whose leaves (were) fair, and the fruit

7. *Traffic, market,* עִזָּבוֹן *izzabon.*
Eze. 27. 12 with silver..they traded in thy fairs
27. 14 the house of Togarmah traded in thy fairs
27. 16, 22 they occupied in thy fairs with
27. 19 going to and fro occupied in thy fairs
27. 27 Thy riches, and thy fairs, thy merchandise

8. *To be or act graciously,* חָנַן *chanan,* 3. [*See* **SPEAK.**]
Prov. 26. 25 When he speaketh fair, believe him not

9. *Fair of form,* יְפַה תֹאַר [*yapheh*].
Esth. 2 7 and the maid (was) fair and beautiful

10. *Belonging to the town, agreeable,* ἀστεῖος *asteios*
Acts 7. 20 Moses was born, and was exceeding fair

FAIR, to be —

To be fair, beauteous, יָפָה *yaphah.*
Song 4. 10 How fair is thy love, my sister
7. 6 How fair and how pleasant art thou, O
Eze. 31. 7 Thus was he fair in his greatness, in the

FAIR, to make self —

To make or show self fair, יָפָה *yaphah,* 7.
Jer. 4. 30 in vain shalt thou make thyself fair

FAIR, very —

Very fair, יְפֵה־פִיָּה *yepheh-phiyyah.*
Jer. 46. 20 Egypt..a very fair heifer..destruction

FAIR colours —

Red ore, stibium, ruby, פּוּךְ *puk.*
Isa. 54. 11 I will lay thy stone. with fair colours

FAIR one —

Fair, beauteous one, יָפֶה *yapheh.*
Song 2. 10 my love, my fair one; 2. 13

FAIR show, to make a —

To make a fair face, εὐπροσωπέω *euprosōpeō.*
Gal. 6. 12 As many as desire to make a fair show in

FAIR speech —

1. *A taking, reception, doctrine,* לֶקַח *leqach.*
Prov. 7. 21 With her much fair speech she caused him

2. *Easy discourse,* εὐλογία *eulogia.*
Rom 16. 18 by good words and fair speeches deceive

FAIR weather —

1. *Gold, shining, fair weather,* זָהָב *zahab.*
Job 37. 22 Fair weather cometh out of the north

2. *Fine weather,* εὐδία *eudia.*
Matt 16. 2 ye say, (It will be) fair weather; for the

FAIR word —

Good, טוֹב *tob.*
Jer. 12. 6 though they speak fair words unto thee

FAIRER, to be —

To become fair, be made fair, יָפָה *yaphah,* 4.
Psa. 45. 2 Thou art fairer than the children of men

FAIREST —

Fair, beauteous one, יָפֶה *yapheh.*
Song 1. 8 O thou fairest among women, go thy way
5. 9 O thou fairest among women? what (is)
6. 1 O thou fairest among women? whither

FAIR HAVENS, καλοὶ λιμένες *kaloi limenes.*
A harbour in the island of Crete, not mentioned in any other ancient writing. It was on the S. and was practically the harbour of Lasæa, about five miles to the E. of Cape Matala, the most conspicuous headland on the S. coast of the island.
Acts 27. 8 a place which is called The Fair Havens

FAITH —

1. *Faithfulness, steadiness,* אֵמֻן *emun.*
Deut 32. 20 very froward..children in whom (is) no f.

2. *Faithfulness, stability,* אֱמוּנָה *emunah.*
Hab. 2. 4 but the just shall live by his faith

3. *Hope,* ἐλπίς *elpis.*
Heb. 10. 23 hold fast the profession of (our) faith

4. *Faith, faithfulness, steadfastness,* πίστις *pistis.*
Matt. 8. 10 not found so great faith, no, not in Israel
9. 2 Jesus, seeing their faith, said unto the
9. 22 Daughter..thy faith hath made thee who.
9. 29 According to your faith be it unto you
15. 28 woman, great (is) thy faith: be it unto
17. 20 If ye have faith as a grain of mustard
21. 21 If ye have faith, and doubt not, ye shall
23. 23 of the law, judgment, mercy, and faith
Mark 2. 5 Jesus saw their faith, he said unto the
4. 40 he said..how is it that ye have no faith?
5. 34 thy faith hath made thee whole; go in
10. 52 Go thy way; thy faith hath made thee
11. 22 Jesus answering saith..Have faith in God
Luke 5. 20 when he saw their faith, he said unto him
7. 9 not found so great faith, no, not in Israel
7. 50 Thy faith hath saved thee; go in peace
8. 25 And he said unto them, Where is your f.?
8. 48 thy faith hath made thee whole; go in
17. 5 And the apostles said..Increase our faith
17. 6 If ye had faith as a grain of mustard
17. 19 go thy way; thy faith hath made thee
18. 8 shall he find faith on the earth?
18. 42 Receive thy sight..faith hath saved thee
22. 32 prayed for thee, that thy faith fail not
Acts 3. 16 his name through faith in his name hath
3. 16 the faith which is by him hath given him
6. 5 man full of faith and of the Holy Ghost
6. 7 the priests were obedient to the faith
6. 8 Stephen, full of [faith] and power, did
11. 24 and full of the Holy Ghost and of faith
13. 8 to turn away the deputy from the faith
14. 9 perceiving that he had faith to be healed
14. 22 exhorting them to continue in the faith
14. 27 opened the door of faith unto the Gentiles
15. 9 purifying their hearts by faith
16. 5 the churches established in the faith
20. 21 and faith toward our Lord Jesus Christ
24. 24 heard him concerning the faith in Christ
26. 18 are sanctified by faith that is in me
Rom 1. 5 obedience to the faith among all nations
1. 8 your faith is spoken of throughout the
1. 12 by the mutual faith both of you and me
1. 17 righteousness..revealed from faith to fa.
1. 17 is written, The just shall live by faith
3. 3 shall their unbelief make the faith of
3. 22 righteousness of God (which is) by faith
3. 25 propitiation through faith in his blood
3. 27 of works? Nay; but by the law of faith
3. 28 justified by faith without the deeds of
3. 30 faith, and uncircumcision through faith
3. 31 we then make void the law through fai.?
4. 5 his faith is counted for righteousness
4. 9 that faith was reckoned to Abraham for
4. 11 righteousness of the faith, which (he had
4. 12 steps of that faith of our father Abraham
4. 13 but through the righteousness of faith
4. 14 faith is made void, and the promise
4. 16 (it is) of faith, that (it might be) by grace
4. 16 that also which is of the faith of Abrah.
4. 19 being not weak in faith, he considered
4. 20 was strong in faith, giving glory to God
5. 1 being justified by faith, we have peace
5. 2 access by [faith] into this grace wherein
9. 30 even the righteousness which is of faith
9. 32 (they sought it) not by faith, but as it
10. 6 righteousness which is of faith speaketh
10. 8 that is, the word of faith, which we pre.
10. 17 faith (cometh) by hearing, and hearing
11. 20 thou standest by faith. Be not high
12. 3 dealt to every man the measure of faith
12. 6 according to the proportion of faith
14. 1 Him that is weak in the faith receive ye
14. 22 Hast thou faith? have (it) to thyself
14. 23 damned..because (he eateth) not of faith
14. 23 for whatsoever (is) not of faith is sin
16. 26 all nations for the obedience of faith
1 Co. 2. 5 your faith should not stand in the wisdom
12. 9 To another faith by the same Spirit
13. 2 though I have all faith, so that I could
13. 13 now abideth faith, hope, charity, these
15. 14 preaching vain, and your faith (is)..vain
15. 17 Christ be not raised, your faith (is) vain
16. 13 stand fast in the faith, quit you like men
2 Co. 1. 24 that we have dominion over your faith
1. 24 helpers of your joy: for by faith ye stand
4. 13 having the same spirit of faith, according
5. 7 For we walk by faith, not by sight
8. 7 (in) faith, and utterance, and knowledge
10. 15 when your faith is increased, that we shall
13. 5 Examine..whether ye be in the faith
Gal. 1. 23 preacheth the faith which once he destr.
2. 16 by the faith of Jesus Christ, even we have
2. 16 might be justified by the faith of Christ
2. 20 I live by the faith of the Son of God
3. 2, 5 by the works..or by the hearing of faith?
3. 7 they which are of faith, the same are the
3. 8 would justify the heathen through faith
3. 9 they which be of faith are blessed with
3. 11 evident: for, The just shall live by faith
3. 12 the law is not of faith: but, The man that
3. 14 the promise of the Spirit through faith
3. 22 promise by faith of Jesus Christ might
3. 23 before faith came, we were kept under
3. 23 the faith which should afterwards
3. 24 that we might be justified by faith
3. 25 after that faith is come, we are no longer
3. 26 children of God by faith in Christ Jesus
5. 5 for the hope of righteousness by faith
5. 6 but faith which worketh by love
5. 22 long suffering, gentleness, goodness, faith
6. 10 them who are of the household of faith
Eph. 1. 15 I heard of your faith in the Lord Jesus
2. 8 For by grace are ye saved through faith
3. 12 access with confidence by the faith of
3. 17 Christ may dwell in your hearts by faith
4. 5 One Lord, one faith, one baptism
4. 13 we all come in the unity of the faith
6. 16 taking the shield of faith, wherewith ye
6. 23 love with faith, from God the Father
Phil. 1. 25 for your furtherance and joy of faith
1. 27 striving together for the faith of the
2. 17 the sacrifice and service of your faith
3. 9 righteousness which is of God by faith
3. 9 that which is through the faith of Christ
Col. 1. 4 Since we heard of your faith in Christ
1. 23 If ye continue in the faith grounded and
2. 5 the stedfastness of your faith in Christ
2. 7 stablished in the faith, as ye have been
2. 12 through the faith of the operation of God
1 Th. 1. 3 Remembering..your work of faith, and
1. 8 your faith to God ward is spread abroad
3. 2 and to comfort you concerning your faith
3. 5 I sent to know your faith, lest by some
3. 6 good tiding of your faith and charity
3. 7 we were comforted over you..by your f.
3. 10 that which is lacking in your faith?
5. 8 putting on the breastplate of faith and
2 Th. 1. 3 your faith groweth exceedingly, and the
1. 4 for your patience and faith in all your

2 Th. 1. 11 goodness, and the work of faith with po
3. 2 be delivered..for all (men) have not faith
1 Ti. 1. 2 Unto Timothy, (my) own son in the faith
1. 4 than godly edifying which is in faith
1. 5 a good conscience, and (of) faith unfeig.
1. 14 faith and love which is in Christ Jesus
1. 19 Holding faith, and a good conscience
1. 19 concerning faith have made shipwreck
2. 7 a teacher of the Gentiles in faith and
2. 15 if they continue in faith and charity and
3. 9 mystery of the faith in a pure conscience
3. 13 in the faith which is in Christ Jesus
4. 1 some shall depart from the faith, giving
4. 6 the words of faith and of good doctrine
4. 12 in charity, in spirit, in faith, in purity
5. 8 he hath denied the faith, and is worse
5. 12 they have cast off their first faith
6. 10 have erred from the faith, and pierced
6. 11 godliness, faith, love, patience, meekness
6. 12 Fight the good fight of faith, lay hold
6. 21 some..have erred concerning the faith
2 Ti. 1. 5 the unfeigned faith that is in thee
1. 13 faith and love which is in Christ Jesus
2. 18 and overthrow the faith of some
2. 22 follow righteousness, faith, charity, peace
3. 8 corrupt..reprobate concerning the faith
3. 10 faith, long suffering, charity, patience
3. 15 through faith which is in Christ Jesus
4. 7 finished (my) course, I have kept the faith
Titus 1. 1 according to the faith of God's elect, and
1. 4 Titus, (mine) own son after the common f.
1. 13 that they may be sound in the faith
2. 2 sound in faith, in charity, in patience
3. 15 Greet them that love us in the faith
Phm 5 Hearing of thy love and faith, which thou
6 the communication of thy faith may bec.
Heb. 4. 2 mixed with faith in them that heard (it)
6. 1 from dead works, and of faith toward G.
6. 12 through faith and patience inherit the
10. 22 in full assurance of faith, having our
10. 38 the just shall live by faith: but if (any)
11. 1 faith is the substance of things hoped
11. 3 Through faith we understand that the
11. 4 By faith Abel offered unto God a more
11. 5 By faith Enoch was translated that he
11. 6 without faith (it is) impossible to please
11. 7 By faith Noah, being warned of God of
11. 7 the righteousness which is by faith
11. 8 By faith Abraham, when he was called to
11. 9 By faith he sojourned in the land of
11. 11 Through faith also Sara herself received
11. 13 all died in faith, not having received
11. 17 By faith Abraham, when he was tried
11. 20 By faith Isaac blessed Jacob and Esau
11. 21 By faith Jacob, when he was a dying
11. 22 By faith Joseph, when he died, made
11. 23 By faith Moses, when he was born, was
11. 24 By faith Moses, when he was come to
11. 27 By faith he forsook Egypt, not fearing
11. 28 Through faith he kept the passover, and
11. 29 By faith they passed through the Red sea
11. 30 By faith the walls of Jericho fell down
11. 31 By faith the harlot Rahab perished not
11. 33 through faith subdued kingdoms, wrought
11. 39 obtained a good report through faith
12. 2 the author and finisher of (our) faith
13. 7 whose faith follow, considering the end
Jas. 1. 3 trying of your faith worketh patience
1. 6 But let him ask in faith, nothing wavering
2. 1 have not the faith of our Lord Jesus
2. 5 the poor of this world rich in faith
2. 14 hath faith, and have not works? can fa.
2. 17 faith, if it hath not works, is dead, being
2. 18 Thou hast faith..show me thy faith
2. 18 and I will show thee my faith by my
2. 20 know..that faith without works is dead?
2. 22 Seest thou how faith wrought with his
2. 22 and by works was faith made perfect
2. 24 that by works..and not by faith only
2. 26 so faith without works is dead also
5. 15 the prayer of faith shall save the sick
1 Pe. 1. 5 through faith unto salvation ready to be
1. 7 the trial of your faith, being much more
1. 9 Receiving the end of your faith, (even)
1. 21 that your faith and hope might be in God
5. 9 Whom resist stedfast in the faith, know
2 Pe. 1. 1 that have obtained like precious faith
1. 5 add to your faith virtue; and to virtue
1 Jo. 5. 4 that overcometh the world, (even) our fa.
Jude 3 the faith which was once delivered unto
20 building up..on your most holy faith
Rev. 2. 13 hast not denied my faith, even in those
2. 19 and faith, and thy patience, and thy
13. 10 the patience and the faith of the saints
14. 12 commandments of God, and the faith of

FAITH, of little —

Little of faith, ὀλιγόπιστος oligopistos.

Matt 6. 30 more (clothe) you, O ye of little faith?
8. 26 Why are ye fearful, O ye of little faith?
14. 31 O thou of little faith, wherefore didst
16. 8 O ye of little faith, why reason ye among
Luke 12. 28 how much more..you, O ye of little faith?

FAITHFUL —

1. *Faithfulness, truth, אֵמוּן emun.*

Prov 13. 17 but a faithful ambassador (is) health
14. 5 A faithful witness will not lie: but a
20. 6 but a faithful man who can find?

2. *Faithfulness, stability, אֱמוּנָה emunah.*

Psa. 119. 86 All thy commandments (are) faithful
119. 138 Thy testimonies..(are)..very faithful

3. *To be steady, faithful, אָמַן aman.*

2 Sa. 20. 19 (that are) peaceable (and) faithful in Isr
Psa. 12. 1 faithful fail from among the children of
31. 23 (for) the LORD preserveth the faithful

4. *To be steady, faithful, אָמַן aman, 5.*

Dan. 6. 4 forasmuch as he (was) faithful, neither

5. *Truth, stedfastness, אֱמֶת emeth.*

Neh. 7. 2 he (was) a faithful man, and feared God

6. *Faithful, steady, πιστός pistos.*

Matt 24. 45 Who then is a faithful and wise servant
25. 21, 23 faithful servant: thou hast been fait.
Luke 12. 42 Who then is that faithful and wise stew.
16. 10 faithful in that which is least..faithful
16. 11 been faithful in the unrighteous mam.
16. 12 faithful in that which is another man's
19. 17 thou hast been faithful in a very little
Acts 16. 15 judged me to be faithful to the Lord
1 Co. 1. 9 God (is) faithful, by whom ye were called
4. 2 required..that a man be found faithful
4. 17 my beloved son, and faithful in the Lord
7. 25 obtained mercy of the Lord to be faithful
10. 13 God (is) faithful, who will not suffer you
Gal. 3. 9 they..are blessed with faithful Abraham
Eph. 1. 1 and to the faithful in Christ Jesus
6. 21 brother and faithful minister in the Lord
Col. 1. 2 faithful brethren in Christ which are at
1. 7 is for you a faithful minister of Christ
4. 7 faithful minister and fellow servant in
4. 9 Onesimus, a faithful and beloved brother
1 Th. 5. 24 Faithful (is) he that calleth you, who also
2 Th. 3. 3 the Lord is faithful, who shall stablish
1 Ti. 1. 12 he counted me faithful, putting me into
1. 15 This (is) a faithful saying, and worthy of
3. 11 not slanderers..faithful in all things
4. 9 This (is) a faithful saying, and worthy of
6. 2 they are faithful and beloved, partakers
2 Ti. 2. 2 the same commit thou to faithful men
2. 11 (It is) a faithful saying: For if we be
2. 13 abideth faithful: he cannot deny himself
Titus 1. 6 having faithful children, not accused of
1. 9 the faithful word as he hath been taught
3. 8 (This is) a faithful saying, and these
Heb. 2. 17 a merciful and faithful High Priest in
3. 2 was faithful to him that appointed him
3. 5 Moses verily (was) faithful in all his
10. 23 for he (is) faithful that promised
11. 11 she judged him faithful who had promi.
1 Pe. 4. 19 commit..(to him)..as unto a faithful Crea.
5. 12 By Silvanus, a faithful brother unto you
1 Jo. 1. 9 he is faithful and just to forgive us (our)
Rev. 1. 5 (who is) the faithful Witness, (and) the
2. 10 be thou faithful unto death, and I will
2. 13 wherein Antipas (was) my faithful martyr
3. 14 the faithful and true Witness, the begin.
17. 14 and they that are with him (are)..faithful
19. 11 he that sat..(was) called Faithful and Tr.
21. 5 for these words are true and faithful
22. 6 These sayings (are) faithful and true: and

FAITHFUL, to be —

To be faithful, steady, אָמַן aman, 2.

Num 12. 7 My servant Moses..who (is) faithful in all
Deut. 7. 9 Know..he (is) God, the faithful God
1 Sa. 2. 35 And I will raise me up a faithful priest
22. 14 who (is so) faithful among all thy servants
Neh. 9. 8 And foundest his heart faithful before
13. 13 for they were counted faithful; and their
Psa. 89. 37 and (as) a faithful witness in heaven
101. 6 Mine eyes (shall be) upon the faithful of
Prov 11. 13 he that is of a faithful spirit concealeth
25. 13 (so is) a faithful messenger to them that
27. 6 Faithful (are) the wounds of a friend: but
Isa. 1. 21 How is the faithful city become an har.!
1. 26 thou shalt be called..The faithful city
8. 2 I took unto me faithful witnesses to rec.
49. 7 because of the LORD that is faithful, (and)
Jer. 42. 5 be a true and faithful witness between us
Hos. 11. 12 but Judah..is faithful with the saints

FAITHFUL (man) —

Faithfulness, stability, אֱמוּנָה emunah.

Prov 28. 20 A faithful man shall abound with bless.

FAITHFULLY —

1. *Faithfulness, stability, אֱמוּנָה emunah.*

2 Ki. 12. 15 they reckoned not..for they dealt faith.
22. 7 no reckoning..because they dealt faith.
2 Ch. 19. 9 faithfully, and with a perfect; 31. 12, 34. 12.

1a. *Trustworthiness, אֱמֶת emeth.*

Jer. 23. 28 let him speak my word faithfully

2. *Faithful, steady, πιστός pistos.*

3 Jo. 5 Beloved, thou doest faithfully whatsoever

FAITHFULNESS —

1. *Faithfulness, stability, אֱמוּנָה emunah.*

1 Sa. 26. 23 render to every man..his faithfulness: for
Psa. 36. 5 thy faithfulness (reacheth) unto the clou.
40. 10 I have declared thy faithfulness and thy
88. 11 (or) thy faithfulness in destruction?
89. 1 will I make known thy faithfulness to all
89. 2 thy faithfulness shalt thou establish in
89. 5 thy faithfulness also in the congregation
89. 8 or to thy faithfulness round about thee?
89. 24 my faithfulness and my mercy (shall be)
89. 33 nor suffer my faithfulness to fail
92. 2 To show forth..thy faithfulness every
119. 75 (that) thou in faithfulness hast afflicted me
119. 90 Thy faithfulness (is) unto all generations
143. 1 in thy faithfulness answer me, (and) in
Isa. 11. 5 and faithfulness the girdle of his reins
Isa. 25. 1 counsels of old (are) faithfulness (and)
Lam. 3. 23 new every morning: great (is) thy faith.
Hos. 2. 20 even betroth thee unto me in faithfulness

2. *To be prepared, established, ready, כּוּן kun, 2.*

Psa. 5. 9 For (there is) no faithfulness in their mo.

FAITHLESS —

Unsteadfast, unfaithful, ἄπιστος apistos.

Matt 17. 17 O faithless and perverse generation, how
Mark 9. 19 O faithless generation, how long shall I be
Luke 9. 41 O faithless and perverse generation! how
John 20. 27 and be not faithless, but believing

FALL —

1. *Stumbling, כִּשָּׁלוֹן kishshalon.*

Prov. 16. 18 and an haughty spirit before a fall

2. *Fall, carcase, מַפֶּלֶת mappeleth.*

Prov. 29. 16 but the righteous shall see their fall
Eze. 26. 15 isles shake at the sound of thy fall
26. 18 the isles tremble in the day of thy fall
31. 16 nations to shake at the sound of his fall
32. 10 at (every) moment..in the day of thy fall

3. *To fall, נָפַל naphal.*

Jer. 49. 21 earth is moved at the noise of their fall

4. *A falling aside, παράπτωμα paraptōma.*

Rom 11. 11 through their fall salvation (is come)
11. 12 Now if the fall of them (be) the riches of

5. *Fall, downfall, πτῶσις ptōsis.*

Matt. 7. 27 and it fell: and great was the fall of it
Luke 2. 34 Behold, this (child) is set for the fall and

FALL (among), to —

1. *To be, הָיָה hayah.*

Josh 22. 20 wrath fell on all the congregation of Is.?

2. *To go or come out, יָצָא yatsa.*

Num 33. 54 shall be in the place where his lot falleth
Josh 16. 1 the lot of the children of Joseph fell from

3. *To go or come down, יָרַד yarad.*

Num 11. 9 when the dew fell..the manna fell upon

4. *To bend or bow the knee, כָּרַע kara.*

2 Ki. 1. 13 came and fell on his knees before Elijah
Ezra 9. 5 I fell upon my knees, and spread out my

5. *To stumble, be feeble, כָּשַׁל kashal.*

Lev. 26. 37 they shall fall one upon another, as it
Isa. 28. 13 go, and fall backward, and be broken
31. 3 both he that helpeth shall fall, and he
Jer. 6. 21 and the sons together shall fall upon them
46. 16 He made many to fall, yea, one..upon
Lam. 5. 13 and the children fell under the wood
Hos. 4. 5 Therefore shalt thou fall in the day, and
4. 5 the prophet also shall fall with thee in
5. 5 therefore..Judah also shall fall with them
14. 1 for thou hast fallen by thine iniquity

6. *To stumble, be feeble, כָּשַׁל kashal, 2.*

Psa. 9. 3 they shall fall and perish at thy presence
Prov. 24. 16 but the wicked shall fall into mischief
Isa. 40. 30 and the young men shall utterly fall
Eze. 33. 12 he shall not fall thereby in the day that
Dan. 11. 14 exalt themselves..but they shall fall
11. 33 yet they shall fall by the sword, and by
11. 34 when they shall fall, they shall be holpen
11. 35 (some) of them..shall fall, to try them
Hos. 5. 5 therefore shall Israel..fall in; 14. 9.

7. *To be stumbled, לָבַט labat, 2.*

Prov 10. 8, 10 but a prating fool shall fall; Hos. 4. 14.

7a. *Be moved, מוֹט mot, 2.*

Psa. 140. 10 let burning coals fall upon them

8. *To cause to pour out or run over, נָגַר nagar, 5.*

Psa. 63. 10 They shall fall by the sword; they shall

9. *To fall, נָפַל naphal.*

Gen. 4. 5 was very wroth, and his countenance fell
4. 6 LORD said..why is thy countenance fallen?
14. 10 and the kings of Sodom..fell there; and
15. 12 a deep sleep fell upon Abram; and, lo, an
15. 12 horror of great darkness fell upon him
17. 3 And Abram fell on his face: and God
17. 17 Abraham fell upon his face, and laughed
33. 4 Esau ran..and fell on his neck, and kissed
44. 14 and they fell before him on the ground
45. 14 he fell upon his brother Benjamin's neck
46. 29 Joseph..fell on his neck, and wept on his
49. 17 so that his rider shall fall backward
50. 1 Joseph fell upon his father's face, and
Exod 15. 16 Fear and dread shall fall upon them; by
21. 33 dig a pit..and an ox or an ass fall therein
32. 28 there fell..that day about three thousand
Lev. 9. 24 they shouted, and fell on their faces
11. 32 upon whatsoever (any) of them..doth fall
11. 33 every earthen vessel whereinto (any)..f.
11. 35 whereupon (any part) of their carcase fall.
11. 37 if (any part) of their carcase fall upon any
11. 38 and (any part) of their carcase fall thereon
26. 7 they shall fall before you by the sword
26. 8 your enemies shall fall before you by the
26. 36 and they shall fall when none pursueth
Num 14. 3 brought us unto this land, to fall by the
14. 5 Moses and Aaron fell on their faces before
14. 29 Your carcases shall fall in this wilderness
14. 32 carcases, they shall fall in this wilderness
14. 43 ye shall fall by the sword: because ye are
16. 4 when Moses heard (it), he fell upon his f.
16. 22 they fell upon their faces, and said, O God
16. 45 consume..And they fell upon their faces
20. 6 Moses and Aaron..fell upon their faces
34. 2 the land that shall fall unto you for an

Deut 22. 8 that thou bring not blood..if any man f.
Josh. 5. 14 Joshua fell on his face to the earth, and
7. 6 Joshua..fell to the earth upon his face
8. 25 And (so) it was, (that) all that fell that day
11. 7 So Joshua came..and they fell upon them
17. 5 And there fell ten portions to Manasseh
Judg. 4. 16 all the host of Sisera fell upon the edge
5. 27 he fell..at her feet he bowed, he fell
7. 13 smote it that it fell, and overturned it
8. 10 there fell an hundred and twenty thous.
12. 6 there fell at that time of the Ephraimites
13. 20 Manoah and his wife looked..and fell on
15. 18 fall into the hand of the uncircumcised?
16. 30 the house fell upon the lords, and upon
18. 1 inheritance had not fallen unto them
20. 44 there fell..eighteen thousand men: all
20. 46 So that all which fell that day of Benja.
Ruth 2. 10 Then she fell on her face, and bowed her.
3. 18 until thou know how the matter will fall
1 Sa. 4. 10 there fell of Israel thirty thousand footm.
4. 18 he fell from off the seat backward by the
11. 7 the fear of the LORD fell on the people
14. 13 fell before Jonathan; and his armour b.
14. 45 there shall not one hair of his head fall
17. 49 and he fell upon his face to the earth
20. 41 fell on his face to the ground, and bowed
25. 23 fell before David on her face, and bowed
25. 24 fell at his feet, and said, Upon me, my
26. 20 let not my blood fall to the earth before
28. 20 Saul fell straightway all along on the ea.
29. 3 I have found no fault in him since he fell
31. 4 Therefore Saul took a sword, and fell upon
31. 5 his armour bearer..fell likewise upon his
2 Sa. 1. 2 when he came..he fell to the earth, and
3. 29 or that falleth on the sword, or that
3. 34 falleth before wicked men, (so) fellest
4. 4 it came to pass..that he fell, and became
9. 6 he fell on his face, and did reverence. And
11. 17 there fell (some) of the people of the ser.
14. 4 she fell on her face to the ground, and
14. 11 there shall not one hair of thy son fall to
14. 22 Joab fell to the ground on his face, and
17. 12 we will light upon him as the dew falleth
20. 8 a girdle..as he went forth it fell out
21. 9 they fell (all) seven together, and were
21. 22 fell by the hand of David, and by the hand
24. 14 let us fall now..let me not fall into
1 Ki. 1. 52 there shall not an hair of him fall to the
18. 7 he knew him, and fell on his face, and
18. 38 the fire of the LORD fell, and consumed
18. 39 when all the people saw (it), they fell on
20. 30 a wall fell upon twenty and seven thous.
22. 20 that he may go up and fall at Ramoth-g.?
2 Ki. 2. 13 He took..the mantle..that fell
2. 14 he took the mantle..that fell from him
4. 37 Then she went in, and fell at his feet
6. 5 the ax head fell into the water: and
6. 6 And the man of God said, Where fell it?
7. 4 let us fall unto the host of the Syrians
10. 10 there shall fall unto the earth nothing
14. 10 that thou shouldest fall..thou, and Judah
1 Ch. 5. 10 with the Hagarites, who fell by their hand
10. 4 So Saul took a sword, and fell upon it
10. 5 when his armour bearer saw..he fell lik.
12. 19 And there fell (some) of Manasseh to D.
12. 19 saying, He will fall to his master Saul
12. 20 there fell to him of Manasseh, Adnah
20. 8 they fell by the hand of David, and by
21. 13 let me fall now..let me not fall into
21. 14 there fell of Israel seventy thousand men
21. 16 clothed in sackcloth, fell upon their faces
26. 14 And the lot eastward fell to Shelemiah
2 Ch. 15. 9 for they fell to him out of Israel in abun.
18. 19 that he may go up and fall at Ramoth-g.?
20. 18 inhabitants of Jerusalem fell before the
25. 19 that thou shouldest fall..thou, and Jud.
29. 9 lo, our fathers have fallen by the sword
Esth. 6. 13 before whom thou hast begun to fall
6. 13 but shalt surely fall before him
8. 17 for the fear of the Jews fell upon them
9. 2 for the fear of them fell upon all people
9. 3 because the fear of Mordecai fell upon
Job 1. 15 And the Sabeans fell..and took them
1. 19 fell upon the young men, and they are
4. 13 the visions..when deep sleep falleth
13. 11 Shall not..his dread fall upon you?
31. 22 let mine arm fall from my shoulder blade
33. 15 when deep sleep falleth upon men
Psa. 5. 10 let them fall by their own counsels; cast
10. 10 that the poor may fall by his strong ones
27. 2 and my foes..they stumbled and fell
35. 8 into that very destruction let him fall
37. 24 Though he fall, he shall not be utterly
45. 5 arrows (are) sharp..the people fall under
78. 64 Their priest fell by the sword; and their
82. 7 But ye shall..fall like one of the princes
91. 7 A thousand shall fall at thy side, and ten
105. 38 for the fear of them fell upon them
118. 13 that I might fall: but the LORD helped me
141. 10 Let the wicked fall into their own nets
145. 14 The LORD upholdeth all that fall, and
Prov 11. 5 the wicked shall fall by his own wicked.
11. 14 Where no counsel (is), the people fall
11. 28 He that trusteth in his riches shall fall
13. 17 A wicked messenger falleth into mischief
17. 20 he that hath a perverse tongue falleth
22. 14 he that is abhorred of the LORD shall fall
24. 16 For a just (man) falleth seven times
24. 17 Rejoice not when thine enemy falleth
26. 27 Whoso diggeth a pit shall fall therein
28. 10 he shall fall himself into his own pit
28. 14 he that hardeneth his heart shall fall into
Prov 28. 18 but..perverse (in his) ways shall fall at
Eccl. 4. 10 if they fall, the one will lift up his fellow
4. 10 woe to him (that is) alone when he falle.
9. 12 when it falleth suddenly upon them
10. 8 He that diggeth a pit shall fall into it
11. 3 and if the tree fall toward the south
11. 3 in the place where the tree falleth, there
Isa. 3. 25 Thy men shall fall by the sword, and thy
8. 15 many among them shall stumble, and fall
10. 4 Without me..they shall fall under the
10. 34 and Lebanon shall fall by a mighty one
13. 15 every one that is joined..shall fall by the
22. 25 be removed, and be cut down, and fall
24. 18 fleeth from the noise of the fear shall fa.
24. 20 and it shall fall, and not rise again
26. 18 neither have the inhabitants..fallen
30. 25 And there shall be..when the towers fall
31. 8 Then shall the Assyrian fall with the swo.
47. 11 Therefore..mischief shall fall upon thee
54. 15 whosoever..against thee shall fall for thy
Jer. 6. 15 they shall fall among them that fall
8. 4 Shall they fall, and not arise? shall he
8. 12 shall they fall among them that fall
9. 22 men shall fall as dung upon the open field
20. 4 they shall fall by the sword of their
21. 9 he that goeth out, and falleth to the C.
23. 12 they shall be driven on, and fall therein
25. 27 Drink ye..spue, and fall, and rise no more
25. 34 and ye shall fall like a pleasant vessel
39. 9 and those that fell away, that fell to him
39. 18 thou shalt not fall by the sword, but thy
44. 12 and they shall all..fall in the land of Eg.
46. 6 they shall stumble, and fall toward the
46. 16 one fell upon another; and they said
48. 44 He that fleeth from the fear shall fall
49. 26 Therefore her young men shall fall in her
50. 30 Therefore shall her young men fall in the
50. 32 the most proud shall stumble and fall
51. 4 Thus the slain shall fall in the land of the
51. 44 yea, the wall of Babylon shall fall
51. 47 all her slain shall fall in the midst of her
51. 49 Babylon (hath caused) the slain..to fall
51. 49 so at Babylon shall fall the slain of all
52. 15 residue..that fell to the king of Babylon
Lam. 1. 7 when her people fell into the hand of the
Eze. 1. 28 when I saw (it), I fell upon my face, and I
3. 23 behold the glory..and I fell on my face
5. 12 a third part shall fall by the sword round
6. 7 the slain shall fall in the midst of you
6. 11 they shall fall by the sword, by the fami.
6. 12 and he that is near shall fall by the sword
8. 1 the hand of the Lord GOD fell there upon
9. 8 I fell upon my face, and cried, and said
11. 5 And the Spirit of the LORD fell upon me
11. 10 Ye shall fall by the sword: I will judge
13. 11 Say unto them..it shall fall: there shall
13. 11 and ye, O great hail stones, shall fall
13. 14 the foundation thereof..shall fall, and ye
17. 21 with all his bands shall fall by the sword
23. 25 and thy remnant shall fall by the sword
24. 6 bring it out piece by piece; let no lot fall
24. 21 your daughters..shall fall by the sword
25. 13 they of Dedan shall fall by the sword
27. 27 shall fall into the midst of the seas in the
27. 34 all thy company in the midst..shall fall
29. 5 thou shalt fall upon the open fields
30. 4 when the slain shall fall in Egypt, and
30. 5 the men of the land..shall fall with them
30. 6 They also that uphold Egypt shall fall
30. 6 shall they fall in it by the sword, saith
30. 17 The young men..shall fall by the sword
32. 20 They shall fall in the midst of..slain by
33. 27 they that (are) in the wastes shall fall by
35. 8 shall they fall that are slain with the swo.
38. 20 steep places shall fall, and every wall s. f.
39. 4 Thou shalt fall upon the mountains of Is.
39. 5 Thou shalt fall upon the open field; for
39. 23 gave them..so fell they all by the sword
43. 3 that I saw..and I fell upon my face
44. 4 behold, the glory..and I fell upon my face
47. 14 this land shall fall unto you for inherita.
Dan. 8. 17 I was afraid, and fell upon my face: but
10. 7 a great quaking fell upon them, so that
11. 19 he shall stumble and fall, and not be
Hos. 7. 16 their princes shall fall by the sword for
10. 8 they shall say..to the hills, Fall on us
13. 16 they shall fall by the sword; their infants
Joel 2. 8 they fall upon the sword, they shall not
Amos 3. 5 Can a bird fall in a snare upon the earth
3. 14 horns of the altar shall be cut off, and fall
7. 17 thy sons and thy daughters shall fall by
8. 14 they shall fall, and never rise up again
9. 9 yet shall not the least grain fall upon the
Jon. 1. 7 they cast lots, and the lot fell upon Jonah
Mic. 7. 8 Rejoice not..when I fall, I shall arise
Nah. 3. 12 they shall even fall into the mouth of the

10. *To cause or let self to fall*, נָפַל *naphal*, 7.
Gen. 43. 18 that he may seek..and fall upon us

11. *To fall*, נְפַל *nephal.*
Dan. 2. 46 king Nebuchadnezzar fell upon his face
4. 31 there fell a voice from heaven..O king N.
7. 20 before whom three fell; even (of) that

12. *To go up*, עָלָה *alah.*
Lev. 16. 9 the goat upon which the LORD's lot fell
16. 10 the goat, on which the lot fell, to be the

13. *To fall upon*, פָּגַע *paga.*
Judg. 8. 21 Rise thou, and fall upon us; for as the
15. 12 that ye will not fall upon me yourselves
1 Sa. 22. 17 **to fall upon the priests of the LORD**
1 Sa. 22. 18 fall upon the priests..and he fell upon the
2 Sa. 1. 15 David..said, Go near, (and) fall upon him
1 Ki. 2. 25 and he fell upon him that he died
2. 29 Solomon sent..saying, Go, fall upon him
2. 31 Do as he hath said, and fall upon him
2. 34 Benaiah..went up, and fell upon him
2. 46 Benaiah..which went out, and fell upon

14. *To become, come into being*, γίνομαι *ginomai.*
Rev. 16. 2 there fell a noisome and grie.; Acts 1. 18.

15. *To fall out*, ἐκπίπτω *ekpiptō.*
Mark 13. 25 the stars of heaven [shall fall], and the
Acts 27. 17 fearing lest they should fall into the
27. 29 fearing lest we should have fallen upon
Jas. 1. 11 the flower thereof falleth, and the grace
2 Pe. 3. 17 lest ye also..fall from your own sted.

16. *To fall in or into*, ἐμπίπτω εἰς *empiptō eis.*
Matt 12. 11 and if it fall into a pit on the sabbath day
Luke 10. 36 was neighbour unto him that fell among
14. 5 Which of you shall have an..ox [fallen
1 Ti. 3. 6 lest being lifted up with pride he fall
3. 7 lest he fall into reproach and the snare
6. 9 they that will be rich fall into temptation
Heb 10. 31 (It is) a fearful thing to fall into the ha

17. *To fall upon*, ἐπιπίπτω *epipiptō.*
Luke 1. 12 he was troubled, and fear fell upon him
15. 20 ran, and fell on his neck, and kissed him
Acts 8. 16 as yet he was fallen upon none of them
10. 10 while they made ready, [he fell] into a
10. 44 the Holy Ghost [fell on] all them which
11. 15 as I began to speak, the Holy Ghost fell
13. 11 there [fell on] him a mist and a darkness
19. 17; 20. 10; 20. 37; Rom. 15. 3.

18. *To cast upon*, ἐπιβάλλω *epiballō.*
Luke 15. 12 give me the portion of goods that falleth

19. *To come down*, καταβαίνω *katabaino.*
Rev. 16. 21 there fell upon men a great hail out of

20. *To fall down*, καταπίπτω *katapiptō.*
Acts 26. 14 when we were all fallen to the earth

21. *To bear down*, καταφέρω *katapherō.*
Acts 20. 9 Eutychus, being fallen into a deep sleep

22. *To fall*, πίπτω *piptō.*
Matt. 7. 25 beat upon that house; and it fell not
7. 27 and beat upon that house; and it fell
10. 29 one of them shall not fall on the ground
13. 4 some..fell by the wayside, and the fowls
13. 5 Some fell upon stony places, where
13. 7 some fell among thorns; and the thorns
13. 8 other fell into good ground, and bro.
15. 14 Let them alone..both shall fall into the
15. 27 crumbs which fall from their masters'
17. 6 they fell on their face, and were sore afr.
17. 15 ofttimes he falleth into the fire, and oft
21. 44 whosoever shall fall on the stone
21. 44 on whomsoever it shall fall, it will grind
24. 29 and the stars shall fall from heaven
26. 39 he went a little farther, and fell on his
Mark 4. 4 as he sowed, some fell by the way side
4. 5 some fell on stony ground, where it had
4. 7 some fell among thorns, and the thorns
4. 8 other fell on good ground, and did yield
5. 22 and when he saw him, he fell at his feet
9. 20 fell on the ground, and wallowed foaming
14. 35 fell on the ground, and prayed that, if it
Luke 5. 12 a man full of leprosy..fell on (his) face
6. 39 shall they not both fall into the ditch?
6. 49 stream did beat..and immediately [it fell]
8. 5 and as he sowed, some [fell] by the way
8. 6 some fell upon a rock; and as soon as it
8. 7 some fell among thorns; and the thorns
8. 8 other fell on good ground, and sprang up
8. 14 And that which fell among thorns are they
10. 18 I beheld Satan as lightning fall from he.
11. 17 a house (divided) against a house falleth
13. 4 upon whom the tower in Siloam fell, and
16. 21 crumbs which fell from the rich man's
20. 18 Whosoever shall fall..shall be broken
20. 18 on whomsoever it shall fall, it will grind
21. 24 they shall fall by the edge of the sword
23. 30 begin to say..Fall on us; and to the hills
John 12. 24 Except a corn of wheat fall into the ground
18. 6 they went backward, and fell to the gro.
Acts 1. 26 the lot fell upon Matthias; and he was
9. 4 he fell to the earth, and heard a voice
22. 7 I fell unto the ground, and heard a voice
27. 34 there shall not an hair [fall] from the head
Rom 11. 11 Have they stumbled that they should fall?
11. 22 on them which fell, severity; but toward
14. 4 to his own master he standeth or falleth
1 Co. 10. 8 fell in one day three and twenty thousand
10. 12 Wherefore let him..take heed lest he fall
Heb. 3. 17 whose carcases fell in the wilderness?
4. 11 lest any man fall after the same example
Jas. 5. 12 let your yea be yea..lest ye fall into con.
Rev. 1. 17 when I saw him, I fell at his feet as dead
2. 5 Remember..from whence [thou art fallen]
6. 13 the stars of heaven fell unto the earth
6. 16 Fall on us, and hide us from the face of
7. 11 and fell before the throne on their faces
8. 10 and there fell a great star from heaven
8. 10 it fell upon the third part of the rivers
9. 1 and I saw a star fall from heaven unto
11. 11 great fear [fell] upon them which saw them
11. 13 the tenth part of the city fell, and in the
11. 16 fell upon their faces, and worshipped God
14. 8 Babylon is fallen, [is fallen], that great city
16. 19 cities of the nations fell: and great Bab.

Rev. 17. 10 five are fallen, and one is, (and) the other
18. 2 Babylon the great is fallen, [is fallen], and
19. 10 I fell at his feet to worship him. And he

23. *To stumble*, πταίω *ptaiō*.
2 Pe. 1. 10 if ye do these things, ye shall never fall

FALL among, to —
To fall around, περιπίπτω *peripiptō*.
Luke10. 30 A certain (man) . fell among thieves, which

FALL at, to —
To fall toward, προσπίπτω *prospiptō*.
Mark 7. 25 a (certain) woman . . came and fell at his

FALL away, to —
1. *To fall*, נָפַל *naphal*.
2 Ki.25. 11 fugitives that fell away to the king of
Jer. 37. 13 saying, Thou fallest away to the Chaldeans
37. 14 (It is) false ; I fall not away to the Chal.
39. 9 those that fell away . . with the rest of the
52. 15 those that fell away . . and the rest of the

2. *To place away*, ἀφίστημι *aphistēmi*.
Luke 8. 13 and in time of temptation fall away

3. *To fall out*, ἐκπίπτω *ekpiptō*.
1 Pe. 1. 24 and the flower thereof falleth away

4. *To fall beyond, amiss*, παραπίπτω *parapiptō*.
Heb. 6. 6 If they shall fall away, to renew them

FALL, to cause to —
1. *To cause to stumble*, כָּשַׁל *kashal*, 5.
Prov. 4. 16 sleep not . . unless they cause (some) to fall
Eze. 36. 15 shalt thou cause thy nations to fall any

2. *To cause to fall*, נָפַל *naphal*, 5.
Gen. 2. 21 God caused a deep sleep to fall upon Adam
2 Ki.19. 7 I will cause him to fall by the sword in
Isa. 37. 7 I will cause him to fall by the sword in
Jer. 3. 12 I will not cause mine anger to fall upon
15. 8 I have caused (him) to fall upon it sudd.
19. 7 I will cause them to fall by the sword
Eze. 30. 22 I will cause the sword to fall out of his
32. 12 will I cause thy multitude to fall, the
39. 3 will cause thine arrows to fall out of thy

FALL, caused to —
A stumbling block, מִכְשׁוֹל *mikshol*.
Eze. 44. 12 caused the house of Israel to fall into in.

FALL down, to —
1. *To stumble*, כָּשַׁל *kashal*.
Psa.107. 12 they fell down, and (there was) none to

2. *To fade, wear away*, נָבֵל *nabel*.
Isa. 34. 4 all their host shall fall down, as the leaf

3. *To fall*, נָפַל *naphal*.
Gen. 50. 18 his brethren also went and fell down be.
Deut22. 4 Thou shalt not see . his ox fall down by
Josh. 6. 5 the wall of the city shall fall down flat
6. 20 the wall fell down flat, so that the people
Judg. 5. 27 where he bowed, there he fell down dead
19. 26 Then came the woman . . and fell down at
1 Sa. 17. 52 the wounded of the Philistines fell down
31. 1 the men . . fell down slain in mount Gilboa
2 Sa. 2. 16 so they fell down together : wherefore
2. 23 he fell down there, and died in the same
2. 23 to the place where Asahel fell down and
19. 18 the son of Gera fell down before the king
2 Ki. 1. 2 Ahaziah fell down through a lattice in his
1 Ch. 5. 22 For there fell down many slain, because
10. 1 the men . fell down slain in mount Gilboa
2 Ch.13. 17 so there fell down . five hundred thousand
Esth. 8. 3 Esther spake . . and fell down at his feet
Job 1. 20 fell down upon the ground, and worship.
Isa. 9. 10 The bricks are fallen down, but we will
31. 3 he that is holpen shall fall down, and
Eze. 11. 13 Then fell I down upon my face, and cried
30. 25 and the arms of Pharaoh shall fall down
Dan. 11. 26 overflow ; and many shall fall down slain

4. *To cause self to fall*, נָפַל *naphal*, 7.
Deut. 9. 18 I fell down before the LORD, as at the
9. 25 fell down before the LORD . . as I fell down

5. *To fall*, נְפַל *nephal*.
Dan. 3. 5, 10 fall down and worship the golden
3. 6, 11 whoso falleth not down and worship
3. 7 fell down (and) worshipped the golden im.
3. 15 fall down and worship the image which
3. 23 these three men . . fell down bound into

6. *To bow down, do obeisance*, סָגַד *sagad*.
Isa. 44. 15 he maketh a god . . and falleth down
44. 17 he falleth down unto it, and worshippeth
44. 19 shall I fall down to the stock of a tree?
46. 6 he maketh it a god : they fall down, yea

7. *To crouch, lie down*, רָבַץ *rabats*.
Num22. 27 she fell down under Balaam : and Balaam's

8. *To bow self, do obeisance, worship*, שָׁחָה *shachah*, 7.
2 Sa. 18. 28 he fell down to the earth upon his face
Psa. 72. 11 yea, all kings fall down before him
Isa. 45. 14 they shall fall down unto thee, they shall

9. *To go or come down*, καταβαίνω *katabainō*.
Luke22. 44 drops of blood falling down to the ground

10. *To fall down*, καταπίπτω *katapiptō*.
Acts 28. 6 swollen, or fallen down dead suddenly

11. *To fall*, πίπτω *piptō*.
Matt. 2. 11 they saw the young child . . and fell down
4. 9 if thou wilt fall down and worship me
18. 26 servant therefore fell down, and worship.
18. 29 his fellow-servant fell down at his feet
Luke 8. 41 he fell down at Jesus' feet, and besought
17. 16 fell down on (his) face at his feet, giving
John11. 32 she fell down at his feet, saying unto him
Acts 5. 5 Ananias hearing these words fell down
5. 10 Then fell she down straightway at his
10. 25 Cornelius met him, and fell down at his
15. 16 tabernacle of David, which is fallen down
20. 9 fell down from the third loft, and was
1 Co. 14. 25 so falling down on (his) face he will wor.
Heb. 11. 30 By faith the walls of Jericho fell down
Rev. 4. 10 The four and twenty elders fall down bef.
5. 8 four (and) twenty elders fell down before
5. 14 the four (and) twenty elders fell down and
19. 4 the four and twenty elders . fell down
22. 8 I fell down to worship before the feet of

FALL down at, to —
To fall toward, προσπίπτω *prospiptō*.
Luke 5. 8 When Simon Peter saw (it), he fell d. at

FALL down, to let —
To cause or let go down, יָרַד *yarad*, 5.
1 Sa. 21. 13 let his spittle fall down upon his beard

FALL down before, to —
To fall toward, προσπίπτω *prospiptō*.
Mark 3. 11 unclean spirits . fell down before him
5. 33 the woman . fell down before him, and
Luke 8. 28 he cried out, and fell down before him
8. 47 she came trembling, and falling down
Acts 16. 29 came trembling, and fell down before

FALL down from Jupiter, which —
Fallen from Zeus, i.e., *heaven*, Διοπετής *Diopetēs*.
Acts 19. 35 of the (image) which fell down from Ju.?

FALL flat, to —
To bow self, do obeisance, worship, שָׁחָה *shachah*, 7.
Num22. 31 bowed down his head, and fell flat on his f.

FALL from, to —
1. *To fall off from*, ἀποπίπτω *apopiptō*.
Acts 9. 18 immediately there fell from his eyes as it

2. *To fall out of*, ἐκπίπτω *ekpiptō*.
Gal. 5. 4 justified by the law ; ye are fallen from
2 Pe. 3. 17 lest ye . . fall from your own stedfastness

FALL grievously, to —
To revolve, חִיל, חוּל *chul, chil*.
Jer. 23. 19 it shall fall grievously upon the head of

FALL headlong, to —
Becoming prostrate, πρηνὴς γενόμενος *prēnēs gen.*
Acts 1. 18 falling headlong, he burst asunder in the

FALL into, to —
To fall around, περιπίπτω *peripiptō*.
Acts 27. 41 falling into a place where two seas met
Jas. 1. 2 count it all joy when ye fall into divers

FALL, to let —
1. *To spread out, leave*, נָטַשׁ *natash*.
Num11. 31 let (them) fall by the camp, as it were a

2. *To let or cause to fall*, נָפַל *naphal*, 5.
1 Sa. 3. 19 let none of his words fall to the ground
Psa. 78. 28 And he let (it) fall in the midst of their

3. *To spoil*, שָׁלַל *shalal*.
Ruth 2. 16 And let fall also (some) of the handfuls

FALL, to make —
1. *To cause to fall*, נָפַל *naphal*, 5.
1 Sa. 18. 25 Saul thought to make David fall by the

2. *To cause to stumble*, כָּשַׁל *kashal*, 5.
2 Ch.25. 8 God shall make thee fall before the enemy
Psa. 64. 8 they shall make their own tongue to fall
Lam. 1. 14 hath made my strength to fall, the LORD

FALL off, to —
1. *To fade, wear away*, נָבֵל *nabel*.
Isa. 34. 4 as the leaf falleth off from the vine, and

2. *To fall off*, ἐκπίπτω *ekpiptō*.
Acts 12. 7 And his chains fell off from (his) hands
27. 32 Then the soldiers cut . . and let her fall off

FALL out, to —
1. *To go or come out*, יָצָא *yatsa*.
2 Ch.21. 19 his bowels fell out by reason of his sickn.

2. *To meet, happen*, קָרָא *qara*.
Exod. 1. 10 when there falleth out any war, they join

3. *To be angry*, רָגַז *ragaz*.
Gen. 45. 24 See that ye fall not out by the way

4. *To come*, ἔρχομαι *erchomai*.
Phil. 1. 12 things (which happened) . . have fallen out

FALL, ready to —
To fall, נָפַל *naphal*.
Isa. 30. 13 shall be to you as a breach ready to fall

FALL upon, to —
1. *To fall upon*, פָּגַע *paga*.
Exod. 5. 3 lest he fall upon us with pestilence, or
1 Ki. 2. 32 who fell upon two men more righteous

2. *To push out, strip*, פָּשַׁט *pashat*.
2 Ch.25. 13 the soldiers . . fell upon the cities of Judah
Job 1. 17 The Chaldeans . . fell upon the camels, and

FALL with pain, to —
To revolve, חִיל, חוּל *chul, chil*.
Jer. 30. 23 it shall fall with pain upon the head of

FALLEN, to be —
1. *To come in*, בּוֹא *bo*.
Num32. 19 our inheritance is fallen to us on this side

2. *To stumble*, כָּשַׁל *kashal*.
Isa. 59. 14 for truth is fallen in the street, and equi

3. *To fall*, נָפַל *naphal*.
Gen. 4. 6 and why is thy countenance fallen?
Josh. 2. 9 that your terror is fallen upon us, and
8. 24 they were all fallen on the edge of the
Judg. 3. 25 their lord (was) fallen down dead on the
19. 27 the woman his concubine was fallen down
1 Sa. 5. 3, 4 Dagon (was) fallen upon his face to the
26. 12 because a deep sleep . . was fallen upon
31. 8 found Saul and his three sons fallen in
2 Sa. 1. 4 many of the people also are fallen and
1. 10 could not live after that he was fallen
1. 12 because they were fallen by the sword
1. 19 high places : how are the mighty fallen!
1. 25 How are the mighty fallen in the midst
1. 27 How are the mighty fallen, and the weap.
3. 38 and a great man fallen this day in Israel?
22. 39 yea, they are fallen under my feet
1 Ch.10. 8 they found Saul and his sons fallen in
2 Ch.20. 24 they (were) dead bodies fallen to the earth
Esth. 7. 8 Haman was fallen upon the bed whereon
Job 1. 16 The fire of God is fallen from heaven, and
Psa. 7. 15 and is fallen into the ditch (which) he
16. 6 The lines are fallen unto me in pleasant
18. 38 were not able to rise : they are fallen
20. 8 They are brought down and fallen : but
36. 12 There are the workers of iniquity fallen
55. 4 and the terrors of death are fallen upon
57. 6 into the midst whereof they are fallen
69. 9 the reproaches of them . . are fallen upon
Isa. 3. 8 Jerusalem is ruined, and Judah is fallen
14. 12 How art thou fallen from heaven, O Luci.
16. 9 for the shouting . . for thy harvest is fallen
21. 9 and said, Babylon is fallen, is fallen ; and
Jer. 38. 19 I am afraid of the Jews that are fallen to
46. 12 mighty, (and) they are fallen both togeth.
48. 32 the spoiler is fallen upon thy . . fruits and
50. 15 her foundations are fallen, her walls are
51. 8 Babylon is suddenly fallen and destroyed
Lam. 2. 21 my young men are fallen by the sword
5. 16 The crown is fallen (from) our head : woe
Eze. 13. 12, 31. 12, 31. 22, 23, 24, 32. 27.
Hos. 7. 7 ; Amos 5. 2, 9. 11 ; Zech. 11. 2.

4. *To fall out of*, ἐκπίπτω *ekpiptō*.
Rev. 2. 5 Remember . . from whence thou art fall.

FALLEN in decay, be —
His hand wavers, מָטָה יָדוֹ [*yad*].
Lev. 25. 35 waxen poor and fallen in decay with thee

FALLING —
1. *Overthrow, falling*, דְּחִי *dechi*.
Psa. 56. 13 (wilt) not (thou deliver) my feet from fal.
116. 8 thou hast delivered . . my feet from falling

2. *To fall*, נָפַל *naphal*.
Num24. 4, 16 falling (into a trance), but having his
Job 14. 18 the mountain falling cometh to nought

3. *To stumble*, כָּשַׁל *kashal*.
Job 4. 4 words have upholden him that was falling

4. *To fade, wear away*, נָבֵל *nabel*.
Isa. 34. 4 and as a falling (fig) from the fig tree

FALLING away —
The falling away, ἡ ἀποστασία *hē apostasia*.
2 Th. 2. 3 except there come a falling away first

FALLING down —
To move, slip, fail, מוֹט *mot*.
Prov.25. 26 A righteous man falling down before the

FALLING, from —
Unfalling, without falling, ἄπταιστος *aptaistos*.
Jude 24 him that is able to keep you from falling

FALLOW deer —
Fallow deer, brown goat or gazelle, יַחְמוּר *yachmur*.
Deut.14. 5 the roebuck, and the fallow deer, and
1 Ki. 4. 23 harts, and roebucks, and fallow deer

FALLOW ground —
Broken up ground, tillage, נִיר *nir*.
Jer. 4. 3 Break up your fallow ground, and sow
Hos. 10. 12 reap in mercy; break up your fallow gro.

FALSE —
1. *Vanity, iniquity*, אָוֶן *aven*.
Prov.17. 4 A wicked doer giveth heed to false lips

2. *Violence*, חָמָס *chamas*.
Psa. 35. 11 False witnesses did rise up ; they laid to

3. *A lie, deceit*, כָּזָב *kazab*.
Prov.21. 28 A false witness shall perish: but the man

4. *Deceit*, מִרְמָה *mirmah*.
Prov.11. 1 A false balance (is) abomination to the
20. 23 Divers weights . . and a false balance (is)

5. *Deceit*, רְמִיָּה *remiyyah*.
Psa.120. 3 what shall be done unto thee, thou false

6. *Emptiness, vanity, falsehood*, שָׁוְא *shav*.
Exod.23. 1 Thou shalt not raise a false report ; put
Deut. 5. 20 Neither shalt thou bear false witness
Lam. 2. 14 but have seen for thee false burdens and
Eze. 21. 23 it shall be unto them as a false divinati.
Zech.10. 2 and the diviners . . have told false dreams

7. *Falsehood,* שֶׁקֶר *sheqer.*
Exod 20. 16 Thou shalt not bear false witness
23. 7 Keep thee far from a false matter
Deut 19. 18 behold (if) the witness (be) a false witness
2 Ki. 9. 12 And they said, (It is) false; tell us now
Job 36. 4 For truly my words (shall) not (be) false
Psa. 27. 12 false witnesses are risen up against me
119. 104 I get..therefore I hate every false way
119. 128 Therefore..I hate every false way
Prov 12. 17 showeth..righteousness, but a false wit.
14. 5 A faithful witness will not lie: but a fal.
19. 5, 9 A false witness shall not be unpunish.
25. 14 Whoso boasteth himself of a false gift
25. 18 A man that beareth false witness against
Jer. 14. 14 they prophesy unto you a false vision and
23. 32 I (am) against them that prophesy false
37. 14 (It is) false; I fall not away to the Chald.
Zech. 8. 17 let none..imagine evil..love no false oath
Mal. 3. 5 And I will come near to..false swearers

8. *False, lying,* ψευδής *pseudēs.*
Acts 6. 13 And set up false witnesses, which said

[*See also* Accusation, accuser, apostle, brethren, christs, prophet, witness.]

FALSEHOOD —

1. *Transgression,* מַעַל *maal.*
Job 21. 34 in your answers there remaineth falseho.

2. *Falsehood,* שֶׁקֶר *sheqer.*
2 Sa. 18. 13 Otherwise I should have wrought falseh.
Psa. 7. 14 Behold, he..brought forth falsehood
119. 118 them that err..for their deceit (is) fals.
144. 8, 11 right hand (is) a right hand of falseh.
Isa. 28. 15 under falsehood have we hid ourselves
57. 4 (are) ye not..a seed of falsehood?
59. 13 uttering from the heart words of falseh.
Jer. 10. 14 for his molten image (is) falsehood, and
13. 25 thou hast forgotten me, and trusted in f.
51. 17 for his molten image (is) falsehood, and
Hos. 7. 1 for they commit falsehood, and the thief
Mic. 2. 11 If a man walking in the spirit and falseh.

FALSELY —

1. *Emptiness, vanity,* שָׁוְא *shav.*
Hos. 10. 4 swearing falsely in making a covenant

2. *Falsehood,* שֶׁקֶר *sheqer.*
Lev. 6. 5 all that about which he hath sworn fals.
19. 12 ye shall not swear by my name falsely
Deut 19. 18 hath testified falsely against his brother
Jer. 5. 2 The LORD liveth; surely they swear fals.
5. 31 The prophets prophesy falsely, and the
6. 13 unto the priest every one dealeth falsely
7. 9 Will ye..swear falsely, and burn incense
8. 10 from the prophet..every one dealeth fal.
29. 9 For they prophesy falsely unto you in my
40. 16 for thou speakest falsely of Ishmael
43. 2 saying unto Jeremiah, Thou speakest fa.
Zech. 5. 4 the house of him that sweareth falsely

3. *Over a falsehood,* עַל־שֶׁקֶר *al-sheqer.*
Lev. 6. 3 lieth concerning it, and sweareth falsely

4. *To speak falsely, lie,* ψεύδομαι *pseudomai.*
Matt. 5. 11 say all manner of evil against you falsely

FALSELY so called —

Falsely named, ψευδώνυμος *pseudōnumos.*
1 Ti. 6. 20 oppositions of science falsely so called

FALSELY, to deal —

1. *To lie, act deceitfully,* כָּחַשׁ *kachash,* 3.
Lev. 19. 11 ye shall not steal, neither deal falsely

2. *To lie, utter falsehood,* שָׁקַר *shaqar.*
Gen. 21. 23 that thou wilt not deal falsely with me

3. *To lie, deal falsely,* שָׁקַר *shaqar,* 3.
Psa. 44. 17 neither have we dealt falsely in thy cov.

FALSIFYING —

To pervert, עָוַת *avath,* 3.
Amos 8. 5 and falsifying the balances by deceit?

FAME —

1. *Voice,* קוֹל *qol.*
Gen. 45. 16 the fame thereof was heard in Pharaoh's

2. *Name,* שֵׁם *shem.*
1 Ki. 4. 31 his fame was in all nations round about
1 Ch. 14. 17 the fame of David went out into all
22. 5 the house..exceeding magnifical, of fame
Zeph 3. 19 and I will get them praise and fame in

3. *Hearing, fame, report,* שְׁמוּעָה *shemuah.*
1 Ki. 10. 7 prosperity exceedeth the fame which
2 Ch. 9. 6 (for) thou exceedest the fame that I heard

4. *Hearing, fame, report,* שֵׁמַע *shema.*
Num 14. 15 the nations which have heard the fame of
1 Ki. 10. 1 the queen of Sheba heard of the fame
2 Ch. 9. 1 the queen of Sheba heard of the fame
Job 28. 22 We have heard the fame thereof with
Isa. 66. 19 that have not heard my fame, neither

5 *Hearing, fame,* שֹׁמַע *shoma.*
Josh. 6. 27 and his fame was (noised) throughout all
9. 9 for we have heard the fame of him, and
Esth. 9. 4 For Mordecai (was) great..and his fame
Jer. 6. 24 We have heard the fame thereof; our

6. *Hearing,* ἀκοή *akoē.*
Matt. 4. 24 And his fame went throughout all Syria
14. 1 Herod the tetrarch heard of the fame of
Mark 1. 28 And immediately his fame spread abroad

7. *A sound, noise,* ἦχος *ēchos.*
Luke 4. 37 And the fame of him went out into every

8. *Word,* λόγος *logos.*
Luke 5. 15 But so much the more went there a fame

9. *Fame, saying,* φήμη *phēmē.*
Matt. 9. 26 And the fame hereof went abroad into
Luke 4. 14 there went out a fame of him through

FAME, to spread abroad one's —

To say throughout, everywhere, διαφημίζω *diaphē.*
Matt. 9. 31 But they..spread abroad his fame in all

FAMILIAR —

Peace, prosperity, completeness, שָׁלוֹם *shalom.*
Psa. 41. 9 Yea, mine own familiar friend, in whom
Jer. 20. 10 All my familiars watched for my halting

FAMILIAR friend —

To be known, acquainted with, יָדַע *yada,* 4.
Job 19. 14 my familiar friends have forgotten me

FAMILIAR spirit —

A necromancer, אוֹב *ob.*
Lev. 19. 31 Regard not them that have familiar spir.
20. 6 the soul that turneth after..familiar spi.
20. 27 A man also..that hath a familiar spirit
Deut 18. 11 or a consulter with familiar spirits, or a
1 Sa. 28. 3 had put away those that had familiar sp.
28. 7 Seek me a woman that hath a familiar sp.
28. 7 Behold..a woman that hath a familiar s.
28. 8 divine unto me by the familiar spirit
28. 9 hath cut off those that have familiar spi.
2 Ki 21. 6 dealt with familiar spirits and wizards
23. 24 Moreover the (workers with) familiar sp.
1 Ch. 10. 13 for asking (counsel) of..a familiar spirit
2 Ch. 33. 6 dealt with a familiar spirit, and with wiz.
Isa. 8. 19 Seek unto them that have familiar spirits
19. 3 seek..to them that have familiar spirits
29. 4 as of one that hath a familiar spirit, out

FAMILIES —

Infants, household, טַף *taph.*
Gen. 47. 12 with bread according to (their) families

FAMILY —

1. *A thousand,* אֶלֶף *eleph.*
Judg. 6. 15 behold, my family (is) poor in Manasseh

2. *House, household,* בַּיִת *bayith.*
1 Ch. 13. 14 the ark of God remained with the family
2 Ch. 35. 5, 12 to the divisions of the families of the
Psa. 68. 6 God setteth the solitary in families: he

3. *Family,* מִשְׁפָּחָה *mishpachah.*
Gen. 10. 5 every one..after their families, in their
10. 18 and afterward were the families of the
10. 20 the sons of Ham, after their families
10. 31 the sons of Shem, after their families
10. 32 These..the families of the sons of Noah
12. 3 in thee shall all families of the earth be
28. 14 in thy seed shall all the families of the
36. 40 These..the names..according to their fa.
Exod. 6. 14 Carmi: these (be) the families of Reuben
6. 15 Shaul..these (are) the families of Simeon
6. 17 Libni and Shimi, according to their fam.
6. 19 these (are) the families of Levi according
6. 24 these (are) the families of the Korhites
6. 25 these..the heads..according to their fa.
12. 21 take you a lamb according to your fami.
Lev. 20. 5 I will set my face..against his family
25. 10 ye shall return every man unto his family
25. 41 and shall return unto his own family
25. 45 and of their families that (are) with you
25. 47 or to the stock of the stranger's family
25. 49 or (any) that is nigh..of his family may
Num. 1. 2 Take ye the sum of all..after their fami.
1. 18 declared their pedigrees after their fami.
1. 20 of the children of..after their families
[So in v. 22, 24, 26, 28, 30, 32, 34, 36, 38, 40, 42.]
2. 34 they set forward, every one after their f.
3. 15 Number the children..by their families
3. 18 these (are) the names..by their families
3. 19 the sons of Kohath by their families
3. 20 the sons of Merari by their families
3. 20 These (are) the families of the Levites
3. 21 Of Gershon..the family of the Libnites
3. 21 and the family of the Shimites..families
3. 23 The families of the Gershonites shall
3. 27 And of Kohath..the family of the A.
3. 27 and the family of the Izeharites
3. 27 and the family of the Hebronites
3. 27 and the family of the Uzzielites
3. 27 these (are) the families of the Kohathites
3. 29 The families of the sons of Kohath shall
3. 30 And the chief..of the families of the Ko.
3. 33 Of Merari..the family of the Mahlites
3. 33 and the family of the Mushites
3. 33 these (are) the families of Merari
3. 35 And the chief..of the families of Merari
3. 39 throughout their families, all the males
4. 2 the sons of Levi, after their families, by
4. 18 Cut ye not off the tribe of the families of
4. 22 of the sons of Gershon..by their families
4. 24, 28, 33 This (is) the service of the families of
4. 29 thou shalt number them after their families
4. 34 numbered the sons..after their families
4. 36 those that were numbered..by their famil.
4. 37 These..they that were numbered of the f.
4. 38 the sons of Gershon, throughout their f.
4. 40 numbered of them, throughout their fam.
4. 41 they that were numbered of the families
4. 42, 45 those that were numbered of the families
Num. 4. 42 sons of Merari, throughout their families
4. 44 those that were numbered..after their f.
4. 46 numbered of the Levites..after their fa.
11. 10 heard the people weep throughout their fa.
26. 5 of Reuben; Hanoch..the family of the H.
26. 5 of Pallu, the family of the Palluites
26. 6 Of Hezron, the family of the Hezronites
26. 6 of Carmi, the family of the Carmites
26. 7 These (are) the families of the Reubenites
26. 12 The sons of Simeon after their families
26. 12 of Nemuel, the family of the Nemuelites
26. 12 of Jamin, the family of the Jaminites
26. 12 of Jachin, the family of the Jachinites
26. 13 Of Zerah, the family of the Zarhites
26. 13 of Shaul, the family of the Shaulites
26. 14 These (are) the families of the Simeonites
26. 15 The children of Gad after their families
26. 15 of Zephon, the family of the Zephonites
26. 15 of Haggi, the family of the Haggites
26. 15 of Shuni, the family of the Shunites
26. 16 Of Ozni, the family of the Oznites
26. 16 of Eri, the family of the Erites
26. 17 Of Arod, the family of the Arodites
26. 17 of Areli, the family of the Arelites
26. 18 These (are) the families of the children of
26. 20 the sons of Judah after their families
26. 20 of Shelah, the family of the Shelanites
26. 20 of Pharez, the family of the Pharzites
26. 20 of Zerah, the family of the Zarhites
26. 21 of Hezron, the family of the Hezronites
26. 21 of Hamul, the family of the Hamulites
26. 22 These (are) the families of Judah according
26. 23 the sons of Issachar, after their families
26. 23 (of) Tola, the family of the Tolaites
26. 23 of Pua, the family of the Punites
26. 24 of Jashub, the family of the Jashubites
26. 24 of Shimron, the family of the Shimronites
26. 25 These (are) the families of Issachar
26. 26 the sons of Zebulun after their families
26. 26 of Sered, the family of the Sardites
26. 26 of Elon, the family of the Elonites
26. 26 of Jahleel, the family of the Jahleelites
26. 27 These (are) the families of the Zebulunites
26. 28 The sons of Joseph after their families
26. 29 of Machir, the family of the Machirites
26. 29 of Gilead..the family of the Gileadites
26. 30 (of) Jeezer, the family of the Jeezerites
26. 30 of Helek, the family of the Helekites
26. 31 And (of) Asriel, the family of the Asrielites
26. 31 and (of) Shechem, the family of the Shec.
26. 32 And (of) Shemida, the family of the Shem.
26. 32 and (of) Hepher, the family of the Heph.
26. 34 These (are) the families of Manasseh
26. 35 the sons of Ephraim after their families
26. 35 of Shuthelah, the family of the Shuthalí
26. 35 of Becher, the family of the Bachrites
26. 35 of Tahan, the family of the Tahanites
26. 36 of Eran, the family of the Eranites
26. 37 These (are) the families of the sons of Eph.
26. 37 the sons of Joseph after their families
26. 38 The sons of Benjamin after their families
26. 38 of Bela, the family of the Belaites
26. 38 of Ashbel, the family of the Ashbelites
26. 38 of Ahiram, the family of the Ahiramites
26. 39 Of Shupham, the family of the Shupham.
26. 39 of Hupham, the family of the Huphamit.
26. 40 (Of Ard), the family of the Ardites
26. 40 of Naaman, the family of the Naamites
26. 41 the sons of Benjamin after their families
26. 42 These..the sons of Dan after their famil.
26. 42 of Shuham, the family of the Shuhamites
26. 42 These..the families of Dan after their fa.
26. 43 All the families of the Shuhamites, accord.
26. 44 the children of Asher after their families
26. 44 of Jimna, the family of the Jimnites
26. 44 of Jesui, the family of the Jesuites
26. 44 of Beriah, the family of the Beriites
26. 45 of Heber, the family of the Heberites
26. 45 of Malchiel, the family of the Malchielit.
26. 47 These..the families of the sons of Asher
26. 48 the sons of Naphtali after their families
26. 48 of Jahzeel, the family of the Jahzeelites
26. 48 of Guni, the family of the Gunites
26. 49 of Jezer, the family of the Jezerites
26. 49 of Shillem, the family of the Shillemites
26. 50 families of Naphtali acc. to their families
26. 57 And these..of the Levites after their fa.
26. 57 of Gershon, the family of the Gershonites
26. 57 of Kohath, the family of the Kohathites
26. 57 of Merari, the family of the Merarites
26. 58 These (are) the families of the Levites
26. 58 the family of the Libnites, the family of
26. 58 the family of the Mahlites, the family of
26. 58 the family of the Korathites
27. 1 of the families of Manasseh the son of J.
27. 4 be done away from among his family
27. 11 kinsman that is next to him of his family
33. 54 shall divide the land..among your fami.
36. 1 the chief fathers of the families of the
36. 1 of the families of the sons of Joseph
36. 6 only to the family of the tribe of their
36. 8 shall be wife unto one of the family of
36. 12 they were married into the families of
36. 12 their inheritance remained in..the family
Deut 29. 18 Lest there should be among you..family
Josh. 7. 14 the tribe..shall come according to the f.
7. 14 and the family which the LORD shall take
7. 17 And he brought the family of Judah
7. 17 and he took the family of the Zarhites
7. 17 and he brought the family of the Zarhites
13. 15 Moses gave..according to their families
13. 23 This..of Reuben after their families

Josh. 13. 24 tribe of Gad..according to their families
13. 28 inheritance..of Gad after their families
13. 29 the half tribe of Manasseh..by their fa.
13. 31 one half..of Machir by their families
15. 1 the tribe..of Judah by their families
15. 12, 20 of Judah..according to their families
16. 5 Ephraim according to their families
16. 8 the children of Ephraim by their families
17. 2 the children of Manasseh by their families
17. 2 male children..of Joseph by their fami.
18. 11, 20, 21, 28 Benjamin..according to their f.
19. 1, 8 Simeon according to their families
19. 10, 16 Zebulun according to their families
19. 17, 23 Issachar according to their families
19. 24, 31 of Asher according to their families
19. 32, 39 Naphtali according to their families
19. 40, 48 of Dan according to their families
21. 4 And the lot came out for the families of
21. 5 Kohath (had) by lot out of the families
21. 6 of Gershon (had) by lot out of the families
21. 7 The children of Merari by their families
21. 10 the children of Aaron, (being) of the fa.
21. 20 the families of the children of Kohath
21. 26 All the cities (were) ten..for the families
21. 27 children of Gershon, of the families of
21. 33 of the Gershonites according to their fa.
21. 34 unto the families of the children of Merari
21. 40 for the children of Merari, by their fam.
21. 40 which were remaining of the families of
Judg. 1. 25 but they let go the man and all his family
9. 1 communed with them, and..all the fam.
13. 2 a certain man of Zorah, of the family of
17. 7 there was a young man..of the family of
18. 2 the children of Dan sent of their family
18. 11 there went from thence of the family of
18. 19 thou be a priest unto a..family in Israel?
21. 24 every man to his tribe and to his family
Ruth 2. 1 a mighty man of wealth, of the family of E.
1 Sa. 9. 21 and my family the least of all the families
10. 21 to come near by their families, the family
18. 18 what (is) my life, (or) my father's family
20. 6 a yearly sacrifice there for all the family
20. 29 Let me go, I pray thee; for our family
2 Sa. 14. 7 the whole family is risen against thine
16. 5 thence came out a man of the family of
1 Ch. 2. 53 the families of Kirjath-jearim; the Ithr.
2. 55 the families of the scribes which dwelt
4. 2 These (are) the families of the Zorathites
4. 8 the families of Aharhel the son of Harum
4. 21 the families of the house of them that
4. 27 neither did all their family multiply, like
4. 38 These mentioned..princes in their fami.
5. 7 his brethren by their families, when the
6. 19 these are the families of the Levites acc.
6. 54 of the families of the Kohathites; for
6. 60 All their cities throughout their families
6. 61 sons of Kohath..left of the family of
6. 62 sons of Gershom, throughout their fami.
6. 63 sons of Merari..throughout their famil.
6. 66 And..of the families of the sons of Koh.
6. 70 Bileam with her suburbs, for the family
6. 71 out of the family of the half tribe of Ma.
7. 5 their brethren among all the families of
Neh. 4. 13 I even set the people after their families
Esth. 9. 28 every family, every province, and every
Job 31. 34 or did the contempt of families terrify
Psa. 107. 41 and maketh (him) families like a flock
Jer. 1. 15 I will call all the families of the kingdo.
2. 4 Hear..all the families of the house of I.
3. 14 I will take you one of a city..two of a f.
8. 3 residue of them that remain of this evil f.
10. 25 Pour out thy fury..upon the families that
25. 9 I will send and take all the families of
31. 1 will I be the God of all the families of Is.
33. 24 The two families which the LORD hath
Eze. 20. 32 We will be as the heathen, as the families
Amos 3. 1 children of Israel, against the whole fam.
3. 2 You only have I known of all the families
Mic. 2. 3 saith the LORD; Behold, against this fa.
Nah. 3. 4 selleth..families through her witchcrafts
Zech. 12. 12 the land shall mourn, every family apart
12. 12 the family of the house of David apart
12. 12 the family of the house of Nathan apart
12. 13 The family of the house of Levi apart
12. 13 the family of Shimei apart, and their
12. 14 All the families that remain, every family
14. 17 whoso will not come up of (all) the fami.
14. 18 And if the family of Egypt go not up

4. *Family (one's own)*, πατριά *patria*.
Eph. 3. 15 Of whom the whole family in heaven and

FAMINE —

1. *Famine, hunger*, כָּפָן *kaphan*.
Job 5. 22 At destruction and famine thou shalt la.
30. 3 For want and famine..solitary; fleeing

2. *Hunger, famine*, רָעָב *raab*.
Gen. 12. 10 there was a famine in the land: and A.
12. 10 for the famine (was) grievous in the land
26. 1 And there was a famine in the land
26. 1 beside the first famine that was in the
41. 27 seven empty..shall be seven years of fa.
41. 30 there shall arise..seven years of famine
41. 30 and the famine shall consume the land
41. 31 shall not be known..by reason of that f.
41. 36 store..against the seven years of famine
41. 36 that the land perish not through the fam.
41. 50 born two sons before the years of famine
41. 56 the famine was over all the face of the
41. 56 the famine waxed sore in the land of Eg.
41. 57 because that the famine was (so) sore in
42. 5 for the famine was in the land of Canaan
Gen. 43. 1 And the famine (was) sore in the land
45. 6 For these two years (hath) the famine
45. 11 for yet (there are) five years of famine
47. 4 for the famine (is) sore in the land of Ca.
47. 13 the famine (was) very sore, so that the
47. 13 of Canaan, fainted by reason of the famine
47. 20 because the famine prevailed over them
Ruth 1. 1 came to pass..that there was a famine
2 Sa. 21. 1 there was a famine in the days of David
24. 13 Shall seven years of famine come unto
1 Ki. 8. 37 If there be in the land famine, if there be
18. 2 And (there was) a sore famine in Samaria
2 Ki. 6. 25 And there was a great famine in Samaria
7. 4 then the famine (is) in the city, and we
8. 1 for the LORD hath called for a famine
25. 3 And on the ninth..the famine prevailed
1 Ch. 21. 12 Either three years' famine; or three mo.
2 Ch. 20. 9 If..evil cometh upon us..or famine, we
32. 11 Hezekiah persuade you..to die by famine
Job 5. 20 In famine he shall redeem thee from
Psa. 33. 19 and to keep them alive in famine
105. 16 Moreover he called for a famine upon the
Isa. 14. 30 I will kill thy root with famine, and he
51. 19 the famine, and the sword: by whom
Jer. 5. 12 neither shall we see sword nor famine
11. 22 sons and their daughters shall die by fa.
14. 12 but I will consume them..by the famine
14. 13 neither shall ye have famine; but I will
14. 15 say, Sword and famine shall not be in this
14. 15 By sword and famine shall those prophets
14. 16 because of the famine and the sword
14. 18 behold them that are sick with famine!
15. 2 such as (are) for the famine, to the famine
16. 4 and they shall be consumed..by famine
18. 21 deliver up their children to the famine
21. 7 I will deliver Zedekiah..from the famine
21. 9 He that abideth..shall die..by the famine
24. 10 I will send the sword, the famine, and
27. 8 that nation will I punish..with the fam.
27. 13 Why will ye die..by the famine, and by
29. 17 will send upon them the sword, the fam
29. 18 I will persecute them..with the famine
32. 24 because of the sword, and of the famine
32. 36 It shall be delivered..by the famine, and
34. 17 liberty..to the pestilence, and to the fa.
38. 2 He that remaineth..shall die..by the fa.
42. 16 the famine, whereof ye were afraid, shall
42. 17 they shall die by the sword, by the famine
42. 22 know..that ye shall die..by the famine
44. 12 they shall..be consumed..by the famine
44. 12 they shall die..by the sword and..famine
44. 13 I have punished Jerusalem..by the fam.
44. 18 and have been consumed..by the famine
44. 27 men of Judah..shall be consumed..by..f.
52. 6 the famine was sore in the city, so that
Lam. 5. 10 Our skin was black..because of the..fa.
Eze. 5. 12 with famine shall they be consumed in
5. 16 I shall send..the evil arrows of famine
5. 16 I will increase the famine upon you
5. 17 So will I send upon you famine and evil
6. 11 they shall fall by the sword, by the fam.
6. 12 he that..is besieged shall die by the fam
7. 15 and the pestilence and the famine within
7. 15 he that (is) in the city, famine and pestil.
12. 16 I will leave a few men..from the famine
14. 13 and will send famine upon it, and will
14. 21 send my four sore judgments..famine
36. 29 I will also save you..and lay no famine
36. 30 ye shall receive no more reproach of fam.
Amos 8. 11 that I will send a famine in the land
8. 11 not a famine of bread, nor a thirst for w.

3. *Hunger, famine*, רְעָבוֹן *reabon*.
Gen. 42. 19 carry corn for the famine of your houses
42. 33 take (food for) the famine of your house.
Psa. 37. 19 in the days of famine they shall be satis.

4. *Hunger, famine*, λιμός *limos*.
Matt 24. 7 there shall be famines, and pestilences
Mark 13. 8 and there shall be famines and troubles
Luke 4. 25 widows were in Israel..when great fam.
15. 14 there arose a mighty famine in that land
21. 11 great earthquakes shall be..and famines
Rom. 8. 35 famine, or nakedness, or peril, or sword?
Rev. 18. 8 shall her plagues come in one day..fam.

FAMISH, to —

To make lean, famish, רָזָה *razah*.
Zeph. 2. 11 for he will famish all the gods of the earth

FAMISH, to suffer to —

To cause to hunger, רָעֵב *raeb*, 5.
Prov. 10. 3 LORD will not suffer the soul..to famish

FAMISHED —

Hunger, רָעָב *raab*.
Isa. 5. 13 and their honourable men (are) famished

FAMISHED, to be —

To be hungry, רָעֵב *raeb*.
Gen. 41. 55 when all the land of Egypt was famished

FAMOUS —

1. *Honourable*, אַדִּיר *addir*.
Psa. 136. 18 And slew famous kings: for his mercy
Eze. 32. 18 and the daughters of the famous nations

2. *Called*, קָרִיא [V.L. קרוא].
Num 26. 9 Dathan and Abiram..famous in the con.

3. *Called*, קָרִיא *qari*.
Num 16. 2 famous in the congregation, men of ren.

4. *Men of names*, אַנְשֵׁי שֵׁמוֹת [*anashim*].
1 Ch. 12. 30 famous throughout the house of their

5. *Of name*, שֵׁם *shem*.
1 Ch. 5. 24 mighty men of valour, famous men
Eze. 23. 10 and she became famous among women

FAMOUS, to be —

1. *To be known*, יָדַע *yada*, 2. Psa. 74. 5.
2. *To be called*, קָרָא *qara*, 2. Ruth 4. 14.
3. *To call a name*, קָרָא שֵׁם *qara shem*.
Ruth 4. 11 Ephratah, and be famous in Bethlehem

FAN —

1. *Fan*, מִזְרֶה *mizreh*.
Isa. 30. 24 winnowed with the shovel and..the fan
Jer. 15. 7 I will fan them with a fan in the gates

2. *Fan*, πτύον *ptuon*.
Matt. 3. 12 Whose fan (is) in his hand, and he will
Luke 3. 17 Whose fan (is) in his hand, and he will

FAN, to —

1. *To scatter, fan, winnow*, זָרָה *zarah*.
Isa. 41. 16 Thou shalt fan them, and the wind shall
Jer. 4. 11 A dry wind..not to fan, nor to cleanse
15. 7 I will fan them with a fan in the gates

2. *To scatter, winnow*, זָרָה *zarah*, 3.
Jer. 51. 2 send unto Babylon fanners, that shall fan

FANNER —

To be strange, זוּר *zur*.
Jer. 51. 2 And will send unto Babylon fanners, that

FAR —

1. *Might, exceedingly*, מְאֹד *meod*.
Judg 19. 11 when they (were) by Jebus, the day was f.
Psa. 97. 9 LORD..thou art exalted far above all gods
Jer. 49. 30 Flee, get you far off, dwell deep, O ye in.

2. *Far off*, מֶרְחָק *merchaq*.
2 Sa. 15. 17 and tarried in a place that was far off
Prov. 25. 25 so (is) good news from a far country
Isa. 8. 9 and give ear, all ye of far countries: gird
10. 3 desolation (which) shall come from far?
17. 13 they shall flee far off, and shall be chased
30. 27 the name of the LORD cometh from far
46. 11 man that executeth my counsel from a far
Jer. 4. 16 watchers come from a far country, and
5. 15 I will bring a nation upon you from far
6. 20 and the sweet cane from a far country?
Eze. 23. 40 ye have sent for men to come from far

3. *Far, far off, afar*, רָחוֹק *rachoq*.
Deut 28. 49 bring a nation against thee from far, from
29. 22 the stranger that shall come from a far
Josh. 9. 6 We be come from a far country: now
9. 9 From a very far country thy servants are
9. 22 We (are) very far from you; when ye dw.
Judg 18. 7 and they (were) far from the Zidonians
18. 28 no deliverer, because it (was) far from Z.
1 Ki. 8. 41 a stranger, that..cometh out of a far co.
8. 46 they carry them away captives..far or
2 Ki. 20. 14 Hezekiah said, They are come from a far
2 Ch. 6. 32 stranger..is come from a far country for
Neh. 4. 19 we are separated..one far from another
Esth. 9. 20 sent letters unto all..(both) nigh and far
Psa. 22. 1 (why art thou so) far from helping me
119. 155 Salvation (is) far from the wicked: for
Prov 15. 29 The LORD (is) far from the wicked: but
31. 10 virtuous woman? for her price (is) far
Eccl. 7. 23 I will be wise; but it (was) far from me
Isa. 5. 26 lift up an ensign to the nations from far
22. 3 bound together, (which)..fled from far
39. 3 Hezekiah said, They are come from a far
43. 6 bring my sons from far, and my daught.
46. 12 ye stout hearted, that (are) far from
49. 1 hearken, ye people, from far; The LORD
49. 12 Behold, these shall come from far; and
60. 4 thy sons shall come from far, and thy da.
60. 9 to bring thy sons from far, their silver
Jer. 12. 2 thou (art) near in their mouth, and far
25. 26 all the kings of the north, far and near
48. 24 upon all the cities..of Moab, far or near
Eze. 22. 5 (Those that be) near, and (those that be) f.
Hab. 1. 8 and their horsemen shall come from far

4. *Far, far off, afar*, רָחִיק *rachiq*.
Ezra 6. 6 Now (therefore)..be ye far from thence

5. *To be far*, רָחַק *rachaq*.
Josh. 3. 16 upon an heap very far from the city Adam
Psa. 103. 12 As far as the east is from the west, (so)

6. *Far off, a long way off*, μακράν *makran*.
Mar. 12. 34 Thou art not far from the kingdom of God
Luke 7. 6 when he was now not far from the house
John 21. 8 they were not far from land, but as it
Acts 17. 27 though he be not far from every one of us

7. *Far, far off*, μακρός *makros*.
Luke 15. 13 took his journey into a far country, and
19. 12 certain nobleman went into a far country

8. *Forwards, far off*, πόῤῥω *porrhō*.
Matt 15. 8 This people..but their heart is far from
Mark 7. 6 This people..but their heart is far from

9. *Much more*, πολλῷ μᾶλλον *pollō mallon*.
Phil. 1. 23 and to be with Christ; which is far better

10. *From before*, מִנֶּגֶד *min-neged*.
Judg. 9. 17 adventured his life far, and delivered

11. *Separation, impurity*, נִדָּה *niddah*.
Eze. 7. 20 therefore have I set it far from them

[*See also* Above, away, drive, flee, go, keep, put, remove, thus, withdraw.]

FAR above —
Over above, ὑπεράνω *huperanō.*
Eph. 1. 21 Far above all principality, and power
4. 10 the same also that ascended up far above

FAR abroad —
Afar, far, far off, רָחוֹק *rachoq.*
2 Ch.26. 15 his name spread far abroad; for he was

FAR away, to be —
To be far off, רָחַק *rachaq.*
Isa. 49. 19 they that swallowed thee up..be far away

FAR away, to put —
To put far off, רָחַק *rachaq,* 5.
Job 11. 14 iniquity (be) in thine hand, put it far away
Psa. 88. 8 put away mine acquaintance far from me

FAR, be —
1. *Profanation,* חָלִילָה *chalilah.*
Gen. 18. 25 That be far from thee to do after this
18. 25 be as the wicked, that be far from thee
1 Sa. 2. 30 Be it far from me; for them that honour
20. 9 Far be it from thee: for if I knew
22. 15 enquire of God for him? be it far from me
2 Sa. 20. 20 Far be it, far be it from me, that I sh.
23. 17 Be it far from me, O LORD, that I should
Job 34. 10 Far be it from God, (that he should do)

2. *(Be) kind to thyself,* ἵλεώς σοι *hileōs soi.*
Matt16. 22 Be it far from thee, Lord: this shall not

FAR, to be —
To be far off, רָחַק *rachaq.*
Job 5. 4 His children are far from safety, and they
21. 16 the counsel of the wicked is far from me
22. 18 the counsel of the wicked is far from me
Psa. 22. 11 Be not far from me; for trouble (is) near
22. 19 But be not thou far from me, O LORD
35. 22 keep not silence..LORD, be not far from
38. 21 Forsake me not..my God, be not far from
71. 12 be not far from me: O my God, make
109. 17 delighted not in blessing, so let it be far
119. 150 They draw nigh..they are far from thy
Prov 22. 5 he that doth keep his soul shall be far
Isa. 54. 14 thou shalt be far from oppression; for
59. 9 Therefore is judgment far from us, neither
Lam. 1. 16 because the comforter..is far from me

FAR country —
Afar, far off, מֶרְחָק *merchaq.*
Zech.10. 9 they shall remember me in far countries

FAR, dwell in —
Afar, far off, מֶרְחָק *merchaq.*
Jer. 8. 19 because of them that dwell in a far country

FAR, to get —
To be far off, רָחַק *rachaq.*
Eze. 11. 15 Get you far from the LORD: unto us is

FAR hence —
A long way, far off, μακράν *makran.*
Acts 22. 21 I..send thee far hence unto the Gentiles

FAR off —
1. *Afar, far off,* מֶרְחָק *merchaq.*
Isa. 17. 13 and they shall flee far off, and shall be

2. *Far, far off,* רָחוֹק *rachoq.*
Deut.13. 7 nigh unto thee, or far off from thee, from
20. 15 cities (which are) very far off from thee
30. 11 it (is) not hidden..neither (is) it far off
2 Ch. 6. 36 away captives unto a land far off or near
Prov 27. 10 a neighbour..near than a brother far off
Eccl. 7. 24 That which is far off, and exceeding deep
Isa. 33 13 Hear, ye (that are) far off, what I have
57. 9 didst send thy messengers far off, and didst
57. 19 Peace, peace to (him that is) far off, and
Eze. 6. 12 He that is far off shall die of the pestil.
12. 27 prophesieth of the times (that are) far off
Dan. 9. 7 unto all Israel..(that are) far off, through
Joel 3. 8 sell them to the Sabeans, to a people far off
Zech. 6. 15 they (that are) far off shall come and build

3. *From before,* מִנֶּגֶד *min-neged.*
Num. 2. 2 far off about the tabernacle of the congre.

4. *To put far off,* רָחַק *rachaq,* 5.
Gen. 44. 4 gone out of the city, (and) not (yet) far off

5. *A long way, far off,* μακράν *makran.*
Eph. 2. 13 ye who sometime were far off are made

FAR, from —
From far off, μακρόθεν *makrothen.*
Mark 8. 3 faint..for divers of them came from far

FAR, thus —
Up to this, ἕως τούτου *heōs toutou.*
Luke22. 51 And Jesus answered..Suffer ye thus far

FAR off, to be —
To be far off, רָחַק *rachaq.*
Isa. 46. 13 it shall not be far off, and my salvation
59. 11 for salvation, (but) it is far off from us

FAR off, to cast —
To put far off, רָחַק *rachaq,* 5.
Eze. 11. 16 I have cast them far off among the heat.

FAR off, very —
Afar, far off, מֶרְחָק *merchaq.*
Isa. 33. 17 shall behold the land that is very far off

FAR off, to (wander) —
To put far off, רָחַק *rachaq,* 5.
Psa. 55. 7 Lo, (then) would I wander far off, (and)

FAR passed —
Much, many, πολύς *polus.*
Mark 6. 35 disciples..said..now the time (is) far pa.

FAR, to put —
To put far off, רָחַק *rachaq,* 5.
Job 19. 13 He hath put my brethren far from me
Psa. 88. 18 Lover and friend hast thou put far from
Prov. 4. 24 and perverse lips put far from thee

FAR removed, to be —
To be far off, רָחַק *rachaq.*
Mic. 7. 11 that day shall the decree be far removed

FAR richer, to be —
To make great wealth, עָשָׂה עֹשֶׁר גָּדוֹל *asah osher gadol.*
Dan. 11. 2 fourth shall be far richer than (they) all

FAR spent — πολύς *polus.*
Mark 6. 35 when the day was now far spent, his dis.

FAR, that are —
Far off, afar, רָחֵק *racheq.*
Psa. 73. 27 they that are far from thee shall perish

FAR, to be too —
To be far off, רָחַק *rachaq.*
Deut 12. 21 If the place..there be too far from thee
14. 24 if the place be too far from thee, which

FARE —
Peace, prosperity, completeness, שָׁלוֹם *shalom.*
1 Sa. 17. 18 look how thy brethren fare, and take their

FARE —
Hire, reward, שָׂכָר *sakar.*
Jon. 1. 3 so he paid the fare thereof, and went

FARE, to —
To make merry, εὐφραίνω *euphrainō.*
Luke16. 19 clothed..and fared sumptuously every day

FAREWELL, or FARE YE WELL —
1. *To make strong,* ῥώννυμι *rhōnnumi.*
Acts 15. 29 abstain..ye shall do well. Fare ye well
23. 30 what they had against him. [Farewell]

2. *To rejoice,* χαίρω *chairō.*
2 Co. 13. 11 Finally, brethren, farewell. Be perfect

FAREWELL, to bid —
To arrange off from, ἀποτάσσομαι *apotassomai.*
Luke 9. 61 bid them farewell, which are at home at
Acts 18. 21 bade them farewell, saying, I must by all

FARM —
Field (cultivated), ἀγρός *agros.*
Matt22. 5 one to his farm, another to his merchan.

FARTHER side, the —
The other side, beyond, τὸ πέραν *to peran.*
Mark10. 1 the coasts..by the farther side of Jordan

FARTHING —
1. *Assarion,* (1-*tenth of a denarius*), ἀσσάριον.
Matt 10. 29 Are not two sparrows sold for a farthing?
Luke12. 6 Are not five sparrows..for two farthings?

2. *Quadrans,* (1-*fourth of an as.*), κοδράντης *kodra.*
Matt. 5. 26 till thou hast paid the uttermost farthing
Mark12. 42 threw in two mites, which make a farth.

FASHION —
1. *Likeness,* דְּמוּת *demuth.*
2 Ki. 16. 10 the fashion of the altar, and the pattern

2. *Judgment, rule,* מִשְׁפָּט *mishpat.*
Exod26. 30 the tabernacle according to the fashion
1 Ki. 6. 38 and according to all the fashion of it
Eze. 42. 11 (were) both according to their fashions

3. *Preparation, establishment,* תְּכוּנָה *tekunah.*
Eze. 43. 11 form of the house, and the fashion thereof

4. *Thing seen, sight, appearance,* εἶδος *eidos.*
Luke 9. 29 fashion of his countenance was altered

5. *Face, countenance,* πρόσωπον *prosōpon.*
Jas. 1. 11 the grace of the fashion of it perisheth

6. *Scheme,* σχῆμα *schēma.*
1 Co. 7. 31 the fashion of this world passeth away
Phil. 2. 8 being found in fashion as a man, he hum.

7. *Type, model,* τύπος *tupos.*
Acts 7. 44 according to the fashion that he had seen

FASHION, on this —
Thus, οὕτως *houtōs.*
Mark 2. 12 saying, We never saw it on this fashion

FASHION, to —
1. *To form, frame,* יָצַר *yatsar.*
Psa. 33. 15 He fashioneth their hearts alike; he con.
Isa. 22. 11 respect unto him that fashioned it long
44. 12 fashioneth it with hammers, and worketh
45. 9 Shall the clay say to him that fashioneth

2. *To prepare, set up,* כּוּן *kun,* 3a.
Job 31. 15 and did not one fashion us in the womb?
Psa.119. 73 Thy hands have made me and fashioned

3. *To do,* עָשָׂה *asah.*
Job 10. 8 Thine hands have made me, and fashioned

4. *To fashion, compress,* צוּר *tsur.*
Exod32. 4 fashioned it with a graving tool, after

FASHION one's self according to, to —
To form with, conform to, συσχηματίζω *suschēma.*
1 Pe. 1. 14 not fashioning yourselves according to

FASHIONED, to be —
1. *To be formed,* יָצַר *yatsar,* 4.
Psa.139. 16 (which) in continuance were fashioned

2. *To be prepared, set up,* כּוּן *kun,* 2.
Eze. 16. 7 (thy) breasts are fashioned, and thine

FASHIONED like unto, to be —
Having same form with, σύμμορφος *summorphos.*
Phil. 3. 21 be fashioned like unto his glorious body

FAST —
1. *Speedily, diligently, carefully,* אָסְפַּרְנָא *osparna.*
Ezra 5. 8 this work goeth fast on, and prospereth

2. *To bind,* אָסַר *asar.*
Judg15. 13 we will bind thee fast, and deliver thee
16. 11 If they bind me fast with new ropes that

3. *Might, (with),* מְאֹד *meod.*
Jer. 48. 16 calamity..and his affliction hasteth fast

4. *To restrain, keep in,* עָצַר *atsar.*
Gen. 20. 18 the LORD had fast closed up all the wombs

5. *A fast,* צוֹם *tsom.*
1 Ki. 21. 9 Proclaim a fast, and set Naboth on high
21. 12 They proclaimed a fast, and set Naboth
2 Ch.20. 3 proclaimed a fast throughout all Judah
Ezra 8. 21 I proclaimed a fast there, at the river
Isa. 58. 3 in the day of your fast ye find pleasure
58. 5 Is it such a fast that I have chosen?
58. 5 thou call this a fast, and an acceptable
58. 6 (Is) not this the fast that I have chosen?
Jer. 36. 9 they proclaimed a fast before the LORD
Joel 1. 14 Sanctify ye a fast, call a solemn assembly
2. 15 sanctify a fast, call a solemn assembly
Jon. 3. 5 proclaimed a fast, and put on sackcloth
Zech. 8. 19 The fast of the fourth (month), and the f.
8. 19 the fast of the seventh, and the fast

6. *A fasting, fast,* νηστεία *nēsteia.*
Acts 27. 9 because the fast was now already past

[*See also* Abide, asleep, cleave, hold, keep, set, stand, stick.]

FAST, to —
1. *To fast,* צוּם *tsum.*
Judg.20. 26 and fasted that day until even, and
1 Sa. 7. 6 And they..fasted on that day, and said
31. 13 they took their bones..and fasted seven
2 Sa. 1. 12 mourned and wept, and fasted until even
12. 21 Thou didst fast and weep for the child
12. 22 While the child was yet alive, I fasted and
12. 23 now he is dead, wherefore should I fast?
1 Ki. 21. 27 fasted, and lay in sackcloth, and went
1 Ch.10. 12 buried their bones..and fasted seven d.
Ezra 8. 23 So we fasted, and besought our God for
Neh. 1. 4 and mourned (certain) days, and fasted
Esth. 4. 16 gather together all the Jews..and fast ye
4. 16 I also and my maidens will fast likewise
Isa. 58. 3 Wherefore have we fasted, (say they)
58. 4 Behold, ye fast for strife and debate
58. 4 ye shall not fast as (ye do this) day, to
Jer. 14. 12 When they fast, I will not hear their cry
Zech. 7. 5 When ye fasted and mourned in the fifth
7. 5 did ye at all fast unto me, (even) to me?

2. *To fast a fast,* צוּם צוֹם *tsum tsom.*
2 Sa. 12. 16 David fasted, and went in, and lay all

3. *To fast,* νηστεύω *nēsteuō.*
Matt. 4. 2 when he had fasted forty days and forty
6. 16 Moreover, when ye fast, be not, as the
6. 16 that they may appear unto men to fast
6. 17 But thou, when thou fastest, anoint thine
6. 18 That thou appear not unto men to fast
9. 14 Pharisees fast oft, but thy disciples fast
9. 15 days will come..and then shall they fast
Mark 2. 18 the Pharisees fast, but thy disciples fast
2. 19 [Can..children of the bridechamber fa.]
2. 19 as long as they have..they cannot fast
2. 20 and then shall they fast in those days
Luke 5. 33 Why do the disciples of John fast often
5. 34 Can ye make the children..fast while the
5. 35 and then shall they fast in those days
18. 12 I fast twice in the week, I give tithes of
Acts 10. 30 Four days ago I was [fasting] until this
13. 2 As they ministered to the Lord, and fast.
13. 3 And when they had fasted and prayed

FAST, used to —
They were fasting, ἦσαν νηστεύοντες [*nēsteuō*].
Mark 2. 18 And the disciples of John..used to fast

FAST, to make —
To make firm, fixed, sure, ἀσφαλίζω *asphalizō.*
Acts 16. 24 and made their feet fast in the stocks

FASTEN, to —
1. *To lay hold,* אָחַז *achaz.*
1 Ki. 6. 6 (the beams) should not be fastened in the
Esth. 1. 6 fastened with cords of fine linen and pu.

2. *To strengthen, harden, fix,* חָזַק *chazaq,* 3.
Isa. 41. 7 he fastened it with nails, (that) it should
Jer. 10. 4 they fasten it with nails and with ham.

3. *To give,* נָתַן *nathan.*
Exod28. 14 fasten the wreathen chains to the ouches
28. 25 two wreathen (chains) thou shalt fasten
39. 18 two ends..they fastened in the two ouc.
39. 31 to fasten (it) on high upon the mitre ; as
40. 18 Moses reared up the tabernacle, and fas.

4. *To cause to alight, to fasten,* צָנַח *tsanach.*
Judg. 4. 21 smote the nail..and fastened it into the

5. *To strike, fix,* תָּקַע *taqa.*
Judg16. 14 she fastened (it) with the pin, and said
1 Sa. 31. 10 and they fastened his body to the wall of
1 Ch.10. 10 fastened his head in the temple of Dagon
Isa. 22. 23 I will fasten him (as) a nail in a sure
22. 25 the nail that is fastened in the sure place

FASTEN on, to —
To fit or fix down on, καθάπτω *kathaptō.*
Acts 28. 3 a viper out of the heat, and fastened on

FASTEN one's eyes, to —
To look intently, ἀτενίζω *atenizō.*
Luke 4. 20 eyes of all..in the synagogue were faste.
Acts 3. 4 Peter, fastening his eyes upon him with
11. 6 when I had fastened mine eyes, I consid.

FASTENED —
1. *To be prepared, set up, established,* כּוּן *kun,* 6.
Eze. 40. 43 within (were) hooks, an hand broad, fas.

2. *To plant,* נָטַע *nata.*
Eccl. 12. 11 words of the wise (are)..as nails fastened

3. *To be joined, coupled, fastened,* צָמַד *tsamad,* 4.
2 Sa.20. 8 upon it a girdle (with) a sword fastened

FASTENED, to be —
1. *To be laid hold of,* אָחַז *achaz,* 6.
2 Ch. 9. 18 six steps..(which were) fastened to the

2. *To be sunk,* טָבַע *taba,* 6.
Job 38. 6 are the foundations thereof fastened? or

FASTING —
1. *Fasting,* טְוָת *tevath.*
Dan. 6. 18 Then the king..passed the night fasting

2. *Fasting,* צוֹם *tsom.*
Neh. 9. 1 children of Israel were assembled with f.
Esth. 4. 3 mourning among the Jews, and fasting
9. 31 the matters of the fastings and their cry
Psa. 35. 13 I humbled my soul with fasting; and my
69. 10 I wept, (and chastened) my soul with fas.
109. 24 My knees are weak through fasting; and
Jer. 36. 6 in the LORD'S house upon the fasting day
Dan. 9. 3 to seek by prayer and..with fasting, and
Joel 2. 12 Turn ye (even) to me with..fasting, and

3. *Fasting, without food,* ἄσιτος *asitos.*
Acts 27. 33 ye have tarried and continued fasting

4. *A fasting, fast,* νηστεία *nēsteia.*
Matt17. 21 [kind goeth not out but by prayer and fas.]
Mark 9. 29 can come forth by nothing but by..[fas.]
Luke 2. 37 but served (God) with fastings and pray.
Acts 14. 23 when they had..prayed with fasting, they
1 Co. 7. 5 that ye may give yourselves to [fasting]
2 Co. 6. 5 in labours, in watchings, in fastings
11. 27 in fastings often, in cold and nakedness

5. *Fasting, not eating,* νῆστις *nēstis.*
Matt15. 32 and I will not send them away fasting
Mark 8. 3 if I send them away fasting to their own

FAT —
1. *Fat, firm,* בְּרִי *beri.*
Eze. 34. 20 I, will judge between the fat cattle and

2. *Fat, firm,* בָּרִיא *bari.*
Gen. 41. 4 eat up the seven well favoured and fat k.
41. 18 seven kine, fat fleshed and well favoured
41. 20 the lean..eat up the first seven fat kine
Judg. 3. 17 king of Moab : and Eglon (was) a very fat
1 Ki. 4. 23 Ten fat oxen, and twenty oxen out of the
Zech 11. 16 he shall eat the flesh of the fat, and tear

3. *Fat, opulent,* דָּשֵׁן *dashen.*
Psa. 22. 29 All (they that be) fat upon earth shall eat
92. 14 they shall be fat and flourishing
Isa. 30. 23 it shall be fat and plenteous : in that day

4. *Fat, best part, marrow,* חֵלֶב, חֶלֶב *cheleb.*
Gen. 4. 4 firstlings of his flock, and of the fat ther.
45. 18 and ye shall eat the fat of the land
Exod23. 18 neither shall the fat of my sacrifice rem.
29. 13 thou shalt take all the fat that covereth
29. 13 two kidneys, and the fat that (is) upon
29. 22 Also thou shalt take of the ram the fat
29. 22 the rump, and the fat that covereth the
29. 22 two kidneys, and the fat that (is) upon
Lev. 3. 3, 9, 14 the fat that covereth the inwards
3. 3, 9, 14 all the fat that (is) upon the inwar.
3. 4 the two kidneys, and the fat that (is) on
3. 9 the fat thereof, (and) the whole rump, it
3. 10, 15 two kidneys, and the fat that (is) upon
3. 16 for a sweet savour. All the fat (is) the L.
3. 17 statute..that ye eat neither fat nor blood
4. 8 he shall take off from it all the fat of the
4. 8 the fat that covereth..and all the fat that
4. 9 two kidneys, and the fat that (is) upon
4. 19 he shall take all his fat from him, and b.
4. 26 he shall burn all his fat upon the altar
4. 26 as the fat of the sacrifice of peace offer.
4. 31, 35 he shall take away all the fat thereof
4. 31 as the fat is taken away from off the
4. 35 as the fat of the lamb is taken away
6. 12 burn thereon the fat of the peace offer.
Lev. 7. 3 he shall offer of it all the fat thereof
7. 3 the rump, and the fat that covereth the
7. 4 two kidneys, and the fat that (is) on them
7. 23 Ye shall eat no manner of fat, of ox, or
7. 24 the fat of the beast..and the fat of that
7. 25 For whosoever eateth the fat of the beast
7. 30 the fat with the breast, it shall he bring
7. 31 priest shall burn the fat upon the altar
7. 33 the sons of Aaron that offereth..the fat
8. 16, 25 all the fat that (was) upon the inwards
8. 16, 25 and the two kidneys, and their fat
8. 25 And he took the fat, and the rump, and
8. 26 put (them) on the fat, and upon the right
9. 10 But the fat, and the kidneys, and the ca.
9. 19 And the fat of the bullock and of the ram
9. 20 And they put the fat..and he burnt the f.
9. 24 and consumed upon the altar..the fat
10. 15 the offerings made by fire of the fat, to
16. 25 fat of the sin offering shall he burn upon
17. 6 burn the fat for a sweet savour unto the
Num18. 17 shalt burn their fat (for) an offering made
Deut32. 14 with fat of lambs, and..fat of kidneys of
32. 38 Which did eat the fat of their sacrifices
Judg. 3. 22 the fat closed upon the blade, so that he
1 Sa. 2. 15 Also before they burnt the fat, the priest's
2. 16 Let them not fail to burn the fat presently
15. 22 (and) to hearken than the fat of rams
2 Sa. 1. 22 from the fat of the mighty, the bow of
1 Ki. 8. 64, 64 and the fat of the peace offerings
2 Ch. 7. 7 he offered burnt offerings, and the fat of
7. 7 to receive the burnt offerings..and the f.
29. 35 offerings (were) in abundance, with the f.
35. 14 in offering of burnt offerings and the fat
Psa. 17. 10 They are inclosed in their own fat : with
Isa. 1. 11 I am full of the..fat of fed beasts ; and
34. 6 with the fat of the kidneys of rams : for
43. 24 neither hast thou filled me with the fat
Eze. 34. 3 ye eat the fat, and ye clothe you with the
39. 19 ye shall eat fat till ye be full, and drink
44. 7 when ye offer my bread, the fat and the
44. 15 they shall stand..to offer unto me the fat

5. *Preciousness,* יְקָר *yaqar.*
Psa. 37. 20 enemies of the LORD (shall be) as the fat

6. *Fat oily substances,* מַשְׁמַנִּים *mashmannim.*
Neh. 8. 10 he said unto them, Go your way, eat the f.

7. *Grease, fat,* פֶּדֶר *peder.*
Lev. 1. 8 the priests, Aaron's sons, shall lay..the f.
1. 12 he shall cut it..with his head and his fat
8. 20 and Moses burnt the head..and the fat

8. *Oily,* שָׁמֵן *shamen.*
Gen. 49. 20 Out of Asher his bread (shall be) fat, and
Num13. 20 what the land (is), whether it (be) fat or
1 Ch. 4. 40 And they found fat pasture and good, and
Neh. 9. 25 And they took strong cities, and a fat la.
9. 35 and in the large and fat land which thou
Eze. 34. 14 and (in) a fat pasture shall they feed upon
34. 16 but I will destroy the fat and the strong
Hab. 1. 16 because by them their portion (is) fat, and

9. *A stall, fattening,* מַרְבֵּק *marbeq.*
1 Sa. 28. 24 And the woman had a fat calf in the ho.

10. *Oil,* שֶׁמֶן *shemen.*
Isa. 28. 1 which (are) on the head of the fat valleys
28. 4 beauty, which (is) on the head of the fat

FAT, to be —
To be fat, insensate, טָפַשׁ *taphash.*
Psa.119. 70 Their heart is as fat as grease ; (but) I

FAT beast or cattle —
Fatling, מְרִיא *meri.*
1 Ki. 1. 9 Adonijah slew sheep and oxen and fat ca.
1. 19, 25 hath slain oxen and fat cattle and sheep
Amos 5. 22 regard the peace offerings of your fat be.

FAT, to become —
To make or become fat, שָׁמַן *shaman,* 5.
Neh. 9. 25 and became fat, and delighted themselves

FAT, to be made —
1. *To be made fat,* דָּשֵׁן *dashen,* 4.
Prov 11. 25 The liberal soul shall be made fat; and he
13. 4 the soul of the diligent shall be made fat
28. 25 that putteth his trust..shall be made fat
Isa. 34. 7 and their dust made fat with fatness

2. *To be made fat,* דָּשֵׁן *dashen,* 7b.
Isa. 34. 6 it is made fat with fatness, (and) with the

FAT, to make —
1. *To fatten,* דָּשֵׁן *dashen,* 3.
Prov.15. 30 (and) a good report maketh the bones fat

2. *To arm,* חָלַץ *chalats,* 5.
Isa. 58. 11 And the LORD shall..make fat thy bones

3. *To make fat or oily,* שָׁמַן *shaman,* 5.
Isa. 6. 10 Make the heart of this people fat, and

FAT, to make selves —
To make fat, בָּרָא *bara,* 5.
1 Sa. 2. 29 to make yourselves fat with the chiefest

FAT ones —
1. *Fat ones,* מֵחִים *mechim.*
Isa. 5. 17 and the waste places of the fat ones shall

2. *Fatness, fat one,* מִשְׁמָן *mishman.*
Isa. 10. 16 send among his fat ones leanness ; and

FAT things —
Oil, fatness, שֶׁמֶן *shemen.*
Isa. 25. 6 make unto all people a feast of fat things
25. 6 fat things full of marrow, of wines on the

FAT, to wax —
1. *To be or become fat,* דָּשֵׁן *dashen.*
Deut31. 20 and they shall have eaten..and waxen fat

2. *To be or become fat, oily,* שָׁמַן *shaman.*
Deut32. 15 But Jeshurun waxed fat, and kicked

FAT, to be waxen —
To be or become fat, oily, שָׁמַן *shaman.*
Deut 32 15 thou art waxen fat, thou art grown thick
Jer. 5. 28 They are waxen fat, they shine : yea, they

FAT fleshed —
Fat in flesh, בְּרִיא בָשָׂר *beri basar.*
Gen. 41. 2, 18 seven well favoured kine and fat fleshed

FATHER —
1. *Father, ancestor, source, inventor,* אָב *ab.*
Gen. 2. 24 Therefore shall a man leave his father and
4. 20 And Adah bare Jabal : he was the father
4. 21 he was the father of all such as handle
9. 18 Japheth : and Ham (is) the father of C.
9. 22 the father of Canaan, saw..his father, and
9. 23 and covered the nakedness of their father
9. 23 and they saw not their father's nakedness
10. 21 Unto Shem also, the father of all the chil.
11. 28 Haran died before his father Terah in
11. 29 father of Milcah, and the father of Iscah
12. 1 Get thee out..from thy father's house
17. 4 and thou shalt be a father of many na.
17. 5 a father of many nations have I made
19. 31 Our father (is) old, and (there is) not a
19. 32 Come, let us make our father drink wine
19. 33 they made their father drink wine that
19. 34 Behold, I lay yesternight with my father
19. 35 they made their father drink wine that
19. 36 the daughters..with child by their father
19. 37 the same (is) the father of the Moabites
19. 38 the same (is) the father of the children of
20. 12 she (is) the daughter of my father, but
20. 13 God caused me to wander from my fath.
22. 7 Abraham his father, and said, My father
22. 21 Huz..and Kemuel the father of Aram
24. 7 God..which took me from my father's h.
24. 23 is there room (in) thy father's house for
24. 38 But thou shalt go unto my father's house
24. 40 thou shalt take a wife..of my father's h.
26. 3 oath which I sware unto Abraham thy f.
26. 15 For all the wells which his father's serv.
26. 15 digged in the days of Abraham his father
26. 18 they had digged in the days of..his father
26. 18 after the names by which his father had
26. 24 I (am) the God of Abraham thy father
27. 6 I heard thy father speak unto Esau thy
27. 9 I will make..savoury meat for thy father
27. 10 thou shalt bring (it) to thy father, that
27. 12 My father peradventure will feel me, and
27. 14 savoury meat, such as his father loved
27. 18 came unto his father, and said, My fath.
27. 19 Jacob said unto his father, I (am) Esau
27. 22 And Jacob went near unto Isaac his father
27. 26 his father Isaac said unto him, Come near
27. 30 Jacob was..scarce gone out from..his f.
27. 31 savoury meat, and brought it unto his f.
27. 31 and said unto his father, Let my father
27. 32 Isaac his father said unto him, Who (art)
27. 34 when Esau heard the words of his father
27. 34 and said unto his father..O my father!
27. 38 And Esau said unto his father
27. 38 Hast thou but one blessing, my father?
27. 38 bless me, (even) me also, O my father!
27. 39 Isaac his father answered and said unto
27. 41 because of the blessing wherewith his fa.
27. 41 The days of mourning for my father are
28. 2 the house of Bethuel, thy mother's father
28. 7 And that Jacob obeyed his father and his
28. 8 daughters of Canaan pleased not..his fa.
28. 13 I (am) the LORD God of Abraham thy fa.
28. 21 So that I come again to my father's house
29. 9 Rachel came with her father's sheep; for
29. 12 Jacob told Rachel that he (was) her fath.
29. 12 and she ran and told her father
31. 1 Jacob hath taken..all that (was) our fa.
31. 1 of (that) which (was) our father's hath he
31. 5 said unto them, I see your father's coun.
31. 5 the God of my father hath been with me
31. 6 with all my power I have served your f.
31. 7 your father hath deceived me, and changed
31. 9 God hath taken..the cattle of your father
31. 14 (Is there) yet any portion..in our father's
31. 16 the riches..God hath taken from our fa.
31. 18 to go to Isaac his father in the land of C.
31. 19 had stolen the images that (were) her fa.
31. 29 but the God of your father spake unto me
31. 30 because thou sore longedst after thy fath.
31. 35 she said to her father, Let it not displease
31. 42 Except the God of my father, the God of
31. 53 the God of their father, judge betwixt us
31. 53 Jacob sware by the Fear of his father Is.
32. 9 O God of my father..God of my father I.
33. 19 at the hand of..Hamor, Shechem's father
34. 4 Shechem spake unto his father Hamor
34. 6 Hamor the father of Shechem went out
34. 11 Shechem said unto her father and unto
34. 13 sons of Jacob answered..Hamor his fath.
34. 19 honourable than all the house of his fath.
35. 18 Ben-oni : but his father called him Benj.
35. 22 Reuben went and lay with Bilhah his fa.
35. 27 Jacob came unto Isaac his father unto
36. 9 Esau the father of the Edomites in mount
36. 24 as he fed the asses of Zibeon his father
36. 43 he (is) Esau the father of the Edomites

Gen. 37. 1 dwelt in the land wherein his father was
37. 2 and with the sons of Zilpah, his father's
37. 2 Joseph brought unto his father their evil
37. 4 when his brethren saw that their father
37. 10 he told (it) to his father, and to his breth.
37. 10 his father rebuked him, and said unto h.
37. 11 but his father observed the saying
37. 12 his brethren went to feed their father's
37. 22 to deliver him to his father again
37. 32 they brought (it) to their father; and said
37. 35 Thus his father wept for him
38. 11 Remain a widow at thy father's house
38. 11 Tamar went and dwelt in her father's h.
41. 51 God..hath made me forget all..my fath.
42. 13 the youngest (is) this day with our father
42. 29 they came unto Jacob their father unto
42. 32 We..twelve brethren, sons of our father
42. 32 the youngest (is) this day with our father
42. 35 they and their father saw the bundles of
42. 36 Jacob their father said unto them, Me
42. 37 Reuben spake unto his father, saying
43. 2 their father said unto them, Go again
43. 7 (Is) your father yet alive? have ye
43. 8 Judah said unto Israel his father, Send
43. 11 And their father Israel said unto them
43. 23 the God of your father, hath given you
43. 27 (Is) your father well, the old man of
43. 28 And they answered, Thy servant our fat.
44. 17 get you up in peace unto your father
44. 19 saying, Have ye a father, or a brother?
44. 20 We have a father, an old man, and a
44. 20 he alone is left..and his father loveth him
44. 22 we said..The lad cannot leave his father
44. 22 for (if) he should leave his father, (his f.)
44. 24 we came up unto thy servant my father
44. 25 our father said, Go again..buy us a little
44. 27 And thy servant my father said unto us
44. 30 when I come to thy servant my father
44. 31 the gray hairs of thy servant our father
44. 32 became surety for the lad unto my father
44. 32 I shall bear the blame to my father for
44. 34 For how shall I go up to my father
44. 34 I see the evil that shall come on my fat.
45. 3 I (am) Joseph: doth my father yet live?
45. 8 he hath made me a father to Pharaoh
45. 9 Haste ye, and go up to my father, and
45. 13 ye shall tell my father of all my glory in
45. 18 take your father, and your households
45. 19 this do ye..bring your father, and come
45. 23 And to his father he sent after this
45. 23 bread and meat for his father by the way
45. 25 and came into..Canaan unto..their fat.
45. 27 the spirit of Jacob their father revived
46. 1 sacrifices unto the God of his father Isaac
46. 3 I (am) God, the God of thy father: fear
46. 5 sons of Israel carried Jacob their father
46. 29 Joseph..went up to meet Israel his father
46. 31 And Joseph said..unto his father's house
46. 31 My brethren, and my father's house
47. 1 My father and my brethren..are come
47. 5 Thy father and thy brethren are come
47. 6 in the best of the land make thy father
47. 7 And Joseph brought in Jacob his father
47. 11 Joseph placed his father and his brethren
47. 12 And Joseph nourished his father, and
48. 1 told Joseph, Behold, thy father (is) sick
48. 9 Joseph said unto his father, They (are)
48. 17 when Joseph saw that his father laid his
48. 17 he held up his father's hand, to remove
48. 18 Joseph said unto his father, Not so, my f.
48. 19 his father refused, and said, I know (it)
49. 2 and hearken unto Israel your father
49. 4 because thou wentest up to thy father's
49. 8 thy father's children shall bow down bef.
49. 25 by the God of thy father, who shall help
49. 26 The blessings of thy father have prevail.
49. 28 this (is it) that their father spake unto
50. 1 Joseph fell upon his father's face, and
50. 2 commanded..physicians to embalm his f.
50. 5 My father made me swear, saying, Lo, I
50. 5 therefore let me go up..and bury my fa.
50. 6 Pharaoh said, Go up and bury thy father
50. 7 Joseph went up to bury his father: and
50. 8 the house of Joseph..and his father's h.
50. 10 he made a mourning for his father seven
50. 14 his father, after he had buried his father
50. 15 when Joseph's brethren saw that their f.
50. 16 Thy father did command before he died
50. 17 forgive the..servants of the God of thy fa.
50. 22 Joseph dwelt in Egypt, he..his father's
Exod. 2. 16 filled the troughs to water their father's
2. 18 And when they came to Reuel their fat.
3. 6 he said, I (am) the God of thy father, the
15. 2 my father's God, and I will exalt him
18. 4 for the God of my father..(was) mine
20. 12 Honour thy father and thy mother: that
21. 15 he that smiteth his father, or his mother
21. 17 he that curseth his father, or his mother
22. 17 If her father utterly refuse to give her
40. 15 as thou didst anoint their father, that
Lev. 16. 32 to minister in the priest's office in his f.
18. 7 The nakedness of thy father, or the nak.
18. 8 The nakedness of thy father's wife shalt
18. 8 it (is) thy father's nakedness
18. 9 nakedness of..the daughter of thy fath.
18. 11 The nakedness of thy father's wife's dau.
18. 11 begotten of thy father, she (is) thy sister
18. 12 not uncover the nakedness of thy fathe.
18. 12 she (is) thy father's near kinswoman
18. 14 not uncover the nakedness of thy father's
19. 3 Ye shall fear every man his..father
20. 9 every one that curseth his father or his m.

Lev. 20. 9 he hath cursed his father or his mother
20. 11 the man that lieth with his father's wife
20. 11 hath uncovered his father's nakedness
20. 17 if a man shall take his sister, his father's
20. 19 not uncover the nakedness..of thy fath.
21. 2 for his mother, and for his father, and
21. 9 she profaneth her father: she shall be
21. 11 Neither shall he..defile himself for his f.
22. 13 and is returned unto her father's house
22. 13 she shall eat of her father's meat
Num. 3. 4 ministered..in the sight of..their father
3. 24, 30, 35 the chief of the house of the fath.
6. 7 not make himself unclean for his father
12. 14 If her father had but spit in her face
17. 6 gave..according to their fathers' houses
18. 1 Thou and thy sons and thy father's house
18. 2 the tribe of thy father, bring thou with
27. 3 Our father died in the wilderness, and he
27. 4 Why should the name of our father be
27. 4 possession among the brethren of our fa.
27. 7 inheritance among their father's brethren
27. 7 shalt cause the inheritance of their father
27. 10 shall give his inheritance unto his father's
27. 11 if his father have no brethren, then ye
30. 3 (being) in her father's house in her youth
30. 4 And her father hear her vow, and her
30. 4 and her father shall hold his peace at her
30. 5 But if her father disallow her in the day
30. 5 LORD shall forgive her, because her father
30. 16 between the father and his daughter
36. 6 to the family of the tribe of their father
36. 8 one of the family of the tribe of her fath.
36. 12 in the tribe of the family of their father
Deut. 5. 16 Honour thy father and thy mother, as
21. 13 bewail her father and her mother a full
21. 18 which will not obey the voice of his fath.
21. 19 Then shall his father and his mother lay
22. 15 Then shall the father of the damsel, and
22. 16 the damsel's father shall say unto the eld.
22. 19 and give..unto the father of the damsel
22. 21 the damsel to the door of her father's h.
22. 21 to play the whore in her father's house
22. 29 man..shall give unto the damsel's father
22. 30 A man shall not take his father's wife
22. 30 nor discover his father's skirt
26. 5 A Syrian ready to perish (was) my father
27. 16 Cursed (be) he that setteth light by his f
27. 20 Cursed (be) he that lieth with his father's
27. 20 because he uncovereth his father's skirt
27. 22 lieth with..the daughter of his father
32. 6 (is) not he thy father (that) hath bought
32. 7 ask thy father, and he will show thee
33. 9 Who said unto his father and to his moth.
Josh. 2. 12 ye will..show kindness unto my father's
2. 13 ye will save alive my father, and my moth.
2. 18 thou shalt bring thy father, and thy
2. 18 all thy father's household, home unto thee
6. 23 men..brought out Rahab, and her father
6. 25 Joshua saved Rahab..and her father's h.
15. 13 the city of Arba the father of Anak, which
15. 18 she moved him to ask of her father a field
17. 1 Machir the first born of Manasseh, the fa.
17. 4 gave..among the brethren of their father
19. 47 Dan, after the name of Dan their father
21. 11 they gave them the city of Arba the father
24. 2 Your fathers dwelt on the other side of
24. 2 Terah, the father of Abraham, and the f.
24. 3 I took your father Abraham from the
24. 32 sons of Hamor the father of Shechem for
Judg. 1. 14 she moved him to ask of her father a field
6. 15 and I (am) the least in my father's house
6. 25 Take thy father's young bullock, even the
6. 25 the altar of Baal that thy father hath
6. 27 because he feared his father's household
8. 32 buried in the sepulchre of Joash his fat.
9. 1 family of the house of his mother's father
9. 5 he went unto his father's house at Ophrah
9. 17 my father fought for you, and adventured
9. 18 ye are risen up against my father's h.
9. 28 serve the men of Hamor the father of S.
9. 56 which he did unto his father, in slaying
11. 36 And she said unto him, My father
11. 37 she said unto her father, Let this thing
11. 39 she returned unto her father, who did
14. 2 he came up, and told his father and his
14. 3 his father and his mother said unto him
14. 3 Samson said unto his father, Get her for
14. 4 his father and his mother knew not that
14. 5 Then went Samson down, and his father
14. 6 he told not his father or his mother what
14. 9 went..and came to his father and mother
14. 10 So his father went down unto the woman
14. 15 lest we burn thee and thy father's house
14. 16 I have not told (it) my father nor my mo.
14. 19 and he went up to his father's house
15. 1 her father would not suffer him to go in
15. 2 her father said, I verily thought that thou
15. 6 came up, and burned her and her father
16. 31 brethren, and all the house of his father
16. 31 in the burying place of Manoah his father
17. 10 Dwell with me, and be unto me a father
18. 19 go..and be to us a father and a priest
18. 29 Dan, after the name of Dan their father
19. 2 went away from him unto her father's
19. 3 she brought him unto her father's house
19. 3 when the father of the damsel saw him
19. 4 and his father in law, the damsel's father
19. 5 the damsel's father said unto his son in
19. 6 the damsel's father had said unto the man
19. 8 the damsel's father said, Comfort thine
19. 9 his father in law, the damsel's father, said
Ruth 2. 11 thou hast left thy father and thy mother

Ruth 4. 17 he (is) the father of Jesse, the father of D.
1 Sa. 2. 25 they hearkened not unto..their father
2. 27 Did I..appear unto the house of thy fath.
2. 28 did I give unto the house of thy father
2. 30 thy house, and the house of thy father
2. 31 I will cut off..the arm of thy father's h.
9. 3 And the asses of Kish Saul's father were
10. 2 thy father hath left the care of the asses
10. 12 But who (is) their father? Therefore it
14. 1 let us go over..But he told not his father
14. 27 Jonathan heard not when his father ch.
14. 28 Thy father straitly charged the people
14. 29 Then said Jonathan, My father hath tro.
14. 51 Kish (was) the father of Saul..Ner the f.
17. 15 David went..to feed his father's sheep at
17. 25 and make his father's house free in Israel
17. 34 Thy servant kept his father's sheep, and
18. 2 would let him go no more..to his father's
18. 18 what (is) my life, (or) my father's family
19. 2 Saul my father seeketh to kill thee: now
19. 3 I will go out and stand beside my father
19. 3 I will commune with my father of thee
19. 4 spake good of David unto Saul his father
20. 1 and what (is) my sin before thy father
20. 2 behold, my father will do nothing either
20. 2 why should my father hide this thing
20. 3 Thy father certainly knoweth that I have
20. 6 If thy father at all miss me, then say
20. 8 why shouldest thou bring me to thy fat.?
20. 9 that evil were determined by my father
20. 10 what (if) thy father answer thee roughly?
20. 12 when I have sounded my father about
20. 13 but if it please my father (to do) thee evil
20. 13 with thee, as he hath been with my father
20. 32 Jonathan answered Saul his father, and
20. 33 knew that it was determined of his father
20. 34 was grieved for David, because his father
22. 1 when..all his father's house heard (it)
22. 3 Let my father and my mother, I pray
22. 11 Ahimelech..and all his father's house
22. 15 (nor) to all the house of my father: for
22. 16 Thou shalt surely die..and all thy father's
22. 22 of all the persons of thy father's house
23. 17 Fear not: for the hand of Saul my father
23. 17 and that also Saul my father knoweth
24. 11 Moreover, my father, see, yea, see the
24. 21 wilt not destroy my name out of my fat.
2 Sa. 2. 32 buried him in the sepulchre of his father
3. 7 Wherefore hast thou gone in unto my f.
3. 8 kindness this day unto the house of..thy f.
3. 29 Let it rest..on all his father's house
6. 21 the LORD, which chose me before thy fa.
7. 14 I will be his father, and he shall be my
9. 7 I will..show..kindness for..thy father's
9. 7 will restore..all the land of Saul thy fa.
10. 2 as his father showed kindness unto me
10. 2 David sent to comfort him..for his father
10. 3 thou that David doth honour thy father
13. 5 when thy father cometh to see thee, say
14. 9 the iniquity (be) on me, and on my father's
15. 34 (as) I (have been) thy father's servant hi.
16. 3 shall..restore..the kingdom of my father
16. 19 as I have served in thy father's presence
16. 21 Go in unto thy father's concubines, which
16. 22 Absalom went in unto his father's concu.
17. 8 For, said Hushai, thou knowest thy father
17. 8 thy father (is) a man of war, and will not
17. 10 for all Israel knoweth that thy father (is)
17. 23 was buried in the sepulchre of his father
19. 28 For all (of) my father's house were but
19. 37 by the grave of my father, and of my
21. 14 Zelah, in the sepulchre of Kish his father
24. 17 Let thine hand..be against..my father's
1 Ki. 1. 6 his father had not displeased him at any
2. 12 Solomon upon the throne of..his father
2. 24 set me on the throne of David my father
2. 26 barest the ark..before David my father
2. 26 been afflicted in all wherein my father
2. 31 from me, and from the house of my fat.
2. 32 and slew them with the sword, my father
2. 44 that thou didst to David my father
3. 3 walking in the statutes of David his fat.
3. 6 Thou..showed unto thy servant..my fa.
3. 7 thy servant king instead of..my father
3. 14 as thy father David did walk, then I will
5. 1 anointed him king in the room of his fa.
5. 3 Thou knowest how that David my father
5. 5 as the LORD spake unto David my father
6. 12 which I spake unto David thy father
7. 14 his father (was) a man of Tyre, a worker
7. 51 brought in the things which D. his father
8. 15 spake with his mouth unto David my fa.
8. 17 it was in the heart of David my father to
8. 18 And the LORD said unto David my father
8. 20 I am risen up in the room of D. my father
8. 24 Who hast kept with thy servant D. my f.
8. 25 God..keep with thy servant David my f.
8. 26 thou spakest unto thy servant D. my fa.
9. 4 as David thy father walked, in integrity
9. 5 as I promised to David thy father, saying
11. 4 as (was) the heart of David his father
11. 6 went not fully after the LORD, as..his fa.
11. 12 I will not do it for David thy father's sake
11. 17 certain Edomites of his father's servants
11. 27 repaired the breaches of the city of..his f.
11. 33 have not walked..as (did) David his father
11. 43 slept with his fathers..of David his fat.
12. 4 Thy father made our yoke grievous: now
12. 4 make thou the grievous service of thy f.
12. 6 men, that stood before Solomon his father
12. 9 Make the yoke which thy father did put
12. 10 Thy father made our yoke heavy, but make

1 Ki. 12. 10 shall be thicker than my father's loins
12. 11 now whereas my father did lade you with
12. 11 my father hath chastised you with whips
12. 14 My father made your yoke heavy, and I
12. 14 my father (also) chastised you with whips
13. 11 them they told also to their father
13. 12 their father said unto them, What way
15. 3 he walked in all the sins of his father
15. 3 not perfect..as the heart of David his f.
15. 11 Asa did..right..as (did) David his father
15. 15 he brought in the things which his father
15. 19 (and) between my father and thy father
15. 24 in the city of David his father, and
15. 26 and walked in the way of his father, and
18. 18 but thou, and thy father's house, in that
19. 20 Let me, I pray thee, kiss my father and
20. 34 cities which my father took from thy fa.
20. 34 thou shalt make streets..as my father
22. 43 walked in all the ways of Asa his father
22. 46 which remained in the days of his father
22. 50 was buried..in the city of David his fath.
22. 52 walked in the way of his father, and in
22. 53 according to all that his father had done
2 Ki. 2. 12 My father, my father! the chariot of Isr.
3. 2 he wrought evil..but not like his father
3. 2 put away the image of Baal that his father
3. 13 get thee to the prophets of thy father
4. 18 he went out to his father to the reapers
4. 19 he said unto his father, My head, my he.
5. 13 My father, (if) the prophet had bid thee
6. 21 My father, shall I smite (them)? shall I
9. 25 rode together after Ahab his father, the
10. 3 set (him) on his father's throne, and fight
13. 14 O my father, my father! the chariot of I.
13. 25 out of the hand of Jehoahaz his father by
14. 3 yet not like David his father: he did
14. 3 according to all things as Joash his father
14. 5 slew his servants which had slain..his fa.
14. 21 and made him king instead of his father
15. 3 according to all that his father Amaziah
15. 34 he did according to all that his father U.
15. 38 was buried..in the city of David his fat.
16. 2 did not..right..like David his father
18. 3 according to all that David his father did
20. 5 Thus saith..the God of David thy father
21. 3 the high places which Hezekiah his fath.
21. 20 he did..evil..as his father Manasseh did
21. 21 he walked in all the way that his father
21. 22 And he forsook the LORD God of his fat.
22. 2 walked in all the way of David his father
23. 30 and made him king in his father's stead
23. 34 king in the room of Josiah his father, and
24. 9 according to all that his father had done
1 Ch. 2. 17 the father of Amasa (was) Jether the Ish.
2. 21 to the daughter of Machir the father of
2. 23 (belonged) to the sons of Machir, the fat.
2. 24 Hezron's wife, bare him Ashur the father
2. 42 Mesha his first born, which (was) the fat.
2. 42 the sons of Mareshah the father of Heb.
2. 44 Shema begat Raham the father of Jorko.
2. 45 and Maon (was) the father of Beth-zur
2. 49 She bare also Shaaph the father of Mad.
2. 49 Sheva the father of Machbenah, and the f.
2. 50, 52 Shobal the father of Kirjath-jearim
2. 51 father of Bethlehem, Hareph the father
2. 55 Hemath, the father of the house of Rec.
4. 3 these (were of) the father of Etam; Jezr.
4. 4 the father of Gedor, and Ezer the father
4. 5 Ashur the father of Tekoa had two wives
4. 11 begat Mehir, which (was) the father of Es.
4. 12 and Tehinnah the father of Irnahash
4. 14 Joab, the father of the valley of Charas.
4. 17 and Ishbah the father of Eshtemoa
4. 18 Jehudijah bare Jered the father of Gedor
4. 18 father of Socho, and Jekuthiel the father
4. 19 the father of Keilah the Garmite, and Es.
4. 21 father of Lecah, and Laadah, the father
5. 1 forasmuch as he defiled his father's bed
7. 14 the Aramitess bare Machir the father of
7. 22 And Ephraim their father mourned many
7. 31 Malchiel, who (is) the father of Birzavith
7. 40 children of Asher, heads of (their) father's
8. 29 And at Gibeon dwelt the father of Gibeon
9. 19 his brethren, of the house of his father
9. 35 And in Gibeon dwelt the father of Gibeon
12. 28 of his father's house twenty and two cap.
17. 13 I will be his father, and he shall be my
19. 2 because his father showed kindness to me
19. 2 sent..to comfort him concerning his fat.
19. 3 Thinkest..that David doth honour thy f.
21. 17 Let thine hand..be on me, and on my fa.
22. 10 shall be my son, and I (will be) his father
23. 11 one reckoning, according to (their) fath.
24. 2 Nadab and Abihu died before their father
24. 19 orderings..under Aaron their father, as
25. 3 under the hands of their father Jeduthun
25. 6 these (were) under the hands of their fat.
26. 6 ruled throughout the house of their fat.
26. 10 he was not the first born, yet his father
28. 4 chose me before all the house of my fath.
28. 4 the house of Judah the house of my fat.
28. 4 among the sons of my father he liked me
28. 6 have chosen him..and I will be his father
28. 9 my son, know thou the God of thy father
29. 10 Blessed (be) thou, LORD God of Israel our f.
29. 23 Solomon sat..instead of David his father
2 Ch. 1. 8 showed great mercy unto David my fath.
1. 9 let thy promise unto David my father be
2. 3 As thou didst deal with David my father
2. 7 men..whom David my father did provide
2. 13 sent a cunning man..of Huram my fath.
2. 14 his father (was) a man of Tyre, skilful to
2 Ch. 2. 14 cunning men of my lord David thy father
2. 17 numbering wherewith David his father
3. 1 LORD appeared unto David his father, in
4. 16 The pots also..did Huram his father
5. 1 brought..the things that David his father
6. 4 which he spake with his mouth to my fa.
6. 7 Now it was in the heart of David my fat.
6. 8 But the LORD said to David my father
6. 10 risen up in the room of David my father
6. 15, 16 with thy servant David my father that
7. 17 if thou wilt walk..as David thy father
7. 18 as I have covenanted with David thy fat.
8. 14 according to the order of David his father
9. 31 was buried in the city of David his father
10. 4 Thy father made our yoke grievous: now
10. 4 ease..the grievous servitude of thy father
10. 6 that had stood before Solomon his father
10. 9 Ease somewhat the yoke that thy father
10. 10 Thy father made our yoke heavy, but
10. 10 (finger) shall be thicker than my father's
10. 11 For whereas my father put a heavy yoke
10. 11, 14 my father chastised you with whips
10. 14 My father made your yoke heavy, but I
15. 18 he brought..the things that his father
16. 3 (there was) between my father and thy f.
17. 3 cities of Ephraim, which Asa his father
17. 4 But sought to the LORD God of his father
20. 32 And he walked in the way of Asa his fa.
21. 3 And their father gave them great gifts of
21. 4 was risen up to the kingdom of his father
21. 12 saith the LORD God of David thy father
21. 12 not walked in the ways of..thy father
21. 13 hast slain thy brethern of thy father's ho.
22. 4 counsellors, after the death of his father
24. 22 the kindness which Jehoiada his father
25. 3 slew his servants that had killed..his fat.
26. 1 made him king in the room of his father
26. 4 according to all that his father Amaziah
27. 2 according to all that his father Uzziah did
28. 1 he did not..right..like David his father
29. 2 according to all that David his father had
33. 22 he did..evil..as did Manasseh his father
33. 22 carved images which Manasseh his father
33. 23 humbled not himself..as Manasseh his f.
34. 2 walked in the ways of David his father
34. 3 to seek after the God of David his father
36. 1 made him king in his father's stead in
Neh. 1. 6 both I and my father's house have sinned
Esth. 2. 7 for she had neither father nor mother
2. 7 when her father and mother were dead
4. 14 and thy father's house shall be destroyed
Job 15. 10 very aged men, much elder than thy fat.
17. 14 have said to corruption, Thou (art) my f.
29. 16 I (was) a father to the poor: and the
31. 18 he was brought up with me, as (with) a f.
38. 28 Hath the rain a father? or who hath
42. 15 their father gave them inheritance among
Psa. 27. 10 When my father and my mother forsake
45. 10 forget..thine own people, and thy father's
68. 5 A father of the fatherless, and a judge of
89. 26 Thou (art) my Father, my God, and the
103. 13 Like as a father pitieth (his) children, (so)
Prov. 1. 8 My son, hear the instruction of thy father
3. 12 even as a father the son (in whom) he
4. 1 Hear..the instruction of a father, and
4. 3 For I was my father's son, tender and
6. 20 My son, keep thy father's commandment
10. 1 A wise son maketh a glad father: but a
13. 1 A wise son (heareth) his father's instruc.
15. 5 A fool despiseth his father's instruction
15. 20 A wise son maketh a glad father: but a
17. 21 and the father of a fool hath no joy
17. 25 A foolish son (is) a grief to his father
19. 13 foolish son (is) the calamity of his father
19. 26 He that wasteth (his) father, (and) chaseth
20. 20 Whoso curseth his father or his mother
23. 22 Hearken unto thy father that begat thee
23. 24 The father of the righteous shall greatly
23. 25 Thy father and thy mother shall be glad
27. 10 Thine own friend, and thy father's friend
28. 7 companion of riotous (men) shameth his f.
28. 24 Whoso robbeth his father or his mother
29. 3 Whoso loveth wisdom rejoiceth his father
30. 11 a generation (that) curseth their father
30. 17 The eye (that) mocketh at (his) father
Isa. 3. 6 his brother, of the house of his father
7. 17 LORD shall bring..upon thy father's ho.
8. 4 For before the child..cry, My father, and
9. 6 The mighty God, The everlasting Father
22. 21 he shall be a father to the inhabitants of
22. 23 be for a glorious throne to his father's ho.
22. 24 all the glory of his father's house, the
38. 5 saith the LORD, the God of David thy fa.
38. 19 the father to the children shall make
43. 27 Thy first father hath sinned, and thy tea.
45. 10 Woe unto him that saith unto (his) father
51. 2 Look unto Abraham your father, and unto
58. 14 feed thee with the heritage of..thy father
63. 16 Doubtless thou (art) our Father, though
63. 16 thou, O LORD, (art) our Father, our Red.
64. 8 But now, O LORD, thou (art) our Father
Jer. 2. 27 Saying to a stock, Thou (art) my father
3. 19 I said, Thou shalt call me, My father
12. 6 thy brethren, and the house of thy father
16. 7 cup of consolation to drink for their fath.
20. 15 the man who brought tidings to my fath.
22. 11 which reigned instead of Josiah his father
22. 15 Did not thy father eat and drink, and do
31. 9 for I am a father to Israel, and Ephraim
35. 6 for Jonadab the son of Rechab our father
35. 8 have we obeyed..the son of Rechab our f.
35. 10 according to all that Jonadab our father
Jer. 35. 14 they drink none, but obey their father's
35. 16 performed the commandment of their fa.
35. 18 Because ye have obeyed..your father
Eze. 16. 3 thy father (was) an Amorite, and thy m.
16. 45 an Hittite, and your father an Amorite
18. 4 as the soul of the father, so also the soul
18. 14 a son, that seeth all his father's sins
18. 17 shall not die for the iniquity of his father
18. 18 his father, because he cruelly oppressed
18. 19 doth not the son bear the iniquity of the f.
18. 20 son shall not bear the iniquity of the fath.
18. 20 neither shall the father bear the iniquity
22. 7 In thee have they set light by father and
22. 10 In thee have they discovered their fath.
22. 11 hath humbled his sister, his father's dau.
44. 25 but for father, or for mother, or for son
Amos 2. 7 a man and his father will go in unto the
Mic. 7. 6 For the son dishonoureth the father, the
Zech. 13. 3 his father and his mother that begat him
Mal. 1. 6 A son honoureth (his) father, and a serv.
1. 6 if then I (be) a father, where (is) mine h.
2. 10 Have we not all one father? hath not one

2. *Father, ancestor*, אַב *ab.*

Dan. 5. 2 golden and silver vessels which his father
5. 11 and in the days of thy father, light and
5. 11 whom the king Nebuchadnezzar thy fath.
5. 11 thy father, made master of the magicians
5. 13 whom the king my father brought out of
5. 18 God gave Nebuchadnezzar thy father a

3. *Father, ancestor*, πατήρ *patēr.*

Matt. 2. 22 did reign in Judea in the room of his fa.
3. 9 We have Abraham to (our) father: for I
4. 21 in a ship with Zebedee their father
4. 22 immediately left the ship and their fath.
5. 16 and glorify your Father which is in heav.
5. 45 That ye may be the children of your Fat.
5. 48 Be ye therefore perfect, even as your Fa.
6. 1 otherwise ye have no reward of your Fa.
6. 4 thy Father which seeth in secret himself
6. 6 pray to thy Father which is in secret
6. 6 and thy Father which seeth in secret
6. 8 for your Father knoweth what things ye
6. 9 pray ye, Our Father which art in heaven
6. 14 your heavenly Father will also forgive
6. 15 neither will your Father forgive your
6. 18 but unto thy Father which is in secret
6. 18 and thy Father, which seeth in secret
6. 26 yet your heavenly Father feedeth them
6. 32 for your heavenly Father knoweth that
7. 11 how much more shall your Father which
7. 21 but he that doeth the will of my Father
8. 21 Lord, suffer me first to go and bury my f.
10. 20 but the Spirit of your Father which spea.
10. 21 brother shall deliver up..and the father
10. 29 not fall on the ground without your Fat.
10. 32 him will I confess also before my Father
10. 33 him will I also deny before my Father
10. 35 I am come to set a man..against his fat.
10. 37 He that loveth father or mother more
11. 25 said..O Father, Lord of heaven and earth
11. 26 Even so, Father: for so it seemed good in
11. 27 All..are delivered unto me of my Father
11. 27 no man knoweth the Son, but the Father
11. 27 neither knoweth any man the Father, save
12. 50 For whosoever shall do the will of my F.
13. 43 as the sun in the kingdom of their Father
15. 4 saying, Honour thy father and mother
15. 4 He that curseth father or mother, let
15. 5 Whosoever shall say to..father or..mot.
15. 6 And honour not his father or his mother
15. 13 Every plant, which my heavenly Father
16. 17 hath not..but my Father which is in he.
16. 27 the Son..shall come in the glory of his F.
18. 10 behold the face of my Father which is in
18. 14 Even so it is not the will of your Father
18. 19 it shall be done for them of my Father
18. 35 So likewise shall my heavenly Father do
19. 5 For this cause shall a man leave father
19. 19 Honour thy father and (thy) mother; and
19. 29 [every one that hath forsaken father or m.]
20. 23 for whom it is prepared of my Father
21. 31 Whether of them..did the will of..father?
23. 9 And call no (man) your father upon the
23. 9 for one is your Father, which is in heaven
24. 36 not the angels of heaven, but my Father
25. 34 Come, ye blessed of my Father, inherit
26. 29 when I drink it new with you in my Fat.
26. 39 prayed, saying, O my Father, if it be pos.
26. 42 O my Father if this cup may not pass aw.
26. 53 Thinkest..that I cannot..pray to my F.
28. 19 baptizing them in the name of the Father
Mark 1. 20 they left their father Zebedee in the ship
5. 40 taketh the father and the mother of the
7. 10 Moses said, Honour thy father and thy
7. 10 Whoso curseth father or mother, let him
7. 11 If a man shall say to his father or mother
7. 12 suffer him no more to do ought for his f.
8. 38 when he cometh in the glory of his Fath.
9. 21 he asked his father, How long is it ago
9. 24 straightway the father of the child cried
10. 7 For this cause shall a man leave his fat.
10. 19 Thou knowest..Honour thy father and m.
10. 29 There is no man that hath left house..or f
11. 10 Blessed (be) the kingdom of our father
11. 25 that your Father also which is in heaven
11. 26 [If ye do not forgive, neither will your F.]
13. 12 brother shall betray..and the father the
13. 32 of that day..knoweth no man..but the F
14. 36 Abba, Father, all things (are) possible
15. 21 they compel one Simon..father of Alexa.
Luke 1. 32 God shall give..him the throne of his fa.

Luke 1. 59 Zacharias, after the name of his father
1. 62 they made signs to his father, how he
1. 67 his father Zacharias was filled with the
1. 73 The oath which he sware to our father A.
2. 48 thy father and I have sought thee sorrow.
2. 49 wist ye not that I must be about my Fat.
3. 8 We have Abraham to (our) father: for I
6. 36 Be ye..merciful, as your Father also is
8. 51 the father and the mother of the maiden
9. 26 come in his own glory, and (in his) Fath.
9. 42 and delivered him again to his father
9. 59 Lord, suffer me first to go and bury my f.
10. 21 I thank thee, O Father, Lord of heaven
10. 21 even so, Father; for so it seemed good
10. 22 All things are delivered to me of my Fat.
10. 22 no man knoweth who the Son is, but the F.
11. 2 When ye pray, say, Our Father which art
11. 11 If a son shall ask bread of..a father, will
11. 13 how much more shall..heavenly Father
12. 30 your Father knoweth that ye have need
12. 32 it is your Father's good pleasure to give
12. 53 The father shall be divided against the
12. 53 and the son against the father; the mot.
14. 26 If any..come to me, and hate not his fat.
15. 12 younger of them said to (his) father, Fat.
15. 17 How many hired servants of my father's
15. 18 I will arise and go to my father, and will
15. 18 Father, I have sinned against Heaven
15. 20 And he arose and came to his father
15. 20 when he was yet a great way off, his fat.
15. 21 the son said unto him, Father, I have s.
15. 22 the father said to his servants, Bring
15. 27 thy father hath killed the fatted calf
15. 28 therefore came his father out, and entrea.
15. 29 And he answering said to (his) father, Lo
16. 24 And he cried and said, Father Abraham
16. 27 Then he said, I pray thee therefore, fat.
16. 27 thou wouldest send him to my father's h.
16. 30 And he said, Nay, father Abraham: but
18. 20 Thou knowest..Honour thy father and
22. 29 as my Father hath appointed unto me
22. 42 Saying, Father, if thou be willing, remove
23. 34 [Then said Jesus, Father, forgive them]
23. 46 Father, into thy hands I commend my
24. 49 I send the promise of my Father upon you
John 1. 14 glory as of the only begotten of the Fath.
1. 18 Son, which is in the bosom of the Father
2. 16 make not my Father's house an house of
3. 35 The Father loveth the Son, and hath giv.
4. 12 Art thou greater than our father Jacob
4. 21 nor yet at Jerusalem, worship the Father
4. 23 the true worshippers shall worship the F.
4. 23 for the Father seeketh such to worship
4. 53 So the father knew that (it was) at the
5. 17 My Father worketh hitherto, and I work
5. 18 but said also that God was his Father
5. 19 nothing..but what he seeth the Father
5. 20 For the Father loveth the Son, and show.
5. 21 For as the Father raiseth up the dead, and
5. 22 For the Father judgeth no man, but hath
5. 23 the Son, even as they honour the Father
5. 23 honoureth not the Father which hath
5. 26 For as the Father hath life in himself
5. 30 but the will of [the Father] which hath
5. 36 for the works which the Father hath
5. 36 bear witness of me, that the Father hath
5. 37 the Father himself, which hath sent me
5. 43 I am come in my Father's name, and ye
5. 45 Do not think..I will accuse..to the Fath.
6. 27 Son..for him hath God the Father sealed
6. 32 but my Father giveth you the true bread
6. 37 All that the Father giveth me shall come
6. 39 And this is the [Father's] will which hath
6. 42 Is not this Jesus..whose father and mot.
6. 44 No man can come to me, except the Fat.
6. 45 and hath learned of the Father, cometh
6. 46 Not that any man hath seen the Father
6. 46 he which is of God, he hath seen the Fat.
6. 57 Father hath sent me, and I live by the F.
8. 16 not alone, but I and the Father that sent
8. 18 the Father that sent me beareth witness
8. 19 said they unto him, Where is thy Father?
8. 19 Ye neither know me, nor my Father: if
8. 19 ye should have known my Father also
8. 27 understood not that he spake..of the Fat.
8. 28 but as my Father hath taught me, I speak
8. 29 [the Father] hath not left me alone; for
8. 38 I speak that..I have seen with my Fath.
8. 38 ye do that..ye have seen with your father
8. 39 They answered..him, Abraham is our fa.
8. 41 Ye do the deeds of your father. Then said
8. 41 born of fornication; we have one Father
8. 42 If God were your Father, ye would love
8. 44 Ye are of (your) father the devil, and the
8. 44 lusts of your father ye will do. He was
8. 44 a lie..for he is a liar, and the father of it
8. 49 I honour my Father, and ye do dishonour
8. 53 Art thou greater than our father Abraham
8. 54 it is my Father that honoureth me; of
8. 56 Your father Abraham rejoiced to see my;
10. 15 As the Father knoweth me, even so know
10. 17 Therefore doth my Father love me, beca.
10. 18 This commandment..I received of my F.
10. 25 the works that I do in my Father's name
10. 29 My Father, which gave (them) me, is
10. 29 is able to pluck..out of my Father's hand
10. 30 I and (my) Father are one
10. 32 Many..works have I showed..from my F.
10. 36 say ye of him, whom the Father hath
10. 37 If I do not the works of my Father, beli.
10. 38 ye may know and believe that the Father
11. 41 Father, I thank thee that thou hast heard
John 12. 26 if any man serve me, him will (my) Father
12. 27 what shall I say? Father, save me from
12. 28 Father, glorify thy name. Then came
12. 49 the Father which sent me, he gave me a
12. 50 I speak therefore, even as the Father said
13. 1 depart out of this world unto the Father
13. 3 Jesus knowing that the Father had given
14. 2 In my Father's house are many mansions
14. 6 no man cometh unto the Father, but by
14. 7 ye should have known my Father also
14. 8 Lord, show us the Father, and it sufficeth
14. 9 he that hath seen me hath seen the Fath.
14. 9 how sayest thou (then), Show us the Fa.
14. 10 that I am in the Father, and the Father
14. 10 I speak not of myself: but the Father
14. 11 that I (am) in the Father, and the Father
14. 12 greater..because I go unto my Father
14. 13 that the Father may be glorified in the
14. 16 I will pray the Father, and he shall give
14. 20 ye shall know that I (am) in my Father
14. 21 he that loveth me shall be loved of my F.
14. 23 my Father will love him, and we will come
14. 24 not mine, but the Father's which sent me
14. 26 But the Comforter..whom the Father
14. 28 I go unto the Father; for my Father is
14. 31 the world may know that I love the Fa.
14. 31 as the Father gave me commandment
15. 1 I am the true vine, and my Father is the
15. 8 Herein is my Father glorified, that ye
15. 9 As the Father hath loved me, so have I
15. 10 as I have kept my Father's command.
15. 15 all things that I have heard of my Father
15. 16 whatsoever ye shall ask of the Father in
15. 23 He that hateth me hateth my Father also
15. 24 now have they..hated both me and my F.
15. 26 whom I will send unto you from the F.
15. 26 truth, which proceedeth from the Father
16. 3 because they have not known the Father
16. 10 Of righteousness, because I go to my F.
16. 15 All things that the Father hath are mine
16. 16 [ye shall see me; because I go to the F.]
16. 17 What is this..Because I go to the Father?
16. 23 Whatsoever ye shall ask the Father in
16. 25 but I shall show you plainly of the Father
16. 26 I say not..I will pray the Father for you
16. 27 For the Father himself loveth you, beca.
16. 28 I came forth from the Father, and am
16. 28 I leave the world, and go to the Father
16. 32 yet I am not alone, because the Father
17. 1 Father, the hour is come; glorify thy Son
17. 5 And now, O Father, glorify thou me with
17. 11 Holy Father, keep through thine own
17. 21 That they all may be one; as thou, Father
17. 24 Father, I will that they also whom thou
17. 25 O righteous Father, the world hath not
18. 11 the cup which my Father hath given me
20. 17 for I am not yet ascended to my Father
20. 17 I ascend unto my Father, and your Father
20. 21 as (my) Father hath sent me, even so send
Acts 1. 4 but wait for the promise of the Father
1. 7 which the Father hath put in his own
2. 33 having received of the Father the promise
7. 2 The God of glory appeared unto our fa.
7. 4 from thence, when his father was dead
7. 14 Then sent Joseph, and called his father
7. 20 Moses was..nourished up in his father's
16. 1 the son of a..Jewess,..but his father
16. 3 they knew all that his father was a Greek
28. 8 it came to pass, that the father of Publius
Rom. 1. 7 Grace to you and peace from God our F.
4. 1 What shall we then say that..our [father]
4. 11 that he might be the father of all them
4. 12 the father of circumcision to them who
4. 12 in the steps of that faith of our father
4. 16 of Abraham; who is the father of us all
4. 17 I have made thee a father of many natio.
4. 18 might become the father of many nations
6. 4 from the dead by the glory of the Father
8. 15 the spirit..whereby we cry, Abba, Father
9. 10 Rebecca..conceived..by our father Isaac
15. 6 even the Father of our Lord Jesus Christ
1 Co. 1. 3 Grace..and peace, from God our Father
5. 1 that one should have his father's wife
8. 6 But to us..one God, the Father, of whom
15. 24 delivered up the kingdom to..the Father
2 Co. 1. 2 Grace..and peace from God our Father
1. 3 Blessed (be) God, even the Father of our
1. 3 the Father of mercies, and the God of all
6. 18 And will be a Father unto you, and ye
11. 31 The God and Father of our Lord Jesus C.
Gal. 1. 1 but by Jesus Christ, and God the Father
1. 3 Grace..and peace from God the Father
1. 4 according to the will of God and our Fa.
4. 2 until the time appointed of the father
4. 6 sent forth the spirit..crying, Abba, Fath.
Eph. 1. 2 Grace..and peace, from God our Father
1. 3 Blessed (be) the God and Father of our L.
1. 17 the God of our Lord Jesus Christ, the Fa.
2. 18 have access by one Spirit unto the Fath.
3. 14 I bow my knees unto the Father of our L.
4. 6 One God and Father of all, who (is) above
5. 20 Giving thanks..unto God and the Father
5. 31 For this cause shall a man leave his fat.
6. 2 Honour thy father and mother; which
6. 23 love with faith, from God the Father and
Phil. 1. 2 Grace..and peace, from God our Father
2. 11 confess..to the glory of God the Father
2. 22 as a son with the father, he hath served
4. 20 Now unto God and our Father (be) glory
Col. 1. 2 Grace..and peace, from God our Father
1. 3 We give thanks to God and the Father of
1. 12 Giving thanks unto the Father, which
Col. 2. 2 [of God, and of the Father, and of Christ]
3. 17 giving thanks to God and the Father by
1 Th. 1. 1 of the Thessalonians..in God the Father
1. 1 Grace..and peace, from God [our Father]
1. 3 in the sight of God and our Father
2. 11 we exhorted..as a father (doth) his chil.
3. 11 Now God himself and our Father, and our
3. 13 God, even our Father, at the coming of
2 Th. 1. 1 God our Father and the Lord Jesus Chr.
1. 2 Grace..and peace, from God our Father
2. 16 God, even our Father, which hath loved
1 Ti. 1. 2 peace, from God our Father and Jesus
5. 1 Rebuke not an elder, but entreat..as a fa.
2 Ti. 1. 2 peace, from God the Father and Christ
Titus 1. 4 peace, from God the Father and the
Phm. 3 peace, from God our Father and the L.
Heb. 1. 5 I will be to him a Father, and he shall be
7. 10 he was yet in the loins of his father when
12. 7 what son is he whom the father chasten
12. 9 be in subjection unto the Father of
Jas. 1. 17 Every good gift..cometh down from the F.
1. 27 Pure religion..before God and the Fath.
2. 21 Was not Abraham our father justified by
3. 9 Therewith bless we God, even the Father
1 Pe. 1. 2 according to the foreknowledge of..the F.
1. 3 Blessed (be) the God and Father of our L
1. 17 if ye call on the Father, who without
2 Pe. 1. 17 For he received from God the Father ho
1 Jo. 1. 2 that eternal life which was with the Fath.
1. 3 truly our fellowship (is) with the Father
2. 1 we have an advocate with the Father
2. 13 because ye have known the Father
2. 15 world, the love of the Father is not in him
2. 16 the pride of life, is not of the Father, but
2. 22 he is antichrist, that denieth the Father
2. 23 denieth the Son, the same hath not the F.
2. 24 shall continue in the Son, and in the Fat.
3. 1 Behold what manner of love the Father
4. 14 do testify that the Father sent the Son
5. 7 in heaven, the Father, the Word, and the
2 Jo. 3 peace, from God the Father, and from the
3 Jesus Christ, the Son of the Father, in
4 have received a commandment from the F.
9 he hath both the Father and the Son
Jude 1 them that are sanctified by God the Fath.
Rev. 1. 6 made us..priests unto God and his Fath.
2. 27 rule..even as I received of my Father
3. 5 I will confess his name before my Father
3. 21 and am set down with my Father in his
14. 1 having his Father's name written in their

FATHER, whose —

Son of, בֵּן *ben.*

Lev. 24. 10 whose father (was) an Egyptian, went out

FATHER, murderer of a —

Smiter of a father, πατραλῴας *patralōas.*

1 Ti. 1. 9 for murderers of fathers and murderers

FATHER, without —

Without a father, ἀπάτωρ *apatōr.*

Heb. 7. 3 Without father, without mother, without

FATHER (in) law —

1. *Husband's father,* חָם *cham.*

Gen. 38. 13 Behold, thy father in law goeth up to
38. 25 she sent to her father in law, saying, By
1 Sa. 4. 19 and that her father in law and her husb.
4. 21 because of her father in law and her hus.

2. *Wife's father,* חֹתֵן *chothen.*

Exod. 3. 1 Moses kept the flock of..his father in law
4. 18 Moses..returned to Jethro his father in l.
18. 1 When Jethro..Moses' father in law, heard
18. 2 Then Jethro, Moses' father in law, took
18. 5 Moses' father in law, came with his sons
18. 6 I thy father in law Jethro am come unto
18. 7 Moses went out to meet his father in law
18. 8 Moses told his father in law all that the
18. 12 Moses' father in law, took a burnt offering
18. 12 came..to eat..with Moses' father in law
18. 14 when Moses' father in law saw all that he
18. 15 Moses said unto his father in law, Because
18. 17 Moses' father in law said unto him, The
18. 24 Moses hearkened to..his father in law
18. 27 And Moses let his father in law depart
Num 10. 29 said unto Hobab..Moses' father in law
Judg. 1. 16 children of the Kenite, Moses' father in l.
4. 11 of the children of Hobab, the father in law
19. 4 And his father in law, the damsel's father
19. 7 when the man rose up..his father in law
19. 9 his father in law, the damsel's father, said

3. *Father in law,* πενθερός *pentheros.*

John 18. 13 to Annas first: for he was father in law

FATHERLESS —

1. *Orphan, fatherless,* יָתוֹם *yathom.*

Exod 22. 24 shall be widows, and your children fath.
Deut 10. 18 He doth execute the judgment of the fa.
14. 29 the fatherless, and the widow, which (are)
16. 11, 14 the fatherless, and the widow, that
24. 17 Thou shalt not pervert..the fatherless
24. 19, 20, 21 shall be for the stranger, for the f.
26. 12 and hast given (it) unto..the fatherless
26. 13 also have given them..to the fatherless
27. 19 Cursed (be) he that perverteth..the fath.
Job 6. 27 Yea, ye overwhelm the fatherless, and ye
22. 9 the arms of the fatherless have been
24. 3 They drive away the ass of the fatherless
24. 9 They pluck the fatherless from the breast
29. 12 Because I delivered the..fatherless
31. 17 and the fatherless hath not eaten thereof
31. 21 If I have lifted up..against the fatherless

Psa. 10. 14 for..thou art the helper of the fatherless
10. 18 To judge the fatherless and the oppressed
68. 5 A father of the fatherless, and a judge of
82. 3 Defend the poor and fatherless: do just.
94. 6 They slay..and murder the fatherless
109. 9 Let his children be fatherless, and his
109. 12 neither let there be any to favour his fa.
146. 9 The LORD..relieveth the fatherless and
Prov 23. 10 enter not into the fields of the fatherless
Isa. 1. 17 judge the fatherless, plead for the widow
1. 23 they judge not the fatherless, neither
9. 17 neither shall have mercy on their father.
10. 2 and (that) they may rob the fatherless!
Jer. 5. 28 they judge not the cause..of the fatherl.
7. 6 (If) ye oppress not the stranger, the fath.
22. 3 do no violence to the stranger, the fath.
49. 11 Leave thy fatherless children, I will pre.
Eze. 22. 7 in thee have they vexed the fatherless
Hos. 14. 3 for in thee the fatherless findeth mercy
Zech. 7. 10 And oppress not the widow, nor the fath.
Mal. 3. 5 against those that oppress..the fatherless

2. *There is not a father*, אֵין אָב *en ab.*
Lam. 5. 3 We are orphans and fatherless, our mot.

3. *Orphan*, ὀρφανός *orphanos.*
Jas. 1. 27 To visit the fatherless and widows in their

FATHERLESS child —
Orphan, fatherless, יָתוֹם *yathom.*
Exod 22. 22 shall not afflict any..fatherless child

FATHER'S brother —
Father's brother, uncle, דּוֹד *dod.*
Num 36. 11 were married unto their father's brothers'
2 Ki. 24. 17 made Mattaniah his father's brother king

FATHER'S sister —
Father's sister, aunt, דּוֹדָה *dodah.*
Exod. 6. 20 And Amram took..his father's sister, to

FATHERS —
1. *Fathers, ancestors*, אָבוֹת *aboth.*
Gen. 15. 15 And thou shalt go to thy fathers in peace
31. 3 Return unto the land of thy fathers, and
46. 34 even until now, both we..also our fathers
47. 3 Thy servants (are) shepherds..also our f.
47. 9 the years of the life of my fathers in the
47. 30 I will lie with my fathers, and thou shalt
48. 15 God, before whom my fathers Abraham
48. 16 and the name of my fathers Abraham and
48. 21 bring you again unto the land of your fa.
Exod. 3. 13 The God of your fathers hath sent me
3. 15, 16 The LORD God of your fathers, the G.
4. 5 believe that the LORD God of their fathers
6. 14 These (be) the heads of their fathers' ho.
6. 25 these (are) the heads of the fathers of the
10. 6 neither thy fathers, nor thy father's fat.
12. 3 according to the house of (their) fathers
13. 5 which he sware unto thy fathers to give
13. 11 as he sware unto thee and to thy fathers
20. 5 visiting the iniquity of the fathers upon
34. 7 visiting the iniquity of the fathers upon
Lev. 25. 41 unto the possession of his fathers shall
26. 39 in the iniquities of their fathers shall
26. 40 confess..the iniquity of their fathers
Num. 1. 2 by the house of their fathers, with the
1. 4 every one head of the house of his fathers
1. 16 princes of the tribes of their fathers, heads
1. 18 their families, by the house of their fath.
[So in v. 20, 22, 24, 26, 28, 30, 32, 34, 36, 38, 40, 42.]
1. 44 each one was for the house of his fathers
1. 45 by the house of their fathers, from twenty
1. 47 the Levites after the tribe of their fathers
2. 2 Every man..with the ensign of their fa.
2. 32 numbered..by the house of their fathers
2. 34 according to the house of their fathers
3. 15 Number..after the house of their fathers
3. 20 Levites according to the house of their f.
4. 2, 29, 38, 40, 42 by the house of their fathers
4. 22 throughout the houses of their fathers, by
4. 34, 46 and after the house of their fathers
7. 2 heads of the house of their fathers
11. 12 land which thou swarest unto their fath.
13. 2 of every tribe of their fathers shall ye
14. 18 visiting the iniquity of the fathers upon
14. 23 the land which I sware unto their fathers
17. 2 according to the house of (their) fathers
17. 3 for the head of the house of their fathers
17. 6 according to their fathers' houses, (even)
20. 15 How our fathers went down into Egypt
20. 15 and the Egyptians vexed us and our fat.
26. 2 throughout their fathers' house, all that
26. 55 the names of the tribes of their fathers
31. 26 and the chief fathers of the congregation
32. 8 Thus did your fathers, when I sent them
32. 14 ye are risen up in your fathers' stead, an
32. 28 chief fathers of the tribes of the children
33. 54 according to the tribes of your fathers
34. 14, 14 according to the house of their fathe.
36. 1 And the chief fathers of the families of
36. 1 the chief fathers of the children of Israel
36. 3 taken from the inheritance of our fathe.
36. 4, 7 inheritance of the tribe of our fathers
Deut. 1. 8 land..the LORD sware unto your fathe.
1. 11 The LORD God of your fathers make you
1. 21 as the LORD God of thy fathers hath said
1. 35 which I sware to give unto your fathers
4. 1 which the LORD God of your fathers giv.
4. 31 nor forget the covenant of thy fathers
4. 37 because he loved thy fathers, therefore he
5. 3 made not this covenant with our fathers
5. 9 visiting the iniquity of the fathers upon
Deut. 6. 3 as the LORD God of thy fathers hath pro.
6. 10 the land which he sware unto thy fathers
6. 18 which the LORD sware unto thy fathers
6. 23 the land which he sware unto our fathers
7. 8 oath which he had sworn unto your fath.
7. 12 the mercy which he sware unto thy fat.
7. 13 the land which he sware unto thy fathe.
8. 1 the land..the LORD sware unto your fat.
8. 3 humbled thee..neither did thy fathers
8. 16 with manna, which thy fathers knew not
8. 18 covenant which he sware unto thy fathe.
9. 5 the word..the LORD sware unto thy fat.
10. 11 the land, which I sware unto their fathe.
10. 15 the LORD had a delight in thy fathers to
10. 22 Thy fathers went down into Egypt with
11. 9, 21 which the LORD sware unto your fat.
12. 1 the land which the LORD God of thy fat.
13. 6 thou hast not known, thou, nor thy fath.
13. 17 as he hath sworn unto thy fathers
19. 8 as he hath sworn unto thy fathers, and
19. 8 land which he promised..unto thy fathers
24. 16 The fathers shall not be put to death for
24. 16 neither shall the children..for the fathe.
26. 3 which the LORD sware unto our fathers
26. 7 we cried unto the LORD God of our fath.
26. 15 as thou swarest unto our fathers, a land
27. 3 the LORD God of thy fathers hath promi.
28. 11 the land..the LORD sware unto thy fathe.
28. 36, 64 which neither thou nor thy fathers
29. 13 and as he hath sworn unto thy fathers
29. 25 covenant of the LORD God of their fathe.
30. 5 into the land which thy fathers possessed
30. 5 and multiply thee above thy fathers
30. 9 rejoice..as he rejoiced over thy fathers
30. 20 the land..the LORD sware unto thy fath.
31. 7 the LORD hath sworn unto their fathers
31. 16 Behold, thou shalt sleep with thy fathers
31. 20 the land which I sware unto their fathers
32. 17 to new (gods that) came..whom your fa.
Josh. 1. 6 the land which I sware unto their fathers
4. 21 When your children shall ask their fath.
5. 6 which the LORD sware unto their fathers
14. 1 and the heads of the fathers of the tribes
18. 3 land, which the LORD God of your fathers
19. 51 the heads of the fathers of the tribes of
21. 1 Then came near the heads of the fathers
21. 1 unto the heads of the fathers of the trib.
21. 43 which he sware to give unto their fathers
21. 44 to all that he sware unto their fathers
22. 14 an head of the house of their fathers
22. 28 Behold the pattern..which our fathers
24. 2 Thus saith the LORD..Your fathers dwelt
24. 6 And I brought your fathers out of Egypt
24. 6 Egyptians pursued after your fathers
24. 14 and put away the gods which your fath.
24. 15 whether the gods which your fathers
24. 17 the LORD..brought us up and our fathe.
Judg. 2. 10 generation were gathered unto their fat.
2. 12 they forsook the LORD God of their fath.
2. 17 turned..out of the way which their fath.
2. 19 corrupted (themselves) more than their f.
2. 20 my covenant..I commanded their fathers
2. 22 they will keep the way..as their fathers
3. 4 which he commanded their fathers by
6. 13 where (be) all his miracles which our fa.
21. 22 And it shall be, when their fathers or
1 Sa. 12. 6 brought your fathers up out of the land
12. 7 which he did to you and to your fathers
12. 8 and your fathers cried unto the LORD
12. 8 Moses..which brought forth your fathers
12. 15 against you, as (it was) against your fat.
2 Sa. 7. 12 and thou shalt sleep with thy fathers
1 Ki. 1. 21 when my lord..shall sleep with his fath.
2. 10 So David slept with his fathers, and was
8. 1 the chief of the fathers of the children
8. 21 covenant..which he made with our fath.
8. 34, 48 land which thou gavest unto their f.
8. 40 the land which thou gavest unto our fat.
8. 53 when thou broughtest our fathers out of
8. 57 as he was with our fathers: let him not
8. 58 statutes..which he commanded our fath.
9. 9 God, who brought forth their fathers out
11. 21 heard..that David slept with his fathers
11. 43 Solomon slept with his fathers, and was
13. 22 not come unto the sepulchre of thy fath.
14. 15 good land, which he gave to their fathers
14. 20 and he slept with his fathers, and Nadab
14. 22 above all that their fathers had done
14. 31 And Rehoboam slept with his fathers, and
14. 31 was buried with his fathers in the city of
15. 8 Abijam slept with his fathers; and they
15. 12 removed all the idols that his fathers
15. 24 And Asa slept with his fathers, and was
15. 24 buried with his fathers in the city of Da.
16. 6 Baasha slept with his fathers, and was
16. 28 Omri slept with his fathers, and was bu.
19. 4 for I (am) not better than my fathers
21. 3 give the inheritance of my fathers unto
21. 4 give thee the inheritance of my fathers
22. 40 So Ahab slept with his fathers; and Ah.
22. 50 And Jehosaphat slept with his fathers
22. 50 and was buried with his fathers in the
2 Ki. 8. 24 And Joram slept with his fathers, and
8. 24 was buried with his fathers in the city of
9. 28 buried him in his sepulchre with his fat.
10. 35 Jehu slept with his fathers: and they b.
12. 18 his fathers, kings of Judah, had dedicated
12. 21 they buried him with his fathers in the
13. 9 Jehoahaz slept with his fathers; and they
13. 13 Joash slept with his fathers; and Jerob.
14. 6 The fathers shall not be put to death for
14. 6 nor the children..for the fathers; but
2 Ki. 14. 16 Jehoash slept with his fathers, and was
14. 20 and he was buried..with his fathers in
14. 22 after that the king slept with his fathers
14. 29 Jeroboam slept with his fathers, (even)
15. 7 So Azariah slept with his fathers; and
15. 7 they buried him with his fathers in the
15. 9 he did..evil..as his fathers had done
15. 22 And Menahem slept with his fathers
15. 38 And Jotham slept with his fathers, and
15. 38 was buried with his fathers in the city of
16. 20 And Ahaz slept with his fathers, and was
16. 20 buried with his fathers in the city of Da.
17. 13 the law which I commanded your fathers
17. 14 like to the neck of their fathers, that did
17. 15 covenant that he made with their fathers
17. 41 as did their fathers, so do they unto this
19. 12 delivered them which my fathers have
20. 17 that which thy fathers have laid up
20. 21 And Hezekiah slept with his fathers: and
21. 8 out of the land which I gave their fathers
21. 15 since the day their fathers came forth out
21. 18 And Manasseh slept with his fathers, and
21. 22 And he forsook the LORD God of his fath.
22. 13 because our fathers have not hearkened
22. 20 I will gather thee unto thy fathers, and
23. 32, 37 according to all that his fathers had
24. 6 So Jehoiakim slept with his fathers: and
1 Ch. 4. 38 the house of their fathers increased gre.
5. 13 brethren of the house of their fathers
5. 15 Ahi..chief of the house of their fathers
5. 24, 24 heads of the house of their fathers
5. 25 transgressed against the God of their fa.
6. 19 of the Levites according to their fathers
7. 2 and Shemuel, heads of their father's house
7. 4 after the house of their fathers, (were)
7. 7, 9 heads of the house of (their) fathers,
7. 11 All these..by the heads of their fathers
8. 6 heads of the fathers of the inhabitants
8. 10 These (were) his sons, heads of the fathers
8. 28 These (were) heads of the fathers, by
9. 9 All these men (were) chief of the fathers
9. 13 brethren, heads of the house of their fat.
9. 19 and their fathers, (being) over the host of
9. 33 these (are) the singers, chief of the fathers
9. 34 These chief fathers of the Levites (were)
12. 17 the God of our fathers look (thereon), and
12. 30 famous throughout the house of their fa.
15. 12 Ye (are) the chief of the fathers of the L.
17. 11 that thou must go (to be) with thy fathers
23. 9 These (were) the chief of the fathers of
23. 24 their fathers; (even) the chief of the fat.
24. 4 chief men of the house of (their) fathers
24. 4 according to the house of their fathers
24. 6 and (before) the chief of the fathers of
24. 30 Levites after the house of their fathers
24. 31 and the chief of the fathers of the priests
24. 31 even the principal fathers over against
26. 13 according to the house of their fathers
26. 21 chief fathers, (even) of Laadan the Ger.
26. 26 and the chief fathers, the captains over
26. 31 to the generations of his fathers
26. 32 brethren..(were) two thousand..chief fa.
27. 1 the chief fathers and captains of thous.
29. 6 Then the chief of the fathers and princes
29. 15 and sojourners, as (were) all our fathers
29. 18 our fathers, keep this for ever in the
29. 20 blessed the LORD God of their fathers
2 Ch. 1. 2 in all Israel, the chief of the fathers
5. 2 Solomon assembled..the chief of the fat.
6. 25 land..thou gavest to them and to their f.
6. 31 land which thou gavest unto our fathers
6. 38 land, which thou gavest unto their fathers
7. 22 they forsook the Lord GOD of their fath.
9. 31 Solomon slept with his fathers, and he
11. 16 sacrifice unto the LORD God of their fa.
12. 16 And Rehoboam slept with his fathers
13. 12 not against the..God of your fathers
13. 18 relied upon the LORD God of their fathers
14. 1 So Abijah slept with his fathers, and they
14. 4 Judah to seek the..God of their fathers
15. 12 to seek the LORD God of their fathers
16. 13 Asa slept with his fathers, and died in
17. 14 according to the house of their fathers
19. 4 back unto the LORD God of their fathers
19. 8 and of the chief of the fathers of Israel
20. 6 O LORD God of our fathers, (art) not thou
20. 33 their hearts unto the God of their fathers
21. 1 Jehoshaphat slept with his fathers
21. 1 and was buried with his fathers in the ci.
21. 10 had forsaken the LORD God of his fathers
21. 19 no burning..like the burning of his fath.
23. 2 and the chief of the fathers of Israel
24. 18 left the house of the..God of their fathers
24. 24 had forsaken the LORD God of their fath.
25. 4 The fathers shall not die for the children
25. 4 neither shall the children die for the fath.
25. 5 according to the house of (their) fathers
25. 28 buried him with his fathers in the city of
26. 2 after that the king slept with his fathers
26. 12 whole number of the chief of the fathers
26. 23 So Uzziah slept with his fathers
26. 23 and they buried him with his fathers
27. 9 Jotham slept with his fathers, and they
28. 6 had forsaken the..God of their fathers
28. 9 because the LORD God of your fathers was
28. 25 provoked to anger the..God of his fathers
28. 27 Ahaz slept with his fathers, and they
29. 5 the house of the LORD God of your fathers
29. 6 For our fathers have trespassed, and done
29. 9 lo, our fathers have fallen by the sword
30. 7 be not ye like your fathers, and like your
30. 7 against the LORD God of their fathers

2 Ch. 30. 8 be ye not stiffnecked, as your fathers
30. 19 to seek God, the LORD God of his fathers
30. 22 confession to the..God of their fathers
31. 17 priests by the house of their fathers
32. 13 Know ye not what I and my fathers have
32. 14 the gods of those nations that my fathers
32. 15 and out of the hand of my fathers
32. 33 Hezekiah slept with his fathers, and they
33. 8 land which I..appointed for your fathers
33. 12 humbled himself..before the God of his f.
33. 20 Manasseh slept with his fathers, and they
34. 21 because our fathers have not kept the
34. 28 Behold, I will gather thee to thy fathers
34. 32 covenant of God, the God of their fathers
34. 33 following the LORD, the God of their fat.
35. 4 And prepare..by the houses of your fath.
35. 5 of the fathers of your brethren the people
35. 24 buried in..the sepulchres of his fathers
36. 15 the LORD God of their fathers sent to
Ezra 1. 5 Then rose up the chief of the fathers of
2. 59 they could not show their fathers' house
2. 68 And..of the chief of the fathers, when
3. 12 of the priests..and chief of the fathers
4. 2 they came..to the chief of the fathers
4. 3 and the rest of the chief of the fathers of
7. 27 Blessed (be) the LORD God of our fathers
8. 1 These (are) now the chief of their fathers
8. 28 offering unto the LORD God of your fath.
8. 29 before the..chief of the fathers of Israel
9. 7 Since the days of our fathers (have) we
10. 11 confession unto the..God of your fathers
10. 16 And Ezra..(with) certain chief of the fat.
10. 16 after the house of their fathers, and all
Neh. 2. 3 when..the place of my fathers' sepulchres
2. 5 unto the city of my fathers' sepulchres
7. 61 they could not show their fathers' house
7. 70, 71 some of the chief of the fathers gave
8. 13 the chief of the fathers of all the people
9. 2 confessed..the iniquities of their fathers
9. 9 didst see the affliction of our fathers in
9. 16 But they and our fathers dealt proudly
9. 23 which thou hadst promised to their fath.
9. 32 come..on our fathers, and on all thy peo.
9. 34 Neither have..our fathers, kept thy law
9. 36 the land that thou gavest unto our fath.
10. 34 after the houses of our fathers, at times
11. 13 And his brethren, chief of the fathers
12. 12 were priests, the chief of the fathers
12. 22 The Levites..recorded chief of the fathers
12. 23 sons of Levi, the chief of the fathers
13. 18 Did not your fathers thus, and did not
Job 8. 8 prepare thyself to the search of their fa.
15. 18 Which wise men have told from their fa.
30. 1 have me in derision, whose fathers I
Psa. 22. 4 Our fathers trusted in thee: they trusted
39. 12 a stranger..a sojourner, as all my fathers
44. 1 O God, our fathers have told us, (what)
45. 16 Instead of thy fathers shall be thy child.
49. 19 He shall go to the generation of his fath.
78. 3 which..our fathers have told us
78. 5 which he commanded our fathers, that
78. 8 And might not be as their fathers, a stub.
78. 12 things did he in the sight of their fathers
78. 57 and dealt unfaithfully like their fathers
95. 9 When your fathers tempted me, proved
106. 6 We have sinned with our fathers, we ha.
106. 7 Our fathers understood not thy wonders
109. 14 Let the iniquity of his fathers be reme.
Prov 17. 6 the glory of children (are) their fathers
19. 14 House and riches..the inheritance of fa.
22. 28 the ancient landmark, which thy fathers
Isa. 14. 21 for the iniquity of their fathers; that
37. 12 delivered them which my fathers have
39. 6 which thy fathers have laid up in store
64. 11 Our holy..house, where our fathers prai.
65. 7 and the iniquities of your fathers togeth.
Jer. 2. 5 What iniquity have your fathers found
3. 18 given for an inheritance unto your fathe.
3. 24 shame hath devoured the labour of our f.
3. 25 we have sinned..we and our fathers
6. 21 the fathers and the sons together shall
7. 7 in the land that I gave to your fathers
7. 14 which I gave to you and to your fathers
7. 18 The children gather wood, and the fathe.
7. 22 For I spake not unto your fathers, nor
7. 25 Since the day that your fathers came for.
7. 26 Yet..they did worse than their fathers
9. 14 after Baalim, which their fathers taught
9. 16 whom neither they nor their fathers hav.
11 4 Which I commanded your fathers in the
11. 5 oath which I have sworn unto your fath.
11. 7 I earnestly protested unto your fathers
11. 10 covenant which I made with their fathe.
13. 14 And I will dash..the fathers and the so.
14. 20 We acknowledge..the iniquity of our fa.
16. 3 concerning their fathers that begat them
16. 11 Because your fathers have forsaken me
16. 12 And ye have done worse than your fathe.
16. 13 ye know not, (neither) ye nor your fathe.
16. 15 their land that I gave unto their fathers
16. 19 Surely our fathers have inherited lies
17. 22 the sabbath day, as I commanded your f.
19. 4 whom neither they nor their fathers ha.
23. 27 as their fathers have forgotten my name
23. 39 the city that I gave you and your father.
24. 10 that I gave unto them and to their fathe.
25. 5 and to your fathers for ever and ever
30. 3 to the land that I gave to their fathers
31. 29 The fathers have eaten a sour grape, an.
31. 32 the covenant that I made with their fat.
32. 18 recompensest the iniquity of the fathers
32. 22 which thou didst swear to their fathers

Jer. 34. 5 and with the burnings of thy fathers
34. 13 I made a covenant with your fathers in
34. 14 but your fathers hearkened not unto me
35. 15 I have given to you and to your fathers
44. 3 whom they knew not..nor your fathers
44. 9 forgotten the wickedness of your fathers
44. 10 that I set before you and before your fa.
44. 17 our fathers, our kings, and our princes
44. 21 ye, and your fathers, your kings, and you.
47. 3 fathers shall not look back to..children
50. 7 even the LORD, the hope of their fathers
Lam. 5. 7 Our fathers have sinned, (and are) not
Eze. 2. 3 they and their fathers have transgressed
5. 10 Therefore the fathers shall eat the sons
5. 10 and the sons shall eat their fathers
18. 2 The fathers have eaten sour grapes, and
20. 4 to know the abominations of their fathe.
20. 18 Walk ye not in the statutes of your fath.
20. 24 their eyes were after their fathers' idols
20. 27 Yet in this your fathers have blaspheme.
20. 30 polluted after the manner of your fathers?
20. 36 Like as I pleaded with your fathers in
20. 42 lifted up mine hand to give it to your fa.
36. 28 in the land that I gave to your fathers
37. 25 dwell in the land..wherein your fathers
47. 14 lifted up mine hand to give it unto your f.
Dan. 9. 6 which spake in thy name to..our father.
9. 8 to us..confusion of face..and to our fat.
9. 16 and for the iniquities of our fathers
11. 24 he shall do (that) which his fathers have
11. 37 Neither shall he regard the God of his fa.
11. 38 a god whom his fathers knew not shall
Hos. 9. 10 I saw your fathers as the first ripe in the
Joel 1. 2 Hath this been..in the days of your fat.?
Amos 2. 4 after the which their fathers have walk.
Mic. 7. 20 which thou hast sworn unto our fathers
Zec. 1. 2 hath been sore displeased with your fat.
1. 4 Be ye not as your fathers, unto whom
1. 5 Your fathers, where (are) they? and the
1. 6 did they not take hold of your fathers?
8. 14 when your fathers provoked me to wrath
Mal. 2. 10 profaning the covenant of our fathers?
3. 7 Even from the days of your fathers ye
4. 6 he shall turn the heart of the fathers to
4. 6 the heart of the children to their fathers

2. *Fathers, ancestors,* אֲבָהָן *abahan.*
Ezra 4. 15 the book of the records of thy fathers
5. 12 But after that our fathers had provoked
Dan. 2. 23 I thank thee..O thou God of my fathers

3. *Fathers, ancestors,* πατέρες *pateres.*
Matt 23. 30 If we had been in the days of our fathe.
23. 32 Fill ye up..the measure of your fathers
Luke 1. 17 to turn the hearts of the fathers to the
1. 55 As he spake to our fathers, to Abraham
1. 72 To perform the mercy..to our fathers
6. 23 for in the like manner did their fathers
6. 26 for so did their fathers to the false pro.
11. 47 ye build..and your fathers killed them
11. 48 that ye allow the deeds of your fathers
John 4. 20 Our fathers worshipped in this mounta.
6. 31 Our fathers did eat manna in the desert
6. 49 Your fathers did eat manna in the wilde.
6. 58 not as your fathers; 7. 22, but of the f.
Acts 3. 13 the God of our fathers, hath glorified his
3. 22 [For Moses truly said unto the fathers]
3. 25 covenant which God made with our fath.
5. 30 The God of our fathers raised up Jesus
7. 2 And he said, Men, brethren, and fathers
7. 11 and our fathers found no sustenance
7. 12 Jacob heard..he sent out our fathers first
7. 15 So Jacob..died, he, and our fathers
7. 19 The same..evil entreated our fathers, so
7. 32 I (am) the God of thy fathers, the God of
7. 39 To whom our fathers would not obey, but
7. 44 Our fathers had the tabernacle of witness
7. 45 Which also our fathers that came after
7. 45 God drave out before the face of our fat.
7. 51 ye do always..as your fathers (did), so (do)
7. 52 Which of the prophets have not your fat.
13. 17 The God of this people..chose our fathers
13. 32 the promise which was made unto the fa.
13. 36 David..was laid unto his fathers, and saw
15. 10 which neither our fathers nor we were
22. 1 Men, brethren, and fathers, hear ye my
22. 14 And he said, The God of our fathers hath
26. 6 of the promise made of God unto our fa.
28. 25 Well spake the Holy Ghost..unto our fa.
Rom. 9. 5 Whose (are) the fathers, and of whom as
11. 28 (they are) beloved for the fathers' sakes
15. 8 to confirm the promises..unto the fathers
1 Co. 4. 15 yet (have ye) not many fathers: for in Ch.
10. 1 how that all our fathers were under the
Eph. 6. 4 And, ye fathers, provoke not your children
Col. 3. 21 Fathers, provoke not your children (to a.)
Heb. 3. 9 When your fathers tempted me, proved
8. 9 the covenant that I made with their fat.
12. 9 Furthermore we have had fathers of our
2 Pe. 3. 4 for since the fathers fell asleep, all things
1 Jo. 2. 13 I write unto you, fathers, because ye have
2. 14 I have written unto you, fathers, because

FATHERS, of the, or of one's —
1. *Paternal, ancestral,* πατρικός *patrikos.*
Gal. 1. 14 zealous of the traditions of my fathers

2. *Paternal,* πατρῷος *patrōos.*
Acts 22. 3 the perfect manner of the law of the fat.
24. 14 so worship I the God of my fathers, beli.
28. 17 against the people or customs of our fa.

FATHERS, by tradition from the —
Given over by ancestors, πατροπαράδοτος *patropa.*
1 Pe. 1. 18 conversation..by tradition from your fa.

FATHOM —
Fathom, (length of outstretched arms), ὀργυιά.
Acts 27. 28 sounded, and found (it) twenty fathoms
27. 28 sounded again, and found (it) fifteen fath.

FATLING —
1. *Fat ones,* מֵחִים *mechim.*
Psa. 66. 15 I will offer..burnt sacrifices of fatlings

2. *Fat, firm,* מְרִיא *meri.*
2 Sa. 6. 13 had gone..he sacrificed oxen and fatlings
Isa. 11. 6 the young lion and the fatling together
Eze. 39. 18 bullocks, all of them fatlings of Bashan

3. *Second, (younger and later),* מִשְׁנֶה *mishneh.*
1 Sa. 15. 9 spared..of the fatlings, and the lambs, and

4. *Fattened, fed up,* σιτιστός *sitistos.*
Matt 22. 4 my oxen and (my) fatlings (are) killed

FATNESS —
1. *Fatness,* דֶּשֶׁן *deshen.*
Judg. 9. 9 Should I leave my fatness, wherewith by
Job 36. 16 should be set on thy table..full of fatness
Psa. 36. 8 They shall be..satisfied with the fatness
63. 5 My soul shall be satisfied as (with)..fatn.
65. 11 goodness, and thy paths drop fatness
Isa. 55. 2 and let your soul delight itself in fatness
Jer. 31. 14 And I will satiate the soul..with fatness

2. *Fat, best part, marrow,* חֵלֶב *cheleb.*
Job 15. 27 he covereth his face with his fatness
Psa. 73. 7 Their eyes stand out with fatness: they
Isa. 34. 6 it is made fat with fatness..with the blood
34. 7 and their dust made fat with fatness

3. *Fatness, fat one,* מִשְׁמָן *mishman.*
Gen. 27. 28 the fatness of the earth, and plenty of corn
27. 39 thy dwelling shall be the fatness of the
Isa. 17. 4 and the fatness of his flesh shall wax lean

4. *Fatness, oil,* שֶׁמֶן *shemen.*
Psa. 109. 24 weak..and my flesh faileth of fatness

5. *Fatness, fat,* πιότης *piotēs.*
Rom 11. 17 with them partakest of the root and fat.

FATS —
Press or vat for oil or wine, יֶקֶב *yeqeb.*
Joel 2. 24 the fats shall overflow with wine and oil
3. 13 for the press is full, the fats overflow

FATTED —
1. *To be fattened,* אָבַס *abas.*
1 Ki. 4. 23 roebucks, and fallow deer, and fatted fowl

2. *Fattened, stall,* מַרְבֵּק *marbeq.*
Jer. 46. 21 her hired men (are)..like fatted bullocks

3. *Fattened, fed up,* σιτευτός *siteutos.*
Luke 15. 23 And bring hither the fatted calf, and kill
15. 27 thy father hath killed the fatted calf
15. 30 thou hast killed for him the fatted calf

FATTER —
Fat, firm, בָּרִיא *bari.*
Dan. 1. 15 countenances appeared fairer and fatter

FATTEST (places) —
Fatness, fat one, מִשְׁמָן *mishman.*
Psa. 78. 31 slew the fattest of them, and smote down
Dan. 11. 24 He shall enter..even upon the fattest pl.

FAULT —
1. *Error, failure, sin,* חָטָא *chata.*
Exod. 5. 16 but the fault (is) in thine own people

2. *Error, failure, sin,* חֵטְא *chet.*
Gen. 41. 9 saying, I do remember my faults this day

3. *What and what, whatever,* מְאוּמָה *meumah.*
1 Sa. 29. 3 I have found no fault in him since he

4. *Perversity, iniquity,* עָוֹן *avon.*
2 Sa. 3. 8 that thou chargest me to day with a fault
Psa. 59. 4 prepare themselves without (my) fault

5. *Wrongness, wickedness,* רִשְׁעָה *rishah.*
Deut 25. 2 and to be beaten..according to his fault

6. *To corrupt,* שָׁחַת *shechath.*
Dan. 6. 4 they could find none occasion nor fault
6. 4 neither was there any error or fault found

7. *Cause, case,* αἰτία *aitia.*
John 18. 38 Pilate saith..I find in him no fault (at all)
19. 4 that ye may know that I find no fault in
19. 6 Pilate saith..I find no fault in him

8. *Cause, case,* αἴτιον *aition.*
Luke 23. 4 Then said Pilate..I find no fault in this
23. 14 I..have found no fault in this man

9. *Lack, failure, defect,* ἥττημα *hettēma.*
1 Co. 6. 7 Now therefore there is utterly a fault am.

10. *A falling aside, mishap,* παράπτωμα *paraptōma.*
Gal. 6. 1 if a man be overtaken in a fault, ye which
Jas. 5. 16 Confess..[faults] one to another, and pray

FAULT, to find —
To blame, μέμφομαι *memphomai.*
Mark 7. 2 with unwashen hands, they found fault
Rom. 9. 19 Thou wilt say..Why doth he yet find fault?
Heb. 8. 8 For, finding fault with them, he saith

FAULT, to tell one's —
To convict, ἐλέγχω elegchō.
Matt. 18. 15 go and tell him his fault between thee

FAULT, without —
Without blemish, blame, spot, ἄμωμος amōmos.
Rev. 14. 5 they are without fault before the throne

FAULTLESS —
1. *Without blame, ἄμεμπτος amemptos.*
Heb. 8. 7 For if that first (covenant) had been fault.
2. *Without blemish, blame, spot, ἄμωμος amōmos.*
Jude 24 to present..faultless before the presence

FAULTS, for your —
To miss, err, sin, ἁμαρτάνω hamartanō.
1 Pe. 2. 20 if, when ye be buffeted for your faults, ye

FAULTY, one which is —
Guilty, אָשֵׁם ashem.
2 Sa. 14. 13 the king doth speak..as one which is fau.

FAULTY, to be found —
To be or become guilty, אָשַׁם asham.
Hos. 10. 2 now shall they be found faulty: he shall

FAVOUR —
1. *Grace, favour, חֵן chen.*
Gen. 18. 3 My Lord, if now I have found favour in
30. 27 I pray thee, if I have found favour in
39. 21 gave him favour in the sight of the keeper
Exod. 3. 21 I will give this people favour in the sight
11. 3 the LORD gave the people favour in the si.
12. 36 the LORD gave the people favour in the
Num. 11. 11 wherefore have I not found favour in thy
11. 15 if I have found favour in thy sight
Deut. 24. 1 it come to pass that she find no favour
Ruth 2. 13 she said, Let me find favour in thy sight
1 Sa. 16. 22 for he hath found favour in my sight
20. 29 now, if I have found favour in thine eyes
25. 8 Wherefore let the young men find favour
2 Sa. 15. 25 if I shall find favour in the eyes of the L.
1 Ki. 11. 19 Hadad found great favour in the sight of
Esth. 2. 15 Esther obtained favour in the sight of all
5. 2 the king saw Esther..she obtained favour
5. 8 If I have found favour in the sight of the
7. 3 If I have found favour in thy sight, O
8. 5 and if I have found favour in his sight
Prov. 3. 4 So shalt thou find favour and good und.
13. 15 Good understanding giveth favour: but
22. 1 loving favour rather than silver and gold
28. 23 He that rebuketh..shall find more favour
31. 30 Favour (is) deceitful, and beauty (is) vain
Eccl. 9. 11 nor yet favour to men of skill; but time
2. *Grace, favour, חֲנִינָה chaninah.*
Jer. 16. 13 a land..where I will not show you favour
3. *Kindness, חֶסֶד chesed.*
Esth. 2. 17 she obtained grace and favour in his sight
Job 10. 12 Thou hast granted me life and favour
Dan. 1. 9 Now God had brought Daniel into favour
4. *Delighting, חָפֵץ chaphets.*
Psa. 35. 27 Let them..be glad, that favour my righ.
5. *Face, פָּנִים panim.*
Psa. 45. 12 (even) the rich..shall entreat thy favour
119. 58 I entreated thy favour with (my) whole
Prov. 19. 6 Many will entreat the favour of the prince
29. 26 Many seek the ruler's favour: but (every)
6. *Pleasure, good will, רָצוֹן ratson.*
Deut. 33. 23 O Naphtali, satisfied with favour, and f.
Psa. 5. 12 with favour wilt thou compass him as
30. 5 in his favour (is) life: weeping may endure
30. 7 LORD, by thy favour thou hast made my
89. 17 in thy favour our horn shall be exalted
106. 4 Remember me, O LORD, with the favour
Prov. 8. 35 and shall obtain favour of the LORD
11. 27 He that..seeketh good procureth favour
12. 2 A good (man) obtaineth favour of the LORD
14. 9 but among the righteous (there is) favour
14. 35 The king's favour (is) toward a wise serv.
16. 15 his favour (is) as a cloud of the latter ra.
18. 22 (Whoso) findeth a wife..obtaineth favour
19. 12 but his favour (is) as dew upon the grass
Isa. 60. 10 in my favour have I had mercy on thee
7. *Peace, prosperity, completeness, שָׁלוֹם shalom.*
Song 8. 10 then was I..as one that found favour
8. *Grace, favour, תְּחִנָּה techinnah.*
Josh. 11. 20 that they might have no favour, but that
9. *Grace, χάρις charis.*
Luke 1. 30 Fear not, Mary; for thou hast found fav.
2. 52 Jesus increased..in favour with God and
Acts 2. 47 Praising God, and having favour with all
7. 10 gave him favour and wisdom in the sight
7. 46 Who found favour before God, and desir.
25. 3 And desired favour against him, that he

FAVOUR, (be in) to —
1. *To incline or be gracious to, חָנַן chanan.*
Psa. 102. 13 the time to favour her, yea, the set time
109. 12 neither let there be any to favour his fa.
Lam. 4. 16 they respected not..they favoured not
2. *To incline or be gracious to, חָנַן chanan, 3a.*
Psa. 102. 14 For thy servants..favour the dust thereof
3. *To have delight in, חָפֵץ chaphets.*
2 Sa. 20. 11 He that favoureth Joab, and he that (is)
Psa. 41. 11 By this I know that thou favourest me
4. *Good in the eyes of, טוֹב בְּעֵינֵי tob be-ene.*
1 Sa. 2. 26 was in favour both with the LORD, and
29. 6 nevertheless the lords favour thee not

FAVOUR, to find —
1. *To find grace or favour, חָנַן chanan, 6.*
Prov. 21. 10 his neighbour findeth no favour in his
2. *To be or become good, יָטַב yatab.*
Neh. 2. 5 if thy servant have found favour in thy

FAVOUR, to have a —
To be pleased with, רָצָה ratsah.
Psa. 44. 3 because thou hadst a favour unto them

FAVOUR, to show —
To incline or be gracious to, חָנַן chanan.
Deut. 28. 50 shall not regard..nor show favour to the
Psa. 112. 5 A good man showeth favour, and lendeth
Isa. 27. 11 he that formed..will show them no favo.

FAVOUR, to be showed —
To find grace or favour, חָנַן chanan, 6.
Isa. 26. 10 Let favour be showed to the wicked

FAVOURABLE, to be —
1. *To incline or be gracious to, חָנַן chanan.*
Judg. 21. 22 Be favourable unto them for our sakes
2. *To be pleased with, רָצָה ratsah.*
Job 33. 26 he will be favourable unto him; and he
Psa. 77. 7 and will he be favourable no more?
85. 1 LORD, thou hast been favourable unto

FAVOURED, well —
1. *Fair of appearance, יְפַת־מַרְאֶה yephath mareh.*
Gen. 29. 17 but Rachel was beautiful and well favou.
39. 6 And Joseph was..goodly..and well favo.
41. 2 there came up..seven well favoured kine
41. 4 did eat up the seven well favoured and f.
2. *Fair of form, יְפֵה־תֹאַר [yapheh].*
Gen. 41. 18 seven kine, fat fleshed and well favoured
3. *Good in appearance, טוֹב מַרְאֶה tob mareh.*
Dan. 1. 4 well favoured, and skilful in all wisdom
4. *Good of grace, טוֹב חֵן tob chen.*
Nah. 3. 4 the well favoured harlot, the mistress of

FAVOURED, highly —
To give grace to, treat graciously, χαριτόω charitoō.
Luke 1. 28 Hail..highly favoured, the Lord (is) with

FEAR —
1. *Terror, אֵימָה emah.*
Exod. 15. 16 Fear and dread shall fall upon them
23. 27 I will send my fear before thee, and will
Ezra 3. 3 fear (was) upon them because of the peo.
Job 9. 34 from me, and let not his fear terrify me
Prov. 20. 2 The fear of a king (is) as the roaring of a
2. *Fear, sorrow, דְּאָגָה deagah.*
Josh. 22. 24 if we have not..done it for fear of (this)
3. *Trembling, חֲרָדָה charadah.*
Prov. 29. 25 The fear of man bringeth a snare: but
Isa. 21. 4 my pleasure hath he turned into fear
4. *Fright, terror, חַת chath.*
Job 41. 33 not his like, who is made without fear
5. *Fear, reverence, יִרְאָה yirah.*
Gen. 20. 11 Surely, the fear of God (is) not in this
Exod. 20. 20 and that his fear may be before your fa.
Deut. 2. 25 This day will I begin to put..the fear
2 Sa. 23. 3 (must be) just, ruling in the fear of God
2 Ch. 19. 9 Thus shall ye do in the fear of the LORD
Neh. 5. 9 ought ye not to walk in the fear of our
5. 15 so did not I, because of the fear of God
Job 4. 6 (Is) not (this) thy fear, thy confidence
6. 14 he forsaketh the fear of the Almighty
15. 4 Yea, thou castest off fear, and restraine.
22. 4 Will he reprove thee for fear of thee?
28. 28 the fear of the LORD, that (is) wisdom
Psa. 2. 11 Serve the LORD with fear, and rejoice
5. 7 in thy fear will I worship toward thy
19. 9 The fear of the LORD (is) clean, enduring
34. 11 I will teach you the fear of the LORD
90. 11 even according to thy fear, (so is) thy wr.
111. 10 The fear of the LORD (is) the beginning of
119. 38 thy servant, who (is devoted) to thy fear
Prov. 1. 7 The fear of the LORD (is) the beginning of
1. 29 and did not choose the fear of the LORD
2. 5 Then shalt thou understand the fear of
8. 13 The fear of the LORD (is) to hate evil: pr.
9. 10 The fear of the LORD (is) the beginning of
10. 27 The fear of the LORD prolongeth days: but
14. 26 In the fear of the LORD (is) strong confid.
14. 27 The fear of the LORD (is) a fountain of life
15. 16 Better (is) little with the fear of the LORD
15. 33 The fear of the LORD (is) the instruction
16. 6 by the fear of the LORD (men) depart from
19. 23 The fear of the LORD (tendeth) to life; and
22. 4 By humility, (and) the fear of the LORD
23. 17 in the fear of the LORD all the day long
Isa. 7. 25 there shall not come thither the fear of
11. 2 of the fear of; 11. 3, 29. 13, 33. 6, 63. 17.
Jer. 32. 40 I will put my fear in their hearts, that
Eze. 30. 13 I will put a fear in the land of Egypt
Jon. 1. 16 Then the men feared the LORD exceed.
6. *Fear, מָגוֹר magor.*
Psa. 31. 13 fear (was) on every side: while they took
Isa. 31. 9 shall pass over to his strong hold for fear
Jer. 6. 25 the sword of the enemy (and) fear (is) on
20. 10 I heard the defaming of many, fear on
46. 5 fear (was) round about, saith the LORD
49. 29 they shall cry..Fear (is) on every side
7. *Fear, מְגוֹרָה megorah.*
Prov. 10. 24 The fear of the wicked, it shall come upon
8. *Fear, מְגוּרָה megurah.*
Psa. 34. 4 and delivered me from all my fears
Isa. 66. 4 will bring their fears upon them; because
9. *Fear, reverence, מוֹרָא mora.*
Gen. 9. 2 the fear of you and the dread of you shall
Isa. 8. 12 neither fear ye their fear, nor be afraid
8. 13 (let) him (be) your fear, and (let) him (be)
Mal. 1. 6 and if I (be) a master, where (is) my fear?
2. 5 I gave them to him (for) the fear wherew.
10. *Fear, מוֹרָה morah.*
Psa. 9. 20 Put them in fear, O LORD; (that) the
11. *Dread, fear, פַּחַד pachad.*
Gen. 31. 42 Except..the Fear of Isaac, had been with
31. 53 Jacob sware by the Fear of his father Isaac
Deut. 11. 25 the LORD your God shall lay the fear of
28. 67 for the fear of thine heart wherewith thou
1 Sa. 11. 7 the fear of the LORD fell on the people
1 Ch. 14. 17 the LORD brought the fear of him upon
2 Ch. 14. 14 for the fear of the LORD came upon them
17. 10 the fear of the LORD fell upon all the
19. 7 now let the fear of the LORD be upon you
20. 29 the fear of God was on all the kingdoms
Esth. 8. 17 for the fear of the Jews fell upon them
9. 2 for the fear of them fell upon all people
9. 3 because the fear of Mordecai fell upon
Job 4. 14 Fear came upon me, and trembling
21. 9 Their houses (are) safe from fear, neither
22. 10 snares..and sudden fear troubleth thee
25. 2 Dominion and fear (are) with him; he
39. 16 her labour is in vain without fear
39. 22 He mocketh at fear, and is not affrighted
Psa. 31. 11 I was..a fear to mine acquaintance
36. 1 (that there is) no fear of God before his
53. 5 were they..(where) no fear was: for God
64. 1 preserve my life from fear of the enemy
105. 38 for the fear of them fell upon them
119. 120 My flesh trembleth for fear of thee; and
Prov. 1. 26 I will mock when your fear cometh
1. 27 When your fear cometh as desolation
1. 33 and shall be quiet from fear of evil
3. 25 Be not afraid of sudden fear, neither of
Song 3. 8 every man..his sword..because of fear
Isa. 2. 10 hide thee in the dust, for fear of the LORD
2. 19 they shall go into the holes..for fear of
2. 21 for fear of the LORD, and for the glory of
24. 17 Fear, and the pit, and the snare, (are)
24. 18 he who fleeth from the noise of the fear
Jer. 30. 5 We have heard a voice of..fear, and not
48. 43 Fear, and the pit, and the snare..upon
48. 44 He that fleeth from the fear shall fall into
49. 5 Behold, I will bring a fear upon thee
Lam. 3. 47 Fear and a snare is come upon us, des.
12. *Dread, fear, פַּחְדָּה pachdah.*
Jer. 2. 19 and that my fear (is) not in thee, saith
13. *Rage, anger, trembling, רֹגֶז rogez.*
Isa. 14. 3 LORD shall give thee rest..from thy fear
14. *Fear, terror, trembling, רֶטֶט retet.*
Jer. 49. 24 Damascus is waxed feeble..fear hath
15. *Trembling, רְעָדָה readah.*
Psa. 48. 6 Fear took hold upon them there, (and)
16. *Timidity, δειλία deilia.*
2 Ti. 1. 7 God hath not given us the spirit of fear
17. *Fear, terror, φόβος phobos.*
Matt. 14. 26 It is a spirit: and they cried out for fear
28. 4 for fear of him the keepers did shake
28. 8 they departed quickly..with fear and
Luke 1. 12 when Zacharias saw..fear fell upon him
1. 65 fear came on all that dwelt round about
5. 26 were all amazed..and were filled with f.
7. 16 there came a fear on all: and they glori.
8. 37 for they were taken with great fear: And
21. 26 Men's hearts failing them for fear, and
John 7. 13 no man spake openly of him for fear of
19. 38 a disciple of Jesus, but secretly for fear
20. 19 the disciples were assembled for fear of
Acts 2. 43 fear came upon every soul: and many
5. 5 great fear came on all them that heard
5. 11 great fear came upon all the church, and
9. 31 walking in the fear of the Lord, and in
19. 17 fear fell on them all, and the name of the
Rom. 3. 18 There is no fear of God before their eyes
8. 15 not received the spirit of bondage..to fe.
13. 7 fear to whom fear; honour to whom hon.
1 Co. 2. 3 I was with you in weakness, and in fear
2 Co. 7. 1 perfecting holiness in the fear of God
7. 5 without (were) fightings, within (were) f.
7. 11 (what) indignation, yea, (what) fear, yea
7. 15 how with fear and trembling ye received
Eph. 5. 21 Submitting..one to another in the fear of
6. 5 with fear and trembling, in singleness of
Phil. 2. 12 work out your own salvation with fear
Heb. 2. 15 And deliver them who through fear of
1 Pe. 1. 17 pass the time of your sojourning..in fear
2. 18 subject to (your) masters with all fear
3. 2 your chaste conversation (coupled) with f.
3. 15 an answer..with meekness and fear
1 Jo. 4. 18 There is no fear in love; but perfect
4. 18 love casteth out fear: because fear hath
Jude 23 others save with fear, pulling..out of
Rev. 11. 11 great fear fell upon them which saw them

Rev. 18. 10 Standing afar off for the fear of her tor.
18. 15 shall stand afar off for the fear of her

FEAR, to —

1. *To be afraid*, גּוּר *gur.*
Deut 32. 27 Were it not that I feared the wrath of the
Psa. 22. 23 and fear him, all ye the seed of Israel
Hos. 10. 5 The inhabitants of Samaria shall fear

2. *To be afraid*, דְּחַל *dechal.*
Dan. 5. 19 all people, nations, and languages..feared
6. 26 in every dominion..men tremble and fear

3. *To be pained*, חִיל, חוּל *chul, chil.*
1 Ch. 16. 30 Fear before him, all the earth: the world
Psa. 96. 9 O worship..fear before him, all the earth

4. *To be afraid*, יָגֹר *yagor.*
Psa. 119. 39 Turn away my reproach which I fear; for
Jer. 22. 25 into the hand of..whose face thou fearest

5. *To fear, reverence*, יָרֵא *yare.*
Gen. 15. 1 Fear not, Abram: I (am) thy shield, (and)
19. 30 he feared to dwell in Zoar: and he dwelt
21. 17 What aileth thee, Hagar? fear not; for
26. 7 for he feared to say, (She is) my wife; lest
26. 24 I (am) the God of Abraham thy father: f.
35. 17 the midwife said unto her, Fear not
43. 23 And he said, Peace (be) to you, fear not
46. 3 fear not to go down into Egypt; for I
50. 19 And Joseph said unto them, Fear not
50. 21 Now therefore fear ye not: I will nour.
Exod. 1. 17 the midwives feared God, and did not
1. 21 came to pass, because the midwives fea.
2. 14 Moses feared, and said, Surely this thing
9. 30 I know that ye will not yet fear the LORD
14. 13 Moses said unto the people, Fear ye not
14. 31 the people feared the LORD, and believ.
20. 20 Moses said unto the people, Fear not
Lev. 19. 3 Ye shall fear every man his mother and
19. 14 but shalt fear thy God: I (am) the LORD
19. 32 Thou shalt rise up..and fear thy God
25. 17 but thou shalt fear thy God: for I (am)
25. 36 Take thou no usury of him..but fear
25. 43 Thou shalt not rule..but shalt fear thy
Num 14. 9 neither fear ye the people..fear them
21. 34 the LORD said unto Moses, Fear him not
Deut. 1. 21 possess..fear not, neither be discouraged
3. 2 the LORD said unto me, Fear him not
3. 22 Ye shall not fear them: for the LORD
4. 10 that they may learn to fear me all the
5. 29 an heart in them, that they would fear
6. 2 that thou mightest fear the LORD thy God
6. 13 Thou shalt fear the LORD thy God, and
6. 24 these statutes, to fear the LORD our God
8. 6 to walk in his ways, and to fear him
10. 12 to fear the LORD thy God, to walk in all
10. 20 Thou shalt fear the LORD thy God; him
13. 4 Ye shall walk after the LORD..and fear
13. 11 all Israel shall hear, and fear, and shall
14. 23 that thou mayest learn to fear the LORD
17. 13 And all the people shall hear, and fear
17. 19 that he may learn to fear the LORD his
19. 20 those which remain shall hear, and fear
20. 3 let not your hearts faint; fear not, and do
21. 21 and all Israel shall hear, and fear
28. 58 that thou mayest fear this glorious and
31. 6 Be strong, and of a good courage, fear
31. 8 he will not fail thee..fear not, neither
31. 12 fear the LORD your God, and observe to
31. 13 hear, and learn to fear the LORD your
Josh. 4. 14 they feared him, as they feared Moses
4. 24 that ye might fear the LORD your God
8. 1 the LORD said unto Joshua, Fear not
10. 2 That they feared greatly, because Gibeon
10. 8 the LORD said unto Joshua, Fear them
10. 25 Joshua said unto them, Fear not, nor be
24. 14 fear the LORD, and serve him in sincerity
Judg. 4. 18 Turn in, my lord, turn in to me; fear not
6. 10 fear not the gods of the Amorites, in
6. 23 Peace (be) unto thee; fear not: thou
6. 27 because he feared his father's household
8. 20 youth drew not his sword; for he feared
Ruth 3. 11 now, my daughter, fear not; I will do to
1 Sa. 3. 15 And Samuel feared to show Eli the vision
4. 20 said..Fear not; for thou hast born a son
12. 14 If ye will fear the LORD, and serve him
12. 18 all the people greatly feared the LORD
12. 20 Samuel said unto the people, Fear not
12. 24 Only fear the LORD, and serve him in
14. 26 no man put..for the people feared the
15. 24 because I feared the people, and obeyed
22. 23 Abide thou with me, fear not; for he
23. 17 he said unto him, Fear not; for the hand
2 Sa. 3. 11 could not answer..because he feared him
9. 7 David said unto him, Fear not: for I will
10. 19 So the Syrians feared to help the children
12. 18 the servants of David feared to tell him
13. 28 I say unto you, Smite Amnon..fear not
1 Ki. 1. 50 And Adonijah feared because of Solomon
1. 51 Behold, Adonijah feareth king Solomon
3. 28 and they feared the king: for they saw
8. 40 That they may fear thee all the days that
8. 43 to fear thee, as (do) thy people Israel
17. 13 And Elijah said unto her, Fear not; go
18. 12 I thy servant fear the LORD from my youth
2 Ki. 6. 16 And he answered, Fear not; for they that
17. 7 the children of Israel..had feared other
17. 25 they feared not the LORD: therefore the
17. 28 taught them how they should fear the L.
17. 35 Ye shall not fear other gods, nor bow
17. 36 the LORD..him shall ye fear, and him
17. 37 and ye shall not fear other gods
17. 38 not forget; neither shall ye fear other
2 Ki. 17. 39 But the LORD your God ye shall fear; and
25. 24 Fear not to be the servants of the Chald.
1 Ch. 28. 20 fear not, nor be dismayed; for the LORD
2 Ch. 6. 31 That they may fear thee, to walk in thy
6. 33 know..and fear thee, as..thy people Isr.
20. 3 Jehoshaphat feared, and set himself to
20. 17 fear not, nor be dismayed; to morrow
Neh. 1. 11 thy servants, who desire to fear thy name
7. 2 a faithful man, and feared God above
Job 1. 9 said, Doth Job fear God for nought?
9. 35 (Then) would I speak, and not fear him
11. 15 thou shalt be stedfast, and shalt not fear
37. 24 Men do therefore fear him: he respecteth
Psa. 23. 4 I will fear no evil: for thou (art) with me
27. 1 The LORD (is) my light..whom shall I fe.?
27. 3 my heart shall not fear: though war
33. 8 Let all the earth fear the LORD: let all
34. 9 O fear the LORD, ye his saints: for (there
40. 3 many shall see (it), and fear, and shall
46. 2 Therefore will not we fear, though the
49. 5 Wherefore should I fear in the days of
52. 6 The righteous also shall see, and fear, and
55. 19 they have no changes, therefore they fear
56. 4 I will not fear what flesh can do unto me
64. 4 suddenly do they shoot at him, and fear
64. 9 all men shall fear, and shall declare the
67. 7 all the ends of the earth shall fear him
72. 5 They shall fear thee as long as the sun
76. 8 to be heard..the earth feared, and was
86. 11 LORD..unite my heart to fear thy name
102. 15 So the heathen shall fear the name of the
112. 1 Blessed (is) the man (that) feareth the L.
118. 6 The LORD (is) on my side; I will not fear
119. 63 I (am) a companion of all..that fear thee
Prov. 3. 7 fear the LORD, and depart from evil
24. 21 My son, fear thou the LORD and the king
Eccl. 3. 14 God doeth (it), that (men) should fear
5. 7 also (divers) vanities: but fear thou God
8. 12 well with them..which fear before him
12. 13 Fear God, and keep his commandments
Isa. 7. 4 Take heed, and be quiet; fear not, neither
8. 12 A confederacy; neither fear ye their fear
25. 3 the city of the terrible nations shall fear
35. 4 Be strong, fear not: behold, your God
41. 5 The isles saw (it), and feared; the ends
41. 10 Fear thou not; for I (am) with thee; be
41. 13 saying unto thee, Fear not; I will help
41. 14 Fear not, thou worm Jacob, (and) ye men
43. 1 O Israel, Fear not: for I have redeemed
43. 5 Fear not; for I (am) with thee: I will
44. 2 Fear not, O Jacob, my servant; and thou
51. 7 fear ye not the reproach of men, neither
54. 4 Fear not; for thou shalt not be ashamed
54. 14 far from oppression; for thou shalt not f.
57. 11 of whom hast thou been afraid or feared
57. 11 even of old, and thou fearest me not?
59. 19 So shall they fear the name of the LORD
Jer. 3. 8 yet her treacherous sister Judah feared
5. 22 Fear ye not me? saith the LORD: will ye
5. 24 Let us now fear the LORD our God, that
10. 7 Who would not fear thee, O king of
23. 4 they shall fear no more, nor be dismayed
30. 10 Therefore fear thou not, O my servant
32. 39 that they may fear me for ever, for the
40. 9 Fear not to serve the Chaldeans: dwell
44. 10 neither have they feared, nor walked in
46. 27 But fear not thou, O my servant Jacob
46. 28 Fear thou not, O Jacob my servant, saith
51. 46 lest your heart faint, and ye fear for the
Lam. 3. 57 I called upon thee..thou saidst, Fear not
Eze. 3. 9 fear them not, neither be dismayed at
11. 8 Ye have feared the sword; and I will
Dan. 10. 12 Then said he unto me, Fear not, Daniel
10. 19 O man greatly beloved, fear not: peace
Hos. 10. 3 We have no king, because we feared not
Joel 2. 21 Fear not, O land; be glad and rejoice
Amos 3. 8 The lion hath roared, who will not fear?
Jon. 1. 16 Then the men feared the LORD exceedin.
Mic. 7. 17 our God, and shall fear because of thee
Zeph. 3. 7 I said, Surely thou wilt fear me, thou
3. 16 it shall be said to Jerusalem, Fear thou
Hag. 1. 12 and the people did fear before the LORD
2. 5 my spirit remaineth among you: fear ye
Zech. 8. 13 fear not, (but) let your hands be strong
8. 15 and to the house of Judah: fear ye not
9. 5 Ashkelon shall see (it), and fear; Gaza
Mal. 2. 5 wherewith he feared me, and was afraid
3. 5 and fear not me, saith the LORD of hosts

6. *Fearing, reverencing*, יָרֵא *yare.*
Gen. 22. 12 now I know that thou fearest God, seeing
32. 11 I fear him, lest he will come and smite me
42. 18 This do, and live; (for) I fear God
Exod. 9. 20 He that feared the word of the LORD am.
18. 21 provide..able men, such as fear God
Deut 25. 18 How he met thee..and he feared not God
Judg. 7. 10 But if thou fear to go down, go thou with
1 Ki. 18. 3 Now Obadiah feared the LORD greatly
2 Ki. 4. 1 thou knowest that thy servant did fear
17. 32 So they feared the LORD, and made unto
17. 33 They feared the LORD, and served their
17. 34 they fear not the LORD, neither do they
17. 41 So these nations feared the LORD, and se.
Job 1. 1 one that feared God, and eschewed evil
1. 8 an upright man, one that feareth God, and
2. 3 an upright man, one that feareth God, and
Psa. 15. 4 but he honoureth them that fear the LORD
22. 23 Ye that fear the LORD, praise him; all ye
22. 25 I will pay my vows before them that fear
25. 12 What man (is) he that feareth the LORD?
25. 14 secret of the LORD (is) with them that f.
31. 19 which thou hast laid up for them that f.
Psa. 33. 18 the eye of the LORD (is) upon them that f.
34. 7 encampeth round about them that fear
34. 9 for..no want to them that fear him
60. 4 Thou hast given a banner to them that f.
61. 5 given (me) the heritage of those that fear
66. 16 Come..hear, all ye that fear God, and I
85. 9 his salvation (is) nigh them that fear him
103. 11 great is his mercy toward them that fear
103. 13 the LORD pitieth them that fear him
103. 17 the mercy..is..upon them that fear him
111. 5 He hath given meat unto them that fear
115. 11 Ye that fear the LORD, trust in the LORD
115. 13 He will bless them that fear the LORD
118. 4 Let them now that fear the LORD say, that
119. 74 They that fear thee will be glad when they
119. 79 Let those that fear thee turn unto me, and
128. 1 Blessed (is) every one that feareth the L.
128. 4 thus shall the man be blessed that fear.
135. 20 ye that fear the LORD, bless the LORD
145. 19 will fulfil the desire of them that fear him
147. 11 LORD taketh pleasure in them that fear
Prov. 13. 13 he that feareth the commandment shall
14. 2 He that walketh in his uprightness fear.
14. 16 A wise (man) feareth, and departeth from
31. 30 a woman (that) feareth the LORD, she sh.
Eccl. 7. 18 he that feareth God shall come forth of
8. 12 shall be well with them that fear God
8. 13 because he feareth not before God
9. 2 he that sweareth, as (he) that feareth an
Isa. 50. 10 Who (is) among you that feareth the L.
Jer. 26. 19 did he not fear the LORD, and besought
42. 16 the sword, which ye feared, shall over.
Dan. 1. 10 And the prince..said unto Daniel, I fear
Jon. 1. 9 I (am) an Hebrew; and I fear the LORD
Mal. 3. 16 Then they that feared the LORD spake
3. 16 a book..was written..for them that feared
4. 2 But unto you that fear my name shall

7. *To fear, be afraid, terrified*, עָרַץ *arats.*
Job 31. 34 Did I fear a great multitude, or did the
Isa. 29. 23 sanctify..and shall fear the God of Israel

8. *To fear, be afraid*, פָּחַד *pachad.*
Deut 28. 66 thou shalt fear day and night, and shalt
28. 67 of thine heart wherewith thou shalt fear
Job 3. 25 For the thing which I greatly feared is
Psa. 78. 53 led them on safely, so that they feared
Isa. 19. 16 it shall be afraid and fear, because of the
44. 8 Fear ye not, neither be afraid: have not
44. 11 they shall fear..they shall be ashamed
60. 5 thine heart shall fear, and be enlarged
Jer. 33. 9 they shall fear and tremble for all the
Hos. 3. 5 shall fear the LORD and his goodness in

9. *To fear, be afraid*, פָּחַד *pachad*, 3.
Prov 28. 14 Happy (is) the man that feareth alway
Isa. 51. 13 and hast feared continually every day

10. *To fear, be afraid, frightened*, שָׂעַר *saar.*
Deut 32. 17 new (gods)..whom your fathers feared not

11. *To be circumspect, cautious*, εὐλαβέομαι *eulabeo.*
Acts 23. 10 the chief captain, [fearing] lest Paul should

12. *To cause fear, terrify*, φοβέω *phobeō.*
Matt. 1. 20 Joseph, thou son of David, fear not to
10. 26 Fear them not therefore: for there is
10. 28 And fear not them which kill the body
10. 28 but rather fear him which is able to des.
10. 31 Fear ye not therefore, ye are of more val.
14. 5 he feared the multitude, because they
21. 26 if we shall say, Of men; we fear the peo.
21. 46 they feared the multitude, because they
27. 54 they feared greatly, saying, Truly this
28. 5 the angel answered..Fear not ye; for I
Mark 4. 41 they feared exceedingly, and said one to
5. 33 But the woman, fearing and trembling
6. 20 For Herod feared John, knowing that he
11. 18 they feared him, because all the people
11. 32 if we shall say, Of men; they feared the
12. 12 they sought to lay hold on him, but fear.
Luke 1. 13 But the angel said unto him, Fear not
1. 30 And the angel said unto her, Fear not
1. 50 his mercy (is) on them that fear him
2. 10 the angel said unto them, Fear not: for
5. 10 And Jesus said unto Simon, Fear not
8. 50 when Jesus heard (it), he answered..Fe.
9. 34 they feared as they entered into the
9. 45 they feared to ask him of that saying
12. 5 I will forewarn you whom ye shall fear
12. 5 Fear him..I say unto you..Fear him
12. 7 Fear not therefore: ye are of more value
12. 32 Fear not, little flock; for it is your Fath.
18. 2 There was in a city a judge, which feared
18. 4 Though I fear not God, nor regard man
19. 21 For I feared thee, because thou art an
20. 19 they feared the people; for they percei.
22. 2 might kill him; for they feared the people
23. 40 Dost not thou fear God, seeing thou art
John 9. 22 These..spake his parents, because they f.
12. 15 Fear not, daughter of Sion: behold, thy
Acts 5. 26 for they feared the people, lest they
10. 2 A devout (man), and one that feared God
10. 22 Cornelius the centurion..one that feareth
10. 35 But in every nation he that feareth him
13. 16 Men of Israel, and ye that fear God, give
13. 26 whosoever among you feareth God, to
16. 38 they feared, when they heard that they
27. 17 fearing lest they should fall into the
27. 24 Fear not, Paul; thou must be brought
27. 29 fearing lest we should have fallen upon
Rom. 11. 20 Well..Be not high-minded, but fear
2 Co. 11. 3 I fear, lest, by any means, as the serpent
12. 20 I fear, lest, when I come, I shall not find

Gal. 2. 12 withdrew and separated himself, fearing
Col. 3. 22 but in singleness of heart, fearing God
Heb. 4. 1 Let us therefore fear, lest, a promise
11. 27 By faith he forsook Egypt, not fearing
13. 6 I will not fear what man shall do unto
1 Pe. 2. 17 Honour all..Fear God. Honour the
1 Jo. 4. 18 He that feareth is not made perfect in
Rev. 1. 17 Fear not; I am the first and the last
2. 10 Fear none of those things which thou
11. 18 them that fear thy name, small and gre.
14. 7 Saying with a loud voice, Fear God, and
15. 4 Who shall not fear thee, O Lord, and
19. 5 Praise our God, all..ye that fear him

13. *To have fear*, φόβον ἔχω *phobon echō.*
1 Ti. 5. 20 that sin rebuke..that others also may fear

FEAR exceedingly, to —
To be greatly afraid, terrified, ἔκφοβος εἶναι.
Heb. 12. 21 Moses said, I exceeedingly fear and quake

FEAR, to be in —
To fear, be afraid, פָּחַד *pachad.*
Psa. 14. 5 There were they in great fear: for God
53. 5 There were they in great fear, (where) no

FEAR, without —
Fearlessly, without fear, ἀφόβως *aphobōs.*
Luke 1. 74 we, being delivered..serve him without f.
1 Co. 16. 10 see that he may be with you without fear
Phil. 1. 14 more bold to speak the word without fe.
Jude 12 feeding themselves without fear: clouds

FEAR of —
Face of, פְּנֵי *pene.*
Judg. 9. 21 Jotham ran away..for fear of Abimelech
1 Sa. 21. 10 David arose, and fled that day for fear of
23. 26 David made haste to get away for fear of
Jer. 35. 11 Come, and let us go to Jerusalem for fear of
35. 11 and for fear of the army of the Syrians
37. 11 was broken up from Jerusalem for fear of
41. 9 which Asa the king had made for fear of
50. 16 for fear of the oppressing sword they shall

FEAR, to put in —
To make afraid, יָרֵא *yare*, 3.
Neh. 6. 14 the rest..that would have put me in fear
6. 19 Tobiah sent letters to put me in fear

FEARED, to be —
1. *To be feared, reverenced*, יָרֵא *yare*, 2.
1 Ch. 16. 25 he also (is) to be feared above all gods
Psa. 76. 7 Thou..thou, (art) to be feared: and who
96. 4 the LORD..he (is) to be feared above all
130. 4 forgiveness..that thou mayest be feared

2. *To fear, be afraid, terrified*, עָרַץ *arats*, 2.
Psa. 89. 7 God is greatly to be feared in the assem.

FEARED, that ought to be —
Fear or reverence, (an object of), מוֹרָא *mora.*
Psa. 76. 11 presents unto him that ought to be feared

FEARETH, in that (one) —
From or on account of his cautiousness, ἀπὸ τῆς εὐλαβείας *apo tēs eulabeias.*
Heb. 5. 7 to save..and was heard in that he feared

FEARFUL —
1. *To be feared, reverenced*, יָרֵא *yare*, 2.
Exod. 15. 11 LORD..fearful (in) praises, doing wond ?
Deut. 28. 58 mayest fear this glorious and fearful na.

2. *Fearing*, יָרֵא *yare.*
Deut. 20. 8 What man..fearful and faint hearted?
Judg. 7. 3 Whosoever (is) fearful and afraid, let

3. *To be hasty, hastened*, מָהַר *mahar*, 2.
Isa. 35. 4 Say to them..of a fearful heart, Be strong

4. *Timid*, δειλός *deilos.*
Matt. 8. 26 Why are ye fearful, O ye of little faith?
Mark 4. 40 he said unto them, Why are ye so fear.?
Rev. 21. 8 But the fearful, and unbelieving, and

5. *Fearful, terrible*, φοβερός *phoberos.*
Heb. 10. 27 But a certain fearful looking for of judg.

FEARFUL sight —
What is fearful or terrible, φόβητρον, φόβηθρον.
Luke 21. 11 fearful sights and great signs shall there

FEARFUL thing —
Fearful, terrible, φοβερός *phoberos.*
Heb. 10. 31 a fearful thing to fall into the hands of

FEARFULLY —
To be feared, reverenced, יָרֵא *yare*, 2.
Psa. 139. 14 I will praise thee; for I am fearfully (and)

FEARFULNESS —
1. *Fear, reverence*, יִרְאָה *yirah.*
Psa. 55. 5 Fearfulness and trembling are come upon

2. *Trembling, horror, fright*, פַּלָּצוּת *pallatsuth.*
Isa. 21. 4 My heart panted, fearfulness affrighted

3. *Trembling*, רְעָדָה *readah.*
Isa. 33. 14 fearfulness hath surprised the hypocrites

FEARING —
Fearing, reverencing, יָרֵא *yare.*
Josh. 22. 25 make our children cease from fearing the

FEARS —
Terrors, חַתְחַתִּים *chathchattim.*
Eccl. 12. 5 fears (shall be) in the way, and the almon.

FEAST —
1. *Festival*, חַג, חָג *chag.*
Exod. 10. 9 for we (must hold) a feast unto the LORD
12. 14 and ye shall keep it a feast to the LORD
13. 6 in the seventh day..a feast to the LORD
23. 15 Thou shalt keep the feast of unleavened
23. 16 the feast of harvest, the first fruits of thy
23. 16 the feast of ingathering..in the end of the
32. 5 said, To morrow (is) a feast to the LORD
34. 18 The feast of unleavened bread shalt thou
34. 22 thou shalt observe the feast of weeks, of
34. 22 the feast of ingathering at the year's end
34. 25 neither shall the sacrifice of the feast of
Lev. 23. 6 on the fifteenth day..(is) the feast of unl.
23. 34 The fifteenth day..(shall be) the feast of
23. 39 ye shall keep a feast unto the LORD seven
23. 41 ye shall keep it a feast unto the LORD
Num 28. 17 the fifteenth day of this month (is) the fe.
29. 12 ye shall keep a feast unto the LORD seven
Deut 16. 10 thou shalt keep the feast of weeks unto
16. 13 Thou shalt observe the feast of tabernac.
16. 14 thou shalt rejoice in thy feast, thou, and
16. 16 Three times..in the feast of unleavened
16. 16 in the feast of weeks, and in the feast
31. 10 seven years..in the feast of tabernacles
Judg 21. 19 a feast of the LORD in Shiloh yearly
1 Ki. 8. 2 all the men of Israel..at the feast in
8. 65 And at that time Solomon held a feast
12. 32 Jeroboam ordained a feast in the eighth
12. 32 like unto the feast that (is) in Judah, and
12. 33 ordained a feast unto the children of
2 Ch. 5. 3 the men of Israel assembled..in the feast
7. 8 at the same time Solomon kept the feast
7. 9 for they kept..the feast seven days
8. 13 in the feast of unleavened bread
8. 13 in the feast of weeks, and in the feast of
30. 13 assembled..much people to keep the fe.
30. 21 children of Israel..kept the feast of
35. 17 the feast of unleavened bread seven
Ezra 3. 4 They kept also the feast of tabernacles
6. 22 kept the feast of unleavened bread seven
Neh. 8. 14 should dwell in booths in the feast of
8. 18 they kept the feast seven days; and on
Eze. 45. 17 in the feasts, and in the new moons, and
45. 21 ye shall have the passover, a feast of
45. 23 seven days of the feast he shall prepare
45. 25 shall he do the like in the feast of the se.
46. 11 in the feasts and in the solemnities, the
Hos. 9. 5 What will ye do..in the day of the feast
Amos 8. 10 And I will turn your feasts into mourning
Zech 14. 16 and to keep the feast of tabernacles
14. 18, 19 not up to keep the feast of tabernacles

2. *Bread, eating*, לֶחֶם *lechem.*
Dan. 5. 1 Belshazzar the king made a great feast to

3. *An appointed meeting*, מוֹעֵד *moed.*
Lev. 23. 2 feasts of the LORD..these (are) my feasts
23. 4, 37 These (are) the feasts of the LORD
23. 44 Moses declared..the feasts of the LORD
2 Ch. 30. 22 they did eat throughout the feast seven
Zech. 8. 19 joy and gladness, and cheerful feasts

4. *Contortion, perversion*, מָעוֹג *maog.*
Psa. 35. 16 With hypocritical mockers in feasts, they

5. *Feast, drinking*, מִשְׁתֶּה *mishteh.*
Gen. 19. 3 he made them a feast, and did bake
21. 8 Abraham made a great feast the..day
26. 30 he made them a feast, and they did eat
29. 22 Laban gathered..the men..and made a f.
40. 20 he made a feast unto all his servants
Judg 14. 10 Samson made there a feast; for so used
14. 12 declare..within the seven days of the fe.
14. 17 And she wept..while their feast lasted
1 Sa. 25. 36 held a feast in his house, like the feast of
2 Sa. 3. 20 David made Abner, and the men..a feast
1 Ki. 3. 15 Solomon..made a feast to all his servants
Esth. 1. 3 third year of his reign, he made a feast
1. 5 the king made a feast unto all the people
1. 9 Also Vashti the queen made a feast for
2. 18 made a great feast..(even) Esther's feast
8. 17 the Jews had joy..a feast and a good day
Prov. 15. 15 a merry heart (hath) a continual feast
Isa. 5. 12 the harp..and wine, are in their feasts
25. 6 in this mountain shall..make..a feast
25. 6 a feast of wines on the lees, of fat things
Jer. 51. 39 In their heat I will make their feasts

6. *Supper*, δεῖπνον *deipnon.*
Matt 23. 6 love the uppermost rooms at feasts, and
Mark 12. 39 seats..and the uppermost rooms at feasts
Luke 20. 46 the scribes..love..the chief rooms at fe.

7. *Reception*, δοχή *dochē.*
Luke 5. 29 Levi made him a great feast in his own
14. 13 when thou makest a feast, call the poor

8. *Feast, festival*, ἑορτή *heortē.*
Matt 26. 5 Not on the feast..lest there be an uproar
27. 15 at (that) feast the governor was wont to
Mark 15. 6 at (that) feast he released unto them one
Luke 2. 41 to Jerusalem every year at the feast of
2. 42 to Jerusalem after the custom of the feast
22. 1 the feast of unleavened bread drew nigh
23. 17 [must release one unto them at the feast]
John 4. 45 at the feast: for they..went unto the feast
5. 1 After this there was a feast of the Jews
6. 4 the passover, a feast of the Jews, was
7. 2 the Jews' feast of tabernacles was at hand
7. 8 this feast: I go not up..unto this feast
7. 10 then went he also up unto the feast, not
7. 11 the Jews sought him at the feast, and
7. 14 about the midst of the feast, Jesus went
John 7. 37 In..that great (day) of the feast, Jesus
11. 56 that he will not come to the feast?
12. 12 much people that were come to the feast
12. 20 that came up to worship at the feast
13. 1 before the feast of the passover, when
13. 29 that we have need of against the feast
Acts 18. 21 [I must by all means keep this feast that]

FEAST of the dedication —
Dedications, ἐγκαίνια *egkainia.*
John 10. 22 at Jerusalem the feast of the dedication

FEAST, to —
To make a feast, עָשָׂה מִשְׁתֶּה *asah mishteh.*
Job 1. 4 his sons went and feasted (in their) houses

FEAST (day) —
1. *Festival*, חַג, חָג *chag.*
Hos. 2. 11 I will..cause..to cease, her feast days
Amos 5. 21 I hate, I despise your feast days, and I

2. *Feast, festival*, ἑορτή *heortē.*
Mark 14. 2 Not on the feast (day), lest there be an
John 2. 23 in the feast (day), many believed in his

FEAST, to hold or keep (a solemn) —
1. *To hold, keep or observe a festival*, חָגַג *chagag.*
Exod. 5. 1 that they may hold a feast unto me in the
12. 14 ye shall keep it a feast by an ordinance
23. 14 Three times thou shalt keep a feast unto
Lev. 23. 39 ye shall keep a feast unto the LORD seven
Deut 16. 15 Seven days shalt thou keep a solemn feast

2. *To hold a feast*, ἑορτάζω *heortazō.*
1 Co. 5. 8 let us keep the feast, not with old leaven

FEAST, set —
Appointed meeting, מוֹעֵד *moed.*
Num 29. 39 ye shall do..in your set feasts, beside your
1 Ch. 23. 31 all burnt sacrifices..on the set feasts
2 Ch. 31. 3 for the new moons, and for the set feasts
Ezra 3. 5 set feasts of the LORD that were consecr.
Neh. 10. 33 for the set feasts..and (for) all the work

FEAST, solemn —
1. *A festival*, חַג, חָג *chag.*
Psa. 81. 3 Blow up the trumpet..on our solemn fe.
Nah. 1. 15 keep thy solemn feasts, perform thy vows
Mal. 2. 3 (even) the dung of your solemn feasts

2. *Appointed meeting*, מוֹעֵד *moed.*
Num 15. 3 or in your solemn feasts, to make a sweet
2 Ch. 2. 4 the solemn feasts of the LORD our God
Lam. 1. 4 because none come to the solemn feasts
2. 6 the LORD hath caused the solemn feasts
2. 7 a noise..as in the day of a solemn feast
Eze. 36. 38 the flock of Jerusalem in her solemn fea.
46. 9 before the LORD in the solemn feasts
Hos. 2. 11 I will..cause..to cease..her solemn fea.
12. 9 dwell..as in the days of the solemn feasts

3. *Appointed meeting*, מוֹעָדָה *moadah.*
2 Ch. 8. 13 on the solemn feasts, three times in the

FEAST with, to —
To hold well with, συνευωχέω *suneuōcheō.*
2 Pe. 2. 13 sporting..with..while they feast with you
Jude 12 they feast with you, feeding themselves

FEASTING —
Feast, drinking, מִשְׁתֶּה *mishteh.*
Esth. 9. 17, 18 made it a day of feasting and gladness
9. 19 gladness and feasting, and a good day
9. 22 that they should make them days of feas.
Job 1. 5 when the days of..feasting were gone ab.
Eccl. 7. 2 mourning than..to the house of feasting
Jer. 16. 8 Thou shalt not..go into the house of fea.

FEATHER —
1. *Wing*, אֶבְרָה *ebrah.*
Psa. 68. 13 dove..and her feathers with yellow gold
91. 4 He shall cover thee with his feathers

2. *Feather*, נוֹצָה *notsah.*
Eze. 17. 3 full of feathers, which had divers colours
17. 7 another great eagle with..many feathers
Job 39. 13 or wings and feathers unto the ostrich?

3. *Feather*, נֹצָה *notsah.*
Lev. 1. 16 shall pluck away his crop with his feath.

FEATHERED —
Wing, כָּנָף *kanaph.*
Psa. 78. 27 He rained..feathered fowls like as the
Eze. 39. 17 Speak unto every feathered fowl, and to

FED (beast) —
1. *Fat, firm*, בָּרִיא *bari.*
Eze. 34. 3 Ye eat the fat..kill them that are fed

2. *To be fed*, זוּן *zun*, 6 [V.L. יָזַן].
Jer. 5. 8 They were (as) fed horses in the morning

3. *Fatling*, מְרִיא *meri.*
Isa. 1. 11 I am full of..the fat of fed beasts; and I

FED, to be — זוּן *zun*, 2. *to be fed.*
Dan. 4. 12 boughs thereof, and all flesh was fed of it

1. *To feed*, רָעָה *raah.*
Psa. 37. 3 Trust in the LORD..verily thou shalt be f.

2. *To fatten, satisfy*, χορτάζω *chortazō.*
Luke 16. 21 desiring to be fed with the crumbs which f.

FEEBLE —
1. *Weak*, אֲמֵלָל *amelal.*
Neh. 4. 2 What do these feeble Jews? will they f.

2. *To be feeble,* חָשַׁל *chashal,* 2.
Deut 25. 18 he..smote..all..feeble behind thee, when
3. *To bend or bow the knee,* כָּרַע *kara.*
Job 4. 4 thou hast strengthened the feeble knees
4. *To stumble,* כָּשַׁל *kashal.*
2 Ch. 28. 15 carried all the feeble of them upon asses
Psa. 105. 37 not one feeble (person) among their tribes
Isa. 35. 3 weak hands, and confirm the feeble knees
5. *To be stumbled,* כָּשַׁל *kashal,* 2.
Zech. 12. 8 he that is feeble among them at that day
6. *Not abundant, great, mighty,* לוֹא כַּבִּיר *lo kabbir.*
Isa. 16. 14 and the remnant..very small..feeble
7. *Not strong or bony,* לֹא־עֲצוּם *lo atsum.*
Prov 30. 26 The conies..a feeble folk, yet make they
8. *Without strength,* ἀσθενής *asthenēs.*
1 Co. 12. 22 members..which seem to be more feeble
9. *To loose, disjoin,* παραλύω *paraluō.*
Heb. 12. 12 Wherefore lift up..the feeble knees

FEEBLE, to be —
1. *To be feeble, covered,* עָטַף *ataph,* 5.
Gen. 30. 42 But when the cattle were feeble, he put
2. *To faint, cease, be feeble,* פּוּג *pug,* 2.
Psa. 38. 8 I am feeble and sore broken: I have roar.
3. *To be or become feeble,* רָפָה *raphah.*
2 Sa. 4. 1 his hands were feeble, and all the Israel.
Eze. 7. 17 All hands shall be feeble, and all knees
21. 7 all hands shall be feeble, and every spirit

FEEBLE, to wax —
To be or become feeble, רָפָה *raphah.*
Jer. 6. 24 our hands wax feeble: anguish hath tak.
49. 24 Damascus is waxed feeble, (and) turneth
50. 43 hath heard..and his hands waxed feeble

FEEBLE, to be waxed —
To be or become weak, אָמַל *amal,* 4b.
1 Sa. 2. 5 she that hath..children is waxed feeble

FEEBLE minded —
Of a little soul, faint-hearted, ὀλιγόψυχος *oligops.*
1 Th. 5. 14 comfort the feebleminded, support the

FEEBLENESS —
Feebleness, רִפְיוֹן *riphyon.*
Jer. 47. 3 not look back..for feeblenesss of hands

FEEBLER —
To be feeble, עָטַף *ataph.*
Gen. 30. 42 so the feebler were Laban's, and the

FEED, to (bestow to) —
1. *To eat,* אָכַל *akal.*
Lam. 4. 5 They that did feed delicately are desolate
Dan. 11. 26 they that feed..of his meat shall destroy
2. *To cause to burn, consume,* בָּעַר *baar,* 3.
Exod 22. 5 and shall feed in another man's field; of
3. *To taste,* טָעַם *team.*
Dan. 5. 21 they fed him with grass like oxen, and
4. *To cause to tear, feed,* טָרַף *taraph,* 5.
Prov. 30. 8 feed me with food convenient for me
5. *To sustain, nourish,* כּוּל *kul,* 3a.
2 Sa. 19. 33 Come thou over with me, and I will feed
20. 3 the king..put them in ward, and fed them
1 Ki. 17. 4 I have commanded the ravens to feed
18. 4 took an hundred prophets..and fed them
18. 13 I hid an hundred men..and fed them with
Zech 11. 16 nor feed that that standeth still; but he
6. *To feed, give to eat,* לָעַט *laat,* 5.
Gen. 25. 30 Esau said to Jacob, Feed me, I pray thee
7. *To lead, tend, feed,* נָהַל *nahal,* 3.
Gen. 47. 17 he fed them with bread for all their cattle
8. *To feed,* רָעָה *raah.*
Gen. 29. 7 water ye the sheep, and go (and) feed
30. 31 I will again feed (and) keep thy flock
30. 36 Jacob fed the rest of Laban's flocks
36. 24 as he fed the asses of Zibeon his father
37. 12 his brethren went to feed their father's fl.
37. 13 Do not thy brethren feed..in Shechem?
37. 16 tell me, I pray thee, where they feed
41. 2 well favoured kine..fed in a meadow
41. 18 seven kine..and they fed in a meadow
48. 15 the God which fed me all my life long
Exod 34. 3 neither let the flocks nor herds feed befo.
1 Sa. 17. 15 David went..to feed his father's sheep at
2 Sa. 5. 2 Thou shalt feed my people Israel, and
7. 7 whom I commanded to feed my people I.
1 Ch. 11. 2 Thou shalt feed my people Israel, and
17. 6 whom I commanded to feed my people
27. 29 And over the herds that fed in Sharon
Job 24. 2 they violently take away flocks, and feed
Psa. 28. 9 Save thy people..feed them also, and lift
49. 14 laid in the grave; death shall feed on
78. 71 he brought him to feed Jacob his people
78. 72 So he fed them according to the integrity
Prov 10. 21 The lips of the righteous feed many: but
15. 14 the mouth of fools feedeth on foolishness
Song 1. 7 Tell me..where thou feedest, where thou
1. 8 O thou fairest among women..feed thy
2. 16 My beloved..feedeth among the lilies
4. 5 young roes..which feed among the lilies
6. 2 My beloved is gone down..to feed in the
6. 3 my beloved (is) mine: he feedeth among
Isa. 5. 17 Then shall the lambs feed after their man.
11. 7 And the cow and the bear shall feed
14. 30 the first born of the poor shall feed, and
27. 10 there shall the calf feed, and there shall
30. 23 in that day shall thy cattle feed in large
40. 11 He shall feed his flock like a shepherd; he
44. 20 He feedeth on ashes: a deceived heart
49. 9 They shall feed in the ways, and their
61. 5 strangers shall stand and feed your flocks
65. 25 the wolf and the lamb shall feed together
Jer. 3. 15 pastors..which shall feed you with know.
6. 3 they shall feed every one in his place
23. 2 against the pastors that feed my people
23. 4 set up shepherds..which shall feed them
50. 19 he shall feed on Carmel and Bashan, and
Eze. 34. 2 Woe (be) to the shepherds..that do feed
34. 2 should not the shepherds feed the flocks?
34. 3 Ye eat the fat..(but) ye feed not the flock
34. 8 the shepherds fed themselves, and fed not
34. 10 cause them to cease from feeding the flock
34. 10 neither shall the shepherds feed themsel.
34. 13 I will..feed them upon the mountains of
34. 14 I will feed them in a good pasture, and
34. 14 a fat pasture shall they feed upon the
34. 15 I will feed my flock, and I will cause them
34. 16 the fat..I will feed them with judgment
34. 23 one Shepherd..and he shall feed them
34. 23 he shall feed them, and he shall be their
Hos. 4. 16 now the LORD will feed them as a lamb
9. 2 floor and the wine press shall not feed
12. 1 Ephraim feedeth on wind, and followeth
Jon. 3. 7 flock..let them not feed, nor drink water
Mic. 5. 4 he shall stand and feed in the strength of
7. 14 Feed thy people with thy rod, the flock of
7. 14 let them feed (in) Bashan and Gilead, as
Zeph. 2. 7 they shall feed thereupon: in the houses
3. 13 they shall feed and lie down, and none
Zech 11. 4 saith..Feed the flock of the slaughter
11. 7 I will feed the flock of slaughter..you, O
11. 7 And I took..two staves..and I fed the
11. 9 Then said I, I will not feed you: that
9. *To feed, pasture,* βόσκω *boskō.*
Matt. 8. 30 there was..an herd of many swine feed.
Mark 5. 11 there was..a great herd of swine feeding
5. 14 they that fed the swine fled, and told (it)
Luke 8. 32 there was..an herd of many swine feed.
8. 34 When they that fed..saw what was done
15. 15 he sent him into his fields to feed swine
John 21. 15 He saith unto him, Feed my lambs
21. 17 Jesus saith unto him, Feed my sheep
10. *To tend as a shepherd,* ποιμαίνω *poimainō.*
John 21. 16 He saith unto him, Feed my sheep
Acts 20. 28 Take heed..to feed the church of God
1 Co. 9. 7 or who feedeth a flock, and eateth not of
1 Pe. 5. 2 Feed the flock of God which is among
Jude 12 they feast..feeding themselves without f.
Rev. 7. 17 For the Lamb..shall feed them, and shall
11. *To nourish,* τρέφω *trephō.*
Matt. 6. 26 yet your heavenly Father feedeth them
25. 37 LORD, when saw we thee..and fed (thee)?
Luke 12. 24 Consider the ravens..God feedeth them
Rev. 12. 6 that they should feed her there a thousand
12. *To feed with bits as a child,* ψωμίζω *psōmizō.*
Rom 12. 20 if thine enemy hunger, feed him; if he
1 Co. 13. 3 though I bestow all my goods to feed

FEED cattle, to —
To tend as a shepherd, ποιμαίνω *poimainō.*
Luke 17. 7 having a servant..feeding cattle, will say

FEED to the full, to —
To satisfy, fill, שָׂבַע *saba,* 5.
Jer. 5. 7 when I had fed them to the full, they

FEED with, to —
1. *To cause or give to eat,* אָכַל *akal,* 5.
Exod 16. 32 see the bread wherewith I have fed you
Deut. 8. 3 he humbled thee..and fed thee with m.
8. 16 Who fed thee in the wilderness with m.
1 Ki. 22. 27 feed him with bread of affliction, and with
2 Ch. 18. 26 feed him with bread of affliction and with
Psa 80. 5 Thou feedest them with the bread of tears
81. 16 He should have fed them also with the
Isa. 49. 26 I will feed them..with their own flesh
58. 14 I will..feed thee with the heritage of Jac.
Jer. 9. 15 I will feed them..with wormwood, and
23. 15 I will feed them with wormwood, and
Eze. 16. 19 oil, and honey, (wherewith) I fed thee
2. *To give to drink, to water,* ποτίζω *potizō.*
1 Co. 3. 2 I have fed you with milk, and not with

FEEDING —
To feed, רָעָה *raah.*
Gen. 37. 2 Joseph..was feeding the flock with his
Job 1. 14 oxen were plowing, and the asses feeding

FEEDING place —
Feeding place, מִרְעֶה *mireh.*
Nah. 2. 11 Where (is)..the feeding place of the young

FEEL, to —
1. *To understand, feel,* בִּין *bin.*
Psa. 58. 9 Before your pots can feel the thorns, he
2. *To know,* יָדַע *yada.*
Job 20. 20 Surely he shall not feel quietness in his
Prov 23. 35 they have beaten me, (and) I felt (it) not
Eccl. 8. 5 keepeth the commandment shall feel no
3. *To feel, touch, grope,* מוּשׁ *mush* 5, [V.L. מֵשׁ;].
Judg 16. 26 Suffer me that I may feel the pillars where.
4. *To feel, touch,* מוּשׁ *mush.*
Gen. 27. 21 Come near, I pray thee, that I may feel
5. *To feel, search, grope,* מָשַׁשׁ *mashash.*
Gen. 27. 12 My father peradventure will feel me, and
27. 22 Jacob went near..and he felt him, and
6. *To begin to know,* γινώσκω *ginōskō.*
Mark 5. 29 she felt in..body that she was healed of
7. *To suffer,* πάσχω *paschō.*
Acts 28. 5 he shook off the beast..and felt no harm

FEEL after, to —
To touch, handle, feel after, ψηλαφάω *psēlaphaō.*
Acts 17. 27 if haply they might feel after him, and

FEELING, to be past —
To put away pain, ἀπαλγέω *apalgeō.*
Eph. 4. 19 Who being past feeling have given them.

FEELING of, to be touched with the —
To suffer along with, συμπαθέω *sumpatheō.*
Heb. 4. 15 cannot be touched with the feeling of our

FEET —
1. *Feet (place of the),* מַרְגְּלוֹת *margeloth.*
Ruth. 3. 4 thou shalt go in, and uncover his feet, and
3. 7 she came softly, and uncovered his feet
3. 8 and, behold, a woman lay at his feet
3. 14 And she lay at his feet until the morning
Dan. 10. 6 his feet like in colour to polished brass
2. *Ancles, joints (of the feet),* קַרְסֻלַּיִם *qarsullayim.*
2 Sa. 22. 37 my steps..so that my feet did not slip
Psa. 18 36 enlarged my steps..that my feet did not
3. *Feet,* רַגְלַיִם *raglayim.*
Gen. 18. 4 wash your feet, and rest yourselves under
19. 2 tarry all night, and wash your feet, and
24. 32 to wash his feet, and the men's feet that
43. 24 gave..water, and they washed their feet
49. 10 nor a lawgiver from between his feet, un.
49. 33 he gathered up his feet into the bed, and
Exod. 3. 5 put off thy shoes from off thy feet, for
4. 25 cast (it) at his feet, and said, Surely a bl.
12. 11 loins girded, your shoes on your feet, and
24. 10 under his feet as it were a paved work of
25. 26 four corners that (are) on the four feet
30. 19 his sons shall wash..their feet thereat
30. 21 they shall wash their hands and their feet
37. 13 the four corners that (were) in the four f.
40. 31 and his sons washed..their feet thereat
Lev. 8. 24 upon the great toes of their right feet; and
11. 21 which have legs above their feet, to leap
11. 23 creeping things, which have four feet
11. 42 whatsoever hath more feet among all cr.
Num 20. 19 I will only..go through on my feet
Deut. 2. 28 only I will pass through on my feet
11. 24 whereon the soles of your feet shall tread
28. 57 one that cometh out from between her f.
33. 3 they sat down at thy feet; (every one) sh.
Josh. 3. 13 the feet of the priests that bare the
4. 3 place where the priest's feet stood firm
4. 9 in the place where the feet of the priests
4. 18 the soles of the priests' feet were lifted
9. 5 old shoes and clouted upon their feet, and
10. 24 put your feet upon the necks of these ki.
10. 24 they..put their feet upon the necks of
14. 9 land whereon thy feet have trodden shall
Judg. 3. 24 Surely he covereth his feet in his summer
4. 10 with ten thousand men at his feet: and
4. 15 so that Sisera..fled away on his feet
4. 17 Sisera fled away on his feet to the tent of
5. 27 At her feet he bowed..at her feet he bo.
19. 21 they washed their feet, and did eat and
1 Sa. 2. 9 He will keep the feet of his saints, and
14. 13 Jonathan climbed up upon..his feet, and
24. 3 Saul went in to cover his feet: and David
25. 24 fell at his feet, and said, Upon me, my
25. 41 handmaid (be) a servant to wash the feet
2 Sa. 3. 34 Thy hands (were) not bound, nor thy feet
4. 4 Jonathan..had a son..lame of (his) feet
4. 12 they..cut off their hands and their feet
9. 3 hath yet a son, (which is) lame on (his) f.
9. 13 Mephibosheth..was lame on both his feet
11. 8 Go down to thy house, and wash thy feet
19. 24 had neither dressed his feet, nor trimmed
22. 10 came down; and darkness (was) under his f.
22. 34 He maketh my feet like hinds' (feet); and
22. 39 yea, they are fallen under my feet
1 Ki. 2. 5 and in his shoes that (were) on his feet
5. 3 until the LORD put them under..his feet
14. 6 when Ahijah heard the sound of her feet
14. 12 when thy feet enter into the city, the ch.
15. 23 Nevertheless..he was diseased in his feet
2 Ki. 4. 27 when she came..she caught him by the f.
4. 37 Then she went in, and fell at his feet, and
6. 32 (is) not the sound of his master's feet be.
9. 35 they found no more of her than..the feet
13. 21 he revived, and stood upon his feet
21. 8 Neither will I make the feet of Israel mo.
1 Ch. 28. 2 Then David the king stood up upon his f.
2 Ch. 3. 13 and they stood on their feet, and their f.
16. 12 And Asa..was diseased in his feet, until
Neh. 9. 21 waxed not old, and their feet swelled not
Esth. 8. 3 Esther spake..and fell down at his feet
Job 12. 5 He that is ready to slip with (his) feet (is
13. 27 Thou puttest my feet also in the stocks
13. 27 settest a print upon the heels of my feet
18. 8 For he is cast into a net by his own feet
18. 11 Terrors..shall drive him to his feet
29. 15 I was eyes to the blind, and feet (was) I
30. 12 they push away my feet, and they raise

Job 33. 11 He putteth my feet in the stocks, he ma.
Psa. 8. 6 thou hast put all (things) under his feet
18. 9 came down..darkness (was) under his f.
18. 33 He maketh my feet like hinds' (feet), and
18. 38 not able..they are fallen under my feet
22. 16 they pierced my hands and my feet
25. 15 for he shall pluck my feet out of the net
31. 8 thou hast set my feet in a large room
40. 2 He..set my feet upon a rock, (and) estab.
47. 3 He shall subdue..the nations under our f.
56. 13 (wilt) not (thou deliver) my feet from fal.
66. 9 and suffereth not our feet to be moved
73. 2 my feet were almost gone; my steps had
105. 18 Whose feet they hurt with fetters: he
115. 7 feet have they, but they walk not; neith.
116. 8 eyes from tears, (and) my feet from falling
119. 59 and turned my feet unto thy testimonies
119. 101 refrained my feet from every evil way
119. 105 Thy word (is) a lamp unto my feet, and
122. 2 Our feet shall stand within thy gates, O
Prov. 1. 16 their feet run to evil, and make haste to
4. 26 Ponder the path of thy feet, and let all
5. 5 Her feet go down to death; her steps ta.
6. 13 he speaketh with his feet, he teacheth
6. 18 feet that be swift in running to mischief
6. 28 upon hot coals, and his feet not be burn.?
7. 11 her feet abide not in her house
19. 2 and he that hasteth with (his) feet sinne.
26. 6 sendeth a message..cutteth off the feet
Song 5. 3 I have washed my feet; how shall I defi.
Isa. 3. 16 and making a tinkling with their feet
6. 2 with twain he covered his feet, and with
7. 20 shave..the head, and the hair of the feet
23. 7 own feet shall carry her afar off to sojou.
26. 6 foot shall tread it down, (even) the feet
28. 3 The crown..shall be trodden under feet
32. 20 (thither) the feet of the ox and the ass
41. 3 way (that) he had not gone with his feet
49. 23 and lick up the dust of thy feet; and thou
52. 7 feet of him that bringeth good tidings
59. 7 feet run to evil, and they make haste to
60. 13 will make the place of my feet glorious
60. 14 themselves down at the soles of thy feet
Jer. 13. 16 before your feet stumble upon the dark
14. 10 they have not refrained their feet
18. 22 pit to take me, and hid snares for my f.
38. 22 thy feet are sunk in the mire, (and) they
Lam. 1. 13 he hath spread a net for my feet; he hath
3. 34 crush under his feet all the prisoners of
Eze. 1. 7 their feet (were) straight feet; and the
1. 7 sole of their feet (was) like..calf's foot
2. 1 stand upon thy feet, and I will speak unto
2. 2 set me upon my feet, that I heard him
3. 24 set me upon my feet, and spake with me
16. 25 hast opened thy feet to every one that
24. 17 put on thy shoes upon thy feet, and cover
24. 23 and your shoes upon your feet: ye shall
25. 6 stamped with the feet, and rejoiced in
32. 2 troubledst the waters with thy feet, and
34. 18 tread down with your feet the residue of
34. 18 ye must foul the residue with your feet?
34. 19 that which ye have trodden with your feet
34. 19 that which ye have fouled with your feet
37. 10 stood up upon their feet, an exceeding
43. 7 the place of the soles of my feet, where
Nah. 1. 3 and the clouds (are) the dust of his feet
1. 15 feet of him that bringeth good tidings
Hab. 3. 5 and burning coals went forth at his feet
3. 19 and he will make my feet like hinds'
Zech. 14. 4 his feet shall stand in that day upon
14. 12 consume..while they stand upon their f.
Mal. 4. 3 ashes under the soles of your feet in the

4. *Foot,* רְגַל *regal.*
Dan. 2. 33 his feet part of iron and part of clay
2. 34 upon his feet (that were) of iron and clay
2. 41 thou sawest the feet and toes, part of
2. 42 (as) the toes of the feet (were) part of iron
7. 4 made stand upon the feet as a man, and a
7. 7 stamped the residue with the feet of it
7. 19 and stamped the residue with his feet

5. *Foot,* πούς *pous.*
Matt. 7. 6 lest they trample them under their feet
10. 14 depart..shake off the dust of your feet
15. 30 came..and cast them down at Jesus' feet
18. 8 two feet to be cast into everlasting fire
18. 29 [this fellow servant fell down at his feet]
28. 9 they came and held him by the feet, and
Mark 5. 22 and when he saw him, he fell at his feet
6. 11 shake off the dust under your feet for a
7. 25 heard of him..came and fell at his feet
9. 45 than having two feet to be cast into hell
Luke 1. 79 to guide our feet into the way of peace
7. 38 stood at his feet..began to wash his feet
7. 38 kissed his feet, and anointed (them) with
7. 44 thou gavest me no water for my feet
7. 44 she hath washed my feet with tears, and
7. 45 woman..hath not ceased to kiss my feet
7. 46 woman hath anointed [my feet] with oint.
8. 35 sitting at the feet of Jesus, clothed, and
8. 41 he fell down at Jesus' feet, and besought
9. 5 shake off the very dust from your feet
10. 39 Mary, which also sat at Jesus' feet, and
15. 22 ring on his hand, and shoes on (his) feet
17. 16 fell down on (his) face at his feet, giving
24. 39 Behold my hands and my feet, that it is I
24. 40 [showed them (his) hands and (his) feet]
John 11. 2 and wiped his feet with her hair, whose
11. 32 she fell down at his feet, saying unto him
12. 3 anointed the feet..and wiped his feet
13. 5 began to wash the disciples feet, and to
13. 6 Peter saith..Lord, dost thou wash my f.?
John 13. 8 saith..Thou shalt never wash my feet
13. 9 not my feet only, but also (my) hands and
13. 10 He..needeth not save to wash (his) [feet]
13. 12 after he had washed their feet, and had
13. 14 If I then, (your) Lord..washed your feet
13. 14 ye also ought to wash one another's feet
20. 12 one at the head, and the other at the feet
Acts 4. 35 And laid (them) down at the apostles' feet
4. 37 money, and laid (it) at the apostles' feet
5. 2 a..part, and laid (it) at the apostles' feet
5. 9 the feet of them which have buried thy
5. 10 fell she down straightway at his feet
7. 33 Put off thy shoes from thy feet: for the
7. 58 laid..their clothes at a young man's feet
10. 25 fell down at his feet, and worshipped (him)
13. 25 whose shoes of (his) feet I am not worthy
13. 51 shook off the dust of their feet against
14. 8 impotent in his feet, being a cripple from
14. 10 Stand upright on thy feet. And he leaped
16. 24 and made their feet fast in the stocks
21. 11 and bound his own hands and feet, and
22. 3 yet brought up..at the feet of Gamaliel
26. 16 stand upon thy feet: for I have appeared
Rom. 3. 15 Their feet (are) swift to shed blood
10. 15 feet of them that preach the gospel of
16. 20 bruise Satan under your feet shortly
1 Co. 12. 21 nor again the head to the feet, I have no
15. 25 he hath put all enemies under his feet
15. 27 For he hath put all things under his feet
Eph. 1. 22 hath put all (things) under his feet, and
6. 15 your feet shod with the preparation of
1 Ti. 5. 10 if she have washed the saints' feet, if she
Heb. 2. 8 all things in subjection under his feet
12. 13 make straight paths for your feet, lest
Rev. 1. 15 his feet like unto fine brass, as if they
1. 17 when I saw him, I fell at his feet as dead
2. 18 and his feet (are) like fine brass
3. 9 them to come and worship before thy feet
10. 1 the sun, and his feet as pillars of fire
11. 11 into them, and they stood upon their feet
12. 1 a woman..with..the moon under her feet
13. 2 was like unto a leopard, and his feet were
19. 10 I fell at his feet to worship him. And he
22. 8 to worship before the feet of the angel

6. *Stepping, foot, basis,* βάσις *basis.*
Acts 3. 7 feet and ancle bones received strength

FEIGN, to —

1. *To devise, feign,* בָּדָא *bada.*
Neh. 6. 8 thou feignest them out of thine own heart

2. *To pretend, be judged under a mask,* ὑποκρίνομαι *hupokrinomai.*
Luke 20. 20 which should feign themselves just men

FEIGN self to be another, to —

To make self a stranger, נָכַר *nakar,* 7.
1 Ki. 14. 5 shall feign herself (to be) another (woman)
14. 6 why feignest thou thyself (to be) another?

FEIGN self to be a mourner, to —

To show self a mourner, אָבַל *abal,* 7.
2 Sa. 14. 2 I pray..feign thyself to be a mourner

FEIGNED —

1. *Deceit,* מִרְמָה *mirmah.*
Psa. 17. 1 prayer, (that goeth) not out of feigned

2. *Shaped, formed,* πλαστός *plastos.*
2 Pe. 2. 3 with feigned words make merchandise of

FEIGNEDLY —

Falsehood, שֶׁקֶר *sheqer.*
Jer. 3. 10 not..with her whole heart, but feignedly

FE'-LIX, Φῆλιξ *phēlix, (from Latin felix), happy.*
A cruel Roman procurator of Judæa, appointed (after Cumanus) by the emperor Claudius, whose freedman he was. A.D. 51–58.
Acts 23. 24 and bring (him) safe unto F. the governor
23. 26 Claudius Lysias unto the..governor F.
24. 3 We accept (it) always..most noble F.
24. 22 When F. heard these things..he deferred
24. 24 after certain days, when F. came with
24. 25 as he reasoned of righteousness. F.
24. 27 after two years P. Festus came into F.
25. 14 There is a certain man left in bonds by F.

FELL, to —

To cause to fall, נָפַל *naphal,* 5.
2 Ki. 3. 19 shall fell every good tree, and stop all
3. 25 and they..felled all the good trees: only

FELLER —

To cut off, כָּרַת *karath.*
Isa. 14. 8 Since thou..no feller is come up against us

FELLING —

To cause to fall, נָפַל *naphal,* 5.
2 Ki. 6. 5 as one was felling a beam, the ax headf.

FELLOES —

Spokes (of a wheel), חִשֻּׁקִים *chishshuqim.*
1 Ki. 7. 33 felloes, and their spokes, (were) all molten

FELLOW —

1. *A man, individual,* אִישׁ *ish.*
1 Sa. 29. 4 Make this fellow return, that he may go

2. *A man,* אֱנוֹשׁ *enosh.*
Judg 18. 25 lest angry fellows run upon thee, and thou

3. *Companion,* חָבֵר *chaber.*
Psa. 45. 7 God..hath anointed thee..above thy fel.
Eccl. 4. 10 they fall, the one will lift up his fellow
Isa. 44. 11 all his fellows shall be ashamed; and
Eze. 37. 19 and the tribes of Israel his fellows, and

4. *Companion,* חַבַר *chabar.*
Dan. 2. 13 sought Daniel and his fellows to be slain
2. 18 that Daniel and his fellows should not

5. *Companion,* חַבְרָה *chabrah.*
Dan. 7. 20 whose look..more stout than his fellows

6. *Fellow, fellowship,* עָמִית *amith.*
Zech 13. 7 Awake..against the man (that is) my fell.

7. *Friend,* רֵעַ *rea.*
Exod. 2. 13 Wherefore smitest thou thy fellow?
Judg. 7. 13 a man that told a dream unto his fellow
7. 14 And his fellow answered and said, This
7. 22 set every man's sword against his fellow
1 Sa. 14. 20 every man's sword was against his fellow
2 Sa. 2. 16 caught every one his fellow by the head
2. 16 and (thrust) his sword in his fellow's side
Isa. 34. 14 and the satyr shall cry to his fellow
Jon. 1. 7 they said every one to his fellow, Come
Zech. 3. 8 thou, and thy fellows that sit before thee

8. *Friend,* רְעָה *reah* [V.L. רַעְיָה *rayah*].
Judg 11. 37 and bewail my virginity, I and my fellows

9. *A man,* ἀνήρ *anēr.*
Acts 17. 5 certain lewd fellows of the baser sort

10. *Companion, comrade,* ἑταῖρος *hetairos.*
Matt. 11. 16 like..children..calling unto their [fell.]

11. *Partner, holding with others,* μέτοχος *metochos.*
Heb. 1. 9 God..hath anointed thee..above thy fel.

FELLOWSHIP —

1. *Fellowship, deposit,* תְּשׂוּמֶת יָד *tesumeth yad.*
Lev. 6. 2 commit a trespass..in fellowship, or in

2. *Fellowship, communion,* κοινωνία *koinōnia.*
Acts 2. 42 in the apostles' doctrine and fellowship
1 Co. 1. 9 by whom ye were called unto the fellow.
2 Co. 8. 4 the fellowship of the ministering to the
Gal. 2. 9 they gave..the right hands of fellowship
Eph. 3. 9 see what (is) the [fellowship] of the mys.
Phil. 1. 5 For your fellowship in the Gospel from
2. 1 if any fellowship of the Spirit, if any
3. 10 That I may know..the fellowship of his
1 Jo. 1. 3 that ye also may have fellowship with us
1. 3 truly our fellowship (is) with the Father
1. 6 If we say that we have fellowship with
1. 7 we have fellowship one with another, and

3. *Partnership, a holding with,* μετοχή *metochē.*
2 Co. 6. 14 what fellowship hath righteousness with

[*See also* Base, citizen, disciple, heir, helper, labourer, pestilent, prisoner, servant, soldier, such, this, work, worker, yoke.]

FELLOWSHIP with, to have —

1. *To be joined,* חָבַר *chabar,* 4.
Psa. 94. 20 Shall..iniquity have fellowship with

2. *To become a partaker,* κοινωνὸς γίνομαι *koinōnos g.*
1 Co. 10. 20 that ye should have fellowship with dev.

3. *To be a joint partaker with,* συγκοινωνέω *sugko.*
Eph. 5. 11 have no fellowship with the unfruitful

FELT, to be —

To (cause to) feel, touch, grope, מָשַׁשׁ *mashash,* 5.
Exod. 10. 21 there..be darkness..(which) may be felt

FEMALE —

1. *A woman, female, wife,* אִשָּׁה *ishshah.*
Gen. 7. 2 male and his female..male and his fem.

2. *A female,* נְקֵבָה *neqebah.*
Gen. 1. 27 God created man..male and female crea.
5. 2 Male and female created he them; and
6. 19 living thing..they shall be male and fem.
7. 3 Of fowls also..the male and the female
7. 9 There went in..the male and the female
7. 16 they that went in, went in male and fem.
Lev. 3. 1 whether..a male or female, he shall offer
3. 6 male or female, he shall offer it without
4. 28 he shall bring..a female without blemish
4. 32 he shall bring..a female without blemish
5. 6 he shall bring..a female from the flock
12. 7 the law for her that hath born..a female
27. 4 if it (be) a female, then thy estimation
27. 5 thy estimation shall be..for the female
27. 6 for the female thy estimation..three sh.
27. 7 thy estimation..for the female ten shekels
Num. 5. 3 Both male and female shall ye put out
Deut. 4. 16 and make..the likeness of male or fem.

3. *Female, (from* θηλή, *teat),* θῆλυς *thēlus.*
Matt 19. 4 that he..made them male and female
Mark 10. 6 But..God made them male and female
Gal. 3. 28 there is neither male nor female: for ye

FEN —

Mire, swamp, בִּצָּה *bitstsah.*
Job 40. 21 lieth..in the covert of the reed, and fens

FENCE —

Hedge, wall, גָּדֵר *gader.*
Psa. 62. 3 shall be..as a bowing wall..a tottering f.

FENCE, to —

1. *To fence,* עָזַק *azaq,* 3.
Isa. 5. 2 he fenced it, and gathered out the stones

2. *To hedge, fence,* שׂוּךְ *suk,* 3a.
Job 10. 11 Thou..hast fenced me with bones and

FENCE up, to —
To hedge or wall up, גָּדַר *gadar.*
Job 19. 8 He hath fenced up my way that I cannot

FENCED —
1. *To fence, cut off,* בָּצַר *batsar.*
Deut. 3. 5 All these cities (were) fenced with high
9. 1 to possess..cities great, and fenced up to
28. 52 until thy high and fenced walls come
Josh. 14. 12 (that) the cities (were) great (and) fenced
2 Sa. 20. 6 lest he get him fenced cities, and escape
2 Ki. 18. 13 did..come up against all the fenced cities
19. 25 thou shouldst be to lay waste fenced cit.
2 Ch. 17. 2 he placed forces in all the fenced cities
19. 5 throughout all the fenced cities of Judah
32. 1 and encamped against the fenced cities
33. 14 put captains of war in all the fenced cit.
Isa. 2. 15 every high tower, and..every fenced wall
Jer. 15. 20 I will make thee..a fenced brasen wall
Eze. 36. 35 ruined cities (are become) fenced, (and)
Hos. 8. 14 and Judah hath multiplied fenced cities
Zeph. 1. 16 A day of..alarm against the fenced cities
2. *Fenced place,* מִבְצָר *mibtsar.*
Num 32. 17 shall dwell in the fenced cities because
32. 36 Beth-nimrah, and Beth-haran, fenced cit.
Josh. 10. 20 that the rest..entered into fenced cities
19. 35 the fenced cities (are) Ziddim, Zer, and
1 Sa. 6. 18 of fenced cities, and of country villages
2 Ki. 3. 19 ye shall smite every fenced city, and ev.
10. 2 chariots..a fenced city also, and armour
17. 9 the tower of the watchmen to the fenced
18. 8 the tower of the watchmen to the fenced
2 Ch. 17. 19 whom the king put in the fenced cities
Jer. 5. 17 they shall impoverish thy fenced cities
3. *Bulwark,* מָצוֹר *matsor.*
2 Ch. 8. 5 fenced cities, with walls, gates, and bars
4. *Bulwark,* מְצוּרָה *metsurah.*
2 Ch. 11. 23 he dispersed of all..unto every fenced c.
12. 4 And he took the fenced cities which
14. 6 he built fenced cities in Judah: for the
21. 3 their father gave them..fenced cities in

FENCED, to be —
To be or become full, מָלֵא *male,* 2.
2 Sa. 23. 7 But the man..must be fenced with iron

FENCED city —
Bulwark, מְצוּרָה *metsurah.*
2 Ch. 11. 10 in Judah and in Benjamin fenced cities

FENCED, most —
Fenced place, מִבְצָר *mibtsar.*
Dan. 11. 15 king..shall..take the most fenced cities

FERRET —
A ferret, hedgehog, אֲנָקָה *anaqah.*
Lev. 11. 30 And the ferret, and the chameleon, and

FERRY boat —
Ferry boat, עֲבָרָה *abarah.*
2 Sa. 19. 18 there went over a ferry boat to carry over

FERVENT —
1. *Extended, stretched out,* ἐκτενής *ektenēs.*
1 Pe. 4. 8 above all things have fervent charity am.
2. *To boil, be hot, fervid,* ζέω *zeō.*
Rom 12. 11 Not slothful..fervent in spirit; serving

FERVENT, to be —
To boil, be hot, fervid, ζέω *zeō.*
Acts 18. 25 being fervent in the spirit, he spake and

FERVENT mind —
Zeal, fervour, ζῆλος *zēlos.*
2 Co. 7. 7 told us..your fervent mind toward me

FERVENTLY —
In an outstretched manner, ἐκτενῶς *ektenōs.*
1 Pe. 1. 22 love one another with a pure heart ferv.

FES'-TUS, Φῆστος *(from Latin festus).*
Porcius Festus, the successor of Felix as procurator of Judæa. A.D. 58-62.
Acts 24. 27 after two years Porcius F. came into F.'
25. 1 when F. was come into the province
25. 4 F. answered, that Paul should be kept at
25. 9 F., willing to do the Jews a pleasure
25. 12 F., when he had conferred with the cou.
25. 13 Bernice came unto Cæsarea to salute F.
25. 14 F. declared Paul's cause unto the king
25. 22 Then Agrippa said unto F., I would also
25. 23 at F.'s commandment Paul was brought
25. 24 F. said, King Agrippa, and all men which
26. 24 F. said with a loud voice, Paul, thou art
26. 25 But he said, I am not mad, most noble F.
26. 32 Then said Agrippa unto F., This man

FETCH, to —
1. *To gather,* אָסַף *asaph.*
2 Sa. 11. 27 David sent and fetched her to his house
2. *To cause to come in, bring in,* בּוֹא *bo,* 5.
Neh. 8. 15 Go forth unto the mount, and fetch olive
3. *To take, receive,* לָקַח *laqach.*
Gen. 18. 5 I will fetch a morsel of bread, and comf.
18. 7 Abraham..fetched a calf tender and good
27. 9 Go now to the flock, and fetch me from
27. 13 only obey my voice, and go fetch me
27. 14 And he went, and fetched, and brought
27. 45 I will send and fetch thee from thence
42. 16 Send one of you, and let him fetch your
Exod. 2. 5 saw the ark..she sent her maid to fetch
Deut 19. 12 the elders of his city shall send and fetch
24. 19 thou shalt not go again to fetch it: it
30. 4 and from thence will he fetch thee
Judg 11. 5 the elders of Gilead went to fetch Jeph.
18. 18 these..fetched the carved image, the
20. 10 to fetch victual for the people, that they
1 Sa. 4. 3 Let us fetch the ark of the covenant of
10. 23 And they ran and fetched him thence
16. 11 Samuel said unto Jesse, Send and fetch
20. 31 now send and fetch him unto me, for he
26. 22 one of the young men come..and fetch it
2 Sa. 4. 6 (as though) they would have fetched wh.
9. 5 David..fetched him out of the house of
14. 2 Joab sent to Tekoah, and fetched thence
1 Ki. 7. 13 Solomon sent and fetched Hiram out of
9. 28 they came to Ophir, and fetched from
17. 10 Fetch me..a little water in a vessel, that
17. 11 as she was going to fetch (it), he called to
2 Ki. 6. 13 spy where he (is), that I may send and f.
11. 4 Jehoiada sent and fetched the rulers over
Isa. 56. 12 I will fetch wine, and we will fill ourselves
Jer. 36. 21 So the king sent Jehudi to fetch the roll
4. *To lift up,* נָשָׂא *nasa.*
2 Ch. 12. 11 the guard came and fetched them, and
Job 36. 3 I will fetch my knowledge from afar, and

FETCH (a pledge), to —
To obtain a pledge, עָבַט *abat.*
Deut 24. 10 not go into his house to fetch his pledge

FETCH a stroke, to —
To be driven away, נָדַח *nadach,* 2.
Deut 19. 5 his hand fetcheth a stroke with the ax to

FETCH about, to —
To go or bring round about, סָבַב *sabab,* 3.
2 Sa. 14. 20 To fetch about this form of speech hath

FETCH forth, to —
To cause to come out, bring out, יָצָא *yatsa,* 5.
Jer. 26. 23 they fetched forth Urijah out of Egypt

FETCH home again, to —
To cause to come back, שׁוּב *shub,* 5.
2 Sa. 14. 13 in that the king doth not fetch home again

FETCH out —
1. *To cause to come out,* יָצָא *yatsa,* 5.
Num 20. 10 must we fetch you water out of this rock?
2. *To lead out,* ἐξάγω *exagō.*
Acts 16. 37 let them come themsel. and fetch us out

FETCH up, to —
1. As No. 2.
2 Ch. 1. 17 they fetched up, and brought forth out
2. *To cause to come up,* עָלָה *alah,* 5.
1 Sa. 6. 21 come ye down, (and) fetch it up to you
7. 1 the men..fetched up the ark of the LORD

FETCHED, to be —
To be taken, לָקַח *laqach,* 6.
Gen. 18. 4 Let a little water, I pray you, be fetched

FETTER —
1. *Fetter,* כֶּבֶל *kebel.*
Psa. 105. 18 Whose feet they hurt with fetters: he
149. 8 To bind..their nobles with fetters of iron
2. *Chains, fetters,* זִקִּים *ziqqim.*
Job 36. 8 And if..bound in fetters..be holden in
3. *Brass,* נְחֹשֶׁת *nechosheth.*
2 Sa. 3. 34 not bound, nor thy feet put into fetters
2 Ch. 33. 11 and bound him with fetters, and carried
36. 6 Nebuchadnezzar..bound him in fetters
4. *Fetter (for the feet),* πέδη *pedē.*
Mark 5. 4 he had been often bound with fetters and
5. 4 and the fetters broken in pieces: neither
Luke 8. 29 was kept bound with chains and in fetters

FETTER of brass —
Brass, נְחֹשֶׁת *nechosheth.*
Judg 16. 21 took..and bound him with fetters of brass
2 Ki. 25. 7 and bound him with fetters of brass

FEVER —
1. *Fever, burning heat,* קַדַּחַת *qaddachath.*
Deut 28. 22 The LORD shall smite thee..with a fever
2. *Fiery heat, fever,* πυρετός *puretos.*
Matt. 8. 15 he touched her hand, and the fever left
Mark 1. 31 the fever left her, and she ministered
Luke 4. 38 wife's mother was taken with a great fev.
4. 39 he stood over her, and rebuked the fever
John 4. 52 at the seventh hour the fever left him
Acts 28. 8 the father of Publius lay sick of a fever

FEVER, to be sick of a —
To be in a fever, πυρέσσω *puressō.*
Matt. 8. 14 he saw his wife's mother..sick of a fever
Mark 1. 30 Simon's wife's mother lay sick of a fever

FEW —
1. *Single ones,* אֲחָדִים *achadim.*
Gen. 27. 44 tarry with him a few days, until thy broth.
29. 20 and they seemed unto him..a few days
Dan. 11. 20 but within few days he shall be destro.
2. *Few, a small company,* מִזְעָר *mizar.*
Isa. 24. 6 inhabitants..are burned, and few men
3. *A little, few,* מְעַט *meat.*
Gen. 47. 9 few and evil have the days of..my life been
Lev. 25. 52 if there remain but few years unto the
Num 13. 18 whether they..strong or weak, few or m.
26. 54 to few thou shalt give the less inheritance
26. 56 shall..be divided between many and few
35. 8 from (them that have) few ye shall give
Josh. 7. 3 make not all..to labour..for they..few
1 Sa. 14. 6 no restraint..to save by many or by few
17. 28 with whom hast thou left those few sheep
1 Ch. 16. 19 When ye were..even a few, and strangers
2 Ch. 29. 34 the priests were too few, so that they
Neh. 7. 4 the people (were) few therein, and the
Job 10. 20 (Are) not my days few? cease..let me
Psa. 109. 8 Let his days be few..let another take his
Eccl. 5. 2 God (is) in heaven..let thy words be few
9. 14 a little city, and few men within it; and
Isa. 10. 7 off nations not a few; Jer. 42. 2; Eze. 5. 3.
3a. *Men of fewness,* מְתֵי מְעַט [*methim*].
Deut 26. 5 sojourned there with a few, and became
28. 62 ye shall be left few in number, whereas
4. *Men,* מְתִים *methim.*
Gen. 34. 30 I..few in number, they shall gather them.
Deut. 4. 27 ye shall be left few in number; Ps. 105. 12.
4a. *Men of number,* מְתֵי מִסְפָּר [*methim*].
1 Ch. 16. 19 When ye were but few..and strangers in
5. *Short,* קָצֵר *qatser.*
Job 14. 1 Man..born of a woman (is) of few days
6. *A number,* מִסְפָּר *mispar.*
Num. 9. 20 when the cloud was a few days upon the
Deut 33. 6 Let Reuben live..let (not) his men be few
Job 16. 22 When a few years are come, then I shall
Isa. 10. 19 the rest of the trees..shall be few, that
Eze. 12. 16 I will leave a few men of them from the
7. *Little, few,* ὀλίγος *oligos.*
Matt. 7. 14 which leadeth unto life, and few there be
9. 37 truly..plenteous, but the labourers..few
15. 34 they said, Seven, and a few little fishes
20. 16 [for many be called, but few chosen]
22. 14 For many are called, but few..chosen
Mark 6. 5 he laid his hands upon a few sick folk
8. 7 they had a few small fishes: and he bles
Luke 10. 2 truly (is) great, but the labourers (are) few
13. 23 Lord, are there few that be saved? And
Acts 17. 4 Greeks..and of the chief women not a few
17. 12 of honourable women..of men, not a few
Heb. 12. 10 For they verily for a few days chastened
1 Pe. 3. 20 wherein few, that is, eight souls were
Rev. 3. 4 Thou hast a few names even in Sardis

FEW, few things —
Little, few, ὀλίγος *oligos.*
Matt 25. 21, 23 hast been faithful over a few things
Luke 12. 48 that knew not..shall be beaten with few
Rev. 2. 14, 20 I have a few things against thee, beca.

FEW words, a —
Concisely, briefly, συντόμως *suntomōs.*
Acts 24. 4 that thou wouldest hear..a few words

FEW words, in (a) —
1. *In (or through) short space,* διὰ βραχέων *dia brach.*
Heb. 13. 22 I have written a letter..in a few words
2. *In a little, briefly,* ἐν ὀλίγῳ *en oligō.*
Eph. 3. 3 the mystery; as I wrote afore in few wo.

FEW, to be, borrow, or give —
1. *To be or become few,* מָעַט *maat.*
Jer 30. 19 multiply them, and they shall not be few
2. *To become few,* מָעַט *maat,* 3.
Eccl. 12. 3 the grinders cease, because they are few
3. *To make few,* מָעַט *maat,* 5.
Num. 35. 8 ye shall give few: every one shall give
2 Ki. 4. 3 borrow thee vessels..borrow not a few

FEW in number, to make —
To make few, מָעַט *maat,* 5.
Lev. 26. 22 beasts..which shall..make you few in n.

FEW, some or very —
A few, מְעַט *meat.*
Neh. 2. 12 I arose in the night, I and some few men
Psa. 105. 12 When they were (but)..very few, and str.

FEWER, FEWEST —
Few, מְעַט *meat.*
Num. 33. 54 to the fewer ye shall give the less inher.
Deut. 7. 7 for ye (were) the fewest of all people

FEWNESS —
To be few, מָעַט *maat.*
Lev. 25. 16 according to the fewness of years thou

FIDELITY —
Faith, stedfastness, πίστις *pistis.*
Titus 2. 10 Not purloining, but showing all..fidelity

FIELD —
1. *Earth, land,* אֶרֶץ *erets.*
Eze. 29. 5 I have given..to the beasts of the field
2. *Field, open country,* בַּר *bar.*
Dan. 2. 38 the beasts of the field..hath he given
4. 12 beasts of the field had shadow under it
4. 15, 23 leave the stump..in..grass of the fie.
4. 21 under which the beasts of the field dwelt
4. 23 his portion (be) with..beasts of the field
4. 25, 32 thy dwelling..with..beasts of the fie.
3. *Without, out place,* חוּץ *chuts.*
Job 5. 10 Who..sendeth waters upon the fields
Prov. 8. 26 While as yet he had not made..the fields

4. *Portion,* חֶלְקָה *chelqah.*
2 Sa. 14. 30 Joab's field (is) near mine, and he hath
14. 30 Absalom's servants set the field on fire
14. 31 have thy servants set my field on fire?

5. *Level place, field,* שָׂדֶה *sadeh.*
Gen. 2. 5 every plant of the field before it was in
2. 5 every herb of the field before it grew
2. 19 LORD God formed every beast of the field
2. 20 gave names to. .every beast of the field
3. 1 more subtile than any beast of the field
3. 14 cursed..above every beast of the field
3. 18 and thou shalt eat the herb of the field
4. 8 came to pass, when they were in the fie.
23. 9 the cave..which (is) in the end of his fi.
23. 11 the field give I thee, and the cave that
23. 13 I will give thee money for the field ; take
23. 17 the field of Ephron, which (was) in Mac.
23. 17 the field, and the cave which (was) there.
23. 17 and all the trees that (were) in the field
23. 19 buried Sarah..in the cave of the field
23. 20 the field, and the cave..were made sure
24. 63 Isaac went out to meditate in the field
24. 65 What man..walketh in the field to meet
25. 9 in the field of Ephron..which (is) before
25. 10 The field which Abraham purchased of
25. 27 was a cunning hunter, a man of the field
25. 29 Esau came from the field, and he (was)
27. 3 take..thy weapons..and go out to the f.
27. 5 Esau went to the field to hunt (for) veni.
27. 27 the smell..(is) as the smell of a field
29. 2 he looked, and behold a well in the field
30. 14 Reuben..found mandrakes in the field
30. 16 Jacob came out of the field in the even.
31. 4 Jacob..called Rachel..to the field unto
33. 19 he bought a parcel of a field, where he
34. 5 his sons were with his cattle in the field
34. 7 the sons of Jacob came out of the field
34. 28 They took..that which (was) in the field
36. 35 who smote Midian in the field of Moab
37. 7 we (were) binding sheaves in the field
37. 15 and, behold, (he was) wandering in the f.
39. 5 blessing..was upon all he had..in the fi.
41. 48 the food of the field, which (was) round
47. 20 the Egyptians sold every man his field
47. 24 shall be your own, for seed of the field
49. 29, 30 in the cave that (is) in the field of
49. 30 which Abraham bought with the field of
49. 32 The purchase of the field and of the cave
50. 13 buried him in the cave of the field of
50. 13 which Abraham bought with the field
Exod. 1. 14 and in all manner of service in the field
8. 13 and the frogs died..out of the fields
9. 3 upon thy cattle which (is) in the field
9. 19 gather..all that thou hast in the field
9. 19 every man and beast..found in the field
9. 21 left his servants and his cattle in the fie.
9. 22 may be hail .upon every herb of the fie.
9. 25 the hail smote..all that (was) in the field
9. 25 the hail smote every herb of the field
9. 25 the hail..brake every tree of the field
10. 5 which groweth for you out of the field
10. 15 remained not any..thing..in..the field
16. 25 to day ye shall not find it in the field
22. 5 If a man shall cause a field..to be eaten
22. 5 his beast..feed in another man's field
22. 5 of the best of his own field..shall he
22. 6 If fire break out..so that..the field, be
22. 31 flesh (that is) torn of beasts in the field
23. 11 what they leave the beasts of the field
23. 16 labours, which thou hast..in the field
23. 16 gathered in thy labours out of the field
23. 29 lest..the beast of the field multiply
Lev. 14. 7 let the living bird loose into the..field
14. 53 let go the living bird..into the open fields
17. 5 which they offer in the open field, even
19. 9 thou shalt not wholly reap..thy field
19. 19 thou shalt not sow thy field with mingled
23. 22 thou shalt not make clean..thy field
25. 3 Six years thou shalt sow thy field, and
25. 4 thou shalt neither sow thy field, nor
25. 12 ye shall eat the increase..out of the field
25. 31 villages..shall be counted as the fields of
25. 34 the field of the suburbs of their cities
26. 4 the trees of the field shall yield their
27. 16 if a man shall sanctify..of a field of his
27. 17 If he sanctify his field from the year of
27. 18 if he sanctify his field after the jubilee
27. 19 if he that sanctified the field will in any
27. 20 And if he will not redeem the field, or if
27. 20 if he have sold the field to another man
27. 21 But the field..shall be..as a field devoted
27. 22 a field..which (is) not of the fields of his
27. 24 the field shall return unto him of whom
27. 28 no devoted thing..of the field..shall be
Num16. 14 or..inheritance of fields and vineyards
19. 16 one..slain with a sword in the open fields
20. 17 we will not pass through the fields, or
21 22 we will not turn into the fields, or into
22. 4 as the ox licketh up the grass of the field
22. 23 the ass turned..and went into the field
23. 14 he brought him into the field of Zophim
Deut. 5. 21 shalt thou covet thy neighbour's. .field
7. 22 lest the beasts of the field increase upon
11. 15 I will send grass in thy field for thy cattle
14. 22 that the field bringeth forth year by year
20. 19 for the tree of the field (is) man's (life)
21. 1 If (one) be found slain..lying in the field
22. 25 But if a man find a. .damsel in the field
22. 27 he found her in the field..the betrothed
24. 19 When thou cuttest down..in thy field
24. 19 and hast forgot a sheaf in the field, thou
Deut28. 3 and blessed (shalt) thou (be) in the field
28. 16 and cursed (shalt) thou (be) in the field
28. 38 Thou shalt carry..seed out into the field
Josh. 8. 24 all the inhabitants of Ai in the field, in
15. 18 that she moved him to ask..a field
21. 12 But the fields..gave they to Caleb the son
Judg. 1. 14 that she moved him to ask..a field
5. 4 when thou marchedst out of the field of
5. 18 people..jeoparded their lives..in..the fi.
9. 27 they went out into the fields, and gath.
9. 32 thou and the people..lie in wait in the fi.
9. 42 that the people went out into the field
9. 43 he took..and laid wait in the field, and
9. 44 ran upon all..that (were) in the fields
13. 9 the angel..came..as she sat in the field
19. 16 there came an old man..out of the field
20. 31 of which one goeth. .to Gibeah in the fie.
Ruth 2. 2 Let me now go to the field, and glean
2. 3 she. .gleaned in the field after the reap.
2. 3 her hap was to light on a part of the fie.
2. 8 Go not to glean in another field, neither
2. 9 (Let) thine eyes (be) on the field that
2. 17 So she gleaned in the field until even
2. 22 that they meet thee not in any other field
4. 5 What day thou buyest the field of the
1 Sa 4. 2 they slew of the army in the field about
6. 14 the cart came into the field of Joshua, a
6. 18 unto this day in the field of Joshua, the
8. 14 he will take your fields, and your viney.
11. 5 Saul came after the herd out of the field
14. 15 was trembling in the host, in the field
17. 44 I will give thy flesh..to..beasts of the fi.
19. 3 stand beside my father in the field where
20. 5 that I may hide myself in the field unto
20. 11 Come, and let us go out into the field
20. 11 they went out both of them into the field
20. 24 So David hid himself in the field : and
20. 35 Jonathan went out into the field at the
22. 7 will the son of Jesse give..you fields and
25. 15 with them, when we were in the fields
30. 11 And they found an Egyptian in the field
2 Sa. 1. 21 neither..rain upon you, nor fields of
10. 8 Syrians of Zoba..by themselves in the fi.
11. 11 servants..are encamped in the open fields
11. 23 the men..came out unto us into the field
14. 6 and they two strove together in the field
17. 8 as a bear robbed of her whelps in the field
18. 6 So the people went out into the field
20. 12 he removed Amasa..into the field, and
21. 10 day, nor the beasts of the field by night
1 Ki. 2. 26 Get..to Anathoth, unto thine own fields
11. 29 and they two (were) alone in the field
14. 11 him that dieth in the field shall the fowls
16. 4 him that dieth of his in the fields shall
21. 24 him that dieth in the field shall the fowls
2 Ki. 4. 39 one went out into the field to gather he.
7. 12 are they gone..to hide..in the field
8. 6 Restore..all the fruits of the field since
9. 25 cast him in the portion of the field of N.
9. 37 shall be as dung upon the face of the field
18. 17 which (is) in the highway of the fuller's fi.
19. 26 they were (as) the grass of the field, and
1 Ch. 1. 46 which smote Midian in the field of Moab
6. 56 the fields..they gave to Caleb the son of
16. 32 let the fields rejoice, and all that (is)
19. 9 kings that were come (were)..in the field
27. 25 over the store houses in the fields, in the
27. 26 over them that did the work of the field
2 Ch. 26. 23 they buried him..in the field of the burial
31. 5 brought..of all the increase of the field
31. 19 in the fields of the suburbs of their cities
Neh. 11. 25 And for the villages, with their fields
11. 30 at Lachish, and the fields thereof, at Az.
12. 29 out of the fields of Geba and Azmaveth
12. 44 to gather into them out of the fields of
13. 10 Levites..were fled every one to his field
Job 5. 23 be in league with the stones of the field
5. 23 the beasts of the field shall be at peace
24. 6 They reap..his corn in the field : and they
40. 20 where all the beasts of the field play
Psa. 78. 12 Marvellous things did he in..the field of
78. 43 wrought..his wonders in the field of Zoan
103. 15 as a flower of the field, so he flourisheth
107. 37 And sow the fields, and plant vineyards
132. 6 we found it in the fields of the wood
Prov 23. 10 enter not into the fields of the fatherless
24. 27 and make it fit for thyself in the field
24. 30 I went by the field of the slothful, and by
27. 26 and the goats (are) the price of the field
31. 16 She considereth a field, and buyeth it
Eccl. 5. 9 the king (himself) is served by the field
Song 2. 7 I charge you..by the hinds of the field
3. 5 I charge you. .by the hinds of the field
7. 11 Come. .let us go forth into the field; let
Isa. 5. 8 Woe unto them. .(that) lay field to field
7. 3 pool in the highway of the fuller's field
32. 12 They shall lament. .for the pleasant fields
36. 2 pool in the highway of the fuller's field
37. 27 they were (as) the grass of the field, and
40. 6 all the goodliness. .as the flower of the fi.
43. 20 The beast of the field shall honour me
55. 12 all the trees of the field shall clap. .hands
Jer. 6. 12 fields and wives together: for I will
6. 25 Go not forth into the field, nor walk by
7. 20 poured out. .upon the trees of the field
8. 10 I give. .their fields to them that shall
9. 22 shall fall as dung upon the open field
12. 4 shall. .the herbs of every field wither
12. 9 assemble all the beasts of the field, come
13. 27 abominations on the hills in the field
14. 5 the hind also calved in the field, and
14. 18 If I go forth into the field, then behold
Jer. 17. 3 O my mountain in the field, I will give
26. 18 Zion shall be plowed. .a field, and Jeru.
27. 6 the beasts of the field have I given him
28. 14 I have given him the beasts of the field
32. 7 Buy thee my field that (is) in Anathoth
32. 8 Buy my field, I pray thee, that (is) in A.
32. 9 I bought the field of Hanameel my uncle's
32. 15 Houses and fields..shall be possessed
32. 25 Buy thee the field for money, and take
32. 43 And fields shall be bought in this land
32. 44 Men shall buy fields for money, and sub.
35. 9 neither have we vineyard, nor field, nor
40. 7, 13 all the captains of the forces..in the fi.
41. 8 we have treasures in the field, of wheat
Eze. 7. 15 he that (is) in the field shall die with the
16. 5 but thou wast cast out in the open field
16. 7 thee to multiply as the bud of the field
17. 5 seed..and planted it in a fruitful field
17. 24 all the trees of the field shall know that I
20. 46 prophesy against the forest of the..field
26. 6 her daughters which (are) in the field
26. 8 He shall slay. .thy daughters in the field
29. 5 thou shalt fall upon the open fields ; thou
31. 4 little rivers unto all the trees of the field
31. 5 was exalted above all the trees of the fi.
31. 6 did all the beasts of the field bring forth
31. 13 all the beasts of the field shall be upon
31. 15 all the trees of the field fainted for him
32. 4 I will cast thee forth upon the open field
33. 27 him that (is) in the open field will I give
34. 5 became meat to all the beasts of the field
34. 8 became meat to every beast of the field
34. 27 the tree of the field shall yield her fruit
36. 30 I will multiply. .the increase of the field
38. 20 the beasts of the field. .shall shake at my
39. 4 give thee unto. .the beasts of the field to
39. 5 Thou shall fall upon the open field : for I
39. 10 they shall take no wood out of the field
39. 17 Speak unto. .every beast of the field
Hos. 2. 12 and the beasts of the field shall eat them
2. 18 a covenant. .with the beasts of the field
4. 3 with the beasts of the field, and with the f.
Joel 1. 10 The field is wasted, the land mourneth
1. 11 because the harvest of the field is perished
1. 12 all the trees of the field, are withered
1. 19 flame hath burned all the trees of the fi.
1. 20 The beasts of the field cry also unto thee
Obad. 19 possess the fields of Ephraim, and the fi.
Mic. 1. 6 will make Samaria as an heap of the field
2. 2 they covet fields, and take..by violence
2. 4 turning away he hath divided our fields
3. 12 Therefore shall Zion..be plowed..a field
4. 10 thou shalt dwell in the field, and thou
Zech. 10. 1 the LORD shall..give..grass in the field
Mal. 3. 11 your vine cast her fruit..in the field

6. *Level places,* שָׂדַי *sadai.*
Deut32. 13 that he might eat the increase of the field
Psa. 8. 7 All..oxen, yea, and the beasts of the field
50. 11 and the wild beasts of the field (are) mine
80. 13 the wild beast of the field doth devour it
96. 12 Let the field be joyful, and all that (is)
104. 11 They give drink to every beast of the fi.
Isa. 56. 9 All ye beasts of the field, come to devour
Jer. 4. 17 As keepers of a field, are they against her
18. 14 of Lebanon..from the rock of the field?
Lam. 4. 9 pine away..for..the fruits of the field
Hos. 10. 4 as hemlock in the furrows of the field
12. 11 their altars (are) as heaps in..the fields
Joel 2. 22 Be not afraid, ye beasts of the field : for

7. *Field,* שְׁדֵמָה *shedemah.*
Deut32. 32 For their vine (is)..of the fields of Gom.
2 Ki.23. 4 he burned them..in the fields of Kidron
Isa. 16. 8 the fields of Heshbon languish..the vine
Hab. 3. 17 the fields shall yield no meat; the flock

8. *Fields (cultivated),* יְגֵבִים *yegebim.*
Jer. 39. 10 Nebuzar-adan..gave them..fields at the

9. As No. 7 [V.L. שרמות].
Jer. 31. 40 all the fields unto the brook of Kidron

10. *Field,* ἀγρός *agros.*
Matt. 6. 28 Consider the lilies of the field, how they
6. 30 if God so clothe the grass of the field
13. 24 a man which sowed good seed in his field
13. 27 didst not thou sow good seed in thy field?
13. 31 which a man took, and sowed in his field
13. 36 Declare..the parable of the tares of the fi.
13. 38 The field is the world ; the good seed are
13. 44 is like unto treasure hid in a field
13. 44 selleth all..he hath, and buyeth that field
24. 18 Neither let him which is in the field return
24. 40 Then shall two be in the field ; the one
27. 7 bought with them the potter's field, to
27. 8 that field was called, The field of blood
27. 10 gave them for the potter's field, as the L.
Mark13. 16 let him that is in the field not turn back
Luke12. 28 the grass, which is to day in the field, and
15. 15 he sent him into his fields to feed swine
15. 25 Now his elder son was in the field : and
17. 7 when he is come from the field, Go and
17. 31 he that is in the field, let him likewise
17. 36 [Two..shall be in the field ; the one sh.]

11. *A space, open country,* χώρα *chōra.*
John 4. 35 Lift up your eyes, and look on the fields
Jas. 5. 4 labourers who..reaped down your fields

12. *A little space or place,* χωρίον *chōrion.*
Acts 1. 18 Now this man purchased a field with the
1. 19 that field is called..The field of blood

FIERCE —

1. *Fierce,* אַכְזָר *akzar.*
Job 41. 10 None (is so) fierce that dare stir him up

2. *Heat,* חָרוֹן *charon.*
Exod 32. 12 Turn from thy fierce wrath, and repent of
Num 25. 4 that the fierce anger of the LORD may be
32. 14 to augment yet the fierce anger of the L.
1 Sa. 28. 18 nor executedst his fierce wrath upon Am.
2 Ch. 28. 11 the fierce wrath of the LORD (is) upon you
28. 13 and (there is) fierce wrath against Israel
29. 10 that his fierce wrath may turn away from
Psa. 88. 16 Thy fierce wrath goeth over me; thy ter.
Isa. 13. 9 cruel both with wrath and fierce anger
13. 13 remove..in the day of his fierce anger
Jer. 4. 8 the fierce anger of the LORD is not turned
4. 26 cities..were broken down..by his fierce
12. 13 ashamed..because of the fierce anger of
25. 37 are cut down because of the fierce anger
25. 38 is desolate..because of his fierce anger
30. 24 The fierce anger of the LORD shall not re.
49. 37 I will bring evil upon them..my fierce a.
51. 45 deliver..from the fierce anger of the LORD
Lam. 1. 12 LORD hath afflicted..in..his fierce anger
4. 11 he hath poured out his fierce anger, and
Jon. 3. 9 God will..turn away from his fierce an.
Zeph. 2. 2 before the fierce anger of the LORD come
3. 8 to pour upon them..all my fierce anger

3. *Heat,* חֳרִי *chori.*
1 Sa. 20. 34 So Jonathan arose..in fierce anger, and
Isa. 7. 4 for the fierce anger of Rezin with Syria
Lam. 2. 3 He hath cut off in..fierce anger all the

4. *To be strong,* יָעַז *yaaz,* 2.
Isa. 33. 19 Thou shalt not see a fierce people, a peo.

5. *Strong,* עַז *az.*
Gen. 49. 7 Cursed (be) their anger, for (it was) fierce
Deut 28. 50 A nation of fierce countenance, which
Isa. 19. 4 and a fierce king shall rule over them
Dan. 8. 23 a king of fierce countenance..shall stand

6. *Not mild, savage,* ἀνήμερος *anēmeros.*
2 Ti. 3. 3 false accusers, incontinent, fierce, desp.

7. *Hard,* σκληρός *sklēros.*
Jas. 3. 4 Behold also the ships..driven of fierce

8. *Dangerous, fierce, injurious,* χαλεπός *chalepos.*
Matt. 8. 28 exceeding fierce, so that no man might

FIERCE, to be —
To be sharp, acute, light, חָדַד *chadad.*
Hab. 1. 8 Their horses..are more fierce than..wol.

FIERCE, to be the more —
To be strong upon, ἐπισχύω *epischuō.*
Luke 23. 5 And they were the more fierce, saying

FIERCE lion —
A (roaring) lion, שַׁחַל *shachal.*
Job 4. 10 the voice of the fierce lion, and the teeth
10. 16 Thou huntest me as a fierce lion; and
28. 8 not trodden..nor the fierce lion passed by

FIERCENESS —

1. *Heat,* חָרוֹן *charon.*
Deut. 13. 17 that the LORD may turn from the fierce.
Josh. 7. 26 So the LORD turned from the fierceness
2 Ki. 23. 26 the LORD turned not from the fierceness
2 Ch. 30. 8 that the fierceness of his wrath may turn
Psa. 78. 49 He cast upon them the fierceness of his
85. 3 thou hast turned..from the fierceness of
Jer. 25. 38 is desolate because of the fierceness of the
Hos. 11. 9 I will not execute the fierceness of mine
Nah. 1. 6 who can abide in the fierceness of his a.?

2. *Shaking, trembling,* רַעַשׁ *raash.*
Job 39. 24 He swalloweth the ground with fierceness

3. *Wrath,* θυμός *thumos.*
Rev. 16. 19 the cup of the wine of the fierceness of his
19. 15 the wine press of the fierceness and wrath

FIERCER, to be —
To be sharp, hard, קָשָׁה *qashah.*
2 Sa. 19. 43 the words of the men of Judah were fier.

FIERY —

1. *Fire,* אֵשׁ *esh.*
Psa. 21. 9 Thou shalt make them as a fiery oven in

2. *Fire,* נוּר *nur.*
Dan. 3. 6, 11, 15 into the midst of a burning fiery f.
3. 17 to deliver us from the burning fiery furn.
3. 20 to cast (them) into the burning fiery fur.
3. 21 cast into the midst of the burning fiery f.
3. 23 fell down bound into..the burning fiery f.
3. 26 came near to..the burning fiery furnace
7. 9 his throne..the fiery flame..his wheels
7. 10 A fiery stream..came forth from before

3. *Burning one,* שָׂרָף *saraph.*
Num 21. 6 the LORD sent fiery serpents among the
Deut. 8. 15 fiery serpents, and scorpions, and drought

4. *Fire,* πῦρ *pur.*
Heb. 10. 27 But a certain fearful looking for of..fiery

5. *To be set on fire,* πυρόομαι *puroomai.*
Eph. 6. 16 ye shall be able to quench all the fiery

FIERY serpent —
Burning one, שָׂרָף *saraph.*
Num. 21. 8 Make thee a fiery serpent, and set it upon
Isa. 14. 29 his fruit (shall be) a fiery flying serpent
30. 6 whence..the viper and fiery flying serpent

FIERY trial —
A burning, πύρωσις *purōsis.*
1 Pe. 4. 12 concerning the fiery trial which is to try

FIFTEEN —

1. *Five (and) ten,* חֲמִשָּׁה עָשָׂר *or* חֲמֵשׁ עֶשְׂרֵה [*chamesh*].
Gen. 5. 10 Enos lived..eight hundred and fifteen ye.
7. 20 Fifteen cubits upward did the waters pre.
Exod 27. 14 The hangings of one side..fifteen cubits
27. 15 on the other side..hangings fifteen (cubi.)
38. 14 The hangings of the one side..fifteen cu.
38. 15 on this..and that..hangings of fifteen cub.
Lev. 27. 7 then thy estimation shall be fifteen she.
Judg. 8. 10 their hosts with them, about fifteen tho.
2 Sa. 9. 10 Ziba had fifteen sons and twenty servants
19. 17 Ziba..his fifteen sons and his twenty
1 Ki. 7. 3 (lay) on forty five pillars, fifteen (in) a row
2 Ki. 14. 17 Amaziah..lived after..Jehoash..fifteen y.
20. 6 And I will add unto thy days fifteen yea.
2 Ch. 25. 25 of Jehoahaz king of Israel, fifteen years
Isa. 38. 5 I will add unto thy days fifteen years
Eze. 45. 12 five and twenty shekels, fifteen shekels
Hos. 3. 2 So I bought her to me for fifteen..of sil.

2. *Five and ten,* חֲמֵשׁ וְעֶשֶׂר *chamesh ve-asar.*
Gen. 25. 7 an hundred threescore and fifteen years
Exod 38. 25 seven hundred and threescore and fifteen
Num 31. 37 six hundred and threescore and fifteen

3. *Ten (and) five,* δεκαπέντε *dekapente.*
John 11. 18 Bethany was..about fifteen furlongs off
Acts 27. 28 they sounded again, and found (it) fifteen
Gal. 1. 18 to see Peter, and abode with him fifteen

4. *Seventy five,* ἑβδομήκοντα πέντε. [*hebdomēkonta*].
Acts 7. 14 all his kindred, threescore and fifteen

FIFTEENTH —

1. *Five (and) ten,* חֲמִשָּׁה עָשָׂר *chamishshah asar.*
Exod 16. 1 on the fifteenth day of the second month
Lev. 23. 6 on the fifteenth day..the feast of unleav.
23. 34 The fifteenth day of the seventh month
23. 39 Also in the fifteenth day..ye shall keep a
Num 28. 17 in the fifteenth day of this month (is) the f.
29. 12 on the fifteenth day..ye shall have an
33. 3 they departed..on the fifteenth day of
1 Ki. 12. 32 ordained a feast..on the fifteenth day of
12. 33 the fifteenth day of the eighth month
2 Ki. 14. 23 In the fifteenth year of Amaziah the son
1 Ch. 24. 14 The fifteenth to Bilgah, the sixteenth to
25. 22 The fifteenth to Jeremoth..his sons, and
2 Ch. 15. 10 they gathered..together..in the fifteenth
Esth. 9. 18 on the fifteenth..of the same they rested
9. 21 and the fifteenth day of the same, yearly
Eze. 32. 17 in the fifteenth..of the month..the word
45. 25 in the fifteenth day of the month, shall

2. *Five and tenth,* πεντεκαιδέκατος *pentekaidekatos.*
Luke 3. 1 in the fifteenth year of the reign of Tiber.

FIFTH —

1. *Fifth,* חֲמִשִׁי, חֲמִישִׁי *chamishshi, chamishi.*
Gen. 1. 23 the evening and..morning were the fifth
30. 17 she conceived, and bare Jacob the fifth
47. 24 that ye shall give the fifth..unto Pharaoh
Lev. 19. 25 in the fifth year shall ye eat of the fruit
22. 14 he shall put the fifth..thereof unto it
27. 13 he shall add a fifth..thereof unto thy
27. 15, 19 he shall add the fifth..of the money
27. 27 he..shall add a fifth (part) of it thereto
27. 31 he shall add thereto the fifth..thereof
Num. 5. 7 he shall..add unto it the fifth..thereof
7. 36 On the fifth day Shelumiel the son of Z.
29. 26 on the fifth day nine bullocks, two rams
33. 38 died..in the first (day) of the fifth month
Josh. 19. 24 the fifth lot came out for the tribe..of A.
Judg. 19. 8 he arose early..on the fifth day to depart
2 Sa. 3. 4 the fifth, Shephatiah the son of Abital
1 Ki. 14. 25 it came to pass, in the fifth year of king R.
2 Ki. 25. 8 in the fifth month..came Nebuzar-adan
1 Ch. 2. 14 Nethaneel the fourth, Raddai the fifth
3. 3 The fifth, Shephatiah of Abital; the sixth
8. 2 Nohah the fourth, and Rapha the fifth
12. 10 Mishmannah the fourth, Jeremiah..fifth
24. 9 The fifth to Malchijah, the sixth to Mij.
25. 12 The fifth to Nethaniah..his sons, and his
26. 3 Elam the fifth, Jehohanan the sixth, Eli.
26. 4 Sacar the fourth, and Nethaneel the fifth
27. 8 The fifth (captain) for the fifth month
2 Ch. 12. 2 in the fifth year..Shishak..came up
Ezra 7. 8 he came to Jerusalem in the fifth month
7. 9 on the first..of the fifth month came he
Jer. 1. 3 of Jerusalem captive in the fifth month
28. 1 it came to pass..in the fifth month, (that)
36. 9 it came to pass in the fifth year of Jehoi.
52. 12 in the fifth month..came Nebuzar-adan
Eze. 1. 2 fifth..of the month, which (was) the fifth
20. 1 it came to pass..in the fifth (month)
Zech. 7. 3 Should I weep in the fifth month..as I
7. 5 When ye fasted and mourned in the fifth
8. 19 the fast of the fifth..shall be..joy and

2. *Five,* חָמֵשׁ, חֲמִשָּׁה *chamesh, chamishshah.*
2 Ki. 8. 16 in the fifth year..Jehoram..began to
Neh. 6. 15 the wall was finished in the twenty and fi.
Eze. 1. 1 in the fifth..of the month..the heavens
1. 2 In the fifth..of the month..the fifth yea.
8. 1 in the sixth (month), in the fifth..of the
33. 21 in the tenth (month), in the fifth..of the

3. *Fifth,* πέμπτος *pemptos.*
Rev. 6. 9 when he had opened the fifth seal, I saw
9. 1 the fifth angel sounded, and I saw a star f.
16. 10 the fifth angel poured out his vial upon
21. 20 The fifth, sardonyx; the sixth, sardius

FIFTH part —
Fifth, חֲמִשִׁי, חֲמִישִׁי *chamishshi, chamishi.*
Lev. 5. 16 he..shall add the fifth part thereto, and
6. 5 he..shall add the fifth part more thereto
1 Ki. 6. 31 the lintel (and) side posts (were) a fifth p.

FIFTH part, to take up the —
To take fifth part, rank or place, חָמַשׁ *chamesh,* 3.
Gen. 41. 34 Let Pharaoh..take up the fifth part of

FIFTH (rib) —
Fifth (part or rib), חֹמֶשׁ *chomesh.*
2 Sa. 2. 23 Abner..smote him under the fifth (rib)
3. 27 Joab..smote him there under the fifth (r.)
4. 6 and they smote him under the fifth (rib)
20. 10 so he smote him therewith in the fifth (r.)

FIFTH time —
Fifth, חֲמִשִׁי, חֲמִישִׁי *chamishshi, chamishi.*
Neh. 6. 5 Then sent Sanballat..the fifth time with

FIFTIES, by —
By fifty, ἀνὰ πεντήκοντα *ana pentēkonta.*
Mark 6. 40 And they sat down in ranks..by fifties
Luke 9. 14 Make them sit down by fifties in a comp.

FIFTIETH —
Fifty, חֲמִשִּׁים *chamishshim.*
Lev. 25. 10 ye shall hallow the fiftieth year, and proc.
25. 11 A jubile shall that fiftieth year be unto
2 Ki. 15. 23 In the fiftieth year of Azariah king of J.
15. 27 In the two and fiftieth year of Azariah

FIFTY —

1. *Fifty,* חֲמִשִּׁים *chamishshim.*
Gen. 6. 15 the breadth of it fifty cubits, and the
7. 24 upon the earth an hundred and fifty days
8. 3 after the end of the hundred and fifty da.
9. 28 Noah lived..three hundred and fifty years
9. 29 days..were nine hundred and fifty years
18. 24 Peradventure there be fifty righteous
18. 24 for the fifty righteous that (are) therein?
18. 26 If I find in Sodom fifty righteous within
18. 28 there shall lack five of the fifty righteous
Exod 18. 21, 25 rulers of fifties, and rulers of tens
26. 5 Fifty loops shalt thou make in the one
26. 5 fifty loops shalt thou make in the edge
26. 6 And thou shalt make fifty taches of gold
26. 10 thou shalt make fifty loops on the edge
26. 10 fifty loops in the edge of the curtain
26. 11 thou shalt make fifty taches of brass, and
27. 12 on the west side..hangings of fifty cubits
27. 13 the breadth of the court..(shall be) fifty
30. 23 Take..cinnamon..two hundred and fifty
30. 23 sweet calamus two hundred and fifty
36. 12 Fifty loops made he in one curtain, and fi.
36. 13 he made fifty taches of gold, and coupled
36. 17 fifty loops upon..and fifty loops made he
36. 18 he made fifty taches (of) brass to couple
38. 12 for the west side..hangings of fifty cubits
38. 13 for the east side eastward fifty cubits
38. 26 three thousand and five hundred and fifty
Lev. 23. 16 unto the morrow..shall ye number fifty
27. 3 thy estimation shall be fifty shekels of si.
27. 16 an homer of barley seed..at fifty shekels
Num. 1. 23 Those..numbered of them..(were) fifty
1. 25 forty..five thousand six hund. and fifty
1. 29 fifty and four thousand and four hundred
1. 31 fifty and seven thousand and four hundred
1. 43 fifty and three thousand and four hundred
1. 46 three thousand..five hundred and fifty
2. 6 fifty and four thousand and four hundred
2. 8 fifty and seven thousand and four hundred
2. 13 fifty and nine thousand and three hundred
2. 15 five thousand and six hundred and fifty
2. 16 fifty and one thousand..four hund. and f.
2. 30 fifty and three thousand and four hundred
2. 31 an hundred thousand and fifty and seven
2. 32 three thousand and five hundred and fifty
4. 3, 23, 30, 35, 39, 43, 47 From..until fifty years
4. 36 were two thousand seven hundred and fi.
8. 25 from the age of fifty years they shall cease
16. 2 two hundred and fifty princes of the ass.
16. 17 two hundred and fifty censers; thou also
16. 35 consumed the two hundred and fifty men
26. 10 fire devoured two hundred and fifty men
26. 34 fifty and two thousand and seven hundred
26. 47 fifty and three thousand and four hundred
31. 30 thou shalt take one portion of fifty, of the
31. 47 Moses took one portion of fifty..of man
31. 52 sixteen thousand seven hundred and fifty
Deut. 1. 15 captains over fifties, and captains over
22. 29 Then the man..shall give..fifty..of silver
Josh. 7. 21 a wedge of gold of fifty shekels weight
1 Sa. 6. 19 he smote of the people fifty thousand and
8. 12 he will appoint..captains over fifties
2 Sa. 15. 1 Absalom prepared..fifty men to run before
24. 24 David bought..the oxen for fifty shekels of
1 Ki. 1. 5 he prepared..fifty men to run before him
7. 2 the breadth thereof fifty cubits, and the
7. 6 the length thereof..fifty cubits, and the
9. 23 five hundred and fifty, which bare rule
10. 29 and an horse for an hundred and fifty
18. 19 prophets of Baal four hundred and fifty
18. 22 Baal's prophets..four hundred and fifty
2 Ki. 1. 9 king sent..a captain of fifty with his fifty
1. 10 Elijah answered..the captain of fifty, If I
1. 10 then let fire..consume thee and thy fifty
1. 10 came..fire..and consumed him and his fi.
1. 11 another captain of fifty with his fifty

2 Ki. 1. 12 let fire..consume thee and thy fifty
1. 12 fire..came..and consumed him and his fl.
1. 13 he sent..a captain of..fifty with his fifty
1. 13 And the third captain of fifty went up
1. 13 let..the life of these fifty thy servants
1. 14 captains of the..fifties with their fifties
2. 7 fifty men of the sons of the prophets went
2. 16 there be with thy servants fifty strong
2. 17 Send. They sent therefore fifty men
13. 7 Neither did he leave..but fifty horsemen
15. 2 he reigned two and fifty years in Jerusalem
15. 20 Menahem exacted..of each man fifty sh.
15. 25 and with him fifty men of the Gileadites
21. 1 Manasseh..reigned fifty and five years in
1 Ch. 5. 21 they took..of their camels fifty thousand
5. 21 sheep two hundred and fifty thousand
8. 40 sons, and sons' sons, an hundred and fifty
9. 9 brethren..nine hundred and fifty and six
12. 33 Of Zebulun..fifty thousand, which could
2 Ch. 1. 17 and an horse for an hundred and fifty
2. 17 they were found an hundred and fifty th.
3. 9 the weight of the nails (was) fifty shekels
8. 10 two hundred and fifty, that bare rule over
8. 18 took..four hundred and fifty talents of
26. 3 he reigned fifty and two years in Jerusa.
33. 1 he reigned fifty and five years in Jerusa.
Ezra 2. 7 a thousand two hundred fifty and four
2. 14 children of Bigvai, two thousand fifty and
2. 15 children of Adin, four hundred fifty and f.
2. 22 The men of Netophah, fifty and six
2. 29 The children of Nebo, fifty and two
2. 30 children of Magbish, an hundred fifty and
2. 31 Elam, a thousand two hundred fifty and
2. 37 children of Immer, a thousand fifty and
2. 60 children of Nekoda, six hundred fifty and
8. 3 with him..of the males an hundred and f.
8. 6 the son of Jonathan, and with him fifty
8. 26 six hundred and fifty talents of silver
Neh. 5. 17 an hundred and fifty of the Jews and ru.
6. 15 So the wall was finished..in fifty and two
7. 10 The children of Arah, six hundred fifty
7. 12 a thousand two hundred fifty and four
7. 20 children of Adin, six hundred fifty and fl.
7. 33 The men of the other Nebo, fifty and two
7. 34 a thousand two hundred fifty and four
7. 40 children of Immer, a thousand fifty and
7. 70 The Tirshatha gave..fifty basons, five h.
Esth. 5. 14 Let a gallows be made of fifty cubits high
7. 9 Behold also, the gallows, fifty cubits high
Isa. 3. 3 The captain of fifty, and the honourable
Eze. 40. 15 from the..gate..unto the..porch..fifty
40. 21, 25, 36 the length..fifty cubits, and the
40. 29, 33 fifty cubits long, and five and twenty
42. 2 north door, and the breadth..fifty cubits
42. 7 chambers, the length thereof..fifty cub.
42. 8 the length of the chambers..(was) fifty
45. 2 fifty cubits round about for the suburbs
48. 17 toward the north two hundred and fifty
48. 17 toward the south two hundred and fifty
48. 17 toward the east two hundred and fifty
48. 17 toward the west two hundred and fifty
Hag. 2. 16 for to draw out fifty..out of the press

2. *Fifty* πεντήκοντα *pentēkonta.*
Luke 7. 41 five hundred pence, and the other fifty
16. 6 Take thy bill, and sit down..write fifty
John 8. 57 Thou art not yet fifty years old, and hast
21. 11 great fishes, an hundred and fifty and th.
Acts 13. 20 about the space of four hundred and fifty

FIFTY every where —
Fifty by fifty, חֲמִשִּׁים בַּחֲמִשִּׁים [*chamishshim*].
Exod 27. 18 and the breadth fifty every where, and

FIFTY, by —
Fifty men (i.e. *each*), חֲמִשִּׁים אִישׁ *chamishshim ish.*
1 Ki. 18. 4 Obadiah..hid them by fifty in a cave, and f.
18. 13 I hid an hundred men..by fifty in a cave

FIG —
1. *Fig, fig tree,* תְּאֵנָה *teenah.*
Gen. 3. 7 they sewed fig leaves together, and made
Num 13. 23 and..of the pomegranates and of the figs
20. 5 it (is) no place of seed, or of figs, or of vi.
2 Ki. 20. 7 Isaiah said, Take a lump of figs. And
Neh. 13. 15 as also wine, grapes, and figs, and all
Isa. 38. 21 Isaiah..said, Let them take a lump of fl.
Jer. 24. 1 two baskets of figs..set before the temple
24. 2 very good figs..figs..first ripe..naughty fl.
24. 3 And I said, Figs; the good figs, very good
24. 5 Like these good figs, so will I acknowled.
24. 8 as the evil figs, which cannot be eaten
29. 17 I will..make them like vile figs, that ca.

2. *Fig,* σῦκον *sukon.*
Matt. 7. 16 Do men gather grapes of thorns, or figs of
Mark 11. 13 nothing but leaves; for the time of figs
Luke 6. 44 For of thorns men do not gather figs, nor
Jas. 3. 12 either a vine, figs? so (can) no fountain

FIG, green —
Green, hard, unripe fig, פַּג *pag.*
Song. 2. 13 The fig tree putteth forth her green figs

FIG, untimely —
Unripe fig, ὄλυνθος *olunthos.*
Rev. 6. 13 as a fig tree casteth her untimely figs

FIG tree —
1. *Fig tree, fig,* תְּאֵנָה *teenah.*
Deut. 8. 8 A land of wheat..and fig trees, and pom.
Judg. 9. 10 the trees said to the fig tree, Come thou
9. 11 But the fig tree said unto them, Should
1 Ki. 4. 25 man under his vine and under his fig tree
2 Ki. 18. 31 eat ye..every one of his fig tree, and dr.
Psa. 105. 33 He smote their vines..and their fig trees
Prov 27. 18 Whoso keepeth the fig tree shall eat the f.
Song 2. 13 The fig tree putteth forth her green figs
Isa. 34. 4 down..as a falling (fig) from the fig tree
36. 16 eat ye..every one of his fig tree, and dr.
Jer. 5. 17 shall eat up thy vines and thy fig trees
8. 13 nor figs on the fig tree, and the leaf shall
Hos. 2. 12 I will destroy her vines and her fig trees
9. 10 as the first ripe in the fig tree at her first
Joel 1. 7 He hath..barked my fig tree: he hath
1. 12 The vine is dried up, and the fig tree la.
2. 22 the fig tree and the vine do yield their
Amos 4. 9 your fig trees and your olive trees increased
Mic. 4. 4 shall sit every man..under his fig tree
Nah. 3. 12 All thy strongholds (shall be like) fig trees
Hab. 3. 17 Although the fig tree shall not blossom
Hag. 2. 19 the vine, and the fig tree, and the pome.
Zech. 3. 10 call..under the vine and under the fig tree

2. *Fig, fig tree,* συκέα, συκῆ *sukea, sukē.*
Matt 21. 19 when he saw a fig tree in the way, he came
21. 19 presently the fig tree withered away
21. 20 How soon is the fig tree withered away!
21. 21 shall not only do this..to the fig tree
24. 32 Now learn a parable of the fig tree: When
Mark 11. 13 seeing a fig tree afar off having leaves, he
11. 20 they saw the fig tree dried up from the
11. 21 the fig tree which thou cursedst is wither.
13. 28 Now learn a parable of the fig tree; When
Luke 13. 6 A certain (man) had a fig tree planted in
13. 7 years I come seeking fruit on this fig tree
21. 29 Behold the fig tree, and all the trees
John 1. 48 when thou was under the fig tree, I saw
1. 50 I saw thee under the fig tree, believest
Jas. 3. 12 Can the fig tree..bare olive berries?
Rev. 6. 13 as a fig tree casteth her untimely figs

FIGHT —
1. *Order, rank, arranging,* מַעֲרָכָה *maarakah.*
1 Sa. 17. 20 as the host was going forth to the fight

2. *Public conflict,* ἀγών *agōn.*
1 Ti. 6. 12 Fight the good fight of faith, lay hold on
2 Ti. 4. 7 I have fought a good fight, I have finish.

3. *A contest, struggle,* ἄθλησις *athlēsis.*
Heb. 10. 32 ye endured a great fight of afflictions

4. *War, battle, fight,* πόλεμος *polemos.*
Heb. 11. 34 waxed valiant in fight, turned to flight

FIGHT, to —
1. *To fight, consume,* לָחַם *lacham.*
Psa. 35. 1 fight against them that fight against me
56. 1 for man..he fighting daily oppresseth
56. 2 for (they be) many that fight against me

2. *To fight, be consumed,* לָחַם *lacham,* 2.
Exod. 1. 10 join..our enemies, and fight against us
14. 14 The LORD shall fight for you, and ye
14. 25 the LORD fighteth for them against the
17. 8 Then came Amalek, and fought with Is.
17. 9 Choose us out men, and go out, fight with
17. 10 So Joshua..fought with Amalek: and M.
Num 21. 1 he fought against Israel, and took..of
21. 23 he came to Jahaz, and fought against Is.
21. 26 Sihon..had fought against the former
Deut. 1. 30 The LORD your God..he shall fight for
1. 41 We have sinned..we will go up and fight
1. 42 Say unto them, Go not up, neither fight
3. 22 the LORD your God he shall fight for you
20. 4 to fight for you against your enemies, to
20. 10 thou comest nigh unto a city to fight
Josh. 9. 2 they gathered themselves together, to fl.
10. 14 hearkened..for the LORD fought for Isr.
10. 25 all your enemies against whom ye fight
10. 29 Then Joshua..and all Israel..fought
10. 31, 34 encamped against it, and fought
10. 36 Joshua..and all Israel..fought against it
10. 38 Joshua returned..to Debir, and fought
10. 42 the LORD God of Israel fought for Israel
11. 5 pitched together..to fight against Israel
19. 47 the children of Dan went up to fight
23. 3 your God (is) he that hath fought for you
23. 10 the LORD your God, he (it is) that fighte.
24. 8 they fought with you: and I gave them
24. 11 and the men of Jericho fought against
Judg. 1. 1 Who shall go up..to fight against them?
1. 3 Come up with me..that we may fight
1. 5 they fought against him, and they slew
1. 8 the children of Judah had fought against
1. 9 children of Judah went down to fight
5. 19 The kings came (and) fought, then fought
5. 20 They fought..the stars in their courses f.
8. 1 when thou wentest to fight with the M.?
9. 17 For my father fought for you, and adven.
9. 38 go out, I pray now, and fight with them
9. 39 Gaal went out..and fought with Abimel.
9. 45 Abimelech fought against the city all
9. 52 Abimelech came unto the tower, and fou.
10. 9 passed over Jordan to fight also against J.
10. 18 What man (is he) that will begin to fight
11. 6 that we may fight with the children of
11. 8 and fight against the children of Ammon
11. 9 If ye bring me home again to fight against
11. 12 that thou art come against me to fight in
11. 20 Sihon..pitched in Jahaz, and fought
11. 25 Balak..did he ever fight against them
11. 32 Jephthah passed over..to fight against
12. 1 Wherefore passedst thou over to fight
12. 3 then are ye come up..to fight against me?
12. 4 gathered..all the men..and fought with
1 Sa. 4. 9 quit yourselves like men, and fight
1 Sa. 4. 10 the Philistines fought, and Israel was
8. 20 go out before us, and fight our battles
12. 9 the Philistines..fought against them
13. 5 the Philistines gathered..to fight with I.
14. 47 Saul..fought against all his enemies on
15. 18 fight against them until they be consum.
17. 9 If he be able to fight with me, and to kill
17. 10 give me a man, that we may fight toget.
17. 19 in the valley of Elah, fighting with the P.
17. 32 thy servant will go and fight with this P.
17. 33 Thou art not able to go..to fight with
18. 17 be thou valiant for me, and fight the
19. 8 David went out and fought with the Ph.
23. 1 the Philistines fight against Keilah, and
23. 5 David and his men..fought with the Ph.
25. 28 my lord fighteth the battles of the LORD
28. 1 Philistines gathered their armies..to fig.
29. 8 that I may not go fight against the enem.
31. 1 Now the Philistines fought against Israel
2 Sa. 2. 28 the people stood still..neither fought
8. 10 because he had fought against Hadad.
10. 17 Syrians set themselves in array..and fo.
11. 17 And the men of the city..fought with J.
11. 20 approached ye so nigh..when ye did fl.?
12. 26 Joab fought against Rabbah of the child.
12. 27 I have fought against Rabbah, and have
12. 29 David..fought against it, and took it
21. 15 David went down..and fought against
1 Ki. 12. 21 to fight against the house of Israel, to
12. 24 Ye shall not go up, nor fight against
20. 23 but let us fight against them in the plain
20. 25 we will fight against them in the plain
22. 31 Fight neither with small nor great, save
22. 32 And they turned aside to fight against
2 Ki. 3. 21 that the kings were come up to fight aga.
8. 29 when he fought against Hazael king of S.
9. 15 when he fought with Hazael king of Syr.
10. 3 even out..and fight for your master's ho.
12. 17 Hazael..fought against Gath, and took it
13. 12 his might wherewith he fought against A.
14. 15 how he fought with Amaziah king of Ju.
19. 9 he is come out to fight against thee
1 Ch. 10. 1 Now the Philistines fought against Israel
18. 10 because he had fought against Haderezer
19. 17 against the Syrians, they fought with him
2 Ch. 11. 1 to fight against Israel, that he might bri.
11. 4 Ye shall not go up, nor fight against your
13. 12 O..fight ye not against the LORD God of
18. 30 Fight ye not with small or great, save
18. 31 they compassed about him to fight: but
20. 17 Ye shall not (need) to fight in this (battle)
20. 29 that the LORD fought against the enemies
22. 6 when he fought with Hazael king of Syria
27. 5 He fought also with the king of the Amo.
32. 8 with us (is) the LORD..to fight our battles
35. 20 Necho king of Egypt came up to fight
35. 22 disguised himself, that he might fight
35. 22 came to fight in the valley of Megiddo
Neh. 4. 8 to fight against Jerusalem, and to hinder
4. 14 remember the LORD..and fight for your
4. 20 resort ye thither..God shall fight for us
Psa. 109. 3 They..fought against me without a cause
Isa. 19. 2 they shall fight every one against his bro.
20. 1 Tartan came..and fought against Ashdod
30. 32 in battles of shaking will he fight with it
63. 10 therefore he was turned..he fought
Jer. 1. 19 they shall fight against thee; but they
15. 20 they shall fight against thee, but they
21. 4 wherewith ye fight against the king of B.
21. 5 I myself will fight against you with an
32. 5 though ye fight with the Chaldeans, ye
32. 24 into the hand of the Chaldeans, that fight
32. 29 the Chaldeans, that fight against this city
33. 5 They come to fight with the Chaldeans
34. 1 and all the people, fought against Jeru.
34. 7 the king of Babylon's army fought again.
34. 22 and they shall fight against it, and take
37. 8 And the Chaldeans shall..fight against
37. 10 whole army of the Chaldeans that fight
41. 12 they took all the men, and went to fight
51. 30 The..men of Babylon have forborn to fig.
Dan. 10. 20 now will I return to fight with the prince
11. 11 the king of the south shall..fight with
Zech 10. 5 they shall fight, because the LORD (is)
14. 3 Then shall the LORD go forth, and fight
14. 3 as when he fought in the day of battle
14. 14 Judah also shall fight at Jerusalem: and

3. *To assemble, war, serve,* צָבָא *tsaba.*
Isa. 29. 7 the multitude of all the nations that fight
29. 8 so shall..the nations be that fight against
31. 4 so shall the LORD..come down to fight
Zech 14. 12 all the people that have fought against

4. *To war,* צָבָה *tsabah.*
Isa. 29. 7 even all that fight against her and her

5. *War, warfare, battle,* מִלְחָמָה *milchamah.*
Deut. 2. 32 Sihon came out against us..to fight at J.
Judg 20. 20 Israel put themselves in array to fight
1 Ki. 20. 26 went up to Aphek, to fight against Israel
2 Ch. 32. 2 that he was purposed to fight against J.
Psa. 144. 1 my hands to war, (and) my fingers to fight

6. *To agonize, contest publicly,* ἀγωνίζομαι *agōnizo.*
John 18 36 then would my servants fight, that I shou.
1 Ti. 6. 12 Fight the good fight of faith, lay hold on
2 Ti. 4. 7 I have fought a good fight, I have finished

7. *To fight, strive,* μάχομαι *machomai.*
Jas. 4. 2 ye fight and war, yet ye have not, because

8. *To war, battle, fight,* πολεμέω *polemeō.*
Rev. 2. 16 I..will fight against them with the sword

Rev. 12. 7 Michael and his angels fought against
12. 7 and the dragon fought and his angels
9. *To box*, πυκτεύω *pukteuō*.
1 Co. 9. 26 so fight I, not as one that beateth the air

FIGHT against God, to —
1. *To fight with God*, θεομαχέω *theomacheō*.
Acts 23. 9 find no evil..let us not fight against God
2. *Fighting with God*, θεομάχος *theomachos*.
Acts 5. 39 haply ye be found even to fight against G.

FIGHT with beasts, to —
To fight with wild beasts, θηριομαχέω *thēriomacheō*.
1 Co.15. 32 if..I have fought with beasts at Ephesus

FIGHTING —
A fight, striving, μάχη *machē*.
2 Co. 7. 5 without (were) fightings, within (were)
Jas. 4. 1 From whence (come) wars and fightings

FIGHTING men —
To do or make war, עָשָׂה מִלְחָמָה *asah milchamah*.
2 Ch.26. 11 Uzziah had an host of fighting men, that

FIGURE —
1. *Figure, idol*, סֶמֶל, סֵמֶל *semel*.
Deut. 4. 16 the similitude of any figure, the likeness
2. *Form, building*, תַּבְנִית *tabnith*.
Isa. 44. 13 he..maketh it after the figure of a man
3. *Antitype, corresponding impression*, ἀντίτυπον.
Heb. 9. 24 the holy places..the figures of the true
4. *A parable, placing alongside*, παραβολή *parabolē*.
Heb. 9. 9 Which (was) a figure for the time then
11. 19 whence also he received him in a figure
5. *A type, impression*, τύπος *tupos*.
Acts 7. 43 ye took up..figures which ye made to
Rom. 5. 14 who is the figure of him that was to come

FIGURE, like —
Antitype, ἀντίτυπον *antitupon*.
1 Pe. 3. 21 The like figure whereunto (even) baptism

FIGURES, carved —
Carving, graving, מִקְלַעַת *miqlaath*.
1 Ki. 6. 29 carved all the walls..with carved figures

FILE —
File, notched edge, פְּצִירָה פִּים *petsirah pim*.
1 Sa. 13. 21 Yet they had a file for the mattocks, and

FILL —
1. *Full*, מָלֵא *male*.
Jer. 23. 24 do not I fill heaven and earth? saith the
2. *Fulness*, מְלֹא *melo*.
Exod16. 32 Fill an omer of it to be kept for your gen.
Isa. 8. 8 stretching out of his wings shall fill..thy
3. *Satiety, fulness*, שֹׂבַע *soba*.
Lev. 25. 19 ye shall eat your fill, and dwell therein
Deut23. 24 thou mayest eat grapes thy fill at thine

FILL, to —
1. *To fill, complete, be full*, מָלֵא *male*.
Gen. 1. 22 multiply, and fill the waters in the seas
Exod10. 6 they shall fill thy houses, and the houses
40. 34, 35 glory of the LORD filled the tabernacle
1 Ki. 8. 10 the cloud filled the house of the LORD
8. 11 glory of the LORD had filled the house of
18. 33 Fill four barrels with water, and pour(it)
2 Ch. 5. 14 glory of the LORD had filled the house of
7. 1 and the glory of the LORD filled the house
7. 2 because the glory of the LORD had filled
Psa 110. 6 shall fill (the places) with the dead bodies
Isa. 14. 21 nor fill the face of the world with cities
27. 6 Israel shall..fill the face of the world
Jer. 16. 18 they have filled mine inheritance with
19. 4 they..filled this place with the blood of
46. 12 and thy cry hath filled the land: for the
Eze. 8. 17 for they have filled the land with violence
10. 3 and the cloud filled the inner court
28. 16 they have filled..thee with violence, and
30. 11 they shall..fill the land with the slain
43. 5 the glory of the LORD filled the house
44. 4 the glory of the LORD filled the house of
2. *To fill*, מָלֵא *male*, 3.
Gen. 21. 19 went and filled the bottle with water, and
24. 16 she went down..and filled her pitcher
26. 15 had stopped them, and filled them with
42. 25 commanded to fill their sacks with corn
44. 1 Fill the men's sacks (with) food, as much
Exod. 2. 16 they..filled the troughs to water their f.
28. 3 whom I have filled with the spirit of wis.
31. 3 I have filled him with the spirit of God
35. 31 he hath filled him with the spirit of God
35. 35 Them hath he filled with wisdom of heart
Deut. 6. 11 houses..which thou filledst not, and wells
Josh. 9. 13 these bottles of wine, which we filled
1 Sa. 16. 1 Fill thine horn with oil, and go, I will
1 Ki. 18. 35 and he filled the trench also with water
20. 27 but the Syrians filled the country
2 Ki. 3. 25 cast every man his stone, and filled it
21. 16 till he had filled Jerusalem from one end
23. 14 he..filled their places with the bones of
24. 4 he filled Jerusalem with innocent blood
Ezra 9. 11 abominations, which have filled it from
Job 3. 15 Or with princes..who filled their houses
8. 21 Till he fill thy mouth with laughing, and
15. 2 Should a wise man..fill his belly with the
20. 23 (When) he is about to fill his belly, (God)
Job 22. 18 Yet he filled their houses with good
23. 4 I would..fill my mouth with arguments
38. 39 Wilt thou..fill the appetite of the young
41. 7 Canst thou fill his skin with barbed irons?
Psa. 17. 14 whose belly thou fillest with thy hid (tr.)
80. 9 cause it to take deep root, and it filled
81. 10 open thy mouth wide, and I will fill it
83. 16 Fill their faces with shame; that they
107. 9 he..filleth the hungry soul with goodness
129. 7 Wherewith the mower filleth not his hand
Prov. 1 13 we shall fill our houses with spoil
8. 21 to inherit substance; and I will fill their
Isa. 33. 5 he hath filled Zion with judgment and
65. 20 an old man that hath not filled his days
Jer. 13. 13 I will fill all the inhabitants of this land
15. 17 for thou hast filled me with indignation
33. 5 to fill them with the dead bodies of men
41. 9 Ishmael the son of Nethaniah filled it
51. 14 Surely I will fill thee with men, as with
51. 34 he hath filled his belly with my delicates
Eze. 3. 3 fill thy bowels with this roll that I give
7. 19 shall not satisfy their souls, neither fill
9. 7 Defile the house, and fill the courts with
10. 2 and fill thine hand with coals of fire from
11. 6 ye have filled the streets thereof with the
24. 4 Gather the pieces..fill (it) with the choice
32. 5 I will..fill the valleys with thy height
35. 8 I will fill his mountains with his slain
Nah. 2. 12 The lion..filled his holes with prey, and
Zeph. 1. 9 which fill their master's houses with vio.
Hag. 2. 7 I will fill this house with glory, saith the
Zech. 9. 13 When I have..filled the bow with Ephr.
3. *To fill*, מְלָא *mela*.
Dan. 2. 35 the stone that smote the image..filled the
4. *To cover*, עָטָה *atah*.
Psa. 84. 6 make it a well; the rain also filleth the
5. *To fill, satisfy, water*, רָוָה *ravah*, 5.
Isa. 43. 24 neither hast thou filled me with the fat
6. *To satisfy, satiate, fill*, שָׂבַע *saba*, 5.
Job 9. 18 He will not suffer..but filleth me with
Psa.147 14 filleth thee with the finest of the wheat
Lam. 3. 15 He hath filled me with bitterness, he hath
Eze. 27 33 thou filledst many people; thou didst
32. 4 I will fill the beasts of the whole earth
7. *To fill, load*, γεμίζω *gemizō*.
Luke14 23 to come in, that my house may be filled
15 16 he would fain have filled his belly with
John 2. 7 Fill the waterpots..And they filled
6. 13 they..filled twelve baskets with the frag.
Rev. 8. 5 the angel..filled it with fire of the altar
15. 8 temple was filled with smoke from the
8. *To fill in, make quite full*, ἐμπίπλημι *empiplēmi*.
Luke 1. 53 He hath filled the hungry with good thi.
John 6. 12 When they were filled, he said unto his
Rom 15. 24 if first I be somewhat filled with your
9. *To fill in*, ἐμπιπλάω *empiplaō*.
Acts 14. 17 filling our hearts with food and gladness
10. *To mingle, mix*, κεράννυμι *kerannumi*, -ύω.
Rev. 18 6 cup which she hath filled fill to her double
11. *To fill, make full*, πίμπλημι, πλήθω *plēthō*.
Matt 27. 48 took a sponge, and filled (it) with vinegar
Luke 1. 15 he shall be filled with the Holy Ghost
1. 41 Elisabeth was filled with the Holy Ghost
1. 67 Zacharias was filled with the Holy Ghost
4. 28 all they in the synagogue..were filled
5. 7 filled both the ships, so that they began
5. 26 they were all amazed..and were filled
6. 11 were filled with madness; and communed
John19. 29 they filled a sponge with vinegar, and
Acts 2. 4 they were all filled with the Holy Ghost
3. 10 they were filled with wonder and amaze.
4. 8 Then Peter, filled with the Holy Ghost
4. 31 and they were all filled with the Holy G.
5. 17 and all they..were filled with indignation
9. 17 that thou mightest..be filled with the
13. 9 Saul..filled with the Holy Ghost, set his
13. 45 they were filled with envy, and spake
19. 29 the whole city was filled with confusion
12. *To fill, make full*, πληρόω *plēroō*.
Luke 2. 40 waxed strong in spirit, filled with wisdom
3. 5 Every valley shall be filled, and every
John 12. 3 was filled with the odour of the ointment
16. 6 because I have said..sorrow hath filled
Acts 2. 2 and it filled all the house where they
5. 3 why hath Satan filled thine heart to lie
5. 28 have filled Jerusalem with your doctrine
13. 52 the disciples were filled with joy, and
Rom. 1. 29 Being filled with all unrighteousness
15. 13 the God of hope fill you with all joy and
15. 14 ye also are..filled with all knowledge
2 Co. 7. 4 I am filled with comfort, I am exceeding
Eph. 1. 23 the fulness of him that filleth all in all
3. 19 might be filled with all the fulness of God
4. 10 ascended up..that he might fill all things
5. 18 be not drunk..but be filled with the Spirit
Col. 1. 9 that ye might be filled with the knowledge
2 Ti. 1. 4 desiring to see thee..that I may be filled
13. *To fill together or thoroughly*, συμπληρόω *sumpl.*
Luke 8. 23 they were filled..and were in jeopardy
14. *To feed*, χορτάζω *chortazō*.
Matt. 5. 6 Blessed (are) they..for they shall be filled
14. 20 they did all eat, and were filled: and they
15. 33 so much bread..as to fill so great a mul.?
15. 37 they did all eat, and were filled: and they
Mark 6. 42 And they did all eat, and were filled
Mark 7. 27 Jesus said..Let the children first be filled
8. 8 So they did eat, and were filled: and they
Luke 6. 21 Blessed are (ye)..for ye shall be filled
9. 17 And they did eat, and were all filled: and
John 6. 26 ye did eat of the loaves, and were filled
Jas. 2. 16 Depart in peace, be (ye) warmed and filled
Rev. 19. 21 all the fowls were filled with their flesh

FILL full, to —
To fill, load, γεμίζω *gemizō*.
Mark15. 36 one ran and filled a sponge full of vinegar

FILL selves, to —
1. *To suck in, satiate*, סָבָא *saba*.
Isa. 56. 12 we will fill ourselves with strong drink
2. *To satisfy, satiate*, שָׂבַע *saba*.
Deut31. 20 they shall have eaten and filled themsel.

FILL, to take the —
To be filled, satisfied, watered, רָוָה *ravah*.
Prov. 7. 18 let us take our fill of love until the mor.

FILL or be filled up, to —
1. *To fill up*, ἀναπληρόω *anaplēroō*.
1 Th. 2. 16 might be saved, to fill up their sins alway
2. *To fill up instead of*, ἀνταναπληρόω *antanaplēr*.
Col. 1. 24 Who..fill up that which is behind of the
3. *To fill, make full*, πληρόω *plēroō*.
Matt23. 32 Fill ye up then the measure of your fath.
4. *To end*, τελέω *teleō*.
Rev. 15. 1 for in them is filled up the wrath of God

FILL up, which is put in to —
That which fills up, πλήρωμα *plērōma*.
Matt 9. 16 that which is put in to fill it up taketh

FILLED —
Full, מָלֵא *male*.
Isa. 6. 1 lifted up, and his train filled the temple

FILLED, to be —
1. *To be full*, מָלֵא *male*.
Gen. 6. 13 the earth is filled with violence through
2 Ch. 5. 13 the house was filled with a cloud, (even)
Zech. 9. 15 they shall be filled like bowls, (and) as
2. *To be filled*, מָלֵא *male*, 2.
Eccl. 6. 7 and yet the appetite is not filled
Hab. 2. 14 earth shall be filled with the knowledge
3. *To fill*, מָלֵא *male*, 3.
2 Ch.16. 14 in the bed which was filled with sweet
4. *To be satisfied, satiated*, שָׂבַע *saba*.
Deut 26. 12 may eat within thy gates, and be filled
Neh. 9. 25 so they did eat, and were filled, and
Psa. 78. 29 So they did eat, and were well filled: for
Prov. 1. 31 and be filled with their own devices
14. 14 The backslider..shall be filled with his
Eccl. 6. 3 If..his soul be not filled with good, and
Eze. 39. 20 ye shall be filled..with horses and char.
Hos. 13. 6 so were they filled; they were filled, and

FILLED full, to be —
To be satisfied, satiated, שָׂבַע *saba*.
Lam. 3. 30 He giveth..he is filled full with reproach

FILLED with —
Full, מָלֵא *male*.
Eze. 36. 38 the..cities be filled with flocks of men

FILLED with, to be —
1. *To be full*, מָלֵא *male*.
Psa. 38. 7 For my loins are filled with a loathsome
Prov 12. 21 but the wicked shall be filled with misc.
Isa. 21. 3 Therefore are my loins filled with pain
34. 6 The sword of the LORD is filled with blo.
Jer. 51. 5 their land was filled with sin against the
2. *To be full*, מָלֵא *male*, 2.
Gen. 6. 11 and the earth was filled with violence
Exod. 1. 7 and the land was filled with them
Num14. 21 all the earth shall be filled with the
1 Ki. 7. 14 was filled with wisdom and understand.
2 Ki. 3. 17 yet that valley shall be filled with water
3. 20 and the country was filled with water
Psa.126. 2 Then was our mouth filled with laughter
Prov. 3. 10 So shall thy barns be filled with plenty
20. 17 his mouth shall be filled with gravel
24. 4 be filled with all precious and pleasant
Eccl. 1. 8 not satisfied..nor the ear filled with hea
Song 5. 2 for my head is filled with dew, (and) my
Isa. 6. 4 and the house was filled with smoke
Jer. 13. 12, 12 Every bottle shall be filled with wine
Eze. 10. 4 the house was filled with the cloud, and
23. 33 Thou shalt be filled with drunkenness
3. *To be satisfied, satiated*, שָׂבַע *saba*.
Exod16. 12 in the morning ye shall be filled with br.
Psa.104. 28 openest thine hand, they are filled with
123. 3 we are exceedingly filled with contempt
123. 4 Our soul is exceedingly filled with the
Prov. 5. 10 Lest strangers be filled with thy wealth
18. 20 (and) with the increase..shall he be filled
25. 16 lest thou be filled therewith, and vomit
30. 16 the earth (that) is not filled with water
30. 22 and a fool when he is filled with meat
Hab. 2. 16 Thou art filled with shame for glory
4. *To fill up, make full*, πληρόω *plēroō*.
Phil. 1. 11 Being filled with the fruits of righteous.

FILLET —
Thread, cord, חוּט *chut*.
Jer. 52. 21 a fillet of twelve cubits did compass it

FILLET, to —
To fillet or fasten, חָשַׁק *chashaq,* 3.
Exod 38. 28 overlaid their chapiters, and filleted them
FILLETED, to be —
To be filleted or fastened, חָשַׁק *chashaq,* 4.
Exod 27. 17 the pillars..(shall be) filleted with silver
38. 17 pillars of the court (were) filleted with
FILLED up, piece that —
That which fills up, πλήρωμα *plērōma.*
Mark 2. 21 else the new piece that filled it up taketh
FILLETS —
Fillets, fastenings, חֲשֻׁקִים *chashuqim.*
Exod 27. 10 the hooks..and their fillets (shall be of) s.
27. 11 the hooks of the pillars and their fillets
36. 38 overlaid their chapiters and their fillets
38. 10, 11, 12, 17 hooks of the pillars and..fillets
38. 19 the overlaying of..their fillets (of) silver
FILTH —
1. *Filth, excrement,* צֹאָה *tsoah.*
Isa. 4. 4 Lord shall have washed away the filth of
2. *Cleansings, offscourings,* περικάθαρμα, *perikath.*
1 Co. 4. 13 we are made as the filth of the world
3. *Filth, dirt,* ῥύπος *rhupos.*
1 Pe. 3. 21 the putting away of the filth of the flesh
FILTHINESS —
1. *Uncleanness,* טֻמְאָה *tumah.*
Ezra 6. 21 from the filthiness of the heathen of the
Lam. 1. 9 Her filthiness (is) in her skirts; she rem.
Eze. 22. 15 I..will consume thy filthiness out of thee
24. 11 the filthiness of it may be molten in it
24. 13 In thy filthiness (is) lewdness: because I
24. 13 shalt not be purged from thy filthiness
36. 25 from all your filthiness..will I cleanse
2. *Impurity,* נִדָּה *niddah.*
2 Ch. 29. 5 carry forth the filthiness out of the holy
Ezra 9. 11 unclean..with the filthiness of the people
3. *Brass, impudence,* נְחֹשֶׁת *nechosheth.*
Eze. 16. 36 Because thy filthiness was poured out
4. *Excrement, filth,* צֹאָה *tsoah.*
Prov. 30. 12 and (yet) is not washed from their filthi
Isa. 28. 8 tables are full of vomit (and) filthiness
5. *Baseness, obscenity,* αἰσχρότης *aischrotēs.*
Eph. 5. 4 Neither filthiness, nor foolish talking
6. *Uncleanness,* ἀκαθάρτης *akathartēs.*
Rev. 17. 4 having a golden cup..full of..filthiness
7. *A soiling, defilement,* μολυσμός *molusmos.*
2 Co. 7. 1 cleanse ourselves from all filthiness of
8. *Dirt, filth,* ῥυπαρία *rhuparia.*
Jas. 1. 21 lay apart all filthiness and superfluity of
FILTHY —
1. *To be filthy,* אָלַח *alach,* 2.
Job 15. 16 much more abominable and filthy (is)
2. *Things passing away,* עִדִּים *iddim.*
Isa. 64. 6 all our righteousnesses (are) as filthy rags
3. *Filth,* צוֹא *tso.*
Zech. 3. 3 Joshua was clothed with filthy garments
3. 4 Take away the filthy garments from him
4. *Shameful,* αἰσχρός *aischros.*
Titus 1. 11 teaching things..for filthy lucre's sake
5. *Lasciviousness,* ἀσέλγεια *aselgeia.*
2 Pe. 2. 7 vexed with the filthy conversation of the
FILTHY communication —
Shameful discourse, αἰσχρολογία *aischrologia.*
Col. 3. 8 put off..blasphemy, filthy communicat.
FILTHY, to be —
1. *To be rebellious,* מָרָא *mara.*
Zeph. 3. 1 Woe to her that is filthy and polluted, to
2. *To make filthy, act filthily,* ῥυπόω *rhupoō.*
Rev 22. 11 he which is [filthy], let him [be filthy] still
FILTHY, to become —
To be filthy, אָלַח *alach,* 2.
Psa. 14. 3 they are (all) together become filthy
53. 3 they are altogether become filthy; (there
FIN —
Fin, סְנַפִּיר *senappir.*
Lev. 11. 9 whatsoever hath fins and scales in the w.
11. 10 that have not fins and scales in the seas
11. 12 hath no fins nor scales in the waters
Deut 14. 9 all that have fins and scales shall ye
14. 10 whatsoever hath not fins and scales ye
FINALLY —
1. *What is left, remaining,* λοιπόν *loipon.*
2 Co. 13. 11 Finally, brethren, farewell. Be perfect
Eph. 6. 10 Finally, my brethren, be strong in the L.
Phil. 3. 1 Finally, my brethren, rejoice in the Lord
4. 8 Finally, brethren, whatsoever things are
2 Th. 3. 1 Finally, brethren, pray for us, that the
2. *End, completion,* τέλος *telos.*
1 Pe. 3. 8 Finally, (be ye) all of one mind, having
FIND, to —
1. *To find,* מָצָא *matsa.*
Gen. 4. 14 every one that findeth me shall slay me
6. 8 Noah found grace in the eyes of the LORD

Gen. 8. 9 dove found no rest for the sole of her foot
11. 2 they found a plain in the land of Shinar
16. 7 angel of the LORD found her by a fountain
18. 3 if now I have found favour in thy sight
18. 26 If I find in Sodom fifty righteous within
18. 28 If I find there forty and five, I will not
18. 30 I will not do (it), if I find thirty there
19. 11 they wearied themselves to find the door
19. 19 thy servant hath found grace in thy sight
26. 19 and found there a well of springing water
26. 32 and said unto him, We have found water
27. 20 How (is it)..thou hast found (it) so quick.
30. 14 found mandrakes in the field, and brou.
30. 27 if I have found favour in thine eyes
31. 32 With whomsoever thou findest thy gods
31. 33 went into Jacob's tent..he found (them)
31. 34 searched all the tent, but found (them)
31. 35 And he searched, but found not the ima.
31. 37 what hast thou found of all thy household
32. 5 sent..that I may find grace in thy sight
32. 19 shall ye speak unto Esau, when ye find
33. 8 to find grace in the sight of my lord
33. 10 if now I have found grace in thy sight
33. 15 let me find grace in the sight of my lord
34. 11 Let me find grace in your eyes, and what
36. 24 that found the mules in the wilderness
37. 15 a certain man found him, and, behold, he
37. 17 went after his brethren, and found them
37. 32 This have we found: know now whether
38. 20 from the woman's hand; but he found
38. 22 he returned..and said, I cannot find her
38. 23 I sent this kid, and thou hast not found
39. 4 Joseph found grace in his sight, and he
41. 38 Can we find (such a one) as this (is), a man
44. 8 the money which we found in our sack's
44. 16 found out the iniquity of thy servants
47. 25 let us find grace in the sight of my lord
47. 29 If now I have found grace in thy sight
50. 4 If now I have found grace in your eyes
Exod. 5. 11 Go ye, get you straw where ye can find it
15. 22 they went three days..and found no wa.
16. 25 to day ye shall not find it in the field
16. 27 went..for to gather, and they found none
33. 12 thou hast also found grace in my sight
33. 13 if I have found grace in thy sight, show
33. 16 thy people have found grace in thy sight?
33. 17 thou hast found grace in my sight, and I
34. 9 If now I have found grace in thy sight, O
Lev. 6. 3 have found that which was lost, and lieth
6. 4 restore..the lost thing which he found
Num 11. 11 have I not found favour in thy sight
11. 15 kill me..if I have found favour in thy
15. 32 they found a man that gathered sticks
15. 33 And they that found him gathering sti.
32. 5 if we have found grace in thy sight, let
35. 27 the revenger of blood find him without
Deut. 4. 29 thou shalt find (him), if thou seek him w.
22. 3 which he hath lost, and thou hast found
22. 14 when I came to her, I found her not a m.
22. 17 saying, I found not thy daughter a maid
22. 23 a man find her in the city, and lie with
22. 25 man find a betrothed damsel in the field
22. 27 found her in the field, (and) the betrothed
22. 28 If a man find a damsel (that is) a virgin
24. 1 it come to pass that she find no favour in
24. 1 he hath found some uncleanness in her
32. 10 He found him in a desert land, and in the
Josh. 2. 22 throughout all the way, but found (them)
Judg. 1. 5 they found Adoni-bezek in Bezek: and
6. 17 If now I have found grace in thy sight
15. 15 he found a new jawbone of an ass, and
17. 8 to sojourn where he could find a (place)
17. 9 go to sojourn where I may find a (place)
21. 12 they found among the inhabitants of
Ruth 1. 9 The LORD grant you that ye may find rest
2. 2 (him) in whose sight I shall find grace
2. 10 Why have I found grace in thine eyes
2. 13 Let me find favour in thy sight, my lord
1 Sa. 1. 18 Let thine handmaid find grace in thy sig.
9. 4 land of Shalisha, but they found (them)
9. 4 through the land..but they found (them)
9. 11 found young maidens going out to draw
9. 13 ye shall straightway find him, before he
9. 13 for about this time ye shall find him
10. 2 shalt find two men by Rachel's sepulchre
12. 5 that ye have not found ought in my hand
14. 30 spoil of their enemies which they found?
16. 22 for he hath found favour in my sight
20. 3 that I have found grace in thine eyes
20. 29 if I have found favour in thine eyes, let
23. 17 for the hand of Saul..shall not find thee
24. 19 if a man find his enemy, will he let him
25. 8 let the young men find favour in thine ey.
27. 5 If I have now found grace in thine eyes
29. 3 have found no fault in him since he fell
29. 6 I have not found evil in thee since the
29. 8 what hast thou found in thy servant so
30. 11 they found an Egyptian in the field, and
31. 8 they found Saul and his three sons fallen
2 Sa. 7. 27 therefore hath thy servant found in his
14. 22 I have found grace in thy sight, my lord
15. 25 shall find favour in the eyes of the LORD
16. 4 I may find grace in thy sight, my lord, O
17. 20 when they had sought and could not find
1 Ki. 1. 3 found Abishag a Shunammite, and brou.
11. 19 Hadad found great favour in the sight of
11. 29 Ahijah the Shilonite found him in the
13. 14 and found him sitting under an oak
13. 28 found his carcase cast in the way, and
18. 5 find grass to save the horses and mules
18. 10 took an oath..that they found thee not
18. 12 and he cannot find thee, he shall slay me

1 Ki. 19. 19 found Elisha the son of Shaphat, who
20. 36 was departed from him, a lion found him
20. 37 he found another man, and said, Smite
21. 20 Hast thou found me, O mine enemy?
21. 20 I have found (thee); because thou hast
2 Ki. 2. 17 they sought three days, but found him
4. 39 found a wild vine, and gathered thereof
9. 35 they found no more of her than the skull
17. 4 And the king..found conspiracy in Hosh.
19. 8 found the king of Assyria warring against
22. 8 I have found the book of the law in the
23. 24 book that Hilkiah the priest found in the
1 Ch. 4. 40 they found fat pasture and good, and the
10. 8 found Saul and his sons fallen in mount
17. 25 found (in his heart) to pray before thee
20. 2 found it to weigh a talent of gold, and
2 Ch. 20. 16 shall find them at the end of the brook
20. 25 they found among them in abundance
22. 8 found the princes of Judah, and the sons
25. 5 found them three hundred thousand ch.
29. 16 uncleanness that they found in the temp.
32. 4 kings of Assyria come, and find much wat.
34. 14 Hilkiah the priest found a book of the
34. 15 I have found the book of the law in the
Ezra 8. 15 and found there none of the sons of Levi
Neh. 5. 8 their peace, and found nothing (to answer)
7. 5 I found a register..and found written ther.
8. 14 they found written in the law which the
9. 8 foundest his heart faithful before thee
Esth. 5. 8 found favour in the sight of the king
7. 3 If I have found favour in thy sight, O
8. 5 and if I have found favour in his sight
Job 3. 22 are glad, when they can find the grave?
17. 10 for I cannot find (one) wise (man) among
23. 3 Oh that I knew where I might find him!
31. 29 or lifted up myself when evil found him
32. 3 found no answer, and (yet) had condemn.
32. 13 ye should say, We have found out wisdom
33. 10 findeth occasions against me, he counteth
33. 24 saith, Deliver him..I have found a rans.
37. 23 (Touching) the Almighty, we cannot find
Psa. 10. 15 seek..his wickedness (till) thou find none
17. 3 thou hast tried me, (and) shalt find noth.
69. 20 I looked..for comforters, but I found no.
76. 5 none of the men..have found their hands
84. 3 the sparrow hath found an house, and
89. 20 I have found David my servant; with my
107. 4 They wandered..they found no city to dw.
116. 3 hold upon me: I found trouble and sorr.
119. 162 rejoice..as one that findeth great spoil
132. 6 we found it in the fields of the wood
Prov. 1. 13 We shall find all precious substance, we
1. 28 seek me early, but they shall not find me
2. 5 Then shalt thou..find the knowledge of
3. 4 So shalt thou find favour and good
3. 13 Happy (is) the man (that) findeth wisdom
4. 22 they (are) life unto those that find them
7. 15 to seek thy face, and I have found thee
8. 9 and right to them that find knowledge
8. 17 those that seek me early shall find me
8. 35 whoso findeth me findeth life, and shall
16. 20 that handleth a matter wisely shall find
17. 20 that hath a froward heart findeth no good
18. 22 (Whoso) findeth a wife findeth a good (th.)
19. 8 he that keepeth understanding shall find
20. 6 but a faithful man who can find?
21. 21 He that followeth..mercy findeth life
24. 14 when thou hast found (it), then there
25. 16 Hast thou found honey? eat so much as
28. 23 shall find more favour than he that
31. 10 Who can find a virtuous woman? for her
Eccl. 7. 14 that man should find nothing after him
7. 26 I find more bitter than death the woman
7. 27 this have I found, saith the Preacher
7. 28 Which yet my soul seeketh, but I find not
7. 28 one man among a thousand have I found
7. 28 a woman among all those have I not found
7. 29 this only have I found, that God hath
8. 17 man cannot find out the work that is done
8. 17 yet he shall not find..not be able to find
9. 10 Whatsoever thy hand findeth to do, do
11. 1 for thou shalt find it after many days
Song 3. 1, 2 I sought him, but I found him not
3. 3 watchmen that go about the city found
3. 4 but I found him whom my soul loveth
5. 6 I sought him, but I could not find him
5. 7 watchmen that went about the city found
5. 8 if ye find my beloved, that ye tell him
8. 1 I should find thee without, I would kiss
8. 10 then was I in his eyes as one that found
Isa. 10. 10 hand hath found the kingdoms of the idols
10. 14 hath found as a nest the riches of the pe.
34. 14 and find for herself a place of rest
37. 8 found the king of Assyria warring against
41. 12 shalt seek them, and shalt not find them
57. 10 thou hast found the life of thine hand
58. 3 in the day of your fast ye find pleasure
Jer. 2. 5 What iniquity have your fathers found in
2. 24 in her month they shall find her
2. 34 I have not found it by secret search, but
5. 1 if ye can find a man, if there be (any) that
6. 16 and ye shall find rest for your souls
10. 18 distress them, that they may find (it so)
14. 3 they came to the pits, (and) found no w.
23. 11 in my house have I found their wicked.
29. 13 And ye shall seek me, and find (me)
31. 2 The people..found grace in the wildern.
41. 12 found him by the great waters that (are)
45. 3 fainted in my sighing, and I find no rest
50. 7 All that found them have devoured them
Lam. 1. 3 among the heathen, she findeth no rest
1. 6 become like harts (that) find no pasture

Lam. 2. 9 prophets also find no vision from the LORD
2. 16 looked for; we have found, we have seen
Eze. 3. 1 eat that thou findest; eat this roll, and go
22. 30 And I sought for a man..but I found
Dan. 1. 20 he found them ten times better than all
Hos. 2. 6 make a wall, that she shall not find her
2. 7 shall seek them, but shall not find (them)
5. 6 they shall not find (him); he hath withd.
9. 10 found Israel like grapes in the wilderness
12. 4 found him (in) Beth-el, and there he spa.
12. 8 I have found me out substance; (in) all
12. 8 find none iniquity in me that (were) sin
Amos 8. 12 word of the LORD, and shall not find (it)
Jon. 1. 3 he found a ship going to Tarshish: so he

2. *To find*, שְׁכַח *shekach*, 5.
Ezra 4. 15 so shalt thou find in the book of the rec.
7. 16 that thou canst find in all the province
Dan. 2. 25 I have found a man of the captives of
6. 4 sought to find occasion against Daniel
6. 4 they could find none occasion nor fault
6. 5 not find any occasion against this Daniel
6. 5 we find (it) against him concerning the
6. 11 found Daniel praying and making suppli.

3. *To find out*, ἀνευρίσκω *aneuriskō*.
Luke 2. 16 found Mary and Joseph, and the babe
Acts 21. 4 finding disciples, we tarried there seven

4. *To find*, εὑρίσκω *heuriskō*.
Matt. 1. 18 was found with child of the Holy Ghost
2. 8 when ye have found (him), bring me word
7. 7 seek, and ye shall find; knock, and it
7. 8 he that seeketh findeth; and to him
7. 14 the way..and few there be that find it
8. 10 I have not found so great faith, no, not
10. 39 He that findeth his life shall lose it
10. 39 loseth his life for my sake shall find it
11. 29 and ye shall find rest unto your souls
12. 43 dry places, seeking rest, and findeth none
12. 44 he findeth (it) empty, swept, and garnish.
13. 44 which when a man hath found, he hideth
13. 46 when he had found one pearl of great
16. 25 lose his life for my sake shall find it
17. 27 thou shalt find a piece of money: that
18. 13 if it so be that he find it, verily I say
18. 28 found one of his fellow-servants, which
20. 6 found others standing idle, and saith unto
21. 2 shall find an ass tied, and a colt with her
21. 19 found nothing thereon, but leaves only
22. 9 as many as ye..find, bid to the marriage
22. 10 as many as they found, both bad and good
24. 46 lord when he cometh shall find so doing
26. 40 findeth them asleep, and saith unto Peter
26. 43 And he came and found them asleep again
26. 60 found none: yea, though many false
26. 60 false witnesses came, (yet) [found they]
27. 32 they found a man of Cyrene, Simon by
Mark 1. 37 when they had found him, they said unto
7. 30 she found the devil gone out, and her
11. 2 find a colt tied, whereon never man sat
11. 4 and found the colt tied by the door with.
11. 13 haply he might find any thing thereon
11. 13 came to it, he found nothing but leaves
13. 36 Lest coming suddenly he find you sleeping
14. 16 came..and found as he had said unto them
14. 37 and findeth them sleeping, and saith unto
14. 40 he found them asleep again, for their eyes
14. 55 sought for witness..and found none
Luke 1. 30 for thou hast found favour with God
2. 12 shall find the babe wrapped in swaddling
2. 45 when they found him not, they turned
2. 46 they found him in the temple, sitting in
4. 17 he found the place where it was written
5. 19 when they could not find by what (way)
6. 7 they might find an accusation against him
7. 9 I have not found so great faith, no, not
7. 10 found the servant whole that had been
8. 35 found the man, out of whom the devils
9. 36 the voice was past, Jesus was found alone
11. 9 seek, and ye shall find; knock, and it
11. 10 he that seeketh findeth; and to him that
11. 24 finding none, he saith, I will return unto
11. 25 cometh, he findeth (it) swept and garnished
12. 37 lord when he cometh shall find watching
12. 38 find (them) so, blessed are those servants
12. 43 lord when he cometh shall find so doing
13. 6 and sought fruit thereon, and found none
13. 7 seeking fruit on this fig tree, and find none
15. 4 after that which is lost, until he find it?
15. 5 when he hath found (it), he layeth (it) on
15. 6 for I have found my sheep which was lost
15. 8 and seek diligently till she find (it)?
15. 9 when she hath found (it), she calleth (her)
15. 9 I have found the piece which I had lost
15. 24 he was lost, and is found. And they began
15. 32 is alive again; and was lost, and is found
17. 18 There are not found that returned to give
18. 8 cometh, shall he find faith on the earth?
19. 30 shall find a colt tied, whereon yet never
19. 32 and found even as he had said unto them
22. 13 went, and found as he had said unto them
22. 45 he found them sleeping for sorrow
23. 2 found this (fellow) perverting the nation
23. 4 said Pilate..I find no fault in this man
23. 14 have found no fault in this man touching
23. 22 I have found no cause of death in him
24. 2 they found the stone rolled away from
24. 3 and found not the body of the Lord Jesus
24. 23 when they found not his body, they came
24. 24 found (it) even so as the woman had said
24. 33 found the eleven gathered together, and
John 1. 41 He first findeth his own brother Simon
1. 41 We have found the Messias, which is
1. 43 findeth Philip, and saith unto him; Fol.
1. 45 Philip findeth Nathanael, and saith unto
1. 45 We have found him, of whom Moses in
2. 14 found in the temple those that sold oxen
5. 14 Jesus findeth him in the temple, and said
6. 25 found him on the other side of the sea
7. 34, 36 Ye shall seek me, and shall not find
7. 35 Whither will he go, that we shall not find
9. 35 when he had found him, he said unto him
10. 9 and shall go in and out, and find pasture
11. 17 he found that he had (lain) in the grave
12. 14 when he had found a young ass, sat the.
18. 38 and saith..I find in him no fault (at all)
19. 4 ye may know that I find no fault in him
19. 6 crucify (him): for I find no fault in him
21. 6 right side of the ship, and ye shall find
Acts 4. 21 finding nothing how they might punish
5. 10 and found her dead, and, carrying (her)
5. 22 found them not in the prison, they retu.
5. 23 prison truly found we shut with all safety
5. 23 when we had opened, we found no man
5. 39 ye be found even to fight against God
7. 11 and our fathers found no sustenance
7. 46 Who found favour before God, and desired
7. 46 to find a tabernacle for the God of Jacob
8. 40 Philip was found at Azotus: and passing
9. 2 if he found any of this way, whether they
9. 33 found a certain man named Æneas, which
10. 27 and found many that were come together
11. 26 when he had found him, he brought him
12. 19 found him not, he examined the keepers
13. 6 they found a certain sorcerer, a false
13. 22 I have found David the (son) of Jesse, a
13. 28 they found no cause of death (in him), yet
17. 6 when they found them not, they drew J.
17. 23 I found an altar with this inscription, To
17. 27 if haply they might..find him, though he
18. 2 found a certain Jew named Aquila, born
19. 1 came to Ephesus: and finding certain d.
19. 19 counted the price..and found (it) fifty
21. 2 finding a ship sailing over unto Phenicia
23. 9 We find no evil in this man: but if a
24. 5 we have found this man (a) pestilent (fel.)
24. 12 neither found me in the temple disputing
24. 18 Jews..found me purified in the temple
24. 20 if they have found any evil doing in me
27. 6 found a ship of Alexandria sailing into
27. 28 And sounded, and found (it) twenty fath.
27. 28 they sounded again, and found (it) fifteen
28. 14 Where we found brethren, and were de.
Rom. 4. 1 What shall we say..Abraham..hath f.?
7. 10 (ordained) to life, I found (to be) unto d.
7. 18 to perform that which is good [I find]
7. 21 I find then a law, that, when I would do
10. 20 I was found of them that sought me not
1 Co. 4. 2 in stewards, that a man be found faithful
15. 15 and we are found false witnesses of God
2 Co. 2. 13 I found not Titus my brother: but taking
5. 3 being clothed we shall not be found naked
9. 4 find you unprepared, we..should be ash.
11. 12 that..they may be found even as we
12. 20 I shall not find you such as I would, and
12. 20 (that) I shall be found unto you such as
Gal. 2. 17 we ourselves also are found sinners
Phil. 2. 8 being found in fashion as a man, he hu.
3. 9 And be found in him, not having mine
2 Ti. 1. 17 sought me out very diligently, and found
1. 18 he may find mercy of the Lord in that d.
Heb. 4. 16 and find grace to help in time of need
11. 5 was not found, because God had transla.
12. 17 he found no place of repentance, though
1 Pe. 1. 7 the trial..might be found unto praise and
2. 22 Who did no sin, neither was guile found
2 Pe. 3. 14 ye may be found of him in peace, without
2 John 4 I found of thy children walking in truth
Rev. 2. 2 hast tried..and hast found them liars
3. 2 not found thy works perfect before God
5. 4 no man was found worthy to open and
9. 6 men seek death, and shall not find it
12. 8 neither was their place found any more
14. 5 And in their mouth was found no guile
16. 20 and the mountains were not found
18. 14 and thou shalt find them no more at all
18. 21 Babylon..shall be found no more at all
18. 22 shall be found any more in thee
18. 24 in her was found the blood of prophets
20. 11 and there was found no place for them
20. 15 whosoever was not found written in the

5. *To take thoroughly*, καταλαμβάνω *katalambanō*.
Acts 25. 25 I found that he had committed nothing

FIND, can —
To find, εὑρίσκω *heuriskō*.
Luke 19. 48 could not find what they might do: for

FIND, to cause to —
To cause to find, מָצָא *matsa*, 5.
Job 34. 11 cause every man to find accor. to (his) ways

FIND occasion, to —
To find, מָצָא *matsa*.
Judg. 9. 33 do to them as thou shalt find occasion

FIND out, to —
1. *To think out*, חָשַׁב *chashab*.
2 Ch. 2. 14 to find out every device which shall be

2. *To find*, מָצָא *matsa*.
Gen. 44. 16 God hath found out the iniquity of thy
Num 32. 23 and be sure your sin will find you out
Judg 14. 12 certainly declare it me..and find (it) out
14. 18 If ye had not ploughed..ye had not fo. out
1 Sa. 20. 21 send a lad, (saying), Go, find out the arr.
20. 36 Run, find out now the arrows which I sh.
Job 11. 7 Canst thou by searching find out God?
11. 7 canst thou find out the Almighty unto
Psa. 21. 8 Thine hand shall find out all thine enem.
21. 8 right hand shall find out those that hate
132. 5 Until I find out a place for the LORD
Prov. 8. 12 and find out knowledge of witty invent.
Eccl. 3. 11 no man can find out the work that God
7. 24 That which is far..who can find it out?
7. 27 (counting)..to find out the account
8. 17 a man cannot find out the work that is
12. 10 Preacher sought to find out acceptable

FINDING (out) —
1. *To find*, מָצָא *matsa*.
Gen. 4. 15 lest any finding him should kill him
Isa. 58. 13 nor finding thine own pleasure, nor spe.

2. *Search, searching*, חֵקֶר *cheqer*.
Job 9. 10 Which doeth great things past finding o.

FINDING out, past —
Not to be traced out, ἀνεξιχνίαστος *anexichniastos*.
Rom. 11. 33 judgments, and his ways past finding out!
[*See also* Ease, favour, mercy.]

FINE, finest —
1. *Fatness*, חֵלֶב *cheleb*.
Psa. 81. 16 should have fed them also with the finest
147. 14 filleth thee with the finest of the wheat

2. *Good*, טָב *tab*.
Dan. 2. 32 image's head (was) of fine gold, his breast

3. *Good*, טוֹב *tob*.
2 Ch. 3. 5 which he overlaid with fine gold, and set
3. 8 he overlaid it with fine gold, (amounting)

4. *Fine combed*, שָׂרִיק *sariq*.
Isa. 19. 9 they that work in fine flax, and they that

5. *To be made to shine*, צָהַב *tsahab*, 6.
Ezra 8. 27 vessels of fine copper, precious as gold

FINE, to —
To refine, זָקַק *zaqaq*.
Job 28. 1 and a place for gold (where) they fine (it)

FINE flour —
1. *Fine flour (rolled or crushed small)*, סֹלֶת *soleth*.
Lev. 2. 1 his offering shall be (of) fine flour; and he
2. 4 cakes of fine flour mingled with oil
2. 5 fine flour unleavened, mingled with oil
2. 7 it shall be made (of) fine flour with oil
5. 11 of an ephah of fine flour for a sin offering
6. 20 fine flour for a meat offering perpetual
7. 12 cakes mingled with oil, of fine flour, fried
14. 10 deals of fine flour (for) a meat offering
14. 21 fine flour mingled with oil for a meat offer.
23. 13 tenth deals of fine flour mingled with oil
23. 17 they shall be of fine flour; they shall be
24. 5 shalt take fine flour, and bake twelve
Num. 6. 15 cakes of fine flour mingled with oil, and
7. 13, 19, 25, 31, 37 fine flour mingled with oil
7. 43, 49, 55, 61 fine flour mingled with oil
7. 67, 73, 79 of fine flour mingled with oil
8. 8 fine flour mingled with oil, and another
1 Ki. 4. 22 was thirty measures of fine flour, and
2 Ki. 7. 1 measure of fine flour (be sold) for a shekel
7. 16 a measure of fine flour was (sold) for a
7. 18 and a measure of fine flour for a shekel
1 Ch. 9. 29 the fine flour, and the wine, and the oil
23. 29 for the fine flour for meat offering, and
Eze. 16. 13 thou didst eat fine flour, and honey, and
16. 19 fine flour, and oil, and honey (wherewith)
46. 14 hin of oil, to temper with the fine flour

2. *Fine flour*, σεμίδαλις *semidalis*.
Rev. 18. 13 fine flour, and wheat, and beasts, and

FINE brass —
Fine frankincense or brass, χαλκολίβανον *chalk.*
Rev. 1. 15 his feet like unto fine brass, as if they
2. 18 flame of fire, and his feet (are) like fine b.

FINE gold —
Fine gold, חָרוּץ *charuts*.
Prov. 3. 14 and the gain thereof than fine gold
Zech. 9. 3 and fine gold as the mire of the streets

FINE linen —
1. *Fine linen, braided or twisted yarn*, אֵטוּן *etun*.
Prov. 7. 16 carved (works), with fine linen of Egypt

2. *Fine white linen, byssus*, בּוּץ *buts*.
1 Ch. 4. 21 the house of them that wrought fine linen
15. 27 (was) clothed with a robe of fine linen
2 Ch. 2. 14 in blue, and in fine linen, and in crimson
3. 14 fine linen, and wrought cherubim thereon
Esth. 1. 6 fastened with cords of fine linen and
8. 15 with a garment of fine linen and purple
Eze. 27. 16 purple, and broidered work, and fine li.

3. *Byssus, fine white linen*, βύσσινος *bussinos*.
Rev. 18. 16 that was clothed in fine linen, and purple
19. 8 be arrayed in fine linen, clean and white
19. 8 fine linen is the righteousness of saints
19. 14 clothed in fine linen, white and clean

4. *Fine linen, muslin*, σινδών *sindōn*.
Mark 15. 46 he bought fine linen, and took him down

5. *Byssus, fine white linen,* βύσσος *bussos.*
Luke 16. 19 clothed in purple and fine linen; Rev 18. 12.

FINE meal. *See* **MEAL.**

FINER —

To refine, צָרַף *tsaraph.*
Prov. 25. 4 there shall come..a vessel for the finer

FINGER —

1. *Finger,* אֶצְבַּע *etsba.*
Exod. 8. 19 magicians said..This (is) the finger of God
29. 12 put (it) upon the horns..with thy finger
31. 18 tables..written with the finger of God
Lev. 4. 6 priest shall dip his finger in the blood
4. 17 shall dip his finger (in some) of the blood
4. 25, 34 shall take of the blood..with his fing.
4. 30 take of the blood thereof with his finger
8. 15 put (it) upon the horns..with his finger
9. 9 he dipped his finger in the blood, and
14. 16 the priest shall dip his right finger in
14. 16 shall sprinkle of the oil with his finger
14. 27 priest shall sprinkle with..right finger
16. 14 and sprinkle (it) with his finger upon the
16. 14 sprinkle of the blood with his finger
16. 19 sprinkle of the blood..with his finger
Num 19. 4 shall take of her blood with his finger
Deut. 9. 10 tables..written with the finger of God
2 Sa. 21. 20 that had on every hand six fingers, and
1 Ch. 20. 6 whose fingers and toes (were) four and
Psa. 8. 3 consider..heavens, the work of thy fingers
144. 1 strength which teacheth..my fingers to
Prov. 6. 13 with his feet, he teacheth with his fingers
7. 3 Bind them upon thy fingers, write them
Song 5. 5 and my fingers (with) sweet smelling
Isa. 2. 8 that which their own fingers have made
17. 8 respect (that) which his fingers have made
58. 9 the yoke, the putting forth of the finger
59. 3 with blood, and your fingers with iniquity
Jer. 52. 21 the thickness thereof (was) four fingers

2. *Fingers,* אֶצְבְּעָן *etsbean.*
Dan. 5. 5 In the same hour came forth fingers of a

3. *Finger,* δάκτυλος *daktulos.*
Matt 23. 4 will not move..with one of their fingers
Mark 7. 33 put his fingers into his ears, and he spit
Luke 11. 20 I with the finger of God cast out devils
11. 46 touch not the burdens with..your fingers
16 24 he may dip the tip of his finger in water
John 8. 6 [and with (his) finger wrote on the ground]
20. 25 put my finger into the print of the nails
20. 27 Reach hither thy finger, and behold my

FINING pot —

Refining vessel, מַצְרֵף *matsreph.*
Prov. 17. 3 The fining pot (is) for silver, and the fur.
27. 21 (As) the fining pot for silver, and the fur.

FINISH, to —

1. *To cut off,* בָּצַע *batsa,* 3.
Zech. 4. 9 his hands shall also finish it; and thou

2. *To shut, restrain, finish,* כָּלָא *kala,* 3.
Dan. 9. 24 to finish the transgression, and to make

3. *To complete, finish,* כָּלָה *kalah.*
1 Ch. 28. 20 until thou hast finished all the work for

4. *To finish, complete,* כָּלָא *kalah,* 3.
Gen. 6. 16 and in a cubit shalt thou finish it above
Exod 40. 33 So Moses finished the work
Ruth 3. 18 until he have finished the thing this day
1 Ki. 6. 9 So he built the house, and finished it
6. 14 Solomon built the house, and finished it
7. 1 and he finished all his house
9. 1 finished the building of the house of the
1 Ch. 27. 24 he finished not, because there fell wrath
2 Ch. 7. 11 Solomon finished the house of the LORD
24. 14 when they had finished (it), they brought
31. 7 and finished (them) in the seventh month

5. *To complete, finish,* כְּלַל *kelal,* 5a.
Ezra 6. 14 finished (it), according to the commandm.

6. *To finish, complete,* שָׁלַם *shalam,* 3.
1 Ki. 9. 25 before the LORD. So he finished the house

7. *To finish, complete,* שְׁלַם *shelam,* 5.
Dan. 5. 26 numbered thy kingdom, and finished it

8. *To end fully,* ἀποτελέω *apoteleō.*
Jas. 1. 15 when it is finished, bringeth forth death

9. *To finish throughout,* διανύω *dianuō.*
Acts 21. 7 when we had finished (our) course from

10. *To end fully,* ἐκτελέω *ekteleō.*
Luke 14. 29 foundation, and is not able to finish (it)
14. 30 began to build, and was not able to finish

11. *To end besides or upon,* ἐπιτελέω *epiteleō.*
2 Co. 8. 6 would also finish in you the same grace

12. *To end together or wholly,* συντελέω *sunteleō.*
Rom. 9. 28 he will finish the work, and cut (it) short

13. *To end, finish,* τελειόω *teleioō.*
John 4. 34 is to do the will..and to finish his work
5. 36 which the Father hath given me to finish
17. 4 I have finished the work which thou gav.
Acts 20. 24 I might finish my course with joy, and

14. *The things toward completion,* τὰ πρὸς ἀπαρτισμόν *ta pros apartismon.*
Luke 14. 28 whether he have (sufficient) to [finish]

15. *To end, finish,* τελέω *teleō.*
Matt 13. 53 when Jesus had finished these parables
19. 1 when Jesus had finished these sayings
Matt 26. 1 when Jesus had finished all these sayings
John 19. 30 he said, It is finished: and he bowed
2 Ti. 4. 7 I have finished (my) course, I have kept
Rev. 10. 7 the mystery of God should be finished
11. 7 they shall have finished their testimony
20. 5 until the thousand years were finished

16. *To complete doing,* כַּלֵּה לַעֲשׂוֹת *kalah la-asoth.*
2 Ch. 4. 11 Huram finished the work that he was to

FINISHED, to be —

1. *To cause to go out,* יָצָא *yetsa,* 5a.
Ezra 6. 15 this house was finished on the third day

2. *To be complete, finished,* כָּלָה *kalah.*
Exod 39. 32 Thus was all the work..finished; and the
1 Ki. 6. 38 was the house finished throughout all
2 Ch. 8. 16 was prepared..and until it was finished
29. 28 until the burnt offering was finished
Dan. 12. 7 when..all these (things) shall be finished

3. *To be completed, finished,* כָּלָה *kalah,* 4.
Gen. 2. 1 the heavens and the earth were finished
2 Ch. 31. 1 when all this was finished, all Israel

4. *To be finished, complete,* שָׁלַם *shalam.*
2 Ch. 5. 1 all the work..for the house..was finished
Neh. 6. 15 the wall was finished in the twenty and

5. *To be finished, complete,* שְׁלַם *shelam.*
Ezra 5. 16 in building, and (yet) it is not finished

6. *To become, happen,* γίνομαι *ginomai.*
Heb. 4. 3 works were finished from the foundation

FINISHER —

Finisher, ender, completer, τελειωτής *teleiōtēs.*
Heb. 12. 2 the author and finisher of (our) faith

FIR —

1. *Fir, cypress, pine,* בְּרוֹשׁ *berosh.*
2 Sa. 6. 5 all manner of (instruments..of) fir wood
1 Ki. 5. 8 of cedar, and concerning timber of fir
5. 10 gave Solomon cedar trees and fir trees
6. 15 the floor of the house with planks of fir
6. 34 the two doors (were of) fir tree: the two
9. 11 with cedar trees and fir trees, and with
2 Ch. 3. 5 the greater house he ceiled with fir tree

2. *Cypresses, firs, pines,* בְּרוֹתִים *berothim.*
Song 1. 17 beams..(are) cedar, (and) our rafters of f.

FIR tree —

Fir, cypress, or pine tree, בְּרוֹשׁ *berosh.*
2 Ki. 19. 23 cut down..the choice fir trees thereof
2 Ch. 2. 8 fir trees, and algum trees, out of Lebanon
Psa. 104. 17 (as for) the stork, the fir trees (are) her
Isa. 14. 8 the fir trees rejoice at thee, (and) the
37. 24 cut down..the choice fir trees thereof
41. 19 I will set in the desert the fir tree..pine
55. 13 Instead of the thorn shall come..fir tree
60. 13 the fir tree, the pine tree, and the box
Eze. 27. 5 all thy (ship) boards of fir trees of Senir
31. 8 the fir trees were not like his boughs
Hos. 14. 8 I (am) like a green fir tree. From me is
Nah. 2. 3 and the fir trees shall be terribly shaken
Zech 11. 2 Howl, fir tree; for the cedar is fallen

FIRE —

1. *Light, fire,* אוּר *ur.*
Isa. 24. 15 Wherefore glorify ye the LORD in the fires
31. 9 whose fire (is) in Zion, and his furnace in
44. 16 saith, Aha, I am warm, I have seen the f
47. 14 coal to warm at, (nor) fire to sit before it
Eze. 5. 2 Thou shalt burn with fire a third part in

2. *Fire,* אֵשׁ *esh.*
Gen. 19. 24 and fire from the LORD out of heaven
22. 6 he took the fire in his hand, and a knife
22. 7 Behold the fire and the wood: but where
Exod. 3. 2 a flame of fire out of the midst of a bush
3. 2 the bush burned with fire, and the bush
9. 23 and the fire ran along upon the ground
9. 24 fire mingled with the hail, very grievous
12. 8 eat the flesh in that night, roast with fire
12. 9 nor sodden at all..but roast (with) fire
12. 10 which remaineth..ye shall burn with fire
13. 21 in a pillar of fire, to give them light
13. 22 by day, nor the pillar of fire by night
14. 24 the pillar of fire and of the cloud, and
19. 18 because the LORD descended..in fire
22. 6 If fire break out, and catch in thorns, so
24. 17 glory of the LORD (was) like devouring fire
29. 14 thou burn with fire without the camp
29. 34 thou shalt burn the remainder with fire
32. 20 and burnt (it) in the fire, and ground (it)
32. 24 I cast it into the fire, and there came out
35. 3 Ye shall kindle no fire throughout your
40. 38 fire was on it by night, in the sight of all
Lev. 1. 7 the priest shall put fire upon the altar
1. 7 and lay the wood in order upon the fire
1. 12 that (is) on the fire which (is) upon the al.
1. 17 upon the wood that (is) upon the fire
2. 14 green ears of corn dried by the fire, (even)
3. 5 which (is) upon..wood that (is) on the fi.
4. 12 burn him on the wood with fire: where
6. 9 the fire of the altar shall be burning in it
6. 10 and take up the ashes which the fire hath
6. 12 fire upon the altar shall be burning in it
6. 13 fire shall ever be burning upon the altar
6. 30 sin offering..it shall be burnt in the fire
7. 17 the remainder..shall be burnt with fire
7. 19 it shall be burnt with fire: and as for
8. 17 dung, he burnt with fire without the camp
8. 32 that which remaineth..ye burn with fire
9. 11 hide he burnt with fire without the camp
9. 24 there came a fire out from before the LORD
Lev. 10. 1 took..his censer, and put fire therein, and
10. 1 offered strange fire before the LORD, which
10. 2 went out fire from the LORD, and devoured
13. 52 garment..it shall be burnt in the fire
13. 55 thou shalt burn it in the fire; it (is) fret
13. 57 burn that wherein the plague (is) with fire
16. 12 take a censer full of burning coals of fire
16. 13 the incense upon the fire before the LORD
16. 27 they shall burn in the fire their skins
19. 6 the third day, it shall be burnt in the fire
20. 14 shall be burnt with fire, both he and they
21. 9 she profaneth..she shall be burnt with fire
Num. 3. 4 they offered strange fire before the LORD
6. 18 and put (it) in the fire which (is) under
9. 15 as it were the appearance of fire, until
9. 16 and the appearance of fire by night
11. 1 the fire of the LORD burnt among them
11. 2 prayed unto the LORD, the fire was quen
11. 3 the fire of the LORD burnt among them
14. 14 goest before..in a pillar of fire by night
16. 7 put fire therein, and put incense in them
16. 18 put fire in them, and laid incense thereon
16. 35 there came out a fire from the LORD, and
16. 37 scatter thou the fire yonder; for they are
16. 46 put fire therein from off the altar, and
18. 9 most holy things, (reserved) from the fire
21. 28 For there is a fire gone out of Heshbon, a
26. 10 fire devoured two hundred and fifty men
26. 61 they offered strange fire before the LORD
31. 10 burnt..all their goodly castles, with fire
31. 23 Every thing that may abide the fire
31. 23 ye shall make (it) go through the fire, and
31. 23 all that abideth not the fire ye shall make
Deut. 1. 33 in fire by night, to show you by what way
4. 11 the mountain burned with fire unto the
4. 12 spake unto you out of the midst of the fire
4. 15 you in Horeb out of the midst of the fire
4. 24 the LORD thy God (is) a consuming fire
4. 33 God speaking out of the midst of the fire
4. 36 upon earth he showed thee his great fire
4. 36 his words out of the midst of the fire
5. 4 LORD talked..out of the midst of the fire
5. 5 ye were afraid by reason of the fire, and
5. 22 LORD spake..out of the midst of the fire
5. 23 for the mountain did burn with fire
5. 24 heard his voice out of the midst of the fire
5. 25 for this great fire will consume us: if we
5. 26 God speaking out of the midst of the fire
7. 5 and burn their graven images with fire
7. 25 images of their gods..ye burn with fire
9. 3 (as) a consuming fire he shall destroy them
9. 10 out of the midst of the fire in the day of
9. 15 the mount burned with fire: and the two
9. 21 and burnt it with fire, and stamped it
10. 4 out of the midst of the fire in the day of
12. 3 burn their groves with fire; and ye shall
12. 31 they have burnt in the fire to their gods
13. 16 shalt burn with fire the city, and all the
18. 10 or his daughter to pass through the fire
18. 16 neither let me see this great fire any
32. 22 fire is kindled in mine anger, and shall
Josh. 6. 24 they burnt the city with fire, and all
7. 15 accursed thing shall be burnt with fire
7. 25 and burned them with fire, after they had
8. 8 (that) ye shall set the city on fire
8. 19 and hasted and set the city on fire
11. 6 thou shalt..burn their chariots with fire
11. 9 and burnt their chariots with fire
11. 11 smote all..and he burnt Hazor with fire
Judg. 1. 8 and smitten it..and set the city on fire
6. 21 there rose up fire out of the rock, and
9. 15 let fire come out of the bramble, and
9. 20 if not, let fire come out from Abimelech
9. 20 let fire come out from the men of Shech.
9. 49 and set the hold on fire upon them
9. 52 hard unto the door..to burn it with fire
12. 1 will burn thine house upon thee with fire
14. 15 burn thee and thy father's house with fi.
15. 5 And when he had set the brands on fire
15. 6 and burnt her and her father with fire
15. 14 became as flax that was burnt with fire
16. 9 tow is broken when it toucheth the fire
18. 27 they smote..and burnt the city with fire
20. 48 also they set on fire all the cities that
1 Sa. 30. 1 smitten Ziklag, and burnt it with fire
30. 3 and, behold, (it was) burned with fire
30. 14 of Caleb; and we burned Ziklag with fire
2 Sa. 14. 30 See, Joab's field..go and set it on fire
14. 30 Absalom's servants set the field on fire
14. 31 have thy servants set my field on fire?
22. 9 fire out of his mouth devoured: coals were
22. 13 before him were coals of fire kindled
23 7 they shall be utterly burned with fire in
1 Ki. 9. 16 and taken Gezer, and burnt it with fire
16. 18 Zimri..burnt the king's house..with fire
18. 23, 23 lay (it) on wood, and put no fire
18 24 and the God that answereth by fire, let
18. 25 and call on..your gods, but put no fire
18. 38 the fire of the LORD fell, and consumed
19. 12 And after the earthquake a fire
19 12 not in the fire: and after the fire a still
2 Ki. 1. 10, 12 let fire come down from heaven, and
1. 10, 14 there came down fire from heaven
1. 12 the fire of God came down from heaven
2. 11 a chariot of fire, and horses of fire, and
6. 17 full of horses and chariots of fire round
8. 12 their stronghold wilt thou set on fire
16. 3 made his son to pass through the fire
17. 17 caused their sons..to pass through..fire
17. 31 Sepharvites burnt their children in fire
19. 18 And have cast their gods into the fire
21. 6 he made his son pass through the fire

2 Ki.23. 10 make his son..to pass through the fire
23. 11 burned the chariots of the sun with fire
25. 9 every great..house burnt he with fire
1 Ch.14. 12 And..their gods..were burned with fire
21. 26 he answered him from heaven by fire
2 Ch. 7. 1 fire came down from heaven, and consu.
7. 3 all..Israel saw how the fire came down
28. 3 and burnt his children in the fire, after
33. 6 to pass through the fire in the valley of
35. 13 And they roasted the passover with fire
36. 19 burnt all the palaces thereof with fire
Neh. 1. 3 the gates thereof are burned with fire
2. 3, 13, 17 gates thereof..consumed with fire?
9. 12 in the night by a pillar of fire, to give
9. 19 neither the pillar of fire by night, to shew
Job 1. 16 The fire of God is fallen from heaven, and
15. 34 fire shall consume the tabernacles of brib.
18. 5 and the spark of his fire shall not shine
20. 26 a fire not blown shall consume him; it
22. 20 the remnant of them the fire consumeth
28. 5 and under it is turned up as it were fire
31. 12 a fire (that) consumeth to destruction
41. 19 go burning lamps..sparks of fire leap out
Psa. 11. 6 he shall rain..fire and brimstone, and an
18. 8 fire out of his mouth devoured: coals
18. 12 clouds passed, hail..and coals of fire
18. 13 gave his voice; hail..and coals of fire
21. 9 in his wrath, and the fire shall devour
29. 7 voice of the LORD divideth..flames of fire
39. 3 while I was musing the fire burned
46. 9 he burneth the chariot in the fire
50. 3 a fire shall devour before him, and it
66. 12 we went through fire and through water
68. 2 as wax melteth before the fire, (so) let
74. 7 They have cast fire into thy sanctuary
78. 14 and all the night with a light of fire
78. 21 a fire was kindled against Jacob, and
78. 63 The fire consumed their young men; and
79. 5 LORD?..shall thy jealousy burn like fire?
80. 16 burned with fire, (it is) cut down: they
83. 14 As the fire burneth a wood, and as the
89. 46 LORD?..shall thy wrath burn like fire?
97. 3 A fire goeth before him, and burneth up
104. 4 Who maketh..his ministers a flaming fire
105. 32 He gave them..flaming fire in their land
105. 39 and fire to give light in the night
106. 18 And a fire was kindled in their company
118. 12 they are quenched as the fire of thorns
140. 10 let them be cast into the fire; into deep
148. 8 Fire, and hail; snow, and vapours; stormy
Prov. 6. 27 Can a man take fire in his bosom, and his
16. 27 and in his lips (there is) as a burning fire
26. 20 Where no wood is..the fire goeth out
26. 21 (As)..wood to fire; so (is) a contentious
30. 16 and the fire (that) saith not, (It is) enough
Song 8. 6 the coals thereof (are) coals of fire
Isa. 1. 7 your cities (are) burned with fire: your
4. 5 and the shining of a flaming fire by night
5. 24 as the fire devoureth the stubble, and
9. 5 but..shall be with burning..fuel of fire
9. 18 For wickedness burneth as the fire: it
9. 19 people shall be as the fuel of the fire
10. 16 a burning like the burning of a fire
10. 17 the light of Israel shall be for a fire
26. 11 fire of thine enemies shall devour them
29. 6 tempest, and the flame of devouring fire
30. 14 a sherd to take fire from the hearth
30. 27 and his tongue as a devouring fire
30. 30 and (with) the flame of a devouring fire
30. 33 the pile thereof (is) fire and much wood
33. 11 your breath, (as) fire, shall devour you
33. 12 (as) thorns..shall they be burned in the fi.
33. 14 who..shall dwell with the devouring fire?
37. 19 And have cast their gods into the fire
43. 2 when thou walkest through the fire, thou
44. 16 He burneth part thereof in the fire; with
44. 19 I have burned part of it in the fire; yea
47. 14 Behold..the fire shall burn them; they
50. 11 Behold, all ye that kindle a fire, that
50. 11 walk in the light of your fire, and in the
54. 16 smith that bloweth the coals in the fire
64. 2 As (when) the melting fire burneth, the fi.
64. 11 our beautiful house..is burnt up with fire
65. 5 These (are) a smoke in my nose, a fire
66. 15 behold, the LORD will come with fire
66. 15 to render..his rebuke with flames of fire
66. 16 For by fire..will the LORD plead with all
66. 24 neither shall their fire be quenched; and
Jer. 4. 4 lest my fury come forth like fire, and
5. 14 I will make my words in thy mouth fire
6. 29 lead is consumed of the fire; the founder
7. 18 the fathers kindle the fire, and the wom.
7. 31 to burn..their daughters in the fire
11. 16 he hath kindled fire upon it, and the
15. 14 for a fire is kindled in mine anger, (which)
17. 4 for ye have kindled a fire in mine anger
17. 27 then will I kindle a fire in the gates there.
19. 5 burn their sons with fire (for) burnt offe.
20. 9 as a burning fire shut up in my bones
21. 10 this city..he shall burn it with fire
21. 12 lest my fury go out like fire, and burn
21. 14 I will kindle a fire in the forest thereof
22. 7 and they shall..cast (them) into the fire
23. 29 (Is) not my word like as a fire? saith the
29. 22 the king of Babylon roasted in the fire
32. 29 Chaldeans..shall come and set fire on this
34. 2 this city..he shall burn it with fire
34. 22 and they shall..burn it with fire: and I
36. 23 he cut it..and cast (it) into the fire that
36. 23 until all the roll was consumed in the fi.
36. 32 which Jehoiakim..had burnt in the fire
37. 8 Chald. shall come..and burn it with fire
Jer. 37. 10 (yet) should they..burn this city with fire
38. 17 this city shall not be burned with fire
38. 18 they shall burn it with fire, and thou
38. 23 cause this city to be burned with fire
39. 8 Chaldeans burned..the houses..with fire
43. 12 I will kindle a fire in the houses of the
43. 13 and the houses..shall he burn with fire
48. 45 a fire shall come forth out of Heshbon
49. 2 and her daughters shall be burnt with fi.
49. 27 will kindle a fire in the wall of Damascus
50. 32 I will kindle a fire in his cities, and it
51. 32 the reeds they have burned with fire, and
51. 58 her high gates shall be burned with fire
51. 58 folk in the fire, and they shall be weary
52. 13 and all the houses..burned he with fire
Lam. 1. 13 From above hath he sent fire into my bo.
2. 3 burned against Jacob like a flaming fire
2. 4 he stood..he poured out his fury like fi.
4. 11 hath kindled a fire in Zion, and it hath
Eze. 1. 4 a great cloud, and a fire infolding itself
1. 4 of amber, out of the midst of the fire
1. 13 like burning coals of fire, (and) like the
1. 13 the fire was bright, and out of the fire
1. 27 I saw..the appearance of fire round
1. 27 I saw as it were the appearance of fire
5. 4 cast them into the midst of the fire, and
5. 4 burn them in the fire; (for) thereof shall
5. 4 fire come forth into all the house of Israel
8. 2 lo, a likeness as the appearance of fire
8. 2 from the appearance of his loins..fire
10. 2 and fill thine hand with coals of fire from
10. 6 Take fire from between the wheels, from
10. 7 the fire that (was) between the cherubim
15. 4 it is cast into the fire..the fire devoureth
15. 5 when the fire hath devoured it, and it is
15. 6 which I have given to the fire for fuel
15. 7 go out from (one) fire, and (another) fire
16. 41 they shall burn thine houses with fire
19. 12 and withered; the fire consumed them
19. 14 fire is gone out of a rod of her branches
20. 31 make your sons to pass through the fire
20. 47 Behold, I will kindle a fire in thee, and
21. 31 I will blow against thee in the fire of my
21. 32 Thou shalt be for fuel to the fire; thy
22. 20 to blow the fire upon it, to melt (it); so
22. 21 blow upon you in the fire of my wrath
22. 31 I have consumed them with the fire of
23. 25 thy residue shall be devoured by the fire
23. 47 and burn up their houses with fire
24. 10 Heap on wood, kindle the fire, consume
24. 12 wearied..her scum (shall be) in the fire
28. 14 walked..in the midst of the stones of fire
28. 16 from the midst of the stones of fire
28. 18 therefore will I bring forth a fire from
30. 8 when I have set a fire in Egypt, and
30. 14 will set fire in Zoan, and will execute
30. 16 I will set fire in Egypt: Sin shall have
36. 5 in the fire of my jealousy have I spoken
38. 19 in the fire of my wrath have I spoken
38. 22 and great hailstones, fire, and brimstone
39. 6 I will send a fire on Magog, and among
39. 9 shall set on fire and burn the weapons
39. 10 they shall burn the weapons with fire
Dan. 10. 6 his eyes as lamps of fire, and his arms
Hos. 7. 6 the morning it burneth as a flaming fire
8. 14 but I will send a fire upon his cities
Joel 1. 19, 20 the fire hath devoured the pastures of
2. 3 A fire devoureth before them; and behind
2. 5 a flame of fire that devoureth the stubble
2. 30 show..blood, and fire, and pillars of sm.
Amos 1. 4 I will send a fire into the house of Hazael
1. 7, 10 I will send a fire on the wall of
1. 12 I will send a fire upon Teman, which
1. 14 I will kindle a fire in the wall of Rabbah
2. 2, 5 But I will send a fire..and it shall dev.
5. 6 lest he break out like fire in the house of
7. 4 the LORD God called to contend by fire
Obad. 18 And the house of Jacob shall be a fire
Mic. 1. 4 as wax before the fire, (and) as the waters
1. 7 the hires..shall be burned with the fire
Nah. 1. 6 his fury is poured out like fire, and the
3. 13 Behold..the fire shall devour thy bars
3. 15 There shall the fire devour thee; the sw.
Hab. 2. 13 the people shall labour in the very fire
Zeph. 1. 18 shall be devoured by the fire of his jealo.
3. 8 shall be devoured with the fire of my jea.
Zech. 2. 5 For I..will be..a wall of fire round about
3. 2 not this a brand plucked out of the fire?
9. 4 Behold..she shall be devoured with fire
11. 1 Open thy doors..that the fire may devour
12. 6 like an hearth of fire among the wood
12. 6 like a torch of fire in a sheaf; and they
13. 9 I will bring the third part through the fi.
Mal. 3. 2 like a refiner's fire, and like fullers' sope

3. *Fire*, אֶשָּׁה *eshshah*. **[V.L. for *esh*.]**
Jer. 6. 29 the lead is consumed of the fire; the fo.

4. *Burning*, בְּעֵרָה *beerah*.
Exod22. 6 he that kindled the fire shall surely make

5. *Fire*, נוּר *nur*.
Dan. 3. 22 the flame of the fire slew those men that
3. 24 Did not we cast three men..into..the fi.?
3. 25 four men..walking in the midst of the fi.
3. 26 came forth of the midst of the fire
3. 27 upon whose bodies the fire had no power
3. 27 nor the smell of fire had passed on them
7. 9 fiery flame..his wheels (as) burning fire

6. *Fire*, πῦρ *pur*.
Matt. 3. 10 tree..is hewn down, and cast into the fire
3. 11 baptize you with the Holy Ghost, and..fire
Matt. 3. 12 burn up the chaff with unquenchable fire
5. 22 Thou fool, shall be in danger of hell fire
7. 19 tree..is hewn down, and cast into the fire
13. 40 As..the tares are..burned in the fire; so
13. 42 shall cast them into a furnace of fire
13. 50 shall cast them into the furnace of fire
17. 15 for oft times he falleth into the fire, and
18. 8 two feet to be cast into everlasting fire
18. 9 having two eyes to be cast into hell fire
25. 41 Depart from me..into everlasting fire
Mark 9. 22 oft times it hath cast him into the fire
9. 43, 45 [the fire that shall never be quenched]
9. 44, 46, 48 [and the fire is not quenched]
9. 47 having two eyes to be cast into hell [fire]
9. 49 For every one shall be salted with fire
Luke 3. 9 tree..is hewn down, and cast into the fire
3. 16 baptize..with the Holy Ghost and with fi.
3. 17 the chaff he will burn with fire unquench.
9. 54 that we command fire to come down from
12. 49 I am come to send fire on the earth
17. 29 it rained fire and brimstone from heaven
22. 55 when they had kindled a fire in the midst
John15. 6 men..cast..into the fire, and they are bur.
Acts 2. 3 cloven tongues like as of fire, and it sat
2. 19 blood, and fire, and vapour of smoke
7. 30 an angel..in a flame of fire in a bush
28. 5 he shook off the beast into the fire, and
Rom.12. 20 thou shalt heap coals of fire on his head
1 Co. 3. 13 because it shall be revealed by fire
3. 13 the fire shall try every man's work of
3. 15 himself shall be saved; yet so as by fire
2 Th. 1. 8 In flaming fire taking vengeance on them
Heb. 1. 7 Who maketh..his ministers a flame of fi.
11. 34 Quenched the violence of fire, escaped
12. 18 the mount..that burned with fire, nor
12. 29 For our God (is) a consuming fire
Jas. 3. 5 how great a matter a little fire kindleth!
3. 6 the tongue (is) a fire, a world of iniquity
5. 3 and shall eat your flesh as it were fire
1 Pe. 1. 7 your faith..though it be tried with fire
2 Pe. 3. 7 reserved unto fire against the day of
Jude 7 suffering the vengeance of eternal fire
23 pulling..out of the fire; hating even the
Rev. 1. 14 and his eyes (were) as a flame of fire
2. 18 who hath his eyes like unto a flame of fire
3. 18 to buy of me gold tried in the fire
4. 5 seven lamps of fire burning before the
8. 5 filled it with fire of the altar, and cast
8. 7 there followed hail and fire mingled with
8. 8 a great mountain burning [with fire] was
9. 17 out of their mouths issued fire and smoke
9. 18 by the fire, and by the smoke, and by the
10. 1 mighty angel..his feet as pillars of fire
11. 5 fire proceedeth out of their mouth, and
13. 13 so that he maketh fire come down from h.
14. 10 he shall be tormented with fire and brim.
14. 18 another angel..which had power over fire
15. 2 as it were a sea of glass mingled with fire
16. 8 given unto him to scorch men with fire
17. 16 shall eat her flesh, and burn her with fire
18. 8 she shall be utterly burned with fire
19. 12 His eyes..as a flame of fire, and on his
19. 20 both were cast alive into a lake of fire
20. 9 fire came down from God out of heaven
20. 10 the devil..was cast into the lake of fire
20. 14 And death and hell were cast into..fire
20. 15 not found..was cast into the lake of fire
21. 8 in the lake which burneth with fire and

7. *Fire, pyre*, πυρά *pura*.
Acts 28. 2 for they kindled a fire, and received us
28. 3 And when Paul..laid (them) on the fire

8. *Light*, φῶς *phōs*.
Mark14. 54 he sat..and warmed himself at the fire
Luke22. 56 maid beheld him as he sat by the fire

FIRE, to be on —
To be set on fire, πυρόομαι *puroomai*.
2 Pe. 3. 12 wherein the heavens being on fire shall

FIRE, of —
Of fire, fiery, πύρινος *purinos*.
Rev. 9. 17 having breastplates of fire, and of jacinth

FIRE, to set or be set on — [*See* SET.]
1. *To kindle, burn*, יָצַת *yatsath*, 5.
2 Sa. 14. 31 have thy servants set my field on fire?

2. *To set on fire, burn*, לָהַט *lahat*, 3.
Deut32. 22 and set on fire the foundations of the m.
Psa. 57. 4 (even among) them that are set on fire
83. 14 the flame setteth the mountains on fire
Isa. 42. 25 and it hath set him on fire round about

3. *To set in a blaze*, φλογίζω *phlogizō*.
Jas. 3. 6 setteth on fire..and it is set on fire of hell

FIRE, sign of —
Uplifted signal, מַשְׂאֵת *maseth*.
Jer. 6. 1 set up a sign of fire in Beth-haccerem

FIRE brand—
1. *Brand*, אוּד *ud*.
Isa. 7. 4 for the two tails of these smoking fireb.
Amos 4. 11 ye were as a firebrand plucked out of the

2. *Sparks*, זִקִּים *ziqqim*.
Prov.26. 18 As a mad (man) who casteth firebrands

3. *Lamp*, לַפִּיד *lappid*.
Judg15. 4 took firebrands, and turned tail to tail
15. 4 and put a firebrand in the midst between

FIRE pan —
Fire pan, censer, snuff dish, מַחְתָּה *machtah.*
Exod27. 3 and his flesh hooks, and his fire pans
38. 3 (and) the flesh hooks, and the fire pans
2 Ki. 25. 15 the fire pans, and the bowls. . such things
Jer. 52. 19 the fire pans, and the bowls, and the cal.

FIRKIN —
A measure, μετρητής *metrētēs.*
John 2. 6 containing two or three firkins apiece

FIRM —
1. *Firm, fat,* בָּרִיא *bari.*
Psa. 73. 4 in their death; but their strength (is) firm

2. *To prepare, establish, set up,* כּוּן *kun,* 5.
Josh. 3. 17 the priests. . stood firm on dry ground in
4. 3 the place where the priests' feet stood firm

3. *Steadfast, firm, sure,* βέβαιος *bebaios.*
Heb. 3. 6 rejoicing of the hope firm unto the end

FIRM, to be (as) —
To be firm, יָצַק *yatsaq.*
Job 41. 23 they are firm in themselves; they cannot
41 24 His heart is as firm as a stone; yea, as

FIRM, to make —
To make strong, תָּקֵף *teqeph,* 3.
Dan. 6. 7 to make a firm decree, that whosoever

FIRMAMENT —
Expanse, רָקִיעַ *raqia.*
Gen. 1. 6 God said, Let there be a firmament in the
1. 7 God made the firmament, and divided
1. 7 the waters which (were) under the firm.
1. 7 waters which (were) above the firmament
1. 8 And God called the firmament Heaven
1. 14 Let there be lights in the firmament of
1. 15 let them be for lights in the firmament of
1. 17 And God set them in the firmament of
1. 20 fly above the earth in the open firmament
Psa. 19. 1 the firmament showeth his handywork
150. 1 praise him in the firmament of his power
Eze. 1. 22 And the likeness of the firmament upon
1. 23 under the firmament (were) their wings
1. 25 there was a voice from the firmament that
1. 26 above the firmament that (was) over their
10. 1 the firmament that (was) above the head
Dan. 12. 3 shine as the brightness of the firmament

FIRST —
1. *One,* אֶחָד *echad.*
Gen. 1. 5 evening and the morning were the first
2. 11 The name of the first (is) Pison: that (is)
8. 5 on the first. . of the month, were the tops
8. 13 in the six hundredth and first year
8. 13 the first. . of the month, the waters were
Exod40. 2 On the first day of the. . month shalt thou
40. 17 on the first. . of the month. . the tabernacle
Lev. 23 24 In the seventh month, in the first. . of the
Num. 1. 1 on the first. . of the second month, in the
1. 18 on the first. . of the second month, and
29. 1 in the seventh month, on the first . of the
33. 38 died. . in the first. . of the fifth month
Deut. 1. 3 in the eleventh month, on the first. . of
1 Ki. 16. 23 In the thirty and first year of Asa king of
2 Ch.29 17 Now they began on the first. . of the. . mo.
36. 22 in the first year of Cyrus king of Persia
Ezra 1. 1 in the first year of Cyrus king of Persia
3. 6 From the first day of the seventh month
7. 9 For upon the first. . of the. . month
7. 9 on the first. . of the fifth month came he
10. 16 sat down in the first day of the tenth
10. 17 made an end. . by the first day of the
Neh. 8. 2 upon the first day of the seventh month
Job 42. 14 he called the name of the first, Jemima
Eze. 26. 1 in the eleventh year, in the first. . of the
29. 17 in the first. . of the month, the word
31. 1 in the third (month), in the first. . of the
32. 1 in the twelfth month, in the first. . of the
45. 18 in the first. . of the month, thou shalt
Dan. 1. 21 Daniel continued. . unto the first year of
9. 1 In the first year of Darius the son of A.
9. 2 In the first year of his reign, I Daniel
11. 1 Also I, in the first year of Darius the Mede
Hag. 1. 1 in the sixth month, in the first day of

2. *One,* חַד *chad.*
Ezra 5. 13 in the first year of Cyrus the king of B.
6. 3 in the first year of Cyrus the king
Dan. 6. 2 three presidents, of whom Daniel. . first
7. 1 In the first year of Belshazzar king of Ba.

3. *Former,* קַדְמַי *qadmai.*
Dan. 7. 4 The first. . like a lion, and had eagle's win.
7. 8 there were three of the first horns plucked
7. 24 and he shall be diverse from the first

4. *Head, first,* רִאשׁוֹן *reishon.*
Josh.21. 10 of Levi, had. for their's was the first lot
Job 15. 7 (Art) thou the first man (that) was born?

5. *Head, principal,* רֹאשׁ *rosh.*
1 Ch.12. 9 Ezer the first, Obadiah the second, Eliab
16 7 David delivered first. . to thank the L.
23. 19 Of the sons of Hebron; Jeriah the first
23. 20 Of the sons of Uzziel; Micah the first
24. 21 sons of Rehabiah, the first. . Isshiah
Amos 6. 7 now shall they go captive with the first

6. *Head, first,* רִאשׁוֹן *rishon.*
Gen. 8. 13 in the first (month). . the waters were dr.
13. 4 which he had made there at the first
25. 25 the first came out red, all over like an
26. 1 beside the first famine that was in the
28. 19 name of that city. . Luz at the first
38. 28 a scarlet thread, saying, This came out fi.
41. 20 the ill favoured kine did eat up the first
Exod. 4. 8 neither hearken to the voice of the first
12. 2 it. . the first month of the year to you
12. 15 the first day ye shall put away leaven out
12. 15 from the first day until the seventh day
12. 16 in the first day. . an holy convocation
12. 18 In the first. . on the fourteenth day of the
34. 1 Hew. . tables of stone like unto the first
34. 1 the words that were in the first tables
34. 4 two tables of stone like unto the first
40. 2 On the. . day of the first month shalt thou
40. 17 in the first month in the second year, on
Lev. 4. 21 burn him as he burned the first bullock
5. 8 offer (that) which (is) for. . sin offering fi.
9. 15 slew it, and offered it for sin, as the first
23. 5 In the fourteenth. . of the first month at
23. 7 In the first day ye shall have an holy
23. 35 On the first day. . an holy convocation: ye
23. 39 on the first day. . a sabbath, and on the
23. 40 ye shall take you on the first day the
Num. 2. 9 camp of Judah. . These shall first set forth
7. 12 he that offered his offering the first day
9. 1 in the first month of the second year after
9. 5 on the fourteenth day of the first month
10. 13 they first took their journey according to
10. 14 In the first (place) went the standard of
20. 1 into the desert of Zin in the first month
28. 16 in the fourteenth day of the first month
28. 18 In the first day. . an holy convocation
33 3 they departed from Rameses in the first
33. 3 on the fifteenth day of the first month
Deut. 9. 18 I fell down. . as at the first, forty days
10. 1, 3 tables of stone like unto the first
10. 2 the words that were in the first tables
10. 4 wrote. . according to the first writing
10. 10 I stayed. . according to the first time, fo.
13. 9 thine hand shall be first upon him to put
16. 4 which thou sacrificedst the first day at
17. 7 The hands of the witnesses shall be first
Josh. 4. 19 on the tenth. . of the first month, and
8 5 it shall come to pass. . as at the first, that
8. 6 say, They flee before us, as at the first
Judg18. 29 name of the city (was) Laish at the first
20. 22 they put themselves in array the first day
20. 32 They (are) smitten down. . as at the first
20. 39 they are smitten. . as (in) the first battle
1 Sa. 14. 14 that first slaughter. . was about twenty
2 Sa. 19. 20 I am come the first this day of all the
19. 43 that our advice should not be first had
21. 9 they. . were put to death. . in the first
1 Ki. 17. 13 but make me thereof a little cake first
18. 25 Choose. . one bullock. . and dress (it) first
20. 9 All that thou didst send for. . at the first
20. 17 And the young men. . went out first; and
1 Ch. 9. 2 Now the first inhabitants. . in their poss.
11. 6 Whosoever smiteth the Jebusites first
11. 6 So Joab the son of Zeruiah went first up
12. 15 they that went over Jordan in the first
15. 13 For because ye (did it) not at the first
24. 7 the first lot came forth to Jehoiarib
25. 9 the first lot came forth for Asaph to Jos.
27. 2 Over the first course for the first month
27. 3 the captains of the host for the first mo.
29. 29 the acts of David the king, first and last
2 Ch. 3. 3 The length by cubits after the first mea.
9. 29 the rest of the acts of Solomon, first and
12. 15 Now the acts of Rehoboam, first and last
16. 11 the acts of Asa, first and last, lo, they
17. 3 he walked in the first ways of his father
20. 34 the rest of the acts of Jehoshaphat, first
25. 26 the rest of the acts of Amaziah, first and
26. 22 the rest of the acts of Uzziah, first and
28. 26 rest of his acts and of all his ways, first
29. 3 He, in the first year. . in the first month
29. 17 they began on. . the first month to sanctify
29. 17 in the sixteenth day of the first month
35. 1 on the fourteenth. . of the first month
35. 27 And his deeds, first and last, behold
Ezra 3. 12 ancient men, that had seen the first house
6. 19 upon the fourteenth. . of the first month
7. 9 For upon. . the first month began he to
8. 31 on the twelfth. . of the first month, to go
10. 17 they made an end. . by the. . first month
Neh. 7. 5 found. . of them which came up at the fi.
8. 18 from the first day unto the last day, he
Esth. 1. 14 (and) which sat the first in the kingdom
3. 7 In the first month, that (is), the month N.
3. 12 on the thirteenth day of the first month
Prov.18. 17 first in his own cause. . just; but his
Isa. 1. 26 I will restore thy judges as at the first
9. 1 when at the first he [Heb. *eth rishon.*]
41. 4 I the LORD, the first, and with the last
41. 27 The first (shall say) to Zion, Behold
43. 27 Thy first father hath sinned, and thy
44. 6 I (am) the first, and I (am) the last; and
48. 12 Hearken. . I (am) the first, I also (am) the
60. 9 the ships of Tarshish first, to bring thy
Jer. 7. 12 Shiloh, where I set my name at the first
16. 18 first I will recompense their iniquity and
33. 7 I. . will build them, as at the first
33. 11 For I will cause to return. . as at the first
50. 17 first the king of Assyria hath devoured
Eze. 29. 17 in the first (month). . the word of the Lo.
30. 20 in the first (month) in the seventh. . of
40. 21 were after the measure of the first gate
45. 18 In the first (month). . thou shalt take a
45. 21 In the first (month), in the fourteenth
Dan. 8. 21 and the great horn. . (is) the first king
10. 4 the first month, as I was by the side of
10. 12 from the first day. . thy words were heard
Hos. 2. 7 I will go and return to my first husband
Joel 2. 23 cause to come. . the latter rain in the first
Mic. 4. 8 unto thee shall it come, even the first
Hag. 2. 3 Who. . saw this house in her first glory?
Zech. 6. 2 In the first chariot (were) red horses, and
12. 7 The LORD also shall save. . Judah first
14. 10 unto the place of the first gate, unto the

7. *Beginning, first,* רִאשֹׁנִי *rishoni.*
Jer. 25. 1 the first year of Nebuchadrezzar king of

8. *Foremost, first,* רֵאשִׁית *reshith.*
Exod23. 19 The first of the first fruits of thy land
34. 26 The first of the first fruits of thy land
Num 15. 20 Ye shall offer up a cake of the first of your
15. 21 Of the first of your dough ye shall give
24. 20 said, Amalek. . the first of the nations
Deut.18. 4 and the first of the fleece of thy sheep
26. 2 That thou shalt take of the first of all the
Eze. 44. 30 And the first of all the first fruits of all
44. 30 ye shall. . give unto the priest the first of

9. *Commencement, first,* תְּחִלָּה *techillah.*
Judg. 1. 1 Who shall go up for us. . first, to fight
20. 18 Which of us shall go up first to the battle
20. 18 the LORD said, Judah (shall go up) first
2 Sa. 17. 9 some of them be overthrown at the first
Dan. 8. 1 after that which appeared. . at the first

10. *To begin,* חָלַל *chalal,* 5.
1 Sa. 14. 35 the same was the first altar that he built

11. *Its* (Heb. pron. = Eng. *the first*).
Lev. 14. 10 one ewe lamb of the first year without
Num. 6. 14 one ewe lamb of the first year without
15. 27 he shall bring a she goat of the first year

12. *Beginning, principal point,* ἀρχή *archē.*
Heb. 5. 12 the first principles of the oracles Ac. 26. 4

13. *One,* μία *mia.*
Titus 3. 10 after the first and second admonition

14. *Prior,* πρότερον *proteron.*
Heb. 4. 6 they to whom it was first preached
7. 27 to offer up sacrifice, first for his own sins

15. *First,* πρῶτον, *or* τὸ πρῶτον *prōton, or to prōton.*
Matt. 5. 24 first be reconciled to thy brother, and
6. 33 But seek ye first the kingdom of God
7. 5 first cast out the beam out of thine own
8. 21 suffer me first to go and bury my father
12. 29 except he first bind the strong man?
13. 30 Gather ye together first the tares, and
17. 10 Why then say. . that Elias must first come?
17. 11 Elias truly shall [first] come, and restore
23. 26 cleanse first that. . within the cup and
Mark 3. 27 except he will first bind the strong man
4. 28 first the blade, then the ear, after that
7. 27 Let the children first be filled: for it is
9. 11 Why say the scribes that Elias must first
9. 12 he answered. . Elias verily cometh first
13. 10 the Gospel must first be published among
16. 9 [he appeared first to Mary Magdalene]
Luke 6. 42 cast out first the beam out of thine own
9. 59 suffer me first to go and bury my father
9. 61 but let me first go bid them farewell
10. 5 into whatsoever house ye enter, first say
11. 38 he had not first washed before dinner
14. 28 For which of you. . sitteth not down first
14. 31 Or what king. . sitteth not down first, and
17. 25 But first must he suffer many things
21. 9 for these things must first come to pass
John 18. 13 led him away to Annas first; for he was
Acts 3. 26 Unto you first God, having raised up his
7. 12 in Egypt, he sent out our fathers first
11. 26 disciples were called Christians first in A.
13. 46 word of God should first have been spoken
26. 20 But showed first unto them of Damascus
Rom. 1. 8 First, I thank my God through Jesus Ch.
1. 16 to the Jew [first], and also to the Greek
2. 9 of the Jew first, and also of the Gentile
2. 10 to the Jew first, and also to the Gentile
15. 24 if first I be somewhat filled with your
1 Co. 12. 28 first apostles, secondarily prophets, third.
15. 46 that (was) not first which is spiritual, but
2 Co. 8. 5 first gave their own selves to the Lord
Eph. 4. 9 he also descended [first] into the lower
1 Th. 4. 16 and the dead in Christ shall rise first
2 Th. 2. 3 except there come a falling away first
1 Ti. 2. 1 I exhort therefore, that, first of all
3. 10 let these also first be proved; then let
5. 4 let them learn first to show piety at home
2 Ti. 1. 5 which dwelt first in thy grandmother L.
Heb. 7. 2 first being by interpretation King of
Jas. 3. 17 wisdom that is from above is first pure
1 Pe. 4. 17 if (it) first (begin) at us, what shall the
2 Pe. 1. 20 Knowing this first, that no prophecy of
3. 3 Knowing this first, that there shall come

16. *Foremost, first,* πρῶτος *prōtos.*
Matt 10. 2 The first, Simon, who is called Peter, and
12. 45 last. . of that man is worse than the first
17. 27 take up the fish that first cometh up; and
19. 30 first shall be last; and the last. . first
20. 8 beginning from the last unto the first
20. 10 But when the first came, they supposed
20. 16 the last shall be first, and the first last
21. 28 he came to the first, and said, Son, go
21. 31 They say unto him, The [first]. Jesus saith
21. 36 sent other servants more than the first
22. 25 the first. . left his wife unto his brother
22. 38 This is the first and great comm 26. 17.
27. 64 last error shall be worse than the first
Mark 9. 35 If any man desire to be [first], (the same)
10. 31 first shall be last; and the last first
12. 20 first took a wife, and dying left no seed

Mark12. 28 Which is the first commandment of all?
12. 29 The first of all the commandments (is)
12. 30 [This (is) the first command.] 14. 22; 16. 9.
Luke 2. 2 this taxing was first made when Cyrenius
11. 26 the last (state)..is worse than the first
13. 30 which shall be first, and there are first
14. 18 The first said unto him, I have bought a
16. 5 said unto the first, How much owest thou
19. 16 Then came the first, saying, Lord, thy
20. 29 the first took a wife, and died without
John 1. 41 He [first] findeth his own brother Simon
5. 4 [whosoever then first..stepped in was]
8. 7 He that is without sin..[let him first cast]
19. 32 soldiers..brake the legs of the first, and
20. 4 the other disciple..came first to the sep.
20. 8 disciple which came first to the sepulchre
Acts 12. 10 When they were past the first..ward
20. 18 from the first day that I came into Asia
26. 23 he should be the first that should rise
27. 43 cast (themselves) first (into the sea), and
Rom 10. 19 First Moses saith, I will provoke you to
1 Co. 14. 30 If (any thing) be revealed..let the first
15. 45 The first man Adam was made a living
15. 47 The first man (is) of the earth
Eph. 6. 2 which is the first commandment with
Phil. 1. 5 For your fellowship..from the first day
1 Ti. 1. 16 in me first Jesus Christ might show forth
2. 13 For Adam was first formed, then Eve
5. 12 because they have cast off their first faith
2 Ti. 2. 6 husbandman that laboureth must be first
4. 16 At my first answer no man stood with me
Heb. 8. 7 if that first (covenant) had been faultless
8. 13 new (covenant), he hath made the first
9. 1 the first (covenant) had also ordinances
9. 2 the first, wherein (was) the candlestick
9. 6 priests went..into the first tabernacle
9. 8 as the first tabernacle was yet standing
9. 15 (that were) under the first testament
9. 18 neither the first (testament) was dedica.
10. 9 He taketh away the first, that he may est.
1 Jo. 4. 19 We love him, because he first loved us
Rev. 1. 11 Alpha and Omega, [the first and the last]
1. 17 Fear not; I am the first and the last
2. 4 because thou hast left thy first love
2. 5 repent, and do the first works; or else I
2. 8 These things saith the First and the Last
2. 19 and the last (to be) more than the first
4. 1 the first voice which I heard (was) as it
4. 7 the first beast (was) like a lion, and the
8. 7 The first angel sounded, and there fol.
13. 12 exerciseth all the power of the first beast
13. 12 causeth..them..to worship the first beast
16. 2 the first went, and poured out his vial
20. 5 finished. This (is) the first resurrection
20. 6 he that hath part in the first resurrection
21. 1 for the first heaven and the first earth
21. 19 The first foundation..jasper; the second
22. 13 Alpha and Omega..the first and the last

FIRST, at (the) —

1. *First*, πρῶτον *prōton.*
John10. 40 into the place where John at first bapti.
12. 16 understood not his disciples at the first
19. 39 which at the first came to Jesus by night
Acts 15 14 how God at the first did visit the Gentiles

2. *Prior*, πρότερον *proteron.*
Gal. 4. 13 how..I preached..unto you at the first

FIRST, to be —

To lie or be laid before, πρόκειμαι *prokeimai.*
2 Co. 8. 12 For if there be first a willing mind, (it is)

FIRST child, to bring forth —

To bring forth a first born, בָּכַר *bakar*, 5.
Jer. 4. 31 of her that bringeth forth her first child

FIRST (day) —

1. *One.* μία *mia.*
Matt28. 1 as it began to dawn toward the first (day)
Mark16. 2 the first (day) of the week, they came
Luke24. 1 upon the first (day) of the week, very e.
John20. 1 The first (day) of the week cometh Mary
20. 19 being the first (day) of the week, when
Acts 20. 7 upon the first (day) of the week, when
1 Co. 16. 2 Upon the first (day) of the week Tit. 3. 10.

2. *Foremost, first*, πρῶτος *prōtos.*
Matt26. 17 Now the first (day) of the..unleavened
Mark14. 12 And the first day of unleavened bread
16. 9 [risen early the first (day) of the week]

FIRST estate —

Beginning, principality, ἀρχή *archē.*
Jude 6 angels which kept not their first estate

FIRST, from the very —

From above, from the first, ἄνωθεν *anōthen.*
Luke 1. 3 understanding of all..from the very first

FIRST of all —

1. *Among the foremost*, ἐν πρώτοις *en prōtois.*
1 Co. 15. 3 I delivered unto you first of all that which

2. *First*, πρῶτον *prōton.*
Luke 12. 1 began to say unto his disciples first of a.
1 Co. 11. 18 For first of all, when ye come together

FIRST begotten —

First born, πρωτότοκος *prōtotokos.*
Heb. 1. 6 when he bringeth in the first begotten
Rev. 1. 5 Jesus Christ..the first begotten of the d.

FIRST, of the —

Son, produce, בֵּן *ben.*
Exod12. 5 without blemish, a male of the first year
29. 38 two lambs of the first year day by day co.
Lev. 9. 3 of the first year, without blemish, for a
12. 6 she shall bring a lamb of the first year for
23. 12 he lamb without blemish of the first year
23. 18 lambs without blemish of the first year
23. 19 two lambs of the first year for a sacrifice
Num. 6. 12 shall bring a lamb of the first year for a
6. 14 one he lamb of the first year without ble.
6. 14 one ewe lamb of the first year without bl.
7. 15 one ram, one lamb of the first year
[So in v. 21, 27, 33, 39, 45, 51, 57, 63, 69, 75, 81.]
7. 17 he goats, five lambs of the first year
[So in v. 23, 29, 35, 41, 47, 53, 59, 65, 71, 77, 83.]
7. 87 the lambs of the first year twelve, with
7. 88 the lambs of the first year sixty
28. 3, 9 lambs of the first year without spot
28. 11, 19, 27 one ram, seven lambs of the first
29. 2 lambs of the first year, without blemish
29. 8, 13 lambs of the first year; they shall be
29. 17, 20, 23, 26, 29, 32 fourteen lambs of the fir.
29. 36 seven lambs of the first year, without bl.
Eze. 46. 13 a lamb of the first year without blemish

FIRST part or time —

1. *Beginning, first or best*, רֵאשִׁית *reshith.*
Deut 33. 21 he provided the first part for himself
Hos. 9. 10 as the first ripe in the fig tree at her first t.

2. *Commencement*, תְּחִלָּה *techillah.*
Gen. 43. 18 returned in our sacks at the first time are
43. 20 we came indeed down at the first time

FIRST born —

1. *First born, firstling*, בְּכוֹר *bekor.*
Gen. 10. 15 Canaan begat Sidon his first born, and
22. 21 Huz his first born, and Buz his brother
25. 13 first born of Ishmael, Nebajoth; and Ked.
27. 19 I (am) Esau thy first born; I have done
27. 32 he said, I (am) thy son, thy first born, Esau
35. 23 Reuben, Jacob's first born, and Simeon
36. 15 sons of Eliphaz the first born..of Esau
38. 6 Judah took a wife for Er his first born
38. 7 Er, Judah's first born, was wicked in the
41. 51 Joseph called the name of the first born
43. 33 the first born according to his birthright
46. 8 and his sons: Reuben, Jacob's first born
48. 14 wittingly; for Manasseh (was) the first bo.
48. 18 Not so, my father: for this (is) the first b.
49. 3 Reuben, thou (art) my first born, my might
Exod. 4. 22 saith..Israel (is) my son..my first born
4. 23 I will slay thy son..thy first born
6. 14 sons of Reuben the first born of Israel
11. 5 all the first born in the land of Egypt shall
11. 5 from the first born of Pharaoh that sitteth
11. 5 unto the first born of the maidservant
11. 5 and all the first born of beasts
12. 12 I..will smite all the first born in the land
12. 29 the LORD smote all the first born in the
12. 29 from the first born of Pharaoh that sat on
12. 29 unto the first born of the captive that
12. 29 and all the first born of cattle
13. 2 Sanctify unto me all the first born, what.
13. 13 all the first born of man among thy chil.
13. 15 that the LORD slew all the first born in
13. 15 the first born of man, and the first born
13. 15 all the first born of my children I redeem
22. 29 the first born of thy sons shalt thou give
34. 20 All the first born of thy sons thou shalt
Num. 3. 2 Nadab the first born, and Abihu, Eleazar
3. 12 instead of all the first born that openeth
3. 13 Because all the first born (are) mine
3. 13 on the day that I smote all the first born
3. 13 I hallowed unto me all the first born in I.
3. 40 Number all the first born of the males
3. 41 instead of all the first born among the c.
3. 42 And Moses numbered..all the first born
3. 43 all the first born males by the number
3. 45 Take the Levites instead of all the first b.
3. 46, 50 of the first born of the children of Isr.
8. 16 the first born of all the children of Israel
8. 17, 18 all the first born of the children of Is.
8. 17 I smote every first born in the land of E.
18. 15 the first born of man shalt thou surely
33. 4 For the Egyptians buried all..first born
Deut21. 15 and..the first born son be her's that was
21. 16 the son of the hated..the first born
21. 17 son of the hated (for) the first born
25. 6 the first born which she beareth shall
Josh. 6. 26 shall lay the foundation..in his first born
17. 1 Manasseh; for he (was) the first born of
17. 1 for Machir the first born of Manasseh
Judg. 8. 20 he said unto Jether his first born, Up
1 Sa. 8. 2 first born [Heb. *ben bekor, first born son*]
17. 13 Eliab the first born; and next unto him, A.
2 Sa. 3. 2 his first born was Amnon, of Ahinoam
1 Ki. 16. 34 laid the foundation..in..his first born
1 Ch. 1. 13 Canaan begat Zidon his first born, and H.
1. 29 first born of Ishmael, Nebaioth; then K.
2. 3 Er, the first born of Judah, was evil in
2. 13 Jessie begat his first born Eliab, and A.
2. 25 sons of Jerahmeel the first born of Hez.
2. 27 sons of Ram the first born of Jerahmeel
2. 42 Mesha his first born, which (was) the fa.
2. 50 the son of Hur, the first born of Ephratah
3. 1 the first born Amnon, of Ahinoam the
3. 15 sons of Josiah..the first born Johanan
4. 4 sons of Hur, the first born of Ephratah
5. 1 sons of Reuben, the first born of Israel
1 Ch. 5. 3 sons..of Reuben the first born of Israel
6. 28 sons of Samuel; the first born Vashni
8. 1 Now Benjamin begat Bela his first born
8. 30 And his first born son Abdon, and Zur
8. 39 Ulam his first born, Jehush the second
9. 5 Shilonites; Asaiah the first born, and his
9. 31 the first born of Shallum the Korahite
9. 36 And his first born son Abdon, then Zur
26. 2 Zechariah the first born, Jediael the sec.
26. 4 Shemaiah the first born, Jehozabad the
26. 10 he was not the first born, yet his father
2 Ch. 21. 3 to Jehoram, because he (was) the first b.
Neh. 10. 36 Also the first born of our sons, and of our
Job 18. 13 the first born of death shall devour his
Psa. 78. 51 And smote all the first born in Egypt
89. 27 I will make him (my) first born, higher
105. 36 He smote also all the first born in their
135. 8 Who smote the first born of Egypt, both
136. 10 To him that smote Egypt in their first b.
Isa. 14. 30 And the first born of the poor shall feed
Jer. 31. 9 I am a father..and Ephraim (is) my first b
Mic. 6. 7 shall I give my first born (for) my transg.
Zech. 12. 10 as one that is in bitterness for..first born

2. *Birthright*, בְּכֹרָה *bekorah.*
Deut 21. 17 son of the hated..the right of the first b.

3. *First born*, בְּכִירָה *bekirah.*
Gen. 19. 31 And the first born said unto the younger
19. 33 the first born went in, and lay with her
19. 34 that the first born said unto the younger
19. 37 the first born bare a son, and called his
29. 26 to give the younger, before the first born
1 Sa. 14. 49 name of the first born Merab, and the

4. *First born*, πρωτότοκος *prōtotokos.*
Matt. 1. 25 till she had brought forth her [first born]
Luke 2. 7 And she brought forth her first born son
Rom. 8. 29 that he might be the first born among
Col. 1. 15 Who is..the first born of every creature
1. 18 who is..the first born from the dead
Heb. 11. 28 lest he that destroyed the first born sho.
12. 23 To the general assembly..of the first born

FIRST born, to make —

To constitute first born, בָּכַר *bakar*, 3.
Deut 21. 16 not make the son of the beloved first born

FIRST fruit —

1. *First or earliest fruit*, בִּכּוּר *bikkur.*
Exod23. 16 the first fruits of thy labours, which thou
23. 19 The first of the first fruits of thy land thou
34. 22 of the first fruits of wheat harvest, and
34. 26 The first of the first fruits of thy land
Lev. 2. 14 if thou offer a meat offering of thy first f.
2. 14 for the meat offering of thy first fruits
23. 17 (they are) the first fruits unto the LORD
23. 20 with the bread of the first fruits, (for) a
Num28. 26 in the day of the first fruits, when ye bri.
2 Ki. 4. 42 brought the man of God bread of the f. f.
Neh. 10. 35 And to bring the first fruits of our ground
10. 35 and the first fruits of all fruit of all trees
13. 31 and for the first fruits. Remember me, O
Eze. 44. 30 And the first of all the first fruits of all

2. *First or principal*, רֵאשִׁית *reshith.*
Lev. 2. 12 As for the oblation of the first fruits, ye
23. 10 ye shall bring a sheaf of the first fruits
Num 18. 12 the first fruits of them which they shall
Deut 18. 4 The first fruit..of thy corn, of thy
26. 10 first fruits [Heb. *reshith peri, first of fruit*]
2 Ch. 31. 5 brought in abundance the first fruits of
Neh. 10. 37 we should bring the first fruits of our d.
12. 44 for the first fruits, and for the tithes, to
Prov. 3. 9 and with the first fruits of all thine incr.
Jer. 2. 3 the first fruits of his increase: all that
Eze. 20. 40 the first fruits of your oblations, with all
48. 14 nor alienate the first fruits of the land

3. *First fruits*, ἀπαρχή *aparchē.*
Rom. 8. 23 which have the first fruits of the Spirit
11. 16 For if the first fruit (be) holy, the lump
16. 5 who is the first fruits of Achaia unto Ch.
1 Co. 15. 20 become the first fruits of them that slept
15. 23 Christ the first fruits; afterward they
16. 15 that it is the first fruits of Achaia, and
Jas. 1. 18 that we should be a kind of first fruits of
Rev. 14. 4 the first fruits unto God and to the Lamb

FIRST ripe —

1. *First ripe fruit*, בִּכּוּר *bikkur.*
Num. 13. 20 the time (was) the time of the first ripe
18. 13 whatsoever is first ripe in the land, which

2. *First ripe fruit*, בִּכּוּרָה *bikkurah.*
Hos. 9. 10 I saw your fathers as the first ripe in the

3. *First ripe fruit*, בַּכּוּרָה *bakkurah.*
Jer. 24. 2 very good figs..like the figs..first ripe

FIRST ripe fig —

First ripe fruit, בִּכּוּר *bikkur.*
Nah. 3. 12 fig trees with the first ripe figs: if they

FIRST ripe fruit —

First ripe fruit, בִּכּוּרָה *bikkurah.*
Mic. 7. 1 Woe..my soul desired the first ripe fruit

FIRSTLING —

1. *Firstling, first born*, בְּכוֹר *bekor.*
Lev. 27. 26 Only the firstling of the beasts, which
Num. 3. 41 instead of all the firstlings among the ca.
18. 15 the firstling of unclean beasts shalt thou
18. 17 But the firstling of a cow, or the firstling
Deut15. 19 All the firstling males that come of thy

Deut 15. 19 thou shalt do no work with the firstling
15. 19 nor shear the firstling of thy sheep
33. 17 His glory (is like) the firstling of his bul.

2. *Firstling, first born,* בְּכוֹרָה *bekorah.*
Gen. 4. 4 Abel, he also brought of the firstlings of
Deut 12. 6 the firstlings of your herds and of your
12. 17 the firstlings of thy herds, or of thy flock
14. 23 the firstlings of thy herds and of thy flocks
Neh. 10. 36 the firstlings of our herds and of our flocks

3. *What opens (the womb),* פֶּטֶר *peter.*
Exod 13. 12 every firstling that cometh of a beast
13. 13 every firstling of an ass thou shalt redeem
34. 19 every firstling among thy cattle..ox or
34. 20 But the firstling of an ass thou shalt red.

FIRSTLING, to be—
To be made a firstling, בָּכַר *bakar,* 4.
Lev. 27. 26 which should be the LORD'S firstling, no

FISH —
1. *Fish,* דָּג [V.L. דָּאג] *dag.*
Neh. 13. 16 There dwelt men..which brought fish

2. *Fish,* דָּג *dag.*
Gen. 9. 2 shall be..upon all the fishes of the sea
Num 11. 22 or shall all the fish of the sea be gathered
1 Ki. 4. 33 he spake also of beasts..and of fishes
2 Ch. 33. 14 even to the entering in at the fish gate
Neh. 3. 3 the fish gate did the sons of Hassenaah
12. 39 And from..above the fish gate..even unto
Job 12. 8 the fishes of the sea shall declare unto
41. 7 Canst thou fill..his head with fish spears?
Psa. 8. 8 The fowl of the air, and the fish of the
Eccl. 9. 12 as the fishes that are taken in an evil net
Eze. 38. 20 So that the fishes of the sea, and the fowls
Hos. 4. 3 the fishes of the sea also shall be taken
Jon. 1. 17 LORD had prepared a great fish to swallow
1. 17 Jonah was in the belly of the fish three
2. 10 LORD spake unto the fish, and it vomited
Hab. 1. 14 And makest men as the fishes of the sea
Zeph. 1. 3 I will consume..the fishes of the sea, and
1. 10 the noise of a cry from the fish gate, and

3. *Fish,* דָּגָה *dagah.*
Gen. 1. 26, 28 have dominion over the fish of the sea
Exod 7. 18 And the fish that (is) in the river shall
7. 21 And the fish that (was) in the river died
Num 11. 5 We remember the fish which we did eat
Deut. 4. 18 likeness of any fish that (is) in the waters
Psa. 105. 29 turned..waters into blood, and slew..fish
Isa. 50. 2 their fish stinketh, because..no water, and
Eze. 29. 4 I will cause the fish of thy rivers to stick
29. 4 all the fish of thy rivers shall stick unto
29. 5 leave..thee and all the fish of thy rivers
47. 9 there shall be a..great multitude of fish
47. 10 their fish shall be according to their kinds
47. 10 as the fish of the great sea, exceeding
Jon. 2. 1 Then Jonah prayed..out of the fish's belly

4. *Soul, breathing creature,* נֶפֶשׁ *nephesh.*
Isa. 19. 10 all that make sluices (and) ponds for fish

5. *Fish,* ἰχθύς *ichthus.*
Matt. 7. 10 if he ask a fish, will he give him a serpe.?
14. 17 We have here..five loaves, and two fishes
14. 19 took the five loaves, and the two fishes
15. 36 he took the seven loaves and the fishes
17. 27 and take up the fish that first cometh up
Mark 6. 38 they knew, they say, Five, and two fishes
6. 41 had taken the five loaves and the two fish.
6. 41 the two fishes divided he among them all
6. 43 full of the fragments, and of the fishes
Luke 5. 6 they inclosed a great multitude of fishes
5. 9 draught of the fishes which they had taken
9. 13 We have..but five loaves and two fishes
9. 16 he took the five loaves and the two fishes
11. 11 or if..a fish, will he for a fish give him
24. 42 they gave him a piece of a broiled fish
John 21. 6 able to draw it for the multitude of fishes
21. 8 came..dragging the net with fishes
21. 11 drew the net to land full of great fishes
1 Co. 15. 39 another of fishes (and) another of birds

6. *A little or small fish,* ὀψάριον *opsarion.*
John 6. 11 likewise of the fishes as much as they
21. 9 they saw a fire of coals there, and fish laid
21. 10 Bring of the fish which ye have now cau.
21. 13 cometh, and taketh bread..and fish likew.

FISH, little or small —
1. *A little or small fish,* ἰχθύδιον *ichthudion.*
Matt 15. 34 they said, Seven, and a few little fishes
Mark 8. 7 they had a few small fishes: and he bles.

2. *A little or small fish,* ὀψάριον *opsarion.*
John 6. 9 five barley loaves, and two small fishes

FISH, to —
To fish, דִּיג *dig.*
Jer. 16. 16 for many fishers..and they shall fish them

FISH hook —
Fish hook, thorn, סִיר דּוּגָה *sir dugah.*
Amos 4. 2 will take..your posterity with fish hooks

FISHER —
1. *Fisher,* דַּוָּג *davvag.* [V.L. דַּיָּג in Jer.]
Jer. 16. 16 I will send for many fishers, saith the L.
Eze. 47. 10 the fishers shall stand upon it from E.-g.

2. *Fisher,* דַּיָּג *dayyag.*
Isa. 19. 8 The fishers also shall mourn, and all they

3. *Fisher,* ἁλιεύς *halieus.*
Matt. 4. 18 a net into the sea: for they were fishers
Matt. 4. 19 and I will make you fishers of men
Mark 1. 16 a net into the sea: for they were fishers
1. 17 and I will make you..fishers of men

FISHER'S coat —
A tunic, cloak, ἐπενδύτης *ependutēs.*
John 21. 7 he girt (his) fisher's coat..for he was naked

FISHERMAN —
Fisher, ἁλιεύς *halieus.*
Luke 5. 2 but the fishermen were gone out of them

FISHING, a —
To fish, ἁλιεύω *halieuō.*
John 21. 3 Peter saith unto them, I go a fishing

FISHPOOL —
Blessing, pool, pond, בְּרֵכָה *berekah.*
Song 7. 4 thine eyes..the fishpools in Heshbon

FIST —
1. *Fist,* אֶגְרֹף *egroph.*
Exod 21. 18 and one smite another..with (his) fist
Isa. 58. 4 and to smite with the fist of wickedness

2. *Two hands, fists,* חָפְנַיִם *chophnayim.*
Prov. 30. 4 who hath gathered the wind in his fists?

FIT —
1. *Ready, fit, opportune,* עִתִּי *itti.*
Lev. 16. 21 by the hand of a fit man into the wilder.

2. *Well or conveniently placed,* εὔθετος *euthetos.*
Luke 9. 62 No man..looking back, is fit for the kin.
14. 35 It is neither fit for the land, nor yet for

3. *Coming down, becoming, suitable,* καθῆκον *kath.*
Acts 22. 22 Away with such..for it is not [fit] that he

FIT, to —
1. *To do,* עָשָׂה *asah.*
Isa. 44. 13 he fitteth it with planes, and he marketh

2. *To make fully ready,* καταρτίζω *katartizō.*
Rom. 9. 22 the vessels of wrath fitted to destruction

FIT, to be —
To come up, be becoming, suitable, ἀνήκω *anēkō.*
Col. 3. 18 submit yourselves..as it is fit in the Lord

FIT, to make —
To make ready, עָתַד *athad,* 3.
Prov 24. 27 and make it fit for thyself in the field

FIT to go out —
Going out, יָצָא *yatsa* (partic.).
1 Ch. 7. 11 fit to go out for war and battle

FITCHES —
1. *Prickly, spelt,* כֻּסֶּמֶת *kussemeth.*
Eze. 4. 9 Take thou also unto thee..fitches, and put

2. *Black cumin,* קֶצַח *qetsach.*
Isa. 28. 25 doth he not cast abroad the fitches, and
28. 27 the fitches are not threshed with a thres.
28. 27 the fitches are beaten out with a staff

FITLY —
1. *At its times or circumstances,* עַל־אָפְנָיו [*al*].
Prov 25. 11 A word fitly spoken (is like) apples of gold

2. *On the fillings up,* עַל־מְלֵאת *al milleth.*
Song 5. 12 His eyes..washed with milk..fitly set

FITTED —
To be made straight, יָשַׁר *yashar,* 4.
1 Ki. 6. 35 with gold fitted upon the carved work

FITTED, to be —
To be prepared, set up, established, כּוּן *kun,* 2.
Prov 22. 18 they shall withal be fitted in thy lips

FIVE —
1. *Five,* חָמֵשׁ ,חֲמִשָּׁה *chamishshah, chamesh.*
Gen. 5. 6 Seth lived an hundred and five years
5. 11 days of Enos were nine hundred and five
5. 15 And Mahalaleel lived sixty and five years
5. 17 were eight hundred ninety and five years
5. 21 Enoch lived sixty and five years, and
5. 23 were three hundred sixty and five years
5. 30 five hundred ninety and five years
5. 32 And Noah was five hundred years old
11. 11 Shem lived..five hundred years, and
11. 12 Arphaxad lived five and thirty years, and
11. 32 were two hundred and five years: and T.
12. 4 Abram..seventy and five years old when
14. 9 king of Ellasar; four kings with five
18. 28 Peradventure there shall lack five of the
18. 28 wilt thou destroy all..for (lack of) five?
18. 28 If I find there forty and five, I will not
43. 34 was five times so much as any of theirs
45. 6 yet..five years, in the which..neither
45. 11 for yet..five years of famine; lest thou
45. 22 to Benjamin..five changes of raiment
47. 2 he took some of his brethren..five men
Exod 22. 1 he shall restore five oxen for an ass
26. 3 The five curtains shall be coupled toge.
26. 3 and..five curtains..coupled one to anot.
26. 9 thou shalt couple five curtains by thems.
26. 26 five for the boards of the one side of the
26. 27, 27 five bars for the boards of the
26. 37 make..five pillars..and..cast five sockets
27. 1 five cubits long, and five cubits broad
27. 18 the height five cubits (of) fine twined lin.
30. 23 Take..of pure myrrh five hundred
30. 24 And of cassia five hundred..after the
36. 10 the five curtains; 36. 10, 16, 31, 32, 32.
Exod 36. 38 the five pillars of it with their hooks
36. 38 but their five sockets (were of) brass
38. 1 five cubits..the length..and five cubits
38. 18 the height in the breadth (was) five cub.
38. 26 three thousand and five hundred and fif.
38. 28 of the..five..he made hooks for the pill.
Lev. 26. 8 five of you shall chase an hundred, and
27. 5 from five years old even unto twenty yea.
27. 6 from a month old even unto five years
27. 6 shall be of the male five shekels of
Num. 1. 21 forty and six thousand and five hundred
1. 25 of Gad, (were) forty and five thousand
1. 33 of Ephraim..forty thousand and five hu.
1. 37 of Benjamin..thirty and five thousand
1. 41 forty and one thousand and five hundred
1. 46 three thousand and five hundred and fif.
2. 11 forty and six thousand and five hundred
2. 15 forty and five thousand and six hundred
2. 19 his host..forty thousand and five hund.
2. 23 thirty and five thousand and four hund.
2. 28 forty and one thousand and five hundred
2. 32 three thousand and five hundred and fif.
3. 22 (were) seven thousand and five hundred
3. 50 three hundred and threescore and five
4. 48 were eight thousand and five hundred
7. 17 five rams, five he goats, five lambs of the
[So in v. 23, 29, 35, 41, 47, 53, 59, 65, 71, 77, 83.]
8. 24 from twenty and five years old and
11. 19 Ye shall not eat one day..nor five days
18. 16 for the money of five shekels, after the
26. 18 of Gad..forty thousand and five hundred
26. 22 and sixteen thousand and five hundred
26. 27 threescore thousand and five hundred
26. 37 thirty and two thousand and five hun
26. 41 forty and five thousand and six hundred
26. 50 forty and five thousand and four hundred
31. 8 and Hur, and Reba, five kings of Midian
31. 28 one soul of five hundred..of the persons
31. 32 seventy thousand and five thousand she.
31. 36 thirty thousand and five hundred sheep
31. 39 (were) thirty thousand and five hundred
31. 43 seven thousand and five hundred sheep
31. 45 thirty thousand asses and five hundred
Josh. 8. 12 And he took about five thousand men
10. 5 Therefore the five kings of the Amorites
10. 16 these five kings fled, and hid themselves
10. 17 The five kings are found hid in a cave at
10. 22 bring out those five kings unto me out of
10. 23 brought forth those five kings unto him
10. 26 slew them, and hanged them on five trees
13. 3 five lords of the Philistines; the Gazat.
14. 10 forty and five years..fourscore and five
Judg. 3. 3 five lords of the Philistines, and all the
18. 2 Dan sent of their family five men from
18. 7 the five men departed, and came to Laish
18. 14 Then answered the five men that went to
18. 17 the five men that went to spy out the
20. 35 twenty and five thousand and an hundred
20. 45 they gleaned of them..five thousand men
20. 46 twenty and five thousand men that drew
1 Sa. 6. 4 Five golden emerods, and five golden mi.
6. 16 when the five lords of the Philistines had
6. 18 all the cities..(belonging) to the five lords
17. 5 the weight..(was) five thousand shekels
17. 40 And he..chose him five smooth stones
21. 3 give (me) five (loaves of) bread in mine
22. 18 slew on that day fourscore and five per.
25. 18 five sheep ready dressed, and five measu.
25. 42 with five damsels of hers that went after
2 Sa. 4. 4 He was five years old when the tidings
21. 8 five sons of Michal the daughter of Saul
24. 9 of Judah..five hundred thousand men
1 Ki. 4. 32 and his songs were a thousand and five
6. 6 The nethermost chamber (was) five cu.
6. 10 he built chambers..five cubits high
6. 24 five cubits..the one..and five cubits the
7. 3 (lay) on forty five pillars, fifteen (in) a
7. 16 the height..five cubits..height..five
7. 23 his height (was) five cubits; and a line of
7. 39 he put five bases on the right side of the
7. 39 and five on the left side of the house
7. 49 five on the right..and five on the left
9. 23 five hundred and fifty, which bare rule
22. 42 Jehoshaphat (was) thirty and five years
22. 42 he reigned twenty and five years in Jer
2 Ki. 6. 25 fourth part of a cab..for five (pieces) of
7. 13 take, I pray thee, five of the horses that
13. 19 Thou shouldest have smitten five or six
14. 2 He was twenty and five years old when
15. 33 Five and twenty years old was he when
18. 2 Twenty and five years old was he when
19. 35 an hundred fourscore and five thousand
21. 1 and reigned fifty and five years in Jerus.
23. 36 Jehoiakim (was) twenty and five years old
25. 19 five men of them that were in the king's
1 Ch. 2. 4 All the sons of Judah (were) five
2. 6 and Calcol, and Dara: five of them in
3. 20 Ohel..and Hasadiah, Jushab-hesed, five
4. 32 Rimmon, and Tochen, and Ashan, five ci
4. 42 five hundred men, went to mount Seir
7. 3 Joel, Ishiah, five: all of them chief men
7. 7 and Uzziel, and Jerimoth, and Iri, five
11. 23 he slew an Egyptian..five cubits high
29. 7 And gave..of gold five thousand talents
2 Ch. 3. 11 one wing..five cubits..other wing..five
3. 12 wing of the other..five cubits..five cub.
3. 15 two pillars of thirty and five cubits high
3. 15 the chapiter..of each..(was) five cubits
4. 2 a molten sea..five cubits the height ther.
4. 6, 7, 8 five on the right hand, and five on
6. 13 of five cubits long, and five cubits broad
13. 17 fell..five hundred thousand chosen men

2 Ch. 15. 19 the five and thirtieth year of the reign of
20. 31 thirty and five years old when he began
20. 31 he reigned twenty and five years in Jer.
25. 1 Amaziah (was) twenty and five years old
26. 13 and seven thousand and five hundred
27. 1 Jotham (was) twenty and five years old
27. 8 He was five and twenty years old when
29. 1 Hezekiah..(was) five and twenty years
33. 1 he reigned fifty and five years in Jer.
35. 9 five thousand..and five hundred oxen
36. 5 Jehoiakim (was) twenty and five years old
Ezra 1. 11 vessels..five thousand and four hundred
2. 5 of Arah, seven hundred seventy and five
2. 8 of Zattu, nine hundred forty and five
2. 20 The children of Gibbar, ninety and five
2. 33 of Lod..seven hundred twenty and five
2. 34 of Jericho, three hundred forty and five
2. 66 their mules, two hundred forty and five
2. 67 camels, four hundred thirty and five
2. 69 five thousand pounds of silver, and one
Neh. 7. 13 of Zattu, eight hundred forty and five
7. 20 of Adin, six hundred fifty and five
7. 25 The children of Gibeon, ninety and five
7. 36 Jericho, three hundred forty and five
7. 67 two hundred forty and five singing men
7. 68 their mules, two hundred forty and five
7. 69 camels, four hundred thirty and five
7. 70 five hundred and thirty priests' garments
Esth. 9. 6 the Jews..destroyed five hundred men
9. 12 Jews have..destroyed five hundred men
9. 16 of their foes seventy and five thousand
Job 1. 3 and five hundred yoke of oxen, and
1. 3 five hundred she asses, and a very great
Isa 7. 8 within threescore and five years shall
17. 6 five in the outmost fruitful branches
19. 18 In that day shall five cities in the land of
30. 17 at the rebuke of five shall ye flee: till
37. 36 a hundred and fourscore and five thous
Jer. 52. 22 and the height of one..(was) five cubits
52. 30 seven hundred forty and five persons
52. 31 in the five and twentieth..of the month
Eze. 8. 16 about five and twenty men, with their
11. 1 at the door of the gate five and twenty
40. 1 In the five and twentieth year of our cap
40. 7 between the little chambers..five cubits
40. 13 the breadth (was) five and twenty cubits
40. 21, 25 and the breadth five and twenty cubits
40. 29 fifty cubits long, and five and twenty cu.
40. 30 five and twenty cubits long, and five cub.
40. 33 fifty cubits long, and five and twenty cub.
40. 36 and the breadth five and twenty cubits
40. 48 five cubits on this side, and five cubits on
41. 2 five cubits on the one side, and five cubits
41. 9 The thickness of the wall..(was) five cub.
41. 11 breadth of the place..(was) five cubits
41. 12 the wall of the building (was) five cubits
42. 16, 17, 18, 19 He measured..five hundred re
42. 20 five hundred..long, and five hundred br.
45. 1 the length of five and twenty thousand
45. 2 five hundred..with five hundred..square
45. 3 the length of five and twenty thousand
45. 5 the five and twenty thousand of length
45. 6 possession of the city five thousand broad
45. 6 and five and twenty thousand long
45. 12 twenty shekels, five and twenty shekels
48. 8, 9, 10, 13, 15 five and twenty thousand
48. 15 And the five thousand (that are) left in the
48. 16, 16, 16, 16, 30, 33, 34 four thousand and five
48. 20 five and twenty thousand by five and
48. 21, 21 over against the five and twenty thou
Dan. 12. 12 three hundred and five and thirty days

2. *Five*, πέντε *pente*.
Matt 14. 17 We have here but five loaves, and two fi.
14. 19 took the five loaves, and the two fishes
16. 9 remember the five loaves of the five thou.
25. 2 five of them were wise, and five..foolish
25. 15 unto one he gave five talents, to another
25. 16 he that had received the five talents went
25. 16 traded..and made..other five talents
25. 20 And so he that had received five talents
25. 20 came and brought other five talents
25. 20 thou deliveredst..five..have gained..five
Mark 6. 38 when they knew, they say, Five, and two
6. 41 when he had taken the five loaves and the
8. 19 When I brake the five loaves among five
Luke 1. 24 his wife..hid herself five months, saying
9. 13 We have no more but five loaves and two
9. 16 Then he took the five loaves and the two
12. 6 Are not five sparrows sold for two farth.?
12. 52 there shall be five in one house divided
14. 19 I have bought five yoke of oxen, and I go
16. 28 I have five brethren; that he may testify
19. 18 Lord, thy pound hath gained five pounds
19. 19 And he said..Be thou also over five cities
John 4. 18 thou hast had five husbands; and he
5. 2 is called..Bethesda, having five porches
6. 9 which hath five barley loaves, and two
6. 13 the fragments of the five barley loaves
6. 19 So when they had rowed about five and
Acts 4. 4 and the number..was about five thousand
20. 6 and came unto them to Troas in five days
24. 1 after five days Ananias..descended with
1 Co. 14. 19 Yet..I had rather speak five words with
Rev. 9. 5 they should be tormented five months
9. 10 their power (was) to hurt men five months
17. 10 there are seven kings: five are fallen, and

FIVE apiece —
Five five, חֲמֵשֶׁת חֲמֵשֶׁת *chamesheth chamesheth.*
Num 3. 47 Thou shalt..take five shekels apiece by

FIVE times —
Five times, πεντάκις *pentakis.*
2 Co. 11. 24 Of the Jews five times received I forty

FIX, to —
To set fast, στηρίζω *stērizō.*
Luke 16. 26 between us and you there is a great gulf fi.

FIXED, to be —
To be prepared, set up, established, כּוּן *kun*, 2.
Psa. 57. 7 My heart is fixed, O God, my heart is fixed
108. 1 O God, my heart is fixed; I will sing and give
112. 7 his heart is fixed, trusting in the LORD

FLAG —
1. *Reed*, אָחוּ *achu.*
Job 8. 11 can the flag grow without water?
2. *Weed*, סוּף *suph.*
Exod. 2. 3 she laid (it) in the flags by the river's br.
2. 5 and when she saw the ark among the flags
Isa. 19. 6 and dried up: the reeds and flags shall

FLAGON —
1. *A cake of grapes*, אֲשִׁישָׁה *ashishah.*
2 Sa. 6. 19 And he dealt..to every one..a flagon (of w.)
1 Ch. 16. 3 And he dealt to every one..a flagon (of w.)
Song 2. 5 Stay me with flagons, comfort me with a.
Hos. 3. 1 the children of Israel..love flagons of w.
2. *Bottle*, נֶבֶל, נֵבֶל *nebel.*
Isa. 22. 24 of cups, even to all the vessels of flagons

FLAKES —
Refuse, flake, מַפָּל *mappal.*
Job 41. 23 The flakes of his flesh are joined together

FLAME —
1. *Fire*, אֶשָּׁא *eshsha.*
Dan. 7. 11 and his body..given to the burning flame
2. *Completeness*, כָּלִיל *kalil.*
Judg. 20. 40 the flame of the city ascended up to hea.
3. *Heart, middle*, לַבָּה *labbah.*
Exod. 3. 2 the Angel..appeared..in a flame of fire
4. *Flame*, לַהַב *lahab.*
Judg. 13. 20 when the flame went up toward heaven
13. 20 that the angel..ascended in the flame of
Job 41. 21 and a flame goeth out of his mouth
Isa. 13. 8 at another; their faces (shall be as) fla.
29. 6 tempest, and the flame of devouring fire
30. 30 the flame of a devouring fire..scattering
66. 15 to render..his rebuke with flames of fire
Joel 2. 5 a flame of fire that devoureth the stubble
5. *Flame*, לֶהָבָה, לַהֶבֶת *lehabah, lahebeth.*
Num 21. 28 a flame from the city of Sihon: it hath
Psa. 29. 7 The voice..divideth the flames of fire
83. 14 as the flame setteth the mountains on fire
106. 18 company; the flame burned up the wicked
Isa. 5. 24 Therefore as..the flame consumeth the
10. 17 his Holy One for a flame: and it shall
43. 2 neither shall the flame kindle upon thee
47. 14 themselves from the power of the flame
Jer. 48. 45 and a flame from the midst of Sihon
Eze. 20. 47 the flaming flame shall not be quenched
Dan. 11. 33 yet they shall fall..by flame, by captivity
Joel 1. 19 the flame hath burnt all the trees of
2. 3 behind them a flame burneth: the land
Obad. 18 the house of Joseph a flame, and the
6. *Uplifted signal*, מַשְׂאֵת *maseth.*
Judg. 20. 40 when the flame began to arise up out of
7. *Spark, flame*, שְׁבִיב *shebib.*
Dan. 3. 22 the flame of the fire slew those men that
7. 9 his throne..the fiery flame..his wheels
8. *Flame*, שַׁלְהֶבֶת *shalhebeth.*
Job 15. 30 the flame shall dry up his branches; and
Song 8. 6 coals of fire..a most vehement flame
9. *Flame*, φλόξ *phlox.*
Luke 16. 24 mercy..for I am tormented in this flame
Acts 7. 30 angel of the Lord in a flame of fire in a
Heb. 1. 7 Who maketh..his ministers a flame of fi.
Rev. 1. 14 and his eyes (were) as a flame of fire
2. 18 who hath his eyes like unto a flame of fire
19. 12 His eyes (were) as a flame of fire, and on

FLAME, great —
Uplifted signal, מַשְׂאֵת *maseth.*
Judg. 20. 38 that they should make a great flame

FLAMING —
1. *Fire*, אֵשׁ *ish.*
Nah. 2. 3 the chariots..with flaming torches in the
2. *Flame*, לֶהָבָה, לַהֶבֶת *lehabah, lahebeth.*
Psa. 105. 32 He gave them..flaming fire in their land
Isa. 4. 5 and the shining of a flaming fire by night
Lam. 2. 3 burned against Jacob like a flaming fire
Hos. 7. 6 in the morning it burneth as a flaming fi.
3. *To flame, flash*, לָהַט *lahat.*
Psa. 104. 4 Who maketh..his ministers a flaming fire
4. *Flame, flashing*, לַהַט *lahat.*
Gen. 3. 24 a flaming sword which turned every way
5. *Flame*, φλόξ *phlox.*
2 Th. 1. 8 In flaming fire taking vengeance on them
6. *Flame*, שַׁלְהֶבֶת *shalhebeth.*
Eze. 20. 47 the flaming flame shall not be quenched

FLANKS —
Flank, loin, כֶּסֶל *kesel.*
Lev. 3. 4, 10, 15 which (is) by the flanks, and the
4. 9 which (is) by the flanks, and the caul
7. 4 which (is) by the flanks, and the caul
Job 15. 27 and maketh collops of fat on (his) flanks

FLAT —
Under, תַּחַת *tachath.*
Josh. 6. 5 and the wall..shall fall down flat

FLAT nose, to have a —
To be compressed, חָרַם *charam.*
Lev. 21. 18 or a lame, or he that hath a flat nose

FLATTER, to —
1. *To make smooth, flatter*, חָלַק *chalaq*, 5.
Psa. 5. 9 open sepulchre; they flatter with their
36. 2 For he flattereth himself in his own eyes
Prov. 2. 16 the stranger..flattereth with her words
7. 5 the stranger..flattereth with her words
28. 23 than he that flattereth with the tongue
29. 5 A man that flattereth his neighbour
2. *To make simple, entice*, פָּתָה *pathah*, 3.
Psa. 78. 36 they did flatter him with their mouth

FLATTERETH, that —
To be or make simple, entice, פָּתָה *pathah.*
Prov 20. 19 meddle not with him that flattereth

FLATTERIES —
1. *Smoothnesses, flatteries*, חֲלַקּוֹת *chalaqqoth.*
Dan. 11. 32 And such..shall he corrupt by flatteries
2. *Smoothnesses, flatteries*, חֲלַקְלַקּוֹת *chalaqlaqqoth.*
Dan. 11. 21 and obtain the kingdom by flatteries
11. 34 many shall cleave to them with flatteries

FLATTERING —
1. *Smooth, flattering*, חָלָק *chalaq.*
Prov. 26. 28 and a flattering mouth worketh ruin
Eze. 12. 24 nor flattering divination within the house
2. *Smoothness*, חֵלֶק *cheleq.*
Prov. 7. 21 with the flattering of her lips she forced
3. *Smoothness, flattery*, חֶלְקָה *chelqah.*
Psa. 12. 2 flattering lips..with a double heart, do
12. 3 The LORD shall cut off all flattering lips
4. *Flattery, adulation*, κολακεία *kolakeia.*
1 Th. 2. 5 neither at any time used we flattering

FLATTERING titles, to give —
To surname, give flattering title, כָּנָה *kanah*, 3.
Job 32. 21 neither let me give flattering titles unto
32. 22 For I know not to give flattering titles

FLATTERY —
1. *Smoothness, flattery*, חֵלֶק *cheleq.*
Job 17. 5 He that speaketh flattery to (his) friends
2. *Smoothness, flattery*, חֶלְקָה *chelqah.*
Prov. 6. 24 from the flattery of the tongue of a stra.

FLAX —
1. *Flax, wick*, פִּשְׁתָּה *pishtah.*
Exod. 9. 31 And the flax and the barley was smitten
9. 31 (was) in the ear, and the flax (was) bolled
Isa. 42. 3 the smoking flax shall he not quench
2. *Flax, linen*, פִּשְׁתֶּה *pishteh.*
Josh. 2. 6 hid them with the stalks of flax, which she
Judg 15. 14 became as flax that was burnt with fire
Prov 31. 13 She seeketh wool and flax, and worketh
Isa. 19. 9 they that work in fine flax, and they that
Eze. 40. 3 with a line of flax in his hand, and a
Hos. 2. 5 my wool and my flax, mine oil and my
2. 9 and will recover my wool and my flax
3. *Flax*, λίνον *linon.*
Matt 12. 20 and smoking flax shall he not quench

FLAY, to —
To strip off, פָּשַׁט *pashat*, 5.
Lev. 1. 6 he shall flay the burnt offering, and cut
2 Ch. 29. 34 they could not flay all the burnt offerings
35. 11 from their hands, and the Levites flayed
Mic. 3. 3 Who also..flay their skin from off them

FLEA —
Flea, פַּרְעֹשׁ *parosh.*
1 Sa. 24. 14 after whom dost thou pursue..after a flea
26. 20 for the king..is come out to seek a flea

FLED, to be —
1. *To flee*, בָּרַח *barach.*
Gen. 31. 22 it was told Laban..that Jacob was fled?
1 Sa. 27. 4 it was told Saul that David was fled to G.
2 Sa. 19. 9 now he is fled out of the land for Absalom
1 Ki. 12. 2 he was fled from the presence of..Solom.
Neh. 13. 10 singers..were fled every one to his field
2. *To move, wander, flee away*, נָדַד *nadad.*
Isa. 22. 3 All thy rulers are fled together, they are
Jer. 4. 25 all the birds of the heavens were fled
9. 10 both the fowl..and the beast are fled
3. *To hasten, flee*, נוּס *nus.*
Gen. 39. 13 he had left his garment..and was fled
Num 35. 25, 26 city of his refuge, whither he was fled
35. 32 him that is fled to the city of his refuge
1 Sa. 4. 17 Israel is fled before the Philistines, and
2 Sa. 1. 4 That the people are fled from the battle
10. 14 Ammon saw that the Syrians were fled
1 Ki. 2. 29 that Joab was fled unto the tabernacle
1 Ch. 19. 15 Ammon saw that the Syrians were fled

Isa. 10. 29 Ramah is afraid; Gibeah of Saul is fled
Jer. 46. 5 their mighty ones..are fled apace, and

FLEE, to —

1. *To flee,* בָּרַח *barach.*

Gen. 16. 6 dealt hardly with her, she fled from her
16. 8 I flee from the face of my mistress Sarai
27. 43 flee thou to Laban my brother to Haran
31. 20 in that he told him not that he fled
31. 21 So he fled with all that he had; and he
35. 1 when thou fleddest from the face of Esau
35. 7 when he fled from the face of his brother
Exod. 2. 15 Moses fled from the face of Pharaoh
14. 5 it was told the king..that the people fled
Num 24. 11 Therefore now flee thou to thy place
Judg 11. 3 Jephthah fled from his brethren, and dw.
1 Sa. 19. 12 and he went, and fled, and escaped
19. 18 So David fled, and escaped, and came to
20. 1 David fled from Naioth in Ramah, and
21. 10 David..fled that day for fear of Saul, and
22. 17 and because they knew when he fled
22. 20 Abiathar, escaped, and fled after David
23. 6 when Abiathar the son of Ahimelech fled
2 Sa. 4. 3 the Beerothites fled to Gittaim, and were
13. 34 But Absalom fled. And the young man
13. 37 Absalom fled, and went to Talmai, the
13. 38 Absalom fled, and went to Geshur, and
15. 14 And David said..Arise, and let us flee
1 Ki. 2. 7 for so they came to me when I fled beca.
11. 17 That Hadad fled, he and certain Edomites
11. 23 which fled from his lord Hadadezer king
11. 40 Jeroboam arose, and fled into Egypt, unto
2 Ch. 10. 2 whither he had fled from the presence of
Neh. 6. 11 And I said, Should such a man as I flee?
Job 14. 2 he fleeth also as a shadow, and continueth
20. 24 He shall flee from the iron weapon
27. 22 he would fain flee out of his hand
Psa. 3. *title.* when he fled from Absalom his son
57. *title.* when he fled from Saul in the cave
139. 7 or whither shall I flee from thy presence?
Isa. 22. 3 are bound..(which) have fled from far
48. 20 flee ye from the Chaldeans, with a voice
Jer. 4. 29 The whole city shall flee for the noise of
26. 21 when Urijah heard it, he..fled, and went
39. 4 then they fled, and went forth out of the
52. 7 all the men of war fled, and went forth
Dan. 10. 7 so that they fled to hide themselves
Hos. 12. 12 Jacob fled into the country of Syria; and
Jon. 1. 3 Jonah rose up to flee unto Tarshish from
1. 10 that he fled from the presence of the LORD
4. 2 Therefore I fled before unto Tarshish

2. *To move, wander, flee away,* נָדַד *nadad.*

Psa. 31. 11 they that did see me without fled from
Isa. 21. 14 prevented with their bread him that fled
21. 15 For they fled from the swords, from the
33. 3 At the noise of..tumult the people fled
Hos. 7. 13 Woe unto them! for they have fled from
Nah. 3. 7 all they that look upon thee shall flee

3. *To move self off,* נוּד *nud.*

Psa. 11. 1 how say ye..Flee (as) a bird to your mo.?

4. *To hasten, flee,* נוּס *nus.*

Gen. 14. 10 the kings of Sodom and Gomorrah fled
14. 10 they that remained fled to the mountain
19. 20 Behold now, this city (is) near to flee unto
39. 12 he left his garment in her hand, and fled
39. 15, 18 he left his garment with me, and fled
Exod. 4. 3 a serpent; and Moses fled from before it
14. 25 Let us flee from the face of Israel; for the
14. 27 the Egyptians fled against it; and the L.
21. 13 appoint..a place whither he shall flee
Lev. 26. 17 and ye shall flee when none pursueth you
26. 36 they shall flee, as fleeing from a sword
Num 10. 35 let them that hate thee flee before thee
16. 34 And all Israel..fled at the cry of them
35. 6 cities for refuge..that he may flee thither
35. 11 that the slayer may flee thither, which
35. 15 that killeth any person unawares may fl.
Deut. 4. 42 That the slayer might flee thither, which
19. 3 parts, that every slayer may flee thither
19. 4 of the slayer which shall flee thither, that
19. 5 he shall flee unto one of those cities, and
19. 11 if any man..fleeth into one of these cities
28. 7 they shall..flee before thee seven ways
28. 25 thou shalt..flee seven ways before them
Josh. 7. 4 and they fled before the men of Ai
8. 5 it shall come to pass..we will flee
8. 6 will say, They flee..therefore we will flee
8. 15 and fled by the way of the wilderness
8. 20 they had no power to flee this way or
8. 20 the people that fled..turned back upon
10. 11 it came to pass, as they fled from before
10. 16 these five kings fled, and hid themselves
20. 3 That the slayer..unawares..may flee
20. 4 when he that doth flee unto one of those
20. 6 return..unto the city from whence he fled
20. 9 whosoever killeth..unawares might flee
Judg. 1. 6 Adoni-bezek fled; and they pursued after
4. 15 so that Sisera..fled away on his feet
7. 22 the host fled to Beth-shittah in Zererath
8. 12 when Zebah and Zalmunna fled, he purs.
9. 21 Jotham ran away and fled and went to B.
9. 40 Abimelech chased him, and he fled before
9. 51 and thither fled all the men and women
20. 32 Let us flee, and draw them from the city
20. 45 they..fled toward the wilderness unto the
20. 47 six hundred men turned and fled to the
1 Sa. 4. 10 and they fled every man into his tent
4. 16 I fled to day out of the army. And he said
14. 22 they heard that the Philistines fled, every
17. 24 all the men of Israel..fled from him, and
1 Sa. 17. 51 And when the Philistines saw..they fled
19. 8 great slaughter; and they fled from him
19. 10 and David fled, and escaped that night
30. 17 four hundred young men, which..fled
31. 1 the men of Israel fled from before the P.
31. 7 Israel..saw that the men of Israel fled
31. 7 they forsook the cities, and fled, and the
2 Sa. 4. 4 and his nurse took him up, and fled
4. 4 as she made haste to flee, that he fell
10. 13 Joab drew nigh..and they fled before him
10. 14 then fled they also before Abishai, and
10. 18 the Syrians fled before Israel; and David
13. 29 then all the king's sons arose..and fled
17. 2 the people that (are) with him shall flee
18. 3 for if we flee away, they will not care for
18. 17 and all Israel fled every one to his tent
19. 3 people..steal away when they flee in batt.
19. 8 for Israel had fled every man to his tent
23. 11 and the people fled from the Philistines
24. 13 or wilt thou flee..before thine enemies
1 Ki. 2. 28 Joab fled unto the tabernacle of the LORD
12. 18 Rehoboam made speed..to flee to Jerus.
20. 20 the Syrians fled, and Israel pursued them
20. 30 But the rest fled to Aphek, into the city
20. 30 Benhadad fled, and came into the city
2 Ki. 3. 24 so that they fled before them: but they
7. 7 they arose, and fled in the twilight, and
7. 7 left their tents..and fled for their life
8. 21 and the people fled into their tents
9. 3 open the door and flee, and tarry not
9. 10 And he opened the door, and fled
9. 23 Joram turned his hands, and fled, and
9. 27 he fled by the way of the garden house
9. 27 and he fled to Megiddo, and died there
14. 12 and they fled every man to their tents
14. 19 he fled to Lachish; but they sent after
1 Ch. 10. 1 the men of Israel fled from before the P.
10. 7 when all the men..saw that they fled
10. 7 then they forsook their cities, and fled
11. 13 people fled from before the Philistines
19. 14 Joab..drew nigh..and they fled before
19. 15 they likewise fled before Abishai his bro.
19. 18 the Syrians fled before Israel; and David
2 Ch. 10. 18 Rehoboam made speed..to flee to Jeru.
13. 16 the children of Israel fled before Judah
14. 12 before Judah; and the Ethiopians fled
25. 22 and they fled every man to his tent
25. 27 he fled to Lachish: but they sent to Lac.
Psa. 68. 1 let them also that hate him flee before him
104. 7 At thy rebuke they fled; at the voice of
114. 3 The sea saw (it), and fled: Jordan was
114. 5 What (ailed) thee..that thou fleddest?
Prov 28. 1 The wicked flee when no man pursueth
28. 17 A man that doeth violence..shall flee to
Isa. 10. 3 to whom will ye flee for help? and where
13. 14 they shall..flee every one into his own
17. 13 they shall flee far off, and shall be chased
20. 6 whither we flee for help to be delivered
24. 18 he who fleeth from the noise of the fear
30. 16 will flee upon horses; therefore shall ye
30. 17 at the rebuke of five shall ye flee
31. 8 he shall flee from the sword, and his
Jer. 48. 6 Flee, save your lives, and be like the
48. 19 ask him that fleeth, and her that escapeth
48. 45 They that fled stood under the shadow of
49. 8 Flee ye, turn back..O inhabitants of De.
49. 24 Damascus..turneth herself to flee, and
49. 30 Flee, get you far off, dwell deep, O ye
50. 16 they shall flee every one to his own land
50. 28 The voice of them that flee and escape out
51. 6 Flee out of the midst of Babylon, and
Amos 5. 19 As if a man did flee from a lion, and a
9. 1 he that fleeth of them shall not flee away
Zech. 2. 6 flee from the land of the north, saith the
14. 5 ye shall flee (to) the valley of the moun.
14. 5 ye shall flee, like as ye fled from before

5. *To (cause to) flee,* נוּס *nus,* 5.

Judg. 7. 21 and all the host ran, and cried, and fled

6. *To go forth, flee,* נָצָא *natsa.*

Jer. 48. 9 Give wings unto Moab, that it may flee

7. *To flee out,* ἐκφεύγω *ekpheugō.*

Acts 16. 27 supposing..the prisoners had been fled
19. 16 so that they fled out of that house naked

8. *To flee down,* καταφεύγω *katapheugō.*

Acts 14. 6 They were ware of (it), and fled unto L.
Heb. 6. 18 who have fled for refuge to lay hold upon

9. *To flee,* φεύγω *pheugō.*

Matt. 2. 13 take the young child..and flee into Egypt
3. 7 who hath warned you to flee from the
8. 33 they that kept them fled, and went their
10. 23 flee ye into another: for verily I say unto
24. 16 Then let them which be in Judea flee
26. 56 all the disciples forsook him, and fled
Mark 5. 14 they that fed the swine fled, and told (it)
13. 14 then let them that be in Judea flee to
14. 50 And they all forsook him, and fled
14. 52 he left the linen cloth, and fled from
16. 8 they went out quickly, and fled from the
Luke 3. 7 who hath warned you to flee from the
8. 34 they fled, and went and told (it) in the
21. 21 let them which are in Judea flee to the
John 10. 5 will they not follow, but will flee from
10. 12 he that is an hireling..fleeth: and the
10. 13 The hireling fleeth, because he..careth
Acts 7. 29 Then fled Moses at this saying, and was
27. 30 as the shipmen were about to flee out of
1 Co. 6. 18 Flee fornication. Every sin that a man
10. 14 my dearly beloved, flee from idolatry
1 Ti. 6. 11 thou, O man of God, flee these things
2 Ti. 2. 22 Flee also youthful lusts: but follow
Jas. 4. 7 Resist the devil, and he will flee from you
Rev. 9. 6 to die, and death shall flee from them
12. 6 the woman fled into the wilderness, where

FLEE apace, to —

To move, wander, flee away, נָדַד *nadad.*

Psa. 68. 12 Kings of armies did flee apace; and she

FLEE away, to —

1. *To flee,* בָּרַח *barach.*

Gen. 31. 27 Wherefore didst thou flee away secretly
Job 9. 25 my days..they flee away, they see no good
Amos 7. 12 flee thee away into the land of Judah

2. *To move, wander, flee away,* נָדַד *nadad,* 3b.

Nah. 3. 17 when the sun ariseth they flee away, and

3. *To move self off,* נָדַד *nadad,* 7a.

Psa. 64. 8 all that see them shall flee away

4. *To flee,* נוּס *nus.*

Judg. 4. 17 Sisera fled away on his feet to the tent of
Song 2. 17 Until..the shadows flee away, turn, my
4. 6 Until..the shadows flee away, I will get
Isa. 35. 10 and sorrow and sighing shall flee away
51. 11 sorrow and mourning shall flee away
Jer 46. 6 Let not the swift flee away, nor the
46. 21 they also are turned..are fled away tog.
Amos 2. 16 among the mighty shall flee away naked
9. 1 of them shall not flee away, and he that
Nah. 2. 8 yet they shall flee away. Stand, stand

5. *To flee forth,* נוּץ *nuts.*

Lam. 4. 15 when they fled away and wandered, they

6. *To flee, be weary,* עוּף *uph.*

Nah. 3. 16 the cankerworm spoileth, and fleeth away

7. *To flee,* φεύγω *pheugō.*

Rev. 16. 20 every island fled away, and the moun.
20. 11 from whose face..the heaven fled away

FLEE before, to —

To go or come before, קָדַם *qadam,* 3. [*See* FLEE 1].

Jon. 4. 2 Therefore I fled before unto Tarshish

FLEE far, to —

To be far off, רָחַק *rachaq.*

Job 30. 10 They abhor me, they flee far from me, and

FLEE to hide, to —

To cover self, כָּסָה *kasah,* 3.

Psa. 143. 9 LORD..I flee unto thee to hide me

FLEE, to make —

1. *To cause to flee,* בָּרַח *barach,* 5.

Job 41. 28 The arrow cannot make him flee: sling

2. *To cause to flee,* נוּס *nus,* 5.

Exod. 9. 20 He..made his servants and his cattle flee

FLEE, way to —

Refuge (place of), flight, מָנוֹס *manos.*

Jer. 25. 35 the shepherds shall have no way to flee

FLEECE —

1. *Fleece, mowings of grass,* גֵּז *gez.*

Deut 18. 4 the first of the fleece of thy sheep, shalt
Job 31. 20 (not) warmed with the fleece of my sheep

2. *Fleece, mowings of grass,* גִּזָּה *gizzah.*

Judg. 6. 37 I will put a fleece of wool in the floor
6. 37 if the dew be on the fleece only, and
6. 38 for he..thrust the fleece together, and
6. 38 wringed the dew out of the fleece, a bowl
6. 39 let me prove..this once with the fleece
6. 39 let it now be dry only upon the fleece
6. 40 for it was dry upon the fleece only, and

FLEEING —

1. *Flight,* מְנוּסָה *menusah.*

Lev. 26. 36 they shall flee, as fleeing from a sword

2. *To flee,* נוּס *nus.*

Deut. 4. 42 and that fleeing unto one..he might live

3. *To flee,* עָרַק *araq.*

Job 30. 3 fleeing into the wilderness in former time

FLEETH, that —

One fleeing, נִיס *nis.*

Jer. 48. 44 He that fleeth from the fear shall fall into

FLESH —

1. *Flesh,* בָּשָׂר *basar.*

Gen. 2. 21 he..closed up the flesh instead thereof
2. 23 said, This (is) now..flesh of my flesh: she
2. 24 unto his wife: and they shall be one flesh
6. 3 strive with man, for that he also (is) flesh
6. 12 for all flesh had corrupted his way upon
6. 13 The end of all flesh is come before me
6. 17 waters upon the earth, to destroy all flesh
6. 19 And of every living thing of all flesh, two
7. 15 of all flesh, wherein (is) the breath of life
7. 16 went in male and female of all flesh, as
7. 21 all flesh died that moved upon the earth
8. 17 all flesh, (both) of fowl, and of cattle, and
9. 4 flesh with the life..shall ye not eat
9. 11 neither shall all flesh be cut off any more
9. 15 you and every living creature of all flesh
9. 15 no more become a flood to destroy all fle.
9. 16 and every living creature of all flesh that
9. 17 me and all flesh that (is) upon the earth

Gen. 17. 11 circumcise the flesh of your foreskin; and
17 13 my covenant shall be in your flesh for an
17. 14 man child whose flesh..is not circumcised
17. 23 circumcised the flesh of their foreskin in
17. 24, 25 when he was circumcised in the flesh
29. 14 Surely thou (art) my bone and my flesh
37. 27 for he (is) our brother (and) our flesh
40. 19 the birds shall eat thy flesh from off thee
Exod. 4. 7 it was turned again as his (other) flesh
12. 8 they shall eat the flesh in that night
12. 46 thou shalt not carry forth..flesh abroad
16. 3 when we sat by the flesh pots, (and) when
16. 8 the LORD shall give you..flesh to eat, and
16. 12 saying, At even ye shall eat flesh, and in
21. 28 and his flesh shall not be eaten ; but the
22. 31 neither shall ye eat (any) flesh (that is)
29. 14 flesh of the bullock..shalt thou burn with
29. 31 and seethe his flesh in the holy place
29. 32 Aaron and his sons shall eat the flesh of
29. 34 And if ought of the flesh..remain unto the
30. 32 Upon man's flesh shall it not be poured
Lev. 4. 11 and all his flesh, with his head, and with
6. 10 breeches shall he put upon his flesh, and
6. 27 Whatsoever shall touch the flesh thereof
7. 15, 18 the flesh of the sacrifice of his peace
7. 17 remainder of the flesh..shall be burnt
7. 19 the flesh that toucheth any unclean (thing)
7. 19 as for the flesh, all that be clean shall eat
7. 20, 21 flesh of the sacrifice of peace offerings
8. 17 But the bullock, and his hide, his flesh
8. 31 Boil the flesh (at) the door of the tabern.
8. 32 And that which remaineth of the flesh
9. 11 the flesh and the hide he burnt with fire
11. 8 Of their flesh shall ye not eat, and their
11. 11 ye shall not eat of their flesh, but ye shall
12. 3 flesh of his foreskin shall be circumcised
13. 2 shall have in the skin of his flesh a rising
13. 2 and it be in the skin of his flesh (like) the
13. 3 on the plague in the skin of the flesh
13. 3 (be) deeper than the skin of his flesh, it
13. 4 spot (be) white in the skin of his flesh
13. 10 (there be) quick raw flesh in the rising
13. 11 an old leprosy in the skin of his flesh
13. 13 the leprosy have covered all his flesh, he
13. 14 But when raw flesh appeareth in him, he
13. 15 And the priest shall see the raw flesh, and
13. 15 the raw flesh (is) unclean : it (is) a leprosy
13. 16 Or if the raw flesh turn again..he shall
13. 18 The flesh also, in which..was a boil, and
13. 24 Or if there be (any) flesh, in the skin
13. 38 in the skin of their flesh bright spots
13. 39 bright spots in the skin of their flesh
13. 43 the leprosy..in the skin of the flesh
14. 9 also he shall wash his flesh in water, and
15. 2 hath a running issue out of his flesh
15. 3 whether his flesh run..or his flesh be
15. 7 he that toucheth the flesh of him that
15. 13 shall..bathe his flesh in running water
15. 16 then he shall wash all his flesh in water
15. 19 if..her issue in her flesh be blood
16. 4 have the linen breeches upon his flesh
16. 4 therefore shall he wash his flesh in water
16. 24 he shall wash his flesh with water in the
16. 26, 28 And he..shall..bathe his flesh in wat.
16. 27 they shall burn in the fire..their flesh
17. 11 For the life of the flesh (is) in the blood
17. 14 For (it is) the life of all flesh ; the blood
17. 14 shall eat the blood of no manner of flesh
17. 14 for the life of all flesh (is) the blood the.
17. 16 if he wash (them) not, nor bathe his flesh
19. 28 any cuttings in your flesh for the dead
21. 5 nor make any cuttings in their flesh
22. 6 unless he wash his flesh with water
26. 29 eat the flesh of your sons, and the flesh
Num. 8. 7 and let them shave all their flesh, and
11. 4 and said, Who shall give us flesh to eat?
11 13 Whence should I have flesh to give unto
11. 13 saying, Give us flesh, that we may eat
11. 18 ye shall eat flesh : for ye have wept in
11. 18 saying, Who shall give us flesh to eat?
11. 18 therefore the LORD will give you flesh, and
11. 21 thou hast said, I will give them flesh
11. 33 the flesh (was) yet between their teeth
12 12 of whom the flesh is half consumed when
16. 22 the God of the spirits of all flesh, shall
18. 15 that openeth the matrix in all flesh
18. 18 the flesh of them shall be thine, as the
19. 5 her skin, and her flesh, and her blood
19. 7 and he shall bathe his flesh in water
19. 8 And he..shall ..bathe his flesh in water
27 16 God of the spirits of all flesh, set a man
Deut. 5. 26 who (is there of) all flesh, that hath heard
12. 15 thou mayest..eat flesh in all thy gates
12. 20 thou shalt say, I will eat flesh, because
12. 20 longeth to eat flesh, thou mayest eat flesh
12. 23 mayest not eat the life with the flesh
12. 27 thou shalt offer..the flesh and..blood
12. 27 thy God, and thou shalt eat the flesh
14. 8 ye shall not eat of their flesh, nor touch
16. 4 neither shall..flesh..remain all night
28. 53 thou shalt eat..the flesh of thy sons and
28. 55 that he will not give..of the flesh of his
32. 42 and my sword shall devour flesh ; (and
Judg. 6. 19 the flesh he put in a basket, and he
6. 20 Take the flesh and the unleavened cakes
6. 21 Then the angel..touched the flesh and
6. 21 fire..consumed the flesh and the unleav.
8. 7 I will tear your flesh with the thorns
9. 2 also that I (am) your bone and your flesh
1 Sa 2. 13 while the flesh was in seething, with a
2. 15 said..Give flesh to roast for the priest
2. 15 he will not have sodden flesh of thee, but

1 Sa. 17. 44 I will give thy flesh unto the fowls of the
2 Sa. 5. 1 Behold, we (are) thy bone and thy flesh
19. 12 my brethren, ye (are) my bones and my fl.
19. 13 (Art) thou not of my bone, and of my fl.?
1 Ki. 17. 6 the ravens brought him bread and flesh
17. 6 bread and flesh in the evening ; and he
19. 21 boiled their flesh..and gave unto the pe.
21. 27 that he..put sackcloth upon his flesh, and
2 Ki. 4. 34 and the flesh of the child waxed warm
5. 10 and thy flesh shall come again to thee
5. 14 his flesh came again like unto the flesh of
6 30 (he had) sackcloth within upon his flesh
9. 36 shall dogs eat the flesh of Jezebel
1 Ch. 11. 1 Behold, we (are) thy bone and thy flesh
2 Ch. 32. 8 With him (is) an arm of flesh ; but with
Neh. 5. 5 our flesh (is) as the flesh of our brethren
Job 2. 5 touch his bone and his flesh, and he will
4. 15 passed before my face ; the hair of my fl.
6. 12 strength of stones? or (is) my flesh of br.?
7. 5 My flesh is clothed with worms and clods
10. 4 Hast thou eyes of flesh? or seest thou as
10. 11 Thou hast clothed me with skin and flesh
13. 14 Wherefore do I take my flesh in my teeth
14. 22 But his flesh upon him shall have pain
19. 20 My bone cleaveth..to my flesh, and I am
19. 22 and are not satisfied with my flesh?
19. 26 destroy this (body), yet in my flesh shall
21. 6 and trembling taketh hold on my flesh
31. 31 said not, Oh that we had of his flesh! we
33. 21 His flesh is consumed away, that it cannot
33. 25 His flesh shall be fresher than a child's
34. 15 All flesh shall perish together, and man
41. 23 The flakes of his flesh are joined together
Psa. 16. 9 my flesh also shall rest in hope
27. 2 came upon me to eat up my flesh, they
38. 3, 7 (There is) no soundness in my flesh
50. 13 Will I eat the flesh of bulls, or drink the
56. 4 I will not fear what flesh can do unto me
63. 1 my flesh longeth for thee in a dry..land
65. 2 hearest prayer, unto thee shall all flesh
78. 39 he remembered that they (were but) flesh
79. 2 the flesh of thy saints unto the beasts of
84. 2 and my flesh crieth out for the living God
109. 24 My knees are weak..my flesh faileth of
119. 120 My flesh trembleth for fear of thee ; and
136. 25 Who giveth food to all flesh : for his me.
145. 21 let all flesh bless his holy name for ever
Prov. 4. 22 For they (are)..health to all their flesh
5. 11 when thy flesh and thy body are consu.
14. 30 A sound heart (is) the life of the flesh
23. 20 Be not..among riotous eaters of flesh
Eccl. 4. 5 The fool..eateth his own flesh
5. 6 Suffer not thy mouth to cause thy flesh
11. 10 Therefore..put away evil from thy flesh
12. 12 and much study (is) a weariness of the fl.
Isa 9. 20 they shall eat every man the flesh of his
17. 4 and the fatness of his flesh shall wax
22. 13 killing sheep, eating flesh, and drinking
31. 3 and their horses flesh, and not spirit
40. 5 and all flesh shall see (it) together : for
40. 6 All flesh (is) grass, and all the goodliness
44. 16 with part thereof he eateth flesh ; he
44. 19 I have roasted flesh, and eaten (it) : and
49. 26 that oppress thee with their own flesh
49. 26 and all flesh shall know that I the LORD
58. 7 thou hide not thyself from thine own fl.?
65. 4 which eat swine's flesh, and broth of ab.
66. 16 sword will the LORD plead with all flesh
66. 17 eating swine's flesh, and the abomination
66. 23 shall all flesh come to worship before me
66. 24 they shall be an abhorring unto all flesh
Jer. 7. 21 Put..unto your sacrifices, and eat flesh
11. 15 and the holy flesh is passed from thee?
12. 12 end of the land : no flesh shall have peace
17. 5 trusteth in man, and maketh flesh his
19. 9 I will cause them to eat the flesh of their
19. 9 sons, and the flesh of their daughters
19. 9 they shall eat every one the flesh of his
25. 31 for the LORD..will plead with all flesh
32. 27 I (am) the LORD, the God of all flesh : is
45. 5 I will bring evil upon all flesh, saith the
Lam. 3. 4 My flesh and my skin hath he made old
Eze. 4. 14 neither came there abominable flesh into
11. 3 (city is) the caldron, and we (be) the flesh
11. 7 they (are) the flesh, and this (city is) the
11. 11 neither shall ye be the flesh in the midst
11. 19 will take the stony heart out of their fle.
11. 19 and will give them an heart of flesh
16. 26 Egyptians thy neighbours, great of flesh
20. 48 all flesh shall see that I the LORD have
21. 4 shall my sword go forth..against all flesh
21. 5 That all flesh may know that I the LORD
23. 20 whose flesh (is as) the flesh of asses, and
24. 10 consume the flesh, and spice it well, and
32. 5 I will lay thy flesh upon the mountains
36. 26 take..the stony heart out of your flesh
36. 26 and I will give you an heart of flesh
37. 6 And I will..bring up flesh upon you
37. 8 the sinews and the flesh came up upon
39. 17 That ye may eat flesh, and drink blood
39. 18 Ye shall eat the flesh of the mighty
40. 43 upon the tables (was) the flesh of the off.
44. 7 uncircumcised in flesh, to be in my sanc.
44. 9 No stranger..uncircumcised in flesh
Dan. 1. 15 fatter in flesh than all the children which
10. 3 neither came flesh nor wine in my mouth
Hos. 8. 13 They sacrifice flesh (for) the sacrifices of
Joel 2. 28 I will pour out my Spirit upon all flesh
Mic. 3. 3 and as flesh within the caldron
Hag. 2. 12 If one bear holy flesh in the skirt of his
Zech. 2. 13 Be silent, O all flesh, before the LORD
11. 9 let the rest eat every one the flesh of

Zech 11. 16 he shall eat the flesh of the fat, and
14. 12 Their flesh shall consume away while they

2. *Flesh*, בְּשַׂר *besar.*

Dan. 2. 11 the gods, whose dwelling is not with fle
4. 12 meat for all..and all flesh was fed of it
7. 5 and they said..Arise, devour much flesh

3. *Slaughtered food*, טִבְחָה *tibchah.*

1 Sa. 25. 11 my flesh that I have killed for my shear.

4. *Flesh, meat, food*, לְחוּם *lechum.*

Zeph. 1. 17 blood..as dust, and their flesh as the d.

5. *Flesh, (remainder, remains)*, שְׁאֵר *sheer.*

Psa. 73. 26 My flesh and my heart faileth..God (is)
78. 20 Behold..can he provide flesh for his pe.?
78. 27 He rained flesh also upon them as dust
Prov. 11. 17 but (he that is) cruel troubleth his own
Jer. 51. 35 The violence done to me and to my flesh
Mic. 3. 2 and their flesh from off their bones
3. 3 Who also eat the flesh of my people, and

6. *Flesh, meat*, κρέας *kreas.*

Rom. 14. 21 good neither to eat flesh, nor to drink w.
1 Co. 8. 13 I will eat no flesh while the world stand

7. *Flesh*, σάρξ *sarx.*

Matt 16. 17 flesh and blood hath not revealed (it)
19. 5 And said..and they twain shall be one fl.?
19. 6 they are no more twain, but one flesh
24. 22 there should no flesh be saved : but for
26. 41 the spirit..(is) willing, but the flesh (is)
Mark 10. 8 And they twain shall be one flesh : so
10. 8 they are no more twain, but one flesh
13. 20 no flesh should be saved : but for the
14. 38 The spirit..(is) ready, but the flesh (is)
Luke 3. 6 all flesh shall see the salvation of God
24. 39 for a spirit hath not flesh and bones, as
John 1. 13 nor of the will of the flesh, nor of the will
1. 14 the Word was made flesh, and dwelt
3. 6 That which is born of the flesh is flesh
6. 51 the bread that I will give is my flesh
6. 52 How can this man give us (his) flesh to
6. 53 Except ye eat the flesh of the Son of man
6. 54 Whoso eateth my flesh..hath eternal life
6. 55 my flesh is meat indeed, and my blood is
6. 56 He that eateth my flesh..dwelleth in me
6. 63 the flesh profiteth nothing : the words
8. 15 Ye judge after the flesh ; I judge no man
17. 2 thou hast given him power over all flesh
Acts 2. 17 I will pour out of my Spirit upon all fle.
2. 26 moreover also my flesh shall rest in hope
2. 30 [according to the flesh, he would raise]
2. 31 neither his flesh did see corruption
Rom. 1. 3 of the seed of David according to the fle.
2. 28 circumcision which is outward in the fl.
3. 20 there shall no flesh be justified in his
4. 1 our father, as pertaining to the flesh
6. 19 because of the infirmity of your flesh
7. 5 when we were in the flesh, the motions of
7. 18 that in me that is, in my flesh, dwelleth
7. 25 but with the flesh the law of sin
8. 1 [to them..who walk not after the flesh]
8. 3 in that it was weak through the flesh
8. 3 likeness of sinful flesh..sin in the flesh
8. 4 in us, who walk not after the flesh, but
8. 5 after the flesh do mind..things of the fle.
8. 8 they that are in the flesh cannot please
8. 9 ye are not in the flesh, but in the Spirit
8. 12 not to the flesh, to live after the flesh
8. 13 if ye live after the flesh, ye shall die
9. 3 for..my kinsmen according to the flesh
9. 5 of whom as concerning the flesh Christ
9. 8 They which are the children of the flesh
11 14 I may provoke to emulation..my flesh
13. 14 and make not provision for the flesh
1 Co. 1. 26 that not many wise men after the flesh
1. 29 That no flesh should glory in his presence
5. 5 for the destruction of the flesh, that the
6. 16 for two, saith he, shall be one flesh
7. 28 such shall have trouble in the flesh : but
10. 18 Behold Israel after the flesh : are not
15. 39 All flesh (is) not the same flesh : but
15. 39 but..one..[flesh] of men, another [flesh]
15. 50 flesh and blood cannot inherit the kingd.
2 Co. 1. 17 do I purpose according to the flesh, that
4. 11 might be made manifest in our mortal fl.
5. 16 henceforth know we no man after the fl.
5. 16 we have known Christ after the flesh
7. 1 from all filthiness of the flesh and spirit
7. 5 when we were come..our flesh had no
10. 2 as if we walked according to the flesh
10. 3 the flesh, we do not war after the flesh
11. 18 Seeing that many glory after the flesh
12. 7 there was given to me a thorn in the fle.
Gal. 1. 16 I conferred not with flesh and blood
2. 16 for by..the law shall no flesh be justified
2. 20 the life which I now live in the flesh I
3. 3 are ye now made perfect by the flesh?
4. 13 through infirmity of the flesh I preached
4. 14 my temptation which was in my flesh ye
4. 23 was born after the flesh ; but he of the
4. 29 as then he that was born after the flesh
5. 13 not liberty for an occasion to the flesh
5. 16 ye shall not fulfil the lust of the flesh
5. 17 For the flesh lusteth against the Spirit
5. 17 and the Spirit against the flesh : and
5. 19 Now the works of the flesh are manifest
5. 24 have crucified the flesh with the affect.
6. 8 that soweth to his flesh shall of the flesh
6. 12 as desire to make a fair show in the flesh
6. 13 but..that they may glory in your flesh
Eph. 2. 3 conversation..in the lusts of our flesh

Eph. 2. 3 fulfilling the desires of the flesh and of
2. 11 (being) in time past Gentiles in the flesh
2. 11 the Circumcision in the flesh made by
2. 15 Having abolished in his flesh the enmity
5. 29 For no man ever yet hated his own flesh
5. 30 [For we are members..of his flesh]
5. 31 his wife, and they two shall be one flesh
6. 5 that are..masters according to the flesh
6. 12 we wrestle not against flesh and blood
Phil. 1. 22 if I live in the flesh, this (is) the fruit of
1. 24 Nevertheless to abide in the flesh (is)
3. 3 For we..have no confidence in the flesh
3. 4 I might..have confidence in the flesh
3. 4 hath whereof he might trust in the flesh
Col. 1. 22 In the body of his flesh through death, to
1. 24 afflictions..in my flesh for his body's
2. 1 as have not seen my face in the flesh
2. 5 For though I be absent in the flesh, yet
2. 11 in putting off..the sins of the flesh by
2. 13 and the uncircumcision of your flesh
2. 23 any honour to the satisfying of the flesh
3. 22 obey..masters according to the flesh
1 Ti. 3. 16 God was manifest in the flesh, justified
Phm. 16 a brother..in the flesh, and in the Lord?
Heb. 2. 14 as the children are partakers of flesh and
5. 7 Who in the days of his flesh, when he
9. 13 sanctifieth to the purifying of the flesh
10. 20 through the veil, that is to say, his flesh
12. 9 we have had fathers of our flesh which
Jas. 5. 3 and shall eat your flesh as it were fire
1 Pe. 1. 24 For all flesh (is) as grass, and all the glo.
3. 18 Christ..being put to death in the flesh
3. 21 the putting away of the filth of the flesh
4. 1 Christ hath suffered for us in the flesh
4. 1 for he that hath suffered in the flesh
4. 2 live the rest of (his) time in the flesh
4. 6 be judged according to men in the flesh
2 Pe. 2. 10 chiefly them that walk after the flesh in
2. 18 they allure through the lusts of the flesh
1 Jo. 2. 16 the lust of the flesh, and the lust of the
4. 2, 3 that Jesus Christ is come in the flesh
2 Jo. 7 that Jesus Christ is come in the flesh
Jude 7 and the cities..going after strange flesh
8 these (filthy) dreamers defile the flesh
23 even the garment spotted by the flesh
Rev. 17. 16 shall eat her flesh, and burn her with
19. 18 flesh of kings, and the flesh of captains
19. 18 the flesh of mighty men, and the flesh of
19. 18 the flesh of all (men, both) free and bond
19. 21 all the fowls were filled with their flesh

FLESH hook —

1. *Hook, fork,* מַזְלֵג *mazleg.*
1 Sa. 2. 13 a flesh hook of three teeth in his hand
2. 14 all that the flesh hook brought up the

2. *Hooks, forks,* מִזְלָגוֹת *mizlagoth.*
Exod27. 3 and his flesh hooks, and his fire pans
38. 3 (and) the flesh hooks, and the fire pans
Num. 4. 14 the flesh hooks, and the shovels, and the
1 Ch. 28. 17 gold for the flesh hooks, and the bowls
2 Ch. 4. 16 the flesh hooks, and all their instruments

FLESHLY, fleshy —

1. *Fleshly, fleshlike,* σαρκικός *sarkikos.*
2 Co. 1. 12 not with fleshly wisdom, but by the grace
1 Pe. 2. 11 abstain from fleshly lusts, which war aga.

2. *Of flesh,* σάρκινος *sarkinos.*
2 Co. 3. 3 not in tables of stone, but in fleshy tables

3. *Flesh,* σάρξ *sarx.*
Col. 2. 18 vainly puffed up by his fleshly mind

FLIES, divers sorts of —

Beetle, dog fly, עָרֹב *arob.*
Psa. 78. 45 He sent divers sorts of flies among them
105. 31 there came divers sorts of flies, (and) lice

FLIETH, that —

Flying fowl or bird, עוֹף *oph.*
Deut14. 19 And every creeping thing that flieth (is)

FLIGHT —

1. *Flight,* מָנוֹס *manos.*
Amos 2. 14 the flight shall perish from the swift

2. *Flight,* מְנוּסָה *menusah.*
Isa. 52. 12 not go out with haste, nor go by flight

3. *Flight,* φυγή *phugē.*
Matt 24. 20 that your flight be not in the winter
Mark13. 18 that [your flight] be not in the winter

FLIGHT, to put to —

1. *To cause to flee,* בָּרַח *barach,* 5.
1 Ch.12. 15 put to flight all (them) of the valleys

2. *To cause to flee,* נוּס *nus,* 5.
Deut32. 30 two put ten thousand to flight, except

3. *To pursue,* רָדַף *radaph.*
Lev. 26. 8 you shall put ten thousand to flight

FLINT —

1. *Flint,* חַלָּמִישׁ *challamish.*
Deut. 8. 15 brought..water out of the rock of flint
Psa.114. 8 turned..the flint into a fountain of waters
Isa. 50. 7 therefore have I set my face like a flint

2. *Rock,* צֹר *tsor.*
Eze. 3. 9 harder than flint have I made thy forehe.

FLINTY —

Flint, חַלָּמִישׁ *challamish.*
Deut32. 13 to suck..oil out of the flinty rock

FLOATS —

Floats or rafts (of timber), דֹּבְרוֹת *dobroth.*
1 Ki. 5. 9 I will convey them by sea in floats unto

FLOCK —

1. *Cattle, acquisition,* מִקְנֶה *miqneh.*
Num32. 26 our flocks, and all our cattle, shall be

2. *Flock, drove, herd,* עֵדֶר *eder.*
Gen. 29. 2 (were) three flocks of sheep lying by it
29. 2 out of that well they watered the flocks
29. 3 And thither were all the flocks gathered
29. 8 until all the flocks be gathered together
30. 40 he put his own flocks by themselves, and
Judg. 5. 16 to hear the bleatings of the flocks?
1 Sa. 17. 34 a bear, and took a lamb out of the flock
2 Ch.32. 28 all manner of beasts, and cotes for flocks
Job 24. 2 they violently take away flocks, and feed
Psa. 78. 52 guided them in..wilderness like a flock
Song 1. 7 turneth..by the flocks of thy companions
4. 1 thy hair (is) as a flock of goats, that
4. 2 like a flock (of sheep that are even) shorn
6. 5 thy hair (is) as a flock of goats that
6. 6 as a flock of sheep which go up from the
Isa. 17. 2 they shall be for flocks, which shall lie
32. 14 a joy of wild asses, a pasture of flocks
40. 11 He shall feed his flock like a shepherd
Jer. 6. 3 shepherds with their flocks shall come
13. 17 the LORD'S flock is carried away captive
13. 20 where (is) the flock (that) was given thee
31. 10 keep him, as a shepherd (doth) his flock
31. 24 and they (that) go forth with flocks
51. 23 also break..the shepherd and his flock
Eze. 34. 12 As a shepherd seeketh out his flock in
Joel 1. 18 yea, the flocks of sheep are made desolate
Mic. 2. 12 as the flock in the midst of their fold
4. 8 O tower of the flock, the strong hold of
5. 8 as a young lion among the flocks of sheep
Zeph. 2. 14 flocks shall lie down in the midst of her
Zech.10. 3 hath visited his flock the house of Judah
Mal. 1. 14 which hath in his flock a male, and vow.

3. *Sheep, flock,* צֹאן *tson.*
Gen. 4. 4 brought of the firstlings of his flock
13. 5 Lot also..had flocks, and herds, and tents
21. 28 set seven ewe lambs of the flock by thems.
24. 35 he hath given him flocks, and herds, and
26. 14 he had possession of flocks, and possession
27. 9 Go now to the flock, and fetch me from
29. 2 there (were) three flocks of sheep lying by
29. 10 the flock of Laban his mother's brother
30. 31 I will again feed (and) keep thy flock
30. 32 I will pass through all thy flock to day
30. 36 and Jacob fed the rest of Laban's flocks
30. 38 which he had pilled before the flocks in
30. 38 when the flocks came to drink, that they
30. 39 the flocks conceived before the rods, and
30. 40 set the faces of the flocks toward the
30. 40 and all the brown in the flock of Laban
31. 4 called Rachel and Leah..unto his flock
31. 38 the rams of thy flock have I not eaten
32. 5 I have oxen, and asses, flocks, and men
32. 7 the flocks, and herds, and the camels
33. 13 flocks and herds with young (are) with
33. 13 overdrive them..all the flock will die
37. 2 was feeding the flock with his brethren
37. 12 to feed their father's flock in Shechem
37. 14 see whether it be well..with the flocks
38. 17 I will send (thee) a kid from the flock
45. 10 thy flocks, and thy herds and all that
46. 32 they have brought their flocks, and their
47. 1 and their flocks, and their herds, and all
47. 4 servants have no pasture for their flocks
47. 17 the flocks [Heb. *miqneh tson, possession*
50. 8 their flocks, and their herds [*of flocks*]
Exod. 2. 16 the troughs to water their father's flock
2. 17 and helped them, and watered their flock
2. 19 (water) enough for us, and watered the fl.
3. 1 the flock of Jethro his father in law
3. 1 the flock to the backside of the desert
10. 9 We will go..with our flocks and with
10. 24 let your flocks and your herds be stayed
12. 32 Also take your flocks and your herds, as
12. 38 flocks, and herds..very much cattle
34. 3 neither let the flocks nor herds feed bef.
Lev 1. 2 the cattle..of the herd, and of the flock
1. 10 And if his offering (be) of the flocks
3. 6 And if his offering..(be) of the flock
5. 6 a female from the flock, a lamb or a kid
5. 15, 18 a ram without blemish out of the flo.
6. 6 a ram without blemish out of the flock
27. 32 And concerning the tithe of..the flock
Num 11. 22 Shall the flocks and the herds be slain
15. 3 to make a sweet savour..of the flock
31. 30 take one portion of fifty..of the flocks
Deut. 8. 13 And..thy herds and thy flocks multiply
12. 6 firstlings of your herds and of your flocks
12. 17 firstlings of thy herds, or of thy flock
12. 21 then thou shalt kill..of thy flock, which
14. 23 firstlings of thy herds and of thy flocks
15. 14 Thou shalt furnish him..out of thy flock
15. 19 and of thy flock thou shalt sanctify unto
16. 2 Thou shalt..sacrifice..of the flock and
1 Sa. 30. 20 David took all the flocks and the herds
2 Sa. 12. 2 The rich..had exceeding many flocks and
12. 4 he spared to take of his own flock, and of
1 Ch. 4. 39 they went..to seek pasture for their flo.
4. 41 (there was) pasture there for their flocks
27. 31 over the flocks (was) Jaziz the Hagarite
2 Ch.17. 11 and the Arabians brought him flocks
32. 29 and possessions of flocks and herds in
35. 7 Josiah gave to the people, of the flock

Ezra 10. 19 a ram of the flock for their tresspass
Neh. 10. 36 firstlings of our herds and of our flocks
Job 21. 11 send forth their little ones like a flock
30. 1 to have set with the dogs of my flock
Psa. 65. 13 The pastures are clothed with flocks
77. 20 Thou leddst thy people like a flock by
80. 1 thou that leadest Joseph like a flock
107. 41 and maketh (him) families like a flock
Prov 27. 23 diligent to know the state of thy flocks
Song 1. 8 go..forth by the footsteps of the flock
Isa. 60. 7 the flocks..shall be gathered together
61. 5 And strangers shall..feed your flocks
63. 11 of the sea with the shepherd of his flock?
65. 10 And Sharon shall be a fold of flocks
Jer. 3. 24 their flocks and their herds, their sons
5. 17 they shall eat up thy flocks and thine
13. 20 where (is)..thy beautiful flock?
23. 2 Ye have scattered my flock, and driven
23. 3 I will gather the remnant of my flock
25. 34 wallow yourselves..ye principal of the fl.
25. 35 nor the principal of the flock to escape
25. 36 an howling of the principal of the flock
31. 12 for the young of the flock and of the herd
33. 12 shepherds causing (their) flocks to lie do.
33. 13 shall the flocks pass again under the ha.
49. 20 Surely the least of the flock shall draw
49. 29 and their flocks shall they take away
50. 8 and be as the he goats before the flocks
50. 45 Surely the least of the flock shall draw
Eze. 24. 5 Take the choice of the flock, and burn
25. 5 the Ammonites a couching place for flo.
34. 2 should not the shepherds feed the flocks?
34. 3 ye eat the fat..ye feed not the flock
34. 6 my flock was scattered upon all the face
34. 8 my flock became a prey, and my flock b.
34. 8 search for my flock..fed not my flock
34. 10 I will require my flock at their hand
34. 10 cause..to cease from feeding the flock
34. 10 I will deliver my flock from their mouth
34. 15 I will feed my flock, and I will cause
34. 17 O my flock, thus saith the LORD God
34. 19 my flock, they eat that which ye have
34. 22 Therefore will I save my flock, and they
34. 31 And ye my flock, the flock of my pasture
36. 37 I will increase them with men like a flock
36. 38 As the holy flock, as the flock of Jerusalem
36. 38 so shall..waste cities be filled with flocks
43. 23, 25 a ram out of the flock, without blem.
45. 15 one lamb out of the flock, out of two hu.
Hos. 5. 6 They shall go with their flocks and with
Amos 6. 4 and eat the lambs out of the flock
7. 15 the LORD took me as I followed the flock
Jon. 3. 7 Let neither..herd nor flock, taste any
Mic. 7. 14 Feed..the flock of thine heritage, which
Hab. 3. 17 the flock shall be cut off from the fold
Zeph. 2. 6 the sea coast shall be..folds for flocks
Zech. 9. 16 save them..as the flock of his people
10. 2 therefore they went their way as a flock
11. 4 saith..Feed the flock of the slaughter
11. 7 And I will feed the flock of slaughter
11. 7 O poor of the flock..And I fed the flock
11. 11 the poor of the flock that waited upon me
11. 17 the idol shepherd that leaveth the flock!

4. *A flock,* ποίμνη *poimnē.*
Matt26. 31 the sheep of the flock shall be scattered
Luke 2. 8 keeping watch over their flock by night
1 Co. 9. 7 a flock, and eateth not of..the flock?

5. *A little flock,* ποίμνιον *poimnion.*
Luke12. 32 Fear not, little flock; for it is your
Acts20. 28 Take heed therefore..to all the flock
20. 29 grievous wolves..not sparing the flock
1 Pe. 5. 2 Feed the flock of God which is among you
5. 3 lords..but being ensamples to the flock

FLOCK, little —

A bare or exposed flock, חָשִׂף *chasiph.*
1 Ki.20. 27 pitched..like two little flocks of kids

FLOCKS —

1. *Pasturing, feeding flock,* מַרְעִית *marith.*
Jer. 10. 21 and all their flocks shall be scattered

2. *Multiplications,* עַשְׁתָּרוֹת *ashtaroth.*
Deut. 7. 13 he will..bless..the flocks of thy sheep
28. 4 Blessed (shall be)..the flocks of thy sheep
28. 18 Cursed (shall be)..the flocks of thy sheep
28. 51 shall not leave thee..flocks of thy sheep

FLOOD —

1. *A brook, flood,* אֹר *or.*
Amos 8. 8 and it shall rise up wholly as a flood

2. *Inundation, flood, storm,* זֶרֶם *zerem.*
Isa. 28. 2 as a flood of mighty waters overflowing

3. *A brook, flood,* יְאֹר *yeor.*
Jer. 46. 7 Who (is) this (that) cometh up as a flood
46. 8 Egypt riseth up like a flood, and (his) w.
Amos 8. 8 it shall be..drowned, as (by) the flood of
9. 5 and it shall rise up wholly like a flood
9. 5 and shall be drowned, as (by) the flood of

4. *A flood, deluge,* מַבּוּל *mabbul.*
Gen. 6. 17 behold, I, even I, do bring a flood of wa.
7. 6 when the flood of waters was upon the e
7. 7 ark, because of the waters of the flood
7. 10 waters of the flood were upon the earth
7. 17 the flood was forty days upon the earth
9. 11 cut off any more by the waters of a flood
9. 11 neither shall there any more be a flood to
9. 15 the waters shall no more become a flood
9. 28 And Noah lived after the flood three
10. 1 unto them were sons born after the flood

Gen. 10. 32 divided in the earth after the flood
11. 10 begat Arphaxad two years after the flood
Psa. 29. 10 The LORD sitteth upon the flood; yea

5. *A river*, נָהָר *nahar*.
Josh. 24. 2 dwelt on the other side of the flood in
24. 3 Abraham from the other side of the flood
24. 14 served on the other side of the flood
24. 15 that (were) on the other side of the flood
Job 14. 11 and the flood decayeth and drieth up
20. 17 He shall not see the rivers, the floods
22. 16 foundation was overflown with a flood
28. 11 He bindeth the floods from overflowing
Psa. 24. 2 For he..established it upon the floods
66. 6 they went through the flood on foot
93. 3 The floods have lifted up, O LORD
93. 3 the floods have lifted up their voice
93. 3 the floods lift up their waves
98. 8 Let the floods clap..hands: let the hills
Song 8. 7 neither can the floods drown it: if a man
Isa. 59. 19 When the enemy shall come in like a flood
Eze. 31. 15 I restrained the floods thereof, and the
Jon. 2. 3 the floods compassed me about: all thy

6. *To flow*, נָזַל *nazal*.
Exod. 15. 8 the floods stood upright as an heap
Psa. 78. 44 their floods, that they could not drink
Isa. 44. 3 I will pour..floods upon the dry ground

7. *A brook*, נַחַל *nachal*.
2 Sa. 22. 5 floods of ungodly men made me afraid
Job 28. 4 The flood breaketh out from the inhabi.
Psa. 18. 4 floods of ungodly men made me afraid
74. 15 didst cleave the fountain and the flood
Jer. 47. 2 waters..shall be an overflowing flood

8. *Flood, stream*, שִׁבֹּלֶת *shibboleth*.
Psa. 69. 2 waters, where the floods overflow me
69. 15 Let not the water flood overflow me

9. *Overflowing, flood*, שֶׁטֶף, שֵׁטֶף *sheteph*.
Psa. 32. 6 surely in the floods of great waters they
Dan. 9. 26 and the end thereof..with a flood, and
11. 22 with the arms of a flood shall they be ov.
Nah. 1. 8 with an overrunning flood he will make

10. *Deluge, washing down*, κατακλυσμός *kataklu.*
Matt 24. 38 in the days that were before the flood
24. 39 knew not until the flood came, and took
Luke 17. 27 the flood came, and destroyed them all
2 Pe. 2. 5 bringing in the flood upon the world of

11. *Flood tide, full flowing*, πλημμύρα *plēmmura.*
Luke 6. 48 when the flood arose, the stream beat

12. *River flood, stream*, ποταμός *potamos*.
Matt. 7. 25 the rain descended, and the floods came
7. 27 the rain descended, and the floods came
Rev. 12. 15 the serpent cast out..water as a flood
12. 16 the flood which the dragon cast out of his

FLOOD, carried away of the —
Borne on by the stream, ποταμοφόρητος *potamoph.*
Rev. 12. 15 cause her to be carried away of the flood

FLOOR —
1. *Threshing floor, forum*, גֹּרֶן *goren*.
Gen. 50. 11 saw the mourning in the floor of Atad
Deut 15. 14 Thou shalt furnish him..out of thy floor
Judg. 6. 37 I will put a fleece of wool in the floor
Ruth 3. 3 Wash..and get thee down to the floor
3. 6 And she went down unto the floor, and
3. 14 known that a woman came into the floor
Isa. 21. 10 O my threshing, and the corn of my floor
Hos. 9. 1 hast loved a reward upon every corn flo.
9. 2 The floor..shall not feed them, and the
13. 3 chaff (that) is driven..out of the floor, and
Joel 2. 24 floors shall be full of wheat, and the fats
Mic. 4. 12 for he shall gather them..into the floor

2. *Floor, bottom*, קַרְקַע *qarqa*.
Num. 5. 17 of the dust that is in the floor of the
1 Ki. 6. 15 he built..both the floor of the house, and
6. 15 covered the floor of the house with planks
6. 16 he built..both the floor and the walls
6. 30 the floor of the house he overlaid with

3. *Floor, barn*, ἅλων *halōn*.
Matt. 3. 12 and he will throughly purge his floor
Luke 3. 17 he will throughly purge his floor, and
[*See also* Barn floor, corn floor, threshing floor.]

FLOOR, to —
To join, cause to meet, קָרָה *qarah*, 3.
2 Ch. 34. 11 and to floor the houses which the kings

FLOOR, one side of the —
Floor, bottom, קַרְקַע *qarqa*.
1 Ki. 7. 7 with cedar from one side of the floor to

FLOTES —
Floats, rafts, רַפְסֹדוֹת *raphsodoth*.
2 Ch. 2. 16 we will bring it to thee in flotes by sea to

FLOUR —
1. *Dough*, בָּצֵק *batseq*.
2 Sa. 13. 8 she took flour, and kneaded (it), and made

2. *Fine crushed flour*, סֹלֶת *soleth*.
Exod 29. 2 (of) wheaten flour shalt thou make them
29. 40 a tenth deal of flour mingled with the fo.
Lev. 2. 2 and he shall take..of the flour thereof
6. 15 he shall take..of the flour of the meat
Num 15. 4 a tenth deal of flour mingled with the
15. 6, 9 tenth deals of flour mingled with
28. 5 a tenth (part) of an ephah of flour for a
28. 9 two tenth deals of flour..mingled with
28. 12, 12 tenth deals of flour (for) a meat offer.
Num 28. 13 a several tenth deal of flour mingled with
28. 20 meat offering (shall be of) flour mingled
28. 28 their meat offering of flour mingled with
29. 3, 9, 14 meat offering (shall be of) flour mi.

3. *Rubbed grain, meal*, קֶמַח *qemach*.
Judg. 6. 19 unleavened cakes of an ephah of flour
1 Sa. 1. 24 she took..one ephah of flour, and a bottle
28. 24 and she..took flour, and kneaded (it), and
2 Sa. 17. 28 Brought beds..and barley, and flour, and

FLOUR, fine —
Fine flour, (*Lat. simila, similago*,) σεμίδαλις.
Rev. 18. 13 and fine flour, and wheat, and beasts, and

FLOURISH, to —
1. *To flourish* (*become despised?*) נָאַץ *naats*, 5.
Eccl. 12. 5 the almond tree shall flourish, and the

2. *To break forth, flourish*, פָּרַח *parach*.
Psa. 72. 7 In his days shall the righteous flourish
92. 12 The righteous shall flourish like the palm
Prov 11. 28 the righteous shall flourish as a branch
Song 6. 11 (and) to see whether the vine flourished
7. 12 let us see if the vine flourish, (whether)
Isa. 66. 14 your bones shall flourish like an herb

3. *To (cause to) flourish*, פָּרַח *parach*, 5.
Psa. 92. 13 Those..shall flourish in the courts of our
Prov. 14. 11 tabernacle of the upright shall flourish

4. *To blossom, flourish*, צוּץ *tsuts*, 5.
Psa. 72. 16 (they)..shall flourish like grass of the ea.
90. 6 In the morning it flourisheth, and growe.
92. 7 all the workers of iniquity do flourish
103. 15 as a flower of the field, so he flourisheth
132. 18 upon himself shall his crown flourish

FLOURISH, to make to —
To cause to break forth or flourish, פָּרַח *parach*, 5.
Isa. 17. 11 shalt thou make thy seed to flourish
Eze. 17. 24 and have made the dry tree to flourish

FLOURISH again, to —
To flourish, or shoot up again, ἀναθάλλω *anathal.*
Phil. 4. 10 your care of me hath flourished again

FLOURISHING —
1. *Fresh, flourishing*, רַעֲנָן *raanan*.
Psa. 92. 14 they shall be fat and flourishing

2. *Fresh, flourishing*, רַעֲנַן *raanan*.
Dan. 4. 4 Nebuchadnezzar was..flourishing in my

FLOW, to —
1. *To flow, issue*, זוּב *zub*.
Exod. 3. 8, 17 land flowing with milk and honey
[So in 13. 5; 33. 3; Lev. 20. 24; Num. 13. 27; 14. 8; 16.
13, 14; Deut. 6. 3; 11. 9; 26. 9, 15; 27. 3; 31. 20; Josh.
5. 6, Jer. 11. 5; 32. 22; Ezek. 20. 6, 15.]
Jer. 49. 4 Wherefore gloriest thou in..thy flowing

2. *To go on*, יְלַךְ *yalak*.
Josh. 4. 18 the waters..flowed over all his banks, as
Joel 3. 18 the hills shall flow with milk, and all the
3. 18 rivers of Judah shall flow with waters

3. *To flow, become bright*, נָהַר *nahar*.
Isa. 2. 2 above the hills; and all nations shall flow
Mic. 4. 1 above the hills; and people shall flow

4. *To flow*, נָזַל *nazal*.
Psa. 147. 18 causeth..to blow, (and) the waters flow

5. *To flow, overflow*, צוּף *tsuph*.
Lam. 3. 54 Waters flowed over mine head; (then) I

6. *To flow*, ῥέω *rheō*.
John 7. 38 out of his belly shall flow rivers of living

FLOW away, to —
To be poured out, spread out, נָגַר *nagar*, 2.
Job 20. 28 shall flow away in the day of his wrath

FLOW, to cause to —
To cause to flow, נָזַל *nazal*, 5.
Isa. 48. 21 caused the waters to flow out of the rock

FLOW down, to —
To flow, tremble, זָלַל *zalal*, 2.
Isa. 64. 1 that the mountains might flow down at
64. 3 mountains flowed down at thy presence

FLOW out, to —
To flow, flow on, נָזַל *nazal*.
Song 4. 16 (that) the spices thereof may flow out

FLOW together, to —
To flow, become bright, נָהַר *nahar*.
Isa. 60. 5 Then thou shalt see, and flow together
Jer. 31. 12 they shall come..and shall flow together
51. 44 nations shall not flow together any more

FLOWER —
1. *Tower, towering plant*, מִגְדָּל *migdal*.
Song 5. 13 His cheeks (are)..(as) sweet flowers; his

2. *Blossom, flower*, נִצָּה *nitsah*.
Job 15. 33 and shall cast off his flower as the olive
Isa. 18. 5 the sour grape is ripening in the flower

3. *Blossom, flower*, נִצָּן *nitsan*.
Song 2. 12 The flowers appear on the earth; the ti.

4. *Flower, flourishing*, פֶּרַח *perach*.
Exod 25. 31 and his flowers, shall be of the same
25. 33 (with) a knop and a flower in one branch
25. 33 and three bowls..(with) a knop and a fl.
25. 34 bowls..(with) their knops and their flow.
Exod 37. 17 knops, and his flowers, were of the same
37. 19 in one branch, a knop and a flower
37. 19 and three bowls..a knop and a flower: so
37. 20 four bowls..his knops, and his flowers
Num. 8. 4 unto the flowers thereof, (was) beaten
1 Ki. 7. 26 brim..was wrought..with flowers of lilies
7. 49 with the flowers, and the lamps, and the
2 Ch. 4. 5 and the brim..with flowers of lilies
4. 21 the flowers, and the lamps, and the tongs
Nah. 1. 4 and the flower of Lebanon languisheth

5. *Blossom, flower*, צִיץ *tsits*.
1 Ki. 6. 18 carved with knops and open flowers: all
6. 29 palm trees and open flowers, within and
6. 32 carved upon them carvings of..flowers
6. 35 And he carved (thereon)..open flowers
Job 14. 2 He cometh forth like a flower, and is cut
Psa. 103. 15 as a flower of the field, so he flourisheth
Isa. 28. 1 whose glorious beauty (is) a fading flower
40. 6 all the goodliness thereof (is) as the flower
40. 7, 8 The grass withereth, the flower fadeth

6. *Blossom, flower*, צִיצָה *tsitsah*.
Isa. 28. 4 glorious beauty..shall be a fading flower

7. *A flower*, ἄνθος *anthos*.
Jas. 1. 10 because as the flower..he shall pass away
1. 11 and the flower thereof falleth, and the
1 Pe. 1. 24 the glory of man as the flower of grass
1. 24 and the flower thereof falleth away

FLOWER of one's age, to pass the —
To be beyond the point, εἰμὶ ὑπέρακμος. [*eimi*].
1 Co. 7. 36 if she pass the flower of (her) age, and

FLOWER of their age, in the —
Men, אֲנוֹשִׁים *enoshim*.
1 Sa. 2. 33 all..shall die in the flower of their age

FLOWERS —
Impurity, separation, נִדָּה *niddah*.
Lev. 15. 24 lie with her..and her flowers be upon him
15. 33 of her that is sick of her flowers, and of

FLOWING —
1. *To send or flow forth*, נָבַע *naba*.
Prov 18. 4 wellspring of wisdom (as) a flowing brook

2. *To flow*, נָזַל *nazal*.
Jer. 18. 14 shall the cold flowing waters that come

3. *To overflow*, שָׁטַף *shataph*.
Isa. 66. 12 the glory of the Gentiles like a flowing

FLUTE —
Flute, pipe, reed, מַשְׁרוֹקִיתָא *mashroqitha*.
Dan. 3. 5, 15 ye hear the sound of the cornet, flute
3. 7 the people heard the sound of the..flute
3. 10 that shall hear the sound of the..flute

FLUTTER, to —
To move, flutter, shake, רָחַף *rachaph*, 3.
Deut. 32. 11 As an eagle..fluttereth over her young

FLUX —
Dysentery, δυσεντερία *dusenteria*.
Acts 28. 8 the father..lay sick..of a bloody flux

FLY —
Fly, זְבוּב *zebub*.
Eccl. 10. 1 Dead flies cause the ointment..to send
Isa. 7. 18 the LORD shall hiss for the fly that (is) in

FLY, to —
1. *To use the wing*, אָבַר *abar*, 5.
Job 39. 26 Doth the hawk fly by thy wisdom

2. *To fly*, דָּאָה *daah*.
Deut 28. 49 the end of the earth..as the eagle flieth
Psa. 18. 10 he did fly upon the wings of the wind
Jer. 48. 40 he shall fly as an eagle, and shall spread
49. 22 he shall come up and fly as the eagle

3. *To fly*, עוּף *uph*.
Deut. 4. 17 of any winged fowl that flieth in the air
2 Sa. 22. 11 And he rode upon a cherub, and did fly
Job 5. 7 unto trouble, as the sparks fly upward
Psa. 18. 10 And he rode upon a cherub, and did fly
91. 5 (nor) for the arrow (that) flieth by day
Isa. 6. 6 Then flew one of the seraphim unto me
11. 14 they shall fly upon the shoulders of the P.
60. 8 Who (are) these (that) fly as a cloud, and
Hab. 1. 8 they shall fly as the eagle (that) hasteth

4. *To fly*, עוּף *uph*, 3a.
Gen. 1. 20 and fowl..may fly above the earth in the
Isa. 6. 2 covered his feet..with twain he did fly

5. *To be ravenous*, עִיט *it*.
1 Sa. 15. 19 didst fly upon the spoil, and didst evil in

6. As No. 5 [V.L. עָשָׂה *asah*].
1 Sa. 14. 32 the people flew upon the spoil, and took

7. *To fly, expand the wings*, πετάομαι *petaomai*.
Rev. 4. 7 the fourth beast..like a [flying] eagle
8. 13 And I beheld, and heard an angel [flying]
14. 6 I saw another angel [fly] in the midst of
19. 17 all the fowls that [fly] in the midst of h.

8. *To fly, expand the wings*, πέτομαι *petomai*.
Rev. 12. 14 that she might fly into the wilderness

FLY away, to —
1. *To fly*, עוּף *uph*.
Job 20. 8 He shall fly away as a dream, and shall
Psa. 55. 6 then) would I fly away, and be at rest
90. 10 for it is soon cut off, and we fly away

2. *To (cause to) fly,* עוּף *uph,* 1 [V.L. 5].
Prov.23. 5 they fly away as an eagle toward heaven
3. *To show self flying,* עוּף *uph,* 7a.
Hos. 9. 11 their glory shall fly away like a bird, from
FLY, to be caused to —
To be caused to fly, יָעַף *yaaph,* 6.
Dan. 9. 21 being caused to fly swiftly, touched me
FLY, to make —
To cause to break out, פָּרַח *parach.*
Eze. 13. 20 ye..hunt the souls to make (them) fly
13. 20 souls that ye hunt to make (them) fly
FLYING —
1. *Wing (with),* כָּנָף *kanaph.*
Psa.148. 10 cattle; creeping things, and flying fowl
2. *To fly,* עוּף *uph.*
Prov 26. 2 as the swallow by flying, so the curse
Isa. 31. 5 As birds flying, so will the LORD of hosts
Zech. 5. 1 Then I..looked, and, behold, a flying roll
5. 2 And I answered, I see a flying roll; the
3. *To fly,* עוּף *uph,* 3a.
Isa. 14. 29 and his fruit..a fiery flying serpent
30. 6 whence (come) the..fiery flying serpent
4. *Fowl,* עוֹף *oph.*
Lev. 11. 21 of every flying creeping thing that goeth
11. 23 all..flying creeping things, which have
FOAL —
1. *Son,* בֵּן *ben.*
Zech. 9. 9 riding..upon a colt the foal of an ass
2. *Foal, colt of an ass,* עַיִר *ayir.*
Gen. 32. 15 ten bulls, twenty she asses, and ten foals
49. 11 Binding his foal unto the vine, and his
3. *Son,* υἱός *huios.*
Matt. 21. 5 upon an ass, and a colt the foal of an ass
FOAM —
Chip, foam, קֶצֶף *qetseph.*
Hos. 10. 7 her king is cut off as the foam upon the
FOAM, to —
To foam, froth, ἀφρίζω *aphrizō.*
Mark 9. 18 he foameth, and gnasheth with his teeth
9. 20 fell on the ground, and wallowed foaming
FOAM out, to —
To foam upon, or about, ἐπαφρίζω *epaphrizō.*
Jude 13 waves..foaming out their own shame
FOAMETH again, that he —
With foam, μετὰ ἀφροῦ *meta aphrou.*
Luke 9. 39 it teareth him that he foameth again
FODDER —
Provender, בְּלִיל *belil.*
Job 6. 5 grass? or loweth the ox over his fodder?
FOE —
1. *Enemy,* אֹיֵב *oyebh.*
Psa. 27. 2 mine enemies and my foes, came upon
30. 1 hast not made my foes to rejoice over me
2. *Adversary, straitener, distresser,* צַר, צָר *tsar.*
1 Ch.21. 12 months to be destroyed before thy foes
Psa. 89. 23 I will beat down his foes before his face
3. *To hate,* שָׂנֵא *sane.*
Esth. 9. 16 But the other Jews..slew of their foes
4. *Enemy,* ἐχθρός *echthros.*
Matt10. 36 a man's foes..they of his own household
Acts 2. 35 Until I make thy foes thy footstool
FOLD —
1. *Hedged or fenced place,* גְּדֵרָה *gederah.*
Num32. 16 We will build sheep folds here for our cat.
32. 24 Build you..folds for your sheep; and do
32. 36 And..fenced cities: and folds for sheep
Zeph. 2. 6 the sea coast shall be..folds for flocks
2. *Pasture land, fold,* דֹּבֶר *dober.*
Mic. 2. 12 as the flock in the midst of their fold
3. *Restrained place, fold,* מִכְלָה *miklah.*
Psa. 50. 9 I will take no..he goats out of thy folds
78. 70 David..and took him from the sheep fol.
Hab. 3. 17 the flock shall be cut off from the fold
4. *Home, comely place,* נָוֶה *naveh.*
Isa. 65. 10 And Sharon shall be a fold of flocks
Jer. 23. 3 and will bring them again to their folds
Eze. 34. 14 upon..high mountains..shall their fold
34. 14 there shall they lie in a good fold, and
5. *Court, yard,* αὐλή *aulē.*
John10. 16 sheep I have, which are not of this fold
6. *A flock,* ποίμνη *poimnē.*
John10. 16 there shall be one fold..one shepherd
FOLD, to —
To clasp, חָבַק *chabaq.*
Eccl. 4. 5 The fool foldeth his hands together, and
FOLD, to make a —
To cause to crouch, רָבַץ *rabats,* 5.
Isa. 13. 20 shall the shepherds make their fold there
FOLD up, to —
To roll or fold up, ἑλίσσω *helissō.*
Heb. 1. 12 And as a vesture shalt thou fold them up

FOLDEN together —
To wrap together, סָבַךְ *sabak.*
Nah. 1. 10 For while..folden together (as) thorns
FOLDING —
1. *Folding,* גָּלִיל *galil.*
1 Ki. 6. 34, 34 the two leaves of the..door..folding
2. *Clasping,* חִבֻּק *chibbuq.*
Prov. 6. 10 a little folding of the hands to sleep
24. 33 a little folding of the hands to sleep
FOLK —
1. *Nation, people,* לְאֹם *leom.*
Jer. 51. 58 folk in the fire, and they shall be weary
2. *People,* עַם *am.*
Gen. 33. 15 leave..of the folk that (are) with me
Prov 30. 26 The conies..a feeble folk, yet make they
FOLLOW —
Foot (at the foot of), רֶגֶל *regel.*
Exod11. 8 Get thee out, and all..that follow thee
Judg. 8. 5 bread unto the people that follow me
1 Sa. 25. 27 unto the young men that follow my lord
1 Ki. 20. 10 handfuls for all the people that follow
2 Ki. 3. 9 and for the cattle that followed them
FOLLOW, to —
1. *After,* אַחַר *achar,* אַחֲרֵי *achare.*
Num14. 24 because he..hath followed me fully, him
32. 11 because they have not wholly followed
32. 12 for they have wholly followed the LORD
Deut. 1. 36 because he hath wholly followed the Lo.
12. 30 thou be not snared by following them
Josh.14. 8 but I wholly followed the LORD my God
14. 9 because thou hast wholly followed the
14. 14 wholly followed the LORD God of Israel
Judg. 9. 3 their hearts inclined to follow Abim.
1 Sa. 13. 7 all the people followed him trembling
2 Sa. [2. 19 in going he turned not..from following]
17. 9 slaughter among the people that follow
1 Ki[12. 20 none that followed the house of David]
16. 22 the people that followed Omri prevailed
16. 22 against the people that followed Tibni
20. 19 came..and the army which followed
Neh. 4. 23 nor the men of the guard which followed
Psa. 45. 14 the virgins her companions that follow
Jer. 17. 16 I have not hastened..to follow thee
Eze. 16. 34 none followeth thee to commit whoredoms
Amos 7. 15 the LORD took me as I followed the flock
2. *To pursue,* רָדַף *radaph.*
Gen. 44. 4 Up, follow after the men; and when thou
Exod14. 4 that he shall follow after them; and I
Deut 16. 20 That which is..just shalt thou follow
Judg. 3. 28 And he said unto them, Follow after me
2 Ki. 5. 21 So Gehazi followed after Naaman. And
9. 27 Jehu followed after him, and said, Smite
Psa. 23. 6 goodness and mercy shall follow me all
38. 20 because I follow (the thing that) good (is)
Isa. 5. 11 early..(that) they may follow strong dri.
3. *To pursue,* רָדַף *radaph,* 3.
Prov.12. 11 he that followeth vain (persons is) void
4. *To follow,* ἀκολουθέω *akoloutheō.*
Matt. 4. 20 they straightway left..and followed him
4. 22 And they..left the ship..and followed
4. 25 And there followed him great multitudes
8. 1 was come..great multitudes followed
8. 10 and said to them that followed, Verily I
8. 19 Master, I will follow thee whithersoever
8. 22 But Jesus said unto him, Follow me
8. 23 into a ship, his disciples followed him
9. 9 Follow me. And he arose, and followed
9. 19 And Jesus arose, and followed him, and
9. 27 two blind men followed him, crying, and
10. 38 that taketh not his cross, and followeth
12. 15 great multitudes followed him, and he
14. 13 they followed him on foot out of the cities
16. 24 let him..take up his cross, and follow me
19. 2 great multitudes followed him; and he
19. 21 Jesus said unto him..come..follow me
19. 27 we have forsaken all, and followed thee
19. 28 I say..That ye which have followed me
20. 29 from Jericho, a great multitude followed
20. 34 received sight, and they followed him
21. 9 the multitudes..that followed, cried
26. 58 Peter followed him afar off unto the high
27. 55 women..which followed Jesus from Gal.
Mark 1. 18 they forsook their nets, and followed
2. 14 Follow me. And he arose and followed
2. 15 there were many, and they followed him
3. 7 a great multitude from Galilee [followed]
5. 24 and much people followed him, and
6. 1 he went out..and his disciples follow him
8. 34 let him..take up his cross, and follow me
9. 38 [in thy name, and he followeth not us]
9. 38 [forbad him, because he followeth not us]
10. 21 come, take up the cross, and follow me
10. 28 we have left all, and have followed thee
10. 32 and as they followed, they were afraid
10. 52 he received his sight, and followed Jesus
11. 9 they that followed, cried, saying, Hosan.
14. 13 there shall meet you a man..follow him
14. 51 there [followed] him a certain young man
14. 54 Peter followed him afar off, even into
15. 41 Who also..followed him and ministered
Luke 5. 11 land, they forsook all, and followed him
5. 27 and he said unto him, Follow me
5. 28 he left all, rose up, and followed him
7. 9 said unto the people that followed him
9. 11 the people..followed him: and he

Luke 9. 23 take up his cross daily, and follow me
9. 49 because he followeth not with us
9. 57 LORD, I will follow thee whithersoever
9. 59 And he said unto another, Follow me
9. 61 LORD, I will follow thee; but let me first
18. 22 sell all..thou hast..and come, follow me
18. 28 Lo, we have left all, and followed thee
18. 43 he received his sight, and followed him
22. 10 follow him into the house where he
22. 39 and his disciples also followed him
22. 54 house. And Peter followed afar off
23. 27 there followed him a great company of
John 1. 37 heard him speak, and they followed Jes.
1. 38 Jesus turned, and saw them following
1. 40 One of the two which..followed him
1. 43 findeth Philip, and saith unto him, Foll.
6. 2 a great multitude followed him, because
8. 12 he that followeth me shall not walk in
10. 4 he goeth before..and the sheep follow
10. 5 a stranger will they not follow, but will
10. 27 and I know them, and they follow me
11. 31 The Jews then..followed her, saying, She
12. 26 If any man serve me, let him follow me
13. 36 Whither I go, thou canst not follow me
13. 36 but thou shalt follow me afterwards
13. 37 Lord, why cannot I follow thee now? I
18. 15 And Simon Peter followed Jesus, and (so
20. 6 Then cometh Simon Peter following him
21. 19 had spoken this, he saith unto him, Foll.
21. 20 the disciple whom Jesus loved following
21. 22 what (is that) to thee? Follow thou me
Acts 12. 8 Cast thy garment about thee, and follow
12. 9 he went out, and followed him; and
13. 43 many of the Jews..followed Paul and B.
21. 36 the multitude of the people followed
1 Co.10. 4 of that spiritual Rock..followed them
Rev. 6. 8 Death, and Hell followed with him
14. 4 These are they which follow the Lamb
14. 8 And there followed another angel, saying
14. 9 the third angel followed them, saying
14. 13 labours; and their works do follow them
19. 14 the armies..in heaven followed him upon
5. *To become, begin to be,* γίνομαι *ginomai.*
Rev. 8. 7 there followed hail and fire mingled with
6. *To pursue,* διώκω *diōkō.*
Luke17. 23 See here..go not after (them), nor follow
1 Th. 5. 15 but ever follow that which is good, both
2 Ti. 2. 22 follow righteousness, faith, charity
Heb.12. 14 Follow peace with all (men), and holiness
7. *Come behind,* δεῦτε ὀπίσω *deute opisō.*
Matt. 4. 19 Follow me, and I will make you fishers
8. *To be after,* εἰμὶ μετά *eimi meta.*
Matt.27. 62 that followed the day of the preparation
9. *To follow out,* ἐξακολουθέω *exakoloutheō.*
2 Pe. 1. 16 we have not followed cunningly devised
2. 2 many shall follow their pernicious ways
2. 15 following the way of Balaam..of Bozor
10. *To follow upon* ἐπακολουθέω *epakoloutheō.*
Mark16. 20 [confirming the words with signs follow.]
1 Ti. 5. 10 if she have diligently followed every good
1 Pe. 2. 21 example, that ye should follow his steps
11. *To follow down or thoroughly,* κατακολουθέω.
Acts 16. 17 The same followed Paul and us, and
12. *To mimic, imitate,* μιμέομαι *mimeomai.*
2 Th. 3. 7 yourselves know how ye ought to follow
3. 9 make..an ensample unto you to follow
Heb.13. 7 whose faith follow, considering the end
3 Jo. 11 follow not that which is evil, but that
13. *To follow alongside of,* παρακολουθέω *parakol.*
Mark16. 17 [signs shall follow them that believe]
14. *To follow along with,* συνακολουθέω *sunakolo.*
Mark 5. 37 he suffered no man [to follow] him, save
Luke23. 49 the women that followed him from Gali.
15. *To go in after,* בּוֹא אַחַר *bo achar.*
Exod14. 17 they shall follow them: and I will get
2 Ki.11. 15 him that followeth her kill with the
2 Ch.23. 14 whoso followeth her, let him be slain
16. *To be after,* הָיָה אַחַר *hayah achar.*
Exod23. 2 Thou shalt not follow a multitude to
1 Sa.12. 14 continue following the LORD your God
2 Sa. 2. 10 But the house of Judah followed David
1 Ki.16. 21 half of the people followed Tibni; 12. 20.
17. *To go on after,* הָלַךְ אַחַר *halak achar.*
Gen. 32. 19 so commanded he..all that followed the
Deut. 4. 3 for all the men that followed Baal-peor
Josh. 6. 8 the ark of the covenant of the LORD foll
1 Sa. 17. 13, 14 and the three eldest..followed Saul
2 Sa. 3. 31 And king David (himself) followed the
1 Ki.14. 8 and who followed me with all his heart
18. *To go on habitually after,* הָלַךְ אַחַר *halak achar,* 7.
1 Sa. 25. 27 unto the young men that follow my lord
19. *To go on after,* יָלַךְ אַחַר *yalak achar.*
Gen. 24. 5, 8 the woman will not be willing to follow
24. 39 Peradventure the woman will not follow
24. 61 And Rebekah arose..and followed the
Num16. 25 and the elders of Israel followed him
Judg. 2. 12 And they forsook..and followed other g.
9. 4 vain and light persons, which followed
9. 49 all the people..followed Abimelech
Ruth 3. 10 inasmuch as thou followedst not young
1 Sa. 30. 21 faint that they could not follow David
1 Ki. 18. 18 forsaken..and thou hast followed Baalim
18. 21 God, follow him: but if Baal..follow him
19. 20 Kiss..my mother, and..I will follow thee

2 Ki. 4. 30 leave thee. And he arose, and followed
6. 19 neither (is) this the city: follow me, and
13. 2 he..followed the sins of Jeroboam the
17. 15 they followed vanity, and became vain
Eze. 10. 11 whither the head looked they followed it
13. 3 that follow their own spirit, and have

20. *To go out*, יָצָא *yatsa.*
2 Sa. 11. 8 there followed him a mess...from the ki.

FOLLOW after, to —

1. *To pursue*, רָדַף *radaph.*
Psa.119. 150 They draw nigh that follow after misch.
Prov 21. 21 He that followeth after righteousness and
Isa. 1. 23 every one loveth gifts and followeth after
51. 1 ye that follow after righteousness, ye
Hos. 12. 1 Ephraim..followeth after the east wind

2. *To pursue*, רָדַף *radaph*, 3.
Prov 15. 9 he loveth him that followeth after righ.
28. 19 he that followeth after vain (persons)
Hos. 2. 7 she shall follow after her lovers, but she

3. *To pursue*, διώκω *diōkō.*
Rom. 9. 30 which followed not after righteousness
9. 31 Israel, which followed after..righteousn.
14. 19 Let us therefore follow after the things
1 Co.14. 1 Follow after charity, and desire spiritual
Phil. 3. 12 I follow after, if that I may apprehend
1 Ti. 6. 11 But thou..follow after righteousness

4. *To follow upon*, ἐπακολουθέω *epakoloutheō.*
1 Ti. 5. 24 and some (men) they follow after

5. *In order*, καθεξῆς *kathexēs.*
Acts 3. 24 from Samuel and those that follow after

6. *To pursue thoroughly*, καταδιώκω *katadiōkō.*
Mark 1. 36 they that were with him followed after

7. *To follow thoroughly*, κατακολουθέω *katakolouth.*
Luke23. 55 And the women also..followed after, and

FOLLOW, that should —

After these (things), μετὰ ταῦτα *meta tauta.*
1 Pe. 1. 11 and the glory that should follow

FOLLOW, what would —

What is about to be, τὸ ἐσόμενον *to esomenon.*
Luke22. 49 When they..saw what would follow, they

FOLLOW close or hard, to —

To cleave, adhere to, דָּבַק *dabeq.*
Psa. 63. 8 My soul followeth hard after thee: thy
Jer. 42. 16 the famine..shall follow close after you

FOLLOW hard (after or upon), to —

To (cause to) cleave or adhere to, דָּבַק *dabeq*, 5.
1 Sa. 14. 22 they also followed hard after them in
31. 2 the Philistines followed hard upon Saul
2 Sa. 1. 6 and horsemen followed hard after him
1 Ch.10. 2 the Philistines followed hard after Saul

FOLLOW on, to —

To pursue, רָדַף *radaph.*
Hos. 6. 3 (if) we follow on to know the LORD

FOLLOWED, to be —

To be done, עָשָׂה *asah*, 2.
2 Sa. 17. 23 saw that his counsel was not followed

FOLLOWER —

Imitator, μιμητής *mimētēs.*
1 Co. 4. 16 I beseech you, be ye followers of me
11. 1 Be ye followers of me, even as I also (am)
Eph. 5. 1 Be ye therefore followers of God, as dear
1 Th. 1. 6 ye became followers of us, and of the L.
2. 14 became followers of the churches of God
Heb. 6. 12 That ye be not slothful, but followers of
1 Pe. 3. 13 if ye be [followers] of that which is good?

FOLLOWER together —

Joint imitator, συμμιμητής *summimētēs.*
Phil. 3. 17 be followers together of me, and mark

FOLLOWING (after) —

1. *After, afterward*, אַחַר *achar.*
Deut. 7. 4 they will turn away..from following me
Josh.22. 16, 18 turn away..from following the LORD
22. 23 an altar to turn from following the LORD
22. 29 turn this day from following the LORD
Ruth 1. 16 to return from following after thee
1 Sa. 12. 20 turn not aside from following the LORD
14. 46 Saul went up from following the Philis.
15. 11 for he is turned back from following me
24. 1 Saul was returned from following the P.
2 Sa. 2. 21 Asahel would not turn aside from follow.
2. 22 said..Turn thee aside from following
2. 26 return from following their brethren?
2. 27 every one from following his brother
2. 30 Joab returned from following Abner: and
7. 8 I took thee..from following the sheep, to
1 Ki. 1. 7 and they following Adonijah helped (him)
9. 6 if ye shall at all turn from following me
2 Ki.17. 21 drave Israel from following the LORD
18. 6 departed not from following him, but
1 Ch.17. 7 I took thee..from following the sheep
2 Ch.25. 27 did turn away from following the LORD
34. 33 departed not from following the LORD
Psa. 78. 71 From following the ewes..he brought him

2. *Another*, אַחֵר *acher.*
Psa 109. 13 in the generation following let their name

3. *Behind*, אַחֲרוֹן *acharon.*
Psa. 48. 13 ye may tell (it) to the generation follow.

4. *On the coming (night)*, τῇ ἐπιούσῃ *tē epiousē.*
Acts 23. 11 the night following, the Lord stood by

5. *To go on after*, הָלַךְ אַחַר *yalak achar.*
Judg. 2. 19 in following other gods to serve them
1 Ki. 21. 26 did very abominably in following idols

6. *Afterwards*, אַחֲרֵי־כֵן *achare ken.*
Gen. 41. 31 by reason of that famine following; for

FOLLOWING, the day —

1. *Upon the morrow*, τῇ ἐπαύριον *tē epaurion.*
John 1. 43 The day following Jesus would go forth
6. 22 The day following, when the people which

2. *The coming (day)*, τῇ ἐπιούσῃ *tē epiousē.*
Acts 21. 18 the (day) following Paul went in with us

3. *The succeeding (day)*, τῇ ἑξῆς *tē hexēs.*
Acts21. 1 we came..the (day) following unto Rhod.

4. *The adjoining (day)*, τῇ ἐχομένῃ *tē echomenē.*
Luke13. 33 I must walk to day..and the (day) follo.

FOLLY —

1. *Folly*, אִוֶּלֶת *ivveleth.*
Prov. 5. 23 in the greatness of his folly he shall go
13. 16 but a fool layeth open (his) folly
14. 8 his way: but the folly of fools (is) deceit
14. 18 The simple inherit folly: but the prudent
14. 24 (but) the foolishness of fools (is) folly
14. 29 (he that is) hasty of spirit exalteth folly
15. 21 Folly (is) joy to (him that is) destitute of
16. 22 but the instruction of fools (is) folly
17. 12 a man, rather than a fool in his folly
18. 13 before he heareth (it), it (is) folly and
26. 4 Answer not a fool according to his folly
26. 5 Answer a fool according to his folly, lest
26. 11 As a dog..(so) a fool returneth to his folly

2. *Self confidence, folly*, כֶּסֶל *kesel.*
Psa. 49. 13 This their way (is) their folly: yet their
Eccl. 7. 25 and to know the wickedness of folly

3. *Self confidence, folly*, כִּסְלָה *kislah.*
Psa. 85. 8 but let them not turn again to folly, even

4. *Emptiness, folly*, נְבָלָה *nebalah.*
Gen. 34. 7 because he had wrought folly in Israel
Deut22. 21 because she hath wrought folly in Israel
Josh. 7. 15 because he hath wrought folly in Israel
Judg19. 23 do not (so) wickedly..do not this folly
20. 6 for they have committed..folly in Israel
20. 10 folly that they have wrought in Israel
1 Sa. 25. 25 Nabal (is) his name, and folly (is) with
2 Sa. 13. 12 Nay, my brother..do not thou this folly
Job 42. 8 lest I deal with you (after your) folly, in
Isa. 9. 17 and every mouth speaketh folly. For all

5. *Thickheadedness*, סֶכֶל *sekel.*
Eccl. 10. 6 Folly is set in great dignity, and the rich

6. *Thickheadedness*, סִכְלוּת *sikluth.*
Eccl. 2. 3 to lay hold on folly, till I might see what
2. 12 And I turned myself to behold..folly: for
2. 13 Then I saw that wisdom excelleth folly
10. 1 (so doth) a little folly him that is in rep.

7. *Thickheadedness*, שִׂכְלוּת *sikluth.*
Eccl. 1. 17 And I gave my heart to know..folly: I

8. *Folly, (light?)* תָּהֳלָה *toholah.*
Job 4. 18 and his angels he charged with folly

9. *Insipidity, folly*, תִּפְלָה *tiphlah.*
Job 24. 12 crieth out: yet God layeth not folly (to
Jer. 23. 13 And I have seen folly in the prophets of

10. *Senselessness*, ἄνοια *anoia.*
2 Ti. 3. 9 for their folly shall be manifest unto all

11. *Heedlessness, foolishness*, ἀφροσύνη *aphrosunē.*
2 Co.11. 1 could bear with me a little in (my) folly

FOOD —

1. *To eat*, אָכַל *akal.*
Gen. 47. 24 four parts shall be your own..food for

2. *Eating, food*, אֹכֶל *okel.*
Gen. 41. 35 And let them gather all the food of those
41. 35 and let them keep food in the cities
41. 36 that food shall be for store to the land
41. 48 he gathered up all the food of the seven
41. 48 laid up the food in the cities: the food
42. 7 From the land of Canaan to buy food
42. 10 but to buy food are thy servants come
43. 2 father said..Go again, buy us a little fo.
43. 4 we will go down and buy thee food
43. 20 O sir, we came indeed down..to buy food
43. 22 other money have we brought..to buy f.
44. 1 saying, Fill the men's sacks (with) food
44. 25 said, Go again, (and) buy us a little food
47. 24 seed of the field, and for your food
Prov 13. 23 Much food (is in) the tillage of the poor

3. *Eating food*, אָכְלָה *oklah.*
Gen. 6. 21 shall be for food for thee, and for them

4. *Increase, food*, בּוּל *bul.*
Job 40. 20 the mountains bring him forth food

5. *Bread, food*, לֶחֶם *lechem.*
Lev. 3. 11, 16 the food of the offering made by fire
22. 7 of the holy things; because it (is) his food
Deut10. 18 loveth..in giving him food and raiment
1 Sa. 14. 24, 28 Cursed..the man that eateth (any) f.
14. 24 So none of the people tasted (any) food
2 Sa. 9. 10 thy master's son may have food to eat
1 Ki. 5. 9 accomplish my desire, in giving food for

Job 24. 5 wilderness (yieldeth) food for them (and)
Psa. 78. 25 Man did eat angels' food: he sent them
104. 14 may bring forth food out of the earth
136. 25 Who giveth food to all flesh: for his mer.
146. 7 which giveth food to the hungry. The
147. 9 He giveth to the beast his food, (and) to
Prov.27. 27 (thou shalt have) goats' milk..for thy f.
27. 27 for the food of thy household, and (for)
28. 3 a sweeping rain which leaveth no food
30. 8 feed me with food convenient for me
31. 14 ships; she bringeth her food from afar
Eze. 48. 18 for food unto them that serve the city

6. *Eating, food*, מַאֲכָל *maakal.*
Gen. 2. 9 to grow every tree that is..good for food
3. 6 saw that the tree (was) good for food, and
6. 21 take thou unto thee of all food that is e.
Lev. 19. 23 planted all manner of trees for food
Prov. 6. 8 (and) gathereth her food in the harvest

7. *Eating, food*, מַכֹּלֶת *makkoleth.*
1 Ki. 5. 11 of wheat (for) food to his household, and

8. *Hunting, venison*, צַיִד *tsayid.*
Job 38. 41 Who provideth for the raven his food?

9. *Food, flesh*, שְׁאֵר *sheer.*
Exod21. 10 her food..and her duty of marriage, shall

10. *Eating, the act of eating*, βρῶσις *brōsis.*
2 Co. 9. 10 both minister bread for (your) food, and

11. *Thorough nourishment*, διατροφή *diatrophē.*
1 Ti. 6. 8 having food..let us be therewith content

12. *Nourishment*, τροφή *trophē.*
Acts 14. 17 filling our hearts with food and gladness
Jas. 2. 15 If a brother..be..destitute of daily food

FOOL —

1. *Fool*, אֱוִיל *evil.*
Psa107. 17 Fools, because of their transgression and
Prov. 1. 7 (but) fools despise wisdom and instruc.
7. 22 as a fool to the correction of the stocks
10. 8, 10 but a prating fool shall fall
10. 21 feed many: but fools die for want of wis.
11. 29 the fool (shall be) servant to the wise of
12. 15 The way of a fool (is) right in his own eyes
12. 16 A fool's wrath is presently known: but a
14. 9 Fools make a mock at sin: but among
15. 5 A fool despiseth his father's instruction
16. 22 but the instruction of fools (is) folly
17. 28 Even a fool, when he holdeth his peace
20. 3 strife: but every fool will be meddling
24. 7 Wisdom (is) too high for a fool: he open.
27. 3 a fool's wrath (is) heavier than them both
27. 22 Though thou shouldest bray a fool in a
Isa. 19. 11 Surely the princes of Zoan (are) fools, the
35. 8 wayfaring men, though fools, shall not err
Hos. 9. 7 the prophet (is) a fool, the spiritual man

2. *Boaster*, הָלַל *halal.*
Psa. 75. 4 I said unto the fools, Deal not foolishly

3. *Self confident*, כְּסִיל *kesil.*
Psa. 49. 10 the fool and the brutish person perish
92. 6 neither doth a fool understand this
94. 8 and (ye) fools, when will ye be wise?
Prov. 1. 22 scorning, and fools hate knowledge?
1. 32 the prosperity of fools shall destroy them
3. 35 but shame shall be the promotion of fools
8. 5 ye fools, be ye of an understanding heart
10. 18 and he that uttereth a slander, (is) a fool
10. 23 (It is) as sport to a fool to do mischief
12. 23 the heart of fools proclaimeth foolishness
13. 16 dealeth with knowledge: but a fool lay.
13. 19 abomination to fools to depart from evil
13. 20 a companion of fools shall be destroyed
14. 8 his way: but the folly of fools (is) deceit
14. 16 but the fool rageth, and is confident
14. 24 (but) the foolishness of fools (is) folly
14. 33 but (that which is) in the midst of fools
15. 2 mouth of fools poureth out foolishness
15. 14 the mouth of fools feedeth on foolishness
17. 10 more than an hundred stripes into a fool
17. 12 meet a man, rather than a fool in his folly
17. 16 price in the hand of a fool to get wisdom
17. 21 He that begetteth a fool (doeth it) to his
17. 24 eyes of a fool (are) in the ends of the
18. 2 A fool hath no delight in understanding
18. 6 A fool's lips enter into contention, and
18. 7 A fool's mouth (is) his destruction, and
19. 1 perverse in his lips, and is a fool
19. 10 Delight is not seemly for a fool; much
19. 29 and stripes for the back of fools
23. 9 Speak not in the ears of a fool; for he
26. 1 so honour is not seemly for a fool
26. 3 for the ass, and a rod for the fool's back
26. 4 Answer not a fool according to his folly
26. 5 Answer a fool according to his folly, lest
26. 6 sendeth a message by the hand of a fool
26. 7, 9 so (is) a parable in the mouth of fools
26. 8 so (is) he that giveth honour to a fool
26. 10 The great (God)..both rewardeth the fool
26. 11 As a dog..(so) a fool returneth to his
26. 12 (there is) more hope of a fool than of him
28. 26 that trusteth in his own heart is a fool
29. 11 A fool uttereth all his mind: but a wise
29. 20 (there is) more hope of a fool than of him
Eccl. 2. 14 the fool walketh in darkness: and I my.
2. 15 As it happeneth to the fool, so it hap.
2. 16 of the wise more than of the fool for ever
2. 16 And how dieth the wise (man)? as the f.
4. 5 fool foldeth his hands together, and eateth
5. 1 to hear than to give the sacrifice of fools

Eccl. 5. 3 and a fool's voice (is known) by..words
5. 4 pay it; for (he hath) no pleasure in fools
6. 8 what hath the wise more than the fool?
7. 4 the heart of fools (is) in the house of
7. 5 than for a man to hear the song of fools
7. 6 crackling..so (is) the laughter of the fo.
7. 9 for anger resteth in the bosom of fools
9. 17 the cry of him that ruleth among fools
10. 2 right hand; but a fool's heart at his left
10. 12 the lips of a fool will swallow up himself

4. *Empty person, fool,* נָבָל *nabal.*
2 Sa. 3. 33 and said, Died Abner as a fool dieth?
13. 13 thou shalt be as one of the fools in Israel
Job 30. 8 (They were) children of fools, yea, child.
Psa. 14. 1 The fool hath said in his heart, (There is)
53. 1 The fool hath said in his heart, (There is)
Prov 17. 7 Excellent speech becometh not a fool
17. 21 and the father of a fool hath no joy
30. 22 and a fool when he is filled with meat
Jer. 17. 11 leave them..and at his end shall be a f.

5. *Thickheaded,* סָכָל *sakal.*
Eccl. 2. 19 whether he shall be a wise (man) or a f.?
10. 3 when he that is a fool walketh by the
10. 3 he saith to every one (that) he (is) a fool
10. 14 A fool also is full of words: a man can.

6. *Thoughtless,* ἀνόητος *anoētos.*
Luke 24. 25 O fools, and slow of heart to believe all

7. *Unwise,* ἄσοφος *asophos.*
Eph. 5. 15 See then that ye walk..not as fools, but

8. *Heedless, witless,* ἄφρων *aphrōn.*
Luke 11. 40 fools, did not he that made that which is
12. 20 fool, this night thy soul shall be required
1 Co. 15. 36 (Thou) fool, that which thou sowest is
2 Co. 11. 16 I say again, Let no man think me a fool
11. 16 if otherwise, yet as a fool receive me
11. 19 For ye suffer fools gladly, seeing ye..are
12. 6 I shall not be a fool; for I will say the
12. 11 I am become a fool in glorying; ye have

9. *Fool, (or as in Hebrew, a rebel),* μωρός *mōros.*
Matt. 5. 22 whosoever shall say, Thou fool! shall
23. 17, 19 (Ye) fools, and blind! for whether is
1 Co. 3. 18 let him become a fool, that he may be
4. 10 We (are) fools for Christ's sake, but ye

FOOL, to speak as a —
To think amiss or wrongly, παραφρονέω *paraphr.*
2 Co. 11. 23 I speak as a fool, I (am) more: in labours

FOOL, to become a —
To make foolish, μωραίνω *mōrainō.*
Rom. 1. 22 Professing..to be wise, they became fools

FOOL, to play the —
To act foolishly, סָכַל *sakal,* 5.
1 Sa. 26. 21 behold, I have played the fool, and have

FOOLISH —
1. *Fool, foolish,* אֱוִיל *evil.*
Job 5. 2 wrath killeth the foolish man, and envy
5. 3 I have seen the foolish taking root: but
Prov 10. 14 the mouth of the foolish (is) near destru.
14. 3 In the mouth of the foolish (is) a rod of
29. 9 a wise man contendeth with a foolish man
Jer. 4. 22 my people (is) foolish, they have not kn.

2. *Foolish,* אֱוִלִי *evili.*
Zech 11. 15 the instruments of a foolish shepherd

3. *Brutish,* בַּעַר *baar.*
Psa. 73. 22 So foolish (was) I, and ignorant: I was

4. *To boast,* הָלַל *halal.*
Psa. 5. 5 The foolish shall not stand in thy sight
73. 3 For I was envious at the foolish, (when)

5. *Self confident,* כְּסִיל *kesil.*
Prov 10. 1 but a foolish son (is) the heaviness of his
14. 7 Go from the presence of a foolish man
15. 7 the heart of the foolish (doeth) not so
15. 20 but a foolish man despiseth his mother
17. 25 A foolish son (is) a grief to his father, and
19. 13 foolish son (is) the calamity of his father
21. 20 but a foolish man spendeth it up
Eccl. 4. 13 an old and foolish king, who will no more
10. 15 The labour of the foolish wearieth every

6. *Self confidence,* כְּסִילוּת *kesiluth.*
Prov. 9. 13 foolish woman (is) clamorous; (she is) si.

7. *Empty, foolish,* נָבָל *nabal.*
Deut 32. 6 O foolish people and unwise? (is) not he
32. 21 provoke them to anger with a foolish na.
Psa. 39. 8 make me not the reproach of the foolish
74. 18 foolish people have blasphemed thy name
74. 22 the foolish man reproacheth thee daily
Eze. 13. 3 Woe unto the foolish prophets, that

8. *Thickheaded,* סָכָל *sakal.*
Eccl. 7. 17 neither be thou foolish: why shouldest
Jer. 5. 21 Hear now this, O foolish people, and

9. *Simple,* פְּתִי *pethi.*
Prov. 9. 6 Forsake the foolish, and live; and go in

10. *Thoughtless,* ἀνόητος *anoētos.*
Gal. 3. 1 O foolish Galatians, who hath bewitched
3. 3 Are ye so foolish? having begun in the S.
1 Ti. 6. 9 (into) many foolish and hurtful lusts, wh.
Titus 3. 3 For we ourselves also were..foolish, dis.

11. *Unintelligent,* ἀσύνετος *asunetos.*
Rom. 1. 21 and their foolish heart was darkened
10. 19 (and) by a foolish nation I will anger you

12. *Heedless, senseless,* ἄφρων *aphrōn.*
Rom. 2. 20 An instructor of the foolish, a teacher of
1 Pe. 2. 15 put to silence the ignorance of foolish

13. *Foolish, dull, slow,* μωρός *mōros.*
Matt. 7. 26 shall be likened unto a foolish man
25. 2 five..were wise, and five (were) foolish
25. 3 They that (were) foolish took their lamps
25. 8 the foolish said unto the wise, Give us of
2 Ti. 2. 23 But foolish and unlearned questions av.
Titus 3. 9 avoid foolish questions, and genealogies

FOOLISH, to be —
1. *To be or become foolish,* יָאַל *yaal,* 2.
Jer. 5. 4 Surely these (are) poor; they are foolish

2. *To be self confident, foolish,* כָּסַל *kasal.*
Jer. 10. 8 But they are..brutish and foolish; the

FOOLISH, to make —
1. *To make foolish,* סָכַל *sakal,* 3.
Isa. 44. 25 and maketh their knowledge foolish

2. *To make foolish,* μωραίνω *mōrainō.*
1 Co. 1. 20 hath not God made foolish the wisdom of

FOOLISH talking or things —
1. *Insipid, untempered,* תָּפֵל *taphel.*
Lam. 2. 14 Thy prophets have seen..foolish things

2. *Foolish discourse,* μωρολογία *mōrologia.*
Eph. 5. 4 Neither filthiness, nor foolish talking

3. *Foolish,* μωρός *mōros.*
1 Co. 1. 27 But God hath chosen the foolish things

FOOLISH woman —
Empty, foolish woman נְבָלָה *nebalah.*
Job 2. 10 as one of the foolish women speaketh

FOOLISHLY —
1. *Folly,* אִוֶּלֶת *ivveleth.*
Prov. 14. 17 (He that is) soon angry dealeth foolishly

2. *Folly,* תִּפְלָה *tiphlah.*
Job 1. 22 Job sinned not, nor charged God foolishly

3. *In senselessness,* ἐν ἀφροσύνῃ *en aphrosunē.*
2 Co. 11. 17 That which I speak, I speak..foolishly
11. 21 is bold, I speak foolishly, I am bold also

FOOLISHLY, to deal —
To boast, הָלַל *halal.*
Psa. 75. 4 I said unto the fools, Deal not foolishly

FOOLISHLY, to do —
1. *To be or become foolish,* יָאַל *yaal,* 2.
Num 12. 11 wherein we have done foolishly, and

2. *To be empty, foolish,* נָבֵל *nabel.*
Prov 30. 32 If thou hast done foolishly in lifting up

3. *To act foolishly,* סָכַל *sakal,* 2.
1 Sa. 13. 13 Samuel said..Thou hast done foolishly
2 Sa. 24. 10 take away..for I have done very foolishly
1 Ch. 21. 8 do away..for I have done very foolishly
2 Ch. 16. 9 Herein thou hast done foolishly: therefore

4. *To act foolishly,* סָכַל *sakal,* 5.
Gen. 31. 28 Thou hast now done foolishly in (so) doing

FOOLISHNESS —
1. *Folly,* אִוֶּלֶת *ivveleth.*
Psa. 38. 5 are corrupt because of my foolishness
69. 5 O God, thou knowest my foolishness
Prov 12. 23 the heart of fools proclaimeth foolishness
14. 24 (but) the foolishness of fools (is) folly
15. 2 mouth of fools poureth out foolishness
15. 14 the mouth of fools feedeth on foolishness
19. 3 foolishness of man perverteth his way
22. 15 Foolishness (is) bound in the heart of a
24. 9 The thought of foolishness (is) sin: and
27. 22 (yet) will not his foolishness depart from

2. *Folly,* סִכְלוּת *sikluth.*
Eccl. 7. 25 of folly, even of foolishness (and) madness
10. 13 The beginning..(is) foolishness; and the

3. *Senselessness,* ἀφροσύνη *aphrosunē.*
Mark 7. 22 evil eye, blasphemy, pride, foolishness

4. *Folly,* μωρία *mōria.*
1 Co. 1. 18 preaching of the cross is..foolishness
1. 21 foolishness of preaching to save them
1. 23 and unto the Greeks foolishness
2. 14 of God: for they are foolishness unto
3. 19 the wisdom of this world is foolishness

5. *That which is foolish,* τὸ μωρόν *to mōron.*
1 Co. 1. 25 the foolishness of God is wiser than men

FOOLISHNESS, to turn into —
To make foolish, סָכַל *sakal,* 3.
2 Sa. 15. 31 turn the counsel of A. into foolishness

FOOLS, to become or make —
1. *To boast, praise,* הָלַל *halal,* 3a.
Job 12. 17 he leadeth..and maketh the judges fools

2. *To be or become foolish,* יָאַל *yaal,* 2.
Isa. 19. 13 The princes of Zoan are become fools

FOOT —
1. *Base, station,* כֵּן *ken.*
Exod 30. 18 Thou shalt..make..his foot (also of) br.
30. 28 all his vessels, and the laver and his foot
31. 9 his furniture, and the laver and his foot
35. 16 and all his vessels, the laver and his foot
38. 8 he made..the foot of it (of) brass, of the
39. 39 and all his vessels, the laver and his foot
Exod 40. 11 thou shalt anoint the laver and his foot
Lev. 8. 11 his vessels, both the laver and his foot

2. *Step,* פַּעַם *paam.*
2 Ki. 19. 24 with the sole of my feet have I dried up
Psa. 58. 10 wash his feet in the blood of the wicked
74. 3 Lift up thy feet unto the perpetual deso.
Prov 29. 5 flattereth..spreadeth a net for his feet
Song 7. 1 How beautiful are thy feet with shoes, O
Isa. 37. 25 with the sole of my feet have I dried up

3. *Foot,* רֶגֶל *regel.*
Gen. 8. 9 found no rest for the sole of her foot, and
41. 44 shall no man lift up his hand or foot
Exod 21. 24 tooth for tooth, hand for hand, foot for f.
29. 20 upon the great toe of their right foot, and
Lev. 8. 23 and upon the great toe of his right foot
13. 12 the plague from his head even to his foot
14. 14, 17, 25, 28 upon the great toe of his right f.
Num 22. 25 crushed Balaam's foot against the wall
Deut. 2. 5 no, not so much as a foot breadth; beca.
8. 4 neither did thy foot swell, these forty ye.
11. 10 wateredst (it) with thy foot, as a garden
19. 21 tooth for tooth, hand for hand, foot for f.
25. 9 loose his shoe from off his foot, and spit
28. 35 from the sole of thy foot unto the top of
28. 56 set the sole of her foot upon the ground
28. 65 shall the sole of thy foot have rest: but
29. 5 thy shoe is not waxen old upon thy foot
32. 35 their foot shall slide in (due) time: for
33. 24 brethren, and let him dip his foot in oil
Josh. 1. 3 that the sole of your foot shall tread upon
5. 15 Loose thy shoe from off thy foot; for the
2 Sa. 2. 18 Asahel (was as) light of foot as a wild roe
14. 25 from the sole of his foot even to the cro.
2 Ch. 33. 8 Neither will I any more remove the foot
Job 2. 7 from the sole of his foot unto his crown
28. 4 (even the waters) forgotten of the foot
39. 15 forgetteth that the foot may crush them
Psa. 9. 15 in the net..is their own foot taken
26. 12 My foot standeth in an even place: in the
36. 11 Let not the foot of pride come against me
38. 16 when my foot slippeth, they magnify..ag.
68. 23 That thy foot may be dipped in the blood
91. 12 lest thou dash thy foot against a stone
94. 18 When I said, My foot slippeth; thy mer.
Prov. 1. 15 My son..refrain thy foot from their path
3. 23 walk in thy way safely, and thy foot
3. 26 and shall keep thy foot from being taken
4. 27 Turn not..remove thy foot from evil
25. 17 Withdraw thy foot from thy neighbour's
25. 19 Confidence..(is like)..a foot out of joint
Eccl. 5. 1 Keep thy foot when thou goest to the h.
Isa. 1. 6 From the sole of the foot even unto the
20. 2 and put off thy shoe from thy foot. And
26. 6 The foot shall tread it down, (even) the f.
41. 2 Who..called him to his foot, gave the
58. 13 If thou turn away thy foot from the sab.
Jer. 2. 25 Withhold thy foot from being unshod
Eze. 6. 11 stamp with thy foot, and say, Alas for all
29. 11 No foot of man..nor foot of beast shall
32. 13 neither shall the foot of man trouble them
Amos 2. 15 (he that is) swift of foot shall not deliver

4. *Foot,* πούς *pous.*
Matt. 4. 6 lest..thou dash thy foot against a stone
18. 8 if thy hand or thy foot offend thee, cut
22. 13 Bind him hand and foot, and take him
Mark 9. 45 if thy foot offend thee, cut it off: it is
Luke 4. 11 lest..thou dash thy foot against a stone
John 11. 44 bound hand and foot with grave clothes
1 Co. 12. 15 If the foot shall say, Because I am not
Rev. 10. 2 and he set his right foot upon the sea, and
[*See also* Trample, tread under, trodden, trodden under.

FOOT, on —
1. *Foot,* רֶגֶל *regel.*
Judg. 5. 15 he was sent on foot into the valley. For
Psa. 66. 6 they went through the flood on foot

2. *Foot soldier,* רַגְלִי *ragli.*
Exod 12. 37 about six hundred thousand on foot (that

3. *On foot, by land,* πεζῇ *pezē.*
Matt 14. 13 they followed him on foot out of the cities

FOOT on, to set one's —
Foot step, foot breadth, βῆμα ποδός *bēma podos.*
Acts 7. 5 no, not (so much as) to set his foot on

FOOT, garment down to the —
Reaching the foot, ποδήρης *podērēs.*
Rev. 1. 13 clothed with a garment down to the foot

FOOT, to tread under —
1. *To tread down,* בּוּס *bus.*
Isa. 14. 25 upon my mountains tread him under foot

2. *To tread down,* בּוּס *bus,* 3a.
Jer. 12. 10 have trodden my portion under foot, they

3. *To be trodden down,* בּוּס *bus,* 6.
Isa. 14. 19 the pit; as a carcase trodden under foot

FOOTMAN —
1. *Footman,* רַגְלִי *ragli.*
Num 11. 21 people..six hundred thousand footmen
1 Sa. 4. 10 for there fell..thirty thousand footmen
15. 4 two hundred thousand footmen, and ten
2 Sa. 10. 6 the Syrians..twenty thousand footmen
1 Ki. 20. 29 slew..an hundred thousand footmen in
2 Ki. 13. 7 ten chariots, and ten thousand footmen
Jer. 12. 5 If thou hast run with the footmen, and

2. *To run,* רוץ *ruts.*
1 Sa. 22. 17 the king said unto the footmen that stood

3. *Footman, man on foot,* אִישׁ רַגְלִי *ish ragli.*
Judg 20. 2 four hundred thousand footmen that drew
2 Sa. 8. 4 horsemen, and twenty thousand footmen
1 Ch. 18. 4 and twenty thousand footmen; 19. 18.

FOOTSTEP —

1. *Heel, trace, footstep,* עָקֵב *aqeb.*
Psa. 77. 19 waters, and thy footsteps are not known
89. 51 they have reproached the footsteps of
Song 1. 8 go thy way forth by the footsteps of the

2. *Movement, step, foot, anvil, time, now,* פַּעַם *paam.*
Psa. 17. 5 in thy paths, (that) my footsteps slip not

FOOTSTOOL —

1. *Footstool, place for treading on,* כֶּבֶשׁ *kebesh.*
2 Ch. 9. 18 six steps..with a footstool of gold

2. *A stool for the foot,* הֲדֹם רֶגֶל *hadom regel.*
1 Ch. 28. 2 for the footstool of our God, and had
Psa. 99. 5 our God, and worship at his footstool
110. 1 until I make thine enemies thy footstool
132. 7 we will worship at his footstool
Isa. 66. 1 my throne, and the earth (is) my footstool
Lam. 2. 1 remembered not his footstool in the day

3. *Footstool, what is under the foot,* ὑποπόδιον.
Jas. 2. 3 there, or sit here under my footstool

4. *Footstool of the feet,* ὑποπόδιον τῶν ποδῶν.
Matt. 5. 35 Nor by the earth; for it is his footstool
22. 44 till I make thine enemies [thy footstool]?
Mark 12. 36 till I make thine enemies thy footstool
Luke 20. 43 Till I make thine enemies thy footstool
Acts 2. 35 Until I make thy foes thy footstool
7. 49 earth (is) my footstool: what house will
Heb. 1. 13 until I make thine enemies thy footstool?
10. 13 till his enemies be made his footstool

FOR —

1. *Then,* אָז *az.*
2 Ki. 5. 3 for he would recover him of his leprosy

2. *Unto,* אֶל *el.*
Exod. 8. 25 Pharaoh called for Moses and for Aaron

3. *Because, for,* בַּאֲשֶׁר *ba-asher.*
Eccl. 7. 2 for that (is) the end of all men; and the

4. *The, that, at, with,* אֵת *eth.*
Lev. 5. 7 then he shall bring for his trespass..two

5. *In (that which),* בְּמוֹ *bemo.*
Isa. 25. 10 straw is trodden down for the dunghill

6. *For, through, up, over, by, in behalf of,* בְּעַד *bead.*
Gen. 20. 7 he shall pray for thee, and thou shalt
Exod. 8. 28 shall not go very far away: entreat for
32. 30 I shall make an atonement for your sin
Lev. 16. 6 and make an atonement for himself, and
Jer. 7. 16 neither lift up cry nor prayer for them
21. 2 Enquire, I pray thee, of the LORD for us

7. *Because of, for the sake of,* גָּלָל *galal.*
Jer. 11. 17 for the evil of the house of Israel, and of

8. *Because, for,* דִּי *di.*
Ezra 7. 23 for why should there be wrath against

9. *Because, for,* כִּי *ki.*
Gen. 2. 5 for..God had not caused it to rain upon
29. 32 for she said, Surely the LORD hath looked
Exod 13. 17 for God said, Lest peradventure the peop.

10. *To, for,* לְמוֹ *lemo.*
Job 27. 14 be multiplied, (it is) for the sword: and

11. *From,* מִן *min.*
Dan. 2. 20 Blessed be the name of God for ever and
5. 19 for the majesty that he gave him, all

12. *For the sake of,* לְמַעַן *le-maan.*
Gen. 18. 24 for the fifty righteous that (are) therein?

13. *Over against,* נֹכַח *nokach.*
Gen. 25. 21 And Isaac entreated the LORD for his

14. *For the purpose of,* בַּעֲבוּר *ba-abur.*
Exod. 9. 16 have I raised thee up, for to show (in)

15. *Unto, till,* עַד *ad.*
Gen. 13. 15 to thee will I give it, and to thy seed for
Dan. 6. 7 ask a petition of any god or man for
7. 12 yet their lives were prolonged for a sea.
7. 18 possess the kingdom for ever, even for

16. *In reference to, for,* עַל *al.*
Gen. 19. 17 that he said, Escape for thy life; look not
Ezra 4. 15 for which cause was this city destroyed
6. 11 let his house be made a dunghill for this
6. 17 and for a sin offering for all Israel, twelve
6. 18 in their courses, for the service of God
Dan. 6. 23 Then was the king exceeding glad for

17. *In consequence of,* עֵקֶב *eqeb.*
Isa. 5. 23 Which justify the wicked for reward, and

18. *In exchange for,* חֵלֶף *cheleph.*
Num 18. 21 all the tenth in Israel for an inheritance
18. 31 it (is) your reward for your service in

19. *Over against, in behalf of,* ἀντί *anti.*
Matt. 5. 38 An eye for an eye, and a tooth for a tooth
17. 27 take, and give unto them for me and thee
20. 28 and to give his life a ransom for many
Mark 10. 45 and to give his life a ransom for many
Luke 11. 11 will he for a fish give him a serpent?
John 1. 16 have all we received, and grace for grace
Rom 12 17 Recompense to no man evil for evil
1 Co. 11. 15 for (her) hair is given her for a covering
1 Th. 5. 15 See that none render evil for evil unto
Heb. 12. 2 who for the joy that was set before him
12. 16 who for one morsel of meat sold his birth.
Jas. 4. 15 For that ye (ought) to say, If the Lord
1 Pe. 3. 9 Not rendering evil for evil, or railing for

20. *From, on account of,* ἀπό *apo.*
Matt 13. 44 for joy thereof goeth and selleth all that
14. 26 is a spirit: and they cried out for fear
28. 4 for fear of him the keepers did shake
Luke 19. 3 could not for the press, because he was
21. 26 Men's hearts failing them for fear, and
22. 45 he found them sleeping for sorrow
24. 41 while they yet believed not for joy, and
John 21. 6 were not able to draw it for the multitude
Acts 12. 14 she opened not the gate for gladness, but
22. 11 when I could not see for the glory of

21. *During, until,* ἄχρι *achri.*
Luke 4. 13 he departed from him for a season
Acts 13. 11 be blind, not seeing the sun for a season

22. *Verily, therefore,* γάρ *gar.*
Matt. 1. 20 for that which is conceived in her is of
1. 21 for he shall save his people from their
2. 2 for we have seen his star in the east, and
2. 5 for thus it is written by the prophet
2. 6 for out of thee shall come a Governor
2. 13 for Herod will seek the young child to
2. 20 for they are dead which sought the young
3. 2, 3, 9, 15; 4. 6, 10, 17, 18; 5. 12, 18, 20, 29, 30, 46; 6. 7, 8, 14, 16, 21, 24, 32, 34; 7. 2, 8, 12, 25, 29; 9. 5, 13, 16, 21, 24; 10. 10, 17, [19], 20, [23], 26, 35; 11. [10], 13, 18, 30; 12. 8, 33, 34, 37, 40, 50; 13. 12, 15, 17; 14. 3, 4, 24; 15. 2, 4, 19; 16. 2, 3, 25, 26, 27; 17. 15, 20; 18. 7, 10, [11], 20; 19. 12, 14, 22; 20. 1, [16]; 21. 26, 32; 22. 14, 16, 28, 30; 23. 3, [4], 8, 9, [10], 13, 17, 29, 39; 24. 5, 6, 7, 21, 24, 27, [28], 38; 25. 14, 29, 35, 42; 26. 9, 10, 11, 12, 28, 31, 43, 52; 27. 18, 19, 43; 28. 2, 5, 6.
Mark 1. 16, 22, 38; 2. 15; 3. 10, 21, [35]; 4. 22, 25, [28]; 5. 8, 28, 42; 6. 14, 17, 18, 20, 31, [36], 48, 50, 52, [52]; 7. 3, [8], 10, 21, [25], 27; 8. [3], 35, 36; 9. 6, 6, 31, 34, 39, 40, 41, 49; 10. 14, 22, [27]; 11. 13, 18, [23], 32; 12. 12, 14, 23, 25, [36], 44; 13. [6], [7], 8, [9], 11, 19, 22, 33, 35; 14. 5, 7, 40, 56; 15. 10; 16. 4, 8.
Luke 1. 15, 18, 30, 44, 48, 76; 2. 10; 3 8; 4. [8], 10; 5. 9, 39; 6. 23, 23, 26, 38, 43, 44, 44, 45, [48]; 7. 5, 6, [28], 33; 8. 17, 18, 29, 29, 40, 46; 9. 14, 24, 25, 26, 44, 48, 50, [56]; 10. 7, 24; 11. 10, 30; 12. 12, 30, 34, 52, 58; 14. 14, 24, 28; 16. 2, 13, 28; 17. 21, 24; 18. 16, 23, 25, 32; 19. 5, 10, 21, [26], 48; 20. 6, 19, 33, 36, 38; 21. 4, 8, 9, 15, 23, 26, 35; 22. 2, 16, 18, 27, 37, 71; 23. 8, 12, 15, 34, 41
John 2. 25; 3. 2, 16, 17, 20, 24, 34, 34; 4. 8, 9, 18, 42, 44, 45, 47; 5. [4], 13, 19, 20, 21, 22, 26, 36, 46, 46; 6. 6, 27, 33, 55, 64, 71; 7. 1, 4, 5, 39; 8. 24, 42; 9. 22; 11. 39; 12. 8, 43, 47; 13. 11, 13, 15, 29; 14. 30; 16. 7, 13, 27; 18. 13; 19. 6, 31, 36; 20. 9, 17; 21. 7, 8. Acts 1. 20; 2. 15, 25, 34, 39; 3 [22]; 4. 3, 12, 16, 20, 22, 27, 34; 5. 26, 36; 6. 14; 7. 33, 40; 8. 7, 16, 21, 23; 9. 11, 16; 10. 46; 13. 8, 27, 36, 47; 15. 21, 28; 16. 3, 28; 17. 20, 23, 28, 28; 18. [3], [15], 18, 28; 19. 24, 32, 37; 20. 10, 13, 16, 16, 27, [29]; 21. 3, 13, 22, 29, 36; 22. 22, 26; 23. 5, 8, 11, 17, 21; 24. 5; 25. [11], 27; 26. 16, 26, 26, 26; 27. 22 23, 25, 34, 34; 28. 2, 22, 27.
Rom. 1. 9, 11, 16, 16, 17, 18, 19, 20, 26; 2. 1, 1, 11, 12, 13, 14, 24, 25. 28; 3. 3, 7, 9. 20, 22, 23; 4. 2, 3, 9, 13, 14, [15]; 5. 6, 7, 10, 13, 15, 16, 17, 19; 6. 5, 7, 10, 14, 14, 19, 20, 21, 23; 7. 1, 2, 5, 7, 8, 11, [14], 15, 15, 18, 18, 19, 22; 8. 2, 3, 5, 6, 7, 13, 14, 15, 18, 19, 20, 22, 24, 24, 26, 38; 9. 3, 6, 9, 11, 15, 17, 19, 28, [32]; 10. 2, 3, 4, 5, 10, 11, 12, 12, 13, 16; 11. 1, [13], 15, 21, 23, 24, 25, 29, 30, 32, 34; 12. 3, 4, 19, 20; 13. 1, 3, 4, 4, 4, 6, 6, 8 9, 11; 14. 3, 4, 6, 7, 8, 9, 10, 11, 17, 18; 15. 3, 4, 18, [24], 26, 27; 16. 18, 19.
1 Co. 1. 11, 17, 18, 19, 21, 26; 2. 2, 8, 10, 11, 14, 16; 3. 2, 3, 3, 3, 4, 9, 11, 13, 17, 19, 19, 21; 4. 4, 7, 9, 15, 15, 20; 5. 3, 12; 6. 16, 20; 7. [7], 9, 14, 16, 22, 31; 8. [8], 10; 9 2, 9, 15, 16, 16, 17, 19; 10. 4, 5, 17, 26, [28], 29; 11. 5, 6, 7, 8, 12, 18, 19, 21, 23, 26, 29, [31]; 12. 8, 12; 13 [9], [12]; 14. 2, 2, [5], 9, [14], 17, 31, 33, 34, 35; 15. 3, 9, 16, 21, 22, 25, 27, 32, 34, 41 52, 53; 16. 5, 7, 9, 10, 11, 18. 2 Co. 1. 8, 12, 13, 19, 20, 24; 2. 2, 4, 9, 11, 17; 3. 6, 9, 11, 14; 4. 5, 11, 15, 17. 18; 5. 1, 2, 7, 10, [12], 13, 14 [21]; 6. 2, 14, 16; 7. 3, [8], 9, 10, 11; 8. 9, 10, 12, 13; 9. 1, 2. 7; 10. 3, 4, 8, 12, 14, 14 18; 11. 2, 2, 4, [5], 9, 13, 14, 19. 20; 12. 6, 6, 9, 10, 11, 11, 13, 14, 14, 20; 13. 4, 8, 9.
Gal. 1. 10, [10], 12, 13; 2. 6, 8, 12, 18, 19, 21; 3. 10, 10, [13], 18, 21, 26, 27, 28; 4. 15, 22, 24, 25, 27, 30; 5. 5, 6, 13, 14, 17; 6. 3, 5, 7, 9, 13, 15, 17. Eph. 2. 8, 10, 14; 5. 5, 6, 8, 9, 12, 13, 29; 6. 1. Phil. 1. 8, 19, 21, [23]; 2. 13, 20, 21, 27; 3. 3, 18, 20; 4. 11. Col. 2. 1, 5; 3. 3, 20, [24]; 4. 13. 1 Th. 1. 8, 9; 2. 1, 3, 5, 9, [9], 14, 19, 20; 3. 3, 4, 9; 4. 2, 3, 7, 9, 14, 15; 5. 2, [3], 7, 18. 2 Th. 2. 7; 3. 2, 7, 10, 11. 1 Ti. 2. [3], 5, 13; 3. 13; 4. 5, 8, 10, 16; 5. 4, 11, 15, 18; 6. 7, 10. 2 Ti. 1. 7, 12; 2. 11, 16; 3. 2, 6, 9; 4. 3, 6, 10, 11, 15. Titus 1. 7, 10; 2. 11; 3. 9, 12. Phm. 7, 15, 22.
Heb. 1. 5; 2. 2, 5, 8, 10, 11, 16, 18; 3. 3, 4, 14, 16; 4. 3, 4, 8, 10, 12, 15; 5. 1, 13, 13; 6. 4, 7, 10, 13, 16; 7. 1, 10, 11, 12, 13, 14, 17, 18, 19, 21, 26, 27, 28; 8. 3, [4], 5, 7, 8; 9. 2, 13, 16, 17, 19, 24; 10. 1, 4, 14, 15, 23, 26, 30, 36, 37; 11. 2, 5, 6, 10, 14, 16, 26, 27, 32; 12. 3, 6. 7, 10, 17, 17, 18, 20, 25; 13. 2, 5, 9, 11, 14, 16, 17, 17, 18.
Jas. 1. 6, 7, 11, 13, 20, 24; 2. 2, 10, 11, 13, 26; 3. 2, 7, 16; 4. 14. 1 Pe. 2. 19, 20, 21, 25; 3. 5, 10, 17; 4. 3, 6. 2 Pe. 1. 8, 10, 11, 16, 17, 21; 2. 4, 8, 18, 19, 20, 21; 3. 4, 5. 1 Jo. 2. 19; 4. 20; 5. 3. 2 Jo. 11. 3 Jo. 3. Jude 4. Rev. 1. 3; 3. 2; 9. 19, 19; 13. 18; 14. 4, [5]; 16. [6], 14; 17. 17; 19. 8, 10; 21. 1, 22, 23, 25; 22. [9], [18].

23. *Through, by means of,* διά *(gen.) dia.*
Rom 15. 30 Now I beseech you brethren, for the L.

24. *Because of this,* διότι *dioti.*
Luke 1. 13 Fear not, Zacharias: for thy prayer is
21. 28 lift up your heads; for your redemption
Acts 10. 20 doubting nothing: for I have sent them
18. 10 For I am with thee..for I have much
22. 18 for they will not receive thy testimony
Gal. 2. 16 for by the works of the law shall no flesh
1 Pe. 1. 24 For all flesh (is) as grass, and all the glory

25. *But, now, moreover,* δέ *de.*
Mark 16. 8 for they trembled and were amazed
Luke 23. 17 For of necessity he must release one unto

26. *With a view to,* εἰς *eis.*
Matt. 5. 13 it is thenceforth good for nothing, but to
6. 34 Take therefore no thought for the morr.
8. 4 offer the gift..for a testimony unto them
10. 10 Nor scrip for (your) journey, neither two
10. 18 for a testimony against them and the G.
24. 14 gospel..shall be preached..for a witness
26. 13 shall also this..be told for a memorial of
26. 28 which is shed..for the remission of sins
27. 10 gave them for the potter's field, as the L
Mark 1. 4 preach the baptism of repentance for the
1. 44 offer..those things..for a testimony unto
6. 8 they should take nothing for (their) jour.
6. 11 shake off the dust..for a testimony agai.
13. 9 brought..for a testimony against them
14. 9 shall be spoken of for a memorial of her
Luke 2. 34 set for the fall and rising again of many
2. 34 for a sign which shall be spoken against
3. 3 preaching the baptism of repentance for
5. 4 and let down your nets for a draught
5. 14 and offer..for a testimony unto them
9. 3 Take nothing for (your) journey, neither
9. 5 shake off the very dust..for a testimony
9. 13 we should go and buy meat for all this p
9. 62 No man..looking back, is fit [for] the
12. 19 thou hast..goods laid up for many years
14. 35 It is neither fit for the land, nor yet for
21. 13 And it shall turn to you for a testimony
John 1. 7 The same came for a witness, to bear
9. 39 For judgment I am come into this world
Acts 2. 38 be baptized..for the remission of sins
7. 5 he would give it to him for a possession
7. 21 took him up, and nourished him for her
10. 4 are come up for a memorial before God
13. 2 for the work whereunto I have called
13. 47 for salvation unto the ends of the earth
14. 26 recommended..for the work which they
23. 30 how that the Jews laid wait for the man
Rom. 1 5 for obedience to the faith among all nat.
2. 26 uncircumcision be counted for circumci.
4. 3 was counted unto him for righteousness
4. 5 his faith is counted for righteousness
4. 9 that faith was reckoned to Abraham for
4. 22 it was imputed to him for righteousness
8. 28 that all things work together for good to
9. 8 the children..are counted for the seed
10. 4 the end of the law for righteousness to
13. 4 is the minister of God to thee for good
15. 2 please (his) neighbour for (his) good to e.
15. 4 were written for our learning; that we
15. 26 for the poor saints which are at Jerusal.
15. 31 my service which (I have) [for] Jerusalem
16. 26 made known..for the obedience of faith
1 Co. 5. 5 to deliver..for the destruction of the fl.
11. 17 not for the better, but for the worse
14. 22 Wherefore tongues are for a sign, not to
16. 1 the collection for the saints, as I have gi.
2 Co. 5. 5 he that hath wrought us for the selfsame
8. 14 abundance (may be a supply) for their
8. 14 abundance also may be (a supply) for your
9. 10 both minister bread for (your) food, and
10. 8 for edification, and not for your destruc.
Gal. 3. 6 it was accounted to him for righteousness
5. 13 only (use) not liberty for an occasion to
Eph. 2. 22 are builded together for an habitation of
4. 12 for the work of the ministry, for the edi.
5. 2 a sacrifice to God for a sweet smelling
6. 22 I have sent unto you for the same purp.
Phil. 1. 17 I am set for the defence of the Gospel
1. 25 for your furtherance and joy of faith
Col. 1. 16 things were created by him, and for him
1. 25 which is given to me for you, to fulfil
2 Ti. 4. 11 he is profitable to me for the ministry
Titus 3. 14; Heb. 3. 5; 6. 16; 9. 9; 9. 15; 11. 8; Jas. 2. 23; 1 Pe. 1. 4; 2. 14; Rev 9. 15; 22. 2.

27. *Because,* διά *(acc.) dia.*
Matt. 6 25; 12. 27; 13. 13, 52; 14. 2; 18. 23; 21. 43; 23. 14; 24. 44; Mark 6. 14; 11. 24; 12. 24; Luke 11. 19, 49; 12. 22; 14. 20; John 1. 31; 5. 6, 18; 6. 65; 7 22; 8. 47; 9. 23; 10. 17; 12. 39; 13. 11; 15. 19; 16. 15; 19 11; Acts 2. 26; Rom. 4. 16; 2 Co. 4. 1; 7. 13; 13. 10; 1 Th. 3. 7; 2 Ti. 2. 10; Phm. 15; Heb. 1. 9; 2. 1; 1 Jo. 3. 1; 4. 5; Rev. 7. 15; 12. 12; 18. 8.

28. *Out of, from,* ἐκ *ek.*
Matt 20. 2 agreed with the labourers for a penny a
Rev. 16. 10 and they gnawed their tongues for pain

29. *In,* ἐν *en.*
Matt 6. 7 shall be heard for their much speaking
Luke 1. 44 the babe leaped in my womb for joy
Phil. 1. 26 be more abundant in Jesus Christ for me
1 Ti. 5. 10 Well reported of for good works; if she
Jas. 5. 3 treasure together for the last days
1 Pe. 4. 14 ye be reproached for the name of Christ

30. *Because of, on account of,* ἕνεκα *heneka.*
Acts 28. 20 for the hope of Israel I am bound with
Rom 14. 20 For meat destroy not the work of God

30. *Since truly, inasmuch as,* ἐπειδή *epeidē.*
Luke 11. 6 For a friend of mine in his journey is
1 Co. 1. 22 For the Jews require a sign, and the
Phil. 2. 26 For he longed after you all, and was full

31. *Upon, about, for,* ἐπί (*dat.*) *epi.*
Matt 19. 9 put away..except (it be) for fornication
Mark 3. 5 being grieved for the hardness of their
Luke 2. 20 for all the things that they had heard
13. 17 rejoiced for all the glorious things that
Acts 4. 21 glorified God for that which was done
15. 14 to take out of them a people [for] his name
15. 31 they rejoiced for the consolation
20. 38 most of all for the words which he spake
26. 6 for the hope of the promise made of God
1 Co. 1. 4 for the grace of God which is given you
2 Co. 7. 13 the more joyed we for the joy of Titus
9. 13 glorify God for your professed subjection
9. 15 Thanks..unto God for his unspeakable
Phil. 1. 5 For your fellowship in the Gospel from
3. 12 that for which also I am apprehended of
1 Th. 3. 9 render..for all the joy wherewith we joy
Jas 5. 1 howl for your miseries that shall come
5. 7 and hath long patience for it, until he
Rev. 18. 9 lament [for] her, when they shall see the

32. *Upon, for,* ἐπί (*acc.*) *epi.*
Luke 7. 44 thou gavest me no water for my feet
18. 4 he would not for a while: but afterward
23. 28 for me, but weep for yourselves, and for
John 19. 24 and for my vesture they did cast lots
Phil. 3. 14 [for] the prize of the high calling of God
Heb. 12. 10 but he for (our) profit, that (we) might be
1 Pe. 1. 13 for the grace that is to be brought unto

33. *And,* καί *kai.*
Luke 6. 32 For if ye love them which love you, what
Rom 11. 27 For this (is) my covenant unto them, when
1 Jo. 3. 4 for sin is the transgression of the law

34. *And verily indeed,* καὶ γάρ *kai gar.*
Matt. 8. 9 For I am a man under authority, having
26. 73 Surely thou..for thy speech bewrayeth
Mark 14. 70 for thou art a Galilæan, and thy speech
Luke 6. 32 for sinners also love those that love
6. 33 for sinners also do even the same
22. 59 also was with him; for he is a Galilæan
John 4. 23 for the Father seeketh such to worship
Acts 19. 40 For we are in danger to be called in
Rom. 16. 2 for she hath been a succourer of many
1 Co. 8. 5 For though there be that are called gods
12. 13 For by one Spirit are we all baptized
12. 14 For the body is not one member, but many
14. 8 For if the trumpet give an uncertain
2 Co. 2. 10 for if I forgave anything, to whom I
3. 10 For even that which was made glorious
5. 4 For we that are in (this) tabernacle do
7. 5 For, when we were come into Macedonia
13. 4 For though he was crucified through
Heb. 4. 2 For unto us was the Gospel preached, as
5. 12 For when..the time ye ought to be teach.
10. 34 For ye had compassion of me in my bonds
12. 29 For our God (is) a consuming fire
13. 22 for I have written a letter unto you in

35. *Down upon, or along,* κατά (*acc.*) *kata.*
Matt 19. 3 man to put away his wife for every cause

36. *Of the,* τοῦ *tou.*
Luke 2. 21 for the circumcising of the child, his name

37. *That, because,* ὅτι *hoti.*
Matt. 6. 26 for they sow not, neither do they reap
Mark 1. 27 [for with authority commandeth he even]
12. 32 for there is one God; and there is none
Luke 1. 45 for there shall be a performance of those
1. 48 for, behold, from henceforth all generat.
4. 36 for with authority and power he comm.
7. 39 what manner of woman..for she is a sin.
8. 25 for he commandeth even the winds and
12. 24 the ravens: for they neither sow nor reap
15. 6 for I have found my sheep which was lost
15. 9 for I have found the piece which I had
John 4. 35 for they are white already to harvest
5. 28 for the hour is coming, in the which all
7. 52 for out of Galilee ariseth no prophet
14. 17 for he dwelleth with you, and shall be in
Acts 8. 33 for his life is taken from the earth
22. 15 For thou shalt be his witness unto all
1 Co. 16. 17 for that which was lacking on your part
2 Co. 1. 5 For as the sufferings of Christ abound
2. 15 For we are unto God a sweet savour of
7. 14 For if I have boasted anything to him
8. 3 For to (their) power, I bear record, yea
Gal. 4. 27 for the desolate hath many more 3. 11.
Eph. 2. 18 For through him we both have access by
Phil. 4. 16 For even in Thessalonica ye sent once and
1 Th. 1. 5 For our gospel came not unto you in word
2 Th. 3. 7 for we behaved not ourselves disorderly
1 Jo. 3. 2 like him; for we shall see him as he is
3. 20 [For] if our heart condemn us, God is
4. 8 [loveth not knoweth not God; for God is]
Rev. 12. 12 for the devil is come down unto you
18. 20 Rejoice..for God hath avenged you on
19. 7 for the marriage of the Lamb is come, and
21. 5 for these words are true and faithful

38. *Because,* ὅτι *hoti* (*causal*).
Matt. 5. 3, 10 for their's is the kingdom of heaven
5. 4 that mourn: for they shall be comforted
5. 5 meek: for they shall inherit the earth
5. 6 which do hunger..for they shall be filled
5. 7 the merciful: for they shall obtain mercy
5. 8 the pure in heart: for they shall see God
5. 9 for they shall be called the children v. 10.
Matt. 5. 12 for great (is) your reward in heaven
5. 34 neither by heaven; for it is God's throne
5. 35 Nor by the earth; for it is his footstool
5. 35 for it is the city of the great King
5. 45 for he maketh his sun to rise on the evil
6. 5 for they love to pray standing in the
6. 13 [For thine is the kingdom, and the power]
7. 13 for wide (is) the gate, and broad (is) the
11. 21 for if the mighty works, which were done
11. 23 for if the mighty works, which have been
11. 26 for so it seemed good in thy sight
11. 29 for I am meek and lowly in heart: and
12. 42 for she came from the uttermost parts of
13. 16 for they see: and your ears, for they hear
15. 23 Send her away; for she crieth after us
16. 17 for flesh and blood hath not revealed (it)
16. 23 for thou savourest not the things that be
17. 15 have mercy on my son: for he is lunatic
23. 13 for ye shut up the kingdom of heaven
23. 14 [for ye devour widows' houses, and for a]
23. 15 for ye compass sea and land to make one
23. 23 for ye pay tithe of mint and anise and
23. 25 for ye make clean the outside of the cup
23. 27 for ye are like unto whited sepulchres
24. 42 for ye know not what hour your Lord doth
24. 44 for in such an hour as ye think not the S.
25. 8 Give us of your oil; for our lamps are
25. 13 for ye know neither the day nor the hour
Mark 5. 9 My name (is) Legion: for we are many
6. 17 Philip's wife; for he had married her
8. 33 for thou savourest not the things that be
14. 27 for it is written, I will smite the Shepherd
Luke 1. 37 For with God nothing shall be impossible
1. 49 For he that is mighty hath done to me
1. 68 for he hath visited and redeemed his
2. 11 For unto you is born this day..a Saviour
2. 30 For mine eyes have seen thy salvation
4. 6 for that is delivered unto me; and to wh.
4. 32 his doctrine: for his word was with power
4. 41 speak: for they knew that he was Christ
4. 43 other cities also: for therefore am I sent
5. 8 Depart from me; for I am a sinful man
6. 19 for there went virtue out of him, and
6. 20 Blessed..for your's is the kingdom of God
6. 21 for ye shall be filled..for ye shall laugh
6. 24 for ye have received your consolation
6. 25 for ye shall hunger..for ye shall mourn
6. 35 for he is kind unto the unthankful and (to)
7. 47 sins..are forgiven; for she loved much
8. 37 for they were taken with great fear. And
8. 42 For he had one only daughter, about twel.
9. 12 get victuals: for we are here in a desert
9. 38 look upon my son: for he is mine only ch.
10. 13 for if the mighty works had been done in
10. 21 Father; for so it seemed good in thy sight
11. 31 for she came from the utmost parts of
11. 32 for they repented at the preaching of J.
11. 42 for ye tithe mint and rue and all manner
11. 43 for ye love the uppermost seats in the
11. 44 for ye are as graves which appear not
11. 46 for ye lade men with burdens grievous to
11. 47 for ye build the sepulchres of the proph.
11. 48 for they indeed killed them, and ye build
11. 52 for ye have taken away the key of know.
12. 15 for a man's life consisteth not in the
12. 32 for it is your Father's good pleasure to
12. 40 for the Son of man cometh at an hour
13. 24 for many..will seek to enter in, and shall
13. 31 depart hence: for Herod will kill thee
13. 33 for it cannot be that a prophet perish out
14. 11 For whosoever exalteth himself shall be
14. 14 for they cannot recompense thee..thou
14. 17 Come; for all things are now ready
15. 24 For this my son was dead, and is alive
15. 32 for this thy brother was dead, and is alive
16. 3 for my lord taketh away from me the
16. 8 for the children of this world are..wiser
16. 15 for that which is highly esteemed among
16. 24 tongue; for I am tormented in this flame
18. 14 for every one that exalteth himself shall
19. 4 to see him: for he was to pass that (way)
19. 43 For the days shall come upon thee, that
21 22 For these be the days of vengeance, that
23. 29 For, behold, the days are coming, in the
23. 31 For if they do these things in a green tree
24. 29 for it is toward evening, and the day is f.
24. 39 for a spirit hath not flesh and bones, as
John 1. 15, 30 preferred before me: for he was befo.
1. 17 For the law was given by Moses, (but)
4. 22 we know what we worship: for salvation
5. 38 for whom he hath sent, him ye believe
5. 39 for in them ye think ye have eternal life
6. 38 For I came down from heaven, not to do
7. 8 I go not up yet..for my time is not yet
7. 29 for I am from him, and he hath sent me
8. 14 for I know whence I came, and whither
8. 16 For I am not alone, but I and the Father
8. 20 no man laid hands on him; for his hour
8. 29 for I do always those things that please
8. 44 for he is a liar, and the father of it
10. 4 sheep follow him: for they know his voi.
10. 5 for they know not the voice of strangers
11. 47 What do we? for this man doeth many
12. 49 For I have not spoken of myself; but
14. 28 I go unto the Father: for my Father is
15. 5 for without me ye can do nothing
15. 15 for the servant knoweth not what his lord
15. 15 for all things that I have heard of my F.
16. 14 for he shall receive of mine, and shall
17. 8 For I have given unto them the words
17. 9 which thou hast given me; for they are
17. 24 for thou lovedst me before the foundation
John 18. 2 for Jesus oft times resorted thither with
18. 18 had made a fire of coals; for it was cold
19. 20 for the place..was nigh to the city: and
19. 42 for the sepulchre was nigh at hand
Acts 1. 5 For John truly baptized with water; but
1. 17 For he was numbered with us, and had
2. 25 for he is on my right hand, that I should
4. 21 for all (men) glorified God for that which
5. 38 for if this counsel or this work be of men
9. 15 for he is a chosen vessel unto me, to bear
10. 14 for I have never eaten anything that is
10. 38 went about doing good..for God was with
11. 8 for nothing common..hath..entered into
11. 24 For he was a good man, and full of the
13. 41 for I work a work in your days, a work
22. 21 Depart: for I will send thee far hence
Rom. 8. 29 For whom he did foreknow, he also did
11. 36 For of him, and through him, and to him
1 Co. 4. 9 for we are made a spectacle unto the
10. 17 For we (being) many are one bread, (and)
11. 15 for (her) hair is given her for a covering
2 Co. 4. 6 For God..hath shined in our hearts, to
7. 8 For though I made you sorry with a letter
8. 17 For indeed he accepted the exhortation
10. 10 For (his) letters..(are) weighty and pow.
Gal 3. 11 evident: for, The just shall live by faith
4. 12 be as I (am); for I (am) as ye (are): ye
4. 20 desire to be present..for I stand in doubt
6. 8 For he that soweth to his flesh shall of
Eph 4. 25 for we are members one of another
5. 23 For the husband is the head of the wife
5. 30 For we are members of his body, of his
6. 12 For we wrestle not against flesh and blo.
Phil. 1. 29 For unto you it is given in the behalf of
Col. 1. 16 For by him were all things created, that
1. 19 For it pleased (the Father) that in him
2. 9 For in him dwelleth all the fulness of the
1 Th. 2. 14 for ye also have suffered like things of
3. 8 For now we live, if ye stand fast in the
4. 16 For the Lord himself shall descend from
5. 9 For God hath not appointed us to wrath
2 Th. 2. 3 for (that day shall not come), except there
1 Ti. 4. 4 For every creature of God (is) good, and
2 Ti. 1. 16 for he oft refreshed me, and was not
Heb. 8. 10 For this (is) the covenant that I will make
8. 11 for all shall know me, from the least to
8. 12 For I will be merciful to their unright.
Jas. 1. 12 for when he is tried, he shall receive the
1. 23 For if any be a hearer of the word, and not
5. 8 for the coming of the Lord draweth nigh
1 Pe 1. 16 it is written, Be ye holy; for I am holy
2. 15 For so is the will of God, that with well
3. 12 For the eyes of the Lord (are) over the
3. 18 For Christ also hath once suffered for
4. 1 for he that hath suffered in the flesh hath
4. 8 for charity shall cover the multitude of
4. 14 for the Spirit of glory..resteth upon you
4. 17 For the time (is come) that judgment
5. 5 for God resisteth the proud, and giveth
5. 7 Casting all your care upon him; for he
1 Jo 2. 16 For all that (is) in the world, the lust of
3. 8 for the devil sinneth from the beginning
3. 9 for his seed remaineth in him: and he
3. 11 For this is the message that ye heard from
4. 7 love one another: for love is of God; and
5. 4 For whatsoever is born of God overcometh
5. 7 For there are three that bear record in
5. 9 for this is the witness of God which he
2 Jo. 7 For many deceivers are entered into the
Jude 11 for they have gone in the way of Cain
Rev. 3. 4 walk with me in white: for they are wor.
3. 8 for thou hast a little strength, and hast
4. 11 for thou hast created all things, and
5. 9 for thou wast slain, and hast redeemed
6. 17 For the great day of his wrath is come
7. 17 For the Lamb..shall feed them, and shall
11. 2 for it is given unto the Gentiles: and the
12. 10 for the accuser..is cast down, which
12. 12 for the devil is come down unto you
14. 7 for the hour of his judgment is come: and
14. 15 for the time is come for thee to reap; for
14. 18 gather the clusters..for her grapes are
15. 1 for in them is filled up the wrath of God
15. 4 for (thou) only (art) holy: for all nations
15. 4 for thy judgments are made manifest
16. 6 For they have shed the blood of saints
16. 21 for the plague thereof was..great
17. 14 for he is Lord of lords, and King of kings
18. 3 For all nations have drunk of the wine
18. 5 For her sins have reached unto heaven
18. 7 for she saith in her heart, I sit a queen
18. 8 for strong (is) the Lord..who judgeth her
18. 10 for in one hour is thy judgment come
18. 11 for no man buyeth their merchandise any
18. 17 For in one hour so great riches is come to
18. 19 for in one hour is she made desolate
18. 23 for thy merchants were the great men of
18. 23 for by thy sorceries were..nations deceiv.
19. 2 For true and righteous (are) his judgments
19. 2 for he hath judged the great whore, which
19. 6 for the Lord God omnipotent reigneth
21. 4 neither..any more pain: [for] the former
22. 5 for the Lord God giveth them light: and
22. 10 prophecy of this book: [for] the time is

39. *Concerning, about,* περί (*gen.*) *peri.*
Matt. 2. 8 and search diligently for the young child
6. 28 And why take ye thought for raiment?
22. 16 Master..neither carest thou for any
26. 28 this is my blood..which is shed for many
Mark 1. 44 offer for thy cleansing those things which
12. 14 we know that thou..carest for no man

Mark14. 24 blood of the new testament..shed [for]
Luke 2. 27 to do for him after the custom of the law
3. 19 reproved by him for Herodias..and for
4. 38 mother..and they besought him for her
5. 14 offer for thy cleansing, according as M.
12. 26 is least, why take ye thought for the rest?
19. 37 praise God..for all the mighty works that
22. 32 But I have prayed for thee, that thy
John 9. 21 ask him: he shall speak for himself
10. 13 The hireling..careth not for the sheep
10. 33 For a good work we stone thee not
10. 33 but for blasphemy; and because that thou
12. 6 This..not that he cared for the poor; but
15. 22 now they have no cloak for their sin
16. 26 I say not..I will pray the Father for you
17. 9 I pray for them..not for the world, but f.
17. 20 Neither pray I for these alone, but for
19. 24 but cast lots for it, whose it shall be
Acts 8. 15 Who..prayed for them, that they might
19. 40 be called in question for this day's uproar
24. 21 Except it be for this one voice, that I
Rom. 8. 3 and for sin, condemned sin in the flesh
Eph. 6. 18 Praying always..in the spirit .for all
Col. 1. 3 We give thanks..praying always [for] you
2. 1 what great conflict I have [for] you, and
4. 3 praying also for us, that God would open
1 Th. 1. 2 We give thanks to God always for you all
3. 9 what thanks can we render to God..for
5. 25 Brethren, pray for us
2 Th. 1. 3 We are bound to thank God always for
1. 11 Wherefore also we pray always for you
2. 13 to give thanks alway to God for you
3. 1 Finally, brethren, pray for us, that the
Phm. 10 I beseech thee for my son Onesimus
Heb. 5. 3 he ought, as for the people, so also for
10. 6 In burnt offerings..for sin thou hast had
10. 8 burnt offerings..for sin thou wouldest not
10. 18 these (is, there is) no more offering for sin
10. 26 there remaineth no more sacrifice for sins
11. 40 God..provided some better thing for us
13. 11 is brought into the sanctuary..[for] sin
13. 18 Pray for us: for we trust we have a good
1 Pe. 3. 18 Christ also hath once suffered for sins, the
5. 7 Casting all..upon him; for he careth for
1 Jo. 2. 2 for our sins..for our's only, but also for
4. 10 his Son..the propitiation for our sins
5. 16 I do not say that he shall pray for it

40. *Toward, leading to,* πρός *(gen.) pros.*
Acts 27. 34 take..meat; for this is for your health

41. *Toward, in consideration of,* πρός *(acc.) pros.*
Matt 26. 12 on my body, she did (it) for my burial
Mark10. 5 For the hardness of your heart he wrote
Luke 8. 13 have no root, which for a while believe
John 5. 35 ye were willing for a season to rejoice in
Acts 3. 10 they knew that it was he which sat for
13. 15 any word of exhortation for the people
1 Co. 7. 5 except..with consent for a time, that ye
7. 35 And this I speak for your own profit
7. 35 but for that which is comely, and that
10. 11 and they are written for our admonition
2 Co. 2. 16 And who (is) sufficient for these things?
7. 8 made you sorry, though..but for a season
Gal. 2. 5 we gave place..no, not for an hour
Eph. 4. 12 For the perfecting of the saints..the wo.
1 Th. 2. 17 being taken from you for a short time in
1 Ti. 1. 16 for a pattern to them which should
2 Ti. 3. 16 for doctrine, for reproof, for correction f.
Phm. 15 perhaps he..departed for a season, that
Heb. 12. 10 they verily for a few days chastened
12. 11 no chastening for the present seemeth

42. *In behalf of,* ὑπέρ *(gen.) huper.*
Matt. 5. 44 pray for them which..persecute you
Luke 6. 28 pray [for] them which despitefully use
9. 50 said..he that is not against us is for us
22. 19 This is my body, which is given for you
22. 20 in my blood, which is shed for you
John 6. 51 which I will give for the life of the world
10. 11 good shepherd giveth his life for the she.
10. 15 and I lay down my life for the sheep
11. 4 but for the glory of God, that the Son of
11. 50 that one man should die for the people
11. 51 that Jesus should die for that nation
11. 52 not for that nation only, but that also
15. 13 that a man lay down his life for his friends
18. 14 that one man should die for the people
Acts 5. 41 counted worthy to suffer shame for his
8. 24 Pray ye to the Lord for me, that none of
12. 5 but prayer was made..unto God [for] him
15 26 have hazarded their lives for the name of
21. 13 to die..for the name of the Lord Jesus
21. 26 should be offered for every one of them
26. 1 Thou art permitted to speak [for] thyself
Rom. 1. 5 obedience..among all nations, for his na.
1. 8 First, I thank my God..[for] you all, that
5. 6 in due time Christ died for the ungodly
5. 7 scarcely for a righteous man will one die
5. 7 for a good man some would even dare
5. 8 while..yet sinners, Christ died for us
8. 26 the Spirit itself maketh intercession [for]
8. 27 he maketh intercession for the saints acc.
8. 31 If God (be) for us, who (can be) against
8. 32 but delivered him up for us all, how shall
8. 34 Christ..who also maketh intercession for
9. 3 were accursed from Christ for my breth.
10. 1 Brethren, my..prayer to God for Israel
14. 15 Destroy not him..for whom Christ died
15. 8 was a minister of the circumcision for the
15. 9 Gentiles might glorify God for (his) mercy
15. 30 with me in (your) prayers to God for me
16. 4 Who have for my life laid down their own

1 Co. 1. 13 was Paul crucified [for] you? or were ye
4. 6 that no one of you be puffed up for one
5. 7 For even Christ..is sacrificed [for] us
10. 30 evil spoken of..for which I give thanks?
11. 24 this is my body, which is broken for you
12. 25 should have the same care one for anoth.
15. 3 how that Christ died for our sins accord.
15. 29 they do which are baptized for the dead
15. 29 why are they then baptized for the dead?
2 Co. 1. 6 for your consolation..for your consola.
1. 11 also helping together by prayer for us
5. 14 if one died for all, then were all dead
5. 15 And..he died for all, that they which
5. 15 unto him which died for them, and rose
5. 20 Now then we are ambassadors for Christ
5. 21 he hath made him..sin for us, who knew
7. 12 but that our care for you in the sight of
8. 16 put..care into the heart of Titus for you
9. 14 by their prayer for you, which long after
12. 8 For this thing I besought the Lord thrice
12. 15 I will very gladly..be spent for you
12. 19 all things, dearly beloved, for your edify.
13. 8 nothing against the truth, but for the
Gal. 1. 4 Who gave himself [for] our sins, that he
2. 20 Son of God, who..gave himself for me
3. 13 Christ..being made a curse for us: for it
Eph. 1. 16 Cease not to give thanks for you, making
3. 1 Paul, the prisoner of Jesus Christ for you
3. 13 ye faint not at my tribulations for you
5. 2 hath given himself for us an offering and
5. 20 Giving thanks always for all things unto
5. 25 even as Christ also..gave himself for it
6. 19 And for me, that utterance may be given
6. 20 For which I am an ambassador in bonds
Phil. 1. 4 in every prayer of mine for you all making
Col. 1. 7 who is for you a faithful minister of Chr.
1. 9 do not cease to pray for you, and to desire
1 24 Who now rejoice in my sufferings for you
4. 12 labouring fervently for you in prayers
4. 13 that he hath a great zeal for you, and them
1 Th. 5. 10 Who died for us, that, whether we wake
2 Th. 1. 4 we..glory in you..for your patience and
1. 5 kingdom of God, for which ye also suffer
1 Ti. 2. 1 giving of thanks, be made for all men
2. 2 For kings, and..all..in authority
2. 6 Who gave himself a ransom for all, to be
Titus 2. 14 Who gave himself for us, that he might
Heb. 2. 9 that he..should taste death for every man
5. 1 every high priest..is ordained for men in
5. 1 that he may offer..sacrifices for sins
5. 3 And..he ought..to offer [for] sins
6. 20 Whither the forerunner is for us entered
7. 25 ever liveth to make intercession for them
7. 27 offer up sacrifice, first for his own sins
9. 7 not without blood, which he offered for
9. 24 to appear in the presence of God for us
10. 12 after he had offered one sacrifice for sins
13. 17 they watch for your souls, as they that
Jas. 5. 16 and pray one for another, that ye may be
1 Pe 2. 21 because Christ also suffered for us, leaving
3. 18 the just for the unjust, that he might
4. 1 as Christ..suffered [for] us in the flesh
1 Jo. 3. 16 because he laid down his life for us: and
3. 16 to lay down (our) lives for the brethren

43. *As, like as,* ὡς *hōs.*
Matt21. 46 because they took him for a prophet
1 Pe. 2. 16 and not using..liberty for a cloke of

[*See also* Aloud, as, call, care, shout, sing, wait, waited, why.]

FOR all —

1. *Even,* גַּם *gam.*
Lev. 26. 44 And yet for all that, when they be in the

2. *With,* עִם *im.*
Neh. 5. 18 yet for all this required not I the bread of

FOR all that —

Thus, so, οὕτω *houtō.*
1 Co.14. 21 yet for all that will they not hear me

FOR...cause —

1. *Over against this,* ἀντὶ τούτου *anti toutou.*
Eph. 5. 31 For this cause shall a man leave his f.

2. *Through this, on account of this,* διὰ τοῦτο.
John 12. 18 For this cause the people also met him
12. 27 but for this cause came I unto this hour
Acts 28. 20 For this cause..have I called for you, to
Rom. 1. 26 For this cause God gave them up unto
13. 6 For, for this cause pay ye tribute also
15. 9 For this cause I will confess to thee
1 Co. 4. 17 For this cause have I sent unto you Tim.
11. 10 For this cause ought the woman to have
11. 30 For this cause many (are) weak and sick.
Col. 1. 9 For this cause we also, since the day we
1 Th. 2. 13 For this cause also thank we God without
3. 5 For this cause, when I could no longer
2 Th. 2. 11 for this cause God shall send them strong
1 Ti. 1. 16 Howbeit for this cause I obtained mercy
Heb. 9. 15 for this cause he is the mediator of the

3. *With a view to this,* εἰς τοῦτο *eis touto.*
John 18. 37 and for this cause came I into the world
1 Pe. 4. 6 for this cause was the gospel preached

4. *Because of, on account of,* ἕνεκα *heneka.*
Matt19. 5 For this cause shall a man leave father
Mark10. 7 For this cause shall a man leave his fa.
Acts 26. 21 For these causes the Jews caught me in
2 Co. 7. 12 not for his cause that had done the wrong
7. 12 nor for his cause that suffered wrong, but

5. *For the sake of this,* τούτου χάριν *toutou charin.*
Eph. 3. 1 For this cause I Paul, the prisoner of J.
3. 14 For this cause I bow my knees unto the
Titus 1. 5 For this cause left I thee in Crete, that

6. *For you,* ὑμῖν *(dat.) humin.*
2 Co. 5. 13 whether we be sober, [it is] for your cause

FOR ever —

All the days, כָּל־הַיָּמִים *kol-hay-yamim.*
Gen. 43. 9 then let me bear the blame for ever
44. 32 shall bear the blame to my father for ev.
Deut. 4. 40 prolong (thy) days upon the earth..for e.
18. 5 minister in the name of the LORD..for e.
Josh. 4. 24 ye might fear the LORD your God for ev.
1 Sa. 28. 2 make thee keeper of mine head for ever
1 Ki. 12. 7 then they will be thy servants for ever
2 Ch. 21. 7 a light to him and to his sons for ever
Psa. 23. 6 will dwell in the house of the LORD for e.
Jer. 31. 36 from being a nation before me for ever
32. 39 that they may fear me for ever, for the
35. 19 want a man to stand before me for ever

FOR...sake —

1. *Because of, for the sake of,* גָּלָל *galal.*
Gen 30. 27 the LORD hath blessed me for thy sake
39. 5 LORD blessed the..house for Joseph's sa.
Deut. 1. 37 LORD was angry with me for your sakes
Mic. 3. 12 shall Zion for your sake be plowed..a fi

2. *On account of,* διά *(acc.) dia (gen.)*
Matt10. 22 shall be hated of all..for my name's sake
14. 3 and put..in prison for Herodias' sake
14. 9 nevertheless for the oath's sake, and
19. 12 eunuchs for the kingdom of heaven's sa.
24. 9 hated of all nations for my name's sake
24. 22 for the elect's sake those days shall be
Mark 4. 17 persecution ariseth for the word's sake
6. 17 bound him in prison for Herodias' sake
6. 26 sorry; (yet) for his oath's sake, and for
13. 13 be hated of all..for my name's sake
13. 20 for the elect's sake, whom he hath chosen
Luke21. 17 ye shall be hated..for my name's sake
John12. 9 they came not for Jesus' sake only, but
14. 11 or else believe me for the very work's sake
15. 21 will they do unto you for my name's sake
Rom. 4. 23 Now it was not written for his sake alone
13. 5 for wrath, but also for conscience' sake
15. 30 for..Christ's sake, and for the love of the
1 Co. 4. 10 We (are) fools for Christ's sake, but ye
9. 23 And this I do for the Gospel's sake, that
10. 25, 27 asking no question for conscience' sake
2 Co. 4. 5 ourselves your servants for Jesus' sake
4. 11 alway delivered unto death for Jesus' sake
Col. 3. 6 [For which things' sake] the wrath of
1 Th. 5. 13 esteem them..in love for their work's sak.
1 Ti. 5. 23 use a little wine for thy stomach's sake
2 Ti. 2. 10 I endure all things for the elect's sakes
Phm. 9 Yet for love's sake I rather beseech being
1 Pe. 2. 13 Submit yourselves..for the Lord's sake
3. 14 and if ye suffer for righteousness' sake
1 Jo. 2. 12 sins are forgiven you for his name's sake
2 Jo. 2 For the truth's sake, which dwelleth in

3. *On account of us,* δι' ἡμᾶς *di hēmas.*
1 Co. 9. 10 Or saith he (it) altogether for our sakes?
9. 10 For our sakes, no doubt, (this) is written

4. *On account of you,* δι' ὑμᾶς *di humas.*
John11. 15 I am glad for your sakes that I was not
12. 30 This voice came not..but for your sakes
Rom. 11. 28 for your sakes..beloved for the fathers' sa.
1 Co. 4. 6 transferred to myself..for your sakes
2 Co. 2. 10 for your sakes..in the person of Christ
4. 15 For all things (are) for your sakes, that
8. 9 yet for your sakes he became poor, that
1 Th. 1. 5 what manner of men we were..for your s.
3. 9 we joy for your sakes before our God

5. *On account of that one,* δι' ἐκεῖνον *di ekeinon.*
1 Co. 10. 28 eat not for his sake that showed it, and

6. *In,* ἐν *en.*
Eph. 4. 32 God for Christ's sake hath forgiven you

7. *Because of, on account of,* ἕνεκα *heneka.*
Matt. 5. 10 are persecuted for righteousness' sake
5. 11 say all..evil against you..for my sake
10. 18 brought before governors..for my sake
10. 39 he that loseth his life for my sake shall
16. 25 whosoever will lose his life for my sake
19. 29 hath forsaken houses..for my name's sa.
Mark 8. 35 whosoever shall lose his life for my sake
10. 29 left house..for my sake, and the gospel's
13. 9 shall be brought before..kings for my sa.
Luke 6. 22 shall reproach..for the Son of man's sake
9. 24 whosoever will lose his life for my sake
18. 29 left house..for the kingdom of God's sake
21. 12 brought before kings..for my name's sake
Rom. 8. 36 For thy sake we are killed all the day long

8. *Around, about, concerning,* περί *peri (gen.)*
Acts 26. 7 For which hope's sake, king Agrippa, I

9. *In behalf of,* ὑπέρ *huper (gen.)*
John13. 37 Lord..I will lay down my life for thy sake
13. 38 Wilt thou lay down thy life for my sake?
17. 19 for their sakes I sanctify myself, that they
Acts 9. 16 things he must suffer for my name's sake
2 Co. 12. 10 pleasure..in distresses, for Christ's sake
Phil. 1. 29 not only..but also to suffer for his sake
Col. 1. 24 for his body's sake, which is the church
3 Jo. 7 that for his name's sake they went forth

10. *For the sake of,* χάριν *charin.*
Titus 1. 11 teaching things..for filthy lucre's sake

FOR that —

1. *If, since,* εἰ *ei.*
Heb. 7. 15 for that after the similitude of Melchised.

2. *Since, seeing that,* ἐπεί *epei.*
Heb. 5. 2 for that he himself also is compassed with

3. *Since truly,* ἐπειδή *epeidē.*
2 Co. 5. 4 not [for that] we would be unclothed

4. *Upon, about, for,* ἐπί (*dat.*) *epi.*
Rom. 5. 12 so death passed upon all men, [for that]

5. *Because,* ὅτι *hoti.*
John 12. 18 the people..met him, for that they heard
2 Co. 1. 24 Not for that we have dominion over your
1 Ti. 1. 12 for that he counted me faithful, putting

FOR that...ought to say —

Instead of saying, ἀντὶ τοῦ λέγειν, *anti tou legein.*
Jas. 4. 15 For that ye (ought) to say, If the Lord

FOR then —

1. *Since, seeing that,* ἐπεί *epei.*
Rom. 3. 6 for then how shall God judge the world?
Heb. 9. 26 For then must he often have suffered
10. 2 For then would they not have ceased to

2. *Seeing that then,* ἐπεὶ ἄρα *epei ara.*
1 Co. 5. 10 for then must ye needs go out of the wor.

FOR to —

1. *In order to,* לְמַעַן *le-maan.*
Jer. 43. 3 for to deliver us into the hand of the

2. *With a view to the,* εἰς τό *eis to.*
Rom 11. 11 Gentiles, for to provoke them to jealousy

3. *In order that, to the end that, so that,* ἵνα *hina.*
Mark 3. 10 they pressed upon him for to touch him
John 10. 10 The thief cometh not, but for to steal
11. 53 took counsel..for to put him to death
Acts 17. 15 receiving a commandment..for to come
22. 5 to bring them..bound..for to be punish.
Eph. 2. 15 for to make in himself of twain one new
Rev. 9. 15 loosed..for to slay the third part of men
12. 4 the dragon stood..for to devour her child

4. *Toward the,* πρὸς τό *pros to.*
Matt 23. 5 all their works they do for to be seen of

[*See also* Call, cause, ever, evermore, hope, intent, lay, lie, little, look, make, purpose, season, seek, send, tarry, time, wait.]

FORASMUCH as —

1. *After,* אַחַר *achar.*
Gen. 41. 39 Forasmuch as God hath showed thee all

2. *After that,* אַחֲרֵי אֲשֶׁר *achare asher.*
Judg 11. 36 forasmuch as the LORD hath taken veng.
2 Sa. 19. 30 forasmuch as my lord the king is come

3. *Because,* יַעַן *yaan.*
Amos 5. 11 Forasmuch therefore as your treading (is)

4. *Because that,* יַעַן אֲשֶׁר *yaan asher.*
1 Ki. 14. 7 Forasmuch as I exalted thee from among

5. *Because that,* יַעַן כִּי *yaan ki.*
1 Ki. 13. 21 Forasmuch as thou hast disobeyed the
Isa. 8. 6 Forasmuch as this people refuseth the
29. 13 Forasmuch as this people draw near (me)

6. *That, because,* כִּי *ki.*
Deut 12. 12 forasmuch as he hath no part nor inher.

7. *Because that,* כִּי עַל־כֵּן *ki al ken.*
Num 10. 31 forasmuch as thou knowest how we are

8. *Because that,* כָּל־קֳבֵל דִּי *kol qebel di.*
Ezra 7. 14 Forasmuch as thou art sent of the king
Dan. 2. 40 forasmuch as iron breaketh..and subdueth
2. 41 forasmuch as thou sawest the iron mixed
2. 45 Forasmuch as thou sawest that the stone
4. 18 forasmuch as all the wise (men) of my
5. 12 Forasmuch as an excellent spirit, and
6. 4 forasmuch as he (was) faithful, neither
6. 22 forasmuch as..innocency was found in

9. *Till,* עַד *ad.*
Josh. 17. 14 forasmuch as the LORD hath blessed me

10. *If, since,* εἰ *ei.*
Acts 11. 17 Forasmuch then as God gave them the

11. *Since, seeing that,* ἐπεί *epei.*
1 Co. 14. 12 Even so ye, forasmuch as ye are zealous
Heb. 2. 14 Forasmuch then as the children are par.

12. *Since indeed,* ἐπειδήπερ, ἐπειδή *epeidēper.*
Luke 1. 1 Forasmuch as many have taken in hand
Acts 15. 24 Forasmuch as we have heard, that certain

FORASMUCH as...was —

Being, ὤν *ōn.*
Acts 9. 38 forasmuch as Lydda was nigh to Joppa

FORBEAR, to —

1. *To be silent, cease, stand still,* דָּמַם *damam.*
Eze. 24. 17 Forbear to cry, make no mourning for

2. *To cease, leave off, forbear,* חָדַל *chadal.*
Exod 23. 5 and wouldest forbear to help him; thou
Num. 9. 13 and forbeareth to keep the passover, even
Deut 23. 22 if thou shalt forbear to vow, it shall be
1 Sa. 23. 13 told Saul..and he forbare to go forth
1 Ki. 22. 6 Shall I go..to battle, or shall I forbear?
22. 15 shall we go..to battle, or shall we forb.?
2 Ch. 18. 5, 14 Shall we go..to battle, or shall I for.?
25. 16 forbear; why shouldest thou be smitten?
25. 16 Then the prophet forbare, and said, I
2 Ch. 35. 21 forbear thee from..God, who (is) with me
Job 16. 6 and (though) I forbear, what am I eased?
Jer. 40. 4 but if it seem ill unto thee..forbear
41. 8 So he forbare, and slew them not among
51. 30 The mighty men of Babylon have forborne
Eze. 2. 5, 7 they will hear, or whether they will fo.
3. 11 they will hear, or whether they will forb.
3. 27 let him forbear: for they (are) a rebellious
Zech 11. 12 give (me) my price; and if not, forbear

3. *To keep back, spare, withhold,* חָשַׂךְ *chasak.*
Prov 24. 11 If thou forbear to deliver..drawn unto

4. *To draw or stretch out,* מָשַׁךְ *mashak.*
Neh. 9. 30 Yet many years didst thou forbear them

5. *To hold self back or up,* ἀνέχομαι *anechomai.*
Eph. 4. 2 with long suffering, forbearing one anot.
Col. 3. 13 Forbearing..and forgiving one another

6. *To send back, let away,* ἀνίημι *aniēmi.*
Eph. 6. 9 forbearing threatening: knowing that

7. *To spare,* φείδομαι *pheidomai.*
2 Co. 12. 6 but..I forbear, lest any man should think

FORBEAR working, to —

Not to work, μὴ ἐργάζεσθαι *mē ergazesthai.*
1 Co. 9. 6 have not we power to forbear working?

FORBEAR, can —

To cover, conceal, forbear, στέγω *stegō.*
1 Th. 3. 1 when we could no longer forbear, we
3. 5 when I could no longer forbear, I sent

FORBEARANCE —

A holding back, ἀνοχή *anochē.*
Rom. 2. 4 riches of his goodness and forbearance
3. 25 past, through the forbearance of God

FORBEARETH, he that —

Ceasing, leaving off, forbearing, חָדֵל *chadel.*
Eze. 3. 27 him hear; and he that forbeareth, let

FORBEARING —

1. *Temper,* אַף *aph.*
Prov 25. 15 By long forbearing is a prince persuaded

2. *To contain, sustain,* כּוּל *kul,* 3a.
Jer. 20. 9 I was weary with forbearing, and I could

FORBID —

Profanation, חָלִילָה *chalilah.*
1 Sa. 24. 6 The LORD forbid that I should do this
26. 11 The LORD forbid that I should stretch fo.
1 Ki. 21. 3 Naboth said to Ahab, The LORD forbid
1 Ch. 11. 19 And said, My God forbid it me, that I

FORBID (to take), to —

1. *To restrain, shut up,* כָּלָא *kala.*
Num 11. 28 Joshua..said, My lord Moses, forbid the.

2. *To set up, command, lay a charge,* צָוָה *tsavah,* 3.
Deut. 2. 37 whatsoever the LORD our God forbade us
4. 23 the LORD thy God hath forbidden thee

3. *To cut short, thoroughly, restrain,* διακωλύω.
Matt 3. 14 John forbade him, saying, I have need to

4. *To cut short, restrain,* κωλύω *kōluō.*
Matt 19. 14 and forbid them not, to come unto me
Mark 9. 38 he followeth not us: and we forbade him
9. 39 Jesus said, Forbid him not: for there is
10. 14 and forbid them not: for of such is the k.
Luke 6. 29 him that taketh away thy cloke forbid
9. 49 we forbade him, because he followeth not
9. 50 And Jesus said unto him, Forbid..not
18. 16 forbid them not: for of such is the king.
23. 2 forbidding to give tribute to Cesar, say.
Acts 10. 47 Can any man forbid water, that these
16. 6 forbidden of the Holy Ghost to preach the
24 23 should forbid none of his acquaintance to
1 Co. 14. 39 and forbid not to speak with tongues
1 Th. 2. 16 Forbidding us to speak to the Gentiles
1 Ti. 4. 3 Forbidding to marry..to abstain from m.
2 Pe. 2. 16 voice forbade the madness of the prophet
3 Jo. 10 forbiddeth them that would, and casteth

FORBID, God —

1. *Profanation,* חָלִילָה *chalilah.*
Gen. 44. 7 God forbid that thy servants should do
44. 17 he said, God forbid that I should do so
Josh 22. 29 God forbid that we should rebel against
24. 16 God forbid that we should forsake the
1 Sa. 12. 23 God forbid that I should sin against the
14. 45 Shall Jonathan die..God forbid: (as) the
20. 2 God forbid; thou shalt not die: behold
Job 27. 5 God forbid that I should justify you: till

2. *Let it not be,* μὴ γένοιτο *mē genoito.*
Luke 20. 16 when they heard (it), they said, God for.
Rom. 3. 4 God forbid: yea, let God be true, but ev.
3. 6 God forbid: for then how shall God jud.
3. 31 God forbid: yea, we establish the law
6. 2 God forbid. How shall we, that are dead
6. 15 What then? shall we sin..God forbid
7. 7 (Is) the law sin? God forbid. Nay, I had
7. 13 Was..good made death unto me? God f.
9. 14 (Is)..unrighteousness with God? God fo.
11. 1 Hath God cast away his people? God fo.
11. 11 God forbid: but..through their fall salv.
1 Co. 6. 15 make..members of an harlot? God forbid
Gal. 2. 17 (is)..Christ the minister of sin? God for.
3. 21 God forbid: for if there had been a law
6. 14 God forbid that I should glory, save in

FORBIDDEN, to be —

Not, לֹא *lo.*
Lev. 5. 17 any of these things which are forbidden

FORBIDDING, no man —

Uncut off, unrestrained, ἀκωλύτως *akōlutōs.*
Acts 28. 31 and teaching..no man forbidding him

FORCE —

1. *Arm, force,* אֶדְרָע *edra.*
Ezra 4. 23 made them to cease by force and power

2. *Strength,* אוֹן *on.*
Job 40. 16 and his force (is) in the navel of his belly

3. *Might,* גְּבוּרָה *geburah.*
Jer. 23. 10 course is evil, and their force (is) not

4. *Strength,* חָזְקָה *chozqah.*
1 Sa. 2. 16 give..and if not, I will take (it) by force
Eze. 34. 4 with force and with cruelty have ye ruled

5. *Hand,* יָד *yad.*
Jer. 18. 21 pour out..(blood) by the force of the sw.
Eze. 35. 5 by the force of the sword in the time of

6. *Power,* כֹּחַ *koach.*
Job 30. 18 By the great force..is my garment chan.
Jer. 48. 45 They that fled stood..because of the force
Amos 2. 14 the strong shall not strengthen his force

FORCE, of —

Steadfast, firm, βέβαιος *bebaios.*
Heb. 9. 17 For a testament (is) of force after men

FORCE, to —

1. *To take hold,* חָזַק *chazaq,* 5.
Deut 22. 25 the man force her, and lie with her

2. *To subdue,* כָּבַשׁ *kabash.*
Esth. 7. 8 Will he force the queen also before me in

3. *To press, crush,* לָחַץ *lachats.*
Judg. 1. 34 the Amorites forced the children of Dan

4. *To drive or force away,* נָדַח *nadach,* 5.
Prov. 7. 21 with the flattering of her lips she forced

5. *To afflict, humble,* עָנָה *anah,* 3.
Judg 20. 5 my concubine have they forced, that she
2 Sa. 13. 12 Nay, my brother, do not force me; for no
13. 14 but, being stronger than she, forced her
13. 22 because he had forced his sister Tamar
13. 32 from the day..he forced his sister Tamar

FORCE self, to —

To refrain or force self, אָפַק *aphaq,* 7.
1 Sa. 13. 12 I forced myself therefore, and offered a

FORCE, to take by —

To snatch away, seize, ἁρπάζω *harpazō.*
Matt 11. 12 kingdom..and the violent take it by force
John 6. 15 they would come and take him by force
Acts 23. 10 to take him by force from among them

FORCES —

1. *Strength, force, army,* חַיִל *chayil.*
2 Ch. 17. 2 he placed forces in all the fenced cities of
Isa. 60. 5 the forces of the Gentiles shall come unto
60. 11 may bring..the forces of the Gentiles
Jer. 40. 7, 13 all the captains of the forces
41. 11, 13, 16 the captains of the forces that
42. 1 Then all the captains of the forces, and
42. 8 and all the captains of the forces which
43. 4, 5 and all the captains of the forces
Obad. 11 strangers carried away captive his forces

2. *Strong ones, forces,* מַאֲמַצִּים *maamatstsim.*
Job 36. 19 not gold, nor all the forces of strength

3. *Stronghold, strength,* מָעוֹז *maoz.*
Dan. 11. 38 shall he honour the God of forces: and a

FORCES, great —

Strength, force, army, חַיִל *chayil.*
Dan. 11. 10 shall assemble a multitude of great forces

FORCIBLE, to be —

To be powerful (or sweet), מָרַץ *marats,* 2.
Job 6. 25 How forcible are right words! but what

FORCING —

1. *Wringing out, churning,* מִיץ *mits.*
Prov 30. 33 the forcing of wrath bringeth forth strife

2. *To drive or force away,* נָדַח *nadach.*
Deut 20 19 destroy..by forcing an ax against them

FORD —

1. *Passage, ford,* מַעֲבָר *maabar.*
Gen. 32. 22 rose..and passed over the ford Jabbok

2. *Passage, ford,* מַעְבָּרָה *mabarah.*
Josh. 2. 7 them the way to Jordan unto the fords
Judg. 3. 28 took the fords of Jordan toward Moab
Isa. 16. 2 Moab shall be at the fords of Arnon

FORECAST, to —

1. *To think, devise, design,* חָשַׁב *chashab.*
Dan. 11. 25 they shall forecast devices against him

2. *To think, devise, design,* חָשַׁב *chashab,* 3.
Dan. 11. 24 he shall forecast his devices against the

FOREFATHER —

1. *First father,* אָב רִאשׁוֹן *ab rishon.*
Jer. 11. 10 to the iniquities of their forefathers

2. *Earlier born ones, progenitors,* πρόγονοι *progon.*
2 Ti. 1. 3 God, whom I serve from (my) forefathers

FORE-FRONT —

1. *Over against the face,* מוּל פָּנִים *mul panim.*
Exod 26. 9 double..in the fore-front of the taberna.

Exod28. 37 upon the fore-front of the mitre it shall be
Lev. 8. 9 upon his fore-front, did he put the golden
2 Sa. 11. 15 Set ye Uriah in the fore-front of the hot.

2. *Face*, פָּנִים *panim*.
2 Ki.16. 14 from the fore-front of the house, from
Eze. 40. 19 from the fore-front of the lower gate
40. 19 unto the fore-front of the inner court
47. 1 for the fore-front of the house (stood) to.

3. *Head*, רֹאשׁ *rosh*.
2 Ch. 20. 27 Jehoshaphat in the fore-front of them

4. *Tooth*, שֵׁן *shen*.
1 Sa. 14. 5 The fore-front of the one (was) situate

FOREHEAD —

1. *Nose*, אַף *aph*.
Eze. 16. 12 I put a jewel on thy forehead, and earr.

2. *Forehead*, מֵצַח *metsach*.
Exod28. 38 it shall be upon Aaron's forehead, that
28. 38 it shall be always upon his forehead
1 Sa. 17. 49 smote the Philistine in his forehead
17. 49 that the stone sunk into his forehead
2 Ch. 26. 19 the leprosy even rose up in his forehead
26. 20 behold, he (was) leprous in his forehead
Jer. 3. 3 thou hadst a whore's forehead, thou ref.
Eze. 3. 8 thy forehead strong against their forehea.
3. 9 harder than flint have I made thy foreh.
9. 4 set a mark upon the foreheads of the men

3. *Forehead, between the eyes*, μέτωπον *metōpon*.
Rev. 7. 3 have sealed the servants..in their foreh.
9. 4 have not the seal of God in their foreheads
13. 16 all..to receive a mark..in their foreheads
14. 1 Father's name written in their foreheads
14. 9 receive (his) mark in his forehead, or in
17. 5 And upon her forehead (was) a name
20. 4 received (his) mark upon their foreheads
22. 4 and his name (shall be) in their foreheads

FOREHEAD, bald —
With bald forehead, גִּבֵּחַ *gibbeach*.
Lev. 13. 41 fallen off..he (is) forehead bald: (yet is)

FOREIGNER —

1. *Unknown, stranger*, נָכְרִי *nokri*.
Deut 15. 3 Of a foreigner thou mayest exact (it aga.)
Obad. 11 foreigners entered into his gates, and

2. *Settler*, תּוֹשָׁב *toshab*.
Exod12. 45 A foreigner and an hired servant shall

3. *Sojourner, one dwelling near*, πάροικος *paroikos*.
Eph. 2. 19 ye are no more strangers and foreigners

FOREKNOW, to —
To begin to know first or beforehand, προγινώσκω.
Rom. 8. 29 whom he did foreknow, he also did pred.
11. 2 cast away his people whom he foreknew

FOREKNOWLEDGE —
A knowing first or beforehand, πρόγνωσις *prognō.*
Acts 2. 23 determinate counsel and foreknowledge
1 Pe. 1. 2 Elect according to the foreknowledge of

FOREMOST —
First, former, foremost, רִאשׁוֹן *rishon*.
Gen. 32. 17 he commanded the foremost, saying
33. 2 put the handmaids and their children f.
2 Sa. 18. 27 Me thinketh the running of the foremost

FOREORDAIN, to —
To begin to know beforehand, προγινώσκω *progin.*
1 Pe. 1. 20 Who verily was foreordained before the f.

FORE PART —

1. *Face*, פָּנִים *panim*.
Exod28. 27 toward the fore part thereof, over against
39. 20 underneath, toward the fore part of it
1 Ki. 6. 20 the oracle in the fore part..twenty cub.
Eze. 42. 7 toward the outer court on the fore part

2. *Fore part, prow*, πρῷρα *prōra*.
Acts 27. 41 the fore part stuck fast, and remained

FORERUNNER —
One that runs before, πρόδρομος *prodromos*.
Heb. 6. 20 Whither the forerunner is for us entered

FORESEE, to —
To see, behold, רָאָה *raah*.
Prov22. 3 a prudent (man) foreseeth the evil, and
27. 12 A prudent (man) foreseeth the evil, (and)

FORESEE, see before, to —
To see before, προεῖδον; Acts 2. 25 προορώμαι.
Acts 2. 31 He, seeing this before, spake of the
Gal. 3. 8 the Scripture, foreseeing that God would

FORESHIP —
Prow (of a ship), πρῷρα *prōra*.
Acts 27 30 would have cast anchors out of the fores.

FORESKIN —
Uncircumcision, foreskin, עָרְלָה *orlah*.
Gen. 17. 11 shall circumcise the flesh of your foreskin
17. 14 whose flesh of his foreskin is not circum.
17. 23 circumcised the flesh of their foreskin
17. 24, 25 circumcised in the flesh of his foreskin
Exod. 4. 25 cut off the foreskin of her son, and cast
Lev 12. 3 in the eighth day the flesh of his foreskin
Deut10. 16 Circumcise..the foreskin of your heart
Josh. 5. 3 circumcised..at the hill of the foreskins
1 Sa. 18. 25 an hundred foreskins of the Philistines
18. 27 David brought their foreskins, and they
2 Sa. 3. 14 I espoused to me for an hundred foresk.
Jer. 4. 4 take away the foreskins of your heart

FORESKIN uncovered, to be —
To be uncircumcised, עָרֵל *arel*, 2.
Hab. 2. 16 let thy foreskin be uncovered: the cup

FOREST —

1. *Forest, thicket*, חֹרֶשׁ *choresh*.
2 Ch.27. 4 in the forests he built castles and towers

2. *Forest, out-spread place*, יַעַר *yaar*.
1 Sa. 22. 5 David..came into the forest of Hareth
1 Ki. 7. 2 He built also the house of the forest of
10. 17, 21 the house of the forest of Lebanon
2 Ki. 19. 23 I will enter into..the forest of his Carmel
2 Ch. 9. 16, 20 the house of the forest of Lebanon
Psa. 50. 10 every beast of the forest (is) mine..the
104. 20 all the beasts of the forest do creep
Isa. 9. 18 shall kindle in the thickets of the forest
10. 18 shall consume the glory of his forest
10. 19 the rest of the trees of his forest shall be
10. 34 shall cut down the thickets of the forests
21. 13 In the forest in Arabia shall ye lodge, O
22. 8 to the armour of the house of the forest
29. 17 fruitful field shall be esteemed as a forest?
32. 15 the fruitful field be counted for a forest
32. 19 it shall hail, coming down on the forest
37. 24 I will enter into..the forest of his Carmel
44. 14 Cypress..among the trees of the forest
44. 23 break forth..O forest, and every tree th.
56. 9 to devour..all ye beasts in the forest
Jer. 5. 6 a lion out of the forest shall slay them
10. 3 for (one) cutteth a tree out of the forest
12. 8 heritage is unto me as a lion in the forest
21. 14 I will kindle a fire in the forest thereof
26. 18 the house as the high places of a forest
46. 23 They shall cut down her forest, saith the
Eze. 15. 2, 6 vine tree..among the trees of the for.?
20. 46 prophesy against the forest of the south
20. 47 say to the forest of the south, Hear the
39. 10 neither cut down (any) out of the forests
Hos. 2. 12 I will make them a forest, and the beasts
Amos 3. 4 Will a lion roar in the forest, when he
Mic. 3. 12 the house as the high places of the forest
5. 8 as a lion among the beasts of the forest
Zech 11. 2 the forest of the vintage is come down

3. *Forest, out spread place*, יַעְרָה *yaarah*.
Psa. 29. 9 maketh..to calve..discovereth the forests

4. *Paradise, park or garden ground*, פַּרְדֵּס *pardes*.
Neh. 2. 8 unto Asaph the keeper of the king's forest

FOREST of Arabia, יַעַר בַּעְרָב *yaar baarab*.
Its situation is quite unknown.
Isa. 21. 13 In the forest in A. shall ye lodge

FOREST of Carmel, יַעַר כַּרְמִל *yaar karmel*.
South of Accho, in Zebulun, on the S. border of Asher.
2 Ki. 19. 23 will enter into..the forest of his C.
Isa. 37. 24 will enter into..the forest of his C.

FOREST of Hareth, יַעַר חֶרֶת *yaar chereth*.
Somewhere on the border of the Philistine plain in the S. of Judah.
1 Sa. 22. 5 departed, and came into the forest of H.

FOREST of Lebanon, יַעַר הַלְּבָנוֹן *yaar hallebanon*.
The "House of the forest of Lebanon" was so called probably from being fitted up with cedar. It was built by Solomon for an armoury, in Jerusalem, with forest-like rows of the cedars of Lebanon.
1 Ki. 7. 2 built also the house of the forest of L.
10. 17 put them in the house of the forest of L.
10. 21 the vessels of the house of the forest of L.
2 Ch. 9. 16 put them in the house of the forest of L.
9. 20 the vessels of the house of the forest of L.

FORETELL —

1. *To say beforehand*, προεῖπον *proeipon*.
Mark13. 23 behold, I have foretold you all things

2. *To announce beforehand*, προκαταγγέλλω.
Acts 3. 24 have likewise [foretold] of these days

3. *To lay before, tell before*, προλέγω *prolegō.*
2 Co. 13. 2 I told you before, and foretell you, as if

FOREWARN, to —

1. *To say before*, προεῖπον *proeipon*.
1 Th. 4. 6 as we also have forewarned you and testi.

2. *To show secretly*, ὑποδείκνυμι *hupodeiknumi*.
Luke12. 5 I will forewarn you whom ye shall fear

FORFEITED, to be —
To be devoted, חָרַם *charam*, 6.
Ezra 10. 8 all his substance should be forfeited, and

FORGE, to —
To stitch or sew on, טָפַל *taphal*.
Job 13. 4 ye (are) forgers of lies, ye (are) all physi.
Psa.119. 69 The proud have forged a lie against me

FORGET —
Forgetful, forgetting, שָׁכֵחַ *shakeach*.
Psa. 9. 17 into hell..all the nations that forget God
Isa. 65. 11 ye (are) they that..forget my holy moun.

FORGET, to —

1. *To forget*, נָשָׁה *nashah*.
Jer. 23. 39 behold, I, even I, will utterly forget you
Lam. 3. 17 thou hast removed my soul..I forgat

2. *To forget*, שָׁיָה *shayah*.
Deut 32. 18 and hast forgotten God that formed thee

3. *To forget, neglect*, שָׁכַח *shakach*.
Gen. 27. 45 and he forget (that) which thou hast done
40. 23 did not..remember Joseph, but forgat
Deut. 4. 9 keep thy soul diligently, lest thou forget
4. 23 lest ye forget the covenant of the LORD
4. 31 nor forget the covenant of thy fathers
6. 12 beware lest thou forget the LORD, which
8. 11 Beware that thou forget not the LORD thy
8. 14 and thou forget the LORD thy God, which
8. 19 if thou do at all forget the LORD thy God
9. 7 Remember..forget not, how thou provo.
24. 19 and hast forgot a sheaf in the field
25. 19 thou shalt blot out..thou shalt not forget
26. 13 commandments, neither have I forgotten
Judg. 3. 7 forgat the LORD their God, and served
1 Sa. 1. 11 remember me, and not forget thine
12. 9 when they forgat the LORD their God, he
2 Ki. 17. 38 And the covenant..ye shall not forget
Job 8. 13 So (are) the paths of all that forget God
9. 27 If I say, I will forget my complaint
11. 16 Because thou shalt forget (thy) misery
19. 14 my familiar friends have forgotten me
24. 20 The womb shall forget him; the worm
39. 15 forgetteth that the foot may crush them
Psa. 9. 12 he forgetteth not the cry of the humble
10. 11 hath said in his heart, God hath forgotten
10. 12 Arise, O LORD..forget not the humble
13. 1 How long wilt thou forget me, O LORD?
42. 9 Why hast thou forgotten me? why go I
44. 17 yet have we not forgotten thee, neither
44. 20 If we have forgotten the name of our God
44. 24 forgettest our affliction and our oppres.?
45. 10 forget also thine own people, and thy fa.
50. 22 Now consider this, ye that forget God
59. 11 Slay them not, lest my people forget
74. 19 forget not the congregation of thy poor
74. 23 Forget not the voice of thine enemies
77. 9 Hath God forgotten to be gracious?
78. 7 and not forget the works of God, but
78. 11 And forgat his works, and his wonders
102. 4 My heart is smitten..so that I forget to
103. 2 Bless the LORD..forget not all his benefits
106. 13 They soon forgat his works; they waited
106. 21 They forgat God their Saviour, which
119. 16 thy statutes: I will not forget thy word
119. 61 robbed me..I have not forgotten thy law
119. 83 like a bottle..do I not forget thy statutes
119. 93 I will never forget thy precepts: for with
119. 109 in my hand: yet do I not forget thy law
119. 139 mine enemies have forgotten thy words
119. 141 despised; (yet) do not I forget thy prec.
119. 153 Consider..for I do not forget thy law
119. 176 for I do not forget thy commandments
137. 5 If I forget..let my right hand forget
Prov. 2. 17 and forgetteth the covenant of her God
3. 1 My son, forget not my law; but let thine
4. 5 get understanding: forget (it) not; neith.
31. 5 Lest they drink, and forget the law, and
31. 7 Let him drink, and forget his poverty
Isa. 17. 10 Because thou hast forgotten the God of
49. 14 Zion said..my Lord hath forgotten me
49. 15 Can a woman forget her sucking child
49. 15 they may forget, yet will I not forget
51. 13 forgettest the LORD thy Maker, that hath
54. 4 thou shalt forget the shame of thy youth
Jer. 2. 32 Can a maid forget her ornaments
2. 32 yet my people have forgotten me days
3. 21 they have forgotten the LORD their God
13. 25 thou hast forgotten me, and trusted in
18. 15 my people hath forgotten me, they have
23. 27 as their fathers have forgotten my name
30. 14 All thy lovers have forgotten thee
44. 9 Have ye forgotten the wickedness of
50. 6 they have forgotten their resting place
Lam. 5. 20 Wherefore dost thou forget us for ever
Eze. 22. 12 and hast forgotten me, saith the Lord G.
23. 35 Because thou hast forgotten me, and
Hos. 2. 13 she went after her lovers, and forgat me
4. 6 thou hast forgotten the law of thy God
4. 6 I will also forget thy children
8. 14 For Israel hath forgotten his Maker
13. 6 filled..therefore have they forgotten me
Amos 8. 7 I will never forget any of their works

4. *To forget about*, ἐπιλανθάνομαι *epilanthanomai*.
Matt16. 5 his disciples..had forgotten to take bread
Mark 8. 14 (the disciples) had forgotten to take bre.
Luke12. 6 not one of them is forgotten before God
Phil. 3. 13 forgetting those things which are behind
Heb. 6. 10 God (is) not unrighteous to forget your
13. 16 to do good and to communicate forget
Jas. 1. 24 forgetteth what manner of man he was

5. *To forget utterly*, ἐκλανθάνομαι *eklanthanomai*.
Heb. 12. 5 ye have forgotten the exhortation which

6. *To receive forgetfulness*, λαμβάνω λήθην *lambanō*.
2 Pe. 1. 9 hath forgotten that he was purged from

FORGET, to cause to —
To cause to forget, שָׁכַח *shakach*, 5.
Jer. 23. 27 Which think to cause my people to forget

FORGET, to make —
To cause to forget, נָשָׁה *nashah*, 3.
Gen. 41. 51 God..hath made me forget all my toil

FORGETFUL —
Forgetfulness, ἐπιλησμονή *epilēsmonē*.
Jas. 1. 25 he being not a forgetful hearer, but a

FORGETFUL, to be —
To forget also or besides, ἐπιλανθάνομαι *epilantha.*
Heb. 13. 2 Be not forgetful to entertain strangers

FORGETFULNESS —
Forgetfulness, נְשִׁיָּה *neshiyyah.*
Psa. 88. 12 thy righteousness in the land of forget.?

FORGIVE, to —
1. *To cover,* כָּפַר *kaphar,* 3.
Psa. 78. 38 But he..full of compassion, forgave (their)
Jer. 18. 23 forgive not their iniquity, neither blot out

2. *To lift up or away,* נָשָׂא *nasa.*
Gen. 50. 17 Forgive..the trespass..forgive the tresp.
Exod10. 17 Now therefore forgive, I pray thee, my
32. 32 Yet now, if thou wilt forgive their sin
Num 14. 19 and as thou hast forgiven this people
Josh 24. 19 he will not forgive your transgressions
1 Sa. 25. 28 forgive the trespass of thine handmaid
Psa. 25. 18 Look upon..and forgive all my sins
32. 5 and thou forgavest the iniquity of my sin
85. 2 Thou hast forgiven the iniquity of thy p.
99. 8 thou wast a God that forgavest them
Isa. 2. 9 humbleth..therefore forgive them not

3. *To send away, let go,* סָלַח *salach.*
Num30. 5, 8, 12 and the LORD shall forgive her
1 Ki. 8. 30 hear thou..and when thou hearest, forgive
8. 34 forgive the sin of thy people Israel
8. 36 forgive the sin of thy servants, and of thy
8. 39 in heaven thy dwelling-place, and forgive
8. 50 And forgive thy people that have sinned
2 Ch. 6. 21 hear..and when thou hearest forgive
6. 25 hear thou from the heavens, and forgive
6. 27 hear..and forgive the sin of thy servants
6. 30 forgive, and render unto every man acco.
6. 39 and forgive thy people which have sinned
7. 14 will forgive their sin, and will heal their
Psa. 103. 3 Who forgiveth all thine iniquities; who
Jer. 31. 34 I will forgive their iniquity, and I will re.
36. 3 that I may forgive their iniquity and
Dan. 9. 19 O Lord, forgive; O Lord, hearken and
Amos 7. 2 O Lord GOD, forgive, I beseech thee: by

4. *To loose away,* ἀπολύω *apoluō.*
Luke 6. 37, 37 forgive, and ye shall be forgiven

5. *To be gracious to,* χαρίζομαι *charizomai.*
Luke 7. 43 I suppose..(he) to whom he forgave most
2 Co. 2. 7 So that..ye (ought) rather to forgive (him)
2. 10 To whom ye forgive..for if I forgave
2. 10 any thing, to whom I forgave (it), for your
12. 13 not burdensome to you? forgive me this
Eph. 4. 32 tender-hearted, forgiving one another
4. 32 as God for Christ's sake hath forgiven
Col. 2. 13 quickened..having forgiven you all tres.
3. 13 forgiving one another..as Christ forgave

6. *To send or let off or away,* ἀφίημι *aphiēmi.*
Matt. 6. 12 And forgive us our debts, as we forgive
6. 14 For if ye forgive men their trespasses
6. 14 your heavenly Father will..forgive you
6. 15 if ye forgive not men their trespasses
6. 15 neither will your Father forgive your tr.
9. 2 Son, be of good cheer; thy sins be forgi.
9. 5 sins be forgiven thee; or to say, Arise
9. 6 hath power on earth to forgive sins
12. 31 All manner of sin..shall be forgiven
12. 31 the blasphemy..shall not be forgiven unto
12. 32 the Son of man, it shall be forgiven him
12. 32 it shall not be forgiven him, neither in
18. 21 Lord, how oft shall..I forgive him? till
18. 27 loosed him, and forgave him the debt
18. 32 I forgave thee all that debt, because thou
18. 35 [if ye from your hearts forgive not every]
Mark 2. 5 he said..Son, thy sins be forgiven thee
2. 7 who can forgive sins but God only?
2. 9 sins be forgiven thee; or to say, Arise
2. 10 hath power on earth to forgive sins
3. 28 All sins shall be forgiven unto the sons
4. 12 and (their) sins should be forgiven them
11. 25 forgive..that your Father..may forgive
11. 26 [do not forgive, neither will your F. f.]
Luke 5. 20 said..Man, thy sins are forgiven thee
5. 21 Who can forgive sins, but God alone?
5. 23 Thy sins be forgiven thee; or to say
5. 24 Son of man hath power..to forgive sins
7. 47 Her sins, which are many, are forgiven
7. 47 but to whom little is forgiven..loveth
7. 48 he said unto her, Thy sins are forgiven
7. 49 Who is this that forgiveth sins also?
11. 4 forgive us our sins: for we also forgive
12. 10 shall be forgiven him..it shall not be fo.
17. 3 Take heed..if he repent, forgive him
17. 4 saying, I repent; thou shalt forgive him
23. 34 [Then said Jesus, Father, forgive them]
Acts 8. 22 if perhaps the thought..may be forgiven
Rom. 4. 7 Blessed..they whose iniquities are forgi.
Jas. 5. 15 committed sins, they shall be forgiven
1 Jo. 1. 9 he is faithful and just to forgive us
2. 12 because your sins are forgiven you for

FORGIVE frankly, to —
To be gracious to, χαρίζομαι *charizomai.*
Luke 7. 42 nothing..he frankly forgave them both

FORGIVE, ready to —
Sending away, letting go, סַלָּח *sallach.*
Psa. 86. 5 thou, LORD, (art) good, and ready to forg.

FORGIVEN —
To lift up or away, נָשָׂא *nasa.*
Psa. 32. 1 (is he whose) transgression (is) forgiven
Isa. 33. 24 the people..(shall be) forgiven..iniquity

FORGIVEN, to be —
1. *To be covered,* כָּפַר *kaphar,* 7.
Deut21. 8 And the blood shall be forgiven them

2. *To be sent away, let go,* סָלַח *salach,* 2.
Lev. 4. 20, 26, 31, 35 and it shall be forgiven
5. 10, 13, 16, 18 and it shall be forgiven him
6. 7 it shall be forgiven him for any thing
19. 22 the sin..he hath done shall be forgiven
Num15. 25, 26, 28, and it shall be forgiven

FORGIVENESS —
1. *A sending away, letting go,* סְלִיחָה *selichah.*
Psa. 130. 4 But..forgiveness with thee, that thou
Dan. 9. 9 To the Lord our God..forgivenesses

2. *A sending away, letting go,* ἄφεσις *aphesis.*
Mark 3. 29 hath never forgiveness, but is in danger
Acts 5. 31 a Saviour..to give..forgiveness of sins
13. 38 is preached unto you the forgiveness of
26. 18 that they may receive forgiveness of sins
Eph. 1. 7 In whom we have..the forgiveness of
Col. 1. 14 In whom we have..the forgiveness of

FORGIVING —
1. *To lift up or away,* נָשָׂא *nasa.*
Exod34. 7 forgiving iniquity and transgression
Num14. 18 forgiving iniquity and transgression

2. *To be gracious to,* χαρίζομαι *charizomai.*
Eph. 4. 32 tender-hearted, forgiving one another
Col. 3. 13 Forbearing..and forgiving one another

FORGOTTEN —
To be forgotten, שָׁכַח *shakach,* 2.
Job 28. 4 forgotten of the foot: they are dried up

FORGOTTEN, to be —
1. *To be forgotten,* נָשָׁה *nashah,* 2.
Isa. 44. 21 O Israel, thou shalt not be forgotten of

2. *To be forgotten,* שָׁכַח *shakach,* 2.
Gen. 41. 30 the plenty shall be forgotten in the land
Deut31. 21 shall not be forgotten out of the
Psa. 9. 18 the needy shall not alway be forgotten
31. 12 I am forgotten as a dead man out of
Eccl. 2. 16 that which now (is)..shall all be forgot.
9. 5 for the memory of them is forgotten
Isa. 23. 15 Tyre shall be forgotten seventy years
23. 16 thou harlot that hast been forgotten
65. 16 because the former troubles are forgotten
Jer. 20. 11 everlasting confusion shall never be forg.
23. 40 shame, which shall not be forgotten
50. 5 covenant (that) shall not be forgotten

3. *To be or become forgotten,* שָׁכַח *shakach,* 7.
Eccl. 8. 10 they were forgotten in the city where

FORGOTTEN, to cause to be —
To cause to forget, שָׁכַח *shakach,* 3.
Lam. 2. 6 hath caused the..sabbaths to be forgot.

FORK —
Triple fork, שְׁלֹשׁ קִלְּשׁוֹן *shelosh qilleshon.*
1 Sa. 13. 21 for the coulters, and for the forks, and

FORM —
1. *Sight, appearance, vision,* מַרְאֶה *mareh.*
Job 4. 16 I could not discern the form thereof

2. *Judgment, rule,* מִשְׁפָּט *mishpat.*
2 Ch. 4. 7 candlesticks..according to their form

3. *Face,* פָּנִים *panim.*
2 Sa. 14. 20 To fetch about this form of speech hath

4. *Form, sharp outline,* צוּרָה *tsurah.*
Eze. 43. 11 show them the form of the house, and the
43. 11 the forms thereof..all the forms thereof
43. 11 that they may keep the whole form ther.

5. *Image, shadow,* צֶלֶם *tselem.*
Dan. 3. 19 the form of his visage was changed against

6. *Appearance, sight,* רֵו *rev.*
Dan. 2. 31 image..and the form thereof (was) terri.
3. 25 form of the fourth is like the Son of God

7. *Form, visage,* תֹּאַר *toar.*
1 Sa. 28. 14 he said unto her, What form (is) he of?
Isa. 52. 14 and his form more than the sons of men
53. 2 For..he hath no form nor comeliness

8. *Pattern, form, building,* תַּבְנִית *tabnith.*
Eze. 8. 3 he put forth the form of an hand, and
8. 10 behold, every form of creeping things
10. 8 appeared..the form of a man's hand

9. *Form,* μορφή *morphē.*
Mark16. 12 [he appeared in another form unto two]
Phil. 2. 6 Who, being in the form of God, thought
2. 7 took upon him the form of a servant

10. *Form, appearance,* μόρφωσις *morphōsis.*
Rom. 2. 20 which hast the form of knowledge and of
2 Ti. 3. 5 Having a form of godliness, but denying

11. *Type, impress,* τύπος *tupos.*
Rom. 6. 17 that form of doctrine which was delivered

12. *Under type, outline,* ὑποτύπωσις *hupotupōsis.*
2 Ti. 1. 13 Hold fast the form of sound words, which

FORM, to —
1. *To bring forth (in pain),* חִיל, חוּל *chil,* 3*a.*
Deut32. 18 and hast forgotten God that formed thee
Job 26. 13 his hand..formed the crooked serpent
Psa. 90. 2 or ever thou hadst formed the earth and
Prov. 26. 10 The great (God), that formed all..both

2. *To form, fashion, frame, constitute,* יָצַר *yatsar.*
Gen. 2. 7 the LORD God formed man (of) the dust
2. 8 there he put the man..he had formed
2. 19 God formed every beast of the field
2 Ki. 19. 25 of ancient times that I have formed it?
Psa. 94. 9 he that formed the eye, shall he not see?
95. 5 and his hands formed the dry (land)
Isa. 27. 11 he that formed them will show them no
37. 26 Hast thou not heard..that I..formed it?
43. 1 thus saith..he that formed thee, O Israel
43. 7 I have formed him; yea, I have made
43. 21 This people have I formed for myself
44. 2 LORD that made thee, and formed thee
44. 10 Who hath formed a god, or molten a
44. 21 I have formed thee; thou (art) my servant
44. 24 he that formed thee from the womb
45. 7 I form the light, and create darkness
45. 18 God himself that formed the earth and
45. 18 he formed it to be inhabited: I (am) the
49. 5 And now, saith the LORD that formed me
Jer. 1. 5 Before I formed thee in the belly I knew
10. 16 [he (is) the former of all..and Israel (is)]
33. 2 the LORD that formed it, to establish it
Amos 4. 13 For, lo, he that formeth the mountains
7. 1 he formed grasshoppers in the beginning
Zech. 12. 1 formeth the spirit of man within him

3. *To form,* μορφόω *morphoō.*
Gal. 4. 19 I travail in birth..until Christ be formed

4. *To shape, mould,* πλάσσω *plassō.*
Rom. 9. 20 say to him that formed (it), Why hast thou
1 Ti. 2. 13 For Adam was first formed, then Eve

FORM, without —
A ruin, vacancy, תֹּהוּ *tohu.*
Gen. 1. 2 And the earth was without form, and
Jer. 4. 23 and, lo, (it was) without form and void

FORMED, thing —
Thing moulded or shaped, πλάσμα *plasma.*
Rom. 9. 20 Shall the thing formed say..Why hast

FORMED, to be —
1. *To be brought forth (in pain),* חִיל, חוּל *chil,* 4*a.*
Job 26. 5 Dead (things) are formed from under

2. *To be formed, fashioned, framed,* יָצַר *yatsar,* 2.
Isa. 43. 10 before me there was no God formed

3. *To be formed, fashioned, framed,* יָצַר *yatsar,* 6.
Isa. 54. 17 No weapon that is formed against thee

4. *To be moved, kneaded, formed,* קָרַץ *qarats,* 4.
Job 33. 6 Behold..I also am formed out of the clay

FORMER —
1. *To form, constitute, fashion, frame,* יָצַר *yatsar.*
Jer. 51. 19 for he (is) the former of all; Jer. 10. 16

2. *Before, eastern, ancient,* קַדְמֹנִי *qadmoni.*
Zech 14. 8 half of them toward the former sea
Mal. 3. 4 pleasant unto the LORD..as in former ye.

3. *First, former, foremost,* רִאשׁוֹן *rishon.*
Gen. 40. 13 after the former manner when thou wast
Num 21. 26 who had fought against the former king
Deut 24. 4 Her former husband, which sent her
1 Sa. 17. 30 answered him..after the former manner
2 Ki. 1. 14 the two captains of the former fifties with
17. 34 Unto this day they do after the former
17. 40 but they did after their former manner
Neh. 5. 15 But the former governors that (had been)
Psa. 79. 8 O remember not against us former iniqui.
89. 49 where (are) thy former loving kindnesses
Eccl. 1. 11 (There is) no remembrance of former
7. 10 that the former days were better than
Isa. 41. 22 let them show the former things, what
42. 9 the former things are come to pass
43. 9 who..can..show us former things? let
43. 18 Remember ye not the former things
46. 9 Remember the former things of old: for
48. 3 I have declared the former things from
61. 4 shall raise up the former desolations
65. 7 therefore will I measure their former
65. 16 because the former troubles are forgot.
65. 17 and the former shall not be remembered
Jer. 34. 5 the former kings which were before thee
36. 28 and write in it all the former words that
Dan. 11. 29 but it shall not be as the former, or as the
Hag. 2. 9 shall be greater than of the former, saith
Zech. 1. 4 unto whom the former prophets have
7. 7 LORD hath cried by the former prophets
7. 12 sent in his Spirit by the former prophets
8. 11 I (will) not (be)..as in the former days

4. *First, former,* רִישׁוֹן *rishon.*
Job 8. 8 enquire, I pray thee, of the former age

5. *Before, first,* πρότερος *proteros, -ον.*
Eph. 4. 22 concerning the former conversation, the
Heb. 10. 32 call to remembrance the former days, in
1 Pe. 1. 14 according to the former lusts in your ig.

6. *First, foremost,* πρῶτος *prōtos.*
Acts 1. 1 The former treatise have I made, O The.
Rev. 21. 4 for the former things are passed away

FORMER estate —
Former state or condition, קַדְמָה *qadmah.*
Eze. 16. 55, 55 shall return to their former estate
16. 55 shall return to your former estate

FORMER (rain) —
1. *Sprinkling rain,* מוֹרֶה *moreh.*
Joel 2. 23 given you the former rain..former rain

2. *Sprinkling rain,* יוֹרֶה *yoreh.*
Jer. 5. 24 giveth rain, both the former and the latter
3. *To be abundant, flow over,* יָרָה *yarah.*
Hos. 6. 3 as the latter (and) former rain unto the

FORMER things —
First, former, foremost, רִאשׁוֹן *rishon.*
Isa. 41. 22 let them show the former things, what
42. 9 Behold, the former things are come to p.
43. 9 who..can..show us former things? let
43. 18 Remember ye not the former things
46. 9 Remember the former things of old: for
48. 3 I have declared the former things from

FORMER time —
Face, front, פָּנִים *panim.*
Ruth 4. 7 Now this (was the manner) in former time

FORMER time, in —
Yesternight, former time, אֶמֶשׁ *emesh.*
Job 30. 3 wilderness in former time desolate and

FORNICATION —
1. *Fornication, whoredom,* תַּזְנוּת *taznuth.*
Eze. 16. 15 pouredst out thy fornications on every
16. 29 Thou hast..multiplied thy fornication
2. *Fornication, whoredom,* πορνεία *porneia.*
Matt. 5. 32 saving for the cause of fornication, cause.
15. 19 For out of the heart proceed..fornicatio.
19. 9 put away his wife, except..for fornica.
Mark 7. 21 from within..proceed..fornications, mu.
John. 8. 41 We be not born of fornication; we have
Acts 15. 20 that they abstain from..fornication, and
15. 29 that ye abstain..from fornicatior: from
21. 25 only that they keep themselves..from fo.
Rom. 1. 29 Being filled with..[fornication], wicked.
1 Co. 5. 1 (that there is) fornication among you
5. 1 fornication as is not so much as named
6. 13 Now the body (is) not for fornication, but
6. 18 Flee fornication. Every sin that a man
7. 2 (to avoid) fornication, let every man have
2 Co. 12. 21 have not repented of the..fornication
Gal. 5. 19 Now the works of the flesh..are..fornic.
Eph. 5. 3 But fornication..let it not be once named
Col. 3. 5 fornication..inordinate affection, evil
1 Th. 4. 3 that ye should abstain from fornication
Rev. 2. 21 space to repent of her fornication; and
9. 21 Neither repented..of their fornication
14. 8 the wine of the wrath of her fornication
17. 2 drunk with the wine of her fornication
17. 4 abominations and filthiness of her forni.
18. 3 the wine of the wrath of her fornication
19. 2 did corrupt the earth with her fornicati.

FORNICATION, to cause to commit —
To cause to commit fornication, זָנָה *zanah,* 5.
2 Ch. 21. 11 caused the inhabitants..to commit forn.

FORNICATION, to commit —
1. *To commit fornication,* זָנָה *zanah.*
Isa. 23. 17 and shall commit fornication with all
Eze. 16. 26 Thou hast also committed fornication
2. *To commit fornication,* πορνεύω *porneuō.*
1 Co. 6. 18 but he that committeth fornication sin.
10. 8 Neither let us commit fornication, as
Rev. 2. 14 sacrificed unto idols, and to commit forn.
2. 20 to teach..to commit fornication, and to
17. 2 With whom the kings..have committed f.
18. 3 have committed fornication with her, and
18. 9 kings..who have committed fornication

FORNICATION, to give one's self over to —
To commit much fornication, ἐκπορνεύω *ekporneuō.*
Jude 7 giving themselves over to fornication

FORNICATOR —
Fornicator, πόρνος *pornos.*
1 Co. 5. 9 I wrote..not to company with fornicators
5. 10 Yet not altogether with the fornicators
5. 11 if any man..be a fornicator, or covetous
6. 9 neither fornicators, nor idolators, nor
Heb. 12. 16 Lest there (be) any fornicator, or profane

FORSAKE, to —
1. *To cease, leave off, forbear,* חָדַל *chadal.*
Judg 9. 11 Should I forsake my sweetness, and my
2. *To leave, spread out,* נָטַשׁ *natash.*
Deut 32. 15 then he forsook God (which) made him
Judg. 6. 13 but now the LORD hath forsaken us, and
1 Sa. 12. 22 the LORD will not forsake his people for
1 Ki. 8. 57 let him not leave us, nor forsake us
2 Ki. 21. 14 And I will forsake the remnant of mine
Psa. 78. 60 So that he forsook the tabernacle of S.
Prov. 1. 8 and forsake not the law of thy mother
6. 20 and forrake not the law of thy mother
Isa. 2. 6 Therefore thou hast forsaken thy people
Jer. 7. 29 the LORD hath rejected and forsaken the
15. 6 Thou hast forsaken me, saith the LORD
23. 33 I will even forsake you, saith the LORD
23. 39 I will forsake you, and the city that I
3. *To forsake, leave, leave off,* עָזַב *azab.*
Deut 12. 19 Take heed to thyself that thou forsake n.
14. 27 the Levite..thou shalt not forsake him
28. 20 doings, whereby thou hast forsaken me
29. 25 Because they have forsaken the covenant
31. 6 he will not fail thee, nor forsake thee
31. 8 he will not fail thee, neither forsake thee
31. 16 will forsake me, and break my covenant
31. 17 I will forsake them, and I will hide my f.
Josh. 1. 5 I will not fail thee, nor forsake thee
24. 16 God forbid that we should forsake the
24. 20 If ye forsake the LORD, and serve strange
Judg. 2. 12 forsook the LORD God of their fathers
2. 13 they forsook the LORD, and served Baal
10. 6 forsook the LORD, and served not him
10. 10 we have forsaken our God, and also served
10. 13 Yet ye have forsaken me, and served ot.
1 Sa. 8. 8 wherewith they have forsaken me, and
12. 10 because we have forsaken the LORD, and
31. 7 they forsook the cities, and fled; and the
1 Ki. 6. 13 and will not forsake my people Israel
9. 9 Because they forsook the LORD their God
11. 33 Because that they have forsaken me, and
12. 8 But he forsook the counsel of the old m.
12. 13 the king..forsook the old men's counsel
18. 18 in that ye have forsaken the commandm.
19. 10, 14 the children of Israel have forsaken
2 Ki 21. 22 he forsook the Lord GOD of his fathers
22. 17 Because they have forsaken me, and have
1 Ch. 10. 7 then they forsook their cities, and fled
28. 9 if thou forsake him, he will cast thee off
28. 20 will not fail thee, nor forsake thee, until
2 Ch. 7. 19 But if ye turn away, and forsake my
7. 22 Because they forsook the LORD God of
10. 8 he forsook the counsel which the old men
10. 13 king Rehoboam forsook the counsel of
12. 1 he forsook the law of the LORD, and all
12. 5 Thus saith the LORD, Ye have forsaken me
13. 10 we have not forsaken him; and the priests
13. 11 we keep the charge..but ye have forsaken
15. 2 if ye forsake him, he will forsake you
21. 10 because he had forsaken the LORD God of
24. 20 forsaken the LORD, he hath also forsaken
24. 24 because they had forsaken the LORD God
28. 6 because they had forsaken the LORD God
29. 6 For our fathers..have forsaken him, and
34. 25 Because they have forsaken me, and have
Ezra 8. 22 his wrath (is) against all them that forsake
9. 9 yet our God hath not forsaken us in our
9. 10 for we have forsaken thy commandments
Neh. 9. 17 ready to pardon..and forsookest them
9. 19 thou..forsookest them not in the wilder.
9. 31 thou didst not utterly..forsake them; for
10. 39 we will not forsake the house of our God
Job 6. 14 he forsaketh the fear of the Almighty
20. 13 (Though) he spare it, and forsake it not
20. 19 he hath oppressed (and) forsaken the poor
Psa. 9. 10 for thou, LORD, hast not forsaken them
22. 1 My God, my God, why hast thou forsaken
27. 9 leave me not, neither forsake me, O God
27. 10 When my father and my mother forsake
37. 8 Cease from anger, and forsake wrath. fret
37. 28 For the LORD..forsaketh not his saints
38. 21 Forsake me not, O LORD: O my God, be
71. 9 forsake me not when my strength faileth
71. 11 Saying, God hath forsaken him: persecute
71. 18 forsake me not, until I have showed thy
89. 30 If his children forsake my law, and walk
94. 14 neither will he forsake his inheritance
119. 8 I will keep thy statutes: O forsake me
119. 53 because of the wicked that forsake thy
119. 87 had almost consumed..but I forsook not
Prov. 2. 17 Which forsaketh the guide of her youth
3. 3 Let not mercy and truth forsake thee
4. 2 good doctrine, forsake ye not my law
4. 6 Forsake her not, and she shall preserve
9. 6 Forsake the foolish, and live; and go in
15. 10 grievous unto him that forsaketh the way
27. 10 thy father's friend, forsake not; neither
28. 4 They that forsake the law praise the wi.
28. 13 whoso confesseth and forsaketh (them)
Isa. 1. 4 forsaken the LORD, they have provoked
1. 28 and they that forsake the LORD shall be
41. 17 the God of Israel will not forsake them
42. 16 will I do unto them, and not forsake them
49. 14 The LORD hath forsaken me, and my Lord
54. 7 For a small moment have I forsaken thee
55. 7 Let the wicked forsake his way, and the
58. 2 forsook not the ordinance of their God
65. 11 But ye (are) they that forsake the LORD
Jer. 1. 16 against them..who have forsaken me, and
2. 13 they have forsaken me, the fountain of
2. 17 in that thou hast forsaken the LORD thy
2. 19 thou hast forsaken the LORD thy God, and
5. 7 thy children have forsaken me, and sworn
5. 19 Like as ye have forsaken me, and served
9. 13 the LORD saith, Because they have forsa.
9. 19 because we have forsaken the land
12. 7 I have forsaken mine house, I have left
14. 5 and forsook (it), because there was no
16. 11 Because your fathers have forsaken me
16. 11 have forsaken me, and have not kept my
17. 13 all that forsake thee shall be ashamed
17. 13 because they have forsaken the LORD, the
19. 4 Because they have forsaken me, and have
22. 9 Because they have forsaken the covenant
25. 38 He hath forsaken his covert, as the lion
51. 9 forsake her, and let us go every one into
Lam. 5. 20 Wherefore dost thou..forsake us so long
Eze. 8. 12 the LORD hath forsaken the earth
9. 9 The LORD hath forsaken the earth, and
20. 8 neither did they forsake the idols of Eg.
Dan. 11. 30 intelligence with them that forsake the
Jon. 2. 8 They that observe lying vanities forsake
4. *To fail, let alone, desist,* רָפָה *raphah,* 5.
Deut. 4. 31 he will not forsake thee, neither destroy
Psa. 138. 8 forsake not the works of thine own hands
5. *Apostacy from,* ἀποστασία ἀπό *apostasia apo.*
Acts 21. 21 thou teachest all the Jews..to forsake M.
6. *To arrange (self) off or away,* ἀποτάσσομαι *apotas.*
Luke 14. 33 whosoever he be of you that forsaketh not
7. *To send or let away,* ἀφίημι *aphiēmi.*
Matt 19. 27 we have forsaken all, and followed thee
19. 29 And every one that hath forsaken houses
26. 56 Then all the disciples forsook him, and
Mark 1. 18 And straightway they forsook their nets
14. 50 And they all forsook him, and fled
Luke 5. 11 they forsook all, and followed him
8. *To leave down in,* ἐγκαταλείπω *egkataleipō.*
Matt 27. 46 My God! my God! why hast thou forsa.
Mark 15. 34 My God! my God! why hast thou forsa.
2 Co. 4. 9 Persecuted, but not forsaken; cast down
2 Ti. 4. 10 For Demas hath forsaken me, having lov.
4. 16 but all (men) forsook me: (I pray God)
Heb. 10. 25 Not forsaking the assembling of ourselves
13. 5 I will never leave thee, nor forsake thee
9. *To leave down or thoroughly,* καταλείπω *katale.*
Heb. 11. 27 By faith he forsook Egypt, not fearing
2 Pe. 2. 15 Which have forsaken the right way, and

FORSAKEN —
1. *Widowed, forsaken one,* אַלְמָן *alman.*
Jer. 51. 5 For Israel (hath) not (been) forsaken, nor
2. *To forsake, leave,* עָזַב *azab.*
Isa. 17. 2 cities of Aroer (are) forsaken: they shall
17. 9 his strong cities be as a forsaken bough
54. 6 hath called thee as a woman forsaken
60. 15 thou hast been forsaken and hated, so
62. 4 Thou shalt be no more termed Forsaken
Jer. 4. 29 every city (shall be) forsaken, and not a
Zeph. 2. 4 For Gaza shall be forsaken, and Ashkelon
3. *To be sent away, let alone,* שָׁלַח *shalach,* 4.
Isa. 27. 10 (and) the habitation forsaken, and left like

FORSAKEN, to be —
1. *To be left, spread out,* נָטַשׁ *natash,* 2.
Amos 5. 2 she is forsaken upon her land; (there is)
2. *To be left, spread out,* נָטַשׁ *natash,* 4.
Isa. 32. 14 Because the palaces shall be forsaken
3. *To fail, be plucked away,* נָתַשׁ *nathash,* 2.
Jer. 18. 14 shall the cold flowing waters..be forsak.?
4. *To be forsaken, left,* עָזַב *azab,* 2.
Neh. 13. 11 said, Why is the house of God forsaken?
Job 18. 4 shall the earth be forsaken for thee? and
Psa. 37. 25 yet have I not seen the righteous forsaken
Isa. 7. 16 land..shall be forsaken of both her kings
62. 12 be called, Sought out, A city not forsaken
Eze. 36. 4 saith..to the cities that are forsaken

FORSAKING —
Forsaking, abandonment, עֲזוּבָה *azubah.*
Isa. 6. 12 and (there be) a great forsaking in the

FORSOMUCH as —
Because that, καθότι *kathoti.*
Luke 19. 9 forsomuch as he also is a son of Abraham

FORSWEAR oneself, to —
To swear against or falsely, ἐπιορκέω *epiorkeō.*
Matt. 5. 33 Thou shalt not forswear thyself, but shalt

FORT —
1. *Fort, fortification,* דָּיֵק *dayeq.*
2 Ki. 25. 1 they built forts against it round about
Jer. 52. 4 and built forts against it round about
Eze. 4. 2 build a fort against it, and cast a mount
17. 17 and building forts, to cut off many pers.
21. 22 to cast a mount, (and) to build a fort
26. 8 and he shall make a fort against thee
2. *Stronghold,* מָעוֹז *maoz.*
Dan. 11. 19 he shall turn his face toward the fort of
3. *Stronghold, fortress,* מְצָד *metsad.*
Eze. 33. 27 they that (be) in the forts and in the caves
4. *Stronghold, fortress,* מְצוּדָה *metsudah.*
2 Sa. 5. 9 So David dwelt in the fort, and called it
5. *Bulwark,* מְצוּרָה *metsurah.*
Isa. 29. 3 and I will raise forts against thee
6. *Fort, high or secret place,* עֹפֶל *ophel.*
Isa. 32. 14 the forts and towers shall be for dens for

FORT, high —
High place, tower, מִשְׂגָּב *misgab.*
Isa. 25. 12 the fortress of the high fort of thy walls

FORTH —
1. *To go on,* הָלַךְ *halak.*
Psa. 126. 6 He that goeth forth and weepeth, bearing
2. *Without, outside,* חוּץ *chuts.*
Gen. 39. 13 garment in her hand, and was fled forth
Judg 19. 25 so the man took..and brought her forth
4. *A breach, breaking forth,* פֶּרֶץ *perets.*
Gen. 38. 29 and she said, How hast thou broken fo.?
5. *Into the midst,* εἰς τὸ μέσον *eis to meson.*
Mark 3. 3 And he saith unto the man..Stand forth
6. *Without, forth,* ἔξω *exō.*
John 11. 43 cried with a loud voice, Lazarus, come fo.
15. 6 abide not in me, he is cast forth as a bra.
19. 4 Pilate therefore went forth again, and
19. 4 I bring him forth to you, that ye may k.
19. 5 Then came Jesus forth, wearing the cro
19. 13 he brought Jesus forth, and sat down in

Acts 5. 34 and commanded to put the apostles forth
9. 40 Peter put them all forth, and kneeled

[*See also* Break, breaking, bring, brought, bud, call, called, carry, cast, come, conduct, draw, driven, fetch, fruit, get, give, go, going, have, hold, joy, launch, lead, led, let, look, manifest, order, pass, proceed, poured, put, putting, reach, send, sending, set, setter, shed, shew, shine, shoot, show, sing, speak, spread, spreadest spring, stand, stretch, stretched, take, thousands, write.]

FORTH of or without —

1 *Unto from the house of,* אֶל־מִבֵּית *el mib-beth.*
2 Ki. 11. 15 Have her forth without the ranges: and
2 Ch. 23. 14 Have her forth of the ranges: and whoso

2. *From on,* מֵעַל *me-al.*
Amos 7. 17 Israel shall..go into captivity forth of

FORTHWITH —

1. *Speedily, diligently, carefully,* אָסְפַּרְנָא *osparna.*
Ezra 6. 8 forthwith expences be given unto these

2. *Straightway,* εὐθέως *eutheōs.*
Matt 13. 5 and forthwith they sprung up, because
26. 49 forthwith he came to Jesus, and said, Ha.
Mark 1. 29 forthwith, when they were come out of
1. 43 charged him, and [forthwith] sent him
5. 13 And forthwith Jesus gave them leave
Acts 12. 10 forthwith the angel departed from him
21. 30 and forthwith the doors were shut

3. *Straightway,* εὐθύς *euthus.*
John 19. 34 forthwith came thereout blood and wat.

4. *With the thing itself, therewith,* παραχρῆμα *par.*
Acts 9. 18 he received sight [forthwith], and arose

FORTIETH —

Forty, אַרְבָּעִים *arbaim.*
Num 33. 38 in the fortieth year after the children of
Deut. 1. 3 it came to pass in the fortieth year, in
1 Ch. 26. 31 In the fortieth year of the reign of David
2 Ch. 16. 13 died in the one and fortieth year of his

FORTIFIED —

Bulwark, מָצוֹר *matsor.*
Mic. 7. 12 the fortified cities, and from the fortress

FORTIFY, to —

1. *To strengthen, harden,* אָמֵץ *amats,* 3.
Nah. 2. 1 make..loins strong, fortify..power migh.

2. *To fence,* בָּצַר *batsar,* 3.
Isa. 22. 10 the houses have ye broken down to forti
Jer. 51. 53 and though she should fortify the height

3. *To strengthen,* חָזַק *chazaq,* 3.
2 Ch. 11. 11 he fortified the strongholds, and put
26. 9 Uzziah built towers..and fortified them
Nah. 3. 14 fortify thy strongholds: go into clay

4. *To leave,* עָזַב *azab.*
Neh. 3. 8 they fortified Jerusalem unto the broad
4. 2 will they fortify themselves? will they

5. *To bind together, fortify,* צוּר *tsur.*
Judg 9. 31 behold, they fortify the city against thee

FORTRESS —

1. *Fenced place,* מִבְצָר *mibtsar.*
Isa. 17. 3 The fortress also shall cease from Ephra.
25. 12 the fortress of the high fort of thy walls
34. 13 nettles and brambles in the fortresses
Jer. 6. 27 I have set thee..a tower..a fortress am.
Hos. 10. 14 all thy fortresses shall be spoiled, as Sh.
Amos 5. 9 spoiled shall come against the fortress

2 *Stronghold,* מָעוֹז *maoz.*
Jer. 16. 19 O LORD, my strength, and my fortress
Dan. 11. 7 and shall enter into the fortress of the
11. 10 return, and be stirred up..to his fortress

3. *Fortress, bulwark,* מְצוּדָה *metsudah.*
2 Sa. 22. 2 The LORD (is) my rock, and my fortress
Psa. 18. 2 the LORD (is) my rock and my fortress
31. 3 For thou (art) my rock and my fortress
71. 3 for thou (art) my rock and my fortress
91. 2 (He is) my refuge and my fortress
144. 2 My goodness, and my fortress; my high

4. *Bulwark,* מָצוֹר *matsor.*
Jer. 10. 17 Gather up..O inhabitant of the fortress
Mic. 7. 12 and from the fortress even to the river

FOR-TU-NA'-TUS, Φορτουνάτος *(from Latin), fortunate.*

A Corinthian Christian mentioned by Paul.
1 Co. 16. 17 I am glad of the coming of..F. and Ach.

FORTY —

1. *Forty,* אַרְבָּעִים *arbaim.*
Gen. 5. 13 Cainan lived..eight hundred and forty
7. 4, 12 upon the earth forty days and forty
7. 17 the flood was forty days upon the earth
8. 6 it came to pass at the end of forty days
18. 28 And he said, If I find there forty and five
18. 29 Peradventure there shall be forty found
18. 29 he said, I will not do (it) for forty's sake
25. 20 Isaac was forty years old when he took
26. 34 Esau was forty years old when he took
32. 15 forty kine, and ten bulls, twenty she asses
47. 28 age of Jacob was an hundred forty and se.
50. 3 forty days were fulfilled for him; for so
Exod 16. 35 children of Israel did eat manna forty
24. 18 in the mount forty days and forty nights
26. 19 thou shalt make forty sockets of silver
26. 21 their forty sockets (of) silver; two sockets
Exod 34. 28 with the LORD forty days and forty nights
36. 24 forty sockets of silver he made under
36. 26 their forty sockets of silver; two sockets
Lev. 25. 8 shall be unto thee forty and nine years
Num. 1. 21 of the tribe of Reuben..forty and six
1. 25 of the tribe of Gad..forty and five
1. 33 of the tribe of Ephraim..forty thousand
1. 41 of the tribe of Asher..forty and one tho.
2. 11 And his host..forty and six thousand
2. 15 And his host..forty and five thousand
2. 19 And his host..forty thousand and five
2. 28 And his host..forty and one thousand
13. 25 And they returned..after forty days
14. 33 your children shall wander..forty years
14. 34 in which ye searched the land..forty days
14. 34 shall ye bear your iniquities..forty years
26. 7 of them were forty and three thousand
26. 18 of them, forty thousand and five hundred
26 41, 50 were numbered of them..forty and
32. 13 he made them wander..forty years, until
35. 6 to them ye shall add forty and two cities
35. 7 give to the Levites..forty and eight cities
Deut. 2. 7 these forty years the LORD thy God (hath
8. 2 LORD thy God led thee these forty years
8. 4 neither did thy foot swell, these forty ye.
9. 9 then I abode..forty days and forty nights
9. 11 at the end of forty days and forty nights
9. 18, 25 fell down..forty days and forty nights
10. 10 I stayed..forty days and forty nights
25. 3 Forty stripes he may give him..not exceed
29. 5 I have led you forty years in the wilder.
Josh. 4. 13 About forty thousand prepared for war
5. 6 the children of Israel walked forty years
14. 7 Forty years old (was) I when Moses the
14. 10 the LORD hath kept me alive..these forty
21. 41 All the cities..forty and eight cities with
Judg. 3. 11 And the land had rest forty years. And
5. 8 was there a shield..seen among forty th.
5. 31 And the land had rest forty years
8. 28 the country was in quietness forty years
12. 6 and there fell..forty and two thousand
12. 14 he had forty sons and thirty nephews
13. 1 into the hand of the Philistines forty ye.
1 Sa 4. 18 And he had judged Israel forty years
17. 16 the Philistine..presented himself forty
2 Sa. 2. 10 Ish-bosheth, Saul's son, (was) forty years
5. 4 David..thirty years old..reigned forty
10. 18 David slew..forty thousand horsemen
15. 7 it came to pass after forty years, that Ab
1 Ki. 2. 11 David reigned over Israel..forty years
4. 26 Solomon had forty thousand stalls of
6. 17 the temple before it, was forty cubits
7. 3 the beams, that (lay) on forty five pillars
7. 38 one laver contained forty baths..every la.
11. 42 Solomon reigned in Jerusalem..forty ye.
14. 21 Rehoboam..forty and one years old when
15. 10 forty and one reigned he in Jerusalem
19. 8 went..forty days and forty nights unto
2 Ki. 2. 24 and tare forty and two children of them
8. 9 of every good thing of Damascus, forty
10. 14 two and forty men; neither left he any
12. 1 and forty years reigned he in Jerusalem
14. 23 began to reign in Samaria..forty and one
1 Ch. 5. 18 four and forty thousand seven hundred
12. 36 of Asher..expert in war, forty thousand
19. 18 David slew..forty thousand footmen
29. 27 he reigned over Israel..forty years; seven
2 Ch. 9. 30 Solomon reigned in Jerusalem..forty ye.
12. 13 Rehoboam (was) one and forty years old
22. 2 Forty and two years old (was) Ahaziah
24. 1 and he reigned forty years in Jerusalem
Ezra 2. 8 of Zattu, nine hundred forty and five
2. 10 of Bani, six hundred forty and two
2. 24 the children of Azmaveth, forty and two
2. 25 seven hundred and forty and three
2. 34 of Jericho, three hundred forty and five
2. 38 Pashur, a thousand two hundred forty
2. 66 their mules, two hundred forty and five
Neh. 5. 15 and wine, besides forty shekels of silver
7. 13 of Zattu, eight hundred forty and five
7. 15 of Binnui, six hundred forty and eight
7. 28 The men of Beth-azmaveth, forty and two
7. 29 Buroth, seven hundred forty and three
7. 36 of Jericho, three hundred forty and five
7. 41 of Pashur, a thousand two hundred forty
7. 44 The singers..an hundred forty and eight
7. 62 of Nekoda, six hundred forty and two
7. 67 and they had two hundred forty and five
7. 68 their mules, two hundred forty and five
9. 21 forty years didst thou sustain them in the
11. 13 chief of the fathers, two hundred forty
Job 42. 16 lived Job an hundred and forty years
Psa. 95. 10 Forty years long was I grieved with (this)
Jer. 52. 30 captive of the Jews seven hundred forty
Eze. 4. 6 iniquity of the house of Judah forty
29. 11 neither shall it be inhabited forty years
29. 12 the cities..shall be desolate forty years
29. 13 At the end of forty years will I gather the
41. 2 he measured the length thereof, forty
46. 22 courts joined of forty..long, and thirty
Amos 2. 10 led you forty years through the wilder.
5. 25 Have ye offered..offerings..forty years
Jon. 3. 4 Yet forty days, and Nineveh shall be

2. *Forty,* τεσσαράκοντα *tessarakonta,* τεσσεράκον.
Matt. 4. 2 had fasted forty days and forty nights
Mark 1. 13 he was there in the wilderness forty
Luke 4. 2 Being forty days tempted of the devil
John 2. 20 Then said the Jews, Forty and six years
Acts 1. 3 being seen of them forty days, and speak.
4. 22 For the man was above forty years old
7. 30 when forty years were expired, there ap.
Acts 7. 36 wonders..in the wilderness forty years
7. 42 sacrifices..forty years in the wilderness?
13. 21 gave..Saul..by the space of forty years
23. 13 they were more than forty which had
23. 21 for there lie in wait for him..forty men
2 Co. 11. 24 Of the Jews five times received I forty
Heb. 3. 9 proved me, and saw my works forty years
3. 17 But with whom was he grieved forty yea.?
Rev 7. 4 sealed an hundred (and) forty..four thou.
11. 2 holy city shall they tread under foot forty
13. 5 unto him to continue forty..two months
14. 1 and with him an hundred forty..four
14. 3 could learn that song but the hundred..f.
21. 17 he measured..an hundred..forty..four c.

FORTY...thousand —

Four myriad, אַרְבַּע רִבּוֹא (*or* רִבּוֹ) *arba ribbo.*
Ezra 2. 64 The whole..forty and two thousand three
Neh. 7. 66 The whole..forty and two thousand three

FORTY years old —

Forty years' time, τεσσαρακονταετὴς χρόνος.
Acts 7. 23 when he was full forty years old, it came

FORTY years, of —

Forty years, τεσσαρακονταετής *tessarakontaetēs.*
Acts 13. 18 about the time of forty years suffered he

FORWARD —

1. *Yonder, beyond, henceforth,* הָלְאָה *haleah.*
Num 32. 19 not..on yonder side Jordan, or forward
1 Sa. 10. 3 Then shalt thou go on forward from the.
18. 9 Saul eyed David from that day..forward
Eze. 39. 22 LORD their God from that day and forw.
43. 27 and (so) forward, the priests shall make

2. *To go on,* הָלַךְ *halak.*
Gen. 26 13 went forward, and grew until he became

3. *And upward,* וּמָעְלָה *u-malah.*
1 Sa. 16. 13 came upon David from that day forward
30. 25 it was (so) from that day forward, that

4. *To the front,* לְפָנִים *le-phanim.*
Jer. 7. 24 and went backward, and not forward
Eze. 10. 22 they went every one straight forward

5. *Before,* קֶדֶם *qedem.*
Job 23. 8 Behold, I go forward, but he (is) not

6. *Speedy, hasty,* σπουδαῖος *spoudaios.*
2 Co. 8. 17 being more forward, of his own accord

FORWARD, to be —

1. *To wish, will,* θέλω *thelō.*
2 Co. 8. 10 to do, but also to be forward a year ago

2. *To hasten, make speed,* σπουδάζω *spoudazō.*
Gal. 2. 10 the same which I also was forward to do

FORWARD, to go —

To lift up, remove, journey, נָסַע *nasa.*
Exod 14. 15 children of Israel, that they go forward
Num. 2. 24 they shall go forward in the third rank
10. 5 that lie on the east parts shall go forward

FORWARD, to set —

1. *To cause to go up, advance, promote,* יָעַל *yaal,* 5.
Job 30. 13 They mar my path, they set forward my

2. *To remove, lift up, journey,* נָסַע *nasa.*
Num. 1. 51 when the tabernacle setteth forward, the
2. 17 Then the tabernacle..shall set forward
2. 17 as they encamp, so shall they set forward
2. 34 and so they set forward, every one after
4. 5 And when the camp setteth forward, Aa.
4. 15 sanctuary, as the camp is to set forward
10. 17 the sons of Merari set forward bearing
10. 18 the standard..of Reuben set forward ac.
10. 21 the Kohathites set forward, bearing the
10. 22 the standard..of Ephraim set forward ac.
10. 25 the standard..of Dan set forward
10. 28 the journeyings..when they set forward
10. 35 came to pass, when the ark set forward
21. 10 the children of Israel set forward, and
22. 1 the children of Israel set forward, and

FORWARDNESS —

Speed, haste, σπουδή *spoudē.*
2 Co. 8. 8 but by occasion of the forwardness of

FORWARDNESS of mind —

Readiness of mind, προθυμία *prothumia.*
2 Co. 9. 2 For I know the forwardness of your mind

FOUL —

Unclean, ἀκάθαρτος *akathartos.*
Mark 9. 25 he rebuked the foul spirit, saying unto
Rev. 18. 2 the hold of every foul spirit, and a cage

FOUL weather —

Winter, a pouring out (of rain), χειμών *cheimōn.*
Matt 16. 3 And in the morning..foul weather to day

FOUL, to —

To foul, trample, trouble, רָפַשׂ *raphas.*
Eze. 32. 2 camest forth..and fouledst their rivers
34. 18 but ye must foul the residue with your

FOUL, to be —

To smear, become smeared, חָמַר *chamar,* 4a.
Job 16. 16 My face is foul with weeping, and on

FOULED, that which.. have —

Foul or trampled thing, מִרְפָּשׂ *mirpas.*
Eze. 34. 19 they drink that which ye have fouled

FOUND, to —

1. *To found, lay a foundation,* יָסַד *yasad.*

Psa. 24. 2 For he hath founded it upon the seas, and
89. 11 the fulness thereof, thou hast founded
104. 8 unto the place which thou hast founded
119. 152 that thou hast founded them for ever
Prov. 3. 19 The LORD by wisdom hath founded the
Isa. 14. 32 LORD hath founded Zion, and the poor of
23. 13 the Assyrian founded it for them that
Amos 9. 6 and hath founded his troop in the earth

2. *To found,* θεμελιόω *themelioō.*

Matt. 7. 25 it fell not : for it was founded upon a r.
Luke. 6. 48 not shake it..[for it was founded upon a r.]

FOUND, to be — [*See also* **FIND.**]

1. *To find, be found,* מָצָא *matsa.*

Gen. 2. 20 but for Adam there was not found an h.
Job 20. 8 He shall fly away..and..not be found
Psa. 32. 6 in a time when thou mayest be found
36. 2 until his iniquity be found to be hateful
Eccl. 9. 15 Now there was found in it a poor wise

2. *To be found,* מָצָא *matsa,* 2.

Gen. 18. 29, 30, 31 Peradventure there shall be..fou.
18. 32 Peradventure ten shall be found there
44. 9 whomsoever of thy servants it be found
44. 10 he with whom it is found shall be my
44. 12 the cup was found in Benjamin's sack
44. 16 and (he) also with whom the cup is found
44. 17 the man in whose hand the cup is found
47. 14 gathered up all the money that was found
Exod. 9. 19 every man and beast which shall be found
12. 19 Seven days shall there be no leaven found
21. 16 or if he be found in his hand, he shall
22. 2 If a thief be found breaking up, and be
22. 4 If the theft be certainly found in his h.
22. 7 if the thief be found, let him pay double
22. 8 If the thief be not found, then the master
35. 23 And every man, with whom was found
35. 24 every man, with whom was found shittim
Deut 17. 2 If there be found among you, within any
18. 10 There shall not be found among you
20. 11 all the people..found therein shall be tri.
21. 1 If (one) be found slain in the land which
22. 20 virginity be not found for the damsel
22. 22 If a man be found lying with a woman
22. 28 and lie with her, and they be found
24. 7 If a man be found stealing any of his
Josh. 10. 17 The five kings are found hid in a cave at
1 Sa. 9. 20 set not thy mind on them..they are found
10. 2 The asses..thou wentest to seek are fou.
10. 16 He told us..that the asses were found
10. 21 they sought him, he could not be found
13. 19 Now there was no smith found through.
13. 22 there was neither sword nor spear found
13. 22 and with Jonathan his son was there fo.
25. 28 and evil hath not been found in thee
2 Sa. 17. 12 in some place where he shall be found
17. 13 until there be not one small stone found
1 Ki. 1. 52 but if wickedness shall be found in him
14. 13 because in him there is found (some) good
2 Ki. 12. 5 wheresoever any breach shall be found
12. 10 told the money that was found in the ho.
12. 18 all the gold (that was) found in the treasu.
14. 14 all the vessels that were found in the ho.
16. 8 silver and gold that was found in the ho.
18. 15 Hezekiah gave..all..(that was) found
20. 13 and all that was found in his treasures
22. 9 gathered the money that was found in
22. 13 concerning..this book that is found : for
23. 2 book of the covenant which was found in
25. 19 and five men..which were found in the
25. 19 and threescore men of the people..found
1 Ch. 4. 41 the habitations that were found there
24. 4 there were more chief men found of the
26. 31 there were found among them mighty
28. 9 if thou seek him, he will be found of thee
29. 8 they with whom..stones were found gave
2 Ch. 2. 17 they were found an hundred and fifty
15. 2 if ye seek him, he will be found of you
15. 4 and sought him, he was found of them
15. 15 Judah..sought..and he was found of th.
19. 3 Nevertheless there are good things found
21. 17 all the substance that was found in the
25. 24 all the vessels that were found in the
34. 17 gathered..the money that was found in
34. 21 the words of the book that is found
34. 30 the book of the covenant that was found
36. 8 that which was found in him, behold they
Ezra 2. 62 their register..but they were not found
10. 18 among..sons of the priest there were fo.
Neh. 7. 64 their register..but it was not found
13. 1 and therein was found written, that the
Esth. 6. 2 it was found written, that Mordecai had
Job 19. 28 seeing the root of the matter is found in
28. 12 But where shall wisdom be found?
28. 13 neither is it found in the land of the living
42. 15 in all the land were no women found
Psa. 37. 36 I sought him, but he could not be found
Prov. 6. 31 But (if) he be found, he shall restore sev.
10. 13 In the lips of him..wisdom is found
16. 31 (if) it be found in the way of righteous.
Isa. 13. 15 Every one that is found shall be thrust
22. 3 all that are found in thee are bound
30. 14 so that there shall not be found in the
35. 9 it shall not be found there ; but the
39. 2 and all that was found in his treasures
51. 3 joy and gladness shall be found therein
55. 6 Seek ye the LORD while he may be found
65. 1 I am found of (them that) sought me not
65. 8 As the new wine is found in the cluster
Jer. 2. 26 As the thief is ashamed when he is found
2. 34 Also in thy skirts is found the blood of
2. 34 I have not found it by secret search, but
5. 26 For among my people are found wicked
11. 9 A conspiracy is found among the men of
15. 16 Thy words were found, and I did eat them
29. 14 And I will be found of you, saith the L.
41. 3 and the Chaldeans that were found there
41. 8 But ten men were found among them that
48. 27 Israel..was he found among thieves? for
50. 20 sins of Judah, and they shall not be found
50. 24 O Babylon..thou art found, and also cau.
52. 25 seven men..which were found in the city
52. 25 that were found in the midst of the city
Eze. 26. 21 yet shalt thou never be found again
28. 15 perfect..till iniquity was found in thee
Dan. 1. 19 among them all was found none like Da.
11. 19 shall stumble and fall, and not be found
12. 1 every one that shall be found written in
Hos. 14. 8 Ephraim..From me is thy fruit found
Mic. 1. 13 the transgressions of Israel were found in
Zeph. 3. 13 neither shall a deceitful tongue be found
Zech. 10. 10 and (place) shall not be found for them
Mal. 2. 6 and iniquity was not found in his lips

3. *To be found,* שְׁכַח *shekach,* 5.

Ezra 4. 19 it is found that this city of old time hath

4. *To be found,* שְׁכַח *shekach,* 2.

Ezra 6. 2 there was found at Achmetha, in the pa.
Dan. 2. 35 that no place was found for them : and
5. 11 light..and wisdom..was found in him
5. 12 of doubts, were found in the same Daniel
5. 14 and excellent wisdom is found in thee
5. 27 Thou art weighed..and art found wanting
6. 4 neither was there any..fault found in him
6. 22 before him innocency was found in me
6. 23 no manner of hurt was found upon him

5. *To become,* γίνομαι *ginomai.*

2 Co. 7. 14 our boasting..before Titus, is found a

FOUND out, to be —

1. *To be searched out,* חָקַר *chaqar,* 2.

1 Ki. 7. 47 neither was the weight of the brass f. out
2 Ch. 4. 18 the weight of the brass could not be f. out

2. *To be found,* מָצָא *matsa,* 2.

Esth. 2. 23 inquisition was made..it was found out

FOUNDATION —

1. *Socket,* אֶדֶן *eden.*

Job 38. 6 Whereupon are the foundations thereof

2. *Foundation,* אָשִׁישׁ *ashish.*

Isa. 16. 7 for the foundations of Kir-hareseth shall

3. *To be founded,* יָסַד *yasad,* 2.

Exod 9. 18 since the foundation thereof even until

4. *To be founded,* יָסַד *yasad,* 4.

1 Ki. 7. 10 the foundation..costly stones, even great

5. *Foundation,* יְסוֹד *yesod.*

2 Ch. 23. 5 a third part at the gate of the foundation
Job 4. 19 them..whose foundation (is) in the dust
22. 16 whose foundation was overflown with a
Psa. 137. 7 Rase (it), rase..to the foundation thereof
Prov. 10. 25 the righteous (is) an everlasting founda.
Lam. 4. 11 it hath devoured the foundations thereof
Eze. 13. 14 so that the foundation thereof shall be
30. 4 her foundations shall be broken down
Mic. 1. 6 I will discover the foundations thereof
Hab. 3. 13 by discovering the foundation unto the

6. *Foundation,* יְסוּדָה *yesudah.*

Psa. 87. 1 His foundation (is) in the holy mountains

7. *Foundation,* מוּסָד *musad.*

2 Ch. 8. 16 prepared unto the day of the foundation
Isa. 28. 16 Behold, I lay in Zion..a sure foundation

8. *Foundation,* מוּסָדָה *musadah.*

Eze. 41. 8 the foundations of the side chambers

9. *Base,* מָכוֹן *makon.*

Psa 104. 5 (Who) laid the foundations of the earth

10. *Foundation,* מַסָּד *massad.*

1 Ki. 7. 9 even from the foundation unto the coping

11. *Foundation, prince, column,* שָׁת *shath.*

Psa. 11. 3 If the foundations be destroyed, what can

12. *Foundation, anything laid,* θεμέλιος *themelios.*

Luke 6. 48 digged deep, and laid the foundation on
6. 49 is like a man that without a foundation
14. 29 Lest haply, after he hath laid the founda.
Acts 16. 26 so that the foundations of the prison were
Rom 15. 20 I should build upon another man's foun.
1 Co. 3. 10 I have laid the foundation, and another
3. 11 For other foundation can no man lay
3. 12 if any man build upon this foundation
Eph. 2. 20 are built upon the foundation of the ap.
1 Ti. 6. 19 Laying up..a good foundation against
2 Ti. 2. 19 the foundation of God standeth sure
Heb. 6. 1 not laying again the foundation of repe.
11. 10 he looked for a city which hath foundations
Rev. 21. 14 the wall of the city had twelve founda.
21. 19 the foundations of the wall of the city
21. 19 The first foundation (was) jasper ; the

13. *A casting or laying down, founding,* καταβολή *katabolē.*

Matt 13. 35 kept secret from the foundation of the
25. 34 prepared for you from the foundation of
Luke 11. 50 which was shed from the foundation of
John 17. 24 thou lovedst me before the foundation of
Eph. 1. 4 in him before the foundation of the world
Heb. 4. 3 were finished from the foundation of the
9. 26 suffered since the foundation of the world
1 Pe. 1. 20 foreordained before the foundation of the
Rev. 13. 8 slain from the foundation of the world
17. 8 not written..from the foundation of the

FOUNDATION to be laid —

1. *To be founded,* יָסַד *yasad,* 2.

Isa. 44. 28 even saying..Thy foundation shall be laid

2. *To be founded,* יָסַד *yasad,* 4.

1 Ki. 6. 37 fourth year was the foundation..laid
Ezra 3. 6 But the foundation..was not..laid
Hag. 2. 18 the foundation of the..temple was laid
Zech. 8. 9 the foundation of the house..was laid

3. *To be founded,* יָסַד *yasad,* 6.

Ezra 3. 11, 12 the foundation of the house was laid

FOUNDATION, to lay for a —

To found, lay as a foundation, יָסַד *yasad,* 3.

Isa. 28. 16 I lay in Zion for a foundation a stone

FOUNDATION, to lay the —

1. *To found, lay a foundation,* יָסַד *yasad.*

2 Ch. 31. 7 they began to lay the foundation of the
Job 38. 4 when I laid the foundations of the earth?
Psa. 102. 25 Of old hast thou laid the foundation of
Isa. 48. 13 Mine hand also hath laid the foundation
51. 13 and laid the foundations of the earth
51. 16 and lay the foundations of the earth
54. 11 and lay thy foundations with sapphires
Zec. 12. 1 and layeth the foundation of the earth

2. *To found, lay a foundation,* יָסַד *yasad,* 3.

Josh. 6. 26 he shall lay the foundation thereof in his
1 Ki. 5. 17 stones, to lay the foundation of the house
16. 34 he laid the foundation thereof in Abiram
Ezra 3. 10 when the builders laid the foundation of
3. 12 when the foundation of this house was
Zech. 4. 9 have laid the foundation of this house

FOUNDATION of, to lay the —

To found, lay foundation of, θεμελιόω *themelioō.*

Heb. 1. 10 Thou..hast laid the foundation of the ea.

FOUNDATIONS —

1. *Foundations,* אֻשְׁיוֹת *oshyoth.*

Jer. 50. 15 her foundations are fallen, her walls are

2. *Foundations,* אֻשִּׁין *ushshin.*

Ezra 4. 12 have set up..and joined the foundations
5. 16 laid the foundation of the house of God
6. 3 let the foundations thereof be strongly

3. *Foundations,* מוֹסָדוֹת *mosadoth.*

Deut 32. 22 and set on fire the foundations of the
2 Sa. 22. 8 the foundations of heaven moved and
22. 16 the foundations of the world were disco.
Psa. 18. 7 the foundations also of the hills moved
18. 15 the foundations of the world were disco.
82. 5 all the foundations of the earth are out
Prov. 8. 29 when he appointed the foundations of the
Isa. 24. 18 the foundations of the earth do shake
40. 21 have ye not understood from the founda.
58. 12 thou shalt raise up the foundations of
Jer. 31. 37 and the foundations of the earth searched
51. 26 for a corner, nor a stone for foundations
Mic. 6. 2 Hear..ye strong foundations of the earth

FOUNDER —

To refine, purify, צָרַף *tsaraph.*

Judg 17. 4 and gave them to the founder, who made
Jer. 6. 29 the founder melteth in vain : for the wic.
10. 9 the work..of the hands of the founder
10. 14 every founder is confounded by the grav.
51. 17 every founder is confounded by the grav.

FOUNTAIN —

1. *Well, cistern,* [V.L. בּוֹר], בַּיִר *bayir.*

Jer. 6. 7 As a fountain casteth out her waters, so

2. *Fountain,* מַבּוּעַ *mabbua.*

Eccl. 12. 6 or the pitcher be broken at the fountain

3. *Spring, fountain,* מַעְיָן *mayan.*

Gen. 7. 11 the same day were all the fountains of
8. 2 The fountains also of the deep and the
Lev. 11. 36 Nevertheless a fountain or pit, (wherein
Josh. 15. 9 unto the fountain of the water of Nepht.
1 Ki. 18. 5 Go..unto all fountains of water, and unto
2 Ch. 32. 4 who stopped all the fountains, and the
Psa. 74. 15 Thou didst cleave the fountain and the fl.
114. 8 turned..the flint into a fountain of waters
Prov. 5. 16 Let thy fountains be dispersed abroad
8. 24 when..no fountains abounding with wa.
25. 26 a troubled fountain, and a corrupt spring
Song 4. 12 a spring shut up, a fountain sealed
4. 15 A fountain of gardens, a well of living w
Isa. 41. 18 and fountains in the midst of the valleys
Hos. 13. 15 and his fountain shall be dried up : he
Joel 3. 18 a fountain shall come forth of the house

4. *Fountain,* מָקוֹר *maqor.*

Lev. 20. 18 he hath discovered her fountain, and
20. 18 she hath uncovered the fountain of her
Psa. 36. 9 For with thee (is) the fountain of life
68. 26 Bless..the Lord, from the fountain of Is.
Prov. 5. 18 Let thy fountain be blessed : and rejoice
13. 14 The law of the wise (is) a fountain of life
14. 27 The fear of the LORD (is) a fountain of life
Jer. 2. 13 they have forsaken me, the fountain of
9. 1 and mine eyes a fountain of tears, that
17. 13 the LORD, the fountain of living waters
Hos. 13. 15 his fountain shall be dried up : he shall
Zech. 13. 1 In that day there shall be a fountain

5. *Spring, fountain,* עַיִן *ayin.*
Gen. 16. 7 angel..found her by a fountain of water
16. 7 by the fountain in the way to Shur
Num 33. 9 and in Elim..twelve fountains of water
Deut. 8. 7 a land of brooks of water, of fountains
33. 28 the fountain of Jacob..upon a land of
1 Sa. 29. 1 the Israelites pitched by a fountain which
2 Ch. 32. 3 to stop the waters of the fountains which
Neh. 2. 14 Then I went on to the gate of the fount.
3. 15 But the gate of the fountain repaired
12. 37 at the fountain gate, which was over aga.
Prov. 8. 28 when he strengthened the fountains of

6. *Fount, source,* πηγή *pēgē.*
Mark 5. 29 straightway the fountain of her blood
Jas. 3. 11 Doth a fountain send forth at the same
3. 12 [so (can) no fountain both yield salt water]
Rev. 7. 17 shall lead them unto living fountains of
8. 10 and upon the fountains of waters
14. 7 made heaven..and the fountains of waters
16. 4 poured out his vial upon the..fountains of
21. 6 of the fountain of the water of life freely

FOUR —

1. *Four,* (אַרְבָּעָה,) אַרְבַּע *arba.*
Gen. 2. 10 it was parted, and became into four heads
11. 13, 15 lived..four hundred and three years
11. 16 Eber lived four and thirty years, and be.
11. 17 Eber lived..four hundred and thirty yea.
14. 9 king of Ellasar; four kings with five
15. 13 they shall afflict them four hundred years
23. 15 the land (is worth) four hundred shekels
23. 16 four hundred shekels of silver, current
32. 6 to meet thee, and four hundred men with
33. 1 Esau came, and with him four hundred
47. 24 four parts shall be your own, for seed of
Exod 12. 40 sojourning..(was) four hundred and thirty
12. 41 it came to pass at the end of the four hu.
22. 1 he shall restore..four sheep for a sheep
25. 12 thou shalt cast four rings of gold for it
25. 12 and put (them) in the four corners there.
25. 26 thou shalt make for it four rings of gold
25. 26 four corners that (are) on the four feet
25. 34 in the candlestick (shall be) four bowls
26. 2, 8 the breadth of one curtain four cubits
26. 32 thou shalt hang it upon four pillars of
26. 32 gold, upon the four sockets of silver
27. 2 horns of it upon the four corners thereof
27. 4 make four brasen rings in the four corners
27. 16 their pillars..four, and their sockets four
28. 17 thou shalt set in it..four rows of stones
36. 9 the breadth of one curtain four cubits
36. 15 and four cubits (was) the breadth of one
36. 36 made thereunto four pillars (of) shittim
36. 36 and he cast for them four sockets of silv.
37. 3, 13 And he cast for it four rings of gold
37. 3 (to be set) by the four corners of it; even
37. 13 put the rings upon the four corners that
37. 20 in the candlestick (were) four bowls made
38. 2 he made the horns..on the four corners
38. 5 he cast four rings for the four ends of the
38. 19 pillars (were) four, and their sockets..four
38. 29 and two thousand and four hundred she.
39. 10 And they set in it four rows of stones
Lev. 11. 20 All fowls that creep, going upon (all) four
11. 21 creeping thing that goeth upon (all) four
11. 23 creeping things, which have four feet
11. 27 all manner of beasts that go on (all) four
11. 42 whatsoever goeth upon (all) four, or what.
Num. 1. 29 fifty and four thousand and four hund.
1. 31 fifty and seven thousand and four hund.
1. 37 thirty and five thousand and four hund.
1. 43 fifty and three thousand and four hund.
2. 6 fifty and four thousand and four hund.
2. 8 fifty and seven thousand and four hund.
2. 9 six thousand and four hundred, through.
2. 16 fifty and one thousand and four hund.
2. 23 (were) thirty and five thousand and four
2. 30 fifty and three thousand and four hund.
7. 7 Two wagons and four oxen he gave unto
7. 8 four wagons and eight oxen he gave unto
7. 85 two thousand and four hundred (shekels)
7. 88 peace offerings, (were) twenty and four
25. 9 those that died..were twenty and four
26. 25, 43 threescore and four thousand and
26. 47 fifty and three thousand and four hund.
26. 50 forty and five thousand and four hund.
Deut. 3. 11 four cubits the breadth of it, after the
22. 12 make thee fringes upon the four quarters
Josh 19. 7 Ether, and Ashan; four cities and their
21. 18 and Almon with her suburbs; four cities
21. 22 Beth-horon with her suburbs; four cities
21. 24 Gath-rimmon with her suburbs; four cit.
21. 29 En-gannim with her suburbs; four cities
21. 31 and Rehob with her suburbs; four cities
21. 35 Nahalal with her suburbs; four cities
21. 39 Jazer with her suburbs; four cities in all
Judg. 9. 34 they laid wait against Shechem in four
11. 40 went yearly to lament..four days in a ye.
19. 2 and was there four whole months
20. 2 four hundred thousand footmen that
20. 17 were numbered four hundred thousand
20. 47 abode in the rock Rimmon four months
21. 12 they found..four hundred young virgins
1 Sa. 4. 2 and they slew..about four thousand men
22. 2 there were with him about four hundred
25. 13 there went up after David about four h.
27. 7 David dwelt..a full year and four months
30. 10 David pursued, he and four hundred men
30. 17 save four hundred young men, which rode
2 Sa. 21. 20 four and twenty in number; and he also
21. 22 These four were born to the giant in Gath
1 Ki. 6. 1 And it came to pass, in the four hundred
7. 2 upon four rows of cedar pillars, with ce.
7. 19 (were) of lily work in the porch, four cu.
7. 27 four cubits (was) the length of one base
7. 27 and four cubits the breadth thereof, and
7. 30 And every base had four brasen wheels
7. 30 the four corners thereof had undersetters
7. 32 And under the borders (were) four wheels
7. 34 four undersetters to the four corners of
7. 38 every laver was four cubits..upon every
7. 42 four hundred pomegranates for the two
9. 28 gold, four hundred and twenty talents
10. 26 he had a thousand and four hundred
15. 33 to reign over all Israel..twenty and four
18. 19 the prophets of Baal four hundred and
18. 19 the prophets of the groves four hundred
18. 22 but Baal's prophets (are) four hundred
18. 33 Fill four barrels with water, and pour
22. 6 about four hundred men, and said unto
2 Ki. 7. 3 And there were four leprous men at the
14. 13 unto the corner gate, four hundred cubits
1 Ch. 3. 5 four, of Bath-shua the daughter of Ammon
5. 18 four and forty thousand seven hundred
7. 1 Tola, and Puah, Jashub, and Shimrom, fo.
7. 7 and two thousand and thirty and four
9. 24 In four quarters were the porters, toward
9. 26 For these Levites, the four chief porters
12. 26 Of the children of Levi, four thousand
20. 6 whose fingers and toes..four and twenty
21. 5 Judah (was) four hundred threescore and
21. 20 his four sons with him hid themselves
23. 4 Of which, twenty and four thousand
23. 5 Moreover, four thousand (were) porters
23. 5 and four thousand praised the LORD with
23. 10 These (four) were the sons of Shimei
23. 12 Amram, Izhar, Hebron, and Uzziel, four
24. 18 the four and twentieth to Maaziah
25. 31 The four and twentieth to Romanti-ezer
26. 17 northward four a day, southward four a
26. 18 At Parbar westward, four at the causeway
27. 1 of every course..twenty and four thous.
27. 2, 4, 5, 7, 8, 9 his course (were) twenty and f.
27. 10, 11, 12, 13, 14, 15 his course..twenty and f.
2 Ch. 1. 14 he had a thousand and four hundred
4. 13 four hundred pomegranates on the two
8. 18 took thence four hundred and fifty talents
9. 25 Solomon had four thousand stalls for
13. 3 with..four hundred thousand chosen men
18. 5 gathered..of prophets four hundred men
25. 23 to the corner gate, four hundred cubits
Ezra 1. 10 basons of a second..four hundred and
1. 11 All..five thousand and four hundred
2. 7 a thousand two hundred fifty and four
2. 15 of Adin, four hundred fifty and four
2. 31 a thousand two hundred fifty and four
2. 40 Levites..of Hodaviah, seventy and four
2. 67 Their camels, four hundred thirty and
Neh. 6. 4 they sent unto me four times after this
7. 12 a thousand two hundred fifty and four
7. 23 of Bezai, three hundred twenty and four
7. 34 a thousand two hundred fifty and four
7. 43 Levites..of Hodevah, seventy and four
7. 69 camels, four hundred thirty and five
11. 6 four hundred threescore and eight valiant
11. 18 Levites..two hundred fourscore and four
Job 1. 19 and smote the four corners of the house
42. 16 Job..saw..his sons' sons..four generati.
Prov 30. 15 (yea), four (things) say not, (It is) enough
30. 18 too wonderful for me, yea, four which I
30. 21 disquieted, and for four..it cannot bear
30. 24 There be four..little upon the earth, but
30. 29 three..which go well, yea, four are comely
Isa. 11. 12 gather..from the four corners of the earth
17. 6 four..five in the outmost fruitful branches
Jer. 15. 3 I will appoint over them four kinds, saith
36. 23 when Jehudi had read three or four leaves
49. 36 the four winds from the four quarters of
52. 21 the thickness thereof (was) four fingers
52. 30 all the persons (were) four thousand and
Eze. 1. 5 the likeness of four living creatures
1. 6 And every one had four faces
1. 6 and every one had four wings
1. 8 under their wings on their four sides
1. 8 they four had their faces and their wings
1. 10 they four had the face of a man, and
1. 10 they four had the face of an ox on the
1. 10 they four also had the face of an eagle
1. 15 by the living creatures, with his four f.
1. 16 they four had one likeness: and their
1. 17 they went upon their four sides
1. 18 rings..full of eyes round about them four
7. 2 the end is come upon the four corners of
10. 9 when I looked, behold the four wheels
10. 10 they four had one likeness, as if a wheel
10. 11 they went upon their four sides; they
10. 12 wheels..the wheels that they four had
10. 14 And every one had four faces: the first f.
10. 21 Every one had four faces..four wings
14. 21 when I send my four sore judgments upon
37. 9 Come from the four winds, O breath, and
40. 41 Four tables (were) on this side, and four
40. 42 And the four tables (were) of hewn stone
41. 5 the breadth of..side chamber, four cubits
42. 20 He measured it by the four sides: it had
43. 14 to the greater settle (shall be) four cubits
43. 15 So the altar (shall be) four cubits; and
43. 15 from the altar and upward..four horns
43. 16 altar..square in the four squares thereof
43. 17 and fourteen broad in the four squares
43. 20 on the four horns..and on the four corn.
45. 19 upon the four corners of the settle of the
46. 21 caused me to pass by the four corners of
Eze. 46. 22 In the four corners of the court..courts
46. 22 these four corners (were) of one measure
46. 23 And..a row..round about them four
48. 16, 16, 16, 16, 30, 32, 33, 34 four thousand and
Dan. 1. 17 As for these four children, God gave them
8. 8 for it came up four notable ones t. t. four
8. 22 whereas four stood up for it, four kingd.
10. 4 in the four and twentieth day of the first
11. 4 shall be divided toward the four winds of
Amos 1. 3, 6, 9, 11, 13 For three trans...and for four
2. 1, 4, 6 For three transgressions..and for four
Hag. 1. 15 In the four and twentieth day of the sixth
2. 10 In the four and twentieth (day) of the
2. 18 from the four and twentieth day of the
2. 20 the word..came unto Haggai in the four
Zech. 1. 7 Upon the four and twentieth day of the
1. 18 Then..I..saw, and behold four horns
1. 20 And the LORD showed me four carpenters
2. 6 I have spread you abroad as the four wi.
6. 1 there came four chariots out from betw.
6. 5 These (are) the four spirits of the heavens

2. *Four,* (אַרְבָּעָה,) אַרְבַּע *arba.*
Ezra 6. 17 two hundred rams, four hundred lambs
Dan. 3. 25 I see four men loose, walking in the midst
7. 2 the four winds of the heaven strove upon
7. 3 four great beasts came up from the sea
7. 6 upon the back of it four wings of a fowl
7. 6 the beast had also four heads; and dom.
7. 17 These..beasts, which are four, (are) four

3. *Four,* τέσσαρες *tessares.*
Matt 24. 31 shall gather together..from the four winds
Mark 2. 3 sick of the palsy, which was borne of four
13. 27 shall gather together..from the four winds
Luke 2. 37 a widow of about fourscore and four years
John 11. 17 he had (lain) in the grave four days already
19. 23 made four parts, to every soldier a part
Acts 10. 11 a great sheet knit at the four corners
11. 5 let down from heaven by four corners
12. 4 delivered (him) to four quaternions of
21. 9 the same man had four daughters, virgins
21. 23 We have four men which have a vow on
27. 29 they cast four anchors out of the stern
Rev. 4. 4 round about the throne (were) four and
4. 4 and upon the seats I saw four and twenty
4. 6 round about the throne, (were) four bea.
4. 8 the four beasts had each of them six wi.
4. 10 The four and twenty elders fall down be.
5. 6 in the midst..of the four beasts, and in
5. 8 when he had taken the book, the four
5. 8 and four (and) twenty elders fell down
5. 14 And the four beasts said, Amen. And
5. 14 the four (and) twenty elders fell down
6. 1 I heard..one of the four beasts saying
6. 6 I heard a voice in the midst of the four
7. 1 I saw four angels standing on the four c
7. 1 holding the four winds of the earth
7. 2 cried with a loud voice to the four angels
7. 4 sealed an hundred..forty..four thousand
7. 11 and (about) the elders, and the four beas.
9. 13 I heard a voice from the [four] horns of
9. 14 Loose the four angels which are bound in
9. 15 the four angels were loosed, which were
11. 16 the four and twenty elders which sat
14. 1 with him an hundred forty..four thousa.
14. 3 and before the four beasts, and the elders
14. 3 but the hundred..forty..four thousand
15. 7 one of the four beasts gave unto the seven
19. 4 the four and twenty elders, and the four
20. 8 the nations which are in the four quarters
21. 17 measured..an hundred..forty..four cub.

4. *Fourth,* τέταρτος *tetartos.*
Acts 10. 30 Four days ago I was fasting until this h.

FOUR (days, months, hundred, thousand) —

1. *Four months, (the space of),* τετράμηνον, -ος.
John 4. 35 Say not ye, There are yet four months

2. *Belonging to fourth day,* τεταρταῖος *tetartaios.*
John 11. 39 he stinketh: for he hath been (dead) four d.

3. *Four thousand,* τετρακισχίλιοι *tetrakischilioi.*
Matt 15. 38 they that did eat were four thousand men
16. 10 Neither the seven loaves of the four tho.
Mark 8. 9 they that had eaten were about four tho.
8. 20 when the seven among four thousand
Acts 21. 38 leddest out..four thousand men that

4. *Four hundred,* τετρακόσιοι *tetrakosioi.*
Acts 5. 36 to whom a number of men, about four h
7. 6 and entreat (them) evil four hundred ye.
13. 20 about the space of four hundred and fifty
Gal. 3. 17 the law, which was four hundred and th.

FOUR and twenty —

Twenty four, εἰκοσιτέσσαρες *eikositessares.*
Rev. 5. 14 the [four (and) twenty elders] fell down

FOUR fold —

1. *Four fold,* אַרְבַּעְתַּיִם *arbatayim.*
2 Sa. 12. 6 he shall restore the lamb four fold, beca.

2. *Four fold,* τετραπλόος *tetraploos.*
Luke 19. 8 by false accusation, I restore..four fold

FOUR footed beast —

Four footed, quadruped, τετράπους *tetrapous.*
Acts 10. 12 Wherein..all manner of four footed bea.
11. 6 I considered, and saw four footed beasts
Rom. 1. 23 and four footed beasts, and creeping

FOURSCORE —

1. *Eighty,* שְׁמֹנִים *shemonim.*
Gen. 16. 16 Abram (was) fourscore and six years old

Gen. 35. 28 Isaac were an hundred and fourscore y.
Exod. 7. 7 Moses (was) fourscore..Aaron fourscore
Num. 2. 9 an hundred thousand and fourscore tho.
4. 48 eight thousand and five hundred and fou.
Josh 14. 10 I (am) this day fourscore and five years
Judg. 3. 30 And the land had rest fourscore years
1 Sa. 22. 18 slew on that day fourscore and five per.
2 Sa. 19. 32 Barzillai was a very aged man..fourscore
19. 35 I (am) this day fourscore years old..can
1 Ki. 5. 15 fourscore thousand hewers in the moun.
12. 21 hundred and fourscore thousand chosen
2 Ki. 6. 25 until an ass's head was (sold) for fourscore
10. 24 Jehu appointed fourscore men without
19. 35 an hundred fourscore and five thousand
1 Ch. 7. 5 reckoned in all..fourscore and seven th.
15. 9 Eliel the chief, and his brethren fourscore
25. 7 all..was two hundred fourscore and eight
2 Ch. 2. 2 fourscore thousand to hew in the moun.
2. 18 fourscore thousand (to be) hewers in the
11. 1 hundred and fourscore thousand chosen
14. 8 two hundred and fourscore thousand
17. 15 two hundred and fourscore thousand
17. 18 an hundred and fourscore thousand
26. 17 with him fourscore priests of the LORD
Ezra 8. 8 Zebadiah..and with him fourscore males
Neh. 7. 26 Netophah, an hundred fourscore and
11. 18 Levites..two hundred fourscore and four
Esth. 1. 4 many days..an hundred and fourscore
Psa. 90. 10 and if by reason of strength..fourscore
Song 6. 8 There are threescore queens, and foursc.
Isa. 37. 36 a hundred and fourscore and five thou.
Jer. 41. 5 there came..from Samaria..fourscore

2. *Eighty*, ὀγδοήκοντα *ogdoēkonta.*
Luke 2. 37 And she (was) a widow of about fourscore
16. 7 he said..Take thy bill, and write fours.

FOURSQUARE —

1. *Fourth*, רְבִיעִי *rebii.*
Eze. 48. 20 ye shall offer the holy oblation foursquare

2. *To be foursquare*, רָבַע *raba.*
Exod 27. 1 the altar shall be foursquare: and the
28. 16 Foursquare it shall be, (being) doubled
30. 2 foursquare shall it be; and two cubits
37. 25 he made the incense altar..foursquare
38. 1 And he made the altar..foursquare
39. 9 It was foursquare; they made the

3. *To be foursquare*, רָבַע *raba*, 4.
1 Ki. 7. 31 gravings with their borders, foursquare
Eze. 40. 47 and an hundred cubits broad, foursquare

4. *Four cornered*, τετράγωνος *tetragōnos.*
Rev. 21. 16 the city lieth foursquare, and the length

FOURTEEN —

1. *Four (and) ten*, אַרְבָּעָה עָשָׂר (אַרְבַּע) *arba (arbaah) asar.*
Gen. 31. 41 I served thee fourteen years for thy two
46. 22 sons of Rachel..all the souls (were) fou.
Num. 1. 27 threescore and fourteen thousand and
2. 4 threescore and fourteen thousand and
16. 49 Now they that died..were fourteen tho.
29. 13, 17, 20, 23, 26, 29, 32 fourteen lambs of the
29. 15 tenth..to each lamb of the fourteen lambs
Josh 15. 36 of Judah..fourteen cities with their vil.
18. 28 of Benjamin..fourteen cities with their
1 Ki. 8. 65 seven days and seven days..fourteen days
1 Ch. 25. 5 God gave to Heman fourteen sons and
2 Ch. 13. 21 Abijah..married fourteen wives, and
Job 42. 12 for he had fourteen thousand sheep
Eze. 43. 17 settle..fourteen..long and fourteen br.

2. *Fourteen*, δεκατέσσαρες *dekatessares.*
Matt. 1. 17 from Abraham to David..fourteen gener.
1. 17 away into Babylon (are) fourteen genera.
1. 17 unto Christ (are) fourteen generations
2 Co. 12. 2 I knew a man in Christ above fourteen
Gal. 2. 1 Then fourteen years after I went up again

FOURTEENTH —

1. *Four (and) ten*, אַרְבַּע עֶשְׂרֵה, אַרְבָּעָה עָשָׂר *arbaah asar.*
Gen. 14. 5 in the fourteenth year came Chedorlaomer
Exod 12. 6 shall keep it up until the fourteenth day
12. 18 In the first (month), on the fourteenth day
Lev. 23. 5 In the fourteenth..of the first month at
Num. 9. 3 In the fourteenth day of this month, at
9. 5 they kept the passover on the fourteenth
9. 11 The fourteenth day of the second month
28. 16 in the fourteenth day of the first month
Josh. 5. 10 kept the passover on the fourteenth day
2 Ki. 18. 13 in the fourteenth year of king Hezekiah
1 Ch. 24. 13 to Huppah, the fourteenth to Jeshebeab
25. 21 The fourteenth to Mattithiah..his sons
2 Ch. 30. 15 they killed the passover on the fourteenth
35. 1 they killed the passover on the fourteenth
Ezra 6. 19 kept the passover upon the fourteenth
Esth. 9. 15 on the fourteenth day also of the month
9. 17 on the fourteenth day of the same rested
9. 18 Jews..assembled..on the fourteenth th.
9. 19 made the fourteenth day of the month
9. 21 they should keep the fourteenth day of
Isa. 36. 1 Now it came to pass in the fourteenth ye.
Eze. 40. 1 in the fourteenth year after that the city
45. 21 in the fourteenth day of the month, ye

2. *Four and tenth*, τεσσαρεσκαιδέκατος *tessareska.*
Acts 27. 27 But when the fourteenth night was come
27. 33 This day is the fourteenth day that ye

FOURTH —

1. *Four*, אַרְבַּע *arba.*
1 Ki. 22. 41 in the fourth year of Ahab king of Israel
2 Ch. 3. 2 he began to build..in the fourth year of
Neh. 9. 1 Now in the twenty and fourth day of this
Zech. 7. 1 it came to pass in the fourth year of
7. 1 in the fourth (day) of the ninth month

2. *Fourth*, רְבִיעִי *rebii.*
Gen. 1. 19 the evening and the morning were the f.
2. 14 And the fourth river (is) Euphrates
15. 16 But in the fourth generation they shall
Exod 28. 20 And the fourth row a beryl, and an onyx
39. 13 And the fourth row, a beryl, an onyx, and
Lev. 19. 24 But in the fourth year all the fruit ther.
Num. 7. 30 On the fourth day Elizur the son of She.
29. 23 And on the fourth day ten bullocks, two
Josh. 19. 17 the fourth lot came out to Issachar, for
Judg 19. 5 it came to pass on the fourth day, when
2 Sa. 3. 4 the fourth, Adonijah the son of Haggith
1 Ki. 6. 1 in the fourth year of Solomon's reign over
6. 33 posts (of) olive tree, a fourth part (of the
6. 37 In the fourth year was the foundation of
2 Ki. 10. 30 thy children of the fourth (generation)
15. 12 saying, Thy sons shall sit..unto the fourth
18. 9 And it came to pass in the fourth year of
1 Ch. 2. 14 Nethaneel the fourth, Raddai the fifth
3. 2 the fourth, Adonijah the son of Haggith
3. 15 the third Zedekiah, the fourth Shallum
8. 2 Nohah the fourth, and Rapha the fifth
12. 10 Mishmannah the fourth, Jeremiah the fi.
23. 19 Jahaziel the third, and Jekameam the fo.
24. 8 The third to Harim, the fourth to Seorim
24. 23 Jahaziel the third, Jekameam the fourth
25. 11 The fourth to Izri, (he), his sons, and his
26. 2 Zebadiah the third, Jathniel the fourth
26. 4 Sacar the fourth, and Nethaneel the fifth
26. 11 Tebaliah the third, Zechariah the fourth
27. 7 The fourth (captain) for the fourth month
2 Ch. 20. 26 And on the fourth day they assembled
Ezra 8. 33 Now on the fourth day was the silver and
Jer. 25. 1 in the fourth year of Jehoiakim the son
28. 1 in the fourth year, (and) in the fifth mo.
36. 1 it came to pass, in the fourth year of
39. 2 in the fourth month, the ninth (day) of
45. 1 in the fourth year of Jehoiakim the son
46. 2 in the fourth year of Jehoiakim the son
51. 59 into Babylon in the fourth year of his re.
52. 6 And in the fourth month, in the ninth
Eze. 1. 1 it came to pass..in the fourth (month)
10. 14 and the fourth the face of an eagle
Dan. 11. 2 and the fourth shall be far richer than
Zech. 6. 3 in the fourth chariot grisled and bay
8. 19 The fast of the fourth (month), and the

3. *Fourth*, רְבִיעַי *rebii.*
Dan 2. 40 And the fourth kingdom shall be strong
3. 25 form of the fourth is like the Son of God
7. 7 and behold a fourth beast, dreadful and
7. 19 I would know the truth of the fourth b.
7. 23 said, The fourth beast shall be the fourth

4. *Fourth, (those of the)*, רִבֵּעִים *ribbeim.*
Exod 20. 5 unto the third and fourth (generation) of
34. 7 unto the third and to the fourth (gener.)
Num 14. 18 unto the third and fourth (generation)
Deut. 5. 9 unto the third and fourth (generation) of

5. *Fourth*, τέταρτος *tetartos.*
Matt 14. 25 in the fourth watch of the night Jesus
Mark. 6. 48 and about the fourth watch of the night
Rev. 4. 7 the fourth beast (was) like a flying eagle
6. 7 And when he had opened the fourth seal
6. 7 I heard the voice of the fourth beast say
8. 12 And the fourth angel sounded, and the t.
16. 8 the fourth angel poured out his vial upon
21. 19 third, a chalcedony; the fourth, an emer.

FOURTH (part) —

1. *Fourth*, רְבִיעִי *rebii.*
Exod 29. 40 and the fourth part of an hin of wine (for)
Lev. 23. 13 (shall be) of wine, the fourth (part) of an
Num 15. 4 with the fourth (part) of an hin of oil
15. 5 the fourth (part) of an hin of wine for a
28. 5 mingled with the fourth (part) of an hin
28. 7 And the drink..(shall be) the fourth (pa.)
28. 14 and a fourth (part) of an hin unto a lamb
Neh. 9. 3 read in the book..(one) fourth part of the
9. 3 and (another) fourth part they confessed

2. *Fourth*, רֶבַע *reba.*
Exod 29. 40 the fourth part of an hin of beaten oil
1 Sa. 9. 8 I have here at hand the fourth part of a

3. *Fourth*, רֹבַע *roba.*
Num 23. 10 the number of the fourth (part) of Israel?
2 Ki 6. 25 the fourth part of a cab of dove's dung

4. *Fourth*, τέταρτος *tetartos.*
Rev. 6. 8 power was given..over the fourth part of

FOWL —

1. *Choice or fat geese*, בַּרְבֻּרִים *barburim.*
1 Ki. 4. 23 roebucks, and fallow deer, and fatted fowl

2. *Fowl*, עוֹף *oph.*
Gen. 1. 20 fowl (that) may fly above the earth in the
1. 21 and every winged fowl after his kind: and
1. 22 fill the waters in the seas, and let fowl
1. 26, 28 and over the fowl of the air, and over
1. 30 to every fowl of the air, and to every
2. 19 the LORD God formed..every fowl of the
2. 20 gave names..to the fowl of the air, and
6. 7 I will destroy..the fowls of the air; for
6. 20 Of fowls after their kind, and of cattle
7. 3 Of fowls also of the air by sevens, the m.
7. 8 of fowls, and of every thing that creepeth
7. 14 every fowl after his kind, every bird of
7. 21 And all flesh died..both of fowl, and of
7. 23 creeping things, and the fowl of the he.
Gen. 8. 17 Bring forth with thee..(both) of fowl
8. 19 every creeping thing, and every fowl
8. 20 took..of every clean fowl, and offered
9. 2 upon every fowl of the air, upon all that
9. 10 of the fowl, of the cattle, and of every
Lev. 1. 14 And if the burnt sacrifice..(be) of fowls
7. 26 ye shall eat no manner..of fowl or of
11. 13 shall have in abomination among the fo.
11. 20 All fowls that creep, going upon (all)
11. 46 of the fowl, and of every living creature
17. 13 catcheth any beast or fowl that may be
20. 25 and between unclean fowls and clean
20. 25 abominable by beast, or by fowl, or by
Deut 14. 20 (But of) all clean fowls ye may eat
28. 26 thy carcase shall be meat unto all fowls
1 Sa. 17. 44 I will give thy flesh unto the fowls of the
17. 46 give the carcases..this day unto the fowls
1 Ki. 4. 33 he spake also of beasts, and of fowl, and
14. 11 him that dieth..shall the fowls of the air
16. 4 him that dieth..shall the fowls of the
21. 24 and him that dieth..shall the fowls..eat
Job 12. 7 But ask now..the fowls of the air, and
28. 21 and kept close from the fowls of the air
35. 11 maketh us wiser than the fowls of heav.?
Psa. 50. 11 I know all the fowls of the mountains
78. 27 feathered fowls like as the sand of the sea
79. 2 given (to be) meat unto the fowls of the
104. 12 By them shall the fowls of the heaven
Jer. 7. 33 carcases..shall be meat for the fowls of
9. 10 both the fowl of the heavens and the
15. 3 the fowls of the heaven, and the beasts
16. 4 carcases shall be meat for the fowls of
19. 7 will I give to be meat for the fowls of
34. 20 bodies shall be for meat unto the fowls
Eze. 29. 5 I have given thee for meat..to the fowls
31. 6 All the fowls of heaven made their nests
31. 13 Upon his ruin shall all the fowls of the
32. 4 will cause all the fowls of the heaven to
38. 20 fowls of the heaven, and the beasts of
44. 31 shall not eat..whether it be fowl or beast
Hos. 2. 18 with the fowls of heaven, and (with) the
4. 3 shall languish..with the fowls of heaven
7. 12 I will bring them down as the fowls of
Zeph. 1. 3 I will consume the fowls of the heaven

3. *Fowl*, עוֹף *oph.*
Dan. 2. 38 and the fowls of the heaven hath he
7. 6 had upon the back of it four wings of a f.

4. *Ravenous fowl*, עַיִט *ayit.*
Gen. 15. 11 the fowls came down upon the carcases
Job 28. 7 (There is) a path which no fowl knoweth
Isa. 18. 6 left..unto the fowls..and the fowls

5. *Bird, sparrow, fowl*, צִפּוֹר *tsippor.*
Deut. 4. 17 likeness of any winged fowl that flieth
Neh. 5. 18 also fowls were prepared for me, and
Psa. 8. 8 The fowl of the air, and the fish of the
148. 10 cattle; creeping things, and flying fowl
Eze. 17. 23 under it shall dwell all fowl of every wi.
39. 17 Speak unto every feathered fowl, and to

6. *Bird, sparrow, fowl*, צִפַּר *tsippar.*
Dan. 4. 12 fowls of the heaven dwelt in the boughs
4. 14 and the fowls from his branches
4. 21 upon whose branches the fowls of the

7. *Bird, fowl*, ὄρνεον *orneon.*
Rev. 19. 17 saying to all the fowls that fly in the
19. 21 all the fowls were filled with their flesh

8. *Winged fowl*, πετεινόν *peteinon.*
Matt. 6. 26 Behold the fowls of the air: for they sow
13. 4 and the fowls came and devoured them
Mark 4. 4 fowls of the air came and devoured it up
4. 32 so that the fowls of the air may lodge
Luke 8. 5 and the fowls of the air devoured it
12. 24 much more are ye better than the fowls?
13. 19 the fowls of the air lodged in the bran.
Acts 10. 12 and creeping things, and fowls of the air
11. 6 and creeping things, and fowls of the air

FOWLER —

1. *Fowler, ensnarer*, יָקוֹשׁ *yaqosh.*
Hos. 9. 8 the prophet (is) a snare of a fowler in all

2. *Fowler, ensnarer*, יָקוּשׁ *yaqush.*
Psa. 91. 3 he shall deliver thee from..the fowler
Prov. 6. 5 and as a bird from the hand of the fowler

3. *To lay a snare, ensnare*, יָקשׁ *yaqosh.*
Psa. 124. 7 as a bird out of the snare of the fowlers

FOX —

1. *Fox, jackal*, שׁוּעָל *shual.*
Judg 15. 4 Samson..caught three hundred foxes, and
Neh. 4. 3 if a fox go up, he shall even break down
Psa. 63. 10 they shall be a portion for foxes
Song 2. 15 Take us the foxes, the little foxes, that
Lam. 5. 18 which is desolate, the foxes walk upon
Eze. 13. 4 thy prophets are like the foxes in the

2. *Fox*, ἀλώπηξ *alōpēx.*
Matt. 8. 20 The foxes have holes, and the birds of
Luke 9. 58 Foxes have holes, and birds of the air
13. 32 Go ye, and tell that fox, Behold, I cast

FRAGMENT —

Fragment, broken piece, κλάσμα *klasma.*
Matt 14. 20 and they took up of the fragments that
Mark 6. 43 twelve baskets full of the fragments, and
8. 19, 20 how many baskets full of fragments
Luke 9. 17 and there was taken up of fragments
John 6. 12 Gather up the fragments that remain
6. 13 filled twelve baskets with the fragments

FRAIL —
Left, forbearing, frail, חָדֵל *chadel.*
Psa. 39. 4 LORD..(that) I may know how frail I (am)

FRAME—
1. *Frame, formation, imagination,* יֵצֶר *yetser.*
Psa.103. 14 For he knoweth our frame; he rememb.
2. *Building, frame,* מִבְנֶה *mibneh.*
Eze. 40. 2 by which (was) as the frame of a city on

FRAME, to —
1. *To frame, constitute,* יָצַר *yatsar.*
Psa. 94. 20 iniquity..which frameth mischief by a
Isa. 29. 16 shall..say of him that framed it, He
Jer. 18. 11 Behold, I frame evil against you, and
2. *To prepare, establish,* כּוּן *kun,* 5.
Judg.12. 6 for he could not frame to pronounce (it)
3. *To give,* נָתַן *nathan.*
Hos. 5. 4 They will not frame their doings to turn
4. *To couple, join together,* צָמַד *tsamad,* 5.
Psa. 50. 19 to evil, and thy tongue frameth deceit
5. *To make thoroughly fit,* καταρτίζω *katartizō.*
Heb. 11. 3 that the worlds were framed by the word

FRAME together, to fitly —
To lay out fitly together, συναρμολογέω *sunarmol.*
Eph. 2. 21 whom all the building, fitly framed toge.

FRAMED, thing —
Frame, form, imagination. יֵצֶר *yetser.*
Isa. 29. 16 or shall the thing framed say of him that

FRANKINCENSE —
1. *Frankincense,* לְבוֹנָה *lebonah.*
Exod30. 34 sweet spices with pure frankincense
Lev. 2. 1 and he shall..put frankincense thereon
2. 15 And thou shalt..lay frankincense thereon
2. 16 with all the frankincense thereof
5. 11 neither shall he put (any) frankincense
6. 15 and all the frankincense which (is) upon
24. 7 thou shalt put pure frankincense upon
Num. 5. 15 nor put frankincense thereon; for it (is)
1 Ch. 9. 29 and the frankincense, and the spices
Neh. 13. 5 they laid..the frankincense, and the ve.
13. 9 with the meat offering and the frankin.
Song 3. 6 perfumed with myrrh and frankincense
4. 6 I will get me..to the hill of frankincense
4. 14 cinnamon, with all trees of frankincense
2. *Frankincense,* λίβανος *libanos.*
Matt 2. 11 they presented unto him..frankincense
Rev. 18. 13 ointments, and frankincense, and wine

FRAUD —
Fraud, oppression, תֹּךְ *tok.*
Psa. 10. 7 His mouth is full of cursing..and fraud

FRAUD, to keep back by —
To deprive of, ἀποστερέω *apostereō.*
Jas. 5. 4 hire..which is of you kept back by fraud

FRAY (away), to —
To cause to tremble, trouble, חָרַד *charad,* 5.
Deut28. 26 the beasts..and no man shall fray..away
Jer. 7. 33 the beasts..and none shall fray..away
Zech. 1. 21 but these are come to fray them, to cast

FREE —
1. *Gratis, for nought,* חִנָּם *chinnam.*
Exod21. 11 then shall she go out free without money
2. *Free,* חָפְשִׁי *chophshi.*
Exod 21. 2 in the seventh he shall go out free for no.
21. 5 I love..my children; I will not go out free
21. 26 he shall let him go free for his eye's sake
21. 27 he shall let him go free for his tooth's
Deut 15. 12 seventh year thou shalt let him go free
15. 13 And when thou sendest him out free from
15. 18 when thou sendest him away free from
1 Sa. 17. 25 and make his father's house free in Isra.
Job 3. 19 and the servant (is) free from his master
39. 5 Who hath sent out the wild ass free? or
Psa. 88. 5 Free among the dead, like the slain that
Isa. 58. 6 (Is) not this..to let the oppressed go free
Jer. 34. 9 man should let his man servant..go free
34. 10 and every one his maid servant, go free
34. 11 whom they had let go free, to return
34. 14 thou shalt let him go free from thee
3. *Willing, liberal, noble,* נָדִיב *nadib.*
2 Ch.29. 31 and as many as were of a free heart
Psa. 51. 12 Restore..and uphold me (with thy) free
4. *Acquitted,* נָקִי *naqi.*
Deut 24. 5 he shall be free at home one year, and
5. *Open, let away, free,* פָּטַר, פָּטִיר *patar* or *patir.*
1 Ch. 9. 33 (who remaining) in the chambers (were) f.
6. *Free, at liberty,* ἐλεύθερος *eleutheros.*
Matt17. 26 Jesus saith..Then are the children free
John 8. 33 how sayest thou, Ye shall be made free?
8. 36 if the Son..ye shall be free indeed
Rom. 6. 20 ye were the servants of sin, ye were free
7. 3 she is free from that law; so that she is
1 Co. 7. 21 if thou mayest be made free, use (it)
7. 22 he that is called, (being) free, is Christ's
9. 1 Am I not an apostle? am I not free?
9. 19 For though I be free from all (men), yet
12. 13 whether (we) be bond or free; and have
Gal. 3. 28 there is neither bond nor free, there is
4. 26 But Jerusalem which is above is free
4. 31 So then brethren, we are..of the free
Eph. 6. 8 receive of the Lord whether..bond or fr.
Col. 3. 11 Barbarian, Scythian, bond (nor) free: but
1 Pe. 2. 16 As free, and not using..liberty for a
Rev. 13. 16 And he causeth all..free and bond, to
19. 18 and the flesh of all..free and bond, both

FREE, to be —
1. *To be or become free,* חָפַשׁ *chaphash,* 4.
Lev. 19. 20 be put to death, because she was not fr.
2. *To be or become acquitted,* נָקָה *naqah,* 2.
Num. 5. 19 be thou free from this bitter water that
5. 28 then she shall be free, and shall conceive

FREE, to let go —
To open, loose, פָּתַח *pathach,* 3.
Psa.105. 20 the ruler of the people, and let him go f.

FREE, to make —
To free, make free, ἐλευθερόω *eleutheroō.*
John 8. 32 know..and the truth shall make you free
8. 36 If the Son therefore shall make you free
Rom. 6. 18 Being then made free from sin, ye beca.
6. 22 But now being made free from sin, and
8. 2 in Christ Jesus hath made me free from
Gal. 5. 1 wherewith Christ hath made us free, and

FREE gift —
A grace, gift, χάρισμα *charisma.*
Rom. 5. 15 not as the offence, so also (is) the free g.
5. 16 the free gift is of many offences unto ju.

FREE offering —
Willing offering, נְדָבָה *nedabah.*
Exod36. 3 they brought yet unto him free offerings
Amos.4. 5 proclaim..publish the free offerings; for

FREE man or woman —
1. *One fully freed,* ἀπελεύθερος *apeleutheros.*
1 Co. 7. 22 (being) a servant, is the Lord's free man
2. *Free person,* ἐλεύθερος *eleutheros.*
Gal. 4. 22 by a bond maid, the other by a free wo.
4. 23 but he of the free woman (was) by promi.
4. 30 not be heir with the son of the free woman
Rev. 6. 15 every free man, hid themselves in the dens

FREED, to be —
1. *To be cut off,* כָּרַת *karath,* 2.
Josh. 9. 23 there shall none of you be freed from
2. *To justify, declare just,* δικαιόω *dikaioō.*
Rom. 6. 7 For he that is dead is freed from sin

FREEDOM —
1. *Freedom,* חֻפְשָׁה *chuphshah.*
Lev. 19. 20 not at all redeemed, nor freedom given
2. *Citizenship,* πολιτεία *politeia.*
Acts 22. 28 With a great sum obtained I this freedom

FREELY —
1. *Gratis, for nought,* חִנָּם *chinnam.*
Num11. 5 the fish which we did eat in Egypt freely
2. *Willing offering,* נְדָבָה *nedabah.*
Psa. 54. 6 I will freely sacrifice unto thee: I will
Hos. 14. 4 I will love them freely: for mine anger
3. *Freely, gratis,* δωρεάν *dōrean.*
Matt10. 8 Heal..freely ye have received, freely give
Rom. 3. 24 Being justified freely by his grace through
2 Co.11. 7 I have preached to you the gospel..freely?
Rev. 21. 6 of the fountain of the water of life freely
22. 17 let him take the water of life freely
4. *With full speech,* μετὰ παῤῥησίας *meta parrhēsias.*
Acts 2. 29 let me freely speak unto you of the pat.
5. *To use full speech or ease,* παῤῥησιάζομαι *parrhē.*
Acts 26. 26 before whom also I speak freely: for I am

FREEWILL, to be minded of one's own —
To offer willingly, נָדַב *nedab,* 2.
Ezra 7. 13 which are minded of their own free will

FREEWILL offering —
1. *To offer willingly,* נָדַב *nedab,* 2.
Ezra 7. 16 with the freewill offering of the people
2. *Willing offering,* נְדָבָה *nedabah.*
Lev. 22. 18 for all his freewill offerings, which
22. 21 or a freewill offering in beeves or sheep
22. 23 mayest thou offer (for) a freewill offering
23. 38 and beside all your freewill offerings
Num15. 3 or in a freewill offering, or in your solemn
29. 39 your vows, and your freewill offerings
Deut 12. 6 your freewill offerings, and the firstlings
12. 17 nor thy freewill offerings, or heave
16. 10 a tribute of a freewill offering of thine
23. 23 a freewill offering, according as thou
2 Ch.31. 14 Kore..(was) over the freewill offerings of
Ezra 1. 4 beside the freewill offering for the house
3. 5 that willingly offered a freewill offering
8. 28 silver and the gold (are) a freewill offer.
Psa.119. 108 Accept..the freewill offerings of my

FREQUENT, more —
More abundantly, περισσοτέρως *perissoterōs.*
2 Co.11. 23 in prisons more frequent, in deaths oft.

FRESH —
1. *New, fresh,* חָדָשׁ *chadash.*
Job 29. 20 My glory (was) fresh in me, and my bow
2. *Moisture, freshness,* לְשַׁד *leshad.*
Num11. 8 the taste of it was as the taste of fresh oil
3. *Fresh,* רַעֲנָן *raanan.*
Psa. 92. 10 my horn..I shall be anointed with fresh
4. *Sweet,* γλυκύς *glukus.*
Jas. 3. 12 no fountain both yield salt water and fre.

FRESH, to be —
To be fresh, רֻטֲפַשׁ *rutaphash.*
Job 33. 25 His flesh shall be fresher than a child's

FRET, to —
1. *To be wroth, sad, morose,* זָעַף *zaaph.*
Prov19. 3 and his heart fretteth against the LORD
2. *To be angry,* רָגַז *ragaz.*
Eze. 16. 43 but hast fretted me in all these (things)

FRET inward —
A hollow, fretting, corrosion, פְּחֶתֶת *pechetheth.*
Lev.13. 55 it (is) fret inward, (whether) it (be) bare

FRET, to make to —
To cause to thunder or trembling, רָעַם *raam,* 5.
1 Sa. 1. 6 for to make her fret, because the LORD

FRET selves, to —
1. *To fret self,* חָרָה *charah,* 7.
Psa. 37. 1 Fret not thyself because of evil doers
37. 7 fret not thyself because of him who prosp.
37. 8 fret not thyself in any wise to do evil
Prov.24. 19 Fret not thyself because of evil (men)
2. *To (be or) show self wroth,* קָצַף *qatsaph,* 7.
Isa. 8. 21 they shall fret themselves, and curse the.

FRETTING —
To fret, prick, מָאַר *maar,* 5.
Lev. 13. 51 the plague (is) a fretting leprosy; it (is)
13. 52 for it (is) a fretting leprosy; it shall be
14. 44 it (is) a fretting leprosy in the house: it

FRIED, (that which is) —
To be fried, רָבַךְ *rabak,* 6.
Lev. 7. 12 cakes mingled with oil, of fine flour, fried
1 Ch. 23. 29 for that which is fried, and for all man.

FRIEND —
1. *To love,* אָהַב *ahab.*
2 Sa. 19. 6 In that thou..hatest thy friends: for thou
2 Ch. 20. 7 to the seed of Abraham thy friend for
Esth. 5. 10 Haman..sent and called for his friends
5. 14 Then said..all his friends unto him, Let
6. 13 And Haman told..all his friends every
Prov 14. 20 poor is hated..but the rich (hath) many f.
18. 24 a friend (that) sticketh closer than a bro.
27. 6 Faithful (are) the wounds of a friend
Isa. 41. 8 But thou..the seed of Abraham my fri.
Jer. 20. 4 a terror to thyself, and to all thy friends
20. 6 buried there, thou, and all thy friends
2. *To love,* אָהַב *ahab,* 3.
Zech.13. 6 I was wounded (in) the house of my fri.
3. *Men of peace,* אַנְשֵׁי שָׁלוֹם *aneshe shalom.*
Jer. 38. 22 Thy friends have set thee on, and have
4. *Leader,* אַלֻּף, אַלּוּף *alluph.*
Prov 16. 28 and a whisperer separateth chief friends
17. 9 that repeateth a matter separateth..fr.
5. *Friend,* מֵרֵעַ *merea.*
Gen. 26. 26 Abimelech..and Ahuzzath one of his fri.
2 Sa. 3. 8 show..to his brethren, and to his friends
Prov 19. 7 how much more do his friends go far from
6. *Friend,* רֵיעַ *rea.*
Job 6. 27 ye overwhelm..ye dig..for your friend
7. *Friend,* רֵעַ *rea.*
Gen. 38. 12 he and his friend Hirah the Adullamite
38. 20 sent the kid by the hand of his friend the
Exod33. 11 spake..as a man speaketh unto his friend
1 Sa. 30. 26 he sent of the spoil..to his friends, saying
2 Sa. 13. 3 But Amnon had a friend, whose name
16. 17 said..(Is) this thy kindness to thy friend?
16. 17 why wentest thou not with thy friend?
1 Ki. 16. 11 neither of his kinsfolks, nor of his friends
Job 2. 11 Now when Job's three friends heard of
6. 14 pity (should be showed) from his friend
16. 20 My friends scorn me..mine eye poureth
17. 5 He that speaketh flattery to..friends
19. 21 have pity upon me, O ye my friends
32. 3 Also against his three friends was his
42. 7 against thee, and against thy two friends
42. 10 LORD turned..when he prayed for his fr.
Psa. 35. 14 as though (he had been) my friend (or)
38. 11 My lovers and my friends stand aloof
88. 18 Lover, and friend hast thou put far from
Prov. 6. 1 My son, if thou be surety for thy friend
6. 3 thou art come into the hand of thy friend
6. 3 humble thyself and make sure thy friend
17. 17 A friend loveth at all times, and a brother
17. 18 becometh surety in the presence of his f.
18. 24 A man (that hath) friends must show him.
19. 4 Wealth maketh many friends: but the
19. 6 every man (is) a friend to him that giveth
22. 11 the grace of his lips the king..his friend
27. 9 so (doth) the sweetness of a man's friend
27. 10 Thine own friend, and thy father's friend
27. 14 He that blesseth his friend with a loud
27. 17 so a man..the countenance of his friend
Song 5. 1 eat, O friends; drink, yea, drink abund.
5. 16 This (is) my beloved, and this (is) my fri.
Jer. 6. 21 the neighbour and his friend shall perish
19. 9 shall eat every one the flesh of his friend
Lam. 1. 2 all her friends have dealt treacherously

Hos. 3. 1 Go yet, love a woman beloved of (her) fr.
Mic. 7. 5 Trust ye not in a friend, put ye not con.

8.*Friend*, רֵעֶה *reeh*.
2 Sa. 15. 37 So Hushai, David's friend, came into the
16. 16 when Hushai the Archite, David's friend
1 Ki. 4. 5 Zabud..principal officer..king's friend

9.*Comrade*, ἑταῖρος *hetairos*.
Matt 20. 13 Friend, I do thee no wrong: didst not
22. 12 Friend, how camest thou in hither not
26. 50 said..Friend, wherefore art thou come?

10.*Friend*, φίλος *philos*.
Matt 11. 19 Behold..a friend of publicans and sinners
Luke 7. 6 the centurion sent friends to him, saying
7. 34 Behold..a friend of publicans and sinners
11. 5 a friend, and shall go..Friend, lend me
11. 6 For a friend of mine in his journey is
11. 8 not..give him because he is his friend, yet
12. 4 I say unto you my friends, Be not afraid
14. 10 he may say unto thee, Friend, go up hi.
14. 12 call not thy friends, nor thy brethren
15. 6 calleth together..friends and neighbours
15. 9 she calleth..friends and..neighbours
15. 29 that I might make merry with my friends
16. 9 Make to yourselves friends of the mam.
21. 16 ye shall be betrayed both by..friends
23. 12 Pilate and Herod were made friends tog.
John 3. 29 but the friend of the bridegroom, which
11. 11 Our friend Lazarus sleepeth; but I go
15. 13 that a man lay down his life for his fri.
15. 14 Ye are my friends, if ye do whatsoever
15. 15 but I have called you friends; for all
19. 12 let this man go, thou art not Cesar's fri.
Acts 10. 24 Cornelius..had called together his..fri.
19. 31 And certain..which were his friends
27. 3 gave..liberty to go unto his friends to re.
Jas. 2. 23 and he was called the Friend of God
4. 4 a friend of the world is the enemy of God
3 John 14 (Our) friends salute thee. Greet the frien.

FRIEND, to make one a —
To persuade, πείθω *peithō*.
Acts 12. 20 having made Blastus..their friend, des.

FRIEND, to use as —
To treat as a friend, רָעָה *raah*, 3.
Judg 14. 20 companion, whom he had used as his fr.

FRIENDLY —
Heart, לֵב *leb*.
Judg 19. 3 went after her, to speak friendly unto
Ruth 2. 13 thou hast spoken friendly unto thine ha.

FRIENDLY, to show self —
To show self a friend, רָעַע *raa*, 7*a*.
Prov 18. 24 A man..must show himself friendly; and

FRIENDS (his) —
Men, מְתִים *methim*.
Job 19. 19 All my inward friends abhorred me: and
Female friend, φίλη *philē*. Luke 15. 9.
Those beside him, οἱ παρ' αὐτοῦ *hoi par autou*.
Mark 3. 21 when his friends heard..they went out

FRIENDS, thy —
Those belonging to, or with thee, οἱ σοὶ *hoi soi*.
Mark 5. 19 Go home to thy friends, and tell them

FRIENDSHIP —
Friendship, φιλία *philia*.
Jas. 4. 4 know ye not that the friendship of the

FRIENDSHIP with, to make —
To show self a friend, רָעָה *raah*, 7.
Prov 22. 24 Make no friendship with an angry man

FRINGE —
1.*Fringe, lock (of hair)*, צִיצִת *tsitsith*.
Num 15. 38 bid them that they make them fringes in
15. 38 and that they put upon the fringe of the
15. 39 it shall be unto you for a fringe, that ye

2.*Fringes, wreaths*, גְּדִלִים *gedilim*.
Deut 22. 12 Thou shalt make thee fringes upon the

FRO —
To turn back, שׁוּב *shub*.
Gen. 8. 7 a raven, which went forth to and fro
[*See also* Driven, go, going, reel, removing, run, running, to, toss, tossed, tossing, walk to.]

FROG —
1.*Frog*, צְפַרְדֵּעַ *tsephardea*.
Exod. 8. 2 I will smite all thy borders with frogs
8. 3 the river shall bring forth frogs abunda
8. 4 the frogs shall come up both on thee, and
8. 5 cause frogs to come up upon the land of
8. 6 the frogs came up, and covered the land
8. 7 and brought up frogs upon the land of
8. 8 that he may take away the frogs from me
8. 9 to destroy the frogs from thee and thy
8. 11 the frogs shall depart from thee, and
8. 12 because of the frogs which he had broug.
8. 13 the frogs died out of the houses, out of
Psa. 78. 45 He sent..frogs, which destroyed them
105. 30 Their land brought forth frogs in abund.

2.*Frog*, βάτραχος *batrachos*.
Rev. 16. 13 And I saw three unclean spirits like frogs

FROM —
1.*From then*, מֵאָז *me-az*.
Ruth 2. 7 came, and hath continued even from the

2. *From after*, מֵאַחֲרֵי *me-acharé*.
2 Sa. 11. 15 retire ye from him, that he may be smit.

2*a*.*From the hand (power) of*, מִיַּד [*min yad*].
2 Ch. 30. 6 from the king; Ps. 141. 9 from the snares

3.*Unto*, אֶל *el*.
Exod 36. 22 tenons equally distant one from another

4.*From (being) beside*, מֵאֵצֶל *me-etsel*.
1 Sa. 17. 30 And he turned from him toward another

5.*With*, אֵת *eth*.
Gen. 4. 1 said, I have gotten a man from the LORD

6.*So as not*, לְבִלְתִּי *le bilti*.
Josh. 22. 25 our children cease from fearing the LORD

7.*From the sufficiency of*, מִדֵּי *mid-de*.
1 Sa. 7. 16 he went from year to year in circuit to
2 Ch. 24. 5 to repair the house of your God from ye.
Isa. 66. 23 from one..to another..from one..to an.
Zech 14. 16 shall even go up from year to year to wor.

8. *Over against*, מוּל *mul*.
Lev. 5. 8 wring off his head from his neck, but

9.*Even from*, לְמִן *le-min*.
Deut. 9. 7 from the day that thou didst depart out

10.*From, out of*, מִן *min*.
Gen. 2. 6 But there went up a mist from the earth
Ezra 4. 12 the Jews which came up from thee to us
4. 21 until..commandment shall be given from
6. 6 your companions..be ye far from thence
6. 11 let timber be pulled down from his house
Dan. 2. 5 The thing is gone from me: if ye will not
2. 8 because ye see the thing is gone from me
3. 17 our God..is able to deliver us from the
4. 13 and an holy one came down from heaven
4. 14 get away from under it..from his branch
4. 16 Let his heart be changed from man's, and
4. 23 an holy one coming down from heaven
4. 25 That they shall drive thee from men
4. 31 there fell a voice from heaven..O king
4. 31 The kingdom is departed from thee
4. 32 And they shall drive thee from men, and
4. 33 he was driven from men, and did eat
5. 20 he was deposed from his kingly throne
5. 21 And he was driven from the sons of men
6. 20 is..God..able to deliver thee from the
6. 27 delivered Daniel from the power of the
7. 3 from the sea, diverse one from another
7. 4 and it was lifted up from the earth
7. 7 it (was) diverse from all the beasts that
7. 10 A fiery stream issued..forth from before
7. 19 which was diverse from all the others
7. 23 which shall be diverse from all kingdoms
7. 24 and he shall be diverse from the first

11.*From before*, מִן קֳדָם *min qodam*.
Dan. 2. 15 Why (is) the decree (so) hasty from the

12. *From on*, מֵעַל *me-al*.
Gen. 4. 14 thou hast driven me out this day from the

13.*Over*, עַל *al*.
Dan. 6. 18 Then the king..his sleep went from him

14.*From (being) with*, מֵעִם *me-im*.
Gen. 44. 29 if ye take this also from me, and mischief

15.*With*, עִם *im*.
Dan. 4. 3 his dominion (is) from generation to gen.
4. 34 his kingdom (is) from generation to gen.

16.*From with me*, מֵעִמָּדִי *me-immad-i*.
1 Sa. 10. 2 When thou art departed from me to day

17.*From before*, (מִלִּפְנֵי) מִפְּנֵי *mip-pene* (*mil-li-phene*).
Num 22. 33 and turned from me; [Heb., לְפָנַי *before*.]
22. 33 unless she had turned from me, surely
1 Sa. 17. 24 all the men of Israel..fled from him, and
19. 8 David went out..and they fled from him
25. 10 break away every man from his master
2 Sa. 15. 14 for we shall not..escape from Absalom
2 Ki. 11. 2 hid him..in the bedchamber from Atha.
Esth. 1. 19 let there go a royal commandment from
Job 13. 20 then will I not hide myself from thee
Psa. 61. 3 thou hast been..a strong tower from the
Eccl. 10. 5 as an error..proceedeth from the ruler
Isa. 20. 6 to be delivered from the king of Assyria
21. 15 For they fled from the swords, from the
21. 15 bent bow, and from the grievousness of
Jer. 41. 15 But Ishmael..escaped from Johanan with
48. 44 He that fleeth from the fear shall fall
Eze. 30. 9 shall messengers go forth from me in sh.
Hos. 11. 2 they called them, so they went from them
Amos 5. 19 As if a man did flee from a lion, and a

18.*Before*, קֳדָם *qodam*.
Dan. 5. 24 Then was the part of the hand sent from

19.*From over against*, מִנֶּגֶד *min-neged*.
Jer. 16. 17 neither is their iniquity hid from mine e.

20. *From over*, מֵעֵבֶר *me-eber*.
Job 1. 19 there came a great wind from the wilde.

21.*Between...between*, בֵּין...בֵּין *ben...ben*.
Gen. 1. 4 God divided the light from the darkness

22.*From between*, מִבֵּין *mib-ben*.
Eze. 47. 18 shall measure from..and from..and from
47. 18 from the land..from the border unto the

23.*From, away from*, ἀπό *apo*.
Matt 1. 17 So all the generations from Abraham to
1. 17 from David until the carrying away into
1. 17 from the carrying away into Babylon un.
1. 21 for he shall save his people from their s.
1. 24 Then Joseph, being raised from sleep, did

Matt. 2. 1 there came wise men from the east to Je.
2. 16 slew all..from two years old and under
3. 7 who hath warned you to flee from the w
3. 13 Then cometh Jesus from Galilee to Jor.
4. 17 From that time Jesus began to preach
4. 25 great multitudes of people from Galilee
5. 18 one tittle shall in no wise pass from the
5. 29, 30 and cast (it) from thee: for it is pro.
6. 13 lead us not into..but deliver us from evil
7. 23 depart from me, ye that work iniquity
8. 1 When he was come down from the moun.
8. 11 That many shall come from the east and
8. 30 there was a good way off from them an
9. 15 when the bridegroom shall be taken from
9. 16 that which is put in..taketh from the
9. 22 the woman was made whole from that h.
11. 12 from the days of John the Baptist until
11. 25 thou hast hid these things from the wise
12. 38 Master, we would see a sign from thee
13. 12 whosoever hath not, from him shall be
13. 35 kept secret from the foundation of the
14. 2 This is John the Baptist: he is risen from
15. 8 This people..their heart is far from me
15. 27 dogs eat of the crumbs which fall from
15. 28 her daughter was made whole from that
17. 9 as they came down [from] the mountain
17. 18 the child was cured from that very hour
18. 8, 9 and cast..from thee: it is better for
18. 35 if ye from your hearts forgive not every
19. 1 he departed from Galilee, and came into
19. 8 but from the beginning it was not so
20. 8 beginning from the last unto the first
20. 29 as they departed from Jericho, a great
21. 8 others cut down branches from the trees
21. 43 The kingdom of God shall be taken from
22. 46 neither durst any..from that day forth
23. 34 and persecute (them) from city to city
23. 35 from the blood of righteous Abel unto
24. 1 Jesus went out, and departed [from] the
24. 29 the stars shall fall from heaven, and the
24. 31 gather..from one end of heaven to the
25. 28 Take therefore the talent from him, and
25. 29 [from] him that hath not shall be taken
25. 32 he shall separate them one from another
25. 32 as a shepherd divideth..sheep from the
25. 34 the kingdom prepared for you from the
25. 41 Depart from me, ye cursed, into everlas.
26. 16 from that time he sought opportunity to
26. 39 if it be possible, let this cup pass from
26. 42 if this cup may not pass away [from me]
26. 47 from the chief priests and elders of the
27. 40 If..the Son of God, come down from the
27. 42 let him now come down from the cross
27. 45 Now from the sixth hour there was dark
27. 51 rent in twain from the top to the bottom
27. 55 women..which followed Jesus from Gal.
27. 64 He is risen from the dead; so the last error
28. 2 came and rolled back the stone [from] the
28. 7 tell his disciples that he is risen from the
28. 8 they departed quickly from the sepulch.
Mark 1. 9 that Jesus came from Nazareth of Galilee
1. 42 the leprosy departed from him, and he
2. 20 the bridegroom shall be taken away from
3. 7 multitude from Galilee..and from
3. 8 And from Jerusalem, and from Idumæa
3. 22 the scribes which came down from Jeru.
4. 25 from him shall be taken even that which
5. 35 there came from the ruler of the synagog.
7. 1 certain of the scribes, which came from
7. 4 And..from the market, except they wash
7. 6 This people..their heart is far from me
7. 17 when he was entered into the house from
7. 33 he took him aside from the multitude, and
8. 11 seeking of him a sign from heaven, temp.
9. 9 as they came down [from] the mountain
10. 6 But from the beginning of the creation
11. 12 when they were come from Bethany, he
12. 34 Thou art not far from the kingdom of G.
13. 19 such as was not from the beginning of
13. 27 from the uttermost part of the earth to
14. 35 if..possible, the hour might pass from him
14. 36 Father..take away this cup from me
14. 52 he left the linen cloth, and fled [from]
15. 30 Save thyself, and come down from the cr.
15. 32 Let Christ..descend now from the cross
15. 38 rent in twain from the top to the bottom
16. 8 they went out quickly, and fled from the
Luke 1. 2 which from the beginning were eye witn.
1. 38 And the angel departed from her
1. 48 from henceforth all generations shall call
1. 52 He hath put down the mighty from (their)
2. 4 Joseph also went up from Galilee, out of
2. 15 as the angels were gone away from them
2. 36 and had lived..seven years from her vir.
2. 37 which departed not [from] the temple
3. 7 who hath warned you to flee from the w
4. 1 Jesus..returned from Jordan, and was
4. 13 the devil..departed from him for a season
4. 42 that he should not depart from them
5. 3 he would thrust out a little from the land
5. 8 Depart from me; for I am a sinful man
5. 10 from henceforth thou shalt catch men
5. 13 immediately the leprosy departed from
5. 35 the bridegroom shall be taken away from
7. 6 when he was now not far from the house
8. 18 whosoever hath not, from him shall be
8. 37 multitude..besought him to depart from
9. 5 shake off the very dust from your feet
9. 33 it came to pass, as they departed from
9. 37 when they were come down from the hill
9. 39 bruising him hardly departeth from him
9. 45 it was hid from them, that they perceived

Luke 9. 54 command fire to come down [from] heav.
10. 21 thou hast hid these things from the wise
10. 30 A certain (man) went down from Jerusa.
10. 42 which shall not be taken away from her
11. 4 [lead us not..but deliver us from evil]
11. 50 which was shed from the foundation of
11. 51 From the blood of Abel unto the blood of
12. 52 For from henceforth there shall be five
12. 58 that thou mayest be delivered from him
13. 15 on the sabbath loose his ox or..ass from
13. 16 be loosed from this bond on the sabbath
13. 27 depart from me, all (ye) workers of iniqu.
13. 29 come from the east..and [from] the north
16. 3 for my lord taketh away from me the
16. 18 marrieth her that is put away [from] (her)
16. 21 crumbs which fell from the rich man's
16. 30 but if one went unto them from the dead
17. 29 it rained fire and brimstone from heaven
18. 34 this saying was hid from them, neither
19. 24 Take from him the pound, and give (it)
19. 26 from him that hath not..taken away [from]
19. 39 some of the Pharisees from among the
19. 42 but now they are hid from thine eyes
21. 11 and great signs shall there be from heav.
22. 41 he was withdrawn from them about a
22. 42 remove this cup from me: nevertheless
22. 43 [there appeared an angel unto him from]
22. 45 when he rose up from prayer, and was
23. 5 beginning from Galilee to this place
23. 49 the women that followed him from Gal.
24. 2 they found the stone rolled away from
24. 9 And returned from the sepulchre, and told
24. 13 which was from Jerusalem..threescore fu.
24. 51 he was parted from them, and carried up
John 3. 2 thou art a teacher come from God
8. 44 He was a murderer from the beginning
10. 5 but will flee from him; for they know
10. 18 No man taketh it from me, but I lay it
11. 53 Then from that day forth they took cou.
12. 36 departed, and did hide himself from them
13. 3 that he was come from God, and went to
14. 7 from henceforth ye know him, and hath
15. 27 ye have been with me from the beginning
16. 22 and your joy no man taketh from you
16. 30 we believe that thou camest forth from
18. 28 Then led they Jesus from Caiaphas unto
19. 27 from that hour that disciple took her unto
21. 8 they were not far from land, but as it
Acts 1. 4 they should not depart from Jerusalem
1. 11 this same Jesus, which is taken up from
1. 12 from the mount called Olivet, which is
1. 22 Beginning from the baptism of John, unto
1. 22 that he was taken up from us, must one
2. 40 Save yourselves from this untoward gene.
3. 19 of refreshing shall come from the presen.
3. 24 Yea, and all the prophets from Samuel
3. 26 in turning away every one of you from his
5. 38 Refrain from these men, and let them
5. 41 they departed from the presence of the c.
8. 10 from the least to the greatest, saying
8. 26 unto the way that goeth down from Jer.
8. 33 declare..for his life is taken from the
9. 3 shined round about him a light [from] h.
9. 8 Saul arose from the earth; and when his
9. 18 immediately there fell from his eyes as it
10. 17 the men which were sent from Corneli..s
10. 21 [which were sent unto him from Cornel.]
10. 23 certain brethren from Joppa accompanied
10. 37 began from Galilee, after the baptism
11. 11 three men..sent from Cesarea unto me
11. 27 came prophets from Jerusalem unto An.
12. 10 forthwith the angel departed from him
12. 19 And he went down from Judea to Cesarea
13. 8 seeking to turn away the deputy from
13. 13 when Paul and his company loosed from
13. 13 John departing from them, returned to J.
13. 14 when they departed from Perga, they
13. 29 they took..down from the tree, and laid
13. 31 which came up with him from Galilee
13. 39 all that believe are justified from all
14. 15 ye should turn from these vanities unto
14. 19 there came thither..Jews from Antioch
15. 1 certain men which came down from Jud.
15. 18 Known unto God are all his works from
15. 20 that they abstain [from] pollutions of id.
15. 33 they were let go in peace from the bret.
15. 38 who departed from them from Pamphylia
15. 39 that they departed asunder one from the
16. 11 Therefore loosing from Troas, we came
17. 27 though he be not far from every one of
18. 2 a certain Jew..lately come from Italy
18. 5 when Silas and Timotheus were come fr.
18. 6 from henceforth I will go unto the Gen.
18. 16 And he drave them from the judgment
18. 21 And he sailed from Ephesus
19. 9 he departed from them, and separated
19. 12 So that from his body were brought unto
19. 12 and the diseases departed from them
20. 6 we sailed away from Philippi after the
20. 9 Eutychus..fell down from the third loft
20. 17 from Miletus he sent to Ephesus, and
20. 18 Ye know, from the first day that I came
20. 26 that I (am) pure from the blood of all
21. 1 after we were gotten from them, and
21. 7 when we had finished..course from Tyre
21. 10 there came down from Judea a certain
22. 22 said, Away with such..from the earth
22. 29 Then straightway they departed from
22. 30 he loosed him [from..bands,] and com.
23. 21 ready, looking for a promise from thee
24. 18 Whereupon certain Jews from Asia found
25. 1 he ascended from Cesarea to Jerusalem

Acts 25. 7 the Jews which came down from Jerusa.
26. 18 To open their eyes..to turn..from dark.
27. 21 ye should..not have loosed from Crete
28. 23 persuading them..from morning till ev.
Rom. 1. 7 Grace to you and peace from God our F.
1. 18 the wrath of God is revealed from heaven
1. 20 the invisible things of him from the cre.
5. 9 we shall be saved from wrath through
5. 14 Nevertheless death reigned from Adam
6. 7 For he that is dead is freed from sin
6. 18 Being then made free from sin, ye became
6. 22 But now being made free from sin, and
7. 2 she is loosed from the law of (her) husb.
7. 3 if her husband be dead, she is free from
7. 6 now we are delivered from the law, that
8. 2 hath made me free from the law of sin
8. 21 shall be delivered from the bondage of
8. 35 Who shall separate us from the love of C.?
8. 39 shall be able to separate us from the love
9. 3 were accursed from Christ for my breth.
11. 26 and shall turn away ungodliness from J.
15. 19 so that from Jerusalem, and round about
15. 31 That I may be delivered from them that
1 Co. 1. 3 Grace (be) unto you, and peace, from God
7. 10 Let not the wife depart from (her) husba.
7. 27 Art thou loosed from a wife? seek not a
10. 14 Wherefore, my dearly beloved, flee from
14. 36 What! came the word of God out from y.?
2 Co. 1. 2 Grace (be) to you, and peace, from God
3. 18 are changed into the same image from
5. 6 in the body, we are absent from the Lord
7. 1 let us cleanse ourselves from all filthiness
11. 3 so your minds should be corrupted from
11. 9 the brethren which came from Macedo.
12. 8 I besought..that it might depart from
Gal. 1. 3 Grace (be) to you, and peace, from God
1. 6 that ye are so soon removed from him
2. 12 For before that certain came from James
4. 24 one from the mount Sinai, which gender.
Eph. 1. 2 Grace (be) to you, and peace, from God
3. 9 which from the beginning of the world
4. 31 Let all..evil speaking, be put away from
6. 23 and love with faith, from God the Father
Phil. 1. 2 Grace (be) to you, and peace, from God
1. 5 For your fellowship in the Gospel from
4. 15 when I departed from Macedonia, no
Col. 1. 2 Grace (be) unto you, and peace, from God
1. 23 not moved away from the hope of the
1. 26 which hath been hid from ages and from
2. 20 if ye be dead with Christ from the rudi.
1 Th. 1. 1 [Grace (be) unto you, and peace, from G]
1. 8 For from you sounded out the word of
1. 9 how ye turned to God from idols to serve
1. 10 which delivered us from the wrath to
2. 17 being taken from you for a short time in
3. 6 when Timotheus came from you unto us
4. 3 that ye should abstain from fornication
4. 16 the Lord himself shall descend from hea.
5. 22 Abstain from all appearance of evil
2 Th. 1. 2 Grace unto you, and peace, from God
1. 7 the Lord Jesus shall be revealed from h.
1. 9 destruction from the presence..and from
2. 13 because God hath [from the beginning]
3. 2 that we may be delivered from unreason.
3. 3 who shall stablish you, and keep..from
3. 6 that ye withdraw yourselves from every
1 Ti. 1. 2 Grace, mercy..peace, from God our Fa.
6. 5 corrupt minds..[from such withdraw th.]
6. 10 they have erred from the faith, and pier.
2 Ti. 1. 2 Grace, mercy..peace, from God the Father
1. 3 God, whom I serve from (my) forefathers
2. 19 that nameth the name of Christ depart f.
2. 21 If a man therefore purge himself from
3. 15 that from a child thou hast known the
4. 4 they shall turn away (their) ears from the
4. 18 the Lord shall deliver me from every evil
Titus 1. 4 Grace, mercy..peace, from God the Fa.
2. 14 that he might redeem us from all iniquity
Phm. 3 Grace to you, and peace, from God our F.
Heb. 3. 12 evil heart..in departing from the living
4. 3 although the works were finished from
4. 4 God did rest the seventh day from all his
4. 10 ceased from his own works, as God..from
6. 1 the foundation of repentance from dead
6. 7 the earth..receiveth blessing from God
7. 1 who met Abraham returning from the
7. 26 harmless, undefiled, separate from sin.
8. 11 all shall know me, from the least to the
9. 14 purge your conscience from dead works
10. 22 having our hearts sprinkled from an evil
11. 15 mindful of that..from whence they came
12. 25 if we turn..from him that (speaketh) fr.
Jas. 1. 17 cometh down from the Father of lights
1. 27 to keep himself unspotted from the world
4. 7 Resist the devil, and he will flee from you
5. 19 if any of you do err from the truth, and
1 Pe. 1. 12 with the Holy Ghost sent down from he.
3. 10 let him refrain his tongue from evil, and
2 Pe. 3. 4 continue..from the beginning of the crea.
1 Jo. 1. 1 That which was from the beginning
1. 7 Christ his Son cleanseth us from all sin
1. 9 and to cleanse us from all unrighteous.
2. 7 an old commandment which ye had from
2. 7 is the word which ye have heard [from]
2. 13, 14 ye have known him..from the begin.
2. 20 ye have an unction from the Holy One
2. 24 which ye have heard from the beginning
2. 24 If that which ye have heard from the b.
3. 8 for the devil sinneth from the beginning
3. 11 this is the message that ye have heard f.
3. 17 and shutteth up his bowels..from him
4. 21 And this commandment have we from

1 Jo. 5. 21 Little children keep yourselves from idols
2 Jo. 5 but that which we had from the begin.
6 That, as ye have heard from the begin.
Jude 14 Enoch also, the seventh from Adam
Rev. 1. 4 from him which is..and from the seven
1. 5 And from Jesus Christ..the faithful wit.
1. 5 washed us [from] our sins in his own
3. 12 which cometh down out of heaven from
6. 4 to take peace [from] the earth, and that
6. 16 hide us from the face..and from the
7. 2 I saw another angel ascending from the
7. 17 God shall wipe away all tears [from] their
9. 6 shall desire..and death shall flee from
12. 14 nourished..from the face of the serpent
13. 8 slain from the foundation of the world
14. 3 which were redeemed from the earth
14. 4 These were redeemed from among men
16. 17 there came a great voice..from the th.
17. 8 written..from the foundation of the world
18. 14 And the fruits..are departed from thee
18. 14 and all things..are departed from thee
20. 9 fire came down [from God] out of heaven
20. 11 from whose face the earth and the heaven
21. 2 new Jerusalem, coming down from God
21. 4 God shall wipe away all tears [from] their
21. 10 city..descending out of heaven [from]
22. 19 if any man shall take away from the

24. *Through*, διά (*gen.*) *dia*.
2 Th. 2. 2 nor by word, nor by letter as from us, as

25. *Near, nigh*, ἐγγύς *eggus*.
Acts 1. 12 from Jerusalem a sabbath day's journey

26. *Out of, from*, ἐκ *ek*, ἐξ *ex*.
Matt 3. 17 And lo a voice from heaven, saying
12. 42 for she came from the uttermost parts of
15. 18 those things..come forth from the heart
16. 1 he would show them a sign from heaven
17. 9 Son of man be risen again from the dead
19. 12 which were so born from (their) mother's
21. 25 whence was it? from heaven, or of men?
21. 25 If we shall say, From heaven; he will say
24. 31 gather together his elect from the four
28. 2 the angel of the Lord descended from h.
Mark 1. 11 And there came a voice from heaven
6. 14 That John the Baptist was risen from the
6. 16 It is John..he is risen [from the dead]
7. 31 And again, departing from the coasts of
9. 9 till the Son of man were risen from the
9. 10 what the rising from the dead should
10. 20 all these have I observed from my youth
11. 20 they saw the fig tree dried up from the
11. 30 The baptism of John, was (it) from hea.
11. 31 If we shall say, From heaven; he will
12. 25 For when they shall rise from the dead
13. 27 gather together his elect from the four
16. 3 Who shall roll us away the stone [from]
Luke 1. 15 be filled..even from his mother's womb
1. 71 That we should be saved from our enem.
1. 71 and from the hand of all that hate us
1. 78 whereby the dayspring from on high
3. 22 and a voice came from heaven, which
9. 7 was said..that John was risen from the
10. 7 remain..Go not from house to house
10. 18 I beheld Satan as lightning fall from he.
11. 16 others..sought of him a sign from heav.
11. 31 she came from the utmost parts of the
12. 36 when he will return from the wedding
16. 31 neither..though one rose from the dead
17. 7 will say..when he is come from the field
20. 4 The baptism of John, was it from heaven
20. 5 If we shall say, From heaven; he will say
20. 35 to obtain..the resurrection from the d.
23. 55 the women..which came with him from
24. 46 and to rise from the dead the third day
24. 49 until ye be endued with power from on
John 1. 19 when the Jews sent..Levites from Jerus.
1. 32 I saw the Spirit descending from heaven
2. 22 When therefore he was risen from the d.
3. 13 but he that came down from heaven
3. 27 except it be given him from heaven
3. 31 He that cometh from heaven is above all
5. 24 not come..but is passed from death unto
6. 23 there came other boats from Tiberias
6. 31 He gave them bread from heaven to eat
6. 32 bread from heaven..true bread from he.
6. 33 is he which cometh down from heaven
6. 38 For I came down [from] heaven, not to
6. 41 I am the bread which came down from h.
6. 42 that he saith, I came down from heaven?
6. 50 the bread which cometh down from hea.
6. 51, 58 bread which came down from heaven
6. 64 For Jesus knew from the beginning who
8. 23 Ye are from beneath; I am from above.
8. 42 for I proceeded forth and came from G.
9. 1 he saw a man which was blind from
10. 32 Many good works have I showed you from
12. 1 Lazarus..whom he raised from the dead
12. 9 Lazarus..whom he had raised from the d.
12. 17 Lazarus..and raised him from the dead
12. 27 Father, save me from this hour: but for
12. 28 Then came there a voice from heaven
12. 32 And I, if I be lifted up from the earth
13. 4 He riseth from supper, and laid aside his
17. 15 but that thou shouldest keep them from
18. 3 having received a band..from the chief
19. 23 coat..woven from the top throughout
20. 1 Mary..seeth the stone taken away from
20. 9 that he must rise again from the dead
21. 14 after that he was risen from the dead
Acts 1. 25 [from] which Judas by transgression fell
2. 2 And suddenly there came a sound from

Acts 3. 2 a certain man lame from his mother's
3. 15 whom God hath raised from the dead
4. 2 preached..the resurrection from the dead
4. 10 Jesus..whom God raised from the dead
10. 41 with him after he rose from the dead
11. 5 let down from heaven by four corners
11. 9 But the voice answered me again from h.
12. 7 And his chains fell off from (his) hands
12. 25 Barnabas and Saul returned from Jerus.
13. 30 But God raised him from the dead
13. 34 And..that he raised him up from the d.
14. 8 being a cripple from his mother's womb
15. 24 that certain which went out from us
15. 29 from which if ye keep yourselves ye shall
17. 3 Christ must needs have..risen again from
17. 31 in that he hath raised him from the dead
18. 1 After these things Paul departed from A.
18. 2 commanded all Jews to depart [from] R.
22. 6 suddenly there shone from heaven a
26. 4 My manner of life from my youth, which
26. 17 Delivering thee from the people, and..the
27. 34 for there shall not an hair fall [from] the
28. 17 yet was I delivered prisoner from Jerus.
Rom. 1. 17 righteousness of God revealed from faith
4. 24 that raised up Jesus our Lord from the d
6. 4 that like as Christ was raised up from
6. 9 Knowing that Christ being raised from
6. 13 as those that are alive from the dead
6. 17 but ye have obeyed from the heart that
7. 4 to him who is raised from the dead
7. 24 who shall deliver me from the body of
8. 11 of him that raised up Jesus from the d.
8. 11 he that raised up Christ from the dead
10. 7 to bring up Christ again from the dead
10. 9 that God hath raised him from the dead
11. 15 what..the receiving..but life from the
1 Co. 9. 19 For though I be free from all (men), yet
15. 12 if Christ be preached that he rose from
15. 20 But now is Christ risen from the dead
15. 47 the second man (is) the Lord from heaven
2 Co. 1. 10 Who delivered us from so great a death
3. 1 or (letters) of commendation from you?
5. 2 clothed upon with our house which is fr.
5. 8 willing rather to be absent from the body
Gal. 1. 1 God the Father, who raised him from the
1. 4 that he might deliver us from this present
1. 8 though we, or an angel from heaven, pre.
1. 15 who separated me from my mother's wo.
3. 13 Christ hath redeemed us from the curse
Eph. 1. 20 when he raised him from the dead, and
4. 16 From whom the whole body fitly joined
5. 14 arise from the dead, and Christ shall give
6. 6 doing the will of God from the heart
Phil. 3. 20 from whence also we look for the Saviour
Col. 1. 13 Who hath delivered us from the power
1. 18 the beginning, the first born from the de.
2. 12 God, who hath raised him from the dead
2. 19 not holding the Head, from which all the
4. 16 ye likewise read the (epistle) from Laodi.
1 Th. 1. 10 And to wait for his Son from heaven
1. 10 whom he raised from the dead, (even) J.
2 Ti. 2. 8 was raised from the dead according to
Heb. 5. 7 unto him that was able to save..from
7. 6 he whose descent is not counted from
11. 19 able to raise..up, even from the dead
13. 20 that brought again from the dead our L.
Jas. 5. 20 he which converteth the sinner from the
5. 20 shall save a soul from death, and shall
1 Pe. 1. 3 by the resurrection of Jesus Christ from
1. 18 redeemed..from your vain conversation
1. 21 God, that raised him up from the dead
2 Pe. 1. 18 this voice which came from heaven we
2. 21 [to turn from the holy commandment]
1 Jo. 2. 19 They went out from us, but they were
3. 14 We know that we have passed from death
Rev. 3. 10 I also will keep thee from the hour of
8. 10 and there fell a great star from heaven
9. 1 and I saw a star fall from heaven unto
9. 13 I heard a voice from the four horns of
10. 1 I saw another..angel come down from h.
10. 4 I heard a voice from heaven saying unto
10. 8 the voice which I heard from heaven sp.
11. 11 the Spirit of life from God entered into
11. 12 they heard a great voice from heaven
13. 13 he maketh fire come down from heaven
14. 2 I heard a voice from heaven, as the voice
14. 13 I heard a voice from heaven saying unto
14. 13 that they may rest from their labours
14. 18 another angel came out from the altar
15. 8 from the glory of God, and from his pow.
18. 1 I saw another angel come down from h.
18. 4 I heard another voice from heaven, say.
20. 1 I saw an angel come down from heaven

27. *From, from beside,* παρά *(gen.) para.*
Mark 12. 2 that he might receive from the husband.
14. 43 from the chief priests and the scribes and
Luke 1. 45 of those things which were told her from
2. 1 there went out a decree from Cesar Au.
8. 49 there cometh one [from] the ruler of the
John 1. 6 There was a man sent from God, whose
5. 34 But I receive not testimony from man
5. 41 I receive not honour from men
5. 44 and seek not the honour that (cometh) fr.
7. 29 for I am from him, and he hath sent me
15. 26 whom I will send unto you from the Fat.
15. 26 of truth, which proceedeth from the Fat.
16. 27 and have believed that I came out from
16. 28 I came forth [from] the Father, and am
17. 8 and have known that I came out from
Acts 9. 14 here he hath authority from the chief
22. 5 from whom also I received letters unto
26. 10 having received authority from the chief
26. 12 authority and commission [from] the ch.
Phil. 4. 18 having received of E. the things..from you
2 Pe. 1. 17 For he received from God the Father ho.
2 John 3 from God..and from the Lord Jesus Ch.
4 we have received a commandment from

28. *Of the,* τοῦ *tou.*
Rom 15. 22 I have been much hindered from coming

29. *By,* ὑπό *(gen.) hupo.*
Luke 1. 26 the angel Gabriel was sent [from] God
2 Pe. 1. 17 a voice to him from the excellent glory

FROM among (or up) —
1. *From, out of,* מִן *min.*
Eze. 36. 24 I will take you from among the heathen

2. *From (being) with,* מֵעִם *me-im.*
Ruth 4. 10 name of the dead be not cut off from am.

3. *From,* ἀπό *apo.*
Acts 15. 19 them which from among the Gentiles

4. *Out of,* ἐκ (μέσου) *ek mesou*
Matt 13. 49 and sever the wicked from among 19. 20.
Acts 3. 23 shall be destroyed from among Lu. 18. 21.
17. 33 So Paul departed from among them
23. 10; 1 Co. 5. 2, 13; 2 Co. 6. 17; Heb. 5. 1.

FROM thence, that place — ἐκεῖθεν *ekeithen.*
Matt. 4. 21; 9. 9; 12. 15; 15. 29; Mark 6. 1, 10; 7. 24; 10. 1; Luke 16. 26; Acts 7. 4; 13. 4; 16. 12; 21. 1; 27. 4; 38. 15.

FROM beside —
From (being) beside, מֵאֵצֶל *me-etsel.*
1 Ki. 3. 20 took my son from beside me, while thine
Eze. 10. 16 wheels also turned not from beside them

FROM between —
From (being) with, מֵעִם *me-im.*
Gen. 48. 12 Joseph brought them out from between

FROM off —
From on, מֵעַל *me-al.*
Gen. 7. 4 will I destroy from off the face of the ea.

FROM the midst —
From between, מִבֵּין *mib-ben.*
Jer. 48. 45 and a flame from the midst of Sihon

FRONT —
Face, פָּנִים *panim.*
2 Sa. 10. 9 When Joab saw that the front of the bat.
2 Ch. 3. 4 And the porch that (was) in the front

FRONTIER —
End, extremity, קָצֶה *qatseh.*
Eze. 25. 9 from his cities..on his frontiers, the glory

FRONTLETS —
Frontlets, טוֹטָפוֹת *totaphoth.*
Exod 13. 16 and for frontlets between thine eyes
Deut. 6. 8 they shall be as frontlets between thine
11. 18 that they may be as frontlets between yo.

FROST —
1. *Frost, hail stones,* חֲנָמַל *chanamal.*
Psa. 78. 47 and their sycamore trees with frost

2. *Cold, frost, ice,* קֶרַח *qerach.*
Gen. 31. 40 consumed me, and the frost by night
Job 37. 10 By the breath of God frost is given
Jer. 36. 30 shall be cast out..in the night to the fr.

FROWARD —
1. *Froward, tortuous,* הֲפַכְפַּךְ *haphakpak.*
Prov 21. 8 The way of man (is) froward and strange

2. *To be perverse, perverted,* לוּז *luz,* 2.
Prov. 2. 15 crooked, and (they) froward in their paths
3. 32 For the froward (is) abomination to the

3. *Perverse,* עִקֵּשׁ *iqqesh.*
2 Sa. 22. 27 with the froward thou wilt show thyself
Psa. 18. 26 with the froward thou wilt show thyself
101. 4 A froward heart shall depart from me
Prov 11. 20 They that are of a froward heart (are) ab.
17. 20 He that hath a froward heart findeth
22. 5 snares (are) in the way of the froward

4. *To be a wrestler,* פָּתַל *pathal,* 2.
Job 5. 13 and the counsel of the froward is carried
Prov. 8. 8 nothing froward or perverse in them

5. *Perverseness, frowardness,* תַּהְפֻּכוֹת *tahpukoth.*
Prov 8. 13 pride..and the froward mouth, do I hate
10. 31 but the froward tongue shall be cut out
16. 28 A froward man soweth strife; and a whis.

6. *Perverse, perversities,* עִקְּשׁוּת *iqqeshuth.*
Prov. 4. 24 Put away from thee a froward mouth
6. 12 a wicked man, walketh with a froward

7. *Crooked, perverse,* σκολιός *skolios.*
1 Pe. 2. 18 not only to the good..but also to the fro.

FROWARD, to show self —
To show self a wrestler, פָּתַל *pathal,* 7.
Psa. 18. 26 froward thou wilt show thyself froward

FROWARD, very, (thing) —
Perverseness, frowardness, תַּהְפֻּכוֹת *tahpukoth.*
Deut 32. 20 for they (are) a very froward generation
Prov. 2. 12 from the man that speaketh froward thi.
16. 30 He shutteth his eyes to devise froward t.

FROWARDLY —
Turning back, שׁוֹבָב *shobab.*
Isa. 57. 17 he went on frowardly in the way of his h.

FROWARDNESS —
Perverseness, frowardness, תַּהְפֻּכוֹת *tahpukoth.*
Prov 2. 14 delight in the frowardness of the wicked
6. 14 Frowardness (is) in his heart, he deviseth
10. 32 the mouth of the wicked..frowardness

FROZEN, to be —
To become caught or struck together, לָכַד *lakad,* 7.
Job 38. 30 and the face of the deep is frozen

FRUIT —
1. *Fruit, budding,* אֵב *eb.*
Song 6. 11 I went down..to see the fruits of the va.

2. *Fruit, budding,* אֵב *eb.*
Dan. 4. 12, 21 and the fruit thereof much, and in it
4. 14 shake off his leaves, and scatter his fruit

3. *Increase,* יְבוּל *yebul.*
Deut 11. 17 and that the land yield not her fruit
Hab. 3. 17 neither (shall) fruit (be) in the vines; the
Hag. 1. 10 and the earth is stayed (from) her fruit

4. *Child,* יֶלֶד *yeled.*
Exod 21. 22 so that her fruit depart..and yet no

5. *Bread, food,* לֶחֶם *lechem.*
Jer. 11. 19 Let us destroy the tree with the fruit

6. *Eating, food,* מַאֲכָל *maakal.*
Neh. 9. 25 vineyards..and fruit trees in abundance

7. *Fulness,* מְלֵאָה *meleah.*
Deut 22. 9 the fruit of thy seed which thou hast sown

8. *Fruit, utterance,* נִיב *nib* [V.L. נוב].
Isa. 57. 19 I create the fruit of the lips; Peace

9. *Fruit, utterance,* נִיב *nib.*
Mal. 1. 12 The table..(is) polluted; and the fruit

10. *Fruit,* פְּרִי *peri.*
Gen. 1. 11 the fruit tree yielding fruit..whose seed
1. 12 and the tree yielding fruit, whose seed
1. 29 every tree, in the which (is) the fruit of
3. 2 We may eat of the fruit of the trees of the
3. 3 But of the fruit of the tree which (is) in
3. 6 she took of the fruit thereof, and did eat
4. 3 Cain brought of the fruit of the ground
30. 2 withheld from thee..fruit of the womb?
Exod 10. 15 they did eat..all the fruit of the trees
Lev. 19. 23 then ye shall count the fruit thereof as
19. 24 all the fruit thereof shall be holy, to
19. 25 in the fifth year shall ye eat of the fruit
25. 19 And the land shall yield her fruit, and ye
26. 4 the trees of the field shall yield their fruit
26. 20 neither shall the trees..yield their fruits
27. 30 (whether) of the seed..(or) of the fruit of
Num 13. 20 and bring of the fruit of the land. Now
13. 26 and showed them the fruit of the land
13. 27 came unto the land..and this (is) the fr.
Deut. 1. 25 they took of the fruit of the land in their
7. 13 bless the fruit of thy womb, and the fruit
26. 2 of the first of all the fruit of the earth
28. 4 Blessed (shall be) the fruit of thy body
28. 4 fruit of thy ground, and the fruit of thy
28. 11 plenteous..in the fruit of thy body, and
28. 11 the fruit of thy cattle, and in the fruit of
28. 18 the fruit of thy body, and the fruit of thy
28. 33 The fruit of thy land, and all thy labours
28. 42 All thy trees and fruit of thy land shall
28. 51 eat the fruit of thy cattle, and the fruit
28. 53 thou shalt eat the fruit of thine own body
30. 9 plenteous..in the fruit of thy body, and
30. 9 fruit of thy cattle, and in the fruit of thy
2 Ki. 19. 29 plant vineyards, and eat the fruits there.
19. 30 take root downward, and bear fruit upw.
Neh. 9. 36 to eat the fruit thereof and the good the.
10. 35 of all fruit of all trees, year by year, unto
10. 37 and the fruit of all manner of trees, of
Psa. 1. 3 that bringeth forth his fruit in his season
21. 10 Their fruit shalt thou destroy from the
72. 16 the fruit thereof shall shake like Lebanon
104. 13 is satisfied with the fruit of thy works
105. 35 and devoured the fruit of their ground
107. 37 which may yield fruits of increase
127. 3 the fruit of the womb (is his) reward
132. 11 Of the fruit of thy body will I set upon
Prov. 1. 31 they eat of the fruit of their own way
8. 19 My fruit (is) better than gold, yea, than
11. 30 The fruit of the righteous (is) a tree of
12. 14 be satisfied..by the fruit of (his) mouth
13. 2 A man shall eat good by the fruit of (his)
18. 20 be satisfied with the fruit of his mouth
18. 21 they that love it shall eat the fruit there.
27. 18 Whoso keepeth the..tree shall eat the f.
31. 16 with the fruit of her hands she planteth
31. 31 Give her of the fruit of her hands; and
Eccl. 2. 5 planted trees in them of all (kind of) fr.
Song 2. 3 and his fruit (was) sweet to my taste
4. 13 plants (are) an orchard..with pleasant fr.
4. 16 Let my beloved..eat his pleasant fruits
8. 11 every one for the fruit thereof was to br.
8. 12 those that keep the fruit..two hundred
Isa. 3. 10 they shall eat the fruit of their doings
4. 2 the fruit of the earth (shall be) excellent
10. 12 I will punish the fruit of the stout heart
13. 18 have no pity on the fruit of the womb
14. 29 and his fruit (shall be) a fiery flying serp.
27. 9 this (is) all the fruit to take away his sin
37. 30 plant vineyards, and eat the fruit thereof
37. 31 again take root..and bear fruit upward

Isa. 65. 21 plant vineyards, and eat the fruit of them
Jer. 2. 7 to eat the fruit..and the goodness there.
6. 19 the fruit of their thoughts, because they
7. 20 poured out upon..the fruit of the ground
11. 16 A green olive tree, fair, (and) of goodly f.
12. 2 they grow, yea, they bring forth fruit
17. 8 neither shall cease from yielding fruit
17. 10 (and) according to the fruit of his doings
21. 14 will punish you according to the fruit of
29. 5, 28 plant gardens, and eat the fruit of
32. 19 and according to the fruit of his doings
Lam. 2. 20 Shall the women eat their fruit, (and)
Eze. 17. 8 It was planted..that it might bear fruit
17. 9 shall he not..cut off the fruit thereof
17. 23 and bear fruit, and be a goodly cedar: and
19. 12 the east wind dried up her fruit; her
19. 14 fire..hath devoured her fruit, so that
25. 4 they shall eat thy fruit, and..drink thy
34. 27 the tree of the field shall yield her fruit
36. 8 yield your fruit to my people of Israel
36. 30 I will multiply the fruit of the tree, and
47. 12 neither shall the fruit..be consumed: it
47. 12 the fruit thereof shall be for meat, and
Hos. 9. 16 root is dried up, they shall bear no fruit
10. 1 he bringeth forth fruit unto himself
10. 1 according to the multitude of his fruit
10. 13 ye have eaten the fruit of lies: because
14. 8 From me is thy fruit found
Joel 2. 22 for the tree beareth her fruit, the fig tree
Amos 2. 9 yet I destroyed his fruit from above, and
6. 12 the fruit of righteousness into hemlock
9. 14 make gardens, and eat the fruit of them
Mic. 6. 7 fruit of my body (for) the sin of my soul?
7. 13 be desolate..for the fruit of their doings
Zech. 8. 12 the vine shall give her fruit, and the
Mal. 3. 11 not destroy the fruits of your ground

11. *Incoming, fruit,* תְּבוּאָה *tebuah.*
Exod 23. 10 and shalt gather in the fruits thereof
Lev. 23. 39 when ye have gathered in the fruit of the
25. 3 and gather in the fruit thereof
25. 15 unto the number of years of the fruits he
25. 16 number..of the fruits doth he sell unto
25. 21 it shall bring forth fruit for three years
25. 22 and eat..of old fruit until the ninth year
25. 22 until her fruits come in ye shall eat..the
Deut 22. 9 and the fruit of thy vineyard, be defiled
33. 14 for the precious fruits..by the sun
Josh. 5. 12 they did eat of the fruit of the land of
2 Ki. 8. 6 Restore all..the fruits of the field since
Prov 10. 16 to life: the fruit of the wicked to sin

12. *Fruit, increase,* תְּנוּבָה *tenubah.*
Judg. 9. 11 Should I forsake..my good fruit, and go
Isa. 27. 6 and fill the face of the world with fruit
Lam. 4. 9 stricken through for..the fruits of the fl.

13. *Produce,* γέννημα *gennēma.*
Matt 26. 29 I will not drink henceforth of this fruit
Mark 14. 25 I will drink no more of the fruit of the v.
Luke 12. 18 there will I bestow all my [fruits] and my
22. 18 I will not drink of the fruit of the vine
2 Co. 9. 10 increase the fruits of your righteousness

14. *Fruit,* καρπός *karpos.*
Matt. 3. 8 Bring forth therefore fruits meet for v. 10.
7. 16 Ye shall know them by their fruits. Do
7. 17 every good tree bringeth forth good fruit
7. 17 a corrupt tree bringeth forth evil fruit
7. 18 A good tree cannot bring forth evil fruit
7. 18 neither (can) a corrupt tree..good fruit
7. 19 tree that bringeth not forth good fruit
7. 20 Wherefore by their fruits ye shall know
12. 33 Either make the tree good, and his fruit
12. 33 fruit corrupt: for the tree is known by..f.
13. 8 brought forth fruit, some an hundred fold
13. 26 was sprung up, and brought forth fruit
21. 19 Let no fruit grow on thee henceforward
21. 34 And when the time of the fruit drew near
21. 34 that they might receive the fruits of it
21. 41 which shall render him the fruits in their
21. 43 given to a nation bringing forth the fruits
Mark 4. 7 thorns..choked it, and it yielded no fruit
4. 8 did yield fruit that sprang up and incre.
4. 29 But when the fruit is brought forth
11. 14 No man eat fruit of thee hereafter for ev.
12. 2 might receive..of the fruit of the vineya.
Luke 1. 42 and blessed (is) the fruit of thy womb
3. 8 Bring forth therefore fruits worthy of re.
3. 9 which bringeth not forth good fruit is
6. 43 good tree bringeth not forth corrupt fruit
6. 43 neither doth a corrupt tree..good fruit
6. 44 For every tree is known by his own fruit
8. 8 sprang up, and bare fruit an hundred fold
12. 17 I have no room where to bestow my fru.?
13. 6 he came and sought fruit thereon, and
13. 7 these three years I come seeking fruit on
13. 9 And if it bear fruit..and if not..after th.
20. 10 that they should give him of the fruit of
John 4. 36 and gathereth fruit unto life eternal
12. 24 but if it die, it bringeth forth much fruit
15. 2 Every branch in me that beareth not fru.
15. 2 purgeth it, that it may bring forth more f.
15. 4 As the branch cannot bear fruit of itself
15. 5 the same bringeth forth much fruit: for
15. 8 that ye bear much fruit; so shall ye be
15. 16 that ye should go and bring forth fruit
15. 16 and (that) your fruit should remain
Acts 2. 30 that of the fruit of his loins, according to
Rom. 1. 13 that I might have some fruit among you
6. 21 What fruit had ye then in those things
6. 22 ye have your fruit unto holiness, and the
15. 28 and have sealed to them this fruit, I will
1 Co. 9. 7 and eateth not of the fruit thereof? or
Gal. 5. 22 But the fruit of the Spirit is love, joy
Eph. 5. 9 the fruit of the Spirit (is) in all goodness
Phil. 1. 11 Being filled with the fruits of righteous.
1. 22 But if I live in the flesh, this (is) the fruit
4. 17 I desire fruit that may abound to your ac.
2 Ti. 2. 6 husbandm...must be..partaker of the fr.
Heb. 12. 11 it yieldeth the peaceable fruit of righte.
13. 15 the fruit of (our) lips giving thanks to his
Jas. 3. 17 gentle..full of mercy and good fruits
3. 18 the fruit of righteousness is sown in peace
5. 7 waiteth for the precious fruit of the ea.
5. 18 and the earth brought forth her fruit
Rev. 22. 2 which bare twelve (manner of) fruits
22. 2 (and) yielded her fruit every month
[*See also* Cast, first ripe, hasty, new, summer, sycamore.]

FRUIT, best —
What is praised, זִמְרָה *zimrah.*
Gen. 43. 11 take of the best fruits in the land in your

FRUIT, to bear —
To bear fruit, καρποφορέω *karpophoreō.*
Matt 13. 23 which also beareth fruit, and bringeth fo.

FRUIT, to bring —
To be fruitful, פָּרָה *parah.*
Eze. 36. 11 and they shall increase and bring fruit

FRUIT, to bring forth —
1 *To bring forth, increase,* נוּב *nub.*
Psa. 92. 14 They shall still bring forth fruit in old
2. *To bear fruit,* καρποφορέω *karpophoreō.*
Mark 4. 20 and receive (it), and bring forth fruit
4. 28 the earth bringeth forth fruit of herself
Luke 8. 15 keep..and bring forth fruit with patience
Rom. 7. 4 that we should bring forth fruit unto God
7. 5 did work..to bring forth fruit unto death
Col. 1 6 and bringeth forth fruit, as .also in you

FRUIT, first of ripe —
Fulness, מְלֵאָה *meleah.*
Exod 22. 29 the first of thy ripe fruits, and of thy liq.

FRUIT, without —
Without fruit, ἄκαρπος *akarpos.*
Jude 12 without fruit, twice dead, plucked up by

FRUIT withereth, whose —
Withering autumnal fruit, φθινοπωρινός *phthino.*
Jude 12 trees whose fruit withereth..twice dead

FRUITFUL —
1. *Seed,* זֶרַע *zera.*
Eze. 17. 5 took..and planted it in a fruitful field
2. *To be fruitful,* פָּרָה *parah.*
Gen. 49. 22 a fruitful bough..a fruitful bough by a
Psa. 128. 3 Thy wife..as a fruitful vine by the sides
Isa. 17. 6 four (or) five in the outmost fruitful bra.
32. 12 They shall lament..for the fruitful vine
Eze. 19. 10 she was fruitful and full of branches by
3. *Of fruit,* פְּרִי *peri.*
Psa. 107. 34 A fruitful land into barrenness, for the
148. 9 and all hills; fruitful trees, and all ced.
4. *Fruit bearing,* καρποφόρος *karpophoros.*
Acts 14. 17 gave us rain from heaven, and fruitful

FRUITFUL, to be —
1. *To produce fruit,* פָּרָא *para*, 5.
Hos. 13. 15 Though he be fruitful among..brethren
2. *To be fruitful,* פָּרָה *parah.*
Gen. 1. 22 Be fruitful, and multiply, and fill the wat.
1. 28 God said unto them, Be fruitful, and mu.
8. 17 that they may breed..and be fruitful
9. 1 Be fruitful, and multiply, and replenish
9. 7 And you, be ye fruitful, and multiply
26. 22 and we shall be fruitful in the land
35. 11 And God said..be fruitful and multiply
Exod. 1. 7 And the children of Israel were fruitful
Jer. 23. 3 and they shall be fruitful and increase
3. *To bear fruit,* καρποφορέω *karpophoreō.*
Col. 1. 10 being fruitful in every good work, and

FRUITFUL, to cause to be —
To make fruitful, פָּרָה *parah*, 5.
Gen 41. 52 For God hath caused me to be fruitful in

FRUITFUL field —
Fruitful place or field, כַּרְמֶל *karmel.*
Isa. 10. 18 of his fruitful field, both soul and body
29. 17 Lebanon shall be turned into a fruitful fl.
29. 17 the fruitful field shall be esteemed as a f.
32. 15 and the wilderness be a fruitful field
32. 15 the fruitful field be counted for a forest
32. 16 righteousness remain in the fruitful field

FRUITFUL, to make —
To make fruitful, פָּרָה *parah*, 5.
Gen. 17. 6 I will make thee exceeding fruitful, and
17. 20 I..will make him fruitful, and will mult.
28. 3 God..bless thee, and make thee fruitful
48. 4 I will make thee fruitful, and multiply
Lev. 26. 9 I will..make you fruitful, and multiply

FRUITFUL place —
Fruitful place or field, כַּרְמֶל *karmel.*
Jer. 4. 26 the fruitful place (was) a wilderness, and

FRUITFUL, very —
A son of oil, בֶּן־שֶׁמֶן *ben shemen.*
Isa. 5. 1 hath a vineyard in a very fruitful hill

FRUITS —
1. *Power,* כֹּחַ *koach.*
Job 31. 39 If I have eaten the fruits thereof without
2. *Ripe or full fruits,* ὀπώρα *opōra.*
Rev. 18. 14 the fruits that thy soul lusted after are

FRUSTRATE, to —
1. *To break, make void,* פָּרַר *parar*, 5.
Ezra 4. 5 to frustrate their purpose, all the days
Isa. 44. 25 That frustrateth the tokens of the liars
2. *To put aside,* ἀθετέω *atheteō.*
Gal. 2. 21 I do not frustrate the grace of God: for

FRYING pan —
Frying pan, kettle, מַרְחֶשֶׁת *marchesheth.*
Lev. 2. 7 if..a meat offering (baken) in the frying p.
7. 9 and all that is dressed in the frying pan

FUEL —
1. *Eating, food,* אָכְלָה *oklah.*
Eze. 15. 4 Behold, it is cast into the fire for fuel
15. 6 which I have given to the fire for fuel
21. 32 Thou shalt be for fuel to the fire; thy
2. *Eating, food,* מַאֲכֹלֶת *maakoleth.*
Isa. 9. 5 but..shall be with burning..fuel of fire
9. 19 shall be as the fuel

FUGITIVE —
1. *One fleeing, a fugitive,* בָּרִיחַ *bariach.*
Isa. 15. 5 his fugitives..unto Zoar, an heifer of
2. *One fleeing, a fugitive,* מִבְרָח *mibrach.*
Eze. 17. 21 all his fugitives with all his bands shall
3. *To move, shake, stagger, wander,* נוּעַ *nua.*
Gen. 4. 12 a fugitive and a vagabond shalt thou be
4. 14 I shall be a fugitive and a vagabond
4. *To fall,* נָפַל *naphal.*
2 Ki. 25. 11 the fugitives that fell away to the king of
5. *One who slips out,* פָּלִיט *palit.*
Judg 12. 4 Ye Gileadites (are) fugitives of Ephraim

FULFIL, to —
1. *To cut off,* בָּצַע *batsa*, 3.
Lam. 2. 17 he hath fulfilled his word that he had
2. *To complete, finish,* כָּלָה *kalah*, 3.
Exod. 5. 13 Fulfil your works..daily tasks, as when
5. 14 Wherefore have ye not fulfilled your task
3. *To fill up or in,* מָלֵא *male.*
Job 36. 17 thou hast fulfilled the judgment of the w.
4. *To fill in or up,* מָלֵא *male*, 3.
Gen. 29. 27 Fulfil her week, and we will give thee
29. 28 And Jacob did so, and fulfilled her week
Exod 23. 26 the number of thy days I will fulfil
1 Ki. 2. 27 that he might fulfil the word of the LORD
8. 15 and hath with his hand fulfilled (it), say.
8. 24 and hast fulfilled (it) with thine hand, as
2 Ch. 6. 4 who hath with his hands fulfilled (that)
6. 15 and hast fulfilled (it) with thine hand, as
36. 21 To fulfil the word of the LORD by the m.
36. 21 desolate..to fulfil threescore and ten ye.
Psa. 20. 5 banners: the LORD fulfil all thy petitions
Jer. 44. 25 and fulfilled with your hand, saying
5. *To do,* עָשָׂה *asah.*
2 Sa. 14. 22 in that the king hath fulfilled the request
1 Ch. 22. 13 if thou takest heed to fulfil the statutes
Psa. 145. 19 He will fulfil the desire of them that fear
148. 8 vapour; stormy wind fulfilling his word
6. *To fill up,* ἀναπληρόω *anaplēroō.*
Matt 13. 14 And in them is fulfilled the prophecy of
Gal. 6. 2 Bear ye..and so fulfil the law of Christ
7. *To fill out,* ἐκπληρόω *ekplēroō.*
Acts 13. 33 God hath fulfilled the same unto us their
8. *To fill, make full,* πληρόω *plēroō.*
Matt. 3. 15 for thus it becometh us to fulfil all righ.
4. 14 That it might be fulfilled which was sp.
5. 17 I am not come to destroy, but to fulfil
Acts 12. 25 returned..when they had fulfilled..min.
13. 25 And as John fulfilled his course, he said
13. 27 voices..they have fulfilled..in condemn.
14. 26 recommended..for the work which they f.
Rom. 13. 8 he that loveth another hath fulfilled
Phil. 2. 2 Fulfil ye my joy, that ye be like minded
Col. 1. 25 made a minister..to fulfil the word of G.
4. 17 And say..Take heed..that thou fulfil it
2 Th. 1. 11 fulfil all the good pleasure of (his) good.
9. *To do, make,* ποιέω *poieō.*
Acts 13. 22 a man..which shall fulfil all my will
Eph. 2. 3 fulfilling the desires of the flesh and of
Rev. 17. 17 in their hearts to fulfil his will, and to
10. *To accomplish, end,* τελειόω *teleioō.*
Luke 2. 43 And when they had fulfilled the days, as
John 19. 28 that the Scripture might be fulfilled, saith
11. *To end,* τελέω *teleō.*
Acts 13. 29 when they had fulfilled all that was wri
Rom. 2. 27 if it fulfil the law, judge thee, who by
Gal. 5. 16 ye shall not fulfil the lust of the flesh
Jas. 2. 8 If ye fulfil the royal law according to the
Rev. 15. 8 till the seven plagues..were fulfilled
17. 17 until the words of God shall be fulfilled
20. 3 till the thousand years should be fulfilled
12. *To end together,* συντελέω *sunteleō.*
Mark 13. 4 sign when all these things shall be fulfil.

FULFILLED, to be —

1. *To be complete, finished,* כָּלָה *kalah.*
Ezra 1. 1 that the word of the LORD..might be ful.

2. *To be full,* מָלֵא *male.*
Gen. 25. 24 when her days to be delivered were ful.
29. 21 Give..my wife, for my days are fulfilled
50. 3 And forty days were fulfilled for him
50. 3 for so are fulfilled the days of those that
Lev. 12. 4 the days of her purifying be fulfilled
12. 6 when the days of her purifying are ful.
Num. 6. 5 until the days be fulfilled, in the which
6. 13 when the days of his separation are ful.
2 Sa. 7. 12 when thy days be fulfilled, and thou
Lam. 4. 18 our end is near, our days are fulfilled
Eze. 5. 2 when the days of the siege are fulfilled
Dan. 10. 3 till three whole weeks were fulfilled

3. *To be filled, completed,* מָלֵא *male,* 2.
Exod. 7. 25 And seven days were fulfilled, after that

4. *To be ended,* סוּף *suph.*
Dan. 4. 33 The same hour was the thing fulfilled

5. *To become, come to pass,* γίνομαι *ginomai.*
Matt. 5. 18 shall in no wise pass..till all be fulfilled
24. 34 shall not pass, till all these things be f.
Luke21. 32 shall not pass away, till all be fulfilled

6. *To fill, make full,* πληρόω *plēroō.*
Matt 1. 22 this was done, that it might be fulfilled
2. 15 it might be fulfilled which was spoken of
2. 17 Then was fulfilled that which was spoken
2. 23 that it might be fulfilled which was spo.
8. 17 That it might be fulfilled which was spo.
12. 17 That it might be fulfilled which was spo.
13. 35 That it might be fulfilled which was spoken
21. 4 All this was done, that it might be ful.
26. 54 how then shall the scriptures be fulfilled
26. 56 scriptures of the prophets might be ful.
27. 9 Then was fulfilled that which was spoken
27. 35 [that it might be fulfilled which was sp.]
Mark 1. 15 The time is fulfilled, and the kingdom of
14. 49 but the scriptures must be fulfilled
15. 28 [And the scripture was fulfilled, which]
Luke 1. 20 my words, which [shall be fulfilled] in
4. 21 This day is this scripture fulfilled in your
21. 22 that all things..written [may be fulfilled]
21. 24 until the times of the Gentiles be fulfilled
22. 16 until it be fulfilled in the kingdom of God
24. 44 that all things must be fulfilled, which
John 3. 29 voice; this my joy therefore is fulfilled
12. 38 That the saying..might be fulfilled, which
13. 18 but that the scripture may be fulfilled
15. 25 that the word might be fulfilled that is
17. 12 that the scripture might be fulfilled
17. 13 that they might have my joy fulfilled
18. 9 That the saying might be fulfilled, which
18. 32 That the saying of Jesus might be fulfil.
19. 24 that the scripture might be fulfilled
19. 36 done, that the scripture should be ful.
Acts 1. 16 this scripture must needs have been ful.
3. 18 But those things..he hath so fulfilled
9. 23 And after that many days were fulfilled
Rom. 8. 4 righteousness..might be fulfilled in us
2 Co. 10. 6 disobedience, when your obedience is fu.
Gal. 5. 14 For all the law is fulfilled in one word
Jas. 2. 23 the scripture was fulfilled which saith
Rev. 6. 11 and their brethren..should be fulfilled

FULFILLING, (be)—

Fulness, πλήρωμα *plērōma.*
Rom.13. 10 therefore love (is) the fulfilling of the

FULL —

1. *Full,* מָלֵא *male.*
Gen. 41. 7 ears devoured the seven rank and full
41. 22 seven ears came up in one stalk, full and
Num. 7. 13 both of them..full of fine flour mingled
7. 14, 20 One spoon of..gold, full of incense
7. 19 full of fine flour mingled with oil, for a
[So in v. 25, 31, 37, 43, 49, 55, 61, 67, 73, 79].
7. 26, 32, 38, 44, 50 golden spoon..full of ince.
7. 56, 62, 68, 74, 80 golden spoon..full of incen.
7. 86 The golden spoons..twelve, full of incen.
Deut. 6. 11 houses full of all good..which thou fille.
33. 23 and full with the blessing of the LORD
34. 9 Joshua..was full of the spirit of wisdom
Ruth. 1. 21 I went out full, and the LORD hath brou.
2 Sa. 23. 11 where was a piece of ground full of lenti.
2 Ki. 4. 4 and thou shalt set aside that which is full
7. 15 all the way (was) full of garments and v.
1 Ch. 11. 13 where was a parcel of ground full of bar.
21. 22 thou shalt grant it me for the full price
21. 24 but I will verily buy it for the full price
Neh. 9. 25 and possessed houses full of all goods
Psa. 73. 10 waters of a full (cup) are wrung out to
75. 8 a cup, and the wine is red; it is full of mi.
144. 13 our garners..full, affording all manner
Prov.17. 1 than an house full of sacrifices..strife
Eccl. 1. 7 run into the sea; yet the sea (is) not full
Isa. 1. 21 the faithful city..it was full of judgment
22. 2 Thou that art full of stirs, a tumultuous
51. 20 they are full of the fury of the LORD, the
Jer. 4. 12 a full wind from those..shall come unto
5. 27 cage is full of birds, so (are) their houses f.
6. 11 the aged with (him that is) full of days
35. 5 And I set..pots full of wine, and cups
Eze. 1. 18 rings..full of eyes round about them four
10. 12 and the wheels full of eyes round about
17. 3 full of feathers, which had divers colours
28. 12 Thou..full of wisdom, and perfect in be.
37. 1 midst of the valley which (was) full of b.
Amos 2. 13 as a cart is pressed (that is) full of sheaves
Nah. 3. 1 it (is) all full of lies..robbery; the prey

2. *Fulness,* מְלוֹא, מְלֹא *melo.*
Exod16. 33 Take a pot, and put an omer full of man.
Lev. 16. 12 he shall take a censer full of burning
16. 12 hands full of sweet incense beaten small
Num22. 18 If Balak would give me his house full of
24. 13 If Balak would give me his house full of
Judg. 6. 38 wringed the dew..a bowl full of water
2 Sa. 8. 2 measured..with one full line to keep ali.
2 Ki. 4. 39 gathered thereof wild gourds his lap full
Eccl. 4. 6 than both the hands full (with) travail
Isa. 6. 3 Holy..the whole earth (is) full of his glo.
Eze. 32. 15 be destitute of that whereof it was full
41. 8 foundations..a full reed of six great cub.

3. *Many, much, great,* רַב *rab.*
Lam. 1. 1 How doth the city sit solitary (that was) f.

4. *Satisfied, satiated,* שָׂבֵעַ *sabea.*
Gen. 25. 8 Then Abraham..died..an old man, and f.
1 Sa. 2. 5 full have hired out themselves for bread
Prov 27. 7 The full soul loatheth an honey comb: b.

5. *Satiety,* שֹׂבַע *soba.*
Exod16. 3 when we did eat bread to the full; for
Lev. 26. 5 ye shall eat your bread to the full, and
Psa. 78. 25 angels' food: he sent them meat to the f.

6. *To complete,* שָׁלַם *shalam,* 3.
Exod22. 3 he should make full restitution: if he

7. *Finished, perfect,* שָׁלֵם *shalem.*
Gen. 15. 16 the iniquity of the Amorites (is) not yet f.
Ruth 2. 12 a full reward be given thee of the LORD

8. *Bone, essence,* עֶצֶם *etsem.*
Job 21. 23 One dieth in his full strength, being wh.

9. *Perfect, complete,* תָּמִים *tamim.*
Lev. 25. 30 not redeemed within the space of a full

10. *Days,* יָמִים *yamim.*
Dan. 10. 2 I Daniel was mourning three full weeks

11. *To satiate, satisfy,* κορέννυμι *korennumi.*
1 Co. 4. 8 Now ye are full, now ye are rich, ye have

12. *Replete, stored, full,* μεστός *mestos.*
Matt23. 28 within ye are full of hypocrisy and ini.
John19. 29 Now there was set a vessel full of vinegar
21. 11 drew the net to land full of great fishes
Rom. 1. 29 full of envy, murder, debate, deceit, ma.
15. 14 that ye also are full of goodness, filled
Jas. 3. 8 (it is) an unruly evil, full of deadly poison
3. 17 full of mercy and good fruits, without
2 Pe. 2. 14 Having eyes full of adultery, and that

13. *To replete, store, fill,* μεστόω *mestoō.*
Acts 2. 13 Others..said, These men are full of new

14. *Full,* πλήρης *plērēs.*
Matt14. 20 up of the fragments..twelve baskets full
15. 37 broken (meat)..was left seven baskets f.
Mark 4. 28 ear, after that the full corn in the ear
6. 43 And they took up twelve baskets full of
8. 19 how many baskets full of fragments took
Luke 4. 1 And Jesus, being full of the Holy Ghost
5. 12 behold a man full of leprosy; who seeing
John 1. 14 dwelt among us..full of grace and truth
Acts 6. 3 men..full of the Holy Ghost and wisdom
6. 5 they chose Stephen, a man full of faith
6. 8 Stephen, full of faith and power, did
7. 55 he, being full of the Holy Ghost, looked
9. 36 this woman was full of good works and
11. 24 he was a good man, and full of the Holy
13. 10 O full of all subtilty and all mischief
19. 28 they were full of wrath, and cried out
2 John 8 lose not..but that we receive a full rew.

15. *To make full,* πληρόω *plēroō.*
John16. 24 ye shall receive, that your joy may be full
1 Jo. 1. 4 write we unto you that your joy may be f.
2 John 12 speak face to face, that our joy may be f.

16. *Fulness,* πλήρωμα *plērōma.*
Mark 8. 20 how many baskets full of fragments took
[*See also* Age, branches, ears, end, feed, filled, weight.]

FULL, to be (or have) —

1. *To be full,* מָלֵא *male.*
Exod. 8. 21 houses of the Egyptians shall be full of
Judg16. 27 Now the house was full of men and wo.
2 Ki. 4. 6 came to pass, when the vessels were full
6. 17 the mountain (was) full of horses and ch.
Job 20. 11 His bones are full..of his youth, which
21. 24 His breasts are full of milk, and his bones
32. 18 For I am full of matter, the spirit within
36. 16 should be set on thy table..full of fatness
Psa. 10. 7 His mouth is full of cursing and deceit
26. 10 and their right hand is full of bribes
33. 5 earth is full of the goodness of the LORD
48. 10 thy right hand is full of righteousness
65. 9 the river of God..is full of water: thou
74. 20 dark places..are full of the habitations
104. 24 O LORD..the earth is full of thy riches
119. 64 The earth, O LORD, is full of thy mercy
Eccl. 9. 3 also the heart..is full of evil, and mad.
Isa. 1. 15 will not hear: your hands are full of bl.
11. 9 the earth shall be full of the knowledge
13. 21 houses shall be full of doleful creatures
15. 9 the waters of Dimon shall be full of blood
22. 7 thy choicest valleys shall be full of char.
28. 8 For all tables are full of vomit..filthiness
Isa. 30. 27 his lips are full of indignation, and his
Jer. 6. 11 I am full of the fury of the LORD; I am
23. 10 For the land is full of adulterers; for
Eze. 7. 23 is full of bloody crimes, and the city is f.
9. 9 land is full of blood, and the city full of
10. 4 the court was full of the brightness of the
Joel 2. 24 the floors shall be full of wheat, and the
3. 13 for the press is full, the fats overflow
Mic. 3. 8 truly I am full of power by the spirit of
6. 12 For the rich men thereof are full of vio.
Hab. 3. 3 God came..the earth was full of his pra.

2. *To be filled,* מָלֵא *male,* 2.
2 Ki. 10. 21 the house of Baal was full from one end
Esth. 3. 5 bowed not..then was Haman full of wra.
5. 9 he was full of indignation against Morde.
Eccl.11. 3 If the clouds be full of rain, they empty
Isa. 2. 7 Their land also is full of silver and gold
2. 7 their land is also full of horses, neither
2. 8 Their land also is full of idols; they wor.
Eze. 9. 9 the land is full of blood, and the city full
32. 6 thy blood..and the rivers shall be full of
Zech. 8. 5 the streets of the city shall be full of boys

3. *To fill in or up,* מָלֵא *male,* 3.
Psa.127. 5 Happy..the man that hath his quivers f.

4. *To be filled,* מְלָא *mela,* 4.
Dan. 3. 19 Then was Nebuchadnezzar full of fury

5. *To be satisfied, satiated,* שָׂבַע *saba.*
Deut. 6. 11 when thou shalt have eaten and be full
8. 10 When thou hast eaten and art full, then
8. 12 Lest..thou hast eaten and art full, and
11. 15 grass..that thou mayest eat, and be full
1 Ch.23. 1; Psa. 104. 16; Prov. 27. 20; 30. 9.

6. *To be fed,* χορτάζομαι *chortazomai.*
Phil. 4. 12 I am instructed both to be full and to

7. *To fill, load, freight,* γεμίζω *gemizō.*
Mark 4. 37 beat into the ship, so that it was now full

8. *To fill in, make full,* ἐμπίπλημι *empiplēmi.*
Luke 6. 25 Woe unto you that are full! for ye shall

9. *To make full,* πληρόω *plēroō.*
Matt13. 48 Which, when it was full, they drew to sh.
John15. 11 might remain..and..your joy might be f.
Acts 7. 23 And when he was full forty years old
Phil. 4. 18 I am full, having received of Epaphrodi.

FULL, to become —

To be or become full, מָלֵא *male.*
Lev. 19. 29 and the land become full of wickedness

FULL, to be come to the —

To perfect, finish, תָּמַם *tamam,* 5.
Dan. 8. 23 when..transgressors are come to the full

FULL, to draw —

To fill up, מָלֵא *male,* 3.
2 Ki. 9. 24 Jehu drew a bow with his full strength

FULL of —

1. *Satisfied, satiated,* שָׂבֵעַ *sabea.*
Gen. 35. 29 Isaac gave up the ghost..old and full of
1 Ch.29. 28 he died..full of days, riches and honour
Job 10. 15 (I am) full of confusion; therefore see
14. 1 Man..(is) of few days, and full of trouble
42. 17 So Job died..old, and full of days

2. *To be full, replete, loaded,* γέμω *gemō.*
Rev. 4. 6 four beasts full of eyes before and behind
5. 8 golden vials full of odours, which are the
15. 7 golden vials full of the wrath of God
17. 3 full of names of blasphemy, having seven
17. 4 having a golden cup in her hand full of
21. 9 seven vials full of the seven last plagues

FULL of, to be —

1. *To make many,* רָבָה *rabah,* 5.
Eccl.10. 14 A fool also is full of words: a man cannot

2. *To be satiated,* שָׂבַע *saba.*
2 Ch.24. 15 Jehoiada..was full of days when he died
Job 7. 4 and I am full of tossings to and fro unto
Psa. 17. 14 they are full of children, and leave the
88. 3 For my soul is full of troubles: and my
Isa. 1. 11 I am full of the burnt offerings of rams

3. *To be full, replete,* γέμω *gemō.*
Matt23. 25 within they are full of extortion and
23. 27 but are within full of dead..bones, and
Luke11. 39 your inward part is full of ravening and
Rom. 3. 14 Whose mouth (is) full of cursing and
Rev. 4. 8 And the four beasts..full of eyes within
[*See also* Compassion, heaviness, labour, marrow.]

FULL, to make —

To make full, πληρόω *plēroō.*
Acts 2. 28 thou shalt make me full of joy with thy

FULL come, to be —

To make full, πληρόω *plēroō.*
John 7. 8 not up yet..for my time is not yet full c.

FULL tale, to give in —

To fill up, מָלֵא *male,* 3.
1 Sa. 18. 27 they gave them in full tale to the king

FULL, till be —

Satiety, שָׂבְעָה *sobah.*
Eze. 39. 19 ye shall eat fat till ye be full, and drink

FULL, to the —
To be satisfied, satiated, שָׂבָע *saba.*
Exod16. 8 give you..in the morning bread to the f.
FULL (time) came —
To fill full, πλήθω *plēthō.*
Luke 1. 57 Now Elizabeth's full time came that she
FULL year —
Days, יָמִים *yamim.*
Lev. 25. 29 within a..full year may he redeem it
FULLER —
1. *To wash,* כָּבַס *kabas.*
2 Ki. 18. 17 which (is) in the high way of the fuller's f.
Isa. 7. 3 pool in the high way of the fuller's field
36. 2 stood..in the high way of the fuller's field
2. *To wash,* כָּבַס *kabas,* 3.
Mal. 3. 2 like a refiner's fire, and like fuller's sope
3. *A fuller, cloth dresser,* γναφεύς *gnapheus.*
Mark 9. 3 so as no fuller on earth can white them
FULLY —
1. *To finish,* כָּלָה *kalah,* 3.
Num. 7. 1 on the day that Moses had fully set up
2. *Full,* מָלֵא *male.*
Nah. 1. 10 they shall be devoured as stubble fully
3. *To fill in or up,* מָלֵא *male,* 3.
Num14. 24 because he..hath followed me fully, him
4. *To be put before,* נָגַד *nagad,* 6.
Ruth 2. 11 It hath fully been showed me all that
FULLY preach, to —
To make full, πληρόω *plēroō.*
Rom15. 19 I have fully preached the gospel of Christ
FULLY, to go —
To fill up, complete, מָלֵא *male,* 3.
1 Ki.11. 6 Solomon..went not fully after the LORD
FULLY set, to be —
To be full, fill in, מָלֵא *male.*
Eccl. 8. 11 the heart..of men is fully set in them
FULNESS —
1. *To be full, fill in, complete,* מָלֵא *mala.*
Job 20. 22 In the fulness of his sufficiency he shall
2. *Fulness,* מְלֹא *melo.*
Deut33. 16 the precious things of the earth and ful.
1 Ch.16. 32 Let the sea roar, and the fulness thereof
Psa. 24. 1 The earth (is) the LORD'S, and the fulness
50. 12 the world (is) mine, and the fulness ther.
89. 11 the world and the fulness thereof, thou
96. 11 let the sea roar, and the fulness thereof
98. 7 Let the sea roar, and the fulness thereof
Eze. 19. 7 the land was desolate, and the fulness
3. *Fulness,* מְלֵאָה *meleah.*
Num18. 27 as though..the fulness of the wine press
4. *Satiety,* שֹׂבַע *soba.*
Psa. 16. 11 in thy presence (is) fulness of joy; at thy
5. *Satiety,* שִׂבְעָה *sibah.*
Eze. 16. 49 fulness of bread, and abundance of idlen.
6. *Fullness,* πλήρωμα *plērōma.*
John 1. 16 And of his fulness have all we received
Rom.11. 12 if the fall..how much more their fulness!
11. 25 until the fulness of the Gentiles be come
15. 29 I shall come in the fulness of the blessing
1 Co. 10. 26, 28 the earth (is) the Lord's, and the ful.
Gal. 4. 4 But when the fulness of the time was
Eph. 1. 10 That in the dispensation of the fulness
1. 23 the fulness of him that filleth all in all
3. 19 that ye might be filled with all the fulness
4. 13 the measure of the stature of the fulness
Col. 1. 19 pleased..that in him should all fulness
2. 9 For in him dwelleth all the fulness of
[*See also* Assured, come, know, known, persuaded, ripe.]
FURBISH, to —
1. *To polish,* מָרַט *marat.*
Eze. 21. 9 a sword is sharpened, and also furbished
21. 11 he hath given it to be furbished, that it
21. 28 sword..for the slaughter (it is) furbished
2. *To scour, polish,* מָרַק *maraq.*
Jer. 46. 4 furbish the spears..put on the brigan.
FURBISHED —
To be polished, מָרַט *marat,* 4.
Eze. 21. 10 it is furbished that it may glitter
21. 11 and it is furbished, to give it into the
FURIOUS —
1. *Heat, fury,* חֵמָה *chemah.*
Prov 22. 24 and with a furious man thou shalt not go
29. 22 and a furious man aboundeth in trans.
Eze. 5. 15 execute judgments..in furious rebukes
25. 17 vengeance upon them with furious rebu.
2. *Possessor of heat,* בַּעַל חֵמָה *baal chemah.*
Nah. 1. 2 God..the LORD revengeth, and (is) fur.
FURIOUS, to be —
To be wroth, קָצַף *qetsaph.*
Dan. 2. 12 For this cause the king was..very fur.
FURIOUSLY —
1. *In heat,* בְּחֵמָה *be-chemah.*
Eze. 23. 25 and they shall deal furiously with thee
2. *With madness, fury,* בְּשִׁגָּעוֹן *be-shiggaon.*
2 Ki. 9. 20 driving of Jehu..for he driveth furiously
FURLONG —
A stade, (one tenth of English mile, one eighth of Roman), στάδιον *stadion.*
Luke24. 13 was from Jerusalem..threescore furlongs
John 6. 19 about five and twenty or thirty furlongs
11. 18 Bethany was nigh..about fifteen furlongs
Rev. 14. 20 space of a thousand..six hundred furlo.
21. 16 with the reed, twelve thousand furlongs
FURNACE —
1. *Furnace, oven,* אַתּוּן *attun.*
Dan. 3. 6, 11, 15 the midst of a burning fiery furnace
3. 17 to deliver us from the burning fiery fur.
3. 19 should heat the furnace one seven times
3. 20 to cast..into the burning fiery furnace
3. 21, 23 the midst of the burning fiery furnace
3. 22 and the furnace exceeding hot, the flame
3. 26 to the mouth of the burning fiery furnace
2. *Furnace, smelting oven,* כִּבְשָׁן *kibshan.*
Gen. 19. 28 smoke..went up as the smoke of a fur.
Exod. 9. 8 Take to you handfuls of ashes of the fur.
9. 10 they took ashes of the furnace, and stood
19 18 smoke..ascended as the smoke of a fur.
3. *Furnace, a crucible,* כּוּר *kur.*
Deut. 4. 20 brought you forth out of the iron furnace
1 Ki. 8. 51 from the midst of the furnace of iron
Prov 17. 3 pot (is) for silver, and the furnace for gold
27. 21 the fining pot for silver, and the furnace
Isa. 48. 10 I have chosen thee in the furnace of
Jer. 11. 4 I brought them..from the iron furnace
Eze. 22. 18 they (are) brass..in the midst of the fur.
22. 20 they gather..into the midst of the fur.
22. 22 As silver is melted in the..furnace, so
4. *Furnace,* עֲלִיל *alil.*
Psa. 12. 6 silver tried in a furnace of earth, puri.
5. *An oven,* תַּנּוּר *tannur.*
Gen. 15. 17 a smoking furnace, and a burning lamp
Neh. 3. 11 Hashub..repaired..the tower of the fur.
12. 38 from beyond the tower of the furnaces
Isa. 31. 9 LORD, whose fire (is) in Zion, and his fur.
6. *Furnace,* κάμινος *kaminos.*
Matt13. 42 shall cast them into a furnace of fire
13. 50 shall cast them into the furnace of fire
Rev. 1. 15 his feet..as if they burned in a furnace
9. 2 smoke..as the smoke of a great furnace
FURNISH, to —
1. *To fill in or up, complete,* מָלֵא *male,* 3.
Isa. 65. 11 furnish the drink offering unto that num.
2. *To lift up,* נָשָׂא *nasa,* 3.
1 Ki 9. 11 Hiram..had furnished Solomon with
3. *To encircle as with a chain,* עָנַק *anaq,* 5.
Deut.15. 14 Thou shalt furnish him liberally out of
4. *To set in array,* עָרַךְ *arak.*
Psa 78. 19 Can God furnish a table in the wilderness?
Prov. 9. 2 wine; she hath also furnished her table
5. *To make a vessel,* עָשָׂה כְּלִי *asah keli.*
Jer. 46. 19 furnish thyself to go into captivity; for
6. *To be filled,* πλήθομαι *plēthomai.*
Matt22. 10 and the wedding was furnished with
7. *To spread out,* στρώννυμι *strōnnumi.*
Mark14. 15 he will show you a large upper room f.
Luke22. 12 he shall show you a large upper room f.
FURNISH thoroughly, to —
To fit out, ἐξαρτίζω *exartizō.*
2 Ti. 3. 17 throughly furnished unto all good works
FURNITURE —
1. *Vessel, implement,* כְּלִי *keli.*
Exod31. 7 and all the furniture of the tabernacle
31. 8 And the table and his furniture, and the
31. 8 pure candlestick with all his furniture
31. 9 altar of burnt offering with all his furni.
35. 14 The candlestick also..and his furniture
39. 33 the tent, and all his furniture, his taches
Nah. 2. 9 glory out of all the pleasant furniture
2. *Bolster,* כַּר *kar.*
Gen. 31. 34 Rachel..put them in the camel's furni.
FURROW —
1. *Cutting, furrow,* גְּדוּד *gedud.*
Psa. 65. 10 thou settlest the furrows thereof: thou
2. *Furrow,* מַעֲנָה, מַעֲנִית *maanah, maanith.*
Psa.129. 3 The plowers..they made long their fur.
3. *Furrow,* עוֹנָה *onah* [V.L. עינה].
Hos. 10. 10 shall bind themselves in their two fur.
4. *Bed, furrow,* עֲרוּגָה *arugah.*
Eze. 17. 7 that he might water it by the furrows
17. 10 it shall wither in the furrows where it
5. *Furrow, ridge,* תֶּלֶם *telem.*
Job 31. 38 or that the furrows likewise..complain
39. 10 Canst thou bind the unicorn..in the f.?
Hos. 10. 4 springeth up as hemlock in the furrows
12. 11 their altars (are) as heaps in the furrows
FURTHER —
1. *Further, moreover,* יוֹתֵר *yother.*
Eccl. 12. 12 And further, by these, my son, be admo.
2. *Again, yet, any more,* עוֹד *od.*
Esth. 9. 12 what (is) thy request further? and it shall
3. *Yet, further,* ἔτι *eti.*
Matt26. 65 what further need have we of witnesses!
Acts 21. 28 and further brought Greeks also into the
Heb. 7. 11 what further need..that another priest
4. *Yet further,* ἐπὶ πλεῖον *epi pleion.*
Acts 4. 17 But that it spread no further among the
24. 4 that I be not further tedious unto thee
2 Ti. 3. 9 But they shall proceed no further, for
5. *Further,* πορρώτερω *porrhōterō.*
Luke24. 28 made as though he would have gone fur.
6. *To add,* יָסַף *yasaph.*
Deut20. 8 the officers shall speak further unto the
7. *To add,* יָסַף *yasaph,* 5.
Num22. 26 the angel of the LORD went further, and
Job 38. 11 Hitherto shalt thou come, but no further
FURTHER, any —
Yet, still, further, ἔτι *eti.*
Mark 5. 35 why troublest thou the Master any fur.?
14. 63 What need we any further witnesses?
Luke22. 71 What need we any further witness? for
FURTHER, to (go) —
1. *To lift up,* נָשָׂא *nasa,* 3.
Ezra 8. 36 they furthered the people, and the house
2. *To bring out,* פּוּק *puq,* 5.
Psa.140. 8 further not his wicked device, (lest) they
3. *To set apart,* διΐστημι *diistēmi.*
Acts 27. 28 when they had gone a little further, they
FURTHERANCE —
A striking forward, advance, προκοπή *prokopē.*
Phil. 1. 12 have fallen out rather unto the furthera.
1. 25 abide..for your furtherance and joy of f.
FURTHERMORE —
1. *Again, yet, any more,* עוֹד *od.*
Exod. 4. 6 And the LORD said furthermore unto him
2. *Then, so then,* εἶτα *eita.*
Heb. 12. 9 Furthermore we have had fathers of our
3. *As to what is left,* τὸ λοιπόν *to loipon.*
1 Th. 4. 1 Furthermore then we beseech you, bret.
4. *And,* וְ *va.*
Eze. 8. 6 He said furthermore unto me, Son of m.
FURTHERMORE, and —
Also, אַף *aph.*
Eze. 23. 40 And furthermore, that ye have sent for
FURY —
1. *Heat, fury,* חֵמָא *chema.*
Dan. 11. 44 he shall go forth with great fury to dest.
2. *Heat, fury,* חֲמָא *chama.*
Dan. 3. 13 Then Nebuchadnezzar in..rage and fury
Dan. 3. 19 Then was Nebuchadnezzar full of fury
3. *Heat, fury,* חֵמָה *chemah.*
Gen. 27. 44 tarry..until thy brother's fury turn away
Lev. 26. 28 I will walk contrary unto you..in fury
Isa. 27. 4 Fury (is) not in me: who would set the
34. 2 and..fury upon all their armies: he hath
42. 25 he hath poured upon him the fury of his
51. 13 because of the fury of the oppressor, as
51. 13 and where (is) the fury of the oppressor?
51. 17 which hast drunk..the cup of his fury
51. 20 they are full of the fury of the LORD, the
51. 22 the dregs of the cup of my fury; thou
59. 18 he will repay, fury to his adversaries
63. 3 for I will..trample them in my fury; and
63. 5 therefore..my fury, it upheld me
63. 6 I will..make them drunk in my fury, and
66. 15 to render his anger with fury, and his
Jer. 4. 4 lest my fury come forth like fire, and
6. 11 I am full of the fury of the LORD; I am
7. 20 mine anger and my fury shall be poured
10. 25 Pour out thy fury upon the heathen that
21. 5 in anger, and in fury, and in great wrath
21. 12 lest my fury go out like fire, and burn
23. 19 whirlwind of the LORD is gone forth in f
25. 15 Take the wine cup of this fury at my
30. 23 the whirlwind..goeth forth with fury
32. 31 city hath been..a provocation..of my fu.
32. 37 whither I have driven them..in my fury
33. 5 of men, whom I have slain..in my fury
36. 7 for great (is) the anger and the fury that
42. 18 As..my fury hath been poured forth
42. 18 so shall my fury be poured forth upon
44. 6 my fury and mine anger was poured for.
Lam. 2. 4 he stood..he poured out his fury like fire
4. 11 The LORD hath accomplished his fury
Eze. 5. 13 I will cause my fury to rest upon them
5. 13 when I have accomplished my fury in
5. 15 in anger and in fury and in furious rebu.
6. 12 thus will I accomplish my fury upon
7. 8 Now will I shortly pour out my fury
8. 18 Therefore will I also deal in fury: mine
9. 8 in thy pouring out of thy fury upon Jer.?
13. 13 rend (it) with a stormy wind in my fury
13. 13 great hailstones in (my) fury, to consume
14. 19 and pour out my fury upon it in blood
16. 38 I will give thee blood in fury and jealo.
16. 42 So will I make my fury toward thee to
19. 12 she was plucked up in fury, she was cast
20. 8 I said, I will pour out my fury upon
20. 13, 21 I said, I would pour out my fury

Eze. 20. 33 with fury poured out, will I rule over
20. 34 I will bring you..with fury poured out
21. 17 I will cause my fury to rest: I the LORD
22. 20 so will I gather (you)..in my fury, and I
22. 22 that I the LORD have poured out my fury
24. 8 That it might cause fury to come up to
24. 13 till I have caused my fury to rest upon
25. 14 according to mine anger and..to my fury
30. 15 I will pour out my fury upon Sin, the
36. 6 I have spoken..in my fury, because ye
36. 18 I poured my fury upon them for the blo.
38. 18 it shall come to pass..my fury shall come
Dan. 8. 6 and ran unto him in the fury of his pow.
9. 16 let..thy fury be turned away from thy
Mic. 5. 15 in anger and fury upon the heathen
Nah. 1. 6 his fury is poured out like fire, and the
Zech. 8. 2 and I was jealous for her with great fury

4. *Heat, fierceness, wrath,* חָרוֹן *charon.*
Job 20. 23 shall cast the fury of his wrath upon him

G

GA'-AL, גַּעַל *rejection.*
A son of Ebed who aided the Shechemites against Abimelech. B.C. 1209.
Judg. 9. 26 G. the son of Ebed came with his breth.
9. 28 G. the son of Ebed said, Who (is) Abim.
9. 30 when Zebul..heard the words of G. the
9. 31 Behold, G...and his brethren be come to
9. 35 And G. the son of E. went out, and stood
9. 36 And when G. saw the people, he said
9. 37 G. spake again and said, See there come
9. 39 And G. went out before the men of She.
9. 41 and Zebul thrust out G. and his brethren

GA'-ASH, גַּעַשׁ *quaking.*
More accurately Mount Gaash in the district of Mount Ephraim. On the N. side of the hill was Timnath-serah (or cheres), the city given to Joshua.
Josh 24. 30 buried..on the north..of the hill of G.
Judg. 2. 9 buried..on the north..of the hill G.
2 Sa. 23. 30 Benaiah..Hiddai of the brooks of G.
1 Ch. 11. 32 Hurai of the brooks of G., Abiel the Ar.

GA'-BA, גֶּבַע *height.*
A Levitical city in Benjamin near Ramah, five miles from Gofna (now called Gifna), towards Neapolis. It was the N. border of Judah, as Rimmon was the southern.
Josh 18. 24 Chephar-haammonai, and Ophni, and G.
Ezra 2. 26 The children of Ramah and G., six hun.
Neh. 7. 30 The men of Ramah and G., six hundred

GAB'-BAI, גַּבַּי *ingatherer.*
A chief among the Benjamites after the return from exile. B.C. 445.
Neh. 11. 8 after him G., Sallai, nine hundred twenty

GAB-BA'-THA, Γαββαθᾶ, *(from Heb.), elevated place.*
The tribunal or place of judgment in Jerusalem, called in Greek Λιθόστρωτον, the "pavement."
John 19. 13 called..Pavement, but in the Hebrew, G.

GAB-RI'-EL, גַּבְרִיאֵל, Γαβριήλ *God is mighty.*
A divine messenger sent to Daniel, to Mary, and to Zacharias.
Dan. 8. 16 G., make this (man) to understand the
9. 21 the man G., whom I had seen in the vision
Luke 1. 19 I am G., that stand in the presence of G.
1. 26 in the sixth month the angel G. was sent

GAD, גָּד, Γάδ, *the seer, lot, fortune.*
1. Jacob's seventh son, first born of Zilpah, Leah's maid, and uterine brother of Asher. B.C. 1749.
Gen. 30. 11 troop cometh: and she called his name G.
35. 26 sons of Zilpah, Leah's handmaid; G. and
46. 16 sons of G.; Ziphion, and Haggi, Shuni
49. 19 G., a troop shall overcome him: but he
Exod. 1. 4 Dan, and Naphtali, G., and Asher
1 Ch. 5. 11 the children of G. dwelt over against th.

2. The tribe that sprang from Gad and the territory they inhabited.
Num. 1. 14 Of G.; Eliasaph the son of Deuel
1. 24 Of the children of G., by their genera.
1. 25 of the tribe of G...forty and five thou
2. 14 tribe of G...the captain of the sons of G
7. 42 son of Deuel, prince of the children of G.
10. 20 over the host of the tribe of..G. (was) E.
13. 15 Of the tribe of G., Geuel the son of Machi.
26. 15 The children of G. after their families
26. 18 These..the families of the children of G.
32. 1 the children of G. had a very great mul.
32. 2 The children of G...came and spake unto
32. 6 And Moses said unto the children of G.
32. 25 And the children of G...spake unto M.
32. 29 If the children of G..will pass with you
32. 31 the children of G...answered, saying, As
32. 33 Moses gave..to the children of G...the
32. 34 the children of G. built Dibon, and Atar.
34. 14 the tribe of the children of G. according
Deut 27. 13 Reuben, G., and Asher, and Zebulun, D.
33. 20 of G...Blessed (be) he that enlargeth G.
Josh. 4. 12 the children of G...passed over armed
13. 24 unto the tribe of G...the children of G.
13. 28 This..inheritance of the children of G.
18. 7 G., and Reuben, and half the tribe of M.
20. 8 Ramoth in Gilead out of the tribe of G.
21. 7 out of the tribe of G., and out of the tribe
21. 38 out of the tribe of G., Ramoth in Gilead
22. 9 children of G...returned, and departed
Josh. 22. 10 children of G...built there an altar by J.
22. 11 children of G...built an altar over against
22. 13 sent..to the children of G...Phinehas
22. 15 And they came unto..the children of G.
22. 21 the children of G...said unto the heads of
22. 25 ye children of Reuben and children of G.
22. 30 the words that the children..of G...spake
22. 31 Phinehas..said unto the children..of G.
22. 32 returned from the children..of G., out
22. 33 to destroy the land wherein..G. dwelt
22. 34 the children of G. called the altar (Ed)
1 Sa. 13. 7 the Hebrews went over..to the land of G.
2 Sa. 24. 5 the city..in the midst of the river of G.
1 Ch. 2. 2 and Benjamin, Naphtali, G., and Asher
6. 63 out of the tribe of G., and out of the tribe
6. 80 out of the tribe of G.; Ramoth in Gilead
12. 14 These..of the sons of G., captains of the
Jer. 49. 1 why (then) doth their king inherit G.
Eze. 48. 27 from the east side unto the west side G.
48. 28 by the border of G., at the south side
48. 34 one gate of G., one gate of Asher, one
Rev. 7. 5 Of the tribe of G. (were) sealed twelve
The following localities were in the territory of Gad: Aroer, Ataroth, Atroth, Shophan, Beth-aram or Haran, Beth-nimrah, Betonim, Debir, Dibon, Jogbethah, Karkor, Magdala, Zaphon, Minnith, Peniel, Ramoth-Gilead, &c.

3. A prophet who joined David when in "the hold," and by whose advice he quitted it for the Forest of Hareth.
1 Sa. 22. 5 And the prophet G. said unto David
2 Sa. 24. 11 the word of the LORD came unto..G.
24. 13 So G. came to David, and told him, and
24. 14 David said unto G., I am in a great strait
24. 18 G. came that day to David, and said unto
24. 19 David, according to the saying of G., went
1 Ch. 21. 9 the LORD spake unto G., David's seer
21. 11 So G. came to David, and said unto him
21. 13 David said unto G., I am in a great strait
21. 18 the angel of the LORD commanded G to
21. 19 And David went up at the saying of G.
29. 29 and in the book of G. the seer
2 Ch. 29. 25 according to the commandment of..G.

GAD about, to —
To go away or about, אָזַל *azal.*
Jer. 2. 36 Why gaddest thou about so much to ch.

GA-DA-RE-NES, Γαδαρηνοί.
The people of Gadara, the capital of Peræa; E. of the Jordan opposite Tiberias and Scythopolis (now called *Om-keis*); S.E. from S. end of the Sea of Tiberias, and near the river *Hieromax.*
Mark 5. 1 came over..into the country of the [G.]
Luke 8. 26 they arrived at the country of the [G.]
8. 37 the [G.] round about besought him to de.

GAD'-DI, גַּדִּי *belonging to fortune.*
Son of Susi, and a chief of Manasseh, sent with others to spy out the land. B.C. 1490.
Num 13. 11 Of the tribe of Joseph..G. the son of Susi

GAD-DI'-EL, גַּדִּיאֵל *Gad is fortune bringer.*
Son of Sodi, and a chief of Zebulun sent out with others to spy the land. B.C. 1490.
Num 13. 10 Of the tribe of Zebulun, G. the son of S.

GA'-DI, גָּדִי *fortunate.*
Father of Menahem who killed Shallum, and succeeded him as king of Israel B.C. 772.
2 Ki. 15. 14 Menahem, the son of G. went up from T.
15. 17 began Menahem the son of G. to reign

GAD-ITE (the), הַגָּדִי *haggadi.*
Patronymic of the tribe of Gad.
Deut. 3. 12 the cities thereof, gave I unto..the G.
3. 16 unto the G. I gave from Gilead..unto the
4. 43 and Ramoth in Gilead, of the G.; and
29. 8 took their land, and gave..to the G.
Josh. 1. 12 to the Reubenites, and to the G...spake
12. 6 LORD gave it..a possession unto the..G.
13. 8 With whom..the G have received their
22. 1 Joshua called the Reubenites, and the G.
2 Sa. 23. 36 the son of Nathan of Zobah, Bani the G.
2 Ki. 10. 33 Jordan eastward, all the land of..the G.
1 Ch. 5 18 The sons of Reuben, and the G., and half
5. 26 he carried them away, even..the G., and
12. 8 of the G. there separated themselves unto
12. 37 on the other side of Jordan, of the..G.
26. 32 made rulers over the Reubenites, the G.

GA'-HAM, גַּחַם *blackness.*
A son of Nahor by his concubine Reumah. B.C. 1860.
Gen. 22. 24 she bare also Tebah, and G., and Thahash

GA'-HAR, גַּחַר *prostration, concealment.*
One of the Nethinim whose posterity came up with Zerubbabel to Jerusalem B.C. 447.
Ezra 2. 47 children of Giddel, the children of G.
Neh. 7. 49 children of Giddel, the children of G.

GAIN —
1. *Dishonest gain,* בֶּצַע *betsa.*
Judg 5. 19 then fought the kings..they took no gain
Job 22. 3 (is it) gain (to him), that thou makest thy
Prov. 1. 19 ways of every one that is greedy of gain
15 27 He that is greedy of gain troubleth his
Isa. 33. 15 he that despiseth the gain of oppressions
56. 11 every one for his gain, from his quarter
Mic. 4. 13 I will consecrate their gain unto the L.

2. *Price, hire,* מְחִיר *mechir.*
Dan. 11. 39 and shall divide the land for gain

3. *Increase, fruit,* תְּבוּאָה *tebuah.*
Prov. 3. 14 and the gain thereof than fine gold

4. *Work,* ἐργασία *ergasia.*
Acts 16. 16 brought her masters much gain by sooths.
16. 19 saw that the hope of their gains was gone
19. 24 brought no small gain unto the craftsmen

5. *Gain,* κέρδος *kerdos.*
Phil. 1. 21 to me to live (is) Christ, and to die (is) g.
3. 7 But what things were gain to me, those I

6. *A providing, getting,* πορισμός *porismos.*
1 Ti. 6. 5 supposing that gain is godliness: from
6. 6 godliness with contentment is great gain

GAIN, dishonest —
Dishonest gain, בֶּצַע *betsa.*
Eze. 22. 13 smitten thine hand at thy dishonest gain
22. 27 to destroy souls, to get dishonest gain

GAIN, to —
1. *To gain dishonestly,* בָּצַע *batsa.*
Job 27. 8 what (is) the hope..though he hath gai.

2. *To gain, buy,* זְבַן *zeban.*
Dan. 2. 8 ye would gain the time, because ye see

3. *To gain, make gain,* κερδαίνω *kerdainō.*
Matt 16. 26 if he shall gain the whole world, and lose
18. 15 if he shall hear thee, thou hast gained
25. 17 he that (had received) two, he also gained
25. 20 behold, I have gained..five talents more
25. 22 behold, I have gained two other talents
Mark 8. 36 if he shall gain the whole world, and lose
Luke. 9. 25 if he gain the whole world, and lose him.
Acts 27. 21 and to have gained this harm and loss
1 Co. 9. 19 made myself servant..that I might gain
9. 20 became as a Jew, that I might gain the
9. 20 might gain them that are under the law
9. 21 I might gain them that are without law
9. 22 became I as weak, that I might gain the

4. *To do, make,* ποιέω *poieō.*
Luke 19 18 Lord, thy pound hath gained five pounds

5. *To work toward,* προσεργάζομαι *prosergazomai.*
Luke 19. 16 Lord, thy pound hath gained ten pounds

GAIN, to get —
To make gain, κερδαίνω *kerdainō.*
Jas. 4. 13 continue..and buy and sell, and get gain

GAIN of, to make a —
To get advantage of, πλεονεκτέω *pleonekteō.*
2 Co. 12. 17 Did I make a gain of you by any of them
12. 18 Did Titus make a gain of you? walked we

GAIN greedily, to —
To gain dishonestly, בָּצַע *batsa,* 3.
Eze. 22. 12 thou hast greedily gained..by extortion

GAIN by trading, to —
To do in business, διαπραγματεύομαι *diapragmate.*
Luke 19. 15 how much every man had gained by tra.

GAINSAY, to —
1. *To say against,* ἀντεῖπον *anteipon.*
Luke 21. 15 shall not be able to gainsay nor resist

2. *To speak over against,* ἀντιλέγω *antilegō.*
Rom 10. 21 unto a disobedient and gainsaying people

GAINSAYER —
To speak over against, ἀντιλέγω *antilegō.*
Titus 1. 9 to exhort and to convince the gainsayers

GAINSAYING —
A speech over against, ἀντιλογία *antilogia.*
Jude 11 and perished in the gainsaying of Core

GAINSAYING, without —
Without objection, ἀναντιῤῥήτως *anantirrhētōs.*
Acts 10. 29 Therefore came I..without gainsaying

GAI'-US, Γάϊος *(from Latin) Caius.*
1. A native of Macedonia, and companion of Paul.
Acts 19. 29 having caught G. and Aristarchus..they

2. A man of Derbe in Lycaonia, and companion of Paul.
Acts 20. 4 G. of Derbe, and Timotheus; and of Asia

3. A Corinthian whom Paul baptised.
Rom 16. 23 G. mine host, and of the whole church
1 Co. 1. 14 that I baptised none..but Crispus and G.

4. Person to whom John's third Epistle was written.
3 John 1 The elder unto the well beloved G., whom

GA'-LAL, גָּלָל *great, rolling.*
1. A Levite who came up from exile. B.C. 445.
1 Ch. 9. 15 Bakbakkar, Heresh, and G., and Mattan.

2. A Levite who came up from exile. B.C. 445.
1 Ch. 9 16 Obadiah..son of Shemaiah, the son of G.
Neh. 11. 17 Shammua, the son of G., the son of Jed.

GA-LA-TIA, Γαλατία.
The *Gallia* of the East; Roman writers call its inhabitants *Galli,* just as Greek writers call the people of ancient France *Galatia.* Galatia, the Roman province, was the central region of the peninsula of Asia Minor, with the provinces of Asia on the W., Cappadocia on the E., Pamphylia and Cilicia on the S., and Bithynia and Pontus on the N. The exact limits were frequently changing.
Acts 16. 6 had gone throughout..the region of G.
18. 23 went over (all) the country of G. and Phr.
1 Co. 16. 1 I have given order to the churches of G.

Gal. 1. 2 which are with me, unto the churches..G.
2 Ti. 4. 10 Crescens to G., Titus unto Dalmatia
1 Pe. 1. 1 the strangers scattered throughout..G.

GA-LA-TI-ANS, Γαλάται. *Inhabitants of Galatia.*
Gal. 3. 1 O foolish G., who hath bewitched you

GALBANUM —
Galbanum, a Syrian gum, חֶלְבְּנָה *chelbenah.*
Exod30. 34 Take unto thee sweet spices..galbanum

GAL'-EED, גַּלְעֵד *heap of witness.*
A name given by Jacob to the heap that he and Laban made on Mount Gilead as an evidence of the covenant between them.
Gen. 31. 47 Jegar-sahadutha: but Jacob called it G.
31. 48 Therefore was the name of it called G.

GAL-I-LE-ANS, Γαλιλαῖοι. *Inhabitants of Galilee.*
Mark14. 70 for thou art a G., and thy speech agreeth
Luke13. 1 There were..some that told him of the G.
13. 2 these G. were sinners above all the G.
22. 59 this..also was with him; for he is a G.
23. 6 he asked whether the man were a G.
John 4. 45 the G. received him, having seen all the
Acts 2. 7 Behold, are not all..which speak G.?

GA-LI'-LEE, הַגָּלִיל, הַגָּלִילָה, Γαλιλαία, *the circle.*
A district of Naphtali; after the captivity it embraced all Canaan N. of Samaria and W. of the Jordan, and was spoken of as Upper or N. and Lower or S. Galilee.
Josh.20. 7 they appointed Kedesh in G. in mount
21. 32 Kedesh in G. with her suburbs, (to be) a
1 Ki. 9. 11 gave Hiram twenty cities in the land of G.
2 Ki.15. 29 Hazor, and Gilead, and G., all the land
1 Ch. 6. 76 Kedesh in G. with her suburbs, and Ha.
Isa. 9. 1 beyond Jordan, in G. of the nations
Matt. 2. 22 he turned aside into the parts of G.
3. 13 Then cometh Jesus from G. to Jordan un.
4. 12 when Jesus had heard..he departed into G.
4. 15 (by) the way of the sea..G. of the Gentiles
4. 18 Jesus, walking by the sea of G., saw two
4. 23 Jesus went about all G., teaching in their
4. 25 there followed him..multitudes..from G.
15. 29 departed..and came..unto the sea of G.
17. 22 while they abode in G., Jesus said unto
19. 1 Jesus had finished..he departed from G.
21. 11 This is..the prophet of Nazareth of G.
26. 32 But..again, I will go before you unto G.
26. 69 saying, Thou also wast with Jesus of G.
27. 55 women..which followed Jesus from G.
28. 7 and, behold, he goeth before you into G.
28. 10 go tell my brethren that they go into G.
28. 16 the eleven disciples went away into G.
Mark 1 9 came to pass..that Jesus came from..G.
1. 14 Jesus came into G., preaching the gospel
1. 16 Now as he walked by the sea of G., he
1. 28 throughout all the region round about G.
1. 39 preached in..synagogues throughout..G.
3. 7 a great multitude from G. followed him
6. 21 his lords, high captains, and chief..of G.
7. 31 he came unto the sea of G., through the
9. 30 departed thence, and passed through G.
14. 28 I am risen, I will go before you into G.
15. 41 Who also, when he was in G., followed
16. 7 tell..disciples..he goeth before you into G.
Luke 1. 26 Gabriel was sent from G. unto a city of G.
2. 4 Joseph also went up from G., out of the
2. 39 had performed all things..returned into G.
3. 1 Herod being tetrarch of G., and his broth.
4. 14 returned in the power of the spirit into G.
4. 31 came down to Capernaum, a city of G.
4. 44 And he preached in the synagogues of G.
5. 17 which were come out of every town of G.
8. 26 the Gadarenes, which is over against G.
17. 11 passed through the midst of Sam. and G.
23. 5 throughout all Jewry, beginning from G.
23. 6 When Pilate heard of G., he asked whet.
23. 49 the women that followed him from G.
23. 55 women also, which came with him from G.
24. 6 he spake unto you when he was yet in G.
John 1. 43 day following Jesus would go..into G.
2. 1 there was a marriage in Cana of G.
2. 11 beginning of miracles did Jesus in..G.
4. 3 He left Judea, and departed..into G.
4. 43 Now after two days he..went into G.
4. 45 Then when he was come into G., the Ga.
4. 46 So Jesus came again into Cana of G.
4. 47 Jesus was come out of Judea into G.
4. 54 when he was come out of Judea into G.
6. 1 Jesus went over the sea of G., which is
7. 1 After these things Jesus walked in G.
7. 9 had said these words..he abode..in G.
7. 41 some said, Shall Christ come out of G.?
7. 52 Art thou also of G.? Search, and look
7. 52 for out of G. ariseth no prophet
12. 21 Philip, which was of Bethsaida of G., and
21. 2 Didymus, and Nathanael of Cana in G.
Acts 1. 11 Ye men of G., why stand ye gazing up
5. 37 After this man rose up Judas of G.
9. 31 the churches rest throughout all..G. and
10. 37 That word, (I say), ye know..from G.
13. 31 which came up with him from G. to Jer.

GALL —
1. *Gall, bitter thing, bitterness,* מְרֹרָה *merorah.*
Job 20. 14 turned, (it is) the gall of asps within him
20. 25 glittering sword cometh out of his gall

2. *Gall, bladder,* מְרֵרָה *mererah.*
Job 16. 13 he poureth out my gall upon the ground

3. *Venom, a poisonous herb,* רֹאשׁ *rosh.*
Deut 29. 18 a root that beareth gall and wormwood
Psa. 69. 21 They gave me also gall for my meat; and
Jer. 8. 14 God hath..given us water of gall to dri.
9. 15 and give them water of gall to drink
23. 15 and make them drink the water of gall
Lam. 3. 5 and compassed (me) with gall and
3. 19 Remembering..the wormwood and the g.
Amos 6. 12 for ye have turned judgment into gall

4. *Gall, venom,* רוֹשׁ *rosh.*
Deut32. 32 their grapes (are) grapes of gall, their clu.

5. *Gall, bile, anything bitter,* χολή *cholē.*
Matt 27. 34 vinegar to drink mingled with gall: and
Acts 8. 23 that thou art in the gall of bitterness

GALLANT —
Honourable, glorious, אַדִּיר *addir.*
Isa. 33. 21 neither shall gallant ship pass thereby

GALLERY —
1. *Gallery, portico,* [V.L. אַתּוּק], אַתִּיק *attiq.*
Eze. 41. 15 and the galleries thereof on the one side

2. *Gallery, portico,* אַתִּיק *attiq.*
Eze. 41. 16 the galleries round about on their three
42. 3 gallery against gallery in three (stories)
42. 5 for the galleries were higher than these

3. *Flowings, ringlet,* רַהַט *rahat.*
Song 7. 5 the king (is) held in the galleries

GALLEY —
Ship, navy, אֳנִי *oni.*
Isa. 33. 21 wherein shall go no galley with oars, ne.

GAL'-LIM, גַּלִּים *fountains or heaps.*
A city of Benjamin, N. of Jerusalem.
1 Sa. 25. 44 Phalti the son of Laish, which..of G.
Isa. 10. 30 Lift up thy voice, O daughter of G.

GAL-LI'-O, Γαλλίων.
Seneca's younger brother, a careless Roman proconsul of Achaia. His full name was *Junius Annæus Gallio.* There is no authority for his being put to death by Nero.
Acts 18. 12 And when G. was the deputy of Achaia
18. 14 G. said unto the Jews, If it were a matter
18. 17 And G. cared for none of those things

GALLOWS —
Wood, tree, עֵץ *ets.*
Esth. 5. 14 Let a gallows be made of fifty cubits high
5. 14 and he caused the gallows to be made
6. 4 to hang Mordecai on the gallows that he
7. 9 Behold also, the gallows, fifty cubits high
7. 10 So they hanged Haman on the gallows
8. 7 and him they have hanged upon the gal.
9. 13 Haman's..sons be hanged upon the gall.
9. 25 he and his sons..be hanged on the gallows

GA-MA-LI'-EL, גַּמְלִיאֵל Γαμαλιήλ *God is recompenser.*
1. A chief of Manasseh chosen to aid in taking the census in the wilderness. B.C. 1490.
Num. 1. 10 of Manasseh; G. the son of Pedahzur
2. 20 the captain..of Manasseh..G. the son of
7. 54 On the eighth day..G. the son of Pedah.
7. 59 this..the offering of G. the son of Pedah.
10. 23 And over the host..G. the son of Pedah.

2. A celebrated teacher among the Jews.
Acts 5. 34 a Pharisee, named G., a doctor of the law
22. 3 brought up in this city at the feet of G.

GAM-MA'-DIM, גַּמָּדִים.
This word occurs only once, and has been said to mean "pigmies, warriors, giants, Cappadocians," &c. The LXX. has "guards or watchmen."
Eze. 27. 11 the G. were in thy towers: they hanged

GA'-MUL, גָּמוּל *weaned, matured.*
A priest, the leader of the twenty second course in the service of the Sanctuary B.C. 1015
1 Ch. 24. 17 to Jachin, the two and twentieth to G.

GAP —
Breach, פֶּרֶץ *perets.*
Eze. 13. 5 Ye have not gone up into the gaps, neit.
22. 30 stand in the gap before me for the land

GAPE, to —
1. *To open, gape,* פָּעַר *paar.*
Job 16. 10 They have gaped upon me with their mo.

2. *To open wide, gape,* פָּצָה *patsah.*
Psa. 22. 13 They gaped upon me (with) their mouths

GARDEN —
1. *Garden,* גַּן *gan.*
Gen. 2. 8 God planted a garden eastward in Eden
2. 9 tree of life..in the midst of the garden
2. 10 And a river went out..to water the gar.
2. 15 and put him into the garden of Eden
2. 16 Of every tree of the garden thou mayest
3. 1 shall not eat of every tree of the garden?
3. 2 We may eat..of the trees of the garden
3. 3 tree which (is) in the midst of the garden
3. 8 heard..the LORD God walking in the ga.
3. 8 hid..amongst the trees of the garden
3. 10 he said, I heard thy voice in the garden
3. 23 sent him forth from the garden of Eden
3. 24 he placed at the east of the garden of E.
13. 10 well watered..as the garden of the LORD
Deut 11. 10 and wateredst (it)..as a garden of herbs
1 Ki. 21. 2 that I may have it for a garden of herbs
2 Ki 9. 27 he fled by the way of the garden house
21. 18 garden of his own house, in the garden
21. 26 in his sepulchre in the garden of Uzz
2 Ki.25. 4 the gate..which (is) by the king's garden
Neh. 3. 15 of the pool of Siloah by the king's garden
Song 4. 12 A garden inclosed (is) my sister, (my) sp.
4. 15 A fountain of gardens, a well of..waters
4. 16 Awake, O north wind..blow upon my g.
4. 16 Let my beloved come into his garden, and
5. 1 I am come into my garden, my sister, (my)
6. 2 My beloved is gone down into his garden
6. 2 to feed in the gardens..to gather lilies
8. 13 Thou that dwellest in the gardens, the
Isa. 51. 3 her desert like the garden of the LORD
58. 11 thou shalt be like a watered garden, and
Jer. 31. 12 their soul shall be as a watered garden
39. 4 went..by the way of the king's garden
52. 7 the gate..which (was) by the king's gar.
Lam. 2. 6 his tabernacle, as (if it were of) a garden
Eze. 28. 13 Thou hast been in Eden the garden of G.
31. 8 The cedars in the garden of God could
31. 8 nor any tree in the garden of God was li.
31. 9 the trees..in the garden of God, envied
36. 35 land..is become like the garden of Eden
Joel 2. 3 the land (is) as the garden of Eden before

2. *Garden,* גַּנָּה *gannah.*
Num24. 6 spread forth, as gardens by the river's si.
Job 8. 16 his branch shooteth forth in his garden
Eccl. 2. 5 I made me gardens and orchards, and I
Isa. 1. 29 ye shall be confounded for the gardens
1. 30 and as a garden that hath no water
61. 11 as the garden causeth the things that are
65. 3 A people..that sacrificeth in gardens, and
66. 17 purify themselves in the gardens behind
Jer. 29. 5, 28 plant gardens, and eat the fruit of
Amos 4. 9 when your gardens and your vineyards
9. 14 they shall also make gardens, and eat the

3. *Garden,* גִּנָּה *ginnah.*
Esth. 1. 5 court of the garden of the king's palace
7. 7 the king..(went) into the palace garden
7. 8 the king returned out of the palace gar.
Song 6. 11 I went down into the garden of nuts to

4. *Garden, orchard, plantation,* κῆπος *kēpos.*
Luke13. 19 which a man took, and cast into his gar.
John18. 1 over the brook Cedron, where was a gar.
18. 26 Did not I see thee in the garden with him?
19. 41 there was a garden; and in the garden a

GARDENER —
Gardener, κηπουρός *kēpouros.*
John20. 15 She, supposing him to be the gardener

GA'-REB, גָּרֵב *reviler, despiser.*
1. One of David's worthies, the son of Jether, or an inhabitant of Jathir, in the mountainous district of Judah. B.C. 1048.
2 Sa. 23. 38 Ira an Ithrite, G. an Ithrite
1 Ch.11. 40 Ira the Ithrite, G. the Ithrite

2. A hill near Jerusalem.
Jer. 31. 39 go forth over against it upon the hill G.

GARLAND —
Garland, wreath, chaplet, στέμμα *stemma.*
Acts 14. 13 brought oxen and garlands unto the ga.

GARLICK —
Garlick, שׁוּם *shum.*
Num11. 5 the leeks, and the onions, and the garli.

GARMENT —
1. *Honourable, glorious mantle,* אַדֶּרֶת *addereth.*
Gen. 25. 25 came out red, all over like an hairy gar.
Josh. 7. 21 When I saw..a goodly Babylonish gar.
7. 24 silver, and the garment, and the wedge
Zech13. 4 neither shall they wear a rough garment

2. *Cloak, garment, covering,* בֶּגֶד *beged.*
Gen. 38. 14 she put her widow's garments off from
38. 19 put on the garments of her widowhood
39. 12 And she caught him by his garment, sa.
39. 12 and he left his garment in her hand, and
39. 13 when she saw that he had left his garm.
39. 15 he left his garment with me, and fled
39. 16 she laid up his garment by her until his
39. 18 he left his garment with me, and fled out
Exod28. 2 thou shalt make holy garments for Aaron
28. 3 that they may make Aaron's garments to
28. 4 these..the garments which they shall
28. 4 they shall make holy garments for Aaron
29. 5 thou shalt take the garments, and put
29. 21 take..oil, and sprinkle..upon his garmen.
29. 21 upon the garments of his sons with him
29. 21 he shall be hallowed, and his garments
29. 21 his sons, and his sons' garments with him
29. 29 the holy garments of Aaron shall be his
31. 10 the holy garments for Aaron the priest
31. 10 the garments of his sons, to minister in
35. 19 the holy garments for Aaron the priest
35. 19 the garments of his sons, to minister in
35. 21 for all his service, and for the holy garm.
39. 1 and made the holy garments for Aaron
39. 41 the holy garments for Aaron the priest
39. 41 and his sons' garments, to minister in
40. 13 thou shalt put upon Aaron the holy gar.
Lev. 6. 11 And he shall put off his garments
6. 11 and put on other garments, and carry fo
6. 27 of the blood thereof upon any garment
8. 2 the garments, and the anointing oil, and
8. 30 sprinkled (it) upon Aaron..upon his gar.
8. 30 and upon his sons' garments with him
8. 30 and sanctified Aaron, (and) his garments
8. 30 his sons, and his sons' garments with him
13. 47 The garment also that the plague of lep.

Lev. 13. 47 a woollen garment, or a linen garment
13. 49 if the plague be..reddish in the garment
13. 51 if the plague be spread in the garment
13. 52 He shall therefore burn that garment
13. 53 the plague be not spread in the garment
13. 56 then he shall rend it out of the garment
13. 57 And if it appear still in the garment
13. 58 And the garment, either warp or woof
13. 59 leprosy in a garment of woollen or linen
14. 55 for the leprosy of a garment, and of a
15. 17 every garment, and every skin, whereon
16. 4 these (are) holy garments; therefore shall
16. 23 Aaron..shall put off the linen garments
16. 24 and put on his garments, and come forth
16. 32 put on the linen clothes..the holy gar.
19. 19 neither shall a garment mingled of linen
21. 10 that is consecrated to put on the garments
Num 15. 38 fringes in the borders of their garments
20. 26 strip Aaron of his garments, and put
20. 28 Moses stripped Aaron of his garments
Judg 14 12 I will give you..thirty change of garments
14. 13 shall ye give..thirty change of garments
2 Sa. 13. 31 Then the king arose, and tare his gar.
2 Ki. 5. 22 give them, I pray..two changes of gar.
5. 23 two bags, with two changes of garments
5. 26 (Is it) a time to receive money, and..gar.
7. 15 all the way (was) full of garments and
9. 13 they hasted, and took every man his gar.
25. 29 And changed his prison garments: and
Ezra 9. 3 I rent my garment and my mantle, and
9. 5 having rent my garment and my mantle
Job 13. 28 consumeth, as a garment that is moth-ea.
37. 17 How thy garments (are) warm, when he
Psa. 22. 18 They part my garments among them, and
45. 8 All thy garments..of myrrh, and aloes
102. 26 all of them shall wax old like a garment
109. 19 Let it be unto him as the garment
Prov 20. 16 Take his garment that is surety (for) a
25. 20 (As) he that taketh away a garment in
27. 13 Take his garment that is surety for a
Eccl. 9. 8 Let thy garments be always white; and
Isa. 50. 9 lo, they all shall wax old as a garment
51. 6 the earth shall wax old like a garment
51. 8 the moth shall eat them up like a garm.
52. 1 put on thy beautiful garments, O Jeru.
59. 6 Their webs shall not become garments
59. 17 he put on the garments of vengeance
61. 10 clothed me with the garments of salva.
63. 1 cometh .with dyed garments from Bo.?
63. 2 thy garments like him that treadeth in
63. 3 blood shall be sprinkled upon my gar.
Jer. 36. 24 they were not afraid, nor rent their gar.
43. 12 as a shepherd putteth on his garment
52. 33 And changed his prison garments: and
Eze. 16. 16 of thy garments thou didst take, and
16 18 tookest thy broidered garments, and
18. 7. 16 hath covered the naked with a gar.
26. 16 princes..put off their broidered garments
42. 14 but there they shall lay their garments
42. 14 and shall put on other garments, and
44. 17 they shall be clothed with linen garments
44. 19 they shall put off their garments wherein
44. 19 and they shall put on other garments
44. 19 not sanctify the people with their garm.
Joel 2. 13 rend your heart, and not your garments
Hag. 2. 12 one bear holy flesh in the skirt of his gar
Zech. 3. 3 Joshua was clothed with filthy garments
3. 4 Take away the filthy garments from him
3. 5 So they..clothed him with garments

3. *A coat,* כְּתֹנֶת, כֻּתֹּנֶת *kethoneth, kuttoneth.*
2 Sa. 13. 18 And (she had) a garment of divers colours
13. 19 and rent her garment of divers colours
Ezra 2. 69 They gave..one hundred priests' garments
Neh. 7. 70 five hundred and thirty priests' garments
7. 72 threescore and seven priests' garments

4. *Clothing,* לְבוּשׁ *lebush.*
Gen. 49. 11 he washed his garments in wine, and his
Job 30 18 is my garment changed: it bindeth me
38. 9 When I made the cloud the garment the.
38. 14 It is turned..and they stand as a garment
41. 13 Who can discover the face of his garment?
Psa 69. 11 I made sackcloth also my garment; and
104. 6 Thou coveredst it..as (with) a garment
Lam. 4. 14 that men could not touch their garments
Mal. 2. 16 for (one) covereth violence with his gar.

5. *Clothing,* לְבוּשׁ *lebush.*
Dan. 3. 21 bound in..their hats, and their..garme.
7. 9 whose garment..white as snow, and the

6. *Long robe,* מַד *mad.*
Lev. 6. 10 the priest shall put on his linen garment
1 Sa. 18. 4 stripped himself of..his garments, even to
2 Sa. 20. 8 And Joab's garment that he had put on
Psa. 109. 18 with cursing like as with his garment

7. *Long robe,* מִדָּה *middah.*
Psa. 133. 2 that went down to the skirts of his gar.

8. *Long robe,* מֶדֶו *medev.*
2 Sa. 10. 4 and cut off their garments in the middle
1 Ch. 19. 4 and cut off their garments in the midst

9. *Covering, wrapping,* מַעֲטֶה *maateh.*
Isa. 61. 3 the garment of praise for the spirit of

10. *Outer garment,* שַׂלְמָה *salmah.*
Josh. 9. 5 old shoes..and old garments upon them
9. 13 our garments and our shoes are become
1 Ki. 10. 25 And they brought..garments, and armour
11. 29 he had clad himself with a new garment
11, 30 And Ahijah caught the new garment that
Psa. 104. 2 Who coverest (thyself) with light as..a g.
Song 4. 11 the smell of thy garments (is) like the
Mic. 2. 8 ye pull off the robe with the garment

11. *Outer garment, raiment,* שִׂמְלָה *simlah.*
Gen. 9. 23 And Shem and Japheth took a garment
35. 2 and be clean, and change your garments
Deut 22. 5 neither..a man put on a woman's garment
Judg. 8. 25 they spread a garment, and did cast ther.
Prov 30. 4 who hath bound the waters in a garment?
Isa. 9. 5 with..noise, and garments rolled in blood

12. *Covering, dress,* שִׁית *shith.*
Psa. 73. 6 violence covereth them (as) a garment

13. *Garment,* תַּכְרִיךְ *takrik.*
Esth. 8. 15 with a garment of fine linen and purple

14. *Any thing put on,* ἔνδυμα *enduma.*
Matt 22. 11 which had not on a wedding garment
22. 12 camest thou..not having a wedding gar.?

15. *Clothing,* ἔσθησις *esthēsis.*
Luke 24. 4 two men stood by them in shining gar.

16. *Garment,* ἱμάτιον *himation.*
Matt. 9. 16 a piece of new cloth unto an old garment
9. 16 for that..put in..taketh from the garm.
9. 20 came..and touched the hem of his garm.
9. 21 If I may but touch his garment, I shall
14. 36 might only touch the hem of his garment
21. 8 a very great multitude spread their gar.
23. 5 and enlarge the borders [of their garme.]
27. 35 [and parted his garments, casting lots]
27. 35 [They parted my garments among them]
Mark 2. 21 a piece of new cloth on an old garment
5. 27 came..behind, and touched his garment
6. 56 touch if it were but the border of his g.
10. 50 And he, casting away his garment, rose
11. 7 brought the colt..and cast their garments
11. 8 many spread their garments in the way
13. 16 not turn back..to take up his garment
15. 24 they parted his garments, casting lots
Luke 5. 36 No man putteth a piece of a new garment
8. 44 Came..and touched the border of his g.
19. 35 they cast their garments upon the colt
22. 36 let him sell his garment, and buy one
John 13. 4 He riseth..and laid aside his garment
13. 12 So after he had..taken his garments, and
19. 23 Then the soldiers..took his garments, and
Acts 9. 39 showing the coats and garments which D.
12. 8 Cast thy garment about thee, and follow
Heb. 1. 11 and they all shall wax old as doth a gar.
Jas. 5. 2 Your riches are corrupted, and your gar.
Rev. 3. 4 a few..which have not defiled their gar.
16. 15 Blessed (is) he that..keepeth his garme.

17. *Coat, inner vest,* χιτών *chitōn.*
Jude 23 hating even the garment spotted by the

GARMENT down to the foot —
Joining or touching the feet, ποδήρης *podērēs.*
Rev. 1. 13 clothed with a garment down to the foot

GARMENT, long —
Long robe, stole, στολή *stolē.*
Mark 16. 5 young man..clothed in a long white gar.

GARMENT of divers sorts —
A mixed cloth, שַׁעַטְנֵז *shaatnez.*
Deut 22. 11 shalt not wear a garment of divers sorts

GAR-MITE, הַגַּרְמִי *the strong or bony one.*
Patronymic of Keilah, son of Nahum of the tribe of Judah through Caleb the son of Jephunneh. B.C. 1400.
1 Ch 4. 19 father of Keilah the G., and Eshtemoa

GARNER —
1. *Treasury,* אוֹצָר *otsar.*
Joel 1. 17 the garners are laid desolate, the barns

2. *Garner,* מָזֶו *mezev.*
Psa. 144. 13 our garners..full, affording all manner of

3. *Barn, repository,* ἀποθήκη *apothēkē.*
Matt. 3. 12 and gather his wheat into the garner
Luke 3. 17 and will gather the wheat into his garner

GARNISH, to —
1. *To overlay, cover,* צָפָה *tsaphah,* 3.
2 Ch. 3. 6 And he garnished the house with precious

2. *Splendour* שִׁפְרָה *shiphrah.*
Job 26. 13 By his spirit he hath garnished the heav.

3. *To set in order, adorn, beautify,* κοσμέω *kosmeō.*
Matt 12. 44 he findeth (it) empty, swept, and garnish.
23. 29 garnish the sepulchres of the righteous
Luke 11. 25 when he cometh, he findeth (it)..garnis.
Rev 21. 19 garnished with all manner of precious

GARRISON —
1. *Station, garrison,* מַצָּב *matstsab.*
1 Sa. 13. 23 And the garrison of the Philistines went
14. 1 let us go over to the Philistines' garrison
14. 4 to go over unto the Philistines' garrison
14. 6 let us go over unto the garrison of these
14. 11 discovered themselves unto the garrison
14. 15 the garrison, and the spoilers, they also
2 Sa. 23. 14 the garrison of the Philistines (was) then

2. *Station,* מַצָּבָה *matstsabah.*
1 Sa. 14. 12 And the men of the garrison answered

3. *Station,* מַצֶּבָה *matstsebah.*
Eze. 26. 11 thy strong garrisons shall go down to the

4. *Station, garrison,* נְצִיב *netsib.*
1 Sa. 10. 5 where (is) the garrison of the Philistines
13. 3 And Jonathan smote the garrison of the
1 Sa. 13. 4 heard say..Saul had smitten a garrison
2 Sa. 8. 6 Then David put garrisons in Syria of D.
8. 14 garrisons in..all Edom put he garrisons
1 Ch. 11. 16 the Philistines' garrison was (then) at
18. 13 he put garrisons in Edom; and all the E.
2 Ch. 17. 2 and set garrisons in the land of Judah

GARRISON, to keep with a —
To keep watch or guard, φρουρέω *phroureō.*
2 Co. 11. 32 the governor..kept the city..with a garr.

GASH'-MU, גַּשְׁמוּ *corporealness.*
An influential Samaritan in Nehemiah's time. Perhaps the same as *Geshem.* B.C. 445.
Neh. 6. 6 It is reported among the heathen, and G.

GA'-TAM, גַּעְתָּם *burnt valley.*
Fourth son of Eliphaz son of Esau. B.C. 1680.
Gen. 36. 11 Teman, Omar, Zepho, and G., and Kenaz
36. 16 Duke Korah, duke G., (and) duke Ama.
1 Ch. 1. 36 Teman, and Omar, Zephi, and G., Kenaz

GATE —
1. *Door,* דֶּלֶת *deleth.*
Deut. 3. 5 these cities..fenced with high walls, gates
Josh. 6 26 in his youngest..shall he set up the gates
1 Sa. 23. 7 by entering into a town that hath gates
1 Ki. 16. 34 set up the gates thereof in his youngest
2 Ch. 8. 5 fenced cities, with walls, gates, and bars
14. 7 make about (them) walls, and towers, gates
Neh. 13. 19 I commanded that the gates should be
Psa. 107. 16 For he hath broken the gates of brass, and
Prov. 8. 34 watching daily at my gates, waiting at
Isa. 45. 2 I will break in pieces the gates of brass
Jer. 49. 31 neither gates nor bars, (which) dwell alone
Eze. 26. 2 Aha! she is broken..the gates of the pe.
38. 11 all of them..having neither bars nor gates

2. *Threshold,* סַף *saph.*
1 Ch. 9. 19 keepers of the gates of the tabernacle
9. 22 All..chosen to be porters in the gates

3. *Opening,* פֶּתַח *pethach.*
1 Ki. 17. 10 And when he came to the gate of the city
1 Ch 19. 9 put the battle in array before the gate of
Esth. 5. 1 sat..over against the gate of the house
Prov. 17. 19 he that exalteth his gate seeketh destru.
Song 7. 13 at our gates (are) all manner of pleasant
Isa. 3. 26 And her gates shall lament and mourn
13. 2 that they may go into the gates of the

4. *Gate,* שַׁעַר *shaar.*
Gen. 19. 1 and Lot sat in the gate of Sodom: and
22. 17 thy seed shall possess the gate of his ene.
23. 10 of all that went in at the gate of his city
23. 18 before all that went in at the gate of his
24. 60 let thy seed possess the gate of those
28 17 How dreadful..this (is) the gate of heaven
34. 20 came unto the gate of their city, and com.
34. 24 the gate of his city . . the gate of his city
Exod 20. 10 nor thy stranger that (is) within thy gates
27. 16 for the gate of the court..an hanging of
32. 26 Moses stood in the gate of the camp, and
32. 27 go in and out from gate to gate throughout
38. 15 And for the other side of the court gate
38. 18 And the hanging for the gate of the court
38. 31 the sockets of the court gate, and all the
39. 40 the hanging for the court gate, his cords
40. 8 hang up the hanging at the court gate
40. 33 and set up the hanging of the court gate
Num. 4. 26 the hanging for the door of the gate of
Deut. 5. 14 nor thy stranger that (is) within thy gates
6. 9 And thou shalt write them..on thy gates
11. 20 And thou shalt write them..upon thy g.
12. 12 and the Levite that (is) within your gates
12. 15 mayest kill and eat flesh in all thy gates
12. 17 Thou mayest not eat within thy gates the
12. 18 and the Levite that (is) within thy gates
12. 21 thou shalt eat in thy gates whatsoever thy
14. 21 unto the stranger that (is) in thy gates
14. 27 And the Levite that (is) within thy gates
14. 28 tithe..and shalt lay (it) up within thy gates
14. 29 which (are) within thy gates, shall come
15. 7 of thy brethren within any of thy gates
15. 22 Thou shalt eat it within thy gates: the
16. 5 within any of thy gates, which the LORD
16. 11 and the Levite that (is) within thy gates
16. 14 the fatherless..that (are) within thy gates
16. 18 officers shalt thou make..in all thy gates
17. 2 within any of thy gates which the LORD
17. 5 Then shalt thou bring..unto thy gates.
17. 8 matters of controversy within thy gates
18. 6 if a Levite come from any of thy gates
21. 19 bring him out..unto the gate of his place
22. 15 unto the elders of the city in the gate
22. 24 bring them..unto the gate of that city
23. 16 which he shall choose in one of thy gates
24. 14 strangers..in thy land within thy gates
25. 7 let his brother's wife go up to the gate
26. 12 that they may eat within thy gates, and
28. 52, 52 he shall besiege thee in all thy gates
28. 55 enemies shall distress thee in all thy ga.
28. 57 enemy shall distress thee in thy gates
31. 12 and thy stranger that (is) within thy gat.
Josh. 2. 5 (about the time) of shutting of the gate
2. 7 they..were gone out, they shut the gate
7. 5 chased them..before the gate..unto She.
8. 29 cast it at the entering of the gate of the
20. 4 at the entering of the gate of the city
Judg. 5. 8 chose new gods; then (was) war in the g.
5. 11 the people of the LORD go down to the g.
9. 35 in the entering of the gate of the city
9. 40 chased him..unto the entering of the ga.

Judg. 9. 44 stood in the entering of the gate of the
16. 2 laid wait for him all night in the gate of
16. 3 Samson..took the doors of the gate of
18. 16 And..stood by the entering of the gate
18. 17 priest stood in the entering of the gate
Ruth 4. 1 Then went Boaz up to the gate, and sat
4. 10 be not cut off..from the gate of his place
4. 11 And all the people that (were) in the ga.
1 Sa. 4. 18 fell..backward by the side of the gate
9. 18 Saul drew near to Samuel in the gate
17. 52 until thou come to..the gates of Ekron
21. 13 and scrabbled on the doors of the gate
2 Sa. 3. 27 Joab took him aside in the gate to speak
10. 8 in array at the entering in of the gate
11. 23 them even unto the entering of the gate
15. 2 Absalom..stood beside the way of the g.
18. 4 the king stood by the gate side, and all
18. 24 And David sat between the two gates
18. 24 went up to the roof over the gate unto
18. 33 went up to the chamber over the gate
19. 8 Then the king arose, and sat in the gate
19. 8 Behold, the king doth sit in the gate
23. 15, 16 well of Beth-lehem, which (is) by the g.
1 Ki. 22. 10 in the entrance of the gate of Samaria
2 Ki. 7. 1 two..of barley for a shekel, in the gate of
7. 3 leprous men at the entering in of the ga.
7. 17 the lord..to have the charge of the gate
7. 17 the people trode upon him in the gate
7. 18 to morrow about this time in the gate of
7. 20 the people trode upon him in the gate
9. 31 And as Jehu entered in at the gate, she
10. 8 two heaps at the entering in of the gate
11. 6 And a third part..at the gate of Sur
11. 6 a third part at the gate behind the guard
11. 19 came by the way of the gate of the guard
14. 13 the gate of Ephraim unto the corner gate
15. 35 He built the higher gate of the house of
23. 8 brake down the high places of the gates
23. 8 in the entering in of the gate of Joshua
23. 8 on a man's left hand at the gate of the
25. 4 by the way of the gate between two walls
1 Ch. 9. 18 Who hitherto..in the king's gate eastw.
9. 23 the oversight of the gates of the house of
11. 17, 18 well of Beth-lehem, that (is) at the ga.
22. 3 for the nails for the doors of the gates
26. 13 And they cast lots..for every gate
26. 16 westward, with the gate Shallecheth, by
2 Ch. 8. 14 porters also by their courses at every ga.
18. 9 at the entering in of the gate of Samaria
23. 5 a third part at the gate of the foundation
23. 15 to the entering of the horse gate by the
23. 19 And he set the porters at the gates of the
23. 20 through the high gate into the king's ho.
24. 8 at the gate of the house of the LORD
25. 23 the gate of Ephraim to the corner gate
26. 9 at the corner gate, and at the valley gate
27. 3 He built the high gate of the house of
31. 2 to praise in the gates of the tents of the
32. 6 in the street of the gate of the city
33. 14 even to the entering in at the fish gate
35. 15 and the porters (waited) at every gate
Neh. 1. 3 and the gates thereof are burnt with fire
2. 3 the gates thereof are consumed with fire?
2. 8 timber to make beams for the gates of the
2. 13 I went out by night by the gate of the
2. 13 and the gates..were consumed with fire
2. 14 I went on to the gate of the fountain, and
2. 15 and entered by the gate of the valley
2. 17 and the gates thereof are burnt with fire
3. 1 they builded the sheep gate; they sanct.
3. 3 But the fish gate did the sons of Hassen.
3. 6 Moreover the old gate repaired Jehoiada
3. 13 The valley gate repaired Hanun, and the
3. 13 cubits on the wall unto the dung gate
3. 14 the dung gate repaired Malchiah the son
3. 15 the gate of the fountain repaired Shallun
3. 26 over against the water gate toward the
3. 28 From above the horse gate repaired the
3. 29 also Shemaiah..the keeper of the east g.
3. 31 repaired..over against the gate Miphkad
3. 32 unto the sheep gate repaired the goldsmi.
6. 1 had not set up the doors upon the gates
7. 3 Let not the gates of Jerusalem be opened
8. 1 the street that (was) before the water gate
8. 3 the street that (was) before the water gate
8. 16 and in the street of the water gate
8. 16 and in the street of the gate of Ephraim
11. 19 and their brethren that kept the gates
12. 25 the ward at the thresholds of the gates
12. 30 and purified the people, and the gates
12. 31 upon the wall toward the dung gate
12. 37 And at the fountain gate, which was
12. 37 went up..unto the water gate eastward
12. 39 And from above the gate of Ephraim
12. 39 above the old gate..above the fish gate
12. 39 unto the sheep gate..in the prison gate
13. 19 when the gates of Jerusalem began to be
13. 19 and (some) of my servants set I at the g.
13. 22 and..they should come (and) keep the g.
Esth. 2. 19 then Mordecai sat in the king's gate
2. 21 while Mordecai sat in the king's gate
3. 2, 3 servants, that (were) in the king's gate
4. 2 And came even before the king's gate
4. 2 for none (might) enter into the king's ga.
4. 6 street..which (was) before the king's gate
5. 9 Haman saw Mordecai in the king's gate
5. 13 Mordecai the Jew sitting at the king's g.
6. 10 the Jew, that sitteth at the king's gate
6. 12 Mordecai came again to the king's gate
Job 5. 4 His children..are crushed in the gate
29. 7 When I went out to the gate through the
31. 21 If I have..when I saw my help in the g.
Job 38. 17 Have the gates of death been opened
Psa. 9. 13 that liftest me up from the gates of death
9. 14 may show forth all thy praise in the ga.
24. 7, 9 Lift up your heads, O ye gates
69. 12 They that sit in the gate speak against
87. 2 The LORD loveth the gates of Zion more
100. 4 Enter into his gates with thanksgiving
107. 18 they draw near unto the gates of death
118. 19 Open to me the gates of righteousness
118. 20 This gate of the LORD, into which the
122. 2 Our feet shall stand within thy gates, O J.
127. 5 shall speak with the enemies in the gate
147. 13 hath strengthened the bars of thy gates
Prov. 1. 21 She crieth..in the openings of the gates
8. 3 She crieth at the gates, at the entry of
14. 19 the wicked at the gates of the righteous
22. 22 neither oppress the afflicted in the gate
24. 7 he openeth not his mouth in the gate
31. 23 Her husband is known in the gates, when
31. 31 let her own works praise her in the gates
Song 7. 4 in Heshbon, by the gate of Bath-rabbim
Isa. 14. 31 Howl, O gate; cry, O city; thou, whole P.
22. 7 shall set themselves in array at the gate
24. 12 and the gate is smitten with destruction
26. 2 Open ye the gates, that the righteous
28. 6 to them that turn the battle to the gate
29. 21 a snare for him that reproveth in the g.
38. 10 I said..I shall go to the gates of the grave
45. 1 to open..and the gates shall not be shut
54. 12 I will make..thy gates of carbuncles
60. 11 Therefore thy gates shall be open conti.
60. 18 but thou shalt call..thy gates Praise
62. 10 Go through, go through the gates; pre.
Jer. 1. 15 at the entering of the gates of Jerusalem
7. 2 Stand in the gate of the LORD'S house
7. 2 that enter in at these gates to worship
14. 2 Judah mourneth, and the gates thereof
15. 7 I will fan them with a fan in the gates of
17. 19 Go and stand in the gate of the children
17. 19 and in all the gates of Jerusalem
17. 20 Hear ye..all..that enter in by these gates
17. 21 nor bring (it) in by the gates of Jerusa.
17. 24 to bring in no burden through the gates
17. 25 Then shall there enter into the gates of
17. 27 entering in at the gates of Jerusalem on
17. 27 then will I kindle a fire in the gates th.
19. 2 which (is) by the entry of the east gate
20. 2 in the stocks that (were) in the high gate
22. 2 thy people that enter in by these gates
22. 4 then shall there enter in by the gates of
22. 19 cast forth beyond the gates of Jerusalem
26. 10 sat down in the entry of the new gate of
31. 38 from the tower of Hananeel unto the gate
31. 40 unto the corner of the horse gate toward
36. 10 at the entry of the new gate of the LORD'S
37. 13 And when he was in the gate of Benja.
38. 7 the king..sitting in the gate of Benjamin
39. 3 princes..came in, and sat in the middle g.
39. 4 fled..by the gate betwixt the two walls
51. 58 her high gates shall be burnt with fire
52. 7 by the way of the gate between the two
Lam. 1. 4 all her gates are desolate: her priests
2. 9 Her gates are sunk into the ground; he
4. 12 have entered into the gates of Jerusalem
5. 14 The elders have ceased from the gate
Eze. 8. 3 to the door of the inner gate that looketh
8. 5 northward at the gate of the altar this
8. 14 he brought me to the door of the gate of
9. 2 came from the way of the higher gate
10. 19 stood at the door of the east gate of the
11. 1 the spirit..brought me unto the east gate
11. 1 at the door of the gate five and twenty
21. 15 have set..the sword against all their gates
21. 22 to appoint..rams against the gates, to
26. 10 when he shall enter into thy gates, as
40. 3 behold..a man..and he stood in the gate
40. 6 Then came he unto the gate which look.
40. 6 and measured the threshold (of the gate)
40. 7 of the gate by the porch of the gate
40. 8 He measured also the porch of the gate
40. 9 Then measured he the porch of the gate
40. 9 and the porch of the gate (was) inward
40. 10 And the little chambers of the gate east.
40. 11 the breadth of the entry of the gate
40. 11 the length of the gate, thirteen cubits
40. 13 He measured then the gate from the roof
40. 14 the post of the court round about the gate
40. 15 And from the face of the gate of the ent.
40. 15 the face of the porch of the inner gate
40. 16 and to their posts within the gate round
40. 18 And the pavement by the side of the gates
40. 18 over against the length of the gates, (was)
40. 19 from the fore-front of the lower gate unto
40. 20 And the gate of the outward court that
40. 21 were after the measure of the first gate
40. 22 after the measure of the gate that looketh
40. 23 And the gate of the inner court (was)
40. 23 over against the gate toward the north
40. 23 and he measured from gate to gate an
40. 24 and, behold, a gate toward the south
40. 27 And..a gate in the inner court toward
40. 27 he measured from gate to gate toward
40. 28 to the inner court by the south gate
40. 28 he measured the south gate according to
40. 32 and he measured the gate according to
40. 35 And he brought me to the north gate
40. 38 by the posts of the gates, where they
40. 39 in the porch of the gate (were) two tables
40. 40 goeth up to the entry of the north gate
40. 40 which (was) at the porch of the gate
40. 41 by the side of the gate; eight tables
40. 44 without the inner gate (were) the cham.
Eze. 40. 44 which (was) at the side of the north gate
40. 44 one at the side of the east gate (having)
40. 48 the breadth of the gate (was) three cubits
42. 15 he brought me forth toward the gate
43. 1 he brought me to the gate..the gate that
43. 4 by the way of the gate whose prospect
44. 1 brought me back the way of the gate of
44. 2 This gate shall be shut, it shall not be
44. 3 enter by the way of the porch of (that) g.
44. 4 brought he me the way of the north gate
44. 11 (having) charge at the gates of the house
44. 17 when they enter in at the gates of the
44. 17 whiles they minister in the gates of the
45. 19 upon the posts of the gate of the inner
46. 1 The gate of the inner court that looketh
46 2 by the way of the porch of (that) gate
46. 2 and shall stand by the post of the gate
46. 2 shall worship at the threshold of the gate
46. 2 the gate shall not be shut until the eve.
46. 3 shall worship at the door of this gate
46. 8 go in by the way of the porch of (that) g.
46. 9 entereth in by the way of the north gate
46. 9 shall go out by the way of the south gate
46. 9 that entereth by the way of the south g.
46. 9 go forth by the way of the north gate
46. 9 he shall not return by the way of the g.
46. 12 shall then open him the gate that looketh
46. 12 after his going forth..shall shut the gate
46. 19 through the entry..at the side of the ga.
47. 2 out of the way of the gate northward
47. 2 and led me..unto the utter gate by the
48. 31 the gates of the city..after the names of
48. 31 three gates northward; one gate of Reu.
48. 31 one gate of Judah, one gate of Levi
48. 32 and three gates; and one gate of Joseph
48. 32 one gate of Benjamin, one gate of Dan
48. 33 and three gates; one gate of Simeon
48. 33 one gate of Issachar, one gate of Zebulun
48. 34 (with) their three gates; one gate of Gad
48. 34 one gate of Asher, one gate of Naphtali
Amos 5. 10 They hate him that rebuketh in the gate
5. 12 and they turn aside the poor in the gate
5. 15 establish judgment in the gate: it may
Obad. 11 foreigners entered into his gates, and cast
13 not have entered into the gate of my p.
Mic. 1. 9 he is come unto the gate of my people
1. 12 came down from the LORD unto the gate
2. 13 have passed through the gate, and are
Nah. 2. 6 The gates of the rivers shall be opened
3. 13 the gates of thy land shall be set wide
Zeph. 1. 10 the noise of a cry from the fish gate, and
Zech. 8. 16 judgment of truth and peace in your gates
14. 10 from Benjamin's gate unto..the first gate
14. 10 unto the corner gate, and (from) the tower

5. *Gate*, תְּרַע *tera.*
Dan. 2. 49 but Daniel (sat) in the gate of the king

6. *A door*, θύρα *thura.*
Acts 3. 2 at the gate of the temple which is called

7. *A gate*, (*wing of a double gate*), πύλη *pulē.*
Matt. 7. 13 Enter ye in at the straight gate: for
7. 13 wide (is) [the gate], and broad (is) the
7. 14 Because strait (is) the [gate], and narrow
16. 18 the gates of hell shall not prevail against
Luke 7. 12 when he came nigh to the gate of the city
13. 24 Strive to enter in at the straight [gate]
Acts 3. 10 sat..at the Beautiful gate of the temple
9. 24 they watched the gates day and night to
12. 10 they came unto the iron gate that leadeth
Heb. 13. 12 Jesus also..suffered without the gate

8. *Gate, gateway*, πυλών *pulōn.*
Luke 16. 20 which was laid at his gate, full of sores
Acts 10. 17 behold, the men..stood before the gate
12. 13 as Peter knocked at the door of the gate
12. 14 she opened not the gate for gladness
12. 14 and told how Peter stood before the gate
14. 13 brought oxen and garlands unto the gates
Rev. 21. 12 a wall great and high (and)..twelve gates
21. 12 [at the gates twelve angels, and names]
21. 13 east, three gates; on the north, three ga.
21. 13 south, three gates..the west, three gates
21. 15 to measure the city, and the gates thereof
21. 21 And the twelve gates (were) twelve pearls
21. 21 every several gate was of one pearl
21. 25 the gates of it shall not be shut at all by
22. 14 enter in through the gates into the city

GATES, two leaved —

Double door, דְּלָתַיִם *delathayim.*
Isa. 45. 1 to open before him the two leaved gates

GATH, גַּת *wine press, fortune.*

One of the five royal cities of the Philistines and native place of Goliath. It stood upon the conspicuous hill now called *Tell-es-Safiêh.* This hill is at the foot of the mountains of Judah, ten miles E. of Ashdod and ten S. by E. of Ekron. The ruins are very extensive.

Josh 11. 22 Gaza, in G and in Ashdod, there remained
1 Sa. 5. 8 Let the ark of..God..be carried..unto G.
6. 17 a trespass offering unto the LORD..for G.
7. 14 restored to Israel, from Ekron..unto G.
17. 4 went out a champion..Goliath, of G.
17. 23 there came up..the Philistine of G.
17. 52 Israel..pursued the Philistines..unto G.
21. 10 D. arose..and went to Achish..king of G.
21. 12 D...was sore afraid of Achish the king of G.
27. 2 D...passed over..unto Achish..king of G.
27. 3 And David dwelt with Achish at G., he
27. 4 it was told Saul that David was fled to G.
27. 11 to bring (tidings) to G., saying, Lest they
2 Sa. 1. 20 Tell (it) not in G. publish (it) not in the

2 Sa. 15. 18 six hundred men which came..from G.
21. 20 And there was yet a battle in G.
21. 22 These four were born to the giant in G.
1 Ki. 2. 39 servants of Shimei ran..unto A...of G.
2. 39 they told Shimei..thy servants (be) in G.
2. 40 And Shimei arose..and went to G.
2. 40 went, and brought his servants from G.
2. 41 told Solomon..Shimei had gone..to G.
2 Ki. 12. 17 Hazael king of Syria..fought against G.
1 Ch. 7. 21 Shuthelah..whom the men of G...slew
8. 13 Shema..drove away the inhabitants of G.
18. 1 David smote the Philistines..and took G.
20. 6 And yet again there was war at G.
20. 8 These were born unto the giant in G.
2 Ch. 11. 8 And G., and Mareshah, and Ziph
26. 6 he went..and brake down the wall of G.
Psa. 56. *title* Michtam..the Philistines took him in G.
Amos 6. 2 then go down to G. of the Philistines
Mic. 1. 10 Declare ye (it) not at G., weep ye not at

GATHER —

A gathering, קְבֻצָה *qebutsah.*
Eze. 22. 20 they gather silver, and brass, and iron

GATHER, to —

1. *To gather,* אָגַר *agar.*
Deut. 28. 39 shalt neither drink (of) the wine, nor ga.
Prov. 6. 8 (and) gathereth her food in the harvest
10. 5 He that gathereth in summer (is) a wise

2. *To gather together or up,* אָסַף *asaph.*
Gen. 6. 21 food that is eaten, and thou shalt gather
Exod 23. 10 and shalt gather in the fruits thereof
Lev. 25. 3 shalt prune..and gather in the fruit
Num 11. 16 Gather unto me seventy men of the eld.
11. 24 gathered the seventy men of the elders
11. 32 stood up..and they gathered the quails
11. 32 he that gathered least gathered ten
19. 9 shall gather up the ashes of the heifer
19. 10 he that gathereth the ashes of the heifer
Josh. 24. 1 Joshua gathered all the tribes of Israel
Judg. 3. 13 he gathered unto him the children of A.
Ruth 2. 7 let me glean and gather after the reapers
1 Sa. 5. 8 They sent therefore, and gathered all the
2 Sa. 21. 13 they gathered the bones of them that were
2 Ki. 22. 4 which the keepers..have gathered of the
22. 20 I will gather thee unto thy fathers, and
23. 1 they gathered unto him all the elders of
1 Ch. 19. 17 he gathered all Israel, and passed over
2 Ch. 1. 14 Solomon gathered chariots and horsemen
24. 11 Thus they..gathered money in abundance
29. 15 they gathered their brethren, and sanct
29. 20 the king rose early, and gathered the rul.
34. 9 money..which the Levites..had gathered
34. 28 I will gather thee to thy fathers, and thou
Job 34. 14 (if) he gather unto himself his spirit and
39. 12 he will bring home thy seed, and gather
Psa. 26. 9 Gather not my soul with sinners, nor my
39. 6 and knoweth not who shall gather them
Prov 30. 4 who hath gathered the wind in his fists?
Eccl. 2. 26 giveth travail, to gather and to heap up
Isa. 10. 14 as one gathereth eggs..have I gathered
17. 5 when the harvest man gathereth the corn
Jer. 10. 17 Gather up thy wares out of the land
40. 10 gather ye wine, and summer fruits, and
40. 12 gathered wine and summer fruits very
Eze. 24. 4 Gather the pieces thereof into it..every
Joel 1. 14 gather the elders..all the inhabitants of
2. 16 Gather the people..gather the children
Hab. 1. 9 they shall gather the captivity as the sand
1. 15 and gather them in their drag: therefore
2. 5 but gathereth unto him all nations, and
Zeph. 3. 8 to gather the nations, that I may assem.
3. 18 I will gather (them that are) sorrowful
Zech. 14. 2 For I will gather all nations against Jer.

3. *To gather,* אָסַף *asaph,* 3.
Isa. 62. 9 they that have gathered it shall eat it
Jer. 9. 22 as the handful..none shall gather (them)

4. *Gathering,* אֹסֶף *oseph.*
Mic. 7. 1 as when they have gathered the summer

5. *To pluck,* אָרָה *arah.*
Song 5. 1 I have gathered my myrrh with my spice

6. *To take the spoil,* בָּזַז *bazaz.*
2 Ch. 20. 25 they were three days in gathering of the

7. *To cut off,* בָּצַר *batsar.*
Lev. 25. 5 neither gather the grapes of thy vine un.
25. 11 nor gather..in it of thy vine undressed
Deut 24. 21 When thou gatherest the grapes of thy
Judg. 9. 27 they went out into the fields, and gathe.

8. *To hatch, brood,* דָּגַר *dagar.*
Isa. 34. 15 and hatch, and gather under her shadow

9. *To heap up,* כָּנַס *kanas.*
Neh. 12. 44 to gather into them, out of the fields of
Psa. 33. 7 He gathereth the waters of the sea
Eccl. 2. 8 I gathered me also silver and gold, and

10. *To heap up,* כָּנַס *kanas,* 3.
Eze. 22. 21 Yea, I will gather you, and blow upon
39. 28 I have gathered them unto their own la.

11. *To glean,* לָקַט *laqat.*
Gen. 31. 46 Jacob said..Gather stones; and they took
Exod 16. 4 and gather a certain rate every day, that
16. 5 it shall be twice as much as they gather
16. 16 Gather of it every man according to his
16. 17 the children of Israel did so, and gathered
16. 18 they gathered every man according to
16. 21 And they gathered it every morning
16. 22 on the sixth day they gathered twice as
16. 26 Six days ye shall gather it; but on the
16. 27 went..on the seventh day for to gather
Num 11. 8 gathered (it), and ground (it) in mills, or
Psa. 104. 28 (That) thou givest them they gather
Song 6. 2 My beloved is gone down..to gather lilies

12. *To glean,* לָקַט *laqat,* 3.
Lev. 19. 9 neither shalt thou gather the gleanings of
19. 10 neither shalt thou gather (every) grape of
23. 22 neither shalt thou gather any gleaning
Judg. 1. 7 kings..gathered (their meat) under my
2 Ki. 4. 39 one went out into the field to gather herbs
4. 39 and gathered thereof wild gourds his lap
Isa. 17. 5 it shall be as he that gathereth ears in the
Jer. 7. 18 The children gather wood, and the fathers

13. *To glean,* לָקַשׁ *laqash,* 3.
Job 24. 6 they gather the vintage of the wicked

14. *To fill in,* מָלֵא *male.*
Jer. 51. 11 gather the shields: the LORD hath raised

15. *To pour out,* נָתַךְ *nathak,* 5.
2 Ki. 22. 9 Thy servants have gathered the money

16. *To cause to flee,* עוּז *uz,* 5.
Exod. 9. 19 Send therefore now..gather thy cattle

17. *To do, make,* עָשָׂה *asah.*
1 Sa 14. 48 he gathered an host, and smote the A.

18. *To heap up,* צָבַר *tsabar.*
Gen. 41. 49 Joseph gathered corn as the sand of the

19. *To cry or call together,* צָעַק *tsaaq,* 2.
2 Ki. 3. 21 they gathered all that were able to put

20. *To gather, assemble, collect,* קָבַץ *qabats.*
Gen 41. 35 let them gather all the food of those good
Deut 13. 16 thou shalt gather all the spoil of it into
1 Sa. 7. 5 Samuel said, Gather all Israel to Mizpeh
2 Sa. 3. 21 will gather all Israel unto my Lord the k.
1 Ki. 11. 24 he gathered men unto him, and became
18. 19 gather to me all Israel unto mount Carmel
2 Ki. 6. 24 Ben-hadad..gathered all his host, and
2 Ch. 15. 9 And he gathered all Judah and Benjamin
23. 2 gathered the Levites out of all the cities
24. 5 gather of all Israel money to repair the
Psa. 41. 6 his heart gathereth iniquity to itself
Prov 13. 11 he that gathereth by labour shall increase
Eze. 22. 19 I will gather you into the midst of Jeru.
22. 20 so will I gather (you) in mine anger and

21. *To gather, assemble, collect,* קָבַץ *qabats,* 3.
Deut 30. 3 and gather thee from all the nations
30. 4 thence will the LORD thy God gather thee
Neh. 1. 9 (yet) will I gather them from thence, and
Psa. 106. 47 and gather us from among the heathen
107. 3 gathered them out of the lands, from the
Prov 28. 8 he shall gather it for him that will pity
Isa. 34. 16 and his spirit it hath gathered them
40. 11 he shall gather the lambs with his arm
43. 5 I will..gather thee from the west
54. 7 but with great mercies will I gather thee
56. 8 The Lord GOD which gathereth the outc.
56. 8 Yet will I gather..to him, besides those
66. 18 that I will gather all nations and tongues
Jer. 23. 3 I will gather the remnant of my flock out
29. 14 I will gather you from all the nations, and
31. 8 I will..gather them from the coasts of
31. 10 He that scattered Israel will gather him
32. 37 I will gather them out of all countries
Eze. 11. 17 I will even gather you from the people
16. 37 therefore I will gather all thy lovers, with
16. 37 I will even gather them round about ag.
20. 34 I will..gather you out of the countries
20. 41 when I..gather you out of the countries
28. 25 When I shall have gathered the house of
29. 13 At the end of forty years will I gather the
34. 13 I will..gather them from the countries
36. 24 I will..gather you out of all countries
37. 21 I will..gather them on every side, and
39. 27 gathered them out of their enemies'
Hos. 8. 10 now will I gather them, and they shall
Joel 2. 6 pained; all faces shall gather blackness
3. 2 I will also gather all nations, and will
Mic. 1. 7 for she gathered (it) of the hire of an ha.
2. 12 I will surely gather the remnant of Israel
4. 6 I will gather her that is driven out
4. 12 he shall gather them as the sheaves into
Nah. 2. 10 and the faces of them all gather blackness
3. 18 people is scattered..and no man gathere.
Zeph. 3. 19 I will..gather her that was driven out
3. 20 even in the time that I gather you: for
Zech 10. 8 I will hiss for them, and gather them; for
10. 10 I will..gather them out of Assyria; and

22. *To cause to congregate, convene,* קָהַל *qahal,* 5.
Num 16. 19 Korah gathered all the congregation aga.
Deut 31. 28 Gather unto me all the elders of your tri.
2 Ch. 11. 1 he gathered of the house of Judah and B.
Eze. 38. 13 hast thou gathered thy company to take

23. *To gather,* קָשַׁשׁ *qashash,* 3a.
Exod 5. 7 let them go and gather straw for them.
5. 12 scattered..to gather stubble instead of
Num 15. 32 they found a man that gathered sticks

24. *To acquire, gain,* רָכַשׁ *rakash.*
Gen. 12. 5 all their substance that they had gath.

25. *To lead together also,* ἐπισυνάγω *episunagō.*
Matt. 23. 37 even as a hen gathereth her chickens

26. *To lay together,* συλλέγω *sullegō.*
Matt. 7. 16 Do men gather grapes of thorns, or figs
13. 40 As therefore the tares are gathered and
13. 41 they shall gather out of his kingdom all
13. 48 gathered the good into vessels, but cast
Luke 6. 44 For of thorns men do not gather figs, nor

27. *To lead together,* συνάγω *sunagō.*
Matt. 3. 12 and gather his wheat into the garner; but
6. 26 neither do they reap, nor gather into bar.
12. 30 he that gathereth not with me scattereth
13. 30 but gather the wheat into my barn
13. 47 unto a net, that..gathered of every kind
25. 24 gathering where thou hast not strawed
25. 26 and gather where I have not strawed
27. 27 and gathered unto him the whole band
Mark 5. 21 much people gathered unto him: and he
Luke 3. 17 and will gather the wheat into his garner
11. 23 he that gathereth not with me scattereth
John 4. 36 and gathereth fruit unto life eternal
11. 47 Then gathered the chief priests and the
15. 6 men gather them, and cast..into the fire
Rev. 16. 14 to gather them to the battle of that great

28. *To roll or twist together,* συστρέφω *sustrephō.*
Acts 28. 3 when Paul had gathered a bundle of sticks

29. *To gather in ripe fruit,* τρυγάω *trugaō.*
Luke 6. 44 nor of a bramble bush gather they grapes
Rev. 14. 18 gather the clusters of the vine of the earth
14. 19 and gathered the vine of the earth, and

30. *To cause to come together, infer,* συμβιβάζω.
Acts 16. 10 assuredly gathering that the Lord had

GATHER in, to —

To gather together or up, אָסַף *asaph.*
Exod 23. 16 when thou hast gathered in thy labours
Lev. 23. 39 when ye have gathered in the fruit of the
25. 20 we shall not sow, nor gather in our incre.
Deut 11. 14 that thou mayest gather in thy corn, and
16. 13 after that thou hast gathered in thy corn
28. 38 and shalt gather..little in; for the locust

GATHER out (stones), to —

To cast out stones, סָקַל *saqal,* 3.
Isa. 5. 2 he fenced it, and gathered out the stones
62. 10 gather out the stones; lift up a standard

GATHER self in troops, to —

To gather self together, גָּדַד *gadad,* 7a.
Mic. 5. 1 Now gather thyself in troops, O daughter

GATHER selves, to —

1. *To gather together or up,* אָסַף *asaph.*
2 Sa. 10. 15 the Syrians..gathered themselves together
Eze. 39. 17 gather yourselves on every side to my

2. *To be met by appointment,* יָעַד *yaad,* 2.
Num 10. 4 then the princes..shall gather themselves

3. *To fill or set self,* מָלֵא *male,* 7.
Job 16. 10 they have gathered themselves together

4. *To cause to flee, strengthen self, hasten,* עוּז *uz,* 5.
Jer. 6. 1 gather yourselves to flee out of the midst

5. *To be gathered, assembled,* קָבַץ *qabats,* 2.
1 Ch. 11. 1 Then all Israel gathered themselves to D.
13. 2 that they may gather themselves unto us

6. *To press, gather or assemble self,* קָבַץ *qabats,* 7.
Josh. 9. 2 they gathered themselves together, to
1 Sa. 22. 2 gathered themselves unto him; and he

GATHER selves to flee, to —

To cause to flee, strengthen self, hasten, עוּז *uz,* 5.
Isa. 10. 31 inhabitants..gather themselves to flee

GATHER selves together, to —

1. *To be gathered,* אָסַף *asaph,* 2.
Gen. 34. 30 they shall gather themselves together
49. 1 Gather yourselves together, that I may
Exod 32. 26 the sons of Levi gathered themselves tog.
Josh. 10. 5 five kings..gathered themselves together
Judg 20. 14 children of Benj. gathered themselv. tog.
1 Sa. 13. 5 gathered themselves together to fight
13. 11 gathered themselves together at Michm.
1 Ch. 19. 7 of Ammon gathered themselves together
2 Ch. 30. 3 the people gathered themselves together
Ezra 3. 1 gathered themselves together as one man
Neh. 8. 1 the people gathered themselves together
12. 28 the singers gathered themselves together
Psa. 35. 15 and gathered themselves together
35. 15 the abjects gathered themselves together
104. 22 they gather themselves together, and lay

2. *To gather together, decree,* גָּדַר *gadad.*
Psa. 94. 21 They gather themselves together against

3. *To assemble,* גּוּר *gur.*
Psa. 56. 6 They gather themselves together, they

4. *To be met by appointment,* יָעַד *yaad,* 2.
Num 27. 3 of them that gathered themselves together

5. *To be cried or called together,* צָעַק *tsaaq,* 2.
Judg. 7. 23, 24 the men..gathered themselves togeth.
12. 1 gathered themselves together, and went

6. *To be pressed together, gathered,* קָבַץ *qabats,* 2.
Gen. 49. 2 Gather yourselves together, and hear
1 Sa. 28. 4 gathered themselves together, and came
2 Ch. 15. 10 So they gathered themselves together at
20. 4 Judah gathered themselves together, to
Ezra 10. 7 should gather themselves together unto
10. 9 gathered themselves together unto Jerus.
Isa. 49. 18 all these gather themselves together
60. 4 all they gather themselves together, they
Joel 3. 11 gather yourselves together round about

7. *To press (or gather) self together,* קָבַץ *qabats,* 7.
1 Sa. 8. 4 gathered themselves together, and came
2 Sa. 2. 25 gathered themselves together after Abner

8. *To be congregated,* קָהַל *qahal,* 2.
Exod32. 1 the people gathered themselves together
Num16. 3 they gathered themselves together against
20. 2 they gathered themselves together against
Josh 22. 12 gathered themselves together at Shiloh
Esth. 8. 11; 9. 2; 9. 15; 9. 16.

9. *To be led or brought together,* συνάγομαι *sunago.*
Mark 6. 30 gathered themselves together, Rev. 19. 17.

10. *To gather self together,* קָשַׁשׁ *qashash,* 7a.
Zeph. 2. 1 Gather yourselves together..O nation not

GATHER the grape thereof, to —

To make common, חָלַל *chalal,* 3.
Deut28. 30 and shalt not gather the grapes thereof

GATHER together, to —

1. *To gather together or up,* אָסַף *asaph.*
Gen. 29. 22 Laban gathered together all the men of
Exod. 3. 16 Go, and gather the elders of Israel toget.
4. 29 gathered together all the elders of the
Num21. 16 Gather the people together, and I will
21. 23 Sihon gathered all his people together
Judg. 9. 6 all the men of Shechem gathered together
11. 20 but Sihon gathered all his people together
16. 23 lords of the Philistines gathered them to.
1 Sa. 5. 11 and gathered together all the lords of
17. 1 the Philistines gathered together their ar.
2 Sa. 10. 17 he gathered all Israel together, and pas.
12. 28 gather the rest of the people together
12. 29 David gathered all the people together
1 Ki.10. 26 Solomon gathered together chariots and
1 Ch.23. 2 he gathered together all the princes of I.
2 Ch.28. 24 Ahaz gathered together the vessels of the
29. 4 gathered them together into the east
34. 29 sent and gathered together all the elders
Psa. 50. 5 Gather my saints together unto me

2. *To assemble,* גּוּר *gur.*
Isa. 54. 15 they shall surely gather together..not
54. 15 whosoever shall gather together against

3. *To (cause to) cry or call together,* זָעַק *zaaq,* 5.
Judg. 4. 13 Sisera gathered together all his chariots

4. *To heap up, gather,* כָּנַס *kanas.*
1 Ch.22. 2 commanded to gather together the stra.
Esth. 4. 16 Go, gather together all the Jews (that are)
Eccl. 3. 5 and a time to gather stones together

5. *To heap up, gather,* כָּנַס *kanas,* 3.
Psa.147. 2 he gathereth together the outcasts of Is.

6. *To gather, heap up,* כְּנַשׁ *kenash.*
Dan. 3. 2 king sent to gather together the princes

7. *To fill in or up, complete,* מָלֵא *male,* 3.
Jer. 4. 5 gather together, and say, Assemble your.

8. *To draw away or out,* נָתַךְ *nathak,* 5.
2 Ch.34. 17 they have gathered together the money

9. *To heap up,* צָבַר *tsabar.*
Exod. 8. 14 they gathered them together upon heaps

10. *To press together, gather, assemble,* קָבַץ *qabats.*
Judg.12. 4 Jephthah gathered together all the men
1 Sa. 28. 1 gathered their armies together for warf.
28. 4 and Saul gathered all Israel together
29. 1 gathered together all their armies to A.
2 Sa. 2. 30 when he had gathered all the people tog.
1 Ki.18. 20 gathered the prophets together unto mo.
20. 1 Ben-hadad..gathered all his host togeth.
22. 6 gathered the prophets together, about
2 Ki.10. 18 Jehu gathered all the people together
2 Ch.18. 5 gathered together of prophets four hun.
24. 5 he gathered together the priests and the
25. 5 Amaziah gathered Judah together, and
32. 6 and gathered them together to him in
Ezra 7. 28 I gathered together out of Israel chief
8. 15 I gathered them together to the river
Neh. 7. 5 to gather together the nobles, and the ru.
Esth. 2. 3 that they may gather together all the

11. *To be gathered, assembled,* קָבַץ *qabats,* 2.
1 Sa. 7. 6 they gathered together to Mizpeh, and

12. *To press, gather or collect together,* קָבַץ *qabats,* 3.
1 Ch.16. 35 gather us together, and deliver us from
Neh.13. 11 I gathered them together, and set them
Isa. 11. 12 gather together the dispersed of Judah
22. 9 ye gathered together the waters of the

13. *To press or gather self together,* קָבַץ *qabats,* 7.
Jer. 49. 14 Gather ye together, and come against

14. *To cause to congregate, convene,* קָהַל *qahal,* 5.
Exod35. 1 gathered all the congregation..together
Lev. 8. 3 gather thou all the congregation together
Num. 8. 9 shalt gather the whole assembly..toget.
20. 8 gather thou the assembly together, thou
20. 10 gathered the congregation together before
Deut. 4. 10 Gather me the people together, and I will
31. 12 Gather the people together, men, and
1 Ch.13. 5 So David gathered all Israel together
15. 3 And David gathered all Israel together
Job 11. 10 If he cut off..or gather together, then

15. *To gather,* קָשַׁשׁ *qashash.*
Zeph. 2. 1 gather together, O nation not desired

16. *To cause to hear, summon,* שָׁמַע *shamea,* 3.
1 Sa. 15. 4 Saul gathered the people together, and

17. *To lead or bring together,* ἐπισυνάγω *episunagō.*
Matt.24. 31 they shall gather together his Mt. 23. 37.
Mark 1. 33 all the city was gathered together at the
Mark13. 27 shall gather together his elect from the
Luke12. 1 when there were gathered together an
13. 34 gathered thy children together, as a hen

18. *To lay together,* συλλέγω *sullegō.*
Matt.13. 30 Gather ye together first the tares, and

19. *To lead together,* συνάγω *sunagō.*
Matt. 2. 4 gathered all the chief priests..together, he
22. 10 gathered together all as many as they
25. 32 before him shall be gathered all 22. 34.
Mark 4. 1 there was gathered unto him a great
6. 30 the apostles gathered themselves toget.
Luke15. 13 the younger son gathered all together
John 6. 13 Therefore they gathered..together, and
11. 52 but that also he should gather together
Acts 14. 27 and had gathered the church together
15. 30 they had gathered the multitude togeth.
Rev. 16. 16 he gathered them together into a place
20. 8 nations..to gather them together to bat.

20. *To crowd or assemble together,* συναθροίζω *sun.*
Luke24. 33 and found the eleven [gathered together]
Acts 12. 12 where many were gathered together pr.

21. *To add, increase, continue,* יָסַף *yasaph,* 5.
2 Sa. 6. 1 David gathered together all (the) chosen

GATHER together in one, to —

To make up under one head, ἀνακεφαλαιόομαι.
Eph. 1. 10 he might gather together in one all

GATHER up, to —

1. *To gather together or up,* אָסַף *asaph.*
Gen. 49. 33 he gathered up his feet into the bed

2. *To glean, gather,* לָקַט *laqat,* 3.
Gen. 47. 14 Joseph gathered up all the money that
1 Sa. 20. 38 Jonathan's lad gathered up the arrows

3. *To press or gather together,* קָבַץ *qabats.*
Gen. 41. 48 he gathered up all the food of the seven

4. *To press, gather or collect together,* קָבַץ *qabats,* 3.
Jer. 49. 5 none shall gather up him that wandereth
Hos. 9. 6 Egypt shall gather them up, Memphis

5. *To lay together,* συλλέγω *sullegō.*
Matt.13. 28 Wilt thou then that we..gather them up?
13. 29 Nay; lest, while ye gather up the tares

6. *To lead together,* συνάγω *sunagō.*
John 6. 12 Gather up the fragments that remain

GATHERED, to be —

1. *To be gathered (together or up,)* אָסַף *asaph,* 2.
Gen. 25. 8 Then Abraham..was gathered to his
25. 17 Ishmael..was gathered unto his people
29. 3 And thither were all the flocks gathered
35. 29 Isaac..died, and was gathered unto his
49. 29 I am to be gathered unto my people
49. 33 Jacob..was gathered unto his people
Num20. 24 Aaron shall be gathered unto his people
20. 26 Aaron shall be gathered..and shall die
27. 13 thou also shalt be gathered unto thy pe.
27. 13 as Aaron thy brother was gathered
31. 2 afterward shalt thou be gathered unto
Deut32. 50 die..and be gathered unto thy people
32. 50 as Aaron..was gathered unto his people
Judg. 2. 10 all..were gathered unto their fathers
6. 33 the children of the east were gathered
20. 11 So all the men of Israel were gathered
2 Sa. 17. 11 I counsel that all Israel be..gathered
2 Ki.22. 20 thou shalt be gathered into thy grave in
2 Ch.34. 28 thou shalt be gathered to thy grave in
Job 27. 19 The rich man..shall not be gathered: he
Prov27. 25 and herbs of the mountains are gathered
Isa. 49. 5 Though Israel be not gathered, yet shall
Jer. 8. 2 they shall not be gathered, nor be buried
25. 33 they shall not be..gathered, nor buried
Mic. 4. 11 many nations are gathered against thee

2. *To be gathered (together or up),* אָסַף *asaph,* 4.
Isa. 24. 22 And they shall be gathered together
33. 4 your spoil shall be gathered..the gather.
Eze. 38. 12 the people..gathered out of the nations
Hos. 10. 10 the people shall be gathered against them

3. *To assemble,* גּוּר *gur.*
Psa. 59. 3 the mighty are gathered against me; not
140. 2 continually are they gathered together

4. *To be cried or called together,* זָעַק *zaaq,* 2.
Judg. 6. 34 and Abi-ezer was gathered after him
6. 35 Manasseh; who also was gathered after

5. *To be gleaned, gathered,* לָקַט *laqat,* 4.
Isa. 27. 12 ye shall be gathered one by one, O ye ch.

6. *To gather self together,* לָקַט *laqat,* 7.
Judg. 11. 3 there were gathered vain men to Jeph.

7. *To press, gather, assemble,* קָבַץ *qabats.*
Neh. 5. 16 all my servants..gathered thither unto

8. *To be pressed, gathered, assembled,* קָבַץ *qabats,* 2.
2 Ch.13. 7 And there are gathered unto him vain
Isa. 34. 15 there shall the vultures also be gathered
56. 8 beside those that are gathered unto him
Jer. 40. 15 that all the Jews which are gathered unto
Eze. 29. 5 shalt not be brought together, nor gath.

9. *To be pressed, gathered or assembled,* קָבַץ *qabats,* 4.
Eze. 38. 8 gathered out of many people, against

10. *To be congregated,* קָהַל *qahal,* 2.
Num16. 42 the congregation was gathered against
Jer. 26. 9 all the people were gathered against Je.

11. *To be gathered or bound together,* קָוָה *qavah,* 2.
Jer. 3. 17 all the nations shall be gathered unto it

GATHERED together, to be —

1. *To be gathered,* אָסַף *asaph,* 2.
Gen. 29. 7 that the cattle should be gathered toget.
29. 8 until all the flocks be gathered together
Lev. 26. 25 when ye are gathered together within
Num11. 22 shall all the fish of the sea be gathered t.
1 Sa. 17. 1 and were gathered together at Shochoh
17. 2 Saul and..Israel were gathered together
2 Sa. 23. 9 were there gathered together to battle
23. 11 were gathered together into a troop
1 Ch.11. 13 there the Philistines were gathered toge.
2 Ch.12. 5 princes..that were gathered together to
Neh. 8. 13 on the second day were gathered togeth
Psa. 47. 9 princes of the people are gathered toget.
Isa. 13. 4 of the kingdoms of nations gathered tog.
Zech.12. 3 though all the people..be gathered toge.

2. *To be gathered,* אָסַף *asaph,* 4.
Zech.14. 14 the wealth..shall be gathered together

3. *To gather self together,* אָסַף *asaph,* 7.
Deut33. 5 the tribes of Israel were gathered toget.

4. *To be cried or called together,* זָעַק *zaaq,* 2.
Judg18. 22 the men..were gathered together, and

5. *To be met together by appointment,* יָעַד *yaad,* 2.
Num14. 35 that are gathered together against me
16. 11 all thy company (are) gathered together

6. *To be heaped up, gathered together,* כְּנַשׁ *kenash,* 4
Dan. 3. 3 were gathered together unto the dedica.
3. 27 And the princes..being gathered togeth.

7. *To be added, joined together,* סָפַח *saphach,* 4.
Job 30. 7 under the nettles they were gathered to.

8. *To be heaped together,* עָרַם *aram,* 2.
Exod15. 8 the waters were gathered together, the

9. *To be cried or called together,* צָעַק *tsaaq,* 2.
Judg10. 17 the children of Ammon were gathered t.

10. *To be gathered, assembled,* קָבַץ *qabats,* 2.
Josh.10. 6 all the kings..are gathered together aga.
1 Sa. 25. 1 all the Israelites were gathered together
2 Ch.32. 4 there was gathered much people together
Esth. 2. 8 when many maidens were gathered toge.
2. 19 when the virgins were gathered together
Psa.102. 22 When the people are gathered together
Isa. 43. 9 Let all the nations be gathered together
60. 7 the flocks of Kedar shall be gathered to.
Hos. 1. 11 the children of Israel be gathered toget.

11. *To press self together,* קָבַץ *qabats,* 7.
Judg. 9. 47 that all the men..were gathered togeth.
1 Sa. 7. 7 were gathered together to Mizpeh, the
Isa. 44. 11 let them all be gathered together, let

12. *To be congregated,* קָהַל *qahal,* 2.
Lev. 8. 4 the assembly was gathered together unto
Judg.20. 1 the congregation was gathered together

13. *To be gathered, bound together,* קָוָה *qavah,* 2.
Gen. 1. 9 Let the waters..be gathered together

14. As No. 12 [V.L. קלה].
2 Sa. 20. 14 they were gathered together, and went

15. *To lead together,* συνάγω *sunagō.*
Matt13. 2 great multitudes were gathered together
18. 20 For where two or three are gathered tog.
22. 41 While the Pharisees were gathered tog.
24. 28 there will the eagles be gathered together
27. 17 when they were gathered together, Pilate
Mark 2. 2 many were gathered together, insomuch
Luke17. 37 thither will the eagles be [gathered toge.]
Acts 4. 6 were gathered together at Jerusalem
4. 26 the rulers were gathered together against
4. 27 the people of Israel, were gathered toge.
20. 8 chamber, where they were gathered toge.
1 Co. 5. 4 when ye are gathered together, and my
Rev. 19. 19 gathered together to make war against

16. *To go (or come) together,* σύνειμι *suneimi.*
Luke 8. 4 when much people were gathered together

GATHERED together, is to be —

To (cause to) congregate, convene, קָהַל *qahal,* 5.
Num 10. 7 the congregation is to be gathered toge.

GATHERED thick together, to be —

To throng or gather upon, ἐπαθροίζομαι *epathroiz.*
Luke11. 29 the people were gathered thick together

GATHERED up again, to be —

To be gathered, אָסַף *asaph,* 2.
2 Sa. 14. 14 water..which cannot be gathered up ag.

GATHERER —

To cultivate, gather, or seek out figs, בָּלַס *balas.*
Amos 7. 14 but I (was)..a gatherer of sycamore fruit

GATHERING —

1. *Gathering,* אֹסֶף *oseph.*
Isa. 32. 10 shall fail, the gathering shall not come
33. 4 gathered..the gathering of the caterpillar

2. *Obedience, expectation, hope,* יִקְּהָה *yiqqehah.*
Gen. 49. 10 and unto him..the gathering of the people

3. *To gather,* קָשַׁשׁ *qashash,* 3a.
Num 15. 33 And they that found him gathering sticks
1 Ki. 17. 10 the widow woman (was) there gathering
17. 12 and, behold, I (am) gathering two sticks

4. *Laying aside, collection,* λογία *logia.*
1 Co. 16. 2 that there be no gatherings when I come

GATHERING together —
1. *Collection,* מִקְוֶה *miqveh.*
Gen. 1. 10 the gathering together of the waters
2. *Leading together unto,* ἐπισυναγωγή *episunagōgē.*
2 Th. 2. 1 and (by) our gathering together unto him

GATH HE'-PHER, גַּת חֵפֶר *wine press of the well.*
A city of Zebulun, not far from Japhia (now called *Yafa*); the native place of the prophet Jonah, whose reputed tomb is shown at the village of *El-Meshhad* on the top of a hill, two miles E. of *Sufurieh.* It is called *Gittah-hepher,* in Josh. 19. 13.
2 Ki.14. 25 which he spake by..Jonah..of G. H.

GATH RIM'-MON, גַּת רִמּוֹן *wine press of Rimmon.*
1. A Levitical city of Dan on the plain of Philistia near Joppa.
Josh 19. 45 And Jehud, and Beneberak, and G.
2. A Levitical town of the half tribe of Manasseh W. of the Jordon. In 1 Ch. 6. 70, it is called *Bileam.*
Josh 21. 25 Taanach with her suburbs, and G. 21.24.
1 Ch. 6. 69 Aijalon with her suburbs, and G. with

GAY —
Bright, λαμπρός *lampros.*
Jas. 2. 3 to him that weareth the gay clothing

GA'-ZA, עַזָּה, Γάζα, *the strong place.*
1. One of the five chief cities of the Philistines, and still called *Ghuzzeh* or *Azzah.* Like Damascus it is remarkable for its existence from the remotest times. It is still a place of importance, and even yet larger than Jerusalem.
Gen. 10. 19 the border of the Canaanites was..unto G.
Josh.10. 41 smote them from Kadesh-barnea..unto G.
11. 22 only in G...and in Ashdod, there rema.
15. 47 G. with her towns and her villages
Judg. 1. 18 Also Judah took G. with the coast thereof
16. 1 Then went Samson to G., and saw there
16. 21 the Philistines..brought him down to G.
1 Sa. 6. 17 trespass offering unto the LORD..for G.
2 Ki 18. 8 He smote the Philistines..unto G.
Jer. 47. 1 that came..before that Pharoah smote G.
47. 5 Baldness is come upon G.; Ashkelon is
Amos 1. 6 For three transgressions of G...I will not
1. 7 I will send a fire on the wall of G., which
Zeph. 2. 4 G. shall be forsaken, and Ashkelon a des
Zech. 9. 5 G. also..and be..sorrowful; and Ekron
9. 5 the king shall perish from G., and Ashk.
Acts 8. 26 that goeth down from Jerusalem unto G.
2. A city of Ephraim.
Judg. 6. 4 increase of..earth, till thou come unto G.
1 Ch. 7. 28 Shechem also and the towns..unto G.

GAZ'-ZAM, גַּזָּם *devourer, swaggerer.*
The sons of Gazzam were among the families of the Nethinim who returned from the exile with Zerubbabel. B.C. 536.
Ezra 2. 48 children of Nekoda, the children of G.
Neh. 7. 51 The children of G., the children of Uzza

GA-ZA-THITES, GA-ZITES, עַזָּתִים.
The inhabitants of Gaza or Azzah.
Josh.13. 3 five lords of the Philistines; the G., and
Judg 16. 2 (And it was told) the G., saying, Samson

GAZE, to —
1. *To see, look, behold,* רָאָה *raah.*
Exod 19. 21 lest they break through..to gaze, and
2. *To look into,* ἐμβλέπω *emblepō.*
Acts 1. 11 why stand ye gazing up into heaven? this

GA'-ZER, גָּזֶר *precipice.* See GEZER.
The difference in the orthography arises from the Hebrew accent being here attended to, though neglected in other places where the same form occurs.
2 Sa. 5. 25 smote..from Geba until thou come to G.
1 Ch. 14. 16 smote..Philistines from Gibeon..to G.

GA'-ZEZ, גָּזֵז *shearer.*
1. A son of Caleb by Ephah his concubine. B.C. 1520.
1 Ch. 2. 46 Ephah..bare Haran, and Moza, and G.
2. Grandson of Caleb son of Jephunneh. B.C. 1500.
1 Ch. 2. 46 bare Haran..and Haran begat G.

GAZING stock —
Sight, appearance, רֳאִי *roi.*
Nah. 3. 6 And I..will set thee as a gazing stock

GAZING stock, to make a —
To make a spectacle, θεατρίζω *theatrizō.*
Heb. 10. 33 whilst ye were made a gazing stock both

GE'-BA, גֶּבַע, Γαβαά, *height, hill.*
A Levitical city of Benjamin. In the cities along the N. boundary the name is given as *Gaba* (a change due to the emphasis in Hebrew before a pause), and the same change occurs in Ezra 2. 26; Neh. 7. 30 and 11. 31; 2 Sa. 5. 25; 2 Ki. 23. 8; the last three of these being in the Common Version *Geba.* In one place the name Geba is used as the northern landmark of the kingdom of Judah and Benjamin, in the expression "from Geba to Benjamin" (2 Ki. 23. 8.); and also as an eastern limit to Gazer (2 Sa. 5. 25).
Josh 21. 17 Gibeon with her suburbs, G. with her
1 Sa. 13. 3 the garrison of the Philistines..in G.
2 Sa. 5. 25 and smote the Philistines from G...to
1 Ki. 15. 22 king Asa built with them G. of Benjamin
2 Ki. 23. 8 the priests had burnt incense, from G.
1 Ch. 6. 60 out of the tribe of Benjamin; G.
1 Ch. 8. 6 of the fathers of the inhabitants of G.
2 Ch. 16. 6 and he built therewith G. and Mizpah
Neh. 11. 31 The children also of Benjamin from G.
12. 29 out of the fields of G. and Azmaveth
Isa. 10. 29 they have taken up their lodging at G.
Zech 14. 10 a plain from G. to Rimmon south of Jer.

GE'-BAL, גְּבַל *border, hilly.*
1. The city Bibylus, between Beirut and Tripolis.
Eze. 27. 9 The ancients of G...were in thee thy
2 A district between the S. end of the Salt Sea and Petra, inhabited by Edom [גְּבָל].
Psa. 83. 7 G., and Ammon, and Amalek; the Phili.

GE'-BER, גֶּבֶר *strong.*
1. "The son of Geber," who had charge of Havoth-Jair and the district of Argob for Solomon. B.C. 1014.
1 Ki. 4. 13 The son of G., in Ramoth-gilead; to him
2. Geber, the son of Uri, had "the land of Gilead," a district S. of the former—the country originally possessed by Sihon and Og—probably the modern *Belka,* the great pasture lands of the tribes E. of the Jordan.
1 Ki. 4. 19 G. the son of Uri..in the country of Gil.

GE'-BIM, גֵּבִים *springs, cisterns, ditches.*
A city of Benjamin, between Anathoth and the ridge on which Nob was situated. Compare *Gob.*
Isa. 10. 31 the inhabitants of G. gather themselves

GE-DAL'-IAH, גְּדַלְיָהוּ, גְּדַלְיָה *Jah is great.*
1. Son of Ahikam and grandson of Shaphan king Josiah's secretary. After the destruction of the temple (B.C. 588) Nebuchadnezzar left Gedaliah with a Chaldæan guard at Mizpeh, six miles N. of Jerusalem, to govern the vine-dressers and husbandmen left in the land.
2 Ki. 25. 22 over them he made G. the son of Ahikam
25. 23 the king of Babylon had made G. gover.
25. 23 there came to G. to Mizpah, even Ish.
25. 24 G. sware to them, and to their men, and
25. 25 Ishmael the son of Nethaniah..smote G.
Jer. 39. 14 Even they sent..committed him unto G.
40. 5 Go back also to G. the son of Ahikam
40. 6 Then went Jeremiah unto G. the son of
40. 7 the king of Babylon had made G...gover.
40. 8 Then they came to G. to Mizpah, even Is.
40. 9 And G. the son of Ahikam..sware unto
40. 11 he had set over them G. the son of Ahi.
40. 12 Jews..came to the land of Judah, to G.
40. 13 and all the captains..came to G. to M.
40. 14 But G. the son of Ahikam believed them
40. 15 Then Johanan..spake to G. in Mizpah
40. 16 But G. the son of Ahikam said unto Jo.
41. 1 Ishmael..came unto G. the son of Ahi.
41. 2 Then arose Ishmael..and smote G. the son
41. 3 also slew all the Jews that were..with G.
41. 4 And it came to pass..after he had slain G.
41. 6 he said..Come to G. the son of Ahikam
41. 9 the men, whom he had slain because of G.
41. 10 Nebuzar-adan..had committed to G.
41. 16 after (that) he had slain G. the son of A.
41. 18 because Ishmael..had slain G. the son
43. 6 every person..Nebuzar-adan..left with G.
2. A Levite, one of the six sons of Jeduthun.
1 Ch.25. 3 the sons of Jeduthun; G., and Zeri, and
25. 9 the second to G., who with his brethren
3. A priest that had taken a strange wife in the exile. B.C. 456.
Ezra 10. 18 Maaseiah, and Eliezer, and Jarib, and G.
4. Grandfather of Zephaniah the prophet. B.C. 700.
Zeph. 1. 1 Cushi, the son of G., the son of Amariah
5. A prince who caused Jeremiah to be imprisoned. B.C. 590.
Jer. 38. 1 G. the son of Pashur..heard the words

GE-DE'-ON, Γεδεών, *Greek form of the Heb. Gideon.*
Heb. 11. 32 for the time would fail me to tell of G.

GE'-DER, גֶּדֶר *walled.*
A royal city of the Canaanites taken by Joshua. It was on the W. of the Jordan, in the extreme S. It was not the same as *Gedor* which was between Hebron and Bethlehem; nor was it *Gederah* in the low country; but may be the *Gedor* named in 1 Ch. 4. 39, in connection with the Simeonites.
Josh.12. 13 king of Debir, one; the king of G., one

GE-DE'-RAH, הַגְּדֵרָה *sheep cote.*
A city in the lowlands of Judah.
Josh.15. 36 Sharaim, and Adithaim, and G., and Ged.

GE-DE-RA-THITE, גְּדֵרָתִי. *Inhabitant of Gederah.*
1 Ch.12. 4 Jahaziel, and Johanan, and Jozabad the G.

GE-DE-RITE, גְּדֵרִי. *An inhabitant of Geder.*
1 Ch.27. 28 in the low plains..Baal-hanan the G

GE-DE-ROTH, גְּדֵרוֹת *sheepcotes.*
A town in the lowlands of Judah.
Josh.15. 41 G., Beth-dagon, and Naamah, and Mak.
2 Ch.28. 18 G., and Shocho with the villages thereof

GE-DE-RO-THA-IM, גְּדֵרֹתַיִם *two sheepfolds.*
A town in the pastureland of Judah.
Josh.15. 36 Sha., and Adhitaim, and Gederah, and G.

GE'-DOR, גְּדוֹר, גְּדֹר.
1. A city in the mountainous part of Judah a few miles N. of Hebron. It is now called *Jedûr,* and half-way between Bethlehem and Hebron; but the *Gœdur* of Eusebius is more likely, and is ten miles S. of Diospolis (now called *Lûdd*).
Josh.15. 58 Halhul, Beth-zur, and G.
2. The town of Jeroham whose sons were among the mighty men of Benjamin who joined David at Ziklag.
1 Ch.12. 7 Joelah, and Zeb the sons of Jeroham of G.
3. The son of Jehiel father of Gibeon, and an ancestor of Saul. B.C. 1100.
1 Ch. 8. 31 And G., and Ahio, and Zacher
9. 37 G., and Ahio, and Zechariah, and Mikloth
4. This name occurs twice in the genealogies of Judah,—in the former *Penuel* is called the father of Gedor, and in the latter *Jered* is in the same relation. In the Targum both these names (with others) are given to Moses by Jehudijah, who is identified with the daughter of Pharaoh.
1 Ch. 4. 4 Penuel the father of G., and Ezer the fa.
4. 18 Jehudijah bare Jered the father of G.
5. A place in the tribe of Simeon, in the extreme S. of Judah, and different from that named under No. 1. It was between the S. of Judah and Mount Seir, *i.e.* Petra.
1 Ch. 4. 39 And they went to the entrance of G.

GE-HA'-ZI, גֵּיחֲזִי *denier, diminisher.*
The servant of the prophet Elisha. B.C. 894.
2 Ki. 4. 12 And he said to G. his servant, Call this
4. 14 G. answered, Verily she hath no child
4. 25 to G. his servant, Behold..that Shuna.
4. 27 but G. came near to thrust her away
4. 29 Then he said to G., Gird up thy loins
4. 31 G. passed on before them, and laid the
4. 36 he called G., and said, Call this Shunam.
5. 20 G., the servant of Elisha the man of God
5. 21 So G. followed after Naaman
5. 25 And Elisha said unto him, Whence..G.?
8. 4 the king talked with G., the servant of the
8. 5 G. said..O king, this (is) the woman, and

GE-LI'-LOTH, גְּלִילוֹת *circles.*
A place named among the points marking the S. boundary line of Benjamin. This boundary went from Enshemesh towards Geliloth over against the ascent of Adummin. In Josh. 15. 7, Gilgal is substituted for Geliloth.
Josh 18. 17 G., which (is) over against the going up of

GE-MAL'-LI, גְּמַלִּי *camel owner.*
A Danite, father of Ammiel, ruler of his tribe, and one of the twelve men sent out to explore the land. B.C. 1490.
Num13. 12 Of the tribe of Dan, Ammiel the son of G.

GE-MAR'-IAH, גְּמַרְיָהוּ, גְּמַרְיָה.
1. Son of Shaphan and father of Micaiah. B.C. 599.
Jer. 36. 10 in the chamber of G. the son of Shaphan
36. 11 When Michaiah the son of G...had heard
36. 12 all the princes sat there, (even)..G., the
36. 25 G., had made intercession to the king that
2. Son of Hilkiah, sent (B.C. 597) by king Zedekiah as ambassador to Nebuchadnezzar, and the bearer of Jeremiah's letter to the captive Jews.
Jer. 29. 3 By the hand of..G. the son of Hilkiah

GENDER, to —
1. *To beget,* יָלַד *yalad.*
Job 38. 29 the hoary frost..who hath gendered it?
2. *To cause to pass through,* עָבַר *abar,* 3.
Job 21. 10 Their bull gendereth, and faileth not
3. *To beget,* γεννάω *gennaō.*
Gal. 4. 24 which gendereth to bondage, which is A.
2 Ti. 2. 23 knowing that they do gender strifes

GENDER, to let —
To cause to lie down, רָבַע *raba,* 5.
Lev. 19. 19 Thou shalt not let thy cattle gender with

GENEALOGIES —
Genealogy, γενεαλογία *genealogia.*
1 Ti. 1. 4 Neither give heed to..endless genealogies

GENEALOGIES, to be reckoned by —
To reckon by genealogy, יָחַשׂ *yachas.*
1 Ch. 5. 17 All these were reckoned by genealogies
9. 1 So all Israel were reckoned by genealo.

GENEALOGY —
1. *To be reckoned by genealogy,* יָחַשׂ *yachas,* 7.
1 Ch. 4. 33 These..their habitations, and their gene.
7. 5 reckoned in all by their genealogies four.
7. 7 were reckoned by their genealogies twenty
7. 9 after their genealogy by their generations
7. 40 the number throughout the genealogy of
2 Ch. 12. 15 written in the book..concerning genea.?
31. 16 Beside their genealogy of males, from
31. 17 Both to the genealogy of the priests by
31. 18 And to the genealogy of all their little
31. 19 to all that were reckoned by genealogies
Ezra 2. 62 those that were reckoned by genealogy
8. 1 the genealogy of them that went up with
Neh. 7. 64 those that were reckoned by genealogy
2. *Genealogy,* יַחַשׂ *yachas.*
Neh. 7. 5 I found a register of the genealogy of
3. *Genealogy,* γενεαλογία *genealogia.*
Titus 3. 9 But avoid..genealogies, and contention

GENEALOGY, to be reckoned —
To be reckoned by genealogy, יָחַשׂ *yachas,* 7.
1 Ch. 5. 1 the genealogy is not to be reckoned afte.
5. 7 families, when the genealogy..was reck
9. 22 These were reckoned by their genealogy in
Ezra 8. 3 were reckoned by genealogy of the males
Neh. 7. 5 that they might be reckoned by genea.

GENERAL —
Prince, head, chief, captain, שַׂר *sar.*
1 Ch. 27. 34 the general of the king's army (was) J.

GENERALLY —
To be gathered, אָסַף *asaph,* 2.
2 Sa. 17. 11 Israel be generally gathered unto thee

GENERATION —
1. *Circle, generation,* דּוֹר *dor.*
Gen. 6. 9 a just man (and) perfect in his generations
7. 1 righteous before me in this generation
9. 12 which I make..for perpetual generations
15. 16 But in the fourth generation they shall
17. 7, 9 thy seed after thee in their generations
17. 12 every man child in your generations, he
Exod. 1. 6 And Joseph died..and all that generation
3. 15 this (is) my memorial unto all generations
12. 14 a feast..throughout your generations
12. 17 observe this day in your generations by
12. 42 to be observed..in their generations
16. 32, 33 an omer..to be kept for your genera.
17. 16 war with Amalek from generation to gen.
27. 21 a statute for ever unto their generations
29. 42 offering throughout your generations, (at)
30. 8 perpetual incense..throughout your gen.
30. 10 atonement..throughout your generations
30. 21 to his seed throughout their generations
30. 31 oil unto me throughout your generations
31. 13 a sign..throughout your generations; that
31. 16 observe the sabbath throughout their ge.
40. 15 priesthood throughout their generations
Lev. 3. 17 a perpetual statute for your generations
6. 18 a statute for ever in your generations
7. 36 for ever throughout their generations
10. 9 a statute..throughout your generations
17. 7 unto them throughout their generations
21. 17 thy seed in their generations that hath
22. 3 of all your seed among your generations
23. 14, 31 for ever throughout your generations
23. 21 a statute..throughout your generations
23. 41 a statute for ever in your generations: ye
23. 43 That your generations may know that I
24. 3 a statute for ever in your generations
25. 30 established..throughout his generations
Num 10. 8 ordinance for ever throughout your gen.
15. 14 whosoever (be) among you in your gener.
15. 15 an ordinance for ever in your generations
15. 21 an heave offering in your generations
15. 23 henceforward among your generations
15. 38 fringes..throughout their generations
18. 23 for ever throughout your generations
32. 13 forty years, until all the generation, that
35. 29 unto you throughout your generations
Deut. 1. 35 not one of these men of this evil genera.
2. 14 until all the generation of the men of war
7. 9 keepeth covenant..to a thousand genera.
23. 2 even to his tenth generation shall he not
23. 3 even to their tenth generation shall they
23. 8 children..shall enter..in their third gen.
29. 22 So that the generation to come..shall say
32. 5 a perverse and crooked generation
32. 7 consider the years of many generations
32. 20 for they (are) a very froward generation
Josh 22. 27 our generations after us, that we might
22. 28 say..to our generations in time to come
Judg. 2. 10 all that generation were gathered unto
2. 10 and there arose another generation after
3. 2 Only that the generations..might know
1 Ch. 16. 15 he commanded to a thousand generations
Esth. 9. 28 and kept throughout every generation
Job 42. 16 lived Job..and saw..(even) four genera.
Psa. 12. 7 preserve them from this generation for
14. 5 God (is) in the generation of the righteous
22. 30 it shall be accounted..for a generation
24. 6 the generation of them that seek him
33. 11 the thoughts of his heart to all genera.
45. 17 name to be remembered in all generations
48. 13 ye may tell (it) to the generation follow.
49. 11 their dwelling places to all generations
49. 19 He shall go to the generation of his fath.
61. 6 wilt prolong..his years as many genera.
71. 18 showed thy strength unto (this) genera.
72. 5 They shall fear thee..throughout all gen.
73. 15 I should offend (against) the generation
78. 4 showing to the generation to come the
78. 6 That the generation to come might know
78. 8 rebellious generation; a generation (that)
79. 13 show forth thy praise to all generations
85. 5 draw out thine anger to all generations?
89. 1 make known thy faithfulness to all gen.
89. 4 build up thy throne to all generations
90. 1 been our dwelling place in all generations
95. 10 long was I grieved with (this) generation
100. 5 and his truth (endureth) to all generations
102. 12 and thy remembrance unto all generations
102. 18 be written for the generation to come
102. 24 thy years (are) throughout all generations
105. 8 he commanded to a thousand generations
106. 31 for righteousness unto all generations for
109. 13 in the generation following let their name
112. 2 the generation of the upright shall be
119. 90 Thy faithfulness (is) unto all generations
135. 13 thy memorial..throughout all generations
145. 4 One generation shall praise thy works to
145. 13 dominion (endureth) throughout all gen.
146. 10 The LORD shall reign..unto all genera.
Prov 27. 24 doth the crown (endure) to every gener.?
30. 11 a generation (that) curseth their father
30. 12 generation (that are) pure in their own
30. 13 a generation, O how lofty are their eyes!
30. 14 a generation, whose teeth (are as) swords
Eccl. 1. 4 generation passeth away, and..generation
Isa. 13. 20 dwelt in from generation to generation
34. 10 from generation to generation it shall lie
34. 17 from generation to generation shall they
41. 4 calling the generations from the beginn.?
51. 8 my salvation from generation to genera.
51. 9 awake, as in the ancient days, in the gen.
53. 8 and who shall declare his generation?
58. 12 shalt raise up the foundations of many g.
60. 15 I will make thee..a joy of many genera.?
61. 4 repair..the desolations of many generat.
Jer. 2. 31 O generation, see ye the word of the LORD
7. 29 and forsaken the generation of his wrath
50. 39 dwelt in from generation to generation
Lam. 5. 19 thy throne from generation to generation
Joel 1. 3 and their children another generation
2. 2 any more..to the years of many generat.
3. 20 Jerusalem from generation to generation

2. *Circle, generation,* דָּר *dar.*
Dan. 4. 3 his dominion (is) from generation to gen.
4. 34 his kingdom (is) from generation to gene.

3. *Generation,* γενεά *genea.*
Matt. 1. 17 all the generations..(are) fourteen gene.
1. 17 into Babylon (are) fourteen generations
1. 17 unto Christ (are) fourteen generations
11. 16 whereunto shall I liken this generation?
12. 39 An evil..generation seeketh after a sign
12. 41 shall rise in judgment with this generat.
12. 42 rise up in the judgment with this gener.
12. 45 Even so..also unto this wicked generation
16. 4 A wicked and adulterous generation seek.
17. 17 O faithless and perverse generation, how
23. 36 All..shall come upon this generation
24. 34 This generation shall not pass, till all
Mark 8. 12 Why doth this generation seek after a sign?
8. 12 There shall no sign be given unto this ge.
8. 38 in this adulterous and sinful generation
9. 19 O faithless generation, how long shall I
13. 30 this generation shall not pass, till all
Luke 1. 48 henceforth all generations shall call me
7. 31 shall I liken the men of this generation?
9. 41 O faithless and perverse generation, how
11. 29 This is an evil generation: they seek a
11. 30 so shall..the Son of man be to this gene.
11. 31 rise up..with the men of this generation
11. 32 rise up in the judgment with this gener.
11. 50 blood..may be required of this generat.
11. 51 It shall be required of this generation
16. 8 are in their generation wiser than the
17. 25 first must he..be rejected of this genera.
21. 32 This generation shall not pass away
Acts 2. 40 Save yourselves from this..generation
8. 33 and who shall declare his generation?
13. 36 David, after he had served his own gen.
Col. 1. 26 mystery..hid from ages and from genera.
Heb. 3. 10 I was grieved with that generation, and

4. *Birth, origin,* γένεσις *genesis.*
Matt. 1. 1 The book of the generation of Jesus Chr.

5. *Progeny, produce,* γέννημα *gennēma.*
Matt. 3. 7 O generation of vipers, who hath warned
12. 34 O generation of vipers, how can ye, being
23. 33 serpents..generation of vipers, how can
Luke 3. 7 O generation of vipers, who hath warned

6. *Race, kind,* γένος *genos.*
1 Pe. 2. 9 But ye..a chosen generation, a royal

GENERATION to generation, from —
To generations of generations, εἰς γενεὰς γενεῶν.
Luke 1. 50 that fear him [from generation to gener.]

GENERATIONS —
Generations, births, תּוֹלְדוֹת *toledoth.*
Gen. 2. 4 These (are) the generations of the heav.
5. 1 This (is) the book of the generations of
6. 9 These (are) the generations of Noah: No.
10. 1 the generations of the sons of Noah
10. 32 after their generations, in their nations
11. 10 These (are) the generations of Shem
11. 27 Now these (are) the generations of Terah
25. 12 Now these (are) the generations of Ishm.
25. 13 by their names, according to their gener.
25. 19 And these (are) the generations of Isaac
36. 1 Now these (are) the generations of Esau
36. 9 these (are) the generations of Esau the
37. 2 These (are) the generations of Jacob
Exod. 6. 16 the names..according to their generati.
6. 19 the families..according to their generat.
Num. 1. 20 by their generations, after their families
[So in v. 22, 24, 26, 28, 30, 32, 34, 36, 38, 40.]
1. 42 throughout their generations, after their
3. 1 These also (are) the generations of Aaron
Ruth 4. 18 Now these (are) the generations of Pharez
1 Ch. 1. 29 These (are) their generations: The first b.
5. 7 when the genealogy of their generations
7. 2 valiant men of might in their generations
7. 4 And with them, by their generations
7. 9 after their genealogy by their generations
8. 28 heads of the fathers, by their generations
9. 9 their brethren, according to their gener.
9. 34 These..(were) chief throughout their ge.
26. 31 chief..according to the generations of

GEN-NE-SA'-RET, (Sea of), Γεννησαρέτ.
In the Old Testament it is called the "Sea of Chinnereth *or* Cinneroth," from a town of that name on its shore. It is also called the "Sea of Galilee," and the "Lake *or* Sea of Tiberias."
Matt 14. 34 gone over, they came into the land of [G.]
Mark 6. 53 they came into the land of G., and drew
Luke 5. 1 came to pass..he stood by the lake of G.

GENTILE —
1. *Nation, a collective body,* גּוֹי *goi.*
Gen. 10. 5 By these were the isles of the Gentiles
Judg. 4. 2 which dwelt in Harosheth of the Gentiles
4. 13 from Harosheth of the Gentiles unto the
4. 16 pursued..unto Harosheth of the Gentiles
Isa. 11. 10 to it shall the Gentiles seek: and his rest
42. 1 he shall bring forth judgment to the Ge.
42. 6 and give thee..for a light of the Gentiles
49. 6 I will also give thee for a light to the G.
49. 22 I will lift up mine hand to the Gentiles
54. 3 and thy seed shall inherit the Gentiles
60. 3 And the Gentiles shall come to thy light
60. 5 forces of the Gentiles shall come unto
60. 11 may bring unto thee the forces of the G.
60. 16 Thou shalt..suck the milk of the Gentil.
61. 6 ye shall eat the riches of the Gentiles
61. 9 their seed shall be known among the Ge.
62. 2 the Gentiles shall see thy righteousness
66. 12 the glory of the Gentiles like a flowing
66. 19 shall declare my glory among the Gentil.
Jer. 4. 7 the destroyer of the Gentiles is on his
14. 22 Are there..among the vanities of the Ge.
16. 19 the Gentiles shall come unto thee from
46. 1 The word of the LORD..against the Gen.
Lam. 2. 9 her princes (are) among the Gentiles: the
Eze. 4. 13 eat their defiled bread among the Genti.
Hos. 8. 8 now shall they be among the Gentiles as
Joel 3. 9 Proclaim ye this among the Gentiles
Mic. 5. 8 the remnant..shall be among the Gent.
Zech. 1. 21 to cast out the horns of the Gentiles
Mal. 1. 11 my name (shall be) great among the Ge.

2. *Nation,* ἔθνος *ethnos.*
Matt. 4. 15 beyond Jordan, Galilee of the Gentiles
6. 32 For after all these things do the Gentiles
10. 5 Go not into the way of the Gentiles, and
10. 18 a testimony against them and the Genti.
12. 18 he shall show judgment to the Gentiles
12. 21 And in his name shall the Gentiles trust
20. 19 shall deliver him to the Gentiles to mock
20. 25 Ye know that the princes of the Gentiles
Mark 10. 33 and shall deliver him to the Gentiles
10. 42 are accounted to rule over the Gentiles
Luke 2. 32 A light to lighten the Gentiles, and the
18. 32 For he shall be delivered unto the Genti.
21. 24 shall be trodden down of the Gentiles
21. 24 until the times of the Gentiles be fulfilled
22. 25 The kings of the Gentiles exercise lords.
Acts 4. 27 Herod, and Pontius Pilate, with the Ge.
7. 45 into the possession of the Gentiles, whom
9. 15 to bear my name before the Gentiles, and
10. 45 because that on the Gentiles also was po.
11. 1 heard that the Gentiles had also received
11. 18 Then hath God also to the Gentiles gran.
13. 42 [the Gentiles] besought that these words
13. 46 first..to you..lo, we turn to the Gentiles
13. 47 I have set thee to be a light of the Gen.
13. 48 when the Gentiles heard this, they were
14. 2 the unbelieving Jews stirred up the Gen.
14. 5 was an assault made both of the Gentiles
14. 27 opened the door of faith unto the Gentil.
15. 3 declaring the conversion of the Gentiles
15. 7 that the Gentiles..should hear the word
15. 12 God had wrought among the Gentiles by
15. 14 how God at the first did visit the Gentiles
15. 17 all the Gentiles, upon whom my name is
15. 19 which from among the Gentiles are tur.
15. 23 unto the brethren which are of the Gen.
18. 6 from henceforth I will go unto the Gent.
21. 11 shall deliver..into the hands of the Ge.
21. 19 what..God had wrought among the Gen.
21. 21 the Jews which are among the Gentiles
21. 25 As touching the Gentiles which believe
22. 21 I will send thee far hence unto the Gen.
26. 17 Delivering thee from..the Gentiles, unto
26. 20 to the Gentiles, that they should repent
26. 23 and should show light..to the Gentiles
28. 28 the salvation of God is sent unto the Ge.
Rom. 1. 13 among you also, even as among other G.
2. 14 For when the Gentiles, which have not
2. 24 God is blasphemed among the Gentiles
3. 29 not also of the Gentiles? Yes, of the G.
9. 24 not of the Jews only, but also of the Ge.?
9. 30 That the Gentiles, which followed not
11. 11 salvation (is come) unto the Gentiles, for
11. 12 of them the riches of the Gentiles how
11. 13 For I speak to you Gentiles, inasmuch as
11. 13 as I am the apostle of the Gentiles, I
11. 25 until the fulness of the Gentiles be come
15. 9 that the Gentiles might glorify God for
15. 9 I will confess to thee among the Gentiles
15. 10 saith, Rejoice, ye Gentiles, with his peo.
15. 11 Praise the Lord, all ye Gentiles; and
15. 12 he that shall rise to reign over the Gent.
15. 12 in him shall the Gentiles trust
15. 16 the minister of Jesus Christ to the Gent.
15. 16 that the offering up of the Gentiles might
15. 18 to make the Gentiles obedient, by word
15. 27 if the Gentiles have been made partakers
16. 4 also all the churches of the Gentiles
1 Co. 5. 1 is not so much as named among the Ge.
10. 20 that the things which [the Gentiles] sac.
12. 2 Ye know that ye were Gentiles, carried
Gal. 2. 2 gospel which I preach among the Genti.
2. 8 was mighty in me toward the Gentiles
2. 12 For before..he did eat with the Gentiles
2. 14 why compellest thou the Gentiles to live
2. 15 Jews by nature, and not sinners of the G.
3. 14 the blessing..might come on the Gentiles
Eph. 2. 11 in time past Gentiles in the flesh, who
3. 1 the prisoner of Jesus Christ for you Gen.

Eph. 3. 6 That the Gentiles should be fellow heirs
3. 8 that I should preach among the Gentiles
4. 17 that ye henceforth walk not as other G.
Col. 1. 27 glory of this mystery among the Gentiles
1 Th. 2. 16 Forbidding us to speak to the Gentiles
4. 5 even as the Gentiles which know not God
1 Ti. 2. 7 teacher of the Gentiles in faith and veri.
3. 16 preached unto the Gentiles, believed on
2 Ti. 1. 11 I am appointed..a teacher of the Gentiles
4. 17 and..all the Gentiles might hear: and I
1 Pe. 2. 12 your conversation honest among the Ge.
4. 3 to have wrought the will of the Gentiles
3 John 7 went forth, taking nothing [of the Gen.]
Rev. 11. 2 for it is given unto the Gentiles: and

Hellenes, Greeks, Ἕλλην *Hellēn.*
John 7. 35 among the Gentiles, and teach the Gen.?
Rom. 2. 9 of the Jew first, and also of the Gentile
2. 10 to the Jew first, and also to the Gentile
3. 9 have before proved both Jews and Gen.
1 Co. 10. 32 Give none offence..to the Gentiles, nor
12. 13 whether..Jews or Gentiles, whether..b.

GENTILES, after the manner of —
In the manner of the nations, ἐθνικῶς *ethnikōs.*
Gal. 2. 14 If thou..livest after the manner of Gen.

GENTLE —
1. *Yielding, pliant,* ἐπιεικής *epieikēs.*
Titus 3. 2 gentle, showing all meekness unto all
Jas. 3. 17 gentle..easy to be entreated, full of
1 Pe. 2. 18 not only to the good and gentle, but also

2. *Gentle, mild,* ἤπιος *ēpios.*
1 Th. 2. 7 But we were [gentle] among you, even as
2 Ti. 2. 24 be gentle unto all..apt to teach, patient

GENTLENESS —
1. *To be humble,* עָנָה *anah.*
2 Sa. 22. 36 and thy gentleness hath made me great

2. *Humility,* עֲנָוָה, עַנְוָה *anavah, anvah.*
Psa. 18. 35 and thy gentleness hath made me great

3. *Gentleness, yielding,* ἐπιείκεια *epieikeia.*
2 Co. 10. 1 beseech you by the..gentleness of Christ

4. *Kindness, usefulness,* χρηστότης *chrēstotēs.*
Gal. 5. 22 the fruit of the spirit is..gentleness, go.

GENTLY —
Gently, לְאַט *leat.*
2 Sa. 18. 5 gently for my sake with the young man

GE-NU'-BATH, גְּנֻבַת.
Son of Hadad the Edomite by an Egyptian princess, the sister of Tahpenes the Queen of the Pharaoh who governed Egypt near the end of David's reign. B.C. 1000.
1 Ki. 11. 20 the sister of Tahpenes bare him G. his
11. 20 and G. was in Pharaoh's household among

GE'-RA, גֵּרָא *enmity.*
A son of Bela. The text of 1 Ch. 8. 3 is corrupt, and the different Geras there named may be reduced to one, the son of Bela. The Gera of Judges 3. 15, as the ancestor of Ehud, and in 2 Sa. 16. 5 as the ancestor of Shimei, is probably also this same person. B.C. 1650.
Gen. 46. 21 the sons of Benjamin.. G., and Naaman
Judg. 3. 15 a deliverer, Ehud the son of G., a Benja.
2 Sa. 16. 5 whose name (was) Shemei, the son of G.
19. 16 Shimei the son of G., a Benjamite, which
19. 18 Shimei the son of G. fell down before the
1 Ki. 2. 8 behold..with thee Shimei the son of G.
1 Ch. 8. 3 the sons of Bela were, Addar, and G., and
8. 5 And G., and Shephuphan, and Huram
8. 7 Naaman, and Ahiah, and G., he removed

GE'-RAH —
Gerah, a small coin, גֵּרָה *gerah.*
Exod. 30. 13 a shekel (is) twenty gerahs: an half she.
Lev. 27. 25 shekel..twenty gerahs shall be the shekel
Num. 3. 47 shekel..the shekel (is) twenty gerahs
18. 16 after the shekel..which (is) twenty gerahs
Eze. 45. 12 And the shekel (shall be) twenty gerahs

GE'-RAR, גְּרָר *circle.*
An ancient city S. of Gaza, probably the birthplace of Isaac. *Joorf-el-Gerar*, as now existing, is three hours S.S.E. of Gaza, and limits the northern boundary of the territory, if not the actual site of the town. The *Wady-el-Ain*, is perhaps the site of the ancient *Gerar* where the wells were digged by Abraham and reopened by Isaac (Gen. 26. 18 22.)
Gen. 10. 19 from Sidon, as thou comest to G., unto
20. 1 Abraham journeyed..and sojourned in G.
20. 2 Abimelech king of G. sent, and took S.
26. 1 And Isaac went unto Abimelech..unto G.
26. 6 And Isaac dwelt in G.
26. 17 Isaac..pitched his tent in the valley of G.
26. 20 the herdmen of G. did strive with Isaac's
26. 26 Then Abimelech went to him from G.
2 Ch. 14. 13 Asa and the people..pursued them unto G.
14. 14 they smote all the cities round about G.

GER-GE-SEN'-ES, Γεργεσηνοί.
The inhabitants of a district S.E. of the Lake of Tiberias. In some MSS. the reading is Gadarenoi
Matt. 8. 28 he was come..into the country of the [G.]

GE-RI'-ZIM, גְּרִזִּים *waste places.*
A mountain of the Gerizzites, or dwellers in a "shorn" land ("a desert"), possibly the tribe subdued by David. In conjunction with Mount Ebal it was the scene of a great solemnity upon the entrance of Israel into Canaan.
Deut. 11. 29 shalt put the blessing upon mount G.
27. 12 These shall stand upon mount G. to bless
Josh. 8. 33 half of them over against mount G., and
Judg. 9. 7 he went and stood in the top of mount G.

GER'-SHOM, גֵּרְשֹׁם *a stranger there.*
1. First born son of Moses and Zipporah. B.C. 1500.
Exod. 2. 22 bare..a son, and he called his name G.
18. 3 sons; of which the name of the one...G.
1 Ch. 23. 15 The sons of Moses..G., and Eliezer
23. 16 Of the sons of G., Shebuel (was) the chief
26. 24 the son of G... (was) ruler of the treasures

2. Gershom eldest son of Levi. B.C. 1700.
1 Ch. 6. 16 The sons of Levi; G., Kohath, and Merari
6. 17 these (be) the names of the sons of G.; L.
6. 20 Of G.; Libni his son, Jahath his son
6. 43 son of Jahath, the son of G., the son of
6. 62 And to the sons of G...thirteen cities
6. 71 Unto the sons of G...out of the family of
15. 7 Of the sons of G.; Joel the chief, and his

3. One of the family of Phinehas. B.C. 536.
Ezra. 8. 2 Of the sons of Phinehas; G.: of the sons

4. Father of Jonathan, a Levite that became priest to the Danites that settled at Laish in the time of the Judges.
Judg. 18. 30 Jonathan, the son of G...he and his sons

GER'-SHON, גֵּרְשׁוֹן.
Another form of Gershom, son of Levi, found in the following passages:—
Gen. 46. 11 the sons of Levi; G., Kohath, and Mera.
Exod. 6. 16 G., and Kohath, and Merari: and the
6. 17 sons of G.; Libni, and Shimi, according
Num. 3. 17 sons of Levi..G., and Kohath, and Mera.
3. 18 these (are) the names of the sons of G.
3. 21 Of G...the family of the Libnites, and the
3. 25 And the charge of the sons of G. in the
4. 22 Take also the sum of the sons of G.
4. 28 This (is) the service..of the sons of G. 4. 41.
4. 38 those that were numbered of the sons of G.
7. 7 four oxen he gave unto the sons of G.
10. 17 the sons of G. and the sons of Merari
26. 57 of G., the family of the Gershonites: of
Josh. 21. 6 the children of G. (had) by lot..thirteen
1 Ch. 6. 1 The sons of Levi; G., Kohath, and Mer.
23. 6 the sons of Levi, (namely), G., Kohath

GER-SHON-ITES, גֵּרְשֻׁנִּי.
Patronymic of the descendants of Gershon son of Levi.
Num. 3. 21 Shimites: these (are) the families of the G.
3. 23 The families of the G. shall pitch behind
3. 24 the chief..of the G...Eliasaph the son of
4. 24 the service of the families of the G.
4. 27 be all the service of the sons of the G.
26. 57 family of the G.: of Kohath, the family
Josh. 21. 33 All the cities of the G...(were) thirteen
1 Ch. 23. 7 Of the G. (were), Laadan, and Shimei
26. 21 the sons of the G. Laadan..(were) Jehieli
26. 21 chief fathers, (even) of Laadan the G.
29. 8 treasure..by the hand of Jehiel the G.
2 Ch. 29. 12 of the G.; Joah the son of Zimmah

GE'-SHAM, גֵּישָׁן (*prop. Geshan*), *firm, strong.*
A son of Jahdai of the family of Caleb. B.C. 1470.
1 Ch. 2. 47 Regem, and Jotham, and G., and Pelat

GE'-SHEM, גֶּשֶׁם *corporealness.*
An Arabian who with others opposed Nehemiah. B.C. 445.
Neh. 2. 19 But when..G. the Arabian, heard (it)
6. 1 G. the Arabian..heard that I had builded
6. 2 That Sanballat and G. sent unto me, say.

GE'-SHUR, גְּשׁוּר *bridge-land.*
A kingdom in the N.E. of Bashan adjoining Argob and Aram, and on the eastern slope of Hermon.
2 Sa. 3. 3 Maacah the daughter of Talmai king of G.
13. 37 But Absalom fled..to Talmai..king of G.
13. 38 So Absalom fled, and went to G., and
14. 23 So Joab arose and went to G., and brou.
14. 32 to say, Wherefore am I come from G.?
15. 8 thy servant vowed..while I abode at G.
1 Ch. 2. 23 he took G., and Aram, with the towns of
3. 2 Maachah the daughter of Talmai k. of G.

GE-SHU'-RI and GESHURITES, גְּשׁוּרִי.
1. The inhabitants of Geshur.
Deut. 3. 14 took all the country..unto the coasts of G.
Josh. 12. 5 And reigned..unto the border of the G.
13. 11 Gilead, and the border of the G. and Ma.
13. 13 the children of Israel expelled not the G.
13. 13 but the G...dwell among the Israelites

2. A tribe dwelling between Arabia and Philistia.
Josh. 13. 2 the borders of the Philistines, and all G.
1 Sa. 27. 8 David and his men..invaded the G., and

GET (into), to—
1. *To come or go in,* בּוֹא *bo.*
Gen. 45. 17 and go, get you into the land of Canaan
1 Sa. 22. 5 depart, and get thee into the land of Ju.
2 Sa. 19. 3 the people gat them by stealth that day
1 Ki. 1. 13 Go and get thee in unto king David, and
2 Ki. 7. 12 catch them alive, and get into the city
Isa. 22. 15 Go, get thee unto this treasurer..unto S.
47. 5 Sit thou silent, and get thee into dark.
Eze. 3. 4 go, get thee unto the house of Israel, and
3. 11 go, get thee to them of the captivity, unto

2. *To cause to come,* בּוֹא *bo,* 5.
Lam. 5. 9 We gat our bread with..our lives because

3. *To cut off, gain dishonestly,* בָּצַע *batsa.*
Eze. 22. 27 to destroy souls, to get dishonest gain

4. *To seek,* בָּקַשׁ *baqash,* 3.
Eccl. 3. 6 A time to get, and a time to lose; a time

5. *To go on,* יָלַךְ *yalak.*
Gen. 12. 1 Get thee out of thy country, and from
22. 2 and get thee into; Ex. 5. 4, 7. 15, 10. 28.
Num. 22. 13 Get you into your land; for the LORD
Josh. 2. 16 Get you to the mountain, lest the pursu.
22. 4 return ye, and get you into; Judg. 19. 28.
2 Sa. 4. 7 and gat them away through; 2 Sa. 17. 23.
1 Ki. 2. 26 Get thee to Anathoth, unto thine own fi.
14. 12 Arise thou therefore, get thee to thine
17. 3 Get thee hence, and turn thee eastward
17. 9 Arise, get thee to Zarephath, which
2 Ki. 3. 13 get thee to the prophets of thy father
Jer. 5. 5 I will get me unto the great men, and

6. *To take, receive,* לָקַח *laqach.*
Gen. 34. 4 Shechem spake..Get me this damsel to
Exod. 5. 11 Go ye, get you straw where ye can find it
Judg. 14. 2 now therefore get her for me to wife
14. 3 Get her for me; for she pleaseth me well
Prov. 9. 7 He that reproveth a scorner getteth to
22. 25 Lest thou learn..and get a snare to thy

7. *To find,* מָצָא *matsa.*
Num. 31. 50 what every man hath gotten, of jewels of
2 Sa. 20. 6 lest he get him fenced cities, and escape us
Job 31. 25 and because mine hand had gotten much
Prov. 6. 33 A wound and dishonour shall he get; and

8. *To move (off),* נוּד *nud.*
Jer. 49. 30 Flee, get you far off, dwell deep, O ye in.

9. *To remove, journey,* נָסַע *nasa.*
Num. 14. 25 turn you, and get you into the wilderness

10. *To (cause to) reach, attain, overtake,* נָשַׂג *nasag,* 5.
Num. 6. 21 beside (that) that his hand shall get

11. *To do, make,* עָשָׂה *asah.*
Gen. 12. 5 the souls that they had gotten in Haran
31. 1 of..our father's hath he gotten all this
Deut. 8. 17 My power..hath gotten me this wealth
8. 18 he that giveth thee power to get wealth
2 Sa. 8. 13 David gat..a name when he returned fr.
Neh. 9. 10 So didst thou get thee a name, as (it is)
Eccl. 2. 8 I gat me men singers and women singers
Isa. 15. 7 Therefore the abundance they have got.
Jer. 17. 11 he that getteth riches, and not by right
48. 36 the riches..he hath gotten are perished
Eze. 28. 4 With..wisdom..thou hast gotten thee
28. 4 and hast gotten gold and silver into thy
38. 12 people..which have gotten cattle and
Dan. 9. 15 hast gotten thee renown, as at this day

12. *To cause to come out, bring out,* פּוּק *puq,* 5.
Prov. 3. 13 and the man (that) getteth understanding

13. *To get, obtain,* קָנָה *qanah.*
Gen. 4. 1 said, I have gotten a man from the LORD
Prov. 4. 5 Get wisdom, get understanding: forget
4. 7 get wisdom: and with all..get understa.
15. 32 he that heareth reproof getteth understa.
16. 16 How much better..to get wisdom than g.?
16. 16 to get understanding rather to be chosen
17. 16 a price in the hand of a fool to get wisd.
18. 15 The heart of the prudent getteth know.
19. 8 He that getteth wisdom loveth his own
Eccl. 2. 7 I got..servants and maidens, and had
Jer. 13. 1 Go, and get thee a linen girdle, and put
13. 2 So I got a girdle, according to the word of
13. 4 Take the girdle that thou hast got, which
19. 1 Go and get a potter's earthen bottle, and

14. *To acquire, gain,* רָכַשׁ *rakash.*
Gen. 31. 18 and all his goods which he had gotten
31. 18 which he had gotten in Padan-aram
36. 6 which he had got in the land of Canaan
46. 6 which they had gotten in the land of Ca.

15. *To place, set, put, appoint,* שׂוּם, שִׂים *sim, sum.*
Zeph. 3. 19 I will get them praise and fame in every

16. *To go up into,* ἐμβαίνω *embainō.*
Matt. 14. 22 to get into a ship, and to go before him
Mark 6. 45 constrained his disciples to get into the

17. *To go out or forth,* ἔξειμι *exeimi.*
Acts 27. 43 cast..first (into the sea), and get to land

18. *To begin to find,* εὑρίσκω *heuriskō.*
Luke 9. 12 that they may go..and get victuals: for
[*See also* Deceitfully, early, far, heat, possession, stealth, understanding, victory.]

GET, to be able to —
To cause to reach, attain, overtake, נָשַׂג *nasag,* 5.
Lev. 14. 22, 31 such as he is able to get..the one
14. 32 whose hand is not able to get..to his cle.

GET away, to —
1. *To go on,* יָלַךְ *yalak.*
1 Sa. 23. 26 David made haste to get away for fear of S.
26. 12 and they gat them away, and no man saw
2 Sa. 4. 7 gat them away through the plain all night

2. *To go out,* יָצָא *yatsa.*
Jer. 48. 9 unto Moab, that it may flee and get away

3. *To move (off),* נוּד *nud.*
Dan. 4. 14 let the beasts get away from under it

GET, can —
To cause to reach, attain, overtake, נָשַׂג *nasag,* 5.
Lev. 14. 21 if he (be) poor, and cannot get so much
14. 30 And he shall offer..such as he can get

GET down, to —
1. *To go down,* יָרַד *yarad.*
Gen. 42. 2 get you down thither, and buy for us
Exod19. 24 Away, get thee down, and thou shalt
32. 7 Go, get thee down; for thy people, which
Deut. 9. 12 Arise, get thee down quickly from hence
Judg. 7. 9 Arise, get thee down unto the host; for
Ruth 3. 3 anoint thee..and get thee down to the fl.
1 Sa. 15. 6 get you down from among the Amalekites
1 Ki. 18. 44 get thee down, that the rain stop thee n.
Joel 3. 13 come, get you down; for the press is full
2. *To go down,* καταβαίνω *katabainō.*
Acts 10. 20 Arise therefore, and get thee down, and

GET thee, to —
To go away or under, ὑπάγω *hupagō.*
Matt16. 23 Get thee behind me, Satan: thou art an
Mark 8. 33 Get thee behind me, Satan: for thou sa.
Luke 4. 8 [said..Get thee behind me, Satan]

GET forth, to —
To go out, יָצָא *yatsa.*
Exod12. 31 Rise up..get you forth from among my p.

GET hence, to —
1. *To go on,* יָלַךְ *yalak.*
Zech. 6. 7 Get you hence, walk to and fro through
2. *To go out,* יָצָא *yatsa.*
Isa. 30. 22 thou shalt say unto it, Get thee hence
3. *To go away or under,* ὑπάγω *hupagō.*
Matt. 4. 10 Get thee hence, Satan: for it is written

GET (him), to —
1. *To be gathered,* אָסַף *asaph,* 2.
Num 11. 30 Moses gat him into the camp, he and the
2. *To go on,* יָלַךְ *yalak.*
Judg 19. 28 man rose up, and gat him unto his place
2 Sa. 17. 23 arose, and gat him home to his house

GET hold upon, to —
To find, מָצָא *matsa.*
Psa. 116. 3 the pains of hell gat hold upon me: I fo.

GET honour, to —
To be or become honoured, weighty, כָּבֵד *kabed,* 2.
Exod14. 17 and I will get me honour upon Pharaoh
14. 18 when I have gotten me honour upon Ph.

GET more, to —
To add, יָסַף *yasaph,* 5.
Eccl. 1. 16 and have gotten more wisdom than all

GET (self back) again, to —
To turn back, שׁוּב *shub.*
Num22. 34 now therefore..I will get me back again
Deut. 5. 30 Go say..Get you into your tents again

GET (self) up, to —
1. *To ride,* רָכַב *rakab.*
2 Sa. 13. 29 every man gat him up upon his mule
2. *To be gone up,* רָמַם *ramam,* 2.
Num16. 45 Get you up from among this congregation

GET out, to —
1. *To go out,* יָצָא *yatsa.*
Gen. 19. 14 Up, get you out of this place; for the
31. 13 arise, get thee out from this land, and
Exod11. 8 Get thee out, and all the people that fol.
2. *To go out or forth,* ἐξέρχομαι *exerchomai.*
Luke13. 31 Get thee out, and depart hence: for H.
Acts 7. 3 Get thee out of thy country, and from
22. 18 Make haste, and get thee quickly out of

GET over, to —
To go over, עָבַר *abar.*
Deut. 2. 13 Now rise up..get you over the brook Z.

GET thee, to —
To go on, הָלַךְ *halak.*
1 Ki.14. 2 get thee to Shiloh: behold, there (is) A.

GET up, to —
1. *To touch, come upon, strike,* נָגַע *naga.*
2 Sa. 5. 8 Whosoever getteth up to the gutter, and
2. *To go up,* עָלָה *alah.*
Gen. 44. 17 as for you, get you up in peace unto your
Exod. 1. 10 fight..and..get them up out of the land
24. 18 Moses went..and gat him up into the m.
Num13. 17 Get you up this..southward, and go up
14. 40 gat them up into the top of the mount.
27. 12 Get thee up into this mount Abarim, and
Deut. 3. 27 Get thee up into the top of Pisgah, and
17. 8 get thee up into the place which the LORD
32. 49 Get thee up into this mountain Abarim
Josh.17. 15 get thee up to the wood..and cut down
Judg. 9. 48 Abimelech gat him up to mount Zalmon
9. 51 and gat them up to the top of the tower
1 Sa. 9. 13 Now therefore get you up; for about this
13. 15 Samuel arose, and gat him up from Gil.
24. 22 David and his men gat them up unto the h.
25. 5 Get you up to Carmel, and go to Nabal
1 Ki.12. 18 made speed to get him up to his chariot
18. 41 Get thee up, eat and drink; for..a sound
2 Ch.10. 18 made speed to get him up to (his) chariot
Isa. 40. 9 O Zion..get thee up into the high moun.
Jer. 46. 4 get up, ye horsemen, and stand forth
49. 31 Arise, get you up unto the wealthy nation
3. *To be gone up,* עָלָה *alah,* 2.
Num16. 24 Get you up from about the tabernacle of
16. 27 So they gat up from the tabernacle of K.

4. *To rise,* קוּם *qum.*
Josh. 7. 10 Get thee up; wherefore liest thou thus

GET (you) —
To turn aside, סוּר *sur.*
Isa. 30. 11 Get you out of the way, turn aside out

GE'-THER, גֶּתֶר.
The third in order of the sons of Aram, but in 1 Ch. 1. 17 reckoned among the sons of Shem. B.C. 2200.
Gen. 10. 23 And the children of Aram..G., and Ma.
1 Ch. 1. 17 Aram, and Uz, and Hul, and G., and M.

GETH-SE-MA'-NE, Γεθσημανῆ (*from Heb.*) *wine press and oil* (*farm*).
A place beyond the Kedron, at the foot of Olivet, to the N.W., and nearly a mile from the walls of Jerusalem. Attached to it was a garden or orchard.
Matt.26. 36 Then cometh Jesus..to a place called [G].
Mark14. 32 they came to a place which was named G.

GETTING —
1. *Acquisition,* פֹּעַל *poal.*
Prov.21. 6 The getting of treasures by a lying tong.
2. *Getting, obtaining,* קִנְיָן *qinyan.*
Gen. 31. 18 he carried away..the cattle of his getting
Prov. 4. 7 with all thy getting get understanding

GE-U'-EL, גְּאוּאֵל *God of salvation.*
A son of Machi, a prince of Gad, and one of those sent out to search the land. B.C. 1490.
Num.13. 15 Of the tribe of Gad, G. the son of Machi

GE'-ZER, גֶּזֶר *a precipice.*
An ancient city of Canaan whose king Horam or Elam was slain, with all his people, by Joshua and Israel. The town itself was not destroyed but formed one of the boundary marks of Ephraim on the W. limit of the tribe, and was allotted to the Kohathites. It was near lower Beth-horon and the sea, and is now called *Jimzu,* the ancient Gimzo, four miles N. of Nicopolis (*Amwâs*).
Josh 10. 33 Horam king of G. came up to help Lach.
12. 12 The king of Eglon, one; the king of G.
16. 3 unto the coast of Beth-horon..and to G.
16. 10 drave not out the Cana. that dwelt in G.
21. 21 they gave them..G. with her suburbs
Judg. 1. 29 drive out the Canaanites that dwelt in G.
1. 29 but the Canaanites dwelt in G. among
1 Ki. 9. 15 Jerusalem..Hazor, and Megiddo, and G.
9. 16 Pharaoh king of Egypt had..taken G.
9. 17 Solomon built G., and Beth-horon the
1 Ch. 6. 67 they gave unto them..G. with her sub.
7. 28 and westward G., with the towns thereof
20. 4 there arose war at G. with the Philistines

GEZRITES, גִּרְזִי, גִּזְרִי. *The inhabitants of Gezer.*
1 Sa. 27. 8 David and his men..invaded..the G.

GHOST — (*See also* Holy).
1. *Soul, animal breath,* נֶפֶשׁ *nephesh.*
Job 11. 20 their hope..the giving up of the ghost
Jer. 15. 9 she hath given up the ghost; her sun is
2. *Spirit,* πνεῦμα *pneuma.*
Matt27. 50 when he had cried..yielded up the ghost
John19. 30 he bowed his head, and gave up the ghost

GHOST, to give or yield up the —
1. *To gasp out, expire,* גָּוַע *gava.*
Gen. 25. 8 Abraham gave up the ghost, and died in
25. 17 Ishmael..gave up the ghost and died
35. 29 Isaac gave up the ghost, and died, and
49. 33 Jacob..yielded up the ghost, and was gat.
Job 3. 11 (why) did I (not) give up the ghost when
10. 18 Oh that I had given up the ghost, and no
13. 19 if I hold my tongue, I..give up the ghost
14. 10 man giveth up the ghost, and where (is)
Lam. 1. 19 mine elders gave up the ghost in the city
2. *To breathe out,* ἐκπνέω *ekpneō.*
Mark15. 37 And Jesus cried..and gave up the ghost
15. 39 that he so cried out, and gave up the g.
Luke23. 46 and having said thus, he gave up the gh.
3. *To breathe out, expire,* ἐκψύχω *ekpsuchō.*
Acts 5. 5 Ananias..fell down, and gave up the gh.
5. 10 yielded up the ghost: and the young
12. 23 was eaten of worms, and gave up the gh.

GI'-AH, גִּיחַ *waterfall, ravine or glen.*
A place on the way to the wilderness of Gibeon of Benjamin.
2 Sa. 2. 24 the hill of Ammah, that (lieth) before G.

GIANT —
1. *Mighty, strong one,* גִּבּוֹר *gibbor.*
Job 16. 14 He breaketh..runneth upon me like a g.
2. *Fearful one, giant,* רָפָא *rapha.*
Deut. 2. 11 Which also were accounted giants, as
2. 20 That also was accounted a land of giants
2. 20 giants dwelt therein in old time; and
3. 11 only Og..remained of the remnant of g.
3. 13 Bashan, which was called the land of gia.
Josh.12. 4 Og..of the remnant of the giants, that
13. 12 who remained of the remnant of the gia.
15. 8 the end of the valley of the giants north.
17. 15 land of the Perizzites and of the giants
18. 16 in the valley of the giants on the north
1 Ch 20. 4 Sippai..of the children of the giant
20. 6 he also was the son of the giant
20. 8 These were born unto the giant in Gath

3. *A fearful one, giant,* רָפָה *raphah.*
2 Sa. 21. 16 Ishbi-benob..of the sons of the giant
21. 18 Saph, which (was) of the sons of the giant
21. 20 and he also was born to the giant
21. 22 These four were born to the giant in Gath
4. *Fallen ones, fellers,* נְפִילִים *nephilim.*
Gen. 6. 4 There were giants in the earth in those
Num13. 33 And there we saw the giants, the
13. 33 sons of Anak, (which come) of the giants

GIB'-BAR, גִּבָּר *high, mighty.*
One who came up with Zerubbabel. B.C. 536.
Ezra 2. 20 The children of G., ninety and five

GIB-BE'-THON, גִּבְּתוֹן *height.*
A town of Dan given to the Kohathites.
Josh 19. 44 And Eltekeh, and G., and Baalath
21. 23 of the tribe of Dan..G. with her suburbs
1 Ki. 15. 27 and Baasha smote him at G., which
15. 27 for Nadab and all Israel laid siege to G.
16. 15 the people (were) encamped against G.
16. 17 Omri went up from G., and all Israel with

GIB'-EA, גִּבְעָא *highlander.*
Son of Sheva, a descendant of Judah. But perhaps the city Gibeah in Judah is meant.
1 Ch. 2. 49 Sheva..and the father of G.: and the da.

GIB'-EAH, GIB'-EATH, גִּבְעַת, גֶּבַע, גָּבַע, גִּבְעָה *height.*
A city in the mountains of Judah, now *el-Ful.*
Josh. 15. 57 Cain, G., and Timnah; ten cities with
18. 28 Jebusi, which (is) Jerusalem, G., (and) K.
Judg 19. 12 city..of Israel; we will pass over to G.
19. 13 draw near to one of these places..in G.
19. 14 the sun went down..by G., which
19. 15 turned aside..to go in..to lodge in G.
19. 16 and he sojourned in G.: but the men of
20. 4 I came into G. that (belongeth) to Benja.
20. 5 And the men of G. rose against me
20. 9 this..the thing which we will do to G.
20. 10 when they come to G. of Benjamin, acc.
20. 13 the children of Belial, which (are) in G.
20. 14 gathered..tog. out of the cities unto G.
20. 15 beside the inhabitants of G., which were
20. 19 children of Israel..encamped against G.
20. 20 put..in array to fight against them at G.
20. 21 children of Benjamin came forth out of G.
20. 25 Benjamin went forth..out of G. the sec.
20. 29 Israel set liers in wait round about G.
20. 30 and put themselves in array against G.
20. 31 and the other to G. in the field, about
20. 33 the liers..came..out of the meadows of G.
20. 34 there came against G. ten thousand
20. 36 the liers in wait..they had set beside G.
20. 37 liers in wait hasted, and rushed upon G.
20. 43 trode them down with ease over against G.
1 Sa. 10. 26 Saul also went home to G.; and there
11. 4 Then came the messengers to G. of Saul
13. 2 and a thousand were with Jonathan in G.
13. 15 and gat him up from Gilgal unto G.
13. 16 And Saul..abode in G. of Benjamin
14. 2 Saul tarried in the uttermost part of G.
14. 5 and the other southward over against G.
14. 16 watchmen of Saul in G. of Benjamin look.
15. 34 Saul went up to his house to G. of Saul
22. 6 Saul abode in G. under a tree in Ramah
23. 19 Then came up the Ziphites to Saul to G.
26. 1 And the Ziphites came unto Saul to G.
2 Sa. 6. 3, 4 the house of Abinadab that (was) in G.
21. 6 will hang them up unto the LORD in G.
23. 29 Ittai the son of Ribai out of G. of the
1 Ch.11. 31 Ithai the son of Ribai of G., (that pertai.)
2 Ch.13. 2 Michaiah the daughter of Uriel of G.
Isa. 10. 29 Ramah is afraid; G. of Saul is fled
Hos. 5. 8 Blow ye the cornet in G...the trumpet
9. 9 corrupted (themselves), as in the days of G.
10. 9 thou hast sinned from the days of G.
10. 9 the battle in G...did not overtake them

GIB-EA-THITE, גִּבְעָתִי. *An inhabitant of Gibeah.*
1 Ch.12. 3 then Joash, the sons of Shemaah the G.

GIB-E'-ON, גִּבְעוֹן *hill, height.*
One of the four cities of the Hivites that made a league with Joshua to escape the fate of Jericho and Ai. It was given to Benjamin and made a Levitical city. It is now called *El-Jib,* on the northern camel road from Jerusalem to Jaffa, and stands on the more northern of two mamelons, just at the spot where the road to the sea parts into two branches. The road passes to the N. of the base of the hill *El-Jib,* four miles from Bethel.
Josh. 9. 3 when the inhabitants of G. heard what J.
9. 17 Now their cities (were) G., and Chephirah
10. 1 the inhabitants of G. had made peace
10. 2 they feared greatly, because G. (was) a
10. 4 Come..and help me, that we may smite G.
10. 5 and all their hosts..encamped before G.
10. 6 the men of G. sent unto Joshua..saying
10. 10 slew them with a great slaughter at G.
10. 12 he said..Sun, stand thou still upon G.
10. 41 And Joshua smote them..even unto G.
11. 19 save the Hivites, the inhabitants of G.
18. 25 G., and Ramah, and Beeroth
21. 17 out of the tribe of Benjamin, G. with her
2 Sa. 2. 12 servants..went out from Mahanaim to G.
2. 13 went..and met together by the pool of G.
2. 16 was called Helkath-hazzurim..in G.
2. 24 Giah by the way of the wilderness of G.
3. 30 he had slain their brother Asahel at G.
20. 8 When..at the great stone which (is) in G.
1 Ki. 3. 4 the king went to G. to sacrifice there
3. 5 In G. the LORD appeared to Solomon in

1 Ki. 9. 2 time, as he had appeared unto him at G.
1 Ch. 8. 29 And at G. dwelt the father of G.; whose
9. 35 And in G. dwelt the father of G., Jehiel
14. 16 smote the host of the Philistines from G.
16. 39 tabernacle..in the high place..at G.
21. 29 For..at that season in the high place at G.
2 Ch. 1. 3 Solomon..went to the high place..at G.
1. 13 Solomon came (from)..the high pl...at G.
Neh. 3. 7 repaired..the men of G., and of Mizpah
7. 25 The children of G. ninety and five
Isa. 28. 21 he shall be wroth as (in) the valley of G.
Jer. 28. 1 Azur the prophet, which (was) of G.
41. 12 found him by the great waters..in G.
41. 16 eunuchs, whom he had brought..from G.

GIBEONITES, גִּבְעֹנִי. *The inhabitants of Gibeon.*
2 Sa. 21. 1 (It is) for Saul..because he slew the G.
21. 2 the king called the G., and said unto
21. 2 the G. (were) not of the children of Israel
21. 3 Wherefore David said unto the G., What
21. 4 the G. said unto him, We will have no sil.
21. 9 delivered them into the hands of the G.
1 Ch. 12. 4 Ismaiah the G., a mighty man among the
Neh. 3. 7 next unto them repaired Melatiah the G.

GIB-LITES, גִּבְלִי.
The inhabitants of Gebal or Bibylus, a city in Phœnicia, on the sea shore. In 1 Kings 5. 18, Hebrew *Giblite* is rendered in English stonesquarer. *See* Gebal.
Josh. 13. 5 the land of the G., and all Lebanon

GID-DAL'-TI, גִּדַּלְתִּי *I have magnified.*
One of the sons of Heman, "the king's seer," and hence a Kohathite. His office was, with thirteen of his brethren, to sound the horn in the service of the tabernacle. He had also charge of the twenty-second course. B.C. 1015.
1 Ch. 25. 4 Jerimoth, Hananiah, Hanani, Eliath., G.
25. 29 The two and twentieth to G., (he), his

GID'-DEL, גִּדֵּל *very great.*
1. One whose children came up with Zerubbabel. B.C. 536.
Ezra 2. 47 the children of G., the children of Gahar
Neh. 7. 49 children of Hanan, the children of G.
2. Sons of Giddel; were also among the servants of Solomon who came up in the same company with No. 1.
Ezra 2. 56 children of Darkon, the children of G.
Neh. 7. 58 children of Darkon, the children of G.

GID'-EON, גִּדְעוֹן *feller, hewer,* i.e. *great warrior.*
A son of Joash a Manassehite. He delivered Israel from Midian. He is also called *Jerubbaal*, and judged Israel forty years as the fifth judge. B.C. 1256.
Judg. 6. 11 his son G. threshed wheat by the wine p.
6. 13 G. said unto him, Oh my Lord, if the Lo.
6. 19 And G. went in, and made ready a kid
6. 22 when G. perceived that he (was) an angel
6. 22 G. said, Alas, O Lord GOD! for because I
6. 24 Then G. built an altar there unto the L.
6. 27 Then G. took ten men of his servants
6. 29 G. the son of Joash hath done this thing
6. 34 But the Spirit of the LORD came upon G
6. 36 G. said unto God, If thou wilt save Isra.
6. 39 G. said..Let not thine anger be hot aga.
7. 1 G., and all the people..rose up early, and
7. 2 the LORD said unto G., The people that
7. 4 the LORD said unto G., The people (are)
7. 5 the LORD said unto G., Every one that
7. 7 the LORD said unto G., By the three hun
7. 13 when G. was come, behold, (there was)
7. 14 This (is) nothing else save the sword of G.
7. 15 when G. heard the telling of the dream
7. 18 say, (The sword) of the LORD, and of G
7. 19 So G., and the hundred men that (were)
7. 20 cried, The sword of the LORD, and of G.
7. 24 G. sent messengers throughout all mount
7. 25 brought the heads of Oreb and Zeeb to G.
8. 4 G. came to Jordan, (and) passed over, he
8. 7 G. said, Therefore, when the LORD hath
8. 11 G. went up by the way of them that
8. 13 G. the son of Joash returned from battle
8. 21 G. arose, and slew Zebah and Zalmunna
8. 22 Then the men of Israel said unto G.
8. 23 G. said unto them, I will not rule over
8. 24 G. said..I would desire a request of you
8. 27 G. made an ephod thereof, and put it in
8. 27 which thing became a snare unto G., and
8. 28 country was in quietness..in..days of G.
8. 30 G had threescore and ten sons of his
8. 32 G the son of Joash died in a good old a.
8. 33 it came to pass, as soon as G. was dead
8. 35 showed they kindness to the house of..G.

GID-EO'-NI, גִּדְעֹנִי.
Father of Abidan, a prince of Benjamin, and one of those appointed to take the census at Sinai. B.C. 1490.
Num. 1. 11 Of Benjamin; Abidan the son of G.
2. 22 and the captain..Abidan the son of G.
7. 60 On the ninth day Abidan the son of G.
7. 65 this..the offering of Abidan the son of G.
10. 24 over the host..Abidan the son of G.

GID'-OM, גִּדְעֹם *desolation.*
A place named as the limit to which the pursuit of Benjamin extended after the battle of Gibeah. Hence it was between Gibeah and the cliff Rimmon (now called *Rummon*), about three miles E of Bethel.
Judg. 20. 45 pursued hard after them unto G., and slew

GIER EAGLE —
1. *Parti-coloured vulture, gier eagle,* רָחָם *racham.*
Lev. 11. 18 swan, and the pelican, and the gier eagle
2. *Parti-coloured vulture, gier eagle,* רָחָמָה *rachamah.*
Deut 14. 17 the pelican, and the gier eagle, and the

GIFT —
1. *A reward,* אֶשְׁכָּר *eshkar.*
Psa. 72. 10 kings of Sheba and Seba shall offer gifts
2. *Offering, present,* מִנְחָה *minchah.*
2 Sa. 8. 2 became D.'s servants, (and) brought gifts
8. 6 became servants to D., (and) brought gifts
1 Ch. 18. 2, 6 became D.'s servants, (and) brought gifts
2 Ch. 26. 8 And the Ammonites gave gifts to Uzziah
32. 23 many brought gifts unto the LORD to Jer.
Psa. 45. 12 the daughter..(shall be there) with a gift
3. *Lifting up, gift, burden,* מַשְׂאֵת *maseth.*
Esth. 2. 18 Then the king..gave gifts, according to
4. *Gift,* מַתָּן *mattan.*
Gen. 34. 12 Ask me never so much dowry and gift
Num 18. 11 the heave offering of their gift, with all
Prov 18. 16 A man's gift maketh room for him
21. 14 A gift in secret pacifieth anger, and a re.
5. *Gift,* מַתְּנָא *mattena.*
Dan. 2. 6 ye shall receive of me gifts and rewards
2. 48 the king..gave him many great gifts
5. 17 Let thy gifts be to thyself, and give thy
6. *Gift,* מַתָּנָה *mattanah.*
Gen. 25. 6 Abraham gave gifts, and sent them away
Exod 28. 38 Israel shall hallow in all their holy gifts
Lev. 23. 38 beside your gifts, and beside all your vows
Num 18. 6 to you (they are) given..a gift for the L.
18. 7 given your priest's office..a service of gift
18. 29 Out of all your gifts ye shall offer every
2 Ch. 21. 3 their father gave them great gifts of silver
Esth. 9. 22 days..of sending..gifts to the poor
Psa. 68. 18 thou hast received gifts for men; yea
Prov 15. 27 troubleth..but he that hateth gifts shall
Eccl. 7. 7 and a gift destroyeth the heart
Eze. 20. 26 I polluted them in their own gifts, in
20. 31 when ye offer your gifts; 20. 39, 46: 16, 17.
6a. *Gifted,* נְתֻנִים [*nathan*].
Num. 8. 19 I have given the Levites (as) a gift to
7. *Gift,* מַתַּת *mattath.*
Prov 25. 14 Whoso boasteth himself of a false gift
Eccl. 3. 13 of all his labour, it (is) the gift of God
5. 19 in his labour; this (is) the gift of God
8. *A separation or impure gift,* נֵדֶה *nedeh.*
Eze. 16. 33 They give gifts to all whores; but thou
9. *A separating or impure gift,* נָדָן *nadan.*
Eze 16. 33 but thou givest thy gifts to all thy lovers
10. *Gift, thing lifted up,* נִשֵּׂאת *nisseth.*
2 Sa. 19. 42 have we eaten..or hath he given us any g?
11. *Bribe, bribery, reward,* שֹׁחַד *shochad.*
Exod 23. 8 And thou shalt take no gift: for the gift
Deut 16. 19 neither take a gift: for a gift doth blind
2 Ch. 19. 7 nor respect of persons, nor taking of gifts
Prov. 6. 35 rest content, though thou givest many g
17. 8 A gift (is as) a precious stone in the eyes
17. 23 A wicked (man) taketh a gift out of the
Isa 1. 23 every one loveth gifts, and followeth after
Eze 22. 12 In thee have they taken gifts to shed bl.
12. *Gift, bribe, thing lifted up,* תְּרוּמָה *terumah.*
Prov. 29. 4 he that receiveth gifts overthroweth it
13. *A thing put up or devoted to God,* ἀνάθημα.
Luke 21. 5 how it was adorned with goodly..gifts
14. *A gift,* δόμα *doma.*
Matt. 7. 11 know how to give good gifts unto your
Luke 11 13 know how to give good gifts unto your
Eph. 4. 8 he led captivity captive, and gave gifts
Phil. 4. 17 Not because I desire a gift: but I desire
15. *A giving, the act of giving,* δόσις *dosis.*
Jas. 1 17 Every good gift..cometh down from the
16. *A free gift, present,* δωρεά *dōrea.*
John 4 10 If thou knewest the gift of God, and who
Acts 2. 38 ye shall receive the gift of the Holy Ghost
8 20 thou hast thought that the gift of God
10. 45 was poured out the gifts of the Holy Ghost
11 17 as God gave them the like gift as..unto
Rom. 5 15 the grace of God, and the gift by grace
5. 17 they which receive..[the gift] of righteo.
2 Co. 9. 15 Thanks ..unto God for his unspeakable g.
Eph. 3. 7 according to the gift of the grace of God
4. 7 according to the measure of the gift of C.
Heb. 6. 4 tasted of the heavenly gift, and were
17. *A free gift, what is given,* δώρημα *dōrēma.*
Rom. 5. 16 not as..by one that sinned, (so is) the gift
Jas 1 17 every perfect gift is from above, and com.
18. *A gift,* δῶρον *dōron.*
Matt. 2. 11 they presented unto him gifts; gold, and
5. 23 if thou bring thy gift to the altar, and
5. 24 Leave there thy gift before the altar, and
5. 24 be reconciled..then come and offer thy g.
8. 4 offer the gift that Moses commanded, for
15. 5 a gift, by whatsoever thou mightest be
23. 18 whosoever sweareth by the gift that is
23. 19 gift, or the altar that sanctifieth the gift?
Mark 7. 11 Corban, that is to say, a gift, by whatsoe.
Luke 21. 1 rich men casting their gifts into the tre.
Eph. 2. 8 not of yourselves; (it is) the gift of God
Heb. 5. 1 that he may offer both gifts and sacrifices
8. 3 is ordained to offer gifts and sacrifices
8. 4 priests that offer gifts according to the
9. 9 in which were offered both gifts and sa.
11. 4 God testifying of his gifts: and by it he
Rev. 11. 10 and shall send gifts one to another
19. *Distribution, parting,* μερισμός *merismos.*
Heb. 2. 4 divers miracles, and gifts of the Holy G.
20. *Grace, favour, free gift,* χάρις *charis.*
2 Co. 8. 4 Praying..that we would receive the gift
21. *Grace, favour, kindness,* χάρισμα *charisma.*
Rom. 1. 11 I may impart unto you some spiritual g.
6. 23 gift of God (is) eternal life through J. C.
11. 29 For the gifts and calling of God (are)
12. 6 Having then gifts differing according to
1 Co. 1. 7 So that ye come behind in no gift; wait.
7. 7 But every man hath his proper gift of G.
12. 4 there are diversities of gifts, but the same
12. 9 to another the gifts of healing by the same
12. 28 after that miracles, then gifts of healings
12. 30 Have all the gifts of healing? do all speak
12. 31 covet earnestly the best gifts: and yet
2 Co. 1. 11 that for the gift (bestowed) upon us by
1 Ti. 4. 14 Neglect not the gift that is in thee, which
2 Ti. 1. 6 that thou stir up the gift of God, which is
1 Pe. 4. 10 As every man hath received the gift

GIFT, free —
Grace, favour, kindness, χάρισμα *charisma.*
Rom. 5. 15 not as the offence, so also (is) the free g.
5. 16 the free gift (is) of many offences unto

GIFTS, giveth —
A man of gifts, אִישׁ מַתָּן *ish mattan.*
Prov 19. 6 man (is) a friend to him that giveth gifts

GI'-HON, גִּחוֹן, גִּיחוֹן *stream.*
1. The second river of the Garden of Eden, variously supposed to have been the Oxus (or Araxes), the Pyramus, the Ganges, or the Nile.
Gen. 2. 13 And the name of the second river (is) G.
2. A place near Jerusalem where Solomon was anointed and proclaimed king. Here in the valley of Gihon was a fountain which had likely been named after the place, or *vice-versa.*
1 Ki. 1. 33 Solomon..to ride..and bring him..to G.
1. 38 Solomon to ride..and brought him to G.
1. 45 the prophet have anointed him king in G.
2 Ch. 32. 30 also stopped the upper water course of G.
33. 14 he built a wall..on the west side of G

GI-LA'-LAI, גִּלֲלַי *rolling, weighty.*
One of a party of priests who played on David's instruments at the consecration of the wall of Jerusalem in the company under Ezra. B.C. 445.
Neh 12 36 G..with the musical instruments of D.

GIL-BO'-A, גִּלְבֹּעַ *bubbling fountain.*
A hilly district of Manasseh W. of the Jordan, in Issachar, where Saul was slain The mount is six miles from Beth-shean, and at its foot lay Shunem and Aphek; at its back is a village now called *Gelbon.*
1 Sa. 28. 4 gathered all Israel..and they pitched in G.
2 Sa. 21. 12 when the Philistines had slain Saul in G.

GIL'-EAD, גִּלְעָד *strong, rocky.*
1. A mountainous district E. of the Jordan, occupied by Reuben, Gad, and Manasseh. It was afterwards called *Peræa.*
Gen. 37. 25 a company of Ishmeelites came from G.
Num 32. 1 they saw the land of Jazer, and..of G.
32. 26 our cattle, shall be..in the cities of G.
32. 29 then ye shall give them the land of G. for
32. 39 the children of Machir..went to G., and
32. 40 Moses gave G unto Machir the son of M.
Deut. 2. 36 the city that (is) by the river..unto G.
3. 10 All the cities of the plain, and all G., and
3. 13 G..gave I unto the half tribe of Manasseh
3. 15 And I gave G. unto Machir
3. 16 unto the Gadites I gave from G. even
4. 43 and Ramoth in G., of the Gadites; and
34. 1 the LORD showed him all the land of G.
Josh. 12. 2 from half G., even unto the river Jabbok
12. 5 half G., the border of Sihon king of Hesh.
13. 11 G., and the border of the Geshurites and
13. 25 their coast..Jazer, and all the cities of G.
13. 31 half G., and Ashtaroth, and Edrei, cities
17. 1 he was a man of war, therefore he had G.
17. 5 there fell..to Manasseh..the land of G.
17. 6 of Manasseh's sons had the land of G.
20. 8 and Ramoth in G. out of the tribe of Gad
21. 38 out of the tribe of Gad, Ramoth in G.
22. 9 departed..to go unto the country of G.
22. 13 child. of Israel sent..into the land of G
22. 15 they came..unto the land of G., and they
22. 32 Phinehas..returned..out of the land of G.
Judg 5 17 G. abode beyond Jordan: and why did
10. 4 thirty cities..which (are) in the land of G.
10. 8 the land of the Amorites, which (is) in G.
10. 17 the children of Ammon..encamped in G.
10 18 the people (and) princes of G. said one
10. 18 be head over all the inhabitants of G.
11. 5 the elders of G. went to fetch Jephthah
11. 7 And Jephthah said unto the elders of G.
11. 8 And the elders of G. said unto Jephthah
11. 8 be our head over all the inhabitants of G.
11 9 And Jephthah said unto the elders of G.
11. 11 Then Jephthah went with the elders of G.
11. 29 came upon Jephthah..he passed over G.
11. 29 Manasseh, and passed over Mizpeh of G.
11. 29 from Mizpeh of G he passed over (unto)
12. 4 Then Jephthah gathered..the men of G.
12. 4 the men of G. smote Ephraim, because
12. 5 the men of G. said unto him, (Art) thou

Judg 12. 7 and was buried in (one of) the cities of G.
20. 1 even to Beer-sheba, with the land of G.
1 Sa. 13. 7 went over Jordan to the land of..G.
2 Sa. 2. 9 made him king over G., and over the A.
17. 26 So Israel and Absalom pitched in..G.
24. 6 they came to G., and to the land of Taht.
1 Ki. 4. 13 him..the towns of Jair..which (are) in G.
4. 19 Geber the son of Uri..in the country of G.
17. 1 Elijah..of the inhabitants of G., said unto
22. 3 Know ye that Ramoth in G. (is) ours, and
2 Ki. 10. 33 From Jordan eastward, all the land of G.
10. 33 which (is) by the river Arnon, even G.
15. 29 Tiglath-pileser..took..Hazor, and G., and
1 Ch. 2. 22 three and twenty cities in the land of G.
5. 9 cattle were multiplied in the land of G.
5. 10 they dwelt in their tents throughout..G.
5. 16 they dwelt in G. in Bashan, and in her
6. 80 out of the tribe of Gad; Ramoth in G.
26. 31 found..mighty men of valour at Jazer of G.
27. 21 Of the half (tribe) of Manasseh in G., Iddo
Psa. 60. 7 G. (is) mine, and Manasseh (is) mine
108. 8 G. (is) mine; Manasseh (is) mine; Ephr.
Song 6. 5 as a flock of goats that appear from G.
Jer. 8. 22 (Is there) no balm in G.; (is there) no
22. 6 Thou (art) G. unto me, (and) the head of
46. 11 Go up into G., and take balm, O virgin
50. 19 and his soul shall be satisfied upon..G.
Eze. 47. 18 the east side ye shall measure..from G.
Hos. 6. 8 G. (is) a city of them that work iniquity
12. 11 (Is there) iniquity (in) G.? surely they are
Amos 1. 3 they have threshed G. with threshing in.
1. 13 have ripped up the woman with child of G.
Obad. 19 and Benjamin (shall possess) G.
Mic. 7. 14 let them feed (in) Bashan and G., as in
Zech. 10. 10 I will bring them into the land of G.

2. Perhaps the name of a mountain W. of the Jordan near Jezreel, but the true reading may be Gilboa. Gideon encamped at the "Spring of Herod," which is at the base of Gilboa.

Judg. 7. 3 let him..depart early from mount G.

3. Son of Machir, grandson of Manasseh. B.C. 1620.

Num. 26. 29 Machir begat G.: of G. (come) the family
26. 30 These (are) the sons of G.: (of) Jeezer
27. 1 the son of Hepher, the son of G., the son
36. 1 chief fathers of the families of..G.
Josh. 17. 1 a lot for..Machir..the father of G.
17. 3 Zelophehad..son of Hepher, the son of G.
1 Ch 2. 21 the daughter of Machir, the father of G.
2 23 these..the sons of Machir, the father of G.
7. 14 concubine..bare Machir the father of G.
7. 17 These (were) the sons of G., the son of M.

4. Father of Jephthah, judge of Israel B.C. 1200.

Judg. 11. 1 the son of an harlot: and G. begat Jeph.
11. 2 G.'s wife bare him sons: and his wife's

5. A chief of a family of Gad. B.C. 1300.

1 Ch. 5. 14 Huri, the son of Jaroah, the son of G.

GIL-EAD-ITES, הַגִּלְעָדִי. *Descendants of Gilead.*

Num. 26. 29 of Gilead (come) the family of the G.
Judg. 10. 3 after him arose Jair, a G., and judged
11. 1 Now Jephthah the G. was a mighty man
11. 40 lament the daughter of Jephthah the G.
12. 5 And the G. took the passages of Jor. v. 4.
12. 7 Then died Jephthah the G., and was
2 Sa. 17. 27 Shobi..and Barzillai the G. of Rogelim
19. 31 Barzillai the G. came down from Rogel
1 Ki. 2. 7 kindness unto the sons of Barzillai the G.
2 Ki. 15. 25 Pekah..and with him fifty men of the G.
Ezra 2. 61 wife of the daughters of Barzillai the G.
Neh. 7. 63 of the daughters of Barzillai the G. to wife

GIL'-GAL, גִּלְגָּל *circle, wheel.*

1. A place W. of the Jordan, near Jericho, in Benjamin, where Israel spent the first night after crossing the Jordan.

Deut. 11. 30 dwell in the champaign over against G.
Josh. 4. 19 the people came up..and encamped in G.
4. 20 those twelve stones..Joshua pitch in G.
5. 9 Wheref. the name of the place is called G.
5. 10 And the children of Israel encamped in G.
9. 6 they went to Joshua unto the camp at G.
10. 6 men..sent unto Joshua to the camp to G.
10. 7 So Joshua ascended from G., he, and all
10. 9 Joshua..went up from G. all night
10. 15 Joshua returned..unto the camp to G.
10. 43 And Josh. returned..unto the camp to G.
14. 6 children of Judah came unto Joshua in G.
15. 7 toward G., that (is) before the going up
Judg. 2. 1 an angel of the LORD came up from G.
3. 19 turned again from the quarries..by G.
1 Sa. 7. 16 went from year to year in circuit to..G.
10. 8 And thou shalt go down before me to G.
11. 14 said Samuel. Come, and let us go to G.
11. 15 And all the people went to G.; and
11. 15 they made Saul king before the LORD in G.
13. 4 the people were called together..to G.
13. 7 Saul..(was) yet in G., and all the people
13. 8 but Samuel came not to G.; and the pe.
13. 12 Philistines will come down now..to G.
13. 15 And Samuel arose, and gat him up from G.
15. 12 he set him up a place, and is gone..to G.
15. 21 to sacrifice unto the LORD thy God in G.
15. 33 And Samuel hewed Agag in pieces..in G.
2 Sa. 19. 15 Judah came to G., to go to meet the king
19. 40 Then the king went on to G., and Chim.
2 Ki. 2. 1 that Elijah went with Elisha from G.
4. 38 And Elisha came again to G.: and
Neh. 12. 29 Also from the house of G., and out of the
Hos. 4. 15 and come not ye unto G., neither go ye
9. 15 All their wickedness (is) in G.; for their
Hos. 12. 11 are vanity: they sacrifice bullocks in G.
Amos 4. 4 at G. multiply transgression; and bring
5. 5 But seek not Beth-el, nor enter into G.
5. 5 for G. shall surely go into captivity, and
Mic. 6. 5 answered him from Shittim unto G.

2. A city between Dor and Tirsa.

Josh. 12. 23 the king of the nations of G., one

3. A city N. of Joppa, near the sea (now called *Jidjulah*), near Antipatris.

Josh. 9. 6 they went to Joshua unto the camp at G.
10. 6 sent unto Joshua to the camp to G.
10. 7 So Joshua ascended from G., he, and all
10. 9 Joshua therefore..went up from G. all
10. 15, 43 Jos. returned..unto the camp to G.

4. A place twelve miles S. of Ebal and Gerizim (now called *Jiljiliah*).

2 Ki. 2. 1 that Elijah went with Elisha from G.
4. 38 And Elisha came again to G.: and (there

GI'-LOH, גִּלֹה *circle.*

A town in the mountains of Judah near Hebron, and Ahithophel's native place.

Josh. 15. 51 Goshen, and Holon, and G.; eleven cities
2 Sa. 15. 12 Absalom sent for Ahithophel..from G.

GI-LO'-NITE, גִּילֹנִי, גִּלֹנִי.

A inhabitant of Giloh. B.C. 1023.

2 Sa. 15. 12 And Absalom sent for Ahithophel the G.
23. 34 Eliam the son of Ahithophel the G.

GIM'-ZO, גִּמְזוֹ *sycamore.*

A city in the N. of Judah, two or three miles S.W. of Lydda and S. of the road between Jerusalem and Jaffa. Here is *Jimzu* a large village on an eminence and well surrounded with trees.

2 Ch. 28. 18 G. also and the villages thereof: and they

GIN —

1. *A snare,* מוֹקֵשׁ *moqesh.*

Psa. 140 5 The proud..they have set gins for me. S.
141 9 and the gins of the workers of iniquity
Amos 3. 5 Can a bird fall..where no gin (is) for him?

2. *Gin, snare,* פַּח *pach.*

Job 18. 9 The gin shall take (him) by the heel, (and)
Isa. 8. 14 for a gin and for a snare to the inhabi.

GI'-NATH, גִּינַת *protection.*

The father of Tibni who disputed the throne of Israel with Omri after the death of Zimri. B.C. 926.

1 Ki. 16. 21 half..followed Tibni the son of G.
16. 22 people that followed Tibni the son of G.

GIN-NE'-THON, גִּנְּתוֹן, גִּנְּתוֹי, גִּנְּתוֹ *great protection.*

Or Ginnetho, a prince or priest who, with Nehemiah, sealed the covenant. B.C. 445.

Neh. 10. 6 Daniel, G., Baruch
12. 4 Iddo, Ginnetho, Abijah
12. 16 Of Iddo, Zechariah; of G., Meshullam

GIRD, to —

1. *To gird,* אָזַר *azar,* 3.

Psa. 18. 32 God that girdeth me with strength, and
Isa. 45 5 I girded thee, though thou hast not

2. *To bind,* אָסַר *asar.*

Job 12. 18 and girdeth their loins with a girdle

3. *To put on,* אָפַד *aphad.*

Exod 29. 5 gird him with the curious girdle of the

4. *Girdle,* חֲגוֹרָה *chagorah.*

Isa. 32. 11 make you bare, and gird..upon..loins

5. *To gird, restrain,* חָגַר *chagar.*

Exod 29. 9 And thou shalt gird them with girdles
Lev. 8. 7 girded him with the girdle, and clothed
8. 7 he girded him with the curious girdle of
8. 13 girded them with girdles, and put bonnets
Judg. 3. 16 he did gird it under his raiment upon his
1 Sa. 17. 39 David girded his sword upon his armour
2 Sa. 3. 31 gird you with sackcloth, and mourn be.
1 Ki. 20. 32 So they girded sackcloth on their loins
Psa. 45. 3 Gird thy sword upon (thy) thigh, O (Most)
Prov 31. 17 She girdeth her loins with strength, and
Isa. 22. 12 to baldness, and to girding with sack.
Jer. 4. 8 For this gird you with sackcloth, lament
6. 26 gird (thee) with sackcloth, and wallow
49. 3 gird you with sackcloth; lament, and run
Eze. 7. 18 They shall also gird (themselves) with s.
27. 31 gird them with sackcloth, and they shall
44. 18 they shall not gird (themselves) with any

6. *To gird,* ζώννυμι *zōnnumi,* ζωννύω *zōnnuō.*

John 21. 18 When thou wast young, thou girdedst
21. 18 another shall gird thee, and carry..whi.

7 *To gird thoroughly,* διαζώννυμι, *diazōnnumi.*

John 13. 4 He riseth..took a towel, and girded him.
13. 5 with the towel wherewith he was girded
21. 7 he girt (his) fisher's coat (unto him)

GIRD about, to —

To bind, bind up, חָבַשׁ *chabash.*

Eze. 16. 10 and I girded thee about with fine linen

GIRD on, to —

To gird, חָגַר *chagar.*

Deut. 1. 41 when ye had girded on every man his w.
1 Sa. 25. 13 said..Gird ye on every man his sword
25 13 And they girded on every man his sword
25. 13 and David also girded on his sword
1 Ki. 20. 11 Let not him that girdeth on..boast him.

GIRD self, to —

1. *To gird self,* אָזַר *azar,* 7.

Psa. 93. 1 he hath girded himself: the world also is
Isa. 8. 9, 9 gird yourselves, and ye shall be broken

2. *To gird, be restrained,* חָגַר *chagar.*

Isa. 15. 3 In their streets they shall gird themselves
Lam. 2. 10 they have girded themselves with sack.
Joel 1. 13 Gird yourselves, and lament, ye priests

3. *To gird around,* περιζώννυμι *perizōnnumi.*

Luke 12. 37 he shall gird himself, and make them to
17. 8 gird thyself, and serve me, till I have
Acts 12. 8 Gird thyself, and bind on thy sandals

GIRD up —

1. *To gird,* אָזַר *azar.*

Job 38. 3 Gird up now thy loins like a man; for I
40. 7 Gird up thy loins now like a man: I will
Jer. 1. 17 Thou therefore gird up thy loins, and

2. *To gird, be restrained,* חָגַר *chagar.*

2 Ki. 4. 29 Gird up thy loins, and take my staff in
9. 1 Gird up thy loins, and take this box of

3. *To gird up, compress,* שָׁנַס *shanas,* 3.

1 Ki. 18. 46 he girded up his loins, and ran before A.

4. *To gird up,* ἀναζώννυμι *anazōnnumi.*

1 Pe. 1. 13 gird up the loins of your mind, be sober

[**GIRD unto one's self, to —**
To gird thoroughly, διαζώννυμι *diazōnnumi.*
John 21. 7 he girt (his) fisher's coat, for he was na.]

GIRD with, to —

To gird, אָזַר *azar,* 3.

2 Sa. 22. 40 For thou hast girded me with strength
Psa. 18. 39 For thou hast girded me with strength
30. 11 thou hast put off..and girded me with g.

GIRDED, to be —

1. *To be girded,* אָזַר *azar.*

1 Sa. 2. 4 they that stumbled are girded with str.

2. *To become girded,* אָזַר *azar,* 2.

Psa. 65. 6 setteth fast the mountains..girded with

3. *To bind,* אָסַר *asar.*

Neh. 4. 18 every one had his sword girded by his

4. *To gird,* חָגַר *chagar.*

Exod 12. 11 your loins girded, your shoes on your feet
Lev. 16. 4 and shall be girded with a linen girdle
1 Sa. 2. 18 Samuel..a child, girded with a linen ep.
2 Sa. 6. 14 David (was) girded with a linen ephod
20. 8 Joab's garment..was girded unto him
21. 16 he, being girded with a new (sword), tho.
Psa. 109. 19 and for a girdle wherewith he is girded
Dan. 10. 5 whose loins (were) girded with fine gold
Joel 1. 8 Lament like a virgin girded with sackcloth

GIRDED with —

Girded, חָגוֹר *chagor.*

Eze. 23. 15 Girded with girdles upon their loins, exc.

GIRDED about, to be —

To gird round about, περιζώννυμι *perizōnnumi.*

Luke 12. 35 Let your loins be girded about, and (your)

GIRDED, to have —

To gird round about, περιζώννυμι περί *perizōnnumi.*

Rev. 15. 6 having their breasts girded with golden g.

GIRDING —

Girding, מַחֲגֹרֶת *machagoreth.*

Isa. 3. 24 instead of a stomacher a girding of sack.

GIRDLE —

1. *Girdle, sash,* אַבְנֵט *abnet.*

Exod 28. 4 a broidered coat, a mitre, and a girdle
28. 39 thou shalt make the girdle (of) needle-w
28. 40 thou shalt make for them girdles, and b
29. 9 And thou shalt gird them with girdles
39. 29 a girdle (of) fine twined linen, and blue
Lev. 8. 7 girded him with the girdle, and clothed
8. 13 girded them with girdles, and put bonnets
16. 4 and shall be girded with a linen girdle
Isa. 22. 21 I will..strengthen him with thy girdle

2. *Girdle,* אֵזוֹר *ezor.*

2 Ki. 1. 8 with a girdle of leather about his loins
Job 12. 18 and girdeth their loins with a girdle
Isa. 5. 27 neither shall the girdle of their loins be
11. 5 righteousness shall be the girdle of his
11. 5 and faithfulness the girdle of his reins
Jer. 13. 1 Go and get thee a linen girdle, and put
13. 2 So I got a girdle, according to the word
13. 4 Take the girdle that thou hast got, which
13. 6 Arise, go..and take the girdle from then.
13. 7 and took the girdle from the place where
13. 7 the girdle was marred, it was profitable
13 10 as this girdle, which is good for nothing
13. 11 For as the girdle cleaveth to the loins of
Eze. 23. 15 Girded with girdles upon their loins

3. *Girdle,* חָגוֹר *chagor.*

1 Sa. 18. 4 stripped himself..even..to his girdle
2 Sa. 20. 8 upon it a girdle (with) a sword fastened
Prov 31. 24 She..delivereth girdles unto the merch.

4. *Girdle,* חֲגוֹרָה *chagorah.*

2 Sa. 18. 11 given..ten (shekels) of silver, and a girdle
1 Ki. 2. 5 put the blood of war upon his girdle that
Isa. 3. 24 instead of a girdle a rent; and instead of

5. *Girdle, band,* מֵזַח, (מְזִיחַ) *mezach.*
Psa. 109. 19 and for a girdle wherewith he is girded
6. *Girdle, zone, belt,* ζώνη *zōnē.*
Matt. 3. 4 a leathern girdle about his loins; and his
Mark 1. 6 with a girdle of skin about his loins
Acts 21. 11 took Paul's girdle, and bound his own
21. 11 bind the man that owneth this girdle, and
Rev. 1. 13 girt about the paps with a golden girdle
15. 6 having their breasts girded with golden g.

GIRDLE, curious —
Device, devised work, חֵשֶׁב *chesheb.*
Exod 28. 8, 27, 28 the curious girdle of the ephod
29. 5 with the curious girdle of the ephod
39. 5, 20, 21 the curious girdle of his ephod
Lev. 8. 7 with the curious girdle of the ephod

GIR-GA-SHITES, גִּרְגָּשִׁי.
A tribe early in possession of part of Canaan. It is uniformly plural in the Common Version except twice, Gen. 10. 16, and 1 Ch. 1. 14; in the former it is *Girgasite.*
Gen. 10. 16 Jebusite, and the Amorite, and the G.
15. 21 Amorites, and the Canaanites, and the G.
Deut. 7. 1 the Hittites, and the G., and the Amor.
Josh. 3. 10 the Hivites, and the Perizzites, and the G.
24. 11 men of Jericho fought against..the G.
1 Ch. 1. 14 Jebusite also, and the Amorite, and the G.
Neh. 9. 8 the land of the..Jebusites, and the G.

GIRL —
Child, female, lass, girl, יַלְדָּה *yaldah.*
Joel 3. 3 they have..sold a girl for wine, that they
Zech. 8. 5 full of boys and girls playing in the stre.

GIRT — [*See also* **GIRD** 7.]
To be girded, אָזַר *azar.*
2 Ki. 1. 8 an hairy man, and girt with a girdle of l.

GIRT, to be —
To gird round about, περιζώννυμι *perizōnnumi.*
Rev. 1. 13 girt about the paps with a golden girdle

GIRT about, to have —
To gird round about, περιζώννυμι *perizōnnumi.*
Eph. 6. 14 having your loins girt about with truth

GIS'-PA (or GISH'-PA), גִּשְׁפָּא *listening, attentive.*
An overseer of the Nethinim in "the Ophel," after the exile. B.C. 445.
Neh. 11. 21 Ziha and G. (were) over the Nethinims

GIT-TAH HE'-PHER, גִּתָּה חֵפֶר.
A town in Zebulun, also called *Gath-hepher.*
Josh. 19. 13 passeth on along on the east to G.

GIT-TA'-IM, גִּתַּיִם *two wine presses.*
1. A place of refuge near Beeroth.
2 Sa. 4. 3 And the Beerothites fled to G., and were
2. A place near Gath inhabited by Benjamites after the return from exile. This and No. 1. may be the same place, as this latter is N W. of Jerusalem.
Neh. 11. 33 Hazor, Ramah, G.

GIT-TITES, גִּתִּי, גִּתִּים.
Inhabitants of Gath, six hundred of whom followed David as a body guard under Ittai Gittite may also be an inhabitant of Gittaim, or of Gath-rimmon.
Josh. 13. 3 the Eshkalonites, the G., and the Ekron.
2 Sa. 6. 10 into the house of Obed-edom the G.
6. 11 cont. in the house of Obed-edom the G.
15. 18 and all the G...passed on before the king
15. 19 Then said the king to Ittai the G
15. 22 Ittai the G. passed over, and all his men
18. 2 third part under the hand of Ittai the G.
21. 19 Elhanan..slew (the bro. of) Goliath the G.
1 Ch. 13. 13 into the house of Obed-edom the G.
20. 5 slew Lahmi the brother of Goliath the G.

GIT'-TITH, הַגִּתִּית *from or of Gath.*
A musical instrument manufactured at Gath. When David was in exile there he probably became acquainted with it and adopted it in the musical part of the service of the tabernacle
Psa. 8. *title.* To the chief musician upon G., A Psalm
81. ,, To the chief musician upon G., (A Ps.)
84. ,, To the chief musician upon G., A Psa.

GIVE, to —
1. *To cause to come in,* בּוֹא *bo,* 5.
Psa. 78. 29 they did eat..for he gave them their own
2. *To speak,* דָּבַר *dabar,* 3.
2 Ki. 25. 6 So they took..and they gave judgment
Jer. 4. 12 now also will I give sentence against them
39. 5 Riblah..where he gave judgment upon
52. 9 Riblah..where he gave judgment upon
3. *To turn,* הָפַךְ *haphak.*
1 Sa. 10. 9 when he had turned..God gave him ano.
4. *To apportion,* חָלַק *chalaq.*
Deut 29. 26 gods whom..he had not given unto them
5. *To give,* יְהַב *yahab.*
Gen. 29. 21 Jacob said unto Laban, Give..my wife
30. 1 Rachel..said..Give me children, or else
47. 15 all the Egyptians..said, Give us bread
47. 16 And Joseph said, Give your cattle; and I
Josh 18. 4 Give out from among you three men for
Judg. 1. 15 she said unto him, Give me a blessing
20. 7 Behold..give here your advice and coun.
1 Sa. 14. 41 Therefore Saul said..Give a perfect (lot)
2 Sa. 16. 20 Give counsel among you what we shall do
1 Ch. 16. 28 Give unto the LORD, ye kindreds of the
16. 28 give unto the LORD glory and strength
16. 29 Give unto the LORD the glory (due) unto
Psa. 29. 1 Give unto the LORD, O ye mighty, give
29. 2 Give unto the LORD the glory due unto
60. 11 Give us help from trouble: for vain (is)
96. 7 Give unto the LORD, O ye kindreds of the
96. 7 give unto the LORD glory and strength
96. 8 Give unto the LORD the glory (due unto)
108. 12 Give us help from trouble: for vain (is)
Prov 30. 15 hath two daughters, (crying), Give, give
Hos. 4. 18 her rulers (with) shame do love, Give ye
Zech 11. 12 If ye think good, give..my price; and if
6. *To give,* יְהַב *yehab.*
Ezra 5. 12 he gave them into the hand of Nebucha.
Dan. 2. 21 he giveth wisdom unto the wise, and
2. 23 who hast given me wisdom and might
2. 37 God of heaven hath given thee a kingdom
2. 38 the fowls of the heaven hath he given
2. 48 the king..gave him many..gifts, and
5. 17 give thy rewards to another; yet I will
5. 18 God gave Nebuchadnezzar thy father a
5. 19 And for the majesty that he gave him, all
6. 2 that the princes might give accounts unto
7. *To do good, benefit,* יָטַב *yatab,* 5.
1 Sa. 2. 32 (the wealth) which (God) shall give Israel
8. *To a man of gifts,* לְאִישׁ מַתָּן *le-ish mattan.*
Prov 19. 6 every man (is) a friend to him that giveth
9. *To lift up,* נָשָׂא *nasa,* 3.
2 Sa. 19. 42 have we eaten..or hath he given us any
10. *To give,* נָתַן *nathan.*
Gen. 1. 29 I have given you every herb bearing seed
3. 6 and gave also unto her husband with her
3. 12 The woman whom thou gavest..with me
3. 12 she gave me of the tree, and I did eat
9. 3 as the green herb have I given you all
12. 7 said, Unto thy seed will I give this land
13. 15 to thee will I give it, and to thy seed for
13. 17 the land..for I will give it unto thee
14. 20 And he gave him tithes of all
14. 21 Give me the persons, and take the goods
15. 2 Lord GOD, what wilt thou give me, seeing
15. 3 Behold, to me thou hast given no seed
15. 7 brought thee..to give thee this land to
15. 18 Unto thy seed have I given this land, from
16. 3 gave her to her husband Abram to be his
16. 5 I have given my maid into thy bosom
17. 8 I will give unto thee, and to thy seed af.
17. 16 I will bless her, and give thee a son also
18. 7 fetched a calf tender and good, and gave
20. 14 and gave..unto Abraham, and restored
20. 16 I have given thy brother a thousand
21. 14 and took bread..and gave (it) unto Hagar
21. 27 Abraham took sheep and oxen, and gave
23. 4 give me a possession of a burying place
23. 9 That he may give me the cave of Machp.
23. 9 he shall give it me for a possession of a
23. 11 Nay..hear me: the field give I thee
23. 11 the cave that (is) therein, I give it thee
23. 11 in the presence of..my people give I it
23. 13 I will give thee money for the field; take
24. 7 Unto thy seed will I give this land; he
24. 32 gave straw and provender for the camels
24. 35 he hath given him flocks, and herds, and
24. 36 unto him hath he given all that he hath
24. 41 if they give not thee (one), thou shalt be
24. 53 gold, and raiment, and gave..to Rebekah
24. 53 he gave also to her brother and to her
25. 5 Abraham gave all that he had unto Isaac
25. 6 Abraham gave gifts, and sent them away
25. 34 Jacob gave Esau bread and pottage of le.
26. 3 unto thee..I will give all these countries
26. 4 will give unto thy seed all these countries
27. 17 she gave the savoury meat and the bread
27. 28 God give thee of the dew of heaven, and
27. 37 all his brethren have I given to him for
28. 4 And give thee the blessing of Abraham, to
28. 4 the land..which God gave unto Abraham
28. 13 to thee will I give it, and to thy seed
28. 20 and will give me bread to eat, and raim.
28. 22 of all that thou shalt give me I will sure.
29. 19 (It is) better that I give her to thee
29. 19 than that I should give her to another
29. 24 Laban gave unto his daughter Leah Zilp.
29. 26 to give the younger before the first born
29. 27 Fulfil her week, and we will give thee
29. 28 he gave him Rachel his daughter to wife
29. 29 Laban gave to Rachel his daughter Bilh.
29. 33 he hath therefore given me this (son) also
30. 4 she gave him Bilhah her handmaid to w.
30. 6 God..heard my voice, and hath given me
30. 9 she took Zilpah..and gave her Jacob to
30. 14 Give me, I pray thee, of thy son's mand.
30. 18 Leah said, God hath given me my hire
30. 18 because I have given my maiden to my
30. 26 Give..my wives and my children, for
30. 28 Appoint me thy wages, and I will give
30. 31 And he said, What shall I give thee?
30. 31 Jacob said, Thou shalt not give me any
30. 35 and gave..into the hand of his sons
31. 9 hath taken away the cattle..and given
34. 8 saying..I pray you give her him to wife
34. 9 give your daughters unto us, and take
34. 11 and what ye shall say unto me I will give
34. 12 I will give according as ye shall say unto
34. 12 but give me the damsel to wife
34. 14 We cannot do this..to give our sister to
34. 16 Then will we give our daughters unto you
34. 21 and let us give them our daughters
Gen. 35. 4 they gave unto Jacob all the strange gods
35. 12 the land which I gave..to thee I will give
35. 12 to thy seed after thee will I give the land
38. 9 lest that he should give seed to his broth.
38. 16 What wilt thou give me, that thou may.
38. 17 Wilt thou give..a pledge till thou send
38. 18 he said, What pledge shall I give thee?
38. 18 he gave (it) her, and came in unto her
38. 26 because..I gave her not to Shelah my son
39. 21 gave him favour in the sight of the keeper
40. 11 and I gave the cup into Pharaoh's hand
40. 21 and he gave the cup into Pharaoh's hand
41. 45 he gave him to wife Asenath the daughter
42. 25 and to give them provision for the way
42. 27 to give his ass provender in the inn, he
43. 14 God Almighty give you mercy before the
43. 23 your God..hath given you treasure in
43. 24 and gave..water, and they washed their
43. 24 and he gave their asses provender
45. 18 I will give you the good of the land of E.
45. 21 Joseph gave them wagons, according to
45. 21 and gave them provision for the way
45. 22 To all of them he gave each man changes
45. 22 but to Benjamin he gave three hundred
46. 18 whom Laban gave to Leah his daughter
46. 25 which Laban gave unto Rachel his daug.
47. 11 gave them a possession in the land of E.
47. 16 your cattle; and I will give you for your
47. 17 Joseph gave them bread..for horses, and
47. 19 and give..seed, that we may live, and
47. 22 eat their portion which Pharaoh gave
47. 24 that ye shall give the fifth..unto Pharaoh
48. 4 and will give this land to thy seed after
48. 9 They..my sons, whom God hath given
48. 22 Moreover I have given to thee one porti.
49. 21 a hind let loose: he giveth goodly words
Exod. 2. 9 nurse it for me, and I will give..thy wages
2. 21 and he gave Moses Zipporah his daughter
3. 21 I will give this people favour in the sight
5. 7 Ye shall no more give the people straw to
5. 10 Thus saith Pharaoh, I will not give you
6. 4 to give them the land of Canaan, the land
6. 8 I did swear to give it to Abraham, to I.
6. 8 and I will give it you for an heritage
10. 25 Moses said, Thou must give us also sacri.
11. 3 the LORD gave the people favour in the
12. 25 to the land which the LORD will give you
12. 36 the LORD gave the people favour in the
13. 5 which he sware unto thy fathers to give
13. 11 bring thee into the land..and shall give it
16. 8 when the LORD shall give you in the eve.
16. 15 the bread which the LORD hath given you
16. 29 for that the LORD hath given you the sa.
16. 29 he giveth you on the sixth day the bread
17. 2 said, Give us water that we may drink
20. 12 the land which the LORD thy God giveth
21. 4 If his master have given him a wife, and
21. 23 if..mischief follow, then thou shalt give
21. 30 he shall give for the ransom of his life
21. 32 he shall give unto their master thirty sh.
22. 17 If her father utterly refuse to give her
22. 29 the first born of thy sons shalt thou give
22. 30 on the eighth day thou shalt give it me
24. 12 I will give thee tables of stone, and a law
25. 16, 21 the testimony..I shall give thee
30. 12 then shall they give every man a ransom
30. 13 This they shall give, every one that passe.
30. 14 every one..shall give an offering unto the
30. 15 The rich shall not give more, and
30. 15 the poor shall not give less, than half
30. 15 when (they) give an offering unto the Lo.
31. 6 I have given with him Aholiab the son
31. 18 he gave unto Moses..two tables of testi.
32. 13 this land that I have spoken of will I give
32. 24 So they gave (it) me: then I cast it into
33. 1 saying, Unto thy seed will I give it
Lev. 5. 16 give it unto the priest: and the priest
6. 5 give it unto him to whom it appertaineth
6. 17 I have given it..their portion of my offer.
7. 32 the right shoulder shall ye give unto the
7. 34 have given them unto Aaron the priest
10. 17 and (God) hath given it you to bear the
14. 34 into the land of Canaan, which I give to
15. 14 and come..and give them unto the priest
17. 11 I have given it to you upon the altar to
20. 2 that giveth..of his seed unto Molech, he
20. 3 because he hath given of his seed unto M.
20. 4 when he giveth of his seed unto Molech
20. 24 and I will give it unto you to possess it
22. 14 and shall give (it) unto the priest with
23. 10 When ye be come into the land which I
23. 38 all your freewill offerings, which ye give
25. 2 When ye come into the land which I give
25. 37 Thou shalt not give him thy money upon
25. 38 to give you the land of Canaan..to be
26. 4 Then I will give you rain in due season
26. 6 I will give peace in the land, and ye shall
27. 9 all that (any man) giveth of such unto the
27. 23 he shall give thine estimation in that day
Num. 3. 9 thou shalt give the Levites unto Aaron
3. 48 thou shalt give the money, wherewith
3. 51 Moses gave the money of them that were
5. 7 give (it) unto (him) against whom he hath
5. 10 whatsoever any man giveth the priest, it
7. 5 thou shalt give them unto the Levites, to
7. 6 took the wagons and the oxen, and gave
7. 7 Two wagons and four oxen he gave unto
7. 8 four wagons and eight oxen he gave unto
7. 9 But unto the sons of Kohath he gave no.
8. 19 I have given the Levites..a gift to Aaron
10. 29 of which the LORD said, I will give it you
11. 13 Whence should I have flesh to give unto

Num 11. 13 saying, Give us flesh, that we may eat
11. 18 therefore the LORD will give you flesh
11. 21 and thou hast said, I will give them flesh
11. 25 and gave (it) unto the seventy elders: and
13. 2 which I give unto the children of Israel
14. 8 he will bring us into this land, and give
15. 2 When ye be come into the land..I give
15. 21 Of the first of your dough ye shall give
16. 14 or given us inheritance of fields and vin.
17 6 every one of their princes gave him a rod
18 7 I have given your priest's office..a serv.
18. 8 I also have given thee the charge of mine
18. 8 unto thee have I given them, by reason
18. 11 I have given them unto thee, and to thy
18. 12 the first fruits of them..have I given thee
18. 19 All the heave offerings..have I given
18. 21 I have given the children of Levi all the
18. 24 tithes..I have given to the Levites to in.
18. 26 the tithes which I have given you from
18. 28 ye shall give thereof the LORD'S heave o.
19. 3 ye shall give her unto Eleazar the priest
20. 12 into the land which I have given them
20. 21 Edom refused to give Israel passage
20. 24 into the land which I have given unto
21. 16 Gather the people together, and I will g.
21. 29 he hath given his sons that escaped, and
22. 13 the LORD refuseth to give me leave to go
22. 18 If Balak would give me his house full of
24. 13 If Balak would give me his house full of
25. 12 I give unto him my covenant of peace
27. 4 Give unto us..a possession among the b.
27. 7 thou shalt surely give them a possession
27. 9 ye shall give his inheritance unto his br.
27. 10 ye shall give his inheritance unto his fat.
27. 11 ye shall give his inheritance unto his ki.
27. 12 and see the land which I have given unto
31. 29 Take..and give (it) unto Eleazar the pri.
31. 30 give them unto the Levites, which keep
31. 41 Moses gave the tribute..the LORD'S hea.
31. 47 gave them unto the Levites, which kept
32. 7, 9 the land which the LORD hath given
32. 29 ye shall give them the land of Gilead for
32. 33 Moses gave unto them..to the children
32. 40 Moses gave Gilead unto Machir the son
33. 53 I have given you the land to possess it
34. 13 commanded to give unto the nine tribes
35. 2 Command..that they give unto the Lev.
35. 2 ye shall give..unto the Levites suburbs
35. 4 which ye shall give unto the Levites
35. 6 which ye shall give unto the Levites
35. 7 all the cities which ye shall give to the
35. 8 And the cities which ye shall give (shall
35. 8 every one shall give of his cities unto the
35. 13 of these cities which ye shall give, six
35 14 Ye shall give three cities on this side Jo.
35 14 three cities shall ye give in the land of C.
36. 2 LORD commanded my lord to give the la.
36. 2 to give the inheritance of Zelophehad
Deut. 1. 8 to give unto them and to their seed after
1. 20 which the LORD our God doth give
1. 25 which the LORD our God doth give
1. 35 which I sware to give unto your fathers
1. 36 to him will I give the land that he hath
1. 39 unto them will I give it, and they shall
2. 5 for I will not give you of their land, no
2. 5 because I have given mount Seir unto E.
2. 9 for I will not give thee of their land
2. 9 I have given Ar unto the children of Lot
2. 12 the land..which the LORD gave unto
2. 19 for I will not give thee of the land of the
2. 19 I have given it unto the children of Lot
2. 24 I have given into thine hand Sihon the
2. 28 give me water for money, that I may dr.
2. 29 the land which the LORD our God giveth
2. 31 I have begun to give Sihon and his land
3. 12 gave I unto the Reubenites and to the G
3. 13 gave I unto the half tribe of Manasseh
3. 15 And I gave Gilead unto Machir
3. 16 unto the Gadites I gave from Gilead even
3. 18 The LORD your God hath given you this
3. 19 abide in your cities which I have given
3. 20 Until the LORD have given rest unto your
3. 20 your God hath given them beyond Jor.
3. 20 unto his possession, which I have given
4. 1 the land which the LORD God..giveth
4. 21 thy God giveth thee..an inheritance
4. 38 to give thee their land..an inheritance
4. 40 which the LORD thy God giveth thee, for
5. 16 in the land which the LORD thy God giv.
5. 31 in the land which I give them to possess
6. 10 to give thee great and goodly cities
6. 23 to give us the land which he sware unto
7. 3 thy daughter thou shalt not give unto
7. 13 which he sware unto thy fathers to give
8. 10 for the good land which he hath given
8. 18 he that giveth thee power to get wealth
9. 6 God giveth thee not this good land to
9. 11 the LORD gave me the two tables of stone
9. 23 possess the land which I have given you
10. 4 tables..and the LORD gave them unto me
10. 11 the land which I sware..to give unto
11. 9 to give unto them, and to their seed
11. 14 I will give (you) the rain of your land
11. 17 the good land which the LORD giveth you
11. 21 sware unto your fathers to give them, as
11. 31 the land..the LORD your God giveth you
12. 1 land..the LORD..giveth thee to possess it
12. 9 to the inheritance..the LORD..giveth you
12. 15 the blessing..which he hath given thee
12. 21 thy flock, which the LORD hath given thee
13. 1 If..a prophet..giveth thee a sign or a w.
13. 12 cities, which the LORD thy God hath given
Deut 14. 21 thou shalt give it unto the stranger that
15. 4 which..God giveth thee..an inheritance
15. 7 thy land which the LORD thy God giveth
15. 9 and thou givest him nought; and he cry
15. 10 Thou shalt surely give him, and thine
15. 10 shall not be grieved when thou givest
15. 14 of thy flock..thou shalt give unto him
16. 5 gates, which the LORD thy God giveth
16. 10 thou shalt give..according as the LORD
16. 17 the blessing..which he hath given thee
16. 18 gates, which the LORD thy God giveth
16. 20 the land which the LORD thy God giveth
17. 2 which the LORD thy God giveth thee
17. 14 which the LORD thy God giveth thee
18. 3 they shall give unto the priest the shoul.
18. 4 first of the fleece..shalt thou give him
18. 9 land which the LORD thy God giveth thee
19. 1 whose land the LORD thy God giveth thee
19. 2 land, which the LORD thy God giveth
19. 8 and give thee all the land which he
19. 8 he promised to give unto thy fathers
19. 10 land, which the LORD thy God giveth
19. 14 that the LORD thy God giveth thee to
20. 14 which the LORD thy God hath given thee
20. 16 which the LORD thy God doth give thee
21. 1 the LORD thy God giveth thee to possess
21. 23 the LORD thy God giveth thee to possess
22. 16 I gave my daughter unto this man to wife
22. 19 give..unto the father of the damsel
22. 29 man..shall give unto the damsel's father
24. 1 give (it) in her hand, and send her out of
24. 3 giveth (it) in her hand, and sendeth her
24. 4 which the LORD thy God giveth thee (for)
24. 15 At his day thou shalt give (him) his hire
25. 15, 19 in the land which the LORD..giveth
25. 19 when the LORD..hath given thee rest
26. 1 which the LORD thy God giveth thee (for)
26. 2 land that the LORD thy God giveth thee
26. 3 LORD sware unto our fathers for to give us
26. 9 hath given us this land..a land that flo.
26. 10 the land which thou, O LORD, hast given
26. 11 which the LORD thy God hath given unto
26. 12 hast given (it) unto the Levite, the stra.
26. 13 and also have given them unto the Levite
26. 14 nor given (ought) thereof for the dead
26. 15 and the land which thou hast given us
27. 2, 3 land which the LORD thy God giveth
28. 8 in the land which the LORD..giveth thee
28. 11 LORD sware unto thy fathers to give thee
28. 12 the heaven to give the rain unto thy land
28. 52, 53 which the LORD thy God hath given
28. 55 So that he will not give to any of them of
28. 65 the LORD shall give thee there a trembl.
29. 4 Yet the LORD hath not given you an heart
29. 8 we took their land, and gave it for an in.
30. 20 land which the LORD sware..to give them
31. 7 which the LORD hath sworn..to give them
32. 49, 52 which I give..the children of Israel
34. 4 saying, I will give it unto thy seed
Josh. 1. 2 unto the land which I do give to them
1. 3 have I given unto you, as I said unto M.
1. 6 the land which I sware..to give them
1. 11 which the LORD..giveth you to possess it
1. 13 God hath given you rest, and hath given
1. 14 remain in the land which Moses gave you
1. 15 Until the LORD have given your brethren
1. 15 land which the LORD your God giveth
1. 15 which Moses the LORD'S servant gave you
2. 9 I know that the LORD hath given you the
2. 12 show kindness..and give me a true token
2. 14 when the LORD hath given us the land
5. 6 which the LORD sware..he would give us
6. 2 I have given into thine hand Jericho, and
6. 16 Shout; for the LORD hath given you the
8. 1 I have given into thy hand the king of Ai
8. 18 for I will give it into thine hand
9. 24 to give you all the land, and to destroy
11 23 Joshua gave it for an inheritance unto I.
12. 6 Moses the servant of the LORD gave it
12 7 which Joshua gave unto the tribes of Is.
13 8 their inheritance, which Moses gave them
13 8 as Moses the servant of the LORD gave
13 14 Only unto the tribe of Levi he gave none
13 15 Moses gave unto..the children of Reuben
13. 24 Moses gave..unto the tribe of Gad..unto
13 29 Moses gave..unto the half tribe of Man.
13 33 But unto the tribe of Levi Moses gave not
14 3 For Moses had given the inheritance of
14 3 unto the Levites he gave none inherit.
14 4 they gave no part unto the Levites in the
14 12 Now therefore give me this mountain
14 13 Joshua..gave unto Caleb..Hebron for an
15 13 And unto Caleb..he gave a part among
15 16 to him will I give Achsah my daughter
15 17 he gave him Achsah his daughter to wife
15 19 Give me a blessing; for thou hast given me
15 19 give me also springs of water. And he g.
17 4 to give us an inheritance among our bret.
17. 4 he gave them an inheritance among the
17. 14 Why hast thou given me (but) one lot and
18. 3 the land, which the LORD..hath given
18. 7 which Moses the servant of the LORD ga.
19 49 gave an inheritance to Joshua the son of
19 50 they gave him the city which he asked
20. 4 give him a place, that he may dwell amo.
21. 2 commanded..to give us cities to dwell in
21. 3 children of Israel gave unto the Levites
21. 8 gave by lot unto the Levites these cities
21. 9 they gave out of the tribe of the child.
21. 11 they gave them the city of Arba the fath.
21. 12 But the fields..gave they to Caleb the son
21. 13 Thus they gave to the children of Aaron
Josh 21. 21 they gave them Shechem with her subur.
21. 43 the LORD gave unto Israel all the land
21. 43 which he sware to give unto their fathers
22. 4 God hath given rest unto your brethren
22. 4 which Moses the servant of the LORD ga.
22 7 Moses had given (possession) in Bashan
22. 7 unto the (other) half thereof gave Joshua
23. 13 this good land..the LORD..hath given
23. 15 this good land..the LORD..hath given
23. 16 the good land which he hath given unto
24. 3 multiplied his seed, and gave him Isaac
24. 4 And I gave unto Isaac Jacob and Esau
24. 4 I gave unto Esau mount Seir, to possess
24. 8 I gave them into your hand, that ye mig.
24. 13 I have given you a land for which ye did
Judg. 1 12 to him will I give Achsah my daughter
1. 13 he gave him Achsah his daughter to wife
1. 15 me a blessing: for thou hast given me a
1. 15 give me also springs..And Caleb gave he
1. 20 they gave Hebron unto Caleb, as Moses
3. 6 and gave their daughters to their sons
5. 25 He asked water..she gave..milk; she br
6. 9 drave them out..and gave you their land
7. 2 to give the Midianites into their hands
8. 5 Give, I pray you, loaves of bread unto the
8. 6 that we should give bread unto thine ar?
8. 15 that we should give bread unto thy men
8. 24 that ye would give me every man the
8. 25 they answered, We will willingly give
9. 4 And they gave him threescore and ten
14. 9 and he gave them, and they did eat: but
14 12 I will give you thirty sheets and thirty
14 13 then shall ye give me thirty sheets and
14 19 and gave change of garments unto them
15. 2 therefore I gave her to thy companion
15 6 because he had..given her to his compan
15 18 Thou hast given this great deliverance
16. 5 we will give thee, every one of us, eleven
17 4 and gave them to the founder, who made
17. 10 I will give thee ten..of silver by the year
18. 10 for God hath given it into your hands
20. 36 Israel gave place to the Benjamites
21. 1 there shall not any of us give his daugh.
21 7 we will not give them of our daughters
21. 14 they gave them wives which they had
21. 18 we may not give them wives of our daug.
21. 18 Cursed (be) he that giveth a wife to Ben.
21 22 ye did not give unto them at this time
Ruth 2. 18 gave to her that she had reserved after
3 17 These six (measures) of barley gave he me
4. 7 plucked off his shoe, and gave (it) to his
4. 12 of the seed which the LORD shall give
4. 13 LORD gave her conception, and she bare
1 Sa. 1. 4 he gave to Peninnah his wife, and to all
1. 5 But unto Hannah he gave a worthy por.
1. 11 wilt give unto thine handmaid a man ch.
1. 11 then I will give him unto the LORD all
1. 27 LORD hath given me my petition which I
2. 10 he shall give strength unto his king, and
2. 15 Give flesh to roast for the priest; for he
2 16 thou shalt give..now: and if not, I will
2 28 did I give unto the house of thy father all
6 5 ye shall give glory unto the God of Israel
8. 6 Give us a king to judge us. And Samuel
8. 14 take..the best..and give..to his servants
8. 15 take..of your vineyards, and give to his
9. 8 will I give to the man of God to tell us
9. 23 Bring the portion which I gave thee, of
10. 4 they will salute thee, and give thee two
15 28 hath given it to a neighbour of thine
17. 10 give me a man, that we may fight together
17. 25 the king..will give him his daughter, and
17. 44 I will give thy flesh unto the fowls of the
17. 46 I will give the carcases of the host of the
17. 47 and he will give you into our hands
18. 4 Jonathan..gave it to David, and his gar.
18. 17 my elder daughter Merab, her will I give
18. 21 I will give him her, that she may be a
18. 27 Saul gave him Michal his daughter to wi.
20. 40 Jonathan gave his artillery unto his lad
21 3 give (me) five (loaves of) bread in mine
21. 6 So the priest gave him hallowed (bread)
21. 9 said, (There is) none like that; give it me
22 7 will the son of Jesse give every one of you
22 10 And he..gave him victuals, and gave
22. 13 in that thou hast given him bread, and a
25 8 give, I pray thee, whatsoever cometh to
25. 11 and give (it) unto men whom I know not
25. 44 But Saul had given Michal his daughter
27 5 let them give me a place in some town
27 6 Then Achish gave him Ziklag that day
28 17 and given it to thy neighbour..to David
30. 11 and gave him bread, and he did eat
30 12 they gave him a piece of a cake of figs
30. 22 we will not give them..of the spoil that
30. 23 with that which the LORD hath given us
2 Sa. 4. 10 that I would have given him a reward
9 9 I have given unto thy master's son all
12 8 And I gave thee thy master's house
12. 8 and gave thee the house of Israel and of
12. 11 I will..give..unto thy neighbour, and he
18. 11 I would have given thee ten (shekels) of
21. 6 And the king said, I will give (them)
22. 36 Thou hast also given me the shield of thy
22 41 Thou hast also given me the necks of
24 9 Joab gave up the sum of the number of
24 23 All these..did Araunah..give unto the
1 Ki. 1. 48 which hath given (one) to sit on my throne
2. 17 give me Abishag the Shunammite to wife
3. 5 and God said, Ask what I shall give thee
3. 6 that thou hast given him a son to sit on
3. 9 Give..thy servant an understanding hea.

1 Ki. 3. 12 lo, I have given thee a wise..heart; so that
3. 13 I have also given thee that which thou
3. 25 give half to the one, and half to the other
3. 26 O my lord, give her the living child, and
3. 27 Give her the living child, and in no wise
4. 29 God gave Solomon wisdom and under.
5. 6 unto thee will I give hire for thy servants
5. 7 which hath given unto David a wise son
5. 10 So Hiram gave Solomon cedar trees and
5. 11 Solomon gave Hiram twenty thousand
5. 11 thus gave Solomon to Hiram year by year
5. 12 the LORD gave Solomon wisdom, as he had
8. 32 to give him according to his righteous.
8. 34 which thou gavest unto their fathers
8. 36 and give rain upon thy land, which thou
8. 36 hast given to thy people for an inheritan.
8. 39 give to every man according to his ways
8. 40 the land which thou gavest unto our fat.
8. 48 land which thou gavest unto their fath.
8. 50 give them compassion before them who
8. 56 Blessed (be) the LORD, that hath given
9. 7 out of the land which I have given them
9. 11 king Solomon gave Hirim twenty cities
9. 12 to see the cities which Solomon had given
9. 13 What..(are) these which thou hast given
9. 16 and given it..a present unto his daughter
10. 10 she gave the king an hundred and twenty
10. 10 the queen of Sheba gave to king Solomon
10. 13 king Solomon gave unto the queen of Sh.
10. 13 besides (that) which Solomon gave her of
11. 11 rend..from thee, and will give it to thy
11. 13 will give one tribe to thy son for David
11. 18 gave him an house..and gave him land
11. 19 so that he gave him to wife the sister of
11. 31 Behold, I will..give ten tribes to thee
11. 35 and will give it unto thee..ten tribes
11. 36 unto his son will I give one tribe, that D.
11. 38 be with thee..and will give Israel unto
13. 3 And he gave a sign the same day, saying
13. 5 the sign which the man of God had given
13. 7 refresh thyself, and I will give thee a rew.
13. 8 If thou wilt give me half thine house, I
14. 8 And rent the kingdom..and gave it thee
14. 15 good land, which he gave to their fathers
14. 16 he shall give Israel up because of the sins
15. 4 for David's sake did the LORD..give him
17. 19 And he said unto her, Give me thy son
18. 23 Let them therefore give us two bullocks
19. 21 gave unto the people, and they did eat
21. 2 Give me thy vineyard, that I may have
21 2 I will give thee for it a better vineyard
21. 2 I will give thee the worth of it in money
21. 3 LORD forbid it me, that I should give the
21. 4 I will not give thee the inheritance of my
21. 6 said..Give me thy vineyard for money
21. 6 or else if it please thee, I will give thee
21. 6 answered, I will not give thee my vineya.
21. 7 I will give thee the vineyard of Naboth
21. 15 which he refused to give thee for money
2 Ki. 4. 42 Give unto the people, that they may eat
4. 43 Give the people, that they may eat: for
5. 1 by him the LORD hath given deliverance
5. 22 give them, I pray thee, a talent of silver
6. 28 This woman said unto me, Give thy son
6. 29 Give thy son, that we may eat him; and
8. 19 as he promised him to give him alway a
8. 29 wounds which the Syrians had given him
10. 15 give (me) thine hand. And he gave (him)
11. 10 did the priest give king David's spears
12. 11 they gave the money, being told, into the
12. 14 they gave that to the workmen, and rep.
13. 5 LORD gave Israel a saviour, so that they
14. 9 Give thy daughter to my son to wife
15. 19 Menahem gave Pul a thousand talents of
15. 20 of silver, to give to the king of Assyria
18. 15 Hezekiah gave..all the silver (that was)
18. 16 cut off..and gave it to the king of Assyr.
21. 8 out of the land which I gave their fathers
22. 5 let them give it to the doers of the work
22. 8 And Hilkiah gave the book to Shaphan
23. 11 that the kings of Judah had given to the
23. 35 Jehoiakim gave the silver and the gold
23. 35 but he taxed the land to give the money
23. 35 exacted the silver and the gold..to give
1 Ch. 2. 35 Sheshan gave his daughter to Jarha his
6. 55 they gave them Hebron in the land of J.
6. 56 the fields of the city..they gave to Caleb
6. 57 to the sons of Aaron they gave the cities
6. 64 the children of Israel gave to the Levites
6. 65 they gave by lot out of the tribe of the
6. 67 they gave unto them, (of) the cities of re.
16. 18 Unto thee will I give the land of Canaan
21. 5 Joab gave the sum of the number of the
21. 23 I give (thee) the oxen (also) for burnt off.
21. 23 wheat for the meat offering; I give it all
21. 25 So David gave to Ornan for the place six
22. 9 I will give him rest from all his enemies
22. 9 will give peace and quietness unto Israel
22. 12 Only the LORD give thee wisdom and
22. 18 hath he (not) given you rest on every side?
22. 18 for he hath given the inhabitants of the
25. 5 God gave to Heman fourteen sons and
28. 5 for the LORD hath given me many sons
28. 11 David gave to Solomon his son the patt.
29. 3 (which) I have given to the house of my
29. 7 gave for the service of the house of God
29. 8 they..gave (them) to the treasure of the
29. 14 and of thine own have we given thee
29. 19 give unto Solomon my son a perfect hea.
2 Ch 1. 7 said unto him, Ask what I shall give thee
1. 10 Give me now wisdom and knowledge
1. 12 I will give thee riches, and wealth, and

2 Ch. 2. 10 I will give to thy servants, the hewers
2. 12 who hath given to David the king a wise
6. 25 which thou gavest to them and to their
6. 27 which thou hast given unto thy people
6. 31 the land which thou gavest unto our fat.
6. 38 which thou gavest unto their fathers, and
7. 20 out of my land which I have given them
9. 9 she gave the king an hundred and twen.
9. 9 as the queen of Sheba gave king Solomon
9. 12 king Solomon gave to the queen of Sheba
11. 23 and he gave them victual in abundance
13. 5 gave the kingdom over Israel to David
20. 7 gavest it to the seed of Abraham thy fri.
21. 3 their father gave them great gifts of silver
21. 3 the kingdom gave he to Jehoram, because
21. 7 as he promised to give a light to him and
24. 12 Jehoiada gave it to such as did the work
25. 9 which I have given to the army of Israel?
25. 9 The LORD is able to give thee much more
25. 18 Give thy daughter to my son to wife: and
26. 8 the Ammonites gave gifts to Uzziah: and
27. 5 the children of Ammon gave him the same
28. 21 gave (it) unto the king of Assyria: but he
30. 7 (who) therefore gave them up to desolat.
30. 12 the hand of God was to give them one h.
31. 4 to give the portion of the priests and the
31. 15 to give to their brethren by courses, as
31. 19 to give portions to all the males among
32. 11 Doth not Hezekiah persuade you to give
32. 24 he spake unto him, and he gave him a
32. 29 God had given him substance very much
34. 10 they gave it to the workmen that wrought
34. 11 to the artificers and builders gave they
34. 18 Hilkiah the priest hath given me a book
35. 8 gave unto the priests for the passover off.
35. 12 that they might give according to the
36. 17 had no compassion..he gave (them) all
36. 23 hath the LORD God of heaven given me
Ezra 1. 2 The LORD God of heaven hath given me
2. 69 They gave after their ability unto the tre.
3. 7 They gave money also unto the masons
7. 6 which the LORD God of Israel had given
7. 11 king Artaxerxes gave unto Ezra the pri.
9. 8 to give us a nail in his holy place, that
9. 8 God may..give us a little reviving in our
9. 9 to give us a reviving, to set up the house
9. 9 to give us a wall in Judah and in Jerusa.
9. 12 give not your daughters unto their sons
9. 13 and hast given us (such) deliverance as
10. 19 they gave their hands that they would
Neh. 2. 1 I took up the wine, and gave (it) unto the
2. 7 let letters be given me to the governors
2. 8 that he may give me timber to make be.
2. 9 I came..and gave them the king's letters
4. 4 give them for a prey in the land of capti.
7. 70 some of the chief of the fathers gave unto
7. 70 The Tirshatha gave to the treasure a th.
7. 71 the chief of the fathers gave to the trea.
7. 72 (that) which the rest of the people gave
9. 8 a covenant with him, to give the land of
9. 8 give..to his seed, and hast performed thy
9. 13 gavest them right judgments, and true
9. 15 gavest them bread from heaven for their
9. 15 land which thou hadst sworn to give them
9. 20 gavest also thy good Spirit..and gavest
9. 22 gavest them kingdoms and nations, and
9. 24 gavest them into their hands, with their
9. 27 thou gavest them saviours, who saved
9. 30 therefore gavest thou them into the hand
9. 35 thy great goodness that thou gavest them
9. 35 fat land which thou gavest before them
9. 36 the land that thou gavest unto our fath.
10. 30 that we would not give our daughters un.
12. 47 all Israel..gave the portions of the sing.
13. 25 Ye shall not give your daughters unto
Esth. 1. 19 let the king give her royal estate unto
1. 20 all the wives shall give to their husbands
2. 3 let their things for purification be given
2. 9 speedily gave her her things for purifica.
2. 9 meet to be given her, out of the king's h.
2. 18 Then the king..gave gifts, according to
3. 10 gave it unto Haman the son of Hammed.
4. 8 he gave him the copy of the writing of
8. 1 give the house of Haman, the Jews' ene.
8. 2 And the king..gave it unto Mordecai
8. 7 I have given Esther the house of Haman
Job 1. 21 the LORD gave, and the LORD hath taken
2. 4 all that a man hath will he give for his
5. 10 Who giveth rain upon the earth, and
35. 7 If thou be righteous, what givest thou h.?
35. 10 Where (is) God my maker, who giveth
36. 6 preserveth not..but giveth right to the
36. 31 For by them..he giveth meat in abunda.
38. 36 who hath given understanding to the h.?
39. 19 Hast thou given the horse strength? hast
42. 11 every man also gave him a piece of mon.
42. 15 their father gave them inheritance among
Psa. 2. 8 Ask of me, and I shall give (thee) the he.
18. 13 the Highest gave his voice; hail (stones)
18. 35 Thou hast also given me the shield of thy
18. 40 Thou hast also given me the necks of
21. 2 Thou hast given him his heart's desire
21. 4 He asked life of thee, (and) thou gavest
28. 4 Give them according..give them after
29. 11 The LORD will give strength unto his pe.
37. 4 shall give thee the desires of thine heart
37. 21 the righteous showeth mercy, and giveth
44. 11 Thou hast given us like sheep..for meat
49. 7 nor give to God a ransom for him
51. 16 desirest not sacrifice, else would I give
60. 4 Thou hast given a banner to them that
61. 5 thou hast given (me) the heritage of those

Psa. 68. 11 LORD gave the word; great (was) the
68. 35 the God of Israel (is) he that giveth stre.
69. 21 They gave me also gall for my meat; and
72. 1 Give the king thy judgments, O God, and
72. 15 to him shall be given of the gold of Sheba
74. 14 gavest him (to be) meat to the people inh.
78. 20 can he give bread also? can he provide
78. 24 and had given them of the corn of heav.
78. 46 gave also their increase unto the caterp.
79. 2 given (to be) meat unto the fowls of the
84. 11 the LORD will give grace and glory: no
85. 12 LORD shall give (that which is) good; and
86. 16 give thy strength unto thy servant, and
99. 7 they kept..the ordinance (that) he gave
104. 27 that thou mayest give (them) their meat
104. 28 (That) thou givest them they gather: thou
105. 11 Unto thee will I give the land of Canaan
105. 32 He gave tham hail for rain..flaming
105. 44 And gave them the lands of the heathen
106. 15 he gave them their request; but sent
106. 41 he gave them into the hand of the heath.
111. 5 He hath given meat unto them that fear
111. 6 may give them the heritage of the heath.
112. 9 He hath dispersed, he hath given to the
115. 1 but unto thy name give glory, for thy m.
115. 16 the earth hath he given to the children
124. 6 who hath not given us (as) a prey to their
127. 2 (for) so he giveth his beloved sleep
132. 4 will not give sleep to mine eyes, (or) slu.
135. 12 gave their land (for) an heritage, an her.
136. 21 gave their land for an heritage: for his
136. 25 Who giveth food to all flesh: for his me.
144. 10 (It is he) that giveth salvation unto kings
145. 15 thou givest them their meat in due sea.
146. 7 which giveth food to the hungry. The
147. 9 He giveth to the beast his food, (and) to
147. 16 He giveth snow like wool: he scattereth
Prov. 1. 4 To give subtilty to the simple, to the yo.
2. 6 For the LORD giveth wisdom: out of his
3. 28 come again, and to morrow I will give
3. 34 scorneth the scorners: but he giveth gr.
4. 2 For I give you good doctrine, forsake ye
4. 9 She shall give to thine head an ornament
5. 9 Lest thou give thine honour unto others
6. 4 Give not sleep to thine eyes, nor slumber
6. 31 shall give all the substance of his house
9. 9 Give (instruction) to a wise (man), and he
13. 15 Good understanding giveth favour: but
21. 26 but the righteous giveth and spareth not
22. 9 for he giveth of his bread to the poor
22. 16 he that giveth to the rich, (shall) surely
23. 26 My son, give me thine heart, and let
23. 31 when it giveth his colour in the cup
26. 8 so (is) he that giveth honour to a fool
28. 27 He that giveth unto the poor shall not
29. 15 The rod and reproof give wisdom: but
29. 17 Correct thy son, and he shall give thee
29. 17 yea, he shall give delight unto thy soul
30. 8 give me neither poverty nor riches; feed
31. 3 Give not thy strength unto women, nor
31. 6 Give strong drink unto him that is ready
31. 15 and giveth meat to her household, and
31. 31 Give her of the fruit of her hands; and
Eccl. 1. 13 I gave my heart to seek and search out
1. 13 this sore travail hath God given to the
1. 17 I gave my heart to know wisdom, and
2. 26 For (God) giveth to a man that (is) good in
2. 26 to the sinner he giveth travail, to gather
2. 26 he may give to (him that is) good before
3. 10 which God hath given to the sons of men
5. 1 more ready to hear than to give the sac.
5. 18 which God giveth him; for it (is) his po.
5. 19 Every man also to whom God hath given
5. 19 and hath given him power to eat thereof
6. 2 God hath given..yet God giveth him not
8. 15 life, which God giveth him under the sun
9. 9 which he hath given thee under the sun
11. 2 Give a portion to seven, and also to eight
12. 7 spirit shall return unto God who gave it
Song 2. 13 vines (with) the tender grape give a (good)
7. 12 vineyards..there will I give thee my loves
7. 13 mandrakes give a smell, and at our gates
8. 7 if a man would give all the substance of
Isa. 3. 4 I will give children (to be) their princes
7. 14 the LORD himself shall give you a sign
8. 18 the children whom the LORD hath given
30. 20 the LORD give you the bread of adversity
30. 23 Then shall he give the rain of thy seed
36. 8 Now therefore give pledges, I pray thee
36. 8 and I will give thee two thousand horses
40. 29 He giveth power to the faint; and to
41. 2 Who..gave the nations before him, and
41. 2 he gave (them) as the dust to his sword
41. 27 I will give to Jerusalem one that bring.
42. 5 he that giveth breath unto the people
42. 6 give thee for a covenant of the people
42. 8 and my glory will I not give to another
42. 24 Who gave Jacob for a spoil, and Israel
43. 3 I gave Egypt (for) thy ransom, Ethiopia
43. 4 therefore will I give men for thee, and
43. 20 because I give waters in the wilderness
43. 28 have given Jacob to the curse, and Israel
45. 3 I will give thee the treasures of darkness
47. 6 I have..given them into thine hand: thou
48. 11 and I will not give my glory unto another
49. 6 I will also give thee for a light to the G.
49. 8 I will..give thee for a covenant of the
50. 4 The Lord GOD hath given me the tongue
50. 6 I gave my back to the smiters, and my
55. 4 I have given him (for) a witness to the
55. 10 that it may give seed to the sower, and
56. 5 Even unto them will I give in mine ho.

Isa. 56. 5 I will give them an everlasting name
61. 3 to give unto them beauty for ashes, the
62. 7 give him no rest, till he establish, and
62. 8 Surely I will no more give thy corn (to
Jer. 3. 8 I had..given her a bill of divorce ; yet
3. 15 I will give you pastors according to mine
3. 18 to the land that I have given for an
3. 19 give thee a pleasant land, a goodly herit.
4. 16 give out their voice against the cities of J.
5. 24 fear the LORD our God, that giveth rain
7. 7 in the land that I gave to your fathers
7. 14 unto the place which I gave to you and
8. 10 Therefore will I give their wives unto
8. 13 (the things that) I have given them
11. 5 to give them a land flowing with milk
12. 7 I have given the dearly beloved of my
13. 16 Give glory to the LORD your God, before
14. 13 will give you assured peace in this place
14. 22 can the heavens give showers? (Art) not
15. 13 thy treasures will I give to the spoil with.
16 15 their land that I gave unto their fathers
17 3 I will give thy substance (and) all thy
17 4 from thine heritage that I gave thee ; and
17. 10 even to give every man according to his
19. 7 their carcases will I give to be meat for
20. 4 I will give all Judah into the hand of
20. 5 all the treasures..will I give into the
22. 13 without wages, and giveth him not for
22. 25 I will give thee into the hand of them
23. 39 the city that I gave you and your fathers
24. 7 I will give them an heart to know me
24. 8 So will I give Zedekiah the king of Judah
24. 10 from off the land that I gave unto them
25. 5 in the land that the LORD hath given
25. 31 he will give them (that are) wicked to
26. 24 that they should not give him into the
27. 5 have given it unto whom it seemed meet
27. 6 now have I given all these lands into the
27. 6 the beasts of the field have I given him
28. 14 I have given him the beasts of the field
29. 6 give your daughters to husbands, that
29. 11 not of evil, to give you an expected end
30. 3 to the land that I gave to their fathers
30. 16 all that prey upon thee will I give for a
31. 35 which giveth the sun for a light by day
32. 3, 28 I will give this city into the hand of
32. 12 I gave the evidence of the purchase unto
32. 19 to give every one according to his ways
32 22 hast given them this land, which thou
32. 22 to give them, a land flowing with milk
32. 39 I will give them one heart, and one way
34 2 I will give this city into the hand of the
34. 18 I will give the men that have transgress.
34. 20 I will even give them into the hand of
34. 21 princes, will I give into the hand of their
35 15 dwell in the land which I have given to
36. 32 gave it to Baruch the scribe, the son of
37 21 that they should give him daily a piece
38. 16 neither will I give thee into the hand of
39. 10 land of Judah, and gave them vineyards
40. 5 captain of the guard gave him victuals
44. 30 I will give Pharaoh-hophra king of Egypt
44. 30 as I gave Zedekiah king of Judah into the
45. 5 but thy life will I give unto thee for a pr.
48 9 Give wings unto Moab, that it may flee
50. 15 she hath given her hand : her foundations
Lam. 1. 11 they have given their pleasant things for
2. 18 give thyself no rest ; let not the apple of
3 30 He giveth (his) cheek to him that smiteth
3. 65 Give them sorrow of heart, thy curse unto
5 6 We have given the hand (to) the Egyp.
Eze. 2. 8 open thy mouth, and eat that I give thee
3. 3 with this roll that I give thee Then did
4. 15 Then he said unto me, Lo, I have given
7. 21 I will give it into the hands of the stra.
11 17 and I will give you the land of Israel
11. 19 I will give them one heart, and I will
11. 19 and will give them an heart of flesh
15. 6 which I have given to the fire for fuel, so
15. 6 will I give the inhabitants of Jerusalem
16. 17 which I had given thee, and madest to
16. 19 My meat also which I gave thee, fine fl.
16. 33 give gifts to all whores ; but thou givest
16. 34 in that thou givest a reward, and no re.
16 36 children. which thou didst give unto
16. 38 I will give thee blood in fury and jealo.
16. 39 I will also give thee into their hand, and
16. 41 thou also shalt give no hire any more
16. 61 I will give them unto thee for daughters
17. 15 that they might give him horses and
17. 18 he had given his hand, and hath done all
18. 7 hath given his bread to the hungry, and
18. 8 He (that) hath not given forth upon usury
18. 13 Hath given forth upon usury, and hath
18. 16 hath given his bread to the hungry, and
20. 11 I gave them my statutes, and showed
20. 12 also I gave them my sabbaths, to be a sign
20. 15 the land which I had given (them), flow.
20. 25 I gave them also statutes..not good, and
20. 28, 42 I lifted up mine hand to give it to
21. 11 he hath given it to be furbished, that it
21. 11 to give it into the hand of the slayer
21. 27 whose right it is ; and I will give it (him)
23. 31 therefore will I give her cup into thine
23. 46 will give them to be removed and spoiled
25. 10 will give them in possession, that the
28. 25 that I have given to my servant Jacob
29. 5 I have given thee for meat to the beasts
29. 19 I will give the land of Egypt unto Nebu.
29. 20 I have given him the land of Egypt (for)
29. 21 I will give thee the opening of the mouth
33. 27 will I give to the beasts to be devoured

Eze. 36. 26 A new heart also will I give you, and a
36. 26 and I will give you an heart of flesh
36. 28 that I gave to your fathers ; and ye shall
37. 25 that I have given unto Jacob my servant
39. 4 I will give thee unto the ravenous birds
39. 11 I will give unto Gog a place there of gra.
39. 23 gave them into the hand of their enemies
43. 19 thou shalt give to the priests the Levites
44. 28 ye shall give them no possession in Israel
44. 30 ye shall also give unto the priest the
45. 8 shall they give to the house of Israel
46. 16 If the prince give a gift unto any of his
46. 17 if he give a gift of his inheritance to one
47. 14 to give it unto your fathers : and this
47. 23 there shall ye give (him) his inheritance
Dan. 1. 2 the LORD gave Jehoiakim king of Judah
1. 12 let them give us pulse to eat, and water
1. 16 they should drink, and gave them pulse
1. 17 God gave them knowledge and skill in
8. 13 to give both the sanctuary and the host
11. 17 he shall give him the daughter of women
11. 21 shall not give the honour of the kingdom
Hos. 2. 5 that give (me) my bread and my water
2. 8 did not know that I gave her corn, and
2. 12 that my lovers have given me : and I will
2. 15 I will give her her vineyards from thence
9. 14 Give them..what wilt thou give? give
13. 10 thou saidst, Give me a king and princes?
13. 11 I gave thee a king in mine anger, and
Joel 2. 17 give not thine heritage to reproach, that
2. 23 for he hath given you the former rain
3. 3 have given a boy for an harlot, and sold
Amos 4. 6 I also have given you cleanness of teeth
9. 15 their land which I have given them, saith
Mic. 1. 14 shalt thou give presents to Moresheth-g.
6. 7 shall I give my first born (for) my transg.
Hag. 2. 9 in this place will I give peace, saith the
Zech. 3. 7 I will give thee places to walk among
8. 12 vine shall give..shall give her..shall give
10. 1 give them showers of rain, to every one
Mal. 2. 2 lay (it) to heart, to give glory unto my
2. 5 I gave them to him (for) the fear where.

11. *To give*, נְתַן *nethan*.

Dan. 2. 16 the king that he would give ; 4. 17, 25, 32.

11*a*. *To call*, קְרָא *qara*.

Gen. 2 20 gave names to all cattle, and to the fowl

12. *To lift up, exalt*, רוּם *rum*, 5.

2 Ch. 30 24 Hezekiah king of Judah did give to the
30. 24 and the princes gave to the congregation
35. 7 Josiah gave to the people, of the flock
35. 8 his princes gave willingly unto the peo.
35. 9 gave unto the Levites for the passover off.

13. *To put, place*, שׂוּם *sum*.

Num. 6. 26 LORD lift up his countenance..give thee
Deut 22 14 give occasions of speech against her, and
22. 17 he hath given occasions of speech (against
Josh. 7. 19 My son, give, I pray thee, glory to the L.
1 Sa. 2. 20 LORD give thee seed of this woman, for
Ezra 4. 21 Give ye now commandment to cause
Neh. 8. 8 gave the sense, and caused..to underst.
9. 7 and gavest him the name of Abraham
Prov. 8. 29 When he gave to the sea his decree, that
Isa. 42 12 Let them give glory unto the LORD, and
Dan. 1. 7 Unto whom the prince of the eunuchs g.
1. 7 for he gave unto Daniel (the name) of B.

14. *To give away (from oneself)*, ἀποδίδωμι *apodid.*

Matt 12. 36 they shall give account thereof in the d.
20. 8 give them (their) hire, beginning from
Luke 16. 2 give an account of thy stewardship ; for
Acts 4. 33 with great power gave the apostles wit.
19. 40 no cause whereby [we may give] an account
2 Ti. 4. 8 the righteous Judge, shall give me at that
Heb. 13. 17 as they that must give account, that they
1 Pe. 4. 5 Who shall give account to him that is
Rev. 22. 12 to give every man according as his work

15. *To apportion, portion off*, ἀπονέμω *aponemō.*

1 Pe. 3. 7 giving honour unto the wife, as unto the

16. *To give throughout*, διαδίδωμι *diadidōmi.*

Rev. 17. 13 [shall give] their power and strength unto

17. *To give*, δίδωμι *didōmi.*

Matt. 4. 9 All these things will I give thee, if thou
5. 31 let him give her a writing of divorcement
5. 42 Give to him that asketh thee, and from
6. 11 Give us this day our daily bread
7. 6 Give not that which is holy unto the dogs
7. 7 Ask, and it shall be given you ; seek, and
7. 11 know how to give good gifts unto your
7. 11 give good things to them that ask him
9. 8 which had given such power unto men
10. 1 he gave them power (against) unclean
10. 8 freely ye have received, freely give
10. 19 [it shall be given you in that same hour]
12. 39 there shall no sign be given to it, but the
13. 11 Because it is given unto you to know the
13. 11 but to them it is not given
13. 12 whosoever hath, to him shall be given
14. 7 he promised..to give her whatsoever she
14. 8 Give me here John Baptist's head in a
14. 9 the king..commanded (it) to be given
14. 11 was brought in a charger, and given to
14. 16 They need not depart ; give ye them to
14. 19 gave the loaves to (his) disciples, and the
15. 36 gave to his disciples, and the disciples to
16. 4 there shall no sign be given unto it, but
16. 19 I will give unto thee the keys of the king.
16. 26 what shall a man give in exchange for his

Matt 17. 27 that take, and give unto them for me
19. 7 command to give a writing of divorcem.
19. 11 cannot receive..save..to whom it is given
19. 21 give to the poor, and thou shalt have
20. 4 and whatsoever is right I will give you
20. 14 I will give unto this last even as unto
20. 23 to sit on my right..is not mine to give
20. 28 and to give his life a ransom for many
21. 23 and who gave thee this authority?
21. 43 given to a nation bringing forth the fru.
22. 17 Is it lawful to give tribute unto Cesar
24. 29 the moon shall not give her light, and
24. 45 to give them meat in due season
25. 8 Give us of your oil ; for our lamps are
25. 15 unto one he gave five talents, to another
25. 28 give (it) unto him which hath ten talents
25. 29 For unto every one that hath shall be gi.
25. 35 For I was an hungered, and ye gave me
25. 42 For I was an hungered, and ye gave me no
26. 9 might have been sold for much, and giv.
26. 15 What will ye give me, and I will deliver
26. 26 and gave (it) to the disciples, and said
26. 27 and gave (it) to them, saying, Drink ye
26. 48 he that betrayed him gave them a sign
27. 10 gave them for the potter's field, as the
27. 34 They gave him vinegar to drink mingled
28. 12 they gave large money unto the soldiers
28. 18 All power is given unto me in heaven
Mark 2. 26 gave also to them which were with him
4. 11 Unto you it is given to know the mystery
4. 25 For he that hath, to him shall be given
5. 43 that something should be given her to
6. 2 what wisdom (is) this which is given unto
6. 7 and gave them power over unclean spirits
6. 22 whatsoever thou wilt, and I will give (it)
6. 23 I will give (it) thee, unto the half of my
6. 25 I will that thou give me by and by in a
6. 28 brought his head in a charger, and gave
6. 28 and the damsel gave it to her mother
6. 37 said unto them, Give ye them to eat
6. 37 Shall we go and buy..and give them to
6. 41 gave (them) to his disciples to set before
8. 6 and gave to his disciples to set before
8. 12 There shall no sign be given unto this g.
8. 37 Or what shall a man give in exchange
10. 21 sell whatsoever thou hast, and give to the
10. 40 to sit on my right..is not mine to give
10. 45 and to give his life a ransom for many
11. 28 who gave thee this authority to do these
12. 9 and will give the vineyard unto others
12. 14 Is it lawful to give tribute to Cesar, or
12. 15 Shall we give, or shall we not give? But
13. 11 whatsoever shall be given you in that
13. 24 and the moon shall not give her light
13. 34 gave authority to his servants, and to
14. 5 might have been sold..and have been gi.
14. 11 they were glad, and promised to give
14. 22 gave to them, and said, Take, eat : this
14. 23 he gave (it) to them ; and they all drank
14. 44 he that betrayed him had given them a
15. 23 they gave him to drink wine mixed with
Luke 1. 32 the Lord God shall give unto him the
1. 77 To give knowledge of salvation unto his
4. 6 All this power will I give thee, and the
4. 6 and to whomsoever I will I give it
6. 4 gave also to them that were with him
6. 30 Give to every man that asketh of thee
6. 38 Give, and it shall be given unto you
6. 38 good measure..shall men give into your
7. 44 thou gavest me no water for my feet : but
7. 45 Thou gavest me no kiss : but this woman
8. 10 Unto you it is given to know the myster.
8. 18 whosoever hath, to him shall be given
8. 55 and he commanded to give her meat
9. 1 gave them power and authority over all
9. 13 he said unto them, Give ye them to eat
9. 16 and gave to the disciples to set before
10. 19 I give unto you power to tread on serpe.
10. 35 gave..to the host, and said unto him
11. 3 Give us day by day our daily bread
11. 7 Trouble me not..I cannot rise and give
11. 8 Though he will not rise and give him
11. 8 because of..he will rise and give him as
11. 9 Ask, and it shall be given you ; seek, and
11. 13 know how to give good gifts unto your
11. 13 give the Holy Spirit to them that ask him?
11. 29 there shall no sign be given it, but the
11. 41 But rather give alms of such things as ye
12. 32 your Father's good pleasure to give you
12. 33 Sell that ye have, and give alms ; prov.
12. 42 to give..portion of meat in due season?
12. 48 For unto whomsoever much is given, of
12. 51 Suppose ye that I am come to give peace
12. 58 give diligence that thou mayest be deliv.
14. 9 Give this man place ; and thou begin
15. 12 Father, give me the portion of goods
15. 16 the husks..and no man gave unto him
15. 29 yet thou never gavest me a kid, that I
16. 12 who shall give you that which is your own?
17. 18 are not found that returned to give glory
18. 43 all the people..gave praise unto God
19. 8 the half of my goods I give to the poor
19. 15 these servants..to whom he had given
19. 23 Wherefore then gavest not thou my mo.
19. 24 and give (it) to him that hath ten pounds
19. 26 unto every one which hath shall be given
20. 2 or who is he that gave thee this authority
20 10 that they should give him of the fruit
20 16 and shall give the vineyard to others
20. 22 Is it lawful for us to give tribute unto C.
21. 15 I will give you a mouth and wisdom
22. 5 they were glad, and covenanted to give

Luke22. 19 and brake..and gave unto them, saying
22. 19 This is my body, which is given for you
23. 2 forbidding to give tribute to Cesar
John 1. 12 to them gave he power to become the
1. 17 For the law was given by Moses, (but)
1. 22 that we may give an answer to them
3. 16 that he gave his only begotten Son, that
3. 27 can receive nothing, except it be given
3. 34 for God giveth not the spirit by measure
3. 35 and hath given all things into his hand
4. 5 ground that Jacob gave to his son Joseph
4. 7 Jesus saith unto her, Give me to drink
4. 10 who it is that saith to thee, Give me to
4. 10 he would have given thee living water
4. 12 our father Jacob, which gave us the well
4. 14 drinketh of the water that I shall give
4. 14 [but the water that I shall give him shall]
4. 15 Sir, give me this water, that I thirst not
5. 26 so hath he given to the Son to have life in
5. 27 hath given him authority to execute
5. 36 works which the Father hath given me to
6. 27 which the Son of man shall give unto you
6. 31 He gave them bread from heaven to eat
6. 32 Moses gave you not that bread from heav.
6. 32 but my Father giveth you the true bread
6. 33 the bread..giveth life unto the world
6. 34 Lord, evermore give us this bread
6. 37 All that the Father giveth me shall come
6. 39 that of all which he hath given me I should
6. 51 and the bread that I will give is my flesh
6. 51 which I will give for the life of the world
6. 52 How can this man give us..flesh to eat?
6. 65 except it were given unto him of my Fat.
7. 19 Did not Moses give you the law, and
7. 22 Moses therefore gave unto you circumci.
9. 24 said unto him, Give God the praise: we
10. 28 I give unto them eternal life; and they
10. 29 My Father, which gave..me, is greater
11. 22 thou wilt ask of God, God will give (it)
11. 57 Pharisees had given a commandment, that
12. 5 three hundred pence, and given to the
12. 49 he gave me a commandment, what I
13. 3 the Father had given all things into his
13. 15 I have given you an example, that ye
13. 26 when he had dipped the sop, he gave (it)
13. 29 he should give something to the poor
13. 34 A new commandment I give unto you
14. 16 he shall give you another Comforter, that
14. 27 my peace I give unto you: not as the
14. 27 giveth, give I unto you. Let not your
15. 16 the Father in my name, he may give it
16. 23 the Father in my name, he will give (it)
17. 2 thou hast given him power over all flesh
17. 2 that he should give..to as many as thou
17. 4 the work which thou gavest me to do
17. 6 men which thou gavest me out of the
17. 6 thou gavest them me; and they have
17. 7 whatsoever thou hast given me are of
17. 8 I have given unto..which thou gavest me
17. 9 which thou hast given me; for they are
17. 11 whom thou hast given me, that they may
17. 12 those that thou gavest me I have kept
17. 14 I have given them thy word; and the
17. 22 glory which thou gavest me I have given
17. 24 they also whom thou hast given me, be
17. 24 my glory, which thou hast given me: for
18. 9 them which thou gavest me have I lost
18. 11 Father hath given me, shall I not drink
19. 9 Whence art thou? But Jesus gave him
19. 11 except it were given thee from above
21. 13 cometh, and taketh bread, and giveth
Acts 2. 4 as the spirit gave them utterance
3. 6 such as I have give I thee: In the name
3. 16 hath given him this perfect soundness
4. 12 other name under heaven given among
5. 31 for to give repentance to Israel, and
5. 32 whom God hath given to them that obey
7. 5 he gave him none inheritance in it, no
7. 5 would give it to him for a possession, and
7. 8 he gave him the covenant of circumcis.
7. 10 gave him favour and wisdom in the sight
7. 38 the lively oracles to give unto us
8. 18 Holy Ghost was given, he offered them
8. 19 Saying, Give me also this power, that on
9. 41 he gave her (his) hand, and lifted her up
11. 17 as God gave them the like gift as (he did)
12. 23 he gave not God the glory: and he was
13. 20 [he gave..judges about the space of four]
13. 21 God gave unto them Saul the son of Cis
13. 34 I will give you the sure mercies of David
14. 17 did good, and gave us rain from heaven
15. 8 giving them the Holy Ghost, even as (he
17. 25 he giveth to all life, and breath, and all
20. 32 and to give you an inheritance among
20. 35 It is more blessed to give than to receive
24. 26 money should have been given him of P.
Rom. 4. 20 was strong in faith, giving glory to God
5. 5 by the Holy Ghost which is given unto us
11. 8 God hath given them the spirit of slumber
12. 3 For I say, through the grace given unto
12. 6 according to the grace that is given to us
12. 19 give place unto wrath: for it is written
14. 12 every one of us shall give account of
15. 15 of the grace that is given to me of God
1 Co. 1. 4 grace of God which is given you by J. C.
3. 5 even as the Lord gave to every man?
3. 10 the grace of God which is given unto me
7. 25 yet I give my judgment, as one that hath
11. 15 for (her) hair is given her for a covering
12. 7 is given to every man to profit withal
12. 8 is given by the spirit the word of wisdom
12. 24 having given more abundant honour to

1 Co. 14. 7 giving sound, whether pipe or harp
14. 7 give a distinction in the sounds, how
14. 8 if the trumpet give an uncertain sound
15. 38 God giveth it a body as it hath pleased
15. 57 which giveth us the victory through our
2 Co. 1. 22 and given the earnest of the spirit in our
5. 5 hath given unto us the earnest of the
5. 12 but give you occasion to glory on our
5. 18 and hath given to us the ministry of
6. 3 Giving no offence in anything, that the
8. 5 first gave their own selves to the Lord
8. 10 I give (my) advice: for this is expedient
9. 9 hath given to the poor: his righteousness
10. 8 the Lord hath given us for edification
12. 7 there was given to me a thorn in the fl.
13. 10 hath given me to edification, and not to
Gal. 1. 4 gave himself for our sins, that he might
2. 9 that was given unto me, they gave to me
3. 21 if there had been a law given which could
3. 22 might be given to them that believe
4. 15 out your own eyes, and have given them
Eph. 1. 17 may give unto you the spirit of wisdom
1. 22 gave him (to be) the head over all (things)
3. 2 grace of God which is given me to you
3. 7 grace of God given unto me by the effec.
3. 8 is this grace given, that I should preach
4. 7 is given grace according to the measure
4. 8 captivity captive, and gave gifts unto
4. 11 gave some, apostles; and some, prophets
4. 27 Neither give place to the devil
6. 19 may be given unto me, that I may open
Col. 1. 25 dispensation of God which is given to me
1 Th. 4. 2 what commandments we gave you by the
4. 8 who hath also given unto us his Holy Sp.
2 Th. 2. 16 and hath given (us) everlasting consolat.
3. 16 give you peace always by all means
1 Ti. 2. 6 Who gave himself a ransom for all, to be
4. 14 gift..which was given thee by prophecy
5. 14 give none occasion to the adversary to
2 Ti. 1. 7 God hath not given us the spirit of fear
1. 9 grace, which was given us in Christ Jesus
1. 16 The Lord give mercy unto the house of
2. 7 the Lord give thee understanding in all
2. 25 if God peradventure will give them
Titus 2. 14 Who gave himself for us, that he might
Heb. 2. 13 the children which God hath given me
7. 4 even..Abraham gave the tenth of the sp.
Jas. 1. 5 ask of God, that giveth to all (men) liber.
1. 5 upbraideth not; and it shall be given him
2. 16 notwithstanding ye give them not those
4. 6 But he giveth more grace. Wherefore he
4. 6 but giveth grace unto the humble
5. 18 prayed again, and the heaven gave rain
1 Pe. 1. 21 gave him glory; that your faith and hope
5. 5 for God..giveth grace to the humble
2 Pe. 3. 15 according to the wisdom given unto him
1 Jo. 3. 23 and love one another, as he gave us com.
3. 24 in us, by the spirit which he hath given
4. 13 because he hath given us of his
5. 11 that God hath given to us eternal life
5. 16 he shall give him life for them that sin
5. 20 hath given us an understanding, that
Rev. 1. 1 which God gave unto him, to show unto
2. 7, 17 To him that overcometh will I give
2. 10 and I will give thee a crown of life
2. 17 will give him a white stone, and in the
2. 21 I gave her space to repent of her fornica.
2. 23 I will give unto every one of you accord.
2. 26 to him will I give power over the nations
2. 28 And I will give him the morning star
4. 9 when those beasts give glory and honour
6. 2 and a crown was given unto him: and he
6. 4 was given to him that sat thereon to take
6. 4 there was given unto him a great sword
6. 8 power was given unto them over the fou.
6. 11 white robes were given unto every one of
7. 2 to whom it was given to hurt the earth
8. 2 and to them were given seven trumpets
8. 3 there was given unto him much incense
9. 1 to him was given the key of the bottom.
9. 3 unto them was given power, as the scor.
9. 5 to them it was given that they should not
10. 9 said unto him, Give me the little book
11. 1 there was given me a reed like unto a rod
11. 2 for it is given unto the Gentiles: and the
11. 3 I will give .unto my two witnesses, and
11. 13 and gave glory to the God of heaven
11. 18 that thou shouldest give reward unto thy
12. 14 to the woman were given two wings of a
13. 2 the dragon gave him his power, and his
13. 4 the dragon which gave power unto the b.
13. 5 there was given unto him a mouth
13. 5 and power was given unto him to con.
13. 7 [it was given unto him to make war with]
13. 7 power was given him over all kindreds
13. 15 he had power to give life unto the image
14. 7 Fear God, and give glory to him; for the
15. 7 one of the four beasts gave unto the seven
16. 6 thou hast given them blood to drink; for
16. 8 power was given unto him to scorch men
16. 9 and they repented not to give him glory
16. 19 to give unto her the cup of the wine of
17. 17 give their kingdom unto the beast, until
18. 7 so much torment and sorrow give her
19. 7 Let us be glad and rejoice, and give hon.
20. 4 and judgment was given unto them: and
21. 6 I will give unto him that is athirst of the

18. *To give as a gift*, δωρέομαι *dōreomai.*
Mark15. 45 when he knew...he gave the body to
2 Pe. 1. 3 as his divine power hath given unto us
1. 4 Whereby are given unto us exceeding

19. *To give upon or over to* ἐπιδίδωμι *epididōmi.*
Matt. 7. 9 if his son ask bread, will he give him a s.?
7. 10 if he ask a fish, will he give him a serp.?
Luke11. 11 If a son shall ask..will he give him a st.?
11. 11 a fish, will he for a fish give him a serp.?
24. 30 and blessed (it), and brake, and gave to
24. 42 they gave him a piece of a broiled fish
John13. 26 [He it is, to whom I shall give a sop, when]

20. *To give testimony or witness*, μαρτυρέω *martur.*
1 Jo. 5. 10 believeth not the record that God gave of

21. *To give a share*, μεταδίδωμι *metadidōmi.*
Rom12. 8 he that giveth, (let him do it) with simp.
Eph. 4. 28 that he may have to give to him that

22. *From*, παρά *para* (*gen.*).
Luke10. 7 eating and drinking such things as they g.

23. *To give over to*, παραδίδωμι *paradidōmi.*
1 Co.13. 3 though I give my body to be burned, and
Gal. 2. 20 Son of God, who loved me, and gave him.
Eph. 5. 2 hath given himself for us an offering and
5. 25 even as Christ also..gave himself for it

24. *To bear into beside*, παρεισφέρω *pareispherō.*
2 Pe. 1. 5 giving all diligence, add to your faith vir.

25. *To hold alongside of*, παρέχω *parechō.*
Acts 17. 31 he hath given assurance unto all (men)
Col. 4. 1 give unto (your) servants that which is
1 Ti. 6. 17 who giveth us richly all things to enjoy

26. *To do, make*, ποιέω *poieō.*
Jude 3 when I gave all diligence to write unto you

27. *To put, set, place*, τίθημι *tithēmi.*
John10. 11 shepherd giveth his life for the sheep

28. *To grant as a favour*, χαρίζομαι *charizomai.*
Luke 7. 21 and unto many..blind he gave sight
Acts 27. 24 hath given thee all them that sail with
Gal. 3. 18 but God gave (it) to Abraham by promise
Phil. 1. 29 is given in the behalf of Christ, not only
2. 9 given him a name which is above every
Phm. 22 through your prayers I shall be given

29. *To be chorus leader, to supply*, χορηγέω *chor.*
1 Pe. 4. 11 ability which God giveth: that God in all

30. *To draw out, prolong*, מָשַׁךְ *mashak.*
Eccl. 2. 3 to give myself unto wine, yet acquainting

31. *To cause to turn back*, שׁוּב *shub*, 5.
2 Ki.17. 3 became his servant, and gave; Ex. 21. 34

32. *To send forth, out or away*, שָׁלַח *shalach.*
Psa. 50. 19 Thou givest thy mouth to evil, and thy

[*See also* Account, answer, charge, commandment, counsel, drink, ear, eat, few, flattering tittles, heat, inherit, knowledge, law, leave, less, life, light, many, marriage, more, name, passages, pledges, possess, power, praise, provender, quietness, respite, rest, reward, shout, sixth part, skill, speedily, stripes, such, thanks, understanding, warning, witness.]

GIVE again, to —

1. *To cause to turn back*, שׁוּב *shub*, 5.
Lev. 25. 51 he shall give again the price of his
25. 52 accord. unto his years shall he give him a

2. *To finish, complete, recompense*, שָׁלַם *shalam*, 3.
Eze. 33. 15 give again that he had robbed, walk in

3. *To give away*, ἀποδίδωμι *apodidōmi.*
Luke 4. 20 gave (it) again to the minister, and sat

GIVE against, to —

To bear against or down, καταφέρω *katapherō.*
Acts 26. 10 put to death, I ga. my voice against (them)

GIVE commandment or charge, to —

1. *To say*, אָמַר *amar.*
1 Ch.14. 12 David gave a commandment, and they

2. *To enjoin on*, ἐντέλλομαι *entellomai.*
Matt. 4. 6 He shall give his angels charge concern.
Luke 4. 10 He shall give his angels charge over thee
John14. 31 as the Father gave me commandment
Acts 1. 2 after that he..had given commandments
Heb. 11. 22 gave commandment concerning his bones

GIVE (counsel) to —

To give counsel, יָעַץ *yaats.*
2 Sa. 17. 7 that A. hath giv. (is) not good at this time
1 Ki. 12. 8 they had given him, and consulted with
12. 13 the old men's counsel that they gave him
2 Ch.10. 8 old men gave him, and took counsel with

GIVE first, to —

To give forth or foremost, προδίδωμι *prodidōmi.*
Rom 11. 35 who hath first given to him, and it shall

GIVE forth, to —

1. *To give*, נָתַן *nathan.*
Num20. 8 it shall give forth his water, and thou

2. *To give*, δίδωμι *didōmi.*
Acts 1. 26 they gave forth their lots; and the lot

GIVE freely, to —

To grant (as a favour), χαρίζομαι *charizomai.*
Rom. 8. 32 shall he not..freely give us all things?

GIVE, graciously to —

To grace, favour, חָנַן *chanan.*
Gen. 33. 5 God hath graciously given thy servant

GIVE (light), to — [*See* LIGHT.]

1. *To (cause to) give light, shine*, אוֹר *or*, 5.
Eze. 32. 7 and the moon shall not give her light

2. *To cause to shine,* הָלַל *halal,* 5.
Isa. 13. 10 For the stars..shall not give their light

GIVE (meat) **to —**
To give or cause to eat, בָּרָה *barah,* 5.
2 Sa. 13. 5 give me meat, and dress the meat in my

GIVE more, **to —**
To put or place toward, προστίθημι *prostithēmi.*
Mark 4. 24 [unto you that hear shall more be given]

GIVE moreover, **to —**
To (cause to) add, increase, continue, יָסַף *yasaph,* 5.
2 Sa. 12. 8 I would moreover have given unto thee

GIVE name, **to —**
1. *Call by names,* קָרָא בְּשֵׁמוֹת [*qara*] ; Num. 32. 38.
2. *Call a name to,* קָרָא שֵׁם לְ [*qara*] ; Ruth 4. 17.

GIVE one's self to, **to —**
To have leisure, σχολάζω *scholazō.*
1 Co. 7. 5 ye may give yourselves to fasting and

GIVE out, to —
To lay out, say, λέγω *legō.*
Acts 8. 9 giving out that himself was some great

GIVE over, to —
1. *To give,* נָתַן *nathan.*
Psa. 118. 18 he hath not given me over unto death
2. *To (cause to) shut up or in,* סָגַר *sagar,* 5.
Psa. 78. 50 gave their life over to the pestilence
78. 62 He gave his people over..unto the sword
3. *To shut up or in,* סָכַר *sakar,* 3.
Isa. 19. 4 will I give over into the hand of a cruel
4. *To give over,* παραδίδωμι *paradidōmi.*
Rom. 1. 28 God gave them over to a reprobate mind
Eph. 4. 19 have given themselves over unto lasciv.

GIVE place, to —
1. *To come, or draw nigh,* נָגַשׁ *nagash.*
Isa. 49. 20 for me: give place to me that I may dwell
2. *To give place, go back, withdraw,* ἀναχωρέω.
Matt. 9. 24 Give place; for the maid is not dead, but
3. *To yield,* εἴκω *eikō.*
Gal. 2. 5 To whom we gave place by subjection, no

GIVE presently, to —
To place beside, παρίστημι *paristēmi.*
Matt 26. 53 he shall presently give me more than

GIVE self wholly to, to —
To be in (a thing), εἶναι ἐν *einai en.*
1 Ti. 4. 15 give thyself wholly to them; that thy

GIVE to eat —
To cause or give to eat, אָכַל *akal,* 5.
Num 11. 4 and said, Who shall give us flesh to eat?
11. 18 Who shall give us flesh to eat?..well with
2 Ch. 28. 15 gave them to eat and to drink, and anoi.
Prov 25. 21 hungry, give him bread to eat; and if

GIVE up, to —
1. *To blow, breathe out, boil,* נָפַח *naphach.*
Jer. 15. 9 she hath given up the ghost: her sun is
2. *To give,* נָתַן *nathan.*
Deut 23. 14 and to give up thine enemies before thee
31. 5 the LORD shall give them up before your
Isa. 43. 6 I will say to the north, Give up; and to
Hos. 11. 8 How shall I give thee up, Ephraim?..sh.
Mic. 5. 3 Therefore will he give them up, until the
6. 14 which thou deliverest will I give up to
3. *To (cause to) shut up or in,* סָגַר *sagar,* 5.
Lam. 2. 7 he hath given up into the hand of the
Psa. 78. 48 He gave up their cattle also to the hail
4. *To send forth, out, or away,* שָׁלַח *shalach,* 3.
Psa. 81. 12 I gave them up unto their own hearts'
5. *To give,* δίδωμι *didōmi.*
Rev. 20. 13 the sea gave up the dead which were in
6. *To give over,* παραδίδωμι *paradidōmi.*
John 19. 30 bowed his head, and gave up the ghost
Acts 7. 42 God turned, and gave them up to worship
Rom. 1. 24 God also gave them up to uncleanness
1. 26 For this cause God gave them up unto

GIVE reverence, to —
To turn toward, in or back, ἐντρέπομαι *entrepomai.*
Heb. 12. 9 we have had fathers..we gave..reverence

GIVE self continually, to —
To be firm or strong toward, προσκαρτερέω *prosk.*
Acts 6. 4 we will give ourselves continually to pr.

GIVE stripes, to —
To (cause to) smite, נָכָה *nakah,* 5.
Deut 25. 3 Forty stripes he may give him, (and) not

GIVE willingly, to —
To give willingly, נָדַב *nadab.*
Exod 25. 2 every man that giveth it willingly with

GIVEN, to be —
1. *To give place, ascribe,* יְהַב *yehab.*
Dan. 5. 28 Thy kingdom is..given to the Medes and
7. 4 as a man, and a man's heart was given to
7. 6 four heads; and dominion was given to
7. 11 and his body..given to the burning flame
Dan. 7. 14 there was given him dominion, and glory
7. 22 judgment was given to the saints of the
7. 27 shall be given to the people of the saints
2. *To be given,* יְהַב *yehab,* 2.
Ezra 6. 4 let the expenses be given out of the king's
6. 8 forthwith expenses be given unto these
6. 9 let it be given them day by day without
7. 19 The vessels also that are given thee for
Dan. 4. 16 let a beast's heart be given unto him; and
7. 25 they shall be given into his hand until
3. *To give,* נָתַן *nathan.*
Lev. 7. 36 the LORD commanded to be given them
1 Sa. 18. 19 when Merab..should have been given to
4. *To be given,* נָתַן *nathan,* 2.
Gen. 38. 14 she was not given unto him to wife
Exod. 5. 16 There is no straw given unto thy servants
5. 18 for there shall no straw be given you, yet
Lev. 10. 14 are given out of the sacrifices of peace
19. 20 not at all redeemed, nor freedom given
Num 26. 62 was no inheritance given them among
Josh 24. 33 which was given him in mount Ephraim
1 Sa. 18. 19 she was given unto Adriel the Meholath.
25. 27 let it even be given unto the young men
2 Ki. 25. 30 a continual allowance given him of the
1 Ch. 5. 1 his birthright was given unto the sons
Neh. 10. 29 which was given by Moses the servant of
Neh. 13. 10 of the Levites had not been given..for
Esth. 2. 13 whatsoever she desired was given her to
3. 14 for a commandment to be given in every
3. 15 the decree was given in Shushan the pa.
4. 8 the decree that was given at Shushan to
5. 3 it shall be even given thee to the half of
7. 3 let my life be given me at my petition
8. 13 a commandment to be given in every
8. 14 the decree was given at Shushan the pa.
9. 14 the decree was given at Shushan; and
Job 9. 24 The earth is given into the hand of the
15. 19 Unto whom alone the earth was given
Eccl. 12. 11 The words..are given from one shepherd
Isa. 9. 6 a child is born, unto us a son is given
33. 16 bread shall be given him: his waters
35. 2 the glory of Lebanon shall be given unto
37. 10 Jerusalem shall not be given into the
Jer. 13. 20 where (is) the flock (that) was given thee
21. 10 it shall be given into the hand of the
32. 24, 25, 43 is given into the hand of the Cha.
38. 3 This city shall surely be given into the
38. 18 shall this city be given into the hand
39. 17 thou shalt not be given into the hand of
52. 34 there was a continual diet given him of
Eze. 11. 15 unto us is this land given in possession
16. 34 no reward is given unto thee, therefore
33. 24 the land is given us for inheritance
35. 12 desolate, they are given us to consume
47. 11 not be healed; they shall be given to salt
Dan. 8. 12 And an host was given..against the daily
11. 11 multitude shall be given into his hand
5. *To be given, put,* נָתַן *nathan,* 6.
Num 26. 54 shall his inheritance be given according
32. 5 let this land be given unto thy servants
1 Ki. 2. 21 Let Abishag the Shunammite be given to
2 Ki. 5. 17 Shall there not then, I pray thee, be giv.
6. *To be placed, appointed,* שׂוּם *sum,* 2.
Ezra 4. 21 commandment shall be given from me

GIVEN, that which he hath —
Recompense, deserving, benefit, deed, גְּמוּל *gemul.*
Prov 19. 17 that which he hath given will he pay him

GIVEN to —
1. *To enslave,* δουλόω *douloō.*
Titus 2. 3 not given to much wine, teachers of good
2. *To pursue,* διώκω *diōkō.*
Rom 12. 13 the necessity of saints; given to hospita.

GIVEN to, to be —
To hold toward, προσέχω *prosechō.*
1 Ti. 3. 8 not given to much wine, not greedy of fi.

GIVEN, the things that are freely —
The things granted as a favour, τὰ χαρισθέντα.
1 Co. 2. 12 the things that are freely given to us of

GIVEN to covetousness —
To cut off, gain dishonestly, בָּצַע *batsa.*
Jer. 6. 13 For..every one (is) given to covetousness
8. 10 the greatest is given to covetousness, from

GIVEN to it, those that are —
Master, owner, בַּעַל *baal.*
Eccl. 8. 8 neither..deliver those that are given to it

GIVEN up, to be —
To be given, נָתַן *nathan,* 2.
Dan. 11. 6 but she shall be given up, and they that

GIVEN (wholly) **—**
To give, נָתַן *nathan.*
Num. 3. 9 they (are) wholly given unto him out of
8. 16 they (are) wholly given unto me from am.
18. 6 to you (they are) given (as) a gift for the
Deut 28. 31 thy sheep (shall be) given unto thine ene.

GIVEN, (wounds) **to be —**
To (cause to) smite, נָכָה *nakah,* 5.
2 Ki. 8. 29 which the Syrians had given him at Ram.
9. 15 which the Syrians had given him, when
2 Ch. 22. 6 which were given him at Ramah, when

GIVER —
Giver, δότης *dotēs.*
2 Co. 9. 7 necessity: for God loveth a cheerful giver

GIVETH GIFTS —
A man of gifts, אִישׁ מַתָּן *ish mattan.*
Prov 19. 6 man (is) a friend to him that giveth gifts

GIVING —
1. *To give,* נָתַן *nathan.*
Deut 10. 18 stranger, in giving him food and raiment
21. 17 by giving him a double portion of all that
Ruth 1. 6 visited his people in giving them bread
1 Ki. 5. 9 my desire, in giving food for my househ.
2 Ch. 6. 23 by giving him according to his righteous.
2. *A giving, a gift,* δόσις *dosis.*
Phil. 4. 15 concerning giving and receiving, but ye

GIVING up —
Breathing out, puff, מַפָּח *mappach.*
Job 11. 20 hope (shall be as) the giving up of the g.

GI-ZO-NITE, גִּזוֹנִי.
Patronymic of one whose sons were among David's guard. B.C. 1048.
1 Ch. 11. 34 sons of Hashem the G., Jonathan the son

GLAD —
1. *Good,* טוֹב *tob.*
1 Ki. 8. 66 glad of heart, for all the goodness that
Esth. 5. 9 that day joyful and with a glad heart
2. *Rejoicing,* שָׂמֵחַ *sameach.*
2 Ch. 7. 10 glad and merry in heart for the goodness
Esth. 8. 15 the city of Shushan rejoiced and was glad
Psa. 126. 3 hath done great things for us..we are gl.
Prov 17. 5 he that is glad at calamities shall not be

GLAD, to be —
1. *To rejoice, joy,* גִּיל, גּוּל *gul, gil.*
Psa. 31. 7 I will be glad and rejoice in thy mercy
48. 11 let..Judah be glad, because of thy judg.
96. 11 let the earth be glad; let the sea roar
Prov 24. 17 let not thine heart be glad when he stu.
Song 1. 4 we will be glad and rejoice in thee; we
Isa. 25. 9 we will be glad and rejoice in his salva.
66. 10 and be glad with her, all ye that love her
Joel 2. 21 be glad and rejoice: for the LORD will do
2. 23 Be glad then, ye children of Zion, and
Hab. 1. 15 catch..therefore they rejoice and are gl.
2. *To be good,* טְאֵב *teeb.*
Dan. 6. 23 Then was the king exceeding glad for
3. *To be or become good,* יָטַב *yatab.*
Judg 18. 20 the priest's heart was glad; and he took
4. *To enjoy, rejoice,* שִׂישׂ, שׂוּשׂ *sus, sis.*
Job 3. 22 are glad, when they can find the grave?
Isa. 35. 1 the solitary place shall be glad for them
65. 18 But be ye glad and rejoice for ever (in
Lam. 1. 21 they are glad that thou hast done (it)
5. *To rejoice,* שָׂמֵחַ *sameach.*
Exod. 4. 14 when he seeth thee, he will be glad in
1 Sa. 11. 9 to the men of Jabesh; and they were gl.
1 Ch. 16. 31 Let the heavens be glad, and let the ea.
Job 22. 19 The righteous see..and are glad; and
Psa. 9. 2 I will be glad and rejoice in thee: I will
14. 7 shall rejoice, (and) Israel shall be glad
16. 9 my heart is glad, and my glory rejoiceth
32. 11 Be glad in the LORD, and rejoice, ye right.
34. 2 the humble shall hear..and be glad
35. 27 Let them shout for joy, and be glad
40. 16 that seek thee rejoice and be glad in thee
53. 6 Jacob shall rejoice..Israel shall be glad
64. 10 The righteous shall be glad in the LORD
67. 4 let the nations be glad, and sing for joy
68. 3 But let the righteous be glad: let them
69. 32 The humble shall see (this, and) be glad
70. 4 that seek thee rejoice and be glad in thee
90. 14 that we may rejoice and be glad all our
97. 1 rejoice; let the multitude of isles be glad
97. 8 Zion heard, and was glad; and the daug.
104. 34 shall be sweet: I will be glad in the Lo.
105. 38 Egypt was glad when they departed; for
107. 30 Then are they glad because they be quiet
118. 24 hath made; we will rejoice and be glad
119. 74 They that fear thee will be glad when
122. 1 I was glad when they said unto me, Let
Prov 23. 25 thy mother shall be glad, and she that
Isa. 39. 2 Hezekiah was glad of them, and showed
Jer. 41. 13 that (were) with him, then they were glad
50. 11 Because ye were glad, because ye rejoiced
Lam. 4. 21 Rejoice and be glad, O daughter of Edom
Jon. 4. 6 So Jonah was exceeding glad of the gourd
Zeph. 3. 14 be glad and rejoice with all the heart, O
Zech 10. 7 yea, their children shall see..and be glad
6. *To leap much, be glad,* ἀγαλλιάομαι *agalliaomai.*
Acts 2. 26 my heart rejoice, and my tongue was glad
7. *To rejoice, be of good cheer,* χαίρω *chairō.*
Mark 14. 11 when they heard..they were glad, and
Luke 15. 32 It was meet that we should..be glad: for
22. 5 they were glad, and covenanted to give
23. 8 Herod saw Jesus, he was exceeding glad
John 8. 56 to see my day; and he saw..and was glad
11. 15 I am glad for your sakes that I was not
20. 20 Then were the disciples glad when they
Acts 11. 23 and had seen the grace of God, was glad
13. 48 the Gentiles heard this, they were glad
Rom 16. 19 I am glad therefore on your behalf: but
1 Co. 16. 17 I am glad of the coming of Stephanas and
2 Co. 13. 9 For we are glad when we are weak, and

1 Pe. 4. 13 ye may be glad also with exceeding joy
Rev. 19. 7 Let us be glad and rejoice, and give hon.

GLAD, to be exceeding —

To leap much, be glad, ἀγαλλιάομαι *agalliaomai.*
Matt. 5. 12 Rejoice, and be exceeding glad; for great

GLAD, to make —

1. *To make joyful,* חָדָה *chadah,* 3.
Psa. 21. 6 thou hast made him exceeding glad with

2. *To make joyful or glad,* שָׂמַח *sameach,* 3.
Psa. 45. 8 palaces, whereby they have made thee g.
46. 4 the streams whereof shall make glad the
90. 15 Make us glad according to the days..thou
92. 4 For thou, LORD, hast made me glad thro.
104. 15 wine..maketh glad the heart of man,(and)
Prov 10. 1 A wise son maketh a glad father: but a
12. 25 it stoop: but a good word maketh it glad
15. 20 A wise son maketh a glad father: but a
27. 11 My son, be wise, and make my heart glad
Jer. 20. 15 is born unto thee, making him very glad
Hos. 7. 3 They make the king glad with their wick.

3. *To make glad, cheer,* εὐφραίνω *euphrainō.*
2 Co. 2. 2 who is he then that maketh me glad, but

GLAD tidings, to bring, declare, show —

To tell good news, εὐαγγελίζομαι *euaggelizomai.*
Luke 1. 19 am sent..to show thee these glad tidings
8. 1 showing the glad tidings of the kingdom
Acts 13. 32 we declare unto you glad tidings, how
Rom 10. 15 and bring glad tidings of good things

GLADLY —

1. *Gladly, readily, joyfully,* ἀσμένως *asmenōs.*
Acts 2. 41 they that [gladly] received his word were
21. 17 were come..the brethren received us gl.

2. *Sweetly, with relish,* ἡδέως *hēdeōs.*
Mark 6. 20 he did many things, and heard him gladly
12. 37 And the common people heard him gladly
2 Co. 11. 19 For ye suffer fools gladly, seeing ye..are

GLADLY, most or very —

Most sweetly, ἥδιστα *hēdista.*
2 Co. 12. 9 Most gladly therefore will I rather glory
12. 15 I will very gladly spend and be spent for

GLADNESS —

1. *Joy,* גִּיל *gil.*
Joel 1. 16 joy and gladness from the house of our

2. *Gladness,* חֶדְוָה *chedvah.*
1 Ch. 16. 27 strength and gladness (are) in his place

3. *Goodness,* טוּב *tub.*
Deut 28. 47 with gladness of heart, for the abundance

4. *Loud cry, proclamation, singing,* רִנָּה *rinnah.*
Psa. 105. 43 brought forth his..chosen with gladness

5. *Rejoicing, joy, gladness, mirth,* שִׂמְחָה *simchah.*
Num 10. 10 in the day of your gladness, and in your
2 Sa. 6. 12 ark..into the city of David with gladness
1 Ch. 29. 22 the LORD on that day with great gladness
2 Ch. 29. 30 they sang praises with gladness, and they
30. 21 kept the feast..seven days with great gl.
30. 23 and they kept..seven days with gladness
Neh. 8. 17 And there was very great gladness
12. 27 to keep the dedication with gladness, both
Esth. 8. 16 The Jews had light, and gladness, and joy
9. 17, 18 made it a day of feasting and gladness
9. 19 gladness and feasting, and a good day, and
Psa. 4. 7 Thou hast put gladness in my heart, more
30. 11 sackcloth, and girded me with gladness
45. 15 With gladness and rejoicing (shall) they
51. 8 Make me to hear joy and gladness; (that)
97. 11 and gladness for the upright in heart
100. 2 Serve the LORD with gladness: come bef.
106. 5 that I may rejoice in the gladness of thy
Prov 10. 28 The hope of the righteous..gladness; but
Song 3. 11 in the day of the gladness of his heart
Isa. 16. 10 gladness is taken away, and joy out of
22. 13 joy and gladness, slaying oxen and killing
30. 29 and gladness of heart, as when one goeth
35. 10 they shall obtain joy and gladness, and
51. 3 joy and gladness shall be found therein
Jer. 7. 34 the voice of gladness, the voice of the br.
16. 9 the voice of gladness, the voice of the br.
25. 10 the voice of gladness, the voice of the br.
31. 7 Sing with gladness for Jacob, and shout
33. 11 the voice of gladness; the voice of the br.
Zech. 8. 19 be to the house of Judah joy and gladness

6. *Joy, rejoicing, gladness,* שָׂשׂוֹן *sason.*
Esth. 8. 17 the Jews had joy and gladness, a feast
Psa. 45. 7 with the oil of gladness above thy fellows
Isa. 51. 11 they shall obtain gladness and joy: (and)

7. *Much leaping, gladness,* ἀγαλλίασις *agalliasis.*
Luke 1. 14 thou shalt have joy and gladness; and
Acts 2. 46 eat..with gladness and singleness of h.
Heb. 1. 9 with the oil of gladness above thy fellows

8. *Cheer, gladness,* εὐφροσύνη *euphrosunē.*
Acts 14. 17 filling our hearts with food and gladness

9. *Joy,* χαρά *chara.*
Mark 4. 16 immediately receive it with gladness
Acts 12. 14 she opened not the gate for gladness, but
Phil. 2. 29 in the Lord with all gladness; and hold

GLASS — [*See* BEHOLD.]

1. *Roll, tablet, mirror,* גִּלָּיוֹן *gillayon.*
Isa. 3. 23 The glasses, and the fine linen, and the

2. *Mirror, looking glass,* ἔσοπτρον *esoptron.*
1 Co. 13. 12 For now we see through a glass, darkly
Jas. 1. 23 man beholding his natural face in a glass

3. *Glass, anything transparent,* ὕαλος *hualos.*
Rev. 21. 18 and the city (was)..like unto clear glass
21. 21 pure gold, as it were transparent glass

GLASS, of —

Made of glass, ὑάλινος *hualinos.*
Rev. 4. 6 before the throne..a sea of glass like
15. 2 I saw as it were a sea of glass mingled
15. 2 stand on the sea of glass, having the harps

GLASS, looking —

Vision, looking glass, מַרְאָה *marah.*
Exod 38. 8 the foot of it (of) brass, of the looking g.

GLEAN, to —

1. *To gather, glean,* לָקַט *laqat.*
Ruth 2. 8 Go not to glean in another field, neither go

2. *To gather, glean,* לָקַט *laqat,* 3.
Ruth 2. 2 and glean ears of corn after (him) in
2. 3 came, and gleaned in the field after the
2. 7 I pray you, let me glean and gather after
2. 15 And when she was risen up to glean, B.
2. 15 Let her glean even among the sheaves
2. 16 that she may glean..and rebuke her not
2. 17 So she gleaned in the field until even
2. 17 and beat out that she had gleaned
2. 18 her mother in law saw what she had gle.
2. 19 Where hast thou glean to day? and
2. 23 by the maidens of Boaz to glean unto the

3. *To roll, glean, suck,* עָלַל *alal,* 3a.
Lev. 19. 10 And thou shalt not glean thy vineyard
Deut 24. 21 thou shalt not glean (it) afterward: it
Judg 20. 45 and they gleaned of them in the highways
Jer. 6. 9 They shall throughly glean the remnant

GLEANING —

Gleaning, לֶקֶט *leqet.*
Lev. 19. 9 neither shalt thou gather the gleanings of
23. 22 neither shalt thou gather any gleaning of

GLEANING (of the) grapes —

Gleanings, עֹלֵלוֹת *oleloth.*
Judg. 8. 2 (Is) not the gleaning of the grapes of E.
Isa. 17. 6 Yet gleaning grapes shall be left in it
24. 13 as the gleaning grapes when the vintage
Jer. 49. 9 would they not leave..gleaning grapes?
Mic. 7. 1 I am..as the grape gleanings of the vin.

GLEDE —

Vulture, hawk, glede, רָאָה *raah.*
Deut. 14. 13 the glede, and the kite, and the vulture

GLISTER, to —

To flash as lightning, ἐξαστράπτω *exastraptō.*
Luke 9. 29 and his raiment (was) white (and) glist.

GLISTERING —

Lead ore, stibium, ruby, פּוּךְ *puk.*
1 Ch. 29. 2 and (stones) to be set, glistering stones

GLITTER —

Brightness, lightning, בָּרָק *baraq.*
Eze. 21. 10 it is furbished that it may glitter: should

GLITTERING —

1. *Brightness, lightning,* בָּרָק *baraq.*
Deut 32. 41 If I whet my glittering sword, and mine
Job 20. 25 the glittering sword cometh out of his g.
Eze. 21. 28 to consume because of the glittering
Nah. 3. 3 the bright sword and the glittering spear
Hab. 3. 11 at the shining of thy glittering spear

2. *Flame, blade,* לַהַב *lahab.*
Job 39. 23 the glittering spear and the shield

GLOOMINESS —

Thick darkness, gloominess, אֲפֵלָה *aphelah.*
Joel 2. 2 A day of darkness and of gloominess, a
Zeph. 1. 15 a day of darkness and gloominess, a day

GLORIFIED, to be —

1. *To be weighty, heavy, honoured,* כָּבֵד *kabed.*
Isa. 66. 5 Let the LORD be glorified: but he shall

2. *To be or become heavy, honoured,* כָּבֵד *kabed,* 2.
Lev. 10. 3 before all the people I will be glorified
Isa. 26. 15 O LORD..thou art glorified: thou hast
Eze. 28. 22 and I will be glorified in the midst of
39. 13 a renown, the day that I shall be glorified
Hag. 1. 8 and I will be glorified, saith the LORD

3. *To beautify self,* פָּאַר *paar,* 7.
Isa. 49. 3 my servant..in whom I will be glorified
60. 21 work of my hands, that I may be glori.
61. 3 of the LORD, that he might be glorified

4. *To be glorified,* ἐνδοξάζομαι *endoxazomai.*
2 Th. 1. 10 When he shall come to be glorified in
1. 12 That the name..may be glorified in you

GLORIFIED together, to be —

To glorify together, συνδοξάζω *sundoxazō.*
Rom. 8. 17 that we may be also glorified together

GLORIFY, to —

1. *To honour, adorn,* הָדַר *hadar,* 3.
Dan. 5. 23 and the God..hast thou not glorified

2. *To make heavy, give honour,* כָּבֵד *kabed,* 3.
Psa. 22. 23 all ye the seed of Jacob, glorify him; and
50. 15 I will deliver thee, and thou shalt glorify
50. 23 Whoso offereth praise glorifieth me: and
86. 9 O Lord; and shall glorify thy name
86. 12 and I will glorify thy name for evermore
Isa. 24. 15 Wherefore glorify ye the LORD in the fir.
25. 3 Therefore shall the strong people glorify

3. *To make heavy, give honour,* כָּבֵד *kabed,* 5.
Jer. 30. 19 I will also glorify them, and they shall

4. *To beautify,* פָּאַר *paar,* 3.
Isa. 55. 5 for the Holy One..for he hath glorified
60. 7 and I will glorify the house of my glory
60. 9 Holy One..because he hath glorified thee

5. *To glorify, honour,* δοξάζω *doxazō.*
Matt. 5. 16 and glorify your Father which is in heav.
9. 8 they marvelled, and glorified God, which
15. 31 and they glorified the God of Israel
Mark 2. 12 all amazed, and glorified God, saying
Luke 2. 20 the shepherds returned, glorifying and
4. 15 And he taught..being glorified of all
5. 25 departed to his own house, glorifying God
5. 26 they glorified God, and were filled with
7. 16 they glorified God, saying, That a great
13. 13 she was made straight, and glorified God
17. 15 turned..and with a loud voice glorified
18. 43 and followed him, glorifying God: and
23. 47 he glorified God, saying, Certainly this
John 7. 39 because that Jesus was not yet glorified
11. 4 that the Son of God might be glorified
12. 16 but when Jesus was glorified, then rem.
12. 23 that the Son of man should be glorified
12. 28 Father, glorify thy name. Then came
12. 28 I have both glorified..and will glorify (it
13. 31 Now is the Son..[glorified]..God is glori.
13. 32 If God be glorified..God shall..glorify
13. 32 and shall straightway glorify him
14. 13 that the Father may be glorified in the
15. 8 Herein is my Father glorified, that ye bear
16. 14 He shall glorify me; for he shall receive
17. 1 Father, the hour is come; glorify thy Son
17. 1 that thy Son also may glorify thee
17. 4 I have glorified thee on the earth: I have
17. 5 O Father, glorify thou me with thine own
17. 10 thine are mine; and I am glorified in
21. 19 signifying by what death he should glorify
Acts 3. 13 God ..hath glorified his Son Jesus; whom
4. 21 for all..glorified God for that which was
11. 18 they held their peace, and glorified God
13. 48 and glorified the word of the Lord: and
21. 20 when they heard (it), they glorified the L.
Rom. 1. 21 they glorified (him) not as God, neither
8. 30 whom he justified, them he also glorified
15. 6 That ye may with..one mouth glorify God
15. 9 that the Gentiles might glorify God for
1 Co. 6. 20 therefore glorify God in your body, and in
2 Co. 9. 13 they glorify God for your professed sub.
Gal. 1. 24 And they glorified God in me
2 Th. 3. 1 and be glorified, even as (it is) with you
Heb. 5. 5 So also Christ glorified not himself to be
1 Pe. 2. 12 glorify God in the day of visitation
4. 11 that God in all things may be glorified
4. 14 [evil spoken of, but on your part he is g.]
4. 16 but let him glorify God on this behalf
Rev. 15. 4 Who shall not fear thee..and glorify thy
18. 7 How much she hath glorified herself, and

GLORIFY self, to —

To beautify self, פָּאַר *paar,* 7.
Isa. 44. 23 for the LORD..glorified himself in Israel

GLORIOUS —

1. *Honourable,* אַדִּיר *addir.*
Isa. 33. 21 But there the glorious LORD (will be)

2. *To become honourable,* אָדַר *adar,* 2.
Exod 15. 11 who (is) like thee, glorious in holiness

3. *To become light,* אוֹר *or,* 2.
Psa. 76. 4 Thou (art) more glorious (and) excellent

4. *To honour, adorn,* הָדַר *hadar.*
Isa. 63. 1 Who (is)..this (that is) glorious in his

5. *Honour, beauty, majesty, adornment,* הָדָר *hadar.*
Psa. 111. 3 His work (is) honourable and glorious

6. *Honour, beauty, majesty,* הוֹד *hod.*
Isa. 30. 30 the LORD shall cause his glorious voice to

7. *To be or become heavy, honoured,* כָּבֵד *kabed,* 2.
Deut. 28. 58 that thou mayest fear this glorious and
Psa. 87. 3 Glorious things are spoken of thee, O

8. *Honour, heaviness, wealth,* כָּבוֹד *kabod.*
Neh. 9. 5 and blessed be thy glorious name, which
Esth. 1. 4 When he showed the riches of his glorio.
Psa. 66. 2 Sing forth..make his praise glorious
72. 19 And blessed (be) his glorious name for ev.
145. 5 I will speak of the glorious honour of thy
145. 12 and the glorious majesty of his kingdom
Isa. 4. 2 shall the branch of the LORD be..glorious
11. 10 a root of Jesse..his rest shall be glorious
22. 23 he shall be for a glorious throne to his
Jer. 17. 12 A glorious high throne from the beginni.

9. *Beauty, desire,* צְבִי *tsebi.*
Isa. 28. 1 whose glorious beauty (is) a fading flower
28. 4 And the glorious beauty, which (is) on
Dan. 11. 16 and he shall stand in the glorious land
11. 41 He shall enter also into the glorious land
11. 45 between the seas in the glorious holy m.

10. *Beauty, glory,* תִּפְאֶרֶת, תִּפְאָרָה *tiphereth, tipharah.*
1 Ch. 29. 13 we thank thee, and praise thy glorious n.
Isa. 63. 12 right hand of Moses with his glorious arm
63. 14 so didst thou..to make thyself a glorious

11. *Glorious, of glory*, τῆς δόξης *tēs doxēs.*
Rom. 8. 21 into the glorious liberty of the children
2 Co. 4. 4 lest the light of the glorious gospel of C.
Phil. 3. 21 be fashioned like unto his glorious body
Col. 1. 11 according to his glorious power, unto all
1 Ti. 1. 11 According to the glorious gospel of the
Titus 2. 13 Looking for..the glorious appearing of

12. *Through glory*, διὰ δόξης *dia doxēs.*
2 Co. 3. 11 if that which is done away (was) glorious

13. *In glory*, ἐν δόξῃ *en doxē.*
2 Co. 3. 7 if the ministration of death..was glorious
3. 8 the ministration of the spirit be rather g.?
3. 11 much more that which remaineth (is) gl.

14. *Glorious, in glory*, ἔνδοξος *endoxos.*
Luke 13. 17 rejoiced for all the glorious things that
Eph. 5. 27 That he might present it to himself a gl.

GLORIOUS, to be —
To be or become heavy, honoured, כָּבֵד *kabed*, 2.
2 Sa. 6. 20 How glorious was the king of Israel to.
Isa. 49. 5 yet shall I be glorious in the eyes of the

GLORIOUS, all —
Heaviness, honour, כְּבוּדָּה *kebuddah.*
Psa. 45. 13 The king's daughter (is) all glorious with.

GLORIOUS, to become —
To become honourable, adorned, אָדַר *adar*, 2.
Exod. 15. 6 Thy right hand..is become glorious in

GLORIOUS, to be made —
1. *To be heavy, honoured*, כָּבַד *kabed.*
Eze. 27. 25 made very glorious in the midst of the
2. *To be glorified*, δοξάζομαι *doxazomai.*
2 Co. 3. 10 For even that which was made glorious

GLORIOUS, to make —
To make heavy, give honour, כָּבֵד *kabed*, 3.
Isa. 60. 13 I will make the place of my feet glorious

GLORIOUS things —
To become heavy, honoured, כָּבֵד *kabed*, 2.
Psa. 87. 3 Glorious things are spoken of thee, O city

GLORIOUSLY —
1. *To rise, triumph*, גָּאָה *gaah.*
Exod. 15. 1, 21 for he hath triumphed gloriously
2. *Heaviness, honour*, כָּבוֹד *kabod.*
Isa. 24. 23 shall reign..before his ancients gloriously

GLORY —
1. *Adornment*, אַדֶּרֶת *addereth.*
Zech. 11. 3 for their glory is spoiled: a voice of th
2. *Honour, adornment*, הָדָר *hadar.*
Deut 33. 17 His glory (is like) the firstling of his bul.
Psa. 90. 16 and thy glory unto their children
Isa. 2. 10, 19, 21 and for the glory of his majesty
5. 14 their glory, and their multitude, and
Mic. 2. 9 have ye taken away my glory for ever
3. *Honour, adornment*, הֶדֶר *heder.*
Dan. 11. 20 a raiser of taxes (in) the glory of the
4. *Honour, beauty, majesty*, הוֹד *hod.*
1 Ch. 16. 27 Glory and honour (are) in his presence
Job 39. 20 the glory of his nostrils (is) terrible
40. 10 and array thyself with glory and beauty
Psa. 8. 1 who hast set thy glory above the heavens
45. 3 thy sword..with thy glory and thy maj.
148. 13 his glory (is) above the earth and heaven
Jer. 22. 18 shall not lament for him..Ah his glory!
Hab. 3. 3 His glory covered the heavens, and the
Zech. 6. 13 he shall bear the glory, and shall sit and
5. *Cleanness, purity*, טְהָר *tohar.*
Psa. 89. 44 Thou hast made his glory to cease, and
6. *Preciousness, rarity*, יְקָר *yeqar.*
Dan. 2. 37 a kingdom, power, and strength, and gl.
4. 36 for the glory of my kingdom, mine hono.
5. 18 a kingdom, and majesty, and glory, and
5. 20 was deposed..and they took his glory
7. 14 there was given him dominion, and glory
7. *Weight, heaviness, honour*, כָּבוֹד *kabod.*
Gen. 31. 1 of..our father's hath he gotten all this g.
45. 13 ye shall tell my father of all my glory
Exod 16. 7 then ye shall see the glory of the LORD
16. 10 the glory of the LORD appeared in the
24. 16 the glory of the LORD abode upon mount
24. 17 And the sight of the glory of the LORD
28. 2 holy garments..for glory and for beauty
28. 40 and bonnets..for glory and for beauty
29. 43 and..shall be sanctified by my glory
33. 18 said, I beseech thee, show me thy glory
33. 22 it shall come to pass, while my glory
40. 34, 35 the glory of the LORD filled the tab.
Lev. 9. 6 the glory of the LORD shall appear unto
9. 23 the glory of the LORD appeared unto all
Num. 14. 10 the glory of the LORD appeared in the
14. 21 the earth shall be filled with the glory
14. 22 all those men which have seen my glory
16. 19, 42 and the glory of the LORD appeared
20. 6 the glory of the LORD appeared unto
Deut. 5. 24 LORD our God hath showed us his glory
Josh. 7. 19 give, I pray thee, glory to the LORD God
1 Sa. 2. 8 to make them inherit the throne of glory
4. 21, 22 The glory is departed from Israel
6. 5 ye shall give glory unto the God of Israel
1 Ki. 8. 11 for the glory of the LORD had filled the
1 Ch. 16. 24 Declare his glory among the heathen
16. 28 give unto the LORD glory and strength

1 Ch. 16. 29 Give unto the LORD the glory (due) unto
2 Ch. 5. 14 for the glory of the LORD had filled the
7. 1 and the glory of the LORD filled the house
7. 2 because the glory of the LORD had filled
7. 3 the glory of the LORD upon the house
Esth. 5. 11 Haman told them of the glory of his riches
Job 19. 9 He hath stripped me of my glory, and
29. 20 My glory (was) fresh in me, and my bow
Psa. 3. 3 my glory, and the lifter up of mine head
4. 2 how long (will ye turn) my glory into
8. 5 hast crowned him with glory and honour
16. 9 my glory rejoiceth: my flesh also shall
19. 1 The heavens declare the glory of God
21. 5 His glory (is) great in thy salvation: hon.
24. 7, 9 and the King of glory shall come in
24. 8, 10 Who (is) this King of glory? The Lo.
24. 10 The LORD of hosts, he (is) the King of g.
29. 1 give unto the LORD glory and strength
29. 2 Give unto the LORD the glory due unto
29. 3 the God of glory thundereth: the LORD
29. 9 his temple doth every one speak of..glo.
30. 12 To the end that..glory may sing praise
49. 16 when the glory of his house is increased
49. 17 For..his glory shall not descend after
57. 5, 11 (let) thy glory (be) above all the earth
57. 8 Awake up, my glory; awake, psaltery
62. 7 In God (is) my salvation and my glory
63. 2 To see thy power and thy glory, so (as)
72. 19 let the whole earth be filled (with) his g.
73. 24 Thou shalt..afterward receive me (to) g.
79. 9 Help us..for the glory of thy name; and
84. 11 For..the LORD will give grace and glory
85. 9 salvation (is) nigh..that glory may dwell
96. 3 Declare his glory among the heathen, his
96. 7 give unto the LORD glory and strength
96. 8 Give unto the LORD the glory (due unto)
97. 6 and all the people see his glory
102. 15 and all the kings of the earth thy glory
102. 16 the LORD..shall appear in his glory
104. 31 The glory of the LORD shall endure for e.
106. 20 Thus they changed their glory into the
108. 1 I will..give praise, even with my glory
108. 5 and thy glory above all the earth
113. 4 The LORD (is) high..his glory above the
115. 1 but unto thy name give glory, for thy
138. 5 they shall sing..for great (is) the glory
145. 11 They shall speak of the glory of thy kin.
149. 5 Let the saints be joyful in glory: let
Prov. 3. 35 The wise shall inherit glory: but shame
25. 2 (It is) the glory of God to conceal a thing
25. 27 to search their own glory (is not) glory
Isa. 3. 8 to provoke the eyes of his glory
4. 5 for upon all the glory (shall be) a defence
6. 3 Holy..the whole earth (is) full of his glo.
8. 7 the king of Assyria, and all his glory
10. 3 and where will ye leave your glory?
10. 16 under his glory he shall kindle a burning
10. 18 And shall consume the glory of his forest
14. 18 all of them, lie in glory, every one in his
16. 14 and the glory of Moab shall be contemned
17. 3 they shall be as the glory of the children
17. 4 the glory of Jacob shall be made thin
21. 16 and all the glory of Kedar shall fail
22. 18 the chariots of thy glory..the shame of
22. 24 they shall hang upon him all the glory of
35. 2 the glory of Lebanon shall be given unto
35. 2 they shall see the glory of the LORD, (and)
40. 5 the glory of the LORD shall be revealed
42. 8 my glory will I not give to another
42. 12 Let them give glory unto the LORD, and
43. 7 for I have created him for my glory
48. 11 I will not give my glory unto another
58. 8 the glory of the LORD shall be thy rerew.
59. 19 and his glory from the rising of the sun
60. 1 the glory of the LORD is risen upon thee
60. 2 and his glory shall be seen upon thee
60. 13 The glory of Lebanon shall come unto
61. 6 in their glory shall ye boast yourselves
62. 2 and all kings thy glory: and thou shalt
66. 11 be delighted with the abundance of her g.
66. 12 the glory of the Gentiles like a flowing s.
66. 18 and they shall come, and see my glory
66. 19 nor heard..neither have seen my glory
66. 19 they shall declare my glory among the G.
Jer. 2. 11 my people have changed their glory for
13. 16 Give glory to the LORD your God, before
14. 21 do not disgrace the throne of thy glory
48. 18 come down from..glory, and sit in thirst
Eze. 1. 28 of the likeness of the glory of the LORD
3. 12 Blessed (be) the glory of the LORD from
3. 23 behold, the glory of the LORD stood there
3. 23 as the glory which I saw by the river of
8. 4 behold, the glory of the God of Israel
9. 3 the glory of the God of Israel was gone
10. 4 Then the glory of the LORD went up from
10. 4 full of the brightness of the LORD'S glory
10. 18 Then the glory of the LORD departed
10. 19 the glory of the God of Israel (was) over
11. 22 the glory of the God of Israel (was) over
11. 23 the glory of the LORD went up from the
31. 18 To whom art thou thus like in glory
39. 21 I will set my glory among the heathen
43. 2 the glory of the God of Israel came from
43. 2 and the earth shined with his glory
43. 4 the glory of the LORD came into the house
43. 5 the glory of the LORD filled the house
44. 4 the glory of the LORD filled the house of
Dan. 11. 39 whom he shall..increase with glory
Hos. 4. 7 will I change their glory into shame
9. 11 Ephraim, their glory shall fly away like a
10. 5 for the glory thereof, because it is depar.
Mic. 1. 15 he shall come unto Adullam the glory of

Nah. 2. 9 none end of..glory out of all the pleasant
Hab. 2. 14 the knowledge of the glory of the LORD
2. 16 Thou art filled with shame for glory
2. 16 shameful spewing (shall be) on thy glory
Hag. 2. 3 Who..that saw this house in her first gl.?
2. 7 and I will fill this house with glory, saith
2. 9 The glory of this latter house shall be
Zech. 2. 5 For I..will be the glory in the midst of
2. 8 After the glory hath he sent me unto the
Mal. 2. 2 to give glory unto my name, saith the Lo.
8. *Beauty, desire*, צְבִי *tsebi.*
Isa. 13. 19 Babylon, the glory of kingdoms, the bea.
23. 9 to stain the pride of all glory..to bring
24. 16 have we heard songs..glory to the right.
28. 5 LORD of hosts be for a crown of glory
Eze. 20. 6, 15 a land..which (is) the glory of all lands
25. 9 on his frontiers, the glory of the country
26. 20 I shall set glory in the land of the living
9. *Beauty, glory*, תִּפְאֶרֶת, תִּפְאָרָה *tiphereth, tipharah.*
1 Ch. 22. 5 of fame and of glory throughout all coun.
29. 11 the power, and the glory, and the victory
Psa. 78. 61 delivered..his glory into the enemy's hand
89. 17 For thou (art) the glory of their strength
Prov. 4. 9 a crown of glory shall she deliver to thee
16. 31 The hoary head (is) a crown of glory, (if) it
17. 6 and the glory of children (are) their fath.
19. 11 and (it is) his glory to pass over a trans.
20. 29 The glory of young men (is) their strength
28. 12 When righteous..do rejoice..great glory
Isa. 10. 12 I will punish..the glory of his high looks
20. 5 they shall be afraid..of Egypt their glory
46. 13 place salvation in Zion for Israel my glory
60. 7 and I will glorify the house of my glory
60. 19 everlasting light, and thy God thy glory
62. 3 Thou shalt also be a crown of glory in the
63. 15 habitation of thy holiness and of thy glo.
Jer. 13. 11 a name, and for a praise, and for a glory
13. 18 come down..the crown of your glory
Eze. 24. 25 the joy of their glory, the desire of their
Zech 12. 7 glory of the house of David and the glory
10. *Honour*, כָּבוֹד *kabod.*
Psa. 79. 9 for the glory of thy name: and deliver us
11. *Glory*, δόξα *doxa.*
Matt. 4. 8 the kingdoms..and the glory of them
6. 13 [and the power, and the glory, for ever]
6. 29 That even Solomon in all his glory was
16. 27 the Son of man shall come in the glory of
19. 28 the Son..shall sit in the throne of his gl.
24. 30 clouds of heaven with power and great g.
25. 31 the Son of man shall come in his glory
25. 31 shall he sit upon the throne of his glory
Mark 8. 38 when he cometh in the glory of his F.
10. 37 the other on thy left hand, in thy glory
13. 26 in the clouds with great power and glory
Luke 2. 9 the glory of the Lord shone round about
2. 14 Glory to God in the highest, and on earth
2. 32 and the glory of thy people Israel
4. 6 will I give thee, and the glory of them
9. 26 when he shall come in his own glory, and
9. 31 Who appeared in glory, and spake of his
9. 32 they saw his glory, and the two men that
12. 27 Solomon in all his glory was not arrayed
17. 18 that returned to give glory to God, save
19. 38 peace in heaven, and glory in the highest
21. 27 in a cloud, with power and great glory
24. 26 Ought not Christ..to enter into his glory?
John 1. 14 we beheld his glory, the glory as of the
2. 11 and manifested forth his glory; and his
7. 18 speaketh of himself seeketh his own glory
7. 18 but he that seeketh his glory that sent
8. 50 I seek not mine own glory: there is one
11. 4 but for the glory of God, that the Son of
11. 40 that..thou shouldest see the glory of G.?
12. 41 when he saw his glory, and spake of him
17. 5 with the glory which I had with thee
17. 22 the glory which thou gavest me I have
17. 24 that they may behold my glory, which
Acts 7. 2 The God of glory appeared unto our fat.
7. 55 saw the glory of God, and Jesus standing
12. 23 smote..because he gave not God the glory
22. 11 And when I could not see for the glory
Rom. 1. 23 changed the glory of the uncorruptible
2. 7 seek for glory and honour and immorta.
2. 10 But glory, honour, and peace, to every
3. 7 abounded through my lie unto his glory
3. 23 all have sinned, and come short of the g.
4. 20 was strong in faith, giving glory to God
5. 2 and rejoice in hope of the glory of God
6. 4 raised up from the dead by the glory of
8. 18 with the glory which shall be revealed
9. 4 the adoption, and the glory, and the
9. 23 he might make known the riches of his g.
9. 23 which he had afore prepared unto glory
11. 36 all things: to whom (be) glory for ever
15. 7 as Christ also received us, to the glory of
16. 27 To God only wise, (be) glory through J. C.
1 Co. 2. 7 hidden..which God ordained..unto our g.
2. 8 would not have crucified the Lord of glory
10. 31 whatsoever ye do, do all to the glory of
11. 7 as he is the image and glory of God
11. 7 but the woman is the glory of the man
11. 15 it is a glory to her: for..hair is given her
15. 40 but the glory of the celestial (is) one, and
15. 41 one glory of the sun, and another glory
15. 41 and another glory of the stars..in glory
15. 43 sown in dishonour; it is raised in glory
2 Co. 1. 20 in him Amen, unto the glory of God by
3. 7 behold..for the glory of his countenance
3. 9 ministration of condemnation (be) glory

2 Co. 3. 9 ministration of righteousness exceed. in g.
3. 10 by reason of the glory that excelleth
3. 18 beholding as in a glass the glory of the
3. 18 into the same image from glory to glory
4. 6 light of the knowledge of the glory of G.
4. 15 grace might..redound to the glory of God
4. 17 worketh for us..eternal weight of glory
8. 19 administered by us to the glory of the
8. 23 messengers of the churches..the glory of
Gal. 1. 5 To whom (be) glory for ever and ever. A.
Eph. 1. 6 To the praise of the glory of his grace
1. 12 we should be to the praise of his glory
1. 14 is the earnest..unto the praise of his g.
1. 17 That the God..the Father of glory, may
1. 18 what the riches of the glory of his inher
3. 13 my tribulations for you, which is your g.
3. 16 grant..according to the riches of his glory
3. 21 Unto him (be) glory in the church by C.
Phil. 1. 11 filled..unto the glory and praise of God
2. 11 confess..to the glory of God the Father
3. 19 Whose..glory (is) in their shame, who
4. 19 according to his riches in glory by Christ
4. 20 Now unto God and our Father (be) glory
Col. 1. 27 make known what (is) the riches of the g.
1. 27 which is Christ in you, the hope of glory
3. 4 shall ye also appear with him in glory
1 Th. 2. 6 Nor of men sought we glory, neither of
2. 12 who hath called you unto his..glory
2. 20 For ye are our glory and joy
2 Th. 1. 9 destruction..from the glory of his power
2. 14 to the obtaining of the glory of our Lord
1 Ti. 1. 17 (be) honour and glory for ever and ever
3. 16 believed..in the world, received..into gl.
2 Ti. 2. 10 which is in Christ Jesus with eternal gl.
4. 18 to whom (be) glory for ever and ever A.
Heb. 1. 3 Who being the brightness of (his) glory
2. 7 thou crownedst him with glory and hon.
2. 9 Jesus..crowned with glory and honour
2. 10 bringing many sons unto glory, to make
3. 3 this..was counted worthy of more glory
9. 5 over it the cherubim of glory shadowing
13. 21 to whom (be) glory for ever and ever. A.
Jas. 2. 1 of our Lord Jesus Christ, (the Lord) of g.
1 Pe. 1. 7 might be found unto praise..and glory
1. 11 testified before hand..the glory that
1. 21 that raised him up..and gave him glory
1. 24 all the glory of man as the flower of
4. 13 that, when his glory shall be revealed, ye
4. 14 the spirit of glory and of God resteth
5. 1 a partaker of the glory that shall be
5. 4 ye shall receive a crown of glory that fa.
5. 10 who hath called us unto his eternal glory
5. 11 To him (be) [glory and] dominion for ever
2 Pe. 1. 3 him that hath called us to glory and vir.
1. 17 he received from God..honour and glory
1. 17 a voice to him from the excellent glory
3. 18 To him (be) glory both now and for ever
Jude 24 faultless before the presence of his glory
25 glory and majesty dominion and power
Rev. 1. 6 to him (be) glory and dominion for ever
4. 9 when those beasts give glory and honour
4. 11 to receive glory and honour and power
5. 12 to receive..honour, and glory, and bless.
5. 13 Blessing, and honour, and glory, and po.
7. 12 Blessing, and glory, and wisdom, and th.
11. 13 and gave glory to the God of heaven
14. 7 Fear God, and give glory to him; for the
15. 8 filled with smoke from the glory of God
16. 9 and they repented not to give him glory
18. 1 and the earth was lightened with his gl.
19. 1 Salvation, and glory, and honour, and
21. 11 Having the glory of God: and her light
21. 23 for the glory of God did lighten it, and
21. 24 and the kings..do bring their glory and
21. 26 they shall bring the glory and honour

12. *Celebrity*, κλέος *kleos*.
1 Pe. 2. 20 For what glory..if, when ye be buffeted

GLORY, desirous of vain —
Vain glorious, full of empty glory, κενόδοξος.
Gal. 5. 26 Let us not be desirous of vain glory

GLORY, full of —
To be glorified, δοξάζομαι *doxazomai*.
1 Pe. 1. 8 rejoice with joy unspeakable and full of g.

GLORY, to have —
To be glorified, δοξάζομαι *doxazomai*.
Matt. 6. 2 hypocrites..that they may have glory of
2 Co. 3. 10 had no glory in this respect, by reason of

GLORY, to —
1. *To boast self*, הָלַל *halal*, 7.
1 Ch. 16. 10 Glory ye in his holy name: let the heart
Psa. 63. 11 every one that sweareth by him shall gl.
64. 10 and all the upright in heart shall glory
105. 3 Glory ye in his holy name: let the heart
106. 5 that I may glory with thine inheritance
Isa. 41. 16 shalt glory in the Holy One of Israel
45. 25 seed of Israel be justified, and shall glory
Jer. 4. 2 and the nations..in him shall they glory
9. 23 Let not the wise..glory in his wisdom
9. 23 neither let the mighty..glory in his might
9. 23 let not the rich..glory in his riches
9. 24 But let him that glorieth glory in this
49. 4 Wherefore gloriest thou in the valleys

2. *To become heavy, honoured*, כָּבַד *kabed*, 2.
2 Ki. 14. 10 glory..and tarry at home: for why sho.

3. *To beautify self*, פָּאַר *paar*, 7.
Exod. 8. 9 Moses said unto Pharaoh, Glory over me

4. *To praise self*, שָׁבַח *shabach*, 7.
1 Ch. 16. 35 we may give thanks..(and) glory in thy

5. *To boast against*, κατακαυχάομαι *katakauchaomai*.
Jas. 3. 14 glory not, and lie not against the truth

6. *To boast*, καυχάομαι *kauchaomai*.
Rom. 5. 3 And not only (so), but we glory in tribu.
1 Co. 1. 29 That no flesh should glory in his presence
1. 31 He that glorieth, let him glory in the
3. 21 Therefore let no man glory in men. For
4. 7 why dost thou glory, as if thou hadst not
2 Co. 5. 12 them which glory in appearance, and not
10. 17 he that glorieth, let him glory in the Lord
11. 12 wherein they glory they may be found
11. 18 Seeing that many glory..I will glory also
11. 30 If I must needs glory, I will glory of the
12. 1 not expedient for me doubtless to glory
12. 5 will I glory: yet of myself I will not gl.
12. 6 though I would desire to glory, I shall
12. 9 Most gladly therefore will I rather glory
Gal. 6. 13 that they may glory in your flesh
6. 14 God forbid that I should glory, save in
2 Th. 1. 4 we ourselves glory in you in the churches

7. *Boasting*, καύχημα *kauchēma*.
Rom. 4. 2 he hath..to glory; but not before God
2 Co. 5. 12 give you occasion to glory on our behalf

GLORY of, to have nothing to —
Not a matter of boasting, οὐ καύχημα *ou kauchēma*.
1 Co. 9. 16 I have nothing to glory of: for necessity

GLORY, whereof I may —
Boasting, (the act), καύχησις *kauchēsis*.
Rom. 15. 17 I have therefore whereof I may glory

GLORYING —
1. *Boasting, (the subject matter)*, καύχημα *kauchēma*.
1 Co. 5. 6 Your glorying (is) not good. Know ye not
9. 15 any man should make my glorying void

2. *Boasting, (the act)*, καύχησις *kauchēsis*.
2 Co. 7. 4 great (is) my glorying of you: I am filled

GLORYING, in —
To boast, καυχάομαι *kauchaomai*.
2 Co. 12. 11 I am become a fool [in glorying]; ye have

GLUTTON —
To be gluttonous, vile, lightly esteemed, זָלַל *zalal*.
Deut 21. 20 This our son (is)..a glutton, and a drunk.
Prov. 23. 21 For the drunkard and the glutton shall

GLUTTONOUS —
An eater, φάγος *phagos*.
Matt 11. 19 Behold a man gluttonous, and a wine bi.
Luke 7. 34 Behold a gluttonous man, and a wine bi.

GNASH, to —
1. *To gnash*, חָרַק *charaq*.
Job 16. 9 gnasheth upon me with his teeth; mine
Psa. 35. 16 they gnashed upon me with their teeth
37. 12 The wicked..gnasheth upon him with his
112. 10 he shall gnash with his teeth, and melt
Lam. 2. 16 they hiss and gnash the teeth: they say

2. *To bite, gnash*, βρύχω *bruchō*.
Acts 7. 54 and they gnashed on him with (their) te.

GNASH with, to —
To creak, gnash, τρίζω *trizō*.
Mark 9. 18 he foameth, and gnasheth with his teeth

GNASHING —
A biting, gnashing, βρυγμός *brugmos*.
Matt. 8. 12 there shall be weeping and gnashing of
13. 42, 50 there shall be wailing and gnashing
22. 13 there shall be weeping and gnashing of
24. 51 there shall be weeping and gnashing of
25. 30 there shall be weeping and gnashing of
Luke 13. 28 There shall be weeping and gnashing of

GNAT —
Gnat, mosquito, κώνωψ *kōnōps*.
Matt 23. 24 blind guides, which strain at a gnat, and

GNAW, to —
To chew, gnaw, μασσάομαι *massaomai*.
Rev. 16. 10 and they gnawed their tongues for pain

GNAW the bone, to —
To gnaw a bone, גָּרַם *garam*.
Zeph. 3. 3 they gnaw not the bones till the morrow

GO —
1. *To step*, צָעַד *tsaad*.
2 Sa. 6. 13 when they that bare the ark..had gone
Prov 30. 29 There be three (things) which go well, yea

2. *Procession, going*, הֲלִיכָה *tahalukah*.
Neh. 12. 31 went on the right hand upon the wall

GO, to —
1. *To go away or about*, אֲזַל *azal*.
Ezra 4. 23 they went up in haste to Jerusalem unto
5. 8 we went into the province of Judea, to
5. 15 Take these vessels, go, carry them into
Dan. 2. 17 Then Daniel went to his house, and made
2. 24 he went and said thus unto him; Destroy
6. 18 Then the king went to his palace, and
6. 19 and went in haste unto the den of lions

2. *To travel*, אָרַח *arach*.
Job 34. 8 Which goeth in company with the work.

3. *To go straight or right*, אָשַׁר *ashar*.
Prov. 9. 6 and go in the way of understanding

4. *To declare happy, go straight or right*, אָשַׁר *ashar*, 3.
Prov. 4. 14 Enter not..and go not in the way of evil

5. *To go in*, בּוֹא *bo*.
Gen. 10. 19 as thou goest, unto Sodom, and Gomorrah
10. 30 as thou goest, unto Sephar, a mount of the
15. 15 thou shalt go to thy fathers in peace
25. 18 they dwelt..as thou goest toward Assyria
31. 18 to go to Isaac his father in the land of C.
31. 33 Laban went into Jacob's tent, and into
37. 30 The child (is) not..whither shall I go?
39. 11 went into the house to do his business
Exod. 7. 23 Pharaoh turned and went into his house
8. 1 Go unto Pharaoh, and say unto him, Thus
8. 1 Let my people go, that they may serve me
14. 16 and the children of Israel shall go on dry
14. 22 the children of Israel went into the midst
15. 19 For the horse of Pharaoh went in with
18. 23 all this people shall also go to their place
24. 18 Moses went into the midst of the cloud
30. 20 When they go into the tabernacle of the
34. 12 of the land whither thou goest, lest it be
40. 32 When they went into the tent of the c.
Lev. 9. 23 Moses and Aaron went into the taberna.
10. 9 Do not drink wine..when ye go into the
14. 36 before the priest go..to see the plague
14. 46 Moreover he that goeth into the house
16. 23 garments which he put on when he went
Num. 5. 22 And this water..shall go into thy bowels
8. 22 after that went the Levites in to do their
14. 24 bring into the land whereunto he went
17. 8 Moses went into the tabernacle of witn.
20. 6 Moses and Aaron went from the presence
22. 14 they went unto Balak, and said, Balaam
25. 8 he went after the man of Israel into the
31. 21 the men of war which went to the battle
32. 6 Shall your brethren go to war, and shall
32. 9 that they should not go into the land
Deut. 1. 7 and go to the mount of the Amorites
4. 5 do so in the land whither ye go to poss.
4. 34 Or hath God assayed to go (and) take him
7. 1 the land whither thou goest to possess it
9. 5 dost thou go to possess their land; but
11. 29 the land whither thou goest to possess it
12. 26 and go unto the place which the LORD
12. 29 whither thou goest to possess them, and
19. 5 As when a man goeth into the wood with
23. 20 the land whither thou goest to possess it
24. 10 thou shalt not go into his house to fetch
26. 3 thou shalt go unto the priest that shall
28. 21, 63 the land whither thou goest to possess
30. 16 the land whither thou goest to possess it
30. 18 passest over Jordan to go to possess it
31. 7 for thou must go with this people unto
31. 16 the land whither they go (to be) among
32. 52 thou shalt not go thither unto the land
Josh. 6. 22 Go into the harlot's house, and bring out
18. 3 How long (are) ye slack to go to possess
Judg. 4. 21 went softly unto him, and smote the nail
9. 5 he went unto his father's house at Ophr.
9. 27 went into the house of their god, and did
18. 10 When ye go, ye shall come unto a people
18. 18 these went into Micah's house, and fetch.
18. 20 and went in the midst of the people
Ruth. 2. 18 she took (it) up, and went into the city
3. 7 he went to lie down at the end of the
3. 15 laid (it) on her: and she went into the
3. 17 Go not empty unto thy mother in law
1 Sa. 17. 12 the man went among men (for) an old
21. 10 arose..and went to Achish the king of G.
25. 5 Get you up to Carmel, and go to Nabal
27. 8 as thou goest to Shur, even unto the land
29. 8 that I may not go fight against the enemi.
2 Sa. 11. 11 shall I then go into mine house, to eat and
18. 9 the mule went under the thick boughs of
20. 3 and fed them, but went not in unto them
20. 8 at the great stone..Amasa went before
20. 14 he went through all the tribes of Israel
20. 14 they were gathered together, and went
20. 22 Then the woman went unto all the people
1 Ki. 2. 19 Bath-sheba therefore went unto king Sol.
14. 3 take with thee ten loaves..and go to him
14. 28 when the king went into the house of the
16. 18 he went into the palace of the king's ho.
17. 13 Fear not; go..do as thou hast said: but
20. 33 Then he said, Go ye, bring him. Then B.
22. 25 when thou shalt go into an inner chamber
22. 30 disguised himself, and went into the bat.
2 Ki. 5. 5 go, and I will send a letter unto the king
5. 18 when my master goeth into the house of
7. 5 to go unto the camp of the Syrians
7. 8 they went into one tent, and did eat and
7. 9 that we may go and tell the king's house.
9. 6 And he arose, and went into the house
10. 23 Jehu went, and Jehonadab the son of R.
11. 16 she went by the way by the which the
11. 18 all the people of the land went into the
18. 21 it will go into his hand, and pierce it
19. 1 and went into the house of the LORD
2 Ch. 8. 18 they went with the servants of Solomon
14. 11 in thy name we go against this multitude
18. 24 when thou shalt go into an inner chamb.
18. 29 I will disguise myself, and will go to the
23. 17 all the people went to the house of Baal
25. 7 let not the army of Israel go with thee
25. 8 But if thou wilt go, do (it), be strong for
26. 16 went into the temple of the LORD to burn
29. 16 the priests went into the inner part of the
Ezra 9. 11 The land, unto which ye go to possess it
Neh. 6. 11 would go into the temple to save his life?
Esth. 2. 13 to go with her out of the house of the
2. 14 In the evening she went, and on the mor.

Job 37. 8 Then the beasts go into dens, and remain
Psa. 43. 4 Then will I go unto the altar of God
49. 19 He shall go to the generation of his fath.
66. 12 we went through fire and through water
66. 13 I will go into thy house with burnt offer.
71. 16 I will go in the strength of the Lord GOD
73. 17 Until I went into the sanctuary of God
118. 19 I will go into them..I will praise the L.
132. 7 We will go into his tabernacles; we will
Prov. 7. 22 as an ox goeth to the slaughter, or as a f.
22. 24 and with a furious man thou shalt not go
23. 30 they that go to seek mixed wine
27. 10 neither go into thy brother's house in the
Isa. 2. 19 they shall go into the holes of the rocks
2. 21 To go into the clefts of the rocks, and
13. 2 that they may go into the gates of the
30. 8 Now go, write it before them in a table
36. 6 it will go into his hand, and pierce it
37. 1 and went into the house of the LORD
41. 3 the way..he had not gone with his feet
Jer. 4. 5 and let us go into the defenced cities
4. 29 they shall go into thickets, and climb
16. 8 Thou shalt not also go into the house of
26. 21 was afraid, and fled, and went into Egypt
27. 18 vessels..at Jerusalem, go not to Babylon
28. 4 with all the captives of Judah, that went
34. 3 not escape..and thou shalt go to Babylon
35. 11 Come, and let us go to Jerusalem for fear
36. 5 I cannot go into the house of the LORD
36. 6 Therefore go thou, and read in the roll
38. 11 went into the house of the king under
40. 6 Then went Jeremiah unto Gedaliah the
42. 14 but we will go into the land of Egypt
42. 15 enter into Egypt, and go to sojourn there
42. 19 ye remnant of Judah; Go ye not into E.
42. 22 whither ye desire to go (and) to sojourn
43. 2 Go not into Egypt to sojourn there
Eze. 3. 24 said..Go, shut thyself within thine house
20. 29 What (is) the high place whereunto ye go?
36. 20 whither they went, they profaned my
36. 21 among the heathen whither they went
36. 22 which ye have profaned, whither ye went
38. 11 I will go to them that are at rest, that
41. 3 Then went he inward, and measured the
42. 9 as one goeth into them from the..court
44. 27 in the day that he goeth into the sanctu.
47. 8 These waters issue out..and go
47. 15 the way of Hethlon, as men go to Zedad
48. 1 the way of Hethlon, as one goeth to Ha.
Hos. 9. 10 they went to Baal-peor, and separated
Amos 5. 19 or went into the house, and leaned his
Jon. 1. 3 to go with them unto Tarshish from the
Nah. 3. 14 go into clay, and tread the mortar
Mic. 4. 10 shalt dwell in the field, and thou shalt go
Zech. 6. 10 go into the house of Josiah the son of Z.

6. *To tread,* דָּרַךְ *darak.*

Isa. 59. 8 whosoever goeth therein shall not know

7. *To go,* הָלַךְ *halak.*

Ezra 7. 13 that all they of the people..go with thee

8. *To go on,* הָלַךְ *halak.*

Gen. 2. 14 that (is) it which goeth toward the east
12. 9 Abram journeyed, going on still toward
13. 5 Lot also, which went with Abram, had
14. 24 the portion of the men which went with
15. 2 seeing I go childless, and the steward of
18. 16 Abraham went with them to bring them
24. 42 if now thou do prosper my way which I go
26. 26 Then Abimelech went to him from Gerar
28. 20 will keep me in this way that I go, and
31. 19 Laban went to shear his sheep: and R.
32. 1 Jacob went on his way, and the angels of
32. 20 appease him with the present that goeth
35. 3 and was with me in the way which I went
Exod. 3. 19 that the king of Egypt will not let you go
10. 8 he said..(but) who (are) they that shall go?
13. 21 LORD went before them by day in a pill.
14. 19 angel..which went before the camp of I.
15. 19 Israel went on dry (land) in the midst of
17. 5 thy rod..take in thine hand, and go
33. 15 If thy presence go not..carry us not
Lev. 11. 21 every flying creeping thing that goeth
11. 27 whatsoever goeth upon his paws, among
11. 27 all manner of beasts that go on (all) four
11. 42 Whatsoever goeth upon the belly, and
11. 42 whatsoever goeth upon (all) four, or
Num. 14. 14 they have heard..thou goest before them
14. 38 of the men that went to search the land
22. 13 refuseth to give me leave to go with you
22. 22 God's anger was kindled because he went
24. 1 he went not, as at other times, to seek
24. 14 And now, behold, I go unto my people
24. 25 Balaam rose up..and Balak also went his
32. 41 Jair the son of Manasseh went and took
32. 42 Nobah went and took Kenath, and
Deut. 1. 30 The LORD your God, which goeth before
1. 31 in all the way that ye went, until ye came
1. 33 Who went in the way before you, to
6. 18 that thou mayest go in and possess the
14. 25 and shalt go unto the place which the
16. 7 thou shalt turn in the morning, and go
20. 4 LORD your God (is) he that goeth with
24. 2 she may go and be another man's (wife)
26. 2 shalt go unto the place which the LORD
31. 6 LORD thy God, he (it is) that doth go
31. 8 LORD, he (it is) that doth go before thee
Josh. 2. 5 whither the men went I wot not: pursue
3. 3 then ye shall remove..and go after it
6. 9 the armed men went before the priests
6. 13 went on continually..went before them

Josh. 10. 24 said unto the captains..which went with
18. 8 Joshua charged them that went to desc.
23. 16 have gone and served other gods, and
24. 17 preserved us in all the way .we went
Judg. 1. 3 I likewise will go with thee into thy lot
4. 8 If thou wilt..with me, then I will go
8. 1 thou calledst us not when thou wentest
9. 8 The trees went forth..to anoint a king
9. 11 and go to be promoted over the trees?
9. 13 and go to be promoted over the trees?
11. 8 that thou mayest go with us, and fight
14. 3 that thou goest to take a wife of the
14. 19 he went down to Ashkelon, and slew
17. 9 and I go to sojourn where I may find
18. 5 whether our way which we go shall be
18. 14 the five men that w. to spy out the coun.
18. 17 the five men that w. to spy out the
19. 9 get you early..that thou mayest go home
19. 18 I went to Beth-lehem-judah, but..going
21. 21 catch..and go to the land of Benjamin
Ruth 2. 9 go thou after them: have I not charged
2. 9 when thou art athirst, go unto the vessels
1 Sa. 2. 20 And they went unto their own home
6. 8 the cart..and send it away, that it may go
6. 12 lowing as they went..the lords..went
7. 16 he went from year to year in circuit to
9. 6 he can show us our way that we should go
10. 2 The asses which thou wentest to seek
10. 14 Whither went ye? And he said, To seek
10. 26 And Saul also went home to Gibeah; and
14. 46 the Philistines went to their own place
17. 7 and one bearing a shield went before
17. 13 the names of his three sons that went to
17. 15 David went and returned from Saul
20. 13 that thou mayest go in peace: and the
23. 18 David abode..Jonathan went to his house
23. 23 come ye again..and I will go with you
25. 42 five damsels of hers that went after her
30. 22 wicked men..of those that went with D.
30. 22 Because they went not with us, we will
2 Sa. 6. 4 ark of God: And Ahio went before the
7. 9 I was with thee whithersoever thou went
7. 23 whom God went to redeem for a people
8. 6 preserved David whithersoever he went
8. 14 preserved David whithersoever he went
12. 23 I shall go to him, but he shall not return
15. 11 with Absalom went..men..they went
15. 20 seeing I go whither I may, return thou
15. 30 he went barefoot: and all the people
16. 13 and cursed as he went, and threw stones
16. 17 why wentest thou not with thy friend?
17. 11 that thou go to battle in thine own person
17. 17 and a wench went and told them
19. 25 Wherefore wentest not thou with me, M.
23. 17 the blood of the men that went in jeopa.
24. 12 Go and say unto David, Thus saith the L.
1 Ki. 2. 2 I go the way of all the earth: be thou st.
2. 41 it was told Solomon that Shimei had gone
9. 6 but go and serve other gods, and worship
13. 12 What way went he?..the man of God
18. 6 Ahab went one way by himself, and
18. 6 Obadiah went another way by himself
19. 4 he himself went a day's journey into the
22. 48 they went not; for the ships were broken
2 Ki. 1. 3 ye go to enquire of Baal-zebub the god of
2. 7 fifty men of the sons of the prophets went
4. 23 Wherefore wilt thou go to him to day?
5. 10 Go and wash in Jordan seven times
5. 25 And he said, Thy servant went no whither
5. 26 Went not mine heart..when the man
1 Ch. 4. 42 And (some) of them..went to mount Seir
6. 15 And Jehozadak went..when the LORD
15. 25 So David..went to bring up the ark of
17. 21 whom God went to redeem (to be) his own
18. 6 preserved David whithersoever he went
18. 13 preserved David whithersoever he went
2 Ch. 7. 19 and shall go and serve other gods, and
8. 17 Then went Solomon to Ezion-geber, and
9. 21 For the king's ships went to Tarshish
18. 12 the messenger that went to call Micaiah
Neh. 2. 16 the rulers knew not whither I went, or
12. 38 And the other..went over against
Job 1. 4 his sons went and feasted (in their) houses
16. 22 then I shall go the way..I shall not ret.
23. 8 Behold, I go forward, but he (is) not
41. 19 Out of his mouth go burning lamps
Prov. 7. 22 He goeth after her straightway, as an ox
Eccl. 1. 6 The wind goeth toward the south, and
3. 20 All go unto one place; all are of the dust
6. 6 seen no good: do not all go to one place
9. 10 no work..in the grave, whither thou go.
12. 5 man goeth to his long home; and the mo.
Song 7. 9 the best wine for my beloved, that goeth
Isa. 2. 3 many people shall go and say, Come ye
2. 21 To go into the clefts of the rocks, and
8. 6 refuseth the waters of Shiloah that go
8. 7 he shall come..and go over all his banks
30. 29 as when one goeth with a pipe to come
38. 5 Go and say to Hezekiah, Thus saith the L.
45. 16 they shall go to confusion together (that
52. 12 LORD will go before you, and the God of
58. 8 thy righteousness shall go before thee
Jer. 2. 23 I am not polluted, I have not gone after
3. 1 and she go from him, and become another
3. 12 Go and proclaim these words toward the
11. 10 they went after other gods to serve [them
11. 12 inhabitants of Jerusalem go and cry unto
13. 1 Go and get thee a linen girdle, and put it
17. 19 Go and stand in the gate of the children
19. 1 Go and get a potter's earthen bottle, and
19. 10 in the sight of the men that go with thee
28. 13 Go and tell Hananiah, saying, Thus saith

Jer. 29. 12 ye shall go and pray unto me, and I will
31. 2 Israel, when I went to cause him to rest
31. 21 the way..thou wentest: turn again, O vi.
34. 2 Go and speak to Zedekiah king of Judah
35. 2 Go unto the house of the Rechabites, and
35. 13 Go and tell the men of Judah, and the
39. 16 Go and speak to Ebed-melech the Eth.
41. 6 weeping all along as he went: and it ca.
48. 11 Moab..neither hath he gone into captiv.
50. 4 of Israel shall come..going and weeping
50. 6 they have gone from mountain to hill
Eze. 7. 14 but none goeth to the battle: for my wr.
20. 16 for their heart went after their idols
33. 31 their heart goeth after their coveteousness
Hos. 7. 11 they call to Egypt, they go to Assyria
11. 2 they called them, so they went from them
Amos 1. 15 their king shall go into captivity: he and
Nah. 3. 10 she went into captivity: her young chil.
Zech. 2. 2 Then said I, Whither goest thou? And he
8. 21 the inhabitants of one (city) shall go to
9. 14 and shall go with whirlwinds of the south

9. *To go on,* הָלַךְ *halak, 3.*

1 Ki. 21. 27 Ahab..lay in sackcloth, and went softly
Job 30. 28 I went mourning without the sun: I
Psa. 38. 6 I am troubled..I go mourning all the day
85. 13 Righteousness shall go before him, and
104. 26 There go the ships..that leviathan..thou
Prov. 6. 28 Can one go upon hot coals, and his feet
Hab. 3. 11 at the light of thine arrows they went

10. *To go on habitually,* הָלַךְ *halak, 7.*

Josh. 18. 4 they shall rise and go through the land
1 Sa. 23. 13 and went whithersoever they could go
1 Ch. 16. 20 they went from nation to nation, and fr.
21. 4 Joab departed, and went throughout all
Psa. 43. 2 why go I mourning because of the oppr.
105. 13 When they went from one nation to an.
Prov. 6. 22 When thou goest, it shall lead thee

11. *To go on,* יָלַךְ *yalak.*

Gen. 3. 14 upon thy belly shalt thou go, and dust
7. 18 the ark went upon the face of the waters
9. 23 Shem and Japheth..went backward, and
11. 31 to go into the land of Canaan; and they
12. 4 So Abram departed..and Lot went
12. 5 they went forth to go into the land of C.
12. 19 behold thy wife, take (her), and go thy
13. 3 he went on his journeys from the south
16. 8 and whither wilt thou go? And she said
18. 22 the men turned their faces..and went
21. 16 she went, and sat her down over against
21. 19 she went and filled the bottle with water
22. 3 went unto the place of which God had
22. 5 I and the lad will go yonder and worship
22. 6 and they went both of them together
22. 8 so they went both of them together
22. 13 Abraham went and took the ram, and offe
22. 19 rose up and went together to Beer-sheba
24. 4 thou shalt go unto my country, and to
24. 10 and he arose, and went to Mesopotamia
24. 38 thou shalt go unto my father's house
24. 51 Rebekah (is) before thee, take..and go
24. 55 at the least ten; after that she shall go
24. 56 send me away that I may go to my mas.
24. 58 Wilt thou go..And she said, I will go
25. 22 And she went to enquire of the LORD
26. 1 Isaac went unto Abimelech king of the P.
26. 13 the man waxed great, and went forward
26. 16 Abimelech said unto Isaac, Go from us
27. 5 Esau went to the field to hunt..venison
27. 9 Go now to the flock, and fetch me from
27. 13 only obey my voice, and go fetch me
27. 14 And he went, and fetched, and brought
28. 2 Arise, go to Padan-aram, to the house of
28. 5 he went to Padan-aram unto Laban, son
28. 9 Then went Esau unto Ishmael, and took
28. 10 Jacob went out from Beer-sheba and went
28. 15 in all (places) whither thou goest
29. 7 water ye the sheep, and go..feed (them)
30. 14 Reuben went in the days of wheat harv.
30. 25 Send me away, that I may go unto mine
30. 26 for whom I have served thee, and let me g.
32. 17 Whose (art) thou? and whither goest thou?
33. 12 and let us go, and I will go before thee
35. 22 Reuben went and lay with Bilhah his fa.
36. 6 went into the country from the face of
37. 12 his brethren went to feed their father's fl.
37. 14 said to him, Go, I pray thee, see whether
37. 17 I heard them say, Let us go to Dothan
37. 17 Joseph went after his brethren, and found
38. 11 Tamar went and dwelt in her father's ho.
41. 55 Go unto Joseph; what he saith to you, do
42. 19 go ye, carry corn for the famine of your
42. 38 befall him by the way in the which ye go
43. 8 Send the lad with me, and we will..go
45. 17 lade your beasts, and go, get you unto the
45. 28 Israel said..I will go and see him before I
50. 18 his brethren also went and fell down bef
Exod. 2. 1 there went a man of the house of Levi
2. 7 Shall I go and call to thee a nurse of the
2. 8 And Pharaoh's daughter said to her, Go
2. 8 the maid went and called the child's m.
3. 11 Who (am) I, that I should go unto Phar.
3. 16 Go, and gather the elders of Israel toge.
3. 18 and now let us go, we beseech thee, three
3. 21 that, when ye go, ye shall not go empty
4. 12 Now therefore go, and I will be with thy
4. 18 Moses went and returned to Jethro his
4. 18 Let me go, I pray thee, and return unto
4. 18 And Jethro said to Moses, Go in peace
4. 19 Go, return into Egypt: for all the men
4. 21 When thou goest to return into Egypt

Exod. 4. 27 Go into the wilderness to meet Moses
4. 27 he went, and met him in the mount of
4. 29 Moses and Aaron went and gathered
5. 3 let us go, we pray thee, three days' jour.
5. 7 let them go and gather straw for them.
5. 8 saying, Let us go..sacrifice to our God
5. 11 Go ye, get you straw where ye can find
5. 17 Let us go (and) do sacrifice to the LORD
5. 18 Go therefore now..work: for there shall
8. 25 Go ye, sacrifice to your God in the land
8. 27 We will go three days' journey into the
8. 28 Pharaoh said, I will let you go, that ye
8. 28 only ye shall not go very far away: ent.
10. 8 Go, serve the LORD your God..who (are)
10. 9 We will go..with our herds will we go
10. 11 Not so: go now ye..men, and serve the L.
10. 24 Go ye, serve the LORD; only let your fl.
10. 24 let your little ones also go with you
10. 26 Our cattle also shall go with us; there
12. 31 and go, serve the LORD, as ye have said
13. 21 the LORD..before them..to go by day
14. 19 the angel..removed and w. behind them
14. 21 the LORD caused the sea to go..by a
15. 22 they went out into the wilderness of Shur
15. 22 they went three days in the wilderness
18. 27 and he went his way into his own land
19. 10 Go unto the people, and sanctify them
23. 23 mine Angel shall go before thee, and bring
32. 1 make us gods, which shall go before us
32. 23 make us gods, which shall go before us
32. 7 the LORD said unto Moses, Go, get thee
32. 34 Therefore now go, lead the people unto
32. 34 behold, mine Angel shall go before thee
33. 14 My presence shall go..and I will give
33. 16 (Is it) not in that thou goest with us?
34. 9 let my Lord, I pray thee, go among us
Num. 10. 30 he said unto him, I will not go; but I
10. 32 it shall be, if thou go with us, yea, it
13. 26 they went and came to Moses, and to A.
16. 25 Moses rose up, and went unto Dathan
16. 46 go quickly unto the congregation, and
20. 17 we will go by the king's (high) way, we
21. 22 we will go along by the king's..way
22. 12 Thou shalt not go with them; thou shalt
22. 20 rise up..go with them; but yet the
22. 21 Balaam..went with the princes of Moab
22. 23 And the ass saw..and went into the field
22. 35 Go with the men..So Balaam went with
22. 39 Baalam went with Balak, and they came
23. 3 Stand by thy burnt offering, and I will go
23. 3 And he went to an high place
24. 25 Baalam rose up, and went and returned
32. 39 the son of Manasseh went to Gilead, and
33. 8 went three days' journey in the wilder.
Deut. 1. 19 we went through all that great and ter.
1. 33 to show you by what way ye should go
2. 27 I will go along by the high way, I will
5. 30 Go say to them, Get you into your tents
6. 14 Ye shall not go after other gods, of the
11. 28 to go after other gods, which ye have not
13. 2 Let us go after other gods, which thou
13. 6 Let us go and serve other gods, which
13. 13 Let us go and serve other gods, which thou
17. 3 hath gone and served other gods, and w.
20. 5, 6 let him go and return to [unto] his hou.
20. 7, 8 let him go and return unto his house
28. 14 to go after other gods to serve them
28. 41 not enjoy..for they shall go into captivi.
29. 18 to go..serve the gods of these nations
29. 26 they went and served other gods, and
31. 1 Moses went and spake these words unto
31. 14 Moses and Joshua went, and presented
Josh. 1. 7 mayest prosper whithersoever thou goest
1. 9 God (is) with thee whithersoever thou go.
1. 16 whithersoever thou sendest us we will go
2. 1 saying, Go view the land, even Jericho
2. 1 they went, and came into an harlot's ho.
2. 16 hide..and afterward may ye go your w.
2. 22 they went, and came unto the mountain
3. 4 ye may know the way by which ye..go
3. 6 took up..and went before the people
5. 13 Joshua went unto him, and said unto him
8. 9 they went to lie in ambush, and abode
8. 13 Joshua went that night into the midst
9. 4 They did work wilily, and went and made
9. 6 they went to Joshua unto the camp at G.
9. 11 go to meet them, and say unto them
9. 12 on the day we came forth to go unto you
16. 7 And it went down from Janohah to A.
18. 8 Go and walk through the land, and des.
18. 9 the men went and passed through the
22. 6 sent them away: and they went unto
22. 9 to go unto the country of Gilead, to the
Judg. 1. 3 Come up with me..So Simeon went with
1. 10 Judah went against the Canaanites that
1. 11 from thence he went against the inhabit.
1. 16 they went and dwelt among the people
1. 17 Judah went with Simeon his brother
1. 26 the man went into the land of the Hitti.
2. 6 when Joshua had let the people go, the
2. 6 the children of Israel went every man
3. 13 went and smote Israel, and possessed
4. 6 Go and draw toward mount Tabor, and
4. 8 If thou wilt go with me, then I will
4. 8 if thou wilt not go with me..I will not go
4. 9 And she said, I will surely go with thee
4. 9 Deborah arose, and went with Barak to
6. 14 Go in this thy might, and thou shalt save
7. 4 This shall go with thee, the same shall go
7. 4 This shall not go..the same shall not go
7. 7 let all the..people go every man unto his
8. 29 the son of Joash went and dwelt in his
Judg. 9. 1 the son of Jerubbaal went to Shechem
9. 6 and went and made Abimelech king
9. 7 he went and stood in the top of mount
9. 21 and went to Beer, and dwelt there, for
9. 50 Then went Abimelech to Thebez, and en.
10. 14 Go and cry unto the gods which ye have
11. 5 the elders of Gilead went to fetch Jepht.
11. 11 Jephthah went with the elders of Gilead
11. 18 they went along through the wilderness
11. 37 that I may go up and down upon the
11. 38 And he said, Go. And he sent her away
11. 38 she went with her companions, and bew.
11. 40 the daughters of Israel went yearly to
12. 1 and didst not call us to go with thee?
13. 11 Manoah arose, and went after his wife
14. 9 went on eating, and came to his father
15. 4 Samson went and caught three hundred
16. 1 Then went Samson to Gaza, and saw there
17. 10 Dwell with me..So the Levite went in
18. 2 Go, search the land: who when they ca.
18. 6 the priest said unto them, Go in peace
18. 6 before the LORD (is) your way wherein ye g.
18. 9 be not slothful to go..to enter to possess
18. 19 lay thine hand upon thy mouth, and go
18. 26 And the children of Dan went their way
19. 3 her husband arose, and went after her, to
19. 17 Whither goest thou? and whence comest
19. 18 I went to Beth-lehem-judah, but..going
19. 27 and went out to go his way; and, behold
19. 28 said unto her, Up, and let us be going
20. 8 We will not any (of us) go to his tent, ne.
21. 10 Go and smite the inhabitants of Jabesh-g.
21. 20 saying, Go and lie in wait in the vineyards
21. 23 they went and returned unto their inher.
Ruth 1. 1 a certain man of Beth-lehem-judah went
1. 7 they went on their way to return unto the
1. 8 Go, return each to her mother's house
1. 11 why will ye go with me? (are) there yet
1. 12 Turn again, my daughters, go..for I am
1. 16 for whither thou goest, I will go; and w.
1. 18 When she saw that she was..to go with
1. 19 So they two went until they came to
2. 2 Let me now go to the field, and glean
2. 2 And she said unto her, Go, my daughter
2. 3 And she went, and came, and gleaned
2. 8 Go not to glean in another field, neither
1 Sa. 1. 17 Then Eli answered and said, Go in peace
1. 18 So the woman went her way, and did eat
2. 11 Elkanah went to Ramah to his house
3. 5 lie down again. And he went and lay
3. 6 arose and w. to Eli, and said, Here (am) I
3. 8 arose and w. to Eli, and said, Here (am) I
3. 9 Eli said unto Samuel, Go, lie down: and
3. 9 So Samuel went and lay down in his pla.
8. 22 Samuel said..Go ye every man unto his
9. 3 Take now..and arise, go seek the asses
9. 6 now let us go thither; peradventure he
9. 7 But, behold, (if) we go, what shall we
9. 9 when a man went to enquire of God
9. 9 Come, and let us go to the seer: for (he
9. 10 Well said; come, let us go. So they went
10. 9 when he had turned his back to go from
10. 26 home to Gibeah; and there went with him
11. 14 Come, and let us go to Gilgal, and renew
11. 15 all the people went to Gilgal; and there
14. 16 the multitude melted away, and they went
14. 19 that the noise..went on and increased
15. 3 Now go and smite Amalek, and utterly
15. 6 Go, depart, get you down from among the
15. 18 Go and utterly destroy the sinners the A.
15. 20 and have gone the way which the LORD
15. 34 Then Samuel went to Ramah; and Saul
16. 1 Fill thine horn with oil, and go, I will
16. 2 Samuel said, How can I go? if Saul hear
16. 13 So Samuel rose up, and went to Ramah
17. 13 the three eldest sons of Jesse went (and)
17. 20 and went, as Jesse had commanded him
17. 20 as the host was going forth to the fight
17. 32 thy servant will go and fight with this P.
17. 33 Thou art not able to go against this Phil.
17. 37 Saul said unto David, Go, and the LORD
17. 39 he assayed to go; for he had not proved
17. 39 David said unto Saul, I cannot go with
18. 27 Wherefore David arose and went, he
19. 12 and he went, and fled, and escaped
19. 18 he and Samuel went and dwelt in Naioth
19. 22 Then went he also to Ramah, and came
19. 23 he went thither to Naioth in Ramah
19. 23 he went on and prophesied, until he came
20. 21 Go, find out the arrows. If I expressly
20. 40 Jonathan..said..Go, carry (them) to the
20. 42 Jonathan said to David, Go in peace
22. 3 David went thence to Mizpeh of Moab
23. 2 Shall I go and smite these Philistines?
23. 2 Go and smite the Philistines, and save K.
23. 5 So David and his men went to Keilah
23. 16 Jonathan..went to David into the wood
23. 22 Go, I pray you, prepare yet, and know
23. 24 they arose, and went to Ziph before Saul
23. 25 Saul also and his men went to seek (him)
23. 26 Saul went on this side of the mountain
23. 28 Saul..went against the Philistines
24. 2 went to seek David and his men upon the
24. 7 Saul rose up out of the cave, and went on
24. 22 Saul went home; but David and his men
25. 42 she went after the messengers of David
26. 11 take..the cruse of water, and let us go
26. 19 of the LORD, saying, Go, serve other gods
26. 25 So David went on his way, and Saul
28. 7 that I may go to her, and enquire of her
28. 8 he went, and two men with him, and they
28. 22 mayest have strength when thou goest
1 Sa. 29. 7 Wherefore now return, and go in peace
30. 2 carried (them) away, and went on their
30. 9 So David went, he and the six hundred
31. 12 All the valiant men arose, and went all
2 Sa. 2. 29 went through all Bithron, and they
2. 32 Joab and his men went all night, and
3. 16 her husband went with her along weeping
3. 16 Then said Abner unto him, Go, return
3. 19 Abner went also to speak in the ears of
3. 21 I will arise and go, and will gather all
3. 21 sent Abner away; and he went in peace
4. 5 Rechab and Baanah, went, and came
5. 6 the king and his men went to Jerusalem
6. 2 David arose, and went with all the people
6. 12 So David went and brought up the ark
7. 3 Go, do all that (is) in thine heart; for
7. 5 Go and tell my servant David, Thus
8. 3 as he went to recover his border at the
11. 22 So the messenger went, and came and
12. 29 David..went to Rabbah, and fought
13. 7 Go now to thy brother Amnon's house
13. 8 So Tamar went to her brother Amnon's
13. 19 hand on her head, and went on crying
13. 24 let the king..and his servants, go with
13. 25 Nay, my son, let us not all now go, lest
13. 25 howbeit he would not go, but blessed
13. 26 If not..let my brother Amnon go with
13. 26 king said..Why should he go with thee
13. 37 Absalom fled, and went to Talmai, the
13. 38 So Absalom fled, and went to Geshur
14. 8 Go to thine house, and I will give charge
14. 21 go therefore, bring the young man Absa.
14. 23 So Joab arose, and went to Geshur, and
14. 30 go and set it on fire. And Absalom's
15. 7 let me go and pay my vow, which I have
15. 9 And the king said unto him, Go in peace
15. 9 So he arose, and went to Hebron
15. 19 Wherefore goest thou also with us? return
15. 20 should I this day make thee go up and
15. 22 And David said to Ittai, Go and pass over
16. 13 as David and his men went by the way
17. 17 and they went and told king David
17. 21 went and told king David, and said unto
18. 21 Go tell the king what thou hast seen
18. 24 the watchman went up to the roof over
18. 33 as he went, thus he said, O my son A.
19. 15 Judah came to Gilgal, to go to meet the k.
19. 26 that I may ride thereon, and go to the
20. 5 So Amasa went to assemble..Judah
21. 12 David went and took the bones of Saul
24. 1 to say, Go, number Israel and Judah
1 Ki. 1. 13 Go and get thee in unto king David, and
1. 49 and rose up, and went every man his way
1. 50 went, and caught hold on the horns of
1. 53 Solomon said unto him, Go to thine house
2. 8 in the day when I went to Mahanaim
2. 29 Solomon sent..saying, Go, fall upon him
2. 40 Shimei arose..and went to Gath to Ach.
2. 40 Shimei went, and brought his servants
3. 4 the king went to Gibeon to sacrifice there
8. 66 went unto their tents joyful and glad of
10. 13 so she turned, and went to her own cou.
11. 5 Solomon went after Ashtoreth the godd.
11. 10 that he should not go after other gods
11. 21 Let me depart, that I may go to mine
11. 22 thou seekest to go to thine own country
11. 22 Nothing: howbeit let me go in any wise
11. 24 they went to Damascus, and dwelt therein
12. 1 Rehoboam went to Shechem: for all Is.
12. 30 for the people went..before the one
13. 10 So he went another way, and returned
13. 14 went after the man of God, and found him
13. 17 nor turn again to go by the way that
13. 28 he went and found his carcase cast in the
14. 4 Jeroboam's wife..went to Shiloh, and
14. 7 Go, tell Jeroboam, Thus saith the LORD
14. 9 for thou hast gone and made thee other
16. 31 went and served Baal, and worshipped
17. 5 So he went and did according unto the
17. 5 he went and dwelt by the brook Cherith
17. 10 So he arose and went to Zarephath
17. 15 she went, and did according to the say.
18. 1 Go, show thyself unto Ahab; and I will
18. 2 Elijah went to show himself unto Ahab
18. 5 Go into the land, unto all fountains of
18. 8 go, tell thy lord, Behold, Elijah (is here)
18. 11 go, tell thy lord, Behold, Elijah (is here)
18. 14 go, tell thy lord, Behold, Elijah (is here)
18. 16 Obadiah went to meet Ahab..Ahab went
18. 45 And Ahab rode, and went to Jezreel
19. 3 he arose, and went for his life, and came
19. 8 went in the strength of that meat forty d.
19. 15 Go, return on thy way to the wilderness
19. 20 he said unto him, Go back again: for
19. 21 Then he arose, and went after Elijah
20. 22 Go, strengthen thyself, and mark, and see
20. 27 the children of Israel..went against them
20. 43 king of Israel went to his house heavy
22. 4 Wilt thou go with me to battle to Ramo.
22. 6 Shall I go against Ramoth-gilead to battle
22. 15 Micaiah, shall we go against Ramoth-gil.
22. 48 Jehoshaphat made ships..to go to Ophir
22. 49 Let my servants go with thy servants
2 Ki. 1. 2 Go, enquire of Baal-zebub the god of Ek.
1. 6 Go, turn again unto the king that sent
2. 1 that Elijah went with Elisha from Gilgal
2. 6 not leave thee. And they two went on
2. 16 let them go, we pray thee, and seek thy
2. 18 he said..Did I not say unto you, Go not?
2. 25 he went from thence to mount Carmel
3. 7 he went and sent to Jehoshaphat the king
3. 7 wilt thou go with me against Moab to

2 Ki. 3. 9 So the king of Israel went, and the king
4. 3 Then he said, Go, borrow thee vessels ab.
4. 5 So she went from him, and shut the door
4. 7 he said, Go, sell the oil, and pay thy debt
4. 24 Drive, and go forward; slack not..riding
4. 25 So she went, and came unto the man of
4. 29 Gird up thy loins..and go thy way: if
5. 19 And he said unto him, Go in peace
6. 2 Let us go, we pray thee, unto Jordan, and
6. 2 where we may dwell. And he answered, Go
6. 3 go with thy serv...he answered, I will go
6. 4 So he went with them. And when they
6. 13 he said, Go and spy where he (is), that I
6. 22 that they may eat..and go to their
6. 23 he sent..and they went to their master
7. 8 and carried thence (also), and went and
7. 14 and the king sent..saying, Go and see
7. 15 And they went after them unto Jordan
8. 1 Arise, and go thou and thine household
8. 2 she went with her household, and sojou.
8. 8 go, meet the man of God, and enquire of
8. 9 So Hazael went to meet him, and took a
8. 10 Go, say unto him, Thou mayest certainly
8. 28 he went with Joram the son of Ahab to
9. 1 take this box..and go to Ramoth-gilead
9. 4 So..the prophet, went to Ramoth-gilead
9. 15 out of the city to go to tell (it) in Jezreel
9. 16 Jehu rode in a chariot, and went to Jezr.
9. 18 So there went one on horseback to meet
9. 35 they went to bury her; but they found
10. 25 and went to the city of the house of Baal
16. 10 king Ahaz went to Damascus to meet
17. 27 let them go and dwell there, and let him
19. 36 So Sennacherib..went and returned, and
22. 13 Go ye, enquire of the LORD for me, and
22. 14 went unto Huldah the prophetess, the
23. 29 Pharaoh-nechoh..king Josiah went again.
25. 4 and (the king) went the way toward the
1 Ch. 4. 39 And they went to the entrance of Gedor
11. 4 David and all Israel went to Jerusalem
12. 20 As he went to Ziklag, there fell to him
17. 4 Go and tell David my servant, Thus saith
17. 11 that thou must go (to be) with thy fathers
18. 3 as he went to stablish his dominion by
19. 5 Then there went (certain), and told David
21. 2 Go, number Israel from Beer-sheba even
21. 10 Go and tell David, saying, Thus saith the
21. 30 David could not go before it to enquire of
2 Ch. 1. 3 So Solomon..went to the high place that
8. 3 Solomon went to Hamath-zobah, and pr.
10. 1 Rehoboam went to Shechem: for to She.
10. 16 So all Israel went to their tents
11. 4 returned from going against Jeroboam
16. 3 go, break thy league with Baasha king
18. 3 Wilt thou go with me to Ramoth-gilead?
18. 5 Shall we go to Ramoth-gilead to battle
18. 14 Micaiah, shall we go to Ramoth-gilead
20. 36 joined..to make ships to go to Tarshish
20. 37 that they were not able to go to Tarshish
22. 5 went with Jehoram the son of Ahab king
25. 10 Amaziah separated them..to go home
25. 11 went to the valley of Salt, and smote of
25. 13 that they should not go with him to
30. 6 So the posts went with the letters from
34. 21 Go, enquire of the LORD for me, and for
34. 22 Hilkiah..went to Huldah the prophetess
Ezra 8. 31 Then we departed..to go unto Jerusalem
10. 6 Ezra..went into the chamber of Johanan
Neh. 8. 12 all the people went their way to eat, and
9. 12 light in the way wherein they should go
9. 19 and the way wherein they should go
12. 32 after them went Hoshaiah, and half of
Esth. 4. 16 Go, gather together all the Jews (that are)
Job 10. 21 Before I go (whence) I shall not return
38. 35 that they may go, and say unto thee
42. 8 go to my servant Job, and offer up for
42. 9 went and did according as the LORD co.
Psa. 32. 8 teach..in the way which thou shalt go
39. 13 spare me..before I go hence, and be no
42. 9 why go I mourning because of the oppr.
84. 7 They go from strength to strength
97. 3 A fire goeth before him, and burneth up
107. 7 that they might go to a city of habitation
122. 1 Let us go into the house of the LORD
139. 7 Whither shall I go from thy spirit?
Prov. 3. 28 Say not unto thy neighbour, Go, and come
4. 12 When thou goest, thy steps shall not be
6. 3 go, humble thyself, and make sure thy fr.
6. 6 Go to the ant, thou sluggard; consider
14. 7 Go from the presence of a foolish man
15. 12 scorner..neither will he go unto the wise
30. 29 three..four are comely in going
Eccl. 2. 1 Go to now, I will prove thee with mirth
5. 1 Keep thy foot when thou goest to the
5. 15 naked shall he return to go as he came
5. 16 in all points as he came, so shall he go
7. 2 better to go to the house of mourning
7. 2 than to go to the house of feasting: for
8. 3 Be not hasty to go out of his sight: stand
10. 15 he knoweth not how to go to the city
Isa. 3. 16 walking and mincing (as) they go, and
6. 8 Whom shall I send, and who will go for
6. 9 And he said Go, and tell this people
18. 2 Go, ye swift messengers, to a nation sca.
20. 2 Go and loose the sackcloth from off thy
21. 6 Go, set a watchman, let him declare what
22. 15 Go, get thee unto this treasurer..unto S.
28. 13 that they might go, and fall backward
33. 21 wherein shall go no galley with oars
37. 37 So Sennacherib..went and returned, and
38. 10 I shall go to the gates of the grave
45. 2 I will go before thee, and make the croo.

Isa. 48. 17 leadeth..by the way..thou shouldest go
52. 12 For ye shall not..go by flight: for the L.
57. 17 he went on frowardly in the way of his
Jer. 1. 7 thou shalt go to all that I shall send thee
2. 25 loved strangers, and after them will I go
3. 8 Judah feared not, but went and played
7. 12 But go ye now unto my place which
9. 2 that I might leave my people, and go
13. 4 arise, go to Euphrates, and hide it there
13. 5 So I went, and hid it by Euphrates, as
13. 6 Arise, go to Euphrates, and take the
13. 7 Then I went to Euphrates, and digged
15. 6 thou art gone backward: therefore will I
16. 5 neither go to lament nor bemoan them
20. 6 all that dwell in thine house shall go into
22. 22 thy lovers shall go into captivity: surely
25. 6 go not after other gods to serve them
28. 11 And the prophet Jeremiah went his way
30. 16 every one of them, shall go into captivity
35. 15 go not after other gods to serve them
36. 19 Go, hide thee, thou and Jeremiah; and
37. 12 to go into the land of Benjamin, to sep.
40. 4 whither it seemeth good..to go, thither
40. 5 or go where..convenient unto thee to go
40. 15 Let me go, I pray thee, and I will slay
41. 12 went to fight with Ishmael the son of Ne.
41. 14 went unto Johanan the son of Kareah
41. 15 escaped..and went to the Ammonites
41. 17 they departed..to go to enter into Egypt
44. 3 they went to burn incense..to serve other
45. 5 thy life will I give..whither thou goest
46. 22 The voice thereof shall go like a serpent
49. 3 for their king shall go into captivity
50. 4 they shall go, and seek the LORD their
51. 9 forsake her, and let us go every one into
51. 59 when he went with Zedekiah the king of
52. 7 and they went by the way of the plain
Lam. 4. 18 hunt..that we cannot go in our streets
Eze. 1. 9 joined..they turned not when they went
1. 9 they went every one straight forward
1. 12 And they went every one straight
1. 12 whither the spirit was to go, they went
1. 12 they turned not when they went
1. 17 they turned not when they went
1. 17 When they went, they went upon their
1. 19 when the..creatures went, the wheels
1. 20 Whithersoever the spirit was to go
1. 20 they went, thither (was their) spirit to go
1. 21 When those went, (these) went; and when
1. 24 when they went, I heard the noise of their
3. 1 and go speak unto the house of Israel
3. 4 Son of man, go, get thee unto the house
3. 11 go, get thee to them of the captivity, unto
3. 14 I went in bitterness, in the heat of my
10. 11 When they went, they went upon their
10. 11 they turned not as they went
10. 11 they turned not as they went
10. 16 when the cherubim went, the wheels we.
10. 22 they went every one straight forward
12. 11 they shall remove, (and) go into captivity
20. 39 Go ye, serve ye every one his idols, and
30. 17 and these..shall go into captivity
30. 18 and her daughters shall go into captivity
Hos. 1. 2 Go, take unto thee a wife of whoredoms
1. 3 So he went and took Gomer the daughter
2. 5 for she said, I will go after my lovers
2. 7 I will go and return to my first husband
2. 13 she went after her lovers, and forgat me
3. 1 Go yet, love a woman beloved of (her) fr.
5. 6 They shall go with their flocks and with
5. 13 then went Ephraim to the Assyrian, and
5. 15 I will go (and) return to my place, till they
7. 12 When they shall go, I will spread my net
Amos 2. 7 a man and his father will go in unto the
6. 2 and from thence go ye to Hamath the
7. 12 O thou seer, go, flee thee away into the
7. 15 Go, prophesy unto my people Israel
9. 4 though they go into captivity before their
Jon 1. 2 Arise, go to Nineveh, that great city, and
3. 2 Arise, go unto Nineveh, that great city
3. 3 So Jonah arose, and went unto Nineveh
Mic. 1. 8 I will go stripped and naked: I will make
2. 3 neither shall ye go haughtily: for this
Hab. 3. 5 Before him went the pestilence, and bur.
Zech. 6. 7 the bay..sought to go that they might
8. 21 Let us go speedily to pray..I will go also
8. 23 We will go with you; for we have heard

12. *To (cause to) go on.* הָלַךְ *yalak*, 5.
Num16. 46 go quickly unto the congregation, and

13. *To go out,* יָצָא *yatsa.*
Lev. 15. 32 This (is) the law of him..whose seed goeth
22. 4 or a man whose seed goeth from him
Esth. 1. 19 let there go a royal commandment from
Psa. 41. 6 his heart gathereth..he goeth abroad
Zech. 6. 8 these that go toward the north country

14. *To remove, journey,* נָסַע *nasa.*
Exod14. 19 the pillar of the cloud went from before
Num. 2. 31 They shall go hindmost with their stand.
10. 14 In the first (place) went the standard of
10. 33 the ark..went before them in the three
Judg18. 11 there went from thence of the family of

15. *To go aside,* סוּר *sur.*
Judg16. 17 my strength will go from me, and I shall
1 Sa. 22. 14 goeth at thy bidding, and is honourable

16. *To go over,* עָבַר *abar.*
Gen. 41. 46 and went throughout all the land of Egy.
Exod38. 26 for every one that went to be numbered
Lev. 26. 6 neither shall the sword go through your
Num13. 32 through which we have gone to search it

Num22. 26 the angel of the LORD went further, and
32. 21 And will go all of you armed over
Deut. 6. 1 in the land whither ye go to possess it
11. 8 the land whither ye go to possess it
11. 11 the land whither ye go to possess it
30. 13 Who shall go over the sea for us, and br.
Judg12. 1 went northward, and said unto Jephthah
Ruth 2. 8 neither go from hence, but abide here fast
2 Sa. 20. 14 he went through all the tribes of Israel
1 Ki. 22. 24 Which way went the spirit of the LORD
22. 36 there went a proclamation throughout
2 Ch. 18. 23 Which way went the spirit of the LORD
Neh. 9. 11 so that they went through the midst of
Job 9. 11 Lo, he goeth by me, and I see (him) not
21. 29 Have ye not asked them that go by the
Psa. 42. 4 for I had gone with the multitude; I
66. 6 they went through the flood on foot
Prov. 24. 30 I went by the field of the slothful, and
Isa. 54. 9 the waters of Noah should no more go
Jer. 49. 17 every one that goeth by it shall be aston.
50. 13 every one that goeth by Babylon shall
Eze. 9. 5 Go ye after him through the city, and sm.
14. 17 Sword, go through the land; so that I cut

17. *To go up,* עָלָה *alah.*
Num20. 19 We will go by the high way: and if I and
1 Ki. 22. 15 Go, and prosper: for the LORD shall deli.
Job 6. 18 The paths..they go to nothing and perish

18. *To (cause to) go up,* עָלָה *alah*, 5.
1 Ki. 10. 16 six hundred..of gold went to one target
10. 17 three pound of gold went to one shield
2 Ch. 9. 15 six hundred..of beaten gold went to
9. 16 three hundred..went to one shield

19. *To step, go apart,* פָּשַׂע *pasa.*
Isa. 27. 4 I would go through them, I would burn

20. *To step,* צָעַד *tsaad.*
Prov. 7. 8 and he went the way to her house
Jer. 10. 5 needs be borne, because they cannot go

21. *To go or come near,* קָרַב *qarab.*
Lev. 9. 7 Go unto the altar, and offer thy sin offer.
9. 8 Aaron therefore went unto the altar, and
22. 3 that goeth unto the holy things, which
Isa. 8. 3 I went unto the prophetess; and she con.

22. *To go to and fro,* שׁוּט *shut.*
2 Sa. 24. 8 So when they had gone through all the

23. *To go about, or singing,* שׁוּר *shur.*
Isa. 57. 9 thou wentest to the king with ointment

24. *To go, lead,* ἄγω *agō.*
Matt26. 46 Rise, let us be going: behold, he is at
Mark 1. 38 Let us go into the next towns, that I may
14. 42 Rise up, let us go; lo, he that betrayeth
John 11. 7 saith he..Let us go into Judea again
11. 15 not there..nevertheless let us go unto him
11. 16 Let us also go, that we may die with him
14. 31 even so I do. Arise, let us go hence

25. *To go up,* ἀναβαίνω *anabainō.*
Luke 5. 19 they went upon the house top, and let him

26. *To go away or off,* ἄπειμι *apeimi.*
Acts 17. 10 who coming..went into the synagogue of

27. *To go off or away,* ἀπέρχομαι *aperchomai.*
Matt. 2. 22 when he heard..he was afraid to go thit.
4. 24 And his fame went throughout all Syria
8. 19 I will follow thee whithersoever thou g.
8. 21 suffer me first to go and bury my father
8. 32 they went into the herd of swine: and
10. 5 Go not into the way of the Gentiles, and
13. 28 Wilt thou then that we go and gather
13. 46 went and sold all that he had, and bought
14. 15 that they may go into the villages, and
14. 25 Jesus [went] unto them, walking on the
16. 21 how that he must go unto Jerusalem
18. 30 went and cast him into prison, till he
21. 29 but afterward he repented, and went
21. 30 answered and said, I (go), sir; and went
25. 10 while they went to buy, the bridegroom
25. 18 he that had received one went and digged
25. 25 and went and hid thy talent in the earth
26. 36 Sit ye here, while I go and pray yonder
27. 5 departed, and went and hanged himself
28. 10 go tell my brethren that they go into G.
Mark 1. 20 they left their father..and went after him
5. 24 And (Jesus) went with him; and much
6. 27 he went and beheaded him in the prison
6. 36 that they may go into the country round
6. 37 Shall we go and buy two hundred penny.
7. 24 went into the borders of Tyre and Sidon
9. 43 than having two hands to go into hell
14. 10 Judas Iscariot, one of the twelve, went
14. 12 Where wilt thou that we go and prepare
16. 13 [they went and told (it) unto the residue]
Luke 5. 14 go, and show thyself to the priest, and offer
8. 34 [went and] told (it) in the city and in the
9. 12 that [they may go] into the towns and co.
9. 57 I will follow thee whithersoever thou go.
9. 59 suffer me first to go and bury my father
9. 60 go thou and preach the kingdom of God
17. 23 See here! or, see there! go not after (the.)
22. 13 they went, and found as he had said unto
24. 24 certain of them..went to the sepulchre
John 4. 47 he went unto him, and besought him that
6. 1 After these things Jesus went over the
6. 68 Lord, to whom shall we go? thou hast
9. 7 He went his way therefore, and washed
9. 11 I went and washed, and I received sight
11. 54 went thence unto a country near to the
12. 19 said..behold, the world is gone after him
18. 6 they went backward, and fell to the gro.

Acts 5. 26 then went the captain with the officers
Gal. 1. 17 I went into Arabia, and returned again
Jude 7 going after strange flesh are set forth
Rev. 10. 9 I went unto the angel, and said unto him
12. 17 went to make war with the remnant of
16. 2 the first went, and poured out his vial

28. *To go through*, διέρχομαι *dierchomai.*
Luke 2. 15 Let us now go even unto Bethlehem, and
Acts 11. 22 Barnabas, that [he should go] as far as A.
20. 25 among whom I have gone preaching the

29. *To go into*, εἰσέρχομαι *eiserchomai.*
Luke 19. 7 That he was gone to be Mr. 10. 25, Lu. 18. 25.

30. *To pass out of*, ἐκπορεύομαι ἐκ or ἔξω, or ἀπό
Mark 10. 46 as he went out of Jericho with his disci.
11. 19 when even was come, he went out of the
13. 1 as he went out of the temple, one of his
Rev. 1. 16 out of his mouth went a sharp two edged
19. 15 out of his mouth goeth a sharp sword

31. *To go out or forth*, ἐξέρχομαι *exerchomai.*
Matt. 15. 21 Then Jesus went thence, and departed
Luke 14. 18 I must needs go and see it: I pray thee
Acts 16. 10 we endeavoured to go into Macedonia
16. 19 saw that the hope of their gains was gone
Rom. 10. 18 verily, their sound went into all the earth
2 Co. 2. 13 but..I went from thence into Macedonia
8. 17 but..of his own accord he went unto you

32. *To go in unto*, εἴσειμι εἰς *eiseimi eis.*
Acts 3. 3 Peter and John about to go into the tem.
Heb. 9. 6 the priests went always into the first tab.

33. *To go on*, ἔρχομαι *erchomai.*
Matt. 12. 9 when he was departed thence, he went
13. 36 Then Jesus..went into the house: and
14. 12 and buried it, and went and told Jesus
14. 29 Peter..walked on the water, to go to Jes.
Mark 3. 19 and they went into an house
Luke 2. 44 But they..went a day's journey; and
14. 1 as he went into the house of one of the
John 4. 45 seen all..for they also went unto the feast
6. 17 went over the sea toward Capernaum
21. 3 They say unto him, We also go with thee
Acts 4. 23 being let go, they went to their own com.
28. 14 to tarry..and so we went toward Rome
Heb. 11. 8 obeyed..not knowing whither he went

34. *To go in unto*, ἐμβαίνω εἰς *embainō eis.*
Matt. 13. 2 so that he went into a ship, and sat
Luke 8. 22 that he went into a ship with his discip.

35. *To go back, pass*, μεταβαίνω *metabainō.*
Luke 10. 7 remain..Go not from house to house

36. *To go or pass along*, παραπορεύομαι *paraporeu.*
Mark 2. 23 he went through the corn fields on the

37. *To become alongside*, παραγίνομαι *paraginomai.*
Acts 23. 16 he went and entered into the castle

38. *To make way*, ποιέω ὁδόν *poieō hodon.*
Mark 2. 23 as they went, to pluck the ears of corn

39. *To go near or alongside*, παρέρχομαι *parercho.*
Luke 17. 7 will say..Go and sit down to meat?

40. *To walk round about*, περιπατέω *peripateō.*
Mark 12. 38 scribes, which love to go in long clothing

41. *To go or pass on*, πορεύομαι *poreuomai.*
Matt. 2. 8 Go and search diligently for the young
2. 20 go into the land of Israel: for they are
8. 9 I say to this (man), Go, and he goeth
9. 13 But go ye and learn what (that) meaneth
10. 6 go rather to the lost sheep of the house
10. 7 as ye go, preach, saying The kingdom
11. 4 Go and show John again those things
12. 1 At that time Jesus went on the sabbath
12. 45 Then goeth he, and taketh with himself
17. 27 go thou to the sea, and cast an hook
18. 12 goeth into the mountains, and seeketh
21. 2 Go into the village over against you, and
21. 6 the disciples went, and did as Jesus com.
22. 9 Go ye therefore into the highways, and
22. 15 Then went the Pharisees, and took coun.
25. 9 go ye rather to them that sell, and buy
25. 16 Then he..went and traded with the same
26. 14 Then one of the twelve..went unto the
27. 66 So they went, and made the sepulchre
28. 7 go quickly, and tell his disciples that
28. 9 [And as they went to tell his disciples]
28. 19 Go ye therefore, and teach all nations
Mark 16. 10 [she went and told them that had been]
16. 12 [as they walked, and went into the coun.]
16. 15 [Go ye into all the world, and preach the]
Luke 1. 39 and went into the hill country with haste
2. 3 all went to be taxed, every one into his
2. 41 his parents went to Jerusalem every year
4. 42 departed and went into a desert place
5. 24 take up thy couch, and go into thine ho.
7. 6 Then Jesus went with them. And when
7. 8 and I say unto one, Go, and he goeth
7. 11 that he went into a city called Nain; and
7. 50 Thy faith hath saved thee; go in peace
8. 48 Daughter, be of good comfort..go in peace
9. 13 except we should go and buy meat for all
9. 51 he stedfastly set his face to go to Jerusa.
9. 52 they went, and entered into a village of
9. 53 face was as though he would go to Jeru.
9. 56 And they went to another village
9. 57 that, as they went in the way, a certain
10. 37 Then said Jesus..Go, and do thou likew.
10. 38 it came to pass, as they went, that he
11. 5 shall go unto him at midnight, and say
11. 26 Then goeth he, and taketh..seven other
13. 32 Go ye, and tell that fox, Behold, I cast
14. 10 when thou art bidden, go and sit down in
14. 19 five yoke of oxen, and I go to prove them
14. 31 Or what king, going to make war against
15. 4 go after that which was lost, until he
15. 15 he went and joined himself to a citizen
15. 18 I will arise and go to my father, and will
16. 30 but if one went unto them from the dead
17. 11 it came to pass, as he went to Jerusalem
17. 14 said..Go show yourselves unto the priest
19. 12 A certain nobleman went into a far cou.
19. 28 he went before, ascending up to Jerusal.
19. 36 as he went, they spread their clothes in
21. 8 Take heed..go ye not therefore after
22. 8 Go and prepare us the passover, that we
22. 22 truly the Son of man goeth, as it was
22. 33 am ready to go with thee, both into prison
22. 39 he came out, and went, as he was wont
24. 13 two of them went that same day to a vil.
24. 28 drew nigh unto the village whither they w.
24. 28 as though he would have gone further
John 7. 35 Whither will he go, that we shall not fi.
7. 35 will he go unto the dispersed among the G.
7. 53 [And every man went unto his own house]
8. 1 [Jesus went unto the mount of Olives]
8. 11 [Neither do I condemn thee: go, and sin]
10. 4 he goeth before them, and the sheep fol.
11. 11 I go, that I may awake him out of sleep
14. 2 I would have told you. I go to prepare a
14. 3 if I go and prepare a place for you, I will
14. 12 greater..because I go unto my Father
14. 28 I go unto the Father: for my Father is
16. 28 I leave the world, and go to the Father
20. 17 go to my brethren, and say unto them
Acts 1. 11 come..as ye have seen him go into heav.
1. 25 take part..that he might go to his own
5. 20 Go, stand and speak in the temple to the
8. 26 Arise, and go toward the south, unto the
8. 27 he arose and went: and, behold, a man
8. 36 as they went on (their) way, they came
8. 39 the eunuch..went on his way rejoicing
9. 11 Arise, and go into the street which is
10. 20 go with them, doubting nothing: for I
12. 17 departed, and went into another place
16. 7 they assayed to go into Bithynia: but the
16. 16 it came to pass, as we went to prayer, a
16. 36 now therefore depart, and go in peace
17. 14 sent away Paul, to go as it were to the
18. 6 from henceforth I will go unto the Gent.
19. 21 Paul purposed in the spirit..to go to Je.
20. 1 and departed for to go into Macedonia
20. 22 I go bound in the spirit unto Jerusalem
22. 5 went to Damascus, to bring them which
22. 10 Arise, and go into Damascus; and there
23. 23 Make ready two hundred soldiers to go
23. 32 they left the horsemen [to go] with him
25. 12 unto Cesar? unto Cesar shalt thou go
25. 20 I asked..whether he would go to Jerus.
26. 12 Whereupon, as I went to Damascus with
27. 3 gave..liberty to go unto his friends to
28. 26 Go unto this people, and say, Hearing
Rom. 15. 25 now I go unto Jerusalem to minister
1 Co. 10. 27 and ye be disposed to go, whatsoever is
16. 4 if it be meet that I go also, they shall go
16. 6 bring me on my journey whithersoever I g.
1 Ti. 1. 3 As I besought..when I went into Maced.
Jas. 4. 13 we will go into such a city, and continue
1 Pe. 3. 19 By which also he went and preached
3. 22 Who is gone into heaven, and is on the
Jude 11 for they have gone in the way of Cain

42. *To go toward*, προσέρχομαι *proserchomai.*
Acts 22. 26 he went and told the chief captain, saying

43. *To go away*, ὑπάγω *hupagō.*
Matt. 5. 41 compel thee to go a mile, go with him
8. 32 And he said unto them, Go. And when
9. 6 take up thy bed, and go unto thine ho.
13. 44 for joy thereof goeth and selleth all that
18. 15 go and tell him his fault between thee and
19. 21 go..sell that thou hast, and give to the
20. 4 Go ye also into the vineyard, and whats.
20. 7 Go ye also into the vineyard; and whats.
21. 28 said, Son, go work to day in my vineyard
26. 18 Go into the city to such a man, and say
26. 24 The Son of man goeth as it is written of
28. 10 go tell my brethren that they go into G
Mark 5. 19 Go home to thy friends, and tell them
5. 34 go in peace, and be whole of thy plague
6. 31 for there were many coming and going
6. 38 How many loaves have ye? go and see
14. 13 Go ye into the city, and there shall meet
14. 21 The Son of man indeed goeth, as it is
Luke 8. 42 [But as he went the people thronged]
12. 58 When thou goest with thine adversary
17. 14 that, as they went, they were cleansed
19. 30 Go ye into the village over against
John 3. 8 but canst not tell..whither it goeth
4. 16 Go, call thy husband, and come hither
6. 21 the ship was at the land whither they w.
7. 3 Depart hence, and go into Judæa, that
7. 33 and (then) I go unto him that sent me
8. 14 I know whence I came, and whither I go
8. 14 tell whence I come, and whither I go
8. 21 said Jesus..whither I go, ye cannot come
8. 22 he saith Whither I go, ye cannot come
9. 7 said..Go, wash in the pool of Siloam
9. 11 Go to the pool of Siloam, and wash: and
11. 8 stone thee; and goest thou thither again?
11. 31 She goeth unto the grave to weep there
11. 44 Jesus saith..Loose him, and let him go
12. 35 that walketh..knoweth not whither he goeth
13. 3 he was come from God, and went to God
John 13. 33 Whither I go, ye cannot come; so now I
13. 36 Simon Peter said..Lord, whither goest
13. 36 Whither I go, thou canst not follow me
14. 4 whither I go ye know, and the way ye
14. 5 Lord, we know not whither thou goest
15. 16 that ye should go and bring forth fruit
16. 5 none of you asketh me, Whither goest
16. 10 because I go to my Father, and ye see
16. 16 [ye shall see me; because I go to the Fa.]
16. 17 What is this..Because I go to the Father?
21. 3 Peter saith unto them, I go a fishing
1 Jo. 2. 11 knoweth not whither he goeth, because
Rev. 10. 8 Go..take the little book which is open
13. 10 He that leadeth into captivity shall go
14. 4 follow the Lamb whithersoever he goeth
17. 8 and shall ascend..and go into perdition
17. 11 the beast that was..goeth into perdition

44. *To give way*, χωρέω *chōreō.*
Matt. 15. 17 whatsoever entereth in at the mouth go.

[*See also* Armed, astray, captive, captivity, forward, free fully, ill, let, letting, near, nigh, right on, well, well with, whoring.]

GO, able to —

To go out or forth, יָצָא *yatsa.*
Num. 26. 2 all that are able to go to war in Israel

GO aboard, to —

To go up upon, ἐπιβαίνω *epibainō.*
Acts 21. 2 finding a ship..we went aboard, and set

GO about, to —

1. *To go on*, הָלַךְ *halak.*
Prov. 20. 19 He that goeth about (as) a talebearer re.

2. *To withdraw self, turn about*, חָמַק *chamaq*, 7.
Jer. 31. 22 How long wilt thou go about, O thou

3. *To go round about*, סָבַב *sabab.*
Josh. 16. 6 and the border went about eastward unto
1 Sa. 15. 12 he set him up a place, and is gone about
2 Ki. 3. 25 the slingers went about (it), and smote it
2 Ch. 17. 9 went about throughout all the cities of J.
23. 2 they went about in Judah, and gathered
Eccl. 2. 20 I went about to cause my heart to despair
Song 3. 3 The watchmen that go about the city fo.
5. 7 The watchmen that went about the city

4. *To go round about*, סָבַב *sabab*, 3a.
Psa. 55. 10 Day and night they go about it upon the
Song 3. 2 I will rise now, and go about the city in

5. *To go about, trade*, סָחַר *sachar.*
Jer. 14. 18 both the prophet and the priest go about

6. *To do, make*, עָשָׂה *asah.*
Deut. 31. 21 know their imagination which they go ab.

7. *To go to and fro*, שׁוּט *shut.*
Num. 11. 8 the people went about, and gathered (it)

8. *To go through*, διέρχομαι *dierchomai.*
Acts 10. 38 who went about doing good, and healing

9. *To put hands on, attempt*, ἐπιχειρέω *epicheireō.*
Acts 9. 29 Grecians: but they went about to slay

10. *To seek, desire*, ζητέω *zēteō.*
John 7. 19 none of you keepeth..Why go ye about to
7. 20 Thou hast a devil: who goeth about to
Acts 21. 31 as they went about to kill him, tidings
Rom. 10. 3 and going about to establish their own

11. *To try, attempt*, πειράζω *peirazō.*
Acts 24. 6 Who also hath gone about to profane the

12. *To try, attempt*, πειράομαι *peiraomai.*
Acts 26. 21 caught me in the temple, and went about

13. *To go round about*, περιάγω *periagō.*
Matt. 4. 23 Jesus went about all Galilee, teaching in
9. 35 And Jesus went about all the cities and
Acts 13. 11 he went about seeking some to lead him

GO abroad, to —

1. *To go on habitually*, הָלַךְ *halak*, 7.
Psa. 77. 17 sent out a sound: thine arrows also went a.

2. *To go out or forth*, יָצָא *yatsa.*
Deut. 23. 10 then shall he go abroad out of the camp

3. *To go through*, διέρχομαι *dierchomai.*
Luke 5. 15 went there a fame abroad of him

4. *To go out or forth*, ἐξέρχομαι *exerchomai.*
Matt. 9. 26 the fame hereof went abroad into all that
John 21. 23 Then went this saying abroad among the

GO again, to —

1. *To go back*, שׁוּב *shub.*
Gen. 43. 2 said unto them, Go again, buy us a little
43. 13 Take also your brother, and arise, go ag.
44. 25 our father said, Go again, (and) buy us
Num. 23. 16 said, Go again unto Balak, and say thus
Deut. 24. 19 thou shalt not go again to fetch it: it
1 Sa. 5. 11 let it go again to his own place, that it
25. 12 So David's young men..went again, and
29. 4 that he may go again to his place which
1 Ki. 12. 27 and go again to Rehoboam king of Judah
18. 43 And he said, Go again seven times
19. 20 he said unto him, Go back again: for
2 Ki. 4. 31 wherefore he went again to meet him
2 Ch. 19. 4 and he went out again through the people
Jer. 46. 16 Arise, and let us go again to our own pe.

2. *To turn upon or about*, ἐπιστρέφω *epistrephō.*
Acts 15. 36 Let us go again and visit our brethren in

GO along, to —
To go on, הָלַךְ *halak.*
Josh.17. 7 the border went along on the right hand
2 Sa. 16. 13 Shimei went along on the hill's side over

GO and meet, to —
To come opposite to, ὑπαντάω *hupantaō.*
John11. 20 Martha..went and met him: but Mary

GO aside, to —
1. *To go aside,* סוּר *sur.*
Deut 28. 14 thou shalt not go aside from any of the
2. *To go aside,* שָׂטָה *satah.*
Num. 5. 12 If any man's wife go aside, and commit
5. 19 if thou hast not gone aside to unclean.
5. 20 But if thou hast gone aside (to another)
5. 29 when a wife goeth aside (to another) ins.
3. *To give space, withdraw,* ἀναχωρέω *anachōreō.*
Acts 23. 19 went (with him) aside privately, and asked
26. 31 when they were gone aside, they talked
4. *To go away,* ἀπέρχομαι *aperchomai.*
Acts 4. 15 commanded them to go aside out of the
5. *To give space, withdraw,* ὑποχωρέω *hupochōreō.*
Luke 9. 10 went aside privately into a desert place

GO astray, to —
1. *To be driven or forced away,* נָדַח *nadach,* 2.
Deut 22. 1 shalt not see thy brother's ox..go astray
2. *To err, go astray through ignorance,* שָׁגַג *shagag.*
Psa.119. 67 Before I was afflicted I went astray; but
3. *To err, go astray through ignorance,* שָׁגָה *shagah.*
Prov. 5. 23 greatness of his folly he shall go astray
4. *To go astray, err,* πλανάομαι *planaomai.*
Matt18. 12 be gone astray..which is gone astray
18. 13 ninety and nine which went not astray
1 Pe. 2. 25 For ye were as sheep going astray; but
2 Pe. 2. 15 are gone astray, following the way of B.

GO astray, to cause to —
To cause to err through ignorance, שָׁגָה *shagah,* 5.
Prov 28. 10 causeth the righteous to go astray in an

GO away, to —
1. *To go on,* הָלַךְ *halak.*
Jer. 22. 10 weep sore for him that goeth away: for
51. 50 Ye that have escaped the sword go away
Hos. 6. 4 and as the early dew it goeth away
2. *To go on,* יָלַךְ *yalak.*
Gen. 38. 19 she arose, and went away, and laid by
Exod12. 28 children of Israel went away, and did as
Josh.18. 8 men arose, and went away: and Joshua
Judg19. 2 went away from him unto her father's h.
1 Sa. 15. 27 And as Samuel turned about to go away
28. 25 they rose up, and went away that night
2 Ki. 5. 11 But Naaman was wroth, and went away
5. 12 So he turned, and went away in a rage
Hos. 5. 14 I, (even) I, will tear and go away; I will
3. *To go out,* יָצָא *yatsa.*
Deut 15. 16 I will not go away from thee; because
4. *To remove, journey,* נָסַע *nasa.*
Judg16. 3 and went away with them, bar and all
16. 14 and went away with the pin of the beam
5. *To be removed,* נָסַע *nasa,* 2.
Job 4. 21 Doth not their excellency..go away?
6. *To go on or over,* עָבַר *abar.*
2 Sa. 18. 9 the mule that (was) under him went away
7. *To go up,* עָלָה *alah.*
2 Ki. 12. 18 and he went away from Jerusalem
8. *To turn the face,* פָּנָה *panah.*
Jer. 6. 4 Woe unto us! for the day goeth away, for
9. *To turn,* הָפַךְ *haphak.*
2 Ch. 9. 12 went away to her own land, she and her
10. *To go away or off,* ἀπέρχομαι *aperchomai.*
Matt. 8. 31 [suffer us to go away into the herd of sw.]
19. 22 he went away sorrowful: for he had gr.
25. 46 And these shall go away into everlasting
26. 42 He went away again the second time, and
26. 44 he left them, and went away again, and
Mark10. 22 And he was sad..and went away grieved
14. 39 And again he went away, and prayed
Luke 2. 15 as the angels were gone away from them
John 4. 8 For his disciples were gone away unto the
6. 22 (that) his disciples were gone away alone
10. 40 went away again beyond Jordan, into
16. 7 It is expedient for you that I go away
16. 7 for if I go not away, the Comforter will
20. 10 Then the disciples went away again unto
11. *To go out or forth,* ἐξέρχομαι *exerchomai.*
Acts 10. 23 on the morrow Peter went away with th.
12. *To pass on,* πορεύομαι *poreuomai.*
Matt28. 16 Then the eleven disciples went away into
13. *To go away,* ὑπάγω *hupagō.*
John 6. 67 Then said Jesus..Will ye also go away?
12. 11 many of the Jews went away, and belie.
14. 28 I go away, and come (again) unto you

GO back, to —
1. *To depart, remove, fall off from,* מוּשׁ *mush,* 5.
Job 23. 12 Neither have I gone back from the comm.
2. *To go back,* סוּג *sug.*
Psa. 80. 18 So will not we go back from thee: quick.
3. *To be or keep free,* פָּרַע *para.*
Eze. 24 14 I will not go back, neither will I spare
4. *To go back,* שׁוּב *shub.*
Judg11. 35 opened my mouth..and I cannot go back
18. 26 he turned and went back unto his house
1 Ki. 13. 19 So he went back with him, and did eat
2 Ki. 2. 13 went back, and stood by the bank of Jo.
8. 29 And king Joram went back to be healed

GO before, to —
1. *To go before,* קָדַם *qadam,* 3.
Psa. 68. 25 The singers went before, the players on
89. 14 mercy and truth shall go before thy face
2. *To go before,* προάγω *proagō.*
Matt. 2. 9 and, lo, the star..went before them, till
14. 22 and to go before him unto the other side
21. 9 And the multitudes that went before
21. 31 go into the kingdom of God before you
26. 32 But after..I will go before you into Galilee
28. 7 behold, he goeth before you into Galilee
Mark 6. 45 to go to the other side before unto Beths.
10. 32 and Jesus went before them: and they
11. 9 And they that went before, and they that
14. 28 But after..I will go before you into Galil.
16. 7 tell..Peter that he goeth before you into
Luke18. 39 And they which [went before] rebuked
1 Ti. 1. 18 to the prophecies which went before on
5. 24 going before to judgment; and some (men)
Heb. 7. 18 the commandment going before for the
3. *To go before or first,* προέρχομαι *proerchomai.*
Luke 1. 17 And he shall go before him in the spirit
22. 47 one of the twelve, went before them
Acts 20. 5 These going before, tarried for us at Tro.
20. 13 And we went before to ship, and sailed
2 Co. 9. 5 that they would go before unto you
4. *To pass before,* προπορεύομαι *proporeuomai.*
Luke 1 76 for thou shalt go before the face of the L.
Acts 7. 40 Make us gods to go before us: for (as for

GO beyond, to —
1. *To go over or beyond,* עָבַר *abar.*
Num24. 13 I cannot go beyond the commandment
2. *To go over or beyond,* ὑπερβαίνω *huperbainō.*
1 Th. 4. 6 That no (man) go beyond and defraud

GO by, to —
To go over or beyond, עָבַר *abar.*
Job 21. 29 Have ye not asked them that go by the
Psa.129. 8 Neither do they which go by say, The

GO captive, to —
To remove into exile, גָּלָה *galah.*
Amos 6. 7 Therefore now shall they go captive with

GO, to cause or make to —
1. *To make to go on,* הָלַךְ *halak,* 3.
Job 24. 10 They cause (him) to go naked without
2. *To cause to go on,* יָלַךְ *yalak,* 5.
Exod14. 21 LORD caused the sea to go (back) by a st.
Lev. 26. 13 broken the bands..and made you go upri.
2 Sa. 13. 13 whither shall I cause my shame to go?

GO down, to —
1. *To go in,* בּוֹא *bo.*
Gen. 15. 17 when the sun went down, and it was d.
Exod22. 26 it unto him by that the sun goeth down
Deut24. 13 the pledge again when the sun goeth do.
24. 15 neither shall the sun go down upon it
Josh10. 13 and hasted not to go down about a whole
Judg14 18 the seventh day before the sun went down
19. 14 and the sun went down upon them
2 Sa 2. 24 the sun went down when they were come
Eccl 1. 5 the sun goeth down, and hasteth to his
Isa. 60. 20 Thy sun shall no more go down; neither
Jer. 15. 9 her sun is gone down while..yet day; she
Mic. 3. 6 the sun shall go down over the prophets
2. *To be cast down,* חָתַת *chathath,* 2.
Job 21. 13 and in a moment go down to the grave
3. *To go down,* יָרַד *yarad.*
Gen. 11. 7 Go to, let us go down, and there confound
12. 10 Abram went down into Egypt to sojourn
18. 21 I will go down now, and see whether
24. 16 she went down to the well, and filled
24. 45 she went down unto the well, and drew
26. 2 Go not down into Egypt; dwell in the
37. 35 I will go down into the grave unto my s.
38. 1 that Judah went down from his brethren
42. 3 Joseph's ten brethren went down to buy
42. 38 My son shall not go down with you; for
43. 4 wilt send..we will go down and buy thee
43. 5 thou wilt not send..we will not go down
43. 15 rose up, and went down to Egypt, and
44. 26 We cannot go down..will we go down
46. 3 fear not to go down into Egypt; for I
46. 4 I will go down with thee into Egypt; and
Exod19. 14 Moses went down from the mount unto
19. 21 Go down, charge the people, lest they
19. 25 Moses went down unto the people, and
32. 15 Moses turned, and went down from the
Num16. 30 and they go down quick into the pit; then
16. 33 They..went down alive into the pit, and
20. 15 How our fathers went down into Egypt
34. 11 And the coast shall go down from S.
Deut 10. 22 Thy fathers went down into Egypt with
26. 5 he went down into Egypt, and sojourned
Josh15. 10 went down to Beth-shemesh, and passed
16. 3 And goeth down westward to the coast
16. 7 it went down from Janohah to Ataroth
18. 18 northward, and went down unto Arabah
Josh 24. 4 Jacob and his children went down into E.
Judg. 1. 9 the children of Judah went down to fight
3. 27 the children of Israel went down with
3. 28 they went down after him, and took the
4. 14 So Barak went down from mount Tabor
5. 11 then shall the people of the LORD go down
7. 10 But if thou fear to go down, go thou with
7. 10 go thou with Phurah thy servant down
7. 11 shall thine hands be strengthened to go d.
7. 11 Then went he down with Phurah his ser.
11. 37 that I may go up and down upon the
14. 1 Samson went down to Timnath, and saw
14. 5 Then went Samson down, and his father
14. 7 he went down and talked with the wom.
14. 10 So his father went down unto the woman
14. 19 he went down to Ashkelon, and slew thi.
15. 8 he went down and dwelt in the top of the
Ruth 3. 6 she went down unto the floor, and did
1 Sa. 10. 8 thou shalt go down before me to Gilgal
13. 20 all the Israelites went down to the Phili.
14. 36 Let us go down after the Philistines by
14. 37 Shall I go down after the Philistines?
15. 12 passed on, and gone down to Gilgal
20. 19 thou shalt go down quickly, and come to
22. 1 his father's house heard (it), they went d.
23. 4 Arise, go down to Keilah; for I will del.
23. 8 to go down to Keilah, to besiege David
25. 1 David arose, and went down to the wild.
26. 2 Saul arose, and went down to the wilder.
26. 6 Who will go down with me to Saul to the
26. 6 Abishai said, I will go down with thee
29. 4 let him not go down with us to battle
2 Sa. 5. 17 David heard..and went down to the hold
11. 8 Go down to thy house, and wash thy feet
11. 9 But Uriah..went not down to his house
11. 10 Uriah went not down unto his house
11. 10 why..didst thou not go down unto thine
11. 13 went out..but went not down to his ho.
17. 18 had a well..whither they went down
19. 20 come..to go down to meet my lord the
21. 15 David went down, and his servants with
23. 13 three of the thirty chief went down, and
23. 20 he went down also and slew a lion in
23. 21 he went down to him with a staff, and
1 Ki. 1. 38 Cherethites, and the Pelethites, went do.
21. 16 that Ahab rose up to go down to the
21. 18 Arise, go down to meet Ahab king of I.
2 Ki. 1. 15 Go down with him; be not afraid of him
1. 15 he arose, and went down with him unto
2. 2 I will not leave thee. So they went down
3. 12 and the king of Edom went down to him
5. 14 Then went he down, and dipped himself
8. 29 Ahaziah..went down to see Joram the
10. 13 we go down to salute the children of the
12. 20 house of Millo, which goeth down to Sil.
20. 11 by which it had gone down in the dial of
1 Ch 11. 15 three of the thirty captains went down
11. 22 he went down and slew a lion in a pit
11. 23 and he went down to him with a staff
2 Ch.18. 2 And..he went down to Ahab to Samaria
20. 16 To morrow go ye down against them
22. 6 Azariah..went down to see Jehoram the
Neh. 3. 15 unto the stairs that go down from the
Job 7. 9 so he that goeth down to the grave shall
17. 16 They shall go down to the bars of the pit
Psa 22. 29 all they that go down to the dust shall
28. 1 I become like them that go down into
30. 3 kept..that I should not go down to the
30. 9 What profit..when I go down to the pit?
55. 15 let them go down quick into hell: for
88. 4 I am counted with them that go down
104. 8 they go down by the valleys unto the
107. 23 They that go down to the sea in ships
107 26 they go down again to the depths: their
115. 17 neither any that go down into silence
133. 2 went down to the skirts of his garments
143. 7 lest I be like unto them that go down
Prov. 1. 12 whole, as those that go down into the pit
5. 5 Her feet go down to death; her steps
18. 8 they go down into the innermost parts
26. 22 they go down into the innermost parts
Song 6. 11 I went down into the garden of nuts to
Isa. 14. 19 that go down to the stones of the pit
30. 2 That walk to go down into Egypt, and
31. 1 Woe to them that go down to Egypt for
38. 18 they that go down into the pit cannot
42. 10 ye that go down to the sea, and all that
52. 4 My people went down aforetime into Eg.
63. 14 As a beast goeth down into the valley
Jer. 18. 2 Arise, and go down to the potter's house
18. 3 Then I went down to the potter's house
22. 1 Go down to the house of the king of J.
36. 12 Then he went down into the king's house
48. 15 his chosen young men are gone down to
50. 27 let them go down to the slaughter: woe
Eze. 26. 11 thy strong garrisons shall go down to the
26. 20 with them that go down to the pit, that
31. 14 death..with them that go down to the
31. 15 In the day when he went down to the
31. 17 They also went down into hell with him
32. 18, 24, 25, 29, 30 with them that go down to
32. 19 go down, and be thou laid with the uncir.
47. 8 These waters..go down into the desert
Amos 6. 2 then go down to Gath of the Philistines
Jon. 1. 3 Jonah rose up..and went down to Joppa
1. 3 went down into it, to go with them unto
2. 6 I went down to the bottoms of the mou.
4. *To be taken or brought down,* יָרַד *yarad,* 6.
1 Sa. 30. 24 as his part (is) that goeth down to the
5. *To go down,* נָחַת *nachath.*
Job 21. 13 and in a moment go down to the grave

6. *To stretch out,* נָטָה *natah.*
Num21. 15 that goeth down to the dwelling of Ar.
2 Ki.20. 10 light thing for the shadow to go down

7. *To go in upon,* ἐπιδύω ἐπὶ *epiduō epi.*
Eph. 4. 26 let not the sun go down upon your wrath

8. *To go down,* καταβαίνω *katabainō.*
Mark13. 15 let him..not go down into the house
Luke 2. 51 he went down with them, and came to
10. 30 A certain (man) went down from Jerus.
18. 14 this man went down to his house justified
John 2. 12 After this he went down to Capernaum
4. 51 as he was now going down, his servants
5. 4 [an angel went down at a certain season]
6. 16 his disciples went down unto the sea
Acts 7. 15 So Jacob went down into Egypt, and died
8. 26 unto the way that goeth down from Jer.
8. 38 they went down both into the water, both
10. 21 Then Peter went down to the men which
14. 25 had preached..they went down into A.
18. 22 had landed..he went down to Antioch
20. 10 Paul went down, and fell on him, and
23. 10 commanded the soldiers to go down, and
25. 6 had tarried..he went down unto Cesarea

9. *To go down,* κατέρχομαι *katerchomai.*
Acts 8. 5 Then Philip went down to the city of S.
12. 19 he went down from Judea to Cesarea

GO down with, to —
To go down with, συγκαταβαίνω *sugkatabainō.*
Acts 25. 5 go down with (me), and accuse this man

GO every where, to —
To go throughout, διέρχομαι *dierchomai.*
Acts 8. 4 they..went every where preaching the w.

GO downward, to —
To go down, יָרַד *yarad.*
Eccl. 3. 21 the spirit of the beast that goeth downw.

GO far (off), to —
1. *To be or keep far off,* רָחַק *rachaq.*
Prov.19. 7 how much more do his friends go far from
Eze. 8. 6 that I should go far off from my sanctuary
2. *To go or put far off,* רָחַק *rachaq,* 5.
Josh. 8. 4 go not very far from the city, but be ye

GO far away, to —
To go or put far off, רָחַק *rachaq,* 5.
Exod 8. 28 only ye shall not go very far away: entr.

GO farther, to —
1. *To go forward or forth,* προβαίνω *probainō.*
Mark 1. 19 when he had gone a little farther thence
2. *To go forward, or forth,* προέρχομαι *proerchomai.*
Matt26. 39 [he went a little farther,] and fell on his

GO forth, to —
1. *To go forth or out,* יָצָא *yatsa.*
Gen. 8. 7 he sent forth a raven, which went forth
8. 16 Go forth of the ark, thou, and thy wife
8. 18 Noah went forth, and his sons, and his
8. 19 Every beast..went forth out of the ark
9. 18 the sons of Noah, that went forth of the
10. 11 Out of that land went forth Asshur, and
11. 31 they went forth with them from Ur of
12. 5 they went forth to go into the land of C.
42. 15 By the life of Pharaoh ye shall not go fo.
Lev. 14. 3 the priest shall go forth out of the camp
Num26. 4 which went forth out of the land of E.
31. 13 went forth to meet them without the ca.
33. 1 which went forth out of the land of E.
Deut21. 10 When thou goest forth to war against
23. 9 When the host goeth forth against thine
23. 12 a place..whither thou shalt go forth abr.
Josh 18. 17 went forth to En-shemesh, and went forth
Judg. 3. 23 Then Ehud went forth through the porch
5. 31 as the sun when he goeth forth in his m.
20. 25 Benjamin went forth against them out of
Ruth 1. 7 Wherefore she went forth out of the place
1 Sa. 17. 55 when Saul saw David go forth against the
18. 30 the princes of the Philistines went forth
18. 30 and it came to pass, after they went forth
23. 13 was told Saul..and he forbare to go forth
30. 21 they went forth to meet David, and to m.
2 Sa. 11. 1 it came..at the time when kings go forth
13. 39 king David longed to go forth unto Abs.
15. 16 the king went forth, and all his househo.
15. 17 the king went forth, and all the people
18. 2 I will surely go forth with you myself also
18. 3 Thou shalt not go forth: for if we flee
19. 7 Now therefore arise, go forth, and speak
19. 7 if thou go not forth, there will not tarry
20. 8 a sword..as he went forth it fell out
1 Ki. 2. 36 dwell there, and go not forth thence any
19. 11 And he said, Go forth, and stand upon
22. 22 said, I will go forth..go forth, and do so
2 Ki. 2. 21 he went forth unto the spring of the wa.
8. 3 she went forth to cry unto the king for
9. 15 let none go forth (nor) escape out of the
11. 7 two parts of all you that go forth on the
18. 7 he prospered whithersoever he went forth
19. 31 out of Jerusalem shall go forth a remnant
1 Ch. 12. 33, 36 such as went forth to battle, expert in
2 Ch. 20. 20 went forth into the wilderness of Tekoa
20. 20 as they went forth, Jehoshaphat stood
25. 5 three hundred thousand..to go forth to
26. 6 he went forth and warred against the Ph.
Neh. 8. 15 Go forth unto the mount, and fetch olive
8. 16 So the people went forth, and brought
Esth. 4. 6 So Hatach went forth to Mordecai unto
Esth. 5. 9 Then went Haman forth that day joyful
Job 1. 12 So Satan went forth from the presence of
2. 7 So Satan went forth from the presence of
24. 5 go they forth to their work; rising betim.
39. 4 they go forth, and return not unto them
Psa. 44. 9 But thou..goest not forth with our armi.
68. 7 when thou wentest forth before thy peop.
104. 23 Man goeth forth unto his work and to
108. 11 wilt not thou, O God, go forth with our
146. 4 His breath goeth forth, he returneth to
Prov.25. 8 Go not forth hastily to strive, lest (thou
30. 27 yet go they forth all of them by bands
Song 1. 8 go thy way forth by the footsteps of the
3. 11 Go forth, O ye daughters of Zion, and
7. 11 let us go forth into the field; let us lodge
Isa. 2. 3 for out of Zion shall go forth the law, and
7. 3 Go forth now to meet Ahaz, thou, and S.
37. 32 out of Jerusalem shall go forth a remna.
37. 36 Then the angel of the LORD went forth
42. 13 The LORD shall go forth as a mighty man
48. 3 they went forth out of my mouth, and I
48. 20 Go ye forth of Babylon, flee ye from the
49. 9 Go forth; to them that (are) in darkness
49. 17 they that made thee waste shall go forth
55. 11 So shall my word be that goeth forth out
62. 1 until the righteousness thereof go forth
66. 24 they shall go forth, and look upon the
Jer. 2. 37 Yea, thou shalt go forth from him, and
6. 25 Go not forth into the field, nor walk by
14. 18 If I go forth into the field, then behold
15. 1 cast..out of my sight let them go forth
15. 2 Whither shall we go forth? then thou
19. 2 go forth unto the valley of the son of H.
22. 11 Shallum..which went forth out of this pl.
25. 32 evil shall go forth from nation to nation
30. 23 the whirlwind of the LORD goeth forth
31. 4 and shalt go forth in the dances of them
31. 39 the measuring line shall yet go forth over
37. 12 Then Jeremiah went forth out of Jerusa.
38. 2 he that goeth forth to the Chaldeans shall
38. 8 Ebed-melech went forth out of the king's
38. 17 If thou wilt assuredly go forth unto the
38. 18 But if thou wilt not go forth to the king
38. 21 But if thou refuse to go forth, this (is)
39. 4 went forth out of the city by night, by
41. 6 Ishmael..went forth from Mizpah to
43. 12 he shall go forth from thence in peace
44. 17 whatsoever thing goeth forth out of our
48. 7 Chemosh shall go forth into captivity
50. 8 go forth out of the land of the Chaldeans
52. 7 went forth out of the city by night, by
Eze. 1. 13 and out of the fire went forth lightning
3. 22 Arise, go forth into the plain, and I will
3. 23 Then I arose, and went forth into the pl.
9. 7 he said..go ye forth. And they went forth
12. 4 thou shalt go forth at even in their sight
12. 12 the prince..shall bear..and shall go forth
16. 14 thy renown went forth among the heathen
21. 4 shall my sword go forth out of his sheath
24. 12 her great scum went not forth out of her
27. 33 When thy wares went forth out of the
30. 9 In that day shall messengers go forth from
39. 9 they that dwell in the cities..shall go forth
44. 19 when they go forth into the utter court
46. 2 then he shall go forth; but the gate shall
46. 8 and he shall go forth by the way thereof
46. 9 shall go forth by the way of the north ga.
46. 9 but shall go forth over against it
46. 10 and when they go forth, shall go forth
46. 12 then he shall go forth; and after his
47. 3 And when the man..went forth eastward
Dan. 11. 44 therefore he shall go forth with great
Hos. 6. 5 (are as) the light (that) goeth forth
Joel 2. 16 let the bridegroom go forth of his cham.
3. 18 and a fountain shall come forth of the
Amos 5. 3 and that which went forth (by) an hundr.
Mic. 4. 2 for the law shall go forth of Zion, and the
4. 10 for now shalt thou go forth out of the
Hab. 1. 4 and judgment doth never go forth; for
3. 5 and burning coals went forth at his feet
3. 13 Thou wentest forth for the salvation of
Zech. 2. 3 the angel that talked with me went forth
5. 3 This (is) the curse that goeth forth over
5. 5 the angel that talked with me went forth
5. 5 and see what (is) this that goeth forth
5. 6 This (is) an ephah that goeth forth. He
6. 5 which go forth from standing before
6. 6 The black horses..go forth into the north
6. 6 and the white go forth after them
6. 6 and the grisled go forth toward the south
6. 7 And the bay went forth, and sought to go
9. 14 his arrow shall go forth as the lightning
14. 2 and half of the city shall go forth into
14. 3 Then shall the LORD go forth, and fight
Mal. 4. 2 and ye shall go forth, and grow up as

2. *To remove, journey,* נָסַע *nasa.*
Num11. 31 And there went forth a wind from the L.
Jer. 31. 24 and they (that) go forth with flocks

3. *To go forth,* נְפַק *nephaq.*
Dan. 2. 13 And the decree went forth that the wise

4. *To go over or beyond,* עָבַר *abar.*
2 Ch.21. 9 Then Jehoram went forth with his princes
Isa. 28. 19 From the time that it goeth forth it shall

5. *To go on out of,* ἐκπορεύομαι *ekporeuomai.*
Mark10. 17 And when he was gone forth into the way
Rev. 16. 14 (which) [go forth] unto the kings of the

6. *To go forth or out of,* ἐξέρχομαι *exerchomai.*
Matt13. 3 Behold, a sower went forth to sow
14. 14 And Jesus went forth, and saw a great
Matt24. 26 he is in the desert; go not forth
25. 1 and went forth to meet the bridegroom
Mark 2. 12 and went forth before them all: insomuch
2. 13 And he went forth again by the sea side
3. 6 And the Pharisees went forth, and straig.
6. 24 And she went forth, and said unto her
14. 16 And his disciples went forth, and came
16. 20 [And they went forth, and preached every]
Luke 5. 27 And after these things he went forth
7. 17 this rumour of him went forth througho.
8. 27 And when he went forth to land, there
John 1. 43 Jesus would go forth into Galilee, and
12. 13 and went forth to meet him, and cried
18. 1 he went forth with his disciples over
18. 4 Jesus..went forth, and said unto them
19. 4 Pilate therefore went forth again, and
19. 17 And he bearing his cross went forth into
20. 3 Peter therefore went forth, and that
21. 3 They went forth, and entered into a ship
Acts 16. 3 Him would Paul have to go forth with
Heb. 13. 13 Let us go forth therefore unto him with.
3 Jo. 7 for his name's sake they went forth
Rev. 6. 2 and he went forth conquering, and to co.

7. *To go or pass on,* πορεύομαι *poreuomai.*
Luke 8. 14 when they have heard, go forth, and are

GO (forth), able to —
To go forth or out of, יָצָא *yatsa.*
Num. 1. 3 all that are able to go forth to war in
1. 20 all that were able to go forth to war
[So also 22, 24, 26, 28, 30, 32, 34, 36, 38, 40, 42, 45.]
26. 2 all that are able to go to war in Israel

GO forth, to cause to —
To cause to go forth, יָצָא *yatsa,* 5.
Eze. 20. 10 I caused them to go forth out of the land

GO forth, to make to —
To cause to remove or journey, נָסַע *nasa,* 5.
Psa. 78. 52 But made his own people to go forth like

GO forward, to —
1. *To go on,* הָלַךְ *halak.*
2 Ki. 20. 9 shall the shadow go forward ten degrees
2. *To (cause to) smite,* נָכָה *nakah,* 5.
2 Ki. 3. 24 but they went forward smiting the Moab.
3. *To lift up,* נָסַע *nasa.*
Exod14. 15 speak unto..Israel, that they go forward
Num. 2. 24 they shall go forward in the third rank
10. 5 that lie on the east parts shall go forward
4. *To go forward,* προέρχομαι *proerchomai.*
Mark14. 35 And [he went forward] a little, and fell on

GO further, to —
To put asunder, διΐστημι *diistēmi.*
Acts 27. 28 and when they had gone a little further

GO from, to —
To move, wander, flee away, נָדַד *nedad.*
Dan. 6. 18 Then the king..his sleep went from him

GO hard, to —
To be or go nigh, נָגַשׁ *nagash.*
Judg 9. 52 and went hard unto the door of the tow.

GO home, to —
To go back, שׁוּב *shub.*
1 Sa. 18. 2 and would let him go no more home to

GO in, to —
1. *To go in,* בּוֹא *bo.*
Gen. 7. 7 And Noah went in, and his sons, and his
7. 9 There went in two and two unto Noah
7. 15 And they went in unto Noah into the ark
7. 16 they that went in, went in male and female
16. 2 I pray thee, go in unto my maid; it may
16. 4 And he went in unto Hagar, and she
19. 33 and the first born went in, and lay with
19. 34 go thou in, (and) lie with him, that we
23. 10, 18 all that went in at the gate of his city
29. 21 my days are fulfilled, that I may go in
29. 23 brought her to him; and he went in unto
29. 30 he went in also unto Rachel, and he loved
30. 3 Behold my maid Bilhah, go in unto her
30. 4 gave him Bilhah..and Jacob went in unto
38. 2 and he took her, and went in unto her
38. 8 Go in unto thy brother's wife, and marry
38. 9 he went in unto his brother's wife, that he
Exod. 5. 1 Moses and Aaron went in, and told Phar.
6. 11 Go in, speak unto Pharaoh king of Egypt
7. 10 Moses and Aaron went in unto Pharaoh
9. 1 Go in unto Pharaoh, and tell him, Thus
10. 1 Go in unto Pharaoh: for I have hardened
14. 23 the Egyptians pursued, and went in after
28. 29, 35 when he goeth in unto the holy (place)
28. 30 when he goeth in before the LORD: and
34. 34 when Moses went in before the LORD to
34. 35 until he went in to speak with him
Lev. 14. 36 the priest shall go in to see the house
16. 17 when he goeth in to make an atonement
21. 11 Neither shall he go in to any dead body
21. 23 he shall not go in unto the veil, nor come
Num. 4. 19 Aaron and his sons shall go in, and appo.
4. 20 they shall not go in to see when the holy
8. 15 after that shall the Levites go in to do
8. 24 they shall go in to wait upon the service
27. 17 which may go in before them, and which
Deut. 1. 8 go in and possess the land which the L.
1. 37 saying, Thou also shalt not go in thither
1. 38 Joshua the son of Nun..shall go in thit.

Deut. 1. 39 they shall go in thither, and unto them
4. 1 go in and possess the land which the Lo.
4. 21 that I should not go in unto that good
6. 18 that thou mayest go in and possess the
8. 1 go in and possess the land which the Lo.
9. 1 to go in to possess nations greater and
10. 11 that they may go in and possess the land
11. 8 and go in and possess the land whither
11. 10 the land whither thou goest to possess it
11. 11 the land, whither ye go to possess it, (is) a
11. 31 ye shall pass over Jordan to go in to
21. 13 after that thou shalt go in unto her
22. 13 If any man take a wife, and go in unto
25. 5 her husband's brother shall go in unto
27. 3 that thou mayest go in unto the land
Josh. 1. 11 to go in to possess the land, which the
6. 23 the young men that were spies went in
23. 12 and go in unto them, and they to you
Judg. 3. 22 the haft also went in after the blade
6. 19 Gideon went in, and made ready a kid
15. 1 I will go in to my wife into the chamber
15. 1 would not suffer him to go in
16. 1 saw there an harlot, and went in unto her
19. 15 they turned aside thither, to go in (and)
19. 15 when he went in, he sat him down in a s.
Ruth 3. 4 thou shalt go in, and uncover his feet
4. 13 when he went in unto her, the LORD gave
1 Sa. 24. 3 Saul went in to cover his feet: and David
2 Sa. 3. 7 Wherefore hast thou gone in unto my
7. 18 Then went king David in, and sat before
12. 16 David fasted, and went in, and lay all
12. 24 David comforted Bath-sheba..and went in
16. 21 Go in into thy father's concubines, which
16. 22 Absalom went in unto his father's concu.
17. 25 Ithra, an Israelite, that went in to Abigail
1 Ki. 1. 15 Bath-sheba went in unto the king into
11. 2 Ye shall not go in to them, neither shall
13. 8 I will not go in with thee, neither will
13. 16 I may not return..nor go in with thee
16. 10 Zimri went in and smote him, and killed
17. 12 that I may go in and dress it for me and
2 Ki. 4. 33 He went in therefore, and shut the door
4. 37 she went in, and fell at his feet, and
5. 4 went in, and told his lord, saying, Thus
5. 25 he went in, and stood before his master
9. 2 go in, and make him arise up from among
10. 24 when they went in to offer sacrifices and
10. 25 Go in..slay them; let none come forth
1 Ch. 2. 21 Hezron went in to the daughter of Mac.
7. 23 when he went in to his wife, she concei.
2 Ch. 23. 6 they shall go in, for they (are) holy: but
26. 17 Azariah the priest went in after him, and
29. 18 they went in to Hezekiah the king, and
Neh 6. 11 would go into the temple..I will not go in
9. 15 they should go in to possess the land
9. 23 that they should go in to possess (it)
9. 24 the children went in and possessed the
Esth. 2. 12 when every maid's turn was come to go in
2. 15 the turn of Esther..was come to go in
4. 8 to charge her that she should go in unto
4. 16 so will I go in unto the king, which (is)
5. 14 then go thou in merrily with the king
Psa 26. 4 neither will I go in with dissemblers
51. *title.* after he had gone in to Bath-sheba
Prov. 6 29 So he that goeth in to his neighbour's
Jer. 36. 20 they went in to the king into the court
Eze. 8. 9 Go in, and behold the wicked abomina.
8. 10 I went in and saw; and, behold, every
9. 2 they went in, and stood beside the braz.
10. 2 Go in between the wheels, (even) under
10. 2 And he went in in my sight
10. 3 Cherubim stood..when the man went in
10. 6 he went in, and stood beside the wheels
23. 44 went in..as they go in..so went they in
46. 8 he shall go in by the way of the porch of
46. 10 when they go in, shall go in; and when

2. *To go over or beyond,* עָבַר *abar.*
Exod 32. 27 go in and out from gate to gate through.

3. *To go up,* עָלַל *alal.*
Dan. 2. 16 Then Daniel went in, and desired of the
2. 24 Daniel went in unto Arioch, whom the k.
6. 10 when Daniel knew..he went in to his ho.

4. *To go in into,* εἴσειμι *eiseimi.*
Acts 21. 18 Paul went in with us unto James; and

5. *To go into,* εἰσέρχομαι *eiserchomai.*
Matt. 7. 13 and many there be which go in thereat
9. 25 he went in, and took her by the hand, and
23. 13 go in..neither suffer ye them..to go in
25. 10 they that were ready went in with him to
26. 58 went in, and sat with the servants, to see
Mark 14. 14 wheresoever he shall go in, say ye to the
15. 43 Joseph..came, and went in boldly unto P.
Luke 8. 51 he suffered no man to go in, save Peter
11. 37 and he went in, and sat down to meat
15. 28 And he was angry, and would not go in
24. 29 And he went in to tarry with them
John 10. 9 and shall go in and out, and find pasture
20. 5 stooping down..saw..yet went he not in
20. 8 Then went in also that other disciple
Acts 1. 21 all the time that the Lord Jesus went in
9. 6 Arise, and go into the city, and it shall
10 27 he went in, and found many that were
11. 3 Thou wentest in to men uncircumcised
17 2 Paul, as his manner was, went in unto

GO in with, to —
To go in with, συνεισέρχομαι *suneiserchomai.*
John 18. 15 that disciple..went in with Jesus into

GO into, to —
1. *To go in,* בּוֹא *bo.*
1 Ki. 11. 17 That Hadad fled..to go into Egypt
1 Sa. 20. 42 he arose..and Jonathan went into the c.
Jer. 42. 17 the men that set their faces to go into E.
44. 12 that have set their faces to go into the

2. *To go into,* εἰσέρχομαι *eiserchomai.*
Matt 15. 11 Not that which goeth into the mouth
21. 12 And Jesus went into the temple of God
27. 53 went into the holy city, and appeared
Mark 2. 26 How he went into the house of God in
8. 26 Neither go into the town, nor tell (it) to
Luke 1. 9 when he went into the temple of the L.
4. 16 went into the synagogue on the sabbath
6. 4 How he went into the house of God, and
7. 36 he went into the Pharisee's house, and
19. 45 he went into the temple, and began to
John 18. 28 went not into the judgment hall, lest
19. 9 went again into the judgment hall, and
20. 6 went into the sepulchre, and seeth the
Acts 9. 6; 13. 14; 14. 1; 19. 8.

3. *To go into,* εἴσειμι *eiseimi.*
Acts 3. 3 seeing Peter..about to go into; Heb. 9. 6.

4. *To enter into,* εἰσπορεύομαι *eisporeuomai.*
Mark 1. 21 went into Capernaum; and straightway

GO into with, to —
To go in with, συνεισέρχομαι *suneiserchomai.*
John 6. 22 Jesus went not with his disciples into

GO, to let —
1. *To become feeble, desist,* רָפָה *raphah.*
Exod. 4. 26 So he let him go: then she said, A bloody

2. *To loose off or away,* ἀπολύω *apoluō.*
Luke 14. 4 he took..and healed him, and let him go
22. 68 if I also ask (you), [ye will not..let (me) go]
23. 22 therefore chastise him, and let (him) go
John 19. 12 If thou let this man go, thou art not Ce.
Acts 3. 13 when he was determined to let (him) go
4. 21 they let them go, finding nothing how they
4. 23 being let go, they went to their own co.
5. 40 And..they commanded..and let them go
15. 33 were let go in peace from the brethren
16. 35 sent..saying, Let those men go
16. 36 The magistrates have sent to let you go
17. 9 when they had taken..they let them go
28. 18 Who..would have let (me) go, because

GO, to make to —
1. *To cause to tread,* דָּרַךְ *darak,* 5.
Psa. 119. 35 Make me to go in the path of thy com.
Isa. 11. 15 The LORD shall..make..go over dry shod

2. *To cause to pass over,* עָבַר *abar,* 5.
Num 31. 23 ye shall make (it) go through the fire, and
31. 23 ye shall make go through the water

GO near, to —
1. *To go near,* קָרַב *qarab.*
Lev. 10. 5 So they went near, and carried them in
Deut. 5 27 Go thou near, and hear all that the LORD

2. *To go near,* קָרַב *qarab,* 3.
Job 31. 37 as a prince would I go near unto him

3. *To go toward,* προσέρχομαι *proserchomai.*
Acts 8. 29 Then the Spirit said..Go near, and join

GO on, to —
1. *To go on,* הָלַךְ *halak.*
Gen. 19. 2 shall rise up early, and go on your ways

2. *To go forth or out,* יָצָא *yatsa.*
Num 34. 4 shall go on to Hazar-addar, and pass on
34. 9 the border shall go on to Ziphron, and the
Job 39. 21 he goeth on to meet the armed men

3. *To lift up the foot,* נָשָׂא רֶגֶל *nasa regel.*
Gen. 29. 1 Then Jacob went on his journey, and ca.

4. *To be done,* עֲבַד *abad,* 2.
Ezra 5. 8 this work goeth fast on, and prospereth

5. *To go over or beyond,* עָבַר *abar.*
Exod 17. 5 LORD said unto Moses, Go on before the
1 Sa. 25. 19; 2 Sa. 19. 40, 20. 13; Neh. 2. 14.

5a. *Break up (camp), wander,* נָסַע *nasa.*
Gen. 12. 9 going on still toward the south

6. *To go forward,* προβαίνω *probainō.*
Matt. 4. 21 going on from thence, he saw other two

7. *To bear on,* φέρω *pherō.*
Heb. 6. 1 let us go on unto perfection; not laying

GO on forward, to —
To pass or change, חָלַף *chalaph.*
1 Sa. 10. 3 Then shalt thou go on forward from the.

GO one way or other, to —
To unite self, take possession, אָחַד *achad,* 7.
Eze. 21. 16 Go thee one way or other..on the right

GO (one's) way, to —
1. *To go on,* יָלַךְ *yalak.*
Gen. 14. 11 took all the goods..and went their way
18. 33 And the LORD went his way, as soon as
25. 34 eat and drink..rose up, and went his w.
Judg 19. 5 Comfort thine heart..afterward go your w.
Neh. 8. 10 Then he said unto them, Go your way, eat
Eccl. 9. 7 Go thy way, eat thy bread with joy, and

Dan. 12. 9 And he said, Go thy way, Daniel: for the
12. 13 go thou thy way till the end..for thou

2. *To go off or away,* ἀπέρχομαι *aperchomai.*
Matt. 8 33 and went their ways into the city, and
13. 25 his enemy..sowed tares..and went his w.
20. 4 Go ye also..And they went their way
22. 5 they made light of (it), and went their w.
22. 22 marvelled, and left him, and went their w.
Mark 11. 4 they went their way, and found the colt
12. 12 and they left him, and went their way
Luke 8. 39 he went his way, and published through.
19. 32 they that were sent went their way, and
22. 4 he went his way, and communed with
John 4. 28 The woman..went her way into the c. 7.
11. 28 she went her way, and called Mary her
11. 46 some of them went their ways to the Ph.
Acts 9. 17 Ananias went his way, and entered into
Jas. 1. 24 For he beholdeth himself, and goeth his w.

3. *To go or pass on,* πορεύομαι *poreuomai.*
Luke 4. 30 But he passing through..went his way
7. 22 Go your way, and tell John what things
17. 19 go thy way: thy faith hath made thee
John 4. 50 Go thy way..and he went his way
Acts 9. 15 But the Lord said unto him, Go thy way
21. 5 we departed and went our way; and
24. 25 Go thy way for this time; when I have a

4. *To go away,* ὑπάγω *hupagō.*
Matt. 5. 24 Leave there thy gift..and go thy way
8. 4 but go thy way, show thyself to the priest
8. 13 Go thy way; and as thou hast believed
20. 14 Take (that) thine (is), and go thy way: I
27. 65 go your way, make (it) as sure as ye can
Mark 1. 44 go thy way, show thyself to the priest
2. 11 Arise..and go thy way unto thine house
7. 29 And he said..For this saying go thy way
10. 21 go thy way, sell whatsoever thou hast
10. 52 Jesus said unto him, Go thy way; thy fa.
11. 2 Go your way into the village over against
16. 7 But go your way, tell his disciples and P.
Luke 10. 3 Go your ways: behold, I send you forth
John 8. 21 I go my way, and ye shall seek me, and
16. 5 But now I go my way to him that sent
18. 8 if..ye seek me, let these go their way
Rev. 16. 1 Go your ways, and pour out the vials of

GO onward, to —
To remove, journey, נָסַע *nasa.*
Exod 40. 36 the children of Israel went onward in all

GO on journey, to —
To go on the way, ὁδοιπορέω *hodoiporeō.*
Acts 10. 9 as they went on their journey, and drew

GO out, out of, —
1. *To go on,* הָלַךְ *halak.*
Ruth 1. 21 I went out full, and the LORD hath brou.
Esth. 9. 4 his fame went out throughout all the

2. *To go on,* יָלַךְ *yalak.*
Josh 16. 8 the goings out thereof were at the sea

3. *To go forth or out,* יָצָא *yatsa.*
Gen. 2. 10 a river went out of Eden to water the g.
4. 16 Cain went out from the presence of the
9. 10 from all that go out of the ark, to every
14. 8 there went out the king of Sodom, and
14. 17 the king of Sodom went out to meet him
15. 14 afterward shall they come out with great
17. 6 nations..and kings shall come out of thee
19. 6 Lot went out at the door unto them, and
19. 14 Lot went out, and spake unto his sons
24. 11 the time that women go out to draw (w.)
24. 63 Isaac went out to meditate in the field
27. 3 go out to the field, and take me..venison
28. 10 Jacob went out from Beer-sheba and w.
30. 16 Leah went out to meet him, and said
31. 33 Then went he out of Leah's tent, and
34. 1 Dinah..went out to see the daughters of
34. 6 Hamor..went out unto Jacob to commu.
34. 24, 24 all that went out of the gate of his c.
34. 26 took D. out of Shechem's house, and went
41. 45 Joseph went out over (all) the land of E.
41. 46 Joseph went out from the presence of P.
43 31 he washed his face, and went out, and
44. 28 And the one went out from me, and I
47. 10 Jacob..went out from before Pharaoh
Exod. 2. 11 he went out unto his brethren, and look.
2. 13 when he went out the second day, beho.
5. 10 the taskmasters of the people went out
7. 15 he goeth out unto the water; and thou
8. 12 And Moses and Aaron went out from P.
8. 29 I go out from thee, and I will entreat the
8. 30 Moses went out from Pharaoh, and entr.
9 33 Moses went out of the city from Pharaoh
10. 6 he turned himself, and went out from P.
10. 18 he went out from Pharaoh, and entreated
11. 4 About midnight will I go out into the
11. 8 Get thee out..after that I will go out
11. 8 he went out from Pharaoh, in a great an
12. 22 none of you shall go out at the door of
12. 41 all the hosts of the LORD went out from
14. 8 the children of Israel went out with an
15 20 all the women went out after her with
15 22 they went out into the wilderness of Sh.
16. 4 the people shall go out and gather a cer.
16 27 there went out..of the people on the se.
16. 29 let no man go out of his place on the se.
17. 9 Choose us out men, and go out, fight with
18. 7 Moses went out..and did obeisance, and
21. 2 in the seventh he shall go out free for
21. 3 he shall go out by himself: if he were

Exod21. 3 then his wife shall go out with him
21. 4 master's, and he shall go out by himself
21. 5 I love my master..I will not go out free
21. 7 she shall not go out as the men servants
21. 11 then shall she go out free without money
33. 7 every one which sought the LORD went o.
Lev. 8. 33 ye shall not go out of the door of the ta.
10. 2 there went out fire from the LORD, and
10. 7 ye shall not go out from the door of the
14. 38 the priest shall go out of the house to
15. 16 if any man's seed..go out from him, then
16. 18 he shall go out unto the altar that (is)
21. 12 Neither shall he go out of the sanctuary
24. 10 went out among the children of Israel
25. 28 in the jubilee it shall go out, and he
25. 30 it shall not go out in the jubilee
25. 31 and they shall go out in the jubilee
25. 33 the house..the city..shall go out in..jub.
25. 54 then he shall go out in the year of jubilee
27. 21 the field, when it goeth out in the jubilee
Num11. 24 Moses went out, and told the people the
11. 26 but went not out unto the tabernacle
21. 23 went out against Israel into the wilder.
21. 33 Og the king of Bashan went out against
22. 32 I went out to withstand thee, because
22. 36 he went out to meet him unto a city of
27. 17 Which may go out before them, and
27. 21 at his word shall they go out, and at his
31. 27 between them..who went out to battle
31. 28 of the men of war which went out to bat.
31. 36 the portion of them that went out to war
33. 3 the children of Israel went out with an
Deut20. 1 When thou goest out to battle against
24. 5 he shall not go out to war, neither shall
28. 6 blessed (shalt) thou (be) when thou goest o.
28. 19 cursed (shalt) thou (be) when thou goest o.
28. 25 thou shalt go out one way against them
31. 2 I can no more go out and come in: also
Josh. 2. 5 it came to pass..that the men went out
2. 19 whosoever shall go out of the doors of
6. 1 shut up..none went out, and none came
8. 14 the men of the city went out against Isr.
8. 17 not a man..that went not out after Isra.
11. 4 they went out, they and all their hosts
14. 11 for war, both to go out, and to come in
15. 3 it went out to the south side to Maaleh
15. 4 and went out unto the river of Egypt
15. 9 went out to the cities of mount Ephron
15. 11 went out into the..went out unto Jab.
16. 2 goeth out from Bethel to Luz, and
16. 6 the border went out toward the sea to
16. 7 came to Jericho, and went out at Jordan
18. 15 went out on the west, and went out to
19. 12 then goeth out to Daberath, and..to J.
19. 13 goeth out to Remmon-methoar, to Neah
19. 27 and goeth out to Cabul on the left hand
19. 34 and goeth out from thence to Hukkok
19. 47 the coast of the children of Dan went out
Judg. 2. 15 Whithersoever they went out, the hand
3. 10 and he judged Israel, and went out to
3. 19 all that stood by him went out from him
4. 18 Jael went out to meet Sisera, and said
5. 4 LORD, when thou wentest out of Seir, when
9. 27 they went out into the fields, and gather.
9. 35 Gaal the son of Ebed went out, and stood
9. 38 Go out, I pray now, and fight with them
9. 39 Gaal went out before the men of Shech.
9. 42 that the people went out into the field
11. 3 gathered vain men..and went out with him
16. 20 I will go out, as at other times before, and
19. 23 the master of the house, went out unto
19. 27 her lord rose up..and went out to go his
20. 1 Then all the children of Israel went out
20. 14 go out to battle against the children of I.
20. 20 the men of Israel went out to battle aga.
20. 28 Shall I yet again go out to battle against
20. 31 the children of Benjamin went out agai.
21. 24 they went out from thence every man to
Ruth 2. 22 that thou go out with his maidens, that
1 Sa. 4. 1 Israel went out against the Philistines to
7. 11 the men of Israel went out of Mizpeh
8. 20 go out before us, and fight our battles
9. 26 they went out both of them, he and Sam.
13. 10 Saul went out to meet him, that he might
13. 23 the garrison of the Philistines went out
17. 4 there went out a champion out of the
17. 35 I went out after him, and smote him, and
18. 5 David went out whithersoever Saul sent
18. 13 he went out and came in before the peo.
18. 16 because he went out and came in before
19. 3 I will go out and stand beside my father
19. 8 David went out and fought with the Ph.
20. 11 Come, and let us go out into the field
20. 11 they went out both of them into the field
20. 35 Jonathan went out into the field at the
24. 8 David also arose afterward, and went out
28. 1 thou shalt go out with me to battle, thou
2 Sa. 2. 12 Abner..went out from Mahanaim to Gib.
2. 13 And Joab..went out, and met together
5. 24 for then shall the LORD go out before thee
11. 13 at even he went out to lie on his bed with
11. 17 the men of the city went out and fought
13. 9 And they went out every man from him
18. 6 So the people went out into the field ag.
19. 19 the day that my lord the king went out
20. 7 there went out after him Joab's men, and
20. 7 they went out of Jerusalem, to pursue
21. 17 Thou shalt go no more out with us to ba.
24. 4 the captains of the host went out from
24. 7 they went out to the south of Judah
24. 20 Araunah went out, and bowed himself
1 Ki. 2. 37 on the day thou goest out, and passest

1 Ki. 2. 42 on the day thou goest out, and walkest
2. 46 which went out, and fell upon him, that
3. 7 I know not (how) to go out or come in
8. 44 If thy people go out to battle against
10. 29 a chariot came up and went out of Egypt
11. 29 when Jeroboam went out of Jerusalem
12. 25 Then Jeroboam..went out from thence
15. 17 not suffer any to go out or come in to A.
19. 13 Elijah..went out, and stood in the enter.
20. 16 And they went out at noon: but Ben-hadad
20. 17 And the young men..went out first; and
20. 21 And the king of Israel went out, and
20. 31 let us, I pray thee..go out to the king of
20. 39 Thy servant went out into the midst of
2 Ki. 3. 6 king Jehoram went out of Samaria the
4. 18 it fell on a day, that he went out to his
4. 21 shut (the door) upon him, and went out
4. 37 and took up her son, and went out
4. 39 And one went out into the field to gather
5. 2 the Syrians had gone out by companies
5. 27 he went out from his presence a leper
7. 16 the people went out, and spoiled the tents
9. 21 Joram..and Ahaziah..went out, each in
9. 24 the arrow went out at his heart, and he
10. 9 he went out, and stood, and said to all
11. 8 be ye with the king as he goeth out and
11. 9 with them that should go out on the
13. 5 they went out from under the hand of
19. 35 the angel of the LORD went out, and
24. 12 Jehoiachin..went out to the king of Ba.
1 Ch. 5. 18 of valiant men..that went out to the
7. 11 (soldiers), fit to go out to war (and) battle
12. 17 David went out to meet them, and answ.
14. 8 David heard..and went out against them
14. 15 then thou shalt go out to battle: for God
14. 17 the fame of David went out into all lands
20. 1 at the time that kings go out..Joab led
21. 21 went out of the threshing floor, and bowed
27. 1 which came in and went out month by
2 Ch. 1. 10 that I may go out and come in before
6. 34 If thy people go out to war against their
14. 10 Asa went out against him, and they set
15. 2 he went out to meet Asa, and said unto
15. 5 no peace to him that went out, nor to
16. 1 might let none go out or come in to Asa
18. 21 he said, I will go out..go out, and do..so
19. 2 Jehu..went out to meet him, and said to
19. 4 he went out again through the people
20. 17 to morrow go out against them: for the
20. 21 praise..as they went out before the army
22. 7 he went out with Jehoram against Jehu
23. 7 when he cometh in, and when he goeth o.
23. 8 with them that were to go out on the s.
24. 5 Go out unto the cities of Judah, and gat.
26. 11 fighting men, that went out to war by
26. 18 go out of the sanctuary; for thou hast tr.
26. 20 himself hasted also to go out, because the
28. 9 he went out before the host that came to
31. 1 all Israel..went out to the cities of Judah
35. 20 Necho..and Josiah went out against him
Neh. 2. 13 I went out by night by the gate of the
Esth. 3. 15 The posts went out, being hastened by
4. 1 and went out into the midst of the city
7. 8 As the word went out of the king's mouth
8. 14 the posts that rode upon mules..went out
8. 15 Mordecai went out from the presence of
Job 29. 7 I went out to the gate through the city
31. 34 I kept silence..went not out of the door?
37. 2 and the sound..goeth out of his mouth
41. 20 Out of his nostrils goeth smoke, as..of a
41. 21 His breath..a flame goeth out of his mo.
Psa. 60. 10 God..didst not go out with our armies
81. 5 when he went out through the land of E.
114. 1 When Israel went out of Egypt, the house
Prov22. 10 contention shall go out; yea, strife and
Isa. 52. 11 go ye out from thence..go ye out of the
52. 12 ye shall not go out with haste, nor go by
55. 12 ye shall go out with joy, and be led forth
Jer. 5. 6 every one that goeth out thence shall be
17. 19 whereby the kings of Judah..go out, and
21. 9 he that goeth out, and falleth to the Ch.
21. 12 lest my fury go out like fire, and burn
37. 4 Jeremiah came in and went out among
39. 4 and he went out the way of the plain
51. 45 My people, go ye out of the midst of her
Eze. 3. 25 and thou shalt not go out among them
10. 7 into..hands..who took..and went out
10 19 when they went out, the wheels also (were)
15. 7 they shall go out from (one) fire, and (an.)
42. 14 then shall they not go out of the holy
44. 3 and shall go out by the way of the same
46. 9 shall go out by the way of the south gate
Amos 4. 3 And ye shall go out at the breaches
5. 3 The city that went out (by) a thousand
Jon. 4. 5 So Jonah went out of the city, and sat
Zech. 2. 3 and another angel went out to meet him
8. 10 neither..peace to him that went out or
14. 8 living waters shall go out from Jerusalem

4. *To be quenched,* כָּבָה *kabah.*
Lev. 6. 13 burning upon the altar..shall never go o.
1 Sa. 3. 3 And ere the lamp of God went out in the
Prov 26. 20 Where no wood is..the fire goeth out
31. 18 good: her candle goeth not out by night

5. *To remove, journey,* נָסַע *nasa.*
Num10. 34 by day, when they went out of the camp

6. *To go away,* ἀπέρχομαι *aperchomai.*
Luke 8. 31 not command them to go out into the

7. *To go from,* ἀποβαίνω *apobainō.*
Luke 5. 2 but the fishermen were gone out of them

8. *To pass out or forth,* ἐκπορεύομαι *ekporeuomai.*
Matt. 3. 5 Then went out to him Jerusalem, and all
17. 21 [this kind goeth not out but by prayer]
Mark 1. 5 there went out unto him all the land of J.
7. 19 goeth out into the draught, purging all
Luke 4. 37 the fame of him went out into every place
Acts 9. 28 he was with them coming in and going o.

9. *To go forth or out,* ἔξειμι *exeimi.*
Acts 13. 42 when the Jews were gone out of the syn.

10. *To go forth or out,* ἐξέρχομαι *exerchomai.*
Matt. 9. 32 As they went out, behold, they brought
11. 7 What went ye out into the wilderness to
11. 8 But what went ye out for to see? A man
11. 9 But what went ye out for to see? A pro.
12. 14 the Pharisees went out, and held a coun.
12. 43 When the unclean spirit is gone out of a
13. 1 The same day went Jesus out of the house
18. 28 the same servant went out, and found one
20. 1 which went out early in the morning to
20. 3 he went out about the third hour, and
20. 5 he went out about the sixth and ninth
20. 6 about the eleventh hour he went out, and
21. 17 he left them, and went out of the city
22. 10 those servants went out into the highways
24. 1 Jesus went out, and departed from the
25. 6 the bridegroom cometh; go ye out to meet
26. 30 they went out unto the mount of Olives
26. 71 And when he was gone out into the porch
26. 75 And he went out, and wept bitterly
Mark 1. 35 he went out, and departed into a solitary
1. 45 But he went out, and began to publish
3. 21 they went out to lay hold on him: for
4. 3 Behold, there went out a sower to sow
5. 13 the unclean spirits went out, and entered
5. 14 [they went out] to see what it was that was
5. 30 knowing in himself..virtue had gone out
6. 1 And he went out from thence, and came
6. 12 they went out, and preached that men
7. 29 the devil is gone out of thy daughter
7. 30 she found the devil gone out, and her da.
8. 27 And Jesus went out, and his disciples
11. 11 he went out unto Bethany with the twel.
14. 26 they went out into the mount of Olives
14. 68 he went out into the porch; and the cock
16. 8 they went out quickly, and fled from the
Luke 2. 1 there went out a decree from Cesar Aug.
4. 14 there went out a fame of him through all
6. 12 it came to pass..that he went out into
6. 19 there went virtue out of him, and healed
7. 24 What went ye out into the wilderness for
7. 25, 26 But what went ye out for to see? A
8. 2 Magdalene, out of whom went seven dev.
8. 5 A sower went out to sow his seed: and
8. 33 Then went the devils out of the man, and
8. 35 Then they went out to see what was done
8. 46 I perceive that virtue is gone out of me
9. 5 when ye go out of that city, shake off the
10. 10 go your ways out into the streets of the
11. 14 when the devil [was gone out], the dumb
11. 24 When the unclean spirit is gone out of a
14. 21 Go out quickly into the streets and lanes
14. 23 Go out into the highways and hedges, and
17. 29 the same day that Lot went out of Sodom
21. 37 at night he went out, and abode in the
22. 62 And Peter went out and wept bitterly
John 4. 30 they went out of the city, and came unto
8. 9 [And they..went out one by one, beginn.]
8. 59 went out of the temple, going through
10. 9 and shall go in and out, and find pasture
11. 31 that she rose up hastily and went out
13. 30 He then having received the sop went..out
13. 31 when he was gone out, Jesus said, Now
18. 16 Then went out that other disciple, which
18. 29 Pilate then went out unto them, and said
18. 38 he went out again unto the Jews, and
Acts 1. 21 the Lord Jesus went in and out among us
12. 9 And he went out, and followed him; and
12. 10 they went out, and passed on through one
15. 24 that certain which went out from us have
16. 13 on the sabbath we went out of the city
16. 40 they went out of the prison, and entered
19. 12 and the evil spirits [went out of] them
1 Co. 5. 10 for then must ye needs go out of the wor.
Heb. 11. 8 when he was called to go out into a place
11. 8 he went out, not knowing whither he we.
1 Jo. 2. 19 They went out from us, but they were
4. 1 because many false prophets are gone out
Rev. 3. 12 a pillar..and he shall go no more out
6. 4 And there went out another horse..red
20. 8 shall go out to deceive the nations which

11. *To quench,* σβέννυμι *sbennumi.*
Matt25. 8 Give us..oil; for our lamps are gone out

12. *To turn back,* שׁוּב *shub.*
Exod32. 27 go in and out from gate to gate through.

GO out, to cause or let —

To cause to go forth or out, יָצָא *yatsa,* 5.
Gen. 45. 1 cried, Cause every man to go out from
Job 15. 13 and lettest..words go out of thy mouth?

GO out of the way, to —

To bend or incline out, ἐκκλίνω *ekklinō.*
Rom. 3. 12 They are all gone out of the way, they

GO over, to —

1. *To go over or beyond,* עָבַר *abar.*
Deut. 2. 13 and we went over the brook Zered
3. 25 I pray thee, let me go over and see the
3. 27 for thou shalt not go over this Jordan
3. 28 for he shall go over before this people

Deut. 4. 14 the land whither ye go over to possess it
4. 21 sware that I should not go over Jordan
4. 22 I must not go over..ye shall go over
4. 26 the land whereunto ye go over Jordan to
9. 3 God (is) he which goeth over before thee
12. 10 ye go over Jordan, and dwell in the land
31. 2 hath said..Thou shalt not go over this J.
31. 3 he will go over..he shall go over before
31. 13 in the land whither ye go over Jordan to
32. 47 in the land whither ye go over Jordan to
34. 4 said..but thou shalt not go over thither
Josh. 1. 2 go over this Jordan, thou, and all this p.
18. 13 the border went over from thence toward
24. 11 ye went over Jordan, and came unto Jer.
Judg. 6. 33 went over, and pitched in the valley of
9. 26 Gaal the son of Ebed..went over to She.
12. 5 when those..said, Let me go over; that
1 Sa. 13. 7 the Hebrews went over..to the land of G
14. 1 let us go over to the Philistines' garrison
14. 4 to go over unto the Philistines' garrison
14. 6 let us go over unto the garrison of these
26. 13 David went over to the other side, and
30. 10 they could not go over the brook Besor
2 Sa. 2. 15 there arose and went over by number tw.
16. 9 let me go over, I pray thee, and take off
19. 18 there went over a ferry boat to carry over
19. 31 and went over Jordan with the king, to
19. 36 Thy servant will go a little way over Jo.
19. 37 let him go over with my lord the king
19. 38 Chimham shall go over with me, and I
19. 39 And all the people went over Jordan
2 Ki. 2. 8 so that they two went over on dry ground
2. 14 they parted hither..and Elisha went over
8. 21 So Joram went over to Zair, and all the
1 Ch. 12. 15 These (are) they that went over Jordan in
29. 30 the times that went over him, and over
Psa. 88. 16 Thy fierce wrath goeth over me; thy ter.
124. 4 the stream had gone over our soul
124. 5 the proud waters had gone over our soul
Isa. 8. 8 he shall overflow and go over; he shall
51. 23 have said..Bow down, that we may go o.
51. 23 and as the street, to them that went over
54. 9 waters of Noah should no more go over
Jer. 41. 10 departed to go over to the Ammonites

2. *To go prosperously,* צָלֵחַ *tsaleach.*
2 Sa. 19. 17 they went over Jordan before the king

3. *To pass through,* διαπεράω *diaperaō.*
Matt 14. 34 when they were gone over, they came into

4. *To go through,* διέρχομαι *dierchomai.*
Luke 8. 22 Let us go over unto the other side of the
Acts 18. 23 went over..the country of Galatia and P.
20. 2 when he had gone over those parts, and

5. *To end,* τελέω *teleō.*
Matt 10. 23 Ye shall not have gone over the cities of

GO over, to make —
To cause to tread, דָּרַךְ *darak,* 5.
Isa. 11. 15 and shall..make (men) go over dry shod

GO round (about), to —
1. *To (cause to) go round,* נָקַף *naqaph,* 5.
Josh. 6. 3 ye shall..go round about the city once
Psa. 48. 12 Walk..and go round about her: tell the

2. *To go round about,* סָבַב *sabab,* 3a.
Psa. 59. 6 They return..and go round about the ci.
59. 14 let them..go round about the city

3. *To go round about,* περιάγω *periagō.*
Mark 6. 6 he went round about the villages, teach.

GO see, to —
To look after, פָּקַד *paqad.*
2 Ki. 9. 34 Go, see now this cursed..and bury her

GO softly, to —
To go softly, lovingly, דָּדָה *dadah,* 7.
Isa. 38. 15 I shall go softly all my years in the bitt.

GO, to teach to —
To cause to go on foot, רָגַל *ragal,* 5a.
Hos. 11. 3 I taught Ephraim also to go, taking them

GO thence, to —
To go forth or out, ἐξέρχομαι *exerchomai.*
Matt 10. 11 enquire..and there abide till ye go thence

GO through or throughout, to —
1. *To go over or beyond,* עָבַר *abar.*
Num 20. 19 I will only..go through on my feet
20. 20 And he said, Thou shalt not go through
Josh. 3. 2 that the officers went through the host
Isa. 60. 15 forsaken and hated, so that no man w. th.
62. 10 Go through, go through the gates; pre.
Eze. 9. 4 Go through the midst of the city, throu.
Mic. 5. 8 who, if he go through, both treadeth do.

2. *To go to and fro,* שׁוּט *shut.*
2 Sa. 24. 2 Go now through all the tribes of Israel

3. *To go on through,* διαπορεύομαι *diaporeuomai.*
Luke 6. 1 that he went through the corn fields; and
13. 22 And he went through the cities and vil.
Acts 16. 4 as they went through the cities, they de.

4. *To go through,* διέρχομαι *dierchomai.*
Matt 19. 24 It is easier for a camel to go through the
Luke 9. 6 went through the towns, preaching the
John 4. 4 And he must needs go through Samaria
8. 59 going through the midst of them, and so
Acts 13. 6 when they had gone through the isle un.
15. 41 he went through Syria..confirming the
16. 6 when they had gone throughout Phrygia

5. *To go in through,* διοδεύω *diodeuō.*
Luke 8. 1 he went throughout every city and villa.

6. *To go into,* εἰσέρχομαι *eiserchomai.*
Mark 10. 25 It is easier for a camel to go through the

GO to, to —
1. *To give help,* יָהַב *yahab.*
Gen. 11. 3 Go to, let us make brick, and burn them
11. 4 Go to, let us build us a city and a tower
11. 7 Go to, let us go down, and there confou.
38. 16 Go to, I pray thee, let me come in unto

2. *To go on,* יָלַךְ *yalak.*
2 Ki. 5. 5 the king of Syria said, Go to..I will send

3. *Pray, please,* נָא *na.*
Judg 7. 3 Now therefore go to, proclaim in the ears

4. *Go,* ἄγε *age.*
Jas. 4. 13 Go to now, ye that say, To day or to mor.
5. 1 Go to now..rich men, weep and howl for

5. *To go toward,* προσέρχομαι *proserchomai.*
Matt 27. 58 He went to Pilate, and begged the body
Luke 10. 34 went to (him), and bound up his wounds

GO to and fro, to —
1. *To go about or away,* אָזַל *azal,* 4.
Eze. 27. 19 Dan also and Javan going to and fro occ.

2. *To go to and fro,* שׁוּט *shut.*
Job 1. 7 From going to and fro in the earth, and
2. 2 From going to and fro in the earth, and

GO up —
A going up, ascent, מַעֲלָה *maalah.*
Ezra 7. 9 upon the first (day)..began he to go up

GO up, to —
1. *To go away,* אָזַל *azal.*
Ezra 4. 23 they went up in haste to Jerusalem unto

2. *To go,* הָלַךְ *halak.*
Ezra 7. 13 of their own free will to go up to Jerus.

3. *To go nigh, approach,* נָגַשׁ *nagash.*
Judg 20. 23 Shall I go up again to battle against the

4. *To go up,* עָלָה *alah.*
Gen. 2. 6 But there went up a mist from the earth
13. 1 Abram went up out of Egypt, he, and
17. 22 left off..and God went up from Abraham
19. 28 the smoke of the country went up as the
19. 30 Lot went up out of Zoar, and dwelt in
26. 23 he went up from thence to Beer-sheba
35. 1 Arise, go up to Beth-el, and dwell there
35. 3 And let us arise, and go up to Beth-el
35. 13 God went up from him in the place whe.
38. 12 went up unto his sheep shearers to Tim.
38. 13 thy father in law goeth up to Timnath
44. 33 and let the lad go up with his brethren
44. 34 For how shall I go up to my father, and
45. 9 Haste ye, and go up to my father, and
45. 25 they went up out of Egypt, and came in.
46. 29 Joseph..went up to meet Israel his fath.
46. 31 I will go up, and show Pharaoh, and say
49. 4 thou wentest up..he went up to my cou.
50. 5 let me go up, I pray thee, and bury my f.
50. 6 Go up and bury thy father, according as
50. 7 Joseph went up..and with him went up
50. 9 there went up with him both chariots and
50. 14 all that went up with him to bury his
Exod. 8. 3 which shall go up and come into thine
10. 14 the locusts went up over all the land of
12. 38 a mixed multitude went up also with th.
13. 18 the children of Israel went up harnessed
17. 10 Moses, Aaron, and Hur, went up to the
19. 3 Moses went up unto God, and the LORD
19. 12 Take heed..go (not) up into the mount
19. 20 LORD called Moses..and Moses went up
20. 26 Neither shalt thou go up by steps unto
24. 2 neither shall the people go up with him
24. 9 Then went up Moses, and Aaron, Nadab
24. 13 and Moses went up into the mount of G.
24. 15 Moses went up into the mount, and a cl.
32. 30 and now I will go up unto the LORD
33. 1 Depart..go up hence, thou and the peo.
33. 3 I will not go up in the midst of thee
34. 4 went up unto mount Sinai, as the LORD
34. 24 when thou shalt go up to appear before
Num 13. 17 Get you up..and go up into the mountain
13. 21 they went up, and searched the land from
13. 30 Let us go up at once, and possess it; for
13. 31 But the men that went up with him said
13. 31 We be not able to go up against the peo.
14. 40 and will go up into the place which the
14. 42 Go not up, for the LORD (is) not among you
14. 44 they presumed to go up unto the hill top
20. 27 they went up into mount Hor in the sight
21. 33 they turned, and went up by the way of
32. 9 when they went up unto the valley of E.
33. 38 Aaron the priest went up into mount H.
Deut. 1. 21 go up..possess..as the LORD God of thy f.
1. 22 by what way we must go up, and into
1. 24 they turned and went up into the moun.
1. 26 ye would not go up, but rebelled against
1. 28 Whither shall we go up? our brethren
1. 41 we will go up and fight, according to all
1. 41 ye were ready to go up into the hill
1. 42 Say unto them, Go not up, neither fight
1. 43 and went presumptuously up into the hill
3. 1 we turned, and went up the way to Bas.
5. 5 ye were afraid..and went not up into the
9. 23 Go up and possess the land which I have
10. 3 went up into the mount, having the two
25. 7 let his brother's wife go up to the gate

Deut 30. 12 Who shall go up for us to heaven, and
32. 50 die in the mount whither thou goest up
34. 1 Moses went up from the plains of Moab
Josh. 6. 20 the people went up into the city, every
7. 2 spake..saying, Go up and view the coun.
7. 2 And the men went up and viewed Ai
7. 3 and said..Let not all the people go up
7. 3 let about two or three thous. men go up
7. 4 So there went up thither of the people
8. 1 arise, go up to Ai: see, I have given into
8. 3 So Joshua arose..to go up against Ai
8. 10 and went up, he and the elders of Israel
8. 11 all the people..went up, and drew nigh
10. 5 went up, they and all their hosts, and
10. 9 Joshua..went up from Gilgal all night
10. 36 Joshua went up from Eglon, and all Isr.
11. 17 from the mount Halak, that goeth up to S
12. 7 the mount Halak, that goeth up to Seir
14. 8 my brethren that went up with me made
15. 3 went up to Adar, and fetched a compass
15. 6 the border went up to Beth-hogla, and
15. 6 the border went up to the stone of Bohan
15. 7 the border went up toward Debir from
15. 8 the border went up by the valley of the
15. 8 the border went up to the top of the mo.
15. 15 he went up thence to the inhabitants of
16. 1 to the wilderness that goeth up from J.
18. 12 the border went up to the side of Jericho
18. 12 went up through the mountains westwar.
19. 11 their border went up toward the sea, and
19. 12 goeth out to Daberath, and goeth up to J.
19. 47 Dan went up to fight against Leshem, and
22. 12 at Shiloh, to go up to war against them
22. 33 did not intend to go up against them in
Judg. 1. 1 Who shall go up for us against the Can.
1. 2 LORD said, Judah shall go up: behold, I
1. 4 Judah went up; and the LORD delivered
1. 16 went up out of the city of palm trees
1. 22 they also went up against Beth-el: and
4. 10 he went up..and Deborah went up with
8. 8 he went up thence to Penuel, and spake
8. 11 Gideon went up by the way of them that
8. 20 he said unto Jether..Up, (and) slay them
13. 20 when the flame went up toward heaven
14. 19 and he went up to his father's house
15. 9 the Philistines went up, and pitched in J.
18. 9 Arise, that we may go up against them
18. 12 they went up, and pitched in Kirjath-j.
18. 17 men that went to spy out..land went up
20. 18 the children of Israel arose, and went up
20. 18 Which of us shall go up first to the battle
20. 23 the children of Israel went up and wept
20. 23 And the LORD said, Go up against him
20. 26 all the children of Israel..went up, and
20. 28 Go up; for to morrow I will deliver them
20. 30 the children of Israel went up against
20. 31 of which one goeth up to the house of G
21. 19 the highway that goeth up from Beth-el
Ruth 4. 1 Then went Boaz up to the gate, and sat
1 Sa. 1. 3 this man went up out of his city yearly
1. 7 when she went up to the house of the
1. 21 man Elkanah, and all his house, went up
1. 22 But Hannah went not up; for she said
5. 12 and the cry of the city went up to heaven
6. 9 see, if it goeth up by the way of his own
6. 20 and to whom shall he go up from us?
7. 7 the lords of the Philistines went up agai.
9. 11 as they went up the hill to the city, they
9. 13 before he go up to the high place to eat
9. 14 they went up into the city..when they
9. 14 came out..for to go up to the high place
9. 19 go up before me unto the high place; for
14. 9 stand still..and will not go up unto them
14. 10 if they say thus..then we will go up: for
14. 21 which went up with them into the camp
14. 46 Saul went up from following the Philist.
15. 34 Saul went up to his house to Gibeah of S.
23. 29 David went up from thence, and dwelt in
25. 13 there went up after David about four hu.
25. 35 Go up in peace to thine house; see, I
27. 8 David and his men went up, and invaded
29. 9 He shall not go up with us to the battle
29. 11 and the Philistines went up to Jezreel
2 Sa. 2. 1 Shall I go up into any of the cities of Ju.?
2. 1 And the LORD said unto him, Go up. And
2. 1 David said, Whither shall I go up? And
2. 2 So David went up thither, and his two
5. 19 Shall I go up to the Philistines? wilt thou
5. 19 And the LORD said unto David, Go up
5. 23 Thou shalt not go up..fetch a compass be.
15. 24 Abiathar went up, until all the people
15. 30 David went up..and wept as he went up
15. 30 and..went up, weeping as they went up
18. 33 went up to the chamber over the gate
19. 34 that I should go up with the king unto J.
20. 2 So every man of Israel went up from after
22. 9 There went up a smoke out of his nostrils
24. 18 Go up, rear an altar unto the LORD in the
24. 19 David..went up, as the LORD commanded
1 Ki. 2. 34 So Benaiah the son of Jehoiada went up
6. 8 they went up with winding stairs into
9. 16 Pharaoh king of Egypt had gone up and
10. 5 his ascent by which he went up unto the
12. 24 Ye shall not go up, nor fight against your
12. 27 If this people go up to..sacrifice in the h.
12. 28 It is too much for you to go up to Jeru.
15. 17 Baasha king of Israel went up against J.
16. 17 Omri went up from Gibbethon, and all I.
18. 42 So Ahab went up to eat and to drink
18. 42 And Elijah went up to the top of Carmel
18. 43 And said..Go up now, look toward the
18. 43 And he went up, and looked, and said

1 Ki. 18. 44 he said, Go up, say unto Ahab, Prepare
20. 1 he went up and besieged Samaria, and
20. 26 Ben-hadad..went up to Aphek, to fight a.
22. 6 Go up; for the LORD shall deliver (it) into
22. 12 Go up to Ramoth-gilead, and prosper
22. 20 that he may go up and fall at Ramoth.
22. 29 the king of Israel..went up to Ramoth-g.
2 Ki. 1. 3 go up to meet the messengers of the king
1. 9 And he went up to him; and, behold, he
1. 13 the third captain of fifty went up, and
2. 11 Elijah went up by a whirlwind into hea.
2. 23 And he went up from thence unto Beth-el
2. 23 as he was going up by the way, there
2. 23 Go up, thou bald head; go up, thou bald h.
3. 7 And he said, I will go up: I..as thou
3. 8 And he said, Which way shall we go up?
4. 21 she went up, and laid him on the bed of
4. 34 he went up, and lay upon the child, and
4. 35 went up, and stretched himself upon him
6. 24 Ben-hadad..went up, and besieged Sama.
12. 17 Hazael king of Syria went up, and fought
12. 17 Hazael set his face to go up to Jerusalem
14. 11 Therefore Jehoash king of Israel went up
15. 14 Menahem the son of Gadi went up from T.
16. 9 the king of Assyria went up against Da.
17. 5 Then the king of Assyria..went up to S.
18. 17 and they went up and came to Jerusalem
18. 25 Go up against this land, and destroy it
19. 14 Hezekiah went up into the house of the L.
20. 5 thou shalt go up unto the house of the L.
20. 8 that I shall go up into the house of the L.
22. 4 Go up to Hilkiah the high priest, that he
23. 2 the king went up into the house of the L.
23. 29 Pharaoh-nechoh king of Egypt went up
1 Ch. 11. 6 So Joab the son of Zeruiah went first up
13. 6 David went up, and all Israel, to Baalah
14. 8 all the Philistines went up to seek David
14. 10 Shall I go up against the Philistines?
14. 10 Go up; for I will deliver them into thine
14. 14 Go not up after them; turn away from
21. 18 that David should go up, and set up an
21. 19 David went up at the saying of Gad, which
2 Ch. 9. 4 by which he went up into the house of
11. 4 Ye shall not go up, nor fight against your
18. 2 and persuaded him to go up .to Ramoth.
18. 5 Go up; for God will deliver (it) into the
18. 11 Go up to Ramoth-gilead, and prosper
18. 14 Go ye up, and prosper, and they shall be
18. 19 that he may go up and fall at Ramoth-g
18. 28 So the king of Israel..went up to Ramoth.
25. 21 So Joash the king of Israel went up; and
29. 20 Hezekiah..went up to the house of the L.
34. 30 the king went up into the house of the L.
36. 23 LORD..(be) with him, and let him go up
Ezra 1. 3 let him go up to Jerusalem, which (is) in J.
1. 5 to go up to build the house of the LORD
2. 1 the children..that went up out of the
2. 59 And these (were) they which went up
7. 6 This Ezra went up from Babylon; and
7. 7 there went up..of the children of Israel
7. 28 out of Israel chief men to go up with me
8. 1 genealogy of them that went up with me
Neh. 2. 15 Then went I up in the night by the brook
4. 3 if a fox go up, he shall even break down
7. 6 that went up out of the captivity, of those
7. 61 these..they which went up..from Telm.
12. 1 the priests and the Levites that went up
12. 37 they went up by the stairs of the city of
Psa. 18. 8 There went up a smoke out of his nost.
104. 8 They go up by the mountains; they go
122. 4 Whither the tribes go up, the tribes of
132. 3 I will not come..nor go up into my bed
Prov 26. 9 a thorn goeth up into the hand of a dru.
Song 6. 6 as a flock of sheep which go up from the
7. 8 I will go up to the palm tree, I will take
Isa. 2. 3 let us go up to the mountain of the LORD
5. 24 and their blossom shall go up as dust
7. 1 went up toward Jerusalem to war against.
7. 6 Let us go up against Judah, and vex it
15. 5 with weeping shall they go it up; for in
21. 2 Go up, O Elam: besiege, O Media: all the
34. 10 the smoke thereof shall go up for ever
35. 9 nor (any) ravenous beast shall go up the.
36. 10 Go up against this land, and destroy it
37. 14 Hezekiah went up unto the house of the
38. 22 that I shall go up to the house of the L.?
57. 7 thither wentest thou up to offer sacrifice
Jer. 5. 10 Go ye up upon her walls, and destroy
6. 4 Prepare..arise, and let us go up at noon
6. 5 Arise, and let us go by night, and let us
21. 2 Nebuchadrezzar..that he may go up from
22. 20 Go up to Lebanon, and cry; and lift up
31. 6 Arise ye, and let us go up to Zion unto
46. 8 saith, I will go up, (and) will cover the
46. 11 Go up into Gilead, and take balm, O virgin
48. 5 of Luhith continual weeping shall go up
49. 28 Arise ye, go up to Kedar, and spoil the
50. 21 Go up against the land of Merathaim
Eze. 8. 11 and a thick cloud of incense went up
11. 23 the glory of the LORD went up from the
11. 24 the vision that I had seen went up from
13. 5 Ye have not gone up into the gaps, neit
38. 11 I will go up to the land of unwalled vill.
40. 6 went up the stairs thereof, and measured
40. 22 and they went up unto it by seven steps
40. 40 as one goeth up to the entry of the north
40. 49 by the steps whereby they went up to it
Hos. 4. 15 neither go ye up to Beth-aven, nor swear
Mic. 4. 2 let us go up to the mountain of the LORD
Hag. 1. 8 Go up to the mountain, and bring wood
Zech. 14. 16 shall even go up from year to year to w.
14. 18 if the family of Egypt go not up, and come

5. *To be gone up*, עָלָה *alah*, 2.
2 Sa. 2. 27 the people had gone up every one from

6. *To (cause to) go up*, עָלָה *alah*, 5.
2 Ch. 1. 6 Solomon went up thither to the brasen

7. *To be or go high*, רוּם *rum*.
Eze. 10. 4 the glory of the LORD went up from the

8. *To go up*, ἀναβαίνω *anabainō*.
Matt. 3. 16 Jesus, when he was baptized, went up
5. 1 he went up into a mountain: and when
14. 23 he went up into a mountain apart to pray
15. 29 went up into a mountain, and sat down
20. 17 Jesus going up to Jerusalem took the tw.
20. 18 Behold, we go up to Jerusalem; and the
Mark 3. 13 he goeth up into a mountain, and calleth
6. 51 And he went up unto them into the ship
10. 32 they were in the way going up to Jeru.
10. 33 Behold, we go up to Jerusalem; and the
Luke 2. 4 Joseph also went up from Galilee, out of
2. 42 he was twelve years old, they went up
9. 28 and went up into a mountain to pray
18. 10 Two men went up into the temple to pr.
18. 31 Behold, we go up to Jerusalem, and all
John 2. 13 passover was at hand, and Jesus went up
5. 1 After this..Jesus went up to Jerusalem
7. 8 Go ye up..I go not up yet unto this feast
7. 10 were gone up, then went he also up unto
7. 14 Jesus went up into the temple, and taug.
11. 55 many went out of the country up to Je.
21. 11 Simon Peter went up, and drew the net
Acts 1. 13 they went up into an upper room, where
3. 1 Peter and John went up together into
10. 9 Peter went up upon the housetop to pray
15. 2 should go up to Jerusalem, unto the ap
18. 22 when he had landed..and gone up, and
21. 4 said..that he should not go up to Jeru.
21. 12 besought him not to go up to Jerusalem
21. 15 after those days we..went up to Jerusa.
24. 11 since I went up to Jerusalem for to wo.
25. 9 Wilt thou go up to Jerusalem, and there
Gal. 2. 1 I went up again to Jerusalem with Barn.
2. 2 I went up by revelation, and communica.
Rev. 20. 9 they went up on the breadth of the earth

9. *To go up*, ἀνέρχομαι *anerchomai*.
John 6. 3 Jesus went up into a mountain, and there
Gal. 1. 17 Neither went I up to Jerusalem to them
1. 18 I went up to Jerusalem to see Peter, and

10. *To go up toward*, προσαναβαίνω *prosanabainō*.
Luke 14. 10 he may say unto thee, Friend, go up high.

11. *To go or pass on*, πορεύομαι *poreuomai*.
Acts 1. 10 as he went up, behold, two men stood by

12. *To go up into*, ἐμβαίνω *embainō*.
Luke 8. 37 he went up into the ship, and returned

GO unto, to —

1. *To go in*, בּוֹא *bo*.
Prov. 2. 19 None that go unto her return again, nei.

2. *To go toward or to*, προσέρχομαι *proserchomai*.
Luke 23. 52 This (man) went unto Pilate, and begged
Acts 9. 1 And Saul..went unto the high priest

GO up and down, to —

1. *To go up and down*, הָלַךְ *halak*, 7.
Eze. 1. 13 it went up and down among the living
19. 6 And he went up and down among the

2. *To go on*, יָלַךְ *yalak*.
Lev. 19. 16 Thou shalt not go up and down..a tale b.

GO up and down, to make —

To cause to move, נוּעַ *nua*, 5.
2 Sa. 15. 20 should I this day make thee go up and d.

GO up, to make to —

To cause to go up, עָלָה *alah*, 5.
Judg. 2. 1 I made you to go up out of Egypt, and

GO up to, to —

Going up, ascent, עֹלָה *olah*.
Eze. 40. 26 And..seven steps to go up to it, and

GO upward, to —

To go up, עָלָה *alah*.
Eccl. 3. 21 Who knoweth the spirit..that goeth up.

GO.. way, to —

1. *To go on*, יָלַךְ *yalak*.
Gen. 24. 61 servant took Rebecca, and went his way
Judg 19. 14 they passed on and went their way
1 Sa. 20. 22 go thy way: for the LORD hath sent thee

2. *To remove, journey*, נָסַע *nasa*.
Zech 10. 2 therefore they went their way as a flock

3. *To go on, over or beyond*, עָבַר *abar*.
Esth. 4. 17 So Mordecai went his way, and did acco.

GO with, to —

1. *To go gently, lovingly*, דָּדָה *dadah*, 7.
Psa. 42. 4 I went with them to the house of God

2. *To go on with*, συμπορεύομαι *sumporeuomai*.
Luke 7. 11 many of his disciples went with him, and
14. 25 And there went great multitudes with
24. 15 Jesus himself drew near, and went with

3. *To go with*, συνέρχομαι *sunerchomai*.
Acts 9. 39 Then Peter arose and went with them
11. 12 the spirit bade me go with them, nothing
15. 38 and went not with them to the work
21. 16 There went with us also..of the disciples

GOAD —

1. *A goad, prick*, דָּרְבָן *dorban*.
1 Sa. 13. 21 and for the axes, and to sharpen the goa.

2. *A teacher, goad, prick*, מַלְמָד *malmad*.
Judg. 3. 31 slew..six hundred men with an ox goad

GOADS —

Goads, pricks, דָּרְבֹנוֹת *dorbonoth*.
Eccl. 12. 11 The words of the wise (are) as goads, and

GOAT —

1. *A goat, she goat*, עֵז *ez*.
Gen. 27. 9 Go now to the flock, and fetch me..goats
27. 16 she put the skins of the kids of the goats
30. 32 the spotted and speckled among the go.
30. 33 not speckled and spotted among the go.
37. 31 killed a kid of the goats, and dipped the
Exod 12. 5 take (it) out from the sheep, or..the go.
25. 4 purple and scarlet, and fine linen, and g.
26. 7 And thou shalt make curtains (of) goats'
35. 6, 23 purple..scarlet, and fine linen, and g.
35. 26 And all the women..in wisdom spun go.
36. 14 he made curtains (of) goats' (hair) for the
Lev 1. 10 if his offering (be)..of the goats, for a
3. 12 if his offering (be) a goat, then he shall
4. 23, 28 shall bring his offering, a kid of the g.
5. 6 a lamb, or a kid of the goats, for a sin
7. 23 ye shall eat no manner of fat..of goat
9. 3 Take ye a kid of the goats for a sin off.
16. 5 two kids of the goats for a sin offering
17. 3 that killeth..lamb, or goat, in the camp
22. 19 of the beeves, of the sheep, or of the go.
22. 27 When a bullock, or a sheep, or a goat
23. 19 ye shall sacrifice one kid of the goats for
Num. 7. 16 one kid of the goats for a sin offering
[So also v. 22, 28, 34, 40, 46, 52, 58, 64, 70, 76, 82.]
7. 87 kids of the goats for sin offering twelve
15. 24 one kid of the goats for a sin offering
18. 17 the firstling of a goat, thou shalt not red.
28. 15 one kid of the goat's for a sin offering
28. 30 one kid of the goats, to make an atone.
29. 5, 11, 16, 19, 25 And one kid of the goats
31. 20 all work of goats' (hair), and all things
Deut 14. 4 ye shall eat: The ox, the sheep, and the g.
1 Sa. 19. 13, 16 a pillow of goats' (hair) for his bolster
25. 2 three thousand sheep, and a thousand g.
Prov. 27. 27 And..goats' milk enough for thy food
Song 4. 1 thy hair (is) as a flock of goats, that app.
6. 5 thy hair (is) as a flock of goats, that app.
Eze. 43. 22 thou shalt offer a kid of the goats with
45. 23 and a kid of the goats daily..a sin offer.

2. *He goat, chief*, עַתּוּד *attud*.
Num. 7. 17 two oxen, five rams, five he goats, five
[So also v. 23, 29, 35, 41, 47, 53, 59, 65, 71, 77, 83.]
7. 88 the rams sixty, the he goats sixty, the
Deut 32. 14 goats, with the fat of kidneys of wheat
Psa. 50. 9 I will take no..he goats out of thy fold
50. 13 Will I eat..or drink the blood of goats?
66. 15 I will offer bullocks with goats. Selah
Prov 27. 26 and the goats (are) the price of the field
Isa. 1. 11 I delight not in the blood of..he goats
34. 6 with the blood of lambs and goats, with
Jer. 50. 8 and be as the he goats before the flocks
51. 40 I will bring them down like..he goats
Eze. 27. 21 they occupied with thee in..rams and g.
34. 17 I judge..between the rams and..he go.
39. 18 of rams, of lambs, and of goats, of bullo.
Zech 10. 3 Mine anger..and I punished the goats: for

3. *He goat*, צָפִיר *tsaphir*.
Dan. 8. 5 the goat..a notable horn between his ey.
8. 21 And the rough goat (is) the king of Grecia

4. *Goat, kid, hairy one*, שָׂעִיר *sair*.
Lev. 4. 24 lay his hand upon the head of the goat
9. 15 the goat, which (was) the sin offering
10. 16 Moses diligently sought the goat of the
16. 7 he shall take the two goats, and present
16. 8 Aaron shall cast lots upon the two goats
16. 9 Aaron shall bring the goat upon which
16. 10 the goat, on which the lot fell to be the s.
16. 15 Then shall he kill the goat of the sin off.
16. 18 and shall take..of the blood of the goat
16. 20 made an end..he shall bring the live goat
16. 21 his hands upon the head of the live goat
16. 21 putting them upon the head of the goat
16. 22 the goat shall bear upon him all their
16. 22 he shall let go the goat in the wilderness
16. 26 he that let go the goat for the scape goat
16. 27 the goat (for) the sin offering, whose blo.
Num 28. 22 one goat..a sin offering, to make an ato.
29. 22, 28, 31, 34, 38 And one goat..a sin offeri.
Eze. 43. 25 days shalt thou prepare every day a goat

5. *A young kid*, ἐρίφιον *eriphion*.
Matt 25. 33 he shall set..the goats on the left

6. *A kid, young goat*, ἔριφος *eriphos*.
Matt 25. 32 shepherd divideth..sheep from the goats

7. *A he goat*, τράγος *tragos*.
Heb. 9. 12 Neither by the blood of goats and calves
9. 13 if the blood of bulls and of goats, and the
9. 19 he took the blood of calves and of goats
10. 4 that the blood of bulls and of goats should

GOAT, he —

1. *Goat, kid, hairy one*, שָׂעִיר *sair*.
2 Ch. 29. 23 they brought forth the he goats..the sin

2. *He goat*, צְפִיר *tsaphir*.
Ezra 8. 35 offered..twelve he goats..a sin offering

2a. *He goat of goats*, צְפִיר עִזִּים [*tsaphir*].
2 Ch. 29. 21 seven lambs, and seven he goats, for a sin
Ezra 6. 17 twelve he goats, according; Dan. 8. 5, 8.

3. *He goat,* תַּיִשׁ *tayish.*
Gen. 30. 35 he removed that day the he goats that
32. 14 twenty he goats, two hundred ewes, and
2 Ch. 17. 11 seven thousand and seven hundred he g.
Prov 30. 31 A greyhound; an he goat also; and a ki.

GOAT, she —
Goat, עֵז *ez.*
Gen. 15. 9 a she goat of three years old, and a ram
30. 35 all the she goats that were speckled and
31. 38 thy ewes and thy she goats have not ca.
32. 14 Two hundred she goats, and twenty he
Num 15. 27 he shall bring a she goat of the first year

GO'-ATH, GO'-AH, גֹּעָה *constance.*
A place on the E. of Jerusalem, and near it: named in connection with the hill Gareb.
Jer. 31. 39 measuring line..shall compass about to G.

GOATS, wild —
Mountain goats, יְעֵלִים *yeelim.*
1 Sa. 24. 2 David..upon the rocks of the wild goats
Job 39. 1 when the wild goats of the rock bring
Psa. 104. 18 high hills (are) a refuge for the wild goats

GOAT SKIN —
Goat skin, δέρμα αἴγειον *derma aigeion.*
Heb. 11. 37 wan. about in sheep skins and goat skins

GOB, גֹּב, גּוֹב *a pit or hollow.*
A locality where David had two encounters with the Philistines. In 1 Ch. 20. 4 the place of the first encounter is given as *Gezer;* whereas the LXX. and Syriac have *Gath.* The third fight all agree took place at Gath.
2 Sa. 21. 18 again a battle with the Philistines at G.
21. 19 again a battte in G. with the Philistines

GOBLET —
Basin, אַגָּן *aggan.*
Song 7. 2 Thy navel..a round goblet..wanteth not

GOD —
1. As No. 6.
Hab. 3. 19 The LORD God is my strength, and he will
2. *Mighty one,* אֵל *el.*
Gen. 14. 18 and he..the priest of the most high God
14. 19 Blessed (be) Abram of the most high God
14. 20 And blessed (be) the most high God, wh.
14. 22 the most high God, the possessor of hea.
16. 13 Thou God seest me: for she said, Have
17. 1 I (am) the Almighty God; walk before
21. 33 and called there on the..everlasting G.
28. 3 God Almighty bless thee, and make thee
31. 13 I (am) the God of Beth-el, where thou
35. 1 make there an altar unto God, that
35. 3 I will make there an altar unto God, who
35. 11 I (am) God Almighty; be fruitful and
43. 14 God Almighty gave you mercy before
46. 3 I (am) God..fear not to go down into E.
48. 3 God Almighty appeared unto me at Luz
49. 25 by the God of thy father, who shall help
Exod. 6. 3 God Almighty; but by my name Jehovah
15. 2 he (is) my God, and I will prepare him an
15. 11 Who (is) like unto thee..among the gods?
20. 5 I the LORD..(am) a jealous God, visiting
34. 6 The LORD God, merciful and gracious
34. 14 For thou shalt worship no other god
34. 14 LORD, whose name (is) Jealous, (is) a..God
Num 12. 13 Heal her now, O God, I beseech thee
16. 22 fell upon their faces, and said, O God
23. 8 How shall I curse, whom God hath not
23. 19 God (is) not a man, that he should lie
23. 22 God brought them out of Egypt: he
23. 23 shall be said..What hath God wrought!
24. 4 which heard the words of God, which saw
24. 8 God brought him forth out of Egypt
24. 16 which heard the words of God, and knew
24. 23 Alas! who shall live when God doeth
Deut. 3. 24 what God..in heaven or in earth that
4. 24 LORD..(is) a consuming fire..jealous God
4. 31 For the LORD..(is) a merciful God; he will
5. 9 the LORD..a jealous God, visiting the
6. 15 For the LORD..(is) a jealous God among
7. 9 the faithful God, which keepeth covenant
7. 21 among you, a mighty God and terrible
10. 17 a great God, a mighty, and a terrible
32. 4 a God of truth, and without iniquity, just
32. 12 and (there was) no strange god with him
32. 18 and hast forgotten God that formed thee
32. 21 to jealousy with (that which is) not God
33. 26 none like unto the God of Jeshurun
Josh. 3. 10 know that the living God (is) among you
22. 22 God..the LORD God..he knoweth, and I.
24. 19 he (is) a jealous God; he will not forgive
Judg. 9. 46 into an hold of the house of the god Ber.
1 Sa. 2. 3 LORD (is) a God of knowledge, and by him
2 Sa. 22. 31 God, his way (is) perfect; the word of the
22. 32 For who (is) God, save the LORD? and who
22. 33 God (is) my strength..power: and he
22. 48 It (is) God that avengeth me, and that br.
23. 5 Although my house (be) not so with God
Neh. 1. 5 the great and terrible God, that keepeth
9. 31 for thou (art) a gracious and merciful God
9. 32 the great, the mighty, and the terrible G.
Job 5. 8 I would seek unto God, and..commit my
8. 3 Doth God pervert judgment? or doth the
8. 5 If thou wouldest seek unto God betimes
8. 13 So (are) the paths of all that forget God
8. 20 Behold, God will not cast away a perfect
9. 2 but how should man be just with God?
12. 6 and they that provoke God are secure
13. 3 Surely I would..desire to reason with G.
13. 7 Will ye speak wickedly for God? and
Job 13. 8 Will ye accept..will ye contend for God?
15. 4 Yea, thou..restrainest prayer before God
15. 11 (Are) the consolations of God small with
15. 13 That thou turnest thy spirit against God
15. 25 he stretcheth out his hand against God
16. 11 God hath delivered me to the ungodly
18. 21 this..place (of him that) knoweth not G.
19. 22 Why do ye persecute me as God, and are
20. 15 God shall cast them out of his belly
20. 29 the portion..appointed unto him by God
21. 14 they say unto God, Depart from us; for
21. 22 Shall (any) teach God knowledge? seeing
22. 2 Can a man be profitable unto God, as he
22. 13 And thou sayest, How doth God know?
22. 17 Which said unto God, Depart from us
23. 16 For God maketh my heart soft, and the
25. 4 then can man be justified with God?
27. 2 God liveth, (who) hath taken away my
27. 9 Will God hear his cry when trouble co.
27. 11 I will teach you by the hand of God
27. 13 the portion of a wicked man with God
31. 14 What then shall I do when God riseth up?
31. 23 For destruction (from) God (was) a terror
31. 28 for I should have denied the God..above
32. 13 should say..God thrusteth him down, not
33. 4 The spirit of God hath made me, and the
33. 6 I (am) according to thy wish in God's
33. 14 God speaketh once, yea twice, (yet man)
33. 29 all these..worketh God often times with
34. 5 and God hath taken away my judgment
34. 10 hearken unto me..Far be it from God
34. 12 surely God will not do wickedly, neither
34. 23 he should enter into judgment with God
34. 31 Surely it is meet to be said unto God
34. 37 and multiplieth his words against God
35. 2 My righteousness (is) more than God's?
35. 13 Surely God will not hear vanity, neither
36. 5 Behold, God (is) mighty, and despiseth not
36. 22 God exalteth by his power: who teacheth
36. 26 God (is) great, and we know (him) not
37. 5 God thundereth marvellously with his
37. 10 By the breath of God frost is given; and
37. 14 and consider the wondrous works of God
38. 41 when his young ones cry unto God, they
40. 9 Hast thou an arm like God? or canst thou
40. 19 He (is) the chief of the ways of God: he
Psa. 5. 4 thou (art) not a God that hath pleasure
7. 11 God is angry (with the wicked) every day
10. 11 God hath forgotten: he hideth his face
10. 12 O God, lift up thine hand: forget not
16. 1 Preserve me, O God: for in thee do I put
17. 6 I have called..thou wilt hear me, O God
18. 2 my God, my strength, in whom I will
18. 30 God, his way (is) perfect: the word of..L.
18. 32 God that girdeth me with strength, and
18. 47 God that avengeth me, and subdueth the
19. 1 The heavens declare the glory of God
22. 1 My God, my God, why hast thou forsaken
22. 10 thou (art) my God from my mother's be.
29. 3 the God of glory thundereth: the LORD
31. 5 thou hast redeemed me, O LORD God of
42. 2 My soul thirsteth..for the living God
42. 8 (and) my prayer unto the God of my life
42. 9 I will say unto God my rock, Why hast
43. 4 Then will I go..unto God my exceeding
44. 20 stretched out our hands to a strange god
52. 1 the goodness of God (endureth) continu.
52. 5 God shall likewise destroy thee for ever
55. 19 God shall hear, and afflict them, even he
57. 2 unto God that performeth..for me
63. 1 thou (art) my God; early will I seek
68. 19 the LORD..the God of our salvation. Se.
68. 20 our God (is) the God of salvation; and
68. 24 the goings of my God, my king, in the
68. 35 the God of Israel (is) he that giveth str.
73. 11 And they say, How doth God know? and
73. 17 Until I went into the sanctuary of God
74. 8 burnt up all the synagogues of God
77. 9 Hath God forgotten to be gracious? hath
77. 13 in the sanctuary: who (is so) great a G.
77. 14 Thou (art) the God that doest wonders
78. 7 and not forget the works of God, but
78. 8 whose spirit was not stedfast with God
78. 18 they tempted God in their heart, by ask.
78. 19 Can God furnish a table in the wilderness?
78. 34 they returned and enquired early after G.
78. 35 they remembered..the high God their Re.
78. 41 they turned back, and tempted God, and
81. 9 There shall no strange god be in thee
81. 9 neither shalt thou worship any strange g.
83. 1 hold not thy peace..be not still, O God
84. 2 my flesh crieth out for the living God
85. 8 I will hear what God the LORD will speak
86. 15 But thou, O LORD, (art) a God full of
89. 7 God is greatly to be feared in the assem.
89. 26 Thou (art) my Father, my God, and the
90. 2 everlasting to everlasting, thou (art) God
94. 1 LORD God, to whom vengeance belongeth
94. 1 O God, to whom vengeance belongeth
95. 3 For the LORD (is) a great God, and a
99. 8 thou wast a God that forgavest them
102. 24 O my God, take me not away in the midst
104. 21 The young lions..seek their meat from G
106. 14 lusted..and tempted God in the desert
106. 21 They forgat God their saviour, which
107. 11 they rebelled against the words of God
118. 27 God (is) the LORD, which hath showed us
118. 28 Thou (art) my God, and I will praise thee
136. 26 O give thanks unto the God of heaven
139. 17 O God! how great is the sum of them!
139. 23 Search me, O God, and know my heart
140. 6 I said unto the LORD, Thou (art) my God
Psa. 146. 5 Happy (is he) that (hath) the God of Jac.
149. 6 (Let) the high (praises) of God (be) in
150. 1 Praise God in his sanctuary: praise him
Isa. 5. 16 God, (that is) holy, shall be sanctified in
8. 10 Take counsel together..for God (is) with
9. 6 The mighty God, The everlasting Father
10. 21 remnant..return..unto the mighty God
12. 2 God (is) my salvation; I will trust, and
14. 13 exalt my throne above the stars of God
31. 3 Now the Egyptians (are) men, and not G.
40. 18 To whom then will ye liken God? or
42. 5 Thus saith God the LORD, he that created
43. 10 before me there was no God formed, nei.
43. 12 ye (are) my witnesses..that I (am) God
44. 10 Who hath formed a god, or molten a gr.
44. 15 yea, he maketh a god, and worshippeth
44. 17 the residue thereof he maketh a god
44. 17 saith, Deliver me; for thou (art) my god
45. 14 Surely God (is) in thee; and (there is)
45. 15 Verily thou (art) a God that hidest thys.
45. 20 and pray unto a god (that) cannot save
45. 21 a just God, and a Saviour; (there is) none
45. 22 for I (am) God, and (there is) none else
46. 6 he maketh it a god: they fall down, yea
46. 9 I (am) God, and (there is) none else
Jer. 32. 18 the mighty God, the LORD of hosts, (is)
51. 56 LORD God of recompences shall surely
Lam. 3. 41 Let us lift up..(our) hands unto God
Eze. 10. 5 as the voice of the Almighty God when
28. 2 thou hast said, I (am) a god, I sit (in) the
28. 2 yet thou (art) a man, and not God, though
28. 9 but thou (shalt be) a man, and no god, in
Dan. 9. 4 O Lord, the great and dreadful God
11. 36 and magnify himself above every god, and
11. 36 speak..things against the God of gods
Hos. 1. 10 be said..(Ye are) the sons of the living G.
11. 9 for I (am) God, and not man; the Holy
11. 12 Judah yet ruleth with God, and is faithf.
Jon. 4. 2 I knew that thou (art) a gracious God, and
Mic. 7. 18 Who (is) a God like unto thee, that pard.
Nah. 1. 2 God (is) jealous, and the LORD revengeth
Zech. 7. 2 they had sent unto the house of God
Mal. 1. 9 now, I pray you, beseech God that he
2. 10 hath not one God created us? why do we
2. 11 married the daughter of a strange god

3. *God, an object of worship,* אֱלָהּ *elah.*
Ezra 4. 24 Then ceased the work of the house of G.
5. 1 prophesied..in the name of the God of I.
5. 2 began to build the house of God which
5. 2 with them..the prophets of God helping
5. 5 the eye of their God was upon the elders
5. 8 to the house of the great God, which is
5. 11 We are the servants of the God of heaven
5. 12 provoked the God of heaven unto wrath
5. 13 made a decree to build this house of God
5. 14 And the vessels also..of the house of G.
5. 15 let the house of God be builded in his
5. 16 laid the foundation of the house of God
5. 17 to build this house of God at Jerusalem
6. 3 (concerning) the house of God at Jerusal.
6. 5 and silver vessels of the house of God
6. 5 and place (them) in the house of God
6. 7 Let the work of this house of God alone
6. 7 let..build this house of God in his place
6. 8 for the building of this house of God
6. 9 for the burnt offerings of the God of hea.
6. 10 sweet savours unto the God of heaven
6. 12 the God that hath caused his name to
6. 12 to destroy this house of God which (is)
6. 14 the commandment of the God of Israel
6. 16 kept the dedication of this house of God
6. 17 at the dedication of this house of God an
6. 18 for the service of God, which (is) at Jeru.
7. 12 a scribe of the law of the God of heaven
7. 14 according to the law of thy God which
7. 15 have freely offered unto the God of Israel
7. 16 for the house of their God which (is) in
7. 17 upon the altar of the house of your God
7. 18 to do..that do after the will of your God
7. 19 for the service of the house of thy God
7. 19 deliver thou before the God of Jerusalem
7. 20 shall be needful for the house of thy G.
7. 21 the scribe of the law of the God of heaven
7. 23 Whatsoever is commanded by the God
7. 23 for the house of the God of heaven
7. 24 or ministers of this house of God, it
7. 25 after the wisdom of thy God that (is) in
7. 25 all such as know the laws of thy God
7. 26 whosoever will not do the law of thy God
Jer. 10. 11 The gods that have not made the heave.
Dan. 2. 11 except the gods, whose dwelling is not
2. 18 would desire mercies of the God of heav.
2. 19 Then Daniel blessed the God of heaven
2. 20 Blessed be the name of God for ever and
2. 23 I thank thee, and praise thee, O thou G.
2. 28 there is a God in heaven that revealeth
2. 37 for the God of heaven hath given thee a
2. 44 shall the God of heaven set up a kingdom
2. 45 the great God hath made known to the k.
2. 47 that your God (is) a God of gods, and a L.
3. 12 they serve not thy gods, nor worship the
3. 14 do not ye serve my gods, nor worship the
3. 15 who (is) that God that shall deliver you
3. 17 our God whom we serve is able to deliver
3. 18 we will not serve thy gods, nor worship
3. 25 form of the fourth is like the Son of God
3. 26 servants of the most high God, come
3. 28 Blessed (be) the God of Shadrach, Mesh.
3. 28 nor worship any god except their own G.
3. 29 speak any thing amiss against the God of
3. 29 no other god that can deliver after this

Dan. 4. 2 that the high God hath wrought toward
4. 8 according to the name of my god, and
4. 8 in whom (is) the spirit of the holy gods
4. 9, 18 the spirit of the holy gods (is) in thee
5. 3 out of the temple of the house of God
5. 4 They drank wine, and praised the gods
5. 11 in whom (is) the spirit of the holy gods
5. 11 wisdom, like the wisdom of the gods, was
5. 14 that the spirit of the gods (is) in thee
5. 18 O thou king, the most high God gave N.
5. 21 that the most high God ruled in the kin.
5. 23 thou hast praised the gods of silver, and
5. 23 and the God in whose hand thy breath
5. 26 God hath numbered thy kingdom
6. 5 against him concerning the law of his G.
6. 7 whosoever shall ask a petition of any god
6. 10 gave thanks before his God, as he did
6. 11 and making supplication before his God
6. 12 that shall ask (a petition) of any god or
6. 16 Thy God, whom thou servest continually
6. 20 O Daniel..is thy God whom thou servest
6. 22 My God hath sent his angel, and hath
6. 23 was found..because he believed in his G.
6. 26 the God of Daniel; for he (is) the living G.

4. *God, gods, objects of worship,* אֱלֹהִים *elohim.*

Gen. 1. 1 In the beginning God created the heaven
1. 2 the spirit of God moved upon the face of
1. 3 God said, Let there be light: and there
1. 4 God saw the light, that (it was) good
1. 4 God divided the light from the darkness
1. 5 God called the light Day, and the dark.
1. 6 God said, Let there be a firmament
1. 7 God made the firmament, and divided
1. 8 God called the firmament Heaven
1. 9 God said, Let the waters under the heav.
1. 10 God called the dry (land) Earth; and the
1. 10, 12, 21, 25 God saw that (it was) good
1. 11 God said, Let the earth bring forth grass
1. 14 God said, Let there be lights in the
1. 16 God made two great lights; the greater
1. 17 God set them in the firmament of the h.
1. 20 God said, Let the waters bring forth
1. 21 God created great whales, and every
1. 22 God blessed them, saying, Be fruitful
1. 24 God said, Let the earth bring forth the
1. 25 God made the beast of the earth after
1. 26 God said, Let us make man in our image
1. 27 So God created man in his (own) image
1. 27 in the image of God created he him; male
1. 28 God blessed them, and God said unto
1. 29 God said..I have given you every herb
1. 31 God saw every thing that he had made
2. 2 on the seventh day God ended his work
2. 3 God blessed the seventh day, and sancti.
2. 3 rested from all his work which God cre.
2. 4 in the day that the LORD God made the
2. 5 the LORD God had not caused it to rain
2. 7 LORD God formed man (of) the dust of
2. 8 LORD God planted a garden eastward in
2. 9 out of the ground made the LORD God to
2. 15 LORD God took the man, and put him
2. 16 LORD God commanded the man, saying
2. 18 LORD God said, (It is) not good that
2. 19 LORD God formed every beast of the field
2. 21 LORD God caused a deep sleep to fall up.
2. 22 which the LORD God had taken from man
3. 1 any beast of the field which the LORD G.
3. 1 Yea, hath God said, Ye shall not eat of
3. 3 God hath said, Ye shall not eat of it, nei.
3. 5 God doth know that in the day ye eat
3. 8 they heard the voice of the LORD God
3. 8 from the presence of the LORD God amo.
3. 9 LORD God called unto Adam, and said
3. 13 LORD God said unto the woman, What
3. 14 LORD God said unto the serpent, Because
3. 21 did the LORD God make coats of skins
3. 22 LORD God said, Behold, the man is become
3. 23 LORD God sent him forth from the garden
4. 25 God..hath appointed me another seed
5. 1 In the day that God created man
5. 1 in the likeness of God made he him
5. 22 Enoch walked with God after he begat
5. 24 Enoch walked with God..God took him
6. 2 the sons of God saw the daughters of m.
6. 4 when the sons of God came in unto the
6. 9 N. was a just man (and)..walked with G.
6. 11 The earth also was corrupt before God
6. 12 God looked upon the earth, and, behold
6. 13 God said..The end of all flesh is come
6. 22 Thus did Noah; according to all that G.
7. 9 There went in..as God had commanded
7. 16 as God had commanded him: and the L.
8. 1 God remembered Noah..and God made
8. 15 And God spake unto Noah, saying
9. 1 God blessed Noah and his sons, and said
9. 6 for in the image of God made he man
9. 8 God spake unto Noah, and to his sons
9. 12 God said, This (is) the token of the cove.
9. 16 everlasting covenant between God and
9. 17 God said..This (is) the token of the cov.
9. 26 said, Blessed (be) the LORD God of Shem
9. 27 God shall enlarge Japheth, and he shall
17. 3 Abram fell on his face: and God talked
17. 7 a God unto thee, and to thy seed after
17. 8 I will give..and I will be their God
17. 9 God said..Thou shalt keep my covenant
17. 15 God said..As for Sarai thy wife, thou
17. 18 Abraham said unto God, O that Ishmael
17. 19 God said, Sarah thy wife shall bear thee
17. 22 left off talking..and God went up from A.
17. 23 the selfsame day, as God had said unto

Gen. 19. 29 God destroyed the cities of the plain, that
19. 29 God remembered Abraham, and sent Lot
20. 3 God came to Abimelech in a dream by
20. 6 God said unto him in a dream, Yea, I
20. 11 Surely the fear of God (is) not in this pl.
20. 13 when God caused me to wander from my
20. 17 So Abraham prayed unto God: and God
21. 2 at the set time of which God had spoken
21. 4 circumcised..as God had commanded
21. 6 Sarah said, God hath made me to laugh
21. 12 God said..Let it not be grievous in thy
21. 17 God heard the voice of the lad; and the
21. 17 angel of God called to Hagar out of
21. 17 for God hath heard the voice of the lad
21. 19 God opened her eyes, and she saw a well
21. 20 God was with the lad; and he grew, and
21. 22 God (is) with thee in all that thou doest
21. 23 swear unto me here by God, that thou
22. 1 God did tempt Abraham, and said unto
22. 3 the place of which God had told him
22. 8 My son, God will provide himself a lamb
22. 9 to the place which God had told him of
22. 12 for now I know that thou fearest God
24. 3 the God of heaven, and the God of the
24. 7 The LORD God of heaven, which took me
24. 12, 27, 42, 48 LORD God of my master Abr.
25. 11 God blessed his son Isaac: and Isaac
26. 24 I (am) the God of Abraham thy father
27. 20 Because the LORD thy God brought (it)
27. 28 God give thee of the dew of heaven, and
28. 4 inherit the land..which God gave unto
28. 12 behold the angels of God ascending and
28. 13 I (am) the LORD God of Abraham thy fa.
28. 13 and the God of Isaac: the land whereon
28. 17 this (is) none other but the house of God
28. 20 If God will be with me, and will keep me
28. 21 in peace, then shall the LORD be my God
28. 22 this stone..shall be God's house: and of
30. 2 (Am) I in God's stead, who hath withheld
30. 6 Rachel said, God hath judged me, and
30. 17 God hearkened unto Leah, and she conc.
30. 18 Leah said, God hath given me my hire
30. 20 God hath endued me (with) a good dow.
30. 22 And God remembered Rachel, and God
30. 23 said, God hath taken away my reproach
31. 5 the God of my father hath been with me
31. 7 but God suffered him not to hurt me
31. 9 God hath taken away the cattle of your
31. 11 the angel of God spake unto me in a dre.
31. 16 all the riches which God hath taken from
31. 16 whatsoever God hath said unto thee, do
31. 24 God came to Laban the Syrian in a dream
31. 29 but the God of your father spake unto
31. 42 the God of my father, the God of Abraham
31. 42 God hath seen mine affliction and the
31. 50 God (is) witness betwixt me and thee
31. 53 The God of Abraham, and the God of N.
31. 53 the God of their father, judge betwixt
32. 1 Jacob went..and the angels of God met
32. 2 he said, This (is) God's host: and he cal.
32. 9 O God of my father Abraham, and God
32. 28 for as a prince hast thou power with God
32. 30 for I have seen God face to face, and my
33. 5 The children which God hath..given thy
33. 10 though I had seen the face of God, and
33. 11 God hath dealt graciously with me, and
35. 1 God said..Arise, go up to Beth-el, and
35. 5 and the terror of God was upon the cities
35. 7 there God appeared unto him, when he
35. 9 God appeared unto Jacob again, when
35. 10 God said..Thy name (is) Jacob: thy
35. 11 God said unto him..be fruitful and multi.
35. 13 God went up from him in the place whe.
35. 15 called the name of the place where God
39. 9 how..can I do this..and sin against God?
40. 8 (Do) not interpretations (belong) to God?
41. 16 God shall give Pharaoh an answer of pe.
41. 25 God hath showed Pharaoh what he (is)
41. 28 What God (is) about to do he showeth unto
41. 32 because the thing (is) established by God
41. 32 and God will shortly bring it to pass
41. 38 a man in whom the spirit of God (is)?
41. 39 Forasmuch as God hath showed thee all
41. 51 For God..hath made me forget all my
41. 52 God hath caused me to be fruitful in
42. 18 Joseph said..This do, and live..I fear G.
42. 28 What (is) this..God hath done unto us?
43. 23 your God, and the God of your father
43. 29 said, God be gracious unto thee, my son
44. 16 God hath found out the iniquity of thy
45. 5 God did send me before you to preserve
45. 7 God sent me before you to preserve you
45. 8 not you (that) sent me hither, but God
45. 9 God hath made me lord of all Egypt
46. 1 offered sacrifices unto the God of his fat.
46. 2 God spake unto Israel in the visions of the
46. 3 I (am)..the God of thy father: fear not
48. 9 my sons, whom God hath given me in
48. 11 lo, God hath showed me also thy seed
48. 15 God, before whom my fathers Abraham
48. 15 the God which fed me all my life long
48. 20 God make thee as Ephraim, and as Man.
48. 21 God shall be with you, and bring you
50. 17 of the servants of the God of thy father
50. 19 Fear not; for (am) I in the place of God?
50. 20 God meant it unto good, to bring to pass
50. 24 God will surely visit you, and bring you
50. 25 God will surely visit you, and ye shall
Exod. 1. 17 the midwives feared God, and did not as
1. 20 God dealt well with the midwives: and
1. 21 because the midwives feared God, that
2. 23 their cry came up unto God by reason

Exod. 2. 24 God heard their groaning, and God rem.
2. 25 God looked upon..Israel, and God had
3. 1 came to the mountain of God..to Horeb
3. 4 God called unto him out of the midst of
3. 6 I (am) the God of thy father, the God of
3. 6 the God of Isaac, and the God of Jacob
3. 6 for he was afraid to look upon God
3. 11 Moses said unto God, Who (am) I, that I
3. 12 ye shall serve God upon this mountain
3. 13 The God of your fathers hath sent me
3. 14 God said unto Moses, I am that I am
3. 15 God said moreover unto Moses, Thus
3. 15 LORD God of your fathers, the God of
3. 15 the God of Isaac, and the God of Jacob
3. 16 LORD God of your fathers, the God of A.
3. 18 LORD God of the Hebrews hath met with
3. 18 that we may sacrifice to the LORD our G.
4. 5 LORD God of their fathers, the God of
4. 5 the God of Isaac, and the God of Jacob
4. 16 and thou shalt be to him instead of God
4. 20 Moses took the rod of God in his hand
4. 27 went, and met him in the mount of God
5. 1 Thus saith the LORD God of Israel, Let
5. 3 The God of the Hebrews hath met with
5. 3 sacrifice unto the LORD our God; lest he
5. 8 saying, Let us go..sacrifice to our God
6. 2 God spake unto Moses, and said unto him
6. 7 I will take you..I will be to you a God
6. 7 shall know that I (am) the LORD your G
7. 1 See, I have made thee a god to Pharaoh
7. 16 LORD God of the Hebrews hath sent me
8. 10 that..none like unto the LORD our God
8. 19 magicians said..This (is) the finger of G
8. 25 Go ye, sacrifice to your God in the land
8. 26 we shall sacrifice..to the LORD our God
8. 27 sacrifice to the LORD our God, as he shall
8. 28 that ye may sacrifice to the LORD your G.
9. 1, 13 Thus saith the LORD God of the Heb.
9. 30 that ye will not yet fear the LORD God
10. 3 the LORD God of the Hebrews
10. 7 that they may serve the LORD their God
10. 8 Go, serve the LORD your God..who (are),
10. 16 I have sinned against the LORD your God
10. 17 entreat the LORD your God, that he may
10. 25 we may sacrifice unto the LORD our God
10. 26 must we take to serve the LORD our God
13. 17 God led them not..the way of the land
13. 17 for God said, Lest peradventure the peo.
13. 18 God led the people about..the way of the
13. 19 God will surely visit you; and ye shall
14. 19 the angel of God, which went before the
15. 2 my father's God, and I will exalt him
15. 26 hearken to the voice of the LORD thy G.
16. 12 shall know that I (am) the LORD your G.
17. 9 stand..with the rod of God in mine hand
18. 1 heard of all that God had done for Moses
18. 4 for the God of my father..(was) mine he.
18. 5 where he encamped at the mount of God
18. 12 a burnt offering and sacrifices for God
18. 12 eat..with Moses' father in law before G.
18. 15 people come unto me to enquire of God
18. 16 do make (them) know the statutes of God
18. 19 Hearken..and God shall be with thee
18. 19 Be thou for the people to God ward
18. 19 thou mayest bring the causes unto God
18. 21 able men, such as fear God, men of truth
18. 23 If thou..do this thing, and God command
19. 3 Moses went up unto God, and the LORD
19. 17 people out of the camp to meet with God
19. 19 Moses spake, and God answered him by
20. 1 And God spake all these words, saying
20. 2 I (am) the LORD thy God, which have
20. 5 for I the LORD thy God (am) a jealous
20. 7 Thou shalt not take the name of..God in
20. 10 (is) the sabbath of the LORD thy God
20. 12 upon the land which the LORD thy God
20. 19 but let not God speak with us, lest we d.
20. 20 Fear not: for God is come to prove you
20. 21 near unto the thick darkness where God
21. 13 but God deliver (him) into his hand; then
22. 20 He that sacrificeth unto (any) god, save
23. 19 bring into the house of the LORD thy God
23. 25 ye shall serve the LORD your God, and he
24. 10 And they saw the God of Israel: and
24. 11 also they saw God, and did eat and drink
24. 13 and Moses went up into the mount of God
29. 45 And I will dwell..and will be their God
29. 46 shall know that I (am) the LORD their G.
29. 46 among them: I (am) the LORD their God
31. 3 I have filled him with the spirit of God
31. 18 two tables..written with the finger of G.
32. 11 Moses besought the LORD his God, and
32. 16 And the tables (were) the work of God
32. 16 and the writing (was) the writing of God
32. 27 Thus saith the LORD God of Israel, Put
34. 23 before the LORD God, the God of Israel
34. 24 before the LORD thy God thrice in the
34. 26 bring unto the house of the LORD thy God
35. 31 he hath filled him with the spirit of God
Lev. 2. 13 suffer the salt of the covenant of thy God
4. 22 the commandments of the LORD his God
11. 44 For I (am) the LORD your God: ye shall
11. 45 that bringeth you up..to be your God
18. 2, 4, 30 I (am) the LORD your God
18. 21 shalt thou profane the name of thy God
19. 2 for I the LORD your God (am) holy
19. 3, 4, 10, 25, 31, 34, 36 (am) the LORD your G.
19. 12 neither shalt..profane the name of thy G.
19. 14 but shalt fear thy God: I (am) the LORD
19. 32 and fear thy God: I (am) the LORD
20. 7 be ye holy: for I (am) the LORD your God
20. 24 I (am) the LORD your God, which have

Lev. 21. 6 They shall be holy unto their God
21. 6 and not profane the name of their God
21. 6 the bread of their God, they do offer
21. 7 her husband: for he (is) holy unto his G.
21. 8 he offereth the bread of thy God: he
21. 12 nor profane the sanctuary of his God
21. 12 the anointing oil of his God (is) upon him
21. 17 not approach to offer the bread of his God
21. 21 not come nigh to offer the bread of his G.
21. 22 He shall eat the bread of his God
22. 25 shall ye offer the bread of your God of
22. 33 That brought you out..to be your God
23. 14 have brought an offering unto your God
23. 22, 43 I (am) the LORD your God
23. 28 atonement..before the LORD your God
23. 40 shall rejoice before the LORD your God
24. 15 Whosoever curseth his God shall bear his
24. 22 one..law..for I (am) the LORD your God
25. 17 fear thy God: for I (am) the LORD your G.
25. 36 Take thou no usury..but fear thy God
25. 38 I (am) the LORD your God, which brought
25. 38 to give you the land..to be your God
25. 43 rule..with rigour, but shalt fear thy G.
25. 55 my servants..I (am) the LORD your God
26. 1 no idols..for I (am) the LORD your God
26. 12 I will walk..and will be your God, and
26. 13 I (am) the LORD your God, which brought
26. 44 I will not..for I (am) the LORD their God
26. 45 I might be their God: I (am) the LORD
Num. 6. 7 consecration of his God (is) upon his
10. 9 remembered before the LORD your God
10. 10 before your God: I (am) the LORD your G.
15. 40 remember..and be holy unto your God
15. 41, 41 I (am) the LORD your God
15. 41 brought you out..to be your God
16. 9 that the God of Israel hath separated you
16. 22 the God of the spirits of all flesh, shall
21. 5 the people spake against God, and again.
22. 9 God came unto Balaam, and said, What
22. 10 Balaam said unto God, Balak the son of
22. 12 God said unto Balaam, Thou shalt not go
22. 18 go beyond the word of the LORD my God
22. 20 God came unto Balaam at night, and said
22. 22 God's anger was kindled because he went
22. 38 the word that God putteth in my mouth
23. 4 God met Balaam: and he said unto him
23. 21 the LORD his God (is) with him, and the
23. 27 peradventure it will please God that thou
24. 2 and the spirit of God came upon him
25. 13 he was zealous for his God, and made an
27. 16 the God of the spirits of all flesh, set a
Deut. 1. 6 LORD our God spake unto us in Horeb
1. 10 LORD your God hath multiplied you, and
1. 11 LORD God of your fathers make you a
1. 17 for the judgment (is) God's: and the
1. 19 as the LORD our God commanded
1. 20 which the LORD our God doth give unto
1. 21 LORD thy God hath set the land before
1. 21 as the LORD God of thy fathers hath said
1. 25 a good land which the LORD our God doth
1. 26 the commandment of the LORD your God
1. 30 The LORD your God, which goeth before
1. 31 seen how that the LORD thy God bare
1. 32 ye did not believe the LORD your God
1. 41 all that the LORD our God commanded us
2. 7 the LORD thy God hath blessed thee in
2. 7 these forty years the LORD thy God (hath
2. 29 the land which the LORD our God giveth
2. 30 the LORD thy God hardened his spirit
2. 33 the LORD our God delivered him before
2. 36 the LORD our God delivered all unto us
2. 37 whatsoever the LORD our God forbade us
3. 3 So the LORD our God delivered into our
3. 18 LORD your God hath given you this land
3. 20 which the LORD your God hath given
3. 21 all that the LORD your God hath done
3. 22 the LORD your God he shall fight for you
4. 1 the LORD God of your fathers giveth you
4. 2 the commandments of the LORD your God
4. 3 God hath destroyed them from among
4. 4 that did cleave unto the LORD your God
4. 5 as the LORD my God commanded me
4. 7 who (hath) God..nigh..the LORD our God
4. 10 stoodest before the LORD thy God in Hor.
4. 19 the LORD thy God hath divided unto all
4. 21 which the LORD thy God giveth thee (for)
4. 23 forget the covenant of the LORD your God
4. 23 which the LORD thy God hath forbidden
4. 24 the LORD thy God (is) a consuming fire
4. 25 evil in the sight of the LORD thy God
4. 29 if..thou shalt seek the LORD thy God
4. 30 if thou turn to the LORD thy God, and
4. 31 the LORD thy God (is) a merciful God
4. 32 since the day that God created man upon
4. 33 Did..people hear the voice of God speak.
4. 34 Or hath God assayed to go (and) take him
4. 34 according to all that the LORD your God
4. 35 mightest know that the LORD he (is) God
4. 39 the LORD he (is) God in heaven above
4. 40 earth, which the LORD thy God giveth
5. 2 The LORD our God made a covenant with
5. 6 I (am) the LORD thy God, which brought
5. 9 for I the LORD thy God (am) a jealous
5. 11 not take the name of the LORD thy God
5. 12, 16 as the LORD thy God hath commanded
5. 14 day (is) the sabbath of the LORD thy God
5. 15 the LORD thy God brought thee out then.
5. 15 the LORD thy God commanded thee to
5. 16 land which the LORD thy God giveth thee
5. 24 LORD our God hath showed us his glory
5. 24 God doth talk with man, and he liveth
5. 25 if we hear the voice of the LORD our God

Deut. 5. 26 the voice of the living God speaking out
5. 27 hear all that the LORD our God shall say
5. 27 all that the LORD our God shall speak
5. 32, 33 LORD your God hath commanded you
6. 1 LORD your God commanded to teach you
6. 2 thou mightest fear the LORD thy God, to
6. 3 as the LORD God of thy fathers hath pro.
6. 4 The LORD our God (is) one LORD
6. 5 thou shalt love the LORD thy God with
6. 10 when the LORD thy God shall have brou.
6. 13 Thou shalt fear the LORD thy God, and
6. 15 For the LORD thy God (is) a jealous
6. 15 lest the anger of the LORD thy God be ki.
6. 16 Ye shall not tempt the LORD your God
6. 17 commandments of the LORD your God
6. 20 which the LORD our God hath command.
6. 24 to fear the LORD our God, for our good
6. 25 to do all these..before the LORD our God
7. 1 When the LORD thy God shall bring thee
7. 2 when the LORD thy God shall deliver them
7. 6 an holy people unto the LORD thy God
7. 6 the LORD thy God hath chosen thee to be
7. 9 Know..that the LORD thy God, he (is) G.
7. 12 the LORD thy God shall keep unto thee
7. 16 which the LORD thy God shall deliver
7. 18 remember what the LORD thy God did
7. 19 whereby the LORD thy God brought thee
7. 19 so shall the LORD thy God do unto all the
7. 20 the LORD thy God will send the hornet
7. 21 LORD thy God (is) among you, a mighty
7. 22 LORD thy God will put out those nations
7. 23 LORD thy God shall deliver them unto
7. 25 an abomination to the LORD thy God
8. 2 way which the LORD thy God led thee
8. 5 (so) the LORD thy God chasteneth thee
8. 6 the commandments of the LORD thy God
8. 7 LORD thy God bringeth thee into a good
8. 10 then thou shalt bless the LORD thy God
8. 11 that thou forget not the LORD thy God
8. 14 and thou forget the LORD thy God, which
8. 18 thou shalt remember the LORD thy God
8. 19 if thou do at all forget the LORD thy God
8. 20 unto the voice of the LORD your God
9. 3 LORD thy God (is) he which goeth over
9. 4 LORD thy God hath cast them out from
9. 5 LORD thy God doth drive them out from
9. 6 LORD thy God giveth thee not this good
9. 7 how thou provokedst the LORD thy God
9. 10 tables..written with the finger of God
9. 16 had sinned against the LORD your God
9. 23 the commandment of the LORD your God
10. 9 according as the LORD thy God promised
10. 12 what doth the LORD thy God require of
10. 12 but to fear the LORD thy God, to walk in
10. 12 to serve the LORD thy God with all thy
10. 14 heaven of heavens, (is) the LORD'S thy G.
10. 17 For the LORD your God (is) God of gods
10. 20 Thou shalt fear the LORD thy God
10. 21 He (is) thy praise, and he (is) thy God
10. 22 LORD thy God hath made thee as the stars
11. 1 thou shalt love the LORD thy God, and
11. 2 the chastisement of the LORD your God
11. 12 A land which the LORD thy God careth
11. 12 the eyes of the LORD thy God (are)
11. 13 to love the LORD your God, and to serve
11. 22 to love the LORD your God, to walk in
11. 25 LORD your God shall lay the fear of
11. 27, 28 commandments of the LORD your God
11. 29 when the LORD thy God hath brought
11. 31 which the LORD your God giveth you
12. 1 land which the LORD God of thy fathers
12. 4 Ye shall not do so unto the LORD your G.
12. 5 unto the place which the LORD your God
12. 7 ye shall eat before the LORD your God
12. 7 wherein the LORD thy God hath blessed
12. 9 inheritance which the LORD your God giv.
12. 10 land which the LORD your God giveth
12. 11 a place which the LORD your God shall
12. 12 shall rejoice before the LORD your God
12. 15 to the blessing of the LORD thy God
12. 18 must eat them before the LORD thy God
12. 18 in the place which the LORD thy God
12. 18 shalt rejoice before the LORD thy God in
12. 20 When the LORD thy God shall enlarge
12. 21 If the place which the LORD thy God hath
12. 27, 27 upon the altar of the LORD thy God
12. 28 right in the sight of the LORD thy God
12. 29 When the LORD thy God shall cut off the
12. 31 shalt not do so unto the LORD thy God
13. 3 the LORD your God proveth you, to know
13. 3 whether ye love the LORD your God
13. 4 Ye shall walk after the LORD your God
13. 5 turn (you) away from the LORD your God
13. 5 way which the LORD thy God commanded
13. 10 thrust thee away from the LORD thy God
13. 12 cities, which the LORD thy God hath given
13. 16 thereof every whit, for the LORD thy God
13. 18 hearken to the voice of the LORD thy God
13. 18 right in the eyes of the LORD thy God
14. 1 Ye (are) the children of the LORD your G.
14. 2, 21 an holy people unto the LORD thy G.
14. 23 thou shalt eat before the LORD thy God
14. 23 mayest learn to fear the LORD thy God
14. 24, 25 which the LORD thy God shall choose
14. 24 when the LORD thy God hath blessed
14. 26 shalt eat there before the LORD thy God
14. 29 that the LORD thy God may bless thee in
15. 4 land which the LORD thy God giveth thee
15. 5 unto the voice of the LORD thy God, to
15. 6 the LORD thy God blesseth thee, as he
15. 10, 18 the LORD thy God shall bless thee
15. 14 the LORD thy God hath blessed thee

Deut 15. 15 and the LORD thy God redeemed thee
15. 19 shalt sanctify unto the LORD thy God
15. 20 shalt eat (it) before the LORD thy God
15. 21 not sacrifice it unto the LORD thy God
16. 1, 2 the passover unto the LORD thy God
16. 5 which the LORD thy God giveth thee
16. 6, 7 which the LORD thy God shall choose
16. 8 a solemn assembly to the LORD thy God
16. 10 unto the LORD thy God with a tribute
16. 10 according as the LORD thy God hath bl.
16. 11 shalt rejoice before the LORD thy God
16. 11 which the LORD thy God hath chosen
16. 15 unto the LORD thy God in the place
16. 15 the LORD thy God shall bless thee in all
16. 16 males appear before the LORD thy God
16. 17 to the blessing of the LORD thy God
16. 18, 20 which the LORD thy God giveth thee
16. 21 unto the altar of the LORD thy God
16. 22 image; which the LORD thy God hateth
17. 1 not sacrifice unto the LORD thy God
17. 1 an abomination unto the LORD thy God
17. 2, 14 which the LORD thy God giveth thee
17. 2 in the sight of the LORD thy God, in
17. 8 which the LORD thy God shall choose
17. 12 minister there before the LORD thy God
17. 15 whom the LORD thy God shall choose
17. 19 he may learn to fear the LORD his God
18. 5 the LORD thy God hath chosen him out
18. 7 minister in the name of the LORD his God
18. 9 land which the LORD thy God giveth
18. 12 LORD thy God doth drive them out from
18. 13 shalt be perfect with the LORD thy God
18. 14 LORD thy God hath not suffered thee so
18. 15 LORD thy God will raise up unto thee
18. 16 desiredst of the LORD thy God in Horeb
18. 16 hear again the voice of the LORD my God
19. 1 When the LORD thy God hath cut off
19. 1, 2, 3, 10, 14 the LORD thy God giveth thee
19. 8 if the LORD thy God enlarge thy coast
19. 9 to love the LORD thy God, and to walk
20. 1 LORD thy God (is) with thee, which brou.
20. 4 LORD your God (is) he that goeth with you
20. 13 LORD thy God hath delivered it into
20. 14 which the LORD thy God hath given thee
20. 16 which the LORD thy God doth give thee
20. 17 as the LORD thy God hath commanded
20. 18 should ye sin against the LORD your God
21. 1, 23 which the LORD thy God giveth thee
21. 5 them the LORD thy God hath chosen to
21. 10 LORD thy God hath delivered them into
21. 23 for he that is hanged (is) accursed of God
22. 5 abomination unto the LORD thy God
23. 5 LORD thy God would not hearken unto
23. 5 but the LORD thy God turned the curse
23. 5 because the LORD thy God loved thee
23. 14 LORD thy God walketh in the midst of thy
23. 18 into the house of the LORD thy God for
23. 18 abomination unto the LORD thy God
23. 20 that the LORD thy God may bless thee in
23. 21 shalt vow a vow unto the LORD thy God
23. 21 LORD thy God will surely require it of
23. 23 thou hast vowed unto the LORD thy God
24. 4 which the LORD thy God giveth thee
24. 9 Remember what the LORD thy God did
24. 13 shall be..unto thee before the LORD thy G.
24. 18 the LORD thy God redeemed thee thence
24. 19 that the LORD thy God may bless thee in
25. 15, 19 land which the LORD thy God giveth
25. 16 an abomination unto the LORD thy God
25. 18 faint and weary; and he feared not God
25. 19 when the LORD thy God hath given thee
26. 1, 2 land..the LORD thy God giveth thee
26. 2 place which the LORD thy God shall cho.
26. 3 I profess this day unto the LORD thy God
26. 4 down before the altar of the LORD thy G.
26. 5 speak and say before the LORD thy God
26. 7 when we cried unto the LORD God of our
26. 10 thou shalt set it before the LORD thy God
26. 10 and worship before the LORD thy God
26. 11 which the LORD thy God hath given unto
26. 13 thou shalt say before the LORD thy God
26. 14 hearkened to the voice of the LORD my G.
26. 16 This day the LORD thy God hath comman.
26. 17 to be thy God, and to walk in his ways
26. 19 an holy people unto the LORD thy God
27. 2, 3 land which the LORD thy God giveth
27. 3 as the LORD God of thy fathers hath pro.
27. 5 build an altar unto the LORD thy God, an
27. 6 shalt build the altar of the LORD thy God
27. 6 shalt offer..thereon unto the LORD thy G.
27. 7 and rejoice before the LORD thy God
27. 9 become the people of the LORD thy God
27. 10 obey the voice of the LORD thy God, and
28. 1, 2, 15, 45 the voice of the LORD thy God
28. 1 LORD thy God will set thee on high above
28. 8 land which the LORD thy God giveth thee
28. 9 13 the commandments of the LORD thy G.
28. 47 thou servedest not the LORD thy God with
28. 52, 53 which the LORD thy God hath given
28. 58 fear this..fearful name, The LORD thy G.
28. 62 not obey the voice of the LORD thy God
29. 6 might know that I (am) the LORD your G.
29. 10 stand..all of you before the LORD your G.
29. 12 enter into covenant with the LORD thy G.
29. 12 which the LORD thy God maketh with
29. 13 he may be unto thee a God, as he hath
29. 15 with us this day before the LORD our G.
29. 18 turneth..this day from the LORD our God
29. 25 forsaken the covenant of the LORD God
29. 29 secret (things belong) unto the LORD..G.
30. 1 whither the LORD thy God hath driven
30. 2 And shalt return unto the LORD thy God

Deut 30. 3 LORD thy God will turn thy captivity, and
30. 3 whither the LORD thy God hath scattered
30. 4 will the LORD thy God gather thee
30. 5 LORD thy God will bring thee into the land
30. 6 LORD thy God will circumcise thine heart
30. 6 to love the LORD thy God with all thine
30. 7 LORD thy God will put all these curses
30. 9 LORD thy God will make thee plenteous
30. 10 hearken unto the voice of the LORD thy G.
30. 10 if thou turn unto the LORD thy God with
30. 16 I command thee..to love the LORD thy G.
30. 16 LORD thy God shall bless thee in the land
30. 20 That thou mayest love the LORD thy G.
31. 3 The LORD thy God, he will go over before
31. 6 LORD thy God, he (it is) that doth go
31. 11 to appear before the LORD thy God in
31. 12 may learn, and fear the LORD your God
31. 13 and learn to fear the LORD your God
31. 17 Are not these evils..because our God (is)
31. 26 ark of the covenant of the LORD your G.
32. 3 ascribe ye greatness unto our God
32. 39 and (there is) no god with me: I kill, and
33. 1 wherewith Moses the man of God blessed
33. 27 The eternal God (is thy) refuge, and un.
Josh. 1. 9 LORD thy God (is) with thee whithersoever
1. 11, 15 land, which the LORD your God giveth
1. 13 The LORD your God hath given you rest
1. 17 only the LORD thy God be with thee, as
2. 11 LORD your God, he (is) God in heaven
3. 3 ark of the covenant of the LORD your G.
3. 9 and hear the words of the LORD your God
4. 5 over before the ark of the LORD your God
4. 23 LORD your God dried up the waters of J.
4. 23 as the LORD your God did to the Red sea
4. 24 that ye might fear the LORD your God for
7. 13 for thus saith the LORD God of Israel
7. 19 give, I pray thee, glory to the LORD God
7. 20 I have sinned against the LORD God of I.
8. 7 LORD your God will deliver it into your
8. 30 Joshua built an altar unto the LORD God
9. 9 because of the name of the LORD thy God
9. 18 had sworn unto them by the LORD God of
9. 19 We have sworn unto them by the LORD G.
9. 23 drawers of water for the house of my God
9. 24 LORD thy God commanded his servant
10. 19 LORD your God hath delivered them into
10. 40 as the LORD God of Israel commanded
10. 42 the LORD God of Israel fought for Israel
13. 14 the sacrifices of the LORD God of Israel
13. 33 LORD God of Israel (was) their inheritan.
14. 6 LORD said unto Moses the man of God
14. 8, 9 wholly followed the LORD my God
14. 14 he wholly followed the LORD God of Isr.
18. 3 land, which the LORD God of your fathers
18. 6 cast lots for you..before the LORD our G.
22. 3 the commandment of the LORD your God
22. 4 LORD your God hath given rest unto your
22. 5 to love the LORD your God, and to walk in
22. 16 that ye have committed against the God
22. 19 altar besides the altar of the LORD our G.
22. 24 What have ye to do with the LORD God
22. 29 besides the altar of the LORD our God that
22. 33 the children of Israel blessed God, and
22. 34 a witness between us that the LORD (is) G.
23. 3 ye have seen all that the LORD your God
23. 3 LORD your God (is) he that hath fought
23. 5 LORD your God, he shall expel them from
23. 5 as the LORD your God hath promised unto
23. 8 But cleave unto the LORD your God, as
23. 10 LORD your God, he (it is) that fighteth for
23. 11 Take..heed..that ye love the LORD..God
23. 13 LORD your God will no more drive out
23. 13, 15 land which the LORD your God hath
23. 14 good things which the LORD your God
23. 15 which the LORD your God promised you
23. 16 the covenant of the LORD your God
24. 1 and they presented themselves before G.
24. 2 Thus saith the LORD God of Israel, Your
24. 17 the LORD our God, he (it is) that brought
24. 18 will we..serve the LORD; for he (is) our G.
24. 19 for he (is) an holy God; he (is) a jealous
24. 23 incline your heart unto the LORD God of I.
24. 24 LORD our God will we serve, and his voice
24. 26 Joshua wrote..in the book..the law of G.
24. 27 a witness unto you, lest ye deny your G.
Judg. 1. 7 as I have done, so God hath requited me
2. 12 they forsook the LORD God of their fath.
3. 7 forgat the LORD their God, and served B.
3. 20 Ehud said, I have a message from God
4. 6 Hath not the LORD God of Israel com.
4. 23 So God subdued on that day Jabin the
5. 3 I will sing..to the LORD God of Israel
5. 5 Sinai from before the LORD God of Israel
6. 8 Thus saith the LORD God of Israel, I br.
6. 10 I (am) the LORD your God; fear not the
6. 20 the angel of God said unto him, Take
6. 26 build an altar unto the LORD thy God
6. 31 if he (be) a god, let him plead for himself
6. 36 Gideon said unto God, If thou wilt save
6. 39 Gideon said unto God, Let not thine anger
6. 40 God did so that night: for it was dry up.
7. 14 into his hand hath God delivered Midian
8. 3 God hath delivered into your hands the
8. 33 Israel..went..and made Baal-ber. their g.
8. 34 remembered not the LORD their God, who
9. 7 Hearken..that God may hearken unto
9. 9 wherewith by me they honour God and
9. 13 my wine, which cheereth God and man
9. 23 God sent an evil spirit between Abime.
9. 27 went into the house of their god, and
9. 56 God rendered the wickedness of Abime.
9. 57 the evil of the men of Shechem did God

Judg 10. 10 we have forsaken our God, and also ser.
11. 21 LORD God of Israel delivered Sihon and
11. 23 LORD God of Israel hath dispossessed..A.
11. 24 possess that which Chemosh thy god giv.
11. 24 LORD our God shall drive out from before
13. 5, 7 the child shall be a Nazarite unto God
13. 6 A man of God came unto me, and his co.
13. 6 like the countenance of an angel of God
13. 8 let the man of God which thou didst send
13. 9 God hearkened to the voice of Manoah
13. 9 the angel of God came again unto the wo.
13. 22 We shall..die, because we have seen God
15. 19 God clave an hollow place that (was) in
16. 17 for I..a Nazarite unto God from my mo.
16. 23 offer a great sacrifice unto Dagon their g.
16. 23 Our god hath delivered Samson our ene.
16. 24 when the people saw..they praised their g.
16. 28 strengthen me..only this once, O God
18. 5 Ask counsel, we pray thee, of God, that
18. 10 for God hath given it into your hands
18. 31 all the time that the house of God was in
20. 2 in the assembly of the people of God
20. 18 and asked counsel of God, and said, Which
20. 27 the ark of the covenant of God (was)
21. 2 and abode there till even before God
21. 3 O LORD God of Israel, why is this come
Ruth. 1. 16 people..my people, and thy God my God
2. 12 of the LORD God of Israel, under whose
1 Sa. 1. 17 the God of Israel grant..thy petition that
2. 2 neither (is there) any rock like our God
2. 27 there came a man of God unto Eli, and
2. 30 LORD God of Israel saith, I said indeed
3. 3 ere the lamp of God went out in the
3. 3 temple of the LORD, where the ark of G.
3. 17 God do so to thee, and more also, if thou
4. 4 with the ark of the covenant of God
4. 7 for they said, God is come into the camp
4. 11 the ark of God was taken; and the two
4. 13 for his heart trembled for the ark of God
4. 17 are dead, and the ark of God is taken
4. 18 when he made mention of the ark of God
4. 19 the tidings that the ark of God was taken
4. 21 because the ark of God was taken, and
4. 22 glory is departed..for the ark of God is
5. 1 the Philistines took the ark of God
5. 2 the Philistines took the ark of God, they
5. 7 The ark of the God of Israel shall not
5. 7 his hand is sore..upon Dagon our god
5. 8 What shall we do with the ark of the God
5. 8 Let the ark of the God of Israel be carr.
5. 8 they carried the ark of the God of Israel
5. 10 Therefore they sent the ark of God to E.
5. 10 it came to pass, as the ark of God came to
5. 10 have brought about the ark of the God
5. 11 Send away the ark of the God of Israel
5. 11 the hand of God was very heavy there
6. 3 If ye send away the ark of the God of I.
6. 5 ye shall give glory unto the God of Isra.
6. 20 to stand before this holy LORD God?
7. 8 Cease not to cry unto the LORD our God
9. 6 Behold now..in this city a man of God
9. 7 not a present to bring to the man of God
9. 8 will I give to the man of God to tell us
9. 9 when a man went to enquire of God, thus
9. 10 went unto the city where the man of God
9. 27 that I may show thee the word of God
10. 3 meet thee three men going up to God to
10. 5 thou shalt come to the hill of God, where
10. 7 do as occasion serve thee; for God (is)
10. 9 had turned..God gave him another heart
10. 10 the spirit of God came upon him, and he
10. 18 Thus saith the LORD God of Israel, I br.
10. 19 ye have this day rejected your God, who
10. 26 a band..whose hearts God had touched
11. 6 the spirit of God came upon Saul when
12. 9 when they forgat the LORD their God, he
12. 12 when the LORD your God (was) your king
12. 14 continue following the LORD your God
12. 19 Pray for thy servants unto the L. thy God
13. 13 the commandment of the LORD thy God
14. 18 Saul said..Bring hither the ark of God
14. 18 the ark of God was at that time with the
14. 36 said..Let us draw near hither unto God
14. 37 Saul asked counsel of God, Shall I go
14. 41 Saul said unto the LORD God of Israel
14. 44 God do so and more also: for thou shalt
14. 45 for he hath wrought with God this day
15. 15 spared..to sacrifice..the LORD thy God
15. 21 to sacrifice unto the LORD thy God in Gi.
15. 30 turn..that I may worship..LORD thy God
16. 15 an evil spirit from God troubleth thee
16. 16 when the evil spirit from God is upon
16. 23 when the..spirit from God was upon Sa.
17. 26 should defy the armies of the living God?
17. 36 hath defied the armies of the living God
17. 45 the God of the armies of Israel, whom
17. 46 may know that there is a God in Israel
18. 10 the evil spirit from God came upon Saul
19. 20 the spirit of God was upon the messeng.
19. 23 the spirit of God was upon him also, and
20. 12 O LORD God of Israel, when I have soun.
22. 3 with you, till I know what God will do
22. 13 and hast enquired of God for him, that he
22. 15 Did I then begin to enquire of God for
23. 7 God hath delivered him into mine hand
23. 10 O LORD God of Israel, thy servant hath
23. 11 O LORD God of Israel, I beseech thee
23. 14 but God delivered him not into his hand
23. 16 Jonathan..strengthened his hand in God
25. 22 So and more also do God unto the enem.
25. 29 the bundle of life with the LORD thy God
25. 32 Blessed (be) the LORD God of Israel, whi.

1 Sa. 25. 34 the LORD God of Israel liveth, which ha.
26. 8 God hath delivered thine enemy into thi.
28. 15 God is departed from me, and answereth
29. 9 good in my sight, as an angel of God
30. 6 encouraged himself in the LORD his God
30. 15 Swear unto me by God, that thou wilt
2 Sa. 2. 27 Joab said, (As) God liveth, unless thou
3. 9 So do God to Abner, and more also, exc.
3. 35 So do God to me, and more also, if I taste
5. 10 and the LORD God of hosts (was) with hi.
6. 2 to bring up from thence the ark of God
6. 3 they set the ark of God upon a new cart
6. 4 accompanying the ark of God: and Ahio
6. 6 Uzzah put forth..to the ark of God, and
6. 7 and God smote him there for (his) error
6. 7 and there he died by the ark of God
6. 12 hath blessed..because of the ark of God
6. 12 D. went and brought up the ark of God
7. 2 the ark of God dwelleth within curtains
7. 22 Wherefore thou art great, O LORD God
7. 22 neither (is there any) God beside thee
7. 23 like Israel, whom God went to redeem
7. 24 and thou, LORD, art become their God
7. 25 And now, O LORD God, the word that thou
7. 26 The LORD of hosts (is) the God over Israel
7. 27 thou, O LORD of hosts, God of Israel
7. 28 thou (art) that God, and thy words be
9. 3 that I may show the kindness of God
10. 12 play the men..for the cities of our God
12. 7 Thus saith the LORD God of Israel, I ano.
12. 16 David therefore besought God for the ch.
14. 11 let the king remember the LORD thy God
14. 13 such a thing against the people of God?
14. 14 neither doth God respect (any) person
14. 16 together out of the inheritance of God
14. 17 as an angel of God, so (is) my lord the
14. 17 therefore the LORD thy God will be with
14. 20 accord. to the wisdom of an angel of God
15. 24 bearing the ark of the covenant of God
15. 24 and they set down the ark of God; and A.
15. 25 Carry back the ark of God into the city
15. 29 Abiathar carried the ark of God again
15. 32 come to the top..where he worshipped G.
16. 23 as if a man..enquired at the oracle of God
18. 28 Blessed (be) the LORD thy God, which
19. 13 God do so to me, and more also, if thou be
19. 27 my lord the king (is) as an angel of God
21. 14 after that God was entreated for the land
22. 3 The God of my rock; in him will I trust
22. 7 called upon the LORD, and cried to my G.
22. 22 have not wickedly departed from my God
22. 30 by my God have I leaped over a wall
22. 32 and who (is) a rock, save our God?
22. 47 exalted be the God of the rock of my sal.
23. 1 the anointed of the God of Jacob, and
23. 3 The God of Israel said, the Rock of Israel
23. 3 that ruleth..just, ruling in the fear of G.
24. 3 the LORD thy God add unto the people
24. 23 Araunah said.. The LORD thy God accept
24. 24 burnt offerings unto the LORD my God of
1 Ki. 1. 17 thou swarest by the LORD thy God unto
1. 30 as I sware unto thee by the LORD God of
1. 36 the LORD God of my lord the king say so
1. 47 God make the name of Solomon better
1. 48 Blessed (be) the LORD God of Israel, which
2. 3 keep the charge of the LORD thy God, to
2. 23 God do so to me, and more also, if Adon.
3. 5 and God said, Ask what I shall give thee
3. 7 O LORD my God, thou hast made thy ser.
3. 11 God said unto him, Because thou hast a.
3. 28 saw that the wisdom of God (was) in him
4. 29 God gave Solomon wisdom and understa.
5. 3 unto the name of the LORD his God, for
5. 4 LORD my God hath given me rest on ev.
5. 5 house unto the name of the LORD my God
8. 15 Blessed (be) the LORD God of Israel, wh.
8. 17, 20 an house for the name of the LORD G.
8. 23 LORD God of Israel..no God like thee
8. 25 LORD God of Israel, keep with thy ser.
8. 26 O God of Israel, let thy word, I pray thee
8. 27 But will God indeed dwell on the earth?
8. 28 Yet have thou respect..O LORD my God
8. 57 The LORD our God be with us, as he was
8. 59 be nigh unto the LORD our God day and
8. 60 That all..may know that the LORD (is) G.
8. 61 be perfect with the LORD our God, to wa.
8. 65 before the LORD our God, seven days and
9. 9 Because they forsook the LORD their God
10. 9 Blessed be the LORD thy God, which
10. 24 wisdom, which God had put in his heart
11. 4 was not perfect with the LORD his God
11. 9 his heart was turned from the LORD God
11. 23 God stirred him up (another) adversary
11. 31 thus saith the LORD, the God of Israel
11. 33 Chemosh the god..and Milcom the god of
12. 22 word of God came unto..the man of God
13. 1 there came a man of God out of Judah by
13. 4 heard the saying of the man of God
13. 5 acc. to the sign which the man of God
13. 6 answered and said unto the man of God
13. 6 Entreat now the face of the LORD thy G.
13. 6 the man of God besought the LORD, and
13. 7 the king said unto the man of God, Come
13. 8 the man of God said unto the king, If th.
13. 11 all the works that the man of God had d.
13. 12 had seen what way the man of God went
13. 14 went after the man of God, and found
13. 14 (Art) thou the man of God that camest
13. 21 he cried unto the man of God that came
13. 21 which the LORD thy God commanded thee
13. 26 It (is) the man of God, who was disobed.
13. 29 took up the carcase of the man of God

1 Ki 13. 31 wherein the man of God (is) buried; lay
14. 7 Go..Thus saith the LORD God of Israel
14. 13 good thing toward the LORD God of Isr.
15. 3 was not perfect with the LORD his God
15. 4 did the LORD his God give him a lamp
15. 30 he provoked the LORD God of Israel to
16. 13 in provoking the LORD God of Israel to
16. 26, 33 to provoke the LORD God of Israel
17. 1 (As) the LORD God of Israel liveth, before
17. 12 (As) the LORD thy God liveth, I have not
17. 14 thus saith the LORD God of Israel, The
17. 18 O thou man of God? art thou come unto
17. 20 O LORD my God, hast thou also brought
17. 21 O LORD my God, I pray thee, let this ch.
17. 24 by this I know..thou (art) a man of God
18. 10 (As) the LORD thy God liveth, there is
18. 21 if the LORD (be) God, follow him: but if
18. 24 the God that answereth..let him be God
18. 27 Cry aloud; for he (is) a god: either he is
18. 36 LORD God of Abraham, Isaac, and of Isr.
18. 36 let it be known this day that thou (art) G.
18. 37 may know that thou (art) the LORD God:
18. 39 he (is) the God! the LORD, he (is) the God!
19. 8 forty nights unto Horeb the mount of G.
19. 10, 14 been very jealous for the LORD God
20. 28 there came a man of God, and spake unto
20. 28 LORD (is) God of the hills..he (is) not G.
21. 10 Thou didst blaspheme God and the king
21. 13 Naboth did blaspheme God and the king
22. 53 provoked to anger the LORD God of Isra.
2 Ki. 1. 2 enquire of Baal-zebub the God of Ekron
1. 3 not a God..(that) ye go to..the god of E.?
1. 6 not a God..(that) thou sendest to..the god
1. 9 Thou man of God, the king hath said
1. 10 If I (be) a man of God, then let fire come
1. 11 O man of God, thus hath the king said
1. 12 If I (be) a man of God, let fire come down
1. 12 the fire of God came down from heaven
1. 13 O man of God I pray thee, let my life
1. 16 to enquire of Baal-zebub the god of Ekron
1. 16 no God in Israel to enquire of his word?
2. 14 Where (is) the LORD God of Elijah? And
4. 7 Then she came and told the man of God
4. 9 I perceive..this (is) an holy man of God
4. 16 Nay, my lord..man of God, do not lie
4. 21 laid him on the bed of the man of God
4. 22 that I may run to the man of God, and
4. 25 she went, and came unto the man of God
4. 25 when the man of God saw her afar off
4. 27 when she came to the man of God to the
4. 27 the man of God said, Let her alone; for
4. 40 O..man of God..death in the pot. And
4. 42 brought the man of God bread of the first
5. 7 (Am) I God, to kill and to make alive
5. 8 when Elisha the man of God had heard
5. 11 call on the name of the LORD his God
5. 14 accord. to the saying of the man of God
5. 15 he returned to the man of God, he and
5. 15 no God in all the earth, but in Israel
5. 20 the servant of Elisha the man of God
6. 6 And the man of God said, Where fell it?
6. 9 the man of God sent unto the king of Is.
6. 10 which the man of God told him and war.
6. 15 when the servant of the man of God was
6. 31 God do so and more also to me, if the h.
7. 2 answered the man of G., and said, Behold
7. 17 and he died, as the man of God had said
7. 18 as the man of God had spoken to the king
7. 19 that lord answered the man of God, and
8. 2 did after the saying of the man of God
8. 4 with Gehazi, the servant of the man of G.
8. 7 saying, The man of God is come hither
8. 8 go, meet the man of God, and enquire of
8. 11 he was ashamed: and the man of God w.
9. 6 Thus saith the LORD God of Israel, I
10. 31 walk in the law of the LORD God of Israel
13. 19 the man of God was wroth with him, and
14. 25 according to the word of the LORD God
16. 2 right in the sight of the LORD his God
17. 7 had sinned against the LORD their God
17. 9 not right against the LORD their God
17. 14 did not believe in the LORD their God
17. 16, 19 commandments of the LORD their G.
17. 26, 26, 27 the manner of the God of the land
17. 39 But the LORD your God ye shall fear
18. 5 He trusted in the LORD God of Israel
18. 12 not the voice of the LORD their God
18. 22 if ye say..We trust in the LORD our God
19. 4 It may be the LORD thy God will hear
19. 4 king..sent to reproach the living God
19. 4 the words which the LORD thy God hath
19. 10 Let not thy God in whom thou trustest
19. 15 O LORD God of Israel, which dwellest
19. 15 thou art the God..thou alone, of all the
19. 16 hath sent him to reproach the living G.
19. 19 Now therefore, O LORD our G., I beseech
19. 19 that thou (art) the LORD God..thou only
19. 20 saying, Thus saith the LORD God of Israel
19. 37 as he was..in the house of Nisroch his g.
20. 5 Thus saith the LORD, the God of David
21. 12 Therefore thus saith the LORD God of I.
21. 22 he forsook the LORD God of his fathers
22. 15, 18 Thus saith the LORD God of Israel
23. 16 which the man of God proclaimed, who
23. 17 the man of God, which came from Judah
23. 21 Keep the passover unto..your God, as (it
1 Ch. 4. 10 Jabez called on the God of Israel, saying
4. 10 God granted him that which he request.
5. 20 they cried to God in the battle, and he
5. 22 many slain, because the war (was) of God
5. 25 they transgressed against the God of
5. 25 people..whom God destroyed before

1 Ch. 5. 26 the God of Israel stirred up the spirit of
6. 48 of the tabernacle of the house of God
6. 49 Moses the servant of God had comman.
9. 11 of Ahitub, the ruler of the house of God
9. 13 work of the service of the house of God
9. 26 over the chambers..of the house of God
9. 27 they lodged round about the house of G.
11. 2 LORD thy God said unto thee, Thou shalt
11. 19 My God forbid it me, that I should do
12. 17 the God of our fathers look (thereon)
12. 18 peace (be) unto thee..thy God helpeth
12. 22 until..a great host, like the host of God
13. 2 If..good unto you, and..the LORD our G.
13. 3 let us bring again the ark of our God to us
13. 5 to bring the ark of God from Kirjath-jear.
13. 6 to bring up thence the ark of God the L.
13. 7 they carried the ark of God in a new
13. 8 and all Israel played before God with all
13. 10 and there he died before God
13. 12 David was afraid of God that day, saying
13. 12 How shall I bring the ark of God..to me?
13. 14 the ark of God remained with the family
14. 10 And David enquired of God, saying, Shall
14. 11 God hath broken in upon mine enemies
14. 14 Therefore David enquired again of God
14. 14 God said unto him, Go not up after them
14. 15 God is gone forth before thee, to smite
14. 16 David therefore did as God commanded
15. 1 prepared a place for the ark of God, and
15. 2 None ought to carry the ark of God but
15. 2 hath the L. chosen to carry the ark of G.
15. 12 may bring up the ark of the LORD God of
15. 13 the LORD our God made a breach upon
15. 14 to bring up the ark of the LORD God of I.
15. 15 the Levites bare the ark of God upon
15. 24 with the trumpets before the ark of God
15. 26 when God helped the Levites that bare
16. 1 So they brought the ark of God, and set
16. 1 sacrifices and peace offerings before God
16. 4 to thank and praise the LORD God of Isr.
16. 6 before the ark of the covenant of God
16. 14 He (is) the LORD our God; his judgments
16. 35 Save us, O God of our salvation, and
16. 36 Blessed (be) the LORD God of Israel for
16. 42 and with musical instruments of God
17. 2 Do all that (is) in thine heart; for God
17. 3 the word of God came to Nathan, saying
17. 16 Who (am) I, O LORD God, and what (is)
17. 17 this was a small thing in thine eyes, O G.
17. 17 and hast regarded me..O LORD God
17. 20 neither..God beside thee, according to
17. 21 whom God went to redeem (to be) his own
17. 22 and thou, LORD, becamest their God
17. 24 The LORD of hosts (is) the God of Israel
17. 24 a God to Israel: and (let) the house of D.
17. 25 For thou, O my God, hast told thy serva.
17. 26 And now, LORD, thou art God, and hast
19. 13 valiantly..for the cities of our God: and
21. 7 And God was displeased with this thing
21. 8 David said unto God, I have sinned grea
21. 15 God sent an angel unto Jerusalem to de.
21. 17 David said unto God, (Is it) not I (that)
21. 17 Let thine hand..O LORD my God, be on
21. 30 could not go before it to enquire of God
22. 1 This (is) the house of the LORD God, and
22. 2 wrought stones to build the house of G.
22. 6 to build an house for the LORD God of I.
22. 7 house unto the name of the LORD my G.
22. 11 build the house of the LORD thy God, as
22. 12 mayest keep the law of the LORD thy G.
22. 18 (Is) not the LORD your God with you?
22. 19 set..your soul to seek the LORD your God
22. 19 build ye the sanctuary of the LORD God
22. 19 to bring..the holy vessels of God, into the
23. 14 Now..Moses the man of God, his sons
23. 25 LORD God of Israel hath given rest unto
23. 28 work of the service of the house of God
24. 5 and governors (of the house) of God, were
24. 19 as the LORD God of Israel had comman.
25. 5 in the words of God, to lift up the horn
25. 5 God gave to Heman fourteen sons and
25. 6 for the service of the house of God, accord.
26. 5 Peulthai the eighth: for God blessed him
26. 20 over the treasures of the house of God
26. 32 for every matter pertaining to God
28. 2 an house..for the footstool of our God
28. 3 God said unto me, Thou shalt not build
28. 4 LORD God of Israel chose me before all
28. 8 in the audience of our God, keep and seek
28. 8 the commandments of the LORD your God
28. 9 know thou the God of thy father, and
28. 12 of the treasures of the house of God, and
28. 20 God..my God, (will be) with thee; he
28. 21 for all the service of the house of God
29. 1 my son, whom alone God hath chosen
29. 1 (is) not for man, but for the LORD God
29. 2 all my might for the house of my God
29. 3 set my affection to the house of my God
29. 3 I have given to the house of my God, over
29. 7 gave for the service of the house of God
29. 10 Blessed (be) thou, LORD God of Israel
29. 13 our God, we thank thee, and praise thy
29. 16 O LORD our God, all this store that we
29. 17 I know also, my God, that thou triest
29. 18 O LORD God of Abraham, Isaac, and of
29. 20 said..Now bless the LORD your God. And
29. 20 blessed the LORD God of their fathers, and
2 Ch. 1. 1 LORD his God (was) with him, and magni.
1. 3 the tabernacle of the congregation of God
1. 4 the ark of God had David brought up
1. 7 In that night did God appear unto Sol.
1. 8 Solomon said unto God, Thou hast show.

2 Ch. 1. 9 Now, O LORD God, let thy promise unto
1. 11 God said to Solomon, Because this was
2. 4 house to the name of the LORD my God
2. 4 on the solemn feasts of the LORD our God
2. 5 (is) great; for great (is) our God above all
2. 12 Blessed (be) the LORD God of Israel, that
3. 3 for the building of the house of God. The
4. 11 for king Solomon for the house of God
4. 19 vessels that (were for) the house of God
5. 1 among the treasures of the house of God
5. 14 for the glory..had filled the house of G.
6. 4 Blessed (be) the LORD God of Israel, who
6. 7, 10 for the name of the LORD God of Isr.
6. 14 O LORD God..no God like thee in the he.
6. 16 O LORD God..keep with thy servant Da.
6. 17 O LORD God of Israel, let thy word be
6. 18 will God in very deed dwell with men on
6. 19 Have respect..O LORD my God, to heark.
6. 40 Now, my God, let..thine eyes be open
6. 41 Now therefore arise, O LORD God, into
6. 41 let thy priests, O LORD God, be clothed
6. 42 O LORD God, turn not away the face of
7. 5 all the people dedicated the house of G
7. 22 Because they forsook the LORD God of
8. 14 had David the man of God commanded
9. 8 Blessed be the LORD thy God, which
9. 8 king for the LORD thy God: because..G.
9. 23 to hear his wisdom, that God had put in
10. 15 for the cause was of God, that the LORD
11. 2 came to Shemaiah the man of God, saying
11. 16 to seek the LORD God of Israel came to
11. 16 to sacrifice unto the LORD God of their
13. 5 Ought ye not to know that the LORD God
13. 10 as for us, the LORD (is) our God, and we
13. 11 we keep the charge of the LORD our God
13. 12 God himself (is) with us for (our) captain
13. 12 fight ye not against the LORD God of your
13. 15 that God smote Jeroboam and all Israel
13. 16 and God delivered them into their hand
13. 18 they relied upon the LORD God of their f.
14. 2 and right in the eyes of the LORD his God
14. 4 to seek the LORD God of their fathers
14. 7 because we have sought the LORD our G.
14. 11 Asa cried unto the LORD his God, and
14. 11 help us, O LORD our God; for we rest on
14. 11 O LORD, thou (art) our God; let not man
15. 1 the spirit of God came upon Azariah the
15. 3 Israel (hath been) without the true God
15. 4 did turn unto the LORD God of Israel, and
15. 6 for God did vex them with all adversity
15. 9 saw that the LORD his God (was) with him
15. 12 to seek the LORD God of their fathers with
15. 13 whosoever would not seek the LORD God
15. 18 he brought into the house of God the
16. 7 and not relied on the LORD thy God, there.
17. 4 But sought to the..God of his father, and
18. 5 Go up; for God will deliver (it) into the ki.
18. 13 even what my God saith, that will I speak
18. 31 and God moved them (to depart) from him
19. 3 and hast prepared thine heart to seek God
19. 4 brought them back unto the LORD God of
19. 7 no iniquity with the LORD our God, nor
20. 6 LORD God of our fathers, (art) not thou G.
20. 7 (Art) not thou our God, (who) didst drive
20. 12 our God, wilt thou not judge them? for
20. 15 for the battle (is) not yours, but God's
20. 19 stood up to praise the LORD God of Israel
20. 20 Believe in the LORD your God, so shall ye
20. 29 the fear of God was on all the kingdoms
20. 30 for his God gave him rest round about
20. 33 not prepared their hearts unto the God of
21. 10 he had forsaken the LORD God of his fath.
21. 12 Thus saith the LORD God of David thy f.
22. 7 the destruction of Ahaziah was of God, by
22. 12 was with them hid in the house of God
23. 3 covenant with the king in the house of G.
23. 9 shields..which (were) in the house of God
24. 5 money to repair the house of your God
24. 7 sons..had broken up the house of God
24. 9 collection (that) Moses the servant of G.
24. 13 they set the house of God in his state, and
24. 16 both toward God, and toward his house
24. 18 they left the house of the LORD God of
24. 20 the spirit of God came upon Zechariah
24. 20 Thus saith God, Why transgress ye the
24. 24 because they had forsaken the LORD God
24. 27 and the repairing of the house of God
25. 7 there came a man of God to him, saying
25. 8 God shall make thee fall before the ene.
25. 8 God hath power to help, and to cast down
25. 9 Amaziah said to the man of God, But
25. 9 the man of God answered, The LORD is
25. 16 I know that God hath determined to
25. 20 it (came) of God, that he might deliver
25. 24 that were found in the house of God with
26. 5 he sought God in the days of Zechariah
26. 5 had understanding in the visions of God
26. 5 as long as he sought the LORD, God made
26. 7 God helped him against the Philistines
26. 16 transgressed against the LORD his God
26. 18 neither..thine honour from the LORD God
27. 6 prepared his ways before the LORD his G.
28. 5 the LORD his God delivered him into the
28. 6 because they had forsaken the LORD God
28. 9 because the LORD God of your fathers
28. 10 with you, sins against the LORD your God?
28. 24 the vessels of the house of God, and cut
28. 24 in pieces the vessels of the house of God
28. 25 provoked to anger the LORD God of his
29. 5 sanctify..the house of the LORD God of
29. 6 evil in the eyes of the LORD our God, and
29. 7 in the holy (place) unto the God of Israel

2 Ch. 29. 10 a covenant with the LORD God of Israel
29. 36 that God had prepared the people: for
30. 1, 5 to keep the passover unto the LORD G.
30. 6 turn again unto the LORD God of Abra.
30. 7 trespassed against the LORD God of their
30. 8 serve the LORD your God, that the fierce.
30. 9 the LORD your God (is) gracious and mer.
30. 12 the hand of God was to give them one
30. 16 acord. to the law of Moses the man of God
30. 19 to seek God, the LORD God of his fathers
30. 22 making confession to the LORD God of
31. 6 consecrated unto the LORD their God
31. 13 and Azariah the ruler of the house of G.
31. 14 (was) over the freewill offerings of God
31. 20 right and truth before the LORD his God
31. 21 began in the service of the house of God
31. 21 in the commandments, to seek his God
32. 8 with us (is) the LORD our God to help us
32. 11 LORD our God shall deliver us out of the
32. 14 your God should be able to deliver you
32. 15 how much less shall your God deliver you
32. 16 servants spake yet..against the LORD G.
32. 17 letters to rail on the LORD God of Israel
32. 17 so shall not the God of Hezekiah deliver
32. 19 they spake against the God of Jerusalem
32. 21 he was come into the house of his god
32. 29 God had given him substance very much
32. 31 God left him, to try him, that he might
33. 7 which he had made, in the house of God
33. 7 of which God had said to David and to S.
33. 12 he besought the LORD his God. and
33. 12 humbled himself greatly before the God
33. 13 Manasseh knew that the LORD he (was) G.
33. 16 commanded Judah to serve the LORD God
33. 17 sacrifice..unto the LORD their God only
33. 18 his prayer unto his God, and the words
33. 18 in the name of the LORD God of Israel
34. 3 he began to seek after the God of David
34. 8 to repair the house of the LORD his God
34. 9 that was brought into the house of God
34. 23, 26 Thus saith the LORD God of Israel
34. 27 thou didst humble thyself before God
34. 32 to the covenant of God, the God of their
34. 33 made all..to serve the LORD their God
34. 33 from following the LORD. the God of
35. 3 serve now the LORD your God, and his
35. 8 rulers of the house of God, gave unto the
35. 21 for God commanded me to make haste
35. 21 forbear thee from (meddling with) God
35. 22 words of Necho from the mouth of God
36. 5, 12 evil in the sight of the LORD his God
36. 13 who had made him swear by God: but
36. 13 from turning unto the LORD God of Israel
36. 15 the LORD God of their fathers sent to them
36. 16 they mocked the messengers of God, and
36. 18 all the vessels of the house of God, great
36. 19 they burnt the house of God, and brake
36. 23 hath the LORD God of heaven given me
36. 23 LORD his God (be) with him, and let him
Ezra 1. 2 LORD God of heaven hath given me all the
1. 3 his God be with him, and let him go up
1. 3 the LORD God of Israel he (is) the God
1. 4 for the house of God that (is) in Jerusale
1. 5 with all..whose spirit God had raised
2. 68 offered freely for the house of God to set
3. 2 builded the altar of the God of Israel, to
3. 2 written in the law of Moses the man of G
3. 8 of their coming unto the house of God at
3. 9 forward the workmen in the house of G
4. 1 builded the temple unto the LORD God of
4. 2 build with you: for we seek your God, as
4. 3 do with us to build an house unto our G.
4. 3 we..will build unto the LORD God of Is.
6. 21 separated themselves..to seek the L. God
6. 22 in the work of the house of God, the God
7. 6 which the LORD God of Israel had given
7. 6 according to the hand of the LORD his G.
7. 9 according to the good hand of his God
7. 27 Blessed (be) the LORD God of our fathers
7. 28 as the hand of the LORD my God (was)
8. 17 bring..ministers for the house of our God
8. 18 by the good hand of our God upon us
8. 21 we might afflict ourselves before our God
8. 22 The hand of our God (is) upon all them
8. 23 So we fasted, and besought our God for
8. 25 the offering of the house of our God, which
8. 28 offering unto the LORD God of your fath.
8. 30 to Jerusalem, unto the house of our God
8. 31 the hand of our God was upon us, and he
8. 33 vessels weighed in the house of our God
8. 35 offered burnt offerings unto the God of I.
8. 36 furthered the people, and the house of G.
9. 4 trembled at the words of the God of Isr.
9. 5 spread out my hands unto the LORD my G.
9. 6 O my God, I am ashamed and blush to
9. 6 lift up my face to thee, my God: for
9. 8 grace hath been..from the LORD our God
9. 8 that our God may lighten our eyes, and
9. 9 yet our God hath not forsaken us in our
9. 9 to set up the house of our God, and to
9. 10 O our God, what shall we say after this?
9. 13 seeing that thou our God hast punished
9. 15 God of Israel, thou (art) righteous; for
10. 1 casting..down before the house of God
10. 2 We have trespassed against our God, and
10. 3 let us make a covenant with our God to
10. 3 tremble at the commandment of our God
10. 6 Ezra rose up from before the house of G.
10. 9 people sat in the street of the house of G.
10. 11 make confession unto the LORD God of
10. 14 until the fierce wrath of our God for this
Neh. 1. 4 and prayed before the God of heaven

Neh 1. 5 I beseech thee, O LORD God of heaven, the
2. 4 So I prayed to the God of heaven
2. 8 according to the good hand of my God
2. 12 what my God had put in my heart to do
2. 18 I told them of the hand of my God which
2. 20 The God of heaven, he will prosper us
4. 4 Hear, O our God; for we are despised: and
4. 9 we made our prayer unto our God, and
4. 15 God had brought their counsel to nought
4. 20 resort ye thither..our God shall fight for
5. 9 ought ye not to walk in the fear of our G.
5. 13 So God shake out every man from his ho.
5. 15 so did not I, because of the fear of God
5. 19 Think upon me, my God, for good, (acco.)
6. 10 Let us meet together in the house of God
6. 12 I perceived that God had not sent him
6. 14 My God, think thou upon Tobiah and S.
6. 16 that this work was wrought of our God
7. 2 faithful man, and feared God above many
7. 5 my God put into mine heart to gather
8. 6 Ezra blessed the LORD, the great God: and
8. 8 they read in the book, in the law of God
8. 9 This day (is) holy unto the LORD your G.
8. 16 and in the courts of the house of God
8. 18 he read in the book of the law of God
9. 3 the book of the law of the LORD their G.
9. 3 and worshipped the LORD their God
9. 4 with a loud voice unto the LORD their G.
9. 5 Stand up..bless the LORD your God for
9. 7 Thou (art) the LORD the God, who didst
9. 18 This (is) thy god that brought thee up out
9. 32 our God, the great, the mighty, and the
10. 28 separated themselves..unto the law of G.
10. 29 entered..into an oath, to walk in God's
10. 29 which was given by M. the servant of God
10. 32 for the service of the house of our God
10. 33 (for) all the work of the house of our G.
10. 34 to bring (it) into the house of our God
10. 34 to burn upon the altar of the LORD our G.
10. 36 to bring to the house of our God, unto the
10. 36 that minister in the house of our God
10. 37 to the chambers of the house of our God
10. 38 of the tithes unto the house of our God
10. 39 we will not forsake the house of our God
11. 11 Seraiah..the ruler of the house of God
11. 16 the outward business of the house of G.
11. 22 over the business of the house of God
12. 24 commandment of David the man of G.
12. 36 instruments of David the man of God
12. 40 So stood the two..in the house of God
12. 43 God had made them rejoice with great
12. 45 the porters kept the ward of their God
12. 46 songs of praise and thanksgiving unto G.
13. 1 not come into the congregation of God
13. 2 our God turned the curse into a blessing
13. 4 of the chamber of the house of our God
13. 7 chamber in the courts of the house of God
13. 9 brought..the vessels of the house of God
13. 11 Why is the house of God forsaken? And
13. 14 Remember me, O my God, concerning
13. 14 that I have done for the house of my God
13. 18 did not our God bring all this evil upon
13. 22 Remember me, O my God, (concerning)
13. 25 made them sware by God..Ye shall not
13. 26 Solomon..who was beloved of his God
13. 26 and God made him king over all Israel
13. 27 to transgress against our God in marrying
13. 29 Remember them, O my God, because they
13. 31 Remember me, O my God, for good
Job 1. 1 one that feared God, and eschewed evil?
1. 5 It may be that my sons have..cursed God
1. 6 when the sons of God came to present
1. 8 one that feareth God, and escheweth ev.?
1. 9 Satan..said, Doth Job fear God for nou.?
1. 16 The fire of God is fallen from heaven, and
1. 22 In all this Job sinned not, nor charged G.
2. 1 when the sons of God came to present
2. 3 one that feareth God, and escheweth ev.?
2. 9 Then said his wife..curse God, and die
2. 10 shall we receive good at the hand of God
5. 8 and unto God would I commit my cause
20. 29 This..the portion of a wicked man from G.
28. 23 God understandeth the way thereof, and
32. 2 he justified himself rather than God
34. 9 that he should delight himself with God
38. 7 and all the sons of God shouted for joy?
Psa. 3. 2 (There is) no help for him in God. Selah
3. 7 Arise, O LORD; save me, O my God: for
4. 1 Hear me when I call, O God of my righ.
5. 2 Hearken unto the voice of my cry..my G.
5. 10 Destroy thou them, O God; let them fall
7. 1 O LORD my God, in thee do I put my tru.
7. 3 O LORD my God, if I have done this; if
7. 9 the righteous God trieth the hearts and
7. 10 My defence (is) of God, which saveth the
7. 11 God judgeth the righteous, and..is angry
9. 17 (and) all the nations that forget God
10. 4 The wicked..God (is) not in all his thoug.
10. 13 Wherefore doth the wicked contemn G.?
13. 3 Consider..hear me, O LORD my God
14. 1 The fool hath said in his heart..no God
14. 2 any that did understand, (and) seek God
14. 5 God (is) in the generation of the righteous
18. 6 In my distress I..cried unto my God: he
18. 21 have not wickedly departed from my God
18. 28 LORD my God will enlighten my darkness
18. 29 and by my God have I leaped over a wall
18. 31 or who (is) a rock save our God?
18. 46 and let the God of my salvation be exalt.
20. 1 the name of the God of Jacob defend thee
20. 5 in the name of our God we will set up
20. 7 remember the name of the LORD our G.

Psa. 22. 2 O my God, I cry in the day time, but thou
24. 5 righteousness from the God of his salva.
25. 2 O my God, I trust in thee: let me not
25. 5 thou art the God of my salvation; on thee
25. 22 Redeem Israel, O God, out of all his tro.
27. 9 neither forsake me, O God of my salva.
30. 2 O LORD my God, I cried unto thee, and
30. 12 O LORD my God, I will give thanks unto
31. 14 I trusted in thee..Thou (art) my God
33. 12 Blessed (is) the nation whose God (is) the
35. 23 awake..unto my cause, my God..my L.
35. 24 Judge me, O LORD my God, according to
36. 1 (that there is) no fear of God before his
36. 7 excellent (is) thy loving kindness, O God!
37. 31 The law of his God (is) in his heart; none
38. 15 For..thou wilt hear, O LORD my God
38. 21 O LORD: O my God, be not far from me
40. 3 hath put a new song..praise unto our G.
40. 5 Many, O LORD my God, (are) thy wonder.
40. 8 I delight to do thy will, O my God: yea
40. 17 my help..make no tarrying, O my God
41. 13 Blessed (be) the LORD God of Israel from
42. 1 so panteth my soul after thee, O God
42. 2 soul thirsteth for God, for the living G
42. 2 when shall I come and appear before G.?
42. 3 continually say unto me, Where (is)..G.?
42. 4 I went with them to the house of God, with
42. 5 hope thou in God; for I shall yet praise
42. 6 O my God, my soul is cast down within
42. 10 they say daily unto me, Where (is) thy G.?
42. 11 the health of my countenance, and my G.
43 1 Judge me, O God, and plead my cause
43. 2 For thou (art) the God of my strength
43. 4 Then will I go unto the altar of God, u. G.
43. 4 upon the harp will I praise..O God, my G.
43. 5 hope in God; for I shall yet praise him
43. 5 the health of my countenance, and my G.
44. 1 We have heard with our ears, O God, our
44. 4 Thou art my King, O God: command de.
44. 8 In God we boast all the day long, and
44. 20 If we have forgotten the name of our G.
44. 21 Shall not God search this out? for he
45. 2 therefore God hath blessed thee for ever
45. 6 Thy throne, O God, (is) for ever and ever
45. 7 therefore God, thy God hath anointed th.
46. 1 God (is) our refuge and strength, a very
46. 4 streams..shall make glad the city of G.
46. 5 God (is) in the midst of her; she shall not
46. 5 God shall help her, (and that) right early
46. 7, 11 the God of Jacob (is) our refuge. Sel.
46. 10 Be still, and know that I (am) God: I will
47. 1 shout unto God with the voice of triumph
47. 5 God is gone up with a shout, the LORD
47. 6 Sing praises to God, sing praises; sing
47. 7 For God (is) the King of all the earth, sing
47. 8 God reigneth over the heathen: God sit.
47. 9 (even) the people of the God of Abraham
47. 9 the shields of the earth (belong) unto G.
48. 1 to be praised in the city of our God..the
48. 3 God is known in her palaces for a refuge
48. 8 God will establish it for ever. Selah
48. 9 We have thought..O God, in the midst
48. 10 According to thy name, O God, so (is) thy
48. 14 this God (is) our God for ever and ever
49. 7 None..can..give to God a ransom for
49. 15 God will redeem my soul from the pow
50. 1 The mighty God..the LORD, hath spoken
50. 2 Out of Zion, the perfection of beauty, G.
50. 3 Our God shall come, and shall not keep
50. 6 the heavens shall declare..God (is) judge
50. 7 Hear, O my people..I (am) God..thy G.
50. 14 Offer unto God thanksgiving; and pay
50. 16 unto the wicked God saith, What hast
50. 23 to him..will I show the salvation of G
51. 1 Have mercy upon me, O God, according
51. 10 Create in me a clean heart, O God; and
51. 14 Deliver me..O God, thou God of my sal.
51. 17 The sacrifices of God (are) a broken spirit
51. 17 a contrite heart, O God, thou wilt not
52. 7 Lo, (this is) the man (that) made not God
52. 8 like a green olive tree in the house of G.
52. 8 I trust in the mercy of God for ever and
53. 1 The fool hath said in his heart..no God
53. 2 God looked down from heaven upon the
53. 2 that did understand, that did seek God
53. 4 of iniquity..they have not called upon G
53. 5 God hath scattered the bones of him that
53. 5 shame, because God hath despised them
53. 6 When God bringeth back the captivity
54. 1 Save me, O God, by thy name, and judge
54. 2 Hear my prayer, O God; give ear to the
54. 3 they have not set God before them. Sel.
54. 4 God (is) mine helper: the LORD (is) with
55. 1 Give ear to my prayer, O God; and hide
55. 14 walked unto the house of God in company
55. 16 As for me, I will call upon God; and the
55. 19 no changes, therefore they fear not God
55. 23 thou, O God, shalt bring them down into
56. 1 Be merciful unto me, O God; for man
56. 4 In God I will praise his word: in God I
56. 7 (thine) anger cast down the people, O G.
56. 9 turn back: this I know; for God (is) for
56. 10 In God will I praise (his) word; in the L
56. 11 In God have I put my trust: I will not
56. 12 Thy vows (are) upon me, O God: I will
56. 13 that I may walk before God in the light
57. 1 Be merciful unto me, O God, be merciful
57. 2 I will cry unto God most high; unto God
57. 3 God shall send forth his mercy and his
57. 5 Be thou exalted, O God, above the heav.
57. 6 My heart is fixed, O God, my heart is
57. 11 Be thou exalted, O God, above the heav.

Psa. 58. 6 Break their teeth, O God, in their mouth
58. 11 he is a God that judgeth in the earth
59. 1 Deliver me from mine enemies, O my God
59. 5 O LORD God of hosts, the God of Israel
59. 9 I wait upon thee: for God (is) my defence
59. 10 The God of my mercy shall prevent me
59. 10 God shall let me see (my desire) upon
59. 13 that God ruleth in Jacob unto the ends
59. 17 my defence, (and) the God of my mercy
60. 1 O God, thou hast cast us off, thou hast
60. 6 God hath spoken in his holiness; I will
60. 10 (Wilt) not thou, O God..(thou), O God
60. 12 Through God we shall do valiantly: for
61. 1 Hear my cry, O God; attend unto my
61. 5 For thou, O God, hast heard my vows
61. 7 He shall abide before God for ever: O
62. 1 Truly my soul waiteth upon God: from
62. 5 My soul, wait thou only upon God; for
62. 7 In God (is) my salvation and my glory
62. 7 the rock of my strength..(is) in God
62. 8 Trust in him..God (is) a refuge for us
62. 11 God hath spoken..(belongeth) unto God
63. 1 O God..early will I seek thee; my soul
63. 11 the king shall rejoice in God; every one
64. 1 Hear my voice, O God, in my prayer: pre.
64. 7 God shall shoot at them (with) an arrow
64. 9 and shall declare the work of God; for
65. 1 Praise waiteth for thee, O God, in
65. 5 wilt thou answer us, O God of our salva.
65. 9 greatly enrichest it with the river of God
66. 1 Make a joyful noise unto God, all ye
66. 3 Say unto God, How terrible (art thou)
66. 5 Come and see the works of God: (he is)
66. 8 O bless our God, ye people, and make
66. 10 For thou, O God, hast proved us: thou
66. 16 Come (and) hear, all ye that fear God
66. 19 verily God hath heard..he hath attended
66. 20 Blessed (be) God, which hath not turned
67. 1 God be merciful unto us, and bless us
67. 3 Let the people praise thee, O God; let all
67. 5 Let the people praise thee, O God; let all
67. 6 God, (even) our own God, shall bless us
67. 7 God shall bless us; and all the ends of
68. 1 Let God arise, let his enemies be scattered
68. 2 the wicked perish at the presence of God
68. 3 let them rejoice before God; yea, let th.
68. 4 Sing unto God, sing praises to his name
68. 5 A father of the fatherless..(is) God in his
68. 6 God setteth the solitary in families: he
68. 7 O God, when thou wentest forth before
68. 8 heavens..dropped at the presence of God
68. 8 at the presence of God, the God of Israel
68. 9 Thou, O God, didst send a plentiful rain
68. 10 thou, O God, hast prepared..for the poor
68. 15 The hill of God (is as) the hill of Bashan
68. 16 the hill (which) God desireth to dwell in
68. 17 The chariots of G. (are) twenty thousand
68. 18 the LORD God might dwell (among them)
68. 21 God shall wound the head of his enemies
68. 24 They have seen thy goings, O God; (even)
68. 26 Bless ye God in the congregations, (even)
68. 28 Thy God hath commanded thy strength
68. 28 strengthen, O God, that which thou hast
68. 31 shall..stretch out her hands unto God
68. 32 Sing unto God, ye kingdoms of the earth
68. 34 Ascribe ye strength unto God: his excel.
68. 35 God, (thou art) terrible out of thy holy pl.
68. 35 power unto (his) people. Blessed (be) God
69. 1 Save me, O God; for the waters are come
69. 3 mine eyes fail while I wait for my God
69. 5 O God, thou knowest my foolishness; and
69. 6 confounded for my sake, O God of Israel
69. 13 O God, in the multitude of thy mercy
69. 29 let thy salvation, O God, set me up on
69. 30 I will praise the name of God with a so.
69. 32 and your heart shall live that seek God
69. 35 For God will save Zion, and will build the
70. 1 (Make haste), O God, to deliver me; ma.
70. 4 say continually, Let God be magnified
70. 5 I (am) poor..make haste unto me, O God
71. 4 Deliver me, O my God, out of the hand of
71. 11 Saying, God hath forsaken him: persec.
71. 12 O God, be not far from me: O my God
71. 17 O God, thou hast taught me from my
71. 18 Now also..O God, forsake me not, until
71. 19 Thy righteousness also, O God, (is) very
71. 19 things: O God, who (is) like unto thee!
71. 22 (even) thy truth, O my God: unto thee
72. 1 Give the king thy judgments, O God, and
72. 18 Blessed (be) the LORD God, the God of I.
73. 1 Truly God (is) good to Israel, (even) to
73. 26 God (is) the strength of my heart, and
73. 28 (it is) good for me to draw near to God
74. 1 O God, why hast thou cast (us) off for
74. 10 God, how long shall the adversary repr.
74. 12 God (is) my king of old, working salvati.
74. 22 Arise, O God, plead thine own cause: re.
75. 1 Unto thee, O God, do we give thanks
75. 7 God (is) the judge: he putteth down one
75. 9 I will sing praises to the God of Jacob
76. 1 In Judah (is) God known; his name (is)
76. 6 At thy rebuke, O God of Jacob, both the
76. 9 When God arose to judgment, to save all
76. 11 Vow, and pay unto the LORD your God
77. 1 I cried unto God with my voice, (even)
77. 3 I remembered God, and was troubled: I
77. 13 O God..who (is so) great..as (our) God?
77. 16 The waters saw thee, O God, the waters
78. 7 That they might set their hope in God
78. 10 They kept not the covenant of God, and
78. 19 Yea, they spake against God; they said
78. 22 they believed not in God, and trusted
Psa. 78. 31 The wrath of God came upon them, and
78. 35 And they remembered that God (was) th.
78. 56 provoked the most high God, and kept
78. 59 When God heard (this), he was wroth
79. 1 O God, the heathen are come into thine
79. 9 Help us, O God of our salvation, for the
79. 10 the heathen say, Where (is) their God?
80. 3 Turn us again, O God, and cause thy face
80. 4 O LORD God of hosts, how long wilt thou
80. 7 Turn us again, O God of hosts, and cause
80. 14 Return, we beseech thee, O God of hosts
80. 19 Turn us again, O LORD God of hosts, ca.
81. 1 Sing aloud unto God our strength
81. 1 make a joyful noise unto the God of Jac.
81. 4 statute for Israel, (and) a law of the God
81. 10 I (am) the LORD thy God, which brought
82. 1 God standeth in the congregation of the
82. 8 Arise, O God, judge the earth: for thou
83. 1 keep not thou silence, O God: hold not
83. 12 Let us take to ourselves the houses of God
83. 13 O my God, make them like a wheel; as
84. 3 O LORD of hosts, my King, and my God
84. 7 (every one of them)..appeareth before G.
84. 8 O LORD God of hosts..give ear, O God
84. 9 Behold, O God our shield, and look upon
84. 10 be a doorkeeper in the house of my God
84. 11 For the LORD God (is) a sun and shield
85. 4 Turn us, O God of our salvation, and ca.
86. 2 O thou my God, save thy servant that
86. 10 For thou (art) great..thou (art) God alone
86. 12 I will praise thee, O LORD my God, with
86. 14 O God, the proud are risen against me
87. 3 Glorious things are spoken..O city of G.
88. 1 LORD God of my salvation, I have cried
89. 8 O LORD God of hosts, who (is) a strong L.
90. *title.* A Prayer of Moses the man of God
90. 17 let the beauty of the LORD our God be
91. 2 (He is) my refuge and my fortress: my G.
92. 13 shall flourish in the courts of our God
94. 7 neither shall the God of Jacob regard (it)
94. 22 and my God (is) the rock of my refuge
94. 23 (yea), the LORD our God shall cut them
95. 7 he (is) our God; and we (are) the people
98. 3 all..have seen the salvation of our God
99. 5 Exalt ye the LORD our God, and worship
99. 8 Thou answeredst them, O LORD our God
99. 9 Exalt the LORD our God, and worship
99. 9 holy hill; for the LORD our God (is) holy
100. 3 Know ye that the LORD he (is) God: (it
104. 1 O LORD my God, thou art very great
104. 33 I will sing praise to my God while I have
105. 7 He (is) the LORD our God: his judgments
106. 47 Save us, O LORD our God, and gather us
106. 48 Blessed (be) the LORD God of Israel from
108. 1 O God, my heart is fixed; I will sing and
108. 5 Be thou exalted, O God, above the heav.
108. 7 God hath spoken in his holiness; I will
108. 11 (Wilt) not (thou), O God, (who) hast cast
108. 11 wilt not thou, O God, go forth with our
108. 13 Through God we shall do valiantly: for
109. 1 Hold not thy peace, O God of my praise
109. 26 Help me, O LORD my God: O save me
113. 5 Who (is) like unto the LORD our God
115. 2 the heathen say, Where (is) now their G.?
115. 3 But our God (is) in the heavens: he hath
116. 5 Gracious (is) the LORD..yea, our God (is)
119. 115 I will keep the commandments of my G.
122. 9 Because of the house of the LORD our G.
123. 2 so our eyes (wait) upon the LORD our G.
135. 2 in the courts of the house of our God
136. 2 O give thanks unto the God of gods: for
143. 10 for thou (art) my God: thy spirit (is) good
144. 9 I will sing a new song unto thee, O God
144. 15 (is that) people, whose God (is) the LORD
145. 1 I will extol thee, my God, O King; and I
146. 2 I will sing praises unto my God while I
146. 5 whose hope (is) in the LORD his God
146. 10 LORD shall reign for ever, (even) thy God
147. 1 good to sing praises unto our God; for
147. 7 sing praise upon the harp unto our God
147. 12 Praise the LORD..praise thy God, O Zion
Prov. 2. 5 and find the knowledge of God
2. 17 and forgetteth the covenant of her God
3. 4 understanding in the sight of God and
25. 2 (It is) the glory of God to conceal a thing
30. 9 and take the name of my God (in vain)
Eccl. 1. 13 this sore travail hath God given to the
2. 24 I saw, that it (was) from the hand of God
2. 26 may give to (him that is) good before God
3. 10 which God hath given to the sons of men
3. 11 that God maketh from the beginning to
3. 13 enjoy the good..it (is) the gift of God
3. 14 I know that whatsoever God doeth, it
3. 14 God doeth (it), that (men) should fear
3. 15 and God requireth that which is past
3. 17 God shall judge the righteous and the
3. 18 that God might manifest them, and that
5. 1 thou goest to the house of God, and
5. 2 to utter (any) thing before God: for God
5. 4 When thou vowest a vow unto God
5. 6 wherefore should God be angry at thy
5. 7 also (divers) vanities: but fear thou God
5. 18 all the days of his life, which God giveth
5. 19 to whom God hath given riches and wea.
5. 19 to rejoice..this (is) the gift of God
5. 20 God answereth (him) in the joy of his he.
6. 2 A man to whom God hath given riches
6. 2 God giveth him not power to eat thereof
7. 13 Consider the work of God: for who can
7. 14 God..hath set the one over against the
7. 18 he that feareth God shall come forth of
7. 26 whoso pleaseth God shall escape from
Eccl. 7. 29 that God hath made man upright; but
8. 2 and (that) in regard of the oath of God
8. 12 it shall be well with them that fear God
8. 13 because he feareth not before God
8. 15 which God giveth him under the sun
8. 17 Then I beheld all the work of God, that
9. 1 their works, (are) in the hand of God: no
9. 7 for God now accepteth thy works
11. 5 so thou knowest not the works of God
11. 9 for all these (things) God will bring thee
12. 7 spirit shall return unto God who gave it
12. 13 Fear God, and keep his commandments
12. 14 For God shall bring every work into
Isa. 1. 10 give ear unto the law of our God, ye peo.
2. 3 Come ye..to the house of the God of Ja.
7. 11 Ask thee a sign of the LORD thy God; ask
7. 13 weary men, but will ye weary my God
8. 19 should not a people seek unto their God?
8. 21 curse their king and their God, and look
13. 19 shall be as when God overthrew Sodom
17. 6 thereof, saith the LORD God of Israel
17. 10 Because thou hast forgotten the God of
21. 10 the LORD of hosts, the God of Israel
21. 17 for the LORD God of Israel hath spoken
24. 15 the name of the LORD God of Israel in the
25. 1 O LORD, thou (art) my God; I will exalt
25. 9 Lo, this (is) our God; we have waited for
26. 13 O LORD our God, (other) lords beside
28. 26 his God doth instruct him to discretion
29. 23 sanctify..and shall fear the God of Israel
30. 18 for the LORD (is) a God of judgment
35. 2 they shall see..the excellency of our God
35. 4 God will come (with) vengeance, (even) G.
36. 7 We trust in the LORD our God: (is it) not
37. 4 the LORD thy God will hear the words of
37. 4 sent to reproach the living God, and will
37. 4 words which the LORD thy God hath
37. 10 Let not thy God..deceive thee, saying
37. 16 O LORD of hosts, God of Israel, that dw.
37. 16 thou (art) the God, (even) thou alone, of
37. 17 which hath sent to reproach the living G.
37. 20 O LORD our God, save us from his hand
37. 21 Thus saith the LORD God of Israel, Whe.
37. 38 in the house of Nisroch his god, that Ad.
38. 5 the God of David thy father, I have heard
40. 1 comfort ye my people, saith your God
40. 3 make..in the desert a highway for our G.
40. 8 the word of our God shall stand for ever
40. 9 be not afraid; say..Behold your God!
40. 27 my judgment is passed over from my G.?
40. 28 the everlasting God, the LORD, the Crea.
41. 10 Fear thou not..for I (am) thy God: I
41. 13 For I the LORD thy God will hold thy ri.
41. 17 the God of Israel will not forsake them
43. 3 I (am) the LORD thy God, the Holy One
44. 6 the last; and beside me (there is) no G.
45. 3 I the LORD..(am) the God of Israel
45. 5 (there is) no God beside me: I girded
45. 14 and (there is) none else, (there is) no God
45. 15 hidest thyself, O God of Israel, the Savi.
45. 18 God himself that formed the earth, and
45. 21 and (there is) no God else beside me; a
46. 9 (I am) God, and (there is) none like me
48. 1 make mention of the God of Israel, (but)
48. 2 and stay themselves upon the God of Is.
48. 17 the LORD thy God which teacheth thee to
49. 4 with the LORD, and my work with my G.
49. 5 and my God shall be my strength
50. 10 let him trust..and stay upon his God
51. 15 But I (am) the LORD thy God, that divid.
51. 20 they are full of..the rebuke of thy God
51. 22 God (that) pleadeth the cause of his peo.
52. 7 that saith unto Zion, Thy God reigneth!
52. 10 all..shall see the salvation of our God
52. 12 the God of Israel (will be) your rereward
53. 4 esteem him stricken, smitten of God, and
54. 5 The God of the whole earth shall he be
54. 6 when thou wast refused, saith thy God
55. 5 because of the LORD thy God, and for the
55. 7 to our God, for he will abundantly pardon
57. 21 (There is) no peace, saith my God, to the
58. 2 forsook not the ordinance of their God
58. 2 they take delight in approaching to God
59. 2 between you and your God, and your
59. 13 departing away from our God, speaking
60. 9 unto the name of the LORD thy God, and
60. 19 but the LORD..and thy God thy glory
61. 2 and the day of vengeance of our God; to
61. 6 shall call you the Ministers of our God
61. 10 my soul shall be joyful in my God; for
62. 3 a royal diadem in the hand of thy God
62. 5 the bride, (so) shall thy God rejoice over
64. 4 neither hath the eye seen, O God, beside
65. 16 shall bless himself in the God of truth
65. 16 shall swear by the God of truth; because
66. 9 shall I cause to bring forth..saith thy G.
Jer. 2. 17, 19 thou hast forsaken the LORD thy God
2. 19 my fear (is) not in thee, saith the Lord G.
3. 13 thou hast transgressed against..God, and
3. 21 they have forgotten the LORD their God
3. 22 come..for thou (art) the LORD our God
3. 23 truly in the LORD our God (is) the salva.
3. 25 have sinned against the LORD our God
3. 25 not obeyed the voice of the LORD our G.
5. 4 know not..the judgment of their God
5. 5 have known the judgment of their God
5. 14 thus saith the LORD God of hosts, Becau
5. 19 Wherefore doeth the LORD our God all
5. 24 Let us now fear the LORD our God, that
7. 3, 21 the LORD of hosts, the God of Israel
7. 23 and I will be your God, and ye shall be
7. 28 obeyeth not the voice of the LORD..God

Jer. 8. 14 the LORD our God hath put us to silence
9. 15 saith the LORD of hosts, the God of Israel
10. 10 LORD (is) the true G., he (is) the living G.
11. 3 Thus saith the LORD God of Israel; Cur.
11. 4 ye be my people, and I will be your God
13. 12 Thus saith the LORD God of Israel, Every
13. 16 Give glory to the LORD your God, before
14. 22 (Art) not thou he, O LORD our God? the.
15. 16 called by thy name, O LORD God of hosts
16. 9 saith the LORD of hosts, the God of Israel
16. 10 have committed against the LORD our G.
19. 3, 15 the LORD of hosts, the God of Israel
21. 4 Thus saith the LORD God of Israel, Behold
22. 9 forsaken the covenant of the LORD..God
23. 2 thus saith the LORD God of Israel against
23. 23 God at hand, saith the LORD, and not a G.
23. 36 living God, of the LORD of hosts our G.
24. 5 Thus saith the LORD, the God of Israel
24. 7 be my people, and I will be their God
25. 15 saith the LORD God of Israel unto me
25. 27 saith the LORD of hosts, the God of Israel
26. 13 and obey the voice of the LORD your God
26. 16 to us in the name of the LORD our God
27. 4, 21 Thus saith the LORD..God of Israel
28. 2 Thus speaketh the LORD..God of Israel
28. 14 For thus saith the LORD..God of Israel
29. 4, 8, 21 Thus saith the LORD..God of Israel
29. 25 Thus speaketh the LORD..God of Israel
30. 2 Thus speaketh the LORD God of Israel
30. 9 they shall serve the LORD their God, and
30. 22 be my people, and I will be your God
31. 1 will I be the God of all the families of I.
31. 6 let us go up to Zion unto the LORD..God
31. 18 turned; for thou (art) the LORD my God
31. 23 Thus saith the LORD..God of Israel, As
31. 33 be their God, and they shall be my people
32. 14, 15 Thus saith the LORD..God of Israel
32. 27 I (am) the LORD, the God of all flesh: is
32. 36 thus saith the LORD, the God of Israel
32. 38 be my people, and I will be their God
33. 4 For thus saith the LORD, the God of Is.
34. 2, 13 Thus saith the LORD, the God of Israel
35. 4 the son of Igdaliah, a man of God, which
35. 13, 17, 18, 19 Thus saith the LORD..God of I.
37. 3 Pray now unto the LORD our God for us
37. 7 Thus saith the LORD, the God of Israel
38. 17 Thus saith..the God of Israel; If thou
39. 16 saith the LORD of hosts, the God of Israel
40. 2 thy God hath pronounced this evil upon
42. 2 and pray for us unto the LORD thy God
42. 3 the LORD thy God may show us the way
42. 4 I will pray unto the LORD your God acc.
42. 5 the LORD thy God shall send thee to us
42. 6, 6 obey the voice of the LORD our God
42. 9 Thus saith the LORD, the God of Israel
42. 13 obey the voice of the LORD your God
42. 15, 18 saith the LORD of hosts, the God of Is.
42. 20 when ye sent me unto the LORD your God
42. 20 Pray for us unto the LORD our God; and
42. 20 unto all that the LORD our God shall say
42. 21 obeyed the voice of the LORD your God
43. 1 all the words of the LORD their God, for
43. 1 the LORD their God had sent him to them
43. 2 the LORD our God hath not sent thee to
43. 10 the LORD of hosts, the God of Israel
44. 2 saith the LORD of hosts, the God of Israel
44. 7 the God of hosts, the God of Israel
44. 11, 25 the LORD of hosts, the God of Israel
45. 2 saith the LORD, the God of Israel, unto
46. 25 the God of Israel, saith; Behold, I will
48. 1 saith the LORD of hosts, the God of Israel
50. 4 they shall go, and seek the LORD their G.
50. 18 saith the LORD of hosts, the God of Israel
50. 28 the vengeance of the LORD our God, the
50. 40 God overthrew Sodom and Gomorrah and
51. 5 nor Judah of his God, of the LORD of ho.
51. 10 in Zion the work of the LORD our God
51. 33 saith the LORD of hosts, the God of Israel
Eze. 1. 1 were opened, and I saw visions of God
8. 3 and brought me in the visions of God to
8. 4 the glory of the God of Israel (was) there
9. 3 the glory of the God of Israel was gone
10. 19 the glory of the God of Israel (was) over
10. 20 that I saw under the God of Israel by the
11. 20 be my people, and I will be their God
11. 22 the glory of the God of Israel (was) over
11. 24 brought me in a vision by..spirit of God
14. 11 and I may be their God, saith the LORD
20. 5 them, saying, I (am) the LORD your God
20. 7 and defile not..I (am) the LORD your God
20. 19 I (am) the LORD your God; walk in my
20. 20 may know that I (am) the LORD your G.
28. 2 I sit (in) the seat of God, in the midst of
28. 2, 6 set thine heart as the heart of God
28. 9 before him that slayeth thee, I (am) God
28. 13 Thou hast been in Eden the garden of G.
28. 14 thou wast upon the holy mountain of G.
28. 16 as profane out of the mountain of God
28. 26 shall know that I (am) the LORD their G.
31. 8 The cedars in the garden of God could
31. 8 nor any tree in the garden of God was
31. 9 the trees..that (were) in the garden of G.
34. 24 the LORD will be their God, and my ser.
34. 30 that I the LORD their God (am) with them
34. 31 (and) I (am) your God, saith the LORD G.
36. 28 shall be my people, and I will be your G.
37. 23 they be my people, and I will be their G.
37. 27 I will be their God, and they shall be my
39. 22 I (am) the LORD their God from that day
39. 28 they know that I (am) the LORD their God
40. 2 In the visions of God brought he me into
43. 2 the glory of the God of Israel came from

Eze. 44. 2 the God of Israel, hath entered in by it
Dan. 1. 2 part of the vessels of the house of God
1. 2 which he carried..to the house of his god
1. 2 brought into the treasure house of his god
1. 9 God had brought Daniel into favour and
1. 17 God gave them knowledge and skill in
9. 3 I set my face unto the Lord God, to seek
9. 4 I prayed unto the LORD my God, and
9. 9 To the Lord our God (belong) mercies
9. 10 we obeyed the voice of the LORD our G.
9. 11 in the law of Moses the servant of God
9. 13 not our prayer before the LORD our God
9. 14 our God (is) righteous in all his works
9. 15 now, O Lord our God, that hast brought
9. 17 O our God, hear the prayer of thy servant
9. 18 O my God, incline thine ear, and hear
9. 19 defer not, for thine own sake, O my God
9. 20 my God for the holy mountain of my God
10. 12 and to chasten thyself before thy God,
11. 32 people that do know their God shall be
11. 37 Neither shall he regard the God of his
Hos. 1. 7 will save them by the LORD their God
2. 23 and they shall say, (Thou art) my God
3. 5 seek the LORD their God, and David their
4. 1 nor knowledge of God in the land
4. 6 thou hast forgotten the law of thy God
4. 12 have gone a whoring from under their G.
5. 4 frame their doings to turn unto their G.
6. 6 and the knowledge of God more than
7. 10 they do not return to the LORD their God
8. 2 shall cry unto me, My God, we know thee
8. 6 workman made it; therefore it (is) not G.
9. 1 thou hast gone a whoring from thy God
9. 8 watchman of Ephraim (was) with my God
9. 8 (and) hatred in the house of his God
9. 17 My God will cast them away, because
12. 3 by his strength he had power with God
12. 5 the LORD God of hosts; the LORD (is) his
12. 6 turn thou to thy God: keep mercy and
12. 6 and wait on thy God continually
12. 9 the LORD thy God from the land of Egypt
13. 4 the LORD thy God from the land of Egypt
13. 4 and thou shalt know no god but me: for
13. 16 for she hath rebelled against her God
14. 1 return unto the LORD thy God; for thou
Joel 1. 13 come, lie all night..ministers of my God
1. 13 is withholden from the house of your God
1. 14 (into) the house of the LORD your God, and
1. 16 and gladness from the house of our God
2. 13 turn unto the LORD your God: for he (is)
2. 14 a drink offering unto the LORD your God
2. 17 say among the people, Where (is) their G.?
2. 23 Be glad..and rejoice in the LORD your G.
2. 26 and praise the name of the LORD your G.
2. 27 (that) I (am) the LORD your God, and none
3. 17 I (am) the LORD your God dwelling in Zion
Amos 2. 8 condemned (in) the house of their God
3. 13 Hear..saith the LORD God, the God of h.
4. 11 as God overthrew Sodom and Gomorrah
4. 12 prepare to meet thy God, O Israel
4. 13 The LORD, The God of hosts, (is) his name
5. 14 the God of hosts, shall be with you, as ye
5. 15 the LORD God of hosts will be gracious
5. 16 the God of hosts, the LORD, saith thus
5. 26 your images, the star of your God, which
5. 27 the LORD, whose name (is) The God of h.
6. 8 saith the LORD the God of hosts, I abhor
6. 14 saith the LORD the God of hosts; and they
8. 14 that swear..and say, Thy God, O Dan
9. 15 I have given them, saith the LORD thy G.
Jon. 1. 5 and cried every man unto his god, and c.
1. 6 call upon thy God, if so be that God will
1. 9 the God of heaven, which hath made the
2. 1 Jonah prayed unto the LORD his God out
2. 6 thou brought up my life..O LORD my G.
3. 5 the people of Nineveh believed God, and
3. 8 let man and beast..cry mightily unto God
3. 9 Who can tell (if) God will turn and repent
3. 10 God saw their works, that they turned
3. 10 God repented of the evil, that he had said
4. 6 the LORD God prepared a gourd, and
4. 7 God prepared a worm when the morning
4. 8 that God prepared a vehement east wind
4. 9 God said to Jonah, Doest thou well to be
Mic. 3. 7 ashamed..for (there is) no answer of God
4. 2 and to the house of the God of Jacob
4. 5 will walk every one in the name of his god
4. 5 will walk in the name of the LORD our G.
5. 4 majesty of the name of the LORD his God
6. 6 (and) bow myself before the high God?
6. 8 and to walk humbly with thy God?
7. 7 wait for the God of my salvation: my G.
7. 10 Where is the LORD thy God? mine eyes
7. 17 they shall be afraid of the LORD our God
Hab. 1. 12 O LORD my God, mine Holy One? we
3. 18 I will joy in the God of my salvation
Zeph. 2. 7 their God shall visit them, and turn away
2. 9 saith the LORD of hosts, the God of Israel
3. 2 trusted not..she drew not near to her G.
3. 17 thy God in the midst of thee (is) mighty
Hag. 1. 12 obeyed the voice of the LORD their God
1. 12 as the LORD their God had sent him, and
1. 14 the house of the LORD of hosts, their God
Zech. 6. 15 obey the voice of the LORD your God
8. 8 and I will be their God, in truth and
8. 23 for we have heard (that) God (is) with
9. 7 he that remaineth..(shall be) for our God
9. 16 their God shall save them in that day as
10. 6 I (am) the LORD their God, and will hear
11. 4 Thus saith the LORD my God; Feed the
12. 5 strength in the LORD of hosts their God
12. 8 the house of David (shall be) as God, as

Zech. 13. 9 and they shall say, The LORD (is) my God
14. 5 my God shall come, (and) all the saints
Mal. 2. 16 the God of Israel, saith that he hateth
2. 17 or, Where (is) the God of judgment?
3. 8 Will a man rob God? Yet ye have robbed
3. 14 Ye have said, It (is) vain to serve God
3. 15 (they that) tempt God are even delivered
3. 18 between him that serveth God and him

5. *God, object of worship,* אֱלוֹהַּ *eloah.*

Deut. 32. 15 he forsook God (which) made him, and
32. 17 They sacrificed unto devils, not to God
2 Ch. 32. 15 for no God of any nation or kingdom
Neh. 9. 17 thou (art) a God ready to pardon, gracio.
Job 3. 4 let not God regard it from above, neither
3. 23 (given) to a man..whom God hath hedged
4. 9 By the blast of God they perish, and by
4. 17 Shall mortal man be more just than God
5. 17 happy (is) the man whom God correcteth
6. 4 the terrors of God do set themselves in
6. 8 that God would grant (me) the thing that
6. 9 that it would please God to destroy me
9. 13 (If) God will not withdraw his anger, the
10. 2 I will say unto God, Do not condemn me
11. 5 oh that God would speak, and open his
11. 6 that God exacteth of thee (less) than thi.
11. 7 Canst thou by searching find out God?
12. 4 who calleth upon God, and he answereth
12. 6 into whose hand God bringeth (abund.)
15. 8 Hast thou heard the secret of God? and
16. 20 (but) mine eye poureth out (tears) unto G.
16. 21 that one might plead for a man with God
19. 6 Know now that God hath overthrown me
19. 21 for the hand of God hath touched me
19. 26 destroy..yet in my flesh shall I see God
21. 9 neither (is) the rod of God upon them
21. 19 God layeth up his iniquity for his child.
22. 12 (Is) not God in the height of heaven? and
22. 26 and shalt lift up thy face unto God
24. 12 crieth..yet God layeth not folly (to them)
27. 3 and the spirit of God (is) in my nostrils
27. 8 hath gained, when God taketh away his
27. 10 Almighty? will he always call upon God?
29. 2 as (in) the days (when) God preserved me
29. 4 the secret of God (was) upon my tabernacle
31. 2 what portion of God (is there) from above?
31. 6 weighed..that God may know mine integ.
33. 12 I will answer thee, that God is greater
33. 26 He shall pray unto God, and he will be
35. 10 none saith, Where (is) God my maker
36. 2 that (I have) yet to speak on God's behalf
37. 15 Dost thou know when God disposed them
37. 22 Fair weather..with God (is) terrible maj.
39. 17 God hath deprived her of wisdom, neith.
40. 2 he that reproveth God, let him answer
Psa. 18. 31 For who (is) God save the LORD? or who
50. 22 Now consider this, ye that forget God, lest
114. 7 Tremble..at the presence of the God of
139. 19 Surely thou wilt slay the wicked, O God
Prov. 30. 5 Every word of God (is) pure: he (is) a shi.
Isa. 44. 8 Is there a God beside me? yea, (there is)
Dan. 11. 37 nor regard any god: for he shall magnify
11. 38 shall he honour the God of forces: and
11. 39 Thus shall he do..with a strange god
Hab. 1. 11 (imputing) this his power unto his god
3. 3 God came from Teman, and the Holy One

6. *Jehovah,* יְהוִֹה [read by Jews *elohim*, prob. *Yahweh*].

Gen. 15. 2 Abram said, Lord GOD, what wilt thou
15. 8 he said, Lord GOD, whereby shall I know
Deut. 3. 24 O Lord GOD, thou hast begun to show thy
9. 26 O Lord GOD, destroy not thy people and
Josh. 7. 7 Joshua said, Alas, O Lord GOD, wherefore
Judg. 6. 22 Gideon said, Alas, O Lord GOD! for bec.
16. 28 O Lord GOD, remember me, I pray thee
2 Sa. 7. 18 he said, Who (am) I, O Lord GOD? and
7. 19 yet a small thing in thy sight, O Lord GOD
7. 19 (is) this the manner of man, O Lord GOD?
7. 20 for thou, Lord GOD, knowest thy servant
7. 28 now, O Lord GOD, thou (art) that God
7. 29 thou, O Lord GOD, hast spoken (it): and
1 Ki. 2. 26 thou barest the ark of the Lord GOD bef.
8. 53 our fathers out of Egypt, O Lord GOD
Psa. 68. 20 unto GOD the Lord (belong) the issues
69. 6 O Lord GOD of hosts, be ashamed for my
71. 5 For thou (art) my hope, O Lord GOD: (th.
71. 16 I will go in the strength of the Lord GOD
73. 28 I have put my trust in the Lord GOD, that
109. 21 do thou for me, O GOD the Lord, for thy
141. 8 mine eyes (are) unto thee, O GOD the Lord
Isa. 3. 15 What mean ye..saith the Lord GOD of
7. 7 Thus saith the Lord GOD, It shall not
10. 23 For the Lord GOD of hosts shall make a
10. 24 thus saith the Lord GOD of hosts, O my
22. 5 a day of..perplexity by the Lord GOD of
22. 12 in that day did the Lord GOD of hosts call
22. 14 Surely this..saith the Lord GOD of hosts
22. 15 Thus saith the Lord GOD of hosts, Go, get
25. 8 the Lord GOD will wipe away tears from
28. 16 thus saith the Lord GOD, Behold, I lay in
28. 22 I have heard from the Lord GOD of hosts
30. 15 thus saith the Lord GOD, the Holy One of
40. 10 the Lord GOD will come with strong (hand
48. 16 now the Lord GOD, and his spirit, hath
49. 22 Thus saith the Lord GOD, Behold, I will
50. 4 The Lord GOD hath given me the tongue
50. 5 The Lord GOD hath opened mine ear, and
50. 7 the Lord GOD will help me; therefore
50. 9 the Lord GOD will help me; who (is) he
52. 4 thus saith the Lord GOD, My people went
56. 8 The Lord GOD which gathereth the outc.
61. 1 The spirit of the Lord GOD (is) upon me
61. 11 so the LORD God will cause righteousness

Isa. 65. 13 thus saith the Lord GOD, Behold, my ser
65. 15 the Lord GOD shall slay thee, and call his
Jer. 1. 6 Then said I, Ah, Lord GOD! behold, I can.
2. 19 my fear (is) not in thee, saith the Lord G.
2. 22 iniquity is marked..saith the Lord GOD
4. 10 Then said I, Ah, Lord GOD! surely thou
7. 20 thus saith the Lord GOD; Behold, mine
14. 13 Then said I, Ah, Lord GOD! behold, the
32. 17 Ah Lord GOD! behold, thou hast made the
32. 25 O Lord GOD, Buy thee the field for money
44. 26 land of Egypt, saying, The Lord GOD liv.
46. 10 this (is) the day of the Lord GOD of hosts
46. 10 the Lord GOD of hosts hath a sacrifice in
49. 5 I will bring a fear..saith the Lord GOD
50. 25 this (is) the work of the Lord GOD of hosts
50. 31 I (am) against thee..saith the Lord GOD
Eze. 2. 4 say unto them, Thus saith the Lord GOD
3. 11 tell them, Thus saith the Lord GOD, whet.
3. 27 say unto them, Thus saith the Lord GOD
4. 14 Then said I, Ah Lord GOD! behold, my
5. 5 Thus saith the Lord GOD; This (is) Jerus.
5. 7 thus saith the Lord GOD; Because ye
5. 8 thus saith the Lord GOD; Behold, I, (even)
5. 11 Wherefore, (as) I live, saith the Lord GOD
6. 3 mountains..hear the word of the Lord G.
6. 3 Thus saith the Lord GOD to the mountains
6. 11 Thus saith the Lord GOD; Smite with thine
7. 2 thus saith the Lord GOD unto the land of
7. 5 Thus saith the Lord GOD; An evil, an
8. 1 the hand of the Lord GOD fell there upon
9. 8 Ah Lord GOD! wilt thou destroy all the
11. 7 thus saith the Lord GOD, Your slain, whom
11. 8 I will bring a sword..saith the Lord GOD
11. 13 Ah Lord GOD! wilt thou make a full end
11. 16 Thus saith the Lord GOD; Although I
11. 17 Thus saith the Lord GOD; I will even
11. 21 I will recompense..saith the Lord GOD
12. 10 thou unto them, Thus saith the Lord GOD
12. 19 Thus saith the Lord GOD of the inhabit.
12. 23 Thus saith the Lord GOD; I will make
12. 25 and will perform it, saith the Lord GOD
12. 28 Thus saith the Lord GOD; There shall
12. 28 word..shall be done, saith the Lord GOD
13. 3 Thus saith the Lord GOD; Woe unto the
13. 8 thus saith the Lord GOD; Because ye have
13. 8 I (am) against you, saith the Lord GOD
13. 9 and ye shall know that I (am) the Lord G.
13. 13 thus saith the Lord GOD; I will even
13. 16 and (there is) no peace, saith the Lord G.
13. 18 Thus saith the Lord GOD; Woe to the (w.)
13. 20 thus saith the Lord GOD; Behold, I (am)
14. 4 Thus saith the Lord GOD; Every man of
14. 6 Thus saith the Lord GOD; Repent, and
14. 11 and I may be their GOD, saith the Lord G.
14. 14 by their righteousness, saith the Lord GOD
14. 16, 18, 20 (as) I live, saith the Lord GOD, they
14. 21 thus saith the Lord GOD; How much more
14. 23 that I have done in it, saith the Lord G.
15. 6 thus saith the Lord GOD; As the vine
15. 8 I will make the land..saith the Lord G.
16. 3 Thus saith the Lord GOD unto Jerusalem
16. 8 a covenant with thee, saith the Lord G.
16. 14 I had put upon thee, saith the Lord GOD
16. 19 and (thus) it was, saith the Lord GOD
16. 23 woe, woe unto thee! saith the Lord G.
16. 30 How weak is thine heart, saith the Lord G.
16. 36 Thus saith the Lord GOD; Because thy
16. 43 I..will recompense..saith the Lord GOD
16. 48 (As) I live, saith the Lord GOD, Sodom
16. 59 thus saith the Lord GOD; I will even
16. 63 that thou hast done, saith the Lord GOD
17. 3 Thus saith the Lord GOD; A great eagle
17. 9 Thus saith the Lord GOD; Shall it pros.?
17. 16 (As) I live, saith the Lord GOD, surely
17. 19 thus saith the Lord GOD; (As) I live, su.
17. 22 Thus saith the Lord GOD; I will also take
18. 3 (As) I live, saith the Lord GOD, ye shall
18. 9 he shall surely live, saith the Lord GOD
18. 23 Have I any pleasure..saith the Lord G.
18. 30 I will judge you..saith the Lord GOD
18. 32 I have no pleasure..saith the Lord GOD
20. 3 Thus saith the Lord GOD; Are ye come to
20. 3 (As) I live, saith the Lord GOD, I will not
20. 5 Thus saith the Lord GOD; In the day
20. 27 Thus saith the Lord GOD; Yet in this
20. 30 Thus saith the Lord GOD; Are ye pollut.
20. 31 (As) I live, saith the Lord GOD, I will not
20. 33 (As) I live, saith the Lord GOD, surely
20. 36 will I plead with you, saith the Lord G.
20. 39 O house of Israel, thus saith the Lord G.
20. 40 in mine holy mountain..saith the Lo. G.
20. 44 O ye house of Israel, saith the Lord GOD
20. 47 Thus saith the Lord GOD; Behold, I will
20. 49 Then said I, Ah Lord GOD! they say of
21. 7 behold, it cometh..saith the Lord GOD
21. 13 it shall be no (more), saith the Lord GOD
21. 24 thus saith the Lord GOD; Because ye have
21. 26 Thus saith the Lord GOD; Remove the
21. 28 Thus saith the Lord GOD concerning the
22. 3 Thus saith the Lord GOD; The city shed.
22. 12 and hast forgotten me, saith the Lord G.
22. 19 thus saith the Lord GOD; Because ye are
22. 28 Thus saith the Lord GOD, when the LORD
22. 31 have I recompensed..saith the Lord GOD
23. 22 O Aholibah, thus saith the Lord GOD
23. 28 For thus saith the Lord GOD; Behold, I
23. 32 Thus saith the Lord GOD; Thou shalt
23. 34 for I have spoken (it), saith the Lord G.
23. 35 thus saith the Lord GOD; Because thou
23. 46 thus saith the Lord GOD; I will bring up
23. 49 and ye shall know that I (am) the Lo. G.
24. 3 Thus saith the Lord GOD; Set on a pot

Eze. 24. 6, 9 thus saith the Lord GOD; Woe to the
24. 14 shall they judge thee, saith the Lord G.
24. 21 Thus saith the Lord GOD; Behold, I will
24. 24 ye shall know that I (am) the Lord GOD
25. 3 of the Lord GOD; Thus saith the Lord G.
25. 6 thus saith the Lord GOD; Because thou
25. 8 Thus saith the Lord GOD; Because that
25. 12 Thus saith the Lord GOD; Because that
25. 13 thus saith the Lord GOD; I will also
25. 14 they shall know my..saith the Lord GOD
25. 15 Thus saith the Lord GOD; Because the
25. 16 thus saith the Lord GOD; Behold, I will
26. 3 thus saith the Lord GOD; Behold, I (am)
26. 5 I have spoken (it), saith the Lord GOD
26. 7 thus saith the Lord GOD; Behold, I will
26. 14 the Lord have spoken (it), saith the L. G.
26. 15 Thus saith the Lord GOD to Tyrus; Shall
26. 19 thus saith the Lord GOD; When I shall
26. 21 never be found again, saith the Lord G.
27. 3 Thus saith the Lord GOD; O Tyrus, thou
28. 2 Thus saith the Lord GOD; Because thine
28. 6 thus saith the Lord GOD; Because thou
28. 10 for I have spoken (it), saith the Lord G.
28. 12 Thus saith the Lord GOD; Thou sealest
28. 22 Thus saith the Lord GOD; Behold, I (am)
28. 24 they shall know that I (am) the Lord G.
28. 25 Thus saith the Lord GOD; When I shall
29. 3 Thus saith the Lord GOD; Behold, I (am)
29. 8 thus saith the Lord GOD; Behold, I will
29. 13 thus saith the Lord GOD; At the end of
29. 16 they shall know that I (am) the Lord G.
29. 19 thus saith the Lord GOD; Behold, I will
29. 20 they wrought for me, saith the Lord GOD
30. 2 Thus saith the Lord GOD; Howl ye; Woe
30. 6 fall in it by the sword, saith the Lord G.
30. 10 Thus saith the Lord GOD; I will also make
30. 13 Thus saith the Lord GOD; I will also dest.
30. 22 thus saith the Lord GOD; Behold, I (am)
31. 10 thus saith the Lord GOD; Because thou
31. 15 Thus saith the Lord GOD; In the day when
31. 18 This (is) Pharaoh and..saith the Lord G.
32. 3 Thus saith the Lord GOD; I will therefore
32. 8 set darkness upon thy..saith the Lord G.
32. 11 thus saith the Lord GOD; The sword of
32. 14 rivers to run like oil, saith the Lord GOD
32. 16 for all her multitude, saith the Lord GOD
32. 31 army slain by..sword, saith the Lord G.
32. 32 and all his multitude, saith the Lord GOD
33. 11 (As) I live, saith the Lord GOD, I have no
33. 25 Thus saith the Lord GOD; Ye eat with
33. 27 Thus saith the Lord GOD; (As) I live
34. 2 Thus saith the Lord GOD unto the sheph.
34. 8 (As) I live, saith the Lord GOD, surely
34. 10 Thus saith the Lord GOD; Behold, I (am)
34. 11 thus saith the Lord GOD; Behold, I, (even)
34. 15 cause them to lie down, saith the Lord G.
34. 17 thus saith the Lord GOD; Behold, I judge
34. 20 thus saith the Lord GOD unto them; Be.
34. 30 Israel, (are) my people, saith the Lord G.
34. 31 (and) I (am) your God, saith the Lord GOD
35. 3 Thus saith the Lord GOD; Behold, O
35. 6 (as) I live, saith the Lord GOD, I will pr.
35. 11 (as) I live, saith the Lord GOD, I will even
35. 14 Thus saith the Lord GOD; When the wh.
36. 2 Thus saith the Lord GOD; Because the
36. 3 Thus saith the Lord GOD; Because they
36. 4 mountains..hear the word of the Lord G.
36. 4 Thus saith the Lord GOD to the mounta.
36. 5 thus saith the Lord GOD; Surely in the
36. 6 Thus saith the Lord GOD; Behold, I have
36. 7 thus saith the Lord GOD; I have lifted up
36. 13 Thus saith the Lord GOD; Because they
36. 14 neither bereave thy..saith the Lord GOD
36. 15 to fall any more, saith the Lord GOD
36. 22 Thus saith the Lord GOD; I do not (this)
36. 23 know..I (am) the LORD, saith the Lord G.
36. 32 Not for your sakes..saith the Lord GOD
36. 33 Thus saith the Lord GOD; In the day that
36. 37 Thus saith the Lord GOD; I will yet
37. 3 And I answered, O Lord GOD, thou know.
37. 5 Thus saith the Lord GOD unto these bones
37. 9 Thus saith the Lord GOD; Come from the
37. 12 Thus saith the Lord GOD; Behold, O my
37. 19, 21 Thus saith the Lord GOD; Behold, I
38. 3 Thus saith the Lord GOD; Behold, I (am)
38. 10 Thus saith the Lord GOD; It shall also
38. 14 Thus saith the Lord GOD; In that day
38. 17 Thus saith the Lord GOD; (Art) thou he
38. 18 it shall come to pass..saith the Lord GOD
38. 21 for a sword against him..saith the Lord G.
39. 1 Thus saith the Lord GOD; Behold, I (am)
39. 5 for I have spoken (it), saith the Lord GOD
39. 8 Behold, it is come..saith the Lord GOD
39. 10 those that robbed them, saith the Lord G.
39. 13 I shall be glorified, saith the Lord GOD
39. 17 thou son of man, thus saith the Lord G.
39. 20 with all men of war, saith the Lord GOD
39. 25 thus saith the Lord GOD; Now will I br.
39. 29 poured out my spirit..saith the Lord G.
43. 18 Son of man, thus saith the Lord GOD
43. 19 to minister unto me, saith the Lord GOD
43. 27 and I will accept you, saith the Lord GOD
44. 6 Thus saith the Lord GOD; O ye house of
44. 9 Thus saith the Lord GOD; No stranger
44. 12 I lifted up mine hand..saith the Lord G.
44. 15 and they shall stand..saith the Lord GOD
44. 27 offer his sin offering, saith the Lord GOD
45. 9 Thus saith the Lord GOD; Let it suffice
45. 9 and execute judgment..saith the Lord G.
45. 15 to make reconciliation..saith the Lord G.
45. 18 Thus saith the Lord GOD; In the first
46. 1 Thus saith the Lord GOD; The gate of

Eze. 46. 16 Thus saith the Lord GOD; If the prince)
47. 13 Thus saith the Lord GOD; This (shall be
47. 23 there shall ye give..saith the Lord GOD
48. 29 these..their portions, saith the Lord G.
Amos 1. 8 remnant..shall perish, saith the Lord G.
3. 7 Surely the Lord GOD will do nothing, but
3. 8 the Lord GOD hath spoken, who can but
3. 11 Thus saith the Lord GOD; An adversary
3. 13 Hear ye, and testify..saith the Lord GOD
4. 2 The Lord GOD hath sworn by his holiness
4. 5 for this liketh you..saith the Lord GOD
5. 3 thus saith the Lord GOD; The city that
6. 8 The Lord GOD hath sworn by himself
7. 1 Thus hath the Lord GOD showed unto me
7. 2 then I said, O Lord GOD, forgive, I bese.
7. 4 Thus hath the Lord GOD showed unto me
7. 4 behold, the Lord GOD called to contend
7. 5 Then said I, O Lord GOD, cease, I beseech
7. 6 This also shall not be, saith the Lord G.
8. 1 Thus hath the Lord GOD showed unto me
8. 3 howlings in that day, saith the Lord GOD
8. 9 it shall come to pass..saith the Lord GOD
8. 11 the days come, saith the Lord GOD, that
9. 5 the Lord GOD of hosts (is) he that touch.
9. 8 the eyes of the Lord GOD (are) upon the
Obad. 1 Thus saith the Lord GOD concerning Ed.
Mic. 1. 2 let the Lord GOD be witness against you
Zeph. 1. 7 Hold thy peace at the..of the Lord GOD
Zech. 9. 14 The Lord GOD shall blow the trumpet

7. *A rock,* צוּר *tsur.*

Isa. 44. 8 yea, (there is) no God; I know not (any)

8. *God, a god, object of worship,* θεός *theos.*

Matt. 1. 23 Emmanuel..which..interpreted, is, God
3. 9 God is able of these stones to raise up
3. 16 the spirit of God descending like a dove
4. 3 If thou be the son of God, command that
4. 4 that proceedeth out of the mouth of God
4. 6 If thou be the Son of God, cast thyself
4. 7 Thou shalt not tempt the Lord thy God
4. 10 Thou shalt worship the Lord thy God, and
5. 8 the pure in heart..they shall see God
5. 9 they shall be called the children of God
5. 34 neither by heaven; for it is God's throne
6. 24 Ye cannot serve God and mammon
6. 30 If God so clothe the grass of the field
6. 33 seek ye first the kingdom of God, and his
8. 29 to do with thee, Jesus, thou son of God?
9. 8 they marvelled and glorified God, which
12. 4 How he entered into the house of God, and
12. 28 if I cast out devils by the spirit of God
12. 28 then the kingdom of God is come unto
14. 33 saying, Of a truth thou art the Son of God
15. 3 transgress the commandment of God by
15. 4 For God commanded, saying, Honour thy
15. 6 have ye made the commandment of God
15. 31 to see: and they glorified the God of Israel
16. 16 art the Christ, the Son of the living God
16. 23 savourest not the things that be of God
19. 6 What therefore God hath joined together
19. 17 none good but one, (that is), God: but if
19. 24 rich man to enter into the kingdom of G.
19. 26 but with God all things are possible
21. 12 Jesus went into the temple of God, and
21. 31 go into the kingdom of God before you
21. 43 The kingdom of God shall be taken from
22. 16 thou art true, and teachest the way of G.
22. 21 and unto God the things that are God's
22. 29 Ye do err, not knowing the..power of G.
22. 30 but are as the angels of God in heaven
22. 31 that which was spoken unto you by God
22. 32 God of A...God of Isaac..God of Jacob
22. 32 God is not the God of the dead, but of
22. 37 Thou shalt love the Lord thy God with
23. 22 sweareth by the throne of God, and by
26. 61 I am able to destroy the temple of God
26. 63 I adjure thee by the living God, that thou
26. 63 whether thou be the Christ, the Son of G.
27. 40 If thou be the Son of God, come down
27. 43 He trusted in God; let him deliver him
27. 43 for he said, I am the son of God
27. 46 that is to say, My God! My God! why hast
27. 54 saying, Truly this was the Son of God
Mark 1. 1 gospel of Jesus Christ, the Son of God
1. 14 preaching the gospel of the kingdom of G.
1. 15 the kingdom of God is at hand: repent
1. 24 know..who thou art, the Holy One of G.
2. 7 Why..who can forgive sins but God only?
2. 12 all amazed, and glorified God, saying, We
2. 26 How he went into the house of God in
3. 11 and cried, saying, Thou art the Son of G.
3. 35 For whosoever shall do the will of God
4. 11 know the mystery of the kingdom of God
4. 26 So is the kingdom of God, as if a man
4. 30 shall we liken the kingdom of God? or
5. 7 Jesus, (thou) Son of the most high God?
5. 7 I adjure thee by God, that thou torment
7. 8 laying aside the commandment of God
7. 9 ye reject the commandment of God, that
7. 13 Making the word of God of none effect
8. 33 savourest not the things that be of God
9. 1 till they have seen the kingdom of God
9. 47 to enter into the kingdom of God with
10. 6 But..God made them male and female
10. 9 What therefore God hath joined together
10. 14 Suffer..for of such is the kingdom of God
10. 15 shall not receive the kingdom of God as
10. 18 (there is) none good but one, (that is), God
10. 23 have riches enter into the kingdom of G.!
10. 24 in riches to enter into the kingdom of G.!
10. 25 rich man to enter into the kingdom of G.

Mark 10. 27 but not with God: for with God all things
11. 22 Jesus answering saith..Have faith in G.
12. 14 but teachest the way of God in truth: Is
12. 17 and to God the things that are God's
12. 24 because ye know not..the power of God?
12. 26 how in the bush God spake unto him, say
12. 26 God of Abraham..God of Isaac..God of,
12. 27 He is not the God of the dead, but the G.
12. 29 O Israel; The Lord our God is one Lord
12. 30 thou shalt love the Lord thy God with all
12. 32 hast said the truth: for there is one God
12. 34 Thou art not far from the kingdom of G.
13. 19 which God created unto this time, neither
14. 25 I drink it new in the kingdom of God
15. 34 which is, being interpreted, My G.! my G.!
15. 39 he said, Truly this man was the Son of G.
15. 43 which also waited for the kingdom of God
16. 19 and sat on the right hand of God
Luke 1. 6 both righteous before God, walking in all
1. 8 executed the priest's office before God
1. 16 many..shall he turn to the Lord their G.
1. 19 stand in the presence of God; and am
1. 26 the angel Gabriel was sent from God unto
1. 30 for thou hast found favour with God
1. 32 God shall give unto him the throne of
1. 35 holy thing..shall be called the Son of G.
1. 37 For with God nothing shall be impossible
1. 47 my spirit hath rejoiced in God my Saviour
1. 64 opened..and he spake, and praised God
1. 68 Blessed (be) the Lord God of Israel; for
1. 78 Through the tender mercy of our God
2. 13 the heavenly host praising God, and say.
2. 14 Glory to God in the highest, and on earth
2. 20 the shepherds returned..praising God for
2. 28 Then took he him..and blessed God, and
2. 40 and the grace of God was upon him
2. 52 and in favour with God and man
3. 2 word of God came unto John the son of
3. 6 all flesh shall see the salvation of God
3. 8 God is able..to raise up children unto A.
3. 38 was..Adam, which was (the son) of God
4. 3 If thou be the son of God command this
4. 4 by bread alone, but by every word of G.
4. 8 Thou shalt worship the Lord thy God
4. 9 If thou be the Son of God, cast thyself
4. 12 Thou shalt not tempt the Lord thy God
4. 34 I know thee..the Holy One of God
4. 41 Thou art Christ, the Son of God. And he
4. 43 I must preach the kingdom of God to
5. 1 pressed..to hear the word of God, he
5. 21 Who can forgive sins but God alone?
5. 25 departed to his own house, glorifying G.
5. 26 were all amazed, and they glorified God
6. 4 went into the house of God, and did take
6. 12 and continued all night in prayer to God
6. 20 Blessed..for yours is the kingdom of God
7. 16 and they glorified God, saying, That a
7. 16 and, That God hath visited his people
7. 28 he that is least in the kingdom of God is
7. 29 the publicans, justified God, being bap.
7. 30 and lawyers rejected the counsel of God
8. 1 glad tidings of the kingdom of God: and
8. 10 the mysteries of the kingdom of God: but
8. 11 the parable..The seed is the word of God
8. 21 which hear the word of God, and do it
8. 28 Jesus, (thou) Son of God most high? I
8. 39 how great things God hath done unto
9. 2 to preach the kingdom of God, and to
9. 11 spake unto them of the kingdom of God
9. 20 Peter answering said, The Christ of God
9. 27 not taste..till they see the kingdom of G.
9. 43 all amazed at the mighty power of God
9. 60 go thou and preach the kingdom of God
9. 62 looking back, is fit for the kingdom of God
10. 9, 11 kingdom of God is come nigh unto you
10. 27 Thou shalt love the Lord thy God with all
11. 20 I with the finger of God cast out devils
11. 20 the kingdom of God is come upon you
11. 28 they that hear the word of God, and keep
11. 42 pass over judgment and the love of God
11. 49 Therefore also said the wisdom of God, I
12. 6 not one of them is forgotten before God
12. 8 also confess before the angels of God
12. 9 shall be denied before the angels of God
12. 20 God said..(Thou) fool, this night thy soul
12. 21 layeth up..and is not rich toward God
12. 24 God feedeth them: how much more are
12. 28 If then God so clothe the grass, which is
12. 31 rather seek ye the kingdom of God; and
13. 13 she was made straight, and glorified God
13. 18 Unto what is the kingdom of God like?
13. 20 Whereunto..I liken the kingdom of God?
13. 28 see Abraham..in the kingdom of God
13. 29 and shall sit down in the kingdom of God
14. 15 shall eat bread in the kingdom of God
15. 10 in the presence of the angels of God
16. 13 Ye cannot serve God and mammon
16. 15 men; but God knoweth your hearts: for
16. 15 that..is abomination in the sight of God
16. 16 the kingdom of God is preached, and
17. 15 and with a loud voice glorified God
17. 18 that returned to give glory to God, save
17. 20 when the kingdom of God should come
17. 20 The kingdom of God cometh not with
17. 21 the kingdom of God is within you
18. 2 a judge, which feared not God, neither
18. 4 Though I fear not God, nor regard man
18. 7 shall not God avenge his own elect, which
18. 11 God, I thank thee, that I am not as other
18. 13 Saying, God be merciful to me a sinner
18. 16 children..of such is the kingdom of God
18. 17 shall not receive the kingdom of God as
Luke 18. 19 none (is) good, save one, (that is), God
18. 24 have riches enter into the kingdom of G!
18. 25 rich man to enter into the kingdom of G.
18. 27 impossible with men are possible with G.
18. 29 or children, for the kingdom of God's sake
18. 43 immediately..followed him, glorifying G.
18. 43 when they saw (it), gave praise unto God
19. 11 kingdom of G. should immediately appear
19. 37 disciples began to rejoice and praise G.
20. 21 but teachest the way of God truly
20. 25 and unto God the things which be God's
20. 36 the children of God, being the children
20. 37 he calleth the Lord the God of Abraham
20. 37 the God of Isaac, and the God of Jacob
20 38 he is not a God of the dead, but of the
21. 4 have .cast in unto the offerings of God
21. 31 that the kingdom of God is nigh at hand
22. 16 it be fulfilled in the kingdom of God
22. 18 until the kingdom of God shall come
22. 69 sit on the right hand of the power of G.
22. 70 said they..Art thou then the Son of God?
23 35 save .if he be Christ, the chosen of God
23. 40 Dost not thou fear God, seeing thou art
23. 47 he glorified God, saying, Certainly this
23. 51 himself waited for the kingdom of God
24 19 mighty in deed and word before God and
24. 53 in the temple, praising and blessing God
John 1. 1 Word was with God, and the Word was G.
1. 2 The same was in the beginning with God
1. 6 There was a man sent from God, whose
1. 12 gave he power to become the sons of God
1. 13 flesh, nor of the will of man, but of God
1. 18 No man hath seen God at any time; the
1. 29 Behold the Lamb of God, which taketh
1. 34 bare record that this is the Son of God
1. 36 looking..he saith, Behold the Lamb of G!
1. 49 thou art the Son of God; thou art the K.
1. 51 angels of God ascending and descending
3. 2 that thou art a teacher come from God
3. 2 that thou doest, except God be with him
3. 3 he cannot see the kingdom of God
3. 5 he cannot enter into the kingdom of God
3. 16 God so loved the world, that he gave his
3. 17 God sent not his Son into the world to
3. 18 the name of the only begotten Son of God
3. 21 manifest, that they are wrought in God
3. 33 He..hath set to his seal that God is true
3. 34 God hath sent speaketh the words of God
3. 34 God giveth not the spirit by measure
3. 36 but the wrath of God abideth on him
4. 10 If thou knewest the gift of God, and who
4. 24 God (is) a spirit: and they that worship
5. 18 because he..said also that God was his
5. 18 Father, making himself equal with God
5. 25 shall hear the voice of the Son of God
5. 42 that ye have not the love of God in you
5. 44 not the honour that (cometh) from God
6. 27 for him hath God the Father sealed
6. 28 do, that we might work the works of God?
6. 29 This is the work of God, that ye believe
6. 33 the bread of God is he which cometh down
6. 45 And they shall be all taught of God. Every
6. 46 save he which is of God, he hath seen the
6. 69 art that Christ, the Son of the living God
7. 17 whether it be of God, or (whether) I spe.
8. 40 told..the truth, which I have heard of G.
8. 41 said they..we have one Father, (even) G.
8. 42 If God were your Father, ye would love
8. 42 I proceeded forth and came from God
8. 47 He that is of God heareth God's words
8. 47 hear (them) not, because ye are not of G.
8. 54 of whom ye say, that he is your God
9. 3 the works of God should be made mani.
9. 16 This man is not of God, because he keep.
9. 24 Give God the praise: we know that this
9, 29 We know that God spake unto Moses
9. 31 we know that God heareth not sinners
9. 33 If this man were not of God, he could do
9. 35 Dost thou believe on the Son of God?
10. 33 that thou, being a man, makest thyself G.
10. 35 unto whom the word of God came, and the
10. 36 because I said, I am the Son of God?
11. 4 for the glory of God, that the Son of God
11. 22 wilt ask of God, God will give (it) thee
11. 27 the Son of God, which should come into
11. 40 thou shouldest see the glory of God?
11. 52 the children of God that were scattered
12. 43 praise of men more than the praise of G.
13. 3 he was come from God, and went to God
13. 31 the Son..glorified, and God is glorified in
13. 32 If God be glorified in him, God shall also
14. 1 ye believe in God, believe also in me
16. 2 will think that he doeth God service
16. 27 have believed that I came out from God
16. 30 believe that thou camest forth from God
17. 3 they might know thee the only true God
19. 7 because he made himself the Son of God
20. 17 your Father; and (to) my God, and your G.
20. 28 and said unto him, My Lord and my God
20. 31 that Jesus is the Christ, the Son of God
21. 19 by what death he should glorify God. And
Acts 1. 3 things pertaining to the kingdom of God
2. 11 in our tongues the wonderful works of G.
2. 17 come to pass in the last days, saith God
2. 22 man approved of God among you by mir.
2. 22 which God did by him in the midst of you
2. 23 by the..counsel and foreknowledge of G.
2. 24 Whom God hath raised up, having loosed
2. 30 knowing that God had sworn with an oath
2. 32 This Jesus hath God raised up, whereof
2. 33 being by the right hand of God exalted
2. 36 God hath made that same Jesus, whom
Acts 2. 39 as many as the Lord our God shall call
2. 47 Praising God, and having favour with all
3. 8 walking, and leaping, and praising God
3. 9 people saw him walking and praising God
3. 13 The God of Abraham..the God of our fa.
3. 15 whom God hath raised from the dead
3. 18 those things, which God before had
3. 21 which God hath spoken by the mouth of
3. 22 A prophet shall the Lord your God raise
3. 25 covenant which God made with our fath.
3. 26 God, having raised up his Son Jesus, sent
4. 10 whom God raised from the dead..by him
4. 19 Whether it be right in the sight of God to
4. 19 unto you more than unto God, judge ye
4. 21 all..glorified God for that which was done
4. 24 lifted up their voice to God with one acc.
4. 24 Lord, thou (art) God, which hast made h.
4. 31 they spake the word of God with boldness
5. 4 thou hast not lied unto men, but unto G.
5. 29 We ought to obey God rather than men
5. 30 The God of our fathers raised up Jesus
5. 31 Him hath God exalted with his right ha.
5. 32 also the Holy Ghost, whom God hath giv.
5. 39 if it be of God, ye cannot overthrow it
6. 2 that we should leave the word of God
6. 7 the word of God increased; and the nu.
6. 11 blasphemous words against Mos., and..G.
7. 2 The God of glory appeared unto our fath.
7. 6 God spake on this wise, That his seed
7. 7 nation..in bondage will I judge, said God
7. 9 sold Joseph into Egypt: but God was with
7. 17 the time..which God had sworn to Abra.
7. 25 how that God by his hand would deliver
7. 32 I (am) the God of thy fathers, the God of
7. 32 the God of Isaac, and the God of Jacob
7. 35 the same did God send (to be) a ruler and
7. 37 A prophet shall the Lord your God raise
7. 42 God turned, and gave them up to worship
7. 43 the star of your god Remphan, figures
7. 45 Gentiles, whom God drave out before the
7. 46 Who found favour before God, and desi.
7. 46 to find a tabernacle for the God of Jacob
7. 55 looked up..and saw the glory of God, and
7. 55 Jesus standing on the right hand of God
7. 56 man standing on the right hand of God
8. 10 This man is the great power of God
8. 12 the things concerning the kingdom of G.
8. 14 Samaria had received the word of God
8. 20 that the gift of God may be purchased
8. 21 thy heart is not right in the sight of God
8. 22 Repent therefore..and pray God, if per.
8. 37 I believe that Jesus C. is the Son of God;
9. 20 preached Christ..that he is the Son of G.
10. 2 one that feared God with all his house
10. 2 to the people, and prayed to God alway
10. 3 saw..an angel of God coming in to him
10. 4 are come up for a memorial before God
10. 15 What God hath cleansed..call not thou
10. 22 one that feareth God, and of good report
10. 28 God hath showed me that I should not
10. 31 are had in remembrance in the sight of G.
10. 33 are we all here present before God, to
10. 33 things that are commanded thee of God
10. 34 I perceive that God is no respecter of pe.
10. 38 How God anointed Jesus of Nazareth with
10. 38 and healing all..for God was with him
10. 40 Him God raised up the third day, and
10. 41 but unto witnesses chosen before of God
10. 42 he which was ordained of God..the judge
10. 46 them speak with tongues, and magnify G.
11. 1 Gentiles had also received the word of G.
11. 9 What God hath cleansed..call not thou
11. 17 as God gave them the like gift as..unto
11. 17 what was I, that I could withstand God?
11. 18 they held their peace, and glorified God
11. 18 Then hath God also to the Gentiles gran.
11. 23 Who, when he..had seen the grace of G.
12. 5 but prayer was made..unto God for him
12. 22 (It is) the voice of a god, and not of a man
12. 23 smote him, because he gave not God the
12. 24 But the word of God grew and multiplied
13. 5 preached the word of God in the synago.
13. 7 and desired to hear the word of God
13. 16 Men of Israel, and ye that fear God, give
13. 17 The God of this people of Israel chose our
13. 21 God gave unto them Saul the son of Cis
13. 23 Of this man's seed hath God, according to
13. 26 and whosoever among you feareth God
13. 30 But God raised him from the dead
13. 33 God hath fulfilled the same unto us their
13. 36 served his..generation by the will of God
13. 37 But he, whom G. raised again, saw no corr.
13. 43 persuaded..continue in the grace of God
13. 44 whole city together to hear the word of G.
13. 46 It was necessary that the word of God
14. 15 from these vanities unto the living God
14. 22 tribulation enter into the kingdom of G.
14. 26 been recommended to the grace of God
14. 27 rehearsed all that God had done with th.
15. 4 declared all things that God had done
15. 7 good while ago God made choice among
15. 8 God, which knoweth the hearts, bare them
15. 10 why tempt ye God, to put a yoke upon the
15. 12 God had wrought among the Gentiles by
15. 14 God at the first did visit the Gentiles, to
15. 18 Known unto God are all his works from
15. 19 from among the Gentiles are turned to G.
15. 40 by the brethren unto the grace of God
16. 14 a certain woman..which worshipped God
16. 17 are the servants of the most high God
16. 25 Silas prayed, and sang praises unto God
16. 34 believing in God with all his house

Acts 17. 13 word of God was preached of Paul at B.
17. 23 this inscription, TO THE UNKNOWN GOD
17. 24 God that made the world and all things
17. 29 as we are the offspring of God, we ought
17. 30 the times of this ignorance God winked
18. 7 (one) that worshipped God, whose house
18. 11 teaching the word of God among them
18. 13 men to worship God contrary to the law
18. 21 I will return again unto you, if God will
18. 26 unto him the way of God more perfectly
19. 8 the things concerning the kingdom of G.
19. 11 God wrought special miracles by the han.
20. 21 repentance toward God, and faith toward
20. 24 testify the gospel of the grace of God
20. 25 I have gone preaching the kingdom of G.
20. 27 declare unto you all the counsel of God
20. 28 to feed the church of God, which he hath
20. 32 I commend you to God, and to the word
21. 19 what things God had wrought among the
22. 3 zealous toward God, as ye all are this d.
22. 14 The God of our fathers hath chosen thee
23. 1 good conscience before God until this d.
23. 3 God shall smite thee, (thou) whited wall
23. 4 said, Revilest thou God's high priest?
24. 14 worship I the God of my fathers, believ.
24. 15 And have hope toward God, which they
24. 16 a conscience void of offence toward God
26. 6 the promise made of God unto our fath.
26. 8 that God should raise the dead?
26. 18 (from) the power of Satan unto God, that
26. 20 that they should repent and turn to God
26. 22 Having therefore obtained help of God
26. 29 I would to God, that not only thou, but
27. 23 stood by me this night the angel of God
27. 24 God hath given thee all them that sail
27. 25 I believe God, that it shall be even as
27. 35 thanks to God in presence of them all
28. 6 and said that he was a god
28. 15 Paul saw, he thanked God, and took cou.
28. 23 testified the kingdom of God, persuading
28. 28 salvation of God..sent unto the Gentiles
28. 31 Preaching the kingdom of God, and teach.
Rom. 1. 1 apostle, separated unto the gospel of God
1. 4 declared (to be) the Son of God with pow.
1. 7 To all that be in Rome, beloved of God
1. 7 peace from God our Father, and the L.
1. 8 I thank my God through Jesus Christ
1. 9 God is my witness, whom I serve with
1. 10 a prosperous journey by the will of God
1. 16 it is the power of God unto salvation to
1. 17 righteousness of God revealed from faith
1. 18 the wrath of God is revealed from heaven
1. 19 that which may be known of God is mani.
1. 19 for God hath showed (it) unto them
1. 21 knew God, they glorified (him) not as G.
1. 23 changed..glory of the uncorruptible God
1. 24 God also gave them up to uncleanness
1. 25 Who changed the truth of God into a lie
1. 26 God gave them up unto vile affections
1. 28 like to retain God in (their) knowledge
1. 28 God gave them over to a reprobate mind
1. 32 Who knowing the judgment of God
2. 2 the judgment of God is according to tru.
2. 3 thou shalt escape the judgment of God?
2. 4 that the goodness of God leadeth thee to
2. 5 of the righteous judgment of God
2. 11 there is no respect of persons with God
2. 13 hearers of the law (are) just before God
2. 16 In the day when God shall judge the
2. 17 and restest..and makest thy boast of G.
2. 23 breaking the law dishonourest thou G?
2. 24 the name of God is blasphemed among
2. 29 whose praise (is) not of men, but of God
3. 2 were committed the oracles of God
3. 3 make the faith of God without effect?
3. 4 yea, let God be true, but every man a li.
3. 5 commend the righteousness of God
3. 5 (Is) God unrighteous who taketh venge.
3. 6 for then how shall God judge the world?
3. 7 if the truth of God hath more abounded
3. 11 there is none that seeketh after God
3. 18 There is no fear of God before their
3. 19 the world may become guilty before God
3. 21 the righteousness of God without the law
3. 22 the righteousness of God (which is) by
3. 23 sinned, and come short of the glory of G.
3. 25 God hath set forth (to be) a propitiation
3. 25 are past, through the forbearance of God
3. 29 (Is he) the God of the Jews only? (is he)
3. 30 (it is) one God which shall justify the
4. 2 (whereof) to glory; but not before God
4. 3 Abraham believed God, and it was coun.
4. 6 unto whom God imputeth righteousness
4. 17 before him whom he believed, (even) G.
4. 20 He staggered not at the promise of God
4. 20 was strong in faith, giving glory to God
5. 1 we have peace with God through our L.
5. 2 and rejoice in hope of the glory of God
5. 5 the love of God is shed abroad in our h.
5. 8 But God commendeth his love toward us
5. 10 we were reconciled to God by the death
5. 11 we also joy in God through our Lord Jesus
5. 15 much more the grace of God, and the gift
6. 10 but in that he liveth, he liveth unto God
6. 11 but alive unto God through Jesus Christ
6. 13 but yield yourselves unto God, as those
6. 13 instruments of righteousness unto God
6. 17 But God be thanked, that ye were the ser.
6. 22 and become servants to God, ye have
6. 23 but the gift of God (is) eternal life through
7. 4 that we should bring forth fruit unto G.
7. 22 I delight in the law of God after the in.

Rom. 7. 25 I thank God through Jesus Christ our L.
7. 25 with the mind I..serve the law of God
8. 3 God, sending his own Son in the likeness
8. 7 the carnal mind (is) enmity against God
8. 7 for it is not subject to the law of God
8. 8 they that are in the flesh cannot please G.
8. 9 if so be that the spirit of God dwell in
8. 14 as many as are led by the spirit of God
8. 14 they are the sons of God
8. 16 witness..that we are the children of God
8. 17 heirs of God, and joint heirs with Christ
8. 19 for the manifestation of the sons of God
8. 21 the glorious liberty of the children of G.
8. 27 maketh intercession..according to..God
8. 28 work..for good to them that love God
8. 31 If God (be) for us, who (can be) against us?
8. 33 of God's elect? (It is) God that justifieth
8. 34 who is even at the right hand of God
8. 39 able to separate us from the love of God
9. 5 who is over all, God blessed for ever. A.
9. 6 Not as though the word of God hath taken
9. 8 these (are) not the children of God
9. 11 that the purpose of God according to
9. 14 What..(Is there) unrighteousness with G.?
9. 16 that runneth, but of God that showeth
9. 20 who art thou that repliest against God?
9. 22 if God, willing to show..wrath, and to
9. 26 be called the children of the living God
10. 1 my heart's desire and prayer to God for I.
10. 2 bear..record that they have a zeal of God
10. 3 they being ignorant of God's righteous.
10. 3 submitted..unto the righteousness of G.
10. 9 that God hath raised him from the dead
10. 17 by hearing, and hearing by the word of G.
11. 1 I say then, Hath God cast away his peo.?
11. 2 God hath not cast away his people which
11. 2 how he maketh intercession to God aga.
11. 8 God hath given them the spirit of slumber
11. 21 if God spared not the natural branches
11. 22 Behold..the goodness and severity of G.
11. 23 for God is able to graff them in again
11. 29 the gifts and calling of God (are) without
11. 30 as ye in times past have not believed God
11. 32 God hath concluded them all in unbelief
11. 33 both of the wisdom and knowledge of G.!
12. 1 I beseech you..by the mercies of God
12. 1 living sacrifice, holy, acceptable unto G.
12. 2 and acceptable, and perfect will of God
12. 3 according as God hath dealt to every man
13. 1 For there is no power but of God
13. 1 the powers that be are ordained of God
13. 2 Whosoever..resisteth the ordinance of G.
13. 4 he is the minister of God to thee for good
13. 4 he is the minister of God, a revenger to
13. 6 they are God's ministers, attending con.
14. 3 that eateth: for God hath received him
14. 4 he shall be holden up; for God is able to
14. 6 eateth to the Lord, for he giveth God th.
14. 6 to the Lord he eateth not, and giveth G.
14. 11 and every tongue shall confess to God
14. 12 every one..shall give account..to God
14. 17 the kingdom of God is not meat and drink
14. 18 (is) acceptable to God, and approved of
14. 20 For meat destroy not the work of God
14. 22 have (it) to thyself before God. Happy (is)
15. 5 the God of patience and consolation grant
15. 6 That ye may with one mind..glorify God
15. 7 Christ also received us, to the glory of G.
15. 8 of the circumcision for the truth of God
15. 9 that the Gentiles might glorify God for
15. 13 the God of hope fill you with all joy and
15. 15 of the grace that is given to me of God
15. 16 ministering the gospel of God, that the
15. 17 have..in those things which pertain to G.
15. 19 signs..by the power of the spirit of God
15. 30 strive together with me in..prayers to G.
15. 32 come unto you with joy by the will of G.
15. 33 Now the God of peace (be) with you all.
16. 20 the God of peace shall bruise Satan under
16. 26 the commandment of the everlasting G.
16. 27 To God only wise, (be) glory through Jesus
1 Co. 1. 1 Paul..an apostle..through the will of G.
1. 2 Unto the church of God which is at Cor.
1. 3 Grace..unto you, and peace, from God
1. 4 I thank my God always on your behalf
1. 4 for the grace of God which is given you
1. 9 God (is) faithful, by whom ye were called
1. 14 I thank God that I baptized none of you
1. 18 us which are saved it is the power of God
1. 20 hath not God made foolish the wisdom
1. 21 For after that in the wisdom of God
1. 21 the world by wisdom knew not God
1. 21 it pleased God by the foolishness of pre.
1. 24 the power of God, and the wisdom of God
1. 25 the foolishness of God is wiser than men
1. 25 the weakness of God is stronger than men
1. 27 God hath chosen the foolish things of the
1. 27 God hath chosen the weak things of the
1. 28 base things..hath God chosen..things
1. 30 who of God is made unto us wisdom, and
2. 1 declaring unto you the testimony of God
2. 5 should not stand..but in the power of G
2. 7 But we speak the wisdom of God in a
2. 7 which God ordained before the world
2. 9 things which God hath prepared for them
2. 10 God hath revealed (them) unto us by his
2. 10 all things, yea, the deep things of God
2. 11 knoweth no man, but the spirit of God
2. 12 but the spirit which is of God; that we
2. 12 things that are freely given to us of God
2. 14 not the things of the spirit of God: for
3. 6 I have planted..but God gave the incre.

1 Co. 3. 7 anything..but God, that giveth the incre.
3. 9 For we are labourers together with God
3. 9 ye are God's husbandry..God's building
3. 10 According to the grace of God which is
3. 16 Know ye not that ye are the temple of G.
3. 16 and (that) the spirit of God dwelleth in
3. 17 If any man defile the temple of God, him
3. 17 shall God destroy: for the temple of God
3. 19 wisdom of this world is foolishness..G.
3. 23 And ye are Christ's; and Christ (is) God's
4. 1 and stewards of the mysteries of God
4. 5 then shall every man have praise of God
4. 9 I think that God hath set forth us the
4. 20 the kingdom of God (is) not in word, but
5. 13 But them that are without God judgeth
6. 9 shall not inherit the kingdom of God?
6. 10 Nor thieves..shall inherit the kingd. of G.
6. 11 Lord Jesus, and by the spirit of our God
6. 13 but God shall destroy both it and them
6. 14 God hath both raised up the Lord, and
6. 19 Holy Ghost..in you, which ye have of God
6. 20 therefore glorify God in your body
6. 20 and in your spirit, which are God's
7. 7 But every man hath his proper gift of G.
7. 15 in such..but God hath called us to peace
7. 17 as God hath distributed to every man, as
7. 19 the keeping of the commandments of God
7. 24 let every man..therein abide with God
7. 40 I think also that I have the spirit of God
8. 3 if any man love God, the same is known
8. 4 and that (there is) none other God but
8. 6 But to us..one God, the Father, of whom
8. 8 But meat commendeth us not to God
9. 9 of the ox..Doth God take care for oxen?
9. 21 being not without law to God, but under
10. 5 with many..God was not well pleased
10. 13 God (is) faithful, who will not suffer you
10. 20 they sacrifice to devils, and not to God
10. 31 whatsoever ye do, do all to the glory of G.
10. 32 to the Gentiles, nor to the church of God
11. 3 the man; and the head of Christ (is) God
11. 7 as he is the image and glory of God: but
11. 12 so (is) the man..but all things of God
11. 13 is it comely that a woman pray unto God
11. 16 such custom, neither the churches of God
11. 22 despise ye the church of God, and shame
12. 3 that no man speaking by the spirit of God
12. 6 it is the same God which worketh all in
12. 18 now hath God set the members every one
12. 24 but God hath tempered the body together
12. 28 God hath set some in the church, first
14. 2 speaketh not unto men, but unto God
14. 18 I thank my God, I speak with tongues
14. 25 will worship God, and report that God is
14. 28 and let him speak to himself, and to God
14. 33 For God is not..of confusion, but of pe.
14. 36 What? came the word of God out from
15. 9 because I persecuted the church of God
15. 10 But by the grace of God I am what I am
15. 10 but the grace of God which was with me
15. 15 and we are found false witnesses of God
15. 15 because we have testified of God that he
15. 24 shall have delivered up the kingdom to G.
15. 28 Son..be subject..that God may be all in
15. 34 some have not the knowledge of God
15. 38 God giveth it a body as it hath pleased
15. 50 blood cannot inherit the kingdom of God
15. 57 thanks (be) to God, which giveth us the
2 Co. 1. 1 apostle of Jesus Christ by the will of G.
1. 1 unto the church of God which is at Corinth
1. 2 Grace (be) unto you and peace from God
1. 3 Blessed (be) God, even the Father of our
1. 3 the Father of mercies, and the God of all
1. 4 comfort..we ourselves are comforted of G.
1. 9 not trust..but in God which raiseth the
1. 12 by the grace of God, we have had our co.
1. 18 God (is) true, our word toward you was
1. 19 the Son of God, Jesus Christ, who was p.
1. 20 all the promises of God in him (are) yea
1. 20 in him Amen, unto the glory of God by
1. 21 he which stablisheth us with you..(is) G.
1. 23 Moreover I call God for a record upon my
2. 14 thanks (be) unto God, which always caus.
2. 15 we are unto God a sweet savour of Christ
2. 17 as many, which corrupt the word of God
2. 17 but as of God, in the sight of God speak
3. 3 but with the spirit of the living God; not
3. 4 such trust have we through Christ to God
3. 5 of ourselves; but our sufficiency (is) of G.
4. 2 nor handling the word of God deceitfully
4. 2 every man's conscience in the sight of G.
4. 4 In whom the god of this world hath blin.
4. 4 of Christ, who is the image of God, should
4. 6 God, who commanded the light to shine
4. 6 light of the knowledge of the glory of God
4. 7 the excellency of the power may be of G.
4. 15 grace might..redound to the glory of God
5. 1 we have a building of God, an house not
5. 5 he that hath wrought us..(is) God, who
5. 11 but we are made manifest unto God; and
5. 13 we be beside ourselves, (it is) to God
5. 18 all things (are) of God, who hath recon.
5. 19 To wit, that God was in Christ, reconcil.
5. 20 as though God did beseech (you) by us
5. 20 we pray (you)..be ye reconciled to God
5. 21 might be made the righteousness of God
6. 1 that ye receive not the grace of God in
6. 4 approving ourselves as..ministers of God
6. 7 the word of truth, by the power of God
6. 16 what agreement hath the temple of God
6. 16 for ye are the temple of the living God
6. 16 as God hath said..I will be their God

2 Co 7. 1 perfecting holiness in the fear of God
7. 6 God, that comforteth those that are cast
7. 12 that our care for you in the sight of God
8. 1 we do you to wit of the grace of God
8. 5 to the Lord, and unto us by the will of G.
8. 16 thanks (be) to God, which put the same
9. 7 necessity: for God loveth a cheerful giver
9. 8 God (is) able to make all grace abound
9. 11 causeth through us thanksgiving to God
9. 12 also by many thanksgivings unto God
9. 13 they glorify God for your professed sub.
9. 14 for the exceeding grace of God in you
9. 15 Thanks (be) unto God for his unspeakable
10. 4 not carnal, but mighty through God to
10. 5 exalteth itself against the knowledge of G.
10. 13 rule which God hath distributed to us
11. 7 I have preached to you the gospel of God
11. 11 because I love you not? God knoweth
11. 31 The God and Father of our Lord Jesus C.
12. 2, 3 out of the body, I cannot tell: God kno.
12. 19 Again..we speak before God in Christ
12. 21 lest, when I come again, my God will
13. 4 yet he liveth by the power of God
13. 4 with him by the power of God toward you
13. 7 Now I pray to God that ye do no evil
13. 11 the God of love and peace shall be with
13. 14 the love of God..(be) with you all. Amen
Gal. 1. 1 but by Jesus Christ, and God the Father
1. 3 Grace (be) to you and peace from God
1. 4 according to the will of God and our Fa.
1. 10 For do I now persuade men, or God?
1. 13 I persecuted the church of God, and was.
1. 15 when it pleased God, who separated me
1. 20 unto you, behold, before God, I lie not
1. 24 And they glorified God in me
2. 6 God accepteth no man's person
2. 19 dead to the law, that I might live unto G.
2. 20 I live by the faith of the Son of God, who
2. 21 I do not frustrate the grace of God: for
3. 6 Even as Abraham believed God, and it
3. 8 the Scripture, forseeing that God would
3. 11 is justified by the law in the sight of God
3. 17 that was confirmed before of God in Chr.
3. 18 but God gave (it) to Abraham by promise
3. 20 a mediator is not..of one; but God is one
3. 21 the law then against the promises of God?
3. 26 ye are all the children of God by faith in
4. 4 God sent forth his Son, made of a woman
4. 6 God hath sent forth the spirit of his Son
4. 7 if a son, then an heir of God through Ch.
4. 8 Howbeit then, when ye knew not God
4. 9 But now, after that ye have known God
4. 9 or rather are known of God, how turn ye
4. 14 received me as an angel of God..as Christ
5. 21 such..shall not inherit the kingdom of G.
6. 7 Be not deceived; God is not mocked
6. 16 and mercy, and upon the Israel of God
Eph. 1. 1 Paul, an apostle..by the will of God, to
1. 2 Grace (be) to you, and peace, from God
1. 3 Blessed (be) the God and Father of our
1. 17 That the God of our Lord Jesus Christ
2. 4 God, who is rich in mercy, for his great
2. 8 that not of yourselves; (it is) the gift of G.
2. 10 which God hath before ordained that we
2. 16 reconcile both unto God in one body by
2. 19 the saints, and of the household of God
2. 22 for an habitation of God through the sp.
3. 2 of the dispensation of the grace of God
3. 7 according to the gift of the grace of God
3. 9 which..hath been hid in God, who creat.
3. 10 be known..the manifold wisdom of God
3. 19 might be filled with all the fulness of God
4. 6 One God and Father of all, who (is) above
4. 13 and of the knowledge of the Son of God
4. 18 being alienated from the life of God thr.
4. 24 which after God is created in righteous.
4. 30 grieve not the Holy Spirit of God, whereby
4. 32 as God for Christ's sake hath forgiven you
5. 1 Be ye..followers of God, as dear children
5. 2 sacrifice to God for a sweet smelling sav.
5. 5 in the kingdom of Christ and of God
5. 6 cometh the wrath of God upon the chil.
5. 20 Giving thanks..unto God and the Father
5. 21 Submitting yourselves..in the fear of G.
6. 6 doing the will of God from the heart
6. 11 Put on the whole armour of God, that ye
6. 13 take unto you the whole armour of God
6. 17 sword of the spirit, which is the word of G.
6. 23 from God the Father and the Lord Jesus
Phil. 1. 2 Grace (be) unto you, and peace, from God
1. 3 I thank my God upon every remembrance
1. 8 God is my record, how greatly I long af.
1. 11 which are..unto the glory and praise of G.
1. 28 but to you of salvation, and that of God
2. 6 Who, being in the form of God, thought
2. 6 thought it not robbery to be equal with G.
2. 9 God also hath highly exalted him, and
2. 11 confess..to the glory of God the Father
2. 13 For it is God which worketh in you both
2. 15 That ye may be..the sons of God, witho.
2. 27 God had mercy on him; and not on him
3. 3 the circumcision, which worship God in
3. 9 the righteousness which is of God by fai.
3. 14 for the prize of the high calling of God
3. 15 God shall reveal even this unto you
3. 19 whose god (is their) belly, and (whose)
4. 6 your requests be made known unto God
4. 7 the peace of God, which passeth all und.
4. 9 and the God of peace shall be with you
4. 18 a sacrifice acceptable, well pleasing to G.
4. 19 But my God shall supply all your need
4. 20 unto God and our Father (be) glory for

Col. 1. 1 Paul, an apostle..by the will of God
1. 2 from God our Father and the Lord Jesus
1. 3 We give thanks to God and the Father of
1. 6 heard..and knew the grace of God in tr.
1. 10 and increasing in the knowledge of God
1. 15 Who is the image of the invisible God
1. 25 according to the dispensation of God wh.
1. 25 is given to me..to fulfil the word of God
1. 27 To whom God would make known what
2. 2 acknowledgment of the mystery of God
2. 12 through the faith of the operation of G.
2. 19 body..increaseth with the increase of G.
3. 1 Christ sitteth on the right hand of God
3. 3 and your life is hid with Christ in God
3. 6 wrath of God cometh on the children
3. 12 as the elect of God, holy and beloved
3. 15 let the peace of God rule in your hearts
3. 17 giving thanks to God and the Father
3. 22 but in singleness of heart, fearing God
4. 3 that God would open unto us a door of
4. 11 fellow workers unto the kingdom of God
4. 12 perfect and complete in all the will of G.
1 Th. 1. 1 unto the church..in God the Father and
1. 1 Grace (be) unto you, and peace, from G.
1. 2 We give thanks to God always for you
1. 3 work..in the sight of God and our Fath.
1. 4 Knowing, brethren..your election of G.
1. 8 in every place your faith to God-ward
1. 9 and how ye turned to God from idols
1. 9 to serve the living and true God
2. 2 in our God to speak..the gospel of God
2. 4 as we were allowed of God to be put in
2. 4 not as pleasing men, but God, which
2. 5 used we flattering words..God (is) witness
2. 8 not the gospel of God only, but also our
2. 9 we preached unto you the gospel of God
2. 10 Ye (are) witnesses, and God (also), how
2. 12 That ye would walk worthy of God, who
2. 13 For this cause also thank we God witho.
2. 13 when ye received the word of God which
2. 13 but, as it is in truth, the word of God
2. 14 became followers of the churches of God
2. 15 they please not God; and are contrary
3. 2 sent..our brother, and minister of God
3. 9 what thanks can we render to God again
3. 9 we joy for your sakes before our God
3. 11 Now God himself..direct our way unto
3. 13 unblameable in holiness before God
4. 1 how ye ought to walk and to please God
4. 3 this is the will of God..your sanctification
4. 5 even as the Gentiles which know not G.
4. 7 God hath not called us unto uncleanness
4. 8 He therefore..despiseth not man, but G.
4. 14 even so them also..will God bring with
4. 16 with a shout..and with the trump of G.
5. 9 For God hath not appointed us to wrath
5. 18 this is the will of God in Christ Jesus
5. 23 the very God of peace sanctify you wholly
2 Th 1. 1 in God our Father and the Lord Jesus C.
1. 2 from God our Father and the Lord Jesus
1. 3 We are bound to thank God always for
1. 4 we..glory in you in the churches of God
1. 5 token of the righteous judgment of God
1. 5 counted worthy of the kingdom of God
1. 6 Seeing (it is) a righteous thing with God
1. 8 vengeance on them that know not God
1. 11 that our God would count you worthy
1. 12 according to the grace of our God and
2. 4 that is called God, or that is worshipped
2. 4 he as God sitteth in the temple of God
2. 4 showing himself that he is God
2. 11 God shall send them strong delusion, that
2. 13 we are bound to give thanks alway to G.
2. 13 because God hath..chosen you to salvat.
2. 16 our Lord Jesus Christ himself, and God
3. 5 direct your hearts into the love of God
1 Ti. 1. 1 by the commandment of God our Saviour
1. 2 from God our Father and Jesus Christ
1. 11 the glorious gospel of the blessed God
1. 17 immortal, invisible, the only wise God
2. 3 acceptable in..sight of God our Saviour
2. 5 one God, and one mediator between G.
3. 5 shall he take care of the church of God?
3. 15 God, which is the church of the living G.
3. 16 God was manifest in the flesh, justified
4. 3 which God hath created to be received
4. 4 every creature of God (is) good, and
4. 5 sanctified by the word of God and prayer
4. 10 we trust in the living God, who is the
5. 4 that is good and acceptable before God
5. 5 widow indeed, and desolate, trusteth in G.
5. 21 I charge (thee) before God, and the Lord
6. 1 the name of God and (his) doctrine be not
6. 11 man of God, flee these things; and follow
6. 13 I give thee charge in the sight of God
6. 17 in the living God, who giveth us richly
2 Ti. 1. 1 an apostle of Jesus..by the will of God
1. 2 from God the Father and Christ Jesus
1. 3 I thank God, whom I serve from (my)
1. 6 that thou stir up the gift of God, which
1. 7 God hath not given us the spirit of fear
1. 8 the Gospel according to the power of G.
2. 9 but the word of God is not bound
2. 15 Study to show thyself approved unto G.
2. 19 foundation of God standeth sure
2. 25 if God peradventure will give..repentance
3. 17 the man of God may be perfect, through.
4. 1 I charge (thee) therefore before God, and
Titus 1. 1 a servant of God, and an apostle of Jesus
1. 1 according to the faith of God's elect, and
1. 2 which God, that cannot lie, promised be.
1. 3 to the commandment of God our Saviour

Titus 1. 4 from God the Father and the Lord Jesus
1. 7 must be blameless, as the steward of God
1. 16 They profess that they know God; but
2. 5 that the word of God be not blasphemed
2. 10 adorn the doctrine of God our Saviour
2. 11 the grace of God that bringeth salvation
2. 13 the glorious appearing of the great God
3. 4 the kindness and love of God our Saviour
3. 8 they which have believed in God might
Phm. 3 from God our Father and the Lord Jesus
4 I thank my God, making mention of thee
Heb. 1. 1 God, who at sundry times and in divers
1. 6 let all the angels of God worship him
1. 8 Thy throne, O God, (is) for ever and ever
1. 9 God, (even) thy God, hath anointed thee
2. 4 God also bearing (them) witness, both
2. 9 that he by the grace of God should taste
2. 13 and the children which God hath given
2. 17 high priest in things (pertaining) to God
3. 4 but he that built all things (is) God
3. 12 unbelief, in departing from the living God
4. 4 God did rest the seventh day from all his
4. 9 remaineth..a rest to the people of God
4. 10 from his own works, as God (did) from
4. 12 the word of God (is) quick, and powerful
4. 14 into the heavens, Jesus the Son of God
5. 1 for men in things (pertaining) to God
5. 4 but he that is called of God, as (was)
5. 10 Called of God an high priest after the
5. 12 first principles of the oracles of God
6. 1 from dead works, and of faith toward G.
6. 3 And this will we do, if God permit
6. 5 have tasted the good word of God, and
6. 6 crucify to themselves the Son of God
6. 7 the earth..receiveth blessing from God
6. 10 For God (is) not unrighteous to forget
6. 13 God made promise to Abraham, because
6. 17 Wherein God, willing more abundantly
6. 18 in which (it was) impossible for God to
7. 1 priest of the most high God, who met
7. 3 made like unto the Son of God; abideth
7. 19 by the which we draw nigh unto God
7. 25 to save them..that come unto God by
8. 10 I will be to them a God, and they shall
9. 14 who..offered himself without spot to G.
9. 14 from dead works to serve the living God!
9. 20 testament which God hath enjoined unto
9. 24 to appear in the presence of God for us
10. 7 said I, Lo, I come..to do thy will, O God
10. 9 said he, Lo, I come to do thy will, O God
10. 12 sat down on the right hand of God
10. 21 an high priest over the house of God
10. 29 hath trodden under foot the Son of God
10. 31 to fall into the hands of the living God
10. 36 after ye have done the will of God, ye
11. 3 worlds were framed by the word of God
11. 4 Abel offered unto God a more excellent
11. 4 was righteous, God testifying of his gifts
11. 5 not found, because God had translated
11. 5 he had this testimony, that he pleased G.
11. 6 that cometh to God must believe that he
11. 10 a city..whose builder and maker (is) God
11. 16 God is not ashamed to be called their God
11. 19 God (was) able to raise (him) up, even
11. 25 suffer affliction with the people of God
11. 40 God having provided some better thing
12. 2 at the right hand of the throne of God
12. 7 God dealeth with you as with sons
12. 15 lest any man fail of the grace of God
12. 22 and unto the city of the living God, the
12. 23 God the Judge of all, and to the spirits
12. 28 whereby we may serve God acceptably
12. 29 For our God (is) a consuming fire
13. 4 whoremongers and adulterers God will
13. 7 who have spoken unto you the word of G.
13. 15 let us offer the sacrifice of praise to God
13. 16 for with such sacrifices God is well plea.
13. 20 the God of peace, that brought again
Jas. 1. 1 James, a servant of God and of the Lord
1. 5 let him ask of God, that giveth to all
1. 13 Let no man say..I am tempted of God
1. 13 for God cannot be tempted with evil
1. 20 wrath..worketh not..righteousness of G.
1. 27 Pure religion and undefiled before God
2. 5 Hath not God chosen the poor of this w
2. 19 Thou believest that there is one God
2. 23 which saith, Abraham believed God, and
2. 23 and he was called the friend of God
3. 9 Therewith bless we God, even the Father
3. 9 which are made after the similitude of G.
4. 4 that the friendship..is enmity with God?
4. 4 a friend of the world is the enemy of God
4. 6 he saith, God resisteth the proud, but
4. 7 Submit yourselves therefore to God
4. 8 Draw nigh to God, and he will draw nigh
1 Pe. 1. 2 according to the foreknowledge of God
1. 3 Blessed (be) the God and Father of our L.
1. 5 Who are kept by the power of God thro.
1. 21 Who by him do believe in God, that rai.
1. 21 that your faith and hope might be in G.
1. 23 of incorruptible, by the word of God, wh.
2. 4 disallowed..of men, but chosen of God
2. 5 sacrifices, acceptable to God by Jesus Ch.
2. 10 not a people, but..now the people of God
2. 12 they may..glorify God in the day of visit.
2. 15 so is the will of God, that with well doing
2. 16 As free..but as the servants of God
2. 17 Honour all..Fear God. Honour the king
2. 19 if a man for conscience toward God end.
2. 20 it patiently, this (is) acceptable with God
3. 4 which is in the sight of God of great price
3. 5 the holy women also, who trusted in God

1 Pe. 3. 15 But sanctify the Lord God in your hearts
3. 17 better, if the will of God be so, that ye
3. 18 suffered..that he might bring us to God
3. 20 the long suffering of God waited in the
3. 21 answer of a good conscience toward God
3. 22 and is on the right hand of God; angels
4. 2 to the lusts of men, but to the will of G.
4. 6 but live according to God in the spirit
4. 10 good stewards of the manifold grace of G.
4. 11 If any man speak..as the oracles of God
4. 11 as of the ability which God giveth
4. 11 that God in all things may be glorified
4. 14 the spirit of glory and of God resteth
4. 16 but let him glorify God on this behalf
4. 17 judgment must begin at the house of God
4. 17 of them that obey not the gospel of God?
4. 19 that suffer according to the will of God
5. 2 Feed the flock of God which is among you
5. 5 God resisteth the proud, and giveth grace
5. 6 therefore under the mighty hand of God
5. 10 the God of all grace, who hath called us
5. 12 that this is the true grace of God wherein
2 Pe. 1. 1 through the righteousness of God and our
1. 2 multiplied..through the knowledge of G.
1. 17 he received from God the Father honour
1. 21 holy men of God spake..moved by the
2. 4 if God spared not the angels that sinned
3. 5 by the word of God the heavens were of
3. 12 hasting unto the coming of the day of G.
1 Jo. 1. 5 declare unto you, that God is light, and
2. 5 in him verily is the love of God perfected
2. 14 the word of God abideth in you, and ye
2. 17 he that doeth the will of God abideth for
3. 1 that we should be called the sons of God!
3. 2 Beloved, now are we the sons of God; and
3. 8 the Son of God was manifested, that he
3. 9 Whosoever is born of God doth not com.
3. 9 he cannot sin, because he is born of God.
3. 10 In this the children of God are manifest
3. 10 doeth not righteousness is not of God
3. 17 how dwelleth the love of God in him?
3. 20 God is greater than our heart, and know
3. 21 (then) have we confidence toward God
4. 1 try the spirits whether they are of God
4. 2 Hereby know ye the spirit of God
4. 2 Every spirit that confesseth..is of God
4. 3 spirit that confesseth not..is not of God
4. 4 Ye are of God, little children, and have
4. 6 we are of God: he that knoweth God he
4. 6 he that is not of God heareth not us
4. 7 let us love one another: for love is of G.
4. 7 loveth is born of God, and knoweth God
4. 8 that loveth not knoweth not God; for G.
4. 9 In this was manifested the love of God
4. 9 God sent his only begotten Son into the
4. 10 Herein is love, not that we loved God
4. 11 if God so loved us, we ought also to love
4. 12 No man hath seen God at any time
4. 12 If we love one another, God dwelleth in
4. 15 shall confess that Jesus is the Son of God
4. 15 God dwelleth in him; and he in God
4. 16 known..the love that God hath to us. G.
4. 16 in love dwelleth in God, and God in him
4. 20 If a man say, I love God, and hateth his
4. 20 how can he love God whom he hath not
4. 21 That he who loveth God love his brother
5. 1 Whosoever believeth..is born of God
5. 2 love the children of God, when we love G.
5. 3 For this is the love of God, that we keep
5. 4 whatsoever is born of God overcometh
5. 5 believeth that Jesus is the Son of God?
5. 9 witness of men, the witness of God is gr.
5. 9 this is the witness of God which he hath
5. 10 He that believeth on the Son of God hath
5. 10 he that believeth not God hath made him
5. 10 believeth not the record that God gave
5. 11 that God hath given to us eternal life
5. 12 he that hath not the Son of God hath not
5. 13, 13 believe on the name of the Son of G.
5. 18 that whosoever is born of God sinneth not
5. 18 he that is begotten of God keepeth hims.
5. 19 we know that we are of God, and the whole
5. 20 we know that the Son of God is come, and
5. 20 This is the true God, and eternal life
2 Jo. 3 mercy..peace, from God the Father, and
9 Whosoever transgresseth..hath not God
3 Jo. 11 Beloved..He that doeth good is of God
11 but he that doeth evil hath not seen God
Jude. 1 that are sanctified by G. the Father, and
4 turning the grace of our God into lasci.
4 denying the only Lord God, and our Lo.
21 Keep yourselves in the love of G., looking
25 To the only wise God our Saviour, (be)
Rev. 1. 1 which God gave unto him, to show unto
1. 2 Who bare record of the word of God, and
1. 6 hath made us kings and priests unto G.
1. 9 for the word of God, and for the testim.
2. 7 is in the midst of the paradise of God
2. 18 These things saith the Son of God, who
3. 1 he that hath the seven spirits of God, and
3. 2 not found thy works perfect before God
3. 12 make a pillar in the temple of my God
3. 12 I will write upon him the name of my G.
3. 12 and the name of the city of my God
3. 12 cometh down out of heaven from my G.
3. 14 the beginning of the creation of God
4. 5 lamps..which are the seven spirits of G.
4. 8 Holy, holy, holy, Lord God Almighty
5. 6 which are the seven spirits of God sent
5. 9 hast redeemed us to God by thy blood
5. 10 hast made us unto our God kings and
6. 9 that were slain for the word of God, and

Rev. 7. 2 angel..having the seal of the living God
7. 3 we have sealed the servants of our God
7. 10 Salvation to our God which sitteth upon
7. 11 fell..on their faces, and worshipped God
7. 12 (be) unto our God for ever and ever. Am.
7. 15 are they before the throne of God, and
7. 17 God shall wipe away all tears from their
8. 2 the seven angels which stood before God
8. 4 ascended up before God out of the ang.
9. 4 those men which have not the seal of G.
9. 13 of the golden altar which is before God
10. 7 the mystery of God should be finished
11. 1 Rise, and measure the temple of God
11. 4 These are..standing before the God of
11. 11 the spirit of life from God entered into
11. 13 and gave glory to the God of heaven
11. 16 which sat before God on their seats, fell
11. 16 upon their faces and worshipped God
11. 17 O Lord God Almighty, which art, and
11. 19 the temple of God was opened in hea.
12. 5 and her child was caught up unto God
12. 6 where she hath a place prepared of God
12. 10 strength, and the kingdom of our God
12. 10 which accused them before our God
12. 17 which keep the commandments of God
13. 6 opened his mouth in blasph. against G.
14. 4 first fruits unto God and to the Lamb
14. 5 are without fault before the throne of G.
14. 7 Fear God, and give glory to him; for the
14. 10 shall drink of the wine of the wrath of G.
14. 12 they that keep the commandments of G.
14. 19 the great winepress of the wrath of God
15. 1 for in them is filled up the wrath of God
15. 2 stand on the sea..having the harps of G.
15. 3 sing the song of Moses the servant of G.
15. 3 marvellous (are) thy works, Lord God A.
15. 7 seven golden vials full of the wrath of G.
15. 8 filled with smoke from the glory of God
16. 1 pour out the vials of the wrath of God
16. 7 Even so, Lord God Almighty, true and
16. 9 blasphemed the name of God, which hath
16. 11 And blasphemed the God of heaven beca.
16. 14 battle of that great day of God Almighty
16. 19 Babylon came in remembrance before G.
16. 21 and men blasphemed God because of the
17. 17 For God hath put in their hearts to fulfil
17. 17 until the words of God shall be fulfilled
18. 5 and God hath remembered her iniquities
18. 8 strong (is) the Lord God who judgeth her
18. 20 Rejoice..God hath avenged you on her
19. 1 honour, and power, unto the Lord our G.
19. 4 fell down and worshipped God that sat
19. 5 Praise our God, all ye his servants, and
19. 6 for the Lord God omnipotent reigneth
19. 9 saith..These are the true sayings of God
19. 10 And he said unto me..worship God; for
19. 13 and his name is called The Word of God
19. 15 the fierceness and wrath of Almighty G.
19. 17 Come..unto the supper of the great God
20. 4 for the word of God, and which had not
20. 6 they shall be priests of God and of Christ
20. 9 fire came down from God out of heaven
20. 12 And I saw the dead..stand before God
21. 2 coming down from God out of heaven
21. 3 the tabernacle of God (is) with men, and
21. 3 and God himself shall be..their God
21. 4 God shall wipe away all tears from their
21. 7 I will be his God, and he shall be my son
21. 10 city..descending out of heaven from God
21. 11 Having the glory of God: and her light
21. 22 the Lord God Almighty and the Lamb are
21. 23 the glory of God did lighten it, and the L.
22. 1 proceeding out of the throne of God and
22. 3 the throne of God..shall be in it; and
22. 5 for the Lord God giveth them light: and
22. 6; 22. 9; 22. 18; 22. 19.

9. *A daimon, demon, shade,* δαιμόνιον *daimonion.*
Acts 17. 18 seemeth..a setter forth of strange gods

10. *Lord, master,* κύριος *kurios.*
Acts 19. 20 So mightily grew the word of God and

GOD, to fight against —

1. *To fight with God,* θεομαχέω *theomacheō.*
Acts 23. 9 saying..let us not fight against God

2. *One fighting against God,* θεομάχος *theomachos.*
Acts 5. 39 lest..ye be found even to fight against G.

GOD, taught of —

God taught, θεοδίδακτος *theodidaktos.*
1 Th. 4. 9 ye..are taught of God to love one anoth.

GOD, given by inspiration of —

God breathed, θεόπνευστος *theopneustos.*
2 Ti. 3. 16 Scripture (is) given by inspiration of God

GOD, worshipper of —

One fearing or reverencing God, θεοσεβής *theoseb*
John 9. 31 but if any man be a worshipper of God

GOD, to be admonished of —

To warn by an oracle, χρηματίζω *chrēmatizō.*
Heb. 8. 5 Moses was admonished of God when he

GOD, answer of —

Oracular warning, χρηματισμός *chrēmatismos.*
Rom 11. 4 But what saith the answer of God unto

GOD, hater of —

God hater, θεοστυγής *theostugēs.*
Rom. 1. 30 Backbiters, haters of God, despiteful, pr.

GOD, lover of —

Lover of God, φιλόθεος *philotheos.*
2 Ti. 3. 4 lovers of pleasures more than lovers of G.

GOD forbid —

1. *Profanation! far be it!* חָלִילָה *chalilah.*
Gen. 44. 7 God forbid that thy servants should do
44. 17 God forbid that I should do so..the man
Josh 22. 29 God forbid that we should rebel against
24. 16 God forbid that we should forsake the L.
1 Sa. 12. 23 God forbid that I should sin against the
14. 45 God forbid: (as) the LORD liveth, there
20. 2 he said..God forbid; thou shalt not die
Job 27. 5 God forbid that I should justify you: till

2. *Let it not be!* μὴ γένοιτο *mē genoito.*
Luke 20. 16 when they heard (it), they said, God for.
Rom. 3. 4 God forbid: yea, let God be true, but
3. 6 God forbid: for then how shall God judge
3. 31 God forbid: yea, we establish the law
6. 2 God forbid. How shall we, that are dead
6. 15 What then? shall we sin..God forbid
7. 7 (Is) the law sin? God forbid. Nay, I had
7. 13 Was..good made death..God forbid
9. 14 unrighteousness with God? God forbid
11. 1 Hath God cast away his people? God for.
11. 11 stumbled that they should fall? God for.
1 Co. 6. 15 the members of an harlot? God forbid
Gal. 2. 17 Christ the minister of sin? God forbid
3. 21 against the promises of God? God forbid
6. 14 God forbid that I should glory, save in

GOD save —

To live, let live, give life, חָיָה *chayah.*
1 Sa. 10. 24 shouted, and said, God save the king
2 Sa. 16. 16 God save the king, God save the king
1 Ki. 1. 25 they eat..and say, God save king Adon.
1. 34 blow ye..and say, God save king Solomon
1. 39 all the people said, God save king Solom.
2 Ki. 11. 12 clapped..and said, God save the king
2 Ch. 23. 11 anointed him, and said, God save the ki.

GOD speed —

To rejoice, be of good cheer, χαίρω *chairō.*
2 John 10 receive..not..neither bid him God speed
11 he that biddeth him God speed is partak.

GOD, without —

Atheist, without a god, ἄθεος *atheos.*
Eph. 2. 12 having no hope, and without God in the

(GOD) ward, to —

Over against, מוּל *mul.*
Exod. 18. 19 Be thou for the people to God ward, that

GODDESS —

1. *Gods, a god, object of worship,* אֱלֹהִים *elohim.*
1 Ki. 11. 5, 33 Ashtoreth the goddess of the Zidonians

2. *Goddess,* θεά *thea.*
Acts 19. 27 that the temple of the great goddess Dia.
19. 35 a worshipper of the great [goddess] Diana
19. 37 nor yet blasphemers of your [goddess]

GODHEAD —

1. *The godhead, that which is divine,* τὸ θεῖον [*theios*].
Acts 17. 29 that the Godhead is like unto gold, or si.

2. *Divinity,* θειότης *theiotēs.*
Rom. 1. 20 his eternal power and Godhead; so that

3. *Deity,* θεότης *theotēs.*
Col. 2. 9 dwelleth all the fulness of the Godhead

GODLINESS —

1. *Piety, reverence,* εὐσέβεια *eusebeia.*
1 Ti. 2. 2 peaceable life in all godliness and honesty
3. 16 And..great is the mystery of godliness
4. 7 and exercise thyself (rather) unto godlin.
4. 8 but godliness is profitable unto all things
6. 3 the doctrine which is according to godli.
6. 5 supposing that gain is godliness: from
6. 6 godliness with contentment is great gain
6. 11 follow after righteousness, godliness, fai.
2 Ti. 3. 5 Having a form of godliness, but denying
Titus 1. 1 of the truth which is after godliness
2 Pe. 1. 3 things that (pertain) unto life and godli.
1. 6 patience; and to patience godliness
1. 7 And to godliness brotherly kindness; and
3. 11 ought ye to be in..conversation and god.

2. *Fear or worship of God,* θεοσέβεια *theosebeia.*
1 Ti. 2. 10 which becometh women professing godl.

GODLY —

1. *Kind,* חָסִיד *chasid.*
Psa. 4. 3 hath set apart him that is godly for him.
32. 6 For this shall every one that is godly pray

2. *God, of God,* אֱלֹהִים *elohim.*
Mal. 2. 15 That he might seek a godly seed. There.

3. *Pious, reverential,* εὐσεβής *eusebēs.*
2 Pe. 2. 9 The Lord knoweth how to deliver the g.

4. *Piously, reverentially,* εὐσεβῶς *eusebōs.*
2 Ti. 3. 12 all that will live godly in Christ Jesus
Titus 2. 12 should live soberly, righteously, and go.

5. *Of God,* θεοῦ *theou.*
2 Co. 1. 12 that in simplicity and godly sincerity
11. 2 jealous over you with godly jealousy
1 Ti. 1. 4 rather than godly edifying which is in f.

6. *According to God,* κατὰ θεόν *kata theon.*
2 Co. 7. 10 For godly sorrow worketh repentance to

GODLY man (or fear) —
Kind, חָסִיד *chasid*.
Psa. 12. 1 Help, LORD; for the godly man; He. 12. 28

GODLY manner, after a —
According to God, κατὰ θεόν *kata theon*.
2 Co. 7. 9 were made sorry after a godly manner

GODLY sort, after a —
1. *Worthy of God*, ἀξίως τοῦ θεοῦ *axiōs tou theou*.
3 John 6 bring forward..after a godly sort, thou

2. *According to God*, κατὰ θεόν *kata theon*.
2 Co. 7. 11 that ye sorrowed after a godly sort, what

GODS —
1. *Gods*, אֱלֹהִים *elohim*.
Gen. 3. 5 shall be as gods, knowing good and evil
31. 30 wherefore hast thou stolen my gods?
31. 32 With whomsoever thou findest thy gods
35. 2 Put away the strange gods that (are)
35. 4 strange gods which (were) in their hand
Exod 12. 12 against all the gods of Egypt I will exe.
20. 3 Thou shalt have no other gods before me
20. 23 Ye shall not make with me gods of silver
20. 23 neither shall ye make unto you gods of g.
22. 28 Thou shalt not revile the gods, nor curse
23. 13 no mention of the name of other gods
23. 24 Thou shalt not bow down to their gods
23. 32 shalt make no covenant..with their gods
23. 33 if thou serve their gods, it will surely be
32. 1, 23 make us gods, which shall go before
32. 4, 8 These (be) thy gods, O Israel, which
32. 31 this people..have made them gods of g.!
34. 15 gods, and do sacrifice unto their gods
34. 16 daughters go a whoring after their gods
34. 16 thy sons go a whoring after their gods
34. 17 Thou shalt make thee no molten gods
Lev. 19. 4 nor make to yourselves molten gods
Num 25. 2 unto the sacrifice of their gods: and the
25. 2 and the people..bowed down to their g.
Deut. 4. 28 serve gods, the work of men's hands, wood
5. 7 Thou shalt have no other gods before me
6. 14 shall not go after other gods, of the gods
7. 4 turn away..that they may serve other g.
7. 16 neither shalt thou serve their gods; for
7. 25 graven images of their gods shall ye burn
8. 19 walk after other gods, and serve them
10. 17 For the LORD your God (is) God of gods
11. 28 command..to go after other gods; 11. 16
12. 2 wherein the nations..served their gods
12. 3 hew down the graven images of their g.
12. 30 thou enquire not after their gods, saying
12. 30 How did these nations serve their gods?
12. 31 abomination..have they done unto their g.
12. 31 they have burnt in the fire to their gods
13. 2 saying, Let us go after other gods, which
13. 6, 13 saying, Let us go and serve other go.
13. 7 gods of the people which are round about
17. 3 And hath gone and served other gods, and
18. 20 shall speak in the name of other gods
20. 18 which they have done unto their gods; so
28. 14 not go aside..to go after other gods to
28. 36, 64 and there shalt thou serve other gods
29. 18 to go (and) serve the gods of these nations
29. 26 served other gods..gods whom they knew
30. 17 and worship other gods, and serve them
31. 16 a whoring after the gods of the strangers
31. 18 in that they are turned unto other gods
31. 20 then will they turn unto other gods, and
32. 17 They sacrificed..to gods whom they knew
32. 37 he shall say, Where (are) their gods, (their)
Josh 22. 22 The LORD God of gods, the LORD God of g.
23. 7 make mention of the name of their gods
23. 16 and have gone and served other gods, and
24. 2 fathers dwelt..and they served other gods
24. 14, 15 the gods which your fathers served
24. 15 or the gods of the Amorites, in whose
24. 16 said, God forbid that we..serve other g.
24. 20 serve strange gods, then will he turn and
24. 23 put away..the strange gods which (are)
Judg. 2. 3 and their gods shall be a snare unto you
2. 12 other gods, of the gods of the people that
2. 17 they went a whoring after other gods, and
2. 19 in following other gods to serve them, and
3. 6 gave..to their sons, and served their gods
5. 8 They chose new gods; then (was) war in
6. 10 fear not the gods of the Amorites, in
10. 6 served..the gods of Syria, and the gods
10. 6 gods of Moab, and the gods of the chil.
10. 6 the gods of the Philistines, and forsook
10. 13 ye have forsaken me, and served other g.
10. 14 cry unto the gods which ye have chosen
10. 16 put away the strange gods from among
17. 5 the man Micah had an house of gods, and
18. 24 Ye have taken away my gods which I
Ruth 1. 15 unto her people and unto her gods: return
1 Sa. 4. 8 out of the hand of these mighty gods?
4. 8 the gods that smote the Egyptians with
6. 5 from off your gods, and from off your la.
7. 3 put away the strange gods and Ashtaroth
8. 8 forsaken me, and served other gods, so do
17. 43 the Philistine cursed David by his gods
26. 19 driven me..saying, Go, serve other gods
28. 13 I saw gods ascending out of the earth
2 Sa. 7. 23 Egypt, (from) the nations and their gods?
1 Ki. 9. 6 and serve other gods, and worship them
9. 9 and have taken hold upon other gods
11. 2 will turn away your heart after their go.
11. 4 turned away his heart after other gods
11. 8 wives which burnt incense..unto their g.
1 Ki. 11. 10 that he should not go after other gods
12. 28 behold thy gods, O Israel, which brought
14. 9 hast gone and made thee other gods, and
18. 24 call ye on the name of your gods, and I
18. 25 call on the name of your gods, but put
19. 2 So let the gods do (to me), and more also
20. 10 The gods do so unto me, and more also, if
20. 23 Their gods (are) gods of the hills; theref.
2 Ki. 5. 17 neither burnt..sacrifice unto other gods
17. 7 that the children..had feared other gods
17. 29 every nation made gods of their own
17. 31 burnt their children in fire to..the gods
17. 33 served their own gods, after the manner
17. 35 Ye shall not fear other gods, nor bow yo.
17. 37 observe..and ye shall not fear other gods
17. 38 forget; neither shall ye fear other gods
18. 33 Hath any of the gods..delivered at all
18. 34 Where (are) the gods of Hamath, and of
18. 34 where (are) the gods of Sepharvaim, He.
18. 35 Who (are) they among all the gods of the
19. 12 Have the gods..delivered them which my
19. 18 cast their gods..for they were (no) gods
22. 17 and have burnt incense unto other gods
1 Ch. 5. 25 went a whoring after the gods of the pe.
10. 10 his armour in the house of their gods
14. 12 when they had left their gods there, Da.
16. 25 he also (is) to be feared above all gods
16. 26 For all the gods of the people (are) idols
2 Ch. 2. 5 for great (is) our God above all gods
7. 19 shall go and serve other gods, and worship
7. 22 laid hold on other gods, and worshipped
13. 8 calves, which Jeroboam made you for g.
13. 9 may be a priest of (them that are) no go.
25. 14 brought the gods of the children of Seir
25. 14 set them up (to be) his gods, and bowed
25. 15 Why hast thou sought after the gods of
25. 20 because they sought after the gods of E.
28. 23 he sacrificed unto the gods of Damascus
28. 23 the gods of the kings of Syria help them
28. 25 burn incense unto other gods, and prov.
32. 13 were the gods of the nations of those la.
32. 14 Who (was there) among all the gods of
32. 17 As the gods of the nations of (other) lands
32. 19 as against the gods of the people of the
33. 15 took away the strange gods, and the idol
34. 25 and have burned incense unto other gods
Ezra 1. 7 had put them in the house of his gods
Psa. 82. 1 God standeth..he judgeth among the g.
82. 6 I have said, Ye (are) gods; and all of you
86. 8 Among the gods (there is) none like unto
95. 3 the LORD (is)..a great King above all go.
96. 4 the LORD..(is) to be feared above all go.
96. 5 For all the gods of the nations (are) idols
97. 7 Confounded be all..worship him, all (ye) g.
97. 9 thou, LORD..art exalted far above all gods
135. 5 and (that) our Lord (is) above all gods
136. 2 O give thanks unto the God of gods: for
138. 1 before the gods will I sing praise unto
Isa. 21. 9 images of her gods he hath broken unto
36. 18 Hath any of the gods of the nations deli.
36. 19 Where (are) the gods of Hamath and Ar?.
36. 19 where (are) the gods of Sepharvaim? and
36. 20 Who (are they) among all the gods of
37. 12 Have the gods..delivered them which
37. 19 cast their gods..for they (were) no gods
41. 23 that we may know that ye (are) gods
42. 17 say to the molten images, Ye (are) our g
Jer. 1. 16 have burnt incense unto other gods, and
2. 11 changed (their) gods, which (are) yet no g.?
2. 28 But where (are) thy gods that thou hast
2. 28 number of thy cities are thy gods, O Jud.
5. 7 sworn by (them that are) no gods: when
5. 19 and served strange gods in your land, so
7. 6 neither walk after other gods to your hu.
7. 9 walk after other gods whom ye know not
7. 18 pour out drink offerings unto other gods
11. 10 they went after other gods to serve them
11. 12 go and cry unto the gods unto whom they
11. 13 number of thy cities were thy gods, O J.
13. 10 and walk after other gods, to serve them
16. 11 walked after other gods, and have served
16. 13 there shall ye serve other gods day and
16. 20 man make gods..and they (are) no gods?
19. 4 burnt incense in it unto other gods, wh.
19. 13 poured out drink offerings unto other g.
22. 9 and worshipped other gods, and served
25. 6 And go not after other gods to serve them
32. 29 poured out drink offerings unto other go.
35. 15 go not after other gods to serve them
43. 12 kindle a fire in the houses of the gods of
43. 13 the houses of the gods of the Egyptians
44. 3 to serve other gods, whom they knew not
44. 5 to burn no incense unto other gods
44. 8 burning incense unto other gods in the
44. 15 burnt incense unto other gods, and all
46. 25 No, and Pharaoh..with their gods, and
48. 35 and him that burneth incense to his gods
Dan. 11. 8 also carry captives into Egypt their gods
Hos. 3. 1 who look to other gods, and love flagons
14. 3 neither will we say..(Ye are) our gods
Nah. 1. 14 out of the house of thy gods will I cut
Zeph. 2. 11 he will famish all the gods of the earth

2. *God, a god, object of worship*, θεός *theos*.
John 10. 34 written in your law, I said, Ye are gods?
10. 35 he called them gods unto whom the word
Acts 7. 40 Make us gods to go before us: for (as for)
14. 11 gods are come down to us in the likeness
19. 26 they be no gods which are made with
1 Co. 8. 5 For though there be that are called gods
8. 5 as there be gods many, and lords many
Gal. 4. 8 unto them which by nature are no gods

3. *A little demon, deified spirit*, δαιμόνιον *daimonion*.
Acts 17. 18 to be a setter forth of strange gods

GOETH up, that —
A going up, ascent, מַעֲלֶה *maaleh*.
Josh 10. 10 along the way that goeth up to Beth-hor

GOETH, where —
Entrance, going in, מָבוֹא *mabo*.
Deut 11. 30 by the way where the sun goeth down, in

GOG, גּוֹג *high, mountain*.
1. A Reubenite, and grandson of Joel. B.C. 1600.
1 Ch. 5. 4 Shemaiah his son, G. his son, Sh. his son
2. A prince of Rosh, Meshek, Tubal, and Tiras, in ancient Scythia or Tartary.
Eze. 38. 2 Son of man, set thy face against G., the
38. 3 Behold, I (am) against thee, O G., the
38. 14 son of man, prophesy and say unto G.
38. 16 when I shall be sanctified in thee, O G.
38. 18 when G. shall come against the land of
39. 1 thou son of man, prophesy against G.
39. 1 Behold, I (am) against thee, O G., the
39. 11 I will give unto G. a place there of grav.
39. 11 there shall they bury G., and all his mul.
Rev. 20. 8 G. and Magog, to gather them together to

GOING —
1. *A step, going*, אָשֻׁר *ashur*.
Psa. 17. 5 Hold up my goings in thy paths, (that) my
40. 2 upon a rock, (and) established my goings
Prov 14. 15 the prudent (man) looketh well to his go.

2. *A going, way, company*, הֲלִיכָה *halikah*.
Psa. 68. 24 seen thy goings, O God; (even) the goings

3. *To go on*, יָלַךְ *yalak*.
2 Sa. 2. 19 in going he turned not to the right hand
2 Ch. 11. 4 and returned from going against Jeroboam
Prov 30. 29 go well, yea, four are comely in going

4. *Path, custom*, מַעְגָּלָה *magalah*.
Prov. 5. 21 the LORD, and he pondereth all his goings
Isa. 59. 8 and (there is) no judgment in their goings

5. *A step, going*, מִצְעָד *mitsad*.
Prov 20. 24 Man's goings (are) of the LORD; how can

6. *To go over or beyond*, עָבַר *abar*.
Job 33. 28 deliver his soul from going into the pit

7. *A step, foot*, פַּעַם *paam*.
Psa. 140. 4 who have purposed to overthrow my go.

8. *A step, pace*, צַעַד *tsaad*.
Job 34. 21 ways of man, and he seeth all his goings

9. *Stepping, going*, צְעָדָה *iseadah*.
2 Sa. 5. 24 when thou hearest the sound of a going
1 Ch. 14. 15 when thou shalt hear a sound of going in

GOING about —
To go or set round, נָקַף *naqaph*, 5.
Josh. 6. 11 compassed the city, going about (it) once

GOING down —
1. *To go in*, בּוֹא *bo*.
Gen. 15. 12 when the sun was going down, a deep
Exod 17. 12 steady until the going down of the sun
Deut 16. 6 at the going down of the sun, at the sea.
Josh 10. 27 at the time of the going down of the sun
1 Ki. 22. 36 about the going down of the sun, saying
2 Ch. 18. 34 about the time of the sun going down he

2. *To go down*, יָרַד *yarad*.
Job 33. 24 Deliver him from going down to the pit

3. *Going in, entrance*, מָבוֹא *mabo*.
Josh. 1. 4 sea toward the going down of the sun
Psa. 50. 1 of the sun unto the going down thereof
104. 19 the sun knoweth his going down
113. 3 the sun unto the going down of the same
Mal. 1. 11 unto the going down of the same, my na.

4. *Going down*, מוֹרָד *morad*.
Josh. 7. 5 smote them in the going down: where.
10. 11 (and) were in the going down to Beth-ho.
Jer. 48. 5 in the going down of Horonaim the ene.

5. *Going in or down*, מַעַל *meal*.
Dan. 6. 14 till the going down of the sun to deliver

GOING, to be —
To enter, πορεύομαι *poreuomai*.
Matt 28. 11 when they were going, behold, some of

GOING forth —
1. *To go out or forth*, יָצָא *yatsa*.
Isa. 13. 10 sun shall be darkened in his going forth

2. *A going out or forth*, מוֹצָא *motsa*.
Psa. 19. 6 going forth (is) from the end of the heav.
Eze. 44. 5 with every going forth of the sanctuary
Dan. 9. 25 from the going forth of the commandm.
Hos. 6. 3 going forth is prepared as the morning

3. *Outgoings*, תּוֹצָאוֹת *totsaoth*.
Num 34. 4 the going forth thereof shall be from the
34. 8 the goings forth of the border shall be to

GOING out —
1. *To go out or forth*, יָצָא *yatsa*.
Deut 33. 18 he said, Rejoice, Zebulun, in thy going o.
1 Sa. 29. 6 thy going out and thy coming in with me
2 Ki. 19. 27 thy going out, and thy coming in, and
Isa. 37. 28 thy going out, and thy coming in, and

2. *Going out or forth*, מוֹצָא *motsa*.
Num33. 2 Moses wrote their goings out according
33. 2 journeys according to their goings out
2 Sa. 3. 25 to know thy going out, and thy coming
Eze. 42. 11 their goings out (were) both according to
43. 11 the goings out thereof, and the comings

3. *Outgoings*, תּוֹצָאוֹת *totsaoth*.
Num34. 5, 12 goings out of it shall be at the..sea
34. 9 goings out of it shall be at Hazar-enan
Josh 15. 4 goings out of that coast were at the sea
15. 7 the goings out thereof were at En-rogel
15. 11 goings out of the border were at the sea
16. 3 and the goings out thereof are at the sea
16. 8 the goings out thereof were at the sea
18. 12 goings out thereof were at the wilderness
18. 14 goings out thereof were at Kirjath-baal
Eze. 48. 30 goings out of the city on the north side

GOING over —
To go over or beyond, עָבַר *abar*.
Num32. 7 from going over into the land which the

GOING to and fro,—
1. *To go about*, אָזַל *azal*, 4.
Eze. 27. 19 Dan also and Javan going to and fro occ.
2. *To go to and fro*, שׁוּט *shut*.
Job 1. 7 From going to and fro in the earth, and
2. 2 From going to and fro in the earth, and

GOING up —
1. *A going up, ascent*, מַעֲלֶה *maaleh*.
Josh 15. 7 that (is) before the going up to Adummi.
18. 17 (is) over against the going up of Adumm.
Judg. 1. 36 coast..(was) from the going up to Akra.
2 Ki. 9. 27 (they did so) at the going up to Gur, wh.
Neh.12. 37 at the going up of the wall, above the
Jer. 48. 5 For in the going up of Luhith continual
Eze. 40. 31, 34, 37 the going up to it (had) eight steps
2. *To go up*, עָלָה *alah*.
Neh. 3. 19 over against the going up to the armoury
3. *Upper chamber, gallery, ascent*, עֲלִיָּה *aliyyah*.
Neh. 3. 31 Miphkad, and to the going up of the
3. 32 between the going up of the corner unto

GOINGS forth —
Outgoings, מוֹצָאוֹת *motsaoth*.
Mic. 5. 2 whose goings forth (have been) from of

GO'-LAN, גּוֹלָן *circle*.
A Levitical city of Manasseh in Bashan, and one of the three cities of refuge E. of the Jordan. The village of *Nawa* on the E. border of *Jaulân* is much too far eastward to be Golan.
Deut. 4. 43 and G. in Bashan, of the Manassites
Josh.20. 8 G. in Bashan out of the tribe of Manass.
21. 27 out of..Manasseh, (they gave) G. in Bash.
1 Ch. 6. 71 Unto the sons of Gershom (were given)..G.

GOLD —
1. *Defence, wealth*, בֶּצֶר *betsar*.
Job 36. 19 not gold, nor all the forces of strength
2. *Defence, wealth*, בְּצַר *betser*.
Job 22. 24 shalt thou lay up gold as dust, and the
3. *Gold, (from its shining)*, דְּהַב *dehab*.
Ezra 5. 14 vessels also of gold and silver of the
7. 15 to carry the silver and gold, which the
7. 16 the silver and gold that thou canst find
7. 18 with the rest of the silver and the gold
Dan. 2. 32 This image's head (was) of fine gold, his
2. 35 clay, the brass, the silver, and the gold
2. 38 over them all. Thou(art)this head of gold
2. 45 brass, the clay, the silver, and the gold
3. 1 the king made an image of gold, whose
5. 4 praised the gods of gold, and of silver
5. 7 (have) a chain of gold about his neck,and
5. 16 (have) a chain of gold about thy neck,and
5. 23 hast praised the gods of silver, and gold
5. 29 (put) a chain of gold about his neck, and
4. *Gold (from its shining)*, זָהָב *zahab*.
Gen. 2. 11 whole land of Havilah, where (there is) g.
2. 12 the gold of that land (is) good: there (is)
13. 2 very rich in cattle, in silver, and in gold
24. 22 bracelets..of ten (shekels) weight of gold
24. 35 flocks, and herds, and silver, and gold
24. 53 jewels of silver, and jewels of gold, and
41. 42 and put a gold chain about his neck
44. 8 out of thy lord's house silver or gold?
Exod. 3. 22 of silver, and jewels of gold, and raiment
11. 2 borrow..jewels of silver, and jewels of g.
12. 35 of silver, and jewels of gold, and raiment
20. 23 neither shall ye make..you gods of gold
25. 3 take of them; gold, and silver, and brass
25. 11 And thou shalt overlay it with pure gold
25. 11 make upon it a crown of gold round abo.
25. 12 thou shalt cast four rings of gold for it
25. 13 make staves..and overlay them with g.
25. 17 thou shalt make a mercy seat (of) pure g.
25. 18 thou shalt make two cherubim (of) gold
25. 24 gold, and make thereto a crown of gold
25. 26 thou shalt make for it four rings of gold
25. 28 overlay them with gold, that the table
25. 29 (of) pure gold shalt thou make them
25. 31 shalt make a candlestick (of) pure gold
25. 36 it (shall be) one beaten work (of) pure g.
25. 38 snuff dishes..(shall be of) pure gold
25. 39 a talent of pure gold shall he make it
26. 6 thou shalt make fifty taches of gold, and
26. 29 with gold, and make their rings (of) gold

Exod26. 29 thou shalt overlay the bars with gold
26. 32 with gold: their hooks (shall be of) gold
26. 37 with gold, (and) their hooks (shall be of) g.
28. 5 they shall take gold, and blue, and pur.
28. 6 they shall make the ephod (of) gold, (of) b.
28. 8 gold, (of) blue, and purple, and scarlet
28. 11 make them to be set in ouches of gold
28. 13 And thou shalt make ouches (of) gold
28. 14 And two chains (of) pure gold at the ends
28. 15 (of) gold, (of) blue, and (of) purple, and
28. 20 shall be set in gold in their inclosings
28. 22 the ends (of) wreathen work (of) pure gold
28. 23 upon the breastplate two rings of gold
28. 24 shalt put the two wreathen (chains) of g.
28. 26 thou shalt make two rings of gold, and
28. 27 two (other) rings of gold thou shalt make
28. 33 bells of gold between them round about
28. 36 thou shalt make a plate (of) pure gold
30. 3 thou shalt overlay it with pure gold, the
30. 3 make unto it a crown of gold round about
30. 5 the staves..and overlay them with gold
31. 4 work in gold, and in silver, and in brass
32. 24 Whosoever hath any gold, let them break
32. 31 great sin, and have made them gods of g.!
35. 5 an offering..gold, and silver, and brass
35. 22 and rings, and tablets, all jewels of gold
35. 22 (offered) an offering of gold unto the LORD
35. 32 work in gold, and in silver, and in brass
36. 13 he made fifty taches of gold, and coupled
36. 34 with gold, and made their rings (of) gold
36. 34 and overlaid the bars with gold
36. 36 them with gold: their hooks (were of) g.
36. 38 their chapiters and their fillets with gold
37. 2 he overlaid it with pure gold within and
37. 2 made a crown of gold to it round about
37. 3 he cast for it four rings of gold, (to be set)
37. 4 made staves..and overlaid them with g.
37. 6 And he made the mercy seat (of) pure g.
37. 7 he made two cherubims (of) gold, beaten
37. 11 gold, and made thereunto a crown of g.
37. 12 and made a crown of gold for the border
37. 13 he cast for it four rings of gold, and put
37. 15 overlaid them with gold, to bear the tab.
37. 16 his covers to cover withal, (of) pure gold
37. 17 he made the candlesticks (of) pure gold
37. 22 all..(was) one beaten work (of) pure gold
37. 23 and his snuff dishes, (of) pure gold
37. 24 (Of) a talent of pure gold made he it, and
37. 26 he overlaid it with pure gold, (both) the
37. 26 made unto it a crown of gold round abo.
37. 27 he made two rings of gold for it under
37. 28 the staves..and overlaid them with gold
38. 24 the gold that was occupied for the work
38. 24 the gold of the offering, was twenty and
39. 2 he made the ephod (of) gold, blue, and
39. 3 they did beat the gold into thin plates
39. 5, 8 (of) gold, blue, and purple, and scarlet
39. 6 onyx stones inclosed in ouches of gold
39. 13 in ouches of gold in their inclosings
39. 15 the ends, (of) wreathen work (of) pure g.
39. 16 made two ouches (of) gold, and two gold
39. 17 they put the two wreathen chains of gold
39. 19 they made two rings of gold, and put
39. 25 they made bells (of) pure gold, and put
39. 30 the plate of the holy crown (of) pure go.
40. 5 thou shalt set the altar of gold for the
Num. 7. 14 One spoon of ten (shekels) of gold, full of
7. 20 One spoon of gold of ten (shekels), full
7. 84 twelve silver bowls, twelve spoons of go.
7. 86 the gold of the spoons (was) an hundred
8. 4 And this work..(was of) beaten gold, unto
22. 18 give me his house full of silver and gold
24. 13 give me his house full of silver and gold
31. 22 gold, and the silver, the brass, the iron
31. 50 of jewels of gold, chains, and bracelets
31. 51 Eleazar the priest took the gold of them
31. 52 gold of the offering that they offered up
31. 54 the priest took the gold of the captains
Deut. 7. 25 desire the silver or gold (that is) on them
8. 13 thy silver and thy gold is multiplied, and
17. 17 greatly multiply to himself silver and gold
29. 17 silver and gold, which (were) among them
Josh. 6. 19 gold, and vessels of brass and iron, (are)
6. 24 the gold, and the vessels of brass and of
7. 21 a wedge of gold of fifty shekels weight
7. 24 the garment, and the wedge of gold, and
22. 8 with gold, and with brass, and with iron
Judg. 8. 26 thousand and seven hundred (shekels)..g.
1 Sa. 6. 8 put the jewels of gold, which ye return
6. 11 the coffer with the mice of gold, and the
6. 15 wherein the jewels of gold (were), and
2 Sa. 1. 24 on ornaments of gold upon your apparel
8. 7 David took the shields of gold that were
8. 10 and vessels of gold, and vessels of brass
8. 11 the silver and gold that he had dedicated
12. 30 talent of gold with the precious stones
21. 4 We will have no silver nor gold of Saul
1 Ki. 6. 20 he overlaid it with pure gold; and (so)
6. 21 overlaid the house within with pure gold
6. 21 by the chains of gold before the oracle
6. 21 a partition..and he overlaid it with gold
6. 22 And the whole house he overlaid with g.
6. 22 the whole altar..he overlaid with gold
6. 28 And he overlaid the cherubim with gold
6. 30 floor of the house he overlaid with gold
6. 32 overlaid (them) with gold, and spread g.
6. 35 with gold fitted upon the carved work
7. 48 the altar of gold, and the table of gold
7. 49 the candlesticks of pure gold, five on
7. 49 and the lamps, and the tongs, (of) gold
7. 50 (of) pure gold; and the hinges (of) gold
7. 51 even the silver, and the gold, and the v.

1 Ki. 9. 11 cedar trees and fir trees, and with gold
9. 14 sent to the king sixscore talents of gold
9. 28 fetched from thence gold, four hundred
10. 2 and very much gold, and precious stones
10. 10 an hundred and twenty talents of gold
10. 11 brought gold from Ophir, brought in
10. 14 the weight of gold that came to Solomon
10. 14 hundred threescore and six talents..gold
10. 16 beaten gold: six hundred (shekels) of g.
10. 17 (of) beaten gold; three pound of gold went
10. 18 ivory, and overlaid it with the best gold
10. 21 Solomon's drinking vessels (were of) gold
10. 21 vessels of the house..(were of) pure gold
10. 22 bringing gold, and silver, ivory, and apes
10. 25 vessels of gold, and garments, and armo.
12. 28 made two calves (of) gold, and said unto
14. 26 shields of gold which Solomon had made
15. 15 the house of the LORD, silver, and gold
15. 18 Asa took all the silver and the gold (that
15. 19 unto thee a present of silver and gold
20. 3 Thy silver and thy gold (is) mine; thy
20. 5 thy gold, and thy wives, and thy children
20. 7 he sent..for my silver, and for my gold
22. 48 made ships..to go to Ophir for gold
2 Ki. 5. 5 six thousand..of gold, and ten changes
7. 8 carried thence silver, and gold, and
12. 13 any vessels of gold, or vessels of silver
12. 18 all the gold..found in the treasures of
14. 14 he took all the gold and silver, and all
16. 8 Ahaz took the silver and gold (that was
18. 14 talents of silver, and thirty talents of gold
20. 13 the silver, and the gold, and the spices
23. 33 trib...talents of silver, and a talent of go.
23. 35 gave the silver and the gold to Pharaoh
23. 35 he exacted the silver and the gold of the
24. 13 cut in pieces all the vessels of gold which
25. 15 (and) such things as (were) of gold, (in) g.
1 Ch.18. 7 David took the shields of gold that were
18. 10 all manner of vessels of gold and silver
18. 11 with the silver and the gold that he bro.
20. 2 and found it to weigh a talent of gold
21. 25 six hundred shekels of gold by weight
22. 14 an hundred thousand talents of gold
22. 16 Of the gold, the silver, and the brass, and
28. 14 gave) of gold by weight for (things) of g.
28. 15 the weight for the candlesticks of gold
28. 15 and for their lamps of gold, by weight
28. 16 by weight (he gave) gold for the tables
28. 17 Also pure gold for the flesh hooks, and
28. 18 for the altar of incense refined gold by
28. 18 gold for the pattern of the chariot of the
29. 2 the gold for (things to be made) of gold
29. 3 I have of mine own proper good, of gold
29. 4 three thousand talents of gold, of the g.
29. 5 The gold for (things) of gold, and the sil.
29. 7 of gold five thousand talents and ten
2 Ch. 1. 15 the king made silver and gold at Jerusa.
2. 7 a man cunning to work in gold, and in
2. 14 skilful to work in gold, and in silver, in
3. 4 And he overlaid it within with pure gold
3. 5 fir tree, which he overlaid with fine gold
3. 6 and the gold (was) gold of Parvaim
3. 7 He overlaid also the house..with gold
3. 8 he overlaid it with fine gold..to six hun.
3. 9 weight of the nails (was) fifty shekels of g.
3. 9 he overlaid the upper chambers with gold
3. 10 cherubim..and overlaid them with gold
4. 7 And he made ten candlesticks of gold
4. 8 he made an hundred basins of gold
4. 20 Moreover the candlesticks..of pure gold
4. 21 tongs, (made he of) gold, (and)..perfect g.
4. 22 the spoons, and the censers, (of) pure g.
4. 22 doors of the house of the temp.,(were of) g.
5. 1 the silver, and the gold, and all the inst.
8. 18 four hundred and fifty talents of gold
9. 1 gold in abundance, and precious stones
9. 9 an hundred and twenty talents of gold
9. 10 servants..which brought gold from Ophir
9. 13 the weight of the gold that came to Sol.
9. 13 and threescore and six talents of gold
9. 14 governors..brought gold and silver to S.
9. 15 made two hundred targets (of) beaten g.
9. 15 six hundred..of beaten gold went to one
9. 16 three hundred shields..beaten gold
9. 16 three hundred..of gold went to one shi.
9. 17 throne..and overlaid it with pure gold
9. 18 six steps..with a footstool of gold..fast.
9. 20 And all the drinking vessels..(were of) g.
9. 20 and all the vessels..(were of) pure gold
9. 21 bringing gold, and silver, ivory, and
9. 24 vessels of silver, and vessels of gold, and
12. 9 he carried away also the shields of gold
13. 11 and the candlestick of gold with the lamps
15. 18 he himself had dedicated, silver, and g.
16. 2 Asa brought out silver and gold out of
16. 3 behold, I have sent thee silver and gold
21. 3 great gifts of silver, and of gold, and of
24. 14 and spoons, and vessels of gold and silver
25. 24 all the gold and the silver, and all the
32. 27 and for gold, and for precious stones
36. 3 hundred talents of silver..a talent of g.
Ezra 1. 4, 6 with gold, and with goods, and with
1. 9 thirty chargers of gold, a thousand cha.
1. 10 Thirty basins of gold, silver basins of
1. 11 All the vessels of gold and of silver (were)
2. 69 They gave..one thousand drams of gold
8. 25 the silver, and the gold, and the vessels
8. 26 I even weighed..of gold an hundred tal.
8. 27 Also twenty basins of gold of a thousand
8. 27 vessels of fine copper, precious as gold
8. 28 the silver and the gold (are) a freewill
8. 30 the weight of the silver, and the gold

Ezra 8. 33 the silver and the gold and the vessels
Neh. 7. 70 a thousand drams of gold, fifty basins
7. 71, 72 twenty thousand drams of gold, and
Esth. 1. 6 the beds (were of) gold and silver, upon
1. 7 they gave (them) drink in vessels of gold
8. 15 with a great crown of gold, and with a
Job 3. 15 Or with princes that had gold, who filled
23. 10 hath tried me, I shall come forth as gold
28. 1 and a place for gold (where) they fine (it)
28. 6 of sapphires; and it hath dust of gold
28. 17 The gold and the crystal cannot equal it
31. 24 If I have made gold my hope, or have
42. 11 money, and every one an ear ring of gold
Psa. 19. 10 More to be desired (are they) than gold
45. 13 glorious..her clothing (is) of wrought g.
72. 15 to him shall be given of the gold of Sheba
105. 37 He brought them forth also with..gold
115. 4 Their idols (are) silver and gold, the work
119. 72 better unto me than thousands of gold
119. 127 I love thy commandments above gold
135. 15 idols of the heathen (are) silver and gold
Prov 11. 22 (As) a jewel of gold in a swine's snout
17. 3 pot (is) for silver, and the furnace for g.
20. 15 There is gold, and a multitude of rubies
22. 1 loving favour rather than silver and gold
25. 11 like) apples of gold in pictures of silver
25. 12 (As) an ear ring of gold, and an ornament
27. 21 pot for silver, and the furnace for gold
Eccl. 2. 8 I gathered me also silver and gold, and
Song 1. 11 We will make thee borders of gold, with
3. 10 He made..the bottom thereof (of) gold
5. 14 His hands (are as) gold rings set with the
Isa. 2. 7 Their land also is full of silver and gold
2. 20 his idols of silver, and his idols of gold
13. 17 (as for) gold, they shall not delight in it
30. 22 the ornament of thy molten images of gold
31. 7 his idols of silver, and his idols of gold
39. 2 the silver, and the gold, and the spices
40. 19 the goldsmith spreadeth it over with gold
46. 6 They lavish gold out of the bag, and weigh
60. 6 they shall bring gold and incense; and
60. 9 their silver and their gold with them
60. 17 For brass I will bring gold, and for iron
Jer. 4. 30 thou deckest thee with ornaments of gold
10. 4 They deck it with silver and with gold
10. 9 gold from Uphaz, the work of the work.
52. 19 (that) which (was) of gold (in) gold, and
Lam. 4. 1 How is the gold become dim! (how) is
Eze. 7. 19 their gold shall be removed..their gold
16. 13 Thus wast thou decked with gold and si.
16. 17 fair jewels of my gold and of my silver
27. 22 and with all precious stones, and gold
28. 4 hast gotten gold and silver into thy trea.
28. 13 the emerald, and the carbuncle, and gold
38. 13 to carry away silver and gold, to take
Dan. 11. 8 their precious vessels of silver and of gold
11. 38 shall he honour with gold, and silver, and
11. 43 power over the treasures of gold and of
Hos. 2. 8 and multiplied her silver and gold
8. 4 of their silver and their gold have they
Joel 3. 5 ye have taken my silver and my gold, and
Nah. 2. 9 the spoil of silver, take the spoil of gold
Hab. 2. 19 it (is) laid over with gold and silver, and
Zeph. 1. 18 Neither their silver nor their gold shall
Hag. 2. 8 The silver (is) mine, and the gold (is) mine
Zech. 4. 2 behold, a candlestick all (of) gold, with a
6. 11 take silver and gold, and make crowns
13. 9 and will try them as gold is tried: they
14. 14 gold, and silver, and apparel, in great
Mal. 3. 3 and purge them as gold and silver, that

5. *Best gold*, חָרוּץ *charuts.*
Psa. 68. 13 silver, and her feathers with yellow gold
Prov. 8. 10 and knowledge rather than choice gold
8. 19 My fruit is better than gold, yea, than
16. 16 How much better..to get wisdom than g.?

6. *Pure gold*, כֶּתֶם *kethem.*
Job 28. 16 It cannot be valued with the gold of Op.
Psa. 45. 9 hand did stand the queen in gold of Oph.
Song 5. 11 His head (is as)..gold; his locks (are) bu.

7. *Refined gold*, סְגוֹר *segor.*
Job 28. 15 It cannot be gotten for gold, neither shall

8. *Gold*, χρυσίον *chrusion.*
Acts 3. 6 Peter said, Silver and gold have I none
20. 33 I have coveted no man's silver, or gold
Heb. 9. 4 the ark..overlaid round about with gold
1 Pe. 1. 7 being much more precious than of gold
1. 18 with corruptible things, (as) silver and g.
3. 3 wearing of gold, or of putting on of app.
Rev. 3. 18 I counsel thee to buy of me gold tried in
21. 18 the city (was) pure gold, like unto clear
21. 21 the street of the city (was) pure gold, as

9. *Gold*, χρυσός *chrusos.*
Matt. 2. 11 gifts; gold, frankincense, and myrrh
10. 9 Provide neither gold, nor silver, nor brass
23. 16 whosoever shall swear by the gold of the
23. 17 blind! for whether is greater, the gold
23. 17 or the temple that sanctifieth the gold?
Acts 17. 29 that the Godhead is like unto gold, or si.
1 Co. 3. 12 gold, silver, precious stones, wood, hay
1 Ti. 2. 9 not with broided hair, or gold, or pearls
Jas. 5. 3 Your gold and silver is cankered; and
Rev. 9. 7 on their heads..as it were crowns of gold
9. 20 idols of gold, and silver, and brass, 17. 4.
18. 12 The merchandise of gold, and silver, and
18. 16 scarlet, and decked with gold, and preci.

GOLD, fine —

1. *Best good*, חָרוּץ *charuts.*
Prov. 3. 14 and the gain thereof than fine gold
Zech. 9. 3 and fine gold as the mire of the street

2. *Pure gold*, כֶּתֶם *kethem.*
Job 31. 24 or have said to the fine gold, (Thou art)
Prov 25. 12 and an ornament of fine gold, (so is) a
Lam. 4. 1 (how) is the most fine gold changed! the
Dan. 10. 5 loins (were) girded with fine gold of Up.

3. *Fine gold*, פַּז *paz.*
Job 28. 17 exchange..(shall not be for) jewels of fine g.
Psa. 19. 10 yea, than much fine gold; sweeter also
119. 127 I love thy commandments..above fine g.
Prov. 8. 19 My fruit (is) better..yea, than fine gold
Song 5. 11 His head (is as) the most fine gold; his
5. 15 His legs..set upon sockets of fine gold
Isa. 13. 12 make a man more precious than fine gold
Lam. 4. 2 sons of Zion, comparable to fine gold, how

GOLD, pure —

1. *Pure gold*, כֶּתֶם *kethem.*
Job 28. 19 neither shall it be valued with pure gold

2. *Fine gold*, פַּז *paz.*
Psa. 21. 3 settest a crown of pure gold on his head

GOLD, of —

Golden, of gold, χρύσεος *chruseos.*
2 Ti. 2. 20 there are not only vessels of gold and of
Rev. 4. 4 and they had on their heads crowns of g.
9. 20 idols of gold, and silver, and brass, and

GOLD ring, with a —

Having a gold ring, χρυσοδακτύλιος *chrusodakt.*
Jas. 2. 2 if there come..a man with a gold ring, in

GOLDEN —

1. *Gold*, דְּהַב *dehab.*
Ezra 6. 5 also let the golden and silver vessels of
Dan. 3. 5 fall down and worship the golden image
3. 7 fell down (and) worshipped the golden i.
3. 10 fall down and worship the golden image
3. 12, 14, 18 nor worship the golden image
5. 2 to bring the golden and silver vessels
5. 3 Then they brought the golden vessels

2. *Gold*, זָהָב *zahab.*
Gen. 24. 22 that the man took a golden ear ring of
Exod 25. 25 thou shalt make a golden crown to the
28. 34, 34 A golden bell and a pomegranate
30. 4 two golden rings shalt thou make to it
32. 2 Break off the golden ear rings, which (are)
32. 3 the people brake off the golden ear rings
39. 20 they made two (other) golden rings, and
39. 38 the golden altar, and the anointing oil
40. 26 he put the golden altar in the tent of the
Lev. 8. 9 did he put the golden plate, the holy cr.
Num. 4. 11 upon the golden altar they shall spread
7. 32, 38, 44, 50, 62, 68, 74, 80 One golden spo.
7. 86 The golden spoons (were) twelve, full of
Judg. 8. 24 they had golden ear rings, because they
8. 26 the weight of the golden ear rings that
1 Sa. 6. 4 Five golden emerods, and five golden m.
6. 17 these (are) the golden emerods which the
6. 18 the golden mice..the number of all the
2 Ki. 10. 29 the golden calves that (were) in Beth-el
1 Ch. 28. 17 for the golden basins..by weight for
2 Ch. 4. 19 the golden altar also, and the tables
13. 8 (there are) with you golden calves, which
Esth. 4. 11 king shall hold out the golden sceptre
5. 2 the king held out to Esther the golden
8. 4 the king held out the golden sceptre to.
Eccl. 12. 6 or the golden bowl be broken, or the pi.
Jer. 51 7 Babylon..a golden cup in the LORD's h.
Zech. 4. 12 through the..golden pipes..empty the g.

3. *Golden, of gold*, χρύσεος *chruseos*, -οῦς.
Heb. 9. 4 Which had the golden censer and the a.
9. 4 wherein (was) the golden pot that had
Rev. 1. 12 being turned I saw seven golden candle.
1. 13 girt about the paps with a golden girdle
1. 20 and the seven golden candlesticks. The
2. 1 in the midst of the seven golden candle.
5. 8 golden vials full of odours, which are the
8. 3 And another angel came..having a gold.
8. 3 upon the golden altar which was before
9. 13 from the four horns of the golden altar
14. 14 having on his head a golden crown, and
15. 6 their breasts girded with golden girdles
15. 7 golden vials full of the wrath of God
17. 4 having a golden cup in her hand full of
21. 15 had a golden reed to measure the city

GOLDEN city —

Golden ore, exactress of gold, מַדְהֵבָה *madhebah.*
Isa. 14. 4 hath the oppressor ceased! the golden c.

GOLDEN wedge —

Pure gold, כֶּתֶם *kethem.*
Isa. 13. 12 even a man than the golden wedge of O.

GOLDSMITH —

1. *To refine, try, purify*, צָרַף *tsaraph.*
Neh. 3. 8 Uzziel the son of Harhaiah, of the gold.
3. 32 repaired the goldsmiths and the mercha.
Isa. 40. 19 the goldsmith spreadeth it over with go.
41. 7 so the carpenter encouraged the goldsm.
46. 6 They..hire a goldsmith; and he maketh

2. *Refiner, purifier*, צֹרְפִי *tsorephi.*
Neh. 3. 31 repaired Malchiah the goldsmith's son

GOL-GO'-THA, Γολγοθᾶ *a skull.*
The Hebrew name of the spot at which Christ was crucified. It is so given by three of the evangelists; but Luke, according to his usual practice, gives the Greek equivalent.
Matt. 27. 33 they were come unto a place called G.
Mark 15. 22 And they bring him unto the place G.
John 19. 17 a skull, which is called in the Hebrew, G.

GOL-I'-ATH, גָּלְיָת *an exile or soothsayer.*
A famous giant of Gath, probably a descendant of the Rephaim. He defied the armies of Israel, but was slain and despoiled by David while a stripling. His height was 6 cubits and 1 span; taking the cubit at 21 inches, that would make him 10½ feet high. B.C 1063.
1 Sa. 17. 4 there went out a champion..named G.
17. 23 there came up the champion..G. by name
21. 9 G...whom thou slewest in the valley of
22. 10 and gave him the sword of G. the Philis.
2 Sa. 21. 19 where Elhanan..slew (the brother of) G.
1 Ch. 20. 5 slew Lahmi the brother of G. the Gittite

GO'-MER, גֹּמֶר *completion, heat.*
1. Eldest son of Japheth, and father of Ashkenaz, Riphath, and Togarmah, B.C. 2340. He was progenitor of the Cimerians, Cimbri, and other branches of the Celtic family, as well as of the modern Gael and Cymry, the latter preserving the original name with slight variation.
Gen. 10. 2 sons of Japheth; G., and Magog, and
10. 3 the sons of G.; Ashkenaz, and Riphath
1 Ch. 1. 5 sons of Japheth; G., and Magog, and M.
1. 6 the sons of G.; Ashchenaz, and Riphath
2. The people descended from Gomer. They settled on the N. of the Black Sea, and then spread themselves southward and westward to the extremities of Europe.
Eze. 38. 6 G., and all his bands; the house of Tog.
3. The wife or concubine of Hosea. B.C. 785.
Hos. 1. 3 So he went and took G. the daughter of

GO-MOR'-RAH, עֲמֹרָה *fissure, submersion.* Γόμοῤῥα.
One of the five "cities of the plain" or "vale of Siddim" that were plundered by Chedorlaomer and his allies. All these cities save Zoar were afterwards destroyed with fire from heaven.
Gen. 10. 19 as thou goest, unto Sodom, and G., and
13. 10 before the LORD destroyed Sodom and G.
14. 2 made war..with Birsha king of G., Shin.
14. 8 there went out..the king of G., and the
14. 10 the kings of Sodom and G. fled, and fell
14. 11 they took all the goods of Sodom and G.
18. 20 Because the cry of Sodom and G. is great
19. 24 LORD rained upon Sodom and upon G. br.
19. 28 he looked toward Sodom and G., and
Deut 29. 23 like the overthrow of Sodom, and G., A.
32. 32 For their vine (is)..of the fields of G.: their
Isa. 1. 9 Except..we should have been like unto G.
1. 10 give ear unto the law..ye people of G.
13. 19 as when God overthrew Sodom and G.
Jer. 23. 14 and the inhabitants thereof as G.
49. 18 As in the overthrow of Sodom and G.
50. 40 As God overthrew Sodom and G. and the
Amos 4. 11 of you, as God overthrew Sodom and G.
Zeph. 2. 9 and the children of Ammon as G., (even)
Matt 10. 15 It shall be more tolerable for..G. in the
Mark 6. 11 It shall be more tolerable for..G. in the
Rom. 9. 29 Except..we had..been made like unto G.
2 Pe. 2. 6 turning the cities of Sodom and G. into
Jude 7 Even as Sodom and G., and the cities

GONE, be —

Measure (itself), מִדַּד [*madad*, 3].
Job 7. 4 When shall I arise, and the night be go.?

GONE, to be —

1. *To go away*, אֲזַד *azad.*
Dan. 2. 5 The thing is gone from me: if ye will
2. 8 because ye see the thing is gone from me

2. *To go about or away*, אָזַל *azal.*
Deut 32. 36 when he seeth that (their) power is gone
Prov 20. 14 when he is gone his way, then he boast.

3. *He is not, there is not*, אַיִן *ayin.*
1 Ki. 20. 40 And as thy servant was busy..he was g.
Psa. 38. 10 light of mine eyes, it also is gone from

4. *To go in*, בּוֹא *bo.*
Num. 7. 89 when Moses was gone into the tabernacle
1 Sa. 20. 41 as soon as the lad was gone, David arose
Jer. 44. 8 land of Egypt, whither ye be gone to d.
44. 14 which are gone into the land of Egypt to
44. 28 that are gone into the land of Egypt to

5. *To remove*, גָּלָה *galah.*
Isa. 24. 11 is darkened, the mirth of the land is g.

6. *To go on*, הָלַךְ *halak.*
Gen. 31. 30 now, (though) thou wouldest needs be g.
34. 17 we take our daughter, and we will be g.
1 Sa. 14. 17 Number now, and see who is gone from
1 Ki. 22. 13 the messenger that was gone to call Mi.
Prov. 7. 19 For the goodman..is gone a long journey
Song 2. 11 winter is past, the rain is over (and) gone
6. 1 Whither is thy beloved gone, O thou fa..
Isa. 46. 2 but themselves are gone into captivity
Jer. 2. 23 I am not polluted, I have not gone after
9. 10 the fowl..and the beast..they are gone
Lam. 1. 5 her children are gone into captivity before
1. 18 my young men are gone into captivity
Eze. 37. 21 among the heathen, whither they be gone
Hos. 9. 6 lo, they are gone because of destruction

7. *To be gone*, הָלַךְ *halak*, 2.
Psa. 109. 23 I am gone like the shadow when it decl.

8. *To go on*, יָלַךְ *yalak.*
Gen. 28. 7 Jacob obeyed..and was gone to Padan-a.
42. 33 leave one of your brethren..and be gone
Exod 12. 32 Also take..as ye have said, and be gone

2 Sa. 3. 22 sent him away, and he was gone in peace
3. 23 hath sent him away, and he is gone in pe.
3. 24 hast sent him away, and he is quite gone?
1 Ki. 13. 24 when he was gone, a lion met him by the
18. 12 it shall come to pass..I am gone from thee
Job 19. 10 He hath destroyed me..and I am gone
Jer. 5. 23 this people..they are revolted and gone
15. 6 saith the LORD, thou art gone backward
Lam. 1. 6 they are gone without strength before

9. *To stretch out, turn aside,* נָטָה *natah.*
Psa. 73. 2 But as for me, my feet were almost gone

10. *To go in,* בּוֹא *bo.*
Exod 33. 8 until he was gone into the tabernacle
Num. 7. 89 when Moses was gone into the tabernacle
Jer. 44. 14, 28 which are gone into the land of Eg.

11. *To go over or beyond,* עָבַר *abar.*
Num 13. 32 through which we have gone to search it
Psa. 42. 7 thy waves and thy billows are gone over
Song 5. 6 had withdrawn himself, (and) was gone

GONE (round) about, to be —
To go or set round, נָקַף *naqaph,* 5.
Job 1. 5 when the days of..feasting were gone ab.
Isa. 15. 8 the cry is gone round about the borders

GONE aside, to be —
To turn, be turned aside, סוּר *sur.*
Psa. 14. 3 They are all gone aside, they are (all) to.

GONE away, to be —
1. *To be pressed, estranged,* זוּר *zur,* 2.
Isa. 1. 4 children..they are gone away backward
2. *To move, wander,* נוּעַ *nua.*
Job 28. 4 they are dried up, they are gone away
3. *To go on,* יָלַךְ *yalak.*
Judg 18. 24 Ye have taken..and ye are gone away
4. *To turn aside,* סוּר *sur.*
Mal. 3. 7 ye are gone away from mine ordinances

GONE back, to be —
To turn back, שׁוּב *shub.*
Ruth 1. 15 thy sister in law is gone back unto her

GONE out, that which is —
An out going, מוֹצָא *motsa.*
Deut 23. 23 That which is gone out of thy lips thou

GONE out, thing —
Out going, מוֹצָא *motsa.*
Psa. 89. 34 nor alter the thing that is gone out of my

GONE away far, to be —
To be far off, רָחַק *rachaq.*
Eze. 44. 10 the Levites that are gone away far from

GOOD —
1. *Kind,* חָסִיד *chasid.*
Mic. 7. 2 The good (man) is perished out of the ea.
2. *Good,* טָב *tab.*
Ezra 5. 17 Now therefore, if..good to the king, let
3. *Good,* טוֹב *tob.*
Gen. 1. 4 And God saw the light, that (it was) good
1. 10, 12, 18, 21, 25 and God saw that (it was) g.
1. 31 God saw..and, behold, (it was) very good
2. 9 pleasant to the sight and good for food
2. 9 and the tree of knowledge of good and
2. 12 the gold of that land (is) good: there
2. 17 tree of the knowledge of good and evil
2. 18 God said, (It is) not good that the man
3. 5 shall be as gods, knowing good and evil
3. 6 woman saw that the tree (was) good for
3. 22 is become as one of us, to know good and
15. 15 thou shalt be buried in a good old age
18. 7 fetched a calf tender and good, and gave
19. 8 and do ye to them as (is) good in your ey.
24. 50 we cannot speak unto thee bad or good
25. 8 died in a good old age, an old man, and
26. 29 we have done unto thee nothing but good
27. 9 fetch me from thence two good kids of
30. 20 God hath indued me (with) a good dowry
31. 24, 29 that thou speak not..either good or
40. 16 baker saw that the interpretation was g.
41. 5 seven ears of corn came up ..rank and go.
41. 22 seven ears came up in one ..full and go.
41. 24 the thin ears devoured the seven good e.
41. 26 The seven good kine (are) seven years
41. 26 and the seven good ears (are) seven yea.
41. 35 all the food of those good years that come
44. 4 Wherefore have ye rewarded evil for go.?
49. 15 he saw that rest (was) good, and the land
50. 20 God meant it unto good, to bring to pass
Exod. 3. 8 unto a good land and a large. unto a land
18. 17 The thing that thou doest (is) not good
Lev. 27. 10 a good for a bad, or a bad for a good
27. 12 shall value it, whether it be good or bad
27. 14 shall estimate it, whether it be good or b.
27. 33 He shall not search whether it be good or
Num 10. 29 come thou..and we will do thee good
13. 19 the land..whether it (be) good or bad
14. 7 The land..(is) an exceeding good land
24. 13 to do..good or bad of mine own mind
Deut. 1. 14 The thing which thou hast spoken (is)
1. 25 a good land which the LORD our God
1. 35 there shall not one..see that good land
1. 39 had no knowledge between good and evil
3. 25 see the good land that (is) beyond Jordan
4. 21 that I should not go in unto that good land
4. 22 ye shall go over, and possess that good
6. 18 thou shalt do..right and good in the sig.

Deut. 6. 18 mayest go in and possess the good land
6. 24 to fear the LORD our God, for our good
8. 7 thy God bringeth thee into a good land
8. 10 for the good land which he hath given
9. 6 thy God giveth thee not this good land to
10. 13 which I command thee this day for thy g.?
11. 17 ye perish quickly from off the good land
12. 28 when thou doest..good and right in the
26. 11 thou shalt rejoice in every good (thing)
28. 12 LORD shall open unto thee his good trea.
30. 9 and in the fruit of thy land, for good
30. 9 LORD will again rejoice over thee for g.
30. 15 I have set before thee..life and good, and
Josh. 9. 25 as it seemeth good and right unto thee to
21. 45 There failed not ought of any good thing
23. 13 until ye perish from off this good land
23. 14 not one thing hath failed of all the good
23. 15 as all good things are come upon you
23. 15 from off this good land which the LORD
23. 16 shall perish quickly from off the good la.
Judg. 8. 32 died in a good old age, and was buried in
9. 11 forsake my sweetness, and my good fruit
10. 15 do thou unto us whatsoever seemeth g.
18. 9 seen the land, and, behold, it (is) very g.
19. 24 with them what seemeth good unto you
Ruth 2. 22 good, my daughter, that thou go out with
1 Sa. 1. 23 Do what seemeth thee good; tarry until
2. 24 no good report that I hear: ye make the
3. 18 LORD: let him do what seemeth him good
11. 10 ye shall do with us all that seemeth good
12. 23 I will teach you the good and the right
14. 36 Do whatsoever seemeth good unto thee
14. 40 people said..Do what seemeth good unto
15. 9 the fatlings, and the lambs, and all..good
19. 4 Jonathan spake good of David unto Saul
19. 4 his works (have been) to thee-ward very g.
24. 17 thou hast rewarded me good, whereas I
24. 19 LORD reward thee good for that thou hast
25. 3 a woman of good understanding, and of a
25. 8 we come in a good day: give, I pray thee
25. 15 the men (were) very good unto us, and
25. 21 and he hath requited me evil for good
25. 30 according to all the good that he hath
26. 16 This thing (is) not good that thou hast d.
29. 6 thy coming in with me in the host (is) g.
29. 9 I know that thou (art) good in my sight
2 Sa. 3. 19 seemed good to Israel, and that..seemed
10. 12 LORD do that which seemeth him good
13. 22 And Absalom spake .neither good nor
14. 17 so (is) my lord the king, to discern good
14. 32 good for me (to have been) there still
15. 3 See, thy matters (are) good and right
15. 26 let him do to me as seemeth good unto
16. 12 LORD will requite me good for his cursing
17. 7 The counsel..(is) not good at this time
17. 14 LORD had appointed to defeat the good
18. 27 He (is) a good man, and cometh with g
19. 18 carry over..and to do what he thought g.
19. 27 do therefore (what is) good in thine eyes
19. 35 can I discern between good and evil?
19. 37 do to him what shall seem good unto
19. 38 do..that which shall seem good unto
24. 22 take and offer up what (seemeth) good
1 Ki. 1. 42 thou (art) a valiant man, and bringest g.
2. 38 The saying (is) good: as my lord the king
2. 42 saidst..The word (that) I have heard (is) g.
3. 9 that I may discern between good and bad
8. 36 that thou teach them the good way whe.
8. 56 hath not failed one word of all his good
12. 7 answer them, and speak good words to
14. 13 because in him there is found (some) good
14. 15 he shall root up Israel out of this good l.
21. 2 if it seem good to thee, I will give thee
22. 8 he doth not prophesy good concerning
22. 13 the words of the prophets (declare) good
22. 13 I pray thee..speak (that which is) good
22. 18 he would prophesy no good..but evil?
2 Ki. 3. 19 and shall fell every good tree, and stop
3. 19 mar every good piece of land with stones
3. 25 on every good piece of land cast every
3. 25 wells of water, and felled all the good
10. 5 do thou (that which is) good in thine eyes
20. 3 and have done..good in thy sight
20. 19 Good (is) the word of the LORD which
1 Ch. 4. 40 they found fat pasture and good, and the
16. 34 give thanks unto the LORD; for (he is) g.
19. 13 let the LORD do..good in his sight
21. 23 let my lord the king do..good in his eyes
28. 8 that ye may possess this good land, and
29. 28 he died in a good old age, full of days
2 Ch. 5. 13 praised the LORD, (saying), For (he is) g
6. 27 when thou hast taught them the good
7. 3 praised the LORD, (saying), For (he is) g.
10. 7 please them, and speak good words to
14. 2 Asa did..good and right in the eyes
18. 7 for he never prophesied good unto me
18. 12 the words of the prophets (declare) good
18. 12 be like one of theirs, and speak thou good
18. 17 he would not prophesy good unto me, but
19. 3 there are good things found in thee
19. 11 and the LORD shall be with the good
24. 16 because he had done good in Israel, both
30. 18 saying, The good LORD pardon every one
30. 22 that taught the good knowledge of the L.
31. 20 wrought..good and right and truth before
Ezra 3. 11 because..good, for his mercy (endureth)
7. 9 according to the good hand of his God
8. 18 by the good hand of our God upon us
8. 22 upon all them for good that seek him
Neh. 2. 8 according to the good hand of my God
2. 18 of the hand of my God which was good
2. 18 strengthened their hands for (this) good

Neh. 5. 9 It (is) not good that ye do: ought ye not
5. 19 Think upon me, my God, for good, (acco.)
9. 13 gavest..good statutes and commandments
9. 20 Thou gavest also thy good spirit to instr.
13. 31 Remember me, O my God, for good
Esth. 3. 11 to do with them as it seemeth good to
7. 9 Mordecai, who had spoken good for the
8. 17 and gladness, a feast and a good day
9. 19 gladness and feasting, and a good day
9. 22 was turned..from mourning into a good
Job 2. 10 shall we receive good at the hand of God
7. 7 remember..mine eye shall no more see g.
9. 25 my days..they flee away, they see no good
22. 18 he filled their houses with good..but the
22. 21 be at peace: thereby good shall come
30. 26 When I looked for good, then evil came
34. 4 let us know among ourselves what (is) g.
Psa. 4. 6 many that say, Who will show us..good?
14. 1, 3 (there is) none that doeth good
25. 8 Good and upright (is) the LORD: therefo.
34. 8 O taste and see that the LORD (is) good
34. 10 they that seek..shall not want any good
34. 12 man..loveth..days, that he may see go.?
34. 14 Depart from evil, and do good; seek
35. 12 They rewarded me evil for good, (to) the
36. 4 he setteth himself in a way (that is) not g.
37. 3 Trust in the LORD, and do good; (so) shalt
37. 27 Depart from evil, and do good; and dwell
38. 20 They also that render evil for good are
38. 20 because I follow (the thing that) good (is)
39. 2 I held my peace..from good; and my
45. 1 My heart is inditing a good matter: I
52. 3 Thou lovest evil more than good..lying
52. 9 I will wait..for (it is) good before thy
53. 1, 3 (there is) none that doeth good
54. 6 I will praise thy name, O LORD, for..go.
69. 16 Hear me..for thy loving kindness (is) good
73. 1 Truly God (is) good to Israel, (even) to such
73. 28 But (it is) good for me to draw near to G.
84. 11 no good..will he withhold from them
85. 12 Yea, the LORD shall give..good; and our
86. 5 For thou, Lord, (art) good, and ready to
86. 17 Show me a token for good; that they wh.
92. 1 good (thing) to give thanks unto the LORD
100. 5 For the LORD (is) good; his mercy (is) ever.
103. 5 Who satisfieth thy mouth with good..thy
104. 28 thou openest thine hand, they are f. with g
106. 1 O give thanks unto the LORD; for..good
106. 5 That I may see the good of thy chosen
107. 1 O give thanks unto the LORD, for..good
109. 5 they have rewarded me evil for good, and
109. 21 because thy mercy (is) good, deliver thou
111. 10 a good understanding have all they that
112. 5 A good man showeth favour, and lendeth
118. 1, 29 O give thanks unto the LORD; for..go.
119. 39 Turn away..for thy judgments (are) good
119. 68 Thou (art) good, and doest good: teach
119. 71 good for me that I have been afflicted
119. 122 Be surety for thy servant for good: let
122. 9 Because of the house..I will seek thy g.
125. 4 O LORD, unto (those that be) good, and
133. 1 how good and how pleasant (it is) for br.
135. 3 Praise the LORD; for the LORD (is) good
136. 1 O give thanks unto the LORD; for..good
143. 10 thou (art) my God: thy spirit (is) good
145. 9 The LORD (is) good to all; and his tender
147. 1 for..good to sing praises unto our God
Prov. 2. 9 Then shalt thou understand..every good
2. 20 That thou mayest walk in the way of good
3. 4 good understanding in the sight of God
3. 27 Withhold not good from them to whom
4. 2 I give you good doctrine, forsake ye not
11. 23 The desire of the righteous (is) only good
11. 27 He that diligently seeketh good procureth
12. 2 A good (man) obtaineth favour of the L.
12. 14 A man shall be satisfied with good by the
12. 25 the heart of man..a good word maketh
13. 2 A man shall eat good by the fruit of (his)
13. 15 Good understanding giveth favour: but
13. 21 but to the righteous good shall be repaid
13. 22 A good (man) leaveth an inheritance to
14. 14 a good man (shall be satisfied) from him.
14. 19 The evil bow before the good; and the
14. 22 mercy and truth..to them that devise g.
15. 3 The eyes..beholding the evil and the g.
15. 23 and a word..in due season, how good
15. 30 a good report maketh the bones fat
16. 20 He that handleth..wisely shall find good
16. 29 and leadeth him into the way..not good
17. 13 Whoso rewardeth evil for good, evil shall
17. 20 that hath a froward heart findeth no go.
17. 26 to punish the just (is) not good, (nor) to
18. 5 (It is) not good to accept the person of
18. 22 (Whoso) findeth a wife findeth a good
19. 2 soul (be) without knowledge, (it is) not g.
19. 8 keepeth understanding shall find good
20. 23 and a false balance (is) not good
24. 13 My son, eat thou honey, because (it is) g.
24. 23 (It is) not good to have respect of persons
24. 25 and a good blessing shall come upon
25. 25 so (is) good news from a far country
25. 27 (It is) not good to eat much honey; so
28. 10 but the upright shall have good (things)
28. 21 To have respect of persons (is) not good
31. 12 She will do him good and not evil all
31. 18 perceiveth that her merchandise (is) go.
Eccl. 2. 3 till I might see what (was) that good
2. 24 he should make his soul enjoy good in
2. 26 (God) giveth to a man that (is) good in
2. 26 may give to (him that is) good before God
3. 12 I know that (there is) no good in them
3. 12 to rejoice, and to do good in his life

Eccl. 3. 13 and enjoy the good of all his labour, it
4. 8 do I labour, and bereave my soul of go.?
4. 9 they have a good reward for their labour
5. 18 (it is) good and comely (for one) to eat
5. 18 to enjoy the good of all his labour that
6. 3 his soul be not filled with good, and also
6. 6 thousand years..yet hath he seen no go.
6. 12 knoweth what (is) good for man in (this)
7. 11 Wisdom (is) good with an inheritance
7. 18 (It is) good that thou shouldest take hold
7. 20 just man..that doeth good, and sinneth
9. 2 to the good and to the clean, and to the
9. 2 as (is) the good, so (is) the sinner; (and)
9. 18 but one sinner destroyeth much good
11. 6 or whether they both (shall be) alike go.
12. 14 whether (it be) good, or whether (it be)
Song 1. 3 of the savour of thy good ointments thy
Isa. 5. 20 them that call evil good, and good evil
7. 15, 16 refuse the evil, and choose the good
38. 3 have done (that which is) good in thy
39. 8 Good (is) the word of the LORD which
52. 7 feet of him that bringeth good tidings
55. 2 eat ye (that which is) good, and let your
65. 2 which walketh in a way (that was) not g.
Jer. 5. 25 sins have withholden good (things) from
6. 16 where (is) the good way, and walk there.
8. 15 We looked for peace, but no good (came)
14. 11 Pray not for this people for (their) good
14. 19 we looked for peace, and (there is) no g.
17. 6 shall not see when good cometh; but
18. 10 I will repent of the good wherewith I
18. 20 Shall evil be recompensed for good? for
18. 20 stood before thee to speak good for them
21. 10 for evil, and not for good, saith the LORD
24. 2 One basket (had) very good figs, (even)
24. 3 the good figs, very good; and the evil
24. 5 Like these good figs..will I acknowledge
24. 5 the land of the Chaldeans for (their) go.
24. 6 I will set mine eyes upon them for good
26. 14 with me as seemeth good and meet unto
29. 10 and perform my good word toward you
29. 32 neither shall he behold the good that I
32. 39 the good of them, and of their children
32. 42 all the good that I have promised them
33. 9 hear all the good that I do unto them
33. 11 the LORD (is) good; for his mercy (endu.)
33. 14 I will perform that good thing which I
39. 16 upon this city for evil, and not for good
40. 4 If it seem good unto thee to come with
40. 4 whither it seemeth good and convenient
42. 6 Whether (it be) good, or whether (it be)
44. 27 watch over them for evil, and not for go.
Lam. 3. 25 LORD (is) good unto them that wait for
3. 26 (It is) good that (a man) should both hope
3. 27 (It is) good for a man that he bear the
3. 38 the mouth..proceedeth not evil and go.?
Eze. 17. 8 planted in a good soil by great waters
18. 18 (that) which (is) not good among his peo.
20. 25 I gave them..statutes (that were) not g.
24. 4 (even) every good piece, the thigh, and
34. 14 I will feed them in a good pasture, and
34. 14 there shall they lie in a good fold, and
34. 18 you to have eaten up the good pasture
36. 31 your doings that (were) not good, and
Hos. 4. 13 the shadow thereof (is) good: therefore
8. 3 hath cast off (the thing that is) good
Amos 5. 14 Seek good, and not evil, that ye may live
5. 15 love the good, and establish judgment
9. 4 eyes upon them for evil, and not for go.
Mic. 1. 12 inhabitant..waited carefully for good
3. 2 Who hate the good, and love the evil
6. 8 He hath showed thee, O man, what (is) g.
Nah. 1. 7 The LORD (is) good, a strong hold in the
Zech. 1. 13 (with) good words (and) comfortable wo.
11. 12 If ye think good, give (me) my price; and
Mal. 2. 17 Every one that doeth evil (is) good in the

4. *Good, goodness, good thing,* טוּב *tub.*
Gen. 45. 18 give you the good of the land of Egypt
45. 20 good of all the land of Egypt (is) your's
Deut. 6. 11 houses full of all good (things), which
Ezra 9. 12 eat the good of the land, and leave (it)
Neh. 9. 36 the fruit thereof and the good thereof
Job 21. 16 Lo, their good (is) not in their hand
Psa. 119. 66 Teach me good judgment and knowled.
128. 5 thou shalt see the good of Jerusalem all
Isa. 1. 19 obedient, ye shall eat the good of the la.

5. *Equity, benefit,* כִּשְׁרוֹן *kishron.*
Eccl. 5. 11 what good (is there) to the owners the.

6. *Might, with might,* מְאֹד *meod.*
Deut. 2. 4 take ye good heed unto yourselves there.
4. 15 Take ye therefore good heed unto yours.
Josh. 23. 11 Take good heed therefore unto yoursel.

7. *Good,* ἀγαθός *agathos.*
Matt. 5. 45 sun to rise on the evil and on the good
7. 11 If ye..know how to give good gifts unto
7. 17 every good tree bringeth forth
7. 18 A good tree cannot bring forth evil fruit
12. 35 A good man, out of the good treasure of
19. 16 Good Master, what..shall I do, that I
19. 17 Why callest thou me good?..none good
20. 15 Is thine eye evil, because I am good?
22. 10 as many as they found, both bad and go.
25. 21, 23 Well done..good and faithful servant
Mark 10. 17 Good Master, what shall I do that I may
10. 18 Why callest thou me good?..none good
Luke 6. 45 A good man out of the good treasure of
8. 8 other fell on good ground, and sprang up
8. 15 which in an honest and good heart, having
10. 42 Mary hath chosen that good part, which
Luke 11. 13 If ye..know how to give good gifts unto
18. 18 Good Master, what shall I do to inherit
18. 19 Why callest thou me good? none (is) go.
19. 17 he said..Well, thou good servant: beca.
23. 50 Joseph, a counsellor..a good man, and
John 5. 29 they that have done good, unto the resu.
7. 12 for some said, He is a good man: others
Acts 9. 36 this woman was full of good works and
11. 24 he was a good man, and full of the Holy
23. 1 I have lived in all good conscience before
Rom. 2. 10 to every man that worketh good, to the
3. 8 Let us do evil, that good may come?
5. 7 for a good man some would even dare to
7. 12 the commandment holy, and just, and g.
7. 19 For the good that I would I do not: but
8. 28 work together for good to them that love
9. 11 neither having done any good or evil, that
12. 2 that ye may prove what (is) that good
12. 21 Be not overcome..overcome evil with g.
13. 3 rulers are not a terror to good works, but
13. 4 he is the minister of God to thee for good
14. 16 Let not then your good be evil spoken of
15. 2 Let every one of us please..for..good to
2 Co. 5. 10 to that he hath done..whether..good or
9. 8 that ye..may abound to every good work
Gal. 6. 10 let us do good unto all..especially unto
Eph. 2. 10 created in Christ Jesus unto good works
4. 29 that which is good to the use of edifying
Phil. 1. 6 that he which hath begun a good work in
Col. 1. 10 being fruitful in every good work, and in.
1 Th. 3. 6 ye have good remembrance of us always
2 Th. 2. 16 consolation and good hope through grace
2. 17 stablish you in every good word and work
1 Ti. 1. 5 and (of) a good conscience, and (of) faith
1. 19 Holding faith, and a good conscience
2. 10 But which becometh women..with good
5. 10 have diligently followed every good work
2 Ti. 2. 21 vessel..prepared unto every good work
3. 17 throughly furnished unto all good works
Titus 1. 16 and unto every good work reprobate
2. 5 discreet, chaste, keepers at home, good
2. 10 Not purloining, but showing all good
3. 1 to obey..to be ready to every good work
Heb. 13. 21 Make you perfect in every good work
Jas. 1. 17 Every good gift and every perfect gift
3. 17 full of mercy and good fruits, without
1 Pe. 2. 18 not only to the good and gentle, but also
3. 10 he that will love life, and see good days
3. 11 Let him eschew evil, and do good; let
3. 16 Having a good conscience; that, whereas
3. 16 that falsely accuse your good conversation
3. 21 the answer of a good conscience toward

8. *Life, means of life,* βίος *bios.*
1 Jo. 3. 17 whoso hath this world's good, and seeth

9. *Well, good,* εὖ *eu.*
Mark 14. 7 whensoever ye will ye may do them good

10. *Beautiful, pleasing, good,* καλόν *kalon.*
Rom. 7. 21 when I would do good, evil is present
Heb. 5. 14 exercised to discern both good and evil
Jas. 4. 17 to him that knoweth to do good, and do.

11. *Beautiful, pleasing, good,* καλός *kalos.*
Matt. 3. 10 every tree which bringeth not forth good
5. 16 that they may see your good works, and
7. 17 tree bringeth forth good fruit; but a
7. 18 neither..a corrupt tree bring forth good
7. 19 Every tree that bringeth not forth good
12. 33 make the tree good, and his fruit good
13. 8 other fell into good ground, and brought
13. 23 he that received seed into the good ground
13. 24 a man which sowed good seed in his field
13. 27 didst not thou sow good seed in thy field?
13. 37 He that soweth the good seed is the Son
13. 38 the good seed are the children of the
13. 48 gathered the good into vessels, but cast
17. 4 Lord, it is good for us to be here: if thou
26. 10 she hath wrought a good work upon me
26. 24 it had been good for that man if he had
Mark 4. 8 other fell on good ground, and did yield
4. 20 these are they which are sown on good
9. 5 Master, it is good for us to be here: and
9. 50 Salt (is) good; but if the salt have lost
14. 6 said..she hath wrought a good work on
14. 21 good were it for that man if he had never
Luke 3. 9 which bringeth not forth good fruit is
6. 38 good measure, pressed down, and shaken
6. 43 a good tree bringeth not forth corrupt
6. 43 doth a corrupt tree bring forth good fruit
8. 15 But that on the good ground are they
9. 33 Master, it is good for us to be here: and
14. 34 Salt (is) good: but if the salt have lost
John 2. 10 saith..Every man..doth set forth good
2. 10 thou hast kept the good wine until now
10. 11 I am the good shepherd: the good shep.
10. 14 I am the good shepherd, and know my
10. 32 Many good works have I showed you
10. 33 For a good work we stone thee not; but
Rom. 7. 16 I consent unto the law that (it is) good
14. 21 good neither to eat flesh, nor to drink
1 Co. 5. 6 Your glorying (is) not good. Know ye not
7. 1 (It is) good for a man not to touch a wo.
7. 8 it is good for them if they abide even as
7. 26 I suppose therefore that this is good for
7. 26 (I say), that (it is) good for a man so to
Gal. 4. 18 But..good to be zealously affected alwa.
1 Ti. 1. 8 we know that the law (is) good, if a man
1. 18 thou by them mightest war a good warf.
2. 3 this (is) good and acceptable in the sight
3. 1 desire the office..he desireth a good work
3. 7 he must have a good report of them wh.
3. 13 purchase to themselves a good degree, and
1 Ti. 4. 4 every creature of God (is) good, and no.
4. 6 thou shalt be a good minister of Jesus C.
4. 6 in the words of faith and of good doctr.
5. 4 for that is good and acceptable before G.
5. 10 Well reported of for good works; if she
5. 25 Likewise also the good works..are mani.
6. 12 Fight the good fight of faith, lay hold on
6. 12 hast professed a good profession before
6. 13 who before Pontius Pilate witnessed a g.
6. 18 that they be rich in good works, ready
6. 19 a good foundation against the time to
2 Ti. 1. 14 That good thing which was committed
2. 3 endure hardness, as a good soldier of Je.
4. 7 I have fought a good fight, I have finished
Titus 2. 7 showing thyself a pattern of good works
2. 14 a peculiar people, zealous of good works
3. 8 might be careful to maintain good works
3. 8 These things are good and profitable unto
3. 14 maintain good works for necessary uses
Heb. 6. 5 And have tasted the good word of God
10. 24 to provoke unto love and to good works
13. 18 for we trust we have a good conscience
Jas. 3. 13 let him show out of a good conversation
1 Pe. 2. 12 they may by..good works, which they
4. 10 as good stewards of the manifold grace

12. *Well, fairly, beautifully,* καλῶς *kalōs.*
Matt. 5. 44 [do good to them that hate you, and pray]
Luke 6. 27 Love your enemies, do good to them wh.

13. *Useful, profitable,* χρηστός *chrēstos.*
1 Co 15. 33 evil communications corrupt good mann.

14. *Usefulness, kindness,* χρηστότης *chrēstotēs.*
Rom. 3. 12 there is none that doeth good, no, not one

[*See also* Advice, courage, do, heed, liking, piece, proper, think, tidings, way, what.]

GOOD, to be —

1. *To be good, well,* טוֹב *tob.*
1 Sa. 20. 12 behold, (if there be) good toward David
Job 10. 3 (Is it) good unto thee that thou shouldest
13. 9 Is it good that he should search you out

2. *To be or become good,* יָטַב *yatab.*
Gen. 41. 37 the thing was good in the eyes of Phara.

3. *To be prosperous, profitable,* צָלַח *tsaleach.*
Jer. 13. 10 as this girdle, which is good for nothing

4. *To be strong, have strength,* ἰσχύω *ischuō.*
Matt. 5. 13 it is thenceforth good for nothing, but to

5. *To bear or carry together, conduce,* συμφέρω *sum.*
Matt. 19. 10 If the case..be so..it is not good to

GOOD, can do —

To profit, יָעַל *yaal,* 5.
Job 15. 3 speeches wherewith he can do no good?

GOOD courage, to be of —

To be or become strong or courageous, אָמֵץ *amats.*
Deut 31. 6, 7, 23 Be strong, and of a good courage
Josh. 1. 6, 9, 18 Be strong and of a good courage
10. 25 be strong, and of good courage: for thus
1 Ch. 22. 13 be strong, and of good courage; dread
28. 20 Be strong and of good courage and do (it)

GOOD deed —

1. *Kindness,* חֶסֶד *chesed.*
Neh. 13. 14 wipe not out my good deeds that I have

2. *Good,* טוֹב *tob.*
Neh. 6. 19 they reported his good deeds before me

GOOD, to do —

1. *To do good,* טוֹב *tob,* 5.
Num 10. 29 come..with us, and we will do thee good
Psa. 119. 68 Thou (art) good, and doest good: teach
125. 4 Do good, O LORD, unto (those that be)
Jer. 32. 41 I will rejoice over them to do them good

2. *To do good,* יָטַב *yatab,* 5.
Gen. 32. 12 I will surely do thee good, and make thy
Lev. 5. 4 to do good, whatsoever (it be) that a man
Deut. 8. 16 to do thee good at thy latter end
28. 63 the LORD rejoiced over you to do you go.
30. 5 he will do thee good, and multiply thee
Josh 24. 20 after that he hath done you good
Judg 17. 13 Now know I that the LORD will do me g.
Job 24. 21 and doeth not good to the widow
Psa. 36. 3 hath left off to be wise, (and) to do good
51. 18 Do good in thy good pleasure unto Zion
Prov. 17. 22 A merry heart doeth good (like) a medici.
Isa. 41. 23 do good, or do evil, that we may be dismay.
Jer. 4. 22 but to do good they have no knowledge
10. 5 neither also (is it) in them to do good
13. 23 do good, that are accustomed to do evil
32. 40 not turn away from them, to do..good
Mic. 2. 7 do good to him that walketh uprightly
Zeph. 1. 12 will not do good, neither will he do evil

3. *To do good,* ἀγαθοεργέω *agathoergeō.*
1 Ti. 6 18 That they do good, that they be rich in

4. *To do good,* ἀγαθοποιέω *agathopoieō*
Mark 3. 4 it lawful to do good on the sabbath days
Luke 6. 9 the sabbath days to do good, or to do ev.
6. 33 if ye do good to them which do good to
6. 35 do good, and lend, hoping for nothing
Acts 14. 17 he did good, and gave us rain from heav.
3 Jo. 11 He that doeth good is of God: but

5. *To work well, confer benefits,* εὐεργετέω *euergeteō.*
Acts 10. 38 who went about doing good, and healing

6. *Well doing,* εὐποιΐα *eupoiia.*
Heb. 13. 16 to do good and to communicate forget not

GOOD health —
Peace, שָׁלוֹם *shalom.*
Gen.43. 28 father (is) in good health, he (is) yet alive

GOOD, to make -
1. *To do good,* יָטַב *yatab,* 5.
Jer. 18. 11 and make your ways and your doings good
2. *To cause to rise, confirm,* קוּם *qum,* 5.
Num23. 19 he spoken, and shall he not make it good?
3. *To recompense,* שָׁלַם *shalam,* 3.
Exod21. 34 The owner of the pit shall make (it) good
22. 11, 15 and he shall not make (it) good
22. 13 shall not make good that which was torn
22. 14 it be hurt..he shall surely make it good
Lev. 24. 18 he that killeth a beast shall make it good

GOOD pleasure —
1. *Good will or pleasure,* רָצוֹן *ratson.*
Psa. 51. 18 in thy good pleasure unto Zion: build
2. *Good pleasure,* εὐδοκία *eudokia.*
Eph. 1. 5 according to the good pleasure of his wi.
1. 9 according to his good pleasure which he
Phil. 2. 13 both to will and to do of (his) good pleas.
2 Th. 1. 11 fulfil all the good pleasure of..goodness

GOOD, to seem —
1. *To be or seem good,* טוֹב *tob.*
1 Ch.13. 2 If (it seem) good unto you, and (that it
Esth. 5. 4 If (it seem) good unto the king, let the
2. *To be or become good,* יָטַב *yetab.*
Ezra 7. 18 whatsoever shall seem good to thee, and
3. *To be or go right,* יָשַׁר *yashar.*
Jer. 18. 4 as seemed good to the potter to make (it)

GOOD speed, to send —
To cause to meet, קָרָה *qarah,* 5.
Gen. 24. 12 send me good speed this day, and show

GOOD success, to have —
To cause to act wisely, שָׂכַל *sakal,* 5.
Josh. 1. 8 and then thou shalt have good success

GOOD thing —
1. *Good, goodness, good thing,* טוּב *tub.*
Gen. 45. 23 asses laden with the good things of Egy.
2 Ki 8. 9 of every good thing of Damascus, forty
2. *Good thing,* ἀγαθόν *agathon.*
Matt. 7. 11 give good things to them that ask him!
12. 34 how can ye, being evil, speak good things?
12. 35 of the heart, bringeth forth good things
19. 16 what good thing shall I do, that I may
Luke 1. 53 hath filled the hungry with good things
16. 25 thy lifetime receivedst thy good things
John 1. 46 there any good thing come out of Nazar.
Rom. 7. 18 know that in me..dwelleth no good thing
10. 15 and bring glad tidings of good things!
Gal. 6. 6 unto him that teacheth in all good things
Eph. 6. 8 that whatsoever good thing any man do.
Philem 6 of every g. thing which is in you in Christ
Heb 9. 11 an high priest of good things to come
10. 1 having a shadow of good things to come
3. *Good, beautiful,* καλόν *kalon.*
Gal. 4. 18 zealously affected always in (a) good (thi.)
Heb. 13. 9 For (it is) a good thing that the heart be

GOOD men, lover of —
Lover or friend of good men, φιλάγαθος *philagathos.*
Titus 1. 8 a lover of good men, sober, just, holy

GOOD place, in a —
Well, pleasantly, καλῶς *kalōs.*
Jas. 2. 3 and say..Sit thou here in a good place

GOOD things, teacher of —
Teacher of good, καλοδιδάσκαλος *kalodidaskalos.*
Titus 2. 3 not false. teachers of good things

GOOD, that which is —
1. *That which is good,* τὸ ἀγαθόν *to agathon.*
Luke 6. 45 heart bringeth forth that which is good
Rom. 7. 13 Was then that which is good made death
7. 13 working death in me by that which is go.
12. 9 is evil; cleave to that which is good
13. 3 Do that which is good, and thou shalt
16. 19 have you wise unto that which is good
1 Th. 5. 15 but ever follow that which is good, both
1 Pe. 3. 13 if ye be followers of that which is good?
3 John 11 that which is evil, but that which is good
2. *That which is beautiful,* τὸ καλόν *to kalon.*
Rom. 7. 18 to perform that which is good I find not
1 Th. 5. 21 all things: hold fast that which is good

GOOD, the thing which is —
That which is good, τὸ ἀγαθόν *to agathon.*
Eph. 4. 28 with (his) hands the thing which is good

GOOD tidings, to bring —
To tell good news, εὐαγγελίζομαι *euaggelizomai.*
Luke 2. 10 I bring you good tidings of great joy
1 Th. 3. 6 brought us good tidings of your faith and

GOOD way off, a —
To put far off, רָחַק *rachaq,* 5.
Gen. 21. 16 went, and sat her down..a good way off

GOOD way, a —
To put far off, רָחַק *rachaq,* 5.
Judg18. 22 when they were a good way from the h.

GOOD while —
1. *Again, yet, while, any more,* עוֹד *od.*
Gen. 46. 29 he fell..and wept on his neck a good wh.
2. *Sufficient days,* ἡμέρας ἱκανάς [*hēmera*] Acts18.18
3. *In past days,* ἀφ' ἡμερῶν ἀρχαίων [*hēmera*] Acts15.7

GOOD words —
Courteous language, χρηστολογία *chrēstologia.*
Rom 16. 18 by good words and fair speeches deceive

GOOD WILL —
1. *Good pleasure or will,* רָצוֹן *ratson.*
Deut 33 16 the good will of him that dwelt in the b.
Mal. 2. 13 or receiveth (it) with good will at your
2. *Good pleasure,* εὐδοκία *eudokia.*
Luke 2. 14 on earth peace, good will toward men
Phil. 1. 15 Some indeed preach Christ..of good will
3. *Good will,* εὔνοια *eunoia.*
Eph. 6. 7 With good will doing service, as to the L.

GOODLIER —
Good, טוֹב *tob.*
1 Sa. 9. 2 not among the children of Israel a good.

GOODLIEST —
Good, טוֹב *tob.*
1 Sa. 8. 16 your goodliest young men, and your asses
1 Ki. 20. 3 thy children..the goodliest, (are) mine

GOODLINESS —
Kindness, kindliness, חֶסֶד *chesed.*
Isa. 40. 6 all the goodliness thereof (is) as the flow.

GOODLY —
1. *Honourable, shining,* אַדִּיר *addir.*
Eze. 17. 23 and bear fruit, and be a goodly cedar
2. *Honourable or shining,* אֶדֶר *eder.*
Zech.11. 13 a goodly price that I was prised at of th.
3. *Honourable or shining,* אַדֶּרֶת *addereth.*
Eze. 17. 8 It was planted..that it might be a goodly
4. *Honour, beauty, majesty,* הָדָר *hadar.*
Lev. 23. 40 ye shall take..the boughs of goodly trees
5. *Honour, beauty, majesty,* הוֹד *hod.*
Zech.10. 3 hath made them as his goodly horse in
6. *Desire,* חֶמְדָּה *chemdah.*
2 Ch.36. 10 with the goodly vessels of the house of
7. *Desires, desirable objects,* חֲמוּדוֹת *chamudoth.*
Gen. 27. 15 Rebekah took goodly raiment of her eld.
8. *To be good,* טוֹב *tob.*
Num 24. 5 How goodly are thy tents, O Jacob..thy t.
9. *Good (of form),* (תֹּאַר) טוֹב *tob (toar).*
Exod. 2. 2 when she saw him that he (was a) goodly
Deut. 3. 25 land..that goodly mountain, and Leba.
6. 10 to give thee great and goodly cities, which
8. 12 and hast built goodly houses, and dwelt
Josh. 7. 21 When I saw..a goodly Babylonish garment
1 Sa. 9. 2 Saul, a choice young man, and a goodly
16. 12 of a beautiful countenance, and goodly
1 Ki. 1. 6 and he also (was a) very goodly (man)
Joel 3. 5 have carried into your temples my goodly
10. *Desirable thing,* מַחְמָד *machmad.*
2 Ch.36. 19 destroyed all the goodly vessels thereof
11. *Appearance,* מַרְאֶה *mareh.*
2 Sa. 23. 21 And he slew an Egyptian, a goodly man
12. *Beauty, ornament,* פְּאֵר *peer.*
Exod39. 28 and goodly bonnets (of) fine linen, and
13. *Beauty, desire,* צְבִי *tsebi.*
Jer. 3. 19 a goodly heritage of the hosts of nations?
14. *Beauty,* שֶׁפֶר *shepher.*
Gen. 49. 21 a hind let loose: he giveth goodly words
15. *Fair of form,* יְפֵה תֹאַר [*yapheh*].
Gen. 39. 6 Joseph was (a) goodly (person), and well
Jer. 11. 16 A green olive tree..(and) of goodly fruit
16. *Good, beautiful,* καλός *kalos*
Matt13. 45 a merchant man seeking goodly pearls
Luke21. 5 how it was adorned with goodly stones
17. *Bright, shining,* λαμπρός *lampros.*
Jas. 2. 2 a man with a gold ring in goodly apparel
Rev. 18. 14 all things which were dainty and goodly
18. *God, of might,* אֵל *el.*
Psa. 80. 10 the boughs..(were like) the goodly cedars
19. *Rattling wings, ostriches,* רְנָנִים *renanim.*
Job 39. 13 (Gavest thou) the goodly wings unto the
20. *To be fair, beautiful, good,* שָׁפַר *shaphar*
Psa. 16 6 The lines are fallen..I have a goodly h.

GOODLY, to make
To do or make good, טוֹב *tob,* 5
Hos. 10. 1 his land they have made goodly images

GOOD MAN —
1. *A man,* אִישׁ *ish.*
Prov. 7. 19 the good man (is) not at home, he is gone
2. *House despot, master of the house,* οἰκοδεσπότης.
Luke22. 11 And ye..say unto the good man of the h.

GOOD MAN of the house —
House despot, master of the house, οἰκοδεσπότης.
Matt20. 11 murmured against the good man of the h.
24. 43 if the good man of the house had known
Mark14. 14 say ye to the good man of the house, The
Luke 12. 39 if the good man of the house had known

GOODNESS —
1. *Kindness,* חֶסֶד *chesed.*
Exod34. 6 LORD God..abundant in goodness and
2 Ch.32. 32 the acts of Hezekiah, and his goodness
35. 26 rest of the acts of Josiah, and his goodn.
Psa. 33. 5 earth is full of the goodness of the LORD
52. 1 the goodness of God (endureth) continua.
107. 8, 15, 21, 31 praise the LORD (for) his good.
144. 2 My goodness, and my fortress; my high
Prov20. 6 will proclaim every one his own goodness
Hos. 6. 4 your goodness (is) as a morning cloud, and
2. *Good, goodness,* טוֹב *tob.*
Exod18. 9 Jethro rejoiced for all the goodness which
Num 10. 32 what goodness the LORD shall do unto us
Judg. 8. 35 according to all the goodness which he
2 Sa. 7. 28 thou hast promised this goodness unto
1 Ki. 8. 66 for all the goodness that the LORD had
1 Ch.17. 26 hast promised this goodness unto thy ser.
2 Ch. 6. 41 and let thy saints rejoice in goodness
7. 10 for the goodness that the LORD had sho.
Psa. 16. 2 Thou (art) my LORD: my goodness..not
21. 3 preventest..with the blessings of goodn.
23. 6 goodness and mercy shall follow me all
65. 11 Thou crownest the year with thy goodn.
68. 10 thou, O God, hast prepared of thy goodn.
107. 9 and filleth the hungry soul with goodness
Jer. 33. 9 fear and tremble for all the goodness, and
Hos. 10. 1 according to the goodness of his land they
3. *Good, goodness, good thing,* טוּב *tub.*
Exod33. 19 make all my goodness pass before thee
Neh. 9. 25 delighted themselves in thy great goodn.
9. 35 thy great goodness that thou gavest them
Psa. 25. 7 remember thou me for thy goodness'
27. 13 unless I had believed to see the goodness
31. 19 how great (is) thy goodness, which thou
65. 4 satisfied with the goodness of thy house
145. 7 utter the memory of thy great goodness
Isa. 63. 7 the great goodness toward the house of
Jer. 2. 7 fruit thereof and the goodness thereof
31. 12 flow together to the goodness of the L.
31. 14 shall be satisfied with my goodness, saith
Hos. 3. 5 fear the LORD and his goodness in the
Zech. 9. 17 how great (is) his goodness, and how gre.
4. *Goodness,* ἀγαθωσύνη *agathōsunē.*
Rom 15. 14 ye also are full of goodness, filled with
Gal. 5. 22 long suffering, gentleness, goodness, faith
Eph. 5. 9 all goodness and righteousness and truth
2 Th. 1. 11 all the good pleasure of (his) goodness
5. *Usefulness, benignity,* χρηστότης *chrēstotēs.*
Rom. 2. 4 despisest thou the riches of his goodness
11. 22 Behold therefore the goodness and seve.
11. 22 goodness, if thou continue in (his) good.
6. *Useful, benign,* χρηστός *chrēstos.*
Rom. 2. 4 that the goodness of God leadeth thee

GOODS —
1. *Strength,* אוֹן *on.*
Job 20. 10 and his hands shall restore their goods
2. *Force, wealth,* חַיִל *chayil.*
Num31. 9 and all their flocks, and all their goods
3. *Good, good thing,* טוֹב *tob.*
Deut28. 11 LORD shall make thee plenteous in goods
Eccl. 5. 11 When goods increase, they are increased
4. *Good, goodness, good thing,* טוּב *tub.*
Gen. 24. 10 the goods of his master (were) in his h.
Neh. 9. 25 possessed houses full of all goods, wells
Job 20. 21 therefore shall no man look for his goods
5. *Work, business,* מְלָאכָה *melakah.*
Exod22. 8, 11 put his hand unto his neighbour's go.
6. *Riches, wealth,* נִכְסִין *niksin.*
Ezra 6. 8 of the king's goods, (even) of the tribute
7. 26 confiscation of goods, or to imprisonment
7. *Getting, acquisition,* קִנְיָן *qinyan.*
Eze. 38. 12 which have gotten cattle and goods, that
38. 13 to take away cattle and goods, to take a
8. *Substance, goods,* רְכוּשׁ *rekush.*
Gen. 14. 11 took all the goods of Sodom and Gomor.
14. 12 they took Lot..and his goods, and depa.
14. 16 he brought back all the goods, and also
14. 16 and his goods, and the women also, and
14. 21 Give me..and take the goods to thyself
31. 18 his goods which he had gotten, the cattle
46. 6 their goods, which they had gotten in
Num16. 32 (apperta.) unto Korah, and all (their) g.
35. 3 for their goods, and for all their beasts
2 Ch.21. 14 children, and thy wives, and all thy g.
Ezra 1. 4, 6 with gold, and with goods, and with bea.
9. *Good, good thing,* ἀγαθός *agathos.*
Luke12. 18 will I bestow all my fruits and my goods
12. 19 hast much goods laid up for many years
10. *Essence, substance,* οὐσία *ousia.*
Luke15. 12 the portion of goods that falleth (to me)
11. *Vessel, instrument,* σκεῦος *skeuos.*
Matt12. 29 how can one enter..and spoil his goods
Mark 3. 27 No man can enter..and spoil his goods
12. *The things existing,* τὰ ὑπάρχοντα *ta huparcho.*
Matt24. 47 shall make him ruler over all his goods
25. 14 servants, and delivered unto them his g.
Luke11. 21 keepeth his palace, his goods are in pea.
16. 1 unto him that he had wasted his goods
19. 8 the half of my goods I give to the poor

1 Co.13. 3 I bestow all my goods to feed (the poor)
Heb.10. 34 took joyfully the spoiling of your goods

13. *Existence, substance,* ὕπαρξις *huparxis.*
Acts 2. 45 And sold their possessions and goods, and

GOODS, to be increased with —
To be rich, wealthy, πλουτέω *plouteō.*
Rev. 3. 17 and increased with goods, and have need

GOODS, thy —
The things belonging to thee, τὰ σά *ta sa.*
Luke 6. 30 taketh away thy goods ask (them) not aga.

GOPHER —
Gopher, cedar, cypress, fir wood, גֹּפֶר *gopher.*
Gen. 6. 14 Make thee an ark of gopher wood; rooms

GORE, to —
To push, gore, נָגַח *nagach.*
Exod21. 28 ox gore a man or a woman, that they die
21. 31 Whether he have gored a son, or have g.

GORGEOUS —
Bright, shining, λαμπρός *lampros.*
Luke23. 11 arrayed him in a gorgeous robe, and sent

GORGEOUSLY, most —
Perfection, מִכְלוֹל *miklol.*
Eze. 23. 12 captains..rulers clothed most gorgeously

GORGEOUSLY apparelled, they which are —
Those in splendid garments, οἱ ἐν ἱματισμῷ ἐνδόξῳ ὑπάρχοντες *hoi en himatismō endoxō huparchontes.*
Luke 7. 25 they which are gorgeously apparelled, and

GO'-SHEN, גֹּשֶׁן.
1. The name of a part of Egypt where the Israelites dwelt during their sojourn there. It is usually called the "land of Goshen" but also simply Goshen. "The land of Rameses" seems (Gen. 47. 11) to have been another name for Goshen, unless it be simply a district of it. From Gen. 45. 10 it appears to have been a territory near the palace of Joseph's Pharaoh, who was of the 15th Egyptian dynasty, and resided part of the year at Memphis, and during harvest time at Avaris, on the Bubastite or Pelusiac branch of the Nile. Goshen was probably the extreme province of Egypt towards Canaan (Gen. 46. 28, 29, and 33, 34).
Gen. 45. 10 And thou shalt dwell in the land of G.
46. 28 he sent Judah..to direct his face unto G.
46. 28 and they came into the land of G.
46. 29 went up to meet Israel his father, to G.
46. 34 that ye may dwell in the land of G.: for
47. 1 and, behold, they (are) in the land of G.
47. 4 let thy servants dwell in the land of G.
47. 6 in the land of G. let them dwell: and if
47. 27 And Israel dwelt..in the country of G.
50. 8 little ones..they left in the land of G.
Exod. 8. 22 I will sever in that day the land of G.
9. 26 Only in the land of G...was there no hail

2. A district in southern Canaan, between Gaza and Gibeon, and part of the maritime plain of Judah.
Josh.10. 41 And Joshua smote..all the country of G.
11. 16 So Joshua took..all the land of G., and

3. A town in the mountains of Judah.
Josh.15. 51 And G., and Holon, and Giloh; eleven

GOSPEL —
Good news, tidings, word, εὐαγγέλιον *euaggelion.*
Matt. 4. 23 preaching the gospel of the kingdom, and
9. 35 preaching the gospel of the kingdom, and
24. 14 gospel of the kingdom shall be preached
26. 13 Wheresoever this gospel shall be preach.
Mark 1. 1 beginning of the gospel of Jesus Christ
1. 14 preaching the gospel of the kingdom of
1. 15 at hand: repent ye, and believe the gos.
8. 35 lose his life for my sake and the gospel's
10. 29 or lands, for my sake, and the gospel's
13. 10 the gospel must first be published among
14. 9 Wheresoever this gospel shall be preached
16. 15 [and preach the gospel to every creature]
Acts 15. 7 Gentiles..should hear the word of the g.
20. 24 to testify the gospel of the grace of God
Rom. 1. 1 Paul..separated unto the gospel of God
1. 9 whom I serve with my spirit in the gospel
1. 16 I am not ashamed of the gospel of Christ
2. 16 by Jesus Christ according to my gospel
10. 16 But they have not all obeyed the gospel
11. 28 As concerning the gospel..enemies for
15. 16 ministering the gospel of God, that the
15. 19 I have fully preached the gospel of Christ
15. 29 fulness of the blessing of [the gospel of] C.
16. 25 to stablish you according to my gospel
1 Co. 4. 15 I have begotten you through the gospel
9. 12 lest we should hinder the gospel of Christ
9. 14 preach the gospel should live of the gos.
9. 18 I may make the gospel of Christ without
9. 18 that I abuse not my power in the gospel
9. 23 this I do for the gospel's sake, that I mi.
15. 1 I declare unto you the gospel which I pr.
2 Co. 2. 12 I came to Troas to (preach) Christ's gos.
4. 3 if our gospel be hid, it is hid to them that
4. 4 the light of the glorious gospel of Christ
8. 18 whose praise (is) in the gospel throughout
9. 13 professed subjection unto the gospel of C.
10. 14 to you also in (preaching) the gospel of C.
11. 4 or another gospel, which ye have not acc.
11. 7 because I have preached to you the gos.
Gal. 1. 6 are..removed from him..unto another g.
1. 7 and would pervert the gospel of Christ
1. 11 the gospel which was preached of me is
Gal. 2. 2 that gospel which I preach among
2. 5 that the truth of the gospel might contin.
2. 7 that the gospel of the uncircumcision was
2. 14 not..according to the truth of the gospel
Eph. 1. 13 after that ye heard..the gospel of your
3. 6 of his promise in Christ by the gospel
6. 15 with the preparation of the gospel of pe.
6. 19 to make known the mystery [of the gospel]
Phil. 1. 5 For your fellowship in the gospel from
1. 7 defence and confirmation of the gospel
1. 12 rather unto the furtherance of the gospel
1. 17 that I am set for the defence of the gospel
1. 27 be as it becometh the gospel of Christ
1. 27 striving together for the faith of the gos.
2. 22 a son..he hath served with me in the g.
4. 3 women which laboured with me in the g.
4. 15 that in the beginning of the gospel, when
Col. 1. 5 in the word of the truth of the gospel
1. 23 not moved away from the hope of the g.
1 Th. 1. 5 our gospel came not unto you in word
2. 2 to speak unto you the gospel of God with
2. 4 allowed..to be put in trust with the gos.
2. 8 not the gospel of God only, but also our
2. 9 we preached unto you the gospel of God
3. 2 fellow labourer in the gospel of Christ
2 Th. 1. 8 that obey not the gospel of our Lord Jes.
2. 14 Whereunto he called you by our gospel
1 Ti. 1. 11 According to the glorious gospel of the
2 Ti. 1. 8 partaker of the afflictions of the gospel
1. 10 immortality to light through the gospel
2. 8 raised from the dead according to my go.
Phm. 13 ministered..in the bonds of the gospel
1 Pe. 4. 17 of them that obey not the gospel of God?
Rev. 14. 6 having the everlasting gospel to preach

GOSPEL, to preach before the —
To tell good news before hand, προευαγγελίζομαι.
Gal. 3. 8 preached before the gospel unto Abraham

GOSPEL (of), to preach the —
To tell good news, εὐαγγελίζομαι *euaggelizomai.*
Luke 4. 18 he hath anointed me to preach the gospel
9. 6 preaching the gospel, and healing every
20. 1 as he taught..and preached the gospel
Rom. 1. 15 I am ready to preach the gospel to you
10. 15 of them that [preach the gospel of peace]
15. 20 so have I strived to preach the gospel
1 Co. 1. 17 not to baptize, but to preach the gospel
9. 16 though I preach the gospel, I have noth.
9. 16 woe is unto me, if I preach not the gos.!
9. 18 that, when I preach the gospel, I may
2 Co. 10. 16 To preach the gospel in the (regions) be.
Gal. 1. 8 preach any other gospel unto you than
1. 9 If any..preach any other gospel unto you
4. 13 I preached the gospel unto you at the

GOSPEL into or unto, to preach the —
To tell good news, εὐαγγελίζομαι *euaggelizomai.*
Acts 8. 25 preached the gospel in many villages of
14. 7 And there they preached the gospel
14. 21 when they had preached the gospel to
16. 10 called us for to preach the gospel unto
1 Pe. 1. 12 them that have preached the gospel unto

GOSPEL, to be preached by the —
To tell good news, εὐαγγελίζομαι *euaggelizomai.*
1 Pe. 1. 25 which by the gospel is preached unto you

GOSPEL is preached to or unto, the —
To tell good news, εὐαγγελίζομαι *euaggelizomai.*
Luke 7. 22 to the poor the gospel is preached
Heb. 4. 2 For unto us was the gospel preached, as
1 Pe. 4. 6 for this cause was the gospel preached

GOSPEL preached to, to have the —
To tell good news, εὐαγγελίζομαι *euaggelizomai.*
Matt.11. 5 the poor have the gospel preached to them

GOTTEN, to be —
1. *To be gathered,* אָסַף *asaph,* 2.
2 Sa. 17. 13 Moreover if he be gotten into a city, then
2. *To be given,* נָתַן *nathan,* 6.
Job 28. 15 cannot be gotten for gold, neither shall
3. *To draw away,* ἀποσπάω *apospaō.*
Acts 21. 1 that after we were gotten from them

GOTTEN hastily, to be —
Be hastened, בָּהַל *bahal,* 4 [V.L. בחל, 4].
Prov.20. 21 An inheritance (may be) gotten hastily

GOURD —
1. *Gourd, palma christi,* קִיקָיוֹן *qiqayon.*
Jon. 4. 6 the LORD God prepared a gourd, and
4. 6 So Jonah was exceeding glad of the gou.
4. 7 and it smote the gourd that it withered
4. 9 Doest thou well to be angry for the go.?
4. 10 Thou hast had pity on the gourd, for the
2. *Knobs, gourds, wild cucumbers,* פַּקֻּעֹת *paqquoth.*
2 Ki. 4. 39 gathered thereof wild gourds his lap full

GOVERN, to —
1. *To bind up, gird,* חָבַשׁ *chabash.*
Job 34. 17 Shall even he that hateth right govern?
2. *To lead forth,* נָחָה *nachah,* 5.
Psa. 67. 4 and govern the nations upon earth. Sel.
3. *To do, make, work, use,* עָשָׂה *asah.*
1 Ki.21. 7 Dost thou now govern the kingdom of I.?

GOVERNMENT —
1. *Rule,* מֶמְשָׁלָה *memshalah.*
Isa. 22. 21 I will commit thy government into his
2. *Princely power,* מִשְׂרָה *misrah.*
Isa. 9. 6 the government shall be upon his should.
9. 7 Of the increase of (his) government and
3. *A steering, piloting, directing,* κυβέρνησις *kuber.*
1 Co.12. 28 helps, governments, diversities of tongues
4. *Lordship, power,* κυριότης *kuriotēs.*
2 Pe. 2. 10 walk after the flesh..and depise govern.

GOVERNOR —
1. *A leader,* אַלֻּף, אַלּוּף *alluph.*
Zech. 9. 7 he shall be as a governor in Judah, and
12. 5 the governors of Judah shall say in their
12. 6 In that day will I make the governors of
2. *To grave, decree,* חָקַק *chaqaq.*
Judg. 5. 9 My heart (is) toward the governors of Is.
3. *To decree,* חָקַק *chaqaq,* 3a.
Judg. 5. 14 out of Machir came down governors, and
4. *To rule,* מָשַׁל *mashal.*
Gen. 45. 26 he (is) governor over all the land of Egy.
2 Ch. 23. 20 the governors of the people, and all the
Psa. 22. 28 and he (is) the governor among the nat.
Jer. 30. 21 their governor shall proceed from the
5. *Leader, one going before,* נָגִיד *nagid.*
2 Ch.28. 7 and Azrikam the governor of the house
6. *One lifted up, prince,* נָשִׂיא *nasi.*
2 Ch. 1. 2 to every governor in all Israel, the chief
7. *Governor, captain, viceroy,* פֶּחָה *pechah.*
1 Ki.10. 15 and of the governors of the country
2 Ch. 9. 14 governors of the country, brought gold and
Ezra 8. 36 to the governors on this side the river
Neh. 2. 7 given me to the governors beyond the ri.
2. 9 I came to the governors beyond the river
3. 7 unto the throne of the governor on this
5. 14 to be their governor in the land of Jud.
5. 14 have not eaten the bread of the governor
5. 15 the former governors..were chargeable
5. 18 required not I the bread of the governor
12. 26 in the days of Nehemiah the governor
Esth. 3. 12 governors that (were) over every province
Hag. 1. 1, 14 the son of Shealtiel, governor of Jud.
2. 2 son of Shealtiel, governor of Judah, and
2. 21 Speak to Zerubbabel, governor of Judah
Mal. 1. 8 offer it now unto thy governor; will he
8. *Governor, captain, viceroy,* פֶּחָה *pechah.*
Ezra 5. 3, 6 Tatnai, governor on this side the river
5. 14 Sheshbazzar, whom he had made govern.
6. 6 Now..Tatnai, governor beyond the river
6. 7 let the governor..build this house of G.
6. 13 Then Tatnai, governor on this side the
9. *Overseer, inspector,* פָּקִיד *paqid.*
Jer. 20. 1 who (was) also chief governor in the hou.
10. *Head, prince, chief, captain,* שַׂר *sar.*
1 Ki. 22 26 unto Amon the governor of the city, and
2 Ki. 23. 8 the gate of Joshua the governor of the
1 Ch.24. 5 governors of the sanctuary, and govern.
2 Ch.18. 25 carry him back to Amon the governor
11. *Ruler,* שַׁלִּיט *shallit.*
Gen. 42. 6 Joseph (was) the governor over the land
12. *Ethnarch, ruler of a people,* ἐθνάρχης *ethnarch.*
2 Co. 11. 32 the governor under Aretas the king kept
13. *To make, lead, guide straight,* εὐθύνω *euthunō*
Jas. 3. 4 turned..whithersoever the governor list.
14. *Leader, guide, one going before,* ἡγεμών *hēgemōn.*
Matt.10. 18 ye shall be brought before governors
27. 2 delivered him to Pontius Pilate the gov.
27. 11 stood before the governor: and the gov.
27. 14 insomuch that the governor marvelled
27. 15 the governor was wont to release unto
27. 21 The governor answered and said unto th.
27. 23 [the governor said,] Why, what evil hath
27 27 Then the soldiers of the governor took J.
28. 14 And if this come to the governor's ears
Luke20. 20 unto the power and authority of the gov.
Acts 23. 24 and bring..safe unto Felix [the governor]
23. 26 unto the most excellent governor Felix
23 33 and delivered the epistle to the governor
23. 34 when the governor had read..he asked of
24. 1 who informed the governor against Paul
24. 10 after that the governor had beckoned
26. 30 the king rose up, and the governor, and
1 Pe. 2. 14 Or unto governors, as unto them that are
15. *To lead, guide, go before,* ἡγέομαι *hēgeomai.*
Matt. 2. 6 for out of thee shall come a Governor
Acts 7. 10 he made him governor over Egypt and
16. *House manager,* οἰκονόμος *oikonomos.*
Gal. 4. 2 is under tutors and governors until the

GOVERNOR, to be —
To go before, be leader or guide, ἡγεμονεύω.
Luke 2. 2 made when Cyrenius was governor of S.
3. 1 Pontius Pilate being governor of Judea

GOVERNOR of the feast —
Chief of a triklinium, ἀρχιτρίκλινος *architriklinos.*
John 2. 8 and bear unto the governor of the feast
2. 9 the governor of the feast called the brid.

GOVERNOR, chief —
Leader, one going before, נָגִיד *nagid.*
1 Ch.29. 22 Solomon..and anointed (him)..the chief g.

GOVERNORS —
Prefects, סִגְנִין *sigenin.*
Dan. 2. 48 chief of the governors over all the wise

Dan. 3. 2 the princes, the governors, and the capt.
3. 3 Then the princes, the governors, and cap.
3. 27 the princes, governors, and captains, and
6. 7 the governors, and the princes, the coun.

GO'-ZAN, גּוֹזָן *food.*

The English version makes this name appear to be a river; though it was evidently not a river but a country. Gozan was a place to which Israel was carried away by Pul, Tiglath-Pileser, and Shalmaneser (possibly Sargon). It was perhaps identical with the *Gauzanitis* of Ptolemy, and the *Mygdonia* of other writers. The river Habor (now Khabour), watered and drained it as the great Mesopotamian affluent of the Euphrates.

2 Ki. 17. 6 and placed..in Habor (by) the river of G.
18. 11 put them..in Habor (by) the river of G.
19. 12 G., and Haran, and Rezeph, and the
1 Ch. 5. 26 Hara, and to the river G., unto this day
Isa. 37. 12 G., and Haran, and Rezeph, and the

GRACE —

1. *Grace, favour,* חֵן *chen.*
Gen. 6. 8 Noah found grace in the eyes of the LORD
19. 19 thy servant hath found grace in thy sight
32. 5 sent..that I may find grace in thy sight
33. 8 to find grace in the sight of my lord
33. 10 if now I have found grace in thy sight
33. 15 let me find grace in the sight of my lord
34. 11 Let me find grace in your eyes, and what
39. 4 Joseph found grace in his sight, and he
47. 25 let us find grace in the sight of my lord
47. 29 If now I have found grace in thy sight
50. 4 If now I have found grace in your eyes
Exod 33. 12 and thou hast also found grace in my
33. 13 if I have found grace in thy sight, show
33. 13 know..that I may find grace in thy sight
33. 16 thy people have found grace in thy sight?
33. 17 thou hast found grace in my sight, and I
34. 9 If now I have found grace in thy sight
Num 32. 5 if we have found grace in thy sight, let
Judg. 6. 17 If now I have found grace in thy sight
Ruth 2. 2 after (him) in whose sight I shall find gr.
2. 10 Why have I found grace in thine eyes
1 Sa. 1. 18 Let thine handmaid find grace in thy
20. 3 that I have found grace in thine eyes
27. 5 If I have now found grace in thine eyes
2 Sa. 14. 22 that I have found grace in thy sight, my
16. 4 (that) I may find grace in thy sight, my
Esth. 2. 17 she obtained grace and favour in his sight
Psa. 45. 2 grace is poured into thy lips: therefore
84. 11 the LORD will give grace and glory: no
Prov. 1. 9 For they..an ornament of grace unto thy
3. 22 life unto thy soul, and grace to thy neck
3. 34 Surely..he giveth grace unto the lowly
4. 9 give to thine head an ornament of grace
22. 11 (for) the grace of his lips the king (shall
Jer. 31. 2 The people..found grace in the wilder.
Zech. 4. 7 shoutings, (crying), Grace, grace unto it!
12. 10 the spirit of grace and of supplications

2. *Grace, supplication for grace,* תְּחִנָּה *techinnah.*
Ezra 9. 8 now for a little space grace hath been

3. *Gracefulness, comeliness,* εὐπρέπεια *euprepeia.*
Jas. 1. 11 the grace of the fashion of it perisheth

4. *Grace, graciousness,* χάρις *charis.*
Luke 2. 40 and the grace of God was upon him
John 1. 14 dwelt among us..full of grace and truth
1. 16 And of his fulness..and grace for grace
1. 17 grace and truth came by Jesus Christ
Acts 4. 33 the apostles..great grace was upon them
11. 23 when he came, and had seen the grace of
13. 43 persuaded..to continue in the grace of G.
14. 3 gave testimony unto the word of his grace
14. 26 been recommended to the grace of God
15. 11 that through the grace of the Lord Jesus
15. 40 being recommended..unto the grace of G.
18. 27 them..which had believed through grace
20. 24 to testify the gospel of the grace of God
20. 32 to the word of his grace, which is able
Rom. 1. 5 By whom we have received grace and ap.
1. 7 Grace to you and peace from God our F.
3. 24 Being justified freely by his grace through
4. 4 is the reward not reckoned of grace, but
4. 16 (it is) of faith, that (it might be) by grace
5. 2 access..into this grace wherein we stand
5. 15 the grace of God, and the gift by grace
5. 17 they which receive abundance of grace
5. 20 where sin abounded, grace did much more
5. 21 even so might grace reign through right.
6. 1 Shall we continue in sin, that grace may
6. 14, 15 are not under the law, but under grace
11. 5 remnant according to..election of grace
11. 6 if by grace, then (is it) no more of works
11. 6 otherwise grace is no more grace. But
11. 6 (it be) of works, [then is it no more grace]
12. 3 through the grace given unto me, to every
12. 6 according to the grace that is given to
15. 15 of the grace that is given to me of God
16. 20 The grace of our Lord Jesus Christ
16. 24 [The grace of our Lord Jesus Christ]
1 Co. 1. 3 Grace (be) unto you, and peace, from G.
1. 4 the grace of God which is given you by
3. 10 the grace of God which is given unto me
10. 30 if I by grace be a partaker, why am I evil
15. 10 grace of God I am what I am: and his g.
15. 10 I, but the grace of God which was with
16. 23 grace of our Lord Jesus Christ (be) with
2 Co. 1. 2 Grace (be) to you and peace from God
1. 12 but by the grace of God, we have had our
4. 15 that the abundant grace might through
6. 1 ye receive not the grace of God in vain
8. 1 we do you to wit of the grace of God
2 Co. 8. 6 also finish in you the same grace also
8. 7 (see) that ye abound in this grace also
8. 9 know the grace of our Lord Jesus Christ
8. 19 chosen..to travel with us with this grace
9. 8 able to make all grace abound toward
9. 14 for the exceeding grace of God in you
12. 9 My grace is sufficient for thee; for my
13. 14 The grace of the Lord Jesus Christ, and
Gal. 1. 3 Grace (be) to you and peace from God the
1. 6 the grace of Christ unto another gospel
1. 15 who separated..and called (me) by his g.
2. 9 perceived the grace that was given unto
2. 21 I do not frustrate the grace of God: for
5. 4 by the law; ye are fallen from grace
6. 18 grace of our Lord Jesus Christ (be) with
Eph. 1. 2 Grace (be) to you, and peace, from God
1. 6 To the praise of the glory of his grace
1. 7 according to the riches of his grace
2. 5 together with Christ, by grace ye are sav.
2. 7 show the exceeding riches of his grace in
2. 8 by grace are ye saved through faith; and
3. 2 dispensation of the grace of God which
3. 7 according to the gift of the grace of God
3. 8 least of all saints, is this grace given
4. 7 But unto every one of us is given grace
4. 29 it may minister grace unto the hearers
6. 24 Grace (be) with all them that love our L.
Phil. 1. 2 Grace (be) unto you, and peace, from God
1. 7 ye all are partakers of my grace
4. 23 grace of our Lord Jesus Christ (be) with
Col. 1. 2 Grace (be) unto you, and peace, from God
1. 6 and knew the grace of God in truth
3. 16 singing with grace in your hearts to the
4. 6 Let your speech (be) alway with grace
4. 18 Remember my bonds. Grace (be) with
1 Th. 1. 1 Grace (be) unto you, and peace, from G.
5. 28 grace of our Lord Jesus Christ (be) with
2 Th. 1. 2 Grace unto you, and peace, from God our
1. 12 grace of our God and the Lord Jesus C.
2. 16 consolation and good hope through grace
3. 18 grace of our Lord Jesus Christ (be) with
1 Ti. 1. 2 Grace, mercy, (and) peace, from God our
1. 14 grace of our Lord was exceeding abunda.
6. 21 Grace (be) with thee. Amen
2 Ti. 1. 2 Grace, mercy, (and) peace, from God the
1. 9 according to his own purpose and grace
2. 1 strong in the grace that is in Christ Jesus
4. 22 [Grace (be) with you. Amen]
Titus 1. 4 Grace, mercy, (and) peace, from God the
2. 11 the grace of God that bringeth salvation
3. 7 being justified by his grace, we should
3. 15 Grace (be) with you all. Amen
Phm. 3 Grace to you, and peace, from God our
25 grace of our Lord Jesus Christ (be) with
Heb. 2. 9 by the grace of God should taste death
4. 16 come boldly unto the throne of grace
4. 16 and find grace to help in time of need
10. 29 done despite unto the spirit of grace?
12. 15 lest any man fail of the grace of God
12. 28 let us have grace, whereby we may serve
13. 9 that the heart be established with grace
13. 25 Grace (be) with you all. Amen
Jas. 4. 6 But he giveth more grace. Wherefore he
4. 6 but giveth grace unto the humble
1 Pe. 1. 2 Grace unto you, and peace, be multiplied
1. 10 of the grace (that should come) unto you
1. 13 hope to the end for the grace that is to
3. 7 being heirs together of the grace of life
4. 10 stewards of the manifold grace of God
5. 5 For God..giveth grace to the humble
5. 10 the God of all grace, who hath called us
5. 12 the true grace of God wherein ye stand
2 Pe. 1. 2 Grace and peace be multiplied unto you
3. 18 grow in grace, and (in) the knowledge of
2 Jo. 3 Grace be with you, mercy, (and) peace
Jude 4 the grace of our God into lasciviousness,
Rev. 1. 4 Grace (be) unto you, and peace, from him
22. 21 grace of our Lord Jesus Christ (be) with

GRACIOUS —

1. *Grace, favour,* חֵן *chen.*
Prov. 11. 16 A gracious woman retaineth honour; and
Eccl. 10. 12 words of a wise man's mouth (are) graci.

2. *Gracious,* חַנּוּן *channun.*
Exod 22. 27 that I will hear; for I (am) gracious
34. 6 merciful and gracious, long suffering and
2 Ch. 30. 9 LORD your God (is) gracious and merciful
Neh. 9. 17 gracious and merciful, slow to anger, and
9. 31 for thou (art) a gracious and merciful God
Psa. 86. 15 a God full of compassion, and gracious
103. 8 The LORD (is) merciful and gracious, slow
111. 4 the LORD (is) gracious, and full of comp.
112. 4 gracious, and full of compassion, and ri.
116. 5 Gracious (is) the LORD, and righteous; yea
145. 8 The LORD (is) gracious, and full of comp.
Joel 2. 13 for he (is) gracious and merciful, slow to
Jon. 4. 2 for I knew that thou (art) a gracious God

3. *Grace, graciousness,* χάρις *charis.*
Luke 4. 22 and wondered at the gracious words which

4. *Useful, kind,* χρηστός *chrēstos.*
1 Pe. 2. 3 If..ye have tasted that the Lord (is) gra.

GRACIOUS, to be —

1. *To grace, be gracious,* חָנַן *chanan.*
Gen. 43. 29 said, God be gracious unto thee, my son
Exod 33. 19 will be gracious to whom I will be grac.
Num. 6. 25 shine upon thee, and be gracious unto
2 Ki. 13. 23 LORD was gracious unto them, and had c.
Job 33. 24 Then he is gracious unto him, and saith
Psa. 77. 9 Hath God forgotten to be gracious? hath
Isa. 30. 18 wait, that he may be gracious unto you
30. 19 he will be very gracious unto thee at the
33. 2 O LORD, be gracious unto us; we have
Amos 5. 15 LORD God of hosts will be gracious unto
Mal. 1. 9 beseech God that he will be gracious unto

2. *To be gracious,* חָנַן *chanan,* 2.
Jer. 22. 23 how gracious shalt thou be when pangs

GRACIOUS to, to be —

To be gracious, act graciously, חָנַן *chanan,* 3.
2 Sa. 12. 22 GOD will be gracious to me, that the child

GRACIOUSLY —

Good, טוֹב *tob.*
Hos. 14. 2 receive (us) graciously: so will we render

GRACIOUSLY, to deal, or give —

To be gracious, חָנַן *chanan.*
Gen. 33. 5 children which God hath graciously given
33. 11 God hath dealt graciously with me, and

GRAFF in or into, to —

To engraft, stick in, ἐγκεντρίζω *egkentrizō.*
Rom 11. 17 thou..wert graffed in among them, and
11. 19 broken off, that I might be graffed in
11. 23 And they also..shall be graffed in
11. 23 for God is able to graff them in again
11. 24 and wert graffed contrary to nature into
11. 24 how much more shall these..be graffed in

GRAIN —

A kernel, grain, seed, κόκκος *kokkos.*
Matt 13. 31 The kingdom of heaven is like to a grain
17. 20 If ye have faith as a grain of mustard se.
Mark 4. 31 (It is) like a grain of mustard seed, which
Luke 13. 19 It is like a grain of mustard seed, which
17. 6 If ye had faith as a grain of mustard seed
1 Co. 15. 37 not that body that shall be, but bare gr.

GRAIN, least —

Grain, pebble, צְרוֹר *tseror.*
Amos 9. 9 yet shall not the least grain fall upon the

GRANDMOTHER —

Mamma, grandmother, μάμμη *mammē.*
2 Ti. 1. 5 which dwelt first in thy grandmother

GRANT —

Grant, permission, רִשְׁיוֹן *rishyon.*
Ezra 3. 7 according to the grant that they had of C.

GRANT, to —

1. *To cause to come in,* בּוֹא *bo,* 5.
1 Ch. 4. 10 God granted him that which he requested

2. *To give,* נָתַן *nathan.*
Lev. 25. 24 ye shall grant a redemption for the land
Ruth 1. 9 The LORD grant you that ye may find rest
1 Sa. 1. 17 the God of Israel grant..thy petition that
1 Ch. 21. 22 Grant me the place of (this) threshing flo.
21. 22 thou shalt grant it me for the full price
2 Ch. 12. 7 but I will grant them some deliverance
Ezra 7. 6 and the king granted him all his request
Neh. 1. 11 grant him mercy in the sight of this man
2. 8 the king granted me, according to the go.
Esth. 5. 8 if it please the king to grant my petition
8. 11 Wherein the king granted the Jews which
Job 6. 8 that God would grant..the thing that I
Psa. 20. 4 Grant thee according to thine own heart
85. 7 Show us thy mercy..grant us thy salva.
140. 8 Grant not, O LORD, the desires of the wi.

3. *Do with, show towards, give to,* עָשָׂה עִם *asah im.*
Job 10. 12 Thou hast granted me life and favour

4. *To give,* δίδωμι *didōmi.*
Mark 10. 37 Grant unto us that we may sit, one on
Luke 1. 74 That he would grant unto us, that we
Acts 4. 29 grant unto thy servants, that with all
11. 18 Then hath God also to the Gentiles gr.
14. 3 granted signs and wonders to be done by
Rom 15. 5 grant you to be like minded one toward
Eph. 3. 16 That he would grant you, according to
2 Ti. 1. 18 The Lord grant unto him that he may
Rev. 3. 21 To him that overcometh will I grant to
19. 8 And to her was granted that she should

5. *To say, speak,* εἶπον *eipon.*
Matt 20. 21 Grant that these my two sons may sit

6. *To grant as a favour,* χαρίζομαι *charizomai.*
Acts 3. 14 desired a murderer to be granted unto

GRANT graciously, to —

To be gracious, give grace, favour, חָנַן *chanan.*
Psa. 119. 29 way of lying, and grant me thy law graci.

GRANTED, to be —

1. *To give,* נָתַן *nathan.*
2 Ch. 1. 12 Wisdom and knowledge (is) granted unto
Prov 10. 24 desire of the righteous shall be granted

2. *To be given,* נָתַן *nathan,* 2.
Esth. 5. 6 What (is) thy petition?..it shall be gran.
7. 2 What (is) thy petition..it shall be granted
9. 12 what (is) thy petition..it shall be granted
9. 13 let it be granted to the Jews which (are)

GRAPE —

A part, single berry, פֶּרֶט *peret.*
Lev. 19. 10 neither shalt thou gather (every) grape of

GRAPE, tender —

Tender flower, the bulb, סְמָדַר *semadar.*
Song 2. 13 the vines (with) the tender grape give a
2. 15 the vines: for our vines (have) tender gr.
7. 12 let us see if..the tender grape appear

GRAPE gatherer —
To cut off, gather, בָּצַר *batsar.*
Jer. 6. 9 turn back thine hand as a grape gatherer
49. 9 If grape gatherers come to thee, would
Obad. 5 if the grape gatherers came to thee

GRAPE gleanings, gleaning of grapes —
Gleanings, עֹלֵלוֹת *oleloth.*
Judg. 8. 2 (Is) not the gleaning of the grapes of Ep.
Mic. 7. 1 I am..as the grape gleanings of the vint.

GRAPES —
1. *Gleanings,* עֹלֵלוֹת *oleloth.*
Obad. 5 came..would they not leave (some) gra.?
2. *Grape,* עֵנָב *enab.*
Gen. 40. 11 I took the grapes, and pressed them into
49. 11 and his clothes in the blood of grapes
Lev. 25. 5 neither gather the grapes of thy vine und.
Num. 6. 3 any liquor of grapes, nor eat moist grapes
13. 20 the time (was) the time of the first ripe g.
13. 23 cut..a branch with one cluster of grapes
Deut 23. 24 thou mayest eat grapes thy fill at thine
32. 14 thou didst drink the pure blood of the g.
32. 32 their grapes (are) grapes of gall, their cl.
Neh. 13. 15 as also wine, grapes, and figs, and all
Isa. 5. 2, 4 looked that it should bring forth grapes
Jer. 8. 13 no grapes on the vine, nor figs on the fig
Hos. 9. 10 I found Israel like grapes in the wildern.
Amos 9. 13 the treader of grapes him that soweth
3. *Cluster of grapes,* σταφυλή *staphulē.*
Matt. 7. 16 Do men gather [grapes] of thorns, or figs
Luke 6. 44 nor of a bramble bush gather they grapes
Rev. 14. 18 and gather..for her [grapes] are fully ripe

GRAPES, gleaning —
Gleanings, עֹלֵלוֹת *oleloth.*
Isa. 17. 6 Yet gleaning grapes shall be left in it, as
24. 13 as the gleaning grapes when the vintage
Jer. 49. 9 would they not leave..gleaning grapes?

GRAPES, ripe —
Grape, עֵנָב *enab.*
Gen. 40. 10 clusters thereof brought forth ripe grapes

GRAPES, wild —
Bad grapes, בְּאֻשִׁים *beushim.*
Isa. 5. 2 looked..and it brought forth wild grapes
5. 4 wherefore..brought it forth wild grapes?

GRASS —
1. *Tender grass,* דֶּשֶׁא *deshe.*
Gen. 1. 11 Let the earth bring forth grass, the herb
1. 12 And the earth brought forth grass..herb
Job 6. 5 Doth the wild ass bray when he hath gr.?
Isa. 15. 6 the grass faileth, there is no green thing
Jer. 14. 5 and forsook (it), because there was no gr.
2. *Hay, grass, herb,* חָצִיר *chatsir.*
1 Ki. 18. 5 we may find grass to save the horses and
2 Ki. 19. 26 the grass on the house tops, and..blasted
Job 40. 15 Behold now behemoth..he eateth grass
Psa. 37. 2 they shall soon be cut down like the grass
90. 5 in the morning..like grass (which) grow.
103. 15 man, his days (are) as grass; as a flower
104. 14 He causeth the grass to grow for the cat.
129. 6 Let them be as the grass (upon) the house
147. 8 who maketh grass to grow upon the mou.
Isa. 35. 7 where each lay..grass, with reeds and ru.
37. 27 the grass on the house tops, and..blasted
40. 6 All flesh (is) grass, and all the goodliness
40. 7 The grass withereth, the flower fadeth
40. 7 bloweth upon it: surely the people (is) g.
40. 8 The grass withereth, the flower fadeth
44. 4 they shall spring up..among the grass
51. 12 the son of man..shall be made..grass
3. *Green herb or grass,* יֶרֶק *yereq.*
Num 22. 4 as the ox licketh up the grass of the field
4. *Herb, grass,* עֵשֶׂב *eseb.*
Deut. 11. 15 I will send grass in thy fields for thy cat.
29. 23 nor any grass groweth therein, like the
32. 2 distil..as the showers upon the grass
2 Ki. 19. 26 they were (as) the grass of the field, and
Job 5. 25 thine offspring as the grass of the earth
Psa. 72. 16 city shall flourish like grass of the earth
92. 7 When the wicked spring as the grass, and
102. 4 My heart is smitten..withered like grass
102. 11 like a shadow..I am withered like grass
106. 20 the similitude of an ox that eateth grass
Prov 19. 12 but his favour (is) as dew upon the grass
Isa. 37. 27 they were (as) the grass of the field, and
Jer. 14. 6 their eyes did fail, because..no grass
Amos 7. 2 they had made an end of eating the grass
Mic. 5. 7 as the showers upon the grass, that tarri.
Zech 10. 1 and give..to every one grass in the field
5. *Herb, grass,* עֲשַׂב *asab.*
Dan. 4. 15 with the beasts in the grass of the earth
4. 25, 32 they shall make thee to eat grass as
4. 33 was driven from men, and did eat grass
5. 21 they fed him with grass like oxen, and
6. *Fodder, grass,* χόρτος *chortos.*
Matt. 6. 30 if God so clothe the grass of the field
14. 19 the multitude to sit down on the grass
Mark 6. 39 to make all sit down..upon the green gr.
Luke 12. 28 If then God so clothe the grass, which is
John 6. 10 Now there was much grass in the place
Jas. 1. 10 as the flower of the grass he shall pass
1. 11 it withereth the grass, and the flower
1 Pe. 1. 24 all flesh (is) as grass..as the flower of gr.
1. 24 The grass withereth, and the flower ther.
Rev. 8. 7 fire..and all green grass was burnt up
9. 4 that they should not hurt the grass of

GRASS, at —
Grassing, דְּשָׁא *dasha.*
Jer. 50. 11 ye are grown fat as the heifer at grass

GRASS, tender —
1. *Tender grass,* דֶּשֶׁא *deshe.*
2 Sa. 23. 4 the tender grass (springing) out of the ea.
Prov 27. 25 the tender grass showeth itself, and herbs
2. *Tender grass,* דֶּתֶא *dethe.*
Dan. 4. 15, 23 leave..in the tender grass of the field

GRASSHOPPER —
1. *Locust,* אַרְבֶּה *arbeh.*
Judg. 6. 5 they came as grasshoppers for multitude
7. 12 lay along in the valley like grasshoppers
Job 39. 20 Canst thou make him afraid as a grassh.?
Jer. 46. 23 because they are more than the grasshop.
2. *Locust, grasshopper,* גּוֹב *gob.*
Amos 7. 1 he formed grasshoppers in the beginning
3. *Grasshopper,* חָגָב *chagab.*
Lev. 11. 22 ye may eat..the grasshopper after his
Num 13. 33 we were in our own sight as grasshoppers
Eccl. 12. 5 and the grasshopper shall be a burden
Isa. 40. 22 the inhabitants thereof (are) as grasshop.

GRASSHOPPER, great —
Locust, grasshopper, גּוֹב *gob.*
Nah. 3. 17 thy captains as the great grasshoppers

GRATE —
A grate, anything twisted or woven, מִכְבָּר *mikbar.*
Exod 27. 4 thou shalt make for it a grate of network
35. 16 altar of burnt offering, with his brasen g.
38. 4 he made for the altar a brasen grate of n.
38. 5 cast four rings for the four ends of the g.
38. 30 the brasen altar, and the brasen grate for
39. 39 The brasen altar, and his grate of brass

GRAVE —
1. *Heap, prayer,* בְּעִי *bei.*
Job 30. 24 will not stretch out..hand to the grave
2. *Grave,* קְבוּרָה *qeburah.*
Gen. 35. 20 And Jacob set a pillar upon her grave
35. 20 that (is) the pillar of Rachel's grave unto
Eze. 32. 23 her company is round about her grave
32. 24 all her multitude round about her grave
3. *Grave,* קֶבֶר *qeber.*
Gen. 50. 5 in my grave which I have digged for me
Exod 14. 11 Because..no graves in Egypt, hast thou
Num 19. 16 toucheth..a bone of a man, or a grave
19. 18 touched..one slain, or one dead, or a gr.
2 Sa. 3. 32 the king..wept at the grave of Abner
19. 37 by the grave of my father and of my mo.
1 Ki. 13. 30 And he laid his carcase in his own grave
14. 13 mourn..for he only..shall come to the g.
2 Ki. 22. 20 thou shalt be gathered into thy grave in
23. 6 cast the powder thereof upon the graves
2 Ch. 34. 4 strowed (it) upon the graves of them that
34. 28 thou shalt be gathered to thy grave in
Job 3. 22 are glad, when they can find the grave?
5. 26 Thou shalt come to (thy) grave in a full
10. 19 been carried from the womb to the grave
17. 1 my days are extinct, the graves..for me
21. 32 Yet shall he be brought to the grave, and
Psa. 88. 5 like the slain that lie in the grave, whom
88. 11 Shall thy..kindness be declared in the g.?
Isa. 14. 19 thou art cast out of thy grave like an ab.
53. 9 he made his grave with the wicked, and
65. 4 Which remain among the graves, and
Jer. 8. 1 bring out the bones..out of their graves
20. 17 that my mother might have been my gr.
26. 23 cast his dead body into the graves of the
Eze. 32. 22 his graves (are) about him: all of them
32. 23 Whose graves are set in the sides of the
32. 25, 26 her graves (are) round about him: all
37. 12 O my people, I will open your graves
37. 12 cause you to come up out of your graves
37. 13 when I have opened your graves, O my
37. 13 and brought you up out of your graves
39. 11 I will give unto Gog a place there of gr.
Nah. 1. 14 I will make thy grave; for thou art vile
4. *The unseen state,* שְׁאוֹל *sheol.*
Gen. 37. 35 I will go down into the grave unto my son
42. 38 down my grey hairs with sorrow to the g.
44. 29 down my grey hairs with sorrow to the g.
44. 31 down the grey hairs..with sorrow to the g.
1 Sa. 2. 6 he bringeth down to the g., and bringeth
1 Ki. 2. 6 hoar head go down to the grave in peace
2. 9 bring thou down to the grave with blood
Job 7. 9 he that goeth down to the grave shall
14. 13 O that thou wouldest hide me in the gr.
17. 13 If I wait, the grave (is) mine house: I
21. 13 and in a moment go down to the grave
24. 19 (so doth) the grave (those which) have
Psa. 6. 5 in the grave who shall give thee thanks?
30. 3 hast brought up my soul from the grave
31. 17 the wicked..let them be silent in the g.
49. 14 Like sheep they are laid in the grave; d.
49. 14 their beauty shall consume in the grave
49. 15 redeem my soul from the power of the g.
88. 3 and my life draweth nigh unto the grave
89. 48 deliver his soul from the hand of the g.?
141. 7 Our bones are scattered at the grave's
Prov. 1. 12 Let us swallow them up alive as the grave
30. 16 The grave; and the barren womb, the
Eccl. 9. 10 no work..in the grave, whither thou go.
Song 8. 6 jealousy (is) cruel as the grave: the coals
Isa. 14. 11 Thy pomp is brought down to the grave
38. 10 I said..I shall go to the gates of the gr.
38. 18 For the grave cannot praise thee, death
Eze. 31. 15 In the day..he went down to the grave
Hos. 13. 14 ransom them from the power of the gra.
13. 14 O grave, I will by thy destruction: rep.
5. *Corruption,* שַׁחַת *shachath.*
Job 33. 22 Yea, his soul draweth near unto the gra.
6. *Hades, the unseen state,* ᾅδης *hadēs.*
1 Co. 15. 55 O death..[O gr.,] where (is) thy victory?
7. *Memorial, grave,* μνῆμα *mnēma.*
Rev. 11. 9 not suffer their dead bodies to be put in g.
8. *Memorial, grave,* μνημεῖον *mnēmeion.*
Matt 27. 52 the graves were opened; and many bodies
27. 53 came out of the graves after his resurrec.
Luke 11. 44 for ye are as graves which appear not
John 5. 28 all that are in the graves shall hear his
11. 17 he had (lain) in the grave four days alre.
11. 31 She goeth unto the grave to weep there
11. 38 Jesus therefore..cometh to the grave. It
12. 17 when he called Lazarus out of his grave

GRAVE clothes —
Bandages, κειρίαι *keiriai.*
John 11. 44 bound hand and foot with grave clothes

GRAVE —
Venerable, reverend, grave, σεμνός *semnos.*
1 Ti. 3. 8 Likewise..the deacons..grave, not dou.
3. 11 Even so..wives..grave, not slanderers
Titus 2. 2 That the aged men be sober, grave, tem.

GRAVE, to —
1. *To grave, decree,* חָקַק *chaqaq.*
Isa. 22. 16 that graveth an habitation for himself in
49. 16 I have graven thee upon the palms of
2. *To grave, cut or hew out,* פָּסַל *pasal.*
Hab. 2. 18 that the maker thereof hath graven it
3. *To open up,* פָּתַח *pathach,* 3.
Exod 28. 9 grave on them the names of the children
28. 36 grave upon it..the engravings of a signet
1 Ki. 7. 36 he graved cherubim, lions, and palm tr.
2 Ch. 2. 14 to grave any manner of graving, and to
3. 7 gold: and graved cherubim on the walls
4. *To grave gravings,* פִּתַּח פִּתּוּחִים [*pathach,* 3].
2 Ch. 2. 7 that can skill to grave with the cunning

GRAVEL —
1. *Gravel, halved stone,* חָצָץ *chatsats.*
Prov 20. 17 but..his mouth shall be filled with grav.
2. *Bowels, gravel,* מָעָה *maah.*
Isa. 48. 19 the offspring of thy bowels like the gra.

GRAVEL stone —
Halved stone, gravel, חָצָץ *chatsats.*
Lam. 3. 16 hath..broken my teeth with gravel ston.

GRAVEN —
1. *To plow, grave, devise,* חָרַשׁ *charash.*
Jer. 17. 1 graven upon the table of their heart, and
2. *To grave, plow, devise,* חָרַת *charath.*
Exod 32. 16 the writing of God, graven upon the tab.
3. *To be opened up,* פָּתַח *pathach,* 4.
Exod 39. 6 graven, as signets are..with the names
4. *Something graven, sculptured,* χάραγμα *charagma.*
Acts 17. 29 or stone, graven by art and man's device

GRAVEN, to be —
To be hewn, חָצַב *chatseb,* 2.
Job 19. 24 That they were graven with an iron pen

GRAVEN, are —
Graving, פִּתּוּחַ *pittuach.*
Exod 39. 6 as signets are graven, with the names of

GRAVEN image —
1. *Graven, cut or hewn image,* פֶּסֶל *pesel.*
Exod 20. 4 Thou shalt not make..any graven image
Lev. 26. 1 Ye shall make you no idols nor graven im.
Deut. 4. 16, 23 and make you a graven image
4. 25 and make a graven image..the likeness
5. 8 Thou shalt not make thee..graven image
27. 15 man that maketh..graven or molten im.
Judg 17. 3 to make a graven image, and a molten i.
17. 4 who made thereof a graven image and a
18. 14 teraphim, and a graven image, and a m.
18. 17 took the graven image, and the ephod
18. 20 and the teraphim, and the graven image
18. 30 children of Dan set up the graven image
18. 31 they set them up Micah's graven image
2 Ki. 21. 7 he set a graven image of the grove that
Psa. 97. 7 Confounded be all..that serve graven i.
Isa. 40. 19 The workman melteth a graven image
40. 20 cunning workman to prepare a graven i.
42. 17 that trust in graven images, that say to
44. 9 They that make a graven image (are) all
44. 10 or molten a graven image (that) is profit.
44. 15 he maketh it a graven image, and falleth
44. 17 he maketh a god, (even) his graven image
45. 20 that set up the wood of their graven im.
48. 5 my graven image, and my molten image
Jer. 10. 14 founder is confounded by the graven im
51. 17 founder is confounded by the graven im.
Nah. 1. 14 I cut off the graven image and the molt.
Hab. 2. 18 What profiteth the graven image that the
2. *Graven, cut or hewn images,* פְּסִילִים *pesilim.*
Deut. 7. 5 and burn their graven images with fire

Deut. 7. 25 The graven images of their gods shall ye
12. 3 ye shall hew down the graven images of
2 Ki. 17. 41 and served their graven images, both
2 Ch. 33. 19 set up groves and graven images, before
34. 7 had beaten the graven images into pow.
Psa. 78. 58 moved..to jealousy with their graven im.
Isa. 10. 10 whose graven images did excel them of J.
21. 9 all the graven images of her gods he hath
30. 22 defile..the covering of thy graven imag.
42. 8 LORD..neither my praise to graven ima.
Jer. 8. 19 they provoked me..with their graven im.
50. 38 it (is) the land of graven images, and they
51. 47 I will do judgment upon the graven im.
51. 52 I will do judgment upon her graven im.
Hos. 11. 2 and burnt incense to graven images
Mic. 1. 7 all the graven images thereof shall be
5. 13 Thy graven images also will I cut off, and

GRAVING —

1. *Graving, carving,* מִקְלַעַת *miqlaath.*
1 Ki. 7. 31 upon the mouth of it (were) gravings with
2. *Graving,* פִּתּוּחַ *pittuach.*
2 Ch. 2. 14 to grave any manner of graving, and to
Zech. 3. 9 I will engrave the graving thereof, saith

GRAVING tool —

Graving tool, pen, חֶרֶט *cheret.*
Exod 32. 4 fashioned it with a graving tool, after he

GRAVITY —

Venerableness, gravity, σεμνότης *semnotēs.*
1 Ti. 3. 4 his children in subjection with all gravity
Titus 2. 7 (showing) uncorruptness, gravity, sincer.

GRAY or GREY hairs —

Old age, gray hairs, שֵׂיבָה *sebah.*
Gen. 42. 38 then shall ye bring down my grey hairs
44. 29 ye shall bring down my grey hairs with
44. 31 thy servants shall bring down the grey h.
Deut 32. 25 the suckling..with the man of grey hairs
Hos. 7. 9 grey hairs are here and there upon him

GRAY or GREY headed —

1. *Aged, gray headed,* שִׂיב *sib.*
Job 15. 10 both the grey headed and very aged men
2. *Old age, gray hairs,* שֵׂיבָה *sebah.*
Psa. 71. 18 Now also when I am old and grey headed
Prov 20. 29 and the beauty of old men (is) the grey h.

GRAY or GREY headed, to be —

To be old, gray headed, שִׂיב *sib.*
1 Sa. 12. 2 and I am old and grey headed; and, beh.

GREASE —

Fat, חֵלֶב *cheleb.*
Psa. 119. 70 Their heart is as fat as grease; (but) I

GREAT —

1. *Juncture, joining,* אַצִּיל *atstsil.*
Eze. 41. 8 foundations..a full reed of six great cub.
2. *Master,* בַּעַל *baal.*
Prov 18. 9 is brother to him that is a great waster
3. *Great,* גָּדוֹל *gadol* [V.L. גבול].
Josh. 15. 47 unto the river of Egypt, and the great sea
4. *Great,* גָּדוֹל *gadol.*
Gen. 1. 16 God made two great lights; the greater
1. 21 God created great whales, and every liv.
10. 12 And Resen..the same (is) a great city
12. 2 I will make of thee a great nation, and I
12. 17 plagued Pharaoh..with great plagues be.
15. 12 an horror of great darkness fell upon him
15. 14 shall they come out with great substance
15. 18 unto the great river, the river Euphrates
17. 20 Ishmael..I will make him a great nation
18. 18 shall surely become a great and mighty
19. 11 smote the men..both small and great
20. 9 brought on me and on my kingdom a g.
21. 8 Abraham made a great feast the (same) day
21. 18 Arise..for I will make him a great nation
27. 34 cried with a great and exceeding bitter c.
29. 2 and a great stone..upon the well's mouth
39. 9 how then can I do this great wickedness
41. 29 there come seven years of great plenty
45. 7 to save your lives by a great deliverance
46. 3 for I will there make of thee a great na.
50. 10 with a great and very sore lamentation
Exod. 3. 3 I will..turn aside, and see this great si.
6. 6 I will redeem you..with great judgments
7. 4 out of the land of Egypt by great judg.
11. 3 the man Moses (was) very great in the land
11. 6 there shall be a great cry throughout all
12. 30 and there was a great cry in Egypt; for
14. 31 Israel saw that great work which the L.
18. 22 every great matter they shall bring unto
32. 10 and I will make of thee a great nation
32. 11 with great power, and with a mighty hand
32. 21 thou hast brought so great a sin upon th.?
32. 30 Ye have sinned a great sin: and now I
32. 31 this people have sinned a great sin, and
Num 13. 28 and the cities (are) walled, (and) very gr.
34. 6 ye shall even have the great sea for a bo.
34. 7 from the great sea ye shall point out for.
Deut. 1. 7 unto the great river, the river Euphrates
1. 17 shall hear the small as well as the great
1. 19 we went through all that great and ter.
1. 28 the cities (are) great and walled up to h.
2. 7 thy walking through this great wilderness
2. 10, 21 a people great, and many, and tall, as
4. 6 Surely this great nation (is) a wise and
4. 7, 8 For what nation (is there so) great
4. 32 whether there hath been..as this great
Deut. 4. 34 by great terrors, according to all that the
4. 36 upon earth he showed thee his great fire
5. 22 of the thick darkness, with a great voice
5. 25 this great fire will consume us: if we
6. 10 to give thee great and goodly cities, which
6. 22 LORD showed..wonders, great and sore
7. 19 The great temptations which thine eyes
8. 15 Who led thee through that great and
9. 1 cities great, and fenced up to heaven
9. 2 A people great and tall, the children of
10. 17 Lord of lords, a great God, a mighty, and
10. 21 that hath done for thee these great and
11. 7 your eyes have seen all the great acts of
18. 16 neither let me see this great fire any
25. 13 not have..divers weights, a great and a
25. 14 not..divers measures, a great and a small
26. 5 became there a nation, great, mighty, and
26. 8 with great terribleness, and with signs
27. 2 thou shalt set thee up great stones, and
28. 59 great plagues, and of long continuance
29. 3 The great temptations which thine eyes
29. 3 the signs, and those great miracles
29. 24 what (meaneth) the heat of this great a.?
29. 28 in anger, and in wrath, and in great indi.
34. 12 in all the great terror which Moses show.
Josh. 1. 4 unto the great river, the river Euphrates
1. 4 unto the great sea toward the going down
6. 5 the people shall shout with a great shout
6. 20 the people shouted with a great shout
7. 9 and what wilt thou do unto thy great na?
7. 26 they raised over him a great heap of sto.
8. 29 and raise thereon a great heap of stones
9. 1 in all the coasts of the great sea over
10. 2 because Gibeon (was) a great city, as one
10. 10 slew them with a great slaughter at Gi.
10. 11 the LORD cast down great stones from
10. 18 Roll great stones upon the mouth of the
10. 20 of slaying them with a very great slaug.
10. 27 and laid great stones in the cave's mouth
14. 12 and (that) the cities (were) great (and)
14. 15 (Arba was) a great man among the Ana.
15. 12 And the west border (was) to the great
15. 47 and the great sea, and the border (thereof)
17. 17 Thou..hast great power: thou shalt not
22. 10 an altar by Jordan, a great altar to see to
23. 4 inheritance..unto the great sea westward
23. 9 LORD hath driven out..great nations and
24. 17 which did those great signs in our sight
24. 26 took a great stone, and set it up there
Judg. 2. 7 who had seen all the great works of the
5. 15 divisions of Reuben..great thoughts of
5. 16 divisions of Reuben..great searchings of
11. 33 smote them..with a very great slaughter
15. 8 smote them hip and thigh with a great
15. 18 Thou hast given this great deliverance
16. 5 and see wherein his great strength (lieth)
16. 6, 15 wherein thy great strength (lieth)
16. 23 to offer a great sacrifice unto Dagon their
21. 5 they had made a great oath concerning
1 Sa. 2. 17 the sin of the young men was very great
4. 5 all Israel shouted with a great shout, so
4. 6 What..the noise of this great shout in
4. 10 and there was a very great slaughter
4. 17 there hath been..a great slaughter
5. 9 against the city, with a very great destr.
5. 9 the men of the city both small and great
6. 9 he hath done us this great evil: but if
6. 14 and sto[o]d there, where..a great stone
6. 15 the ark..and put (them) on the great stone
6. 18 even unto the great (stone of) Abel, whe.
6. 19 had smitten..the people with a great sl.
7. 10 LORD thundered with a great thunder on
12. 16 s[ta]nd and see this great thing, which
12. 22 will not forsake his people for his great
14. 20 (and there was) a very great discomfiture
14. 33 he said..roll a great stone unto me this
14. 45 who hath wrought this great salvation in
17. 25 the king will enrich him with great riches
19. 5 LORD wrought a great salvation for all, I.
19. 8 and slew them with a great slaughter
19. 22 came to a great well that (is) in Sechu
20. 2 my father will do nothing, either great or
23. 5 David..smote them with a great slaughter
25. 2 the man (was) very great, and he had
30. 2 they slew not any, either great or small
30. 16 because of all the great spoil that they
30. 19 neither small nor great, neither sons nor
2 Sa. 5. 10 David went on, and grew great, and the
7. 9 and have made thee a great name
7. 9 like unto the name of the great (men) that
18. 7 there was there a great slaughter that
18. 9 went under the thick boughs of a great
18. 17 cast him into a great pit in the wood
18. 17 laid a very great heap of stones upon him
18. 29 I saw a great tumult, but I knew not
19. 32 had provided..for he (was) a very great
23. 8 When they (were) at the great stone
23. 10, 12 and the LORD wrought a great victory
1 Ki. 1. 40 rejoiced with great joy, so that the ea.
3. 4 Gibeon..for that (was) the great high
3. 6 Thou hast showed..my father great mer.
3. 6 thou hast kept for him this great kindn.
4. 13 threescore great cities with walls and
5. 17 they brought great stones, costly stones
7. 9 on the outside toward the great court
7. 10 great stones, stones of ten cubits, and
7. 12 the great court round about (was) with
8. 42 they shall hear of thy great name, and of
8. 65 all Israel with him, a great congregation
10. 18 the king made a great throne of ivory
18. 45 clouds and wind, and there was a great
19. 11 a great and strong wind rent the mount.
1 Ki. 20. 13 Hast thou seen all this great multitude
20. 21 slew the Syrians with a great slaughter
20. 28 will I deliver all this great multitude
22. 31 Fight neither with small nor great, save
2 Ki 3. 27 their was great indignation against Isr.
4. 8 to Shunem, where (was) a great woman
4. 38 Set on the great pot, and seethe pottage
5. 1 Naaman..was a great man with his mas.
5. 13 (if) the prophet had bid thee..great thing
6. 23 And he prepared great provision for them
6. 25 And there was a great famine in Samaria
7. 6 noise of horses..the noise of a great host
8. 13 a dog, that he should do this great thing?
10. 19 for I have a great sacrifice (to do) to Ba.
16. 15 Upon the great altar burn the morning
17. 21 and Jeroboam..made them sin a great
17. 36 with great power, and a stretched out arm
18. 19 Thus saith the great king, the king of A.
18. 28 Hear the word of the great king, the ki.
22. 13 for great (is) the wrath of the LORD that
23. 2 and all the people, both small and great
23. 26 from the fierceness of his great wrath
25. 9 every great (man's) house burnt he with
25. 26 And all the people, both small and great
1 Ch 11. 14 LORD saved (them) by a great deliverance
12. 22 until..a great host, like the host of God
16. 25 great (is) the LORD, and greatly to be pr.
22. 8 and hast made great wars: thou shalt
25. 8 as well the small as the great, the teach
26. 13 cast lots, as well the small as the great
29. 1 young and tender, and the work (is) gre.
29. 9 David the king also rejoiced with great
29. 22 And did eat and drink..with great glad.
2 Ch. 1. 8 Thou hast showed great mercy unto Da.
1. 10 for who can judge this thy people..gre.?
2. 5 the house which I build (is) great; for g.
2. 9 for the house..(shall be) wonderful great
4. 9 the great court, and doors for the court
6. 32 from a far country for thy great name's
7. 8 all Israel with him, a very great congre.
9. 17 the king made a great throne of ivory
15. 13 small or great, whether man or woman
16. 14 they made a very great burning for him
18. 30 Fight ye not with small or great, save
21. 14 with a great plague will the LORD smite
26. 15 to shoot arrows and great stones withal
28. 5 carried away a great multitude of them
28. 5 who smote him with a great slaughter
30. 21 kept the feast..seven days with great gl.
30. 26 So there was great joy in Jerusalem: for
31. 15 to give..as well to the great as to the s.
34. 21 great (is) the wrath of the LORD that is
34. 30 and all the people, great and small
36. 18 all the vessels of the house of God, great
Ezra 3. 11 all the people shouted with a great shout
9. 7 (have) we (been) in a great trespass unto
9. 13 evil deeds, and for our great trespass
Neh. 1. 3 The remnant..(are) in great affliction and
1. 5 the great and terrible God, that keepeth
1. 10 whom thou hast redeemed by thy great
3. 27 over against the great tower that lieth
4. 14 remember the LORD..great and terrible
5. 1 there was a great cry of the people, and
5. 7 And I set a great assembly against them
6. 3 I (am) doing a great work, so that I can.
7. 4 Now the city (was) large and great; but
8. 6 And Ezra blessed the LORD, the great G.
8. 12 send portions, and to make great mirth
8. 17 And there was very great gladness
9. 18, 26 and..wrought great provocations
9. 25 delighted themselves in thy great good.
9. 32 our God, the great, the mighty, and the
9. 37 they have dominion..we (are) in great d.
12. 31 Then I..appointed two great (compan.)
12. 43 Also that day they offered great sacrifi.
12. 43 God had made them rejoice with great
13. 5 he had prepared for him a great chamber
13. 27 to do all this great evil, to transgress
Esth. 1. 5 made a feast..both unto great and small
1. 20 husbands honour, both to great and sm.
2. 18 the king made a great feast unto all his
4. 3 great mourning among the Jews, and
8. 15 with a great crown of gold, and with a
9. 4 Mordecai (was) great in the king's house
10. 3 great among the Jews, and accepted of
Job 1. 19 there came a great wind from the wilde.
3. 19 The small and great are there; and the
Psa. 21. 5 His glory (is) great in thy salvation
47. 2 (he is) a great King over all the earth
48. 1 Great (is) the LORD, and greatly to be p.
57. 10 thy mercy (is) great unto the heavens
76. 1 In Judah (is) God known; his name (is) g.
77. 13 who (is so) great a God as (our) God?
86. 10 thou (art) great, and doest wondrous th?
86. 13 great (is) thy mercy toward me; and
95. 3 LORD (is) a great God, and a great King
96. 4 the LORD (is) great, and greatly to be pr.
99. 2 LORD (is) great in Zion; and he (is) high
99. 3 Let them praise thy great..name; and
104. 25 this great and wide sea, wherein (are)
104. 25 innumerable, both small and great beasts
108. 4 thy mercy (is) great above the heavens
111. 2 The works of the LORD (are) great, sought
115. 13 He will bless them..small and great
135. 5 For I know that the LORD (is) great, and
136. 4 To him who alone doeth great wonders
136. 7 To him that made great lights: for his
136. 17 To him which smote great kings: for his
138. 5 they shall sing..for great (is) the glory of
145. 3 Great (is) the LORD, and greatly to be pr.
145. 8 LORD (is)..slow to anger, and of great
147. 5 Great (is) our Lord, and of great power

Prov 19. 19 A man of great wrath shall suffer punis.
25. 6 and stand not in the place of great (men)
Eccl. 9. 13 wisdom have I seen . . it (seemed) great
9. 14 and there came a great king against it
9. 14 besieged it, and built great bulwarks aga.
10. 4 for yielding pacifieth great offences
Isa. 5. 9 desolate..great and fair, without inhabi.
8. 1 Take thee a great roll, and write in it
9. 2 The people..have seen a great light: they
12. 6 great (is) the Holy One of Israel in the
27. 1 LORD with his sore and great and strong
27. 13 the great trumpet shall be blown, and
29. 6 with earthquake, and great noise, with
34. 6 a great slaughter in the land of Idumea.
36. 4 Thus saith the great king, the king of A.
36. 13 Hear ye the words of the great king, the
54. 7 but with great mercies will I gather
Jer. 4. 6 I will bring evil from the north, and a gr.
5. 5 I will get me unto the great men, and will
6. 1 evil appeareth out of the north, and great
6. 22 a great nation shall be raised from the
10. 6 LORD; thou (art) great, and thy name (is)
10. 22 a great commotion out of the north cou.
11. 16 with the noise of a great tumult he hath
14. 17 my people is broken with a great breach
16. 6 Both the great and the small shall die in
16. 10 hath the LORD pronounced all this great
21. 5 in anger, and in fury, and in great wrath
21. 6 And..they shall die of a great pestilence
22. 8 the LORD done thus unto this great city?
25. 14 many nations and great kings shall serve
25. 32 a great whirlwind shall be raised up from
26. 19 Thus might we procure great evil against
27. 5 by my great power and by my outstretc.
27. 7 many nations and great kings shall serve
28. 8 against great kingdoms, of war, and of
30. 7 Alas! for that day (is) great, so that none
31. 8 a great company shall return thither
32. 17 by thy great power and stretched out arm
32. 18 The Great, the Mighty God, the LORD of
32. 19 Great in counsel, and mighty in work
32. 21 with a stretched out arm, and with great
32. 37 in mine anger, and in my fury, and in g.
32. 42 Like as I have brought all this great evil
33. 3 show thee great and mighty things, which
36. 7 great (is) the anger and the fury that the
43. 9 Take great stones in thine hand, and hide
44. 7 Wherefore commit ye..great evil against
44. 15 a great multitude, even all the people
44. 26 I have sworn by my great name, saith the
48. 3 A voice of crying..spoiling and great
50. 9 an assembly of great nations from the
50. 22 A sound of battle..and of great destruc.
50. 41 and a great nation, and many kings shall
51. 54 great destruction from the land of the C.
51. 55 and destroyed out of her the great voice
52. 13 all the houses of the great..burned he
Lam. 2. 13 for thy breach (is) great like the sea: who
Eze. 1. 4 a great cloud, and a fire infolding itself
3. 12 I heard behind me a voice of a great rush.
3. 13 the wheels..a noise of a great rushing
8. 6 the great abominations that the house
9. 9 The iniquity..(is) exceeding great, and
17. 3 A great eagle with great wings, long wi.
17. 7 another great eagle with great wings and
17. 9 without great power or many people to
21. 14 it (is) the sword of the great slain, which
25. 17 I will execute great vengeance upon them
29. 3 the great dragon that lieth in the midst
29. 18 to serve a great service against Tyrus
36. 23 I will sanctify my great name, which was
37. 10 and stood up..an exceeding great army
38. 13 take away cattle and goods, to take a gr.
38. 15 a great company, and a mighty army
38. 19 in that day..shall be a great shaking in
39. 17 a great sacrifice upon the mountains of I.
47. 10 as the fish of the great sea, exceeding
47. 15 from the great sea, the way of Hethlon
47. 19 (in) Kadesh, the river to the great sea
47. 20 The west side also..the great sea from
48. 28 (and) to the river toward the great sea
Dan. 8. 8 when he was strong, the great horn was
8. 21 the great horn that (is) between his eyes
9. 4 O Lord, the great and dreadful God
9. 12 by bringing upon us a great evil: for
10. 4 as I was by the side of the great river
10. 7 a great quaking fell upon them, so that
10. 8 I was left alone, and saw this great visi.
11. 13 with a great army and with much riches
11. 25 stir up his power..with a great army
11. 25 with a very great and mighty army
11. 28 Then shall he return..with great riches
11. 44 he shall go forth with great fury to des.
12. 1 the great prince which standeth for the
Hos. 1. 11 come up..for great..the day of Jezreel
Joel 2. 11 the day of the LORD (is) great and very
2. 25 my great army which I sent among you
2. 31 before the great and the terrible day of
Amos 6. 11 he will smite the great house with brea.
Jon. 1. 2 Arise, go to Nineveh, that great city, and
1 4 LORD sent out a great wind into the sea
1. 12 I know that for my sake this great tem.
1. 17 LORD had prepared a great fish to swallow
3 2 Arise, go unto Nineveh, that great city
3. 3 Nineveh was an exceeding great city of
4. 11 should not I spare Nineveh, that great
Mic. 7. 3 the great (man), he uttereth his mischiev.
Nah. 1. 3 LORD (is) slow to anger, and great in power
Zeph. 1. 10 and a great crashing from the hills
1. 14 The great day of the LORD (is) near, (it
Zech. 1. 14 I am jealous for..Zion with a great jealou.
4. 7 Who (art) thou, O great mountain? before
Zech. 7. 12 came a great wrath from the LORD of ho.
8. 2 I was jealous for Zion with great jealousy
8. 2 and I was jealous for her with great fury
14. 4 (and there shall be) a very great valley
Mal. 1. 11, 11 my name (shall be) great among the
1. 14 I (am) a great King, saith the LORD of ho.
4. 5 before the coming of the great and dread.

5. *Great*, גָּדַל *gadel*.
2 Ch. 17. 12 And Jehoshaphat waxed great exceeding.
Eze. 16. 26 the Egyptians thy neighbours, great of

6. *Great or rolled stone*, גְּלָל *gelal*.
Ezra 5. 8 which is builded with great stones, and
6. 4 three rows of great stones, and a row of

7. *To commit fornication*, זָנָה *zanah*.
Hos. 1. 2 the land hath committed great whoredom

8. *To be pained*, חוּל, חִיל *chul, chil*.
Eze. 30. 16 Sin shall have great pain and No shall be

9. *To give honour, make heavy*, כָּבֵד *kabed*, 3.
Num 24. 11 I thought to promote thee unto great h.

10. *Heavy, honourable*, כָּבֵד *kabed*.
Gen. 50. 9 chariots and horsemen..a very great co.
1 Ki. 3. 9 who is able to judge this thy so great a
10. 2 she came to Jerusalem with a very great
2 Ki. 6. 14 sent..horses, and chariots, and a great
18. 17 sent..with a great host against Jerusalem
2 Ch. 9. 1 with a very great company, and camels
Isa. 32. 2 as the shadow of a great rock in a weary
36. 2 sent..unto king Hezekiah. with a great

11. *Might, with might*, מְאֹד *meod*.
Deut. 3. 5 All..beside unwalled towns a great many
Judg 12. 2 I and my people were at great strife with
2 Sa. 12. 30 the spoil of the city in great abundance
24. 14 I am in a great strait: let us fall now into
1 Ki. 10. 11 brought in from Ophir great plenty of
11. 19 Hadad found great favour in the sight of
1 Ch. 21. 13 I am in a great strait: let me fall now
2 Ch. 4. 18 Solomon made all these vessels in great
9. 9 of spices great abundance, and precious
Job 35. 15 yet he knoweth (it) not in great extremity
Isa. 47. 9 for the great abundance of thine enchant.
Zech 14. 14 silver, and apparel, in great abundance

12. *Increase, abundance*, מַרְבֶּה *marbeh*.
Isa. 33. 23 then is the prey of a great spoil divided

13. *To make despised*, נָאַץ *naats*, 3.
2 Sa. 12. 14 thou hast given great occasion to the en.

14. *Mighty*, עָצוּם *atsum*.
Num 32. 1 Gad had a very great multitude of cattle

15. *To do, make*, עָשָׂה *asah*.
1 Sa. 26. 25 thou shalt both do great (things), and also

16. *Abundant, much*, רַב *rab*.
Gen. 6. 5 that the wickedness of man (was) great in
7. 11 the fountains of the great deep broken up
13. 6 their substance was great, so that they
18. 20 the cry of Sodom and Gomorrah is great
26. 14 he had..herds, and great store of servants
Num 11. 33 smote the people with a very great plague
14. 18 LORD (is) long suffering, and of great mercy
Josh. 10. 11 LORD cast down great stones from heaven
11. 8 chased them unto great Zidon, and unto
17. 14 seeing I (am) a great people, forasmuch as
17. 15 If thou (be) a great people..get thee up
17. 17 Thou (art) a great people, and hast..power
19. 28 Hammon, and Kanah..unto great Zidon
1 Sa. 12. 17 see that your wickedness (is) great, which
26. 13 afar off, a great space (being) between
2 Sa. 3. 22 and brought in a great spoil with them
24. 14 his mercies (are) great: and let me not
1 Ki. 3. 8 people which thou hast chosen, a great
5. 7 hath given..a wise son over this great peo.
19. 7 because the journey (is) too great for thee
1 Ch. 21. 13 very great (are) his mercies: but let me
2 Ch. 13. 8 ye (be) a great multitude, and..with you
13. 17 Abijah..slew them with a great slaughter
15. 5 great vexations (were) upon all the inhab.
20. 12 we have no might against this great com.
20. 15 Be not afraid..by reason of this great mul.
21. 3 their father gave them great gifts of silver
21. 15 great sickness by disease of thy bowels
24. 25 for they left him in great diseases
28. 13 our trespass is great, and..fierce wrath
Ezra 10. 1 a very great congregation of men and wo.
Neh. 9. 17 slow to anger, and of great kindness, and
9. 31 for thy great mercies' sake thou didst not
9. 35 in thy great goodness that thou gavest
Esth. 1. 20 throughout all his empire, for it is great
Job 1. 3 she asses, and a very great household
5. 25 shalt know also that thy seed (shall be) g.
22. 5 (Is) not thy wickedness great? and thine
31. 25 If I rejoiced because my wealth (was) gr.
31. 34 Did I fear a great multitude, or did the
38. 21 or (because) the number of thy days (is) g.?
39. 11 trust him, because his strength (is) great?
Psa. 19. 11 in keeping of them (there is) great reward
19. 13 I shall be innocent from the great trans.
22. 25 My praise..of thee in the great congreg.
25. 11 LORD, pardon mine iniquity; for it (is) g.
31. 19 how great (is) thy goodness, which thou
32. 6 in the floods of great waters they shall
35. 18 I will give thee thanks in the great cong.
36. 6 thy judgments (are) a great deep: O LORD
40. 9 I have preached righteousness in the gr.
40. 10 and thy truth from the great congregation
48. 2 mount Zion..the city of the great King
68. 11 great (was) the company of those that
71. 20 which hast showed me great and sore
Psa. 77. 19 thy path in the great waters, and thy foot.
78. 15 and gave..drink as..the great depths
107. 23 They..that do business in great waters
119. 156 Great (are) thy tender mercies, O LORD
119. 162 I rejoice..as one that findeth great spoil
119. 165 Great peace have they which love thy
135. 10 Who smote great nations, and slew mighty
144. 7 deliver me out of great waters, from the
145. 7 shall..utter the memory of thy great go.
147. 5 of great power: his understanding (is)
Prov 13. 7 that maketh himself poor, yet (hath) gr.
14. 29 slow to wrath (is) of great understanding
15. 16 than great treasure, and trouble therewi.
22. 1 rather to be chosen than great riches
26. 10 The great (God), that formed all..both
28. 12 When righteous..do rejoice, (there is) gr.
28. 16 that wanteth understanding (is)..a great
Eccl. 2. 21 This also (is) vanity and a great evil
8. 6 the misery of man (is) great upon him
10. 6 Folly is set in great dignity, and the rich
Isa. 6. 12 a great forsaking in the midst of the land
13. 4 The noise..like as of a great people
16. 14 glory of Moab..with all that great mul.
23. 3 And by great waters the seed of Sihor
30. 25 waters in the day of the great slaughter
51. 10 dried the sea, the waters of the great de.
53. 12 will I divide him (a portion) with the gr.
54. 13 and great (shall be) the peace of thy chil.
63. 7 the great goodness toward the house of I.
Jer. 13. 9 will I mar..the great pride of Jerusalem
41. 12 and found him by the great waters that
51. 55 when her waves do roar like great waters
Lam. 1. 1 she (that was) great among the nations
3. 23 new every morning: great (is) thy faith.
Eze. 1. 24 like the noise of great waters, as the vo.
17. 5 he placed (it) by great waters..set it (as)
17. 8 It was planted in a good soil by great w.
17. 17 with (his) mighty army and great company
24. 12 her great scum went not forth out of her
26. 19 the deep..and great waters shall cover
27. 26 Thy rowers have brought thee into great
31. 6 under his shadow dwelt all great nations
31. 7 Thus was he..his root was by great wa.
31. 15 the floods..and the great waters were
32. 13 the beasts thereof from beside the great
38. 4 a great company (with) bucklers and sh.
47. 9 there shall be a very great multitude of
Dan. 9. 18 for our right., but for thy great mercies
11. 3 that shall rule with great dominion, and
11. 5 his dominion (shall be) a great dominion
11. 10 shall assemble a multitude of great forc.
11. 11 and he shall set forth a great multitude
Hos. 9. 7 multitude of thine iniquity, and the great
Joel 2. 2 a great people and a strong; there hath
2. 11 for his camp (is) very great: for (he is)
2. 13 slow to anger, and of great kindness, and
3. 13 fats overflow: for their wickedness (is) g.
Amos 3. 9 and behold the great tumults in the mid.
3. 15 and the great houses shall have an end
6. 2 from thence go ye to Hamath the great
7. 4 it devoured the great deep, and did eat
Jon. 4. 2 slow to anger, and of great kindness, and
Hab. 3. 15 didst walk through..the heap of great w.
Zech 14. 13 a great tumult from the LORD shall be

17. *Abundant, much*, רַב *rab*.
Ezra 4. 10 whom the great and noble Asnapper br.
5. 8 to the house of the great God, which is
5. 11 which a great king of Israel builded and
Dan. 2. 31 This great image, whose brightness (was)
2. 35 and the stone..became a great mountain
2. 45 the great God hath made known to the
4. 30 Is not this great Babylon, that I have
5. 1 Belshazzar the king made a great feast
7. 2 the four winds..strove upon the great sea

18. *Abundance, multitude*, רֹב *rob*.
2 Ch. 24. 24 the LORD delivered a very great host into
30. 13 there assembled..a very great congreg.
Job 23. 6 Will he plead against me with (his) great
30. 18 By the great force..is my garment chan.
36. 18 then a great ransom cannot deliver thee
Psa. 33. 17 neither shall he deliver..by his great
Prov 16. 8 a little with righteousness, than great re.
Lam. 1. 3 because of affliction, and because of great
Eze. 28. 5 By thy great wisdom..by thy traffic hast

19. *To cause to be abundant*, רָבָה *rabah*, 5.
Gen. 15. 1 I (am) thy shield..thy exceeding great
Neh. 4. 1 he was wroth, and took great indignation
4. 19 The work (is) great and large, and we are
Eccl. 1. 16 my heart had great experience of wisdom
2. 7 I had great possessions of..cattle above

20. *Abundant, very great*, רַבְרַב *rabrab*.
Dan. 2. 48 and gave him many great gifts, and made
4. 3 How great (are) his signs! and how mighty
7. 3 four great beasts came up from the sea
7. 7 it had great iron teeth: it devoured and
7. 11 because of the voice of the great words
7. 17 These great beasts, which are four, (are)

21. *Great, much, many*, שַׂגִּיא *saggi*.
Job 36. 26 Behold, God (is) great, and we know (him)

22. *Great, much, many*, שַׂגִּיא *saggi*.
Dan. 2. 6 receive of me gifts and rewards and great
2. 31 Thou..sawest, and, behold, a great image
4. 10 a tree..and the height thereof (was) gre.

23. *God, mighty one*, אֵל *el*.
Psa. 36. 6 Thy righteousness (is) like the great mo.

24. *God*, אֱלֹהִים *elohim*.
Gen. 30. 8 With great wrestlings have I wrestled
1 Sa. 14. 15 quaked: so it was a very great trembling

25. *Conceiving, pregnant,* הָרָה *harah.*
Jer. 20. 17 been my grave, and her womb..always g.

26. *Heat,* חֳרִי *chori.*
Exod. 11. 8 he went out from Pharaoh in a great an.
2 Ch. 25. 10 and they returned home in great anger

27. *Bitter,* מַר *mar.*
Isa. 38. 17 Behold, for peace I had great bitterness

28. *Evil,* רַע *ra.*
Hos. 10. 15 do unto you because of your great wick.

29. *Coming or reaching to, sufficient,* ἱκανός *hikanos.*
Mark 10. 46 his disciples and a great number of peo.
Acts 22. 6 there shone from heaven a great light

30. *Very much,* λίαν *lian.*
Mark 1. 35 rising up a great while before day, he

31. *Great,* μέγας *megas.*
Matt. 2. 10 they rejoiced with exceeding great joy
4. 16 The people..in darkness saw great light
5. 19 the same shall be called great in the ki.
5. 35 Jerusalem; for it is the city of the great
7. 27 and it fell: and great was the fall of it
8. 24 there arose a great tempest in the sea
8. 26 rebuked..the sea; and there was a great
15. 28 O woman, great (is) thy faith: be it unto
20. 26 whosoever will be great among you, let
22. 36 which (is) the great commandment in
22. 38 This is the first and great commandment
24. 21 For then shall be great tribulation, such
24. 24 and shall show great signs and wonders
24. 31 angels with a great sound of a trumpet
27. 60 he rolled a great stone to the door of
28. 2 And, behold, there was a great earthqu.
28. 8 they departed..with fear and great joy
Mark 4. 32 and shooteth out great branches; so that
4. 37 And there arose a great storm of wind
4. 39 the wind ceased, and there was a great
5. 11 there was..a [great] herd of swine feeding
5. 42 astonished with a great astonishment
10. 43 but whosoever will be great among you
13. 2 Seest thou these great buildings? there
16. 4 stone was rolled away: for it was very g.
Luke 1. 15 he shall be great in the sight of the Lord
1. 32 He shall be great, and shall be called the
2. 10 I bring you good tidings of great joy
4. 25 when great famine was throughout all
4. 38 wife's mother was taken with a great fev.
5. 29 Levi made him a great feast in his own
6. 49 and the ruin of that house was great
7. 16 That a great prophet is risen up among
8. 37 to depart..for they were taken with gre.
9. 48 he that is least..the same shall be great
13. 19 and it grew, and waxed a [great] tree
14. 16 A certain man made a great supper, and
16. 26 between us..there is a great gulf fixed
21. 11 great earthquakes shall be in divers pla.
21. 11 and great signs shall there be from heav.
21. 23 there shall be great distress in the land
24. 52 and returned to Jerusalem with great
John 6. 18 the sea arose, by reason of a great wind
7. 37 In the last day, that great (day) of the
21. 11 drew the net to land full of great fishes
Acts 2. 20 before that great and notable day of the
4. 33 with great power gave the apostles witn.
4. 33 and great grace was upon them all
5. 5 great fear came upon all them that heard
5. 11 And great fear came upon all the church
6. 8 Stephen..did great wonders and miracles
7. 11 there came a dearth..and great affliction
8. 1 there was a great persecution against
8. 2 and made great lamentation over him
8. 8 And there was great joy in that city
8. 10 This man is the great power of God
10. 11 as it had been a great sheet knit at the
11. 5 as it had been a great sheet, let down
11. 28 that there should be great dearth
15. 3 they caused great joy unto all the breth.
16. 26 And suddenly there was a great earthqu.
19. 27 that the temple of the great goddess D.
19. 28 saying, Great (is) Diana of the Ephesians
19. 34 cried out, Great (is) Diana of the Ephesi.
19. 35 is a worshipper of the great goddess Dia.
23. 9 And there arose a great cry: and the
26. 22 witnessing both to small and great, say.
Rom. 9. 2 That I have great heaviness and continu.
1 Co. 16. 9 a great door and effectual is opened unto
Eph. 5. 32 This is a great mystery: but I speak
1 Ti. 3. 16 And without controversy great is the my.
6. 6 godliness with contentment is great gain
2 Ti. 2. 20 in a great house there are not only vess.
Titus 2. 13 the glorious appearing of the great God
Heb. 4. 14 Seeing then that we have a great high
10. 35 which hath great recompence of reward
13. 20 Lord Jesus, that great shepherd of the sh.
Jude 6 reserved..unto the judgment of the great
Rev. 1. 10 heard behind me a great voice, as of a
2. 22 that commit adultery with her into great
6. 4 and there was given unto him a great
6. 12 there was a great earthquake; and the
6. 17 the great day of his wrath is come; and
7. 14 they which came out of great tribulation
8. 8 as it were a great mountain burning
8. 10 there fell a great star from heaven, burn.
9. 2 a smoke..as the smoke of a [great] furna.
9. 14 which are bound in the great river Euph.
11. 8 dead bodies..in the street of the great
11. 11 great fear fell upon them which saw
11. 12 they heard a great voice from heaven say.
11. 13 the same hour was there a great earthq.
Rev. 11. 15 and there were great voices in heaven
11. 17 thou hast taken to thee thy great power
11. 18 them that fear thy name, small and great
11. 19 thunderings, and an earthquake, and gr.
12. 1 there appeared a great wonder in heaven
12. 3 behold a great red dragon, having seven
12. 9 the great dragon was cast out, that old
12. 12 having great wrath, because he knoweth
12. 14 were given two wings of a great eagle
13. 2 his power, and his seat, and great auth.
13. 13 he doeth great wonders, so that he mak.
13. 16 he caused all, both small and great, rich
14. 2 I heard..as the voice of a great thunder
14. 8 Babylon is fallen, is fallen, that great city
14. 19 cast (it) into the great wine press of the
15. 1 I saw another sign in heaven, great and
15. 3 Great and marvellous (are) thy works, L.
16. 1 I heard a great voice out of the temple
16. 9 And men were scorched with great heat
16. 12 poured out his vial upon the great river
16. 14 to the battle of that great day of God A.
16. 17 there came a [great] voice out of the tem.
16. 18 there was a great earthquake, such as
16. 18 so mighty an earthquake, (and) so great
16. 19 the great city was divided into three pa.
16. 19 great Babylon came in remembrance bef.
16. 21 there fell upon men a great hail out of
16. 21 for the plague thereof was exceeding gr.
17. 1 the judgment of the great whore that
17. 5 Mystery, Babylon The Great, The Mother
17. 6 when I saw her, I wondered with great
17. 18 the woman which thou sawest is that gr.
18. 1 came down from heaven, having great
18. 2 [Babylon the great is fallen, is fallen, and]
18. 10 that great city Babylon, that mighty city
18. 16 Alas, alas, that great city, that was clot.
18. 18 What (city is) like unto this great city!
18. 19 Alas, alas, that great city, wherein were
18. 21 angel took up a stone like a great millst.
18. 21 Thus with violence shall that great city
19. 1 I heard a great voice of much people in
19. 2 he hath judged the great whore, which
19. 5 and ye that fear him, both small and gr.
19. 17 together unto the supper of the great G.
19. 18 (both) free and bond, both small and gr.
20. 1 having the key..and a great chain in his
20. 11 I saw a great white throne, and him that
20. 12 I saw the dead, small and great, stand
21. 3 I heard a great voice out of heaven, say.
21. 10 he carried me away in the spirit to a gr.
21. 10 and showed me that [great] city, the holy
21. 12 And had a wall great and high, (and) had

32. *Many, numerous,* πολύς *polus.*
Matt. 2. 18 lamentation, and weeping, and great mo.
4. 25 there followed him great multitudes of
5. 12 for great (is) your reward in heaven: for
8. 1 When he was come down..great multitu.
8. 18 when Jesus saw great multitudes about
12. 15 great multitudes followed him, and he
13. 2 great multitudes were gathered together
14. 14 Jesus went forth, and saw a great multi.
15. 30 great multitudes came unto him, having
19. 2 And great multitudes followed him; and
19. 22 sorrowful: for he had great possessions
20. 29 from Jericho, a great multitude followed
24. 30 coming in the clouds..with power and gr.
26. 47 and with him a great multitude with sw.
Mark 3. 7 a great multitude from Galilee followed
3. 8 they about Tyre and Sidon, a great mul.
4. 1 there was gathered unto him a great m.
9. 14 he saw a great multitude about them
10. 22 grieved: for he had great possessions
13. 26 coming in the clouds with great power
14. 43 and with him a [great] multitude with sw.
Luke 2. 36 she was of a great age, and had lived
5. 6 they inclosed a great multitude of fishes
5. 15 great multitudes came together to hear
5. 29 there was a great company of publicans
6. 17 and a great multitude of people out of
6. 23 for, behold, your reward (is) great in
6. 35 your reward shall be great, and ye shall
10. 2 The harvest truly (is) great, but the lab.
14. 25 there went great multitudes with him
21. 27 coming in a cloud, with power and great
23. 27 there followed him a great company of
John 5. 3 In these lay a [great] multitude of impot.
6. 2 a great multitude followed him, because
6. 5 Jesus..saw a great company come unto
Acts 6. 7 a great company of the priests were obe.
11. 21 a great number believed, and turned
14. 1 that a great multitude both of the Jews
17. 4 of the devout Greeks a great multitude
21. 40 And when there was made a great silence
22. 28 With a great sum obtained I this freedom
23. 10 And when there arose a great dissension
24. 2 Seeing that by thee we enjoy great quiet.
24. 7 with great violence took (him) away out
25. 23 Agrippa was come, and Bernice, with gr.
28. 6 but after they had looked a great while
28. 29 [and had great reasoning among themsel.]
2 Co. 3. 12 Seeing..we use great plainness of speech
7. 4 Great (is) my boldness of speech toward
7. 4 great (is) my glorifying of you: I am fill.
8. 2 How that in a great trial of affliction the
8. 22 upon the great confidence which..in you
Eph. 2. 4 for his great love wherewith he loved us
Col. 4. 13 that he hath a great zeal for you, and
1 Th. 2. 17 endeavoured..to see your face with great
1 Ti. 3. 13 great boldness in the faith which is in C.
Phm. 7 we have great joy and consolation in thy
Heb. 10. 32 in which..ye endured a great fight of affl.
Rev. 7. 9 After this I beheld, and lo, a great mul.
19. 6 I heard as it were the voice of a great m.

[*See also* Delight, do, drought, flame, forces, grasshopper, hailstones, how, lion, man, mercies, owl, pain, power, so, stature, teeth, toe, very, while to come, wonders.]

GREAT, to be —

1. *To be mighty, strong,* גָּבַר *gabar.*
Psa. 103. 11 great is his mercy toward them that fear
117. 2 For his merciful kindness is great toward

2. *To be or become great,* גָּדַל *gadal.*
Gen. 48. 19 he also shall be great; but truly his you.
Num 14. 17 let the power of my Lord be great, acco.
2 Sa. 7. 22 Wherefore thou art great, O LORD God
Job 2. 13 for they saw that (his) grief was very gr.
Psa. 92. 5 how great are thy works..thy thoughts
104. 1 thou art very great; thou art clothed
Eccl. 2. 9 So I was great, and increased more than
Mic. 5. 4 for now shall he be great into the ends
Zech 12. 11 In that day shall there be a great mour.

3. *To be bony, substantial,* עָצַם *atsam.*
Psa. 139. 17 thy thoughts..O God! how great is the

GREAT as would contain —
House, בַּיִת *bayith.*
1 Ki. 18. 32 as great as would contain two measures

GREAT, to become —

1. *To be or become great,* גָּדַל *gadal.*
Gen. 24. 35 he is become great: and he hath given
26. 13 the man..grew until he became very gr.
Jer. 5. 27 therefore they are become great, and wax.

2. *To become great,* גָּדַל *gadal,* 5.
Dan. 8. 4 did according to his will, and became g.

GREAT with child —
Pregnant, ἔγκυος *egkuos.*
Luke 2. 5 his espoused wife, being great with child

GREAT (cattle) —
Oxen, herd, cattle, בָּקָר *baqar.*
Eccl. 2. 7 possessions of great and small cattle above

GREAT curse —
A thing devoted, ἀνάθεμα *anathema.*
Acts 23. 14 We have bound ourselves under a great c.

GREAT deal, the more a —
Much more, πολλῷ μᾶλλον *pollō mallon.*
Mark 10. 48 he cried the more a great deal, (Thou)

GREAT deal, so much the more a —
More exceedingly, μᾶλλον περισσότερον *mallon pe.*
Mark 7. 36 so much the more a great deal they pub.

GREAT estate, to come to —
To become great, גָּדַל *gadal,* 5.
Eccl. 1. 16 Lo, I am come to great estate, and have

GREAT, exceeding —
Greatest, μέγιστος *megistos.*
2 Pe. 1. 4 given..exceeding great and precious pr.

GREAT (fear) —
Fear, פַּחַד *pachad.*
Psa. 14. 5 There were they in great fear: 53. 5.

GREAT, to give —
To cause to be great, גָּדַל *gadal,* 5.
Psa. 18. 50 Great deliverance giveth he to his king

GREAT hail (stones) —
Hail, ice, אֶלְגָּבִישׁ *elgabish.*
Eze. 13. 11 and ye, O great hailstones, shall fall
13. 13 and great hailstones, in (my) fury, to co.
38. 22 and great hailstones, fire, and brimstone

GREAT, how —

1. *How great (a degree),* ἡλίκος *hēlikos.*
Jas. 3. 5 how great a matter a little fire kindleth

2. *How great (a degree),* πηλίκος *pēlikos.*
Heb. 7. 4 consider how great this man (was), unto

3. *How great (a quantity),* πόσος *posos.*
Matt. 6. 23 be darkness: how great (is) that darkn.!

GREAT lord —
Warrior, knight, שָׁלִישׁ *shalish.*
Eze 23. 23 great lords and renowned, all of them

GREAT, to make —

1. *To make great,* גָּדַל *gadal,* 3.
Gen. 12. 2 I will bless thee, and make thy name gr.
1 Ch. 29. 12 in thy hand (it is) to make great, and to
Eze. 31. 4 The waters made him great, the deep set

2. *To cause to be great,* גָּדַל *gadal,* 5.
Eccl. 2. 4 I made me great works; I builded me ho.
Eze. 24. 9 I will even make the pile for fire great

3. *To make great or abundant,* רָבָה *rabah,* 5.
Judg 20. 38 that they should make a great flame with
2 Sa. 22. 36 and thy gentleness hath made me great
Psa. 18. 35 and thy gentleness hath made me great

GREAT man —

1. *A man,* אִישׁ *ish.*
Isa. 2. 9 the great man humbleth himself: there.

2. *Great one,* גָּדוֹל *gadol.*
2 Sa. 3. 38 there is a prince and a great man fallen
2 Ki. 10. 6 with the great men of the city, which
10. 11 all his great men, and his kinsfolks, and

1 Ch.17. 8 name of the great men that (are) in the
Neh. 11. 14 Zabdiel, the son of (one of) the great men
Prov18. 16 man's gift..bringeth him before great men
Nah. 3. 10 and all her great men were bound in ch.

3. *Great, mighty, elder,* רַב *rab.*
Job 32. 9 Great men are not (always) wise; neither

4. *Great ones, magnates,* μεγιστᾶνες *megistanes.*
Rev. 6. 15 the kings of the earth, and the great men
18. 23 thy merchants were the great men of the

GREAT man, to make a —
To make great, רְבָה *rebah,* 3.
Dan. 2. 48 Then the king made Daniel a great man

GREAT, man of —
Great, גָּדֹל *gadol* [V.L. גרל].
Prov.19. 19 A man of great wrath shall suffer punis.

GREAT matter —
Great, גָּדוֹל *gadol.*
Psa.131. 1 neither do I exercise myself in great ma.

GREAT measure —
Abundantly, by measure, שָׁלִישׁ *shalish.*
Psa. 80. 5 givest them tears to drink in great mea.

GREAT number —
1. *Heaviness, weight,* כֹּבֶד *kobed.*
Nah. 3. 3 a multitude of slain, and a great number

2. *Abundance,* רֹב *rob.*
2 Ch.30. 24 a great number of priests sanctified them

GREAT number of —
Coming or reaching to, sufficient, ἱκανός *hikanos.*
Mark10. 46 with his disciples and a great number of

GREAT one, (some) —
1. *Great, mighty,* רַב *rab.*
Isa. 19. 20 shall send them a saviour, and a great one

2. *A certain great one,* τις μέγας *tis megas.*
Acts 8. 9 giving out that himself was some great one

3. *The great ones,* οἱ μεγάλοι *hoi megaloi.*
Mark10. 42 their great ones exercise authority upon

GREAT owl —
Owl, crane or heron, ibis, יַנְשׁוּף *yanshuph.*
Lev. 11. 17 and the cormorant, and the great owl
Deut14. 16 The little owl, and the great owl, and the

GREAT, to show —
To make great, magnify, μεγαλύνω *megalunō.*
Luke 1. 58 heard how the Lord had showed great

GREAT, so —
1. *So great (a degree),* τηλικοῦτος *tēlikoutos.*
2 Co. 1. 10 Who delivered us from so great a death
Heb. 2. 3 How shall we escape, if we neglect so g.
Jas. 3. 4 Behold..the ships, which though..so g.

2. *So great (a quantity),* τοσοῦτος *tosoutos.*
Matt. 8. 10 I have not found so great faith, no, not
15. 33 much bread..as to fill so great a multit.?
Luke 7. 9 I have not found so great faith, no, not
Heb. 12. 1 are compassed about with so great a cloud
Rev. 18. 17 in one hour so great riches is come to

GREAT, they that are —
The great ones, οἱ μεγάλοι *hoi megaloi.*
Matt.20. 25 they that are great exercise authority

GREAT thing —
1. *Great,* גָּדוֹל *gadol.*
2 Ki. 8. 4 Tell me, I pray thee, all the great things
Job 5. 9 Which doeth great things and unsearch.
9. 10 Which doeth great things past finding out
37. 5 great things doeth he, which we cannot
Psa. 71. 19 who hast done great things: O God, who
106. 21 which had done great things in Egypt
Jer. 45. 5 And seekest thou great things for thyself?

2. *Greatness,* גְּדוּלָּה, גְּדֻלָּה *gedullah, gedulah.*
2 Sa. 7. 21 hast thou done all these great things, to
7. 23 and to do for you great things and terrible
1 Ch.17. 19 done..making known all (these) great th.

3. *Myriad, greatness,* רִבּוֹא, רִבּוֹ *ribbo.*
Hos. 8. 12 I have written to him the great things of

4. *Very great,* רַבְרְבָן *rabrab.*
Dan. 7. 8 eyes..and a mouth speaking great things

5. *Great thing,* μέγα *mega.*
1 Co. 9. 11 great thing if we shall reap your carnal
2 Co.11. 15 Therefore (it is) no great thing if his min.
Rev. 13. 5 given unto him a mouth speaking great th.

6. *The great things,* τὰ μεγαλεῖα *ta megaleia.*
Luke 1. 49 that is mighty hath done to me [great th.]

GREAT (things), to do —
To make great, גָּדַל *gadal,* 5.
1 Sa.12. 24 consider how great (things) he hath done
Psa.126. 2,3 The LORD hath done great things for them
Joel 2. 20 come up, because he hath done great thi.
2. 21 Fear not..for the LORD will do great thi.

GREAT things, how —
How great (a quantity), ὅσος *hosos.*
Mark 5. 19 how great things the Lord hath done for
5. 20 how great things Jesus had done for him
Luke 8. 39 show how great things God hath done
8. 39 how great things Jesus had done unto
Acts 9. 16 I will show him how great things he must

GREAT things, very —
Very great, רַבְרְבָן *rabrab.*
Dan. 7. 20 and a mouth that spake very great things

GREAT (things), what —
1. *How great (a degree),* ἡλίκος *hēlikos.*
Col. 2. 1 that ye knew what great conflict I have

2. *How great (a quantity),* ὅσος *hosos.*
Mark 3. 8 when they had heard [what great things]

GREAT toes —
Thumbs of the feet, בְּהֹנוֹת רַגְלַיִם *behonoth raglayim.*
Judg. 1. 6 and cut off his thumbs and his great toes
1. 7 their thumbs and their great toes cut off

GREAT, very —
1. *To give honour, weight,* כָּבַד *kabed,* 3.
Num22. 17 I will promote thee unto very great hon.

2. *Very much or numerous,* πάμπολυς *pampolus.*
Mark 8. 1 In those days the multitude [being very g.]

3. *Most,* πλεῖστος *pleistos.*
Matt 21. 8 a very great multitude spread their gar.

GREAT, to wax —
1. *To be or become great,* גָּדַל *gadal.*
Gen. 19. 13 because the cry of them is waxen great
26. 13 the man waxed great, and went forward
Eze. 16. 7 and thou hast increased and waxen great
Dan. 8. 9 a little horn, which waxed exceeding gr.
8. 10 And it waxed great..to the host of heaven

2. *To make or become great,* גָּדַל *gadal,* 5.
Dan. 8. 8 Therefore the he goat waxed very great

GREATER —
1. *Great,* גָּדוֹל *gadol.*
Gen. 1. 16 the greater light to rule the day, and the
4. 13 My punishment (is) greater than I can be.
39. 9 none greater in this house than I; neither
Exod18. 11 I know that the LORD (is) greater than all
Num14. 12 thee a greater nation and mightier than
Deut. 1. 28 The people (is) greater and taller than we
4. 38 nations..greater and mightier than thou
9. 1 to possess nations greater and mightier
11. 23 shall possess greater nations and mightier
Josh.10. 2 because it (was) greater than Ai, and all
2 Sa. 13. 15 greater than the love wherewith he had
13. 16 greater than the other that thou didst
2 Ch. 3. 5 the greater house he ceiled with fir tree
Esth. 9. 4 for..Mordecai waxed greater and greater
Eze. 8. 6, 13, 15 thou shalt see greater abominations
43. 14 from the lesser settle..to the greater set.
Hag. 2. 9 The glory of this..house shall be greater

2. *To go on,* הָלַךְ *halak.*
1 Ch.11. 9 So David waxed greater and greater: for

3. *Many, great,* רַב *rab.*
Deut. 7. 1 nations greater and mightier than thou
9. 14 a nation mightier and greater than they
Dan.11. 13 set..a multitude greater than the former
Amos 6. 2 their border greater than your border?

4. *Greater,* μειζότερος *meizoteros.*
3 John 4 I have no greater joy than to hear that

5. *Greater,* μείζων *meizōn.*
Matt.11. 11 there hath not risen a greater than John
11. 11 least in the kingdom of heaven is greater
12 6 in this place is (one) greater than the tem.
23. 17 whether is greater, the gold, or the tem.
23. 19 whether (is) greater, the gift, or the altar
Mark 4. 32 it groweth up, and becometh greater
12. 31 There is none other commandment grea.
Luke 7. 28 there is a not greater prophet than John
7 28 least in the kingdom of God is greater
12 18 I will pull down my barns, and build gr.
22 27 whether (is) greater, he that sitteth at
John 4. 12 Art thou greater than our father Jacob
5. 20 he will show him greater works than
5. 36 I have greater witness than (that) of Jo.
8. 53 Art thou greater than our father Abrah.
10. 29 My Father, which gave (them) me, is gr.
13. 16 The servant is not greater than his lord
13. 16 neither he that is sent greater than he
14. 12 and greater (works) than these shall he
14. 28 Father: for my Father is greater than I
15. 13 Greater love hath no man than this, that
15. 20 The servant is not greater than his lord
19. 11 he that delivered me unto thee hath the g.
1 Co. 14. 5 greater (is) he that prophesieth than he
Heb. 6. 13 because he could swear by no greater, he
6. 16 men verily swear by the greater; and an
9. 11 by a greater and more perfect tabernacle
11. 26 Esteeming the reproach of Christ greater
Jas. 3. 1 we shall receive the greater condemnat.
2 Pe. 2. 11 angels, which are greater in power and
1 Jo. 3. 20 God is greater than our heart, and know.
4. 4 because greater is he that is in you, than
5. 9 the witness of God is greater: for this

6. *More abundant,* περισσότερος *perissoteros.*
Matt 23. 14 [therefore ye shall receive the greater]
Mark 12. 40 these shall receive greater damnation
Luke 20. 47 the same shall receive greater damnation

7. *More, something more,* πλείων *pleiōn,* πλέον *pleon.*
Matt 12. 41 and, behold, a greater than Jonas (is)
12. 42 and, behold, a greater than Solomon (is)
Luke11. 31 and, behold, a greater than Solomon (is)
11. 32 and, behold, a greater than Jonas (is)
Acts 15. 28 to lay upon you no greater burden than

GREATER part, the —
The more part, the majority, οἱ πλείους *hoi pleious.*
1 Co. 15. 6 of whom the greater part remain unto

GREATER things —
Greater, μείζων *meizōn.*
John 1. 50 thou shall see greater things than these

GREATER, to be (much) —
1. *To be or become great,* גָּדַל *gadal.*
Gen. 41. 40 only in the throne will I be greater than
48. 19 his younger brother shall be greater than
Lam. 4. 6 is greater than the punishment of the sin

2. *To be great,* רָבָה *rabah.*
1 Sa. 14. 30 had there not been now a much greater
Job 33. 12 I will answer thee, that God is greater

GREATEST —
1. *Great, large,* μέγας *megas.*
Acts 8. 10 they all gave heed, from the least to t.g.
Heb. 8. 11 shall know me from the least to the gre.

2. *Greater, larger,* μείζων *meizōn.*
Matt.13. 32 when it is grown, it is the greatest among
18. 1 Who is the greatest in the kingdom of h.?
18. 4 the same is greatest in the kingdom of
23. 11 he that is greatest among you shall be
Mark 9. 34 had disputed..who (should be) the grea.
Luke 9. 46 a reasoning..which of them should be g.
22. 24 which of them should be accounted the g.
22. 26 he that is greatest among you, let him
1 Co.13. 13 these three; but the greatest of these (is)

3. *Great,* גָּדוֹל *gadol.*
1 Ch.12. 14 an hundred, and the greatest over a tho.
Job 1. 3 was the greatest of all the men of the
Jer. 6. 13 from the least of them even unto the gr.
8. 10 every one from the least even unto the g.
31. 34 from the least of them unto the greatest
42. 1, 8 people from the least even unto the g.
44. 12 shall die, from the least even unto the g.
Jon. 3. 5 from the greatest of them even to the

GREATEST part —
Multitude, מַרְבִּית *marbith.*
1 Ch.12. 29 the greatest part of them had kept the

GREATLY —
1. *Might,* מְאֹד *meod.*
Gen. 7. 18 and were increased greatly upon the ea.
19. 3 he pressed upon them greatly; and they
24. 35 LORD hath blessed my master greatly
32. 7 Then Jacob was greatly afraid and distr.
Exod19. 18 and the whole mount quaked greatly
Num11. 10 the anger of the LORD was kindled great.
14. 39 told..Israel: and the people mourned g.
Deut17. 17 neither shall he greatly multiply to him.
Josh 10. 2 they feared greatly, because Gibeon (was)
Judg. 2. 15 for evil..and they were greatly distressed
6. 6 Israel was greatly impoverished because
1 Sa. 11. 6 upon Saul..and his anger was kindled g.
11. 15 and all the men of Israel rejoiced greatly
12. 18 all the people greatly feared the LORD
16. 21 he loved him greatly; and he became his
17. 11 all Israel..were dismayed, and greatly
28. 5 he was afraid, and his heart greatly tre.
30. 6 David was greatly distressed; for the
2 Sa. 10. 5 sent..because the men were greatly ash.
12. 5 David's anger was greatly kindled again.
24. 10 I have sinned greatly in that I have done
1 Ki. 2. 12 Solomon..his kingdom was established g.
5. 7 when Hiram heard..he rejoiced greatly
18. 3 Now Obadiah feared the LORD greatly
1 Ch.16. 25 great (is) the LORD, and greatly to be pr.
19. 5 sent..for the men were greatly ashamed
21. 8 David said unto God, I have sinned grea.
2 Ch.25. 10 their anger was greatly kindled against J.
33. 12 humbled himself greatly before the God
Job 8. 7 yet thy latter end should greatly increase
Psa. 21. 1 in thy salvation how greatly shall he re.!
38. 6 I am troubled; I am bowed down greatly
47. 9 shields..(belong) unto God: he is greatly
48. 1 Great is the LORD, and greatly to be pra
78. 59 he was wroth, and greatly abhorred Isr.
96. 4 For the LORD (is) great, and greatly to be
105. 24 he increased his people greatly, and made
107. 38 He blesseth..that they are multiplied g
109. 30 I will greatly praise the LORD with my
112. 1 delighteth greatly in his commandment
116. 10 therefore have I spoken: I was greatly
119. 51 The proud have had me greatly in deris.
145. 3 Great (is) the LORD, and greatly to be pr.
Jer. 9. 19 we are greatly confounded, because we ha.
20. 11 they shall be greatly ashamed; for they
Eze. 20. 13 and my sabbaths they greatly polluted
Obad. 2 I have made thee small..thou art greatly
Zeph. 1. 14 (it is) near, and hasteth greatly, (even) the
Zech. 9. 9 Rejoice greatly, O daughter of Zion; sh.

2. *Much, abundant, mighty, great,* רַב *rab.*
Psa. 62. 2 my defence; I shall not be greatly moved
65. 9 thou greatly enrichest it with the river
89. 7 God is greatly to be feared in the assem.

3. *Abundance, multitude, greatness,* רֹב *rob.*
1 Ch. 4. 38 the house of their fathers increased gre.

4. *To make many or great,* רָבָה *rabah,* 5.
Gen. 3. 16 I will greatly multiply thy sorrow and

5. *Great, much, many,* שַׂגִּיא *saggi.*
Dan. 5. 9 Then was king Belshazzar greatly troub.

6. *Shame,* בֹּשֶׁת *bosheth.*
Isa. 42. 17 they shall be greatly ashamed, that trust
7. *Joy,* גִּיל *gil.*
Prov23. 24 The father of the righteous shall greatly
8. *Very much, exceedingly,* λίαν *lian.*
Matt27. 14 insomuch that the governor marvelled g.
2 Ti. 4. 15 for he hath greatly withstood our words
2 John 4 I rejoiced greatly that I found of thy ch.
3 John 3 I rejoiced greatly when the brethren ca.
9. *Greatly,* μεγάλως *megalōs.*
Phil. 4. 10 I rejoiced in the Lord greatly, that now
10. *Much, many,* πολύς *polus.*
Mark 5. 23 besought him greatly, saying, My little
5. 38 and seeth..them that wept and wailed g.
12. 27 God of the living: ye therefore do greatly
1 Co.16. 12 I greatly desired him to come unto you
11. *Exceedingly, greatly,* σφόδρα *sphodra.*
Matt 27. 54 they feared greatly, saying, Truly this
Acts 6. 7 the disciples multiplied in Jerusalem g.
12. *With joy,* χαρᾷ *chara.*
John 3. 29 rejoiceth greatly because of the bridegr.

GREATLY (feared), thing —
Fear, פַּחַד *pachad.*
Job 3. 25 the thing which I greatly feared is come

GREATLY rejoice, to —
To sing, cry aloud, רָנַן *ranan,* 3.
Psa. 71. 23 My lips shall greatly rejoice when I sing

GREATNESS —
1. *Great,* גָּדוֹל *gadol.*
Exod15. 16 by the greatness of thine arm they shall
2. *Greatness,* גְּדוּלָּה, גְּדֻלָּה *gedulah, gedullah.*
1 Ch.17. 19 hast thou done all this greatness, in ma.
17. 21 to make thee a name of greatness and
29. 11 Thine, O LORD, (is) the greatness, and
Esth 10. 2 the declaration of the greatness of Mor.
Psa. 71. 21 Thou shalt increase my greatness, and
145. 3 the LORD..his greatness (is) unsearchable
145. 6 thy terrible acts: and I will declare thy g.
3. *Greatness,* גֹּדֶל *godel.*
Num14. 19 according unto the greatness of thy me.
Deut. 3. 24 hast begun to show thy servant thy grea.
5. 24 hath showed us his glory, and his great.
9. 26 thou hast redeemed through thy greatn.
11. 2 LORD your God, his greatness, his mighty
32. 3 the LORD: ascribe ye greatness unto our
Psa. 79. 11 according to the greatness of thy power
150. 2 praise him according to his excellent gre.
Eze. 31. 2 Whom art thou like in thy greatness?
31. 7 Thus was he fair in his greatness, in the
31. 18 and in greatness among the trees of Ed.
4. *Increase, abundance,* מַרְבִּית *marbith.*
2 Ch. 9. 6 the one half of the greatness of thy wisd.
5. *Abundance, multitude, greatness,* רֹב *rob.*
Exod15. 7 in the greatness of thine excellency thou
Neh. 13. 22 spare me according to the greatness of
Psa. 66. 3 through the greatness of thy power shall
Prov. 5. 23 in the greatness of his folly he shall go
Isa. 40. 26 all by names by the greatness of his mi.
57. 10 Thou art wearied in the greatness of thy
63. 1 travelling in the greatness of his strength?
Jer. 13. 22 For the greatness of thine iniquity are
6. *Greatness,* רְבוּ *rebu.*
Dan. 4. 22 thy greatness is grown, and reacheth unto
7. 27 the greatness of the kingdom under the
7. *To be many, abundant,* רָבָה *rabah.*
2 Ch.24. 27 the greatness of the burdens (laid) upon
8. *Greatness,* μέγεθος *megethos.*
Eph. 1. 19 what (is) the exceeding greatness of his

GREAVES —
Frontlet, מִצְחָה *mitschah.*
1 Sa. 17. 6 greaves of brass upon his legs, and a tar.

GRE'-CIA, GREECE, יָוָן *yavan,* Ἑλλάς, *hellas.*
A country of southern Europe lying E. of Italy and W. of Asia Minor, the Isles of the Ionian Archipelago; called *Javan* in Hebrew.
Dan. 8. 21 And the rough goat (is) the king of G.
10. 20 when I am gone..the prince of G. shall
11. 2 shall stir up all against the realm of G.
Zech. 9. 13 thy sons, O Zion, against thy sons, O G.
Acts 20. 2 gone over those parts..he came into G.

GRECIANS—
1. *Sons of the Javanim,* בְּנֵי־הַיְּוָנִים *bene-hayyevanim.*
Joel 3 6 children..have ye sold unto the Grecians
2. *Hellenist, a Jew born out of Canaan,* Ἑλληνιστής.
Acts 6. 1 there arose a murmuring of the Grecians
9. 29 spake..and disputed against the Grecians
11. 20 spake unto [the Grecians], preaching the

GREEDILY —
Desire, תַּאֲוָה *taavah.*
Prov 21. 26 He coveteth greedily all the day long

GREEDINESS —
A having or desiring more, πλεονεξία *pleonexia.*
Eph. 4. 19 to work all uncleanness with greediness

GREEDY —
1. *To heap up,* בָּצַע *batsa.*
Prov. 1. 19 the way of every one that is greedy of g.
15. 27 He that is greedy of gain troubleth his
2. *Strong of soul,* עַז נֶפֶשׁ *az nephesh.*
Isa. 56. 11 greedy dogs (which) can never have eno.

GREEDY, to be —
To have a desire, כָּסַף *kasaph.*
Psa. 17. 12 Like as a lion..is greedy of his prey, and

GREEK —
1. *A native of Greece, not a Jew or barbarian,* Ἕλλην *Hellēn.*
John12. 20 there were certain Greeks among them
Acts 14. 1 a great multitude..of the Greeks believed
16. 1 Jewess, and believed..his father..a Gre.
16. 3 they knew all that his father was a Greek
17. 4 of the devout Greeks a great multitude
18. 4 and persuaded the Jews and the Greeks
18. 17 Then all [the Greeks] took Sosthenes, the
19. 10 all..heard the word..both Jews and Gr.
19. 17 this was known to all the Jews and Gr.
20. 21 Testifying both to the Jews, and..Greeks
21. 28 brought Greeks also into the temple, and
Rom. 1. 14 I am debtor both to the Greeks and to
1. 16 to the Jew first, and also to the Greek
10. 12 no difference between the Jew and the G.
1 Co. 1. 22 the Jews require a sign, and the Greeks
1. 23 Christ crucified..unto the [Greeks] fool.
1. 24 them which are called, both Jews and G.
Gal. 2. 3 Titus, who was with me, being a Greek
3. 28 There is neither Jew nor Greek, there is
Col. 3. 11 Where there is neither Greek nor Jew
2. *Greek, Grecian,* Ἑλληνικός *Hellēnikos.*
Rev. 9. 11 but in the Greek tongue hath (his) name
3. *A Greek female,* Ἑλληνίς *Hellēnis.*
Mark 7. 26 The woman was a Greek, a Syrophenician
Acts 17. 12 also of honourable women which were G.
4. *In Greek,* Ἑλληνιστί *Hellēnisti.*
Acts 21. 37 chief captain..said, Canst thou speak G.?

GREEK, in —
In Greek, Ἑλληνιστί *Hellēnisti.*
John19. 20 it was written in Hebrew, (and) Greek

GREEK, of —
Greek, Grecian, Ἑλληνικός *Hellēnikos.*
Luke23. 38 [in letters of Greek, and Latin, and Heb.]

GREEN —
1. *Tender grass,* דֶּשֶׁא *deshe.*
Psa. 23. 2 He maketh me to lie down in green pas.
2. *Green, green herb,* יָרָק *yaraq.*
2 Ki.19. 26 (as) the green herb, (as) the grass on the
Isa. 37. 27 (as) the green herb, (as) the grass on the
3. *Green herb, greenness,* יֶרֶק *yereq.*
Gen. 1. 30 every green herb for meat: and it was
9. 3 as the green herb have I given you all
Psa. 37. 2 they shall soon..wither as the green herb
4. *Cotton,* כַּרְפַּס *karpas.*
Esth. 1. 6 white, green, and blue (hangings) fasten.
5. *Moist, fresh,* לַח *lach.*
Gen. 30. 37 Jacob took him rods of green poplar, and
Judg16. 7 If they bind me with seven green withs
16. 8 seven green withs which had not been
Eze. 17. 24 have dried up the green tree, and have
20. 47 and it shall devour every green tree in
6. *Wet,* רָטֹב *ratob.*
Job 8. 16 He (is) green before the sun, and his b.
7. *Flourishing, fresh,* רַעֲנָן *raanan.*
Deut 12. 2 upon the hills, and under every green
1 Ki.14. 23 they also built them..under every green
2 Ki.16. 4 and on the hills, and under every green
17. 10 set..up images..under every green tree
2 Ch.28. 4 on the hills, and under every green tree
Job 15. 32 his time, and his branch shall not be gr.
Psa. 37. 35 and spreading himself like a green bay t.
52. 8 I (am) like a green olive tree in the house
Song 1. 16 thou (art) fair..also our bed (is) green
Isa. 57. 5 with idols under every green tree, slaying
Jer. 2. 20 and under every green tree thou wander.
3. 6 she is gone..under every green tree, and
3. 13 to the strangers under every green tree
11. 16 A green olive tree, fair..of goodly fruit
17. 2 their altars and their groves by the green
17. 8 heat cometh, but her leaf shall be green
Eze. 6. 13 under every green tree, and under every
Hos. 14. 8 I (am) like a green fir tree. From me is
8. *Pale green,* χλωρός *chlōros.*
Mark 6. 39 make all sit down..upon the green grass
Rev. 8. 7 trees..and all green grass, was burnt up
9. *Wet, moist,* ὑγρός *hugros.*
Luke23. 31 if they do these things in a green tree

GREEN thing —
1. *Green thing,* יָרוֹק *yaroq.*
Job 39. 8 and he searcheth after every green thing
2. *Greenness, green herb,* יֶרֶק *yereq.*
Exod10. 15 there remained not any green thing in
Isa. 15. 6 the grass faileth, there is no green thing
3. *Pale green,* χλωρός *chlōros.*
Rev. 9. 4 neither any green thing, neither any tree

GREENISH —
Green, yellow, יְרַקְרַק *yeraqraq.*
Lev. 13. 49 if the plague be greenish or reddish in
14. 37 hollow strakes, greenish or reddish, which

GREENNESS —
Greenness, budding, אֵב *eb.*
Job. 8. 12 Whilst it (is) yet in his greenness .. not

GREET, to—
1. *To ask of peace,* שָׁאַל לְשָׁלוֹם *shaal le-shalom.*
1 Sa. 25. 5 go to Nabal, and greet him in my name
2. *To draw to self, clasp, embrace,* ἀσπάζομαι *aspa.*
Rom 16. 3 Greet Priscilla and Aquila my helpers in
16. 6 Greet Mary, who bestowed much labour
16. 8 Greet Amplias my beloved in the Lord
16. 11 Greet them that be of the (household) of
1 Co. 16. 20 All the brethren greet you. Greet ye one
2 Co.13. 12 Greet one another with an holy kiss
Phil. 4. 21 The brethren which are with me greet
Col. 4. 14 Luke, the .. physician, and Demas, greet
1 Th. 5. 26 Greet all the brethren with an holy kiss
2 Ti. 4. 21 Eubulus greeteth thee, and Pudens, and
Titus 3. 15 Greet them that love us in the faith
1 Pe. 5. 14 Greet.. one another with a kiss of charity
2 Jo. 13 The children of thy elect sister greet thee
3 Jo. 14 friends salute thee. Greet the friends by

GREETING —
1. *Drawing to self, salutation,* ἀσπασμός *aspasmos.*
Matt23. 7 greetings in the markets, and to be called
Luke11. 43 for ye love .. greetings in the markets
20. 46 which .. love greetings in the markets
2. *To rejoice, be of good cheer,* χαίρω *chairō.*
Jas. 1. 1 James .. to the twelve tribes .. greeting

GREETING, (send) —
To rejoice, be of good cheer, χαίρω *chairō.*
Acts 15. 23 elders..(send) greeting unto the brethr.
23. 26 Lysias unto..Felix (sendeth) greeting

GREW — [*See* GROW.]
Becoming great, גָּדֵל *gadel.*
Gen. 26. 13 the man..grew until he became very gre
1 Sa 2. 26 the child Samuel grew on, and was in fa.

GREW upon, that which —
Shoot, plant, צֶמַח *tsemach.*
Gen. 19. 25 overthrew..that which grew upon the gr.

GREW, where it —
Shoot, plant, צֶמַח *tsemach.*
Eze. 17. 10 shall wither in the furrows where it grew

GREY head (ed) —
Greyness, שֵׂיבָה *sebah.*
Psa. 71. 18 Now also when I am old and grey headed
Prov.20. 29 and the beauty of old men (is) the grey h.

GREY HOUND —
Stag, girt in the loins, זַרְזִיר מָתְנַיִם *zarzir mothnayim.*
Prov.30. 31 A grey hound; an he goat also; and a ki.

GRIEF —
1. *To become sick, weak, pained,* חָלָה *chalah,* 2.
Isa. 17. 11 a heap in the day of grief and of desperate
2. *Sickness, weakness, pain,* חֳלִי *choli.*
Isa. 53. 3 a man of sorrows..acquainted with grief
53. 4 he hath borne our griefs, and carried our
Jer. 6. 7 before me continually (is) grief and wou.
10. 19 Truly this (is) a grief, and I must bear it
3. *Sorrow, affliction,* יָגוֹן *yagon.*
Psa. 31. 10 my life is spent with grief, and my years
Jer. 45. 3 for the LORD hath added grief to my sor.
4. *Pain,* כְּאֵב *keeb.*
Job 2. 13 for they saw that (his) grief was very gre.
16. 6 Though I speak, my grief is not asswaged
5. *Sadness, provocation, anger,* כַּעַס *kaas.*
1 Sa. 1. 16 out of the abundance of my..grief have
Psa. 6. 7 Mine eye is consumed because of grief
31. 9 LORD..mine eye is consumed with grief
Prov.17. 25 A foolish son (is) a grief to his father
Eccl. 1. 18 in much wisdom (is) much grief; and he
2. 23 his days (are) sorrows..his travail grief
6. *Sadness, provocation, anger,* כַּעַשׂ *kaas.*
Job 6. 2 Oh that my grief were throughly weighed
7. *Pain,* מַכְאוֹב *makob.*
2 Ch. 6. 29 when every one shall know..his own gr.
Psa. 69. 26 they talk to the grief of those whom thou
8. *Bitterness,* מֹרָה *morah.*
Gen. 26. 35 Which were a grief of mind unto Isaac
9. *Stumbling block,* פּוּקָה *puqah.*
1 Sa. 25. 31 That this shall be no grief unto thee, nor
10. *Evil,* רַע *ra.*
Jon. 4. 6 a shadow..to deliver him from his grief
11. *Grief, grievance,* λύπη *lupē.*
1 Pe. 2. 19 for conscience toward God endure grief

GRIEF, to cause or put to —
1. *To afflict, grieve,* יָגָה *yagah,* 5.
Lam. 3. 32 But though he cause grief, yet will he
2. *To make sick,* חָלָה *chalah,* 5.
Isa. 53. 10 he hath put (him) to grief: when thou
3. *To grieve, afflict,* λυπέω *lupeō.*
2 Cor. 2. 5 if any have caused grief, he hath not gr.

GRIEF, with —
To groan, sigh, στενάζω *stenazō.*
Heb. 13. 17 they may do it with joy, and not with g

GRIEVANCE —

Labour, perverseness, misery, עָמָל *amal.*

Hab. 1. 3 dost thou..cause (me) to behold grievance?

GRIEVE, to —

1. *To grieve,* אָדַב *adab,* 5.

1 Sa. 2. 33 to consume thine eyes, and to grieve th.

2. *To be pained,* חִיל, חוּל *chul, chil.*

Jer. 5. 3 thou hast stricken..but they have not g.

3. *To burn, be wroth,* חָרָה *charah.*

1 Sa. 15. 11 it grieved Samuel; and he cried unto

4. *To afflict, grieve,* יָגָה *yagah,* 3.

Lam. 3. 33 he doth not afflict willingly nor grieve

5. *To be or become weary,* לָאָה *laah,* 2.

Prov. 26. 15 it grieveth him to bring it again to his

6. *To grieve,* עָצַב *atsab.*

1 Ch. 4. 10 keep..from evil, that it may not grieve

7. *To grieve,* עָצַב *atsab,* 5.

Psa. 78. 40 How oft did they..grieve him in the de.!

8. *To grieve, afflict,* λυπέω *lupeō.*

2 Co. 2. 5 he hath not grieved me, but in part; that
Eph. 4. 30 grieve not the Holy Spirit of God, where.

GRIEVED, to be —

1. *To pain self, become pained,* חִיל, חוּל *chul, chil,* 7a.

Esth. 4. 4 Then was the queen exceedingly grieved

2. *To be sick, weak,* חָלָה *chalah.*

Isa. 57. 10 hast found..therefore thou wast not gr.

3. *To become sick, weak,* חָלָה *chalah,* 2.

Amos 6. 6 they are not grieved for the affliction of

4. *To show self violent,* חָמֵץ *chamets,* 7.

Psa. 73. 21 Thus my heart was grieved, and I was p.

5. *To be evil,* יָרַע *yera.*

Deut 15. 10 thine heart shall not be grieved when th.
1 Sa. 1. 8 why is thy heart grieved? (am) not I be.
Neh. 2. 10 it grieved them exceedingly that there
13. 8 it grieved me sore: therefore I cast forth

6. *To be pained,* כָּאָה *kaah,* 2.

Dan. 11. 30 he shall be grieved, and return, and have

7. *To be sad, angry,* כָּעַס *kaas.*

Psa. 112. 10 The wicked shall see (it), and be grieved

8. *To be pierced,* כָּרָא *kera,* 2.

Dan. 7. 15 I Daniel was grieved in my spirit in the

9. *To be or become weary,* לָאָה *laah.*

Job 4. 2 to commune with thee, wilt thou be gri.

10. *To be bitter,* מָרַר *marar.*

1 Sa. 30. 6 the soul of all the people was grieved

11. *To be grieved, solicitous,* עָגַם *agam.*

Job 30. 25 was (not) my soul grieved for the poor?

12. *To grieve,* עָצַב *atsab.*

Isa. 54. 6 as a woman forsaken, and grieved in spi.

13. *To be grieved,* עָצַב *atsab,* 2.

Gen. 45. 5 be not grieved nor angry with yourselves
1 Sa. 20. 3 Let not Jonathan know this, lest he be g.
20. 34 for he was grieved for David, because his
2 Sa. 19. 2 how the king was grieved for his son
Neh. 8. 11 the day (is) holy; neither be ye grieved

14. *To grieve self,* עָצַב *atsab,* 7.

Gen. 34. 7 the men were grieved, and they were

15. *To loathe, be weary of,* קוּט *qut.*

Psa. 95. 10 Forty years long was I grieved with (this)

16. *To show self weary of,* קוּט *qut,* 7a.

Psa. 119. 158 I beheld th transgressors, and was gri.
139. 21 am not I grieved with those that rise up

17. *To be vexed, weary,* קוּץ *quts.*

Exod. 1. 12 they were grieved because of the children

18. *To be or become short,* קָצַר *qatsar.*

Judg 10. 16 his soul was grieved for the misery of Is.

19. *To labour through, grieve self,* διαπονέω *diapon.*

Acts 4. 2 Being grieved that they taught the peo.
16. 18 Paul, being grieved, turned and said to

20. *To grieve, afflict,* λυπέω *lupeō.*

Mark 10. 22 And he was sad..and went away grieved
John 21. 17 Peter was grieved because he said unto
Rom 14. 15 if thy brother be grieved with (thy) meat
2 Co. 2. 4 not that ye should b grieved, but that

21. *To grieve at the same time,* συλλυπέω *sullupeō.*

Mark 3. 5 being grieved for the hardness of their

GRIEVED with, to b —

To be grieved at, feel disgust at, προσοχθίζω *pros.*

Heb. 3. 10 I was grieved with that generation, and
3. 17 with whom was he grieved forty years?

GRIEVED, to have sorely —

To make bitter, מָרַר *marar,* 3.

Gen. 49. 23 The archers have sorely grieved him, and

GRIEVED or GRIEVETH, it —

1. *To grieve self,* עָצַב *atsab,* 7.

Gen. 6. 6 made man..and it grieved him at his he.

2. *To be bitter,* מָרַר *marar.*

Ruth 1. 13 for it grieveth me much for your sakes

GRIEVING —

To cause pain, כָּאַב *kaab,* 5.

Eze. 28. 24 there shall be no more..(any) grieving

GRIEVOUS (to be) —

1. *To pain, be pained,* חִיל, חוּל *chul, chil,* 5.

Psa. 10. 5 His ways are always grievous; thy

2. *To pain self,* חִיל, חוּל *chul, chil,* 7a.

Jer. 23. 19 a whirlwind..even a grievous whirlwind

3. *To become sick, weak,* חָלָה *chalah,* 2.

Jer. 10. 19 Woe is me..my wound is grievous: but
14. 17 is broken..with a very grievous blow
30. 12 Thus saith the LORD..thy wound (is) grie.
Nah. 3. 19 (There is) no healing..thy wound is gri.

4. *To be evil,* יָרַע *yera.*

Gen. 21. 11 the thing was very grievous in Abraham's
21. 12 Let it not be grievous in thy sight, beca.
Isa. 15. 4 Moab..his life shall be grievous unto him

5. *To be weighty, heavy,* כָּבֵד *kabed.*

Gen. 12. 10 for the famine (was) grievous in the land
41. 31 not be known..for it (shall be) very gri.
50. 11 This (is) a grievous mourning to the Egy.
Exod. 8. 24 there came a grievous swarm (of flies)
9. 3 (there shall be) a very grievous murrain
9. 18 I will cause it to rain a very grievous hail
9. 24 fire mingled with the hail, very grievous
10. 14 in all the coasts of Egypt · very grievous

6. *To be powerful, grievous,* מָרַץ *marats,* 2.

1 Ki. 2. 8 which cursed me with a grievous curse in

7. *To turn aside,* סוּר *sur.*

Jer. 6. 28 They (are) all grievous revolters, walking

8. *Grievous thing, grieving,* עֶצֶב *etseb.*

Prov. 15. 1 wrath: but grievous words stir up anger

9. *Sharp,* קָשֶׁה *qasheh.*

1 Ki. 12. 4 make thou the grievous service of thy fa.
2 Ch. 10. 4 ease thou somewhat the grievous servit.
Isa. 21. 2 A grievous vision is declared unto me; the

10. *Evil,* רַע *ra.*

Prov. 15. 10 Correction (is) grievous unto him that for.
Eccl. 2. 17 the work that is wrought..(is) grievous

11. *Sicknesses, diseases,* תַּחֲלֻאִים *tachaluim.*

Jer. 16. 4 They shall die of grievous deaths; they

12. *Weighty, heavy,* βαρύς *barus.*

Acts 20. 29 shall grievous wolves enter in among you
25. 7 laid many and grievous complaints again.
1 Jo. 5. 3 and his commandments are not grievous

13. *Of grief,* λύπης *lupēs.*

Heb. 12. 11 seemeth to be joyous, but grievous

14. *Slothful, tedious,* ὀκνηρός *oknēros.*

Phil. 3. 1 To write..to me indeed (is) not grievous

15. *Evil, painful, irksome,* πονηρός *ponēros.*

Rev. 16. 2 there fell a noisome and grievous sore

GRIEVOUS to be borne —

Hard to be borne, δυσβάστακτος *dusbastaktos.*

Matt 23. 4 heavy burdens [and grievous to be borne]
Luke 11. 46 lade..with burdens grievous to be borne

GRIEVOUS, to make —

To make sharp, קָשָׁה *qashah,* 5.

1 Ki. 12. 4 Thy father made our yoke grievous: now
2 Ch. 10. 4 Thy father made our yoke grievous: now

GRIEVOUS things —

Ancient, stiff, עָתָק *athaq.*

Psa. 31. 18 which speak grievous things proudly and

GRIEVOUSLY —

1. *Sin,* חֵטְא *chet.*

Lam. 1. 8 Jerusalem hath grievously sinned; there.

2. *Transgression,* מַעַל *maal.*

Eze. 14. 13 sinneth against me by trespassing griev.

3. *To rebel,* מָרָה *marah.*

Lam. 1. 20 is turned..for I have grievously rebelled

4. *Greatly, vehemently,* δεινῶς *deinōs.*

Matt. 8. 6 sick of the palsy, grievously tormented

5. *Badly, evilly,* κακῶς *kakōs.*

Matt 15. 22 my daughter is grievously vexed with a

GRIEVOUSLY, to fall —

To pain, be in pain, חוּל, חִיל *chul, chil.*

Jer. 23. 19 it shall fall grievously upon the head of

GRIEVOUSNESS —

1. *Weight, heaviness,* כֹּבֶד *kobed.*

Isa. 21. 15 they fled..from the grievousness of

2. *Labour, perverseness, misery,* עָמָל *amal.*

Isa. 10. 1 Woe unto them that..write grievousness

GRIND, to —

1. *Mill, mill stone,* טְחוֹן *techon.*

Lam. 5. 13 They took the young men to grind, and

2. *To grind,* טָחַן *tachan.*

Exod 32. 20 took the calf..and ground (it) to powder
Num 11. 8 gathered (it) and ground (it) in mills, or
Deut. 9. 21 I took..the calf..(and) ground (it) very
Judg 16. 21 and he did grind in the prison house
Job 31. 10 let my wife grind unto another, and let
Isa. 3. 15 and grind the faces of the poor? saith the
47. 2 Take the mill stones, and grind meal: un

3. *To grind,* ἀλήθω *alēthō.*

Matt 24. 41 Two (women shall be) grinding at the m.
Luke 17. 35 Two (women) shall be grinding together

GRIND to powder —

To disperse, scatter, λικμάω *likmaō.*

Matt 21. 44 it shall fall, it will grind him to powder
Luke 20. 18 it shall fall, it will grind him to powder

GRINDER —

To grind, טָחַן *tachan.*

Eccl. 12. 3 the grinders cease, because they are fe

GRINDING —

Grinding, טַחֲנָה *tachanah.*

Eccl. 12. 4 when the sound of the grinding is low

GRISLED —

Grisled, בָּרֹד *barod.*

Gen. 31. 10, 12 rams..ringstraked, speckled, and gri.
Zech. 6. 3 in the fourth chariot grisled and bay ho.
6. 6 the grisled go forth toward the south co.

GROAN, to —

1. *To sigh,* אָנַח *anach,* 2.

Joel 1. 18 How do the beasts groan! the herds of

2. *To groan,* אָנַק *anaq.*

Jer. 51. 52 through..her land the wounded shall gr.

3. *To groan,* נָאַק *naaq.*

Job 24. 12 Men groan from out of the city, and the
Eze. 30. 24 he shall groan before him..with the gro.

4. *To snort, be deeply moved,* ἐμβριμάομαι *embrim.*

John 11. 33 he groaned in the spirit, and was troubled
11. 38 Jesus, therefore, again groaning in him.

5. *To groan, sigh,* στενάζω *stenazō.*

Rom. 8. 23 even we ourselves groan within ourselves
2 Co. 5. 2 in this we groan, earnestly desiring to be
5. 4 we that are in (this) tabernacle do groan

GROAN together, to —

To groan or sigh together, συστενάζω *sustenazō.*

Rom. 8. 22 whole creation groaneth..in pain togeth.

GROANING —

1. *Sighing,* אֲנָחָה *anachah.*

Job 23. 2 my stroke is heavier than my groaning
Psa. 6. 6 I am weary with my groaning; all the
38. 9 Lord..my groaning is not hid from thee
102. 5 By reason of the voice of my groaning

2. *Groaning,* אֲנָקָה *anaqah.*

Psa. 102. 20 To hear the groaning of the prisoner; to

3. *Groaning,* נְאָקָה *neaqah.*

Exod 2. 24 God heard their groaning, and God rem.
6. 5 I have also heard the groaning of the c.
Judg. 2. 18 it repented the LORD because of their g.
Eze. 30. 24 groan..with the groanings of a deadly

4. *Groaning, sighing,* στεναγμός *stenagmos.*

Acts 7. 34 I have heard their groaning, and am come
Rom. 8. 26 for us with groanings which cannot be

GROPE, to —

1. *To feel, grope, draw nigh,* גָּשַׁשׁ *gashash,* 3.

Isa. 59. 10 We grope..like the blind, and we grope

2. *To search, grope,* מָשַׁשׁ *mashash,* 3.

Deut 28. 29 shall grope at noon day, as the blind gr.
Job 5. 14 and grope in the noon day as in the night
12. 25 They grope in the dark without light

GROSS, to wax —

To make fat or thick, παχύνω *pachunō.*

Matt 13. 15 For this people's heart is waxed gross, and
Acts 28. 27 the heart of this people is waxed gross

GROUND —

1. *Soil, ground,* אֲדָמָה *adamah.*

Gen. 2. 5 and (there was) not a man to till the gr.
2. 6 and watered the whole face of the ground
2. 7 formed man (of) the dust of the ground
2. 9 out of the ground made the Lord God to
2. 19 out of the ground the LORD God formed
3. 17 cursed (is) the ground for thy sake; in
3. 19 till thou return unto the ground; for out
3. 23 to till the ground from whence he was
4. 2 sheep, but Cain was a tiller of the ground
4. 3 Cain brought of the fruit of the ground
4. 10 the voice..crieth unto me from the gr.
4. 12 When thou tillest the ground, it shall not
5. 29 because of the ground..the LORD hath
7. 23 which was upon the face of the ground
8. 8 were abated from off the face of the gr.
8. 13 and, behold, the face of the ground was
8. 21 I will not again curse the ground any
19. 25 and that which grew upon the ground
Exod. 3. 5 place whereon thou standest (is) holy gr
8. 21 and also the ground whereon they (are)
Lev. 20. 25 living thing that creepeth on the ground
Num 16. 31 that the ground clave asunder..under
Deut. 4. 18 of anything that creepeth on the ground
28. 4 the fruit of thy ground, and the fruit of
28. 11 plenteous..in the fruit of thy ground, in
1 Sa. 20. 31 as the son of Jesse liveth upon the ground
2 Sa. 17. 12 light upon him as the dew falleth on the g.
1 Ki. 7. 46 did the king cast them, in the clay gro.
1 Ch. 27. 26 the work of the field for tillage of the gr.
2 Ch. 4. 17 in the clay ground between Succoth and Z.
Neh. 10. 35 to bring the first fruits of our ground, and
10. 37 the tithes of our ground unto the Levites
Job 5. 6 neither doth trouble spring out of the g.
Psa. 105. 35 and devoured the fruit of their ground
Isa. 28. 24 doth he open and break the clods of his g.?
30. 23 that thou shalt sow the ground withal
30. 24 the young asses that ear the ground shall

Jer. 7. 20 be poured out..upon the fruit of the gr.
14. 4 the ground is chapt, for there was no rain
25. 33 the slain..shall be dung upon the ground
Hos. 2. 18 (with) the creeping things of the ground
Hag. 1. 11 upon (that) which the ground bringeth f.
Mal. 3. 11 shall not destroy the fruits of your gro.

2. *Earth,* אֶרֶץ *erets.*
Gen. 18. 2 ran..and bowed himself toward the gro.
19. 1 bowed himself with his face toward the g.
33. 3 bowed himself to the ground seven times
38. 9 that he spilled (it) on the ground, lest that
44. 14 and they fell before him on the ground
Exod. 9. 23 hail, and the fire ran along upon the gr.
Deut 15. 23 thou shalt pour it upon the ground as w.
28. 56 to set..her foot upon the ground for del.
Judg. 4. 21 fastened it into the ground..so he died
6. 39 and upon all the ground let there be dew
6. 40 God did so..there was dew on all the gr.
13. 20 and fell on their faces to the ground
Ruth 2. 10 bowed herself to the ground, and said
1 Sa. 3. 19 did let none of his words fall to the gro.
5. 4 fallen upon his face to the ground before
14. 32 took sheep..and slew (them) on the gro.
14. 45 there shall not one hair..fall to the gro.
20. 41 David..fell on his face to the ground
25. 23 Abigail..bowed herself to the ground
26. 7 his spear stuck in the ground at his bol.
28. 14 he stooped with (his) face to the ground
2 Sa. 2. 22 wherefore should I smite thee to the gr.?
8. 2 with a line, casting them down to the gr.
14. 14 as water spilt on the ground, which can.
14. 22 Joab fell to the ground on his face, and
14. 33 bowed himself on his face to the ground
18. 11 didst thou not smite him there to the g.?
20. 10 and shed out his bowels to the ground
24. 20 bowed himself..on his face upon the gr.
1 Ki. 1. 23 bowed himself..with his face to the gro.
2 Ki. 2. 15 bowed themselves to the ground before
4. 37 bowed herself to the ground, and took up
1 Ch. 21. 21 bowed..to David with..face to the gro.
2 Ch. 7. 3 they bowed..with their faces to the gro.
Job 1. 20 fell down upon the ground, and worship.
2. 13 So they sat down with him upon the gro.
16. 13 he poureth out my gall upon the ground
18. 10 The snare (is) laid for him in the ground
39. 24 He swalloweth the ground with fierceness
Psa. 74. 7 the dwelling place of thy name to the g.
89. 39 hast profaned his crown..to the ground
89. 44 and cast his throne down to the ground
107. 35 He turneth..dry ground into water-spr.
143. 3 hath smitten my life down to the ground
147. 6 he casteth the wicked down to the ground
Isa. 3. 26 and she..desolate, shall sit upon the gr.
14. 12 (how) art thou cut down to the ground
21. 9 her gods he hath broken unto the ground
25. 12 bring to the ground, (even) to the dust
26. 5 he layeth it low..to the ground; he brin.
29. 4 And thou..shalt speak out of the ground
29. 4 thy voice shall be..out of the ground, and
47. 1 O virgin daughter of B., sit on the grou.
51. 23 thou hast laid thy body as the ground
53. 2 shall grow up..as a root out of a dry gr.
Jer. 14. 2 the gates..they are black unto the grou.
Lam. 2. 2 he hath brought..down to the ground
2. 9 Her gates are sunk into the ground; he
2. 10 The elders..of Zion..sit upon the ground
2. 10 virgins..hang down their heads to the g.
2. 21 The young and the old lie on the ground
Eze. 12. 6 cover thy..that thou see not the ground
12. 12 that he see not the ground with (his) eyes
13. 14 bring it down to the ground, so that the
19. 12 she was cast down to the ground, and the
19. 13 she (is) planted..in a dry and thirsty gr.
24. 7 she poured it not upon the ground, to
26. 11 thy..garrisons shall go down to the gro.
26. 16 they shall sit upon the ground, and shall
28. 17 I will cast thee to the ground, I will lay
38. 20 and every wall shall fall to the ground
41. 16 from the ground up to the windows, and
41. 20 From the ground unto above the door
43. 14 And from the bottom (upon) the ground
Dan. 8. 5 an he goat came..and touched not the
8. 7 cast him down to the ground, and stam.
8. 10 it cast down..of the stars to the ground
8. 12 and it cast down the truth to the ground
8. 18 in a deep sleep on my face toward the g.
10. 9 on my face, and my face toward the gro.
10. 15 I set my face toward the ground, and I
Amos 3. 14 horns..shall be cut off, and fall to the g.
Obad. 3 Who shall bring me down to the ground?
Zech. 8. 12 the ground shall give her increase, and

3. *Portion, field,* חֶלְקָה *chelqah.*
2 Sa. 23. 12 he stood in the midst of the ground, and

4. *A cutting, ploughing,* חָרִישׁ *charish.*
1 Sa. 8. 12 to ear his ground, and to reap his harvest

5. *Dust,* עָפָר *aphar.*
Job 14. 8 and the stock thereof die in the ground

6. *Field, plain,* שָׂדֶה *sadeh.*
Josh. 24. 32 a parcel of ground which Jacob bought
1 Sa. 14. 25 and there was honey upon the ground
1 Ch. 11. 13 where was a parcel of ground full of bar.

7. *Soil, land,* γῆ *gē.*
Matt. 10. 29 one of them shall not fall [on the ground]
13. 8 other fell into good ground, and brought
13. 23 that received seed into the good ground
15. 35 he commanded..to sit down on the gro.
Mark 4. 8 other fell on good ground, and did yield
4. 20 are they which are sown on good ground
Mark 4. 26 as if a man should cast seed into the gro.
8. 6 he commanded..to sit down on the gro.
9. 20 fell on the ground, and wallowed foam.
14. 35 fell on the ground, and prayed that, if
Luke 8. 8 other fell on good ground, and sprang up
8. 15 that on the good ground are they, which
13. 7 cut it down; why cumbereth it the gro.?
22. 44 [drops of blood falling down to the gro.]
John 8. 6 [and with (his) finger wrote on the grou.]
8. 8 [he stooped down, and wrote on the gro.]
12. 24 Except a corn of wheat fall into the gr.
Acts 7. 33 place where thou standest is holy grou.

8. *Ground, bottom,* ἔδαφος *edaphos.*
Acts 22. 7 I fell unto the ground, and heard a voice

9. *Basis, foundation,* ἑδραίωμα *hedraiōma.*
1 Ti. 3. 15 God, the pillar and ground of the truth

10. *Space, place,* χώρα *chōra.*
Luke 12. 16 The ground of a certain rich man brought

GROUND, to lay even with the —
To lay on the ground, level, ἐδαφίζω *edaphizō.*
Luke 19. 44 shall lay thee even with the ground, and

GROUND, on or to the —
On the ground or earth, χαμαί *chamai.*
John 9. 6 he spat on the ground, and made clay of
18. 6 they went backward, and fell to the gro.

GROUND, parcel or piece of —
1. *Spot, place,* χωρίον *chōrion.*
John 4. 5 to the parcel of ground that Jacob gave

2. *Field,* ἀγρός *agros.*
Luke 14. 18 I have bought a piece of ground, and I

GROUND, to —
To lay a foundation, θεμελιόω *themelioō.*
Eph. 3. 17 ye, being rooted and grounded in love
Col. 1. 23 If ye continue in the faith grounded and

GROUNDED —
Any thing founded, מוּסָדָה *musadah.*
Isa. 30. 32 every place where the grounded staff shall

[*See also* Corn, dry fallow, parched.]

GROVE —
1. *A tamarisk,* אֶשֶׁל *eshel.*
Gen. 21. 33 planted a grove in Beer-sheb., and called

2. *A shrine,* אֲשֵׁרָה, אֲשֵׁירָה *asherah.*
Exod 34. 13 But ye shall..cut down their groves
Deut. 7. 5 cut down their groves, and burn their
12. 3 break their pillars, and burn their groves
16. 21 Thou shalt not plant thee a grove of any
Judg. 3. 7 did evil..and served Baalim and the gr.
6. 25 Take..and cut down the grove that (is)
6. 26 a burnt sacrifice with the wood of the gr.
6. 28 the grove was cut down that (was) by it
6. 30 because he hath cut down the grove that
1 Ki. 14. 15 because they have made their groves, pr.
14. 23 built them high places, and images, and g.
15. 13 because she had made an idol in a grove
16. 33 Ahab made a grove; and Ahab did more
18. 19 the prophets of the groves four hundred
2 Ki. 13. 6 there remained the grove also in Samaria
17. 10 they set them up images and groves in
17. 16 made a grove, and worshipped all the
18. 4 brake the images, and cut down the gr.
21. 3 made a grove, as did Ahab king of Israel
21. 7 he set a graven image of the grove that
23. 4 vessels..made for Baal, and for the grove
23. 6 he brought out the grove from the house
23. 7 where the women wove hangings for the g.
23. 14 brake..the images, and cut down the gr.
23. 15 burned the high place..and burned the g.
2 Ch. 14. 3 brake..the images, and cut down the gr.
15. 16 because she had made an idol in a grove
17. 6 took away the high places and groves
19. 3 in that thou hast taken away the groves
24. 18 And they..served groves and idols: and
31. 1 brake the images..and cut down the gr.
33. 3 reared up altars for Baalim, and made g.
33. 19 set up groves and graven images, before
34. 3, 4 and the groves, and the carved images
34. 7 had broken down the altars and the gro.
Isa. 17. 8 respect..either the groves or the images
27. 9 the groves and images shall not stand
Jer. 17. 2 remember their altars and their groves
Mic. 5. 14 I will pluck up thy groves out of the

GROW, to —
1. *To be or become great,* גָּדַל *gadal.*
Gen. 21. 8 And the child grew, and was weaned: and
21. 20 he grew, and dwelt in the wilderness
25. 27 the boys grew: and Esau was a; 26. 13.
Exod. 2. 10 the child grew, and she brought him
Judg 13. 24 the child grew, and the LORD blessed
1 Sa. 2. 21 the child Samuel grew before the; 2. 26.
3. 19 Samuel grew, and the LORD was with

2. *To increase greatly (as fish),* דָּגָה *dagah.*
Gen. 48. 16 let them grow into a multitude in the

3. *To go on,* יָלַךְ *yalak.*
Jer. 12. 2 they grow, yea, they bring forth fruit

4. *To go out or forth,* יָצָא *yatsa.*
Job 31. 40 Let thistles grow instead of wheat, and

5. *To be or become firm,* יָצַק *yatsaq.*
Job 38. 38 When the dust groweth into hardness

6. *To go up,* עָלָה *alah.*
Deut 29. 23 it is not sown..nor any grass groweth
Isa. 53. 2 he shall grow up before him as a tender
Eze. 47. 12 on this side and on that side, shall grow

7. *To be fruitful,* פָּרָה *parah.*
Gen. 47. 27 Israel..grew, and multiplied exceedingly
Isa. 11. 1 and a Branch shall grow out of his roots

8. *To flourish, break forth,* פָּרַח *parach.*
Lev. 13. 39 it (is) a freckled spot (that) groweth in
Hos. 14. 5 he shall grow as the lily, and cast forth
14. 7 they shall revive (as) the corn, and grow as

9. *To break or burst forth,* פָּרַץ *parats.*
Exod. 1. 12 But..the more they multiplied and grew

10. *To shoot or spring forth,* צָמַח *tsamach.*
Gen. 2. 5 and every herb of the field before it grew
Exod 10. 5 shall eat every tree which groweth for you
Job 8. 19 and out of the earth shall others grow
Eze. 17. 6 it grew, and became a spreading vine of

11. *To become great,* רְבָה *rebah.*
Dan. 4. 11 The tree grew, and was strong, and the
4. 20 The tree that thou sawest, which grew

12. *To become great,* שָׂגָה *sagah.*
Psa. 92. 12 he shall grow like a cedar in Lebanon

13. *To become great,* שְׂגָא *sega.*
Ezra 4. 22 why should damage grow to the hurt of

14. *To increase, grow up,* αὐξάνω *auxanō.*
Matt. 6. 28 the lilies of the field, how they grow
13. 32 when it is grown, it is the greatest amo.
Luke 1. 80 the child grew, and waxed strong in spi.
2. 40 the child grew, and waxed strong in spi.
12. 27 Consider the lilies how they grow: they
13. 19 it grew, and waxed a great tree; and the
Acts 7. 17 the people grew and multiplied in Egypt
12. 24 But the word of God grew and multipl.
19. 20 So mightily grew the word of God and
Eph. 2. 21 groweth unto an holy temple in the Lord
1 Pe. 2. 2 milk of the word, that ye may grow ther.
2 Pe. 3. 18 grow in grace, and (in) the knowledge of

15. *To begin to be, become,* γίνομαι *ginomai.*
Matt 21. 19 Let no fruit grow on thee henceforward
Acts 5. 24 they doubted..whereunto this would gr.

16. *To come or go,* ἔρχομαι *erchomai.*
Mark 5. 26 was nothing bettered, but rather grew

GROW again, to —
To shoot or spring up, צָמַח *tsamach,* 3.
Judg 16. 22 the hair of his head began to grow again

GROW exceedingly, to —
To increase exceedingly, ὑπεραυξάνω *huperauxanō.*
2 Th. 1. 3 because that your faith groweth exceed.

GROW, to cause to —
To cause to shoot or spring up, צָמַח *tsamach,* 5.
Psa. 104. 14 He causeth the grass to grow for the cat.

GROW long, to suffer to —
To send forth, שָׁלַח *shalach,* 3.
Eze. 44. 20 nor suffer their locks to grow long; they

GROW, to make (to) —
1. *To make great, nourish,* גָּדַל *gadal,* 3.
Jon. 4. 10 hast not laboured, neither madest it grow

2. *To cause to shoot or spring up,* צָמַח *tsamach,* 5.
Gen. 2. 9 out of the ground made..God to grow
2 Sa. 23. 5 (my) desire, although he make (it) not to g.
Psa. 147. 8 who maketh grass to grow upon the mo.

3. *To cause to grow,* שׂוּג *sug,* 3a.
Isa. 17. 11 In the day..make thy plant to grow, and

GROW (of selves), such things as —
Self-sown grain, spontaneous growth, סָפִיחַ *saphiach.*
2 Ki. 19. 29 this year such things as grow of themselves
Job 14. 19 thou washest away the things which grow
Isa. 37. 30 eat (this) year such as groweth of itself

GROW to an end, to —
To incline, decline, חָנָה *chanah.*
Judg 19. 9 behold, the day groweth to an end, lodge

GROW together, to —
To increase together, συναυξάνω *sunauxanō.*
Matt 13. 30 Let both grow together until the harvest

GROW up, to —
1. *To rise, triumph,* גָּאָה *gaah.*
Job 8. 11 Can the rush grow up without mire? can

2. *To be or become great, grow up,* גָּדַל *gadal.*
Judg 11. 2 his wife's sons grew up, and they thrust
2 Sa. 12. 3 it grew up together with him, and with

3. *To change, pass on,* חָלַף *chalaph.*
Psa. 90. 5 (they are) like grass (which) groweth up
90. 6 the morning it flourisheth, and groweth up

4. *To increase,* פּוּשׁ *push.*
Mal. 4. 2 ye shall go forth, and grow up as calves

5. *To shoot or spring up,* צָמַח *tsamach.*
Zech. 6. 12 he shall grow up out of his place, and he

6. *To become great,* רָבָה *rabah.*
Job 39. 4 Their young ones..grow up with corn

7. *To draw out or off, pass on, change,* שָׁלַף *shalaph.*
Psa. 129. 6 grass..withereth afore it groweth up

8. *To go up,* ἀναβαίνω *anabainō.*
Mark 4. 7 the thorns grew up, and choked it, and
4. 32 when it is sown, it groweth up, and bec.

9. *To increase,* αὐξάνω *auxanō.*
Eph. 4. 15 may grow up into him in all things, wh.
10. *To lengthen, grow up,* μηκύνω *mēkunō.*
Mark 4. 27 the seed should spring and grow up, he
GROW up, to cause to —
To cause to shoot or spring up, צָמַח *tsamach,* 5.
Jer. 33. 15 will I cause the Branch..to grow up un.
GROWETH of its own accord or of itself, which —
Self-sown grain, spontaneous growth, סָפִיחַ *saphiach.*
Lev. 25. 5 That which groweth of its own accord of
25. 11 neither reap that which groweth of itself
GROWN, to be —
1. *To be or become great,* גָּדַל *gadal.*
Gen. 38. 11 Remain..till Shelah my son be grown
38. 14 she saw that Shelah was grown, and she
Exod. 2. 11 it came to pass..when Moses was grown
Ruth 1. 13 Would ye tarry..till they were grown?
2 Ki. 4. 18 when the child was grown, it fell on a
2. *To shoot or spring up,* צָמַח *tsamach,* 3.
2 Sa. 10. 5 Tarry..until your beards be grown, and
1 Ch. 19. 5 Tarry..until your beards be grown, and
Eze. 16. 7 thine hair is grown, whereas thou (wast)
3. *To be or become great,* רְבָה *rebah.*
Dan. 4. 22 It (is) thou, O king, that art grown and
4. 22 thy greatness is grown, and reacheth
4. 33 till his hairs were grown like eagles' (fe).
GROWN fat, to be —
To increase, פּוּשׁ *push.*
Jer. 50. 11 because ye are grown fat as the heifer at
GROWN over, to be —
To go up, עָלָה *alah.*
Prov 24. 31 And, lo, it was all grown over with thorns
GROWN up —
Standing corn, stalk, קָמָה *qamah.*
2 Ki. 19. 26 and (as corn) blasted before it be grown up
Isa. 37. 27 and (as corn) blasted before it be grown up
GROWN up, to be —
1. *To be or become great,* גָּדַל *gadal.*
1 Ki. 12. 8, 10 the young men that were grown up
Ezra 9. 6 our trespass is grown up unto the heav.
2. *To become great, be nourished,* גָּדַל *gadal,* 4.
Psa. 144. 12 (may be) as plants grown up in their yo.
3. *To shoot or spring up,* צָמַח *tsamach.*
Lev. 13. 37 if..there is black hair grown up therein
GROWN up, not —
Late, behind, not grown up, אָפִיל *aphil.*
Exod. 9. 32 wheat and the rie..(were) not grown up
GROWTH, latter —
Scattering, latter growth, לֶקֶשׁ *leqesh.*
Amos 7. 1 of the shooting up of the latter growth
7. 1 the latter growth after the king's mowi.
GRUDGE, to —
1. *To murmur,* לוּן, לִין *lun, lin.*
Psa. 59. 15 wander..and grudge if they be not satis.
2. *To groan, sigh,* στενάζω *stenazō.*
Jas. 5. 9 Grudge not one against another, brethren
GRUDGE, to bear —
To keep anger, נָטַר *natar.*
Lev. 19. 18 Thou shalt not..bear any grudge against
GRUDGING —
Grudging, murmuring, γογγυσμός *goggusmos.*
1 Pe. 4. 9 Use hospitality one to another without [g.]
GRUDGINGLY —
Out of grief, ἐκ λύπης *ek lupēs.*
2 Co. 9. 7 not grudgingly, or of necessity: for God
GUARD —
1. *Slaughterer, butcher,* טַבָּח *tabbach.*
Gen. 37. 36 Egypt unto Potiphar..captain of the gua.
39. 1 captain of the guard, an Egyptian bought
40. 3 in the house of the captain of the guard
40. 4 the captain of the guard charged Joseph
41. 10 in ward in the captain of the guard's ho.
41. 12 servant to the captain of the guard; and
2 Ki. 25. 8, 11, 20 Nebuzar-adan, captain of the gu.
25. 10 that (were) with the captain of the guard
25. 12 the captain of the guard left of the poor
25. 15 silver, the captain of the guard took away
25. 18 the captain of the guard took Seraiah the
Jer 39. 9, 10, 11, 13 Nebuzar-adan..captain of the g.
40. 1 the captain of the guard had let him go
40. 2 the captain of the guard took Jeremiah
40. 5 So the captain of the guard gave him
41. 10 the captain of the guard had committed
43. 6 the captain of the guard had left with
52. 12 came Nebuzar-adan, captain of the guard
52. 14 that (were) with the captain of the guard
52. 15 captain of the guard carried away captive
52. 16 the captain of the guard left (certain) of
52. 19 silver, took the captain of the guard away
52. 24 the captain of the guard took Seraiah the
52. 26 the captain of the guard took them, and
52. 30 the captain of the guard carried away c.
Dan. 2. 14 to Arioch the captain of the king's guard
2. *Guard,* מִשְׁמַעַת *mishmaath.*
2 Sa. 23. 23 three: and David set him over his guard
1 Ch. 11. 25 three: and David set him over his guard
3. *Watch,* מִשְׁמָר *mishmar.*
Neh. 4. 22 that in the night they may be a guard to
4. 23 the men of the guard which followed me
Eze. 38. 7 prepare..and be thou a guard unto them
4. *To run,* רוּץ *ruts.*
1 Ki. 14. 27 unto the hands of the chief of the guard
14. 28 was (so) that the guard bare them, and
14. 28 brought them back into the guard cham.
2 Ki. 10. 25 Jehu said to the guard and to the capta.
10. 25 the guard and the captains cast (them)
11. 4 with the captains and the guard, and br.
11. 6 a third part at the gate behind the guard
11. 11 the guard stood, every man with his we.
11. 13 when Athaliah heard the noise of the g.
11. 19 the guard, and all the people of the land
11. 19 came by the way of the gate of the guard
2 Ch. 12. 10 to the hands of the chief of the guard
12. 11 entered..the guard came and fetched
12. 11 brought them again into the guard cha.
GUD-GO'-DAH, גֻּדְגֹּדָה *incision.*
A station of the Israelites in the wilderness near Ezion-geber between Mosera and Jotbath: perhaps the same as Hor-hagidgad in Num. 33. 32, 33.
Deut 10. 7 From thence they journeyed unto G.
10. 7 and from G. to Jotbath, a land of rivers
GUEST —
1. *To call, invite,* קָרָא *qara.*
1 Ki. 1. 41, 49 and all the guests that (were) with
Prov. 9. 18 that) her guests (are) in the depths of
Zeph. 1. 7 prepared a sacrifice, he hath bid his guests
2. *To be laid up, received as a guest,* ἀνάκειμαι.
Matt 22. 10 and the wedding was furnished with gu.
22. 11 when the king came in to see the guests
GUEST, to be —
To loose down, rest, καταλύω *kataluō.*
Luke 19. 7 to be guest with a man that is a sinner
GUEST CHAMBER —
Place for resting, khan, κατάλυμα *kataluma.*
Mark 14. 14 Where is the guest chamber, where I shall
Luke 22. 11 Where is the guest chamber, where I shall
GUIDE —
1. *Leader, chief,* אַלֻּף, אַלּוּף *alluph.*
Psa. 55. 13 thou, a man mine equal, my guide, and
Prov. 2. 17 Which forsaketh the guide of her youth
Jer. 3. 4 My father, thou (art) the guide of my y.?
Mic. 7. 5 put ye not confidence in a guide; keep
2. *Captain, ruler, judge,* קָצִין *qatsin.*
Prov. 6. 7 Which having no guide, overseer, or ruler
3. *Guide, conductor,* ὁδηγός *hodēgos.*
Matt 23. 16 Woe unto you, (ye) blind guides, which
23. 24 (Ye) blind guides, which strain at a gnat
Acts 1. 16 which was guide to them that took Jesus
Rom. 2. 19 thou thyself art a guide of the blind, a
GUIDE, to —
1. *To make or declare happy,* אָשַׁר *ashar,* 3.
Prov. 23. 19 be wise, and guide thine heart in the way
2. *To cause to tread,* דָּרַךְ *darak,* 5.
Psa. 25. 9 The meek will he guide in judgment; and
3. *To counsel,* יָעַץ *yaats.*
Psa. 32. 8 shall go: I will guide thee with mine eye
4. *To sustain,* כּוּל *kul,* 3a.
Psa. 112. 5 he will guide his affairs with discretion
5. *To lead, drive,* נָהַג *nahag,* 3.
Psa. 78. 52 guided them in the wilderness like a flock
6. *To lead, tend,* נָהַל *nahal,* 3.
Exod 15. 13 thou hast guided..in thy strength unto
2 Ch. 32. 22 LORD saved..and guided them on every
Psa. 31. 3 for thy name's sake lead me, and guide
Isa. 49. 10 by the springs of water shall he guide
51. 18 none to guide her among all the sons
7. *To lead forth,* נָחָה *nachah.*
Isa. 58. 11 LORD shall guide thee continually, and
8. *To lead forth,* נָחָה *nachah,* 5.
Job 31. 18 I have guided her from my mother's wo.
38. 32 or canst thou guide Arcturus with his s.?
Psa. 73. 24 Thou shalt guide me with thy counsel
78. 72 guided them by the skilfulness of his ha.
Prov 11. 3 The integrity of the upright shall guide
9. *To guide straight,* κατευθύνω *kateuthunō.*
Luke 1. 79 to guide our feet into the way of peace
10. *To show the way, guide,* ὁδηγέω *hodēgeō.*
John 16. 13 is come, he will guide you into all truth
Acts 8. 31 How can I, except some man..guide me
GUIDE, to be —
To lead, נָהַג *nahag,* 3.
Psa. 48. 14 this God..he will be our guide..unto de.
GUILE —
1. *Deceit,* מִרְמָה *mirmah.*
Psa. 34. 13 Keep..from evil..thy lips from speaking g.
55. 11 deceit and guile depart not from her str.
2. *Craftiness, subtilty,* עָרְמָה *ormah.*
Exod 21. 14 if a man come..to slay him with guile
3. *Deceit, sloth,* רְמִיָּה *remiyyah.*
Psa. 32. 2 the man..in whose spirit (there is) no gu.
4. *Bait, guile,* δόλος *dolos.*
John 1. 47 an Israelite indeed, in whom is no guile!
2 Co. 12. 16 But..being crafty, I caught you with gu.
1 Th. 2. 3 For our exhortation (was) not..in guile
1 Pe. 2. 1 laying aside all malice, and all guile, and
2. 22 Who did no sin, neither was guile found
3. 10 and his lips that they speak no guile
Rev. 14. 5 in their mouth was found no [guile]: for
GUILTINESS —
Guilt, אָשָׁם *asham.*
Gen. 26. 10 shouldest have brought guiltiness upon
GUILTLESS —
1. *Innocent, free, acquitted,* נָקִי *naqi.*
Num 32. 22 shall return, and be guiltless before the
Josh. 2. 19 his blood..upon his head, and we..guilt.
2 Sa. 3. 28 and my kingdom (are) guiltless before
14. 9 and the king and his throne (be) guiltless
2. *Without a crime, guiltless,* ἀναίτιος *anaitios.*
Matt 12. 7 ye would not have condemned the guilt.
GUILTLESS, to be —
To be innocent, free, נָקָה *naqah,* 2.
Num. 5. 31 Then shall the man be guiltless from ini.
1 Sa. 26. 9 against the LORD's anointed, and be gui.?
GUILTLESS, to hold —
To declare innocent, נָקָה *naqah,* 3.
Exod 20. 7 LORD will not hold him guiltless that ta.
Deut. 5. 11 LORD will not hold (him) guiltless that
1 Ki. 2. 9 Now therefore hold him not guiltless
GUILTY —
1. *Guilty,* אָשֵׁם *ashem.*
Gen. 42. 21 We (are) verily guilty concerning our br.
Ezra 10. 19 guilty, (they offered) a ram of the flock
2. *Wicked,* רָשָׁע *rasha.*
Num 35. 31 for the life of a murderer, which (is) gui.
3. *Under justice,* ὑπόδικος *hupodikos.*
Rom. 3. 19 all the world may become guilty before G.
GUILTY, to be —
1. *To be guilty,* אָשַׁם *asham.*
Lev. 4. 13, 22 which should not be done, and are g.
4. 27 which ought not to be done, and be gui.
5. 2 he also shall be unclean, and guilty
5. 3 when he knoweth..then he shall be gui.
5. 4 then he shall be guilty in one of these
5. 5 it shall be, when he shall be guilty in
5. 17 though he wist (it) not, yet is he guilty
6. 4 because he hath sinned, and is guilty
Num. 5. 6 against the LORD, and that person be gu.
Judg 21. 22 ye did not give..(that) ye should be guil.
2. *To owe, be indebted,* ὀφείλω *opheilō.*
Matt 23. 18 sweareth by the gift..upon it, he is guilty
GUILTY of —
Held in, subject to, ἔνοχος *enochos.*
Matt 26. 66 What think ye?..He is guilty of death
Mark 14. 64 all condemned him to be guilty of death
1 Co. 11. 27 shall be guilty of the body and blood of
Jas. 2. 10 yet offend in one..he is guilty of all
GUILTY, to become, be found, hold self —
To be guilty, אָשַׁם *asham.*
Prov 30 10 lest he curse thee, and thou be found guil.
Eze. 22. 4 Thou art become guilty in thy blood that
Zech 11. 5 hold themselves not guilty: and they that
GULF —
A chasm, rent, χάσμα *chasma.*
Luke 16. 26 between us..there is a great gulf fixed
GU'-NI, גּוּנִי *protected.*
1. A son of Naphtali, founder of the family of the Gunites. B.C. 1697.
Gen. 46. 24 Jahzeel, and G., and Jezer, and Shillem
Num 26. 48 sons of Naphtali..of G., the family of the
1 Ch. 7. 13 Jahziel, and G., and Jezer, and Shallum
2. Father of Abdiel a chief man of Gad. B.C. 1400.
1 Ch. 5. 15 Ahi the son of Abdiel, the son of G.
GU-NITES, הַגּוּנִי
The family of Guni, son of Naphtali.
Num 26. 48 Naphtali..of Guni, the family of the G.
GUR, גּוּר *dwelling, lion's whelp.*
"The going up to Gur" (*i.e.* "the Ascent or steep of Gur" or of the lion's whelp), a rising ground at which Ahaziah was slain by Jehu. It was at Ibleam, between Jezreel and Beth-haggan, the present *Jenin.*
2 Ki. 9. 27 (And they did so) at the going up to G.
GUR BA'-AL, גּוּר־בַּעַל *dwelling of Baal.*
A place between Canaan and the Arabian peninsula.
2 Ch. 26. 7 against the Arabians that dwelt in G.-b.
GUSH out, to —
1. *To flow, issue,* זוּב *zub.*
Psa. 78. 20 smote the rock, that the waters gushed o.
105. 41 opened the rock, and the water gushed o.
Isa. 48. 21 clave the rock..the waters gushed out
2. *To flow,* נָזַל *nazal.*
Jer. 9. 18 and our eyelids gush out with waters
3. *To shed, or pour out,* שָׁפַךְ *shaphak.*
1 Ki. 18. 28 cut themselves..till the blood gushed o.
4. *To pour out or forth,* ἐκχύνω *ekchunō.*
Acts 1. 18 he burst..and all his bowels gushed out
GUTTER —
1. *Waterspout,* צִנּוֹר *tsinnor.*
2 Sa. 5. 8 Whosoever getteth up to the gutter, and

2. *Gutter, trough,* רַהַט *rahat.*
Gen. 30. 38 he set the rods..in the gutters in the w.
30. 41 Jacob laid the rods..in the gutters, that

H

HA —

He-ah, הֶאָח *heach.*
Job 39. 25 He saith among the trumpets, Ha, ha!

HA-A-HASH-TA'-RI, הָאֲחַשְׁתָּרִי *the courier.*
The Ahashtarite, a man or a family descended from Ashur father of Tekoa, by his second wife Naarah. B.C. 1500.
1 Ch. 4. 6 Naarah bare..Hepher, and Temeni, and H.

HA-BA'-IAH, חֲבָיָה חֳבַיָּה *Jah is protection.*
The Bene-Chabajah were among the sons of the priests who returned from Babylon with Zerubbabel. B.C. 536.
Ezra 2. 61 the children of H., the children of Koz
Neh. 7. 63 And of the priests: the children of H.

HA-BAK'-KUK, חֲבַקּוּק *love's embrace.*
A prophet in Judah whose parentage, birthplace, and era are unrecorded. B.C. 626.
Hab. 1. 1 The burden which H. the prophet did see
3. 1 A prayer of H. the prophet upon Shigio.

HA-BA-ZIN'-IAH, חֲבַצִּנְיָה.
The head of the family of the Rechabites. His descendant Jaazaniah was chief among them in the days of Jeremiah. B.C. 660.
Jer. 35. 3 the son of Jeremiah, the son of H., and

HABERGEON —

1. *Coat of mail* שִׁרְיָה *shiryah.*
Job 41. 26 the spear, the dart, nor the habergeon

2. *Coat of mail,* שִׁרְיוֹן *shiryon.*
2 Ch. 26. 14 spears, and helmets, and habergeons, and
Neh. 4. 16 the shields, and the bows, and the haber.

3. *A linen coat of mail,* תַּחְרָא *tachara.*
Exod 28. 32 as it were the hole of an habergeon, that
39. 23 And..an hole..as the hole of an habergeon

HABITABLE part —

Fruitful or habitable place, תֵּבֵל *tebel.*
Prov. 8. 31 Rejoicing in the habitable part of his e.

HABITATION —

1. *Place of sojourn, habitation,* גֵּרוּת *geruth.*
Jer. 41. 17 habitation of Chimham, which is by Beth.

2. *Habitation,* זְבוּל, זְבֻל *zebul.*
2 Ch. 6. 2 I have built an house of habitation for
Isa. 63. 15 behold from the habitation of thy holi.
Hab. 3. 11 sun..moon stood still in their habitation

3. *Tower,* טִירָה *tirah.*
Psa. 69. 25 Let their habitation be desolate..let

4. *To sit down or still, dwell,* יָשַׁב *yashab.*
Psa. 33. 14 From the place of his habitation he look.
Jer. 9. 6 Thine habitation (is) in the midst of dec.
Obad. 3 whose habitation (is) high; that saith in

5. *Seat, dwelling place,* מוֹשָׁב *moshab.*
Gen. 36. 43 according to their habitations in the land
Exod 12. 20 in all your habitations shall ye eat unlea.
35. 3 shall kindle no fire throughout your hab.
Lev. 13. 46 dwell alone; without the camp..his hab.
23. 17 Ye shall bring out of your habitations two
Num 15. 2 When ye be come into the land of your ha.
1 Ch. 4. 33 These..their habitations, and their gene.
7. 28 their possessions and habitations..Beth.
Psa. 107. 7 that they might go to a city of habitation
107. 36 that they may prepare a city for habitati.
132. 13 the LORD..hath desired (it) for his habit.
Eze. 6. 14 make..desolate..in all their habitations

6. *Fixed place, base,* מָכוֹן *makon.*
Psa. 89. 14 Justice and judgment (are) the habitation
97. 2 righteousness and judgment (are) the h.

7. *Preparation, birth, habitation,* מְכוּרָה *mekurah.*
Eze. 29. 14 return..into the land of their habitation

8. *Espousal,* מְכֵרָה *mekerah.*
Gen. 49. 5 instruments of cruelty (are in) their hab.

9. *Habitation,* מָעוֹן *maon.*
Deut 26. 15 Look down from thy holy habitation, from
1 Sa. 2. 29 which I have commanded (in my) habit.
2. 32 thou shalt see an enemy (in my) habitat.
1 Ch. 4. 41 and the habitations that were found there
Psa. 26. 8 I have loved the habitation of thy house
68. 5 A father..(is) God in his holy habitation
71. 3 Be thou my strong habitation, whereunto
91. 9 hast made..the most high, thy habitation
Jer. 25. 30 and utter his voice from his holy habita.
Zech. 2. 13 for he is raised up out of his holy habit.

10. *Habitation,* מְעוֹנָה *meonah.*
Jer. 21. 13 or who shall enter into our habitations?

11. *Settled dwelling place,* מִשְׁכָּן *mishkan.*
2 Ch. 29. 6 turned away their faces from the habita.
Psa. 78. 28 let (it) fall..round about their habitations
132. 5 an habitation for the mighty (God) of Ja.
Isa. 22. 16 graveth an habitation for himself in a
54. 2 stretch forth the curtains of thine habit.

12. *Settled dwelling place,* מִשְׁכַּן *mishkan.*
Ezra 7. 15 God of Israel, whose habitation (is) in Jer.

13. *Comely or resting place,* נָאָה *naah.*
Psa. 74. 20 dark places of the earth are full of the h
Jer. 9. 10 and for the habitations of the wilderness
25. 37 the peaceable habitations are cut down
Lam. 2. 2 Lord hath swallowed up all the habitat.
Amos 1. 2 the habitations of the shepherds shall

14. *Comely or resting place,* נָוָה *navah.*
Job 8. 6 make the habitation of thy righteousness

15. *Comely or resting place,* נָוֶה *naveh.*
Exod 15. 13 guided..in thy strength unto thy holy h.
2 Sa. 15. 25 and show me (both) it and his habitation
Job 5. 3 the foolish..suddenly I cursed his habit.
5. 24 thou shalt visit thy habitation, and shalt
18. 15 brimstone shall be scattered upon his h.
Prov. 3. 33 but he blesseth the habitation of the just
Isa. 27. 10 the habitation forsaken, and left like a
32. 18 my people shall dwell in a peaceable ha.
33. 20 thine eyes shall see Jerusalem a quiet h.
34. 13 an habitation of dragons..a court for owls
35. 7 in the habitation of dragons, where each
Jer. 10. 25 and have made his habitation desolate
25. 30 he shall mightily roar upon his habitation
31. 23 The LORD bless thee, O habitation of jus.
33. 12 shall be an habitation of shepherds caus.
49. 19 come..against the habitation of the str.
49. 20 shall make their habitations desolate
50. 7 LORD, the habitation of justice, even the
50. 19 I will bring Israel again to his habitation
50. 44 come up..unto the habitation of the str.
50. 45 shall make (their) habitation desolate

16. *Settled dwelling place,* שָׁכֵן *sheken.*
Deut 12. 5 unto his habitation shall ye seek, and

17. *Fold,* ἔπαυλις *epaulis.*
Acts 1. 20 Let his habitation be desolate, and let no

18. *Place of habitation,* κατοικητήριον *katoikētērion.*
Eph. 2. 22 builded together for an habitation of God
Rev. 18. 2 Babylon..is become the habitation of

19. *A dwelling house,* κατοικία *katoikia.*
Acts 17. 26 determined..the bounds of their habita.

20. *Habitation,* οἰκητήριον *oikētērion.*
Jude 6 angels which..left their own habitation

21. *Tent, tabernacle,* σκηνή *skēnē.*
Luke 16. 9 they may receive you into everlasting h.

HABITATION, to have —

1. *To settle down, rest,* שָׁכַן *shaken.*
Psa. 104. 12 the fowls of the heaven have their habit.

2. *To settle down, rest,* שְׁכַן *shekan.*
Dan. 4. 21 the fowls of the heaven had their habit.

HABITATION, to prepare an —

To make to rest, נָוָה *navah,* 5.
Exod. 15. 2 my God, and I will prepare him an hab.

HA'-BOR, חָבוֹר *united.*
The affluent of the Euphrates called by Strabo, Abhorras; by Isidore, Aburas; and by Pliny and Ptolemy, Chaboras. It still bears the name of *Khabour,* which was inserted in an Assyrian inscription in the 9th century before our era. See CHEBAR.
2 Ki. 17. 6 placed them in..Habor (by) the river of
18. 11 put them..in H. (by) the river of Gozan
1 Ch. 5. 26 brought them unto..H., and Hara, and

HA-CHAL'-IAH, חֲכַלְיָה *Jah is hidden.*
Father of Nehemiah the Tirshatha. B.C. 476.
Neh. 1. 1 The words of Nehemiah the son of H.
10. 1 those that sealed (were)..the son of H.

HA-CHI'-LAH, חֲכִילָה *drought.*
A hill in the S. of Judah, in the wilderness of Ziph, facing the Jeshimon (*i.e.* waste and barren) district.
1 Sa. 23. 19 H., which (is) on the south of Jeshimon?
26. 3 And Saul pitched in the hill of H., 26. 1

HACH-MO'-NI, חַכְמוֹנִי *the wise.*
The father of Jehiel who was a companion of the sons of David. B.C. 1080.
1 Ch. 27. 32 Jehiel the son of H. (was) with the king's

HACH-MO-NITE, בֶּן־חַכְמוֹנִי.
That is, the "son of Hachmoni" (according to 1 Ch. 27. 32), where it is rightly translated. See TACHMONITE.
1 Ch. 11. 11 Jashobeam, an H., the chief of the capt.

HAD —

There is, there are, יֵשׁ *yesh.*
Gen. 39. 4 and all (that) he had he put into his hand
39. 5 in his house, and over all that he had
39. 5 all that he had in the house, and in the
Ezra 10. 44 and (some) of them had wives by whom
[*See also* Abomination, charge of.]

HAD, to be —

To become, begin to be, γίνομαι *ginomai.*
Acts 25. 26 that, after examination had, I might have

HAD no, when as yet he —

He not having, οὐκ ὄντος αὐτῷ *ouk ontos autō.*
Acts 7. 5 would give it to him..when..he had no

HAD not —

If not, לוּלֵי *lule.*
Psa. 106. 23 had not Moses his chosen stood before

HA'-DAD, הֲדַד, חֲדַד *mighty.*
1. A son of Bedad, king of Edom. See HADAR. B.C. 1500.
Gen. 36. 35 H. the son of Bedad..reigned in his stead
36. 36 H. died, and Samlah..reigned in his ste.
1 Ch. 1. 46 H. the son of Bedad..reigned in his stead
1. 47 when H. was dead, Samlah..reigned in
2. An Edomite of the royal family who lived in the time of Solomon. B.C. 1015.
1 Ki. 11. 14 And the LORD stirred up..H. the Edomite
11. 17 H. fled..to go into Egypt..H. (being) yet
11. 19 H. found great favour in the sight of Ph.
11. 21 H. heard in Egypt that David slept with his
11. 21 H. said to Pharaoh, Let me depart, that I
11. 25 beside the mischief that H. (did): and he
3. A son of Ishmael, and grandson of Abraham. B.C. 1840.
1 Ch. 1. 30 Mishma, and Dumah, Massa, H., and Tema
4. The last of the early kings of Edom. This name should be *Hadar.* In his childhood he escaped the massacre under Joab in which his father seems to have fallen. B.C. 1015.
1 Ch. 1. 50 when Baal-hanan was dead, H. reigned in
1. 51 H. died also. And the dukes of Edom

HA-DAD-E'-ZER, הֲדַדְעֶזֶר *mighty is the help.*
The king of the Aramite state of Zobah, who was defeated by David and driven across the Euphrates. See HADAREZER. B.C. 1040.
2 Sa. 8. 3 David smote also H., the son of Rehob
8. 5 Syrians of Damascus came to succour H.
8. 7 And David took the shields of gold..of H.
8. 8 from Betah, and from Berothai, cities of H.
8. 9 that David had smitten all the host of H.
8. 10 because he had fought against H...for H.
8. 12 of Amalek, and of the spoil of H., son of
1 Ki. 11. 23 which fled from his lord H. king of Zobah

HA-DAD-RIM'-MON, הֲדַדְרִמּוֹן *Hadad of Rimmon.*
A place in the valley of Megiddo in Issachar where Josiah died, not far from Jezreel; now called *Rummaneh.*
Zech. 12. 11 as the mourning of H. in the valley of M.

HA'-DAR, חֲדַר *enclosing, fire God,* הֲדַר *powerful.*
1. A son of Ishmael and grandson of Hagar. B.C. 1840.
Gen. 25. 15 H., and Tema, Jetur, Naphish, and Ked.
2. The 8th and last of the ancient kings of Edom. B.C. 1500.
Gen. 36. 39 Baal-hanan..died, and H. reigned in his

HA-DAR-E'-ZER, הֲדַרְעֶזֶר *Hader is help.*
The king of Aram-zobah, sometimes called *Hadadezer,* which see. B.C. 1040.
2 Sa. 10. 16 H. sent, and brought out the Syrians that
10. 16 Shobach the captain of the host of H.
10. 19 all the kings (that were) servants to H.
1 Ch. 18. 3 David smote H. king of Zobah unto H.
18. 5 the Syrians of Damascus came to help H.
18. 7 And David took the shields of gold..of H.
18. 8 from Tibhath, and from Chun, cities of H.
18. 9 David had smitten all the host of H. king
18. 10 because he had fought against H...for H.
19. 16 captain of the host of H. (went) before
19. 19 when the servants of H. saw that they

HA-DA'-SHAH, חֲדָשָׁה *new.*
A town of Judah in the maritime low country, near *Gofno,* three miles from Beth-horon.
Josh 15. 37 Zenan, and H., and Migdal-gad

HA-DAS'-SAH, הֲדַסָּה *myrtle.*
The earlier name of Esther the cousin of Mordecai. She became the wife of Ahasuerus (Xerxes). B.C. 518.
Esth. 2. 7 And he brought up H., that (is) Esther

HA-DAT'-TAH, חֲדַתָּה *new.*
An appellation of *Hazor* in Judah—not a separate city as the Common Version has it.
Josh 15. 25 Hazor, H., and Kerioth, (and) Hezron

HA'-DID, חָדִיד *peak, sharp.*
A city of Benjamin near Lod and Ono, now called *el-Hadítheh,* about three miles E. of *Lydd* or Lod.
Ezra 2. 33 The children of Lod, H., and Ono, seven
Neh. 7. 37 The children of Lod, H., and Ono, seven
11. 34 H., Zeboim, Neballat

HAD'-LAI, חַדְלָי *lax.*
An Ephraimite, father of Amasa who was one of the chiefs of the tribe in the reign of Pekah. B.C. 742.
2 Ch. 28. 12 Amasa the son of H., stood up against

HA-DO'-RAM, הֲדוֹרָם *Hadar is high.*
1. A son of Joktan of the family of Shem. B.C. 2210.
Gen. 10. 27 And H., and Uzal, and Diklah
1 Ch. 1. 21 H. also, and Uzal, and Diklah
2. A son of Tou, king of Hamath in the time of David.
1 Ch. 18. 10 He sent H. his son to king David, to en.
3. The intendant of taxes under David, Solomon, and Rehoboam, who lost his life at the revolt at Shechem. In 1 Kings 4. 6, the name is given in the longer form *Adoniram;* in Samuel as *Adoram* (2 Sa. 20. 24). B.C. 975.
2 Ch. 10. 18 Rehoboam sent H. that (was) over the tr

HAD'-RACH, חַדְרָךְ *periodical return.*
Perhaps this name is derived from Hadar. It was a district of Syria, but mentioned only once. Some think that Hadrach is the name of the Syrian god of the seasons, or of a king called after him, and having Damascus as his capital.
Zech. 9. 1 the burden..of the LORD in the land of H.

HAFT —

An haft, shaft, נִצָּב *nitstsab.*
Judg. 3. 22 And the haft also went in after the blade

HA'-GAB, חָגָב *bent.*
The Bene-hagab were among the Nethinim who returned with Zerubbabel to Jerusalem. This name is omitted in Nehemiah's list. B.C. 536.
Ezra 2. 46 The children of H., the children of Shal

HA-GA'-BAH, HAGABA, חֲגָבָא ,חֲגָבָה.
Another returned Nethinim exile. B.C. 536.
Ezra 2. 45 children of Lebanah, the children of H.
Neh. 7. 48 children of Lebana, the children of H.

HA'-GAR, הָגָר, Ἄγαρ *wandering.*
Sarai's Egyptian handmaid who became the mother of Ishmael by Abram. See AGAR. B.C. 1914.
Gen. 16. 1 had an handmaid..whose name (was) H.
16. 3 And Sarai, Abram's wife, took H...and
16. 4 And he went in unto H., and she conce.
16. 8 And he said, H., Sarai's maid, whence c.
16. 15 And H. bare Abram a son
16. 15 Abram called his son's name, which H.
16. 16 when H. bare Ishmael to Abram
21. 9 Sarah saw the son of H. the Egyptian
21. 14 a bottle of water, and gave (it) unto H.
21. 17 the angel of God called to H. out of hea.
21. 17 and said unto her, What aileth thee, H.?
25. 12 Abraham's son, whom H...bare unto A.

HAG-A-RENES, הַגְרִים.
Psa. 83. 6 The tabernacles..of Moab, and the H.

HAG-A-RITES, הַגְרִיאִים.
A people upon whom the Reubenites made war in the time of Saul. They were W. of the Jordan, and E. of Gilead.
1 Ch. 5. 10 the days of Saul..made war with the H.
5. 19 they made war with the H., with Jetur
5. 20 and the H. were delivered into their

HAG-E-RITE, הַגְרִי.
A patronymic of Jaziz whom David set over his flocks.
1 Ch. 27. 31 And over the flocks (was) Jaziz the H

HAG'-GAI, חַגַּי *festive.*
The tenth in order of what are called the minor prophets, and the first of those that prophesied after the captivity.
Ezra 5. 1 H. the prophet..prophesied unto the Je.
6. 14 prospered through the prophesying of H.
Hag. 1. 1 came the word of the LORD by H. the
1. 3 Then came the word of the LORD by H.
1. 12 Joshua..obeyed..the words of H. the
1. 13 Then spake H. the LORD'S messenger in
2. 1 the word of the LORD by the prophet H.
2. 10 the word of the LORD by H. the prophet
2. 13 Then said H., If (one that is) unclean
2. 14 Then answered H., and said, So (is) this
2. 20 again the word of the LORD came unto H.

HAG-GE'-RI, הַגְרִי *wanderer.*
The father of Mibhar, one of David's heroes. B.C. 1040.
1 Ch. 11. 38 brother of Nathan, Mibhar the son of H.

HAG'-GI, חַגִּי *festive.*
The second son of Gad, founder of the Haggites. B.C. 1670. The same name precisely is applied to the family.
Gen. 46. 16 sons of Gad; Ziphion, and H., Shuni
Num 26. 15 of H., the family of the Haggites: of Shuni

HAG-GI'-AH, חַגִּיָּה.
A descendant of Merari the son of Levi. B.C. 1035.
1 Ch. 6. 30 Shimea his son, H. his son, Asaiah his

HAG-GITES, הַחַגִּי *the Haggite.*
The posterity of Haggi the second son of Gad. B.C. 1670.
Num 26. 15 of Haggi, the family of the H.: of Shuni

HAG'-GITH, חַגִּית *festive.*
A wife of king David and mother of his fourth son Adonijah. B.C. 1045.
2 Sa. 3. 4 And the fourth, Adonijah the son of H.
1 Ki. 1. 5 Then Adonijah the son of H. exalted
1. 11 Hast thou not heard that A. the son of H.
2. 13 Adonijah the son of H. came to Bath-sh.
1 Ch. 3. 2 the fourth, Adonijah the son of H.

HA'-I, הָעַי *haai, the heap.*
This is the form in which *Ai* appears in the first instance in the Common Version. This arises from the translators having expressed the definite article (*ha*), with which *Ai* is variably accompanied, in the Hebrew text. It was a city of Benjamin E. of Beth-el. See AI.
Gen. 12. 8 Beth-el on the west, and H. on the east
13. 3 at the beginning, between Beth-el and H.

HAIL —
1. *Hail,* בָּרָד *barad.*
Exod. 9. 18 I will cause it to rain a very grievous h.
9. 19 hail shall come down upon them, and
9. 22 that there may be hail in all the land of
9. 23 LORD sent thunder and hail, and the fire
9. 23 LORD rained hail upon the land of Egypt
9. 24 there was hail, and fire mingled with t.h.
9. 25 the hail smote throughout all the land
9. 25 the hail smote every herb of the field
9. 26 in the land of Goshen..was there no hail
9. 28 there be no..mighty thunderings and h.
9. 29 cease, neither shall there be any more h.
9. 33 the thunders and hail ceased, and the
9. 34 when Pharaoh saw that the rain and the h.
10. 5 which remaineth unto you from the hail
10. 12 eat every herb of the land..all that the h.
10. 15 fruit of the trees which the hail had le.
Job 38. 22 or hast thou seen the treasures of the h.?
Psa. 18. 12, 13 hail (stones) and coals of fire
78. 47 He destroyed their vines with hail, and
78. 48 He gave up their cattle also to the hail
105. 32 He gave them hail for rain..flaming
148. 8 Fire, and hail; snow, and vapour; stormy
Isa. 28. 2 as a tempest of hail..a destroying storm
28. 17 the hail shall sweep away the refuge of
Hag. 2. 17 I smote you with blasting..and with ha.
2. *Hail,* χάλαζα *chalaza.*
Rev. 8. 7 there followed hail and fire mingled with
11. 19 and there were lightnings..and great h.
16. 21 there fell upon men a great hail out of h.
16. 21 men blasphemed God because of..the h.

HAIL, to —
1. *To hail, send hail,* בָּרַד *barad.*
Isa. 32. 19 When it shall hail, coming down on the
2. *To rejoice, be of good cheer,* χαίρω *chairō.*
Matt. 26. 49 and said, Hail, Master! and kissed him
27. 29 mocked him, saying, Hail, King of the J.!
Mark 15. 18 began to salute him, Hail, King of the J.!
Luke 1. 28 Hail!..highly favoured, the Lord (is)
John 19. 3 And said, Hail, King of the Jews! and

HAIL, all —
To rejoice, be of good cheer, χαίρω *chairō.*
Matt. 28. 9 behold, Jesus met them, saying, All ha.!

HAIL STONE —
1. *Stone of hail,* אֶבֶן בָּרָד *eben barad,* Josh 10. 11, Is. 30. 30.
2. *Stone of ice* or *hail,* אֶבֶן אֶלְגָּבִישׁ [*eben*].
Eze. 13. 11, 13; 38. 22.

HAIR —
1. *A lock of hair,* דַּלָּה *dallah.*
Song 7. 5 and the hair of thine head like purple
2. *Separation, chaplet,* נֵזֶר *nezer.*
Jer. 7. 29 Cut off thine hair..and cast (it) away, and
3. *Hair,* שַׂעַר *saar.*
Isa. 7. 20 shave..the head, and the hair of the feet
4. *Hair,* שֵׂעָר *sear.*
Lev. 13. 3 the hair in the plague is turned white
13. 4 and the hair thereof be not turned white
13. 10 and it have turned the hair white, and
13. 20 skin, and the hair thereof be turned wh.
13. 21 and, behold..no white hairs therein
13. 25 the hair in the bright spot be turned wh.
13. 26 no white hair in the bright spot, and it
13. 30 in it a yellow thin hair; then the priest
13. 31 no black hair in it; then the priest shall
13. 32 and there be in it no yellow hair, and the
13. 36 the priest shall not seek for yellow hair
13. 37 and..there is black hair grown up therein
14. 8 shave off all his hair, and wash himself
14. 9 he shall shave all his hair off his head
14. 9 even all his hair he shall shave off: and
Num. 6. 5 let the locks of the hair of his head grow
6. 18 take the hair of the head of his separat.
Judg 16. 22 the hair of his head began to grow again
2 Sa. 14. 26 he weighed the hair of his head at two h.
Ezra 9. 3 I..plucked off the hair of my head and
Song 4. 1 thy hair (is) as a flock of goats, that app.
6. 5 thy hair (is) as a flock of goats that app.
Eze. 16. 7 thine hair is grown, whereas thou (wast)
5. *Hair,* שְׂעַר *sear.*
Dan. 3. 27 nor was an hair of their head singed
4. 33 till his hairs were grown like eagles'
7. 9 and the hair of his head like the pure
6. *Hair,* שַׂעֲרָה *saarah.*
Judg 20. 16 every one could sling stones at an hair
1 Sa. 14. 45 there shall not one hair of his head
2 Sa. 14. 11 shall not one hair of thy son fall to
1 Ki. 1. 52 there shall not an hair of him fall to the
Job 4. 15 a spirit passed..the hair of my flesh sto.
Psa. 40. 12 more than the hairs of mine head
69. 4 are more than the hairs of mine head
7. *Hair,* (*wool, feathers*), θρίξ *thrix.*
Matt. 3. 4 same John had his raiment of camel's h.
5. 36 thou canst not make one hair white or b.
10. 30 the very hairs of your head are all num.
Mark 1. 6 John was clothed with camel's hair, and
Luke 7. 38 and did wipe..with the hairs of her head
7. 44 and wiped (them) with the hairs of her h.
12. 7 the very hairs of your head are all num.
21. 18 there shall not an hair of your head per.
John 11. 2 Mary which..wiped his feet with her h.
12. 3 Then..Mary..wiped his feet with her h.
Acts 27. 34 there shall not an hair fall from the head
1 Pe. 3. 3 not be that outward..of plaiting [the h.]
Rev. 1. 14 His head and..hairs..white like wool, as
9. 8 they had hair as the hair of women, and
8. *Hair* (*of the head*), κόμη *komē.*
1 Co. 11. 15 a glory..for..hair is given her for a cover.

HAIR, broided —
Folded or braided hair, πλέγμα *plegma.*
1 Ti. 2. 9 nor with broided hair, or gold, or pea.

HAIR to be fallen off —
To be peeled, polished, plucked off, מָרַט *marat,* 2.
Lev. 13. 40 the man whose hair is fallen off his head
13. 41 he that hath his hair fallen off from the

HAIR, to pluck off —
To peel, polish, pluck off, מָרַט *marat.*
Neh. 13. 25 plucked off their hair, and made them
Isa. 50. 6 my cheeks to them that plucked off the h.

HAIR, to have long —
To have or let the hair grow long, κομάω *komaō.*
1 Co. 11. 14 man have long hair, it is a shame unto h.
11. 15 if a woman have long hair, it is a glory

HAIR, well (set) —
Wreathed or curled work, מִקְשֶׁה *miqsheh.*
Isa. 3. 24 instead of well set hair baldness; and

HAIR, of —
Made of hair, hairy, τρίχινος *trichinos.*
Rev. 6. 12 sun became black as sackcloth of hair

HAIRY —
1. *Hairy,* שָׂעִיר *sair.*
Gen. 27. 11 Esau my brother (is) a hairy man, and I
27. 23 his hands were hairy, as his brother Esa.
2. *Hair,* שֵׂעָר *sear.*
Gen. 25. 25 the first came out red, all over like an h.
Psa. 68. 21 the hairy scalp of such an one as goeth
3. *Owner of hair,* בַּעַל שֵׂעָר *baal sear.*
2 Ki. 1. 8 hairy man, and girt with a girdle of lea.

HAK-KA'-TAN, הַקָּטָן *the little one.*
The father of Johanan who was chief of the Bene-Azgad returned exiles with Ezra. B.C. 538. The name is simply *Katan,* "little," with the definite article prefixed.
Ezra 8. 12 the son of H., and with him an hundred

HAK'-KOZ, הַקּוֹץ *the nimble.*
A priest, the chief of the 7th course in the service of the sanctuary as appointed by David. B.C. 1015. In Ezra 2. 61, and Neh. 3. 4, 21, the name occurs as that of a family of priests, the prefix in these passages being taken correctly as the definite article. Hence the name appears as *Koz,* which see.
1 Ch. 24. 10 The seventh to H., the eighth to Abijah

HA-KU'-PHA, חֲקוּפָא *incitement.*
The Bene-Chupha were among the Nethinim who returned from Babylon with Zerubbabel. B.C. 536.
Ezra 2. 51 the children of H., the children of Harh.
Neh. 7. 53 the children of H., the children of Harh.

HA'-LAH, חֲלַח.
Probably this is a different place from the *Calah* of Gen. 10. 11; but it may be identified with the Chalcitis of Ptolemy, which is described as between Anthemusia and Gauzanitis. The name seems to remain in the modern *Gla,* a large mound on the Upper *Khabour* above its confluence with the *Jerujer.* Hither a portion of the Israelites were transported by Shalmaneser. B.C. 721.
2 Ki. 17. 6 and placed them in H. and in Habor
18. 11 and put them in H. and in Habor
1 Ch. 5. 26 and brought them unto H., and Habor

HA'-LAK, חָלָק *the smooth (mountain).*
A mountain, named as the southern limit of Joshua's conquests, but which has not yet been identified.
Josh. 11. 17 from the mount H., that goeth up to S.
12. 7 unto the mount H., that goeth up to Seir

HALE, to —
1. *To draw or drag down or along,* κατασύρω *kata.*
Luke 12. 58 lest he hale thee to the judge, and the j.
2. *To draw or drag,* σύρω *surō.*
Acts 8. 3 and haling men and women, committed

HALF —
1. *Half, middle,* חֵצִי ,חֲצִי *chetsi, chatsi.*
Exod 24. 6 Moses took half of the blood, and put
24. 6 half of the blood he sprinkled on the al.
25. 10, 17 two cubits and a half..the length
25. 10, 17 and a cubit and a half the breadth
25. 10, 23 and a cubit and a half the height the.
26. 12 the half curtain that remaineth shall ha.
26. 16 a cubit and a half..the breadth of one
36. 21 the breadth of a board one cubit and a h.
37. 1, 6 two cubits and a half..the length of it
37. 1, 6 and a cubit and a half the breadth of
37. 1, 10 and a cubit and a half the height of
Num 12. 12 of whom the flesh is half consumed when
15. 9 of flour mingled with half an hin of oil
15. 10 bring for a drink offering half an hin of
28. 14 drink offerings shall be half an hin of w.
32. 33 unto half the tribe of Manasseh the son
34. 13 unto the nine tribes, and to the half tri.
34. 14 half the tribe of Manasseh have received
34. 15 two tribes and the half tribe have recei.
Deut. 3. 12 half mount Gilead, and the cities thereof
3. 13 of Og, gave I unto the half tribe of Man.
29. 8 to the Gadites, and to the half tribe of M.
Josh. 1. 12 to half the tribe of Manasseh, spake Jos.
4. 12 half the tribe of Manasseh, passed over
8. 33 half of them over against mount Gerizim
8. 33 and half of them over against mount E.
12. 2 from half Gilead, even unto the river J.
12. 5 and the Maachathites, and half Gilead
12. 6 the Gadites, and the half tribe of Manas.
13. 7 the nine tribes, and the half tribe of Ma.
13. 25 and half the land of the children of Am.
13. 29 Moses gave..unto the half tribe of Man.
13. 29 was..of the half tribe of the children of
13. 31 And half Gilead, and Ashtaroth, and Ed.
13. 31 to the one half of the children of Machir
14. 2 for the nine tribes, and (for) the half tri.
14. 3 and an half tribe on the other side Jor.
18. 7 Gad, and Reuben, and half the tribe of
21. 5 out of the half tribe of Manasseh, ten ci.
21. 6 out of the half tribe of Manasseh in Bas.
21. 27 out of the (other) half tribe of Manasseh
22. 1 the Gadites, and the half tribe of Manas.
22. 7 Now to the (one) half of the tribe of Ma.
22. 7 unto the (other) half thereof gave Joshua

Josh.22. 9 the half tribe of Manasseh, returned, and
22. 10 the half tribe of Manasseh, built there an
22. 11 and the half tribe of Manasseh, have bui.
22. 13 and to the half tribe of Manasseh, into
22. 15 and to the half tribe of Manasseh, unto
22. 21 the half tribe of Manasseh, answered and
1 Sa. 14. 14 within as it were an half acre of land
2 Sa. 10. 4 shaved off the one half of their beards
18. 3 neither if half of us die, will they care for
19. 40 the king, and also half the people of Is.
1 Ki. 3. 25 give half to the one, and half to the other
7. 31 mouth..(was) round..a cubit and an half
7. 32 height of a wheel (was) a cubit and half
7. 35 a round compass of half a cubit high: and
10. 7 and, behold, the half was not told me
13. 8 If thou wilt give me half thine house, I
16. 21 half of the people followed Tibni the son
16. 21 to make him king; and half followed O.
1 Ch. 2. 52 Shobal..had sons; Haroeh..half of the M.
2. 54 and half of the Manahethites, the Zorites
5. 18 the Gadites, and half the tribe of Mana.
5. 23 children of the half tribe of Manasseh
5. 26 and the half tribe of Manasseh, and bro.
6. 61 the half (tribe) of Manasseh, by lot, ten c.
6. 71 out of the family of the half tribe of Ma.
12. 31 of the half tribe of Manasseh eighteen th.
12. 37 and of the half tribe of Manasseh, with
26. 32 made rulers over..the half tribe of Man.
27. 20 of the half tribe of Manasseh; Joel the son
27. 21 Of the half..of Manasseh in Gilead; Iddo
2 Ch. 9. 6 one half of the greatness of thy wisdom
Neh. 3. 9, 12, 16, 17, 18 the ruler of the half part of
4. 6 wall was joined together unto the half
4. 16 half of my servants wrought in the work
4. 16 the other half of them held both the sp.
4. 21 half of them held the spears from the
12. 32 Hoshaiah, and half of the princes of Ju.
12. 38 and the half of the people upon the wall
12. 40 and I, and the half of the rulers with me
13. 24 children spake half in the speech of Ash.
Esth. 5. 3 be even given thee to the half of the ki.
5. 6 to the half of the kingdom it shall be pe.
7. 2 be performed..to the half of the kingdom
Eze. 16. 51 Neither hath Samaria committed half of
40. 42 cubit and an half long..a cubit and an h.
43. 17 and the border about it..half a cubit; and
Dan. 12. 7 for a time, times, and an half; and when
Zech 14. 2 half of the city shall go forth into capti.
14. 4 half of the mountain shall remove toward
14. 4 the north, and half of it toward the south
14. 8 half of them toward..former sea, and half

2.*Half*, מֶחֱצָה *mechetsah.*
Num. 31. 36 the half..the portion of them that went
31. 43 the half (that pertained unto) the congr.

3.*Half*, מַחֲצִית *machatsith.*
Exod30. 13 This they shall give..half a shekel after
30. 13 an half shekel..the offering of the LORD
30. 15 poor shall not give less, than half a she.
38. 26 A bekah for every man..half a shekel
Lev. 6. 20 half of it in the morning, and half thereof
Num31. 29 Take..of their half, and give..unto Elea.
31. 30 of the children of Israel's half, thou shalt
31. 42 of the children of Israel's half, which M.
31. 47 of the children of Israel's half, Moses took
Josh 21. 25 out of the half tribe of Manasseh
1 Ki. 16. 9 Zimri, captain of half (his) chariots, con.
1 Ch. 6. 61 left of the family..out of the half tribe
6. 70 out of the half tribe of Manasseh; Aner

4.*Middle, midst*, תָּוֶךְ *tavek.*
Deut. 3. 16 even unto the river Arnon half the valley

5.*Half*, ἥμισυ *hēmisu.*
Mark 6. 23 I will give (it) thee, unto the half of my
Luke19. 8 the half of my goods I give to the poor
Rev. 11. 9 see their dead bodies three days and an h.
11. 11 after three days and an half the spirit of
12. 14 nourished for a time, and times, and ha.

HALF dead —
Half dead, ἡμιθανής *hēmithanēs.*
Luke 10. 30 wounded..departed, leaving..half dead

HALF hour, *the space of* —
Half an hour, ἡμιώριον *hēmiōrion*, ἡμιώρον.
Rev. 8. 1 silence..about the space of half an hour

HALF, to live out —
To halve, חָצָה *chatsah.*
Psa. 55. 23 deceitful men shall not live out half their

HALF so much —
Half, מַחֲצִית *machatsith.*
Exod 30. 23 Take..of sweet cinnamon half so much

HAL'-HUL, חַלְחוּל *full of hollows.*
A city in the hill country of Judah beside Beth-zur and Gedor, N. of Hebron, and about four miles distant from it. The name is said to be still unchanged, others write it *Hulhal.*
Josh.15. 58 H., Beth-zur, and Gedor

HA'-LI, חֲלִי.
A town on the boundary of Asher, named between Helkath and Beten; but nothing more is known of its situation.
Josh.19. 25 And their border was Helkath, and H.

HALL —
Open court, αὐλή *aulē.*
Mark15. 16 the soldiers led him away into the hall
Luke22. 55 had kindled a fire in the midst of the h.

HALL, common —
Praetor's house or office, πραιτώριον *praitōrion.* (*Lat.*)
Matt 27. 27 took Jesus into the common hall, and g.

HALLOW —
1.*To set apart*, קָדַשׁ *qadesh*, 3.
Exod20. 11 LORD blessed the sabbath day, and hallo.
29. 1 to hallow them, to minister unto me in
40. 9 shalt hallow it, and all the vessels thereof
Lev. 16. 19 hallow it from the uncleanness of the ch.
22. 32 Israel: I (am) the LORD which hallow
25. 10 ye shall hallow the fiftieth year, and pro.
Num. 6. 11 and shall hallow his head that same day
1 Ki. 8. 64 The same day did the king hallow the
2 Ch. 7. 7 Solomon hallowed the middle of the co.
Jer. 17. 22 hallow ye the sabbath day, as I comma.
17. 24 hallow the sabbath day, to do no work
17. 27 to hallow the sabbath day, and not to..b.
Eze. 20. 20 hallow my sabbaths; and they shall be a
44. 24 my laws..they shall hallow my sabbaths

2.*To set apart*, קָדַשׁ *qadesh*, 5.
Exod28. 38 Israel shall hallow in all their holy gifts
Lev. 22. 2 which they hallow unto me: I (am) the L.
22. 3 the children of Israel hallow unto the L.
Num. 3. 13 I hallowed unto me all the first born in I.
1 Ki. 9. 3 I have hallowed this house which thou
9. 7 house, which I have hallowed for my na.
2 Ch.36. 14 the house of the LORD which he had hal.

3.*To set apart, hallow, sanctify*, ἁγιάζω *hagiazō.*
Matt. 6. 9 pray ye: Our Father..Hallowed be thy
Luke11. 2 say, Our Father..Hallowed be thy name

HALLOWED —
A setting apart, separation, קֹדֶשׁ *qodesh.*
1 Sa. 21. 4 there is hallowed bread; if the young
21. 6 So the priest gave him hallowed (bread)

HALLOWED, to be —
1.*To be set apart*, קָדַשׁ *qadash.*
Exod29. 21 he shall be hallowed, and his garments
Num16. 37 take up the censers..for they are hallowed
16. 38 therefore they are hallowed: and they

2.*To be or become set apart*, קָדַשׁ *qadesh*, 2.
Lev. 22. 32 I will be hallowed among the children of

HALLOWED part —
What is set apart, מִקְדָּשׁ *miqdash.*
Num18. 29 (even) the hallowed part thereof out of it

HALLOWED things —
What is set apart, separation, קֹדֶשׁ *qodesh.*
Lev. 12. 4 she shall touch no hallowed thing, nor
19. 8 he hath profaned the hallowed thing of
Num. 5. 10 every man's hallowed things shall be his
18. 8 heave offerings of all the hallowed things
Deut26. 13 I have brought away the hallowed things
2 Ki.12. 18 Jehoash..took all the hallowed things
12. 18 his own hallowed things, and all the gold

HA-LO'-HESH, HAL-LO'-HESH, הַלּוֹחֵשׁ *the whisperer.*
1. Father of Shallum who ruled over part of Jerusalem and helped to rebuild the wall. B.C. 475.
Neh. 3. 12 unto him repaired Shallum the son of H.
2. One or a family that sealed the covenant with Nehemiah. B.C. 475.
Neh. 10. 24 H., Pileha, Shobek

HALT —
Lame, crippled, χωλός *chōlos.*
Matt 18. 8 better..to enter into life halt or maimed
Mark 9. 45 better for thee to enter halt into life
Luke14. 21 bring in hither the poor..and the halt
John 5. 3 great multitude..of blind, halt, withered

HALT, to —
1.*To leap, pass over*, פָּסַח *pasach.*
1 Ki. 18. 21 How long halt ye between two opinions?

2.*To halt*, צָלַע *tsala.*
Gen. 32. 31 the sun rose..and he halted upon his
Mic. 4. 6 will I assemble her that halteth, and I
4. 7 I will make her that halted a remnant
Zeph. 3. 19 I will save her that halteth, and gather

3.*Halting*, צֶלַע *tsela.*
Psa. 38. 17 For I (am) ready to halt, and my sorrow

HALTING —
Halting, צֶלַע *tsela.*
Jer. 20. 10 All my familiars watched for my halting

HAM, הָם *multitude.*
Here Chedorlaomer smote the Zuzim. If these people were the Zamzummim, Ham must have been in what was afterwards the land of the Ammonites. Hence Ham may be but another name of their chief stronghold Rabbah, now *Amman.* Others think it is the modern *Humeimath* one mile above *Rabba*, the ancient Ar-moab, on the Roman road.
Gen. 14. 5 smote..the Zuzims in H., and the Emims

HAM, חָם *swarthy, dark coloured.*
1. The youngest son of Noah, and father of Canaan. The Egyptian word *Kem*, Egypt=Ham, as an adjective, means "black" and "warm." His sons were Cush and Mizraim, Phut and Canaan. Ham was the only son of Noah after whom a country was named. B.C. 2348.
Gen. 5. 32 and Noah begat Shem, H., and Japheth
6. 10 Noah begat three sons, Shem, H., and J.
7. 13 Shem, and H., and Japheth, the sons of
9. 18 the sons of Noah..were Shem, and H.
9. 18 and H. (is) the father of Canaan
9. 22 H...saw the nakedness of his father
Gen. 10. 1 generations of the sons of Noah; Shem, H.
10. 6 the sons of H.; Cush, and Mizraim, and
10. 20 These (are) the sons of H., after their
1 Ch. 1. 4 Noah, Shem, H., and Japheth
1. 8 The sons of H.; Cush, and Mizraim
2. The patronymic of his descendants.
1 Ch. 4. 40 for (they) of H. had dwelt there of old
Psa. 78. 51 (their) strength in the tabernacles of H.
105. 23 and Jacob sojourned in the land of H.
105. 27 showed his..wonders in the land of H.
106. 22 Wondrous works in the land of H., (and)

HA'-MAN, הָמָן *celebrated Haman, Hom.*
The chief minister or vizier of Ahasuerus (Xerxes). B.C. 510. After the failure of his plot to cut off all the Jews in the empire of Persia he was hanged on the gallows which he had erected for Mordecai. He is called the Agagite, as signifying that he was of Amalekitish descent: but in the LXX he is called a *Macedonian* in Esth. 9. 24 (cf. 3. 1), and a *Persian* by Sulpicius Severus.
Esth. 3. 1 After these..did k. Ahasuerus promote H.
3. 2 all the king's servants..reverenced H.
3. 4 they told H., to see whether Mordecai's
3. 5 when H. saw..then was H. full of wrath
3. 6 wherefore H. sought to destroy all the J.
3. 7 they cast Pur, that (is), the lot, before H.
3. 8 H. said unto king Ahasuerus, There is a
3. 10 king took his ring..and gave it unto H.
3. 11 the king said unto H., The silver (is) giv.
3. 12 all that H. had commanded, unto the king's
3. 15 And the king and H. sat down to drink
4. 7 the money that H. had promised to pay
5. 4 let the king and H. come this day unto
5. 5 the king said, Cause H. to make haste
5. 5 So the king and H. came to the banquet
5. 8 let the king and H. come to the banquet
5. 9 Then went H. forth that day joyful and
5. 9 when H. saw Mordecai in the king's gate
5. 10 Nevertheless H. refrained himself, and
5. 11 H. told them of the glory of his riches, and
5. 12 H. said moreover, Yea, Esther..did let
5. 14 the thing pleased H.; and he caused the
6. 4 Now H. was come into the outward court
6. 5 said..Behold, H. standeth in the court
6. 5 So H. came in. And the king said unto
6. 6 H. thought in his heart, To whom would
6. 7 H. answered the king, For the man whom
6. 10 Then the king said to H., Make haste
6. 11 Then took H. the apparel and the horse
6. 12 but H. hasted to his house mourning
6. 13 H. told Zeresh his wife and all his friends
6. 14 and hasted to bring H. unto the banquet
7. 1 So the king and H. came to banquet with
7. 6 The adversary and enemy (is) this..H.
7. 6 Then H. was afraid before the king and
7. 7 H. stood up to make request for his life
7. 8 H. was fallen upon the bed whereon Est.
7. 8 As the word went out..they covered H.'s
7. 9 gallows..which H. had made for Morde.
7. 9 the gallows..standeth in the house of H.
7. 10 So they hanged H. on the gallows that
8. 1 did..Ahasuerus give the house of H...un.
8. 2 his ring, which he had taken from H.
8. 2 Esther set Mordecai over the house of H.
8. 3 besought..to put away the mischief of H.
8. 5 the letters devised by H. the son of Ha.
8. 7 I have given Esther the house of H., and
9. 10 ten sons of H. the son of Hammedatha
9. 12 The Jews have slain..the ten sons of H.
9. 13 let H.'s ten sons be hanged upon the gal.
9. 14 given..and they hanged H.'s ten sons
9. 24 Because H...had devised against the Je.

HA'-MATH, HE'-MATH, חֲמָת *defenced, walled.*
A city of Upper Syria in the valley of the Orontes, about midway between its source (near *Baalbek*) and the bend which it makes at *Jisrhadid.* The Hamathites were a Hamitic race and are included among the desendants of Canaan (Gen. 10. 18.)
Num13. 21 So they went up..as men come to H.
34. 8 shall point out..unto the entrance of H.
Judg. 3. 3 Baal-hermon unto the entering in of H.
2 Sa. 8. 9 Toi king of H. heard that David had sm.
1 Ki. 8. 65 from the entering in of H. unto the river
2 Ki. 14. 25 from the entering of H. unto the sea of
14. 28 how he recovered Damascus, and H...for
17. 24 the king of Assyria brought..from H.
17. 30 and the men of H. made Ashima
18. 34 Where (are) the gods of H., and of Arpa.?
19. 13 Where (is) the king of H., and the king
23. 33 Pharaoh-nechoh put him in bands..in..H
25. 21 slew them at Riblah in the land of H.
1 Ch.13. 5 Shihor of Egypt..unto the entering of H.
18. 3 David smote Hadarezer..unto H., as he
18. 9 Tou king of H. heard how David had sm.
2 Ch. 7. 8 from the entering in of H. unto the river
8. 4 the store cities, which he built in H.
Isa. 10. 9 (is) not H. as Arpad? (is) not Samaria as
11. 11 his people, which shall be left, from..H.
36. 19 Where (are) the gods of H. and Arphad
37. 13 Where (is) the king of H., and the king of
Jer. 39. 5 they brought him up..to Riblah in..H.
49. 23 Concerning Damascus. H. is confounded
52. 9 they took the king..to Riblah in..H.
52. 27 put them to death..in the land of H.
Eze. 47. 16 H., Berothah, Sibraim, which (is) between
47. 16 border of Damascus, and the border of H.
47. 17 north northward and the border of H.
47. 20 border, till a man come over against H.
48. 1 of the way of Hethlon, as one goeth to H

Eze. 48. 1 of Damascus northward, to the coast of H.
Amos 6. 2 and from thence go ye to H. the great
6. 14 shall afflict..from the entering in of H.
Zech. 9. 2 And H. also shall border thereby

HA-MATH-ITE, חֲמָתִי *belonging to Hamath.*
The patronymic of certain descendants of Canaan dwelling on the extreme north of Palestine.
Gen. 10. 18 Arvadite, and the Zemarite, and the H.
1 Ch. 1. 16 Arvadite, and the Zemarite, and the H.

HA-MATH ZO'-BAH, חֲמַת צוֹבָה.
The fuller name of *Hamath.* It is called by the Greeks *Epiphania*: but it is probably *not* Hamath the Great, being distinguished from it by the suffix *Zobah*; as Ramath-*Gilead* is distinguished from Ramah in *Benjamin.*
2 Ch. 8. 3 Solomon went to H., and prevailed against

HAM'-MATH, חַמַּת *warm springs.*
A fortified city in the territory allotted to Naphtali, one mile from Tiberias. Its name indicates that it contained the "hot baths" of Tiberias. Josephus calls it *Emmaus*, a village not far from Tiberias, where Vespasian encamped before Tiberias. The *Hammam*, at present four in number, still send up their hot sulphureous waters (144° Fahr.), at a spot rather more than a mile S. of the modern town, *Tubariyeh*, at the extremity of the ruins of the ancient city.
Josh. 19. 35 the fenced cities..Ziddim, Zer, and H.

HAM-ME-DA'-THA, הַמְּדָתָא *given by Hom.*
The father of Haman the Agagite at the court of Ahasuerus (Xerxes) king of Persia. B.C. 550.
Esth. 3. 1 promote Haman the son of H. the Agagite
3. 10 and gave it unto Haman the son of H.
8. 5 letters devised by Haman the son of H.
9. 10 ten sons of Haman the son of H...slew
9. 24 the son of H...had devised against the

HAM-ME'-LECH, הַמֶּלֶךְ *the king.*
Though this is given in the Common Version as a proper name, it might and perhaps ought to have been translated as the ordinary Hebrew word for "the king"; *i.e.*, in the first case Jehoiakim, and in the latter Zedekiah.
Jer. 36. 26 king commanded Jerahmeel the son of H.
38. 6 the dungeon of Malchiah the son of H.

HAMMER —

1. *Hammer, hammering,* הַלְמוּת *halmuth.*
Judg. 5. 26 She put her hand..to the workmen's ha.

2. *Hammer,* מַקָּבָה *maqqabah.*
1 Ki. 6. 7 there was neither hammer nor ax..heard
Isa. 44. 12 fashioneth it with hammers, and worketh
Jer. 10. 4 they fasten it with nails and with ham.

3. *Hammer,* מַקֶּבֶת *maqqebeth.*
Judg. 4. 21 Then Jael..took an hammer in her hand

4. *Hammer,* פַּטִּישׁ *pattish.*
Isa. 41. 7 he that smootheth (with) the hammer
Jer. 23. 29 a hammer (that) breaketh the rock in pi.
50. 23 How is the hammer..cut asunder and

5. *Hatchets, clubs,* כֵּילַפּוֹת *kelappoth.*
Psa. 74. 6 now they break down..with axes and h.

HAM-MO-LE'-KETH, הַמֹּלֶכֶת *the queen.*
Daughter of Machir and sister of Gilead the grandson of Manasseh. One of her children was Abi-ezer, from whose family sprang the great judge Gideon. She may have ruled over a portion of the land belonging to Gilead; and hence her name. B.C. 1450.
1 Ch. 7. 18 sister H. bare Ishod, and Abiezer, and M.

HAM'-MON, חַמּוֹן *hot spring.*
1. A city of Asher, not far from Zidon-rabbah, or "Great Zidon". It may be *Hamul*, about ten miles from Tyre, and near the coast.
Josh. 19. 28 Rehob, and H., and Kanah..unto great

2. A city allotted to the Levites out of the tribe of Naphtali, and answering to the cities (or city) called Hammath and Hammath-dor.
1 Ch. 6. 76 with her suburbs, and H. with her sub.

HAM-MOTH DOR חַמֹּת דֹּאר.
A city of Naphtali allotted to the Gershonite Levites, and appointed a city of refuge. It is perhaps identical with *Hammath.* In 1 Chr. 6. 76, the name is *Hammon.*
Josh 21. 32 H.-d. with her suburbs, and Kartan with

HA-MO'-NAH, הֲמוֹנָה *multitude.*
The place in or near which the multitudes of Gog are to be buried, after the great slaughter, and which is to derive its name from that circumstance.
Eze. 39. 16 also the name of the city (shall be) H.

HA-MON GOG, הֲמוֹן גּוֹג *multitude by Gog.*
A glen previously known as the "ravine of the passengers on the E. of the Sea," after the burial there of Gog and all his multitude.
Eze. 39. 11 and they shall call (it), The valley of H.-g.
39. 15 have buried it in the valley of H.-g.

HA'-MOR, חֲמוֹר *large jackass.*
The figure employed by Jacob for Issachar; also a Hivite or Horite, who, at the return of Jacob into Palestine, was prince of the city of Shechem, and father of Shechem whose treatment of Dinah brought destruction to himself and all his kindred and city. The name in the Greek form is *Emmor*, and Abraham is said to have bought his sepulchre from the sons of *Emmor.* B.C. 1739.
Gen. 33. 19 at the hand of the children of H.
34. 2 when Shechem the son of H...saw her
34. 4 Shechem spake unto his father H., saying
34. 6 H. the father of Shechem went out unto
34. 8 And H. communed with them, saying
34. 13 sons of Jacob answered Shechem and H.
34. 18 their words pleased H., and Shechem, H.'s
34. 20 H. and Shechem..came unto the gate of
34. 24 unto H., and unto Shechem his son, hear.
34. 26 they slew H. and Shechem his son with
Josh. 24. 32 which Jacob bought of the sons of H. the
Judg 9. 28 Serve the men of H. the father of Shechem

HA-MU'-EL, חַמּוּאֵל *God is a sun.*
A son of Mishma, a Simeonite, of the family of Shaul. B.C. 1200.
1 Ch. 4. 26 the sons of Mishma; H. his son, Zacchur

HA'-MUL, חָמוּל *pity.*
The younger son of Pharez son of Judah by Tamar. He was the head of the Hamulite family. B.C. 1650.
Gen. 46. 12 the sons of Pharez were Hezron and H.
Num 26. 21 of H., the family of the Hamulites
1 Ch. 2. 5 The sons of Pharez; Hezron, and H.

HA-MU-LITES, חָמוּלִי *belonging to Hamul.*
The descendants of Hamul son of Pharez.
Num 26. 21 of Hamul, the family of the H.

HA-MU'-TAL, חֲמוּטַל *God is fresh life; kin to the dew.*
A daughter of Jeremiah of Libnah, one of king Josiah's wives, and mother of Jehoahaz and Mattaniah or Zedekiah. In the last two texts the name is given as *Hamital*, which the LXX. adopts throughout. B.C. 600.
2 Ki. 23. 31 his mother's name (was) H., the daughter
24. 18 his mother's name (was) H., the daughter
Jer. 52. 1 his mother's name (was) H. the daughter

HA-NAM'-EEL, חֲנַמְאֵל *gift or grace of God.*
Son of Shallum and cousin of Jeremiah the prophet who purchased a field from him in full assurance that it would ultimately prove a good investment. B.C. 590.
Jer. 32. 7 H. the son of Shallum thine uncle, shall
32. 8 H., mine uncle's son, came to me in the
32. 9 I bought the field of H., my uncle's son
32. 12 in the sight of H. mine uncle's (son)

HA'-NAN, חָנָן *merciful.*
1. A son of Shashak, a descendant of Benjamin. B.C. 1340.
1 Ch. 8. 23 And Abdon, and Zichri, and H.

2. A son of Azel a Benjamite, through Saul. B.C. 860.
1 Ch. 8. 38 Azel had six sons..Azrikam, Bocheru..H.
9. 44 Azel had six sons..Azrikam, Bochern..H.

3. Son of Maachah, one of the heroes of David's guard. B.C. 1040.
1 Ch. 11. 43 H. the son of Maachah, and Joshaphat

4. A Nethinim returned captive with Zerubbabel. B.C. 536.
Ezra. 2. 46 children of Shalmai, the children of H.
Neh. 7. 49 children of H., the children of Giddel

5. A Levite who assisted Ezra when he read the law. B.C. 445.
Neh. 8. 7 H...caused the people to understand the

6. A Levite who sealed the covenant with Nehemiah and the people. [Perhaps the same as No. 5]. B.C. 445.
Neh. 10. 10 their brethren, Shebaniah, Hodijah..H.
13. 13 next to them (was) H. the son of Zaccur

7. A chief (or the patronymic of a family) who sealed the covenant with Nehemiah. B.C. 445.
Neh. 10. 22 Pelatiah, H., Anaiah

8. Another of the chiefs on the same occasion.
Neh. 10. 26 And Ahijah, H., Anan

9. An officer in the Lord's house whose sons had a chamber in the temple. He was son of Igdaliah. B.C. 600.
Jer. 35. 4 into the chamber of the sons of H., the

HA-NAN'-EEL, חֲנַנְאֵל *God is gracious.*
Hananeel was the builder of the tower near the Sheep-gate of Jerusalem.
Neh. 3. 1 they sanctified it, unto the tower of H.
12. 39 the tower of H., and the tower of Meah
Jer. 31. 38 from the tower of H. unto the gate of the
Zech. 14. 10 the tower of H. unto the king's wine pre.

HA-NA'-NI, חֲנָנִי *gracious.*
1. One of the sons of Heman, David's seer and head of the 18th course of the service of the Sanctuary. B.C. 1015.
1 Ch. 25. 4 Of Heman..Hananiah, H., Eliathah, Gid.
25. 25 H...his sons, and his brethren..twelve

2. A seer who rebuked Asa for buying off Benhadad king of Syria. B.C. 941.
2 Ch. 16. 7 at that time H. the seer came to Asa king

3. The father of Jehu the seer who testified against Baasha and Jehoshaphat. B.C. 930.
1 Ki. 16. 1 the word..came to Jehu the son of H.
16. 7 by the hand of..Jehu the son of H. came
2 Ch. 19. 2 Jehu the son of H. the seer went out to
20. 34 written in the book of Jehu the son of H.

4. A priest who had taken a strange wife. B.C. 456.
Ezra 10. 20 of the sons of Immer; H., and Zebadiah

5. A brother of Nehemiah who returned from Jerusalem to Susa and was afterwards made governor of Jerusalem under Nehemiah. B.C. 446.
Neh. 1. 2 That H., one of my brethren, came, he
7. 2 I gave my brother H...charge over Jeru.

6. A priest and musician who assisted in the ceremonial of purifying the walls of Jerusalem. B.C. 445.
Neh. 12. 36 his brethren, Shemaiah..Judah, H., with

HA-NAN'-IAH, חֲנַנְיָהוּ, חֲנַנְיָה *Jah is gracious.*
1. A son of Heman the singer and chief of the 16th course of the 24 into which the 288 Levite musicians were divided by king David. Heman's sons were especially employed to blow the horns. B.C. 1015.
1 Ch. 25. 4 sons of Heman..H., Hanani, Eliathah
25. 23 H...his sons, and his brethren..twelve

2. A chief captain of king Uzziah's army. B.C. 810.
2 Ch. 26. 11 under the hand of H., (one) of the king's

3. The father of Zedekiah, one of the princes in the reign of Jehoakim king of Judah. B.C. 630.
Jer. 36. 12 sat..the son of H., and all the princes

4. Son of Azur, a Benjamite of Gibeon and false prophet in the reign of Zedekiah king of Judah. B.C. 595. In this year he withstood Jeremiah the prophet.
Jer. 28. 1 H. the son of Azur the prophet..spake
28. 5 prophet Jere. said unto the prophet H.
28. 10 H...took the yoke from off..Jeremiah's
28. 11 H. spake in the presence of all the people
28. 12 after..H. the prophet had broken the
28. 13 Go and tell H., saying, Thus saith the L.
28. 15 Then said the prophet Jeremiah unto H.
28. 15 Hear now, H.; The LORD hath not sent
28. 17 So H. the prophet died the same year, in

5. Grandfather of Irijah, the captain of the ward at the gate of Benjamin. He arrested Jeremiah on a charge of deserting to the Chaldæans. B.C. 596.
Jer. 37. 13 Irijah, the son of Shelemiah..son of H.

6. Son of Shashak and head of a Benjamite house. B.C 1340.
1 Ch. 8. 24 And H., and Elam, and Antothijah

7. The Hebrew name of Shadrach, who was of the house of David. B.C. 607.
Dan. 1. 6 these were, of the children of Judah..H
1. 7 of Belteshazzar; and to H., of Shadrach
1. 11 prince of the eunuchs had set over..H.
1. 19 among..all was found none like Daniel, H
2. 17 Daniel..made the thing known to H.

8. A son of Zerubbabel in the ancestry of Jesus. B.C 500.
1 Ch. 3. 19 sons of Zerubbabel: Meshullam, and H.
3. 21 And the sons of H.; Pelatiah, and Jesai.

9. A son of Bebai, who returned with Ezra from Babylon B.C. 456.
Ezra 10. 28 the sons also of Bebai; Jehohanan, H.

10. An apothecary and priest. B.C. 445.
Neh. 3. 8 Next unto him also repaired H. the son

11. One that repaired a portion of the wall of Jerusalem with Hanun. B.C. 445.
Neh. 3. 30 After him repaired H. the son of Shele.

12. A ruler of the palace at Jerusalem under Nehemiah. B.C. 445.
Neh. 7. 2 I gave..Hanani, and H...charge over J.

13. An individual or family that sealed the covenant. B.C. 445.
Neh. 10. 23 Hoshea, H., Hashub

14. A priest in the time of Jehoiakim. B.C. 630.
Neh. 12. 12 the chief of the fathers..of Jeremiah, H.
12. 41 the priests..Zechariah, (and) H., with

HAND —

1. *Palm of the hand,* אֶכֶף *ekeph.*
Job 33. 7 neither shall my hand be heavy upon

2. *Hand,* יָד *yad.*
Gen. 3. 22 now, lest he put forth his hand, and take
4. 11 receive thy brother's blood from thy hand
5. 29 concerning our work and toil of our han.
8. 9 then he put forth his hand, and took her
9. 2 into your hand are they delivered
9. 5, 5 at the hand of every beast will I require
9. 5 at the hand of man; at the hand of every
14. 20 delivered thine enemies into thy hand
14. 22 I have lift up mine hand unto the LORD
16. 6 Behold, thy maid (is) in thy hand; do to
16. 9 and submit thyself under her hands
16. 12 his hand (will be) against every man, and
16. 12 every man's hand against him; and he
19. 10 the men put forth their hand, and pulled
19. 16 the men laid hold upon his hand, and
19. 16 the hand of his wife, and upon the hand
21. 18 Arise..and hold him in thine hand; for
21. 30 seven ewe lambs shalt thou take of my h.
22. 6 he took the fire in his hand, and a knife
22. 10 And Abraham stretched forth his hand
22. 12 Lay not thine hand upon the lad, neither
24. 2 Put, I pray thee, thy hand under my thi.
24. 9 the servant put his hand under the thigh
24. 10 the goods of his master (were) in his hand
24. 18 and let down her pitcher upon her hand
24. 22 two bracelets for her hands of ten (shek.)
24. 30 and bracelets upon his sister's hands, and
24. 47 and I put..the bracelets upon her hands
25. 26 and his hand took hold on Esau's heel
27. 16 And she put the skins..upon his hands
27. 17 the bread..into the hand of her son Jacob
27. 22 but the hands (are) the hands of Esau
27. 23 his hands were hairy, as..Esau's hands
30. 35 and gave (them) into the hand of his sons
31. 29 It is in the power of my hand to do you
31. 39 of my hand didst thou require it, (whet.)
32. 11 the hand of my brother, from the hand

Gen. 32. 13 took of that which came to his hand a
32. 16 he delivered..into the hand of his serv.
33. 10 then receive my present at my hand; for
33. 19 at the hand of the children of Hamor
35. 4 strange gods which (were) in their hand
37. 21 and he delivered him out of their hands
37. 22 Shed no blood..and lay no hand upon
37. 22 he might rid him out of their hands, to
37. 27 and let not our hand be upon him; for
38. 18 she said..thy staff that (is) in thine hand
38. 20 sent the kid by the hand of his friend
38. 20 receive (his) pledge from the woman's h.
38. 28 to pass..that (the one) put out (his) hand
38. 28 and bound upon his hand a scarlet thread
38. 29 as he drew back his hand, that, behold
38. 30 that had the scarlet thread upon his hand
39. 1 bought him of the hands of the Ishmeel.
39. 3 the LORD made all..to prosper in his ha.
39. 4 and all (that) he had he put into his ha.
39. 6 he left all that he had in Joseph's hand
39. 8 committed all that he hath to my hand
39. 12, 13 left his garment in her hand, and fled
39. 22 committed to Joseph's hand..the prison.
39. 23 looked not to any thing..under his hand
40. 11 And Pharaoh's cup (was) in my hand: and
40. 13 shalt deliver Pharaoh's cup into his hand
41. 35 lay up corn under the hand of Pharaoh
41. 42 Pharaoh took off his ring from his hand
41. 42 put it upon Joseph's hand, and arrayed
41. 44 without thee shall no man lift up his ha.
42. 37 deliver him into my hand, and I will bri.
43. 9 of my hand shalt thou require him: if I
43. 12 And take double money in your hand
43. 12 the money..carry (it) again in your hand
43. 15 they took double money in their hand
43. 21 we have brought it again in our hand
43. 22 we brought down in our hands to buy fo.
43. 26 the present which (was) in their hand
44. 17 the man in whose hand the cup is found
46. 4 Joseph shall put his hand upon thine ey.
47. 29 put, I pray thee, thy hand under my thi.
48. 14 upon Manasseh's head, guiding his hands
48. 17 his right hand upon the head of Ephraim
48. 17 he held up his father's hand, to remove
48. 22 I took out of the hand of the Amorite
49. 8 thy hand (shall be) in the neck of thine e.
49. 24 the arms of his hands were made strong
49. 24 by the hands of the mighty (God) of Ja.
Exod. 2. 19 delivered us out of the hand of the shep.
3. 8 deliver them out of the hand of the Egy.
3. 19 not let you go, no, not by a mighty hand
3. 20 I will stretch out my hand, and smite E.
4. 2 What (is) that in thine hand? And he
4. 4 Put forth thine hand..he put forth his ha.
4. 6 Put now thine hand into thy bosom. And
4. 6 put his hand into his bosom: and when
4. 6 behold, his hand (was) leprous as snow
4. 7 Put thine hand into thy bosom again
4. 7 he put his hand into his bosom again
4. 13 by the hand (of him whom) thou wilt
4. 17 thou shalt take this rod in thine hand
4. 20 and Moses took the rod of God in his h.
4. 21 those wonders..I have put in thine hand
5. 21 to put a sword in their hand to slay us
6. 1 with a strong hand shall he let them go
6. 1 with a strong hand shall he drive them
7. 4 that I may lay my hand upon Egypt
7. 5 when I stretch forth mine hand upon E.
7. 15 the rod..shalt thou take in thine hand
7. 17 smite with the rod that (is) in mine hand
7. 19 stretch out thine hand upon the waters
8. 5 Say unto Aaron, Stretch forth thine hand
8. 6 And Aaron stretched out his hand over
8. 17 Aaron stretched out his hand with his
9. 3 hand of the LORD is upon thy cattle
9. 15 now I will stretch out my hand, that I
9. 22 Stretch forth thine hand toward heaven
10. 12 Stretch out thine hand over the land of
10. 21 Stretch out thine hand toward heaven
10. 22 Moses stretched forth his hand toward h.
12. 11 eat it; (with)..your staff in your hand
13. 3 by strength of hand the LORD brought
13. 9 be for a sign unto thee upon thine hand
13. 9 with a strong hand hath the LORD brou.
13. 14, 16 By strength of hand the LORD brou.
13. 16 it shall be for a token upon thine hand
14. 8 the children..went out with an high ha.
14. 16, 26 stretch out thine hand over the sea
14. 21, 27 Moses stretched..his hand over the
14. 30 saved..out of the hand of the Egyptians
15. 9 will draw my sword, my hand shall dest.
15. 17 O LORD, (which) thy hands have establi.
15. 20 Miriam..took a timbrel in her hand; and
16. 3 died by the hand of the LORD in the land
17. 5 thy rod..take in thine hand, and go
17. 9 stand..with the rod of God in mine hand
17. 11 when Moses held up his hand, that Isra
17. 11 and when he let down his hand, Amalek
17. 12 But Moses' hands (were) heavy; and they
17. 12 stayed up his hands..and his hands were
18. 9, 10 out of the hand of the Egyptians
18. 10 delivered..out of the hand of Pharaoh
18. 10 from under the hand of the Egyptians
19. 13 There shall not an hand touch it, but he
21. 13 but God deliver (him) into his hand; then
21. 16 or if he be found in his hand, he shall
21. 20 with a rod, and he die under his hand
21. 24 tooth for tooth, hand for hand, foot for
22. 4 If the theft be certainly found in his ha
22. 8, 11 put his hand unto his neighbour's go.
23. 1 put not thine hand with the wicked to be
23. 31 inhabitants of the land into your hand
Exod. 24. 11 upon the nobles..he laid not his hand
29. 10, 15, 19 shall put their hands upon the he.
29. 20 and upon the thumb of their right hand
29. 25 thou shalt receive them of their hands
30. 19, 21 shall wash their hands and their feet
32. 4 And he received (them) at their hand
32. 11 with great power, and with a mighty ha?
32. 15 two tables of the testimony..in his hand
32. 19 cast the tables out of his hands, and brake
34. 4 took in his hand the two tables of stone
34. 29 the two tables of testimony in Moses' ha.
35. 25 all the women..did spin with their hands
35. 29 commanded to be made by the hand of
38. 21 by the hand of Ithamar, son to Aaron the
40. 31 washed their hands and their feet there.
Lev. 1. 4 he shall put his hand upon the head of
3. 2, 8, 13 he shall lay his hand upon the head
4. 4 lay his hand upon the bullock's head, and
4. 15 elders..shall lay their hands upon the he.
4. 24, 29, 33 shall lay his hand upon the head
7. 30 His own hands shall bring the offerings
8. 14, 18, 22 laid their hands upon the head of
8. 23 put (it)..upon the thumb of his right ha.
8. 24 upon the thumbs of their right hands
8. 36 the LORD commanded by the hand of M.
9. 22 Aaron lifted up his hand toward the pe.
10. 11 spoken unto them by the hand of Moses
14. 14, 17, 25, 28 upon the thumb of his..hand
14. 32 hand is not able to get (that which per.)
15. 11 and hath not rinsed his hands in water
16. 21 Aaron shall lay both his hands upon the
16. 21 send (him) away by the hand of a fit man
22. 25 Neither from a stranger's hand shall ye
24. 14 that heard..lay their hands upon his he.
25. 14 or buyest (ought) of thy neighbour's ha.
25. 28 remain in the hand of him that..bought
26. 25 be delivered into the hand of the enemy
26. 46 in mount Sinai by the hand of Moses
Num. 4. 28 under the hand of Ithamar; 4. 33.
4. 37 commandment of the LORD by the hand
4. 45 the word of the LORD by the hand of M.
4. 49 they were numbered by the hand of Mo.
5. 18 the priest shall have in his hand the bitter
5. 25 shall take..out of the woman's hand, and
6. 21 beside (that) that his hand shall get: ac.
7. 8 under the hand of Ithamar the son of A.
8. 10 shall put their hands upon the Levites
8. 12 the Levites shall lay their hands upon the
9. 23 commandment of the LORD by the hand
10. 13 commandment of the LORD by the hand
11. 23 Is the LORD'S hand waxed short? thou
15. 23 commanded you by the hand of Moses
16. 40 the LORD said to him by the hand of M.
20. 11 Moses lifted up his hand, and with his
20. 20 with much people, and with a strong ha.
21. 2 wilt..deliver this people into my hand
21. 26 taken all his land out of his hand, even
21. 34 for I have delivered him into thy hand
22. 7 the rewards of divination in their hand
22. 23 his sword drawn in his hand: and the ass
22. 29 I would there were a sword in mine hand
22. 31 his sword drawn in his hand: and he
25. 7 when Phinehas..took a javelin in his ha.
27. 18 Take..Joshua..and lay thine hand upon
27. 23 he laid his hands upon him, and gave him
27. 23 the LORD commanded by the hand of M.
31. 6 and the trumpets to blow in his hand
33. 1 with their armies under the hand of Mo.
33. 3 Israel went out with an high hand in the
35. 18 Or (if) he smite him with an hand weap.
35. 21 Or in enmity smite him with his hand
35. 25 deliver..out of the hand of the revenger
36. 13 the LORD commanded by the hand of M.
Deut. 1. 25 they took of the fruit..in their hands
1. 27 deliver us into the hand of the Amorites
2. 7 blessed thee in all the works of thy hand
2. 15 the hand of the LORD was against them
2. 24 I have given into thine hand Sihon the
2. 30 that he might deliver him into thy hand
3. 2 I will deliver him..into thy hand; and
3. 3 LORD our God delivered into our hands
3. 8 out of the hand of the two kings of the
3. 24 show..thy greatness, and thy mighty ha.
4. 28 shall serve gods, the work of men's hands
4. 34 wonders, and by war, and by a mighty h.
5. 15 brought thee out..through a mighty ha.
6. 8 shalt bind them for a sign upon thine h.
6. 21 brought us out of Egypt with a mighty h.
7. 8 LORD brought you out with a mighty ha.
7. 8 from the hand of Pharaoh king of Egypt
7. 19 the mighty hand, and the stretched out
7. 24 he shall deliver their kings into thine h.
8. 17 the might of (mine) hand hath gotten me
9. 15 two tables of the covenant..in my two h.
9. 17 tables, and cast them out of my two ha.
9. 26 brought..out of Egypt with a mighty ha.
10. 3 up..having the two tables in mine hand
11. 2 your God, his greatness, his mighty hand
11. 18 and bind them for a sign upon your hand
12. 6 heave offerings of your hand, and your
12. 7 rejoice in all that ye put your hand unto
12. 11 the heave offering of your hand, and all
12. 17 offerings, or heave offering of thine hand
12. 18 in all that thou puttest thine hands unto
13. 9 thine hand shall be first upon him to put
13. 9 and afterwards the hand of all the people
13. 17 nought of the cursed thing to thine hand
14. 25 bind up the money in thine hand, and
14. 29 bless thee in all the work of thine hand
15. 3 with thy brother thine hand shall release
15. 7 nor shut thine hand from thy poor brot.
15. 8 thou shalt open thine hand wide unto h.
Deut. 15. 10 and in all that thou puttest thine hand
15. 11 Thou shalt open thine hand wide unto
16. 10 a tribute of a freewill offering of thine h.
16. 15 bless thee..in all the works of thine ha.
17. 7 The hands of the witnesses shall be first
17. 7 and afterward the hands of all the people
19. 5 his hand fetcheth a stroke with the ax to
19. 12 deliver him into the hand of the avenger of
19. 21 tooth for tooth, hand for hand, foot for f.
20. 13 thy God hath delivered it into thine hand
21. 6 shall wash their hands over the heifer
21. 7 Our hands have not shed this blood, nei.
21. 10 God hath delivered them into thine hand
23. 20 in all that thou settest thine hand to in
23. 25 thou mayest pluck the ears with thine h.
24. 1 give (it) in her hand, and send her out of
24. 3 giveth (it) in her hand, and sendeth her
24. 19 may bless thee in..the work of thine hand
25. 11 out of the hand of him that smiteth him
25. 11 putteth forth her hand, and taketh him
26. 4 priest shall take the basket out of thine h.
26. 8 brou. us..out of Egypt with a mighty h.
27. 15 the work of the hands of the craftsman
28. 8, 20 all that thou settest thine hand unto
28. 12 and to bless all the work of thine hand
28. 32 and (there shall be) no might in thine h.
30. 9 thee plenteous in every work of thine h.
31. 29 to anger through the work of your hands
32. 27 lest they should say, Our hand (is) high
32. 39 neither..that can deliver out of my hand
32. 40 I lift up my hand to heaven, and say, I
32. 41 If..mine hand take hold on judgment, I
33. 3 all his saints (are) in thy hand: and they
33. 7 let his hands be sufficient for him; and
33. 11 Bless..and accept the work of his hands
34. 9 for Moses had laid his hands upon him
34. 12 And in all that mighty hand, and in all
Josh. 2. 19 blood..on our head, if (any) hand be upon
2. 24 LORD hath delivered into our hands all
4. 24 That all..might know the hand of the L.
5. 13 a man..with his sword drawn in his hand
6. 2 See, I have given into thine hand Jericho
7. 7 to deliver us into the hand of the Amor.
8. 1 I have given into thy hand the king of A.
8. 7 LORD your God will deliver it into your h.
8. 18 Stretch out the spear that (is) in thy hand
8. 18 for I will give it into thine hand. And J.
8. 18 stretched out the spear..in his hand to.
8. 19 as soon as he had stretched out his hand
8. 26 Joshua drew not his hand back, where.
9. 25 And now, behold, we (are) in thine hand
9. 26 delivered them out of the hand of the c.
10. 6 Slack not thy hand from thy servants
10. 8 for I have delivered them into thine hand
10. 19 God hath delivered them into your hand
10. 30 LORD delivered it also..into the hand of
10. 32 LORD delivered Lachish into the hand of
11. 8 LORD delivered them into the hand of I.
14. 2 as the LORD commanded by the hand of
20. 2 whereof I spake unto you by the hand of
20. 5 not deliver the slayer up into his hand
20. 9 not die by the hand of the avenger of b.
21. 2, 8 LORD commanded by the hand of Mo.
21. 44 LORD delivered..enemies into their hand
22. 9 to the word of the LORD by the hand of
22. 31 children of Israel out of the hand of the
24. 8 I gave them into your hand, that ye mi.
24. 10 Balaam..so I delivered you out of his ha.
24. 11 and I delivered them into your hand
Judg. 1. 2 I have delivered the land into his hand
1. 4 delivered..the Perizzites into their hand
1. 35 the hand of the house of Joseph prevail.
2. 14 into the hands of spoilers that spoiled
2. 14 sold them into the hands of their enem.
2. 15 the hand of the LORD was against them
2. 16 out of the hand of those that spoiled them
2. 18 out of the hand of their enemies all the
2. 23 neither delivered he them into the hand
3. 4 commanded their fathers by the hand of
3. 8 and he sold them into the hand of Chus.
3. 10 of Mesopotamia into his hand; and his h.
3. 15 Ehud..a Benjamite, a man left handed
3. 21 Ehud put forth his left hand, and took
3. 28 your enemies the Moabites into your ha.
3. 30 So Moab was subdued..under the hand
4. 2 LORD sold them into the hand of Jabin
4. 7 and I will deliver him into thine hand
4. 9 shall sell Sisera into the hand of a woman
4. 14 LORD hath delivered Sisera into thine h.
4. 21 Then Jael..took an hammer in her hand
4. 24 the hand of the children of Israel prosp.
5. 26 She put her hand to the nail, and her r.h.
6. 1 them into the hand of Midian seven years
6. 2 the hand of Midian prevailed against Isr.
6. 9 I delivered you out of the hand of the E.
6. 9 out of the hand of all that oppressed you
6. 21 the end of the staff that (was) in his hand
6. 36, 37 thou wilt save Israel by mine hand
7. 2 me to give the Midianites into their hand
7. 2 saying, Mine own hand hath saved me
7. 6 of them that lapped..their hand to
7. 7 and deliver the Midianites into thine h.
7. 8 So the people took victuals in their hand
7. 9 for I have delivered it into thine hand
7. 11 afterward shall thine hands be strength.
7. 14 into his hand hath God delivered Midian
7. 15 LORD hath delivered into your hand the
7. 16 he put a trumpet in every man's hand
7. 19 brake the pitchers that (were) in their h.
7. 20 and held the lamps in their left hands
7. 20 and the trumpets in their right hands to
8. 3 God hath delivered into your hands the

Judg. 8. 6, 15 Are..Zebah and Zalmunna..in thine h.
8. 7 delivered Zebah and Zalmunna into mine h.
8. 22 thou hast delivered us from the hand of
8. 34 out of the hands of all their enemies on
9. 16 according to the deserving of his hands
9. 17 delivered you out of the hand of Midian
9. 29 to God this people were under my hand!
9. 48 Abimelech took an ax in his hand, and
10. 7 sold them into the hands of the Philistines
10. 7 into the hands of the children of Ammon
10. 12 cried..and I delivered you out of their h.
11. 21 Sihon and all his people into the hand of
11. 30 the children of Ammon into mine hands
11. 32 and the LORD delivered them into his h.
12. 2 called..ye delivered me not out of their h.
12. 3 the LORD delivered them into my hand
13. 1 LORD delivered them into the hand of
13. 5 deliver Israel out of the hand of the Ph.
13. 23 received..a meat offering at our hands
14. 6 and (he had) nothing in his hand: but
15. 12 deliver thee into the hand of the Philis.
15. 13 bind thee..and deliver thee into their h.
15. 14 and his bands loosed from off his hands
15. 15 put forth his hand and took it, and slew
15. 17 he cast away the jawbone out of his hand
15. 18 given this great deliverance into the hand
15. 18 and fall into the hand of the uncircum.?
16. 18 came up..and brought money in their h.
16. 23 delivered Samson our enemy into our h.
16. 24 Our god hath delivered into our hands
16. 26 said unto the lad that held him by the h.
17. 3 the silver..from my hand for my son, to
18. 10 for God hath given it into your hands
18. 19 lay thine hand upon thy mouth, and go
19. 27 and her hands (were) upon the threshold
20. 28 Go up..I will deliver them into thine h.
Ruth 1. 13 the hand of the LORD is gone out against
4. 5 What day thou buyest the field of the h.
4. 9 that I have bought all..of the hand of N.
1 Sa. 2. 13 with a flesh hook of three teeth in his h.
4. 8 out of the hand of these mighty gods?
5. 4 the palms of his hands (were) cut off upon
5. 6 the hand of the LORD was heavy upon
5. 7 his hand is sore upon us, and upon Dagon
5. 9 the hand of the LORD was against the city
5. 11 the hand of God was very heavy there
6. 3 known..why his hand is not removed
6. 5 peradventure he will lighten his hand
6. 9 then we shall know that (it is) not his h.
7. 3 he will deliver you out of the hand of the
7. 8 he will save us out of the hand of the P.
7. 13 the hand of the LORD was against the P.
7. 14 did Israel deliver out of the hands of the
9. 8 I have here at hand the fourth part of a
9. 16 he may save my people out of the hand
10. 4 which thou shalt receive of their hands
10. 18 delivered you out of the hand of the Eg.
10. 18 and out of the hand of all kingdoms, (and)
11. 7 sent (them)..by the hands of messengers
12. 3 of whose hand have I received (any) bribe
12. 4 neither..taken ought of any man's hand
12. 5 that ye have not found ought in my hand
12. 9 he sold them into the hand of Sisera, ca.
12. 9 and into the hand of the Philistines
12. 9 and into the hand of the king of Moab
12. 10 deliver us out of the hand of our enemies
12. 11 delivered you out of the hand of your en.
12. 15 then shall the hand of the LORD be again.
13. 22 neither sword nor spear found in the ha.
14. 10 hath delivered them into our hand: and
14. 12 delivered them into the hand of Israel
14. 13 And Jonathan climbed up upon his hands
14. 19 and Saul said..Withdraw thine hand
14. 26 no man put his hand to his mouth: for
14. 27 the end of the rod..in his hand, and dip.
14. 27 and put his hand to his mouth; and his
14. 37 wilt thou deliver them into the hand of I.
14. 43 the end of the rod that (was) in mine ha.
14. 48 out of the hands of them that spoiled
16. 16 that he shall play with his hand, and thou
16. 23 took an harp, and played with his hand
17. 22 left his carriage in the hand of the keeper
17. 37 he will deliver me out of the hand of this
17. 40 he took his staff in his hand, and chose
17. 40 his sling (was) in his hand: and he drew
17. 46 will the LORD deliver thee into mine ha.
17. 47 and he will give you into our hands
17. 49 David put his hand in his bag, and took
17. 50 (there was) no sword in the hand of Da.
17. 57 the head of the Philistine in his hand
18. 10 and David played with his hand, as at
18. 10 and (there was) a javelin in Saul's hand
18. 17 Let not mine hand be upon him, but
18. 17 let the hand of the Philistines be upon h.
18. 21 that the hand of the Philistines may be
18. 25 make David fall by the hand of the Phil.
19. 9 his hand: and David played with (his) h.
20. 16 require (it) at the hand of David's enemies
21. 3 Now therefore what is under thine hand?
21. 3 give (me) five (loaves of) bread in mine hand
21. 4 no common bread under mine hand; but
21. 8 is there not here under thine hand spear
21. 13 and feigned himself mad in their hands
22. 6 now Saul..having his spear in his hand
22. 17 because their hand also (is) with David
22. 17 would not put forth their hand to fall
23. 4 deliver the Philistines into thine hand
23. 6 came down (with) an ephod in his hand
23. 7 God hath delivered him into mine hand
23. 11 Will the men..deliver me..into his hand?
23. 12 me and my men into the hand of Saul?
23. 14 but God delivered him not into his hand
1 Sa. 23. 16 Jonathan..strengthened his hand in God
23. 17 the hand of Saul..shall not find thee
23. 20 to deliver him into the king's hand
24. 4 deliver thine enemy into thine hand, that
24. 6 to stretch forth mine hand against him
24. 10 delivered thee to day into mine hand in
24. 10 not put forth mine hand against my lord
24. 11 see the skirt of thy robe in my hand: for
24. 11 evil nor transgression in mine hand, and
24. 12, 13 but mine hand shall not be upon thee
24. 15 plead..and deliver me out of thine hand
24. 18 the LORD had delivered me into thine h.
24. 20 Israel shall be established in thine hand
25. 8 give..whatsoever cometh to thine hand
25. 26 from avenging thyself with thine own h.
25. 33 from avenging myself with mine own ha.
25. 35 So David receiv d of her hand (that)
25. 39 of my reproach from the hand of Nabal
26. 8 delivered thine enemy into thine hand
26. 9 who can stretch forth his hand against
26. 11 that I should stretch forth mine hand
26. 18 have I done? or what evil (is) in mine h.?
26. 23 for the LORD delivered thee into (my) h.
26. 23 but I would not stretch forth mine hand
27. 1 now perish one day by the hand of Saul
27. 1 despair..so shall I escape out of his hand
28. 17 hath rent the kingdom out of thine hand
28. 19, 19 deliver..into the hand of the Philis.
30. 15 nor deliver me into the hands of my mas.
30. 23 and delivered the company..into our ha.
2 Sa. 1. 14 to stretch forth thine hand to destroy the
2. 7 now let your hands be strengthened, and
3. 8 not delivered thee into the hand of David
3. 12 and, behold, my hand (shall be) with thee
3. 18 saying, By the hand of my servant David
3. 18 save..out of the hand of the Philistines
3. 18 and out of the hand of all their enemies
3. 34 Thy hands (were) not bound, nor thy feet
4. 1 his hands were feeble, and all the Israel.
4. 11 shall I not..require his blood of your h.
4. 12 and cut off their hands and their feet, and
5. 19 wilt thou deliver them into mine hand?
5. 19 deliver the Philistines into thine hand
8. 1 took..out of the hand of the Philistines
10. 2 to comfort him by the hand of his serv.
10. 10 he delivered into the hand of Abishai his
11. 14 wrote a letter..and sent (it) by the hand
12. 7 I delivered thee out of the hand of Saul
12. 25 he sent by the hand of Nathan the prop.
13. 5 that I may see (it), and eat (it) at her ha.
13. 6 in my sight, that I may eat at her hand
13. 10 Bring the meat..that I may eat of thine h.
13. 19 laid her hand on her head, and went on
14. 19 (Is not) the hand of Joab with thee in all
15. 5 he put forth his hand, and took him, and
16. 8 delivered the kingdom into the hand of
16. 21 then shall the hands of all..be strong
18. 2 a third part..under the hand of Joab
18. 2 a third part under the hand of Abishai
18. 2 a third part under the hand of Ittai the
18. 12 put forth mine hand against the king's
18. 28 that lifted up their hand against my lord
20. 9 Amasa by the beard with the right hand
20. 10 took no heed to the sword..in Joab's h.
20. 21 hath lifted up his hand against the king
21. 9 he delivered them into the hands of the G.
21. 20 a man..that had on every hand six fing.
21. 22 fell by the hand of David, and by the ha.
22. 21 according to the cleanness of my hands
22. 35 He teacheth my hands to war; so that a
23. 6 because they cannot be taken with hands
23. 10 until his hand was weary, and his hand
23. 21 and the Egyptian had a spear in his hand
23. 21 plucked the spear out of the Egyptian's h.
24. 14 let us fall now into the hand of the LORD
24. 14 and let me not fall into the hand of man
24. 16 when the angel stretched out his hand
24. 16 said..It is enough; stay now thine hand
24. 17 Let thine hand, I pray thee, be against
1 Ki. 2. 25 king Solomon sent by the hand of Benai.
2. 46 the kingdom was established in the hand
8. 15 and hath with his hand fulfilled (it), say.
8. 24 hast fulfilled (it) with thine hand, as (it is)
8. 42 For they shall hear..of thy strong hand
8. 53 as thou spakest by the hand of Moses thy
8. 56 which he promised by the hand of Moses
11. 12 I will rend it out of the hand of thy son
11. 26 even he lifted up (his) hand against the
11. 27 the cause that he lifted up (his) hand
11. 31 I will rend the kingdom out of the hand
11. 34 not..the whole kingdom out of his hand
11. 35 I will take the kingdom out of his son's h.
13. 4 that he put forth his hand from the altar
13. 4 And his hand..dried up, so that he could
13. 6 that my hand may be restored me again
13. 6 the king's hand was restored him again
14. 18 which he spake by the hand of his serv.
14. 27 unto the hands of the chief of the guard
15. 18 them into the hand his servants
16. 7 also by the hand of the prophet Jehu the
16. 7 provoking him..with the work of his ha.
17. 11 Bring me..a morsel of bread in thine h.
18. 9 wouldest eliver thy servant into the ha.
18. 46 And the hand of the LORD was on Elijah
20. 6 they shall put (it) in their hand, and take
20. 13 I will deliver t in o thine hand this day
20. 28 deliver all this..multitude into thine ha.
20. 42 thou hast let go ut f (thy) hand a man
22. 3 take it not out of he hand of the king of
22. 6, 15 LORD shall deliver (it) into the hand
22. 12 shall deliver (it) into the king's hand
22. 34 Turn thine hand, and carry me out of
2 Ki. 3. 10, 13 to deliver them into the hand of Mo.
3. 11 which poured water on the hands of Eli.
3. 15 that the hand of the LORD came upon him
3. 18 deliver the Moabites also into your hand
4. 29 take my staff in thine hand, and go thy
5. 11 and strike his hand over the place, and
5. 18 he leaneth on my hand, and I bow myse.
5. 20 in not receiving at his hands that which
5. 24 he took (them) from their hand, and besto.
6. 7 And he put out his hand, and took it
7. 2 a lord on whose hand the king leaned
7. 17 appointed the lord on whose hand he le.
8. 8 Take a present in thine hand, and go, meet
8. 20, 22 Edom revolted from under the hand
9. 1 take this box of oil in thine hand, and go
9. 7 avenge the blood..at the hand of Jezebel
9. 23 Joram turned his hands, and fled, and said
9. 35 and the feet, and the palms of (her) hands
10. 15 give..thine hand. And he gave..his ha.
10. 24 men whom I have brought into your ha.
11. 8 every man with his weapons in his hand
11. 11 every man with his weapons in his hand
11. 16 And they laid hands on her; and she went
12. 11 gave the money..into the hands of them
12. 15 the men into whose hand they delivered
13. 3 delivered them into the hand of Hazael
13. 3 and into the hand of Ben-hadad the son
13. 5 they went out from under the hand of the
13. 16 Put thine hand upon..he put his hand
13. 16 Elisha put his hands upon the king's ha.
13. 25 took again out of the hand of Ben-hadad
13. 25 cities which he had taken out of the hand
14. 5 as the kingdom was confirmed in his hand
14. 25 he spake by the hand of his servant Jonah
14. 27 he saved them by the hand of Jeroboam
15. 19 hand..to confirm the kingdom in his hand
17. 7 from under the hand of Pharaoh king of
17. 20 delivered them into the hand of spoilers
17. 39 deliver you out of the hand of all your
18. 29 not be able to deliver you out of his hand
18. 30 shall not be delivered into the hand of
18. 33 delivered at all his land of the hand of
18. 34 they delivered Samaria out of mine hand?
18. 35 delivered their country out of mine hand
18. 35 should deliver Jerusalem out of mine ha.?
19. 10 delivered into the hand of the king of A.
19. 14 Hezekiah received the letter of the hand
19. 18 no gods, but the work of men's hands, wood
19. 19 save thou us out of his hand, that all the
21. 14 deliver them into the hand of their ene.
22. 5 let them deliver it into the hand of the
22. 7 money that was delivered into their hand
22. 9 into the hand of them that do the work
22. 17 provoke me..with..works of their hand
1 Ch. 4. 10 that thine hand might be with me, and
5. 10 with the Hagarites, who fell by their hand
5. 20 Hagarites were delivered into their hand
6. 15 carried..by the hand of Nebuchadnezzar
11. 23 in the Egyptian's hand (was) a spear like
11. 23 plucked the spear out of..Egyptian's hand
13. 9 Uzza put forth his hand to hold the ark
13. 10 he put his hand to the ark: and there he
14. 10 wilt thou deliver them into mine hand?
14. 10 for I will deliver them into thine hand
14. 11 broken in upon mine enemies by mine h.
16. 7 into the hand of Asaph and his brethren
18. 1 towns out of the hand of the Philistines
19. 11 unto the hand of Abishai his brother, and
20. 8 fell by the hand of David, and by the h.
21. 13 let me fall now into the hand of the LORD
21. 13 but let me not fall into the hand of man
21. 15 said..It is enough, stay now thine hand
21. 16 having a drawn sword in his hand stret.
21. 17 Let thine hand, I pray thee, O LORD my
22. 18 inhabitants of the land into mine hand
25. 2 under the hands of Asaph, which proph.
25. 3 under the hands of their father Jeduthun
25. 6 these (were) under the hands of their fa.
26. 28 (it was) under the hand of Shelomith, and
28. 19 understand in writing by (his) hand upon
29. 5 (to be made) by the hands of artificers
29. 8 by the hand of Jehiel the Gershonite
29. 12 hand (is) power and might; and in thine h.
29. 16 this store..(cometh) of thine hand, and
2 Ch. 6. 4 who hath with his hands fulfilled (that)
6. 15 hast fulfilled (it) with thine hand, as (it
6. 32 thy mighty hand, and thy stretched out
8. 18 sent him, by the hands of his servants
10. 15 which he spake by the hand of Ahijah the
12. 5 I also left you in the hand of Shishak
12. 7 out upon Jerusalem by the hand of Shis.
12. 10 to the hands of the chief of the guard
13. 8 kingdom..in the hand of the sons of D.
13. 16 and God delivered them into their hand
15. 7 let not your hands be weak: for your wo.
16. 7 king of Syria escaped out of thine hand
16. 8 LORD, he delivered them into thine hand
17. 5 LORD stablished the kingdom in his hand
18. 5 God will deliver (it) into the king's hand
18. 11 shall deliver (it) into the hand of the king
18. 14 they shall be delivered into your hand
18. 33 Turn thine hand, that thou mayest carry
20. 6 and in thine hand (is there not) power and
21. 10 under the hand of Judah unto this day
21. 10 did Libnah revolt from under his hand
23. 7 every man with his weapons in his hand
23. 10 every man having his weapon in his ha.
23. 15 they laid hands on her: and when she was
23. 18 by the hand of the priests the Levites
24. 11 was brought..by the hand of the Levites
24. 24 delivered a..great host into their hand
25. 15 deliver their own people out of thine ha.?

2 Ch.25. 20 deliver them into the hand (of..enemies)
26. 11 account by the hand of Jeiel the scribe
26. 11 under the hand of Hananiah, (one) of the
26. 13 under their hand (was) an army, three
26. 19 (had) a censer in his hand to burn incense
28. 5 him into the hand of the king of Syria
28. 5 into the hand of the king of Israel, who
28. 9 he hath delivered them into your hand
29. 23 and they laid their hands upon them
30. 12 hand of God was to give them one heart
30. 16 (they received) of the hand of the Levites
31. 13 (were) overseers under the hand of Con.
32. 13 to deliver their lands out of mine hand?
32. 14 could deliver his people out of mine hand
32. 14 be able to deliver you out of mine hand?
32. 15 out of mine hand, and out of the hand of
32. 15 your God deliver you out of mine hand?
32. 17 delivered their people out of mine hand
32. 17 deliver his people out of mine hand
32. 19 (which were) the work of the hands of m.
32. 22 saved..from the hand of Sennacherib the
32. 22 and from the hand of all (other), and
33. 8 and the ordinances by the hand of Moses
34. 9 of the hand of Manasseh and Ephraim
34. 10 they put (it) in the hand of the workmen
34. 17 the hand of..overseers, and to the hand
34. 25 provoke me..with..the works of their ha.
35. 6 the word of the LORD by the hand of M.
35. 11 sprinkled (the blood) from their hands
36. 17 he gave (them) all into his hand
Ezra 1. 6 strengthened their hands with vessels of
1. 8 by the hand of Mithredath the treasurer
4. 4 weakened the hands of the people of Ju.
6. 22 to strengthen their hands in the work of
7. 6 to the hand of the LORD his God upon
7. 9 to the good hand of his God upon him
7. 28 the hand of the LORD my God (was) upon
8. 18 by the good hand of our God upon us
8. 22 The hand of our God (is) upon all them
8. 26 even weighed unto their hand six hundr.
8. 31 the hand of our God was upon us, and
8. 33 by the hand of Meremoth the son of U.
9. 2 the hand of the princes and rulers hath
9. 7 into the hand of the kings of the lands
10. 19 they gave their hands that they would put
Neh. 1. 10 thou hast redeemed..by thy strong hand
2. 8 according to the good hand of my God
2. 18 I told them of the hand of my God which
2. 18 So they strengthened their hands for (this)
4. 17 with one of his hands wrought in the wo.
6. 5 the fifth time with an open letter in his h.
6. 9 Their hands shall be weakened from the
6. 9 Now therefore, (O God,) strengthen my h.
8. 6 Amen, Amen, with lifting up their hands
9. 14 and laws, by the hand of Moses thy serv.
9. 24 and thou..gavest them into their hands
9. 27 into the hand of their enemies, who vex.
9. 27 saved them out of the hand of their ene.
9. 28 leftest thou them in the hand of their en.
9. 30 into the hand of the people of the lands
11. 24 at the king's hand in all matters concer.
13. 21 if ye do (so) again, I will lay hands on you
Esth. 2. 21 sought to lay hand on the king Ahasuer.
3. 6 he thought scorn to lay hands on Morde.
3. 9 to the hands of those that have the char.
3. 10 the king took his ring from his hand, and
5. 2 the golden sceptre that (was) in his hand
6. 2 sought to lay hand on the king Ahasuer.
6. 9 be delivered to the hand of one of the ki.
8. 7 because he laid his hand upon the Jews
9. 2 to lay hand on such as sought their hurt
9. 10 but on the spoil laid they not their hand
9. 15 but on the prey they laid not their hand
9. 16 but they laid not their hands on the prey
Job 1. 10 Thou hast blessed the work of his hands
1. 11 But put forth thine hand now, and touch
1. 12 only upon himself put not forth thine h.
2. 5 But put forth thine hand now, and touch
2. 6 he (is) in thine hand; but save his life
4. 3 and thou hast strengthened the weak ha.
5. 12 so that their hands cannot perform..ent.
5. 15 But he saveth..from the hand of the m.
5. 18 he woundeth, and his hands make whole
6. 9 that he would let loose his hand, and cut
6. 23 Or, Deliver me from the enemy's hand?
6. 23 or, Redeem me from the hand of the mig.?
9. 24 earth is given into the hand of the wick.
9. 33 (that) might lay his hand upon us both
10. 7 none that can deliver out of thine hand
10. 8 Thine hands have made me, and fashion.
11. 14 If iniquity (be) in thine hand, put it far
12. 6 into whose hand God bringeth (abundant.)
12. 9 the hand of the LORD hath wrought this?
12. 10 In whose hand (is) the soul of every living
14. 15 have a desire to the work of thine hand
15. 23 day of darkness is ready at his hand
15. 25 he stretcheth out his hand against God
16. 11 turned me over into the hands of the wi.
17. 3 who (is) he (that) will strike hands with
17. 9 he that hath clean hands shall be strong.
19. 21 for the hand of God hath touched me
20. 10 and his hands shall restore their goods
20. 22 every hand of the wicked shall come
21. 5 be astonished, and lay..hand upon..mo.
21. 16 Lo, their good (is) not in their hand: the
26. 13 his hand hath formed the crooked serpe.
27. 11 I will teach you by the h. of God: (that)
27. 22 spare: he would fain flee out of his hand
28. 9 He putteth forth his hand upon the rock
29. 20 and my bow was renewed in my hand
30. 2 whereto (might) the strength of their h.
30. 21 with thy strong hand thou opposest thy.

Job 30. 24 Howbeit he will not stretch out (his) hand
31. 21 If I have lifted up my hand against the f.
31. 25 and because mine hand had gotten much
31. 27 or my mouth hath kissed my hand
34. 19 for they all (are) the work of his hands
34. 20 mighty shall be taken away without hand
35. 7 givest..or what receiveth he of thine ha.?
37. 7 He sealeth up the hand of every man
40. 4 I will lay mine hand upon my mouth
Psa. 8. 6 dominion over the works of thy hands
10. 12 Arise, O LORD; O God, lift up thine hand
10. 14 mischief..to requite (it) with thy hand
17. 14 From men (which are) thy hand, O LORD
18. *title.* his enemies, and from the hand of Saul
18. 20, 24 according to the cleanness of my ha.
18. 34 He teacheth my hands to war, so that a
21. 8 Thine hand shall find out all thine ene.
22. 16 the wicked..pierced my hands and my
26. 10 In whose hands (is) mischief, and their
28. 2 when I lift up my hands toward thy holy
28. 4 give them after the work of their hands
28. 5 they regard not..the operation of his h.
31. 5 Into thine hand I commit my spirit: thou
31. 8 not shut me up into the hand of the ene.
31. 15 My times (are) in thy hand: deliver me
31. 15 from the hand of mine enemies, and from
32. 4 day and night thy hand was heavy upon
36. 11 let not the hand of the wicked remove
37. 24 for the LORD upholdeth (him with) his h.
37. 33 The LORD will not leave him in his hand
38. 2 fast in me, and thy hand presseth me sore
39. 10 I am consumed by the blow of thine hand
44. 2 didst drive out the heathen with thy hand
55. 20 He hath put forth his hands against such
58. 2 ye weigh the violence of your hands in
68. 31 Ethiopia shall soon stretch out her h.
71. 4 Deliver me..out of the hand of the wic.
73. 23 thou hast holden (me) by my right hand
74. 11 Why withdrawest thou thy hand, even
75. 8 For in the hand of the LORD (there is) a
76. 5 none of the men..have found their hands
77. 20 a flock by the hand of Moses and Aaron
78. 42 They remembered not his hand, (nor) the
78. 61 and his glory into the enemy's hand
80. 17 Let thy hand be upon the man of thy
81. 14 turned my hand against their adversaries
82. 4 rid (them) out of the hand of the wicked
88. 5 and they are cut off from thy hand
89. 13 strong is thy hand, (and) high is thy right
89. 21 With whom my hand shall be established
89. 25 I will set his hand also in the sea, and his
89. 48 deliver his soul from the hand of the g.?
90. 17 establish..the work of our hands upon us
90. 17 yea, the work of our hands establish thou
92. 4 I will triumph in the works of thy hands
95. 4 In his hand (are) the deep places of the
95. 5 he made it; and his hands formed the
95. 7 and we (are)..the sheep of his hand. Tod.
97. 10 delivereth..out of the hand of the wicked
102. 25 and the heavens (are) the work of thy h.
104. 28 thou openest thine hand, they are filled
106. 10 he saved..from the hand of him that ha.
106. 10 redeemed them from the hand of the ene.
106. 26 he lifted up his hand against them, to
106. 41 gave them into the hand of the heathen
106. 42 brought into subjection under their hand
107. 2 redeemed from the hand of the enemy
109. 27 That they may know that this (is) thy h.
111. 7 The works of his hands (are) verity and
115. 4 Their idols (are)..the work of men's hand
115. 7 They have hands, but they handle not
119. 73 Thy hands have made me and fashioned
119. 173 Let thine hand help me: for I have ch.
121. 5 the LORD (is) thy shade upon thy right h.
123. 2 (look) unto the hand of their masters,(and)
123. 2 eyes of a maiden unto the hand of her m.
125. 3 lest the righteous put forth their hands
127. 4 As arrows..in the hand of a mighty man
134. 2 Lift up your hands (in) the sanctuary, and
135. 15 The idols..(are)..the work of men's hands
136. 12 With a strong hand, and..stretched out
138. 7 thou shalt stretch forth thine hand against
138. 8 forsake not the works of thine own hands
139. 10 Even there shall thy hand lead me, and
140. 4 Keep me..from the hands of the wicked
143. 5 thy works; I muse on the work of thy h.
143. 6 I stretch forth my hands unto thee: my
144. 1 the LORD..which teacheth my hands to
144. 7 Send thine hand from above; rid me, and
144. 7 deliver..from the hand of strange child.
144. 11 Rid me..from the hand of strange child.
145. 16 Thou openest thine hand, and satisfiest
149. 6 and a two edged sword in their hand
Prov. 1. 24 I have stretched out my hand, and no m.
3. 27 it is in the power of thine hand to do (it)
6. 5 as a roe from the hand (of the hunter)
6. 5 as a bird from the hand of the fowler
6. 10 slumber, a little folding of the hands to
6. 17 tongue, and hands that shed innocent bl.
10. 4 but the hand of the diligent maketh rich
11. 21 (Though) hand (join) in hand, the wicked
12. 14 the recompence of a man's hands shall be
12. 24 The hand of the diligent shall bear rule
14. 1 foolish plucketh it down with her hands
16. 5 (though) hand (join) in hand, he shall not
17. 16 price in the hand of a fool to get wisdom
19. 24 A slothful (man) hideth his hand in (his)
21. 1 king's heart (is) in the hand of the LORD
21. 25 desire..killeth him; for his hands
24. 33 slumber, a little folding of the hands to
26. 6 sendeth a message by the hand of a fool
26. 9 goeth up into the hand of a drunkard, so

Prov 26. 15 The slothful hideth his hand in (his) bos
30. 28 The spider taketh hold with her hands
30. 32 if thou hast thought evil, (lay) thine hand
31. 19 She layeth her hands to the spindle, and
31. 20 She reacheth forth her hands to the needy
31. 31 Give her of the fruit of her hands; and
Eccl. 2. 11 I looked on..the works..my hands had
2. 24 I saw that it (was) from the hand of God
4. 5 The fool foldeth his hands together, and
5. 6 and destroy the work of thine hands?
5. 14 and (there is) nothing in his hand
5. 15 which he may carry away in his hand
7. 18 also from this withdraw not thine hand
7. 26 snares and nets, (and) her hands (as) ba.
9. 1 the wise..(are) in the hand of God: no
9. 10 Whatsoever thy hand findeth to do, do
10. 18 through idleness of the hands the house
11. 6 in the evening withhold not thine hand
Song 5. 4 My beloved put in his hand by the hole
5. 5 and my hands dropped (with) myrrh, and
5. 14 His hands (are as) gold rings set with the
7. 1 the work of the hands of a..workman
Isa. 1. 12 who hath required this at your hand, to
1. 15 will not hear: your hands are full of bl.
1. 25 will turn my hand upon thee, and purely
2. 8 they worship the work of their own hand
3. 6 and (let) this ruin (be) under thy hand
3. 11 the reward of his hands shall be given him
5. 12 neither consider the operation of his hand
5. 25 stretched forth his hand against them
5. 25 not turned away, but his hand (is) stret.
6. 6 flew one..having a live coal in his hand
8. 11 the LORD spake thus..with a strong hand
9. 12, 17, 21 but his hand (is) stretched out still
10. 4 but his hand (is) stretched out still
10. 5 staff in their hand is mine indignation
10. 10 hand hath found the kingdoms of the idols
10. 13 the strength of my hand I have done (it)
10. 14 my hand hath found as a nest the riches
10. 32 he shall shake his hand (against) the mo.
11. 8 shall put his hand on the cockatrice' den
11. 11 the LORD shall set his hand again the
11. 14 shall lay their hand upon Edom and M.
11. 15 shall he shake his hand over the river
13. 2 shake the hand, that they may go into
13. 7 Therefore shall all hands be faint, and
14. 26 this (is) the hand that is stretched out
14. 27 and his hand (is) stretched out, and who
17. 8 look to the altars, the work of his hands
19. 4 give over into the hand of a cruel lord
19. 16 shaking of the hand of the LORD of hosts
19. 25 Assyria the work of my hands, and Israel
22. 21 will commit thy government into his hand
23. 11 He stretched out his hand over the sea
25. 10 in this mountain shall the hand of the
25. 11 he shall spread forth his hands in the
25. 11 together with the spoils of their hands
26. 11 thy hand is lifted up, they will not see
28. 2 cast down to the earth with the hand
29. 23 the work of mine hands, in the midst of h.
31. 3 the LORD shall stretch out his hand, both
31. 7 own hands have made unto you (for) a
34. 17 hand hath divided it unto them by line
35. 3 Strengthen ye the weak hands, and con.
36. 15 into the hand of the king of Assyria
36. 18 out of the hand of the king of Assyria?
36. 19 they delivered Samaria out of my hand?
36. 20 have delivered their land out of my hand
36. 20 should deliver Jerusalem out of my hand?
37. 10 into the hand of the king of Assyria
37. 14 letter from the hand of the messengers
37. 19 but the work of men's hands, wood and
37. 20 our God, save us from his hand, that all
40. 2 hath received of the LORD'S hand double
41. 20 the hand of the LORD hath done this, and
42. 6 will hold thine hand, and will keep thee
43. 13 (is) none that can deliver out of my hand
44. 5 subscribe (with) his hand unto the LORD
45. 9 makest thou? or thy work, He hath no h.?
45. 11 concerning the work of my hands command
45. 12 my hands, have stretched out the heavens
47. 6 I have..given them into thine hand
48. 13 Mine hand also hath laid the foundation
49. 2 in the shadow of his hand hath he hid me
49. 22 I will lift up mine hand to the Gentiles
50. 2 Is my hand shortened at all, that it can.
50. 11 This shall ye have of mine hand; ye shall
51. 16 covered thee in the shadow of mine hand
51. 17 which hast drunk at the hand of the LORD
51. 18 (is there any) that taketh her by the hand
51. 22 I have taken out of thine hand the cup
51. 23 into the hand of them that afflict thee
53. 10 pleasure of the LORD..prosper in his ha.
56. 2 and keepeth his hand from doing any
57. 10 thou hast found the life of thine hand
59. 1 the LORD'S hand is not shortened, that
60. 21 work of my hands, that I may be glorified
62. 3 Thou shalt..be a crown of glory in the hand

64. 8 and we all (are) the work of thy hand
65. 2 I have spread out my hands all the day
65. 22 shall long enjoy the work of their hands
66. 2 all those (things) hath mine hand made
66. 14 the hand of the LORD shall be known to.
Jer. 1. 9 the LORD put forth his hand, and touched
1. 16 worshipped the works of their own hands
2. 37 thine hands upon thine head: for the L.
6. 9 turn back thine hand as a grape gatherer
6. 12 stretch out my hand upon the inhabitants
6. 24 our hands wax feeble: anguish hath
10. 3 the work of the hands of the workman
10. 9 the work..of the hands of the founder

Jer. 11. 21 Prophesy not..thou die not by our hand
15. 6 will I stretch out my hand against thee
15. 17 I sat alone, because of thy hand: for thou
15. 21 deliver thee out of the hand of the wicked
16. 21 cause them to know mine hand and my
18. 4 vessel..marred in the hand of the potter
18. 6 the potters's hand, so (are) ye in mine h.
19. 7 the hands of them that seek their lives
20. 4 into the hand of the king of Babylon
20. 5 I give into the hand of their enemies
20. 13 soul of the poor from the hand of evil
21. 4 weapons of war that (are) in your hands
21. 5 against you with an outstretched hand
21. 7 hand of Nebuchadrezzar king of Babylon
21. 7 hand of their enemies, and into the hand
21. 10 into the hand of the king of Babylon
21. 12 deliver..out of the hand of the oppressor
22. 3 deliver..out of the hand of the oppressor
22. 24 were the signet upon my right hand, yet
22. 25 into the hand of them that seek thy life
22. 25 the hand of (them) whose face thou fear.
22. 25 the hand of Nebuchadrezzar king of Ba.
22. 25 and into the hand of the Chaldeans
23. 14 strengthen also the hands of evil doers
25. 6, 7 provoke me..with the works of your h.
25. 14 according to the works of their own hands
25. 15 Take the wine cup of this fury at my ha.
25. 17 Then took I the cup at the LORD'S hand
25. 28 refuse to take the cup at thine hand to
26. 14 As for me, behold, I (am) in your hand
26. 24 the hand of Ahikam..was with Jeremiah
26. 24 not give him into the hand of the people
27. 3 by the hand of the messengers which come
27. 6 into the hand of Nebuchadnezzar the ki.
27. 8 until I have consumed them by his hand
29. 3 By the hand of Elasah the son of Shaph.
29. 21 into the hand of Nebuchadrezzar king of
30. 6 every man with his hands on his loins
31. 11 and ransomed him from the hand of (him
31. 32 in the day..I took them by the hand, to
32. 3, 4, 36 into the hand of the king of Babylon
32. 4 shall not escape out of the hand of the C.
32. 21 with wonders, and with a strong hand
32. 24, 25, 28, 43 into the hand of the Chaldeans
32. 28 into the hand of Nebuchadrezzar king
32. 30 provoked me..with the work of their hand
33. 13 pass again under the hands of him that
34. 2 give this city into the hand of the king
34. 3 thou shalt not escape out of his hand
34. 3 shalt..be taken, and delivered into his h.
34. 20 I will even give them into the hand of
34. 20 into the hand of them that seek their life
34. 21 hand of their enemies, and into the hand
34. 21 the hand of the king of Babylon's army
36. 14 Take in thine hand the roll wherein thou
36. 14 took the roll in his hand, and came unto
37. 17 thou shalt be delivered into the hand of
38. 3 This city shall surely be given into the h.
38. 4 thus he weakeneth the hands of the men
38. 4 and the hands of all the people, in speak.
38. 5 the king said, Behold, he (is) in your hand
38. 16 neither will I give thee into the hand of
38. 18 then shall this city be given into the hand
38. 18, 23 thou shalt not escape out of their hand
38. 19 lest they deliver me into their hand, and
38. 23 shalt be taken by the hand of the king of
39. 17 thou shalt not be given into the hand
40. 4 the chains which (were) upon thine hand
41. 5 with offerings and incense in their hand
42. 11 save you, and to deliver you from his h.
43. 3 to deliver us into the hand of the Chalde.
43. 9 Take great stones in thine hand, and hide
44. 8 provoke me..with the works of your hand
44. 25 and fulfilled with your hand, saying, We
44. 30 king of Egypt into the hand of his enem.
44. 30 into the hand of them that seek his life
44. 30 as I gave Zedekiah..into the hand of Ne.
46. 24 shall be delivered into the hand of the
46. 26 I will deliver them into the hand of those
46. 26 and into the hand of Nebuchadrezzar
46. 26 and into the hand of his servants; and
47. 3 shall not look back..for feebleness of h.
48. 37 upon all the hands..cuttings, and upon
50. 15 Shout against her..she hath given her h.
50. 43 his hands waxed feeble: anguish took h.
51. 7 Babylon..a golden cup in the LORD'S hand
51. 25 I will stretch out mine hand upon thee
Lam. 1. 7 when her people fell into the hand of the
1. 10 The adversary hath spread out his hand
1. 14 The yoke..is bound by his hand; they
1. 14 LORD hath delivered me into (their) hand
1. 17 Zion spreadeth forth her hands..none to
2. 7 he hath given up into the hand of the en.
2. 8 he hath not withdrawn his hand from d.
3. 3 he turneth his hand (against me) all the
3. 64 LORD, according to the work of their hand
4. 2 pitchers, the work of the hands of the p.!
4. 6 overthrown..and no hands stayed on her
4. 10 The hands of the pitiful women have so.
5. 6 We have given the hand (to) the Egypti.
5. 8 none that doth deliver..out of their hand
5. 12 Princes are hanged up by their hand: the
Eze. 1. 3 the hand of the LORD was there upon him
1. 8 And..the hands of a man under their w.
2. 9 I looked, behold, an hand (was) sent unto
3. 14 the hand of the LORD was strong upon me
3. 18, 20 his blood will I require at thine hand
3. 22 the hand of the LORD was there upon me
6. 14 So will I stretch out my hand upon them
7. 17 All hands shall be feeble, and all knees
7. 21 I will give it into the hands of the stra.
7. 27 the hands of the people of the land shall

Eze. 8. 1 the hand of the Lord GOD fell there upon
8. 3 he put forth the form of an hand, and
8. 11 with every man his censer in his hand
9. 1 (with) his destroying weapon in his hand
9. 2 every man a slaughter weapon in his ha.
10. 7 cherub stretched forth his hand from be.
10. 8 the form of a man's hand under their w.
10. 12 their whole body..and their hands, and
10. 21 and the likeness of the hands of a man
11. 9 deliver you into the hands of strangers
12. 7 I digged through the wall with mine hand
13. 9 mine hand shall be upon the prophets
13. 21 and deliver my people out of your hand
13. 21 they shall be no more in your hand to be
13. 22 strengthened the hands of the wicked
13. 23 I will deliver my people out of your hand
14. 9 I will stretch out my hand upon him, and
14. 13 then will I stretch out mine hand upon
16. 11 I put bracelets upon thy hands, and a
16. 27 I have stretched out my hand over thee
16. 39 I will also give thee into their hand, and
16. 49 neither did she strengthen the hand of
17. 18 when, lo, he had given his hand, and ha.
18. 8 hath withdrawn his hand from iniquity
18. 17 hath taken off his hand from the poor
20. 5 In the day when I..lifted up mine hand
20. 5 when I lifted up mine hand unto them
20. 6 In the day..I lifted up mine hand unto
20. 15 Yet also I lifted up my hand unto them
20. 22 I withdrew mine hand, and wrought for
20. 23 I lifted up mine hand unto them, also in
20. 28, 42 (for) the which I lifted up mine hand
20. 33 I live..surely with a mighty hand, and
20. 34 I will bring you out..with a mighty hand
21. 7 all hands shall be feeble, and every spirit
21. 11 furbished, to give it into the hand of the
21. 31 deliver thee into the hand of brutish men
22. 14 or can thine hands be strong, in the days
23. 9 into the hand of her lovers, into the hand
23. 28 I will deliver thee into the hand..into t.h.
23. 31 therefore will I give her cup into thine h.
23. 37 blood (is) in their hands, and with their
23. 42 which put bracelets upon their hands, and
23. 45 (are) adulteresses, and blood (is) in their h.
25. 6 Because thou hast clapped..hands, and
25. 7 I will stretch out mine hand upon thee
25. 13 I will also stretch out mine hand upon
25. 14 lay my vengeance upon Edom by the h.
25. 16 I will stretch out mine hand upon the P.
27. 15 many isles..the merchandise of thine h.
28. 9 a man, and no god, in the hand of him
28. 10 Thou shalt die..by the hand of strangers
30. 10 to cease by the hand of Nebuchadrezzar
30. 12 sell the land into the hand of the wicked
30. 12 make the land waste..by the hand of str.
30. 22 will cause the sword to fall out of his h.
30. 24 And I will..put my sword in his hand
30. 25 when I shall put my sword into the hand
31. 11 into the hand of the mighty one of the h.
33. 6 blood will I require at the watchman's h.
33. 8 but his blood will I require at thine hand
33. 22 the hand of the LORD was upon me in the
34. 10 and I will require my flock at their hand
34. 27 delivered them out of the hand of those
35. 3 I will stretch out mine hand against thee
36. 7 thus saith..GOD; I have lifted up mine h.
37. 1 The hand of the LORD was upon me, and
37. 17 and they shall become one in thine hand
37. 19 the stick..which (is) in the hand of Eph.
37. 19 stick, and they shall be one in mine hand
37. 20 the sticks..shall be in thine hand before
38. 12 to turn thine hand upon the desolate pl.
39. 3 I will smite thy bow out of thy left hand
39. 3 thine arrows to fall out of thy right hand
39. 21 and my hand that I have laid upon them
39. 23 and gave them into the hand of their en.
40. 1 in the self same day the hand of the LORD
40. 3 with a line of flax in his hand, and a me.
40. 5 in the man's hand a measuring reed of
44. 12 therefore have I lifted up mine hand
46. 7 according as his hands shall attain unto
47. 3 when the man that had the line in his h.
47. 14 I lifted up mine hand to give it unto your
Dan. 1. 2 LORD gave Jehoiakim..into his hand
8. 4 neither..that could deliver out of his h.
8. 7 none..could deliver the ram out of his h.
8. 25 he shall cause craft to prosper in his hand
8. 25 but he shall be broken without hand
9. 15 of the land of Egypt with a mighty hand
10. 10 And, behold, an hand touched me, which
10. 10 set me upon..the palms of my hands
11. 11 the multitude shall be given into his hand
11. 16 land, which by his hand shall be consumed
11. 41 these shall escape out of his hand..Edom
11. 42 He shall stretch forth his hand also upon
Hos. 2. 10 and none shall deliver her out of mine h.
7. 5 he stretched out his hand with scorners
12. 7 the balances of deceit (are) in his hand
14. 3 neither will..say..to the work of our h.
Joel 3. 8 into the hand of the children of Judah
Amos 1. 8 and I will turn mine hand against Ekron
5. 19 leaned his hand on the wall, and a ser.
7. 7 Lord stood..with a plumb line in his h.
9. 2 into hell, thence shall mine hand take
Mic. 2. 1 because it is in the power of their hand
5. 9 Thine hand shall be lifted up upon thine
5. 12 I will cut off witchcrafts out of thine ha.
5. 13 no more worship the work of thine hands
7. 16 they shall lay..hand upon..mouth, their
Hab. 3. 4 he had horns (coming) out of his hand
3. 10 the deep..lifted up his hands on high
Zeph. 1. 4 I will also stretch out mine hand upon J.

Zeph. 2. 13 he will stretch out his hand against the
2. 15 every one..shall hiss, (and) wag his hand
3. 16 it shall be said to..Zion, Let not thine h.
Hag. 2. 14 so (is) every work of their hands; and
2. 17 I smote you..in all the labours of your h.
Zech. 2. 1 a man with a measuring line in his hand
2. 9 I will shake mine hand upon them, and
4. 9 The hands of Zerubbabel have laid the
4. 9 his hands shall also finish it; and thou
4. 10 shall see the plummet in the hand of Z.
8. 4 every man with his staff in his hand for
8. 9 Let your hands be strong, ye that hear
8. 13 fear not, (but) let your hands be strong
11. 6 into his neighbour's hand, and into the h.
11. 6 and out of their hand I will not deliver
13. 6 What (are) these wounds in thine hands?
13. 7 I will turn mine hand upon the little
14. 13 on the hand of his neighbour, and his h.
14. 13 shall rise up against the hand of his nei.
Mal. 1. 10 neither..accept an offering at your hand
1. 13 should I accept this of your hand? saith
2. 13 receiveth (it) with good will at your hand

3. *Hand*, יד *yad*.
Ezra 5. 8 and this work..prospereth in their hands
5. 12 he gave them into the hand of Nebuch.
6. 12 people that shall put to their hand to
7. 14 the law of thy God which (is) in thine h.
7. 25 wisdom of thy God that (is) in thine hand
Dan. 2. 34 till that a stone was cut out without hand
2. 38 the fowls..hath he given into thine hand
2. 45 was cut out of the mountain without hand
3. 15 God that shall deliver you out of my ha.?
3. 17 he will deliver (us) out of thine hand, O
4. 35 none can stay his hand, or say unto him
5. 5 same hour came..fingers of a man's hand
5. 5 the king saw the part of the hand that
5. 23 God in whose hand thy breath (is), and
5. 24 Then was the part of the hand sent from
7. 25 they shall be given into his hand until a

4. *Palm* (*of the hand*), *sole* (*of the foot*), כף *kaph*.
Gen. 20. 5 in the..innocency of my hands, have I
31. 42 God hath seen..the labour of my hands
40. 11 and I gave the cup into Pharaoh's hand
40. 21 and he gave the cup into Pharaoh's hand
Exod. 4. 4 caught it, and it became a rod in his hand
9. 29 I will spread abroad my hands unto the
9. 33 spread abroad his hands unto the LORD
29. 24 in the hands of Aaron, and in the hands
33. 22 will cover thee with my hand while I
33. 23 I will take away mine hand, and thou
Lev. 8. 27 upon Aaron's hands, and upon his sons' h.
8. 28 Moses took them from off their hands
14. 16 finger in the oil that (is) in his left hand
14. 17 of the rest of the oil that (is) in his hand
14. 18 of the oil that (is) in the priest's hand he
14. 27 of the oil that (is) in his left hand seven t.
14. 28 priest..put of the oil that (is) in his hand
14. 29 rest of the oil that (is) in the priest's hand
Num. 5. 18 put the offering of memorial in her hand
6. 19 shall put..upon the hands of the Nazar.
24. 10 he smote his hands together: and Balak
Deut 25. 12 thou shalt cut off her hand, thine eye
Judg. 6. 13 delivered us into the hands of the Midi.
6. 14 thou shalt save Israel from the hand of
8. 6, 15 (Are) the hands of Zebah and Zalmu.
12. 3 I put my life in my hands, and passed
14. 9 he took thereof in his hands, and went
1 Sa. 4. 3 may save us out of the hand of our ene.
19. 5 he did put his life in his hand, and slew
28. 21 I have put my life in my hand, and have
2 Sa. 14. 16 to deliver his handmaid out of the hand
18. 12 a thousand (shekels) of silver in mine hand
18. 14 he took three darts in his hand, and th.
19. 9 The king saved us out of the hand of our
19. 9 and he delivered us out of the hand of
22. 1 out of the hand of all..out of the hand
1 Ki. 8. 22 and spread forth his hands toward heaven
8. 38 spread forth his hands toward this house
8. 54 from kneeling on his knees with his hand
18. 44 a little cloud out of the sea, like a man's h.
2 Ki. 4. 34 And he..put..his hands upon his hands
11. 12 they clapped their hands, and said, God
16. 7 save me out of the hand of the king of S.
16. 7 and out of the hand of the king of Israel
18. 21 it will go into his hand, and pierce it: so
20. 6 city out of the hand of the king of Assyria
1 Ch. 12. 17 seeing (there is) no wrong in mine hands
2 Ch. 6. 12 And he stood..and spread forth his hands
6. 13 and spread forth his hands toward heaven
6. 29 shall spread forth his hands in this house
30. 6 that are escaped out of the hand of the k
32. 11 shall deliver us out of the hand of the ki.
Ezra 8. 31 he delivered us from the hand of the ene.
9. 5 spread out my hands unto the LORD my
Job 9. 30 and make my hands never so clean
10. 3 shouldest despise the work of thine hands
11. 13 and stretch out thine hands toward him
13. 14 Wherefore do I..put my life in mine h.?
13. 21 Withdraw thine hand far from me; and
16. 17 Not for..injustice in mine hands: also
22. 30 it is delivered by the pureness of thine h.
27. 23 (Men) shall clap their hands at him, and
29. 9 The princes..laid (their) hand on their
31. 7 if any blot hath cleaved to mine hands
41. 8 Lay thine hand upon him, remember the
Psa. 7. 3 O LORD..if there be iniquity in my hands
9. 16 is snared in the work of his own hands
18. *title*. delivered him from the hand of all his
24. 4 He that hath clean hands, and a pure h.
26. 6 I will wash mine hands in innocency: so
44. 20 or stretched out our hands to a strange

Psa. 47. 1 O clap your h.; 63. 4, lift up my h.
71. 4 the hand of the unrighteous and cruel m.
73. 13 I have..washed my hands in innocency
78. 72 guided them by the skilfulness of his ha.
81. 6 his hands were delivered from the pots
88. 9 I have stretched out my hands unto thee
91. 12 They shall bear thee up in (their) hands
98. 8 Let the floods clap (their) hands: let the
119. 48 My hands also will I lift up unto thy com.
119. 109 My soul (is) continually in my hand
128. 2 thou shalt eat the labour of thine hands
129. 7 Wherewith the mower filleth not his hand
139. 5 beset me..and laid thine hand upon me
141. 2 the lifting up of my hands (as) the even.
Prov. 6. 1 thou hast stricken thy hand with a stran.
6. 3 thou art come into the hand of thy friend
10. 4 beco. poor that dealeth (with) a slack h.
17. 18 A man void of understanding striketh h.
22. 26 Be not thou..of them that strike hands
31. 13 and worketh willingly with her hands
31. 16 with the fruit of her hands she planteth
31. 19 the spindle, and her hands hold the dist.
31. 20 She stretcheth out her hand to the poor
Isa. 1. 15 when ye spread forth your hands, I will
28. 4 while it is yet in his hand he eateth it up
33. 15 shaketh his hands from holding of bribes
36. 6 it will go into his hand, and pierce it: so
38. 6 city out of the hand of the king of Assyria
49. 16 graven thee upon the palms of (my) hands
55. 12 all the trees of the field shall clap..hands
59. 3 your hands are defiled with blood, and
59. 6 and the act of violence (is) in their hands
62. 3 and a royal diadem in the hand of thy G.
Jer. 4. 31 spreadeth her hands..Woe (is) me now!
12. 7 I have given..into the hand of her ene.
15. 21 redeem thee out of the hand of the terri.
Lam. 2. 15 All that pass by clap..hands at thee; they
2. 19 lift up thy hands toward him for the life
3. 41 lift up our..hands unto God in the heaven
Eze. 6. 11 Smite with thine hand, and stamp with
21. 14 prophesy, and smite..hands together
21. 17 I will also smite mine hands together
21. 24 ye..come..ye shall be taken with the h.
22. 13 I have smitten mine hand at thy dishon.
29. 7 When they took hold of thee by thy hand
Jon. 3. 8 from the violence that (is) in their hands
Mic. 4. 10 shall redeem thee from the hand of thine
7. 3 That they may do evil with both hands
Nah. 3. 19 all that hear..shall clap the hands over
Hag. 1. 11 a drought..upon all the labour of the hand

5. *Hand* (*and arm*), χείρ *cheir.*
Matt. 3. 12 Whose fan (is) in his hand, and he will
4. 6 in (their) hands they shall bear thee up
5. 30 if thy right hand offend thee, cut it off
8. 3 Jesus put forth (his) hand, and touched
8. 15 he touched her hand, and the fever left
9. 18 come and lay thy hand upon her, and
9. 25 went in, and took her by the hand, and
12. 10 there was a man which had (his) hand
12. 13 Then saith he..Stretch forth thine hand
12. 49 he stretched forth his hand toward his
14. 31 Jesus stretched forth (his) hand, and ca.
15. 2 they wash not their hands when they eat
15. 20 to eat with unwashen hands defileth not
17. 22 shall be betrayed into the hands of men
18. 8 if thy hand or thy foot offend thee, cut
18. 8 rather than having two hands or two feet
19. 13 that he should put (his) hands on them
19. 15 he laid (his) hands on them, and depart.
22. 13 Bind him hand and foot, and take him
26. 23 He that dippeth (his) hand with me in
26. 45 the Son of man is betrayed into the hands
26. 50 Then came they, and laid hands on Jesus
26. 51 stretched out (his) hand, and drew his
27. 24 he took water, and washed (his) hands
Mark 1. 31 he came and took her by the hand, and
1. 41 Jesus..put forth (his) hand, and touched h.
3. 1 was a man there which had a withered h.
3. 3 unto the man which had the withered h.
3. 5 saith unto the man, Stretch forth thine h.
3. 5 his hand was restored whole as the other
5. 23 come and lay thy hands on her, that she
5. 41 he took the damsel by the hand, and said
6. 2 such mighty works are wrought by his h.?
6. 5 save that he laid his hands upon a few
7. 2 with defiled that is..with unwashen hands
7. 3 except they wash (their) hands oft, eat
7. 5 but eat bread with unwashen hands?
7. 32 they beseech him to put his hand upon
8. 23 he took the blind man by the hand, and
8. 23 put his hands upon him, he asked him if
8. 25 he put (his) hands again upon his eyes, and
9. 27 Jesus took him by the hand, and lifted
9. 31 The Son of man is delivered into the hand
9. 43 if thy hand offend thee, cut it off: it is
9. 43 than having two hands to go into hell
10. 16 put (his) hands upon them, and blessed
14. 41 the Son of man is betrayed into the hands
14. 46 they laid their hands on him, and took
16. 18 [they shall lay hands on the sick, and]
Luke 1. 66 And the hand of the Lord was with him
1. 71 and from the hand of all that hate us
1. 74 being delivered out of the hand of our
3. 17 Whose fan (is) in his hand, and he will
4. 11 in (their) hands they shall bear thee up
4. 40 he laid his hands on every one of them
5. 13 he put forth (his) hand, and touched him
6. 1 did eat, rubbing (them) in (their) hands
6. 6 was a man whose right hand was wither.
6. 8 to the man which had the withered hand
6. 10 Stretch forth thy hand. And he did so
Luke 6. 10 his hand was restored whole as the other
8. 54 took her by the hand, and called, saying
9. 44 shall be delivered into the hands of men
9. 62 No man, having put his hand to the plo.
13. 13 he laid (his) hands on her: and immedi.
15. 22 put a ring on his hand, and shoes on (his)
20. 19 the same hour sought to lay hands on
21. 12 they shall lay their hands on you, and
22. 21 the hand of him that betrayeth me (is)
22. 53 ye stretched forth no hands against me
23. 46 Father, into thy hands I commend my s.
24. 7 be delivered into the hands of sinful men
24. 39 Behold my hands and my feet, that it is
24. 40 [he showed them (his) hands and (his) ft.]
24. 50 he lifted up his hands, and blessed them
John 3. 35 and hath given all things into his hand
7. 30 no man laid hands on him, because his h.
7. 44 taken him; but no man laid hands on h.
10. 28 any man pluck them out of my hand
10. 29 able to pluck (them) out of my Father's h.
10. 39 take him: but he escaped out of their h.
11. 44 bound hand and foot with grave clothes
13. 3 had given all things into his hands, and
13. 9 feet only, but also (my) hands and (my)
20. 20 showed unto them (his) hands and his side
20. 25 see in his hands the print of the nails
20. 25 thrust my hand into his side, I will not
20. 27 behold my hands; and reach hither thy h.
21. 18 thou shalt stretch forth thy hands, and
Acts 2. 23 by wicked hands have crucified and slain
3. 7 he took him by the right hand, and lifted
4. 3 they laid hands on them, and put (them)
4. 28 to do whatsoever thy hand and thy coun.
4. 30 By stretching forth thine hand to heal
5. 12 by the hands of the apostles were many
5. 18 laid their hands on the apostles, and put
6. 6 had prayed, they laid (their) hands on th.
7. 25 that God by his hand would deliver them
7. 35 deliverer by the hand of the angel which
7. 41 rejoiced in the works of their own hands
7. 50 Hath not my hand made all these things?
8. 17 Then laid they (their) hands on them, and
8. 18 through laying on of the apostles' hands
8. 19 on whomsoever I lay hands, he may rec.
9. 12 and putting (his) hand on him, that he m.
9. 17 putting his hands on him, said, Brother
9. 41 he gave her (his) hand, and lifted her up
11. 21 the hand of the Lord was with them: and
11. 30 to the elders by the hands of Barnabas
12. 1 the king stretched forth (his) hands to vex
12. 7 And his chains fell off from (his) hands
12. 11 delivered me out of the hand of Herod
12. 17 beckoning unto them with the hand to
13. 3 laid (their) hands on them, they sent (th.)
13. 11 the hand of the Lord (is) upon thee, and
13. 16 beckoning with (his) hand, said, Men of
14. 3 and wonders to be done by their hands
17. 25 Neither is worshipped with men's hands
19. 6 when Paul had laid (his) hands upon them
19. 11 special miracles by the hands of Paul
19. 26 they be no gods which are made with ha.
19. 33 And Alexander beckoned with the hand
20. 34 hands have ministered unto my necessit.
21. 11 bound his own hands and feet, and said
21. 11 deliver (him) into the hands of the Gent.
21. 27 stirred..the people, and laid hands on
21. 40 beckoned with the hand unto the people
23. 19 the chief captain took him by the hand
24. 7 [with..violence took (him)..out of our h.]
26. 1 Paul stretched forth the hand, and ans.
28. 3 came a viper..and fastened on his hand
28. 4 saw the (venomous) beast hang on his h.
28. 8 and laid his hands on him, and healed
28. 17 delivered..into the hands of the Romans
Rom 10. 21 I have stretched forth my hands unto a
1 Co. 4. 12 And labour, working with our own hands
12. 15 I am not the hand, I am not of the body
12. 21 the eye cannot say unto the hand, I have
16. 21 salutation of (me) Paul with mine own h.
2 Co. 11. 33 down by the wall, and escaped his hands
Gal. 3. 19 (it was) ordained by angels in the hand
6. 11 have written unto you with mine own h.
Eph. 4. 28 working with (his) hands the thing which
Col. 4. 18 The salutation by the hand of me Paul
1 Th. 4. 11 and to work with your own hands, as
2 Th. 3. 17 The salutation of Paul with mine own h.
1 Ti. 2. 8 lifting up holy hands, without wrath and
4. 14 laying on of the hands of the presbytery
5. 22 Lay hands suddenly on no man, neither
2 Ti. 1. 6 in thee by the putting on of my hands
Phm. 19 I Paul have written (it) with mine own h.
Heb. 1. 10 the heavens are the works of thine hands
2. 7 [didst set him over the works of thy han.]
6. 2 of laying on of hands, and of resurrection
8. 9 I took them by the hand to lead them out
10. 31 to fall into the hands of the living God
12. 12 lift up the hands which hang down, and
Jas. 4. 8 Cleanse (your) hands, (ye) sinners; and
1 Pe 5. 6 Humble yourselves..under the mighty h.
1 Jo. 1. 1 our hands have handled, of the Word of
Rev. 1. 16 he had in his right hand seven stars; and
1. 17 he laid his right [hand] upon me, saying
6. 5 he..had a pair of balances in his hand
7. 9 with white robes, and palms in their ha.
8. 4 ascended up..out of the angel's hand
9. 20 repented not of the works of their hands
10. 2 he had in his hand a little book open: and
10. 5 the angel..lifted up his hand to heaven
10. 8 in the hand of the angel which standeth
10. 10 the little book out of the angel's hand
13. 16 to receive a mark in their right hand, or
14. 9 (his) mark in his forehead, or in his hand
Rev. 14. 14 having..in his hand a sharp sickle
17. 4 having a golden cup in her hand full of
19. 2 and hath avenged the blood..at her hand
20. 1 angel..having..a great chain in his hand
20. 4 neither..received (his) mark..in their ha.

HAND, at —

1. *Near,* קָרוֹב *qarob.*
Deut 32. 35 for the day of their calamity (is) at hand
Isa. 13. 6 for the day of the LORD (is) at hand; it
Jer. 23. 23 (Am) I a God at hand, saith the LORD
Joel. 1. 15 for the day of the LORD (is) at hand, and
Zeph. 1. 7 for the day of the LORD (is) at hand: for

2. *Nigh,* ἐγγύς *eggus.*
Matt 26. 18 The Master saith, My time is at hand; I
John 2. 13 the Jews' passover was at hand; and Je.
7. 2 the Jews' feast of tabernacles was at hand
Phil. 4. 5 known unto all men. The Lord (is) at h.
Rev. 1. 3 keep those things..for the time (is) at h.
22. 10 he saith unto me..the time is at hand

HAND, to be at hand —

1. *To be near,* קָרַב *qarab.*
Gen. 27. 41 The days of mourning..are at hand; then
Deut 15. 9 saying..the year of release, is at hand
Eze. 12. 23 The days are at hand, and the effect of

2. *To be or come near,* קָרַב *qarab,* 3.
Eze. 36. 8 people of Israel; for they are at hand to

3. *To be or come nigh,* ἐγγίζω *eggizō.*
Matt. 3. 2 Repent..the kingdom of heaven is at hand
4. 17 Repent..the kingdom of heaven is at hand
10. 7 saying, The kingdom of heaven is at hand
26. 45 behold, the hour is at hand, and the Son
26. 46 behold, he is at hand that doth betray me
Mark 1. 15 the kingdom of God is at hand: repent
14. 42 go; lo, he that betrayeth me is at hand
Rom 13. 12 The night is far spent, the day is at hand
1 Pe. 4. 7 But the end of all things is at hand: be

4. *To place in, or upon,* ἐνίστημι *enistēmi.*
2 Th. 2. 2 as that the day of Christ is at hand

5. *To place or set over,* ἐφίστημι *ephistēmi.*
2 Ti. 4. 6 and the time of my departure is at hand

HAND, (some) to lead by the —

1. *To lead by the hand,* χειραγωγέω *cheiragōgeō.*
Acts 9. 8 they led him by the hand, and brought
22. 11 being led by the hand of them that were

2. *One who leads by the hand,* χειραγωγός *cheirag.*
Acts 13. 11 seeking some to lead him by the hand

HAND, out of —

To kill, הָרַג *harag.*
Num 11. 15 kill me, I pray thee, out of hand, if I have

HAND, to take in —

To put hand on, undertake, ἐπιχειρέω *epicheireō.*
Luke 1. 1 many have taken in hand to set forth in

HAND, with one's own —

With one's own hand, αὐτόχειρ *autocheir.*
Acts 27. 19 cast out with our own hands the tackling

HAND BREADTH, hand broad —

1. *Hand breadth,* טֶפַח *tephach.*
1 Ki. 7. 26 it (was) an hand breadth thick, and the
2 Ch 4. 5 the thickness of it (was) an hand breadth
Psa. 39. 5 thou hast made my days (as) an hand br.

2. *Hand breadth,* טֹפַח *tophach.*
Exod 25. 25 a border of an hand breadth round about
37. 12 a border of an handbreath round about
Eze. 40. 5 reed of six cubits..and an hand breadth
40. 43 within (were) hooks, an hand broad, fast.
43. 13 The cubit (is) a cubit and an hand breadth

HANDED. *See* **BROKEN, LEFT, WEAK.**

HANDFUL —

1. *Sheaf,* עָמִיר *amir.*
Jer. 9. 22 as the handful after the harvest man, and

2. *Handful, expansion, superabundance,* פִּסָּה *pissah.*
Psa. 72. 16 There shall be an handful of corn in the

3. *Handful, closed hand,* קֹמֶץ *qomets.*
Gen. 41. 47 the earth brought forth by handfuls
Lev. 6. 15 he shall take of it his handful, of the

4. *Handful, hollow of the hand,* שֹׁעַל *shoal.*
1 Ki. 20. 10 if..dust of Samaria..suffice for handfuls
Eze. 13. 19 handfuls of barley and..pieces of bread

5. *Fulness of the two fists,* מְלֹא חָפְנַיִם [*melo*].
Exod. 9. 8 Take..handfuls of ashes of the furnace

6. *Fulness of the palm of the hand,* מְלֹא כַף *melo kaph.*
Eccl. 4. 6 Better (is) an handful (with) quietness
1 Ki. 17. 12 but an handful of meal in a barrel, and a

7. *Fulness of the closed hand,* מְלֹא קֹמֶץ *melo qomets.*
Lev. 2. 2 take thereout his handful of the flour
5. 12 and the priest shall take his handful of

HANDFUL, to take an —

1. *To take a handful,* קָמַץ *qamats.*
Num. 5. 26 the priest shall take an handful of the

2. *Fill (his) hand,* מלא כפו [*male,* 3]; Lev. 9. 17.

HANDFULS —

Heaps, צְבָתִים *tsebathim.*
Ruth 2. 16 let fall..(some) of the handfuls of purpose

HANDKERCHIEFS —
Napkin, handkerchief, σουδάριον *soudarion.* (*Lat.*)
Acts 19. 12 brought unto the sick handkerchiefs or

HANDLE —
Handle, כַּף *kaph.*
Song 5. 5 dropped..myrrh, upon the handles of the

HANDLE, to — [*See* **SHAMEFULLY.**]
1. *To lay hold,* אָחַז *achaz.*
2 Ch. 25. 5 that could handle spear and shield
2. *To feel, touch,* מוּשׁ *mush,* 5.
Psa. 115. 7 They have hands, but they handle not
3. *To draw out,* מָשַׁךְ *mashak.*
Judg 5. 14 they that handle the pen of the writer
4. *To set in array,* עָרַךְ *arak.*
1 Ch. 12. 8 that could handle shield and buckler
5. *To handle,* תָּפַשׂ *taphas.*
Gen. 4. 21 of all such as handle the harp and organ
Jer. 2. 8 they that handle the law knew me not
46. 9 Libyans, that handle..Lydians, that handl.
50. 16 Cut off..him that handleth the sickle in
Eze. 27. 29 And all that handle the oar, the mariners
38. 4 great company..all of them handling sw.
Amos 2. 15 Neither shall he stand that handleth the
6. *To touch,* θιγγάνω *thigganō.*
Col. 2. 21 Touch not; taste not; handle not
7. *To feel, grope, handle,* ψηλαφάω *psēlaphaō.*
Luke 24. 39 handle me..for a spirit hath not flesh
1 Jo. 1. 1 our hands have handled, of the word

HANDLE deceitfully, to —
To use deceit, δολόω *doloō.*
2 Co. 4. 2 nor handling the word of God deceitfully

HANDLED, to be —
To catch or handle with the palm, תָּפַשׂ בַּכַּף [*taphas*].
Eze. 21. 11 to be furbished, that it may be handled

HANDMAID —
1. *Handmaid,* אָמָה *amah.*
Exod 23. 12 the son of thy handmaid and the stranger
Judg 19. 19 also for me, and for thy handmaid, and
Ruth 3. 9 she answered, I (am) Ruth thine handm.
3. 9 spread..thy skirt over thine handmaid
1 Sa. 1. 11 look on the affliction of thine handmaid
1. 11 remember..and not forget thine handm.
1. 11 wilt give unto thine handmaid a man ch.
1. 16 Count not thine handmaid for a daughter
25. 24 let thine handmaid, I pray thee, speak
25. 24 and hear the words of thine handmaid
25. 25 I thine handmaid saw not the young men
25. 28 forgive the trespass of thine handmaid
25. 31 dealt well..then remember thine handm.
25. 41 Behold, (let) thine handmaid (be) a serv.
2 Sa. 6. 20 eyes of the handmaids of his servants, as
14. 15 will perform the request of his handmaid
14. 16 to deliver his handmaid out of the hand
20. 17 Hear the words of thine handmaid. And
1 Ki. 1. 13 Didst not thou..swear unto thine hand.
1. 17 My lord, thou swarest..unto thine hand.
3. 20 she arose..while thine handmaid slept
Psa. 86. 16 turn..and save the son of thine handm.
116. 16 truly I (am)..the son of thine handmaid
2. *Maid servant,* שִׁפְחָה *shiphchah.*
Gen. 16. 1 and she had an handmaid, an Egyptian
25. 12 Hagar the Egyptian, Sarah's handmaid
29. 24 gave..Zilpah his maid (for) an handmaid
29. 29 gave..Bilhah his handmaid to be her
30. 4 she gave him Bilhah her handmaid to
33. 1 divided the children..unto the two hand.
33. 2 he put the handmaids and their children
35. 25 And the sons of Bilhah, Rachel's handm.
35. 26 And the sons of Zilpah, Leah's handmaid
Ruth 2. 13 has spoken friendly unto thine handm.
1 Sa. 1. 18 Let thine handmaid find grace in thy
25. 27 which thine handmaid hath brought unto
28. 21 thine handmaid hath obeyed thy voice
28. 22 also unto the voice of thine handmaid
2 Sa. 14. 6 thy handmaid had two sons, and they
14. 7 family is risen against thine handmaid
14. 12 Let thine handmaid..speak (one) word
14. 15 thy handmaid said, I will now speak unto
14. 17 Then thine handmaid said, The word of
14. 19 put..words in the mouth of thine hand.
2 Ki. 4. 2 Thine handmaid hath not any thing in
4. 16 Nay..do not lie unto thine handmaid
Prov 30. 23 an handmaid that is heir to her mistress
Isa. 14. 2 possess them..for servants and handm.
Jer. 34. 11 caused the servants and the handmaids
34. 11, 16 brought them into subjection..for h.
34. 16 every man his handmaid, whom he had
Joel 2. 29 upon the servants and..the handmaids
3. *Female slave or servant,* δούλη *doulē.*
Luke 1. 38 Behold the handmaid of the Lord; be it

HAND MAIDEN—
1. *Maid servant,* שִׁפְחָה *shiphchah.*
Gen. 33. 6 Then the handmaidens came near, they
Ruth 2. 13 not like unto one of thine handmaidens
2. *Female slave or servant,* δούλη *doulē.*
Luke 1. 48 regarded the low estate of his handmaiden
Acts 2. 18 on my handmaidens I will pour out in

HANDS on, to lay—
1. *To exercise power,* κρατέω *krateō.*
Matt 18. 28 he laid hands on him, and took (him) by
21. 46 when they sought to lay hands on him
2. *To hold fast, seize,* πιάζω *piazō.*
John 8. 20 no man laid hands on him; for his hour

HANDS, made by or with —
Made by hands, χειροποίητος *cheiropoiētos.*
Mark 14. 58 this temple that is made with hands
Acts 7. 48 dwelleth not in temples made with hands
17. 24 dwelleth not in temples made with hands
Eph. 2. 11 Circumcision in the flesh made by hands
Heb. 9. 11 perfect tabernacle, not made with hands
9. 24 into the holy places made with hands

HANDS, not made with (or without) —
Not made by hands, ἀχειροποίητος *acheiropoiētos.*
Mark 14. 58 I will build another made without hands
2 Co. 5. 1 an house not made with hands, eternal in
Col. 2. 11 with the circumcision made without hands

HANDS, (both) —
Both hands, חָפְנַיִם *chophnayim.*
Lev. 16. 12 hands full of sweet incense beaten small
Eccl. 4. 6 than both the hands full (with) travail
Eze. 10. 2 fill thine hand with coals of fire from
10. 7 into the hands of (him that was) clothed

HAND STAFF —
A staff of the hand, מַקֵּל יָד *maqqel yad.*
Eze. 39. 9 set on fire and burn..the hand staves, and

HAND WRITING —
Written by the hand, χειρόγραφον *cheirographon.*
Col. 2. 14 Blotting out the handwriting of ordinances

HANDY WORK —
Work of the hands, מַעֲשֵׂה יָדַיִם *maaseh yadayim.*
Psa. 19. 1 and the firmament showeth his handywork

HA'-NES, חָנֵס *Mercury.*
A place in Egypt. It is improbable that it was the Heracleopolis Magna in the Heptanomis; but most likely it was identical with Tahpanes, Daphne, a fortified town on the eastern frontier of Egypt.
Isa. 30. 4 at Zoan, and his ambassadors came to H.

HANG, to —
1. *To hang up, disjoint,* יָקַע *yaqa,* 5.
2 Sa. 21. 9 hanged them in the hill before the LORD
2. *To give, put,* נָתַן *nathan.*
Exod 26. 32 shalt hang it upon four pillars of shittim
3. *To spread out,* סָרַח *sarach.*
Exod 26. 12 the half curtain..shall hang over the
26. 13 it shall hang over the sides of the taber.
4. *To hang up,* תָּלָא *tala.*
2 Sa. 21. 12 where the Philistines had hanged them
5. *To hang up,* תָּלָה *talah.*
Gen. 40. 19 Pharaoh..shall hang thee on a tree; and
40. 22 But he hanged the chief baker: as Joseph
41. 13 so it was; me he restored..him he hanged
Deut 21. 22 put to death, and thou hang him on a
Josh. 8. 29 the king of Ai he hanged on a tree until
10. 26 slew them, and hanged them on five trees
2 Sa. 4. 12 hanged (them) up over the pool in Hebron
21. 12 where the Philistines had hanged them
Esth. 6. 4 to speak unto the king to hang Mordecai
7. 9 Then the king said, Hang him thereon
7. 10 So they hanged Haman on the gallows
8. 7 him they have hanged upon the gallows
9. 14 and they hanged Haman's ten sons
Job 26. 7 He..hangeth the earth upon nothing
Psa. 137. 2 We hanged our harps upon the willows
Song 4. 4 whereon there hang a thousand bucklers
Isa. 22. 24 they shall hang upon him all the glory
Eze. 15. 3 a pin of it to hang any vessel thereon?
6. *To hang up,* תָּלָה *talah,* 3.
Eze. 27. 10 they hanged the shield and helmet in the
27. 11 they hanged their shields upon thy walls
7. *To hang up or on,* κρεμάννυμι, κρεμάω.
Matt 18. 6 a millstone were hanged about his neck
22. 40 On these two commandments hang all
Luke 23. 39 one of the malefactors which were hanged
Acts 5. 30 Jesus, whom ye slew and hanged on a tree
10. 39 whom they slew and hanged on a tree
28. 4 saw the (venomous) beast hang on his hand
Gal. 3. 13 Cursed (is) every one that hangeth on a

HANG down, to—
1. *To cause to go down, let down,* יָרַד *yarad,* 5.
Lam. 2. 10 the virgins..hang down their heads to
2. *To let down beside,* παρίημι *pariēmi.*
Heb. 12. 12 lift up the hands which hang down, and

HANG in doubt, to—
To hang up, תָּלָא *tala.*
Deut 28. 66 thy life shall hang in doubt before thee

HANG self, to—
1. *To strangle self,* חָנַק *chanaq,* 2.
2 Sa. 17. 23 Ahithophel..hanged himself and died
2. *To strangle self,* ἀπάγχομαι *apagchomai.*
Matt 27. 5 departed, and went and hanged himself

HANG up, to—
1. *To hang up, disjoint,* יָקַע *yaqa,* 5.
Num 25. 4 Take all the heads..and hang them up
2 Sa. 21. 6 we will hang them up unto the LORD in
2. *To give,* נָתַן *nathan.*
Exod 26. 33 And thou shalt hang up the veil under
40. 8 and hang up the hanging at the court

HANGED (up), to be —
1. *To be hanged or disjointed,* יָקַע *yaqa,* 6.
2 Sa. 21. 13 the bones of them that were hanged
2. *To hang up,* תָּלָה *talah.*
Deut 21. 23 for he that is hanged (is) accursed of God
2 Sa. 18. 10 Behold, I saw Absalom hanged in an oak
Esth. 5. 14 that Mordecai may be hanged thereon
9. 13 and let Haman's ten sons be hanged upon
9. 25 that he and his sons should be hanged
3. *To be hanged up,* תָּלָה *talah,* 2.
Esth. 2. 23 therefore they were both hanged on a
Lam. 5. 12 Princes are hanged up by their hand
4. *To smite, hang up,* מְחָא *mecha,* 2.
Ezra 6. 11 being set up, let him be hanged thereon

HANGED about, to be —
To lie around, περίκειμαι *perikeimai.*
Mark 9. 42 a millstone were hanged about his neck
Luke 17. 2 a millstone were hanged about his neck

HANGING —
1. *Houses,* בָּתִּים [*apparently an error*].
2 Ki. 23. 7 the women wove hangings for the grove
2. *A hanging,* מָסָךְ *masak.*
Exod 26. 36 thou shalt make an hanging for the door
26. 37 thou shalt make for the hanging five pil.
27. 16 an hanging of twenty cubits, (of) blue
35. 15 the hanging for the door at the entering
35. 17 and the hanging for the door of the court
36. 37 an hanging for the tabernacle door (of)
38. 18 the hanging for the gate of the court (was)
39. 38 and the hanging for the tabernacle door
39. 40 and the hanging for the court gate, his
40. 5 the hanging of the door to the tabernacle
40. 8 and hang up the hanging at the court
40. 28 he set up the hanging (at) the door of the
40. 33 set up the hanging of the court gate. So
Num. 3. 25 the hanging for the door of the tabernacle
3. 31 the hanging, and all the service thereof
4. 25 the hanging for the door of the tabernac.
4. 26 the hanging for the door of the gate of
3. *Hangings,* קְלָעִים *qelaim.*
Exod 27. 9 hangings for the court (of) fine twined
27. 11 (be) hangings of an hundred (cubits) long
27. 12 (shall be) hangings of fifty cubits
27. 14 hangings of one side (of the gate shall)
27. 15 the other side (shall be) hangings fifteen
35. 17 The hangings of the court, his pillars
38. 9 hangings of the court (were of) fine twined
38. 12 west side (were) hangings of fifty cubits
38. 14 The hangings of the one side (of the gate)
38. 15 that hand, (were) hangings of fifteen cub
38. 16 the hangings of the court round about
38. 18 answerable to the hangings of the court
39. 40 The hangings of the court, his pillars
Num. 3. 26 the hangings of the court, and the cur.
4. 26 And the hangings of the court, and the h.
4. *To hang,* תָּלָה *talah.*
Josh. 10. 26 they were hanging upon the trees until

HAN'-NAH, חַנָּה *grace.*
One of Elkanah's two wives, and mother of Samuel the prophet, while she also herself was a prophetess, as is proved by the prophecy contained in her hymn of thanksgiving for the birth of her son. It is in the highest order of prophetic poetry. It contains the first designation of the "*Messiah,*" under that name. B.C. 1171.
1 Sa. 1. 2 two wives; the name of the one (was) H.
1. 2 Peninnah had children, but H. had no chil.
1. 5 But unto H. he gave a worthy portion
1. 5 for he loved H.: but the Lord had shut
1. 8 H., why weepest thou? and why eatest
1. 9 H. rose up after they had eaten in Shiloh
1. 13 H., she spake in her heart; only her lips
1. 15 H. answered and said, No, my lord; I (am)
1. 19 Elkanah knew H. his wife; and the Lord
1. 20 the time was come about after H. had
1. 22 H. went not up; for she said unto her h
2. 1 H. prayed, and said, My heart..in the L.
2. 21 the Lord visited H, so that she conceived

HAN-NA'-THON, חַנָּתֹן *dedicated to grace.*
A city of Zebulun at a point apparently on the northern boundary, now called *Hannah.*
Josh. 19. 14 compasseth it on the north side to H.

HAN-NI'-EL, HANIEL, חַנִּיאֵל *God is gracious.*
1. A son of Ephod who, as prince of Manasseh, assisted in the division of the land. In the Hebrew text his name is identical with that of Haniel (No. 2). B.C. 1452.
Num. 34. 23 for the tribe..of Manasseh, H. the son of
2. A son of Ulla, a prince and hero of Asher.
1 Ch. 7. 39 the sons of Ulla; Arah, and H., and Re.

HA'-NOCH, HE'-NOCH, חֲנוֹךְ *dedicated.*
1. The third of the children of Midian and a grandson of Abraham by Keturah. In the parallel list in 1 Ch. 1. 33, the name is *Henoch* (as above). B.C. 1800.
Gen. 25. 4 And the sons of Midian; Ephah..and H.
1 Ch. 1. 33 And the sons of Midian; Ephah..and H.
2. The eldest son of Reuben, and founder of the family of the Hanochites. B.C. 1700.
Gen. 46. 9 sons of Reuben; H., and Phallu, and H.
Exod 6. 14 The sons of Reuben..H., and Pallu, Hez.
Num 26. 5 the children of Reuben; H...the family
1 Ch. 5. 3 The sons..of Reuben..H., and Pallu, He

3. The son of Jared, a descendant of Seth, is once thus named. In Genesis his name is given *Enoch*. B.C. 3382-3017.

1 Ch. 1. 3 H., Methuselah, Lamech

HA-NO-CHITES, חֲנֹכִי *belonging to Chanok.*
A family whose founder was Hanoch, the eldest son of Reuben. B.C. 1700.

Num 26. 5 Hanoch..the family of the H.: of Pallu

HA'-NUN, חָנוּן *gracious.*
1. Son of Nahash, king of Ammon, who dishonoured the ambassadors of David and involved the Ammonites in a disastrous war. B.C. 1037.

2 Sa. 10. 1 died, and H. his son reigned in his stead
10. 2 said David, I will show kindness unto H.
10. 3 the princes of..Ammon said unto H. their
10. 4 Wherefore H. took David's servants, and
1 Ch. 19. 2 David said, I will show kindness unto H.
19. 2 servants of David came..to H., to comfort
19. 3 princes of..Ammon said to H., Thinkest
19. 4 Wherefore H. took David's servants, and
19. 6 H...sent a thousand talents of silver to

2. A son of Zalaph who assisted in the repair of the wall of Jerusalem on the E. side. B.C. 445.

Neh. 3. 30 H. the sixth son of Zalaph, another piece

3. A man, who, with the people of Zanoah, repaired the ravine gate in the wall of Jerusalem. B.C. 445.

Neh. 3. 13 The valley gate repaired H., and the in.

HAP —
Chance, event, מִקְרֶה *miqreh.*
Ruth 2. 3 her hap was to light on a part of the

HAPH-RA'-IM, חֲפָרַיִם *double (two) wells, or two pits.*
A city of Issachar next to Shunem. About six miles N.E. of *Lejjun* and two miles W. of *Solam* (the ancient Shunem) stands the village of *el-Afuleh*, which may be the representative of Chaphâraim, the Arabic *Ain* having been substituted for the Hebrew *Cheth.*

Josh 19. 19 And H., and Shihon, and Anaharath

HAPLY (if) —
1. *If, that,* לוּא, לוּ *lu.*
1 Sa. 14. 30 if haply the people had eaten freely
2. *If then,* εἰ ἄρα *ei ara.*
Mark 11. 13 if haply he might find any thing thereon
3. *If then,* εἴ ἄραγε *ei arage.*
Acts 17. 27 if haply they might feel after him, and

HAPLY, lest —
1. *Lest ever, at any time,* μήποτε *mēpote.*
Luke 14. 29 Lest haply, after he..laid the foundation
Acts 5. 39 lest haply ye be found even to fight
2. *Lest by any way or means,* μήπως *mēpōs.*
2 Co. 9. 4 Lest haply if they of Macedonia come

HAPPEN, to —
1. *To meet, happen, befall,* אָנָה *anah,* 4.
Prov 12. 21 There shall no evil happen to the just
2. *To be,* הָיָה *hayah.*
1 Sa. 6. 9 it (was) a chance (that) happened to us
3. *To come to, touch,* נָגַע *naga,* 5.
Eccl. 8. 14, 14 it happeneth according to the work of
4. *To meet, happen,* קָרָא *qara.*
Jer. 44. 23 this evil is happened unto you, as at this
5. *To meet, happen,* קָרָה *qarah,* 2.
2 Sa. 1. 6 I happened by chance upon mount Gilboa
6. *To become, begin to be,* γίνομαι *ginomai.*
Rom 11. 25 blindness in part is happened to Israel
7. *To go or come up together,* συμβαίνω *sumbainō.*
Mark 10. 32 tell..what things should happen unto him
Luke 24. 14 of all these things which had happened
Acts 3. 10 at that which had happened unto him
1 Co. 10. 11 things happened unto them for ensamples
1 Pe. 4. 12 some strange thing happened unto you
2 Pe. 2. 22 it is happened unto them according to

HAPPEN to be, to —
To meet, happen, come, קָרָא *qara,* 2.
2 Sa. 20. 1 there happened to be there a man of Be.

HAPPEN (to or unto), to —
To meet happen, come, קָרָה *qarah.*
1 Sa. 28. 10 punishment happen to thee for this thing
Esth. 4. 7 told him..all that had happened unto him
Eccl. 2. 14 also that one event happeneth to them
2. 15 it happeneth even to m ; and why was I
9. 11 but time and chance happeneth to them
Isa. 41. 22 and show us what shall happen: let them

HAPPENETH —
Chance, event, מִקְרֶה *miqreh.*
Eccl. 2. 15 As it happeneth to the fool, so it

HAPPY, HAPPIER —
1. *To be happy,* אָשַׁר *ashar,* 4.
Prov. 3. 18 and happy (is every one) that retaineth
2. *Happiness,* אֹשֶׁר *osher.*
Gen. 30. 13 Happy am I, for the daughters will call
3. *Happinesses of,* אַשְׁרֵי *ashere.*
Deut 33. 29 Happy (art) thou, O Israel: who (is) like
1 Ki. 10. 8 Happy (are) thy men, happy (are) these
2 Ch. 9. 7 Happy (are) thy men..happy (are) these
Job 5. 17 happy (is) the man whom God correcteth
Psa. 127. 5 Happy (is) the man that hath his quiver
Psa. 128. 2 happy (shalt) thou (be), and (it shall be)
137. 8 happy (shall he be) that rewardeth thee
137. 9 Happy (shall he be) that taketh and das.
144. 15 Happy (is that) people that is in such a
144. 15 happy (is that) people whose God (is) the
146. 5 Happy (is he) that (hath) the God of Jacob
Prov. 3. 13 Happy (is) the man (that) findeth wisdom
14. 21 that hath mercy on the poor, happy (is) he
16. 20 whoso trusteth in the LORD, happy (is) he
28. 14 Happy (is) the man that feareth alway
29. 18 but he that keepeth the law, happy (is) he
4. *Happy,* μακάριος *makarios.*
John 13. 17 these things, happy are ye if ye do them
Acts 26. 2 I think myself happy, king Agrippa, bec.
Rom 14. 22 Happy (is) he that condemneth not him.
1 Co. 7. 40 she is happier if she so abide, after my
1 Pe. 3. 14 suffer for righteousness' sake, happy (are
4. 14 If ye be reproached..happy (are ye)

HAPPY, to be —
To be at rest, safe, שָׁלָה, שָׁלֵו *shalah, shalav.*
Jer. 12. 1 (wherefore) are all they happy that deal

HAPPY, to call or count —
1. *To declare happy,* אָשַׁר *ashar,* 3.
Mal. 3. 15 we call the proud happy; yea, they that
2. *To declare happy,* μακαρίζω *makarizō.*
Jas. 5. 11 Behold, we count them happy which

HA'-RA, הָרָא *hill country.*
A place utterly unknown unless it is identified with Haran or Charran, the city of Mesopotamia to which Abraham came from Ur. Haran was known to the ancients as *Carrhae.* Hence we may conclude that a portion of the Israelites carried off by Pul and Tiglath-pileser were settled in *Harran* on the *Belik*, while the greater number were conveyed to *Chabora.*

1 Ch. 5. 26 H., and to the river Gozan, unto this day

HA-RA'-DAH, חֲרָדָה *terror.*
A desert station, the twentieth encampment of the Israelites in the wilderness, and the ninth from Sinai. Its position is still unknown.

Num 33. 24 from mount Shapher, and encamped in H.
33. 25 they removed from H., and pitched in M.

HA'-RAN, חָרָן, הָרָן *strong, enlightened.*
1. The third son of Terah, Abraham's father, and hence the youngest brother of Abram. He had three children, Lot, and two daughters, viz., Milcah who married her uncle Nahor, and Iscah of whom we have the name only, though by Josephus and others she is held to be identical with *Sarah.* B.C. 1990.

Gen. 11. 26 Terah lived seventy years, and begat..H.
11. 27 Terah begat Ab., Nahor, and H.; and H.
11. 28 H. died before his father Terah in the
11. 29 Nahor's wife, Milcah, the daughter of H.
11. 31 Lot the son of H. his son's son, and Sarai

2. A Gershonite Levite in David's time, and one of the family of Shimei. B.C. 1015.

1 Ch. 23. 9 sons of Shimei; Shelomith..and H., three

3. *Charan.*—A son of Caleb the spy, by his concubine, Ephah; he had a son named *Gazez.* B.C. 1500.

1 Ch. 2. 46 bare H., and Moza, and Gazez: and H.

4. *Charan.*—The place to which Abram with his family migrated from Ur, and where the descendants of his brother Nahor established themselves. Hence Haran (*i.e.*, Charan) is called "the city of Nahor." It was in Padan-aram, which is the cultivated district at the foot of the hills, a beautiful district which lies between the *Khabour* and the Euphrates. (*See* Padan-aram). About midway in the district is a town still called *Haran*, which seems to have held its name through all changes, and is the Haran or Charran of Scripture. Till a recent date the people of *Harran* retained the Chaldean language, and the worship of the Chaldean deities. *Harran* is upon the *Belik* (the ancient *Bilichus*), a small affluent of the Euphrates, and which falls into it at nearly 39° E. longitude. It was famous among the Romans as being near the scene of the defeat of Crassus. In the N.T. the name is given as *Charran.*

Gen. 11. 31 and they came unto H., and dwelt there
11. 32 and Terah died in H.
12. 4 five years old when he departed out of H.
12. 5 and the souls that they had gotten in H.
27. 43 arise, flee thou to Laban my brother to H.
28. 10 Jacob went..from Beer-sheba..toward H.
29. 4 whence (be) ye? And they said, Of H. (are)
2 Ki. 19. 12 Gozan, and H., and Rezeph, and the ch.
Isa. 37. 12 Gozan, and H., and Rezeph, and the ch.
Eze. 27. 23 H., and Canneh, and Eden, the merchant.

These passages may not all refer to the same place.

HA-RA-RITE, הָרָרִי, הָאֲרָרִי, הַהֲרָרִי *mountaineer.*
Thought to denote a native of the hill-country of Judah or Ephraim. B.C. 1048.

2 Sa. 23. 11 after him..Shammah..son of Agee the H.
23. 33 Shammah the H...son of Sharar the H.
1 Ch. 11. 34 Jonathan the son of Shage the H.
11. 35 Ahiam the son of Sacar the H., Eliph.

HAR-BO'-NA, HAR-BO'-NAH, חַרְבוֹנָא, חַרְבוֹנָה *ass-driver.*
Third of the seven eunuchs or chamberlains that served Ahasuerus (Xerxes), king of Persia. B.C. 510.

Esth. 1. 10 On the seventh day..he commanded..H.
7. 9 H., one of the chamberlains, said before

HARD —
1. *Strong,* אֵיתָן, אֵתָן *ethan.*
Prov 13. 15 but the way of transgressors (is) hard
2. *Weighty, heavy,* כָּבֵד *kabed.*
Eze. 3. 5, 6 strange speech and of an hard language
3. *To be wonderful,* פָּלָא *pala,* 2.
2 Sa. 13. 2 Amnon thought it hard for him to do any
4. *Sharp, hard,* קָשֶׁה *qasheh.*
Exod. 1. 14 made their lives bitter with hard bondage
18. 26 the hard causes they brought unto Moses
Deut 26. 6 afflicted..and laid upon us hard bondage
2 Sa. 3. 39 the sons of Zeruiah (be) too hard for me
Isa. 14. 3 from the hard bondage wherein thou wast
5. *Hard to please,* δύσκολος *duskolos.*
Mark 10. 24 how hard is it for them that trust in
6. *Dried up, stiff,* σκληρός *sklēros.*
Matt 25. 24 I knew thee that thou art an hard man
John 6. 60 This is an hard saying; who can hear it?
Acts 9. 5 [hard for thee to kick against the pricks]
26. 14 hard for thee to kick against the pricks
Jude 15 their hard (speeches) which ungodly sin.
[*See also* Follow, go, lie, pursue.]

HARD, to be —
1. *To be firm,* יָצַק *yatsaq.*
Job 41. 24 hard as a piece of the nether (millstone)
2. *To be sharp or hard,* קָשָׁה *qashah.*
Deut. 1. 17 the cause that is too hard for you, bring

HARD, to arise...too —
To be wonderful, פָּלָא *pala,* 2.
Deut 17. 8 arise a matter too hard for thee in judg.

HARD by —
1. *Near,* אֵצֶל *etsel.*
1 Ki. 21. 1 hard by the palace of Ahab king of Sam.
2. *Over against,* עֻמָּה *ummah.*
Lev. 3. 9 shall he take off hard by the back bone

HARD hearted —
Hard or sharp of heart, קְשֵׁה לֵב [*qasheh*].
Eze. 3. 7 all..Israel (are) impudent and hard hear.

HARD (labour), to have or be in —
1. *To have it hard (in bearing),* קָשָׁה *qashah,* 3.
Gen. 35. 16 Rachel travailed, and she had hard lab.
2. *To have it hard (in bearing),* קָשָׁה *qashah,* 5.
Gen. 35. 17 when she was in hard labour, that the

HARD to be understood or uttered —
Hard to be understood, δυσνόητος *dusnoētos.*
2 Pe. 3. 16 some things hard to be under. Heb. 5. 11

HARD question —
Acute saying, hidden thing, חִידָה *chidah.*
1 Ki. 10. 1 she came to prove him with hard questions
2 Ch. 9. 1 came to prove Solomon with hard quest.

HARD, to seem —
To be sharp or hard, קָשָׁה *qashah.*
Deut 15. 18 It shall not seem hard unto thee when

HARD sentences —
Acute saying, hidden thing, אֲחִידָן *achidan.*
Dan. 5. 12 showing of hard sentences, and dissolving

HARD thing, to (ask) a —
To make hard (in asking), קָשָׁה *qashah,* 5.
2 Ki. 2. 10 Thou hast asked a hard thing: (neverth.)

HARD things —
1. *Ancient, stiff,* עָתָק *athaq.*
Psa. 94. 4 shall they utter (and) speak hard things?
2. *Sharp,* s . קָשֶׁה *qasheh.*
Psa. 60. 3 Thou hast showed thy people hard things

HARD, to be too —
To be wonderful, פָּלָא *pala,* 2.
Gen. 18. 14 Is any thing too hard for the LORD? At the
Jer. 32. 17 (and) there is nothing too hard for thee
32. 27 is there anything too hard for me?

HARDEN, to —
1. *To strengthen, harden,* אָמַץ *amats,* 3.
Deut 15. 7 thou shalt not harden thine heart, nor
2 Ch. 36. 13 hardened his heart from turning unto
2. *To be or become strong,* חָזַק *chazaq.*
Exod 7. 13 hardened Pharaoh's heart, that he heark.
3. *To strengthen, harden,* חָזַק *chazaq,* 3.
Exod 4. 21 I will harden his heart, that he shall no
9. 12 the LORD hardened the heart of Pharaoh
10. 20, 27 But the LORD hardened Pharaoh's h.
11. 10 the LORD hardened Pharaoh's heart, so
14. 4 And I will harden Pharaoh's heart, that
14. 8 the LORD hardened the heart of Pharaoh
14. 17 I will harden the hearts of the Egyptians
Josh 11. 20 it was of the LORD to harden their hearts
4. *To make heavy, weighty, or hard,* כָּבֵד *kabed,* 3.
1 Sa. 6. 6 Wherefore then do ye harden your hearts
6. 6 as the Egyptians..hardened their hearts?
5. *To make heavy, hard,* כָּבֵד *kabed,* 5.
Exod. 8. 15 he hardened his heart, and hearkened not
8. 32 Pharaoh hardened his heart at this time
9. 34 hardened his heart, he and his servants
10. 1 I have hardened his heart, and the heart
6. *To make strong, hard, impudent,* עָזַז *azaz,* 5.
Prov 21. 29 A wicked man hardeneth his face: but
7. *To make sharp, hard,* קָשָׁה *qashah,* 5.
Exod. 7. 3 will harden Pharaoh's heart, and multiply
Deut. 2. 30 thy God hardened his spirit, and made

2 Ki.17. 14 would not hear, but hardened their necks
Neh. 9. 16 dealt proudly, and hardened their necks
9. 17 but hardened their necks, and in their
9. 29 hardened their neck, and would not hear
Job 9. 4 who hath hardened (himself) against him
Psa. 95. 8 Harden not your heart, as in the provo.
Prov.28. 14 he that hardeneth his heart shall fall into
29. 1 often reproved, hardeneth (his) neck, shall
Jer. 7. 26 hardened their neck: they did worse
19. 15 because they have hardened their necks

8.*To harden*, קָשַׁח *qashach*, 5.
Isa. 63. 17 (and) hardened our heart from thy fear?

9.*To make hard or callous*, πωρόω *pōroō*.
Mark 8. 17 he saith..have ye your heart yet harde.?
John12. 40 He hath..hardened their heart; that they

10.*To make dry or stiff*, σκληρύνω *sklērunō*.
Rom. 9. 18 Therefore..whom he will he hardeneth
Heb. 3. 8, 15 Harden not your hearts, as in the pro.
4. 7 will hear his voice, harden not your heart

HARDEN self, to —
To exalt, tread upon, סָלַד *salad*, 3.
Job 6. 10 yea, I would harden myself in sorrow: let

HARDENED —
Heavy, כָּבֵד *kaved*.
Exod. 7. 14 Pharaoh's heart (is) hardened, he refuseth

HARDENED, to be —
1.*To be or become strong, hard*, חָזַק *chazaq*.
Exod. 7. 22 Pharaoh's heart was hardened, neither
8. 19 and Pharaoh's heart was hardened, and
9. 35 the heart of Pharaoh was hardened, nei.

2.*To be or become heavy*, כָּבֵד *kabed*.
Exod. 9. 7 the heart of Pharaoh was hardened, and

3.*To harden*, קָשַׁח *qashach*, 5.
Job 39. 16 She is hardened against her young ones

4.*To be or become strong*, תְּקֵף *teqeph*.
Dan. 5. 20 his mind hardened in pride, he was dep.

5.*To make hard or callous*, πωρόω *pōroō*.
Mark 6. 52 considered not..for their heart was har.

6.*To make hard or stiff*, σκληρύνω *sklērunō*.
Acts 19. 9 when divers were hardened, and believed
Heb. 3. 13 lest any of you be hardened through the

HARDER —
Strong, חָזָק *chazaq*.
Eze. 3. 9 As an adamant harder than flint have I

HARDER, to make —
To strengthen, חָזַק *chazaq*, 3.
Jer. 5. 3 have made their faces harder than a rock

HARDLY —
1.*Hard to please*, δυσκόλως *duskolōs*.
Matt19. 23 rich man shall hardly enter into..heaven
Mark10. 23 How hardly shall they that have riches
Luke18. 24 How hardly shall they that have riches

2. *With labour, pain or trouble*, μόγις *mogis*.
Luke 9. 39 bruising him, hardly departeth from him

3. *With toil and fatigue*, μόλις *molis*.
Acts 27. 8 hardly passing it, came unto a place which

HARDLY bestead —
To be or become hardened or sharpened, קָשָׁה *qashah*, 2.
Isa. 8. 21 pass through it hardly bestead and hung.

HARDLY, would —
To harden, sharpen, קָשָׁה *qashah*, 5.
Exod.13. 15 when Pharaoh would hardly let us go

HARDNESS —
1.*Straitness, hardness*, מוּצָק *mutsaq*.
Job 38. 38 When the dust groweth into hardness

2.*Hardness, callousness*, πώρωσις *pōrōsis*.
Mark 3. 5 grieved for the hardness of their hearts

3.*Dryness, hardness*, σκληρότης *sklērotēs*.
Rom. 2. 5 after thy hardness and impenitent heart

HARDNESS of heart —
Dryness or stiffness of heart, σκληροκαρδία *sklēro*.
Matt 19. 8 because of the hardness of your hearts
Mark10. 5 For the hardness of your heart he wrote
16. 14 with their unbelief and hardness of heart

HARDNESS, to endure —
To suffer evil, κακοπαθέω *kakopatheō*.
2 Ti. 2. 3 endure hardness, as a good soldier of J.

HARE —
A hare, אַרְנֶבֶת *arnebeth*.
Lev. 11. 6 the hare, because he cheweth the cud, but
Deut.14. 7 the hare, and the coney: for they chew

HA'-REPH, חָרֵף *early born*.
A son of Caleb the son of Hur, and father of Beth-gader. In Ezra 2. 18, and Neh. 7. 24, *Hariph* occurs. B.C. 1450.
1 Ch. 2. 51 H. the father of Beth-gader.

HA'-RETH, חֶרֶת *thicket*.
A piece of forest land in the hill country of Judah.
1 Sa. 22. 5 departed, and came into the forest of H.

HAR-HA'-IAH, חַרְהֲיָה *Jah is protecting*.
Father of Uzziel who repaired a part of the wall of Jerusalem after Nehemiah returned from Shushan. B.C. 445.
Neh. 3. 8 Next..him repaired Uzziel the son of H.

HAR'-HAS, חַרְחַס *glitter, splendour*.
Grandfather of Shallum, the husband of Huldah the prophetess, who lived in the time of Josiah, king of Judah. B.C. 700.
2 Ki.22. 14 Tikvah, the son of H., keeper of the ward.

HAR'-HUR, חַרְחוּר *nobility, distinction*.
A Nethinim who returned from exile. B.C. 536.
Ezra 2. 51 children of Hakupha, the children of H.
Neh. 7. 53 children of Hakupha, the children of H.

HA'-RIM, חָרִם *snub-nosed*.
1. A priest who had charge of the third division in the duties of the sanctuary. B.C. 1015.
1 Ch.24. 8 The third to H., the fourth to Seorim
Ezra 2. 39 children of H., a thousand and seventeen
10. 21 of the sons of H.; Maaseiah, and Elijah
Neh. 3. 11 Malchijah the son of H., and Hashub the
This may rather refer to No. 4.
Neh. 7. 42 children of H., a thousand and seventeen

2. A place in Judah or Benjamin, or rather a family of *Bene-harim* which returned from exile.
Ezra 2. 32 children of H., three hundred and twenty
Neh. 7. 35 children of H., three hundred and twenty

3. One whose descendants took strange wives. B.C. 536.
Ezra 10. 31 the sons of H.; Eliezer, Ishijah, Malchiah

4. One that sealed the covenant with Nehemiah. B.C. 445.
Neh. 10. 5 H., Meremoth, Obadiah

5. A family that sealed the covenant with Nehemiah. B.C. 445.
Neh. 10. 27 Malluch, H., Baanah

6. Perhaps the same as No. 4.
Neh. 12. 15 of H., Adna; of Meraioth, Helkai

HA'-RIPH, חָרִף חָרִיף *early born*.
1. A hundred and twelve of the *Bene*-hariph returned from the captivity with Zerubbabel. B.C. 537.
Neh. 7. 24 children of H., an hundred and twelve

2. The head of a family of Jews that sealed the covenant with Nehemiah. B.C. 442. In Ezra (2. 18) this man is called *Jorah*. Several MSS. (as well as the Arabic and Syriac versions) have *Jodah*.
Neh. 10. 19 H., Anathoth, Nebai

HARLOT —
1.*To commit fornication, go a whoring*, זָנָה *zanah*.
Gen. 34. 31 he deal with our sister as with an harlot?
Lev. 21. 14 A widow..(or) an harlot, these shall he
Josh. 2. 1 they went, and came into an harlot's ho.
6. 17 only Rahab the harlot shall live, she and
6. 22 Go into the harlot's house, and bring out
6. 25 Joshua saved Rahab the harlot alive, and
Judg.11. 1 Now Jephthah..(was) the son of an harlot
16. 1 went Samson to Gaza, and saw..an harlot
1 Ki. 3. 16 Then came..two women (that were) harl.
Prov. 7. 10 a woman (with) the attire of an harlot
29. 3 but he that keepeth company with harlots
Isa. 1. 21 How is the faithful city become an har.!
23. 15 after the end..shall Tyre sing as an harlot
23. 16 thou harlot that hast been forgotten
Jer. 5. 7 and assembled..in the harlots' houses
Eze. 16. 31 and hast not been as an harlot, in that
16. 35 Wherefore, O harlot, hear the word of
Joel 3. 3 have given a boy for an harlot, and sold
Mic. 1. 7 for she gathered (it) of the hire of an har.
1. 7 they shall return to the hire of an harlot
Nah. 3. 4 whoredoms of the well favoured harlot

2.*One set apart*, קְדֵשָׁה *qedeshah*.
Gen. 38. 21 Where (is) the harlot?..There was no har.
38. 22 the men..said..there was no harlot in
Hos. 4. 14 for themselves..sacrifice with harlots

3.*One sold, a seller, fornicator*, πόρνη *pornē*.
Matt 21. 31 That the publicans and the harlots go
21. 32 the publicans and the harlots believed
Luke15. 30 hath devoured thy living with harlots
1 Co. 6. 15 and make (them) the members of an ha.?
6. 16 he which is joined to an harlot is one bo.
Heb. 11. 31 By faith the harlot Rahab perished not
Jas. 2. 25 was not Rahab the harlot justified by wo.
Rev. 17. 5 The mother of [harlots] and abominations

HARLOT, to be or play the —
To commit fornication, go a whoring, זָנָה *zanah*.
Gen. 38. 15 he thought her (to be) an harlot; because
38. 24 thy daughter in law hath played the har.
Jer. 2. 20 thou wanderest, playing the harlot
3. 1 hast played the harlot with many lovers
3. 6 gone up..and there hath played the har.
3. 8 but went and played the harlot also
Eze. 16. 15 playedst the harlot because of thy renown
16. 16 and playedst the harlot thereupon
16. 28 thou hast played the harlot with them
16. 41 cause thee to cease from playing the harlot
23. 5 Aholah played the harlot when she was
23. 19 played the harlot in the land of Egypt
23. 44 in unto a woman that playeth the harlot
Hos. 2. 5 their mother hath played the harlot; she
3. 3 thou shalt not play the harlot, and thou
4. 15 Though thou, Israel, play the h.; Am.7.17

HARM —
1.*Evil*, רַע *ra*.
Gen. 31. 52 thou shalt not pass over this..for harm
Num 35. 23 (was) not his enemy, neither sought his h.
Prov. 3. 30 Strive not..if he have done thee no harm
Jer. 39. 12 look well to him, and do him no harm

2.*An evil thing*, דָּבָר רַע *dabar ra*.
2 Ki. 4. 41 And there was no harm in the pot

3.*Anything out of place*, ἄτοπος *atopos*.
Acts 28. 6 and saw no harm come to him, they cha.

4.*Bad*, κακός *kakos*.
Acts 16. 28 Do thyself no harm; for we are all here
28. 5 he shook off the beast..and felt no harm

5.*Evil*, πονηρός *ponēros*.
Acts 28. 21 neither..showed or spake any harm of

6.*Harm, injury, damage*, ὕβρις *hubris*.
Acts 27. 21 and to have gained this harm and loss

HARM, to (do) —
1. *To do evil*, יָרַע *yera*.
2 Sa. 20. 6 Sheba..do us more harm than (did) Abs.

2. *To afflict, do evil*, רָעַע *raa*, 5.
1 Sa. 26. 21 I will no more do thee harm, because my
1 Ch.16. 22 Touch not..and do my prophets no harm
Psa.105. 15 Touch not..and do my prophets no harm

3.*To treat badly*, κακόω *kakoō*.
1 Pe. 3. 13 who (is) he that will harm you, if ye be

HARM he hath done —
To miss the mark, do wrong, sin, חָטָא *chata*.
Lev. 5. 16 harm that he hath done in the holy thing

HARMLESS —
1.*Not bad, harmless*, ἄκακος *akakos*.
Heb. 7. 26 harmless, undefiled, separate from sinn.

2.*Harmless, unmixed*, ἀκέραιος *akeraios*.
Matt10. 16 wise as serpents, and harmless as doves
Phil. 2. 15 ye may be blameless and harmless, the s.

HAR-NE'-PHER, חַרְנֶפֶר.
A son of Zophah of the tribe of Asher. B.C. 1570.
1 Ch. 7. 36 sons of Zophah; Suah, and H., and Shual

HARNESS -
1.*Armour*, נֶשֶׁק נֵשֶׁק *nesheq*.
2 Ch. 9. 24 harness, and spices, horses, and mules, a

2. *Coat of mail*, שִׁרְיָן *shiryan*.
1 Ki.22. 34 smote..between the joints of the harness
2 Ch.18. 33 smote..between the joints of the harness

HARNESS, to —
To bind, harness, אָסַר *asar*.
Jer. 46. 4 Harness the horses; and get up, ye horse.

HARNESSED —
Armed, girded, חֲמֻשִׁים *chamushim*.
Exod13. 18 the children of Israel went up harnessed

HA'-ROD, חֲרֹד *terror, trembling*.
The well of Harod was a fountain by which Gideon and his army encamped before the rout of the Midianites. It is now the *Ain Jalud*; and "the Hill of Moreh" is the *Jabel Duhy*. Harod was in Manasseh W. of the Jordan, in the plain of Jezreel at Gilboa.
Judg. 7. 1 rose up..and pitched beside the well of H.

HA-ROD-ITE, חֲרֹדִי *belonging to Harod*.
Patronymic of two of David's warrior guard,—Shammah and Elika. In 1 Chron. 11. 27 the name is *Harorite*.
2 Sa. 23. 25 Shammah the H., Elika the H.

HA-RO'-EH, הָרֹאֶה *the seer*.
A son of Shobal, father of Kirjath-jearim, of the tribe of Judah. B.C. 1450.
1 Ch. 2. 52 had sons; H...half of the Manahethites

HA-RO-RITE, הֲרוֹרִי *belonging to Haror*.
Patronymic of Shammoth, one of David's valiant men. It is a variation of *Harodite*.
1 Ch.11. 27 Shammoth the H., Helez the Pelonite

HA-RO'-SHETH, חֲרֹשֶׁת *forest*.
"Harosheth of the Gentiles" (so called from the mixed races that inhabited it), was a city of Galilee in the N. of the land of Canaan, supposed to have stood on the W. coast of the lake Merom (*el-Hulêh*) from which the Jordan issues in an unbroken stream. *Harosheth* was the residence of Sisera, captain of Jabin king of Canaan, whose capital Hazor lay N.W. of it. No trace of the site has as yet been found.
Judg. 4. 2 Sisera, which dwelt in H. of the Gentiles
4. 13 from H. of the Gentiles unto the river of
4. 16 Barak pursued after the chariots..unto H.

HARP —
1.*Harp*, כִּנּוֹר *kinnor*.
Gen. 4. 21 of all such as handle the harp and organ
31. 27 and with songs, with tabret, and with h.?
1 Sa. 10. 5 tabret, and a pipe, and a harp, before
16. 16 a man, (who is) a cunning player on an h.
16. 23 took an harp, and played with his hand
2 Sa. 6. 5 harps, and on psalteries, and on timbrels
1 Ki.10. 12 harps also and psalteries for singers
1 Ch.13. 8 with harps, and with psalteries, and with
15. 16 psalteries and harps and cymbals, sound.
15. 21 with harps on the Sheminith to excel
15. 28 making a noise with psalteries and harps
16. 5 Jeiel with psalteries and with harps; but
25. 1 who should prophesy with harps, with
25. 3 who prophesied with a harp, to give thanks
25. 6 harps, for the service of the house of God
2 Ch. 5. 12 having cymbals, and psalteries, and harps
9. 11 and harps and psalteries for singers: and
20. 28 to Jerusalem with psalteries and harps
29. 25 with harps, according to the commandm.
Neh. 12. 27 (with) cymbals, psalteries, and with harps

Job 21. 12 They take the timbrel and harp, and
30. 31 My harp also is (turned) to mourning, and
Psa. 33. 2 Praise the LORD with harp : sing unto h.
43. 4 upon the harp will I praise thee, O God
49. 4 I will open my dark saying upon the harp
57. 8 awake, psaltery and harp : I (myself) will
71. 22 unto thee will I sing with the harp, O
81. 2 bring..the pleasant harp with the psaltery
92. 3 upon the harp with a solemn sound
98. 5 unto the LORD with the harp ; with the h.
108. 2 Awake, psaltery and harp ; I (myself) will
137. 2 We hanged our harps upon the willows
147. 7 sing praise upon the harp unto our God
149. 3 praises unto him with..timbrel and harp
150. 3 praise him with the psaltery and harp
Isa. 5. 12 the harp and the viol, the tabret and pipe
16. 11 bowels shall sound like an harp for Moab
23. 16 Take an harp, go about the city, thou
24. 8 The mirth..the joy of the harp ceaseth
30. 32 (it) shall be with tabrets and harps : and
Eze. 26. 13 sound of thy harp shall be no more heard

2. *Harp*, קִיתָרֹס, קַתְרֹס *githaros, qathros.*
Dan. 3. 5 hear the sound of the cornet, flute, harp
3. 7, 10, 15 cornet, flute, harp, sackbut, psaltery

3. *Harp*, κιθάρα *kithara.*
1 Co. 14. 7 giving sound, whether pipe or harp, exc.
Rev. 5. 8 having every one of them harps, and gol.
14. 2 voice of harpers harping with their harps
15. 2 stand on the sea..having the harps of God

HARP, to —
To use the harp, κιθαρίζω *kitharizō.*
1 Co. 14. 7 how shall it be known what is..harped?
Rev. 14. 2 I heard the voice of harpers harping with

HARPER —
One who plays upon a harp or guitar, κιθαρῳδός.
Rev. 14. 2 I heard the voice of harpers harping with
18. 22 the voice of harpers, and musicians, and

HARROW —
Pike, חָרִיץ *charits.*
2 Sa. 12. 31 put (them) under saws, and under harrows
1 Ch. 20. 3 cut (them) with saws, and with harrows

HARROW, to —
To level, harrow, שָׂדַד *sadad*, 3.
Job 39. 10 or will he harrow the valleys after thee?

HAR'-SHA, חַרְשָׁא *artificer.*
The children of Harsha were among the Nethinim who returned with Zerubbabel from exile. B.C. 536.
Ezra 2. 52 children of Mehida, the children of H.
Neh. 7. 54 children of Mehida, the children of H.

HART —
A hart, אַיָּל *ayyal.*
Deut. 12. 15 as of the roebuck, and as of the hart
12. 22 Even as the roebuck and the hart is eaten
14. 5 The hart, and the roebuck, and the fallow
15. 22 alike, as the roebuck, and as the hart
1 Ki. 4. 23 an hundred sheep, beside harts, and roe.
Psa. 42. 1 As the hart panteth after the water broo.
Song 2. 9 My beloved is like a roe or a young hart
2. 17 be thou like a roe or a young hart upon
8. 14 a young hart upon the mountains of spices
Isa. 35. 6 Then shall the lame (man) leap as an hart
Lam. 1. 6 become like harts (that) find no pasture

HA'-RUM, הָרֻם *elevated.*
Father of Aharhel a descendant of Coz, from Caleb son of Hur. B.C. 1430.
1 Ch. 4. 8 and the families of Aharhel the son of H.

HA-RU'-MAPH, חֲרוּמַף.
Neh. 3. 10 next..them repaired Jedaiah the son of H.

HA-RU-PHITE, חֲרוּפִי [V. L. חֲרִיפִי].
Shephatiah, a Korhite who joined David at Ziklag. B.C. 1048.
1 Ch. 12. 5 and Shemariah, and Shephatiah the H.

HA'-RUZ, חָרוּץ *industrious.*
Father of Meshullemeth, Manasseh's queen, and mother of Amon king of Judah. B.C. 698.
2 Ki. 21. 19 (was) Meshullemeth, the daughter of H.

HARVEST —
1. *Reaping*, קָצִיר *qatsir.*
Gen. 8. 22 seed time and harvest..shall not cease
30. 14 Reuben went in the days of wheat harvest
45. 6 (there shall) neither (be) earing nor har.
Exod. 23 16 the feast of harvest, the first fruits of thy
34. 21 earing time and in harvest thou shalt
34. 22 of the first fruits of wheat harvest, and
Lev. 19. 9 when ye reap the harvest of your land
19. 9 neither..gather the gleanings of thy har.
23. 10 and shall reap the harvest thereof, then
23. 10 sheaf of the first fruits of your harvest
23. 22 when ye reap the harvest of your land
23. 22 neither..gather any gleaning of thy har.
25. 5 groweth of its own accord of thy harvest
Deut. 24. 19 When thou cuttest down thine harvest
Josh 3. 15 Jordan overfloweth..all the time of har.
Judg. 15. 1 in the time of wheat harvest, that Samson
Ruth 1. 22 came..in the beginning of barley harvest
2. 21 until they have ended all my harvest
2. 23 end of barley harvest and of wheat harvest
1 Sa. 6. 13 reaping their wheat harvest in the valley
8. 12 and (will set them)..to reap his harvest
12. 17 (Is it) not wheat harvest to day? I will
2 Sa. 21. 9 were put to death in the days of harvest
21. 9 in the beginning of barley harvest
2 Sa. 21. 10 from the beginning of harvest until water
23. 13 came to David in the harvest time unto
Job 5. 5 Whose harvest the hungry eateth up, and
Prov. 6. 8 (and) gathereth her food in the harvest
10. 5 he that sleepeth in harvest is a son that
20. 4 shall he beg in harvest, and (have) noth.
25. 13 As the cold of snow in the time of harvest
26. 1 As snow in summer, and as rain in harvest
Isa. 9. 3 they joy..according to the joy in harvest
16. 9 thy summer fruits, and for thy harvest, is
17. 11 the harvest (shall be) a heap in the day
18. 4 like a cloud of dew in the heat of harvest
18. 5 afore the harvest, when the bud is perfect
23. 3 the harvest of the river, (is) her revenue
Jer. 5. 17 they shall eat up thine harvest, and thy
5. 24 reserveth..appointed weeks of the harv.
8. 20 The harvest is past, the summer is ended
50. 16 handleth the sickle in the time of harvest
51. 33 and the time of her harvest shall come
Hos. 6. 11 O Judah, he hath set an harvest for thee
Joel 1. 11 because the harvest of the field is perish.
3. 13 Put ye in the sickle ; for the harvest is
Amos 4. 7 yet three months to the harvest : and I

2. *Reaping*, θερισμός *therismos.*
Matt. 9. 37 The harvest truly (is) plenteous, but the
9. 38 Pray ye therefore the Lord of the harvest
9. 38 will send forth labourers into his harvest
13. 30 Let both grow together until the harvest
13. 30 in the time of harvest I will say to the
13. 39 the harvest is the end of the world ; and
Mark 4. 29 in the sickle, because the harvest is come
Luke 10. 2 The harvest truly (is) great, but the lab.
10. 2 pray ye therefore the Lord of the harvest
10. 2 would send forth labourers into his harv.
John 4. 35 four months, and (then) cometh harvest?
4. 35 for they are white already to harvest
Rev. 14. 15 to reap ; for the harvest of the earth is

HARVEST man —
1. *Reaping, reaper*, קָצִיר *qatsir.*
Isa. 17. 5 when the harvest man gathereth the corn

2. *To reap, shorten*, קָצַר *qatsar.*
Jer. 9. 22 as the handful after the harvest man, and

HA-SAD'-IAH, חֲסַדְיָה *Jah is kind.*
A son of Zerubbabel and descendant of Jehoiakim, king of Judah. B.C. 445.
1 Ch. 3. 20 Hashubah..Ohel, and Berechiah, and H.

HA-SE-NU'-AH, הַסְּנֻאָה *the violated.*
A Benjamite of one of the chief families. The name is really *Senuah*, the definite article being prefixed.
1 Ch. 9. 7 Sallu..the son of Hodaviah, the son of H.

HA-SHAB'-IAH, חֲשַׁבְיָה, חֲשַׁבְיָהוּ *Jah is associated.*
1. A Merarite Levite, son of Amaziah in the line of Ethan the singer. B.C. 1150.
1 Ch. 6. 45 The son of H., the son of Amaziah, the
2. Another Merarite Levite. B.C. 470.
1 Ch. 9. 14 Shemaiah..the son of H., of the sons of M.
3. The fourth of the six sons of Jeduthun, who played the harp in the sanctuary, and had charge of the twelfth course. B.C. 1015.
1 Ch. 25. 3 sons of Jeduthun..Zeri..H., and Mattith.
4. A descendant of Hebron son of Kohath. B.C. 1015
1 Ch. 26. 30 of the Hebronites, H. and his brethren
5. A son of Kemuel who was prince of the Levites in the time of David. B.C. 1015.
1 Ch. 27. 17 Of the Levites, H. the son of Kemuel : of
6. Another Levite, a chief of his tribe, and assisted king Josiah at his great passover feast. B.C. 623.
2 Ch. 35. 9 Conaniah also, and Shemaiah..and H.
7. A Merarite Levite who accompanied Ezra from Babylon. B.C. 457.
Ezra 8. 19 H., and with him Jeshaiah of the sons of M.
8. A chief of the priests of the family of Kohath. B.C. 457.
Ezra 8. 24 of the chief of the priests Sherebiah, H.
9. A ruler of half the environs of Keilah. He repaired a portion of the wall under Nehemiah. B.C. 457.
Neh. 3. 17 Next unto him repaired H., the ruler of
10. A Levite that sealed the covenant with Nehemiah. (Perhaps the same man as in Neh. 12. 24).
Neh. 10. 11 Micha, Rehob, H.
11. Another Levite, son of Bunni. B.C. 470.
Neh. 11. 15 Shemaiah..the son of H., the son of Bu.
12. Another Levite, son of Mattaniah and an attendant at the temple. B.C. 457.
Neh. 11. 22 Uzzi..the son of H., the son of Mattaniah
13. A priest of the family of Hilkiah in the days of Joiakim son of Jeshua. B.C. 623.
Neh. 12. 21 Of Hilkiah, H. ; of Jedaiah
14. A chief Levite appointed for thanksgiving after the return from Babylon [same as No. 12?].
Neh. 12. 24 the chief of the Levites : H., Sherebiah

HA-SHAB'-NAH, חֲשַׁבְנָה *Jah is a friend.*
A chief of the people that sealed the covenant with Nehemiah. B.C. 445.
Neh. 10. 25 Rehum, H., Maaseiah

HA-SHAB-NI'-AH, חֲשַׁבְנְיָה *Jah is a friend.*
1. His son Hattush helped to repair the wall of Jerusalem. B.C. 480.
Neh. 3. 10 next..him repaired Hattush the son of H.
2. A Levite who officiated at the great fast under Ezra and Nehemiah when the covenant was sealed. B.C. 445.
Neh. 9. 5 Then the Levites, Jeshua, and..H., Sh.

HASH-BAD'-ANA, חַשְׁבַּדָּנָה.
A man who stood by Ezra on the left while he read the law to the people. B.C. 445.
Neh. 8. 4 on his left hand, Pedaiah..and H., Zech.

HA'-SHEM, הָשֵׁם *shining.*
Father of several of David's valiant guard. B.C. 1048.
1 Ch. 11. 34 sons of H. the Gizonite, Jonathan the son

HASH-MO'-NAH, חַשְׁמֹנָה, *fruitfulness.*
A station of the Israelites next before Moseroth near Mount Hor. It was the twenty-fifth in the wilderness and the fourteenth from Sinai.
Num 33. 29 went from Mithcah, and pitched in H.
33. 30 they departed from H., and encamped at

HA'-SHUB, HAS'-SHUB, חַשּׁוּב *associate.*
1. Father of Shemaiah a descendant of Merari. The Common Version has omitted the doubling of the letter שׁ ; the name is identical with that elsewhere correctly given, *Hasshub.* B.C. 480.
1 Ch. 9. 14 of the Levites ; Shemaiah the son of H.
Neh. 11. 15 of the Levites : Shemaiah the son of H.
2. A son of Pahath Moab who helped to repair the wall of Jerusalem. B.C. 480.
Neh. 3. 11 H. the son of Pahath-Moab, repaired the
3. Another who assisted at another part of the wall. B.C. 445.
Neh. 3. 23 repaired Benjamin and H. over against
4. A head of a family who sealed the covenant with Nehemiah.
Neh. 10. 23 Hoshea, Hananiah, H.

HA-SHU'-BAH, חֲשֻׁבָה *association.*
A son of Zerubbabel and descendant of Jehoiakim, king of Judah. B.C. 500.
1 Ch. 3. 20 And H., and Ohel, and Berechiah, and Ha

HA'-SHUM, חָשֻׁם *shining.*
1. His descendants returned with Zerubbabel from Babylon. B.C. 636.
Ezra 2. 19 children of H., two hundred twenty and
10. 33 Of the sons of H. ; Mattenai, Mattathah
Neh. 7. 22 children of H., three hundred twenty and
2. A priest who stood beside Ezra while he read the law to the people. B.C. 445.
Neh. 8. 4 and on his left hand, Pedaiah..and H.
3. The head of a family that sealed the covenant with Nehemiah. B.C. 445.
Neh. 10. 18 Hodijah, H., Bezai

HAS'-RAH, חַסְרָה *splendour.*
Another form of *Harhas* (2 Kings 22. 14), which see.
2 Ch. 34. 22 Shallum..the son of H., keeper of the ward.

HAS-SE-NA'-AH, הַסְּנָאָה *the thorn hedge.*
The Bene-has-senaah rebuilt the fish gate when the wall of Jerusalem was repaired. The name is no doubt identical with the *Senaah* of Ezra 2. 35 and Neh. 7. 38, having the definite article prefixed. It may have some connection with the cliff *Seneh* of 1 Sam. 14. 4.
Neh. 3. 3 the fish gate did the sons of H. build, who

HAST —
There is, there are, יֵשׁ *yesh.*
2 Ki. 4. 2 tell me, what hast thou in the house?
Job 33. 32 If thou hast any thing to say, answer me
Prov 3. 28 Say not..Go..when thou hast it by thee

HASTE —
1. *To make haste*, חָפַז *chaphaz.*
2 Ki. 7. 15 the Syrians had cast away in their haste
Psa. 31. 22 For I said in my haste, I am cut off from
116. 11 I said in my haste, All men (are) liars

2. *Haste*, חִפָּזוֹן *chippazon.*
Exod. 12. 11 ye shall eat it in haste : it (is) the LORD'S
Deut. 16. 3 thou camest forth out of..Egypt in haste
Isa. 52. 12 For ye shall not go out with haste, nor

3. *Haste*, σπουδή *spoudē.*
Mark 6. 25 she came in..with haste unto the king
Luke 1. 39 and went into the hill country with haste

HASTE, to —
1. *To hasten, press*, אוּץ *uts.*
Exod. 5. 13 And the taskmasters hasted (them) say.
Josh 10. 13 hasted not to go down about a whole day
Prov. 19. 2 he that hasteth with (his) feet sinneth

2. *To be troubled, hastened*, בָּהַל *bahel*, 2.
Prov. 28. 22 He that hasteth to be rich (hath) an evil

3. *To haste, take trouble*, בָּהַל *bahel*, 5.
Esth. 6. 14 hasted to bring Haman unto the banquet

4. *To hasten, press*, דָּחַף *dachaph*, 2.
2 Ch. 26. 20 yea, himself hasted also to go out, beca.
Esth. 6. 12 but Haman hasted to his house mourning

5. *To make haste*, חוּשׁ *chush.*
1 Sa. 20. 38 Jonathan cried..Make speed, haste, stay
Job 31. 5 or if my foot hath hasted to deceit
Psa. 22. 19 O my strength, haste thee to help me
Hab. 1. 8 shall fly as the eagle (that) hasteth to eat

6. *To make haste*, חוּשׁ *chush*, 5.
Judg. 20. 37 And the liers in wait hasted, and rushed

7. *To hasten*, חָפַז *chaphaz*.
Job 40. 23 he drinketh up a river, (and) hasteth not

8. *To dash, hasten*, עוּשׁ *ius*.
Job 9. 26 as the eagle (that) hasteth to the prey

9. *To make haste*, מָהַר *mahar*, 3.
Gen. 18. 7 fetched a calf..and he hasted to dress it
19. 22 Haste thee, escape thither; for I cannot
24. 18 and she hasted, and let down her pitcher
24. 20 And she hasted, and emptied her pitcher
45. 9 Haste ye, and go up to my father, and say
45. 13 ye shall haste and bring down my father
Josh. 4. 10 and the people hasted and passed over
8. 14 that they hasted, and rose up early, and
8. 19 the ambush..hasted and set the city on fire
1 Sa. 17. 48 David hasted, and ran toward the army
23. 27 Haste thee, and come; for the Philistines
25. 23 she hasted, and lighted off the ass, and fell
25. 34 except thou hadst hasted and come to me.
25. 42 And Abigail hasted, and arose, and rode
28. 24 she hasted, and killed it, and took flour
2 Sa. 19. 16 Shimei..hasted and came down with the
1 Ki. 20. 41 And he hasted, and took the ashes away
2 Ki. 9. 13 they hasted, and took every man his gar.
Prov. 7. 23 as a bird hasteth to the snare, and know.
Jer. 48. 16 near to come, and his affliction hasteth fast

10. *Hasting*, מָהֵר *maher*.
Zeph. 1. 14 The great day of the LORD..hasteth gre.

11. *To pant, swallow up*, שָׁאַף *shaaph*.
Eccl. 1. 5 and hasteth to his place where he arose

12. *To hasten*, σπεύδω *speudō*.
Acts 20. 16 for he hasted, if it were possible for him

HASTE away, to —
To be hastened, חָפַז *chaphaz*, 2.
Psa. 48. 5 they were troubled, (and) hasted away
104. 7 at..voice of thy thunder they hasted aw.

HASTE, to cause to make —
To cause to make haste, hasten, מָהַר *mahar*, 3.
Esth. 5. 5 Cause Haman to make haste, that he may

HASTE, in or with —
1. *Haste*, בְּהִילוּ *behilu*.
Ezra 4. 23 they went up in haste to Jerusalem unto

2. *To be hastened*, בְּהַל, *behal*, 4.
Dan. 2. 25 brought..Daniel before the king in haste
3. 24 the king was astonied, and rose..in haste
6. 19 king..went in haste unto the den of lions

3. *To hasten*, מָהַר *mahar*, 3.
Exod 10. 16 Pharaoh called for Moses and Aaron in h.
12. 33 send them out of the land in haste; for

4. *To hasten*, σπεύδω *speudō*.
Luke 2. 16 they came with haste, and found Mary and

HASTE, to make —
1. *To hasten, press*, אוּץ *uts*.
Prov 28. 20 he that maketh haste to be rich shall not

2. *To hasten*, בָּהַל *bahel*, 3.
2 Ch. 35. 21 for God commanded me to make haste

3. *To flee*, בָּרַח *barach*.
Song 8. 14 Make haste, my beloved, and be thou like

4. *To make haste*, חוּשׁ *chush*.
Deut 32. 35 the things that shall come..make haste
Job 20. 2 to answer, and for (this) I make haste
Psa. 38. 22 Make haste to help me, O Lord my salva.
40. 13 deliver..O LORD, make haste to help me
70. 5 make haste unto me, O God: thou (art)
119. 60 I made haste, and delayed not to keep
141. 1 LORD, I cry unto thee: make haste unto

5. *To make haste*, חוּשׁ *chush*, 5.
Isa. 28. 16 he that believeth shall not make haste

6. *To make haste*, חוּשׁ *chush* [V.L. חִישׁ].
Psa. 71. 12 O God..O my God, make haste for my help

7. *To hasten*, חָפַז *chaphaz*.
2 Sa. 4. 4 came to pass, as she made haste to flee, that

8. *To be hastened*, חָפַז *chaphaz*, 2.
1 Sa. 23. 26 David made haste to get away for fear of

9. *To make haste*, מָהַר *mahar*, 3.
Gen. 24. 46 she made haste, and let down her pitcher
43. 30 Joseph made haste; for his bowels did
Exod 34. 8 And Moses made haste, and bowed his h.
Judg. 9. 48 make haste, (and) do as I (have done)
13. 10 And the woman made haste, and ran and
1 Sa. 9. 12 make haste..for he came to day to the
25. 18 Abigail made haste, and took two hund.
Esth. 6. 10 Make haste..take the apparel and..horse
Prov 1. 16 their feet run to evil, and make haste to
Isa. 49. 17 Thy children shall make haste; thy destro.
59. 7 they make haste to shed innocent blood
Jer. 9. 18 let them make haste, and take up a wail.
Nah. 2. 5 they shall make haste to the wall thereof

10. *To hasten*, σπεύδω *speudō*.
Luke 19. 5 Zacchæus, make haste, and come down
19. 6 And he made haste, and came down, and
Acts 22. 18 Make haste, and get thee quickly out of

HASTE, to require —
To be urgent, נָחַץ *nachats*.
1 Sa. 21. 8 because the king's business required haste

HASTE unto, to —
To haste, urge on, σπεύδω *speudō*.
2 Pet. 3. 12 hasting unto the coming of the day of G.

HASTEN, to —
1. *To hasten, press*, אוּץ *uts*, 5.
Gen. 19. 15 then the angels hastened Lot, saying, Ar.
Jer. 17. 16 I have not hastened from (being) a pastor

2. *To haste*, חוּשׁ *chush*.
Eccl. 2. 25 who else can hasten (hereunto), more than

3. *To make haste*, חוּשׁ *chush*, 5.
Psa. 55. 8 I would hasten my escape from the windy
Isa. 5. 19 Let him make speed, (and) hasten his work
60. 22 I the LORD will hasten it in his time

4. *To hasten, speed*, מָהַר *mahar*.
Psa. 16. 4 (that) hasten (after) another (god): their

5. *To make haste*, מָהַר *mahar*, 3.
Gen. 18. 6 Abraham hastened into the tent unto S.
1 Ki. 22. 9 Hasten (hither) Micaiah the son of Imlah
2 Ch. 24. 5 Go out..and see that ye hasten the matter
24. 5 Howbeit the Levites hastened (it) not
Isa. 51. 14 The captive exile hasteneth that he may

6. *To watch*, שָׁקַד *shaqad*.
Jer. 1. 12 for I will hasten my word to perform it

HASTENED, to be —
1. *To be troubled, hastened*, בָּהַל *bahel*, 4.
Esth. 8. 14 the posts..being hastened and pressed

2. *To press*, דָּחַף *dachaph*.
Esth. 3. 15 being hastened by the king's command.

HASTILY —
1. *Hastily, speedily*, מָהֵר *maher*.
Judg. 2. 23 left..without driving them out hastily
Prov 25. 8 Go not forth hastily to strive, lest..what

2. *Haste, speed*, מְהֵרָה *meherah*.
Judg. 9. 54 he called hastily unto the young man his

3. *To make haste*, מָהַר *mahar*, 3.
1 Sa. 4. 14 And the man came in hastily, and told E.
1 Ki. 20. 33 Now the men..did hastily catch (it): and

4. *Quickly, shortly*, ταχέως *tacheōs*.
John 11. 31 saw Mary, that she rose up hastily and

HASTILY, to bring or be gotten —
1. *To be hastened*, בָּהַל *bahel*, 4.
Prov 20. 21 An inheritance (may be) gotten hastily at

2. *To cause to run*, רוּץ *ruts*, 5.
Gen. 41. 14 brought him hastily out of the dungeon

HASTING —
Hasty, hasting, מָהִיר *mahir*.
Isa. 16. 5 seeking judgment, and hasting righteou.

HASTY —
1. *To hasten, press*, אוּץ *uts*.
Prov 21. 5 but of every one (that is) hasty, only to
29. 20 Seest thou a man (that is) hasty in his w.

2. *To be urgent*, חֲצַף *chatsaph*, 5.
Dan. 2. 15 Why (is) the decree (so) hasty from the k.

3. *To be or become hasty, speedy*, מָהַר *maher*, 2.
Hab. 1. 6 Chaldeans, (that) bitter and hasty nation

4. *To be wroth*, קְצַף *qatsaph*.
Prov 14. 29 but (he that is) hasty of spirit exalteth fol.

HASTY, to be —
1. *To be hastened*, בָּהַל *bahal*, 2.
Eccl. 8. 3 Be not hasty to go out of his sight: stand

2. *To haste*, בָּהַל *bahal*, 3.
Eccl. 7. 9 Be not hasty in thy spirit to be angry: for

3. *To make haste*, מָהַר *mahar*, 3.
Eccl. 5. 2 and let not thine heart be hasty to utter

HASTY fruit —
First fruit, בִּכּוּר *bikkur*.
Isa. 28. 4 the hasty fruit before the summer; which

HA-SU'-PHA, HASH-U'-PHA, חֲשׂוּפָא, חֲשֻׂפָא, *nakedness*.
A Nethinim family that returned from exile. In the Common Version of Nehemiah 7. 46 the name is inaccurately given as *Hashupha*.
Ezra 2. 43 children of H., the children of Tabbaoth
Neh. 7. 46 children of Ziha, the children of H., the ch

HAT —
Turban, כַּרְבְּלָא *karbela*.
Dan. 3. 21 these men were bound in their..hats, and

HA'-TACH, הֲתָךְ.
A chamberlain eunuch in the court of Ahasuerus (Xerxes) in immediate attendance on Esther. B.C. 510.
Esth. 4. 5 Then called Esther for H., (one) of the
4. 6 So H. went forth to Mordecai unto the
4. 9 H. came and told Esther the words of M.
4. 10 Again Esther spake unto H., and gave him

HATCH, to —
1. *To cleave, rend, hatch*, בָּקַע *baqa*.
Isa. 34. 15 There shall the great owl..hatch, and ga.

2. *To cleave, rend, hatch*, בָּקַע *baqa*, 3.
Isa. 59. 5 They hatch cockatrice' eggs, and weave

3. *To bear, bring forth*, יָלַד *yalad*.
Jer. 17. 11 partridge sitteth (on eggs), and hatcheth

HATE, to —
1. *To hate, oppose*, שָׂטַם *satam*.
Gen. 27. 41 Esau hated Jacob because of the blessing
49. 23 archers have sorely grieved..and hated
50. 15 Joseph will peradventure hate us, and
Job 16. 9 teareth (me) in his wrath, who hateth me
Psa. 55. 3 cast iniquity..and in wrath they hate me

2. *To hate*, שָׂנֵא *sane*.
Gen. 24. 60 possess the gate of those which hate them
26. 27 Wherefore come ye to me, seeing ye hate
37. 4 hated him, and could not speak peaceably
37. 5, 8 and they hated him yet the more
Exod 18. 21 men of truth, hating covetousness; and
20. 5 and fourth (generation) of them that hate
23. 5 If thou see the ass of him that hateth thee
Lev. 19. 17 Thou shalt not hate thy brother in thine
26. 17 they that hate you shall reign over you
Deut. 4. 42 hated him not in times past; and that
5. 9 fourth (generation) of them that hate me
7. 10 repayeth them that hate him to their face
7. 10 he will not be slack to him that hateth h.
7. 15 will lay them upon all (them) that hate
12. 31 for every abomination..which he hateth
16. 22 image; which the LORD thy God hateth
19. 4 neighbour..whom he hated not in time
19. 6 inasmuch as he hated him not in time
19. 11 if any man hate his neighbour, and lie in
22. 13 a wife, and go in unto her, and hate her
22. 16 unto this man to wife, and he hateth her
24. 3 (if) the latter husband hate her, and write
30. 7 on them that hate thee, which persecuted
Josh. 20. 5 unwittingly, and hated him not beforeti.
Judg 11. 7 Did not ye hate me, and expel me out of
14. 16 Thou dost but hate me, and lovest me not
15. 2 thought that thou hadst utterly hated her
2 Sa. 13. 15 Amnon hated her exceedingly; so that
13. 15 hatred wherewith he hated her (was) gr.
13. 22 Absalom hated Amnon, because he had
19. 6 lovest thine enemies..hatest thy friends
22. 18 He delivered me..from them that hated
1 Ki. 22. 8 I hate him; for he doth not prophesy go.
2 Ch. 18. 7 I hate him; for he never prophesied good
19. 2 love them that hate the LORD? therefore
Esth. 9. 1 Jews had rule over them that hated them
9. 5 did what they would unto those that hated
Job 8. 22 They that hate thee shall be clothed with
34. 17 Shall even he that hateth right govern?
Psa. 5. 5 thou hatest all workers of iniquity
9. 13 trouble (which I suffer) of them that hate
11. 5 him that loveth violence his soul hateth
18. 17 He delivered me..from them which hated
21. 8 hand shall find out those that hate thee
25. 19 many; and they hate me with cruel hat.
26. 5 have hated the congregation of evil doers
31. 6 hated them that regard lying vanities: but
34. 21 that hate the righteous shall be desolate
35. 19 (neither) let them wink..that hate me
38. 19 that hate me wrongfully are multiplied
41. 7 that hate me whisper together against me
45. 7 lovest righteousness, and hatest wicked.
50. 17 thou hatest instruction, and castest my
69. 4 They that hate me without a cause are
69. 14 me be delivered from them that hate me
86. 17 they which hate me may see (it), and be
97. 10 Ye that love the LORD, hate evil: he
101. 3 I hate the work of them that turn aside
105. 25 He turned their heart to hate his people
106. 10 them from the hand of him that hated
106. 41 and they that hated them ruled over them
118. 7 I see (my desire) upon them that hate me
119. 104 therefore I hate every false way
119. 113 hate (vain) thoughts: but thy law do I
119. 128 to be) right; (and) I hate every false
119. 163 I hate and abhor lying: (but) thy law do
120. 6 long dwelt with him that hateth peace
129. 5 confounded and turned back that hate Z.
139. 21 Do not I hate them, O LORD..and am not
139. 22 I hate them with perfect hatred; I count
Prov. 1. 22 How long..will..fools hate knowledge?
1. 29 they hated knowledge, and did not choose
5. 12 How have I hated instruction, and my he.
6. 16 six (things) doth the LORD hate; yea, se.
8. 13 The fear of the LORD (is) to hate evil
8. 13 evil way, and the froward mouth, do I h.
9. 8 Reprove not a scorner, lest he hate thee
11. 15 and he that hateth suretiship is sure
12. 1 but he that hateth reproof (is) brutish
13. 5 A righteous (man) hateth lying: but a
13. 24 He that spareth his rod hateth his son
15. 10 (and) he that hateth reproof shall die
15. 27 but he that hateth gifts shall live
19. 7 the brethren of the poor do hate him; h.
25. 17 lest he be weary of thee, and (so) hate
26. 24 He that hateth dissembleth with his lips
26. 28 A lying tongue hateth (those that are)
28. 16 he that hateth covetousness shall prolong
29. 10 The blood thirsty hate the upright: but
29. 24 partner with a thief hateth his own soul
Eccl. 2. 17 I hated life; because the work that is
2. 18 I hated all my labour which I had taken
3. 8 A time to love, and a time to hate; a time
Isa. 1. 14 and your appointed feasts my soul hateth
61. 8 I hate robbery for burnt offering; and I
66. 5 Your brethren that hated you, that cast
Jer. 12. 8 it crieth out..therefore have I hated it
44. 4 do not this abominable thing that I hate
Eze. 16. 27 unto the will of them that hate thee, the
16. 37 with all (them) that thou hast hated; I will
23. 28 into the hand (of them) whom thou hatest
35. 6 thou hast not hated blood, even blood
Hos. 9. 15 I hated them: for the wickedness of their

Amos 5. 10 They hate him that rebuketh in the gate
5. 15 Hate the evil, and love the good, and
5. 21 I hate, I despise your feast days, and I
6. 8 abhor the excellency..hate his palaces
Mic. 3. 2 Who hate the good, and love the evil
Zech. 8. 17 these (are things) that I hate, saith the
Mal. 1. 3 I hated Esau, and laid his mountains and
2. 16 LORD..saith, that he hateth putting away

3. *To hate*, שָׂנֵא *sane*, 3.
Num 10. 35 let them that hate thee flee before thee
Deut 32. 41 and will reward them that hate me
33. 11 smite..the loins of them..that hate him
2 Sa. 22. 41 that I might destroy them that hate me
Job 31. 29 at the destruction of him that hated me
Psa. 18. 40 that I might destroy them that hate me
44. 7 and hast put them to shame that hated
44. 10 they which hate us spoil for themselves
55. 12 neither (was it) he that hated me (that)
68. 1 let them..that hate him flee before him
83. 2 that hate thee have lifted up the head
89. 23 will beat..and plague them that hate him
139. 21 O LORD, that hate thee? and am not I
Prov. 8. 36 all they that hate me love death

4. *To hate*, שְׂנֵא *sene*.
Dan. 4. 19 the dream (be) to them that hate thee

5. *Hated*, שִׂנְאָה *sinah*.
Deut. 1. 27 the LORD hated us, he hath brought us
9. 28 he hated them, he hath brought them

6. *To hate*, μισέω *miseō*.
Matt. 5. 43 love thy neighbour, and hate thine enemy
5. 44 [do good to them that hate you], and pray
6. 24 he will hate the one, and love the other
10. 22 be hated of all (men) for my name's sake
24. 9 hated of all nations for my name's sake
24. 10 shall betray..and shall hate one another
Mark 13. 13 be hated of all (men) for my name's sake
Luke 1. 71 and from the hand of all that hate us
6. 22 Blessed are ye when men shall hate you
6. 27 But I say..do good to them which hate you
14. 26 hate not his father, and mother, and wife
16. 13 he will hate the one, and love the other
19. 14 his citizens hated him, and sent a message
21. 17 be hated of all (men) for my name's sake
John 3. 20 every one that doeth evil hateth..light
7. 7 The world cannot hate you; but me it h.
12. 25 he that hateth his life in this world shall
15. 18 world hate you, ye know that it hated me
15. 19 chosen you..therefore the world hateth
15. 23 He that hateth me hateth my Father also
15. 24 now have they..hated both me and my
15. 25 written..They hated me without a cause
17. 14 world hath hated them, because they are
Rom. 7. 15 that do I not; but what I hate, that do I
9. 13 Jacob have I loved, but Esau have I hated
Eph. 5. 29 For no man ever yet hated his own flesh
Titus 3. 3 living in malice..(and) hating one another
Heb. 1. 9 loved righteousness, and hated iniquity
1 Jo. 2. 9, 11 He that..hateth his brother, is in da.
3. 13 Marvel not..if the world hate you
3. 15 Whosoever hateth his brother is a murd.
4. 20 If a man say, I love God, and hateth his
Jude 23 hating even the garment spotted by the
Rev. 2. 6 thou hatest the deeds..which I also hate
2. 15 that hold the doctrine..[which thing I h.]
17. 16 And the ten horns..shall hate the whore

HATED, to be —
1. *To hate*, שָׂנֵא *sane*.
Gen. 29. 31 when the LORD saw that Leah (was) hated
29. 33 Because the LORD hath heard..I (was) h.
Deut 21. 15 two wives, one beloved, and another ha.
21. 15 (both) the beloved and the hated
21. 16 first born before the son of the hated
21. 17 he shall acknowledge the son of the hated
2 Sa. 5. 8 the blind, (that are) hated of David's soul
Isa. 60. 15 thou hast been forsaken and hated

2. *To be hated*, שָׂנֵא *sane*, 2.
Prov 14. 17 and a man of wicked devices is hated
14. 20 The poor is hated..of his own neighbour

3. *One hated*, שָׂנִיא *sani*.
Deut 21. 15 the first born son be hers that was hated

HATEFUL, (to be) —
1. *To be hated*, שָׂנֵא *sane*.
Psa. 36. 2 until his iniquity be found to be hateful

2. *To hate*, μισέω *miseō*.
Rev. 18. 2 a cage of every unclean and hateful bird

3. *Hated, abominated*, στυγητός *stugētos*.
Titus 3. 3 living in malice and envy, hateful, (and)

HATEFULLY —
Hatred, שִׂנְאָה *sinah*.
Eze. 23. 29 And they shall deal with thee hatefully

HATER —
To hate, שָׂנֵא *sane*, 3.
Psa. 81. 15 haters of the LORD should have submitted

HATH —
1. *Unto*, אֶל־ *el*.
Gen. 47. 18 my lord also hath our herds of cattle

2. *There is* (*to* or *in*), (לְ or בְּ) יֵשׁ *yesh* (*le* or *be*).
Gen. 39. 8 he hath committed all..he hath to my h.
2 Ch. 25. 8 God hath power to help, and to cast down
Job 38. 28 Hath the rain a father? or who..the dro.
Mal. 1. 14 deceiver, which hath in his flock a male

HATH it, he that —
Its owners, בְּעָלָיו [*baal*].
Prov 16. 22 a well spring of life unto him that hath it
17. 8 stone in the eyes of him that hath it
Eccl. 10. 20 and that which hath wings shall tell the

HATH (life) —
Soul, breath, נֶפֶשׁ *nephesh*.
Gen. 1. 20 the moving creature that hath life, and

HATH, that —
Owner, בַּעֲלָה *baalah*.
1 Sa. 28. 7, 7 a woman that hath a familiar spirit

HATH, such things as one —
The present things, τὰ παρόντα *ta paronta*.
Heb. 13. 5 content with such things as ye have: for

HATH, that one —
1. *My things*, τὰ ἐμά *ta ema*.
Luke 15. 31 And he said..Son..all that I have is thine

2. *The things beside one*, τὰ παρά *ta para*.
Mark 5. 26 had spent all that she had, and was noth.

3. *The present things*, τὰ ὑπάρχοντα *ta huparchonta*.
Matt 19. 21 sell that thou hast, and give to the poor
Luke 12. 33 Sell that ye have, and give alms; provide
12. 44 will make him ruler over all that he hath
14. 33 of you that forsaketh not all that he hath

HA'-THATH, חֲתַת *bruised*.
A son of Othniel the Kenazite and judge of Israel, through Caleb son of Hur. B.C. 1380.
1 Ch. 4. 13 and Seraiah: and the sons of Othniel; H.

HA-TI'-PHA, חֲטִיפָא.
The *Bene*-Hatipha were among the Nethinim that returned from Babylon. B.C. 636.
Ezra 2. 54 children of Neziah, the children of H.
Neh. 7. 56 children of Neziah, the children of H.

HA-TI'-TA, חֲטִיטָא *exploration*.
A porter or gate keeper of the temple whose descendants returned from the exile. B.C. 636.
Ezra 2. 42 children of Akkub, the children of H.
Neh. 7. 45 children of Akkub, the children of H.

HATRED —
1. *Enmity*, אֵיבָה *ebah*.
Eze. 25. 15 vengeance..to destroy (it) for the old ha.
35. 5 Because thou hast had a perpetual hatred

2. *Hatred*, מַשְׂטֵמָה *mastemah*.
Hos. 9. 7 for..thine iniquity, and the great hatred
9. 8 ways, (and) hatred in the house of his God

3. *Hatred*, שִׂנְאָה *sinah*.
Num 35. 20 But if he thrust him of hatred, or hurl
2 Sa. 13. 15 that the hatred wherewith he hated her
Psa. 25. 19 many; and they hate me with cruel ha.
109. 3 compassed me about..with words of ha.
109. 5 they have rewarded me..hatred for my
139. 22 I hate them with perfect hatred; I count
Prov 10. 12 Hatred stirreth up strifes: but love cov.
10. 18 He that hideth hatred (with) lying lips
15. 17 than a stalled ox and hatred therewith
26. 26 hatred is covered by deceit, his wicked.
Eccl. 9. 1 no man knoweth either love or hatred
9. 6 their hatred, and..envy, is now perished
Eze. 35. 11 hast used out of thy hatred against them

4. *Enmity*, ἔχθρα *echthra*.
Gal. 5. 20 Idolatry, witchcraft, hatred, variance, em.

HAT'-TIL, חַטִּיל *decaying*.
The *Bene*-Hattil were among the children of Solomon's slaves who returned from exile. B.C. 636.
Ezra 2. 57 children of Shephatiah, the children of H.
Neh. 7. 59 children of Shephatiah, the children of H.

HAT'-TUSH, חַטּוּשׁ *contender*.
1. A descendant of the kings of Judah, perhaps a son of Shechaniah, in the 4th or 5th generation from Zerubbabel. B.C. 465.
1 Ch. 3. 22 and the sons of Shemaiah; H., and Igeal
2. A descendant of David who went up from Babylon with Ezra in the reign of Artaxerxes. In Neh. 12. 2 he is said to have returned with Zerubbabel.
Ezra 8. 2 Daniel: of the sons of David; H.
Neh. 3. 10 next unto him repaired H. the son of Hash.
10. 4 H., Shebaniah, Malluch
3. A priest who returned with Zerubbabel. B.C. 636.
Neh. 12. 2 Amariah, Malluch, H.

HAUGHTILY —
Loftiness, רוֹמָה *romah*.
Mic. 2. 3 neither shall ye go haughtily: for this

HAUGHTINESS —
1. *Rising, excellency*, גַּאֲוָה *gaavah*.
Isa. 13. 11 lay low the haughtiness of the terrible
16. 6 his haughtiness, and his pride, and his

2. *Loftiness*, רוּם *rum*.
Isa. 2. 11 the haughtiness of men shall be bowed d.
2. 17 the haughtiness of men shall be made low
Jer. 48. 29 his pride, and the haughtiness of his hea.

HAUGHTY —
1. *Height, haughtiness*, גֹּבַהּ *gobah*.
Prov 16. 18 Pride..and an haughty spirit before a fall

2. *High, haughty*, גָּבֹהַּ, גָּבֹהַ *gaboah*.
Isa. 10. 33 hewn down, and the haughty shall be h.

3. *Haughty*, יָהִיר *yahir*.
Prov 21. 24 Proud (and) haughty scorner (is) his name

4. *Height, high place*, מָרוֹם *marom*.
Isa. 24. 4 haughty people of the earth do languish

5. *To be lofty*, רוּם *rum*.
2 Sa. 22. 28 but thine eyes (are) upon the haughty

HAUGHTY, to be —
To be high or haughty, גָּבַהּ *gabah*.
Psa. 131. 1 LORD, my heart is not haughty, nor mine
Prov 18. 12 Before destruction the heart..is haughty
Isa. 3. 16 Because the daughters of Zion are haughty
Eze. 16. 50 were haughty, and committed abomination
Zeph. 3. 11 thou shalt no more be haughty because of

HAUNT —
Foot, רֶגֶל *regel*.
1 Sa. 23. 22 see his place where his haunt is, (and)

HAUNT, to —
To sit down or still, יָשַׁב *yashab*.
Eze. 26. 17 cause their terror..on all that haunt it!

HAUNT, to be wont to —
To go habitually, or up and down, הָלַךְ *halak*, 7.
1 Sa. 30. 31 where David..and his men were wont to h.

HAU'-RAN, חַוְרָן *cave district*.
The modern *Haurân* and the Greek province of Auranitis, S. of Damascus, W. of Golan and Bashan, E. of Trachonitis (now *Ledsha*), and once called Auranitis. In Ezekiel it includes Golan and Bashan W. of the Jordan.
Eze. 47. 16 Hazar-hatticon..(is) by the coast of H.
47. 18 the east side ye shall measure from H.

HAVE, to —
1*a*. *There is to* (or *with*), (עִם or) לְ יֵשׁ *yesh le* (or *im*).
Gen. 33. 9 Esau said, I have enough, my brother
33. 11 Take..my blessing..because I have eno.
43. 7 The man asked us..have ye (another) b.?
44. 19 saying, Have ye a father, or a brother?
44. 20 We have a father, an old man, and a child
Ruth 1. 12 If I should say, I have hope, (if) I should
2 Sa. 19. 28 what right..have I yet to cry any more
1 Ki. 17. 12 I have not a cake, but an handful of meal
1 Ch. 29. 3 I have of mine own proper good, of gold
2 Ch. 16. 9 from henceforth thou shalt have wars
Eccl. 4. 9 they have a good reward for their labour
Isa. 43. 8 Bring forth..the deaf that have ears
Jer. 41. 8 we have treasures in the field, of wheat
1*b*. *To take*, לָקַח *laqach*; Deut. 21. 11; 1 Sa. 2. 15.
1*c*. *There is in* (or *to*), (לְ or) בְּ אִיתַי *ithai be* (or *le*).
Ezra 4. 16 by this means thou shalt have no portion
Dan. 2. 30 for (any) wisdom that I have more than
3. 25 I see four men loose..and they have no h.

2. *Owner*, בַּעַל *baal*.
Eccl. 7. 12 wisdom giveth life to them that have it
Isa. 41. 15 new sharp threshing instrument having
Dan. 8. 20 The ram..having (two) horns (are) the

3. *To be*, הֲוָא *hava*.
Dan. 6. 2 and the king should have no damage

4. *To inherit*, נָחַל *nachal*.
Num 18. 23 a statute..that..they have no inheritance
18. 24 I have said..they shall have no inherita.

5. *To go or come in*, בּוֹא *bo*.
Gen. 43. 23 Peace (be) to you..I had your money
Job 6. 8 Oh that I might have my request; and

6. *To be to*, לְ הָוָה *havah le*.
Eccl. 2. 22 what hath man of all his labour, and of

7. *To be to*, לְ הָיָה *hayah le*.
Gen. 11. 3 they had brick for stone..slime had they

8. *To complete, finish*, כָּלָה *kalah*, 3.
Gen. 43. 2 when they had eaten up the corn which

9. *To be found*, מָצָא *matsa*, 2.
Deut. 21. 17 him a double portion of all that he hath

10. *To give*, נָתַן *nathan*.
Neh. 13. 4 Eliashib the priest, having the oversight

11. *To place, set*, שׂוּם, שִׂים *sum, sim*.
Ezra 10. 44 (some)..had wives by whom they had ch.

[*See also* Abomination, appetite, assurance, bitterness, can, charge, compassion, damage, deeply, delight, derision, desire, do, dominion, done, end, enough, experience, favour, fellowship, fouled, good success, habitation, hair fallen off, hard (labour), heat, hoofs, hope, horns, hunger, indignation, inheritance, intelligence, issue, joy, knowledge, lack, loss, maintenance, many, mastery, mercy, mercy upon, more, need, need of, occasion, over, oversight, pain, part, pity, pity upon, pleasure, plenty, possession, power, profit, respect, rest, rule, running issue, secret, sent back, shadow, sorrow, superfluous, tithes, understanding, vent, well, wholly.]

12. *To interchange*, ἀντιβάλλω *antiballō*.
Luke 24. 17 (are) these that ye have one to another

13. *To hold off or away*, ἀπέχω *apechō*.
Matt. 6. 2, 5, 16 say unto you, They have their rew.
Phil. 4. 18 I have all, and abound: I am full, having

14. *To become, begin to be*, γίνομαι *ginomai*.
Matt 18. 12 If a man have an hundred sheep, and one
Acts 15. 2 and Barnabas had no small dissension
1 Co. 4. 5 then shall every man have praise of God

15. *To be*, εἰμί *eimi*.
Matt 19. 22 sorrowful: for he had great possessions

Matt 19. 27 followed thee; what shall we have there.
Mark 5. 25 which had an issue of blood twelve years
10. 22 went..grieved: for he had great possession
11. 23 he shall have whatsoever he saith
11. 24 What things..ye desire..ye shall have
Luke 1. 7 they had no child, because that Elisabeth
1. 14 thou shalt have joy and gladness; and
6. 32, 33, 34 what thank have ye? for sinners
7. 41 a certain creditor which had two debtors
8. 42 For he had one only daughter, about tw.
8. 43 a woman, having an issue of blood twelve
9. 13 We have no more but five loaves and two
10. 39 she had a sister called Mary, which also
12. 24 which neither have storehouse nor barn
14. 10 shalt thou have worship in the presence
John 18. 39 ye have a custom, that I should release
Acts. 4. 32 his own; but they had all things common
7. 44 Our fathers had the tabernacle of witness
8. 21 hast neither part nor lot in this matter
13. 15 if ye have any word of exhortation for
18. 10 for I have much people in this city
19. 25 that by this craft we have our wealth
21. 9 the same man had four daughters, virgins
21. 23 Do therefore this..We have four men
Rom. 9. 2; 9. 9; 1 Co. 9. 16; Rev. 22. 14.

16. *My, mine,* τὰ ἐμά *ta ema.*

Luke 15. 31 And he said..all that I have is thine

17. *To have,* ἔχω *echō.*

Matt. 3. 4 John had his raiment of camel's hair, and
3. 9 not to say..We have Abraham to (our) f.
3. 14 I have need to be baptized of thee, and
5. 23 that thy brother hath ought against thee
5. 46 love them which love..what reward have
6. 1 ye have no reward of your Father which
6. 8 what things ye have need of before ye ask
7. 29 he taught them as (one) having authority
8. 9 under authority, having soldiers under me
8. 20 The foxes have holes, and the birds of
8. 20 Son of man hath not where to lay (his)
9. 6 Son of man hath power on earth to forgive
9. 36 scattered..as sheep having no shepherd
11. 15 He that hath ears to hear, let him hear
11. 18 nor drinking, and they say, He hath a
12. 10 was a man which had (his) hand withered
12. 11 What man..shall have one sheep, and
13. 5 places, where they had not much earth
13. 5 because they had no deepness of earth
13. 6 they had no root, they withered away
13. 9 Who hath ears to hear, let him hear
13. 12 whosoever hath, to him shall be given
13. 12 but whosoever hath not, from him shall
13. 12 shall be taken away even that he hath
13. 21 Yet hath he not root in himself, but dur.
13. 27 thy field? from whence then hath it tares?
13. 43 Who hath ears to hear, let him hear
13. 44 selleth all that he hath, and buyeth that
13. 46 and sold all that he had, and bought it
14. 4 It is not lawful for thee to have her
14. 17 have here but five loaves, and two fishes
15. 30 having with them (those that were) lame
15. 32 now three days, and have nothing to eat
15. 34 saith unto them, How many loaves have
17. 20 If ye have faith as a grain of mustard
18. 8 than having two hands or two feet to be
18. 9 having two eyes to be cast into hell fire
18. 25 as he had not to pay, his lord commanded
18. 25 his wife and children, and all that he had
19. 16 shall I do, that [I may have] eternal life?
19. 21 thou shalt have treasure in heaven; and
21. 3 ye shall say, The Lord hath need of them
21. 21 If ye have faith, and doubt not, ye shall
21. 28 A (certain) man had two sons; and he
22. 12 in hither not having a wedding garment?
22. 24 If a man die, having no children, his
22. 25 having no issue, left his wife unto his
22. 28 whose..shall she be..they all had her
25. 25 lo, (there) thou hast (that is) thine
25. 28 give (it) unto him which hath ten talents
25. 29 unto every one that hath shall be given
25. 29 but from him that hath not shall be taken
25. 29 be taken away even that which he hath
26. 7 a woman having an alabaster box of very
26. 11 For ye have the poor always with you
26. 11 but me ye have not always
26. 65 what further need have we of witnesses?
27. 16 they had then a notable prisoner, called
27. 65 Ye have a watch: go your way, make (it)
Mark 1. 22 he taught them as one that had authority
2. 10 Son of man hath power on earth to forg.
2. 17 They that are whole have no need of the
2. 19 [as they have the bridegroom with them]
2. 25 when he had need, and was an hungered
3. 1 a man there which had a withered hand
3. 3 unto the man which had the withered h.
3. 10 for to touch him, as many as had plagues
3. 15 to have power to heal sicknesses, and to
3. 22 He hath Beelzebub, and by the prince of
3. 26 divided, he cannot stand, but hath an end
3. 29 hath never forgiveness but is in danger
3. 30 they said, He hath an unclean spirit
4. 5 stony ground, where it had not much earth
4. 5 because it had no depth of earth
4. 6 because it had no root, it withered away
4. 9 He that hath ears to hear, let him hear
4. 17 have no root in themselves, and so endu.
4. 23 any man have ears to hear, let him hear
4. 25 he that hath, to him shall be given; and
4. 25 he that hath not, from him shall be taken
4. 25 shall be taken even that which he hath
4. 40 he said..how is it that ye have no faith?

Mark 5. 3 Who had (his) dwelling among the tombs
5. 15 see him that..[had] the legion, sitting, and
6. 18 lawful for thee to have thy brother's wife
6. 34 they were as sheep not having a shepherd
6. 36 buy..bread: [for they have nothing to eat]
6. 38 saith..How many loaves have ye? go and
7. 16 any man have ears to hear, let him hear
7. 25 young daughter had an unclean spirit
8. 1 the multitude..having nothing to eat
8. 2 been..three days, and have nothing to eat
8. 5 he asked them, How many loaves have
8. 7 they had a few small fishes: and he bless.
8. 14 neither had they in the ship with them
8. 16 saying, (It is) because we have no bread
8. 17 Why reason ye because ye have no bread?
8. 17 have ye your heart yet hardened?
8. 18 Having eyes, see ye not? and having ears
9. 17 brought..my son, which hath a dumb sp.
9. 43 than having two hands to go into hell
9. 45 having two feet to be cast into hell, into
9. 47 than having two eyes to be cast into hell
9. 50 Have salt in yourselves, and have peace
10. 21 sell whatsoever thou hast, and give to the
10. 21 thou shalt have treasure in heaven: and
10. 23 How hardly shall they that have riches
11. 3 say ye that the Lord hath need of him
11. 13 seeing a fig tree afar off having leaves
11. 22 Jesus..saith unto them, Have faith in G.
11. 25 forgive, if ye have ought against any
12. 6 Having yet therefore one son, his wellbe.
12. 23 whose wife..for the seven had her to wife
12. 44 of her want did cast in all that she had
14. 3 woman having an alabaster box of oint.
14. 7 For ye have the poor with you always
14. 7 do them good: but me ye have not alway
Luke 3. 8 not to say..We have Abraham to (our) f.
3. 11 He that hath two coats, let him impart
3. 11 to him that hath none; and he that hath
4. 33 which had a spirit of an unclean devil
4. 40 that had any sick with divers diseases
5. 24 Son of man hath power upon earth to fo.
6. 8 to the man which had the withered hand
7. 8 under authority, having under me soldiers
7. 33 drinking wine; and ye say, He hath a d.
7. 40 Simon, I have somewhat to say unto thee
7. 42 when they had nothing to pay, he frankly
8. 8 He that hath ears to hear, let him hear
8. 13 these have no root, which for a while
8. 18 whosoever hath, to him shall be given
8. 18 whosoever hath not, from him shall be
8. 18 taken even that which he seemeth to have
8. 27 a certain man, which had devils long time
9. 3 he said..neither have two coats a piece
9. 11 and healed them that had need of healing
9. 58 Foxes have holes, and birds of the air
9. 58 Son of man hath not where to lay (his) h.
11. 5 Which of you shall have a friend, and
11. 6 and I have nothing to set before him?
11. 36 (be) full of light, having no part dark, the
12. 4 after that have no more that they can do
12. 5 after he..hath power to cast into hell
12. 17 I have no room where to bestow my fru.
12. 19 hast much goods laid up for many years
12. 50 I have a baptism to be baptized with; and
13. 6 had a fig tree planted in his vineyard
13. 11 had a spirit of infirmity eighteen years
14. 18 go and see it: I pray thee have me excu.
14. 19 prove them: I pray thee have me excused
14. 35 He that hath ears to hear, let him hear
15. 4 What man of you, having an hundred
15. 8 what woman, having ten pieces of silver
15. 11 And he said, A certain man had two sons
16. 1 a certain rich man which had a steward
16. 28 I have five brethren; that he may testify
16. 29 They have Moses and the Prophets; let
17. 6 ye had faith as a grain of mustard seed
17. 7 having a servant plowing or feeding cattle
18. 22 sell all that thou hast, and distribute
18. 22 thou shalt have treasure in heaven: and
18. 24 How hardly shall they that have riches
19. 17 have thou authority over ten cities
19. 24 and give (it) to him that hath ten pounds
19. 25 said unto him, Lord, he hath ten pounds
19. 26 unto every one which hath shall be given
19. 26 from him that hath not, even that he ha.
19. 31 say..Because the Lord hath need of him
19. 34 And they said, The Lord hath need of him
20. 24 Whose image and superscription hath it?
20. 28 If any man's brother die, having a wife
20. 33 whose..is she? for seven had her to wife
21. 4 hath cast in all the living that she had
22. 36 he that hath a purse, let him take (it)
22. 36 he that hath no sword, let him sell his
22. 37 for the things concerning me have an end
24. 39 and see; for a spirit hath not flesh and
24. 39 flesh and bones, as ye see me have
24. 41 he said unto them, Have ye here any m.?
John 2. 3 mother of Jesus saith..They have no wine
3. 15 should not perish, but have eternal life
3. 16 not perish, but have everlasting life
3. 29 He that hath the bride is the bridegroom
3. 36 believeth on the Son hath everlasting
4. 11 thou hast nothing to draw with, and the
4. 11 whence then hast thou that living water?
4. 17 woman answered and said, I have no hus.
4. 17 Jesus said..well said, I have no husband
4. 18 For thou hast had five husbands; and he
4. 18 he whom thou now hast is not thy husba.
4. 32 I have meat to eat that ye know not of
4. 44 prophet hath no honour in his own country
5. 2 a pool..Bethesda, having five porches
5. 5 had an infirmity thirty and eight years

John 5. 7 I have no man, when the water is troubled
5. 24 hath everlasting life, and shall not come
5. 26 the Father hath life in himself, so hath
5. 36 I have greater witness than (that) of John
5. 38 ye have not his word abiding in you: for
5. 39 in them ye think ye have eternal life
5. 40 not come to me, that ye might have life
5. 42 that ye have not the love of God in you
6. 9 which hath five barley loaves, and two
6. 40 believeth on him, may have everlasting
6. 47 believeth on me hath everlasting life
6. 53 drink his blood, ye have no life in you
6. 54 and drinketh my blood, hath eternal life
6. 68 thou hast the words of eternal life
7. 20 hast a devil: who goeth about to kill thee
8. 6 [that they might have to accuse him]
8. 12 but shall have the light of life
8. 26 I have many things to say and to judge
8. 41 said they..we have one Father, (even) G.
8. 48 thou art a Samaritan, and hast a devil?
8. 49 I have not a devil; but I honour my Fa.
8. 52 we know that thou hast a devil. Abrah.
9. 41 If ye were blind, ye should have no sin
10. 10 might have life, and that they might have
10. 16 sheep I have, which are not of this fold
10. 18 I have power to lay it down, and I have
10. 20 He hath a devil, and is mad; why hear
12. 6 had the bag, and bare what was put the
12. 8 always ye have with you; but me ye have
12. 35 Walk while ye have the light, lest dark.
12. 36 While ye have light, believe in the light
12. 48 rejecteth me..hath one that judgeth him
13. 8 wash thee not, thou hast no part with me
13. 29 because Judas had the bag, that Jesus
13. 29 that we have need of against the feast
13. 35 disciples, if ye have love one to another
14. 21 He that hath my commandments, and
14. 30 the prince of this world..hath nothing
15. 13 Greater love hath no man than this, that
15. 22 they had not had sin: but now they have
15. 24 none other man did, they had not had sin
16. 12 I have yet many things to say unto you
16. 15 All things that the Father hath are mine
16. 21 woman when she is in travail hath sorrow
16. 22 And ye now therefore have sorrow: but
16. 33 have peace. In the world ye shall have
17. 5 which I had with thee before the world
17. 13 might have my joy fulfilled in themselves
18. 10 Peter having a sword drew it, and smote
19. 7 We have a law, and by our law he ought
19. 10 I have power to crucify thee, and have
19. 11 thou couldest have..hath the greater sin
19. 15 answered. We have no king but Cesar
20. 31 ye might have life through his name
21. 5 saith unto them, Children, have ye any
Acts 2. 44 were together, and had all things comm.
2. 45 parted..to all (men), as every man had
2. 47 and having favour with all the people
3. 6 such as I have give I thee: In the name
4. 35 unto every man according as he had need
9. 14 he hath authority from the chief priests
9. 31 Then had the churches rest throughout
13. 5 and they had also John to (their) minister
14. 9 perceiving that he had faith to be healed
15. 21 hath in every city them that preach him
18. 18 shorn (his) head in Cenchrea..he had a vow
19. 13 to call over them which had evil spirits
19. 38 if Demetrius..have a matter against any
21. 23 four men which have a vow on them
23. 17 for he hath a certain thing to tell him
23. 18 man..who hath something to say unto
23. 19 asked..What is that thou hast to tell me?
23. 29 have nothing laid to his charge worthy
24. 15 have hope toward God, which they them.
24. 16 have always a conscience void of offence
24. 19 and object, if they had ought against me
24. 23 let (him) have liberty, and that he should
25. 16 accused have the accusers face to face
25. 19 But had certain questions against him of
25. 26 I have no certain thing to write unto my
25. 26 after..I might have somewhat to write
28. 9 others..which had diseases in the island
28. 19 that I had ought to accuse my nation of
28. 29 and had great reasoning among themse.
Rom. 1. 13 that I might have some fruit among you
2. 14 when the Gentiles, which have not the law
2. 14 these, having not the law, are a law unto
2. 20 which hast the form of knowledge and of
4. 2 he hath..to glory; but not before God
5. 1 [we have] peace with God through our L.
5. 2 By whom also we have access by faith
6. 21 What fruit had ye then in those things
6. 22 ye have your fruit unto holiness, and the
8. 9 Now if any man have not the spirit of Ch.
8. 23 which have the first fruits of the spirit
9. 21 Hath not the potter power over the clay
10. 2 I bear them record that they have a zeal
12. 4 For as we have many members in one body
12. 4 and all members have not the same office
12. 6 Having then gifts differing according to
13. 3 and thou shalt have praise of the same
14. 22 Hast thou faith? have (it) to thyself bef.
15. 4 that we through patience..might have h.
15. 17 I have therefore whereof I may glory
15. 23 having no more place..and having a great
1 Co. 2. 16 instruct him? But we have the mind of
4. 7 what hast thou that thou didst not rec.?
4. 15 though ye have ten thousand instructors
5. 1 reported..that one should have his father's
6. 1 Dare any of you, having a matter against
6. 4 If then ye have judgments of things per
6. 19 which ye have of God, and ye are not your

1 Co 7. 2 have his own wife, and let every woman
7. 7 every man hath his proper gift of God
7. 12 If any brother hath a wife that believeth
7. 13 the woman which hath an husband that
7. 25 concerning virgins I have no command.
7. 28 such shall have trouble in the flesh: but
7. 29 they that have wives be as though they
7. 37 having no necessity, but hath power over
7. 40 I think also that I have the spirit of God
8. 1 Now..we know that we all have knowle.
8. 10 if any man see thee which hast knowledge
9. 4 Have we not power to eat and to drink?
9. 5 Have we not power to lead about a sister
9. 6 Or..have not we power to forbear work.
9. 17 if I do this thing willingly, I have a rew.
11. 4 having(his)head covered,dishonoureth his
11. 10 ought the woman to have power on (her)
11. 16 we have no such custom, neither the chu.
11. 22 have ye not houses to eat and to drink in?
11. 22 or despise..and shame them that have
12. 12 as the body is one, and hath many mem.
12. 21 I have no need of thee..I have no need
12. 23 our uncomely (parts) have more abund.
12. 24 our comely (parts) have no need: but
12. 30 Have all the gifts of healing? do all speak
13. 1 Though I speak..and have not charity, I
13. 2 though I have..prophecy..though I have
13. 2 and have not charity, I am nothing
13. 3 and have not charity, it profiteth me not.
14. 26 hath a psalm, hath a doctrine, hath a
14. 26 hath a revelation, hath an interpretation
15. 31 I protest by your rejoicing which I have
15. 34 for some have not the knowledge of God
2 Co. 1. 9 we had the sentence of death in ourselves
1. 15 come..that ye might have a second ben.
2. 3 lest, when I came, I should have sorrow
2. 4 the love which I have more abundantly
2. 13 I had no rest in my spirit, because I fou.
3. 4 such trust have we through Christ to God
3. 12 Seeing then that we have such hope, we
4. 1 Therefore, seeing we have this ministry
4. 7 we have this treasure in earthen vessels
4. 13 We having the same spirit of faith, acco.
5. 1 we have a building of God, an house not
5. 12 that ye may have somewhat to..them
6. 10 having nothing, and (yet) possessing all
7. 1 Having therefore these promises, dearly
7. 5 our flesh had no rest, but we were troub.
8. 11 a performance..out of that which ye have
8. 12 (it is) accepted according to that a man h.
8. 12 (and) not according to that he hath not
9. 8 that ye, always having all sufficiency in
10. 6 having in a readiness to revenge all diso.
10. 15 having hope, when your faith is increased
Gal. 2. 4 our liberty which we have in Christ Jesus
4. 22 Abraham had two sons; the one by a
4. 27 children than she which hath an husband
6. 4 then shall he have rejoicing in himself
6. 10 As we have therefore opportunity, let
Eph. 1. 7 In whom we have redemption through
2. 12 having no hope, and without God in the
2. 18 through him we both have access by one
3. 12 In whom we have boldness and access
4. 28 that he may have to give to him that
5. 5 hath any inheritance in the kingdom of
5. 27 a glorious church, not having spot, or
Phil. 1. 7 because I have you in my heart; inasm.
1. 23 having a desire to depart, and to be with
1. 30 Having the same conflict which ye saw
2. 2 having the same love, (being) of one acc.
2. 20 For I have no man like minded, who will
2. 27 lest I should have sorrow upon sorrow
3. 4 Though I might also have confidence
3. 9 not having mine own righteousness, which
3. 17 which walk so as ye have us for an ensam.
Col. 1. 14 In whom we have redemption through his
2. 1 that ye knew what great conflict I have
2. 23 Which things have indeed a show of wis.
3. 13 if any man have a quarrel against any
4. 1 knowing that ye also have a Master in h.
4. 13 he hath a great zeal for you, and them
1 Th. 1. 9 what manner of entering in we had unto
3. 6 that ye have good remembrance of us al.
4. 12 and (that) ye may have lack of nothing
4. 13 not, even as others which have no hope
5. 1 But..ye have no need that I write unto
2 Th. 3. 9 Not because we have not power, but to
1 Ti. 3. 4 having his children in subjection with all
3. 7 he must have a good report of them wh.
4. 8 having promise of the life that now is
5. 4 if any widow have children or nephews
5. 12 Having damnation, because they have
5. 16 If any man or woman that believeth have
6. 2 they that have believing masters, let them
6. 8 having food and raiment let us be there.
6. 16 Who only hath immortality, dwelling in
2 Ti. 1. 3 I have remembrance of thee in my prayers
2. 19 standeth sure, having this seal, The Lord
3. 5 Having a form of godliness, but denying
Titus 1. 6 having faithful children, not accused of
2. 8 ashamed, having no evil thing to say of
Phm. 5 which thou hast toward the Lord Jesus
7 we have great joy and consolation in thy
Heb. 2. 14 might destroy him that had the power of
3. 3 builded..hath more honour than the house
4. 14 Seeing then that we have a great High P.
4. 15 we have not an high priest which cannot
5. 12 ye have need that one teach you again
5. 12 are become such as have need of milk
5. 14 those who by reason of use have their sen.
6. 18 we might have a strong consolation, who
6. 19 Which..we have as an anchor of the soul

Heb. 7. 3 having neither beginning of days, nor end
7. 5 have a commandment to take tithes of
7. 6 and blessed him that had the promises
7. 24 this (man)..hath an unchangeable priest.
7. 28 maketh men high priests which have infi.
8. 1 We have such an High Priest, who is set
8. 3 that this man have somewhat also to offer
9. 1 the first..had also ordinances of divine
9. 4 Which had the golden censer, and the ark
9. 4 wherein (was) the golden pot that had m.
10. 1 the law having a shadow of good things
10. 2 should have had no more conscience of
10. 19 Having therefore, brethren, boldness to
10. 34 that ye have in heaven a better and an
10. 35 which hath great recompence of reward
10. 36 ye have need of patience, that, after ye
11. 10 he looked for a city which hath founda.
11. 15 And truly..they might have had opport.
12. 9 we have had fathers of our flesh which
12. 28 let us have grace, whereby we may serve
13. 10 We have an altar, whereof they have no
13. 14 here have we no continuing city, but we
13. 18 we trust we have a good conscience, in
Jas. 1. 4 let patience have (her) perfect work, that
2. 1 have not the faith of our Lord Jesus Ch.
2. 14 though a man say he hath faith, and have
2. 17 Even so faith, if it hath no works, is dead
2. 18 Thou hast faith, and I have works
3. 14 if ye have bitter envying and strife in your
4. 2 Ye lust, and have not..ye have not, bec.
1 Pe. 2. 12 Having your conversation honest among
3. 16 Having a good conscience; that, whereas
4. 8 above all things have fervent charity am.
2 Pe. 1. 19 We have also a more sure word of proph.
2. 14 Having eyes full of adultery, and that
2. 14 an heart they have exercised with covetous
1 John 1. 3 that ye also may have fellowship with us
1. 6 If we say that we have fellowship with
1. 7 we have fellowship one with another, and
1. 8 If we say that we have no sin, we deceive
2. 1 we have an advocate with the Father, J.
2. 7 an old commandment which ye had from
2. 20 ye have an unction from the Holy One, and
2. 23 [the same hath not the Father: (but he]
2. 28 when he shall appear, we may have con.
3. 3 every man that hath this hope in him
3. 15 ye know that no murderer hath eternal l.
3. 17 But whoso hath this world's good, and
3. 17 and seeth his brother have need, and sh.
3. 21 (then) have we confidence toward God
4. 16 known and believed the love that God ha.
4. 17 that we may have boldness in the day of
4. 18 love casteth out fear: because fear hath
4. 21 And this commandment have we from
5. 10 He that believeth..hath the witness in
5. 12 He that hath the Son hath life; (and)
5. 12 he that hath not the Son of God hath not
5. 13 that ye may know that ye have eternal
5. 14 this is the confidence that we have in him
5. 15 we know that we have the petitions that
2 John 5 that which we had from the beginning
9 Whosoever transgresseth..hath not God
9 he hath both the Father and the Son
12 Having many things to write unto you, I
3 John 4 I have no greater joy than to hear that
13 I had many things to write, but I will
Jude 19 These be..sensual, having not the Spirit
Rev. 1. 16 And he had in his right hand seven stars
1. 18 and have the keys of hell and of death
2. 3 and hast patience..laboured, and..not f.
2. 4 Nevertheless I have..against thee, beca.
2. 6 this thou hast, that thou hatest the deeds
2. 7, 11, 17, 29 He that hath an ear, let him h.
2. 10 ye shall have tribulation ten days: be
2. 12 which hath the sharp sword with two e.
2. 14, 20 I have a few things against thee, be.
2. 14 thou hast there them that hold the doc.
2. 15 So hast thou also them that hold the do.
2. 18 who hath his eyes like unto a flame of fire
2. 24 as many as have not this doctrine, and
2. 25 that which ye have..hold fast till I come
3. 1 he that hath the seven spirits of God, and
3. 1 that thou hast a name that thou livest
3. 4 Thou hast a few names even in Sardis
3. 6, 13, 22 He that hath an ear, let him hear
3. 7 he that hath the key of David, he that
3. 8 thou hast a little strength and hast kept
3. 11 hold that fast which thou hast, that no
3. 17 thou sayest, I am rich..and have need of
4. 4 [and they had on their heads crowns of]
4. 7 the third beast had a face as a man, and
4. 8 the four beasts had each of them six wi.
5. 6 having seven horns and seven eyes, whic
5. 8 having every one of them harps, and go.
6. 2 he that sat on him had a bow; and a cr.
6. 5 he that sat on him had a pair of balances
7. 2 having the seal of the living God: and
8. 3 stood at the altar, having a golden censer
8. 6 the seven angels which had the seven tr.
8. 9 which were in the sea, and had life, died
9. 3 as the scorpions of the earth have power
9. 4 those men which have not the seal of G.
9. 8 they had hair as the hair of women, and
9. 9 they had breastplates, as it were breastp.
9. 10 they had tails like unto scorpions, and
9. 11 they had a king over them..the angel of
9. 11 in the Greek tongue hath (his) name Ap.
9. 14 to the sixth angel which had the trumpet
9. 17 them that sat on them, having breastpla.
9. 19 like unto serpents, and had heads, and
10. 2 And he had in his hand a little book open
11. 6 These have power to shut heaven, that it

Rev. 11. 6 and have power over waters to turn them
12. 3 having seven heads and ten horns, and
12. 6 where she hath a place prepared of God
12. 12 the devil is come down unto you, having
12. 12 he knoweth that he hath but a short time
12. 17 and have the testimony of Jesus Christ
13. 1 having seven heads and ten horns, and
13. 9 If any man have an ear, let him hear
13. 11 he had two horns like a lamb, and he sp.
13. 14 which had the wound by a sword, and
13. 17 save he that had the mark, or the name
13. 18 Let him that hath understanding count
14. 1 having his Father's name written in their
14. 6 having the everlasting gospel to preach
14. 11 they have no rest day nor night, who wo.
14. 14 having on his head a golden crown, and
14. 17 another angel..he also having a sharp si.
14. 18 another angel..which had power over fire
14. 18 cried..to him that had the sharp sickle
15. 1 angels having the seven last plagues
15. 2 on the sea of glass, having the harps of G.
15. 6 seven angels..having the seven plagues
16. 2 the men which had the mark of the beast
16. 9 God, which hath power over these plagues
17. 1 the seven angels which had the seven vi.
17. 3 beast..having seven heads and ten horns
17. 4 having a golden cup in her hand full of
17. 7 which hath the seven heads and ten ho.
17. 9 And here (is) the mind which hath wisd.
17. 13 These have one mind, and shall give their
18. 1 I saw another angel..having great power
18. 19 were made rich all that had ships in the
19. 10 thy brethren that have the testimony of
19. 12 he had a name written, that no man knew
19. 16 he hath on (his) vesture and on his thigh
20. 1 having the key of the bottomless pit and
20. 6 Blessed and holy (is) he that hath part
20. 6 on such the second death hath no power
21. 9 the seven angels, which had the seven v.
21. 11 Having the glory of God: and her light
21. 12 And had a wall great and high, (and) had
21. 14 the wall of the city had twelve foundat.
21. 15 he that talked with me had a golden reed
21. 23 the city had no need of the sun, neither

18. *To hold down*, κατέχω *katechō.*
John 5. 4 [made whole of whatsoever disease he had]

19. *To take, receive*, λαμβάνω *lambanō.*
Mark 12. 22 And the seven [had her, and] left no seed
Acts 25. 16 and have licence to answer for himself
Heb. 11. 36 others had trial of..mockings and scour.

20. *To receive again*, μεταλαμβάνω *metalambanō.*
Acts 24. 25 when I have a convenient season I will

21. *To begin, possess, have*, ὑπάρχω *huparchō.*
Acts 3. 6 Silver and gold have I none; but such as
4. 37 Having land, sold (it), and brought the

HAVE, can —

1. *To know, be acquainted with*, יָדַע *yada.*
Isa. 56. 11 greedy dogs (which) can never have eno.

2. *To have*, ἔχω *echō.*
John 19. 11 Thou couldest have no power (at all) ag.

HAVE (a dream), to —

To see (a vision), חֲזָא *chaza.*
Dan. 7. 1 Daniel had a dream and visions of his h.

HAVE away, to —

To cause to go or pass over or beyond, עָבַר *abar*, 5.
2 Ch. 35. 23 said..Have me away; for I am sore wo.

HAVE forth or out, to —

To cause to go out, יָצָא *yatsa*, 5.
2 Sa. 13. 9 And Amnon said, Have out all men from
2 Ki. 11. 15 Have her forth without the ranges: and
2 Ch. 23. 14 Have her forth of the ranges; and whoso

HAVE here, to —

To be found, present, מָצָא *matsa*, 2.
1 Sa. 9. 8 I have here at hand the fourth part of a

HAVE (inheritance) to —

1. *To inherit*, נָחַל *nachal.*
Josh 17. 6 the daughters..had an inheritance among

2. *To fall into inheritance* (?), נָפַל בְּנַחֲלָה [*naphal*].
Eze. 47. 22 they shall have inheritance with you am

HAVE (knowledge), to —

To know, be acquainted with, יָדַע *yada.*
Prov. 17. 27 He that hath knowledge spareth his wo.
30. 3 wisdom, nor have the knowledge of the

HAVE on, to —

To go in, envelope, clothe, ἐνδύω *enduō.*
Matt 22. 11 a man which had not on a wedding gar.
Eph. 6. 14 having on the breastplate of righteous.

HAVE (possession) to —

To be kept or held fast, אָחַז *achaz*, 2.
Gen. 47. 27 they had possessions therein, and grew
Num 32. 30 they shall have possessions among you

HAVE (sufficient), to —

To have, ἔχω *echō.*
Luke 14. 28 whether he have (sufficient) to finish (it)

HAVE (understanding), to —

To know, be acquainted with, יָדַע *yada.*
Job 38. 4 if thou hast understanding; 1 Ch 12. 32.

HAVE nothing to do with, to —

Nothing to thee and to, μηδὲν σοὶ καὶ τῷ [*mēden*].
Matt 27. 19 Have thou nothing to do with that just

HAVE to do with, to —

What to me and to thee? τί ἐμοὶ καὶ σοί ? [*ti emoi*].
Matt. 8. 29 What have we to do with thee, Jesus
Mark 1. 24 what have we to do with thee, thou Jesus
5. 7 What have I to do with thee, Jesus..Son
Luke 4. 34 what have we to do with thee..Jesus of
8. 28 What have I to do with thee, Jesus..Son
John 2. 4 Woman, what have I to do with thee?

HAVE to do, with whom we —

Of whom we are speaking, πρὸς ὃν ἡμῖν ὁ λόγος.
Heb. 4. 13 the eyes of him with whom we have to do

HAVEN —

1. *Shore, haven,* חוֹף *choph.*
Gen. 49. 13 Zebulun shall dwell at the haven of the
49. 13 and he (shall be) for an haven of ships

2. *Haven, refuge,* מָחוֹז *machoz.*
Psa. 107. 30 so he bringeth them unto their desired h.

3. *Haven, refuge,* λιμήν *limēn.*
Acts 27. 12 because the haven was not commodious
27. 12 Phenice..an haven of Crete, and lieth

HAVENS, FAIR, Καλοὶ Λιμένες *Kaloi Limenes.*
A haven at the S. of Cape Salmone in Crete.
Acts 27. 8 came unto a place which is called the F.H.

HA-VI'-LAH, חֲוִילָה *circle, district.*
1. A son of Cush, and descendant of Ham. B.C. 2290.
Gen. 10. 7 the sons of Cush; Seba, and H., and Sa.
1 Ch. 1. 9 the sons of Cush; Seba, and H., and Sa.
2. A son of Joktan and descendant of Shem. B.C. 2240.
Gen. 10. 29 And Ophir, and H., and Jobab: all these
1 Ch. 1. 23 And Ophir, and H., and Jobab. All these
3. The land of *Chwalissi* W. of Ural (?).
Gen. 2. 11 which compasseth the whole land of H.
4. A district E. of Amalek.
Gen. 25. 18 they dwelt from H. unto Shur, that (is)
1 Sa. 15. 7 And Saul smote the Amalekites from H.

HAVOC of, to make —

To treat outrageously, λυμαίνομαι *lumainomai.*
Acts 8. 3 As for Saul, he made havoc of the church

HA'-VOTH JA'-IR, חַוֹּת יָאִיר *villages of Jair.*
Certain villages on the E. of the Jordan, in Gilead or Bashan. These villages were taken by Jair son of Manasseh, and Gilead was allotted to his tribe, while he named the villages after himself *Havoth-jair.* In Deut. 3. 14 it is stated that Jair "took all the tract of Argob unto the boundary of the Geshurite and the Maachathite, and called them after his own name *Bashan-havoth-jair.*"
Num 32. 41 took the small towns..and called them H.
Deut. 3. 14 called them after his..name, Bashan-h.-g.
Judg 10. 4 thirty cities, which are called H.-J. unto

HAWK —

Hawk, נֵץ *nets.*
Lev. 11. 16 the cuckow, and the hawk after his kind
Deut 14. 15 the cuckow, and the hawk after his kind
Job 39. 26 Doth the hawk fly by thy wisdom..stretch

HAWK, night —

Owl, swallow, cuckoo, תַּחְמָס *tachmas.*
Lev. 11. 16 And the owl, and the night hawk, and
Deut 14. 15 And the owl, and the night hawk, and

HAY —

1. *Hay, grass, leek,* חָצִיר *chatsir.*
Prov. 27. 25 The hay appeareth, and the tender grass
Isa. 15. 6 the hay is withered away, the grass fail.

2. *Fodder, grass, hay,* χόρτος *chortos.*
1 Co. 3. 12 silver, precious stones, wood, hay, stubble

HA-ZA'-EL, חֲזָאֵל, חֲזָהאֵל *God sees.*
A king of Damascus who reigned from 885 to 840 B.C. He stood in a high official capacity at Ben-hadad's court, and was sent by the latter to Elisha (when he visited Damascus) to ask whether he would recover from the malady from which he was suffering. But Elisha's answer was that Benhadad *might* recover, but *would* certainly die. When Hazael returned he murdered his master and usurped the throne. Elijah had anointed him as king of Syria. B.C. 906.
1 Ki. 19. 15 Go, return..anoint H...king over Syria
19. 17 him that escapeth the sword of H. shall
2 Ki. 8. 8 the king said unto H., Take a present in
8. 9 So H. went to meet him, and took a pre.
8. 12 H. said, Why weepeth my lord? And he
8. 13 H. said, But what! (is) thy servant a dog
8. 15 he died: and H. reigned in his stead
8. 28 he went with Joram..to the war against H.
8. 29 when he fought against H. king of Syria
9. 14 Joram had kept Ram.-gil...because of H.
9. 15 when he fought with H. king of Syria
10. 32 H. smote them in all the coasts of Israel
12. 17 H...went up..and H. set his face to go
12. 18 sent (it) to H. king of Syria: and he went
13. 3 he delivered them into the hand of H.
13. 3 into the hand of Ben-hadad the son of H.
13. 22 H. king of Syria oppressed Israel all the
13. 24 So H. king of Syria died; and Ben-hadad
13. 25 out of the hand of Ben-hadad the son of H.
2 Ch. 22. 5 to war against H. king of Syria at Ramoth
22. 6 Ramah, when he fought with H. king of
Amos 1. 4 I will send a fire into the house of H.

HA-ZA'-IAH, חֲזָיָה *Jah is seeing.*
A man of Judah of the family of the Shilonites, or descendants of Shelah. B.C. 445.
Neh. 11. 5 the son of Col-hozeh, the son of H., the

HA-ZAR AD'-DAR, חֲצַר אַדָּר.
A place on the S. boundary of the promised land, between Kadesh-Barnea and Azmon. The name appears in the shorter form of *Addar* (or *Adar,* in Josh. 15. 3).
Num 34. 4 shall go on to H., and pass on to Azmon

HAZARD, to —

To give over, παραδίδωμι *paradidōmi.*
Acts 15. 26 Men that have hazarded their lives for

HA-ZAR E'-NAN, חֲצַר עֵינָן *court of the fountains.*
The spot at which the N. and E. boundaries of the promised land meet. The place has been identified with the modern *Kuryetein* ("the two cities"), a village more than 60 miles E.N.E. of Damascus. Here are large fountains, the only ones in that vast region.
Num 34. 9 and the goings out of it shall be at H.
34. 10 ye shall point out your east border from H.
Eze. 47. 17 the border from the sea shall be H., the
[In this passage the Hebrew is *Hazar-enon.*]
48 1 H., the border of Damascus northward, to

HA-ZAR GAD'-DAH, חֲצַר גַּדָּה *court of Gad.*
A town in the S. district of Judah, near Heshmon, but not identified with any modern site. Some think *Jurrah* near Moladah (*El-Milh*) is the modern site.
Josh. 15. 27 And H., and Heshmon, and Beth-palet

HA'-ZAR HAT-TI'-CON, חֲצַר הַתִּיכוֹן *middle Hazar.*
A place specified as on the boundary of Hauran, and named by Ezekiel (47. 16) as one of the ultimate boundaries of the land.
Eze. 47. 16 H., which (is) by the coast of Hauran

HA-ZAR-MA'-VETH, חֲצַרְמָוֶת *court of death.*
The third in order of the sons of Joktan of the family of Shem. B.C. 2210. The name is preserved in the Arabic *Hadramawt* and *Hadrumawt,* the appellation of a province and ancient people of southern Arabia. This identification of the settlement of the descendants of Joktan is accepted by most Biblical scholars. It rests not only on the resemblance of name, but is supported by the fact that Joktan settled in the *Yemen,* along the S. coast of Arabia; by the physical characteristics of the people of this region, and by the identification of the name of several others of Joktan's sons. The province of *Hadramawt* is E. of the modern *Yemen;* anciently the limits of the latter province embraced almost the whole of the S. of the peninsula, extending to the districts of *Shihr* and *Mahrek.* Its capital is *Shibâm,* a very ancient city, whose chief ports are *Mirbât, Kâfri,* and *Kisheem,* from which in ancient times a great trade was carried on with India and Africa.
Gen. 10. 26 Almodad, and Sheleph, and H., and Jer.
1 Ch. 1. 20 Almodad, and Sheleph, and H., and Jerah

HA'-ZAR SHU'-AL, חֲצַר שׁוּעָל *fox or jackal village.*
A town in the south of Judah, between Hazar-gaddah and Beer-sheba. The modern *Saweh* is at or about the right spot, and may be a corruption of the old name.
Josh. 15. 28 And H., and Beer-sheba, and Bizjothjah
19. 3 And H., and Balah, and Azem
1 Ch. 4. 28 dwelt at Beer-sheba, and Moladah, and H.
Neh. 11. 27 And at H...and (in) the villages thereof

HA-ZAR SU'-SAH (SUSIM), חֲצַר סוּסָה *horse village.*
A city in the extreme south of Judah, and allotted to Simeon; it stood near Beth-marcaboth, another city of Simeon.
Josh. 19. 5 Beth-marcaboth, and H.; 1 Ch. 4. 31.

HAZAZON. *See* **HAZEZON.**

HAZEL —

Hazel, לוּז *luz.*
Gen. 30. 37 Jacob took..of the hazel and chestnut

HA-ZE-LEL-PO'-NI, הַצְּלֶלְפּוֹנִי *protection of the face of.*
Sister of the sons of Etam in the genealogies of Judah. B.C. 1380.
1 Ch. 4. 3 and the name of their sister (was) H.

HA-ZE'-RIM, חֲצֵרִים *villages, courts.*
A district in the S. of Canaan near *Gaza,* inhabited in ancient times by the Avim (or Avvim), a tribe that tented over the S.W. of Palestine, and are said to have lived in villages (Hazerim) as far as Gaza (Deut. 2. 23) before their expulsion by the Caphtorim.
Deut. 2. 23 And the Avims which dwelt in H.

HA-ZE'-ROTH, חֲצֵרוֹת *courts, villages.*
The station of the Israelites in the desert next to Kibroth-Hattaavah, and perhaps recognisable in the Arabic *Hudhera,* which is about eighteen hours' journey from Sinai on the road to Akabah.
Num 11. 35 from Kibroth unto H.; and abode at H.
12. 16 afterward the people removed from H.
33. 17 And they departed..and encamped at H.
33. 18 they departed from H., and pitched in
Deut. 1. 1 Paran, and Tophel, and Laban, and H.

HA-ZE-ZON TA'-MAR, חַצְצֹן תָּמָר *row of palms.*
The ancient name of *En-gedi.* The Amorites were dwelling in Hazezon-tamar when the four kings (Gen. 14. 7) made their incursion and fought their successful battle with the five kings. The name is interpreted by Gesenius as "the pruning or felling of the palm;" Jerome calls it *Urbs palmarum.* This may have been the "city of palm trees" (Judg. 1. 16).
Gen. 14. 7 smote..the Amorites, that dwelt in H.
2 Ch. 20. 2 behold, they (be) in Hazazon..En-gedi

HA-ZI'-EL, חֲזִיאֵל *God is seeing.*
A Levite of the family of Shimei or Shimi in the time of David. This was the younger branch of the Gershonites. B.C. 1015.
1 Ch. 23. 9 sons of Shimei; Shelomith, and H., and

HA'-ZO, חֲזוֹ *vision, seer.*
A son of Nahor by Milcah his wife. The name has not been perpetuated in either territory or posterity, B.C. 1890. But he must be placed in Ur (of the Chaldees), or the adjacent countries. Chazene by the Euphrates in Mesopotamia, or Chazene in Assyria, is suggested by Bunsen.
Gen. 22. 22 Chesed, and H., and Pildash, and Jidlaph

HA'-ZOR, חָצוֹר *enclosed.*
1. A fortified city allotted to Naphtali. It was between Ramah and Kadesh on the high ground overlooking Lake Merom. It is now *Khurubeh,* "the ruins," near Kedesh and Lake *Huleh.* Jabin was its king, and it was the chief city of the whole of North Palestine, "the head of all those kingdoms" (Josh. 11. 10). Hazor was the only city burnt by Joshua.
Josh. 11. 1 when Jabin king of H. had heard (those
11. 10 Joshua at that time turned..and took H.
11. 10 H...was the head of all those kingdoms
11. 11 they smote..and he burnt H. with fire
11. 13 Israel burned none of them, save H. only
12. 19 king of Madon, one; the king of H., one
19. 36 And Adamah, and Ramah, and H.
Judg. 4. 2 Jabin king of Canaan, that reigned in H.
4. 17 peace between Jabin the king of H. and
1 Sa. 12. 9 hand of Sisera, captain of the host of H.
2 Ki. 15. 29 took..H., and Gilead, and Galilee, all the
2. A city in the extreme south of Judah, named next in order to *Kedesh* (Josh. 15. 23).
Josh 15. 23 And Kedesh, and H., and Ithnan
1 Ki. 9. 15 and H., and Megiddo, and Gezer
3. Hazor-Hadattah, "new Hazor," another of the southern towns of Judah.
Josh 15. 25 and Kerioth, (and) Hezron, which (is) H.
4. A place in which the Benjamites resided after their return from captivity. It was N. of Jerusalem, and not far distant from it. Probably identical with *Baal-hazor.*
Neh. 11. 33 H., Ramah, Gittaim
5. A name given to certain countries in the E. of Arabia.
Jer. 49. 28 and concerning the kingdoms of H., which
49. 30 Flee, get you far off..ye inhabitants of H.
49. 33 And H. shall be a dwelling for dragons

HA-ZOR HA-DAT'-TAH, חָצוֹר חֲדַתָּה *new court or village.*
A city of Judah near Kerioth. (See No. 3, under *Hazor.*)
Josh 15. 25 Hazor Hadattah, and Kerioth, (and) H.

HE —

1. *A man, any one,* אִישׁ *ish.*
Prov. 28. 22 He that hasteth to be rich (hath) an evil
29. 1 He that, being often reproved, hardeneth
29. 4 but he that receiveth gifts overthroweth

2. *He himself,* הוּא *hu.*
Gen. 4. 4 Abel, he also brought of the firstlings of
Isa. 9. 15 ancient and honourable, he (is) the head
9. 15 the prophet that teacheth lies, he (is) the

3. *This one,* זֶה *zeh.*
Exod 15. 2 LORD. is become my salvation: he (is)

4. *Who? he who,* מִי *mi.*
2 Sa. 20. 11 He that favoureth Joab, and he that (is)

5. *Soul, breathing thing,* נֶפֶשׁ *nephesh.*
Psa. 105. 18 Whose feet they hurt..he was laid in iron

6. *The hand,* יָד *yad.*
Lev. 5. 7, 11 And if he be not able · 12 8. 25. 28

7. *He, he himself,* αὐτός *autos.*
Matt. 1. 21 he shall save his people from their sins
3. 11 he that cometh after me is mightier than
8. 24 covered with the waves: but he was asleep
12. 3 when [he] was an hungered, and they that
14. 2 This is John the Baptist: he is risen from
16. 20 should tell no man that he was Jesus the
21. 27 he said unto them, Neither tell I you by
25. 17 And likewise..[he] also gained other two
Mark 1. 8 but he shall baptize you with the Holy G.
2. 25 And he said unto them, Have ye never
2. 25 what David did..he, and they that were
3. 13 called..whom he would: and they came
4. 27 spring and grow up, he knoweth not how
4. 38 he was in the hinder part of the ship, asl.
6. 16 said, It is John..[he] is risen from the dead
6. 45 unto Bethsaida, while he sent away the
6. 47 midst of the sea, and he alone on the land
7. 36 the more [he] charged them, so much the
8. 29 he saith unto them, But whom say ye that
12. 21 [neither left he any seed: and the third]
14. 15 he will show you a large upper room fur.
Luke 1. 17 he shall go before him in the spirit and
1. 22 he beckoned unto them, and remained
2. 28 Then took he him up in his arms, and
3. 15 mused..whether he were the Christ, or
3. 16 he shall baptize you with the Holy Ghost
4. 15 he taught in their synagogues, being glo.
4. 30 he passing through the midst of them
5. 1 of God, he stood by the lake of Gennesaret
5. 14 he charged him to tell no man: but go

Luke 5. 16 he withdrew himself into the wilderness
5. 17 came to pass on a certain day, as he was
6. 8 he knew their thoughts, and said to the
6. 20 he lifted up his eyes on his disciples, and
6. 35 he is kind unto the unthankful and (to)
7. 5 loveth our nation, and he hath built us a
8. 1 that he went throughout every city and
8. 22 that he went into a ship with his disciples
8. 37 he went up into the ship, and returned
8. 41 and [he] was a ruler of the synagogue: and
8. 54 he put them all out, and took her by the h.
9. 51 he stedfastly set his face to go to Jerusal.
10. 38 that he entered into a certain village: and
11. 17 But he, knowing their thoughts, said unto
11. 28 But he said, Yea rather, blessed (are) they
15. 14 when..had spent all..he began to be in
16. 24 he cried and said, Father Abraham, have
17. 11 he passed through the midst of Samaria
18. 39 should hold his peace: but he cried so
19. 9 forasmuch as he also is a son of Abraham
22. 41 he was withdrawn from them about a
23. 9 questioned with him in many words; but
24. 21 he which should have redeemed Israel
24. 25 Then he said unto them, O fools, and slow
24. 28 he made as though he would have gone f.
24. 31 knew him; and he vanished out of their
John 1. 27 [He it is,] who coming after me, is preferred
2. 12 went down to Capernaum, he, and his m.
2. 25 should testify..for he knew what was in
7. 10 then went he also up unto the feast, not
9. 21 he is of age, ask him; [he] shall speak for
12. 49 he gave me a commandment, what I should
14. 10 the Father, that dwelleth in me, he doeth
18. 1 into the which he entered and his discip.
Acts 7. 15 So Jacob..died, he, and our fathers
10. 42 that it is [he] which was ordained of God
14. 12 Mercurius, because he was chief speaker
16. 33 was baptized, he and all his, straightway
17. 25 seeing he giveth to all life, and breath
20. 35 how he said, It is more blessed to give
28. 6 changed their minds, and said that he was
Eph. 2. 14 he is our peace, who hath made both one
4. 11 he gave some, apostles; and some, prop.
5. 23 as Christ..and he is the saviour of the
5. 27 That he might present it to himself a glo.
Col. 1. 17 he is before all things, and by him all
1. 18 And he is the head of the body, the chu.
1. 18 that in all..he might have the pre-emin.
Heb. 1. 5 I will be to him a Father, and he shall be
4. 10 he also hath ceased from his own works
Jas. 1. 13 God cannot..neither tempteth he any
1 Jo. 1. 7 if we walk in the light, as he is in the
2. 2 he is the propitiation for our sins; and
2. 25 this is the promise that he hath promised
3. 24 dwelleth in him, and he in him. And
4. 10 but that he loved us, and sent his Son
4. 13 that we dwell in him, and he in us, beca.
4. 15 confess..God dwelleth in him, and he in
4. 19 We love him, because [he] first loved us
Rev. 3. 20 come..and will sup with him, and he with
14. 17 angel came..he also having a sharp sickle
17. 11 the beast that was, and is not, even he is
19. 15 he shall rule them with a rod of iron
19. 15 he treadeth the wine press of the fiercen.
21. 7 I will be his God, and he shall be my Son

8. *That person there,* ἐκεῖνος *ekeinos.*
John 1. 18 the only begotten Son..he hath declared
2. 21 But he spake of the temple of his body
3. 30 He must increase, but I (must) decrease
4. 25 I know that Messias cometh..when he is
5. 19 what things soever he doeth, these also
5. 35 He was a burning and a shining light: and
5. 38 for whom he hath sent, him ye believe not
5. 46 ye would have believed me: for he wrote
6. 29 that ye believe on him whom he hath se.
7. 11 the Jews sought him..said, Where is he?
8. 42 neither came I of myself, but he sent me
8. 44 He was a murderer from the beginning
9. 9 others (said)..is like him: (but) he said
9. 11 He answered and said A man that is cal.
9. 12 then said they unto him, Where is he?
9. 25 He answered and said, whether..a sinner
9. 36 He answered and said, Who..Lord, that
9. 37 Thou hast both seen him, and it is he th.
13. 25 He then lying on Jesus' breast saith unto
13. 26 He it is to whom I shall give a sop, when
13. 30 He then having received the sop went
14. 21 and keepeth them, he it is that loveth
14. 26 he shall teach you all things, and bring
15. 26 when the Comforter is come..he shall
16. 8 he will reprove the world of sin, and of
16. 13 Howbeit when he, the spirit of truth, is
16. 14 He shall glorify me..shall receive of mine
18. 17 Art not thou also (one)..He saith, I am
18. 25 Art not thou also (one)..He denied (it)
19. 21 but that he said, I am king of the Jews
Acts 3. 13 when [he] was determined to let (him) go
2 Co. 10. 18 For not he that commendeth himself is
2 Ti. 2. 13 If we believe not, (yet) he abideth faithful
1 Jo. 2. 6 ought himself also so to walk, even as he
3. 3 every man..purifieth himself, even as he
3. 5 ye know that he was manifested to take
3. 7 is righteous, even as he is righteous
3. 16 because he laid down his life for us: and
4. 17 because as he is, so are we in this world

9. *This one here,* ὅδε *hode.*
Luke 16. 25 now [he] is comforted, and thou art torm.

10. *This person here,* οὗτος *houtos.*
Matt 13. 22, 23 that received seed..is he that heareth
27. 58 He went to Pilate and begged the body
Luke 1. 32 He shall be great, and shall be called the
19. 2 was the chief..and [he] was r. 20. 28, 30.
23. 22 Why, what evil hath he done? I have fou.
23. 35 let him save himself, if he be Christ, the
John 1. 41 He first findeth his own brother Simon
4. 47 When he heard that Jesus was come out
6. 42 how is it then that [he] saith, I came down
6. 46 which is of God, he hath seen the Father
6. 71 for he it was that should betray him, be.
7. 35 Whither will he go, that we shall not find
18. 30 If he were not a malefactor, we would
Acts 3. 10 they knew that it was he which sat for
4. 9 impotent man, by what means he is made
7. 36 He brought them out, after that..had
9. 15 for he is a chosen vessel unto me, to bear
9. 20 preached Christ..that he is the Son of G.
10. 6 He lodgeth with one Simon a tanner
10. 6 [he shall tell thee what thou oughtest to]
10. 32 he is lodged in the house of..Simon a ta.
10. 36 peace by Jesus Christ: he is Lord of all
17. 24 seeing that he is Lord of heaven and ear.
18. 26 he began to speak boldly in the synagogue
Rom. 8. 9 have not the spirit..he is none of his
Jas. 1. 23 he is like unto a man beholding his natu.
1. 25 [he] being not a forgetful hearer, but a
1 Jo. 2. 22 he is antichrist, that denieth the Father
2 John 9 abideth..he hath both the Father and

11. *Any one, a certain one,* τις *tis.*
Acts 4. 35 unto every man according as he had need
Heb. 10. 28 He that despised Moses' law died without

HE also —
Even that one, κἀκεῖνος *kakeinos.*
John 14. 12 the works that I do shall he do also; and
Acts 5. 37 he also perished; and all..as many as
2 Ti. 2. 12 if we deny (him), he also will deny us

HE himself —
1. *He himself,* αὐτός *autos.*
Luke 10. 1 city and place, whither he himself would
John 6. 6 for he himself knew what he would do
6. 15 he departed again into a mountain hims.
7. 4 and he himself seeketh to be known ope.
Acts 2. 34 he saith himself, The LORD said unto my
18. 19 he himself entered into the synagogue
19. 22 but he himself stayed in Asia for a season
1 Co. 2. 15 he that is spiritual..he himself is judged
3. 15 he himself shall be saved; yet so as by
Heb. 2. 18 in that he himself hath suffered, being
5. 2 he himself also is compassed with infirm.
3 John 10 neither doth he himself receive the bret.
Rev. 19. 12 a name..that no man knew but he him.

2. *This one himself,* αὐτὸς οὗτος *autos houtos* (*gen.*)
Acts 25. 25 he himself hath appealed to Augustus

3. *One's self, himself,* ἑαυτοῦ *heautou.*
Luke 23. 2 saying that he himself is Christ a
Acts 25. 4 that he himself would depart shortly

HE that —
1. *If any one,* εἴ τις *ei tis.*
Rev. 13. 10 He that leadeth into captivity shall go
13. 10 he that killeth with the sword must be

2. *He who,* ὅς *hos.*
Matt 10. 38 he that taketh not his cross, and followeth
Mark 3. 29 he that shall blaspheme against the Holy
4. 25 For he that hath..and he that hath not
9. 40 he that is not against us is on our part

3. *Who at least,* ὅσγε *hosge.*
Rom. 8. 32 He that spared not his own Son, but deli.

4. *Whoever,* ὅστις *hostis.*
Matt 23. 12 he that shall humble himself shall be ex.

HE, (even he,) and —
Even that one, κἀκεῖνος *kakeinos.*
Luke 11. 7 And he from within shall answer and say
22. 12 And he shall show you a large upper room
John 6. 57; 7. 29; 19. 35.
And he, ὁ δέ *ho de.*
Matt. 2. 21 And he arose, and took the; 12. 11

HE be —
There is, there are, יֵשׁ *yesh.*
1 Sa. 23. 23 if he be in the land, that I will search

HE goat —
1. *He goat, vigorous,* עַתּוּד *attud.*
Num. 7. 17 five rams, five he goats, five lambs of the
[So in verse 23, 29, 35, 41, 47, 53, 59, 65, 71, 77, 83.]
7. 88 the rams sixty, the he goats sixty, the
Isa. 1. 11 I delight not in the blood..of he goats
Jer. 50. 8 and be as the he goats before the flocks
51. 40 bring them down like..rams with he go.
Eze. 34. 17 judge..between the rams and the he go.

2. *A young he goat, hairy,* צָפִיר *tsaphir.*
2 Ch. 29. 21 seven he goats, for a sin offering for the
Ezra 8. 35 twelve he goats (for) a sin offering: all
Dan. 8. 8 Therefore the he goat waxed very great

3. *Hairy one of the goats,* צְפִיר עִזִּים [*tsaphir*].
Ezra 6. 17 twelve he goats, according to the number
Dan. 8. 5 an he goat came from the west, on the

HE is —
There is, יֵשׁ *yesh.*
1 Sa. 9. 12 and said, He is; behold (he is) before you

HEAD —
1. *Poll, skull,* גֻּלְגֹּלֶת *gulgoleth.*
1 Ch. 10. 10 fastened his head in the temple of Dagon

2. *Pillow, bolster,* מְרַאֲשֹׁת *meraashoth.*
1 Ki. 19. 6 a cruse of water at his head: and he did

3. *Head,* רֵאשׁ *resh.*
Dan. 2. 28 the visions of thy head upon thy bed, are
2. 32 This image's head (was) of fine gold, his
2. 38 made thee ruler..Thou (art) this head of
3. 27 nor was an hair of their head singed
4. 5 and the visions of my head troubled me
4. 10 the visions of mine head in my bed; I
4. 13 I saw in the visions of my head upon my bed
7. 1 Daniel had a dream and visions of his h.
7. 6 the beast had also four heads; and domin.
7. 9 the hair of his head like the pure wool
7. 15 and the visions of my head troubled me
7. 20 of the ten horns that (were) in his head

4. *Head,* רֹאשׁ *rosh.*
Gen. 2. 10 it was parted, and became into four heads
3. 15 it shall bruise thy head, and thou shalt
40. 13, 19 Yet..shall Pharaoh lift up thine head
40. 16 (I had) three white baskets on my head
40. 17 eat them out of the basket upon my head
40. 20 he lifted up the head of the chief butler
47. 31 Israel bowed himself upon the bed's head
48. 14 Ephraim's head..upon Manasseh's head
48. 17 his right hand upon the head of Ephraim
48. 17 from Ephraim's head unto Manasseh's h.
48. 18 father..put thy right hand upon his head
49. 26 they shall be on the head of Joseph, and
Exod. 6. 14 These (be) the heads of their father's ho.
6. 25 these (are) the heads of the fathers of the
12. 9 but roast (with) fire; his head with his
18. 25 Moses..made them heads over the people
26. 24 above the head of it unto one ring: thus
29. 6 thou shall put the mitre upon his head
29. 7 pour (it) upon his head, and anoint him
29. 10, 15, 19 shall put their hands upon the h.
29. 17 put..unto his pieces, and unto his head
36. 29 coupled together at the head thereof, to
Lev. 1. 4 he shall put his hand upon the head of
1. 8 lay..the head..in order upon the wood
1. 12 his pieces, with his head and his fat: and
1. 15 the priest shall... ring off his head, and
3. 2, 8, 13 he shall lay his hand upon the head
4. 4 lay his hand upon the bullock's head, and
4. 11 with his head, and with his legs, and his
4. 15 shall lay their hands upon the head of the
4. 24, 29, 33 he shall lay his hand upon the head
5. 8 and wring off his head from his neck, but
8. 9 he put the mitre upon his head; also upon
8. 12 And he poured..oil upon Aaron's head
8. 14, 18, 22 laid their hands upon the head of
8. 20 Moses burnt the head, and the pieces, and
9. 13 with the pieces thereof, and the head
10. 6 And Moses said..Uncover not your heads
13. 12 the plague from his head even to his foot
13. 29 If a man..have a plague upon the head
13. 30 (even) a leprosy upon the head or beard
13. 40 the man whose hair is fallen off his head
13. 41 from the part of his head toward his face
13. 44 a leprous man..his plague (is) in his head
13. 45 clothes shall be rent, and his head bare
14. 9 he shall shave all his hair off his head
14. 18, 29 upon the head of him that is to be
16. 21 shall lay both his hands upon the head
16. 21 putting them upon the head of the goat
19. 27 shall not round the corners of your heads
21. 5 shall not make baldness upon their head
21. 10 upon whose head the..oil was poured
21. 10 shall not uncover his head, nor rend his
24. 14 let all..lay their hands upon his head
Num. 1. 4 every one head of the house of his fathers
1. 16 princes..heads of thousands in Israel
5. 18 priest shall..uncover the woman's head
6. 5 there shall no razor come upon his head
6. 5 shall let the locks of the hair of his head
6. 7 consecration of his God (is) upon his head
6. 9 hath defiled the head of his consecration
6. 9 then he shall shave his head in the day
6. 11 and shall hallow his head that same day
6. 18 And the Nazarite shall shave the head of
6. 18 and shall take the hair of the head of his
7. 2 heads of the house of their fathers, who
8. 12 shall lay their hands upon the heads of
10. 4 heads of the thousands of Israel, shall
13. 3 those men (were) heads of the children of
17. 3 the head of the house of their fathers
25. 4 Take all the heads of the people, and ha.
25. 15 he (was) head over a people, (and) of a c.
30. 1 Moses spake unto the heads of the tribes
Deut. 1. 15 and made them heads over you, captains
5. 23 the heads of your tribes, and your elders
21. 12 shall shave her head, and pare her nails
28. 13 the LORD shall make thee the head, and
28. 23 thy heaven that (is) over thy head shall
28. 44 he shall be the head, and thou shalt be
33. 5 the heads of the people (and) the tribes
33. 16 come upon the head of Joseph, and upon
33. 21 he came with the heads of the people
Josh. 2. 19 blood (shall be) upon his head..on our h.
7. 6 and the elders..put dust upon their he.
11. 10 was the head of all those kingdoms
14. 1 the heads of the fathers of the tribes of
19. 51 the heads of the fathers of the tribes of
21. 1 came near the heads..unto the heads
22. 21, 30 heads of the thousands of Israel
23. 2 for their elders, and for their heads, and
24. 1 for their heads, and for their judges, and
Judg. 5. 26 smote Sisera, she smote off his head, when
7. 25 brought the heads of Oreb and Zeeb to G.
8. 28 so..they lifted up their heads no more
9. 53 cast a..millstone upon Abimelech's head

Judg. 9. 57 evil..did God render upon their heads
10. 18 shall be head over all the inhabitants of
11. 8 be our head over all the inhabitants of G.
11. 9 And Jephthah said..shall I be your head?
11. 11 the people made him head and captain
13. 5 no razor shall come on his head: for the
16. 13 weavest the seven locks of my head with
16. 17 hath not come a razor upon mine head
16. 19 to shave off the seven locks of his head
16. 22 the hair of his head began to grow again
1 Sa. 1. 11 there shall no razor come upon his head
4. 12 his clothes rent, and..earth upon his he.
5. 4 head of Dagon and both the palms of his
10. 1 took a vial..and poured (it) upon his he.
14. 45 there shall not one hair of his head fall
15. 17 the head of the tribes of Israel, and the
17. 5 an helmet of brass upon his head, and he
17. 38 he put an helmet of brass upon his head
17. 46 smite thee, and take thine head from thee
17. 51 David..slew him, and cut off his head
17. 54 David took the head of the Philistine, and
17. 57 the head of the Philistine in his hand
25. 39 wickedness of Nabal upon his own head
28. 2 make thee keeper of mine head for ever
29. 4 (should it) not (be) with the heads of these
31. 9 they cut off his head, and stripped off his
2 Sa. 1. 2 his clothes rent, and earth upon his head
1. 10 took the crown that (was) upon his head
1. 16 David said..Thy blood (be) upon thy head
2. 16 caught every one his fellow by the head
3. 8 Abner..said, (Am) I a dog's head, which
3. 29 Let it rest on the head of Joab, and on all
4. 7 beheaded him, and took his head, and gat
4. 8 they brought the head of Ish-bosheth unto
4. 8 Behold the head of Ish-bosheth the son of
4. 12 but they took the head of Ish-bosheth
12. 30 took their king's crown from off his head
12. 30 stones: and it was (set) on David's head
13. 19 Tamar put ashes on her head, and rent h.
13. 19 laid her hand on her head, and went on
14. 26 when he polled his head, for it was at
14. 26 he weighed the hair of his head at two
15. 30 as he went up, and had his head covered
15. 30 all the people..covered every man his h.
15. 32 with his coat rent, and earth upon his h.
16. 9 let me go over..and take off his head
18. 9 his head, caught hold of the oak, and he
20. 21 his head shall be thrown to thee over the
20. 22 they cut off the head of Sheba the son of B.
22. 44 hast kept me (to be) head of the heathen
1 Ki. 2. 32 shall return his blood upon his own head
2. 33 head of Joab, and upon the head of his
2. 37 thy blood shall be upon thine own head
2. 44 return thy wickedness upon thine..head
8. 1 all the heads of the tribes, the chief of
8. 32 bring his way upon his head; and justi.
20. 31 let us..put..ropes upon our heads, and
20. 32 So they..(put) ropes on their heads, and
2 Ki. 2. 3, 5 take..thy master from thy head to day?
4. 19 he said unto his father, My head, my h.!
6. 25 until an ass's head was (sold) for fourscore
6. 31 if the head of Elisha the son of Shaphat
6. 32 hath sent to take away mine head?
9. 3 take..oil, and pour (it) on his head, and
9. 6 he poured the oil on his head, and said
9. 30 she painted her face, and tired her head
10. 6 take ye the heads of..your master's sons
10. 7 put their heads in baskets, and sent him
10. 8 brought the heads of the king's sons
19. 21 Jerusalem hath shaken her head at thee
25. 27 did lift up the head of Jehoiachin king of
1 Ch. 5. 24, 24 heads of the house of their fathers
7. 2, 40 heads of their father's house
7. 7, 9 heads of the house of (their) fathers
7. 11 All these..by the heads of their fathers
8. 6, 13 heads of the fathers of the inhabitants
8. 10 These (were) his sons, heads of the fathers
8. 28 These (were) heads of the fathers, by their
9. 13 heads of the house of their fathers, a tho.
10. 9 they took his head, and his armour, and
12. 19 He will fall..to (the jeopardy of) our he.
12. 32 the heads of them (were) two hundred
20. 2 David took the crown..from off his head
20. 2 it was set upon David's head: and he br.
29. 11 and thou art exalted as head above all
2 Ch. 3. 16 put (them) on the heads of the pillars; and
5. 2 and all the heads of the tribes, the chief
6. 23 recompensing his way upon his own head
28. 12 of the heads of the children of Ephraim
Ezra 9. 3 plucked off the hair of my head and of
9. 6 our iniquities are increased over (our) h.
Neh. 4. 4 turn their reproach upon their own head
Esth. 2. 17 he set the royal crown upon her head
6. 8 the crown royal which is set upon his h.
6. 12 house mourning, and having his head co.
9. 25 should return upon his own head, and
Job 1. 20 Then Job arose..and shaved his head, and
2. 12 and sprinkled dust upon their heads to.
10. 15 (yet) will I not lift up my head. I (am)
16. 4 I could heap up words..and shake mine h.
19. 9 He hath..taken the crown (from) my h.
20. 6 and his head reach unto the clouds
29. 3 When his candle shined upon my head
41. 7 Canst thou fill..his head with fish spears?
Psa. 3. 3 my glory, and the lifter up of mine head
7. 16 mischief shall return upon his own head
18. 43 hast made me the head of the heathen: a
21. 3 settest a crown of pure gold on his head
22. 7 they shoot out the lip, they shake the h.
23. 5 thou anointest my head with oil; my cup
24. 7, 9 Lift up your heads, O ye gates..lift up
27. 6 now shall mine head be lifted up above

Psa. 38. 4 mine iniquities are gone over mine head
40. 12 they are more than the hairs of mine he.
44. 14 a shaking of the head among the people
60. 7 Ephraim also (is) the strength of mine h.
66. 12 hast caused men to ride over our heads
68. 21 God shall wound the head of his enemies
69. 4 are more than the hairs of mine head
74. 13 thou brakest the heads of the dragons
74. 14 Thou brakest the heads of leviathan in
83. 2 they that hate thee have lifted..the head
108. 8 Ephraim..(is) the strength of mine head
109. 25 looked upon me they shaked their heads
110. 6 he shall wound the heads over many cou.
110. 7 drink..therefore shall he lift up the head
118. 22 is become the head (stone) of the corner
133. 2 the precious ointment upon the head
140. 7 thou hast covered my head in the day of
140. 9 the head of those that compass me about
141. 5 oil, (which) shall not break my head: for
Prov. 1. 9 an ornament of grace unto thy head, and
4. 9 shall give to thine head an ornament of
10. 6 Blessings (are) upon the head of the just
11. 26 blessing (shall be) upon the head of him
25. 22 shalt heap coals of fire upon his head, and
Eccl. 2. 14 The wise man's eyes (are) in his head; but
9. 8 and let thy head lack no ointment
Song 2. 6 His left hand (is) under my head, and his
5. 2 for my head is filled with dew, (and) my
5. 11 His head (is as) the most fine gold; his
7. 5 Thine head upon thee (is) like Carmel, and
7. 5 hair of thine head like purple: the king
8. 3 His left hand (should be) under my head
Isa. 1. 5 The whole head is sick, and..heart faint
1. 6 even unto the head (there is) no soundn.
7. 8 For the head of Syria (is) Damascus, and
7. 8 head of Damascus (is) Rezin; and within
7. 9 head of Ephraim..and the head of Sam.
7. 20 the head, and the hair of the feet: and it
9. 14 will cut off from Israel head and tail
9. 15 The ancient and honourable, he (is) the h.
15. 2 on all their heads (shall be) baldness, (and)
19. 15 work..which the head or tail..may do
28. 1 which (are) on the head of the fat valleys
28. 4 which (is) on the head of the fat valley
35. 10 and everlasting joy upon their heads: they
37. 22 daughter..hath shaken her head at thee
51. 11 everlasting joy (shall be) upon their head
51. 20 they lie at the head of all the streets, as
58. 5 (is it) to bow down his head as a bulrush
59. 17 and an helmet of salvation upon his head
Jer. 2. 37 and thine hands upon thine head: for
9. 1 Oh that my head were waters, and mine
14. 3 they were ashamed..and covered their h.
14. 4 were ashamed, they covered their heads
18. 16 every one that passeth..shall..wag his h.
22. 6 Thou (art) Gilead..(and) the head of L.
23. 19 grievously upon the head of the wicked
30. 23 fall with pain upon the head of the wic.
48. 37 For every head (shall be) bald, and every
52. 31 lifted up the head of Jehoiachin king of
Lam. 2. 10 they have cast up dust upon their heads
2. 10 the virgins..hang down their heads to
2. 15 they..wag their head at the daughter of
3. 54 Waters flowed over mine head; (then) I
5. 16 The crown is fallen (from) our head: woe
Eze 1. 22 upon the heads of the living creature
1. 22 stretched forth over their heads above
1. 25, 26 the firmament that (was) over their h.
5. 1 cause (it) to pass upon thine head and
7. 18 faces, and baldness upon all their heads
8. 3 took me by a lock of mine head; and the
9. 10 will recompense their way upon their h.
10. 1 that was above the head of the cherubim
10. 11 whither the head looked they followed it
11. 21 recompense their way upon their own h.
13. 18 kerchiefs upon the head of every stature
16. 12 and a beautiful crown upon thine head
16. 25 thy high place at every head of the way
16. 31 eminent place in the head of every way
16. 43 will recompense thy way upon (thine) h.
17. 19 it will I recompense upon his own head
21. 19 chose (it) at the head of the way to the
21. 21 stood..at the head of the two ways, to
22. 31 have I recompensed upon their heads
23. 15 in dyed attire upon their heads, all of them
23. 42 and beautiful crowns upon their heads
24. 23 And your tires (shall be) upon your heads
27. 30 and shall cast up dust upon their heads
29. 18 every head (was) made bald, and every
32. 27 laid their swords under their heads; but
42. 12 a door in the head of the way, (even) the
44. 18 shall have linen bonnets upon their heads
44. 20 Neither shall they shave their heads, nor
44. 20 grow long; they shall only poll their hea.
Dan. 1. 10 ye make (me) endanger my head to the
Hos. 1. 11 appoint themselves one head, and they
Joel 3. 4, 7 return your recompence upon your..h.
Amos 2. 7 of the earth on the head of the poor
8. 10 I will bring..baldness upon every head
9. 1 and cut them in the head, all of them
Obad. 15 reward shall return upon thine own head
Jon. 2. 5 the weeds were wrapped about my head
4. 6 that it might be a shadow over his head
4. 8 the sun beat upon the head of Jonah, that
Mic. 2. 13 and the LORD on the head of them
3. 1 Hear, I pray you, O heads of Jacob, and
3. 9 Hear this..ye heads of the house of Jacob
3. 11 The heads thereof judge for reward, and
Hab. 3. 13 thou woundest the head out of the house
3. 14 with his staves the head of his villages
Zech. 1. 21 so that no man did lift up his head: but
3. 5 Let them set a fair mitre upon his head

Zech. 3. 5 So they set a fair mitre upon his head
6. 11 set (them) upon the head of Joshua the

5. *The head*, κεφαλή *kephalē*.
Matt. 5. 36 Neither shalt thou swear by thy head, be.
6. 17 when thou fastest, anoint thine head, and
8. 20 Son of man hath not where to lay (his) h.
10. 30 very hairs of your head are all numbered
14. 8 Give me..John Baptist's head in a char.
14. 11 his head was brought in a charger, and
21. 42 the same is become the head of the cor.
26. 7 poured (it) on his head, as he sat (at meat)
27. 29 they put (it) upon his head, and a reed
27. 30 took the reed, and smote him on the head
27. 37 set up over his head his accusation writ.
27. 39 And they..reviled him, wagging their he.
Mark 6. 24 she said, The head of John the Baptist
6. 25 give me..in a charger the head of John
6. 27 and commanded his head to be brought
6. 28 brought his head in a charger, and gave
12. 10 stone..is become the head of the corner
14. 3 brake the box, and poured (it) on his head
15. 19 they smote him on the head with a reed
15. 29 they..railed on him, wagging their heads
Luke 7. 38 did wipe (them) with the hairs of her head
7. 44 wiped (them) with the hairs of her head
7. 46 My head with oil thou didst not anoint
9. 58 Son of man hath not where to lay (his) h.
12. 7 very hairs of your head are all numbered
20. 17 the same is become the head of the cor.
21. 18 shall not an hair of your head perish
21. 28 then look up, and lift up your heads; for
John 13. 9 Lord, not my feet only but also (my)..he.
19. 2 a crown of thorns, and put (it) on his head
19. 30 he bowed his head, and gave up the ghost
20. 7 And the napkin, that was about his head
20. 12 two angels..sitting, the one at the head
Acts 4. 11 which is become the head of the corner
18. 6 Your blood (be) upon your own heads; I
18. 18 having shorn (his) head in Cenchrea: for
21. 24 that they may shave (their) heads: and all
27. 34 shall not an hair fall from the head of any
Rom 12. 20 thou shalt heap coals of fire on his head
1 Co. 11. 3 that the head of every man is Christ; and
11. 3 the head of the woman..and the head
11. 4 (his) head covered, dishonoureth his head
11. 5 head uncovered, dishonoureth her head
11. 7 man indeed ought not to cover (his) head
11. 10 power on (her) head because of the angels
12. 21 nor again the head to the feet, I have no
Eph. 1. 22 gave him (to be) the head over all (things)
4. 15 into him..which is the head, (even) Christ
5. 23 For the husband is the head of the wife
5. 23 even as Christ is the head of the church
Col. 1. 18 he is the head of the body, the church
2. 10 is the head of all principality and power
2. 19 not holding the Head, from which all the
1 Pe. 2. 7 the same is made the head of the corner
Rev. 1. 14 His head and..hairs (were) white like w.
4. 4 they had on their heads crowns of gold
9. 7 on their heads (were) as it were crowns
9. 17 the heads of the horses (were) as the heads
9. 19 like unto serpents, and had heads, and
10. 1 and a rainbow (was) upon his head, and
12. 1 upon her head a crown of twelve stars
12. 3 great red dragon, having seven heads and
12. 3 ten horns, and seven crowns upon his heads
13. 1 beast..having seven heads and ten horns
13. 1 upon his heads the name of blasphemy
13. 3 I saw one of his heads as it were wounded
14. 14 having on his head a golden crown, and
17. 3 beast..having seven heads and ten horns
17. 7 which hath the seven heads and ten horns
17. 9 The seven heads are seven mountains, on
18. 19 they cast dust on their heads, and cried
19. 12 and on his head (were) many crowns; and

HEAD, wound in the —

To bring to a head, κεφαλαιόω *kephalaioō*.
Mark 12. 4 cast stones, and wounded (him) in the h.

[*See also* Ox head, bald, cow, crown, grey, hoar, hoary. top.]

HEAD (of a hatchet or spear) —

1. *Iron*, בַּרְזֶל *barzel*.
Deut 19. 5 and the head slippeth from the helve, and

2. *Flame, blade*, לֶהָבָה *lahebeth*.
1 Sa. 17. 7 spear's head (weighed) six hundred shek.

HEAD BANDS —

Bands, girdle, קִשֻּׁרִים *qishshurim*.
Isa. 3. 20 the head bands, and the tablets, and the

HEADLONG, to cast down —

To cast down a precipice, κατακρημνίζω *katakrēm.*
Luke 4. 29 that they might cast him down headlong

HEADLONG, to fall —

To fall forward, πρηνὴς γίνομαι *prēnēs ginomai.*
Acts 1. 18 falling headlong, he burst asunder in th.

HEAD STONE —

Stone of the head, אֶבֶן רֹאשָׁה *eben roshah.*
Zech. 4. 7 and he shall bring forth the head stone

HEADY —

Falling forward, προπετής *propetēs.*
2 Ti. 3. 4 heady, high minded, lovers of pleasures

HEAL, to —

1. *To heal, repair*, רָפָא *rapha.*
Gen. 20. 17 and God healed Abimelech, and his wife
Exod 15. 26 for I (am) the LORD that healeth thee

Num 12. 13 Heal her now, O God, I beseech thee
Deut 32. 39 and I make alive; I wound, and I heal
2 Ki. 20. 5 I have seen thy tears: behold, I will heal
20. 8 the sign that the LORD will heal me, and
2 Ch. 7. 14 forgive their sin, and will heal their land
30. 20 LORD hearkened..and healed the people
Psa. 6. 2 O LORD, heal me; for my bones are vexed
30. 2 I cried unto thee, and thou hast healed
41. 4 LORD, be merciful unto me: heal my soul
60. 2 heal the breaches thereof; for it shaketh
103. 3 Who forgiveth..who healeth all thy dis.
107. 20 He sent his word, and healed them, and
147. 3 He healeth the broken in heart, and bin.
Eccl. 3. 3 A time to kill, and a time to heal; a time
Isa. 19. 22 he shall smite and heal (it): and they shall
19. 22 be entreated of them, and shall heal them
30. 26 and healeth the stroke of their wound
57. 18 I have seen his ways, and will heal him
57. 19 saith the LORD; and I will heal him
Jer. 3. 22 Return..(and) I will heal your backslid.
17. 14 Heal me, O LORD.. save me, and I shall be
30. 17 I will heal thee of thy wounds, saith the
Lam. 2. 13 thy breach (is) great.. who can heal thee?
Hos. 5. 13 yet could he not heal you, nor cure you
6. 1 he hath torn, and he will heal us; he hath
7. 1 When I would have healed Israel, then
11. 3 but they knew not that I healed them
14. 4 I will heal their backsliding, I will love

2. *To heal*, רָפָא *rapha*, 3.
2 Ki. 2. 21 I have healed these waters; there shall
Jer. 6. 14 They have healed also the hurt (of the
8. 11 they have healed the hurt of the daughter
51. 9 We would have healed Babylon, but she
Eze. 34. 4 neither have ye healed that which was
Zech. 11. 16 nor heal that that is broken, nor feed that

3. *To make thoroughly sound or whole*, διασώζω.
Luke 7. 3 that he would come and heal his servant

4. *With a view to healing*, εἰς ἴασιν *eis iasin*.
Acts 4. 30 By stretching forth thine hand to heal

5. *To attend to, heal*, θεραπεύω *therapeuō*.
Matt. 4. 23 healing all manner of sickness and all
4. 24 that had the palsy; and he healed them
8. 7 saith unto him, I will come and heal him
8. 16 and he..healed all that were sick
9. 35 healing every sickness and every disease
10. 1 to heal all manner of sickness, and all
10. 8 Heal the sick, cleanse the lepers, raise
12. 10 Is it lawful to heal on the sabbath days?
12. 15 followed him, and he healed them all
12. 22 he healed him, insomuch that the blind
14. 14 with compassion..and he healed their sick
15. 30 cast them..at Jesus' feet; and he healed
19. 2 followed him; and he healed them there
21. 14 the lame came to him..and he healed them
Mark 1. 34 he healed many that were sick of divers
3. 2 he would heal him on the sabbath day
3. 10 he had healed many; insomuch that they
3. 15 to have power [to heal] sickness, and to
6. 5 upon a few sick folk, and healed (them)
6. 13 many that were sick, and healed (them)
Luke 4. 23 this proverb, Physician, heal thyself
4. 40 on every one of them, and healed them
5. 15 to be healed by him of their infirmities
6. 7 whether he would heal on the sabbath d.
6. 18 with unclean spirits: and they were he.
8. 2 healed of evil spirits and infirmities
8. 43 physicians, neither could be healed of any
9. 6 preaching..and healing every where
10. 9 heal the sick that are therein; and say
13. 14 Jesus had healed on the sabbath day, and
13. 14 in them therefore come and be healed
14. 3 Is it lawful to heal on the sabbath day?
Acts 4. 14 man which was healed standing with them
5. 16 sick folks..they were healed every one
8. 7 palsies, and that were lame, were healed
28. 9 others..which had diseases..were healed
Rev. 13. 3 his deadly wound was healed: and all the
13. 12 first beast, whose deadly wound was heal.

6. *To heal*, ἰάομαι *iaomai*.
Matt. 8. 8 but speak..and my servant shall be heal.
8. 13 servant was healed in the self same hour
13. 15 be converted, and I should heal them
Mark 5. 29 felt..that she was healed of that plague
Luke 4. 18 [hath sent me to heal the broken-hearted]
5. 17 the power of the Lord was (present) to h.
6. 17 and to be healed of their diseases
6. 19 virtue out of him, and healed (them) all
7. 7 but say..and my servant shall be healed
8. 47 and how she was healed immediately
9. 2 preach the kingdom..and to heal the sick
9. 11 and healed them that had need of healing
9. 42 healed the child, and delivered him again
14. 4 took (him), and healed him, and let him go
17. 15 when he saw that he was healed, turned
22. 51 And he touched his ear, and healed him
John 4. 47 that he would come down, and heal his son
5. 13 And [he that was healed] wist not who it
12. 40 and be converted, and I should heal them
Acts 3. 11 man which [was healed] held Peter and Jo.
10. 38 healing all that were oppressed of the
28. 8 and laid his hands on him, and healed him
28. 27 be converted, and I should heal them
Heb. 12. 13 which is lame..let it rather be healed
Jas. 5. 16 pray..for another, that ye may be healed
1 Pe. 2. 24 by whose stripes ye were healed

7. *To make sound, or whole*, σώζω *sōzō*.
Mark 5. 23 thy hands on her, that she may be healed
Luke 8. 36 he..possessed of the devils was healed
Acts 14. 9 perceiving that he had faith to be healed

HEALED, to be —

1. *To heal, be healed*, רָפָא *rapha*.
Isa. 6. 10 and understand..and convert, and be he.

2. *To be or become healed*, רָפָא *rapha*, 2.
Lev. 13. 18 The flesh..was a boil, and is healed
13. 37 the scall is healed, he (is) clean: and the
14. 3 plague of leprosy be healed in the leper
14. 48 house clean, because the plague is healed
Deut 28. 27 itch, whereof thou canst not be healed
28. 35 a sore botch that cannot be healed, from
1 Sa. 6. 3 ye shall be healed, and it shall be known
2 Ki. 2. 22 So the waters were healed unto this day
Isa. 53. 5 and with his stripes we are healed
Jer. 15. 18 incurable, (which) refuseth to be healed?
17. 14 I shall be healed; save me, and I shall
51. 8 take balm..if so be she may be healed
51. 9 she is not healed; forsake her, and let us
Eze. 47. 8 (being) brought..the waters shall be he.
47. 9 they shall be healed; and every thing shall
47. 11 and the marishes thereof shall not be h.

3. *To let self be healed*, רָפָא *rapha*, 7.
2 Ki. 8. 29 Joram went back to be healed in Jezreel
9. 15 Joram was returned to be healed in Jez.
2 Ch. 22. 6 And he returned to be healed in Jezreel

4. *To give remedies*, נָתַן רְפֻאוֹת *nathan rephuoth*.
Eze. 30. 21 it shall not be bound up to be healed, to

HEALED, to cause to be —

To heal, cause to be healed, רָפָא *rapha*, 3.
Exod 21. 19 shall cause (him) to be thoroughly healed

HEALER —

To bind up, gird, חָבַשׁ *chabash*.
Isa. 3. 7 I will not be an healer; for in my house

HEALING —

1. *Weakening*, כֵּהָה *kehah*.
Nah. 3. 19 (There) is no healing of thy bruise; thy

2. *Healing*, מַרְפֵּא *marpe*.
Jer. 14. 19 (there is) no healing for us? we looked
14. 19 the time of healing, and behold trouble!
Mal. 4. 2 the Sun..arise with healing in his wings

3. *What raises up, strengthens*, תְּעָלָה *tealah*.
Jer. 30. 13 bound up: thou hast no healing medici.

4. *Attendance, healing*, θεραπεία *therapeia*.
Luke 9. 11 and healed them that had need of heal.
Rev. 22. 2 (were) for the healing of the nations

5. *Healing*, ἴαμα *iama*.
1 Co. 12. 9 the gifts of healing by the same spirit
12. 28 then gifts of healings, helps
12. 30 Have all the gifts of healing? do all

6. *Healing*, ἴασις *iasis*.
Acts 4. 22 on whom this miracle of healing was sh.

HEALTH —

1. *Lengthening, prolongation*, אֲרֻכָה, אֲרוּכָה *arukah*.
Isa. 58. 8 thine health shall spring forth speedily
Jer. 8. 22 why then is not the health of the daugh.
30. 17 I will restore health unto thee, and I
33. 6 I will bring it health and cure, and I

2. *Safety*, יְשׁוּעָה *yeshuah*.
Psa. 42. 11 the health of my countenance, and my G.
43. 5 the health of my countenance, and my G.

3. *Healing*, מַרְפֵּא *marpe*.
Prov. 4. 22 For they (are)..health to all their flesh
12. 18 but the tongue of the wise (is) health
13. 17 but a faithful ambassador (is) health
16. 24 sweet to the soul, and health to the bones
Jer. 8. 15 for a time of health, and behold trouble!

4. *Healing*, רִפְאוּת *riphuth*.
Prov. 3. 8 It shall be health to thy navel, and mar.

5. *Peace, completeness*, שָׁלוֹם *shalom*.
2 Sa. 20. 9 Joab said..(Art) thou in health, my bro.?

6. *Soundness, safety*, σωτηρία *sōtēria*.
Acts 27. 34 this is for your health: for there shall

HEALTH, to be in —

To be in health, ὑγιαίνω *hugiainō*.
3 John 2 that thou mayest prosper and be in health

HEAP —

1. *Heap*, גַּל *gal*.
Gen. 31. 46 heap: and they did eat there upon the h.
31. 48 This heap (is) a witness between me and
31. 51 Behold this heap, and behold (this) pillar
31. 52 This heap (be) witness, and (this) pillar
31. 52 I will not pass over this heap to thee
31. 52 over this heap and this pillar unto me
Josh. 7. 26 a great heap of stones unto this day
8. 29 and raise thereon a great heap of stones
2 Sa. 18. 17 laid a very great heap of stones upon him
2 Ki. 19. 25 to lay waste..cities (into) ruinous heaps
Job 8. 17 His roots are wrapped about the heap, (and)
15. 28 houses..which are ready to become heaps
Isa. 25. 2 thou hast made of a city an heap; (of) a
37. 26 lay waste..cities (into) ruinous heaps
Jer. 9. 11 I will make Jerusalem heaps, (and) a den
51. 37 Babylon shall become heaps, a dwelling
Hos. 12. 11 as heaps in the furrows of the fields

2. *Mass*, חֹמֶר *chomer*.
Exod. 8. 14 they gathered them together upon heaps
Hab. 3. 15 walk..(through) the heap of great waters

3. *Heap (of ruins)*, מְעִי *mei*.
Isa. 17. 1 a city, and it shall be a ruinous heap

4. *Heap, mound, wall*, נֵד *ned*.
Exod 15. 8 the floods stood upright as an heap, (and)
Josh. 3. 13 and they shall stand upon an heap
3. 16 upon an heap very far from the city Adam
Psa. 33. 7 the waters of the sea together as an heap
78. 13 he made the waters to stand as an heap
Isa. 17. 11 the harvest (shall be) a heap in the day

5. *Heap (of ruins)*, עִי *i*.
Psa. 79. 1 they have laid Jerusalem on heaps
Jer. 26. 18 and Jerusalem shall become heaps, and the
Mic. 1. 6 will make Samaria as an heap of the field
3. 12 and Jerusalem shall become heaps, and the

6. *Heap*, עֲרֵמָה *aremah*.
Ruth 3. 7 lie down at the end of the heap of corn
2 Ch. 31. 6 of holy things..and laid (them) by heaps
31. 7 began to lay the foundation of the heaps
31. 8 and the princes came and saw the heaps
31. 9 Hezekiah questioned..concerning the h.
Neh. 4. 2 revive the stones out of the heaps of the
Song 7. 2 an heap of wheat set about with lilies
Jer. 50. 26 cast her up as heaps, and destroy her ut.
Hag. 2. 16 (one) came to an heap of twenty (meas.)

7. *Mound, heap, hillock*, תֵּל *tel*.
Deut 13. 16 it shall be an heap for ever; it shall not
Josh 8. 28 burnt Ai, and made it an heap for ever
Jer. 30. 18 city shall be builded upon her own heap
49. 2 Rabbah..shall be a desolate heap, and

HEAP, to —

1. *To put, put down*, חָתָה *chathah*.
Prov 25. 22 thou shalt heap coals of fire upon his h.

2. *To add*, סָפָה *saphah*, 5.
Deut 32. 23 I will heap mischiefs upon them; I will

3. *To heap up*, צָבַר *tsabar*.
Hab. 1. 10 for they shall heap dust, and take it

4. *To press together (with the fingers)*, קָבַץ *qabats*.
Hab. 2. 5 gathereth..and heapeth unto him all

5. *To make much, multiply*, רָבָה *rabah*, 5.
Eze. 24. 10 Heap on wood, kindle the fire, consume

6. *To heap up upon*, ἐπισωρεύω *episōreuō*.
2 Ti. 4. 3 shall they heap to themselves teachers

7. *To heap up*, σωρεύω *sōreuō*.
Rom. 12. 20 for in so doing thou shalt heap coals of

HEAP up, to —

1. *To join, associate, or heap together*, חָבַר *chabar*, 5.
Job 16. 4 I could heap up words against you, and

2. *To gather or heap up*, כָּנַס *kanas*.
Eccl. 2. 26 to gather and to heap up, that he may g.

3. *To heap up*, צָבַר *tsabar*.
Job 27. 16 Though he heap up silver as the dust, and
Psa. 39. 6 he heapeth up (riches), and knoweth not
Zech. 9. 3 Tyrus..heaped up silver as the dust, and

4. *To place, set, put*, שִׂים, שׂוּם *sum, sim*.
Job 36. 13 the hypocrites in heart heap up wrath

HEAP treasure together, to —

To treasure up, θησαυρίζω *thēsaurizō*.
Jas. 5. 3 Ye have heaped treasure together for the

HEAPS (high) —

1. *Twofold heaps*, חֲמוֹר חֲמֹרָתַיִם *chamor chamorathayim*.
Judg 15. 16 heaps upon heaps, with the jaw of an ass

2. *Heaps*, צִבֻּרִים *tsibburim*.
2 Ki. 10. 8 And he said, Lay ye them in two heaps

3. *High heaps (as way marks)*, תַּמְרוּרִים *tamrurim*.
Jer. 31. 21 Set..up way marks, make thee high heaps

HEAR —

Hearing of the ear, שֵׁמַע אֹזֶן *shema ozen*.
Psa. 18. 44 As soon as they hear of me, they shall

HEAR, to —

1. *To give ear*, אָזַן *azan*, 5.
Psa. 135. 17 They have ears, but they hear not, neither
140. 6 hear the voice of my supplications, O L.

2. *To answer, respond*, עָנָה *anah*.
1 Sa. 7. 9 and Samuel cried..and the LORD heard
8. 18 the LORD will not hear you in that day
1 Ki. 18. 26 called on the name of Baal..O Baal, hear
18. 37 Hear me, O LORD, hear me; that this p.
Job 30. 20 I cry unto thee, and thou dost not hear
Psa. 3. 4 he heard me out of his holy hill. Selah
4. 1 Hear me when I call, O God of my right.
13. 3 Consider (and) hear me, O LORD my God
17. 6 for thou wilt hear me, O God: incline
20. 1 The LORD hear thee in the day of trouble
20. 6 he will hear him from his holy heaven
20. 9 LORD: let the King hear us when we call
22. 2 I cry in the day time, but thou hearest
22. 21 for thou hast heard me from the horns of
34. 4 I sought the LORD, and he heard me, and
38. 15 do I hope: thou wilt hear, O Lord my G.
55. 2 Attend unto me, and hear me: I mourn
60. 5 save (with) thy right hand, and hear me
69. 13 in the multitude of thy mercy hear me
69. 16 Hear me, O LORD; for thy loving kindn.
69. 17 for I am in trouble: hear me speedily
86. 1 Bow down thine ear, O LORD, hear me
118. 21 I will praise thee: for thou hast heard
119. 26 I..declared my ways, and thou heardest
119. 145 hear me, O LORD: I will keep thy statutes
120. 1 I cried unto the LORD, and he heard me
143. 7 Hear me speedily, O LORD; my spirit fa.
Isa. 41. 17 LORD will hear them, (I) the God of Israel

Isa. 49. 8 In an acceptable time have I heard thee
Hos. 2. 21 in that day, I will hear, saith the LORD
2. 21 I will hear the heavens, and they shall h.
2. 22 earth shall hear..and they shall hear Je.
14. 8 I have heard (him), and observed him: I
Jon. 2. 2 I cried..unto the LORD, and he heard me
Mic. 3. 4 he will not hear them: he will even hide
Zech 10. 6 I (am) the LORD their God, and will hear
13. 9 they shall call on my name, and I will h.

. Hearing, שָׁמַע *shema.*

Hos. 7. 12 chastise..as their congregation hath he

. To hear, שָׁמֵעַ *shamea.*

Gen. 3. 8 And they heard the voice of the LORD G.
3. 10 he said, I heard thy voice in the garden
4. 23 hear my voice; ye wives of Lamech,hear.
14. 14 Abram heard that his brother was taken
16. 11 because the LORD hath heard thy affliction
17. 20 as for Ishmael, I have heard thee: Behold
18. 10 Sarah heard (it) in the tent door, which
21. 6 (so that) all that hear will laugh with me
21. 17 God heard the voice of the lad; and the
21. 17 for God hath heard the voice of the lad
21. 26 didst thou tell me, neither yet heard I
23. 6 Hear us, my lord: Thou (art) a mighty p.
23. 8 hear me, and entreat for me to Ephron
23. 11 Nay, my lord, hear me: the field give I
23. 13 I pray thee, hear me: I will give thee
24. 30 when he heard the words of Rebekah his
24. 52 when Abraham's servant heard their w.
27. 5 Rebekah heard when Isaac spake to Esau
27. 6 I heard thy father speak unto Esau thy
27. 34 when Esau heard the words of his father
29. 13 when Laban heard the tidings of Jacob
29. 33 Because the LORD hath heard that I (was)
30. 6 God hath judged me, and hath also heard
31. 1 And he heard the words of Laban's sons
34. 5 Jacob heard that he had defiled Dinah his
34. 7 came out of the field when they heard (it)
35. 22 Reuben..lay with Bilhah..and Israel he.
37. 6 Hear, I pray you, this dream which I have
37. 17 for I heard them say, Let us go to Dothan
37. 21 Reuben heard (it), and he delivered him
39. 15 when he heard that I lifted up my voice
39. 19 when his master heard the words of his
41. 15 I have heard say of thee..thou canst un.
42. 2 I have heard that there is corn in Egypt
42. 21 when he besought us, and we would noth.
42. 22 Spake I not unto you..and ye would noth.
43. 25 they heard that they should eat bread
45. 2 he wept..and the house of Pharaoh heard
49. 2 Gather yourselves together, and hear, ye
Exod. 2. 15 when Pharaoh heard this thing, he sought
2. 24 God heard their groaning, and God rem.
3. 7 and have heard their cry by reason of
4. 31 when they heard that the LORD had visit.
6. 5 I have also heard the groaning of the c.
6. 12 how then shall Pharaoh hear me, who
7. 16 behold, hitherto thou wouldest not hear
15. 14 The people shall hear, (and) be afraid
16. 7 for that he heareth your murmurings
16. 8 the LORD heareth your murmurings which
16. 9 LORD: for he hath heard your murmur.
16. 12 I have heard the murmurings of the chi.
18. 1 heard of all that God had done for Moses
19. 9 that the people may hear when I speak
20. 19 Speak thou with us, and we will hear
22. 23 and they cry..I will surely hear their cry
22. 27 when he crieth unto me, that I will hear
32. 17 when Joshua heard the noise of the peo.
32. 18 but the noise of (them that) sing do I hear
33. 4 when the people heard these evil tidings
Lev. 5. 1 if a soul sin, and hear the voice of swear.
10. 20 And when Moses heard (that), he was c.
24. 14 let all that heard (him) lay their hands
Num. 7. 89 he heard the voice of one speaking unto
9. 8 I will hear what the LORD will command
11. 1 the LORD heard (it); and his anger was
11. 10 Then Moses heard the people weep thro.
12. 2 spoken also by us? And the LORD heard
12. 6 Hear now my words: If there be a prop.
14. 13 Then the Egyptians shall hear (it), for
14. 14 they have heard that thou, LORD, (art)
14. 15 the nations which have heard the fame
14. 27 I have heard the murmurings of the chi.
16. 4 when Moses heard (it), he fell upon his f.
16. 8 Moses said..Hear, I pray you, ye sons of
20. 10 Hear now, ye rebels; must we fetch you
20. 16 he heard our voice, and sent an angel
22. 36 when Balak heard that Balaam was come
23. 18 Rise up, Balak, and hear; hearken unto
24. 4, 16 He hath said, which heard the words
30. 4 And her father hear her vow, and her
30. 5 father disallow her in the day that he h.
30. 7, 11 her husband heard (it), and held his
30. 7, 14 held his peace..in the day that he he.
30. 8 disallowed her on the day that he heard
30. 12 utterly made them void on the day he h.
30. 15 make them void after that he hath heard
33. 40 heard of the coming of the children of I.
Deut. 1. 16 Hear..between your brethren, and judge
1. 17 ye shall hear the small as well as the gr.
1. 17 too hard..bring (it) unto me, and I will h.
1. 34 LORD heard the voice of your words and
1. 43 ye would not hear, but rebelled against
2. 25 who shall hear report of thee, and shall
3. 26 LORD was wroth..and would not hear me
4. 6 which shall hear all these statutes, and
4. 10 I will make them hear my words, that
4. 12 ye heard the voice of the words, but saw
4. 28 which neither see, nor hear, nor eat, nor
4. 33 Did..people hear the voice..as thou..h.

Deut. 4. 36 Out of heaven he made thee to hear his
4. 36 thou heardest his words out of the midst
5. 1 Hear, O Israel, the statutes and judgments
5. 23 when ye heard the voice out of the midst
5. 24 we have heard his voice out of the midst
5. 25 if we hear the voice of the LORD our God
5. 26 that hath heard the voice of the living G.
5. 27 hear all that the LORD our God shall say
5. 27 speak thou..and we will hear (it), and do (it)
5. 28 LORD heard the voice of your words, when
5. 28 I have heard the voice of the words of
6. 3 Hear therefore, O Israel, and observe to
6. 4 Hear, O Israel: The LORD our God (is)
9. 1 Hear, O Israel: Thou (art) to pass over
9. 2 thou hast heard..Who can stand before
12. 28 Observe and hear all these words which
13. 11 all Israel shall hear, and fear, and shall
13. 12 If thou shalt hear..in one of thy cities
17. 4 And it be told thee, and thou hast heard
17. 13 all the people shall hear, and fear, and
18. 16 Let me not hear again the voice of the L.
19. 20 those which remain shall hear, and fear
20. 3 Hear, O Israel; ye approach this day un.
21. 21 stone him..and all Israel shall hear, and
26. 7 LORD heard our voice, and looked on our
29. 4 eyes to see, and ears to hear, unto this d.
29. 19 when he heareth the words of this curse
30. 17 heart turn away, so that thou wilt not h.
31. 12 that they may hear, and that they may
31. 13 their children..may hear, and learn to
32. 1 and hear, O earth, the words of my mouth
33. 7 Hear, LORD, the voice of Judah, and bring
Josh. 2. 10 we have heard how the LORD dried up the
2. 11 as we had heard..our hearts did melt
3. 9 Come hither, and hear the words of the L.
5. 1 heard that the LORD had dried up the w.
6. 5 when ye hear the sound of the trumpet
6. 20 when the people heard the sound of the
7. 9 all the inhabitants of the land shall hear
9. 1 when..the Hivite, and the Jebusite, he.
9. 3 heard what Joshua had done unto Jericho
9. 9 we have heard the fame of him, and all
9. 16 they heard that they (were) their neighb.
10. 1 when Adoni-zedek..heard how Joshua
11. 1 when Jabin king of Hazor had heard
14. 12 thou heardest in that day how the Ana.
22. 11 the children of Israel heard say, Behold
22. 12 when the children of Israel heard..the
22. 30 heard the words that the children of Re.
24. 27 it hath heard all the words of the LORD
Judg. 5. 3 Hear, O ye kings; give ear, O ye princes
5. 16 to hear the bleatings of the flocks? For
7. 11 thou shalt hear what they say; and after.
7. 15 when Gideon heard the telling of the dr.
9. 30 when Zebul..heard the words of Gaal the
9. 46 all the men of the tower of Shechem he.
14. 13 Put forth thy riddle, that we may hear it
20. 3 the children of Benjamin heard that the
Ruth 1. 6 she had heard in the country of Moab h.
2. 8 Hearest thou not, my daughter? Go not
1 Sa. 2. 22 heard all that his sons did unto all Israel
2. 23 I hear of your evil dealings by all this peo.
2. 24 for (it is) no good report that I hear: ye
3. 9 say, Speak, LORD; for thy servant heareth
3. 10 answered, Speak; for thy servant heareth
3. 11 both the ears of every one that heareth
4. 6 when the Philistines heard the noise of
4. 14 when Eli heard the noise of the crying
4. 19 when she heard the tidings that the ark
7. 7 when the Philistines heard that the child.
7. 7 when the children of Israel heard (it), they
8. 21 Samuel heard all the words of the people
11. 6 came upon Saul when he heard those tid.
13. 3 Jonathan smote..and the Philistines he.
13. 3 Saul blew..saying, Let the Hebrews hear
13. 4 all Israel heard say (that) Saul had smit.
14. 22 they heard that the Philistines fled, even
14. 27 Jonathan heard not when his father cha.
15. 14 and the lowing of the oxen which I hear?
16. 2 if Saul hear (it), he will kill me. And
17. 11 When Saul and all Israel heard
17. 23 spake..the same words: and David hea.
17. 28 Eliab his eldest brother heard when he
22. 1 his brethren and all his father's house h.
22. 6 When Saul heard that David was discov.
22. 7 Hear now, ye Benjamites; will the son of
22. 12 And Saul said, Hear now, thou son of A.
23. 10 thy servant hath certainly heard that S.
23. 11 come down, as thy servant hath heard?
23. 25 when Saul heard..he pursued after David
24. 9 Wherefore hearest thou men's words, sa.
25. 4 David heard in the wilderness that Nabal
25. 7 now I have heard that thou hast shearers
25. 24 and hear the words of thine handmaid
25. 39 when David heard that Nabal was dead
26. 19 let my lord the king hear the words of
31. 11 heard of that which the Philistines had
2 Sa. 3. 28 afterward when David heard (it), he said
4. 1 when Saul's son heard that Abner was d.
5. 17 when the Philistines heard that they had
5. 17 David heard..and went down to the hold
5. 24 when thou hearest the sound of a going
7. 22 according to all that we have heard with
8. 9 When Toi king of Hamath heard that D.
10. 7 when David heard of (it), he sent Joab
11. 26 heard that Uriah her husband was dead
13. 21 when king David heard of all these things
14. 16 the king will hear, to deliver his handm.
15. 3 but..no man..of the king to hear thee
15. 10 As soon as ye hear the sound of the tru.
15. 35 what thing soever thou shalt hear out of
15. 36 send unto me every thing that ye can hear

2 Sa. 16. 21 all Israel shall hear that thou art abhorred
17. 5 and let us hear likewise what he saith
17. 9 that whosoever heareth it will say, There
18. 5 all the people heard when the king gave
19. 2 the people heard say that day how the
19. 35 can I hear any more the voice of singing
20. 16 Hear, hear! say, I pray you, unto Joab
20. 17 Hear the words..And he answered, I do h.
22. 7 he did hear my voice out of his temple
22. 45 as soon as they hear, [Heb., the ear hears.]
1 Ki. 1. 11 Hast thou not heard that Adonijah the
1. 41 Adonijah, and all the guests..heard (it)
1. 41 when Joab heard the sound of the trum.
1. 45 This (is) the noise that ye have heard
2. 42 saidst..The word (that) I have heard (is)
3. 28 all Israel heard of the judgment which
4. 34 there came of all people to hear the wis.
4. 34 all kings..which had heard of his wisdom
5. 1 he had heard that they had anointed him
5. 7 when Hiram heard the words of Solomon
6. 7 hammer nor ax (nor) any tool of iron h.
8. 30 hear thou..and when thou hearest, forgive
8. 32 hear thou in heaven, and do, and judge
8. 34, 36 hear thou in heaven, and forgive the
8. 39, 43 hear thou in heaven thy dwelling pl.
8. 42 they shall hear of thy great name, and of
8. 45, 49 hear thou in heaven their prayer and
9. 3 I have heard thy prayer and thy supplicat.
10. 1 when the queen of Sheba heard of the fa.
10. 6 It was a true report that I heard in mine
10. 7 wisdom..exceedeth the fame which I he.
10. 8 Happy (are) thy men..that hear thy wis.
10. 24 all the earth sought to Solomon, to hear
11. 21 when Hadad heard in Egypt that David
12. 2 when Jeroboam the son of Nebat..heard
12. 20 when all Israel heard that Jeroboam was
13. 4 when king Jeroboam heard the saying of
13. 26 that brought him back from the way heard
14. 6 when Ahijah heard the sound of her feet
15. 21 when Baasha heard..he left off building
16. 16 the people..encamped heard say, Zimri
17. 22 LORD heard the voice of Elijah; and the
19. 13 when Elijah heard..he wrapped his face
20. 12 when (Ben-hadad) heard this message, as
20. 31 we have heard that the kings of the house
21. 15 when Jezebel heard that Naboth was sto.
21. 16 when Ahab heard that Naboth was dead
21. 27 when Ahab heard those words,.he rent
22. 19 Hear thou therefore the word of the LORD
2 Ki. 3. 21 when all the Moabites heard that the kings
5. 8 when Elisha the man of God had heard
6. 30 when the king heard the words of the w.
7. 1 Elisha said, Hear ye the word of the LORD
9. 30 when Jehu was come..Jezebel heard (of
11. 13 when Athaliah heard the noise of the g.
14. 11 But Amaziah would not hear. Therefore
17. 14 they would not hear, but hardened their
18. 12 and would not hear (them), nor do (them)
18. 28 Hear the word of the great king, the king
19. 1 when king Hezekiah heard..he rent his
19. 4 It may be the LORD thy God will hear all
19. 4 words which the LORD thy God hath he.
19. 6 Be not afraid of the words..thou hast h.
19. 7 he shall hear a rumour, and shall return
19. 8 he had heard that he was departed from
19. 9 when he heard say of Tirhakah king of E.
19. 11 thou hast heard what the kings of Assy.
19. 16 LORD, bow down thine ear, and hear; open
19. 16 hear the words of Sennacherib, which
19. 20 (That) which thou hast prayed..I have h.
19. 25 Hast thou not heard long ago..I have d.
20. 5 I have heard thy prayer, I have seen thy
20. 12 he had heard that Hezekiah had been
20. 16 Isaiah said..Hear the word of the LORD
21. 12 whosoever heareth of it, both his ears
22. 11 when the king had heard the words of
22. 18 (As touching) the words..thou hast heard
22. 19 when thou heardest what I spake against
22. 19 I also have heard (thee), saith the LORD
25. 23 heard that the king of Babylon had made
1 Ch. 10. 11 heard all that the Philistines had done to
14. 8 heard that David was anointed king over
14. 8 David heard..and went out against them
14. 15 when thou shalt hear a sound of going
17. 20 according to all that we have heard with
18. 9 when Tou king of Hamath heard how D.
19. 8 when David heard..he sent Joab, and all
28. 2 Hear me, my brethren, and my people
2 Ch. 6. 21 hear thou..and when thou hearest, forg.
6. 23 hear thou from heaven, and do, and judge
6. 25, 27 hear thou from the heavens, and forg.
6. 30 hear thou from heaven thy dwelling place
6. 33, 39 hear thou from the heavens..from thy
6. 35 hear thou from thine the heavens their prayer
7. 12 I have heard thy prayer, and have chosen
7. 14 then will I hear from heaven, and will
9. 1 when the queen of Sheba heard of the
9. 5 (It was) a true report which I heard in
9. 6 (for) thou exceedest the fame that I heard
9. 7 Happy..thy servants, which..hear thy w.
9. 23 to hear his wisdom, that God had put in
10. 2 when Jeroboam the son of Nebat..heard
13. 4 Hear me, thou Jeroboam, and all Israel
15. 2 Hear ye me, Asa, and all Judah and Benj.
15. 8 when Asa heard these words, and the pr.
16. 5 it came to pass, when Baasha heard (it)
18. 18 Therefore hear the word of the LORD; I
20. 9 (when) evil cometh..thou wilt hear and h.
20. 20 Hear me, O Judah, and ye inhabitants of
20. 29 when they had heard that the LORD fought
23. 12 when Athaliah heard the noise of the pe.
25. 20 But Amaziah would not hear; for it (ca)

2 Ch. 28. 11 hear me therefore, and deliver the captiv.
29. 5 Hear me, ye Levites; sanctify now your.
33. 13 heard his supplication, and brought him
34. 19 when the king had heard the words of
34. 26 (concerning) the words which thou hast h.
34. 27 when thou heardest his words against
34. 27 I have even heard (thee) also, saith the
Ezra 4. 1 heard that the children of the captivity
9. 3 when I heard this thing, I rent my garm.
Neh. 1. 4 it came to pass, when I heard these words
1. 6 that thou mayest hear the prayer of thy
2. 10 Tobiah the servant, the Ammonite, heard
2. 19 But when..Geshem the Arabian, heard
4. 1 when Sanballat heard that we builded
4. 4 Hear, O our God; for we are despised
4. 7 heard that the walls of Jerusalem were
4. 15 when our enemies heard that it was known
4. 20 In what place..ye hear the sound of the
5. 6 I was very angry when I heard their cry
6. 16 all our enemies heard..and all the heath.
8. 2 and all that could hear with understand.
8. 9 all the people wept, when they heard the
9. 9 and heardest their cry by the Red sea
9. 27, 28 they cried..thou heardest..from heav.
9. 29 hardened their neck, and would not hear
13. 3 when they had heard the law, that they s.
Esth. 1. 18 which have heard of the deed of the queen
Job 2. 11 when Job's three friends heard of all this
3. 18 they hear not the voice of the oppressor
4. 16 (there was) silence, and I heard a voice
5. 27 hear it, and know thou (it) for thy good
13. 1 mine ear hath heard and understood it
13. 6 Hear now my reasoning, and hearken to
13. 17 Hear diligently my speech, and my decl.
15. 8 Hast thou heard the secret of God? and
15. 17 I will show thee, hear me; and that..I
16. 2 I have heard many such things: miserab.
20. 3 I have heard the check of my reproach
21. 2 Hear diligently my speech; and let this
22. 27 he shall hear thee, and thou shalt pay thy
27. 9 Will God hear his cry when trouble com.
28. 22 We have heard the fame thereof with
29. 11 When the ear heard (me), then it blessed
31. 35 Oh that one would hear me! behold, my
33. 1 Wherefore, Job, I pray thee, hear my spe.
33. 8 and I have heard the voice of (thy) words
34. 2 Hear my words, O ye wise (men); and give
34. 16 If now..understanding, hear this; heark.
34. 28 and he heareth the cry of the afflicted
35. 13 Surely God will not hear vanity, neither
37. 2 Hear attentively the noise of his voice
42. 4 Hear, I beseech thee, and I will speak: I
42. 5 I have heard of thee by the hearing of the
Psa. 4. 1 Hear me when I call, O God of my right.
4. 1 have mercy upon me, and hear my prayer
4. 3 the LORD will hear when I call unto him
5. 3 My voice shalt thou hear in the morning
6. 8 LORD hath heard the voice of my weeping
6. 9 LORD hath heard my supplication; the L.
10. 17 thou hast heard the desire of the humble
17. 1 Hear the right, O LORD, attend unto my
17. 6 incline thine ear unto me..hear my spee.
18. 6 he heard my voice out of his temple, and
18. 44 As soon as they hear of me, they shall obey
22. 24 but when he cried unto him, he heard
27. 7 Hear, O LORD..I cry with my voice: ha.
28. 2 Hear the voice of my supplications when
28. 6 because he hath heard the voice of my
30. 10 Hear, O LORD, and have mercy upon me
31. 13 For I have heard the slander of many
31. 22 thou heardest the voice of my supplication
34. 2 the humble shall hear (thereof), and be
34. 6 This poor man cried, and the LORD heard
34. 17 cry, and the LORD heareth, and deliver.
38. 13 But I, as a deaf (man), heard not; and
38. 14 Thus I was as a man that heareth not
39. 12 Hear my prayer, O LORD, and give ear
40. 1 he inclined unto me, and heard my cry
44. 1 We have heard with our ears, O God, our f.
48. 8 As we have heard, so have we seen in the
49. 1 Hear this, all..people; give ear, all..in.
50. 7 Hear, O my people, and I will speak; O
54. 2 Hear my prayer, O God; give ear to the
55. 17 Evening, and morning..he shall hear my
55. 19 God shall hear, and afflict them, even he
59. 7 swords (are) in their lips: for who..doth h.?
61. 1 Hear my cry, O God; attend unto my pra.
61. 5 For thou, O God, hast heard my vows
62. 11 twice have I heard this, that power..unto
64. 1 Hear my voice, O God, in my prayer: pre.
65. 2 O thou that hearest prayer, unto thee
66. 16 Come..hear, all ye that fear God, and I
66. 18 If I regard iniquity..LORD will not hear
66. 19 verily God hath heard..he hath attended
69. 33 the LORD heareth the poor, and despiseth
78. 3 Which we have heard and known, and
78. 21 Therefore the LORD heard..and was wroth
78. 59 When God heard..he was wroth, and gr.
81. 5 I heard a language (that) I understood not
81. 8 Hear, O my people, and I will testify unto
84. 8 O LORD God of hosts, hear my prayer: give
85. 8 I will hear what God the LORD will speak
92. 11 mine ears shall hear..of the wicked that
94. 9 He that planted the ear, shall he not h.?
95. 7 To day if ye will hear his voice
97. 8 Zion heard, and was glad; and the daug.
102. 1 Hear my prayer, O LORD, and let my cry
102. 20 To hear the groaning of the prisoner; to
106. 44 regarded their affliction, when he heard
115. 6 They have ears, but they hear not; noses
116. 1 I love the LORD, because he hath heard
119. 149 Hear my voice, according unto thy loving
Psa. 130. 2 Lord, hear my voice; let thine ears be
132. 6 we heard of it at Ephratah; we found it
138. 4 when they hear the words of thy mouth
141. 6 they shall hear my words; for they are
143. 1 Hear my prayer, O LORD, give ear to my
145. 19 he also will hear their cry, and will save
Prov. 1. 5 A wise (man) will hear, and will increase
1. 8 My son, hear the instruction of thy father
4. 1 Hear, ye children, the instruction of a f.
4. 10 Hear, O my son, and receive my sayings
5. 7 Hear me now therefore, O ye children, and
8. 6 Hear; for I will speak of excellent things
8. 33 Hear instruction, and be wise, and refuse
8. 34 Blessed (is) the man that heareth me, wa.
13. 1 A wise son..a scorner heareth not rebuke
13. 8 but the poor heareth not rebuke
15. 29 but he heareth the prayer of the righteous
15. 31 The ear that heareth the reproof of life
15. 32 he that heareth reproof getteth underst.
18. 13 that answereth a matter before he heareth
19. 20 Hear counsel, and receive instruction, that
19. 27 Cease, my son, to hear the instruction..to
20. 12 The hearing ear, and the seeing eye, the
21. 28 the man that heareth speaketh constantly
22. 17 Bow down thine ear, and hear the words
23. 19 Hear thou, my son, and be wise, and gui.
25. 10 Lest he that heareth..put thee to shame
29. 24 he heareth cursing, and bewrayeth (it)
Eccl. 5. 1 be more ready to hear than to give the s.
7. 5 (It is) better to hear the rebuke of the
7. 5 than for a man to hear the song of fools
7. 21 no heed..lest thou hear thy servant curse
12. 13 Let us hear the conclusion of the whole
Isa. 1. 2 Hear, O heavens, and give ear, O earth
1. 10 Hear the word of the LORD, ye rulers of S.
1. 15 when ye make many prayers, I will not h.
6. 8 I heard the voice of the LORD, saying
6. 9 Hear ye indeed, but understand not; and
6. 10 hear with their ears, and understand
7. 13 Hear ye now, O house of David; (Is it) a
16. 6 have heard of the pride of Moab..very p.
18. 3 and when he bloweth a trumpet, hear ye
21. 10 that which I have heard of the LORD of h.
24. 16 have we heard songs..glory to the right.
28. 12 this..refreshing: yet they would not hear
28. 14 hear the word of the LORD, ye scornful
28. 22 I have heard from the Lord GOD of hosts
28. 23 hear my voice; hearken, and hear my
29. 18 in that day shall the deaf hear the words
30. 9 children..will not hear the law of the L.
30. 19 when he shall hear it, he will answer thee
30. 21 thine ears shall hear a word behind thee
32. 3 the ears of them that hear shall hearken
32. 9 hear my voice, ye careless daughters; give
33. 13 Hear, ye..far off, what I have done; and
34. 1 Come near, ye nations, to hear; and he.
34. 1 let the earth hear, and all that is therein
36. 13 Hear ye the words of the great king, the
37. 1 came to pass, when king Hezekiah heard
37. 4 thy God will hear the words of Rabsha.
37. 4 words which the LORD thy God hath he.
37. 6 Be not afraid of the words..thou hast h.
37. 7 he shall hear a rumour, and return to his
37. 8 he had heard that he was departed from L.
37. 9 And he heard say concerning Tirhakah
37. 9 when he heard..he sent messengers to H.
37. 11 thou hast heard what the kings of Assyria
37. 17 Incline thine ear, O LORD, and hear..hear
37. 26 Hast thou not heard long ago..I have
38. 5 I have heard thy prayer, I have seen thy
39. 1 he had heard that he had been sick, and
39. 5 said..Hear the word of the LORD of hosts
40. 21 Have ye not known? have ye not heard?
40. 28 Hast thou not known, hast thou not he.
41. 26 yea, (there is) none that heareth your wo.
42. 18 Hear, ye deaf; and look, ye blind, that
42. 20 opening the ears, but he heareth not
42. 23 will hearken, and hear for the time to c.?
43. 9 or let them hear, and say, (It is) truth
44. 1 Yet now hear, O Jacob my servant; and
47. 8 Therefore hear now this, thou..given to
48. 1 Hear ye this, O house of Jacob, which are
48. 6 Thou hast heard, see all this; and will
48. 7 before the day when thou heardest them
48. 8 thou heardest not; yea, thou knewest not
48. 14 All ye, assemble yourselves, and hear
48. 16 Come ye near unto me, hear ye this; I h.
50. 4 wakeneth mine ear to hear as the learned
51. 21 Therefore hear now this, thou afflicted
52. 15 which they had not heard shall they con.
55. 3 hear, and your soul shall live; and I will
59. 1 neither his ear heavy, that it cannot hear
59. 2 hid (his) face from you, that he will not h.
64. 4 have not heard, nor perceived by the ear
65. 12 when I spake, ye did not hear; but did
65. 24 while they are yet speaking, I will hear
66. 4 when I spake, they did not hear: but
66. 5 Hear the word of the LORD, ye that tremb.
66. 8 Who hath heard such a thing? who hath
66. 19 the isles..that have not heard my fame
Jer. 2. 4 Hear ye the word of the LORD, O house
4. 19 because thou hast heard..the sound of
4. 21 How long shall I..hear the sound of the
4. 31 I have heard a voice as of a woman in
5. 21 Hear now this, O foolish people, and
5. 21 see not; which have ears, and hear not
6. 10 and give warning, that they may hear?
6. 18 Therefore hear, ye nations, and know
6. 19 Hear, O earth: behold, I will bring evil
6. 24 We have heard the fame thereof: our
7. 2 Hear the word of the LORD, all (ye of) J.
7. 13 and I spake unto you..but ye heard not
Jer. 7. 16 Therefore pray not..I will not hear thee
8. 6 I hearkened and heard, (but) they spake
9. 10 neither can (men) hear the voice of the
9. 20 Yet hear the word of the LORD, O ye
10. 1 Hear ye the word which the LORD speaketh
11. 2, 6 Hear ye the words of this covenant
11. 10 refused to hear my words; and they went
11. 14 for I will not hear (them) in the time that
13. 10 evil people, which refuse to hear my wo.
13. 11 and for a glory: but they would not hear
13. 15 Hear ye, and give ear; be not proud: for
13. 17 But if ye will not hear it, my soul shall
14. 12 When they fast, I will not hear their cry
17. 20 Hear ye the word of the LORD, ye kings
17. 23 that they might not hear, nor receive
18. 13 Ask..the heathen, who hath heard such
19. 3 Hear ye the word of the LORD, O kings of
19. 3 which whosoever heareth, his ears shall
19. 15 that they might not hear my words
20. 1 Now Pashur..heard that Jeremiah prop.
20. 10 For I heard the defaming of many, fear
20. 16 and let him hear the cry in the morning
21. 11 touching..(say), Hear ye the word of the
22. 2 Hear the word of the LORD, O king of J.
22. 5 if ye will not hear these words, I swear
22. 21 (but) thou saidst, I will not hear
22. 29 earth, earth, hear the word of the LORD
23. 18 and hath perceived and heard his word?
23. 18 who hath marked his word, and heard
23. 25 I have heard what the prophets said
25. 4 hearkened, nor inclined your ear to hear
25. 8 Because ye have not heard my words
26. 7 all the people heard Jeremiah speaking
26. 10 When the princes of Judah heard these
26. 11 prophesied..as ye have heard with your e.
26. 12 prophesy..all the words that ye have h.
26. 21 and all the princes, heard his words, the
26. 21 but when Urijah heard it, he was afraid
28. 7 hear thou now this word that I speak in
28. 15 Hear now, Hananiah; The LORD hath not
29. 19 but ye would not hear, saith the LORD
29. 20 Hear ye therefore the word of the LORD
30. 5 We have heard a voice of trembling, of
31. 10 Hear the word of the LORD, O ye nations
31. 18 I have surely heard Ephraim bemoaning
33. 9 which shall hear all the good that I do
34. 4 Yet hear the word of the LORD, O Zede.
34. 10 when all the princes..heard that every
35. 17 I have spoken..but they have not heard
36. 3 the house of Judah will hear all the evil
36. 11 When Michaiah..had heard out of the
36. 13 all the words that he had heard, when
36. 16 when they had heard all the words, they
36. 24 were not afraid..that heard all these wo.
36. 25 to the king..but he would not hear them
37. 5 when the Chaldeans..heard tidings of
37. 20 Therefore hear now, I pray thee, O my
38. 1 heard the words that Jeremiah had
38. 7 when Ebed-melech..heard that they had
38. 25 if the princes hear that I have talked
40. 7, 11 heard that the king of Babylon had
41. 11 heard of all the evil that Ishmael the son
42. 4 the prophet said unto them, I have heard
42. 14 nor hear the sound of the trumpet, nor
42. 15 now therefore hear the word of the LORD
44. 24 Hear the word of the LORD, all Judah
44. 26 Therefore hear ye the word of the LORD
46. 12 The nations have heard of thy shame
48. 5 enemies have heard a cry of destruction
48. 29 We have heard the pride of Moab, he is
49. 14 I have heard a rumour from the LORD
49. 20 Therefore hear the counsel of the LORD
49. 23 for they have heard evil tidings: they are
50. 43 king of Babylon hath heard the report of
50. 45 Therefore hear ye the counsel of the LORD
51. 51 because we have heard reproach: shame
Lam. 1. 18 hear, I pray you, all people, and behold
1. 21 They have heard that I sigh; (there is)
1. 21 mine enemies have heard of my trouble
3. 56 Thou hast heard my voice; hide not thi.
3. 61 Thou hast heard their reproach, O LORD
Eze. 1. 24 I heard the noise of their wings, like the
1. 28 and I heard a voice of one that spake
2. 2 that I heard him that spake unto me
2. 5 they, whether they will hear, or whether
2. 7 shalt speak..whether they will hear, or
2. 8 son of man, hear what I say unto thee
3. 10 receive in thine heart, and hear with thine
3. 11 whether they will hear, or whether they
3. 12 and I heard behind me a voice of a great
3. 17 therefore hear the word at my mouth
3. 27 He that heareth, let him hear; and he
6. 3 Ye mountains of Israel, hear the word
8. 18 though they cry..(yet) will I not hear
12. 2 they have ears to hear, and hear not: for
13. 2 say thou unto them..Hear ye the word
13. 19 by your lying to my people that hear (your)
16. 35 Wherefore, O harlot, hear the word of
18. 25 Hear now, O house of Israel; Is not my
19. 4 The nations also heard of him; he was
20. 47 say to the forest..Hear the word of the
25. 3 say unto the Ammonites, Hear the word
33. 4 whosoever heareth the sound of the tru.
33. 5 He heard the sound of the trumpet, and
33. 7 thou shalt hear the word at my mouth
33. 30 and hear what is the word that cometh
33. 31 they hear thy words, but they will not do
33. 32 they hear thy words, but they do them
34. 7 ye shepherds, hear the word of the LORD
34. 9 O ye shepherds, hear the word of the L.
35. 12 I have heard all thy blasphemies which
35. 13 your words against me: I have heard

Eze. 36. 1 Ye mountains of Israel, hear the word of
36. 4 ye mountains of Israel, hear the word of
37. 4 O ye dry bones, hear the word of the LORD
40. 4 behold with thine eyes, and hear with
43. 6 I heard (him) speaking unto me out of
44. 5 behold with thine eyes, and hear with
Dan. 8. 13 Then I heard one saint speaking, and an.
8. 16 I heard a man's voice between (the banks)
9. 17 O our God, hear the prayer of thy servant
9. 18 O my God, incline thine ear, and hear
9. 19 O Lord, hear; O Lord, forgive; O Lord
10. 9 Yet heard I the voice of his words: and
10. 9 when I heard the voice of his words, then
12. 7 And I heard the man clothed in linen
12. 8 I heard, but I understood not: then said
Hos. 4. 1 Hear the word of the LORD, ye children of
5. 1 Hear ye this, O priests; and hearken, ye
Joel 1. 2 Hear this, ye old men, and give ear, all
Amos 3. 1 Hear this word that the LORD hath spoken
3. 13 Hear ye, and testify in the house of Jacob
4. 1 Hear this word, ye kine of Bashan, that
5. 1 Hear ye this word which I take up
5. 23 I will not hear the melody of thy viols
7. 16 therefore hear thou the word of the LORD
8. 4 Hear this, O ye that swallow up the needy
Obad. 1 We have heard a rumour from the LORD
Jon. 2. 2 cried I, (and) thou heardest my voice
Mic. 1. 2 Hear, all ye people; hearken, O earth, and
3. 1 Hear, I pray you, O heads of Jacob, and
3. 9 Hear this, I pray you, ye heads of the h.
5. 15 and fury..such as they have not heard
6. 1 Hear ye now what the LORD saith; Arise
6. 1 contend thou..and let the hills hear thy
6. 2 Hear ye, O mountains, the LORD'S contr.
6. 9 hear ye the rod, and who hath appointed
7. 7 I will wait..my God will hear me
Nah. 3. 19 all that hear the bruit of thee shall clap
Hab. 1. 2 long shall I cry, and thou wilt not hear!
3. 2 O LORD, I have heard thy speech, (and)
3. 16 When I heard, my belly trembled; my
Zeph. 2. 8 I have heard the reproach of Moab, and
Zech. 1. 4 but they did not hear, nor hearken unto
3. 8 Hear now, O Joshua the high priest, thou
7. 11 stopped their ears, that they should not h.
7. 12 lest they should hear the law, and the w.
7. 13 they would not hear..and I would not h.
8. 9 ye that hear in these days these words by
8. 23 for we have heard (that) God (is) with you
Mal. 2. 2 If ye will not hear, and if ye will not lay
3. 16 heard (it), and a book of remembrance

5. *To cause to be heard*, שָׁמַע *shamea*, 5.
Deut 30. 12, 13 bring it unto us, that we may hear it

6. *To hear*, שְׁמַע *shema*.
Dan. 3. 5, 15 at what time ye hear the sound of the
3. 7 when all the people heard the sound of
3. 10 every man that shall hear the sound of
5. 14 I have even heard of thee, that the spirit
5. 16 I have heard of thee, that thou canst ma.
5. 23 which see not, nor hear, nor know: and
6. 14 Then the king, when he heard (these) w.

7. *To give ear, hearken, hear*, ἀκούω *akouō*.
Matt. 2. 3 When Herod the king had heard (these t.)
2. 9 When they had heard the king, they de.
2. 18 In Rama was there a voice heard, lamen.
2. 22 But when he heard that Archelaus did
4. 12 Now when Jesus had heard that John was
5. 21, 27 ye have heard that it was said by them
5. 33, 38, 43 ye have heard that it hath been s.
7. 24 whosoever heareth these sayings of mine
7. 26 every one that heareth these sayings of
8. 10 When Jesus heard (it), he marvelled, and
9. 12 But when Jesus heard..he said unto them
10. 14 whosoever shall not..hear your words
10. 27 what ye hear in the ear..preach ye upon
11. 2 when John had heard in the prison the
11. 4 show John..those things which ye do hear
11. 5 the lepers are cleansed, and the deaf hear
11. 15 He that hath ears [to hear], let him hear
12. 19 neither shall any man hear his voice in
12. 24 when the Pharisees heard (it) they said
12. 42 for she came..to hear the wisdom of Sol.
13. 9 Who hath ears [to hear], let him hear
13. 13 hearing, they hear not, neither do they
13. 14 By hearing ye shall hear, and shall not
13. 15 hear with (their) ears, and should under.
13. 16 blessed are..your ears, for they hear
13. 17 and have not seen (them); and to hear
13. 17 (things) which ye hear, and have not heard
13. 18 Hear ye therefore the parable of the sow.
13. 19 When any one heareth the word of the
13. 20 the same is he that heareth the word, and
13. 22, 23 that received seed..is he that heareth
13. 43 Who hath ears [to hear], let him hear
14. 1 Herod the tetrarch heard of the fame of
14. 13 When Jesus heard..he departed thence
14. 13 when the people had heard..they follow.
15. 10 and said unto them, Hear, and understa.
15. 12 were offended, after they heard this say.
17. 5 This is my beloved Son..hear ye him
17. 6 And when the disciples heard (it), they
18. 15 if he shall hear thee, thou hast gained
18. 16 But if he will not hear..take with thee
19. 22 when the young man heard that saying
19. 25 When his disciples heard (it), they were
20. 24 when the ten heard (it), they were moved
20. 30 when they heard that Jesus passed by
21. 16 said unto him, Hearest thou what these
21. 33 Hear another parable: There was a cert.
21. 45 when the chief priests and Pharisees had h.
22. 7 But when the king [heard]..he was wroth
22. 22 When they had heard..they marvelled
Matt 22. 33 when the multitude heard..they were as.
22. 34 when the Pharisees had heard that he had
24. 6 ye shall hear of wars and rumours of wars
26. 65 behold, now ye have heard his blasphe.
27. 13 Hearest thou not how many things they
27. 47 Some..when they heard..said, This (man)
Mark 2. 17 When Jesus heard (it), he saith unto them
3. 8 when they had heard what great things
3. 21 when his friends heard..they went out to
4. 9 He that hath ears to hear, let him h.
4. 12 hearing they may hear, and not underst.
4. 15 but, when they have heard, Satan cometh
4. 16 who, when they have heard the word, im.
4. 18 sown among thorns; such as hear the wo.
4. 20 such as hear the word, and receive (it)
4. 23 If any man have ears to hear, let him hear
4. 24 he said unto them, Take heed what ye h.
4. 24 unto you that hear shall more be given
4. 33 spake he..as they were able to hear (it)
5. 27 When she had heard of Jesus, came in the
5. 36 As soon as Jesus heard the word that was
6. 2 and many hearing (him) were astonished
6. 11 whosoever shall not..hear you, when ye
6. 14 And king Herod heard (of him); for his
6. 16 But when Herod heard (thereof,) he said
6. 20 when he heard him, he..heard him gladly
6. 29 when his disciples heard..they came and
6. 55 those that were sick, where they heard he
7. 16 If any man have ears to hear, let him he.
7. 25 For a..woman..heard of him, and came
7. 37 he maketh both the deaf to hear, and the
8. 18 and having ears, hear ye not? and do ye
9. 7 saying, This is my beloved Son: hear him
10. 41 when the ten heard (it), they began to be
10. 47 when he heard that it was Jesus of Naza.
11. 14 No man eat fruit..And his disciples heard
11. 18 the scribes and chief priests heard (it), and
12. 28 came, and having heard them reasoning
12. 29 Hear, O Israel; The Lord our God is one
12. 37 And the common people heard him gladly
13. 7 when ye shall hear of wars and rumours
14. 11 when they heard (it), they were glad and
14. 58 We heard him say, I will destroy this tem
14. 64 Ye have heard the blasphemy: what think
15. 35 And some of them..when they heard (it)
16. 11 [when they had heard that he was alive]
Luke 1. 41 when Elisabeth heard the salutation of M.
1. 58 her neighbours and her cousins heard how
1. 66 And all they that heard..laid (them) up
2. 18 all they that heard (it) wondered at those
2. 20 for all the things that they had heard and
2. 46 both hearing them, and asking them que.
2. 47 all that heard him were astonished at his
4. 23 whatsoever we have heard done in Cape.
4. 28 all they in the synagogue, when they heard
5. 1 as the people pressed upon him to hear the
5. 15 great multitudes came together to hear
6. 17 which came to hear him, and to be healed
6. 27 I say unto you which hear, Love your en.
6. 47 Whosoever cometh to me, and heareth
6. 49 he that heareth, and doeth not, is like a
7. 3 when he heard of Jesus, he sent unto him
7. 9 When Jesus heard these things, he marv.
7. 22 tell John what..ye have seen and heard
7. 22 the lepers are cleansed, the deaf hear, the
7. 29 all the people that heard..and the publi.
8. 8 cried, He that hath ears to hear, let him h.
8. 10 and hearing they might not understand
8. 12 Those by the way side are they that hear
8. 13 on the rock (are they), which, when they h.
8. 14 when they have heard, go forth, and are
8. 15 having heard the word, keep (it), and bring
8. 18 Take heed therefore how ye hear: for w.
8. 21 my brethren are these which hear the w.
8. 50 when Jesus heard..he answered him, sa.
9. 7 Herod the tetrarch heard of all that was
9. 9 who is this of whom I hear such things?
9. 35 saying, This is my beloved Son: hear him
10. 16 He that heareth you heareth me; and he
10. 24 many..have desired to..hear those things
10. 24 which ye hear, and have not heard (them)
10. 39 also sat at Jesus' feet, and heard his word
11. 28 blessed (are) they that hear the word of God
11. 31 for she came..to hear the wisdom of Sol.
12. 3 whatsoever ye have spoken..shall be heard
14. 15 And when one of them..heard these things
14. 35 He that hath ears to hear, let him hear
15. 1 the publicans and sinners for to hear him
15. 25 as he came..he heard music and dancing
16. 2 How is it that I hear this of thee? give an
16. 14 the Pharisees also..heard all these things
16. 29 They have..the prophets; let them hear
16. 31 If they hear not Moses and the prophets
18. 6 Lord said, Hear what the unjust judge
18. 22 when Jesus heard these things, he said
18. 23 when he heard this, he was very sorrow.
18. 26 they that heard..said, Who then can be
18. 36 hearing the multitude pass by, he asked
19. 11 as they heard these things, he added and
19. 48 the people were very attentive to hear him
20. 16 And when they heard..they said, God for.
21. 9 when ye shall hear of wars and commot.
21. 38 all the people came early..for to hear him
22. 71 for we ourselves have heard of his own m.
23. 6 When Pilate heard of Galilee, he asked
23. 8 because he had heard many things of him
John 1. 37 the two disciples heard him speak, and
1. 40 One of the two which heard John (speak)
3. 8 and thou hearest the sound thereof, but
3. 29 which standeth and heareth him, rejoice.
3. 32 what he hath seen and heard, that he tes.
4. 1 how the Pharisees had heard that Jesus
John 4. 42 for we have heard..ourselves, and know
4. 47 When he heard that Jesus was come out
5. 24 He that heareth my word, and believeth
5. 25 when the dead shall hear the voice of the
5. 25 Son of God: and they that hear shall live
5. 28 all that are in the graves shall hear his voi.
5. 30 as I hear, I judge: and my judgment is
5. 37 Ye have neither heard his voice at any time
6. 45 Every man therefore that hath heard, and
6. 60 Many therefore..when they had heard
6. 60 This is an hard saying; who can hear it?
7. 32 The Pharisees heard that the people mur.
7. 40 Many of the people..when they heard this
7. 51 Doth our law judge..man before it hear h.
8. 9 [they which heard..being convicted by]
8. 26 I speak..those things which I have heard
8. 40 told..the truth, which I have heard of G.
8. 43 (even) because ye cannot hear my word
8. 47 He that is of God heareth God's words
8. 47 ye therefore hear..not, because ye are not
9. 27 I have told you already, and ye did not h.
9. 27 wherefore would ye hear (it) again? will ye
9. 31 Now we know that God heareth not sin.
9. 31 if any man..doeth his will, him he hear.
9. 32 was it not heard that any man opened the
9. 35 Jesus heard that they had cast him out
9. 40 the Pharisees which were with him heard
10. 3 the sheep hear his voice: and he calleth
10. 8 robbers: but the sheep did not hear them
10. 16 them also I must bring, and they shall h.
10. 20 He hath a devil, and is mad; why hear ye
10. 27 My sheep hear my voice, and I know them
11. 4 When Jesus heard..he said, This sickness
11. 6 When he had heard therefore that he was
11. 20 as soon as she heard that Jesus was com.
11. 29 As soon as she heard..she arose quickly
11. 41 Father, I thank thee that thou hast heard
11. 42 And I knew that thou hearest me always
12. 12 when they heard that Jesus was coming
12. 18 that they heard that he had done this m.
12. 29 people therefore that stood by, and heard
12. 34 We have heard out of the law that Christ
12. 47 if any man hear my words, and believe not
14. 24 the word which ye hear is not mine, but
14. 28 Ye have heard how I said unto you, I go
15. 15 all things that I have heard of my Father
16. 13 whatsoever he shall hear, (that) shall he
18. 21 ask them which heard me, what I have
18. 37 Every one that is of the truth heareth my
19. 8, 13 When Pilate therefore heard that sa.
21. 7 Now when Simon Peter heard that it was
Acts 1. 4 promise..which, (saith he), ye have heard
2. 6 every man heard them speak in his own
2. 8 how hear we every man in our own ton.
2. 11 we do hear them speak in our tongues the
2. 22 Ye men of Israel, hear these words, Jesus
2. 33 shed forth this, which ye now see and h.
2. 37 Now when they heard..they were pricked
3. 22 him shall ye hear in all things whatsoever
3. 23 every soul, which will not hear that pro.
4. 4 many of them which heard the word bel.
4. 20 the things which we have seen and heard
4. 24 when they heard that, they lifted up their
5. 5 Ananias hearing these words fell down
5. 5 fear came on all them that heard these
5. 11 and upon as many as heard these things
5. 21 when they heard..they entered into the
5. 24 when the high priest..heard these things
5. 33 When they heard..they were cut..and to
6. 11 We have heard him speak blasphemous w.
6. 14 we have heard him say, that this Jesus of
7. 12 when Jacob heard that there was corn in
7. 34 I have heard their groaning, and am come
7. 37 A prophet..like unto me; him shall [ye h.]
7. 54 When they heard these things, they were
8. 6 hearing and seeing the miracles which he
8. 14 Now when the apostles..heard that Sam.
8. 30 Philip ran thither..and heard him read
9. 4 and heard a voice saying unto him, Saul
9. 7 the men..stood speechless, hearing a voice
9. 13 Lord, I have heard by many of this man
9. 21 all that heard..were amazed, and said
9. 38 disciples had heard that Peter was there
10. 22 to send for thee..and to hear words of thee
10. 33 to hear all things that are commanded thee
10. 44 Ghost fell on all them which heard the word
10. 46 For they heard them speak with tongues
11. 1 the apostles..heard that the Gentiles had
11. 7 I heard a voice saying unto me, Arise, P.
11. 18 When they heard these things, they held
13. 7 Paulus..desired to hear the word of God
13. 44 whole city together to hear the word of G
13. 48 when the Gentiles heard this, they were
14. 9 The same heard Paul speak: who stedfast.
14. 14 when the apostles, Barnabas and Paul, h.
15. 7 should hear the word of the Gospel, and
15. 24 Forasmuch as we have heard, that certain
16. 14 a certain woman..heard (us): whose he.
16. 38 they feared, when they heard that they
17. 8 they troubled the people..when they h.
17. 21 but either to tell, or to hear some new t.
17. 32 when they heard of the resurrection of the
17. 32 others said, We will hear thee again of this
18. 8 many of the Corinthians hearing believed
18. 26 whom when Aquilla and Priscilla had h.
19. 2 We have not so much as heard whether
19. 5 When they heard..they were baptized in
19. 10 so that all they which dwell in Asia heard
19. 26 Moreover ye see and hear, that not alone
19. 28 when they heard..they were full of wrath
21. 12 when we heard these things, both we, and
21. 20 when they heard..they glorified the Lord

Acts 21. 22 for they will hear that thou art come
22. 1 Men, brethren, and fathers, hear ye my
22. 2 when they heard that he spake in the H.
22. 7 and heard a voice saying unto me, Saul
22. 9 they heard not the voice of him that spake
22. 14 and shouldest hear the voice of his mouth
22. 15 witness..of what thou hast seen and he.
22. 26 When the centurion heard..he went and
23. 16 when Paul's sister's son heard of their ly.
24. 4 I pray thee that thou wouldest hear us of
24. 22 when Felix [heard these things], having
24. 24 and heard him concerning the faith in C.
25. 22 said..I would also hear the man myself
25. 22 To morrow, said he, thou shalt hear him
26. 3 wherefore I beseech thee to hear me pa.
26. 14 I heard a voice speaking unto me, and
26. 29 but also all that hear me this day, were
28. 15 when the brethren heard of us, they ca.
28. 22 we desire to hear of thee what thou thin.
28. 26 Hearing ye shall hear, and shall not und.
28. 27 and hear with (their) ears, and understand
28. 28 unto the Gentiles and..they will hear it
Rom 10. 14 believe in him of whom they have not h.
10. 14 and how shall they hear without a prea.?
10. 18 But I say, Have they not heard? Yes
11. 8 given them..ears that they should not h.
15. 21 they that have not heard shall understand
1 Co. 2. 9 Eye hath not seen, nor ear heard, neither
11. 18 I hear that there be divisions among you
2 Co. 12. 4 and heard unspeakable words, which it is
12. 6 that which he seeth me..or..heareth of
Gal. 1. 13 ye have heard of my conversation in time
1. 23 they had heard only, that he which per.
4. 21 Tell me..[do ye not hear] the law?
Eph. 1. 13 after that ye heard the word of truth, the
1. 15 after I heard of your faith in the Lord J.
3. 2 If ye have heard of the dispensation of the
4. 21 If so be that ye have heard him, and have
Phil. 1. 27 or else be absent, I may hear of your affa.
1. 30 ye saw in me, (and) now hear (to be) in
2. 26 that ye had heard that he had been sick
4. 9 Those things, which ye have both..heard
Col. 1. 4 Since we heard of your faith in Christ J.
1. 6 since the day ye heard..and knew the gr.
1. 9 we also, since the day we heard (it), do not
1. 23 hope of the gospel, which ye have heard
2 Th. 3. 11 For we hear that there are some which w.
1 Ti. 4. 16 both save thyself, and them that hear thee
2 Ti. 1. 13 sound words, which thou hast heard of
2. 2 And the things that thou hast heard of
4. 17 and (that) all the Gentiles might hear
Phm. 5 Hearing of thy love and faith, which thou
Heb. 2. 1 heed to the things which we have heard
2. 3 was confirmed unto us by them that heard
3. 7 Wherefore..To day if ye will hear his vo.
3. 15 To day if ye will hear his voice, harden
3. 16 For some, when they had heard, did pro.
4. 2 being mixed with faith in them that heard
4. 7 To day if ye will hear his voice, harden
12. 19 which (voice) they that heard entreated
Jas. 1. 19 let every man be swift to hear, slow to
5. 11 Ye have heard of the patience of Job, and
2 Pe. 1. 18 this voice which came from heaven we h.
1 Jo. 1. 1 which we have heard, which we have seen
1. 3 That which we have seen and heard decl.
1. 5 is the message which we have heard of h.
2. 7, 24, 24 which ye have heard from the beg.
2. 18 as ye have heard that antichrist shall come
3. 11 this is the message that ye have heard from
4. 3 whereof ye have heard that it should come
4. 5 of the world, and the world heareth them
4. 6 of God: he that knoweth God heareth us
4. 6 he that is not of God heareth not us
5. 14 that, if we ask anything..he heareth us
5. 15 And if we know that he hear us, whatso.
2 John 6 That, as ye have heard from the beginning
3 John 4 I have no greater joy than to hear that
Rev. 1. 3 they that hear the words of this prophecy
1. 10 and heard behind me a great voice, as of
2. 7, 11, 17, 29 He that hath an ear, let him h.
3. 3 [Remember therefore how thou hast..h.]
3. 6, 13, 22 He that hath an ear, let him hear
3. 20 if any man hear my voice, and open the
4. 1 the first voice which I heard (was) as it
5. 11 I heard the voice of many angels round
5. 13 and all that are in them, heard I saying
6. 1 I heard, as it were the noise of thunder
6. 3, 5, 7 I heard the..beast say, Come and see
6. 6 I heard a voice in the midst of the four b.
7. 4 I heard the number of them which were
8. 13 and heard an angel flying through the
9. 13 I heard a voice from the four horns of the
9. 16 horsemen..and I heard the number of
9. 20 which neither can see, nor hear, nor walk
10. 4 I heard a voice from heaven saying unto
10. 8 the voice which I heard from heaven spake
11. 12 they heard a great voice from heaven sa.
12. 10 And I heard a loud voice saying in heaven
13. 9 If any man have an ear, let him hear
14. 2, 13 And I heard a voice from heaven
14. 2 I heard the voice of harpers harping with
16. 1 I heard a great voice out of the temple
16. 5 I heard the angel of the waters say, Thou
16. 7 I heard another out of the altar say, Even
18. 4 I heard another voice from heaven, saying
19. 1 I heard a great voice of much people in h.
19. 6 I heard as it were the voice of a great mul.
21. 3 I heard a great voice out of heaven, saying
22. 8 And I John saw these things, and heard
22. 8 And when I had heard and seen, I fell d.
22. 17 And let him that heareth say, Come
22. 18 I testify unto every man that heareth the

8. *To hear thoroughly*, διακούω *diakouō.*
Acts 23. 35 I will hear thee, said he, when thine ac.

9. *To give ear to, hearken to*, εἰσακούω *eisakouō.*
Matt. 6. 7 they shall be heard for their much speak.
Luke 1. 13 Fear not, Zacharias: for thy prayer is h.
Acts 10. 31 And said, Cornelius, thy prayer is heard
1 Co. 14. 21 yet for all that will they not hear me
Heb. 5. 7 strong crying..and was heard in that he

10. *To give ear, hear, hearken unto*, ἐπακούω *epak.*
2 Co. 6. 2 I have heard thee in a time accepted, and

11. *To hearken unto*, ἐπακροάομαι *epakroaomai.*
Acts 16. 25 sang praises..and the prisoners heard the.

HEAR, to cause to —

1. *Proclamation*, הַשְׁמָעוּת *hashmauth.*
Eze. 24. 26 to cause (thee) to hear (it) with (thine)

2. *To give attention*, קָשַׁב *qashab*, 5.
Psa. 10. 17 LORD..thou wilt cause thine ear to hear

3. *To cause to hear*, שָׁמַע *shamea*, 5.
Psa. 143. 8 Cause me to hear thy loving kindness in
Song 8. 13 the companions hearken..cause me to h.
Jer. 18. 2 there I will cause thee to hear my words
23. 22 and had caused my people to hear my words
Eze. 36. 15 Neither will I cause (men) to hear in thee

HEAR, to let —

To cause to hear, שָׁמַע *shamea*, 5.
Song 2. 14 let me hear thy voice, for sweet (is) thy

HEAR, to make to —

To cause to hear, שָׁמַע *shamea*, 5.
Deut. 4. 10 I will make them hear my words, that they
4. 36 Out of heaven he made thee to hear his v.
2 Ki. 7. 6 had made..the Syrians to hear a noise of
Psa. 51. 8 Make me to hear joy and gladness

HEAR tell, to —

To hear, שָׁמַע *shamea.*
Num. 21. 1 king Arad..heard tell that Israel came

HEAR before, to —

To hear before or formerly, προακούω *proakouō.*
Col. 1. 5 whereof ye heard before in the word of

HEAR, to neglect to —

To hear amiss, disregard, παρακούω *parakouō.*
Matt 18. 17 if he shall neglect to hear them, tell (it)
18. 17 if he neglect to hear the church, let him

HEARD —

To be heard, שָׁמַע *shamea*, 2.
Eccl. 9. 16 the poor man's..words are not heard
9. 17 The words of wise (men are) heard in

HEARD, which... —

Hearing, the thing heard, ἀκοή *akoē.*
1 Th. 2. 13 received the word of God which ye heard

HEARD, to be —

1. *To be answered, responded to*, עָנָה *anah*, 2.
Job 19. 7 I cry out of wrong, but I am not heard
Prov 21. 13 he also shall cry..but shall not be heard

2. *To be heard*, שָׁמַע *shamea*, 2.
Gen. 45. 16 fame thereof was heard in Pharaoh's ho.
Exod 28. 35 his sound shall be heard when he goeth
Deut. 4. 32 whether there..hath been heard like it
1 Sa. 1. 13 she spake..but her voice was not heard
17. 31 when the words were heard which David
1 Ki. 6. 7 (nor) any tool of iron heard in the house
2 Ch. 30. 27 their voice was heard, and their prayer
Ezra 3. 13 people shouted..the noise was heard afar
Neh. 6. 1 when Sanballat..heard that I had builded
12. 43 so that the joy of Jerusalem was heard
Esth. 2. 8 when the king's commandment..was he.
Job 26. 14 but how little a portion is heard of him
37. 4 will not stay them when his voice is hea.
Psa. 19. 3 nor language (where) their voice is not h.
Song 2. 12 voice of the turtle is heard in our land
Isa. 15. 4 their voice shall be heard (even) unto J.
60. 18 Violence shall no more be heard in thy
65. 19 weeping shall be no more heard in her
Jer. 3. 21 A voice was heard upon the high places
6. 7 violence and spoil is heard in her
8. 16 The snorting of his horses was heard from
9. 19 For a voice of wailing is heard out of Z.
31. 15 A voice was heard in Ramah, lamentation
33. 10 Again there shall be heard in this place
49. 21 the noise thereof was heard in the Red s.
50. 46 and the cry is heard among the nations
51. 46 for the rumour that shall be heard in the
Eze. 10. 5 And the sound..was heard (even) to the
19. 9 his voice should no more be heard upon
26. 13 sound of thy harp shall be no more heard
Dan. 10. 12 thy words were heard, and I am come for
Nah. 2. 13 of thy messengers shall no more be heard

HEARD, to cause to be —

1. *To give, cause or rouse attention*, קָשַׁב *qashab*, 5.
Isa. 10. 30 Lift up thy voice..cause it to be heard

2. *To cause to hear*, שָׁמַע *shamea*, 5.
Psa. 76. 8 Thou didst cause judgment to be heard
Isa. 30. 30 cause his glorious voice to be heard, and
42. 2 nor cause his voice to be heard in the
Jer. 48. 4 little ones have caused a cry to be heard
49. 2 I will cause an alarm..to be heard in R.
Eze. 27. 30 cause their voice to be heard against thee

HEARD, to let be —

1. *To be heard*, שָׁמַע *shamea*, 2.
Exod 23. 13 neither let it be heard out of thy mouth
Jer. 18. 22 Let a cry be heard from their houses

2. *To cause to hear*, שָׁמַע *shamea*, 5.
Judg 18. 25 Let not thy voice be heard among us, lest

HEARD, to make to be —

To cause to be heard, שָׁמַע *shamea*, 5.
2 Ch. 5. 13 to make one sound to be heard in praising
Psa. 66. 8 make the voice of his praise to be heard
Isa. 58. 4 to make your voice to be heard on high

HEARER —

1. *To give ear, hear, hearken*, ἀκούω *akouō.*
Eph. 4. 29 it may minister grace unto the hearers
2 Ti. 2. 14 no profit, (but) to the subverting of the h.

2. *A hearer*, ἀκροατής *akroatēs.*
Rom. 2. 13 For not the hearers of the law (are) just
Jas. 1. 22 and not hearers only, deceiving your own
1. 23 For if any be a hearer of the word, and
1. 25 he being not a forgetful hearer, but a doer

HEARING —

1. *Ear*, אֹזֶן *ozen.*
Deut 31. 11 thou shalt read this..in their hearing
2 Sa. 18. 12 for in our hearing the king charged thee
Job 33. 8 Surely thou hast spoken in mine hearing
Eze. 9. 5 to the others he said in mine hearing, Go
10. 13 it was cried unto them in my hearing

2. *Hearing*, מִשְׁמָע *mishma.*
Isa. 11. 3 neither reprove after the hearing of his

3. *Attention*, קֶשֶׁב *qesheb.*
2 Ki. 4. 31 but (there was) neither voice nor hearing

4. *To hear*, שָׁמַע *shamea.*
Prov. 28. 9 turneth away his ear from hearing the
Eccl. 1. 8 satisfied..nor the ear filled with hearing
Isa. 21. 3 I was bowed down at the hearing (of it)
33. 15 that stoppeth his ears from hearing of
Amos 8. 11 but of hearing the words of the LORD

5. *Hearing*, שֵׁמַע *shema.*
Job 42. 5 I have heard of thee by the hearing of

6. *Hearing, the thing heard*, ἀκοή *akoē.*
Matt 13. 14 By hearing ye shall hear, and shall not
Acts 28. 26 Hearing ye shall hear, and shall not und.
Rom. 10. 17 faith (cometh) by hearing, and hearing
1 Co. 12. 17 where..the hearing? if the whole..hear.
Gal. 3. 2, 5 works of the law, or by the hearing of
Heb. 5. 11 many things..seeing ye are dull of hear.
2 Pe. 2. 8 in seeing and hearing, vexed (his) righte.

7. *Thorough knowledge*, διάγνωσις *diagnōsis.*
Acts 25. 21 to be reserved unto the hearing of A.

HEARING, to be dull of —

To hear heavily, βαρέως ἀκούω *bareōs akouō.*
Matt 13. 15 and (their) ears are dull of hearing, and
Acts 28. 27 and their ears are dull of hearing, and

HEARING, place of —

Place of hearing, court room, ἀκροατήριον *akroatē.*
Acts 25. 23 and was entered into the place of hearing

HEARKEN, to —

1. *To give ear*, אָזַן *azan*, 5.
Num 23. 18 hearken unto me, thou son of Zippor
Job 9. 16 believe that he had hearkened unto my
33. 1 Job, I pray thee..hearken to all my wor.
34. 16 hearken to the voice of my words
37. 14 Hearken unto this, O Job: stand still, and

2. *To attend, be attentive*, קָשַׁב *qashab.*
Isa. 32. 3 the ears of them that hear shall hearken

3. *To give attention*, קָשַׁב *qashab*, 5.
1 Sa. 15. 22 better..to hearken than the fat of rams
2 Ch. 20. 15 Hearken ye, all Judah, and ye inhabitants
33. 10 to his people; but they would not hearken
Neh. 9. 34 nor hearkened unto thy commandments
Job 13. 6 and hearken to the pleadings of my lips
Psa. 5. 2 Hearken unto the voice of my cry, my king
Prov. 29. 12 If a ruler hearken to lies, all his servants
Song 8. 13 the companions hearken to thy voice
Isa. 21. 7 he hearkened diligently with much heed
28. 23 Give ye ear..hearken, and hear my speech
34. 1 and hearken, ye people: let the earth hear
42. 23 will hearken, and hear for the time to come?
48. 18 O that thou hadst hearkened to my com.
49. 1 hearken, ye people, from far; The LORD
51. 4 Hearken unto me, my people; and give ear
Jer. 6. 10 and they cannot hearken: behold, the w.
6. 17 Hearken..But they said, We will not he.
6. 19 they have not hearkened unto my words
8. 6 I hearkened and heard, (but) they spake
Dan. 9. 19 O LORD, hearken and do; defer not, for
Hos. 5. 1 hearken, ye house of Israel; and give ye
Mic. 1. 2 hearken, O earth, and all that therein is
Zech. 1. 4 they did not hear, nor hearken unto me
7. 11 But they refused to hearken, and pulled
Mal. 3. 16 and the LORD hearkened, and heard (it)

4. *To hear, hearken*, שָׁמַע *shamea.*
Gen. 3. 17 Because thou hast hearkened unto the v.
16. 2 And Abram hearkened to the voice of S.
21. 12 hearken unto her voice; for in Isaac shall
23. 15 My lord, hearken unto me: the land (is)
23. 16 And Abraham hearkened unto Ephron
30. 17 God hearkened unto Leah, and she conc.
30. 22 God hearkened to her, and opened her
34. 17 But if ye will not hearken unto us, to be
34. 24 unto..his son, hearkened all that went out
39. 10 he hearkened not unto her, to lie by her
49. 2 and hearken unto Israel your father
Exod. 3. 18 And they shall hearken to thy voice: and
4. 1 they will not believe me, nor hearken unto
4. 8, 9 if they will not believe..neither hearken

Exod. 6. 9 hearkened not unto Moses for anguish of
6. 12 Israel have not hearkened unto me; how
6. 30 and how shall Pharaoh hearken unto me?
7. 4 But Pharaoh shall not hearken unto you
7. 13 that he hearkened not unto them; as the
7. 22 neither did he hearken unto them; as the
8. 15, 19 hearkened not unto them; as the Lo.
9. 12 hearkened not unto them; as the LORD h.
11. 9 Pharaoh shall not hearken unto you; that
15. 26 If thou wilt diligently hearken to the vo.
16. 20 Notwithstanding they hearkened not unto
18. 19 Hearken now unto my voice, I will give
18. 24 So Moses hearkened to the voice of his
Lev. 26. 14 But if ye will not hearken unto me, and
26. 18 And if ye will not yet for all this hearken
26. 21 And if ye..will not hearken unto me; I
26. 27 if ye will not for all this hearken unto me
Num 14. 22 and have not hearkened to my voice
21. 3 And the LORD hearkened to the voice of I.
Deut. 1. 45 the LORD would not hearken to your voice
4. 1 Now therefore hearken, O Israel, unto the
7. 12 if ye hearken to these judgments, and keep
9. 19 But the LORD hearkened unto me at
9. 23 ye believed him not, nor hearkened to
10. 10 LORD hearkened unto me at that time also
11. 13 if ye shall hearken diligently unto my
13. 3 Thou shalt not hearken unto the words of
13. 8 Thou shalt not..hearken unto him; neith.
13. 18 shalt hearken to the voice of the LORD
15. 5 Only if thou carefully hearken unto the
17. 12 and will not hearken unto the priest that
18. 14 these nations..hearkened unto observers
18. 15 a Prophet..unto him ye shall hearken
18. 19 whosoever will not hearken unto my words
21. 18 chastened him, will not hearken unto th.
23. 5 the LORD thy God would not hearken unto
26. 14 I have hearkened to the voice of the LORD
26. 17 keep his statutes..and to hearken unto his
27. 9 Take heed, and hearken, O Israel; this day
28. 1 if thou shalt hearken diligently unto
28. 2 if thou shalt hearken unto the voice of the
28. 13 if that thou hearken unto the commandm.
28. 15 if thou wilt not hearken unto the voice of
28. 45 because thou hearkenedst not unto the
30. 10 If thou shalt hearken unto the voice of the
34. 9 the children of Israel hearkened unto him
Josh. 1. 17 According as we hearkened unto Moses
1. 17 so will we hearken unto thee: only the
1. 18 and will not hearken unto thy words in
10. 14 LORD hearkened unto the voice of a man
24. 10 But I would not hearken unto Balaam
Judg. 2. 17 they would not hearken unto their judges
2. 20 and have not hearkened unto my voice
3. 4 know whether they would hearken unto
9. 7 Hearken unto me..that God may hearken
11. 17 but the king of Edom would not hearken
11. 28 Howbeit the king..hearkened not unto
13. 9 God hearkened to the voice of Manoah
19. 25 But the men would not hearken to him
20. 13 But..Benjamin would not hearken to the
1 Sa. 2. 25 they hearkened not unto the voice of
8. 7 Hearken unto the voice of the people in
8. 9 Now therefore hearken unto their voice
8. 22 Hearken unto their voice, and make them
12. 1 I have hearkened unto your voice in all
15. 1 hearken thou unto the voice of the words
19. 6 Saul hearkened unto the voice of Jonat.
25. 35 I have hearkened to thy voice, and have
28. 21 and have hearkened unto thy words wh.
28. 22 hearken thou also unto the voice of thine
28. 23 and he hearkened unto their voice. So he
30. 24 who will hearken unto you in this matter?
2 Sa. 12. 18 and he would not hearken unto our voice
13. 14 he would not hearken unto her voice
13. 16 But he would not hearken unto her
1 Ki. 8. 28 to hearken unto the cry and to the prayer
8. 29 that thou mayest hearken unto the prayer
8. 30 hearken thou to the supplication of thy
8. 52 to hearken unto them in all that they c.
11. 38 if thou wilt hearken unto all that I com.
12. 15 Wherefore the king hearkened not unto
12. 16 when all Israel saw that the king heark.
12. 24 They hearkened therefore to the word of
15. 20 So Ben-hadad hearkened unto king Asa
20. 8 said..Hearken not (unto him), nor cons.
20. 25 he hearkened unto their voice, and did
22. 28 said, Hearken, O people, every one of you
2 Ki. 10. 6 and (if) ye will hearken unto my voice
13. 4 and the LORD hearkened unto him; for he
16. 9 the king of Assyria hearkened unto him
17. 40 Howbeit they did not hearken, but they
18. 31 Hearken not to Hezekiah: for thus saith
18. 32 and hearken not unto Hezekiah, when he
20. 13 Hezekiah hearkened unto them, and sho.
21. 9 But they hearkened not: and Manasseh
22. 13 because our fathers have not hearkened
2 Ch. 6. 19 to hearken unto the cry and the prayer
6. 20 to hearken unto the prayer which thy se.
6. 21 Hearken therefore unto the supplications
10. 15 So the king hearkened not unto the people
10. 16 that the king would not hearken unto
16. 4 And Ben-hadad hearkened unto king Asa
18. 27 And he said, Hearken, all ye people
24. 17 princes..then the king hearkened unto
25. 16 and hast not hearkened unto my counsel
30. 20 And the LORD hearkened to Hezekiah
35. 22 and hearkened not unto the words of N.
Neh. 9. 16, 29 hearkened not to thy commandments
13. 27 Shall we then hearken unto you to do all
Esth. 3. 4 and he hearkened not unto them, that
Job 32. 10 Therefore I said, Hearken to me; I also
33. 31 Mark well, O Job; hearken unto me: hold
Job 33. 33 If not, hearken unto me: hold thy peace
34. 10 Therefore hearken unto me, ye men of
34. 34 and let a wise man hearken unto me
Psa. 34. 11 Come, ye children, hearken unto me; I will
45. 10 Hearken, O daughter, and consider, and
58. 5 Which will not hearken to the voice of
81. 8 O Israel, if thou wilt hearken unto me
81. 11 But my people would not hearken to my
81. 13 Oh that my people had hearkened unto
103. 20 hearkening unto the voice of his word
106. 25 hearkened not unto the voice of the LORD
Prov. 1. 33 whoso hearkeneth unto me shall dwell
7. 24 Hearken unto me now therefore, O ye
8. 32 Now therefore hearken unto me, O ye ch.
12. 15 he that hearkeneth unto counsel (is) wise
23. 22 Hearken unto thy father that begat thee
Isa. 36. 16 Hearken not to Hezekiah; for thus saith
46. 3 Hearken unto me, O house of Jacob, and
46. 12 Hearken unto me, ye stout hearted, that
48. 12 Hearken unto me, O Jacob and Israel, my
51. 1 Hearken to me, ye that follow after right.
51. 7 Hearken unto me, ye that know righteo.
55. 2 hearken diligently unto me, and eat ye
Jer. 7. 24 But they hearkened not, nor inclined
7. 26 Yet they hearkened not unto me, nor inc.
7. 27 but they will not hearken to thee: thou
11. 11 Behold..I will not hearken unto them
16. 12 that they may not hearken unto me
17. 24 if ye diligently hearken unto me, saith
17. 27 But if ye will not hearken unto me to
18. 19 hearken to the voice of them that cont.
23. 16 Hearken not unto the words of the prop.
25. 3 I have spoken..but ye have not hearke.
25. 4 but ye have not hearkened, nor inclined
25. 7 Yet ye have not hearkened unto me, saith
26. 3 If so be they will hearken, and turn every
26. 4 If ye will not hearken to me, to walk in
26. 5 To hearken to the words of my servants
26. 5 and sending (them), but ye have not he.
27. 9 Therefore hearken not ye to your proph.
27. 14 hearken not unto the words of the prop.
27. 16 Hearken not to the words of your prop.
27. 17 Hearken not unto them; serve the king
29. 8 neither hearken to your dreams which ye
29. 12 pray unto me, and I will hearken unto
29. 19 they have not hearkened to my words
32. 33 have not hearkened to receive instruction
34. 14 but your fathers hearkened not unto me
34. 17 Ye have not hearkened unto me, in
35. 13 instruction to hearken to my words? saith
35. 14 have spoken..but ye hearkened not unto
35. 15 inclined your ear, nor hearkened unto me
35. 16 this people hath not hearkened unto me
36. 31 I have pronounced..but they hearkened
37. 2 did hearken unto the words of the LORD
37. 14 he hearkened not to him: so Irijah took
38. 15 counsel, wilt thou not hearken unto me?
44. 16 we will not hearken unto thee
44. 5 they hearkened not, nor inclined their
Eze. 3. 6 they would have hearkened unto thee
3. 7 Israel will not hearken unto thee; for
3. 7 they will not hearken unto me: for all
20. 8 rebelled..and would not hearken unto me
20. 39 (also), if ye will not hearken unto me: but
Dan. 9. 6 hearkened unto thy servants the prophets
Hos. 9. 17 they did not hearken unto him: and they
Zech. 1. 4 they did not hear, nor hearken unto me

5. *To give ear, hearken, hear*, ἀκούω *akouō*.
Mark 4. 3 Hearken; Behold, there went out a sower
7. 14 Hearken unto me every one (of you), and
Acts 4. 19 to hearken unto you more than unto God
7. 2 Men, brethren, and fathers, hearken; The
15. 13 saying, Men (and) brethren, hearken unto
Jas. 2. 5 Hearken, my beloved brethren, Hath not

6. *To hearken a little*, ὑπακούω *hupakouō*.
Acts 12. 13 a damsel came to hearken, named Rhoda

HEARKEN to or unto, to —

1. *To give ear*, אזן *azan*, 5.
Gen. 4. 23 ye wives of Lamech, hearken unto my sp.

2. *To obey authority*, πειθαρχέω *peitharcheō*.
Acts 27. 21 ye should have hearkened unto me, and

3. *To receive in the ear, give ear to*, ἐνωτίζομαι *enōt*.
Acts 2. 14 known unto you, and hearken to my wo.

HEARKENING —

To hear, שָׁמַע *shamea*.
Psa. 103. 20 hearkening unto the voice of his word

HEART —

1. *The heart*, בַּל *bal*.
Dan. 6. 14 set (his) heart on Daniel to deliver him

2. *The heart*, לֵב *leb*.
Gen. 6. 5 imagination of the thoughts of his heart
6. 6 repented..and it grieved him at his heart
8. 21 the LORD said in his heart, I will not
8. 21 imagination of man's heart (is) evil from
17. 17 said in his heart, Shall (a child) be born
18. 5 and comfort ye your hearts; after that ye
24. 45 before I had done speaking in mine heart
27. 41 and Esau said in his heart, The days of
42. 28 their heart failed (them), and they were
45. 26 Jacob's heart fainted, for he believed them
Exod. 4. 14 seeth thee, he will be glad in his heart
4. 21 I will harden his heart, that he shall not
7. 3 will harden Pharaoh's heart, and multiply
7. 13 hardened Pharaoh's heart, that he heark.
7. 14 Pharaoh's heart (is) hardened, he refuseth
7. 22 Pharaoh's heart was hardened, neither did
7. 23 neither did he set his heart to this also
Exod. 8. 15 he hardened his heart, and hearkened no
8. 19 and Pharaoh's heart was hardened, and h
8. 32 Pharaoh hardened his heart at this time
9. 7 the heart of Pharaoh was hardened, and h
9. 12 the LORD hardened the heart of Pharaoh
9. 14 send all my plagues upon thine heart
9. 34 hardened his heart, he and his servants
9. 35 the heart of Pharaoh was hardened, neithe
10. 1 I have hardened his heart, and the hear
10. 20 LORD hardened Pharaoh's heart, so that
10. 27 the LORD hardened Pharaoh's heart, and
11. 10 LORD hardened Pharaoh's heart, so that
14. 4 I will harden Pharaoh's heart, that he
14. 8 the LORD hardened the heart of Pharaoh
14. 17 will harden the hearts of the Egyptians
15. 8 were congealed in the heart of the sea
25. 2 that giveth it willingly with his heart
28. 29 breastplate of judgment upon his heart
28. 30 they shall be upon Aaron's heart when he
28. 30 judgment of the children..upon his heart
31. 6 the hearts of all that are wise hearted
35. 5 whosoever (is) of a willing heart, let him
35. 21 every one whose heart stirred him up
35. 26 the women whose heart stirred them up
35. 29 whose heart made them willing to bring
35. 34 hath put in his heart that he may teach
35. 35 Them hath he filled with wisdom of heart
36. 2 in whose heart the LORD had put wisdom
36. 2 every one whose heart stirred him up to
Num 32. 7 wherefore discourage ye the heart of the
32. 9 discouraged the heart of the children
Deut 28. 65 shall give thee there a trembling heart
29. 4 hath not given you an heart to perceive
29. 19 I walk in the imagination of mine heart
Josh 11. 20 was of the LORD to harden their hearts
14. 8 brethren..made the heart of the people
Judg. 5. 9 heart (is) toward the governors of Israel
5. 15 Reuben (there were) great thoughts of h
5. 16 (there were) great searchings of heart
9. 3 their hearts inclined to follow Abimelech
16. 15 when thine heart (is) not with me? thou
16. 17 told her all his heart, and said unto her
16. 18 saw that he had told her all his heart
16. 18 Come..for he hath showed me all his he.
16. 25 when their hearts were merry, that they
18. 20 the priest's heart was glad; and he took
19. 5 Comfort thine heart with a morsel of bread
19. 6 Be content..and let thine heart be merry
19. 22 as they were making their hearts merry
Ruth 3. 7 his heart was merry, he went to lie down
1 Sa. 1. 13 Now Hannah, she spake in her heart
2. 1 My heart rejoiceth in the LORD; mine h.
4. 13 for his heart trembled for the ark of God
6. 6 as the Egyptians..hardened their hearts?
10. 9 God gave him another heart: and all those
10. 26 a band of men, whose hearts God had tou.
17. 32 Let no man's heart fail because of him
24. 5 David's heart smote him, because he had
25. 31 nor offence of heart unto my lord, either
25. 36 and Nabal's heart (was) merry within him
25. 37 his heart died within him, and he became
27. 1 And David said in his heart, I shall now
28. 5 he was afraid, and his heart greatly trem.
2 Sa. 6. 16 and she despised him in her heart
7. 21 according to thine own heart, hast thou
7. 27 hath thy servant found in his heart to pr.
13. 28 Mark ye now when Amnon's heart is mer.
13. 33 let not my lord..take the thing to..heart
14. 1 that the king's heart (was) toward Absa.
15. 6 so Absalom stole the hearts of the men
15. 13 The hearts of the men of Israel are after A.
17. 10 whose heart (is) as the heart of a lion, sha.
18. 14 thrust them through the heart of Absalom
19. 19 that the king should take it to his heart
24. 10 And David's heart smote him after that
1 Ki. 3. 9 Give..thy servant an understanding hea.
3. 12 lo, I have given thee a wise..heart; so th.
4. 29 God gave Solomon..largeness of heart
8. 23 that walk before thee with all their hea.
8. 66 went unto their tents joyful and glad of h.
9. 3 and mine heart shall be there perpetually
10. 24 his wisdom, which God hath put in his h.
11. 3 and his wives turned away his heart
12. 26 Jeroboam said in his heart, Now shall
12. 27 then shall the heart of this people turn ag.
12. 33 month..he had devised of his own heart
18. 37 thou hast turned their heart back again
21. 7 Arise..eat bread, and let thine heart be m.
2 Ki. 5. 26 he said unto him, Went not mine heart
6. 11 Therefore the heart of the king of Syria
9. 24 and the arrow went out at his heart, and
12. 4 money that cometh into any man's heart
14. 10 and thine heart hath lifted thee up
23. 3 with all (their) heart and all (their) soul, to
1 Ch. 12. 33 (they were) not of double heart
12. 38 the rest also of Israel (were) of one heart
15. 29 and she despised him in her heart
16. 10 let the heart of them rejoice that seek
17. 19 according to thine own heart, hast thou
28. 9 serve him with a perfect heart, and with
29. 9 because with perfect heart they offered
2 Ch. 6. 14 that walk before thee with all their hea.
6. 38 return to thee with all their heart and
7. 10 glad and merry in heart for the goodness
7. 11 all that came into Solomon's heart to make
7. 16 and mine heart shall be there perpetually
9. 23 his wisdom, that God had put in his hea.
12. 14 because he prepared not his heart to seek
17. 6 his heart was lifted up in the ways of the
25. 19 and thine heart lifteth thee up to boast
26. 16 his heart was lifted up to (his) destruction
29. 31 and as many as were of a free heart, bur.

2 Ch.30. 12 was to give them one heart to do the com.
32. 25 for his heart was lifted up: therefore
32. 26 humbled himself for the pride of his he.
Ezra 6. 22 turned the heart of the king of Assyria
7. 27 put (such a thing) as this in the king's h.
Neh. 2. 2 this (is) nothing (else) but sorrow of heart
2. 12 what my God had put in my heart to do
6. 8 thou feignest them out of thine own heart
7. 5 my God put into mine heart to gather
Esth. 1. 10 when the heart of the king was merry with
5. 9 Then went Haman forth..with a glad h.
6. 6 Now Haman thought in his heart, To wh.
7. 5 that durst presume in his heart to do so?
Job 7. 17 thou shouldest set thine heart upon him?
8. 10 and utter words out of their heart?
11. 13 If thou prepare thine heart, and stretch
12. 24 He taketh away the heart of the chief of
15. 12 Why doth thine heart carry thee away?
17. 4 thou hast hid their heart from understa.
23. 16 For God maketh my heart soft, and the A.
29. 13 I caused the widow's heart to sing for joy
31. 7 and mine heart walked after mine eyes
31. 9 If mine heart have been deceived by a
31. 27 my heart hath been secretly enticed, or
33. 3 My words (shall be of)..my heart; and
34. 14 If he set his heart upon man,(if) he gather
36. 13 But the hypocrites in heart heap up wrath
37. 1 At this also my heart trembleth, and is
37. 24 respecteth not any (that are) wise of heart
41. 24 His heart is as firm as a stone; yea, as h.
Psa. 4. 7 Thou hast put gladness in my heart, more
7. 10 of God, which saveth the upright in heart
9. 1 I will praise (thee)..with my whole heart
10. 6 He hath said in his heart, I shall not be
10. 11 He hath said in his heart, God hath for.
10. 13 he hath said in his heart, Thou wilt not
10. 17 thou wilt prepare their heart, thou wilt
11. 2 they may..shoot at the upright in heart
12. 2 (and) with a double heart, do they speak
13. 5 my heart shall rejoice in thy salvation
14. 1 The fool hath said in his heart, (There is)
16. 9 Therefore my heart is glad, and my glory
17. 3 Thou hast proved mine heart; thou hast
19. 8 The statutes..rejoicing the heart: the co.
19. 14 Let..the meditation of my heart, be accept.
21. 2 Thou hast given him his heart's desire
22. 14 my heart is like wax; it is melted in the
26. 2 O LORD..try my reins and my heart
27. 3 my heart shall not fear; though war sho.
27. 8 my heart said unto thee, Thy face, LORD
27. 14 and he shall strengthen thine heart: wait
28. 7 my heart trusted in him, and I am helped
28. 7 therefore my heart greatly rejoiceth; and
32. 11 shout..all (ye that are) upright in heart
33. 11 the thoughts of his heart to all generati.
33. 15 He fashioneth their hearts alike; he con.
33. 21 For our heart shall rejoice in him; becau.
34. 18 nigh unto them that are of a broken hea.
35. 25 Let them not say in their hearts, Ah! so
36. 1 the wicked saith within my heart (that th.)
36. 10 thy righteousness to the upright in heart
37. 4 shall give thee the desires of thine heart
37. 15 sword shall enter into their own heart
37. 31 The law of his God (is) in his heart; none
38. 8 by reason of the disquietness of my heart
38. 10 My heart panteth, my strength faileth me
39. 3 My heart was hot within me; while I was
40. 10 hid thy righteousness within my heart; I
40. 12 they are more..therefore my heart faileth
41. 6 his heart gathereth iniquity to itself; (wh.)
44. 18 Our heart is not turned back, neither have
44. 21 for he knoweth the secrets of the heart
45. 1 My heart is inditing a good matter: I
45. 5 Thine arrows (are) sharp in the heart of
49. 3 and the meditation of my heart (shall be)
51. 10 Create in me a clean heart, O God; and
51. 17 a broken and a contrite heart, O God, thou
53. 1 The fool hath said in his heart, (There is)
55. 4 My heart is sore pained within me; and
55. 21 but war (was) in his heart: his words were
57. 7 My heart is fixed, O God, my heart is fix.
58. 2 Yea, in heart ye work wickedness; ye w.
61. 2 when my heart is overwhelmed: lead me
62. 10 if riches increase, set not your heart (upon)
64. 6 both the inward (thought)..and the heart
64. 10 and all the upright in heart shall glory
66. 18 If I regard iniquity in my heart, the LORD
69. 20 Reproach hath broken my heart, and I am
74. 8 They said in their hearts, Let us destroy
78. 8 a generation (that) set not their heart ar.
78. 37 For their heart was not right with him
81. 12 gave them up unto their own hearts' lust
84. 2 my heart and my flesh crieth out for the
94. 15 all the upright in heart shall follow it
97. 11 and gladness for the upright in heart
102. 4 My heart is smitten, and withered like
105. 3 let the heart of them rejoice that seek
105. 25 He turned their heart to hate his people
107. 12 he brought down their heart with labour
108. 1 O God, my heart is fixed; I will sing
109. 22 and my heart is wounded within me
112. 7 his heart is fixed, trusting in the LORD
112. 8 His heart (is) established, he shall not be
119. 2 (and that) seek him with the whole heart
119. 10 With my whole heart have I sought thee
119. 11 Thy word have I hid in mine heart, that I
119. 32 run..when thou shalt enlarge my heart
119. 34 I shall observe it with (my) whole heart
119. 36 Incline my heart unto thy testimonies
119. 58 I entreated..with (my) whole heart: be
119. 69 will keep thy precepts with (my) whole h.
119. 70 Their heart is as fat as grease; (but) I delig.
Psa.119. 80 Let my heart be sound in thy statutes
119. 111 for they (are) the rejoicing of my heart
119. 112 I have inclined mine heart to perform
119. 145 I cried with (my) whole heart; hear me
119. 161 my heart standeth in awe of thy word
131. 1 LORD, my heart is not haughty, nor mine
138. 1 I will praise thee with my whole heart
140. 2 Which imagine mischiefs in (their) heart
141. 4 Incline not my heart to (any) evil thing
143. 4 Therefore..my heart within me is desola.
147. 3 healeth the broken in heart, and bindeth
Prov. 2. 2 (and) apply thine heart to understanding
2. 10 When wisdom entereth into thine heart
3. 1 let thine heart keep my commandments
3. 3 write them upon the table of thine heart
3. 5 Trust in the LORD with all thine heart
4. 4 Let thine heart retain my words: keep my
4. 23 Keep thy heart with all diligence; for
5. 12 have I hated instruction, and my heart de.
6. 14 Frowardness (is) in his heart, he deviseth
6. 18 An heart that deviseth wicked imaginati.
6. 21 Bind them continually upon thine heart
7. 3 write them upon the table of thine heart
7. 10 there met him a woman..subtil of heart
7. 25 Let not thine heart decline to her ways
8. 5 ye fools, be ye of an understanding heart
10. 8 The wise in heart will receive command.
10. 20 the heart of the wicked (is) little worth
11. 20 They that are of a froward heart (are) ab.
11. 29 fool (shall be) servant to the wise of heart
12. 8 but he that is of a perverse heart shall be
12. 20 Deceit (is) in the heart of them that imag.
12. 23 the heart of fools proclaimeth foolishness
12. 25 Heaviness in the heart of man maketh
13. 12 Hope deferred maketh the heart sick: but
14. 10 The heart knoweth his own bitterness; and
14. 13 Even in laughter the heart is sorrowful
14. 14 The backslider in heart shall be filled with
14. 30 A sound heart (is) the life of the flesh: but
14. 33 Wisdom resteth in the heart of him that
15. 7 but the heart of the foolish (doeth) not so
15. 13 A merry heart maketh a cheerful counte.
15. 13 but by sorrow of the heart the spirit is
15. 14 The heart of him..seeketh knowledge: but
15. 15 he that is of a merry heart (hath) a con.
15. 28 heart of the righteous studieth to answer
15. 30 The light of the eyes rejoiceth the heart
16. 1 The preparations of the heart in man, and
16. 5 Every one (that is) proud in heart (is) an
16. 9 A man's heart deviseth his way: but the
16. 21 The wise in heart shall be called prudent
16. 23 The heart of the wise teacheth his mouth
17. 16 get wisdom, seeing (he hath) no heart (to
17. 20 He that hath a froward heart findeth no
17. 22 A merry heart doeth good (like) a medic.
18. 2 but that his heart may discover itself
18. 12 Before destruction the heart of man is
18. 15 The heart of the prudent getteth knowled.
19. 3 and his heart fretteth against the LORD
19. 21 (There are) many devices in a man's heart
20. 5 Counsel in the heart of man (is like) deep
20. 9 I have made my heart clean, I am pure
21. 1 The king's heart (is) in the hand of the
21. 4 An high look, and a proud heart, (and)
22. 11 He that loveth pureness of heart, (for)
22. 15 Foolishness (is) bound in the heart of a
22. 17 apply thine heart unto my knowledge
23. 7 drink, saith he..but his heart (is) not
23. 12 Apply thine heart unto instruction, and
23. 15 My son, if thine heart be wise, my heart
23. 17 Let not thine heart envy sinners: but
23. 19 be wise, and guide thine heart in the way
23. 26 My son, give me thine heart, and let thine
23. 33 thine heart shall utter perverse things
24. 2 For their heart studieth destruction, and
24. 17 let not thine heart be glad when he stum.
25. 3 and the heart of kings (is) unsearchable
25. 20 he that singeth songs to an heavy heart
26. 23 Burning lips and a wicked heart (are like
26. 25 (there are) seven abominations in his he.
27. 9 Ointment and perfume rejoice the heart
27. 11 My son, be wise, and make my heart glad
27. 19 As in water..so the heart of man to man
28. 14 he that hardeneth his heart shall fall into
28. 26 He that trusteth in his own heart is a fool
31. 11 heart of her husband doth safely trust in
Eccl. 1. 13 I gave my heart to seek and search out
1. 16 I communed with mine own heart, say.
1. 16 my heart had great experience of wisdom
1. 17 I gave my heart to know wisdom, and to
2. 1 I said in mine heart, Go to now, I will
2. 3 I sought in mine heart to give myself unto
2. 3 yet acquainting mine heart with wisdom
2. 10 I withheld not my heart from any joy
2. 10 for my heart rejoiced in all my labour
2. 15 Then said I in my heart, As it happeneth
2. 15 Then I said in my heart, that this also (is)
2. 20 I went about to cause my heart to despair
2. 22 of the vexation of his heart, wherein he
2. 23 his heart taketh not rest in the night
3. 11 also he hath set the world in their heart
3. 17 I said in mine heart, God shall judge the
3. 18 I said in mine heart concerning the estate
5. 2 let not thine heart be hasty to utter (any
5. 20 God answereth (him) in the joy of his h.
7. 2 and the living will lay (it) to his heart
7. 3 for by the sadness..the heart is made bet.
7. 4 heart of the wise (is) in the house of mo.
7. 4 but the heart of fools (is) in the house of
7. 7 man mad; and a gift destroyeth the heart
7. 22 oftentimes also thine own heart knoweth
7. 25 applied mine heart to know, and to search
Eccl. 7. 26 the woman whose heart (is) snares and nets
8. 5 a wise man's heart discerneth both time
8. 9 and applied my heart unto every work
8. 11 therefore the heart of the sons of men is
8. 16 I applied mine heart to know wisdom, and
9. 1 For all this I considered in my heart, ev.
9. 3 also the heart of the sons of men is full of
9. 7 and drink thy wine with a merry heart
10. 2 A wise man's heart..but a fool's heart
11. 9 let thy heart cheer thee in the days of thy
11. 9 walk in the ways of thine heart, and in the
11. 10 Therefore remove sorrow from thy heart
Song 3. 11 in the day of the gladness of his heart
5. 2 I sleep, but my heart waketh: (it is) the
8. 6 Set me as a seal upon thine heart, as a
Isa. 6. 10 Make the heart of this people fat, and
15. 5 heart shall cry out for Moab; his fugitive
29. 13 have removed their heart far from me
32. 6 and his heart will work iniquity, to prac.
33. 18 Thine heart shall meditate terror. Where
35. 4 Say to them (that are) of a fearful heart
38. 3 how I have walked..with a perfect heart
42. 25 it burned him, yet he laid (it) not to heart
44. 19 And none considereth in his heart, neither
44. 20 a deceived heart hath turned him aside
47. 7 didst not lay these (things) to thy heart
47. 10 thou hast said in thine heart, I (am), and
51. 7 the people in whose heart (is) my law
57. 1 perisheth, and no man layeth (it) to heart
57. 11 and hast not..laid (it) to thy heart? have
57. 15 and to revive the heart of the contrite
57. 17 went on frowardly in the way of his heart
59. 13 uttering from the heart words of falsehood
63. 4 For the day of vengeance (is) in mine hea.
63. 17 LORD, why hast thou..hardened our heart
65. 14 my servants shall sing for joy of heart, but
65. 14 ye shall cry for sorrow of heart, and shall
66. 14 when ye see (this), your heart shall rejoice
Jer. 3. 10 not turned unto me with her whole heart
3. 15 give you pastors according to mine heart
3. 17 after the imagination of their evil heart
4. 9 the heart of the king..and the heart of the
4. 14 wash thine heart from wickedness, that
4. 18 because it reacheth unto thine heart
4. 19 I am pained at my very heart; my heart
5. 23 this people hath a revolting..heart; they
7. 24 in the imagination of their evil heart, and
7. 31 (them) not, neither came it into my heart
8. 18 I would comfort myself..my heart (is) fai.
9. 14 after the imagination of their own heart
9. 26 the house..(are) uncircumcised in the he.
11. 8 in the imagination of their evil heart
11. 20 O LORD..that triest the reins and the h.
12. 3 seen me, and tried mine heart toward thee
12. 11 desolate, because no man layeth (it) to he.
13. 10 walk in the imagination of their heart, and
14. 14 they prophesy..the deceit of their heart
16. 12 walk..after the imagination of his evil he.
17. 1 (it is) graven upon the table of their heart
17. 5 and whose heart departeth from the LORD
17. 9 The heart (is) deceitful above all (things)
17. 10 I the LORD search the heart, (I) try the re.
18. 12 will..do the imagination of his evil heart
20. 9 was in mine heart as a burning fire shut
20. 12 seest the reins and the heart, let me see thy
22. 17 But thine eyes and thine heart (are) not
23. 9 Mine heart within me is broken because of
23. 16 they speak a vision of their own heart, (and)
23. 17 after the imagination of his own heart, No
23. 20 have performed the thoughts of his heart
23. 26 How long shall (this) be in the heart of the
23. 26 prophets of the deceit of their own heart
24. 7 I will give them an heart to know me, that
24. 7 return unto me with their whole heart
30. 21 for who (is) this that engaged his heart to
30. 24 have performed the intents of his heart
31. 21 set thine heart toward the highway, (even)
31. 33 write it in their hearts; and will be their
32. 39 I will give them one heart, and one way
32. 41 I will plant them..with my whole heart
48. 29 his pride, and the haughtiness of his heart
48. 36 mine heart shall sound for Moab like pipes
48. 36 and mine heart shall sound like pipes for
48. 41 mighty men's hearts..as the heart of a w.
49. 16 pride of thine heart, O thou that dwellest
49. 22 heart of the mighty..be as the heart of a
Lam. 1. 20 mine heart is turned within me; for I h.
1. 22 my sighs (are) many, and my heart (is) f.
2. 18 Their heart cried unto the LORD, O wall of
2. 19 pour out thine heart like water before the
3. 65 Give them sorrow of heart, thy curse unto
5. 15 The joy of our heart is ceased; our dance
5. 17 For this our heart is faint; for these (th.)
Eze. 6. 9 I am broken with their whorish heart
11. 19 I will give them one heart, and I will put
11. 19 take the stony heart..give them an heart
11. 21 whose heart walketh after the heart of their
13. 2 them that prophesy out of their own heart
13. 17 which prophesy out of their own heart
13. 22 ye have made the heart of the righteous
14. 3 have set up their idols in their heart, and
14. 4, 7 setteth up his idols in his heart, and
14. 5 I may take..Israel in their own heart
18. 31 make you a new heart and a new spirit
20. 16 polluted..for their heart went after their
21. 7 every heart shall melt, and all hands shall
21. 15 that (their) heart may faint, and (their)
22. 14 Can thine heart endure, or can thine
28. 2 Because thine heart (is) lifted up, and thou
28. 2 though thou set thine heart as the heart
28. 6 Because thou hast set..as the heart of G
28. 17 Thine heart was lifted up because of thy

Eze. 32. 9 I will also vex the hearts of many people
33. 31 their heart goeth after their covetousness
36. 26 A new heart also will I give you, and a
36. 26 will take away the stony heart out of your
36. 26 flesh, and I will give you an heart of flesh
40. 4 set thine heart upon all that I shall show
44. 7 strangers, uncircumcised in heart, and
44. 9 No stranger, uncircumcised in heart, nor
Dan. 1. 8 But Daniel purposed in his heart that he
10. 12 first day that thou didst set thine heart to
Hos. 4. 11 wine and new wine take away the heart
7. 6 they have made ready their heart like an
7. 11 Ephraim also..without heart: they call
7. 14 have not cried unto me with their heart
10. 2 Their heart is divided; now shall they be
11. 8 Mine heart is turned within me, my rep.
13. 6 they were filled, and their heart was ex.
13. 8 will rend the caul of their heart, and there
Obad. 3 pride of thine heart hath deceived thee
3 that saith in his heart, Who shall bring
Nah. 2. 10 and the heart melteth, and the knees sm.
Zeph. 3. 14 be glad and rejoice with all the heart
Zech. 7. 12 they made their hearts (as) an adamant
10. 7 their heart shall rejoice..heart shall rej.
12. 5 the governors..shall say in their heart
Mal. 2. 2 and if ye will not lay (it) to heart, to give
2. 2 already, because ye do not lay (it) to heart
4. 6 he shall turn the heart of the fathers to
4. 6 the children, and the heart of the children

3. *The heart*, לֵב *leb*.
Dan. 7. 28 in me: but I kept the matter in my heart

4. *The heart*, לֵבָב *lebab*.
Gen. 20. 5 in the integrity of my heart, and innocency
20. 6 didst this in the integrity of thy heart
Exod 14. 5 heart of Pharaoh and of his servants was
Lev. 19. 17 shalt not hate thy brother in thine heart
26. 36 I will send a faintness into their hearts in
26. 41 if then their uncircumcised hearts be
Num 15. 39 ye seek not after your own heart and your
Deut. 1. 28 our brethren have discouraged our heart
2. 30 and made his heart obstinate, that he mi.
4. 9 lest they depart from thy heart all the
4. 29 if thou seek him with all thy heart and
4. 39 consider (it) in thine heart, that the LORD
5. 29 O that there was such an heart in them
6. 5 shalt love the LORD..with all thine heart
6. 6 And these words..shall be in thine heart
7. 17 If thou shalt say in thine heart, These
8. 2 to know what (was) in thine heart, whether
8. 5 Thou shalt also consider in thine heart
8. 14 Then thine heart be lifted up, and thou
8. 17 And thou say in thine heart, My power
9. 4 Speak not thou in thine heart, after that
9. 5 or for the uprightness of thine heart, dost
10. 12 and to serve the LORD..with all thy heart
10. 16 Circumcise..the foreskin of your heart
11. 13 and to serve him with all your heart and
11. 16 that your heart be not deceived, and ye
11. 18 lay up these my words in your heart and
13. 3 love the LORD..with all your heart and
15. 7 thou shalt not harden thine heart, nor
15. 9 there be not a thought in thy wicked he.
15. 10 and thine heart shall not be grieved when
17. 17 that his heart turn not away: neither sh.
17. 20 That his heart be not lifted up above his
18. 21 And if thou say in thine heart, How shall
19. 6 while his heart is hot, and overtake him
20. 3 let not your hearts faint; fear not, and
20. 8 brethren's heart faint as well as his heart
26. 16 keep and do them with all thine heart
28. 28 shall smite thee with..astonishment of h.
28. 47 servedst not..with gladness of heart, for
28. 67 for the fear of thine heart wherewith thou
29. 18 whose heart turneth away this day from
29. 19 that he bless himself in his heart, saying
30. 2 I command thee..with all thine heart, and
30. 6 will circumcise thine heart, and the heart
30. 6 to love the LORD..with all thine heart
30. 10 turn unto the LORD..with all thine heart
30. 14 But the word (is) very nigh..in thy heart
30. 17 But if thine heart turn away, so that thou
32. 46 Set your hearts unto all the words which
Josh. 2. 11 hearts did melt, neither did there remain
5. 1 that their heart melted, neither was the.
7. 5 wherefore the hearts of the people melted
14. 7 brought him word..as (it was) in mine h.
22. 5 to serve him with all your heart, and with
23. 14 ye know in all your hearts, and in all
24. 23 incline your heart unto the LORD God of I.
Judg 19. 8 Comfort thine heart, I pray thee. And
19. 9 lodge here, that thine heart may be merry
1 Sa. 1. 8 why is thy heart grieved? (am) not I bet.
2. 35 which (is) in mine heart and in my mind
6. 6 Wherefore then do ye harden your hearts
7. 3 If ye do return..with all your hearts
7. 3 and prepare your hearts unto the LORD
9. 19 and will tell thee all that (is) in thine he.
12. 20 but serve the LORD with all your heart
12. 24 and serve him in truth with all your heart
13. 14 sought him a man after his own heart
14. 7 Do all that (is) in thine heart: turn thee
14. 7 I (am) with thee according to thy heart
16. 7 outward..but the LORD looketh on the h.
17. 28 and the naughtiness of thine heart; for
21. 12 David laid up these words in his heart
2 Sa. 7. 3 Go, do all that (is) in thine heart; for the
19. 14 the heart of all the men of Judah, even
1 Ki. 2. 4 to walk..with all their heart and with all
2. 44 all the wickedness which thine heart is
3. 6 and in uprightness of heart with thee; and
8. 17 it was in the heart of David my father to

1 Ki. 8. 18 Whereas it was in thine heart to build an
8. 18 didst well that it was in thine heart
8. 38 which shall know..his own heart, and sp.
8. 39 whose heart thou knowest; for thou, (even)
8. 39 knowest the hearts of all the children of
8. 48 return unto thee with all their heart, and
8. 58 That he may incline our hearts unto him
8. 61 Let your heart therefore be perfect with
9. 4 in integrity of heart, and in uprightness
10. 2 she communed..of all that was in her he.
11. 2 (for) surely they will turn away your he.
11. 4 his wives turned away his heart after other
11. 4 heart was not perfect..as (was) the heart
11. 9 because his heart was turned from the L.
14. 8 and who followed me with all his heart
15. 3 heart was not perfect..as the heart of D.
15. 14 nevertheless Asa's heart was perfect with
2 Ki. 10. 15 heart right, as my heart (is) with thy h.?
10. 30 hast done..all that (was) in mine heart
10. 31 took no heed to walk..with all his heart
20. 3 how I have walked..with a perfect heart
22. 19 Because thine heart was tender, and thou
23. 25 that turned to the LORD with all his heart
1 Ch. 12. 17 mine heart shall be knit unto you: but if
12. 38 All these men..came with a perfect heart
17. 2 Do all that (is) in thine heart; for God (is)
22. 19 Now set your heart and your soul to seek
28. 2 I (had) in mine heart to build an house of
28. 9 searcheth all hearts, and understandeth all
29. 17 I know also..that thou triest the heart
29. 17 in the uprightness of mine heart I have
29. 18 keep this for ever in..the heart of thy pe.
29. 18 and prepare their heart unto thee
2 Ch. 1. 11 Because this was in thine heart, and thou
6. 7 it was in the heart of David my father to
6. 8 Forasmuch as it was in thine heart to build
6. 8 didst well in that it was in thine heart
6. 30 and render unto every man..whose heart
6. 30 for thou only knowest the hearts of the ch.
9. 1 she communed..of all that was in her hea.
11. 16 such as set their hearts to seek the LORD G.
15. 12 to seek the LORD God..with all their heart
15. 15 for they had sworn with all their heart, and
15. 17 nevertheless the heart of Asa was perfect
16. 9 behalf of (them) whose heart (is) perfect
19. 3 and hast prepared thine heart to seek God
19. 9 saying, Thus shall ye do..with a perfect h.
20. 33 the people had not prepared their hearts
22. 9 who sought the LORD with all his heart
25. 2 did..right..but not with a perfect heart
29. 10 Now (it is) in mine heart to make a coven.
29. 34 the Levites (were) more upright in heart to
30. 19 prepareth his heart to seek God, the LORD
31. 21 he did (it) with all his heart, and prospered
32. 31 he might know all (that was) in his heart
34. 27 Because thine heart was tender, and thou
34. 31 and his statutes, with all his heart, and wi.
36. 13 hardened his heart from turning unto the
Ezra 7. 10 Ezra had prepared his heart to seek the law
Neh. 9. 8 And foundest his heart faithful before th.
Job 1. 5 sinned, and cursed God in their hearts
9. 4 (He is) wise in heart, and mighty in streng.
10. 13 these (things) hast thou hid in thine heart
17. 11 broken off, (even) the thoughts of my heart
22. 22 and lay up his words in thine heart
27. 6 my heart shall not reproach (me) so long
Psa. 4. 4 commune with your own heart upon your
13. 2 (having) sorrow in my heart daily? how lo.
15. 2 and speaketh the truth in his heart
20. 4 Grant thee according to thine own heart
22. 26 shall praise..your heart shall live for ever
24. 4 that hath clean hands, and a pure heart
25. 17 The troubles of my heart are enlarged
28. 3 peace..but mischief (is) in their hearts
31. 24 he shall strengthen your heart, all ye that
62. 8 ye people, pour out your heart before him
69. 32 and your heart shall live that seek God
73. 1 good..(even) to such as are of a clean heart
73. 7 they have more than heart could wish
73. 13 Verily I have cleansed my heart (in) vain
73. 21 my heart was grieved, and I was pricked in
73. 26 My flesh and my heart faileth: (but) God
73. 26 the strength of my heart, and my portion
77. 6 I commune with mine own heart; and my
78. 18 they tempted God in their heart, by asking
78. 72 according to the integrity of his heart; and
84. 5 thee; in whose heart (are) the ways (of t.)
86. 11 O LORD..unite my heart to fear thy name
86. 12 I will praise thee..with all my heart; and
90. 12 that we may apply (our) hearts unto wis.
95. 8 Harden not your heart, as in the provoca.
95. 10 It (is) a people that do err in their heart
101. 2 walk within my house with a perfect heart
101. 4 A froward heart shall depart from me
101. 5 him that hath ..a proud heart will not I
104. 15 wine (that) maketh glad the heart of man
104. 15 and bread (which) strengtheneth man's h.
109. 16 he might even slay the broken in heart
111. 1 will praise the LORD with (my) whole heart
119. 7 praise thee with uprightness of heart: and
139. 23 Search me, O God, and know my heart
Prov. 4. 21 keep them in the midst of thine heart
6. 25 Lust not after her beauty in thine heart
Eccl. 9. 3 madness (is) in their heart while they live
Isa. 1. 5 whole head is sick, and the whole heart f.
6. 10 and understand with their heart, and con.
7. 2 his heart was moved, and the heart of his
9. 9 say in the pride and stoutness of heart
10. 7 neither doth his heart think so; but (it is)
10. 7 in his heart to destroy and cut off nations
10. 12 I will punish the fruit of the stout heart
13. 7 be faint, and every man's heart shall melt

Isa. 14. 13 For thou hast said in thine heart, I will
19. 1 heart of Egypt shall melt in the midst of
21. 4 My heart panted, fearfulness affrighted me
30. 29 gladness of heart, as when one goeth with
32. 4 heart also of the rash shall understand
47. 8 that sayest in thine heart, I (am), and no.
49. 21 Then shalt thou say in thine heart, Who
60. 5 and thine heart shall fear, and be enlarged
Jer. 4. 4 take away the foreskins of your heart, ye
5. 24 Neither say they in their heart, Let us
13. 22 if thou say in thine heart, Wherefore co.
15. 16 and thy word was..rejoicing of mine heart
29. 13 ye shall search for me with all your heart
32. 40 but I will put my fear in their hearts
51. 46 lest your heart faint, and ye fear for the
Lam. 3. 41 Let us lift up our heart with (our) hands
Eze. 3. 10 all my words..receive in thine heart, and
28. 5 and thine heart is lifted up because of thy
28. 6 Because thou hast set thine heart as the
31. 10 and his heart is lifted up in his height
36. 5 with the joy of all (their) heart, with des.
Dan. 8. 25 and he shall magnify (himself) in his heart
11. 12 his heart shall be lifted up; and he shall
11. 27 both these kings' hearts (shall be) to do
11. 28 heart (shall be) against the holy covenant
Hos. 7. 2 they consider not in their hearts (that) I
Joel 2. 12 Turn ye (even) to me with all your heart
2. 13 rend your heart, and not your garments
Zeph. 1. 12 that say in their heart, The LORD will not
2. 15 that said in her heart, I (am), and (there
Zech. 7. 10 none of you imagine evil..in your heart
8. 17 none of you imagine evil in your heart

5. *The heart*, לְבַב *lebab*.
Dan. 2. 30 mightest know the thoughts of thy heart
4. 16 Let his heart be changed from man's
4. 16 and let a beast's heart be given unto him
5. 20 But when his heart was lifted up, and his
5. 21 and his heart was made like the beasts
5. 22 thou..hast not humbled thine heart, tho.
7. 4 made stand..and a man's heart was given

6. *Heart*, לִבָּה *libbah*.
Psa. 7. 9 the righteous God trieth the hearts and
125. 4 to (them that are) upright in their hearts
Prov. 15. 11 how much more then the hearts of the ch.
17. 3 for gold: but the LORD trieth the hearts
21. 2 eyes: but the LORD pondereth the hearts
24. 12 doth not he that pondereth the heart con.
Isa. 44. 18 their hearts, that they cannot understand
Eze. 16. 30 How weak is thine heart, saith the LORD

7. *Soul, breath*, נֶפֶשׁ *nephesh*.
Exod 23. 9 for ye know the heart of a stranger, seeing
Lev. 26. 16 consume the eyes, and cause sorrow of h.
Deut 24. 15 for he (is) poor, and setteth his heart upon
1 Sa. 2. 33 consume thine eyes, and to grieve thine h.
2 Sa. 3. 21 mayest reign over all that thine heart
Psa 10. 3 the wicked boasteth of his heart's desire
Prov. 23. 7 For as he thinketh in his heart, so (is) he
28. 25 He that is of a proud heart stirreth up str.
31. 6 wine unto those that be of heavy hearts
Jer. 42. 20 For ye dissemble in your hearts, when ye
Lam. 3. 51 Mine eye affecteth mine heart because of
Eze. 25. 6 and rejoiced in heart with all thy despite
25. 15 with a despiteful heart, to destroy (it) for
27. 31 shall weep for thee with bitterness of heart
Hos. 4. 8 and they set their heart on their iniquity

8. *Covered part*, שֶׂכְוִי *sekvi*.
Job 38. 36 who hath given understanding to the h.?

9. *Bowels*, מֵעִים *meim*.
Psa. 40. 8 O my God..thy law (is) within my heart

10. *Centre, midst*, קֶרֶב *qereb*.
Jer. 9. 8 peaceably..but in heart he layeth his wait

11. *The heart*, καρδία *kardia*.
Matt. 5. 8 Blessed (are) the pure in heart: for they
5. 28 hath committed adultery..in his heart
6. 21 where your treasure is, there..your heart
9. 4 Wherefore think ye evil in your hearts?
11. 29 for I am meek and lowly in heart: and ye
12. 34 for out of the abundance of the heart the
12. 35 out of the good treasure [of the heart]
12. 40 and three nights in the heart of the earth
13. 15 For this people's heart is waxed gross
13. 15 and should understand with (their) heart
13. 19 catcheth..that which was sown in his h.
15. 8 with (their) lips; but their heart is far fr.
15. 18 But those things..come forth from the h.
15. 19 For out of the heart proceed evil thoughts
18. 35 if ye from your hearts forgive not every
22. 37 love the Lord thy God with all thy heart
24. 48 if that evil servant shall say in his heart
Mark 2. 6 sitting there, and reasoning in their hea.
2. 8 Why reason ye these things in your hearts?
3. 5 grieved for the hardness of their hearts
4. 15 [taketh away the word..sown in their he.]
6. 52 considered not..for their heart was har.
7. 6 with (their) lips, but their heart is far from
7. 19 Because it entereth not into his heart
7. 21 out of the heart of men, proceed evil tho.
8. 17 saith..have ye your heart yet hardened?
11. 23 shall not doubt in his heart, but shall
12. 30 love the Lord thy God with all thy heart
12. 33 to love him with all the heart, and with
Luke 1. 17 to turn the hearts of the fathers to the
1. 51 proud in the imagination of their hearts
1. 66 And all they..laid (them) up in their hea.
2. 19 But Mary..pondered (them) in her heart
2. 35 that the thoughts of many hearts may be
2. 51 mother kept all these sayings in her heart
3. 15 all men mused in their hearts of John

Luke 5. 22 said..What reason ye in your hearts?
6. 45 out of the good treasure of his heart bri.
6. 45 [out of the evil treasure of his heart brin.]
6. 45 of the abundance of the heart his mouth
8. 12 taketh away the word out of their hearts
8. 15 in an honest and good heart, having
9. 47 perceiving the thought of their heart, took
10. 27 love the Lord thy God with all thy heart
12. 34 where your treasure is there..your heart
12. 45 But and if that servant say in his heart
16. 15 but God knoweth your hearts: for that
21. 14 Settle (it) therefore in your hearts, not to
21. 34 lest at any time your hearts be overchar.
24. 25 O fools, and slow of heart to believe all
24. 32 Did not our heart burn within us, while
24. 38 and why do thoughts arise in your hearts?
John 12. 40 He hath..hardened their heart; that they
12. 40 nor understand with (their) heart, and be
13. 2 the devil having now put into the heart
14. 1 Let not your heart be troubled: ye believe
14. 27 Let not your heart be troubled, neither let
16. 6 unto you, sorrow hath filled your heart
16. 22 your heart shall rejoice, and your joy no
Acts 2. 26 Therefore did my heart rejoice, and my
2. 37 they were pricked in their heart, and said
2. 46 did eat their meat with gladness..of heart
4. 32 multitude..were of one heart..neither sa.
5. 3 why hath Satan filled thine heart to lie to
5. 4 why hast thou conceived..in thine heart?
7. 23 it came into his heart to visit his brethren
7. 39 in their hearts turned back again into Eg.
7. 51 uncircumcised in heart and ears, ye do
7. 54 they were cut to the heart, and they gna.
8. 21 for thy heart is not right in the sight of G.
8. 22 if perhaps the thought of thine heart may
8. 37 [If thou believest with..thine heart, thou]
11. 23 that with purpose of heart they would cl.
13. 22 I have found David..after mine own heart
14. 17 filling our hearts with food and gladness
15. 9 no difference..purifying their hearts by f.
16. 14 whose heart the Lord opened, that she att.
21. 13 mean ye to weep and to break mine heart?
28. 27 For the heart of this people is waxed gro.
28. 27 understand with (their) heart, and should
Rom. 1. 21 and their foolish heart was darkened
1. 24 through the lusts of their own hearts, to
2. 5 after thy hardness and impenitent heart
2. 15 Which show the work..in their hearts
2. 29 and circumcision (is that) of the heart, in
5. 5 love of God is shed abroad in our hearts by
6. 17 ye have obeyed from the heart that form
8. 27 he that searcheth the hearts knoweth wh.
9. 2 That I have great heaviness..in my heart
10. 1 my heart's desire and prayer to God for
10. 6 Say not in thine heart, Who shall ascend
10. 8 The word is nigh thee..and in thy heart
10. 9 and shalt believe in thine heart that God
10. 10 For with the heart man believeth unto ri.
16. 18 and fair speeches deceive the hearts of
1 Co. 2. 9 neither have entered into the heart of man
4. 5 make manifest the counsels of the hearts
7. 37 he that standeth stedfast in his heart
7. 37 and hath so decreed in his heart that he w.
14. 25 thus are the secrets of his heart made
2 Co. 1. 22 given the earnest of the spirit in our hearts
2. 4 and anguish of heart I wrote unto you
3. 2 Ye are our epistle written in our hearts
3. 3 of stone, but in fleshy tables of the heart
3. 15 Moses is read, the veil is upon their heart
4. 6 hath shined in our hearts, to (give) the
5. 12 which glory in appearance, and not in he.
6. 11 our mouth is open unto you, our heart is
7. 3 ye are in our hearts to die and live with
8. 16 put the same earnest care into the heart of
9. 7 Every man..as he purposeth in his heart
Gal. 4. 6 sent forth the spirit..into your hearts, c.
Eph. 3. 17 Christ may dwell in your hearts by faith
4. 18 because of the blindness of their heart
5. 19 making melody in your heart to the Lord
6. 5 in singleness of your heart, as unto Christ
6. 22 and (that) he might comfort your hearts
Phil. 1. 7 I have you in my heart; inasmuch as both
4. 7 shall keep your hearts and minds through
Col. 2. 2 That their hearts might be comforted
3. 15 let the peace of God rule in your hearts
3. 16 singing with grace in your hearts to the L.
3. 22 but in singleness of heart, fearing God
4. 8 know your estate, and comfort your he.
1 Th. 2. 4 but God, which trieth our hearts
2. 17 being taken from you..not in heart, end.
3. 13 he may stablish your hearts unblameable
2 Th. 2. 17 Comfort your hearts, and stablish you in
3. 5 the Lord direct your hearts into the love
1 Ti. 1. 5 charity out of a pure heart, and (of) a go.
2 Ti. 2. 22 that call on the Lord out of a pure heart
Heb. 3. 8, 15 Harden not your hearts, as in the pro.
3. 10 They do alway err in (their) heart; and
3. 12 lest there be in any of you an evil heart
4. 7 if ye will hear..harden not your hearts
4. 12 and (is) a discerner..of the heart
8. 10 and write them in their hearts; and I will
10. 16 I will put my laws into their hearts, and in
10. 22 Let us draw near with a true heart, in full
10. 22 having our hearts sprinkled from an evil
13. 9 For (it is) a good thing that the heart be
Jas. 1. 26 but deceiveth his own heart, this man's
3. 14 But if ye have bitter..strife in your hearts
4. 8 and purify (your) hearts, (ye) double min.
5. 5 ye have nourished your hearts, as in a day
5. 8 Be ye also patient; stablish your hearts
1 Pe. 1. 22 love one another with a pure heart ferve.
3. 4 (let it be) the hidden man of the heart, in
1 Pe. 3. 15 But sanctify the Lord God in your hearts
2 Pe. 1. 19 and the day star arise in your hearts
2. 14 an heart they have exercised with covet.
1 Jo. 3. 19 and shall assure our hearts before him
3. 20 if our heart condemn us, God is greater
3. 20 than our heart, and knoweth all things
3. 21 Beloved, if our heart condemn us not
Rev. 2. 23 he which searcheth the reins and hearts
17. 17 For God hath put in their hearts to fulfil
18. 7 for she saith in her heart, I sit a queen, and

12. *Soul, life,* ψυχή *psuchē.*
Eph. 6. 6 doing the will of God from the heart

HEART, hardness of —
Dryness or hardness of heart, σκληροκαρδία *sklēr.*
Matt 19. 8 Moses because of the hardness of your h.
Mark 10. 5 For the hardness of your heart he wrote
16. 14 with their unbelief and hardness of heart

HEART, which knoweth the —
Heart knowing, καρδιογνώστης *kardiognōstēs.*
Acts 1. 24 Lord, which knowest the hearts of all (men)
15. 8 God, which knoweth the hearts, bare them

HEARTED —
1. *Heart,* לֵב *leb.*
Exod 28. 3 shalt speak unto all (that are) wise hearted
35. 10 every wise hearted among you shall come
35. 22 and women, as many as were willing hea.
35. 25 the women that were wise hearted did spin
36. 1 every wise hearted man, in whom the LORD
36. 2 every wise hearted man, in whose heart the
36. 8 every wise hearted man among them that
Psa. 76. 5 The stout hearted are spoiled, they have
Isa. 24. 7 languisheth, all the merry hearted do sigh
46. 12 Hearken unto me, ye stout hearted, that
61. 1 sent me to bind up the broken hearted, to
Eze. 2. 4 impudent children, and stiff hearted. I do
3. 7 the house (are) impudent and hard hea.

2. *Heart,* לֵבָב *lebab.*
Deut 20. 8 What man..fearful and faint hearted? let
Isa. 7. 4 neither be faint hearted for the two tails of

3. *Heart,* καρδία *kardia.*
Luke 4. 18 sent me to heal the broken hearted, to

HEARTH —
1. *A stove,* אָח *ach.*
Jer. 36. 22 (a fire) on the hearth burning before him
36. 23 into the fire that (was) on the hearth
36. 23 in the fire that (was) on the hearth

2. *Pan,* כִּיּוֹר *kiyyor.*
Zech. 12. 6 like an hearth of fire among the wood

3. *Burning,* מוֹקֵד *moqed.*
Psa. 102. 3 and my bones are burned as an hearth

HEARTH, from the —
To burn, יָקַד *yaqad.*
Isa. 30. 14 a sherd to take fire from the hearth, or

HEARTILY —
Out of the soul, ἐκ ψυχῆς *ek psuchēs.*
Col. 3. 23 do (it) heartily, as to the Lord, and not

HEARTS (men's) failing from fear —
To breathe away, ἀποψύχω *apopsuchō.*
Luke 21. 26 Men's hearts failing them for fear, and for

HEARTY —
Soul, breath, נֶפֶשׁ *nephesh.*
Prov. 27. 9 the sweetness of a man's friend by hearty

HEAT —
1. *Heat,* חֹם *chom.*
Gen. 8. 22 cold and heat, and summer and winter, and
18. 1 in the tent door in the heat of the day
1 Sa. 11. 11 and slew the Ammonites until the heat of
2 Sa. 4. 5 came about the heat of the day to the
Job 24. 19 Drought and heat consume the snow water
Isa. 18. 4 dwelling place like a clear heat upon
18. 4 a cloud of dew in the heat of harvest
Jer. 17. 8 shall not see when heat cometh, but her
51. 39 In their heat I will make their feasts

2. *Heat,* חַמָּה *chammah.*
Psa. 19. 6 there is nothing hid from the heat thereof

3. *Heat, fury,* חֵמָה *chemah.*
Eze. 3. 14 in bitterness, in the heat of my spirit

4. *Drought,* חֹרֶב *choreb.*
Job 30. 30 and my bones are burnt with heat
Isa. 4. 6 a shadow in the day time from the heat
25. 4 a shadow from the heat, when the blast
25. 5 as the heat in a dry place; (even) the heat
Jer. 36. 30 shall be cast out in the day to the heat

5. *Heat, fury,* חֳרִי *chori.*
Deut. 29. 24 what (meaneth) the heat of this great an.

6. *Heat, mirage,* שָׁרָב *sharab.*
Isa. 49. 10 neither shall the heat nor sun smite them

7. *Warmth, heat,* θέρμη *thermē.*
Acts 28. 3 there came a viper out of the heat, and

8. *Heat,* καῦμα *kauma.*
Rev. 7. 16 shall the sun light on them, nor any heat
16. 9 men were scorched with great heat, and

9. *Burning, heat,* καύσων *kausōn.*
Matt. 20. 12 have borne the burden and heat of the day
Luke 12. 55 ye say, There will be heat; and it cometh

HEAT, burning —
Burning, heat, καύσων *kausōn.*
Jas. 1. 11 is no sooner risen with a burning heat

HEAT, with fervent —
To be set on fire, burn, καυσόομαι *kausoomai.*
2 Pe. 3. 10, 12 elements shall melt with fervent heat

HEAT, to —
1. *To heat,* אֲזָא *aza.*
Dan. 3. 19 they should heat the furnace one seven
3. 19 times more than it was wont to be heated

2. *To be burning,* בָּעַר *baar.*
Hos. 7. 4 as an oven heated by the baker, (who) cease

HEAT, to get —
1. *To be or become warm,* חָמַם *chamam.*
1 Ki. 1. 2 that my lord the king may get heat

2. *To be or become warm,* יָחַם *yacham.*
1 Ki. 1. 1 covered him with clothes..but..gat no h

HEAT, to have —
To be or become warm, חָמַם *chamam.*
Eccl. 4. 11 if two lie together, then they have heat

HEATH —
1. *Naked or destitute object,* עֲרוֹעֵר *aroer.*
Jer. 48. 6 and be like the heath in the wilderness

2. *Naked or destitute object,* עַרְעָר *arar.*
Jer. 17. 6 he shall be like the heath in the desert

HEATHEN —
1. *A nation,* גּוֹי *goi.*
Lev. 25. 44 of the heathen that are round about you
26. 33 I will scatter you among the heathen, and
26. 38 ye shall perish among the heathen, and
26. 45 I brought..in the sight of the heathen
Deut. 4. 27 shall be left few in number among the h.
2 Sa. 22. 44 hast kept me (to be) head of the heathen
22. 50 thanks unto thee, O LORD, among the hea
2 Ki. 16. 3 to the abominations of the heathen
17. 8 And walked in the statutes of the heathen
17. 11 as (did) the heathen whom the LORD car.
17. 15 went after the heathen that (were) round
21. 2 after the abominations of the heathen
1 Ch. 16. 24 Declare his glory among the heathen
16. 35 deliver us from the heathen, that we may
2 Ch. 20. 6 over all the kingdoms of the heathen?
28. 3 after the abominations of the heathen
33. 2 like unto the abominations of the heathen
33. 9 to do worse than the heathen, whom the
36. 14 after all the abominations of the heathen
Ezra 6. 21 the filthiness of the heathen of the land
Neh. 5. 8 the Jews, which were sold unto the hea.
5. 9 the reproach of the heathen our enemies
5. 17 from among the heathen that (are) about
6. 6 is reported among the heathen, and Gas.
6. 16 the heathen that (were) about us saw (these)
Psa. 2. 1 Why do the heathen rage, and the people
2. 8 give..the heathen (for) thine inheritance
9. 5 Thou hast rebuked the heathen, thou hast
9. 15 The heathen are sunk down in the pit
9. 19 let the heathen be judged in thy sight
10. 16 the heathen are perished out of his land
18. 43 thou hast made me the head of the heath.
18. 49 I give thanks..O LORD, among the heathen
33. 10 bringeth the counsel of the heathen to
44. 2 didst drive out the heathen with thy hand
44. 11 and hast scattered us among the heathen
44. 14 Thou makest us a byword among the hea.
46. 6 The heathen raged, the kingdoms were m.
46. 10 I will be exalted among the heathen, I
47. 8 God reigneth over the heathen: God sit.
59. 5 O LORD..awake to visit all the heathen
59. 8 shalt have all the heathen in derision
78. 55 He cast out the heathen also before them
79. 1 heathen are come into thine inheritance
79. 6 Pour out thy wrath upon the heathen
79. 10 Wherefore should the heathen say, Where
79. 10 let him be known among the heathen in
80. 8 hast cast out the heathen, and planted it
94. 10 He that chastiseth the heathen, shall not
96. 3 Declare his glory among the heathen, his
96. 10 Say among the heathen..the LORD reign.
98. 2 openly showed in the sight of the heathen
102. 15 heathen shall fear the name of the LORD
105. 44 gave them the lands of the heathen: and
106. 35 But were mingled among the heathen, and
106. 41 gave them into the hand of the heathen
106. 47 gather us from among the heathen, to g.
110. 6 He shall judge among the heathen, he sh.
111. 6 give them the heritage of the heathen
115. 2 Wherefore should the heathen say, Where
126. 2 then said they among the heathen, The L.
135. 15 The idols of the heathen (are) silver and
149. 7 To execute vengeance upon the heathen
Isa. 16. 8 the lords of the heathen have broken down
Jer. 9. 16 will scatter them also among the heathen
10. 2 Learn not the way of the heathen, and be
10. 2 for the heathen are dismayed at them
10. 25 Pour out thy fury upon the heathen that
18. 13 Ask ye now among the heathen, who hath
49. 14 an ambassador is sent unto the heathen
49. 15 I will make thee small among the heathen
Lam. 1. 3 she dwelleth among the heathen, she
1. 10 she hath seen (that) the heathen entered
4. 15 they said among the heathen, They shall
4. 20 Under his shadow..live among the heath.
Eze. 7. 24 I will bring the worst of the heathen
11. 12 done after the manners of the heathen
11. 16 have cast them far off among the heathen

Eze 12. 16 all their abominations among the heathen
16. 14 went..among the heathen for thy beauty
20. 9, 14 not be polluted before the heathen
20. 22 be polluted in the sight of the heathen
20. 23 I would scatter them among the heathen
20. 32 will be as the heathen, as the families
20. 41 be sanctified in you before the heathen
22. 4 I made thee a reproach unto the heathen
22. 15 I will scatter thee among the heathen
22. 16 in thyself in the sight of the heathen
23. 30 hast gone a whoring after the heathen
25. 7 deliver thee for a spoil to the heathen
25. 8 Judah (is) like unto all the heathen
28. 25 sanctified..in the sight of the heathen
30. 3 it shall be the time of the heathen
31. 11 hand of the mighty one of the heathen
31. 17 under his shadow in..midst of the heathen
34. 28 shall no more be a prey to the heathen
34. 29 bear the shame of the heathen any more
36. 3 possession unto the residue of the heathen
36. 4 derision to the residue of the heathen
36. 5 spoken against the residue of the heathen
36 6 ye have borne the shame of the heathen
36. 7 the heathen that (are) about you, they shall
36. 15 hear..the shame of the heathen any more
36. 19 I scattered them among the heathen, and
36. 20 they entered unto the heathen, whither
36. 21 Israel had profaned among the heathen
36 22 which ye have profaned among the heathen
36. 23 which was profaned among the heathen
36. 23 the heathen shall know that I (am) the LORD
36. 24 I will take you from among the heathen
36. 30 no..reproach of famine among the heathen
36. 36 the heathen that are left round about
37. 21 children of Israel from among the heathen
37. 28 the heathen shall know that I the LORD
38. 16 the heathen may know me, when I shall
39. 7 the heathen shall know that I (am) the Lo.
39. 21 among the heathen, and all the heathen
39. 23 the heathen shall know that the house of
39. 28 be led into captivity among the heathen
Joel 2. 17 that the heathen should rule over them
2. 19 make you a reproach among the heathen
3. 11 come, all ye heathen, and gather yoursel.
3. 12 Let the heathen be wakened, and come up
3. 12 sit to judge all the heathen round about
Amos 9. 12 the heathen, which are called by my name
Obad. 1 an ambassador is sent among the heathen
2 I have made thee small among the heathen
15 day of the LORD (is) near..all the heathen
16 shall all the heathen drink continually
Mic. 5. 15 in anger and fury upon the heathen, such
Hab. 1. 5 Behold ye among the heathen, and regard
3. 12 thou didst thresh the heathen in anger
Zeph. 2. 11 every one..all the isles of the heathen
Hag. 2. 22 strength of the kingdoms of the heathen
Zech. 1. 15 displeased with the heathen (that are) at
8. 13 ye were a curse among the heathen, O h.
9. 10 and he shall speak peace unto the heathen
14. 14 the wealth of all the heathen round about
14. 18 the LORD will smite the heathen that co.
Mal. 1. 11 my name (shall be) great among the hea.
1. 14 my name (is) dreadful among the heathen

2. *Nation*, ἔθνος *ethnos*
Acts 4. 25 Why did the heathen rage, and the people
2 Co. 11. 26 (in) perils by the heathen, (in) perils in the
Gal. 1. 16 that I might preach him among the hea.
2. 9 we (should go) unto the heathen, and they
3. 8 would justify the heathen through faith

3. *Those belonging to the nations*, οἱ ἐθνικοί *hoi ethnikoi*
Matt. 6. 7 use not vain repetitions, as the heathen (do)

HEATHEN man —
Belonging to the nations, ἐθνικός *ethnikos*.
Matt 18. 17 be..as an heathen man and a publican

HEAVE, to —
To make high, lift up high, רוּם *rum*, 5.
Num 15. 20 as (ye do) the..offering..shall ye heave
18. 30 ye have heaved the best thereof from it
18. 32 ye have heaved from it the best of it

HEAVE offering —
A heaved up offering, תְּרוּמָה *terumah*.
Exod 29. 27 the shoulder of the heave offering, which
29. 28 be Aaron's..for it (is) an heave offering
29. 28 it shall be an heave offering from the
29. 28 (even) their heave offering unto the LORD
Lev. 7. 14 (for) an heave offering unto the LORD, (and)
7. 32 unto the priest (for) an heave offering of
Num 15. 19 offer up an heave offering unto the LORD
15. 20 offer up a cake..(for) an heave offering
15. 20 heave offering of the threshing floor, so
15. 21 an heave offering in your generations
18. 8 the charge of mine heave offerings of
18. 11 the heave offering of their gift, with all
18. 19 All the heave offerings of the holy things
18. 24 offer (as) an heave offering unto the LORD
18. 26 ye shall offer up an heave offering of
18. 27 heave offering shall be reckoned unto you
18. 28 ye also shall offer an heave offering
18. 28 LORD'S heave offering to Aaron the priest
18. 29 offer every heave offering of the LORD
31. 29 give..(for) an heave offering of the LORD
31. 41 tribute, (which was) the LORD'S heave off.
Deut 12. 6 heave offerings of your hand, and your
12. 11 the heave offering of your hand, and all
12. 17 offerings, or heave offering of thine hand

HEAVE (shoulder) —
A heaved up offering, תְּרוּמָה *terumah*.
Lev. 7 34 the heave shoulder have I taken of the
10. 14 heave shoulder shall ye eat in a clean place
10. 15 The heave shoulder and the wave breast
Num. 6. 20 with the wave breast and heave shoulder

HEAVED up, to be —
To be made or lifted up high, רוּם *rum*, 6.
Exod 29. 27 which is heaved up, of the ram of the con.

HEAVEN —
1. *Rolling cloud*, גַּלְגַּל *galgal*.
Psa. 77. 18 voice of thy thunder (was) in the heaven

2. *Thin cloud*, שַׁחַק *shachaq*.
Psa. 89. 6 who in the heaven can be compared unto
89. 37 and (as) a faithful witness in heaven

3. *Heavens*, (*heaved up things*), שָׁמַיִם *shamayim*.
Gen. 1. 1 God created the heaven and the earth
1. 8 God called the firmament Heaven. And the
1. 9 the waters under the heaven be gathered
1. 14, 15 lights in the firmament of the heaven
1. 17 set them in the firmament of the heaven
1. 20 may fly..in the open firmament of heaven
6. 17 to destroy all flesh..from under heaven
7. 11 and the windows of heaven were opened
7. 19 hills that (were) under the whole heaven
7. 23 creeping things, and the fowl of the hea.
8. 2 and the windows of heaven were stopped
8. 2 and the rain from heaven was restrained
11. 4 a tower whose top (may reach) unto hea.
14. 19, 22 high God, possessor of heaven and ea.
15. 5 Look now toward heaven, and tell the st.
19. 24 and fire from the LORD out of heaven
21. 17 angel of God called to Hagar out of heaven
22. 11 angel..called unto him out of heaven
22. 15 angel..called unto Abraham out of heaven
22. 17 thy seed as the stars of the heaven, and as
24. 3 the God of heaven, and the God of the
24. 7 The LORD God of heaven, which took me f.
26. 4 seed to multiply as the stars of heaven
27. 28 God give thee of the dew of heaven, and
27. 39 and of the dew of heaven from above
28. 12 and the top of it reached to heaven: and
28. 17 of God, and this (is) the gate of heaven
49. 25 bless thee with blessings of heaven above
Exod. 9. 8 let Moses sprinkle it toward the heaven in
9. 10 and Moses sprinkled it up toward heaven
9. 22 Stretch forth thine hand toward heaven
9. 23 stretched forth his rod toward heaven
10. 21 Stretch out thine hand toward heaven
10. 22 stretched forth his hand toward heaven
16. 4 I will rain bread from heaven for you; and
17. 14 remembrance of Amalek from under hea.
20. 4 any likeness (of any thing) that (is) in hea.
20. 11 (in) six days the LORD made heaven and
20. 22 that I have talked with you from heaven
24. 10 and as it were the body of heaven in (his)
31. 17 for (in) six days the LORD made heaven and
32. 13 multiply your seed as the stars of heaven
Lev. 26. 19 I will make your heaven as iron, and your
Deut. 1. 10 ye (are) this day as the stars of heaven for
1. 28 cities (are) great and walled up to heaven
2. 25 nations (that are) under the whole heaven
3. 24 for what God (is there) in heaven or in earth
4. 11 burned with fire unto the midst of heaven
4. 19 lest thou lift up thine eyes unto heaven
4. 19 (even) all the host of heaven, shouldest be
4. 19 unto all nations under the whole heaven
4. 26 I call heaven and earth to witness against
4. 32 (ask) from the one side of heaven unto the
4. 36 Out of heaven he made thee to hear his
4. 39 God in heaven above, and upon the earth
5. 8 likeness (of any thing) that (is) in heaven
7. 24 destroy their name from under heaven
9. 1 cities great, and fenced up to heaven
9. 14 blot out their name from under heaven
10. 14 the heaven, and the heaven of heavens, (is)
10. 22 hath made thee as the stars of heaven for
11. 11 (and) drinketh water of the rain of heaven
11. 17 he shut up the heaven, that there be no rain
11. 21 as the days of heaven upon the earth
17. 3 or any of the host of heaven, which I have
25. 19 thou shalt blot out..from under heaven
26. 15 Look down..from heaven, and bless thy p.
28. 12 the heaven to give the rain unto thy land
28. 23 thy heaven that (is) over thy head shall be
28. 24 from heaven shall it come down upon thee
28. 62 whereas ye were as the stars of heaven
29. 20 shall blot out his name from under heaven
30. 4 be driven out unto the utmost..of heaven
30. 12 It (is) not in heaven, that thou shouldest say
30. 12 Who shall go up for us to heaven, and bring
30. 19 I call heaven and earth to record this day
31. 28 call heaven and earth to record against
32. 40 For I lift up my hand to heaven, and say
33. 13 for the precious things of heaven, for the d.
33. 26 (who) rideth upon the heaven in thy help
Josh. 2. 11 God in heaven above, and in earth beneath
8. 20 smoke of the city ascended up to heaven
10. 11 LORD cast down great stones from heaven
10. 13 the sun stood still in the midst of heaven
Judg. 5. 20 They fought from heaven; the stars in
13. 20 when the flame went up toward heaven
20. 40 flame of the city ascended up to heaven
1 Sa. 2. 10 out of heaven shall he thunder upon them
5. 12 and the cry of the city went up to heaven
2 Sa. 18. 9 he was taken up between the heaven and
21. 10 water dropped upon them out of heaven
22. 8 the foundations of heaven moved and shook
22. 14 The LORD thundered from heaven, and the
1 Ki. 8. 22 and spread forth his hands toward heaven
8. 23 (there is) no God like thee, in heaven above
8. 27 heaven, and heaven of heavens, cannot
1 Ki. 8. 30, 32, 34, 36, 39, 43, 45, 49 hear thou in heav.
8. 35 When heaven is shut up, and there is no ra.
8. 54 kneeling..with his hands spread up to hea.
18. 45 that the heaven was black with clouds and
22. 19 all the host of heaven standing by him
2 Ki. 1. 10, 12 let fire come down from heaven, and co.
1. 10 And there came down fire from heaven
1. 12 the fire of God came down from heaven
1. 14 Behold, there came fire down from heaven
2. 1 the LORD would take up Elijah into heaven
2. 11 Elijah went up by a whirlwind into heaven
7. 2 the LORD would make windows in heaven
7. 19 the LORD should make windows in heaven
14. 27 blot out the name..from under heaven: b.
17. 16 worshipped all the host of heaven, and ser.
19. 15 O LORD..thou hast made heaven and earth
21. 3 worshipped all the host of heaven, and ser.
21. 5 he built altars for all the host of heaven
23. 4 the grove, and for all the host of heaven
23. 5 the planets, and to all the host of heaven
1 Ch. 21. 16 stand between the earth and the heaven
21. 26 he answered him from heaven by fire upon
29. 11 for all (that is) in the heaven and in the e.
2 Ch. 2. 6 the heaven and heaven of heavens cannot
2. 12 Blessed (be) the LORD..that made heaven
6. 13 and spread forth his hands toward heaven
6. 14 (there is) no God like thee in the heaven
6. 18 heaven and the heaven of heavens cannot
6. 21 hear thou..from heaven; and when thou
6. 23, 27, 30 Then hear thou from heaven, and
6. 25, 33, 35, 39 Then hear thou from the heaven
6. 26 When the heaven is shut up, and there is
7. 1 fire came down from heaven, and consu.
7. 13 If I shut up heaven that there be no rain
7. 14 then will I hear from heaven, and will for.
18. 18 all the host of heaven standing on his
20. 6 O LORD God..(art) not thou God in heaven?
28. 9 in a rage (that) reacheth up unto heaven
30. 27 their prayer came (up..even) unto heaven
32. 20 son of Amoz, prayed and cried to heaven
33. 3 worshipped all the host of heaven, and
33. 5 he built altars for all the host of heaven
36. 23 hath the LORD God of heaven given me
Ezra 1. 2 The LORD God of heaven hath given me
Neh. 1. 4 and prayed before the God of heaven
1. 5 O LORD God of heaven, the great and terri.
1. 9 unto the uttermost part of the heaven
2. 4 So I prayed to the God of heaven
2. 20 The God of heaven, he will prosper us
9. 6 hast made heaven, the heaven of heavens
9. 6 and the host of heaven worshippeth thee
9. 13 and spakest with them from heaven, and
9. 15 gavest them bread from heaven for their
9. 23 Their children also..as the stars of hea.
9. 27 thou heardest (them) from heaven; and
9. 28 thou heardest (them) from heaven; and
Job 1. 16 The fire of God is fallen from heaven, and
2. 12 sprinkled dust upon their heads toward h
11. 8 (It is) as high as heaven; what canst thou
16. 19 Also now, behold, my witness (is) in heav
20. 27 The heaven shall reveal his iniquity
22. 12 (Is) not God in the height of heaven? and
22 14 and he walketh in the circuit of heaven
26. 11 pillars of heaven tremble and are astonish
28. 24 (and) seeth under the whole heaven
35. 11 maketh us wiser than the fowls of heaven?
37. 3 He directeth it under the whole heaven
38. 29 and the hoary frost of heaven, who hath
38. 33 Knowest thou the ordinances of heaven?
38. 37 or who can stay the bottles of heaven
41. 11 (whatsoever is) under the whole heaven is
Psa. 11. 4 the LORD'S throne (is) in heaven: his eyes
14. 2 The LORD looked down from heaven upon
19. 6 going forth (is) from the end of the heaven
20. 6 he will hear him from his holy heaven
33. 13 The LORD looketh from heaven; he beh.
53. 2 God looked down from heaven upon the
57. 3 He shall send from heaven, and save me
69. 34 Let the heaven and earth praise him, the
73. 25 Whom have I in heaven (but thee)? and
76. 8 cause judgment to be heard from heaven
78. 23 above, and opened the doors of heaven
78. 24 and had given them of the corn of heav.
78. 26 caused an east wind to blow in the heaven
79. 2 given (to be) meat unto the fowls of the h.
80. 14 look down from heaven, and behold, and
85. 11 righteousness shall look down from heaven
89. 29 and his throne as the days of heaven
102. 19 from heaven did the LORD behold the earth
103. 11 For as the heaven is high above the earth
104. 12 By them shall the fowls of the heaven h.
105. 40 satisfied them with the bread of heaven
107. 26 They mount up to the heaven, they go d.
113. 6 to behold (the things that are) in heaven
115. 15 of the LORD which made heaven and earth
115. 16 The heaven, (even) the heavens, (are) the
119. 89 O LORD, thy word is settled in heaven
121. 2 the LORD, which made heaven and earth
124. 8 of the LORD, who made heaven and earth
134. 3 LORD that made heaven and earth bless
135. 6 (that) did he in heaven, and in earth, in
136. 26 O give thanks unto the God of heaven: for
139. 8 If I ascend up into heaven, thou (art) there
146. 6 Which made heaven and earth, the sea
147. 8 Who covereth the heaven with clouds, who
148. 13 his glory (is) above the earth and heaven
Prov. 23. 5 they fly away as an eagle toward heaven
25. 3 The heaven for height, and the earth for
30. 4 Who hath ascended up into heaven, or
Eccl. 1. 13 all (things) that are done under heaven
2. 3 which they should do under the heaven all
3. 1 a time to every purpose under the heaven

Eccl. 5. 2 for God (is) in heaven, and thou upon ea.
Isa. 13. 5 They come from..the end of heaven
13. 10 the stars of heaven and the constellations
14. 12 How art thou fallen from heaven, O Luc.
14. 13 I will ascend into heaven, I will exalt my
34. 4 all the host of heaven shall be dissolved
34. 5 For my sword shall be bathed in heaven
37. 16 O LORD..thou hast made heaven and ea.
40. 12 and meted out heaven with the span, and
55. 10 and the snow from heaven, and returneth
63. 15 Look down from heaven, and behold from
66. 1 The heaven (is) my throne, and the earth
Jer. 7. 18 to make cakes to the queen of heaven
7. 33 shall be meat for the fowls of the heaven
8. 2 the host of heaven, whom they have loved
8. 7 Yea, the stork in the heaven knoweth her
10. 2 be not dismayed at the signs of heaven
15. 3 the fowls of the heaven, and the beasts of
16. 4 shall be meat for the fowls of heaven
19. 7 give to be meat for the fowls of the heaven
19. 13 burned incense unto all the host of hea.
23. 24 do not I fill heaven and earth? saith the
31. 37 If heaven above can be measured, and the
32. 17 thou hast made the heaven and the earth
33. 22 As the host of heaven cannot be number
33. 25 appointed the ordinances of heaven and
34. 20 be for meat unto the fowls of the heaven
44. 17 to burn incense unto the queen of heaven
44. 18, 25 to burn incense to the queen of heaven
44. 19 we burnt incense to the queen of heaven
49. 36 winds from the four quarters of heaven
51. 9 for her judgment reacheth unto heaven
51. 15 hath stretched out the heaven by his und.
51. 48 Then the heaven and the earth, and all
51. 53 Babylon should mount up to heaven, and
Lam. 2. 1 cast down from heaven unto the earth the
3. 50 LORD look down, and behold from heaven
4. 19 are swifter than the eagles of the heaven
Eze. 8. 3 spirit lifted me up between the..heaven
29. 5 given thee for meat..to the fowls of the h.
31. 6 All the fowls of heaven made their nests
31. 13 shall all the fowls of the heaven remain
32. 4 will cause all the fowls of the heaven to
32. 7 I will cover the heaven, and make the
32. 8 All the bright lights of heaven will I make
38. 20 the fowls of the heaven, and the beasts of
Dan. 8. 8 came up..toward the four winds of heaven
8. 10 waxed great, (even) to the host of heaven
9. 12 for under the whole heaven hath not been
11. 4 divided toward the four winds of heaven
12. 7 he held up his right hand..unto heaven
Hos. 2. 18 with the fowls of heaven, and (with) the
4. 3 with the fowls of heaven; yea, the fishes
7. 12 bring them down as the fowls of the heaven
Amos 9. 2 though they climb up to heaven, thence
9. 6 he that buildeth his stories in the heaven
Jon. 1. 9 the God of heaven, which hath made the
Nah. 3. 16 multiplied..above the stars of heaven: the
Zeph. 1. 3 I will consume the fowls of the heaven
1. 5 that worship the host of heaven upon the
Hag. 1. 10 Therefore the heaven over you is stayed f.
Zech. 2. 6 spread..as the four winds of the heaven
5. 9 the ephah between the earth and the heav.
Mal. 3. 10 will not open you the windows of heaven

4. *Heavens, (heaved up things)*, שְׁמַיִן *shemayin.*

Ezra 5. 11 We are the servants of the God of heaven
5. 12 fathers had provoked the God of heaven
6. 9 the burnt offerings of the God of heaven
6. 10 offer..sweet savours unto the God of hea.
7. 12, 21 scribe of the law of the God of heaven
7. 23 commanded by the God of heaven, let it
7. 23 done for the house of the God of heaven
Dan. 2. 18 would desire mercies of the God of heaven
2. 19 Then Daniel blessed the God of heaven
2. 28 But there is a God in heaven that reveal.
2. 37 for the God of heaven hath given thee a
2. 38 and the fowls of the heaven hath he given
2. 44 shall the God of heaven set up a kingdom
4. 11 and the height thereof reached unto heav.
4. 12 fowls of the heaven dwelt in the boughs
4. 13, 23 watcher and an holy one..from heaven
4. 15, 23 let it be wet with the dew of heaven
4. 20 whose height reached unto the heaven
4. 21 whose branches the fowls of the heaven
4. 22 reacheth unto heaven, and thy dominion
4. 25 they shall wet thee with the dew of heaven
4. 31 there fell a voice from heaven, (saying), O
4. 33 his body was wet with the dew of heaven
4. 34 lifted up mine eyes unto heaven, and mine
4. 35 doeth..his will in the army of heaven
4. 37 extol and honour the King of heaven, all
5. 21 his body was wet with the dew of heaven
5. 23 lifted up..against the Lord of heaven
6. 27 worketh signs and wonders in heaven and
7. 2 the four winds of the heaven strove upon
7. 13 Son of man came with the clouds of heaven
7. 27 of the kingdom under the whole heaven

5. *Heaven, sky, air*, οὐρανός *ouranos.*

Matt. 3. 2 for the kingdom of heaven is at hand
3. 17 lo a voice from heaven, saying, This is my
4. 17 for the kingdom of heaven is at hand
5. 3, 10 for theirs is the kingdom of heaven
5. 12 great (is) your reward in heaven: for so
5. 16 glorify your Father which is in heaven
5. 18 Till heaven and earth pass, one jot or
5. 19 called the least in the kingdom of heaven
5. 19 be called great in the kingdom of heaven
5. 20 ye shall in no case enter into..heaven
5. 34 neither by heaven; for it is God's throne
5. 45 children of your Father which is in heaven
Matt. 5. 48 even as your Father [which is in heaven]
6. 1 have no reward of your Father..in heaven
6. 9 Our Father which art in heaven, Hallowed
6. 10 Thy will be done in earth, as (it is) in heav.
6. 20 lay up for yourselves treasures in heaven
7. 11 shall your Father which is in heaven give
7. 21 shall enter into the kingdom of heaven
7. 21 the will of my Father which is in heaven
8. 11 shall sit down..in the kingdom of heaven
10. 7 saying, The kingdom of heaven is at hand
10. 32, 33 before my Father which is in heaven
11. 11 he that is least in the kingdom of heaven
11. 12 the kingdom of heaven suffereth violence
11. 23 which art exalted unto heaven, shalt be
11. 25 O Father, Lord of heaven and earth, beca.
12. 50 the will of my Father which is in heaven
13. 11 the mysteries of the kingdom [of heaven]
13. 24 The kingdom of heaven is likened unto a
13. 31 The kingdom of heaven is like to a grain
13. 33, 44, 45, 47, 52 The kingdom of heaven is like
14. 19 looking up to heaven, he blessed, and br.
16. 1 he would show them a sign from heaven
16. 17 but my Father which is in heaven
16. 19 give..the keys of the kingdom of heaven
16. 19 bind on earth shall be bound in heaven
16. 19 loose on earth shall be loosed in heaven
18. 1 Who is..greatest in the kingdom of heav.
18. 3 not enter into the kingdom of heaven
18. 4 same is greatest in the kingdom of heaven
18. 10 in heaven their angels do always behold
18. 10 the face of my Father which is in heaven
18. 14 will of your Father which is in heaven
18. 18 bind on earth, shall be bound in heaven
18. 18 loose on earth shall be loosed in heaven
18. 19 be done..of my Father which is in heaven
18. 23 kingdom of heaven likened unto a certain
19. 12 eunuchs for the kingdom of heaven's sake
19. 14 for of such is the kingdom of heaven
19. 21 thou shalt have treasure in heaven; and
19. 23 hardly enter into the kingdom of heaven
20. 1 the kingdom of heaven is like unto a man
21. 25 baptism of John, whence was it? from h.
21. 25 If we shall say, From heaven; he will say
22. 2 The kingdom of heaven is like unto a
22. 30 but are as the angels of God in heaven
23. 9 one is your Father, [which is in heaven]
23. 13 shut up the kingdom of heaven against men
23. 22 he that shall swear by heaven, sweareth
24. 29 the stars shall fall from heaven, and the
24. 30 the sign of the Son of man in heaven
24. 30 Son of man coming in the clouds of heaven
24. 31 from one end of heaven to the other
24. 35 Heaven and earth shall pass away, but my
24. 36 not the angels of heaven, but my Father
25. 1 the kingdom of heaven be likened unto ten
26. 64 power, and coming in the clouds of heaven
28. 2 angel of the Lord descended from heaven
28. 18 power is given unto me in heaven and in
Mark 1. 11 there came a voice from heaven, (saying)
6. 41 he looked up to heaven, and blessed, and
7. 34 looking up to heaven, he sighed, and saith
8. 11 seeking of him a sign from heaven, temp.
10. 21 thou shalt have treasure in heaven: and
11. 25 your Father also which is in heaven may
11. 26 [neither..your Father which is in heaven]
11. 30 The baptism of John, was (it) from heaven
11. 31 If we shall say, From heaven; he will say
12. 25 are as the angels which are in heaven
13. 25 the stars of heaven shall fall, and the
13. 25 powers that are in heaven shall be shaken
13. 27 the earth to the uttermost part of heaven
13. 31 Heaven and earth shall pass away; but my
13. 32 no not the angels which are in heaven
14. 62 power, and coming in the clouds of heaven
16. 19 [he was received up into heaven, and sat]
Luke 2. 15 were gone away from them into heaven
3. 21 it came to pass..the heaven was opened
3. 22 a voice came from heaven, which said, Thou
4. 25 heaven was shut up three years and six
6. 23 your reward (is) great in heaven: for in the
9. 16 looking up to heaven, he blessed them, and
9. 54 we command fire to come down from he.
10. 15 Capernaum, which art exalted to heaven
10. 18 beheld Satan as lightning fall from heaven
10. 20 because your names are written in heaven
10. 21 O Father, Lord of heaven and earth, that
11. 2 [Our Father which art in heaven, Hallow,]
11. 2 [will be done, as in heaven, so in earth]
11. 16 others..sought of him a sign from heaven
15. 7 joy shall be in heaven over one sinner
15. 18, 21 Father, I have sinned against heaven
16. 17 is easier for heaven and earth to pass
17. 24 lighteneth out..one (part) under heaven
17. 24 shineth unto the other (part) under heaven
17. 29 it rained fire and brimstone from heaven
18. 13 lift up so much as (his) eyes unto heaven
18. 22 thou shalt have treasure in heaven: and
19. 38 peace in heaven, and glory in the highest
20. 4 The baptism of John, was it from heaven
20. 5 If we shall say, From heaven; he will say
21. 11 great signs shall there be from heaven
21. 26 for the powers of heaven shall be shaken
21. 33 Heaven and earth shall pass away; but my
22. 43 [appeared an angel unto him from heaven]
24. 51 [parted from them, and carried..into hea.]
John 1. 32 Spirit descending from heaven like a dove
1. 51 ye shall see heaven open, and the angels
3. 13 heaven, but he that came down from he.
3. 13 (even) the Son of man [which is in heaven]
3. 27 except it be given him from heaven
3. 31 he that cometh from heaven is above all
6. 31 He gave them bread from heaven to eat
John 6. 32 Moses gave you not that bread from hea.
6. 32 giveth you the true bread from heaven
6. 33 is he which cometh down from heaven, and
6. 38 I came down from heaven, not to do mine
6. 41 the bread which came down from heaven
6. 42 that he saith, I came down from heaven?
6. 50 the bread which cometh down from hea.
6. 51 living bread which came down from hea.
6. 58 that bread which came down from heaven
12. 28 Then came there a voice from heaven, (say.)
17. 1 lifted up his eyes to heaven, and said
Acts 1. 10 stedfastly toward heaven as he went up
1. 11 why stand ye gazing up into heaven? this
1. 11 which is taken up from you into heaven
1. 11 come..as ye have seen him go into heaven
2. 2 there came a sound from heaven as of a
2. 5 men, out of every nation under heaven
2. 19 I will show wonders in heaven above, and
3. 21 the heaven must receive until the times
4. 12 there is none other name under heaven
4. 24 God, which hast made heaven, and earth
7. 42 gave them up to worship..host of heaven
7. 49 Heaven (is) my throne, and earth (is) my
7. 55 looked up stedfastly into heaven, and saw
9. 3 shined round about..a light from heaven
10. 11 saw heaven opened, and a certain vessel
10. 16 vessel was received up again into heaven
11. 5 let down from heaven by four corners
11. 9 the voice answered me again from heaven
11. 10 and all were drawn up again into heaven
14. 15 which made heaven, and earth, and the sea
17. 24 seeing..he is Lord of heaven and earth
22. 6 there shone from heaven a great light
Rom. 1. 18 the wrath of God is revealed from heaven
10. 6 Who shall ascend into heaven? that is, to
1 Co. 8. 5 whether in heaven or in earth, as there be
15. 47 the second man (is) the Lord from heaven
2 Co. 5. 2 with our house which is from heaven
12. 2 such an one caught up to the third heaven
Gal. 1. 8 or an angel from heaven, preach any other
Eph. 1. 10 which are in heaven, and which are on
3. 15 Of whom the whole family in heaven and
6. 9 knowing that your Master..is in heaven
Phil. 3. 20 our conversation is in heaven; from when.
Col. 1. 5 hope which is laid up for you in heaven
1. 16 all things created that are in heaven
1. 20 be) things in earth, or things in heaven
1. 23 to every creature which is under heaven
4. 1 that ye also have a Master in heaven
1 Th. 1. 10 to wait for his Son from heaven, whom he
4. 16 shall descend from heaven with a shout
2 Th. 1. 7 Lord Jesus shall be revealed from heaven
Heb. 9. 24 into heaven itself, now to appear in the
10. 34 have [in heaven] a better and an enduring
12. 23 first born, which are written in heaven
12. 25 away from him that (speaketh) from heav.
12. 26 shake not the earth only, but also heaven
Jas. 5. 12 neither by heaven, neither by the earth
5. 18 and the heaven gave rain, and the earth
1 Pe. 1. 4 an inheritance..reserved in heaven for you
1. 12 with the Holy Ghost sent down from heav.
3. 22 Who is gone into heaven, and is on the
2 Pe. 1. 18 voice which came from heaven we heard
1 Jo. 5. 7 are three that bear record in [heaven]
Rev. 3. 12 cometh down out of heaven from my God
4. 1 a door (was) opened in heaven: and the first
4. 2 a throne was set in heaven, and (one) sat
5. 3 no man in heaven, nor in earth, neither
5. 13 every creature which is in heaven, and on
6. 13 the stars of heaven fell unto the earth
6. 14 the heaven departed as a scroll when it
8. 1 there was silence in heaven about the
8. 10 and there fell a great star from heaven
9. 1 a star fall from heaven unto the earth
10. 1 another mighty angel come..from heaven
10. 4 heard a voice from heaven saying unto me
10. 5 the angel..lifted up his hand to heaven
10. 6 who created heaven, and the things that
10. 8 the voice which I heard from heaven spake
11. 6 These have power to shut heaven, that it
11. 12 great voice from heaven saying unto them
11. 12 they ascended up to heaven in a cloud
11. 13 and gave glory to the God of heaven
11. 15 there were great voices in heaven, saying
11. 19 the temple of God was opened in heaven
12. 1 appeared a great wonder in heaven
12. 3 there appeared another wonder in heaven
12. 4 the third part of the stars of heaven, and
12. 7 there was war in heaven: Michael and his
12. 8 neither was their place found..in heaven
12. 10 I heard a loud voice saying in heaven
13. 6 tabernacle, and them that dwell in heaven
13. 13 he maketh fire come down from heaven on
14. 2 I heard a voice from heaven, as the voice
14. 7 worship him that made heaven, and earth
14. 13 heard a voice from heaven saying unto me
14. 17 came out of the temple which is in heaven
15. 1 I saw another sign in heaven, great and
15. 5 the tabernacle of the testimony in heaven
16. 11 blasphemed the God of heaven because of
16. 17 great voice out of the temple [of heaven]
16. 21 fell upon men a great hail out of heaven
18. 1 saw another angel come down from heaven
18. 4 I heard another voice from heaven, saying
18. 5 her sins have reached unto heaven, and God
18. 20 Rejoice over her, (thou) heaven, and (ye)
19. 1 a great voice of much people in heaven
19. 11 I saw heaven opened, and behold a white
19. 14 the armies (which were) in heaven followed
20. 1 I saw an angel come down from heaven
20. 9 fire came down from God out of heaven
20. 11 the earth and the heaven fled away; and

Rev. 21. 1 I saw a new heaven and a new earth: for
21. 1 the first heaven and the first earth were
21. 2 coming down from God out of heaven, pre.
21. 3 I heard a great voice out of [heaven] saying
21. 10 city..descending out of heaven from God

HEAVEN, from —
From heaven, οὐρανόθεν *ouranothen.*
Acts 14. 17 gave us rain from heaven, and fruitful
26. 13 I saw in the way a light from heaven, above

HEAVEN, in —
Heavenly, in or on heaven, ἐπουράνιος *epouranios.*
Phil. 2. 10 of (things) in heaven, and (things) in ea.

HEAVEN, midst of —
Mid heaven, μεσουράνημα *mesouranēma.*
Rev. 8. 13 angel flying through the midst of heaven
14. 6 saw another angel fly in the midst of he.
19. 17 all the fowls that fly in the midst of hea.

HEAVENLY —
1. *Out of heaven,* ἐξ οὐρανοῦ *ex ouranou.*
Luke 11. 13 how much more shall (your) heavenly F.
2. *Heavenly, in or on heaven,* ἐπουράνιος *epouranios.*
Matt. 18. 35 So likewise shall my [heavenly] Father do
1 Co. 15. 48 heavenly, such (are) they also that (are) h.
15. 49 shall also bear the image of the heavenly
Eph. 1. 20 set..at his own right hand in the heavenly
2 Ti. 4. 18 will preserve (me) unto his heavenly kin.
Heb. 3. 1 partakers of the heavenly calling, consi.
6. 4 have tasted of the heavenly gift, and were
11. 16 now they desire a better..that is, an hea.
12. 22 are come unto..the heavenly Jerusalem
3. *Heavenly,* οὐράνιος *ouranios.*
Matt. 6. 14 your heavenly Father will also forgive you
6. 26 the fowls..yet your heavenly Father feed
6. 32 your heavenly Father knoweth that ye ha.
15. 13 Every plant, which my heavenly Father h.
Luke 2. 13 a multitude of the heavenly host praising
Acts 26. 19 was not disobedient unto the heavenly vi.

HEAVENLY (places) —
The heavenlies, τὰ ἐπουράνια *ta epourania.*
Eph. 1. 3 spiritual blessings in heavenly (places) in
2. 6 sit together in heavenly (places) in Christ
3. 10 and powers in heavenly (places) might be

HEAVENLY things —
The things in heaven, τὰ ἐπουράνια *ta epourania.*
John 3. 12 believe, if I tell you (of) heavenly things?
Heb. 8. 5 the example and shadow of heavenly thi.
9. 23 but the heavenly things themselves with

HEAVENS —
1. *Mixed cloud,* עֲרָבָה *arabah.*
Psa 68. 4 extol him that rideth upon the heavens by
2. *Dropping clouds,* עֲרִיפִים *ariphim.*
Isa. 5. 30 the light is darkened in the heavens the.
3. *Heavens, the heaved up things,* שָׁמַיִם *shamayim.*
Gen. 2. 1 Thus the heavens and the earth were fin.
2. 4 the generations of the heavens and of the
2. 4 LORD God made the earth and the heavens
Deut 10. 14 the heaven of heavens, (is) the LORD'S thy
32. 1 Give ear, O ye heavens, and I will speak
33. 28 Israel..his heavens shall drop down dew
Judg. 5. 4 the heavens dropped, the clouds also dr.
2 Sa. 22. 10 He bowed the heavens also, and came down
1 Ki. 8. 27 and heaven of heavens, cannot contain thee
1 Ch. 16. 26 (are) idols: but the LORD made the heavens
16. 31 Let the heavens be glad, and let the earth
27. 23 increase Israel like to the stars of the he.
2 Ch. 2. 6 seeing the..heaven of heavens cannot con.
6. 18 the heaven of heavens cannot contain thee
6. 25, 33, 35, 39 Then hear thou from the heav.
Ezra 9. 6 our trespass is grown up unto the heavens
Neh. 9. 6 the heaven of heavens, with all their host
Job 9. 8 Which alone spreadeth out the heavens
14. 12 till the heavens (be) no more, they shall
15. 15 yea, the heavens are not clean in his sight
20. 6 Though his excellency mount up to the h.
26. 13 By his spirit he hath garnished the heav.
35. 5 Look unto the heavens, and see; and be.
Psa. 2. 4 He that sitteth in the heavens shall laugh
8. 1 who hast set thy glory above the heavens
8. 3 When I consider thy heavens, the work of
18. 9 He bowed the heavens also, and came do.
18. 13 The LORD also thundered in the heavens
19. 1 The heavens declare the glory of God; and
33. 6 By the word of the LORD were the heavens
36. 5 Thy mercy, O LORD, (is) in the heavens
50. 4 He shall call to the heavens from above
50. 6 the heavens shall declare his righteousness
57. 5 Be thou exalted, O God, above the heav.
57. 10 For thy mercy (is) great unto the heavens
57. 11 Be thou exalted, O God, above the heavens
68. 8 the heavens also dropped at the presence
68. 33 To him that rideth upon the heavens of h.
73. 9 They set their mouth against the heavens
89. 2 shalt thou establish in the very heavens
89. 5 And the heavens shall praise thy wonders
89. 11 The heavens (are) thine, the earth also (is)
96. 5 (are) idols: but the LORD made the heav.
96. 11 Let the heavens rejoice, and let the earth
97. 6 The heavens declare his righteousness, and
102. 25 and the heavens (are) the work of thy ha.
103. 19 LORD hath prepared his throne in the h.
104. 2 who stretchest out the heavens like a cu.
108. 4 For thy mercy (is) great above the heavens
108. 5 Be thou exalted, O God, above the heav.
113. 4 LORD (is) high..his glory above the heav.
Psa. 115. 3 But our God (is) in the heavens: he hath
115. 16 the heavens, (are) the LORD'S: but the ea.
123. 1 Unto thee..O thou that dwellest in the h.
136. 5 To him that by wisdom made the heavens
144. 5 Bow thy heavens, O LORD, and come down
148. 1 Praise ye the LORD from the heavens: pr.
148. 4 Praise him, ye heavens of heavens, and ye
148. 4 and ye waters that (be) above the heavens
Prov. 3. 19 by understanding..established the heaven
8. 27 When he prepared the heavens, I (was)
Isa. 1. 2 Hear, O heavens, and give ear, O earth
13. 13 Therefore I will shake the heavens, and
34. 4 the heavens shall be rolled together as a
40. 22 that stretcheth out the heavens as a curt.
42. 5 he that created the heavens, and stretch.
44. 23 Sing, O ye heavens; for the LORD hath
44. 24 that stretcheth forth the heavens alone
45. 8 Drop down, ye heavens, from above, and
45. 12 I..have..stretched out the heavens, and
45. 18 thus saith the LORD that created the he.
48. 13 and my right hand hath spanned the he.
49. 13 Sing, O heavens; and be joyful, O earth
50. 3 I clothe the heavens with blackness, and
51. 6 Lift up your eyes to the heavens, and look
51. 6 for the heavens shall vanish away like sm.
51. 13 the LORD..hath stretched forth the heav.
51. 16 that I may plant the heavens, and lay the
55. 9 For (as) the heavens are higher than the
64. 1 Oh that thou wouldest rend the heavens
65. 17 For, behold, I create new heavens, and a
66. 22 For as the new heavens, and the new earth
Jer. 2. 12 Be astonished, O ye heavens, at this, and
4. 23 I beheld..the heavens, and they (had) no
4. 25 and all the birds of the heavens were fled
4. 28 For this shall..the heavens above be black
9. 10 both the fowl of the heavens and the bea.
10. 12 stretched out the heaven by his discretion
10. 13 a multitude of waters in the heavens, and
14. 22 or can the heavens give showers? Art not
51. 16 a multitude of waters in the heavens; and
Lam. 3. 41 lift up our heart..unto God in the heav.
3. 66 destroy them..from under the heavens of
Eze. 1. 1 the heavens were opened, and I saw visions
Hos. 2. 21 I will hear the heavens, and they shall
Joel 2. 10 the heavens shall tremble: the sun and
2. 30 I will show wonders in the heavens and
3. 16 and the heavens and the earth shall shake
Hab. 3. 3 His glory covered the heavens, and the
Hag. 2. 6 I will shake the heavens, and the earth
2. 21 saying, I will shake the heavens and the
Zech. 6. 5 These (are) the four spirits of the heavens
8. 12 the heavens shall give their dew; and I
12. 1 which stretcheth forth the heavens, and
4. *Heavens, (heaved up things),* שְׁמַיִן *shemayin.*
Jer. 10. 11 The gods that have not made the heaven
10. 11 they shall perish..from under these heav.
Dan. 4. 26 shalt have known that the heavens do rule
5. *Heavens, skies,* οὐρανοί *ouranoi.*
Matt. 3. 16 and, lo, the heavens were opened unto him
24. 29 and the powers of the heavens shall be
Mark 1. 10 he saw the heavens opened, and the spir.
Luke 12. 33 a treasure in the heavens that faileth not
Acts 2. 34 For David is not ascended into the heav.
7. 56 Behold, I see the heavens opened, and the
2 Co. 5. 1 not made with hands, eternal in the hea.
Eph. 4. 10 far above all heavens, that he might fill all
Heb. 1. 10 the heavens are the works of thine hands
4. 14 that is passed into the heavens, Jesus the
7. 26 High Priest..made higher than the heav.
8. 1 set on..the throne of the majesty in the h.
9. 23 the patterns of things in the heavens shou.
2 Pe. 3. 5 that by the word of God the heavens were
3. 7 the heavens and the earth which are now
3. 10 in the which the heavens shall pass away
3. 12 wherein the heavens being on fire shall be
3. 13 we..look for new heavens and a new earth
Rev. 12. 12 Therefore rejoice, (ye) heavens, and ye

HEAVIER —
Weighty, heavy, כָּבֵד *kabed.*
Prov 27. 3 but a fool's wrath (is) heavier than them

HEAVIER, to be —
To be heavy, weighty, כָּבֵד *kabad.*
Job 6. 3 it would be heavier than the sand of the
23. 2 to day..my stroke is heavier than my gr.

HEAVILY —
1. *Heaviness, weight,* כְּבֵדֻת *kebeduth.*
Exod 14. 25 they drave them heavily: so that the Eg.
2. *To be black, mourning,* קָדַר *qadar.*
Psa. 35. 14 I bowed down heavily, as one that mour.

HEAVILY, to lay —
To make heavy or weighty, כָּבֵד *kabed,* 5.
Isa. 47. 6 upon the ancient hast thou..heavily laid

HEAVINESS —
1. *Sorrow, fear,* דְּאָגָה *deagah.*
Prov. 12. 25 Heaviness in the heart of man maketh it
2. *Weakness,* כֵּהָה *kehah.*
Isa. 61. 3 garment of praise for the spirit of heavi.
3. *Face, aspect,* פָּנִים *panim.*
Job 9. 27 I will leave off my heaviness, and comfort
4. *Lamentation, mourning,* תַּאֲנִיָּה *taaniyyah.*
Isa. 29. 2 and there shall be heaviness and sorrow
5. *Affliction, sorrow,* תּוּגָה *tugah.*
Psa. 119. 28 My soul melteth for heaviness: strengthen
Prov 10. 1 a foolish son (is) the heaviness of his
14. 13 and the end of that mirth (is) heaviness
6. *Affliction, humiliation,* תַּעֲנִית *taanith.*
Ezra 9. 5 I arose up from my heaviness; and, having
7. *Dejection of the eye,* κατήφεια *katēpheia.*
Jas. 4. 9 be turned to mourning, and..joy to heav.
8. *Grief,* λύπη *lupē.*
Rom. 9. 2 I have great heaviness and continual
2 Co. 2. 1 that I would not come again to you in he.

HEAVINESS, to be full of —
1. *To be feeble, mortal,* נוּשׁ *nush.*
Psa. 69. 20 and I am full of heaviness: and I looked
2. *To be very heavy, faint,* ἀδημονέω *adēmoneō.*
Phil. 2. 26 For he longed..and was full of heaviness

HEAVINESS, to be in —
To be grieved, λυπέομαι, *lupeomai.*
1 Pe. 1. 6 ye are in heaviness through manifold

HEAVY —
1. *Heavy, weighty,* כָּבֵד *kabed.*
Exod 17. 12 But Moses' hands (were) heavy; and they
18. 18 for this thing (is) too heavy for thee; thou
1 Ki. 12. 4 and his heavy yoke which he put upon us
12. 11 my father did lade you with a heavy yoke
2 Ch. 10. 4 and his heavy yoke that he put upon us
10. 11 my father put a heavy yoke upon you, I
Psa. 38. 4 mine iniquities..as an heavy burden they
2. *Heaviness,* כֹּבֶד *kobed.*
Prov 27. 3 A stone (is) heavy, and the sand weighty
Isa. 30. 27 and the burden (thereof is) heavy: his lips
3. *A bar, yoke,* מוֹטָה *motah.*
Isa. 58. 6 to undo the heavy burdens, and to let the
4. *Bitter,* מַר *mar.*
Prov 31. 6 wine unto those that be of heavy hearts
5. *Sulky, sour,* סַר *sar.*
1 Ki. 20. 43 went to his house heavy and displeased
21. 4 Ahab came into his house heavy and dis.
6. *Sharp, hard,* קָשֶׁה *qasheh.*
1 Ki. 14. 6 for I (am) sent to thee (with) heavy (tid.)
7. *Evil,* רַע *ra.*
Prov 25. 20 he that singeth songs to an heavy heart
8. *Heavy, weighty,* βαρύς *barus.*
Matt 23. 4 For they bind heavy burdens and grievous

HEAVY, to be —
1. *To be heavy, weighty,* כָּבֵד *kabed.*
1 Sa. 4. 18 for he was an old man, and heavy. And he
5. 6 the hand of the LORD was heavy upon them
5. 11 the hand of God was very heavy there
2 Sa. 14. 26 because (the hair) was heavy on him, th.
Neh. 5. 18 because the bondage was heavy upon this
Job 33. 7 neither shall my hand be heavy upon thee
Psa. 32. 4 day and night thy hand was heavy upon
38. 4 For mine iniquities..they are too heavy
Isa. 24. 20 the transgression thereof shall be heavy
59. 1 neither his ear heavy, that it cannot hear
2. *To be heavy, weighed down,* βαρέομαι *bareomai.*
Matt 26. 43 asleep again: for their eyes were heavy
Mark 14. 40 for their eyes were [heavy], neither wist
Luke 9. 32 Peter and they..were heavy with sleep

HEAVY, to be very —
To be very heavy, faint, ἀδημονέω *adēmoneō.*
Matt 26. 37 and began to be sorrowful and very heavy
Mark 14. 33 began to be sore amazed, and to be very h.

HEAVY, to make —
To make heavy, כָּבֵד *kabed,* 5.
1 Ki. 12. 10 Thy father made our yoke heavy, but
12. 14 My father made your yoke heavy, and I
2 Ch. 10. 10 Thy father made our yoke heavy, but make
10. 14 My father made your yoke heavy, but I
Isa. 6. 10 make their ears heavy, and shut their eyes
Lam. 3. 7 cannot get out: he hath made my chain h.

HEAVY, (to be) too —
Heavy, weighty, כָּבֵד *kabed.*
Num 11. 14 I am not able..because (it is) too heavy

HE'-BER, עֵבֶר *shoot, production, shoot.*
1. Head of a family in the tribe of Gad.
1 Ch. 5. 13 Jorai, and Jachan, and Zia, and H., seven
2. A son of Shashak of the tribe of Benjamin.
1 Ch. 8. 22 And Ishpan, and H., and Eliel

HE'-BER, חֶבֶר (Nu. 26. 25 חֵבֶר), חֶבֶר, Ἐβέρ *companion.*
1. A son of Beriah the son of Asher. B.C. 1640.
Gen. 46. 17 and the sons of Beriah; H., and Malchiel
Num 26. 45 Of the sons of Beriah; of H., the family
1 Ch. 7. 31 And the sons of Beriah; H., and Malchiel
7. 32 And H. begat Japhlet, and Shomer, and
Luke 3. 35 Phalec, which was (the son) of H., which
2. The husband of Jael who killed Sisera. He was a Kenite, while Sisera was captain of Jabin's army. B.C. 1360.
Judg. 4. 11 H. the Kenite..of the children of Hobab
4. 17 fled..to the tent of Jael the wife of H.
4. 17 peace between Jabin..and the house of H.
4. 21 Then Jael H.'s wife took a nail of the tent
5. 24 Blessed..shall Jael the wife of H. the K.
3. A son of Ezra, apparently of the family of Caleb son of Jephunneh. B.C. 1400.
1 Ch. 4. 18 And his wife..bare..H. the father of Soc.
4. A son of Elpaal, a Benjamite. B.C. 1400.
1 Ch. 8. 17 and Meshullam, and Hezeki, and H.

HE-BE-RITES, חֶבְרִי *belonging to Heber.*
A family descended from Heber, a descendant of Beriah son of Asher. B.C. 1640.
Num26. 45 of Heber, the family of the H.: of Malchiel

HE'-BREW, עִבְרִי Ἑβραῖος *belonging to Eber.*
1. Patronymic of Abraham and his offspring.
Gen. 14. 13 there came one..and told Abram the H.
39. 14 he hath brought in an H. unto us to mock
39. 17 The H. servant..came in unto me to mock
40. 15 I was stolen..out of the land of the H.
41. 12 And..there with us a young man, an H.
43. 32 Egyptians might not eat bread with the H.
Exod. 1. 15 the king of Egypt spake to the H. midw.
1. 16 ye do the office of a midwife to the H. wo.
1. 19 the H. women (are) not as the Egyptian
2. 6 she..said, This (is one) of the H.'s children
2. 7 Shall I go and call..a nurse of the H. wo.
2. 11 he spied an Egyptian smiting an H., one of
2. 13 behold, two men of the H. strove together
3. 18 The LORD God of the H. hath met with us
5. 3 The God of the H. hath met with us
7. 16 The LORD God of the H. hath sent me unto
9. 1, 13 Thus saith the LORD God of the H.
10. 3 Thus saith the LORD God of the H.
21. 2 If thou buy an H. servant, six years he
Deut15. 12 if..an H. man, or an H. woman, be sold
1 Sa. 4. 6 What..the noise..in the camp of the H.?
4. 9 that ye be not servants unto the H., as
13. 3 Saul blew the trumpet..saying, Let the H.
13. 7 And (some) of the H. went over Jordan to
13. 19 Lest the H. make (them) swords or spears
14. 11 the H. come forth out of the holes where
14. 21 Moreover the H...(turned) to be with the
29. 3 Then said the princes..What (do) these H.
Jer. 34. 9 every man should let..an H. or an Hebr.
34. 14 let ye go every man his brother an H.
Jon. 1. 9 And he said unto them, I (am) an H.
Acts 6. 1 murmuring of the Grecians against the H.
2 Co.11 22 Are they H.? so (am) I. Are they Israe.?
Phil. 3. 5 Circum. the eighth day..an H. of the H.

2. The language spoken by the Jews in Palestine in the time of Christ. It might more accurately have been called *Syro-Chaldee*, being a mixture of the *Aramaean* of Daniel and Ezra with the ancient Hebrew. The Syriac *Peshito* and the Chaldee *Targum* of Onkelos are its substantial representatives. In the schools of the Rabbis after the destruction of Jerusalem an attempt was made to return to the Hebrew of the Old Testament, as may be seen in the *Mishnah*, &c.
Acts 21. 40 he spake unto (them) in the H. tongue
22. 2 they heard that he spake in the H. tongue
26. 14 I heard a voice speaking..in the H. ton.

HEBREW (tongue), in the —
Hebraistic, Ἑβραϊστί *Hebraisti.*
John 5. 2 which is called in the Hebrew tongue B.
19. 13 the Pavement, but in the Hebrew, Gabb.
19. 17 which is called in the Hebrew, Golgotha
19. 20 it was written in Hebrew, (and) Greek, (and)
Rev. 9. 11 whose name in the Hebrew tongue (is) Ab.
16. 16 a place called in the Hebrew tongue A.

HEBREW, (of) —
Hebraic, Ἑβραϊκός *Hebraikos.*
Luke23. 38 in letters of Greek, and Latin, and Hebrew

HEB'-RON, עֶבְרוֹן חֶבְרוֹן *ford, company.*
1. A city of Asher near Rehob, called also *Abdon* (which see). Properly *Ebron.*
Josh.19. 28 H., and Rehob, and Hammon, and Kanah
2. A city of Judah, 22 miles S. of Jerusalem, in a rocky but fertile district; it was also called *Kirjath-arba*, and now *El-khulil.*
Gen. 13. 18 in the plain of Mamre, which (is) in H.
23. 2, 19 the same (is) H. in the land of Canaan
35. 27 which (is) H., where Abraham and Isaac
37. 14 So he sent him out of the vale of H., and
Num13. 22 ascended by the south, and came unto H.
13. 22 H. was built seven years before Zoan in E.
Josh 10. 3 Adoni-zedek..sent unto Hoham king of H.
10. 5 Therefore..the king of H...encamped be.
10. 23 did so, and brought forth..the king of H.
10. 36 And Joshua went up from Eglon..unto H.
10. 39 as he had done to H., so he did to Debir
11. 21 cut off the Anakims..from H., from Debir
12. 10 The king of Jerusalem, one; the king of H.
14. 13 Joshua..gave unto Caleb..H. for an inh.
14. 14 H. therefore became the inheritance of C.
14. 15 the name of H. before (was) Kirjath-arba
15. 13 Caleb..he gave..Arba..which (city is) H.
15. 54 Humtah, and Kirjath-arba, which (is) H.
20. 7 appointed..Kirjath-arba, which (is) H.
21. 11 they gave them..Arba..which (city is) H.
21. 13 they gave to the children of Aaron..H.
Judg. 1. 10 against the Canaanites that dwelt in H.
1. 10 now the name of H. before (was) Kirjath.
1. 20 they gave H. unto Caleb, as Moses said
16. 3 up to the top of an hill, that (is) before H.
1 Sa. 30. 31 to (them) which (were) in H., and to all
2 Sa. 2. 1 Whither shall I go up? And he said..H.
2. 3 and they dwelt in the cities of H.
2. 11 David was king in H...seven years and
2. 32 and they came to H. at break of day
3. 2 And unto David were sons born in H.
3. 5 These were born to David in H.
3. 19 to speak in the ears of David in H.
3. 20 So Abner came to David to H., and twenty
3. 22 but Abner (was) not with David in H.
3. 27 when Abner was returned to H., 3. 32.
4. 1 Saul's son heard..Abner was dead in H.
4. 8 brought the head of Ish-bosheth..to H.
2 Sa. 4. 12 and hanged (them) up over the pool in H.
4. 12 buried (it) in the sepulchre of Abner in H.
5. 1 Then came all the tribes..to David unto H.
5. 3 elders of Israel came to the king to H.
5. 3 king David made a league with them in H.
5. 5 In H. he reigned over Judah seven years
5. 13 took..wives..after he was come from H.
15. 7 which I have vowed unto the LORD, in H
15. 9 Go in peace. So he arose, and went to H.
15. 10 then ye shall say, Absalom reigneth in H.
1 Ki. 2. 11 seven years reigned he in H., and thirty
1 Ch. 3. 1 the sons..which were born unto him in H.
3. 4 (These) six were born unto him in H; and
6. 55 they gave them H. in the land of Judah
6. 57 to the sons of Aaron they gave..H., (the c.)
11. 1 all Israel gathered..to David unto H.
11. 3 came all the elders..to the king to H.
11. 3 David made a covenant with them in H.
12. 23 the bands..ready..came to David to H.
12. 38 these..came with a perfect heart to H.
29. 27 seven years reigned he in H., and thirty
2 Ch.11. 10 Zorah, and Aijalon, and H., which (are) in
3. A son of Kohath, the son of Levi. B.C. 1600.
Exod. 6. 18 And the sons of Kohath..H., and Uzziel
Num. 3. 19 And the sons of Kohath..H., and Uzziel
1 Ch. 6. 2 And the sons of Kohath..H., and Uzziel
6. 18 And the sons of Kohath..H., and Uzziel
23. 12 The sons of Kohath..H., and Uzziel, four
23. 19 Of the sons of H.; Jeriah the first, Ama.
4. The patronymic of Mareshah a descendant of Caleb the son of Hezron. B.C. 1500.
1 Ch. 2. 42 the sons of Mareshah the father of H.
2. 43 And the sons of H.; Korah, and Tappuah
15. 9 Of the sons of H.; Eliel the chief, and his

HE-BRO-NITES, חֶבְרוֹנִי חֶבְרֹנִי.
Patronymic of the family of Hebron the son of Kohath. B.C. 1600.
Num. 3. 27 And of Kohath..the family of the H.
26. 58 families of the Levites..family of the H.
1 Ch.26. 23 Of the Amramites..the Izharites, the H.
26. 30 the H., Hashabiah and his brethren, men
26. 31 Among the H. (was) Jerijah the chief
26. 31 among the H., according to the generat.

HEDGE —
1. *Hedge, fold*, גָּדֵר *gader.*
Psa. 80. 12 Why hast thou..broken down her hedges
Eccl.10. 8 whoso breaketh an hedge, a serpent
Eze. 13. 5 neither made up the hedge for the house
22. 30 that should make up the hedge, and stand
2. *Hedge, fold*, גְּדֵרָה *gederah.*
1 Ch. 4. 23 those that dwelt among plants and hedges
Psa. 89. 40 Thou hast broken down all his hedges
Jer. 49. 3 lament, and run to and fro by the hedges
Nah. 3. 17 which camp in the hedges in the cold day
3. *Hedge*, מְשׂוּכָה *mesukah.*
Prov 15. 19 the slothful (man is) as an hedge of thorns
Isa. 5. 5 I will take away the hedge thereof, and
4. *A hedge*, φραγμός *phragmos.*
Mark12. 1 set an hedge about (it), and digged (a
Luke 14. 23 Go out into the highways and hedges

HEDGE, to —
To hedge about, גָּדַר *gadar.*
Lam. 3. 7 He hath hedged me about, that I cannot

HEDGE in, to —
To shut up, cover in, סָכַךְ *sakak*, 5.
Job 3. 23 to a man..whom God hath hedged in?

HEDGE, to make an —
To make a fence, שׂוּךְ *suk*, 5.
Job 1. 10 Hast not thou made an hedge about him

HEDGE round about, to —
To put a hedge around, περιτίθημι φραγμόν.
Matt21. 33 and hedged it round about, and digged a

HEDGE up, to —
To hedge up, שׂוּךְ *suk.*
Hos. 2. 6 I will hedge up thy way with thorns, and

HEED, to give —
To give attention, קָשַׁב *qashab*, 5.
Prov.17. 4 A wicked doer giveth heed to false lips
Jer. 18. 18 let us not give heed to any of his words
18. 19 Give heed to me, O LORD, and hearken to

HEED to, to give —
To hold toward, προσέχω *prosechō.*
Acts 8. 10 To whom they all gave heed, from the least
1 Ti. 1. 4 Neither give heed to fables and endless
4. 1 giving heed to seducing spirits, and doctri.
Titus 1. 14 Not giving heed to Jewish fables, and

HEED, to give good —
To give ear, אָזַן *azan*, 3.
Eccl.12. 9 he gave good heed, and sought out, (and)

HEED, much —
Attention, קֶשֶׁב *qesheb.*
Isa. 21. 7 he hearkened diligently with much heed

HEED, to take —
1. *To be warned*, זָהַר *zehar.*
Ezra 4. 22 Take heed now that ye fail not to do this
2. *To observe silently*, סָכַת *sakath*, 5.
Deut27. 9 Take heed, and hearken, O Israel; this day
3. *To give the heart*, נָתַן לֵב *nathan leb.*
Eccl. 7. 21 Also take no heed unto all words that are
4. *To see*, רָאָה *raah.*
1 Ch. 28. 10 Take heed now; for the LORD hath chosen
2 Ch. 19. 6 Take heed what ye do: for ye judge not
5. *To watch, observe*, שָׁמַר *shamar.*
Num 23. 12 Must I not take heed to speak that which
Josh 22. 5 take diligent heed to do the commandme.
1 Ki. 2. 4 If thy children take heed to their way, to
8. 25 that thy children take heed to their way
2 Ki. 10. 31 But Jehu took no heed to walk in the law
1 Ch.22. 13 if thou takest heed to fulfil the statutes
2 Ch. 6. 16 so that thy children take heed to their way
19. 7 take heed, and do (it): for (there is) no iniq.
33. 8 they will take heed to do all that I have
Psa. 39. 1 I will take heed to my ways, that I sin
Hos. 4. 10 they have left off to take heed to the LORD
6. *To be watchful*, שָׁמַר *shamar*, 2.
Gen. 31. 24 Take heed that thou speak not to Jacob
31. 29 Take thou heed that thou speak not to Jac
Exod10. 28 Get thee from me, take heed to thyself
19. 12 Take heed to yourselves, (that ye) go (not)
34. 12 Take heed to thyself, lest thou make a cov.
Deut. 4. 9 Only take heed to thyself, and keep thy so.
4. 15 Take ye therefore good heed unto yourselv.
4. 23 Take heed unto yourselves, lest ye forget
11. 16 Take heed to yourselves, that your heart be
12. 13, 19, 30 Take heed to thyself that thou
24. 8 Take heed in the plague of leprosy, that th.
Josh 23 11 Take good heed therefore unto yourselves
1 Sa. 19. 2 take heed to thyself until the morning
2 Sa. 20. 10 But Amasa took no heed to the sword that
Job 36. 21 Take heed, regard not iniquity: for this
Isa. 7. 4 Take heed, and be quiet; fear not, neither
Jer. 9. 4 Take ye heed every one of his neighbour
17. 21 Take heed to yourselves, and bear no burd.
Mal. 2. 15 Therefore take heed to your spirit, and let
2. 16 therefore take heed to your spirit, that ye
7. *To look, look on or to*, βλέπω *blepō.*
Matt24. 4 Take heed that no man deceive you
Mark 4. 24 he saith unto them, Take heed what ye hear
13. 5 Take heed lest any (man) deceive you
13. 23 But take ye heed: behold, I have foretold
13. 33 Take ye heed, watch and pray: for ye
Luke 8. 18 Take heed therefore how ye hear: for who.
21. 8 Take heed that ye be not deceived: for
1 Co. 3. 10 let every man take heed how he buildeth
8. 9 take heed, lest by any means this liberty
10. 12 Wherefore let him..take heed lest he fall
Gal. 5. 15 take heed that ye be not consumed one
Col. 4. 17 Take heed to the ministry which thou hast
Heb. 3. 12 Take heed, brethren, lest there be in any of
8. *To see, see to*, ὁράω *horaō.*
Matt16. 6 Take heed and beware of the leaven of the
18. 10 Take heed that ye despise not one of these
Mark 8. 15 Take heed, beware of the leaven of the
Luke12. 15 Take heed, and beware of covetousness
Acts 22. 26 Take heed what thou doest: for this man
9. *To hold toward*, προσέχω *prosechō.*
Matt. 6. 1 Take heed that ye do not your alms before
2 Pe. 1. 19 whereunto ye do well that ye take heed
10. *To look at or on, mark*, σκοπέω *skopeō.*
Luke11. 35 Take heed therefore that the light which

HEED, taking —
To watch, observe, שָׁמַר *shamar.*
Psa.119. 9 By taking heed (thereto) according to thy

HEED unto self, to take —
To be watchful, שָׁמַר *shamar*, 2.
Deut. 2. 4 take ye good heed unto yourselves therefo.

HEED to, to take — [*See* **TAKE.**]
1. *To look, look on or at*, βλέπω *blepō.*
Mark13. 9 But take heed to yourselves: for they shall
Col. 4. 17 Take heed to the ministry which thou hast
2. *To hold toward*, προσέχω *prosechō.*
Luke17. 3 Take heed to yourselves: If thy brother
21. 34 take heed to yourselves, lest at any time
Acts 5. 35 Ye men of Israel, take heed to yourselves

HEED to, to give the more earnest —
To hold the more toward, περισσοτέρως προσέχω.
Heb. 2. 1 ought to give the more earnest heed to

HEED unto, to give —
1. *To hold upon*, ἐπέχω *epechō.*
Acts 3. 5 gave heed unto them, expecting to rece.
2. *To hold toward*, προσέχω *prosechō.*
Acts 8. 6 the people with one accord gave heed un.

HEED unto, to take —
1. *To hold upon*, ἐπέχω *epechō.*
1 Ti. 4. 16 Take heed unto thyself, and unto the
2. *To hold toward*, προσέχω *prosechō.*
Acts 20. 28 Take heed therefore unto yourselves, and

HEEL —
1. *The heel*, עָקֵב *aqeb.*
Gen. 3. 15 thy head, and thou shalt bruise his heel
25. 26 his hand took hold on Esau's heel; and
49. 17 that biteth the horse heels, so that his
Job 18. 9 The gin shall take (him) by the heel. (and)
Psa. 41. 9 hath lifted up (his) heel against me
49. 5 the iniquity of my heels shall compass me
Jer. 13. 22 discovered, (and) thy heels made bare
2. *A root*, שֹׁרֶשׁ *shoresh.*
Job 13. 27 settest a print upon the heels of my feet
3. *The heel*, πτέρνα *pterna.*
John13. 18 He..hath lifted up his heel against me

HEEL, to take by the —

To circumvent, take by the heel, עָקַב *aqab.*

Hos. 12. 3 took his brother by the heel in the womb

HE'-GE, HE'-GAI, הֵגֵא, הֵגַי, הֵגֶא.

Chief chamberlain of Ahasuerus, king of Persia. B.C. 518.

Esth. 2. 3 unto the custody of H. the king's chamb.
2. 8 were gathered..to the custody of H.
2. 8 Esther was brought..to the custody of H.
2. 15 she required nothing but what H...app.

HEIFER —

1. *Heifer,* עֶגְלָה *eglah* (Deu. 21.3, 1 Sa. 16.2 with בָּקָר).

Gen. 15. 9 Take me an heifer of three years old, and
Deut 21. 3 elders of that city shall take an heifer
21. 4 shall bring down the heifer unto a rough
21. 4 shall strike off the heifer's neck there in
21. 6 shall wash their hands over the heifer
Judg 14. 18 If ye had not ploughed with my heifer, ye
1 Sa. 16. 2 Take an heifer with thee, and say, I am
Isa. 15. 5 unto Zoar, an heifer of three years old
Jer. 46. 20 Egypt (is like) a very fair heifer, (but)
48. 34 uttered..(as) an heifer of three years old
50. 11 ye are grown fat as the heifer at grass
Hos. 10. 11 Ephraim (is as) an heifer (that is) taught

2. *Cow, kine,* פָּרָה *parah.*

Num 19. 2 they bring thee a red heifer without spot
19. 5 (one) shall burn the heifer in his sight
19. 6 the midst of the burning of the heifer
19. 9 shall gather up the ashes of the heifer
19. 10 he that gathereth the ashes of the heifer
Hos. 4. 16 slideth back as a backsliding heifer: now

3. *A tamed heifer,* δάμαλις *damalis.*

Heb. 9. 13 ashes of an heifer sprinkling the unclean

HEIGHT —

1. *Height, high place,* בָּמָה *bamah.*

Isa. 14. 14 ascend above the heights of the clouds

2. *To make high or lofty,* גָּבַהּ *gabah,* 5.

Isa. 7. 11 either in..depth, or in the height above

3. *Loftiness,* גֹּבַהּ *gobah.*

1 Sa. 17. 4 whose height (was) six cubits and a span
2 Ch. 3. 4 and the height (was) an hundred and tw.
Job 22. 12 (Is) not God in the height of heaven? and
Eze. 19. 11 and she appeared in her height with the
31. 10 and his heart is lifted up in his height
31. 14 their trees stand up in their height
41. 8 also the height of the house round about
Amos 2. 9 height (was) like the height of the cedars

4. *Lofty,* גָּבֹהַּ *gaboah.*

1 Sa. 16. 7 Look not..on the height of his stature

5. *High place,* מָרוֹם *marom.*

2 Ki. 19. 23 come up to the height of the mountains
Psa. 102. 19 down from the height of his sanctuary
148. 1 Praise ye the LORD..in the heights
Isa. 37. 24 I come up to the height of the mountains
37. 24 will enter into the height of his border
Jer. 31. 12 shall come and sing in the height of Zion
49. 16 thou..that holdest the height of the hill
51. 53 she should fortify the height of her stren.
Eze. 17. 23 In the mountain of the height of Israel
20. 40 in the mountain of the height of Israel

6. *Stature, height,* קוֹמָה *qomah.*

Gen. 6. 15 and the height of it thirty cubits
Exod 25. 10, 23 a cubit and a half the height thereof
27. 1 the height thereof (shall be) three cubits
27. 18 height five cubits (of) fine twined linen
30. 2 two cubits (shall be) the height thereof
37. 1 and a cubit and a half the height of it
37. 10 and a cubit and a half the height thereof
37. 25 two cubits (was) the height of it; the h.
38. 1 and three cubits the height thereof
38. 18 the height in the breadth (was) five cubits
1 Ki. 6. 2 and the height thereof thirty cubits
6. 20 twenty cubits in the height thereof: and
6. 26 height of the one cherub (was) ten cubits
7. 2 the height thereof thirty cubits, upon
7. 16 height of the one chapiter (was) five cub.
7. 16 the height of the other chapiter (was) five
7. 23 his height (was) five cubits; and a line of
7. 27 and three cubits the height of it
7. 32 height of a wheel (was) a cubit and half a
2 Ki. 25. 17 The height of the one pillar (was) eighteen
25. 17 the height of the chapiter three cubits
2 Ch. 4. 1 he made..ten cubits the height thereof
4. 2 five cubits the height thereof; and a line
Jer. 52. 21 the height of one pillar (was) eighteen cu.
52. 22 the height of one chapiter (was) five cubits
Eze. 31. 5 Therefore his height was exalted above all
31. 10 and his heart is lifted up in his height
31. 14 trees..exalt themselves for their height
40. 5 breadth..one reed; and the height one reed

7. *Head,* רֹאשׁ *rosh.*

Job 22. 12 behold the height of the stars, how high

8. *Height, loftiness,* רוּם *rum.*

Prov. 25. 3 The heaven for height, and the earth for
Ezra 6. 3 the height therefore threescore cubits
Dan 3. 1 an image..whose height (was) threescore
4. 10 a tree..and the height thereof (was) great
4. 11 the height thereof reached unto heaven
4. 20 whose height reached unto the heaven, and

9. *Hugeness,* רָמוּת *ramuth.*

Eze. 32. 5 will lay..and fill the valleys with thy hei.

10. *Height,* ὕψος *hupsos.*

Eph. 3. 18 what (is) the breadth..and depth, and he.
Rev. 21. 16 the breadth, and the height of it are equal

11. *High thing or place,* ὕψωμα *hupsōma.*

Rom. 8. 39 Nor height, nor depth, nor any other crea.

HEIGHT, to raise up to a great —

To make high or lofty, גָּבַהּ *gabah,* 5.

2 Ch. 33. 14 raised it up to a very great height, and

HEINOUS crime —

Wicked thought or device, זִמָּה *zimmah.*

Job 31. 11 For this (is) an heinous crime; yea, it (is)

HEIR —

1. *To possess, occupy, succeed,* יָרַשׁ *yarash.*

Gen. 15. 3 and, lo, one born in my house is mine heir
2 Sa. 14. 7 and we will destroy the heir also: and so
Jer. 49. 1 Hath Israel no sons? hath he no heir? why
49. 2 unto them that were his heirs, saith the
Mic. 1. 15 Yet will I bring an heir unto thee, O inh.

2. *One who receives a lot or portion,* κληρονόμος.

Matt 21. 38 This is the heir; come, let us kill him
Mark 12. 7 This is the heir; come, let us kill him
Luke 20. 14 This is the heir: come, let us kill him
Rom. 4. 13 that he should be the heir of the world
4. 14 For if they which are of the law (be) heirs
8. 17 And if children, then heirs; heirs of God
Gal. 3. 29 and heirs according to the promise
4. 1 say, (That) the heir, as long as he is a child
4. 7 a son, then an heir of God through Christ
Titus 3. 7 we should be made heirs according to
Heb. 1. 2 whom he hath appointed heir of all things
6. 17 willing..to show unto the heirs of prom.
11. 7 became heir of the righteousness which is
Jas. 2. 5 and heirs of the kingdom which he hath p.

HEIR (of), to be —

1. *To possess, occupy, succeed,* יָרַשׁ *yarash.*

Gen. 15. 4 saying, This shall not be thine heir; but
15. 4 he that shall come..shall be thine heir
21. 10 for the son..shall not be heir with my son
Prov 30. 23 an handmaid that is heir to her mistress
Jer. 49. 2 then shall Israel be heir unto them that

2. *To receive a lot or portion,* κληρονομέω *klēronomeō.*

Gal. 4. 30 for the son..shall not be heir with the son
Heb. 1. 14 for them who shall be heirs of salvation?

HEIR together, or with —

One receiving a lot with (another), συγκληρονόμος.

Heb. 11. 9 the heirs with him of the same promise
1 Pe. 3. 7 and as being heirs together of the grace

HEIR, fellow or joint —

One receiving a lot with (another), συγκληρονόμος.

Rom. 8. 17 heirs of God, and joint heirs with Christ
Eph. 3. 6 That the Gentiles should be fellow heirs

HEL'-AH, חֶלְאָה *tenderness.*

A wife of Asher, a descendant of Caleb son of Hur from Judah. B.C. 1560.

1 Ch. 4. 5 the father of Tekoa had two wives, H. and
4. 7 the sons of H. (were) Zereth, and Jezoar

HE'-LAM, חֵילָם, חֵלָאם.

A place E. of the Jordan, but W. of the Euphrates. Perhaps it is identical with *Alamatha,* on the W. of the Euphrates, near Nicephorium.

2 Sa. 10. 16 they came to H.; and Shobach..(went) be.
10. 17 and passed over Jordan, and came to H.

HEL'-BAH, חֶלְבָּה *fertility.*

A town in the tribe of Asher, near Achzib.

Judg. 1. 31 did Asher drive out the inhabitants of. H.

HEL'-BON, חֶלְבּוֹן *fruitful.*

A city celebrated in ancient times for the quality of its wine. It still bears its ancient name *Helbon* and is a village within a few miles of Damascus and still celebrated for producing the finest grapes in the country. The Arabic name *Halbûn* contains the Hebrew equivalents exactly.

Eze. 27. 18 thy merchant..in the wine of H., and white w.

HELD —

To be hidden, חָבָא *chaba,* 2.

Job 29 10 nobles held their peace, and their tongue

HELD in, to be —

To curb, בָּלַם *balam.*

Psa. 32. 9 whose mouth must be held in with bit and

HEL'-DAI, חֶלְדַּי *enduring.*

1. The 12th captain for the monthly service in the sanctuary. He was descended from Othniel and is called "the Netophathite." B.C. 1015.

1 Ch. 27. 15 The..(captain) for the twelfth month..H.

2. An Israelite who returned from captivity and to whom special honour was given. In verse 14 his name appears to be changed to *Helem.* B.C. 519.

Zech. 6. 10 Take of (them of) the captivity..of H.

HE'-LEB, חֵלֶב *fat.* [*See* **HELED.**]

One of David's valiant men, from Netophah, S.E. of Jerusalem. B.C. 1048.

2 Sa. 23. 29 H. the son of Baanah, a Netophathite

HE'-LED, חֵלֶד. *The same as Heleb.*

1 Ch. 11. 30 H. the son of Baanah the Netophathite

HE'-LEK, חֵלֶק *portion.*

Second son of Gilead, and founder of the family of the Helekites, descended from Manasseh, Joseph's son. B.C. 1560.

Num. 26. 30 of H., the family of the Helekites
Josh. 17. 2 for the children of H.. and for the children

HEL-E-KITES, חֶלְקִי.

Descendants of Helek, son of Gilead of the tribe of Manasseh.

Num 26. 30 of Gilead..of Helek, the family of the H.

HE'-LEM, חֵלֶם *strength.*

1. One mentioned among the descendants of Asher, through Heber son of Beriah. B.C. 1600.

1 Ch. 7. 35 the sons of his brother H.; Zophah, and

2. Person mentioned only once, and apparently the same as *Heldai* in verse 10 of the same chapter. B.C. 519.

Zech. 6. 14 the crowns shall be to H., and to Tobijah

HE'-LEPH, חֵלֶף *place of rushes.*

A border town of Naphtali. It is now probably *Beitlif* an ancient site nearly due E. of *Ras Abyad,* and W. of *Kades,* on the edge of a ravine which probably formed part of the boundary between Asher and Naphtali.

Josh. 19. 33 their coast was from H...unto Lakum

HE'-LEZ, חֶלֶץ, חֵלֶץ, חָלֶץ *strength.*

1. The Pelonite, one of the thirty of David's guard. *Paltite* in 2 Sa. 23. 26 is likely a corruption. He was an Ephraimite, and captain of the 7th monthly course. B.C. 1048.

2 Sa. 23. 26 H. the Paltite, Ira the son of Ikkesh the T.
1 Ch. 11. 27 Shammoth the Harorite, H. the Pelonite
27. 10 seventh..for the seventh month (was) H.

2. A man of Judah and son of Azariah, a descendant of Jerahmeel of the great family of Hezron. B.C. 1300.

1 Ch. 2. 39 And Azariah begat H., and H. begat Ele.

HE'-LI, Ἡλί, Ἡλί.

The father of Joseph, the husband of Mary and real brother of Jacob the father of the Virgin Mary herself. This name in the Hebrew is identical with that of *Eli* the high priest.

Luke 3. 23 son of Joseph, which was (the son) of H.

HEL'-KAI, חֶלְקַי *Jah is a portion.*

A priest of the family of Meraioth or Meremoth, who was living in the generation following the return from Babylon under Zerubbabel. See *Hilkiah.* B.C. 500.

Neh. 12. 15 Of Harim, Adna; of Meraioth, H.

HEL'-KATH, חֶלְקַת, חֶלְקָת *portion.*

The town at the starting point of the tribe of Asher's boundary; and allotted to the Gershonite Levites. Some identify it with the modern *Yerka,* 8 miles E. of *Akka.* In 1 Ch. 6. 75, *Hukok* is substituted for Helkath.

Josh 19. 25 their border was H., and Hali, and Beten
21. 31 H. with her suburbs, and Rehob with her

HEL-KATH HAZ-ZU'-RIM, חֶלְקַת הַצֻּרִים *field of rocks.*

A smooth piece of ground, close to the pool of Gibeon, where Joab's men had a fight with Abner's, which ended in the death of the selected combatants, and brought on a general battle.

2 Sa 2. 16 wherefore that place was called H., which

HELL —

1. *The unseen state,* שְׁאוֹל *sheol.*

Deut 32. 22 and shall burn unto the lowest hell, and
2 Sa. 22. 6 The sorrows of hell compassed me about
Job 11. 8 what canst thou do? deeper than hell
26. 6 Hell (is) naked before him, and destruction
Psa. 9. 17 The wicked shall be turned into hell, (and)
16. 10 For thou wilt not leave my soul in hell
18. 5 The sorrows of hell compassed me about
55. 15 (and) let them go down quick into hell: for
86. 13 delivered my soul from the lowest hell
116. 3 and the pains of hell gat hold upon me
139. 8 if I make my bed in hell, behold, thou
Prov. 5. 5 down to death; her steps take hold on h.
7. 27 Her house (is) the way to hell, going down
9. 18 knoweth..her guests (are) in the depths of
15. 11 Hell and destruction (are) before the LORD
15. 24 that he may depart from hell beneath
23. 14 beat..and shalt deliver his soul from hell
27. 20 Hell and destruction are never full; so
Isa. 5. 14 Therefore hell hath enlarged herself, and
14 9 Hell from beneath is moved for thee to
14. 15 Yet thou shalt be brought down to hell, to
28. 15 and with hell are we at agreement; when
28. 18 your agreement with hell shall not stand
57. 9 and didst debase (thyself even) unto hell
Eze. 31. 16 when I cast him down to hell with them
31 17 They also went down into hell with him
32. 21 shall speak to him out of the midst of hell
32. 27 which are gone down to hell with their
Amos 9 2 Though they dig into hell, thence shall
Jon. 2. 2 out of the belly of hell cried I, (and) thou
Hab. 2. 5 who enlargeth his desire as hell, and (is) as

2. *Hades, the unseen world,* ᾅδης *hadēs.*

Matt 11. 23 thou..shalt be brought down to hell: for
16. 18 gates of hell shall not prevail against it
Luke 10. 15 And thou..shalt be thrust down to hell
16. 23 in hell he lifted up his eyes, being in tor.
Acts 2. 27 thou wilt not leave my soul in hell, neither
2. 31 that his soul was not left in hell, neither
Rev. 1. 18 I..have the keys of hell and of death
6. 8 I looked..and Hell followed with him
20. 13 death and hell delivered up the dead
20. 14 death and hell were cast into the lake

3. *Valley of Hinnom, Gehenna,* γέεννα *geenna.*

Matt. 5. 22 shall say..shall be in danger of hell fire
5. 29, 30 thy whole body should be cast into h
10. 28 him which is able to destroy..body in hell
18. 9 having two eyes to be cast into hell fire
23. 15 twofold more the child of hell than your.
23. 33 how can ye escape the damnation of hell?

Mark 9. 43 than having two hands to go into hell
9. 45 than having two feet to be cast into hell
9. 47 having two eyes to be cast into hell fire
Luke12. 5 hath power to cast into hell; yea, I say
Jas. 3. 6 the tongue..and it is set on fire of hell

HELL, to cast down to —
To send into Tartarus, ταρταρόω *tartaroō.*
2 Pe. 2. 4 but cast (them) down to hell, and deliver.

HELM —
An oar, rudder, πηδάλιον *pēdalion.*
Jas. 3. 4 they turned about with a very small helm

HELMET —
1. *Helmet,* כּוֹבַע *koba.*
1 Sa. 17. 5 (had) an helmet of brass upon his head, and
2 Ch.26. 14 Uzziah prepared for them..helmets, and h.
Isa. 59. 17 an helmet of salvation upon his head; and
Jer. 46. 4 stand forth with (your) helmets; furbish
Eze. 27. 10 they hanged the shield and helmet in thee
38. 5 Persia..all of them with shield and helmet
2. *Helmet,* קוֹבַע *qoba.*
1 Sa. 17. 38 he put an helmet of brass upon his head
Eze. 23. 24 shall set..shield and helmet round about
3. *Something around the head,* περικεφαλαία *perik.*
Eph. 6. 17 take the helmet of salvation, and the sw.
1 Th. 5. 8 and for an helmet the hope of salvation

HE'-LON, חֵלֹן *strong.*
Father of Eliab, chief man of the tribe of Zebulun, at the taking of the census in the wilderness at Sinai. B.C. 1520.
Num. 1. 9 Of Zebulun; Eliab the son of H.
2. 7 Eliab the son of H...captain of the chil.
7. 24 On the third day Eliab the son of H...(did
7. 29 this..the offering of Eliab the son of H.
10. 16 over the host..(was) Eliab the son of H.

HELP —
1. *Safety,* יְשׁוּעָה *yeshuah.*
2 Sa. 10. 11 be too strong for me, then thou shalt help
Psa. 3. 2 which say..(There is) no help for him in G.
42. 5 praise him (for) the help of his countena.
2. *Help,* עֵזֶר *ezer.*
Gen. 2. 18 I will make him an help meet for him
2. 20 there was not found an help meet for him
Exod18. 4 God of my father, (said he, was) mine help
Deut33. 7 be thou an help (to him) from his enemies
33. 26 (who) rideth upon the heaven in thy help
33. 29 saved by the LORD, the shield of thy help
Psa. 20. 2 Send thee help from the sanctuary, and
33. 20 soul waiteth for the LORD: he (is) our help
70. 5 thou (art) my help and deliverer; O LORD
89. 19 I have laid help upon (one that is) mighty
115. 9, 10, 11 the LORD: he (is) their help and th.
121. 1 unto the hills, from whence cometh my h.
121. 2 My help (cometh) from the LORD, which
124. 8 Our help (is) in the name of the LORD, who
146. 5 that (hath) the God of Jacob for his help
Isa. 30. 5 nor be an help nor profit, but a shame, and
Eze. 12. 14 all that (are) about him to help him, and
Dan. 11. 34 they shall be holpen with a little help: but
Hos. 13. 9 destroyed thyself; but in me (is) thine help
3. *Help,* עֶזְרָה, עֶזְרַת *ezrath, ezrah.*
Judg. 5. 23 to the help of the LORD, to the help of the
Job 6. 13 (Is) not my help in me? and is wisdom d.
31. 21 I have lifted up..when I saw my help in
Psa. 22. 19 LORD: O my strength, haste thee to help
27. 9 thou hast been my help; leave me not
35. 2 Take hold of shield..stand up for mine h.
38. 22 Make haste to help me, O Lord my salva.
40. 13 to deliver me: O LORD, make haste to h.
40. 17 thou (art) my help and my deliverer; m.
44. 26 Arise for our help, and redeem us for thy
46. 1 God (is)..a very present help in trouble
60. 11 Give us help from trouble: for vain (is)
63. 7 Because thou h.. t been my help, there.
70. 1 O God..make haste to help me, O LORD
71. 12 not far..O my God, make haste for my h.
94. 17 Unless the LORD (had been) my help, my
108. 12 Give us help from trouble: for vain (is)
Isa. 10. 3 to whom will ye flee for help? and where
20. 6 whither we flee for help to be delivered
31. 1 Woe to them that go down to Egypt for h
31. 2 against the help of them that work iniq.
Jer. 37. 7 Pharaoh's army, which is come forth to h.
Lam. 4. 17 our eyes as yet failed for our vain help
4. *Safety,* תְּשׁוּעָה *teshuah.*
1 Sa. 11. 9 (that time) the sun be hot, ye shall have h.
1 Ch.19. 12 then thou shalt help me: but if the chil.
Psa. 60. 11 from trouble: for vain (is) the help of m.
108. 12 from trouble: for vain (is) the help of m.
146. 3 in the son of man, in whom (there is) no h.
5. *A helping, supporting,* ἀντίληψις *antilēpsis.*
1 Co.12. 28 God hath set some in the church..[helps]
6. *Help, succour,* βοήθεια *boētheia.*
Acts 27. 17 when they had taken up, they used helps
7. *Help, aid, assistance,* ἐπικουρία *epikouria.*
Acts 26. 22 Having therefore obtained help of God, I

HELP, to —
1. *To strengthen,* חָזַק *chazaq,* 3.
2 Ch. 29. 34 their brethren the Levites did help them
2. *Strengthen hand of.* הֶחֱזִיק בְּיַד [*chazaq* 5].
Job 8. 20 not cast away neither will he help the
3. *To save, give safety,* יָשַׁע *yasha,* 5.
Exod. 2. 17 Moses stood up and helped them, and
2 Sa. 10. 11 too strong..then I will come and help
10. 19 the Syrians feared to help the children of
14. 4 and did obeisance, and said, Help, O king
2 Ki. 6. 26 there cried a woman unto him, saying, H.
6. 27 the LORD do not help..whence shall I help
1 Ch.19. 12 too strong for thee, then I will help thee
19. 19 neither would the Syrians help the child.
2 Ch.20. 9 we..cry..then thou wilt hear and help
Psa. 12. 1 Help, LORD; for the godly man ceaseth
116. 6 I was brought low, and he helped me
4. *To lift up,* נָשָׂא *nasa,* 3.
Ezra 1. 4 let the men of his place help him with si.
Esth. 9. 3 and officers of the king, helped the Jews
5. *To leave,* עָזַב *azab.*
Exod.23 5 to help him; thou shalt surely help with
6. *To help,* עָזַר *azar.*
Gen. 49. 25 the God of thy father, who shall help thee
Deut.32. 38 let them rise up and help you, (and) be your
Josh. 1. 14 all the mighty men of valour, and help
10. 4 Come up unto me, and help me, that we
10. 6 come up to us quickly, and save us, and h.
10. 33 Horam king of Gezer came up to help La.
1 Sa. 7. 12 saying, Hitherto hath the LORD helped us
1 Ki. 1. 7 and they following Adonijah helped (him)
20. 16 the thirty and two kings that helped him
1 Ch.12. 17 If ye be come peaceably unto me to help me
12. 18 peace (be) unto thee..for thy God helpeth
12. 19 but they helped them not: for the lords
12. 21 they helped David against the band (of the)
12. 22 day by day there came to David to help
15. 26 when God helped the Levites that bare
18. 5 the Syrians of Damascus came to help H.
22. 17 commanded all the princes of Israel to h.
2 Ch.14. 11 nothing with thee to help..help us, O Lo.
18. 31 Jehosaphat cried out, and the LORD hel.
19. 2 Shouldest thou help the ungodly, and lo.
20. 23 every one helped to destroy another
25. 8 for God hath power to help, and to cast
26. 7 God helped him against the Philistines
26. 13 made war..to help the king against the
28. 16 send unto the kings of Assyria to help him
28. 23 I sacrifice to them, that they may help me
32. 3 He took counsel..and they did help him
32. 8 but with us (is) the LORD our God to help
Ezra 8. 22 band of soldiers and horsemen to help us
10. 15 and Shabbethai the Levite helped them
Job 26. 2 How hast thou helped (him that is) with.
29. 12 delivered..(him that had) none to help
Psa. 22. 11 trouble (is) near; for (there is) none to h.
37. 40 LORD shall help them, and deliver them
46. 5 God shall help her, (and that) right early
79. 9 Help us, O God of our salvation, for the
86. 17 because thou, LORD, hast holpen me, and
107. 12 they fell down, and (there was) none to h.
109. 26 Help me, O LORD my God: O save me ac.
118. 7 taketh my part with th.. that help me
118. 13 Thou hast thrust..but the LORD helped
119. 86 they persecute me wrongfully; help thou
119. 173 Let thine hand help me: for I have cho.
119. 175 Let my soul live..let thy judgments help
Isa. 30. 7 the Egyptians shall help in vain, and to
31. 3 both he that helpeth shall fall, and he that
41. 6 They helped every one his neighbour; and
41. 10 I will strengthen thee; yea, I will help
41. 13 saying unto thee, Fear not; I will help
41. 14 I will help thee, saith the LORD, and thy
44. 2 Thus saith the LORD..(which) will help thee
49. 8 in a day of salvation have I helped thee
50. 7 the Lord GOD will help me; therefore
50. 9 Behold, the Lord GOD will help me; who
63. 5 I looked, and (there was) none to help
Lam. 1. 7 when her people fell..none did help her
Eze. 32. 21 the midst of hell with them that help him
Dan. 10. 13 Michael..came to help me; and I remain.
11. 45 come to his end, and none shall help him
Zech. 1. 15 and they helped forward the affliction
7. *To give help,* עָזַר *azar,* 5.
2 Ch.28. 23 the gods of the kings of Syria help them
8. *Help,* עֶזְרָה *ezrah (see under* **HELP,** No. 3).
2 Ch. 28 21 unto the king of Assyria: but he helped
9. *To call, cry,* קָרָא *qara.*
Psa. 59. 4 (my) fault: awake to help me, and behold
10. *Arm,* זְרוֹעַ *zeroa.*
Psa. 83. 8 they have holpen the children of Lot. Se.
11. *To take hold over again, assist,* ἀντιλαμβάνομαι.
Luke 1. 54 He hath holpen his servant Israel, in re.
12. *To help,* βοηθέω *boētheō.*
Matt15. 25 worshipped him, saying, Lord, help me
Mark 9. 22 have compassion on us, and help us
9. 24 Lord, I believe; help thou mine unbelief
Acts 16. 9 saying, Come over into Macedonia, and h.
21. 28 Crying out, Men of Israel, help: This is
Rev. 12. 16 the earth helped the woman; and the ear.
13. *With a view to help,* εἰς βοήθειαν *eis boētheian.*
Heb 4. 16 mercy, and find grace to help in time of
14. *To take hold at the same time,* συλλαμβάνω *sul.*
Luke 5. 7 that they should come and help them
Phil. 4. 3 help those women which laboured with
15. *To throw together, assist,* συμβάλλομαι *sumbal.*
Acts 18. 27 who..helped them much which had bel.
16. *To take hold with one,* συναντιλαμβάνομαι *sun.*
Luke10. 40 bid her therefore that she help me
Rom. 8. 26 the spirit also helpeth our infirmities
[*See* Lift up again.]

HELP together, to —
To work a little together, συνυπουργέω *sunupourgeō.*
2 Co. 1. 11 Ye also helping together by prayer for

HELP up, to —
To cause to rise up, קוּם *qum,* 5.
Deut22. 4 thou shalt surely help him to lift (them) up
Eccl. 4. 10 for (he hath) not another to help him up

HELP with, to —
To work with, or together, συνεργέω *sunergeō.*
1 Co.16. 16 and to every one that helpeth with (us)

HELPED, to be —
To be helped, עָזַר *azar,* 2.
1 Ch. 5. 20 they were helped against them, and the
2 Ch.26. 15 he was marvellously helped, till he was
Psa. 28. 7 my heart trusted in him, and I am helped
Dan.11. 34 they shall be holpen with a little help

HELPER, (fellow) —
1. *To help,* עָזַר *azar.*
2 Ki.14. 26 nor any left, nor any helper for Israel
1 Ch.12. 1 among the mighty men, helpers of the war
12. 18 unto thee, and peace (be) to thine helpers
Job 9. 13 the proud helpers do stoop under him
30. 13 they set forward..they have no helper
Psa. 10. 14 thou art the helper of the fatherless
30. 10 have mercy upon me: LORD, be thou my h.
54. 4 Behold, God (is) mine helper: the LORD (is)
72. 12 the poor also, and (him) that hath no helper
Jer. 47. 4 cut off from Tyrus and Zidon every helper
Eze. 30. 8 (when) all her helpers shall be destroyed
2. *Help,* עֶזְרָה *ezrah.*
Nah. 3. 9 Put and Lubim were thy helpers
3. *Helper,* βοηθός *boēthos.*
Heb.13. 6 we may boldly say, The Lord (is) my help.
4. *Fellow or joint worker,* συνεργός *sunergos.*
Rom16. 3 Greet Priscilla and Aquila my helpers
16. 9 Salute Urbane our helper in Christ, and
2 Co. 1. 24 but are helpers of your joy 8. 23; 3 Jo. 8.

HELPING —
1. *Safety,* יְשׁוּעָה *yeshuah.*
Psa. 22. 1 far from helping me..the words of my
2. *To support,* סְעַד *sead,* 5.
Ezra 5. 2 with them..the prophets of God helping

HELVE —
Wood, עֵץ *ets.*
Deut19. 5 the head slippeth from the helve, and

HEM —
1. *Hem, skirt, train,* שׁוּל *shul.*
Exod28. 33 upon the hem of it..round about the hem
28. 34 upon the hem of the robe round about
39. 24 they made upon the hems of the robe po.
39. 25 the pomegranates upon the hem of the
39. 26 round about the hem of the robe to min
2. *Border, hem,* κράσπεδον *kraspedon.*
Matt. 9. 20 and touched the hem of his garment
14. 36 they might only touch the hem of his ga.

HE'-MAM, הֵימָם *raging.*
A son of Lotan the eldest son of Seir. In 1 Ch. 1. 39 the name is given as *Homam,* the correct form; which see.
Gen. 36. 22 the children of Lotan were Hori and H.

HE'-MAN, הֵימָן *faithful.*
1. A son of Zerah the son of Jacob. B.C. 1640.
1 Ki. 4. 31 he was wiser than all men; than..H., and
1 Ch. 2. 6 the sons of Zerah..H., and Calcol, and D.
2. Son of Joel and grandson of Samuel the prophet, a Kohathite. He was called "the singer" (*i.e.* musician,) and was the first of the three chief Levites to whom was entrusted the conduct of the vocal and instrumental music of the sanctuary in David's time.
1 Ch. 6. 33 of the sons of the Kohathites; H. a singer
15. 17 So the Levites appointed H. the son of J.
15. 19 So the singers, H., Asaph, and Ethan
16. 41, 42 with them H. and Jeduthan, and the rest
25. 1 to the service of the sons of..H., and of
25. 4 Of H.: the sons of H.; Bukkiah, Mattan.
25. 5 All these (were) the sons of H. the king's
25. 5 God gave to H. fourteen sons and three
25. 6 according to the king's order to A...and H.
2 Ch. 5. 12 all of them..of H...arrayed in white linen
29. 14 of the sons of H.; Jehiel, and Shimei
35. 15 according to the command. of D...and H.
Psa. 88. *title.* Maschil of H. the Ezrahite

HE'-MATH, חַמַּת חֵמַת *warmth.*
1. Another form of the name *Hamath,* but not warranted by the Hebrew.
Amos 6. 14 afflict you from the entering in of H. unto
2. A person or place mentioned in the genealogical lists of Judah as the original of the Kenites and the father of the house of Rechab. Hebrew, *Hammath.*
1 Ch. 2. 55 These (are) the Kenites that came of H.

HEM'-DAN, חֶמְדָּן *pleasant.*
Eldest son of Dishon, son of Anah, the Horite. In 1 Ch. 1. 41 the name is *Hamran,* which in the Common Version is given as *Amram,* instead of *Chamran.* B.C. 1700.
Gen. 36. 26 children of Dishon; H., and Eshban, and

HEMLOCK —
1. *Wormwood,* לַעֲנָה *laanah.*
Amos 6. 12 the fruit of righteousness into hemlock

2. *Poisonous herb, venom,* רֹאשׁ *rosh.*
Hos. 10. 4 judgment springeth up as hemlock in the

HEN, חֵן *grace.*
A son of Zephaniah, apparently the same that is called *Josiah* in verse 10. B.C. 519.
Zech. 6. 14 the crowns shall be to..H. the son of

HEN —
Fowl, hen, ὄρνις *ornis.*
Matt 23. 37 as a hen gathereth her chickens under (h.)
Luke 13. 34 as a hen (doth gather) her brood under (h.)

HE'-NA, הֵנַע *low land.*
A chief city that had been reduced by the Assyrian kings shortly before the time of Sennacherib. On the Euphrates, not far from Sippara, now (*Mosiab*), is an ancient town called *Ana* or *Anah*, which is perhaps the site of the ancient *Hena.*
2 Ki. 18. 34 where (are) the gods of Sepharvaim, H.
19. 13 Where (is) the king of..Sepharvaim, of H.
Isa. 37. 13 Where (is) the king of..Sepharvaim, H.

HE-NA'-DAD, חֵנָדָד *Hadad is gracious.*
The head of a Levite family that aided in rebuilding the temple under Jeshua. B.C. 480.
Ezra 3. 9 sons of H...their sons and their brethren
Neh. 3. 18 After him repaired..Bavai the son of H.
3. 24 After him repaired Binnui the son of H.
10. 9 the Levites..Binnui of the sons of H., K.

HENCE, (from) —
1. *From this,* מִזֶּה *miz-zeh.*
Gen. 37. 17 the man said, They are departed hence
2. *From this or that place,* ἐντεῦθεν *enteuthen.*
Matt. 17. 20 shall say unto this mountain, Remove [h.]
Luke 13. 31 Get thee out, and depart hence; 4. 9; 16. 26.
John 2. 16 Take these things hence; make not my
7. 3 said unto him, Depart hence, and go into
14. 31 that the world..let us go hence, 18. 36.
Jas. 4. 1 (come they) not hence, (even) of your lusts
3. *After these,* μετὰ ταύτας *meta tautas.*
Acts 1. 5 with the Holy Ghost not many days hence
[*See also* Get, from.]

HENCEFORTH —
1. *Yet, still,* עוֹד *od.*
Num 18. 22 Neither must the children of Israel hence.
2. *Now,* עַתָּה *attah.*
2 Ch. 16. 9 from henceforth thou shalt have wars
3. *To add, cause to add,* יָסַף *yasaph,* 5.
Gen. 4. 12 it shall not henceforth yield unto thee
4. *From now,* ἀπ' ἄρτι *ap arti.*
Matt 23. 39 Ye shall not see me henceforth, till ye
26. 29 I will not drink henceforth of this Jo. 14. 7.
5. *What is left, remainder,* λοιπόν *loipon.*
2 Ti. 4. 8 Henceforth there is laid up for me a cro.
6. *No more, not again,* μηκέτι *mēketi.*
Acts 4. 17 speak henceforth to no man in this name
7. *Now,* τὸ νῦν *to nun.*
Luke 1. 48 behold, from henceforth all generations
5. 10 Fear not; from henceforth thou shalt cat.
12. 52 from henceforth there shalt be five in one
Acts 18. 6 from henceforth I will go unto the Gentiles
2 Co. 5. 16 henceforth know we no man after the flesh

HENCEFORTH...no more —
No longer, οὐκέτι *ouketi.*
2 Co. 5. 16 yet now henceforth know we (him) no more

HENCEFORTH, from —
1. *From now,* ἀπάρτι *aparti.*
Rev. 14. 13 which die in the Lord [from henceforth]
2. *What is left, remainder,* τοῦ λοιποῦ, τὸ λοιπόν.
Gal. 6. 17 From henceforth let no man trouble me
Heb. 10. 13 From henceforth expecting till his enemies

HENCEFORTH...not —
1. *No more, not again,* μηκέτι *mēketi.*
Rom. 6. 6 that henceforth we should not serve sin
2 Co. 5. 15 should not henceforth live unto themsel.
Eph. 4. 17 that ye henceforth walk not as other Gent.
2. *No more, not again,* οὐκέτι *ouketi.*
John 15. 15 Henceforth I call you not servants; for

HENCEFORWARD —
1. *Yonder, beyond, henceforth,* הָלְאָה *haleah.*
Num 15. 23 and henceforward among your generations
2. *No more, not again,* μηκέτι *mēketi*; Matt. 21. 19.

HENOCH. *See* **ENOCH** *and* **HANOCH.**

HE'-PHER, חֵפֶר *a digging, a well.*
1. The youngest son of Gilead, and head of the family of the Hepherites. B.C. 1600. Hepher was the father of Zelophehad whose daughters first raised the question of the right of a woman having no brother to hold her father's property.
Num 26. 32 and (of) H., the family of the 26. 33.
27. 1 the daughters of Zelophehad, the son of H.
Josh 17. 2 There was also (a lot) for..children of H.
17. 3 Zelophehad, the son of H...had no sons
2. The second son of Naarah one of Ashur's two wives. Tekoa was founded by Ashur in Judah's genealogy. B.C. 1500.
1 Ch. 4. 6 Naarah bare him Ahuzam, and H., and T.
3. A Mecherathite, one of the thirty heroes of David's guard. B.C. 1048.
1 Ch. 11. 36 H. the Mecherathite, Ahijah the Pelonite
4. A royal city of the Canaanites on the W. of the Jordan; so also was the "land of Hepher," one of Solomon's commissariat districts. It lay below Dor, near Sochoh, to the S. of the centre of Palestine.
Josh. 12. 17 The king of Tappuah, one; the king of H.
1 Ki. 4. 10 to him..Sochoh, and all the land of H.

HE-PHER-ITES, חֶפְרִי *belonging to Chepher.*
The family of Hepher son of Gilead.
Num 26. 32 and (of) Hepher, the family of the H.

HEPH-ZI'-BAH, חֶפְצִי־בָהּ *my delight is in her.*
1. The wife of Hezekiah and mother of Manasseh king of Judah. B.C. 710.
2 Ki. 21. 1 Manasseh..his mother's name (was) H.
2. A name to be borne by Jerusalem when restored.
Isa. 62. 4 thou shalt be called H., and thy land B.

HER —
1. *Soul, breath, desire,* נֶפֶשׁ *nephesh.*
Jer. 2. 24 snuffeth up the wind at her pleasure
2. *He, she, it,* αὐτός *autos.*
Matt. 1. 20 that which is conceived in her is of the Holy
3. *He, she, it,* αὐτός (*gen.*) *autos.*
Matt. 1. 25 she had brought forth her first born son
2. 18 Rachel weeping (for) her children, and
11. 19 But wisdom is justified of her children
14. 8 she, being before instructed of her mother
14. 11 the damsel: and she brought (it) to her
20. 20 the mother of Zebedee's children with her
24. 29 and the moon shall not give her light, and
Mark 6. 24 she went forth, and said unto her mother
6. 28 and the damsel gave it to her mother
7. 26 would cast forth the devil out of her daugh.
7. 30 when she was come to her house, she found
10. 12 if a woman shall put away her husband
12. 44 she of her want did cast..(even) all her
13. 24 and the moon shall not give her light
13. 28 When her branch is yet tender, and putteth
Luke 1. 36 hath also conceived a son in her old age
2. 7 she brought forth her first born son, and
2. 19 Mary kept..and pondered (them) in her
2. 36 had lived..seven years from her virginity
2. 51 his mother kept all these sayings in her he.
7. 35 But wisdom is justified of all her children
7. 38, 44 wipe (them) with the hairs of her head
10. 38 woman named Martha received him into h.
12. 53 mother in law against her daughter in law
12. 53 daughter in law against her mother in law
21. 4 but she of her penury hath cast in all
John 4. 28 The woman then left her water pot, and
11. 2 wiped his feet with her hair, whose brot.
11. 28 called Mary her sister secretly, saying
12. 3 wiped his feet with her hair: and the ho.
Acts 9. 40 she opened her eyes: and when she saw P.
16. 16 which brought her masters much gain by
Gal. 4. 25 now is, and is in bondage with her children
Jas. 5. 18 and the earth brought forth her fruit
Rev. 2. 21 I gave..to repent of her fornication; and
6. 13 even as a fig tree casteth her untimely figs
12. 14 fly into the wilderness, into her place, w.
12. 16 the earth opened her mouth, and swallow.
14. 8 the wine of the wrath of her fornication
17. 4 cup in her hand full of..her fornication
17. 5 And upon her forehead (was) a name wr.
18. 7 for she saith in her heart, I sit a queen
19. 2 did corrupt the earth with her fornication
21. 2 prepared as a bride adorned for her husba.
22. 2 yielded her fruit every month: and the
4. *This one,* οὗτος (*acc.*) *houtos,* ταύτην.
Rev. 12. 15 cause her to be carried away of the flood

HER, as for —
She, הִיא *hi.*
Eze. 30. 18 as for her, a cloud shall cover her, and her

HER own (self) —
1. *He, she, it,* αὐτός (*gen.*) *autos.*
Luke 1. 56 three months, and returned to her own h.
2. *Of himself, one's own,* ἑαυτοῦ *heautou.*
Acts 7. 21 took him up, and nourished him for her own
Matt. 9. 21; 23. 37; Luke 13. 34; 1 Co. 11. 5; 1 Th. 2. 7

HERALD —
Crier, herald, כָּרוֹז *karoz.*
Dan. 3. 4 Then an herald cried aloud, To you it is c.

HERB —
1. *Shining herb,* אוֹרָה *orah.*
2 Ki. 4. 39 went out into the field to gather herbs
Isa. 26. 19 for thy dew (is as) the dew of herbs, and
2. *Shining herb,* אוֹר *or.*
Isa. 18. 4 like a clear heat upon herbs, (and) like a
3. *Grass, tender grass,* דֶּשֶׁא *deshe.*
2 Ki. 19. 26 (as) the green herb, (as) the grass on the h.
Psa. 37. 2 For they shall..wither as the green herb
Isa. 37. 27 they were..(as) the green herb, (as) the
66. 14 and your bones shall flourish like an herb
4. *Hay, grass,* חָצִיר *chatsir.*
Job 8. 12 it withereth before any (other) herb
5. *Green herb,* יָרָק *yaraq.*
Deut 11. 10 sowed thy seed..as a garden of herbs
1 Ki. 21. 2 that I may have it for a garden of herbs
Prov. 15. 17 Better (is) a dinner of herbs where love is
6. *Herb,* עֵשֶׂב *eseb.*
Gen. 1. 11 the herb yielding seed, (and) the fruit tree
1. 12 herb yielding seed after his kind, and
1. 29 I have given you every herb bearing seed
1. 30 (I have given) every green herb for meat
2. 5 and every herb of the field before it grew
3. 18 and thou shalt eat the herb of the field
9. 3 even as the green herb have I given you
Exod. 9. 22 upon every herb of the field, throughout
9. 25 the hail smote every herb of the field, and
10. 12 eat every herb of the land, (even) all that
10. 15 they did eat every herb of the land, and
10. 15 or in the herbs of the field, through all the
Psa. 104. 14 herb for the service of man: that he may
105. 35 did eat up all the herbs in their land
Prov 27. 25 and herbs of the mountains are gathered
Isa. 42. 15 I will..dry up all their herbs; and I
Jer. 12. 4 How long shall..the herbs of every field
7. *Herbage, grass,* βοτάνη *botanē.*
Heb. 6. 7 bringeth forth herbs meet for them by
8. *Garden herbs,* λάχανον *lachanon.*
Matt 13. 32 it is the greatest among herbs, and beco.
Mark 4. 32 becometh greater than all herbs, and sho.
Luke 11. 42 tithe mint and rue, and all manner of he.
Rom. 14. 2 another, who is weak, eateth herbs

HERB, tender —
Tender grass, דֶּשֶׁא *deshe.*
Deut 32. 2 as the small rain upon the tender herb, and
Job 38. 27 and to cause the bud of the tender herb

HERD —
1. *Oxen, herd, cattle,* בָּקָר *baqar.*
Gen. 13. 5 Lot also..had flocks, and herds, and tents
18. 7 Abraham ran unto the herd, and fetched a
24. 35 he hath given him flocks, and herds, and
26. 14 For he had..possession of herds, and great
32. 7 he divided..the flocks, and herds, and the
33. 13 the flocks and herds with young (are) with
45. 10 thy flocks, and thy herds, and all that thou
46. 32 they have brought..their herds, and all
47. 1 their herds..are come out of the land of
47. 17 for the cattle of the herds, and for the asses
50. 8 their herds, they left in the land of Goshen
Exod. 10. 9 with our flocks and with our herds will
10. 24 let your flocks and your herds be stayed
12. 32 take your flocks and your herds, as ye
12. 38 and flocks and herds, (even) very much
34. 3 neither let..herds feed before that moun.
Lev. 1. 2 ye shall bring your offering..of the herd
1. 3 offering (be) a burnt sacrifice of the herd
3. 1 if he offer (it) of the herd; whether (it be)
27. 32 concerning the tithe of the herd, or of the
Num. 11. 22 Shall the flocks and the herds be slain
15. 3 a sweet savour unto the LORD, of the herd
Deut. 8. 13 (when) thy herds and thy flocks multiply
12. 6 ye shall bring..firstlings of your herds
12. 17 mayest not eat..firstlings of thy herds
12. 21 thou shalt kill of thy herd and of thy
14. 23 thou shalt eat..firstlings of thy herds
15. 19 the firstling males that come of thy herd
16. 2 Thou shalt therefore sacrifice..the herd
1 Sa. 11. 5 Saul came after the herd out of the field
30. 20 David took all the flocks and the herds
2 Sa. 12. 2 The rich (man) had exceeding many..he.
12. 4 and he spared to take of..his own herd
1 Ch. 27. 29 over the herds..and over the herds (that
2 Ch. 32. 29 he provided him..herds in abundance; for
Isa. 65. 10 the valley of Achor a place for the herds
Jer. 3. 24 For shame hath devoured..their herds
5. 17 they shall eat up thy flocks and..herds
31. 12 for the young of the flock and of the herd
Hos. 5. 6 shall go with their flocks and..herds
Jon. 3. 7 Let neither..herd nor flock, taste any thing
Hab. 3. 17 and (there shall be) no herd in the stalls
2. *Acquisition, possession,* מִקְנֶה *miqneh.*
Gen. 47. 18 my lord also hath our herds of cattle
3. *Flock, drove, herd,* עֵדֶר *eder.*
Prov. 27. 23 Be thou diligent..look well to thy herds
Joel 1. 18 the herds of cattle are perplexed, because
4. *Herd, drove,* ἀγέλη *agelē.*
Matt. 8. 30 there was a good way off from them an h.
8. 31 suffer us to go away into the herd of swine
8. 32 they went into the [herd of] swine: and
8. 32 the whole herd of swine ran violently down
Mark 5. 11 there was there..a great herd of swine
5. 13 the herd ran violently down a steep place
Luke 8. 32 And there was there an herd of many sw.
8. 33 the herd ran violently down a steep place

HERDMAN —
1. *Herdman,* בּוֹקֵר *boqer.*
Amos 7. 14 but I (was) an herdman, and a gatherer of
2. *Herdman, sheep master,* נֹקֵד *noqed.*
Amos 1. 1 Amos, who was among the herdmen of T.
3. *To feed,* רָעָה *raah.*
Gen. 13. 7 the herdmen of Abram's..and the herd.
13. 8 between my herdmen and thy herdmen
26. 20 the herdmen..did strive with..herdmen
1 Sa. 21. 7 an Edomite, the chiefest of the herdmen

HERE —
1. *Here, now,* אֵפוֹא, אֵפוֹ *epho.*
Exod 33. 16 wherein shall it be known here that I and
2. *Here, hither,* הֲלֹם *halom.*
Gen. 16. 13 Have I also here looked after him that
Judg 20. 7 ye (are) all children of Israel; give here

3. *Here, hither,* הֵנָּה *henah.*
Gen. 21. 23 therefore swear unto me here by God
4. *In this (place),* בָּזֶה, בָּזֶה *baz-zeh, ba-zeh.*
Exod 24. 14 Tarry ye here for us, until we come again
1 Sa. 21. 9 take (it)..(there is) no other save that h.
5. *Thus, here, now,* כֹּה *koh.*
Gen. 31. 37 set (it) here before my brethren and thy
Num 23. 15 he said unto Balak, Stand here by thy
2 Sa. 18. 30 said (unto him), Turn aside, (and) stand h.
6. *Here,* פֹּא *po.*
Job 38. 11 and here shall thy proud waves be stayed
7. *Here,* פּוֹ *po,* פֹּה *poh.*
Gen. 19. 12 said unto Lot, Hast thou here any besides?
Isa. 22. 16 hast thou here, and whom hast thou here
22. 16 thou hast hewed thee out a sepulchre h.
8. *Here, there,* αὐτοῦ *autou.*
Matt 26. 36 saith unto the disciples, Sit ye here, while
9. *Hither, here,* ἐνθάδε *enthade.*
Luke 24. 41 he said unto them, Have ye here any m.?
Acts 16. 28 Do thyself no harm; for we are all here
25. 24 both at Jerusalem, and (also) here, crying
10. *Here,* ὧδε *hōde.*
Matt 12. 41 and, behold, a greater than Jonas (is) he.
12. 42 and, behold, a greater than Solomon (is) h.
14. 8 said, Give me here John Baptist's head
14. 17 they say unto him, We have here but five
16. 28 I say unto you, There be some standing h.
17. 4 to be here: if thou wilt, let us make here
20. 6 saith..Why stand ye here all the day idle?
24. 2 There shall not be left here one stone
24. 23 if any man shall say unto you, Lo, here
26. 38 Then saith he unto them..tarry ye here
28. 6 He is not here; for he is risen, as he said
Mark 6. 3 are not his sisters here with us? And they
8. 4 can a man satisfy these..with bread here
9. 1 That there be some of them that stand h.
9. 5 Master, it is good for us to be here: and
13. 21 if any man shall say to you, Lo, here (is)
14. 32 and he saith to his disciples, Sit ye here
14. 34 And saith unto them..tarry ye here, and
16. 6 he is risen; he is not here: behold the
Luke 4. 23 whatsoever we have heard..do also here
9. 12 Send the multitude away..for we are here
9. 27 of a truth, there be some standing [here]
9. 33 Master, it is good for us to be here: and let
11. 31 and, behold, a greater than Solomon (is) h.
11. 32 and, behold, a greater than Jonas (is) here
17. 21 Neither shall they say, Lo here! or, lo there!
17. 23 they shall say to you, See here! or, see there
22. 38 they said, Lord, behold, here (are) two swo.
24. 6 He is not here, but is risen: remember how
John 6. 9 There is a lad here, which hath five barley
11. 21 Lord, if thou hadst been here, my brother
11. 32 Lord, if thou hadst been here, my brother
Acts 9. 14 And here he hath authority from the chief
Col. 4. 9 They shall make known unto you..here
Heb. 7. 8 And here men that die receive tithes; but
13. 14 For here have we no continuing city, but
Jas. 2. 3 Sit thou [here] in a good place..or sit here
Rev. 13. 10 Here is the patience and the faith of the
13. 18 Here is wisdom. Let him that hath under.
14. 12 Here is the patience of the saints: [here]
17. 9 And here (is) the mind which hath wisdom
[*See* Have, present, stand.]

HERE, to be —
1. *To be found,* מָצָא *matsa,* 2.
Gen. 19. 15 take..thy two daughters, which are here
2. *To be beside, present,* πάρειμι *pareimi.*
Acts 24. 19 Who ought to have been here before thee

HERE present, to be —
To be beside, present, πάρειμι *pareimi.*
Acts 10. 33 therefore are we all here present before G.

HERE, to be all —
To be finished, done, תָּמַם *tamam.*
1 Sa. 16. 11 Samuel said unto Jesse, Are here all (thy)

HERE and there, to be —
To be sprinkled, זָרַק *zaraq.*
Hos. 7. 9 yea, grey hairs are here and there upon him

HEREAFTER —
1. *Behind, backward,* אָחוֹר *achor.*
Isa. 41. 23 Show the things that are to come hereafter
2. *Behind, last, furthest,* אַחַר *achar.*
Eze. 20. 39 serve ye every one his idols, and hereafter
3. *After this,* אַחֲרֵי דְנָה *achare den.*
Dan. 2. 29 what should come to pass hereafter; and he
2. 45 what shall come to pass hereafter: and
4. *From now, henceforth,* ἀπ' ἄρτι *ap arti.*
Matt 26. 64 Jesus saith..Hereafter shall ye see the
John 1. 52 I say unto you, [Hereafter] ye shall see
5. *Yet, still,* ἔτι *eti.*
John 14. 30 Hereafter I will not talk much with you
6. *No more, yet again,* μηκέτι *mēketi.*
Mark 11. 14 No man eat fruit of thee hereafter for ever
7. *From now, henceforth,* ἀπὸ τοῦ νῦν *apo tou nun.*
Luke 22. 69 Hereafter shall the Son of man sit on the
8. *After these,* μετὰ ταῦτα *meta tauta.*
John 13. 7 not now; but thou shalt know hereafter
Rev. 1. 19 and the things which shall be hereafter
4. 1 show thee things which must be hereafter
9. 12 behold, there come two woes more hereaf.

HEREBY —
1. *In or by this,* בְּזֹאת *be-zoth.*
Gen. 42. 15 Hereby ye shall be proved: By the life of
2. *Out of this,* ἐκ τούτου *ek toutou.*
1 Jo. 4. 6 Hereby know we the spirit of truth, and
3. *In this,* ἐν τούτῳ *en toutō.*
1 Co. 4. 4 yet am I not hereby justified: but he that
1 Jo. 2. 3 hereby we do know that we know him
2. 5 whoso keepeth his word..hereby know we
3. 16 Hereby perceive we the love (of God), bec.
3. 19 hereby we know that we are of the truth
3. 24 hereby we know that he abideth in us
4. 2 Hereby know ye the spirit of God. Every
4. 13 Hereby know we that we dwell in him, and

HEREIN —
1. *In or by this,* בְּזֹאת *be-zoth.*
Gen. 34. 22 Only herein will the men consent unto us
2. *In this,* ἐν τούτῳ *en toutō.*
John 4. 37 herein is that saying true, One soweth, and
9. 30 herein is a marvellous thing, that ye know
15. 8 Herein is my Father glorified, that ye bear
Acts 24. 16 herein do I exercise myself, to have always
2 Co. 8. 10 herein I give (my) advice: for this is expe.
1 Jo. 4. 10 Herein is love, not that we loved God, but
4. 17 Herein is our love made perfect, that we

HEREOF —
1. *This,* αὕτη *hautē.*
Matt. 9. 26 fame hereof went abroad into all that land
2. *This,* οὗτος *(acc.) houtos.*
Heb. 5. 3 by reason hereof he ought, as for the peo.

HE'-RES, חֶרֶס *heat, sun.*
Mount Heres near Aijalon on the borders of Judah and Dan, inhabited by Amorites.
Judg. 1. 35 the Amorites would dwell in mount H. in

HE'-RESH, חֶרֶשׁ *work, silence.*
The head of a Levite family and attached to the staff of the tabernacle. B.C. 445.
1 Ch. 9. 15 Bakbakkar, H., and Galal, and Mattan.

HERESY —
Choice, opinion, sentiment, αἵρεσις *hairesis.*
Acts 24. 14 that after the way which they call heresy
1 Co. 11. 19 For there must be also heresies among you
Gal. 5. 20 variance..wrath, strife, seditions, heresies
2 Pe. 2. 1 privily shall bring in damnable heresies

HERETIC, that is an —
Opinionative person, heretic, αἱρετικός *hairetikos.*
Titus 3. 10 A man that is an heretic after the first and

HERETOFORE —
1. *Yesterday,* תְּמוֹל *temol.*
Exod. 4. 10 I (am) not eloquent, neither heretofore
5. 7 straw to make brick, as heretofore: let
5. 8 bricks, which they did make heretofore
5. 14 both yesterday and to day, as heretofore?
Josh. 3. 4 ye have not passed (this) way heretofore
Ruth 2. 11 people which thou knewest not heretofore
2. *Yesterday, third day,* אֶתְמוֹל שִׁלְשֹׁם *ethmol shilshom.*
1 Sa. 4. 7 there hath not been such a thing heretofore

HEREUNTO —
With a view to this, εἰς τοῦτο *eis touto.*
1 Pe. 2. 21 hereunto were ye called; because Christ

HEREWITH —
In, by, or with this, בְּזֹאת, בְּזֹאת *ba-zoth, be-zoth.*
Eze. 16. 29 and yet thou wast not satisfied herewith
Mal. 3. 10 prove me now herewith, saith the LORD

HERITAGE —
1. *Possession,* יְרֻשָּׁה *yerushshah.*
Psa. 61. 5 thou hast given (me) the heritage of those
2. *Possession,* מוֹרָשָׁה *morashah.*
Exod. 6. 8 I will give it you for an heritage: I (am)
3. *Inheritance,* נַחֲלָה *nachalah.*
Job 20. 29 the heritage appointed unto him by God
27. 13 the heritage of oppressors, (which) they
Psa. 94. 5 They break..and afflict thine heritage
111. 6 that he may give them the heritage of the
127. 3 Lo, children (are) an heritage of the LORD
135. 12 their land (for) an heritage, an heritage
136. 21 And gave their land for an heritage: for
136. 22 an heritage unto Israel his servant: for
Isa. 49. 8 cause to inherit the desolate heritages
54. 17 This (is) the heritage of the servants of the
58. 14 feed thee with the heritage of Jacob thy
Jer. 2. 7 and made mine heritage an abomination
3. 19 give thee..a goodly heritage of the hosts
12. 7 I have left mine heritage; I have given
12. 8 Mine heritage is unto me as a lion in the
12. 9 Mine heritage (is) unto me (as) a speckled
12. 15 will bring..every man to his heritage, and
17. 4 shalt discontinue from thine heritage
50. 11 O ye destroyers of mine heritage, because
Joel 2. 17 and give not thine heritage to reproach
3. 2 for my people and (for) my heritage Israel
Mic. 2. 2 they oppress..even a man and his heritage
7. 14 the flock of thine heritage, which dwell
7. 18 transgression of the remnant of his herit.
Mal. 1. 3 laid his mountains and his heritage waste
4. *Inheritance,* נַחֲלַת *nachalath.*
Psa. 16. 6 lines are fallen..yea, I have a goodly he.
5. *Lot, allotment,* κλῆρος *klēros.*
1 Pe. 5. 3 Neither as being lords over (God's) herit.

HERITAGE, to take as an —
To have, take or give inheritance, נָחַל *nachal.*
Psa. 119. 111 testimonies have I taken as an heritage

HER'-MAS, Ἑρμᾶς *Mercury, interpreter.*
A person to whom Paul sends greeting in his epistle to the Romans. The name is Greek, as well as the other four mentioned in the verse.
Rom 16. 14 Salute..H., Patrobas, Hermes, and the

HER'-MES, Ἑρμῆς *Mercury, interpreter.*
A Christian Greek in Rome to whom Paul sends salutation.
Rom 16. 14 Salute..Hermas, Patrobas, H., and the

HER-MO-GE'-NES, Ἑρμογένης.
A person who had turned away from Paul in his latest extremities.
2 Ti. 1. 15 turned away..of whom are Phygel. and H.

HER'-MON, חֶרְמוֹן *prominent, rugged.*
A mountain in the N. eastern border of Palestine, over against Lebanon, adjoining the table-land of Bashan. It stands at the southern end, and is the culminating point of the range of Antilibanus, towering high above the ancient city of Dan and the sources of the Jordan. It still retains its name *Harmun* or *Hermun*. The Amorites called it *Shenir*, and the Zidonians *Sirion*. In Deut. 4. 48 it is called *Sion*, which must not be confounded with *Zion* (Zi-yŏn).
Deut. 3. 8 from the river of Arnon unto mount H.
3. 9 (Which) H. the Sidonians call Sirion, and
4. 48 Aroer..unto mount Sion, which (is) H.
Josh 11. 3 the Hivite under H. in the land of Mizpeh
11. 17 in the valley of Lebanon, under mount H.
12. 1 from the river Arnon unto mount H., and
12. 5 reigned in mount H., and in Salcah, and in
13. 5 from Baal-gad under mount H. unto the
13. 11 all mount H., and all Bashan unto Salcah
1 Ch. 5. 23 increased from Bashan..unto mount H.
Psa. 89. 12 Tabor and H. shall rejoice in thy name
133. 3 As the dew of H...that descended upon
Song 4. 8 look..from the top of Shenir and H., from

HER-MO-NITES, חֶרְמוֹנִים.
The inhabitants at the N. of Naphtali and Manasseh on Mount Hermon.
Psa. 42. 6 I remember thee from the land..of the H.

HE'-ROD, Ἡρώδης.
1. Son of Antipater, procurator of Judea under Julius Cæsar and king under Augustus, and was designated Herod the Great. B.C. 47—A.D. 2.
Matt. 2. 1 Jesus was born..in the days of H. the king
2. 3 When H. the king had heard..he was tro.
2. 7 Then H...enquired of them diligently wh.
2. 12 warned..that they should not return to H.
2. 13 H. will seek the young child to destroy
2. 15 And was there until the death of H.: that
2. 16 Then H...slew all the children that were
2. 19 when H. was dead..an angel..appeareth
2. 22 did reign..in the room of his father H., he
Luke 1. 5 There was, in the days of H...a certain pr.
2. Herod Antipas, son of Herod the Great by Malthace, a Samaritan, became tetrarch of Galilee and Peræa: but banished, A.D. 41.
Matt 14. 1 At that time H. the tetrarch heard of
14. 3 H. had laid hold on John, and bound him
14. 6 But when H.'s birthday was kept
14. 6 the daughter of Herodias..pleased H.
Mark 6. 14 king H. heard..and he said, That John
6. 16 when H. heard..he said, It is John, whom
6. 17 H. himself had sent forth and laid hold
6. 18 John had said unto H., It is not lawful for
6. 20 H. feared John, knowing that he was a
6. 21 H., on his birthday, made a supper to his
6. 22 daughter of the said Herodias..pleased H.
8. 15 Take heed, beware of the leaven..of H.
Luke 3. 1 and H. being tetrarch of Galilee, and his
3. 19 H. the tetrarch, being reproved by him for
3. 19 and for all the evils which H. had done
8. 3 Joanna the wife of Chuza H.'s steward, and
9. 7 H. the tetrarch heard of all that was done
9. 9 And H. said, John have I beheaded: but
13. 31 Get thee out, and depart hence: for H. will
23. 7 soon as he knew that he belonged unto H.'s
23. 7 he sent him to H., who himself also was
23. 8 when H. saw Jesus, he was exceeding glad
23. 11 H. with his men of war set him at nought
23. 12 Pilate and H. were made friends together
23. 15 No, nor yet H.: for I sent you to him; and
Acts 4. 27 both H...and the people of Israel, were
13. 1 Manaen..had been brought up with H.
3. The grandson of Herod the Great, and the son of Aristobulus and Berenice. He was Herod Agrippa I. In A.D. 37 Caligula gave him the governments of the tetrarchs Philip and Lysanias with other marks of royal favour. He died, A.D. 44.
Acts 12. 1 H. the king stretched forth..hands to vex
12. 6 And when H. would have brought him forth
12. 11 hath delivered me out of the hand of H.
12. 19 when H. had sought for him, and found h
12. 20 [H.] was highly displeased with them of
12. 21 H., arrayed in royal apparel, sat upon his
23. 35 commanded him to be kept in H.'s judg.

HE-RO-DI-ANS, Ἡρωδιανοί.
A political Jewish party that favoured Greek customs.
Matt 22. 16 sent out unto him their disciples with the H.
Mark 3. 6 the Pharisees..took counsel with the H.
12. 13 they send unto him certain of the..H., to

HE-RO-DI'-AS, 'Ηρωδιάς.
A daughter of Aristobulus, son of Herod the Great. She was married to her uncle, Philip, but left him for his brother Herod the tetrarch of Galilee.
Matt 14. 3 and put (him) in prison for H.'s sake, his
14. 6 the daughter of H. danced before them, and
Mark 6. 17 bound him in prison for H.'s sake, his bro.
6. 19 Therefore H. had a quarrel against him
6. 22 when the daughter of the said H. came in
Luke 3. 19 being reproved by him for H. his brother

HE-RO-DI'-ON, 'Ηρωδίων.
A Christian of Rome and a kinsman of Paul.
Rom 16. 11 Salute [H.] my kinsman. Greet them that

HERON —
Heron, אֲנָפָה *anaphah.*
Lev. 11. 19 the heron after her kind, and the lapwing
Deut 14. 18 the heron after her kind, and the lapwing

HERSELF —
1. *Soul, self, breath*, נֶפֶשׁ *nephesh.*
Isa. 5. 14 hell hath enlarged herself, and opened
2. *Self*, ἑαυτοῦ *heautou.*
Matt. 9. 21 said within herself, If I may but touch
Luke 1. 24 Elizabeth conceived, and hid herself five
Rev. 2. 20 which calleth herself a prophetess, to te.
18. 7 How much she hath glorified [herself] 19.7
3. *Spontaneously*, αὐτόματος *automatos*; Mk. 4. 28.

HE'-SED, חֶסֶד *kindness.*
The Father of one of Solomon's commissariat officers, in Aruboth, in Judah. B.C. 1015.
1 Ki. 4. 10 The son of H., in Aruboth; to him (perta.)

HESH'-BON, חֶשְׁבּוֹן *stronghold.*
A Levitical city of Reuben and Gad. It first belonged to Moab and then to Ammon, and was N. of the lower part of the Arnon. The ruins of *Hesbân*, twenty miles E. of the Jordan on the parallel of the N. end of the Dead Sea mark the site.
Num 21. 25 Israel dwelt in..H., and in all the villages
21. 26 H. (was) the city of Sihon the king of the
21. 27 Come into H., let the city of Sihon be built
21. 28 For there is a fire gone out of H., a flame
21. 30 H. is perished even unto Dibon, and we
21. 34 do to him as thou didst unto Sihon..at H.
32. 3 H., and Elealeh, and Shebam, and Nebo
32. 37 the children of Reuben built H., and Ele.
Deut. 1. 4 After he had slain S...which dwelt in H.
2. 24 I have given into thine hand S..king of H.
2. 26 I sent messengers..unto Sihon king of H.
2. 30 Sihon king of H. would not let us pass by
3. 2 as thou didst unto S..which dwelt at H.
3. 6 as we did unto Sihon king of H., utterly
4. 46 in the land of Sihon..who dwelt at H.
29. 7 Sihon the king of H...came out against us
Josh. 9. 10 all that he did to..Sihon king of H., and
12. 2 S. king of the Amorites, who dwelt in H.
12. 5 Gilead, the border of Sihon king of H.
13. 10 all the cities of Sihon..which reigned in H.
13. 17 H., and all her cities that (are) in the plain
13. 21 kingdom of Sihon..which reigned in H.
13. 26 from H. unto Ramath-mizpeh, and Beto.
13. 27 rest of the kingdom of Sihon king of H.
21. 39 H. with her suburbs, Jazer with her sub.
Judg 11. 19 sent messengers unto Sihon..king of H.
11. 26 While Israel dwelt in H. and her towns
1 Ch. 6. 81 H. with her suburbs, and Jazer with her
Neh. 9. 22 they possessed..the land of the king of H.
Song 7. 4 thine eyes (like) the fishpools in H., by the
Isa. 15. 4 H. shall cry, and Elealeh: their voice shall
16. 8 the fields of H. languish..the vine of Sib.
16. 9 I will water thee with my tears, O H., and
Jer. 48. 2 in H. they have devised evil against it
48. 34 From the cry of H...unto Elealeh..unto
48. 45 they that fled stood under the shadow of H.
48. 45 a fire shall come forth out of H., and a fl.
49. 3 Howl, O H., for Ai is spoiled: cry, ye da.

HESH'-MON, חֶשְׁמוֹן *fruitfulness.*
A town in the extreme south of Judah, between Moladah and Beersheba. It is perhaps the same as *Azmon* (Num. 34. 4).
Josh 15. 27 Hazar-gaddah, and H., and Beth-palet

HETH, חֵת *terrible.*
A second son of Canaan, ancestor of the Hittites. B.C. 2200.
Gen. 10. 15 Canaan begat Sidon his first born, and H.
23. 3 Abraham..spake unto the sons of H., say.
23. 5 the children of H. answered Abraham, say.
23. 7 Abraham..bowed..to the children of H.
23. 10 Ephron dwelt among the children of H.
23. 10 in the audience of the children of H.
23. 16 had named in..audience of the sons of H.
23. 18 in the presence of the children of H. 25. 10.
23. 20 made sure unto Abraham..by..sons of H.
27. 46 I am weary..because of..daughters of H.
27. 46 if Jacob take a wife of the daughters of H.
49. 32 purchase..(was) from the children of H.
1 Ch. 1. 13 Canaan begat Zidon his first born, and H.

HETH'-LON, חֶתְלֹן *lurking place, stronghold.*
A place in the northern border of the promised land. The "way of Hethlon" is the pass at the N. end of Lebanon from the coast of the Mediterranean to the great plain of Hamath, and is hence identical with the "entrance of Hamath" (Num. 34. 8, &c.)
Eze. 47. 15 great sea, the way of H., as men go to Z.
48. 1 north end to the coast of the way of H.

HEW, to —
1. *To cut, hew, carve*, חָטַב *chatab.*
Deut 19. 5 into the wood with his neighbour to hew
2. *To hew, dig*, חָצַב *chatseb.*
1 Ch. 22. 2 and he set masons to hew wrought stones
2 Ch. 2. 2 and fourscore thousand to hew in the
Prov. 9. 1 she hath hewn out her seven pillars
Isa. 10. 15 against him that heweth therewith
Jer. 2. 13 hewed them out cisterns, broken cisterns
Hos. 6. 5 Therefore have I hewed (them) by the pro.
3. *To cut (off or down)*, כָּרַת *karath.*
1 Ki. 5. 6 they hew me cedar..can skill to hew ti.
Jer. 6. 6 the LORD of hosts said, Hew ye down tr.
4. *To grave*, פָּסַל *pasal.*
Exod 34. 1 the LORD said..Hew thee two tables of
34. 4 he hewed two tables of stone like unto
Deut 10. 1 the LORD said..Hew thee two tables of
10. 3 I..hewed two tables of stone like unto
1 Ki. 5. 18 Hiram's builders did hew (them), and
5. *To hew (stone)*, λατομέω *latomeō.*
Matt 27. 60 which he had hewn out in the rock: and
Mark 15. 46 laid him in a sepulchre which was hewn

HEW down, to —
1. *To cut down*, גָּדַד *gedad.*
Dan. 4. 14 Hew down the tree, and cut off his branc.
4. 23 saying, Hew the tree down, and destroy
2. *To cut down, off, asunder*, גָּדַע *gada.*
Isa. 10. 33 high ones of stature (shall be) hewn down
3. *To cut down*, גָּדַע *gada*, 3.
Deut 12. 3 ye shall hew down the graven images of
4. *To cut (off or down)*, כָּרַת *karath.*
Isa. 44. 14 He heweth him down cedars, and taketh
5. *To cut off*, ἐκκόπτω *ekkoptō.*
Matt. 3. 10 bringeth not forth good fruit is hewn do.
7. 19 bringeth not forth good fruit is hewn do.
Luke 3. 9 bringeth not forth good fruit is hewn do.

HEW in pieces, to —
1. *To cut in pieces*, נָתַח *nathach*, 3.
1 Sa. 11. 7 a yoke of oxen, and hewed them in pieces
2. *To hew*, שָׁסַף *shasaph*, 3.
1 Sa. 15. 33 Samuel hewed Agag in pieces before the L.

HEW out, to —
To hew, dig, חָצַב *chatseb.*
Isa. 22. 16 hast hewed thee out..that heweth him out

HEWED —
1. *Hewn work*, גָּזִית *gazith.*
1 Ki. 5. 17 they brought great..hewed stones, to lay
2. *Hewn work*, מַחְצֵב *machtseb.*
2 Ki. 12. 12 to buy timber and hewed stone to repair

HEWER —
1. *To cut, hew, carve*, חָטַב *chatab.*
Deut 29. 11 from the hewer of thy wood unto the dra.
Josh. 9. 21 let them be hewers of wood and drawers
9. 23 hewers of wood and drawers of water for
9. 27 Joshua made them that day hewers of w.
2 Ch. 2. 10 I will give to thy servants, the hewers that
Jer. 46. 22 and come against her..as hewers of wood
2. *To hew, dig*, חָצַב *chatseb.*
1 Ki. 5. 15 fourscore thousand hewers in the mounta.
2 Ki. 12. 12 And to masons, and hewers of stone, and
1 Ch. 22. 15 workmen with thee in abundance, hewers
2 Ch. 2. 18 fourscore thousand (to be) hewers in the

HEWN, to be —
1. *To be hewn, digged*, חָצַב *chatseb*, 4.
Isa. 51. 1 look unto the rock (whence) ye are hewn
2. *Hewn work*, מַחְצֵב *machtseb.*
2 Ki. 22. 6 to buy timber and hewn stone to repair the
2 Ch. 34. 11 to buy hewn stone, and timber for coup.

HEWN in stone —
Hewn out of a rock, λαξευτός *laxeutos.*
Luke 23. 53 laid it in a sepulchre that was hewn in st.

HEWN down, to be —
To wither, be withered, קָמַל *qamal.*
Isa. 33. 9 Lebanon is ashamed (and) hewn down; Sh.

HEWN or hewed stone —
Hewn work, גָּזִית *gazith.*
Exod 20. 25 thou shalt not build it of hewn stone: for
1 Ki. 6. 36 he built the inner court..of hewed stone
7. 9 according to the measures of hewed stones
7. 11 after the measures of hewed stones, and
7. 12 three rows of hewed stones, and a row of
Isa. 9. 10 but we will build with hewn stones
Lam. 3. 9 He hath inclosed my ways with hewn stone
Eze. 40. 42 the four tables (were) of hewn stone for
Amos 5. 11 ye have built houses of hewn stone, but ye

HEZ-E'-KI, חִזְקִי *Jah is strength.*
A son of Elpaal, a descendant of Benjamin. B.C. 1400.
1 Ch. 8. 17 Zebadiah, and Meshullam, and H., and He.

HEZ-E-KI'-AH, חִזְקִיָּה, חִזְקִיָּהוּ *Jah is strength.*
1. Son and successor of Ahaz on the throne of Judah. B.C. 724-697.
2 Ki. 16. 20 Ahaz slept..and H. his son reigned in his
18. 1 H. the son of Ahaz king of Judah began
18. 9 it came to pass in the..year of king H.
18. 10 in the sixth year of H...Samaria was taken
18. 13 in the fourteenth year of king H. did Sen.
2 Ki. 18. 14 H. king of Judah sent to the king of Assy.
18. 14 the king of Assyria appointed unto H. king
18. 15 H. gave..all the silver (that was) found in
18. 16 At that time did H. cut off (the gold from)
18. 16 the pillars which H. king of Judah had
18. 17 the king..sent..to king H. with a great
18. 19 Speak ye now to H., Thus saith the great
18. 22 whose high places..H. hath taken away
18. 29 Thus saith the king, Let not H. deceive
18. 30 Neither let H. make you trust in the LORD
18. 31 Hearken not to H.: for thus saith the king
18. 32 hearken not unto H., when he persuadeth
18. 37 Then came Eliakim..and Shebna..to H.
19. 1 when king H. heard (it), that he rent his
19. 3 Thus saith H., This day (is) a day of trou.
19. 5 So the servants of king H. came to Isaiah
19. 9 he sent messengers again unto H., saying
19. 10 Thus shall ye speak to H. king of Judah
19. 14 H. received the letter..and read it: and H.
19. 15 H. prayed before the LORD, and said, O
19. 20 Then Isaiah the son of Amoz sent to H.
20. 1 In those days was H. sick unto death: and
20. 3 O LORD, remember..And H. wept sore
20. 5 Turn again, and tell H. the captain of my
20. 8 H. said unto Isaiah, What..the sign that
20. 10 H. answered, It is a light thing for the
20. 12 Ber...sent letters and a present unto H.
20. 12 for he had heard that H. had been sick
20. 13 H. hearkened unto them, and showed
20. 13 there was nothing..that H. showed them
20. 14 Then came Isaiah the prophet unto king H.
20. 14 H. said, They are come from a far country
20. 15 H. answered, All..that (are) in mine house
20. 16 Isaiah said unto H., Hear the word of the
20. 19 Then said H. unto Isaiah, Good (is) the word
20. 20 the rest of the acts of H., and all his might
20. 21 H. slept with his fathers: and Manasseh
21. 3 the high places which H. his father had
1 Ch. 3. 13 Ahaz his son, H. his son, Manasseh his
4. 41 written by name came in the days of H.
2 Ch. 28. 27 Ahaz slept..and H. his son reigned in his
29. 1 H. began to reign (when he was) five and
29. 18 Then they went in to H. the king, and
29. 20 H. the king rose early..and went up to the
29. 27 H. commanded to offer the burnt offering
29. 30 H. the king..commanded the Levites to
29. 31 H. answered and said, Now ye have con.
29. 36 H. rejoiced, and all the people, that God
30. 1 H. sent to all Israel and Judah, and wrote
30. 18 H. prayed for them, saying, The good LORD
30. 20 LORD hearkened to H., and healed the
30. 22 H. spake comfortably unto all the Levites
30. 24 H...did give to the congregation a thousa.
31. 2 And H. appointed the courses of the pri.
31. 8 when H. and the princes came and saw
31. 9 H. questioned with the priests..concerning
31. 11 Then H. commanded to prepare chambers
31. 13 overseers..at the commandment of H. the
31. 20 thus did H. throughout all Judah, and
32. 2 when H. saw that Sennacherib was come
32. 8 rested themselves upon the words of H.
32. 9 Sennacherib..send his servants..unto H
32. 11 Doth not H. persuade you to give over
32. 12 Hath not the same H. taken away his high
32. 15 Now therefore let not H. deceive you, nor
32. 16 And his servants spake yet..against..H.
32. 17 so shall not the God of H. deliver his pe.
32. 20 H. the king..prayed and cried to heaven
32. 22 Thus the LORD saved H. and the inhabit
32. 23 many brought..presents to H. king of J.
32. 24 In those days H. was sick to the death
32. 25 H. rendered not again according to the
32. 26 H. humbled himself for the pride of his h.
32. 26 the wrath..came not..in the days of H.
32. 27 H. had exceeding much riches and honour
32. 30 H. also stopped..And H. prospered in all
32. 32 Now the rest of the acts of H., and his
32. 33 H. slept with his fathers, and they buried
33. 3 the high places which H. his father had
Prov 25. 1 which the men of H. king of Judah copied
Isa. 1. 1 which he saw concerning..Ahaz, (and) H.
36. 1 it came to pass in the..year of king H.
36. 2 the king of Assyria sent..unto king H.
36. 4 Say ye now to H., Thus saith the great k.
36. 7 and whose altars H. hath taken away, and
36. 14 Thus saith the king, Let not H. deceive you
36. 15 Neither let H. make you trust in the LORD
36. 16 Hearken not to H.; for thus saith the king
36. 18 lest H. persuade you, saying, The LORD
36. 22 Then came Eliakim..and Shebna..to H.
37. 1 it came to pass, when king H. heard (it)
37. 3 Thus saith H., This day (is) a day of tro
37. 5 So the servants of king H. came to Isaiah
37. 9 when he heard (it), he sent messengers to H.
37. 10 Thus shall ye speak to H. king of Judah
37. 14 H. received the letter..and read it: and H.
37. 15 And H. prayed unto the LORD, saying
37. 21 Isaiah the son of Amoz sent unto H., say.
38. 1 In those days was H. sick unto death
38. 2 Then H. turned his face toward the wall
38. 3 Remember..O LORD..and H. wept sore
38. 5 Go and say to H., Thus saith the LORD
38. 9 The writing of H. king of Judah, when he
38. 22 H. also had said, What (is) the sign that I
39. 1 Merodach..sent letters and a present to H.
39. 2 H. was glad of them, and showed them the
39. 2 there was nothing..that H. showed them
39. 3 Then came Isaiah the prophet unto king H
39. 3 H. said, They are come from a far country
39. 4 H. answered, All that (is) in mine house
39. 5 Then said Isaiah to H., Hear the word of
39. 8 Then said H. to Isaiah, Good (is) the word

Jer. 15. 4 because of Manasseh the son of H. king of
26. 18 Micah..prophesied in the days of H. king
26. 19 Did H...put him at all to death? did he
Hos. 1. 1 in the days of Uzziah..(and) H., kings of
Mic. 1. 1 in the days of Jotham..and H., kings of

2. A son of Neariah, a descendant of the royal family of Judah. B.C. 460.

1 Ch. 3. 23 And..sons of Neariah; Elioenai, and H.

3. The same name is found in Zephaniah, though it is there rendered in the Common Version *Hizkiah*. B.C. 640.

Zeph. 1. 1 Gedaliah..son of Amariah, the son of H.

4. An exile that returned from Babylon.

Ezra 2. 16 children of Ater of H., ninety and eight
Neh. 7. 21 children of Ater of H., ninety and eight

HEZ'-ION, חֶזְיוֹן *vision.*

The grandfather of Benhadad king of Syria in the time of Asa king of Judah. B.C. 970.

1 Ki. 15. 18 H.. king of Syria, that dwelt at Damascus

HE'-ZIR, חֵזִיר *returning home.*

1. A priest, leader of the 17th monthly course in the time of David. B.C. 1015.

1 Ch. 24. 15 The seventeenth to H., the eighteenth to

2. One of the chiefs that sealed the covenant with Nehemiah. B.C. 445.

Neh. 10. 20 Magpiash, Meshullam, H.

HEZ'-RAI, חֶצְרַי *blooming, beautiful* [V.L. חצרו].

A Carmelite, one of David's thirty heroes.

2 Sa. 23. 35 H. the Carmelite, Paarai the Arbite

HEZ'-RO, חֶצְרוֹ *blooming.*

Supposed to be the same as the preceding.

1 Ch. 11. 37 H. the Carmelite, Naarai the son of Ezbai

HEZ'-RON, חֶצְרֹן, חֶצְרוֹן *blooming.*

1. Son of Pharez and grandson of Judah. B.C. 1650.

Gen. 46. 12 And the sons of Pharez were H. and Ham
Num. [Of H., the family of the Hezronites: of C.]
26. 21 Of H., the family of the Hezronites: of H.
Ruth 4. 18 generations of Pharez: Pharez begat H.
4. 19 H. begat Ram, and Ram begat Ammin.
1 Ch. 2. 5 The sons of Pharez; H., and Hamul
2. 9 The sons also of H., that were born unto
2. 18 Caleb the son of H. begat..of Azubah (his)
2. 21 H. went in to the daughter of Machir the
2. 24 after that H. was dead in Caleb-ephratah
2. 24 H.'s wife, bare him Ashur the father of T.
2. 25 sons of Jerahmeel the first born of H. were
4. 1 Pharez, H., and Carmi, and Hur, and Sho.

2. A son of Reuben, and founder of the family of the Hezronites. B.C. 1700. Num. 26. 6.

Gen. 46. 9 Hanoch, and Phallu, and H., and Carmi
Exod. 6. 14 Hanoch, and Pallu, H., and Carmi
1 Ch. 5. 3 Hanoch, and Pallu, H., and Carmi

3. A town on the S. border of the territory of the tribe of Judah (called Hazor in Josh. 15. 25).

Josh 15. 3 passed along to H., and went up to Adar
15. 25 and Kerioth, (and) H., which (is) Hazor

HEZRONITES, הַחֶצְרֹנִי.

Families that sprang from Hezron.

Num 26. 6 Of Hezron, the family of the Hezronites
26. 21 of Hezron, the family of the Hezronites

HID, to be —

1. *To be hidden*, חָבָא *chaba*, 2.

Josh. 10. 17 five kings are found hid in a cave at Ma.
10. 27 into the cave wherein they had been hid
2 Sa. 17. 9 he is hid now in some pit, or in some (other)
Job 5. 21 Thou shalt be hid from the scourge of the

2. *To be hidden*, חָבָא *chaba*, 6.

Isa. 42. 22 they are hid in prison houses: they are for

3. *To hide self*, חָבָא *chaba*, 7.

2 Ki. 11. 3 he was with her hid in the house of the
2 Ch. 22. 9 they caught him, for he was hid in Sam.
22. 12 he was with them hid in the house of G.
Job 38. 30 The waters are hid as (with) a stone. and

4. *To hide, secrete*, טָמַן *taman*.

Deut 33. 19 shall suck.. (of) treasures hid in the sand
Josh. 7. 21 they (are) hid in the earth in the midst of
7. 22 (it was) hid in his tent, and the silver under
Job 20. 26 All darkness (shall be) hid in his secret

5. *To be hid*, כָּחַד *kachad*, 2.

Psa. 69. 5 O God.. my sins are not hid from thee
139. 15 My substance was not hid from thee, when
Hos. 5. 3 I know Ephraim, and Israel is not hid

6. *To be hidden*, סָתַר *sathar*, 2.

Gen. 4. 14 From thy face shall I be hid; and I shall
Job 3. 23 to a man whose way is hid, and whom G.
Psa. 19. 6 there is nothing hid from the heat thereof
38. 9 Lord..my groaning is not hid from thee
Isa. 40. 27 My way is hid from the LORD, and my jud.
65. 16 and because they are hid from mine eyes
Jer. 16. 17 they are not hid from my face, neither is
Hos. 13. 14 repentance shall be hid from mine eyes
Amos 9. 3 though they be hid from my sight in the
Zeph. 2. 3 it may be ye shall be hid in the day of the

7. *To hide self, become hidden*, סָתַר *sathar*, 7.

Isa. 29. 14 and the understanding o. .shall be hid

8. *To be hidden, concealed*, עָלַם *alam*, 2.

Lev. 4. 13 the thing be hid from the eyes of the ass.
5. 3, 4 and it be hid from him; when he kno.
Num. 5. 13 and it be hid from the eyes of her husband
1 Ki. 10. 3 there was not (any) thing hid from the k.
2 Ch. 9. 2 there was nothing hid from Solomon whi.
Job 28. 21 Seeing it is hid from the eyes of all living
Nah. 3. 11 thou shalt be hid, thou also shalt seek

9. *To hide or conceal self*, עָלַם *alam*, 7.

Job 6. 16 reason of the ice.. wherein the snow is hid

10. *To be hidden, laid up*, צָפַן *tsaphan*, 2.

Jer. 16. 17 neither is their iniquity hid from mine eyes

11. *Hidden*, צָפִין [*tsaphan*], [Ps. 17.4, V.L. צָפוּן].

Psa. 17. 14 whose belly thou fillest with thy hid
Hos. 13. 12 The iniquity of Ephraim..his sin (is) hid

12. *Hid away*, ἀπόκρυφος *apokruphos*.

Luke 8. 17 neither..hid, that shall not be known and
Col. 2. 3 In whom are hid all the treasures of

13. *Hidden, hid*, κρυπτός *kruptos*.

Matt 10. 26 there is nothing..hid, that shall not be
Mark 4. 22 there is nothing hid, which shall not be
Luke 12. 2 that shall not be revealed; neither hid

14. *To be or lie hid*, λανθάνω *lanthanō*.

Mark 7. 24 have no man know (it)..he could not be hid
Luke 8. 47 the woman saw that she was not hid, she c.
Acts 26. 26 none of these things are hidden from him

[*See* Treasure.]

HID, (thing that is) —

Secret or hidden thing, תַּעֲלֻמָּה *taalummah*.

Job 28. 11 (the thing that is) hid bringeth he forth to l.

HID'-DAI, הִדַּי *mighty, chief.*

One of David's thirty valiant men, and dwelt in the hill of Gaash B.C. 1048. In 1 Ch. 11. 32 he is called *Hurai*.

2 Sa. 23. 30 Benaiah the Pirathonite, H. of the brooks?

HID-DE'-KEL, חִדֶּקֶל *rapid.*

The ancient name of the Tigris and the river of Eden which flowed eastward to Assyria. *Digla* or *Diglath*, has been a name of the Tigris in all ages. The prefix *hi* or *hai* "lively" is used of running water, Gen. 26. 19. The name now in use in Mesopotamia is *Dijleh*. But *Digla* is a Semitic corruption of *Tigra*, which is the true name of the river, and means in Medo-persic "*an arrow.*" In the inscriptions of Assyria, however, the name is *Tiggar*. See TIGRIS.

Gen. 2. 14 the name of the third river (is) H.: that
Dan. 10. 4 I was by the side of the great river..H.

HIDDEN —

1. *To hide, secrete*, טָמַן *taman*.

Job 3. 16 Or as an hidden untimely birth I had not

2. *To stop, hide*, סָתַם *satham*.

Psa. 51. 6 in the hidden (part) thou shalt make me to

3. *To be wonderful*, פָּלָא *pala*, 2.

Deut 30. 11 this commandment..(is) not hidden from

4. *Hid, hidden*, κρυπτός *kruptos*.

1 Pe. 3. 4 the hidden man of the heart, in that wh.

5. *To hide away*, ἀποκρύπτω *apokruptō*.

1 Co. 2. 7 we speak the wisdom of God..the hidden

HIDDEN, to be —

1. *To be searched out, hidden*, חָפַשׂ *chaphas*, 4.

Prov. 28. 12 but when the wicked rise, a man is hidden

2. *To be hidden, concealed*, עָלַם *alam*, 2.

Lev. 5. 2 (if) it be hidden from him; he also shall be

3. *To be laid up, hidden*, צָפַן *tsaphan*, 2.

Job 15. 20 the number of years is hidden to the opp.
24. 1 Why, seeing times are not hidden from the

HIDDEN one —

To lay up, hide, צָפַן *tsaphan*.

Psa. 83. 3 They..consulted against thy hidden ones

HIDDEN thing —

1. *Laid up or hidden things*, מַצְפֻּנִים *matspunim*.

Obad. 6 (how) are his hidden things sought up!

2. *To keep, reserve*, נָצַר *natsar*.

Isa. 48. 6 I have showed thee..even hidden things

3. *Hid, hidden thing*, κρυπτόν *krupton*.

1 Co. 4. 5 both will bring to light the hidden things of
2 Co. 4. 2 have renounced the hidden things of dis.

HIDE —

Skin, עוֹר *or*.

Lev. 8. 17 the bullock, and his hide, his flesh, and
9. 11 the flesh and the hide he burnt with fire

HIDE, to —

1. *To hide*, חָבָא *chaba*, 5.

Josh. 6. 17, 25 because she hid the messengers that we
1 Ki. 18. 4 Obadiah took..and hid them by fifty in a
18. 13 I hid an hundred men of the LORD'S proph.
2 Ki. 6. 29 that we may eat him; and she hath hid her
Isa. 49. 2 in the shadow of his hand hath he hid me

2. *To darken, keep back, withhold*, חָשַׂךְ *chashak*, 5.

Psa. 139. 12 darkness hideth not from thee; but the ni.

3. *To hide, lay up*, צָפַן *tsaphan*.

Psa. 27. 5 For in the time of trouble he shall hide me

4. *To be hidden*, טָמַן *taman*, 2.

Isa. 2. 10 hide thee in the dust, for fear of the L.

5. *To hide, secrete*, טָמַן *taman*.

Gen. 35. 4 Jacob hid them under the oak which (was)
Exod. 2. 12 slew the Egyptian, and hid him in the sand
Josh. 2. 6 hid them with the stalks of flax, which she
Job 31. 33 by hiding mine iniquity in my bosom
40. 13 Hide them in the dust together..bind their
Psa. 9. 15 in the net which they hid is their own foot
35. 7 without cause have they hid for me their
35. 8 let his net that he hath hid catch himself
140. 5 The proud have hid a snare for me, and
Prov. 19. 24 A slothful (man) hideth his hand in (his)
26. 15 The slothful hideth his hand in (his) bosom
Jer. 13. 4 go to Euphrates, and hide it there in a hole
13. 5 I went, and hid it by Euphrates, as the LORD
13. 6 which I commanded thee to hide there
13. 7 girdle from the place where I had hid it
18. 22 they have digged a pit to take me, and hid
43. 9 Take great stones in thine hand, and hide
43. 10 will set..upon these stones that I have hid

6. *To hide, secrete*, טָמַן *taman*, 5.

2 Ki. 7. 8 and went and hid (it)..and went and hid

7. *To cut off, hide*, כָּחַד *kachad*, 3.

Gen. 47. 18 We will not hide (it) from my lord, how
Josh. 7. 19 tell me now what thou hast done; hide (it)
1 Sa. 3. 17 hide it not from me..if thou hide (any) thi.
3. 18 Samuel told him every whit, and hid noth.
2 Sa. 14. 18 Hide not from me, I pray thee, the thing
Job 15. 18 wise men have told..and have not hid (it)
Psa. 78. 4 We will not hide (them) from their children
Isa. 3. 9 they declare their sin as Sodom, they hide
Jer. 38. 14 I will ask thee a thing; hide nothing from
38. 25 hide it not from us, and we will not put

8. *To cut off, hide*, כָּחַד *kachad*, 5.

Job 20. 12 sweet..(though) he hide it under his tong.

9. *To cover, conceal*, כָּסָה *kasah*, 3.

Gen. 18. 17 Shall I hide from Abraham that thing which
Job 33. 17 That he may..hide pride from man
Psa. 32. 5 mine iniquity have I not hid. I said, I will
40. 10 I have not hid thy righteousness within my
143. 9 Deliver me..I flee unto thee to hide me
Prov. 10. 18 He that hideth hatred (with) lying lips

10. *To hide*, סָתַר *sathar*, 3.

Isa. 16. 3 hide the outcasts; bewray not him that

11. *To hide*, סָתַר *sathar*, 5.

Exod. 3. 6 Moses hid his face; for he was afraid to
Deut 31. 17 I will hide my face from them, and they
31. 18 I will surely hide my face in that day for
32. 20 I will hide my face from them, I will see
1 Sa. 20. 2 why should my father hide this thing from
2 Ki. 11. 2 they hid him, (even) him and his nurse, in
2 Ch. 22. 11 So Jehoshabeath..hid him from Athaliah
Job 3. 10 it shut not up the doors..nor hid sorrow
13. 24 Wherefore hidest thou thy face, and hol.
34. 29 and when he hideth (his) face, who then
Psa. 10. 11 God hath forgotten: he hideth his face
13. 1 how long wilt thou hide thy face from me?
17. 8 hide me under the shadow of thy wings
22. 24 neither hath he hid his face from him; but
27. 5 in..his tabernacle shall he hide me; he
27. 9 Hide not thy face (far) from me; put not
30. 7 thou didst hide thy face, (and) I was trou.
31. 20 Thou shalt hide them in the secret of thy
44. 24 Wherefore hidest thou thy face..forgett.
51. 9 Hide thy face from my sins, and blot out
64. 2 Hide me from the secret counsel of the w.
69. 17 hide not thy face from thy servant; for I
88. 14 LORD..(why) hidest thou thy face from
102. 2 Hide not thy face from me in the day
104. 29 Thou hidest thy face, they are troubled
119. 19 hide not thy commandments from me
143. 7 hide not thy face from me, lest I be like
Isa. 8. 17 I will wait upon the LORD, that hideth
29. 15 Woe unto them that seek deep to hide
49. 2 a polished shaft; in his quiver hath he h.
50. 6 I hid not my face from shame and spitting
53. 3 we hid as it were our faces from him; he
54. 8 In a little wrath I hid my face from thee
57. 17 I hid me and was wroth, and he went on
59. 2 your sins have hid (his) face from you, that
64. 7 thou hast hid thy face from us, and hast
Jer. 33. 5 for all..I have hid my face from this city
36. 26 to take Baruch..but the LORD hid them
Eze. 39. 23 therefore hid I my face from them, and
39. 24 have I done unto them, and hid my face
39. 29 Neither will I hide my face any more from
Mic. 3. 4 he will even hide his face from them at

12. *To hide*, עָלַם *alam*, 5.

Lev. 20. 4 if the people of the land do any ways hide
2 Ki. 4. 27 the LORD hath hid (it) from me, and hath
Job 42. 3 Who (is) he that hideth counsel without
Psa. 10. 1 (why) hidest thou (thyself) in times of tr.?
Prov. 28. 27 he that hideth his eyes shall have many
Isa. 1. 15 I will hide mine eyes from you; yea, when
Lam. 3. 56 hide not thine ear at my breathing, at my
Eze. 22. 26 and have hid their eyes from my sabbaths

13. *To conceal*, עָמַם *amam*.

Eze. 28. 3 there is no secret that they can hide from
31. 8 cedars in the garden of God could not hide

14. *To hide, lay up, conceal*, צָפַן *tsaphan*.

Exod. 2. 2 she saw..he (was) a goodly (child), she hid
Josh. 2. 4 the woman took the two men, and hid them
Job 10. 13 these (things) hast thou hid in thine heart
17. 4 For thou hast hid their heart from under.
Psa. 119. 11 Thy word have I hid in mine heart, that
Prov. 2. 1 if thou wilt receive my words, and hide
27. 16 Whosoever hideth her hideth the wind

15. *To hide*, צָפַן *tsaphan*, 5.

Exod. 2. 3 when she could not longer hide him, she
Job 14. 13 O that thou wouldest hide me in the grave

16. *To cause to flee, remove hastily*, נוּס *nus*, 5.

Judg. 6. 11 Gideon threshed wheat..to hide (it) from

17. *To hide away,* ἀποκρύπτω *apokruptō.*
Matt 11. 25 [thou hast hid] these things from the w.
25. 18 he that had received one..[hid] his lord's
Luke10. 21 thou hast hid these things from the wise
Eph. 3. 9 which from the beginning..hath been hid
Col. 1. 26 the mystery which hath been hid from

18. *To cover, hide,* καλύπτω *kaluptō.*
2 Co. 4. 3 if our gospel be hid, it is hid to them that
Jas. 5. 20 he which converteth the sinner..shall h.

19. *To hide,* κρύπτω *kruptō.*
Matt. 5. 14 A city that is set on an hill cannot be h.
13. 44 like unto treasure hid..which..he hideth
25. 25 I was afraid, and went and hid thy talent
Luke18. 34 this saying was hid from them, neither
19. 42 known..but now they are hid from thine
Col. 3. 3 and your life is hid with Christ in God
1 Ti. 5. 25 and they that are otherwise cannot be hid
Heb. 11. 23 Moses, when he was born, was hid three
Rev. 2. 17 To him..will I give..the hidden manna
6. 15 the kings of the earth..hid themselves in
6. 16 Fall on us, and hide us from the face of

20. *To cover beyond,* παρακαλύπτω *parakaluptō.*
Luke 9. 45 it was hid from them, that they perceived

21. *To hide around,* περικρύπτω *perikruptō.*
Luke 1. 24 Elisabeth conceived, and hid herself five

HIDE in, to —
To hide in, ἐγκρύπτω *egkruptō.*
Matt 13. 33 which a woman took and [hid] in three
Luke13. 21 which a woman took and [hid] in three
[*See* Flee.]

HIDE self, to —
1. *To be hidden,* חָבָא *chaba,* 2.
Gen. 3. 10 he said..I was afraid..and I hid myself
Josh.10. 16 hid themselves in a cave at Makkedah
Judg. 9. 5 yet Jotham..was left; for he hid himself
1 Sa. 10. 22 he hath hid himself among the stuff
19. 2 abide in a secret (place), and hide thyself
2 Ch.18. 24 when thou shalt go..to hide thyself
Job 29. 8 young men saw me, and hid themselves
Dan. 10. 7 so that they fled to hide themselves
Amos 9. 3 they hide themselves in the top of Carmel

2. *To be hidden,* חָבָא *chaba,* 4.
Job 24. 4 the poor of the earth hide themselves to.

3. *To hide self,* חָבָא *chaba,* 7.
Gen. 3. 8 Adam and his wife hid themselves from
1 Sa. 13. 6 the people did hide themselves in caves
14. 11 the holes where they had hid themselves
14. 22 men of Israel which had hid themselves
23. 23 lurking places where he hideth himself
1 Ch.21. 20 his four sons with him hid themselves

4. *To hide,* חָבָה *chabah.*
Isa. 26. 20 hide thyself as it were for a little moment

5. *To be hidden,* חָבָה *chabah,* 2.
Josh. 2. 16 hide yourselves there three days, until
1 Ki. 22. 25 when thou shalt go..to hide thyself
2 Ki. 7. 12 gone out of the camp to hide themselves
Jer. 49. 10 he shall not be able to hide himself: his

6. As No. 7.
Prov 22. 3 foreseeth the evil, and hideth himself

7. *To be hidden,* סָתַר *sathar,* 2.
Deut. 7. 20 hide themselves from thee, be destroyed
1 Sa. 20. 5 that I may hide myself in the field unto
20. 19 the place where thou didst hide thyself
20. 24 David hid himself in the field: and when
1 Ki. 17. 3 hide thyself by the brook Cherith, that
Job 13. 20 then will I not hide myself from thee
34. 22 workers of iniquity may hide themselves
Psa. 55. 12 then I would have hid myself from him
89. 46 wilt thou hide thyself for ever? shall thy
Prov 27. 12 foreseeth the evil, (and) hideth himself
28. 28 When the wicked rise, men hide thems.
Isa. 28. 15 under falsehood have we hid ourselves
Jer. 23. 24 Can any hide himself in secret places
Amos 9. 3 they hide themselves in the top of Carmel

8. *To hide self,* סָתַר *sathar,* 7.
1 Sa. 23. 19 Doth not David hide himself with us in
26. 1 Doth not David hide himself in the hill
Psa. 54. *title.* Doth not David hide himself with us?
Isa. 45. 15 Verily thou (art) a God that hidest thyself

9. *To cover, wrap up,* עָטַף *ataph.*
Job 23. 9 he hideth himself on the right hand, that

10. *To hide self,* עָלַם *alam,* 7.
Deut22. 1, 4 and hide thyself from them: thou shalt
22. 3 do likewise: thou mayest not hide thyself
Psa. 55. 1 hide not thyself from my supplication
Isa. 58. 7 that thou hide not thyself from thine own

11. *To hide,* צָפַן *tsaphan,* 5.
Psa. 56. 6 they hide themselves, they mark my steps

12. *To hide,* κρύπτω *kruptō.*
John 8. 59 Jesus hid himself, and went out of the tem.
12. 36 departed, and did hide himself from them

HIDING —
Hiding, חֶבְיוֹן *chebyon.*
Hab. 3. 4 and there (was) the hiding of his power

HIDING place —
1. *Hiding place,* מַחֲבֵא *machabe.*
Isa. 32. 2 a man shall be as an hiding place from the

2. *Hiding or secret place,* סֵתֶר *sether.*
Psa. 32. 7 Thou (art) my hiding place; thou shalt pre.
119. 114 Thou (art) my hiding place and my shield
Isa. 28. 17 the waters shall overflow the hiding place

HI'-EL, חִיאֵל *God is living.*
A native of Bethel who rebuilt Jericho in the reign of Ahab, B.C. 918, and in whom was fulfilled the curse pronounced by Joshua (6. 26).
1 Ki.16. 34 In his days did H. the Beth-elite build

HI-E-RA'-PO-LIS, Ἱεράπολις *priestly city.*
A city of Phrygia 20 miles W. of Colosse and 6 N. of Laodicea which are all in the basin of the Mæander. It is now called *Pambuk-Kalessi.*
Col. 4. 13 that he hath a great zeal for..them in H.

HIG-GA'-ION, הִגָּיוֹן.
This word occurs three times in the book of Psalms; and from the multiplicity of interpretations suggested, it would seem to have two meanings—one of a general character implying "*thought,*" "*reflection;*" and another in Ps. 9. 16 and 92. 3 of a special technical nature, bearing the import of musical sounds or signs well known in the age of David, but whose import cannot now easily be determined.
Psa. 9. 16 snared in the work of his own hands. H. S.

HIGH (things) —
1. *A man,* אִישׁ *ish.*
Psa. 49. 2 Both low and high, rich and poor, together

2. *Length,* אֹרֶךְ *orek.*
2 Ch. 3. 15 two pillars of thirty and five cubits high

3. *High, lofty,* גָּבַהּ *gabah.*
Psa.101. 5 him that hath an high look and a proud
Eze. 31. 3 the Assyrian (was)..of an high stature

4. *Height, loftiness,* גֹּבַהּ *gobah.*
Job 11. 8 (It is) as high as heaven, what canst thou
Eze. 1. 18 they were so high that they were dreadful
40. 42 a cubit and a half broad, and one cubit h.

5. *High, haughty,* גָּבֹהַּ, גָּבֹהַ *gaboah.*
Gen. 7. 19 all the high hills that (were) under the
Deut. 3. 5 All these cities (were) fenced with high
28. 52 until thy high and fenced walls come down
1 Ki.14. 23 on every high hill, and under every green
2 Ki.17. 10 images and groves in every high hill, and
Esth. 5. 14 a gallows be made of fifty cubits high, and
7. 9 the gallows, fifty cubits high, which Haman
Job 41. 34 He beholdeth all high (things): he (is) a
Psa.104. 18 The high hills (are) a refuge for the wild
Eccl.12. 5 they shall be afraid of (that which is) high
Isa. 2. 15 upon every high tower, and upon every
30. 25 there shall be upon every high mountain
40. 9 get thee up into the high mountain
Jer. 2. 20 upon every high hill and under every
3. 6 she is gone up upon every high mountain
17. 2 by the green trees upon the high hills
51. 58 her high gates shall be burnt with fire
Eze. 17. 22 will plant (it) upon an high mountain and
17. 24 have brought down the high tree, have
21. 26 Thus saith the Lord..abase (him that is) h.
40. 2 set me upon a very high mountain, by
41. 22 The altar of wood (was) three cubits high
Dan. 8. 3 and the (two) horns (were) high; but one
Zeph. 1. 16 fenced cities, and against the high towers

6. *Heights, summits,* גַּבְנֻנִּים *gabnunnim.*
Psa. 68. 15 an high hill, (as) the hill of Bashan
68. 16 Why leap ye, ye high hills? (this is) the

7. *Great,* גָּדוֹל *gadol.*
Gen. 29. 7 Lo, (it is) yet high day, neither (is it) time
Lev. 21. 10 the high priest among his brethren, upon
Num 35. 25 in it unto the death of the high priest
35. 28 high priest..death of the high priest
Josh20. 6 until the death of the high priest that shall
2 Ki.12. 10 king's scribe and the high priest came up
22. 4 Go up to Hilkiah the high priest, that he
22. 8 Hilkiah the high priest said unto Shaphan
23. 4 king commanded Hilkiah the high priest
2 Ch.34. 9 when they came to Hilkiah the high priest
Neh. 3. 1 Eliashib the high priest rose up, with
3. 20 of the house of Eliashib the high priest
13. 28 Joiada, the son of Eliashib the high priest
Hag. 1. 1, 12, 14 Joshua..son of Josedech the high
2. 2, 4 Joshua the son of Josedech, the high p.
Zech. 3. 1 And he showed me Joshua the high priest
3. 8 Hear now, O Joshua the high priest, thou
6. 11 Joshua the son of Josedech, the high pri.

8. *High place, or person,* מָרוֹם *marom.*
Psa. 71. 19 Thy righteousness also, O God, (is) very h.
92. 8 But thou, LORD, (art) most high for ever
Isa. 57. 15 I dwell in the high and holy (place), with
Jer. 17. 12 A glorious high throne from the beginning
Eze. 34. 14 upon the high mountains of Israel shall
Obad 3 whose habitation (is) high; that saith in h.
Mic. 6. 6 bow myself before the high God? shall I

9. *To be lifted up,* נָשָׂא *nasa,* 2.
Isa. 30. 25 there shall be..upon every high hill, rivers
57. 7 Upon a lofty and high mountain hast thou

10. *Most high,* עִלַּי *illai.*
Dan. 4. 2 signs and wonders that the high God hath

11. *High, uppermost, most high,* עֶלְיוֹן *elyon.*
Deut26. 19 to make thee high above all nations which
1 Ki. 9. 8 at this house, (which) is high, every one
2 Ch. 7. 21 this house, which is high, shall be an asto.
23. 20 they came through the high gate into the
27. 3 He built the high gate of the house of the
Neh. 3. 25 which lieth out from the king's high house
Psa. 78. 35 they remembered..the high God their re.
97. 9 thou, LORD, (art) high above all the earth
Jer. 20. 2 put him in the stocks..in the high gate of

12. *Height, stature,* קוֹמָה *qomah.*
1 Ki. 6. 10 he built chambers..five cubits high: and
6. 23 he made two cherubim..ten cubits high
7. 15 he cast two pillars..eighteen cubits high
7. 35 a round compass of half a cubit high: and
2 Ch. 6. 13 a brasen scaffold..three cubits high, and

13. *To be high,* רוּם *rum.*
Exod14. 8 children of Israel went out with an high h.
Num33. 3 children of Israel went out with an high h.
Deut12. 2 nations which..served..upon the high m.
Job. 21. 22 seeing he judgeth those that are high
38. 15 the wicked..the high arm shall be broken
Psa. 18. 27 For thou wilt..bring down high looks
78. 69 he built his sanctuary like high (palaces)
113. 4 The LORD (is) high above all nations, (and)
138. 6 Though the LORD (be) high, yet hath he
Isa. 2. 13 all the cedars of Lebanon, (that are) high
2. 14 upon all the high mountains, and upon all
6. 1 the LORD sitting upon a throne, high and
57. 15 thus saith the high and lofty One that
Eze. 6. 13 round about their altars, upon every high
17. 22 I will also take..of the high cedar, and
20. 28 they saw every high hill, and all the thick
34. 6 My sheep wandered..upon every high hill

14. *Exaltation,* רוֹמָם *romam.*
Psa.149. 6 (Let) the high (praises) of God (be) in their

15. *To be high, set on high,* שָׂגַב *sagab,* 2.
Prov 18. 11 The rich man's wealth (is)..as an high wall
Isa. 30. 13 swelling out in a high wall, whose breaking

16. *To be high,* שָׁפָה *shaphah,* 2.
Isa. 13. 2 Lift ye up a banner upon the high moun.

17. *Height, on high,* רוּם *rum.*
Prov 21. 4 An high look, and a proud heart, (and) the
Isa. 10. 12 I will punish..the glory of his high looks

18. *Up, above, high,* ἄνω *anō.*
Phil. 3. 14 the prize of the high calling of God in C.J.

19. *Great,* μέγας *megas.*
John19. 31 for that sabbath day was an high day
Heb. 10. 21 And..an high priest over the house of God

20. *High,* ὑψηλός *hupsēlos.*
Matt. 4. 8 devil taketh him up into an exceeding high
17. 1 bringeth them up into an high mountain
Mark 9. 2 leadeth them up into an high mountain
Luke 4. 5 [devil, taking him up into an high moun.]
Acts 13. 17 with an high arm brought he them out of
Rom 12. 16 Mind not high things, but condescend to
Heb. 7. 26 such an high priest became us, (who is)
Rev. 21. 10 he carried me..to a great and high mou.
21. 12 had a wall great and high..had twelve g.

[*See also* Captain, exalt, fort, heaps, minded, most, sounding, tower.]

HIGH, to be —
1. *To be high, lofty,* גָּבַהּ *gabah.*
Psa.103. 11 For as the heaven is high above the earth
Isa. 52. 13 be exalted and extolled, and be very high

2. *To be high, exalted,* רוּם *rum.*
Deut32. 27 lest they should say, Our hand (is) high
Job 22. 12 the height of the stars, how high they are!
Psa. 89. 13 strong is thy hand..high is thy right hand
99. 2 The LORD..he (is) high above all people

3. *To be high, set on high,* שָׂגַב *sagab,* 2.
Psa.139. 6 knowledge..it is high, I cannot (attain)

HIGH degree —
1. *A man,* אִישׁ *ish.*
Psa. 62. 9 Surely..men of high degree (are) a lie: to

2. *Going up, ascent, step,* מַעֲלָה *maalah.*
1 Ch.17. 17 according to the estate of a man of high d.

HIGH, to lift up on —
To lift up, exalt, רוּם *rum,* 3a.
2 Sa. 22. 49 thou also hast lifted me up on high above

HIGH, to make —
1. *To make high, go up high,* גָּבַהּ *gabah,* 5.
Jer. 49. 16 though thou..make thy nest as high as

2. *To exalt, lift up,* רוּם *rum,* 5.
Job 39. 27 Doth the eagle..make her nest on high?

HIGH, most —
1. *High place or person,* מָרוֹם *marom.*
Psa. 56. 2 many..fight against me, O thou most High

2. *Most high, above,* עַל, עָל *al.*
Hos. 7. 16 They return, (but) not to the most high
11. 7 though they called them to the most high

3. *Most high,* עִלַּי *illai.*
Dan. 3. 26 ye servants of the most high God, come
4. 17 the living may know that the most High
4. 24 this (is) the decree of the most High, wh.
4. 25, 32 thou know that the most High ruleth in
4. 34 I blessed the most High, and I praised
5. 18 O thou king, the most high God gave Ne.
5. 21 till he knew that the most high God ruled
7. 25 against the most High..of the most High

4. *High, uppermost, most high,* עֶלְיוֹן *elyon.*
Gen. 14. 18 he (was) the priest of the most high God
14. 19 Blessed (be) Abram of the most high God
14. 20 blessed be the most high God, which hath
14. 22 I have lift up mine hand unto..most high
Num 24. 16 and knew the knowledge of the most High
Deut32. 8 When the most High divided to the nations
2 Sa. 22. 14 and the most High uttered his voice
Psa. 7. 17 will sing praise to..the LORD most high

Psa. 9. 2 sing praise to thy name, O thou most High
21. 7 through the mercy of the most High he
46. 4 (place) of the tabernacles of the most High
47. 2 For the LORD most high (is) terrible; (he
50. 14 and pay thy vows unto the most High
57. 2 I will cry unto God most high; unto God
73. 11 and is there knowledge in the most High?
77. 10 years of the right hand of the most High
78. 17 by provoking the most High in the wild.
78. 56 tempted and provoked the most high God
82. 6 all of you (are) the children of the most H.
83. 18 thou.. (art) the most High over all the ea.
91. 1 in the secret place of the most High shall
91. 9 thou hast made..(even) the most High, thy
92. 1 sing praises unto thy name, O most High
107. 11 contemned the counsel of the most High
Isa. 14. 14 clouds: I will be like the most High
Lam. 3. 35 aside.. before the face of the most High
3. 38 Out of the mouth of the most High proce.

5. *High, uppermost, most high,* עֶלְיוֹן *elyon.*

Dan. 7. 18 the saints of the most High shall take
7. 22 was given to the saints of the most High
7. 25 speak (great) words against the most High
7. 27 the people of the saints of the most High

6. *Highest, most high,* ὕψιστος *hupsistos.*

Mark 5. 7 Jesus, (thou) Son of the most high God?
Luke 8. 28 Jesus, (thou) Son of God most high? I
Acts 7. 48 Howbeit the most High dwelleth not in t.
16. 17 These men are the servants of the most h.
Heb. 7. 1 priest of the most high God, who met A.

HIGH, on —

1. *Above, upward,* מַעַל, מִמַּעַל, מִלְמַעְלָה, לְמַעְלָה *[maal].*

Exod 25. 20 shall stretch forth (their) wings on high
37. 9 cherubim spread out (their) wings on high
39. 31 to fasten (it) on high upon the mitre; as
1 Ch. 14. 2 for his kingdom was lifted up on high
2 Ch. 20. 19 to praise.. with a loud voice on high
34. 4 the images, that (were) on high above them

2. *High place or person, on high,* מָרוֹם *marom.*

2 Ki. 19. 22 lifted up thine eyes on high? (even) against
Job 5. 11 To set up on high those that be low; that
16. 19 now, behold.. my record (is) on high
31. 2 inheritance of the Almighty from on high
39. 18 What time she lifteth up herself on high
Psa. 7. 7 for their sakes.. return thou on high
68. 18 Thou hast ascended on high, thou hast
75. 5 Lift not up your horn on high: speak
93. 4 The LORD on high (is) mightier than the
Isa. 22. 16 heweth him out a sepulchre on high
24. 18 the windows from on high are open, and
24. 21 shall punish the host.. (that are) on high
26. 5 bringeth down them that dwell on high
32. 15 spirit be poured upon us from on high
33. 5 is exalted; for he dwelleth on high: he
33. 16 He shall dwell on high; his place of defe.
37. 23 lifted up thine eyes on high? (even) against
40. 26 Lift up your eyes on high, and behold
58. 4 to make your voice to be heard on high
Jer. 25. 30 The LORD shall roar from on high, and
Hab. 2. 9 that he may set his nest on high, that he

3. *Above,* עַל *al.*

2 Sa. 23. 1 the man (who was) raised up on high, the

4. *High, uppermost, most high,* עֶלְיוֹן *elyon.*

Deut 28. 1 the LORD thy God will set thee on high

5. *Head, top,* רֹאשׁ *rosh.*

1 Ki. 21. 9, 12 set Naboth on high among the people

6. *On high,* רוֹם *rom.*

Hab. 3. 10 the deep.. lifted up his hands on high

7. *To lift up, exalt,* רוּם *rum, 3a.*

2 Sa. 22. 49 thou also hast lifted me up on high above

8. *On high,* ἐν ὑψηλοῖς *en hupsēlois.*

Heb. 1. 3 on the right hand of the majesty on high

9. *Height,* (εἰς) ὕψος *(eis) hupsos.*

Luke 1. 78 the day spring from on high hath visited
24. 49 until ye be endued with power from on high
Eph. 4. 8 When he ascended up on high, he led cap.

HIGH, to dwell on —

To go high to dwell, גָּבַהּ לָשֶׁבֶת *[gabah (5) yashab].*

Psa. 113. 5 Who (is) like.. our God, who dwelleth on h.

HIGH ones —

1. *High place or person,* מָרוֹם *marom.*

Isa. 24. 21 LORD shall punish the host of the high o.

2. *To be high, exalted, tall,* רוּם *rum.*

Isa. 10. 33 the high ones of stature (shall be) hewn

HIGH place —

1. *High place, height,* בָּמָה *bamah.*

Lev. 26. 30 I will destroy your high places, and cut
Num 21. 28 (and) the lords of the high places of Arnon
22. 41 brought him up into the high places of B.
33. 52 and quite pluck down all their high places
Deut 32. 13 He made him ride on the high places of
33. 29 thou shalt tread upon their high places
1 Sa. 9. 12 for.. a sacrifice.. to day in the high place
9. 13 before he go up to the high place to eat
9. 14 Samuel came.. to go up to the high place
9. 19 go up before me unto the high place; for
9. 25 when they were come down from the h. p.
10. 5 prophets coming down from the high place
10. 13 had made an end.. he came to the high p.
2 Sa. 1. 19 beauty of Israel is slain upon thy high pl.
1. 25 O Jonathan.. slain in thine high places
22. 34 He.. setteth me upon my high places
1 Ki. 3. 2 Only the people sacrificed in high places

1 Ki. 3. 3 he sacrificed and burnt incense in high pl.
3. 4 Gibeon.. for that (was) the great high pl.
11. 7 Then did Solomon build an high place for
12. 31 he made an house of high places, and
12. 32 he placed in B. the priests of the high pl.
13. 2 shall he offer the priests of the high places
13. 32 against all the houses of the high places
13. 33 priests of the high places.. of the high pl.
14. 23 they also built them high places, and
15. 14 But the high places were not removed
22. 43 the high places.. yet in the high places
2 Ki. 12. 3 But the high places.. in the high places
14. 4 high places.. incense on the high places
15. 4 high places.. still on the high places
15. 35 high places.. still in the high places
16. 4 and burnt incense in the high places, and
17. 9 built them high places in all their cities
17. 11 they burnt incense in all the high places
17. 29 put (them) in the houses of the high pla.
17. 32 of the high places.. houses of the high p.
18. 4 He removed the high places, and brake
18. 22 he whose high places and whose altars H.
21. 3 he built up again the high places which
23. 5 to burn incense in the high places in the
23. 8 high places.. brake down the high places
23. 9 priests of the high places came not up to
23. 13 the high places that (were) before Jerusa.
23. 15 high place which Jeroboam the son of Ne.
23. 15 high place.. and burned the high place
23. 19 all the houses also of the high places that
23. 20 he slew all the priests of the high places
1 Ch. 16. 39 in the high place that (was) at Gibeon
21. 29 at that season in the high place at Gibeon
2 Ch. 1. 3, 13 to the high place that (was) at Gibeon
11. 15 ordained him priests for the high places
14. 3, 5 he took away.. the high places, and
15. 17 the high places were not taken away out
17. 6 he took away the high places and groves
20. 33 the high places were not taken away; for
21. 11 he made high places in the mountains of
28. 4 He.. burnt incense in the high places, and
28. 25 he made high places to burn incense unto
31. 1 threw down the high places and the altars
32. 12 taken away his high places and his altars
33. 3 For he built again the high places which
33. 17 did sacrifice still in the high places, (yet)
33. 19 the places wherein he built high places
34. 3 from the high places, and the groves, and
Psa. 18. 33 and setteth me upon my high places
78. 58 provoked him.. with their high places
Isa. 15. 2 He is gone up to.. the high places, to we.
16. 12 that Moab is weary on the high place
36. 7 whose high places.. Hezekiah hath taken
58. 14 to ride upon the high places of the earth
Jer. 7. 31 they have built the high places of Tophet
17. 3 thy high places for sin, throughout all
19. 5 They have built also the high places of
26. 18 mountain of the house as the high places
32. 35 they built the high places of Baal, which
48. 35 him that offereth in the high places, and
Eze. 6. 3 and I will destroy your high places
6. 6 the high places shall be desolate; that
16. 16 and deckedst thy high places with divers
20. 29 What (is) the high place whereunto ye go?
36. 2 Aha! even the ancient high places are
43. 7 nor by the carcases.. in their high places
Hos. 10. 8 The high places also of Aven, the sin of I.
Amos 4. 13 treadeth upon the high places of the ear.
7. 9 the high places of Isaac shall be desolate
Mic. 1. 3 tread upon the high places of the earth
1. 5 and what (are) the high places of Judah?
3. 12 mountain of the house as the high places
Hab. 3. 19 make me to walk upon mine high places

2. *High place or person,* מָרוֹם *marom.*

Judg. 5. 18 the death in the high places of the field
Job 25. 2 he maketh peace in his high places
Prov. 8. 2 She standeth in the top of high places, by
9. 14 on a seat in the high places of the city

3. *Pit,* צְרִיחַ *tsariach.*

1 Sa. 13. 6 the people did hide.. in high places, and

4. *High place,* רָמָה *ramah.*

Eze. 16. 24 hast made thee an high place in every st.
16. 25 Thou hast built thy high place at every
16. 31 makest thine high place in every street
16. 39 shall break down thy high places: they

5. *Exposed place,* שְׁפִי *shephi.*

Num 23. 3 I will go.. And he went to an high place
Isa. 41. 18 I will open rivers in high places, and
49. 9 their pastures (shall be) in all high places
Jer. 3. 2 Lift up thine eyes unto the high places
3. 21 A voice was heard upon the high places
4. 11 A dry wind of the high places in the wil.
7. 29 take up a lamentation on high places
12. 12 The spoilers are come upon all high places
14. 6 wild asses did stand in the high places

6. *On or in heaven,* ἐπουράνιος *epouranios.*

Eph. 6. 12 against spiritual wickedness in high (places)

HIGH priest —

1. *The head priest,* כֹּהֵן הָרֹאשׁ *kohen harosh.*

2 Ch. 24. 11 the high priest's officer came and emptied

2. *Priest,* ἱερεύς *hiereus.*

Acts 5. 24 when the [high priest] and the captain of

3. *Chief priest,* ἀρχιερεύς *archiereus.*

Matt 26. 3 unto the palace of the high priest, who
26. 51 struck a servant of the high priest, and
26. 57 led (him) away to Caiaphas the high priest
26. 58 followed.. unto the high priest's palace

Matt 26. 62 the high priest arose, and said unto him
26. 63 the high priest answered and said unto
26. 65 Then the high priest rent his clothes, say.
Mark 2. 26 in the days of Abiathar the high priest
14. 47 smote a servant of the high priest, and
14. 53 they led Jesus away to the high priest: and
14. 54 even into the palace of the high priest
14. 60 the high priest stood up in the midst
14. 61 Again the high priest asked him, and said
14. 63 Then the high priest rent his clothes, and
14. 66 cometh one of the maids of the high priest
Luke 3. 2 Annas and Caiaphas being the high priests
22. 50 smote a servant of the high priest, and cut
22. 54 brought him into the high priest's house
John 11. 49 being the high priest that same year
11. 51 but being high priest that year, he proph.
18. 10 smote the high priest's servant, and cut
18. 13 Caiaphas, which was the high priest that
18. 15 the high priest.. palace of the high priest
18. 16 which was known unto the high priest, and
18. 19 The high priest then asked Jesus of his dis.
18. 22 saying, Answerest thou the high priest so?
18. 24 Annas had sent him.. unto.. the high prie.
18. 26 One of the servants of the high priest, being
Acts 4. 6 Annas the high priest, and Caiaphas, and
5. 17 Then the high priest rose up, and all they
5. 21 the high priest came, and they that were
5. 27 council: and the high priest asked them
7. 1 Then said the high priest, Are these things
9. 1 And Saul.. went unto the high priest
22. 5 As also the high priest doth bear me wit.
23. 2 the high priest Ananias commanded them
23. 4 they.. said, Revilest thou God's high priest?
23. 5 I wist not.. that he was the high priest
24. 1 Ananias the high priest descended with the
25. 2 the high priest and the chief of the Jews
Heb. 2. 17 be a merciful and faithful high priest in
3. 1 consider the apostle and high priest of our
4. 14 that we have a great high priest, that is
4. 15 we have not an high priest which cannot
5. 1 every high priest taken from among men
5. 5 not himself to be made an high priest; but
5. 10 Called of God an high priest after the order
6. 20 made an high priest for ever, after the order
7. 26 For such an high priest became us.. holy
7. 27 needeth not daily, as those high priests, to
7. 28 the law maketh men high priests which
8. 1 We have such an high priest, who is set on
8. 3 every high priest is ordained to offer gifts
9. 7 into the second (went) the high priest alone
9. 11 But Christ being come an high priest of good
9. 25 as the high priest entereth into the holy
13. 11 into the sanctuary by the high priest for

HIGH, to set (up) on —

1. *To lift up, exalt,* רוּם *rum, 3a.*

Eze. 31. 4 the deep set him up on high with her

2. *To make high, set on high,* שָׂגַב *sagab,* 3.

Psa. 69. 29 let thy salvation, O God, set me up on h
91. 14 I will set him on high, because he hath
107. 41 Yet setteth he the poor on high from affl.

HIGH thing —

High thing, ὕψωμα *hupsōma.*

2 Co. 10. 5 Casting down.. every high thing that exalt.

HIGH, things too —

To be wonderful, פָּלָא *pala,* 2.

Psa. 131. 1 neither do I exercise.. in things too high

HIGH, too —

To be high, רוּם *rum.*

Prov. 24. 7 Wisdom (is) too high for a fool: he open

HIGH, very —

Above, upward, onward, מַעַל *maal.*

Deut 28. 43 The stranger.. shall get up.. very high

HIGH time —

Hour, ὥρα *hōra.*

Rom 13. 11 knowing the time, that now (it is) high t.

HIGHER —

1. *High,* גָּבֹהַּ *gaboah.*

1 Sa. 9. 2 (he was) higher than any of the people
Eccl. 5. 8 higher than the highest.. higher than they
Dan. 8. 3 one.. higher than the other, and the higher

2. *High, uppermost, most high,* עֶלְיוֹן *elyōn.*

2 Ki. 15. 35 He built the higher gate of the house of
Psa. 89. 27 I will make him (my) first born, higher
Jer. 36. 10 Then read Baruch.. in the higher court, at
Eze. 9. 2 six men came from the way of the higher

3. *Higher,* ἀνώτερον *anōteron.*

Luke 14. 10 Friend, go up higher: then shalt thou

4. *To hold or be above,* ὑπερέχω *huperechō.*

Rom 13. 1 Let every soul be subject unto the higher

5. *High,* ὑψηλός *hupsēlos.*

Heb. 7. 26 high priest.. made higher than the heaven

HIGHER, to be —

1. *To be high,* גָּבַהּ *gabah.*

1 Sa. 10. 23 when he stood.. he was higher than any
Job 35. 5 behold the clouds.. are higher than thou
Isa. 55. 9 the heavens are higher.. so are my ways h.

2. *To be high, lifted up, exalted,* רוּם *rum.*

Num 24. 7 his king shall be higher than Agag, and
Psa. 61. 2 lead me to the rock (that) is higher than

HIGHER place —

1. *Back, upper part, arch,* גַּב *gab.*

Eze. 43. 13 this (shall be) the higher place of the altar

2. *Clean or dry place,* צְחִיחַ, *tsechiach.*
Neh. 4. 13 on the higher places, I even set the people

HIGHEST —
1. *High, uppermost, most high,* עֶלְיוֹן *elyon.*
Psa. 18. 13 the Highest gave his voice; hail..and coals
87. 5 and the Highest himself shall establish her
Eze. 41. 7 the lowest..to the highest by the midst

2. *Highest, most high,* ὕψιστος *hupsistos.*
Matt. 21. 9 Blessed (is) he..Hosanna in the Highest!
Mark 11. 10 Blessed (be) the..Hosanna in the Highest
Luke 1. 32 and shall be called the Son of the Highest
1. 35 the power of the Highest shall overshadow
1. 76 shalt be called the prophet of the Highest
2. 14 Glory to God in the highest, and on earth
6. 35 and ye shall be the children of the Highest
19. 38 peace in heaven, and glory in the highest

HIGHEST branch —
Foliage, highest branch, צַמֶּרֶת *tsammereth.*
Eze. 17. 3 and took the highest branch of the cedar
17. 22 I will also take of the highest branch of

HIGHEST part —
Head, top, רֹאשׁ *rosh.*
Prov. 8. 26 nor the highest part of the dust of the w.

HIGHEST places —
Backs or arches of the high place, גַּפֵּי מְרוֹם [*gaph*].
Prov. 9. 3 crieth upon the highest places of the city

HIGHEST room —
First reclining place, πρωτοκλισία *prōtoklisia.*
Luke 14. 8 sit not down in the highest room; lest a

HIGHEST seat —
First or foremost seat, πρωτοκαθεδρία *prōtokathed.*
Luke 20. 46 the scribes..love..the highest seats in the

HIGHLY —
[See Displeased, esteemed, think].

HIGHLY, very —
Very abundantly, ὑπὲρ ἐκ περισσοῦ *huper ek periss.*
1 Th. 5. 13 to esteem them very highly in love for

HIGH MINDED, to be —
To think high, ὑψηλοφρονέω *hupsēlophroneō.*
Rom. 11. 20 Well..[be not high minded], but fear
1 Ti. 6. 17 Charge them..that they be not high mind.

HIGHNESS —
1. *Rising, excellency, pride,* גַּאֲוָה *gaavah.*
Isa. 13. 3 mighty ones..them that rejoice in my h.
2. *Lifting up,* שְׂאֵת *seeth.*
Job 31. 23 by reason of his highness I could not en.

HIGHWAY —
1. *Customary path,* אֹרַח *orach.*
Judg. 5. 6 the highways were unoccupied, and the
2. *Way,* דֶּרֶךְ דֶּרֶךְ *derek derek.*
Deut. 2. 27 I will go along by the highway, I will nei.
3. *Out place,* חוּץ *chuts.*
Amos 5. 16 they shall say in all the highways, Alas!
4. *Raised up way, highway,* מְסִלָּה *mesillah.*
Num 20. 19 said unto him, We will go by the highway
Judg 20. 31 in the highways, of which one goeth up to
20. 32 draw them from the city unto the highw.
20. 45 they gleaned of them in the highways five
21. 19 on the east side of the highway that goeth
1 Sa. 6. 12 went along the highway, lowing as they
2 Sa. 20. 12 wallowed..in the midst of the highway
20. 12 he removed Amasa out of the highway into
20. 13 he was removed out of the highway, all
2 Ki. 18. 17 which (is) in the highway of the fuller's fi.
Prov 16. 17 The highway of the upright (is) to depart
Isa. 7. 3 pool in the highway of the fuller's field
11. 16 there shall be an highway for the remnant
19. 23 In that day shall there be an highway out
33. 8 The highways lie waste, the wayfaring man
36. 2 pool in the highway of the fuller's field
40. 3 make straight..a highway for our God
49. 11 and my highways shall be exalted
62. 10 cast up, cast up the highway; gather out
Jer. 31. 21 set thine heart toward the highway, (even)
5. *Highway,* מַסְלוּל *maslul.*
Isa. 35. 8 an highway shall be there, and a way, and
6. *Way,* ὁδός *hodos.*
Matt 22. 10 those servants went out into the highways
Mark 10. 46 Timeus, sat by the highway side begging
Luke 14. 23 Go out into the highways and hedges
7. *Crossways of the ways,* διεξόδους τῶν ὁδῶν *diex.*
Matt 22. 9 Go ye therefore into the highways, and as

HI'-LEN, חִילֵן *strong place.*
A city (called in Josh. 15. 51, 21. 15 *Holon*) belonging to Judah, and assigned to the Levites.
1 Ch. 6. 58 H. with her suburbs, Debir with her sub.

HIL-KI'-AH, חִלְקִיָּה, חִלְקִיָּהוּ *Jah is protection.*
1. Father of Eliakim master of the household to king Hezekiah. B.C. 740.
2 Ki. 18. 18 the son of H., which (was) over the house.
18. 26 Then said Eliakim the son of H., and Sh.
18. 37 Then came Eliakim the son of H., which
Isa. 22. 20 will call my servant Eliakim the son of H.
36. 3 Then came forth unto him Eliakim, H.'s
36. 22 Then came Eliakim the son of H., that

2. High priest in the time of Josiah king of Judah. B.C. 650.
2 Ki. 22. 4 Go up to H. the high priest, that he may
22. 8 H. the high priest said unto Shaphan the
22. 8 H. gave the book to Shaphan, and he read
22. 10 H. the priest hath delivered me a book
22. 12 the king commanded H. the priest, and
22. 14 So H. the priest..went unto Huldah the
23. 4 the king commanded H. the high priest
23. 24 the book that H. the priest found in the
1 Ch. 6. 13 Shallum begat H., and H. begat Azariah
9. 11 Azariah the son of H., the son of Meshul.
2 Ch. 34. 9 when they came to H. the high priest, they
34. 14 H. the priest found a book of the law of
34. 15 H. answered and said to Shaphan the scr.
34. 15 And H. delivered the book to Shaphan
34. 18 saying, H. the priest hath given me a book
34. 20 the king commanded H., and Ahikam the
34. 22 H...went to Huldah the prophetess, the
35. 8 H. and Zechariah and Jehiel, rulers of the
Ezra 7. 1 Seraiah, the son of Azariah, the son of H.
Jer. 29. 3 By the hand of..Gemariah the son of H.
3. A descendant of Merari, son of Levi. B.C. 650.
1 Ch. 6. 45 Hashabiah..son of Amaziah, the son of H.
4. A son of Hosah, a descendant of Merari, and a gate keeper of the tabernacle in the time of David. B.C. 1015.
1 Ch. 26. 11 H. the second, Tebaliah the third, Zech.
5. A priest who stood by Ezra while reading the book of the law to the people. B.C. 445.
Neh. 8. 4 Anaiah, and Urijah, and H., and Maaseiah
11. 11 Seraiah the son of H., the son of Meshul.
12. 7 Sallu, Amok, H., Jedaiah. These (were) the
12. 21 Of H., Hashabiah; of Jedaiah, Nethaneel
6. A priest of Anathoth, and father of Jeremiah the prophet. B.C. 650.
Jer. 1. 1 The words of Jeremiah the son of H., of

HILL —
1. *Height, hillock,* גִּבְעָה *gibah.*
Gen. 49. 26 the utmost bound of the everlasting hills
Exod 17. 9 I will stand on the top of the hill with the
17. 10 and Hur, went up to the top of the hill
Num 23. 9 from the hills I behold him: lo, the people
Deut 12. 2 upon the hills, and under every green tree
33. 15 for the precious things of the lasting hills
Josh. 5. 3 Joshua..circumcised..at the hill of the
24. 33 Eleazar..died; and they buried him in a h.
Judg. 7. 1 The Midianites were..by the hill of Moreh
1 Sa. 7. 1 into the house of Abinadab in the hill, and
10. 5 After that thou shalt come to the hill of G.
10. 10 when they came thither to the hill, behold
23. 19 Doth not David hide..in the hill of Hach.
26. 1 Doth not David hide himself in the hill
26. 3 Saul pitched in the hill of Hachilah
2 Sa. 2. 24 when they were come to the hill of Amm.
2. 25 children of B...stood on the top of an h.
1 Ki. 14. 23 they also built..on every high hill, and
2 Ki. 16. 4 he sacrificed..on the hills, and under e.
17. 10 they set..groves in every high hill, and
2 Ch. 28. 4 He sacrificed also..on the hills, and under
Job 15. 7 or wast thou made before the hills?
Psa. 148. 9 Mountains, and all hills; fruitful trees
Prov. 8. 25 before the hills was I brought forth
Song 2. 8 he cometh..skipping upon the hills
4. 6 I will get me..to the hill of frankincense
Isa. 2. 2 and shall be exalted above the hills; and
2. 14 and upon all the hills (that are) lifted up
10. 32 he shall shake his hand against..the hill
30. 17 till ye be left..as an ensign on an hill
30. 25 there shall be..upon every high hill, rivers
31. 4 to fight for mount Zion, and for the hill
40. 4 every mountain and hill shall be made low
40. 12 Who hath..weighed..the hills in a balance
41. 15 Behold..thou..shalt make the hills as ch.
42. 15 I will make waste mountains and hills
54. 10 the mountains shall depart, and the hills
55. 12 the mountains and the hills shall break
65. 7 fathers..blasphemed me upon the hills
Jer. 2. 20 when upon every high hill..thou wanderest
3. 23 Truly in vain..from the hills..the mult.
4. 24 they trembled, and all the hills moved li.
13. 27 I have seen..abominations on the hills
16. 16 they shall hunt them..from every hill
17. 2 and their groves..upon the high hills
31. 39 measuring line..upon the hill Gareb
49. 16 thou..that holdest the height of the hill
50. 6 they have gone from mountain to hill, they
Eze. 6. 3 Thus saith the Lord GOD..to the hills
6. 13 among their idols..upon every high hill
20. 28 they saw every high hill, and all the thick
34. 6 My sheep wandered..upon every high hill
34. 26 the places round about my hill a blessing
35. 8 in thy hills..shall they fall that are
36. 4, 6 and to the hills, to the rivers, and to the
Hos. 4. 13 They sacrifice..upon the hills, under oaks
10. 8 they shall say..to the hills, Fall on us
Joel 3. 18 the hills shall flow with milk, and all the
Amos 9. 13 the days come..and all the hills shall melt
Mic. 4. 1 it shall be exalted above the hills; and
6. 1 Arise..and let the hills hear thy voice
Nah. 1. 5 the hills melt, and the earth is burned at
Hab. 3. 6 the perpetual hills did bow: his ways
Zeph. 1. 10 and a great crashing from the hills
2. *Mount,* הַר *har.*
Gen. 7. 19 all the high hills that (were) under the
Exod 24. 4 Moses..builded an altar under the hill
Num 14. 44 they presumed to go up unto the hill top
14. 45 the Canaanites which dwelt in that hill
Deut. 1. 7 take your journey..in the hills, and in
Deut. 1. 41 ye were ready to go up into the hill
1. 43 and went presumptuously up into the hill
8. 7 depths that spring out of valleys and hills
11. 11 the land, whether ye go..(is) a land of h.
Josh. 9. 1 when all the kings..in the hills, and in
10. 40 Joshua smote all the country of the hills
11. 16 Joshua took all that land, the hills, and
15. 9 the border was..from the top of the hill
17. 16 The hill is not enough for us: and all the
18. 13 the border descended..near the hill that
18. 14 the border..compassed..from the hill
21. 11 they gave them the city of Arba..in the h.
24. 30 they buried him..on..side of the hill of
Judg. 2. 9 they buried him..on the..side of the hill
16. 3 Samson..carried them..to the top of an h.
1 Sa. 25. 20 she came down by the covert of the hill
26. 13 David..stood on the top of an hill afar
2 Sa. 13. 34 came much people by the way of the hill
16. 13 Shimei went along on the hill's side over
21. 9 they hanged them in the hill before the
1 Ki. 11. 7 Then did Solomon build..in the hill that
16. 24 he bought the hill..built on the hill;
16. 24 after the name of Shemer, owner of the h.
20. 23 Their gods (are) gods of the hills; there.
20. 28 The LORD (is) God of the hills, but he (is)
22. 17 I saw all Israel scattered upon the hills
2 Ki. 1. 9 and, behold, he sat on the top of an hill
4. 27 when she came to the man of God to the h.
Psa. 2. 6 Yet have I set my king upon my holy h.
3. 4 I cried..he heard me out of his holy hill
15. 1 LORD..who shall dwell in thy holy hill?
18. 7 the foundations also of the hills moved
24. 3 Who shall ascend into the hill of the L.?
42. 6 will I remember..from the hill Mizar
43. 3 let them bring me unto thy holy hill, and
68. 15 The hill of God (is as) the hill of Bashan
68. 15 an high hill (as) the hill of Bashan
68. 16 Why leap ye, ye high hills?..the hill..G.
80. 10 The hills were covered with the shadow
95. 4 the strength of the hills (is) his also
97. 5 The hills melted like wax at the presence
98. 8 floods clap..let the hills be joyful together
99. 9 Exalt the LORD..worship at his holy hill
104. 10 He sendeth the springs..run among the h.
104. 13 He watereth the hills from his chambers
104. 18 The high hills (are) a refuge for the wild
104. 32 he toucheth the hills, and they smoke
121. 1 I will lift up mine eyes unto the hills
Isa. 5. 25 the hills did tremble, and their carcases
7. 25 all hills that shall be digged with the
3. *Mount, mountain,* הָרָר, הֲרַר *harar, herer.*
Deut. 8. 9 out of whose hills thou mayest dig brass
Psa. 50. 10 (and) the cattle upon a thousand hills
4. *Ascent, going up,* מַעֲלֶה *maaleh.*
1 Sa. 9. 11 as they went up the hill to the city, they
5. *Hill,* βουνός *bounos.*
Luke 3. 5 every mountain and hill shall be brought
23. 30 shall they begin to say..to the hills, Cover
6. *Mount, mountain,* ὄρος *oros.*
Matt. 5. 14 A city that is set on an hill cannot be hid
Luke 4. 29 led him unto the brow of the hill whereon
9. 37 when they were come down from the hill
7. *Horn, promontory,* קֶרֶן *qeren.*
Isa. 5. 1 hath a vineyard in a very fruitful hill

HILL country —
1. *Hill, hill country,* הַר *har.*
Josh 13. 6 the inhabitants of the hill country from
2. *Mountainous,* ὀρεινός *oreinos.*
Luke 1. 39 Mary..went into the hill country with h.
1. 65 throughout all the hill country of Judea

HILLS, little —
A height, hill, גִּבְעָה *gibah.*
Psa. 65. 12 They drop..and the little hills rejoice on
72. 3 bring peace..the little hills, by righteous.
114. 4, 6 skipped like rams..little hills like la.

HIL'-LEL, הִלֵּל *praised greatly.*
Father of Abdon, of the judges of Israel. He was a native of Pirathon in Mount Ephraim. B.C. 1130.
Judg 12. 13 after him Abdon the son of H., a Pirath.
12. 15 Abdon the son of H. the Pirathonite died

HIM —
1. *A man,* אִישׁ *ish.*
Prov 19. 6 every man (is) a friend to him that giveth
2. *He,* הוּא *hu.*
Gen. 4. 26 to Seth, to him also there was born a son
3. *Who,* מִי *mi.*
Eccl. 9. 4 to him that is joined to all the living there
4. *Himself,* αὐτός, *autos.*
Matt. 8. 18 Jesus saw great multitudes about him
Mark 5. 30 knowing..that virtue had gone out of him
Luke 18. 40 to be brought unto him: and when he was
19. 15 these servants to be called unto him, to
John 1. 47 Jesus saw Nathanael coming to him, and
6. 5 Jesus..saw a great company come unto h.
Acts 5. 37 Judas..drew away much people after him
9. 4 he..heard a voice saying unto him, Saul
23. 2 Ananias commanded them that stood by h.
25. 21 I commanded him to be kept till I might
Heb. 12. 2 who for the joy that was set before him
5. *Of himself,* ἑαυτοῦ *heautou.*
Mark 14. 33 he taketh with [him], Lu. 9. 47; 1 Co. 10. 2

6. *That one,* ταυτα *tauta.*
Heb. 11. 12 sprang there even of one, and him as go.

7. *Him,* τοῦτον *touton.*
Matt 27. 32 Simon..him they compelled to bear his
Luke 9. 26 of him shall the Son of man be ashamed
12. 5 Fear him..yea, I say unto you, Fear him
20. 12 they wounded [him] also, and cast(him) o.
20. 13 they will reverence..when they see him
John 5. 6 Jesus saw him lie, and knew that he had
6. 27 Son..for him hath God the Father sealed
21. 21 Peter seeing him saith t Jesus Lord, and
Acts 2. 23 Him, being delivered by the determinate
5. 31 Him hath God exalted with his right hand
10. 40 Him God raised up the third day, and
13. 27 their rulers, because they knew him not
15. 38 Paul thought no goo.. to take him with
16. 3 Him would Paul have to go forth..and
17. 23 Whom..ye ignorantly worship, him decl.
1 Co. 2. 2 not to know..save Jesus Christ, and him
3. 17 If any man defile the temple..[him] shall
Phil. 2. 23 Him therefore I hope to send presently

8. *Of this one,* τούτου *toutou.*
John 9. 31 if any man..doeth his will, him he heareth

9. *To this one,* τούτῳ *toutō.*
Luke 19. 19 said likewise to him, Be thou also over
John 5. 38 for whom he hath sent, him ye believe not
10. 3 To him the porter openeth; and the sheep
13. 24 Simon Peter therefore beckoned to him
Acts 4. 10 by him doth this man stand here before
10. 43 To him give all the prophets witness, that
13. 39 by him all that believe are justified
25. 5 accuse..if there be any wickedness in him
1 Jo. 2. 4 is a liar, and the truth is not in him
2. 5 in him verily is the love of God perfected

10. *A male,* זָכָר *zakar.*
Num 31. 17 woman that hath known..by lying with h.

11. *Him,* ו, הו...*&c.* (a suffix of various forms).
Gen. 2. 15 and put him into the garden of Eden
3. 9 and said unto him Where art thou
4. 7 and thou shalt rule over him
[Very frequent.]

12. *Him,* ה...(Aramaic suff. also freq.).
Ezra 7. 26 let judgment be executed..upon him

13. *His eyes,* עַיִן *ayin.*
Gen. 27. 12 I shall seem to him as a deceiver; and I
29. 20 they seemed unto him..a few days, for the
48. 17 when Joseph saw..it displeased him: and
1 Sa. 3. 18 the LORD: let..do what seemeth him good
18. 8 and the saying displeased him; and he said
18. 20 they told Saul, and the thing pleased him
2 Sa 10. 12 LORD do that which seemeth him good
24. 22 and offer up what (seemeth) good unto him
1 Ki. 9. 12 to see the cities..and they pleased him
Esth 2. 9 the maiden pleased him, and she obtained
Prov. 24. 18 Lest the LORD see (it) and it displease him
Isa. 59. 15 and it displeased him that..no judgment

14. *His face,* פָּנִים *panim.*
Gen. 32. 21 So went the present over before him. and
Exod 34. 6 LORD passed by before him, and proclaim.
1 Sa. 17. 24 all the men of Israel..fled from him
18. 15 when Saul saw..he was afraid of him
19. 8 David went out..and they fled from him
2 Ki. 1. 15 the angel..said..be not afraid of him
2 Ch. 14. 10 Asa went out against him, and they set
19. 2 Jehu..went out to meet him, and said to
Esth. 1. 19 let there go a royal commandment from h.
2. 9 And the maiden..obtained kindness of h.
Job 42. 8 Job shall pray for you; for him will I ac.
Psa. 17. 13 Arise, O LORD, disappoint him, cast..down

15. *His midst,* קֶרֶב *qereb.*
1 Ki. 17. 21 let this child's soul come into him again
17. 22 the soul of the child came into him again

HIM, of —
Concerning or in reference to this, לָזֶה *la-zeh.*
1 Sa. 21. 11 did they not sing one to another of him in

HIM that is —
A man, אִישׁ *ish.*
Lev. 15. 33 and of him that lieth with her that is un.

HIM also, and him —
And that one, κἀκεῖνος *kakeinos.*
Mark 12. 4 and at him they cast stones, and wounded
12. 5 again he sent another; and him they killed
Luke 20. 11 another servant: and they beat him also

HIMSELF —
1. *He,* הוּא *hu.*
Num 35. 19 The revenger of blood himself shall slay

2. *His* (or *its*) *answer,* מַעֲנֶה *maaneh.*
Prov 16. 4 The LORD hath made all..for himself; yea

3. *His life* (*being*), נֶפֶשׁ *nephesh.*
1 Ki. 19. 4 he requested for himself that he might die
Job 18. 4 He teareth himself in his anger: shall the
32. 2 he justified himself rather than God
Amos 6. 8 The LORD God hath sworn by himself, say.

4. *Of himself,* αὑτοῦ *hautou.*
John 9. 21 he is of age; ask..he shall speak for him.
19. 12 whosoever maketh himself a king speak.
Eph. 1. 5 Having predestinated us..to himself, acc.
1. 9 pleasure which he hath purposed in him.
Heb. 9. 26 to put away sin by the sacrifice of himself
12. 3 consider him that endured..against him.

5. *Of himself,* ἑαυτοῦ *heautou.*
Matt 12. 26 he is divided against himself; how shall
12. 45 taketh with himself..other spirits..th. h.
13. 21 Yet hath he not root in himself, but dureth
16. 24 let him deny himself, and take up his cross
18. 4 shall humble himself as this little child
23. 12 whosoever shall exalt himself shall be
23. 12 he that shall humble himself shall be
27. 42 He saved others; himself he cannot save
Mark 3. 26 if Satan rise up against himself, and be
5. 5 crying, and cutting himself with stones
5. 30 knowing in himself that virtue had gone
8. 34 let him deny himself, and take up his cross
12. 33 to love (his) neighbour as himself, is more
15. 31 He saved others; himself he cannot save
Luke 7. 39 he spake within himself, saying, This m.
9. 23 let him deny himself, and take up his cross
9. 25 he gain the whole world, and lose himself
10. 29 he, willing to justify himself, said unto
11. 18 If Satan also be divided against himself
11. 26 other spirits more wicked than himself
12. 17 he thought within himself, saying, What
12. 21 he that layeth up treasure for himself
14. 11 whosoever exalteth himself shall be abased
14. 11 that humbleth himself shall be exalted
15. 17 when he came to himself, he said, How
16. 3 the steward said within himself, What
18. 4 he said within himself, Though I fear not
18. 11 stood and prayed thus with himself, God
18. 14 one that exalteth himself shall be abased
18. 14 he that humbleth himself shall be exalted
19. 12 to receive for himself a kingdom, and to
23. 2 saying that he himself is Christ a king
23. 35 let him save himself, if he be Christ, the
24. 12 [wondering in himself at that which was]
24. 27 expounded..the things concerning [him.]
John 2. 24 Jesus did not commit [himself] unto them
5. 18 his Father, making himself equal with G.
5. 19 The Son can do nothing of himself, but
5. 26 as the Father hath life in himself, so
5. 26 given to the Son to have life in himself
6. 61 Jesus knew in himself that his disciples
7. 18 He that speaketh of himself seeketh his
8. 22 Then said the Jews, Will he kill himself?
11. 38 Jesus therefore, again groaning in himself
11. 51 this spake he not of himself: but being
13. 4 and took a towel, and girded himself
13. 32 God shall also glorify him in himself
16. 13 for he shall not speak of himself; but
19. 7 because he made himself the Son of God
21. 1 Jesus showed himself again to the
21. 7 naked, and did cast himself into the sea
Acts 1. 3 he showed himself alive after his passion
5. 36 Theudas, boasting himself to be somebody
8. 9 giving out that himself was some great
8. 34 speaketh..of himself, or of some other m.?
10. 1 Peter doubted in himself what this vision
12. 11 when Peter was come to himself, he said
14. 17 he left not [himself] without witness, in
16. 27 would have killed himself, supposing that
19. 31 not adventure himself into the theatre
25. 4 he himself would depart shortly (thither)
28. 16 Paul was suffered to dwell by himself
Rom 14. 7 to himself, and no man dieth to himself
14. 12 shall give account of himself to God
14. 22 Happy (is) he that condemneth not himself
15. 3 Christ pleased not himself; but, as it is
1 Co. 3. 18 Let no man deceive himself. If any man
11. 28 let a man examine himself, and so let him
11. 29 eateth and drinketh damnation to himself
14. 4 in an (unknown) tongue edifieth himself
14. 28 and let him speak to himself, and to God
2 Co. 5. 18 reconciled us to himself by Jesus Christ
5. 19 reconciling the world unto himself, not
10. 7 man trust to himself that he is Christ's
10. 7 let him of himself think this again
10. 18 he that commendeth himself is approved
Gal. 1. 4 Who gave himself for our sins, that he
2. 12 he withdrew and separated himself, fear.
2. 20 who loved me, and gave himself for me
6. 3 when he is nothing, he deceiveth himself
6. 4 shall he have rejoicing in himself alone
Eph. 2. 15 to make in himself of twain one new man
5. 2 hath given himself for us an offering
5. 25 loved the church, and gave himself for it
5. 27 present it to himself a glorious church
5. 28 He that loveth his wife loveth himself
5. 33 every one..love his wife even as himself
Phil. 2. 7 made himself of no reputation, and took
2. 8 he humbled himself, and became obedient
3. 21 even to subdue all things unto himself
2 Th. 2. 4 sitteth..showing himself that he is God
1 Ti. 2. 6 Who gave himself a ransom for all, to be
2 Ti. 2. 13 abideth faithful: he cannot deny himself
2. 21 a man therefore purge himself from these
Titus 2. 14 Who gave himself for us, that he might
2. 14 and purify unto himself a peculiar people
Heb. 1. 3 when he had by [himself] purged our sins
5. 3 so also for [himself], to offer for sins
5. 4 no man taketh this honour unto himself
5. 5 Christ glorified not himself to be made
6. 13 swear by no greater, he sware by [himself]
7. 27 he did once, when he offered up himself
9. 7 which he offered for himself, and (for) the
9. 14 who..offered himself without spot to God
9. 25 Nor..that he should offer himself often
Jas. 1. 24 he beholdeth himself, and goeth his way
1. 27 to keep himself unspotted from the world
1 Jo. 3. 3 purifieth himself, even as he is pure
1 Jo. 5. 10 He that believeth..hath the witness in h.
5. 18 he that is begotten of God keepeth hims

HIMSELF, by —
With his person (*back*), גַּף *gaph.*
Exod 21. 3 came in by himself..shall go out by him.
21. 4 be her master's..he shall go out by himself

HIN —
Hin (*liquid measure* = 12 *logs, or* 280 *cub. in.*), הִין *hin.*
Exod 29. 40 the fourth part of an hin of beaten oil
29. 40 fourth part of an hin of wine (for) a drink
30. 24 of cassia five..and of oil olive an hin
Lev. 19. 36 a just ephah, and a just hin, shall ye have
23. 13 (shall be) of wine, the fourth (part) of an h.
Num 15. 4 mingled with the fourth (part) of an hin
15. 5 the fourth (part) of an hin of wine for a
15. 6 mingled with the third (part) of an hin of
15. 7 offer the third (part) of an hin of wine
15. 9 of flour mingled with half an hin of oil
15. 10 for a drink offering half an hin of wine
28. 5 with the fourth (part) of an hin of beaten
28. 7 fourth (part) of an hin for the one lamb
28. 14 half an hin..of an hin..of an hin unto a
Eze. 4. 11 water by measure, the sixth part of an hin
45. 24 for a ram, and an hin of oil for an ephah
46. 5, 7, 11 and an hin of oil to an ephah
46. 14 third part of an hin of oil, to temper

HIND —
1. *Hind,* אַיָּלָה *ayyalah.*
Gen. 49. 21 Naphtali (is) a hind let loose: he giveth
2 Sa. 22. 34 He maketh my feet like hinds' (feet); and
Job 39. 1 canst thou mark when the hinds do calve
Psa. 18. 33 He maketh my feet like hinds' (feet), and
29. 9 voice of the LORD maketh the hinds to
Song 2. 7 I charge you..by the hinds of the field
3. 5 I charge you..by the hinds of the field
Hab. 3. 19 he will make my feet like hinds' (feet)

2. *Hind,* אַיֶּלֶת *ayyeleth.*
Prov. 5. 19 (be as) the loving hind and pleasant roe
Jer. 14. 5 Yea, the hind also calved in the field, and

HINDER —
Behind, last, furthest, אַחֲרוֹן *acharon.*
Zech 14. 8 and half of them toward the hinder sea

HINDER, to —
1. *To hinder, delay,* אָחַר *achar,* 3.
Gen. 24. 56 And he said unto them, Hinder me not

2. *To keep back, withhold, darken,* חָשַׂךְ *chasak.*
Isa. 14. 6 he..is persecuted, (and) none hindereth

3. *To withhold, keep back,* מָנַע *mana,* 2.
Num 22. 16 Let nothing..hinder thee from coming

4. *To cause to go back,* שׁוּב *shub,* 5.
Job 9. 12 Behold, he taketh away, who can hinder

5. *To make an injury,* עָשָׂה תּוֹעָה *asah toah.*
Neh. 4. 8 fight against Jerusalem, and to hinder it

6. *To cut up or back,* ἀνακόπτω *anakoptō.*
Gal. 5. 7 who [did hinder] you that ye should not

7. *To give an interruption,* ἐγκοπὴν δίδωμι [*didōmi*]
1 Co. 9. 12 we should hinder the gospel of Christ

8. *To cut in, interrupt,* ἐγκόπτω *egkoptō.*
Rom 15. 22 been much hindered from coming to you
1 Th. 2. 18 have come unto you..but Satan hindered

9. *To cut off,* ἐκκόπτω *ekkoptō.*
1 Pe. 3. 7 that your prayers be not [hindered]

10. *To hinder,* κωλύω *kōluō.*
Luke 11. 52 them that were entering in ye hindered
Acts 8. 36 See..what doth hinder me to be baptized?

HINDER end —
After, hinder, אָחַר *achar.*
2 Sa. 2. 23 Abner with the hinder end of the spear

HINDER part (of the ship) —
1. *Back or hinder part,* אָחוֹר *achor.*
1 Ki. 7. 25 and all their hinder parts (were) inward
2 Ch. 4. 4 and all their hinder parts (were) inward
Psa. 78. 66 he smote his enemies in the hinder part

2. *End, rear,* סוֹף *soph.*
Joel 2. 20 his hinder part toward the utmost sea

3. *Hinder part, stern,* πρύμνα *prumna.*
Mark 4. 38 he was in the hinder part of the ship
Acts 27. 41 but the hinder part was broken with the

HINDERED, to be —
To cease, cause to cease, בְּטֵל *betel.*
Ezra 6. 8 unto these men, that they be not hindered

HINDERMOST, HINDMOST —
1. *Behind, last, furthest,* אַחֲרוֹן *acharon.*
Gen. 33. 2 And he put..Rachel and Joseph hinder.
Num. 2. 31 shall go hindmost with their standards

2. *Furthest part, latter end,* אַחֲרִית *acharith.*
Jer. 50. 12 the hindermost of the nations (shall be) a

HINDMOST, to smite the —
To smite the tail or rear, זָנַב *zanab,* 3.
Deut 25. 18 smote the hindmost of thee, (even) all
Josh. 10. 19 pursue..and smite the hindmost of them

HINGE —
1. *Hinge, opening,* פֹּת *poth.*
1 Ki. 7. 50 the hinges (of) gold, (both) for the door

2. *Hinge, form,* צִיר *tsir.*
Prov.26.14 (As) the door turneth upon his hinges, so

HIN'-NOM, הִנֹּם *gratis.*
A person of whom nothing is known but that he had a son whose name is not given, from whom a valley that lay on the W. and S.W. of Jerusalem was named, and in which human sacrifices and filth were burnt. See HELL, No. 3.
Josh 15. 8 went up by the valley of the son of H.
15. 8 mountain that (lieth) before the valley..H.
18. 16 mountain that (lieth) before the valley..H.
18. 16 and descended to the valley of H., to the
2 Ki.23. 10 Topheth..in the valley of..children of H.
2 Ch.28. 3 burnt incense in the valley of the son of H.
33. 6 through..fire in the valley of the son of H.
Neh. 11. 30 And they dwelt..unto the valley of H.
Jer. 7. 31 which (is) in the valley of the son of H.
7. 32 Tophet, nor The valley of the son of H.
19. 2 go forth unto the valley of the son of H.
19. 6 Tophet, nor The valley of the son of H.
32. 35 which (are) in the valley of the son of H.

HIP —
Leg, limb, thigh, שׁוֹק *shoq.*
Judg15. 8 he smote them hip and thigh with a great

HI'-RAH, חִירָה *distinction, nobility.*
An Adullamite, the "*friend*" of Judah. B.C. 1727. For "friend" the LXX and Vulgate read "*shepherd.*"
Gen. 38. 1 certain Adullamite, whose name (was) H.
38. 12 went up..he and his friend H. the Adul.

HI'-RAM, חִירָם, חִירוֹם.
1. A king of Tyre who lived on most friendly alliance with both David and Solomon. B.C. 1015.
2 Sa. 5. 11 H. king of Tyre sent messengers to David
1 Ki. 5. 1 H. king of Tyre sent..for H. was ever a l.
5. 2 And Solomon sent to H., saying
5. 7 when H. heard the words of Solomon, that
5. 8 H. sent to Solomon, saying, I have consi.
5. 10 H. gave Solomon cedar trees and fir trees
5. 11 Solomon gave H. twenty thousand meas.
5. 11 thus gave Solomon to H. year by year
5. 12 there was peace between H. and Solomon
5. 18 Solomon's builders and H.'s did hew..and
9. 11 H...had furnished Solomon with cedar t.
9. 11 Solomon gave H. twenty cities in the land
9. 12 H. came out from Tyre to see the cities w.
9. 14 H. sent to the king sixscore talents of gold
9. 27 H. sent in the navy his servants, shipmen
10. 11 the navy also of H., that brought gold from
10. 22 king had at sea a navy..with the navy of H.
1 Ch.14. 1 H. king of Tyre sent messsengers to David
2 Ch. 2. 11 H. the king of Tyre answered in writing
2. 13 I have sent a cunning man..of H. my fa.
8. 2 the cities which H. had restored to Solomon
8. 18 H. sent him, by the hands of his servants
9. 10 the servants also of H...brought algum t.
9. 21 went to Tarshish with the servants of H.
2. A man of eminence and the principal architect sent by King Hiram to Solomon. In Chronicles he is called *Huram,* where also he has the title *Ab* (father or master) given to him. See HURAM.
1 Ki. 7. 13 Solomon sent and fetched H. out of Tyre
7. 40 H. made the lavers, and the shovels
7. 40 H. made an end of doing all the work
7. 45 which H. made to king Solomon for the h.

HIRE —
1. *Gift, hire,* אֶתְנַן, אֶתְנָן *ethnan.*
Deut23. 18 Thou shalt not bring the hire of a whore
Isa. 23. 17 and she shall turn to her hire, and shall
23. 18 and her hire shall be holiness to the LORD
Eze. 16. 31 as an harlot, in that thou scornest hire
16. 41 and thou also shalt give no hire any more
Mic. 1. 7 the hires thereof shall be burnt with
1. 7 she gathered (it) of the hire of an harlot
1. 7 shall return to the hire of an harlot
2. *Price, hire,* מְחִיר *mechir.*
Mic. 3. 11 the priests thereof teach for hire, and
3. *Hire, wage, price, reward, fare,* שָׂכָר *sakar.*
Gen. 30. 18 God hath given me my hire, because I h.
30. 32 spotted cattle..(of such) shall be my hire
30. 33 it shall come for my hire before thy face
31. 8 The ringstraked shall be thy hire; then
Exod22. 15 (be) an hired (thing), it came for his hire
Deut 24. 15 At his day thou shalt give (him) his hire
1 Ki. 5. 6 unto thee..I give hire for thy servants
Zech. 8. 10 no hire for man, nor any hire for beast
4. *Hire, wage, reward,* μισθός *misthos.*
Matt20. 8 give them (their) hire, beginning from the
Luke10. 7 for the labourer is worthy of his hire
Jas. 5. 4 hire of the labourers who have reaped

HIRE, to —
1. *To hire,* סָכַר *sakar.*
Ezra 4. 5 And hired counsellors against them, to
2. *To hire, reward,* שָׂכַר *sakar.*
Gen. 30. 16 I have hired thee with my son's mandra.
Deut23. 4 they hired against thee Balaam the son
Judg. 9. 4 Abimelech hired vain and light persons
18. 4 and hath hired me, and I am his priest
2 Sa. 10. 6 sent and hired the Syrians of Beth-rehob
2 Ki. 7. 6 the king of Israel hath hired against us
1 Ch.19. 6 to hire them chariots and horsemen out
19. 7 hired thirty and two thousand chariots
2 Ch.24. 12 hired masons and carpenters to repair
25. 6 He hired also an hundred thousand mig.
Neh. 6. 12 for Tobiah and Sanballat had hired him
6. 13 Therefore (was) he hired, that I should be
13. 2 hired Balaam against them, that he should
Isa. 46. 6 and weigh silver..(and) hire a goldsmith
3. *To bribe, reward,* שָׁחַד *shachad.*
Eze. 16. 33 hirest them, that they may come unto thee
4. *To give, hire,* תָּנָה *tanah.*
Hos. 8. 10 they have hired among the nations, now
5. *To give, hire,* תָּנָה *tanah,* 5.
Hos. 8. 9 by himself: Ephraim hath hired lovers
6. *To hire,* μισθόομαι *misthoomai.*
Matt20. 1 went..to hire labourers into his vineyard
20. 7 They say..Because no man hath hired us

HIRE out selves, to —
To be hired, שָׂכַר *sakar,* 2.
1 Sa. 2. 5 (They)..have hired out themselves for b.

HIRED (man, servant) —
1. *One hired,* שָׂכִיר *sakir.*
Exod12. 45 an hired servant shall not eat thereof
22. 15 if it (be) an hired (thing), it came for his
Lev. 22. 10 or an hired servant, shall not eat (of) the
25. 6 thy hired servant, and for thy stranger
25. 40 as an hired servant, (and) as a sojourner
25. 50 according to the time of an hired servant
25. 53 as a yearly hired servant shall he be
Deut 15. 18 been worth a double hired servant (to thee)
24. 14 Thou shalt not oppress an hired servant
Jer. 46. 21 her hired men (are) in the midst of her
2. *Hireling, one hired,* μίσθιος *misthios.*
Luke15. 17 How many hired servants of my father's
15. 19 make me as one of thy hired servants
3. *One hired,* μισθωτός *misthōtos.*
Mark 1. 20 in the ship with the hired servants, and
4. *Any thing hired,* μίσθωμα *misthōma.*
Acts 28. 30 two whole years in his own hired house

HIRED, that is —
1. *One hired,* שָׂכִיר *sakir.*
Lev. 19. 13 the wages of him that is hired shall not
2. *What is hired,* שְׂכִירָה *sekirah.*
Isa. 7 20 the LORD shave with a razor that is hired

HIRELING —
1. *One hired,* שָׂכִיר *sakir.*
Job 7. 1 days also like the days of an hireling?
7. 2 hireling looketh for (the reward of) his
14. 6 shall accomplish, as an hireling, his day
Isa. 16. 14 three years, as the years of an hireling
21. 16 according to the years of an hireling
Mal. 3. 5 that oppress the hireling in (his) wages
2. *Hired one, hireling,* μισθωτός *misthōtos.*
John10. 12 he that is an hireling..not the shepherd
10. 13 [hireling] fleeth, because he is an hireling

HIS —
1. *His, of him,* αὐτοῦ *hautou.*
Matt. 1. 21 he shall save his people from their sins
2. *His own, one's own,* ἑαυτοῦ *heautou.*
Luke11. 21 When a strong man armed keepeth his p.
12. 47 that servant which knew his Lord
13. 19 which a man took, and cast into his gard.
14. 26 hate not [his] father, and mother, and wife
15. 5 he layeth (it) on [his] shoulders, rejoicing
15. 20 And he arose and came to [his] father. But
16. 5 So he called every one of his lord's debtors
19. 13 he called his ten servants, and delivered
Rom. 5. 8 But God commendeth his love toward us
1 Co. 7. 37 decreed..that he will keep his virgin, do.
2 Co. 3. 13 put a veil over [his] face, that the children
Gal. 6. 8 he that soweth to his flesh shall of the fl.
Eph. 5. 28 He that loveth his wife loveth himself
5. 33 let every one of you so love his wife even
1 Th. 2. 11 charged..you, as a father (doth) his chil.
2. 12 who hath called you unto his kingdom and
4. 4 should know how to possess his vessel in s.
2 Th. 2. 6 that he might be revealed in his time
Rev. 10. 7 as he hath declared to his servants the pr.
3. *His own proper,* ἴδιος *idios.*
Matt22. 5 went their ways, one to his farm, another
John 5. 18 but said also that God was his Father
1 Ti. 6. 15 Which in his times he shall show, (who is)
Heb. 4. 10 he also hath ceased..as God..from his
2 Pe. 2. 16 But was rebuked for his iniquity: the du.
4. *Of him,* τοῦ *tou.*
Acts 17. 28 have said, For we are also his offspring
[*See also* Acquaintances, bring, company].

HIS own —
1. *His, of him,* αὐτοῦ *hautou.*
Matt16. 26 gain the..world, and lose his own soul?
27. 60 laid it in his own new tomb, which he had
Mark 6. 1 went out..and came into his own country
6. 4 without honour, but in his own country
6. 4 among his own kin, and in his own house
8. 36 gain the..world, and lose his own soul?
Luke 1. 23 accomplished, he departed to his own ho.
5. 25 departed to his own house, glorifying God
5. 29 made him a great feast in his own house
9. 26 when he shall come in his own glory, and
18. 7 shall not God avenge his own elect, which
John 7. 53 And every man went unto his own house
Acts 21. 11 bound his own hands and feet, and said
1 Co. 6. 14 will also raise up us by his own power
Eph. 1. 11 worketh..after the counsel of his own will
1. 20 and set (him) at his own right hand in the
Heb. 3. 6 Christ as a Son over his own house; whose
4. 10 he also hath ceased from his own works
Jas. 1. 26 but deceiveth his own heart, this man's
1 Pe. 2. 24 bare our sins in his own body on the tree
Rev. 1. 5 washed us from our sins in his own blood
2. *Of one's own,* ἑαυτοῦ *heautou.*
Luke14. 26 his own life also, he cannot be my disciple
Rom. 4. 19 he considered not his own body now dead
8. 3 sending his own Son in the likeness of
1 Co. 7. 2 let every man have his own wife, and let
10. 24 Let no man seek his own, but every man
Gal. 6. 4 let every man prove his own work, and
Eph. 5. 29 no man ever yet hated his own flesh; but
Phil. 2. 4 Look not every man on his own things
3. *His own proper,* ἴδιος *idios.*
Matt. 9. 1 passed over, and came into his own city
25. 14 (who) called his own servants, and deliv.
Mark15. 20 put [his own] clothes on him, and led him
Luke 2. 3 to be taxed, every one into [his own] city
6. 41 the beam that is in thine own eye?
6. 44 For every tree is known by his own fruit.
10. 34 set him on his own beast, and brought h.
John 1. 11 He came unto his own, and his own recei.
1. 41 He first findeth his own brother Simon
4. 44 prophet hath no honour in his own coun.
5. 43 if another shall come in his own name
7. 18 speaketh of himself seeketh his own glory
8. 44 he speaketh a lie, he speaketh of his own
10. 3 and he calleth his own sheep by name, and
10. 4 when he putteth forth his own sheep, he
13. 1 loved his own which were in the world
15. 19 the world would love his own: but beca.
16. 32 shall be scattered, every man to his own
19. 27 that disciple took her unto his own (home)
Acts 1. 7 the Father hath put in his own power
1. 25 fell, that he might go to his own place
2. 6 heard them speak in his own language
4. 32 the things which he possessed was his own
13. 36 after he had served his own generation
20. 28 he hath purchased with his own blood
28. 30 two whole years in his own hired house
Rom. 8. 32 He that spared not his own Son, but
14. 4 to his own master he standeth or falleth
14. 5 be fully persuaded in his own mind
1 Co. 3. 8 every man shall receive his own reward
3. 8 reward, according to his own labour
6. 18 but he..sinneth against his own body
7. 4 husband hath not power of his own body
7. 37 hath power over his own will, and hath
9. 7 a warfare any time at his own charges?
11. 21 one taketh before (other) his own supper
15. 23 every man in his own order: Christ the
15. 38 God giveth..to every seed his own body
Gal. 6. 5 For every man shall bear his own burden.
1 Ti. 3. 4 One that ruleth well his own house, hav.
3. 5 a man know not how to rule his own hou.
5. 8 But if any provide not for his own, and
Heb. 7. 27 for his own sins, and then for the people's.
9. 12; 13. 12; Jas. 1. 14; 2 Pe. 2. 22.
4. *Any one,* τις *tis.*
Acts 11. 29 every man according to his ability

HIS several —
His own proper, ἴδιος *idios.*
Matt25. 15 gave..according to his several ability

HISS, to —
To hiss, call, שָׁרַק *sharaq.*
1 Ki. 9. 8 by it shall be astonished, and shall hiss
Job 27. 23 (Men)..shall hiss him out of his place
Isa. 5. 26 hiss unto them from the end of the earth.
7. 18 the LORD shall hiss for the fly that (is)
Jer. 19 8 hiss because of all the plagues thereof
49. 17 and shall hiss at all the plagues thereof
50. 13 astonished, and hiss at all her plagues
Lam. 2. 15 hiss and wag their head at the daughter
2. 16 they hiss and gnash the teeth: they say
Eze. 27. 36 The merchants..shall hiss at thee; thou
Zeph. 2. 15 every one that passeth by her shall hiss
Zech10. 8 I will hiss for them, and gather them

HISSING —
1. *Hissing,* שְׁרִיקוֹת, [V. L. שְׁרוּקֹת] *sheriqoth.*
Jer. 18. 16 To make their land..a perpetual hissing
2. *Hissing,* שְׁרֵקָה *shereqah.*
2 Ch.29. 8 trouble, to astonishment, and to hissing
Jer. 19. 8 make this city desolate, and an hissing
25. 9 and an hissing, and perpetual desolations
25. 18 an hissing, and a curse; as (it is) this day
29. 18 to be a curse..an hissing, and a reproach
51. 37 And Babylon shall become..an hissing
Mic. 6. 16 and the inhabitants thereof an hissing

HIT, to —
To find, מָצָא *matsa.*
1 Sa. 31. 3 archers hit him; and he was sore woun.
1 Ch.10. 3 the archers hit him, and he was wounded

HITHER —
1. *Here, hither,* הֲלֹם *halom.*
Exod. 3. 5 Draw not nigh hither: put off thy shoes
Judg18. 3 said unto him, Who brought thee hither?
Ruth 2. 14 At meal time come thou hither, and eat
1 Sa. 14. 36 said..Let us draw near hither unto God

1 Sa. 14. 38 Draw ye near hither all the chief of the
Psa. 73. 10 Therefore his people return hither; and

2. *Here, hither,* הֵנָּה *henah.*

Gen. 15. 16 they shall come hither again: for the in.
2 Ki. 8. 7 saying, The man of God is come hither

3. *Here,* פּוֹ, פֹּה *po.*

1 Sa. 16. 11 we will not sit down till he come hither

4. *Hither, here,* ἐνθάδε *enthade.*

John 4. 15 thirst not, neither come hither to draw
4. 16 Go, call thy husband, and come hither
Acts 17. 6 crying, These..are come hither also
25. 17 when they were come hither, without any

5. *Hither, here,* ὧδε *hōde.*

Matt. 8. 29 art thou come hither to torment us before
14. 18 He said, Bring them hither to me
17. 17 Jesus answered..Bring him hither to me
22. 12 Friend, how camest thou in hither not
Mark 11. 3 and straightway he will send him hither
Luke 9. 41 Jesus answering said..Bring thy son [hi.]
14. 21 bring in hither the poor, and the maimed
19. 27 mine enemies..bring hither, and slay (th.)
John 6. 25 they said..Rabbi, when camest thou hi.?
20. 27 Reach hither thy finger, and behold my
Acts 9. 21 came hither for that intent, that he might
Rev. 4. 1 Come up hither, and I will show thee th.
11. 12 Come up hither. And they ascended up to

HITHER, to bring —

To cause to come nigh, נָגַשׁ *nagash,* 5.

1 Sa. 13. 9 Bring hither a burnt offering to me, and
14. 18 Saul said..Bring hither the ark of God
14. 34 Bring me hither every man his ox, and
15. 32 Bring ye hither to me Agag the king of
23. 9 he said to Abiathar..Bring hither the ep.
30. 7 I pray thee, bring me hither the ephod

HITHER, to come —

To come nigh, נָגַשׁ *nagash.*

Josh. 3. 9 Come hither, and hear the words of the Lo.
[*See* Come hither].

HITHER, to call —

To call for, μετακαλέομαι *metakaleomai.*

Acts 10. 32 call hither Simon, whose surname is Peter

HITHERTO — [*See also* 1 Sa. 7. 12.]

1. *From then, from that time,* מֵאָז *me-az.*

2 Sa. 15. 34 thy father's servant hitherto, so (will) I

2. *Yonder, beyond,* הָלְאָה *haleah.*

Isa. 18. 7 terrible from their beginning hitherto; a

3. *Unto thus, hitherto,* עַד כֹּה *ad koh.*

Exod. 7. 16 and, behold, hitherto thou wouldest not
Josh. 17. 14 forasmuch as the LORD hath blessed me h.

4. *Unto thus, hitherto,* עַד־כָּה *ad kah.*

Dan. 7. 28 Hitherto (is) the end of the matter. As for

5. *Here, hither,* עַד הֲלֹם *ad halom.*

2 Sa. 7. 18 that thou hast brought me hitherto?
1 Ch. 17. 16 that thou hast brought me hitherto?

6. *Unto here, hitherto,* עַד הֵנָּה *ad henah.*

Judg 16. 13 Hitherto thou hast mocked me, and told

7. *Until here or now,* ἄχρι τοῦ δεῦρο *achri tou deuro.*

Rom. 1. 13 I purposed to come..but was let hitherto

8. *Until now,* ἕως ἄρτι *heōs arti.*

John 5. 17 My Father worketh hitherto, and I work
16. 24 Hitherto have ye asked nothing in my na.

HITHERTO not —

Not yet, οὔπω *oupō.*

1 Co. 3. 2 for hitherto ye were not able (to bear it)

HIT-TITES, חִתִּי.

The descendants of Heth, son of Canaan, and inhabiting the mountainous country of Judah.

Gen. 15. 20 the Hittites, and the Perizzites, and the R.
23. 10 Ephron the H. answered Abraham in the
25. 9 the field of Ephron the son of Zohar the H.
26. 34 he took..Judith..daughter of Beeri the H.
26. 34 Bashemath the daughter of Elon the H.
36. 2 Adah the daughter of Elon the H., and A.
49. 29 cave that (is) in the field of Ephron the H.
49. 30 bought with the field of Ephron the H. for
50. 13 possession of a burying place of E. the H.
Exod. 3. 8, 17 the Canaanites, and the H., and the A.
13. 5 the Canaanites, and the H., and the Am.
23. 23 the Amorites, and the H., and the Periz.
23. 28 drive out the Hivite..Canaanite, and..H.
33. 2 the Canaanite, the Amorite, and the H.
34. 11 the Amorite, and the Canaanite, and the H.
Num 13. 29 the H., and the Jebusites, and the Amor.
Deut. 7. 1 cast out many nations before thee, the H.
20. 17 the H., and the Amorites, the Canaanites
Josh. 1. 4 all the land of the H., and unto the great
3. 10 drive out..the Canaanites, and the H., and
9. 1 the H., and the Amorite, the Canaanite
11. 3 on the west, and (to) the Amorite, and the H.
12. 8 the H., the Amorites, and the Canaanites
24. 11 the Canaanites, and the H., and the Gir.
Judg. 1. 26 the man went into the land of the H., and
3. 5 Israel dwelt among the Canaanites, H., and
1 Sa. 26. 6 Then..David..said to Ahimelech the H.
2 Sa. 11. 3 of Eliam, the wife of Uriah the H.?
11. 6 David sent..(saying), Send..Uriah the H.
11. 17 fell (some) of the people..and Uriah the H.
11. 21, 24 Thy servant Uriah the H. is dead also
12. 9 Thou hast killed Uriah the H. with the s.
12. 10 and hast taken the wife of Uriah the H.
23. 39 Uriah the H.: thirty and seven in all

1 Ki. 9. 20 all the people..left of the Amorites, H.
10. 29 so for all the kings of the H., and for the
11. 1 Ammonites, Edomites, Zidonians, (and) H.
15. 5 save only in the matter of Uriah the H.
2 Ki. 7. 6 hath hired against us the kings of the H.
1 Ch. 11. 41 Uriah the H., Zabad the son of Ahlai
2 Ch. 1. 17 for all the kings of the H., and for the k.
8. 7 (As for) all the people..left of the H., and
Ezra 9. 1 of the Canaanites, the H., the Perizzites
Neh. 9. 8 to give the land of the Canaanites, the H.
Eze. 16. 3 father..an Amorite..thy mother an H.
16. 45 your mother..an H., and your father an A.

HIV-ITES, חִוִּי *villager, midlander.*

This word in the original Hebrew is always in the singular number, and it is quite uncertain whether it refers to a progenitor or a locality. In the common English version it is sometimes kept in the singular,—the "Hivite." The Hivite is named in Gen. 10. 17 and 1 Ch. 1. 15 as descended from Canaan, son of Ham. It is difficult to fix their locality; but at the time of Jacob's return to Canaan they possessed Shechem, Hamor the Hivite being the prince of the land. They were peaceful and commercially inclined (Gen. 34. 21, 23, 28, 29).

Gen. 10. 17 And the H., and the Arkite, and the Sin.
34. 2 when Shechem the son of Hamor the H.
36. 2 of Anah the daughter of Zibeon the H.
Exod. 3. 8, 17 the Perizzites, and the H., and the J.
13. 5 the Amorites, and the H., and the Jebus.
23. 23 the Canaanites, and the H., and the Jebusites
23. 28 which shall drive out the H., the Canaan.
33. 2 I will drive out the..H., and the Jebusi.
34. 11 the Perizzite, and the H., and the Jebu.
Deut. 7. 1 the Perizzites, and the H., and the Jebu.
20. 17 the Perizzites, the H., and the Jebusites
Josh. 3. 10 the Hittites, and the H., and the Perizzi.
9. 1 the Perizzite, the H., and the Jebusite
9. 7 And the men of Israel said unto the H.
11. 3 and (to) the H. under Hermon in the land
11. 19 save the H., the inhabitants of Gibeon
12. 8 the Canaanites, the Perizzites, the H.
24. 11 the Girgashites, the H., and the Jebusite
Judg. 3. 3 and the H. that dwelt in mount Lebanon
3. 5 Amorites, and Perizzites, and H., and J.
2 Sa. 24. 7 And came..to all the cities of the H., and
1 Ki. 9. 20 Hittites, Perizzites, H., and Jebusites
1 Ch. 1. 15 And the H., and the Arkite, and the Sin.
2 Ch. 8. 7 the Perizzites, and the H., and the Jebu.

HIZ-KI'-AH, חִזְקִיָּה *Jah is strong.*

An ancestor of Zephaniah the prophet. In the Hebrew this name is exactly the same as *Hizkijah* and *Hezekiah.* B.C. 640.

Zeph. 1. 1 Gedaliah, the son of Amariah, the son of H.

HIZ-KI'-JAH, חִזְקִיָּה *Jah is strong.*

The Hebrew of this name is identical with *Hezekiah* and *Hizkiah*; and there is no doubt that the name should be taken with that preceding it, as *Ater*-hizkijah, as given in the lists of those that returned from Babylon with Zerubbabel. B.C. 638.

Neh. 10. 17 Ater, H., Azzur

HO! —

Ho! (threatening, grief, exhortation), הוֹי *hoi.*

Isa. 55. 1 Ho, every one that thirsteth, come ye to
Zech. 2. 6 Ho, ho! (come forth), and flee from the

HOAR, HOARY frost —

Hoar frost, כְּפוֹר *kephor.*

Exod 16. 14 (as) small as the hoar frost on the ground
Job 38. 29 hoary frost of heaven, who hath gendered
Psa. 147. 16 he scattereth the hoar frost like ashes

HOAR (or) HOARY hair or head —

Age, gray headedness, שֵׂיבָה *sebah.*

Lev. 19. 32 Thou shalt rise up before the hoary head
1 Ki. 2. 6 let not his hoar head go down to the grave
2. 9 his hoar head bring thou down to the gr.
Prov 16. 31 The hoary head (is) a crown of glory, (if)
Isa. 46. 4 to hoar hairs will I carry (you): I have

HOARY, (to be) —

Age, gray headedness, שֵׂיבָה *sebah.*

Job 41. 32 (one) would think the deep (to be) hoary

HO'-BAB, חֹבָב *beloved.*

This name occurs twice. It is doubtful whether it means the father-in-law of Moses or his son. In Num. 10. 29 he is called the son of Raguel (or Reuel), who is identified with Jethro in Exod. 2. 18 compared with 3. 1, &c. The words of Judg. 4. 11 are in favour of Hobab's identity with Jethro. Yet this is of later date and a more casual statement.

Num 10. 29 Moses said unto H., the son of Raguel
Judg. 4. 11 the children of H., the father in law of M.

HO'-BAH, חוֹבָה *lurking place.*

The place to which Abraham pursued the kings who had pillaged Sodom. It was situated to the N. of Damascus. Three miles N. of Damascus there is a place called *Masjad Ibrahim,* the "prayer place of Abraham;" and the tradition is that this is the spot on which Abraham thanked God after his victory. Behind this spot there is a cleft in the rock wherein according to tradition the patriarch took refuge on one occasion from the giant Nimrod. Hobah signifies "hiding place." The Jews of Damascus hold that the village of *Jôbar,* not far from *Buzzeh,* is the *Hobah* of Scripture, and they have a synagogue there dedicated to Elijah.

Gen. 14. 15 smote them, and pursued them unto H.

HOD, הוֹד *glory.*

A son of Zophah, a descendant of Asher. B.C. 1550.

1 Ch. 7. 37 Bezer, and H., and Shamma, and Shilshah

HO-DA'-IAH, הוֹדַיְוָהוּ, or הוֹדַוְיָהוּ *honourer of Jah.*

This name ought to be given as *Hodaviah* the son of Elioenai, a descendant of the royal line of Judah. B.C. 445.

1 Ch. 3. 24 And the sons of Elioenai (were) H., and

HO-DAV'-IAH, הוֹדַוְיָה.

1. A chief of the half tribe of Manasseh on the E. of the Jordan. B.C. 800.

1 Ch. 5. 24 H., and Jahdiel..heads of the house of

2. The son of Hassenuah a Benjamite. B.C. 445.

1 Ch. 9. 7 Sallu the son of Meshullam, the son of H.

3. A Levite and founder of the family of the Bene-hodaviah. In Nehemiah the name is Hodevah (Neh. 7. 43) B.C. 638.

Ezra 2. 40 of the children of H., seventy and four

HO'-DESH, חֹדֶשׁ *new moon.*

A wife of Shaharaim, a Benjamite. B.C. 1400.

1 Ch. 8. 9 he begat of H. his wife, Jobab, and Zibai

HO-DE'-VAH, הוֹדְוָה [V.L. הוֹדְיָה] *Jah is honour.*

A Levite family that returned from captivity with Zerubbabel. B.C. 638.

Neh. 7. 43 of the children of H., seventy and four

HO-DI'-AH, or HO-DI'-JAH, הוֹדִיָּה.

1. The wife of one Ezra, a man of Judah; she is the same person as *Jehudijah* in 1 Ch 4 18. B.C. 1400.

1 Ch. 4. 19 the sons of (his) wife H., the sister of Na.

2. A Levite in the time of Ezra and Nehemiah. B.C. 445.

Neh. 8. 7 H., Maaseiah, Kelita, Azariah, Jozabad
9. 5 H...said, Stand up..bless the LORD your
10. 10 their brethren, Shebaniah, H., Kelita, Pel.
10. 13 H., Bani, Beninu

3. A chief of the people under Nehemiah. B.C. 445.

Neh. 10. 18 H., Hashum, Bezai

HOG'-LAH, חָגְלָה *magpie.*

The third of the five daughters of Zelophehad. The name is also in Beth-hoglah. B.C. 1450.

Num 26. 33 Mahlah, and Noah, H., Milcah, and Tirz.
27. 1 Noah, and H., and Milcah, and Tirzah
36. 11 Mahlah, Tirzah, and H., and Milcah, and
Josh. 17. 3 Mahlah, and Noah, H., Milcah, and Tirzah

HO'-HAM, הוֹהָם *Jah protects the multitude.*

An Amorite king of Hebron, and one of the five kings captured and put to death by Joshua in the cave of Makkedah. B.C. 1450.

Josh 10. 3 Adoni-zedek..sent unto H. king of Hebron

HOISE up, to —

To lift up, ἐπαίρω *epairō.*

Acts 27. 40 hoised up the mainsail to the wind, and

HOLD —

1. *Stronghold, fortified place,* מְצָד *metsad.*

1 Ch. 12. 8 separated..unto David into the hold to
12. 16 there came of the children..to the hold
Jer. 51. 30 they have remained in (their) holds: their

2. *Stronghold, fortified place,* מְצוּדָה, מְצֻדָה *metsodah.*

1 Sa. 22. 4 all the while that David was in the hold
22. 5 Abide not in the hold; depart, and get
24. 22 and his men gat them up unto the hold
2 Sa. 5. 17 David heard..and went down to the hold
23. 14 David (was) then in an hold, and the gar.
1 Ch. 11. 16 And David (was) then in the hold, and the
Eze. 19. 9 they brought him into holds, that his voice

3. *Pit, cellar, hole,* צְרִיחַ *tsariach.*

Judg. 9. 46 they entered into an hold of the house
9. 49 set the hold on fire upon them: so that

4. *Keeping,* τήρησις *tērēsis.*

Acts 4. 3 put (them) in hold unto the next day: for

5. *Watch, ward,* φυλακή *phulakē.*

Rev. 18. 2 the hold of every foul spirit, and a cage
[*See* Strong].

HOLD, to —

1. *To lay or keep hold on,* אָחַז *achaz.*

Ruth 3. 15 Bring the veil that (thou hast)..and hold
1 Ch. 13. 9 Uzza put forth his hand to hold the ark
Job 17. 9 The righteous also shall hold on his way
23. 11 My foot hath held his steps, his way have
Psa. 73. 23 thou hast holden (me) by my right hand
77. 4 Thou holdest mine eyes waking: I am so
139. 10 Even there..thy right hand shall hold me
Eccl. 2. 3 to lay hold on folly, till I might see what
Song 3. 4 I held him, and would not let him go, until
3. 8 They all hold swords, (being) expert in w.
Isa. 5. 29 lay hold of the prey, and shall carry (it)
Eze. 41. 6 they had not hold in the wall of the house

2. *To bind,* אָסַר *asar.*

Song 7. 5 the king (is) held in the galleries

3. *To lay or keep hold,* חָזַק *chazaq,* 5.

Gen. 21. 18 hold him in thine hand; for I will make
Exod. 9. 2 if thou refuse..and wilt hold them still
Judg. 7. 20 held the lamps in their left hands, and
16. 26 unto the lad that held him by the hand
Neh. 4. 16 other half of them held both the spears
4. 17 and with the other (hand) held a weapon
4. 21 half of them held the spears from the

Isa. 41. 13 God will hold thy right hand, saying unto
42. 6 will hold thine hand, and will keep thee
45. 1 whose right hand I have holden, to subdue
Jer. 50. 42 They shall hold the bow and the lance

4. *To strengthen self,* חָזַק *chazaq,* 7.
Dan. 10. 21 none that holdeth with me in these things

5. *To think, reckon,* חָשַׁב *chashab.*
Job 13. 24 Wherefore..holdest me for thine enemy?

6. *To contain, comprehend,* כּוּל *kul,* 5.
2 Ch. 4. 5 received and held three thousand baths
Jer. 2. 13 broken cisterns, that can hold no water

7. *To keep hold,* קָבַל *qabal,* 5.
Exod 36. 12 the loops held one (curtain) to another

8. *To stand,* קוּם *qum.*
Job 41. 26 The sword..that layeth at him cannot h.

9. *To set, put, place,* שׂוּם, שִׂים *sum, sim.*
Psa. 66. 9 Which holdeth our soul in life, and suffer.

10. *To hold, uphold, retain,* תָּמַךְ *tamak.*
Prov 31. 19 and her hands hold the distaff
Amos 1. 5, 8 and him that holdeth the sceptre from

11. *To catch, keep hold,* תָּפַשׂ *taphas.*
Jer. 49. 16 thou..that holdest the height of the hill
Eze. 30. 21 to make it strong to hold the sword

12. *To have, hold,* ἔχω *echō.*
Matt 21. 26 we fear..for all hold John as a prophet
Phil. 2. 29 Receive him..and [hold] such in reputat.
1 Ti. 1. 19 Holding faith, and a good conscience
3. 9 Holding the mystery of the faith in a pure
Rev. 6. 9 slain..for the testimony which they held

13. *Was,* ἦν *ēn.*
Acts 14. 4 part held with the Jews, and part with the

14. *To hold down or thoroughly,* κατέχω *katechō.*
Rom. 1. 18 who hold the truth in unrighteousness
7. 6 law, that being dead wherein we were h.
Heb. 3. 14 we hold the beginning of our confidence

15. *To lay hold on,* κρατέω *krateō.*
Mark 7. 3 holding the tradition of the elders
7. 4 things..which they have received to hold
7. 8 hold the tradition of men, (as) the washing
Luke 24. 16 their eyes were holden that they should
Acts 2. 24 was not possible..he should be holden of
3. 11 as the lame man which was healed held
Col. 2. 19 not holding the Head, from which all the
2 Th. 2. 15 hold the traditions which ye have been t.
Rev. 2. 1 These things saith he that holdeth the se.
2. 14 thou hast there them that hold the doctri.
2. 15 them that hold the doctrine of the Nicol.
7. 1 holding the four winds of the earth, that

16. *To take, receive,* λαμβάνω *lambanō.*
Matt 12. 14 the Pharisees went out, and held a coun.

17. *To do, make,* ποιέω *poieō.*
Mark 15. 1 the chief priests held a consultation with

18. *To hold at the same time,* συνέχω *sunechō.*
Luke 22. 63 the men that held Jesus mocked him, and
[See Catch, lay, take; also Feast, guiltless, guilty, innocent, peace, tongue].

HOLD back, to —

1. *To lay or keep hold,* אָחַז *achaz,* 3.
Job 26. 9 He holdeth back the face of his throne

2. *To keep back, withhold, darken,* חָשַׂךְ *chasak.*
2 Sa. 18. 16 people returned..for Joab held back the

HOLD by, to —

To lay or keep hold, κρατέω *krateō.*
Matt 28. 9 held him by the feet, and worshipped him

HOLD fast, to —

1. *To lay or keep hold,* חָזַק *chazaq,* 5.
Job 2. 3 still he holdeth fast his integrity, although
8. 15 he shall hold it fast, but it shall not end.
27. 6 My righteousness I hold fast, and will not
Jer. 8. 5 they hold fast deceit, they refuse to return
50. 33 all that took them captives held them fast

2. *To press, crush, hold fast,* לָחַץ *lachats.*
2 Ki. 6. 32 shut the door, and hold him fast at the

3. *To hold over against,* ἀντέχομαι *antechomai.*
Titus 1. 9 Holding fast the faithful word as he hath

4. *To hold down or thoroughly,* κατέχω *katechō.*
1 Th. 5. 21 Prove all..hold fast that which is good
Heb. 3. 6 if we hold fast the confidence and the rej.
10. 23 Let us hold fast the profession of..faith

5. *To lay or keep hold,* κρατέω *krateō.*
Matt 26. 48 shall kiss, that same is he: hold him fast
Heb. 4. 14; Rev. 2. 13; 2. 25; 3. 11.

6. *To have, hold,* ἔχω *echō.*
2 Ti. 1. 13 Hold fast the form of sound words

7. *To watch, observe, keep,* τηρέω *tēreō.*
Rev. 3. 3 [Remember therefore..and hold fast, and]

HOLD forth, to —

To hold upon, ἐπέχω *epechō.*
Phil. 2. 16 Holding forth the word of life; that I may

HOLD (a feast), to —

To do, make, observe, עָשָׂה *asah.*
1 Ki. 8. 65 at that time Solomon held a feast, and all

HOLD, to catch —

1. *To lay or keep hold,* אָחַז *achaz.*
1 Ki. 1. 51 caught hold on the horns of the altar, say.

2. *To make strong, keep hold,* חָזַק *chazaq,* 5.
1 Ki. 1. 50 and caught hold on the horns of the altar
2. 28 and caught hold on the horns of the altar

HOLD (on or upon), to lay —

1. *To lay hold,* אָחַז *achaz.*
2 Sa. 2. 21 lay thee hold on one of the young men, and

2. *To lay or keep hold,* חָזַק *chazaq,* 5.
Gen. 19. 16 men laid hold upon his hand, and upon
Judg 19. 29 laid hold on his concubine, and divided
1 Sa. 15. 27 he laid hold upon the skirt of his mantle
2 Ch. 7. 22 laid hold on other gods, and worshipped
Prov. 3. 18 a tree of life to them that lay hold upon
Isa. 56. 2 and the son of man (that) layeth hold on
Jer. 6. 23 They shall lay hold on bow and spear; they
Zech 14. 13 shall lay hold every one on the hand of his

3. *To catch, capture, lay or keep hold,* תָּפַשׂ *taphas.*
Deut. 21. 19 Then shall his father..lay hold on him
22. 28 If a man find a damsel..and lay hold on
1 Ki. 13. 4 put forth his hand..saying, Lay hold on

4. *To lay or keep hold,* ἐπιλαμβάνομαι *epilambano.*
Luke 23. 26 laid hold upon one Simon, a Cyrenian
1 Ti. 6. 12 lay hold on eternal life, whereunto thou
6. 19 that they may lay hold on eternal life

5. *To lay or keep hold,* κρατέω *krateō.*
Matt. 12. 11 will he not lay hold on it, and lift (it) out?
14. 3 For Herod had laid hold on John, and
26. 55 sat daily with you..and ye laid no hold on
26. 57 And they that had laid hold on Jesus led
Mark 3. 21 they went out to lay hold on him: for they
6. 17 laid hold upon John, and bound him in
12. 12 they sought to lay hold on him, but feared
14. 51 young man..and the young men laid h. on
Heb. 6. 18 fled..to lay hold upon the hope set before
Rev. 20. 2 he laid hold on the dragon, that old serp.

HOLD (of on or upon), to take —

1. *To lay hold,* אָחַז *achaz.*
Gen. 25. 26 his hand took hold on Esau's heel; and
Exod 15. 14 take hold on the inhabitants of Palestina
15. 15 trembling shall take hold upon them; all
Deut 32. 41 and mine hand take hold on judgment, I
2 Sa. 4. 10 I took hold of him, and slew him in Zikl.
6. 6 and took hold of it; for the oxen shook (it)
Job 21. 6 and trembling taketh hold on my flesh
30. 16 days of affliction have taken hold upon
38. 13 it might take hold of the ends of the earth
Psa. 48. 6 Fear took hold upon them there, (and)
119. 53 Horror hath taken hold upon me because
Eccl. 7. 18 good that thou shouldest take hold of this
Song 7. 8 I will take hold of the boughs thereof
Isa. 13. 8 sorrows shall take hold of them; they
21. 3 pangs have taken hold upon me, as the

2. *To take or keep hold,* חָזַק *chazaq,* 5.
2 Sa. 1. 11 Then David took hold on his clothes, and
13. 11 he took hold of her, and said unto her
1 Ki. 9. 9 Because they..have taken hold upon other
2 Ki. 2. 12 took hold of his own clothes, and rent th.
Psa. 35. 2 Take hold of shield and buckler, and sta.
Isa. 4. 1 take hold of one man, saying, We will eat
27. 5 Or let him take hold of my strength, (that)
56. 4 please me, and take hold of my covenant
56. 6 keepeth..and taketh hold of my covenant
64. 7 stirreth up himself to take hold of thee
Jer. 6. 24 anguish hath taken hold of us, (and) pain
8. 21 astonishment hath taken hold on me
50. 43 anguish took hold of him, (and) pangs as
Zech. 8. 23 men shall take hold..shall take hold (of)

3. *To reach, attain, overtake,* נָשַׂג *nasag,* 5.
Job 27. 20 Terrors take hold on him as waters, a te.
Psa. 40. 12 mine iniquities have taken hold upon me
69. 24 let thy wrathful anger take hold of them
Prov. 2. 19 neither take they hold of the paths of life
Zech. 1. 6 did they not take hold of your fathers?

4. *To turn to clasp,* לָפַת *laphath.*
Judg 16. 29 Samson took hold of the two middle pil.

5. *To remove,* נָסַג *nasag,* 5.
Mic. 6. 14 thou shalt take hold, but shalt not deliver

6. *To let receive, cause to take,* קָבַל *qabal,* 5.
Exod 26. 5 that the loops may take hold one of ano.

7. *To hold, uphold, retain,* תָּמַךְ *tamak.*
Job 36. 17 judgment and justice take hold (on thee)
Prov. 5. 5 Her feet go down..her steps..hold on h.

8. *To catch, capture, keep hold,* תָּפַשׂ *taphas.*
Isa. 3. 6 When a man shall take hold of his brother
Eze. 29. 7 When they took hold of thee by thy hand

9. *To catch, capture, keep hold,* תָּפַשׂ *taphas,* 3.
Prov. 30. 28 The spider taketh hold with her hands

10. *To take hold upon,* ἐπιλαμβάνομαι *epilambano.*
Luke 20. 20 that they might take hold of his words
20. 26 they could not take hold of his words before

HOLD, to take fast —

To make strong, take or keep hold, חָזַק *chazaq,* 5.
Prov. 4. 13 Take fast hold of instruction; let (her)

HOLD (one's) peace, to — [*See* PEACE.]

1. *To be silent, deaf,* חָרַשׁ *charash.*
Psa. 39. 12 hold not thy peace at my tears: for I
83. 1 hold not thy peace, and be not still, O G.
109. 1 Hold not thy peace, O God of my praise

2. *To keep silent,* חָרַשׁ *charash,* 5.
Gen. 24. 21 wondering at her held his peace, to wit
34. 5 Jacob held his peace until they were come
Exod 14. 14 fight for you, and ye shall hold your peace
Num 30. 4 her father shall hold his peace at her; then
30. 7 held his peace at her in the day that he
30. 11 husband heard (it), and held his peace at
30. 14 her husband altogether hold his peace at
30. 14 held his peace at her in the day that he
Judg 18. 19 Hold thy peace, lay thine hand upon thy
1 Sa. 10. 27 despised him..But he held his peace
2 Sa. 13. 20 But hold now thy peace, my sister: he (is)
2 Ki. 18. 36 But the people held their peace, and an.
Neh. 5. 8 Then held they their peace, and found no.
Esth. 4. 14 if thou altogether holdest thy peace at
Job 11. 3 Should thy lies make men hold their peace?
13. 5 that ye would altogether hold your peace!
13. 13 Hold your peace, let me alone, that I may
33. 31 hearken unto me: hold thy peace, and I
33. 33 hold thy peace, and I shall teach thee wis.
Prov 11. 12 man of understanding holdeth his peace
Isa. 36. 21 But they held their peace, and answered
Jer. 4. 19 I cannot hold my peace, because thou h.

3. *To keep silence,* σιγάω *sigaō.*
Luke 20. 26 they could not take hold of his words be.
Acts 12. 17 beckoning unto them..to hold their peace
15. 13 after they had held their peace, James
1 Co. 14. 30 to another..let the first hold his peace

4. *To hold one's peace,* σιωπάω *siōpaō.*
Matt 20. 31 because they should hold their peace: but
26. 63 Jesus held his peace. And the high priest
Mark 3. 4 lawful..to kill? But they held their peace
9. 34 they held their peace: for by the way they
10. 48 charged him that he should hold his peace
14. 61 he held his peace, and answered nothing
Luke 18. 39 rebuked him, that he should [hold his pea.]
19. 40 that, if these should hold their peace, the
Acts 18. 9 Be not afraid..and hold not thy peace

5. *To muzzle, put to silence,* φιμόω *phimoō.*
Mark 1. 25 saying, Hold thy peace, and come out of h.
Luke 4. 35 saying, Hold thy peace, and come out of h.

HOLD to, to —

To hold over against, ἀντέχομαι *antechomai.*
Matt. 6. 24 hold to the one, and despise the other
Luke 16. 13 hold to the one, and despise the other

HOLD up, to —

1. *To lift up,* נָשָׂא *nasa.*
2 Sa. 2. 22 then should I hold up my face to Joab

2. *To support,* סָעַד *saad.*
Psa. 18. 35 thy right hand hath holden me up, and thy
94. 18 My foot slippeth; thy mercy..held me up
119. 117 Hold thou me up, and I shall be safe: and

3. *To lift up, exalt,* רוּם *rum,* 5.
Exod 17. 11 when Moses held up his hand, that Israel
Dan. 12. 7 he held up his right hand and his left

4. *To hold, uphold, retain,* תָּמַךְ *tamak.*
Gen. 48. 17 he held up his father's hand, to remove it
Psa. 17. 5 Hold up my goings in thy paths, (that) my

5. *To make to stand,* ἵστημι *histēmi.*
Rom 14. 4 he shall be holden up; for God is able to

HOLD out, to —

To extend, hold out, יָשַׁט *yashat,* 5.
Esth. 4. 11 the king shall hold out the golden sceptre
5. 2 the king held out to Esther the golden
8. 4 held out the golden sceptre toward Esther

HOLD upon, to get or take —

1. *To find,* מָצָא *matsa.*
Psa. 116. 3 the pains of hell gat ho. upon me: I found

2. *To cause to reach, attain, overtake,* נָשַׂג *nasag,* 5.
Psa. 40. 12 mine iniquities have taken hold upon me

HOLDEN, to be —

1. *To be captured, taken,* לָכַד *lakad,* 2.
Job 36. 8 (and) be holden in cords of affliction

2. *To be supported,* סָמַךְ *samak,* 2.
Psa. 71. 6 By thee have I been holden..from the womb

3. *To do, make,* עָשָׂה *asah,* 2.
2 Ki. 23. 22 there was not holden such a passover from
23. 23 this passover was holden to the LORD in

4. *To be held, retained,* תָּמַךְ *tamak,* 2.
Prov. 5. 22 shall be holden with the cords of his sins

HOLDING —

To hold, retain, תָּמַךְ *tamak.*
Isa. 33. 15 shaketh his hands from holding of bribes

HOLDING in —

To contain, כּוּל *kul,* 5.
Jer. 6. 11 I am weary with holding in: I will pour it

HOLE —

1. *Hole, hollowed out place,* חוֹר, חֹר *chor, chur.*
1 Sa. 14. 11 the Hebrews come forth out of the holes
2 Ki. 12. 9 Jehoiada..bored a hole in the lid of it
Song 5. 4 My beloved put in his hand by the hole
Isa. 11. 8 child shall play on the hole of the asp
42. 22 all of them snared in holes, and they are
Eze. 8. 7 when I looked, behold a hole in the wall
Nah. 2. 12 filled his holes with prey, and his dens
Zech 14. 12 eyes shall consume away in their holes

2. *Enclosure,* מִסְגֶּרֶת *misgereth.*
Mic. 7. 17 they shall move out of their holes like

3. *Cave, cavern, den,* מְעָרָה *mearah.*
Isa. 2. 19 they shall go into the holes of the rocks

4. *Hole,* מַקֶּבֶת *maqqebeth.*
Isa. 51. 1 look..to the hole of the pit (whence) ye

5. *Hole, cleft,* נָקִיק *neqiq.*
Isa. 7. 19 shall rest..in the holes of the rocks, and
Jer. 13. 4 and hide it there in a hole of the rock
16. 16 from every hill, and out of the holes of the

6. *Mouth, opening,* פֶּה *peh.*
Exod 28. 32 there shall be an hole in the top of it, in
28. 32 woven work round about the hole of it
39. 23 (there was) an hole in the midst of the
39. 23 as the hole of..round about the hole, that

7. *Pit,* פַּחַת *pachath.*
Jer. 48. 28 her nest in the sides of the hole's mouth

8. *Hole, burrow,* φωλεός *phōleos.*
Matt. 8. 20 The foxes have holes, and the birds of the
Luke 9. 58 Foxes have holes, and birds of the air (h.)

HOLES, with —
To pierce, נָקַב *naqab.*
Hag. 1. 6 wages (to put it) into a bag with holes

HOLIER, to be —
To be set apart, separate, קָדַשׁ *qadesh.*
Isa. 65. 5 come not near to me; for I am holier than

HOLIEST (of all) —
1. *The separate, set apart objects,* τὰ ἅγια *ta hagia.*
Heb. 9. 8 that the way into the holiest of all was
10. 19 boldness to enter into the holiest by the

2. *Holy of holies,* ἅγια ἁγίων *hagia hagiōn.*
Heb. 9. 3 tabernacle wh. is called the Holiest of all

HOLILY —
Kindly, graciously, ὁσίως *hosiōs.*
1 Th. 2. 10 how holily..we behaved ourselves among

HOLINESS —
1. *Separation, place, or thing set apart,* קֹדֶשׁ *qodesh.*
Exod 15. 11 glorious in holiness, fearful (in) praises
28. 36 and grave upon it..Holiness to the LORD
39. 30 wrote upon it..HOLINESS TO THE LORD
1 Ch. 16. 29 worship the LORD in the beauty of holin.
2 Ch. 20. 21 should praise the beauty of holiness, as
31. 18 they sanctified themselves in holiness
Psa. 29. 2 worship the LORD in the beauty of holin.
30. 4 give thanks at the remembrance of his h.
47. 8 God sitteth upon the throne of his holiness
48. 1 praised..(in) the mountain of his holiness
60. 6 God hath spoken in his holiness; I will
89. 35 Once have I sworn by my holiness that I
93. 5 holiness becometh thine house, O LORD
96. 9 O worship the LORD in the beauty of holi.
97. 12 give thanks at the remembrance of his ho.
108. 7 God hath spoken in his holiness; I will
110. 3 in the beauties of holiness from the womb
Isa. 23. 18 and her hire shall be holiness to the LORD
35. 8 and it shall be called, The way of holiness
62. 9 shall drink it in the courts of my holiness
63. 15 behold from the habitation of thy holiness
63. 18 The people of thy holiness have possessed
Jer. 2. 3 Israel (was) holiness to the LORD..the first
23. 9 and because of the words of his holiness
31. 23 The LORD bless thee, O ..mountain of ho.
Amos 4. 2 The Lord GOD hath sworn by his holiness
Obad 17 upon mount Zion..there shall be holiness
Zech. 14. 20 upon the bells..HOLINESS UNTO THE LORD
14. 21 every pot..in Judah shall be holiness unto
Mal. 2. 11 Judah hath profaned the holiness of the

2. *Separation, setting apart,* ἁγιασμός *hagiasmos.*
Rom. 6. 19 servants to righteousness unto holiness
6. 22 ye have your fruit unto holiness, and the
1 Th. 4. 7 not..unto uncleanness, but unto holiness
1 Ti. 2. 15 if they continue in..holiness with sobriety
Heb. 12. 14 Follow peace with all..holiness, without

3. *Separation, setting apart,* ἁγιότης *hagiotēs.*
Heb. 12. 10 that (we) might be partakers of his holin.

4. *Separation, setting apart,* ἁγιωσύνη *hagiōsunē.*
Rom. 1. 4 according to the spirit of holiness, by the
2 Co. 7. 1 perfecting holiness in the fear of God
1 Th. 3. 13 unblameable in holiness before God, even

5. *Reverence,* εὐσέβεια *eusebeia.*
Acts 3. 12 as though by our own power or holiness

6. *Kindness, graciousness,* ὁσιότης *hosiotēs.*
Luke 1. 75 In holiness and righteousness before him
Eph. 4. 24 is created in righteousness and true holi.

HOLINESS, as becometh —
Proper to priests, ἱεροπρεπής *hieroprepēs.*
Titus 2. 3 in behaviour as becometh holiness, not

HOLLOW —
1. *Hollow,* כַּף *kaph.*
Gen. 32. 25 touched the hollow of his thigh; and the h.
32. 32 the hollow of the thigh..touched the hol.

2. *To be hollow,* נָבַב *nabab.*
Exod 27. 8 Hollow with boards shalt thou make it: as
38. 7 he made the altar hollow with boards
Jer. 52. 21 a fillet of twelve cubits..(it was) hollow

HOLLOW of the hand —
Handful, שֹׁעַל *shoal.*
Isa. 40. 12 the waters in the hollow of his hand, and

HOLLOW place —
Hollow place, מַכְתֵּשׁ *maktesh.*
Judg 15. 19 God clave an hollow place that (was) in

HOLLOW strakes —
Hollow strakes or places, שְׁקַעֲרוּרֹת *sheqaarurroth.*
Lev. 14. 37 the walls of the house with hollow strakes

HO'-LON, חֹלֹן, חֹלוֹן *strong place.*
1. A city in Judah's lot, and assigned to the Levites. In 1 Ch. 6. 58 it is called *Hilen.*
Josh. 15. 51 Goshen, and H., and Giloh; eleven cities
21. 15 H. with her suburbs, and Debir with her

2. A city of Moab, a town of the *Mishor* or level downs E. of the Jordan, and named with Jahazah, Dibon and other known places, but not yet identified: probably *Horon.*
Jer. 48. 21 upon H., and upon Jahazah, and upon M.

HOLY —
1. *Kind,* חָסִיד *chasid.*
Deut 33. 8 Thummin and thy Urim (be) with thy holy
Psa. 86. 2 Preserve my soul, for I (am) holy: O thou
145. 17 (is) righteous..and holy in all his works

2. *Separate, set apart,* קָדוֹשׁ *qadosh.*
Exod 19. 6 a kingdom of priests, and an holy nation
29. 31 and seethe his flesh in the holy place
Lev. 6. 16 shall it be eaten in the holy place; in the
6. 26 in the holy place shall it be eaten, in
6. 27 whereon it was sprinkled in..holy place
7. 6 it shall be eaten in the holy place: it
10. 13 ye shall eat it in the holy place, because
11. 44 ye shall be holy; for I (am) holy: neither
11. 45 ye shall therefore be holy, for I (am) holy
16. 24 wash his flesh with water in..holy place
19. 2 be holy: for I the LORD your God (am) h.
20. 7 Sanctify yourselves..and be ye holy: for I
20. 26 be holy unto me; for I the LORD (am) holy
21. 6 They shall be holy unto their God, and not
21. 7 take a wife..for he (is) holy unto his God
21. 8 sanctify him..he shall be holy unto thee
21. 8 for I the LORD, which sanctify you, (am) h.
24. 9 they shall eat it in the holy place: for it (is)
Num. 5. 17 shall take holy water in an earthen vessel
6. 5 he shall be holy, (and) shall let the locks
6. 8 the days of his separation he (is) holy
15. 40 do all my commandments, and be holy un.
16. 3 the congregation (are) holy, every one of
16. 5 will show who (are) his, and (who is) holy
16. 7 whom the LORD doth choose..(shall be) h.
Deut 7. 6 (art) an holy people unto the LORD thy G.
14. 2; 21 a. holy people unto the LORD thy God
23. 14 therefore shall thy camp be holy: that he
26. 19 be an holy people unto the LORD thy God
28. 9 establish thee an holy people unto himself
Josh. 24. 19 he (is) an holy God; he (is) a jealous God
1 Sa. 2. 2 (There is) none holy as the LORD: for (there
6. 20 able to stand before this holy LORD God?
2 Ki. 4. 9 I perceive that this (is) an holy man of
2 Ch. 35. 3 Levites..which were holy unto the LORD
Neh. 8. 9 This day (is) holy unto the LORD your G.
8. 10 for (this) day (is) holy unto our Lord: ne.
8. 11 Hold your peace, for the day (is) holy; ne.
Psa. 22. 3 But thou (art) holy, (O thou) that inhabitest
46. 4 the holy (place) of the tabernacles of the
65. 4 goodness of thy house..of thy holy temp.
99. 3 Let them praise thy..name; (for) it (is) h.
99. 5 Exalt ye the LORD our God..(for) he (is) h.
99. 9 Exalt the LORD..the LORD our God (is) h.
111. 9 He sent..holy and reverend (is) his name
Prov. 9. 10 knowledge of the holy (is) understanding
30. 3 learned..nor have the knowledge of the h.
Eccl. 8. 10 come and gone from the place of the holy
Isa. 4. 3 remaineth in Jerusalem, shall be called h.
5. 16 God, (that is) holy, shall be sanctified in
6. 3 said, Holy, holy, holy (is) the LORD of h.
57. 15 high and lofty One..whose name (is) Holy
57. 15 I dwell in the high and holy (place), with
58. 13 delight, the holy of the LORD, honourable
Eze. 42. 13 there shall they lay..for the place (is) h.
Dan. 8. 24 shall destroy the mighty and the holy pe.

3. *Separate, set apart,* קַדִּישׁ *qaddish.*
Dan. 4. 8 and in whom (is) the spirit of the holy g.
4. 9 I know that the spirit of the holy gods (is)
4. 18 for the spirit of the holy gods (is) in thee
5. 11 in whom (is) the spirit of the holy gods

4. *Separation, object set apart,* קֹדֶשׁ *qodesh.*
Exod 3. 5 place whereon thou standest (is) holy gr.
12. 16 an holy convocation..an holy convocation
15. 13 in thy strength unto thy holy habitation
16. 23 the rest of the holy sabbath unto the Lo.
22. 31 And ye shall be holy men unto me: neither
26. 33 veil shall divide unto you between the h.
28. 2 thou shalt make holy garments for Aaron
28. 4 they shall make holy garments for Aaron
28. 29, 35 when he goeth in unto the holy (place)
28. 38 children..shall hallow in all their holy g.
28. 43 unto the altar to minister in the holy (p.)
29. 6 thou shalt..put the holy crown upon the
29. 29 the holy garments of Aaron shall be his
29. 30 when he cometh..to minister in the holy
29. 33 shall not eat..because they (are) holy
29. 34 it shall not be eaten, because it (is) holy
30. 25 thou shalt make it an oil of holy ointment
30. 25 ointment..it shall be an holy anointing oil
30. 31 This shall be an holy anointing oil unto me
30. 32 it (is) holy, (and) it shall be holy unto you
30. 35 a perfume..tempered together, pure..h.
30. 37 it shall be unto thee holy for the LORD
31. 10 the holy garments for Aaron the priest
31. 11 anointing oil, and sweet incense for the h.
31. 14 keep the sabbath..for it (is) holy unto you
31. 15 (is) the sabbath of rest, holy to the LORD
Exod 35. 19 to do service in the holy (place), the holy
35. 21 all his service, and for the holy garments
37. 29 he made the holy anointing oil, and the
38. 24 work in all the work of the holy (place)
39. 1 the holy (place), and made the holy gar.
39. 30 the plate of the holy crown (of) pure gold
39. 41 to do service in the holy (place), and the h.
40. 9 and shalt hallow it..and it shall be holy
40. 13 shalt put upon Aaron the holy garments
Lev. 6. 30 to reconcile (withal) in the holy (place)
8. 9 he put the golden plate, the holy crown
10. 10 put difference between holy and unholy
10. 17 not eaten the sin offering in the holy place
10. 18 was not brought in within the holy (place)
10. 18 indeed have eaten it in the holy (place)
14. 13 the burnt offering, in the holy (place): for
16. 2 come not at all times into the holy (place)
16. 3 Thus shall Aaron come into the holy (pl.
16. 4 He shall put on the holy linen coat, and
16. 4 these (are) holy garments; therefore shall
16. 16 make an atonement for the holy (place)
16. 17 to make an atonement in the holy (place)
16. 20 an end of reconciling the holy (place)
16. 23 put on when he went into the holy (place)
16. 27 in to make atonement in the holy (place)
16. 32 the linen clothes, (even) the holy garments
16. 33 make an atonement for the holy sanctuary
19. 24 the fruit thereof shall be holy, to praise
20. 3 my sanctuary, and to profane my holy name
21. 6 do offer: therefore they shall be holy
21. 22 (both) of the most holy, and of the holy
22. 2 they profane not my holy name (in those
22. 32 Neither shall ye profane my holy name
23. 2, 37 shall proclaim (to be) holy convocation
23. 3 the sabbath of rest, an holy convocation
23. 4 holy convocations, which ye shall proclaim
23. 7 ye shall have an holy convocation; ye
23. 8 the seventh day (is) an holy convocation
23. 20 shall be holy to the LORD for the priest
23. 21 it may be an holy convocation unto you
23. 24 blowing of trumpets, an holy convocation
23. 27, 36 shall be an holy convocation unto you
23. 35 first day (shall be) an holy convocation
25. 12 it shall be holy unto you: ye shall eat
27. 9 all that (any man) giveth..shall be holy
27. 10 it and the exchange thereof shall be holy
27. 14 his house (to be) holy unto the LORD
27. 21 shall be holy unto the LORD, as a field
27. 23 that day, (as) a holy thing unto the LORD
27. 30 all the tithe..(it is) holy unto the LORD
27. 32 the tenth shall be holy unto the LORD
27. 33 both it and the change thereof shall be h.
Num. 6. 20 this (is) holy for the priest, with the wave
18. 10 every male shall eat it: it shall be holy
18. 17 they (are) holy: thou shalt sprinkle their
28. 7 in the holy (place) shalt thou cause the
28. 18 In the first day..an holy convocation; ye
28. 25, 26 ye shall have an holy convocation; ye
29. 1 ye shall have an holy convocation; ye
29. 7 tenth..of this seventh month an holy con.
29. 12 fifteenth..ye shall have an holy convoca.
31. 6 to the war, with the holy instruments, and
35. 25 priest, which was anointed with the holy
Deut 26. 15 Look down from thy holy habitation, from
Josh 5. 15 for the place whereon thou standest (is) h.
1 Sa. 21. 5 and the vessels of the young men are holy
1 Ki. 8. 4 all the holy vessels..in the tabernacle, ev
8. 8 seen out in the holy (place) before the or.
8. 10 the priests were come out of the holy (p.)
1 Ch. 16. 10 Glory ye in his holy name: let the heart
16. 35 that we may give thanks to thy holy name
22. 19 to bring..the holy vessels of God, into the
23. 32 should keep..the charge of the holy (p.)
29. 3 all that I have prepared for the holy ho.
29. 16 to build thee an house for thine holy name
2 Ch. 5. 5 all the holy vessels that (were) in the ta.
5. 11 when the priests were come out of the h.
8. 11 because (the places are) holy, whereunto
23. 6 they shall go in, for they (are) holy: but
29. 5 carry forth the filthiness out of the holy
29. 7 nor offered burnt offerings in the holy (p.)
30. 27 to his holy dwelling place..unto heaven
35. 3 Put the holy ark in the house which Sol.
35. 5 stand in the holy (place), according to the
35. 13 but the (other) holy (offerings) sod they
Ezra 8. 28 Ye (are) holy..the vessels (are) holy also
9. 2 so that the holy seed have mingled them.
9. 8 to give us a nail in his holy place, that
Neh. 9. 14 madest known unto them thy holy sabb.
10. 31 not buy..on the sabbath, or on the holy
10. 33 for the set feasts, and for the holy (things)
11. 1 one of ten to dwell in Jerusalem the holy
11. 18 All the Levites in the holy city..two hu.
Psa. 2. 6 Yet have I set my king upon my holy hill
3. 4 and he heard me out of his holy hill
5. 7 in thy fear will I worship toward thy hol.
11. 4 The LORD (is) in his holy temple, the L.
15. 1 LORD..who shall dwell in thy holy hill?
20. 6 he will hear him from his holy heaven
24. 3 and who shall stand in his holy place?
28. 2 when I lift up my hands toward thy holy
33. 21 because we have trusted in his holy name
43. 3 let them bring me unto thy holy hill, and
51. 11 and take not thy holy spirit from me
68. 5 judge of the widows (is) God in his holy h.
68. 17 (is) among them, (as in) Sinai, in the holy
79. 1 O God..thy holy temple have they defiled
87. 1 His foundation (is) in the holy mountains
89. 20 with my holy oil have I anointed him
98. 1 his holy arm, hath gotten him the victory
99. 9 worship at his holy hill; for the LORD our
103. 1 all that is within me, (bless) his holy name

Psa. 105. 3 Glory ye in his holy name: let the heart of
105. 42 For he remembered his holy promise, (and)
106. 47 Save us..to give thanks unto thy holy na.
138. 2 I will worship toward thy holy temple
145. 21 let all flesh bless his holy name for ever
Prov 20. 25 the man (who) devoureth (that which is) h.
Isa. 6. 13 the holy seed (shall be) the substance ther.
11. 9 shall not hurt nor destroy in all my holy
27. 13 shall worship the LORD in the holy mount
48. 2 For they call themselves of the holy city
52. 1 Awake, awake..O Jerusalem, the holy
52. 10 The LORD hath made bare his holy arm in
56. 7 them will I bring to my holy mountain
57. 13 but he..shall inherit my holy mountain
58. 13 from..doing thy pleasure on my holy day
62. 12 The holy people, The redeemed of the L.
63. 10 they rebelled, and vexed his Holy Spirit
63. 11 (is) he that put his Holy Spirit within h.?
64. 10 Thy holy cities are a wilderness, Zion is
64. 11 Our holy and our beautiful house, where our
65. 11 ye (are) they..that forget my holy mount.
65. 25 shall not hurt nor destroy in all my holy
66. 20 shall bring..to my holy mountain Jerusa.
Jer. 11. 15 and the holy flesh is passed from thee?
25. 30 and utter his voice from his holy habitation
31. 40 the whole valley..(shall be) holy unto the
Eze. 20. 39 pollute ye my holy name no more with your
20. 40 in mine holy mountain, in the mountain of
22. 26 have put no difference between the holy
28. 14 thou wast upon the holy mountain of God
36. 20 they profaned my holy name, when they s.
36. 21 But I had pity for mine holy name, which
36. 22 but for mine holy name's sake, which ye
36. 38 As the holy flock, as the flock of Jerusalem
39. 7 So will I make my holy name known in the
39. 7 I will not..pollute my holy name any more
39. 25 and will be jealous for my holy name
42. 13 they (be) holy chambers, where the priests
42. 14 not go out of the holy..for they (are) holy
43. 7 my holy name, shall the house of Israel no
43. 8 they have even defiled my holy name by
44. 19 lay them in the holy chambers, and they
44. 23 between the holy and profane, and cause
45. 1 This (shall be) holy in all the borders thereof
45. 4 the holy (portion) of the lands shall be for
45. 6 long, over against the oblation of the holy
45. 7 on the other side of the oblation of the h.
45. 7 the city, before the oblation of the holy
46. 19 into the holy chambers of the priests, whi.
48. 10 And for them..shall be (this) holy oblat.
48. 14 not sell of it..(it is) holy unto the LORD
48. 18 over against the oblation of the holy (po.)
48. 20 ye shall offer the holy oblation four squ.
48. 21 of the holy oblation..be the holy oblation
Dan. 9. 16 from thy city Jerusalem, thy holy moun.
9. 20 my supplication..for the holy mountain
9. 24 upon thy people, and upon thy holy city
11. 28 and his heart..against the holy covenant
11. 30 against the holy covenant..forsake the h.
11. 45 the seas in the glorious holy mountain
12. 7 to scatter the power of the holy people
Joel 2. 1 and sound an alarm in my holy mountain
3. 17 your God dwelling in Zion, my holy moun.
3. 17 then shall Jerusalem be holy, and there
Amos 2. 7 That pant..to profane my holy name
Obad. 16 as ye have drunk upon my holy mountain
Jon. 2. 4 yet I will look again toward thy holy tem.
2. 7 my prayer came..into thine holy temple
Mic. 1. 2 Lord GOD..the Lord from his holy temple
Hab. 2. 20 But the LORD (is) in his holy temple: let
Zeph. 3. 11 be haughty because of my holy mountain
Hag. 2. 12 If one bear holy flesh in the skirt of his
Zech. 2. 12 inherit Judah his portion in the holy land
2. 13 for he is raised up out of his holy habit.
8. 3 mountain of the LORD..the holy mountain

5. *Separate, set apart, holy,* ἅγιος *hagios.*
Matt. 4. 5 the devil taketh him up into the holy city
7. 6 Give not that which is holy unto the dogs
24. 15 see the abomination..stand in the holy p.
25. 31 and all the [holy] angels with him, then
27. 53 went into the holy city, and appeared unto
Mark 6. 20 knowing..he was a just man and an holy
8. 38 the glory of his Father with the holy ang.
Luke 1. 49 For he that is mighty..holy (is) his name
1. 70 As he spake by the mouth of his holy pr.
1. 72 and to remember his holy covenant
2. 23 that openeth the womb shall be called h.
9. 26 (in his) Father's, and of the holy angels
John 17. 11 Holy Father, keep through thine own n.
Acts 3. 21 by the mouth of all his holy prophets si.
4. 27 For of a truth against thy holy child Je.
4. 30 may be done by the name of thy holy ch.
6. 13 words against this holy place, and the law
7. 33 place where thou standest is holy ground
10. 22 was warned from God by an holy angel
21. 28 and further..hath polluted this holy pl.
Rom. 1. 2 Which he had promised..in the holy scr.
7. 12 Wherefore the law (is) holy, and the co. h.
11. 16 if the first fruit (be) holy, the lump (is)
11. 16 if the root (be) holy, so (are) the branches
12. 1 living sacrifice, holy, acceptable unto God
16. 16 Salute one another with an holy kiss. The
1 Co. 3. 17 temple of God is holy, which (temple) ye
7. 14 children unclean; but now are they holy
7. 34 may be holy both in body and in spirit
16. 20 Greet ye one another with an holy kiss
2 Co. 13. 12 Greet one another with an holy kiss
Eph. 1. 4 we should be holy and without blame bef.
2. 21 groweth unto an holy temple in the Lord
3. 5 now revealed unto his holy apostles and
5. 27 it should be holy and without blemish
Col. 1. 22 to present you holy and unblameable and
3. 12 as the elect of God, holy and beloved
1 Th. 5. 26 Greet all the brethren with an holy kiss
5. 27 epistle be read unto..the [holy] brethren
2 Ti. 1. 9 and called (us) with an holy calling, not
Heb. 3. 1 holy brethren, partakers of the heavenly
1 Pe. 1. 15 hath called you is holy, so be ye holy
1. 16 it is written, Be ye holy; for I am holy
2. 5 an holy priesthood, to offer up spiritual
2. 9 ye (are)..an holy nation, a peculiar people
3. 5 in the old time the holy women also, who
2 Pe. 1. 18 when we were with him in the holy mount
1. 21 [holy] men of God spake (as they were) mo.
2. 21; 3. 2, 11; Rev. 3. 7; 4. 8; 6. 10; 11. 2;
[14. 10;] 18. 20; 20. 6; 21. 2, 10; 22. 6, 11, 19.

6. *Priestly,* ἱερός *hieros,* τὰ ἱερά *ta hiera.*
1 Co. 9. 13 they which minister about holy things, live
2 Ti. 3. 15 thou hast known the Holy Scriptures

7. *Kind, gracious,* ὅσιος *hosios.*
1 Ti. 2. 8 lifting up holy hands, without wrath and
Titus 1. 8 of good men, sober, just, holy, temperate
Heb. 7. 26 (who is) holy, harmless, undefiled, separate
Rev. 15. 4 glorify thy name? for (thou) only (art) [h.]

HOLY, to be —
1. *To be separate, set apart,* קָדֵשׁ *qadesh.*
Exod 29. 37 whatsoever toucheth..altar shall be holy
30. 29 whatsoever toucheth them shall be holy
Lev. 6. 18 every one that toucheth..shall be holy
6. 27 whatsoever shall touch..shall be holy
Hag. 2. 12 his skirt do touch bread..shall it be holy?

2. *To separate, set apart,* ἁγιάζω *hagiazō.*
Rev 22. 11 and he that is..let him be holy still

HOLY day —
1. *Separation, separate or set apart object,* קֹדֶשׁ *qodesh.*
Exod 35. 2 there shall be to you an holy day, a sab.

2. *A feast, festival* ἑορτή *heortē.*
Col. 2. 16 in respect of an holy day, or of the new

HOLY day, to keep —
To keep or celebrate a festival, חָגַג *chagag.*
Psa. 42. 4 went with a multitude that kept holy day

HOLY GHOST, ἅγιον πνεῦμα *hagion pneuma.*
Mat. 1. 18, 20; 3. 11; 12. 32; 28. 19; Mark 1. 8; 3. 29;
12. 36; 13. 11; Luke 1. 15, 35, 41, 67; 2. 25, 26; 3. 16,
22; 4. 1; 12. 10, 12; John 1. 33; [7. 39;] 14. 26; 20. 22;
Acts 1. 2, 5, 8, 16; 2. 4, 33, 38; 4. 8, 31; 5. 3, 32; 6. [3,]
5; 7. 51, 55; 8. 15, 17, [18,] 19; 9. 17, 31; 10. 38, 44, 45,
47; 11. 15, 16, 24; 13. 2, 4, 9, 52; 15. 8, 28; 16. 6; 19.
2, 2, 6; 20. 23, 28; 21. 11; 28. 25; Rom. 5. 5; 9. 1; 14.
17; 15. 13, 16; 1 Co. 2. [13]; 6. 19; 12. 3; 2 Co. 6. 6;
13. 14 (13); 1 Th. 1. 5, 6; 2 Ti. 1. 14; Titus 3. 5; Heb.
2. 4; 3. 7; 6. 4; 9. 8; 10. 15; 1 Pe. 1. 12; 2 Pe. 1. 21;
[1 Jo. 5. 7;] Jude 20.

HOLY, (thing or place), most —
1. *Holy of holies,* קֹדֶשׁ הַקֳּדָשִׁים *qodesh haq-qodashim.*
Exod 26. 33 between the holy (place) and the most h.
26. 34 mercy seat upon the ark..in the most holy
29. 37 it shall be an altar most holy: whatsoever
30. 10 atonement..it (is) most holy unto the L.
30. 29 sanctify..that they may be most holy: wh.
30. 36 it shall be unto you most holy
40. 10 sanctify..and it shall be an altar most h.
Lev. 2. 3, 10 a thing most holy of the offerings of
6. 17 it (is) most holy, as (is) the sin offering
6. 25 be killed before the LORD: it (is) most h.
6. 29 males..shall eat thereof: it (is) most holy
7. 1 Likewise this (is) the law..it (is) most h.
7. 6 Every male..shall eat thereof..it (is) m. h.
10. 12 eat it without leaven..for it (is) most h.
10. 17 seeing it (is) most holy, and (God) hath
14. 13 (so is) the trespass offering: it (is) most h.
24. 9 it (is) most holy unto him of the offerings
27. 28 every devoted thing (is) most holy unto
Num. 4. 4 service of the sons..(about) the most h.
4. 19 when they approach unto the most holy
18. 9 This shall be thine of the most holy thing
18. 9 (shall be) most holy for thee and thy sons
18. 10 In the most holy (place) shalt thou eat it
1 Ki. 6. 16 for the oracle, (even) for the most holy (p.)
7. 50 the doors of the inner house, the most h.
8. 6 brought in the ark..to the most holy (p.)
1 Ch. 6. 49 for all the work of the (place) most holy
23. 13 that he should sanctify the most holy th.
2 Ch. 3. 8 he made the most holy house, the length
3. 10 in the most holy house he made two che.
4. 22 the inner doors therefore for the most holy
5. 7 brought in the ark..into the most holy (p.)
Ezra 2. 63 should not eat of the most holy things, till
Neh. 7. 65 should not eat of the most holy things, till
Eze. 41. 4 said unto me, This (is) the most holy (pl.)
43. 12 limit thereof round about (shall be) most h.
45. 3 be the sanctuary (and) the most holy (pl.)
48. 12 most holy by the border of the Levites
Dan. 9. 24 to seal up..and to anoint the most holy

2. *The holy things of the holies,* קָדְשֵׁי הַקֳּדָשִׁים [*qodesh*]
Lev. 21. 22 bread..of the most holy, and of the holy
2 Ch. 31. 14 oblations of the LORD, and the most holy t.
Eze. 42. 13 the priests..shall eat the most holy things
42. 13 there shall they lay the most holy things
44. 13 any of my holy things, in the most holy (p.)

3. *Separate, set apart, holy,* ἅγιος *hagios.*
Jude 20 building up yourselves on your most holy f.

HOLY, to keep —
To separate or set apart, קָדֵשׁ *qadesh,* 3.
Exod 20. 8 Remember the sabbath day, to keep it h.

HOLY one —
1. *Kind, gracious,* חָסִיד *chasid.*
Psa. 16. 10 thou suffer thine holy one to see corruption
89. 19 thou spakest in vision to thy holy one, and

2. *Separate or set apart one,* קָדוֹשׁ *qadosh.*
2 Ki. 19. 22 (even) against the holy (one) of Israel
Job 6. 10 not concealed the words of the holy one
Psa. 71. 22 with the harp, O thou holy one of Israel
78. 41 Yea, they..limited the holy one of Israel
89. 18 and the holy one of Israel (is) our King
Isa. 1. 4 provoked..holy one of Israel unto anger
5. 19 let the counsel of the holy one of Israel
5. 24 despised the word of..holy one of Israel
10. 17 for a fire, and his holy one for a flame
10. 20 stay upon the LORD, the holy one of Israel
12. 6 great (is) the holy one of Israel in the
17. 7 have respect to the holy one of Israel
29. 19 shall rejoice in the holy one of Israel
29. 23 sanctify the holy one of Jacob, and shall
30. 11 cause the holy one of Israel to cease from
30. 12 thus saith the holy one of Israel, Because
30. 15 saith the Lord GOD, the holy one of Israel
31. 1 they look not unto the holy one of Israel
37. 23 (even) against the holy one of Israel
40. 25 or shall I be equal? saith the holy one
41. 14 and thy redeemer, the holy one of Israel
41. 16 (and) shalt glory in the holy one of Israel
41. 20 the holy one of Israel hath created it
43. 3 God, the holy one of Israel, thy saviour: I
43. 14 LORD, your redeemer, the holy one of I.
43. 15 holy one, the creator of Israel, your king
45. 11 LORD, the holy one of Israel, and his m.
47. 4 LORD of hosts (is) his name, the holy one
48. 17 LORD, thy Redeemer, the holy one of Isr.
49. 7 the Redeemer of Israel, (and) his holy one
49. 7 (and) the holy one of Israel, and he shall
54. 5 and thy Redeemer the holy one of Israel
55. 5 thy God, and for the holy one of Israel
60. 9 to the holy one of Israel, because he hath
60. 14 call thee..The Zion of the holy one of Israel
Jer. 50. 29 proud..against the holy one of Israel
51. 5 with sin against the holy one of Israel
Eze. 39. 7 that I (am) the LORD, the holy one in Isr.
Hos. 11. 9 the holy one in the midst of thee: and I
Hab. 1. 12 my God, mine holy one? we shall not die
3. 3 and the holy one from Mount Paran. Selah

3. *One separate or set apart,* קַדִּישׁ *qaddish.*
Dan. 4. 13, 23 an holy one came down from heaven
4. 17 the demand by the word of the holy ones

4. *Separate, set apart, holy* ἅγιος *hagios.*
Mark 1. 24 I know..who thou art, the holy one of G.
Luke. 4. 34 I know..who thou art; the holy one of G.
Acts 3. 14 ye denied the holy one and the just, and
1 Jo. 2. 20 ye have an unction from the holy one, and

5. *Kind, gracious,* ὅσιος *hosios.*
Acts 2. 27 neither wilt thou suffer thine holy one to
13. 35 Thou shalt not suffer thine holy one to see

HOLY place —
1. *Place separate or set apart,* מִקְדָּשׁ *miqdash.*
Psa. 68. 35 (thou art) terrible out of thy holy places
Eze. 21. 2 drop (thy word) toward the holy places, and
45. 4 it shall be..an holy place for the sanctuary

2. *To separate, set apart,* קָדֵשׁ *qadesh,* 3.
Eze. 7. 24 and their holy places shall be defiled

3. *Separate, set apart, holy,* ἅγιον *hagion.*
Heb. 9. 12 in once into the holy place; 9. 24, 9. 25.

HOLY SPIRIT—Lk. 11. 13, Eph. 1. 13, 4. 30,
1 Th. 4. 8. Isa. 63. 10, 11.

HOLY thing —
1. *Separation, separate or set apart object,* קֹדֶשׁ *qodesh.*
Exod 28. 38 may bear the iniquity of the holy things
Lev. 5. 15 and sin..in the holy things of the LORD
5. 16 harm that he hath done in the holy thing
22. 2 the holy things of the children of Israel
22. 3 goeth unto the holy things, which the chil.
22. 4 he shall not eat of the holy things, until
22. 6 shall not eat of the holy things, unless
22. 7 and shall afterward eat of the holy things
22. 10 shall no stranger eat (of) the holy thing
22. 10 servant, shall not eat (of) the holy thing
22. 12 not eat of an offering of the holy things
22. 14 a man eat (of) the holy thing unwittingly
22. 14 give..unto the priest with the holy thing
22. 15 they shall not profane the holy things of
22. 16 iniquity when they eat their holy things
Num. 4. 15 but they shall not touch (any) holy thing
4. 20 to see when the holy things are covered
5. 9 every offering of all the holy things of the
18. 19 All the heave offerings of the holy things
18. 32 neither shall ye pollute the holy things of
Deut. 12. 26 Only thy holy things which thou hast, and
1 Ch. 23. 28 in the purifying of all holy things, and the
2 Ch. 31. 6 the tithe of holy things which were conse.
Neh. 10. 33 for the set feasts, and for the holy (things)
Eze. 20. 40 of your oblations, with all your holy things
22. 8 Thou hast despised mine holy things, and
22. 26 and have profaned mine holy things: they
44. 8 have not kept the charge of mine holy th.
44. 13 nor to come near to any of my holy things

2. *Separate or set apart object,* ἅγιον *hagion.*
Luke 1. 35 that holy thing which shall be born of th.

HOLY portion —
Separation, separate or set apart object, קֹדֶשׁ *qodesh.*
Eze. 45. 1 offer..unto the LORD, an holy portion of

HO'-MAM, הוֹמָם *raging.*
The form under which an Edomite name appears, which, in Gen. 36. 22, is given *Hemam.* Gesenius considers *Homam* the original form. B.C. 1760.
1 Ch. 1. 39 And the sons of Lotan; Hori, and H.

HOME —
1. *Tent,* אֹהֶל *ohel.*
Judg. 19 9 get..on your way, that thou mayest go ho.
2. *House,* בַּיִת *bayith.*
Gen. 39. 16 laid up..garment..until his lord came h.
43. 16 Bring (these) men home, and slay, and ma.
43. 26 when Joseph came home, they brought him
Exod. 9. 19 beast which..shall not be brought home
Lev. 18. 9 born at home, or born abroad..their nak.
Deut 24. 5 he shall be free at home one year, and shall
Josh. 2. 18 all thy father's household, home unto thee
1 Sa. 6. 7 and bring their calves home from them
6. 10 and shut up their calves at home
10. 26 Saul also went home to Gibeah; and there
24. 22 Saul went home; but David and his men
2 Sa. 13. 7 Then David sent home to Tamar, saying,
1 Ki. 5. 14 a month..in Lebanon..two months at ho.
2 Ki. 14. 10 glory..and tarry at home; for why should
2 Ch. 25. 19 abide now at home; why shouldest thou
Esth. 5. 10 when he came home, he sent and called for
Psa. 68. 12 she that tarried at home divided the spoil
Prov. 7. 19 For the goodman (is) not at home, he is
7. 20 (and) will come home at the day appointed
Eccl. 12. 5 because man goeth to his long home; and
Jer. 39. 14 that he should carry him home: so he dw.
Lam. 1. 20 Behold, O LORD..at home (there is) as de.
Hag. 1. 9 when ye brought (it) home, I did blow up.
3. *Place,* מָקוֹם *maqom.*
1 Sa. 2. 20 And they went unto their own home
2 Ch. 25. 10 to go home again..and they returned home
4. *To cause to turn back,* שׁוּב *shub,* 5.
Judg. 11. 9 If ye bring me home again to fight against
Ruth 1. 21 LORD hath brought me home again empty
2 Sa. 14. 13 the king doth not fetch home again his
Job 39. 12 that he will bring home thy seed, and gather
5. *Middle, midst,* תָּוֶךְ, תּוֹךְ *tok, tavek.*
Deut 21. 12 thou shalt bring her home to thine house
6. *One's own proper (house),* ἴδιος (οἶκος) *idios (oikos).*
Acts 21. 6 we took ship; and they returned home
1 Ti. 5. 4 let them learn first to show piety at home
7. *House, household,* οἰκία *oikia.*
Matt. 8. 6 my servant lieth at home sick of the palsy
8. *House, household,* οἶκος *oikos.*
Mark 5. 19 Go home to thy friends, and tell them how
Luke 15. 6 when he cometh home, he calleth together
1 Co. 11. 34 if any man hunger, let him eat at home
14. 35 let them ask their husbands at home: for

HOME, their own—
Their own, ἑαυτούς (acc.) *heautous.*
John 20. 10 disciples went..again unto [their own h.]

HOME, to be at —
To be among one's people, be at home, ἐνδημέω.
2 Co. 5. 6 whilst we are at home in the body, we are

HOME, to go —
To turn back, שׁוּב *shub.*
1 Sa. 18. 2 would let him no more go home to his f.

HOME, to keep at home —
1. *To remain at home,* נָוָה *navah.*
Hab. 2. 5 a proud man, neither keepeth at home
2. *Watching or keeping the house,* οἰκουρός *oikouros.*
Titus 2. 5 [keepers at home], good, obedient to their

HOME again — [*See* Bring, fetch.]

HOME born —
1. *Native, indigenous, aboriginal,* אֶזְרָח *ezrach.*
Exod 12. 49 One law shall be to him that is home born
2. *Born in the house,* יְלִיד בַּיִת *yelid bayith.*
Jer. 2. 14 (is) he a home born (slave)? why is he spoil.?

HOMER —
Homer, (a dry measure = 10 ephahs), חֹמֶר *chomer.*
Lev. 27. 16 an homer of barley seed (shall be valued)
Num 11. 32 that gathered least gathered ten homers
Isa. 5. 10 seed of an homer shall yield an ephah
Eze. 45. 11 may contain the tenth part of an homer
45. 11 the ephah the tenth part of an homer: the
45. 11 measure thereof shall be after the homer
45. 13, 13 sixth part of an ephah of an homer of
45. 14 the cor, (which is) an homer of ten baths
45. 14 for ten baths (are) an homer
Hos. 3. 2 and (for) an homer of barley, and an half

HOMER, half —
Lethek, (a half homer), לֶתֶךְ *lethek.*
Hos. 3. 2 of barley, and an half homer of barley

HONEST (thing) —
1. *Excellent,* καλός *kalos.*
Luke 8. 15 which in an honest and good heart, having
Rom 12. 17 Provide things honest in the sight of
2 Co. 8. 21 Providing for honest things, not only in
1 Pe. 2. 12 conversation honest among the Gentiles
2. *Venerable, grave,* σεμνός *semnos.*
Phil. 4. 8 whatsoever things (are) honest whatsoev.

HONEST, that which is —
That which is excellent, τὸ καλόν *to kalon.*
2 Co. 13. 7 ye should do that which is honest, though

HONESTLY —
1. *Decently, becomingly,* εὐσχημόνως *euschēmonōs.*
Rom 13. 13 Let us walk honestly as in the day; not
1 Th. 4. 12 ye may walk honestly toward them that
2. *Excellently,* καλῶς *kalōs.*
Heb. 13. 18 in all things willing to live honestly

HONESTY —
Gravity, venerableness, σεμνότης *semnotēs.*
1 Ti. 2. 2 peaceable life in..godliness and honesty

HONEY —
1. *Honey,* דְּבַשׁ *debash.*
Gen. 43. 11 a little honey, spices, and myrrh, nuts, and
Exod. 3. 8, 17 a land flowing with milk and honey
13. 5 a land flowing with milk and honey, that
16. 31 taste..(was) like wafers (made) with honey
33. 3 a land flowing with milk and honey: for
Lev. 2. 11 nor any honey, in any offering of the LORD
20. 24 a land that floweth with milk and honey
Num 13. 27 it floweth with milk and honey; and this
14. 8 a land which floweth with milk and honey
16. 13, 14 land that floweth with milk and honey
Deut. 6. 3 land that floweth with milk and honey
8. 8 pomegranates..land of oil olive, and honey
11. 9 a land that floweth with milk and honey
26. 9, 15 land that floweth with milk and honey
27. 3 a land that floweth with milk and honey
31 20 land..that floweth with milk and honey
32. 13 made him to suck honey out of the rock
Josh. 5. 6 a land that floweth with milk and honey
Judg 14. 8 bees and honey in the carcase of the lion
14. 9 the honey out of the carcase of the lion
14. 18 What (is) sweeter than honey? and what
1 Sa. 14. 25 and there was honey upon the ground
14. 26 the honey dropped; but no man put his
14. 29 because I tasted a little of this honey
14. 43 I did but taste a little honey with the
2 Sa. 17. 29 honey, and butter, and sheep, and cheese
1 Ki. 14. 3 And take..a cruse of honey, and go to him
2 Ki. 18. 32 a land of oil olive and of honey, that ye
2 Ch. 31. 5 honey, and..all the increase of the field
Job 20. 17 the floods, the brooks of honey and butter
Psa. 19. 10 sweeter also than honey, and the honey c.
81. 16 with honey out of the rock should I have
119. 103 (yea, sweeter) than honey to my mouth
Prov. 24. 13 My son, eat thou honey, because (it is)
25. 16 Hast thou found honey? eat so much as is
25. 27 (It is) not good to eat much honey; so for
Song 4. 11 honey and milk (are) under thy tongue
5. 1 I have eaten my honey comb with my ho.
Isa. 7. 15 honey shall he eat, that he may know to
7. 22 honey shall every one eat (that is) left in
Jer. 11. 5 a land flowing with milk and honey, a (it)
32. 22 a land flowing with milk and honey
41. 8 and of barley, and of oil, and of honey
Eze. 3. 3 was in my mouth as honey for sweetness
16. 13 thou didst eat fine flour, and honey, and
16. 19 honey, (wherewith) I fed thee, thou hast
20. 6, 15 land..flowing with milk and honey
27. 17 and Pannag, and honey, and oil, and balm
2. *Honey,* μέλι *meli.*
Matt. 3. 4 and his meat was locusts and wild honey
Mark 1. 6 and he did eat locusts and wild honey
Rev. 10. 9 it shall be in thy mouth sweet as honey
10. 10 it was in my mouth sweet as honey: and

HONEY COMB —
1. *Dropping, juice,* נֹפֶת *nopheth.*
Prov. 5. 3 lips of a strange woman drop (as)..honeyc.
24. 13 honey comb, (which is) sweet to thy taste
27. 7 The full soul loatheth an honey comb
Song 4. 11 lips, O (my) spouse, drop (as) the honey co.
2. *Comb of honey,* יַעְרַת הַדְּבַשׁ *yarath had-debash.*
1 Sa. 14. 27 dipped it in an honey comb, and put his
3. *Comb (of honey),* יַעַר *yaar.*
Song 5. 1 I have eaten my honey comb with my honey
4. *Dropping of the flowings,* נֹפֶת צוּפִים [*nopheth*].
Psa. 19. 10 sweeter also than honey, and the honey c.
5. *A flowing of honey,* צוּף־דְּבַשׁ *tsuph debash.*
Prov 16. 24 Pleasant words (are as) an honey comb
6. *An honeycomb,* μελίσσιον κηρίον *melission kērion.*
Luke 24. 42 of a broiled fish, and of an honey comb

HONOUR —
1. *Honour, beauty, majesty,* הָדָר *hadar.*
1 Ch. 16. 27 Glory and honour (are) in his presence
Psa. 8. 5 hast crowned him with glory and honour
145. 5 of the glorious honour of thy majesty
149. 9 this honour have all his saints. Praise
Prov 31. 25 Strength and honour (are) her clothing
2. *Honour, beauty, majesty,* הֲדַר *hadar.*
Dan. 4. 36 honour and brightness returned unto me
5. 18 kingdom, and majesty, and glory, and hon.
3. *Honour, beauty, majesty,* הֲדָרָה *hadarah.*
Prov 14. 28 multitude of people (is) the king's honour
4. *Honour, beauty, brilliancy,* הוֹד *hod.*
Num 27. 20 shalt put (some) of thine honour upon him
Psa. 21. 5 honour and majesty hast thou laid upon
96. 6 Honour and majesty (are) before him
104. 1 thou art clothed with honour and majesty
Prov. 5. 9 Lest thou give thine honour unto others
Dan. 11. 21 shall not give the honour of the kingdom
5. *Preciousness, honour,* יְקָר *yeqar.*
Esth. 1. 4 and the honour of his excellent majesty
1. 20 wives shall give to their husbands honour
6. 3 What honour and dignity hath been done
6. 7, 9, 9, 11 the king delighteth to honour
6. 6 delight to do honour more than to myself?
8. 16 had light, and gladness, and joy, and hono.
Psa. 49. 12 man (being) in honour abideth not: he is
49. 20 Man (that is) in honour, and understandeth
6. *Preciousness, honour,* יְקָר *yeqar.*
Dan. 2. 6 gifts and rewards and great honour
4. 30 power, and for the honour of my majesty?
7. *Weight, heaviness, honour,* כָּבוֹד *kabod.*
Gen. 49. 6 unto their assembly, mine honour, be not
Num 24. 11 the LORD hath kept thee back from honour
1 Ki. 3. 13 also given thee..both riches and honour
1 Ch. 17. 18 to thee for the honour of thy servant?
29. 12 riches and honour (come) of thee, and thou
29. 28 old age, full of days, riches, and honour
2 Ch. 1. 11 hast not asked riches, wealth, or honour
1. 12 give thee riches, and wealth, and honour
17. 5 and he had riches and honour in abundance
18. 1 had riches and honour in abundance, and
26. 18 neither (shall it be) for thine honour from
32. 27 had exceeding much riches and honour
32. 33 inhabitants..did him honour at his death
Psa. 7. 5 yea, let him..lay mine honour in the dust
26. 8 and the place where thine honour dwelleth
66. 2 Sing forth the honour of his name; make
112. 9 his horn shall be exalted with honour
Prov. 3. 16 (and) in her left hand riches and honour
8. 18 Riches and honour (are) with me; (yea)
11. 16 A gracious woman retaineth honour; and
15. 33 wisdom; and before honour (is) humility
18. 12 is haughty, and before honour (is) humil.
20. 3 an honour for a man to cease from strife
21. 21 findeth life, righteousness, and honour
22. 4 By humility..(are) riches, honour, and life
25. 2 honour of kings (is) to search out a matter
26. 1 so honour is not seemly for a fool
26. 8 so (is) he that giveth honour to a fool
29. 23 honour shall uphold the humble in spirit
Eccl. 6. 2 wealth, and h.; 10. 1 wisdom (and) h.
Mal. 1. 6 If..I (be) a father, where (is) mine honour
8. *Beauty, glory,* תִּפְאָרָה, תִּפְאֶרֶת *tipharah, tiphereth.*
Deut 26. 19 in praise, and in name, and in honour
Judg. 4. 9 journey..shall not be for thine honour
Psa. 71. 8 (with) thy praise (and with) thy honour
Jer. 33. 9 an honour before all the nations of the
9. *Glory,* δόξα *doxa.*
John 5. 41 I receive not honour from men
5. 44 which receive honour one of another, and
5. 44 not the honour that (cometh) from God
8. 54 my honour is nothing: it is my Father
2 Co. 6. 8 By honour and dishonour, by evil report
Rev. 19. 7 glad and rejoice, and give honour to him
10. *Weight, honour,* τιμή *timē.*
John 4. 44 prophet hath no honour in his own country
Acts 28. 10 Who also honoured us with many honours
Rom. 2. 7 seek for glory and honour and immortality
2. 10 honour, and peace, to every man that w.
9. 21 power..to make one vessel unto honour
12. 10 in honour preferring one another
13. 7 fear to whom fear; honour to whom honour
1 Co. 12. 23 upon these we bestow more abundant ho.
12. 24 abundant honour to that (part) which lack
Col. 2. 23 not in any honour to the satisfying of
1 Th. 4. 4 to possess..in sanctification and honour
1 Ti. 1. 17 (be) honour and glory for ever and ever
5. 17 be counted worthy of double honour
6. 1 their own masters worthy of all honour
6. 16 to whom (be) honour and power everlast.
2 Ti. 2. 20 some to honour, and some to dishonour
2. 21 he shall be a vessel unto honour, sancti.
Heb. 2. 7 crownedst him with glory and honour
2. 9 Jesus..crowned with glory and honour
3. 3 he who hath builded..hath more honour
5. 4 no man taketh this honour unto himself
1 Pe. 1. 7 found unto praise and honour and glory
3. 7 husbands..giving honour unto the wife
2 Pe. 1. 17 he received from God the Father honour
Rev. 4. 9 give glory and honour and thanks to him
4. 11 to receive glory and honour and power
5. 12 Worthy..to receive..honour, and glory
5. 13 Blessing, and honour, and glory, and po.
7. 12 honour, and power, and might, (be) unto
19. 1 [honour], and power, unto the Lord our G.
21. 24 do bring their glory and honour into it
21. 26 bring the glory [and honour] of the nations

HONOUR, to get —
To be or become honoured or mighty, כָּבֵד *kabed,* 2
Exod 14. 17 I will get me honour upon Pharaoh, and
14. 18 when I have gotten me honour upon Ph.

HONOUR, to —
1. *To honour,* הָדַר *hadar.*
Lev. 19. 15 nor honour the person of the mighty: (but)
19. 32 Thou shalt..honour the face of the old
2. *To honour,* הֲדַר *hadar,* 3.
Dan. 4. 34 I praised and honoured him that liveth
4. 37 Now I..extol and honour the king of he.
3. *To make heavy, weighty, honoured,* כָּבֵד *kabed,* 3.
Exod 20. 12 Honour thy father and thy mother: that

Deut. 5. 16 Honour thy father and thy mother, as the
Judg. 9. 9 wherewith by me they honour God and
1 Sa. 2. 29 and honourest thy sons above me, to make
2. 30 for them that honour me I will honour
15. 30 I have sinned: (yet) honour me now, I
2 Sa. 10. 3 Thinkest thou that David doth honour
1 Ch. 19. 3 Thinkest thou that David doth honour
Psa. 15. 4 but he honoureth them that fear the LORD
91. 15 I will deliver him, and honour him
Prov. 3. 9 Honour the LORD with thy substance, and
14. 31 he that honoureth him hath mercy on the
Isa. 29. 13 this people..with their lips do honour me
43. 20 The beast of the field shall honour me
43. 23 neither hast thou honoured me with thy
58. 13 shalt honour him, not doing thine own
Lam. 1. 8 all that honoured her despise her, because
Dan. 11. 38 in his estate shall he honour the God of
11. 38 and a god..shall he honour with gold
Mal. 1. 6 A son honoureth (his) father, and a serv.

4. *To make glorious,* δοξάζω *doxazō.*
John 8. 54 Jesus answered, If I honour myself, my
8. 54 it is my Father that honoureth me; of

5. *To make heavy, honour,* τιμάω *timaō.*
Matt 15. 4 Honour thy father and mother: and, He
15. 6 honour not his father or his mother, (he)
15. 8 honoureth me with (their) lips; but their
19. 19 Honour thy father and (thy) mother; and
Mark 7. 6 This people honoureth me with (their) lips
7. 10 Honour thy father and thy mother; and
10. 19 Defraud not, Honour thy father and moth.
Luke 18. 20 Honour thy father and thy mother
John 5. 23 should honour the Son, even as they hon.
5. 23 He that honoureth not the Son honoureth
8. 49 I honour my Father, and ye do dishonour
12. 26 man serve me, him will (my) Father hon.
Acts 28. 10 Who also honoured us with many honours
Eph. 6. 2 Honour thy father and mother; which is
1 Ti. 5. 3 Honour widows that are widows indeed
1 Pe. 2. 17 Honour all (men). Love the brotherhood
2. 17 Fear God. Honour the king

HONOUR, without —
Without honour, unhonoured, ἄτιμος *atimos.*
Matt 13. 57 A prophet is not without honour, save in
Mark 6. 4 A prophet is not without honour, but in

HONOUR, to do, bring, or promote to —
To make weighty, heavy, honoured, כָּבֵד *kabed,* 3.
Num 22. 17 I will promote thee unto very great hon.
22. 37 am I not able..to promote thee to honour?
24. 11 I thought to promote thee unto great ho.
Judg 13. 17 sayings come to pass we may do thee ho.?
Prov. 4. 8 she shall bring thee to honour, when thou

HONOUR, to come to, or be had in —
1. *To be or become weighty, honoured,* כָּבֵד *kabed.*
Job 14. 21 His sons come to honour, and he knoweth

2. *To be or become weighty, honoured,* כָּבֵד *kabed,* 2.
2 Sa. 6. 22 maidservants..of them shall I be had in h.

HONOUR self, to —
To reckon self heavy, weighty, honoured, כָּבֵד *kabed,* 7.
Prov. 12. 9 (is) better than he that honoureth himself

HONOURABLE —
1. *Honour, beauty, majesty,* הוֹד *hod.*
Psa. 111. 3 His work (is) honourable and glorious; and

2. *To be or become weighty, honoured,* כָּבֵד *kabed,* 2.
Gen. 34. 19 he (was) more honourable than all the h.
Num 22. 15 sent..princes..more honourable than th.
1 Sa. 9. 6 a man of God, and (he is) an honourable
22. 14 goeth..and is honourable in thine house?
2 Sa. 23. 19 Was he not most honourable of three?
23. 23 He was more honourable than the thirty
1 Ch. 4. 9 was more honourable than his brethren
11. 21 he was more honourable than the two, for
11. 25 he was honourable among the thirty, but
Isa. 3. 5 and the base against the honourable
23. 8 whose traffickers (are) the honourable of
23. 9 bring into contempt all the honourable of

3. *To be made heavy, weighty, honoured,* כָּבֵד *kabed,* 4.
Isa. 58. 13 a delight, the holy of the LORD, honour.

4. *Weight, heaviness, honour,* כָּבוֹד *kabod.*
Isa. 5. 13 and their honourable men (are) famished

5. *Glorious, in glory,* ἔνδοξος *endoxos.*
1 Co. 4. 10 ye (are) honourable, but we (are) despised

6. *Well fashioned,* εὐσχήμων *euschēmōn.*
Mark 15. 43 Joseph..an honourable counsellor, which
Acts 13. 50 stirred up the devout and honourable w.
17. 12 of honourable women which were Greeks

7. *Weighty, honourable,* τίμιος *timios.*
Heb. 13. 4 Marriage (is) honourable in all, and the b.

8. *Lifted up of face,* נְשֻׂא פָנִים *nasa phanim.*
2 Ki. 5. 1 Naaman..was a great man..and honour.
Isa. 3. 3 the honourable man, and the counsellor
9. 15 The ancient and honourable, he (is) the h.

HONOURABLE, less —
Without honour, or weight, ἄτιμος *atimos.*
1 Co. 12. 23 which we think to be less honourable

HONOURABLE, more —
Honourable, in honour, ἔντιμος *entimos.*
Luke 14. 8 lest a more honourable man than thou be

HONOURABLE, to be —
To be or become heavy, weighty, honoured, כָּבֵד *kabed,* 2.
Isa. 43. 4 thou hast been honourable, and I have

HONOURABLE, to make —
To make honourable, אָדַר *adar,* 5.
Isa. 42. 21 magnify the law, and make (it) honour.

HONOURABLE man or woman —
1. *To be heavy, weighty, honourable,* כָּבֵד *kabed,* 2.
Nah. 3. 10 and they cast lots for her honourable men

2. *Lifted up of face,* נְשׂוּא פָנִים [*nasa*].
Job 22. 8 and the honourable man dwelt in it

3. *Precious, rare,* יָקָר *yaqar.*
Psa. 45. 9 (were) among thy honourable women

HONOURED, to be —
1. *To be or become honoured or adorned,* הָדַר *hadar,* 2.
Lam. 5. 12 the faces of elders were not honoured

2. *To be or become weighty, honoured,* כָּבֵד *kabed,* 2.
Exod 14. 4 and I will be honoured upon Pharaoh, and

3. *To be made weighty, heavy, honoured,* כָּבֵד *kabed,* 4.
Prov 13. 18 that regardeth reproof shall be honoured
27. 18 that waiteth on his master shall be hono.

4. *To make glorious,* δοξάζω *doxazō.*
1 Co. 12. 26 or one member be honoured, all the me.

HOOD —
A hood, diadem, צָנִיף *tsaniph.*
Isa. 3. 23 the fine linen, and the hoods, and the ve.

HOOF —
Hoof, פַּרְסָה *parsah.*
Exod 10. 26 there shall not an hoof be left behind: for
Lev. 11. 3 Whatsoever parteth the hoof, and is clo.
11. 4 divide the hoof..divideth not the hoof
11. 5 And the coney..divideth not the hoof; he
11. 6 cheweth the cud, but divideth not the h.
11. 7 the swine, though he divide the hoof, and
11. 26 of every beast which divideth the hoof
Deut 14. 6 every beast that parteth the hoof, and cl.
14. 7 the cloven hoof..but divide not the hoof
14. 8 the swine, because it divideth the hoof
Isa. 5. 28 their horses' hoofs shall be counted like
Jer. 47. 3 noise of the stamping of the hoofs of his
Eze. 26. 11 With the hoofs of his horses shall he tread
32. 13 neither shall..the hoofs of beasts trouble
Mic. 4. 13 I will make thy hoofs brass; and thou sh.

HOOFS, to have —
To divide, have hoofs, פָּרַס *paras,* 5.
Psa. 69. 31 ox (or) bullock that hath horns and hoofs

HOOK —
1. *Reed,* אַגְמוֹן *agmon.*
Job 41. 2 Canst thou put an hook into his nose? or

2. *Hook, peg,* וָו *vav.*
Exod 26. 32 their hooks (shall be of) gold, upon the
26. 37 their hooks (shall be of) gold: and thou
27. 10, 11 the hooks of the pillars and their fill.
27. 17 their hooks (shall be of) silver, and their
36. 36 their hooks (were of) gold; and he cast
36. 38 five pillars of it with their hooks: and he
38. 10, 11, 12, 17 the hooks of the pillars and their
38. 19 their hooks (of) silver, and the overlaying
38. 28 he made hooks for the pillars, and overl.

3. *Hook, chain, ring (for nose),* חָח *chach.*
2 Ki. 19. 28 therefore I will put my hook in thy nose
Isa. 37. 29 therefore will I put my hook in thy nose
Eze. 29. 4 But I will put hooks in thy jaws, and I
38. 4 I will..put hooks into thy jaws, and I will

4. *Angle, hook,* חַכָּה *chakkah.*
Job 41. 1 Canst thou draw..leviathan with an hook?

5. *Thorn, hook,* צִנָּה *tsinnah.*
Amos 4. 2 that he will take you away with hooks

6. *Double hooks,* שְׁפַתַּיִם *shephattayim.*
Eze. 40. 43 within (were) hooks..fastened round

7. *A hook, fishing hook,* ἄγκιστρον *agkistron.*
Matt 17. 27 cast an hook, and take up the fish that

HOOK, fish —
Thorn, fish hook, סִיר דּוּגָה *sir dugah.*
Amos 4. 2 he will take..your posterity with fish h.
[*See also* Pruning hook.]

HOPE —
1. *Confidence,* בֶּטַח *betach.*
Psa. 16. 9 Therefore..my flesh also shall rest in h.

2. *Confidence,* בִּטָּחוֹן *bittachon.*
Eccl. 9. 4 joined to all the living there is hope: for

3. *Confidence, folly,* כֶּסֶל *kesel.*
Job 8. 14 Whose hope shall be cut off, and whose
31. 24 If I have made gold my hope, or have
Psa. 78. 7 That they might set their hope in God, and

4. *Confidence,* מִבְטָח *mibtach.*
Jer. 17. 7 Blessed (is) the man..whose hope the L.

5. *Refuge,* מַחְסֶה *machseh.*
Jer. 17. 17 Be not a terror unto me: thou (art) my h.
Joel 3. 16 the LORD (will be) the hope of his people

6. *Expectation,* מִקְוֶה *miqveh.*
Ezra 10. 2 there is hope in Israel concerning this
Jer. 14. 8 O the hope of Israel, the saviour thereof
17. 13 O LORD, the hope of Israel, all that fors.
50. 7 even the LORD, the hope of their fathers

7. *Hope, waiting,* שֵׂבֶר *seber.*
Psa. 119. 116 and let me not be ashamed of my hope
146. 5 his help, whose hope (is) in the LORD his

8. *Hope, expectation,* תּוֹחֶלֶת *tocheleth.*
Job 41. 9 Behold, the hope of him is in vain: shall
Psa. 39. 7 Lord, what wait I for? my hope (is) in thee
Prov 10. 28 The hope of the righteous (shall be) glad.
11. 7 and the hope of unjust (men) perisheth
13. 12 Hope deferred maketh the heart sick: but
Lam. 3. 18 My strength and my hope is perished from

9. *Hope, expectation,* תִּקְוָה *tiqvah.*
Ruth 1. 12 I have hope, (if) I should have an husband
Job 4. 6 thy hope, and the uprightness of thy ways?
5. 16 the poor hath hope, and iniquity stoppeth
7. 6 My days..are spent without hope
8. 13 and the hypocrite's hope shall perish
11. 18 shalt be secure, because there is hope
11. 20 hope (shall be as) the giving up of the
14. 7 there is hope of a tree, if it be cut down
14. 19 and thou destroyest the hope of man
17. 15 where (is) now my hope? as for my hope
19. 10 mine hope hath he removed like a tree
27. 8 what (is) the hope of the hypocrite, though
Psa. 71. 5 thou (art) my hope, O Lord GOD: (thou art)
Prov. 19. 18 Chasten thy son while there is hope, and
26. 12 (there is) more hope of a fool than of him
29. 20 (there is) more hope of a fool than of him
Jer. 31. 17 there is hope in thine end, saith the LORD
Lam. 3. 29 in the dust, if so be there may be hope
Eze. 19. 5 her hope was lost, then she took another
37. 11 Our bones are dried, and our hope is lost
Hos. 2. 15 the valley of Achor for a door of hope
Zech. 9. 12 to the strong hold, ye prisoners of hope

10. *Hope,* ἐλπίς *elpis.*
Acts 2. 26 moreover also my flesh shall rest in hope
16. 19 saw that the hope of their gains was gone
23. 6 of the hope and resurrection of the dead
24. 15 have hope toward God, which they themse
26. 6 the hope of the promise made of God unto
26. 7 For which hope's sake, king Agrippa, I am
27. 20 all hope that we should be saved was then
28. 20 for the hope of Israel I am bound with
Rom. 4. 18 Who against hope believed in hope, that
5. 2 and rejoice in hope of the glory of God
5. 4 patience, experience; and experience, hope
5. 5 hope maketh not ashamed; because the
8. 20 him who hath subjected (the same) in h.
8. 24 hope: but hope that is seen is not hope
12. 12 Rejoicing in hope; patient in tribulation
15. 4 that we through patience..might have h.
15. 13 the God of hope fill..ye may abound in h.
1 Co. 9. 10 he that ploweth should plow in hope; and
9. 10 [in hope should be partaker of his hope]
13. 13 abideth faith, hope, and charity, these th.
2 Co. 1. 7 our hope of you (is) stedfast, knowing, that
3. 12 Seeing then that we have such hope, we
10. 15 having hope, when your faith is increased
Gal. 5. 5 wait for the hope of righteousness by
Eph. 1. 18 may know what is the hope of his calling
2. 12 no hope, and without God in the world
4. 4 are called in one hope of your calling
Phil. 1. 20 to my earnest expectation and (my) hope
Col. 1. 5 hope which is laid up for you in heaven
1. 23 moved away from the hope of the gospel
1. 27 which is Christ in you, the hope of glory
1 Th. 1. 3 patience of hope in our Lord Jesus Christ
2. 19 For what (is) our hope, or joy, or crown of
4. 13 even as others which have no hope
5. 8 and for an helmet the hope of salvation
2 Th. 2. 16 consolation and good hope through
1 Ti. 1. 1 and Lord Jesus Christ, (which is) our hope
Titus 1. 2 In hope of eternal life, which God, that
2. 13 Looking for that blessed hope, and the
3. 7 according to the hope of eternal life
Heb. 3. 6 rejoicing of the hope firm unto the end
6. 11 the full assurance of hope unto the end
6. 18 to lay hold upon the hope set before us
7. 19 but the bringing in of a better hope (did)
1 Pe. 1. 3 hath begotten us again unto a lively hope
1. 21 that your faith and hope might be in God
3. 15 a reason of the hope that is in you with
1 Jo. 3. 3 And every man that hath this hope in him

HOPE, to —
1. *To be confident, trust, lean on,* בָּטַח *batach.*
Job 6. 20 were confounded because they had hoped

2. *To stay,* חוּל *chul*
Lam. 3. 26 (a man) should both hope and quietly wait

3. *To wait with hope,* יָחַל *yachal,* 3.
Job 6. 11 What (is) my strength, that I should hope?
Psa. 31. 24 courage..all ye that hope in the LORD
33. 18 upon them that hope in his mercy
33. 22 be upon us, according as we hope in thee
71. 14 But I will hope continually, and will yet
119. 43 for I have hoped in thy judgments
119. 49 upon which thou hast caused me to hope
119. 74 glad..because I have hoped in thy word
119. 81 My soul fainteth..(but) I hope in thy word
119. 114 Thou (art)..my shield: I hope in thy wo.
119. 147 prevented..and cried: I hoped in thy wo.
130. 7 Let Israel hope in the LORD: for with the
131. 3 Israel hope in the LORD from henceforth
147. 11 pleasure..in those that hope in his mercy
Eze. 13. 6 hope that they would confirm the word

4. *To wait with hope,* יָחַל *yachal,* 5.
Psa. 38. 15 in thee, O LORD, do I hope: thou wilt hear
42. 5, 11 hope thou in God; for I shall yet praise
43. 5 hope in God: for I shall yet praise him

Psa.130. 5 soul doth wait, in his word do I hope
Lam. 3. 24 my portion. therefore will I hope in him

5. *To hope, wait, look for,* שָׂבַר *sabar,* 3.
Esth. 9. 1 enemies of the Jews hoped to have power
Psa.119. 166 LORD, I have hoped for thy salvation, and
Isa. 38. 18 they that go..cannot hope for thy truth

6. *To hope,* ἐλπίζω *elpizō.*
Luke 6. 34 lend (to them) of whom ye hope to receive
23. 8 he hoped to have seen some miracle done
Acts 24. 26 He hoped also that money should have been
26. 7 Unto which..our twelve tribes..hope to
1 Co.13. 7 hopeth all things, endureth all things
2 Co. 8. 5 not as we hoped, but first gave their own
Phil. 2. 23 Him therefore I hope to send presently
1 Ti. 3. 14 write I..hoping to come unto thee shortly
1 Pe. 1. 13 hope to the end for the grace that is to be

HOPE, to cause or make to —

1. *To cause to lean or trust,* בָּטַח *batach,* 5.
Psa. 22. 9 thou didst make me hope (when I was)

2. *To cause to wait with hope,* יָחַל *yachal,* 3.
Psa.119. 49 upon which thou hast caused me to hope for
Eze. 13. 6 they have made (others) to hope that they

HOPE, to have —

1. *To take refuge, trust,* חָסָה *chasah.*
Prov.14. 32 but the righteous hath hope in his death

2. *To wait with hope,* יָחַל *yachal,* 5.
Lam.3. 21 I recall to my mind, therefore have I hope

3. *To hope,* ἐλπίζω *elpizō.*
1 Co.15. 19 If in this life only we have hope in Christ

HOPE for, to —

To hope, ἐλπίζω *elpizō.*
Rom. 8. 24 what a man seeth, why doth he yet hope for
8. 25 But if we hope for that we see not, (then)

HOPE for again, to —

To hope away from, ἀπελπίζω *apelpizō.*
Luke 6. 35 do good, and lend, hoping for nothing a.

HOPE, to be no —

To be desperate, despairing, יָאַשׁ *yaash,* 2.
Isa. 57. 10 saidst thou not, There is no hope: thou h.
Jer. 2. 25 but thou saidst There is no hope: no; for
18. 12 And they said, There is no hope: but we

HOPED for, thing —

To hope, ἐλπίζω *elpizō.*
Heb. 11. 1 faith is the substance of things hoped for

HOPH'-NI, חָפְנִי *strong.*
A son of Eli the high priest and Judge. B.C. 1141.
1 Sa. 1. 3 And the two sons of Eli, H. and Phinehas
2. 34 that shall come upon thy two sons, on H.
4. 4 the two sons of Eli, H. and Phinehas
4. 11 the two sons of Eli, H. and Phinehas, were
4. 17 thy two sons also, H. and Phinehas, are

HOR, הֹר, הֹר *mountain.*
1. The "mountain of mountains," on which Aaron died. It was on the boundary line of the land of Edom, and was the next halting place of the Israelites after Kadesh.
Num 20. 22 the children of I...came unto mount H.
20. 23 spake unto Moses and Aaron in mount H.
20. 25 Take Aaron and Eleazar..unto mount H.
20. 27 they went up into mount H. in the sight
21 4 they journeyed from mount H. by the way
Deut32. 50 as Aaron thy brother died in mount H.
2. A hill on the northern frontier of Israel [Num. 34. 7, 8].

HO'-RAM, הֹרָם *elevated.*
A king of Gezer at the time of the conquest of the S.W. part of Palestine. B.C. 1451.
Josh.10. 33 H. king of Gezer came up to help Lachish

HO'-REB, חֹרֵב *waste.*
The range of mountains of which Sinai is the chief. *Serbal* is now understood to be the range, and *Jabel-Mûsa* ("mount of Moses") to be Sinai. See *Sinai.*
Exod. 3. 1 and came to the mountain of God..to H.
17. 6 I will stand..there upon the rock in H.
33. 6 Israel stripped themselves..by..mount H.
Deut. 1. 2 eleven days'..from H. by the way of mount
1. 6 The LORD our God spake unto us in H.
1. 19 when we departed from H., we went thr.
4. 10 stoodest before the LORD thy God in H.
4. 15 the LORD spake unto you in H. out of the
5. 2 LORD..God made a covenant with us in H.
9. 8 Also in H. ye provoked the LORD to wrath
18. 16 thou desiredst of the LORD thy God in H.
29. 1 the covenant that he made with them in H.
1 Ki. 8. 9 two tables..which Moses put there at H.
19. 8 forty days and forty nights unto H. the
2 Ch. 5. 10 two tables which Moses put..at H. when
Psa.106. 19 They made a calf in H., and worshipped
Mal. 4. 4 which I commanded unto him in H. for

HO'-REM, חֳרֵם *fortress.*
A fortified place in the territory of Naphtali, named with Iron and Migdalel. It is now called *Hurah,* near *Yarûn,* on a *Tell* at the S. end of the *Wady-el-Ain.*
Josh 19. 38 Iron, and Migdal-el, H., and Beth-anath

HOR HA-GID'-GAD, חֹר הַגִּדְגָּד *hill of the cleft.*
A desert station where the Israelites encamped; probably the same as *Gudgodah* (Deut. 10. 7).
Num 33. 32 And they removed..and encamped at H.
33. 33 they went from H., and pitched in Jotb.

HO'-RI, חוֹרִי, חֹרִי *free, noble.*
1. A Horite, the son of Lotan, son of Seir. B.C. 1780.
Gen. 36. 22 And the children of Lotan were H. and H.
36. 30 these (are) the dukes (that came) of H.
[Here it has the article prefixed, and is precisely the same word as that rendered "*the Horites*" in Gen. 36. 21 and 29].
1 Ch. 1. 39 And the sons of Lotan; H., and Homam
2. A Simeonite whose son Shaphat was one of the spies. B.C. 1450.
Num13. 5 the tribe of Simeon, Shaphat the son of H.

HO'-RIM, HO-RITES, הַחֹרִי, הַחֹרִים *troglodytes.*
The aboriginal inhabitants of Mount Seir, probably related to the Emim and Rephaim. Their excavated dwellings are still found in hundreds in the sandstone cliffs and mountains of Edom, but especially at Petra. Perhaps they are referred to in Job 30. 6, 7.
Gen. 14. 6 the H. in their mount Seir, unto El-paran
36. 20 These (are) the sons of Seir the H., who
36 21 these (are) the dukes of the H., the chil.
36. 29 These (are) the dukes..of the H. dukes
Deut. 2. 12 The H. also dwelt in Seir before time; but
2. 22 when he destroyed the H. from before

HOR'-MAH, חָרְמָה *fortress.*
Under its earlier name *Zephath* it was the chief town of the king of a Canaanitish town on the S. of Palestine. After its reduction by Joshua it became a territory of Judah, but belonged to Simeon whose territory is reckoned as part of the former. It is now called *Es-Sûfa* and is situated in the gap in the mountain barrier running S.W. and N.E., completing the plateau of southern Palestine. See *Zephath.*
Num14. 45 smote them..discomfited them..unto H.
21. 3 and he called the name of the place H.
Deut. 1. 44 and destroyed you in Seir, (even) unto H.
Josh 12. 14 The king of H., one; the king of Arad, one
15. 30 And Eltolad, and Chesil, and H.
19. 4 And Eltolad, and Bethul, and H.
Judg. 1. 17 And the name of the city was called H.
1 Sa. 30. 30 And to (them) which (were) in H., and to
1 Ch. 4. 30 And at Bethuel, and at H., and at Ziklag

HORN —

1. *Horn,* קֶרֶן *qeren.*
Gen. 22. 13 a ram caught in a thicket by his horns: and
Exod27. 2 shalt make the horns..his horns shall be
29. 12 put (it) upon the horns of the altar with
30. 2 the horns thereof (shall be) of the same
30. 3 sides..round about, and the horns thereof
30. 10 make an atonement upon the horns of it
37. 25 the horns thereof were of the same
37. 26 sides..round about, and the horns of it
38. 2 made the horns thereof on the four corn.
38. 2 the horns thereof were of the same: and
Lev. 4. 7, 18, 25, 30, 34 upon the horns of the altar
8. 15 put (it) upon the horns of the altar round
9. 9 put (it) upon the horns of the altar round
16. 18 put (it) upon the horns of the altar, and
Deut33. 17 his horns (are like) the horns of unicorns
Josh. 6. 5 they make a long (blast) with the ram's h.
1 Sa. 2. 1 mine horn is exalted in the LORD; my m.
2. 10 he shall..exalt the horn of his anointed
16. 1 Fill thine horn with oil, and go, I will
16. 13 Samuel took the horn of oil, and anointed
2 Sa. 22. 3 the horn of my salvation, my high tower
1 Ki. 1. 39 took an horn of oil out of the tabernacle
1. 50, 51 caught hold on the horns of the altar
2. 28 and caught hold on the horns of the altar
22. 11 son of Chenanah made him horns of iron
1 Ch.25. 5 All these (were)..to lift up the horn. And
2 Ch.18. 10 Zedekiah..had made him horns of iron, and
Job 16. 15 I have..defiled my horn in the dust
Psa. 18. 2 horn of my salvation, (and) my high tower
22. 21 heard me from the horns of the unicorns
75. 4 and to the wicked, Lift not up the horn
75. 5 Lift not up your horn on high: speak (not)
75. 10 the horns of the wicked..the horns of the
89. 17 in thy favour our horn shall be exalted
89. 24 and in my name shall his horn be exalted
92. 10 But my horn shalt thou exalt like..an
112. 9 his horn shall be exalted with honour
118. 27 cords, (even) unto the horns of the altar
132. 17 There will I make the horn of David to b.
148. 14 He also exalteth the horn of his people
Jer. 17. 1 is) graven..upon the horns of your altars
48. 25 The horn of Moab is cut off, and his arm
Lam. 2. 3 cut off in (his) fierce anger all the horn of I.
2. 17 hath set up the horn of thine adversaries
Eze. 27. 15 (for) a present horns of ivory and ebony.
29. 21 horn of the house of Israel to bud forth
34. 21 pushed all the diseased with your horns
43. 15 the altar and upward (shall be) four horns
43. 20 put (it) on the four horns of it, and on the
Dan. 8. 3 which had (two) horns: and the (two) hor.
8. 5 goat (had) a notable horn between his eyes
8. 6 he came to the ram that had (two) horns
8. 7 and smote the ram, and brake his two h.
8. 8 great horn was broken; and for it came
8. 9 out of one of them came forth a little h.
8. 20 ram which thou sawest having (two) horns
8. 21 the great horn that (is) between his eyes
Amos 3. 14 horns of the altar shall be cut off, and
6. 13 Have we not taken to us horns by our own
Mic. 4. 13 Arise..for I will make thine horn iron
Hab. 3. 4 he had horns (coming) out of his hand
Zech. 1. 18 lifted I up mine eyes..behold, four horns
1. 19, 21 These (are) the horns which have sca.
1. 21 cast out the horns..which lifted up..horn

2. *Horn,* קֶרֶן *qeren.*
Dan. 7. 7 behold a fourth beast..and it had ten h.
7. 8 considered the horns..another little horn
7. 8 three of the first horns..in this horn (w.)
7. 11 voice of the great words which the horn
7. 20 of the ten horns..even (of) that horn that
7. 21 the same horn made war with the saints
7. 24 the ten horns out of this kingdom (are)

3. *Horn,* κέρας *keras.*
Luke 1. 69 hath raised up an horn of salvation for
Rev. 5. 6 lamb..having seven horns and seven eyes
9. 13 a voice from the four horns of the golden
12. 3 dragon, having seven heads and ten horns
13. 1 ten horns, and upon his horns ten crowns
13. 11 he had two horns like a lamb, and he sp.
17. 3 beast..having seven heads and ten horns
17. 7 which hath the seven heads and ten horns
17. 12, 16 And the ten horns which thou sawest

HORN, ink —

Ink horn, קֶסֶת *qeseth.*
Eze. 9. 2 clothed with linen, with a writer's ink horn
9. 3 which (had) the writer's ink horn by his
9. 11 clothed with linen, which (had) the ink h.
[*See also* Ram's horn.]

HORNET —

Hornet, wasp, צִרְעָה *tsirah.*
Exod23. 28 will send hornets before thee, which shall
Deut. 7. 20 the LORD..will send the hornet among
Jos. 24. 12 I sent the hornet before you, which drave

HORNS, to have —

To have or use horns, קָרַן *qaran,* 5.
Psa. 69. 31 ox (or) bullock that hath horns and hoofs

HO-RO-NA'-IM, חֹרֹנַיִם *double caves.*
A town of Moab named with Zoar and Luhith, but no clue has been found to its exact site.
Isa. 15. 5 in the way of H. they shall raise up a cry
Jer. 48. 3 A voice of crying..from H., spoiling and
48. 5 in the going down of H. the enemies have
48. 34 from Zoar..unto H...heifer of three years

HO-RO-NITE, חֹרֹנִי.
A native of Horonaim Sanballat who opposed Nehemiah in the restoration of Jerusalem. Fürst derives it from *Beth-horon.*
Neh. 2. 10 When Sanballat the H...heard..it grieved
2. 19 when Sanballat the H., and Tobiah..he.
13. 28 son in law to Sanballat the H.: therefore

HORRIBLE (thing) —

1. *Horror, heat,* זַלְעָפָה *zilaphah.*
Psa. 11. 6 fire and brimstone, and an horrible tem.

2. *Wasting, desolation, noise,* שָׁאוֹן *shaon.*
Psa. 40. 2 He brought me up..out of an horrible pit

3. *Vile, horrible,* שַׁעֲרוּר *shaarur.*
Jer. 23. 14 I have seen also..an horrible thing: they

4. *Vile, horrible,* שַׁעֲרוּרִי *shaaruri.*
Jer. 18. 13 the virgin..hath done a very horrible th.
Hos. 6. 10 I have seen an horrible thing in..Israel

HORRIBLY —

Fear, fright, trembling, שַׂעַר *saar.*
Eze. 32. 10 their kings shall be horribly afraid for thee

HORRIBLY afraid, to be —

To be whirled away, שָׂעַר *saar.*
Jer. 2. 12 be horribly afraid, be ye very desolate

HORROR —

1. *Terror,* אֵימָה *emah.*
Gen. 15. 12 an horror of great darkness fell upon him

2. *Horror, heat,* זַלְעָפָה *zalaphah.*
Psa.119. 53 Horror hath taken hold upon me because

3. *Trembling, horror, fright,* פַּלָּצוּת *pallatsuth.*
Psa. 55. 5 upon me, and horror hath overwhelmed
Eze. 7. 18 horror shall cover them; and shame (shall

HORSE —

1. *A horse,* סוּס *sus.*
Gen. 47. 17 gave them bread (in exchange) for horses
49. 17 an adder..that biteth the horse heels, so
Exod 9. 3 the hand of the LORD is upon..the horses
14. 9 all the horses (and) chariots of Pharaoh
14. 23 all Pharaoh's horses, his chariots, and his
15. 1, 21 the horse and his rider hath he thrown
15. 19 For the horse..went in with his chariots
Deut11. 4 what he did..unto their horses, and to
17. 16 he shall not multiply horses to himself
17. 16 to the end that he should multiply horses
20. 1 When thou..seest horses and chariots
Josh.11. 4 went..with horses and chariots very many
11. 6 thou shalt hough their horses, and burn
11. 9 Joshua..houghed their horses and burnt
2 Sa. 15. 1 Absalom prepared..chariots and horses
1 Ki. 4. 26 had forty thousand stalls of horses for his
4. 28 Barley also and straw for the horses and
10. 25 horses, and mules, a rate year by year
10. 28 Solomon had horses brought out of Egypt
10. 29 and an horse for an hundred and fifty
18. 5 may find grass to save the horses..alive
20. 1 thirty and two kings with him, and horses
20. 20 king of Syria escaped on an horse with the
20. 21 smote the horses and chariots, and slew
20. 25 horse for horse, and chariot for chariot
22. 4 people as thy people, my horses as thy h.
2 Ki. 2. 11 a chariot of fire, and horses of fire, and
3. 7 as thy people, (and) my horses as thy ho.

2 Ki. 5. 9 Naaman came with his horses and..cha.
6. 14 Therefore sent he thither horses, and ch.
6. 15 host compassed the city both with horses
6. 17 behold, the mountain (was) full of horses
7. 6 a noise of chariots, and a noise of horses
7. 7 left their tents, and their horses, and their
7. 10 horses tied, and asses tied, and the tents
7. 13 take..five of the horses that remain, which
7. 14 They took therefore two chariot horses
9. 33 her blood was sprinkled..on the horses
10. 2 (there are) with you chariots and horses
11. 16 way by the which the horses came into the
14. 20 they brought him on horses; and he was
18. 23 I will deliver thee two thousand horses, if
23. 11 he took away the horses that the kings of
2 Ch. 1. 16 Solomon had horses brought out of Egypt
1. 17 and an horse for an hundred and fifty
9. 24 horses, and mules, a rate year by year
9. 25 had four thousand stalls for horses and
9. 28 they brought unto Solomon horses out of
23. 15 come to the entering of the horse gate by
25. 28 brought him upon horses, and buried him
Ezra 2. 66 Their horses (were) seven hundred thirty
Neh. 3. 28 From above the horse gate repaired the
7. 68 Their horses, seven hundred thirty and six
Esth. 6. 8 and the horse that the king rideth upon
6. 9 let this apparel and horse be delivered to
6. 10 haste, (and) take the apparel and the horse
6. 11 Then took Haman the apparel and the h.
Job 39. 18 she scorneth the horse and his rider
39. 19 Hast thou given the horse strength? hast
Psa. 20. 7 Some (trust) in chariots, and some in hor.
32. 9 Be ye not as the horse, (or) as the mule
33. 17 An horse (is) a vain thing for safety: nei.
76. 6 chariot and horse are cast into a dead sl.
147. 10 delighteth not in the strength of the hor.
Prov. 21 31 horse (is) prepared against the day of b.
26. 3 A whip for the horse, a bridle for the ass
Eccl. 10. 7 I have seen servants upon horses, and
Isa. 2. 7 their land is also full of horses, neither
5. 28 their horses' hoofs..counted like flint, and
30. 16 ye said, No; for we will flee upon horses
31. 1 and stay on horses, and trust in chariots
31. 3 their horses flesh, and not spirit. When
36. 8 I will give thee two thousand horses, if
43. 17 bringeth forth the chariot and horse, the
63. 13 led them..as an horse in the wilderness
66. 20 upon horses..in chariots, and in litters
Jer. 4. 13 his horses are swifter than eagles. Woe
5. 8 They were (as) fed horses in the morning
6. 23 they ride upon horses, set in array as men
8. 6 as the horse rusheth into the battle
8. 16 The snorting of his horses was heard from
12. 5 then how canst thou contend with horses?
17. 25 kings..riding in chariots and on horses
22. 4 kings..riding in chariots and on horses
31. 40 unto the corner of the horse gate toward
46. 4 Harness the horses; and get up, ye horse.
46. 9 Come up, ye horses; and rage, ye chariots
50. 37 A sword (is) upon their horses, and upon
50. 42 they shall ride upon horses, (every one)
51. 21 I break in pieces the horse and his rider
51. 27 cause the horses to come up as the rough
Eze. 17. 15 might give him horses and much people
23. 6, 12 captains and..horsemen riding upon
23. 20 and whose issue (is like) the issue of hor.
23. 23 captains..all of them riding upon horses
26. 7 from the north, with horses, and..chariots
26. 10 By reason of the abundance of his horses
26. 11 With the hoofs of his horses shall he tread
27. 14 They..traded in thy fairs with horses and
38. 4 all thine army, horses and horsemen, all
38. 15 people..all of them riding upon horses
39. 20 with horses and chariots, with mighty men
Hos. 1. 7 will not save them..by horses, nor by
14. 3 we will not ride upon horses; neither will
Joel 2. 4 The appearance of them (is) as..of horses
Amos 2. 15 neither shall he that rideth the horse de.
4. 10 have taken away your horses; and I have
6. 12 Shall horses run upon the rock? will (one)
Mic. 5. 10 I will cut off thy horses out of the midst of
Nah. 3. 2 The noise..of the prancing horses, and
Hab. 1. 8 horses also are swifter than the leopards
3. 8 that thou didst ride upon thine horses, (and)
3. 15 walk through the sea with thine horses
Hag. 2. 22 horses and their riders shall come down
Zech. 1. 8 and behold a man riding upon a red horse
1. 8 behind him (were there) red horses, spec.
6. 2 red horses..in the second..black horses
6. 3 white horses..in the fourth..bay horses
6. 6 The black horses..go forth into the north
9. 10 I will cut off..the horse from Jerusalem
10. 3 made them as his goodly horse in the ba.
10. 5 the riders on horses shall be confounded
12. 4 will smite every horse with astonishment
12. 4 and will smite every horse..with blindness
14. 15 so shall be the plague of the horse, of the
14. 20 shall there be upon the bells of the horses

2. *A horse*, ἵππος *hippos*.
Jas. 3. 3 put bits in the horses' mouths, that they
Rev. 6. 2 I saw, and behold a white horse: and he
6. 4 there went out another horse (that was)
6. 5 I beheld, and lo a black horse: and he that
6. 8 I looked, and behold a pale horse: and his
9. 7 like unto horses prepared unto battle; and
9. 9 as the sound of chariots of many horses
9. 17 the horses..and the heads of the horses
14. 20 blood came..even unto the horse bridles
18. 13 horses, and chariots, and slaves, and souls
19. 11 heaven opened, and behold a white horse
19. 14 the armies..followed him upon white ho.
Rev. 19. 18 That ye may eat..the flesh of horses, and
19. 19 make war against him that sat on the h.
19. 21 the sword of him that sat upon the horse

HORSEBACK, (to bring) on —

1. *A horse*, סוּס *sus*.
Esth. 8. 10 sent letters by posts on horseback, (and)

2. *Riding on a horse*, רֹכֵב סוּס [*rakab*].
2 Ki. 9. 18 there went one on horseback to meet him
9. 19 Then he sent out a second on horseback

3. *To cause to ride*, רָכַב *rakab*, 5.
Esth. 6. 9 bring him on horseback through the street
6. 11 brought him on horseback through the st.

HORSE HOOFS —

Horse heel, עֲקֵב סוּס *aqeb sus*.
Judg. 5. 22 Then were the horse hoofs broken by the

HORSE LEACH —

Leech, עֲלוּקָה *aluqah*.
Prov 30. 15 The horse leach hath two daughters, (cry.)

HORSEMAN —

1. *Horseman*, פָּרָשׁ *parash*.
Gen. 50. 9 there went up..both chariots and horsem.
Exod 14. 9 his horsemen and his army..overtook them
14. 17, 18 upon his chariots, and upon his horse.
14. 23 (even) all Pharoah's horses..and his hors.
14. 26 the waters may come..upon their horse.
14. 28 covered the chariots, and the horsemen
15. 19 went in..with his horsemen into the sea
Josh 24. 6 Egyptians pursued..with..horsemen unto
1 Sa. 8. 11 He will take your sons..(to be) his horsem.
13. 5 six thousand horsemen, and people as the
2 Sa. 8. 4 And David took..seven hundred horsem.
10. 18 David slew..forty thousand horsemen, and
1 Ki. 1. 5 he prepared him chariots and horsemen
4. 26 And Solomon had..twelve thousand hor.
9. 19 cities for his chariots, and..horsemen, and
9. 22 and rulers of his chariots, and his horse.
10. 26 Solomon gathered..chariots and horsem.
10. 26 and twelve thousand horsemen, whom he
20. 20 escaped on an horse with the horsemen
2 Ki. 2. 12 the chariot of Israel, and the horsemen
13. 7 Neither did he leave..but fifty horsemen
13. 14 chariot of Israel, and the horsemen ther.
18. 24 and put thy trust on Egypt for..horsem.?
1 Ch. 18. 4 David took..seven thousand horsemen
19. 6 silver to hire..chariots and horsemen out
2 Ch. 1. 14 Solomon gathered chariots and horsemen
1. 14 he had..twelve thousand horsemen, which
8. 6 the cities of the horsemen, and all that S.
8. 9 and captains of his chariots and horsemen
9. 25 And Solomon had..twelve thousand hor.
12. 3 With..threescore thousand horsemen: a.
16. 8 with very many chariots and horsemen?
Ezra 8. 22 horsemen to help us against the enemy
Neh. 2. 9 sent captains of the army and horsemen
Isa. 21. 7 he saw a chariot (with) a couple of horse.
21. 9 chariot of men, (with) a couple of horse
22. 6 bare the quiver with chariots of..horsem.
22. 7 horsemen shall set themselves in array at
28. 28 because he will not..bruise it (with) his h.
31. 1 trust..in horsemen, because they are very
36. 9 and put thy trust on Egypt for..horsemen?
Jer 4. 29 the noise of the horsemen and bowmen
46. 4 get up, ye horsemen, and stand forth with
Eze. 23. 6, 12 captains and..horsemen riding upon h.
26. 7 with horsemen, and companies, and much
26. 10 walls..shake at the noise of the horsemen
27. 14 traded..with horses and horsemen and
38. 4 horses and horsemen, all of them clothed
Dan. 11. 40 with horsemen, and with many ships; and
Hos. 1. 7 will not save them by bow..nor by horsem.
Joel 2. 4 and as horsemen, so shall they run
Nah. 3. 3 The horseman lifteth up..the..sword
Hab. 1. 8 their horsemen shall spread..their horse.

2. *A rider*, רַכָּב *rakkab*.
2 Ki. 9. 17 Take an horseman, and send to meet them

3. *Owner of a horse*, בַּעַל פָּרָשׁ *baal parash*.
2 Sa. 1. 6 chariots and horsemen followed hard after

4. *Horseman, cavalry*, ἱππικόν *hippikon*.
Rev. 9. 16 the number of the army of the [horsemen]

5. *Horseman*, ἱππεύς *hippeus*.
Acts 23. 23 horsemen threescore and ten, and spearm.
23. 32 they left the horsemen to go with him, and

HORSES, company of —

A mare, סוּסָה *susah*.
Song 1. 9 a company of horses in Pharaoh's chariots

HO'-SAH, חֹסָה *refuge*.

1. A city of the tribe of Asher, and the next land mark on the boundary to Tyre.
Josh 19. 29 and the coast turneth to H.; and the out.

2. A Levite selected by David to be one of the first door-keepers to the ark after its arrival in Jerusalem. B.C. 1042.
1 Ch. 16. 38 Obed-edom also the son of Jeduthun..H.
26. 10 Also H., of the children of Merari, had sons
26. 11 all the sons and brethren of H...thirteen
26. 16 To Shuppim and H...westward, with the

HOSANNA —

Save, we pray thee! (*Heb.* הוֹשַׁע־נָא) ὡσαννά.
Matt 21. 9, 15 saying, Hosanna to the son of David
21. 9 name of the Lord! Hosanna in the highest
Mark 11. 9 Hosanna! Blessed (is) he that cometh in
Mark 11. 10 Blessed (be) the kingdom..Hosanna in th
John 12. 13 Hosanna: Blessed (is) the King of Israel

HO-SE'-A, הוֹשֵׁעַ *Jah is help*.

The first of what are commonly called the "minor prophets," as they appear in the English Bible. The name in the Hebrew is *Hoshea*. He prophesied B.C. 784–725.
Hos. 1. 1 The word of the LORD that came unto H
1. 2 beginning of the word of the LORD by H
1. 2 LORD said to H., Go, take unto thee a wife

HOSEN —

Fine upper garment, פַּטְּשׁ, [V. L. פַּטִּישׁ] *petesh*.
Dan. 3. 21 were bound in their coats, their hosen, and

HO-SHA'-IAH, הוֹשַׁעְיָה.

1. A man who led the princes of Judah in the procession in the ceremony of the dedication of the wall of Jerusalem. B.C. 445.
Neh. 12. 32 after them went H., and half of the princes

2. Father of Jezaniah or Azariah, a man of note in the time of Nebuchadnezzar. B.C. 610.
Jer. 42. 1 Jezaniah the son of H., and all the people
43. 2 Then spake Azariah the son of H., and J.

HO-SHA'-MA, הוֹשָׁמָע *Jah is hearer*.

A son of Jeconiah or Jehoiachin, the last but one of the kings of Judah. B.C. 580.
1 Ch. 3. 18 Shenazar, Jecamiah, H., and Nedabiah

HO-SHE'-A, or OSHEA, הוֹשֵׁעַ *Jah is help*.

1. The original name of Joshua the son of Nun. In Num. 13. 8 it is given *Oshea*. B.C. 1450.
Deut 32. 44 Moses came and spake..he and H. the son

2. The ruler of the tribe of Ephraim in David's time. B.C. 1015.
1 Ch. 27. 20 Of the children of Ephraim, H. the son of

3. The nineteenth, last, and best king of Israel. B.C. 729–720; and was subdued and imprisoned by Sargon king of Assyria.
2 Ki. 15. 30 H. the son of Elah made a conspiracy ag.
17. 1 began H. the son of Elah to reign in Sa.
17. 3 H. became his servant, and gave him pr.
17. 4 king of Assyria found conspiracy in Ho.
17. 6 In the ninth year of H. the king of Assy
18. 1; 18. 9; 18. 10.

4. A Jew who sealed the covenant with Nehemiah.
Neh. 10. 23 H., Hananiah, Hashub.

HOSPITALITY —

Love of strangers, hospitality, φιλοξενία *philoxenia*.
Rom 12. 13 Distributing..given to hospitality

HOSPITALITY, given to, lover of, use —

Lover of strangers, hospitable, φιλόξενος *philoxenos*.
1 Ti. 3. 2 of good behaviour, given to hospitality, apt
Titus 1. 8 a lover of hospitality, a lover of good men
1 Pe. 4. 9 Use hospitality one to another without

HOST —

1. *Strength, wealth, army, force*, חַיִל *chayil*.
Exod 14. 4 I will be honoured..upon all his host; that
14. 17 I will get me honour upon..all his host
14. 28 and covered..all the host of Pharaoh
15. 4 Pharaoh's..host hath he cast into the sea
Num 31. 14 was wroth with the officers of the host
1 Sa. 14. 48 he gathered an host, and smote the Am.
17. 20 as the host was going forth to the fight
2 Sa. 8. 9 had smitten all the host of Hadadezer
24. 2 the king said to..the captain of the host
24. 4 and against the captains of the host
24. 4 Joab and the captains of the host went
1 Ki. 15. 20 the captains of the hosts which he had
20. 1 Ben-haded..gathered all his host togeth.
2 Ki. 6. 14 Therefore sent he thither..a great host
6. 15 behold, an host compassed the city both
7. 6 of horses, (even) the noise of a great host
9. 5 the captains of the host (were) sitting; and
11. 15 commanded..the officers of the host, and
25. 1 Nebuchadnezzar..came, he, and all his h.
1 Ch. 18. 9 heard how David had smitten all the host
2 Ch. 14. 9 with an host of a thousand thousand, and
16. 7 therefore is the host..escaped out of thine
16. 8 Were not the Ethiopians..a huge host
23. 14 the captains..that were set over the host
24. 23 the host of Syria came up against him
24. 24 delivered a very great host into their hand
26. 11 Uzziah had an host of fighting men, that
Psa. 33. 16 no king saved by the multitude of an host
136. 15 But overthrew Pharaoh and his host in the

2. *Strength, wealth, army, force*, חֵיל *chel*.
2 Ki. 18. 17 with a great host against Jerusalem: and
Obad. 20 captivity of this host of the children of

3. *Camp, encampment*, מַחֲנֶה *machaneh*.
Gen. 32. 2 This (is) God's host: and he called the
Exod 14. 24 looked unto the host..troubled the ho
16. 13 and..the dew lay round about the host
Deut. 2. 14 were wasted out from among the host, as
2. 15 to destroy them from among the host
23. 9 When the host goeth forth against thine
Josh. 1. 11 Pass through the host, and command the
3. 2 that the officers went through the host
8. 13 all the host that (was) on the north of the
10. 5 went up, they and all their hosts, and en.
11. 4 they and all their hosts with them, much
18. 9 came..to Joshua to the host at Shiloh
Judg. 4. 15 LORD discomfited Sisera..and all (his) ho.
4. 16 after the host..all the host of Sisera fell
7. 1 so that the host of the Midianites were on
7. 8 host of Midian was beneath him in the
7. 9 Arise, get thee down unto the host: for

Judg. 7. 10 with Phurah thy servant down to the host
7. 11 be strengthened to go down unto the host
7. 11 of the armed men that (were) in the host
7. 13 a cake..tumbled into the host of Midian
7. 14 into his hand..God delivered..all the host
7. 15 the host of Israel..the host of Midian
7. 21 and all the host ran, and cried, and fled
7. 22 throughout all the host: and the host fled
8. 10 and their hosts..all the hosts of the
8. 11 and smote the host: for the host was
8. 12 took..and discomfited all the host
1 Sa. 11. 11 they came into the midst of the host in
14. 15 there was trembling in the host, in the
14. 19 that the noise that (was) in the host of the
17. 46 the carcases of the host of the Philistines
28. 5 when Saul saw the host of the Philistines
28. 19 LORD also shall deliver the host of Israel
29. 6 and thy coming in with me in the host (is)
2 Sa. 5. 24 go out..to smite the host of the Philistines
23. 16 three..men brake through the host of the
1 Ki. 22. 34 carry me out of the host; for I am woun.
22. 36 went a proclamation throughout the host
2 Ki. 3. 9 and there was no water for the host, and
6. 24 Ben-hadad..gathered all his host, and
7. 4 let us fall unto the host of the Syrians: if
7. 6 the LORD had made the host..to hear a
7. 14 the king sent after the host of the Syrians
1 Ch. 9. 19 fathers, (being) over the host of the LORD
11. 15 the host of the Philistines encamped in the
11. 18 brake through the host of the Philistines
12. 22 (it was) a great host, like the host of God
14. 15 gone forth..to smite the host of the Phil.
14. 16 they smote the host of the Philistines from
2 Ch. 14. 13 destroyed before the LORD, and..his host
18. 33 thou mayest carry me out of the host; for
Psa. 27. 3 Though an host should encamp against
Eze. 1. 24 voice of speech, as the noise of an host

4. *Host, warfare, service*, צָבָא *tsaba*.
Gen. 2. 1 were finished, and all the host of them
21. 22, 32 Phichol the chief captain of his host
Exod. 12. 41 all the hosts of the LORD went out from
Num. 1. 52 and every man..throughout their hosts
2. 4, 6, 8, 11, 13, 15, 19, 21, 23, 26, 28, 30 his h.
2. 32 of the camps, throughout their hosts, (we.)
4. 3 all that enter into the host, to do the wo.
10. 14 over his host (was) Nahshon the son of A.
10. 15, 16, 19, 20, 23, 24, 26, 27 over the host of
10. 18, 22, 25 and over his host (was)
31. 48 which (were) over thousands of the host
Deut. 4. 19 stars, (even) all the host of heaven, should.
17. 3 worshipped..any of the host of heaven
Josh. 5. 14 captain of the host of the LORD am I now
5. 15 captain of the LORD'S host said unto Josh.
Judg. 4. 2 the captain of whose host (was) Sisera
1 Sa. 1. 3 and to sacrifice unto the LORD of hosts in
1. 11 vowed a vow, and said, O LORD of hosts
4. 4 ark of the covenant of the LORD of hosts
12. 9 Sisera, captain of the host of Hazor, and
14. 50 the captain of his host (was) Abner, the
15. 2 Thus saith the LORD of hosts

[So in 2 Sa. 7. 8; 1 Ch. 17. 7; Isa. 3. 15; Jer. 6. 9; 7. 3, 21; 9. 7, 15, 17; 11. 22; 16. 9; 19. 3, 11, 15; 23. 15, 16; 25. 8, 27, 28, 29, 32; 26. 18; 27. 4, 19, 21; 28. 14; 29. 4, 8, 17, 21; 31. 23; 32. 14, 15; 33. 12; 35. 13, 17, 18, 19; 39. 16; 42. 15, 18; 43. 10; 44. 2; 44. 11, 25; 49. 7; 50. 18, 33; 51. 33, 58; Hag. 1. 5, 7; 2. 6, 11; Zech. 1. 3, 4, 14, 17; 2. 8; 3. 7; 8. 2, 4, 6, 7, 9, 14, 19, 20, 23; Mal. 1. 4.]

1 Sa. 17. 45 to thee in the name of the LORD of hosts
17. 55 said unto Abner, the captain of the host
26. 5 the son of Ner, the captain of his host.
2 Sa. 2. 8 the son of Ner, captain of Saul's host
3. 23 all the host that (was) with him were come
5. 10 and the LORD God of hosts (was) with him
6. 2 called by the name of The LORD of hosts
6. 18 blessed..in the name of the LORD of hosts
7. 26 The LORD of hosts (is) the God over Israel
7. 27 thou, O LORD of hosts, God of Israel, hast
8. 16 Joab the son of Zeruiah (was) over the host
10. 7 Joab, and all the host of the mighty men
10. 16 captain of the host of Hadarezer (went)
10. 18 smote Shobach the captain of their host
17. 25 Amasa captain of the host instead of Joab
19. 13 if thou be not captain of the host before
20. 23 Joab (was) over all the host of Israel: and
1 Ki. 1. 19 priest, and Joab the captain of the host
1. 25 the captains of the host, and Abiathar
2. 5 the two captains of the hosts of Israel
2. 32 the host of Israel..of the host of Judah
2. 35 put Benaiah..in his room over the host
4. 4 the son of Jehoiada (was) over the host
11. 15, 21 Joab the captain of the host was
16. 16 made Omri, the captain of the host, king
18. 15 (As) the LORD of hosts liveth, before whom
19. 10, 14 very jealous for the LORD God of hosts
22. 19 host of heaven standing by him on his
2 Ki. 3. 14 (As) the LORD of hosts liveth, before whom
4. 13 the king, or to the captain of the host?
5. 1 captain of the host of the king of Syria
17. 16 worshipped all the host of heaven, and
21. 3 worshipped all the host of heaven, and
21. 5 built altars for all the host of heaven
23. 4 the grove, and for all the host of heaven
23. 5 the planets, and to all the host of heaven
25. 19 the principal scribe of the host, which
1 Ch. 11. 9 for the LORD of hosts (was) with him
12. 14 of the sons of Gad, captains of the host
12. 21 mighty men..and were captains in the host
17. 24 The LORD of hosts (is) the God of Israel
18. 15 Joab the son of Zeruiah (was) over the h.
19. 8 Joab, and all the host of the mighty men
1 Ch. 19. 18 Shophach the captain of the host
25. 1 the captains of the host separated to the
26. 26 the captains of the host, had dedicated
27. 3 chief of all the captains of the host for
27. 5 third captain of the host..(was) Benaiah
2 Ch. 18. 18 the host of heaven standing on his right
26. 14 throughout all the host, shields, and spears
28. 9 he went out before the host that came to
33. 3 and worshipped all the host of heaven
33. 5 he built altars for all the host of heaven
33. 11 the captains of the host of the king of A.
Neh. 9. 6 heaven of heavens, with all their host, the
9. 6 the host of heaven worshippeth thee
Psa. 24. 10 The LORD of hosts, he (is) the king of glory
33. 6 all the host of them by the breath of his
46. 7, 11 LORD of hosts (is) with us; the God of
48. 8 seen in the city of the LORD of hosts, in
59. 5 Thou therefore, O LORD God of hosts, the
69. 6 that wait on thee, O Lord GOD of hosts, be
80. 4 O LORD God of hosts, how long wilt thou
80. 7 Turn us again, O God of hosts, and cause
80. 14 Return, we beseech thee, O God of hosts
80. 19 Turn us again, O LORD God of hosts, cause
84. 1 amiable (are) thy tabernacles, O LORD of h.!
84. 3 O LORD of hosts, my king, and my God
84. 8 O LORD God of hosts, hear my prayer: give
84. 12 O LORD of hosts, blessed (is) the man that
89. 8 O LORD God of hosts, who (is) a strong L.
103. 21 Bless ye the LORD, all (ye) his hosts; (ye)
108. 11 wilt not thou, O God, go..with our hosts?
148. 2 all his angels: praise ye him, all his hosts
Isa. 1. 9 Except the LORD of hosts had left unto us
1. 24 the LORD of hosts, the mighty One of Isr.
2. 12 the day of the LORD of hosts (shall be)
3. 1 behold, the Lord, the LORD of hosts, doth
5. 7 For the vineyard of the LORD of hosts (is)
5. 9 In mine ears (said) the LORD of hosts, Of
5. 16 But the LORD of hosts shall be exalted in
5. 24 cast away the law of the LORD of hosts
6. 3 Holy, holy, holy (is) the LORD of hosts: the
6. 5 for mine eyes have seen..the LORD of hosts
8. 13 Sanctify the LORD of hosts himself; and (l.)
8. 18 from the LORD of hosts, which dwelleth in
9. 7 zeal of the LORD of hosts will perform this
9. 13 neither do they seek the LORD of hosts
9. 19 Through the wrath of the LORD of hosts is
10. 16 Therefore shall the..Lord of hosts, send
10. 23 For the Lord GOD of hosts shall make a
10. 24 thus saith the Lord GOD of hosts, O my
10. 26 LORD of hosts shall stir up a scourge for him
10. 33 the LORD of hosts, shall lop the bough
13. 4 LORD of hosts mustereth the host of the
13. 13 in the wrath of the LORD of hosts, and in
14. 22 I will rise up..saith the LORD of hosts
14. 23 I will sweep it..saith the LORD of hosts
14. 24 LORD of hosts hath sworn, saying, Surely
14. 27 For the LORD of hosts hath purposed, and
17. 3 be as the glory..saith the LORD of hosts
18. 7 present be brought unto the LORD of ho.
18. 7 place of the name of the LORD of hosts
19. 4 rule..saith the Lord, the LORD of hosts
19. 12 know what the LORD of hosts hath purp.
19. 16 shaking of the hand of the LORD of hosts
19. 17 the counsel of the LORD of hosts, which he
19. 18 five cities..swear to the LORD of hosts
19. 20 for a witness unto the LORD of hosts in
19. 25 Whom the LORD of hosts shall bless, say.
21. 10 which I have heard of the LORD of hosts
22. 5 of perplexity by the Lord GOD of hosts in
22. 12 did the Lord GOD of hosts call to weeping
22. 14 revealed in mine ears by the LORD of hosts
22. 14 till ye die, saith the Lord GOD of hosts
22. 15 Thus saith the Lord GOD of hosts, Go, get
22. 25 In that day, saith the LORD of hosts, shall
23. 9 The LORD of hosts hath purposed it, to
24. 21 LORD shall punish the host of the high
24. 23 when the LORD of hosts shall reign in m.
25. 6 shall the LORD of hosts make unto all
28. 5 In that day shall the LORD of hosts be for
28. 22 I have heard from the Lord GOD of hosts
28. 29 This..cometh forth from the LORD of ho.
29. 6 visited of the LORD of hosts with thunder
31. 4 so shall the LORD of hosts come down to
31. 5 so will the LORD of hosts defend Jerusalem
34. 4 the host of heaven..all their host shall
37. 16 LORD of hosts, God of Israel, that dwellest
37. 32 zeal of the LORD of hosts shall do this
39. 5 said..Hear the word of the LORD of hosts
40. 26 that bringeth out their host by number
44. 6 and his redeemer the LORD of hosts; I
45. 12 and all their host have I commanded
45. 13 not for price..saith the LORD of hosts
47. 4 the LORD of hosts (is) his name
48. 2 The LORD of hosts (is) his name
51. 15 roared: The LORD of hosts (is) his name
54. 5 thy maker..The LORD of hosts (is) his na.
Jer. 2. 19 not in thee, saith the Lord GOD of hosts
3. 19 a goodly heritage of the hosts of nations?
5. 14 thus saith the LORD God of hosts, Because
6. 6 For thus hath the LORD of hosts said, H.
8. 2 the host of heaven, whom they have loved
8. 3 have driven them, saith the LORD of hosts
10. 16 The LORD of hosts (is) his name
11. 17 the LORD of hosts, that planted thee, hath
11. 20 O LORD of hosts, that judgest righteously
15. 16 called by thy name, O LORD God of hosts
19. 13 burned incense unto..the host of heaven
20. 12 LORD of hosts, that triest the righteous
23. 36 living God, of the LORD of hosts our God
27. 18 make intercession to the LORD of hosts
28. 2 Thus speaketh the LORD of hosts, the G.
29. 25 Thus speaketh the LORD of hosts, the G.
Jer. 30. 8 in that day, saith the LORD of hosts
31. 35 the LORD of hosts (is) his name
32. 18 Great, the Mighty God, the LORD of hosts
33. 11 Praise the LORD of hosts: for the LORD
33. 22 As the host of heaven cannot be number.
38. 17 Thus saith the LORD, the God of hosts
44. 7 the God of hosts, the God of Israel
46. 10 the day of the Lord GOD of hosts
46. 10 the Lord GOD of hosts hath a sacrifice
46. 18 the king, whose name (is) The LORD of h
46. 25 The LORD of hosts, the God of Israel, saith
48. 1 thus saith the LORD of hosts, the God of I
48. 15 the king, whose name (is) The LORD of h
49. 5 Behold..saith the Lord GOD of hosts, from
49. 26, 35 saith the LORD of hosts
50. 25 work of the Lord GOD of hosts in the land
50. 31 saith the Lord GOD of hosts: for thy day is
50. 34 the LORD of hosts (is) his name: he shall
51. 3 and spare ye not..destroy ye..all her h.
51. 5 of his God, of the LORD of hosts; though
51. 14 The LORD of hosts hath sworn by himself
51. 19 the LORD of hosts (is) his name
51. 57 the King, whose name (is) The LORD of h.
52. 25 and the principal scribe of the host, who
Dan. 8. 10 waxed great, (even) to the host of heaven
8. 10 and it cast down (some) of the host and of
8. 11 Yea..even to the prince of the host, and by
8. 12 an host was given (him) against the daily
8. 13 and the host to be trodden under foot?
Hos. 12. 5 Even the LORD God of hosts; the LORD (is)
Amos 3. 13 saith the Lord GOD, the God of hosts
4. 13 The LORD, The God of hosts, (is) his name
5. 14 the God of hosts, shall be with you, as ye
5. 15 Lord GOD of hosts will be gracious unto
5. 16 the God of hosts, the Lord, saith thus
5. 27 the LORD, whose name (is) The God of h.
6. 8 saith the LORD the God of hosts, I abhor
6. 14 saith the LORD the God of hosts; and they
9. 5 Lord GOD of hosts (is) he that toucheth the
Mic. 4. 4 mouth of the LORD of hosts hath spoken
Nah. 2. 13 I (am) against thee, saith the LORD of h.
3. 5 I (am) against thee, saith the LORD of h.
Hab. 2. 13 Behold, (is it) not of the LORD of hosts
Zeph. 1. 5 them that worship the host of heaven
2. 9 (as) I live, saith the LORD of hosts, the God
2. 10 against the people of the LORD of hosts
Hag. 1. 2 Thus speaketh the LORD of hosts, saying
1. 9 Why? saith the LORD of hosts. Because
1. 14 in the house of the LORD of hosts, their G.
2. 4 I (am) with you, saith the LORD of hosts
2. 7 fill..with glory, saith the LORD of hosts
2. 8 the gold (is) mine, saith the LORD of hosts
2. 9 saith the LORD of hosts: and in this place
2. 9 will I give peace, saith the LORD of hosts
2. 23 In that day, saith the LORD of hosts, will
2. 23 have chosen thee, saith the LORD of hosts
Zech. 1. 3 Turn ye unto me, saith the LORD of hosts
1. 3 will turn unto you, saith the LORD of ho.
1. 6 Like as the LORD of hosts thought to do
1. 12 O LORD of hosts, how long wilt thou not
1. 16 be built in it, saith the LORD of hosts, and
2. 9, 11 that the LORD of hosts hath sent me
3. 9 saith the LORD of hosts, and I will remove
3. 10 In that day, saith the LORD of hosts, shall
4. 6 but by my spirit, saith the LORD of hosts
4. 9 that the LORD of hosts hath sent me unto
5. 4 bring it forth, saith the LORD of hosts
6. 12 Thus speaketh the LORD of hosts, saying
6. 15 that the LORD of hosts hath sent me unto
7. 3 in the house of the LORD of hosts, and to
7. 4 Then came the word of the LORD of hosts
7. 9 Thus speaketh the LORD of hosts, saying
7. 12 words which the LORD of hosts hath sent
7. 12 came a great wrath from the LORD of hosts
7. 13 I would not hear, saith the LORD of hosts
8. 1 the word of the LORD of hosts came (to me)
8. 3 and the mountain of the LORD of hosts
8. 6 in mine eyes? saith the LORD of hosts
8. 9 house of the LORD of hosts was laid
8. 11 the former days, saith the LORD of hosts
8. 14 provoked me..saith the LORD of hosts, and
8. 18 the word of the LORD of hosts came unto
8. 21 Let us go..to seek the LORD of hosts; I
8. 22 shall come to seek the LORD of hosts in
9. 15 The LORD of hosts shall defend them; and
10. 3 the LORD of hosts hath visited his flock
12. 5 strength in the LORD of hosts their God
13. 2 in that day, saith the LORD of hosts, (that
13. 7 Awake, O sword..saith the LORD of hosts
14. 16, 17 to worship the King, the LORD of hosts
14. 21 shall be holiness unto the LORD of hosts
14. 21 no more..in the house of the LORD of ho.
Mal. 1. 6 saith the LORD of hosts unto you, O priests
1. 8 accept thy person? saith the LORD of hosts
1. 9 will he regard..saith the LORD of hosts
1. 10 no pleasure in you, saith the LORD of hosts
1. 11 (shall be) great..saith the LORD of hosts
1. 13 ye..snuffed at it, saith the LORD of hosts
1. 14 I (am) a great King saith the LORD of hosts
2. 2 unto my name, saith the LORD of hosts
2. 4 be with Levi, saith the LORD of hosts
2. 7 he (is) the messenger of the LORD of hosts
2. 8 covenant of Levi, saith the LORD of hosts
2. 12 offereth an offering unto the LORD of hosts
2. 16 saith the LORD of hosts: therefore take
3. 1 he shall come, saith the LORD of hosts
3. 5 and fear not me, saith the LORD of hosts
3. 7 will return unto you, saith the LORD of ho
3. 10 prove me now..saith the LORD of hosts
3. 11 time in the field, saith the LORD of hosts
3. 12 delightsome land, saith the LORD of hosts
3. 14 mournfully before the LORD of hosts?

Mal. 3. 17 shall be mine, saith the LORD of hosts, in
4. 1 burn them up, saith the LORD of hosts
4. 3 I shall do (this), saith the LORD of hosts

5. *A stranger, host,* ξένος *xenos.*
Rom 16. 23 Gaius mine host, and of the whole church

6. *One who receives all, innkeeper,* πανδοχεύς *pandoc.*
Luke 10. 35 two pence, and gave (them) to the host

7. *Army, host,* στρατιά *stratia.*
Luke 2. 13 a multitude of the heavenly host praising
Acts 7. 42 gave them up to worship the host of hea.

HOSTAGE —
Son of sureties, pledges, בְּנֵי־תַעֲרֻבוֹת *ben taaruboth.*
2 Ki. 14. 14 he took..hostages, and returned to S m.
2 Ch. 25. 24 hostages also, and returned to Samaria

HOT —
1. *To heat,* אָזָה, אֲזָא *aza, azah.*
Dan. 3. 22 the furnace exceeding hot, the flame of the

2. *Fire,* אֵשׁ *esh.*
Lev. 13. 24 in the skin whereof (there is) a hot burn.

3. *Hot, warm,* חָם *cham.*
Josh. 9. 12 This our bread we took hot (for) our pro.

4. *Heat,* חֹם *chom.*
1 Sa. 21. 6 to put hot bread in the day when it was

5. *Fervent,* ζεστός *zestos.*
Rev. 3. 15 art neither cold nor hot..cold or hot
3. 16 because thou art..neither cold nor hot
[*See also* Thunderbolts.]

HOT displeasure —
Heat, fury, poison, חֵמָה *chemah.*
Deut. 9. 19 I was afraid of the anger and hot displea.
Psa. 6. 1 neither chasten me in thy hot displeasure
38. 1 neither chasten me in thy hot displeasure

HOT, to be or wax —
1. *Heat,* חֹם *chom.*
1 Sa. 11. 9 To morrow, by (that time) the sun be hot
Neh. 7. 3 the gates..be opened until the sun be hot
Job 6. 17 when it is hot, they are consumed out of

2. *To be or become warm,* חָמַם *chamam.*
Exod 16. 21 and when the sun waxed hot, it melted
Psa. 39. 3 My heart was hot within me; while I was

3. *To be or become warm,* חָמַם *chamam,* 2.
Hos. 7. 7 They are all hot as an oven, and have

4. *To burn, be wroth,* חָרָה *charah.*
Exod 22. 24 my wrath shall wax hot, and I will kill
32. 10 my wrath may wax hot against them, and
32. 11 doth thy wrath wax hot against thy people
32. 19 Moses' anger waxed hot, and he cast the
32. 22 Let not the anger of my lord wax hot
Judg. 2. 14, 20 anger of the LORD was hot against Is.
3. 8 anger of the LORD was hot against Israel
6. 39 Let not thine anger be hot against me
10. 7 anger of the LORD was hot against Israel

5. *To be warm, hot,* יָחַם *yacham.*
Deut 19. 6 pursue the slayer, while his heart is hot
Eze. 24. 11 the brass of it may be hot, and may burn

HOT iron, to be seared with a —
To brand, cause to burn in, καυτηριάζω *kautēriazō.*
1 Ti. 4. 2 having their conscience seared with a hot i.

HO'-THAM, חוֹתָם *determination.* **[HOTHAN.]**
1. A son of Heber of the family of Beriah of the tribe of Asher. B.C. 1640.
1 Ch. 7. 32 Heber begat Japhlet, and Shomer, and H.

2. An Aroerite whose two sons Shama and Jehiel were among David's worthies. B.C. 1048. *Hothan* for *Hotham* is an error since the English Version of A.D. 1611.
1 Ch. 11. 44 Shama and Jehiel the sons of H. the Ar.

HO-THIR, הוֹתִיר *abundance.*
Thirteenth son of Heman "the king's seer." He was a Kohathite and had charge of the twenty-first course in the service of the tabernacle. B.C. 1015.
1 Ch. 25. 4 Joshbekashah, Mallothi, H., (and) Mah.
25. 28 The one and twentieth to H...his sons

HOTLY — [*See* Pursue.]

HOTTEST —
Strong, חָזָק *chazaq.*
2 Sa. 11. 15 in the fore front of the hottest battle

HOUGH to —
To root out, עָקַר *aqar,* 3.
Josh. 11. 6 thou shalt hough their horses, and burn
11. 9 he houghed their horses, and burnt their
2 Sa. 8. 4 David houghed all the chariot (horses)
1 Ch. 18. 4 David also houghed all the chariot (horses)

HOUR —
1. *Look, glance, hour,* שָׁעָה *shaah.*
Dan. 3. 6 the same hour be cast into the midst of
3. 15 ye shall be cast the same hour into the
4. 19 Belteshazzar, was astonied for one hour
4. 33 The same hour was the thing fulfilled
5. 5 In the same hour came forth fingers of a

2. *Hour,* ὥρα *hōra.*
Matt. 8. 13 servant was healed in the self same hour
9. 22 the woman was made whole from that h.
10. 19 [it shall be given you in that same hour]
15. 28 daughter was made whole from that..h.
17. 18 the child was cured from that very hour
Matt 20. 3 he went out about the third hour, and saw
20. 5 went out about the sixth and ninth hour
20. 6 about the eleventh [hour] he went out, and
20. 9 that (were hired) about the eleventh hour
20. 12 These last have wrought (but) one hour
24. 36 of that day and hour knoweth no (man)
24. 42 know not what [hour] your Lord doth come
24. 44 in such an hour as ye think not the Son
24. 50 and in an hour that he is not aware of
25. 13 the hour wherein the Son of man cometh
26. 40 What! could ye not watch with me one h.?
26. 45 take (your) rest: behold, the hour is at h.
26. 55 In that same hour said Jesus to the mul.
27. 45 from the sixth hour unto the ninth hour
27. 46 about the ninth hour Jesus cried with a
Mark 13. 11 whatsoever..be given you in that hour
13. 32 of that day and (that) hour knoweth no
14. 35 if it were possible, the hour might pass
14. 37 Simon..couldest not thou watch one hour?
14. 41 it is enough, the hour is come; behold
15. 25 was the third hour, and they crucified him
15. 33 the sixth hour..until the ninth hour
15. 34 at the ninth hour Jesus cried with a loud
Luke 7. 21 [the same] hour he cured many of (their)
10. 21 In that hour Jesus rejoiced in spirit, and
12. 12 teach you in the same hour what ye ought
12. 39 had known what hour the thief would c.
12. 40 cometh at an hour when ye think not
12. 46 and at an hour when he is not aware, and
20. 19 the same hour sought to lay hands on him
22. 14 when the hour was come, he sat down, and
22. 53 this is your hour, and the power of dark.
22. 59 about the space of one hour after, anoth.
23. 44 the sixth hour..until the ninth hour
24. 33 they rose up the same hour, and returned
John 1. 39 and abode..for it was about the tenth h.
2. 4 Jesus saith..Woman..mine hour is not
4. 6 sat thus..(and) it was about the sixth h.
4. 21 Woman, believe me, the hour cometh, w.
4. 23 But the hour cometh, and now is, when
4. 52 the hour..at the seventh hour the fever
4. 53 at the same hour in the which Jesus said
5. 25 The hour is coming, and now is, when the
5. 28 for the hour is coming, in the which all
7. 30 no man laid..because his hour was not
8. 20 no man laid..for his hour was not yet c.
11. 9 Are there not twelve hours in the day?
12. 23 The hour is come, that the Son of man
12. 27 save me from this hour..unto this hour
13. 1 when Jesus knew that his hour was come
16. 21 hath sorrow, because her hour is come
16. 32 Behold, the hour cometh, yea is now come
17. 1 Father, the hour is come; glorify thy Son
19. 14 it was..about the sixth hour: and he saith
19. 27 from that hour that disciple took her unto
Acts 2. 15 seeing it is (but) the third hour of the day
3. 1 went..into the temple at the hour of pr.
5. 7 about the space of three hours after, wh.
10. 3 evidently, about the ninth hour of the day
10. 9 Peter went up..to pray about the sixth h.
10. 30 Four days ago I was fasting until this h.
10. 30 at the ninth [hour] I prayed in my house
16. 18 And he came out the same hour
16. 33 he took them the same hour of the night
19. 34 about the space of two hours cried out, G.
22. 13 And the same hour I looked up upon him
23. 23 Make ready..at the third hour of the night
1 Co. 4. 11 Even unto this present hour we..hunger
15. 30 And why stand we in jeopardy every ho.?
Gal. 2. 5 we gave place..no, not for an hour; that
Rev. 3. 3 thou shalt not know what hour I will co.
3. 10 will keep thee from the hour of tempta.
9. 15 which were prepared for an hour, and a
11. 13 the same [hour] was there a great earthq.
14. 7 for the hour of his judgment is come: and
17. 12 but receive power as kings one hour with
18. 10 for in one hour is thy judgment come
18. 17 For in one hour so great riches is come to
18. 19 Alas..for in one hour is she made desol.

HOUR, half an —
Half an hour, ἡμιώριον *hēmiōrion.*
Rev. 8. 1 silence..about the space of [half an hour]

HOUR, this —
Now, ἄρτι *arti.*
1 Co. 8. 7 unto this hour eat (it) as a thing offered

HOUSE —
1. *House, household,* בַּיִת *bayith.*
Gen. 7. 1 Come thou and all thy house into the ark
12. 1 Get thee..from thy father's house, unto
12. 15 the woman was taken into Pharaoh's ho.
12. 17 the LORD plagued Pharaoh and his house
14. 14 his trained (servants), born in his own h.
15. 2 steward of my house (is) this Eliezer of D.?
15. 3 and, lo, one born in my house is mine h.
17. 12 he that is born in the house, or bought
17. 13 He that is born in thy house, and he that
17. 23 and all that were born in his house, and
17. 23 male among the men of Abraham's house
17. 27 the men of his house, born in the house
19. 2 turn in..into your servant's house, and
19. 3 turned in..and entered into his house; and
19. 4 men of Sodom, compassed the house round
19. 10 pulled Lot into the house to them, and
19. 11 the men that (were) at the door of the h.
20. 13 caused me to wander from my father's h.
20. 18 all the wombs of the house of Abimelech
24. 2 eldest servant of his house, that ruled over
24. 7 which took me from my father's house, and
24. 23 is their room (in) thy father's house for us
Gen. 24. 27 LORD led me to the house of my master's
24. 28 ran, and told (them of) her mother's house
24. 31 for I have prepared the house, and room
24. 32 man came into the house: and he ungir.
24. 38 But thou shalt go unto my father's house
24. 40 thou shalt take a wife..of my father's h.
27. 15 raiment..which (were) with her in the h.
28. 2 to the house of Bethuel thy mother's fa.
28. 17 this (is) none other but the house of God
28. 21 So that I come again to my father's house
28. 22 this stone..shall be God's house: and of
29. 13 kissed him, and brought him to his house
30. 30 when shall I provide for mine own house
31. 14 or inheritance for us in our father's house?
31. 30 thou sore longedst after thy father's house
31. 41 Thus have I been twenty years in thy h.
33. 17 Jacob..built him an house, and made bo.
34. 19 more honourable than all the house of his
34. 26 and took Dinah out of Shechem's house
34. 29 and spoiled even all that (was) in the ho.
34. 30 and I shall be destroyed, I and my house
36. 6 Esau took..all the persons of his house
38. 11 Remain a widow at thy father's house, till
38. 11 Tamar went and dwelt in her father's h.
39. 2 he was in the house of his master the E.
39. 4 and he made him overseer over his house
39. 5 he had made him overseer in his house
39. 5 the LORD blessed the Egyptian's house for
39. 5 all that he had in the house, and in the
39. 8 wotteth not what (is) with me in the house
39. 9 (There is) none greater in this house than
39. 11 went into the house to do his business
39. 11 none of the men of the house there within
39. 14 she called unto the men of her house, and
40. 3 in the house of the captain of the guard
40. 7 with him in the ward of his lord's house
40. 14 But think..and bring me out of this ho.
41. 10 ward in the captain of the guard's house
41. 40 Thou shalt be over my house, and accor.
41. 51 forget..my toil, and all my father's house
42. 19 be bound in the house of your prison
42. 19 carry corn for the famine of your houses
43. 16 he said to the ruler of his house, Bring
43. 17, 24 man brought the men into Joseph's ho.
43. 18 they were brought into Joseph's house
43. 19 of Joseph's house..the door of the house
43. 26 brought him the present..into the house
44. 1 he commanded the steward of his house
44. 8 out of thy lord's house silver or gold?
44. 14 his brethren came to Joseph's house; for
45. 2 Egyptians and the house of Pharaoh heard
45. 8 lord of..his house, and a ruler throughout
45. 16 fame thereof was heard in Pharaoh's ho.
46. 27 the souls of the house of Jacob, which
46. 31 his brethren, and unto his father's house
49. 31 and my father's house, which (were) in the
47. 14 brought the money into Pharaoh's house
50. 4 Joseph spake unto the house of Pharaoh
50. 7 elders of his house, and all the elders
50. 8 the house of Joseph, and his brethren
50. 8 his father's house: only their little ones
50. 22 dwelt in Egypt, he and his father's house
Exod. 1. 21 feared God, that he made them houses
2. 1 there went a man of the house of Levi
3. 22 and of her that sojourneth in her house
6. 14 These..the heads of their fathers' houses
7. 23 Pharaoh turned and went into his house
8. 3 shall go up and come into thine house
8. 3 into the house of thy servants, and upon
8. 9 destroy..frogs from thee and thy houses
8. 11 from thy houses, and from thy servants
8. 13 the frogs died out of the houses, out of
8. 21 into thy houses: and the houses of the
8. 24 swarm (of flies) into the house of Pharaoh
8. 24 (into) his servants' houses, and into all
9. 20 and his cattle flee into the houses
10. 6 they shall fill thy houses, and the houses
10. 6 the houses of all the Egyptians; which
12. 3 house of (their) fathers..lamb for an house
12. 4 his neighbour next unto his house take
12. 7 and on the upper door post of the houses
12. 13 for a token upon the houses where ye (are)
12. 15 shall put away leaven out of your houses
12. 19 there be no leaven found in your houses
12. 22 shall go out at the door of his house
12. 23 to come in unto your houses to smite (you)
12. 27 houses of the children of Israel in Egypt
12. 27 smote the Egyptians..delivered our hous.
12. 30 not a house where (there was) not one dead
12. 46 In one house shall it be eaten; thou shalt
12. 46 of the flesh abroad out of the house
13. 3 from Egypt, out of the house of bondage
13. 14 out from Egypt, from the house of bondage
16. 31 And the house of Israel called the name
19. 3 Thus shalt thou say to the house of Jacob
20. 2 brought thee..out of the house of bondage
20. 17 Thou shalt not covet thy neighbour's house
22. 7 and it be stolen out of the man's house
22. 8 the master of the house shall be brought
23. 19 bring into the house of the LORD thy God
34. 26 bring unto the house of the LORD thy God
40. 38 in the sight of all the house of Israel
Lev. 10. 6 the whole house of Israel, bewail the
14. 34 a house of the land of your possession
14. 35 he that owneth the house shall come and
14. 35 (there is) as it were a plague in the house
14. 36 shall command that they empty the house
14. 36 that all that (is) in the house be not made
14. 36 the priest shall go in to see the house
14. 37 the walls of the house with hollow strakes
14. 38 of the house to the door of the house
14. 38 and shut up the house seven days

Lev. 14. 39 be spread in the walls of the house
14. 41 he shall cause the house to be scraped
14. 42 other mortar, and shall plaster the house
14. 43 break out in the house, after that he hath
14. 43 after he hath scraped the house, and after
14. 44 (if) the plague be spread in the house
14. 44 it (is) a fretting leprosy in the house: it
14. 45 he shall break down the house, the stones
14. 45 shall break down..the mortar of the house
14. 46 he that goeth into the house all the while
14. 47 he that lieth in the house shall wash his
14. 47 he that eateth in the house shall wash his
14. 48 the house, after the house was plastered
14. 48 the priest shall pronounce the house clean
14. 49 shall take to cleanse the house two birds
14. 51 water, and sprinkle the house seven times
14. 52 he shall cleanse the house with the blood
14. 53 make an atonement for the house: and it
14. 55 the leprosy of a garment, and of a house
16. 6, 11 atonement for himself, and..his house
17. 3, 8, 10 (there be) of the house of Israel
22. 11 he that is born in his house: they shall
22. 13 is returned unto her father's house, as
22. 18 Whatsoever (he be) of the house of Israel
25. 29 sell a dwelling house in a walled city
25. 30 house that (is) in the walled city shall
25. 31 the houses of the villages which have no
25. 32 houses of the cities of their possession
25. 33 the house that was sold, and the city of
25. 33 the houses of the cities of the Levites
27. 14 his house (to be) holy unto the LORD
27. 15 he that sanctified..will redeem his house
Num. 1. 2 by the house of their fathers
[So also 18, 20, 22, 24, 26, 28, 30, 32, 34, 36, 38, 40, 42, 45].
1. 4 every one head of..house of his fathers
1. 44 each one was for the house of his fathers
2. 2 with the ensign of their father's house
2. 32 numbered..by the house of their fathers
2. 34 according to the house of their fathers
3. 15 of Levi after the house of their fathers
3. 20 according to the house of their fathers
3. 24, 30, 35 chief of the house of the father
4. 2, 29, 40, 42 by the house of their fathers
4. 22 throughout the houses of their fathers
4. 34, 46 and after the house of their fathers
4. 38 and by the house of their fathers
7. 2 heads of the house of their fathers, who
12. 7 not so, who (is) faithful in all mine house
16. 32 houses, and all the men that (appertained)
17. 2, 2 according to the house of (their) fathers
17. 3 the head of the house of their fathers
17. 6 according to their fathers' houses, (even)
17. 8 the rod of Aaron for the house of Levi
18. 1 thy father's house with thee, shall bear
18. 11, 13 every one that is clean in thy house
20. 29 they mourned..all the house of Israel
22. 18 give me his house full of silver and gold
24. 13 give me his house full of silver and gold
25. 14 of a chief house among the Simeonites
25. 15 a people, (and) of a chief house in Midian
26. 2 throughout their fathers' house, all that
30. 3 (being) in her father's house in her youth
30. 10 if she vowed in her husband's house, or
30. 16 yet) in her youth in her father's house
32. 18 We will not return unto our houses, until
34. 14, 14 according to the house of their fathers
Deut. 5. 6 land of Egypt, from the house of bondage
5. 21 shalt thou covet thy neighbour's house
6. 7 talk..when thou sittest in thine house
6. 9 write them upon the posts of thy house
6. 11 houses full of all good (things), which thou
6. 12 land of Egypt, from the house of bondage
7. 8 redeemed you out of the house of bondmen
7. 26 bring an abomination into thine house
8. 12 built goodly houses, and dwelt (therein)
8. 14 land of Egypt, from the house of bondage
11. 19 when thou sittest in thine house, and wh.
11. 20 write..upon the door posts of thine house
13. 5 redeemed you out of the house of bondage
13. 10 land of Egypt, from the house of bondage
15. 16 he loveth thee and thine house, because
19. 1 dwellest in their cities, and in their houses
20. 5 What man (is ther) that..built a new h.
20. 5 let him go and return to his house, lest
20. 6, 7, 8 let him go and return unto his house
21. 12 thou shalt bring her home to thine house
21. 13 shall remain in thine house, and bewail
22. 2 thou shalt bring it unto thine own house
22. 8 When thou buildest a new house, then
22. 8 thou bring not blood upon thine house
22. 21 damsel to the door of her father's house
22. 21 to play the whore in her father's house
23. 18 into the house of the LORD thy God for
24. 1 give (it)..and send her out of his house
24. 2 when she is departed out of his house
24. 3 and sendeth her out of his house; or if
24. 10 not go into his house to fetch his pledge
25. 9 that will not build up his brother's house
25. 10 house of him that hath his shoe loosed
25. 14 not have in thine house divers measures
26. 11 hath given unto thee, and unto thine house
26. 13 the hallowed things out of (mine) house
28. 30 thou shalt build an house, and thou shalt
Josh. 2. 1 came into an harlot's house, named Rahab
2. 3 men..which are entered into thine house
2. 12 also show kindness unto my father's house
2. 15 for her house (was) upon the town wall
2. 19 the doors of thy house into the street, his
2. 19 whosoever shall be with thee in the house
6. 17 and all that (are) with her in the house
6. 22 Go into the harlot's house, and bring out
6. 24 the treasury of the house of the LORD

Josh. 9. 12 hot (for) our provision out of our houses
9. 23 drawers of water for the house of my God
17. 17 Joshua spake unto the house of Joseph
18. 5 the house of Joseph shall abide in their
20. 6 unto his own house, unto the city from
21. 45 LORD had spoken unto the house of Israel
22. 14 of each chief house a prince throughout
22. 14 each one (was) an head of the house of their
24. 15 as for me and my house, we will serve the
24. 17 land of Egypt, from the house of bondage
Judg. 1. 22 the house of Joseph, they also went up
1. 23 house of Joseph sent to descry Beth-el
1. 35 hand of the house of Joseph prevailed
4. 17 Hazor and the house of Heber the Kenite
6. 8 you forth out of the house of bondage
6. 15 and I (am) the least in my father's house
8. 27 a snare unto Gideon, and to his house
8. 29 Jerubbaal..went and dwelt in his own h.
8. 35 Neither showed they kindness to the house
9. 1 family of the house of his mother's father
9. 4 silver out of the house of Baal-berith
9. 5 he went unto his father's house at Ophrah
9. 6 gathered together, and all the house of
9. 16 dealt well with Jerubbaal and his house
9. 18 risen up against my father's house this d.
9. 19 with Jerubbaal and with his house this
9. 20 men of Shechem, and the house of Millo
9. 20 let fire come..from the house of Millo
9. 27 went into the house of their god, and did
9. 46 an hold of the house of the god Berith
10. 9 to fight..against the house of Ephraim
11. 2 shalt not inherit in our father's house
11. 7 and expel me out of my father's house?
11. 31 cometh forth of the doors of my house to
11. 34 Jephthah came to Mizpeh unto his house
12. 1 will burn thine house upon thee with fire
14. 15 burn thee and thy father's house with fire
14. 19 and he went up to his father's house
16. 21 and he did grind in the prison house
16. 25 called for Samson out of the prison house
16. 26 the pillars whereupon the house standeth
16. 27 Now the house was full of men and women
16. 29 middle pillars upon which the house stood
16. 30 the house fell upon the lords, and upon
16. 31 all the house of his father came down, and
17. 4 and they were in the house of Micah
17. 5 the man Micah had an house of gods, and
17. 8 to mount Ephraim, to the house of Micah
17. 12 became his priest, and was in the house
18. 2 to the house of Micah, they lodged there
18. 3 When they (were) by the house of Micah
18. 13 And they..came unto the house of Micah
18. 14 know that there is in these houses an ep.
18. 15 came to the house of the young man the
18. 15 unto the house of Micah, and saluted him
18. 18 went into Micah's house, and fetched the
18. 19 be a priest unto the house of one man, or
18. 22 when they were a good way from the ho.
18. 22 in the houses near to Micah's house were
18. 26 he turned and went back unto his house
18. 31 all the time that the house of God was in
19. 2 went away from him unto her father's h.
19. 3 she brought him into her father's house
19. 15 no man that took them into his house to
19. 18 going to the house of the LORD; and there
19. 18 no man that receiveth me to house
19. 21 So he brought him into his house, and g.
19. 22 the men..beset the house round about
19. 22 and spake to the master of the house, the
19. 22 the man that came into thine house, that
19. 23 the man, the master of the house, went
19. 23 seeing..this man is come into mine house
19. 26 of the man's house where her lord (was)
19. 27 opened the doors of the house, and went
19. 27 fallen down (at) the door of the house, and
19. 29 when he was come into his house, he took
20. 5 and beset the house round about upon me
20. 8 neither will we any (of us) turn into his h.
Ruth 1. 8 Go, return each to her mother's house: the
1. 9 each (of you) in the house of her husband
2. 7 that she tarried a little in the house
4. 11 the woman that is come into thine house
4. 11 which two did build the house of Israel: and
4. 12 let thy house be like the house of Pharez
1 Sa. 1. 7 went up to the house of the LORD, so she
1. 19 came to their house to Ramah: and Elka.
1. 21 the man Elkanah, and all his house, went
1. 24 brought him unto the house of the LORD
2. 11 And Elkanah went to Ramah to his house
2. 27 Did I plainly appear unto the house of thy
2. 27 when they were in Egypt, in Pharaoh's h.?
2. 28 did I give unto the house of thy father
2. 30 I said indeed, (that) thy house, and the h.
2. 31 cut off..the arm of thy father's house
2. 32 shall not be an old man in thine house
2. 33 the increase of thine house shall die in
2. 35 I will build him a sure house; and he
2. 36 every one that is left in thine house
3. 12 which I have spoken concerning his house
3. 13 I will judge his house for ever for the
3. 14 I have sworn unto the house of Eli, that
3. 14 the iniquity of Eli's house shall not be
3. 15 opened the doors of the house of the LORD
5. 2 they brought it into the house of Dagon
5. 5 nor any that come into Dagon's house
7. 1 brought it into the house of Abinadab in
7. 2 house of Israel lamented after the LORD
7. 3 Samuel spake unto all the house of Israel
7. 17 there (was) his house; and there he judged
9. 18 Tell me, I pray thee, where the seer's ho.
9. 20 on thee, and on all thy father's house?
10. 25 the people away, every man to his house

1 Sa. 15. 34 Saul went up to his house to Gibeah of Saul
17. 25 and make his father's house free in Israel
18. 2 him go no more home to his father's house
18. 10 he prophesied in the midst of the house
19. 9 he sat in his house with his javelin in his
19. 11 also sent messengers unto David's house
20. 15 cut off thy kindness from my house for
20. 16 made (a covenant) with the house of Da.
21. 15 shall this (fellow) come into my house?
22. 1 brethren and all his father's house heard
22. 11 son of Ahitub, and all his father's house
22. 14 bidding, and is honourable in thine house?
22. 15 servant, (nor) to all the house of my fath.
22. 16 Ahimelech, thou, and all thy father's ho.
22. 22 of all the persons of thy father's house
23. 18 David abode..Jonathan went to his house
24. 21 destroy my name out of my father's house
25. 1 and buried him in his house at Ramah
25. 6 peace (be) to thine house, and peace (be)
25. 28 will certainly make my lord a sure house
25 35 Go up in peace to thine house; see, I have
25. 36 he held a feast in his house, like the
28. 24 the woman had a fat calf in the house, and
31. 9 to publish (it in) the house of their idols
31. 10 put his armour in the house of Ashtaroth
2 Sa. 1. 12 for the house of Israel; because they were
2. 4 David king over the house of Judah
2. 7 the house of Judah have anointed me king
2. 10 But the house of Judah followed David
2. 11 king in Hebron over the house of Judah
3. 1, 6 between the house of Saul and the ho.
3. 1 house of Saul waxed weaker and weaker
3. 6 Abner made himself strong for the house
3. 8 do show kindness this day unto the house
3. 10 translate the kingdom from the house of
3. 19 seemed good to the whole house of Benj.
3. 29 Let it rest..on all his father's house; and
3. 29 let there not fail from the house of Joab
4. 5 and came..to the house of Ish-bosheth
4. 6 came thither into the midst of the house
4. 7 when they came into the house, he lay on
4. 11 slain..in his own house upon his bed?
5. 8 the lame shall not come into the house
5. 11 and masons: and they built David an ho.
6. 3, 4 brought it out of the house of Abinadab
6. 5, 15 David and all the house of Israel
6. 10 into the house of Obed-edom the Gittite
6. 11 the ark..continued in the house of Obed.
6. 12 hath blessed the house of Obed-edom, and
6. 12 from the house of Obed-edom into the city
6. 19 the people departed every one to his ho.
6. 21 before thy father, and before all his house
7. 1 when the king sat in his house, and the
7. 2 See now, I dwell in an house of cedar
7. 5 Shalt thou build me an house..to dwell
7. 6 Whereas I have not dwelt in (any) house
7. 7 Why build ye not me an house of cedar?
7. 11 telleth thee that he will make thee an house
7. 13 He shall build an house for my name; and
7. 16 And thine house and thy kingdom shall be
7. 18 what (is) my house, that thou hast brough
7. 19 hast spoken also of thy servant's house
7. 25 concerning his house, establish (it) for ever
7. 26 let the house of thy servant David be
7. 27 saying, I will build thee an house; therefore
7. 29 to bless the house of thy servant, that
7. 29 house of thy servant be blessed for ever
9. 1 yet any that is left of the house of Saul
9. 2 (there was) of the house of Saul a servant
9. 3 (Is) there not yet any of the house of Saul
9. 4 he (is) in the house of Machir, the son of
9. 5 fetched him out of the house of Machir
9. 9 that pertained to Saul and to all his house
9. 12 all that dwelt in the house of Ziba (were)
11. 2 walked upon the roof of the king's house
11. 4 purified..and she returned unto her ho.
11. 8 Go down to thy house, and wash thy feet
11. 8 Uriah departed out of the king's house
11. 9 slept at the door of the king's house with
11. 9 But Uriah..went not down to his house
11. 10 saying, Uriah went not down unto his ho.
11. 10 didst thou not go down unto thine house?
11. 11 shall I then go into mine house, to eat
11. 13 went out..but went not down to his ho.
11. 27 David sent and fetched her to his house
12. 8 gave thee thy master's house, and thy
12. 8 and gave thee the house of Israel and of
12. 10 sword shall never depart from thine hous
12. 11 evil against thee out of thine own house,
12. 15 Nathan departed unto his house. And the
12. 17 the elders of his house arose, and (went)
12. 20 and came into the house of the LORD, and
12. 20 then he came to his own house; and when
13. 7 Go now to thy brother Amnon's house, and
13. 8 Tamar went to her brother Amnon's house
13. 20 desolate in her brother Absalom's house
14. 8 Go to thine house, and I will give charge
14. 9 iniquity (be) on me, and on my father's hou.
14. 24 Let him turn to his own house, and let
14. 24 Absalom returned to his own house, and
14. 31 came to Absalom unto (his) house, and
15. 16 king left ten women..to keep the house
15. 35 thou shalt hear out of the king's house
16. 3 To day shall the house of Israel restore
16. 5 a man of the family of the house of Saul
16. 8 all the blood of the house of Saul, in
16. 21 which he hath left to keep the house
17. 18 came to a man's house in Bahurim, which
17. 20 servants came to the woman to the house
17. 23 and gat him home to his house, to his city
19. 5 Joab came into the house of the king, and
19. 11 last to bring the king back to the house?

2 Sa. 19. 11 is come to the king, (even) to his house
19. 17 the servant of the house of Saul, and his
19. 20 first this day of all the house of Joseph
19. 28 all (of) my father's house were but dead
19. 30 come again in peace unto his own house
20. 3 David came to his house at Jerusalem; and
20. 3 whom he had left to keep the house, and
21. 1 for (his) bloody house, because he slew
21. 4 silver nor gold of Saul, nor of his house
23. 5 Although my house (be) not so with God
24. 17 against me, and against my father's house
1 Ki. 1. 53 Solomon said unto him, Go to thine house
2. 24 who hath made me an house, as he prom.
2. 27 concerning the house of Eli in Shiloh
2. 31 from me, and from the house of my father
2. 33 upon his house, and upon his throne, shall
2. 34 buried in his own house in the wilderness
2. 36 Build thee an house in Jerusalem, and
3. 1 of building his own house, and the house
3. 2 no house built unto the name of the LORD
3. 17 I and this woman dwell in one house; and
3. 17 delivered of a child with her in the house
3. 18 in the house, save we two in the house
5. 3 my father could not build an house unto
5. 5 I purpose to build an house unto the name
5. 5 he shall build an house unto my name
5. 17 stones, to lay the foundation of the house
5. 18 timber and stones to build the house
6. 1 he began to build the house of the LORD
6. 2 the house which king Solomon built for
6. 3 the porch before the temple of the house
6. 3 according to the breadth of the house
6. 3 (was) the breadth thereof before the house
6. 4 for the house he made windows of narrow
6. 5 against the wall of the house he built
6. 5 (against)..walls of the house round about
6. 6 (in the wall) of the house he made narrow.
6. 6 not be fastened in the walls of the house
6. 7 the house, when it was in building, was
6. 7 (nor) any tool of iron heard in the house
6. 8 (was) in the right side of the house: (and)
6. 9 he built the house, and finished it; and
6. 9 covered the house with beams and boards
6. 10 he built chambers against all the house
6. 10 rested on the house with timber of cedar
6. 12 this house which thou art in building
6. 14 Solomon built the house, and finished it
6. 15 he built the walls of the house within
6. 15 the floor of the house, and the walls of
6. 15 covered the floor of the house with planks
6. 16 twenty cubits on the sides of the house
6. 17 the house, that (is), the temple before it
6. 18 the cedar of the house within (was) carved
6. 19 oracle he prepared in the house within
6. 21 overlaid the house within with pure gold
6. 22 the whole house he overlaid with pure gold
6. 22 until he had finished all the house: also
6. 27 set the cherubim within the inner house
6. 27 one another in the midst of the house
6. 29 carved all the walls of the house round
6. 30 floor of the house he overlaid with gold
6. 37 foundation of the house of the LORD laid
6. 38 was the house finished throughout all the
7. 1 was building his own house thirteen years
7. 1 But Solomon..finished all his house
7. 2 also the house of the forest of Lebanon
7. 8 house where he dwelt (had) another court
7. 8 made also an house for Pharaoh's daughter
7. 12 the inner court of the house of the LORD
7. 12 inner court..and for the porch of the house
7. 39 five bases on the right side of the house
7. 39 five on the left side of the house: and he
7. 39 the sea on the right side of the house
7. 40, 45, 51 made..for the house of the LORD
7. 48 that (pertained) unto the house of the Lo.
7. 50 (both) for the doors of the inner house
7. 50 for the doors of the house, (to wit), of the
7. 51 the treasures of the house of the LORD
8. 6 into the oracle of the house, to the most
8. 10 the cloud filled the house of the LORD
8. 11 glory..had filled the house of the LORD
8. 13 surely built thee an house to dwell in, a
8. 16 I chose no city out..to build an house
8. 17 house for the name of the LORD God of
8. 18 build an house unto my name, thou didst
8. 19 thou shalt not build the house; but thy
8. 19 he shall build the house unto my name
8. 20 house for the name of the LORD God of
8. 27 much less this house that I have builded!
8. 29 be open toward this house night and day
8. 31 come before thine altar in this house
8. 33 make supplication unto thee in this house
8. 38 spread forth his hands toward this house
8. 42 he shall come and pray toward this house
8. 43 they may know that this house, which
8. 44, 48 house that I have built for thy name
8. 63 Israel dedicated the house of the LORD
8. 64 that (was) before the house of the LORD
9. 1 the house of the LORD, and the king's ho.
9. 3 hallowed this house which thou hast built
9. 7 this house, which I have hallowed for my
9. 8 this house, (which) is high, every one that
9. 8 done this unto this land..to this house?
9. 10 when Solomon had built the two houses
9. 10 the house of the LORD, and the king's ho.
9. 15 the house of the LORD, and his own house
9. 24 her house which (Solomon) had built for
9. 25 before the LORD. So he finished the house
10. 4 wisdom, and the house that he had built
10. 5 he went up unto the house of the LORD
10. 12 house of the LORD, and for the king's ho.
10. 17, 21 the house of the forest of Lebanon
1 Ki. 11. 18 gave him an house, and appointed him
11. 20 whom Taphenes weaned in Pharaoh's ho.
11. 28 all the charge of the house of Joseph
11. 38 build thee a sure house, as I built for D.
12. 16 see to thine own house, David. So Israel
12. 19 against the house of David unto this day
12. 20 none that followed the house of David but
12. 21 he assembled all the house of Judah, with
12. 21 to fight against the house of Israel, to
12. 23 unto all the house of Judah and Benjamin
12. 24 return every man to his house; for this
12. 26 the kingdom return to the house of David
12. 27 in the house of the LORD at Jerusalem
12. 31 he made an house of high places, and made
13. 2 shall be born unto the house of David
13. 8 If thou wilt give me half thine house, I
13. 18 Bring him back with thee into thine house
13. 19 did eat bread in his house, and drank water
13. 32 the houses of the high places which (are)
13. 34 became sin unto the house of Jeroboam
14. 4 came to the house of Ahijah. But Ahijah
14. 8 the kingdom away from the house of David
14. 10 bring evil upon the house of Jeroboam
14. 10 away the remnant of the house of Jeroboam
14. 12 get thee to thine own house; (and) when
14. 13 (some) good thing..in the house of Jerobo.
14. 14 cut off the house of Jeroboam that day
14. 26 the treasures of the house of the LORD
14. 26 the treasures of the king's house; he even
14. 27 which kept the door of the king's house
14. 28 the king went into the house of the LORD
15. 15 into the house of the LORD, silver, and
15. 18 the treasures of the house of the LORD
15. 18 and the treasures of the king's house, and
15. 27 son of Ahijah, of the house of Issachar
15. 29 he smote all the house of Jeroboam; he
16. 3 of Baasha, and the posterity of his house
16. 3 will make thy house like the house of
16. 7 against his house, even for all the evil
16. 7 in being like the house of Jeroboam; and
16. 9 the house of Arza, steward of (his) house
16. 11 he slew all the house of Baasha: he left
16. 12 did Zimri destroy all the house of Baasha
16. 18 went into the palace of the king's house
16. 18 king's house, and burnt the king's house
16. 32 an altar for Baal in the house of Baal
17. 15 and she..and her house, did eat (many)
17. 17 the mistress of the house, fell sick; and
17. 23 down out of the chamber into the house
18. 3 which (was) the governor of (his) house
18. 18 thy father's house, in that ye have forsaken
20. 6 shall search thine house, and the houses
20. 31 kings of the house of Israel (are) merciful
20. 43 went to his house heavy and displeased
21. 2 it (is) near unto my house: and I will give
21. 4 came into his house heavy and displeased
21. 22 will make thine house like the house of
21. 22 the house of Baasha the son of Ahijah
21. 29 days will I bring the evil upon his house
22. 17 let them return every man to his house in
22. 39 and the ivory house which he made, and
2 Ki. 4. 2 tell me, what hast thou in the house?
4. 2 handmaid hath not anything in the house
4. 32 when Elisha was come into the house, be.
4. 35 Then he returned, and walked in the ho.
5. 9 stood at the door of the house of Elisha
5. 18 when my master goeth into the house of R.
5. 18 I bow myself in the house of Rimmon
5. 24 bestowed (them) in the house: and he let
6. 32 Elisha sat in his house, and the elders sat
7. 11 and they told (it) to the king's house within
8. 3 to cry unto the king for her house and for
8. 5 cried to the king for her house and for her
8. 18 And he walked..as did the house of Ahab
8. 27 he walked in the way of the house of Ahab
8. 27 he (was) the son-in-law of the house of A.
9. 6 he arose, and went into the house; and he
9. 7 thou shalt smite the house of Ahab thy m.
9. 8 For the whole house of Ahab shall perish
9. 9 I will make the house of Ahab like the ho.
9. 9 like the house of Baasha the son of Ahijah
9. 27 he fled by the way of the garden house
10. 3 Look..and fight for your master's house
10. 5 he that (was) over the house, and he that
10. 10 LORD spake concerning the house of Ahab
10. 11 slew all that remained of the house of Ah.
10. 12 as he (was) at the shearing house in the way
10. 14 slew them at the pit of the shearing house
10. 21 And they came into the house of Baal; and
10. 21 the house of Baal was full from one end
10. 23 And Jehu went..into the house of Baal
10. 25 and went to the city of the house of Baal
10. 26 brought..the images out of the house of
10. 27 brake down the house of Baal, and made
10. 30 hast done unto the house of Ahab accord.
11. 3 he was with her hid in the house of the L.
11. 4 brought them to him into the house of the
11. 4 took an oath of them in the house of the
11. 5 be keepers of the watch of the king's ho.
11. 6 so shall ye keep the watch of the house
11. 7 they shall keep the watch of the house of
11. 15 Let her not be slain in the house of the L.
11. 16 way..horses came into the king's house
11. 18 went into the house of Baal, and brake it
11. 18 appointed officers over the house of the
11. 19 they brought down the king from the ho.
11. 19 by the way of the gate..to the king's hou.
11. 20 slew Athaliah..(beside) the king's house
12. 4 cometh..to bring into the house of the L.
12. 5 let them repair the breaches of the house
12. 6 had not repaired the breaches of the ho.
12. 7 Why repair ye not the breaches of the h.?
2 Ki. 12. 7 but deliver it for the breaches of the ho.
12. 8 neither to repair the breaches of the ho.
12. 9 on the right side as one cometh into the h.
12. 9, 13 brought into the house of the LORD
12. 10 the money..found in the house of the LORD
12. 11 that had the oversight of the house of the
12. 11 that wrought upon the house of the LORD
12. 12 to repair the breaches of the house of the
12. 12 all that was laid out for the house to rep.
12. 13 there were not made for the house of the L.
12. 14 and repaired therewith the house of the L.
12. 18 in the treasures of the house of the LORD
12. 18 and in the king's house, and sent (it) to H.
12. 20 servants..slew Joash in the house of Millo
13. 6 not from the sins of the house of Jeroboam
14. 14 the vessels..found in the house of the L.
14. 14 and in the treasures of the king's house
15. 5 was a leper..and dwelt in a several house
15. 5 Jotham the king's son (was) over the house
15. 25 in the palace of the king's house, with Ar.
15. 35 He built the higher gate of the house of
16. 8 gold..found in the house of the LORD
16. 8 and in the treasures of the king's house
16. 14 brasen altar..from the fore front of the h.
16. 14 from between the altar and the house of
16. 18 the covert..they had built in the house
16. 18 turned he from the house of the LORD for
17. 21 For he rent Israel from the house of Da.
17. 29, 32 in the houses of the high places which
18. 15 all the silver..found in the house of the
18. 15 and in the treasures of the king's house
19. 1 Hezekiah..went into the house of the L.
19. 14 Hezekiah went up into the house of the L.
19. 30 the remnant that is escaped of the house
19. 37 was worshipping in the house of Nisroch
20. 1 Set thine house in order; for thou shalt
20. 5, 8 go up unto the house of the LORD
20. 13 showed them all the house of his precious
20. 13 the house of his armour, and all that was
20. 13 there was nothing in his house, nor in all
20. 15 said, What have they seen in thine house?
20. 15 All..that (are) in mine house have they
20. 17 all that (is) in thine house, and that wh.
21. 4 he built altars in the house of the LORD
21. 5 in the two courts of the house of the LORD
21. 7 he set a graven image..in the house, of
21. 7 In this house, and in Jerusalem, which I
21. 13 and the plummet of the house of Ahab
21. 18 was buried in the garden of his own house
21. 23 the servants..slew the king in his own h.
22. 3 the king sent Shaphan..to the house of
22. 4 silver..brought into the house of the Lo.
22. 5, 9 that have the oversight of the house of
22. 5 the work which (is) in the house of the L.
22. 5 to repair the breaches of the house
22. 6 to buy..hewn stone to repair the house
22. 8 I have found the book of the law in the h
22. 9 the money that was found in the house
23. 2 the king went up into the house of the L.
23. 2 of the book..found in the house of the L.
23. 6 he brought out the grove from the house
23. 7 he brake down the houses of the sodom.
23. 7 that (were) by the house of the LORD, where
23. 11 at the entering in of the house of the L.
23. 12 in the two courts of the house of the Lo.
23. 19 all the houses also of the high places that
23. 24 book that Hilkiah..found in the house
23. 27 I have removed..the house of which I sa.
24. 13 all the treasures of the house of the LORD
24. 13 and the treasures of the king's house, and
25. 9 And he burnt the house of the LORD, and
25. 9 and the king's house, and all the houses
25. 9 every great (man's) house burnt he with
25. 13 pillars of brass..in the house of the LORD
25. 13 the brazen sea..in the house of the LORD
25. 16 Solomon had made for the house of the L.
1 Ch. 2. 54 The sons of Salma..the house of Joab, and
2. 55 Hemath, the father of the house of Rechab
4. 21 families of the house..of the house of A.
4. 38 the house of their fathers increased grea.
5. 13 their brethren, of the house of their fath.
5. 15 Guni, chief of the house of their fathers
5. 24, 24 heads of the house of their fathers
6. 31 set over the service of song in the house
6. 32 until Solomon had built the house of the
6. 48 service of the tabernacle of the house of
7. 2 sons of Tola..heads of their father's house
7. 4 with them..after the house of their fath.
7. 7, 9 heads of the house of (their) fathers
7. 23 Beriah, because it went evil with his ho.
7. 40 All these..heads of (their) father's house
9. 9 chief of the fathers in the house of their
9. 11 son of Ahitub, the ruler of the house of G.
9. 13 brethren, heads of the house of their fath.
9. 13 for the work of the service of the house of
9. 19 his brethren, of the house of his father
9. 23 the oversight of the gates of the house of
9. 23 the house of the tabernacle, by wards
9. 26 the chambers and treasuries of the house
9. 27 they lodged round about the house of G.
10. 6 Saul died..and all his house died together
10. 10 they put his armour in the house of their
12. 28 of his father's house twenty and two cap.
12. 29 had kept the ward of the house of Saul
12. 30 famous throughout the house of their fa.
13. 7 they carried the ark..out of the house of
13. 13 carried it aside into the house of Obed-e.
13. 14 the ark of God remained..in his house
13. 14 the LORD blessed the house of Obed-edom
14. 1 masons and carpenters, to build him an h.
15. 1 made him houses in the city of David, and
15. 25 to bring up the ark..out of the house of

2 Ch. 16. 43 And all..departed every man to his house
16. 43 and David returned to bless his house
17. 1 came to pass, as David sat in his house
17. 1 I dwell in an house of cedars, but the ark
17. 4 Thou shalt not build me an house to dw.
17. 5 For I have not dwelt in an house since
17. 6 Why have ye not built me an house of cedar
17. 10 tell thee..the LORD will build thee an ho.
17. 12 He shall build me an house, and I will
17. 14 I will settle him in mine house and in my
17. 16 Who (am) I..and what (is) mine house
17. 17 thou hast..spoken of thy servant's house
17. 23 concerning thy servant, and..his house
17. 24 (let) the house of David..(be) established
17. 25 hast told..thou wilt build him an house
17. 27 let it please thee to bless the house of thy
21. 17 be on me, and on my father's house; but
22. 1 This (is) the house of the LORD God, and
22. 2 he set masons..to build the house of God
22. 5 the house (that is) to be builded for the L.
22. 6 charged him to build an house for the L.
22. 7 it was in my mind to build an house unto
22. 8 thou shalt not build an house unto my
22. 10 He shall build an house for my name
22. 11 build the house of the LORD thy God, as he
22. 14 I have prepared for the house of the LORD
22. 19 into the house that is to be built to the
23. 4 to set forward the work of the house of the
23. 11 reckoning, according to (their) father's ho.
23. 24 sons of Levi after the house of their fath.
23. 24, 28, 32 the service of the house of the L.
23. 28 the work of the service of the house of G.
24. 4 sixteen chief men of the house of (their)
24. 4 eight..according to the house of their fa.
24. 19 in their service to come into the house of
24. 30 of the Levites after the house of their fa.
25. 6 for song (in) the house of the LORD, with c.
25. 6 for the service of the house of God, accord..
26. 6 ruled throughout the house of their father
26. 12 to minister in the house of the LORD
26. 13 according to the house of their fathers
26. 15 and to his sons the house of Asuppim
26. 20 over the treasures of the house of God, and
26. 22 over the treasures of the house of the LORD
26. 27 did they dedicate to maintain the house of
28. 2 I (had) in mine heart to build an house of
28. 3 Thou shalt not build an house for my name
28. 4 chose me before all the house of my father
28. 4 the house of Judah the house of my father
28. 6 he shall build my house and my courts
28. 10 chosen thee to build an house for the san.
28. 11 of the porch, and of the houses thereof
28. 12 of the courts of the house of the LORD, and
28. 12 of the treasuries of the house of God, and
28. 13, 20 the service of the house of the LORD
28. 13 vessels of service in the house of the L.
28. 21 for all the service of the house of God: and
29. 2 I have prepared..for the house of my G.
29. 3 I have set my affections to the house of
29. 3 I have given to the house of my God over
29. 3 all that I have prepared for the holy ho.
29. 4 silver, to overlay the walls of the houses
29. 7 gave for the service of the house of God
29. 8 to the treasure of the house of the LORD
29. 16 to build thee an house for thine holy na.
2 Ch. 2. 1 to build an house for the name of the Lo.
2. 1 of the LORD, and an house for his kingdom
2. 3 cedars to build him an house to dwell th.
2. 4 I build an house to the name of the LORD
2. 5 house which I build (is) great; for great
2. 6 who is able to build him an house, seeing
2. 6 that I should build him an house, save
2. 9 for the house which I am about to build
2. 12 build an house for the LORD, and an h.
3. 1 Then Solomon began to build the house
3. 3 was instructed for the building of the hou.
3. 4 according to the breadth of the house
3. 5 the greater house he ceiled with fir tree
3. 6 he garnished the house with precious st.
3. 7 He overlaid also the house, the beams
3. 8 he made the most holy house, the length
3. 8 according to the breadth of the house
3. 10 in the most holy house he made two che.
3. 11, 12 reaching to the wall of the house
3. 15 he made before the house two pillars of
4. 11 finished the work..for the house of God
4. 16 their instruments..for the house of the L.
4. 19 all the vessels that (were for) the house of
4. 22 the entry of the house, the inner doors
4. 22 and the doors of the house of the temple
5. 1 that Solomon made for the house of the L.
5. 1 among the treasures of the house of God
5. 7 unto his place. to the oracle of the house
5. 13 house was filled with a cloud..the house
5. 14 the glory of the LORD had filled the house
6. 2 I have built an house of habitation for
6. 5 I chose no city..to build an house in, that
6. 7 to build an house for the name of the L.
6. 8 it was in thine heart to build an house for
6. 9 thou shalt not build the house; but thy
6. 9 he shall build the house for my name
6. 10 have built the house for the name of the
6. 18 much less this house which I have built!
6. 20 That thine eyes may be open upon this h.
6. 22 the oath come before thine altar in this h.
6. 24 make supplication before thee in this ho.
6. 29 shall spread forth his hands in this house
6. 32 if they come and pray in this house
6. 33 that this house, which I have built, is cal.
6. 34, 38 house which I have built for thy name
7. 1 and the glory of the LORD filled the house
7. 2 the priests could not enter into the house

2 Ch. 7. 2 glory of the LORD had filled the..house
7. 3 and the glory of the LORD upon the house
7. 5 So the king..dedicated the house of God
7. 7 the court that (was) before the house of
7. 11 the house of the LORD, and the king's h.
7. 11 the house of the LORD, and in his own h.
7. 12 chosen this place to myself for an house
7. 16 now have I chosen and sanctified this ho.
7. 20 and this house, which I have sanctified for
7. 21 this house, which is high, shall be an as.
7. 21 done thus unto this land, and unto this h.
8. 1 built the house of the LORD, and his own h.
8. 11 unto the house that he had built for her
8. 11 My wife shall not dwell in the house of D.
8. 16 the day of the foundation of the house of
8. 16 (So) the house of the LORD was perfected
9. 3 when the queen..had seen..the house that
9. 4 by which he went up into the house of the L.
9. 11 terraces to the house of the LORD, and to
9. 16, 20 the house of the forest of Lebanon
10. 16 (and) now, David, see to thine own house
10. 19 Israel rebelled against the house of David
11. 1 he gathered of the house of Judah and B.
11. 4 return every man to his house; for this
12. 9 the treasures of the house of the LORD
12. 9 and the treasures of the king's house; he
12. 10 that kept the entrance of the king's house
12. 11 when the king entered into the house of the
15. 18 he brought into the house of God the things
16. 2 house of the LORD and of the king's house
16. 10 was wroth..and put him in a prison house
17. 14 according to the house of their fathers: of
18. 16 return..every man to his house in peace
19. 1 the king..returned to his house in peace
19. 11 the ruler of the house of Judah, for all the
20. 5 in the house of the LORD, before the new
20. 9 before this house..thy name (is) in this ho.
20. 28 with..trumpets into the house of the LORD
21. 6 like as did the house of Ahab: for he had
21. 7 LORD would not destroy the house of David
21. 13 like to the whoredoms of the house of A.
21. 13 hast slain thy brethren of thy father's ho.
21. 17 the substance..found in the king's house
22. 3 He also walked in the ways of the house
22. 4 he did evil..like the house of Ahab: for
22. 7 had anointed to cut off the house of Ahab
22. 8 was executing judgment upon the house
22. 9 So the house of Ahaziah had no power to
22. 10 all the seed royal of the house of Judah
22. 12 he was with them hid in the house of God
23. 3 made a covenant with the king in the house
23. 5 a third part (shall be) at the king's house
23. 5 in the courts of the house of the LORD
23. 6 let none come into the house of the LORD
23. 7 whosoever. cometh into the house, he sho.
23. 9 shields..which (were) in the house of God
23. 12 she came to the people unto the house of
23. 14 said, Slay her not in the house of the LORD
23. 15 of the horse gate by the king's house, they
23. 17 all the people went to the house of Baal
23. 18 the offices of the house of the LORD by the
23. 18 had distributed in the house of the LORD
23. 19 he set the porters at the gates of the house
23. 20 brought down the king from the house of
23. 20 through the high gate into the king's house
24. 4 Joash was minded to repair the house of
24. 5 money to repair..house of your God from
24. 7 had broken up the house of God; and also
24. 7 the dedicated things of the house of the L.
24. 8 without at the gate of the house of the Lo.
24. 12 of the service of the house of the LORD
24. 12 to repair the house of the LORD, and also
24. 12 as wrought..to mend the house of the LORD
24. 13 they set the house of God in his state, and
24. 14 whereof were made vessels for the house
24. 14 they offered burnt offerings in the house
24. 16 both toward God, and toward his house
24. 18 they left the house of the LORD God of
24. 21 stoned him..in the court of the house of
24. 27 and the repairing of the house of God
25. 5 captains..according to the houses of..fa.
25. 24 all the vessels that were found in the ho.
25. 24 the treasures of the king's house, the ho.
26. 19 before the priests in the house of the Lo.
26. 21 and dwelt in a several house..a leper
26. 21 he was cut off from the house of the LORD
26. 21 Jotham his son (was) over the king's ho.
27. 3 He built the high gate of the house of the
28. 7 slew..Azrikam the governor of the house
28. 21 a portion (out) of the house of the LORD
28. 21 and (out) of the house of the king, and of
28. 24, 24 the vessels of the house of God
28. 24 shut up the doors of the house of the LORD
29. 3 opened the doors of the house of the LORD
29. 5 sanctify the house of the LORD God of your
29. 15 and came..to cleanse the house of the L.
29. 16 the inner part of the house of the LORD
29. 16 into the court of the house of the LORD
29. 17 they sanctified the house of the LORD in
29. 18 We have cleansed all the house of the L.
29. 20 Hezekiah..went up to the house of the L.
29. 25 he set the Levites in the house of the Lo.
29. 31 bring..offerings into the house of the L.
29. 35 the service of the house of the LORD was
30. 1 they should come to the house of the LORD
30. 15 brought..offerings into the house of the
31. 10 Azariah the chief priest of the house of Z.
31. 10 to bring the offerings into the house of the
31. 11 to prepare chambers in the house of the
31. 13 and Azariah the ruler of the house of God
31. 16 that entereth into the house of the LORD
31. 17 the genealogy of the priests by the house

2 Ch. 31. 21 in the service of the house of God, and in
32. 21 when he was come into the house of his.
33. 4 he built altars in the house of the LORD
33. 5 in the two courts of the house of the LORD
33. 7 he set a carved image..in the house of G.
33. 7 In this house, and in Jerusalem, which I
33. 15 and the idol out of the house of the LORD
33. 15 in the mount of the house of the LORD
33. 20 they buried him in his own house: and A.
33. 24 And his servants. slew him in his own h.
34. 8 when he had purged the land, and the ho.
34. 8 to repair the house of the LORD his God
34. 9, 14 money that was brought into the ho.
34. 10 workmen that had..oversight of the hou
34. 10 that wrought in the house of the LORD
34. 10 gave it..to repair and amend the house
34. 11 to floor the houses which the kings of J.
34. 15 I have found the book of the law in the h.
34. 17 the money that was found in the house of
34. 30 the king went up into the house of the L.
34. 30 book..that was found in the house of the
35. 2 to the service of the house of the LORD
35. 3 Put the holy ark in the house which Sol.
35. 4 prepare..by the houses of your fathers
35. 8 rulers of the house of God, gave unto the
35. 21 but against the house wherewith I have
36. 7 the vessels of the house of the LORD to B.
36. 10 with the goodly vessels of the house of the
36. 14 polluted the house of the LORD which he
36. 17 slew..with the sword in the house of their
36. 18 all the vessels of the house of God, great
36. 18 the treasures of the house of the LORD
36. 19 they burnt the house of God, and brake d.
36. 23 hath charged me to build him an house
Ezra 1. 2 hath charged me to build him an house
1. 3 build the house of the LORD God of Israel
1. 4 freewill offering for the house of God that
1. 5 to go up to build the house of the LORD
1. 7 brought forth the vessels of the house of
1. 7 and had put them in the house of his gods
2. 36 of the house of Jeshua, nine hundred se.
2. 59 they could not show their fathers' house
2. 68 when they came to the house of the LORD
2. 68 offered freely for the house of God to set
3. 8 of their coming unto the house of God at
3. 8 to set forward the work of the house of the
3. 9 to set forward the workmen in the house
3. 11 because the foundation of the house of the
3. 12 ancient men, that had seen the first house
3. 12 when the foundation of this house was laid
4. 3 Ye have nothing to do..to build an house
6. 22 in the work of the house of God, the God
7. 27 to beautify the house of the LORD which
8. 17 bring unto us ministers for the house of
8. 25 the offering of the house of our God, wh.
8. 29 in the chambers of the house of the LORD
8. 30 to Jerusalem, unto the house of our God
8. 33 weighed in the house of our God by the h.
8. 36 they furthered the people, and the house
9. 9 to set up the house of our God, and to
10. 1 casting himself down before the house of
10. 6 Ezra rose up from before the house of God
10. 9 the people sat in the street of the house
10. 16 chief of the fathers, after the house of their
Neh. 1. 6 both I and my father's house have sinned
2. 8 the palace which (appertained) to the house
2. 8 and for the house that I shall enter into
3. 10 repaired Jedaiah..over against his house
3. 16 repaired Nehemiah..unto the house of the
3. 20, 21 the door of the house of Eliashib
3. 21 even to the end of the house of Eliashib
3. 23 After him repaired..over against their h.
3. 23 After him repaired Azariah..by his house
3. 24 from the house of Azariah unto the turn.
3. 25 which lieth out from the king's high house
3. 28 repaired..every one over against his house
3. 29 repaired Zadok..over against his house
4. 14 and fight for..your wives, and your houses
4. 16 the rulers..behind all the house of Judah
5. 3 We have mortgaged our lands..and houses
5. 11 Restore, I pray you, to them .their houses
5. 13 God shake out every man from his house
6. 10 I came unto the house of Shemaiah the son
6. 10 Let us meet together in the house of God
7. 3 and every one (to be) over against his house
7. 4 therein, and the houses (were) not builded
7. 39 the house of Jeshua, nine hundred seventy
7. 61 they could not show their fathers' house
8. 16 in the courts of the house of God, and in
9. 25 possessed houses full of all goods, wells
10. 32 for the service of the house of our God
10. 33 (for) all the work of the house of our God
10. 34 lots..to bring (it) into the house of our G.
10. 34 after the houses of our fathers, at times
10. 35 And to bring..unto the house of the LORD
10. 36 to bring to the house of our God, unto the
10. 36 priests that minister in the house of our
10. 37 to the chambers of the house of our God
10. 38 the tithe of the tithes unto the house of our
10. 38 to the chambers, into the treasure house
10. 39 we will not forsake the house of our God
11. 11 Seraiah..(was) the ruler of the house of
11. 12 their brethren that did the work of the ho.
11. 16 the outward business of the house of God
11. 22 singers..over the business of the house of
12. 29 from the house of Gilgal, and out of the f.
12. 37 above the house of David, even unto the
12. 40 So stood the two..in the house of God, and
13. 4 of the chamber of the house of our God
13. 7 chamber in the courts of the house of G.
13. 9 brought I again the vessels of the house
13. 11 and said, Why is the house of God forsaken

Neh. 13. 14 that I have done for the house of my God
Esth. 1. 8 appointed to..the officers of his house
1. 9 women (in) the royal house which (belo.)
1. 22 every man should bear rule in his..house
2. 3 the house of the women, unto the custody
2. 8 was brought also unto the king's house
2. 9 to be given her, out of the king's house
2. 9 the best (place) of the house of the women
2. 11 before the court of the women's house, to
2. 13 house of the women unto the king's house
2. 14 into the second house of the women, to the
2. 16 unto king Ahasuerus into his house royal
4. 13 thou shalt escape in the king's house more
4. 14 thy father's house shall be destroyed: and
5. 1 king's house, over against the king's house
5. 1 house, over against the gate of the house
6. 4 the outward court of the king's house
6. 12 Haman hasted to his house mourning, and
7. 8 force the queen..before me in the house?
7. 9 gallows..standeth in the house of Haman
8. 1 give the house of Haman, the Jews' enemy
8. 2 set Mordecai over the house of Haman
8. 7 I have given Esther the house of Haman
9. 4 Mordecai (was) great in the king's house
Job 1. 4 his sons went and feasted (in their) houses
1. 10 about his house, and about all that he
1. 13, 18 eating..in their eldest brother's house
1. 19 smote the four corners of the house, and
3. 15 who filled their houses with silver
4. 19 less (in) them that dwell in houses of clay
7. 10 He shall return no more to his house
8. 15 He shall lean upon his house, but it
15. 28 in houses which no man inhabiteth, which
17. 13 the grave (is) mine house: I have made my
19. 15 They that dwell in mine house, and my
20. 19 taken away an house which he builded not
20. 28 The increase of his house shall depart
21. 9 Their houses (are) safe from fear, neither
21. 21 what pleasure (hath) he in his house after
21. 28 say, Where (is) the house of the prince? and
22. 18 he filled their houses with good (things)
24. 16 In the dark they dig through houses, (wh.)
27. 18 He buildeth his house as a moth, and as
30. 23 and (to) the house appointed for all living
38. 20 know the paths (to) the house thereof?
39. 6 Whose house I have made the wilderness
42. 11 did eat bread with him in his house: and
Psa. 5. 7 will come (into) thy house in the multitude
23. 6 dwell in the house of the LORD for ever
26. 8 I have loved the habitation of thy house
27. 4 I may dwell in the house of the LORD all
30. *title.* (at) the dedication of the house of David
31. 2 rock, for an house of defence to save me
36. 8 satisfied with the fatness of thy house
42. 4 I went with them to the house of God
45. 10 forget..own people, and thy father's house
49. 11 (that) their houses (shall continue) for ever
49. 16 when the glory of his house is increased
50. 9 I will take no bullock out of thy house
52. *title.* David is come to the house of Ahime.
52. 8 like a green olive tree in the house of G.
55. 14 walked unto the house of God in company
59. *title.* and they watched the house to kill him
65. 4 satisfied with the goodness of thy house
66. 13 I will go into thy house with..offerings
69. 9 the zeal of thine house hath eaten me up
84. 3 Yea, the sparrow hath found an house
84. 4 Blessed (are) they that dwell in thy house
84. 10 be a doorkeeper in the house of my God
92. 13 Those that be planted in the house of the
93. 5 holiness becometh thine house, O LORD
98. 3 and his truth toward the house of Israel
101. 2 walk within my house with a perfect heart
101. 7 deceit shall not dwell within my house: he
104. 17 (as for) the stork, the fir trees (are) her h.
105. 21 He made him lord of his house, and ruler
112. 3 Wealth and riches (shall be) in his house
113. 9 He maketh the barren woman to keep h.
114. 1 house of Jacob from a people of strange
115. 10 O house of Aaron, trust in the LORD: he
115. 12 The LORD..will bless the house of Israel
115. 12 he will bless the house of Aaron
116. 19 In the courts of the LORD'S house, in the
118. 3 Let the house of Aaron now say, that his
118. 26 we have blessed you out of the house of
119. 54 have been my songs in the house of my
122. 1 Let us go into the house of the LORD
122. 5 set thrones..the thrones of the house of
122. 9 Because of the house of the LORD our God
127. 1 Except the LORD build the house, they
128. 3 fruitful vine by the sides of thine house
132. 3 not come into the tabernacle of my house
134. 1 which by night stand in the house of the
135. 2 Ye that stand in the house of the LORD, in
135. 2 in the courts of the house of our God
135. 19 Bless the LORD, O house of Israel..O house
135. 20 Bless the LORD, O house of Levi: ye that
Prov. 1. 13 we shall fill our houses with spoil
2. 18 For her house inclineth unto death, and
3. 33 curse..(is) in the house of the wicked
5. 8 and come not nigh the door of her house
5. 10 thy labours (be) in the house of a stranger
6. 31 shall give all the substance of his house
7. 6 For at the window of my house I looked
7. 8 Passing..he went the way to her house
7. 11 stubborn; her feet abide not in her house
7. 27 Her house (is) the way to hell, going down
9. 1 Wisdom hath builded her house, she hath
9. 14 she sitteth at the door of her house, on
11. 29 He that troubleth his own house shall
12. 7 the house of the righteous shall stand
14. 1 Every wise woman buildeth her house

Prov. 14. 11 house of the wicked shall be overthrown
15. 6 In the house of the righteous (is) much
15. 25 LORD will destroy the house of the proud
15. 27 He that is greedy..troubleth his own ho.
17. 1 an house full of sacrifices (with) strife
17. 13 evil shall not depart from his house
19. 14 House and riches (are) the inheritance of
21. 9 with a brawling woman in a wide house
21. 12 considereth the house of the wicked
24. 3 Through wisdom is an house builded, and
24. 27 Prepare..and afterwards build thine ho.
25. 17 Withdraw thy foot from..neighbour's ho.
25. 24 with a brawling woman and in a wide ho.
27. 10 neither go into thy brother's house in the
30. 26 yet make they their houses in the rocks
Eccl. 2. 4 builded me houses; I planted me viney.
2. 7 maidens, and had servants born in my h.
5. 1 when thou goest to the house of God, and
7. 2 house of mourning than to go to the house
7. 4 The heart of the wise (is) in the house of
7. 4 heart of fools (is) in the house of mirth
10. 18 through idleness of the hands the house
12. 3 the keepers of the house shall tremble
Song 1. 17 The beams of our house (are) cedar, (and)
2. 4 He brought me to the banqueting house
3. 4 I had brought him into my mother's house
8. 2 bring thee into my mother's house, (who)
8. 7 all the substance of his house for love
Isa. 2. 2 the mountain of the LORD'S house shall be
2. 3 let us..to the house of the God of Jacob
2. 5 O house of Jacob, come ye, and let us walk
2. 6 forsaken thy people the house of Jacob
3. 6 his brother, of the house of his father
3. 7 in my house (is) neither bread nor clothing
3. 14 the spoil of the poor (is) in your houses
5. 7 For the vineyard..(is) the house of Israel
5. 8 Woe unto them that join house to house
5. 9 many houses shall be desolate, (even) gr.
6. 4 cried, and the house was filled with smoke
6. 11 the houses without man, and the land be
7. 2 it was told the house of David, saying
7. 13 O house of David; (Is it) a small thing for
7. 17 upon thy father's house, days that have
8. 14 of offence to both the houses of Israel
8. 17 hideth his face from the house of Jacob
10. 20 such as are escaped of the house of Jacob
13. 16 their houses shall be spoiled, and their
13. 21 houses shall be full of doleful creatures
14. 1 they shall cleave to the house of Jacob
14. 2 the house of Israel shall possess them in
14. 17 opened not the house of his prisoners?
14. 18 lie in glory, every one in his own house
22. 8 the armour of the house of the forest
22. 10 the houses of Jerusalem, and the houses
22. 15 (even) unto Shebna, which (is) over the h.
22. 18 (shall be) the shame of thy lord's house
22. 21 shall be a father..to the house of Judah
22. 22 the key of the house of David will I lay
22. 23 a glorious throne to his father's house
22. 24 all the glory of his father's house, the
23. 1 there is no house, no entering in: from
24. 10 every house is shut up, that no man may
29. 22 concerning the house of Jacob, Jacob
31. 2 arise against the house of the evil doers
32. 13 all the houses of joy (in) the joyous city
36. 3 Hilkiah's son, which was over the house
37. 1 and went into the house of the LORD
37. 14 went up unto the house of the LORD, and
37. 31 that is escaped of the house of Judah
37. 38 he was worshipping in the house of Nisr.
38. 1 Set thine house in order: for thou shalt
38. 20 we will sing..in the house of the LORD
38. 22 I shall go up to the house of the LORD?
39. 2 the house of his precious things, the
39. 2 all the house of his armour, and all that
39. 2 there was nothing in his house, nor in
39. 4 What have they seen in thine house? And
39. 4 All that (is) in mine house have they seen
39. 6 all that (is) in thine house, and (that)
42. 7 sit in darkness out of the prison house
42. 22 they are hid in prison houses: they are
44. 13 figure..that it may remain in the house
46. 3 Hearken unto me, O house of Jacob, and
46. 3 the remnant of the house of Israel, which
48. 1 O house of Jacob, which are called by the
56. 5 unto them will I give in mine house and
56. 7 make them joyful in my house of prayer
56. 7 called an house of prayer for all people
58. 1 and show..the house of Jacob their sins
58. 7 the poor that are cast out to thy house?
60. 7 and I will glorify the house of my glory
63. 7 great goodness toward the house of Israel
64. 11 our beautiful house, where our fathers
65. 21 they shall build houses, and inhabit (them)
66. 1 where (is) the house that ye build unto me?
66. 20 an offering..into the house of the LORD
Jer. 2. 4 the word of the LORD, O house of Jacob
2. 4 all the families of the house of Israel
2. 26 so is the house of Israel ashamed; they
3. 18 house of Judah shall walk with the house
3. 20 treacherously with me, O house of Israel
5. 7 assembled..by troops in..harlots' houses
5. 11 the house of Israel and the house of Judah
5. 15 will bring a nation..O house of Israel
5. 20 Declare this in the house of Jacob, and
5. 27 so (are) their houses full of deceit: there.
6. 12 their houses shall be turned unto others
7. 2 Stand in the gate of the LORD'S house
7. 10 stand before me in this house, which is
7. 11 Is this house, which is called by my name
7. 14 Therefore will I do unto (this) house
7. 30 in the house which is called by my name

Jer. 9. 26 the house of Israel (are) uncircumcised in
10. 1 LORD speaketh unto you, O house of Israel
11. 10 the house of Israel and the house of Judah
11. 15 What hath my beloved to do in mine ho.
11. 17 of the house of Israel, and of the house
12. 6 the house of thy father, even they have
12. 7 I have forsaken mine house, I have left
12. 14 pluck out the house of Judah from among
13. 11 whole house of Israel and the whole house
16. 5 Enter not into the house of mourning
16. 8 not also go into the house of feasting
17. 22 out of your houses on the sabbath day
17. 26 sacrifices..unto the house of the LORD
18. 2 go down to the potter's house, and there
18. 3 I went down to the potter's house; and
18. 6 O house of Israel, cannot I do with you
18. 6 so (are) ye in mine hand, O house of Israel
18. 22 Let a cry be heard from their houses
19. 13 the houses of Jerusalem, and the houses
19. 13 the houses upon whose roofs they have
19. 14 he stood in the court of the LORD'S house
20. 1 chief governor in the house of the LORD
20. 2 which (was) by the house of the LORD
20. 6 all that dwell in thine house, shall go
21. 11 touching the house of the king of Judah
21. 12 O house of David, thus saith the LORD
22. 1 Go down to the house of the king of Jud.
22. 4 enter in by the gates of this house kings
22. 5 that this house shall become a desolation
22. 6 the LORD unto the king's house of Judah
22. 13 buildeth his house by unrighteousness
22. 14 build me a wide house and large chambers
23. 8 which led the seed of the house of Israel
23. 11 in my house have I found their wicked.
23. 34 will even punish that man and his house
26. 2 Stand in the court of the LORD'S house
26. 2 which come to worship in the LORD'S ho.
26. 6 Then will I make this house like Shiloh
26. 7 these words in the house of the LORD
26. 9 This house shall be like Shiloh, and this
26. 9 against Jeremiah in the house of the LORD
26. 10 king's house unto the house of the LORD
26. 12 sent me to prophesy against this house
26. 18 the mountain of the house as the high
27. 16 the vessels of the LORD'S house shall now
27. 18, 21 house of the Lord, and (in) the house
28. 1 spake unto me in the house of the LORD
28. 3 all the vessels of the LORD'S house that
28. 5 that stood in the house of the LORD
28. 6 to bring..the vessels of the LORD'S house
29. 5, 28 Build ye houses, and dwell (in them)
29. 26 be officers in the house of the LORD, for
31. 27 sow the house of Israel, and the house
31. 31 house of Israel, and with the house of I.
31. 33 I will make with the house of Israel
32. 2 which (was) in the king of Judah's house
32. 15 Houses and fields and vineyards shall be
32. 29 burn it with the houses upon whose roofs
32. 34 in the house which is called by
33. 4 concerning the houses of this city, and
33. 4 concerning the houses of the kings of I.
33. 11 sacrifice..into the house of the LORD
33. 14 the house of Israel, and to the house of
33. 17 upon the throne of the house of Israel
34. 13 of Egypt, out of the house of bond men
34. 15 in the house which is called by my name
35. 2 Go unto the house of the Rechabites, and
35. 2 bring them into the house of the LORD
35. 3 and the whole house of the Rechabites
35. 4 brought them into the house of the LORD
35. 5 I set before the sons of the house of the
35. 7 Neither shall ye build house, nor sow seed
35. 9 Nor to build houses for us to dwell in
35. 18 said unto the house of the Rechabites
36. 3 It may be that the house of Judah will
36. 5 I cannot go into the house of the LORD
36. 6 in the LORD'S house upon the fasting day
36. 8 words of the LORD in the LORD'S house
36. 10 Then read Baruch..in the house of the L.
36. 10 entry of the new gate of the LORD'S house
36. 12 he went down into the king's house, into
36. 22 the king sat in the winter house, in the
37. 15, 20 in the house of Jonathan the scribe
37. 17 the king asked him secretly in his house
38. 7 one of the eunuchs..in the king's house
38. 8 went forth out of the king's house, and
38. 11 went into the house of the king under the
38. 14 entry that (is) in the house of the LORD
38. 17 and thou shalt live, and thine house
38. 22 that are left in the king of Judah's house
38. 26 cause me to return to Jonathan's house
39. 8 burned the king's house, and the houses
41. 5 to bring (them) to the house of the LORD
43. 9 the entry of Pharaoh's house in Tahpanhes
43. 12 fire in the houses of the gods of Egypt
43. 13 the houses of the gods of the Egyptians
48. 13 house of Israel was ashamed of Beth-el
51. 51 into the sanctuaries of the LORD'S house
52. 13 the house of the LORD, and the king's h.
52. 13 houses of Jerusalem, and all the houses
52. 17 pillars (were) in the house of the LORD
52. 17 sea that (was) in the house of the LORD
52. 20 Solomon had made in the house of the L.
Lam. 2. 7 made a noise in the house of the LORD
5. 2 turned to strangers, our houses to aliens
Eze. 2. 5 forbear, for they (are) a rebellious house
2. 6 afraid..though they (be) a rebellious ho.
2. 8 not..rebellious like that rebellious house
3. 1 and go speak unto the house of Israel
3. 4 get thee unto the house of Israel, and
3. 5 (art) not sent..(but) to the house of Israel
3. 7 the house of Israel will not hearken unto

Eze. 3. 7 the house of Israel (are) impudent and h.
3. 9 fear them not..they (be) a rebellious ho.
3. 17 a watchman unto the house of Israel
3. 24 said..Go, shut thyself within thine house
3. 26, 27 for they (are) a rebellious house
4. 3 (shall be) a sign to the house of Israel
4. 4, 5 the iniquity of the house of Israel
4. 6 thou shalt bear the iniquity of the house
5. 4 come forth into all the house of Israel
6. 11 evil abominations of the house of Israel!
7. 24 the heathen..shall possess their houses
8. 1 I sat in mine house, and the elders of
8. 6 that the house of Israel committeth here
8. 10 idols of the house of Israel, pourtrayed
8. 11, 12 the ancients of the house of Israel
8. 14 the door of the gate of the LORD'S house
8. 16 into the inner court of the LORD'S house
8. 17 Is it a light thing to the house of Judah
9. 3 gone up..to the threshold of the house
9. 6 ancient men which (were) before the house
9. 7 Defile the house, and fill the courts with
9. 9 The iniquity of the house of Israel and
10. 3 stood on the right side of the house when
10. 4 the threshold of the house; and the house
10. 18 from off the threshold of the house, and
10. 19 door of the east gate of the LORD'S house
11. 1 unto the east gate of the LORD'S house
11. 3 let us build houses: this (city is) the
11. 5 Thus have ye said, O house of Israel: for
11. 15 the house of Israel wholly, (are) they unto
12. 2 dwellest in..midst of a rebellious house
12. 2 hear not: for they (are) a rebellious house
12. 3 though they (be) a rebellious house
12. 6 set..(for) a sign unto the house of Israel
12. 9 the house of Israel, the rebellious house
12. 10 the house of Israel that (are) among them
12. 24 divination within the house of Israel
12. 25 in your days, O rebellious house, will I
12. 27 (they of) the house of Israel say, The
13. 5 neither made up the hedge for the house
13. 9 in the writing of the house of Israel, neither
14. 4 Every man of the house of Israel that
14. 5 I may take the house of Israel in their
14. 6 say unto the house of Israel, Thus saith
14. 7 every one of the house of Israel, or of the
14. 11 the house of Israel may go no more astray
16. 41 they shall burn thine houses with fire, and
17. 2 speak a parable unto the house of Israel
17. 12 Say now to the rebellious house, Know ye
18. 6, 15 to the idols of the house of Israel
18. 25 O house of Israel; Is not my way equal
18. 29 Yet saith the house of Israel, The way of
18. 29 O house of Israel, are not my ways equal?
18. 30 I will judge you, O house of Israel, every
18. 31 for why will ye die, O house of Israel?
20. 5 hand unto the seed of the house of Jacob
20. 13 the house of Israel rebelled against me
20. 27 speak unto the house of Israel, and say
20. 30 say unto the house of Israel, Thus saith
20. 31 I be enquired of by you, O house of Israel?
20. 39 house of Israel, thus saith the Lord GOD
20. 40 all the house of Israel, all of them in the
20. 44 your corrupt doings, O ye house of Israel
22. 18 the house of Israel is to me become dross
23. 39 have they done in the midst of mine house
23. 47 slay..and burn up their house with fire
24. 3 a parable unto the rebellious house, and
24. 21 Speak unto the house of Israel, Thus saith
25. 3 against the house of Judah, when they we.
25. 8 Behold, the house of Judah (is) like unto
25. 12 hath dealt against the house of Judah by
26. 12 they shall..destroy thy pleasant houses
27. 14 They of the house of Togarmah traded in
28. 24 a pricking brier unto the house of Israel
28. 25 have gathered the house of Israel from the
28. 26 shall build houses, and plant vineyards
29. 6 been a staff of reed to the house of Israel
29. 16 no more the confidence of the house of I.
29. 21 horn of the house of Israel to bud forth
33. 7 set..a watchman unto the house of Israel
33. 10 speak unto the house of Israel..saying
33. 11 for why will ye die, O house of Israel?
33. 20 O ye house of Israel, I will judge you every
33. 30 the walls, and in the doors of the houses
34. 30 they..the house of Israel, (are) my people
35. 15 the inheritance of the house of Israel, bec.
36. 10 all the house of Israel, (even) all of it: and
36. 17 when the house of Israel dwelt in their
36. 21 which the house of Israel had profaned
36. 22 Therefore say unto the house of Israel
36. 22 do not (this) for your sakes, O house of Isr.
36. 32 be ashamed and confounded..O house of
36. 37 be enquired of by the house of Israel
37. 11 these bones are the whole house of Israel
37. 16 (for) all the house of Israel his companions
38. 6 the house of Togarmah of the north quar.
39. 12 seven months shall the house of Israel be
39. 22 So the house of Israel shall know that I
39. 23 shall know that the house of Israel went
39. 25 mercy upon the whole house of Israel, and
39. 29 my spirit upon the house of Israel, saith
40. 4 declare all that thou seest to the house of
40. 5 behold a wall on the outside of the house
40. 45 the keepers of the charge of the house
40. 47 and the altar (that was) before the house
40. 48 he brought me to the porch of the house
41. 5 After he measured the wall of the house
41. 5, 10 round about the house on every side
41. 6 into the wall which (was) of the house for
41. 6 they had not hold in the wall of the house
41. 7 for the winding about of the house went
41. 7 upward round about the house: therefore

Eze. 41. 7 breadth of the house (was still) upward
41. 8 I saw also the height of the house round
41. 13 So he measured the house, an hundred c.
41. 14 Also the breadth of the face of the house
41. 17 even unto the inner house, and without
41. 19 made through all the house round about
41. 26 and (upon) the side chambers of the house
42. 15 made an end of measuring the inner house
43. 4 the glory of the LORD came into the house
43. 5 and..the glory of the LORD filled the house
43. 6 speaking unto me out of the house; and
43. 7 shall the house of Israal no more defile
43. 10 show the house to the house of Israel, that
43. 11 show them the form of the house, and the
43. 12 This (is) the law of the house; upon the top
43. 21 burn it in the appointed place of the house
44. 4 way of the north gate before the house
44. 4 the glory of the LORD filled the house of
44. 5 the ordinances of the house of the LORD
44. 5 mark well the entering in of the house
44. 6 thou shalt say..to the house of Israel, Thus
44. 6 O ye house of Israel, let it suffice you of
44. 7 to be in my sanctuary..(even) my house
44. 11 of the house, and ministering to the house
44. 12 caused the house of Israel to fall into in.
44. 14 keepers of the charge of the house, for all
44. 22 maidens of the seed of the house of Israel
44. 30 cause the blessing to rest in thine house
45. 4 it shall be a place for their houses, and
45. 5 the Levites, the ministers of the house
45. 6 it shall be for the whole house of Israel
45. 8 give to the house of Israel according to
45. 17 in all solemnities of the house of Israel
45. 17 make reconciliation for the house of Israel
45. 19 put (it) upon the posts of the house, and
45. 20 simple: so shall ye reconcile the house
46. 24 the ministers of the house shall boil the
47. 1 he brought me..unto the door of the house
47. 1 out from under the threshold of the house
47. 1 the forefront of the house (stood toward)
47. 1 from the right side of the house, at the
48. 21 and the sanctuary of the house (shall be)
Dan. 1. 2 with part of the vessels of the house of G.
1. 2 he carried into..the house of his god; and
1. 2 brought..into the treasure house of his g.
Hos. 1. 4 blood of Jezreel upon the house of Jehu
1. 4 cause to cease the kingdom of the house
1. 6 have mercy upon the house of Israel; but
1. 7 I will have mercy upon the house of Judah
5. 1 and hearken, ye house of Israel; and give
5. 1 house of the king; for judgment (is) tow.
5. 12 and to the house of Judah as rottenness
5. 14 as a young lion to the house of Judah: I
6. 10 seen an horrible thing in the house of Is.
8. 1 as an eagle against the house of the LORD
9. 4 shall not come into the house of the LORD
9. 8 a snare..(and) hatred in the house of his G.
9. 15 I will drive them out of mine house, I will
11. 11 will place them in their houses, saith the
11. 12 house of Israel with deceit: but Judah
Joel 1. 9 is cut off from the house of the LORD; the
1. 13 withholden from the house of your God
1. 14 (into) the house of the LORD your God, and
1. 16 and gladness from the house of our God?
2. 9 they shall climb up upon the houses; they
3. 18 a fountain shall come forth of the house
Amos 1. 4 I will send a fire into the house of Hazael
1. 5 holdeth the sceptre from the house of E.
2. 8 they drink the wine..(in) the house of
3. 13 Hear ye, and testify in the house of Jacob
3. 15 the winter house with the summer house
3. 15 and the houses of ivory shall perish, and
3. 15 the great houses shall have an end, saith
5. 1 (even) a lamentation, O house of Israel
5. 3 that..shall leave ten, to the house of Isr
5. 4 saith the LORD unto the house of Israel
5. 6 lest he break out like fire in the house
5. 11 ye have built houses of hewn stone, but
5. 19 went into the house, and leaned his hand
5. 25 Have ye offered..sacrifices..O house of
6. 1 Woe..to whom the house of Israel came!
6. 9 if there remain ten men in one house, that
6. 10 of the house..by the sides of the house
6. 11 smite the great house..the little house
6. 14 will raise up against you a nation, O house
7. 9 I will rise against the house of Jeroboam
7. 10 against thee in the midst of the house of
7. 16 drop not (thy word) against the house of
9. 8 will not utterly destroy the house of Jacob
9. 9 I will sift the house of Israel among all
Obad. 1. 17 house of Jacob shall possess their posse.
1. 18 house of Jacob shall be a fire, and the h.
1. 18 house of Esau for stubble, and they shall
1. 18 not be (any) remaining of the house of E.
Mic. 1. 5 for the sins of the house of Israel. What
1. 10 in the house of Aphrah roll thyself in the
1. 14 the houses of Achzib (shall be) a lie to the
2. 2 they covet..houses, and take (them) away
2. 2 so they oppress a man and his house, even
2. 7 O (thou that art) named The house of Ja.
2. 9 cast out from their pleasant houses; from
3. 1 ye princes of the house of Israel; (Is it)
3. 9 house of Jacob, and princes of the house
3. 12 mountain of the house as the high places
4. 1 mountain of the house of the LORD shall
4. 2 to the house of the God of Jacob; and he
6. 4 redeemed..out of the house of servants
6. 10 wickedness in the house of the wicked
6. 16 and all the works of the house of Ahab
7. 6 a man's enemies (are)..of his own house
Nah. 1. 14 out of the house of thy gods will I cut off
Hab. 2. 9 coveteth an evil covetousness to his house

Hab. 2. 10 Thou hast consulted shame to thy house
3. 13 woundedst the head out of the house of
Zeph. 1. 9 which fill their masters' houses with..dec.
1. 13 their houses a desolation..build houses
2. 7 be for the remnant of the house of Judah
2. 7 in the houses of Askelon shall they lie
Hag. 1. 2 time that the LORD'S house should be bu.
1. 4 dwell in your ceiled houses, and this ho.
1. 8 bring wood, and build the house; and I
1. 9 Because of mine house that (is) waste, and
1. 9 ye run every man unto his own house
1. 14 did work in the house of the LORD of ho.
2. 3 you that saw this house in her first glory?
2. 7 I will fill this house with glory, saith the
2. 9 The glory of this latter house shall be gr.
Zech. 1. 16 my house shall be built in it, saith the L.
3. 7 then thou shalt also judge my house, and
4. 9 have laid the foundation of this house; his
5. 4 it shall enter into the house of the thief
5. 4 and into the house of him that sweareth
5. 4 it shall remain in the midst of his house
5. 11 To build it an house in the land of Shinar
6. 10 the house of Josiah the son of Zephaniah
7. 2 When they had sent unto the house of G.
7. 3 the priests which (were) in the house of
8. 9 the foundation of the house of the LORD
8. 13 O house of Judah, and house of Israel; so
8. 15 to do well..to the house of Judah: fear
8. 19 to the house of Judah joy and gladness
9. 8 I will encamp about mine house because
10. 3 hath visited his flock the house of Judah
10. 6 strengthen the house..save the house of
11. 13 cast them to the potter in the house of the
12. 4 open mine eyes upon the house of Judah
12. 7 that the glory of the house of David and
12. 8 the house of David (shall be) as God, as
12. 10 And I will pour upon the house of David
12. 12, 12, 13 the family of the house of
13. 1 a fountain opened to the house of David
13. 6 I was wounded (in) the house of my friends
14. 2 the houses rifled, and the women ravished
14. 20 the pots in the LORD'S house shall be like
14. 21 no more..in the house of the LORD of ho.
Mal. 3. 10 that there may be meat in mine house

2. *House*, בַּיִת *bayith*.
Ezra 4. 24 Then ceased the work of the house of God
5. 2 Jeshua..began to build the house of God
5. 3, 9 commanded you to build this house, and
5. 8 to the house of the great God, which is
5. 11 We..build the house that was builded these
5. 12 who destroyed this house, and carried the
5. 13 Cyrus made a decree to build this house
5. 14 the vessels also..of the house of God, which
5. 15 the house of God be builded in his place
5. 16 laid the foundation of the house of God
5. 17 search made in the king's treasure house
5. 17 to build this house of God at Jerusalem
6. 1 search was made in the house of the rolls
6. 3 a decree (concerning) the house of God at
6. 3 Let the house be builded, the place where
6. 4 expenses be given out of the king's house
6. 5 silver vessels of the house of God, which
6. 5 place, and place (them) in the house of G.
6. 7 Let the work of this house of God alone
6. 7 let the governor..build this house of God
6. 8 for the building of this house of God; that
6. 11 let timber be pulled down from his house
6. 11 let his house be made a dunghill for this
6. 12 this house of God which (is) at Jerusalem
6. 15 this house was finished on the third day
6. 16 kept the dedication of this house of God
6. 17 at the dedication of this house of God an
7. 16 offering willingly for the house of their G.
7. 17 offer them upon the altar of the house of
7. 19 for the service of the house of thy God
7. 20 be needful for the house of thy God
7. 20 bestow (it) out of the king's treasure house
7. 23 diligently done for the house of the God of
7. 24 or ministers of this house of God, it shall
Dan. 2. 5 and your houses shall be made a dunghill
2. 17 Then Daniel went to his house, and made
3. 29 and their houses shall be made a dunghill
4. 4 I Nebuchadnezzar was at rest in mine h.
4. 30 I have built for the house of the kingdom
5. 3 of the temple of the house of God which
5. 10 the queen..came into the banquet house
5. 23 brought..vessels of his house before thee
6. 10 he went into his house; and, his windows

3. *Comely place, habitation*, נָאָה *naah*.
Psa. 83. 12 Let us take to ourselves the houses of G.

4. *House, place of habitation*, οἰκητήριον *oikētērion*.
2 Co. 5. 2 with our house which is from heaven

5. *House, household, family, retainers*, οἰκία *oikia*.
Matt. 2. 11 And when they were come into the house
5. 15 giveth light unto all that are in the house
7. 24 wise man, which built his house upon a
7. 25, 27 the winds blew, and beat upon that h.
7. 26 man, which built his house upon the sand
8. 14 when Jesus was come into Peter's house
9. 10 as Jesus sat at meat in the house, behold
9. 23 when Jesus came into the ruler's house
9. 28 when he was come into the house, the
10. 12 And when ye come into an house, salute
10. 13 the house be worthy, let your peace come
10. 14 when ye depart out of that house or city
12. 25 every city or house divided against itself
12. 29 a strong man's house, and spoil his house
13. 1 The same day went Jesus out of the house
13. 36 Then Jesus..went into the house: and his

Matt 13. 57 in his own country, and in his own house
17. 25 when he was come into the house, Jesus
19. 29 every one that hath forsaken houses, or
23. 14 [ye devour widows' houses, and for a pr.]
24. 17 come down to take anything out of his h.
24. 43 would not have suffered his house to be
26. 6 when Jesus was in Bethany, in the house
Mark 1. 29 they entered into the house of Simon and
2. 15 as Jesus sat at meat in his house, many p.
3. 25 if a house be divided..that house cannot
3. 27 a strong man's house, and spoil..his ho.
6. 4 among his own kin, and in his own house
6. 10 what place soever ye enter into an house
7. 24 entered into an house, and would have no
9. 33 and, being in the house, he asked them
10. 10 in the house his disciples asked him again
10. 29 There is no man that hath left house, or
10. 30 he shall receive..now in this time, houses
12. 40 Which devour widows' houses, and for a
13. 15 the [h.]..to take any thing out of his ho.
13. 34 a man taking a far journey, who left his h.
13. 35 ye know not when the master of the house
14. 3 being in Bethany, in the house of Simon
Luke 4. 38 And he arose..and entered into Simon's h.
5. 29 Levi made him a great feast in his own h.
6. 48 which built an house..beat..upon that h.
6. 49 built an house..and the ruin of that house
7. 6 when he was now not far from the house
7. 36 he went into the Pharisee's [house], and
7. 37 (Jesus) sat at meat in the Pharisee's house
7. 44 I entered into thine house, thou gavest
8. 27 neither abode in..house, but in the tombs
8. 51 when he came into the house, he suffered
9. 4 whatsoever house ye enter into, there abide
10. 5 into whatsoever house ye enter, first say
10. 7 in the same house remain, eating and dr.
10. 7 Go not from house to house
15. 8 sweep the house, and seek diligently till
15. 25 he came and drew nigh to the house, he
17. 31 his stuff in the house, let him not come
18. 29 There is no man that hath left house, or
20. 47 Which devour widows' houses, and for a
22. 10 follow him into the house where he ente.
22. 11 shall say unto the goodman of the house
John 4. 53 and himself believed, and his whole house
8. 35 servant abideth not in the house for ever
11. 31 Jews..which were with her in the house
12. 3 the house was filled with the odour of
14. 2 In my Father's house are many mansions
Acts 4. 34 possessors of lands or houses sold them
9. 11 enquire in the house of Judas for (one)
9. 17 entered into the house; and putting his
10. 6 a tanner, whose house is by the sea side
10. 17 men..had made enquiry for Simon's ho.
10. 32 he is lodged in the house of (one) Simon
11. 11 already come unto the house where I was
12. 12 to the house of Mary the mother of John
16. 32 they spake..to all that were in his house
17. 5 assaulted the house of Jason, and sought
18. 7 entered into a certain (man's) house, nam.
18. 7 whose house joined hard to the synagogue
1 Co. 11. 22 have ye not houses to eat and to drink in
16. 15 ye know the house of Stephanas, that it
2 Co. 5. 1 if our earthly house of (this) tabernacle
5. 1 an house not made with hands, eternal
2 Ti. 2. 20 a great house there are not only vessels
3. 6 are they which creep into houses, and
2 John 10 receive him not into (your) house, neither

6.*House*, οἶκος *oikos*.
Matt. 9. 6 take up thy bed, and go unto thine house
9. 7 And he arose, and departed to his house
10. 6 to the lost sheep of the house of Israel
11. 8 wear soft (clothing) are in king's houses
12. 4 he entered into the house of God, and did
12. 44 return into my house from whence I came
15. 24 unto the lost sheep of the house of Israel
21. 13 My house shall be called the house of
23. 38 your house is left unto you desolate
Mark 2. 1 it was noised that he was in the house
2. 11 Arise..and go thy way into thine house
2. 26 How he went into the house of God in the
3. 19 And Judas..and they went into an house
5. 38 the house of the ruler of the synagogue
7. 17 entered into the house from the people
7. 30 when she was come to her house, she
8. 3 send them away fasting to their..houses
8. 26 And he sent him away to his house, say.
9. 28 when he was come into the house, his
11. 17 My house shall be called..house of prayer
Luke 1. 23 that..he departed to his own house
1. 27 a man whose name was Joseph, of the h.
1. 33 he shall reign over the house of Jacob for
1. 40 entered into the house of Zacharias, and
1. 56 And Mary..returned to her own house
1. 69 an horn..in the house of his servant David
2. 4 because he was of the house and lineage
5. 24 take up thy couch, and go into thine house
5. 25 departed to his own house, glorifying God
6. 4 How he went into the house of God, and
7. 10 returning to the house, found the servant
8. 39 Return to thine own house, and show how
8. 41 besought..that he would come into his h.
9. 61 farewell which are at home at my house
10. 5 And..first say, Peace (be) to this house
10. 38 named Martha received him into her ho.
11. 17 and a house (divided) against a house fal.
11. 24 will return unto my house whence I came
12. 39 not have suffered his house to be broken
12. 52 there shall be five in one house divided
13. 35 Behold, your house is left unto you des.
14. 1 as he went into the house of one of the

Luke 14. 23 compel..to come in, that my house may
16. 4 they may receive me into their houses
16. 27 thou wouldest send him to my father's h.
18. 14 this man went down to his house justified
19. 5 Zaccheus..to day I must abide at thy ho.
19. 9 This day is salvation come to this house
19. 46 My house is the house of prayer: but ye
22. 54 brought him into the high priest's [house]
John 2. 16 make not my Father's house an house of
2. 17 The zeal of thine house hath eaten me up
7. 53 [And every man went unto his own house]
11. 20 Martha..went..but Mary sat..in the hou.
Acts 2. 2 it filled all the house where they were sit.
2. 36 let all the house of Israel know assuredly
7. 10 he made him governor over..all his house
7. 20 nourished up in his father's house three
7. 42 O ye house of Israel, have ye offered to me
7. 47 But Solomon built him an house
7. 49 what house will ye build me? saith the L.
10. 2 one that feared God with all his house
10. 22 to send for thee into his house, and to hear
10. 30 at the ninth hour I prayed in my house
11. 12 and we entered into the man's house
11. 13 how he had seen an angel in his house
11. 14 whereby thou and all thy house shall be
16. 15 come into my house, and abide (there)
16. 31 and thou shalt be saved, and thy house
16. 34 when he had brought them into his house
18. 8 believed on the Lord with al his house
19. 16 so that they fled out of that house naked
21. 8 we entered into the house of Philip the ev.
Rom 16. 5 Likewise..the church that is in their house
1 Co. 16. 19 with the church that is in their house
Col. 4. 15 Salute..the church which is in his house
1 Ti. 3. 4 One that ruleth well his own house, having
3. 5 know not how to rule his own house, how
3. 12 ruling their children and their own houses
3. 15 to behave thyself in the house of God
2 Ti. 1. 16 The Lord give mercy unto the house of O.
Titus 1. 11 who subvert whole houses, teaching things
Phm. 2 fellow soldier, and to the church in thy h.
Heb. 3. 2 as also Moses (was faithful) in all his house
3. 3 as he..hath more honour than the house
3. 4 For every house is builded by some (man)
3. 5 Moses verily (was) faithful in all his house
3. 6 over his own house; whose house are we
8. 8 the house of Israel and with the house of
8. 10; 10. 21; 11. 7; 1 Pe. 2. 5; 4. 17.

HOUSE, at thy —
With thee, πρὸς σέ *pros se.*
Matt. 26. 18 I will keep the passover at thy house

HOUSE, draught —
Outgoings, מוֹצָאוֹת *motsaoth, or* מַחֲרָאוֹת *macharaoth.*
2 Ki. 10. 27 and made it a draught house unto this day

HOUSE to house, from —
1.*From house to house*, κατ' οἶκον *kat' oikon.*
Acts 2. 46 and breaking bread from house to house
20. 20 taught you publicly..from house to house
2.*The houses*, τὰς οἰκίας *tas oikias.*
1 Ti. 5. 13 wandering about from house to house; and

HOUSE, in or into every —
From house to house, κατ' οἶκον *kat' oikon.*
Acts 5. 42 in every house, they ceased not to teach
8. 3 entering into every house, and haling men

HOUSE, goodman or master of the —
House despot or ruler, οἰκοδεσπότης *oikodespotēs.*
Matt 10. 25 If they have called the master of the house
20. 11 murmured against the goodman of the h.
24. 43 if the goodman of the house had known
Mark 14. 14 say ye to the good man of the house, The
Luke 12. 39 if the goodman of the house had known
13. 25 When once the master of the house is risen
14. 21 Then the master of the house, being angry

HOUSE, to guide the —
To be a house despot or ruler, οἰκοδεσποτέω *oikod.*
1 Ti. 5. 14 women marry, bear children, guide the h.

HOUSE, hired —
What is hired, μίσθωμα *misthōma.*
Acts 28. 30 dwelt two whole years in his own hired h.

HOUSE, those of his own —
Belonging to the house, οἰκεῖος *oikeios.*
1 Ti. 5. 8 and specially for those of his own house

HOUSE, with all his —
With all his household, πανοικί *panoiki.*
Acts 16. 34 rejoiced, believing in God with all his ho.

HOUSEHOLD —
1.*House, household*, בַּיִת *bayith.*
Gen. 18. 19 he will command..his household after h.
31. 37 what hast thou found of all thy househo.
35. 2 Then Jacob said unto his household, and
42. 33 take (food for) the famine of your house.
45. 11 lest thou, and thy household, and all that
45. 18 take your father, and your households, and
47. 12 nourished..all his father's household, with
47. 24 for them of your households, and for food
Exod. 1. 1 every man and his household came with
12. 4 if the household be too little for the lamb
Lev. 16. 17 made an atonement..for his household
Num 18. 31 shall eat it in every place, ye and your ho.
Deut. 6. 22 and upon all his household, before our eyes
11. 6 swallowed them up, and their households
12. 7 ye and your households, wherein the Lo.
14. 26 thou shalt rejoice, thou, and thine hous.
15. 20 Thou shalt eat..thou and thy household

Josh. 2. 18 thy father's household, home unto thee
6. 25 her father's household, and all that she
7. 14 shall come by households; and the house
7. 18 And he brought his household man by man
Judg. 6. 27 because he feared his father's household
18. 25 lose thy life, with the lives of thy house.
1 Sa. 25. 17 against our master, and against all his ho.
27. 3 he and his men, every man with his hous.
2 Sa. 2. 3 bring up, every man with his household
6. 11 LORD blessed Obed-edom, and all his ho.
6. 20 Then David returned to bless his houshold
15. 16 the king went forth, and all his household
16. 2 The asses (be) for the king's household to
17. 23 put his household in order, and hanged
19. 18 a ferry boat to carry over the king's hou.
19. 41 have brought the king and his household
1 Ki. 4. 6 And Ahishar (was) over the household; and
4. 7 victuals for the king and his household
5. 9 my desire, in giving food for my household
5. 11 measures of wheat (for) food to his house.
11. 20 Genubath was in Pharaoh's household
2 Ki. 7. 9 that we may go and tell the king's house.
8. 1 Arise, and go thou and thine household
8. 2 went with her household, and sojourned
18. 18, 37 Eliakim..which (was) over the house.
19. 2 Eliakim, which (was) over the household
1 Ch. 24. 6 o e principal household being taken for
Neh. 13. 8 I cast forth all the household stuff of T.
Prov. 27. 27 for the food of thy household, and (for)
31. 15 giveth meat to her household, and a port.
31. 21 She is not afraid of the snow for her househ.
31. 21 all her household (are) clothed with scarlet
31. 27 looketh well to the ways of her household
Isa. 36. 22 Eliakim..that (was) over the household
37. 2 Eliakim, who (was) over the household, and

2.*Service, household*, עֲבֻדָּה *abuddah.*
Job 1. 3 a very great household; so that this man

3.*Service, household*, θεραπεία *therapeia.*
Matt 24. 45 his lord hath made ruler over his [house.]
Luke 12. 42 lord shall make ruler over his household

4.*Household*, οἰκία *oikia.*
Phil. 4. 22 chiefly they that are of Cesar's household

5.*House, household*, οἶκος *oikos.*
Acts 16. 15 when she was baptized, and her household
1 Co. 1. 16 I baptized also the household of Stephanas
2 Ti. 4. 19 Salute Prisca and Aquila, and the househo.

HOUSEHOLD, of the —
Belonging to the house, οἰκεῖος *oikeios.*
Gal. 6. 10 especially unto them who are of the ho.
Eph. 2. 19 fellow citizens..and of the household of

HOUSEHOLD servant —
Household servant, domestic, οἰκέτης *oiketēs.*
Acts 10. 7 he called two of his household servants

HOUSEHOLD, they of the —
Belonging to the house, οἰκιακός *oikiakos.*
Matt 10. 25 how much more..them of his household?
10. 36 a man's foes (shall be) they of his own h.

HOUSEHOLDER —
House despot or ruler, οἰκοδεσπότης *oikodespotēs.*
Matt 13. 27 the servants of the householder came and
13. 52 is like unto a man..an householder which
20. 1 is like unto a man..an householder, which
21. 33 There was a certain householder, which

HOUSES, desolate —
Forsaken habitations, אַלְמְנוֹת *almanoth.*
Isa. 13. 22 wild beasts..shall cry in their desolate h.
[*See also* Roof, shearing, summer.]

HOUSE TOP —
1.*Roof, top, pinnacle*, גָּג *gag.*
2 Ki. 19. 26 they were..(as) the grass on the house tops
Psa. 102. 7 am as a sparrow alone upon the house top
129. 6 them be as the grass (upon) the house top
Prov 21. 9 (It is)..to dwell in a corner of the house top
25. 24 (It is)..to dwell in..corner of the house top
Isa. 22. 1 thou art wholly gone up to the house tops?
37. 27 they were..(as) the grass on the house t.
Jer. 48. 38 lamentation..upon all the house tops of
Zeph. 1. 5 worship the host of heaven upon the h. t.

2.*Building*, δῶμα *dōma.*
Matt 10. 27 what ye hear..preach ye upon the house t.
24. 17 Let him which is on the house top not co.
Mark 13. 15 let him that is on the house top not go
Luke 5. 19 they went upon the house top, and let.
12. 3 shall be proclaimed upon the house tops
17. 31 he which shall be upon the house top, and
Acts 10. 9 Peter went up upon the house top to pray

HOW ? —
1.*Where ? how ?* אֵי *e.*
Jer. 5. 7 How shall I pardon thee for this? thy ch.

2.*How ? how*, אֵיךְ *ek.*
Gen. 44. 34 how shall I go up to my father, and the
Judg 16. 15 How canst thou say, I love thee, when

3.*How ? how*, אֵיכָה *ekah.*
Deut. 1. 12 How can I myself alone bear your cumb.
7. 17 These nations..how can I dispossess them?

4.*How ? how*, אֵיכָכָה *ekakah.*
Esth. 8. 6 how can I endure?..or how can I endure?
Song 5. 3 how shall I put it on?..how shall I defile

5.*How ? how*, πῶς *pōs.*
Matt. 6. 28 Consider the lilies of the field, how they
7. 4 Or how wilt thou say to thy brother, Let

Matt 10. 19 take no thought how or what ye shall sp.
12. 4 How he entered into the house of God, and
12. 26 divided..how shall then his kingdom st.?
12. 29 how can one enter into a strong man's h.
12. 34 how can ye, being evil, speak good things?
16. 11 How is it that ye do not understand that
21. 20 How soon is the fig tree withered away!
22. 12 Friend, how camest thou in hither not
22. 43 How then doth David in spirit call him L.
22. 45 If David then call him Lord, how is he his
23. 33 how can ye escape the damnation of hell?
26. 54 how then shall the scriptures be fulfilled
Mark 2. 26 [How] he went into the house of God in
3. 23 and said..How can Satan cast out Satan?
4. 13 and how then will ye know all parables?
4. 40 Why are ye so fearful? how is it that ye
5. 16 told them how it befell to him that was
8. 21 said..How is it that ye do not understand?
9. 12 how it is written of the Son of man, that
10. 23 How hardly shall they that have riches
10. 24 how hard is it for them that trust in riches
11. 18 and sought how they might destroy him
12. 35 How say the scribes that Christ is the son of
12. 41 beheld how the people cast money into the
14. 1 scribes sought how they might take him by
14. 11 sought how he might conveniently betray
Luke 1. 34 How shall this be, seeing I know not a man?
6. 42 Either how canst thou say to thy brother
8. 18 Take heed therefore how ye hear: for w.
10. 26 What is written in the law? how readest
11. 18 how shall his kingdom stand? because ye
12. 11 take ye no thought how or what thing ye
12. 27 Consider the lilies how they grow: they
12. 50 how am I straitened till it be accomplished!
12. 56 how is it that ye do not discern this time?
14. 7 when he marked how they chose out the
18. 24 How hardly shall they that have riches
20. 41 How say they that Christ is David's son?
20. 44 calleth him Lord, how is he then his son?
22. 2 scribes sought how they might kill him
22. 4 how he might betray him unto them
John 3. 4 How can a man be born when he is old?
3. 9 and said unto him, How can these things
3. 12 how shall ye believe, if I tell you (of)
4. 9 How is it that thou, being a Jew, askest
5. 44 How can ye believe, which receive honour
5. 47 writings, how shall ye believe my words?
6. 42 how is it then that he saith, I came down
6. 52 How can this man give us (his) flesh to eat
7. 15 How know. this man letters, having never
8. 33 how sayest thou, Ye shall be made free?
9. 10 said..unto him, How were thine eyes op.?
9. 15 asked him how he had received his sight
9. 16 How can a man that is a sinner do such mir.
9. 19 was born blind? how then doth he now see?
9. 26 What did he..how opened he thine eyes?
11. 36 said the Jews, Behold how he loved him!
12. 34 how sayest thou, The Son of man must be
14. 5 we know not..and how can we know the
14. 9 how sayest thou (then), Show us the Fath.
Acts 2. 8 how hear we every man in our own tongue
4. 21 finding nothing how they might punish
8. 31 How can I, except some man should guide
9. 27 how he had seen the Lord in the way, and
9. 27 how he had preached boldly at Damascus
11. 13 he showed us how he had seen an angel in
12. 17 how the Lord had brought him out of the
15. 36 visit our brethren..(and see) how they do
Rom. 3. 6 for then how shall God judge the world?
4. 10 How was it then reckoned? when he was
6. 2 How shall we, that are dead to sin, live
8. 32 how shall he not with him also freely
10. 14 [How] then shall they call on him in wh.
10. 14 [how] shall they believe in him of whom
10. 14 [how] shall they hear without a preacher?
10. 15 [how] shall they preach except they be
1 Co. 3. 10 let every man take heed how he buildeth
7. 32 he..careth..[how] he may please the L.
7. 33 he..careth..[how] he may please (his) w.
7. 34 careth..[how] she may please (her) husb.
14. 7 how shall it be known what is piped or
14. 9 how shall it be known what is spoken? for
14. 16 how shall he that occupieth the room of
15. 12 how say some among you that there is no
15. 35 How..the dead raised up? and with what
2 Co. 3. 8 How shall not the ministration of the sp.
Gal. 4. 9 how turn ye again to the weak and begg.
Col. 4. 6 know how ye ought to answer every man
1 Th. 1. 9 how ye turned to God from idols to serve
4. 1 how ye ought to walk and to please God
2 Th. 3. 7 yourselves know how ye ought to follow
1 Ti. 3. 5 how shall he take care of the church of G.?
3. 15 thou mayest know how thou oughtest to
Heb. 2. 3 How shall we escape, if we neglect so great
1 Jo. 3. 17 how dwelleth the love of God in him?
4. 20 [how] can he love God whom he hath not
Rev. 3. 3 Remember..how thou hast received and

6. *Wherefore, why, what, how?* τίς *tis.*
Matt 18. 12 How think ye? If a man have an hundred
Mark 2. 16 [How is it] that he eateth and drinketh
Luke 1. 62 made signs..how he would have him cal.
2. 49 How is it that ye sought me? wist ye not
16. 2 How is it that I hear this of thee? give
John 14. 22 how is it that thou wilt manifest thyself
Acts 5. 9 How is it that ye have agreed together to
1 Co. 7. 16 or how knowest thou, O man, whether
14. 26 How is it then, brethren? when ye come
Eph. 6. 21 ye also may know my affairs, (and) how I

HOW —

1. *That which,* אֵת אֲשֶׁר *eth asher.*
Gen. 30. 29 knowest how I have served thee, and how

2. *How?* הֵיךְ *hek.*
1 Ch. 13. 12 How shall I bring the ark of God (home)
Dan. 10. 17 how can the servant of this my lord talk

3. *That,* כִּי *ki.*
Josh. 10. 1 king..had heard how Joshua had taken

4. *Wherefore?* מַדּוּעַ *maddua.*
Exod. 2. 18 How (is it that) ye are come so soon to day?

5. *What! what! what,* מָה *mah.*
Num 23. 8 How shall I curse, whom God hath not

6. *How? according to what?* כַּמָּה *kam-mah.*
Gen. 47. 8 Pharaoh said unto Jacob, How old (art)

7. *What? what,* מֶה *meh.*
2 Sa. 1. 4 How went the matter? I pray thee, tell

8. *According as,* καθώς *kathōs.*
Acts 15. 14 Simeon hath declared how God at the first

9. *How, that, so that,* ὅπως *hopōs.*
Matt 12. 14 against him, how they might destroy him
22. 15 how they might entangle him in (his) talk
Mark 3. 6 took counsel..how they might destroy h.
Luke 24. 20 And how the chief priests and our rulers

10. *That,* ὅτι *hoti.*
Luke 1. 58 her cousins heard how the Lord had sh.
21. 5 how it was adorned with goodly stones
John 4. 1 the Lord knew how the Pharisees had h.
12. 19 Perceive ye how ye prevail nothing? behold
14. 28 Ye have heard how I said unto you, I go
Acts 14. 27 how he had opened the door of faith unto
20. 35 how he said, It is more blessed to give
Gal. 4. 13 Ye know how through infirmity of the
Phm. 19 albeit I do not say to thee how thou owest
Jas. 2. 22 Seest thou how faith wrought with his
Rev. 2. 2 how thou canst not bear them which are

11. *How, as,* ὡς *hōs.*
Mark 4. 27 the seed..grow up, he knoweth not how
12. 26 [how] in the bush God spake unto him
Luke 6. 4 [How] he went into the house of God, and
8. 47 declared..how she was healed immediat.
22. 61 Peter remembered..how he had said unto
23. 55 beheld the sepulchre, and how his body
24. 6 remember [how] he spake unto you when
24. 35 how he was known to them in breaking of
Acts 10. 28 Ye know how that it is an unlawful thing
10. 38 How God anointed Jesus of Nazareth with
11. 16 the word of the Lord, how that he said
20. 20 how I kept back nothing that was profit.
Rom. 10. 15 How beautiful are the feet of them that
11. 2 how he maketh intercession to God agai.
11. 33 how unsearchable (are) his judgments, and
2 Co. 7. 15 how with fear and trembling ye received
1 Th. 2. 10 Ye (are) witnesses, and God (also), how h.
2. 11 As ye know how we exhorted; Phil. 1. 8.

HOW great (things) —

1. *What? what!* מָה *mah.*
Dan. 4. 3 How great (are) his signs! and how mig.

2. *How much,* ὅσος *hosos.*
Mark 5. 19 tell them how great things the Lord hath
5. 20 how great things Jesus had done for him
Luke 8. 39 show how great things..how great things
Acts 9. 16 I will show him how great things he must

3. *How great,* ἡλίκος *hēlikos,* Jas. 3. 5.

4. *How great,* πηλίκος *pēlikos.*
Heb. 7. 4 consider how great this man (was), unto

5. *How great, how much,* πόσος *posos.*
Matt. 6. 23 be darkness, how great (is) that darkness!

HOW greatly —

As, how, ὡς *hōs.*
Phil. 1. 8 how greatly I long after you..in the bow.

HOW it will go with —

The things concerning, τὰ περὶ *ta peri.*
Phil. 2. 23 so soon as I shall see how it will go with

HOW large —

How great, πηλίκος *pēlikos.*
Gal. 6. 11 Ye see how large a letter I have written

HOW long —

1. *According to what,* כַּמָּה *kam-mah.*
Job 7. 19 How long wilt thou not dep.; 2 Sam. 19. 34.

2. *Till when,* ἕως πότε *heōs pote.*
Matt 17. 17 how long shall I be with you? how long s.
Mark 9. 19 how long shall I be with you? how long s.
Luke 9. 41 How long shall I be with you, and suffer
John 10. 24 How long dost thou make us to doubt? If
Rev. 6. 10 How long, O Lord, holy and true, dost thou

3. *How great, how much,* πόσος *posos.*
Mark 9. 21 How long is it ago since this came unto h.?

4. *Till when?* עַד־אָן עַד־אָנָה *ad an, ad anah.*
Job 8. 2 How long wilt thou speak these (things)?
18. 2 How long (will it be ere) ye make an end

5. *Till what?* עַד־מָה *ad mah.*
Psa. 4. 2 how long (will ye turn) my glory into s.
74. 9 neither..among us any that knoweth how lo.

HOW many (things) —

1. *How much,* ὅσος *hosos.*
2 Ti. 1. 18 in how many things he ministered unto

2. *How great, how much,* πόσος *posos.*
Matt 15. 34 Jesus saith unto them, How many loaves
16. 9 remember..how many baskets ye took up?
16. 10 thousand, and how many baskets ye took
Matt 27. 13 Hearest thou not how many things they
Mark 6. 38 saith..How many loaves have ye? go and
8. 5 he asked them, How many loaves have ye?
8. 19, 20 how many baskets full of fragments
15. 4 how many things they witness against thee
Luke 15. 17 How many hired servants of my father's h.
Acts 21. 20 seest, brother, how many thousands of J.

HOW many soever they be —

As they and as they, כָּהֵם וְכָהֵם *ka-hem ve-ka-hem.*
2 Sa. 24. 3 unto the people, how many soever they be

HOW mighty —

What? what! מָה *mah.*
Dan. 4. 3 how mighty (are) his wonders! his king.

HOW much —

1. *How much,* ὅσος *hosos.*
Acts 9. 13 how much evil he hath done to thy saints
Heb. 8. 6 by how much also he is the mediator of
Rev. 18. 7 How much she hath glorified herself, and

2. *How great, how much,* πόσος *posos.*
Matt. 7. 11 how much more shall your Father which
10. 25 how much more..them of his household?
12. 12 How much then is a man better than a s.?
Luke 11. 13 how much more shall (your) heavenly F.
12. 24 how much more are ye better than the f.?
12. 28 how much more..you, O ye of little faith?
16. 5 said..How much owest thou unto my lord?
16. 7 Then said he..And how much owest thou?
Rom 11. 12 the fall of them..how much more their
11. 24 how much more shall these, which be the
Phm. 16 how much more unto thee, both in the flesh
Heb. 9. 14 How much more shall the blood of Christ
10. 29 Of how much sorer punishment, suppose

3. *What,* τίς *tis.*
Luke 19. 15 know how much every man had gained

HOW much, less, more, rather then —

1. *Also,* אַף *aph.*
Job 4. 19 How much less (in) them that dwell in h.

2. *Also that,* אַף כִּי *aph ki.*
1 Sa. 14. 30 How much more, if haply the people had
1 Ki. 8. 27 how much less this house that I have built
2 Ki. 5. 13 how much rather then, when he saith to

3. *Not at all then, much more then,* μήτι γε *mēti ge.*
1 Co. 6. 3 how much more things that pertain to this

HOW oft or often —

1. *According to what,* כַּמָּה *kam-mah.*
Psa. 78. 40 How oft did they provoke him in the w.

2. *How oft,* ποσάκις *posakis.*
Matt 18. 21 how oft shall my brother sin against me
23. 37 how often would I have gathered thy ch.
Luke 13. 34 how often would I have gathered thy ch.

HOW that —

That, ὅτι *hoti.*
Matt 12. 5 how that on the sabbath days the priests
16. 12 Then understood they how that he bade
16. 21 how that he must go into Jerusalem, and
Luke 7. 22 [how that] the blind see, the lame walk
Acts 7. 25 would have understood how that God by
13. 32 how that the promise which was made
15. 7 ye know how that a good while ago God
20. 35 how that so labouring ye ought to support
Rom. 7. 1 Know ye not..how that the law hath dom.
1 Co. 1. 26 how that not many wise men after the flesh
10. 1 how that all our fathers were under the cl.
15. 3 how that Christ died for our sins according
2 Co. 8. 2 How that in a great trial of affliction the
12. 4 How that he was caught up into paradise
13. 5 how that Jesus Christ is in you, except ye
Gal. 1. 13 how that beyond measure I persecuted
Eph. 3. 3 How that by revelation he made known
Heb. 12. 17 ye know how that afterward, when he w.
Jas. 2. 24 Ye see then how that by works a man is
Jude 5 how that the Lord, having saved the peo.
18 How that they told you there should be

HOWBEIT —

1. *But, truly, yet,* אוּלָם *ulam*
Judg 18. 29 howbeit the name of the city (was) Laish at

2. *Only,* אַךְ *ak.*
1 Sa. 8. 9 howbeit yet protest solemnly unto them

3. *End, no more, no further, only,* אֶפֶס *ephes.*
2 Sa. 12. 14 Howbeit, because by this deed thou hast

4. *So, such, thus,* כֵּן *ken.*
2 Ch. 32. 31 Howbeit in (the business of) the ambass.

5. *Only, surely, nevertheless,* רַק *raq.*
1 Ki. 11. 13 Howbeit I will not rend away all the kin

6. *But, save, howbeit,* ἀλλά *alla.*
John 7. 27 Howbeit we know this man whence he is
Acts 7. 48 Howbeit the most high dwelleth not in t.
1 Co. 8. 7 Howbeit..not in every man that knowle.
14. 20 howbeit in malice be ye children, but in
15. 46; Gal. 4. 8; 1 Ti. 1. 16; Heb. 3. 16.

7. *But,* δέ *de.*
John 6. 23 Howbeit there came other boats from T.

8. *Yet, nevertheless,* μέντοι *mentoi.*
John 7. 13 Howbeit no man spake openly of him for

HOWL, to —

1. *To howl,* יָלַל *yalal,* 5.
Isa. 13. 6 Howl ye; for the day of the LORD (is) at
14. 31 Howl, O gate; cry, O city; thou, whole
15. 2 Moab shall howl over Nebo, and over M.

Isa. 15. 3 every one shall howl, weeping abundantly
16. 7 Moab howl for Moab, every one shall ho.
23. 1, 14 Howl, ye ships of Tarshish: for
23. 6 Pass ye over to Tarshish; howl, ye inha.
65. 14 servants..shall howl for vexation of spirit
Jer. 4. 8 gird you with sackcloth, lament and howl
25. 34 Howl, ye shepherds, and cry; and wallow
47. 2 all the inhabitants of the land shall howl
48. 20 howl and cry; tell ye it in Arnon, that M.
48. 31 Therefore will I howl for Moab, and I will
48. 39 They shall howl..How is it broken down!
49. 3 Howl, O Heshbon, for Ai is spoiled: cry
51. 8 Babylon is suddenly fallen..howl for her
Eze. 21. 12 Cry and howl, son of man; for it shall be
30. 2 Thus saith the Lord GOD; Howl ye, Woe
Hos. 7. 14 cried..when they howled upon their beds
Joel 1. 5 howl, all ye drinkers of wine, because of
1. 11 howl, O ye vine dressers, for the wheat and
1. 13 howl, ye ministers of the altar; come, lie
Mic. 1. 8 Therefore I will wail and howl, I will go
Zeph. 1. 11 Howl, ye inhabitants of Maktesh, for all
Zech 11. 2 Howl, fir tree; for the cedar is fallen; be.
11. 2 howl, O ye oaks of Bashan; for the forest

2. *To howl*, ὀλολύζω *ololuzō.*
Jas. 5. 1 howl for your miseries that shall come

HOWL, to make to —

To cause to howl, יָלַל *yalal*, 5.
Isa. 52. 5 they that rule over them make them to h.

HOWLING —

1. *Howling*, יְלֵל *yelel.*
Deut 32. 10 found him..in the waste howling wilde.

2. *Howling*, יְלָלָה *yelalah.*
Isa. 15. 8 the howling thereof unto..and the howl.
Jer. 25. 36 and an howling of the principal of the fl.
Zeph. 1. 10 an howling from the second, and a great
Zech. 11. 3 a voice of the howling of the shepherds; for

HOWLINGS, to be —

To (cause to) howl, יָלַל *yalal*, 5.
Amos 8. 3 the songs of the temple shall be howlings

HOWSOEVER —

1. *All that which*, כֹּל אֲשֶׁר *kol asher.*
Zeph. 3. 7 howsoever I punished them: but they rose

2. *Only, surely, nevertheless*, רַק *raq.*
Judg 19. 20 howsoever (let) all thy wants (lie) upon me

3. *Let it be what*, יְהִי־מָה *[hayah].*
2 Sa. 18. 22 howsoever, let me, I pray thee, also run

HUGE —

Abundance, multitude, greatness, רֹב *rob.*
2 Ch. 16. 8 Were not the Ethiopians..a huge host

HUK'-KOK, חֻקֹּק, *ditch.*

A place on the boundary of Naphtali. It is now called *Yakuk*, a village in the mountains of Naphtali, W. of the upper end of the Sea of Galilee, about seven miles S.S.W. of *Safed*, and at the head of *Wady-el-Amûd*. The Jews have an ancient tradition that Habakkuk's tomb was here.

Josh 19. 34 the coast..goeth out from thence to H.

HU'-KOK, חוּקֹק *ditch.*

A name of a city in Asher which is substituted, in 1 Ch. 6. 75, for *Helkath* in Josh. 21. 31.

1 Ch. 6. 75 H. with her suburbs, and Rehob with her

HUL, חוּל *circle.*

Second son of Aram and grandson of Shem the son of Noah. B.C. 2200. In 1 Ch. 1. 17 he is made a son of Shem.

Gen. 10. 23 the children of Aram; Uz, and H., and G.
1 Ch. 1. 17 and Uz, and H., and Gether, and Meshech

HUL'-DAH, חֻלְדָּה *weasel.*

A prophetess in the time of king Josiah, who consulted her on the book of the law found by Hilkiah. B.C. 641.

2 Ki. 22. 14 Hilkiah the priest..went unto H. the pr.
2 Ch. 34. 22 And H...went to H. the prophetess, the

HUMBLE (person) —

1. *Humble, afflicted, poor*, עָנִי, עָנָו *ani, anav.*
Psa. 9. 12 he forgetteth not the cry of the humble
10. 12 Arise, O LORD..forget not the humble
10. 17 thou hast heard the desire of the humble
34. 2 the humble shall hear (thereof), and be glad
69. 32 The humble shall see (this, and) be glad

2. *Low or humble*, שָׁפָל *shaphal.*
Prov. 16. 19 Better (it is to be) of an humble spirit with
29. 23 honour shall uphold the humble in spirit
Isa. 57. 15 humble spirit, to revive the spirit of the h.

3. *Bent down of eyes, humble*, שַׁח עֵינַיִם *shach enayim.*
Job 22. 29 lifting up; and he shall save the humble p.

4. *Low, lowly*, ταπεινός *tapeinos.*
Jas. 4. 6 saith, God..giveth grace unto the humble
1 Pe. 5. 5 for God..giveth grace to the humble

HUMBLE, to —

1. *To afflict, humble*, עָנָה *anah*, 3.
Deut. 8. 2 to humble thee..to prove thee, to know
8. 3 he humbled thee, and suffered thee to h.
8. 16 that he might humble thee, and that he
21. 14 shalt not..because thou hast humbled her
22. 24 because he hath humbled his neighbour's
22. 29 because he hath humbled her, he may not
Judg 19. 24 humble ye them, and do with them what
Psa. 35. 13 I humbled my soul with fasting; and my
Eze. 22. 10 in thee have they humbled her that was
22. 11 another in thee..humbled his sister, his

2. *To make low or humble*, שְׁפַל *shaphel*, 5
Psa. 113. 6 Who humbleth (himself) to behold (the thi.

3. *To make low or humble*, שְׁפַל *shephal*, 5.
Dan. 5. 22 thou..hast not humbled thine heart, tho.

4. *To make low*, ταπεινόω *tapeinoō.*
Matt 18. 4 Whosoever therefore shall humble hims.
23. 12 he that shall humble himself shall be ex.
Luke 14. 11 he that humbleth himself shall be exalted
18. 14 he that humbleth himself shall be exalted
2 Co. 12. 21 lest..my God will humble me among you
Phil. 2. 8 he humbled himself, and became obedient

HUMBLE self, to —

1. *To be or become humbled*, כָּנַע *kana*, 2.
1 Ki. 21. 29 Seest thou how Ahab humbleth himself
21. 29 Because he humbleth himself before me
2 Ki. 22. 19 thou hast humbled thyself before the LORD
2 Ch. 7. 14 If my people..shall humble themselves
12. 6 princes..and the king humbled themsel.
12. 7 when the LORD saw that they humbled the.
12. 7 saying, They have humbled themselves
12. 12 when he humbled himself, the wrath of
30. 11 humbled themselves, and came to Jerusa.
32. 26 Hezekiah humbled himself for the pride of
33. 12 humbled himself greatly before the God of
33. 23 And humbled not himself before the LORD
33. 23 as Manasseh his father had humbled him.
34. 27 and thou didst humble thyself before God
34. 27 humbledst thyself before me, and didst
36. 12 humbled not himself before Jeremiah the

2. *To be or become humbled*, עָנָה *anah*, 2.
Exod 10. 3 How long wilt thou refuse to humble thy.

3. *To trample on self*, רָפַס *raphas*, 7.
Prov. 6. 3 humble thyself, and make sure thy friend

4. *To bow*, שָׁחַח *shachach.*
Psa. 10. 10 humbleth himself, that the poor may fall

5. *To be or become low or humble*, שָׁפֵל *shaphel.*
Isa. 2. 9 the great man humbleth himself: therefore

6. *To make low or humble*, שְׁפַל *shaphel*, 5.
Jer. 13. 18 Humble yourselves, sit down: for your

7. *To make self low*, ταπεινόομαι *tapeinoomai.*
Jas. 4. 10 Humble yourselves in the sight of the L.
1 Pe. 5. 6 Humble yourselves therefore under the

HUMBLED, to be —

1. *To be bruised, humbled*, דָּכָא *daka*, 4.
Jer. 44. 10 They are not humbled..unto this day

2. *To be or become humbled*, כָּנַע *kana*, 2.
Lev. 26. 41 if..their uncircumcised hearts be humbl.
2 Ch. 33. 19 and set up groves..before he was humb.

3. *To bow down*, שׁוּחַ *shuach*, 5.
Lam. 3. 20 still in remembrance, and is humbled in

4. *To be or become low or humble*, שָׁפֵל *shaphel.*
Isa. 2. 11 The lofty looks of man shall be humbled
5. 15 and the mighty man shall be humbled
5. 15 and the eyes of the lofty shall be humbled
10. 33 Behold..and the haughty shall be humb.

HUMBLENESS of mind —

Lowliness of mind, ταπεινοφροσύνη *tapeinophros.*
Col 3. 12 Put on therefore..humbleness of mind

HUMBLY —

To be lowly, humble, prepared, צָנַע *tsana*, 5.
Mic. 6. 8 to love mercy, and to walk humbly with

HUMBLY beseech, to —

To bow down self, שָׁחָה *shachah*, 7.
2 Sa. 16. 4 I humbly beseech thee..I may find grace

HUMILIATION —

Lowliness, ταπείνωσις *tapeinōsis.*
Acts 8. 33 In his humiliation his judgment was taken

HUMILITY —

1. *Humility, gentleness, affliction*, עֲנָוָה *anavah.*
Prov 15. 33 of wisdom; and before honour (is) humi.
18. 12 is haughty, and before honour (is) humil.
22. 4 By humility..the fear of the LORD, (are)

2. *Lowliness of mind*, ταπεινοφροσύνη *tapeinophros.*
Col. 2. 18 in a voluntary humility and worshipping
2. 23 and humility, and neglecting of the body
1 Pe. 5. 5 Yea, all..be clothed with humility: for

HUMILITY of mind —

Lowliness of mind, ταπεινοφροσύνη *tapeinophros.*
Acts 20. 19 Serving the Lord with all humility of m.

HUM'-TAH, חֻמְטָה, *enclosed place.*

A city of Judah in the hill country next to Hebron.

Josh 15. 54 H.. and Kirjath-arba, which (is) Hebron

HUNDRED —

1. *Hundred*, מֵאָה *meah* [V.L. אמות].
Eze. 42. 16 five hundred reeds, with the measuring

2. *Hundred*, מֵאָה *meah.*
Gen. 5. 3 Adam lived an hundred and thirty years
5. 4 the days of Adam..were eight hundred
5. 5 nine hundred and thirty years: and he
5. 6 Seth lived an hundred and five years, and
5. 7 eight hundred and seven years, and begat
5. 8 nine hundred and twelve years: and he
5. 10 eight hundred and fifteen years, and begat
5. 11 nine hundred and five years: and he died
5. 13 eight hundred and forty years, and begat
5. 14 nine hundred and ten years: and he died
Gen. 5. 16 eight hundred and thirty years, and begat
5. 17 eight hundred ninety and five years, and
5. 18 And Jared lived an hundred sixty and two
5. 19 lived after he begat Enoch eight hundred
5. 20 were nine hundred sixty and two years: and
5. 22 And Enoch walked with God..three hund.
5. 23 were three hundred sixty and five years
5. 25 lived an hundred eighty and seven years
5. 26 lived..seven hundred eighty and two years
5. 27 were nine hundred sixty and nine years
5. 28 lived an hundred eighty and two years, and
5. 30 lived..five hundred ninety and five years
5. 31 were seven hundred seventy and seven y.
5. 32 Noah was five hundred years old: and N.
6. 3 days shall be an hundred and twenty years
6. 15 the ark (shall be) three hundred cubits
7. 6 Noah (was) six hundred years old when the
7. 24 upon the earth an hundred and fifty days
8. 3 after the end of the hundred and fifty days
9. 28 Noah lived..three hundred and fifty years
9. 29 days..were nine hundred and fifty years
11. 10 Shem (was) an hundred years old, and b.
11. 11 Shem lived..five hundred years, and begat
11. 13, 15 lived..four hundred and three years
11. 17 Eber lived..four hundred and thirty years
11. 19 Peleg lived..two hundred and nine years
11. 21 Reu lived..two hundred and seven years
11. 23 Serug lived..two hundred years, and beg.
11. 25 lived..an hundred and nineteen years, and
11. 32 days..were two hundred and five years
14. 14 (servants)..three hundred and eighteen
15. 13 they shall afflict them four hundred years
17. 17 unto him that is an hundred years old?
21. 5 Abraham was an hundred years old when
23. 1 hundred and seven and twenty years old
23. 15 (is worth) four hundred shekels of silver
23. 16 four hundred shekels of silver, current
25. 7 an hundred threescore and fifteen years
25. 17 an hundred and thirty and seven years
32. 6 meet thee, and four hundred men with
32. 14 Two hundred she goats, and twenty he g.
32. 14 two hundred ewes, and twenty rams
33. 1 Esau came, and with him four hundred
33. 19 a field..for an hundred pieces of money
35. 28 days..were an hundred and fourscore y.
45. 22 he gave three hundred (pieces) of silver
47. 9 The days..(are) an hundred and thirty y.
47. 28 age..was an hundred forty and seven years
50. 22 and Joseph lived an hundred and ten years
50. 26 died, (being) an hundred and ten years old
Exod. 6. 16 (were) an hundred thirty and seven years
6. 18 (were) an hundred thirty and three years
6. 20 an hundred and thirty and seven years
12. 37 hundred thousand on foot (that were) men
12. 40 (was) four hundred and thirty years
12. 41 end of the four hundred and thirty years
14. 7 he took six hundred chosen chariots, and
18. 21, 25 rulers of hundreds, rulers of fifties, and
27. 9 of an hundred cubits long for one side
27. 11 be) hangings of an hundred (cubits) long
27. 18 The length..(shall be) an hundred cubits
30. 23 of pure myrrh five hundred (shekels), and
30. 23 (even) two hundred and fifty (shekels), and
30. 23 calamus two hundred and fifty (shekels)
30. 24 of cassia five hundred (shekels), after the
38. 9 of) fine twined linen, an hundred cubits
38. 11 (the hangings were) an hundred cubits
38. 24 seven hundred and thirty shekels, after
38. 25 the silver..(was) an hundred talents, and
38. 25 a thousand seven hundred and threescore
38. 26 for six hundred thousand and three
38. 26 thousand and five hundred and fifty (men)
38. 27 of the hundred talents of silver were cast
38. 27 an hundred sockets of the hundred talents
38. 28 of the thousand seven hundred seventy and
38. 29 two thousand and four hundred shekels
Lev. 26. 8 shall chase an hundred, and an hundred
Num. 1. 21 forty and six thousand and five hundred
1. 23 fifty and nine thousand and three hundred
1. 25 and five thousand six hundred and fifty
1. 27 and fourteen thousand and six hundred
1. 29 fifty and four thousand and four hundred
1. 31 fifty and seven thousand and four hundred
1. 33 (were) forty thousand and five hundred
1. 35 thirty and two thousand and two hundred
1. 37 thirty and five thousand and four hundred
1. 39 and two thousand and seven hundred
1. 41 forty and one thousand and five hundred
1. 43 fifty and three thousand and four hundred
1. 46 all they..were six hundred thousand and
1. 46 three thousand and five hundred and fifty
2. 4 and fourteen thousand and six hundred
2. 6 fifty and four thousand and four hundred
2. 8 fifty and seven thousand and four hundred
2. 9 (were) an hundred thousand and fourscore
2. 9 thousand and six thousand and four hun.
2. 11 forty and six thousand and five hundred
2. 13 fifty and nine thousand and three hundred
2. 15 and five thousand and six hundred and fifty
2. 16 (were) an hundred thousand and fifty and
2. 16 one thousand and four hundred and fifty
2. 19 (were) forty thousand and five hundred
2. 21 thirty and two thousand and two hundred
2. 23 thirty and five thousand and four hund.
2. 24 All..of the camp..(were) an hundred th.
2. 24 eight thousand and an hundred, through.
2. 26 and two thousand and seven hundred
2. 28 forty and one thousand and five hundred
2. 30 fifty and three thousand and four hundr.
2. 31 All they..(were) an hundred thousand and
2. 31 fifty and seven thousand and six hundred
2. 32 all those..(were) six hundred thousand and

Num. 2. 32 three thousand and five hundred and fifty
3. 22 (were) seven thousand and five hundred
3. 28 (were) eight thousand and six hundred
3. 34 (were) six thousand and two hundred
3. 43 two hundred and threescore and thirteen
3. 46 two hundred and threescore and thirteen
3. 50 a thousand three hundred and threescore
4. 36 two thousand seven hundred and fifty
4. 40 two thousand and six hundred and thirty
4. 44 were three thousand and two hundred
4. 48 thousand and five hundred and fourscore
7. 13 whereof (was) an hundred and thirty (sh.)
[So in verse 19, 25, 31, 37, 43, 49, 55, 61, 67, 73, 79, 85.]
7. 85 two thousand and four hundred (shekels)
7. 86 gold..(was) an hundred and twenty (she.)
11. 21 people..(are) six hundred thousand foot.
16. 2 two hundred and fifty princes of the
16. 17 bring ye..two hundred and fifty censers
16. 35 two hundred and fifty men that offered
16. 49 were fourteen thousand and seven hund.
26. 7 thousand and seven hundred and thirty
26. 10 fire devoured two hundred and fifty men
26. 14 twenty and two thousand and two hund.
26. 18 families..forty thousand and five hund.
26. 22 and sixteen thousand and five hundred
26. 25 and four thousand and three hundred
26. 27 threescore thousand and five hundred
26. 34 fifty and two thousand and seven hund.
26. 37 thirty and two thousand and five hundred
26. 41 forty and five thousand and six hundred
26. 43 and four thousand and four hundred
26. 47 fifty and three thousand and four hundr.
26. 50 forty and five thousand and four hundred
26. 51 children of Israel, six hundred thousand
26. 51 and a thousand seven hundred and thirty
31. 14 captains over hundreds, which came from
31. 28 one soul of five hundred, (both) of the
31. 32 hundred thousand and seventy thousand
31. 36 three hundred thousand and seven and
31. 36 thirty thousand and five hundred sheep
31. 37 six hundred and threescore and fifteen
31. 39 (were) thirty thousand and five hundred
31. 43 hundred thousand and thirty thousand
31. 43 seven thousand and five hundred sheep
31. 45 thirty thousand asses and five hundred
31. 48, 52 of thousands, and captains of hundreds
31. 52 thousand seven hundred and fifty shekels
31. 54 captains of thousands and of hundreds
33. 39 Aaron (was) an hundred and twenty and
Deut. 1. 15 captains over hundreds, and captains over
22. 19 in an hundred (shekels) of silver, and
31. 2 I (am) an hundred and twenty years old
34. 7 Moses (was) an hundred and twenty years
Josh. 7. 21 two hundred shekels of silver and a wedge
24. 29 died, (being) an hundred and ten years old
24. 32 bought..for an hundred pieces of silver
Judg. 2. 8 died, (being) an hundred and ten years old
3. 31 which slew of the Philistines six hundred
4. 3, 13 nine hundred chariots of iron, and
7. 6 them that lapped..were three hundred
7. 7 the three hundred men that lapped will
7. 8 retained those three hundred men. And
7. 16 divided the three hundred men (into) th.
7. 19 the hundred men that (were) with him
7. 22 the three hundred blew the trumpets, and
8. 4 the three hundred men that (were) with
8. 10 an hundred and twenty thousand men
8. 26 thousand and seven hundred (shekels) of
11. 26 dwelt in Heshbon..three hundred years?
15. 4 went and caught three hundred foxes, and
16. 5 give thee..eleven hundred (pieces) of sil.
17. 2, 3 The eleven hundred (shekels) of silver
17. 4 mother took two hundred (shekels) of si.
18. 11 hundred men appointed with weapons of
18. 16 the six hundred men appointed with their
18. 17 six hundred men (that were) appointed
20. 2 hundred thousand footmen that drew sw.
20. 10 And we will take ten men of an hundred
20. 10 an hundred of a thousand, and a thousand
20. 15, 16 seven hundred chosen men
20. 17 four hundred thousand men that drew sw.
20. 35 and five thousand and an hundred men
20. 47 six hundred men turned and fled to the
21. 12 four hundred young virgins, that had kn.
1 Sa. 11. 8 children of Israel were three hundred th.
13. 15 present with him, about six hundred men
14. 2 the people..(were) about six hundred m.
15. 4 two hundred thousand footmen, and ten
17. 7 head (weighed) six hundred shekels of iron
18. 25 an hundred foreskins of the Philistines
18. 27 slew of the Philistines two hundred men
22. 2 were with him about four hundred men
22. 7 captains of thousands, and..of hundreds
23. 13 and his men (which were) about six hu.
25. 13 about four hundred men; and two hund.
25. 18 took two hundred loaves, and two bottles
25. 18 and an hundred clusters of raisins, and
25. 18 two hundred cakes of figs, and laid (them)
27. 2 the six hundred men that (were) with him
29. 2 passed on by hundreds and by thousands
30. 9 the six hundred men that (were) with him
30. 10 he and four hundred men: for two hundred
30. 17 four hundred young men, which rode upon
30. 21 David came to the two hundred men, wh.
2 Sa. 2. 31 three hundred and threescore men died
3. 14 an hundred foreskins of the Philistines
8. 4 and seven hundred horsemen, and twenty
8. 4 reserved of them (for) an hundred chariots
10. 18 (of) seven hundred chariots of the Syrians
14. 26 at two hundred shekels after the king's
15. 11 went two hundred men out of Jerusalem
15. 18 six hundred men which came after him

2 Sa. 16. 1 upon them two hundred (loaves) of bread
16. 1 hundred bunches of raisins, and an hun.
18. 1 and set captains..of hundreds over them
18. 4 the people came out by hundreds, and by
21. 16 three hundred (shekels) of brass in weight
23. 8 (lift up his spear) against eight hundred
23. 18 lifted up his spear against three hundred
24. 9 eight hundred thousand valiant men that
24. 9 the men..(were) five hundred thousand
1 Ki. 4. 23 hundred sheep, beside harts, and roebucks
5. 16 three thousand and three hundred, which
6. 1 in the four hundred and eightieth year
7. 2 the length thereof (was) an hundred cubits
7. 20 the pomegranates (were) two hundred, in
7. 42 four hundred pomegranates for the two
8. 63 and an hundred and twenty thousand sh.
9. 23 five hundred and fifty, which bare rule
9. 28 gold, four hundred and twenty talents
10. 10 an hundred and twenty talents of gold
10. 14 six hundred threescore and six talents of
10. 16 made two hundred targets (of) beaten gold
10. 16 six hundred (shekels) of gold went to one
10. 17 (made) three hundred shields (of) beaten
10. 26 had a thousand and four hundred chariots
10. 29 went..for six hundred (shekels) of silver
10. 29 an horse for an hundred and fifty: and so
11. 3 he had seven hundred wives, princesses
11. 3 three hundred concubines: and his wives
12. 21 an hundred and fourscore thousand
18. 4 Obadiah took an hundred prophets, and
18. 13 hid an hundred men of the LORD'S proph.
18. 19 prophets of Baal four hundred and fifty
18. 19 the prophets of the groves four hundred
18. 22 prophets (are) four hundred and fifty men
20. 15 they were two hundred and thirty two
20. 29 slew..an hundred thousand footmen in
22. 6 prophets together, about four hundred
2 Ki. 3. 4 an hundred thousand lambs, and an hun.
3. 26 took..seven hundred men that drew sw.
4. 43 should I set this before an hundred men?
11. 4, 19 rulers over hundreds, with the captains
11. 9 captains over the hundreds did according
11. 10 to the captains over hundreds did the
11. 15 commanded the captains of the hundreds
14. 13 brake down the wall..four hundred cubits
18. 14 appointed..three hundred talents of silver
19. 35 an hundred fourscore and five thousand
23. 33 tribute of an hundred talents of silver
1 Ch. 4. 42 five hundred men, went to mount Seir
5. 18 thousand seven hundred and threescore
5. 21 of sheep two hundred and fifty thousand
5. 21 they took away..men an hundred thous.
7. 2 two and twenty thousand and six hundred
7. 9 (was) twenty thousand and two hundred
7. 11 thousand and two hundred (soldiers), fit
8. 40 sons, and sons' sons, an hundred and fifty
9. 6 and their brethren, six hundred and ninety
9. 9 brethren..nine hundred and fifty and six
9. 13 thousand and seven hundred and threes.
9. 22 porters..(were) two hundred and twelve
11. 11 lifted up his spear against three hundred
11. 20 lifting..his spear against three hundred
12. 14 one of the least (was) over an hundred, and
12. 24 (were) six thousand and eight hundred
12. 25 men..seven thousand and one hundred
12. 26 of Levi, four thousand and six hundred
12. 27 (were) three thousand and seven hundred
12. 30 twenty thousand and eight hundred
12. 32 the heads of them (were) two hundred; and
12. 35 twenty and eight thousand and six hund.
12. 37 an hundred and twenty thousand
13. 1 the captains of thousands and hundreds
15. 5 and his brethren an hundred and twenty
15. 6 and his brethren two hundred and twenty
15. 7 and his brethren an hundred and thirty
15. 8 the chief, and his brethren two hundred
15. 10 and his brethren an hundred and twelve
18. 4 but reserved of them an hundred chariots
21. 3 an hundred times so many more as they
21. 5 an hundred thousand men that drew sword
21. 5 Judah (was) four hundred threescore and
21. 25 six hundred shekels of gold by weight
22. 14 an hundred thousand talents of gold, and
25. 7 was two hundred fourscore and eight
26. 26 the captains over thousands and hundreds
26. 30 a thousand and seven hundred, (were)
26. 32 thousand and seven hundred chief fathers
27. 1 captains of thousands and hundreds, and
28. 1 and captains over the hundreds, and the
29. 6 the captains of thousands and of hundreds
29. 7 and one hundred thousand talents of iron
2 Ch. 1. 2 captains of thousands and of hundreds
1. 14 had a thousand and four hundred chariots
1. 17 chariot for six hundred (shekels) of silver
1. 17 an horse for an hundred and fifty: and so
2. 2 thousand and six hundred to oversee them
2. 17 and they were found an hundred and fifty
2. 17 and three thousand and six hundred
2. 18 six hundred overseers to set the people
3. 4 and the height (was) an hundred and twen.
3. 8 gold, (amounting) to six hundred talents
3. 16 made an hundred pomegranates, and put
4. 8 And he made an hundred basins of gold
4. 13 hundred pomegranates on the two wreaths
5. 12 with them an hundred and twenty priests
7. 5 and an hundred and twenty thousand sh.
8. 10 two hundred and fifty, that bare rule over
8. 18 four hundred and fifty talents of gold
9. 9 an hundred and twenty talents of gold
9. 13 hundred and threescore and six talents of
9. 15 made two hundred targets (of) beaten gold
9. 15 six hundred (shekels) of beaten gold went

2 Ch. 9. 16 hundred shields (made he of) beaten gold
9. 16 three hundred (shekels) of gold went to
11. 1 hundred and fourscore thousand chosen
12. 3 twelve hundred chariots, and threescore
13. 3 (even) four hundred thousand chosen men
13. 3 with eight hundred thousand chosen men
13. 17 fell..five hundred thousand chosen men
14. 8 out of Judah three hundred thousand; and
14. 8 two hundred and fourscore thousand: all
14. 9 with an host..and three hundred chariots
15. 11 hundred oxen and seven thousand sheep
17. 11 seven thousand and seven hundred rams
17. 11 seven thousand and seven hundred he goa.
17. 14 men of valour three hundred thousand
17. 15 with..two hundred and fourscore thousand
17. 16 two hundred thousand mighty men of va.
17. 17 with bow and shield two hundred thousand
17. 18 an hundred and fourscore thousand ready
18. 5 gathered..of prophets four hundred men
23. 1 took the captains of hundreds, Azariah
23. 9 delivered to the captains of hundreds
23. 14 brought out the captains of hundreds
23. 20 he took the captains of hundreds, and the
24. 15 an hundred and thirty years old (was he)
25. 5 captains over hundreds, according to the
25. 5 three hundred thousand choice (men, able)
25. 6 hired also an hundred thousand mighty
25. 6 hired..for an hundred talents of silver
25. 9 what shall we do for the hundred talents
25. 23 brake down the wall..four hundred cub.
26. 12 men..(were) two thousand and six hund.
26. 13 three hundred thousand, and seven thou.
26. 13 five hundred, that made war with mighty
27. 5 same year an hundred talents of silver
28. 6 slew..hundred and twenty thousand in
28. 8 of their brethren two hundred thousand
29. 32 hundred rams, (and) two hundred lambs
29. 33 six hundred oxen and three thousand sh.
35. 8 hundred (small cattle), and three hundred
35. 9 (small cattle), and five hundred oxen
36. 3 an hundred talents of silver and a talent
Ezra 1. 10 of a second (sort) four hundred and ten
1. 11 (were) five thousand and four hundred
2. 3 two thousand an hundred seventy and two
2. 4 children..three hundred seventy and two
2. 5 of Arah, seven hundred seventy and five
2. 6 two thousand eight hundred and twelve
2. 7 a thousand two hundred fifty and four
2. 8 of Zattu, nine hundred forty and five
2. 9 of Zaccai, seven hundred and threescore
2. 10 of Bani, six hundred forty and two
2. 11 of Bebai, six hundred twenty and three
2. 12 a thousand two hundred twenty and two
2. 13 of Adonikam, six hundred sixty and six
2. 15 of Adin, four hundred fifty and four
2. 17 of Bezai, three hundred twenty and three
2. 18 children of Jorah, an hundred and twelve
2. 19 Hashum, two hundred twenty and three
2. 21 Beth-lehem, an hundred twenty and three
2. 23 Anathoth, an hundred twenty and eight
2. 25 Beeroth, seven hundred..forty and three
2. 26 and Gaba, six hundred twenty and one
2. 27 men of Michmas, an hundred twenty and
2. 28 and Ai, two hundred twenty and three
2. 30 of Magbish, an hundred fifty and six
2. 31 a thousand two hundred fifty and four
2. 32 of Harim, three hundred and twenty
2. 33 and Ono, seven hundred twenty and five
2. 34 of Jericho, three hundred forty and five
2. 35 three thousand and six hundred and thi.
2. 36 Jeshua, nine hundred seventy and three
2. 38 a thousand two hundred forty and seven
2. 41 of Asaph, an hundred twenty and eight
2. 42 (in) all an hundred thirty and nine
2. 58 (were) three hundred ninety and two
2. 60 of Nekoda, six hundred fifty and two
2. 64 thousand three hundred (and) threescore
2. 65 thousand three hundred thirty and seven
2. 65 two hundred singing men and singing w.
2. 66 Their horses (were) seven hundred thirty
2. 66 their mules, two hundred forty and five
2. 67 Their camels, four hundred thirty and fi.
2. 67 asses, six thousand seven hundred and
2. 69 They gave..one hundred priests' garments
8. 3 with him..of the males an hundred and
8. 4 Elihoenai..with him two hundred males
8. 5 Jahaziel, and with him three hundred ma.
8. 9 with him two hundred and eighteen males
8. 10 with him an hundred and threescore males
8. 12 and with him an hundred and ten males
8. 20 two hundred and twenty Nethinims: all
8. 26 six hundred and fifty talents of silver
8. 26 and silver vessels an hundred talents
8. 26 (and) of gold an hundred talents
Neh. 5. 17 my table an hundred and fifty of the Jews
7. 8 two thousand an hundred seventy and two
7. 9 Shephatiah, three hundred seventy and
7. 10 children of Arah, six hundred fifty and two
7. 11 two thousand and eight hundred (and) eig.
7. 12 Elam, a thousand two hundred fifty and
7. 13 children of Zattu, eight hundred forty and
7. 14 children of Zaccai, seven hundred and th.
7. 15 children of Binnui, six hundred forty and
7. 16 children of Bebai, six hundred twenty and
7. 17 two thousand three hundred twenty and
7. 18 Adonikam, six hundred threescore and se.
7. 20 children of Adin, six hundred fifty and fi.
7. 22 of Hashum, three hundred twenty and ei.
7. 23 of Bezai, three hundred twenty and four
7. 24 children of Hariph, an hundred and twe.
7. 26 The men..an hundred fourscore and eight
7. 27 Anathoth, an hundred twenty and eight

Neh. 7. 29 Beeroth, seven hundred forty and three
7. 30 of Ramah and Gaba, six hundred twenty
7. 31 of Michmas, an hundred and twenty and two
7. 32 men of..Ai, an hundred twenty and three
7. 34 a thousand two hundred fifty and four
7. 35 children of Harim, three hundred and tw.
7. 36 of Jericho, three hundred forty and five
7. 37 and Ono, seven hundred twenty and one
7. 38 three thousand nine hundred and thirty
7. 39 priests..nine hundred seventy and three
7. 41 a thousand two hundred forty and seven
7. 44 The singers..an hundred forty and eight
7. 45 The porters..an hundred thirty and eight
7. 60 All..(were) three hundred ninety and two
7. 62 The children..six hundred forty and two
7. 66 forty and two thousand three hundred and
7. 67 seven thousand three hundred thirty and
7. 67 two hundred forty and five singing men
7. 68 Their horses, seven hundred thirty and six
7. 68 their mules, two hundred forty and five
7. 69 camels, four hundred thirty and five
7. 69 six thousand seven hundred and twenty
7. 70 five hundred and thirty priests' garments
7. 71 two thousand and two hundred pound of
11. 6 four hundred threescore and eight valiant
11. 8 after him..nine hundred twenty and eight
11. 12 (were) eight hundred twenty and two
11. 13 his brethren..two hundred forty and two
11. 14 their brethren..an hundred twenty and
11. 18 Levites..two hundred fourscore and four
11. 19 porters..(were) an hundred seventy and
Esth. 1. 1 an hundred and seven and twenty provi.
1. 4 many days..an hundred and fourscore
8. 9 an hundred twenty and seven provinces
9. 6 Jews slew and destroyed five hundred
9. 12 The Jews have slain..five hundred men
9. 15 and slew three hundred men at Shushan
6. 30 the hundred twenty and seven provinces
Job 1. 3 five hundred yoke of oxen, and five hun.
42. 16 After this lived Job an hundred and forty
Prov 17. 10 more..than an hundred stripes into a fool
Eccl. 6. 3 If a man beget an hundred (children), and
8. 12 Though a sinner do evil an hundred times
Song 8. 12 those that keep the fruit thereof two hun.
Isa. 37. 36 a hundred and fourscore and five thous.
65. 20 the child shall die an hundred years old
65. 20 the sinner..an hundred years old, shall
Jer. 52. 23 pomegranates..an hundred round about
52. 29 eight hundred thirty and two persons
52. 30 seven hundred forty and five persons
52. 30 all..(were) four thousand and six hundred
Eze. 4. 5, 9 three hundred and ninety days
40. 19 hundred cubits eastward and northward
40. 23, 27 from gate to gate..an hundred cubits
40. 47 an hundred cubits long, and an hundred
41. 13 an hundred cubits long..an hundred cub.
41. 14 Also the breadth..an hundred cubits
41. 15 an hundred cubits, with the inner temple
42. 2 Before the length of an hundred cubits
42. 8 before the temple (were) an hundred cubits
42. 16, 17, 18, 19 He measured..five hundred
42. 20 five hundred..long, and five hundred br.
45. 2 five hundred..with five hundred..square
45. 15 one lamb out of the flock, out of two hu.
48. 16, 16, 16, 16 four thousand and five hund.
48. 30, 32, 33, 34 four thousand and five hundred
48. 17, 17, 17, 17 and toward..two hundred and
Dan. 8. 14 Unto two thousand and three hundred d.
12. 11 a thousand two hundred and ninety days
12. 12 three hundred and five and thirty days
Amos 5. 3 (by) a thousand shall leave an hundred
5. 3 went forth (by) an hundred shall leave

3. *Hundred*, מֵאָה *meah.*
Ezra 6. 17 And offered..an hundred bullocks
6. 17 two hundred rams, four hundred lambs
7. 22 Unto an hundred talents of silver, and to
7. 22 an hundred measures of wheat, and to an
7. 22 hundred baths of wine, and to an hundred
Dan. 6. 1 an hundred and twenty princes, which

4. *Hundred*, ἑκατόν *hekaton.*
Matt 18. 12 If a man have an hundred sheep, and one
18. 28 servants, which owed him an hundred
Mark 4. 8 thirty, and some sixty, and some an hund.
4. 20 thirty fold, some sixty, and some..hund.
Luke 15. 4 What man of you, having an hundred sh.
16. 6 And he said, An hundred measures of oil
16. 7 And he said, An hundred measures of
John 19. 39 and aloes, about an hundred pound (we.)
21. 11 fishes, an hundred and fifty and three
Acts 1. 15 together were about an hundred and tw.
Rev. 7. 4 an hundred (and) forty (and) four thous.
14. 1 an hundred forty (and) four thousand
14. 3 the hundred (and) forty (and) four thou.
21. 17 an hundred (and) forty (and) four cubits

HUNDRED, five —
Five hundred, πεντακόσιοι *pentakosioi.*
Luke 7. 41 one owed five hundred pence, and the other
1 Co. 15. 6 he was seen of above five hundred breth.

HUNDRED, four —
Four hundred, τετρακόσιοι *tetrakosioi.*
Acts 5. 36 men, about four hundred, joined themse.
7. 6 and entreat (them) evil four hundred ye.
13. 20 judges about the space of four hundred
Gal. 3. 17 law, which was four hundred and thirty
[*See* Six, three, two.]

HUNDRED thousand thousand —
Myriads of myriads, μυριάδες μυριάδων.
Rev. 9. 16 (were) two hundred thousand thousand

HUNDRED years old —
Hundred years of age, ἑκατονταέτης *hekatontaetēs.*
Rom. 4. 19 when he was about an hundred years old

HUNDRED FOLD —
1. *Hundred steps, times*, מֵאָה פְעָמִים [*meah paam*].
2 Sa. 24. 3 how many soever they be, an hundred fold
2. *Hundred measures*, מֵאָה שְׁעָרִים [*meah shaar*].
Gen. 26. 12 received in the same year an hundred fold
3. *Hundred fold*, ἑκατονταπλασίων *hekatontaplasiōn.*
Matt 19. 29 shall receive an hundred fold, and shall
Mark 10. 30 he shall receive an hundred fold now in
Luke 8. 8 sprang up, and bare fruit an hundred fold
4. *Hundred*, ἑκατόν *hekaton.*
Matt 13. 8, 23 some an hundredfold, some sixty fold

HUNDREDTH —
Hundred, מֵאָה *meah.*
Gen. 7. 11 In the six hundredth year of Noah's life
8. 13 in the six hundredth and first year, in the
Neh. 5. 11 the hundredth (part) of the money, and

HUNDREDS, by —
By hundreds, a hundred each, ἀνὰ ἑκατόν *ana hek.*
Mark 6. 40 sat down in ranks, [by hundreds]..fifties

HUNGER —
1. *Hunger, famine*, רָעָב *raab.*
Exod. 16. 3 to kill this whole assembly with hunger
Deut. 28. 48 in hunger, and in thirst, and in nakedness
32. 24 burnt with hunger, and devoured with bur.
Neh. 9. 15 bread from heaven for their hunger, and
Jer. 38. 9 he is like to die for hunger in the place
Lam. 2. 19 thy young children, that faint for hunger
4. 9 are better than (they that be) slain with h.
Eze. 34. 29 they shall be no more consumed with hu.
2. *Hunger, famine*, λιμός *limos.*
Luke 15. 17 have bread enough..and I perish with h.
2 Co. 11. 27 hunger and thirst, in fastings often, in c.
Rev. 6. 8 to kill with sword, and with hunger, and

HUNGER, to (have or suffer) —
1. *To hunger, be hungry*, רָעֵב *raeb.*
Psa. 34. 10 The young lions do lack, and suffer hunger
Prov 19. 15 sleep; and an idle soul shall suffer hunger
Isa. 49. 10 They shall not hunger nor thirst; neither
Jer. 42. 14 nor have hunger of bread; and there will
2. *To hunger*, πεινάω *peinaō.*
Matt. 5. 6 Blessed (are) they which do hunger and
21. 18 as he returned into the city, he hungered
Luke 4. 2 when they were ended, he afterward hu.
6. 21 Blessed..that hunger now: for ye shall
6. 25 Woe unto you that are full! for ye shall hu.
John 6. 35 he that cometh to me shall never hunger
Rom. 12. 20 if thine enemy hunger, feed him; if he
1 Co. 4. 11 we both hunger, and thirst, and are naked
11. 34 if any man hunger, let him eat at home
Rev. 7. 16 They shall hunger no more, neither thirst

HUNGER, to suffer to —
To cause or suffer to be hungry, רָעֵב *raeb*, 5.
Deut. 8. 3 suffered thee to hunger, and fed thee with

HUNGER BITTEN —
Hungry, famished, רָעֵב *raeb.*
Job 18. 12 His strength shall be hunger bitten, and

HUNGERED, to be an —
To hunger, πεινάω *peinaō.*
Matt. 4. 2 he had fasted..he was afterward an hung.
12. 1 his disciples were an hungered, and began
12. 3 what David did, when he was an hungered
25. 35 I was an hungered, and ye gave me meat
25. 37 Lord, when saw we thee an hungered, and
25. 42 I was an hungered, and ye gave ..e no meat
25. 44 when saw we thee an hungered, or athirst
Mark 2. 25 when he had need, and was an hungered
Luke 6. 3 what David did, when himself was an hu.

HUNGRY —
1. *Hungry, famished*, רָעֵב *raeb.*
1 Sa. 2. 5 hungry ceased: so that the barren hath
2 Sa. 17. 29 The people (is) hungry, and weary, and
2 Ki. 7. 12 They know that we (be) hungry; therefore
Job 5. 5 Whose harvest the hungry eateth up, and
22. 7 thou hast withholden bread from the h.
24. 10 they take away the sheaf (from) the hun.
Psa. 107. 5 Hungry and thirsty, their soul fainted in
107. 9 and filleth the hungry soul with goodness
107. 36 there he maketh the hungry to dwell, that
146. 7 which giveth food to the hungry. The L.
Prov. 25. 21 If thine enemy be hungry, give him bread
27. 7 to the hungry soul every bitter thing is
Isa. 8. 21 pass through it hardly bestead and hun.
9. 20 snatch on the right hand, and be hungry
29. 8 It shall even be as when an hungry (man)
32. 6 to make empty the soul of the hungry
44. 12 yea, he is hungry, and his strength faileth
58. 7 (Is it) not to deal thy bread to the hungry
58. 10 thou draw out thy soul to the hungry, and
Eze. 18. 7, 16 hath given his bread to the hungry, and
2. *To hunger*, πεινάω *peinaō.*
Luke 1. 53 He hath filled the hungry with good things

HUNGRY, to be —
1. *To hunger, be hungry, famished*, רָעֵב *raeb.*
Psa. 50. 12 If I were hungry, I would not tell thee
Prov. 6. 30 steal to satisfy his soul when he is hungry
Isa. 8. 21 when they shall be hungry, they shall fret
65. 13 my servants shall eat, but ye shall be hun.
2. *To hunger*, πεινάω *peinaō.*
Mark 11. 12 when they were come from B., he was h.
1 Co. 11. 21 and one is hungry, and another is drunken
Phil. 4. 12 both to be full and to be hungry, both to

HUNGRY, very —
Very hungry, πρόσπεινος *prospeinos.*
Acts 10. 10 became very hungry, and would have eaten

HUNT, to —
1. *To hunt, lie in wait*, צָדָה *tsadah.*
1 Sa. 24. 11 not sinned..yet thou huntest my soul to
2. *To hunt, lie in wait*, צוּד *tsud.*
Gen. 27. 5 Esau went to the field to hunt (for) venison
Lev. 17. 13 hunteth and catcheth any beast or fowl
Job 10. 16 Thou huntest me as a fierce lion; and again
38. 39 Wilt thou hunt the prey for the lion, or
Psa. 140. 11 evil shall hunt the violent man to overth.
Prov. 6. 26 the adulteress will hunt for the precious
Jer. 16. 16 they shall hunt them from every mountain
Lam. 4. 18 They hunt our steps, that we cannot go in
Mic. 7. 2 they hunt every man his brother with a
3. *To hunt*, צוּד *tsud*, 3a.
Eze. 13. 18 make kerchiefs upon the head..to hunt
13. 18 Will ye hunt the souls of my people, and
13. 20 wherewith ye there hunt the souls to make
13. 20 the souls that ye hunt to make (them) fly
4. *To pursue*, רָדַף *radaph.*
1 Sa. 26. 20 when one doth hunt a partridge in the m.

HUNTED, to be —
A hunting, object for hunting, מְצוּדָה *metsudah.*
Eze. 13. 21 shall be no more in your hand to be hunt.

HUNTER —
1. *Hunter*, צַיָּד *tsayyad.*
Jer. 16. 16 after will I send for many hunters, and
2. *Hunting*, צַיִד *tsayid.*
Gen. 10. 9 He was a mighty hunter before the LORD
10. 9 Nimrod the mighty hunter before the L.
25. 27 Esau was a cunning hunter, a man of the

HUNTING, (to take in) —
Hunting, צַיִד *tsayid.*
Gen. 27. 30 Esau his brother came in from his hunting
Prov 12. 27 roasteth not that which he took in hunting

HU'-PHAM, חוּפָם *protected.*
A son of Benjamin, founder of the family of the Huphamites. B.C. 1670. In Gen. 46. 21, and 1 Ch. 7. 12, the name is given *Huppim*.
Num 26. 39 of H., the family of the Huphamites

HU-PHA-MITES, חוּפָמִי.
The patronymic of a family that sprang from the preceding.
Num 26. 39 of Hupham, the family of the H.

HUP'-PAH, חֻפָּה *protection.*
A priest in the time of David who had charge of the 13th of the 24 courses in the service of the sanctuary. B.C. 1015.
1 Ch. 24. 13 The thirteenth to H., the fourteenth to

HUP'-PIM, חֻפִּים *protection.*
Head of a Benjamite family; he was either a son of Bela or of Ir or Iri, one of Bela's five sons. B.C. 1670.
Gen. 46. 21 Ehi, and Rosh, Muppim, and H., and Ard
1 Ch. 7. 12 Shuppim also, and H., the children of Ir
7. 15 Machir took to wife (the sister) of H. and

HUR, חוּר *free, noble.*
1. A man who with Aaron stayed up the hands of Moses at Rephidim during the battle with Amalek. The Jewish tradition is that he was the husband of Miriam and the grandfather of Bezaleel. B.C. 1491.
Exod 17. 10 Moses, Aaron, and H., went up to the top
17. 12 Aaron and H. stayed up his hands, the
24. 14 Aaron and H. (are) with you: if any man
2. A son of Caleb the son of Hezron.
Exod 31. 2 Bezaleel the son of Uri, the son of H., of
35. 30 Bezaleel the son of Uri, the son of H., of
38. 22 Bezaleel the son of Uri, the son of H., of
1 Ch. 2. 19 Caleb took..Ephrath, which bare him H.
2. 20 And H. begat Uri, and Uri begat Bezaleel
2 Ch. 1. 5 that Bezaleel the son of Uri, the son of H.
3. The fourth of the five kings of Midian that were slain with Balaam. B.C. 1452.
Num 31. 8 Evi, and Rekem, and Zur, and H., and R.
Josh. 13. 21 Evi, and Rekem, and Zur, and H., and R.
4. A commissariat officer of Solomon in Mount Ephraim. B.C. 1014.
1 Ki. 4. 8 these..their names: The son of H., in
5. The father of Caleb and eldest son of Ephratah. B.C 1490.
1 Ch. 2. 50 These were the sons of Caleb the son of H.
4. 4 These..the sons of H...the father of Bet.
6. A son of Judah; but really a member of a different generation. B.C. 1700.
1 Ch. 4. 1 sons of Judah..Carmi, and H., and Sho.
7. The ruler of half of Jerusalem in the time of Nehemiah. B.C. 460.
Neh. 3. 9 next..repaired Rephaiah the son of H.

HU'-RAI, חוּרַי *free, noble.*
One of David's guard from the torrents of Gaash. B.C. 1048. In 2 Sa. 23. 30 the *r* is changed to *d.*, and the name given there is *Hiddai*.
1 Ch. 11. 32 H. of the brooks of Gaash, Abiel the Arb

HU'-RAM, חוּרָם *noble, free.*
1. Son of Bela son of Benjamin. B.C. 1670.
1 Ch. 8. 5 And Gera, and Shephuphan, and H.
2. The king of Tyre, who is called Hiram in 2 Sa. 5. 11. B.C. 1015.
2 Ch. 2. 3 Solomon sent to H. the king of Tyre, saying
2. 12 H. said moreover, Blessed (be) the LORD
3. The Tyrian artificer employed by Solomon.
2 Ch. 4. 11 H. made the pots..H. finished the work that
4. 16 all their instruments, did H. his father m.

HU'-RI, חוּרִי *linen weaver.*
The father of Abihail a chief man in the time of Gad. B.C. 1240.
1 Ch. 5. 14 These..the children of Abihail the son of H.

HURL, to —
To cast (away, down, off, out), שָׁלַךְ *shalak*, 5.
Num 35. 20 hurl at him by laying of wait, that he die

HURL as a storm, to —
To frighten, שָׂעַר *saar*, 3.
Job 27. 21 and as a storm hurleth him out of his place

HURT —
1. *A thing*, דָּבָר *dabar.*
1 Sa. 20. 21 peace to thee, and no hurt, (as) the LORD
2. *Injury*, חֲבוּלָה *chabulah.*
Dan. 6. 22 also before thee, O king, have I done no h.
3. *Bruise*, חַבּוּרָה *chabburah.*
Gen. 4. 23 for I have slain..a young man to my hurt
4. *Hurt*, חֲבָל *chabal.*
Dan. 3. 25 walking in..the fire, and they have no h
5. *Hurt*, חֲבָל *chabal.*
Dan. 6. 23 no manner of hurt was found upon him
6. *To cause loss*, נְזַק *nezaq*, 5.
Ezra 4. 22 why should damage grow to the hurt of
7. *Evil*, רַע *ra.*
Gen. 26. 29 That thou wilt do us no hurt, as we have
31. 29 It is in..my hand to do you hurt: but the
1 Sa. 24. 9 saying, Behold, David seeketh thy hurt?
2 Sa. 18. 32 all that rise against thee to do (thee) hurt
2 Ki. 14. 10 why shouldest thou meddle to (thy) hurt
2 Ch. 25. 19 why shouldest thou meddle to (thine) hu.
Esth. 9. 2 to lay hand on such as sought their hurt
Psa. 35. 4 brought to confusion that devise my hurt
35. 26 confusion together that rejoice at mine h.
38. 12 they that seek my hurt speak mischievous
41. 7 hate me..against me do they devise my h.
70. 2 and put to confusion, that desire my hurt
71. 13 Let them be confounded..that seek my h.
71. 24 are brought unto shame, that seek my h.
Eccl. 5. 13 kept for the owners thereof to their hurt
8. 9 one man ruleth over another to his own h.
Jer. 7. 6 neither walk after other gods to your hurt
24. 9 I will deliver them..for (their) hurt, (to)
25. 7 provoke me to anger..to your own hurt
38. 4 man seeketh not the welfare..but the hurt
8. *To do or suffer evil*, רָעַע *raa*, 5.
Psa. 15. 4 sweareth to (his own) hurt; and changeth
9. *Fracture, breaking, breach*, שֶׁבֶר, שֶׁבֶר *sheber.*
Jer. 6. 14 They have healed also the hurt..of my p.
8. 11 they have healed the hurt of the daughter
8. 21 For the hurt..of my people
10. 19 Woe is me for my hurt! my wound is griev.
10. *Reproach, injury*, ὕβρις *hubris.*
Acts 27. 10 this voyage will be with hurt and much

HURT, to (do) —
1. *To destroy, injure*, חֲבַל *chabal*, 3.
Dan. 6. 22 that they have not hurt me: forasmuch as
2. *To cause to blush, put to shame*, כָּלַם *kalam*, 5.
1 Sa. 25. 7 now thy shepherds..we hurt them not
3. *To smite, plague*, נָגַף *nagaph.*
Exod 21. 22 If men strive, and hurt a woman with c.
21. 35 if one man's ox hurt another's, that he die
4. *To afflict*, עָנָה *anah*, 3.
Psa. 105. 18 Whose feet they hurt with fetters: he was
5. *To inspect*, פָּקַד *paqad.*
Isa. 27. 3 lest (any) hurt it, I will keep it night and
6. *To do or suffer evil, treat ill, afflict*, רָעַע *raa*, 5.
Gen. 31. 7 your father..God suffered him not to hurt
Num 16. 15 not taken..neither have I hurt one of them
Josh 24. 20 he will turn and do you hurt, and consume
Isa. 11. 9 They shall not hurt nor destroy in all my
65. 25 They shall not hurt nor destroy in all my
Jer. 25. 6 provoke me not..and I will do you no hurt
7. *To do wrong, injustice*, ἀδικέω *adikeō.*
Luke 10. 19 and nothing shall by any means hurt you
Rev. 2. 11 He that overcometh shall not be hurt of
6. 6 and (see) thou hurt not the oil and the
7. 2 to whom it was given to hurt the earth and
7. 3 Hurt not the earth, neither the sea, nor
9. 4 they should not hurt the grass of the earth
9. 10 their power (was) to hurt men five months
9. 19 and had heads..with them they do hurt
11. 5, 5 And if any man will hurt them
8. *To disable, weaken, hurt*, βλάπτω *blaptō.*
Mark 16. 18 [if they drink..it shall not hurt them]
Luke 4. 35 he came out of him, and hurt him not
9. *To do evil, use badly*, κακόω *kakoō.*
Acts 18. 10 and no man shall set on thee to hurt thee

HURT, to be —
1. *To be caused to blush, put to shame*, כָּלַם *kalam*, 6.
1 Sa. 25. 15 we were not hurt, neither missed we any
2. *To be grieved*, עָצַב *atsab*, 2.
Eccl. 10. 9 Whoso removeth stones shall be hurt there.
3. *To be broken, destroyed, hurt*, שָׁבַר *shabar*, 2.
Exod 22. 10 If..it die, or be hurt, or driven away, no
22. 14 if a man borrow..and it be hurt, or die
4. *To be broken, hurt*, שָׁבַר *shabar*, 6.
Jer. 8. 21 For..the daughter of my people am I h.

HURTFUL —
1. *To cause loss*, נְזַק *nezaq*, 5.
Ezra 4. 15 hurtful unto kings and provinces, and that
2. *Evil*, רַע *ra.*
Psa. 144. 10 delivereth..his servant from the hurtful s.
3. *Disabling, weakening, hurtful*, βλαβερός *blab.*
1 Ti. 6. 9 many foolish and hurtful lusts, which dr.

HURTING —
To do or suffer evil, treat ill, afflict, רָעַע *raa*, 5.
1 Sa. 25. 34 which hath kept me back from hurting thee

HUSBAND —
1. *A man*, אִישׁ *ish.*
Gen. 3. 6 and gave also unto her husband with her
3. 16 thy desire (shall be) to thy husband, and he
16. 3 gave her to her husband Abram to be his
29. 32 now therefore my husband will love me
29. 34 Now this time will my husband be joined
30. 15 small matter that thou hast taken my hus.?
30. 18 because I have given my maiden to my hu.
30. 20 now will my husband dwell with me, beca
Lev. 19. 20 a bondmaid, betrothed to an husband
21. 3 for his sister..which hath had no husband
21. 7 take a woman put away from her husband
Num. 5. 13 and it be hid from the eyes of her husband
5. 19, 20, 29 gone aside (to another) instead of h.
5. 20 some man..with thee beside thine husb.
5. 27 and have done trespass against her husb.
30. 6 if she had at all an husband when she
30. 7, 11 her husband heard (it), and held his p.
30. 8 if her husband disallowed her on the day
30. 10 if she vowed in her husband's house, or
30. 12 if her husband hath utterly made them
30. 12 her husband hath made them void; and
30. 13 her husband may establish it, or her hu.
30. 14 if her husband altogether hold his peace
Deut 22. 23 If a damsel..be betrothed unto an husb.
24. 3 And (if) the latter husband hate her, and
24. 3 or if the latter husband die, which took
25. 11 draweth near for to deliver her husband
28. 56 her eye shall be evil toward the husband
Judg 13. 6 the woman came and told her husband
13. 9 Manoah her husband (was) not with her
13. 10 the woman..ran, and showed her husband
14. 15 Entice thy husband, that he may declare
19. 3 her husband arose, and went after her, to
20. 4 the husband of the woman that was slain
Ruth 1. 3 Naomi's husband died; and she was left
1. 5 was left of her two sons and her husband
1. 9 each (of you) in the house of her husband
1. 12 for I am too old to have an husband
1. 12 (if) I should have an husband also to night
1. 13 would ye stay for them from having hu.?
2. 1 And Naomi had a kinsman of her husba.
2. 11 hast done..since the death of thine hus.
1 Sa. 1. 8 Then said Elkanah her husband to her, H.
1. 22 went not up; for she said unto her husband
1. 23 Elkanah her husband said unto her, Do
2. 19 when she came up with her husband to
4. 19, 21 that her father in law and her husband
25. 19 But she told not her husband Nabal
2 Sa. 3. 16 her husband went with her along weeping
11. 26 heard that Uriah her husband was dead
14. 5 widow woman, and mine husband is dead
14. 7 shall not leave to my husband..name nor
2 Ki. 4. 1 Thy servant my husband is dead; and
4. 9 she said unto her husband, Behold now, I
4. 14 she hath no child, and her husband is old
4. 22 she called unto her husband, and said, S.
4. 26 (is it) well with thy husband? (is it) well
Jer. 6. 11 the husband with the wife shall be taken
Eze. 16. 32 taketh strangers instead of her husband!
16. 45 that loatheth her husband and her child.
44. 25 for sister that hath had no husband, they
Hos. 2. 2 she (is) not my wife, neither (am) I her h.
2. 7 I will go and return to my first husband
2. *A man*, אֱנוֹשׁ *enosh.*
Ruth 1. 11 sons..that they may be your husbands?
Jer. 29. 6 give your daughters to husbands, that they
Eze. 16. 45 loathed their husbands and their children
3. *Lord, master, owner, possessor*, בַּעַל *baal.*
Exod 21. 22 as the woman's husband will lay upon him
Deut 22. 22 lying with a woman married to an husb.
24. 4 Her former husband, which sent her away
2 Sa. 11. 26 was dead, she mourned for her husband
Esth. 1. 17 they shall despise their husbands in their
1. 20 all the wives shall give to their husbands h.
Prov 12. 4 A virtuous woman (is) a crown to her h.
31. 11 The heart of her husband doth safely trust
31. 23 Her husband is known in the gates, when
31. 28 her husband (also), and he praiseth her
Joel 1. 8 Lament like a virgin..for the husband of
4. *Son-in-law, bridegroom, husband*, חָתָן *chathan.*
Exod. 4. 25 Surely a bloody husband (art) thou to me
4. 26 she said, A bloody husband..because of
5. *Friend*, רֵעַ *rea.*
Jer. 3. 20 a wife treacherously departeth from her h.
6. *A man*, ἀνήρ *anēr.*
Matt. 1. 16 Jacob begat Joseph the husband of Mary
1. 19 Joseph her husband, being a just (man)
Mark 10. 12 if a woman shall put away her husband
Luke 2. 36 had lived with an husband seven years
16. 18 her that is put away from (her) [husband]
John 4. 16 saith..Go, call thy husband, and come h.
4. 17 I have no husband..well said, I have no h.
4. 18 hast..five husbands..is not thy husband
Acts 5. 9 feet of them which have buried thy hus.
5. 10 the young men..buried (her) by her hus.
Rom. 7. 2 is bound by the law to (her) husband so
7. 2 husband be dead..the law of (her) husb.
7. 3 while (her) husband liveth..if her husband
1 Co. 7. 2 let every woman have her own husband
7. 3 Let the husband..the wife unto the hus.
7. 4 but the husband..the husband hath not
7. 10 Let not the wife depart from (her) husband
7. 11 to (her) husband: and let not the husband
7. 13 the woman which hath an husband that b.
7. 14 the unbelieving husband is sanctified by
7. 14 and the..wife is sanctified by the [husband]
7. 16 O wife, whether thou shalt save (thy) h.?
7. 34 careth..how she may please (her) husband
7. 39 as her husband liveth; but if her husband
14. 35 let them ask their husbands at home: for
2 Co. 11. 2 I have espoused you to one husband, that
Gal. 4. 27 more children than she which hath an h.
Eph. 5. 22 submit yourselves unto your own husba.
5. 23 the husband is the head of the wife, even
5. 24 so (let) the wives (be) to their own husb.
5. 25 Husbands, love your wives, even as Christ
5. 33 the wife (see) that she reverence (her) h.
Col. 3. 18 submit yourselves unto your own husba.
3. 19 Husbands, love (your) wives, and be not
1 Ti. 3. 2 the husband of one wife, vigilant, sober, of
3. 12 Let the deacons be the husbands of one
Titus 1. 6 If any be blameless, the husband of one
2. 5 obedient to their own husbands, that the
1 Pe. 3. 1 in subjection to your own husbands; that
3. 5 being in subjection unto their own husb.
3. 7 Likewise, ye husbands, dwell with (them)
Rev. 21. 2 prepared as a bride adorned for her hus.

HUSBAND, to be or have an —
1. *To rule, possess, have, marry*, בָּעַל *baal.*
Deut 21. 13 shalt go in unto her, and be her husband
Jer. 31. 32 although I was an husband unto them
Isa. 54. 5 For thy Maker (is) thine husband; The L.
2. *One under a man*, ὕπανδρος *hupandros.*
Rom 7. 2 For the woman which hath an husband is

HUSBAND, loving one's —
Lover of a husband, φίλανδρος *philandros.*
Titus 2. 4 to love their husbands, to love their

HUSBANDMAN —
1. *Husbandman, ploughman*, אִכָּר *ikkar.*
2 Ch. 26. 10 husbandmen..and vine dressers in the
Jer. 31. 24 there shall dwell in Judah..husbandmen
51. 23 the husbandman and his yoke of oxen
Joel 1. 11 Be ye ashamed, O ye husbandmen; howl
Amos 5. 16 they shall call the husbandmen to mour.
2. *To be an husbandman*, יָגַב *yagab* [V.L. גבים].
2 Ki. 25. 12 vinedressers and husbandmen; Jer. 52. 16.
3. *A man of the ground or soil*, אִישׁ אֲדָמָה *ish adamah.*
Gen. 9. 20 Noah began (to be) an husbandman, and
4. *A tiller of the ground*, אִישׁ עֹבֵד אֲדָמָה [*ish*].
Zech 13. 5 I (am) no prophet, I (am) an husbandman
5. *Cultivator of the soil*, γεωργός *geōrgos.*
Matt 21. 33 let it out to husbandmen, and went into
21. 34 he sent his servants to the husbandmen
21. 35 the husbandmen took his servants, and
21. 38 when the husbandmen saw the son, they
21. 40 what will he do unto those husbandmen?
21. 41 will let out (his) vineyard unto other hu.
Mark 12. 1 let it out to husbandmen, and went into
12. 2 to the husbandmen..from the husband.
12. 7 those husbandmen said among themselves
12. 9 He will come and destroy the husbandmen
Luke 20. 9 let it forth to husbandmen, and went into
20. 10 to the husbandmen..but the husbandmen
20. 14 when the husbandmen saw him, they rea.
20. 16 He shall come and destroy these husband
John 15. 1 I am the true vine..my Father is the hu.
2 Ti. 2. 6 The husbandman that laboureth must be
Jas. 5. 7 the husbandman waiteth for the precious

HUSBANDRY —
1. *Ground, soil*, אֲדָמָה *adamah.*
2 Ch. 26. 10 Also he built towers..for he loved husba.
2. *Cultivation of the soil*, γεώργιον *geōrgion.*
1 Co. 3. 9 For..ye are God's husbandry..God's bui.

HUSBAND'S brother —
Husband's brother, יָבָם *yabam.*
Deut 25. 5 her husband's brother shall go in unto h.
25. 7 My husband's brother refuseth to raise up

HUSBAND'S brother, to perform the duty of —
To marry a deceased brother's widow, יָבַם *yabam*, 3.
Deut 25. 5, 7 perform the duty of..husband's brother

HU'-SHAH, חוּשָׁה *haste.*
A son of Ezer of the tribe of Judah. B.C. 1450. It may be the name of a place, or the patronymic of a family.
1 Ch. 4. 4 father of Gedor, and Ezer the father of H.

HU'-SHAI, חוּשַׁי *quick.*
An inhabitant of Eric, and the friend of David in assisting to counteract and overthrow the counsels of Ahithophel. B.C. 1024.
2 Sa. 15. 32 H. the Archite came to meet him with
15. 37 So H., David's friend, came into the city
16. 16 H...David's friend, was come unto Absa.
16. 16 H. said unto Absalom, God save the king
16. 17 Absalom said to H., (Is) this thy kindness
16. 18 H. said unto Absalom, Nay; but whom
17. 5 Then said Absalom, Call now H. the Arc.
17. 6 when H. was come to Absalom, Absalom
17. 7 And H. said unto Absalom, The counsel
17. 8 For, said H., thou knowest thy father and
17. 14 The counsel of H. the Archite (is) better
17. 15 Then said H. unto Zadok and to Abiathar
1 Ki. 4. 16 Baanah the son of H. (was) in Asher and
1 Ch. 27. 33 H. the Archite..the king's companion

HU'-SHAM, חֻשָׁם, חוּשָׁם *hasting.*
A Temanite who became king of Edom. B.C. 1500.
Gen. 36. 34 H. of the land of Temani reigned in his
36. 35 H. died, and Hadad..reigned in his stead
1 Ch. 1. 45 H. of the land of the Temanites reigned
1. 46 when H. was dead, Hadad..reigned in his

HU-SHA-THITE, חֻשָׁתִי.
The patronymic of the family of Hushah of the tribe of Judah.
2 Sa. 21. 18 then Sibbechai the H. slew Saph, which
23. 27 Abiezer the Anethothite, Mebunnai the H.
1 Ch. 11. 29 Sibbecai the H., Ilai the Ahohite
20. 4 which time Sibbechai the H. slew Sippai
27. 11 for the eighth month (was) Sibbecai the H.

HU'-SHIM, חוּשִׁים, חֻשִׁים, חֻשִׁם *hasting.*
1. Son of Dan. B.C. 1680. In Num. 26. 42 the name is changed to *Shuham.*
Gen. 46. 23 And the sons of Dan; H.
2. The son of Aher the Benjamite. B.C. 1650.
1 Ch. 7. 12 children of Ir, (and) H., the sons of Aher
3. One of the two wives of Shaharaim, and the mother of two of his sons. B.C. 1400. *Ahitub* is *Abitub* in the Hebrew.
1 Ch. 8. 8 Shaharaim..H. and Baara (were) his wives
8. 11 And of H. he begat Ahitub, and Elpaal

HUSK —
1. *Husk,* זָג *zag.*
Num. 6. 4 nothing..from the kernels even to the hu.
2. *Sack, bag, husk,* צִקְלוֹן *tsiqlon.*
2 Ki. 4. 42 and full ears of corn in the husk thereof
3. *Pod, carob pod,* κεράτιον *keration.*
Luke 15. 16 with the husks that the swine did eat

HUZ, עוּץ *firm.*
This name is elsewhere given as *Uz,* the eldest son of Nahor and Milcah. See BUZ, UZ.
Gen. 22. 21 H. his first born, and Buz his brother, and

HUZ'-ZAB, הֻצַּב *established.*
The "Zab country," or fertile tract of Assyria E. of the Tigris, drained by the upper and lower Zab rivers (*Zab Ala* and *Zab Asfal*)—the A-*diab*-ene of the geographers. This was the most fertile and valuable part of Assyria, and might well stand for Assyria itself, with which Pliny and Ammianus identify it. *Zeb* (as applied to the rivers) is very ancient, being found in the great inscription of Tiglath-Pileser I., which belongs to the middle of the 12th century B.C.
Nah. 2. 7 H. shall be led away captive, she shall be

HY-ME-NÆ'-US, Ὑμέναιος *nuptial.*
One who had fallen into various errors and excommunicated by Paul.
1 Ti. 1. 20 Of whom is H. and Alexander; whom I
2 Ti. 2. 17 a canker: of whom is H. and Philetus

HYMN —
Hymn, song of praise, ὕμνος *humnos.*
Eph. 5. 19 in psalms and hymns and spiritual songs
Col. 3. 16 in psalms and hymns and spiritual songs

HYMN, to sing a —
To sing a song of praise, ὑμνέω *humneō.*
Matt 26. 30 when they had sung an hymn, Mark 14. 26.

HYPOCRISY —
1. *Profanation,* חֹנֶף *choneph.*
Isa. 32. 6 to practise hypocrisy, and to utter error
2. *Hypocrisy, dissimulation,* ὑπόκρισις *hupokrisis.*
Matt 23. 28 within ye are full of hypocrisy and iniq.
Mark 12. 15 he, knowing their hypocrisy, said unto th.
Luke 12. 1 the leaven of the Pharisees, which is hy.
1 Ti. 4. 2 Speaking lies in hypocrisy; having their
1 Pe 2. 1 hypocrisies, and envies, and all evil spea.

HYPOCRITE —
1. *Profane,* חָנֵף *chaneph.*
Job 8. 13 and the hypocrite's hope shall perish
13. 16 for an hypocrite shall not come before him
15. 34 For the congregation of hypocrites (shall)
17. 8 shall stir up himself against the hypocr.
20. 5 the joy of the hypocrite (but) for a mom.?
27. 8 what (is) the hope of the hypocrite, though
36. 13 But the hypocrites in heart heap up wrath
Prov 11. 9 An hypocrite with (his) mouth destroyeth
Isa. 9. 17 every one (is) an hypocrite and an evil doer
33. 14 fearfulness hath surprised the hypocrites
2. *A profane man,* אָדָם חָנֵף *adam chaneph.*
Job 34. 30 That the hypocrite reign not, lest the peo.
3. *Hypocrite, actor,* ὑποκριτής *hupokritēs.*
Matt. 6. 2 as the hypocrites do in the synagogues and
6. 5 thou shalt not be as the hypocrites (are)
6. 16 when ye fast, be not, as the hypocrites, of
7. 5 Thou hypocrite, first cast out the beam out
15. 7 hypocrites, well did Esaias prophesy of
16. 3 [hypocrites], ye can discern the face of the
22. 18 Jesus..said, Why tempt ye me..hypocr.?
23. 13, 15, 25, 26, 27, 29 woe unto you..hypocrites
23. 14 [Woe unto you..Pharisees, hypocrites!]
24. 51 appoint..his portion with the hypocrites
Mark 7. 6 Well hath Esaias prophesied of you hypo.
Luke 6. 42 Thou hypocrite, cast out first the beam
11. 44 [Woe unto you..Pharisees, hypocrites, for]
12. 56 hypocrites, ye can discern the face of the
13. 15 hypocrite, doth not each one of you on the

HYPOCRISY, without —
Without hypocrisy or dissimulation, ἀνυπόκριτος.
Jas. 3. 17 without partiality, and without hypocrisy

HYPOCRITICAL —
Profane, חָנֵף *chaneph.*
Psa. 35. 16 With hypocritical mockers in feasts, they
Isa. 10. 6 I will send him against an hypocritical

HYSSOP —
1. *Hyssop, organy,* אֵזוֹב *ezob.*
Exod 12. 22 ye shall take a bunch of hyssop, and dip
Lev. 14. 4, 49 and cedar wood, and scarlet, and hyssop
14. 6 cedar wood, and the scarlet, and the hyssop
14. 51 cedar wood, and the hyssop, and the scar.
14. 52 with the cedar wood, and with the hyssop
Num 19. 6 take cedar wood, and hyssop, and scarlet
19. 18 shall take hyssop, and dip (it) in the water
1 Ki. 4. 33 the hyssop that springeth out of the wall
Psa. 51. 7 Purge me with hyssop, and I shall be clean
2. *Hyssop,* ὕσσωπος *hussōpos.*
John 19. 29 a sponge with vinegar, and put (it) upon h.
Heb. 9. 19 he took..hyssop, and sprinkled..the book

I

I —
1. *I, I myself,* אֲנָה, אֲנָא *ana, anah.*
Ezra 6. 12 I Darius have made a decree; let it be done
7. 21 I Artaxerxes the king, do make a decree
Dan. 2. 8 I know of certainty that ye would gain the
2. 23 I thank thee, and praise thee, O thou God
3. 25 He answered and said, Lo, I see four men
4. 4 I Nebuchadnezzar was at rest in mine ho.
4. 7 and I told the dream before them; but
4. 9 I know that the spirit of the holy gods (is)
4. 18 This dream I king Nebuchadnezzar have
4. 30 Is not this great Babylon, that I have built
4. 34 at the end of the days I Nebuchadnezzar
4. 37 Now I Nebuchadnezzar praise and extol
5. 16 I have heard of thee, that thou canst make
7. 15 I Daniel was grieved in my spirit in the
2. *I, I myself,* אֲנִי *ani.*
Gen. 6. 17 I..do bring a flood of waters upon the ea.
9. 12 This (is) the token of the covenant which I
3. *I, I myself,* אָנֹכִי *anoki.*
Gen. 3. 10 because I (was) naked; and..hid myself
4. *I, I myself,* ἐγώ *egō.*
Matt. 3. 11 I indeed baptize you with water unto re.
[This word occurs 350 times so translated.]
5. *Me,* ἐμέ *eme.*
John 3. 30 He must increase, but I (must) decrease
9. 4 I must work the works of him that sent
6. *To me,* ἐμοί *emoi.*
Acts 21. 37 And..he said..May I speak unto thee?
22. 6 as I made my journey, and was come nigh
Rom. 7. 21 that, when I would do good, evil is pre.
Gal. 6. 14 But God forbid that I should glory, save
7. *And I, I also,* κἀγώ = *kai egō.*
Acts 26. 29 such as I am, except these bonds
2 Co. 11. 16 as a fool receive me, that I may boast
Gal. 4. 12 for I (am) as ye (are): ye have not injured
1 Th. 3. 5 For this cause, when I could no longer
8. *Me,* μέ *me.*
Matt 16. 13 Whom do men say that I the Son of man
16. 15 He saith unto them..whom say ye that I
26. 32, 35; Mark 8. 27, 29; 10. [36]; 14. 28, 31; Luke 2. 49; 4. 43; 9. 18, 20; 10. 35; 11. 18; 13. 33; 19. 5, 27; 22. 15; John 10. 16; Acts 11. 15; 13. [25]; 16. 30; 18. [21]; 19. 21, 21; 22. 17; 25. 10; Rom. 15. 16, 19; 2 Co. 2. 3, 13; 7. 7; 12. 21; Gal. 4. 18; Eph. 6. 20; Phil. 1. 7; Col. 4. 4.
9. *To me,* μοί *moi.*
Acts 3. 6 Peter said, Silver and gold have I none
18. 10 to hurt thee: for I have much people in
21. 37 he said unto the chief captain, May I sp.
22. 6 as I made my journey, and was come ni.
22. 17 that, when I was come again to Jerusalem
26. 29 altogeth. such as I am, except these bonds
Rom. 7. 10 the commandment..I found (to be) unto
9. 2 That I have great heaviness and continual
1 Co. 5. 12 For what have I to do to judge them also
9. 16 I have nothing to glory of: for necessity
10. *Of me,* μοῦ *mou.*
Matt 3. 11 that cometh after me is mightier than I
Mark 1. 7 There cometh one mightier than I after
Luke 3. 16 one mightier than I cometh, the latchet
22. 53 When I was daily with you in the temple
John 14. 28 rejoice..for my Father is greater than I
Acts 22. 17 while I prayed in the temple, I was in a
24. 20 any evil..while I stood before the council
25. 15 About whom, when I was at Jerusalem
1 Co. 4. 18 some are puffed up, as though I would not
2 Ti. 1. 12 able to keep that which I have commit.
Heb. 8. 9 when I took them by the hand to lead
11. *My heart,* לִבִּי [*leb*].
Neh. 5. 7 Then I consulted with myself, and..reb.
12. *Before me,* קָדָמַי [*qodam*].
Dan. 4. 2 I thought it good to show the signs and
6. 26 I make a decree, That in every dominion
[*See also* And, even, so.]

I also —
And I, I also, κἀγώ = *kai egō.*
Matt. 2. 8 that I may come and worship him also
[*See also* 10. 32, 33; 16. 18; 21. 24; Mark. 11. [29]; Luke 20. 3; Rom. 3. 7; 2 Co. 11. 18, 21; Eph. 1. 15; Phil. 2. 19; Rev. 2. 6; 3. 10; Acts. 10. 26.]
[*See* Even.]

I AM THAT I AM, or I AM, אֶהְיֶה אֲשֶׁר אֶהְיֶה *or* אֶהְיֶה.
A name indicating rather the *unsearchableness* of God than his mere *existence,* as commonly supposed. [*hayah*]
Exod. 3. 14 God said unto Moses, I AM THAT I AM
3. 14 Thus shalt thou say..I AM hath sent me

I in likewise —
And I, I also, κἀγώ = *kai egō.*
Matt 21. 24 I in likewise will tell you by what autho.

I have —
There is, there are, יֵשׁ *yesh.*
Gen. 33. 9 Esau said, I have enough, my brother
33. 11 Take, I pray thee..because I have enough
Ruth. 1. 12 If I should say, I have hope, (if) I should
1 Ki. 17. 12 I have not a cake, but an handful of meal
1 Ch. 29. 3 I have of mine own proper good, of gold

I would —
If, O that, לוּ *lu.*
Gen. 30. 34 I would it might be according to thy word
Num 22. 29 I would there were a sword in mine hand

IB'-HAR, יִבְחָר *chooser.*
A son of David, born in Jerusalem. B.C. 1030.
2 Sa. 5. 15 I. also, and Elishua, and Nepheg, and Ja.
1 Ch. 3. 6 I. also, and Elishama, and Eliphelet
14. 5 And I., and Elishua, and Elpalet

IB-LE'-AM, יִבְלְעָם *place of victory.*
A city of Manasseh, but in the territory of either Issachar or Asher (Josh. 17. 11). It was near the modern *Jenim,* at the place to the N. of it, now called *Jelama.*
Josh. 17. 11 Manasseh had..I. and her towns, and the
Judg. 1. 27 nor the inhabitants of I. and her towns
2 Ki. 9. 27 at the going up to Gur, which (is) by I.

IB-NE'-IAH, יִבְנְיָה *Jah is builder.*
A son of Jeroham a Benjamite and a chief man of the tribe in the first settlement in Jerusalem. B.C. 480.
1 Ch. 9. 8 I. the son of Jeroham, and Elah the son

IB-NI'-JAH, יִבְנִיָּה *Jah is builder.*
A Benjamite whose offspring dwelt in Jerusalem. B.C. 480.
1 Ch. 9. 8 Shephathiah..son of Reuel, the son of I.

IB-RI, עִבְרִי *passer over, Hebrew.*
A Merarite in the time of David. B.C. 1015.
1 Ch. 24. 27 Beno, and Shoham, and Zaccur, and I.

IB'-ZAN, אִבְצָן *splendid.*
A native of Bethlehem and a judge of Israel for seven years, after Jephthah. He had thirty sons and thirty daughters; and having taken home thirty wives for his sons, he sent out his daughters to as many husbands. His Bethlehem was that in the tribe of Zebulon.
Judg 12. 8 after him I. of Beth-lehem judged Israel
12. 10 Then died I., and was buried at Beth-le.

ICE —
Cold, frost, ice, chrystal, קֶרַח, קֹרַח *qorach, qerach.*
Job. 6. 16 Which are blackish by reason of the ice
38. 29 Out of whose womb came the ice? and
Psa. 147. 17 He casteth forth his ice like morsels: who

I-CHA'-BOD, אִי־כָבוֹד *where (is) the honour, inglorious.*
Son of Phinehas and grandson of Eli. B.C. 1141.
1 Sa. 4. 21 she named the child I. saying, The glory
14. 3 Ahiah, the son of Ahitub, I.'s brother, the

I-CO-NI'-UM, Ἰκόνιον.
The modern *Konieh,* on the central plateau of Asia Minor, towards the W. and not far to the N. of the Taurus chain. This level district was anciently called *Lycaonia* (or "domain of Jove").
Acts 13. 51 they shook off the dust..and came unto I.
14. 1 it came to pass in I., that they went both
14. 19 there came..Jews from Antioch and I.
14. 21 they returned again to Lystra, and (to) I.
16. 2 by the brethren that were at Lystra and I.
2 Ti. 3. 11 which came unto me at Antioch, at I., at

ID-A'-LAH, יִדְאֲלָה *memorial of God.*
A town of Zebulun; probably *Kellah-al-chire,* six miles S.W. of *Semuniyeh,* about three miles S. of *Beit-lahm.*
Josh. 19. 15 Nahallal, and Shimron, and I., and Beth.

ID'-BASH, יִדְבָּשׁ *stout, corpulent.*
One of the three sons of Abi-etam, among the families of Judah. B.C. 1400.
1 Ch. 4. 3 father of Etam; Jezreel, and Ishma..I.

ID'-DO, עִדֹּא *festal, opportune.*
Father of Ahinadab, one of Solomon's commissariat officers. B.C. 1014.
1 Ki. 4. 14 Ahinadab the son of I. (had) Mahanaim

ID'-DO, יִדּוֹ *favourite.*
1. A descendant of Gershom, son of Levi. In verse 41 the name is *Adaiah*, where it is seen that he was an ancestor of Asaph the seer. B.C. 1300.
1 Ch. 6. 21 Joah his son, I. his son, Zerah his son, J.
2. A son of Zechariah of the tribe of Manasseh E. of Jordan, in the time of David. B.C. 1015.
1 Ch.27. 21 Of the half (tribe) of Manasseh..I. the son

ID'-DO, עִדּוֹ, יֶעְדּוֹ, יֶעְדִּי *festal, opportune.*
A seer that denounced the wrath of God against Jeroboam the son of Nebat. B.C. 960.
2 Ch. 9. 29 and in the visions of I. the seer against
12. 15 in the book..of I. the seer concerning ge.?
13. 22 (are) written in the story of the prophet I.

ID'-DO, עִדּוֹא, עִדּוֹ *festal, opportune.*
1. Ancestor of Zechariah the prophet. B.C. 600.
Ezra 5. 1 Zechariah the son of I., prophesied unto
6. 14 the prophet and Zechariah the son of I.
Zech. 1. 1, 7 Berechiah, the son of I., the prophet
2. A priest who returned from Babylon. B.C. 576.
Neh. 12. 4 I., Ginnetho, Abijah
12. 16 Of I., Zechariah; of Ginnethon, Meshul.

ID'-DO, אִדּוֹ *honourable.*
Chief of those that assembled at Casiphia at the time of the 2nd migration from Babylon in the reign of Artaxerxes Longimanus. B.C. 458. He was a Nethinim.
Ezra 8. 17 I sent them with commandment unto I.
8. 17 I told them what they should say unto I.

IDLE —
1. *Deceit, sloth,* רְמִיָּה *remiyyah.*
Prov 19. 15 sleep; and an idle soul shall suffer hunger
2. *To be feeble, idle, remiss,* רָפָה *raphah,* 2.
Exod. 5. 8 they (be) idle; therefore they cry, saying
5. 17 Ye (are) idle..idle: therefore ye say, Let
3. *Idle, unprofitable,* ἀργός *argos.*
Matt12. 36 idle word that men shall speak, they shall
20. 3 saw others standing idle in the market
20. 6 went out, and found others standing [idle]
20. 6 saith..Why stand ye here all the day idle?
1 Ti. 5. 13 they learn (to be) idle..and not only idle

IDLE tale —
Idle talk, λῆρος *lēros.*
Luke24. 11 their words seemed to them as idle tales

IDLENESS —
1. *Sloth,* עַצְלוּת *atsluth.*
Prov.31. 27 She..eateth not the bread of idleness
2. *Lowness, idleness,* שִׁפְלוּת *shiphluth.*
Eccl. 10. 18 through idleness of the hands the house
3. *To cause to rest or be quiet,* שָׁקַט *shaqat,* 5.
Eze. 16. 49 abundance of idleness was in her and in h.

IDOL —
1. *Iniquity, vanity,* אָוֶן *aven.*
Isa. 66. 3 burneth incense, (as if) he blessed an idol
2. *Terror, object of terror,* אֵימָה *emah.*
Jer. 50. 38 graven images, and they are mad upon..i.
3. *Mighty one, a god,* אֵל *el.*
Isa. 57. 5 Enflaming yourselves with idols under
4. *Nought, a thing of nought, idol,* אֱלִיל *elil.*
Lev. 19. 4 Turn ye not unto idols, nor make to your.
26. 1 Ye shall make you no idols nor graven
1 Ch. 16. 26 For all the gods of the people (are) idols
Psa. 96. 5 For all the gods of the nations (are) idols
97. 7 that boast themselves of idols: worship
Isa. 2. 8 Their land also is full of idols; they wor.
2. 18 And the idols he shall utterly abolish
2. 20 his idols of silver, and his idols of gold
10. 10 hand hath found the kingdoms of the id.
10. 11 as I have done unto Samaria and her idols
19. 1 the idols of Egypt shall be moved at his
19. 3 they shall seek to the idols, and to the
31. 7 his idols of silver, and his idols of gold
Hab. 2. 18 that..trusteth therein, to make dumb id.?
Zech.11.17 Woe to the idol shepherd that leaveth the
5. *Horror, a cause of trembling,* מִפְלֶצֶת *miphletseth.*
1 Ki.15. 13 because she had made an idol in a grove
15. 13 Asa destroyed her idol, and burnt (it) by
2 Ch.15. 16 because she had made an idol in a grove
15. 16 Asa cut down her idol, and stamped (it)
6. *Figure, idol,* סֶמֶל, סֵמֶל *semel.*
2 Ch.33. 7 he set a carved image, the idol which he
33. 15 he took away..the idol out of the house
7. *Grief, a cause of grief,* עָצָב *atsab.*
1 Sa. 31. 9 to publish (it in) the house of their idols
1 Ch.10. 9 to carry tidings unto their idols, and to
2 Ch.24. 18 served groves and idols: and wrath came
Psa.106. 36 they served their idols which were a snare
106. 38 whom they sacrificed unto the idols of C.
115. 4 Their idols (are) silver and gold, the work
135. 15 The idols of the heathen (are) silver and
Isa. 10. 11 Shall I not..do to Jerusalem and her idols
46. 1 their idols were upon the beasts, and upon
Jer. 50. 2 her idols are confounded, her images are
Hos. 4. 17 Ephraim (is) joined to idols: let him alone
8. 4 of..their gold have they made them idols
Hos. 13. 2 have made them..idols according to their
14. 8 What have I to do any more with idols?
Mic. 1. 7 all the idols thereof will I lay desolate: for
Zech 13. 2 I will cut off the names of the idols out of
8. *Grief, a cause of grief,* עֶצֶב *etseb.*
Jer. 22. 28 this man Coniah a despised broken idol?
9. *Grief, a cause of grief,* עֹצֶב *otseb.*
Isa. 48. 5 Mine idol hath done them, and my graven
10. *Form, idol,* צִיר *tsir.*
Isa. 45. 16 go to confusion..(that are) makers of idols
11. *Idol, image,* εἴδωλον *eidōlon.*
Acts 7. 41 offered sacrifice unto the idol, and rejoice.
15. 20 that they abstain from pollutions of idols
Rom. 2. 22 thou that abhorest idols, dost thou com.
1 Co. 8. 4 we know that an idol (is) nothing in the
8. 7 for some with conscience of the idol unto
10. 19 [What say I then? that the idol is any th.]
12. 2 carried away unto these dumb idols, even
2 Co. 6. 16 what..hath the temple of God with idols?
1 Th. 1. 9 how ye turned to God from idols to serve
1 Jo. 5. 21 Little children, keep yourselves from idols
Rev. 9. 20 they should not worship devils, and idols

IDOL, thing offered (in sacrifice) to or unto an —
What is sacrificed to an idol, εἰδωλόθυτον *eidōlothu.*
Acts 15. 29 ye abstain from meats offered to idols, and
21. 25 keep themselves from (things) offered to i.
1 Co. 8. 1 Now as touching things offered unto idols
8. 4 things that are offered in sacrifice unto i.
8. 7 some..eat (it) as a thing offered unto an i.
8. 10 to eat those things which are offered to i.
10. 19 that which is offered in sacrifice to idols
10. 28 This is [offered in sacrifice unto idols], eat
Rev. 2. 14 to eat things sacrificed unto idols, and to
2. 20 and to eat things sacrificed unto idols

IDOLATER —
Worshipper of idols, εἰδωλολάτρης *eidōlolatrēs.*
1 Co. 5. 10 covetous, or extortioners, or with idolat.
5. 11 if any..that is called a brother be..an id.
6. 9 neither fornicators, nor idolaters, no
10. 7 Neither be ye idolaters, as..some of them
Eph. 5. 5 nor covetous man, who is an idolater, h.
Rev. 21. 8 idolaters, and all liars, shall have their
22. 15 without (are) dogs..and idolaters, and

IDOLATROUS priests —
Servants, ascetics, כְּמָרִים *kemarim.*
2 Ki. 23. 5 he put down the idolatrous priests, whom

IDOLATRY —
1. *Healers, household idols,* תְּרָפִים *teraphim.*
1 Sa. 15. 23 stubbornness (is as) iniquity and idolatry
2. *Worship of idols,* εἰδωλολατρεία *eidōlolatreia.*
1 Co. 10. 14 Wherefore, my dearly beloved, flee from i.
Gal. 5. 20 Idolatry, witchcraft, hatred, variance
Col. 3. 5 evil..and coveteousness, which is idolatry
1 Pe. 4. 3 banquetings, and abominable idolatries

IDOLATRY, wholly given to —
Full of idols, κατείδωλος *kateidōlos.*
Acts 17. 16 when he saw the city wholly given to id.

IDOL'S temple —
Place of an idol, εἰδωλεῖον *eidōleion.*
1 Co. 8. 10 see thee..sit at meat in the idol's temple

IDOLS —
1. *What are rolled about, large idols,* גִּלּוּלִים *gillulim.*
Lev. 26. 30 cast..upon the carcases of your idols, and
Deut 29. 17 seen their abominations, and their idols
1 Ki. 15. 12 removed all the idols that his fathers had
21. 26 he did very abominably in following idols
2 Ki. 17. 12 they served idols, whereof the LORD had
21. 11 hath made Judah also to sin with his idols
21. 21 served the idols that his father served, and
23. 24 the idols, and all the abominations that
Jer. 50. 2 her idols are confounded, her images are
Eze. 6. 4 will cast down your slain..before your i.
6. 5 lay the dead carcases..before their idols
6. 6 and your idols may be broken and cease
6. 9 eyes. which go a whoring after their idols
6. 13 when their slain..shall be among their i.
6. 13 they did offer sweet savour to all their i.
8. 10 all the idols of the house of Israel, pour.
14. 3 these men have set up their idols in their
14. 4 setteth up his idols..multitude of his idols
14. 5 all estranged from me through their idols
14. 6 Repent, and turn..from your idols; and
14. 7 setteth up his idols in his heart, and put.
16. 36 with all the idols of thy abominations, and
18. 6, 15 eyes to the idols of the house of Israel
18. 12 hath lifted up his eyes to the idols, hath
20. 7 defile not yourselves with the idols of Eg.
20. 8 neither did they forsake the idols of Egypt
20. 16 sabbaths: for their heart went after their i.
20. 18 I said..nor defile yourselves with their i.
20. 24 and their eyes were after their fathers' i.
20. 31 ye pollute yourselves with all your idols
20. 39 every one his idols..and with your idols
22. 3 maketh idols against herself to defile her.
22. 4 hast defiled thyself in thine idols which
23. 7 with all their idols she defiled herself
23. 30 because thou art polluted with their idols
23. 37 with their idols have they committed ad.
23. 39 they had slain their children to their idols
23. 49 and ye shall bear the sins of your idols
30. 13 I will also destroy the idols, and I will
33. 25 Ye..lift up your eyes towards your idols
36. 18 for their idols (wherewith) they had poll.
36. 25 and from all your idols, will I cleanse you
Eze. 37. 23 any more with their idols, nor with their
44. 10 went astray away from me after their id.
44. 12 they ministered unto them before their i.
2. *Images (of the sun),* חַמָּנִים *chammanim.*
2 Ch. 34. 7 cut down all the idols throughout all the
3. *Healers, household gods,* תְּרָפִים *teraphim.*
Zech. 10. 2 For the idols have spoken vanity, and the

IDOLS, abominable —
Abominable or detestable thing, שִׁקּוּץ *shiqquts.*
2 Ch. 15. 8 put away the abominable idols out of all

I-DU-ME'-A, אֱדוֹם, Ἰδουμαία *territory of Edom.*
The Greek form of the name of Edom, the "field of Edom," or Mount Seir ("rugged") whose original inhabitants were called *Horites* from Hori the grandson of Seir, also because that name (*Hori*) was descriptive of their name as troglodites or dwellers in caves. See EDOM.
Isa. 34. 5 behold, it shall come down upon I., and
34. 6 hath..a great slaughter in the land of I.
Eze. 35. 15 shalt be desolate, O mount Seir, and all I
36. 5 have I spoken against..all I., which have
Mark 3. 8 from I., and (from) beyond Jordan; and

IF —
1. *Or, if,* אוֹ *o.*
Lev. 26. 41 if then their uncircumcised hearts be hu.
2. *If,* אִם *im.*
Gen. 4. 7 If thou doest well, shalt thou not be acc.?
43. 9 if I bring him not unto thee, and set him
3. *According as, when,* כַּאֲשֶׁר *ka-asher.*
Gen. 43. 14 If I be bereaved (of..children), I am ber.
4. *If, lo, though, whether, or, surely,* הֵן *hen.*
2 Ch. 7. 13 If I shut up heaven that there be no rain
7. 13 or if I command the locusts to devour the
Ezra 5. 17 if..good to the king, let there be search
Dan. 2. 5 if ye will not make known unto me the
3. 15 if ye be ready that at what time ye hear
3. 17 If it be (so), our God whom we serve is
4. 27 if it may be a lengthening of thy tranqu.
5. 16 now if thou canst read the writing, and
5. *That, because,* כִּי *ki.*
Gen. 4. 24 If Cain shall be avenged sevenfold, truly
6. *Though, if, O that,* לֻא *lu.*
2 Sa. 19. 6 I perceive, that if Absalom had lived, and
7. *O that, if,* לוּ *lu.*
Judg. 8. 19 if ye had saved them alive, I would not
13. 23 If the LORD were pleased to kill us, he
Job 16. 4 if your soul were in my soul's stead, I
Eze. 14. 15 If I cause noisome beasts to pass through
Mic. 2. 11 If a man walking in the spirit and false.
8. *If not, unless,* לוּלֵי *lule.*
Psa 124. 1, 2 If (it had not been) the LORD who was on
9. *Heel, consequence, because, seeing,* עֵקֶב *eqeb.*
Deut. 7. 12 if ye hearken to these judgments, and
10. *If,* εἰ *ei.*
Matt. 4. 3 If thou be the Son of God, command that
4. 6 If thou be the Son of God, cast thyself d.
5. 29 if thy right eye offend thee, pluck it out
5. 30 if thy right hand offend thee, cut it off
6. 23, 30; 7. 11; 8. 31; 10. 25; 11. 14, 21, 23; 12. 7, 26, 27, 28; 14. 28; 17. 4; 18. 8, 9; 19. 10, 17, 21; 22. 45; 23. 30; 24. 24, 43; 26. 24, 39, 42; 27. 40, [42,] 43.
Mark 3. 26; 9. 23; 11. 13, 25, [26]; 13. 22; 14. 21, 35; 15. 44.
Luke 4. 3, 9; 6. 32; 7. 39; 9. 23; 10. 13; 11. 13, 19, 20, 36; 12. 26, 28, 39, 49; 16. 11, 12, 31; 17. 6; 19. 42; 22. 42; 23. 31, 35, [37, 39].
John 1. 25; 3. 12; 4. 10; 5. 47; 7. 4, 23; 8. 19, 39, 42 46; 9. 41; 10. 24, 35, 37, 38; 11. 12; 21, [32]; 13. 14, 17 32; 14. 7, 28; 15. 18, 19, 20, 20; 18. 8, 23, 23, 36; 20. 15.
Acts 4. 9; 5. 39; 8. 22, [37]; 13. 15; 16. 15; 17. 27; 18. 14, 15; 19. 38, 39; 20. 16; 23. 9; 25. 11, 11; 27. 39.
Rom. 3. 3, 5, 7; 4. 2, 14; 5. 10, 15, 17; 6. 5, 8; 7. 16, 20; 8. 9, 10, 11; 13. 13, 17, 25, 31; 9. 22; 11. 6, [6,] 12, 15, 16, 16, 17, 18, 21, 24; 12. 18; 14. 15; 15. 27.
1 Co. 3. 12; 6. 2; 7. 9, 15, 36; 8. 2, 3, 13; 9. 2, 11, 11, 12, 17, 17; 10. 27, 30; 11. 6, 6, 16, 31, 34; 12. 17, 17, 19; 14. 35, 38; 15. 2, 12, 13, 14, 16, 17, 19, 29, 32, 32.
2 Co. 2. 2, 5; 3. 7, 9, 11; 5. [14]; 8. 12; 11. 4, 30.
Gal. 1. 10; 2. 14, 17, 18, 21; 3. 18, 21, 29; 4. 7, 15; 5. 11, 15, 18, 25; 6. 3; Phil. 1. 22; Col. 2. 20; 3. 1; 1 Th. 4. 14; 2 Th. 3. 14; 1 Ti. 3. 5; 5. 4, 8, 10, 10, 10, 10, 10; 2 Ti. 2. 11, 12, 12, 13; Phile. 17, 18.
Heb. 2. 2; 4. 3, 5, 8; 7. 11; 8. 4, 7; 9. 13; 11. 15; 12. [7,] 8, 25; Jas. 1. 5, 26; 2. 8 [μέντοι], 9, 11; 3. 14; 4. 11; 1 Pe. 1. 6, 17, 19, 20, 20, 22; 3. 17; 4. 14, 16, 17, 18; 2 Pe. 2. 4, 20; 1 Jo. 2. 19; 3. 13; 4. 11; 5. 9.
11. *If indeed,* εἴγε *eige.*
Eph. 3. 2 If ye have heard of the dispensation of the
Col. 1. 23 If ye continue in the faith grounded and
12. *If also, even if,* εἰ καί *ei kai.*
Luke11. 18 If Satan also be divided against himself
1 Co. 4. 7 now if thou didst receive (it), why dost
7. 21 but if thou mayest be made free, use (it)
2 Co. 4. 3 if our gospel be hid, it is hid to them that
11. 15 no great thing if his ministers also be tra.
13. *If,* εἴτε *eite.*
1 Co.14. 27 If any man speak in an (unknown) tongue
14. *If,* ἐάν *ean.*
Matt. 4. 9 if thou wilt fall down and worship me
5. 13 if the salt have lost his savour, wherewith
5. 23 thou bring thy gift to the altar, and there

Matt. 5. 46 if ye love them which love you, what rewa.
5. 47 if ye salute your brethren only, what do
6. 14, 15, 22, 23; 7. [9, 10]; 8. 2; 9. 21; 10. 13, 13; 12.
11; 15. 14; 16. 26; 17. 20; 18. 12, 15, 15, 16, 17, 17, 19,
35; 21. 3, 21, 24, 25, 26; 22. 24; 24. 23, 26, 48; 28. 14.
Mark 1. 40; 3. 24, 25; 4. [26]; 7. 11; 8. 3, [36]; 9. 43, 45,
47, 50; 10. 12; 11. 3, 31, [32]; 12. 19; 13. 21; 14. 31.
Luke 4. 7; 5. 12; 6. 33, [34]; 10. 6; 11. [12]; 12. [38]; 14. 34;
15. 8; 16. 30; 17. 3, 3, 4; 19. 31. [40]; 20. 5, 28; 22. 67, 68;
John 3. 12; 5. 31, 43; 6. 51; 7. 17, 37; 8. 16, 24, 31, 36,
51, 52, 54, [55]; 9. 22, 31; 10. 9; 11. 9, 10, 40, 48, 57; 12.
24, 26, 26, 32, 47; 13. 8, 17, 35, 14. 3, 14, 15, 23; 15. 6, 7,
10, 14; 19. 7, 7; 19. 12; 21. 22, 23, 25.
Acts 5. 38; 9. 2; 26. 5; Rom. 2. 25, 25, 26; 7. 2, 3, 3; 10.
9; 11. 22, 23; 12. 20, 20; 13. 4; 14. 23; 15. 24; 1 Co. 4.
19; 5. 11; 6. 4; 7. 8, 11, 28, 28, 36, 39, 40; 8. 10; 9, 9,
16; 10. 28; 11. 14, 15; 12. 15, 16; 14. 6, 8, 11, 14, 23, 24,
28, 30; 16. 4, 7, 10; 2 Co. 5. 1; 9. 4; 13. 2.
Gal. 5. 2; 6. 1; Col. 3. 13; 4. 10; 1 Th. 3. [8]; 1 Ti. 1. 8;
2. 15; 2 Ti. 2. 5, 21; Heb. 3. 6, 7, 14, 15; 4. 7; 6. 3; 10.
38; 13. 23; Jas. 2. 2, 15, 17; 4. 15; 5. 19; 1 Pe. 3. 13; 1
Jo. 1. 6, 7, 8, 9, 10; 2. 1, 3, 15, 24, 29; 3. 20, 21; 4. 12,
20; 5. [14,] 15, 16; 3 Jo. 10; Rev. 3. 3, 20; 22. 18, 19.

15. *If also*, ἐὰν καί *ean kai*.
Gal. 6. 1 Brethren, if a man be overtaken in a fa.

16. *If*, ἐάνπερ *eanper*.
Heb. 3. 6 [if] we hold fast the confidence and the
3. 14 made partakers of Christ, if we hold the
6. 3 And this will we do, if God permit
[See also Also, and.]

IF a or any (man, thing) aught —
If any one, εἴ τις *ei tis*.
Matt 16. 24 If any (man) will come after me, let him
Mark 4. 23; 7. 16; 8. 23; 9. 22, 35; Luke 14. 26; 19.
8; Acts 24. 19, [20]; 25. 5; Rom. 13. 9; 1 Co. 3. 14, 15, 17,
18; 7. 12; 14. 37; 16. 22; 2 Co. 2. 10; 5. 17; 7. 14; 10. 7;
11. 20, 20, 20, 20, 20; Gal. 1. 9; Phil. 2. 1, 1, 1, 1; 3. 4,
15; 4. 8, 8; 2 Th. 3. 10; 1 Ti. 1. 10; 3. 1; 5. 16; 6. 3;
Tit. 1. 6; Jas. 1. 23; 3. 2; 1 Pe. 3. 1; 4. 11, 11; 2 Jo. 10;
Rev. 11. 5, [5]; 13. 9; 14. 9; Luke 9. 23; Rom. 8. 9; 1 Co.
3. 12; 7. 36; 8. 2, 3; 10. 27; 11. 16, 34; 14. 38; 2 Co. 2. 5;
Gal. 6. 3; 2 Th. 3. 14; 1 Ti. 3. 5; 5. 4, 8; Jas. 1. 5, 26.

IF by any means —
If any how, εἴ πως *ei pōs*.
Acts 27. 12 If by any means they might attain to Ph.
Rom. 1. 10; 11. 14; Phil. 3. 11.

IF, and —
If, ἐάν *ean*.
John 6. 62 and if ye shall see the Son of man ascend

IF also, also if —
1. *If also, but if also*, εἰ καί, *or* εἰ δὲ καί *ei de kai*.
Luke 11. 18 If Satan also be divided against himself
2 Co. 11. 15 if his ministers also be transformed as the
2. *Also if, even if*, κἄν *kan*.
Matt 21. 21 but also if ye shall say unto this mountain

IF . . but —
If, even if, κἄν *kan*.
Mark 5. 28 If I may touch but his clothes, I shall be
6. 56 if it were but the border of his garment

IF haply —
O that, if, לוּא *lu*.
1 Sa. 14. 30 if haply the people had eaten freely to day

IF, moreover —
If, אִם *im*.
2 Sa. 17. 13 Moreover if he be gotten into a city, then

IF not, (and) —
1. *If not, unless*, לוּלֵא *lule*.
Judg 14. 18 If ye had not ploughed with my heifer
2. *But if not*, εἰ δὲ μή *or* μήγε *ei de mēge*.
Luke 10. 6 rest upon it: if not, it shall turn to you
13. 9 and if not . . after that thou shalt cut it
John 14. 2 many mansions: if (it were) not (so), I w.
3. *If not*, εἰ μή *ei mē*.
John 9. 33 If this man were not of God, he could do
[*See also* 15. 22, 24; 18. 30; Acts 26. 32.]
4. *If not*, ἐὰν μή *ean mē*.
Matt. 6. 15 But if ye forgive not men their trespasses
[*See also* Matt. 10. 13; 18. 16, 35; John 8. 24; 13. 8; 15. 6;
16. 7; Rom. 11. 23; 1 Co. 8. 8; 9. 16; 14. 11, 28; Jas. 2.
17; 1 Jo. 3. 21; Rev. 3. 3.]

IF otherwise —
But if not, εἰ δὲ μήγε *ei de mēge*.
Luke 5. 36 if otherwise, then both the new maketh a
2 Co. 11. 16 if otherwise, yet as a fool receive me, that

IF peradventure —
Lest at any time, μήποτε *mēpote*.
2 Ti. 2. 25 if God peradventure will give them repe.

IF so —
If, ἐάν *ean*.
Matt. 18. 13 if so be that he find it, verily I say unto

IF so be —
If so be, it may be, unless, אוּלַי, אֻלַי *ulai*.
Josh. 14. 12 if so be the LORD (will be) with me, then
Hos. 8. 7 if so be it yield, the strangers shall swall.

IF so be (that) —
1. *If, if indeed, if at least*, εἴγε *eige*.
2 Co. 5. 3 [If so be that] being clothed we shall
Eph. 4. 21 if so be that ye have heard him, and have

2. *If so be*, εἴπερ (ἄρα) *eiper (ara)*.
Rom. 8. 9 if so be that the spirit of God dwell in you
8. 17 if so be that we suffer with (him), that we
1 Co. 15. 15 whom he raised not up, if so be that the
1 Pe. 2. 3 [if so be] ye have tasted that the Lord (is)

IF some —
If any one, εἴ τις *ei tis*.
Rom 11. 17 And if some of the branches be broken off

IF that —
1. *If, or, whether, lo, surely*, הֵן *hen*.
Ezra 4. 13 Be it known now unto the king, that if
4. 16 We certify the king, that if this city be
2. *If also*, εἰ καί *ei kai*.
Phil. 3. 12 if that I may apprehend that for wh.

IF yet —
If, if indeed, εἴγε καί *eige kai*.
Gal. 3. 4 so many things in vain? if (it be) yet in vain

IG'-AL, יִגְאָל *deliverer*.
1. Son of Joseph of the tribe of Issachar; one of the spies sent from Kadesh to search the land. B.C. 1491.
Num 13. 7 Of the tribe of Issachar, I. the son of Jo.
2. One of David's guard, and son of Nathan of Zobah. In 1 Ch. 11. 38 he is called *Joel* the brother of Nathan. *Igeal* is identical. B.C. 1048.
2 Sa. 23. 36 I. the son of Nathan of Zobah, Bani the

IG-E'-AL, יִגְאָל *deliverer*.
This name in the original Hebrew is identical with the preceding *Igal*. He was a son of Shemaiah a descendant of the royal house of Judah.
1 Ch. 3. 22 and the sons of Shemaiah; Hattush, and I.

IG-DAL'-IAH, יִגְדַּלְיָהוּ *Jah is great*.
Properly *Igdaljahu*. He was father of Hanan, who had a chamber in the temple in the days of Jeremiah. B.C. 640.
Jer. 35. 4 Hanan, the son of I., a man of God, which

IGNOMINY —
Shame, confusion, קָלוֹן *qalon*.
Prov. 18. 3 also contempt, and with ignominy repro.

IGNORANCE —
1. *Error, (wandering, going astray)*, שְׁגָגָה *shegagah*.
Lev. 4. 2 If a soul shall sin through ignorance
4. 22 done . . through ignorance (against) any of
4. 27 if any one . . sin through ignorance, while
5. 15 If a soul . . sin through ignorance, in the
5. 18 concerning his ignorance wherein he erred
Num 15. 24 if (ought) be committed by ignorance wi.
15. 25 it shall be forgiven them; for it (is) igno.
15. 25 sin offering before the Lord, for their ign.
15. 26 seeing all the people (were) in ignorance
15. 27 if any soul sin through ignorance, then
15. 28 when he sinneth by ignorance before the L.
15. 29 one law for him that sinneth through igno.
2. *Ignorance, want of knowledge*, ἄγνοια *agnoia*.
Acts. 3. 17 I wot that through ignorance ye did (it)
17. 30 the times of this ignorance God winked
Eph. 4. 18 alienated . . through the ignorance that is
1 Pe. 1. 14 according to the former lusts in your ig.
3. *Ignorance, want of knowledge*, ἀγνωσία *agnōsia*.
1 Pe. 2. 15 put to silence the ignorance of foolish men

IGNORANCE, to sin (ignorantly or) through —
1. *To err, go astray*, שָׁגַג *shagag*.
Num 15. 28 atonement for the soul that sinneth ignor.
2. *To err, go astray*, שָׁגָה *shagah*.
Lev. 4. 13 if the whole congregation . . sin through ig.

IGNORANT, to be —
1. *Not to know*, לֹא יָדַע *lo yada*.
Psa. 73. 22 So foolish (was) I, and ignorant: I was (as)
Isa. 56. 10 they are all ignorant, they (are) all dumb
63. 16 though Abraham be ignorant of us, and I.
2. *To be ignorant, without knowledge*, ἀγνοέω *agnoeō*.
Rom 10. 3 they being ignorant of God's righteousness
11. 25 I would not . . that ye should be ignorant
1 Co. 10. 1 I would not that ye should be ignorant
14. 38 if any man be ignorant, let him be ignor.
2 Co. 2. 11 advantage . . for we are not ignorant of his
1 Th. 4. 13 I would not have you to be ignorant, br.

IGNORANT —
1. *To be ignorant, without knowledge*, ἀγνοέω.
Rom. 1. 13 I would not have you ignorant, brethren
1 Co. 12 1 brethren, I would not have you ignorant
2 Co. 1. 8 we would not, brethren, have you ignorant
Heb. 5. 2 Who can have compassion on the ignorant
2. *A private person, plebeian*, ἰδιώτης *idiōtēs*.
Acts 4. 13 that they were unlearned and ignorant men

IGNORANT of, to be —
To be or lie hid, λανθάνω *lanthanō*.
2 Pe. 3. 5 For this they willingly are ignorant of
3. 8 be not ignorant of this one thing, that one

IGNORANTLY —
1. *Without knowledge*, בִּבְלִי דַעַת *bi-beli daath*.
Deut 19. 4 Whoso killeth his neighbour ignorantly
2. *To be ignorant, without knowledge*, ἀγνοέω *agnoeō*.
Acts 17. 23 Whom therefore ye ignorantly worship
1 Ti. 1. 13 I obtained mercy: because I did (it) ign.

I'-IM, עִיִּים *circles, heaps*.
1. The contracted form of *Ije-Abarim*, the 37th encampment of the Israelites after leaving Egypt, and the 26th from Sinai.
Num 33. 45 they departed from I., and pitched in D.
2. A town in the extreme S. of Judah.
Josh. 15. 29 Baalah, and I., and Azem

I-JE A-BA'-RIM, עִיֵּי הָעֲבָרִים *heaps of the further region*
One of the later halting-places of Israel as they were approaching Palestine. It was on the S. E. boundary of the territory of Moab, in the *Midbar*, i.e., the uncultivated wilderness. See ABARIM.
Num 21. 11 journeyed from Oboth, and pitched at I., in
33. 44 they departed from Oboth, and pitched in I.

I'-JON, עִיּוֹן *heap*.
A town of Naphtali in the N. of Palestine. It is now called *Merj Ayûn*, and is a few miles N.W. of the site of Dan.
1 Ki. 15. 20 Ben-hadad hearkened . . and smote I., and
2 Ki. 15. 29 came Tiglath-pileser . . and took I., and A.
2 Ch. 16. 4 they smote I., and Dan, and Abel-maim

IK'-KESH, עִקֵּשׁ *subtile*.
Father of Ira the Tekoite, one of David's thirty valiant men. B.C. 1070.
2 Sa. 23. 26 Helez the Paltite, Ira the son of I. the T.
1 Ch. 11. 28 Ira the son of I. the Tekoite, Abi-ezer the
27. 9 The sixth (captain . . was) Ira the son of I.

I'-LAI, עִילַי *elevated*.
An Ahohite and one of the heroes of David's guard. B.C. 1048. In 2 Sam. 23. 28 he is called *Zalmon*.
1 Ch. 11. 29 Sibbecai the Hushathite, I. the Ahohite

ILL —
1. *Evil*, רַע *ra*.
Deut 15. 21 if . . lame, or blind, (or have) any ill blem.
Isa. 3. 11 Woe unto the wicked! (it shall be) ill
2. *To be evil*, רָעַע *raa*.
Jer. 40. 4 if it seem ill unto thee to come with me
3. *Evil*, κακός *kakos*.
Rom 13. 10 Love worketh no ill to his neighbour: th

ILL, to deal or behave self —
To do or suffer evil, treat ill, רָעַע *raa*, 5.
Gen. 43. 6 Wherefore dealt ye (so) ill with me, (as)
Mic. 3. 4 as they have behaved themselves ill in

ILL favoured —
1. *Evil*, רַע *ra*.
Gen. 41. 20 the lean and ill favoured kine did; 41. 27.
2. *Evil (poor) in appearance*, רַע מַרְאֶה [*ra*].
Gen. 41. 3 other kine . . ill favoured and lean fleshed
41. 4 the ill favoured and lean fleshed; 41. 21.
3. *Evil (poor) in figure*, רַע תֹּאַר [*ra*].
Gen. 41. 19 poor and very ill favoured and lean fleshed

ILL, to go —
To be evil, יֵרַע *yera*.
Job 20. 26 it shall go ill with him that is left in his t.
Psa. 106. 32 so that it went ill with Moses for their sake

ILL savour —
Stench, צַחֲנָה *tsachanah*.
Joel 2. 20 his ill savour shall come up, because he h.

ILLUMINATE, to —
To make or give light, φωτίζω *phōtizō*.
Heb. 10. 32 after ye were illuminated, ye endured a gr.

IL-LY-RI'-CUM, Ἰλλυρικόν.
An extensive district lying along the E. coast of the Adriatic, from Italy on the N. to Epirus on the S., and contiguous to Mœsia and Macedonia on the E. The Drilo divided it into Illyris Barbara on the N. and Illyris Græca on the S. Within these limits was included Dalmatia, which name was ultimately used for the whole district.
Rom. 15. 19 unto I.; I have fully preached the gospel

IMAGE —
1. *Any thing set up, pillar or idol*, מַצֵּבָה *matstsebah*.
Exod 23. 24 Thou shalt . . quite break down their imag.
34. 13 ye shall destroy their altars, break their i.
Deut. 7. 5 break down their images, and cut down t.
16. 22 Neither shalt thou set thee up (any) image
1 Ki. 14. 23 high places, and images, and groves, on
2 Ki. 3. 2 he put away the image of Baal that his f.
10. 26 they brought forth the images out of the h.
10. 27 they brake down the image of Baal, and b.
17. 10 set them up images and groves in every h.
18. 4 brake the images, and cut down the grov
23. 14 he brake in pieces the images, and cut d
2 Ch. 14. 3 brake down the images, and cut down the
31. 1 brake the images in pieces,
Jer. 43. 13 He shall break also the images of Beth-s.
Hos. 3. 4 without an image, and without an ephod
10. 1 of his land they have made goodly images
10. 2 he shall break down . . shall spoil their im.
2. *Imagery*, מַשְׂכִּית *maskith*.
Lev. 26. 1 neither shall ye set up (any) image of st.
3. *Figure, idol*, סֶמֶל, סֵמֶל *semel*.
Eze. 8. 3 the seat of the image of jealousy, which
8. 5 behold . . this image of jealousy in the en.
4. *Grief, a cause of grief*, עָצָב *atsab*.
2 Sa. 5. 21 there they left their images, and David and

5. *Image,* צֶלֶם *tselem.*
Gen. 1. 26 Let us make man in our image, after our l.
1. 27 man in his..image, in the image of God c.
5. 3 begat..in his own likeness, after his image
9. 6 shed: for in the image of God made he m.
Num33. 52 destroy all their molten images, and quite
1 Sa. 6. 5 make images of your emerods, and images
6. 11 the mice..and the images of their emerods
2 Ki. 11. 18 his altars and his images brake they in p.
2 Ch. 23. 17 brake his altars and his images in pieces
Psa. 73. 20 O Lord..thou shalt despise their image
Eze. 7. 20 they made..images of their abominations
16. 17 madest to thyself images of men, and di.
23. 14 images of the Chaldeans pourtrayed with
Amos 5. 26 your images, the star of your god, which

6. *Image,* צְלֵם *tselem.*
Dan. 2. 31 Thou..sawest, and, behold, a great image
2. 31 This great image, whose brightness (was)
2. 32 This image's head (was) of fine gold, his b.
2. 34 a stone..smote the image upon his feet
2. 35 stone that smote the image became a g.
3. 1 Nebuchadnezzar the king made an image
3. 2 to come to the dedication of the image
3. 3 unto the dedication of the image that N.
3. 3 they stood before the image that Nebuc.
3. 5 ye fall down and worship the golden im.
3. 7 fell down (and) worshipped the golden i.
3. 10 shall fall down and worship the golden i.
3. 12, 14, 18 nor worship the golden image which
3. 15 ye fall down and worship the image which

7. *Similitude, form, likeness,* תְּמוּנָה *temunah.*
Job 4. 16 an image (was) before mine eyes..silence

8. *Image, likeness,* εἰκών *eikōn.*
Matt 22. 20 Whose (is) this image and superscription?
Mark 12. 16 Whose (is) this image and superscription?
Luke 20. 24 Whose image and superscription hath it?
Rom. 1. 23 into an image made like to corruptible man
8. 29 conformed to the image of his Son, that
1 Co. 11. 7 forasmuch as he is the image and glory
15. 49 the image of the earthy..image of the h.
2 Co. 3. 18 are changed into the same image from g.
4. 4 Christ, who is the image of God, should
Col. 1. 15 Who is the image of the invisible God, the
3. 10 after the image of him that created him
Heb. 10. 1 not the very image of the things, can
Rev. 13. 14 that they should make an image to the b.
13. 15 unto the image of the beast, that the im.
13. 15 as many as would not worship the image
14. 9 If any man worship the beast and his im.
14. 11 who worship the beast and his image, and
15. 2 the victory over the beast, and over his i.
16. 2 and (upon) them which worshipped his i.
19. 20 and them that worshipped his image
20. 4 not worshipped the beast, neither his im.
[*See also* Graven, molten.]

IMAGE, carved —
1. *Graven object,* פֶּסֶל *pesel.*
Judg 18. 18 fetched the carved image, the ephod, and
2 Ch. 33. 7 he set a carved image, the idol which he
2. *Graven objects,* פְּסִילִים *pesilim.*
2 Ch. 33. 22 Amon sacrificed unto all the carved im.
34. 3, 4 groves, and the carved images, and the

IMAGE, express —
Impressed character, χαρακτήρ *charaktēr.*
Heb. 1. 3 Who being..the express image of his pers.

IMAGE, standing —
Anything set up, מַצֵּבָה *matstsebah.*
Lev. 26. 1 neither rear you up a standing image
Mic. 5. 13 and thy standing images out of the midst

IMAGE (work) —
Movable work, צַעֲצֻעִים *tsaatsuim.*
2 Ch. 3. 10 he made two cherubim of image work

IMAGERY —
Imagery, מַשְׂכִּית *maskith.*
Eze. 8. 12 every man in the chambers of his imagery

IMAGES —
1. *Images (of the sun),* חַמָּנִים *chammanim.*
Lev. 26. 30 I will..cut down your images, and cast
2 Ch. 14. 5 took away..the high places and the images
34. 4 the images that (were) on high above them
Isa. 17. 8 have made, either the groves or the im.
27. 9 the groves and images shall not stand up
Eze. 6. 4 your images shall be broken; and I will
6. 6 your images may be cut down, and your
2. *Healers, household gods,* תְּרָפִים *teraphim.*
Gen. 31. 19 Rachel had stolen the images that (were)
31. 34 Rachel had taken the images, and put them
31. 35 he searched, but found not the images
1 Sa. 19. 13 Michal took an image, and laid (it) in the
19. 16 behold..an image in the bed, with a pil.
2 Ki. 23. 24 the images, and the idols, and all the ab.
Eze. 21. 21 he consulted with images, he looked in

IMAGINATION —
1. *Formation, imagination,* יֵצֶר *yetser.*
Gen. 6. 5 every imagination of the thoughts of his
8. 21 the imagination of man's heart (is) evil
Deut 31. 21 I know their imagination which they go
1 Ch. 28. 9 understandeth all the imaginations of the
29. 18 keep this for ever in the imagination of
2. *Stubbornness,* שְׁרִירוּת *sheriruth.*
Deut 29. 19 I walk in the imagination of mine heart
Jer. 3. 17 after the imagination of their evil heart
7. 24 in the imagination of their evil heart, and
Jer. 9. 14 after the imagination of their own heart
11. 8 every one in the imagination of their evil
13. 10 walk in the imagination of their heart
16. 12 ye walk every one after the imagination
18. 12 we will every one do the imagination of
23. 17 after the imagination of his own heart
3. *Thought, device,* מַחֲשֶׁבֶת *machashebeth.*
Prov. 6. 18 An heart that deviseth wicked imaginat.
Lam. 3. 60, 61 (and) all their imaginations against me
4. *Reasoning,* διαλογισμός *dialogismos.*
Rom. 1. 21 became vain in their imaginations, and
5. *Mind, understanding,* διάνοια *dianoia.*
Luke 1. 51 he hath scattered the proud in the imag.
6. *Reasoning,* λογισμός *logismos.*
2 Co. 10. 5 Casting down imaginations, and every

IMAGINE, to —
1. *To meditate, utter, mutter,* הָגָה *hagah.*
Psa. 2. 1 Why do..the people imagine a vain thing?
38. 12 and they..imagine deceits all the day lo.
2. *To devise, purpose,* זָמַם *zamam.*
Gen. 11. 6 nothing..which they have imagined to do
3. *To grave, devise, work,* חָרַשׁ *charash.*
Prov 12. 20 Deceit (is) in the heart of them that ima.
4. *To think, devise, reckon,* חָשַׁב *chashab.*
Job 6. 26 Do ye imagine to reprove words, and the
Psa. 10. 2 taken in the devices that they have ima.
21. 11 For..they imagined a mischievous device
140. 2 Which imagine mischiefs in..heart: con.
Nah. 1. 11 There is..come out of thee, that imagin.
Zech. 7. 10 let none of you imagine evil against his b.
8. 17 let none of you imagine evil in your hearts
5. *To think, devise, reckon,* חָשַׁב *chashab,* 3.
Hos. 7. 15 yet do they imagine mischief against me
Nah. 1. 9 What do ye imagine against the LORD?
6. *To care for, meditate,* μελετάω *meletaō.*
Acts 4. 25 Why did..the people imagine vain things?
[*See also* Mischief, wrongfully.]

IM'-LA, IM'-LAH, יִמְלָא, יִמְלָה *fulfilling.*
Progenitor of Michaiah, who was consulted by Ahab and Jehoshaphat before their expedition to Ramoth-gilead. B.C. 930.
1 Ki. 22. 8 (There is) yet one man, Micaiah the son of I.
22. 9 said, Hasten (hither) Micaiah the son of I.
2 Ch. 18. 7 the same (is) Micaiah, the son of I. And
18. 8 said, Fetch quickly Micaiah the son of I.

IM-MA-NU'-EL, עִמָּנוּאֵל *God (is) with us.*
A symbolic name given to the child who was announced to Ahaz and the people of Judah as the sign that God would give them deliverance from their enemies. Matthew applies it similarly to Jesus the Messiah. See EMMANUEL (Matt. 1. 23).
Isa. 7. 14 virgin shall conceive, and..call his name I.
8. 8 wings shall fill the breadth of thy land, O I.

IMMEDIATELY —
1. *From that very (hour),* ἐξαυτῆς *exautēs.*
Acts 10. 33 Immediately therefore I sent to thee; and
11. 11 immediately there were three men already
21. 32 Who immediately took soldiers and cen.
2. *Directly, straightway,* εὐθέως *eutheōs.*
Matt. 4. 22 they immediately left the ship and their
8. 3 And immediately his leprosy was cleansed
14. 31 immediately Jesus stretched forth (his) h.
20. 34 immediately their eyes received sight, and
24. 29 Immediately after the tribulation of those
26. 74 began he to curse..And [immediately] the
Mark 1. 31 [immediately] the fever left her, and she
1. 42 [immediately] the leprosy departed from
2. 8 [immediately] when Jesus perceived in his
2. 12 immediately he arose, took up the bed, and
4. 5 [immediately] it sprang up, because it had
4. 15 Satan cometh [immediately], and taketh
4. 16 [immediately] receive it with gladness
4. 17 affliction..ariseth..[immediately] they are
4. 29 [immediately] he putteth in the sickle, be.
5. 2 [immediately] there met him out of the
5. 30 Jesus, [immediately] knowing in himself
6. 27 [immediately] the king sent an executioner
6. 50 [immediately] he talked with them, and
10. 52 [immediately] he received his sight, and
14. 43 [immediately], while he yet spake, come. J.
Luke 5. 13 immediately the leprosy departed from
6. 49 [immediately] it fell; and the ruin of that
12. 36 that..they may open unto him immedia.
John 5. 9 immediately the man was made whole, and
6. 21 immediately the ship was at the land
13. 30 He..went [immediately] out: and it was
18. 27 Peter then denied again: and immediately
Acts 9. 18 immediately there fell from his eyes as it
9. 34 make thy bed. And he arose immediately
16. 10 immediately we endeavoured to go into
17. 10 the brethren immediately sent away Paul
17. 14 then immediately the brethren sent away
Gal. 1. 16 immediately I conferred not with flesh
Rev. 4. 2 immediately I was in the Spirit: and, be.
3. *Directly, straightway,* εὐθύς *euthus.*
Mark 1. 12 immediately the spirit driveth him into
1. 28 [immediately] his fame spread abroad thr.
John 21. 3 They..entered into a ship [immediately]
4. *Presently, along with the matter,* παραχρῆμα.
Luke 1. 64 his mouth was opened immediately, and
4. 39 immediately she arose and ministered unto
5. 25 immediately he rose up before them, and
Luke 8. 44 immediately her issue of blood stanched
8. 47 declared..how she was healed immediate.
13. 13 immediately she was made straight, and
18. 43 immediately he received his sight, and
19. 11 the kingdom of God should immediately
22. 60 immediately, while he yet spake, the cock
Acts 3. 7 immediately his feet and ancle bones rec.
12. 23 immediately the angel of the Lord smote
13. 11 immediately there fell on him a mist and
16. 26 immediately all the doors were opened

IM'-MER, אִמֵּר *projecting; prominent.*
1. Name of a family of priests who gave their name to the 16th course of the temple service. B.C. 536. See EMMER.
1 Ch. 9. 12 the son of Meshillemith, the son of I.
Ezra 2. 37 The children of I., a thousand fifty and
10. 20 of the sons of I.; Hanani and Zebadiah
Neh. 7. 40 The children of I., a thousand fifty and
11. 13 the son of Meshillemoth, the son of I.
2. A priest in the time of David to whom the charges of the sanctuary were assigned by lot. B.C. 1015.
1 Ch. 24. 14 The fifteenth to Bilgah, the sixteenth to I.
3. One who returned without a genealogy from Babylon. B.C. 536. But it may be the name of a place.
Ezra 2. 59 they which went up from Tel-melah..I.
Neh. 7. 61 Tel-haresha, Cherub, Addon, and I.
4. The father of Zadok. B.C. 536.
Neh. 3. 29 After them repaired Zadok the son of I.
5. A priest in Jeremiah's time. B.C. 630.
Jer. 20. 1 Now Pashur the son of I. the priest, who

IMMORTAL —
Incorruptible, ἄφθαρτος *aphthartos.*
1 Ti. 1. 17 Now unto the king eternal, immortal, in.

IMMORTALITY —
1. *Deathlessness,* ἀθανασία *athanasia.*
1 Co. 15. 53 and this mortal (must) put on immortality
15. 54 this mortal shall have put on immortality
1 Ti. 6. 16 Who only hath immortality, dwelling in
2. *Incorruption,* ἀφθαρσία *aphtharsia.*
Rom. 2. 7 seek for glory and honour and immortality
2 Ti. 1. 10 hath brought life and immortality to light

IMMUTABILITY, IMMUTABLE —
Unchangeable, immutable, ἀμετάθετος *ametathetos.*
Heb. 6. 17 to show..the immutability of his counsel
6. 18 That by two immutable things, in which

IM'-NA, יִמְנָע *withdrawing.*
A son of Helem, an Asherite and prince of the tribe. B.C. 1690.
1 Ch. 7. 35 sons of his brother Helem; Zophah, and I.

IM'-NAH, יִמְנָה *prosperity.*
1. The first born of Asher. In Gen. 46. 17 the name is given as *Jimnah* in the Common Version, though identical with the present. B.C. 1600.
1 Ch. 7. 30 The sons of Asher; I., and Isuah, and
2. Kore Ben-Imnah assisted in the reformation effected by Hezekiah. B.C. 740.
2 Ch. 31. 14 And Kore the son of I. the Levite, the p.

IMPART, to —
1. *To apportion,* חָלַק *chalaq.*
Job 39. 17 neither hath he imparted to her understa.
2. *To give a share of,* μεταδίδωμι *metadidōmi.*
Luke 3. 11 let him impart to him that hath none; and
Rom. 1. 11 that I may impart unto you some spiritual
1 Th. 2. 8 we were willing to have imparted unto

IMPEDIMENT in his speech, having an —
One who speaks with difficulty, μογιλάλος *mogilalos.*
Mark 7. 32 [one that..had an impediment in his sp.]

IMPENITENT —
Without a change of mind, ἀμετανόητος *ametanoē.*
Rom. 2. 5 after thy hardness and impenitent heart

IMPERIOUS —
Ruling, domineering, שַׁלֶּטֶת *shalleteth.*
Eze. 16. 30 the work of an imperious whorish woman

IMPLACABLE —
Implacable, irreconcileable, ἄσπονδος *aspondos.*
Rom. 1. 31 without natural affection, [implacable]

IMPLEAD, to —
To call into (court), ἐγκαλέω *egkaleō.*
Acts 19. 38 the craftsmen..let them implead one an.

IMPORTUNITY —
Barefacedness, ἀναίδεια *anaideia.*
Luke 11. 8 because of his importunity he will rise and

IMPOSE, to —
To impose, cast, throw, רְמָה *remah.*
Ezra 7. 24 to impose toll, tribute, or custom, upon

IMPOSED, to be —
To lie upon, ἐπίκειμαι *epikeimai.*
Heb. 9. 10 carnal ordinances, imposed..until the

IMPOSSIBLE —
1. *Powerless, weak, impossible,* ἀδύνατος *adunatos.*
Matt 19. 26 With men this is impossible; but with G.
Mark 10. 27 With men (it is) impossible, but not with
Luke 18. 27 The things which are impossible with men
Heb. 6. 4 For..impossible for those who were once
6. 18 in which (it was) impossible for God to lie
11. 6 But without faith (it is) impossible to ple.

2. *Not to be received or accepted,* ἀνένδεκτος *anend.*
Luke 17. 1 It is impossible but that offences will

IMPOSSIBLE, to be —
To be powerless, weak, impotent, ἀδυνατέω *aduna.*
Matt 17. 20 and nothing shall be impossible unto you
Luke 1. 37 For with God nothing shall be impossible

IMPOTENT (folk or man) —
1. *Powerless, weak, impotent,* ἀδύνατος *adunatos.*
Acts 14. 8 there sat a certain man at Lystra, impo.
2. *To be without strength,* ἀσθενέω *astheneō.*
John 5. 3 In these lay a..multitude of impotent folk
5. 7 The impotent man answered him, Sir, I
3. *Without strength,* ἀσθενής *asthenēs.*
Acts 4. 9 the good deed done to the impotent man

IMPOVERISH, to —
To make poor, רָשַׁשׁ *rashash, 3a.*
Jer. 5. 17 they shall impoverish thy fenced cities

IMPOVERISHED, to be —
1. *To become lean, poor, thin, weak,* דָּלַל *dalal,* 2.
Judg. 6. 6 Israel was greatly impoverished because
2. *To be impoverished, low,* סָכַן *sakan,* 4.
Isa. 40. 20 He that (is) so impoverished that he hath
3. *To be made poor,* רָשַׁשׁ *rashash,* 4.
Mal. 1. 4 Whereas Edom saith, We are impoverish.

IMPRISON, to —
To imprison, φυλακίζω *phulakizō.*
Acts 22. 19 Lord, they know that I imprisoned and

IMPRISONMENT —
1. *Band, fetter,* אֱסוּר *esur.*
Ezra 7. 26 confiscation of goods, or to imprisonment
2. *Watch, imprisonment,* φυλακή *phulakē.*
2 Co. 6. 5 In stripes, in imprisonments, in tumults
Heb. 11. 36 yea, moreover of bonds and imprisonm.

IMPUDENT —
1. *To make strong, harden,* עָזַז *azaz,* 5.
Prov. 7. 13 (and) with an impudent face said unto him
2. *Strong of forehead,* חֲזַק מֵצַח *chazaq metsach.*
Eze. 3. 7 all the house of Israel (are) impudent and
3. *Sharp of face,* קְשֵׁה פָנִים [*qasheh*].
Eze. 2. 4 For..impudent children, and stiffhearted

IMPUTE, to —
1. *To think, devise, reckon,* חָשַׁב *chashab.*
2 Sa. 19. 19 Let not my lord impute iniquity unto me
Psa. 32. 2 unto whom the LORD imputeth not iniqu.
2. *To put, place, set,* שׂוּם, שִׂים *sum, sim.*
1 Sa. 22. 15 Let not the king impute (any) thing unto
3. *To bring into account,* ἐλλογέω *ellogeō.*
Rom. 5. 13 sin is not imputed when there is no law
4. *To count, account, reckon,* λογίζομαι *logizomai.*
Rom. 4. 6 unto whom God imputeth righteousness
4. 8 man to whom the Lord will not impute
4. 11 that righteousness might be imputed unto
4. 22 therefore it was imputed to him for right.
4. 23 his sake alone, that it was imputed to him
4. 24 for us also, to whom it shall be imputed
2 Co. 5. 19 not imputing their trespasses unto them
Jas. 2. 23 it was imputed unto him for righteousness

IMPUTED, to be —
To be reckoned, חָשַׁב *chashab,* 2.
Lev. 7. 18 neither shall it be imputed unto him that
17. 4 blood shall be imputed unto that man

IM'-RAH, יִמְרָה *height of Jah.*
A chief of the tribe of Asher, and one of the family of Zophah. B.C. 1570.
1 Ch. 7. 36 The sons of Zophah; Suah..and I.

IM'-RI, אִמְרִי *projecting.*
1. A man of Judah through the family of Pharez. B.C. 536.
1 Ch. 9. 4 the son of Omri, the son of I., the son of
2. A progenitor of Zaccur, one of Nehemiah's assistants in rebuilding the wall. B.C. 470.
Neh. 3. 2 next to them builded Zaccur the son of I.

IN —
1. *Unto, to,* אֶל *el.*
Gen. 8. 21 the LORD said in his heart, I will not again
2. *With,* אֵת *eth.*
Gen. 6. 14 rooms shalt thou make in the ark, and
3. *In,* בְּמוֹ *bemo.*
Isa. 44. 16 He burneth part thereof in the fire; with
44. 19 I have burnt part of it in the fire; yea
4. *Sufficiency, for,* דַּי *dai.*
Jer. 51. 58 labour in vain, and the folk in the fire
5. *From, out of,* מִן *min.*
Gen. 21. 15 the water was spent in the bottle, and
6. *On, over, above,* עַל *al.*
Gen. 1. 20 may fly above the earth in the open firm.
Ezra 5. 15 let the house of God be builded in his pl.
6. 7 let..build this house of God in his place
Dan. 3. 16 not careful to answer thee in this matter
3. 28 delivered his servants that trusted in him
4. 8 But at the last Daniel came in before me
4. 10 Thus (were) the visions of mine head in
4. 29 he walked in the palace of the kingdom
Dan. 4. 36 I was established in my kingdom, and
5. 9 his countenance was changed in him, and
6. 4 neither was there any..fault found in him
7. 28 my countenance changed in me: but I
7. *With,* עִם *im.*
Deut. 8. 5 Thou shalt also consider in thine heart
8. *With,* עִמָּד *immad.*
Job 29. 20 My glory (was) fresh in me, and my bow
9. *According to the mouth of,* לְפִי *le-phi.*
Hos. 10. 12 reap in mercy; break up your fallow gr.
10. *Inner part, within,* פְּנִימָה *penimah.*
2 Ch. 29. 18 they went in to Hezekiah the king, and
11. *In the heart, midst,* בְּקֶרֶב *be-qereb.*
Gen. 45. 6 For these two years..the famine..in the
Exod 23. 21 Beware of him..for my name (is) in him
Deut 19. 10 That innocent blood be not shed in thy l.
29. 11 thy stranger that (is) in thy camp, from
Josh. 6. 25 she dwelleth in Israel (even) unto this day
1 Ki. 3. 28 saw that the wisdom of God (was) in him
Isa 7. 22 shall every one eat that is ..in the land
12. *Under,* תַּחַת *tachath.*
Job 30. 14 in the desolation they rolled themselves
13. *Between,* בֵּין *ben.*
Exod 12. 6 congregation..shall kill it in the evening
14. *In the hand of,* בְּיַד *be-yad.*
Neh. 9. 30 testifiedst..by thy spirit in thy prophets
15 *Over against,* לְנֶגֶד *le-neged.*
2 Sa. 22. 25 according to my cleanness in his eye sight
16. *In the middle, middle,* בְּתָוֶךְ *be-thavek.*
Gen. 37. 7 we (were) binding sheaves in the field, and
41. 48 round about every city, laid he up in the
Exod 39. 3 to work (it) in the blue, and in the purple
39. 3 and in the scarlet, and in the fine linen
Lev. 11. 33 whatsoever (is) in it shall be unclean; and
Num 13. 32 the people that we saw in it (are) men of
1 Ki. 6. 19 the oracle he prepared in the house within
1 Ch. 11. 22 also he went down and slew a lion in a pit
Eze. 14. 14 Though..Noah, Daniel, and Job, were in
14. 16 (Though) these three men (were) in it, (as)
14. 18 Though these three men (were) in it, (as)
14. 20 Though Noah, Daniel, and Job (were) in
17. *Up in, among,* ἀνά *ana.*
Rev. 7. 17 the Lamb which is in the midst of the th.
18. *From,* ἀπό *apo.*
2 Th. 2. 2 That ye be not soon shaken in mind, or
19. *Until,* ἄχρι, ἄχρις *achri, achris.*
Acts. 20. 6 and came unto them to Troas in five days
20. *Through,* διά *(gen.) dia.*
Matt 26. 61 able to destroy..and to build it in three
Acts 16. 9 And a vision appeared to Paul in the night
2 Co. 5. 10 every one may receive the things..[in]
1 Th. 4. 14 them also which sleep in Jesus will God
1 Ti. 2. 15 she shall be saved in child bearing, if
Heb. 7. 9 Levi..who receiveth tithes, payed tithes in
13. 22 for I have written..unto you in few words
2 Pe. 3. 5 standing out of the water and in the wa.
21. *Into, to, at,* εἰς *eis.*
Matt. 2. 23 he came and dwelt in a city called Nazar.
4. 13 he came and dwelt in Capernaum, which
10. 9 Provide neither gold..nor brass in your
10. 27 what ye hear in the ear..preach ye upon
10. 41 in the name of a prophet..in the name of
10. 42 whosoever shall give..in the name of a
12. 18 my beloved, [in] whom my soul is well pl.
13. 30 and bind them [in] bundles to burn them
13. 33 which a woman took and hid in three m.
18. 6 one of these little ones which believe in
18. 20 are gathered together in my name, there
26. 67 Then did they spit in his face, and buffet
27. 51 the veil of the temple was rent in twain
28. 19 teach all nations, baptizing them in the
Mark 1. 9 Jesus..was baptized of John in Jordan
2. 1 and it was noised that he was [in] the house
5. 14 and told (it) in the city, and in the coun.
5. 34 Daughter..go in peace, and be whole of
6. 8 that they should take..no money in..pu.
9. 42 one of (these) little ones that believe [in]
11. 8 garments [in] the way..strawed..[in] the w.
13. 9 and in the synagogues ye shall be beaten
13. 16 let him that is in the field not turn back
14. 20 (It is) one..that dippeth with me in the
14. 60 the high priest stood up in the midst, and
15. 38 the veil of the temple was rent in twain
Luke 1. 20 words, which shall be fulfilled in their s.
1. 44 thy salutation sounded in mine ears, the
2. 28 Then took he him up in his arms, and bl.
4. 35 when the devil had thrown him in the m.
6. 8 Rise up, and stand forth in the midst.
7. 1 ended all his sayings in the audience of
7. 50 Thy faith hath saved thee; go in peace
8. 34 and told (it) in the city and in the country
8. 48 thy faith hath made thee whole; go in peace
11. 7 my children are with me in bed; I cannot
11. 33 No man..putteth (it) in a secret place
13. 21 which a woman took and hid in three mea.
14. 8 sit not down in the highest room; lest a
14. 10 go and sit down in the lowest room; that
16. 8 the children of this world are in their g.
21. 14 Settle (it) therefore [in] your hearts, not to
21. 37 at night he went out, and abode in the m.
22. 19 is given..this do in remembrance of me
John 1. 18 the only begotten Son, which is in the b.
2. 23 many believed in his name, when they s.
3. 15, 16 whosoever believeth [in] him should not
John 3. 18 he hath not believed in the name of the
5. 45 there is (one)..(even) Moses, in whom ye
7. 5 For neither did his brethren believe in h.
9. 7 Go, wash in the pool of Siloam, which is
11. 25 he that believeth in me, though he were
11. 26 whosoever..believeth in me shall never
11. 52 that also he should gather together in one
12. 36 believe in the light, that ye may be the c.
14. 1 ye believe in God, believe also in me
17. 23 that they may be made perfect in one; and
19. 13 in a place that is called the Pavement, but
20. 7 but wrapped together in a place by itself
20. 19 came Jesus and stood in the midst, and
20. 26 came Jesus..and stood in the midst, and
Acts 2. 27 thou will not leave my soul in hell, neit.
2. 31 that his soul was not left in hell, neither
4. 3 laid hands on them, and put..in hold unto
8. 16 they were baptized in the name of the Lo.
8. 23 that thou art in the gall of bitterness, and
10. 43 whosoever believeth in him shall receive
12. 4 he put (him) in prison, and delivered (him)
13. 29 they took..and laid (him) in a sepulchre
16. 24 thrust..and made their feet fast in the s.
17. 21 the Athenians..spent their time in nothing
18. 21 [keep this feast that cometh in Jerusalem]
19. 5 they were baptized in the name of the L.
19. 22 but he himself stayed in Asia for a season
23. 11 as thou hast testified of me in Jerusalem
24. 24 and heard him concerning the faith in Ch.
26. 18 which are sanctified by faith that is in me
Rom. 8. 18 with the glory which shall be revealed in
10. 14 call on him in whom they have not beli.?
11. 32 God hath concluded them all in unbelief
1 Co 1. 13 or were ye baptized in the name of Paul?
1. 15 say that I had baptized in mine own name
8. 6 of whom (are) all things, and we in him
11. 24 Take, eat..this do in remembrance of me
11. 25 as oft as ye drink (it), in remembrance of
15. 54 is written, Death is swallowed up in vict.
2 Co. 1. 5 as the sufferings of Christ abound in us, so
1. 10 in whom we trust that he will yet deliver
1. 21 he which stablisheth us with you in Christ
8. 6 he would also finish in you the same grace
8. 22 the great confidence which (I have) in you
10. 16 To preach the gospel in the (regions) bey.
11. 3 corrupted from the simplicity that is in C.
Gal. 2. 16 even we have believed in Jesus Christ
3. 17 that was confirmed before of God [in] Christ
5. 10 I have confidence in you through the Lord
6. 4 rejoicing in himself alone, and not in an.
Eph. 1. 10 That in the dispensation of the fulness
3. 16 with might by his Spirit in the inner man
4. 13 Till we all come in the unity of the faith
Phil. 1. 5 For your fellowship in the gospel from the
2. 16 I may rejoice in the day of Christ, that I
2. 16 not run in vain, neither laboured in vain
2. 22 as a son..he hath served with me in the
Col. 1. 10 and increasing [in] the knowledge of God
2. 5 and the steadfastness of your faith in C.
3. 10 is renewed in knowledge after the image
1 Th. 4. 17 to meet the Lord in the air: and so shall
2 Th. 2. 4 so that he as God sitteth in the temple of
1 Ti. 6. 9 lusts, which drown men in destruction and
Phm. 6 good thing which is in you in Christ Jesus
Heb. 11. 9 By faith he sojourned in the land of pro.
Jas. 3. 3 put bits in the horses' mouths, that they
1 Pe. 1. 8 in whom, though now ye see (him) not
1. 21 Who..do believe in God..hope might be in
2 Pe. 1. 8 in the knowledge of our Lord Jesus Christ
1. 17 This is my beloved Son, in whom I am well
1 Jo. 5. 8 and the blood: and these three agree in
Rev. 1. 11 What thou seest, write in a book, and send
6. 15 themselves in the dens and in the rocks
11. 9 not suffer their dead bodies to be put in
13. 6 he opened his mouth in blasphemy against
17. 17 God hath put in their hearts to fulfil his
22. *Out of,* ἐκ *ek.*
Luke 11. 6 a friend of mine in his journey is come to
Rev. 3. 18 I counsel thee to buy of me gold tried in
23. *In,* ἐν *en.*
Matt. 1. 20 which is conceived in her is of the Holy G.
2. 1 when Jesus was born in Bethlehem of J.
2. 2 we have seen his star in the east, and are
2. 5 they said unto him, In Bethlehem of Ju.
2. 9 the star, which they saw in the east, went
2. 16 children that were in Bethlehem, and in
2. 18 In Rama was there a voice heard, lamen.
2. 19 angel of the Lord appeareth..to Joseph in
3. 1 In those days came John..preaching in
3. 3, 6, 12, 17; 4. 13, 16, 16, 21, 23; 5. 12, 15, 16, 19, 19, 25, 28, 45, [48]; 6. 1, 2, 2, 4, 4, 5, 5, 6, 6, 9, 10, 18, 18, 20, 23, 29; 7. 3, 3, 4, 11, 15, 21, 22; 8. 10, 11, [13,] 24, 32; 9. 4, 10, 31, 33, 35; 10. 11, 15, 16, 17, 19, 20, 23, 27, 27, 28, 32, 33; 11. 1, 2, 6, 8, 8, 11, 16, 21, 21, 21, 23, 23, 24; 12. 5, 5, 19, [21,] 32, 32, 36, 40, 40, 41, 42, 50; 13. 3, 10, 13, 19, 21, 24, 27, 30, 31, 32, 34, 35, 40, 43, 44, 54, 57, 57, 57; 14. 2, 3, 10, 33; 15. 32, 33; 16. 17, 19, 19, 27, 28; 17. 5, 22; 18. 1, 2, 4, 6, 10, 10, 14, 18, 18, 19, 20; 19. 21, 28; 20. 3, 17, 21; 21. 8, 8, 9, 9, 12, 14, 15, 22, 28, 32, 33, 41, 42, 42; 22. 15, 16, 28, 30, 30, 36, 43; 23. 6 7, [9,] 30, 30, 34, 39; 24. 14, 15, 16, 18, 19, 26, 26, 30, 38, 40, 45, 48, 50, 50; 25. 4, 13, [18,] 25, 31, 36, 39, 43, 44; 26. 6, 6, 13, 23, 29, 55, 55, 69; 27. [5,] 40, 60, 60; 28. 18.
Mark 1. 2, 3, 4, 5, 9, 11, 13, 19, 20, 23, [39, 45]; 2. 6, 8 15, 20; 3. 23; 4. 1, 2, 11, [15,] 17, 28, 36; 5. 5 5, 13, 20, 27, 30, 30; 6. 2, 4, 4, [11,] 14, 17, 27, 29, 47, 48, 51, 56; 8. 1 14, 26, 38, 38; 9. 33, 36, 41, 50; 10. [10,] 21, 30, 30, 32, 37, 52; 11. 9, [10,] 10, 15, 23, 25, [26,] 27; 12. 11, 23, 5, 26, 35, 38, 38, 38, 39; 13. 11, 14, 17, 24, 25, 26, 32; 14. 3, 3, 25, [30,] 49, 66; 15. 7, [29,] 41, 46; 16. [12, 17.]

Luke 1. 5, 6, 7, 8, 17, 18, 21, 22, 25, 26, 31, 36, 39, 41, 44, 66, 69, 75, 79, 80; 2. 1, 7, 7, 8, 11, 12, 14, 16, 19, 21, 23, 24, 25, 29, 34, [38,] 43, 44, 46, 46, 51; 3. 1, 2, 4, 4, 15, 17, 20, 22; 4. 2, 5, 14, 15, 20, 21, 23, [23,] 24, 25, 25, 27, 28, 33, [44]; 5. 7, 12, 22, 29, 35; 6. 12, 12, 23, 23, 41, 41, 42, 42, 42; 7. 9, 21, 23, 25, 25, 28, 32, 37, 37; 8. 10, 13, 15, 27, 27; 9. 12, 26, 31, 36, 57; 10. 7, 9, 12, 13, 13, 13, 20, 20, 21, 26; 11. 1, [2, 2,] 21, 31, 32, 35, 43, 43; 12. 1. 3, 3, 3, 12, 15, 27, 28, 33, 38, 38, 42, 45, 46, 52, 58; 13. 4, [4,] 6, 10, 14, 14, 19, 26, 28, 29, 35; 14. 15; 15, 4, 7, 25; 16. 10, 10, 1[illegible], 10, 11, 12, 23, 23, 23, 24, 25; 17. 6, [24,] 26, 26, 28, 31, 31, 31, [36]; 18. 2, 3, 22, 30, 30; 19. 17, 20, 30, 36, 38, 38, 38, [illegible], 44, 45, 47; 20. 1, 33, 42, 46, 46, 46; 21. 6, 19, 21, 2[illegible], 21, 23, 2[illegible], 27, 37, 38; 22. 16, 20, 28, 30, 37, [44,] 53, 55; 23. 4, 9, 14, 19, 22, 29, 31, 31, 40, 43, 53; 24. 4, 6, [18,] 18, 19, 27, 35, 35, 36, 38, 44, 49, 53.

John 1. 1, 2, 4, 5, 10, 23, 28, 45, 47; 2. 1, 11, 14, 19, 20, 23, [23,] 25; 3. [13,] 14, 21, 23; 4. 14, 20, 20, 21, 23, 24, 31, 37, 44, 53; 5. 3, 13, 14, 26, 26, 28, 35, 38, 39, 42, 43, 43; 6. 10, 31, 45, 49, 53, 56, 56, 59, 59, 61; 7. 1, 1, 4, 9, 10, 18 28, 37; 8. [3, 3, 5, 9], 12, 17, 20, 20, 21, 24, 24, 31, 35, 37, 44, 44; 9. 3, 5, 30, 34; 10. 23, 23, 25, 34, 38, 38; 11. 6, 9, 10, 10, 17, 20, 24, 30, 31, 38, 56; 12. 13, 25, 35, 46, 48; 13. 1, 31, [32,] 32; 14. 2, 10, 10, 10, 11, 11, 13, 13, 14, 14, 17, 20, 20, 20, 26, 30; 15. 2, 4, 4, 4, 4, 5, 5, 6, 7, 7, 8, 9, 10, 10, 11, 16, 25; 16. 23, 23, 24, 25, 25, 26, 33, 33; 17. 10, 11, 11, [12,] 12, 13, 13, 21, 21, 21, 23, 23, 26, 26; 18. 20, 20, 20, 26, 38; 19. 4, 6, 41, 41, 41; 20. 12, 25, 30.

Acts 1. 7, 8, [8,] 10, 15, 15, 20, 20; 2. 17, 18, 19, 22, 46; 3. 6, 26; 4. 7, [12,] 24; 5. 4, 4, 12, 18, 20, 22, 25, 25, 34, 37, 42; 6. 1, 1, 7, 15; 7. 2, 2, 4, 5, 6, 7, [12,] 16, 17, 20, 20, 22, [22,] 29, 30, 30, 34, 35, 36, 36, 36, 38, 38, 38, 41, 41, 42, 42, 44, 48; 8. 8, 9, 21, 33; 9. 10, 11, [12,] 17, 20, 21, 25, 27, 27, 29, 37, 37, 43; 10. 1, 3, 12, 17, 30, 30, 32, 35, 39, [39,] 48; 11. 5, 5, 13, 22, 26, 27, 29; 12. 5, 7; 13. 5, 17, 18, 19, 33, 35, 40, 41; 14. 1, 15, 16, 25; 15. 21, 35; 16. 3, 6, 12, 18, 32, 36; 17. 11, 16, 17, 17, 22, 24, 24, 28, 31, 31; 18. 4, 9, 10, 18, 24, 26; 19. 9, 16, 21, 39; 20. 0, 10, 16; 21. 27, 29; 22. 3, 3, 17, 17; 23. 6, 9, 35; 24. 12, 12, [14,] 18, [20]; 25. 5; 26. 10, 21, 26; 27. 21, 27, 31, 37; 28. 7, 9, 11, 11, 18, 30.

Rom. 1. 2, 7, 9, 17, 18, 19, 21, 27, 27, [28]; 2. 1, 12, 15, 16, 19, 20, 28, 29; 3. 4, 16, 24, 25; 4. 10, 10, 10, 10; 5. 2, 3, 5, 11, 13, 17; 6. 2, 4, 12, [12]; 7. 5, 5, 6, 6, 8, 17, 18, 18, 20, 23, 23; 8. 1, 2, 3, 3, 3, 4, 8, 9, 9, 9, 10, 11, 11, 37, 39; 9. 1, 1, 7, 17, 25, 26, [28,] 33; 10. 6, 8, 8, 9; 12. 4, 5; 13. 9, 13; 14. 5, 17, 18, 22; 15. 13, 13, 23, 27, 29, 30, 31; 16. 2, 2, 3, 7, 8, 9, 10, 11, 12, [12,] 13, 22.

1 Co. 1. 2, 2, 5, 5, 6, 7, 8, 10, 10, 21, 30, 31; 2. 3, 3, 3, 4, 5, 5, 7, 11, 13; 3. 1, 16, 18, 19, 21, 4. 2, 6, 10, 15, 15, 17, 17, 17, 20, 20, 21; 5. 4, 5, 9; 6. 4, 11, 19, 20, [20]; 7. 15, 17, 18, 20, 20, 22, 24, 24, 37, 37, 39; 8. 4, 5, 7, 10; 9. 1, 2, 9, 18, 24; 10. 2, 2, 5, 8, 25; 11. 11, 13, 18, 21, 22, 25; 12. 6, 18, 25, 28; 14. 10, 19, 19, 21, 25, 28, 33, 34, 35; 15. 1, 17, 18, 19, 19, 22, 22, 23, 28, 31, 41, 42, 42, 43, 43, 43, 43, 52, 52, 58; 16. 11, 13, 19. 24.

2 Co. 1. 1, 4, 6, 8, 9, 12, 12, 14, 19, 20, [20,] 22; 2. 1, 10, 14, 14, 15, 15, 17; 3. 2, 3, 3, [7, 9,] 10, 14; 4. 2, 4, 6, 6, 7, 10, 10, 11, 12, 12; 5. 1, 2, 4, 6, 11, 12, 17, 19, 21; 6. 2, 3, 4, 4, 4, 4, 4, 5, 5, 5, 5, 5, 5, 12, 12, 16; 7. 1, 3, 9, 11, [11,] 14, 16, 16; 8. 2. 7, 7, 10, 18, 20, 22; 9. 3, 4, 8, 11; 10. 3, 6, 14, 16, 17; 11. 6 9, 10, 10, 12, 17, 23, 23, 23, 23, 25, 26, 26, 26, [27,] 27, 27, 27, 27, 32, 33; 12. 2, 2, 3, 5, 9, 9, 10, 10, 10, 10, 10, 12, [12,] 19; 13. 3, 3, [4,] 5, 5.

Gal. 1. 13, 14, 14, 16, 22, 24; 2. 4, 20, 20; 3. 8, 10, 10, 12, 19, 26, 28; 4. 14, 18, 19, 25; 5. 6, 14, 14; 6. 1, 1, 6, 12, 13, 14, [15,] 17.

Eph. 1. 1, 3, [3,] 4, 4, 6, 6, 7, 8, 9, 10, [10,] 10, 11, 12, 13, 13, 15, 17, 18, 20, 20, 21, 21, 23; 2. 2, 2, 3, 4, 6, 6, 7, 7, 10, 10, 11, 11, 12, 13, 15, 15, 15, 16, 21, 21 22; 3. 3, 4, [5,] 6, 9, 10, 11, 12, 15, 17, 17, 20, 21; 4. 2, 3, 4, 6, 15, 16, 16, 17, 17, 18, 21, 24; 5. 2, 5, 8, 9, 18, 19, 20, 21, 24; 6. [1,] 4, 5, 9, 10, 10, 12, 13, 18, 20, 20, 21, 24.

Phil. 1. 1, 4, 6, 7, 7, 8, 9, 13, 13, 14, 18, 20, 20, 22, [24,] 26, 27, 28, 30, 30; 2. 1, 5, 5, 6, 7, 12, 12, 13, [15,] 15, 19, 24, 29; 3. 1, 3, 3, 4, 4, 6, 9, 14, 19, 20; 4. 1, 2, 3, 3, 4, 6, 9, 10, 11, 12, 15, 16, 19, 21.

Col. 1. 2, 4, 5, 5, 6, 6, 6, 8, 9, 10, 12, 14, 16, 18, 19, 20, 22, 24, 24, 27, 28, 28, 29; 2. 1, 2, 3, 6, 7, [7,] 9, 10, 11, 11, 12, 12, [13,] 15, 16, 16, 16, 18, 20, 23, 23; 3. 3, 4, 7, 7, 11, 15, 15, 16, 16, 17, 17, 18, 22; 4. 1, 2, 5, 7, 12, 12, 13, 13, 15, 16, 17.

1 Th. 1. 1, 5, 5, 5, 5, 6, 7, 8, 8; 2. 2, 3, 13, 14, 14; 3. 2, 8, 13; 4. 4, 5, 6, 10, 16, 17; 5. 2, 4, 12, 13, 18, 18.

2 Th. 1. 1, 4, 4, 4, 8, 10, 10, 10, 12, 12; 2. 6, [10, 12,] 17; 3. 4, 6, 17.

1 Ti. 1. 2, 4, 13, 14, 16; 2. 2, 2, [7,] 7, 9, 11, 12, 14, 15; 3. 4, 9, 11, 13. 13, 15, 16, 16, 16; 4. 1, 2, 12, 12, 12, [12,] 12, 12, 14; 5. 17; 6. 17, [17,] 18.

2 Ti. 1. 1, 3. 5, 5, 5, 6, 9, 13, 13, 14, 15, 17 18; 2. 1, 1 7, 9, 10, 20, 25; 3. 1, 12, 14, 15, 16; 4. 5.

Titus 1. 5, 13; 2. 3, 7, 9, 10, 12; 3. 3, 15.

Phm. 6, 8, 10, 13, 16, 16, 20, 20, 23.

Heb. 2. 8, 12, 18; 3. 2, 5, 8, 8, 11, 12, 12, 15, 17; 4. 3, 5, 7; 5. 6, 7; 6. 17. 18; 7. 10; 8. 1, 5, 9, 9, 13; 9. 2, 4, 23; 10. 3, 7, 22, 32, [34, 34,] 38; 11. 9, 18, 19, [26,] 37, 37, [38]; 12. 23; 13. 3, 4, 9. 18, 21, 21.

Jas. 1. 6, 8, 9, 10, 11, 23, 25, 27; 2. 2, 2, 4, 5, 10, 16; 3. 2, 14, 18; 4. 1, 5, 16; 5. 5, 14.

1 Pet. 1. 4, 5, 6, 11, 14, 15, 17, 22; 2. [6,] 6, 12, 22, 24; 3. 4, 15, 15, 16, 19, 20; 4. [1,] 2, 3, 4, 11, 19; 5. 6, 9, 14.

2 Pet. 1. 4, 12, 13, 18, 19, 19; 2. 10, 12, 13, 18; 3. [illegible], [10,] 10, 10, 11, 13, 14, 16, 16, 16, 18.

1 John 1. 5, 6, 7, 7, 8, 10; 2. 4, 5. 5, 6, 8, 8, 9, 9. 10, 10, 11, 11, 14, 15, 15, 16, 24, 24, 24, [24,] 27, 27, 28; 3. 5, 6, 9, 10, 14, 15, 17, 24, 24, 24; 4. 2, [3,] 3, 4, 4, 9, 10, 12, 12, 13, 13, 15, 15, 16, 16, 16, 17, 17, 17, 18, 18; 5. [7, 8,] 10, 11, 19, 20, 20.

2 John 1. 2, 3, 4, 6, 7, 9, 9; 3 John 1, 3, 4; Jude 10, 12, [18,] 20, 21. Rev. 1. 6, 4, 5, 9, [9,] 9, 10, [11,] 13, 15, 16, 16; 2. 1, 1, 7, 12, [13,] 18, 24; 3. 1, 4, 4, 5, 7, 12, 21, 21; 4. 1, 2, 2, 4. 6; 5, 3, 6, 6, 13, 13; 6. 5, 6: 7. 9, 14, 15; 8. 1, 9; 9. 6, 10, [illegible]. 17, 19, [19]; 10. 2, 6, 6, 6, 7, 8, 9, 10; 11, 1, [6,] 12, 13, 15, [19,] 19; 12. 1, 3, 7, 8, 10, 12; 13. 6, 8, 12; 14. 5, 6, 13, 14, 17; 15. 1, 1, 5; 16. 3; 17. 3, 4; 18. 6, 7, 8, [10,] 19, 19, 22, 22, 22, [23,] 23, 24; 19. 1, 11, 14, 17, 17; 20. 6, 8, 12, 13, 13, 15; 21. 8, 10, [14,] 22, [23, 24,] 27; 22. 2, 3, 18, 19.

24. *On, upon, over,* ἐπί *(gen.) epi.*

Matt. 2. 22 he heard that Archelaus did reign [in] Ju.
4. 6 and in (their) hands they shall bear thee
6. 10 Thy kingdom come. Thy will be done in
18. 16 that in the mouth of two or three witn.
19. 28 when the Son of man shall sit in the thr.
21. 19 when he saw a fig tree in the way, he came
23. 2 The scribes and the Pharisees sit in Moses'
24. 30 coming in the clouds of heaven with po.
26. 64 sitting..and coming in the clouds of hea.
28. 18 power is given unto me in heaven and in
Mark 4. 31 seed, which when it is sown in the earth
4. 31 [is less than all the seeds that be in the]
8. 4 satisfy..with bread here in the wilderness?
12. 14 but teachest the way of God in truth: Is
12. 26 how in the bush God spake unto him, say.
Luke 4. 11 And in (their) hands they shall bear thee
5. 18 men brought in a bed a man which was
6. 17 he came down with them, and stood in the
11. 2 [Thy will be done, as in heaven, so in ea.]
17. 34 night there shall be two (men) in one bed
21. 23 there shall be great distress in the land
John 19. 13 brought Jesus forth, and sat down in the
Acts 8. 28 sitting in his chariot read Esaias the pr.
20. 9 there sat in a window a certain young m.
Rom. 1. 9 make mention of you always in my pray.
1 Co. 8. 5 called gods, whether in heaven or in earth
2 Co. 13. 1 In the mouth of two or three witnesses
Eph. 1. 16 thanks..making mention of you in my p.
Col. 1. 16 that are in heaven, and that are in earth
1. 20 whether..things in earth, or things in h.
1 Th. 1. 2 making mention of you in our prayers
1 Ti. 6. 17 nor trust in uncertain riches, but in the
Phm. 4 making mention of thee..in my prayers
Heb. 1. 2 Hath in these last days spoken unto us by
8. 10 write them in their hearts: and I will be
10. 16 my laws..[in] their minds will write them
1 Pe. 1. 20 was manifest in these last times for you
2 Pe. 3. 3 there shall come in the last days scoffers
Rev. 1. 20 stars which thou sawest [in] my right hand
5. 13 under the earth, and such as are in the
9. 4 have not the seal of God in their forehe.
11. 8 their dead bodies (shall lie) in the street
13. 16 in their right hand, or [in] their foreheads
14. 1 Father's name written in their foreheads
14. 9 and receive (his) mark in his forehead, or
18. 17 all the company in ships, and sailors, and
22. 4 and his name (shall be) in their foreheads

25. *On, upon, over,* ἐπί *(dat.) epi.*

Matt 13. 14 [in] them is fulfilled the prophecy of Esa.
14. 8 Give me..John Baptist's head in a char.
14. 11 his head was brought in a charger, and
18 5 shall receive one such little child in my
24. 5 many shall come in my name, saying, I
Mark 4. 38 he was [in] the hinder part of the ship, asl.
5. 33 knowing what was done [in] her, came and
6. 25 give me by and by in a charger the head
6. 28 brought his head in a charger, and gave
6. 55 began to carry about in beds those that
9. 37 shall receive one of such children in my
9. 39 no man which shall do a miracle in my
10. 24 how hard is it for them that trust in riches
13. 6 many shall come in my name, saying, I
Luke 1. 47 my spirit hath rejoiced in God
9. 48 Whosoever shall receive this child in my
9. 49 we saw one casting out devils in thy name
18. 9 certain which trusted in themselves that
21. 8 many shall come in my name, saying, I am
24. 47 that repentance..should be preached in
Acts 2. 26 moreover also my flesh shall rest in hope
2. 38 be baptised every one of you [in] the name
3. 11 the people ran together unto them in the
4. 17 speak henceforth to no man in this name
4. 18 they..commanded them not to..teach in
5. 28 that ye should not teach in this name? and
5. 40 commanded that they should not speak in
14. 3 therefore abode they speaking boldly in
Rom. 4. 18 Who against hope believed in hope, that
5. 2 By whom also we..rejoice in hope of the
8. 20 him who hath subjected (the same) in hope
15. 12 a root of Jesse..in him shall the Gentiles
1 Co. 9 10 plow in hope..he that thresheth in hope
13. 6 Rejoiceth not in iniquity, but rejoiceth
2 Co. 1. 4 Who comforteth us in all our tribulation
1. 9 not trust in ourselves, but in God which
3. 14 the same veil untaken away in the read.
7. 4 I am exceeding joyful in all our tribulat.
7. 7 wherewith he was comforted in you, when
7. 13 we were comforted in your comfort: yea
9. 14 long..for the exceeding grace of God in
1 Th. 3. 7 we were comforted over you in all our
1 Ti. 4. 10 suffer reproach, because we trust in the
Titus 1. 2 In hope of eternal life, which God that
Phm. 7. we have great joy and consolation in thy
Heb. 2. 13 And again, I will put my trust in him
9. 10 only in meats and drinks, and divers wa.
9. 26 but now once in the end of the world hath
1 Jo. 3. 3 every man that hath this hope in him
Rev. 22. 16 to testify unto you these things [in] 9. 4.

26. *On, upon, over,* ἐπί *(acc.) epi.*

Matt 27. 29 they put..a reed [in] his right hand: and
27. 43 He trusted [in] God; let him deliver him
Mark 15. 1 [in] the morning the chief priests held a c.
Acts 9. 42 was known..and many believed in the L.
27. 20 when neither sun nor stars in many days
2 Co. 2. 3 I ought to rejoice; having confidence in
1 Ti. 5. 5 she that is a widow indeed..trusteth in G.
1 Pe. 3. 5 the holy women also, who trusted [in] God
Rev. 2. 17 in the stone a new name written, which
5. 1 I saw in the right hand of him that sat on
14. 9 image, and receive (his) mark..in his hand
17. 8 names were not written in the book of life
20. 1 an angel..having..a great chain in his h.
20. 4 neither had received (his) mark..in their

27. *Through, throughout, over against,* κατά *(acc.).*

Matt 1. 20 angel of the Lord appeared unto him in
2. 12, 22 being warned of God in a dream
2. 13, 19 of the Lord appeareth to Joseph in a d.
27. 19 I have suffered many things this day in a d.
Luke 6. 23 in the like manner did their fathers unto
15. 14 there arose a mighty famine in that land
Acts 3. 13 denied him in the presence of Pilate, when
3. 22 him shall ye hear in all things whatsoever
11. 1 the apostles and brethren that were in J.
13. 1 Now there were in the church that was
15. 23 brethren which are of the Gentiles in An.
15. 36 Let us go again and visit our brethren in
17. 22 I perceive that in all things ye are too sup.
24. 12 neither raising up the people..nor in the
24. 14 all things which are written in the law and
25. 3 And..laying wait in the way to kill him
26. 11 I punished them oft in every synagogue
26. 13 I saw in the way a light from heaven, ab.
Rom. 5. 6 in due time Christ died for the ungodly
16. 5 Likewise..the church that is in their ho.
1 Co. 14. 40 Let all things be done decently and in or.
16. 19 Aquila.. with the church that is in their
2 Co. 10. 1 who in presence (am) base among you, but
Col. 3. 20 Children, obey..parents in all things: for
3. 22 Servants, obey in all things..masters ac.
4. 15 Salute..the church which is in his house
Phm. 2 Archippus..and to the church in thy ho.
Heb. 1. 10 Thou, Lord, in the beginning hast laid the
2. 17 in all things it behoved him to be made
3. 8 Harden not your hearts, as..in the day
4. 15 but was in all points tempted like as (we
9. 9 in which were offered both gifts and sac.
11. 13 These all died in faith, not having received

28. *With, among,* μετά *(gen.) meta.*

Mark 14. 62 sitting..and coming in the clouds of he.
Acts 15. 33 they were let go in peace from the bret.

29. *By, with,* παρά *(dat.) para.*

Rom. 11. 25 lest ye should be wise in your own concei.
12. 16 Mind not..Be not wise in your own con.

30. *Around, round about,* περί *(acc.) peri.*

Titus 2. 7 In all things showing thyself a pattern of

31. *Toward,* πρός *(acc.) pros.*

Luke 12. 3 and that which ye have spoken in the ear
24. 12 [wondering in himself at that which was]
1 Jo. 5. 14 this is the confidence that we have in him

32. *Under,* ὑπό *(acc.) hupo.*

Acts 5. 21 entered into the temple early in the morn.

33. *Within,* ἔσω *esō.*

Matt 26. 58 But Peter..went in, and sat with the ser.

[*See also* Abide, abundance, act, admiration, adultery, affliction, arms, array, awe, behalf, bondage, bonds, break, breaking, bring, bringing, brought, call, cast, charge, clothed, come, conference, continue, cut, danger, derision, distress, end, entangle, enter, entering, entrance, execution, fear, gather, go, graff, hedge, held, holding, keep, lie, lodge, more, no, order, pool, pour, put, rend, rejoice, ride, run, shut, sleep, sport, spring, step, straight, swim, take, tear, took, thrust, trouble, turn, vain, walk, wrap, write.]

IN, all that is —

Fulness, מְלֹא *melo.*

Isa. 34. 1 let the earth hear, and all that is therein
42. 10 go down to the sea, and all that is therein
Jer. 8. 16 devoured the land, and all that is in it
47. 2 overflow the land, and all that is therein
Eze. 12. 19 may be desolate from all that is therein
30. 12 all that is therein, by the hand of strang.
Amos 6. 8 deliver up the city with all that is therein
Mic. 1. 2 hearken, O earth, and all that therein is

IN a place —

On, upon, over, ἐπί *(gen.) epi.*

Mark 11. 4 a colt tied by the door without in a place

IN among —

Into, to, at, εἰς *eis.*

Acts 14. 14 Paul..ran in among the people, crying out
20. 29 shall grievous wolves enter in among you

IN at —

Into, to, at, εἰς *eis.*

Matt 15. 17 whatsoever entereth in at the mouth go.

IN every —

Through, throughout, over against, κατά *(acc.) kata.*

Acts 14. 23 had ordained them elders in every church
15. 21 For Moses of old time hath in every city
20. 23 that the Holy Ghost witnesseth in every

IN it —

There, שָׁם *sham.*

2 Ch. 6. 11 in it have I put the ark, wherein (is) the

IN (no) wise —

To put to death, מוּת *muth,* 5. [Adv. infin.].

1 Ki. 3. 26, 27 give her the living child, and in no w.

IN presence, (to be) —

1. *To see,* רָאָה *raah.*

2 Ki. 25. 19 of them that were in the king's presence

2. *Before, ἔμπροσθεν emprosthen.*
1 Th. 2. 19 in the presence of our Lord Jesus Christ

IN respect of —
Through, throughout, over against, κατά (acc.) kata.
Phil. 4. 11 Not that I speak in respect of want: for I

IN sight of —
Before, ἔμπροσθεν emprosthen.
1 Th. 1. 3 in the sight of G.; Matt. 11. 26; Lu. 10. 21

IN...stead —
In behalf of, ὑπέρ (gen.) huper.
2 Co. 5. 20 we pray..in Christ's stead, be ye reconcil.
Phm. 13 that in thy stead he might have ministered
[*See also* Instead.]

IN that —
1. *Because, כִּי ki.*
Deut 31. 18 in that they are turned unto other gods
2. *On, upon, because, עַל al.*
Gen. 31. 20 unawares..in that he told him not that
3. *That, because, ὅτι hoti.*
Rom. 5. 8 in that, while we were yet sinners, Christ

IN that they —
Whosoever, ὅστις hostis.
Acts 17. 11 in that they received the word with all

IN the days of —
On, upon, over, ἐπί (gen.) epi.
Mark 2. 26 went into the house of God in the days of
Acts 11. 28 which came to pass in the days of Claudius

IN the time of —
On, upon, over, ἐπί (gen.) epi.
Luke 4. 27 many lepers were in Israel in the time of

IN unto —
Into, to, at, εἰς eis.
Luke 21. 4 these have of their abundance cast in unto
Acts 19. 30 when Paul would have entered in unto

IN (where) —
About, concerning, περί (gen.) peri.
Luke 1. 4 things, wherein thou hast been instructed

INASMUCH as —
1. *Because, כִּי ki.*
Deut 19. 6 inasmuch as he hated him not in time past
2. *In that...not, לְבִלְתִּי le-bilti.*
Ruth 3. 10 inasmuch as thou followedst not young
3. *Inasmuch as, as long as, ἐφ' ὅσον eph hoson.*
Matt 25. 40 Inasmuch as ye have done (it) unto one of
25. 45 Inasmuch as ye did (it) not to one of the
Rom 11. 13 inasmuch as I am the apostle of the Gen.
4. *According as, καθό katho.*
1 Pe. 4. 13 inasmuch as ye are partakers of Christ's
5. *Inasmuch as, as, καθ' ὅσον kath hoson.*
Heb. 3. 3 inasmuch as he who hath builded the house
7. 20 And inasmuch as not without an oath

INCENSE —
1. *Frankincense, לְבוֹנָה lebonah.*
Isa. 43. 23 an offering, nor wearied thee with incense
60. 6 they shall bring gold and incense; and
66. 3 he that burneth incense, (as if) he blessed
Jer. 6. 20 To what purpose cometh there to me in.
17. 26 bringing burnt offerings..and incense
41. 5 with offerings and incense in their hand
2. *Incense, perfume, קְטוֹרָה qetorah.*
Deut 33. 10 they shall put incense before thee, and
3. *To be perfumed, קָטַר qatar, 6.*
Mal. 1. 11 in every place incense (shall be) offered
4. *Incense, perfume, קִטֵּר qitter.*
Jer. 44. 21 The incense that ye burnt in the cities
5. *Incense, perfume, קְטֹרֶת qetoreth.*
Exod 25. 6 spices for anointing oil, and for sweet in.
30. 1 thou shalt make an altar to burn incense
30. 7 Aaron shall burn thereon sweet incense
30. 8 a perpetual incense before the LORD thr.
30. 9 Ye shall offer no strange incense thereon
30. 27 and his vessels, and the altar of incense
31. 8 all his furniture, and the altar of incense
35. 8 for anointing oil, and for the sweet ince.
35. 15 the incense altar..and the sweet incense
35. 28 the anointing oil, and for the sweet ince.
37. 25 he made the incense altar (of) shittim wo.
37. 29 he made..the pure incense of sweet spices
39. 38 the anointing oil, and the sweet incense
40. 5 shalt set the altar of gold for the incense
40. 27 he burned sweet incense thereon; as the
Lev. 10. 1 put incense thereon, and offered strange
16. 12 hands full of sweet incense beaten small
16. 13 he shall put the incense upon the fire be.
16. 13 that the cloud of the incense may cover
Num. 4. 16 sweet incense, and the daily meat offering
7. 14 spoon of ten (shekels) of gold, full of inc.
7. 20 spoon of gold of ten (shekels), full of inc.
7. 26 golden spoon of ten (shekels), full of inc.
[*So also* v. 32, 38, 44, 50, 56, 62, 68, 74, 80.]
7. 86 golden spoons (were) twelve, full of incense
16. 7 and put incense in them before the LORD
16. 17 put incense in them, and bring ye before
16. 18 laid incense thereon, and stood in the door
16. 35 consumed the..men that offered incense
16. 40 come near to offer incense before the Lo.
16. 46 put on incense, and go quickly unto the
16. 47 put on incense, and made an atonement
1 Sa. 2. 28 to burn incense, to wear an ephod before
1 Ch. 6. 49 his sons offered..on the altar of incense
28. 18 the altar of incense refined gold by weight
2 Ch. 2. 4 to burn before him sweet incense, and
13. 11 burn..burnt sacrifices and sweet incense
26. 16 to burn incens upon the altar of incense
26. 19 the priests..from beside the incense altar
29. 7 they..have not burnt incense nor offered
Psa. 66. 15 I will offer unto thee..the incense of rams
141. 2 Let my prayer be set forth..(as) incense
Isa. 1. 13 incense is an abomination unto me; the
Eze. 8. 11 censer..and a thick cloud of incense went
16. 18 thou hast set mine oil and mine incense
23. 41 whereupon thou hast set mine incense
6. *Incense, perfume, θυμίαμα thumiama.*
Luke 1. 10 people were praying..at the time of inc.
1. 11 angel..on the right side of the altar of i.
Rev. 8. 3 there was given unto him much incense
8. 4 the smoke of the incense..ascended up

INCENSE, altars for —
Incense altars, מְקַטְּרוֹת meqatteroth.
2 Ch. 30. 14 and all the altars for incense took they
[*See also* Burn, burning offer, offering, sweet.]

INCENSED, to be —
To be displeased, heated, חָרָה charah, 2.
Isa. 41. 11 all they that were incensed against thee
45. 24 all that are incensed against him shall

INCLINE, to —
1. *To stretch out, turn aside, away, down, נָטָה natah.*
Judg. 9. 3 their hearts inclined to follow Abimelech
Psa. 40. 1 and he inclined unto me, and heard my
119. 112 I have inclined my heart to perform thy
2. *To stretch out, turn aside, away, נָטָה natah, 5.*
Josh. 24. 23 incline your heart unto the LORD God of
1 Ki. 8. 58 That ye may incline our hearts unto him
Psa. 17. 6 thou wilt hear me, O God: incline thine
45. 10 Hearken, O daughter..and incline thine
49. 4 I will incline mine ear to a parable; I
71. 2 Deliver..incline thine ear unto me, and
78. 1 incline your ears to the words of my mo.
88. 2 Let my prayer come before thee: incline
102. 2 Hide not thy face from me..incline thine
116. 2 he hath inclined his ear unto me, theref.
119. 36 Incline my heart unto thy testimonies
141. 4 Incline not my heart to (any) evil thing
Prov. 4. 20 My son..incline thine ear unto my saying
5. 13 nor inclined mine ear to them that instr.
Isa. 37. 17 Incline thine ear, O LORD, and hear; open
55. 3 Incline your ear, and come unto me: hear
Jer. 7. 24 they hearkened not, nor inclined their ear
7. 26 they hearkened not unto me, nor inclined
11. 8 they obeyed not, nor inclined their ear
17. 23 they obeyed not, neither inclined their
25. 4 ye have not hearkened, nor inclined your
34. 14 fathers hearkened not unto me neither in.
35. 15 ye have not inclined your ear, nor hear.
44. 5 they hearkened not, nor inclined their ear
Dan. 9. 18 O my God, incline thine ear, and hear
3. *To cause to attend, קָשַׁב qashab, 5.*
Prov. 2. 2 So that thou incline thine ear into wisd.
4. *To be bowed down, incline, שׁוּחַ shuach.*
Prov. 2. 18 her house inclineth unto death, and her

INCLOSE, to —
1. *To make a hedge or wall, גָּדַר gadar.*
Lam. 3. 9 He hath inclosed my ways with hewn st.
2. *To set round, compass, נָקַף naqaph, 5.*
Psa. 22. 16 the assembly of the wicked have inclosed
3. *To bind, fashion, צוּר tsur.*
Song 8. 9 we will inclose her with boards of cedar
4. *To enclose together, shut up, συγκλείω sugkleiō.*
Luke 5. 6 they inclosed a great multitude of fishes

INCLOSE round, to —
To compass, encircle, כָּתַר kathar, 3.
Judg 20. 43 they inclosed the Benjamites round about

INCLOSED —
1. *To nail, bolt, נָעַל naal.*
Song 4. 12 A garden inclosed (is) my sister, (my) sp.
2. *To be turned round, surrounded, סָבַב sabab, 6.*
Exod 39. 6 they wrought onyx stones inclosed in ouc.
39. 13 inclosed in ouches of gold in their inclos.
3. *To shut up or in, סָגַר sagar.*
Psa. 17. 10 they are inclosed in their own fat: with

INCLOSING —
Fillings, settings, מִלֻּאָה milluah.
Exod 28. 20 they shall be set in gold in their inclosings
39. 13 inclosed in ouches of gold in their inclos.

INCONTINENCY —
Incontinence, want of authority, ἀκρασία akrasia.
1 Co. 7. 5 that Satan tempt you not for your incon.

INCONTINENT —
Incontinent, without strength, ἀκρατής akratēs.
2 Ti. 3. 3 truce breakers, false accusers, incontin.

INCORRUPTIBLE —
Incorruptible, ἄφθαρτος aphthartos.
1 Co. 9. 25 obtain a corruptible crown, but we an in.
15. 52 the dead shall be raised incorruptible, and
1 Pe. 1. 4 To an inheritance incorruptible, and und.
1. 23 not of corruptible seed, but of incorrupt.

INCORRUPTION —
Incorruption, ἀφθαρσία aphtharsia.
1 Co. 15. 42 It is sown in corruption..raised in incor.
15. 50 neither doth corruption inherit incorrup.
15. 53 For this corruptible must put on incorru.
15. 54 when this corruptible shall have put on in.

INCREASE —
1. *Increase, produce, יְבוּל yebul.*
Lev. 26. 4 the land shall yield her increase, and the
26. 20 for your land shall not yield her increase
Deut 32. 22 shall consume the earth with her increase
Judg. 6. 4 destroyed the increase of the earth, till thou
Job 20. 28 The increase of his house shall depart, (and
Psa. 67. 6 (Then) shall the earth yield her increase
78. 46 He gave also their increase unto the cater.
85. 12 and our land shall yield her increase
Eze. 34. 27 the earth shall yield her increase, and
Zech. 8. 12 the ground shall give her increase, and the
2. *Increase, abundance, מַרְבֶּה marbeh.*
Isa. 9. 7 Of the increase of (his) government and
3. *Increase, abundance, multitude, מַרְבִּית marbith.*
Lev. 25. 37 Thou shalt not..lend him..victuals for i.
1 Sa. 2. 33 all the increase of thy house shall die in
4. *Fœtus, what is cast forth, שֶׁגֶר sheger.*
Deut. 7. 13 he will also bless..the increase of thy kine
28. 4, 18 the increase of thy kine, and the flocks
28. 51 the increase of thy kine, or flocks of thy
5. *Increase, fruit, תְּבוּאָה tebuah.*
Gen. 47. 24 it shall come to pass in the increase, that
Lev. 19. 25 that it may yield unto you the increase
25. 7 for thy cattle..shall all the increase ther.
25. 12 ye shall eat the increase thereof out of the
25. 20 we shall not sow, nor gather in our incr.
Num 18. 30 the increase of the..floor..the increase of
Deut 14. 22 Thou shalt truly tithe all the increase of
14. 28 bring forth all the tithe of thine increase
16. 15 God shall bless thee in all thine increase
26. 12 of tithing all the tithes of thine increase
2 Ch. 31. 5 first fruits..of all the increase of the field
32. 28 Storehouses also for the increase of corn
Neh. 9. 37 it yieldeth much increase unto the kings
Job 31. 12 (as) a fire (that)..would root out all mine i.
Psa. 107. 37 vineyards, which may yield fruits of inc.
Prov. 3. 9 with the first fruits of all thine increase
14. 4 much increase (is) by the strength of the
18. 20 with the increase of his life shall he be f.
Eccl. 5. 10 nor he that loveth abundance with incr.
Isa. 30. 23 and bread of the increase of the earth
Jer. 2. 3 Israel (was)..the first fruits of his increase
Eze. 48. 18 the increase thereof shall be for food unto
6. *Increase, fruit, תְּנוּבָה tenubah.*
Deut 32. 13 that he might eat the increase of the fields
Eze. 36. 30 I will multiply..the increase of the field
7. *Increase, תַּרְבּוּת tarbuth.*
Num 32. 14 ye are risen up..an increase of sinful men
8. *Increase, תַּרְבִּית tarbith.*
Lev. 25. 36 Take thou no usury of him, or increase: but
Eze. 18. 8 neither hath taken any increase, (that)
18. 13 forth upon usury, and hath taken increase
18. 17 hath not received usury nor increase, hath
22. 12 thou hast taken usury and increase, and
9. *Increase, αὔξησις auxēsis.*
Eph. 4. 16 maketh increase of the body unto the ed.
Col. 2. 19 the body..increaseth with the increase
[*See* Vineyards.]

INCREASE, to —
1. *To strengthen, harden, אָמַץ amats, 3.*
Prov. 24. 5 yea, a man of knowledge increaseth stre.
2. *To rise, triumph, גָּאָה gaah.*
Job 10. 16 For it increaseth. Thou huntest me as
3. *To make great, גָּדַל gadal, 5.*
Isa. 9. 3 Thou hast..not increased the joy: they
4. *To add, increase, יָסַף yasaph.*
Isa. 26. 15 Thou hast increased..thou hast increased
29. 19 The meek also shall increase..joy in the
5. *To be added, יָסַף yasaph, 2*
Prov. 11. 24 There is that scattereth, and yet increas.
6. *To add, increase, יָסַף yasaph, 5.*
Ezra 10. 10 taken..to increase the trespass of Israel
Prov. 1. 5 A wise (man) will hear, and will increase
9. 9 teach..and he will increase in learning
9. 11 and the years of thy life shall be increas.
16. 21 the sweetness of the lips increaseth lear.
23. 28 and increaseth the transgressors among
Eccl. 1. 18 he that increaseth knowledge increaseth
2. 9 I was great, and increased more than all
Eze. 5. 16 I will increase the famine upon you, and
23. 14 she increased her whoredoms: for when
7. *To bring forth, increase, נוּב nub.*
Psa. 62. 10 if riches increase, set not your heart (upon
8. *To go up, עָלָה alah.*
1 Ki. 22. 35 the battle increased that day; and the k.
2 Ch. 18. 34 the battle increased that day: howbeit
Psa. 74. 23 the tumult..against thee increaseth con
Eze. 41. 7 and so increased (from) the lowest..to
9. *To make or cause to be fruitful, פָּרָה parah, 5.*
Psa. 105. 24 he increased his people greatly; and m.
10. *Many, much, abundant, great, mighty, רַב rab.*
1 Sa. 14. 19 the noise..went on and increased: and S.
2 Sa. 15. 12 the people increased continually with A

11. *To break forth, up, in,* פָּרַץ *parats.*
Gen. 30. 43 the man increased exceedingly, and had
1 Ch. 4. 38 the house of their fathers increased grea.
Hos. 4. 10 they..shall not increase; because they h.

12. *To be or become many,* רָבָה *rabah.*
Gen. 7. 17 the waters increased, and bare up the ark
Deut. 6. 3 that ye may increase mightily, as the L.
7. 22 lest the beasts of the field increase upon
1 Ch. 5. 23 they increased from Bashan unto Baal-h.
Prov 28. 28 but when they perish, the righteous incr.
29. 16 wicked are multiplied, transgression inc.
Eccl. 5. 11 When goods increase..what good (is there)
Jer. 23. 3 and they shall be fruitful and increase
Eze. 16. 7 thou hast increased and waxen great, and
36. 11 they shall increase and bring fruit: and I
Dan. 12. 4 shall run..and knowledge shall be incre.
Zech 10. 8 they shall increase as they have increased

13. *To multiply, make abundant,* רָבָה *rabah,* 5.
Judg. 9. 29 he said to Abimelech, Increase thine army
Psa. 44. 12 Thou sellest..and dost not increase..by

14. *To cause to multiply, make abound,* רָבָה *rabah,* 5.
Lev. 25. 16 thou shalt increase the price thereof, and
1 Ch. 27. 23 LORD had said he would increase Israel
Job 10. 17 and increasest thine indignation upon me
Psa. 71. 21 Thou shalt increase my greatness, and
Prov 13. 11 he that gathereth by labour shall increase
22. 16 He that oppresseth the poor to increase
28. 8 He that by usury..increaseth his substance
Eccl. 6. 11 there be many things that increase vanity
Isa. 40. 29 to (them that have) no might he increaseth
51. 2 for I called him alone..and increased him
57. 9 didst increase thy perfumes, and didst
Lam. 2. 5 hath increased in the daughter of Judah
Eze. 16. 26 hast increased thy whoredoms, to provoke
28. 5 by thy traffic hast thou increased thy ric.
36. 29 I will call for the corn, and will increase
36. 37 I will increase them with men like a flock
Dan. 11. 39 whom he shall acknowledge (and) increase
Hos. 10. 1 he hath increased the altars; according
12. 1 he daily increaseth lies and desolation
Amos 4. 9 your fig trees and your olive trees increased
Hab. 2. 6 Woe to him that increaseth (that which is)

15. *To make great, magnify,* שָׂגָא *saga,* 5.
Job 12. 23 He increaseth the nations, and destroyeth

16. *To be or become great,* שָׂגָה *sagah.*
Job 8. 7 yet thy latter end should greatly increase

17. *To become great,* שָׂגָה *sagah,* 5.
Psa. 73. 12 prosper in the world; they increase (in)

18. *To increase, grow,* αὐξάνω *auxanō.*
Mark 4. 8 yield fruit that sprang up and [increased]
John 3. 30 He must increase, but I (must) decrease
Acts 6. 7 word of God increased; and the number
2 Co. 9. 10 increase the fruits of your righteousness
10. 15 having hope, when your faith is increased
Col. 1. 10 and increasing in the knowledge of God
2. 19 body..increaseth with the increase of God

19. *To be over and above,* περισσεύω *perisseuō.*
Acts 16. 5 And..the churches..increased in number
1 Th. 4. 10 beseech..that ye increase more and more

20. *To strike forward,* προκόπτω *prokoptō.*
Luke 2. 52 Jesus increased in wisdom and stature
2 Ti. 2. 16 for they will increase unto more ungodli.

21. *To put toward, add to,* προστίθημι *prostithēmi.*
Luke 17. 5 And the apostles said..Increase our faith

INCREASE, to give the —
To increase, give increase, αὐξάνω *auxanō.*
1 Co. 3. 6 Apollos watered; but God gave the incr.
3. 7 any thing..but God that giveth the incre.

INCREASE abundantly, to —
To teem, bring forth abundantly, שָׁרַץ *sharats.*
Exod. 1. 7 the children of Israel..increased abund.

INCREASE in strength, to —
To strengthen, put power in, ἐνδυναμόω *endunamoō.*
Acts 9. 22 Saul increased the more in strength, and c.

INCREASE, to make to —
To make or cause to abound, πλεονάζω *pleonazō.*
1 Th. 3. 12 the Lord make you to increase and abound

INCREASE more and more, to —
To add, יָסַף *yasaph,* 5.
Psa. 115. 14 LORD shall increase you more and more

INCREASED, to be —
1. *To be or become mighty, bony, strong,* עָצַם *atsam.*
Jer. 5. 6 because..their backslidings are increased
15. 8 Their widows are increased to me above
30. 14 thine iniquity..thy sins were increased
30. 15 thy sins were increased, I have done these

2. *To be or become fruitful,* פָּרָה *parah.*
Exod 23. 30 until thou be increased, and inherit the l.
Jer. 3. 16 when ye be multiplied and increased in

3. *To break forth, up, in,* פָּרַץ *parats.*
Gen. 30. 30 and it is..increased unto a multitude; and
Job 1. 10 and his substance is increased in the land

4. *Abundance, multitude, greatness,* רֹב *rob.*
Hos. 4. 7 they were increased, so they sinned against

5. *To be many, multiplied,* רָבַב *rabab.*
Psa. 3. 1 LORD, how are they increased that trouble
4. 7 time..their corn and their wine increased
Eccl. 5. 11 they are increased that eat them; and

6. *To be many, multiplied,* רָבָה *rabah.*
Gen. 7. 18 the waters..were increased greatly upon
Psa. 49. 16 when the glory of his house is increased
Ezra 9. 6 for our iniquities are increased over
Jer. 29. 6 that ye may be increased there, and not
Dan. 12. 4 shall run..and knowledge shall be increas.

INCREASED with goods, to be —
To be or wax rich or wealthy, πλουτέω *plouteō.*
Rev. 3. 17 I am rich, and increased with goods, and

INCREDIBLE thing —
Not to be believed, ἄπιστος *apistos.*
Acts 26. 8 Why should it be thought a thing incred.

INCURABLE —
1. *To be sickly, mortal, desperate,* אָנַשׁ *anash.*
Job 34. 6 my wound (is) incurable without transgre.
Jer. 15. 18 Why is my pain..and my wound incurable
30. 12 Thy bruise (is) incurable..thy wound (is)
30. 15 thy sorrow (is) incurable for the multitude
Mic. 1. 9 wound (is) incurable; for it is come unto

2. *There is no healing,* אֵין מַרְפֵּא *en marpe.*
2 Ch. 21. 18 LORD smote him..with an incurable dise.

INDEBTED, to be —
To be indebted, ὀφείλω *opheilō.*
Luke 11. 4 we also forgive every one that is indebted

INDEED —
1. *But, verily,* אֲבָל *abal.*
Gen. 17. 19 Sarah thy wife shall bear thee a son indeed
2 Sa. 14. 5 (am) indeed a widow woman, and mine h.

2. *Surely, truly, indeed,* אָמְנָה *omnah.*
Gen. 20. 12 indeed (she is) my sister; she (is) the da.
Josh. 7. 20 Indeed I have sinned against the LORD G.

3. *Surely, truly, indeed,* אָמְנָם *omnam.*
Job 19. 4 be it indeed (that) I have erred, mine er.
19. 5 If indeed ye will magnify..against me, and

4. *Surely, truly, indeed,* אֻמְנָם *umnam.*
Num 22. 37 am I not able indeed to promote thee to h.
1 Ki. 8. 27 But will God indeed dwell on the earth?
Psa. 58. 1 Do ye indeed speak righteousness, O con.?

5. *Truly,* ἀληθῶς *alēthōs.*
John 1. 47 Behold an Israelite indeed, in whom is no
4. 42 we..know that this is indeed the Christ
6. 55 is meat [indeed,] and my blood is drink in.
7. 26 Do the rulers know indeed that this is the
8. 31 continue..(then) are ye my disciples ind.

6. *But,* ἀλλά *alla.*
2 Co. 11. 1 bear with me..and indeed bear with me

7. *For,* γάρ *gar.*
Rom. 8. 7 for it is not subject..neither indeed can
1 Th. 4. 10 indeed ye do it toward all the brethren

8. *Indeed,* μέν *men.*
Matt. 3. 11 I indeed baptize you with water unto rep.
13. 32 Which indeed is the least of all seeds; but
20. 23 Ye shall drink indeed of my cup, and be
23. 27 like unto whited sepulchres, which indeed
26. 41 spirit indeed (is) willing, but the flesh (is)
Mark 1. 8 I [indeed] have baptized you with water
10. 39 Ye shall [indeed] drink of the cup that I d.
14. 21 The Son of man indeed goeth, as it is wr.
Luke 3. 16 I indeed baptize you with water; but one
11. 48 they indeed killed them, and ye build th.
23. 41 we indeed justly; for we receive the due
Acts 4. 16 that indeed a notable miracle hath been
11. 16 John indeed baptized with water; but ye
22. 9 they that were with me saw indeed the
Rom. 6. 11 to be dead indeed unto sin, but alive unto
14. 20 All things indeed (are) pure; but (it is)
1 Co. 11. 7 a man indeed ought not to cover (his) h.
2 Co. 8. 17 indeed he accepted the exhortation; but
Phil. 1. 15 Some indeed preach Christ even of envy
3. 1; Col. 2. 23; 1 Pe. 2. 4.

9. *And,* καί *kai,* Mark 9. 13; Phil. 2. 27.

10. *Certainly,* ὄντως *ontōs.*
Mark 11. 32 counted John, that he was a prophet ind.
Luke 24. 34 The Lord is risen indeed, and hath appe.
John 8. 36 shall make you free, ye shall be free ind.
1 Ti. 5. 3 Honour widows that are widows indeed
5. 5 she that is a widow indeed, and desolate
5. 16 it may relieve them that are widows ind.
[*See also* Neither.]

IN-DI-A, הֹדּוּ.
This country was the limit of the territories of Ahasuerus in the east, as was Ethiopia in the west. The names in Herodotus are similarly connected. The Hebrew form *Hoddu* is an abbreviation of *Honadu*, which is identical with the names of the Indies, *Hindu*, or *Sindhu*, as well as with the ancient name of the country *Hapta-Hendu*, as it appears in the Vendidad. The India of the book of Esther is the Punjab, and perhaps Sind, *i.e.*, the India which Herodotus described as forming part of the Persian empire under Darius, and the India conquered by Alexander the Great.
Esth. 1. 1 Ahasuerus which reigned from I. even
8. 9 provinces which (are) from I. unto Ethio.

INDIGNATION —
1. *Indignation, insolence,* זַעַם *zaam.*
Psa. 69. 24 Pour out thine indignation upon them, and
78. 49 the fierceness of his anger, wrath, and in.
102. 10 Because of thine indignation and thy wr.
Isa. 10. 5 the staff in their hand is mine indignation
10. 25 the indignation shall cease, and mine an.
Isa. 13. 5 LORD, and the weapons of his indignation
26. 20 hide thyself..until the indignation be over
30. 27 his lips are full of indignation, and his t.
Jer. 10. 10 nations shall not be able to abide his ind.
15. 17 for thou hast filled me with indignation
50. 25 hath brought forth the weapons of his in.
Lam. 2. 6 hath despised in the indignation of his
Eze. 21. 31 I will pour out mine indignation upon
22. 24 nor rained upon in the day of indignation
22. 31 have I poured out mine indignation upon
Dan. 8. 19 what shall be in the last end of the indig.
11. 36 shall prosper till the indignation be acco.
Nah. 1. 6 Who can stand before his indignation? and
Hab. 3. 12 Thou didst march through the land in in.
Zeph. 3. 8 to pour upon them mine indignation..all

2. *To be indignant, insolent,* זָעַם *zaam.*
Isa. 66. 14 and (his) indignation toward his enemies

3. *Wrath, rage, raging,* זַעַף *zaaph.*
Isa. 30. 30 show..with the indignation of (his) anger
Mic. 7. 9 I will bear the indignation of the LORD

4. *Heat, fury,* חֵמָה *chemah.*
Esth. 5. 9 he was full of indignation against Morde.

5. *Anger, sadness, provocation,* כַּעַשׂ *kaas.*
Job 10. 17 and increasest thine indignation upon me

6. *Wrath,* קֶצֶף *qetseph.*
Deut 29. 28 LORD rooted them out..in great indigna.
2 Ki. 3. 27 there was great indignation against Israel
Isa. 34. 2 the indignation of the LORD (is) upon all

7. *Indignation,* ἀγανάκτησις *aganaktēsis.*
2 Co. 7. 11 indignation, yea..fear, yea..vehement de.

8. *Zeal,* ζῆλος *zēlos.*
Acts 5. 17 rose up..and were filled with indignation
Heb. 10. 27 fiery indignation, which shall devour the

9. *Wrath,* θυμός *thumos.*
Rom. 2. 8 obey unrighteousness, indignation and

10. *Anger,* ὀργή *orgē.*
Rev. 14. 10 without mixture into the cup of his indig.

INDIGNATION, to have, be moved with —
1. *To have indignation,* ἀγανακτέω *aganakteō.*
Matt 20. 24 they were moved with indignation against
26. 8 when his disciples saw (it), they had ind.
Mark 14. 4 there were some that had indignation with

2. *To be indignant, insolent,* זָעַם *zaam.*
Dan. 11. 30 have indignation against the holy coven.
Zech. 1. 12 against which thou hast had indignation
Mal. 1. 4 people against whom the LORD hath ind.

INDIGNATION, to take —
To be angry, sad, כָּעַס *kaas.*
Neh. 4. 1 he was wroth, and took great indignation

INDIGNATION, with —
To have indignation, ἀγανακτέω *aganakteō.*
Luke 13. 14 ruler of the synagogue answered with in.

INDITE, to —
To bubble up, bring forth, indite, רָחַשׁ *rachash.*
Psa. 45. 1 My heart is inditing a good matter: I sp.

INDUSTRIOUS —
A doer of work, עֹשֵׂה מְלָאכָה *oseh melakah.* [*asah*].
1 Ki. 11. 28 seeing the young man that he was indus.

INEXCUSABLE —
Without apology or excuse, ἀναπολόγητος *anapolog.*
Rom. 2. 1 thou art inexcusable, O man, whosoever

INFAMOUS —
Unclean or defiled of name, טְמֵאַת הַשֵּׁם [*tame*].
Eze. 22. 5 near..shall mock thee..infamous..much

INFAMY —
Evil account or report, דִּבָּה *dibbah.*
Prov 25. 10 put thee to shame, and thine infamy turn
Eze. 36. 3 taken up in the lips..and (are) an infamy

INFANT —
1. *Suckling infant,* עוּל *ul.*
Isa. 65. 20 There shall be no more thence an infant

2. *Suckling, infant,* עוֹלֵל, עֹלָל *olel, olal.*
1 Sa. 15. 3 slay both man and woman, infant and su.
Job 3. 16 not been; as infants (which) never saw
Hos. 13. 16 their infants shall be dashed in pieces

3. *Babe, infant,* βρέφος *brephos.*
Luke 18. 15 they brought unto him also infants, that

INFERIOR —
1. *Low, lower,* אֲרַע *ara.*
Dan. 2. 39 after..shall arise another kingdom inferior

2. *To fall,* נָפַל *naphal.*
Job 12. 3 I (am) not inferior to you: yea, who kno.
13. 2 do I know also: I (am) not inferior unto

INFERIOR, to be —
To be less, worse, inferior, ἡττάομαι *hēttaomai.*
2 Co. 12. 13 what is it wherein ye were inferior to

INFIDEL —
Not believing, ἄπιστος *apistos.*
2 Co. 6. 15 or what..he that believeth with an infid.
1 Ti. 5. 8 denied the faith, and is worse than an in.

INFINITE —
1. *No number,* אֵין מִסְפָּר *en mispar.*
Psa. 147. 5 of great power: his understanding (is) in

2. *No end*, אֵין קֵץ *en qets.*
Job 22. 5 wickedness great..thine iniquities infinite?
3. *No end*, אֵין קָצָה *en qetseh.*
Nah. 3. 9 Ethiopia and Egypt..strength and..infin.

INFIRMITY —

1. *To be sick, menstruous*, דָּוָה *davah.*
Lev. 12. 2 to the days of the separation for her infi.
2. *To sicken, appease, weaken*, חָלָה *chalah*, 3.
Psa. 77. 10 And I said, This (is) my infirmity..the
3. *Sickness, disease*, מַחֲלֶה *machaleh.*
Prov 18. 14 The spirit of a man will sustain his infir.
4. *Weakness*, ἀσθένεια *astheneia.*
Matt. 8. 17 Himself took our infirmities, and bare (our)
Luke 5. 15 to be healed by him of their infirmities
8. 2 which had been healed of..infirmities
13. 11 there was a woman which had a spirit of in.
13. 12 Woman, thou art loosed from thine infir
John 5. 5 which had an infirmity thirty and eight y.
Rom. 6. 19 because of the infirmity of your flesh: for
8. 26 Likewise the Spirit also helpeth our infir.
2 Co. 11. 30 glory of the things which concern mine in.
12. 5 of myself I will not glory, but in mine in.
12. 9 will I rather glory in my infirmities, that
12. 10 Therefore I take pleasure in infirmities, in
Gal. 4. 13 Ye know how through infirmity of the fl.?
1 Ti. 5. 23 for thy stomach's sake and thine often in.
Heb. 4. 15 be touched with the feeling of our infirm.
5. 2 that he himself also is compassed with in.
7. 28 law maketh..high priests which have in
5. *Weakness*, ἀσθένημα *asthenēma.*
Rom 15. 1 ought to bear the infirmities of the weak
6. *Sickness, disease*, νόσος *nosos.*
Luke 7. 21 in the same hour he cured many of..inf.

INFLAMMATION —

1. *Burning, inflammation*, דַּלֶּקֶת *dalleqeth.*
Deut 28. 22 LORD shall smite thee with..an inflamm.
2. *Burning, inflammation*, צָרֶבֶת *tsarebeth.*
Lev. 13. 28 for it (is) an inflammation of the burning

INFLAME, to —

To cause to burn, inflame, דָּלַק *dalaq*, 5.
Isa. 5. 11 continue until night, (till) wine inflame

INFLUENCES —

Sweet influences, מַעֲדַנּוֹת *maadannoth.*
Job 38. 31 Canst thou bind the sweet influences of P.

INFOLDING —

To take, receive, or catch oneself, לָקַח *laqach*, 7.
Eze. 1. 4 a great cloud, and a fire infolding itself

INFORM, to —

1. *To consider, discern*, בִּין *bin.*
Dan. 9. 22 he informed (me), and talked with me, and
2. *To show, direct, teach*, יָרָה *yarah*, 5.
Deut 17. 10 to do according to all that they inform
3. *To make manifest*, ἐμφανίζω *emphanizō.*
Acts 24. 1 Tertullus, who informed the governor ag.
25. 2 chief of the Jews informed him against P.
25. 15 priests and the elders of the Jews infor.
4. *To sound throughout, teach fully*, κατηχέω *katēch.*
Acts 21. 21 they are informed of thee, that thou tea.
21. 24 whereof they were informed concerning

INGATHERING —

Ingathering, אָסִף ,אָסִיף *asiph.*
Exod 23. 16 the feast of ingathering..in the end of the
34. 22 the feast of ingathering at the year's end

INHABIT, to —

1. *To sit down or still, inhabit, dwell*, יָשַׁב *yashab.*
Gen. 36. 20 These..the sons of Seir the Horite, who i.
Num 35. 34 Defile not..the land which ye shall inh.
Judg. 1. 17 they slew the Canaanites that inhabited
1. 21 did not drive out the Jebusites that inha.
1 Ch. 5. 9 eastward he inhabited unto the entering
Job 15. 28 in houses which no man inhabiteth, which
Psa. 22. 3 (O thou) that inhabitest the praises of I.
Isa. 42. 11 the villages (that) Kedar doth inhabit: let
44. 26 Thou shalt be inhabited; and to the cities
45. 18 he formed it to be inhabited: I (am) the L.
65. 21 they shall build houses, and inhabit..and
65. 22 They shall not build, and another inhabit
Jer. 48. 18 Thou daughter that dost inhabit Dibon
Eze. 33. 24 they that inhabit those wastes of the land
Amos 9. 14 they shall build the waste cities, and in.
Zeph. 1. 13 they shall also build houses, but not inh.
Zech. 7. 7 when Jerusalem was inhabited and in
7. 7 when..inhabited the south and the plain?
2. *To rest, dwell, inhabit, tabernacle*, שָׁכַן *shaken.*
Prov. 10. 30 but the wicked shall not inhabit the earth
Isa. 57. 15 thus saith the high and lofty One that in.
Jer. 17. 6 shall inhabit the parched places in the w.

INHABITANT —

1. *To sojourn*, גּוּר *gur.*
Job 28. 4 The flood breaketh out from the inhabit.
2. *To dwell*, דּוּר *dur.*
Dan. 4. 35 all the inhabitants of the earth (are) repu.
4. 35 in the army of heaven, and..the inhabita.
3. *To sit still, or down, dwell, inhabit*, יָשַׁב *yashab.*
Gen. 19. 25 he overthrew..all the inhabitants of the
34. 30 to make me to stink among the inhabita.
50. 11 when the inhabitants of the land, the Ca.
Exod 15. 14 sorrow shall take hold on the inhabitants
15. 15 the inhabitants of Canaan shall melt away
23. 31 I will deliver the inhabitants of the land
34. 12, 15 lest thou make a covenant with the in.
Lev. 18. 25 and the land itself vomiteth out her inh.
25. 10 proclaim liberty..unto all the inhabitants
Num 13. 32 land that eateth up the inhabitants ther.
14. 14 they will tell (it) to the inhabitants of this
32. 17 because of the inhabitants of the land
33. 52 ye shall drive out all the inhabitants of
33. 55 if ye will not drive out the inhabitants
Deut 13. 13 have withdrawn the inhabitants of their
13. 15 Thou shalt surely smite the inhabitants
Josh. 2. 9 all the inhabitants of the land faint bec.
2. 24 all the inhabitants of the country do faint
7. 9 all the inhabitants of the land shall hear
8. 24 made an end of slaying all the inhabita.
8. 26 utterly destroyed all the inhabitants of Ai
9. 3 when the inhabitants of Gibeon heard
9. 11 our elders and all the inhabitants of our
9. 24 to destroy all the inhabitants of the land
10. 1 the inhabitants of Gibeon had made peace
11. 19 save the Hivites, the inhabitants of Gib.
13. 6 All the inhabitants of the hill country
15. 15 he went up thence to the inhabitants of
15. 63 As for the Jebusites, the inhabitants of J.
17. 7 the border went along..unto the inhabi.
17. 11 the inhabitants of Dor..the inhabitants of
17. 11 the inhabitants of Taanach..the inhabit.
Judg. 1. 11 he went against the inhabitants of Debir
1. 19 could not drive out the inhabitants of the
1. 27 nor the inhabitants of Dor and her towns
1. 27 the inhabitants of Ibleam..the inhabita.
1. 30 the inhabitants of Kitron, nor the inhab.
1. 31 the inhabitants of Accho, nor the inhabi.
1. 32 the Canaanites, the inhabitants of the land
1. 33 inhabitants of Beth-shemesh, nor the in.
1. 33 inhabitants of the land..the inhabitants
2. 2 ye shall make no league with the inhabi.
5. 23 curse ye bitterly the inhabitants thereof
10. 18 he shall be head over all the inhabitants
11. 8 be our head over all the inhabitants of G.
11. 21 Amorites the inhabitants of that country
20. 15 besides the inhabitants of Gibeah, which
21. 9 none of the inhabitants of Jabesh-gilead
21. 10 Go and smite the inhabitants of Jabesh-g.
21. 12 they found among the inhabitants of Ja.
Ruth 4. 4 Buy (it) before the inhabitants, and before
1 Sa. 6. 21 they sent messengers to the inhabitants
23. 5 So David saved the inhabitants of Keilah
27. 8 for those..of old the inhabitants of the l.
31. 11 when the inhabitants of Jabesh-gilead h.
2 Sa. 5. 6 the Jebusites, the inhabitants of the land
1 Ki. 21. 11 who were the inhabitants in his city, did
2 Ki. 19. 26 their inhabitants were of small power
22. 16 will bring evil..upon the inhabitants there.
22. 19 what I spake..against the inhabitants th.
23. 2 all the inhabitants of Jerusalem with him
1 Ch. 8. 6, 13 heads of the fathers of the inhabitants
8. 13 who drove away the inhabitants of Gath
9. 2 the first inhabitants that (dwelt) in their
11. 4 the Jebusites..the inhabitants of the land
11. 5 And the inhabitants of Jebus said to Da.
22. 18 he hath given the inhabitants of the land
2 Ch 15. 5 great vexations..upon all the inhabitants
20. 7 didst drive out the inhabitants of this l.
20. 15 Hearken ye, all Judah, and ye inhabitants
20. 18 the inhabitants of Jerusalem fell before
20. 20 Hear me, O Judah, and ye inhabitants of
20. 23 stood up against the inhabitants of mount
20. 23 when they had made an end of the inha.
21. 11 caused the inhabitants of Jerusalem to c.
21. 13 hast made Judah and the inhabitants of
22. 1 the inhabitants of Jerusalem made Aha.
32. 22 LORD saved Hezekiah and the inhabitants
32. 26 he and the inhabitants of Jerusalem, so
32. 33 all Judah and the inhabitants of Jerusa.
33. 9 So Manasseh made Judah and the inhabit.
34. 24 I will bring evil..upon the inhabitants
34. 27 against this place, and against the inha.
34. 28 bring upon this place, and upon the inh.
34. 30 the king went up..and the inhabitants of
34. 32 the inhabitants of Jerusalem did accord.
35. 18 Josiah..and the inhabitants of Jerusalem
Ezra 4. 6 an accusation against the inhabitants of
Neh. 3. 13 The valley gate repaired..the inhabitants
7. 3 appoint watches of the inhabitants of Je.
9. 24 thou subduedst before them the inhabit.
Psa. 33. 8 let all the inhabitants of the world stand
33. 14 he looketh upon all the inhabitants of the
49. 1 give ear, all (ye) inhabitants of the world
75. 3 The earth and all the inhabitants thereof
83. 7 the Philistines with the inhabitants of T.
Isa. 5. 3 now, O inhabitants of Jerusalem, and men
5. 9 many houses shall be desolate..without in.
6. 11 Until the cities be wasted without inha.
8. 14 and for a snare to the inhabitants of Jer.
9. 9 Ephraim, and the inhabitant of Samaria
10. 13 I have put down the inhabitants like a
10. 31 inhabitants of Gebim gather themselves
12. 6 Cry out and shout, thou inhabitant of Z.
18. 3 All ye inhabitants of the world, and dw.
20. 6 the inhabitant of this isle shall say in that
21. 14 inhabitants of the land of Tema brought
22. 21 he shall be a father to the inhabitants of
23. 2 Be still, ye inhabitants of the isle; thou
23. 6 Tarshish; howl, ye inhabitants of the is.
24. 1 scattereth abroad the inhabitants thereof
24. 5 earth also is defiled under the inhabitants
24. 6 the inhabitants of the earth are burned
24. 17 (are) upon thee, O inhabitant of the earth
26. 9 inhabitants of the world will learn right.
Isa. 26. 18 have the inhabitants of the world fallen
26. 21 to punish the inhabitants of the earth for
37. 27 their inhabitants (were) of small power
38. 11 I shall behold man no more with the inh.
40. 22 the inhabitants thereof (are) as grassho.
42. 10 Sing..the isles, and the inhabitants ther.
42. 11 let the inhabitants of the rock sing, let
49. 19 too narrow by reason of the inhabitants
Jer. 1. 14 shall break forth upon all the inhabitants
2. 15 his cities are burned without inhabitant
4. 4 ye men of Judah and inhabitants of Jer.
4. 7 cities shall be laid waste, without an inh.
6. 12 I will stretch out my hand upon the inh.
8. 1 the bones of the inhabitants of Jerusalem
9. 11 I will make..desolate, without an inhab.
10. 17 Gather up thy wares..O inhabitant of the
10. 18 I will sling out the inhabitants of the land
11. 2 and speak..to the inhabitants of Jerusa.
11. 9 A conspiracy is found..among the inhab.
11. 12 Then shall the..inhabitants of Jerusalem
13. 13 I will fill all the inhabitants of this land
13. 13 all the inhabitants of Jerusalem with dr.
17. 20 the inhabitants of Jerusalem, that enter
17. 25 Then shall there enter..the inhabitants of
18. 11 speak..to the inhabitants of Jerusalem
19. 3 O kings of Judah, and inhabitants of Jeru.
19. 12 Thus will I do..to the inhabitants thereof
21. 6 I will smite the inhabitants of this city
21. 13 I (am) against thee, O inhabitant of the
22. 23 O inhabitant of Lebanon, that makest thy
23. 14 and the inhabitants thereof as Gomorrah
25. 2 the prophet spake..to all the inhabitants
25. 9 will bring them..against the inhabitants
25. 29 I will call for a sword upon all the inhab.
25. 30 shall give a shout..against all the inhab
26. 9 this city shall be desolate without an inh.
26. 15 bring innocent blood..upon the inhabita.
32. 32 the men of Judah, and the inhabitants of
33. 10 without man, and without inhabitant, and
34. 22 the cities..a desolation without an inha.
35. 13 Go and tell the men of Judah, and the inh.
35. 17 I will bring..upon all the inhabitants of
36. 31 I will bring..upon the inhabitants of Jer.
42. 18 hath been poured forth upon the inhabit.
44. 22 land..without an inhabitant, as at this day
46. 8 I will destroy the city and the inhabitants
46. 19 shall be waste and desolate without an in.
47. 2 all the inhabitants of the land shall howl
48. 19 O inhabitant of Aroer, stand by the way
48. 43 the snare, (shall be) upon thee, O inhabit.
49. 8 Flee ye, turn back, dwell deep, O inhabit.
49. 20 that he hath purposed against the inhab.
49. 30 get you far off, dwell deep, O ye inhabitan.
50. 21 Go up..against the inhabitants of Pekod
50. 34 that he may..disquiet the inhabitants of
50. 35 A sword (is)..upon the inhabitants of B.
51. 12 done that which he spake against the in.
51. 24 I will render..to all the inhabitants of C.
51. 29 to make the land of B...without an inha.
51. 35 upon Babylon, shall the inhabitant of Zi.
51. 35 My blood upon the inhabitants of Chald.
51. 37 Babylon shall become heaps..without ani.
Lam. 4. 12 all the inhabitants of the world, would not
Eze. 11. 15 they unto whom the inhabitants of Jerus.
12. 19 Thus saith the Lord GOD of the inhabita.
15. 6 so will I give the inhabitants of Jerusalem
26. 17 she and her inhabitants, which cause their
27. 8 inhabitants of Zidon and Arvad were thy
27. 35 All the inhabitants of the isles shall be
29. 6 the inhabitants of Egypt shall know that
Dan. 9. 7 to the men of Judah, and to the inhabita.
Hos. 4. 1 LORD hath a controversy with the inhab.
Joel 1. 2 give ear, all ye inhabitants of the land
1. 14 gather the elders..all the inhabitants of
2. 1 let all the inhabitants of the land tremble
Amos 1. 5 I will..cut off the inhabitant from the
1. 8 I will cut off the inhabitant from Ashdod
Mic. 1. 11 Pass ye away, thou inhabitant of Saphir
1. 11 inhabitant of Zaanan came not forth in
1. 12 inhabitant of Maroth waited carefully for
1. 13 O thou inhabitant of Lachish, bind the ch.
1. 15 bring an heir unto thee, O inhabitant of M.
6. 12 the inhabitants thereof have spoken lies
6. 16 I should make..the inhabitants thereof
Zeph. 1. 4 stretch out mine hand..upon all the inh.
1. 11 Howl, ye inhabitants of Maktesh, for all
2. 5 Woe unto the inhabitants of the sea coast
2. 5 destroy thee, that there shall be no inha.
3. 6 there is no man, that there is none inhabi.
Zech. 8. 20 there shall come people, and the inhabit.
8. 21 the inhabitants of one (city) shall go to
11. 6 I will no more pity the inhabitants of the
12. 5 The inhabitants of Jerusalem (shall be)
12. 7 the glory of the inhabitants of Jerusalem
12. 8 In that day shall the LORD defend the in.
12. 10 I will pour..upon the inhabitants of Jer.
13. 1 a fountain opened..to the inhabitants of
4. *Inhabitant, neighbour*, שָׁכֵן *shaken.*
Job 26. 5 from under the waters, and the inhabit.
Isa. 33. 24 the inhabitant shall not say, I am sick
Hos. 10. 5 inhabitants of Samaria shall fear because
5. *Sitter, inhabitant, dweller*, תּוֹשָׁב *toshab.*
1 Ki 17. 1 Elijah the Tishbite..of the inhabitants of
6. *To settle down, dwell*, κατοικέω *katoikeō.*
Rev. 17. 2 the inhabitants of the earth have been

INHABITED, to be —

1. *To sit still or down, inhabit, dwell*, יָשַׁב *yashab.*
Isa. 13. 20 It shall never be inhabited, neither shall
45. 18 he formed it to be inhabited: I (am) the

Jer. 17. 6 parched places..a salt land and not inh.
50. 13 it shall not be inhabited, but it shall be
50. 39 and it shall be no more inhabited for ever
Eze. 26. 20 bring thee down..that thou be not inhab.
29. 11 neither shall it be inhabited forty years
36. 35 desolate and ruined cities..are inhabited
Zech. 2. 4 Jerusalem shall be inhabited (as) towns
9. 5 Gaza, and Ashkelon shall not be inhabited
12. 6 shall be inhabited again in her own place
14. 10 it shall be lifted up, and inhabited in her
14. 11 but Jerusalem shall be safely inhabited

2. *To be dwelt in, inhabited,* יָשַׁב *yashab,* 2.
Exod16. 35 manna..until they came to a land inhabi.
Jer. 6. 8 I make thee desolate, a land not inhabit.
22. 6 a wilderness..cities (which) are not inha.
Eze. 12. 20 the cities (that are) inhabited shall be laid
26. 17 How art thou destroyed (that wast) inhab.
26. 19 city, like the cities that are not inhabited
36. 10 the cities shall be inhabited, and the wa.
38. 12 the desolate places (that are now) inhab.

3. *To be caused to be dwelt in,* יָשַׁב *yashab,* 6.
Isa. 44. 26 saith to Jerusalem, Thou shall be inhab.

4. *To rest, tabernacle,* שָׁכַן *shaken.*
Jer. 46. 26 afterward it shall be inhabited, as in the

INHABITED, to make to be —
To cause to inhabit, or be inhabited, יָשַׁב *yashab,* 5.
Isa. 54. 3 and make the desolate cities to be inhab.

INHABITED, not —
Separation, a cutting off, גְּזֵרָה *gezerah.*
Lev. 16. 22 all their iniquities unto a land not inha.

INHABITED place —
Seat, site, מוֹשָׁב *moshab.*
Eze. 34. 13 in all the inhabited places of the country

INHABITERS (of) —
To settle down, dwell, κατοικέω *katoikeō.*
Rev. 8. 13 Woe, woe, woe, to the [inhabiters] of the
12. 12 Woe to the inhabiters of the earth and of

INHABITING the wilderness —
Inhabitants of the dry places, צִיִּים *tsiyyim.*
Psa. 74. 14 meat to the people inhabiting the wilder.

INHERIT, to —
1. *To occupy, possess,* יָרַשׁ *yarash.*
Gen. 15. 7 brought thee..to give thee this land to i.
15. 8 whereby shall I know that I shall inherit
28. 4 that thou mayest inherit the land wherein
Lev. 20. 24 Ye shall inherit their land, and I will give
25. 46 take them..to inherit (them for) a posse.
Deut. 2. 31 begin to possess, that thou mayest inherit
16. 20 that thou mayest liv and inherit the land
Psa. 25. 13 dwell..and his seed shall inherit the earth
37. 9 those that wait..shall inherit the earth
37. 11 the meek shall inherit the earth, and sh.
37. 22 blessed of him shall inherit the earth; and
37. 29 The righteous shall inherit the land, and
37. 34 he shall exalt thee to inherit the land
105. 44 and they inherited the labour of the peo.
Isa. 54. 3 thy seed shall inherit the Gentiles, and
57. 13 possess..and shall inherit my holy mou.
60. 21 they shall inherit the land for ever, the
65. 9 mine elect shall inherit it, and my serva.
Jer. 8. 10 their fields to them that shall inherit
49. 1 why..doth their king inherit Gad, and
Eze. 33. 24 Abraham was one, and he inherited the

2. *To have, take or give inheritance,* נָחַל *nachal.*
Exod23. 30 until thou be increased, and inherit the
32. 13 all this land..and they shall inherit (it)
Num26. 55 according to the names..they shall inh.
32. 19 we will not inherit with them on yonder
35. 8 according to his inheritance which he in.
Deut19. 14 which thou shalt inherit in the land that
Josh 14. 1 which the children of Israel inherited in
Judg11. 2 Thou shalt not inherit..our father's house
Psa. 69. 36 The seed also of his servants shall inherit
82. 8 Arise..for thou shalt inherit all nations
Prov. 3. 35 The wise shall inherit glory: but shame
11. 29 He that troubleth his..house shall inherit
14. 18 The simple inherit folly: but the prudent
Jer. 16. 19 Surely our fathers have inherited lies
Eze. 47. 14 ye shall inherit it, one as well as another
Zech. 2. 12 LORD shall inherit Judah his portion in

3. *To take or leave an inheritance,* נָחַל *nachal,* 7.
Num32. 18 until the children of Israel have inherited
33. 54 to the tribes of your fathers ye shall inh.
34. 13 This (is) the land which ye shall inherit
Eze. 47. 13 This..the border whereby ye shall inherit

4. *Inheritance,* נַחֲלָה *nachalah.*
Num 18. 24 tithes..I have given to the Levites to in.
Josh 17. 14 given me..one lot and one portion to inh.

5. *To obtain by lot,* κληρονομέω *klēronomeō.*
Matt. 5. 5 Blessed..for they shall inherit the earth
19. 29 receive..and shall inherit everlasting life
25. 34 inherit the kingdom prepared for you from
Mark10. 17 what shall I do that I may inherit eternal
Luke10. 25 what shall I do to inherit eternal life?
18. 18 what shall I do to inherit eternal life?
1 Co. 6. 9 that the unrighteous shall not inherit the
6. 10 Nor thieves..shall inherit the kingdom
15. 50 flesh and blood cannot inherit the king.
15. 50 neither doth corruption inherit incorrup.
Gal. 5. 21 they..shall not inherit the kingdom of God
Heb. 6. 12 who through faith and patience inherit
12. 17 when he would have inherited the blessing
1 Pe. 3. 9 knowing..that ye should inherit a blessing
Rev. 21. 7 He that overcometh [shall inherit] all thi.

INHERIT, to cause, give, or make to —
1. *To cause to occupy or possess,* יָרַשׁ *yarash,* 5.
2 Ch.20. 11 possession, which thou hast given us to in.

2. *To cause to inherit, give inheritance,* נָחַל *nachal,* 5.
Deut. 1. 38 Joshua..he shall cause Israel to inherit
3. 28 he shall cause them to inherit the land
12. 10 land..LORD your God giveth you to inh.
19. 3 land..LORD thy God giveth thee to inhe.
21. 16 when he maketh his sons to inherit (that)
31. 7 and thou shalt cause them to inherit it
1 Sa. 2. 8 to make them inherit the throne of glory
Prov. 8. 21 cause those that love me to inherit subst.
Isa. 49. 8 to cause to inherit the desolate heritages
Jer. 12. 14 I have caused my people Israel to inherit

INHERITANCE —
1. *Portion,* חֵלֶק *cheleq.*
Psa. 16. 5 LORD (is) the portion of mine inheritance

2. *Possession, thing or place occupied,* יְרֻשָּׁה *yerushshah.*
Judg21. 17 an inheritance for them that be escaped
Jer. 32. 8 the right of inheritance (is) thine, and the

3. *A possession, thing occupied,* מוֹרָשָׁה *morashah.*
Deut 33. 4 a law..the inheritance of the congregat.
Eze. 33. 24 saying..the land is given for inheritance

4. *Inheritance,* נַחֲלָה *nachalah.*
Gen. 31. 14 yet any portion or inheritance for us in
48. 6 name of their brethren in their inherita.
Exod15. 17 plant them in the mountain of thine inh.
Num16. 14 or given us inheritance of fields and vine.
18. 20 I (am) thy part and thine inheritance
18. 21 all the tenth in Israel for an inheritance
18. 23, 24 the children of I. they have no inhe.
18. 26 which I have given you..for your inheri.
26. 53 the land shall be divided for an inherita.
26. 54 give the more inheritance .. the less inh.
26. 54 to every one shall his inheritance be given
26. 62 because there was no inheritance given
27. 7 give them a possession of an inheritance
27. 7 thou shalt cause the inheritance of their
27. 8 cause his inheritance..unto his daughter
27. 9, 10, 11 ye shall give his inheritance unto
32. 18 have inherited every man his inheritance
32. 19 because our inheritance is fallen to us on
32. 32 that the possession of our inheritance on
33. 54 the more inheritance..give the less inhe.
34. 2 land that shall fall unto you for an inhe.
34. 14, 15 the half tribe..have received their inh.
35. 2 that they give unto the Levites, of the in.
35. 8 give..unto the Levites according to his in.
36. 2 to give the land for an inheritance by lot
36. 2 to give the inheritance of Zelophehad our
36. 3 their inheritance be taken from the inhe.
36. 3 shall be put to the inheritance of the tribe
36. 3 shall it be taken from the lot of our inher.
36. 4 their inheritance be put unto the inherit.
36. 4 inheritance be taken away from the inh.
36. 7 So shall not the inheritance..remove from
36. 7 shall keep himself to the inheritance of
36. 8 every daughter, that possesseth an inherit.
36. 8 may enjoy every man the inheritance of
36. 9 Neither shall the inheritance remove from
36. 9 shall keep himself to his own inheritance
36. 12 their inheritance remained in the tribe of
Deut. 4. 20 to be unto him a people of inheritance, as
4. 21 the LORD thy God giveth thee (for) an in.
4. 38 to give thee their land (for) an inheritance
9. 26, 29 people and thine inheritance, which
10. 9 Levi hath no part nor inheritance with
10. 9 LORD (is) his inheritance, according as the
12. 9 to the inheritance which the LORD your
12. 12 as he hath no part nor inheritance with
14. 27, 29 he hath no part nor inheritance with
15. 4 God giveth thee (for) an inheritance to
18. 1 shall have no part nor inheritance with
18. 1 they shall eat the offerings..and his inh.
18. 2 shall they have no inheritance among
18. 2 LORD (is) their inheritance, as he hath said
19. 10 LORD thy God giveth thee (for) an inher.
19. 14 they of old time have set in thine inherit.
20. 16 thy God doth give thee (for) an inheritance
21. 23 LORD thy God giveth thee (for) an inheri.
[So in 24. 4; 25 19; 26. 1.]
29. 8 we took their land, and gave it for an inh.
32. 9 For..Jacob (is) the lot of his inheritance
Josh. 11. 23 Joshua gave it for an inheritance unto I.
13. 6 only divide thou it by lot..for an inherit.
13. 7 divide this land for an inheritance unto
13. 8 and the Gadites have received their inher.
13. 14 unto the tribe of Levi he gave none inher.
13. 14 sacrifices..made by fire (are) their inherit.
13. 23 This (was) the inheritance of the children
13. 28 This (is) the inheritance of the children of
13. 33 unto..Levi Moses gave not (any) inherit.
13. 33 LORD God of Israel (was) their inheritance
14. 2 By lot (was) their inheritance, as the LORD
14. 3 For Moses had given the inheritance of
14. 3 unto the Levites he gave none inheritance
14. 9 the land..shall be thine inheritance, and
14. 13 gave unto Caleb..Hebron for an inherit.
14. 14 Hebron..became the inheritance of Caleb
15. 20 This (is) the inheritance of the tribe of the
16. 5 even the border of their inheritance on
16. 8 This (is) the inheritance of the tribe of the
16. 9 among the inheritance of the children of
17. 4 to give us an inheritance among our br.
Josh. 17. 4 he gave them an inheritance amo. ; 17.6
18. 2 which had not yet received their inherit.
18. 4 describe it according to the inheritance
18. 7 the priesthood of the LORD (is) their inhe.
18. 7 have received their inheritance beyond J.
18. 20 This (was) the inheritance of the children
18. 28 This (is) the inheritance of the children of
19. 1 their inheritance was within the inherit.
19. 2 they had in their inheritance Beer-Sheba
19. 8 This (is) the inheritance of the tribe of the
19. 9 the inheritance of the children of Simeon
19. 9 Simeon had..within the inheritance of the
19. 10 the border of their inheritance was unto
19. 16 This (is) the inheritance of the children of
19. 23, 31, 39, 48, This (is) the inheritance of the
19. 41 the coast of their inheritance was Zorah
19. 49 the children of Israel gave an inheritance
19. 51 These (are) the inheritances, which Eleazar
21. 3 gave unto the Levites out of their inherit.
23. 4 to be an inheritance for your tribes, from J.
24. 28 let the people..every man unto his inher.
24. 30 they buried him in the border of his inh..
24. 32 it became the inheritance of the children
Judg. 2. 6 went every man unto his inheritance to
2. 9 they buried him in the border of his inh.
18. 1 Danites sought them an inheritance to
18. 1 inheritance had not fallen unto them am.
20. 6 all the country of the inheritance of Israel
21. 23 they went and returned unto their inher.
21. 24 they went at..every man to his inheritance
Ruth 4. 5, 10 the name of the dead upon his inheri.
4. 6 I cannot..lest I mar mine own inheritance
1 Sa. 10. 1 anointed thee..captain over his inherit.?
26. 19 from abiding in the inheritance of the L.
2 Sa. 14. 16 destroy me and my son..out of the inher.
20. 1 neither have we inheritance in the son of J.
20. 19 why wilt thou swallow up the inheritance
21. 3 that ye may bless the inheritance of the L.
1 Ki. 8. 36 thou hast given to thy people for an inh.
8. 51 For they (be) thy people, and thine inhe.
8. 53 separate them..(to be) thine inheritance
12. 16 neither..inheritance in the son of Jesse
21. 3 that I should give the inheritance of my f.
21. 4 I will not give thee the inheritance of my
2 Ki. 21. 14 I will forsake the remnant of mine inhe.
1 Ch.16. 18 the land of Canaan, the lot of your inhe.
2 Ch. 6. 27 thou hast given unto thy people for an in.
10. 16 and..none inheritance in the son of Jesse
Neh. 11. 20 all the cities of Judah, every one in his in
Job 31. 2 inheritance of the Almighty from on high?
42. 15 their father gave them inheritance among
Psa. 2. 8 I shall give..the heathen..thine inherit.
28. 9 Save thy people, and bless thine inherit.
33. 12 people..he hath chosen for his own inhe
37. 18 and their inheritance shall be for ever
47. 4 He shall choose our inheritance for us, the
68. 9 whereby thou didst confirm thine inheri.
74. 2 the rod of thine inheritance..thou hast
78. 55 divided them an inheritance by line, and
78. 62 He..was wroth with his inheritance
78. 71 feed Jacob his people, and Israel his inh.
79. 1 O God, the heathen are come into thine in.
94. 14 neither will he forsake his inheritance
105. 11 the land of Canaan, the lot of your inheri.
106. 5 that I may glory with thine inheritance
106. 40 insomuch that he abhorred his own inhe.
Prov 17. 2 shall have part of the inheritance among
19. 14 House and riches (are) the inheritance of
20. 21 An inheritance..gotten hastily at the be.
Eccl. 7. 11 Wisdom (is) good with an inheritance; and
Isa. 19. 25 saying, Blessed (be)..Israel mine inheri.
47. 6 I have polluted mine inheritance, and g.
63. 17 thy servant's sake, the tribes of thine inh.
Jer. 10. 16 and Israel (is) the rod of his inheritance
12. 14 mine evil neighbours, that touch the inhe.
16. 18 they have filled mine inheritance with the
51. 19 and (Israel is) the rod of his inheritance
Lam. 5. 2 Our inheritance is turned to strangers, our
Eze. 35. 15 As thou didst rejoice at the inheritance
36. 12 thou shalt be their inheritance, and thou
44. 28 it shall be unto them for an inheritance
44. 28 I (am) their inheritance: and ye shall give
45. 1 ye shall divide by lot the land for inheri.
46. 16 the inheritance thereof shall be his sons'
46. 16 it (shall be) their possession by inheritance
46. 17 if he give a gift of his inheritance to one
46. 17 his inheritance shall be his sons' for them
46. 18 prince shall not take of the people's inh.
47. 14 and this land shall fall unto you for inh.
47. 22 ye shall divide it by lot for an inheritance
47. 22 they shall have inheritance with you am.
47. 23 there shall ye give (him) his inheritance.
48. 29 ye shall divide by lot unto..Israel for in.

5. *What is obtained by lot, possession,* κληρονομία.
Matt21. 38 come..and let us seize on his inheritance
Mark12. 7 let us kill him, and the inheritance shall
Luke12. 13 speak..that he divide the inheritance
20. 14 let us kill him, that the inheritance may
Acts 7. 5 he gave him none inheritance in it, no, not
20. 32 to give you an inheritance among all them
Gal. 3. 18 For if the inheritance (be) of..law, (it is)
Eph. 1. 14 Which is the earnest of our inheritance
1. 18 what the riches of the glory of his inher.
5. 5 hath any inheritance in the kingdom of
Col. 3. 24 ye shall receive the reward of the inheri
Heb. 9. 15 might receive the promise of eternal inh.
11. 8 which he should after receive for an inh.
1 Pe. 1. 4 To an inheritance incorruptible, and und.

6. *A lot, possession,* κλῆρος *klēros.*
Acts 26. 18 inheritance among them which are sanc.
Col. 1. 12 made us meet to be partakers of the inh.

INHERITANCE, to distribute for —
To give inheritance, נָחַל *nachal*, 3.
Josh 13. 32 which Moses did distribute for inheritance
14. 1 Joshua..distributed for inheritance to

INHERITANCE, to divide (by or for) —
1. *To have or give inheritance*, נָחַל *nachal*.
Num34. 18 of every tribe, to divide the land by inhe.
Josh.19. 49 made an end of dividing the land for inh.
2. *To give inheritance*, נָחַל *nachal*, 3.
Num 34. 29 the LORD commanded to divide the inhe.
Josh 19. 51 divided for an inheritance by lot in Shiloh
3. *To cause to inherit*, נָחַל *nachal*, 5.
Deut 32. 8 Most High divided to the nations their in.
Josh. 1. 6 shalt thou divide for an inheritance the
4. *To take or leave an inheritance*, נָחַל *nachal*, 7.
Num 33. 54 ye shall divide the land by lot for an inh.

INHERITANCE, to give (for) —
To cause to inherit, נָחַל *nachal*, 5.
Jer. 3. 18 to the land that I have given for an inhe.
Eze. 46. 18 he shall give his sons inheritance out of

INHERITANCE, to have —
Receive possession, (נַחֲלָה) נָחַל *nachal* (*nachalah*).
Num 18. 20 Thou shalt have no inheritance in their
18. 23 that among..Israel they have no inheri.
18. 24 among..Israel they shall have no inheri.
Josh.17. 6 the daughters of Manasseh had an inhe.
19. 9 the children of Simeon had their inheri.

INHERITANCE, to leave (for) —
1. *To cause to occupy, possess or succeed*, יָרַשׁ *yarash*, 5.
Ezra 9. 12 leave (it) for an inheritance to your chil.
2. *To cause to inherit, give inheritance*, נָחַל *nachal*, 5.
1 Ch.28. 8 leave (it) for an inheritance for your chil.
Prov.13. 22 A good (man) leaveth an inheritance to his

INHERITANCE, to obtain (by) —
To obtain by lot, possess, κληρονομέω κληρόω.
Eph. 1. 11 In whom also [we have obtained an inh.]
Heb. 1. 4 as he hath by inheritance obtained a more

INHERITANCE, to take (as or for an) —
1. *To have or give inheritance*, נָחַל *nachal*.
Exod34. 9 pardon..our sin, and take us for thine in.
Josh.16. 4 Manasseh and Ephraim, took their inher.
2. *To give inheritance*, נָחַל *nachal*, 3 (or חלל, 2).
Eze. 22. 16 thou shalt take thine inheritance in thy.
3. *To take or leave an inheritance*, נָחַל *nachal*, 7.
Lev. 25. 46 ye shall take them as an inheritance for

INHERITOR —
To occupy, possess, יָרַשׁ *yarash*.
Isa. 65. 9 out of Judah an inheritor of my mount.

INIQUITY —
1. *Iniquity, vanity*, אָוֶן *aven*.
Num23. 21 He hath not beheld iniquity in Jacob, ne.
1 Sa. 15. 23 stubbornness (is as) iniquity and idolatry
Job 4. 8 Even..they that plow iniquity..reap the
11. 14 If iniquity (be) in thine hand, put it far
21. 19 God layeth up his iniquity for his children
31. 3 strange (punishment) to the workers of in.?
34. 8 goeth in company with the workers of in.
34. 22 where the workers of iniquity may hide
36. 10 commandeth that they return from iniq.
36. 21 Take heed, regard not iniquity: for this
Psa. 5. 5 not stand..thou hatest all workers of in.
6. 8 Depart from me, all ye workers of iniquity
7. 14 he travaileth with iniquity, and hath con.
14. 4 Have all the workers of iniquity no know.
28. 3 with the workers of iniquity, which speak
36. 3 The words of his mouth (are) iniquity and
36. 12 There are the workers of iniquity fallen
41. 6 heart gathereth iniquity to itself; (when)
53. 4 Have the workers of iniquity no knowledge?
55. 3 they cast iniquity upon me, and in wrath
56. 7 Shall they escape by iniquity? in..anger
59. 2 Deliver me from the workers of iniquity
64. 2 from the insurrection of the workers of in.
66. 18 If I regard iniquity in my heart, the LORD
92. 7 when all the workers of iniquity do flourish
92. 9 the workers of iniquity shall be scattered
94. 4 the workers of iniquity boast themselves?
94. 16 will stand..against the workers of iniquity
94. 23 he shall bring upon them their own i iq.
119. 133 let not any iniquity have dominion over
125. 5 lead them forth with the workers of iniq.
141. 4 wicked works with men that work iniquity
141. 9 and the gins of the workers of iniquity
Prov 10. 29 but destruction..to the workers of iniqu.
19. 28 the mouth of the wicked devoureth iniqu.
21. 15 but destruction..to the workers of iniqu.
Isa. 1. 13 (it is) iniquity, even the solemn meeting
29. 20 and all that watch for iniquity are cut off
31. 2 against the help of them that work iniqu.
32. 6 his heart will work iniquity, to practise
59. 4 conceive mischief, and bring forth iniquity
59. 6 their works (are) works of iniquity, and
59. 7 their thoughts (are) thoughts of iniquity
Hos. 6. 8 Gilead (is) a city of them that work iniq.
12. 11 iniquity (in) Gilead? surely they are van.
Mic. 2. 1 Woe to them that devise iniquity..work
Hab. 1. 3 Why dost thou show me iniquity, and
2. *Mischief, calamity, desire*, הַוָּה *havvah*.
Psa 94. 20 Shall the throne of iniquity have fellows.
3. *Perversity, perverseness*, עָוֶל, עֶוֶל *avel, evel*.
Deut 32. 4 a God of truth, and without iniquity, just
Job 34. 10 Far be it from..the Almighty..iniquity
34. 32 If I have done iniquity, I will do no more
Psa. 7. 3 LORD my God..if there be iniquity in my
53. 1 corrupt..and have done abominable iniq.
Jer. 2. 5 What iniquity have your fathers found in
Eze. 3. 20 When a righteous (man) doth..commit in.
18. 8 hath withdrawn his hand from iniquity
18. 24 when the righteous..committeth iniquity
18. 26 committeth iniquity, and dieth in them
18. 26 for his iniquity that he hath done shall he
28. 18 hast defiled thy sanctuaries..by the iniq.
33. 13 if he..commit iniquity, all his righteous.
33. 13 for his iniquity that he hath committed
33. 15 walk..without committing iniquity; he
33. 18 When the righteous..committeth iniqui.
4. *Perversity*, עַוְיָה (עֲוָיָה) *avayyah*.
Dan. 4. 27 break off..thine iniquities by showing
5. *Perverseness, perversity*, עַוְלָה *avlah*.
2 Ch.19. 7 for (there is) no iniquity with the LORD
Job 6. 29 Return, I pray you, let it not be iniquity
6. 30 Is there iniquity in my tongue? cannot
15. 16 man, which drinketh iniquity like water?
22. 23 thou shalt put away iniquity far from thy
36. 23 or who can say, Thou hast wrought iniq.?
Psa. 37. 1 envious against the workers of iniquity
107. 42 and all iniquity shall stop her mouth
119. 3 They also do no iniquity: they walk in
125. 3 righteous put forth their hands unto ini.
Prov 22. 8 He that soweth iniquity shall reap vanity
Eze. 28. 15 Thou (wast) perfect..till iniquity is found
Hos. 10. 13 ye have reaped iniquity; ye have eaten
Mic. 3. 10 They build up..Jerusalem with iniquity
Hab. 2. 12 Woe to him that..stablisheth a city by in.!
Zeph. 3. 5 The just LORD..not do iniquity: every
3. 13 The remnant of Israel shall not do iniq
Mal 2. 6 iniquity was not found in his lips: he
6. *Perverseness, perversity*, עוֹלָה *olah*.
Job 5. 16 So the poor hath hope, and iniquity stop.
Psa. 64. 6 They search out iniquities; they accom.
7. *Perversity*, עָוֹן *avon*.
Gen. 15. 16 iniquity of the Amorites (is) not yet full
19. 15 lest thou be consumed in the iniquity of
44. 16 God hath found out the iniquity of thy
Exod20. 5 visiting the iniquity of the fathers upon
28. 38 may bear the iniquity of the holy things
28. 43 that they bear not iniquity, and die
34. 7 forgiving iniquity and transgression and
34. 7 visiting the iniquity of the fathers upon
34 9 pardon our iniquity and our sin, and take
Lev. 5 1 if he do not utter..he shall bear his iniq.
5. 17 yet is he guilty, and shall bear his iniq.
7. 18 the soul that eateth of it shall bear his in.
10. 17 hath given it you to bear the iniquity
16. 21 confess over him all the iniquities of the
16 22 the goat shall bear upon him all their in.
17. 16 nor bathe his flesh..shall bear his iniqu.
18. 25 I do visit the iniquity thereof upon it, and
19. 8 that eateth it shall bear his iniquity, be.
20. 17 sister's nakedness; he shall bear his iniq.
20. 19 his near kin: they shall bear their iniq.
22. 16 or suffer them to bear the iniquity of tr.
26. 39 shall pine away in their iniquity in your
26. 39 in the iniquities of their fathers shall they
26. 40 shall confess their iniquity, and the iniq.
26. 41, 43 accept of the punishment of their in.
Num. 5. 15 offering..bringing iniquity to remembra.
5. 31 Then shall the man be guiltless from ini.
5. 31 and this woman shall bear her iniquity
14. 18 forgiving iniquity and transgression, and
14. 18 visiting the iniquity of the fathers upon
14. 19 Pardon, I beseech thee, the iniquity of this
14. 34 day for a year, shall ye bear your iniqu.
15. 31 that soul shall utterly be cut off; his ini.
18. 1 shall bear the iniquity of the sanctuary
18. 1 shall bear the iniquity of your priesthood
18. 23 the Levites..they shall bear their iniquity
30. 15 if he shall..then he shall bear her iniqu.
Deut. 5. 9 visiting the iniquity of the fathers upon
19. 15 shall not rise up against a man for any in.
Josh 22. 17 (Is) the iniquity of Peor too little for us
22. 20 that man perished not alone in his iniqu.
1 Sa. 3. 13 will judge..for the iniquity which he kn.
3. 14 the iniquity of Eli's house shall not be p.
20. 1 What have I done? what (is) mine iniquity?
20. 8 if there be in me iniquity, slay me thyself
25. 24 Upon me, my lord..me (let this) iniquity
2 Sa. 14. 9 My lord, O king, the iniquity (be) on me
14. 32 if there be (any) iniquity in me, let him
19. 19 Let not my lord impute iniquity unto me
22. 24 and have kept myself from mine iniquity
24. 10 LORD, take away the iniquity of thy serv.
1 Ch.21. 8 do away the iniquity of thy servant; for
Ezra 9. 6 our iniquities are increased over (our) he.
9. 7 for our iniquities have we, our kings, (and)
9. 13 God hast punished us less than our iniqu.
Neh. 4. 5 cover not their iniquity, and let not their
9. 2 confessed their sins, and the iniquities of
Job 7. 21 why dost thou not..take away mine in.
10. 6 That thou enquirest after mine iniquity
10. 14 thou wilt not acquit me from mine iniqu
11. 6 God exacteth of thee (less) than thine in.
13. 23 How many (are) mine iniquities and sins?
13. 26 makest me to possess the iniquities of my
14. 17 transgression..thou sewest up mine iniq.
15. 5 thy mouth uttereth thine iniquity, and
20. 27 The heaven shall reveal his iniquity; and
22. 5 (Is) not thy wickedness great..thine iniq.
31. 11 this (is) a heinous crime; yea, it (is) an in.
31. 28 This also (were) an iniquity (to be punis.
31. 33 covered..by hiding mine iniquity in my
Job 33. 9 I (am) innocent; neither (is there) iniqu.
Psa. 18. 23 upright..I kept myself from mine iniqu.
25. 11 LORD, pardon mine iniquity; for it (is)
31. 10 my strength faileth because of mine iniq.
32. 2 unto whom the LORD imputeth not iniqu.
32. 5 mine iniquity have I not hid. I said, I
32. 5 and thou forgavest the iniquity of my sin
36. 2 until his iniquity be found to be hateful
38. 4 mine iniquities are gone over mine head
38. 18 I will declare mine iniquity; I will be
39. 11 When thou..dost correct man for iniqui.
40. 12 mine iniquities have taken hold upon me
49. 5 the iniquity of my heels shall compass me
51. 2 Wash me throughly from mine iniquity
51. 5 Behold, I was shapen in iniquity; and in sin
51. 9 Hide thy face..blot out all mine iniquities
65. 3 Iniquities prevail against me..our transg.
69. 27 Add iniquity unto their iniquity: and let
78. 38 But he..full of compassion, forgave..ini.
79. 8 O remember not against us former iniqu.
85. 2 Thou hast forgiven the iniquity of thy pe.
89. 32 Then will I visit..their iniquity with stri.
90. 8 Thou hast set our iniquites before thee
103. 3 Who forgiveth all thine iniquities; who
103. 10 nor rewarded us according to our iniqui.
106. 43 and were brought low for their iniquity
107. 17 and because of their iniquities, are afflic.
109. 14 Let the iniquity of his fathers be remem.
130. 3 If thou, LORD, shouldest mark iniquities
130. 8 he shall redeem Israel from all his iniq.
Prov. 5. 22 His own iniquities shall take the wicked
16. 6 By mercy and truth iniquity is purged
Isa. 1. 4 Ah sinful nation, a people laden with in.
5. 18 Woe unto them that draw iniquity with
6. 7 thine iniquity is taken away, and thy sin
13. 11 I will punish..the wicked for their iniq.
14. 21 slaughter..for the iniquity of their fath.
22. 14 Surely this iniquity shall not be purged
26. 21 punish the inhabitants of the earth for..i.
27. 9 this..shall the iniquity of Jacob be purg.
30. 13 Therefore this iniquity shall be to you as
33. 24 dwell therein (shall be) forgiven (their) in.
40. 2 cry unto her..that her iniquity is pardo.
43. 24 thou hast wearied me with thine iniquit.
50. 1 for your iniquities have ye sold yourself
53. 5 bruised for our iniquities: the chastisem.
53. 6 LORD hath laid on him the iniquity of us
53. 11 justify many; for he shall bear their iniq.
57. 17 For the iniquity of his covetousness was
59. 2 your iniquities have separated between
59. 3 your fingers with iniquity; your lips
59. 12 and (as for) our iniquities, we know them
64. 6 iniquities, like the wind, have taken us
64. 7 hast consumed us, because of our iniqu.
64. 9 neither remember iniquity for ever: beh.
65. 7 Your iniquities, and the iniquities of your
Jer. 2. 22 thine iniquity is marked before me, saith
3. 13 Only acknowledge thine iniquity, that
5. 25 Your iniquities have turned away these
11 10 They are turned back to the iniquities of
13. 22 For the greatness of thine iniquity are thy
14. 7 LORD, though our iniquities testify against
14. 10 he will now remember their iniquity, and
14. 20 We acknowledge..the iniquity of our fa.
16. 10 or what (is) our iniquity? or what (is) our
16. 17 neither is their iniquity hid from mine
16. 18 first I will recompense their iniquity and
18. 23 forgive not their iniquity, neither blot out
25. 12 that nation, saith the LORD, for their ini.
30. 14, 15 for the multitude of thine iniquity
31. 30 every one shall die for his own iniquity
31. 34 I will forgive their iniquity, and I will
32. 18 recompensest the iniquity of the fathers
33. 8 I will cleanse them from all their iniqui.
33. 8 I will pardon all their iniquities, whereby
36. 3 I may forgive their iniquity and their sin
36. 31 his seed and his servants for their iniquity
50. 20 the iniquity of Israel shall be sought for
51. 6 be not cut off in her iniquity; for this (is)
Lam. 2. 14 and they have not discovered thine iniq.
4. 6 the punishment of the iniquity of the d.
4. 13 the iniquities of her priests, that have
4. 22 The punishment of thine iniquity is acc.
4. 22 he will visit thine iniquity, O daughter
5. 7 our fathers..we have born their iniquities
Eze. 3. 18 the same wicked (man) shall die in his i.
3. 19 he shall die in his iniquity; but thou hast
4. 4 lay the iniquity of the house of Israel upon
4. 4 shalt lie upon it thou shalt bear their in.
4. 5 I have laid upon thee the years of their i.
4. 5 so shalt thou bear the iniquity of the
4. 6 thou shalt bear the iniquity of the house of
4. 17 That they may..consume away for their i.
7. 13 strengthen himself in the iniquity of his
7. 16 all..mourning, every one for his iniquity
7. 19 it is the stumbling block of their iniquity
9. 9 The iniquity of the house of Israel and J.
14. 3 put the stumbling block of their iniquity
14. 4, 7 the stumbling block of his iniquity
14. 10 shall bear the punishment of their iniquity
16. 49 this was the iniquity of thy sister Sodom
18. 17 he shall not die for the iniquity of his fa.
18. 18 his father..even he shall die in his iniquity
18. 19 doth not the son bear the iniquity of the
18. 20 The son shall not bear the iniquity of the
18. 20 neither shall the father bear the iniquity
18. 30 Repent..so iniquity shall not be your ruin
21. 23 he will call to remembrance the iniquity
21. 24 ye have made your iniquity to be remem.
21. 25 day is come, when iniquity (shall have)
21. 29 come, when their iniquity (shall have) an
24. 23 but ye shall pine away for your iniquities

Eze. 28. 18 by the multitude of thine iniquities, by the
29. 16 which bringeth..iniquity to remembrance
32. 27 their iniquities shall be upon their bones
33. 6 he is taken away in his iniquity; but his
33. 8 that wicked (man) shall die in his iniquity
33. 9 he shall die in his iniquity; but thou h.
35. 5 in the time (that their) iniquity (had) an
36. 31 for your iniquities and for your abomina.
36. 33 I shall have cleansed you from all your in.
39. 23 Israel went into captivity for their iniq.
43. 10 they may be ashamed of their iniquities
44. 10 the Levites..they shall even bear their i.
44. 12 and caused..Israel to fall into iniquity
44. 12 therefore..they shall bear their iniquity
Dan. 9. 13 that we might turn from our iniquities, and
9. 16 for our sins, and for the iniquities of our
9. 24 to make reconciliation for iniquity, and to
Hos. 4. 8 and they set their heart on their iniquity
5. 5 shall Israel and Ephraim fall in their ini.
7. 1 the iniquity of Ephraim was discovered
8. 13 now will he remember their iniquity, and
9. 7 for the multitude of thine iniquity, and
9. 9 he will remember their iniquity, he will
12. 8 all my labours they shall find none iniqu.
13. 12 The iniquity of Ephraim (is) bound up; his
14. 1 return..for thou hast fallen by thine ini.
14. 2 Take away all iniquity, and receive..gra.
Amos 3. 2 I will punish you for all your iniquities
Mic. 7. 18 a God like unto thee, that pardoneth ini.
7. 19 he will subdue our iniquities; and thou
Zech. 3. 4 I have caused thine iniquity to pass from
3. 9 I will remove the iniquity of that land in
Mal. 2. 6 and did turn many away from iniquity

8. *Perversity*, עַלְוָה *alvah.*
Hos. 10. 9 the battle..against the children of iniqu.

9. *Labour, misery*, עָמָל *amal.*
Hab. 1. 13 and canst not look on iniquity: wherefore

10. *Wrong, wickedness*, רֶשַׁע *resha.*
Eccl. 3. 16 the place of righteousness, (that) iniquity

11. *Word or matter of perversity*, דְּבַר עָוֹן [*dabar*].
Psa. 65. 3 Iniquities prevail against me..our trans.

12. *Unrighteousness, wrong doing*, ἀδίκημα *adikēma.*
Rev. 18. 5 and God hath remembered her iniquities

13. *Unrighteousness, wrong*, ἀδικία *adikia.*
Luke 13. 27 depart from me, all (ye) workers of iniqi.
Acts 1. 18 purchased a field with the reward of ini.
8. 23 I perceive..thou art in..the bond of ini.
1 Co. 13. 6 Rejoiceth not in iniquity, but rejoiceth in
2 Ti. 2. 19 And, let every one..depart from iniquity
Jas. 3. 6 the tongue (is) a fire, a world of iniquity

14. *Lawlessness*, ἀνομία *anomia.*
Matt. 7. 23 depart from me, ye that work iniquity
13. 41 things that offend, and them which do in.
23. 28 within ye are full of hypocrisy and iniqu.
24. 12 because iniquity shall abound, the love of
Rom. 4. 7 Blessed (are) they whose iniquities are
6. 19 to uncleanness and to iniquity unto iniq.
2 Th. 2. 7 the mystery of iniquity doth already work
Titus 2. 14 that he might redeem us from all iniquity
Heb. 1. 9 hast loved righteousness, and hated iniq.
8. 12 their iniquities will I remember no more
10. 17 sins and iniquities will I remember no

15. *Transgression of law*, παρανομία *paranomia.*
2 Pe. 2. 16 was rebuked for his iniquity: the dumb

16. *Evil, wickedness*, πονηρία *ponēria.*
Acts 3. 26 turning away every one of you from his i.

INIQUITY, punishment of —
Iniquity, punishment of iniquity, עָוֹן *avon.*
Lev. 26. 41, 43 accept of the punishment of their ini.
Lam. 4. 6 the punishment of the iniquity of the da.
4. 22 the punishment of thine iniquity is acco.
Eze. 14. 10 they shall bear the punishment of their i.

INIQUITY, to commit —
1. *To do perversely*, עָוָה *avah.*
Dan. 9. 5 We have sinned, and have committed in.

2. *To do perversely, cause perversity*, עָוָה *avah*, 5.
2 Sa. 7. 14 If he commit iniquity, I will chasten him
Psa. 106. 6 we have committed iniquity, we have done
Jer. 9. 5 (and) weary themselves to commit iniqu.

INJOIN or ENJOIN —
1. *To give in charge*, ἐντέλλομαι *entellomai.*
Heb. 9. 20 testament which God hath injoined unto

2. *To set in order upon*, ἐπιτάσσω *epitassō.*
Phm. 8 bold..to injoin thee that which is conven.

INJURE, to —
To do injustice, wrong, injury, ἀδικέω *adikeō.*
Gal. 4. 12 Brethren..ye have not injured me at all

INJURIOUS —
Despiteful, insulting, ὑβριστής *hubristēs.*
1 Ti. 1. 13 Who was before..injurious: but I obtain

INJUSTICE —
Violence, wrong, injury, חָמָס *chamas.*
Job 16. 17 Not for..injustice in mine hands: also

INK —
1. *Ink*, דְּיוֹ *deyo.*
Jer. 36. 18 answered..I wrote (them) with ink in the

2. *Ink*, μέλαν *melan.*
2 Co. 3. 3 written not with ink, but with the spirit
2 John 12 I would not (write) with paper and ink
3 John 13 I will not with ink and pen write unto

INK HORN —
Ink horn, קֶסֶת *qeseth.*
Eze. 9. 2 clothed with linen, with a writer's inkhorn
9. 3 which (had) the writer's inkhorn by his
9. 11 clothed with linen, which (had) the inkh.

INN —
1. *Lodging, place for passing the night*, מָלוֹן *malon.*
Gen. 42. 27 opened..to give his ass provender in the i.
43. 21 it came to pass, when we came to the inn
Exod. 4. 24 it came to pass by the way in the inn, that

2. *Guest chamber*, κατάλυμα *kataluma.*
Luke 2. 7 there was no room for them in the inn

3. *Inn, general receiving house*, πανδοχεῖον *pando.*
Luke 10. 34 brought him to an inn, and took care of

INNER —
1. *Inner*, פְּנִימִי *penimi.*
1 Ki. 6. 27 he set the cherubim within the inner
6. 36 he built the inner court with three rows
7. 12 both for the inner court of the house of
7. 50 for the doors of the inner house, the most
1 Ch. 28. 11 pattern..of the inner parlours thereof, and
2 Ch. 4. 22 the inner doors thereof for the most holy
Esth. 4. 11 shall come unto the king into the inner
5. 1 stood in the inner court of the king's ho.
Eze. 8. 3 to the door of the inner gate that looketh
8. 16 he brought me into the inner court of the
10. 3 and the cloud filled the inner court
40. 15 unto the face of the porch of the inner
40. 19 unto the forefront of the inner court with.
40. 23 the gate of the inner court (was) over ag.
40. 27 a gate in the inner court toward the south
40. 28 he brought me to the inner court by the
40. 32 brought me into the inner court toward
40. 44 And without the inner gate (were) the
40. 44 chambers of the singers in the inner court
41. 15 with the inner temple and the porches of
41. 17 To that above the door, even unto the in.
42. 3 twenty (cubits) which (were) for the inner
42. 15 he had made an end of measuring the in.
43. 5 So the spirit..brought me into the inner
44. 17 when they enter in at the gates of the in.
44. 17 they minister in the gates of the inner
44. 21 drink..when they enter into the inner
44. 27 unto the inner court, to minister in the
45. 19 the posts of the gate of the inner court
46. 1 The gate of the inner court that looketh

2. *Within, inner*, ἔσω *esō.*
Eph. 3. 16 strengthened with might..in the inner

3. *Inner, innermost*, ἐσώτερος *esōteros.*
Acts 16. 24 thrust them into the inner prison, and

INNER chamber —
Inner chamber, חֶדֶר *cheder.*
1 Ki. 20. 30 came into the city, into an inner chamber
22. 25 when thou shalt go into an inner chamber
2 Ki. 9. 2 go in..and carry him to an inner chamber
2 Ch. 18. 24 when thou shalt go into an inner chamber

INNER part—
Inner part, פָּנִים *panim.*
2 Ch. 29. 16 the priests went into the inner part of the

INNERMOST part —
Inner part, חֶדֶר *cheder.*
Prov 18. 8 down into the innermost parts of the belly
26. 22 go down into the innermost parts of the

INNOCENCY —
1. *Purity*, זָכוּ *zaku.*
Dan. 6. 22 as before him innocency was found in me

2. *Innocence, cleanness*, נִקָּיוֹן *niqqayon.*
Gen. 20. 5 and innocency of my hands, have I done
Psa. 26. 6 I will wash mine hands in innocency: so
73. 13 vain, and washed my hands in innocency
Hos. 8. 5 how long. ere they attain to innocency?

INNOCENT (person) —
1. *Gratuitous*, חִנָּם *chinnam.*
1 Ki. 2. 31 thou mayest take away the innocent blood

2. *Safe, covered*, חַף *chaph.*
Job 33. 9 I (am) innocent; neither..iniquity in me

3. *Innocent, clean, free, acquitted*, נָקִי *naqi.*
Exod 23. 7 the innocent and righteous slay thou not
Deut 19. 10 That innocent blood be not shed in thy l.
19. 13 thou shalt put away..innocent blood from
21. 8 lay not innocent blood unto thy people of
21. 9 shalt thou put away the..innocent blood
27. 25 taketh reward to slay an innocent person
1 Sa. 19. 5 wilt thou sin against innocent blood, to
2 Ki. 21. 16 Manasseh shed innocent blood very much
24. 4 also for the innocent blood that he shed
24. 4 he filled Jerusalem with innocent blood
Job 4. 7 who (ever) perished, being innocent? or
9. 23 he will laugh at the trial of the innocent
17. 8 the innocent shall stir up himself against
22. 19 and the innocent laugh them to scorn
22. 30 He shall deliver the island of the innocent
27. 17 and the innocent shall divide the silver
Psa. 10. 8 in the secret places doth he murder the in.
15. 5 nor taketh reward against the innocent
94. 21 righteous, and condemn the innocent bl.
106. 38 And shed innocent blood..the blood of
Prov. 1. 11 let us lurk privily for the innocent with.
6. 17 a lying tongue, and hands that shed inno.
Isa. 59. 7 they make haste to shed innocent blood
Jer. 2. 34 the blood of the souls of the poor innoc.
7. 6 and shed not innocent blood in this place
19. 4 have filled this place with the blood of in.
Jer. 22. 3 neither shed innocent blood in this place
22. 17 for to shed innocent blood, and for oppr.
26. 15 ye shall surely bring innocent blood upon
Jon. 1. 14 lay not upon us innocent blood: for thou

4. *Innocent, clean*, נָקִיא *naqi.*
Joel 3. 19 they have shed innocent blood in their la.

5. *Innocent, guiltless*, ἀθῷος *athōos.*
Matt 27. 4 [in that I have betrayed the innocent bl.]
27. 24 I am innocent of the blood of this just

INNOCENT, to be —
To be innocent, clean, free, acquitted, נָקָה *naqah*, 2.
Psa. 19. 13 I shall be innocent from the great trans.
Prov. 6. 29 whosoever toucheth her shall not be inno.
28. 20 maketh haste to be rich shall not be inno.
Jer. 2. 35 Yet thou sayest, Because I am innocent

INNOCENT, to hold —
To declare innocent, נָקָה *naqah*, 3.
Job 9. 28 I know that thou wilt not hold me inno.

INNUMERABLE —
1. *No number, without number*, אֵין מִסְפָּר *en mispar.*
Job 21. 33 draw..as (there are) innumerable before
Psa. 40. 12 For innumerable evils have compassed me
104. 25 sea, wherein (are) things creeping innum.
Jer. 46. 23 more than the grasshoppers, and..innu.

2. *Not to be numbered*, ἀναρίθμητος *anarithmētos.*
Heb. 11. 12 as the sand which is by the sea shore in.
[*See also* Company, multitude.]

INORDINATE love or affection —
1. *Doting love*, עֲגָבָה *agabah.*
Eze. 23. 11 she was more corrupt in her inordinate l.

2. *Affection, suffering, lust*, πάθος *pathos.*
Col. 3. 5 uncleanness, inordinate affection, evil co.

INQUISITION to be made —
To be sought or searched out, בָּקַשׁ *baqash*,
Esth. 2. 23 when inquisition was made of the matter

INQUISITION, to make —
To seek, inquire, require, דָּרַשׁ *darash.*
Deut 19. 18 the judges shall make diligent inquisition
Psa. 9. 12 When he maketh inquisition for blood, he

INSCRIPTION —
To write above, ἐπιγράφω *epigraphō.*
Acts. 17. 23 For..I found an altar with this inscript.

INSIDE —
House, within, בַּיִת *bayith.*
1 Ki. 6. 15 covered (them) on the inside with wood

INSOMUCH as —
So that, ὥστε *hōste.*
Acts 1. 19 insomuch as that field is called in their

INSOMUCH that —
1. *With a view to which*, εἰς *eis.*
2 Co. 8. 6 Insomuch that we desired Titus, that as

2. *So that*, ὥστε *hōste.*
Matt. 8. 24 insomuch that the ship was covered with
12. 22 he healed him, insomuch that the blind
13. 54 insomuch that they were astonished, and
15. 31 Insomuch that the multitude wondered
24. 24 insomuch that, if (it were) possible, they
27. 14 insomuch that the governor marvelled
Mark 1. 27 insomuch that they questioned among
1. 45 insomuch that Jesus could no more open.
2. 2 insomuch that there was no room to rec.
2. 12 insomuch that they were all amazed, and
3. 10 insomuch that they pressed upon him for
9. 26 insomuch that many said, He is dead
Luke 12. 1 insomuch that they trode one upon anot.
Acts 5. 15 Insomuch that they brought forth the sick
2 Co. 1. 8 insomuch that we despaired even of life
Gal. 2. 13 insomuch that Barnabas also was carried

INSPIRATION —
Breath, נְשָׁמָה *neshamah.*
Job 32. 8 the inspiration of the Almighty giveth

INSPIRATION of God, given by —
God-breathed, θεόπνευστος *theopneustos.*
2 Ti. 3. 16 All scripture..given by inspiration of God

INSTANT —
1. *Moment, instant*, רֶגַע *rega.*
Jer. 18. 7, 9 (At what) instant I shall speak concerni.

2. *Hour*, ὥρα *hōra.*
Luke 2. 38 she coming in that instant gave thanks

INSTANT, at an —
An instant, פֶּתַע *petha.*
Isa. 29. 5 yea, it shall be at an instant suddenly
30. 13 breaking cometh suddenly at an instant

INSTANT, to be —
1. *To lie upon*, ἐπίκειμαι *epikeimai.*
Luke 23. 23 they were instant with loud voices, requ.

2. *To place upon*, ἐφίστημι *ephistēmi.*
2 Ti. 4. 2 be instant in season, out of season; repr.

INSTANT, to continue —
To persevere, continue in, προσκαρτερέω *proskarte.*
Rom. 12. 12 Rejoicing in hope..continuing instant in

INSTANTLY —
1. *Intently*, ἐν ἐκτενείᾳ *en ekteneia.*
Acts 26. 7 Unto which..our twelve tribes, instantly

2. *Hastily, speedily, σπουδαίως spoudaiōs.*
Luke 7. 4 when they came..they besought him ins.

INSTEAD, in the stead of —

1. *Under, instead of,* תַּחַת *tachath.*
Gen. 2. 21 and closed up the flesh instead thereof
4. 25 another seed instead of Abel, whom Cain
22. 13 a burnt offering in the stead of his son.
30. 2 (Am) I in God's stead, who hath withheld
44. 33 let thy servant abide instead of the lad
Exod 29. 30 that son that is priest in his stead shall
Lev. 16. 32 priest..to minister..in his father's stead
Num. 3. 12 instead of all the first born that openeth
3. 41, 45 instead of all the first born among the
3. 41, 45 the cattle of the Levites instead of
5. 19 (with another) instead of thy husband
5. 20 aside (to another) instead of thy husb.
5. 29 aside (to another) instead of her husb.
8. 16 instead of such as open every womb, (even
32. 14 ye are risen up in your father's stead, an
Deut. 2. 12, 23 destroyed..and dwelt in their stead
2. 21, 22 succeeded them, and dwelt in their s.
10. 6 Eleazar his son ministered..in his stead
Josh. 5. 7 children, (whom) he raised up in their ste.
Judg. 15. 2 take her, I pray thee, instead of her
2 Sa. 16. 8 of Saul, in whose stead thou hast reigned
17. 25 Amasa captain of the host instead of Joab
1 Ki. 1. 30 he shall sit upon my throne in my stead
1. 35 he shall be king in my stead : and I have
3. 7 servant king instead of David my father
14. 27 Rehoboam made in their stead brasen sh.
2 Ki. 17. 24 in the cities of Samaria instead of the
1 Ch. 5. 22 dwelt in their steads until the captivity
Esth. 2. 4 the maiden..be queen instead of Vashti
2. 17 and made her queen instead of Vashti
Job 16. 4 if your soul were in my soul's stead, I
31. 40 grow instead of wheat, and cockle instead
34. 24 He shall..set others in their stead
Psa. 45. 16 Instead of thy fathers shall be thy children
Prov. 11. 8 and the wicked cometh in his stead
Eccl. 4. 15 child that shall stand up in his stead
Isa. 3. 24 instead of sweet smell there shall be stink
3. 24 instead of a girdle a rent; and instead of
3. 24 and instead of a stomacher a girding of
3. 24 sackcloth ; (and) burning instead of bea.
55. 13 Instead of the thorn..instead of the brier
Eze. 16. 32 taketh strangers instead of her husband

2. *For, in behalf of,* ὑπέρ (*gen.*) *huper.*
2 Co. 5. 20 we pray (you), in Christ's stead, be ye re.
Phm. 13 that in thy stead he might have minister.

INSTRUCT, to —

1. *To consider, discern, attend,* בִּין *bin,* 5.
Isa. 40. 14 instructed him, and taught him in the
Dan. 11. 33 they that understand..shall instruct many

2. *To cause to understand,* בִּין *bin,* 3*a.*
Deut. 32. 10 he led him about, he instructed him, he

3. *Reprover, instructor,* יִסּוֹר *yissor.*
Job 40. 2 Shall he that contendeth..instruct (him)?

4. *To chasten, instruct,* יָסַר *yasar,* 3.
Deut. 4. 36 to hear his voice, that he might instruct
Job 4. 3 thou hast instructed many, and thou hast
Psa. 16. 7 my reins also instruct me in the night
Isa. 8. 11 instructed me that I should
28. 26 his God doth instruct him to discretion

5. *To show, direct,* יָרָה *yarah,* 5.
2 Ki. 12. 2 his days wherein Jehoiada..instructed

6. *To teach,* לָמַד *lamad,* 3.
Prov. 5. 13 nor inclined mine ear to them that instr.
Song 8. 2 my mother's house, (who) would instruct

7. *To cause to act wisely,* שָׂכַל *sakal,* 5.
Neh. 9. 20 Thou gavest..thy good spirit to instruct
Psa. 32. 8 I will instruct thee and teach thee in the

8. *To sound throughout, instruct,* κατηχέω *katēcheō.*
Luke 1. 4 those things, wherein thou hast been ins.
Acts 18. 25 This man was instructed in the way of the
Rom. 2. 18 excellent, being instructed out of the law

9. *To make a disciple or learner,* μαθητεύω *mathēteuō.*
Matt 13. 52 instructed unto the kingdom of heaven, is

10. *To nurture as a child, instruct,* παιδεύω *paideuō.*
2 Ti. 2. 25 In meekness instructing those that oppose

11. *To cause to go up or unite together,* συμβιβάζω.
1 Co. 2. 16 mind of the Lord, that he may instruct

INSTRUCT before, to —

To cause to go up before, προβιβάζω *probibazō.*
Matt 14. 8 she, being before instructed of her mother

INSTRUCTED, to be —

1. *To become known,* יָדַע *yada,* 2.
Jer. 31. 19 after that I was instructed, I smote upon

2. *To be founded, instructed,* יָסַד *yasad,* 6.
2 Ch. 3. 3 Solomon was instructed for the building

3. *To be chastised, instructed,* יָסַר *yasar,* 2.
Psa. 2. 10 be instructed, ye judges of the earth
Jer. 6. 8 Be thou instructed, O Jerusalem, lest my

4. *To be taught,* לָמַד *lamad,* 4.
1 Ch. 25. 7 their brethren that were instructed in the

5. *To cause to act wisely,* שָׂכַל *sakal,* 5.
Prov. 21. 11 when the wise is instructed, he receiveth

6. *To initiate into mysteries,* μυέω *mueō.*
Phil. 4. 12 in all things I am instructed both to be

INSTRUCTION —

1. *Chastisement, instruction,* מוּסָר *musar.*
Psa. 50. 17 Seeing thou hatest instruction, and cast.
Prov. 1. 2 To know wisdom and instruction ; to per.
1. 3 To receive the instruction of wisdom, jus.
1. 7 (but) fools despise wisdom and instruction
1. 8 My son, hear the instruction of thy father
4. 1 Hear, ye children, the instruction of a f.
4. 13 Take fast hold of instruction ; let (her) not
5. 12 How have I hated instruction, and my h.
5. 23 He shall die without instruction ; and in
6. 23 reproofs of instruction (are) the way of life
8. 10 Receive my instruction, and not silver; and
8. 33 Hear instruction, and be wise, and refuse
10. 17 He..the way of life that keepeth instruc.
12. 1 Whoso loveth instruction loveth knowled.
13. 1 A wise son (heareth) his father's instruction
13. 18 Poverty..to him that refuseth instruction
15. 5 A fool despiseth his father's instruction
15. 32 He that refuseth instruction despiseth his
15. 33 The fear of the LORD (is) the instruction
16. 22 well spring..but the instruction of fools
19. 20 Hear counsel, and receive instruction, that
19. 27 Cease, my son, to hear the instruction
23. 12 Apply thine heart unto instruction, and
23. 23 wisdom, and instruction, and understand.
24. 32 I looked upon (it, and) received instruction
Jer. 17. 23 that they might not hear, nor receive ins.
32. 33 they have not hearkened to receive inst.
35. 13 Will ye not receive instruction to hearken
Eze. 5. 15 an instruction and an astonishment unto
Zeph. 3. 7 I said, Surely..thou wilt receive instruc.

2. *Instruction,* מוּסָר *mosar.*
Job 33. 16 openeth the ears of men..sealeth their in.

3. *Nurture, instruction,* παιδεία *paideia.*
2 Ti. 3. 16 profitable..for instruction in righteous.

INSTRUCTOR —

1. *To whet, sharpen,* לָטַשׁ *latash.*
Gen. 4. 22 an instructor of every artificer in brass

2. *Child conductor,* παιδαγωγός *paidagōgos.*
1 Co. 4. 15 though ye have ten thousand instructors

3. *One who nurtures or instructs,* παιδευτής *paideut.*
Rom. 2. 20 An instructor of the foolish, a teacher of

INSTRUMENT —

1. *Vessel, instrument,* כְּלִי *keli.*
Gen. 49. 5 instruments of cruelty..their habitations
Exod 25. 9 the pattern of all the instruments thereof
Num. 3. 8 they shall keep all the instruments of the
4. 12 shall take all the instruments of minis.
4. 26 and all the instruments of their service
4. 32 with all their instruments, and with all
4. 32 by name ye shall reckon the instruments
7. 1 and all the instruments thereof, both the
31. 6 with the holy instruments, and the trum.
35. 16 if he smite him with an instrument of iron
1 Sa. 8. 12 his instruments of war, and instruments
2 Sa. 24. 22 and (other) instruments of the oxen for
1 Ki. 19. 21 boiled their flesh with the instruments
1 Ch. 9. 29 to oversee the vessels and all the instrum.
12. 33 expert in war, with all instruments of war
12. 37 with all manner of instruments of war for
15. 16 the singers with instruments of music
16. 42 and with musical instruments of God
23. 5 praised the LORD with the instruments
28. 14 all instruments of all manner of service
28. 14 for all instruments of silver by weight
28. 14 all instruments of every kind of service
2 Ch. 4. 16 the flesh hooks, and all their instruments
5. 1 all the instruments, put he among the
5. 13 with the trumpets, and cymbals, and ins.
7. 6 Levites also with instruments of music of
23. 13 also the singers with instruments of mu.
29. 26 the Levites stood with the instruments of
29. 27 with the instruments (ordained) by David
30. 21 (singing) with loud instruments unto the L.
34. 12 all that could skill of instruments of mu.
Neh. 12. 36 with the musical instruments of David the
Psa. 7. 13 He hath also prepared for him the instr.
Isa. 32. 7 instruments also of the churl (are) evil
54. 16 bringeth forth an instrument for his work
Eze. 40. 42 whereupon also they laid the instruments
Amos 6. 5 invent to themselves instruments of music
Zech 11. 15 Take..the instruments of a foolish sheph.

2. *Weapons, armour,* ὅπλα *hopla.*
Rom. 6. 13 instruments of unrighteousness unto sin
6. 13 instruments of righteousness unto God
[*See also* Musical, threshing, ten strings.]

INSTRUMENT of music —

1. *A trichord,* שָׁלִישׁ *shalish.*
1 Sa. 18. 6 came out..with instruments of music

2. [*Meaning uncertain*], דַּחֲוָן *dachavan.*
Dan. 6. 18 neither were instruments of music brou.

INSTRUMENT, to sing to the stringed —

To play a stringed instrument, נָגַן [*nagan,* 3].
Isa. 38. 20 we will sing my songs to the stringed in.

INSTRUMENT, stringed —

1. *Stringed instrument,* נְגִינָה *neginah.*
Hab. 3. 19 To the chief singer on my stringed instr.

2. *Stringed instrument,* מִנִּים *minnim.*
Psa. 150. 4 praise him with stringed instruments and

INSTRUMENT, play(er) on —

1. *To pipe, play on instruments,* חָלַל *chalal.*
Psa. 87. 7 As well the singers as the players on ins.

To play on a stringed instrument, נָגַן *nagan,* 1, 2.
Psa. 68. 25 the players on instruments ; Eze. 33. 32.

INSURRECTION —

1. *Assembly, company,* רִגְשָׁה *rigshah.*
Psa. 64. 2 from the insurrection of the workers of

2. *A standing up, uprising,* στάσις *stasis.*
Mark 15. 7 who had committed murder in the insur.

INSURRECTION against, to make —

1. *To lift up self,* נְשָׂא *nesa,* 4.
Ezra 4. 19 of old time hath made insurrection against

2. *To place on against,* κατεφίστημι *katephistēmi.*
Acts 18. 12 the Jews made insurrection..against Paul

INSURRECTION with, to make —

An aider or abetter, συστασιαστής *sustasiastēs.*
Mark 15. 7 them that [had made insurrection with]

INTEGRITY —

1. *Perfection, integrity, simplicity,* תֹּם *tom.*
Gen. 20. 5 in the integrity of my heart..have I done
20. 6 I know that thou didst this in the integ.
1 Ki. 9. 4 in integrity of heart, and in uprightness
Psa. 7. 8 and according to mine integrity..in me
25. 21 Let integrity and uprightness preserve me
26. 1 I have walked in mine integrity : I have
26. 11 as for me, I will walk in mine integrity
41. 12 as for me, thou upholdest me in mine in.
78. 72 So he fed them according to the integrity
Prov 19. 1 Better..the poor that walketh in his int.
20. 7 The just (man) walketh in his integrity

2. *Perfection, integrity,* תֻּמָּה *tummah.*
Job 2. 3 still he holdeth fast his integrity, although
2. 9 said..Dost thou still retain thine integ.?
27. 5 till I die I will not remove mine integrity
31. 6 weighed..that God may know mine inte.
Prov 11. 3 The integrity of the upright shall guide

INTELLIGENCE, to have —

To cause to understand, בִּין *bin,* 5.
Dan. 11. 30 have intelligence with them that forsake

INTEND, to —

1. *To say,* אָמַר *amar.*
Exod 2. 14 Intendest thou to kill me, as thou killedst
Josh 22. 33 did not intend to go up against them in
2 Ch. 28. 13 ye intend to add..to our sins and to our

2. *To stretch out, turn aside,* נָטָה *natah.*
Psa. 21. 11 they intended evil against thee ; they im.

3. *To will, be minded, counselled,* βούλομαι *boulomai.*
Acts 5. 28 intend to bring this man's blood upon us
12. 4 intending after Easter to bring him forth

4. *To will, wish,* θέλω *thelō.*
Luke 14. 28 which of you, intending to build a tower

5. *To be about,* μέλλω *mellō.*
Acts 5. 35 take heed to yourselves what ye intend to
20. 13 unto Assos, there intending to take in P.

INTENT —

1. *Order, condition, intent, sake,* דִּבְרָה *dibrah.*
Dan. 4. 17 to the intent that the living may know

2. *Device,* מְזִמָּה *mezimmah.*
Jer. 30. 24 until he have performed the intents of his

3. *Intent, intention, mind,* ἔννοια *ennoia.*
Heb. 4. 12 a discerner of the thoughts and intents

4. *Word, matter, thing,* λόγος *logos.*
Acts 10. 29 I ask..for what intent ye have sent for

INTENT (that), to the or for that —

1. *In order to,* לְמַעַן *le-maan.*
Eze. 40. 4 for to the intent that I might show (them)

2. *For the purpose of,* לְבַעֲבוּר *le-baabur.*
2 Sa. 17. 14 to the intent that the LORD might bring

3. *To this thing,* εἰς τοῦτο *eis touto.*
Acts 9. 21 came hither for that intent, that he might

4. *With a view to,* εἰς *eis.*
1 Co. 10. 6 to the intent we should not lust after evil

5. *That, so that,* ἵνα *hina.*
John 11. 15 I was not there, to the intent ye may bel.
Eph. 3. 10 To the intent that now unto the princip.

6. *For what?* πρὸς τί *pros ti.*
John 13. 28 no man..knew for what intent he spake

INTERCESSION —

A meeting between, intercession, ἔντευξις *enteuxis.*
1 Ti. 2. 1 that..intercessions..be made for all men

INTERCESSION, to make —

1. *To come or fall upon, meet,* פָּגַע *paga.*
Jer. 7. 16 neither make intercession to me : for I
27. 18 let them now make intercession to the L.

2. *To cause to come or fall upon, meet,* פָּגַע *paga,* 5.
Isa. 53. 12 made intercession for the transgressors
Jer. 36. 25 had made intercession to the king that he

3. *To meet with, come between, intercede,* ἐντυγχάνω.
Rom. 8. 27 because he maketh intercession for the
8. 34 Christ..who also maketh intercession for
11. 2 how he maketh intercession to God agai.
Heb. 7. 25 ever liveth to make intercession for them

INTERCESSION for, to make —
To meet with in behalf of one, ὑπερεντυγχάνω *huper.*
Rom. 8. 26 the spirit itself maketh intercession for

INTERCESSOR —
To cause to come or fall upon, meet, פָּגַע *paga,* 5.
Isa. 59. 16 wondered that (there was) no intercessor

INTERMEDDLE, to —
1. *To intermeddle, mix up self,* גָּלַע *gala,* 7.
Prov 18. 1 seeketh (and) intermeddleth with all wi.
2. *To mix up self with something,* עָרַב *arab,* 7.
Prov. 14. 10 a stranger doth not intermeddle with his

INTERMISSION —
Cessation, הֲפוּגָה *haphugah.*
Lam. 3. 49 ceaseth not, without any intermission

INTERPRET, to —
1. *To interpret, explain,* פָּתַר *pathar.*
Gen. 40. 22 hanged..as Joseph had interpreted to th.
41. 8 none that could interpret them unto Ph.
41. 12 and he interpreted to us..he did interpret
41. 13 as he interpreted to us, so it was; me he
41. 15 none that can interpret it..to interpret it
2. *To interpret or explain thoroughly,* διερμηνεύω.
1 Co. 12. 30 all speak with tongues? do all interpret?
14. 5 except he interpret, that the church may
14. 13 Wherefore let him..pray that he may in.
14. 27 and (that) by course; and let one interpr.
3. *To interpret or explain,* ἑρμηνεύω *hermēneuō.*
John 1. 38 which is to say, [being interpreted,] Master

INTERPRETATION —
1. *Sweetness, moral, interpretation,* מְלִיצָה *melitsah.*
Prov. 1. 6 To understand a proverb, and the interp.
2. *Interpretation, explanation,* פֵּשֶׁר *pesher.*
Eccl. 8. 1 who knoweth the interpretation of a thing
3. *Interpretation, explanation,* פְּשַׁר *peshar.*
Dan. 2. 4 tell..the dream, and we will show the in.
2. 5 the dream, with the interpretation thereof
2. 6 if ye show the dream, and the interpreta.
2. 6 show me the dream, and the interpretation
2. 7 and we will show the interpretation of it
2. 9 that ye can show me the interpretation
2. 16 that he would show the king the interpr.
2. 24 I will show unto the king the interpreta.
2. 25 that will make known..the interpretation
2. 26 the dream which I have seen, and the in.
2. 30 that shall make known the interpretation
2. 36 we will tell the interpretation thereof be.
2. 45 the dream (is) certain, and the interpret.
4. 6 they might make known unto me the int.
4. 7 they did not make known unto me the in.
4. 9 my dream..and the interpretation thereof
4. 18 declare the interpretation thereof, foras.
4. 18 not able to make known unto me the int.
4. 19 let not the dream, or the interpretation
4. 19 the interpretation thereof to thine enem.
4. 24 This (is) the interpretation, O king, and
5. 7 and show me the interpretation thereof
5. 8 nor make known to the king the interpr.
5. 12 let Daniel be called..he will show the in.
5. 15 and make known unto me the interpreta.
5. 15 but they could not show the interpretation
5. 16 that thou canst make interpretations
5. 16 and make known to me the interpretation
5. 17 and make known to him the interpretation
5. 26 This (is) the interpretation of the thing
7. 16 So he told me, and made me know the in.
4. *To interpret, explain,* פָּתַר *pathar.*
Gen. 40. 16 When the chief baker saw that the inter.
5. *Interpretation, explanation,* פִּתְרוֹן *pithron.*
Gen. 40. 5 each man according to the interpretation
40. 8 (Do) not interpretations (belong) to God?
40. 12, 18 This (is) the interpretation..The three
41. 11 dreamed each man according to the inte.
6. *A fracture, breaking, interpretation,* שֶׁבֶר, שֵׁבֶר *sheber.*
Judg. 7. 15 heard the telling of the dream, and the in.
7. *Unloosing,* ἐπίλυσις *epilusis.*
2 Pe. 1. 20 no prophecy..is of any private interpret
8. *Interpretation, explanation,* ἑρμηνεία *hermēneia.*
1 Co. 12. 10 to another the [interpretation] of tongues
14. 26 every one of you..hath an interpretation

INTERPRETATION, to be by —
1. *To interpret, explain,* ἑρμηνεύω *hermēneuō.*
John 1. 42 Cephas, which is by interpretation, A
9. 7 Siloam, which is by interpretation, Sent
Heb. 7. 2 first being by interpretation King of righ.
2. *To be interpreted, explained,* μεθερμηνεύομαι.
Acts 13. 8 sorcerer, for so is his name by interpreta.
3. *To interpret or explain fully,* διερμηνεύω *dierm.*
Acts 9. 36 Tabitha, which by interpretation is called

INTERPRETED, to be —
1. *To cast over, interpret, explain,* תַּרְגֵּם *targem.*
Ezra 4. 7 written..and interpreted in the Syrian
2. *To be interpreted, or explained,* μεθερμηνεύομαι.
Matt. 1. 23 Emmanuel, which being interpreted, is, G.
Mark 5. 41 Talitha cumi, which is, being interpreted
15. 22 Golgotha, which is, being interpreted, The
15. 34 Eloi..which is, being interpreted, My God
John 1. 41 Messias, which is, being interpreted, the C.
Acts 4. 36 Barnabas, which is, being interpreted, The

INTERPRETER —
1. *To treat as a scorner or foreigner,* לִיץ לוּץ *luts,* 5.
Gen. 42. 23 for he spake unto them by an interpreter
Job 33. 23 an interpreter, one among a thousand, to
2. *To interpret, explain,* פָּתַר *pathar.*
Gen. 40. 8 a dream, and (there is) no interpreter of
3. *One who interprets or explains fully,* διερμηνευτής.
1 Co. 14. 28 if there be no [interpreter], let him keep

INTERPRETING —
To interpret, explain, פְּשַׁר *peshar,* 3.
Dan. 5. 12 interpreting of dreams, and showing of

INTO —
1. *To, unto,* אֶל *el.*
Gen. 6. 18 thou shalt come into the ark, thou, and
2. *With, near, at, even, by,* אֵת *eth.*
Exod 39. 3 they did beat the gold into thin plates, and
3. *Into,* בְּמוֹ *bemo.*
Job 37. 8 Then the beasts go into dens, and remain
4. *Unto,* עַד *ad.*
Judg 11. 19 Let us pass..through thy land into my
5. *Middle, midst,* תָּוֶךְ *tavek.*
Deut 23. 11 sun is down, he shall come into the camp
6. *Unto, up to,* ἄχρι *achri.*
Acts 20. 4 there accompanied him into Asia, Sopater
7. *Into, to, at,* εἰς *eis.*
Matt. 2. 11 when they were come into the house, they
2. 12 they departed into their own country an.
2. 13 flee into Egypt, and be thou there until I
2. 14 When he arose he took..and departed into
2. 20 Arise..and go into the land of Israel: for
2. 21 he arose..and came into the land of Israel
2. 22 he turned aside into the parts of Galilee
Matt. 3. 10, 12; 4. 1, 5, 8, 12, 18; 5. 1, 20, 25, 29, 30;
6. 6, 13, 26, 30; 7. 19, 21; 8. 5, 12, 14, 23, 28, 31, 32, 32,
33; 9. 1, 1, 17, 17, 23, 26, 28, 38; 10. 5, 5, 11, 12, 23; 11.
7; 12. 4, 9, 11, 29, 44; 13. 2, 30, 36, 42, 47, 48, 50, 54; 14.
13, 15, 22, 23, 32, [34], 35; 15. 11, 14, 17, 17, 21, 29, 39; 16.
13; 17. 1, 15, 15, 22, 25; 18. 3, 8, 8, 9, 9, 30; 19. 1, 17, 23,
24; 20. 1, 2, 4, 7; 21. 2, 10, 12, 17, 18, 21, 23, 31; 22. 10,
13; 24. 38; 25. 21, 23, 30, 41, 46, 46; 26. 18, 30, 32, 41,
45, 52, 71; 27. 6, 27, 53; 28. 7, 10, 11, 16, 16.
Mark 1. 12, 14, 21, 21, 29, 35, 38, 45; 2. 1, 11, 22, [22,]
26; 3. 1, 13, 19, 27; 4. 1, 37; 5. 1, 12, 12, 13, 13, 18; 6. 1,
10, 31, 32, 36, 45, 46, 51, 56; 7. 15, 17, 18, 19, 19, 19, 24,
24, 33; 8. 10, 10, [13,] 26, 27; 9. 2, 22, 22, 25, 28, 31, 42, 43,
[43,] 43, 45, [45,] 45, 47, 47; 10. 1, 17, 23, 24, 25; 11. 2, 2, 11,
11, 23; 12. 41, 43; 13. [15]; 14. 13, 16, 26, 28, 38, 41, 54,
68; 15. 41; 16. 5, 7, [12, 15, 19.]
Luke 1. 9, 39, 39, 40, 79; 2. 3, 4, 15, 27, 39; 3. 3, 9, 17;
4. [1, 5,] 14, 16, 37, 38, 42; 5. 3, 4, 19, 37, 38; 6. 4, 6, 12, 38,
39; 7. 1, 11, 24, 36, 44; 8. 22, 29, 30, 31, 32, 33, 33, 37,
41, 51; 9. 10, 12, 28, 34, 44, 44, 52; 10. 1, 2, 5, 8, 10, 10,
38, 38; 11. 4; 12. 5, 28, 58; 13. 19; 14. 1, 5, 21, 23; 15.
13, 15; 16. 4, 9, 16, 22, 28; 17. 2, 12, 27; 18. 10, 24, 25;
19. 12, 30, 45; 21. 1, 21, 24; 22. 3, 10, 10, 33, 40, 46, 54, 66;
23. [19,] 25, 46; 24. 7, 26, [51].
John 1. 9, 43; 3. 4, 5, 17, 19, 22, 24; 4. 3, 14, 28, 38, 43,
45, 46, 47, 54; 5. 7, 24; 6. 3, 14, 15, 17, 21, 22, 22; 7. 3, 14;
8. [2]; 9. 39; 10. 1, 36, 40; 11. 7, 27, 30, 54; 12. 24, 46;
13. 2, 3, 5, 27; 15. 6; 16. [13,] 20, 21, 28; 17. 18, 18; 18. 1,
11, 15, 28, 33, 37; 19. 9, 17; 20. 6, 11, 25, 25, 27; 21. 3, 7,
Acts 1. 11, 11, 11, 13; 2. 20, 20, 34; 3. 1, 2, 3, 8; 5. 21;
7. 3, 4, 9, [15,] 16, 34, 39, 55; 8. 38; 9. 6, 8, 17, 39; 10. 16,
22, 24; 11. 8, 10, 12; 12. 17; 13. 14; 14. 1, 20, 22, 25; 16. 9,
10, 15, 19, 23, 24, 34, 37, [40]; 17. 10; 18. 7, 18, 19, 27; 19.
8, 22, 29, 31; 20. 1, 2, 3, 18; 21. 3, 8, 11, 26, 28, 29, 34,
37, 38; 22. 4, 10, 11, 23, 24; 23. 10, 16, 20, 28; 25. 23; 27.
1, 6, 17, 30, 38, 39, 41; 28. 5, 17, 23.
Rom. 1. 26; 5. 2, 12; 6. 3, 3, 4; 8. 21; 10. 6, 7, 18; 11.
24; 15. 24, 28.
1 Co. 12. 13, [13]; 14. 9.
2 Co. 1. 16; 2. 13; 7. 5; 11. 13, 14; 12. 4; Gal. 1. 17, 21;
3. 27; 4. 6; Eph. 4. 9, 15; Col. 1. 13; 2 Th. 3. 5, 5; 1 Ti.
1. 3, 12, 15; 3. 6, 7; 6. 7, 9; 2 Ti. 3. 6; Heb. 1. 6; 3. 11,
18; 4. 1, 3, 3, 5, 10, 11; 6. 19; 8. 10; 9. 6, 7, 12, 24, 24, 25;
10. 5, 31; 11. 8; 13. 11; Jas. 1. 25; 4. 13; 5. 4, 12; 1 Pe.
1. 12; 2. 9; 3. 22; 2 Pe. 1. 11; 1 Jo. 4. 1, 9; 2 Jo. 7, 10;
Jude 4; Rev. 2. 10, 22, 22; 5. 6; 8. 5, 8; 12. 6, 9, 14,
14; 13. 10; 14. 19, 19; 15. 8; 16. 16, [17,] 19; 17. 3, 8, 11;
18. 21; 19. 20; 20. 3, 10, 14, 15; 21. 24, 26, 27; 22. 14.
8. *In, into,* ἐν *en.*
Mark 1. 16 he saw Simon..casting a net into the sea
Luke 5. 16 he withdrew himself into the wilderness
23. 42 remember me when thou comest [into] thy
John 3. 35 and hath given all things into his hand
5. 4 [angel went down at a certain season into]
Acts 7. 45 into the possession of the Gentiles, whom
Rom. 1. 23 into an image made like to corruptible man
1. 25 Who changed the truth of God into a lie
2 Co. 8. 16 put the same earnest care into the heart
Gal. 1. 6 removed from him that called you into
1 Ti. 3. 16 believed on in the world, received up into
9. *On, upon, over,* ἐπί (*gen.*) *epi.*
Mark 4. 26 as if a man should cast seed into the gro.
Heb. 10. 16 I will put my laws into their hearts, and
10. *On, upon, over,* ἐπί (*acc.*) *epi.*
Matt 13. 8 other fell into good ground, and brought
13. 20 that received the seed into stony places
13. 23 he that received seed into the good ground
18. 12 goeth into the mountains, and seeketh that
22. 9 Go ye therefore into the highways, and
24. 16 let them which be in Judea flee [into] the
Mark 6. 53 they came into the land of Gennesaret, and
Luke 19. 4 climbed up into a sycomore tree to see
Luke 19. 23 gavest not thou my money into the bank
Acts 7. 23 it came into his heart to visit his brethren
9. 11 Arise, and go into the street which is
1 Co. 2. 9 neither have entered into the heart of man
11. 20 When ye come together therefore into one
14. 23 the whole church be come together into
Rev. 11. 11 life from God entered [into] them
11. *Down, down throughout,* κατά (*acc.*) *kata.*
Acts 5. 15 brought forth the sick [into] the streets
16. 7 they assayed to go [into] Bithynia: but the
12. *Within,* ἔσω *esō.*
Mark 14. 54 even into the palace of the high priest
15. 16 the soldiers led him away into the hall
13. *Under,* ὑπό (*acc.*) *hupo.*
Jas. 5. 12 Swear not..lest ye fall into condemnation
[*See also*, Ashes, bear, beat, bondage, bring, captivity, carrying, east, come, contempt, desolation, enter, entering, entrance, fall, foolishness, get, go, graff, joy, lead, look, scatter, sleep, snare, spread, subjection, take.]

INTREAT or ENTREAT, to —
1. *To smooth down, appease, weaken,* חָלָה *chalah,* 3.
1 Ki. 13. 6 Intreat now the face of the LORD thy God
Psa. 45. 12 rich among the people shall intreat thy
119. 58 I intreated thy favour with (my) whole
Prov 19. 6 Many will intreat the favour of the prince
2. *To be gracious, entreat grace or favour,* חָנַן *chanan.*
Job 19. 17 though I intreated for the children's (sake)
3. *To show self gracious,* חָנַן *chanan,* 7.
Job 19. 16 I called..intreated him with my mouth
4. *To entreat abundantly,* עָתַר *athar.*
Gen. 25. 21 Isaac intreated the LORD for his wife
Exod. 8. 30 Moses went out from Pharaoh, and intre.
10. 18 he went out from Pharaoh, and intreated
Judg 13. 8 Then Manoah intreated the LORD, and
5. *To make abundant intreaty,* עָתַר *athar,* 5.
Exod. 8. 8 Entreat the LORD, that he may take away
8. 9 Glory over me: when shall I entreat for
8. 28 I will let you go..only..entreat for me
8. 29 I will entreat the LORD that the swarms
9. 28 Entreat the LORD, for (it is) enough, that
10. 17 entreat the LORD your God, that he may
6. *To come or fall upon, meet,* פָּגַע *paga.*
Gen. 23. 8 intreat for me to Ephron the son of Zohar
Ruth 1. 16 Intreat me not to leave thee, (or) to retu.
7. *To cause to come or fall upon, meet,* פָּגַע *paga,* 5.
Jer. 15. 11 verily I will cause the enemy to entreat
8. *To cast self down,* פָּלַל *palal,* 7.
1 Sa. 2. 25 if a man sin..who shall intreat for him?
9. *To ask,* ἐρωτάω *erōtaō.*
Phil. 4. 3 I intreat thee also, true yokefellow, help
10. *To ask, crave a little,* παραιτέομαι *paraiteomai.*
Heb. 12. 19 they that heard intreated that the word
11. *To call for, entreat,* παρακαλέω *parakaleō.*
Luke 15. 28 therefore came his father out, and intre
1 Co. 4. 13 Being defamed, we intreat: we are made
1 Ti. 5. 1 Rebuke not an elder, but intreat (him) as

INTREATED, to be —
To be abundantly intreated, עָתַר *athar,* 2.
Gen. 25. 21 the LORD was intreated of him, and Reb.
2 Sa. 21. 14 after that God was intreated for the land
24. 25 So the LORD was intreated for the land, and
1 Ch. 5. 20 he was intreated of them; because they
2 Ch. 33. 13 he was intreated of him, and heard his s.
33. 19 (how God) was intreated of him, and all
Ezra 8. 23 besought..God..and he was intreated of
Isa. 19. 22 he shall be intreated of them, and shall

INTREATED, easy to be —
Easily persuaded, εὐπειθής *eupeithēs.*
Jas. 3. 17 easy to be intreated, full of mercy and

INTREATY —
1. *Supplication for grace,* תַּחֲנוּנִים *tachanunim.*
Prov 18. 23 The poor useth intreaties; but the rich
2. *A calling for, alongside of, entreaty,* παράκλησις.
2 Co. 8. 4 Praying us with much intreaty that we

INTRUDE into, to —
To go or tread in upon, ἐμβατεύω *embateuō.*
Col. 2. 18 intruding into those things which he hath

INVADE, to —
1. *To cut, assault,* גּוּד *gud.*
Hab. 3. 16 when he cometh up..he will invade them
2. *To strip,* פָּשַׁט *pashat.*
1 Sa. 23. 27 for the Philistines have invaded the land
27. 8 David..invaded the Geshurites, and the
30. 1 that the Amalekites had invaded the south
2 Ch. 28. 18 The Philistines also had invaded the cities
3. *To come or go in,* בּוֹא בְּ *bo be.*
2 Ki. 13. 20 bands of the Moabites invaded the land
2 Ch. 20. 10 whom thou wouldest not let Israel invade

INVASION, to make an —
To strip, פָּשַׁט *pashat.*
1 Sa. 30. 14 We made an invasion (upon) the south of

INVENT, to —
To think, devise, design, חָשַׁב *chashab.*
Amos 6. 5 invent to themselves instruments of music

INVENTED —
Device, design, מַחֲשֶׁבֶת *machashebeth.*
2 Ch. 26. 15 engines, invented by cunning men, to be

INVENTIONS —

1. *Devices, designs,* חִשְּׁבֹנוֹת *chishshebonoth.*

Eccl. 7. 29 they have sought out many inventions

2. *A doing, deed,* מַעֲלָל *maalal.*

Psa.106. 29 they provoked..to anger with their inve.
106. 39 went a whoring with their own inventions

3. *Doing, deed,* עֲלִילָה *alilah.*

Psa. 99. 8 though thou tookest vengeance of their i.

INVENTIONS, witty —

Device, מְזִמָּה *mezimmah.*

Prov. 8. 12 and find out knowledge of witty inventions

INVENTOR —

One who finds out (something) more, ἐφευρετής.

Rom. 1. 30 inventors of evil things, disobedient to p.

INVISIBLE —

Unseen, ἀόρατος *aoratos.*

Rom. 1. 20 the invisible things of him from the crea.
Col. 1. 15 Who is the image of the invisible God, the
1. 16 visible and invisible, whether..thrones
1 Ti. 1. 17 unto the king eternal, immortal, invisible
Heb. 11. 27 he endured, as seeing him who is invisible

INVITE, to —

To call, קָרָא *qara.*

1 Sa. 9. 24 since I said, I have invited the people. So
2 Sa. 13 23 and Absalom invited all the king's sons
Esth. 5. 12 to morrow am I invited unto her also with

INWARD, INWARDS —

1. *House, within,* בַּיִת *bayith.*

Exod28. 26 which (is) in the side of the ephod inward
39. 19 which (was) on the side of the ephod inw.
2 Sa. 5. 9 built round about from Millo and inward
1 Ki. 7. 25 oxen..and all their hinder parts (were) i.
2 Ch. 3. 13 they stood..and their faces (were) inward
4. 4 oxen..and all their hinder parts (were) i.
Eze. 40. 9 porch..and the porch of the gate (was) i.

2. *Secret, assembly, counsel,* סוֹד *sod.*

Job 19. 19 All my inward friends abhorred me; and

3. *Inner part, within,* פְּנִים *penim.*

Eze. 40. 16 and windows (were) round about inward
41. 3 Then went he inward, and measured the

4. *Inner part, within,* פְּנִימִי *penimi.*

Eze. 42. 4 walk of ten cubits breadth inward, a way

5. *Heart, middle, midst,* קֶרֶב *qereb.*

Exod29. 13, 22 the fat that covereth the inwards, and
29. 17 wash the inwards of him, and his legs, and
Lev. 1. 9 his inwards and his legs shall he wash in
1. 13 he shall wash the inwards and the legs
3. 3, 9, 14 the fat that covereth the inwards
3. 3, 9, 14 all the fat that (is) upon the inwards
4. 8 the fat that covereth the inwards, and
4. 8 all the fat that (is) upon the inwards
4. 11 with his legs, and his inwards, and his
7. 3 rump, and the fat that covereth the inw.
8. 16, 25 all the fat that (was) upon the inwards
8. 21 he washed the inwards and the legs in w.
9. 14 he did wash the inwards and the legs, and
Psa. 64. 6 the inward..of every one..and the heart

6. *Within,* ἔσω *esō.*

Rom. 7. 22 I delight in the law of God after the inw.

7. *From within,* ἔσωθεν *esōthen.*

2 Co. 4. 16 yet the [inward] (man) is renewed day by

INWARD affection—

Bowels, σπλάγχνα *splagchna.*

2 Co.7. 15 his inward affection is more abundant tow.

INWARD (fret) —

A hollow fretting, corrosion, פְּחֶתֶת *pechetheth.*

Lev. 13. 55 shalt burn it in the fire; it (is) fret inw.

INWARD part or thought —

1. *Inner part,* חֶדֶר *cheder.*

Prov.20. 27 searching all the inward parts of the belly
20. 30 so..stripes the inward part of the belly

2. *Covered, concealed parts, reins,* טֻחוֹת *tuchoth.*

Job 38. 36 Who hath put wisdom in the inward p.?
Psa. 51. 6 thou desirest truth in the inward parts

3. *Heart, middle, midst,* קֶרֶב *qereb.*

Psa. 5. 9 their inward part (is) very wickedness; their
49. 11 Their inward thought (is, that) their ho.
Isa. 16. 11 and mine inward parts for Kir-haresh
Jer. 31. 33 I will put my law in their inward parts

4. *From within,* ἔσωθεν *esōthen.*

Luke11. 39 your inward part is full of ravening and

INWARDLY —

1. *Heart, middle, midst,* קֶרֶב *qereb.*

Psa. 62. 4 they bless..but they curse inwardly. Sel.

2. *In the hidden or concealed part,* ἐν τῷ κρυπτῷ.

Rom. 2. 29 But he (is) a Jew, which is one inwardly

3. *From within,* ἔσωθεν *esōthen.*

Matt. 7. 15 but inwardly they are ravening wolves

IPH-E-DE-IAH, יִפְדְיָה *Jah is freeing.*

A son of Shashak, a Benjamite; a chief of the tribe, and residing in Jerusalem. B.C. 1300.

1 Ch. 8. 25 And I., and Penuel, the sons of Shashak

IR, עִיר, *watcher.*

A Benjamite, the father of Machir. B.C. 1670.

1 Ch. 7. 12 Shup. also, and Hup.. the children of I.

I'-RA, עִירָא *watcher.*

1. A priest to David, and named among his great officers. B.C. 1048.

2 Sa. 20. 26 I. also the Jairite was a chief ruler about

2. Ira the Ithrite (or Jathrite), one of David's guard. B.C. 1048.

2 Sa. 23. 38 I. an Ithrite, Gareb an Ithrite
1 Ch.11. 28 I. the son of Ikkesh the Tekoite, Abi-ezer
27. 9 The sixth (captain..was) I. the son of I.

3. Another member of David's guard,—a Tekoite and son of Ikkesh. He was leader of the 6th monthly course of the 24,000, priests appointed by David. B.C. 1048.

2 Sa. 23. 26 Helez the Paltite, I. the son of Ikkesh the
1 Ch.11. 40 I. the Ithrite, Gareb the Ithrite

I'-RAD, עִירָד.

Son of Enoch and grandson of Cain. B.C. 3840.

Gen. 4. 18 And unto Enoch was born I.: and I. begat

I'-RAM, עִירָם.

A duke of Edom of the family of Esau. B.C. 1470.

Gen. 36. 43 Duke Magdiel, duke I.: these (be) the du.
1 Ch. 1. 54 Duke Magdiel, duke I. These (are) the

I'-RI, עִירִי *Jah is watcher.*

A son of Bela son of Benjamin. B.C. 1670.

1 Ch. 7. 7 And the sons of Bela; Ezbon..and I., five

IR-I'-JAH, יִרְאִיָּה *Jah is seeing.*

A captain of the guard in Jerusalem, who met Jeremiah at the gate of Benjamin and led him back to the princes. B.C. 600.

Jer. 37. 13 captain..(was) there, whose name (was) I.
37. 14 I. took Jeremiah, and brought him to the

IR-NA'-HASH, עִיר־נָחָשׁ *serpent city; magic city.*

A descendant of Chelub from Judah through Caleb son of Hur; or it may be a city.

1 Ch. 4. 12 Eshton begat..Tehinnah the father of I.

IR'-ON, יִרְאוֹן *place of terror.*

A city of Naphtali, probably now *Yarûn*, between Enhazor and Migdal-el.

Josh.19. 38 I., and Migdal-el, Horem, and Beth-anath

IRON —

1. *Iron,* בַּרְזֶל *barzel.*

Gen. 4. 22 an instructor of every artificer in..iron
Lev. 26. 19 I will make your heaven as iron, and your
Num31. 22 the brass, the iron, the tin, and the lead
35. 16 if he smite him with an instrument of i.
Deut. 3. 11 his bedstead (was) a bedstead of iron; (is)
4. 20 brought you forth out of the iron furnace
8. 9 a land whose stones (are) iron, and out of
27. 5 thou shalt not lift up (any) iron..upon
28. 23 the earth that (is) under thee (shall be) i.
28. 48 he shall put a yoke of iron upon thy neck
33. 25 Thy shoes (shall be) iron and brass; and
Josh. 6. 19 silver..gold, and vessels of brass and iron
6. 24 the vessels of brass and of iron, they put
8. 31 over which no man hath lift up (any) iron
17. 16 all the Canaanites..have chariots of iron
17. 18 Canaanites, though they have iron c.
22. 8 and with iron, and with very much raim.
Judg. 1. 19 could not..because they had chariots of i.
4. 3, 13 nine hundred chariots of iron
1 Sa. 17. 7 head (weighed) six hundred shekels of iron
2 Sa. 12. 31 under harrows of iron, and under axes of i.
23. 7 fenced with iron and the staff of a spear
1 Ki. 6. 7 (nor) any tool of iron heard in the house
8. 51 forth..from the midst of the furnace of i.
22. 11 Zedekiah..made him horns of iron: and
2 Ki. 6. 6 cast (it) in thither; and the iron did swim
1 Ch.20. 3 saws, and with harrows of iron, and with
22. 3 David prepared iron in abundance for the
22. 14 of brass and iron without weight; for it
22. 16 of..the silver, and the brass, and the iron
29. 2 iron for (things) of iron, and wood for
29. 7 and one hundred thousand talents of iron
2 Ch. 2. 7 in silver, and in brass, and in iron, and in
2. 14 skilful to work in gold, and..in iron, in
18. 10 Zedekiah..had made him horns of iron
24. 12 such as wrought iron and brass to mend
Job 19. 24 That they were graven with an iron pen
20. 24 He shall flee from the iron weapon, (and)
28. 2 Iron is taken out of the earth, and brass
40. 18 of brass; his bones (are) like bars of iron
41. 27 He esteemeth iron as straw..brass as ro.
Psa. 2. 9 Thou shalt break them with a rod of iron
105. 18 they hurt with fetters: he was laid in iron
107. 10 Such as sit..bound in affliction and iron
107. 16 For he hath..cut the bars of iron in sun.
149. 8 To bind..their nobles with fetters of iron
Prov 27. 17 Iron sharpeneth iron; so a man sharpen.
Eccl.10. 10 If the iron be blunt, and he do not whet
Isa. 10. 34 he shall cut down the..thickets with iron
45. 2 I will..cut in sunder the bars of iron
48. 4 thy neck (is) an iron sinew, and thy brow
60. 17 for iron I will bring silver..for stones iron
Jer. 1. 18 I have made thee this day..an iron pillar
6. 28 (they are) brass and iron; they (are) all
11. 4 I brought them forth..from the iron fur.
15. 12 Shall iron break the northern iron and the
17. 1 written with a pen of iron..the point of a
28. 13 but thou shalt make for them yokes of ir.
28. 14 I have put a yoke of iron upon the neck
Eze. 4. 3 Moreover take thou unto thee an iron p.
4. 3 set it..a wall of iron between thee and
22. 18 all they (are) brass, and tin, and iron, and
22. 20 (As) they gather silver, and brass, and iron
27. 12 with silver, iron, tin and lead, they traded
27. 19 bright iron, cassia, and calamus, were in
Amos 1. 3 threshed..threshing instruments of iron
Mic. 4. 13 I will make thine horn iron, and I will

2. *Iron,* פַּרְזֶל *parzel.*

Dan. 2. 33 His legs of iron, his feet part of iron, and
2. 34 upon his feet (that were) of iron and clay
2. 35 Then was the iron, the clay, the brass, the
2. 40 the fourth kingdom shall be strong as iron
2. 40 forasmuch as iron breaketh in pieces and
2. 40 as iron that breaketh all these, shall it br.
2. 41 part of potter's clay, and part of iron, the
2. 41 shall be in it of the strength of the iron
2. 41 thou sawest the iron mixed with miry c.
2. 42 the toes of the feet (were) part of iron
2. 43 whereas thou sawest iron mixed with miry
2. 43 not cleave..even as iron is not mixed with
2. 45 it break in pieces the iron, the brass, the
4. 15, 23 with a band of iron and brass, in the
5. 4 praised the gods..of iron, of wood, and
5. 23 hast praised the gods of..iron, wood, and
7. 7 it had great iron teeth: it devoured and
7. 19 whose teeth (were of) iron, and his nails

3. *Made of iron,* σιδήρεος *sidēreos.*

Acts 12. 10 they came unto the iron gate that leadeth
Rev. 2. 27 And he shall rule them with a rod of iron
9. 9 they had breastplates, as it were..of iron
12. 5 was to rule all nations with a rod of iron
19. 15 and he shall rule them with a rod of iron

4. *Iron,* σίδηρος *sidēros.*

Rev. 18. 12 all manner vessels of..brass, and iron, and

IRONS, barbed —

A pointed weapon, dart, שֻׂכָּה *sukkah.*

Job 41. 7 Canst thou fill his skin with barbed irons?

IR-PE'-EL, יִרְפְּאֵל *God (is) healer, or restored by God.*

A city of Benjamin.

Josh.18. 27 And Rekem, and I., and Taralah

IR SHE'-MESH, עִיר שֶׁמֶשׁ *city of the sun.*

A city of Dan, probably identical with Beth-shemesh, but certainly connected with Mount *Heres*, "the mount of the sun."

Josh.19. 41 the coast..was Zorah, and Eshtaol, and I.

I'-RU, עִירוּ *watch.*

Eldest son of Caleb, the spy. This name is probably IR, the *u* being the conjunction "*and*," and belonging to the following name. B.C. 1450.

1 Ch. 4. 15 sons of Caleb the son of Jephunneh; I

IS —

There is, he, she, or it is, יֵשׁ *yesh.*

Gen. 28. 16 Surely the LORD is in this place; and I
Judg18. 14 Do ye know that there is in these houses
1 Sa. 9. 11 found..and said unto them, Is the seer
2 Ki. 3. 12 The word of the LORD is with him. So the
10. 15 Is thine heart right, as my heart (is) with
2 Ch.25. 9; Job 9. 33; Mic. 2. 1.

To be in, ἔνειμι *eneimi.*

Gal. 3. 28, 28, 28; Col. 3. 11; Jas 1. 17.

IS, that which, thing as it —

Substance, תּוּשִׁיָּה *tushiyyah.*

Job 11. 6 secrets..(they are) double to that wh. is
26. 3 thou plentifully declared the thing as it is?

IS to say, that —

That is, ὅ ἐστι *ho esti.*

Mark 7. 11 Corban, that is to say, a gift, by whatso.

IS'-AAC, יִצְחָק, יִשְׂחָק 'Ισαάκ, *laughter.*

The son born to Abraham by Sarah in the hundredth year of his age, at Gerar, B.C. 1896. At the age of twenty-five he was directed to be sacrificed by his father. When forty years old he married his cousin Rebekah, by whom, when sixty years of age, he had two sons, Esau and Jacob. He died at Hebron aged 180, and was buried by his two sons in the cave of Machpelah, beside his father. B.C. 1716.

Gen. 17. 19 and thou shalt call his name I.: and I will
17. 21 my covenant will I establish with I.
21. 3 Abraham called the name of his son..I.
21. 4 Abraham circumcised his son I. being ei.
21. 5 old when his son I. was born unto him
21. 8 feast the (same) day that I. was weaned
21. 10 shall not be heir with my son, (even) with I
21. 12 for in I. shall thy seed be called
22. 2 thy son, thine only (son) I., whom thou lo.
22. 3 his young men with him, and I. his son
22. 6 took the wood..and laid (it) upon I. his son
22. 7 I. spake unto Abraham his father, and said
22. 9 bound I. his son, and laid him on the altar
24. 4 shalt go..and take a wife unto my son I.
24. 14 (that) thou hast appointed for thy servant I.
24. 62 I. came from the way of the well Lahai-roi
24. 63 I. went out to meditate in the field at
24. 64 when she saw I., she lighted off the camel
24. 66 servant told I. all things that he had done
24. 67 I. brought her into his mother Sarah's
24. 67 I. was comforted after his mother's (de.)
25. 5 And Abraham gave all that he had unto I.
25. 6 sent them away from I. his son, while he
25. 9 I. and Ishmael buried him in the cave of
25. 11 God blessed his son I.; and I. dwelt by the
25. 19 of I., Abraham's son. Abraham begat I.
25. 20 I. was forty years old when he took Reb.
25. 21 I. entreated the LORD for his wife, because
25. 26 I. (was) threescore years old when she b.
25. 28 I. loved Esau, because he did eat of (his)
26. 1 And I. went unto Abimelech king of the
26. 6 And I. dwelt in Gerar
26. 8 I. (was) sporting with Rebekah his wife

Gen. 26. 9 Abimelech called I., and said, Behold, of
26. 9 I. said unto him, Because I said, Lest I die
26. 12 I. sowed in that land, and received in the
27. 16 Abimelech said unto I., Go from us; for
26. 17 I. departed thence, and pitched his tent
26. 18 I. digged again the wells of water which
26. 19 I.'s servants digged in the valley, and
26. 20 the herdmen..did strive with I.'s herdmen
26. 25 and there I.'s servants digged a well
26. 27 I. said unto them, Wherefore come ye to
26. 31 I. sent them away, and they departed from
26. 32 I.'s servants came, and told him concern.
26: 35 a grief of mind unto I. and to Rebekah
27. 1 I. was old, and his eyes were dim, so that
27. 5 Rebekah heard when I. spake to Esau
27. 20 I. said unto his son, How (is it) that thou
27. 21 I. said unto Jacob, Come near, I pray thee
27. 22 Jacob went near unto I. his father; and
27. 26 I. said unto him, Come near now, and kiss
27. 30 as I. had made an end of blessing Jacob
27. 30 out from the presence of I. his father
27. 32 I. his father said unto him, Who (art) thou?
27. 33 I. trembled very exceedingly, and said, W.?
27. 37 I. answered and said unto Esau, Behold, I
27. 39 I. his father answered and said unto him
27. 46 Rebekah said to I., I am weary of my life
28. 1 I. called Jacob, and blessed him, and ch.
28. 5 I. sent away Jacob: and he went to Padan.
28. 6 I. had blessed Jacob, and sent him away
28. 8 the daughters of Canaan pleased not I. his
28. 13 of Abraham thy father, and the God of I.
31. 18 for to go to I. his father in the land of Can.
31. 42 the God of Abraham, and the fear of I.
31. 53 Jacob sware by the fear of his father I.
32. 9 And Jacob said, O...God of my father I.
35. 12 And the land which I gave Abraham and I.
35. 27 And Jacob came unto I. his father unto
35. 27 which (is) Hebron, where Abraham and I.
35. 28 the days of I. were an hundred and four.
35. 29 I. gave up the ghost, and died, and was
46. 1 offered sacrifices unto the God of his f. I.
48. 15 before whom my fathers Abraham and I.
48. 16 the name of my fathers Abraham and I.
49. 31 there they buried I. and Rebekah his wife
50. 24 land which he sware to Abraham, to I.
Exod. 2. 24 God remembered his covenant with..I.
3. 6 Moreover he said, I (am)..the God of I.
3. 15 God of I...hath sent me unto you: this
3. 16 the God of..I., and of Jacob, appeared
4. 5 the God of I., and the God of Jacob, hath
6. 3 And I appeared unto Abraham, unto I.
6. 8 I did swear to give it to Abraham, to I.
32. 13 Remember Abraham, I., and Israel, thy
33. 1 land which I sware unto Abraham, to I.
Lev. 26. 42 will I remember..my covenant with I., and
Num 32. 11 shall see the land which I sware unto..I.
Deut. 1. 8 LORD sware unto your fathers, Abraham, I.
6. 10 which he sware unto thy fathers, to..I.
9. 5 LORD sware unto thy fathers, Abraham, I.
9. 27 Remember thy servants, Abraham, I., and
29. 13 hath sworn unto thy fathers, to..I., and
30. 20 sware unto thy fathers, to Abraham, to I.
34. 4 I sware unto Abraham, unto I., and unto
Josh. 24. 3 and multipled his seed, and gave him I.
24. 4 And I gave unto I. Jacob and Esau: and
1 Ki. 18. 36 LORD God of Abraham, I., and of Israel
2 Ki. 13. 23 because of his covenant with Abraham, I.
1 Ch. 1. 28 The sons of Abraham; I., and Ishmael
1. 34 And Abraham begat I., The sons of I.; E.
16. 16 (Even of the covenant)..of his oath unto I.
29. 18 O LORD God of Abraham, I., and of Israel
2 Ch. 30. 6 turn again unto the LORD God of..I., and
Psa. 105. 9 made with Abraham, and his oath unto I.
Jer. 33. 26 (to be) rulers over the seed of Abraham, I.
Amos 7. 9 And the high places of I. shall be desolate
7. 16 drop not (thy word) against the house of I.
Matt. 1. 2 Abraham begat I.; and I. begat Jacob; and
8. 11 shall sit down with Abraham, and I., and
22. 32 I am the God of Abraham, and the God of I.
Mark 12. 26 (am) the God of Abraham, and the God of I.
Luke 3. 34 (the son) of Jacob, which was (the son) of I.
13. 28 when ye shall see Abraham, and I., and
20. 37 when he calleth the Lord..the God of I.
Acts 3. 13 The God of Abraham, and of I., and of J.
7. 8 (Abraham) begat I., and circumcised him
7. 8 and I. (begat) Jacob; and Jacob (begat)
7. 32 the God of Abraham, and the God of I.
Rom. 9. 7 but, In I. shall thy seed be called
9. 10 R. also had conceived by..our father I.
Gal. 4. 28 Now we..as I. was, are the children of
Heb. 11. 9 dwelling in tabernacles with I. and Jacob
11. 17 Abraham, when he was tried, offered up I.
11. 18 said, That in I. shall thy seed be called
11. 20 By faith I. blessed Jacob and Esau conc.
Jas. 2. 21 he had offered I. his son upon the altar?

I-SA'-IAH, יְשַׁעְיָהוּ *Jah (is) helper.*
The son of *Amoz*, of whom nothing else is known, but who must not be confounded with *Amos* the prophet. The duration of Isaiah's ministry must have been about sixty years. B.C. 759-690.

2 Ki. 19. 2 And he sent Eliakim..to I. the prophet
19. 5 the servants of king Hezekiah came to I.
19. 6 I. said unto them, Thus shall ye say to your
19. 20 Then I. the son of Amoz sent to Hezekiah
20. 1 And the prophet I. the son of Amoz came
20. 4 afore I. was gone out into the middle court
20. 7 I. said, Take a lump of figs. And they took
20. 8 Hezekiah said unto I., What (shall be) the
20. 9 I. said, This sign shalt thou have of the L.
20. 11 I. the prophet cried unto the LORD; and
20. 14 Then came I. the prophet unto king H.
2 Ki. 20. 16 I. said unto Hezekiah, Hear the word of
20. 19 said Hezekiah unto I., Good (is) the word
2 Ch. 26. 22 acts of Uzziah..did I. the prophet..write
32. 20 the prophet I...prayed and cried to hea.
32. 32 they (are) written in the vision of I. the
Isa. 1. 1 The vision of I. the son of Amoz, which he
2. 1 The word that I. the son of Amoz saw con.
7. 3 Then said the LORD unto I., Go forth now
13. 1 The burden of Babylon, which I...did see
20. 2 At the same time spake the LORD by I. the
20. 3 I. hath walked naked and barefoot three
37. 2 he sent Eliakim..unto I. the prophet, the
37. 5 So the servants of king Hezekiah came to I.
37. 6 I. said unto them, Thus shall ye say unto
37. 21 Then I. the son of Amoz sent unto Heze.
38. 1 I. the prophet, the son of Amoz, came unto
38. 4 Then came the word of the LORD to I.
38. 21 I. had said, Let them take a lump of figs
39. 3 Then came I. the prophet unto king Hez.
39. 5 Then said I...Hear the word of the LORD
39. 8 Then said Hezekiah to I., Good (is) the

IS'-CAH, יִסְכָּה *Jah (is) looking.*
A daughter of Haran the brother of Abram. She was sister of Milcah and Lot. In the Jewish traditions as found in Josephus, she is identified with *Sarai.* B.C 1898.

Gen. 11. 29 the father of Milcah, and the father of I.

IS-CA-RI'-OT, Ἰσκαριώτης *man of Kerioth (?).*
He is sometimes called "the son of *Simon*." This name has received various interpretations, *e.g.*, it has been derived from *Kerioth* (Josh. 15. 25) in the tribe of Judah; from *Kartha*, in Galilee (*Kartan*, Josh. 21. 32); from *καρωίδες*, date groves near Jerusalem and Jericho; from *Scortea*, a "leathern apron," applied to him as the bearer of the bag, *i.e.*, "Judas with the apron;" and from the Hebrew *Ascara*, strangling (angina) given him after his death. He was that apostle and disciple who betrayed his Master. See JUDAS (ISCARIOT).

ISH'-BAH, יִשְׁבָּח *appeaser.*
Father of Eshtemoa in the line of Judah. A probable conjecture is that he was son of Mered by his Egyptian wife Bithiah. B.C. 1400.

1 Ch. 4. 17 and she bare..I. the father of Eshtemoa

ISH'-BAK, יִשְׁבָּק *free.*
A son of Abraham by Keturah, and progenitor of a tribe in northern Arabia. Their locality may have been in the valley of *Sabâk* or *Sibak* in the *Dahnâ*, a fertile and extensive tract in *Nejd* in the high land of Arabia, in the N.E. of it and on the borders of the great desert. B.C. 1853.

Gen. 25. 2 she bare him Zimran..and I., and Shuah
1 Ch. 1. 32 she bare Zimran..Midian, and I., and S.

ISH-BI BE'-NOB, יִשְׁבִּי בְּנֹב *dweller on the mount.*
A son of Rapha one of the race of the Philistine giants. He attacked David in battle but was slain by Abishai. B.C. 1019.

2 Sa. 21. 16 and I., which (was) of the sons of the g.

ISH-BO'-SHETH, אִישׁ־בֹּשֶׁת *man of shame.*
A son of Saul, made king over Israel by Abner, but at last murdered in his bed. B.C. 1048.

2 Sa. 2. 8 But Abner..took I. the son of Saul, and
2. 10 I., Saul's son, (was) forty years old when
2. 12 the servants of I...went out from Maha.
2. 15 twelve..which (pertained) to I. the 3. 7.
3. 8 was Abner very wroth for the words of I.
3. 14 And David sent messengers to I., Saul's
3. 15 And I. sent, and took her from (her) hus.
4. 5 came..to the house of I., who lay on a bed
4. 8 they brought the head of I. unto David to
4. 8 Behold the head of I. the son of Saul th.
4. 12 they took the head of I., and buried (it)

ISH'-I, יִשְׁעִי *my help.*
1. A son of Appaim, a descendant of Pharez son of Judah. B.C. 1420.

1 Ch. 2. 31 sons of Appaim; I. And the sons of I.

2. A descendant of Judah through Caleb the spy. B.C. 1400.

1 Ch. 4. 20 the sons of I. (were) Zoheth and Ben-zo

3. One of the Simeonites who led their tribe against Amalek. B.C. 740.

1 Ch. 4. 42 and Rephaiah, and Uzziel, the sons of I.

4. One of the heads of Manasseh on the E. of the Jordan. B.C. 800.

1 Ch. 5. 24 their fathers, even Epher, and I., and E.

I'-SHI, אִישִׁי *my husband.*
A symbolic name which God's people were to give to him when they returned to him.

Hos. 2. 16 saith the LORD, (that) thou shalt call me I.

ISH-I'-AH, IS-SHI'-AH, ISH-I'-JAH, יִשִּׁיָּה *Jah exists.*
1. The 5th of the five sons of Izrahiah; one of the heads of Issachar in the time of David.

1 Ch. 7. 3 Michael, and Obadiah, and Joel, I., five

2. A descendant of Moses. B.C. 1015.

1 Ch. 24. 21 of the sons of Rehabiah, the first (was) I.

3. A descendant of Levi. B.C. 1015.

1 Ch. 24. 25 brother of Michah (was) I.: of the sons of I.

4. One of the Bene-Harim who had married a strange woman. B.C. 445.

Ezra 10. 31 the sons of Harim; Eliezer, I., Malchiah

ISH'-MA, יִשְׁמָא *high, elevated.*
A descendant of Caleb the son of Hur. B.C. 1400.

1 Ch. 4. 3 of Etam; Jezreel, and I., and Idbash: and

ISH-MA'-EL, יִשְׁמָעֵאל *God (is) hearing.*
1. Son of Abraham by Hagar Sarah's maid. When Ishmael was born Abraham was eighty-six years of age (B.C. 1911), and dwelling in the plain of Mamre. Ishmael was circumcised at the age of thirteen years along with his father and his servants. A promise was given by God that Ishmael should beget twelve princes and become a great nation. He met Isaac, once at least after being sent away, at the burial of Abraham their father. He died aged 137 years. B.C. 1774.

Gen. 16. 11 bear a son, and shalt call his name I.; be.
16. 15 called his son's name, which Hagar bare I.
16. 16 fourscore and six..when Hagar bare I. to
17. 18 Abraham said..that I. might live before
17. 20 as for I., I have heard thee: Behold, I
17. 23 Abraham took I. his son, and all that were
17. 25 I. his son (was) thirteen years old when
17. 26 was Abraham circumcised, and I. his son
25. 9 his sons Isaac and I. buried him in the
25. 12 Now these (are) the generations of I., A.
25. 13 these (are) the names of the sons of I., by
25. 13 the first born of I., Nebajoth; and Kedar
25. 16 These (are) the sons of I., and these (are)
25. 17 these (are) the years of the life of I., an
28. 9 Then went Esau unto I., and took unto
28. 9 Mahalath the daughter of I., Abraham's
36. 3 Bashemath, I.'s daugher, sister of Nebaj.
1 Ch. 1. 28 The sons of Abraham; Isaac, and I.
1. 29 The first born of I., Nebaioth; then Kedar
1. 31 Je...Kedemah. These are the sons of I.

2. A descendant of Zebadiah who was ruler of the house of Judah in Jehoshaphat's time. B.C. 880.

2 Ch. 19. 11 Zebadiah the son of I., the ruler of the

3. A son of Azel a Benjamite, of Saul's family. B.C. 880.

1 Ch. 8. 38 whose names (are) these, Azrikam..and I.
9. 44 whose names (are) these, Azrikam..and I.

4. One of the captains of hundreds who assisted in raising Joash to the throne. B.C. 878.

2 Ch. 23. 1 and I. the son of Jehohanan, and Azariah

5 A priest who had taken a foreign wife. B.C. 450.

Ezra 10. 22 of the sons of Pashur..Maaseiah, I., [Neth.

6. Son of Nethaniah. His vile acts and character are fully given by Jeremiah. B.C. 588.

2 Ki. 25. 23 there came to Gedaliah..even I. the son
25. 25 I. the son of Nethaniah..of the seed royal
Jer. 40. 8 they came to Gedaliah..even I. the son of
40. 14 Baalis..hath sent I. the son of Nethaniah
40. 15 Let me go..and I will slay I. the son of N.
40. 16 Thou shalt not..thou speakest falsely of I.
41. 1 I. the son of Nethaniah..of the seed royal
41. 2 Then arose I. the son of Nethaniah, and
41. 3 I. also slew all the Jews that were with
41. 6 I. the son of Nethaniah went forth from
41 7 that I. the son of Nethaniah slew them
41. 8 were found among them that said unto I.
41. 9 Now the pit wherein I. had cast all the
41. 9 I. the son of Nethaniah filled it with (th.
41. 10 I. carried away captive all the residue of
41. 10 I. the son of Nethaniah carried them away
41. 11 the evil that I. the son of Nethaniah had
41. 12 took all the men, and went to fight with I
41. 13 all the people which (were) with I. saw J.
41. 14 all the people that I. had carried away
41. 15 I. the son of Nethaniah escaped from Jo.
41. 16 remnant..whom he had recovered from I.
41. 18 I. the son of Nethaniah had slain Gedaliah

ISH-MA-EL-ITE, ISH-ME-EL-ITE, יִשְׁמְעֵאלִי.
Patronymic of the tribes descended from Ishmael. In Gen. 37 28 they seem to be also called *Midianites.*

Gen. 37. 25 behold, a company of I. came from Gilead
37. 27 Come, and let us sell him to the I., and
37. 28 they..sold Joseph to the I. for twenty
39. 1 Potiphar..bought him of the hands of the I.
Judg. 8. 24 had golden ear rings, because they (were) I.
1 Ch. 2. 17 the father of Amasa (was) Jether the I.
27. 30 Over the camels also (was) Obil the I.: and
Psa. 83. 6 The tabernacles of Edom, and the I.; of

ISH-MA'-IAH, יִשְׁמַעְיָהוּ *Jah (is) hearing.*
A prince of Zebulun in David's reign. B.C. 1048.

1 Ch. 27. 19 Of Zebulun; I. the son of Obadiah: of Nap.

ISH-ME'-RAI, יִשְׁמְרַי *Jah (is) keeper.*
A descendant of Benjamin, and one of the chief men of the tribe. B.C. 1400.

1 Ch. 8. 18 I. also, and Jezliah, and Jobab, the sons

I'-SHOD, אִישְׁהוֹד *man of honour.*
Properly *Ish-hod.* One of the tribe of Manasseh on the E. of the Jordan, and son of Hammoleketh, "the queen." From his near relationship to Gilead he was probably an influential person. B.C. 1400.

1 Ch. 7. 18 his sister Hammoleketh bare I., and Ab

ISH'-PAN, יִשְׁפָּן *firm, strong.*
A son of Shashak, a chief Benjamite. B.C. 1300.

1 Ch. 8. 22 And I., and Heber, and Eliel

ISH TOB, אִישׁ טוֹב *man of Tob.*
A small state that formed part of *Aram.* It was here that Jephthah fled when thrust out by his brethren. B.C. 1150.

2 Sa. 10. 6 sent and hired..of I. twelve thousand
10. 8 I., and Maacah (were) by themselves in

ISH-U'-AH, I-SU'-AH, ישׁוה *self-answering or satis.*
The second son of Asher, B.C. 1680. In 1 Ch. 7. 30, the orthography is *Isuah* in the Common Version, though it is identical with the Hebrew word in Gen. 46. 17.

Gen 46. 17 the sons of Asher; Jimnah, and I., and
1 Ch. 7. 30 sons of Asher; Imnah, and I., and Ishuai

ISH'-UI, ISH-U'-AI, IS'-UI, JES'-UI, ישׁוי.
1. The third son of Asher, and founder of the family of the *Jesuites.* B.C. 1680.

Gen. 46. 17 sons of Asher; Jimnah, and Ishuah, and I.
Num.26. 44 of J., the family of the Jesuites: of Ber.
1 Ch. 7. 30 sons of Asher; Imnah, and Isuah, and I.

2. Second son of Saul by his wife Ahinoam. B.C. 1060.

1 Sa. 14. 49 the sons of Saul were Jonathan, and I.

ISLAND, isle —

1. *Isle, sea coast,* אי *i.*
Gen. 10. 5 By these were the isles of the Gentiles
Esth.10. 1 upon the land, and..the isles of the sea
Job 22. 30 He shall deliver the island of the innocent
Psa. 72. 10 kings of Tarshish and of the isles shall
97. 1 rejoice; let the multitude of isles be glad
Isa. 11. 11 from Hamath, and..the islands of the sea
20. 6 the inhabitant of this isle shall say in that
23. 2 Be still, ye inhabitants of the isle; thou
23. 6 Tarshish; howl, ye inhabitants of the isle
24. 15 LORD God of Israel in the isles of the sea
40. 15 he taketh up the isles as a very little thing
41. 1 Keep silence before me, O islands; and
41. 5 The isles saw (it), and feared; the ends
42. 4 judgment..and the isles shall wait for his
42. 10 Sing..the isles, and the inhabitants there.
42. 12 Let them..declare his praise in the islands
42. 15 I will make the rivers islands, and I will
49. 1 Listen, O isles, unto me; and hearken, ye
51. 5 the isles shall wait upon me, and on mine
59. 18 to the islands he will repay recompence
60. 9 Surely the isles shall wait for me, and the
66. 19 isles afar off, that have not heard my fa.
Jer. 2. 10 For pass over the isles of Chittim, and
25. 22 kings of the isles which (are) beyond the
31. 10 and declare (it) in the isles afar off, and
50. 39 with the wild beasts of the islands shall
Eze. 26. 15 Shall not the isles shake at the sound of
26. 18 Now shall the isles tremble in the day of
26. 18 the isles that (are) in the sea shall be tro.
27. 3 a merchant of the people for many isles
27. 6 benches (of) ivory..out of the isles of Ch.
27. 7 blue and purple from the isles of Elishah
27. 15 many isles..the merchandise of thine hand
27. 35 All the inhabitants of the isles shall be
39. 6 them that dwell carelessly in the isles
Dan. 11. 18 After this shall he turn..unto the isles
Zeph. 2. 11 every one from his place..all the isles of

2. *Isle, a small island,* νησίον *nēsion.*
Acts 27. 16 running under a certain island which is

3. *Island,* νῆσος *nēsos.*
Acts 13. 6 when they had gone through the isle unto
27. 26 Howbeit we must be cast upon a certain is.
28. 1 they knew that the island was called M.
28. 7 possessions of the chief man of the island
28. 9 others..which had diseases in the island
28. 11 in a ship..which had wintered in the isle
Rev. 1. 9 was in the isle that is called Patmos, for
6. 14 every mountain and island were moved
16. 20 every island fled away, and the mountains

ISLAND, wild beast of the —

Those inhabiting the islands, איים *iyyim.*
Isa. 13. 22 the wild beasts of the island shall cry in
34. 14 shall..meet with the wild beasts of the is.
Jer. 50. 39 with the wild beasts of the islands shall

IS-MACH'-IAH, יסמכיהו *Jah (is) supporter.*
An overseer of the dedicated things at the temple in the time of Hezekiah. B.C. 726.

2 Ch. 31. 13 I., and Mahath..(were) overseers under

IS-MA'-IAH ישׁמעיה *Jah (is) hearing.*
A Gibeonite warrior who joined David at Ziklag. He was among the thirty valiant men, and over them.

1 Ch. 12. 4 I. the Gibeonite, a mighty man among

IS-PAH, ישׁפה *firm, strong.*
A son of Beriah the Benjamite. B.C. 1400.

1 Ch. 8. 16 Michael, and I., and Joha, the sons of B.

IS-RA'-EL, ישׂראל Ἰσραήλ *ruling with God.*
1. The new name given to Jacob. B.C. 1739.

Gen. 32. 28 name shall be called no more Jacob, but I.
35. 10 shall not be called any more Jacob, but I.
35. 10 be thy name: and he called his name I.
35. 21 I. journeyed, and spread his tent beyond
35. 22 it came to pass, when I. dwelt in that land
35. 22 Reuben went and lay with Billah..and I.
37. 3 Now I. loved Joseph more than all his
37. 13 I. said..Do not thy brethren feed (the fl.)
42. 5 the sons of I. came to buy (corn) among
43. 6 I. said, Wherefore dealt ye (so) ill with
43. 8 Judah said unto I. his father, Send the
43. 11 their father I. said unto them, If (it must
45. 21 the children of I. did so: and Joseph
45. 28 I said, (It is) enough; Joseph my son (is)
46. 1 I. took his journey with all that he had
46. 2 God spake unto I. in the visions of the
46. 5 and the sons of I. carried Jacob their fat.
46. 8 these (are) the names of the children of I.
46. 29 Joseph..went up to meet I. his father, to
46. 30 I. said unto Joseph, Now let me die, since
47. 27 I. dwelt in the land of Egypt, in the cou.
47. 29 And the time drew nigh that I. must die
Gen. 47. 31 And I. bowed himself upon the bed's head
48. 2 I. strengthened himself, and sat upon the
48. 8 I. beheld Joseph's sons, and said, Who
48. 10 Now the eyes of I. were dim for age, (so
48. 11 I. said unto Joseph, I had not thought to
48. 13 Ephraim in his right hand toward I.'s left
48. 13 Manasseh in his left hand toward I.'s right
48. 14 I. stretched out his right hand, and laid
48. 21 I. said unto Joseph, Behold, I die; but
49. 2 Gather yourselves toget...hearken unto I.
50. 2 commanded..the physicians embalmed I.
Exod. 1. 1 these (are) the names of the children of I.
1. 7 children of I. were fruitful, and increased
6. 14 The sons of Reuben the first born of I.
32. 13 Remember Abraham, Isaac, and I., thy ser.
Num. 1. 20 And the children of Reuben, I.'s eldest
26. 5 Reuben, the eldest son of I.: the children
Judg18. 29 of Dan their father, who was born unto I.
1 Ki.18. 31 the word..came, saying, I. shall be thy
18. 36 God of Abraham, Isaac, and of I. let it
2Ki. 17. 34 the children of Jacob, whom he named I.
1 Ch. 1. 34 The sons of Isaac; Esau, and I.
2. 1 These (are) the sons of I.; Reuben, Sime.
5. 1 Now the sons of Reuben, the first born of I.
5. 1 given unto the sons of Joseph the son of I.
5. 3 The sons..of Reuben the first born of I.
6. 38 of Kohath, the son of Levi, the son of I.
7. 29 dwelt the children of Joseph the son of I.
29. 10 Blessed (be) thou, LORD God of I. our fa.
29. 18 O LORD God of Abraham, Isaac, and of I.
2 Ch.30. 6 God of Abraham, Isaac, and of I.
Ezra 8. 18 of Mahli, the son of Levi, the son of I.

2. The nation that sprang from Jacob and the land in which they dwelt.

Gen. 32. 32 Therefore the children of I. eat not (of)
34. 7 he had wrought folly in I., in lying with
36. 31 reigned any king over the children of I.
48. 20 In thee shall I. bless, saying, God make
49. 7 I will divide them..and scatter them in I.
49. 16 judge his people, as one of the tribes of I.
49. 24 thence (is) the shepherd, the stone of I.
49. 28 All these (are) the twelve tribes of I.: and
50. 25 Joseph took an oath of the children of I.
Exod. 1. 9 people of the children of I. (are)..mighti.
1. 12 were grieved because of the children of I.
1. 13 Egyptians made the children of I. to serve
2. 23 the children of I. sighed by reason of the
2. 25 God looked upon the children of I., and
3. 9 behold, the cry of the children of I. is co.
3. 10 thou mayest bring..the children of I. out
3. 11 I should bring forth the children of I. out
3. 13 Behold..I come unto the children of I.
3. 14, 15 shalt thou say unto the children of I.
3. 16 Go, and gather the elders of I. together
3. 18 thou shalt come, thou and the elders of I.
4. 22 Thus saith the LORD, I. (is) my son, (even)
4. 29 gathered..the elders of the children of I.
4. 31 the LORD had visited the children of I.
5. 1 Thus saith the LORD God of I., Let my p.
5. 2 that I should obey his voice to let I. go?
5. 2 I know not the LORD, neither will I let I. go
5. 14, 15, 19 the officers of the children of I.
6. 5 heard the groaning of the children of I.
6. 6 Wherefore say unto the children of I., I
6. 9 Moses spake so unto the children of I.
6. 11 that he let the children of I. go out of his
6. 12 the children of I. have not hearkened unto
6. 13 gave them a charge unto the children of I.
6. 13 bring the children of I. out of the land
6. 26 Bring out the children of I. from the land
6. 27 to bring out the children of I. from Egypt
7. 2 that he send the children of I. out of his
7. 4 bring forth..my people the children of I.
7. 5 when I..bring out the children of I. from
9. 4 LORD shall sever between the cattle of I.
9. 4 nothing die..(that is) the children's of I.
9. 6 of the cattle of the children of I. died not
9. 26 where the children of I. (were), was there
9. 35 neither would he let the children of I. go
10. 20 that he would not let the children of I.
10. 23 all the children of I. had light in their d.
11. 7 against..the children of I. shall not a dog
11. 7 a difference between the Egyptians and I.
11. 10 he would not let the children of I. go out
12. 3 Speak ye unto all the congregation of I.
12. 6 the congregation of I. shall kill it in the
12. 15 day, that soul shall be cut off from I.
12. 19 cut off from the congregation of I., whet.
12. 21 Then Moses called for all the elders of I.
12. 27 passed over the houses of the children of I.
12. 28 children of I. went away, and did as the
12. 31 Rise up..both ye and the children of I.
12. 35 children of I. did according to the word
12. 37 children of I. journeyed from Rameses
12. 40 Now the sojourning of the children of I.
12.42 to be observed of all the children of I. in
12. 47 All the congregation of I. shall keep it
12. 50 Thus did all the children of I.; as the L.
12. 51 LORD did bring the children of I. out of
13. 2 openeth the womb among the children of I.
13. 18 children of I. went up harnessed out of
13. 19 he had straitly sworn the children of I.
14. 2 Speak unto the children of I., that they
14. 3 For Pharaoh will say of the children of I.
14. 5 said, Why have we..let I. go from serving
14. 8 he pursued after the children of I.: and
14. 8 children of I. went out with an high hand
14. 10 the children of I. lifted up their eyes, and
14. 10 and the children of I. cried out unto the
14. 15 speak unto the children of I., that they
14. 16 and the children of I. shall go on dry
14. 19 angel..which went before the camp of I.
Exod14. 20 camp of the Egyptians and the camp of I.
14. 22 children of I. went into the midst of the
14. 25 said, Let us flee from the face of I.; for
14. 29 But the children of I. walked upon dry
14. 30 Thus the LORD saved I. that day out of
14. 30 I. saw the Egyptians dead upon the sea
14. 31 I. saw that great work which the LORD
15. 1 Then sang Moses and the children of I.
15. 19 but the children of I. went on dry (land)
15. 22 So Moses brought I. from the Red Sea
16. 1, 2, 9, 10 congregation of the children of I.
16. 3 children of I. said unto them, Would to
16. 6 and Aaron said unto all the children of I.
16. 12 heard the murmurings of the children of I.
16. 15 when the children of I. saw (it), they said
16. 17 And the children of I. did so, and gathered
16. 31 house of I. called the name thereof Man.
16. 35 children of I. did eat manna forty years
17. 1 all the congregation of the children of I.
17. 5 Go..and take with thee of the elders of I.
17. 6 Moses did..in the sight of the elders of I.
17. 7 because of the chiding of the children of I.
17. 8 Then came Amalek, and fought with I. in
17. 11 Moses held up his hand, that I. prevailed
18. 1 heard of all that God had done..for I. his
18. 1 that the LORD had brought I. out of Egypt
18. 8 told..all that the LORD had done..for I.'s
18. 9 the goodness which the LORD had done to I.
18. 12 and Aaron came, and all the elders of I.
18. 25 Moses chose able men out of all I., and
19. 1 the children of I. were gone forth out of
19. 2 in the wilderness: and there I. camped
19. 3 Thus shalt thou..tell the children of I.
19. 6 thou shalt speak unto the children of I.
20. 22 thou shalt say unto the children of I., Ye
24. 1 Come up..and seventy of the elders of I.
24. 4 builded..according to the..tribes of I.
24. 5 he sent young men of the children of I.
24. 9 Then went up..seventy of the elders of I
24. 10 they saw the God of I.: and (there was)
24. 11 upon the nobles of the children of I. he
24. 17 fire..in the eyes of the children of I.
25. 2 Speak unto the children of I., that they
25. 22 I will give thee..unto the children of I.
27. 20 thou shalt command the children of I., that
27. 21 on the behalf of the children of I.
28. 1 take..from among the children of I., that
28. 9 and grave..the names of the children of I.
28. 11 with the names of the children of I.: thou
28. 12 stones of memorial unto the children of I.
28. 21 be with the names of the children of I.
28.29 shall bear the names of the children of I.
28. 30 bear the judgment of the children of I.
28. 38 holy things, which the children of I. shall
29. 28 by a statute..from the children of I.; for
29. 28 an heave offering from the children of I.
29. 43 there I will meet with the children of I.
29. 45 I will dwell among the children of I., and
30. 12 thou takest the sum of the children of I.
30. 16 the atonement money of the children of I.
30. 16 a memorial unto the children of I. before
30. 31 shalt speak unto the children of I., saying
31. 13 Speak thou also unto the children of I.
31. 16 Wherefore the children of I. shall keep
31. 17 sign between me and the children of I
32. 4, 8 These (be) thy gods, O I. which brou.
32. 20 and made the children of I. drink (of it)
32. 27 Thus saith the LORD God of I., Put every
33. 5 Say unto the children of I., Ye (are) a st.
33. 6 the children of I. stripped themselves of
34. 23 men children appear before..the God of I.
34. 27 have made a covenant with thee and with I.
34. 30 when Aaron and all the children of I. saw
34. 32 afterward all the children of I. came nigh
34. 34 came out, and spake unto the children of I.
34. 35 the children of I. saw the face of Moses
35. 1, 4, 20 the congregation of the children of I.
35. 29 children of I. brought a willing offering
35. 30 Moses said unto the children of I., See
36. 3 the offering which the children of I. had
39. 6 with the names of the children of I.
39. 7 for a memorial to the children of I.; as the
39. 14 the names of the children of I., twelve
39. 32 children of I. did according to all that the
39. 42 so the the children of I. made all the wo.
40. 36 the children of I. went onward in all their
40. 38 fire..in the sight of all the house of I.
L 1. 2 Speak unto the children of I., and say
4. 2 Speak unto the children of I., saying, If
4. 13 if the whole congregation of I. sin through
7. 23, 29 Speak unto the children of I., saying
7. 34 have I taken of the children of I. from off
7. 34 by a statute..from among the children of I.
7. 36 to be given them of the children of I., in
7. 38 he commanded the children of I. to offer
9. 1 Moses called Aaron..and the elders of I.
9. 3 unto the children of I. thou shalt speak
10. 6 let your brethren, the whole house of I.
10. 11 that ye may teach the children of I. all
10. 14 of the sacrifices..of the children of I.
11. 2 Speak unto the children of I., saying, Th
12. 2 Speak unto the children of I., saying, If
15. 2 Speak unto the children of I., and say
15. 31 Thus shall ye separate the children of I.
16. 5 of the congregation of the children of I.
16. 16 of the uncleanness of the children of I.
16. 17 atonement..for all the congregation of I.
16. 19 from the uncleanness of the children of I.
16. 21 all the iniquities of the children of I.
16. 34 make an atonement for the children of I.
17. 2 his sons, and unto all the children of I.
17. 3, 8, 10, 13 man (there be) of the house of I.

Lev. 17. 5 children of I. may bring their sacrifices
17. 12 Therefore I said unto the children of I.
17. 14 I said unto the children of I., Ye shall
18. 2 Speak unto the children of I., and say
19. 2 the congregation of the children of I.
20. 2 Again, thou shalt say to the children of I.
20. 2 I., or of the strangers that sojourn in I.
21. 24 his sons, and unto all the children of I.
22. 2 from the holy things of the children of I.
22. 3 the children of I. hallow unto the LORD
22. 15 the holy things of the children of I.
22. 18 his sons, and unto all the children of I.
22. 18 the house of I., or of the strangers in I.
22. 32 will be hallowed among the children of I.
23. 2, 10 Speak unto the children of I., and say
23. 24, 34 Speak unto the children of I., saying
23. 43 made the children of I. to dwell in booths
23. 44 Moses declared unto the children of I. the
24. 2 Command the children of I., that they
24. 8 (being taken) from the children of I. by an
24. 10 son..went out among the children of I.
24. 10 a man of I. strove together in the camp
24. 15 thou shalt speak unto the children of I.
24. 23 Moses spake unto the children of I., that
24. 23 children of I. did as the LORD commanded
25. 2 Speak unto the children of I., and say
25. 33 their possession among the children of I.
25. 46 over your brethren the children of I. ye
25. 55 unto me the children of I. (are) servants
26. 46 made between him and the children of I.
27. 2 Speak unto the children of I., and say
27. 34 commanded Moses for the children of I.
Num. 1. 2 the congregation of the children of I.
1. 3 all that are able to go forth to war in I.
1. 16 These (were) the..heads of thousands in I.
1. 44 and the princes of I., (being) twelve men
1. 45 that were numbered of the children of I.
1. 45 that were able to go forth to war in I.
1. 49 the sum of them among the children of I.
1. 52 the children of I. shall pitch their tents
1. 53 the congregation of the children of I.
1. 54 the children of I. did according to all that
2. 2 Every man of the children of I. shall
2. 32 which were numbered of the children of I.
2. 33 not numbered among the children of I.
2. 34 the children of I. did according to all that
3. 8 keep..the charge of the children of I.
3. 9 given unto him out of the children of I.
3. 12 Levites from among the children of I.
3. 12 openeth the matrix among..children of I.
3. 13 hallowed unto me all the first born in I.
3. 38 for the charge of the children of I.; and
3. 40 of the males of the children of I. from
3. 41, 42, 45 first born among the children of I.
3. 41 among the cattle of the children of I.
3. 46, 50 of the first born of the children of I.
4. 46 and Aaron and the chief of I. numbered
5. 2 Command the children of I., that they put
5. 4 the children of I. did so, and put them out
5. 4 as the LORD spake..did the children of I.
5. 6 Speak unto the children of I., When a man
5. 9 all the holy things of the children of I.
5. 12 Speak unto the children of I., and say
6. 2 Speak unto the children of I., and say
6. 23 ye shall bless the children of I., saying
6. 27 shall put my name upon the children of I.
7. 2 the princes of I., heads of the house of their
7. 84 when it was anointed, by the princes of I.
8. 6, 14 Levites from among the children of I.
8. 9 assembly of the children of I. together
8. 10 the children of I. shall put their hands
8. 11 (for) an offering of the children of I.
8. 16 unto me from among the children of I.
8. 16, 17, 18 first born of all the children of I.
8. 19 I., to do the service of the children of I.
8. 19 make an atonement for the children of I.
8. 19 the children of I., when the children of I.
8. 20 the congregation of the children of I.
8. 20 so did the children of I. unto them
9. 2 the children of I. also keep the passover
9. 4 Moses spake unto the children of I., that
9. 5 according to all..did the children of I.
9. 7 appointed season among..children of I.?
9. 10 Speak unto the children of I. saying, If
9. 17 after that the children of I. journeyed
9. 17 the children of I. pitched their tents
9. 18 the children of Israel journeyed, and at
9. 19 the children of I. kept the charge of the
9. 22 the children of I. abode in their tents
10. 4 (which are) heads of the thousands of I.
10. 12 the children of I. took their journeys out
10. 28 (were) the journeyings of the children of I.
10. 29 the LORD hath spoken good concerning I.
10. 36 Return..unto the many thousands of I.
11. 4 the children of I. also wept again, and
11. 16 Gather..seventy men of the elders of I.
11. 30 gat..into the camp, he and the elders of I.
13. 2 Canaan, which I give..the children of I.
13. 3 those men (were) heads of the children of I.
13. 24 grapes which the children of I. cut down
13. 26 the congregation of the children of I.
13. 32 an evil report..unto the children of I.
14. 2 the children of I. murmured against Mos.
14. 5 of the congregation of the children of I.
14. 7 unto all the company of the children of I.
14. 10 appeared..before all the children of I.
14. 27 heard the murmurings of the children of I.
14. 39 sayings unto all the children of I.; and the
15. 2, 18, 38 Speak unto the children of I., and
15. 26 the congregation of the children of I. v. 25.
15. 29 him that is born among the children of I.
15. 32 the children of I. were in the wilderness

Num 16. 2 with certain of the children of I., two
16. 9 (but) a small thing..the God of I. hath
16. 9 separated you from the congregation of I.
16. 25 rose up..and the elders of I. followed
16. 34 I. that (were) round about them fled at the
16. 38 shall be a sign unto the children of I.
16. 40 (To be) a memorial unto the children of I.
16. 41 the children of I. murmured against Mo.
17. 2 Speak unto the children of I., and take
17. 5 the murmurings of the children of I.
17. 6 Moses spake unto the children of I., and
17. 9 before the LORD unto..the children of I.
17. 12 the children of I. spake unto Moses, saying
18. 5 no wrath any more upon the children of I.
18. 6 the Levites from among the children of I.
18. 8 the hallowed things of the children of I.
18. 11 the wave offerings of the children of I.
18. 14 Every thing devoted in I. shall be thine
18. 19 the children of I. offer unto the LORD
18. 20 thine inheritance among the children of I.
18. 21 all the tenth in I. for an inheritance
18. 22 Neither must the children of I. henceforth
18. 23, 24 among the children of I. they have no
18. 24 the tithes of the children of I., which
18. 26 When ye take of the children of I. the
18. 28 which ye receive of the children of I.
18. 32 the holy things of the children of I.
19. 2 Speak unto the children of I., that they
19. 9 for the congregation of the children of I.
19. 10 it shall be unto the children of I., and
19. 13 that soul shall be cut off from I.: because
20. 1 Then came the children of I., (even) the
20. 12 sanctify me in the eyes of..children of I.
20. 13 the children of I. strove with the LORD
20. 14 Thus saith thy brother I., Thou knowest
20. 19 the children of I. said unto him, We will
20. 21 to give I. passage through his border
20. 21 wherefore I. turned away from him
20. 22 the children of I., (even) the whole congre.
20. 24 which I have given unto the children of I.
20. 29 they mourned..(even) all the house of I.
21. 1 that I. came by the way of the spies
21. 1 he fought against I., and took (some) of
21. 2 I. vowed a vow unto the LORD, and said, If
21. 3 the LORD hearkened to the voice of I., and
21. 6 bit the people; and much people of I. died
21. 10 the children of I. set forward, and pitched
21. 17 I. sang this song, Spring up, O well; sing
21. 21 I. sent messengers unto Sihon king of the
21. 23 not suffer I. to pass through his border
21. 23 but Sihon..went out against I. into the
21. 23 he came to Jahaz, and fought against I.
21. 24 I. smote him with the edge of the sword
21. 25 And I. took all these cities: and I. dwelt in
21. 31 Thus I. dwelt in the land of the Amorites
22. 1 the children of I. set forward, and pitched
22. 2 saw all that I. had done to the Amorites
22. 3 distressed because of the children of I.
23. 7 Come, curse me Jacob, and come, defy I.
23. 10 and the number of the fourth (part) of I.?
23. 21 neither hath he seen perverseness in I.
23. 23 neither (is there) any divination against I.
23. 23 it shall be said of Jacob and of I., What
24. 1 saw that it pleased the LORD to bless I.
24. 2 Balaam lifted up his eyes, and he saw I.
24. 5 How goodly are..thy tabernacles, O I.!
24. 17 a sceptre shall rise out of I., and shall
24. 18 Edom shall be a possession..and I. shall
25. 1 I. abode in Shittim, and the people began
25. 3 I. joined himself unto Baal-peor: and the
25. 3 anger of the LORD was kindled against I.
25. 4 fierce anger..may be turned away from I.
25. 5 Moses said unto the judges of I., Slay ye
25. 6 one of the children of I. came and brou.
25. 6 all the congregation of the children of I.
25. 8 he went after the man of I. into the tent
25. 8 thrust..them through, the man of I.
25. 8 plague was stayed from the children of I.
25. 11 turned my wrath..from the children of I.
25. 11 I consumed not the children of I. in my
25. 13 made an atonement for the children of I.
26. 2 Take the sum of all..the children of I.
26. 2 Take..all that are able to go to war in I.
26. 4 the LORD commanded..the children of I.
26. 51 numbered of the children of I., six hun.
26. 62 not numbered among the children of I.
26. 62 no inheritance given..the children of I.
26. 63 priest, who numbered the children of I.
26. 64 when they numbered the children of I.
27. 8 thou shalt speak unto the children of I.
27. 11 shall be unto the children of I. a statute
27. 12 which I have given unto the children of I.
27. 20 that all..the children of I. may be obed.
27. 21 (both) he, and all the children of I. with
28. 2 Command the children of I., and say unto
29. 40 Moses told the children of I. according to
30. 1 Moses spake..concern. the children of I.
31. 2 Avenge the children of I. of the Midian.
31. 4 throughout all the tribes of I., shall ye
31. 5 were delivered out of the thousands of I.
31. 9 children of I. took (all) the women..cap.
31. 12 the congregation of the children of I.
31. 16 these caused the children of I...to com.
31. 30, 42 And of the children of I.'s half
31. 47 Even of the children of I.'s half, Moses
31. 54 a memorial for the children of I. before
32. 4 LORD smote before the congregation of I.
32. 7 discourage..heart of the children of I.
32. 9 discouraged the heart of the children of I
32. 13 the LORD's anger was kindled against I.
32. 14 to augment..anger of the LORD toward I.
32. 17 go ready armed before the children of I.

Num 32. 18 until the children of I. have inherited
32. 22 shall return, and be guiltless before..I.
32. 28 the chief fathers..of the children of I.
33. 1 journeys of the children of I., which went
33. 3 children of I. went out with an high hand
33. 5 the children of I. removed from Rameses
33. 38 children of I. were come out of the land
33. 40 heard of the coming of the children of I.
33. 51 Speak unto the children of I., and say
34. 2 Command the children of I., and say unto
34. 13 Moses commanded the children of I., say
34. 29 to divide..unto the children of I. in the
35. 2 Command the children of I., that they
35. 8 of the possession of the children of I.
35. 10 Speak unto the children of I., and say
35. 15 for the children of I., and for the strang.
35. 34 I the LORD dwell among the children of I.
36. 1 the chief fathers of the children of I.
36. 2 inheritance by lot to the children of I.
36. 3 of the (other) tribes of the children of I.
36. 4 when the jubilee of the children of I. shall
36. 5 commanded the children of I. according
36. 7 not the inheritance of the children of I.
36. 7 every one of the children of I. shall keep
36. 8 an inheritance in any tribe of the child. of I.
36. 8 that the children of I. may enjoy every
36. 9 every one of the tribes of the children of I.
36. 13 LORD commanded..unto the children of I.
Deut. 1. 1 the words which Moses spake unto all I.
1. 3 Moses spake unto the children of I., acc.
1. 38 encourage him; for he shall cause I. to
2. 12 as I. did unto the land of his possession
3. 18 pass over armed before..the children of I.
4. 1 hearken, O I., unto the statutes and unto
4. 44 which Moses set before the children of I.
4. 45 which Moses spake unto the children of I.
4. 46 whom Moses and the children of I. smote
5. 1 And Moses called all I., and said unto
5. 1 Hear, O I., the statutes and judgments
6. 3 Hear therefore, O I., and observe to do
6. 4 Hear, O I.: The LORD our God (is) one L.
9. 1 Hear, O I.: Thou (art) to pass over Jordan
10. 6 the children of I. took their journey from
10. 12 I., what doth the LORD thy God require.
11. 6 substance that (was)..in the midst of all I.
13. 11 all I. shall hear, and fear, and shall do
17. 4 certain..such abomin. is wrought in I.
17. 12 and thou shalt put away the evil from I.
17. 20 he, and his children, in the midst of I.
18. 1 shall have no part nor inheritance with I.
18. 6 come from any of thy gates out of all I.
19. 13 away (the guilt of) innocent blood from I.
20. 3 Hear, O I.; ye approach this day unto ba.
21. 8 Be merciful, O LORD, unto thy people I.
21. 8 lay not innocent blood unto..I.'s charge
21. 21 put evil away..all I. shall hear, and fear
22. 19 brought..an evil name upon a virgin of I.
22. 21 she hath wrought folly in I., to play the
22. 22 so shalt thou put away evil from I.
23. 17 of I., nor a sodomite of the sons of I.
24. 7 any of his brethren of the children of I.
25. 6 that his name be not put out of I.
25. 7 to raise up unto his brother a name in I.
25. 10 his name shall be called in I., The house
26. 15 bless thy people I., and the land which
27. 1 And Moses with the elders of I. comman.
27. 9 Israel, saying, Take heed, and hearken, O I.
27. 14 say unto all the men of I. with a loud
29. 1 the children of I. in the land of Moab
29. 2 Moses called unto all I., and said unto
29. 10 and your officers, (with) all the men of I.
29. 21 unto evil out of all the tribes of I., accordi.
31. 1 went and spake these words unto all I.
31. 7 said unto him in the sight of all I., Be
31. 9 delivered it..unto all the elders of I.
31. 11 When all I. is come to appear before the
31. 11 thou shalt read this law before all I. in
31. 19 for you, and teach it the children of I.
31. 19 witness for me against the children of I.
31. 22 Moses..wrote..taught it the children of I.
31. 23 thou shalt bring the children of I. into
31. 30 in the ears of all the congregation of I.
32. 8 according to..number of the children of I.
32. 45 end of speaking all these words to all I.
32. 49 unto the children of I. for a possession
32. 51 among the children of I. at the waters of
32. 51 ye sanctified me not in the midst of..I.
32. 52 the land which I give the children of I.
33. 1 the man of God blessed the children of I.
33. 5 the tribes of I. were gathered together
33. 10 teach Jacob thy judgments, and I. thy law
33. 21 he executed..his judgments with I.
33. 28 I. then shall dwell in safety alone: the
33. 29 Happy (art) thou, O I.: who (is) like unto
34. 8 the children of I. wept for Moses in the
34. 9 the children of I. hearkened unto him
34. 10 not a prophet since in I. like unto Moses
34. 12 which Moses showed in the sight of all I.
Josh. 1. 2 give to them, (even) to the children of I.
2. 2 in hither to night of the children of I.
3. 1 to Jordan, he and all the children of I.
3. 7 to magnify thee in the sight of all I.
3. 9 Joshua said unto the children of I., Come
3. 12 take you twelve men out of the tribes of I.
4. 4 whom he had prepared of the children of I.
4. 5, 8 of the tribes of the children of I.
4. 7 memorial unto the children of I.
4. 8 children of I. did so as Joshua commanded
4. 12 passed over armed before the children of I.
4. 14 magnified Joshua in the sight of all I.
4. 21 he spake unto the children of I., saying
4. 22 I. came over this Jordan on dry land

Josh. 5. 1 dried up the waters of Jordan..before..I.
5. 1 any more, because of the children of I.
5. 2 circumcise again the children of I. the
5. 3 circumcised the children of I. at the hill
5. 6 the children of I. walked forty years in
5. 10 the children of I. encamped in Gilgal, and
5. 12 neither had the children of I. manna any
6. 1 shut up because of the children of I.
6. 18 make the camp of I. a curse, and trouble
6. 23 and left them without the camp of I.
6. 25 and she dwelleth in I. (even) unto this day
7. 1 the children of I. committed a trespass
7. 1 was kindled against the children of I.
7. 6 fell to the earth..he and the elders of I.
7. 8 when I. turneth their backs before their
7. 11 I. hath sinned, and they have also trans.
7. 12 the children of I. could not stand before
7. 13 thus saith the LORD God of I., (There is)
7. 13 accursed thing in the midst of thee, O I.
7. 15 and because he hath wrought folly in I.
7. 16 brought I. by their tribes; and the tribe
7. 19 give, I pray..glory to the LORD God of I.
7. 20 I have sinned against the LORD God of I.
7. 23 Joshua, and unto all the children of I.
7. 24 all I. with him, took Achan the son of Z.
7. 25 I. stoned him with stones, and burned
8. 10 went up, he and the elders of I., before
8. 14 and the men..went out against I. to battle
8. 15 I. made as if they were beaten before them
8. 17 not a man left..that went not out after I.
8. 17 left the city open, and pursued after I.
8. 21 all I. saw that the ambush had taken the
8. 22 so they were in the midst of I., some on
8. 24 when I. had made an end of slaying all
8. 27 spoil of that city, I. took for a prey unto
8. 30 built an altar unto the LORD God of I. in
8. 31 As Moses..commanded the children of I.
8. 32 wrote in the presence of the children of I.
8. 33 all I...stood on this side the ark and on
8. 33 commanded..should bless the people of I.
8. 35 read not before all the congregation of I.
9. 2 to fight with Joshua and with I., with one
9. 6 said unto him, and to the men of I., We
9. 7 men of I. said unto the Hivites, Peradven.
9. 17 the children of I. journeyed, and came
9. 18 children of I. smote them not, because the
9. 18 princes..had sworn..by the LORD God..I.
9. 19 sworn unto them by the LORD God of I.
9. 26 and delivered them out of the hand of..I.
10. 1 inhabitants..had made peace with I., and
10. 4 hath made peace..with the children of I.
10. 10 LORD discomfited them before I., and slew
10. 11 came to pass, as they fled from before I.
10. 11 whom the children of I. slew with the
10. 12 the Amorites before the children of I., and
10. 12 said in the sight of I., Sun, stand thou still
10. 14 hearkened..for the LORD fought for I.
10. 15 Joshua returned, and all I. with him, unto
10. 20 Joshua and the children of I. had made
10. 21 moved..against any of the children of I.
10. 24 that Joshua called for all the men of I.
10. 29, 31, 34 Joshua passed..and all I. with him
10. 30 delivered it also..into the hand of I.; and
10. 32 LORD delivered Lachish into the hand of I.
10. 36 Joshua went up from Eglon, and all I.
10. 38, 43 And Joshua returned, and all I. with
10. 40 destroyed..as the LORD God of I. comm.
10. 42 because the LORD God of I. fought for I.
11. 5 and pitched together..to fight against I.
11. 6 will I deliver them up all slain before I.
11. 8 LORD delivered them into the hand of I.
11. 13 I. burned none of them, save Hazor only
11. 14 the children of I. took for a prey unto
11. 16 So Joshua took..the mountain of I., and
11. 19 that made peace with the children of I.
11. 20 that they should come against I. in battle
11. 21 and cut off..from all the mountains of I.
11. 22 none..left in the land of the children of I.
11. 23 Joshua gave it for an inheritance unto I.
12. 1 the kings..which the children of I. smote
12. 6 Them did Moses..and the children of I.
12. 7 kings..which Joshua and the children of I.
12. 7 which Joshua gave unto the tribes of I.
13. 6 I drive out from before the children of I.
13. 13 children of I. expelled not the Geshurites
13. 14 sacrifices of the LORD God of I. made by
13. 22 the soothsaye did the children of I. slay
13. 33 the LORD God of I. (was) their inheritance
14. 1 which the children of I. inherited in the
14. 1 heads of the..tribes of the children of I.
14. 5 LORD commanded .so the children of I.
14. 10 while..I. wandered in the wilderness: and
14. 14 he wholly followed the LORD God of I.
17. 13 when the children of I. were waxen strong
18. 1 the children of I. assembled together at
18. 2 there remained among the children of I.
18. 3 Joshua said unto the children of I., How
18. 10 divided the land unto the children of I.
19. 49 the children of I. gave an inheritance to
19. 51 fathers of the tribes of the children of I.
20. 2 Speak to the children of . saying, Appoint
20. 9 appointed for all the children of I., and
21. 1 fathers of the tribes of the children of I.
21. 3 children of I. gave unto the Levites out of
21. 8 children of I. gave by lot unto the Levites
21. 41 within the possession of the children of I.
21. 43 the LORD gave unto I. all the land which
21. 45 the LORD had spoken unto the house of I.
22. 9 departed from the children of I. out of S.
22. 11 children of I. heard say, Behold, the chi.
22. 11 Jordan, at the passage of the children of I.
22. 12 the children of I. heard (of it), the whole
Josh.22. 12 children of I. gathered themselves toget.
22. 13 children of I. sent unto the children of R.
22. 14 a prince throughout all the tribes of I.
22. 14 of their fathers among the thousands of I.
22. 16 ye have committed against the God of I.
22. 18 be wroth with the whole congregation of I.
22. 20 wrath fell on all the congregation of I.
22. 21 said unto the heads of the thousands of I.
22. 22 he knoweth, and I. he shall know; if (it)
22. 24 What have ye..with the LORD God of I.?
22. 30 heads of the thousands of I. which (were)
22. 31 ye have d livered the children of I. out
22. 32 the land of Canaan, to the children of I.
22. 33 the thing pleased the children of I.; and
22. 33 children of I. blessed God, and did not
23. 1 after that the LORD had given rest unto I.
23. 2 Joshua called for I., (and) for their elders
24. 1 gathered all the tribes of I. to Shechem
24. 1 called for the elders of I., and for their
24. 2 Thus saith the LORD God of I., Your fath.
24. 9 and warred against I., and sent and called
24. 23 incline your heart unto the LORD God of I.
24. 31 I. served the LORD all the days of Joshua
24. 31 works of the LORD, that he had done for I.
24. 32 children of I. brought up out of Egypt
Judg. 1. 1 the children of I. asked the LORD, saying
1. 28 when I. was strong, that they put the
2. 4 these words unto all the children of I.
2. 6 the children of I. went every man unto his
2. 7 great works of the LORD that he did for I.
2. 10 nor..the works which he had done for I.
2. 11 the children of I. did evil in the sight
2. 14, 20 anger of the LORD was hot against I.
2. 22 I may prove I., whether they will keep the
3. 1 which the LORD left, to prove I. by them
3. 2 generations of the children of I. might
3. 4 they were to prove I. by them, to know
3. 5 children of I. dwelt among the Canaanites
3. 7 the children of I. did evil in the sight
3. 8 the anger of the LORD was hot against I.
3. 8 children of I. served Chushan-rishathaim
3. 9, 15 the children of I. cried unto the LORD
3. 9 raised up a deliverer to the children of I.
3. 10 he judged I., and went out to war: and
3. 12 the children of I. did evil again in the
3. 12 strengthened Eglon the king..against I.
3. 13 went and smote I., and possessed the city
3. 14 the children of I. served Eglon the v. 15.
3. 27 the children of I. went down with him from
3. 30 was subdued that day under the hand of I.
3. 31 after him was Shamgar..also delivered I.
4. 1 the children of I. again did evil in the
4. 3 the children of I. cried unto the LORD
4. 3 he mightily oppressed the children of I.
4. 4 And Deborah..she judged I. at that time
4. 5 the children of I. came up to her for
4. 6 Hath not the LORD God of I. commanded
4. 23 the king of Canaan before the children of I.
4. 24 the children of I. prospered, and prevailed
5. 2 Praise ye the LORD for the avenging of I.
5. 3 I will sing (praise) to the LORD God of I.
5. 5 that Sinai from before the LORD God of I.
5. 7 they ceased in I., until that I Deborah
5. 7 I arose a mother in I.
5. 8 or spear seen among forty thousand in I.?
5. 9 My heart (is) toward the governors of I.
5. 11 (the inhabitants) of his villages in I.
6. 1 the children of I. did evil in the sight
6. 2 the hand of Midian prevailed against I.
6. 2 the children of I. made them the dens
6. 3 when I. had sown, that the Midianites ca.
6. 4 left no sustenance for I., neither sheep
6. 6 I. was greatly impoverished because of
6. 6, 7 the children of I. cried unto the LORD
6. 8 sent a prophet unto the children of I.
6. 8 Thus saith the LORD God of I., I brought
6. 14 thou shalt save I. from the hand of the
6. 15 wherewith shall I save I.? behold, my fam.
6. 36, 37 thou wilt save I. by mine hand, as thou
7. 2 lest I. vaunt themselves against me, saying
7. 8 he sent all (the rest of) I. every man unto
7. 14 of Gideon the son of Joash, a man of I.
7. 15 and returned into the host of I., and said
7. 23 the men of I. gathered themselves togeth.
8. 22 the men of I. said unto Gideon, Rule thou
8. 27 I. went thither a whoring after it: which
8. 28 Midian subdued before the children of I.
8. 33 the children of I. turned again, and went
8. 34 the children of I. remembered not the L.
8. 35 the goodness which he had showed unto I.
9. 22 Abimelech had reigned three years over I.
9. 55 the men of I. saw that Abimelech was
10. 1 after Abimelech there arose, to defend I.
10. 2 he judged I. twenty and three years, and
10. 3 and judged I. twenty and two years
10. 6 the children of I. did evil again in the
10. 7 the anger of the LORD was hot against I.
10. 8 I. eighteen years, all the children of I.
10. 9 to fight..so that I. was sore distressed
10. 10 the children of I. cried unto the LORD
10. 11 the LORD said unto the children of I.
10. 15 the children of I. said unto the LORD
10. 16 his soul was grieved for the misery of I.
10. 17 the children of I. assembled themselves
11. 4, 5 the children of Ammon made war against I.
11. 13 I. took away my land, when they came up
11. 15 I. took not away the land of Moab, nor the
11. 16 I. came up from Egypt, and walked thro.
11. 17 I. sent messengers unto the king of Edom
11. 17 would not (consent): and I. abode in Ka.
11. 19 I. sent messengers unto Sihon king of the
11. 19 I. said unto him, Let us pass, we pray thee
Judg 11. 20 trusted not I. to pass through his coast
11. 20 pitched in Jahaz, and fought against I.
11. 21 the LORD God of I. delivered Sihon and all
11. 21 into the hand of I.,...so I possessed all
11. 23 the LORD God of I. hath dispossessed the
11. 23 the Amorites from before his people I.
11. 25 did he ever strive against I., or did he
11. 26 I. dwelt in Heshbon and her towns, and in
11. 27 children of I. and the children of Ammon
11. 33 were subdued before the children of I.
11. 39 she returned..And it was a custom in I.
11. 40 the daughters of I. went yearly to lament
12. 7 J phthah judged I. six years. Then died
12. 8 after him Ibzan of Beth-lehem judged I.
12. 9 and he judged I. seven years
12. 11 Elon..judged I.; and he judged I. ten
12. 13 the son of Hillel, a Pirathonite, judged I.
12. 14 and he judged I. eight years
13. 1 the children of I. did evil again in the
13. 5 he shall begin to deliver I. out of the
14. 4 the Philistines had dominion over I.
15. 20 judged I. in the days of the Philistines
16. 31 buried him..And he judged I. twenty
17. 6 In those days (there was) no king in I.
18. 1 In those days (there was) no king in I.
18. 1 fallen unto them among the tribes of I.
18. 19 a priest unto a tribe and a family in I.?
19. 1 when (there was) no king in I., that there
19. 12 stranger, that (is) not of the children of I.
19. 29 and sent her into all the coasts of I.
19. 30 the children of I. came up out of the land
20. 1 all the children of I. went out, and the
20. 2 the tribes of I., presented themselves in
20. 3 the children of I. were gone...child. of I.
20. 6 all the country of the inheritance of I.
20. 6 have committed lewdness and folly in I.
20. 7 ye (are) all children of I.; give here you
20. 10 ten men..throughout all the tribes of I.
20. 10 the folly that they have wrought in I.
20. 11 the men of I. were gathered against the
20. 12 the tribes of I. sent men through all the
20. 13 put..to death, and put away evil from I.
20. 13 voice of their brethren the children of I.
20. 14 out to battle against the children of I.
20. 17 men of I., beside Benjamin, were v. 18 19.
20. 20 the men of I. went out to battle against
20. 20 the men of I. put themselves in array to
20. 22 the people, the men of I., encouraged them.
20. 23 the children of I. went up and wept before
20. 24 the children of I. came near against the
20. 25 down to the ground of the children of I.
20. 26 the children of I., and all the people
20. 27 the children of I. enquired of the LORD
20. 29 I. set liers in wait round about Gibeah
20. 30 the children of I. went up against the
20. 31 began to smite..about thirty men of I
20. 32 the children of I. said, Let us flee, and
20. 33 the men of I. rose up out of their place
20. 33 the liers in wait of I. came forth out of
20. 34 ten thousand chosen men out of all I.
20. 35 Benjamin before I.: and the children of I.
20. 36 the men of I. gave place to the Benjamites
20. 38 an appointed sign between the men of I.
20. 39 men of I. retired in the battle, Benjamin.
20. 39 B. began to smite (and) kill of the men of I.
20. 41 when the men of I. turned again, the men
20. 42 turned (their backs) before the men of I.
20. 48 the men of I. turned again upon the child.
21. 1 the men of I. had sworn in Mizpeh, saying
21. 3 God of I., why is this come to pass in I.
21. 3 should be to day one tribe lacking in I.?
21. 5 And the children of I. said, Who (is there)
21. 5 the tribes of I. that came not up with
21. 6 children of I. repented them for Benjamin
21. 6 There is one tribe cut off from I. this
21. 8 What one (is there) of the tribes of I. that
21. 15 LORD had made a breach in the tribes of I.
21. 17 that a tribe be not destroyed out of I.
21. 18 for the children of I. have sworn, saying
21. 24 the children of I. departed thence at that
21. 25 In those days (there was) no king in I.
Ruth 2. 12 reward be given thee of the LORD God of I.
4. 7 in former time in I. concerning redeeming
4. 7 and this (was) a testimony in I.
4. 11 which two did build the house of I.
4. 14 kinsman, that his name may be famous in I.
1 Sa. 1. 17 the God of I. grant (thee) thy petition
2. 22 heard all that his sons did unto all I.
2. 28 I chose him out of all the tribes of I.
2. 28 offerings made by fire of..children of I.?
2. 29 of all the offerings of I. my people?
2. 30 the LORD God of I. saith, I said indeed
2. 32 all (the wealth) which (God) shall give I.
3. 11 I will do a thing in I., at which both the
3. 20 I. from Dan even to Beer-sheba, knew that
4. 1 the word of Samuel came to all I. Now I.
4. 2 against I.: and when they joined battle, I.
4. 3 the elders of I. said, Wherefore hath the
4. 5 I. shouted with a great shout, so that the
4. 10 I. was smitten, and they fled every man
4. 10 there fell of I. thirty thousand footmen
4. 17 I. is fled before the Philistines, and
4. 18 he died..And he had judged I. forty years
4. 21, 22 The glory is departed from I.: because
5. 7 The ark of the God of I. shall not abide
5. 8 shall we do with the ark of the God of I.?
5. 8 Let the ark of the God of I. be carried
5. 8 they carried the ark of the God of I. about
5. 10 brought about the ark of the God of I. to
5. 11 Send away the ark of the God of I., and
6. 3 If ye send away the ark of the God of I.
6. 5 ye shall give glory unto the God of I.

1 Sa. 7. 2 the house of I. lamented after the LORD
7. 3 Samuel spake unto all the house of I.
7. 4 the children of I. did put away Baalim and
7. 5 Gather all I. to Mizpeh, and I will pray
7. 6 Samuel judged the children of I. in Mizpeh
7. 7 the children of I. were gathered together
7. 7 up against I. And when the children of I.
7. 8 the children of I. said to Samuel, Cease
7. 9 Samuel cried unto the LORD for I.; and
7. 10 Philistines drew near to battle against I.
7. 10 and they were smitten before I.
7. 11 men of I. went out of Mizpeh, and pursued
7. 13 they came no more into the coast of I.
7. 14 had taken from I. were restored to I.
7. 14 the coasts thereof did I. deliver out of
7. 14 there was peace between I. and the Am.
7. 15 Samuel judged I. all the days of his life
7. 16 he went..and judged I. in all those places
7. 17 there he judged I.; and there he built an
8. 1 that he made his sons judges over I.
8. 4 elders of I. gathered themselves together
8. 22 Samuel said unto the men of I., Go ye
9. 2 (there was) not among the children of I.
9. 9 in I., when a man went to enquire of God
9. 16 anoint..(to be) captain over my people I.
9. 20 on whom (is) all the desire of I.? (Is i)
9. 21 of the smallest of the tribes of I. and
10. 18 And said unto the children of I., Thus
10. 18 saith the LORD God of I., I brought up I.
10. 20 caused all the tribes of I. to come near
11. 2 and lay it (for) a reproach upon all I.
11. 3 send messengers unto all the coasts of I.
11. 7 sent (them) throughout all the coasts of I.
11. 8 children of I. were three hundred thous.
11. 13 the LORD hath wrought salvation in I.
11. 15 and all the men of I. rejoiced greatly
12. 1 And Samuel said unto all I., Behold, I
13. 1 and when he had reigned two years over I.
13. 2 Saul chose him three thousand (men) of I.
13. 4 all I. heard say (that) Saul had smitten a
13. 4 I. also was had in abomination with the
13. 5 gathered..together to fight with I., thirty
13. 6 men of I. saw that they were in a strait
13. 13 established thy kingdom upon I. for ever
13. 19 smith found throughout all the land of I.
14. 12 hath delivered them into the hand of I.
14. 18 was at that time with the children of I.
14. 22 the men of I. which had hid themselves in
14. 23 the LORD saved I. that day: and the battle
14. 24 the men of I. were distressed that day: for
14. 37 wilt thou deliver them into the hand of I.?
14. 39 the LORD liveth, which saveth I., though
14. 40 Then said he unto all I., Be ye on one side
14. 41 Saul said unto the LORD God of I., Give
14. 45 hath wrought this great salvation in I.?
14. 47 Saul took the kingdom over I., and fought
14. 48 delivered I. out of the hands of them that
15. 1 thee (to be) king over his people, over I.
15. 2 I remember (that) which Amalek did to I.
15. 6 showed kindness to all the children of I.
15. 17 I., and the LORD anointed thee king over I.?
15. 26 hath rejected thee from being king over I.
15. 28 hath rent the kingdom of I. from thee this
15. 29 the strength of I. will not lie nor repent
15. 30 the elders of my people, and before I., and
15. 35 repented that he..made Saul king over I.
16. 1 I have rejected him from reigning over I.
17. 2 the men of I. were gathered together, and
17. 3 I stood on a mountain on the other side
17. 8 cried unto the armies of I., and said unto
17. 10 I defy the armies of I. this day; give me
17. 11 I. heard those words of the Philistine
17. 19 the men of I., (were) in the valley of Elah
17. 21 I. and the Philistines had put the battle
17. 24 the men of I., when they saw the man
17. 25 the men of I. said, Have ye seen this man
17. 25 to defy I. is he come up: and it shall be
17. 25 and make his father's house free in I.
17. 26 taketh away the reproach from I.? for
17. 45 the God of the armies of I., whom thou
17. 46 earth may know that there is a God in I.
17. 52 men of I. and of Judah arose, and shout.
17. 53 the children of I. returned from chasing
18. 6 the women came out of all cities of I.
18. 16 I. and Judah loved David, because he we.
18. 18 what (is) my life, (or) my father's f. in I.
19. 5 LORD wrought a great salvation for all I.
20. 12 O LORD God of I., when I have sounded
23. 10 LORD God of I., thy servant hath certain.
23. 11 O LORD God of I., I beseech thee, tell thy
23. 17 thou shalt be king over I., and I shall be
24. 2 three thousand chosen men out of all I.
24. 14 After whom is the king of I. come out?
24. 20 the kingdom of I. shall be established in
25. 30 and shall have appointed thee ruler over I.
25. 32 Blessed (be) the LORD God of I., which sent
25. 34 (as) the LORD God of I. liveth, which hath
26. 2 three thousand chosen men of I. with him
26. 15 who (is) like to thee in I.? wherefore then
26. 20 the king of I. is come out to seek a flea
27. 1 to seek me any more in any coast of I.
27. 12 made his people I. utterly to abhor him
28. 1 together for warfare, to fight with I.
28. 3 all I. had lamented him, and buried him
28. 4 Saul gathered all I. together, and they
28. 19 the LORD will also deliver I. with thee
28. 19 LORD also shall deliver the host of I.
29. 3 the servant of Saul the king of I., which
30. 25 and an ordinance for I. unto this day
31. 1 fought against I.: and the men of I. fled
31. 7 the men of I. that (were) on the other side
31. 7 saw that the men of I. fled, and that Saul

2 Sa. 1. 3 said..Out of the camp of I. am I escaped
1. 12 people of the LORD, and for the house of I.
1. 19 The beauty of I. is slain upon thy high
1. 24 daughters of I., weep over Saul, who clo.
2. 9 Ephraim..over Benjamin, and over all I.
2. 10 forty years..when he began to reign over I.
2. 17 Abner was beaten, and the men of I., be.
2. 28 pursued after I. no more, neither fought
3. 10 to set up the throne of David over I., and
3. 12 with thee, to bring about all I. unto thee
3. 17 had communication with the elders of I.
3. 18 I will save my people I. out of the hand
3. 19 also to speak..all that seemed good to I.
3. 21 will gather all I. unto my lord the king
3. 37 I., understood that day, that it was not of
3. 38 and a great man fallen this day in I.?
5. 1 Then came all the tribes of I. to David
5. 2 he that leddest out and broughtest in I.
5. 2 I., and thou shalt be a captain over I.
5. 3 elders of I. came to the king to Hebron
5. 3 and they anointed David king over I.
5. 5 thirty and three years over all I. and
5. 12 the LORD had established him king over I.
5. 12 exalted his kingdom for his people I.
5. 17 that they had anointed David king over I.
6. 1 gathered together all..chosen (men) of I.
6. 5 the house of I. played before the LORD on
6. 15 the house of I. brought up the ark of the
6. 19 among the whole multitude of I., as well
6. 20 How glorious was the king of I. to day
6. 21 ruler over the people of the LORD, over I.
7. 6 brought up the children of I. out of Egypt
7. 7 I have walked with all the children of I.
7. 7 I., whom I command. to feed my people I.
7. 8 I took..to be ruler over my people, over I.
7. 10 I will appoint a place for my people I.
7. 11 commanded judges..over my people I.
7. 23 I., whom God went to redeem for a people
7. 24 I. (to be) a people unto thee for ever
7. 26 The LORD of hosts (is) the God over I.: and
7. 27 thou, O LORD of hosts, God of I., hast re.
8. 15 And David reigned over all I.; and David
10. 9 he chose of all the choice (men) of I., and
10. 15 saw that they were smitten before I., they
10. 17 he gathered all I. together, and passed
10. 18 the Syrians fled before I.; and David slew
10. 19 smitten before I., they made peace with I.
11. 1 Joab, and his servants with him, and all I.
11. 11 I., and Judah, abide in tents; and my l.
12. 7 Thus saith the..GOD of I., King over I.
12. 8 gave thee the house of I. and of Judah; and
12. 12 but I will do this thing before all I., and
13. 12 no such thing ought to be done in I.: do
13. 13 thou shalt be as one of the fools in I.
14. 25 in all I. there was none to be so much
15. 2 Thy servant (is) of one of the tribes of I.
15. 6 on this manner did Absalom to all I. that
15. 6 Absalom stole the hearts of the men of I.
15. 10 sent spies throughout all the tribes of I.
15. 13 hearts of the men of I. are after Absalom
16. 3 To day shall the house of I. restore me
16. 15 men of I., came to Jerusalem, and Ahith.
16. 18 this people, and all the men of I., choose
16. 21 I. shall hear that thou art abhorred of thy
16. 22 And Absalom went in..in the sight of..I.
17. 4 pleased Absalom..and all the elders of I.
17. 10 I. knoweth that thy father (is) a mighty
17. 11 all I. be generally gathered unto thee
17. 13 I. bring ropes to that city, and we will
17. 14 the men of I. said, The counsel of Hushai
17. 15 counsel Absalom and the elders of I.; and
17. 24 he and all the men of I. with him
17. 26 So I. and Absalom pitched in the land of
18. 6 people went out into the field against I.
18. 7 the people of I. were slain before the serv.
18. 16 the people returned from pursuing after I.
18. 17 and all I. fled every one to his tent
19. 8 for I. had fled every man to his tent
19. 9 at strife throughout all the tribes of I.
19. 11 the speech of all I. is come to the king
19. 22 any man be put to death this day in I.?
19. 22 I know that I (am) this day king over I.?
19. 40 the king, and also half the people of I.
19. 41 the men of I. came to the king, and said
19. 42 the men of Judah answered the men of I.
19. 43 the men of I. answered the men of Judah
19. 43 fiercer than the words of the men of I.
20. 1 and said..every man to his tents, O I.
20. 2 every man of I. went up from after David
20. 14 through all the tribes of I. unto Abel, and
20. 19 them that are) peaceable..faithful in I.
20. 19 to destroy a city and a mother in I.: why
20. 23 Now Joab (was) over all the host of I.: and
21. 2 Gibeonites (were) not of the children of I.
21. 2 the children of I. had sworn unto them
21. 2 his zeal to the children of I. and Judah
21. 4 neither for us shalt thou kill any..in I.
21. 5 from remaining in any of the coasts of I.
21. 15 the Philistines had yet war again with I.
21. 17 that thou quench not the light of I.
21. 21 And when he defied I., Jonathan the son
23. 1 David..the sweet psalmist of I., said
23. 3 The God of I. said, the Rock of I. spake
23. 9 and the men of I. were gone away
24. 1 anger of the LORD was kindled against I.
24. 2 Go now through all the tribes of I., from
24. 4 Joab..went..to number the people of I.
24. 9 there were in I. eight hundred thousand
24. 15 the LORD sent a pestilence upon I., from
24. 25 entreated..the plague was stayed from I.

1 Ki. 1. 3 damsel throughout all the coasts of I., and
1. 20 the eyes of all I. (are) upon thee, that thou
1. 30 I sware unto thee by the LORD God of I.
1. 34 the prophet anoint him there king over I
1. 35 him to be ruler over I. and over Judah
1. 48 Blessed (be) the LORD God of I., which hath
2. 4 not fail thee..a man on the throne of I.
2. 5 did to the two captains of the host of I.
2. 11 the days that David reigned over I. (were)
2. 15 I. set their faces on me, that I should
2. 32 captain of the host of I., and Amasa the
3. 28 I. heard of the judgment which the king
4. 1 So king Solomon was king over all I.
4. 7 Solomon had twelve officers over all I.
5. 13 Solomon raised a levy out of all I.; and
6. 1 after the children of I. were come out of
6. 1 the fourth year of Solomon's reign over I.
6. 13 of I., and will not forsake my people I.
8. 1 Solomon assembled the elders of I., and
8. 1 chief of the fathers of the children of I.
8. 2 the men of I. assembled themselves unto
8. 3 the elders of I. came, and the priests
8. 5 the congregation of I., that were assem.
8. 9 made (a covenant) with the children of I.
8. 14 of I., and all the congregation of I. stood
8. 15 Blessed (be) the LORD God of I., which
8. 16 I brought forth my people I. out of Egypt
8. 16 chose no city out of all the tribes of I.
8. 16 but I chose David to be over my people I.
8. 17, 20 house for..name of the LORD God of I.
8. 20 and sit on the throne of I., as the LORD
8. 22 presence of all the congregation of I., and
8. 23 LORD God of I., (there is) no God like thee
8. 25 LORD God of I., keep with thy servant D.
8. 25 in my sight to sit on the throne of I.; so
8. 26 O God of I., let thy word, I pray thee, be
8. 30 of thy servant, and of thy people I., when
8. 33 When thy people I. be smitten down bef.
8. 34 forgive the sin of thy people I., and bring
8. 36 sin of thy servants, and of thy people I.
8. 38 (made) by any man, (or) by all thy people I.
8. 41 a stranger, that (is) not of thy people I.
8. 43 to fear thee, as (do) thy people I.; and that
8. 52 and unto the supplication of thy people I.
8. 55 and blessed all the congregation of I. with
8. 56 that hath given rest unto his people I., ac.
8. 59 he maintain..the cause of his people I. at
8. 62 king, and all I. with him, offered sacrifice.
8. 63 all the children of I. dedicated the house
8. 65 Solomon held a feast, and all I. with him
8. 66 goodness that the LORD had done..for I.
9. 5 I will establish the throne..upon I. for
9. 5 not fail thee a man upon the throne of I.
9. 7 Then will I cut off I. out of the land which
9. 7 I. shall be a proverb and a byword among
9. 20 all..which (were) not of the children of I.
9. 21 the children of I. also were not able utterly
9. 22 of the children of I. did Solomon make no
10. 9 to set thee on the throne of I.: because the
10. 9 LORD loved I. for ever, therefore made he
11. 2 LORD said unto the children of I., Ye shall
11. 9 heart was turned from the LORD God of I.
11. 16 six months did Joab remain..with all I.
11. 25 he was an adversary to I. all the days of
11. 25 and he abhorred I., and reigned over Syria
11. 31 thus saith the LORD, the God of I., Behold
11. 32 the city which I have chosen out of all..I.
11. 37 thou shalt reign..and shall be king over I.
11. 38 I will be with thee..and will give I. unto
11. 42 Solomon reigned in Jerusalem over all I.
12. 1 all I. were come to Shechem to make him
12. 3 Jeroboam and all the congregation of I.
12. 16 I. saw that the king hearkened not unto
12. 16 What portion have we..to your tents, O I.
12. 16 now see..So I. departed unto their tents
12. 17 the children of I. which dwelt in the cit.
14. 7 Thus saith the LORD God of I., Forasmuch
14. 7 and made thee prince over my people I.
14. 13 good thing toward the LORD God of I.
14. 21 did choose out of all the tribes of I., to
14. 24 LORD cast out before the children of I.
15. 30 provoked the LORD GOD of I. to
16. 13 in provoking the LORD GOD of I. 16, 33.
17. 1 (As) the LORD God of I. liveth, before whom
17. 14 For thus saith the LORD God of I., The
18. 36 be known this day that thou (art) God in I.
22. 53 provoked to anger the LORD God of I., acc.

2 Ki. 2. 12 My father, my father! the chariot of I.
9. 6 Thus saith the LORD God of I., 10. 21.
10. 31 to walk in the law of the LORD God of I.
14. 25 He restored the coast of I. from the ent.
18. 4 the children of I. did burn incense to it
18. 5 He trusted in the LORD God of I.; so that
19. 15 O LORD God of I., which dwellest (between)
19. 20 Thus saith the LORD God of I., (That) which
19. 22 lifted up..(even) against the holy (one) of I.
21. 2 the LORD cast out before the children of I.
21. 7 I have chosen out of all tribes of I., will I
21. 8 Neither will I make the feet of I. move
21. 9 LORD destroyed before the children of I.
21. 12 Therefore thus saith the Lord GOD of I.
22. 15 Thus saith the Lord GOD of I., Tell the
22. 18 Thus saith the Lord GOD of I.
23. 13 which Solomon the king of I. had builded
23. 22 from the days of the judges that judged I.
24. 13 which Solomon king of I. had made in

1 Ch. 1. 43 (any) king reigned over the children of I.
2. 7 Achar, the troubler of I., who transgressed
4. 10 Jabez called on the God of I., saying, Oh
5. 26 God of I. stirred up the spirit of Pul king
6. 49 to make an atonement for I., according to
6. 64 children of I. gave to the Levites (these)
9. 1 So all I. were reckoned by genealogies
10. 1 Now the Philistines fought against I.; and

1 Ch. 10. 1 men of I. fled from before the Philistines
10. 7 the men of I. that (were) in the valley saw
11. 1 Then all I. gathered themselves to David
11. 2 he that leddest out and broughtest in I.
11. 2 thy God said..Thou shalt feed my people I.
11. 2 and thou shalt be ruler over my people I.
11. 3 Therefore came all the elders of I. to the
11. 3 they anointed David king over I., according
11. 4 David and all I. went to Jerusalem, which
11. 10 who strengthened themselves with..all I.
11. 10 king, according to the word..concerning I.
12. 32 to know what I. ought do; the heads of
12. 38 to Hebron, to make David king over all I.
12. 38 the rest also of I. (were) of one heart to
12. 40 sheep abundantly; for there was joy in I.
13. 2 David said unto all the congregation of I.
13. 2 our brethren..left in all the land of I., and
13. 5 So David gathered all I. gether, from
13. 6 David went up, and all I., to Baalah, (that
13. 8 David and all I. played before God with
14. 2 LORD had confirmed him king over I.; for
14. 2 lifted up on high, because of his people I.
14. 8 that David was anointed king over all I.
15. 3 David gathered all I. together to Jerusal.
15. 12 bring up the ark of the LORD God of I.
15. 14 bring up the ark of the LORD God of I.
15. 25 the elders of I., and the captains over
15. 28 I. brought up the ark of the covenant of
16. 3 he dealt to every one of I., both man and
16. 4 to thank and praise the LORD God of I.
16. 13 ye seed of I. his servant, ye children of
16. 17 (and) to I. (for) an everlasting covenant
16. 36 Blessed be the LORD God of I. for ever
16. 40 written in the law..which he command. I.
17. 5 day that I brought up I. unto this day
17. 6 Wheresoever I have walked with all I.
17. 6 spake I a word to any of the judges of I.
17. 7 thou shouldest be ruler over my people I.
17. 9 I will ordain a place for my people I., and
17. 10 command. judges (to be) over my people I.
17. 21 nation in the earth (is) like thy people I.
17. 22 thy people I. didst thou make thine own
17. 24 LORD..(is) the God of I., (even) a G. to I.
18. 14 David reigned over all I., and executed
19. 10 he chose out of all the choice of I., and
19. 16 that they were put to the worse before I.
19. 17 he gathered all I., and passed over Jordan
19. 18 the Syrians fled before I.; and David slew
19. 19 that they were put to the worse before I.
20. 7 when he defied I., Jonathan the son of
21. 1 against I., and provoked David to numb. I.
21. 2 number I. from Beer-sheba even to Dan
21. 3 why will he be a cause of trespass to I.?
21. 4 and went throughout all I., and came to
21. 7 God was displeased..therefore he smo. I.
21. 12 destroying throughout all the coasts of I.
21. 14 pestilence upon I.: and there fell of I.
22. 1 this (is) the altar of the burnt offering for I.
22. 2 the strangers that (were) in the land of I.
22. 6 to build an house for the LORD God of I.
22. 9 peace and quietness unto I. in his days
22. 10 the throne of his kingdom over I. for ever
22. 12 give thee charge concerning I., that thou
22. 13 the LORD charged Mos. with concerning I.
22. 17 David also commanded all the princes of I.
23. 1 he made Solomon his son king over I.
23. 2 gathered together all the princes of I.
23. 25 The LORD God of I. hath given rest unto
24. 19 as the LORD God of I. had commanded
26. 29 sons (were) for the outward business over I.
26. 30 (were) officers among them of I. on this
27. 1 the children of I. after their number, (to)
27. 16 Furthermore over the tribes of I.: the
27. 22 These (were) the princes of the tribes of I.
27. 23 the LORD had said he would increase I.
27. 24 there fell wrath for it against I.; neither
28. 1 David assembled all the princes of I., the
28. 4 the LORD God of I. chose me before all
28. 4 chose me..to be king over I. for ever: for
28. 4 he liked me to make (me) king over all I.
28. 5 upon the throne of the kingdom..over I.
28. 8 in the sight of all I. the congregation of
29. 6 the chief..and princes of the tribes of I.
29. 21 and sacrifices in abundance for all I.
29. 23 sat on the throne..and all I. obeyed him
29. 25 magnified Solomon..in the sight of all I.
29. 25 had not been on any king before him in I.
29. 26 David the son of Jesse reigned over all I.
29. 27 time that he reigned over I. (was) forty
29. 30 the times that went over him, and over I.
2 Ch. 1. 2 Solomon spake unto all I., to the captains
1. 2 to every governor in all I., the chief of
1. 13 Then Solomon came..and reigned over I.
2. 4 This (is an ordinance) for ever to I.
2. 12 Blessed (be) the LORD God of I., that ma.
2. 17 the strangers that (were) in the land of I.
5. 2 Solomon assembled the elders of I., and
5. 2 chief of the fathers of the children of I.
5. 3 all the men of I. assembled themselves
5. 4 the elders of I. came; and the Levites
5. 6 the congregation of I. that were assembl.
5. 10 made (a covenant) with the children of I.
6. 3 I.: and all the congregration of I. stood
6. 4 Blessed (be) the LORD God of I., who hath
6. 5 chose no city among all the tribes of I.
6. 5 any man to be a ruler over my people I.
6. 6 have chosen David to be over my people I.
6. 7, 10 for the name of the LORD God of I.
6. 10 am set on the throne of I., as the LORD
6. 11 that he made with the children of I.
6. 12 presence of all the congregation of I.
6. 13 kneeled. before all the congregation of I.
2 Ch. 6. 14 LORD God of I., (there is) no God like thee
6. 16 O LORD God of I., keep with thy servant
6. 16 a man..to sit upon the throne of I.; yet
6. 17 O LORD God of I., let thy word be verified
6. 21 thy servant, and of thy people I., which
6. 24 thy people I. be put the worse before
6. 25 forgive the sin of thy people I., and bring
6. 27 sin of thy servants, and of thy people I.
6. 29 made of any man, or of all thy people I.
6. 32 stranger, which is not of thy people I., but
6. 33 fear thee, as (doth) thy people I., and may
7. 3 children of I. saw how the fire came down
7. 6 sounded trumpets before them, and all I.
7. 8 I. with him, a very great congregation
7. 10 David, and to Solomon, and to I. his peo.
7. 18 not fail thee a man (to be) ruler in I.
8. 2 caused the children of I. to dwell there
8. 7 and the Jebusites, which (were) not of I.
8. 8 whom the children of I. consumed not
8. 9 of the children of I. did Solomon make no
8. 11 dwell in the house of David king of I., beca.
9. 8 God loved I., to establish them for ever
9. 30 Solomon reigned in Jerusalem over all I.
10. 1 to Shechem were..I. come to make him
10. 3 I. came and spake to Rehoboam, saying
10. 16 I. (saw) that the king would not hearken
10. 16 every man to your tents, O I.: (and) now
10. 16 So all I. went to their tents
10. 17 children of I. that dwelt in the cities of J.
11. 3 Speak unto..all I. in Judah and Benjamin
11. 16 their hearts to seek the LORD God of I.
12. 1 he forsook the law of the LORD, and all I.
12. 6 the princes of I. and the king humbled
12. 13 had chosen out of all the tribes of I., to put
13. 5 LORD God of I. gave the kingdom over I.
15. 3 I. (hath been) without the true God, and
15. 4 turn unto the Lord GOD of I., and sought
15. 13 whosoever would not seek..LORD God of I.
19. 8 of the chief of the fathers of I., for the
20. 7 (who) drive out..before thy people I., and
20. 10 whom thou wouldest not let I. invade
20. 19 to praise the LORD God of I. with a loud
20. 29 LORD fought against the enemies of I.
23. 2 chief of the fathers of I., and they came
24. 5 gather of all I. money to repair the house
24. 6 of the LORD, and of the congregation of I.
24. 9 Moses..(laid) upon I. in the wilderness
24. 16 he had done good in I., both toward God
28. 3 had cast out before the children of I.
28. 23 they were the ruin of him, and of all I.
28. 27 into the sepulchres of the kings of I.
29. 7 burnt offerings..unto the God of I.
29. 10 make a covenant with the LORD God of I.
29. 24 to make an atonement for all I.: for the
29. 24 sin offering (should be made) for all I.
30. 1, 5 the passover unto the LORD God of I.
30. 5 to make proclamation throughout all I.
30. 6 children of I., turn again unto the LORD
30. 26 of Solomon the son of David king of I.
31. 1 all I. that were present went out to the
31. 1 the children of I. returned, every man to
31. 5 the children of I. brought in abundance
31. 8 they blessed the LORD, and his people I.
32. 17 also letters to rail on the LORD God of I.
33. 2 had cast out before the children of I.
33. 7 I have chosen before all the tribes of I.
33. 8 will I any more remove the foot of I.
33. 9 had destroyed before the children of I.
33. 16 commanded Judah..serve..LORD God of I.
33. 18 that spake to him in the name of..God of I.
33. 18 written) in the book of the kings of I.
34. 7 the idols throughout all the land of I.
34. 23 Thus saith the LORD God of I., Tell ye the
34. 26 Thus saith the Lord GOD of I. (concerning)
34. 33 that (pertained) to the children of I., and
34. 33 made all that were present in I. to serve
35. 3 said unto the Levites that taught all I.
35. 3 the son of David king of I. did build
35. 3 now the LORD your God, and his people I.
35. 4 according to..writing of David king of I.
35. 17 the children of I. that were present kept
35. 18 was no passover like to that kept in I.
35. 18 neither did all the kings of I. keep such
35. 18 Judah and I. that were present, and the
35. 25 day, and made them an ordinance in I.
36. 13 heart from turning unto..LORD God of I.
Ezra 1. 3 and build the house of the LORD God of I.
2. 2 The number of the men of the people of I.
2. 59 and their seed, whether they (were) of I.
2. 70 dwelt in their cities, and all I. in their
3. 1 and the children of I. (were) in the cities
3. 2 builded the altar of the God of I., to offer
3. 10 after the ordinance of David king of I.
3. 11 his mercy (endureth) for ever toward I.
4. 1 builded the temple unto..LORD God of I.
4. 3 the rest of the chief of the fathers of I.
4. 3 we..will build unto the LORD God of I.
5. 1 prophesied..in the name of the God of I.
5. 11 which a great king of I. builded and set up
6. 14 to the commandment of the God of I.
6. 16 the children of I., the priests, and the
6. 17 for a sin offering for all I., twelve he.
6. 17 according to..number of the tribes of I.
6. 21 the children of I., which were come again
6. 21 had separated..to seek the LORD God of I.
6. 22 work of the house of God, the God of I.
7. 6 law..which the LORD God of I. had given
7. 7 there went up (some) of the children of I.
7. 10 and to teach in I. statutes and judgments
7. 11 of the LORD, and of his statutes to I.
7. 13 all they of the people of I., and (of) his
7. 15 counsellors..offered unto the God of I.
Ezra 7. 28 I gathered together out of I. chief men
8. 25 his lords, and all I. (there) present, had
8. 29 the Levites, and chief of the fathers of I.
8. 35 offered burnt offerings unto the God of I.
8. 35 twelve bullocks for all I., ninety and six
9. 1 The people of I...have not separated th.
9. 4 trembled at the words of the God of I.
9. 15 O LORD God of I., thou (art) righteous
10. 1 there assembled unto him out of I. a very
10. 2 yet now there is hope in I. concerning
10. 5 Then arose Ezra..and all I., to swear that
10. 10 have taken..to increase the trespass of I.
10. 25 Moreover of I.: of the sons of Parosh; R.
Neh. 1. 6 I pray..for the children of I. thy servants
1. 6 confess the sins of the children of I., wh.
2. 10 to seek the welfare of the children of I.
7. 7 number..of the men of the people of I.
7. 61 could not show..whether they (were) of I.
7. 73 the Nethinims, and all I., dwelt in their
7. 73 seventh month..the children of I. (were)
8. 1 law..which the LORD had commanded..I.
8. 14 the children of I. should dwell in booths
8. 17 that day had not the children of I. done
9. 1 children of I. were assembled with fasti.
9. 2 seed of I. separated themselves from all
10. 33 sin offerings to make an atonement for I.
10. 39 children of I...shall bring the offering of
11. 3 I., the priests, and the Levites, and the
11. 20 residue of I...(were) in all the cities of J.
12. 47 all I. in the days of Zerubbabel..gave the
13. 2 Because they met not the children of I.
13. 3 separated from I. all the mixed multitu.
13. 18 yet ye bring more wrath upon I. by prof.
13. 26 Did not Solomon king of I. sin by these
13. 26 God made him king over all I.: neverthe.
Psa. 14. 7 Oh that the salvation of I. (were come)
14. 7 Jacob shall rejoice, (and) I. shall be glad
22. 3 (O thou) that inhabitest the praises of I.
22. 23 and fear him, all ye the seed of I.
25. 22 Redeem I., O God, out of all his troubles
41. 13 Blessed (be) the LORD God of I. from ev.
50. 7 O I., and I will testify against thee: I
53. 6 Oh that the salvation of I. (were come) out
53. 6 Jacob shall rejoice, (and) I. shall be glad
59. 5 LORD God of hosts, the God of I., awake
68. 8 (was moved) at the presence of..the G. of I.
68. 26 Bless ye God..from the fountain of I.
68. 34 his excellency (is) over I., and his streng.
68. 35 the God of I. (is) he that giveth strength
69. 6 let not those..be confounded..O God of I.
71. 22 unto thee will I sing..thou holy one of I.
72. 18 Blessed (be) the LORD God, the God of I.
73. 1 Truly God (is) good to I., (even) to such
76. 1 (is) God known; his name (is) great in I.
78. 5 For he..appointed a law in I., which he
78. 21 Jacob, and anger also came up against I.
78. 31 God..smote down the chosen (men) of I.
78. 41 they turned..and limited the holy one of I.
78. 55 made the tribes of I. to dwell in their te.
78. 59 God heard (this), he..greatly abhorred I.
78. 71 he brought him to feed..I. his inheritance
80. 1 O Shepherd of I., thou that leadest Jose.
81. 4 For this (was) a statute for I., (and) a law
81. 8 will testify..O I., if thou wilt hearken
81. 11 would not hearken..and I. would none
81. 13 hearkened unto me, (and) I. had walked
83. 4 that the name of I. may be no more in r.
89. 18 our defence; and the holy one of I. (is)
98. 3 hath remembered..toward the house of I.
103. 7 made known..unto the children of I.
105. 10 confirmed..to I. (for) an everlasting cov
105. 23 I. also came into Egypt; and Jacob sojo.
106. 48 Blessed (be) the LORD God of I. from ev.
114. 1 When I. went out of Egypt, the house of
114. 2 Judah was his sanctuary, (and) I. his do.
115. 9 O I., trust thou in the LORD: he (is) their
115. 12 he will bless the house of I.; he will ble.
118. 2 Let I. now say, that his mercy (endureth)
121. 4 he that keepeth I. shall neither slumber
122. 4 the tribes go up..unto the testimony of I.
124. 1 the LORD who was on our side, now may I.
125. 5 LORD shall lead..peace (shall be) upon I.
128. 6 children's children, (and) peace upon I.
129. 1 afflicted me from my youth, may I. now
130. 7 Let I. hope in the LORD: for with the L.
130. 8 he shall redeem I. from all his iniquities
131. 3 Let I. hope in the LORD from henceforth
135. 4 LORD hath chosen..I. for his peculiar tr.
135. 12 gave their land (for)..an heritage unto I.
135. 19 Bless the LORD, O house of I.: bless the
136. 11 brought out I. from among them: for
136. 14 made I. to pass through the midst of it
136. 22 an heritage unto I. his servant: for his
147. 2 he gathereth together the outcasts of I.
147. 19 his statutes and his judgments unto I.
148. 14 of the children of I., a people near unto
149. 2 Let I. rejoice in him that made him: let
Prov. 1. 1 of Solomon the son of David, king of I.
Eccl. 1. 12 the preacher was king over I. in Jerusal.
Song 3. 7 men (are) about it, of the valiant of I.
Isa. 1. 3 (but) I. doth not know, my people doth not
1. 4 provoked the holy one of I. unto anger
1. 24 the LORD of hosts, the mighty one of I.
4. 2 comely for them that are escaped of I.
5. 7 vineyard of the LORD..(is) the house of I.
5. 19 let the counsel of the holy one of I. draw
5. 24 despised the word of the holy one of I.
8. 14 rock of offence to both the houses of I.
8. 18 for wonders in I. from the LORD of hosts
9. 8 sent a word..and it hath lighted upon I.
9. 12 and they shall devour I. with open mouth
9. 14 LORD will cut off from I. head and tail

Isa. 10. 17 the light of I. shall be for a fire, and
10. 20 the remnant of I., and such as are escaped
10. 20 stay upon the LORD, the holy one of I., in
10. 22 thy people I. be as the sand of the sea
11. 12 shall assemble the outcasts of I., and
11. 16 like as it was to I. in the day that he
12. 6 great (is) the holy one of I. in the midst
14. 1 will yet choose I., and set them in their
14. 2 the house of I. shall possess them in the
17. 3 be as the glory of the children of I.
17. 6 branches thereof, saith the LORD God of I.
17. 7 shall have respect to the holy one of I.
17. 9 they left because of the children of I.
19. 24 that day shall I. be the third with Egypt
19. 25 work of my hands, and I. mine inheritance
21. 10 heard of the LORD of hosts, the God of I.
21. 17 for the LORD God of I. hath spoken (it)
24. 15 name of the LORD God of I. in the isles
27. 6 I. shall blossom and bud, and fill the face
27. 12 gathered one by one, O ye children of I.
29. 19 poor..shall rejoice in the holy one of I.
29. 23 sanctify..and shall fear the God of I.
30. 11 cause the holy one of I. to cease from
30. 12 thus saith the holy one of I., Because ye
30. 15 thus saith the Lord GOD, the holy one of I.
30. 29 into the mountain..to the mighty one of I.
31. 1 but they look not unto the holy one of I.
31. 6 unto (him from) whom the children of I.
37. 16 O LORD of hosts, God of I., that dwellest
37. 21 Thus saith the LORD God of I., Whereas
37. 23 voice..(even) against the holy one of I.
40. 27 sayest thou, O Jacob, and speakest, O I.
41. 8 thou, I., (art) my servant, Jacob whom I
41. 14 Fear not, thou worm Jacob..ye men of I.
41. 14 LORD, and thy redeemer, the holy one of I.
41. 16 (and) shalt glory in the holy one of I.
41. 17 (I) the God of I. will not forsake them
41. 20 and the holy one of I. hath created it
42. 24 Who gave Jacob for a spoil, and I. to the
43. 1 thus saith..he that formed thee, O I., v. 3.
43. 14 the LORD, your redeemer, the holy one of I.
43. 15 the LORD, your holy one, the creator of I.
43. 22 but thou hast been weary of me, O I.
43. 28 Jacob to the curse, and I. to reproaches
44. 1 Jacob my servant; and I., whom I have
44. 5 and surname (himself) by the name of I.
44. 6 Thus saith the LORD the King of I., and
44. 21 Remember these, O Jacob and I.; for thou
44. 21 O I., thou shalt not be forgotten of me
44. 23 redeemed Jacob, and glorified himself in I.
45. 3 that I..which call(thee)..(am)the God of I.
45. 4 For Jacob my servant's sake, and I. mine
45. 11 the LORD, the holy one of I., and his ma.
45. 15 (art) a God that hidest thyself, O God of I.
45. 17 (But) I. shall be saved in the LORD with
45. 25 In the LORD shall all the seed of I. be
46. 3 the remnant of the house of I., which are
46. 13 place salvation in Zion for I. my glory
47. 4 LORD of hosts (is) his name..holy one of I.
48. 1 Jacob, which are called by the name of I.
48. 1 make mention of the God of I., (but) not in
48. 2 and stay themselves upon the God of I.
48. 12 Hearken unto me, O Jacob and I., my called
48. 17 the LORD, thy redeemer, the holy one of I.
49. 3 Thou (art) my servant, O I., in whom I
49. 5 Though I. be not gathered, yet shall I be
49. 6 raise..and to restore the preserved of I.
49. 7 LORD, the Redeemer of I., (and) his holy
49. 7 that is faithful, (and) the holy one of I.
52. 12 and the God of I. (will be) your rereward
54. 5 thy redeemer the holy one of I.; The God
55. 5 the holy one of I.; for he hath glorified
56. 8 GOD which gathereth the outcasts of I.
60. 9 thy God, and to the holy one of I.
60. 14 The city..The Zion of the holy one of I.
63. 7 the great goodness toward the house of I.
63. 16 ignorant of us, and I. acknowledge us
66. 20 the children of I. bring an offering in a
Jer. 2. 3 I. (was) holiness unto the LORD, (and) the
2. 4 and all the families of the house of I.
2. 14 (Is) I. a servant? (is) he a home born (slave)?
3. 20 dealt treacherously with me, O house of I.
3. 21 (and) supplications of the children of I.
3. 23 LORD our God (is) the salvation of I.
4. 1 If thou wilt return, O I., saith the LORD
5. 15 a nation upon you from far, O house of I.
6. 9 throughly glean..remnant of I. as a vine
7. 3, 21 saith the LORD of hosts, the God of I.
7. 12 I did..for the wickedness of my people I.
9. 15 thus saith the LORD of hosts, the God of I.
10. 1 The LORD speaketh unto you, O house of I.
10. 16 I. (is) the rod of his inheritance. The LORD
11. 3 Thus saith the LORD God of I.; Cursed (be)
12. 14 I have caused my people I. to inherit
13. 11 to cleave unto me the whole house of I.
13. 12 Thus saith the LORD God of I., Every bot.
14. 8 the hope of I., the saviour thereof in
16. 9 Thus saith the LORD of hosts, the God of I.
16. 14, 15 that brought up the children of I.
17. 13 O LORD, the hope of I., all that forsake
18. 6 O house of I., cannot I do with you as this
18. 6 so (are) ye in mine hand, O house of I.
18. 13 virgin of I. hath done a very horrible
19. 3, 15 saith the LORD of hosts, the God of I.
21. 4 Thus saith the LORD God of I.; Behold, I
23. 2 thus saith the LORD God of I. against the
23. 7 which brought up the children of I. out
23. 8 which led the seed of the house of I. out
23. 13 prophesied..and caused my people I. to
24. 5 Thus saith the LORD, the God of I.; Like
25. 15 thus saith the LORD God of I. unto me
25. 27 Thus saith the LORD of hosts, the God of I.
Jer. 27. 4, 21 saith the LORD of hosts, the God of I.
28. 2 speaketh the LORD of hosts, the God of I.
28. 14 thus saith the LORD of hosts, the God of I.
29. 4, 8, 21 saith the LORD of hosts, the God of I.
29. 23 they have committed villany in I., and
29. 25 speaketh the LORD of hosts, the God of I.
30. 2 Thus speaketh the LORD God of I., saying
30. 3 I will bring again the captivity of my p. I.
30. 4 words that the LORD spake concerning I.
30. 10 neither be dismayed, O I.: for, lo, I will
31. 1 I be the God of all the families of I.
31. 2 (even) I., when I went to cause him to rest
31. 4 thou shalt be built, O virgin of I.: thou
31. 7 O LORD, save thy people, the remnant of I.
31. 9 I am a father to I., and Ephraim (is) my
31. 10 He that scattered I. will gather him, and
31. 21 virgin of I., turn again to these thy cities
31. 23 Thus saith the LORD of hosts, the God of I.
31. 33 that I will make with the house of I.
31. 36 the seed of I. also shall cease from being
31. 37 I will also cast off all the seed of I.
32. 14, 15 Thus saith the LORD of hosts, the God of I.
32. 20 Which hast set signs and wonders..in I.
32. 21 hast brought forth thy people I. out of
32. 30 children of I. have only provoked me to
32. 36 saith the LORD, the God of I., concerning
33. 4 saith the LORD, the God of I., concerning
33. 7 captivity of Judah, and the captivity of I.
33. 14 which I have promised unto the house of I.
33. 17 to sit upon the throne of the house of I.
34. 2, 13 Thus saith the LORD, the God of I.
35. 13, 17, 18, 19 the LORD of hosts, the God of I.
36. 2 that I have spoken unto thee against I.
37. 7 Thus saith the LORD, the God of I.; Thus
38. 17 the LORD, the God of hosts, the God of I.
39. 16 Thus saith the LORD of hosts, the God of I.
42. 9 Thus saith the LORD, the God of I., unto
42. 15, 18 saith the LORD of hosts, the God of I.
43. 10 Thus saith the LORD of hosts, the God of I.
44. 2 Thus saith the LORD of hosts, the God of I.
44. 7 the LORD, the God of hosts, the God of I.
44. 11, 25 saith the LORD of hosts, the God of I.
45. 2 Thus saith the LORD, the God of I., unto
46. 25 the God of I., saith; Behold, I will punish
46. 27 be not dismayed, O I.: for, behold, I will
48. 1 saith the LORD of hosts, the God of I.
48. 27 was not I. a derision unto thee? was he
49. 1 Hath I. no sons? hath he no heir? why (th.)
49. 2 then shall I. be heir unto them that
50. 4 the children of I. shall come, they and
50. 17 I. (is) a scattered sheep; the lions have
50. 18 thus saith the LORD of hosts, the God of I.
50. 19 I will bring I. again to his habitation
50. 20 the iniquity of I. shall be sought for
50. 29 against the LORD, against..holy one of I.
51. 5 I. (hath) not (been) forsaken, nor Judah
51. 5 filled with sin against the holy one of I.
51. 33 thus saith the LORD of hosts, the God of I.
51. 49 Babylon (hath caused) the slain of I. to
Lam. 2. 1 cast down from heaven..the beauty of I.
2. 3 He hath cut off..all the horn of I.
2. 5 hath swallowed up I., he hath swallowed
Eze. 2. 3 I send thee to the children of I., to a
3. 1 and go speak unto the house of I.
3. 4 get thee unto the house of I., and speak
3. 5 thou (art) not sent..(but) to the house of I.
3. 7 the house of I. will not hearken unto thee
3. 7 house of I. (are) impudent and hard hear.
3. 17 made thee a watchman unto the house of I.
4. 3 This (shall be) a sign to the house of I.
4. 13 thus shall the children of I. eat their
5. 4 fire come forth into all the house of I.
6. 2 set thy face toward the mountains of I.
6. 3 Ye mountains of I., hear the word of the
6. 5 the dead carcases of the children of I.
6. 11 the evil abominations of the house of I.!
7. 2 saith the Lord GOD unto the land of I.
8. 4 the glory of the God of I. (was) there
8. 6 great abominations that the house of I.
8. 10 the idols of the house of I., pourtrayed
8. 11 men of the ancients of the house of I.
8. 12 ancients of the house of I. do in the dark
9. 3 the glory of the God of I. was gone up
9. 8 wilt thou destroy all the residue of I.
10. 19 the glory of the God of I. (was) over them
10. 20 creature that I saw under the God of I.
11. 5 Thus have ye said, O house of I.: for I.
11. 10 I will judge you in the border of I.; and
11. 13 thou make a full end of the remnant of I.?
11. 15 the house of I. wholly, (are) they unto
11. 17 and I will give you the land of I.
11. 22 the glory of the God of I. (was) over them
12. 6 set thee (for) a sign unto the house of I.
12. 9 hath not the house of I., the rebellious
12. 10 all the house of I. that (are) among them
12. 19 Thus saith the Lord..of the land of I.
12. 22 that proverb (that) ye have in the land of I.
12. 23 shall no more use it as a proverb in I.
12. 24 flattering divination within..house of I.
12. 27 (they of) the house of I. say, The vision
13. 2 against the prophets of I. that prophesy
13. 4 O I., thy prophets are like the foxes in
13. 5 made up the hedge for the house of I. to
13. 9 written in the writing of the house of I.
13. 9 neither shall they enter..the land of I.
13. 16 prophets of I., which prophesy concerning
14. 1 came certain of the elders of I. unto me
14. 4 Every man of the house of I. that setteth
14. 5 take the house of I. in their own heart
14. 6 say unto the house of I., Thus saith the
14. 7 For every one of the house of I., or of
14. 7 the stranger that sojourneth in I., which
Eze. 14. 9 destroy him from the midst of my people I.
14. 11 house of I. may go no more astray from
17. 2 and speak a parable unto the house of I.
17. 23 In the mountain of the height of I. will I
18. 2 this proverb concerning the land of I.
18. 3 any more to use this proverb in I.
18. 6 his eyes to the idols of the house of I. v. 15.
18. 25 O house of I.; Is not my way equal? are
18. 29 Yet saith the house of I., The way of the
18. 29 house of I., are not my ways equal? are
18. 30 I will judge you, O house of I., every one
18. 31 for why will ye die, O house of I.?
19. 1 a lamentation for the princes of I.
19. 9 no more be heard upon the mountains of I.
20. 1 certain of the elders of I. came to enquire
20. 3 speak unto the elders of I., and say unto
20. 5 In the day when I chose I., and lifted up
20. 13 the house of I. rebelled against me in
20. 27 speak unto the house of I., and say unto
20. 30 say unto the house of I., Thus saith the
20. 31 shall I be enquired of by you..house of I.?
20. 38 they shall not enter into the land of I.
20. 39 O house of I., thus saith the Lord GOD
20. 40 in the mountain of the height of I., saith
20. 40 there shall all the house of I., all of
20. 42 I shall bring you into the land of I., into
20. 44 to your corrupt doings, O ye house of I.
21. 2 and prophesy against the land of I.
21. 3 say to the land of I., Thus saith the LORD
21. 12 it (shall be) upon all the princes of I.
21. 25 thou, profane wicked prince of I., whose
22. 6 the princes of I., every one were in thee
22. 18 the house of I. is to me become dross: all
24. 21 Speak unto the house of I., Thus saith the
25. 3 against the land of I., when it was desolate
25. 6 all thy despite against the land of I.
25. 14 vengeance..by the hand of my people I.
28. 24 a pricking brier unto the house of I.
28. 25 When I shall have gathered the house of I.
29. 6 been a staff of reed to the house of I.
29. 16 the confidence of the house of I., which
29. 21 the horn of the house of I. to bud forth
33. 7 set thee a watchman unto the house of I.
33. 10 speak unto the house of I.; Thus ye speak
33. 11 for why will ye die, O house of I.?
33. 20 ye house of I., I will judge you every
33. 24 inhabit those wastes of the land of I.
33. 28 the mountains of I. shall be desolate
34. 2 Son..prophesy against the shepherds of I.
34. 2 Woe (be) to the shepherds of I. that do
34. 13 feed them upon the mountains of I. by
34. 14 upon the high mountains of I. shall their
34. 14 shall they feed upon the mountains of I.
34. 30 they, (even) the house of I., (are) my peo.
35. 5 hast shed (the blood of) the children of I.
35. 12 hast spoken against the mountains of I.
35. 15 at the inheritance of the house of I., bec.
36. 1 prophesy unto the mountains of I., and
36. 1, 4 mountains of I., hear the word of the L.
36. 6 Prophesy..concerning the land of I., and
36. 8 O mountains of I., ye shall shoot forth
36. 8 yield your fruit to my people of I.; for
36. 10 multiply men upon you, all the house of I.
36. 12 men to walk upon you, (even) my people I.
36. 17 when the house of I. dwelt in their own
36. 21 which the house of I. had profaned among
36. 22 Therefore say unto the house of I., Thus
36. 22 I do not (this) for your sakes, O house of I.
36. 32 ashamed..for your own ways, O house of I.
36. 37 I will..be enquired of by the house of I.
37. 11 these bones are the whole house of I.: be.
37. 12 come up..and bring you into the land..I.
37. 16 and (for) all the house of I. his
37. 19 tribes of I. his fellows, and will put them
37. 21 I will take the children of I. from among
37. 22 make them one nation in the land..of I.
37. 28 shall know that I the LORD do sanctify I.
38. 8 the mountains of I., which have been al.
38. 14 In that day when my people of I. dwelleth
38. 16 thou shalt come up against my people of I.
38. 17 spoken..by my servants the prophets of I.
38. 18 when Gog shall come against the land of I.
38. 19 shall be a great shaking in the land of I.
39. 2 will bring thee upon the mountains of I.
39. 4 Thou shalt fall upon the mountains of I.
39. 7 make..known in the midst of my people I.
39. 7 shall know that I (am)..the holy one in I.
39. 9 they that dwell in the cities of I. shall go
39. 11 give unto Gog a place..of graves in I., the
39. 12 seven months shall the house of I. be bu.
39. 17 a great sacrifice upon the mountains of I.
39. 22 So the house of I. shall know that I (am)
39. 23 house of I. went into captivity for their
39. 25 have mercy upon the whole house of I.
39. 29 poured out my spirit upon the house of I.
40. 2 brought he me into the land of I., and set
40. 4 declare all..thou seest to the house of I.
43. 2 the glory of the God of I. came from the
43. 7 dwell in the midst of the children of I.
43. 7 my holy name, shall the house of I. no
43. 10 show the house to the house of I., that
44. 2 God of I., hath entered in by it, therefore
44. 6 thou shalt say..to the house of I.
44. 6 O ye house of I., let it suffice you of all
44. 9 stranger that (is) among the children of I.
44. 10 when I. went astray, which went astray
44. 12 caused the house of I. to fall into iniquity
44. 22 maidens of the seed of the house of I., or
44. 28 and ye shall give them no possession in I.
44. 29 every dedicated thing in I. shall be theirs
45. 6 it shall be for the whole house of I.
45. 8 In the land shall be his possession in I.

Eze. 45. 8 land shall they give to the house of I. ac.
45. 9 Let it suffice you, O princes of I.: remove
45. 15 out of the fat pastures of I., for a meat
45. 16 give this oblation for the prince in I.
45. 17 in all solemnities of the house of I.: he
45. 17 to make reconciliation for the house of I.
47. 13 land, according to the twelve tribes of I.
47. 18 from the land of I. (by) Jordan, from the
47. 21 this land..according to the tribes of I.
47. 22 the country among the children of I.; they
47. 22 have inheritance..among the tribes of I.
48. 11 went not astray when the children of I.
48. 19 they..serve it out of all the tribes of I.
48. 29 shall divide by lot unto the tribes of I.
48. 31 gates..after the names of the tribes of I.
Dan. 1. 3 should bring (certain) of the children of I.
9. 7 men of Judah..and unto all I., (that are)
9. 11 Yea, all I. have transgressed thy law, even
9. 20 and confessing..the sin of my people I.
Hos. 1. 1 of Jeroboam the son of Joash, king of I.
1. 4 and will cause to cease the kingdom..of I.
1. 5 break the bow of I. in the valley of Jezr.
1. 6 no more have mercy upon the house of I.
1. 10 number of the children of I. shall be as
3. 1 love of the LORD toward the children of I.
3. 4 children of I. shall abide many days with.
3. 5 Afterward shall the children of I. return
4. 1 Hear the word of the LORD..children of I.
4. 15 Though thou, I., play the harlot, (yet) let
4. 16 For I. slideth back as a backsliding heifer
5. 1 Hear ye this..ye house of I.; and give ye
5. 3 I know Ephraim, and I. is not hid from
5. 3 thou committest whoredom, (and) I. is
5. 5 pride of I. doth testify to his face: there.
5. 5 shall I. and Ephraim fall in their iniquity
5. 9 among the tribes of I. have I made known
6. 10 seen an horrible thing in the house of I.
6. 10 there (is) the whoredom of Ephraim, I. is
7. 1 When I would have healed I., then the
7. 10 pride of I. testifieth to his face: and they
8. 2 I. shall cry unto me, My God, we know
8. 3 I. hath cast off (the thing that is) good
8. 6 For from I. (was) it also: the workman
8. 8 I. is swallowed up: now shall they be
8. 14 For I. hath forgotten his maker, and buil.
9. 1 Rejoice not, O I., for joy, as (other) peo.
9. 7 I. shall know (it): the prophet (is) a fool
9. 10 found I. like grapes in the wilderness; I
10. 1 I. (is) an empty vine, he bringeth forth fr.
10. 6 and I. shall be ashamed of his own counsel
10. 8 the sin of I., shall be destroyed: the thorn
10. 9 O I., thou hast sinned from the days of G.
10. 15 in a morning shall the king of I. utterly
11. 1 When I. (was) a child, then I loved him
11. 8 (how) shall I deliver thee, I.? how shall I
11. 12 and the house of I. with deceit: but Jud.
12. 12 I. served for a wife, and for a wife he kept
12. 13 by a prophet the LORD brought I. out of
13. 1 he exalted himself in I.; but when he
13. 9 O I., thou hast destroyed thyself; but in
14. 1 O I., return unto the LORD thy God; for
14. 5 I will be as the dew unto I.: he shall
Joel 2. 27 shall know that I (am) in the midst of I.
3. 2 will plead with them..(for) my heritage I.
3. 16 (will be)..the strength of the children of I.
Amos 1. 1 he saw concerning I. in the days of Uzziah
1. 1 of Jeroboam the son of Joash king of I.
2. 6 For three transgressions of I., and for four
2. 11 (Is it) not even thus, O ye children of I.?
3. 1 Hear this word..O children of I., against
3. 12 so shall the children of I. be taken out
3. 14 I shall visit the transgressions of I. upon
4. 5 this liketh you, O ye children of I., saith
4. 12 Therefore thus will I do unto thee, O I.
4. 12 (and)..prepare to meet thy God, O I.
5. 1 which I take up against you..O house of I.
5. 2 The virgin of I. is fallen; she shall no
5. 3 hundred shall leave ten, to the house of I.
5. 4 thus saith the LORD unto the house of I.
5. 25 offered unto me sacrifices..O house of I.?
6. 1 of the nations, to whom the house of I.
6. 14 will raise up..a nation, O house of I., saith
7. 8 a plumb line in the midst of my people I.
7. 9 the sanctuaries of I. shall be laid waste
7. 10 Amaziah..sent to Jeroboam king of I.
7. 10 conspired against thee in the midst of..I.
7. 11 I. shall surely be led away captive out of
7. 15 unto me, Go, prophesy unto my people I.
7. 16 Thou sayest, Prophesy not against I., and
7. 17 I. shall surely go into captivity forth of
8. 2 end is come upon my people of I.; I will
9. 7 (Are) ye not as children..O children of I.?
9. 7 Have not I brought up I. out of the land
9. 9 I will sift the house of I. among all nat.
9. 14 bring..the captivity of my people of I.
Obad. 20 captivity of this host of the children of I.
Mic. 1. 5 for the sins of the house of I. What (is)
1. 13 for the transgressions of I. were found in
1. 14 houses..(shall be) a lie to the kings of I.
1. 15 shall come unto Adullam the glory of I.
2. 12 I will surely gather the remnant of I.
3. 1 Hear..ye princes of the house of I.; (Is
3. 8 to declare unto Jacob..and to I. his sin
3. 9 Hear this..ye..princes of the house of I.
5. 1 they shall smite the judge of I. with a rod
5. 2 unto me (that is) to be ruler in I.; whose
5. 3 then the remnant..shall return unto..I.
6. 2 hath a controversy..he will plead with I.
Nah. 2. 2 hath turned away..as the excellency of I.
Zeph. 2. 9 (as) I live, saith the LORD..the God of I.
3. 13 The remnant of I. shall not do iniquity
3. 14 Sing, O daughter of Zion; shout, O I.; be

Zeph. 3. 15 the king of I...(is) in the midst of thee
Zech. 9. 1 all the tribes of I., (shall be) toward the L.
12. 1 The burden of the word of the LORD for I.
Mal. 1. 1 The burden of the word of the LORD to I.
1. 5 will be magnified from the border of I.
2. 16 the God of I., saith that he hateth putting
4. 4 I commanded unto him in Horeb for all I.
Matt. 2. 6 a Governor, that shall rule my people I.
2. 20 Saying, Arise..and go into the land of I.
2. 21 And he arose..and came into the land of I.
8. 10 have not found so great faith, no, not in I.
9. 33 saying, It was never so seen in I.
10. 6 go rather to the..sheep of the house of I.
10. 23 not have gone over the cities of I., till
15. 24 but unto the lost sheep of the house of I.
15. 31 wondered..and they glorified the God of I.
19. 28 shall sit..judging the twelve tribes of I.
27. 9 whom they of the children of I. did value
27. 42 If he be the king of I., let him now come
Mark 12. 29 Hear, O I.; The Lord our God is one Lord
15. 32 Let Christ the king of I. descend now from
Luke 1. 16 the children of I. shall he turn to the L.
1. 54 He hath holpen his servant I., in rememb.
1. 68 Blessed (be) the Lord God of I.; for he
1. 80 till the day of his showing unto I.
2. 25 devout, waiting for the consolation of I.
2. 32 A light..and the glory of thy people I.
2. 34 the fall and rising again of many in I.: and
4. 25 many widows were in I. in the days of E.
4. 27 many lepers were in I. in the time of E.
7. 9 have not fonnd so great faith, no, not in I.
22. 30 and sit..judging the twelve tribes of I.
24. 21 been he which should have redeemed I.
John 1. 31 but that he should be made manifest to I.
1. 49 art the Son of God; thou art the king of I.
3. 10 Art thou a master of I., and knowest not
12. 13 Blessed (is) the king of I. that cometh in
Acts 1. 6 this time restore again the kingdom to I.?
2. 22 Ye men of I., hear these words; Jesus of
2. 36 Therefore let all the house of I. know as.
3. 12 Ye men of I., why marvel ye at this? or
4. 8 said unto them, Ye rulers..elders [of I.]
4. 10 Be it known unto..all the people of I.
4. 27 Gentiles, and the people of I., were gath.
5. 21 all the senate of the children of I., and
5. 31 give repentance to I., and forgiveness of
5. 35 Ye men of I., take heed to yourselves
7. 23 into his heart to visit..children of I.
7. 37 Moses which said unto the children of I.
7. 42 O ye house of I., have ye offered to me
9. 15 bear my name before..the children of I.
10. 36 word..(God) sent unto the children of I.
13. 16 Men of I., and ye that fear God, give
13. 17 God of this people [of I.] chose our fathers
13. 23 hath God..raised unto I. a Saviour, Jesus
13. 24 first preached..to all the people of I.
21. 28 Crying out, Men of I., help: This is the
28. 20 for the hope of I. I am bound with this
Rom. 9. 6 For they (are) not all I. which are of I.
9. 27 Esaias also crieth concerning I., Though
9. 27 children of I. be as the sand of the sea, a
9. 31 But I., which followed after the law of
10. 1 [my heart's desire and prayer to God for I.]
10. 19 But I say, Did not I. know? First Moses
10. 21 But to I. he saith, All day long I have
11. 2 he maketh intercession to God against I.
11. 7 I. hath not obtained that which he seek.
11. 25 blindness in part is happened to I., until
11. 26 so all I. shall be saved: as it is written
1 Co. 10. 18 Behold I. after the flesh: are not they
2 Co. 3. 7, 13 that the children of I. could not stedf.
Gal. 6. 16 peace (be) on them..and upon the I. of
Eph. 2. 12 being aliens from the commonwealth of I.
Phil. 3. 5 Circumcise..of the stock of I., (of) the
Heb. 8. 8 make a new covenant with the house of I.
8. 10 that I will make with the house of I. after
11. 22 of the departing of the children of I.; and
Rev. 2. 14 a stumblingblock before the children of I.
7. 4 of all the tribes of the children of I.
21. 12 of the twelve tribes of the children of I.

3. On the revolt of the ten tribes (1 Ki. 12. 1-9) B.C. 975, Canaan was divided into the two kingdoms of *Israel* and *Judah*. The former lasted from 975 till 721 B.C. In 974 Jeroboam sets up the two golden calves, 1 Ki. 12. 28, 29; in 956 Ahijah denounces Jeroboam, 1 Ki. 14. 7; in 953 Nadab is slain, 1 Ki. 15. 27; in 940 the king of Syria invades Israel, 2 Ch. 16. 4; in 929 confusion prevails in Israel, 1 Ki. 16. 9-20; in 918 Jericho is rebuilt, 16. 34; in 910 Elijah destroys the priests of Baal, 18. 40; in 901 the Syrians are miraculously defeated; in 895 Elijah is translated, 2 Ki. 2. 11; in 894 Elisha heals Naaman; in 893 he performs various miracles; in 892 the king of Syria besieges Samaria, 2 Ki. 6. 24; in 891 Elisha restores the Shunamite's son, 4. 32-35; in 885 Hazael kills the king of Syria, 8. 15; in 850 Jonah goes to Nineveh, Jonah 1. 2; 2. 4; in 847 Israel oppressed by the king of Syria, 2 Ki. 8. 3; in 842 is delivered from him, 13. 5; in 838 invaded by Moab, Elisha dies; in 822 Jeroboam II. restores the territory of Israel, 2 Ki. 14. 25; in 793 Amos prophesies; in 784 interregnum of 11 years; in 771 Pul invades Israel; 2 Ki. 15. 19; in 740 Tiglath-pileser carries off captives, 15. 29; in 725 the captivity of ten tribes foretold; in 723 Samaria besieged by Shalmanezer, 18. 9; in 721 the ten tribes carried off into Assyria, 17. 6.

1 Ki. 4. 20 Judah and I. (were) many, 2 Sa. 24. 1.
4. 25 Judah and I. dwelt safely, every man un.
12. 18 all I. stoned him with stones, that he died
12. 19 So I. rebelled against the house of David
12. 20 all I. heard that Jeroboam was come again
12. 20 they sent..and made him king over all I.
12. 21 warriors, to fight against the house of I.

1 Ki. 12. 24 against your brethren the children of I.
12. 28 behold thy gods, O I., which brought thee
12. 33 ordained a feast unto the children of I.
14. 10 (and) him that is shut up and left in I.
14. 13 all I. shall mourn for him, and bury him
14. 14 the LORD shall raise him up a king over I.
14. 15 For the LORD shall smite I., as a reed is
14. 15 he shall root up I. out of this good land
14. 16 he shall give I. up because of the sins of
14. 16 Jeroboam, who did sin, and..made I. to
14. 18 all I. mourned for him, according to the
14. 19 book of the chronicles of the king of I.
15. 9 the twentieth year of Jeroboam king of I.
15. 16 war between Asa and Baasha king of I.
15. 17 Baasha king of I. went up against Judah
15. 19 break thy league with Baasha king of I.
15. 20 sent the captains..against the cities of I.
15. 25 the son of Jeroboam began to reign over I.
15. 25 And Nadab..reigned over I. two years
15. 26, 34 his sin wherewith he made I. to sin
15. 27 Nadab and all I. laid seige to Gibbethon
15. 30 which he sinned, and which he made I.
15. 30 he provoked the LORD God of I. to anger
15. 31 book of the chronicles of the king of I.?
15. 32 war between Asa and Baasha king of I.
15. 33 the son of Ahijah to reign over all I. in
16. 2 made thee prince over my people I.; and
16. 2 hast made my people I. to sin, to provoke
16. 5, 14, 20, 27 chronicles of the kings of I.?
16. 8 Elah the son of Baasha to reign over I.
16. 13 by which they made I. to sin, in provoking
16. 16 all I. made Omri, the captain of the host
16. 16 king over I. that day in the camp
16. 17 went up from Gibbethon, and all I. with
16. 19 in his sin which he did, to make I. to sin
16. 21 the people of I. divided into two parts
16. 23 began Omri to reign over I., twelve years
16. 26 I. to sin, to provoke the LORD GOD of I.
16. 29 began Ahab the son of Omri to reign over I.
16. 29 the son of Omri reigned over I. in Samaria
16. 33 God of I. to anger than all the kings of I.
18. 17 Ahab said..(Art) thou he that troubleth I.
18. 18 I have not troubled I.; but thou and thy
18. 19 gather to me all I. unto mount Carmel, and
18. 20 Ahab sent unto all the children of I., and
19. 10 children of I. have forsaken thy covenant
19. 14 children of I. have forsaken thy covenant
19. 16 Jehu..shalt thou anoint (to be) king over I.
19. 18 I have left (me) seven thousand in I., all
20. 2 he sent messengers to Ahab king of I. into
20. 4, 11 And the king of I. answered and said
20. 7 king of I. called all the elders of the land
20. 13 there came a prophet unto Ahab king of I.
20. 15 the people, (even) all the children of I.
20. 20 the Syrians fled; and I. pursued them; and
20. 21 king of I. went out, and smote the horses
20. 22 the prophet came to the king of I., and
20. 26 and went up to Aphek, to fight against I.
20. 27 children of I. were numbered, and were
20. 27 the children of I. pitched before them
20. 28 spake unto the king of I., and said, Thus
20. 29 the children of I. slew of the Syrians an
20. 31 heard that the kings of the house of I.
20. 31 let us, I pray..go out to the king of I.
20. 32 came to the king of I., and said, Thy ser.
20. 40 the king of I. said unto him, So (shall) thy
20. 41 the king of I. discerned him that he (was)
20. 43 the king of I. went to his house heavy
21. 7 Dost thou now govern the kingdom of I.?
21. 18 go down to meet Ahab king of I., which
21. 21 and him that is shut up and left in I.
21. 22 provoked (me) to anger, and made I. to
21. 26 LORD cast out before the children of I.
22. 1 contin. without war between Syria and I.
22. 2 king of Judah came down to the king of I.
22. 3 the king of I. said unto his servants, Know
22. 4, 5 Jehoshaphat said to the king of I.
22. 6 king of I. gathered the prophets together
22. 8 king of I. said unto Jehoshaphat, (There)
22. 9 the king of I. called an officer, and said
22. 10, 29 the king of I. and Jehoshaphat the
22. 17 I saw all I. scattered upon the hills, as
22. 18, 30 the king of I. said unto Jehoshaphat
22. 26 the king of I. said, Take Micaiah, and carry
22. 30 the king of I. disguised himself, and went
22. 31 saying, Fight..only with the king of I.
22. 32 that they said, Surely it (is) the king of I.
22. 33 perceived that it (was) not the king of I.
22. 34 smote the king of I. between the joints
22. 39 book of the chronicles of the kings of I.?
22. 41 in the fourth year of Ahab king of I.
22. 44 Jehoshap. made peace with the king of I
22. 51 the son of Ahab began to reign over I. in
22. 51 Ahaziah..reigned two years over I.
22. 52 the son of Nebat, who made I. to sin
2 Ki. 1. 1 Moab rebelled against I. after the death
1. 3, 6, 16 not because (there is) not a God in I.
1. 18 book of the chronicles of the kings of I.?
3. 1 the son of Ahab began to reign over I. in
3. 3 the son of Nebat, which made I. to sin
3. 4 rendered unto the king of I. an hundred
3. 5 the king..rebelled against the king of I.
3. 6 Jehoram went out..and numbered all I.
3. 9 the king of I. went, and the king of Jud.
3. 10 the king of I. said, Alas! that the LORD
3. 11 one of the king of I.'s servants answered
3. 12 the king of I. and Jehoshaphat the king
3. 13 Elisha said unto the king of I., What have
3. 13 the king of I. said unto him, Nay: for the
3. 24 And when they came to the camp of I.
3. 27 there was great indignation against I.
5. 2 brought away captive out of the land of I.

2 Ki. 5. 4 said the maid that (is) of the land of I.
5. 5 I will send a letter unto the king of I.
5. 6 he brought the letter to the king of I.
5. 7 when the king of I. had read the letter
5. 8 that the king of I. had rent his clothes
5. 8 shall know that there is a prophet in I.
5. 12 Abana..better than all the waters of I.?
5. 15 (there is) no God in all the earth, but in I.
6. 8 the king of Syria warred against I., and
6. 9 the man of God sent unto the king of I.
6. 10 the king of I. sent to the place which the
6. 11 show me which of us (is) for the king of I.?
6. 12 prophet that (is) in I., telleth the king of I.
6. 21 the king of I. said unto Elisha, when he
6. 23 bands..came no more into the land of I.
6. 26 king of I. was passing by upon the wall
7. 6 the king of I. hath hired against us the
7. 13 they (are) as all the multitude of I. that
8. 12 that thou wilt do unto the children of I.
8. 16, 25 of Joram the son of Ahab king of I.
8. 18 he walked in the way of the kings of I.
8. 26 Athaliah, the daughter of Omri king of I.
9. 3, 12 saith..I have anointed thee king over I.
9. 6 over the people of the LORD, (even) over I.
9. 8 and him that is shut up and left in I.
9. 14 Joram..kept Ramoth-gilead, he and all I.
9. 21 Joram king of I. and Ahaziah king of Ju.
10. 28 Thus Jehu destroyed Baal out of I.
10. 29 the son of Nebat, who made I. to sin
10. 30 thy children..shall sit on the throne of I.
10. 31 the sins of Jeroboam, which made I. to sin
10. 32 those days the LORD began to cut I. short
10. 32 Hazael smote them in all the coasts of I.
10. 34 book of the chronicles of the kings of I.?
10. 36 time that Jehu reigned over I. in Samaria
13. 1 the son of Jehu began to reign over I. in
13. 2 the son of Nebat, which made I. to sin
13. 3 anger of the LORD was kindled against I.
13. 4 he saw the oppression of I., because the
13. 5 the LORD gave I. a saviour, so that they
13. 5 the children of I. dwelt in their tents, as
13. 6 Jeroboam, who made I. sin, (but) walked
13. 8, 12 of the chronicles of the kings of I.?
13. 10 began Jehoash..to reign over I. in Sama.
13. 11 Jeroboam the son of Nebat, who made I.
13. 13 was buried in Samaria with the kings of I.
13. 14 the king of I. came down unto him, and
13. 14 chariot of I., and the horsemen thereof!
13. 16 he said to the king of I., Put thine hand
13. 18 he said unto the king of I., Smite upon the
13. 22 king of Syria oppressed I. all the days of
13. 25 beat him, and recovered the cities of I.
14. 1 year of Joash son of Jehoahaz king of I.
14. 8 the son of Jehoahaz, son of Jehu, king of I.
14. 9 the king of I. sent to Amaziah king of J.
14. 11 Jehoash king of I. went up; and he and
14. 12 Judah was put to the worse before I.; and
14. 13 king of I. took Amaziah king of Judah
14. 15, 28 of the chronicles of the kings of I.?
14. 16 was buried in Samaria with the kings of I.
14. 17 of Jehoash, son of Jehoahaz king of I.
14. 23 the son of Joash king of I. began to reign
14. 24 the son of Nebat, who made I. to sin
14. 25 restored the coast of I. from the entering
14. 26 the LORD saw the affliction of I., (that it
14. 26 shut up, nor any left, nor any helper for I.
14. 27 he would blot out the name of I. from under
14. 28 recovered Damascus, and Hamath..for I.
14. 29 with his fathers, (even) with the kings of I.
15. 1 and seventh year of Jeroboam king of I.
15. 8 son of Jeroboam reign over I. in Samaria
15. 9, 18, 24, 28 son of Nebat, who made I. to s.
15. 11, 15, 21, 26, 31 chronicles of the kings of I.
15. 12 Thy sons shall sit on the throne of I. unto
15. 17 Menahem the son of Gadi to reign over I.
15. 20 Menahem exacted the money of I., (even)
15. 23 the son of Menahem began to reign over I.
15. 27 the son of Remaliah began to reign over I.
15. 29 In the days of Pekah king of I. came
15. 32 of Pekah the son of Remaliah king of I.
16. 3 he walked in the way of the kings of I.
16. 3 cast out from before the children of I.
16. 5 Pekah son of Remaliah king of I. came
16. 7 out of the hand of the king of I., which
17. 1 son of Elah to reign in Samaria over I.
17. 2 as the kings of I. that were before him
17. 6 carried I. away into Assyria, and placed
17. 7 the children of I. had sinned against the
17. 8 the children of I., and of the kings of I.
17. 9 And the children of I. did secretly (those)
17. 13 the LORD testified against I. and against
17. 18 the LORD was very angry with I., and re.
17. 19 in the statutes of I. which they made
17. 20 the LORD rejected all the seed of I., and
17. 21 he rent I. from the house of David; and
17. 21 Jeroboam drave I. from following the L.
17. 22 the children of I. walked in all the sins
17. 23 the LORD removed I. out of his sight, as
17. 23 So was I. carried away out of their own
17. 24 placed (them)..instead of the child. of I.
18. 1, 9 year of Hoshea son of Elah king of I.
18. 4 the children of I. did burn incense to it
18. 10 (is) the ninth year of Hoshea king of I.
18. 11 the king of Assyria did carry away I. un.
21. 3 made a grove, as did Ahab king of I.; and
23. 15 the son of Nebat, who made I. to sin, had
23. 19 the kings of I. had made to provoke (the
23. 22 nor in all the days of the kings of I.
23. 27 also out of my sight, as I have removed I.
1 Ch 5. 17 and in the days of Jeroboam king of I.
9. 1 in the book of the kings of I. and
21. 5 (they of) I. were a thousand thousand and

2 Ch. 10. 18 the children of I. stoned him with stones
10. 19 I. rebelled against the house of David
11. 1 which were warriors, to fight against I.
11. 3 and to all I. in Judah and Benjamin, saying
11. 13 the Levites that (were) in all I. resorted
11. 16 after them out of all the tribes of I.
13. 4 said, Hear me, thou Jeroboam, and all I.
13. 12 children of I., fight ye not against the
13. 15 that God smote Jeroboam and all I. before
13. 16 the children of I. fled before Judah: and
13. 17 there fell down slain of I. five hundred
13. 18 the children of I. were brought under at
15. 9 they fell to him out of I. in abundance
15. 17 high places were not taken away out of I.
16. 1 Baasha king of I. came up against Judah
16. 3 break thy league with Baasha king of I.
16. 4 sent..captains..against the cities of I.
16. 11 the book of the kings of Judah and I.
17. 1 and strengthened himself against I.
17. 4 and walked..not after the doings of I.
18. 3 Ahab king of I. said unto Jehoshaphat
18. 4 And Jehoshaphat said unto the king of I.
18. 5 king of I. gathered together of prophets
18. 7 the king of I. said unto Jehoshaphat, (There
18. 8 king of I. called for one (of his) officers
18. 9, 28 the king of I. and Jehoshaphat king
18. 16 see all I. scattered upon the mountains
18. 17 the king of I. said to Jehoshaphat, Did I
18. 19 Who shall entice Ahab king of I., that he
18. 25 the king of I. said, Take ye Micaiah, and
18. 29 the king of I. said unto Jehoshaphat, I
18. 29 the king of I. disguised himself; and they
18. 30 Fight ye..save only with the king of I.
18. 31 that they said, It (is) the king of I. Therefo.
18. 32 perceived that it was not the king of I.
18. 33 smote the king of I. between the joints
18. 34 the king of I. stayed (himself) up in (his)
20. 34 mentioned in the book of the kings of I.
20. 35 king..join himself with Amaziah king of I.
21. 2 (were) the sons of Jehoshaphat king of I.
21. 4 and slew..(divers) also of the princes of I.
21. 6 he walked in the way of the kings of I.
21. 13 hast walked in the way of the kings of I.
22. 5 with Jehoram the son of Ahab king of I. to
25. 6 thousand mighty men of valour out of I.
25. 7 let not the army of I. go with thee
25. 7 for the LORD (is) not with I...all the childr.
25. 9 which I have given to the army of I.?
25. 17 of Jehoahaz, the son of Jehu, king of I.
25. 18 Joash king of I. sent to Amaziah king of
25. 21 Joash the king of I. went up; and they
25. 22 Judah was put to the worse before I., and
25. 23 the king of I. took Amaziah king of Judah?
25. 25 death of Joash, son of Jehoahaz king of I.
25. 26 in the book of the kings of Judah and I.?
27. 7 in the book of the kings of I. and Judah
28. 2 he walked in the ways of the kings of I.
28. 5 delivered into the hand of the king of I.
28. 8 the children of I. carried away captive of
28. 13 and (there is) fierce wrath against I.
28. 19 brought Judah low because of..king of I.
28. 26 in the book of the kings of Judah and I.
30. 1 keep the passover unto the Lord GOD of I.
30. 6 throughout all I. and Judah,
30. 21 the children of I. that were present at
30. 25 the congregation..that came out of I., and
30. 25 strangers that came out of the land of I.
31. 6 (concerning) the children of I. and Judah
32. 32 in the book of the kings of Judah and I.
33. 18 written) in the book of the kings of I.
34. 9 the remnant of I., and of all Judah and
34. 21 for them that are left in I. and in Judah
35. 18 all Judah and I. that were present, and the
35. 18 neither did all the kings of I. keep such
35. 27 in the book of the kings of I. and Judah
36. 8 in the book of the kings of I. and Judah
Isa. 7. 1 king of I., went up toward Jerusalem to
Jer. 2. 26 As the thief..is the house of I. ashamed
2. 31 Have I been a wilderness unto I.? a land
3. 6 Hast thou seen (that) which backsliding I.
3. 8 whereby backsliding I. committed adult.
3. 11 backsliding I. hath justified herself more
3. 12 Return, thou backsliding I., saith the LO.
3. 18 house of Judah..walk with the house of I.
5. 11 the house of I. and the house of Judah
9. 26 house of I. (are) uncircumcised in the heart
11. 10 the house of I and the house of Judah
11. 17 for the evil of the house of I., and of the
23. 6 shall be saved, and I. shall dwell safely
31. 27 I will sow the house of I. and the house
31. 31 make a new covenant with the house of I.
32. 30 children of I. and the children of Judah
32. 32 Because of all the evil of the children of I.
41. 9 had made for fear of Baasha king of I.
48. 13 house of I. was ashamed of Beth-el their
50. 33 the children of I. and the children of
Eze. 4. 4 lay the iniquity of the house of I. upon it
4. 5 thou bear the iniquity of the house of I.
9. 9 The iniquity of the house of I. and Judah
27. 17 and the land of I., they (were) thy merch.
37. 16 Judah, and (for) all the children of I. his
44. 15 the children of I. went astray from me
Hos. 1. 1 Jeroboam the son of Joash, king of I., v. 11.
Zech. 1. 19 have scattered Judah, I., and Jerusalem
8. 13 O house of Judah, and house of I.; so will
11. 14 the brotherhood between Judah and I.
Mal. 2. 11 an abomination is committed in I. and in

IS-RA-EL-ITE, ISRAELITISH, יִשְׂרְאֵלִי ,יִשְׂרְאֵלִית ,יִשְׂרָאֵל, 'Ισραηλίτης.
One belonging to the tribes of Israel.
Exod. 9. 7 was not one of the cattle of the I. dead
Lev. 23. 42 all that are I. born shall dwell in booths
24. 10 the son of an I. woman, whose father (was)
24. 10 this son of the I. (woman) and a man of
24. 11 the I. woman's son blasphemed the name
Num 25. 14 the name of the I. that was slain, (even)
Josh. 3. 17 the I. passed over on dry ground, until
8. 24 the I. returned unto Ai, and smote it with
13. 6 divide thou it by lot unto the I. for an
13. 13 Maachathites dwell among the I. until this
Judg 20. 21 destroyed down to the ground of the I.
1 Sa. 2. 14 they did in Shiloh unto all the I. that
13. 20 the I. went down to the Philistines, to
14. 21 they also (turned) to be with the I. that
25. 1 the I. were gathered together, and lame.
29. 1 the I. pitched by a fountain which (is) in
2 Sa. 4. 1 were feeble, and all the I. were troubled
17. 25 an I., that went in to Abigail the daugh.
2 Ki. 3. 24 the I. rose up and smote the Moabites, so
7. 13 they (are)..as all the multitude of the I.
1 Ch. 9. 2 first inhabitants that (dwelt..were) the I.
John 1. 47 Behold an I. indeed, in whom is no guile!
Rom. 9. 4 Who are I.; to whom (pertaineth) the ad.
11. 1 I also am an I., of the seed of Abraham
2 Co. 11. 22 Are they I.? so (am) I. Are they the seed

IS-SA'-CHAR, יִשָּׂשכָר, 'Ισαχάρ, *bearing hire, reward.*
1. The invariable form of the name in Hebrew is *Isascar*, but the Masorites have pointed it so as to supersede the second *s*. He was the ninth son of Jacob and the fifth by Leah. Of Issachar as an individual not a word is recorded after his birth. B.C. 1746.
Gen. 30. 18 given me my hire..she called his name I.
35. 23 and Levi, and Judah, and I., and Zebulun
46. 13 the sons of I.; Tola, and Phuvah, and Job
49. 14 I. (is) a strong ass couching down between
Exod. 1. 3 I., Zebulun, and Benjamin
1 Ch. 2. 1 Simeon, Levi, and Judah, I., and Zebulun
7. 1 the sons of I. (were) Tola, and Puah, Jashub

2 The tribe that was descended from Issachar, as well as that allotment of Canaan which they inherited.
Num. 1. 8 Of I.; Nethaneel the son of Zuar
1. 28 Of the children of I., by their generations
1. 29 numbered of them, (even) of the tribe of I.
2. 5 pitch next unto him (shall be) the tribe of I.
2. 5 (shall be) captain of the children of I.
7. 18 Nethaneel the son of Zuar, prince of I.
10. 15 host of the tribe of the children of I. (was)
13. 7 Of the tribe of I., Igal the son of Joseph
26. 23 (Of) the sons of I., after their families: (of)
26. 25 These (are) the families of I. according to
34. 26 prince of the tribe of the children of I.
Deut. 27. 12 and Judah, and I., and Joseph, and Ben.
33. 18 in thy going out; and, I., in thy tents
Josh 17. 10 Asher on the north, and in I. on the east
17. 11 Manasseh had in I. and in Asher, Beth.
19. 17 lot came out to I., for the children of I.
19. 23 of the tribe of the children of I. according
21. 6 out of the families of the tribe of I., and
21. 28 out of the tribe of I., Kishon with her
Judg. 5. 15 princes of I. (were) with Deborah; even I.
10. 1 son of Puah, the son of Dodo, a man of I.
1 Ki. 4. 17 Jehoshaphat the son of Paruah in I.
15. 27 the son of Ahijah, of the house of I., con.
1 Ch. 6. 62 out of the tribe of I., and out of the tribe
6. 72 out of the tribe of I.; Kedesh with her
7. 5 brethren among all the families of I. (we.)
12. 32 the children of I., (which were men) that
12. 40 (even) unto I. and Zebulun and Naphtali
27. 18 of David: of I., Omri the son of Michael
2 Ch. 30. 18 I., and Zebulun, had not cleansed them.
Eze. 48. 25 east side unto the west side, I. a (portion)
48. 26 by the border of I., from the east side
48. 33 Simeon, one gate of I., one gate of Zebulun
Rev. 7. 7 Of the tribe of I. (were) sealed twelve thou.
The following localities were in the territory of Issachar:—Abez, Anaharath, Anem, Aphek, Beth-pazzez, Beth-shemesh, Chesulloth, En-gannim, En-haddah, Haphraim, Harod, Jarmuth, Jezreel, Kedesh, Megiddo, Rabbith, Shahazimah, Shikon, Shunem, &c.
3. A porter of the tabernacle in David's time. B.C. 1040.
1 Ch. 26. 5 sixth, I. the seventh, Peulthai the eighth

ISSHIAH. *See* **ISHIAH.**

ISSUE —

1. *A flowing*, זוֹב *zob.*
Lev. 15. 2 a running..(because of) his issue he (is)
15. 3 this shall be his uncleanness in his issue
15. 3 whether his flesh run with his issue, or
15. 3 his flesh be stopped from his issue, it (is)
15. 13 when he..is cleansed of his issue; then he
15. 15 shall make an atonement for him..his issue
15. 19 her issue in her flesh be blood, she shall
15. 25 all the days of the issue of her unclean.
15. 26 whereon she lieth all the days of her issue
15. 28 if she be cleansed of her issue, then she s.
15. 30 atonement..for the issue of her unclean.

2. *Flowing, issue*, זִרְמָה *zirmah.*
Eze. 23. 20 and whose issue (is like) the issue of horses

3. *Birth, what is born*, מוֹלֶדֶת *moledeth.*
Gen. 48. 6 And thy issue, which thou begettest after

4. *Fountain*, מָקוֹר *maqor.*
Lev. 12. 7 she shall be cleansed from the issue of her

5. *Issue, produce*, צְפִיעוֹת *tsephioth.*
Isa. 22. 24 the offspring and the issue, all vessels of

6. *Outgoings*, תּוֹצָאוֹת *totsaoth.*
Psa. 68. 20 unto GOD the Lord (belong) the issues from
Prov. 4. 23 keep thy heart..out of it (are) the issues

7. *A running, issue,* ῥύσις *rhusis.*
Mark 5. 25 a certain woman, which had an issue of
Luke 8. 43 a woman, having an issue of blood twelve
8. 44 immediately her issue of blood

8. *Seed,* σπέρμα *sperma.*
Matt 22. 25 having no issue, left his wife unto his br.

ISSUE, to —

1. *To go forth, issue,* נְגַד *negad,* 3.
Dan. 7. 10 a fiery stream issued and came forth from

2. *To pass out,* ἐκπορεύομαι *ekporeuomai.*
Rev. 9. 17 out of their mouths issued fire and smoke
9. 18 brimstone, which issued out of their mo.

ISSUE of blood, to be diseased with —

To run with blood, αἱμοῤῥοέω *haimorrhoeō.*
Matt. 9. 20 was diseased with an issue of blood twelve

ISSUE, to have a (running) —

To flow, issue, זוּב *zub.*
Lev. 15. 2 When any man hath a running issue out
15. 4 whereon he lieth that hath the issue is
15. 6 thing whereon he sat that hath the issue
15. 7 toucheth the flesh of him that hath the i.
15. 8 if he that hath the issue spit upon him
15. 9 saddle..he rideth upon that hath the issue
15. 11 whomsoever he toucheth that hath the i.
15. 12 vessel..he toucheth which hath the issue
15. 13 when he that hath an issue is cleansed of
15. 19 And if a woman have an issue, (and) her
15. 25 if a woman have an issue of her blood
15. 32 This (is) the law of him that hath an issue
15. 33 and of him that hath an issue, of the man
22. 4 What man soever..hath a running issue
Num. 5. 2 every one that hath an issue, and whoso.
2 Sa. 3. 29 one that hath an issue, or that is a leper

ISSUE out or from, to —

To go forth or out, יָצָא *yatsa.*
Josh. 8. 22 the other issued out of the city against
2 Ki. 20. 18 thy sons that shall issue from thee, which
Job 38. 8 when it brake forth..it had issued out of
Isa. 39. 7 of thy sons that shall issue from thee
Eze. 47. 1 waters issued out from under the thresh.
47. 8 These waters issue out toward the; 47. 12.

ISUAH, ISUI. *See* **ISHUAH, ISHUI.**

IT —

1. *He, it,* הוּא *hu.*
Gen. 3. 6 and that it (was) pleasant to the eyes, and

2. *She, it,* הִיא *hi.*
Gen. 19. 20 this city (is) near to flee unto, and it (is)
Dan. 2. 44 set up a kingdom..and it shall stand for
7. 7 and it (was) diverse from all the beasts

3. *They,* הֵם *hem.*
Psa. 38. 10 the light of mine eyes, it also is gone

4. *This,* זֹאת *zoth.*
Num 14. 35 I will surely do it unto all this evil cong.
1 Ch. 27. 24 because there fell wrath for it against Is.

5. *This,* זֶה *zeh.*
Gen. 32. 29 Wherefore (is) it (that) thou dost ask after

6. *This,* זֹה *zoh.*
Eccl. 2. 2 I said..mad; and of mirth, What doeth it

7. *Her face,* פָּנֶיהָ *paneha.*
Exod 25. 37 that they may give light over against it

8. *He, he himself,* αὐτός *autos.*
Matt 10. 11 enquire who in it is worthy; and there
John 8. 44 own: for he is a liar, and the father of it

9. *That one,* ἐκεῖνος *ekeinos.*
1 Jo. 5. 16 sin..I do not say that he shall pray for it

10. *This one,* οὗτος *houtos.*
Mark 6. 16 [It is] John, whom I beheaded: he is risen

11. *By this,* ἐν ταύτῃ *en tautē;* ταύτην *tautēn.*
Heb. 11. 2 For by it the elders obtained; 1 Co. 6. 13.

12. *This, that,* τοῦτο *touto.*
Matt 12. 11 if it fall into a pit on the sabbath day
Mark 5. 43 charged them..no man should know it
14. 5 For it might have been sold for more than
Luke 18. 36 And hearing..he asked what it meant
Heb. 13. 17 they may do it with joy, and not with gr.

13. *Of this, of that,* τούτου *toutou.*
John 6. 61 knew..that his disciples murmured at it

IT, of —

Of him, of it, αὐτοῦ *autou.*
Rev. 8. 12 the day shone not for a third part of it

IT be —

1. *It is, there is,* אִיתַי *ithai.*
Ezra 5. 17 whether it be (so), that a decree was made

2. *It is, there is,* יֵשׁ *yesh.*
Gen. 23. 8 If it be your mind that I should bury my
1 Sa. 14. 39 though it be in Jonathan my son, he shall
2 Ki. 9. 15 Jehu said, If it be your minds..let none
10. 15 If it be, give..thine hand. And he gave

IT is —

It is, there is, יֵשׁ *yesh.*
Gen. 31. 29 It is in the power of my hand to do you
2 Ki. 10. 15 And Jehonadab answered, It is. If it be

IT was —

It is, there is, יֵשׁ *yesh.*
Num. 9. 20 And (so) it was, when the cloud was a few
9. 21 And (so) it was, when the cloud abode fr.

ITALIAN, Ἰταλικός *belonging to Italy.*
Acts 10. 1 centurion of the band called the Italian

ITALY, Ἰταλία.
The country of which Rome is the capital; it has the Alps on the N., the Mediterranean on the S., Gulf of Venice on the E., and France and the Mediterranean on the W. In 2450 B.C. the mythic reign of Saturn is said to begin; in 1710 a colony of Arcadians, under Œnotrus, settle in Italy and found the state of Magna Graecia; in 1293 a Pelasgian colony passes from Greece into Italy; in 1253 Evander leads an Arcadian colony into Italy; in 1240 Latinus reigns; in 1181 Æneas arriving, founds Lavinia; in 1152 Ascanius builds Alba Longa; in 895 Tiberinus being defeated, drowns himself in the Albula, whence called the Tiber; in 753 (April 21), Romulus founds Rome; in A.D. 476 Odoacer abolishes the W. empire, and founds the Gothic kingdom of Italy.
Acts 18. 2 lately come from I., with his wife Priscilla
27. 1 determined that we should sail into I.
27. 6 found a ship of Alexandria sailing into I.
Heb. 13. 24 Salute all them..They of I. salute you

ITCH —

Heat, sun, itch, חֶרֶס *cheres.*
Deut 28. 27 emerods, and with the scab, and with the i.

ITCHING, to have —

To itch, κνήθομαι *knēthomai.*
2 Ti. 4. 3 shall they heap..teachers, having itching

I-THAI, אִיתַי *being, existing.*
One of David's thirty valiant men. In 2 Sam. 23. 29 he is called *Ittai.* B.C. 1048.
1 Ch. 11. 31 I. the son of Ribai of Gibeah, (that perta.)

I-THA'-MAR, אִיתָמָר.
The youngest son of Aaron. B.C. 1491.
Exod 6. 23 bare him Nadab, and Abihu, Eleazar, and I.
28. 1 and Abihu, Eleazar and I., Aaron's sons
38. 21 by the hand of I., son to Aaron the priest
Lev. 10. 6, 12 unto Aaron, and..Eleazar and unto I.
10. 16 he was angry with Eleazar and I., the sons
Num. 3. 2 the first born, and Abihu, Eleazar, and I.
3. 4 I. ministered in the priest's office in the
4. 28 their charge (shall be) under the hand of I.
4. 33 under the hand of I. the son of Aaron the
7. 8 the hand of I. the son of Aaron the priest
26. 60 born Nadab and Abihu, Eleazar and I.
1 Ch. 6. 3 Aaron; Nabab..Abihu, Eleazar, and I.
24. 1 of Aaron; Nadab..Abihu, Eleazar, and I.
24. 2 Eleazar and I. executed the priest's office
24. 3 Ahimelech of the sons of I., according to
24. 4 there were more..than of the sons of I.
24. 4 eight among the sons of I. according to
24. 5 the sons of Eleazar, and of the sons of I.
24. 6 taken for Eleazar, and (one) taken for I.
Ezra 8. 2 of the sons of I.; Daniel: of the sons of

I-THI'-EL, אִיתִיאֵל *God is.*
1. A Benjamite, the son of Jesaiah. B.C. 536.
Neh. 11. 7 Maaseiah, the son of I., the son of Jesaiah
2. One of the two persons to whom *Agur* delivered his discourse.
Prov. 30. 1 the man speak unto I., even unto I. and

ITH'-MAH, יִתְמָה *purity.*
A Moabite, and one of the thirty valiant men of David's guard. B.C. 1048.
1 Ch. 11. 46 the sons of Elnaam, and I. the Moabite

ITH'-NAN, יִתְנָן *strong place.*
A town in the extreme S. of Judah, on the borders of the desert if not actually in it.
Josh 15. 23 And Kedesh, and Hazor, and I.

ITH'-RA, יִתְרָא *excellence.*
The father of Absalom's captain Amasa. B.C. 1048. He is called also *Jether* (1 Kings 2. 5).
2 Sa. 17. 25 a man's son whose name (was) I., an Isra.

ITH'-RAN, יִתְרָן *excellent.*
1. A son of Dishon (or Dishan), son of Seir the Horite. B.C. 1700.
Gen. 36. 26 Hemdan, and Eshban, and I., and Cheran
1 Ch. 1. 41 Amram, and Eshban, and I., and Cheran
2. A son of Zophah an Ashorite. B.C. 1550.
1 Ch. 7. 37 Shamma, and Shilshah, and I., and Beera

ITH-RE'-AM, יִתְרְעָם *remnant of the people.*
Sixth son of David by his wife Eglah. He was born at Hebron. Eglah was *Michal,* and died in giving birth to Ithream. B.C. 1046.
2 Sa. 3. 5 And the sixth, I., by Eglah, David's wife
1 Ch. 3. 3 fifth, Shephatiah of Abital; the sixth, I.

ITH-RITES, יִתְרִי *belonging to Jether.*
The patronymic of the family of Jether. The designation of two of the members of David's guard—Ira and Gareb—who belonged to Judah. Those heroes may have come from Jattir in the mountains of Judah where David had friends.
2 Sa. 23. 38 Ira an I., Gareb an I.
1 Ch. 2. 53 the I., and the Puhites, and the Shuma.
11. 40 Ira the I., Gareb the I.

ITSELF, (of) —

1. *This,* זֶה *zeh.*
Psa. 68. 8 Sinai itself..at the presence of God, the

2. *He, he himself,* αὐτός *autos.*
Rom. 8. 16 the spirit itself beareth witness with our
8. 21 the creature itself also shall be delivered
8. 26 the spirit itself maketh intercession for
1 Co. 11. 14 Doth not even nature [itself] teach you, th.
3 John 12 hath good report of all..of the truth itself

3. *Of one's self,* ἑαυτοῦ *heautou.*
Matt. 6. 34 shall take thought for the things of itself
12. 25 Every kingdom divided against itself is b.
12. 25 every city or house divided against itself
Mark 3. 24 if a kingdom be divided against itself, that
3. 25 if a house be divided against itself, that
Luke 11. 17 Every kingdom divided against itself is
John 15. 4 As the branch cannot bear fruit of itself
Eph. 4. 16 maketh increase..unto the edifying of itse.
Rom 14. 14 that (there is) nothing unclean [of itself]

ITSELF, by —

Apart, χωρίς *chōris.*
John 20. 7 but wrapped together in a place by itself

ITSELF, dead of —

Fallen thing, carcase, dead body, נְבֵלָה *nebelah.*
Eze. 44. 31 of any thing that is dead of itself, or torn

ITSELF, dieth of —[*See* Dieth of, growth of itself.]

IT-TAH KA'-ZIN, עִתָּה קָצִין *kindred of the extremity.*
A landmark of the boundary of Zebulun, near Gath-hepher (Gattah-hepher).
Josh 19. 13 thence passeth on along on the east to..I.

IT'-TAI, אִתַּי *being, living.*
1. The Gittite (or inhabitant of Gath), a Philistine in David's army when he fled from Jerusalem in Absalom's rebellion. B.C. 1048.
2 Sa. 15. 19 Then said the king to I. the Gittite, Wh.
15. 21 I. answered the king, and said, (As) the L.
15. 22 David said to I., Go and pass over. And I.
18. 2 a third part under the hand of I. the Git.
18. 5 king commanded Joab and Abishai and I.
18. 12 the king charged thee and Abishai and I.
2. A son of Ribai, a valiant Benjamite in David's army. He is called *Ithai* in 1 Ch. 11. 31.
2 Sa. 23. 29 I. the son of Ribai out of Gibeah of..Be.

I-TU-RE'-A, Ἰτουραία *Ituræa.*
A small province in the N.W. border of Palestine lying along the base of Mount Hermon. It probably derived its name from *Jetur* a son of Ishmael. The tribe of Manasseh having conquered it, dwelt in the land, and increased from Bashan unto Baal-hermon.
Luke 3. 1 his brother Philip tetrarch of I. and of

I'-VAH, עִוָּה *hamlet, or the god Iva, sky.*
A district in Babylonia conquered by the Assyrians near Cuthah, probably identical with *Hit,*—the Is of Herodotus on the Euphrates between *Sippara* (Sepharvaim) and *Anah* (Hena), with which it was politically united before the time of Sennacherib. It is probably the *Ahava* of Ezra 8. 15. See *Ava* or *Avva.*
2 Ki. 18. 34 the gods of Sepharvaim, Hena, and I.?
19. 13 (is) the king of Hamath..Hena, and I.?
Isa. 37. 13 (is) the king of Hamath..Hena, and I.?

IVORY —

1. *A tooth, ivory,* שֵׁן *shen.*
1 Ki. 10. 18 the king made a great throne of ivory, and
22. 39 the ivory house which he made, and all
2 Ch. 9. 17 the king made a great throne of ivory, and
Psa. 45. 8 out of the ivory palaces, whereby they
Song 5. 14 (is as) bright ivory overlaid (with) sapph.
7. 4 thy neck (is) as a tower of ivory: thine
Eze. 27. 6 have made thy benches (of) ivory..out of
27. 15 brought thee..a present horns of ivory
Amos 3. 15 the houses of ivory shall perish, and the
6. 4 That lie upon beds of ivory, and stretch

2. *Elephant's tooth, ivory,* שֶׁנְהַבִּים *shenhabbim.*
1 Ki. 10. 22 bringing gold, and silver, ivory, and apes
2 Ch. 9. 21 bringing gold, and silver, ivory, and apes

3. *Made of ivory,* ἐλεφάντινος *elephantinos.*
Rev. 18. 12 all manner vessels of ivory, and all man.

IZ'-HAR, IZE-HAR, יִצְהָר *shining.*
A son of Kohath, and grandson of Levi. B.C. 1491.
Exod. 6. 18 sons of Kohath; Amram, and I., and He.
6. 21 the sons of I.; Korah, and Nepheg, and Z.
Num. 3. 19 And the sons of Kohath..Amram, and I.
16. 1 Korah, the son of I., the son of Kohath
1 Ch. 6. 2 sons of Kohath; Amram, I., and Hebron
6. 18 the sons of Kohath (were) Amram, and I.
6. 38 The son of I., the son of Kohath, the son
23. 12 The son of Kohath; Amram, I., Hebron
23. 18 Of the sons of I.; Shelomith the chief

IZ-HAR-ITES, יִצְהָרִי *belonging to Izhar.*
Family of Izhar, son of Kohath (Num. 3. 27, Izeharites).
Num. 3. 27 of Kohath (was)..the family of the I., and
1 Ch. 24. 22 Of the I.; Shelomith: of the sons of Shelo.
26. 23 Of the Amramites, (and) the I., the Heb.
26. 29 Of the I., Chenaniah and his sons (were)

IZ-RAH'-IAH יִזְרַחְיָה *Jah (is) appearing.*
A grandson of Tola son of Issachar. B.C. 1600. See *Jezrahiah.*
1 Ch. 7. 3 sons of Uzzi; I.: and the sons of I.; Mic.

IZ-RAH-ITE, יִזְרָח.
The patronymic of Shamhuth, one of David's thirty valiant men. B.C. 1048.
1 Ch. 27. 8 for the fifth month (was) Shamhuth the I.

IZ'-RI, יִצְרִי *creator, former.*
Perhaps the same as *Zeri* (1 Ch. 35. 3), a Levite set over the service of song by David. B.C. 1015.
1 Ch. 25. 11 fourth to I., (he), his sons, and his breth

J

JA-A'-KAN, JA'-KAN, יַעֲקָן *intelligent.*
He is called *Akan* in Gen. 36. 27; a son of Ezer son of Seir. B.C. 1780.
Deut 10. 6 from Beeroth of the children of J. to Mo.
1 Ch. 1. 42 sons of Ezer; Bilhan, and Zavan, (and) J.

JA-A-KO'-BAH, יַעֲקֹבָה *to Jacob.*
A descendant of Simeon, third son of Jacob. B.C. 1048.
1 Ch. 4. 36 Elioenai, and J., and Jeshohaiah, and A.

JA-A'-LA, *Ja-a'-lah,* יַעֲלָא, יַעֲלָה *elevation.*
A servant of Solomon whose descendants returned from exile with Zerubbabel. B.C. 536.
Ezra 2. 56 The children of J., the children of Darkon
Neh. 7. 58 The children of J., the children of Darkon

JAA'-LAM, יַעְלָם.
A son of Seir by Aholibamah, daughter of Anah. B.C. 1740.
Gen. 36. 5 Aholibamah bare Jeush, and J., and Ko.
36. 14 she bare to Esau Jeush, and J., and Korah
36. 18 duke Jeush, duke J., duke Korah: these
1 Ch. 1. 35 The sons of Esau..Jeush, and J., and K.

JAA'-NAI, יַעְנַי *answerer.*
A Gadite that dwelt in Bashan. B.C. 1070.
1 Ch. 5. 12 Joel the chief..and J., and Shaphat in B.

JA-A-RE O-RE'-GIM, יַעְרֵי אֹרְגִים *foresters.*
The father of Elhanan who killed the brother of Goliath of Gath. B.C. 1080. OREGIM, "weavers," ought not to be a part of the name. In 1 Ch. 20. 5 he is called *Jair.*
2 Sa. 21. 19 where Elhanan the son of J., a Bethlehe.

JA-A'-SAU, יַעֲשַׂי *maker* [V.L. יעשו].
One of the family of Bani who had taken a strange wife after the captivity. B.C. 457.
Ezra 10. 37 Mattaniah, Mattenai, and J.

JA-A-SI'-EL, JA-SI'-EL, יַעֲשִׂיאֵל *God is maker.*
1. One of David's valiant men. B.C. 1048.
1 Ch. 11. 47 Eliel, and Obed, and J. the Mesobaite
2. A son of Abner, Saul's cousin. B.C. 1015.
1 Ch. 27. 21 son of Zechariah: of Benjamin; J. the son

JA-A-ZAN'-IAH, יַאֲזַנְיָה, יַאֲזַנְיָהוּ *Jah is hearing.*
1. A Jewish captain, and a Maachathite. B.C. 588.
2 Ki. 25. 23 J. the son of a Maachathite, they and their
2. A chief Rechabite. B.C. 600.
Jer. 35. 3 Then I took J. the son of Jeremiah, the
3. A visionary exciting to idolatry. B.C. 594.
Eze. 8. 11 in the midst of them stood J. the son of
4. A wicked prince of Judah seen in vision by Ezekiel. B.C. 594.
Eze. 11. 1 among whom I saw J. the son of Azur, and

JA-A'-ZER, JA'-ZER, יַעְזֵר, יַעֲזֵיר *fortified.*
A city in Gilead, wrested from the Ammonites, allotted to Gad, and given to the Levites. It afterwards fell to Moab, and was celebrated for its wine. It is now in ruins, and called Szir six hours from *Heshbon,* and four from *Rabbah.*
Num 21. 32 Moses sent to spy out J., and they took
32. 1 when they saw the land of J., and the
32. 3 Ataroth, and Dibon, and J., and Nimrah
32. 35 And Atroth, Shophan, and J., and Jogbe.
Josh 13. 25 their coast was J., and all the cities of G.
21. 39 Heshbon with her suburbs, J. with her
2 Sa. 24. 5 midst of the river of Gad, and toward J.
1 Ch. 6. 81 Hesbon with her suburbs, and J. with her
26. 31 there were found..mighty men..at J. of
Isa. 16. 8 they are come (even) unto J., they wand.
16. 9 I will bewail with the weeping of J. the
Jer. 48. 32 will weep for thee with the weeping of J.
48. 32 they reach (even) to the sea of J.: the sp.

JA-A-ZI'AH, יַעֲזִיָּהוּ *Jah is determining.*
A descendant of Merari in the days of Solomon. B.C. 1010.
1 Ch. 24. 26 Mahli and Mushi: the sons of J.; Beno
24. 27 The sons of Merari by J.; Beno, and Sho.

JA-A-ZI'-EL, יַעֲזִיאֵל *God is determining.*
A Levite in the time of David. B.C. 1015. He is called *Aziel* in 1 Ch. 15. 20.
1 Ch. 15. 18 Zechariah, Ben, and J., and Shemiramoth

JA'-BAL, יָבָל *moving.*
A son of Adah, one of Lamech's wives. B.C. 3870.
Gen. 4. 20 Adah bare J.: he was the father of such

JAB'-BOK, יַבֹּק *running, flowing.*
A small brook rising in the hills of Bashan, forming the border of Ammon towards Israel, opposite Shechem, and falling into the Jordan midway between the Dead Sea and the Sea of Tiberias. Now called *Wady Zerka.*
Gen. 32. 22 he rose up..and passed over the ford J.
Num 21. 24 and possessed his land from Arnon unto J.
Deut. 2. 37 camest not..unto any place of the river J.
3. 16 the border even unto the river J., (which
Josh 12. 2 Sihon..ruled..even unto the river J.
Judg 11. 13 Israel took away my land..even unto J.
11. 22 they possessed all the coasts..even unto J.

JA'-BESH, יָבֵשׁ *dry place.*
1. The abbreviated name of Jabesh-Gilead.
1 Sa. 11. 1 all the men of J. said unto Nahash, Make a
11. 3 the elders of J. said unto him; Give us
11. 5 they told him the tidings of the men of J.
1 Sa. 11. 9 came and showed (it) to the men of J.; and
11. 10 Therefore the men of J. said, To morrow
31. 12 All the valiant men arose..and came to J.
31. 13 they..buried (them) under a tree at J.
1 Ch. 10. 12 They arose..and brought them to J.
10. 12 and buried their bones under the oak in J.
2. The father of Shallum who slew Zechariah and reigned in his stead. B.C. 810.
2 Ki. 15. 10 Shallum the son of J. conspired against him
15. 13 Shallum the son of J. began to reign in the
15. 14 Menahem..smote Shallum the son of J. in

JA-BESH GIL'-EAD, יָבֵשׁ גִּלְעָד *or* יָבֵישׁ.
A city in Gad, on a river of the same name, near Beth-shean, six miles from Pella towards Gerasha. Its name is preserved in the *Wady Jabes (or Yabes),* which enters the Jordan below Bethshan and Scythopolis. Perhaps *Ed-Deir* on the S. of the Wady still marks its site.
Judg 21. 8 behold, there came..to the camp from J.
21. 9 (there were) none of the inhabitants of J.
21. 10 Go and smite the inhabitants of J. with
21. 12 And they found among..inhabitants of J.
21. 14 they had saved alive of the women of J.
1 Sa. 11. 1 the Ammonite..encamped against J.: and
11. 9 Thus shall ye say unto the men of J., To m.
31. 11 when the inhabitants of J. heard of that
2 Sa. 2. 4 the men of J. (were they) that buried Sa.
2. 5 David sent messengers unto the men of J.
21. 12 took..the bones..from the men of J., wh.
1 Ch. 10. 11 J. heard all that the Philistines had done

JA-BEZ, יַעְבֵּץ *height.*
1. A city of Judah; but not yet identified.
1 Ch. 2. 55 families of the scribes which dwelt at J.
2. The head of a family of the tribe of Judah. B.C 1444.
1 Ch. 4. 9 J. was more honourable than his brethren
4. 9 his mother called his name J., saying, Be.
4. 10 J. called on the God of Israel, saying, Oh

JA'-BIN, יָבִין *intelligent.*
1. A king of Hazor, defeated by Joshua near the Lake Merom. B.C. 1450.
Josh. 11. 1 when J. king of Hazor had heard (those
2. Another king of Hazor, who oppressed Israel for twenty years; and whose army was defeated by Deborah and Barak. B.C. 1316.
Judg. 4. 2 the LORD sold them into the hand of J.
4. 7 I will draw unto thee..the captain of J.'s
4. 17 (there was) peace between J. the king of
4. 23 God subdued on that day J. the king of C.
4. 24 Israel prospered, and prevailed against J.
4. 24 until they had destroyed J. king of Canaan
Psa. 83. 9 as (to) Sisera, as (to) J., at the brook of K.

JAB-NE'-EL, יַבְנְאֵל *God is builder.*
1. A city in the S.W. of Judah, now called *Jebna,* one hour N.W. of *Akar* or Ekron.
Josh. 15. 11 and the border..went out unto J.; and
2. A border city of Naphtali S. of the Sea of Galilee; it is called *Jamnia* or *Jamnih* by Josephus.
Josh. 19. 33 And their coast was from..J., unto Lakum

JAB'-NEH, יַבְנֶה *building.*
A Philistine city between Joppa and Ashdod, afterwards called *Jamnia* or *Jamneia,* 240 stadia from Jerusalem, and 12 miles from Diospolis on the Mediterranean, now called *Jebna,* 2 miles from the sea shore.
2 Ch 26. 6 the wall of J., and the wall of Ashdod, and

JA'-CHAN, יַעְכָּן *afflicting.*
The head of a Gadite family. B.C. 1100.
1 Ch. 5. 13 and Jorai, and J., and Zia, and Heber, sev.

JA'-CHIN, יָכִין *founding.*
1. A son of Simeon. B.C. 1700. Called *Jarib,* 1 Ch. 4. 24.
Gen. 46. 10 and J., and Zohar, and Shaul the son of a
Exod. 6. 15 and J., and Zohar, and Shaul the son of a
Num 26. 12 of J., the family of the Jachinites
2. The name of a pillar in Solomon's temple.
1 Ki. 7. 21 right pillar, and called the name thereof J.
2 Ch. 3. 17 called the name of that on..right hand J.
3. A priest in Jerusalem after the captivity. B.C. 445.
1 Ch. 9. 10 the priests; Jedaiah, and Jehoiarib, and J.
Neh. 11. 10 the priests: Jedaiah the son of Joiarib, J.
4. A head of one of the families of the sons of Aaron. B.C. 1015.
1 Ch. 24. 17 The one and twentieth to J., the two and

JA-CHI-NITE, הַיָּכִינִי *the Jachinite.*
The patronymic of the family of Jachin, a Simeonite.
Num 26. 12 of Jachin, the family of the J.

JACINTH, or of JACINTH —
Jacinth, ὑάκινθος *huakinthos,* ὑακίνθινος *huakinthi.*
Rev. 9. 17 having breastplates of fire, and of jacinth
21. 20 the eleventh, a jacinth; the twelfth, an

JA'-COB, יַעֲקֹב, *following after, supplanter,* Ἰακώβ.
1. The second son of Isaac and Rebekah, and a twin brother of Esau. B.C. 1770.
Gen. 25. 26 on Esau's heel; and his name was called J.
25. 27 and J. (was) a plain man, dwelling in tents
25. 28 Isaac loved Esau..but Rebekah loved J.
25. 29 J. sod pottage: and Esau came from the
25. 30 Esau said to J., Feed me, I pray thee, with
25. 31 J. said, Sell me this day thy birth right
25. 33 J. said, Swear to me this day; and he sware
25. 33 and he sold his birth right unto J.
25. 34 J. gave Esau bread and pottage of lentiles
27. 6 Rebekah spake unto J. her son, saying
27. 11 J. said to Rebekah his mother, Behold, E.
Gen. 27. 15 and put them upon J. her younger son
27. 17 and the bread..into the hand of her son J.
27. 19 J. said unto his father, I (am) Esau thy
27. 21 Isaac said unto J., Come near, I pray thee
27. 22 J. went near unto Isaac his father; and
27. 22 The voice (is) J.'s voice, but the hands (are)
27. 30 had made an end of blessing J., and J.
27. 36 Is not he rightly named J.? for he hath
27. 41 Esau hated J. because of the blessing
27. 41 are at hand; then will I slay my brother J.
27. 42 called J. her younger son, and said unto
27. 46 if J. take a wife of the daughters of Heth
28. 1 Isaac called J., and blessed him, and char.
28. 5 Isaac sent away J.: and he went to Padan
28. 5 brother of Rebekah, J.'s and Esau's moth.
28. 6 Esau saw that Isaac had blessed J., and
28. 7 J. obeyed his father and his mother, and
28. 10 J. went out from Beer-sheba and went
28. 16 J. awaked out of his sleep, and he said
28. 18 J. rose up early in the morning, and took
28. 20 J. vowed a vow, saying, If God will be
29. 1 J. went on his journey, and came into the
29. 4 J. said unto them, My brethren, whence
29. 10 J. saw Rachel the daughter of Laban his
29. 10 J. went near, and rolled the stone from
29. 11 J. kissed Rachel, and lifted up his voice
29. 12 J. told Rachel that he (was) her father's
29. 13 heard the tidings of J. his sister's son
29. 15 Laban said unto J., Because thou (art) my
29. 18 J. loved Rachel; and said, I will serve
29. 20 J. served seven years for Rachel; and
29. 21 J. said unto Laban, Give (me) my wife, for
29. 28 J. did so, and fulfilled her week: and
30. 1 Rachel saw that she bare J. no children
30. 1 said unto J., Give me children, or else I
30. 2 J.'s anger was kindled against Rachel
30. 4 handmaid to wife: and J. went in unto
30. 5 And Bilhah conceived, and bare J. a son
30. 7 conceived again, and bare J. a second son
30. 9 Zilpah her maid, and gave her J. to wife
30. 10 And Zilpah, Leah's maid, bare J. a son
30. 12 And Zilpah, Leah's maid, bare J. a second
30. 16 J. came out of the field in the evening
30. 17 she conceived, and bare J. the fifth son
30. 19 conceived again, and bare J. the sixth son
30. 25 J. said unto Laban, Send me away, that I
30. 31 J. said, Thou shalt not give me anything
30. 36 journey betwixt himself and J.: and J.
30. 37 J. took him rods of green poplar, and of
30. 40 J. did separate the lambs, and set the faces
30. 41 J. laid the rods before the eyes of the
30. 42 feebler were Laban's, and the stronger J.'s
31. 1 J. hath taken away all that (was) our fa.
31. 2 J. beheld the countenance of Laban, and
31. 3 the LORD said unto J., Return unto the
31. 4 J. sent and called Rachel and Leah to the
31. 11 angel..spake unto me in a dream, (say.), J.
31. 17 J. rose up, and set his sons and his wives
31. 20 J. stole away unawares to Laban the Sy.
31. 22 told Laban on the third day that J...fled
31. 24, 29 thou speak not to J. either good or
31. 25 Laban overtook J. Now J. had pitched
31. 26 Laban said to J., What hast thou done
31. 31 J. answered and said to Laban, Because I
31. 32 J. knew not that Rachel had stolen them
31. 33 Laban went into J.'s tent, and into Leah's
31. 36 J. was wroth..chode with Laban: and J.
31. 43 And Laban answered and said unto J.
31. 45 J. took a stone, and set it up (for) a pillar
31. 46 J. said unto his brethren, Gather stones
31. 47 Jegar-saha-dutha: but J. called it Galeed
31. 51 Laban said to J. Behold this heap, and
31. 53 J. sware by the fear of his father Isaac
31. 54 J. offered sacrifice upon the mount, and
32. 1 J. went on his way, and the angels of God
32. 2 when J. saw them, he said, This (is) God's
32. 3 J. sent messengers before him to Esau
32. 4 J. saith thus, I have sojourned with Lab.
32. 6 the messengers returned to J., saying, We
32. 7 J. was greatly afraid and distressed: and
32. 9 J. said, O God of my father Abraham, and
32. 18 (They be) thy servant J.'s; it (is) a present
32. 20 J. (is) behind us. For he said, I will ap.
32. 24 J. was left alone; and there wrestled a
32. 25 the hollow of J.'s thigh was out of joint
32. 27 said..What (is) thy name? And he said, J.
32. 28 Thy name shall be called no more J., but
32. 29 J. asked (him), and said, Tell (me), I pray
32. 30 J. called the name of the place Peniel
32. 32 he touched the hollow of J.'s thigh in
33. 1 J. lifted up his eyes, and looked, and
33. 10 J. said, Nay, I pray thee, if now I have
33. 17 J. journeyed to Succoth, and built him an
33. 18 J. came to Shalem a city of Shechem
34. 1 daughter of Leah, which she bare unto J.
34. 3 soul clave unto Dinah the daughter of J.
34. 5 J. heard that he had defiled Dinah his
34. 5 J. held his peace until they were come
34. 6 went out unto J. to commune with him
34. 7 the sons of J. came out of the field when
34. 7 wrought folly..in lying with J.'s daugh.
34. 13 the sons of J. answered Shechem and H.
34. 19 he had delight in J.'s daughter: and he
34. 25 that two of the sons of J., Simeon and L.
34. 27 The sons of J. came upon the slain, and
34. 30 J. said to Simeon and Levi, Ye have tro.
35. 1 God said unto J., Arise, go up to Beth-el
35. 2 J. said unto his household, and to all
35. 4 they gave unto J. all the strange gods
35. 4 J. hid them under the oak which (was)
35. 5 they did not pursue after the sons of J.
35. 6 J. came to Luz, which (is) in the land of

Gen. 35. 9 God appeared unto J. again, when he came
35. 10 J...name shall not be called any more J.
35. 14 J. set up a pillar in the place where he
35. 15 J. called the name of the place where G.
35. 20 J. set a pillar upon her grave: that (is)
35. 22 Now the sons of J. were twelve
35. 23 J.'s first born, and Simeon, and Levi, and
35. 26 these (are) the sons of J., which were born
35. 27 J. came unto Isaac his father unto Mamre
35. 29 died..and his sons Esau and J. buried
36. 6 and went..from the face of..J.
37. 1 J. dwelt in the land wherein his father
37. 2 These (are) the generations of J. Joseph
37. 34 J. rent his clothes, and put sackcloth upon
42. 1 J. saw that there was corn in Egypt, J.
42. 4 Benjamin..J. sent not with his brethren
42. 29 they came unto J. their father unto the
42. 36 J. their father said unto them, Me have
45. 25 and came into..Canaan unto J. their fat.
45. 26 J.'s heart fainted, for he believed them
45. 27 the spirit of J. their father revived
46. 2 in the visions of the night, and said, J., J.
46. 5 And J. rose up from Beer-sheba
46. 5 the sons of Israel carried J. their father
46. 6 into Egypt, J., and all his seed with him
46. 8 into Egypt, J. and his sons: Reuben, J.'s
46. 15 sons..which she bare unto J. in Padan-a.
46. 18 these she bare unto J., (even) sixteen so.
46. 19 The sons of Rachel, J.'s wife; Joseph
46. 22 the sons of Rachel, which were born to J.
46. 25 she bare these unto J.: all the souls (we.)
46. 26 the souls that came with J. into Egypt
46. 26 besides J.'s sons' wives, all the souls (we.)
46. 27 the souls of the house of J., which came
47. 7 Joseph brought in J. his father, and set
47. 7, 10 before Pharaoh: and J. blessed Pha.
47. 8 And Pharaoh said unto J., How old (art)
47. 9 J. said unto Pharaoh, The days of the
47. 28 J. lived in the land of Egypt seventeen
47. 28 the whole age of J. was an hundred forty
48. 2 (one) told J., and said, Behold, thy son J.
48. 3 J. said unto Joseph, God Almighty appe.
49. 1 J. called unto his sons, and said, Gather
49. 2 hear, ye sons of J.; and hearken unto Is.
49. 7 I will divide them in J., and scatter them
49. 24 strong by..hands of the mighty (G.) of J.
49. 33 J. had made an end of commanding his
50. 24 he sware to Abraham, to Isaac, and to J.
Exod. 1. 1 every man and his household came with J.
1. 5 souls that came out of the loins of J.
2. 24 with Abraham, with Isaac, and with J.
3. 6 I (am)..God of Isaac, and the God of J.
3. 15 and the God of J., hath sent me unto you
3. 16 the God of Abraham, of Isaac, and of J.
4. 5 and the God of J., hath appeared unto
6. 3 appeared unto Abraham..Isaac, and..J.
6. 8 to give it to Abraham, to Isaac, and to J.
19. 3 Thus shalt thou say to the house of J., and
33. 1 I sware unto Abraham, to Isaac, and to J.
Lev. 26. 42 Then will I remember my covenant with J.
Num32. 11 sware unto Abraham, unto Isaac, and..J.
Deut. 1. 8 unto your fathers, Abraham, Isaac, and J.
6. 10 fathers, to Abraham, to Isaac, and to J.
9. 5 unto thy fathers, Abraham, Isaac, and J.
9. 27 Remember thy servants, Ab. Isaac, and J.
29. 13 fathers, to Abraham, to Isaac, and to J.
30. 20 fathers, to Abraham, to Isaac, and to J.
34. 4 sware unto Abraham, unto Isaac, and..J.
Josh 24. 4 I gave unto Isaac J. and Esau: and I gave
24. 4 J. and his children went down into Egypt
24. 32 a parcel of ground which J. bought of the
1 Sa. 12. 8 When J. was come into Egypt, and your
2 Ki. 13. 23 his covenant with Abraham, Isaac, and J.
Mal. 1. 2 J.'s brother? saith the LORD; yet I loved J.
Matt. 1. 2 Isaac begat J.; and J. begat Judas and
8. 11 sit down with Abraham, and Isaac, and J.
22. 32 and the God of Isaac, and the God of J.?
Mark12. 26 and the God of Isaac, and the God of J.?
Luke 1. 33 shall reign over the house of J. for ever
3. 34 Which was (the son) of J., which was (the
13. 28 J., and all the prophets, in the kingdom
20. 37 and the God of Isaac, and the God of J.
John 4. 5 of ground that J. gave to his son Joseph
4. 6 J.'s well was there. Jesus therefore, being
4. 12 Art thou greater than our father J., which
Acts 3. 13 God of Abraham, and of Isaac, and of J.
7. 8 and Isaac (begat) [J.]; and J. (begat) the
7. 12 J. heard that there was corn in Egypt, he
7. 14 called his father [J.] to (him), and all his
7. 15 J. went down into Egypt, and died, he, and
7. 32 and the God of Isaac, and the God of J.
7. 46 to find a tabernacle for the God of J.
Rom. 9. 13 J. have I loved, but Esau have I hated
11. 26 and shall turn away ungodliness from J.
Heb. 11. 9 dwelling in tabernacles with Isaac and J.
11. 20 Isaac blessed J. and Esau concerning th.
11. 21 J., when he was a dying, blessed both the

2. The father of Joseph the husband of Mary.
Matt. 1. 15 Eleazar begat Matthan..Matthan begat J.
1. 16 J. begat Joseph the husband of Mary, of

The descendants of Jacob;—the Israelites.
Num23. 7 Come, curse me J., and come, defy Israel
23. 10 Who can count the dust of J., and the
23. 21 He hath not beheld iniquity in J., neither
23. 23 (there is) no enchantment against J., ne.
23. 23 time it shall be said of J. and of Israel
24. 5 How goodly are thy tents, O J., (and) thy
24. 17 there shall come a Star out of J., and a
24. 19 Out of J. shall come he that shall have
Deut 32. 9 J. (is) the lot of his inheritance
Deut 33. 4 the inheritance of the congregation of J.
33. 10 They shall teach J. thy judgments, and
33. 28 the fountain of J. (shall be) upon a land
2 Sa. 23. 1 the anointed of the God of J., and the
1 Ki. 18. 31 number of the tribes of the sons of J.
2 Ki. 17. 34 the LORD commanded the children of J.
1 Ch. 16. 13 ye children of J., his chosen ones
16. 17 hath confirmed the same to J. for a law
Psa. 14. 7 J. shall rejoice, (and) Israel shall be glad
20. 1 the name of the God of J. defend thee
22. 23 the seed of J., glorify him; and fear him
24. 6 that seek him, that seek thy face, O J.
44. 4 King, O God: command deliverances for J.
46. 7, 11 with us; the God of J. (is) our refuge
47. 4 for us, the excellency of J., whom he loved
53. 6 J. shall rejoice, (and) Israel shall be glad
59. 13 let them know that God ruleth in J. unto
75. 9 But..I will sing praises to the God of J.
76. 6 O God of J., both the chariot and horse
77. 15 thy people, the sons of J. and Joseph
78. 5 For he established a testimony in J., and
78. 21 a fire was kindled against J., and anger
78. 71 he brought him to feed J. his people, and
79. 7 they have devoured J., and laid waste his
81. 1 make a joyful noise unto the God of J.
81. 4 for Israel, (and) a law of the God of J.
84. 8 hear my prayer: give ear, O God of J.
85. 1 thou hast brought back the captivity of J.
87. 2 Zion more than all the dwellings of J.
94. 7 neither shall the God of J. regard (it)
99. 4 executest judgment..righteousness in J.
105. 6 his servant, ye children of J. his chosen
105. 10 confirmed the same unto J. for a law, (and)
105. 23 and J. sojourned in the land of Ham
114. 1 the house of J. from a people of strange
114. 7 the Lord, at the presence of the God of J.
132. 2 (and) vowed unto the mighty (God) of J.
132. 5 an habitation for the mighty (God) of J.
135. 4 LORD hath chosen J. unto himself, (and)
146. 5 (he) that (hath) the God of J. for his help
147. 19 He showeth his word unto J., his statutes
Isa. 2. 3 of the LORD, to the house of the God of J.
2. 5 O house of J., come ye and let us walk in
2. 6 hast forsaken thy people the house of J.
8. 17 that hideth his face from the house of J.
9. 8 The Lord sent a word into J., and it hath
10. 20 such as are escaped of the house of J.
10. 21 remnant shall return..the remnant of J.
14. 1 the LORD will have mercy on J., and will
14. 1 and they shall cleave to the house of J.
17. 4 the glory of J. shall be made thin, and
27. 6 cause them that come of J. to take root
27. 9 shall the iniquity of J. be purged; and
29. 22 concerning the house of J., J. shall
29. 23 sanctify the holy one of J., and shall fear
40. 27 Why sayest thou, O J., and speakest, O
41. 8 J. whom I have chosen, the seed of Abra.
41. 14 Fear not, thou worm J., (and) ye men of I.
41. 21 your strong (reasons), saith the King of J.
42. 24 Who gave J. for a spoil, and Israel to the
43. 1 saith the LORD that created thee, O J.
43. 22 thou hast not called upon me, O J.; but
43. 28 have given J. to the curse, and Israel to
44. 1 hear, O J. my servant; and Israel, whom
44. 2 Fear not, O J., my servant; and thou, J.
44. 5 another shall call (himself) by..name of J.
44. 21 Remember these, O J. and Israel; for
44. 23 the LORD hath redeemed J., and glorified
45. 4 For J. my servant's sake, and Israel mine
45. 19 I said not unto the seed of J., Seek ye me
46. 3 O house of J., and all the remnant of the
48. 1 Hear ye this, O house of J., which are
48. 12 Hearken unto me, O J. and Israel, my
48. 20 The LORD hath redeemed his servant J.
49. 5 (be) his servant, to bring J. again to him
49. 6 my servant to raise up the tribes of J.
49. 26 and thy Redeemer, the mighty One of J.
58. 1 show my people..the house of J. their
58. 14 feed..with the heritage of J. thy father
59. 20 them that turn from transgression in J.
60. 16 thy Redeemer, the mighty One of J.
65. 9 I will bring forth a seed out of J., and
Jer. 2. 4 O house of J., and all the families of the
5. 20 Declare this in the house of J., and publ.
10. 16 The portion of J. is not like them: for
10. 25 they have eaten up J., and devoured him
30. 7 it (is) even the time of J.'s trouble.
30. 10 fear thou not, O my servant J., saith the
30. 10 J. shall return, and shall be in rest, and
30. 18 bring again the captivity of J.'s tents
31. 7 Sing with gladness for J., and shout among
31. 11 the LORD hath redeemed J., and ransom.
33. 26 Then will I cast away the seed of J.
33. 26 the seed of Abraham, and Isaac, and J.
46. 27 fear not thou, O my servant J., and be not
46. 27 J. shall return, and be in rest and
46. 28 Fear thou not, O J. my servant, saith the
51. 19 The portion of J. (is) not like them; for
Lam. 1. 17 the LORD hath commanded concerning J.
2. 2 swallowed up all the habitations of J.
2. 3 he burned against J. like a flaming fire
Eze. 20. 5 lifted up mine hand unto the seed of..J.
28. 25 land that I have given to my servant J.
37. 25 land that I have given unto J. my servant
39. 25 Now will I bring again the captivity of J.
Hos. 10. 11 shall plow, (and) J. shall break his clods
12. 2 and will punish J. according to his ways
12. 12 And J. fled into the country of Syria; and
Amos 3. 13 testify in the house of J., saith the Lord
6. 8 I abhor the excellency of J., and hate his
7. 2 by whom shall J. arise? for he (is) small
7. 5 by whom shall J. arise? for he (is) small
Amos 8. 7 LORD hath sworn by the excellency of J.
9. 8 will not utterly destroy the house of J.
Obad. 10 For (thy) violence against thy brother J.
17 house of J. shall possess their possessions
18 the house of J. shall be a fire, and the
Mic. 1. 5 For the transgression of J. (is) all this
1. 5 What (is) the transgression of J.? (is it)
2. 7 (thou that art) named The house of J., is
2. 12 I will surely assemble, O J., all of thee
3. 1 Hear, I pray you, O heads of J., and ye
3. 8 to declare unto J. his transgression, and
3. 9 Hear, I pray..ye heads of the house of J.
4. 2 let us go..to the house of the God of J.
5. 7 the remnant of J. shall be in the midst
5. 8 remnant of J. shall be among the Gentiles
7. 20 Thou wilt perform the truth to J., (and)
Nah. 2. 2 LORD hath turned..the excellency of J.
Mal. 2. 12 the scholar, out of the tabernacles of J.
3. 6 therefore ye sons of J. are not consumed

JA'-DA, יָדָע *knowing.*
A grandson of Jerahmeel the son of Hezron. B.C. 1450.
1 Ch. 2. 28 the sons of Onam were Shammai, and J.
2. 32 the sons of J. the brother of Shammai;

JA'-DAU, יַדּוֹ, יַדַּי *favourite, friend.*
This name is correctly *Jaddai.* One of the family of Nebo who had married a strange wife. B.C. 457.
Ezra 10. 43 Zabad, Zebina, J., and Joel Benaiah

JAD-DU'-A, יַדּוּעַ *very knowing.*
1. A Levite who sealed the covenant with Nehemiah. B.C. 445.
Neh. 10. 21 Meshezabeel, Zadok, J.
2. A descendant of Jeshua the high priest at the end of the captivity. B.C. 520.
Neh. 12. 11 Joiada begat Jonathan, and Jonathan..J.
12. 22 The Levites, in the days of..J., (were) re.

JA'-DON, יָדוֹן *judging.*
One that helped to repair the wall of Jerusalem. B.C. 445.
Neh. 3. 7 next unto them repaired..J. the Merono.

JA'-EL, יָעֵל *chamois.*
The wife of Heber the Kenite who treacherously killed Sisera. B.C. 1316.
Judg. 4. 17 fled away on his feet to the tent of J. the
4. 18 J. went out to meet Sisera, and said unto
4. 21 J., Heber's wife, took a nail of the tent, and
4. 22 J. came out to meet him, and said unto
5. 6 in the days of J., the highways were uno.
5. 24 Blessed above women shall J. the wife of

JA'-GUR, יָגוּר *dwelling.*
A town in the S. part of the lot of the tribe of Judah.
Josh. 15. 21 uttermost cities..Kabzeel, and Eder..J.

JAH, יָהּ *An abbreviation of Jehovah.*
Psa. 68. 4 extol him..by his name J., and rejoice

JA'-HATH, יַחַת, נַחַת *comfort, revival.*
1. A descendant of Shobal the son of Judah. B.C. 1600.
1 Ch. 4. 2 Reaiah the son of Shobal begat J.; and J.
2. A descendant of Gershom, son of Levi. B.C. 1450.
1 Ch. 6. 20 Of Gershom; Libni his son, J. his son, Z.
6. 43 The son of J., the son of Gershom, the son
3. A descendant of Gershom, son of Levi. B.C. 1015.
1 Ch. 23. 10 And..sons of Shimei (were) J., Zina, and J.
23. 11 J. was the chief, and Zizah the second
4. A descendant of Kohath, son of Levi. B.C. 1015.
1 Ch. 24. 22 Shelomoth: of the sons of Shelomoth; J.
5. A descendant of Merari the son of Levi. B.C. 634.
2 Ch. 34. 12 the overseers of them (were) J. and Obad.

JA'-HAZ, JA-HA'-ZA, JA-HA'-ZAH, יַהַץ, יַהְצָה
A Levitical city in Reuben where Sihon king of the Amorites had been conquered. B.C. 1452. (*See* Jahzah.)
Num 21. 23 he came to J., and fought Deut. 2. 32
Josh. 13. 18 And J., and Kedemoth, and Mephaath
21. 36 out of the tribe of Reuben..J. with her
Judg 11. 20 and pitched in J., and fought against Isr.
Isa. 15. 4 their voice shall be heard (even) unto J.
Jer. 48. 21 upon Holon, and upon J., and upon Mep.
48. 34 From the cry of Heshbon..(even) unto J.
[Jos. 21. 36, 37 are wanting in the Hebrew text.]

JA-HAZ'-IAH, יַחְזְיָה *Jah reveals.*
One who was employed to enumerate those who had taken strange wives during the captivity or after the return. B.C. 457.
Ezra 10. 15 Asahel and J...were employed about this

JA-HA-ZI'-EL, יַחֲזִיאֵל *God reveals.*
1. One that joined David at Ziklag. B.C. 1058.
1 Ch. 12. 4 Jeremiah, and J., and Johanan, and Joz.
2. A priest who assisted in bringing up the ark from the house of Obed-edom. B.C. 1042.
1 Ch. 16. 6 Benaiah also and J. the priests with tru
3. A son of Hebron the Kohathite. B.C. 1015.
1 Ch. 23. 19 Amariah the second, J. the third, and Jeka.
24. 23 Amariah the second, J. the third, Jekahme.
4. A Levite that encouraged Jehoshaphat's army against the Moabites. B.C. 896.
2 Ch. 20. 14 Then upon J. the son of Zechariah, the son
5. A chief man whose son returned with Ezra from Babylon. B.C. 487.
Ezra 8. 5 the son of J., and with him three hund.

JAH'-DAI, יָהְדַּי *leader, guide.*
One of the family of Caleb the spy. B.C. 1500
1 Ch. 2. 47 And the sons of J.; Regem, and Jotham

JAH-DI'-EL, יַחְדִּיאֵל *union of God.*
The head of a family of the half tribe of Manasseh E. of the Jordan. B.C. 771.
1 Ch. 5. 24 Hodaviah, and J., mighty men of valour

JAH'-DO, יַחְדוֹ *union.*
Son of Buz the Gadite and father of Jeshishai. B.C. 1450.
1 Ch. 5. 14 son of Jeshishai, the son of J., the son of

JAH-LE'-EL, יַחְלְאֵל *God waits.*
A son of Zebulun—the third of the three. B.C. 1700.
Gen. 46. 14 And the sons of Zebulun..Elon, and J.
Num26. 26 of J., the family of the Jahleelites

JAH-LE-E-LITES, יַחְלְאֵלִי.
A family of Zebulunites founded by Jahleel.
Num26. 26 of Jahleel, the family of the J.

JAH'-MAI, יַחְמַי *Jah protects.*
A son of Tola son of Issachar, Jacob's ninth son and fifth by Leah. B.C. 1700.
1 Ch. 7. 2 And the sons of Tola..Jeriel, and J., and

JAH'-ZAH, יַהְצָה *trodden down.*
A city of Reuben, but afterwards assigned to the Levites. It is called also *Jahaz, Jahaza, Jahazah.*
1 Ch. 6. 78 out of the tribe of Reuben..J. with her

JAH-ZE'-EL, JAH-ZI'-EL, יַחְצְאֵל, יַחְצִיאֵל *God apportions.*
A son of Naphtali the sixth son of Jacob, but his second by Bilhah. B.C. 1700.
Gen. 46. 24 the sons of Naphtali; J., and Guni, and
Num26. 48 of J., the family of the Jahzeelites: of G.
1 Ch. 7. 13 The sons of Naphtali; J., and Guni, and G.

JAH-ZE-E-LITES, יַחְצְאֵלִי.
The patronymic of a family of Naphtalites whose founder was Jahzeel.
Num26. 48 of Jahzeel, the family of the J.: of Guni

JAH-ZE'-RAH, יַחְזֵרָה *Jah protects.*
A priest of the family of Immer whose descendants dwelt in Jerusalem. B.C. 500.
1 Ch. 9. 12 Adiel, the son of J., the son of Meshullam

JAILOR —
Guard of a prison, δεσμοφύλαξ *desmophulax.*
Acts 16. 23 charging the jailor to keep them safely

JA'-IR, יָאִיר *Jah enlightens.*
1. A man descended from Judah through his father Segub, and from Manasseh through his mother the daughter of Machir. B.C. 1452. By Moses he is called "son of Manasseh" (Num. 32. 41; Deut. 3. 14). In 1 Ch. 2. 23 he is called a "son of Machir the father of Gilead."
Num32. 41 J...went and took the small towns thereof
Deut. 3. 14 J...took all the country of Argob unto
1 Ki. 4. 13 to him (pertained) the towns of J. the son
1 Ch. 2. 22 J., who had three and twenty cities in the
2. A Gileadite judge of Israel between Tola and Jephthah. He judged Israel twenty-three years. He may have been a descendant of No. 1. B.C. 1180.
Judg10. 3 after him arose J...and judged Israel tw.
10. 5 And J. died, and was buried in Camon
3. Used briefly for HAVOTH JAIR, which see.
Josh 13. 30 and all the towns of J., which (are) in B.
1 Ch. 2. 23 took Geshur..Aram, with the towns of J.
4. A Benjamite whose son Mordecai was Esther's cousin. B.C. 550.
Esth. 2. 5 whose name (was) Mordecai, the son of J.

JA'-IR, יָעִיר *forest.*
The father of Elhanan who slew Lachmi the brother of Goliath. B.C. 1080. In 2 Sa. 21. 19 he is called *Jaare-Oregim.*
1 Ch.20. 5 the son of J. slew Lahmi the brother of G.

JA-I-RITE, יָאִירִי.
The patronymic of Jair's (No. 1) descendants.
2 Sa. 20. 26 Ira also the J. was a chief ruler about D.

JAI'-RUS, Ἰάειρος.
A ruler of a synagogue in a town of Galilee near the lake of Tiberias.
Mark 5. 22 And, behold, there cometh one..[J.] by
Luke 8. 41 behold, there came a man named J., and

JAKAN. *See* **JAAKAN.**

JA'-KEH, יָקֶה *hearkening.*
The father of Agur. B.C. 1000.
Prov30. 1 The words of Agur the son of J., (even) the

JA'-KIM, יָקִים *a setter up.*
1. Son of Shimhi, a Benjamite. B. C. 1400.
1 Ch. 8. 19 And J., and Zichri, and Zabdi
2. A head of a family of the Aaronites. B.C. 1015.
1 Ch.24. 12 The eleventh to Eliashib, the twelfth to J.

JA'-LON, יָלוֹן *Jah abides.*
A son of Ezra through Caleb the spy. B.C. 1400.
1 Ch. 4. 17 Jether, and Mered, and Epher, and J.

JAM'-BRES, Ἰαμβρῆς.
Probably an Egyptian magician at the court of Pharaoh. He is mentioned along with *Jannes* by the apostle Paul as having withstood Moses. B.C. 1491.
2 Ti. 3. 8 as Jannes and J. withstood Moses, so do

JAMES, Ἰάκωβος.
1 A son of Zebedee and brother of John the apostle.
Matt. 4. 21 J. (the son) of Zebedee, and John his br.
10. 2 J. (the son) of Zebedee, and John his br.
Matt17. 1 Jesus taketh Peter, J., and John his bro.
Mark 1. 19 he saw J. the (son) of Zebedee, and John
1. 29 the house of Simon and Andrew, with J.
3. 17 J. the (son) of Zebedee, and..brother of J.
5. 37 Peter, and J., and John the brother [of J.]
9. 2 taketh (with him) Peter, and J., and John
10. 35 J. and John, the sons of Zebedee come
10. 41 to be much displeased with J. and John
13. 3 J. and John and Andrew asked him priv.
14. 33 he taketh with him Peter and J. and John
Luke 5. 10 so (was) also J. and John, the sons of Ze.
6. 14 J. and John, Philip and Bartholomew
8. 51 J. and John, and the father and the mot.
9. 28 he took Peter and John and J., and went
9. 54 when his disciples J. and John saw (this)
Acts 1. 13 J., and John, and Andrew, Philip, and T.
12. 2 he killed J. the brother of John with the
2. A son of Alpheus.
Matt10. 3 J. (the son) of Alpheus, and Lebbeus
Mark 3. 18 J. the (son) of Alpheus, and Thaddeus, and
Luke 6. 15 J. the (son) of Alpheus, and Simon called
Acts 1. 13 J. (the son) of Alpheus, and Simon Zelo.
3. The brother of the Lord Jesus.
Matt13. 55 brethren, J., and Joses, and Simon, and
Mark 6. 3 of J., and Joses, and of Juda, and Simon
Acts 12. 17 Go show these things unto J.
15. 13 J. answered, saying, Men (and) brethren
21. 18 Paul went in with us unto J.; and all the
1 Co. 15. 7 he was seen of J.; then of all the apostles
Gal. 1. 19 saw I none, save J. the Lord's brother
2. 9 J., Cephas, and John, who seemed to be
2. 12 before that certain came from J., he did
Jas. 1. 1 J., a servant of God and of the Lord Jesus
4. The son of Mary. He is also called the Little.
Matt27. 56 Mary the mother of J. and Joses, and the
Mark15. 40 Mary the mother of J. the less and; 16. 1.
Luke24. 10 Mary the (mother) of J., and other (wo.
5. James the brother of the apostle Jude.
Luke 6. 16 (the brother) of J., and Judas; Acts 1. 13.
Jude 1 brother of J., to them that are sanctified

JA'-MIN, יָמִין *right hand, prosperity.*
1. A son of Simeon the second son of Jacob. B.C. 1700.
Gen. 46. 10 J., and Ohad, and Jachin, and Zohar, and
Exod.6. 15 J., and Ohad, and Jachin, and Zohar, and
Num26. 12 of J., the family of the Jaminites: of Ja.
1 Ch. 4. 24 (were) Nemuel, and J., Jarib, Zerah, (and)
2. A descendant of Hezron, son of Pharez. B.C. 1470.
1 Ch. 2. 27 sons of Ram..were Maaz, and J., and E.
3. A priest who explained the law to the people when Ezra read it. B.C. 445.
Neh. 8. 7 J., Akkub, Shabbethai, Hodijah, Maaseiah

JA-MIN-ITES, יָמִינִי.
The family of Jamin, son of Simeon.
Num26. 12 of Jamin, the family of the J.: of Jachin

JAM'-LECH, יַמְלֵךְ *Jah rules.*
A princely descendant of Simeon. B.C. 800.
1 Ch. 4. 34 And Moshobab, and J., and Joshah the

JANGLING, vain —
Vain discourse, ματαιολογία *mataiologia.*
1 Ti. 1. 6 some..have turned aside unto vain jang.

JAN'-NA, Ἰαννά.
An ancestor of Joseph the husband of Mary the mother of Jesus.
Luke 3. 24 (the son) of [J.], which was (the son) of

JAN'-NES, Ἰαννῆς.
One who, with *Jambres*, withstood Moses.
2 Ti. 3 8 as J. and Jambres withstood Moses, so do

JA-NO'-AH, יָנוֹחַ *resting place.*
A city in the N. of Naphtali, near Abel-beth-maachah.
2 Ki. 15. 29 took Ijon, and Abel-beth-maachah, and J.

JA-NO'-HAH, יָנוֹחָה.
A city between Ephraim and Manasseh; perhaps the same as the preceding.
Josh 16. 6 the border..passed by it on the east to J.
16. 7 it went down from J. to Ataroth, and to

JA'-NUM, יָנִים, יָנוּם *propagation.*
A city in Judah.
Josh.15. 53 And J., and Beth-tappuah, and Aphekah

JA'-PHETH, יֶפֶת *the extender, or fair.*
The second son of Noah, whose descendants spread over the N. and W. regions of the earth. B.C. 2448. He is probably the original of *Japetus* whom the Greeks considered as the ancestor of the human race.
Gen. 5. 32 and Noah begat Shem, Ham, and J.
6. 10 Noah begat three sons, Shem, Ham, and J.
7. 13 Ham, and J., the sons of Noah, and Noah's
9. 18 sons of Noah..were Shem,..Ham, and J.
9. 23 J. took a garment, and laid (it) upon both
9. 27 God shall enlarge J., and he shall dwell
10. 1 of the sons of Noah; Shem, Ham, and J.
10. 2 sons of J.; Gomer, and Magog, and Madai
10. 21 Unto Shem..the brother of J. the elder
1 Ch. 1. 4 Noah, Shem, Ham, and J.
1. 5 The sons of J.; Gomer, Magog, and Madai

JA-PHI'-A, יָפִיעַ *high.*
1. The Amorite king of Lachish who was defeated by Joshua at Gibeon. B.C. 1451.
Josh.10. 3 unto J. king of Lachish, and unto Debir
2. A town near Carmel between Accho and Cæsarea on the coast (Sykamenos).
Josh.19. 12 goeth out to Daberath, and goeth up to J.
3. A son born to David after he began to reign at Jerusalem. B.C. 1040.
2 Sa. 5. 15 Ibhar also, and Elishua, and Nepheg..J.
1 Ch. 3. 7 And Nogah, and Nepheg, and J
14. 6 And Nogah, and Nepheg, and J.

JAPH'-LET, יַפְלֵט *Jah causes to escape.*
A grandson of Beriah, son of Asher. B.C. 1600.
1 Ch. 7. 32 Heber begat J., and Shomer, and Hotham
7. 33 sons of J.; Pasach, and Bimhal, and Ash.
7. 33 These (are) the children of J.

JAPH-LE'-TI, יַפְלֵטִי.
A place unknown; perhaps *Bethpalet.*
Josh.16. 3 goeth down westward to the coast of J.

JA'-PHO, יָפוֹ *high.*
A city on the coast of the Mediterranean, which belonged to the Philistines, and bordered on the territory of the Danites. It is now called *Jafa* (or Joppa), 150 stadia from Antipatris, 6 miles W. of Rama, and 10 hours from Jerusalem at the W. end of the mountain road.
Josh.19. 46 and Rakkon, with the border before J.

JA'-RAH, יַעְרָה *unveiler.*
A son of Ahaz of the family of Saul the Benjamite. B.C. 960. He is *Jehoadah* in 1 Ch. 8. 36.
1 Ch. 9. 42 And Ahaz begat J.; and J. begat Alem

JA'-REB, יָרֵב *contender, avenger.*
An appellation of a king of Asshur (Assyria).
Hos. 5. 13 then went Ephraim..and sent to king J.
10. 6 be also carried..(for) a present to king J.

JA'-RED, JE'-RED, יֶרֶד, יָרֶד, Ἰαρέδ, *descending.*
1. A descendant of Seth and son of Mahalaleel. B.C. 3544–2582.
Gen. 5. 15 lived sixty and five years, and begat J.
5. 16 Mahalaleel lived after he begat J. eight
5. 18 J. lived an hundred sixty and two years
5. 19 J. lived after he begat Enoch eight hun.
5. 20 the days of J. were nine hundred sixty
1 Ch. 1. 2 Kenan, Mahalaleel, Jered
2. An ancestor of Jesus.
Luke 3. 37 Enoch, which was (the son) of [J.], which

JA-RES-I'AH, יַעֲרֶשְׁיָה *Jah gives a couch.*
A son of Jeroham, a Benjamite. B.C. 1300.
1 Ch. 8. 27 J., and Eliah, and Zichri..sons of Jeroh.

JAR'-HA, יַרְחָע.
An Egyptian servant and husband of Ahlai the daughter of Sheshan. B.C. 1400.
1 Ch. 2. 34 a servant, an Egyptian, whose name..J.
2. 35 gave his daughter to J. his servant to

JA'-RIB, יָרִיב *striving.*
1. A son of Simeon, B.C. 1720; called *Jachin* in Gen. 46. 10, and Exod. 6. 15.
1 Ch. 4. 24 (were) Nemuel, and Jamin, J... Zerah, (and)
2. A chief man who accompanied Ezra to Jerusalem. B.C. 457.
Ezra 8. 16 for J., and for Elnathan, and for Nathan
3. A priest who had married a strange wife. B.C. 457.
Ezra 10. 18 Maaseiah and Eliezer, and J., and Geda

JAR'-MUTH, יַרְמוּת *height.*
1. A city in Judah, formerly belonging to the Amorites, whose king was slain by Joshua. It is now called *Yarmûk*, 2 miles from *Beitnetif* or 10 from *Beit-gibrin.*
Josh.10. 3 unto Piram king of J., and unto Japhia
10. 5 the king of J., the king of Lachish, the
10. 23 the king of J., the king of Lachish, (and)
12. 11 The king of J., one; the king of Lachish
15. 35 J. and Adullam, Socoh, and Azekah
Neh. 11. 29 at En-rimmon, and at Zareah, and at J.
2. A Levitical city in Issachar, called also *Remeth* (Josh. 19. 21), and *Remoth* (1 Ch. 6. 73).
Josh.21. 29 J. with her suburbs, En-gannim with her

JA-RO'-AH, יָרוֹחַ *new moon.*
A descendant of Gad. B.C. 1270.
1 Ch. 5. 14 Abihail the son of Huri, the son of J.

JA'-SHEN, יָשֵׁן *shining.*
The father of one of David's worthies. B.C. 1085.
2 Sa. 23. 32 Eliahba the Shaalbonite, of the sons of J.

JA'-SHER, יָשָׁר *upright.*
A book of songs celebrating the glory of Israel.
Josh.10. 13 (Is) not this written in the book of J.?
2 Sa. 1. 18 behold, (it is) written in the book of J.

JA-SHO'-BEAM, יָשָׁבְעָם *the people return.*
1. Son of Zabdiel a Hachmonite and one of David's captains. B.C. 1048.
1 Ch.11. 11 J., an Hachmonite, the chief of the cap.
27. 2 for the first month (was) J. the son of
2. A Korahite descended from Kohath.
1 Ch.12. 6 Azareel, and Joezer, and J., the Korhites

JA'-SHUB, יָשׁוּב, *turning back* [V.L. ישיב in 1 Ch.]
1. The third of the four sons of Issachar. B.C. 1692.
Num 26. 24 Of J., the family of the Jashubites: of
1 Ch. 7. 1 (were) Tola, and Puah, J., and Shimron

2. One of the family of Bani who had taken a strange wife in exile. B.C. 457.

Ezra 10. 29 Malluch, and Adaiah, J., and Sheal, and

JA-SHU-BI LE'-HEM, יָשֻׁבִי לֶחֶם *turning back to Bethle.*
A descendant of Shelah, son of Judah. B.C. 1300.

1 Ch. 4. 22 Saraph..had the dominion in Moab, and J.

JA-SHUB-ITES, יָשֻׁבִי.
The family of Jashub, son of Issachar. Num. 26. 24.

JASIEL. *See* **JAASIEL.**

JA'-SON, Ἰάσων *healing.*
1. A believer in Thessalonica hospitable to Paul and Silas.

Acts 17. 5 assaulted the house of J., and sought to
17. 6 they drew J. and certain brethren unto
17. 7 Whom J. hath received: and these all do
17. 9 when they had taken security of J., and

2. A kinsman of Paul whose salutation Paul sent to Rome.

Rom 16. 21 J., and Sosipater, my kinsmen, salute you

JASPER —

1. *Jasper*, יָשְׁפֵה ,יָשְׁפֶה *yashepheh.*

Exod28. 20 fourth row, a beryl, and an onyx, and a j.
39. 13 fourth row, a beryl, an onyx, and a jasper
Eze. 28. 13 the jasper, the sapphire, the emerald, and

2. *Jasper*, ἴασπις *iaspis.*

Rev. 4. 3 he that sat was to look upon like a jasper
21. 11 even like a jasper stone, clear as crystal
21. 18 the building of the wall of it was (of) jas.
21. 19 The first foundation (was) jasper; the se.

JATH-NI'-EL, יַתְנִיאֵל *God is giving.*
A son of Meshelemiah of the house of Asaph or Ebiasaph (1 Chr. 9. 19). He was a gatekeeper at the tabernacle. B.C. 1015.

1 Ch.26. 2 the second, Zebadiah the third, J. the fo.

JAT'-TIR, יַתִּר *wide.*
A Levitical city in the hill country of Judah. Now called *Attir*, S. of Hebron.

Josh.15. 48 in the mountains, Shamir, and J., and
21. 14 J. with her suburbs, and Eshtemoa with
1 Sa. 30. 27 Ramoth, and to (them) which (were) in J.
1 Ch. 6. 57 and J., and Eshtemoa, with their suburbs

JA'-VAN, יָוָן.
1. The fourth son of Japheth. B.C. 2298.

Gen. 10. 2 J., and Tubal, and Meshech, and Tiras
10. 4 the sons of J.; Elishah, and Tarshish, K.
1 Ch. 1. 5 and J., and Tubal, and Meshech, and Tiras
1. 7 the sons of J.; Elishah, and Tarshish, K.

2. His descendants and their lands, Ionia, Macedonia, Greece, Syria, &c.

Isa. 66. 19 (to) Tubal, and J., (to) the isles afar off

3. A city in S. Arabia, *Yemen*, whither the Phenicians traded. It is perhaps the same as *Uzal.*

Eze. 27. 13 J., Tubal, and Meshech, they (were)..me.
27. 19 J. going to and fro occupied in thy fairs

JAVELIN —

1. *Spear, javelin*, חֲנִית *chanith.*

1 Sa. 18. 10 and (there was) a javelin in Saul's hand
18. 11 Saul cast the javelin; for he said, I will s.
19. 9 as he sat in his house with his javelin in
19. 10 Saul sought to smite David..with the ja.
19. 10 and he smote the javelin into the wall
20. 33 And Saul cast a javelin at him to smite

2. *Javelin, spear, dart*, רֹמַח *romach.*

Num 25. 7 Phinehas..rose..and took a javelin in

JAW, jaw bone, jaw teeth —

1. *Cheek, cheek bone*, לְחִי *lechi.*

Judg 15. 15 he found a new jaw bone of an ass, and
15. 16 With the jaw bone of an ass, heaps upon
15. 16 with the jaw of an ass have I slain a tho.
15. 17 he cast away the jaw bone out of his hand
15. 19 clave an hollow place that (was) in the j.
Job 41. 2 canst thou..bore his jaw through with a
Isa. 30. 28 a bridle in the jaws of the people, causing
Eze. 29. 4 I will put hooks in thy jaws, and I will
38. 4 I will..put hooks into thy jaws, and I will
Hos. 11. 4 they that take off the yoke on their jaws

2. *Jaw*, מַלְקוֹחַ *malqoach.*

Psa. 22. 15 my tongue cleaveth to my jaws; and thou

3. *Jaw teeth*, מְתַלְּעוֹת *methalleoth.*

Job 29. 17 I brake the jaws of the wicked, and pluc.
Prov.30. 14 their jaw teeth (as) knives, to devour the

JAZER. *See* **JAAZER.**

JA'-ZIZ, יָזִיז *shining.*
David's chief shepherd. B.C. 1020.

1 Ch. 27. 31 And over the flocks (was) J. the Hagerite

JEALOUS —

1. *Zealous, jealous*, קַנָּא *qanna.*

Exod20. 5 I the LORD thy God (am) a jealous God
34. 14 LORD, whose name (is) Jealous, (is) a jea.
Deut. 4. 24 thy God (is) a consuming fire..a jealous G.
5. 9 for I the LORD thy God (am) a jealous God
6. 15 LORD thy God (is) a jealous God among

2. *Zealous, jealous*, קַנּוֹא *qanno.*

Josh 24. 19 he (is) a jealous God; he will not forgive
Nah. 1. 2 God (is) jealous, and the LORD revengeth

JEALOUS, to be —

To be zealous, jealous, קָנָא *qana*, 3.

Num. 5. 14 he be jealous of his wife, and she be
5. 14 he be jealous of his wife, and she be not
Num. 5. 30 he be jealous over his wife, and shall set
1 Ki. 19. 10, 14 I have been very jealous for the LORD
Eze. 39. 25 and will be jealous for my holy name
Joel 2. 18 Then will the LORD be jealous for his land
Zech. 1. 14 I am jealous for Jerusalem and for Zion
8. 2 I was jealous for Zion..I was jealous for

JEALOUS over, to be —

To be zealous, ζηλόω *zēloō*

2 Co. 11. 2 For I am jealous over you with godly jeal.

JEALOUSY —

1. *Zeal, jealousy*, קִנְאָה *qinah.*

Num. 5. 14, 14 the spirit of jealousy come upon him
5. 15 it (is) an offering of jealousy, an offering
5. 18 the offering..which (is) the jealousy offer.
5. 25 the priest shall take the jealousy offering
5. 29 This (is) the law of jealousies, when a wife
5. 30 Or when the spirit of jealousy cometh upon
25. 11 that I consumed not..Israel in my jealou.
Deut29. 20 his jealousy shall smoke against that man
Psa. 79. 5 How long..shall thy jealousy burn like
Prov. 6. 34 For jealousy (is) the rage of a man; there.
Song 8. 6 jealousy (is) cruel as the grave: the coals
Isa. 42. 13 he shall stir up jealousy like a man of war
Eze. 8. 3 where (was) the seat of the image of jeal.
8. 5 at the gate..this image of jealousy in the
16. 38 I will give thee blood in fury and jealousy
16. 42 my jealousy shall depart from thee, and
23. 25 I will set my jealousy against thee, and
36. 5 Surely in the fire of my jealousy have I
36. 6 Behold, I have spoken in my jealousy and
38. 19 in my jealousy (and) in the fire of my wr.
Zeph. 1. 18 land shall be devoured by the fire of his j.
3. 8 shall be devoured with the fire of my jeal.
Zech. 1. 14 I am jealous..for Zion with a great jealou.
8. 2 I was jealous for Zion with great jealousy

2. *Zeal*, ζῆλος *zēlos.*

2 Co. 11. 2 I am jealous over you with godly jealo.

JEALOUSY, to move or provoke to —

1. *To make zealous or jealous*, קָנָא *qana*, 3.

Deut 32. 21 They have moved me to jealousy with
1 Ki. 14. 22 they provoked him to jealousy with their

2. *To cause zeal or jealousy*, קָנָא *qana*, 5.

Deut 32. 16 They provoked him to jealousy with stra.
32. 21 and I will move them to jealousy with
Psa. 78. 58 moved him to jealousy with their graven

3. *To cause zeal or jealousy*, קָנָה *qanah*, 5.

Eze. 8. 3 seat of the image..which provoketh to j.

4. *To make very zealous or jealous*, παραζηλόω.

Rom 10. 19 Moses saith, I will provoke you to jealousy
11. 11 to provoke them to jealousy; 1 Co. 10. 22

JEARIM, יְעָרִים *woods.* Name of hill in Josh. 15. 10

JE-A-TE'-RAI, יְאָתְרַי *steadfast.*
A descendant of Gershom son of Levi. B.C. 1250.

1 Ch. 6. 21 Iddo his son, Zerah his son, J. his son

JE-BE-RECH-I'AH, יְבֶרֶכְיָהוּ *Jah is blessing.*
The father of Zechariah. B.C. 770.

Isa. 8. 2 the priest, and Zechariah the son of J.

JE'-BUS, JE-BU'-SI, יְבוּסִי ,יְבוּס *trodden down.*
The city afterwards called *Jerusalem.*

Josh.18. 16 to the valley of Hinnom, to the side of J.
18. 28 J., which (is) Jerusalem, Gibeath, (and)
Judg19. 10 and came over against J., which (is) Jer.
19. 11 when they (were) by J., the day was far
1 Ch.11. 4 Israel went to Jerusalem, which (is) J.
11. 5 the inhabitants of J. said to David, Thou

JE-BU-SITES, יְבוּסִי *belonging to Jebus.*
The descendants of a son of Canaan, son of Ham. They dwelt chiefly around Jerusalem, which they held till the time of David.

Gen. 10. 16 the J., and the Amorite, and the Girgas.
15. 21 Canaanites, and the Girgashites, and..J.
Exod. 3. 8, 17 Perizzites, and the Hivites, and the J.
13. 5 the Amorites, and the Hivites, and the J.
23. 23 and the Canaanites, the Hivites, and the J.
33. 2 and the Perizzite, the Hivite, and the J.
34. 11 the Perizzite, and the Hivite, and the J.
Num13. 29 J., and the Amorites, dwell in the moun.
Deut. 7. 1 the Perizzites, and the Hivites, and the J.
20. 17 the Perizzites, the Hivites, and the J.
Josh. 3. 10 Girgashites, and the Amorites, and the J.
9. 1 the Hivite, and the J., heard (thereof)
11. 3 the J. in the mountains, and (to) the Hi.
12. 8 the Perizzites, the Hivites, and the J.
15. 8 border went..unto the south side of..J.
15. 63 the J. the inhabitants of Jerusalem, the
15. 63 the J. dwell with the children of Judah
24. 11 the Girgashites, the Hivites, and the J.
Judg. 1. 21 J. that inhabited Jerusalem; but the J.
3. 5 Amorites, and Perizzites, and Hivites..J.
19. 11 let us turn in into this city of the J., and
2 Sa. 5. 6 his men went to Jerusalem unto the J.
5. 8 smiteth the J., and the lame and the bli.
24. 16 by the threshing place of Araunah the J.
24. 18 in the threshing floor of Araunah the J.
1 Ki. 9. 20 J., which (were) not of the children of I.
1 Ch. 1. 14 J. also, and the Amorite, and the Girga.
11. 4 where the J. (were), the inhabitants of
11. 6 Whosoever smiteth the J. first shall be
21. 15, 18, 28 the threshing floor of Ornan the J.
2 Ch. 3. 1 in the threshing floor of Ornan the J.
8. 7 and the J., which (were) not of Israel
Ezra 9. 1 the J., the Ammonites, the Moabites, the
Neh. 9. 8 Perizzites, and the J., and the Girgashites
Zech. 9. 7 as a governor in Judah, and Ekron as a J.

JE-CA-MI'-AH, יְקַמְיָה.
A son of Neri. B.C. 580. See *Jekamiah.*

1 Ch. 3. 18 and Shenazar, J., Hoshama, and Nedab

JE-CHOL-I'AH, יְכָלְיָה *Jah is able.*
A woman of Jerusalem, and mother of Azariah (or Uzziah) king of Judah. B.C. 810.

2 Ki. 15. 2 And his mother's name (was) J. of Jeru.
2 Ch.26. 3 His mother's name also (was) J. of Jeru.

JE-CHON-I'AS, Ἰεχονίας—See *Jechoniah.*

Matt. 1. 11 Josias begat J. and his brethren
1. 12 J. begat Salathiel; and Salathiel begat

JE-CON-I'AH, יְכָנְיָה ,יְכָנְיָהוּ *Jah (is) establishing.*
The altered form of *Jehoiachin* the last but one of the kings of Judah. In Matt. 1. 11, 12, it is Jeconias. B.C. 599.

1 Ch. 3. 16 of Jehoiakim: J. his son, Zedekiah his son
3. 17 And the sons of J.; Assir, Salathiel his s.
Esth. 2. 6 had been carried away with J. king of J.
Jer. 24. 1 J. the son of Jehoiakim king of Judah
27. 20 J. the son of Jehoiakim the king of Jud.
28. 4 J. the son of Jehoiakim king of Judah
29. 2 J. the king, and the queen, and the eun.

JE-DA-I'AH, יְדָיָה *Jah is praise.*
1. A descendant of Simeon. B.C. 1080.

1 Ch. 4. 37 the son of J., the son of Shimri, the son

2. One who helped to repair the wall of Jerusalem B.C. 445.

Neh. 3. 10 And next unto them repaired J. the son

JE-DA-I'AH, יְדַעְיָה *Jah (is) knowing.*
1. A priest in Jerusalem, some of whose descendants came up from Jerusalem. B.C. 1015.

1 Ch. 9. 10 the priests; J., and Jehoiarib, and Jac.
24. 7 came forth to Jehoiarib, the second to J
Ezra 2. 36 the children of J., of the house of Jeshua
Neh. 7. 39 the children of J., of the house of Jeshua

2. A priest who returned with Zerubbabel. B.C. 536

Neh. 11. 10 the priests: J. the son of Joiarib, Jachin
12. 6 Shemaiah, and Joiarib, J.
12. 19 And of Joiarib, Mattenai; of J., Uzzi
Zech. 6. 10 of Tobijah, and of J., which are come
6. 14 to J., and to Hen the son of Zephaniah

3. Another priest that returned with Zerubbabel. B.C. 536.

Neh. 12. 7 Sallu, Amok, Hilkiah, J. These (were)
12. 21 Of Hilkiah, Hashabiah; of J. Nethaneel

JE-DI-A'-EL, יְדִיעֲאֵל *God knows.*
1. A son of Benjamin. B.C. 1700. Also called *Ashbel*

1 Ch. 7. 6 of Benjamin; Bela, and Becher, and J.
7. 10 The sons also of J.; Bilhan: and the sons
7. 11 these the sons of J., by the heads of their

2. The son of Shimri, one of David's valiant guard of thirty. B.C. 1048.

1 Ch.11. 45 J. the son of Shimri, and Joha his brother

3. A warrior that joined David in Ziklag. B.C. 1048.

1 Ch.12. 20 J., and Michael, and Jozabad, and Elihu

4. Son of Meshelemiah a descendant of Korah. B.C. 1015.

1 Ch.26. 2 And the sons of Meshelemiah (were)..J.

JE-DI'-DAH, יְדִידָה *beloved.*
The wife of Amon and mother of Josiah, kings of Judah. B.C. 641.

2 Ki. 22. 1 his mother's name (was) J., the daughter

JE-DI-DI'-AH, יְדִידְיָה *Jah is a friend.*
The name given to Solomon by Nathan through the word of the Lord. B.C. 1015.

2 Sa. 12. 25 he called his name J., because of the L.

JE-DU'-THUN, יְדוּתוּן ,יְדִתוּן *a choir of praise.*
A Levite chief singer in the temple. B.C. 1015.

1 Ch. 9. 16 Shemaiah, the son of Galal, the son of J.
16. 38 Obed-edom also the son of J., and Hosah
16. 41 And with them Heman and J., and the
16. 42 Heman and J...And the sons of J. (were)
25. 1 the sons of Asaph, and of Heman, and of J.
25. 3 Of J.: the sons of J.; Gedaliah, and Zeri
25. 3 six, under the hands of their father J.
25. 6 according to the king's order to Asaph, J.
2 Ch. 5. 12 all of them of Asaph, of Heman, of J., with
29. 14 and of the sons of J.; Shemaiah and Uzziel
35. 15 according to the commandment of..J. the
Neh. 11. 17 of Shammua, the son of Galal, the son of J.
Psa. 39. *title.* To the chief Musician, (even) to J., A.
62 „ To the chief Musician, to J., A Psalm
77. „ To the chief Musician, to J., A Psalm

JE-E'-ZER, אִיעֶזֶר, *contracted from* אֲבִיעֶזֶר.
A son of Gilead, grandson of Manasseh. B.C. 1450. See *Abiezer.*

Num26. 30 (of) J., the family of the J.; of Helek, the f.

JE-EZ-ER-ITES, אִיעֶזְרִי.
The patronymic of a family that sprang from Jeezer the son of Gilead.

Num26. 30 of Jeezer, the family of the J.: of Helek

JE-GAR SA-HA-DU'-THA, יְגַר שָׂהֲדוּתָא *heap of testi.*
The name given by Laban to the heap of stones that Jacob called Galeed. B.C. 1740.

Gen. 31. 47 And Laban called it J.: but Jacob called

JE-HAL-EL'-EEL, *Jehalelel*, יְהַלֶּלְאֵל *God is praised.*
1. A descendant of Judah through Caleb the spy. B.C 1400.

1 Ch. 4. 16 And the sons of J.; Ziph, and Ziphah, Tiri.

2. A descendant of Merari in the time of Hezekiah. B.C. 756.

2 Ch.29. 12 Abdi, and Azariah the son of J.: and of the

JEH-DE-I'AH, יֶחְדְּיָהוּ *union of Jah.*

1. The son of Shubael a descendant of Levi in David's time. B.C. 1020.

1 Ch. 24. 20 Amram; Shubael: of the..of Shubael; J.

2. An overseer of the asses in the time of David. B.C. 1020.

1 Ch.27. 30 and over the asses (was) J. the Meronot.

JE-HEZ-E'-KEL, יְחֶזְקֵאל *God is strong.*

One of the priests to whom the charges of the sanctuary were distributed by lot in the time of David. B.C. 1015.

1 Ch. 24. 16 nineteenth to Pethahiah..twentieth to J.

JE-HI'-AH, יְחִיָּה *Jah (is) living.*

A Levite gatekeeper of the ark when brought from the house of Obed-edom. B.C. 1040.

1 Ch.15. 24 Obed-edom and J. (were) door keepers for

JE-HI'-EL, יְחִיאֵל *God is living.*

1. A Levite singer in the tabernacle in David's time. B.C. 1015.

1 Ch.15. 18, 20 and Shemiramoth, and J., and Unni
16. 5 Shemiramoth, and J., and Mattithiah, and

2. A Gershonite. B.C. 1040.

1 Ch.23. 8 The sons of Laadan; the chief (was) J., and
29. 8 gave (them)..by the hand of J. the Ger.

3. A companion of David's sons. B.C. 1030.

1 Ch.27. 32 J...son of Hachmoni (was) with the king's

4. A son of Jehoshaphat, king of Judah. B.C. 889.

2 Ch. 21. 2 the sons of Jehoshaphat, Azariah, and J.

5. A son of Heman the singer in the time of Hezekiah. B.C. 726. [V.L. יחואל].

2 Ch.29. 14 And of the sons of Heman; J. and Shimei

6. A Levite set over the dedicated things in the days of Hezekiah. B.C. 726.

2 Ch.31. 13 And J., and Azaziah, and Nahath, and A.

7. A chief priest in the days of Josiah. B.C. 623.

2 Ch.35. 8 Hilkiah and Zechariah and J., rulers of the

8. The father of Obadiah who returned from exile with Ezra. B.C. 458.

Ezra 8. 9 Obadiah the son of J., and with him two

9. The father of Shechaniah who first acknowledged the guilt of taking strange wives. B.C. 457.

Ezra 10. 2 Shechaniah the son of J., (one) of the sons

10. A priest who had taken a strange wife. B.C. 457.

Ezra 10. 21 and Elijah, and Shemaiah, and J., and Uz.

11. A man of Elam's family who had done the same thing. B.C. 457.

Ezra 10. 26 and J., and Abdi, and Jeremoth, and Eli.

JE-HI-E'-LI, יְחִיאֵלִי.

A son of Laadan the Gershonite, set over the treasures of the sanctuary in the time of David. B.C. 1015.

1 Ch.26. 21 sons of the Gershonite Laadan..(were) J.
26. 22 The sons of J.; Zetham, and Joel his

JE-HIZ-KI'-AH, יְחִזְקִיָּהוּ *Jah is strong.*

A son of Shallum, and a strong opponent of making his brethren slaves in the days of Ahaz. B.C. 742.

2 Ch. 28. 12 J. the son of Shallum, and Amasa the son

JE-HO-A'-DAH, יְהוֹעַדָּה *Jah unveils.*

Son of Ahaz, the great grandson of Jonathan, Saul's son. B.C. 940. Called also *Jarah.*

1 Ch. 8. 36 And Ahaz begat J.; and J. begat Alemeth

JE-HO-AD'-DAN יְהוֹעַדִּין יְהוֹעַדָּן *Jah gives delight.*

The mother of Amaziah and wife of Joash, kings of Judah. B.C. 850.

2 Ki. 14. 2 And his mother's name (was) J. of Jeru.
2 Ch. 25. 1 And his mother's name (was) J. of Jeru.

JE-HO-A'-HAZ, יְהוֹאָחָז יוֹאָחָז *Jah upholds.*

1. A son of Jehu and father of Joash, kings of Israel. B.C. 885.

2 Ki.10. 35 And J. his son reigned in his stead
13. 1 J. the son of Jehu began to reign over
13. 4 J. besought the LORD, and the LORD hea.
13. 7 Neither did he leave of the people to J.
13. 8 the rest of the acts of J., and all that
13. 9 J. slept with his fathers; and they buried
13. 10 began Jehoash the son of J. to reign over
13. 22 king..oppressed Israel all the days of J.
13. 25 the son of J. took again out of the hand
13. 25 which he had taken out of the hand of J.
14. 1 In the second year of Joash son of J. king
14. 8 the son of J., son of Jehu, king of Israel
14. 17 death of Jehoash, son of J., king of Israel
2 Ch.25. 17 the son of J., the son of Jehu, king of I.
25. 25 death of Joash, son of J. king of Israel

2. A son of Josiah who was deposed by Pharaoh Necho. B.C. 610. Called also *Shallum.*

2 Ki. 23. 30 the people of the land took J. the son of
23. 31 J. (was) twenty and three years old when
23. 34 turned his..to Jehoiakim, and took J. aw.
2 Ch.36. 1 the people of the land took J. the son of
36. 2 J. (was) twenty and three years old when
36. 4 Necho took J. his brother, and carried him

3. The son and successor of Jehoram and father of Joash, kings of Judah. B.C. 885. Called also *Ahaziah.*

2 Ch.21. 17 there was never a son left him, save J.
25. 23 took..the son of Joash, the son of J.

JE-HO'-ASH, יְהוֹאָשׁ יוֹאָשׁ *Jah supports.*

1. Son of Ahaziah and father of Amaziah, all kings of Judah. B.C. 850.

2 Ki. 11. 21 Seven years old (was) J. when he began to
12. 1 In the seventh year of Jehu, J. began to
12. 2 J. did (that which was) right in the sight
12. 4 J. said to the priests, All the money of
12. 6 the three and twentieth year of king J.
12. 7 J. called for Jehoiada the priest, and the
12. 18 J. king of Judah took all the hallowed
14. 13 took..the son of J., the son of Ahaziah

2. The son and successor of Jehoahaz on the throne of Israel. He was father of Jeroboam II. See *Joash.* B.C. 840.

2 Ki. 13. 10 began J. the son of Jehoahaz to reign over
13. 25 J. the son of Jehoahaz took again out
14. 8 Amaziah sent messengers to J., the son of
14. 9 J. the king of Israel sent to Amaziah king
14. 11 J. king of Israel went up..he and Amaz.
14. 13 J. king of Israel took Amaziah king of
14. 15 the rest of the acts of J. which he did
14. 16 J. slept with his fathers, and was buried
14. 17 And Amaziah..lived after the death of J.

JE-HO-HA'-NAN, יְהוֹחָנָן *Jah is gracious.*

1. A Kohathite gatekeeper of the tabernacle in David's reign. B.C. 1015

1 Ch.26. 3 Elam the fifth, J. the sixth, Elioenai the

2. A chief captain of Judah in the days of Jehoshaphat. B.C. 900.

2 Ch.17. 15 next to him (was) J. the captain, and with

3. Father of Ishmael, a captain that aided Jehoiada. B.C. 878.

2 Ch.23. 1 and Ishmael the son of J., and Azariah

4. A son of Bebai who had taken a strange wife. B.C. 457.

Ezra 10. 28 Of the sons also of Bebai; J., Hananiah

5. A priest who returned with Zerubbabel. B.C. 536.

Neh. 12. 13 Of Ezra, Meshullam; of Amariah, J.

6. A singer at the purification of the wall of Jerusalem. B.C. 445.

Neh. 12. 42 Eleazar, and Uzzi, and J., and Malchijah

JE-HOI-A'-DA, יְהוֹיָדָע *Jah knows.*

1. The father of Benaiah one of David's officers. B.C. 1048.

2 Sa. 8. 18 Benaiah the son of J. (was over) both the
20. 23 Benaiah the son of J. (was) over the Che.
23. 20 Benaiah the son of J...slew two..men of
23. 22 These (things) did Benaiah the son of J.
1 Ki. 1. 8 Zadok the priest, and Benaiah the son of J.
1. 26 Benaiah the son of J...hath he not called
1. 32 Call me..Benaiah the son of J. And they
1. 36 Benaiah the son of J. answered the king
1. 38 Benaiah the son of J...brought him to G.
1. 44 the king hath sent..Benaiah the son of J.
2. 25 sent by the hand of Benaiah the son of J.
2. 29 Then Solomon sent Benaiah the son of J.
2. 34 So Benaiah the son of J. went up, and
2. 35 king put Benaiah the son of J. in his room
2. 46 the king commanded Benaiah the son of J.
4. 4 Benaiah the son of J. (was) over the host
1 Ch.11. 22 Benaiah the son of J...had done many
11. 24 These (things) did Benaiah the son of J.
18. 17 Benaiah the son of J. (was) over the Che.
27. 5 third captain..(was) Benaiah the son of J.

2. The high priest who made Joash king. B.C. 878.

2 Ki.11. 4 J. sent and fetched the rulers over hund.
11. 9 captains..did..all (things) that J. the pr.
11. 9 took every man his men..and came to J.
11. 15 But J. the priest commanded the captains
11. 17 J. made a covenant between the LORD and
12. 2 days wherein J. the priest instructed him
12. 7 Then king Jehoash called for J. the priest
12. 9 But J. the priest took a chest, and bored
2 Ch 22. 11 wife of J. the priest..hid him from Atha.
23. 1 in the seventh year J. strengthened hims.
23. 8 all things that J. the priest had comman.
23. 8 for J. the priest dismissed not the courses
23. 9 J. the priest delivered to the captains
23. 11 J. and his sons anointed him, and said
23. 14 Then J. the priest brought out the capt.
23. 16 J. made a covenant between him, and be.
23. 18 J. appointed the offices of the house of the
24. 2 Joash did..right..all the days of J. the
24. 3 J. took for him two wives; and he begat
24. 6 the king called for J. the chief, and said
24. 12 J. gave it to such as did the work of the
24. 14 brought the rest of the money before..J.
24. 14 offered..continually all the days of J.
24. 15 But J. waxed old, and was full of days
24. 17 after the death of J. came the princes of
24. 20 spirit..came upon Zechariah the son of J.
24. 22 kindness which J. his father had done to
24. 25 for the blood of the sons of J. the priest

3. A leader of the Aaronites who joined David at Ziklag. B.C. 1048.

1 Ch.12. 27 J. (was) the leader of the Aaronites, and

4. Son of Benaiah, son of Jehoiada, the third of David's counsellors. B.C. 1030.

1 Ch.27. 34 after Ahithophel (was) J. the son of Ben.

5. One of the family of Paseach who repaired a gate of Jerusalem. B.C. 445. (Heb. יוֹיָדָע = Joiada.)

Neh. 3. 6 the old gate repaired J. the son of Paseah

6. A priest in Jerusalem before the exile, but displaced by Zephaniah. B.C. 600.

Jer. 29. 26 hath made thee priest in the stead of J. the

JE-HO-IA'-CHIN, יְהוֹיָכִין יוֹיָכִין *Jah establishes.*

A son of Jehoiakim king of Judah. He was set on the throne by Nebuchadnezzar. B.C. 600.

2 Ki. 24. 6 and J. his son reigned in his stead
24. 8 J. (was) eighteen years old when he began
24. 12 J. the king..went out to the king of Bab.
24. 15 And he carried away J. to Babylon, and
25. 27 thirtieth year of the captivity of J. king
25. 27 he..did lift up the head of J...out of pr.
2 Ch.36. 8 and J. his son reigned in his stead
36. 9 J. (was) eight years old when he began to
Jer. 52. 31 thirtieth year of the captivity of J. king
52. 31 Evil-merodach..lifted up the head of J.
Eze. 1. 2 which (was) the fifth year of king J.'s cap.

JE-HO-IA'-KIM, יְהוֹיָקִים *Jah sets up.*

The name given by Pharaoh-Necho to Eliakim son of Josiah king of Judah, whom he made king instead of Jehoahaz. B.C. 610-600.

2 Ki. 23. 34 Pharaoh-nechoh..turned his name to J.
23. 35 J. gave the silver and the gold to Pharaoh
23. 36 J. (was) twenty and five years old when he
24. 1 and J. became his servant three years
24. 5 the acts of J...(are)..written in the book
24. 6 J. slept with his fathers: and Jehoiachin
24. 19 he did..according to all that J. had done
1 Ch. 3. 15 second J., the third Zedekiah, the fourth
3. 16 the sons of J.; Jeconiah his son, Zedekiah
2 Ch.36. 4 the king of Egypt..turned his name to J.
36. 5 J. (was) twenty and five years old when he
36. 8 rest of the acts of J., and his abomina.
Jer. 1. 3 It came also in the days of J. the son of
22. 18 thus saith the LORD concerning J. the son
22. 24 though Coniah the son of J. king of Judah
24. 1 Jeconiah the son of J. king of Judah
25. 1 in the fourth year of J. the son of Josiah
26. 1 In the beginning of the reign of J. the
26. 21 J. the king, with all his mighty men, and
26. 22 J. the king sent men into Egypt, (namely)
26. 23 brought him unto J. the king; who slew
27. 1 In the beginning of the reign of J. the
27. 20 away captive Jeconiah the son of J.
28. 4 Jeconiah the son of J. king of Judah, with
35. 1 in the days of J. the son of Josiah king
36. 1 in the fourth year of J. the son of Josiah
36. 9 it came to pass in the fifth year of J.
36. 28 which J. the king of Judah hath burnt
36. 29 thou shalt say to J. king of Judah, Thus
36. 30 thus saith the LORD of J. king of Judah
36. 32 the book which J...of Judah had burnt
37. 1 reigned instead of Coniah the son of J.
45. 1 of J. the son of Josiah king of Judah
46. 2 of J. the son of Josiah king of Judah
52. 2 he did..according to all that J. had done
Dan. 1. 1 third year of..reign of J. king of Judah
1. 2 the LORD gave J. king of Judah into his

JE-HO-IA'-RIB, יְהוֹיָרִיב *Jah contends.*

1. A priest in Jerusalem. B.C. 445.

1 Ch. 9. 10 the priests; Jedaiah, and J., and Jachin

2. The head of an Aaronite family when David allotted the charges of the sanctuary. B.C. 1015.

1 Ch.24. 7 the first lot came forth to J the second

JE-HO-NA'-DAB, יְהוֹנָדָב *Jah is liberal.*

A son of Rechab. B.C. 884. See *Jonadab.*

2 Ki. 10. 15 lighted on J. the son of Rechab (coming)
10. 15 J. answered, It is. If it be, give (me) thine
10. 23 Jehu went, and J. the son of Rechab, into

JE-HO-NA'-THAN, יְהוֹנָתָן *Jah gives.*

1. An overseer of the storehouses in the days of David. B.C. 1030.

1 Ch.27. 25 in the castles, (was) J. the son of Uzziah

2. A Levite sent by Jehoshaphat with his princes to teach the people. B.C. 912.

2 Ch. 17. 8 Shemiramoth, and J., and Adonijah, and

3. A priest in the days of Joiakim son of Jeshua. B.C. 536. He is called *Jonathan* in Neh. 12. 35.

Neh. 12. 18 Of Bilgah, Shammua; of Shemaiah, J.

JE-HO'-RAM, יְהוֹרָם *Jah is high.*

1. A son of Jehoshaphat who succeeded him on the throne. B.C. 893–885. See *Joram.*

1 Ki.22. 50 and Jehoram his son reigned in his stead
2 Ki. 1. 17 J. the son of Jehoshaphat king of Judah
8. 16 J. the son of Jehoshaphat king of Judah
8. 25 did Ahaziah the son of J. king of Judah
8. 29 the son of J. king of Judah went down
12. 18 J., and Ahaziah, his fathers, kings of Jud.
2 Ch.21. 1 and J. his son reigned in his stead
21. 3 the kingdom gave he to J., because he
21. 4 when J. was risen up to the kingdom of
21. 5 J. (was) thirty and two years old when he
21. 9 J. went forth with his princes, and all
21. 16 the LORD stirred up against J. the spirit
22. 1 Ahaziah the son of J. king of Judah rei.
22. 6 the son of J. king of Judah went down
22. 11 daughter of king J., the wife of Jehoiada

2. A Son of Ahab, slain by Jehu. B.C. 896–884.

2 Ki. 1. 17 J. reigned in his stead in the second year
3. 1 J. the son of Ahab began to reign over
3. 6 J. went out of Samaria the same time, and

2 Ki. 9. 24 smote J. between his arms, and the arrow
2 Ch.22. 5 went with J. the son of Ahab king of Is.
22. 6 down to see J. the son of Ahab at Jezreel
22. 7 he went out with J. against Jehu the son

3. A priest sent by Jehoshaphat with Elishama to teach Judah. B.C. 900.
2 Ch.17. 8 and with them Elishama and J., priests

JE-HO-SHAB'-EATH, יְהוֹשַׁבְעַת *Jah makes oath.*
A daughter of Jehoram, king of Judah. She concealed Joash son of Ahaziah. B.C. 885. In 2 K. 11. 2 she is called *Jehosheba.*
2 Ch.22. 11 J., the daughter of the king, took Joash
22. 11 J., the daughter of king Jehoram, the

JE-HO-SHA'-PHAT, יְהוֹשָׁפָט *Jah is judge.*
1. David's recorder. B.C. 1030.
2 Sa. 8. 16 and Jehoshaphat the son of Ahilud (was)
20. 24 and Jehoshaphat the son of Ahilud (was)
1 Ki. 4. 3 scribes; J. the son of Ahilud, the recorder
1 Ch.18. 15 and J. the son of Ahilud, recorder

2. A commissariat officer of Solomon's. B.C. 1015.
1 Ki. 4. 17 J. the son of Paruah in Issachar

3. A son of Asa who succeeded his father as king of Judah. B.C. 900.
1 Ki.15. 24 and J. his son reigned in his stead
22. 2 J. the king of Judah came down to the
22. 4 he said unto J., Wilt thou go with me to
22. 4 J. said to the king of Israel, I (am) as thou
22. 5 J. said unto the king of Israel, Enquire
22. 7 J. said, (Is there) not here a prophet of
22. 8 the king of Israel said unto J., (There is)
22. 8 And J. said, Let not the king say so
22. 10 the king of Israel and J...sat each on his
22. 18 the king of Israel said unto J., Did I not
22. 29 the king of Israel and J. the king of Jud.
22. 30 the king of Israel said unto J., I will
22. 32 the captains of the chariots saw J., that
22. 32 to fight against him: and J. cried out
22. 41 And J. the son of Asa began to reign over
22. 42 J. (was) thirty and five years old when he
22. 44 And J. made peace with the king of Israel
22. 45 acts of J., and his might that he showed
22. 48 J. made ships of Tharshish to go to Ophir
22. 49 Then said Ahaziah..son of Ahab unto J.
22. 49 Let my servants go with..but J. would not
22. 50 J. slept with his fathers, and was buried
22. 51 the seventeenth year of J. king of Judah
2 Ki. 1. 17 Jehoram the son of J. king of Judah
3. 1 the eighteenth year of J. king of Judah
3. 7 sent to J. the king of Judah, saying, The
3. 11 J. said, (Is there) not here a prophet of
3. 12 J. said, The word of the LORD is with him
3. 12 J. and the king of Edom went down to
3. 14 regard the presence of J. the king of Ju.
8. 16 J. (being) then king of Judah, Jehoram
8. 16 son of J. king of Judah began to reign
12. 18 J., and Jehoram, and Ahaziah, his fathers
1 Ch. 3. 10 Abia his son, Asa his son, J. his son
2 Ch.17. 1 And J. his son reigned in his stead, and
17. 3 the LORD was with J., because he walked
17. 5 Judah brought to J. presents; and he had
17. 10 so that they made no war against J.
17. 11 (some) of the Philistines brought J. pre.
17. 12 J. waxed great exceedingly; and he built
18. 1 J. had riches and honour in abundance
18. 3 king of Israel said unto J. king of Judah
18. 4 J. said unto the king of Israel, Enquire
18. 6 J. said, (Is there) not here a prophet of
18. 7 the king of Israel said unto J., (There is)
18. 7 And J. said, Let not the king say so
18. 9 the king of Israel and J king of Judah
18. 17 the king of Israel said to J., Did I not
18. 28 and J. the king of Judah went up to Ram.
18. 29 the king of Israel said unto J., I will
18. 31 the captains of the chariots saw J., that
18. 31 J. cried out, and the LORD helped him; and
19. 1 J. the king of Judah returned to his house
19. 2 said to king J., Shouldest thou help the
19. 4 J. dwelt at Jerusalem: and he went out
19. 8 in Jerusalem did J. set of the Levites
20. 1 the Ammonites, came against J. to battle
20. 2 there came some that told J., saying There
20. 3 J. feared, and set himself to seek the LORD
20. 5 J. stood in the congregation of Judah and
20. 15 thou king J., Thus saith the LORD unto
20. 18 J. bowed his head with (his) face to the
20. 20 J. stood and said, Hear me, O Judah, and
20. 25 J. and his people came to take away the
20. 27 J. in the fore front of them, to go again
20. 30 the realm of J. was quiet; for his God gave
20. 31 J. reigned over Judah; He (was) thirty and
20. 34 the acts of J., first and last, behold, they
20. 35 And after this did J. king of Judah join
20. 37 Eliezer..prophesied against J., saying
21. 1 J. slept with his fathers, and was buried
21. 2 he had brethren the sons of J., Azariah
21. 2 these (were) the sons of J. king of Israel
21. 12 not walked in the ways of J. thy father
22. 9 he (is) the son of J., who sought the LORD

4. The father of Jehu who conspired against Joram son of Ahab king of Israel. B.C. 900.
2 Ki. 9. 2 look out there Jehu the son of J., the son
9. 14 the son of J. the son of Nimshi conspired

5. A priest who assisted in bringing the ark from Obed-edom. B.C. 1042.
1 Ch.15. 24 J., and Nethaneel, and Amasai, and Zec.

6. A valley E. of Jerusalem, between it and the Mount of Olives.
Joel 3. 2 will bring them down into the valley of J.
3. 12 come up to the valley of J.: for there will

JE-HO-SHE'-BA, יְהוֹשֶׁבַע *Jah makes oath.*
The daughter of Joram king of Judah. She concealed her nephew Joash to prevent his being slain by Athaliah. See *Jehoshabeath.* B.C. 885.
2 Ki.11. 2 J., the daughter of king Joram, sister of

JE-HO-SHU'-A, יְהוֹשֻׁעַ *Jah saves.*
A name sometimes given to Joshua the son of Nun (or Non). B.C. 1451.
Num.13. 16 Moses called Oshea the son of Nun, J.
1 Ch. 7. 27 Non his son, J. his son

JE-HO'-VAH, יְהוָֹה *the existing one.*
The incommunicable name of the God of Israel. In the Common Version of the English Bible it is generally, though improperly, translated by "the LORD," *which see.*
Exod. 6. 3 but by my name J. was I not known to
Psa. 83. 18 thou, whose name alone (is) J., (art) the
Isa. 12. 2 J. (is) my strength and (my) song; he also
26. 4 in the LORD J. (is) everlasting strength

JE-HO-VAH JIR'-EH, יְהוָֹה יִרְאֶה *Jehovah will provide.*
A place in Jerusalem afterwards called *Moriah.*
Gen. 22. 14 Abraham called the name of that place J.

JE-HO-VAH NIS'-SI, יְהוָֹה נִסִּי *Jehovah is my banner.*
An altar erected by Moses to commemorate the defeat of the Amalekites. B.C. 1491.
Exod17. 15 an altar, and called the name of it J.

JE-HO-VAH SHA'-LOM, יְהוָֹה שָׁלוֹם *Jehovah is peace.*
An altar built by Gideon. B.C. 1256.
Judg. 6. 24 altar there unto the LORD, and called it J.

JE-HO-ZA'-BAD, יְהוֹזָבָד *Jah endows.*
1. The son of Shomer or Shimrith from Moab. He was one of those that slew Jehoash. B.C. 839.
2 Ki.12. 21 son of Shimeath, and J. the son of Shomer
2 Ch.24. 26 and J. the son of Shimrith a Moabitess
2. A son of Obed-edom, a Korathite gatekeeper. B.C. 1040.
1 Ch.26. 4 J. the second, Joah the third, and Sacar
3. A Benjamite, chief captain of Jehoshaphat king of Judah. B.C. 900.
2 Ch.17. 18 next him (was) J., and with him an hun.

JE-HO-ZA'-DAK, יְהוֹצָדָק *Jah is just.*
The grandson of Hilkiah who was high priest at the exile. B.C. 588.
1 Ch. 6. 14 Azariah begat Seraiah..Seraiah begat J.
6. 15 And J. went (into captivity), when the L.

JE'-HU, יֵהוּא *Jah is he.*
1. A son of Hanani, the prophet who announced the Lord's wrath against Baasha king of Israel. B.C. 930.
1 Ki. 16. 1 the word of the LORD came to J. the son
16. 7 by the hand of the prophet J. the son of
16. 12 he spake against Baasha by J. the prophet
2 Ch.19. 2 J. the son of Hanani the seer went out to
20. 34 written in the book of J...son of Hanani
2. The son or grandson of Nimshi. He was anointed by Elijah as king in the room of Ahab. B.C. 884–856.
1 Ki. 19. 16 J. the son of Nimshi shalt thou anoint
19. 17 escapeth the sword of Hazael shall J. slay
19. 17 him that escapeth from the sword of J.
2 Ki. 9. 2 look out there J. the son of Jehoshaphat
9. 5 J. said, Unto which of all us? And he said
9. 11 J. came forth to the servants of his lord
9. 13 and blew with trumpets, saying, J. is king
9. 14 J. the son of Jehoshaphat the son of Ni.
9. 15 J. said, If it be your minds, (then) let none
9. 16 J. rode in a chariot, and went to Jezreel
9. 17 he spied the company of J. as he came, and
9. 18 J. said, What hast thou to do with peace?
9. 19 J. answered, What hast thou to do with
9. 20 the driving (is) like the driving of J. the
9. 21 they went out against J., and met him in
9. 22 Joram saw J...he said, (Is it) peace, J.?
9. 24 J. drew a bow with his full strength, and
9. 27 J. followed after him, and said, Smite him
9. 30 when J. was come to Jezreel, Jezebel he.
9. 31 J. entered in at the gate, she said, (Had)
10. 1 J. wrote letters, and sent to Samaria, unto
10. 5 sent to J., saying, We (are) thy servants
10. 11 J. slew all that remained of the house of
10. 13 J. met with the brethren of Ahaziah king
10. 18 J. gathered all the people together, and
10. 18 Baal a little, (but) J. shall serve him much
10. 19 J. did (it) in subtilty, to the intent that
10. 20 J. said, Proclaim a solemn assembly for
10. 21 J. sent through all Israel; and all the
10. 23 J. went, and Jehonadab the son of Rec.
10. 24 J. appointed four score men without, and
10. 25 J. said to the guard and to the captains
10. 28 Thus J destroyed Baal out of Israel
10. 29 J. departed not from after them, (to wit)
10. 30 the LORD said unto J., Because thou hast
10. 31 J. took no heed to walk in the law of the
10. 34 the acts of J., and all that he did, and
10. 35 J. slept with his fathers: and they buried
10. 36 the time that J. reigned over Israel in
12. 1 In the seventh year of J., Jehoash began
13. 1 the son of J. began to reign over Israel
14. 8 son of Jehoahaz, son of J., king of Israel
15. 12 word of the LORD which he spake unto J.
2 Ch.22. 7 he went out with Jehoram against J. the
22. 8 J. was executing judgment upon the house
2 Ch.22. 9 they caught him..and brought him to J.
25. 17 son of Jehoahaz, the son of J., king of I.
Hos. 1. 4 the blood of Jezreel upon the house of J.
3. A son of Obed and descendant of Hezron. B.C. 1355.
1 Ch. 2. 38 And Obed begat J., and J. begat Azariah
4. A son of Josibiah, a Simeonite. B.C. 850.
1 Ch. 4. 35 J. the son of Josibiah, the son of Seraiah
5. A Benjamite who joined David at Ziklag. B.C. 1058.
1 Ch.12. 3 and Berachah, and J. the Antothite

JE-HUB'-BAH (doubtful reading of יחבה, V.L. חֻבָּה)
A descendant of Shamer, an Asherite. B.C. 1610.
1 Ch. 7. 34 sons of Shamer; Ahi, and Rohgah, J., and

JE-HU'-CAL, JU'-CAL, יְהוּכַל, יוּכַל *Jah is able.*
A son of Shelemiah, sent by Zedekiah to Jeremiah to entreat his prayers for the people. B.C. 590.
Jer. 37. 3 the king sent J. the son of Shelemiah, and
38. 1 J. the son of Shelemiah, and Pashur the

JE'-HUD, יְהֻד *honourable.*
A city of Dan, near Bene-berak.
Josh 19. 45 And J., and Bene-berak, and Gath-rimmon

JE-HU'-DI, יְהוּדִי *a Jew.*
One employed by the princes of Judah to bring Baruch before them. B.C. 606.
Jer. 36. 14 the princes sent J. the son of Nethaniah
36. 21 the king sent J. to fetch the roll: and he
36. 21 J. read it in the ears of the king, and in
36. 23 when J. had read three or four leaves, he

JE-HU-DI'-JAH, יְהֻדִיָּה *the Jewess.*
The wife of Ezra, and a descendant of Judah through Caleb the spy. B.C. 1400.
1 Ch. 4. 18 J. bare Jered the father of Gedor, and H

JE'-HUSH, יְעוּשׁ *collector.*
A Benjamite of the family of Saul. B.C. 860.
1 Ch. 8. 39 J. the second, and Eliphelet the third

JE-I'-EL, JE-HI'-EL, יְעִיאֵל, *God snatches away.*
1. A chief Reubenite. B.C. 1200.
1 Ch. 5. 7 brethren..(were) the chief, J., and Zech.
2. A Benjamite, the father of Gibeon, progenitor of Saul. B.C. 1180. [V.L. Jeuel.]
1 Ch. 9. 35 father of Gibeon, J., whose wife's name
3. One of David's valiant men. B.C. 1048. [V.L. Jeuel.]
1 Ch.11. 44 Shama and J...sons of Hothan the Aro.
4. A Levite gatekeeper and singer in David's reign. B.C. 1040.
1 Ch.15. 18 and Mikneiah, and Obed-edom, and J.
15. 21 J., and Azaziah, with harps on the Shem.
16. 5 J., and Shemiramoth and Jehiel, and Ma.
5. A Levite of the sons of Asaph. B.C. 1040.
2 Ch.20. 14 son of J., the son of Mattaniah, a Levite
6. A principal scribe or recorder of king Uzziah. B.C. 810. [V.L. Jeuel.]
2 Ch.26. 11 their account by the hand of J. the scribe
7. A Levite of the family of Elizaphan in the time of Hezekiah. B.C. 726. [V.L. Jeuel.]
2 Ch.29. 13 of the sons of Elizaphan; Shimri and J.
8. A chief Levite in the days of Josiah of Judah. B.C. 623.
2 Ch.35. 9 J., and Jozabad, chief of the Levites, gave
9. A son of Adonikam who returned with Ezra. B.C. 458. [V.L. Jeuel.]
Ezra 8. 13 J., and Shemaiah, and with them threesc.
10. One of the family of Nebo who had married a strange wife. B.C. 457.
Ezra 10. 43 J., Mattithiah, Zabad, Zebina, Jadan, and

JE-KAB-ZE'-EL, יְקַבְצְאֵל *God gathers.*
A city in the S. of Judah, near Edom. See *Kabzeel.*
Neh. 11. 25 and at J., and (in) the villages thereof

JE-KAM'-EAM, יְקַמְעָם *standing of the people.*
A son of Hebron, grandson of Levi. B.C. 1015.
1 Ch.23. 19 Jahaziel the third, and J. the fourth
24. 23 Jahaziel the third, J. the fourth

JE-KAM-I'AH, יְקַמְיָה *Jah is standing.*
A descendant of Jerahmeel, grandson of Pharez. B.C. 1280.
1 Ch. 2. 41 Shallum begat J., and J. begat Elishama

JE-KU-THI'-EL, יְקוּתִיאֵל *God is mighty.*
A son of Ezra, a descendant of Caleb the spy. B.C. 1400.
1 Ch. 4. 18 father of Socho, and J...father of Zanoah

JE-MI'-MA, יְמִימָה, *pure, fortunate, day.*
The eldest of the three daughters born to Job after his restoration to health and prosperity. B.C. 1520.
Job 42. 14 he called the name of the first, J.; and

JE-MU'-EL, יְמוּאֵל *God is light.*
A son of Simeon. B.C. 1700. In Num. 26. 12, and 1 Ch. 4. 24, the name is *Nemuel.*
Gen. 46. 10 J., and Jamin, and Ohad, and Jachin, and
Exod. 6. 15 J., and Jamin, and Ohad, and Jachin, and

JEOPARD, to —
To reproach (i.e. despise), חָרַף *charaph*, 3.
Judg. 5. 18 jeoparded their lives unto the death in

JEOPARDY, to put life in, or to go in —
To go on with the soul, הָלַךְ בְּנֶפֶשׁ *halak be-nephesh.*
2 Sa. 23. 17 men that went in jeopardy of their lives?
1 Ch. 11. 19 men that have put their lives in jeopardy?

JEOPARDY, to be or stand in —
To be in danger or peril, κινδυνεύω *kinduneuō.*
Luke 8. 23 and they were filled..and were in jeopar.
1 Co. 15. 30 And why stand we in jeopardy every hour?

JEPH'-THAH, JEPH'-THAE, יִפְתָּח *an opposer,* Ἰεφθάε.
A Gileadite judge of Israel. He delivered it from the Ammonites. B.C. 1150. In the Epistle to the Heb. 11. 32 he is called *Jephthæ.*
Judg 11. 1 J. the Gileadite was a mighty man of val.
11. 1 the son of an harlot: and Gilead begat J.
11. 2 they thrust out J., and said unto him
11. 3 J. fled from his brethren, and dwelt in
11. 3 there were gathered vain men to J.
11. 5 went to fetch J. out of the land of Tob
11. 6 they said unto J., Come, and be our cap.
11. 7 J. said unto the elders of Gilead, Did
11. 8, 10 And the elders of Gilead said unto J., Th.
11. 9 J. said unto the elders of Gilead, If ye
11. 11 J. went with the elders of Gilead, and
11. 11 J. uttered all his words before the LORD
11. 12 J. sent messengers unto the king of the
11. 13 king..answered unto the messengers of J.
11. 14 J. sent messengers again unto the king
11. 15 Thus saith J., Israel took not away the
11. 28 not unto the words of J. which he sent
11. 29 the Spirit of the LORD came upon J., and
11. 30 J. vowed a vow unto the LORD, and said
11. 32 J. passed over unto the children of Amm.
11. 34 J. came to Mizpeh unto his house, and
11. 40 lament the daughter of J. the Gileadite
12. 1 said unto J., Wherefore passedst thou
12. 2 J. said unto them, I and my people were
12. 4 J. gathered together all the men of Gilead
12. 7 J. judged Israel six years. Then died J.
1 Sa. 12. 11 sent Jerubbaal, and Bedan, and J., and
Heb. 11. 32 (of) Barak, and (of) Samson, and (of) J.

JE-PHUN'-NEH, יְפֻנֶּה, *appearing.*
1. A man of the tribe of Judah, and father of Caleb the spy. B.C. 1500.
Num 13. 6 Of the tribe of Judah, Caleb the son of J.
14. 6 the son of Nun, and Caleb the son of J.
14. 30 the son of J., and Joshua the son of Nun
14. 38 the son of Nun, and Caleb the son of J.
26. 65 the son of J., and Joshua the son of Nun
32. 12 son of J. the Kenezite, and Joshua the
34. 19 Of the tribe of Judah, Caleb the son of J.
Deut. 1. 36 Save Caleb the son of J.; he shall see it
Josh. 14. 6 the son of J. the Kenezite said unto him
14. 13 gave unto Caleb the son of J. Hebron
14. 14 the inheritance of Caleb the son of J.
15. 13 unto Caleb the son of J. he gave a part
21. 12 fields..gave they to Caleb the son of J. for
1 Ch. 4. 15 sons of Caleb the son of J.; Iru, Elah, and
6. 56 fields..they gave to Caleb the son of J.
2. An Asherite, head of a family. B.C. 1500.
1 Ch. 7. 38 the sons of Jether; J., and Pispah, and

JE'-RAH, יֶרַח *moon.*
A son of Joktan of the family of Shem. B.C. 2210.
Gen. 10. 26 Joktan begat Almodad..and J.
1 Ch. 1. 20 Joktan begat Almodad, and S..and J.

JE-RAH-ME'-EL, יְרַחְמְאֵל *God is merciful.*
1. A son of Hezron, grandson of Judah. B.C. 1540.
1 Ch. 2. 9 sons also of Hezron..J., and Ram, and
2. 25 the sons of J. the first born of Hezron were
2. 26 J. had also another wife, whose name (was)
2. 27 sons of Ram the first born of J. were Maaz
2. 33 Peleth, and Zaza. These were the sons of J.
2. 42 Now the sons of Caleb the brother of J.
2. A son of Kish, a Merarite. B.C. 1015.
1 Ch. 24. 29 Concerning Kish: the son of Kish (was) J.
3. An officer of Jehoiakim, king of Judah. B.C. 606.
Jer. 36. 26 the king commanded J. the son of Ham.

JE-RAH-ME-E-LITES, יְרַחְמְאֵלִי.
The family of Jerahmeel, son of Hezron.
1 Sa. 27. 10 against the south of the J., and against
30. 29 to (them) which (were) in the cities of the J.

JE'-RED, יֶרֶד *low, flowing.*
A son of Ezra a descendant of Caleb the spy. B.C. 1400.
1 Ch. 4. 18 his wife Jehudijah bare J. the father of

JE-RE'-MAI, יְרֵמַי *Jah is high.*
One of the family of Hashum who had taken a strange wife. B.C. 456.
Ezra 10. 33 Of the sons of Hashum..J., Manasseh, (and)

JE-RE-MI'-AH, יִרְמְיָהוּ ,יִרְמְיָה, *Jah is high* Ἰερεμίας.
1. An inhabitant of Libnah, whose daughter Hamutal was the wife of Josiah and mother of Jehoahaz, kings of Judah. B.C. 660.
2 Ki. 23. 31 name (was) Hamutal, the daughter of J.
24. 18 name (was) Hamutal, the daughter of J.
Jer. 52. 1 name (was) Hamutal the daughter of J.
2. A Manassehite, head of a family. B.C. 800.
1 Ch. 5. 24 Azriel, and J., and Hodaviah, and Jahdiel
3. One that joined David at Ziklag. B.C. 1058.
1 Ch. 12. 4 and J., and Jahaziel, and Johanan, and
4. A Gadite who also joined David at Ziklag.
1 Ch. 12. 10 Mishmannah the fourth, J. the fifth
5. Another Gadite that also joined David there.
1 Ch. 12. 13 J. the tenth, Machbanai the eleventh
6. Son of Hilkiah. The prophet from Anathoth in the days of Josiah. B.C. 628. He was of the line of *Abiathar.*
2 Ch. 35. 25 J. lamented for Josiah; and all the singing
36. 12 humbled not himself before J. the prophet
36. 21 To fulfil the word..by the mouth of J.
36. 22 the word of the LORD..by the mouth of J.
Ezra 1. 1 the word of the LORD by the mouth of J.
Jer. 1. 1 The words of J. the son of Hilkiah, of the
1. 11 saying, J., what seest thou? And I said, I
7. 1 The word that came to J. from the LORD
11. 1 The word that came to J. from the LORD
14. 1 The word..that came to J. concerning the
18. 1 The word which came to J. from the LORD
18. 18 Come, and let us devise devices against J.
19. 14 Then came J. from Tophet, whither the L.
20. 1 Now Pashur..heard that J. prophesied
20. 2 Then Pashur smote J. the prophet, and
20. 3 that Pashur brought forth J. out of the
20. 3 Then said J. unto him, The LORD hath not
21. 1 The word which came unto J. from the
21. 3 Then said J. unto them, Thus shall ye say
24. 3 Then said the LORD..What seest thou, J.?
25. 1 word that came to J. concerning all the
25. 2 which J. the prophet spake unto all the
25. 13 which J. hath prophesied against all the
26. 7 all the people heard J. speaking these
26. 8 when J. had made an end of speaking al.
26. 9 all the people were gathered against J. in
26. 12 Then spake J. unto all the princes, and
26. 20 prophesied..according to all the words of J.
26. 24 hand of Ahikam..son of Shapham..with J.
27. 1 came this word unto J. from the LORD
28. 5 Then the prophet J. said unto the prophet
28. 6 Even the prophet J. said, Amen: the LORD
28. 10 took the yoke from off the prophet J.'s
28. 11 And the prophet J. went his way
28. 12 Then the word of the LORD came unto J.
28. 12 prophet had broken the yoke from off..J.
28. 15 Then said the prophet J. unto Hananiah
29. 1 letter that J. the prophet sent from Jer.
29. 27 therefore why hast thou not reproved J.
29. 29 priest read this letter in the ears of J. the
29. 30 Then came the word of the LORD unto J.
30. 1 The word that came to J. from the LORD
32. 1 The word that came to J. from the LORD
32. 2 J. the prophet was shut up in the court
32. 6 J. said, The word of the LORD came unto
32. 26 Then came the word of the LORD unto J.
33. 1 the word of the LORD came unto J. the
33. 19 the word of the LORD came unto J., saying
33. 23 Moreover the word of the LORD came to J.
34. 1 The word which came unto J. from the L.
34. 6 Then J. the prophet spake all these words
34. 8 (This is) the word that came unto J. from
34. 12 Therefore the word of the LORD came to J.
35. 1 The word which came unto J. from the L.
35. 12 Then came the word of the LORD unto J.
35. 18 J. said unto the house of the Rechabites
36. 1 this word came unto J. from the LORD
36. 4 Then J. called Baruch the son of Neriah
36. 4 Baruch wrote from the mouth of J. all
36. 5 J. commanded Baruch, saying, I (am) shut
36. 8 And Baruch..did according to all that J.
36. 10 read Baruch in the book the words of J.
36. 19 Go, hide thee, thou and J.; and let no
36. 26 to take Baruch the scribe, and J. the pro.
36. 27 Then the word of the LORD came to J.
36. 27 words..Baruch wrote at the mouth of J.
36. 32 Then took J. another roll, and gave it to
36. 32 who wrote therein, from the mouth of J.
37. 2 words..which he spake by the prophet J.
37. 3 the king sent Jehucal..to the prophet J.
37. 4 Now J. came in and went out among the
37. 6 the word of the LORD unto the prophet J.
37. 12 Then J. went forth out of Jerusalem to go
37. 13 and he took J. the prophet, saying, Thou
37. 14 Then said J...I fall not away to the Cha.
37. 14 Irijah took J., and brought him to the pri.
37. 15 Wherefore the princes were wroth with J.
37. 16 When J. was entered into the dungeon
37. 16 and J. had remained there many days
37. 17 Is there (any) word from the LORD? And J.
37. 18 Moreover J. said unto king Zedekiah
37. 21 that they should commit J. into the court
37. 21 Thus J. remained in the court of the pris.
38. 1 Pashur..heard the words that J. had sp.
38. 6 Then took they J., and cast him into the
38. 6 they let down J. with cords..so J. v. 9.
38. 7 Ebed-melech..heard that they had put J.
38. 10 Take..hence thirty men..and take up J.
38. 11 took the men..and let them down..to J.
38. 12 Ethiopian said unto J...And J. did so
38. 13 So they drew up J. with cords, and took
38. 13 J. remained in the court of the prison
38. 14 Then Zedekiah..took J...unto him into
38. 14 the king said unto J., I will ask thee a th.
38. 15 Then J. said unto Zedekiah, If I declare
38. 16 Zedekiah the king sware secretly unto J.
38. 17 Then said J. unto Zedekiah, Thus saith
38. 19 Zedekiah the king said unto J., I am af.
38. 20 But J. said, They shall not deliver (thee)
38. 24 Then said Zedekiah unto J., Let no man
38. 27 Then came all the princes unto J., and
38. 28 So J. abode in the court of the prison
39. 11 Nebuchadr...gave charge concerning J.
Jer. 39. 14 they sent, and took J. out of the court of
39. 15 Now the word of the LORD came unto J.
40. 1 The word which came to J. from the LORD
40. 2 the captain of the guard took J., and said
40. 6 Then went J. unto Gedaliah the son of A.
42. 2 said unto J. the prophet, Let, we beseech
42. 4 Then J. the prophet said unto them, I
42. 5 Then they said to J., The LORD be a true
42. 7 that the word of the LORD came unto J.
43. 1 J. had made an end of speaking unto all
43. 2 Then spake Azariah..unto J., Thou
43. 6 J. the prophet, and Baruch the son of N.
43. 8 Then came the word of the LORD unto J.
44. 1 word that came to J. concerning all the J.
44. 15 all the women that stood by..answered J.
44. 20 Then J. said unto all the people, to the
44. 24 Moreover J. said unto all the people, and
45. 1 The word that J. the prophet spake unto
45. 1 these words in a book at the mouth of J.
46. 1 word of the LORD which came to J. the
46. 13 word that the LORD spake to J. the prop.
47. 1 word of the LORD that came to J. the pr.
49. 34 word of the LORD that came to J. the pr.
50. 1 word that the LORD spake..by J. the pr.
51. 59 which J. the prophet commanded Seraiah
51. 60 J. wrote in a book all the evil that should
51. 61 J. said to Seraiah, When thou comest to
51. 64 Thus far (are) the words of J.
Dan. 9. 2 the word of the LORD came to J. the pro.
Matt. 2. 17 that which was spoken by J. the prophet
16. 14 Elias; and others, J., or one of the prop.
27. 9 that which was spoken by J. the prophet
7. A priest who sealed the covenant with Nehemiah. B.C. 445.
Neh. 10. 2 Seraiah, Azariah, J.
12. 1 of Shealtiel, and Jeshua: Seraiah, J., E.
12. 12 fathers: of Seraiah, Meraiah; of J., Ha.
12. 34 Judah, and Benjamin..Shemaiah, and J.
8. A descendant of Jonadab, son of Rechab. B.C. 600.
Jer. 35. 3 the son of J., the son of Habazaniah, and

JE-RE'-MOTH, יְרֵמוֹת *elevation.*
1. A son of the Benjamite Beriah. B.C. 1400.
1 Ch. 8. 14 And Ahio, Shashak, and J.
2. One who married a foreigner in Ezra's time.
Ezra 10. 26 and Jehiel, and Abdi, and J., and Eliah
3. One who married a foreigner in Ezra's time.
Ezra 10. 27 Mattaniah, and J., and Zabad, and Aziza
4. The same as Jerimoth, No. 4. 1 Ch. 23. 23.
5. The same as Jerimoth, No. 5. 1 Ch. 25. 22.

JE-RI'-AH, JE-RI'-JAH, יְרִיָּהוּ ,יְרִיָּה *Jah is foundation.*
A descendant of Hebron, grandson of Levi, in the days of David. B.C. 1030.
1 Ch. 23. 19 J. the first, Amariah the second, Jahaziel
24. 23 J.(...first), Amariah the second, Jahaziel
26. 31 Among the Hebronites (was) J. the chief

JE-RI'-BAI, יְרִיבַי *Jah contends.*
A valiant man of David's guard. B.C. 1048.
1 Ch. 11. 46 J. and Joshaviah, the sons of Elnaam

JE-RI'-CHO, יְרֵחוֹ ,יְרִיחוֹ ,יְרִחֹה *fragrant,* Ἰεριχώ.
A famous city of Benjamin in the plain and on the W. of the Jordan, twenty-five miles N.E. of Jerusalem. It is now called *Er Kiha.* It was taken by Joshua 1451 B.C., and rebuilt 918 B.C. by Hiel. It is also called "the city of palm trees," and was reduced by Vespasian, A.D. 68.
Num 22. 1 plains of Moab on this side Jordan (by) J.
26. 3, 63 the plains of Moab, by Jordan (near) J.
31. 12 of Moab, which (are) by Jordan (near) J.
33. 48, 50 the plains of Moab, by Jordan (near) J
34. 15 on this side Jordan (near) J. eastward
35. 1 in the plains of Moab by Jordan (near) J.
36. 13 in the plains of Moab by Jordan (near) J.
Deut 32. 49 the land of Moab, that (is) over against J.
34. 1 the top of Pisgah, that (is) over against J.
34. 3 the plain of the valley of J., the city of
Josh. 2. 1 Go view the land, even J. And they went
2. 2 it was told the king of J., saying, Behold
2. 3 And the king of J. sent unto Rahab, say.
3. 16 the people passed over right against J.
4. 13 forty thousand..passed..the plains of J.
4. 19 encamped in Gilgal, in the east border of J.
5. 10 and kept the passover..in the plains of J.
5. 13 when Joshua was by J., that he lifted up
6. 1 J. was straitly shut up because of the
6. 2 I have given into thine hand J., and the
6. 25 messengers which Joshua sent to spy...J.
6. 26 that riseth up and buildeth this city J.
7. 2 Joshua sent men from J. to Ai, which (is)
8. 2 as thou didst unto J. and her king: only
9. 3 what Joshua had done unto J. and to Ai
10. 1 as he had done to J. and her king, so he
10. 28 and he did..as he did unto the king of J.
10. 30 but did..as he did unto the king of J.
12. 9 The king of J., one; the king of Ai, which
13. 32 on the other side Jordan, by J., eastward
16. 1 fell from Jordan by J. unto the water of J.
16. 1 to the wilderness that goeth up from J.
16. 7 and came to J., and went out at Jordan
18. 12 the border went up to the side of J. on
18. 21 according to their families were J., and
20. 8 the other side Jordan by J. eastward, they
24. 11 and came unto J.: and the men of J. fought
2 Sa. 10. 5 Tarry at J. until your beards be grown
1 Ki. 16. 34 his days did Hiel the Beth-elite build J.
2 Ki. 2. 4 the LORD hath sent me to J. And he
2. 4 I will not leave thee. So they came to J.
2. 5 sons of the prophets that (were) at J. came

2 Ki. 2. 15 sons of..prophets..(were) to view at J.
2. 18 they came again to him, for he tarried at J.
25. 5 overtook him in the plains of J.: and all
1 Ch. 6. 78 on the other side Jordan by J.. on the
19. 5 Tarry at J. until your beards be grown
2 Ch.28. 15 brought them to J., the city of palm trees
Ezra 2. 34 The children of J., three hundred forty
Neh. 3. 2 And next unto him builded the men of J.
7. 36 The children of J., three hundred forty
Jer. 39. 5 overtook Zedekiah in the plains of J.: and
52. 8 overtook Zedekiah in the plains of J.; and
Matt 20. 29 as they departed from J., a great multit.
Mark10. 46 they came to J.: and as he went out [of J.]
Luke10. 30 certain (man) went..from Jerusalem to J.
18. 35 as he was come nigh unto J., a certain blind
19. 1 And (Jesus) entered and passed through J.
Heb. 11. 30 the walls of J. fell down, after they were

JE-RI'-EL, יְרִיאֵל *foundation of God.*
A son of Tola, son of Issachar. B.C. 1650. 1 Ch. 7. 2.

JERIJAH. *See* **JERIAH.**

JE-RI'-MOTH, יְרִימוֹת *elevation.*
1. A son of Bela, son of Benjamin. B.C. 1650.
1 Ch. 7. 7 and Uzzi, and Uzziel, and J., and Iri, five
2. A son of Becher, son of Benjamin. B.C. 1650. (יְרֵמוֹת.)
1 Ch. 7. 8 and J., and Abiah, and Anathoth, and A.
3. A valiant man who joined David at Ziklag. B.C. 1058.
1 Ch.12 5 and J., and Bealiah, and Shemariah, and
4. A son of Mushi, grandson of Levi. B.C. 1015.
1 Ch.23. 23 sons of Mushi; Mahli, and Eder, and J.
24. 30 sons also of Mushi; Mahli, and Eder..J.
5. A son of Heman, appointed by David for the service of song. B.C. 1015. (*See* Jeremoth.)
1 Ch.25. 4 J., Hananiah, Hanani, Eliathah, Giddalti
6. A ruler in Naphtali in the days of David. B.C. 1020.
1 Ch.27. 19 Obadiah: of Naphtali; J. the son of Azriel
7. A son of David, not elsewhere mentioned. B.C. 1015.
2 Ch.11 18 daughter of J. the son of David to wife

JE-RI'-OTH, יְרִיעוֹת *tremulousness.*
A wife or concubine of Caleb son of Hezron. B.C. 1580.
1 Ch. 2. 18 (children) of Azubah (his) wife, and of J.

JE-ROB-O'-AM, יָרָבְעָם *enlarger.*
1. A son of Nebat from Zereda in Manasseh. He became the first king of the ten tribes of Israel. B.C. 970.
1 Ki. 11. 26 J. the son of Nebat, an Ephrathite of Zer.
11. 28 J. (was) a mighty man of valour: and So.
11. 29 at that time when J. went out of Jerusa.
11. 31 he said to J., Take thee ten pieces; for
11. 40 Solomon sought therefore to kill J.: and J.
12. 2 J. the son of Nebat, who was yet in Egypt
12. 2 for he was fled..and J. dwelt in Egypt
12. 3 J. and all the congregation of Israel came
12. 12 J. and all the people came to Rehoboam
12. 15 LORD spake by Ahijah the Shilonite unto J.
12. 20 all Israel heard that J. was come again
12. 25 J. built Shechem in mount Ephraim, and
12. 26 J. said in his heart, Now shall the king.
12. 32 J. ordained a feast in the eighth month
13. 1 and J. stood by the altar to burn incense
13. 4 J. heard the saying of the man of God
13. 33 J. returned not from his evil way, but
13. 34 this thing became sin unto the house of J.
14. 1 that time Abijah the son of J. fell sick
14. 2 J. said to his wife, Arise, I pray thee, and
14. 2 thou be not known to be the wife of J.
14. 4 J.'s wife did so, and arose, and went to
14. 5 the wife of J. cometh to ask a thing of
14. 6 Come in, thou wife of J.; why feignest
14. 7 tell J., Thus saith the LORD God of Israel
14. 10 the house of J., and will cut off from J.
14. 10 take away the remnant of the house of J.
14. 11 Him that dieth of J. in the city shall
14. 13 for he only of J. shall come to the grave
14. 13 (some) good thing..in the house of J.
14. 14 who shall cut off the house of J. that day
14. 16 give Israel up because of the sins of J.
14. 17 J.'s wife arose, and departed, and came
14. 19 the acts of J., how he warred, and how he
14. 20 the days which J. reigned (were) two and
14. 30 war between Rehoboam and J. all (their)
15. 1 eighteenth year of king J. the son of Ne.
15. 6 there was war between Rehoboam and J.
15. 7 And there was war between Abijam and J.
15. 9 the twentieth year of J. king of Israel
15. 25 the son of J. began to reign over Israel
15. 29 smote all the house of J.; he left not to J.
15. 30 Because of the sins of J. which he sinned
15. 34 walked in the way of J., and in his sin
16. 2 thou hast walked in the way of J., and
16. 3 like the house of J. the son of Nebat
16. 7 provoking him..in being like..house of J.
16. 19 walking in the way of J., and in his sin
16. 26 in all the way of J. the son of Nebat, and
16. 31 walk in the sins of J. the son of Nebat
21. 22 like the house of J. the son of Nebat
22. 52 in the way of J. the son of Nebat, who
2 Ki. 3. 3 unto the sins of J. the son of Nebat
9. 9 like the house of J. the son of Nebat
10. 29 (from) the sins of J. the son of Nebat, who
10. 31 he departed not from the sins of J., which
13. 2 followed the sins of J. the son of Nebat
13. 6 departed not from the sins of..house of J.
13. 11 from all the sins of J. the son of Nebat
14. 24 from all the sins of J. the son of Nebat
15. 9, 18, 24 from the sins of J. the son of Nebat
15. 28 he departed not from the sins of J. the
2 Ki.17. 21 they made J. the son of Nebat king: and J.
17. 22 walked in all the sins of J. which he did
23. 15 the high place which J. the son of Nebat
2 Ch. 9. 29 visions of Iddo the seer against J. the
10. 2 when J. the son of Nebat, who (was) in E.
10. 2 came to pass..that J. returned out of E.
10. 3 J. and..Israel came and spake to Rehob.
10. 12 J. and all the people came to Rehoboam
10. 15 by the hand of Ahijah the Shilonite to J.
11. 4 obeyed..returned from going against J.
11. 14 J. and his sons had cast them off from
12. 15 wars between Rehoboam and J. contin.
13. 1 in the eighteenth year of king J. began
13. 2 And there was war between Abijah and J.
13. 3 J. also set the battle in array against
13. 4 and said, Hear me, thou J., and all Israel
13. 6 J. the son of Nebat, the servant of Solomon
13. 8 golden calves, which J. made you for gods
13. 13 But J. caused an ambushment to come
13. 15 God smote J. and all Israel before Abijah
13. 19 Abijah pursued after J., and took cities
13. 20 Neither did J. recover strength again in
2. A son of Joash or Jehoash the grandfather of Jehu. B.C. 825.
2 Ki.13. 13 J. sat upon his throne: and Joash was
14. 16 and J. his son reigned in his stead
14. 23 J. the son of Joash king of Israel began
14. 27 saved..by the hand of J. the son of Joash
14. 28 the acts of J., and all that he did, and
14. 29 J. slept with his fathers, (even) with the
15. 1 the twenty and seventh year of J. king of
15. 8 did Zachariah the son of J. reign over
1 Ch. 5. 17 All these were reckoned..in the days of J.
Hos. 1. 1 and in the days of J. the son of Joash
Amos 1. 1 in the days of J. the son of Joash king
7. 9 I will rise against the house of J. with
7. 10 priest of Beth-el sent to J. king of Israel
7. 11 J. shall die by the sword, and Israel shall

JE-RO'-HAM, יְרֹחָם *loved.*
1. A Levite, the grandfather of Samuel. B.C. 1190.
1 Sa. 1. 1 the son of J., the son of Elihu, the son of
1 Ch. 6. 27 Eliab his son, J. his son, Elkanah his son
6. 34 son of J., the son of Eliel, the son of Toah
2. The head of a Benjamite family. B.C. 1300.
1 Ch. 8. 27 Jaresiah..Eliah, and Zichri, the sons of J.
3. A descendant of Benjamin in Jesusalem. B.C. 470.
1 Ch. 9. 8 the son of J., and Elah the son of Uzzi
4. A priest whose son Adaiah lived in Jerusalem after the exile. B.C. 445.
1 Ch. 9. 12 the son of J., the son of Pashur, the son
Neh. 11. 12 the son of J., the son of Pelaliah, the son
5. One whose two sons joined David at Ziklag. B.C. 1058.
1 Ch.12. 7 Joelah, and Zebadiah..sons of J. of Gedor
6. The father of Azareel, prince of Dan in the days of David. B.C. 1048.
1 Ch. 27. 22 Of Dan; Azareel the son of J. These (were)
7. The father of Azariah, who helped Jehoiada to set Joash on the throne of Judah. B.C. 800.
2 Ch.23. 1 the son of J., and Ishmael the son of

JE-RUB-BA'-AL, יְרֻבַּעַל *contender with Baal.*
The name given to Gideon by his father Joash. B.C. 1256.
Judg. 6. 32 he called him J., saying, Let Baal plead
7. 1 J., who (is) Gideon, and all the people that
8. 29 J. the son of Joash went and dwelt in his
8. 35 showed they kindness to the house of J.
9. 1 the son of J. went to Shechem unto his
9. 2 the sons of J., (which are) threescore and
9. 5 slew his brethren the sons of J., (being)
9. 5 Jotham the youngest son of J. was left
9. 16 ye have dealt well with J. and his house
9. 19 have dealt truly and sincerely with J.
9. 24 (done) to the three score and ten sons of J.
9. 28 (Is) not (he) the son of J.? and Zebul his
9. 57 came the curse of Jotham the son of J.
1 Sa. 12. 11 And the LORD sent J., and Bedan, and J.

JE-RUB-BE'-SHETH, יְרֻבֶּשֶׁת *contender with the idol.*
Another name of Gideon, given to him by those who wished to avoid pronouncing the name of *Baal* in the former name. Compare Ishbosheth with Eshbaal, &c.
2 Sa. 11. 21 Who smote Abimelech the son of J.? did

JE-RU'-EL, יְרוּאֵל *foundation of God.*
A wilderness in the S. of Judah, west of the hill of Ziph.
2 Ch.20. 16 of the brook, before the wilderness of J.

JE-RU-SA'-LEM, יְרוּשָׁלַם ,יְרוּשָׁלַיִם ,ירושלם ,ירושלים ,יְרוּשְׁלֶם Ἱεροσόλυμα, Ἱερουσαλήμ, *possession of peace.*
A city of the Amorites called Jebus, on the N. of Judah, but counted to Benjamin; it is 15 miles from Jordan and Salt Sea, and 31 from the Mediterranean; it was built on four hills—Zion, Acra, Moriah, and Bezetha; it was surrounded on the E., W., and S. by a valley, which was environed with hills; it had three walls with towers, and was about 4½ miles in circumference. It was first taken by Judah, Judg. 1. 8, but only in part, v. 21, and finally by David, B.C. 1049, 2 Sa. 5. 6; during 1011–1004 its temple was built; in 970 it was plundered by Shishak; and in 884 by the Philistines and Arabs in the days of Jehoram; in 808 by the Israelites; in 710 besieged by Sennacherib; in 610 taken by Pharaoh-Necho; in 598 plundered by Nebuchadnezzar; in 588 rebels against him; in 587 the temple was burnt; in 538 Cyrus encourages its rebuilding; in 515 it is dedicated; in 445 Nehemiah rebuilds the wall; in 332 it is visited by Alexander the Great; in 320 captured by Ptolemy Soter; in 302 annexed to Egypt; in 170 its walls razed by Antiochus Epiphanes; in 63 taken by Pompey; in 44 its walls rebuilt by Antipater, father of Herod the Great: on Sept. 8., A.D. 70, it was destroyed by the Romans; in 130 rebuilt by Hadrian; in 335 Constantine founded the Church of the Holy Sepulchre; in 614 taken by the Persians; in 637 by the Saracens; in 1076 by the Turks; in 1098 assigned to Egypt; in 1099 taken by the Crusaders; in 1187 by Saladin; in 1228 assigned to the Christians; in 1243 taken by the Carizmians; in 1517 by the Ottomans; in 1832 assigned to Egypt; and in 1841 to Turkey.
Josh.10. 1 when Adoni-zedec king of J. had heard
10. 3 king of J. sent unto Hoham king of Hebron
10. 5 Therefore..the king of J...went up..and
10. 23 the king of J., the king of Hebron, the king
12. 10 The king of J., one; the king of Hebron
15. 8 south side of the Jebusite; the same (is) J.
15. 63 the inhabitants of J., the children of
15. 63 dwell with the children of Judah at J.
18. 28 and Jebusi, which (is) J., Gibeath, (and)
Judg. 1. 7 they brought him to J., and there he died
1. 8 children of Judah had fought against J.
1. 21 drive out the Jebusites that inhabited J.
1. 21 dwell with the children of Benjamin in J.
19. 10 and came over against Jebus, which (is) J.
1 Sa. 17. 54 David took the head..and brought it to J.
2 Sa. 5. 5 in J. he reigned thirty and three years
5. 6 his men went to J. unto the Jebusites, the
5. 13 took..more concubines and wives out of J.
5. 14 of those that were born unto him in J.
8. 7 took the shields..and brought them to J.
9. 13 Mephibosheth dwelt in J.; for he did eat
10. 14 from the children of Ammon..came to J.
11. 1 But David tarried still at J.
11. 12 Uriah abode in J. that day and the morr.
12. 31 David and all the people returned unto J.
14. 23 went to Geshur, and brought Absalom to J.
14. 28 Absalom dwelt two full years in J., and
15. 8 the LORD shall bring me again indeed to J.
15. 11 with Absal. went two hundred men..of J.
15. 14 all his servants that (were) with him at J.
15. 29 Abiathar carried the ark of God again to J.
15. 37 into the city, and Absalom came into J.
16. 3 he abideth at J.: for he said, To day shall
16. 15 men of Israel, came to J., and Ahithoph.
17. 20 could not find (them), they returned to J.
19. 19 day that my lord the king went out of J.
19. 25 when he was come to J. to meet the king
19. 33 with me, and I will feed thee with me in J.
19. 34 that I should go up with the king unto J.?
20. 2 clave unto their king, from Jordan..to J.
20. 3 David came to his house at J.; and the
20. 7 they went out of J., to pursue after Sheba
20. 22 And Joab returned to J. unto the king
24. 8 they came to J. at the end of nine months
24. 16 stretched..his hand upon J. to destroy it
1 Ki. 2. 11 thirty and three years reigned he in J.
2. 36 Build thee an house in J., and dwell there
2. 38 And Shimei dwelt in J. many days
2. 41 Shimei had gone from J. to Gath, and was
3. 1 the house..and the wall of J. round about
3. 15 he came to J., and stood before the ark of
8. 1 children of Israel, unto king Solomon in J.
9. 15 the wall of J., and Hazor, and Megiddo
9. 19 that which Solomon desired to build in J.
10. 2 she came to J. with a very great train
10. 26 whom he bestowed..with the king at J.
10. 27 the king made silver (to be) in J. as stones
11. 7 high place..in the hill that (is) before J.
11. 13 and for J.'s sake, which I have chosen
11. 29 time when Jeroboam went out of J., that
11. 32 for J.'s sake, the city which I have chosen
11. 36 may have a light alway before me in J.
11. 42 the time that Solomon reigned in J. over
12. 18 get him up to his chariot, to flee to J.
12. 21 when Rehoboam was come to J., he asse.
12. 27 sacrifice in the house of the LORD at J.
12. 28 It is too much for you to go up to J.
14. 21 he reigned seventeen years in J., the city
14. 25 Shishak king of Egypt came up against J.
15. 2 Three years reigned he in J.: and his
15. 4 did the LORD his God give him a lamp in J.
15. 4 set..his son after him, and to establish J.
15. 10 And forty and one years reigned he in J.
22. 42 he reigned twenty and five years in J.
2 Ki. 8. 17 and he reigned eight years in J.
8. 26 he reigned one year in J. And his mother's
9. 28 servants carried him in a chariot to J.
12. 1 forty years reigned he in J. And his
12. 17 and Hazael set his face to go up to J.
12. 18 sent (it) to Hazael..he went away from J.
14. 2 and reigned twenty and nine years in J.
14. 2 his mother's name (was) Jehoaddan of J.
14. 13 came to J., and brake down the wall of J.
14. 19 they made a conspiracy against him in J.
14. 20 he was buried at J. with his fathers in
15. 2 J. And his mother's name..Jecoliah of J.
15. 33 he reigned sixteen years in J. And his
16. 2 reigned sixteen years in J., and did not
16. 5 Pekah..king of Israel came up to J. to
18. 2 he reigned twenty and nine years in J.
18. 17 against J...they went up, and came to J.
18. 22 J., Ye shall worship before this altar in J.?
18. 35 LORD should deliver J. out of mine hand?
19. 10 J. shall not be delivered into the hand
19. 21 the daughter of J. hath shaken her head
19. 31 out of J. shall go forth a remnant, and
21. 1 reigned fifty and five years in J. And his
21. 4 the LORD said, In J. will I put my name
21. 7 in J., which I have chosen out of all tribes
21. 12 I (am) bringing (such) evil upon J. and
21. 13 I will stretch over J. the line of Samaria
21. 13 and I will wipe J. as (a man) wipeth a dish

2 Ki. 21. 16 he had filled J. from one end to another
21. 19 reigned two years in J. And his mother's
22. 1 and he reigned thirty and one years in J.
22. 14 she dwelt in J. in the college; and they
23. 1 unto him all the elders of Judah and of J.
23. 2 the inhabitants of J. with him, and the
23. 4 he burned them without J. in the fields of
23. 5 Judah, and in the places round about J.
23. 6 from the house of the LORD, without J.
23. 9 came not up to the altar of the LORD in J.
23. 13 high places that (were) before J., which
23. 20 burned men's bones..and returned to J.
23. 23 this passover was holden to..LORD in J.
23. 24 were spied in the land of Judah and in J.
23. 27 will cast off this city J. which I have
23. 30 brought him to J., and buried him in his
23. 31 and he reigned three months in J. And his
23. 33 put him..that he might not reign in J.
23. 36 and he reigned eleven years in J. And his
24. 4 he filled J. with innocent blood; which
24. 8 and he reigned in J. three months. And
24. 8 Nehushta, the daughter of Elnathan of J.
24. 10 the servants..came up against J., and
24. 14 he carried away all J., and all the princes
24. 15 (those) carried he into captivity from J.
24. 18 and he reigned eleven years in J. And his
24. 20 it came to pass in J. and Judah, until he
25. 1 his host, against J., and pitched against
25. 8 a servant of the king of Babylon, unto J.
25. 9 houses of J., and every great (man's)
25. 10 brake down the walls of J. round about
1 Ch. 3. 4 in J. he reigned thirty and three years
3. 5 these were born unto him in J.: Shimea
6. 10 in the temple that Solomon built in J.
6. 15 the LORD carried away Judah and J. by
6. 32 had built the house of the LORD in J.
8. 28 (were)..chief (men). These dwelt in J.
8. 32 also dwelt with their brethren in J.
9. 3 in J. dwelt the children of Judah, and
9. 34 These chief fathers..dwelt at J. 9. 38
11. 4 Israel went to J., which (is) Jebus, where
14. 3 And David took more wives at J.: and D.
14. 4 names of (his) children which he had in J.
15. 3 David gathered all Israel together to J.
18. 7 took the shields..and brought them to J.
19. 15 entered into the city. Then Joab came to J.
20. 1 David tarried at J. And Joab smote Rab.
20. 3 David and all the people returned to J.
21. 4 went throughout all Israel, and came to J.
21. 15 And God sent an angel unto J. to destroy
21. 16 sword in his hand stretched out over J.
23. 25 people, that they may dwell in J. for ever
28. 1 men, and with all the valiant men, unto J.
29. 27 thirty and three (years) reigned he in J.
2 Ch. 1. 4 for he had pitched a tent for it at J.
1. 13 the high place that (was) at Gibeon to J.
1. 14 which he placed..with the king at J.
1. 15 the king made silver and gold at J. (as
2. 7 men that (are) with me in Judah and in J.
2. 16 to Joppa, and thou shalt carry it up to J.
3. 1 house of the LORD at J. in mount Moriah
5. 2 Solomon assembled the elders..unto J.
6. 6 I have chosen J., that my name might be
8. 6 all that Solomon desired to build in J.
9. 1 prove Solomon with hard questions at J.
9. 25 the chariot cities, and with the king at J.
9. 27 the king made silver in J. as stones, and
9. 30 And Solomon reigned in J. over all Israel
10. 18 to get him up to (his) chariot, to flee to J.
11. 1 when Rehoboam was come to J., he gath.
11. 5 Rehoboam dwelt in J., and built cities for
11. 14 Levites left..and came to Judah and J.
11. 16 such as set their hearts..came to J., to
12. 2, 9 Shishak king of Egypt came..against J.
12. 4 he took the fenced cities..and came to J.
12. 5 that were gathered together to J. because
12. 7 shall not be poured out upon J. by the
12. 13 Rehoboam strengthened himself in J., and
12. 13 and he reigned seventeen years in J., the
13. 2 He reigned three years in J. His mother's
14. 15 carried away sheep..and returned to J.
15. 10 they gathered themselves together at J.
17. 13 men of war, mighty men of valour..in J.
19. 1 returned to his house in peace to J.
19. 4 Jehoshaphat dwelt at J.: and he went out
19. 8 in J. did Jehoshaphat set of the Levites
19. 8 controversies, when they returned to J.
20. 5 stood in the congregation of Judah and J.
20. 15 inhabitants of J., and thou king Jehosh.
20. 17 the salvation of the LORD with you..J.
20. 18 the inhabitants of J. fell before the LORD
20. 20 Hear me, O Judah..ye inhabitants of J.
20. 27 every man of Judah and J., and Jehosh.
20. 27 to go again to J. with joy; for the LORD
20. 28 they came to J. with psalteries and harps
20. 31 he reigned twenty and five years in J.
21. 5 Jehoram..reigned eight years in J.
21. 11 caused the inhabitants of J. to commit
21. 13 hast made Judah and the inhabitants of J.
21. 20 he reigned in J. eight years, and departed
22. 1 the inhabitants of J. made Ahaziah his
22. 2 he reigned one year in J. His mother's
23. 2 went about in Judah..they came to J.
24. 1 he reigned forty years in J. His mother's
24. 6 out of Judah and out of J., the collection
24. 9 a proclamation through Judah and J.
24. 18 wrath came upon Judah and J. for this
24. 23 they came to Judah and J., and destroyed
25. 1 he reigned twenty and nine years in J.
25. 1 his mother's name (was) Jehoaddan of J.
25. 23 to J., and brake down the wall of J. from
25. 27 they made a conspiracy against him in J.
2 Ch. 26. 3 and he reigned fifty and two years in J.
26. 3 mother's name also (was) Jecoliah of J.
26. 9 built towers in J. at the corner gate, and
26. 15 he made in J. engines, invented by cunn.
27. 1 reigned sixteen years in J. His mother's
27. 8 to reign, and reigned sixteen years in J.
28. 1 he reigned sixteen years in J.: but he did
28. 10 keep under the children of Judah and J.
28. 24 he made him altars in every corner of J.
28. 27 they buried him in the city, (even) in J.
29. 1 he reigned nine and twenty years in J.
29. 8 wrath of the LORD was upon Judah and J.
30. 1 should come to the house of the L. at J.
30. 2 the congregation in J., to keep the pass.
30. 3 people gathered themselves together to J.
30. 5 passover unto the LORD God of Israel at J.
30. 11 Zebulun humbled themselves..came to J.
30. 13 there assembled at J. much people to ke.
30. 14 took away the altars that (were) in J.
30. 21 children of Israel that were present at J.
30. 26 there was great joy in J.: for since the
30. 26 since the time..was) not the like in J.
31. 4 commanded the people that dwelt in J.
32. 2 that he was purposed to fight against J.
32. 9 king of Assyria send his servants to J.
32. 9 unto all Judah that (were) at J., saying
32. 10 Whereon do ye trust, that ye abide..in J.?
32. 12 and commanded Judah and J., saying
32. 18 the people of J. that (were) on the wall
32. 19 they spake against the God of J., as aga.
32. 22 saved Hezekiah and the inhabitants of J.
32. 23 many brought gifts unto the LORD to J.
32. 25 wrath upon him, and upon Judah and J.
32. 26 (both) he and the inhabitants of J., so
32. 33 the inhabitants of J. did him honour at
33. 1 and he reigned fifty and five years in J.
33. 4 had said, In J. shall my name be for ever
33. 7 in J., which I have chosen before all the
33. 9 Judah and the inhabitants of J. to err
33. 13 brought him again to J. into his kingdom
33. 15 mount of the house of the LORD, and in J.
33. 21 began to reign..reigned two years in J.
34. 1 and he reigned in J. one and thirty years
34. 3 purge Judah and J. from the high places
34. 5 burnt the bones..cleansed Judah and J.
34. 7 he had broken down..he returned to J.
34. 9 delivered the money..they returned to J.
34. 22 she dwelt in J. in the college; and they
34. 29 together all the elders of Judah and J.
34. 30 the inhabitants of J., and the priests, and
34. 32 he caused all that were present in J. and
34. 32 the inhabitants of J. did according to
35. 1 Josiah kept a passover..the LORD in J.
35. 18 were present, and the inhabitants of J.
35. 24 and they brought him to J., and he died
35. 24 all Judah and J. mourned for Josiah
36. 1 made him king in his father's stead in J.
36. 2 and he reigned three months in J.
36. 3 the king of Egypt put him down at J., and
36. 4 Eliakim his brother king..Judah and J.
36. 5 reigned eleven years in J.: and he did
36. 9 reigned three months and ten days in J.
36. 10 Zedekiah his brother..over Judah and J.
36. 11 Zedekiah..reigned eleven years in J.
36. 14 of the LORD which he..hallowed in J.
36. 19 brake down the wall of J., and burnt all
36. 23 charged me to build him an house in J.
Ezra 1. 2 charged me to build him an house at J.
1. 3 and let him go up to J., which (is) in Ju.
1. 3 house of the LORD God..which (is) in J.
1. 4 offering for..house of God that (is) in J.
1. 5 build..house of the LORD which (is) in J.
1. 7 Nebuchadnezzar..brought forth out of J.
1. 11 were brought up from Babylon unto J.
2. 1 came again unto J. and Judah, every one
2. 68 to the house of the LORD which (is) at J.
3. 1 gathered themselves..as one man to J.
3. 8 their coming unto the house of God at J.
3. 8 were come out of the captivity unto J.
4. 6 against the inhabitants of Judah and J.
4. 8 the scribe wrote a letter against J. to
4. 12 came up from thee..are come unto J.
4. 20 There have been mighty kings also over J.
4. 23 they went up in haste to J. unto the Jews
4. 24 work of the house of God which (is) at J.
5. 1 unto the Jews that (were) in Judah and J.
5. 2 to build the house of God which (is) at J.
5. 14 took out of the temple that (was) in J.
5. 15 carry them into the temple that (is) in J.
5. 16 foundation of..house of G. which (is) in J.
5. 17 decree..to build this house of God at J.
6. 3 decree (concerning) the house of God at J.
6. 5 took..out of the temple which (is) at J.
6. 5 brought again unto..temple which (is) at J.
6. 9 appointment of the priests which (are) at J.
6. 12 destroy this house of God which (is) at J.
6. 18 for the service of God, which (is) at J.
7. 7 the porters, and the Nethinims, unto J.
7. 8 he came to J. in the fifth month, which
7. 9 first (day) of the fifth month came he to J.
7. 13 of their own free will to go up to J., go
7. 14 enquire concerning Judah and J., accord.
7. 15 God of Israel, whose habitation (is) in J.
7. 16, 17 the house of their God which (is) in J.
7. 19 (those) deliver thou before the God of J.
7. 27 the house of the LORD which (is) in J.
8. 29 at J., in the chambers of the house of the
8. 30 to bring (them) to J., unto the house of
8. 31 twelfth (day) of..first month, to go unto J.
8. 32 we came to J., and abode there three days
9. 9 and to give us a wall in Judah and in J.
10. 7 made proclamation throughout J. and J.
Ezra 10. 7 should gather themselves together unto J.
10. 9 together unto J. within three days. It
Neh. 1. 2 asked them concerning the Jews..and..J.
1. 3 the wall of J. also (is) broken down, and
2. 11 So I came to J., and was there three days
2. 12 my God had put in my heart to do at J.
2. 13 viewed the walls of J., which were broken
2. 17 J. (lieth) waste, and the gates thereof are
2. 17 let us build up the wall of J., that we be
2. 20 portion, nor right, nor memorial, in J.
3. 8 and they fortified J. unto the broad wall
3. 9 son of Hur, the ruler of the half part of J.
3. 12 the ruler of the half part of J., he and
4. 7 heard that the walls of J. were made up
4. 8 (and) to fight against J., and to hinder it
4. 22 every one with his servant lodge within J.
6. 7 appointed prophets to preach of thee at J.
7. 2 the ruler of the palace, charge over J.
7. 3 Let not the gates of J. be opened until
7. 3 appoint watches of the inhabitants of J.
7. 6 came again to J. and to Judah, every one
8. 15 proclaim in all their cities, and in J.
11. 1 And the rulers of the people dwelt at J.
11. 1 one of ten to dwell in J. the holy city
11. 2 willingly offered themselves to dwell at J.
11. 3 chief of the province that dwelt in J.
11. 4 at J. dwelt (certain) of the children of
11. 6 the sons of Perez that dwelt at J. (were)
11. 22 The overseer also of the Levites at J. (was)
12. 27 at the dedication of the wall of J., they
12. 27 to bring them to J., to keep the dedication
12. 28 out of the plain country round about J.
12. 29 had builded them villages round about J.
12. 43 that the joy of J. was heard even afar off
13. 6 in all this (time) was not I at J.: for in
13. 7 I came to J., and understood of the evil
13. 15 they brought into J. on the sabbath day
13. 16 sold..unto the children of Judah, and in J.
13. 19 the gates of J. began to be dark before
13. 20 merchants..lodged without J. once or tw.
Esth. 2. 6 Who had been carried away from J. with
Psa. 51. 18 Do good..build thou the walls of J.
68. 29 Because of thy temple at J. shall kings
79. 1 they defiled; they have laid J. on heaps
79. 3 have they shed like water round about J.
102. 21 To declare the name..and his praise in J.
116. 19 in the midst of thee, O J. Praise ye the
122. 2 Our feet shall stand within thy gates, O J.
122. 3 J. is builded as a city that is compact
122. 6 Pray for the peace of J.: they shall pros.
125. 2 (As) the mountains (are) round about J.
128. 5 thou shalt see the good of J. all the days
135. 21 LORD out of Zion, which dwelleth at J.
137. 5 O J., let my right hand forget (her cunn.)
137. 6 if I prefer not J. above my chief joy
137. 7 the children of Edom in the day of J.; who
147. 2 The LORD doth build up J.: he gathereth
147. 12 Praise the LORD, O J.; praise thy God, O
Eccl. 1. 1 the Preacher, the son of David, king in J.
1. 12 I the Preacher was king over Israel in J.
1. 16 all (they) that have been before me in J.
2. 7 above all that were in J. before me
2. 9 more than all that were before me in J.
Song 1. 5 black, but comely, O ye daughters of J.
2. 7 I charge you, O ye daughters of J., by
3. 5 I charge you, O ye daughters of J., by
3. 10 paved (with) love, for the daughters of J.
5. 8 I charge you, O daughters of J., if ye find
5. 16 and this (is) my friend, O daughters of J.
6. 4 (art) beautiful, O my love..comely as J.
8. 4 I charge you, O daughters of J., that ye
Isa. 1. 1 which he saw concerning Judah and J.
2. 1 that Isaiah..saw concerning Judah and J.
2. 3 the law, and the word of the LORD from J.
3. 1 doth take away from J. and from Judah
3. 8 For J. is ruined, and Judah is fallen; be.
4. 3 (he that) remaineth in J., shall be called
4. 3 one (that is) written among the living in J.
4. 4 LORD..shall have purged the blood of J.
5. 3 now, O inhabitants of J...judge, I pray
7. 1 went up toward J. to war against it, but
8. 14 and for a snare to the inhabitants of J.
10. 10 graven images did excel them of J. and
10. 11 Shall I not..so do to J. and her idols
10. 12 his whole work upon mount Zion and on J.
10. 32 shake his hand (against) .the hill of J.
22. 10 And ye have numbered the houses of J.
22. 21 shall be a father to the inhabitants of J.
24. 23 LORD..shall reign in mount Zion, and in J.
27. 13 worship the LORD in the holy mount at J.
28. 14 men, that rule this people which (is) in J.
30. 19 the people shall dwell in Zion at J.: thou
31. 5 As birds flying, so will the LORD..defend J.
31. 9 whose fire (is) in Zion, and his furnace in J.
33. 20 thine eyes shall see J. a quiet habitation
36. 2 king..sent Rabshakeh from Lachish to J.
36. 7 said to Judah and to J., Ye shall worship
36. 20 the LORD should deliver J. out of my ha.
37. 10 J. shall not be given into the hand of the
37. 22 daughter of J. hath shaken her head at
37. 32 out of J. shall go forth a remnant, and
40. 2 Speak ye comfortably to J., and cry unto
40. 9 O J., that bringest good tidings, lift up
41. 27 I will give to J. one that bringeth good
44. 26 that saith to J., Thou shalt be inhabited
44. 28 saying to J., Thou shalt be built; and to
51. 17 O J., which hast drunk at the hand of the
52. 1 put on thy beautiful garments, O J., the
52. 2 sit down, O J.: loose thyself from the ba.
52. 9 sing together, ye waste places of J.: for
52. 9 comforted his people,..hath redeemed J.
62. 1 for J.'s sake I will not rest, until the

Isa. 62. 6 I have set watchmen upon thy walls, O J.
62. 7 and till he make J. a praise in the earth
64. 10 Zion is a wilderness, J. a desolation
65. 18 I create J. a rejoicing, and her people a
65. 19 I will rejoice in J., and joy in my people
66. 10 Rejoice ye with J., and be glad with her
66. 13 comfort you..ye shall be comforted in J.
66. 20 upon swift beasts, to my holy mountain J.
Jer. 1. 3 the carrying away of J. captive in the
1. 15 throne at the entering of the gates of J.
2. 2 cry in the ears of J., saying, Thus saith
3. 17 they shall call J. the throne of the LORD
3. 17 unto it, to the name of the LORD, to J.
4. 3 saith the LORD to the men of Judah and J.
4. 4 ye men of Judah and inhabitants of J.
4. 5 publish in J.; and say, Blow ye the trum.
4. 10 hast greatly deceived this people and J.
4. 11 shall it be said to this people and to J.
4. 14 O J., wash thine heart from wickedness
4. 16 publish against J., (that) watchers come
5. 1 ye to and fro through the streets of J.
6. 1 gather yourselves to flee out of..J., and
6. 6 cast a mount against J.: this (is) the city
6. 8 Be thou instructed, O J., lest my soul de.
7. 17 cities of Judah, and in the streets of J.?
7. 34 from the streets of J., the voice of mirth
8. 1 the bones of the inhabitants of J., out of
8. 5 Why (then) is this people of J. slidden
9. 11 I will make J. heaps, (and) a den of dra.
11. 2 men of Judah, and to the inhabitants of J.
11. 6 cities of Judah, and in the streets of J.
11. 9 A conspiracy..among..inhabitants of J.
11. 12 inhabitants of J. go and cry unto the gods
11. 13 (according to)..number of the streets of J.
13. 9 pride of Judah, and the great pride of J.
13. 13 prophets, and all the inhabitants of J.
13. 27 O J.! wilt thou not be made clean? when
14. 2 Judah mourneth..the cry of J. is gone up
14. 16 shall be cast out in the streets of J.
15. 4 be removed..for (that) which he did in J.
15. 5 who shall have pity upon thee, O J.? or
17. 19 Go and stand..in all the gates of J.
17. 20 the inhabitants of J., that enter in by
17. 21 bear..nor bring (it) in by the gates of J.
17. 25 men of Judah, and the inhabitants of J.
17. 26 from the places about J., and from the
17. 27 even entering in at the gates of J. on the
17. 27 it shall devour the palaces of J., and it
18. 11 the inhabitants of J., saying, Thus saith
19. 3 O kings of Judah, and inhabitants of J.
19. 7 the counsel of Judah and J. in this place
19. 13 the houses of J., and the houses of
22. 19 drawn and cast forth beyond the gates of J.
23. 14 I have seen also in the prophets of J. an
23. 15 from the prophets of J. is profaneness
24. 1 with the carpenters and smiths, from J.
24. 8 the residue of J., that remain in this land
25. 2 of Judah, and to all the inhabitants of J.
25. 18 J., and the cities of Judah, and the kings
26. 18 J. shall become heaps, and the mountain
27. 3 of the messengers which come to J. unto
27. 18 the house of the king of Judah, and at J.
27. 20 away captive Jeconiah..from J. to Baby.
27. 20 captive..all the nobles of Judah and J.
27. 21 the house of the king of Judah and of J.
29. 1 the prophet sent from J. unto the residue
29. 1 carried away captive from J. to Babylon
29. 2 princes of Judah and J., and the carpen.
29. 2 and the smiths, were departed from J.
29. 4 to be carried away from J. unto Babylon
29. 20 whom I have sent from J. to Babylon
29. 25 letters..unto all the people that (are) at J.
32. 2 the king of Babylon's army besieged J.: and
32. 32 men of Judah, and the inhabitants of J.
32. 44 in the places about J., and in the cities
33. 10 in the streets of J., that are desolate
33. 13 in the places about J., and in the cities
33. 16 J. shall dwell safely: and this (is the name)
34. 1 fought against J., and against all the
34. 6 words unto Zedekiah king of Judah in J.
34. 7 king of Babylon's army fought against J.
34. 8 with all the people that (were) at J.
34. 19 the princes of J., the eunuchs, and the
35. 11 let us go to J. for fear of the army of
35. 11 for fear of the army..so we dwell at J.
35. 13 men of Judah and the inhabitants of J.
35. 17 upon all inhabitants of J. all the evil
36. 9 proclaimed a fast..to all the people in J.
36. 9 that came from the cities of Judah unto J.
36. 31 upon the inhabitants of J., and upon the
37. 5 Chaldeans that besieged J. heard tidings
37. 5 Chaldeans..heard..they departed from J.
37. 11 army..Chaldeans was broken up from J.
37. 12 Jeremiah went forth out of J. to go into
38. 28 J. was taken: and he was (there) when J.
39. 1 Nebuchadnezzar..and..army against J.
39. 8 with fire, and brake down the walls of J.
40. 1 were carried away captive of J. and Judah
42. 18 poured forth upon the inhabitants of J.
44. 2 all the evil that I have brought upon J.
44. 6, 21 of Judah and in the streets of J.
44. 9 land of Judah and in the streets of J.?
44. 13 as I have punished J., by the sword v. 17.
51. 35 My blood upon the inhabitants..shall J.
51. 50 remember..and let J. come into your mind
52. 1 and he reigned eleven years in J. And
52. 3 it came to pass in J. and Judah, till he
52. 4 came, he and all his army, against J., and
52. 12 fifth month..came Nebuzar-adan..into J.
52. 13 the houses of J., and all the houses of the
52. 14 brake down all the walls of J. round about
52. 29 carried away captive from J. eight hund.

Lam. 1. 7 J. remembered in the days of her affliction
1. 8 J. hath grievously sinned; therefore she
1. 17 J. is as a menstruous woman among them
2. 10 the virgins of J. hang down their heads
2. 13 shall I liken to thee, O daughter of J.?
2. 15 and wag their head at the daughter of J.
4. 12 should have entered into the gates of J.
Eze. 4. 1 and pourtray upon it the city, (even) J
4. 7 shall set thy face toward the siege of J.
4. 16 I will break the staff of bread in J.: and
5. 5 This (is) J.: I have set it in the midst of
8. 3 brought me in the visions of God to J.
9. 4 midst of the city, through the midst of J.
9. 8 in thy pouring out of thy fury upon J.?
11. 15 unto whom the inhabitants of J. have
12. 10 This burden (concerneth) the prince in J.
12. 19 the Lord GOD of the inhabitants of J.
13. 16 which prophesy concerning J., and which
14. 21 I send my four sore judgments upon J.
14. 22 the evil that I have brought upon J., (even)
15. 6 so will I give the inhabitants of J.
16. 2 Son..cause J. to know her abominations
16. 3 Thus saith the Lord GOD unto J.; Thy
17. 12 the king of Babylon is come to J., and
21. 2 set thy face toward J., and drop (thy w.)
21. 20 may come..to Judah in J. the defenced
21. 22 his right hand was the divination for J.
22. 19 I will gather you into the midst of J.
23. 4 names; Samaria (is) Aholah, and J. Ahol.
24. 2 set himself against J. this same day
26. 2 that Tyrus hath said against J., Aha! she
33. 21 one that..escaped out of J. came unto me
36. 38 as the flock of J. in her solemn feasts
Dan. 1. 1 Nebuchadnezzar king of Babylon unto J.
5. 2 taken out of the temple which (was) in J.
5. 3 temple of the house of God..(was) at J.
6. 10 windows..open in his chamber toward J.
9. 2 seventy years in the desolations of J.
9. 7 the inhabitants of J., and unto all Israel
9. 12 not been done as hath been done upon J.
9. 16 thy fury be turned away from thy city J.
9. 16 J. and thy people (are become) a reproach
9. 25 to build J. unto the Messiah the Prince
Joel 2. 32 J. shall be deliverance, as the LORD
3. 1 bring again the captivity of Judah and J.
3. 6 the children of J. have ye sold unto the
3. 16 out of Zion, and utter his voice from J.
3. 17 then shall J. be holy, and there shall no
3. 20 and J. from generation to generation
Amos 1. 2 from Zion, and utter his voice from J.
2. 5 and it shall devour the palaces of J.
Obad. 11 entered..his gates..and cast lots upon J.
20 the captivity of J., which (is) in Sepharad
Mic. 1. 1 which he saw concerning Samaria and J.
1. 5 high places of Judah? (are they) not J.?
1. 9 unto the gate of my people, (even) to J.
1. 12 came down from the LORD unto..gate of J.
3. 10 Zion with blood, and J. with iniquity
3. 12 J. shall become heaps, and the mountain
4. 2 of Zion, and the word of the LORD from J.
4. 8 kingdom shall come to the daughter of J.
Zeph. 1. 4 Judah, and upon all the inhabitants of J.
1. 12 I will search J. with candles, and punish
3. 14 rejoice with all the heart..daughter of J.
3. 16 shall be said to J., Fear thou not; (and)
Zech. 1. 12 how long wilt thou not have mercy on J.
1. 14 I am jealous for J. and for Zion with a
1. 16 I am returned to J. with mercies: my h.
1. 16 a line shall be stretched forth upon J.
1. 17 yet comfort Zion, and shall yet choose J.
1. 19 which have scattered Judah, Israel, and J.
2. 2 measure J., to see what (is) the breadth
2. 4 J. shall be inhabited (as) towns without
2. 12 And the LORD..shall choose J. again
3. 2 the LORD that hath chosen J. rebuke thee
7. 7 J. was inhabited and in prosperity, and
8. 3 will dwell in the midst of J.: and J. shall
8. 4 old women dwell in the streets of J., and
8. 8 they shall dwell in the midst of J.; and
8. 15 I thought in these days to do well unto J.
8. 22 shall come to seek the LORD of hosts in J.
9. 9 shout, O daughter of J.: behold, thy King
9. 10 chariot from E., and the horse from J.
12. 2 I will make J. a cup of trembling unto
12. 2 siege both against Judah (and) against J.
12. 3 that day will I make J. a burdensome st.
12. 5 The inhabitants of J. (shall be) my stren.
12. 6 J. shall be inhabited again..(even) in J.
12. 7 the glory of the inhabitants of J. do not
12. 8 the LORD defend the inhabitants of J.
12. 9 all the nations that come against J.
12. 10 upon the inhabitants of J., the spirit of
12. 11 shall there be a great mourning in J., as
13. 1 fountain opened..to the inhabitants of J.
14. 2 gather all nations against J. to battle
14. 4 mount of Olives, which (is) before J. on
14. 8 living waters shall go out from J.; half
14. 10 a plain from Geba to Rimmon south of J.
14. 11 but J. shall be safely inhabited
14. 12 the people that have fought against J.
14. 14 Judah also shall fight at J.: and the we.
14. 16 of all the nations which came against J.
14. 17 not come up of (all) the families..unto J.
14. 21 Yea, every pot in J. and in Judah shall
Mal. 2. 11 abomination..committed in Is. and in J.
3. 4 Then shall the offering of Judah and J.
Matt. 2. 1 there came wise men from the east to J.
2. 3 he was troubled, and all J. with him
3. 5 Then went out to him J., and all Judea
4. 25 (from) J., and (from) Judea, and (from)
5. 35 neither by J.; for it is the city of the
15. 1 scribes and Pharisees, which were of J.

Matt 16. 21 must go unto J., and suffer many things
20. 17 And Jesus going up to J. took the twelve
20. 18 we go up to J.; and the Son of man shall
21. 1 they drew nigh unto J., and were come to
21. 10 when he was come into J., all the city
23. 37 O J., J., (thou) that killest the prophets
Mark 1. 5 all the land of Judea, and they of J., and
3. 8 from J., and from Idumæa, and (from)
3. 22 the scribes which came down from J. said
7. 1 certain of the scribes, which came from J.
10. 32 they were in the way going up to J.; and
10. 33 we go up to J.; and the Son of man shall
11. 1 when they came nigh [to J.], unto Bethph.
11. 11 Jesus entered into J., and into the temple
11. 15 they come to J.: and Jesus went into the
11. 27 they come again to J.: and as he was w.
15. 41 women which came up with him unto J.
Luke 2. 22 they brought him to J., to present (him)
2. 25 there..a man in J., whose name (was) S.
2. 38 all them that looked for redemption in J
2. 41 his parents went to J. every year at the
2. 42 they went up [to J.] after the custom of the
2. 43 the child Jesus tarried behind in J.; and
2. 45 they turned back again to J., seeking him
4. 9 And he brought him to J., and set him
5. 17 of every town of Galilee, and Judea, and J.
6. 17 people out of all Judea and J., and from
9. 31 decease which he should accomplish at J.
9. 51 he stedfastly set his face to go to J.
9. 53 his face was as though he would go to J.
10. 30 A certain (man) went down from J. to Jer.
13. 4 sinners above all men that dwelt in J.?
13. 22 went..teaching, and journey. toward [J.]
13. 33 cannot be that a prophet perish out of J.
13. 34 O J., J., which killest the prophets, and
17. 11 as he went to J., that he passed through
18. 31 we go up [to J.], and all things that are
19. 11 because he was nigh to J., and because they
19. 28 he went before, ascending up to J.
21. 20 when ye shall see J. compassed with arm.
21. 24 J. shall be trodden down of the Gentiles
23. 7 who himself also was at J. at that time
23. 28 Daughters of J., weep not for me, but weep
24. 13 which was from J. (about) threescore fur.
24. 18 Art thou only a stranger in J., and hast
24. 33 and returned to J., and found the eleven
24. 47 among all nations, beginning at J.
24. 49 tarry ye in the city of [J.], until ye be endued
24. 52 and returned to J. with great joy
John 1. 19 priests and Levites from J. to ask him
2. 13 passover was at hand..Jesus went..to J.
2. 23 he was in J. at the passover, in the feast
4. 20 J. is the place where men ought to wors.
4. 21 neither in this mountain, nor yet at J.
4. 45 the things that he did at J. at the feast
5. 1 feast of the Jews; and Jesus went up to J.
5. 2 there is at J., by the sheep (market), a pool
7. 25 Then said some of them of J., Is not this
10. 22 it was at J. the feast of the dedication
11. 18 Bethany was nigh unto J., about fifteen
11. 55 and many went out of the country up to J.
12. 12 they heard that Jesus was coming to J.
Acts 1. 4 they should not depart from J., but wait
1. 8 ye shall be witnesses unto me both in J.
1. 12 Then returned they unto J. from the mo.
1. 12 which is from J. a sabbath day's journey
1. 19 it was known unto all the dwellers at J.
2. 5 there were dwelling at J. Jews, devout
2. 14 (ye) that dwell at J., be this known unto
4. 6 and as many..were gathered together at J.
4. 16 (is) manifest to all them that dwell in J.
5. 16 (out) of the cities round about unto J.
5. 28 ye have filled J. with your doctrine, and
6. 7 the disciples multiplied in J. greatly; and
8. 1 persecution against..which was at J.
8. 14 the apostles which were at J. heard that
8. 25 returned [to J.], and preached the gospel
8. 26 the way that goeth down from J. unto Ga.
8. 27 an eunuch..had come to J. for to worship
9. 2 he might bring them bound unto J.
9. 13 much evil he hath done to thy saints at J.
9. 21 which called on this name in J., and came
9. 26 when Saul was come to J., he assayed to
9. 28 with them coming in and going out at J.
10. 39 both in the land of the Jews, and in J.
11. 2 when Peter was come up [to J.], they that
11. 22 the ears of the church which was [in J.]
11. 27 in these days came prophets from J.
12. 25 Barnabas and Saul returned from J., when
13. 13 John departing from them returned to J.
13. 27 they that dwell at J., and their rulers
13. 31 which came up with him from Galilee to J.
15. 2 should go up to J. unto the apostles and
15. 4 And when they were come to J., they were
16. 4 the apostles and elders which were [at J.]
18. 21 [I must..keep this feast that cometh in J.]
19. 21 Paul purposed in spirit..to go [to J.], saying
20. 16 hasted..to be [at J.] the day of Pentecost
20. 22 go bound in the spirit unto J., not know.
21. 4 who said..that he should not go up [to J.]
21. 11 So shall the Jews at J. bind the man that
21. 12 and they..besought him not to go up to J.
21. 13 die at J. for the name of the Lord Jesus
21. 15 took up our carriages, and went up [to J.]
21. 17 And when we were come to J., the breth.
21. 31 tidings came..that all J. was in an uproar
22. 5 bring them which were..bound unto J.
22. 17 when I was come again to J., even while
22. 18 get thee quickly out of J.: for they will
23. 11 as thou hast testified of me in J., so must
24. 11 twelve days since I went up to J. for to
25. 1 three days he ascended from Cesarea to J.

Acts 25. 3 he would send for him to J., laying wait
25. 7 the Jews which came down from J., stood
25. 9 Wilt thou go up to J., and there be judged
25. 15 when I was at J., the chief priests and the
25. 20 I asked (him) whether he would go to J.
25. 24 have dealt with me, both at J., and (also)
26. 4 at the first among mine own nation at J.
26. 10 Which thing I also did in J.: and many of
26. 20 and at J., and throughout all the coasts
28. 17 yet was I delivered prisoner from J. into
Rom 15. 19 from J., and round about unto Illyricum
15. 25 I go unto J. to minister unto the saints
15. 26 contribution for the..saints which are at J.
15. 31 that my service which (I have) for J. may
1 Co. 16. 3 I send to bring your liberality unto J.
Gal. 1. 17 Neither went I up to J. to them which
1. 18 I went up to J. to see Peter, and abode
2. 1 I went up again to J. with Barnabas, and
4. 25 mount Sinai in Arabia, and answereth to J.
4. 26 But J. which is above is free, which is the
Heb. 12. 22 the city of the living God, the heavenly J.
Rev. 3. 12 of the city of my God, (which is) New J.
21. 2 John saw the holy city, new J., coming
21. 10 and showed me that great city, the holy J.

JE-RU'-SHA, JE-RU'-SHAH, ירושא, ירושה *possession.*
The daughter of Zadok and wife of Uzziah, and mother of Jotham, kings of Judah. B.C. 760.
2 Ki. 15. 33 his mother's name (was) J., the daughter
2 Ch. 27. 1 His mother's name also (was) J., the dau.

JE-SA-I'AH, JE-SHA-I'AH, ישעיהו, ישעיה *Jah is helper.*
1. A grandson of Zerubbabel. B.C. 470.
1 Ch. 3. 21 the sons of Hananiah; Pelatiah, and J.
2. A son of Jeduthun, and one appointed to the service of song. B.C. 1015.
1 Ch. 25. 3 Zeri, and J., Hashabiah, and Mattithiah
25. 15 eighth to J., (he), his sons, and his brethr.
3. A grandson of Eliezer, son of Moses, and ancestor of Shelomith. B.C. 1015.
1 Ch. 26. 25 J. his son, and Joram his son, and Zichri
4. One of the family of Elam that returned with Ezra. B.C. 447.
Ezra 8. 7 J. the son of Athaliah, and with him sev.
5. A Merarite who joined Ezra. B.C. 447.
Ezra 8. 19 and with him J. of the sons of Merari, his
6. A Benjamite whose posterity dwelt in Jerusalem. B.C. 447.
Neh. 11. 7 Maaseiah, the son of Ithiel, the son of J.

JE-SHA'-NAH, ישנה *ancient.*
A city near Bethel and Ephraim on the N. of Benjamin.
2 Ch. 13. 19 J. with the towns thereof, and Ephraim

JE-SHAR-E'-LAH, ישראלה *of Jesharel.*
A Levite who presided over the service of song. B.C. 1015.
1 Ch. 25. 14 The seventh to J., (he), his sons, and his

JE-SHEB-E'-AB, ישבאב *seat of the father.*
The head of the 14th course of the priests in the service of the sanctuary. B.C. 1015.
1 Ch. 24. 13 thirteenth to Huppah, the fourteenth to J.

JE'-SHER, ישר *rightness.*
A son of Caleb, son of Hezron. B.C. 1540.
1 Ch. 2. 18 sons (are) these; J., and Shobab, and Ard.

JE-SHI'-MON, ישמן, ישימן *a waste, a desert.*
1. A place in the Sinaitic peninsula on the E. of Jordan.
Num 21. 20 the top of Pisgah, which looketh toward J.
23. 28 the top of Peor, that looketh toward J.
2. A place in the desert of Judah on the W. of Jordan.
1 Sa. 23. 24 of Maon, in the plain on the south of J.
26. 1 the hill of Hachilah, (which is) before J.?

JE-SHI'-SHAI, ישישי *Jah is ancient.*
An ancestor of a Gadite family. B.C. 1400.
1 Ch. 5. 14 son of J., the son of Jahdo, the son of B.

JE-SHO-HA-I'AH, ישוחיה *humbled by Jah.*
A descendant of Simeon. B.C. 800.
1 Ch. 4. 36 J., and Asaiah, and Adiel, and Jesimiel

JE-SHU'-A, JE-SHU'-AH, ישוע *Jah is help.*
1. A priest of the sanctuary. B.C. 1015.
1 Ch. 24. 11 The ninth to J., the tenth to Shecaniah
Ezra 2. 36 of the house of J., nine hundred seventy
Neh. 7. 39 of the house of J., nine hundred seventy
2. A Levite in the days of Hezekiah. He managed the tithes. B.C. 720.
2 Ch. 31. 15 J., and Shemaiah, Amariah, and Shecan.
Ezra 2. 40 children of J., and Kadmiel, of the children
Neh. 7. 43 The Levites: the children of J., of Kad.
3. A priest who returned with Zerubbabel. B.C. 536.
Ezra 2. 2 J., Nehemiah, Seraiah, Reelaiah, Morde.
3. 2 Then stood up J. the son of Jozadak, and
3. 8 J. the son of Jozadak, and the remnant of
3. 9 Then stood J. (with) his sons and..breth.
4. 3 J., and the rest of the chief of the fathers
5. 2 son of Shealtiel, and J. the son of Jozadak
10. 18 of the sons of J. the son of Jozadak, and
Neh. 7. 7 J., Nehemiah, Azariah, Raamiah, Nahama.
12. 1 Zerubbabel the son of Shealtiel, and J.
12. 7 and of their brethren in the days of J.
12. 10 And J. begat Joiakim, Joiakim also begat
12. 26 (were) in the days of Joiakim the son of J.
4. The father of Jozabad the Levite that weighed the vessels of the sanctuary. B.C. 536.
Ezra 8. 33 with them (was) Jozabad the son of J.
5. A son of Pahath-Moab whose descendants returned with Zerubbabel. B.C. 536.
Ezra 2. 6 the children of J. (and) Joab, two thous.
Neh. 7. 11 the children of J. and Joab, two thousand
6. The father of Ezer who helped to repair the wall. B.C. 445
Neh. 3. 19 next to him repaired Ezer the son of J.
7. A Levite who explained the law to the people when Ezra read it. B.C. 445.
Neh. 8. 7 Also J., and Bani, and Sherebiah, Jamin
9. 4 of the Levites, J., and Bani, Kadmiel, Sh.
9. 5 Then the Levites, J., and Kadmiel, Bani
12. 8 Moreover the Levites: J., Binnui, Kadm.
12. 24 Sherebiah, and J. the son of Kadmiel
8. The name of Joshua the son of Nun is in one passage thus spelt. B.C. 1491.
Neh. 8. 17 since the days of J. the son of Nun unto
9. The son of Azariah, a Levite, who sealed the covenant. B.C. 445.
Neh. 10. 9 J. the son of Azaniah, Binnui of the sons
10. A city of Benjamin, near Moladah.
Neh. 11. 26 at J., and at Moladah and at Beth-phe.

JE-SHU'-RUN, JE-SU'-RUN, ישרון *the darling upright.*
A poetical appellation of the people of Israel.
Deut 32. 15 J. waxed fat, and kicked: thou art waxen
33. 5 he was king in J., when the heads of the
33. 26 (There is) none like unto the God of J.
Isa. 44. 2 Fear not..thou, J.; whom I have chosen

JE-SI'-AH, ישיהו, ישיה *Jah exists.*
1. One that joined David at Ziklag. B.C. 1058.
1 Ch. 12. 6 J., and Azareel, and Joezer, and Jashobeam.
2. A Kohathite descendant of Uzziel. B.C. 1015. Called also *Isshiah.*
1 Ch. 23. 20 the sons of Uzziel; Micah the first, and J.

JE-SI-MI'-EL, ישימאל *God sets.*
A descendant of Simeon. B.C. 800.
1 Ch. 4. 36 and Asaiah, and Adiel, and J., and Bena.

JES'-SE, ישי, Ἰεσσαί *Jah exists.*
Son of Obed and father of David, and grandson of Boaz and Ruth. B.C. 1120.
Ruth 4. 17 he (is) the father of J., the father of David
4. 22 And Obed begat J., and J. begat David
1 Sa. 16. 1 I will send thee to J. the Beth-lehemite
16. 3 And call J. to the sacrifice, and I will
16. 5 he sanctified J. and his sons, and called
16. 8 J. called Abinadab, and made him pass
16. 9 Then J. made Shammah to pass by. And
16. 10 J. made seven of his sons to pass before
16. 10 And Samuel said unto J., The LORD hath
16. 11 And Samuel said unto J., Are here all (thy)
16. 11 Samuel said unto J., Send and fetch him
16. 18 I have seen a son of J. the Beth-lehemite
16. 19 Saul sent messengers unto J., and said
16. 20 J. took an ass (laden) with bread, and a
16. 22 Saul sent to J., saying, Let David, I pray
17. 12 of that Ephrathite..whose name (was) J.
17. 13 three eldest sons of J. went (and) follow.
17. 17 J. said unto David his son, Take now for
17. 20 and took, and went, as J. had commanded
17. 58 son of thy servant J. the Beth-lehemite
20. 27 Wherefore cometh not the son of J. to
20. 30 chosen..son of J. to thine own confusion
20. 31 as long as the son of J. liveth upon the
22. 7 will the son of J. give every one of you
22. 8 son hath made a league with the son of J.
22. 9 said, I saw the son of J. coming to Nob
22. 13 consp. against me, thou and the son of J.
25. 10 and who (is) the son of J.? There be many
2 Sa. 20. 1 neither have..inheritance in the son of J.
23. 1 the son of J. said, and the man (who was)
1 Ki. 12. 16 (have we) inheritance in the son of J.: to
1 Ch. 2. 12 And Boaz begat Obed, and Obed begat J.
2. 13 J. begat his first born Eliab, and Abina.
10. 14 turned the kingdom unto David..son of J.
12. 18 Thine (are we)..on thy side, thou son of J.
29. 26 David the son of J. reigned over..Israel
2 Ch. 10. 16 (we have) none inheritance in the son of J.
11. 18 Abihail..daughter of Eliab the son of J.
Psa. 72. 20 The prayers of David the son of J. are
Isa. 11. 1 come forth a rod out of the stem of J.
11. 10 in that day there shall be a root of J.
Matt. 1. 5 Booz begat Obed of Ruth..Obed begat J.
1. 6 J. begat David the king; and David the
Luke 3. 32 Which was (the son) of J., which was
Acts 13. 22 I have found David the (son) of J., a man
Rom 15. 12 There shall be a root of J., and he that

JE'-SUI, ישוי *Jah is satisfied.*
A descendant of Asher. B.C. 1700. *See* Ishui. Num 26. 44.

JESURUN. *See* **JESHURUN.**

JESTING —
Pleasantry, εὐτραπελία *eutrapelia.*
Eph. 5. 4 nor jesting, which are not convenient

JE-SU-ITES, הישוי.
The family of the preceding *Jesui.*
Num 26. 44 of Jesui, the family of the J.: of Beriah

JE'-SUS, Ἰησοῦς, *from Heb.* ישוע *saviour.*
1. The son of the Virgin Mary, a descendant of Abraham through David of the tribe of Judah, the long promised and long expected Messiah, born in Bethlehem-Ephratah, and crucified in Jerusalem. A.D. 29.
Matt. 1. 16 Mary, of whom was born J., who is called
1. 21 thou shalt call his name J.; for he shall
Matt. 1. 25 first born son: and he called his name J
2. 1 J. was born in Bethlehem of Judea, in
3. 13 Then cometh J. from Galilee to Jordan
3. 15 J. answering said unto him, Suffer (it to
3. 16 J., when he was baptized, went up straight
4. 1 Then was J. led up of the spirit into the
4. 7 J. said unto him, It is written again, Thou
4. 10 Then saith J. unto him, Get thee hence, S
4. 12 [J.] had heard that John was cast into
4. 17 J. began to preach, and to say, Repent
4. 18 [J.,] walking by the sea of Galilee, saw two
4. 23 And [J.] went about all Galilee, teaching
7. 28 when J. had ended these sayings, the pe.
8. 3 And [J.] put forth (his) hand, and touched
8. 4 J. saith unto him, See thou tell no man
8. 5 when [J.] was entered into Capernaum
8. 7 [J.] saith unto him, I will come and heal
8. 10 When J. heard (it), he marvelled, and
8. 13 J. said unto the centurion, Go thy way
8. 14 when J. was come into Peter's house, he
8. 18 when J. saw great multitudes about him
8. 20 J. saith unto him, The foxes have holes
8. 22 J. said unto him, Follow me; and let the
8. 29 What have we to do with thee, [J.,] thou
8. 34 the whole city came out to meet J.: and
9. 2 J., seeing their faith, said unto the sick
9. 4 J., knowing their thoughts, said, Wherefore
9. 9 as J. passed forth from thence, he saw a
9. 10 as J. sat at meat in the house, behold
9. 12 when [J.] heard (that), he said unto them
9. 15 J. said unto them, Can the children of the
9. 19 J. arose, and followed him, and (so did)
9. 22 J. turned him about; and when he saw
9. 23 J. came into the ruler's house, and saw
9. 27 And when J. departed thence, two blind
9. 28 J. saith unto them, Believe ye that I am
9. 30 J. straitly charged them, saying, See (that)
9. 35 J. went about all the cities and villages
10. 5 These twelve J. sent forth, and comman.
11. 1 J. had made an end of commanding his
11. 4 J. answered and said unto them, Go and
11. 7 J. began to say unto the multitudes conc.
11. 25 J. answered and said, I thank thee, O F.
12. 1 J. went on the sabbath day through the
12. 15 when J. knew (it,) he withdrew himself
12. 25 [J.] knew their thoughts, and said unto
13. 1 The same day went J. out of the house
13. 34 these things spake J. unto the multitude
13. 36 [J.] sent the multitude away, and went
13. 51 [J. saith unto them, Have ye understood all]
13. 53 when J. had finished these parables, he
13. 57 J. said unto them, A prophet is not with.
14. 1 Herod the tetrarch heard of the fame of J.
14. 12 and buried it, and went and told J.
14. 13 J. had heard (of it), he departed thence by
14. 14 [J.] went forth, and saw a great multitude
14. 16 J. said unto them, They need not depart
14. 22 [J.] constrained his disciples to get into
14. 25 [J.] went unto them, walking on the sea
14. 27 J. spake unto them, saying, Be of good
14. 29 he walked on the water, to go to J.
14. 31 J. stretched forth (his) hand, and caught
15. 1 Then came to J. scribes and Pharisees
15. 16 [J.] said, Are ye also..without understa.?
15. 21 Then J. went thence, and departed into
15. 28 Then J. answered and said unto her, O wo.
15. 29 J. departed from thence, and came nigh
15. 30 cast them down at [J.] feet; and he healed
15. 32 J. called his disciples (unto him), and said
15. 34 J. saith unto them, How many loaves have
16. 6 J. said unto them, Take heed and beware
16. 8 when J. perceived, he said unto them, O
16. 13 J. came into the coasts of Cesarea Philip.
16. 17 J. answered and said unto him, Blessed
16. 20 tell no man that he was [J.] the Christ
16. 21 From that time forth began J. to show
16. 24 Then said J. unto his disciples, If any
17. 1 J. taketh Peter, James, and John his br.
17. 4 Then answered Peter, and said unto J.
17. 7 J. came and touched them, and said, Ar.
17. 8 lifted..their eyes, they saw no man, save J.
17. 9 J. charged them, saying, Tell the vision
17. 11 [J.] answered and said unto them, Elias
17. 17 Then J. answered and said, O faithless
17. 18 J. rebuked the devil; and he departed
17. 19 Then came the disciples to J. apart, and
17. 20 [J.] said unto them, Because of your unb.
17. 22 J. said unto them, The Son of man shall
17. 25 J. prevented him, saying, What thinkest
17. 26 J. saith unto him, Then are the children
18. 1 At the same time came the disciples unto J.
18. 2 [J.] called a little child unto him, and set
18. 22 J. saith unto him, I say not unto thee
19. 1 (that) when J. had finished these sayings
19. 14 J. said, Suffer little children, and forbid
19. 18 J. said, Thou shalt do no murder, Thou
19. 21 J. said unto him, If thou wilt be perfect
19. 23 Then said J. unto his disciples, Verily
19. 26 J. beheld (them), and said unto them
19. 28 J. said unto them, Verily I say unto you
20. 17 J. going up to Jerusalem took the twelve
20. 22 J. answered and said, Ye know not what
20. 25 J. called them (unto him), and said, Ye
20. 30 when they heard that J. passed by, cried
20. 32 J. stood still, and called them, and said
20. 34 J. had compassion (on them), and touched
21. 1 And when they drew nigh..then sent J.
21. 6 disciples went, and did as J. commanded
21. 11 This is J...prophet of Nazareth of Galilee
21. 12 J. went into the temple of God, and cast
21. 16 J. saith unto them, Yea; have ye never
21. 21 J. answered and said unto them, Verily

Matt 21. 24 J. answered and said unto them, I also
21. 27 they answered J., and said, We cannot
21. 31 J. saith unto them, Verily I say unto you
21. 42 J. saith unto them, Did ye never read in
22. 1 J. answered and spake unto them again
22. 18 J. perceived their wickedness, and said
22. 29 J. answered and said unto them, Ye do
22. 37 [J.] said unto him, Thou shalt love the
22. 41 Pharisees were gathered together, J. asked
23. 1 Then spake J. to the multitude, and to
24. 1 J. went out, and departed from the tem.
24. 2 [J.] said unto them, See ye not all these
24. 4 J. answered and said unto them, Take
26. 1 when J. had finished all these sayings
26. 4 consulted..they might take J. by subtilty
26. 6 J. was in Bethany, in the house of Simon
26. 10 When J. understood (it), he said unto them
26. 17 the disciples came to J., saying unto him
26. 19 the disciples did as J. had appointed them
26. 26 J. took bread, and blessed (it), and brake
26. 31 Then saith J. unto them, All ye shall be
26. 34 J. said unto him, Verily I say unto thee
26. 36 Then cometh J. with them unto a place
26. 49 he came to J., and said, Hail, Master!
26. 50 J. said unto him, Friend, wherefore art
26. 50 came they, and laid hands on J., and took
26. 51 one of them which were with J. stretched
26. 52 Then said J. unto him, Put up again thy
26. 55 that same hour said J. to the multitudes
26. 57 they that had laid hold on J. led (him) away
26. 59 sought false witness against J., to put
26. 63 But J. held his peace. And the high pri.
26. 64 J. saith unto him, Thou hast said: never.
26. 69 saying, Thou also wast with J. of Galilee
26. 71 This (fellow) was also with J. of Nazareth
26. 75 Peter remembered the word of J., which
27. 1 counsel against J. to put him to death
27. 11 And J. stood before the governor: and
27. 11 And J. said unto him, Thou sayest
27. 17 Barabbas, or J. which is called Christ?
27. 20 they should ask Barabbas, and destroy J.
27. 22 What shall I do then with J. which is
27. 26 when he had scourged J., he delivered
27. 27 soldiers of the governor took J. into the
27. 37 written, This is J. the king of the Jews
27. 46 J. cried with a loud voice, saying, Eli!
27. 50 J., when he had cried again with a loud
27. 54 they that were with him watching J., saw
27. 55 which followed J. from Galilee, ministe.
27. 57 Joseph, who..himself was J. disciple
27. 58 went to Pilate, and begged the body of J.
28. 5 know that ye seek J., which was crucified
28. 9 J. met them, saying, All hail! And they
28. 10 Then said J. unto them, Be not afraid: go
28. 16 a mountain where J. had appointed them
28. 18 J. came and spake unto them, saying, All
Mark 1. 9 J. came from Nazareth of Galilee, and was
1. 14 J. came into Galilee, preaching the gospel
1. 17 J. said unto them, Come ye after me, and
1. 24 what have we to do with..J. of Nazareth?
1. 25 J. rebuked him, saying, Hold thy peace
1. 41 [J.,] moved with compassion; put forth
1. 45 J. could no more openly enter into the
2. 5 When J. saw their faith, he said unto the
2. 8 J. perceived in his spirit that they so rea.
2. 15 it came to pass, that, as J. sat at meat in
2. 15 sinners sat also together with J. and his
2. 17 When J. heard (it), he saith unto them
2. 19 J. said unto them, Can the children..fast
3. 7 But J. withdrew himself with his disciples
5. 6 when he saw J. afar off, he ran and wors.
5. 7 What have I to do with thee, J., (thou)
5. 13 forthwith [J.] gave them leave. And the
5. 15 they come to J., and see him that was
5. 19 Howbeit [J.] suffered him not, but saith
5. 20 to publish..how great things J. had done
5. 21 when J. was passed over again by ship
5. 27 When she had heard of J., came in the
5. 30 J...turned him about in the press, and
5. 36 As soon as J. heard the word that was
6. 4 But J. said unto them, A prophet is not
6. 30 apostles gathered themselves..unto J.
6. 34 [J.]..was moved with compassion toward
7. 27 [J.] said unto her, Let the children first
8. 1 [J.] called his disciples (unto him), and
8. 17 when [J.] knew (it), he saith unto them
8. 27 J. went out, and his disciples, into the
9. 2 after six days J. taketh (with him) Peter
9. 4 with Moses: and they were talking with J.
9. 5 Peter answered and said to J., Master, it
9. 8 they saw no man any more, save J. only
9. 23 J. said unto him..all things (are) possible
9. 25 J. saw that the people came running tog.
9. 27 But J. took him by the hand, and lifted
9. 39 But J. said, Forbid him not: for there is
10. 5 And J. answered and said unto them, For
10. 14 But when J. saw (it), he was much displ.
10. 18 J. said unto him, Why callest..me good?
10. 21 Then J., beholding him, loved him, and
10. 23 And J. looked round about, and saith unto
10. 24 But J. answereth again, and saith unto
10. 27 J., looking upon them, saith, With men
10. 29 J. answered and said, Verily I say unto
10. 32 J. went before them: and they were am.
10. 38 But J. said unto them, Ye know not what
10. 39 J. said..Ye shall indeed drink of the cup
10. 42 But J. called them (to him), and saith unto
10. 47 when he heard that it was J. of Nazareth
10. 47 J., (thou) son of David, have mercy on me
10. 49 J. stood still, and commanded him to be
10. 50 he, casting away his garment..came to J.
10. 51 J. answered and said unto him, What wilt
Mark 10. 52 J. said unto him, Go thy way; thy faith
10. 52 And immediately he..followed [J.] in the
11. 6 they said unto them even as J. had com.
11. 7 they brought the colt to J., and cast their
11. 11 [J.] entered into Jerusalem, and into the
11. 14 [J.] answered and said unto it, No man
11. 15 [J.] went into the temple, and began to
11. 22 J. answering saith unto them, Have faith
11. 29 J. answered and said unto them, I will
11. 33 they answered and said unto J., We can.
11. 33 J. answering saith unto them, Neither do
12. 17 J. answering said unto them, Render to
12. 24 J. answering said unto them, Do ye not
12. 29 J. answered him, The first of all the com.
12. 34 when J. saw that he answered discreetly
12. 35 J. answered and said, while he taught in
12. 41 [J.] sat over against the treasury, and be.
13. 2 J. answering said unto him, Seest thou
13. 5 J. answering them began to say, Take
14. 6 J. said, Let her alone; why trouble ye her?
14. 18 J. said..One of you which eateth with me
14. 22 [J.] took bread, and blessed, and brake (it)
14. 27 J. saith unto them, All ye shall be offen.
14. 30 J. saith unto him, Verily I say unto thee
14. 48 J. answered and said unto them, Are ye
14. 53 they led J. away to the high priest: and
14. 55 council sought for witness against J. to
14. 60 high priest stood up..and asked J., saying
14. 62 J. said, I am: and ye shall see the Son
14. 67 said, And thou also wast with J. of Naz.
14. 72 Peter called to mind the word that J. said
15. 1 the chief priests..bound J., and carried
15. 5 But J. yet answered nothing; so that Pi.
15. 15 Pilate..delivered J., when he had scour.
15. 34 at the ninth hour J. cried with a loud vo.
15. 37 J. cried with a loud voice, and gave up
15. 43 Joseph of Arimathea..craved..body of J.
16. 6 Ye seek J. of Nazareth, which was cruci.
Luke 1. 31 bring forth a son, and..call his name J.
2. 21 his name was called J., which was so na.
2. 27 when the parents brought in the child J.
2. 43 as they returned, the child J. tarried be.
2. 52 J. increased in wisdom and stature, and
3. 21 J. also being baptised..the heaven was
3. 23 J. himself began to be about thirty years
4. 1 J., being full of the Holy Ghost, returned
4. 4 J. answered him, saying, It is written
4. 8 J. answered and said unto him, Get thee
4. 12 J. answering said unto him, It is said
4. 14 J. returned in the power of the spirit into
4. 34 what have we to do with..J. of Nazareth?
4. 35 J. rebuked him, saying, Hold thy peace
5. 8 he fell down at J. knees, saying, Depart
5. 10 J. said unto Simon, Fear not; from hence.
5. 12 who, seeing J., fell on (his) face, and beso.
5. 19 with (his) couch into the midst before J.
5. 22 But when J. perceived their thoughts, he
5. 31 J. answering said unto them, They that
6. 3 J. answering them said, Have ye not read
6. 9 Then said J. unto them, I will ask you one
6. 11 and communed...what they might do to J.
7. 3 when he heard of J., he sent unto him the
7. 4 when they came to J., they besought him
7. 6 J. went with them. And when he was
7. 9 When J. heard these things, he marvelled
7. 19 sent (them) to J., saying, Art thou he that
7. 22 [J.] answering said unto them, Go your
7. 40 J. answering said unto him, Simon, I have
8. 28 When he saw [J.], he cried out, and fell
8. 28 What have I to do with thee, J., (thou) Son
8. 30 And J. asked him, saying, What is thy
8. 35 came to J., and found the man out of
8. 35 sitting at the feet of J., clothed, and in
8. 38 be with him: but [J.] sent him away, say.
8. 39 how great things J. had done unto him
8. 40 when J. was returned, the people (gladly)
8. 41 he fell down at J. feet, and besought him
8. 45 J. said, Who touched me? When all den.
8. 46 And [J.] said, Somebody hath touched me
8. 50 when J. heard (it), he answered him, say.
9. 33 Peter said unto J., Master, it is good for
9. 36 when the voice was past, J. was found
9. 41 J. answering said, O faithless and perver.
9. 42 J. rebuked the unclean spirit, and healed
9. 43 wondered every one at..things which [J.]
9. 47 J., perceiving the thought of their heart
9. 50 J. said unto him, Forbid (him) not: for
9. 58 And J. said unto him, Foxes have holes
9. 60 [J.] said unto him, Let the dead bury their
9. 62 J. said unto him No man, having put his
10. 21 [J.] rejoiced in spirit, and said, I thank
10. 29 he, willing to justify himself, said unto J.
10. 30 J. answering said, A certain (man) went
10. 37 said J. unto him, Go, and do thou likewise
10. 39 Mary, which also sat at [J.] feet, and heard
10. 41 [J.] answered and said unto her, Martha
13. 2 [J.] answering said unto them, Suppose ye
13. 12 when J. saw her, he called (her to him)
13. 14 that J. had healed on the Sabbath day
14. 3 J. answering spake unto the lawyers and
17. 13 and said, J., Master, have mercy on us
17. 17 And J. answering said, Were there not
18. 16 J. called them (unto him), and said, Suffer
18. 19 J. said unto him, Why callest thou me
18. 22 when J. heard these things, he said unto
18. 24 when J. saw that he was very sorrowful
18. 37 told him, that J. of Nazareth passeth by
18. 38 J., (thou) son of David, have mercy on me!
18. 40 J. stood, and commanded him to be brou.
18. 42 J. said unto him, Receive thy sight: thy
19. 3 he sought to see J. who he was; and could
19. 5 when J. came to the place, he looked up
Luke 19. 9 J. said unto him, This day is salvation
19. 35 they brought him to J.: and they cast
19. 35 garments upon the colt, and set J. thereon
20. 8 J. said unto them, Neither tell I you by
20. 34 J. answering said unto them, The children
22. 47 that was called Judas..drew near unto J.
22. 48 But J. said unto him, Judas, betrayest thou
22. 51 J. answered and said, Suffer ye thus far
22. 52 Then J. said unto the chief priests, and
22. 63 the men that held [J.] mocked him, and
23. 8 when Herod saw J., he was exceeding glad
23. 20 Pilate therefore, willing to release J., spake
23. 25 released..but he delivered J. to their will
23. 26 they laid..that he might bear (it) after J.
23. 28 But J., turning unto them, said, Daughters
23. 34 [Then said J., Father, forgive them; for]
23. 42 he said unto J., Lord, remember me when
23. 43 [J.] said unto him, Verily I say unto thee
23. 46 when J. had cried with a loud voice, he
23. 52 went unto Pilate..begged the body of J.
24. 3 they..found not the body of the Lord [J.]
24. 15 J. himself drew near, and went with them
24. 19 they said unto him, Concerning J. of Na.
24. 36 [J.] himself stood in the midst of them
John 1. 29 The next day John seeth J. coming unto
1. 36 looking upon J. as he walked, he saith
1. 37 two disciples heard..and they followed J.
1. 38 Then J. turned, and saw them following
1. 42 he brought him to J. And when J. beheld
1. 43 The day following [J.] would go forth into
1. 45 have found..J. of Nazareth the son of J.
1. 47 J. saw Nathanael coming to him, and saith
1. 48 J. answered and said unto him, Before
1. 50 J. answered and said unto him, Because
2. 1 Cana of Galilee; and the mother of J. was
2. 2 both J. was called, and his disciples, to the
2. 3 the mother of J. saith unto him, They have
2. 4 J. saith unto her, Woman, what have I to
2. 7 J. saith unto them, Fill the water pots
2. 11 This beginning of miracles did J. in Cana
2. 13 passover was at hand; and J. went up to J.
2. 19 J. answered and said unto them, Destroy
2. 22 and they believed..the word which J. had
2. 24 But [J.] did not commit himself unto them
3. 2 The same came to J. by night, and said
3. 3 J. answered and said unto him, 3. 10
3. 5 J. answered, Verily, verily, I say unto
3. 22 After these things came J. and his discip.
4. 1 the Pharisees had heard that J. made
4. 2 Though J. himself baptized not, but his
4. 6 J. therefore, being wearied..sat thus on
4. 7 J. saith unto her, Give me to drink
4. 10 J. answered and said unto her, If thou
4. 13 J. answered and said unto her, Whosoever
4. 16 [J.] saith unto her, Go, call thy husband
4. 17 J. said unto her, Thou hast well said, I
4. 21 J. saith unto her, Woman, believe me
4. 26 J. saith unto her, I that speaketh unto
4. 34 J. saith unto them, My meat is to do the
4. 44 J. himself testified, that a prophet hath
4. 46 So [J.] came again into Cana of Galilee
4. 47 When he heard that J. was come out of J.
4. 48 Then said J. unto him, Except ye see signs
4. 50 J. saith unto him, Go thy way; thy son
4. 50 the man believed the word that J. had
4. 53 in the which J. said unto him, Thy son
4. 54 This (is) again the second miracle (that) J.
5. 1 there was a feast..and J. went up to Jer.
5. 6 When J. saw him lie..he saith unto him
5. 8 J. saith unto him, Rise, take up thy bed
5. 13 for J. had conveyed himself away, 5. 14
5. 15 told the Jews that it was J. which had
5. 16 therefore did the Jews persecute J., and
5. 17 But J. answered them, My Father worketh
5. 19 Then answered J. and said unto them
6. 1 After these things J. went over the sea
6. 3 J. went up into a mountain, and there he
6. 5 When J. then lifted up (his) eyes, and saw
6. 10 J. said, Make the men sit down. Now there
6. 11 J. took the loaves; and when he had given
6. 14 when they had seen the miracles that [J.]
6. 15 J. therefore perceived that they would
6. 17 it was now dark, and J. was not come to
6. 19 they see J. walking on the sea, and draw.
6. 22 that J. went not with his disciples into
6. 24 When the people therefore saw that J.
6. 24 they..came to Capernaum, seeking for J.
6. 26 J. answered them and said, Verily, verily
6. 29 J. answered and said unto them, This is
6. 32 Then J. said unto them, Verily, verily, I say
6. 35 J. said unto them, I am the bread of life
6. 42 they said, Is not this J., the son of Joseph
6. 43 J. therefore answered and said unto them
6. 53 Then J. said unto them, Verily, verily, I say
6. 61 J. knew in himself that his disciples mur.
6. 64 For J. knew from the beginning who they
6. 67 Then said J. unto the twelve, Will ye also
6. 70 [J.] answered them, Have not I chosen
7. 1 After these things J. walked in Galilee
7. 6 Then J. said unto them, My time is not
7. 14 Now about the midst of the feast, J. went
7. 16 J. answered them, and said, My doctrine
7. 21 J. answered and said unto them, I have
7. 28 Then cried J. in the temple, as he taught
7. 33 Then said J. unto them, Yet a little while
7. 37 J. stood and cried, saying, If any man
7. 39 not yet..because that J. was not yet glor.
7. 50 he that came to J. by night, being one of
8. 1 [J. went unto the mount of Olives.]
8. 6 [But J. stooped down, and with (his) finger]
8. 9 [J. was left alone, and the woman stand.]
8. 10 [When J. had lifted up himself, and saw]

John 8. 11 [J. said unto her, Neither do I condemn]
8. 12 Then spake J. again unto them, saying, I
8. 14 J. answered and said unto them, Though
8. 19 J. answered, Ye neither know me, nor my
8. 20 These words spake [J.] in the treasury, as
8. 21 Then said [J.] again unto them, I go my
8. 25 J. saith unto them, Even (the same) that
8. 28 Then said J. unto them, When ye have
8. 31 Then said J. to those Jews which believed
8. 34 J. answered them, Verily, verily, I say
8. 39 J. saith unto them, If ye were Abraham's
8. 42 J. said unto them, If God were your Father
8. 49 J. answered, I have not a devil; but I
8. 54 J. answered, If I honour myself, my honour
8. 58 J. said unto them, Verily, verily, I say
8. 59 but J. hid himself, and went out of the
9. 3 J. answered, Neither hath this man sinned
9. 11 A man that is called J. made clay, and
9. 14 it was the sabbath day when J. made the
9. 35 J. heard that they had cast him out; and
9. 37 J. said unto him, Thou hast both seen him
9. 39 J. said, For judgment I am come into
9. 41 J. said unto them, If ye were blind, ye sho.
10. 6 This parable spake J. unto them: but
10. 7 Then said J. unto them again, Verily
10. 23 J. walked in the temple, in Solomon's p.
10. 25 J. answered them, I told you, and ye bel.
10. 32 J. answered them, Many good works have
10. 34 J. answered them, Is it not written in
11. 4 When J. heard (that), he said, This sick.
11. 5 J. loved Martha, and her sister, and Laz.
11. 9 J. answered, Are there not twelve hours
11. 13 Howbeit J. spake of his death: but they
11. 14 Then said J. unto them plainly, Lazarus
11. 17 Then when J. came, he found that he had
11. 20 Then Martha, as soon as she heard that J.
11. 21 Then said Martha unto J., Lord, if thou
11. 23 J. saith unto her, Thy brother shall rise
11. 25 J. said unto her, I am the resurrection
11. 30 Now J. was not yet come into the town
11. 32 Then when Mary was come where J. was
11. 33 When J. therefore saw her weeping..he
11. 35 J. wept
11. 38 J. therefore, again groaning in himself
11. 39 J. said, Take ye away the stone. Martha
11. 40 J. saith unto her, Said I not unto thee
11. 41 And J. lifted up (his) eyes, and said, Fath.
11. 44 J. saith unto them, Loose him, and let
11. 45 Jews..had seen the things which [J.] did
11. 46 and told them what things J. had done
11. 51 he prophesied that J. should die for that
11. 54 J. therefore walked no more openly amo.
11. 56 Then sought they for J., and spake among
12. 1 J., six days before the passover, came to
12. 3 Mary..anointed the feet of J., and wiped
12. 7 Then said J., Let her alone: against the
12. 9 they came not for J. sake only, but that
12. 11 many of the Jews went..and believed on J.
12. 12 they heard that J. was coming to Jerusa.
12. 14 And J., when he had found a young ass
12. 16 when J. was glorified, then remembered
12. 21 desired him, saying, Sir, we would see J.
12. 22 and again Andrew and Philip tell J.
12. 23 J. answered them, saying, The hour is come
12. 30 J. answered and said, This voice came not
12. 35 Then J. said unto them, Yet a little while
12. 36 These things spake J., and departed, and
12. 44 J. cried and said, He that believeth on
13. 1 J. knew that his hour was come that he
13. 3 [J.] knowing that the Father had given
13. 7 J. answered and said unto him, What I
13. 8 J. answered him, If I wash thee not, thou
13. 10 J. saith to him, He that is washed needeth
13. 21 When J. had thus said, he was troubled
13. 23 leaning on J. bosom one..whom J. loved
13. 25 He then lying on J. breast saith unto
13. 26 J. answered, He it is to whom I shall give
13. 27 Then said J. unto him, That thou doest
13. 29 some (of them) thought..that J. had said
13. 31 Therefore, when he was gone out, J. said
13. 36 J. answered him, Whither I go, thou
13. 38 J. answered him, Wilt thou lay down thy
14. 6 J. saith unto him, I am the way, and the
14. 9 J. saith unto him, Have I been so long
14. 23 J. answered and said unto him, If a man
16. 19 Now J. knew that they were desirous to
16. 31 J. answered them, Do ye now believe?
17. 1 These words spake J., and lifted up his
18. 1 When J. had spoken these words, he went
18. 2 for J. ofttimes resorted thither with his
18. 4 J. therefore..went forth, and said unto
18. 5 They answered him, J. of Nazareth. [J.]
18. 7 Whom seek ye? And they said, J. of Naz.
18. 8 J. answered, I have told you that I am
18. 11 Then said J. unto Peter, Put up thy sword
18. 12 captain and officers of the Jews took J.
18. 15 Simon Peter followed J., and (so did)
18. 15 That disciple..went in with J. into the p.
18. 19 The high priest then asked J. of his disc.
18. 20 J. answered him, I spake openly to the
18. 22 one of the officers..struck J. with the pa.
18. 23 J. answered him, If I have spoken evil
18. 28 Then led they J. from Caiaphas unto the
18. 32 That the saying of J. might be fulfilled
18. 33 Then Pilate..called J., and said unto him
18. 34 J. answered him, Sayest thou this thing
18. 36 J. answered, My kingdom is not of this
18. 37 J. answered, Thou sayest that I am a king
19. 1 Then Pilate therefore took J. and scour.
19. 5 Then came J. forth, wearing the crown of
19. 9 saith unto J., Whence art thou? But J.
19. 11 J. answered, Thou couldest have no power

John 19. 13 he brought J. forth, and sat down in the
19. 16 [And they took J., and led (him) away]
19. 18 crucified..on either side one, and J. in
19. 19 J. OF NAZARETH THE KING OF THE JEWS
19. 20 the place where J. was crucified was nigh
19. 23 soldiers, when they had crucified J., took
19. 25 there stood by the cross of J. his mother
19. 26 When J. therefore saw his mother, and
19. 28 J. knowing that all things were now
19. 30 When J. therefore had received the vine.
19. 33 they came to J., and saw that he was dead
19. 38 Joseph of Arimathea, being a disciple of J.
19. 38 that he might take away the body of [J.]
19. 38 He came therefore, and took the body of J.
19. 39 which at the first came to [J.] by night
19. 40 Then took they the body of J., and wound
19. 42 There laid they J. therefore, because of
20. 2 to the other disciple whom J. loved, and
20. 12 sitting..where the body of J. had lain
20. 14 J. standing, and knew not that it was J.
20. 15 J. saith unto her, Woman, why weepest
20. 16 J. saith unto her, Mary! She turned hers.
20. 17 J. saith unto her, Touch me not; for I am
20. 19 came J. and stood in the midst, and saith
20. 21 Then said [J.] to them again, Peace (be)
20. 24 Didymus, was not with them when J. came
20. 26 (Then) came J., the doors being shut, and
20. 29 J. saith unto him, Thomas, because thou
20. 30 other signs truly did J. in the presence
20. 31 ye might believe that J. is the Christ
21. 1 [J.] showed himself again to the disciples
21. 4 morning was now come, J. stood on the
21. 4 but the disciples knew not that it was J.
21. 5 [J.] saith unto them, Children, have ye
21. 7 disciple whom J. loved saith unto Peter
21. 10 J. saith unto them, Bring of the fish which
21. 12 J. saith unto them, Come (and) dine. And
21. 13 J. then cometh, and taketh bread, and
21. 14 J. showed himself to his disciples after
21. 15 J. saith to Simon Peter, Simon, (son) of
21. 17 J. saith unto him Feed my sheep
21. 20 seeth the disciple whom J. loved following
21. 21 Peter seeing him saith to J., Lord, and
21. 22 J. saith unto him, If I will that he tarry
21. 23 J. said not unto him, He shall not die; but
21. 25 many other things which J. did, the which
Acts 1. 1 of all that J. began both to do and teach
1. 11 this same J., which is taken up from you
1. 14 with the women, and Mary the mother of J.
1. 16 Judas..was guide to them that took J.
1. 21 that the Lord J. went in and out among us
2. 22 J. of Nazareth, a man approved of God
2. 32 J. hath God raised up, whereof we all are
2. 36 God hath made that same J., whom ye
3. 13 God..hath glorified his Son J.; whom ye
3. 26 God, having raised up his Son [J.,] sent him
4. 2 preached through J. the resurrection from
4. 13 knowledge of them..they had been with J.
4. 18 speak at all nor teach in the name of J.
4. 27 against thy holy child J., whom thou hast
4. 30 be done by the name of thy holy child J.
4. 33 witness of the resurrection of the Lord J.
5. 30 The God of our fathers raised up J., whom
5. 40 they should not speak in the name of J.
6. 14 J. of Nazareth shall destroy this place
7. 55 and J. standing on the right hand of God
7. 59 and saying, Lord J., receive my spirit
8. 16 were baptized in the name of the Lord J.
8. 35 at the same..and preached unto him J.
9. 5 I am J. whom thou persecutest. (It is)
9. 17 [J.,] that appeared unto thee in the way as
9. 27 preached boldly at Damascus..name of J.
9. 29 spake boldly in the name of the Lord [J.]
10. 38 God anointed J. of Nazareth with the Holy
11. 20 unto the Grecians, preaching the Lord J.
13. 23 hath God..raised unto Israel a Saviour, J.
13. 33 in that he hath raised up J. again; as it
17. 3 this J., whom I preach unto you, is Christ
17. 7 saying that there is another king, (one) J.
17. 18 [preached unto them J., and the resur.]
18. 5 testified to the Jews (that) J. (was) Christ
18. 28 showing by..Scriptures that J. was Christ
19. 5 were baptized in the name of the Lord J.
19. 10 they..heard the word of the Lord [J.,] both
19. 13 of the Lord J., saying, We adjure you by J.
19. 15 J. I know, and Paul I know; but who are
19. 17 and the name of the Lord J. was magnified
20. 24 which I have received of the Lord J., to
20. 35 to remember the words of the Lord J., how
21. 13 die at Jerusalem for..name of the Lord J.
22. 8 I am J. of Nazareth, whom thou persecu.
25. 19 J., which was dead, whom Paul affirmed
26. 9 contrary to the name of J. of Nazareth
26. 15 And he said, I am J., whom thou persecu.
28. 23 persuading them concerning J., both out
Rom. 3. 26 the justifier of him which believeth in [J.]
4. 24 that raised up J. our Lord from the dead
8. 11 spirit of him that raised up J. from the
10. 9 shalt confess with thy mouth the Lord J.
14. 14 I know, and am persuaded by the Lord J.
1 Co. 5. 5 may be saved in the day of [the Lord J.]
6. 11 are justified in the name of the Lord J.
11. 23 J. the same night in which he was betr.
12. 3 that no man speaking..calleth J. accursed
12. 3 no man can say that J. is the Lord, but by
2 Co. 1. 14 ye also (are) ours in the day of the Lord J.
4. 5 and ourselves your servants for J. sake
4. 10 of the Lord J., that the life also of J.
4. 11 death for J. sake, that the life also of J.
4. 14 that he which raised up the Lord J. shall
4. 14 raise up us also by J., and shall present
11. 4 if he that cometh preacheth another J.

Gal. 6. 17 bear in my body the marks of the Lord J.
Eph. 1. 15 after I heard of your faith in the Lord J.
4. 21 been taught by him, as the truth is in J.
Phil. 2. 10 That at the name of J. every knee should
2. 19 But I trust in the Lord J. to send
Col. 3. 17 whatsoever ye do..(do) all in the name..J.
1 Th. 1. 10 J., which delivered us from the wrath to
2. 15 Who both killed the Lord J. and their own
4. 1 we..exhort (you) by the Lord J...to walk
4. 2 commandments we gave you by the Lord J.
4. 14 For if we believe that J. died and rose
4. 14 even so them also which sleep in J. will
2 Th. 1. 7 when the Lord J. shall be revealed from
Phm. 5 which thou hast toward the Lord J., and
Heb. 2. 9 But we see J., who was made a little lower
4. 14 we have a great high priest..J. the Son
6. 20 J., made an high priest for ever, after
7. 22 By so much was J. made a surety of a
10. 19 enter into the holiest by the blood of J.
12. 2 Looking unto J., the author and finisher
12. 24 to J. the mediator of the new covenant
13. 12 Wherefore J. also..suffered without the
13. 20 brought again from the dead our Lord J.
2 Pe. 1. 2 through the knowledge of God, and of J.
1 Jo. 2. 22 but he that denieth that J. is the Christ?
4. 15 Whosoever shall confess that J. is the Son
5. 1 Whosoever believeth that J is the Christ
5. 5 but he that believeth that J. is the Son of
Rev. 14. 12 here (are) they that keep..the faith of J.
17. 6 with the blood of the martyrs of J.: and
19. 10 thy brethren that have the testimony of J.
19. 10 the testimony of J. is the spirit of proph.
20. 4 that were beheaded for the witness of J.
22. 16 I J. have sent mine angel to testify unto
22. 20 come quickly. Amen. Even so, come, L. J.

2. Jesus, for *Joshua*, the son of Nun.

Acts 7. 45 with J. into the possession of the Gentiles
Heb. 4. 8 For if J. had given them rest, then would

3. Jesus, called Justus, a Christian who was with Paul at Rome, and with him sent salutations to the Colossians

Col. 4. 11 J., which is called Justus, who are of the

JESUS CHRIST, Ἰησοῦς Χριστός.

Matt. 1. 1 The book of the generation of J. C., the
1. 18 birth of [J.] C. was on this wise: When
Mark 1. 1 of the gospel of J. C., the Son of God
John 1. 17 (but) grace and truth came by J. C.
17. 3 that they might know thee..and J. C.
Acts 2. 38 baptized every one..in the name of J. C.
3. 6 In the name of J. C. of Nazareth rise up
3. 20 shall send J. C., which before was preach.
4. 10 by the name of J. C. of Nazareth..doth
5. 42 they ceased not to teach and preach J. C.
8. 12 preaching..concerning..the name of J. C.
8. 37 said, [I believe that J. C. is the Son of God]
9. 34 Eneas, J. C. maketh thee whole: arise
10. 36 which (God) sent..preaching peace by J. C.
11. 17 unto us, who believed on the Lord J. C.
15. 11 through the grace of the Lord J. C. we sh.
15. 26 hazarded..for the name of our Lord J. C.
16. 18 I command thee in the name of J. C. to
16. 31 they said, Believe on the Lord J. C., and
20. 21 Testifying..faith toward our Lord J. C.
28. 31 those things which concern the Lord J. C.
Rom. 1. 1 a servant of J. C., called (to be) an apostle
1. 3 Concerning his Son J. C. our Lord, which
1. 6 Among whom are ye also the called of J. C.
1. 7 peace from God our Father..the Lord J. C.
1. 8 I thank my God through J. C. for you all
2. 16 God shall judge the secrets of men by J. C.
3. 22 (which is) by faith of J. C. unto all and
5. 1 peace with God through our Lord J. C.
5. 11 we also joy in God through our Lord J. C.
5. 15 by grace, (which is) by one man, J. C.
5. 17 they..shall reign in life by one, J. C.
5. 21 righteousness unto eternal life by J. C
6. 3 so many of us as were baptized into J. C.
6. 11 alive unto God through J. C. our Lord
6. 23 gift of God (is) eternal life through J. C.
7. 25 I thank God through J. C. our Lord. So
13. 14 put ye on the Lord J. C., and make not
15. 6 glorify God..the Father of our Lord J. C.
15. 8 Now I say that [J.] C. was a minister of
15. 16 be the minister of J. C. to the Gentiles
15. 17 whereof I may glory through J. C. in those
15. 30 I beseech you..for the Lord J. C.'s sake
16. 18 that are such serve not our Lord [J.] C.
16. 20 grace of our Lord J. C. (be) with you. A.
16. 24 grace of our Lord J. C. (be) with you all. A.
16. 25 the preaching of J. C., according to the
16. 27 To God only wise, (be) glory through J. C.
1 Co. 1. 1 called (to be) an apostle of J. C. through
1. 2 call upon the name of J. C. our Lord, both
1. 3 God our Father, and (from) the Lord J. C.
1. 4 grace of God which is given you by J. C.
1. 7 waiting for the coming of our Lord J. C
1. 8 blameless in the day of our Lord J. C.
1. 9 called unto the fellowship of his Son J. C
1. 10 beseech you..by the name of our Lord J. C.
2. 2 not to know any thing..save J. C., and
3. 11 no man lay than that is laid which is J. C.
5. 4 In the name of our Lord J. C., when ye
5. 4 spirit, with the power of our Lord J. C.
8. 6 one Lord J. C., by whom (are) all things
9. 1 have I not seen J. C. our Lord? are not ye
15. 57 giveth..victory through our Lord J. C.
16. 22 If any man love not the Lord [J.] C., let
16. 23 The grace of our Lord J. C. (be) with you
2 Co. 1. 1 Paul, an apostle of J. C. by the will of God
1. 2 Grace (be) to you..(from) the Lord J. C.
1. 3 even the Father of our Lord J. C., the F.

2 Co. 1. 19 J. C., who was preached among you by us
4. 6 of the glory of God in the face of [J.] C.
5. 18 who hath reconciled us to himself by [J.] C.
8. 9 know the grace of our Lord J. C., that
11. 31 God and Father of our Lord J. C., which
13. 5 how that J. C. is in you, except ye be rep.?
13. 14 The grace of the Lord J. C., and the love
Gal. 1. 1 by J. C., and God the Father, who raised
1. 3 Grace (be) to you..(from) our Lord J. C.
1. 12 taught (it), but by the revelation of J. C.
2. 16 but by the faith of J. C., even we have
2. 16 believed in J. C., that we might be
3. 1 J. C. hath been evidently set forth, cruci.
3. 14 might come on the Gentiles through J. C.
3. 22 promise by faith of J. C. might be given
5. 6 in J. C. neither circumcision availeth any
6. 14 save in the cross of our Lord J. C., by
6. 18 grace of our Lord J. C. (be) with your sp.
Eph. 1. 1 Paul, an apostle of J. C. by the will of G.
1. 2 Grace (be) to you..(from) the Lord J. C.
1. 3 Blessed (be) the God..of our Lord J. C.
1. 5 Having predestinated us..by J. C. to him.
1. 17 That the God of our Lord J. C...may give
2. 20 J. C. himself being the chief corner (stone)
3. 1 Paul, the prisoner of J. C. for you Gentiles
3. 9 in God, [who created all things by J. C.]
3. 14 [bow my knees unto..Father of our...J.C.]
5. 20 thanks..in the name of our Lord J. C.
6. 23 from God the Father and the Lord J. C.
6. 24 Grace (be) with all them that love..J. C.
Phil. 1. 1 Paul and Timotheus, the servants of J. C
1. 2 Grace (be) unto you..(from) the Lord J. C.
1. 6 he..will perform (it) until the day of J. C.
1. 8 I long after you all in the bowels of J. C.
1. 11 the fruits..which are by J. C., unto the
1. 19 through..the supply of the spirit of J. C.
1. 26 rejoicing may be more abundant in J. C.
2. 11 every tongue should confess that J. C. (is)
2. 21 all seek..not the things which are J. C.'s
3. 20 we look for the Saviour, the Lord J. C.
4. 23 The grace of our Lord J. C. (be) with you
Col. 1. 1 Paul, an apostle of J. C. by the will of God
1. 2 [Grace (be) unto you..from..the Lord J.C.]
1. 3 thanks to..the Father of our Lord J. C.
1 Th. 1. 1 in God the Father and (in) the Lord J. C.
1. 1 [Grace (be) unto you..from..the Lord J. C.]
1. 3 patience of hope in our Lord J. C., in the
2. 19 in the presence of our Lord J. C. at his
3. 11 and our Lord J. C., direct our way unto
3. 13 at the coming of our Lord J. C. with all
5. 9 but to obtain salvation by our Lord J. C.
5. 23 blameless unto..coming of our Lord J. C.
5. 28 The grace of our Lord J. C. (be) with you
2 Th 1. 1 in God our Father and the Lord J. C.
1. 2 Grace unto you..peace, from..Lord J. C.
1. 8 that obey not the gospel of our Lord J. C.
1. 12 That the name of our Lord J. C. may be
1. 12 according to the grace of..the Lord J. C.
2. 1 by the coming of our Lord J. C., and (by)
2. 14 obtaining of the glory of our Lord J. C.
2. 16 Now our Lord J. C. himself, and God
3. 6 command you..in..name of our Lord J. C.
3. 12 command and exhort by our Lord J. C.
3. 18 The grace of our Lord J. C. (be) with you
1 Ti. 1. 1, 1 apostle of J. C. by the commandment
1. 2 Grace, mercy, (and) peace, from..J. C.
1. 16 J. C. might show forth all long suffering
4. 6 thou shalt be a good minister of J. C., no.
5. 21 charge (thee) before God, and the L. J. C.
6. 3 (even) the words of our Lord J. C., and
6. 14 until the appearing of our Lord J. C.
2 Ti. 1. 1 Paul, an apostle of J. C. by the will of G.
1. 10 made manifest by the appearing of..J. C.
2. 3 endure hardness, as a good soldier of J. C.
2. 8 Remember that J. C...was raised from
4. 1 I charge..before God, and the Lord J. C.
4. 22 The Lord [J.] C. (be) with thy spirit. Gr.
Titus 1. 1 a servant of God, and an apostle of J. C.
1. 4 from God the Father and the Lord J. C.
2. 13 glorious appearing of..our Saviour J. C.
3. 6 he shed on us abundantly through J. C.
Phm. 1 Paul, a prisoner of J. C., and Timothy
3 from God our Father and the Lord J. C.
9 being..now also a prisoner of J. C.
25 grace of our Lord J. C. (be) with your sp.
Heb. 10. 10 through the offering of the body of J. C.
13. 8 J. C. the same yesterday, and to day, and
13. 21 is well pleasing in his sight, through J. C.
Jas. 1. 1 a servant of God and of the Lord J. C., to
2. 1 have not the faith of our Lord J. C.
1 Pe. 1. 1 Peter, an apostle of J. C., to the strangers
1. 2 and sprinkling of the blood of J. C.: Gra.
1. 3 the God and Father of our Lord J. C.
1. 3 by the resurrection of J. C. from the de.
1. 7 honour and glory at the appearing of J. C.
1. 13 brought unto you at the revelation of J. C.
2. 5 offer..sacrifices, acceptable to G. by J. C.
3. 21 save us..by the resurrection of J. C.
4. 11 that God..may be glorified through J. C.
2 Pe. 1. 1 a servant and an apostle of J. C., to them
1. 1 righteousness of God and our Saviour J. C.
1. 8 in the knowledge of our Lord J. C.
1. 11 kingdom of our Lord and Saviour J. C.
1. 14 even as our Lord J. C. hath showed me
1. 16 the power and coming of our Lord J. C.
2. 20 knowledge of the Lord and Saviour J. C.
3. 18 knowledge of our Lord and Saviour J. C.
1 Jo. 1. 3 with the Father, and with his Son J. C.
1. 7 blood of J. C...cleanseth us from all sin
2. 1 we have an advocate with the Father, J. C.
3. 23 should believe on the name of his Son J. C.
4. 2 Every spirit that confesseth that J. C. is
1 Jo. 4. 3 every spirit that confesseth not that J. C.
5. 6 he that came by water and blood..J. C.
5. 20 him that is true, (even) in his Son [J.] C.
2 John 3 Grace be with you..from the Lord J. C.
7 who confess not that J. C. is come in the
Jude 1 Jude, the servant of J. C., and brother
1 to them that are..preserved in J. C., (and)
4 denying the..Lord God, and our L. J. C.
17 spoken before of the apostles of..J. C.
21 looking for the mercy of our Lord J. C.
Rev. 1. 1 The revelation of J. C., which God gave
1. 2 Who bare record..of the testimony of J. C.
1. 5 And from J. C., (who is) the faithful wit.
1. 9 and in the kingdom and patience of [J.] C.
1. 9 word of God, and for the testimony of J. C.
12. 17 of God, and have the testimony of J. C.
22. 21 The grace of our Lord J. C. (be) with you

JE'-THER, יֶתֶר *pre-eminent.*

1. Gideon's first born son. B.C. 1249.
Judg. 8. 20 he said unto J. his first born, Up, (and)
2. An Ishmaelite, the father of David's nephew Amasa. B.C. 1048.
1 Ki. 2. 5 and unto Amasa the son of J., whom he
2. 32 Amasa the son of J., captain of the host
1 Ch. 2. 17 the father of Amasa (was) J. the Ishmeel.
3. A son of Jerahmeel, son of Hezron. B.C. 1400.
1 Ch. 2. 32 J., and Jonathan: and J. died without ch.
4. A son of Ezra, a descendant of Caleb the spy. B.C. 1400.
1 Ch. 4. 17 the sons of Ezra (were) J., and Mered
5. A descendant of Asher. B.C. 1540.
1 Ch. 7. 38 the sons of J.; Jephunneh, and Pispah

JE'-THETH, יְתֵת *subjection.*

A duke or prince of Edom of the family of Esau. B.C. 1470.
Gen. 36. 40 duke Timnah, duke Alvah, duke J.
1 Ch. 1. 51 were; duke Timnah, duke Aliah, duke J.

JETH'-LAH, יִתְלָה *height.*

A border city of Dan, now called *Shilta.*
Josh 19. 42 And Shaalabbin, and Ajalon, and J.

JETH'-RO, יִתְרוֹ *pre-eminence.*

The father in law of Moses, and a priest of Midian. B.C. 1500. In Exod. 4. 18 the name is *Jether,* but the Common Version gives *Jethro.* In Exod. 2. 18 he is called *Reuel;* and in Num. 10. 29 we have *Reuel* in the Hebrew, but *Raguel* in the Common Version.
Exod. 3. 1 Moses kept the flock of J. his father in
4. 18 Moses went and returned to J. his father
4. 18 And J. said to Moses, Go in peace
18. 1 J., the priest of Midian, Moses' father in
18. 2 J., Moses' father in law, took Zipporah
18. 5 J., Moses' father in law, came with his
18. 6 I. thy father in law J. am come unto thee
18. 9 J. rejoiced for all the goodness which the
18. 10 J. said, Blessed (be) the LORD, who hath
18. 12 J., Moses' father in law, took a burnt off.

JE'-TUR, יְטוּר.

1. A son of Ishmael, son of Hagar, Abraham's concubine. B.C. 1800.
Gen. 25. 15 Hadar, and Tema, J., Naphish, and Kede.
1 Ch. 1. 31 J., Naphish, and Kedemah. These are
2. The tribe that sprang from *Jetur.*
1 Ch. 5. 19 made war with the Hagarites, with J.

JE-U'-EL, יְעוּאֵל *snatching away.*

A descendant of Zerah, son of Judah. B.C. 445.
1 Ch. 9. 6 of the sons of Zerah; J. and their brethren

JE'-USH, יְעוּשׁ *collector.*

1. Esau's son by Aholibamah. B.C. 1760.
Gen. 36. 5 And Aholibamah bare J., and Jaalam
36. 14 and she bare to Esau J., and Jaalam, and
36. 18 sons of Aholibamah, Esau's wife; duke J.
1 Ch. 1. 35 The sons of Esau; Eliphaz, Reuel, and J.
2. Grandson of Jediael, a Benjamite. B.C. 1630.
1 Ch. 7. 10 the sons of Bilhan; J., and Benjamin
3. A Gershonite and descendant of Shimei, and head of a family. B.C. 1015.
1 Ch. 23. 10 sons of Shimei (were) Jahath, Zina, and J.
23. 11 but J. and Beriah had not many sons
4. A son of Rehoboam, and grandson of king Solomon. B.C. 1000.
2 Ch. 11. 19 Which bare him children; J., and Sham.

JE'-UZ, יְעוּץ *counsellor.*

Son of Shaharaim, a Benjamite. B.C. 1400.
1 Ch. 8. 10 J., and Shachia, and Mirma. These (were)

JEW, יְהוּדִי.

1. A descendant of Judah; in later times also an Israelite. In 2 Ki. 16. 6 this appellation is applied to the *two* tribes; in later days the *twelve* tribes. Strictly speaking, the name is appropriate only to the subjects of the kingdom of the two tribes after the separation of the ten tribes, B.C. 975. In 603 Daniel interprets Nebuchadnezzar's first dream; in 561 Evil-merodach releases Jehoiachin from captivity; in 539 Daniel interprets the handwriting to Belshazzar; in 536 decree of Cyrus in favour of the Jews; in 535 the second temple founded; in 516 it is finished; in 463 Artaxerxes stops the rebuilding of the city; in 458 he marries Esther; in 457 Ezra comes; in 444 Nehemiah becomes governor; in 332 Alexander the Great enters Jerusalem; in 320 Ptolemy Soter storms Jerusalem; in 312 Antigonus wrested Judea from Ptolemy; in 285 the Septuagint translation begun; in 203 Antiochus the Great invades Judea and Phenicia; in 200 the sect of the Sadducees arises; in 199 the country is recovered by the Egyptian general Scopas; in 198 Scopas is defeated; in 170 Antiochus Epiphanes massacres 40,000 in Jerusalem; in 168 Apollonius takes Jerusalem and dedicates the temple to Jupiter Olympius; in 165 Judas Maccabaeus rises in arms; in 163 Judas made governor; in 160 he makes the first treaty with the Romans; in 156 the Syrians withdraw; in 144 Jonathan put to death; in 130 Hyrcanus subdues the Idumeans; in 95 the Pharisees rebel; in 70 Hyrcanus is defeated; in 63 Hyrcanus is restored; in 54 Crassus plunders the temple; in 49 Aristobulus poisoned; in 42 Herod marries Mariamne; in 40 the Parthians invade Judea, and Herod proclaimed king by the Romans; in 37 the Romans take Jerusalem; in 31 a dreadful earthquake; in 29 Mariamne put to death; in 17 Herod begins to rebuild the temple; on Friday, April 5th, four years before the Common Era, Jesus is born.
Esth. 2. 5 Shushan the palace there was a certain J.
3. 4 for he had told them that he (was) a J.
5. 13 I see Mordecai the J. sitting at the king's
6. 10 do even so to Mordecai the J., that sitteth
8. 7 Esther the queen, and to Mordecai the J.
9. 29 Mordecai the J., wrote with all authority
9. 31 according as Mordecai the J...had enjoi.
10. 3 Mordecai the J. (was) next unto king Ah.
Jer. 34. 9 none should serve himself..a J. his brot.
Zech. 8. 23 take hold of the skirt of him that is a J.

2. *Jews,* יְהוּדִים, יְהוּדָיֵא, יְהוּדָאִין *yehudim,* Ἰουδαῖοι.
2 Ki. 16. 6 Rezin..recovered Elath..and drave the J.
25. 25 he died, and the J. and the Chaldees that
2 Ch. 32. 18 they cried with a loud voice in the J.'s sp.
Ezra 4. 12 J. which came up from thee to us are come
4. 23 they went up in haste..unto the J., and
5. 1 prophesied unto the J. that (were) in Ju.
5. 5 But the eye..was upon the elders of the J.
6. 7 governor of the J., and the elders of the J.
6. 8 what ye shall do to the elders of these J
6. 14 elders of the J. builded, and they prosp.
Neh. 1. 2 I asked them concerning the J. that had
2. 16 neither had I as yet told (it) to the J., nor
4. 1 took great indignation, and mocked the J.
4. 2 What do these feeble J.? will they fortify
4. 12 when the J. which dwelt by them came
5. 1 a great cry..against their brethren the J.
5. 8 have redeemed our brethren the J., which
5. 17 an hundred and fifty of the J. and rulers
6. 6 thou and the J. think to rebel: for which
13. 23 In those days also saw I J. (that) had mar.
Esth. 3. 6 Haman sought to destroy all the J. that
3. 10 took his ring..and gave it unto..the J.'s
3. 13 cause to perish, all J., both young and old
4. 3 (there was) great mourning among the J.
4. 7 to pay to the king's treasuries for the J.
4. 13 the king's house more than all the J.
4. 14 shall there..deliverance arise to the J.
4. 16 gather together all the J. (that are) pres.
6. 13 If Mordecai (be) of the seed of the J., before
8. 1 give the house of Haman, the J.'s enemy
8. 3 to put away the mischief..against the J.
8. 5 which he wrote to destroy the J. which
8. 7 because he laid his hand upon the J.
8. 8 Write ye also for the J., as it liketh you
8. 9 that Mordecai commanded unto the J.
8. 9 and to the J. according to their writing
8. 11 the king granted the J. which (were) in
8. 13 that the J. should be ready against that
8. 16 The J. had light, and gladness, and joy
8. 17 J. had joy and gladness, a feast and a good
8. 17 became J.; for the fear of the J. fell upon
9. 1 the enemies of the J. hoped to have power
9. 1 the J. had rule over them that hated them
9. 2 the J. gathered themselves together in
9. 3 officers of the king helped the J.: because
9. 5 the J. smote all their enemies with the
9. 6 the J. slew and destroyed five hundred men
9. 10 the enemy of the J., slew they; but on
9. 12 J. have slain and destroyed five hundred
9. 13 let it be granted to the J. which (are) in
9. 15 J. that (were) in Shushan gathered thems.
9. 16 other J. that (were) in the king's provinces
9. 18 J. that (were) at Shushan assembled tog.
9. 19 the J. of the villages that dwelt in the
9. 20 sent letters unto all the J. that (were) in
9. 22 wherein the J. rested from their enemies
9. 23 the J. undertook to do as they had begun
9. 24 of all the J., had devised against the J.
9. 25 device, which he devised against the J.
9. 27 J. ordained, and took upon them, and
9. 28 days..should not fail from among the J.
9. 30 he sent the letters unto all the J., to the
10. 3 and great among the J., and accepted
Jer. 32. 12 the J. that sat in the court of the prison
38. 19 I am afraid of the J. that are fallen to
40. 11 all the J. that (were) in Moab, and among
40. 12 the J. returned out of all places whither
40. 15 the J. which are gathered unto thee should
41. 3 also slew all the J. that were with him
44. 1 the J. which dwell in the land of Egypt
52. 28 the seventh year three thousand J., and
52. 30 carried away captive of the J. seven hun
Dan. 3. 8 Chaldeans came near, and accused the J.
3. 12 There are certain J. whom thou hast set
Matt. 2. 2 Where is he that is born king of the J.?
27. 11 saying, Art thou the king of the J.? And
27. 29 mocked him, saying, Hail, king of the J.!
27. 37 This is Jesus the king of the J.
28. 15 reported among the J. until this day
Mark 7. 3 the J., except they wash (their) hands oft
15. 2 asked him, Art thou the King of the J.?
15. 9 I release unto you the King of the J.?

Mark15. 12 (unto him) whom ye call the King of the J.?
15. 18 began to salute him, Hail, King of the J.!
15. 26 was written over, The King of the J.
Luke 7. 3 he sent unto him the elders of the J.
23. 3 saying, Art thou the King of the J.? And
23. 37 thou be the king of the J., save thyself
23. 38 superscription..This is the King of the J.
23. 51 (he was) of Arimathæa, a city of the J.
John 1. 19 when the J. sent priests and Levites from
2. 6 the manner of the purifying of the J.
2. 13 the J. passover was at hand, and Jesus
2. 18 Then answered the J. and said unto him
2. 20 Then said the J., Forty and six years was
3. 1 man..named Nicodemus..a ruler of the J.
3. 25 there arose a question..J. about purifying
4. 9 How is it that thou, being a Jew, askest
4. 9 J. have no dealings with the Samaritans
4. 22 we know what..for salvation is of the J.
5. 1 there was a feast of the J.; and Jesus w.
5. 10 The J. therefore said unto him that was
5. 15 told the J. that it was Jesus which had
5. 16 therefore did the J. persecute Jesus, and
5. 18 the J. sought the more to kill him, because
6. 4 the passover, a feast of the J. was nigh
6. 41 The J. then murmured at him, because he
6. 52 The J. therefore strove among themselves
7. 1 Jewry, because the J sought to kill him
7. 2 the J. feast of tabernacles was at hand
7. 11 the J. sought him at the feast, and said
7. 13 spake openly of him for fear of the J.
7. 15 the J. marvelled, saying, How knoweth
7. 35 Then said the J. among themselves, Wh.
8. 22 Then said the J., Will he kill himself?
8. 31 Then said Jesus to those J. which believed
8. 48 Then answered the J., and said unto him
8. 52 Then said the J. unto him, Now we know
8. 57 Then said the J. unto him, Thou art not
9. 18 the J. did not believe concerning him
9. 22 they feared the J.: for the J. had agreed
10. 19 a division therefore again among the J.
10. 24 Then came the J. round about him, and
10. 31 the J. took up stones again to stone him
10. 33 The J. answered him, saying, For a good
11. 8 the J. of late sought to stone thee; and
11. 19 the J. came to Martha and Mary, to
11. 31 The J. then which were with her in the
11. 33 the J. also weeping which came with her
11. 36 Then said the J., Behold how he loved
11. 45 many of the J. which came to Mary, and
11. 54 Jesus..walked no more openly among..J.
11. 55 the J. passover was nigh at hand; and
12. 9 the J. therefore knew that he was there
12. 11 the J. went away, and believed on Jesus
13. 33 I said unto the J., Whither I go, ye can.
18. 12 officers of the J. took Jesus, and bound
18. 14 Caiaphas..he which gave counsel to the J.
18. 20 the temple, whither the J. always resort
18. 31 The J. therefore said unto him, It is not
18. 33 said unto him, Art thou the King of the J.?
18. 35 Pilate answered, Am I a J.? Thine own
18. 36 I should not be delivered to the J.: but
18. 38 he went out again unto the J., and saith
18. 39 I release unto you the King of the J.?
19. 3 said, Hail, King of the J.! and they sm.
19. 7 The J. answered him, We have a law, and
19. 12 the J. cried out, saying, If thou let this
19. 14 and he saith unto the J., Behold your K.!
19. 19 was, Jesus of Nazareth the King of the J.
19. 20 This title then read many of the J.; for
19. 21 J. to Pilate, Write not, The King of the J.
19. 21 but that he said, I am King of the J.
19. 31 The J. therefore, because it was the
19. 38 disciple..but secretly for fear of the J.
19. 40 spices, as the manner of the J. is to bury
19. 42 because of the J.'s preparation (day); for
20. 19 disciples were assembled for fear of..J.
Acts 2. 5 there were dwelling at Jerusalem J., de.
2. 10 and strangers of Rome, J. and proselytes
9. 22 confounded the J. which dwelt at Dama.
9. 23 And after..the J. took counsel to kill him
10. 22 good report among all the nation of the J.
10. 28 for a man that is a J. to keep company
10. 39 he did both in the land of the J., and in
11. 19 the word to none but unto the J. only
12. 3 he saw it pleased the J., he proceeded
12. 11 the expectation of the people of the J.
13. 5 word of God in the synagogues of the J.
13. 6 false prophet, a J., whose name (was) B.
13. 42 [the J. were gone out of the synagogue]
13. 43 the J. and religious proselytes followed
13. 45 when the J. saw the multitudes, they
13. 50 J. stirred up the devout and honourable
14. 1 together into the synagogue of the J.
14. 1 a great multitude both of the J. and also
14. 2 the unbelieving J. stirred up the Gentiles
14. 4 part held with the J., and part with the
14. 5 also of the J. with their rulers, to use
14. 19 (certain) J. from Antioch and Iconium
16. 3 circumcised him because of the J. which
16. 20 These men, being J., do exceedingly trou.
17. 1 to Thessalonica..synagogue of the J.
17. 5 the J. which believed not, moved with envy
17. 10 went into the synagogue of the J.
17. 13 when the J. of Thessalonica had
17. 17 disputed he in the synagogue with the J
18. 2 found a certain J. named Aquila, born in
18. 2 had commanded all J. to depart from R.
18. 4 and persuaded the J. and the Greeks
18. 5 testified to the J. (that) Jesus (was) Christ
18. 12 the J. made insurrection with one accord
18. 14 Gallio said unto the J., If it were a matter
18. 14 O (ye) J., reason would that I should bear
Acts 18. 19 he..entered..and reasoned with the J.
18. 24 certain J. named Apollos, born at Alexa.
18. 28 For he mightily convinced the J., (and
19. 10 heard the word of the Lord Jesus, both J.
19. 13 certain of the vagabond J., exorcists, took
19. 14 there were seven sons of (one) Sceva, a J.
19. 17 this was known to all the J. and Greeks
19. 33 drew Alexander out..J. putting him for.
19. 34 when they knew that he was a J., all with
20. 3 the J. laid wait for him, as he was about
20. 19 befell me by the lying in wait of the J.
20. 21 Testifying both to the J., and also to the
21. 11 So shall the J. at Jerusalem bind the man
21. 20 thousands of J. there are which believe
21. 21 thou teachest all the J. which are among
21. 27 the J. which were of Asia, when they saw
21. 39 I am a man (which am) a J. of Tarsus, (a
22. 3 I am verily a man (which am) a J., born in
22. 12 having a good report of all the J. which
22. 30 certainty wherefore he was accused of..J.
23. 12 certain of the J. banded together, and
23. 20 The J. have agreed to desire thee that
23. 27 This man was taken of the J., and should
23. 30 how that [the J.] laid wait for the man
24. 5 among all the J. throughout the world
24. 9 the J. also assented, saying, that these
24. 18 certain J. from Asia found me purified
24. 27 Felix, willing to show the J. a pleasure
25. 2 chief of the J. informed him against Paul
25. 7 the J. which came down from Jerusalem
25. 8 Neither against the law of the J., neither
25. 9 Festus, willing to do the J. a pleasure
25. 10 to the J. have I done no wrong, as thou
25. 15 the elders of the J. informed (me), desir.
25. 24 multitude of the J. have dealt with me
26. 2 the things whereof I am accused of the J.
26. 3 customs and questions..are among the J.
26. 4 My manner of life..know all the J.
26. 7 which..Agrippa, I am accused of the J.
26. 21 the J. caught me in the temple, and went
28. 17 Paul called the chief of the J. together
28. 19 But when the J. spake against (it), I was
28. 29 [the J.] departed, and had great reasoning
Rom. 1. 16 to the J. first, and also to the Greek
2. 9 of the J. first, and also of the Gentile
2. 10 to the J. first, and also to the Gentile
2. 17 thou art called a J., and restest in the
2. 28 For he is not a J. which is one outwardly
2. 29 But he (is) a J. which is one inwardly; and
3. 1 What advantage then hath the J.? or what
3. 9 have before proved both J. and Gentiles
3. 29 (Is he) the God of the J. only? (is he) not
9. 24 of the Jews only, but also of the Gentiles
10. 12 no difference between the J. and the Gre.
1 Co. 1. 22 the J. require a sign, and the Greeks seek
1. 23 unto the Jews a stumbling block, and unto
1. 24 them which are called, both J. and Greeks
9. 20 And unto the J. I became as a J., that
9. 20 I might gain the J.; to them that are
10. 32 neither to the J., nor to the Gentiles, nor
12. 13 whether (we be) J. or Gentiles, whether
2 Co. 11. 24 Of the J. five times received I forty
Gal. 2. 13 the other J. dissembled likewise with him
2. 14 I said..If thou, being a J., livest after
2. 14 the manner of the G., and not as do the J.
2. 15 We (who are) J. by nature, and not sinners
3. 28 There is neither J. nor Greek, there is
Col. 3. 11 there is neither Greek nor J., circumcision
1 Th. 2. 14 have suffered..even as they (have) of..J.
Rev. 2. 9 which say they are J., and are not, but
3. 9 which say they are J., and are not, but

JEWEL —

1. *Ornament*, חֲלִי *chali.*
Song 7. 1 the joints of thy thighs (are) like jewels

2. *Ornament*, חֶלְיָה *chelyah.*
Hos. 2. 13 she decked herself with her jewels, and

3. *Vessel, instrument*, כְּלִי *keli.*
Gen. 24. 53 jewels of silver, and jewels of gold, and
Exod. 3. 22 jewels of silver, and jewels of gold, and
11. 2 borrow..jewels of silver, and jewels of g.
12. 35 jewels of silver, and jewels of gold, and
35. 22 brought..rings, and tablets, all jewels of
Num31. 50 jewels of gold, chains, and bracelets, rings
31. 51 took the gold of them..all wrought jewels
1 Sa. 6. 8 put the jewels of gold, which ye return
6. 15 wherein the jewels of gold (were), and
2 Ch. 20. 25 precious jewels, which they stripped off
32. 27 treasuries for..all manner of pleasant je.
Job 28. 17 the exchange of it (shall not be for) jewels
Prov 20. 15 the lips of knowledge (are) a precious jew.
Isa. 61. 10 as a bride adorneth (herself) with her je.
Eze. 16. 17 Thou hast also taken thy fair jewels of
16. 39 shall take thy fair jewels, and leave thee
23. 26 They shall also..take away thy fair jewels

4. *A ring for the ear or nose*, נֶזֶם *nezem.*
Prov 11. 22 (As) a jewel of gold in a swine's snout
Isa. 3. 21 The rings, and nose jewels
Eze. 16. 12 I put a jewel on thy forehead, and ear rings

5. *A peculiar treasure or property*, סְגֻלָּה *segullah.*
Mal. 3. 17 in that day when I make up my jewels

JEWESS—*A female Jew*, Ἰουδαία *Ioudaia.*
Acts 16. 1 the son of a certain woman, which was a J
24. 24 with his wife Drusilla, which was a J.

JEW'-ISH, JEWS', יְהוּדִית Ἰουδαϊκός *belonging to a J.*
2 Ki. 18. 26 talk not with us in the J. language in
18. 28 cried with a loud voice in the J. language
2 Ch. 32. 18 they cried with a loud voice in the J. sp.
Neh. 13. 24 their children..could not speak in the J.
Isa. 36. 11 speak not to us in the J. language, in the
36. 13 cried with a loud voice in the J. language
Titus 1. 14 Not giving heed to J. fables, and comman.

JEWRY, Ἰουδαία—See *Judea.*
Luke 23. 5 teaching throughout all J., beginning
John 7. 1 he would not walk in J., because the Jews

JEWS, to become, or live as —

1. *To become, act, or show self a Jew*, יָהַד *yahad*, 7.
Esth. 8. 17 many of the people of the land became J.

2. *To become, act as a Jew*, Ἰουδαΐζω *Ioudaizō.*
Gal. 2. 14 compellest..Gentiles to live as do the J.?

JEWS, as do the —

Judaically, Ἰουδαϊκῶς *Ioudaikōs.*
Gal. 2. 14 manner of Gentiles, and not as do the J.

JEWS' religion —

Judaism, Ἰουδαϊσμός *Ioudaismos.*
Gal. 1. 13 in time past in the J. religion, how
1. 14 profited in the J. religion above many

JE-ZAN-I'AH, יְזַנְיָהוּ *Jah determines.*
A captain of the Jews, generally called *Jaazeniah*, who would not be persuaded to serve the Chaldeans. B.C. 588. Called also *Jaazeniah.*
Jer. 40. 8 and J. the son of a Maachathite, they and
42. 1 and J. the son of Hoshaiah, and all the

JE-ZE'-BEL, אִיזֶבֶל, Ἰεζαβήλ *without cohabitation.*
A daughter of Ethbaal, king of the Zidonians, and the wife of Ahab and mother of Joram kings of Israel. B.C. 884.
1 Ki. 16. 31 he took to wife J., the daughter of Ethb.
18. 4 when J. cut off the prophets of the LORD
18. 13 what I did when J. slew the prophets of
18. 19 the prophets of the groves..which eat at J's
19. 1 Ahab told J. all that Elijah had done, and
19. 2 Then J. sent a messenger unto Elijah, say
21. 5 But J. his wife came to him, and said unto
21. 7 J. his wife said unto him, Dost thou now
21. 11 the men of his city..did as J. had sent
21. 14 Then they sent to J., saying, Naboth is
21. 15 when J. heard..J. said to Ahab, Arise
21. 23 J...The dogs shall eat J. by the wall of
21. 25 none like unto Ahab..whom J. his wife
2 Ki. 9. 7 I may avenge the blood..at the hand of J.
9. 10 the dogs shall eat J. in the portion of Jez.
9. 22 so long as the whoredoms of thy mother J.
9. 30 when Jehu was come to Jezreel, J. heard
9. 36 In the portion..dogs eat the flesh of J.
9. 37 the carcase of J. shall be as dung upon
9. 37 (so) that they shall not say, This (is) J.
Rev. 2. 20 because thou sufferest that woman [J.]

JE'-ZER, יֵצֶר *formation.*
The third son of Naphtali. B.C. 1698.
Gen. 46. 24 And the sons of Naphtali..Guni, and J.
Num26. 49 Of J., the family of the Jezerites: of Shil.
1 Ch. 7. 13 The sons of Naphtali..Guni, and J., and

JE-ZER-ITES, יִצְרִי.
The descendants of the preceding *Jezer.*
Num26. 49 Of Jezer, the family of the J.: of Shillem

JE-ZI'-AH, יִזִּיָּה *Jah unites.*
One of the Parosh family that had taken a strange wife. B.C. 457.
Ezra 10. 25 of the sons of Parosh; Ramiah, and J.

JE-ZI'-EL, יְזִיאֵל *God unites* [V.L. יזואל].
Son of Azmaveth a valiant man who joined David at Ziklag with his brother Pelet. B.C. 1058.
1 Ch. 12. 3 and J., and Pelet, the sons of Azmaveth

JEZ-LI'-AH, יִזְלִיאָה *Jah delivers.*
A son of Elpaal a Benjamite. B.C. 1400.
1 Ch. 8. 18 Ishmerai also, and J., and Jobab, the sons

JE-ZO'-AR, (doubtful reading of יִצְחַר, V.L. צֹחַר).
A son of Helah, wife of Ashur, a descendant of Caleb the son of Hur. B.C. 1500.
1 Ch. 4. 7 And the sons of Helah (were)..J., and E.

JEZ-RAH-I'AH, יִזְרַחְיָה *Jah is shining.*
The overseer of those singing at the purification of the people. B.C. 445. See *Izrahiah.*
Neh. 12. 42 And the singers sang loud, with J. (their)

JEZ-RE'-EL, יִזְרְעֶאל, (יִזְרְעֵאל) *God sows.*
1. A city in the hill country of Judah, near Jokdeam and Zanoah.
Josh. 15. 56 And J., and Jokdeam, and Zanoah
1 Sa. 25. 43 David also took Ahinoam of J.; and they
29. 1 Israelites pitched by a fountain..in J.
29. 11 men rose..the Philistines went up to J

2. A city in the tribe of Issachar, but belonging to Manasseh, between Megiddo and Bethshean near Mount Gilboa;— now called *Zerin* or *Serin.*
Josh. 19. 18 their border was toward J., and Chesul.
2 Sa. 2. 9 made him king over Gilead..and over J.
4. 4 the tidings came of..Jonathan out of J.
1 Ki. 4. 12 Beth-shean..(is) by Zartanah beneath J.
18. 45 great rain. And Ahab rode, and went to J.
18. 46 and ran before Ahab to the entrance of J.
21. 1 Jezreelite had a vineyard, which (was) in J.
21. 23 dogs shall eat Jezebel by the wall of J.
2 Ki. 8. 29 Joram went back to be healed in J. of
8. 29 down to see Joram the son of Ahab in J.
9. 10 shall eat Jezebel in the portion of J.
9. 15 Joram was returned to be healed in J. of

2 Ki. 9. 15 out of the city to go to tell (it) in J.
9. 16 Jehu rode in a chariot, and went to J.; for
9. 17 there stood a watchman on the tower in J.
9. 30 when Jehu was come to J., Jezebel heard
9. 36 In the portion of J. shall dogs eat the
9. 37 face of the field in the portion of J.
10. 1 unto the rulers of J., to the elders, and
10. 6 come to me to J. by to morrow this time
10. 7 heads in baskets..sent him (them) to J.
10. 11 that remained of the house of Ahab in J.
2 Ch.22. 6 he returned to be healed in J. because of
22. 6 down to see Jehoram the son of Ahab at J.

3. The valley or plain in which Jezreel stood.

Josh 17. 16 and (they) who (are) of the valley of J.
Judg. 6. 33 went over, and pitched in the valley of J.
Hos. 1. 5 the bow of Israel in the valley of J.
2. 22 shall hear..the oil; and they shall hear J.

4. A descendant of the father of Etam. B.C. 1400.

1 Ch. 4. 3 J., and Ishma, and Idbash: and the name

5. The symbolic name of the eldest son of Hosea the prophet. B.C. 780.

Hos. 1. 4 Call his name J.; for yet a little (while)

6. A symbolic name of Israel.

Hos. 1. 4 I will avenge the blood of J. upon the
1. 11 for great (shall be) the day of J.

JEZ-RE-EL-ITE, יִזְרְעֵאלִי.

The people of *Jezreel* in Issachar.

1 Ki. 21. 1 the J. had a vineyard, which (was) in Je.
21. 4 word which Naboth the J. had spoken to
21. 6 I spake unto Naboth the J., and said unto
21. 7 give thee the vineyard of Naboth the J.
21. 15 possession of..vineyard of Naboth the J.
21. 16 go down to the vineyard of Naboth the J.
2 Ki. 9. 21 met him in the portion of Naboth the J.
9. 25 the portion of the field of Naboth the J.

JEZ-RE-EL-I-TESS, יִזְרְעֵאלִית.

A female inhabitant of *Jezreel* (in Judah). B.C. 1050.

1 Sa. 27. 3 Ahinoam the J., and Abigail the Carmel.
30. 5 Ahinoam the J., and Abigail the wife of
2 Sa. 2. 2 Ahinoam the J., and Abigail, Nabal's wife
3. 2 first born was Amnon, of Ahinoam the J.
1 Ch. 3. 1 the first born Amnon, of Ahinoam the J.

JIB'-SAM, יִבְשָׂם *lovely sweet.*

A son of Tola, son of Issachar. B.C. 1600.

1 Ch. 7. 2 J., and Shemuel, heads of their father's

JID'-LAPH, יִדְלָף *melting away.*

A son of Nahor and nephew of Abraham. B.C. 1870.

Gen. 22. 22 and Hazo, and Pildash, and J., and Bet.

JIM'-NAH, JIM'-NA, יִמְנָה *prosperity.*

The first born son of Asher, whose descendants were called Jimnites. B.C. 1690. Called *Imnah* in 1 Ch. 7. 30.

Gen. 46. 17 J., and Ishuah, and Isui, and Beriah, and
Num 26. 44 of J., the family of the Jimnites: of Jesui

JIM-NITES, הַיִּמְנָה.

A family that sprang from Jimnah the first born of Asher.

Num 26. 44 of Jimna, the family of the J.: of Jesui

JIPH'-TAH, יִפְתָּח *breaking through.*

A city in Judah, near Ashnah and Nezib.

Josh 15. 43 And J., and Ashnah, and Nezib

JIPH'-THAH-EL, יִפְתַּח־אֵל *God is breaking through.*

A valley in Zebulun, on the border of Asher and Zebulun, now called *Jefat.*

Josh 19. 14 outgoings thereof are in the valley of J.
19. 27 the valley of J. toward the north side of

JO'-AB, יוֹאָב *Jah is father.*

1. David's nephew, the son of his sister Zeruiah. He became a most overbearing captain in his uncle David's army. B.C. 1015.

1 Sa. 26. 6 Abishai the son of Zeruiah, brother to J.
2 Sa. 2. 13 J. the son of Zeruiah, and the servants of
2. 14 Abner said to J., Let the young men now
2. 14 play before us. And J. said, Let them arise
2. 18 sons of Zeruiah there, J., and Abishai, and
2. 22 should I hold up my face to J. thy brot.?
2. 24 J. also and Abishai pursued after Abner
2. 26 Then Abner called to J., and said, Shall
2. 27 J. said, (As) God liveth, unless thou hadst
2. 28 J. blew a trumpet, and all the people
2. 30 J. returned from following Abner: and
2. 32 J. and his men went all night, and they
3. 22 servants of David and J. came from (pur.)
3. 23 J. and all the host that (was) with him
3. 23 they told J., saying, Abner the son of Ner
3. 24 Then J. came to the king, and said, What
3. 26 when J. was come out from David, he sent
3. 27 J. took him aside in the gate to speak
3. 29 Let it rest on the head of J., and on all
3. 29 let there not fail from the house of J.
3. 30 So J. and Abishai his brother slew
3. 31 David said to J., and to all the people
8. 16 J. the son of Zeruiah (was) over the host
10. 7 he sent J., and all the host of the mighty
10. 9 J. saw that the front of the battle was
10. 13 J. drew nigh, and the peo. that (were) with
10. 14 J. returned from the children of Ammon
11. 1 David sent J., and his servants with him
11. 6 David sent to J., (saying), Send me Uriah
11. 6 And J. sent Uriah to David
11. 7 David demanded (of him) how J. did, and

2 Sa. 11. 11 J., and the servants of my lord, are enca
11. 14 David wrote a letter to J., and sent (it) by
11. 16 when J. observed the city, that he assigned
11. 17 men of the city went..and fought with J.
11. 18 Then J. sent and told David all the things
11. 22 showed David all that J. had sent him for
11. 25 Thus shalt thou say unto J., Let not this
12. 26 J. fought against Rabbah of the children
12. 27 J. sent messengers to David, and said, I
14. 1 J. the son of Zeruiah perceived that the
14. 2 J. sent to Tekoah, and fetched thence a
14. 3 So J. put the words in her mouth
14. 19 (Is not) the hand of J. with thee in all
14. 19 J., he bade me, and he put all these words
14. 20 hath thy servant J. done this thing: and
14. 21 the king said unto J., Behold now, I have
14. 22 J. fell to the ground on his face, and
14. 22 J. said, To day thy servant knoweth that
14. 23 J. arose, and went to Geshur, and brought
14. 29 Absalom sent for J., to have sent him to
14. 30 J.'s field is near mine, and he hath barley
14. 31 Then J. arose, and came to Absalom unto
14. 32 Absalom answered J., Behold, I sent unto
14. 33 J. came to the king, and told him: and
17. 25 Amasa captain of the host instead of J.
17. 25 Nahash, sister to Zeruiah, J.'s mother
18. 2 David..a third part..under the hand of J.
18. 2 part under the hand of Abishai..J.'s bro.
18. 5 king commanded J. and Abishai and Ittai
18. 10 and told J., and said, Behold, I saw Abs.
18. 11 J. said unto the man that told him, And
18. 12 the man said unto J., Though I should
18. 14 Then said J., I may not tarry thus with
18. 15 ten young men that bare J.'s armour
18. 16 J. blew the trumpet, and the people retur.
18. 16 after Israel: for J. held back the people
18. 20 And J. said unto him, Thou shalt not bear
18. 21 Then said J. to Cushi, Go tell the king
18. 21 And Cushi bowed himself unto J., and ran
18. 22 Then said Ahimaaz..yet again to J., But
18. 22 J. said, Wherefore wilt thou run, my son
18. 29 When J. sent the king's servant, and (me)
19. 1 it was told J., Behold, the king weepeth
19. 5 J. came into the house to the king, and
19. 13 before me continually in the room of J.
20. 7 there went out after him J.'s men, and
20. 8 J.'s garment that he had put on was girded
20. 9 J. said to Amasa, (Art) thou in health, my
20. 9 J. took Amasa by the beard with the right
20. 10 heed to the sword that (was) in J.'s hand
20. 10 J. and Abishai his brother pursued after
20. 11 one of J.'s men stood by him, and said
20. 11 He that favoureth J...(let him go) after J.
20. 13 the people went on after J., to pursue
20. 15 people that (were) with J. battered the
20. 16 say, I pray you, unto J., Come near hither
20. 17 the woman said, (Art) thou J.? And he
20. 20 J. answered and said, Far be it, far be it
20. 21 the woman said unto J., Behold, his head
20. 22 cut off the head..and cast (it) out to J.
20. 22 J. returned to Jerusalem unto the king
20. 23 J. (was) over all the host of Israel: and
23. 18 the brother of J., the son of Zeruiah, was
23. 24 the brother of J., (was) one of the thirty
23. 37 armour bearer to J. the son of Zeruiah
24. 2 the king said to J. the captain of the
24. 3 J. said unto the king, Now the LORD thy
24. 4 the king's word prevailed against J., and
24. 4 J. and the captains of the host went out
24. 9 J. gave up the sum of the number of the
1 Ki. 1. 7 he conferred with J. the son of Zeruiah
1. 19 the priest, and J. the captain of the host
1. 41 when J. heard the sound of the trumpet
2. 5 what J. the son of Zeruiah did to me, (and)
2. 22 the priest, and for J. the son of Zeruiah
2. 28 tidings came to J.: for J. had turned after
2. 28 J. fled unto the tabernacle of the LORD
2. 29 it was told king Solomon that J. was fled
2. 30 saying, Thus said J., and thus he answered
2. 31 take away the innocent blood, which J.
2. 33 blood shall..return upon the head of J.
11. 15 J. the captain of the host was gone up to
11. 16 For six months did J. remain there with
11. 21 Hadad heard..that J. the captain of the
1 Ch. 2. 16 And the sons of Zeruiah; Abishai, and J.
11. 6 J. the son of Zeruiah went first up, and
11. 8 round about: and J. repaired the rest of
11. 20 Abishai the brother of J., he was chief of
11. 26 valiant men..(were) Asahel..brother of J.
11. 39 Naharai..the armour bearer of J. the son
18. 15 J. the son of Zeruiah (was) over the host
19. 8 when David heard (of it), he sent J., and
19. 10 J. saw that the battle was set against him
19. 14 So J...drew near before the Syrians unto
19. 15 entered into the city. Then J. came to
20. 1 J. led forth the power of the army, and
20. 1 And J. smote Rabbah, and destroyed it
21. 2 David said to J., and to the rulers of the
21. 3 J. answered, The LORD make his people
21. 4 the king's word prevailed against J.: wh.
21. 4 J. departed, and went throughout all Is.
21. 5 J. gave the sum of the number of the pe.
21. 6 for the king's word was abominable to J.
26. 28 all that..J. the son of Zeruiah, had dedi.
27. 7 fourth..(was) Asahel the brother of J.
27. 24 J. the son of Zeruiah began to number
27. 34 the general of the king's army (was) J.
Psa. 60. *title.* J. returned, and smote of Edom..twe.

2. A descendant of Caleb the son of Hur, of the tribe of Judah.

1 Ch. 2. 54 Ataroth, the house of J., and half of the

3. A grandson of Kenaz, of the tribe of Judah. B.C. 1450.

1 Ch. 4. 14 and Seraiah begat J., the father of the

4. An Israelite whose posterity went up from Babylon with Zerubbabel. B.C. 538.

Ezra 2. 6 of the children of Jeshua (and) J., two
Neh. 7. 11 of the children of Jeshua and J., two th.

5. One whose descendants went up from Babylon with Ezra. B.C. 458.

Ezra 8. 9 Of the sons of J; Obadiah the son of Je.

JO'-AH, יוֹאָח *Jah is brother.*

1. A son of Asaph the recorder in the time of Hezekiah. B.C. 713.

2 Ki. 18. 18, 37 Shebna the scribe, and J. the son of
18. 26 Then said..J...Speak, I pray thee, to thy
Isa. 36. 3 Shebna the scribe, and J., Asaph's son
36. 11 Then said Eliakim and Shebna and J.
36. 22 Shebna the scribe, and J., the son of As.

2. A descendant of Gershom, son of Levi. B.C. 1380.

1 Ch. 6. 21 J. his son, Iddo his son, Zerah his son,
2 Ch.29. 12 J. the son of Zimmah..Eden the son of J.

3. A son of Obed-edom (a descendant of Kohath), a porter in the tabernacle. B.C. 1015.

1 Ch.26. 4 J. the third, and Sacar the fourth, and N.

4. A Levite commissioned by Josiah to repair the house of the Lord. B.C. 621.

2 Ch. 34. 8 J. the son of Joahaz the recorder, to rep.

JO-A'-HAZ, יוֹאָחָז *Jah helps.*

Father of Joah the recorder under king Josiah. B.C. 624.

2 Ch.34. 8 Joah the son of J. the recorder, to repair

JO-AN'-NA, Ἰωάννα, Ἰωαννᾶς.

1. A female disciple, the wife of an officer in Herod's household.

Luke 8. 3 And J. the wife of Chuza Herod's steward
24. 10 and J...told these things unto the apostles

2. The grandson of Zerubbabel, an ancestor of Joseph the husband of Mary, in the line given by Luke.

Luke 3. 27 Which was (the son) of [J.], which was (the

JO'-ASH, יוֹאָשׁ, יֹאָשׁ *Jah supports.* (יוֹעָשׁ, Nos. 1–2).

1. A son of Becher, son of Benjamin. B.C. 1650.

1 Ch. 7. 8 the sons of Becher; Zemira, and J., and

2. Keeper of the stores of oil in David's time. B.C. 1015.

1 Ch.27. 28 and over the cellars of oil (was) J.

3. The father of Gideon, of the tribe of Manasseh. B.C. 1250.

Judg. 6. 11 under an oak..that (pertained) unto J.
6. 29 Gideon the son of J. hath done this thing
6. 30 Then the men of the city..unto J., Bring
6. 31 J. said unto all that stood against him
7. 14 nothing else save the sword of..son of J.
8. 13 Gideon the son of J. returned from battle
8. 29 Jerubbaal the son of J. went and dwelt in
8. 32 Gideon the son of J. died in a good old
8. 32 was buried in the sepulchre of J. his fa.

4. A son of Ahab, king of Israel. B.C. 896.

1 Ki. 22. 26 and carry him back..to J. the king's son
2 Ch.18. 25 and carry him back..to J. the king's son

5. A son of Ahaziah, king of Judah. B.C. 850. He called also *Jehoash.*

2 Ki. 11. 2 But Jehosheba..took J. the son of Ahaz
12. 19 the rest of the acts of J., and all that he
12. 20 his servants arose..and slew J. in the
13. 1 In the three and twentieth year of J. the
13. 10 In the thirty and seventh year of J. king
14. 1 reigned Amaziah the son of J. king of J.
14. 3 he did according to all things as J. his
14. 17 Amaziah the son of J...lived after the
14. 23 fifteenth year of Amaziah the son of J.
1 Ch. 3. 11 Joram his son, Ahaziah his son, J. his son
2 Ch.22. 11 But Jehoshabeath..took J. the son of Ah.
24. 1 J. (was) seven years old when he be. v. 2.
24. 4 J. was minded to repair the house of the
24. 22 Thus J. the king remembered not the kin.
24. 24 So they executed judgment against J.
25. 23 took Amaziah king of Judah, the son of J.
25. 25 Amaziah the son of J...lived after the death

6. A son of Jehoahaz, and grandson of Jehu. B.C. 840.

2 Ki.13. 9 slept..J. his son reigned in his stead
13. 12 the rest of the acts of J., and all that he
13. 13 J. slept with his fathers..and J. was bur.
13. 14 J. the king of Israel came down unto him
13. 25 three times did J. beat him, and recovered
14. 1 In the second year of J. son of Jehoahaz
14. 23 Jeroboam the son of J. king of Israel be.
14. 27 by the hand of Jeroboam the son of J.
2 Ch.25. 17 Then Amaziah..sent to J., the son of Jeh.
25. 18 J. king of Israel..to Amaziah king of Ju.
25. 21 So J. the king of Israel went up; and they
25. 23 J...took Amaziah king of Judah, the son
25. 25 Amaziah..lived after the death of J., son
Hos. 1. 1 in the days of Jeroboam the son of J., king
Amos 1. 1 in the days of Jeroboam the son of J. king

7. A descendant of Shelah, son of Judah. B.C. 1200.

1 Ch. 4. 22 J., and Saraph, who had the dominion in

8. The second in command of those that joined David at Ziklag. B.C. 1058.

1 Ch.12. 3 The chief (was) Ahiezer, then J., the sons

JO-A'-THAM, Ἰωάθαμ.

A progenitor of Joseph the husband of Mary, as enumerated in Matthew's gospel.

Matt. 1. 9 Ozias begat J.; and J. begat Achaz; and

JOB, אִיּוֹב, Ἰώβ *hated.*

A descendant of Aram, son of Shem, dwelling in Uz, in the N. of Arabia, or in E. of Edom and Moab; supposed to have been contemporaneous with Abraham. The Book of Job was probably introduced to the knowledge of Israel by Moses, who may have written the introduction (chap. i., ii,) and the conclusion (xlii. 9–17). The object of the book is twofold, to show *first,* that true religion is not based on selfish considerations, or an answer to the question, Does Job serve God for nought? and *second,* that temporal calamities are not always the consequences of sin. The character of Job is described in ch. i. 1–5; his first trial in i. 5–22; his second trial in ii. 1–10; his friends' visit, 11–13; his complaint in iii.; Eliphaz's remonstrance in iv., v.; Job's reply in vi. vii.; Bildad's remonstrance in viii.; Job's reply in ix. x.; Zophar's remonstrance in xi.; Job's reply xii, xiii. xiv.; Eliphaz responds in xv.; Job refutes him in xvi. xvii.; Bildad responds in xviii.; Job refutes him in xix.; Zophar responds in xx.; Job refutes him in xxi.; Eliphaz attacks Job in xxii.; Job refutes him in xxiii., xxiv.; Bildad attacks Job in xxv.; Job refutes him in xxvi. xxxi.; Elihu interposes in xxxii.–xxxvii.; God interposes in xxxviii. xxxix, xl. 1, 2; Job humbles himself in xl. 3–5; God resumes, and concludes in xl. 6–xli.; Job's submission, xlii. 1, 6; his friends' submission, 7–9; his latter end, 10–17. He dies, aged about 240 years.

Job 1. 5 it was so..that J., sent and sanctified v. 1.
1. 5 J. said, It may be..Thus did J. continua.
1. 8 Hast thou considered my servant J., that
1. 9 Satan answered..and said, Doth J. fear
1. 14 there came a messenger unto J., and said
1. 20 Then J. arose, and rent his mantle, and
1. 22 In all this J. sinned not, nor charged G.
2. 3 Hast thou considered my servant J., that
2. 7 So went Satan forth..and smote J. with
2. 10 In all this did not J. sin with his lips
2. 11 Now when J.'s three friends heard of all
3. 1 After this J. opened his mouth, and cursed
3. 2 J. spake, and said
6. 1 J. answered and said
[Also in 9. 1; 12. 1; 16. 1; 19. 1; 21. 1; 23. 1; 26. 1.]
27. 1 Moreover J. continued his parable, and
29. 1 Moreover J. continued his parable, and
31. 40 Let thistles grow..The words of J. are
32. 1 So these three men ceased to answer J.
32. 2 against J. was his wrath kindled, because
32. 3 no answer, and (yet) had condemned J.
32. 4 Now Elihu had waited till J. had spoken
32. 12 (there was) none of you that convinced J.
33. 1 Wherefore, J., I pray thee hear my spee.
33. 31 Mark well, O J.; hearken unto me: hold
34. 5 For J. hath said, I am righteous: and God
34. 7 What man (is) like J., (who) drinketh up
34. 35 J. hath spoken without knowledge, and
34. 36 My desire (is, that) J. may be tried unto
35. 16 Therefore doth J. open his mouth in vain
37. 14 Hearken unto this, O J.: stand still, and
38. 1 Then the LORD answered J. out of the
40. 1 Moreover the LORD answered J., and said
40. 3 Then J. answered the LORD, and said
40. 6 Then answered the LORD unto J. out of
42. 1 Then J. answered the LORD, and said
42. 7 the LORD had spoken these words unto J.
42. 7 ye have not spoken..as my servant J.
42. 8 take..seven rams, and go to my servant J.
42. 8 my servant J. shall pray for you; for him
42. 8 ye have not spoken..like my servant J.
42. 9 commanded them: the LORD..accepted J.
42. 10 turned..captivity of J...the LORD gave J.
42. 12 So the LORD blessed the latter end of J.
42. 15 no women..(so) fair as the daughters of J.
42. 16 After this lived J. an hundred and forty
42. 17 So J. died, (being) old, and full of days
Eze. 14. 14 Though these..men, Noah, Daniel, and J.
14. 20 Though Noah, Daniel, and J., (were) in
Jas. 5. 11 Ye have heard of the patience of J., and

JOB, יוֹב *returning.*

The third son of Issachar, called in another genealogy (Num. 26. 24) *Jashib,* and (1 Ch. 7. 1) *Jashub.* B.C. 1692.

Gen. 46. 13 the sons of Issachar..Phuvah, and J., and

JO'-BAB, יוֹבָב *howling.*

1. A son of Joktan the Shemite. B.C. 2200.

Gen. 10. 29 Ophir, and Havilah, and J.: all these
1 Ch. 1. 23 Ophir, and Havilah, and J. All these (were)

2. The second king of Edom, and son of Zerah of Bozrah. B.C. 1500.

Gen. 36. 33 J. the son of Zerah..reigned in his stead
36. 34 J. died, and Husham..reigned in his stead
1 Ch. 1. 44 J. the son of Zerah..reigned in his stead
1. 45 when J. was dead, Husham..reigned in

3. A king of Madon, a Canaanitish city conquered by Joshua. B.C. 1450.

Josh 11. 1 came to pass..that he sent to J. king of

4. A son of Shaharaim, a Benjamite. B.C. 1350.

1 Ch. 8. 9 he begat of Hodesh his wife, J., and Zibia

5. A son of Elpaal, a Benjamite. B.C. 1350.

1 Ch. 8. 18 Ishmerai also, and Jezliah, and J., the

JO-CHE'-BED, יוֹכֶבֶד *Jah is honour.*

The wife of Amram, and mother of Miriam, Aaron, and Moses. B.C. 1560.

Exod. 6. 20 Amram took him J. his father's sister to
Num 26. 59 the name of Amram's wife (was) J., the

JO'-ED, יוֹעֵד *Jah is witness.*

A son of Pedaiah, a Benjamite. B.C. 520.

Neh. 11. 7 Sallu the son of Meshullam, the son of J.

JO'-EL, יוֹאֵל, Ἰωήλ *Jah is God.*

1. The first born son of Samuel the prophet; called *Vashni* in 1 Ch. 6. 28. B.C. 1112.

1 Sa. 8. 2 Now the name of his first born was J., and
1 Ch. 6. 33 Heman a singer, the son of J., the son of
15. 17 Levites appointed Heman the son of J.

2. A Simeonite. B.C. 800.

1 Ch. 4. 35 J., and Jehu the son of Josibiah, the son

3. The father of Shemaiah, a Reubenite. B.C. 1570.

1 Ch. 5. 4 The sons of J.; Shemaiah his son, Gog his
5. 8 Azaz, the son of Shema, the son of J., who

4. A chief Gadite. B.C. 1070.

1 Ch. 5. 12 J. the chief, and Shapham the next, and

5. A Kohathite, and ancestor of Samuel the prophet. B.C. 1212.

1 Ch. 6. 36 son of Elkanah, the son of J., the son of

6. A descendant of Tola, son of Issachar. B.C. 1500.

1 Ch. 7. 3 Michael, and Obadiah, and J., Ishiah, five

7. One of David's valiant men and a brother of Nathan. B.C. 1048.

1 Ch. 11. 38 J. the brother of Nathan, Mibhar the son

8. A Gershonite in the days of David. B.C. 1015.

1 Ch. 15. 7 J. the chief, and his..an hundred and th.
15. 11 Asaiah, and J., Shemaiah, and Eliel, and
23. 8 the chief (was) Jehiel, and Zetham, and J.

9. A Gershonite, keeper of the treasures of the house of the Lord in the days of David. B.C. 1015.

1 Ch. 26. 22 Zetham, and Joel his brother, (which were)

10. A prince of Manasseh, W. of the Jordan, in the days of David. B.C. 1015.

1 Ch. 27. 20 of the half tribe of Manasseh; J. the son

11. A Kohathite that aided in cleansing the temple in the days of Hezekiah. B.C. 726.

2 Ch. 29. 12 J. the son of Azariah, of the sons of the

12. One of Nebo's family who had taken a strange wife during the exile. B.C. 457.

Ezra 10. 43 Mattithiah, Zabad, Zebina, Jadau..J., B.

13. A son of Zichri, and overseer of the Benjamites in Jerusalem. B.C. 445.

Neh. 11. 9 J. the son of Zichri (was) their overseer

14. Son of Pethuel, and prophet in the days of Uzziah king of Judah. B.C. 800–750.

Joel 1. 1 word..that came to J. the son of Pethuel
Acts 2. 16 this is that which was spoken by..[J.]

JO-E'-LAH, יוֹעֵאלָה *God is snatching.*

A son of Jeroham of Gedor who joined David in Ziklag. B.C. 1058.

1 Ch. 12. 7 J. and Zebadiah, the sons of Jeroham of

JO-E'-ZER, יוֹעֶזֶר *Jah is help.*

A Korhite who joined David in Ziklag. B.C. 1058.

1 Ch. 12. 6 Azareel, and J., and Jashobeam, the K.

JOG-BE'-HAH, יָגְבְּהָה *height.*

A place in Gad, now called *Kanuat.*

Num 32. 35 And Atroth, Shophan, and Jaazer, and J.
Judg. 8. 11 dwelt in tents on the east of Nobah and J.

JOG'-LI, יָגְלִי *exiled.*

Father of Bukki and a prince of Dan, chosen to divide the land W. of the Jordan. B.C. 1530.

Num 34. 22 And the prince..Bukki the son of J.

JO'-HA, יוֹחָא *Jah is living.*

1. A son of Beriah, grandson of Shaharaim, a Benjamite. B.C. 1350.

1 Ch. 8. 16 Michael, and Ispah, and J...sons of Beriah

2. One of David's valiant men. B.C. 1048.

1 Ch. 11. 45 son of Shimri, and J. his brother, the Ti.

JO-HA'-NAN, יוֹחָנָן, *Jah is gracious.*

1. A son of Kareah or Careah, a captain of the Jews. B.C. 600.

2 Ki. 25. 23 J. the son of Careah, and Seraiah the son
Jer. 40. 8 J. and Jonathan the sons of Kareah, and
40. 13 J. the son of Kareah, and all the captains
40. 15 J. the son of Kareah spake to Gedaliah in
40. 16 the son of Ahikam said unto J. the son
41. 11, 13 J. the son of Kareah, and all the capt.
41. 14 returned, and went unto J...of Kareah
41. 15 son of Nethaniah escaped from J. with
41. 16 Then took J. the son of Kareah, and all
42. 1 J. the son of Kareah, and Jezaniah the
42. 8 Then called he J. the son of Kareah, and
43. 2 J. the son of Kareah, and all the proud
43. 4, 5 J. the son of Kareah, and all the capt.

2. The eldest son of Josiah, king of Judah. B.C. 610.

1 Ch. 3. 15 the first born J., the second Jehoiakim

3. A son of Elioenai. B.C. 445.

1 Ch. 3. 24 and Akkub, and J., and Dalaiah, and A.

4. A grandson of Ahimaaz, father of Azariah, a Levite. B.C. 900.

1 Ch. 6. 9 Ahimaaz begat Azariah..Azariah begat J.
6. 10 J. begat Azariah, he (it is) that executed

5. A valiant man that joined David at Ziklag. B.C. 1058.

1 Ch. 12. 4 Jahaziel..J., and Jozabad the Gederathite

6. A Gadite that joined David at Ziklag. B.C. 1058.

1 Ch. 12. 12 J. the eighth, Elzabad the ninth

7. An Ephraimite who opposed making slaves of the captives of Judah, in Ahaz's time. B.C. 900. (Heb. *Jehohanan.*)

2 Ch. 28. 12 Azariah the son of J., Berechiah the son

8. A returned exile, son of Hakkatan, in Artaxerxes time. B.C. 457.

Ezra 8. 12 J. the son of Hakkatan, and with him an

9. A priest who, with Ezra, summoned the exiles to Jerusalem. B.C. 458. (Heb. *Jehohanan.*)

Ezra 10. 6 the chamber of J. the son of Eliashib

10. A son of Tobiah the Ammonite, and husband of Meshullam's daughter. B.C. 445. (Heb. *Jehohanan.*)

Neh. 6. 18 J. had taken the daughter of Meshullam

11. A priest in the days of Joiakim, the grandson of Jozadak. B.C. 445.

Neh. 12. 22 days of Eliashib, Joiada, and J., and Ja.
12. 23 until the days of J. the son of Eliashib

JOHN, Ἰωάννης.

1. The son of Zacharias and Elizabeth, who came as the forerunner of the Messiah, and was beheaded by Herod, tetrarch of Galilee. A.D. 28.

Matt. 3. 1 those days came J. the Baptist, preaching
3. 4 J. had his raiment of camel's hair, and a
3. 13 Then cometh Jesus from Galilee..unto J.
3. 14 [J.] forbad him, saying, I have need to be
4. 12 had heard that J. was cast into prison
9. 14 Then came to him the disciples of J., say.
11. 2 J. had heard in the prison the works of
11. 4 show J. again those things which ye do
11. 7 to say unto the multitudes concerning J.
11. 11 not risen a greater than J. the Baptist
11. 12 from the days of J. the Baptist until now
11. 13 prophets and the law prophesied until J.
11. 18 J. came neither eating nor drinking, and
14. 2 This is J. the Baptist: he is risen from the
14. 3 Herod had laid hold on J., and bound him
14. 4 J. said unto him, It is not lawful for thee
14. 8 Give me here J. Baptist's head in a char.
14. 10 And he sent, and beheaded J. in the prison
16. 14 Some (say that thou art) J. the Baptist
17. 13 that he spake unto them of J. the Baptist
21. 25 The baptism of J., whence was it? from
21. 26 fear..people; for all hold J. as a prophet
21. 32 J. came unto you in..way of righteousness
Mark 1. 4 J. did baptize in the wilderness, and pre.
1. 6 J. was clothed with camel's hair, and with
1. 9 came..and was baptised of J. in Jordan
1. 14 after that J. was put in prison, Jesus came
2. 18 the disciples of J. and of the Pharisees
2. 18 disciples of J. and of the Pharisees fast
6. 14 J. the Baptist was risen from the dead
6. 16 It is [J.,] whom I beheaded: he is risen
6. 17 laid hold upon J., and bound him in prison
6. 18 J. had said unto Herod, It is not lawful
6. 20 Herod feared J., knowing that he was a
6. 24 And she said, The head of J. the Baptist
6. 25 in a charger the head of J. the Baptist
8. 28 they answered, J. the Baptist: but some
11. 30 The baptism of J., was (it) from heaven
11. 32 (men) counted J., that he was a prophet
Luke 1. 13 a son, and thou shalt call his name J.
1. 60 and said, Not (so); but he shall be called J.
1. 63 saying, His name is J. And they marvelled
3. 2 the word of God came unto J. the son of
3. 15 men mused in their hearts of J., whether
3. 16 J. answered, saying unto (them) all, I in.
3. 20 this above all, that he shut up J. in prison
5. 33 Why do the disciples of J. fast often, and
7. 18 disciples of J. showed him of all these
7. 19 J. calling (unto him) two of his disciples
7. 20 J. Baptist hath sent us unto thee, saying
7. 22 tell J. what things ye have seen and heard
7. 24 when the messengers of J...concerning J.
7. 28 not a greater prophet than J. the Baptist
7. 29 being baptized with the baptism of J.
7. 33 J. the Baptist came neither eating bread
9. 7 of some, that J. was risen from the dead
9. 9 J. have I beheaded: but who is this of
9. 19 They answering said, J. the Baptist; but
11. 1 to pray, as J. also taught his disciples
16. 16 The law and the prophets (were) until J.
20. 4 The baptism of J., was it from heaven, or
20. 6 they be persuaded that J. was a prophet
John 1. 6 man sent from God, whose name (was) J.
1. 15 J. bare witness of him, and cried, saying
1. 19 this is the record of J., when the Jews
1. 26 J. answered them, saying, I baptize with
1. 28 beyond Jordan, where J. was baptizing
1. 29 [J.] seeth Jesus coming unto him, and
1. 32 J. bare record, saying, I saw the spirit
1. 35 day after, J. stood, and two of his disciples
1. 40 One of the two which heard J. (speak)
3. 23 And J. also was baptizing in Ænon near
3. 24 For J. was not yet cast into prison
3. 25 a question between (some) of J.'s disciples
3. 26 they came unto J., and said unto him, R.
3. 27 J. answered and said, A man can receive
4. 1 made and baptized more disciples than J.
5. 33 Ye sent unto J., and he bare witness unto
5. 36 I have greater witness than (that) of J.
10. 40 into the place where J. at first baptized
10. 41 J. did no miracle: but all things that J.
Acts 1. 5 J. truly baptized with water; but ye shall
1. 22 Beginning from the baptism of J., unto

Acts 10. 37 after the baptism which J. preached
11. 16 J. indeed baptized with water; but ye
13. 24 When J. had first preached before his
13. 25 as J. fulfilled his course, he said, Whom
18. 25 he spake..knowing only the baptism of J.
19. 3 Unto what..And they said, Unto J.'s bap.
19. 4 J. verily baptized with the baptism of

2. A son of Zebedee and younger brother of James, and the beloved disciple of Christ.

Matt. 4. 21 (the son) of Zebedee, and J. his brother
10. 2 James..son) of Zebedee, and J. his broth.
17. 1 Jesus taketh Peter, James, and J. his
Mark 1. 19 the (son) of Zebedee, and J. his brother
1. 29 entered into the house..with James and J.
3. 17 James..and J. the brother of James; and
5. 37 follow him, save Peter, and James, and J.
9. 2 taketh (with him) Peter, and James, and J.
9. 38 J. answered him, saying, Master, we saw
10. 35 James and J., the sons of Zebedee, come
10. 41 began to be much displeased with..J.
13. 3 James and J. and Andrew asked him pr.
14. 33 taketh with him Peter and James and J
Luke 5. 10 also James and J., the sons of Zebedee
6. 14 Simon..and..James and J., Philip and B
8. 51 suffered no man to go in, save..J. and J.
9. 28 after these sayings, he took Peter and J.
9. 49 J. answered and said, Master, we saw one
9. 54 when his disciples James and J. saw (this)
22. 8 he sent Peter and J., saying, Go and pre.
Acts 1. 13 where abode both Peter and James, and J.
3. 1 Peter and J. went up together into the
3. 3 Who seeing Peter and J. about to go into
3. 4 Peter, fastening his eyes upon him with J.
3. 11 the lame man which was healed held..J.
4. 13 when they saw the boldness of Peter and J.
4. 19 Peter and J. answered and said unto them
8. 14 when the apostles..heard..they sent..J.
12. 2 killed James the brother of J. with the
Gal. 2. 9 when James, Cephas, and J...perceived
Rev. 1. 1 he sent and signified..unto his servant J.
1. 4 J. to the seven churches which are in A.
1. 9 I J. who also am your brother, and com.
21. 2 And I [J.] saw the holy city, new Jerusa.
22. 8 And I J. saw these things, and heard (them)

3. A kinsman of Annas the high priest.

Acts 4. 6 Annas the high priest, and Caiaphas, and J.

4. A son of Mary, sister of Barnabas, and surnamed Mark, *which see.*

Acts 12. 12 the mother of J., whose surname was M.
12. 25 took with them J., whose surname was
13. 5 and they had also J. to (their) minister
13. 13 and J. departing from them returned to J.
15. 37 Barnabas determined to take with them J.

JO-IA'-DA, יוֹיָדָע *Jah knows.*
A descendant of Jeshua the priest who returned with Zerubbabel. B.C. 456. See *Jehoiada.*

Neh. 12. 10 also begat Eliashib, and Eliashib begat J.
12. 11 And J. begat Jonathan, and Jonathan
12. 22 days of Eliashib, J., and Johanan, and
13. 28 (one) of the sons of J., the son of Eliashib

JO-IA'-KIM, יוֹיָקִים *Jah sets up.*
The son of Jeshua the priest who returned with Zerubbabel. B.C. 536.

Neh. 12. 10 And Jeshua begat J., J. also begat Elias.
12. 12 in the days of J. were priests, the chief
12. 26 These (were) in the days of J. the son of J.

JO-IA'-RIB, יוֹיָרִיב *Jah contends.*
1. One whom Ezra sent to obtain ministers to return with him to Jerusalem. B.C. 458.

Ezra 8. 16 for J., and for Elnathan, men of unders.

2. A descendant of Pharez whose family dwelt in Jerusalem. B.C. 457.

Neh. 11. 5 the son of Adaiah, the son of J., the son

3. A priest, father of Jedaiah. B.C. 445. See *Jehoiarib.*

Neh. 11. 10 Of the priests: Jedaiah the son of J., Jac.
12. 6 Shemaiah, and J., Jedaiah.
12. 19 And of J., Mattenai; of Jedaiah, Uzzi

JOIN, to —
1. *To be united,* חָבַר *chabar,* 4 [V.L. בחר].
Eccl. 9. 4 to him that is joined to all the living
2. *To sew or join together,* חוּט *chut,* 5.
Ezra 4. 12 have set up the walls..and joined the
3. *To be added,* יָסַף *yasaph,* 2.
Exod. 1. 10 they join also unto our enemies, and fight
4. *To cause to touch,* נָגַע *naga,* 5.
Isa. 5. 8 Woe unto them that join house to house
5. *To bring near,* קָרַב *qarab,* 3.
Eze. 37. 17 join them one to another into one stick

JOIN (battle), to —
1. *To spread out,* נָטַשׁ *natash.*
1 Sa. 4. 2 when they joined battle, Israel was smit.
2. *To set in array,* עָרַךְ *arak.*
Gen. 14. 8 they joined battle with them in the vale

JOIN hard to, to —
To border with, συνομορέω *sunomoreō.*
Acts 18. 7 whose house joined hard to the synagogue

JOIN (in) affinity, to —
To join self in marriage, חָתַן *chathan,* 7.
2 Ch. 18. 1 Now Jehoshaphat..joined affinity with
Ezra 9. 14 Should we..join in affinity with the peo.

JOIN self, to —
1. *To join, become companion,* חָבַר *chabar,* 3.
2 Ch. 20. 36 he joined himself with him to make ships
2. *To join self to,* חָבַר *chabar,* 7.
2 Ch. 20. 35 join himself with Ahaziah king of Israel
20. 37 Because thou hast joined thyself with A.
Dan. 11. 6 they shall join themselves together; for
3. *To be joined,* לָוָה *lavah,* 2.
Esth. 9. 27 all such as joined themselves unto them
Isa. 56. 3 that hath joined himself to the LORD, spe.
56. 6 that join themselves to the LORD, to serve
Jer. 50. 5 Come, and let us join ourselves to the LORD
4. *To be coupled, yoked,* צָמַד *tsamad,* 2.
Num 25. 3 Israel joined himself unto Baal-peor: and
Psa. 106. 28 They joined themselves also unto Baal-p.
5. *To cleave or join self to,* κολλάομαι *kollaomai.*
Luke 15. 15 he went and joined himself to a citizen of
Acts 5. 13 of the rest durst no man join himself to
8. 29 Go near, and join thyself to this chariot
9. 26 he assayed to join himself to the disciples
6. *To cleave or join self to,* προσκολλάομαι *proskol.*
Acts 5. 36 men, about four hundred, [joined thems.]

JOIN selves together, to —
To join self to, become companion, חָבַר *chabar,* 7.
Dan. 11. 6 they shall join themselves together; for

JOIN together, to —
1. *To join together, stir up,* סָכַךְ *sakak,* 3a.
Isa. 9. 11 The LORD shall..join his enemies together
2. *To yoke together,* συζευγνύω *suzeugnuō.*
Matt 19. 6 What therefore God hath joined together
Mark 10. 9 What therefore God hath joined together

JOIN together, to perfectly —
To adjust perfect, or fit thoroughly, καταρτίζω.
1 Co. 1. 10 ye be perfectly joined together in the same

JOINED, to be —
1. *To cleave together, be adhering,* דָּבֵק *dabeq,* 4.
Job 41. 17 They are joined one to another, they stick
2. *To join, be joined,* חָבַר *chabar.*
Exod 28. 7 the two shoulder pieces thereof joined at
Eze. 1. 9 Their wings..joined one to another; they
1. 11 two..of every one..joined one to another
Hos. 4. 17 Ephraim (is) joined to idols: let him alone
3. *To be joined,* חָבַר *chabar,* 4.
Eccl. 9. 4 For to him that is joined to all the living
4. *To rejoice, be joined, become one,* חָדָה *chadah.*
Job 3. 6 let it not be joined unto the days of the
5. *To be united, one,* יָחַד *yachad.*
Isa. 14. 20 Thou shalt not be joined with them in
6. *To be joined,* לָוָה *lavah,* 2.
Gen. 29. 34 Now..will my husband be joined unto me
Num 18. 2 bring..that they may be joined unto thee
18. 4 they shall be joined unto thee, and keep
Psa. 83. 8 Assur also is joined with them: they have
Isa. 14. 1 the strangers shall be joined with them
Zech. 2. 11 many nations shall be joined to the LORD
7. *To be added,* סָפָה *saphah,* 2.
Isa. 13. 15 every one that is joined..shall fall by the
8. *To be coupled, yoked,* צָמַד *tsamad,* 2.
Num 25. 5 his men that were joined unto Baal-peor
9. *To be joined, bound to,* קָטַר *qatar.*
Eze. 46. 22 courts joined of forty..long, and thirty
10. *To be, become, or draw near,* קָרַב *qarab.*
1 Ki. 20. 29 in the seventh day the battle was joined
11. *To be joined, or join self to,* κολλάομαι *kollaom.*
1 Co. 6. 16 know ye not that he which is joined to an
6. 17 he that is joined unto the Lord is one
12. *To be joined, or join self to,* προσκολλάομαι.
Eph. 5. 31 [shall be joined] unto his wife, and they

JOINED together, to be —
1. *To cleave, adhere,* דָּבֵק *dabeq.*
Job 41. 23 flakes of his flesh are joined together
2. *To join, become companion,* חָבַר *chabar.*
Gen. 14. 3 All these were joined together in the vale
3. *To be joined,* חָבַר *chabar,* 4.
Exod 28. 7 thereof; and (so) it shall be joined toget.
4. *To be bound, joined,* קָשַׁר *qashar,* 2.
Neh. 4. 6 all the wall was joined together unto the

JOINED fitly together, to be —
To lay systematically together, συναρμολογέω.
Eph. 4. 16 whom the whole body fitly joined toge.

JOINING —
1. *Cleaving, adhering,* דָּבֵק *dabeq.*
2 Ch. 3. 12 joining to the wing of the other cherub
2. *Couplings,* מְחַבְּרוֹת *mechabberoth.*
1 Ch. 22. 3 prepared iron..for the nails..for the join.

JOINT —
1. *A joining, coupling,* דֶּבֶק *debeq.*
1 Ki. 22. 34 smote..between the joints of the harness
2 Ch. 18. 33 smote..between the joints of the harness
2. *Rounding,* חַמּוּק *chammuq.*
Song 7. 1 the joints of thy thighs (are) like jewels
3. *A knot, joint,* קְטַר *qetar.*
Dan. 5. 6 so that the joints of his loins were loosed
4. *A joint, fitting together,* ἁφή *haphē.*
Eph. 4. 16 compacted by that which every joint sup.
Col. 2. 19 from which all the body by joints and ba.
5. *A joint, fitting together,* ἁρμός *harmos.*
Heb. 4. 12 dividing asunder..of the joints and mar.

JOINT, out of —
Disjointed, tottering, מוּעֶדֶת [*maad,* partic. 4].
Prov 25. 19 (like) a broken tooth, and a foot out of joint

JOINT, to be out of —
1. *To be disjointed, alienated,* יָקַע *yaqa.*
Gen. 32. 25 hollow of Jacob's thigh was out of joint
2. *To separate self, become separated,* פָּרַד *parad,* 7.
Psa. 22. 14 all my bones are out of joint: my heart

JOINT heir —
One who is heir with (another), συγκληρονόμος.
Rom. 8. 17 heirs of God, and joint heirs with Christ

JOK-DE'-AM, יָקְדְעָם *anger of the people.*
A city in the hill country of Judah.

Josh 15. 56 And Jezreel, and J., and Zanoah.

JO'-KIM, יוֹקִים *Jah sets up.*
A descendant of Shelah, son of Judah. B.C. 1200.

1 Ch. 4. 22 And J., and the men of Chozeba, and Jo.

JOK-ME'-AM, יָקְמְעָם *standing of the people.*
A Levitical city of Ephraim, S.W. of Abel Meholah, nearly opposite to the mouth of the Jabbok.

1 Ch. 6. 68 J. with her suburbs, and Beth-horon with

JOK-NE'-AM, יָקְנְעָם *possession of the people*
1. A Levitical city of Zebulun, in the W., near Mount Carmel.

Josh. 12. 22 The king of Kedesh, one; the king of J.
19. 11 and reached to the river that (is) before J.
21. 34 out of the tribe of Zebulun, J. with her

2. Should be *Jokmeam* in Ephraim (in 1 Ki. 4. 12), or *Kibzaim* (in Josh. 21. 2).

1 Ki. 4. 12 (even) unto (the place that is) beyond J.

JOK'-SHAN, יָקְשָׁן *fowler.*
A son of Abraham by Keturah, and father of Sheba and Dedan. B.C. 1848.

Gen. 25. 2 she bare him Zimran, and J., and Medan
25. 3 J. begat Sheba and Dedan. And the sons
1 Ch. 1. 32 she bare Zimran, and J., and Medan
1. 32 And the sons of J.; Sheba, and Dedan

JOK'-TAN, יָקְטָן *little.*
A son of Eber, of the family of Shem. His sons were Almodad, Sheleph, Hazar-maveth, and Jerah. B.C. 2210.

Gen. 10. 25 divided; and his brother's name (was) J.
10. 26 J. begat Almodad, and Sheleph and Haz.
10. 29 and Jobab: all these (were) the sons of J.
1 Ch. 1. 19 Peleg..and his brother's name (was) J.
1. 20 J. begat Almodad..Sheleph, and Hazarm.
1. 23 Havilah, and Jobab..(were) the sons of J.

JOK-THE'-EL, יָקְתְאֵל *God's reward of victory.*
1. A city in the W. of the plain of Judah.

Josh. 15. 38 And Dilean, and Mizpeh, and J.

2. A name given by Amaziah to Selah or Petra in Edom. B.C. 826.

2 Ki. 14. 7 called the name of it J. unto this day

JO-NA'-DAB, יְהוֹנָדָב ,יוֹנָדָב *Jah is liberal.*
1. A son of Shimeah, David's brother. B.C. 1040.

2 Sa. 13. 3 J., the son of Shimeah, D's brother and J
13. 5 J. said unto him, Lay thee down on thy
13. 32 And J., the son of Shimeah, David's bro.
13. 35 J. said unto the king, Behold, the king's

2. The son of Rechab, whom Jehu took with him to show him his zeal for the Lord. B.C. 884. See *Jehonadab.*

Jer. 35. 6 J. the son of Rechab our father comman.
35. 8 Thus have we obeyed the voice of J. the
35. 10 To all that J. our father commanded us
35. 14 The words of J. the son of Rechab, that
35. 16 the sons of J. the son of Rechab have
35. 18 obeyed the commandment of J. your fa.
35. 19 J. the son of Rechab shall not want a

JO'-NAH, יוֹנָה *a dove.*
The son of Amittai, of Gath-Hepher in Zebulun, in the days of Jeroboam II. He was the first Hebrew prophet or missionary sent to a heathen nation. B.C. 825.

2 Ki. 14. 25 he spake by the hand of his servant J.
Jon. 1. 1 word of the LORD came unto J. the son
1. 3 J. rose up to flee unto Tarshish from the
1. 5 J. was gone down into the sides of the
1. 7 they cast lots, and the lot fell upon J.
1. 15 they took up J., and cast him forth into
1. 17 a great fish to swallow up J. And J. was
2. 1 J. prayed unto the LORD his God out of
2. 10 and it vomited out J. upon the dry (land)
3. 1 word of the LORD came unto J. the seco.
3. 3 J. arose, and went unto Nineveh, accord.
3. 4 J. began to enter into the city a day's
4. 1 it displeased J. exceedingly, and he was
4. 5 J. went out of the city, and sat on the
4. 6 made (it) to come up over J., that it might
4. 6 So J. was exceeding glad of the gourd
4. 8 the sun beat upon the head of J., that he
4. 9 God said to J., Doest thou well to be an.

JO'-NAN, Ἰωνάν, Ἰωνάμ.
An ancestor of Joseph the husband of Mary the mother of Jesus.

Luke 3. 30 Joseph, which was (the son) of [J.], which

JO'-NAS, JO'-NA, 'Ιωνᾶς, *from Heb.* יוֹנָה *or from* יוֹחָנָן.

1. The Greek form of the Hebrew Jonah.

Matt 12. 39 given to it, but the sign of the prophet J.
12. 40 J. was three days and three nights in the
12. 41 because they repented at..preaching of J.
12. 41 and, behold, a greater than J. (is) here
16. 4 no sign..but the sign of the prophet J.
Luke 11. 29 given it, but the sign of J. (the prophet)
11. 30 J. was a sign unto the Ninevites, so shall
11. 32 for they repented at the preaching of J.
11. 32 and, behold, a greater than J. (is) here

2. The father of Peter the apostle. In one passage he is called Jona; and in one, Peter is called Barjona (*i.e.* "Son of Jona").

John 1. 42 Thou art Simon the son of J.: thou shalt
21. 15, 16, 17 Simon, (son) of J., lovest thou me?

JO-NATH E-LEM RE-CHO-KIM, יוֹנַת אֵלֶם רְחֹקִים.

Psa. 56. *title*. To the chief musician upon Jonath-el.

JO-NA'-THAN, יְהוֹנָתָן, יוֹנָתָן *Jah is given.*

1. A Levite, son of Gershom, and priest of an idol in Mount Ephraim. B.C. 1406.

Judg 18. 30 J., the son of Gershom, the son of Mana.

2. A son of king Saul, and friend of David. With his father he fell in battle with the Philistines. B.C. 1056.

1 Sa. 13. 2 a thousand..with J. in Gibeah of Benja.
13. 3 J. smote the garrison of the Philistines
13. 16 J. his son, and the people (that were) pr.
13. 22 with Saul and J.: but with Saul and..J.
14. 1 J. the son of Saul said unto the young
14. 3 And the people knew not that J. was gone
14. 4 passages, by which J. sought to go over
14. 6 J. said to the young man that bare his
14. 8 Then said J., Behold, we will pass over
14. 12 the men of the garrison answered J. and
14. 12 J. said unto his armour bearer, Come up
14. 13 J. climbed up upon his hands and upon
14. 13 they fell before J.; and his armour bearer
14. 14 that first slaughter, which J. and his arm.
14. 17 behold, J. and his armour bearer (were)
14. 21 the Israelites that (were) with Saul and J.
14. 27 But J. heard not when his father charged
14. 29 Then said J., My father hath troubled the
14. 39 though it be in J. my son, he shall surely
14. 40 I and J. my son will be on the other side
14. 41 Saul and J. were taken: but the people
14. 42 Cast (lots) between me and J... And J. was
14. 43 Saul said to J., Tell me what thou hast
14. 43 J. told him, and said, I did but taste a
14. 44 God do so..for thou shalt surely die, J.
14. 45 people said unto Saul, Shall J. die, who
14. 45 So the people rescued J., that he died not
14. 49 Now the sons of Saul were J., and Ishui
18. 1 the soul of J... and J. loved him as his own
18. 3 Then J. and David made a covenant, bec.
18. 4 J. stripped himself of the robe that (was)
19. 1 Saul spake to J. his son, and to all his ser.
19. 2 J., Saul's son, delighted much in D.: and J.
19. 4 J. spake good of David unto Saul his fath.
19. 6 Saul hearkened unto the voice of J.: and
19. 7 J. called David, and J. showed him all
19. 7 J. brought David to Saul, and he was in
20. 1 David..came and said before J., What
20. 3 Let not J. know this, lest he be grieved
20. 4 Then said J. unto David, Whatsoever thy
20. 5 David said unto J., Behold, to morrow (is)
20. 9 J. said, Far be it from thee: for if I knew
20. 10 Then said David to J., Who shall tell me?
20. 11 J. said unto David, Come, and let us go out
20. 12 J. said unto David, O LORD God of Israel
20. 13 The LORD do so and much more to J.: but
20. 16 So J. made (a covenant) with the house of
20. 17 J. caused David to swear again, because
20. 18 Then J. said to David, To morrow (is) the
20. 25 and J. arose, and Abner sat by Saul's side
20. 27 Saul said unto J. his son, Wherefore com.
20. 28 J. answered Saul, David earnestly asked
20. 30 Then Saul's anger was kindled against J.
20. 32 J. answered Saul his father, and said unto
20. 33 J. knew that it was determined..to slay D.
20. 34 So J. arose from the table in fierce anger
20. 35 J. went out into the field at the time app.
20. 37 to the place of the arrow which J. had
20. 37 J. cried after the lad, and said, (Is) not
20. 38 J. cried after the lad.. And J.'s lad gath.
20. 39 knew not any thing: only J. and David
20. 40 J. gave his artillery unto his lad, and said
20. 42 J. said to David, Go in peace, forasmuch
20. 42 he arose and departed: and J. went into
23. 16 J., Saul's son, arose, and went to David into
23. 18 David abode in the wood, and J. went to
31. 2 Philistines slew J., and Abinadab, and M.
2 Sa. 1. 4 and Saul and J. his son are dead also
1. 5 How knowest thou that Saul and J. his
1. 12 they mourned..for Saul, and for J. his son
1. 17 David lamented..over Saul and over J.
1. 22 From the blood of the slain..the bow of J.
1. 23 Saul and J. (were) lovely and pleasant in
1. 25 O J., (thou wast) slain in thine high places
1. 26 I am distressed for thee, my brother J.
4. 4 J...had a son (that was) lame of (his) feet
4. 4 the tidings came of Saul and J. out of Jez.
9. 1 that I may show him kindness for J.'s
9. 3 J. hath yet a son, (which is) lame on (his)
9. 6 Now when..the son of J... was come unto
9. 7 I will surely show thee kindness for J. thy
21. 7 king spared Mephibosheth, the son of J.
21. 7 of the LORD's oath that (was) between..J.
21. 12 David went and took..the bones of J.
21. 13 brought up from thence..the bones of J.
2 Sa. 21. 14 the bones of..J. his son buried they in
1 Ch. 8. 33 Saul begat J., and Malchi-shua, and Abin.
8. 34 the son of J. (was) Merib-baal; and Mer.
9. 39 Saul begat J., and Malchi-shua, and Abi.
9. 40 the son of J. (was) Merib-baal: and Mer.
10. 2 Philistines slew J., and Abinadab, and M.

3. A son of Abiathar, a high priest in the time of David. B.C. 1048.

2 Sa. 15. 27 Ahimaaz thy son, and J. the son of Abia.
15. 36 Behold, (they have) there..J., Abiathar's
17. 17 Now J. and Ahimaaz stayed by En-rogel
17. 20 they said, Where (is) Ahimaaz and J.?
1 Ki. 1. 42 behold, J. the son of Abiathar the priest
1. 43 J. answered and said to Adonijah, Verily

4. A son of Shimea, David's brother. B.C. 1050.

2 Sa. 21. 21 J. the son of Shimeah, the brother of Da.
1 Ch. 20. 7 J. the son of Shimea, David's brother

5. One of David's valiant men and son of Jashen (or *Shage* the Hararite). B.C. 1048.

2 Sa. 23. 32 Eliahba..of the sons of Jashen, J.
1 Ch. 11. 34 sons of Hashem..J. the son of Shage the

6. A son of Jada, grandson of Onam. B.C. 1400.

1 Ch. 2. 32 the sons of Jada..Jether, and J.: and Jet.
2. 33 And the sons of J.; Peleth, and Zaza. These

7. An uncle of David. B.C. 1048.

1 Ch. 27. 32 J., David's uncle, was a counsellor, a wise

8. The father of Ebed who returned with Ezra. B.C. 458.

Ezra 8. 6 the son of J., and with him fifty males

9. Son of Asahel, and employed in the matter of the strange wives. B.C. 457.

Ezra 10. 15 J. the son of Asahel and Jahaziah the son

10. A descendant of Jeshua the high priest. B.C. 456.

Neh. 12. 11 And Joiada begat J., and J. begat Jaddua

11. A priest descended from Melicu or Malluchi. B.C. 536.

Neh. 12. 14 Of Melicu, J.; of Shebaniah, Joseph

12. A priest descended from Shemaiah, in the days of Joiakim. B.C. 445. In Neh. 12. 18 he is called *Jehonathan.*

Neh. 12. 35 the son of J., the son of Shemaiah, the son

13. A scribe in whose house Jeremiah was imprisoned. B.C. 589.

Jer 37. 15 in prison in the house of J. the scribe
37. 20 cause me not to return to the house of J.
38. 26 would not cause me to return to J.'s house

14. A son of Kareah who went to Gedaliah the governor. B.C. 588.

Jer. 40. 8 and Johanan and J. the sons of Kareah

JOP'-PA, יָפוֹ, יָפוֹא 'Ιόππη *height, beauty.*

A seaport in Dan, 150 stadia from Antipatris, six miles W. of Rama, and thirty-seven miles N.W. of Jerusalem. See *Japho;* and now called *Jafa.*

2 Ch. 2. 16 bring it to thee in floats by sea to J.
Ezra 3. 7 cedar trees from Lebanon to the sea of J.
Jon. 1. 3 Jonah rose up to flee..and went down to J.
Acts 9. 36 there was at J. a certain disciple named
9. 38 Lydda was nigh to J., and the disciples
9. 42 it was known throughout all J.; and many
9. 43 he tarried many days in J. with one Simon
10. 5 now send men to J., and call for (one) S.
10. 8 when he had declared..he sent them to J.
10. 23 certain brethren from J. accompanied him
10. 32 Send therefore to J., and call hither Simon
11. 5 I was in the city of J. praying: and in a
11. 13 Send men to J., and call for Simon, whose

JO'-RAH, יוֹרָה *harvest-born.*

One whose descendants returned with Zerubbabel from exile. B.C. 536.

Ezra 2. 18 The children of J. an hundred and twelve

JO'-RAI, יוֹרַי.

A Gadite, head of a family. B.C. 1400.

1 Ch. 5. 13 Sheba, and Jorai, and Jachan, and Zia, and

JO'-RAM, יֹרָם, יוֹרָם, יְהוֹרָם *Jah is high,* 'Ιωράμ.

1. A son of Toi, king of Zobah. B.C. 1040.

2 Sa. 8. 10 Toi sent J. his son unto king David, to

2. A son of Jehoshaphat. B.C. 893–885. Called also *Jehoram.*

2 Ki. 8. 21 J. went over to Zair, and all the chariots
8. 23 the acts of J., and all that he did, (are)
8. 24 J. slept with his fathers, and was buried
11. 2 the daughter of king J., sister of Ahaziah
1 Ch. 3. 11 J. his son, Ahaziah his son, Joash his son
Matt. 1. 8 and Josaphat begat J.; and J. begat Ozias

3. A son of Ahab; called also *Jehoram* (which see). B.C. 896–884.

2 Ki. 8. 16 in the fifth year of J. the son of Ahab
8. 25 In the twelfth year of J. the son of Ahab
8. 28 he went with J. the son of Ahab to the
8. 28 against Hazael..the Syrians wounded J.
8. 29 J. went back to be healed in Jezreel of
8. 29 to see J. the son of Ahab in Jezreel
9. 14 son of Nimshi conspired against J. Now J.
9. 15 J. was returned to be healed in Jezreel
9. 16 and went to Jezreel; for J. lay there
9. 16 king of Judah was come down to see J.
9. 17 J. said Take an horseman, and send to
9. 21 J. said, Make ready. And his chariot was
9. 21 And J. king of Israel and Ahaziah king of
9. 22 when J. saw Jehu, that he said, (Is it)
9. 23 J. turned his hands, and fled, and said to
9. 29 in the eleventh year of J. the son of Ahab

4. A descendant of Eliezer the son of Moses. B.C. 1000.

1 Ch. 26. 25 J. his son..Zichri his son, and Shelomith

JOR'-DAN, הַיַּרְדֵּן *the Jordan,* 'Ιορδάνης.

The great river of Palestine, rising from two springs in the valley between Lebanon and Hermon, coming forth from a hollow S. of the city *Dan-jaan.* The upper spring is the *Hasbany,* which rises in the fountain of *Furr,* near *Hasbeiya,* twelve miles N. of *Tell-el-kady.* After flowing three miles through the valley it enters a dark defile of six or seven miles, after which it enters into a marsh of ten miles, terminating in the Lake Merom or *Huleh.* About twelve miles further S. it enters the Sea of Galilee (fourteen miles long and seven broad, and 653 feet below the level of the Mediterranean), and issuing from its S.E. end, flowing on with ever increasing force till it falls into the Salt Sea, 1289 feet below the Mediterranean, and is lost in intense evaporation. The whole length of the Jordan is only 120 miles in a direct line, but in its windings it is above 240 miles. N. of the Sea of Galilee it is called *el-Urdan,* and S. of it to the Salt Sea, it is called *Nahr esh-Sharî'at, i.e.,* the drinking place. The Jordan valley is mild in winter and very hot in summer.

Gen. 13. 10 beheld all the plain of J., that it (was) well
13. 11 Lot chose him all the plain of J.; and Lot
32. 10 with my staff I passed over this J., and
50. 10 threshing floor of Atad..(is) beyond J.
50. 11 called Abel-mizraim, which (is) beyond J.
Num 13. 29 dwell by the sea, and by the coast of J.
22. 1 plains of Moab on this side J. (by) Jericho
26. 3, 63 in the plains of Moab by J. (near) Je.
31. 12 plains of Moab, which (are) by J. (near) J.
32. 5 if we have..grace..bring us not over J.
32. 19 not inherit with them on yonder side J.
32. 19 is fallen to us on this side J. eastward
32. 21 will go all of you armed over J. before
32. 29 children of Reuben..pass with you over J.
32. 32 inheritance on this side J. (may be) ours
33. 48, 50 the plains of Moab, by J. (near) Jericho
33. 49 they pitched by J., from Beth-jesimoth
33. 51 passed over J. into the land of Canaan
34. 12 And the border shall go down to J., and
34. 15 on this side J. (near) Jericho eastward
35. 1 in the plains of Moab by J. (near) Jericho
35. 10 be come over J. into the land of Canaan
35. 14 Ye shall give three cities on this side J.
36. 13 in the plains of Moab by J. (near) Jericho
Deut. 1. 1 spake..on this side J. in the wilderness
1. 5 On this side J., in the land of Moab
2. 29 I shall pass over J., into the land which
3. 8 took..the land that (was) on this side J.
3. 17 J., and the coast (thereof), from Chinner
3. 20 LORD your God hath given them beyond J
3. 25 see the good land that (is) beyond J., that
3. 27 for thou shalt not go over this J.
4. 21 sware that I should not go over J., and
4. 22 I must not go over J.: but ye shall go over
4. 26 land whereunto ye go over J. to possess it
4. 41 Moses severed three cities on this side J.
4. 46 On this side J., in the valley over against
4. 47 the Amorites, which (were) on this side J.
4. 49 the plain on this side J. eastward, even
9. 1 Thou (art) to pass over J. this day, to go
11. 30 (Are) they not on the other side J., by the
11. 31 ye shall pass over J. to go in to possess
12. 10 (when) ye go over J., and dwell in the land
27. 2 ye shall pass over J. unto the land which
27. 4 it shall be when ye be gone over J., (that)
27. 12 bless the people, when ye are come over J.
30. 18 thou passest over J. to go to possess it
31. 2 unto me, Thou shalt not go over this J.
31. 13 land whither ye go over J. to possess it
32. 47 land whither ye go over J. to possess it
Josh. 1. 2 go over this J., thou, and all this people
1. 11 ye shall pass over this J., to go in to
1. 14 land which Moses gave you on this side J.
1. 15 gave you on this side J. toward the sun
2. 7 pursued after them the way to J. unto the
2. 10 Amorites, that (were) on the other side J.
3. 1 and came to J., he and all the children of
3. 8 the water of J., ye shall stand still in J.
3. 11 the ark..passeth over before you into J.
3. 13 in the waters of J., (that) the waters of J.
3. 14 removed from their tents, to pass over J.
3. 15 they that bare the ark were come unto J.
3. 15 J. overfloweth all his banks all the time
3. 17 stood firm on..ground in the midst of J.
3. 17 all the people were passed clean over J.
4. 1 all the people were clean passed over J.
4. 3 Take you hence out of the midst of J., out
4. 5 Pass..before the ark..into the midst of J.
4. 7 the waters of J. were cut off before the
4. 7 when it passed over J., the waters of J.
4. 8 took..twelve stones out of the midst of J.
4. 9 set up twelve stones in the midst of J.
4. 10 For the priests..stood in the midst of J.
4. 16 Command..that they come up out of J.
4. 17 commanded..saying, Come ye up out of J.
4. 18 priests..were come..out of the midst of J.
4. 18 the waters of J. returned into their place
4. 19 the people came up out of J. on the tenth
4. 20 twelve stones, which they took out of J.
4. 22 Israel came over this J. on dry land
4. 23 dried up the waters of J. from before you
5. 1 which (were) on the side of J. westward
5. 1 the LORD had dried up the waters of J.
7. 7 wherefore..brought this people over J.
7. 7 content and dwelt on the other side J.!
9. 1 the kings which (were) on this side J., in
9. 10 kings of..Amorites, that (were) beyond J.
12. 1 other side J. toward the rising of the sun

Josh 12. 7 Israel smote on this side J. on the west
13. 8 which Moses gave them, beyond J. east.
13. 23 border of the children of Reuben was J.
13. 27 J. and (his) border, (even) unto the edge
13. 27 Chinnereth on the other side J. eastward
13. 32 on the other side J., by Jericho, eastward
14. 3 an half tribe on the other side J.: but
15. 5 (was) the salt sea, (even) unto the end of J.
15. 5 of the sea at the uttermost part of J.
16. 1 lot of the children of Joseph fell from J.
16. 7 and came to Jericho, and went out at J.
17. 5 Gilead and Bashan..on the other side J.
18. 7 their inheritance beyond J. on the east
18. 12 their border on the north side was from J.
18. 19 of the salt sea at the south end of J.
18. 20 J. was the border of it on the east side
19. 22 the outgoings of their border were at J.
19. 33 and the outgoings thereof were at J.
19. 34 to Judah upon J. toward the sunrising
20. 8 the other side J. by Jericho eastward, they
22. 4 which Moses..gave you on the other side J.
22. 7 their brethren on this side J. westward
22. 10 they came unto the borders of J., that (are)
22. 10 built there an altar by J., a great altar
22. 11 in the borders of J., at the passage of
22. 25 the LORD hath made J. a border between
23. 4 from J., with all the nations that I have
24. 8 Amorites, which dwelt on the other side J.
24. 11 ye went over J., and came unto Jericho
Judg. 3. 28 and took the fords of J. toward Moab, and
5. 17 Gilead abode beyond J.: and why did Dan
7. 24 take..the waters unto Beth-barah and J.
7. 24 and took the waters unto Beth-barah and J.
7. 25 brought..to Gideon on the other side J.
8. 4 Gideon came to J., (and) passed over, he
10. 8 of Israel that (were) on the other side J.
10. 9 passed over J. to fight also against Judah
11. 13 from Arnon even unto Jabbok, and unto J.
11. 22 and from the wilderness even unto J.
12. 5 the Gileadites took the passages of J.
12. 6 took..and slew him at the passages of J.
1 Sa. 13. 7 (some of) the Hebrews went over J. to the
31. 7 (they) that (were) on the other side J., saw
2 Sa. 2. 29 passed over J., and went through..Bith.
10. 17 he..passed over J., and came to Helam
17. 22 Then David arose..and they passed over J.
17. 22 not one of them that was not gone over J.
17. 24 Absalom passed over J., he and all the
19. 15 king returned, and came to J. And Jud.
19. 15 meet the king, to conduct the king over J.
19. 17 and they went over J. before the king
19. 18 Shimei..fell down..as he was come over J.
19. 31 J. with the king, to conduct him over J.
19. 36 will go a little way over J. with the king
19. 39 the people went over J. And when the
19. 41 brought..David's men with him, over J.
20. 2 unto their king, from J. even to Jerusalem
24. 5 they passed over J., and pitched in Aroer
1 Ki. 2. 8 he came down to meet me at J., and I
7. 46 In the plain of J. did the king cast them
17. 3, 5 by the brook Cherith, that (is) before J.
2 Ki. 2. 6 Tarry..for the LORD hath sent me to J.
2. 7 to view afar off: and they two stood by J.
2. 13 and went back, and stood by the bank of J.
5. 10 wash in J. seven times, and thy flesh shall
5. 14 dipped himself seven times in J., accord.
6. 2 Let us go, we pray thee, unto J., and take
6. 4 when they came to J., they cut down wo.
7. 15 they went after them unto J.: and, lo, all
10. 33 From J. eastward, all the land of Gilead
1 Ch. 6. 78 side J. by Jericho, on the east side of J.
12. 15 These (are) they that went over J. in the
12. 37 on the other side of J., of the Reubenites
19. 17 passed over J., and came upon them, and
26. 30 (were) officers..on this side J. westward
2 Ch. 4. 17 In the plain of J. did the king cast them
Job 40. 23 that he can draw up J. into his mouth
Psa. 42. 6 will I remember thee from the land of J.
114. 3 The sea saw (it), and fled: J. was driven
114. 5 thou J., (that) thou wast driven back?
Isa. 9. 1 sea, beyond J., in Galilee of the nations
Jer. 12. 5 how wilt thou do in the swelling of J.?
49. 19 come..like a lion from the swelling of J.
50. 44 come..like a lion from the swelling of J.
Eze. 47. 18 from the land of Israel (by) J., from the
Zech. 11. 3 a voice..for the pride of J. is spoiled
Matt. 3. 5 Judea, and all the region round about J.
3. 6 were baptized of him in J., confessing
3. 13 cometh Jesus from Galilee to J. unto John
4. 15 the sea, beyond J., Galilee of the Gentiles
4. 25 Jer., and (from) Judea..(from) beyond J
19. 1 came into the coasts of Judea beyond J.
Mark 1. 5 were all baptized of him in the river of J
1. 9 Jesus came..and was bapti. of John in J.
3. 8 Jerusalem, and..Idumea..(from) beyond J.
10. 1 coasts of Judea by the farther side of J.
Luke 3. 3 And he came into all the country about J.
4. 1 returned from J., and was led by the
John 1. 28 These..were done in Bethabara beyond J.
3. 26 he that was with thee beyond J., to whom
10. 40 went away again beyond J., into the place

JO'-RIM, Ἰωρείμ, *from Heb.* יוֹרָם ,יֹרָם.
An ancestor of Jesus through Mary.
Luke 3. 29 J., which was (the son) of Matthat, which

JOR-KO'-AM, יָרְקְעָם *spreading the people.*
A son of Raham, a descendant of Hebron through Caleb the spy; or a city in Judah. 1 Ch. 2. 44.

JOSABAD. *See* **JOZABAD.**

JO-SA'-PHAT, Ἰωσαφάτ. See *Jehoshaphat.*
Matt. 1. 8 Asa begat J.; and J. begat Joram; and

JO'-SE, Ἰωσῆς, *from Heb.* יוֹשֵׁה.
An ancestor of Jesus through Mary.
Luke 3. 29 Which was (the son) of [J.,] which was (the)

JO-SE'-DECH, יְהוֹצָדָק *Jah is righteous.*
The father of Jeshua the priest who helped to rebuild the altar and the temple. B.C. 588. He is also called *Jozadak* in Ezra 3. 2, 8; 5. 2; 10. 18; and Neh. 12. 26.
Hag. 1. 1 to Joshua the son of J. the high priest
1. 12 the son of J., the high priest, with all
1. 14 the spirit of Joshua the son of J., the
2. 2 Joshua the son of J., the high priest, and
2. 4 be strong, O Joshua, son of J...high priest
Zech. 6. 11 upon the head of Joshua the son of J.

JO'-SEPH, יוֹסֵף *increaser*, Ἰωσήφ.
1. The eleventh son of Jacob and first of Rachel. B.C. 1745–1635.
Gen. 30. 24 she called his name J.; and said, The L.
30. 25 when Rachel had born J., that Jacob
33. 2 children after, and Rachel and J. hind.
33. 7 after came J. near and Rachel, and they
35. 24 The sons of Rachel; J. and Benjamin
37. 2 J., (being) seventeen years old, was feed.
37. 2 and J. brought unto his father their evil
37. 3 Israel loved J. more than all his children
37. 5 J. dreamed a dream, and he told (it) his
37. 13 Israel said unto J., Do not thy brethren
37. 17 J. went after his brethren, and found them
37. 23 when J. was come unto his brethren, that
37. 23 they stripped J. out of his coat, (his) coa.
37. 28 lifted up J. out of the pit, and sold J. to
37. 28 and they brought J. into Egypt
37. 29 J. (was) not in the pit; and he rent his
37. 31 they took J.'s coat, and killed a kid of
37. 33 said..J. is without doubt rent in pieces
39. 1 J. was brought down to Egypt; and Poti.
39. 2 LORD was with J., and he was a prosperous
39. 4 J. found grace in his sight, and he served
39. 5 blessed the Egyptian's house for J.'s sake
39. 6 he left all that he had in J.'s hand; and
39. 6 J. was (a) goodly (person), and well favo.
39. 7 his master's wife cast her eyes upon J.
39. 10 as she spake to J. day by day, that he
39. 20 J.'s master took him, and put him into
39. 21 the LORD was with J., and showed him
39. 22 the keeper of the prison committed to J.'s
40. 3 the prison, the place where J. (was) bou.
40. 4 captain of the guard charged J. with them
40. 6 J. came in unto them in the morning, and
40. 8 J. said unto them, (Do) not interpretations
40. 9 the chief butler told his dream to J., and
40. 12 J. said unto him, This (is) the interpreta.
40. 16 he said unto J., I also (was) in my dream
40. 18 J. answered..This (is) the interpretation
40. 22 he hanged..as J. had interpreted to them
40. 23 Yet did not the chief butler remember J.
41. 14 Then Pharaoh sent and called J., and they
41. 15 And Pharaoh said unto J., I have dreamed
41. 16 J. answered Pharaoh, saying, (It is) not
41. 17 Pharaoh said unto J., In my dream, behold
41. 25 J. said unto Pharaoh, The dream of Pha.
41. 39 Pharaoh said unto J., Forasmuch as God
41. 41 Pharaoh said unto J., See, I have set thee
41. 42 ring from his hand, and put it upon J.'s
41. 44 And Pharaoh said unto J., I (am) Pharaoh
41. 45 Pharaoh called J.'s name Zaphnath-paan.
41. 45 And J. went out over (all) the land of Eg.
41. 46 J. (was) thirty years old when he stood
41. 46 J. went out from the presence of Pharaoh
41. 49 J. gathered corn as the sand of the sea
41. 50 And unto J. were born two sons before
41. 51 And J. called the name of the first born
41. 54 began to come, according as J. had said
41. 55 said..Go unto J.; what he saith to you
41. 56 J. opened all the storehouses, and sold
41. 57 came into Egypt to J. for to buy (corn)
42. 3 J.'s ten brethren went down to buy corn
42. 4 J.'s brother, Jacob sent not with his
42. 6 J. (was) the governor over the land, (and)
42. 6 J.'s brethren came, and bowed down
42. 7 J. saw his brethren, and he knew them
42. 8 J. knew his brethren, but they knew not
42. 9 J. remembered the dreams which he dre.
42. 14 J. said unto them, That (is it) that I spa.
42. 18 J. said unto them the third day, This do
42. 23 they knew not that J. understood (them)
42. 25 J. commanded to fill their sacks with corn
42. 36 J. (is) not, and Simeon (is) not, and ye
43. 15 went down to Egypt, and stood before J.
43. 16 when J. saw Benjamin with them, he said
43. 17 And the man did as J. bade; and
43. 17, 24 the man brought the men into J.'s h.
43. 18 they were brought into J.'s house; and
43. 19 came near to the steward of J.'s house
43. 25 they made ready the present against J.
43. 26 when J. came home, they brought him
43. 30 J. made haste; for his bowels did yearn
44. 2 according to the word that J. had spoken
44. 4 J. said unto his steward, Up, follow after
44. 14 Judah and his brethren came to J.'s house
44. 15 J. said unto them, What deed (is) this
45. 1 J. could not refrain himself before all
45. 1 J. made himself known unto his brethren
45. 3 J. said unto his brethren, I (am) J.: doth
45. 4 J. said unto his brethren, Come near to
45. 4 I (am) J. your brother, whom ye sold
45. 9 Thus saith thy son J., God hath made me
45. 16 was heard..saying, J.'s brethren are come
45. 17 Pharaoh said unto J., Say unto thy breth.

Gen. 45. 21 and J. gave them wagons, according to
45. 26 J. (is) yet alive, and he (is) governor over
45. 27 they told him all the words of J., which
45. 27 the wagons which J. had sent to carry
45. 28 J. my son (is) yet alive: I will go and see
46. 4 and J. shall put his hand upon thine eyes
46. 19 sons of Rachel, Jacob's wife; J., and Benj.
46. 20 And unto J. in the land of Egypt were
46. 27 sons of J., which were born him in Egypt
46. 28 he sent Judah before him unto J., to dir.
46. 29 J. made ready his chariot, and went up
46. 30 Israel said unto J., Now let me die, since
46. 31 J. said unto his brethren, and unto his
47. 1 J. came and told Pharaoh, and said, My
47. 5 Pharaoh spake unto J., saying, Thy father
47. 7 J. brought in Jacob his father, and set
47. 11 J. placed his father and his brethren, and
47. 12 J. nourished his father, and his brethren
47. 14 J. gathered up all the money that was
47. 14 J. brought the money into Pharaoh's ho.
47. 15 the Egyptians came unto J., and said, G.
47. 16 J. said, Give your cattle; and I will give
47. 17 they brought their cattle unto J.: and J.
47. 20 J. bought all the land of Egypt for Phar.
47. 23 Then J. said unto the people, Behold, I
47. 26 J. made it a law over the land of Egypt
47. 29 he called his son J., and said unto him
48. 1 (one) told J., Behold, thy father (is) sick
48. 2 thy son J. cometh unto thee: and Israel
48. 3 Jacob said unto J., God Almighty appea.
48. 8 Israel beheld J.'s sons, and said, Who
48. 9 J. said unto his father, They (are) my sons
48. 11 Israel said unto J., I had not thought to
48. 12 J. brought them out from between his
48. 13 J. took them both, Ephraim in his right
48. 15 he blessed J., and said, God, before whom
48. 17 J. saw that his father laid his right
48. 18 J. said unto his father, Not so, my father
48. 21 Israel said unto J., Behold, I die; but
49. 22 J. (is) a fruitful bough, (even) a fruitful
49. 26 they shall be on the head of J., and on
50. 1 J. fell upon his father's face, and wept
50. 2 J. commanded his servants the physicians
50. 4 J. spake unto the house of Pharaoh, saying
50. 7 J. went up to bury his father: and with
50. 8 the house of J., and his brethren, and his
50. 14 J. returned into Egypt, he, and his bret.
50. 15 J.'s brethren saw that their father was
50. 15 said, J. will peradventure hate us, and
50. 16 they sent a messenger unto J., saying
50. 17 So shall ye say unto J., Forgive, I pray
50. 17 And J. wept when they spake unto him
50. 19 J. said unto them, Fear not; for (am) I
50. 22 J. dwelt in Egypt..and J. lived an hund.
50. 23 J. saw Ephraim's children of the third
50. 23 children..were brought up upon J.'s kn.
50. 24 J. said unto his brethren, I die: and God
50. 25 J. took an oath of the children of Israel
50. 26 So J. died, (being) an hundred and ten y.
Exod. 1. 5 seventy souls: for J. was in Egypt (alre.)
1. 6 J. died, and all his brethren, and all that
1. 8 arose up a new king..which knew not J.
13. 19 Moses took the bones of J. with him: for
Num. 1. 10 the children of J.: of Ephraim; Elishama
1. 32 the children of J., (namely), of the children
13. 11 Of the tribe of J., (namely), of the tribe of
26. 28 The sons of J. after their families (were)
26. 37 (are) the sons of J. after their families
27. 1 of the families of Manasseh the son of J.
32. 33 half the tribe of Manasseh the son of J.
34. 23 The prince of the children of J...Hanniel
36. 1 fathers..of the families of the sons of J.
36. 5 The tribe of the sons of J. hath said well
36. 12 families of the sons of Manasseh..son of J.
Deut 27. 12 Judah, and Issachar, and J., and Benja.
33. 13 of J. he said, Blessed of the LORD (be) his
33. 16 let (the blessing) come upon the head of J.
Josh. 14. 4 children of J. were two tribes, Manasseh
16. 1 the lot of the children of J. fell from
16. 4 the children of J., Manasseh and Ephraim
17. 1 he (was) the first born of J.; (to wit,) for
17. 2 male children of Manasseh the son of J.
17. 14 the children of J. spake unto Joshua, say
17. 16 the children of J. said, The hill is not
17. 17 Joshua spake unto the house of J., (even)
18. 5 house of J. shall abide in their coasts
18. 11 children of Judah and the children of J.
24. 32 bones of J., which the children of Israel
24. 32 the inheritance of the children of J.
Judg. 1. 22 the house of J., they also went up against
1. 23 the house of J. sent to descry Beth-el
1. 35 the hand of the house of J. prevailed, so
2 Sa. 19. 20 the first this day of all the house of J.
1 Ki. 11. 28 over all the charge of the house of J.
1 Ch. 2. 2 J., and Benjamin, Naphtali, Gad, and A.
5. 1 birthright was given unto the sons of J.
5. 2 Jud. prevailed..but..birthright (was) J.'s
7. 29 the children of J. the son of Israel
Psa. 77. 15 thy people, the sons of Jacob and J.
78. 67 he refused the tabernacle of J., and chose
80. 1 thou that leadest J. like a flock; thou
81. 5 This he ordained in J. (for) a testimony
105. 17 He sent a man before them, (even) J.
Eze. 37. 16 For J., the stick of Ephraim, and (for) all
37. 19 I will take the stick of J., which (is) in
47. 13 saith the Lord..J. (shall have two) port.
48. 32 one gate of J., one gate of Benjamin, one
Amos 5. 6 he break out like fire in the house of J.
5. 15 will be gracious unto the remnant of J.
6. 6 are not grieved for the affliction of J.
Obad. 18; Zech. 10. 6; Jo. 4. 5; Acts 7. 9, 13, 13, 14, 18; Heb. 11. 21, 22; Rev. 7. 8.

2. The descendants of Joseph son of Jacob.
Deut 33. 13 of J. he said, Blessed of the LORD (be) his
3. The father of Igal of Issachar, one of the spies sent by Moses into Canaan. B.C. 1490.
Num 13. 7 the tribe of Issachar, Igal the son of J.
4. A son of Asaph. B.C. 1015.
1 Ch. 25. 2 J., and Nethaniah, and Asarelah, the sons
25. 9 the first lot came forth for Asaph to J.
5. A man of the family of Bani who had taken a strange wife. B.C. 457.
Ezra 10. 42 Shallum, Amariah, (and) J.
6. A priest of the family of Shebaniah, in the time of Joiakim. B.C. 530.
Neh. 12. 14 Of Melicu, Jonathan; of Shebaniah, J.
7. The husband of Mary the mother of Jesus.
Matt. 1. 16 Jacob begat J. the husband of Mary, of
1. 18 Mary was espoused to J., before they came
1. 19 J. her husband, being a just (man), and
1. 20 J., thou son of David, fear not to take unto
1. 24 J., being raised from sleep, did as the an.
2. 13, 19 the angel..appeareth to J. in a dream
Luke 1. 27 espoused to a man whose name was J.
2. 4 J. also went up from Galilee, out of the
2. 16 found Mary and J., and the babe lying
2. 33 And [J.] and his mother marvelled at
2. 43 [and J. and his mother knew not (of it)]
3. 23 being as was supposed the son of J.
4. 22 And they said, Is not this J.'s son?
John 1. 45 found..Jesus of Nazareth the son of J.
6. 42 Is not this Jesus, the son of J., whose
8. A Jew of Arimathea, a disciple of Jesus, in whose sepulchre the body of Jesus was laid.
Matt 27. 57 there came a rich man of Arimathea..J.
27. 59 when J. had taken the body, he wrapped
Mark 15. 43 J. of Arimathea, an honourable 15. 45
Luke 23. 50 (there was) a man named J., a counsellor
John 19. 38 J. of Arimathea, being a disciple of Jesus
9. Ancestor of Joseph the husband of Mary.
Luke 3. 24 (the son) of Janna..was (the son) of J.
10. Another progenitor of Joseph in the same line.
Luke 3. 26 Semei, which was (the son) of J., which
11. A third and more remote ancestor of Joseph the husband of Mary.
Luke 3. 30 Juda, which was (the son) of J., which
12. A disciple nominated with Matthias to take the place of Judas Iscariot among the apostles.
Acts 1. 23 J. called Barsabas, who was surnamed

JO'-SES, Ἰωσῆς.
1. One of the brethren of Jesus.
Matt 13. 55 brethren, James, and J., and Simon..Ju.?
Mark 6. 3 of James, and J., and of Juda, and Sim.?
2. The son of Mary, probably the same as No. 1.
Matt 27. 56 the mother of James and J., and the mo.
Mark 15. 40 the mother of James the less and of J.
15. 47 (the mother) of J. beheld where he was
3. A Levite of Cyprus, Barnabas, a companion of Paul.
Acts 4. 36 [J.]..by the apostles was surnamed Bar.

JO'-SHAH, יוֹשָׁה *Jah is a gift.*
A descendant of Simeon. B.C. 800.
1 Ch. 4. 34 and Jamlech, and J. the son of Amaziah

JO-SHA'-PHAT, יוֹשָׁפָט *Jah judges.*
One of David's valiant men. B.C. 1048.
1 Ch. 11. 43 the son of Maachah, and J. the Mithnite

JO-SHAV-I'AH, יוֹשַׁוְיָה *Jah is equality.*
One of David's valiant men. B.C. 1048.
1 Ch. 11. 46 Jeribai and J., the sons of Elnaam, and

JOSH-BE-KA'-SHAH, יָשְׁבְּקָשָׁה *seated in hardness.*
A son of Heman, David's leader of song. B.C. 1015.
1 Ch. 25. 4 and Romamti-ezer, J., Mallothi, Hothir
25. 24 The seventeenth to J., (he), his sons, and

JO-SHU'-A, JE-HO-SHU'-A, יְהוֹשֻׁעַ, יְהוֹשׁוּעַ *Jah saves.*
1. The son of Nun and minister and successor of Moses. He led Israel over the Jordan and conquered most of the land and gave inheritance in it to the tribes of Israel. He died aged 110 years and was buried in Timnath-Serah in Mount Ephraim, B.C. 1427. See also *Jehoshuah* and *Oshea.*
Exod 17. 9 Moses said unto J., Choose us out men
17. 10 J. did as Moses had said to him, and fou.
17. 13 J. discomfited Amalek and his people
17. 14 Write..and rehearse (it) in the ears of J.
24. 13 And Moses rose up, and his minister J.
32. 17 J. heard the noise of the people as they
33. 11 his servant J., the son of Nun, a young
Num 11. 28 J. the son of Nun, the servant of Moses
13. 16 And Moses called Oshea the son of N., J.
14. 6 J. the son of Nun, and Caleb the son of
14. 30 son of Jephunneh, and J. the son of Nun
14. 38 J. the son of Nun, and Caleb the son of
26. 65 son of Jephunneh, and J. the son of Nun
27. 18 Take thee J. the son of Nun, a man in
27. 22 took J. and set him before Eleazar the
32. 12 son of Jephunneh..and J. the son of Nun
32. 28 J. the son of Nun, and the chief fathers
34. 17 Eleazar the priest, and J. the son of Nun
Deut. 1. 38 J. the son of Nun, which standeth before
3. 21 I commanded J. at that time, saying, Th.
3. 28 charge J., and encourage him, and stren.
31. 3 J., he shall go over before thee, as the
31. 7 Moses called unto J., and said unto him
31. 14 call J., and present yourselves in the tab.
Deut 31. 14 Moses and J. went, and presented them.
31. 23 he gave J. the son of Nun a charge, and
34. 9 J. the son of Nun was full of the spirit
Josh. 1. 1 that the LORD spake unto J. the son of
1. 10 J. commanded the officers of the people
1. 12 to half the tribe of Manasseh, spake J.
1. 16 And they answered J., saying, All that
2. 1 J. the son of Nun sent out of Shittim two
2. 23 came to J. the son of Nun, and told him
2. 24 they said unto J., Truly the LORD hath
3. 1 J. rose up early in the morning; and they
3. 5 J. said unto the people, Sanctify yourse.
3. 6 J. spake unto the priests, saying, Take up
3. 7 LORD said unto J., This day will I begin
3. 9 J. said unto the children of Israel, Come
3. 10 And J. said, Hereby ye shall know that
4. 1 that the LORD spake unto J., saying
4. 4 Then J. called the twelve men, whom he
4. 5 J. said unto them, Pass over before the
4. 8 Children of Israel did so as J. commanded
4. 8 twelve stones..as the LORD spake unto J.
4. 9 J. set up twelve stones in the midst of
4. 10 LORD commanded J. to speak unto the
4. 10 according to all that Moses commanded J.
4. 14 magnified J. in the sight of all Israel
4. 15 And the LORD spake unto J., saying
4. 17 J. therefore commanded the priests, say.
4. 20 those twelve stones..did J. pitch in Gil.
5. 2 the LORD said unto J., Make thee sharp
5. 3 J. made him sharp knives, and circumci.
5. 4 this (is) the cause why J. did circumcise
5. 7 their children..J. circumcised: for they
5. 9 And the LORD said unto J., This day have
5. 13 when J. was by Jericho, that he lifted up
5. 13 J. went unto him, and said unto him, (Art)
5. 14 J. fell on his face to the earth, and did
5. 15 captain of the LORD'S host said unto J.
5. 15 Loose thy shoe from off..And J. did so
6. 2 the LORD said unto J., See, I have given
6. 6 J. the son of Nun called the priests, and
6. 8 when J. had spoken unto the people, that
6. 10 J. had commanded the people, saying, Ye
6. 12 And J. rose up early in the morning, and
6. 16 J. said unto the people, Shout; for the L.
6. 22 But J. had said unto the two men that had
6. 25 J. saved Rahab the harlot alive, and her
6. 25 messengers which J. sent to spy..Jericho
6. 26 J. adjured (them) at that time, saying, C.
6. 27 LORD was with J.; and his fame was (no.)
7. 2 J. sent men from Jericho to Ai, which (is)
7. 3 they returned to J., and said unto him
7. 6 J. rent his clothes, and fell to the earth
7. 7 J. said, Alas, O Lord GOD, wherefore hast
7. 10 the LORD said unto J., Get thee up; whe.
7. 16 J. rose up early in the morning, and bro.
7. 19 J. said unto Achan, My son, give, I pray
7. 20 Achan answered J., and said, Indeed I
7. 22 J. sent messengers, and they ran unto the
7. 23 brought them unto J., and unto all the
7. 24 J., and all Israel with him, took Achan
7. 25 J. said, Why hast thou troubled us? the L.
8. 1 the LORD said unto J., Fear not, neither
8. 3 J. arose, and all the people of war, to go
8. 3 J. chose out thirty thousand mighty men
8. 9 J. therefore sent them forth: and they
8. 9 but J. lodged that night among the people
8. 10 J. rose up early in the morning, and num.
8. 13 J. went that night into the midst of the
8. 15 J. and all Israel made as if they were
8. 16 pursued after J., and were drawn away
8. 18 the LORD said unto J., Stretch out the
8. 18 J. stretched out the spear that (he had)
8. 21 J. and all Israel saw that the ambush had
8. 23 king..took alive, and brought him to J.
8. 26 J. drew not his hand back, wherewith he
8. 27 word of the LORD which he commanded J.
8. 28 J. burnt Ai, and made it an heap for ever
8. 29 J. commanded that they should take his
8. 30 J. built an altar unto the LORD God of
8. 35 J. read not before all the congregation
9. 2 to fight with J. and with Israel, with one
9. 3 the inhabitants of Gibeon heard what J.
9. 6 they went to J. unto the camp at Gilgal
9. 8 said unto J., We (are) thy servants. And J.
9. 15 J. made peace with them, and made a
9. 22 J. called for them, and he spake unto them
9. 24 they answered J., and said, Because it was
9. 27 J. made them that day hewers of wood and
10. 1 Adoni-zedec..had heard how J. had taken
10. 4 it hath made peace with J. and with the
10. 6 men of Gibeon sent unto J. to the camp
10. 7 So J. ascended from Gilgal, he, and all the
10. 8 the LORD said unto J., Fear them not: for
10. 9 J. therefore came unto them suddenly
10. 12 Then spake J. to the LORD in the day when
10. 15, 38, 43 J. returned, and all Israel with him
10. 17 it was told J., saying, The five kings are
10. 18 J. said, Roll great stones upon the mouth
10. 20 J. and the children of Israel had made an
10. 21 the people returned to the camp to J. at
10. 22 Then said J., Open the mouth of the cave
10. 24 brought out those kings unto J., that J.
10. 25 J. said unto them, Fear not, nor be dism.
10. 26 J. smote them, and slew them, and hanged
10. 27 J. commanded, and they took them down
10. 28 J. took Makkedah, and smote it with the
10. 29 J. passed from Makkedah, and all Israel
10. 31 J. passed from Libnah, and all Israel with
10. 33 J. smote him and his people, until he had
10. 34 J. passed unto Eglon, and all Israel with
10. 36 J. went up from Eglon, and..Israel with
10. 40 J. smote all the country of the hills..and
Josh 10. 41 J. smote them from Kadesh-barnea even
10. 42 and their land did J. take at one time
11. 6 LORD said unto J., Be not afraid because
11. 7 J. came, and all the people of war with
11. 9 J. did unto them as the LORD bade him
11. 10 J. at that time turned back, and took H.
11. 12 the kings of them, did J. take, and smote
11. 13 none..save Hazor only; (that) did J. burn
11. 15 so did Moses command J., and so did J.
11. 16 J. took all that land, the hills, and all
11. 18 J. made war a long time with all those
11. 21 that time came J., and cut off the Anakim
11. 21 J. destroyed them utterly with their cities
11. 23 J. took the whole land, according to all
11. 23 J. gave it for an inheritance unto Israel
12. 7 which J. and the children of Israel smote
12. 7 which J. gave unto the tribes of Israel
13. 1 Now J. was old (and) stricken in years
14. 1 Eleazer the priest, and J. the son of Nun
14. 6 the children of Judah came unto J. in G.
14. 13 J. blessed him, and gave unto Caleb the
15. 13 according to the commandment..to J.
17. 4 and before J. the son of Nun, and before
17. 14 And the children of Joseph spake unto J.
17. 15 J. answered them, If thou (be) a great
17. 17 J. spake unto the house of Joseph, (even)
18. 3 J. said unto the children of Israel, How
18. 8 J. charged them that went to describe the
18. 9 and came (again) to J. to the host at Shi.
18. 10 J. cast lots..in Shiloh..and there J. div.
19. 49 gave an inheritance to J. the son of Nun
19. 51 Eleazer the priest, and J. the son of Nun
20. 1 The LORD also spake unto J., saying
21. 1 unto J. the son of Nun, and unto the heads
22. 1 Then J. called the Reubenites, and the
22. 6 So J. blessed them, and sent them away
22. 7 but unto the (other) half thereof gave J.
22. 7 J. sent them away also unto their tents
23. 1 came to pass..that J. waxed old (and)
23. 2 J. called for all Israel, (and) for their
24. 1 J. gathered all the tribes of Israel to She.
24. 2 J. said unto all the people, Thus saith the
24. 19 J. said unto the people, Ye cannot serve
24. 21 said unto J., Nay; but we will serve the
24. 22 J. said unto the people, Ye (are) witnesses
24. 24 said unto J., The LORD our God will we
24. 25 So J. made a covenant with the people
24. 26 J. wrote these words in the book of the
24. 27 J. said unto all the people, Behold, this
24. 28 So J. let the people depart, every man
24. 29 it came to pass after these things, that J.
24. 31 Israel served the LORD all the days of J.
24. 31 all the days of the elders that overlived J.
Judg. 1. 1 Now after the death of J. it came to pass
2. 6 And when J. had let the people go, the
2. 7 people served the LORD all the days of J.
2. 7 the days of the elders that outlived J.
2. 8 J. the son of Nun..died, (being) an hund.
2. 21 of the nations which J. left when he died
2. 23 neither delivered..them into the hand of J.
1 Ki 16. 34 which he spake by J. the son of Nun
2. A Beth-shemite in the days of Eli. B.C. 1140.
1 Sa. 6. 14 the cart came into the field of J., a Beth.
6. 18 unto this day in the field of J., the Beth.
3. The governor of Jerusalem in the days of Josiah, B.C. 640.
2 Ki. 23. 8 in the entering in of the gate of J. the
4. The son of Josedech and high priest at the rebuilding of the temple. B.C. 520. See *Jeshua.*
Hag. 1. 1, 12, 14 J., the son of Josedech the high priest
2. 2 to J. the son of Josedech, the high priest
2. 4 be strong, O J., son of Josedech, the high
Zech. 3. 1 he showed me J. the high priest standing
3. 3 Now J. was clothed with filthy garments
3. 6 angel of the LORD protested unto J., say.
3. 8 Hear now, O J. the high priest, thou, and
3. 9 the stone that I have laid before J.; upon
6. 11 set (them) upon the head of J. the son of

JO-SI'-AH, יֹאשִׁיָּהוּ, יֹאשִׁיָּה *Jah supports;* Ἰωσίας.
1. A son of Amon king of Judah, B.C. 642-611; prophesied of to Jeroboam, B.C. 970. (In N.T. *Josias.*)
1 Ki. 13. 2 be born unto the house of David, J. by
2 Ki. 21. 24 people..made J. his son king in his stead
21. 26 buried..and J. his son reigned in his stead
22. 1 J. (was) eight years old when he began to
22. 3 in the eighteenth year of king J., (that)
23. 16 as J. turned himself, he spied the sepulc.
23. 19 to provoke (the LORD) to anger, J. took
23. 23 in the eighteenth year of king J., (wherein)
23. 24 did J. put away, that he might perform
23. 28 rest of the acts of J., and all that he did
23. 29 king J. went against him; and he slew
23. 30 Jehoahaz the son of J., and anointed him
23. 34 the son of J. king in the room of J.
1 Ch. 3. 14 Amon his son, J. his son
3. 15 the sons of J. (were), the first born Joha.
2 Ch. 33. 25 people..made J. his son king in his stead
34. 1 J. (was) eight years old when he began to
34. 33 J. took away all the abominations out of
35. 1 Moreover J. kept a passover unto the L.
35. 7 J. gave to the people, of the flock, lambs
35. 16 according to the commandment of king J.
35. 18 keep such a passover as J. kept, and the
35. 19 In the eighteenth year of the reign of J.
35. 20 J. had prepared the temple..and J. went
35. 22 J. would not turn his face from him, but
35. 23 the archers shot at king J.: and the king
35. 24 all Judah and Jerusalem mourned for J.
35. 25 And Jeremiah lamented for J.: and all the

2 Ch.35. 25 the singing women spake of J. in their
35. 26 the acts of J., and his goodness, according
36. 1 the people..took Jehoahaz the son of J.
Jer. 1. 2 word of the LORD came in the days of J.
1. 3 in the days of Jehoiakim the son of J.
1. 3 eleventh year of Zedekiah the son of J.
3. 6 said also unto me in the days of J. the
22. 11 touching Shallum the son of J. king of
22. 11 which reigned instead of J. his father
22. 18 concerning Jehoiakim the son of J. king
25. 1 Jehoiakim the son of J. king of Judah
25. 3 From the thirteenth year of J. the son of
26. 1 Jehoiakim the son of J. king of 27.1
35. 1 of Jehoiakim the son of J. king of Judah
36. 1 of Jehoiakim the son of J. king of Judah
36. 2 from the days of J., even unto this day
36. 9 of Jehoiakim the son of J. king of Judah
37. 1 the son of J. reigned instead of Coniah
45. 1 of Jehoiakim the son of J. king of Judah
46. 2 of Jehoiakim the son of J. king of Judah
Zeph. 1. 1 in the days of J. the son of Amon, king of
Matt. 1. 10 Manasses begat Amon..Amon begat J.
1. 11 J. begat Jechonias and his brethren, about

2. A son of Zephaniah, dwelling in Jerusalem. B.C. 519.
Zech. 6. 10 into the house of J. the son of Zephaniah

JO-SIB-I'AH, יוֹשִׁבְיָה *Jah causes to dwell.*
A Simeonite. B.C. 800.
1 Ch. 4. 35 the son of J., the son of Seraiah, the son

JO-SIPH-I'AH, יוֹסִפְיָה *Jah adds.*
The father of a chief that returned from exile with Ezra. B.C. 457.
Ezra 8. 10 the son of J., and with him an hundred

JOT —
Smallest letter in the Hebrew alphabet, ἰῶτα.
Matt. 5. 18 one jot or one tittle shall in no wise pass

JOT'-BAH, יָטְבָה *excellent for water.*
A place in Judah, same as *Juttah*, now *Jatah*, three miles S. of Hebron, and two miles N.W. of *el-Karmil.*
2 Ki.21. 19 Meshullemeth..daughter of Haruz of J.

JOT-BA'-THAH, JOT'-BATH, יָטְבָתָה.
The 29th encampment of Israel from Egypt, and the 18th from Sinai.
Num33. 33 went from Hor-hagidgad, and pitched in J.
33. 34 removed from J., and encamped at Ebron.
Deut10. 7 from Gudgodah to J., a land of rivers of

JO'-THAM, יוֹתָם *Jah is perfect.*
1. Gideon's youngest son who escaped from Abimelech. B.C. 1209.
Judg. 9. 5 J. the youngest son of Jerubbaal was left
9. 7 when they told (it) to J., he went and stood
9. 21 J. ran away, and fled, and went to Beer
9. 57 came the curse of J. the son of Jerubbaal
2. A son of Azariah (or Uzziah), king of Judah and father of Ahaz king of Judah. B.C. 750.
2 Ki.15. 5 J. the king's son (was) over the house, jud.
15. 7 and J. his son reigned in his stead; v. 30.
15. 32 began J. the son of Uzziah king of Judah
15. 36 the acts of J., and all that he did, (are)
15. 38 J. slept with his fathers, and was buried
16. 1 son of J. king of Judah began to reign
1 Ch. 3. 12 Amaziah his son, Azariah his son, J. his
5. 17 genealogies in the days of J. king of Judah
2 Ch.26. 21 J. his son (was) over the king's house, jud.
26. 23 and J. his son reigned in his stead
27. 1 J. (was) twenty and five years old when
27. 6 J. became mighty, because he prepared
27. 7 the acts of J., and all his wars, and his
27. 9 J. slept with his fathers, and they buried
Isa. 1. 1 Uzziah, J., Ahaz, (and) Hezekiah, kings of
7. 1 in the days of Ahaz the son of J., the son
Hos. 1. 1 Uzziah, J., Ahaz, (and) Hezekiah, kings
Mic. 1. 1 to Micah the Morasthite in the days of J.
3. A son of Jahdai. B.C. 1470.
1 Ch. 2. 47 and J., and Gesham, and Pelet, and Eph.

JOURNEY —
1. *Way, journey,* דֶּרֶךְ *derek.*
Gen. 24. 21 whether the LORD had made his journey
30. 36 he set three days' journey betwixt himself
31. 23 and pursued after him seven days' journey
Exod. 3. 18 go..three days' journey..the wilderness
5. 3 go..three days' journey into the desert
8. 27 We will go three days' journey into the
Num. 9. 10 in a journey afar off, yet he shall keep the
9. 13 the man that (is) clean, and is not in a jour.
10. 33 departed from the mount..three days' j.
10. 33 went before them in the three days' jour.
11. 31 as it were a day's journey on this side, and
11. 31 as it were a day's journey on the other
33. 8 went three days' journey in the wilderness
Josh. 9. 11 Take victuals with you for the journey, and
9. 13 became old by reason of the very long jour.
Judg. 4. 9 the journey that thou takest shall not be
1 Sa. 15. 18 LORD sent thee on a journey, and said, Go
2 Sa. 11. 10 Camest thou not from (thy) journey? why
1 Ki. 18. 27 or he is pursuing, or he is in a journey
19. 4 he himself went a day's journey into the
19. 7 because the journey (is) too great for thee
2 Ki. 3. 9 they fetched a compass of seven days' jo.
Prov. 7. 19 For the goodman..is gone a long journey
2. *A going on, walk, journey,* מַהֲלָךְ *mahalak.*
Neh. 2. 6 For how long shall thy journey be? and
Jon. 3. 3 was a..great city of three days' journey
3. 4 began to enter into the city a day's journey

3. *Journey,* מַסַּע *massa.*
Gen. 13. 3 he went on his journeys from the south
Exod17. 1 after their journeys, according to the com.
40. 36 Israel went onward in all their journeys
40. 38 house of Israel, throughout all their jour.
Num10. 6 they shall blow an alarm for their journ.
10. 12 the children of Israel took their journeys
33. 1 These (are) the journeys of the children
33. 2 according to their journeys by the com.
33. 2 these (are) their journeys according to
Deut10. 11 Arise, take (thy) journey before the people
4. *Way-faring, journeying,* ὁδοιπορία *hodoiporia.*
John 4. 6 Jesus therefore, being wearied with..jour.
5. *Way,* ὁδός *hodos.*
Matt 10. 10 Nor scrip for..journey, neither two coats
Mark 6. 8 they should take nothing for..journey
Luke 2. 44 But they..went a day's journey; and they
9. 3 Take nothing for..journey, neither staves
11. 6 a friend of mine in his journey is come to
Acts 1. 12 Olivet..from Jerusalem a sabbath day's j.

JOURNEY, to —
1. *To lift up, remove, journey,* נָסַע *nasa.*
Gen. 11. 2 it came to pass, as they journeyed from
12. 9 Abram journeyed, going on still toward
13. 11 Lot journeyed east: and they separated
20. 1 Abraham journeyed from thence toward
33. 17 Jacob journeyed to Succoth, and built
35. 5 they journeyed: and the terror of God
35. 16 they journeyed from Beth-el; and there
35. 21 Israel journeyed, and spread his tent be.
Exod12. 37 the children of Israel journeyed from R.
17. 1 Israel journeyed from the wilderness of
40. 37 they journeyed not till the day that it was
Num. 9. 17 after that the children of Israel journeyed
9. 18 the children of Israel journeyed, and at
9. 19 Israel kept the charge..and journeyed
9. 20 to the commandment of the LORD they j.
9. 21 was taken up in the morning, then they j.
9. 21 that the cloud was taken up, they jour.
9. 22 abode in their tents, and journeyed not
9. 22 but when it was taken up, they journeyed
9. 23 at the commandment of the LORD they j.
10. 29 We are journeying unto the place of which
11. 35 the people journeyed from Kibroth-hat.
12. 15 the people journeyed not till Miriam was
20. 22 the whole congregation, journeyed from
21. 4 they journeyed from mount Hor by the
21. 11 they journeyed from Oboth, and pitched
33. 22 they journeyed from Rissah, and pitched
Deut. 10. 7 From thence they journeyed unto Gudgo.
Josh. 9. 17 the children of Israel journeyed, and came
2. *To lift up the feet,* נָשָׂא רַגְלַיִם *nasa raglayim.*
Gen 29. 1 Jacob went on his journey, and came in.
3. *To make a way, progress,* עָשָׂה דֶּרֶךְ *asah derek.*
Judg.17. 8 to the house of Micah, as he journeyed
4. *To journey,* ὁδεύω *hodeuō.*
Luke10. 33 a certain Samaritan, as he journeyed, came
5. *To pass on,* πορεύομαι *poreuomai.*
Acts 9. 3 as he journeyed, he came near Damascus
26. 13 round about me and them which journey.

JOURNEY, to bring forward on one's —
To send forward, προπέμπω *propempō.*
3 John 6 if thou bring forward on their journey

JOURNEY, to go on one's —
To pass on the way, ὁδοιπορέω *hodoiporeō.*
Acts 10. 9 as they went on their journey, and drew

JOURNEY, to have a prosperous —
To have a good journey or passage, εὐοδόομαι *euodo.*
Rom. 1. 10 I might have a prosperous journey by the

JOURNEY, in a —
To pass throughout, διαπορεύομαι *diaporeuomai.*
Rom 15. 24 for I trust to see you in my journey, and

JOURNEY, to make or take a —
1. *To lift up, remove, journey,* נָסַע *nasa.*
Gen. 33. 12 Let us take our journey, and let us go, and
46. 1 Israel took his journey with all that he
Exod13. 20 they took their journey from Succoth
16. 1 they took their journey from Elim, and
Num10. 6 then the camps..shall take their journey
10. 12 the children of Israel took their journeys
10. 13 they first took their journey according to
33. 12 they took their journey out of the wilder.
Deut 1. 7 Turn you, and take your journey, and go
1. 40 take your journey into the wilderness by
2. 1 we turned, and took our journey into the
2. 24 Rise ye up, take your journey, and pass
10. 6 the children of Israel took their journey
2. *To go away from one's people,* ἀποδημέω *apodēmeō.*
Matt25. 15 ever man..and straightway took his jour.
Luke15. 13 took his journey into a far country, and
3. *To pass on,* πορεύομαι *poreuomai.*
Acts 22. 6 it came to pass, that as I made my journey
Rom 15. 24 Whensoever I take my journey into Spain

JOURNEY, taking a far —
Away from one's people, ἀπόδημος *apodēmos.*
Mark13. 34 as a man taking a far journey, who left

JOURNEY with, to —
To journey with, συνοδεύω *sunodeuō.*
Acts 9. 7 the men which journeyed with him stood

JOURNEYING —
1. *Journey,* מַסַּע *massa.*
Num10. 2 use them..for the journeying of the camps
10. 28 Thus (were) the journeyings of the child.
2. *A passing on, journeying,* ὁδοιπορία *hodoiporia.*
2 Co. 11. 26 (In) journeyings often, (in) perils of wat.
3. *To make a passage, progress,* ποιέω πορείαν *poieō.*
Luke13. 22 teaching and journeying toward Jerusa.

JOY —
1. *Joy, rejoicing,* גִּיל *gil.*
Psa. 43. 4 Then will I go..unto God my exceeding j.
Isa. 16. 10 gladness is taken away, and joy out of the
Hos. 9. 1 Rejoice not, O Israel, for joy, as..people
2. *Joy, rejoicing,* גִּילָה *gilah.*
Isa. 35. 2 It shall..rejoice even with joy and singing
3. *Joy,* חֶדְוָה *chedvah.*
Ezra 6. 16 kept the dedication of this house..with joy
Neh. 8. 10 for the joy of the LORD is your strength
4. *Goodness,* טוּב *tub.*
Isa. 65. 14 my servants shall sing for joy of heart, but
5. *Joy, rejoicing,* מָשׂוֹשׂ *masos.*
Job 8. 19 this (is) the joy of his way, and out of the
Psa. 48. 2 the joy of the whole earth, (is) mount Zion
Isa. 24. 8 mirth of tabrets..joy of the harp ceaseth
32. 13 all the houses of joy (in) the joyous city
32. 14 dens..a joy of wild asses, a pasture of flo.
60. 15 I will make thee..a joy of many generat.
65. 18 Jerusalem a rejoicing, and her people a j.
66. 10 rejoice for joy with her, all ye that mourn
Jer. 49. 25 city of praise not left, the city of my joy!
Lam. 2. 15 that (men) call..The joy of the whole earth
5. 15 The joy of our heart is ceased; our dance
Eze. 24. 25 the joy of their glory, the desire of their
6. *Loud cry, proclamation, singing,* רִנָּה *rinnah.*
Psa. 30. 5 weeping may endure for a night, but joy
42. 4 with the voice of joy and praise, with a
126. 5 They that sow in tears shall reap in joy
7. *Rejoicing, joy, gladness, mirth,* שִׂמְחָה *simchah.*
1 Sa. 18. 6 to meet king Saul, with tabrets, with joy
1 Ki. 1. 40 rejoiced with great joy, so that the earth
1 Ch. 12. 40 brought bread..for (there was) joy in Isr.
15. 16 sounding, by lifting up the voice with joy
15. 25 David..went to bring up the ark..with joy
29. 9 David the king also rejoiced with great j.
29. 17 now have I seen with joy thy people, whi.
2 Ch. 20. 27 returned..to go again to Jerusalem with j.
30. 26 So there was great joy in Jerusalem: for
Ezra 3. 12 many..wept..many shouted aloud for joy
3. 13 discern the noise of the shout of joy from
6. 22 And kept the feast..seven days with joy
Neh. 12. 43 God had made them rejoice with great j.
12. 43 the joy of Jerusalem was heard even afar
Esth. 8. 17 the Jews had joy and gladness, a feast and
9. 22 was turned unto them from sorrow to joy
9. 22 make them days of feasting and joy, and
Job 20. 5 and the joy of the hypocrite..for a mom.?
Psa. 16. 11 in thy presence (is) fulness of joy; at thy
137. 6 I prefer not Jerusal. above my chief joy
Prov 12. 20 but to the counsellors of peace (is) joy
14. 10 stranger doth not intermeddle with his j.
15. 21 Folly (is) joy to (him that is) destitute of
15. 23 A man hath joy by the answer of his mo.
21. 15 (It is) joy to the just to do judgment: but
Eccl. 2. 10 I withheld not my heart from any joy; for
2. 26 (God) giveth to a man..knowledge, and j.
5. 20 God answereth (him) in the joy of his he.
9. 7 Go thy way, eat thy bread with joy, and d.
Isa. 9. 3 Thou hast..not increased the joy: they j.
9. 3 before thee according to the joy in harv.
24. 11 all joy is darkened, the mirth of the land is
29. 19 The meek also shall increase..joy in the L.
35. 10 songs, and everlasting joy upon their he.
51. 11 everlasting joy (shall be) upon their head
51. 11 they shall obtain gladness and joy; (and)
55. 12 ye shall go out with joy, and be led forth
61. 7 therefore..everlasting joy shall be unto
66. 5 he shall appear to your joy, and they shall
Jer. 48. 33 joy and gladness is taken from the plent.
Eze. 36. 5 with the joy of all (their) heart, with des.
Joel 1. 16 joy and gladness from the house of our G.
Zeph. 3. 17 he will rejoice over thee with joy; he will
8. *Joy, rejoicing, gladness,* שָׂשׂוֹן *sason.*
Esth. 8. 16 The Jews had light..gladness, and joy
Psa. 51. 8 Make me to hear joy and gladness; (that)
51. 12 Restore unto me the joy of thy salvation
105. 43 And he brought forth his people with joy
Isa. 12. 3 Therefore with joy shall ye draw water
22. 13 behold joy and gladness, slaying oxen, and
35. 10 they shall obtain joy and gladness, and
51. 3 joy and gladness shall be found therein
61. 3 the oil of joy for mourning, the garment of
Jer. 15. 16 thy word was unto me the joy and rejoi
31. 13 I will turn their mourning into joy, and
33. 9 it shall be to me a name of joy, a praise
33. 11 The voice of joy, and the voice of gladness
Joel 1. 12 because joy is withered away from the sons
Zech. 8. 19 shall be to the house of Judah joy and
9. *Shout, shouting,* תְּרוּעָה *teruah.*
Job 33. 26 he shall see his face with joy: for he will
Psa. 27. 6 I offer in his tabernacle sacrifices of joy
10. *Gladness, joy,* ἀγαλλίασις *agalliasis.*
Luke 1. 44 lo..the babe leaped in my womb for joy

11. *Gladness, joy,* εὐφροσύνη *euphrosunē.*
Acts 2. 28 shalt make me full of joy with thy coun.
12. *Joy,* χαρά *chara.*
Matt. 2. 10 they rejoiced with exceeding great joy
13. 20 heareth the word, and anon with joy rece.
13. 44 for joy thereof goeth and selleth all that
25. 21, 23 servant..enter thou into the joy of thy
28. 8 they..quickly..with fear and great joy
Luke 1. 14 thou shalt have joy and gladness; and
2. 10 I bring you good tidings of great joy, which
8. 13 when they hear, receive the word with joy
10. 17 the seventy returned again with joy, say.
15. 7 That likewise joy shall be in heaven over
15. 10 is joy in the presence of the angels of God
24. 41 while they yet believed not for joy, and
24. 52 and returned to Jerusalem with great joy
John 3. 29 rejoiceth greatly..This my joy therefore
15. 11 that my joy might remain..and..your joy
16. 20 but your sorrow shall be turned into joy
16. 21 for joy that a man is born into the world
16. 22 rejoice, and your joy no man taketh from
16. 24 ye shall receive, that your joy may be full
17. 13 might have my joy fulfilled in themselves
Acts 8. 8 And there was great joy in that city
13. 52 the disciples were filled with joy and with
15. 3 they caused great joy unto all the breth.
20. 24 so that I might finish my course [with joy]
Rom 14. 17 and peace, and joy in the Holy Ghost
15. 13 the God of hope fill you with all joy and
15. 32 That I may come unto you with joy by the
2 Co. 1. 24 are helpers of your joy: for by faith ye
2. 3 confidence..that my joy is (the joy) of you
7. 13 the more joyed we for the joy of Titus
8. 2 the abundance of their joy and their deep
Gal. 5. 22 the fruit of the spirit is love, joy, peace
Phil. 1. 4 Always..you all making request with joy
1. 25 you all for your furtherance and joy of
2. 2 Fulfil ye my joy, that ye be like minded
4. 1 beloved and longed for, my joy and crown
1 Th. 1. 6 received the word..with joy of the H. G.
2. 19 For what (is) our hope, or joy, or crown
2. 20 For ye are our glory and joy
3. 9 for all the joy wherewith we joy for your
2 Ti. 1. 4 to see thee..that I may be filled with joy
Heb. 12. 2 who for the joy that was set before him
13. 17 that they may do it with joy, and not with
Jas. 1. 2 My brethren, count it all joy when ye fall
4. 9 to mourning, and (your) joy to heaviness
1 Pe. 1. 8 ye rejoice with joy unspeakable and full
1 Jo. 1. 4 these things write we..that your joy may
2 John 12 speak face to face, that our joy may be
3 John 4 I have no greater joy than to hear that
13. *Grace, thankfulness,* χάρις *charis.*
Phm. 7 we have great [joy] and consolation in thy
[*See also* Aloud, shout for, sing for, skip for.]

JOY, to —
1. *To leap, rejoice, joy, be joyful,* גּוּל ,גִּיל *gil, gul.*
Hab. 3. 18 yet..I will joy in the God of my salvation
Zeph. 3. 17 The LORD..he will joy over thee with sing.
2. *To rejoice, be glad,* שִׂישׂ ,שׂוּשׂ *sus, sis.*
Isa. 65. 19 I will rejoice in Jerusalem, and joy in
3. *To shine, rejoice, joy, be glad,* שָׂמַח *sameach.*
Psa. 21. 1 The king shall joy in thy strength, O L.
Isa. 9. 3 they joy before thee according to the joy
4. *To boast,* καυχάομαι *kauchaomai.*
Rom. 5. 11 we also joy in God through our Lord Je.
5. *To rejoice, joy,* χαίρω *chairō.*
2 Co. 7. 13 exceedingly the more joyed we for the
Phil. 2. 17 if I be offered..I joy and rejoice with
2. 18 For the same cause also do ye joy and
Col. 2. 5 yet am I..joying and beholding your or.
1 Th. 3. 9 wherewith we joy for your sakes before

JOY, to leap for —
To leap, σκιρτάω *skirtaō.*
Luke 6. 23 leap for joy: for, behold, your reward (is)

JOY, exceeding —
Gladness, joy, ἀγαλλίασις *agalliasis.*
Jude 24 is able..to present (you)..with exceeding j.

JOY, to break forth into —
To break forth, פָּצַח *patsach.*
Isa. 52. 9 Break forth into joy, sing together, ye

JOY, to have —
1. *To shine, rejoice, joy, be glad,* שָׂמַח *sameach.*
Prov. 17. 21 a fool..the father of a fool hath no joy
23. 24 that begetteth a wise (child) shall have j.
Isa. 9. 17 Therefore the LORD shall have no joy in
2. *To have joy, pleasure, or advantage,* ὀνίνημι, ὄνημι.
Phm. 20 brother, let me have joy of thee in the L.

JOY, with exceeding —
To be glad, ἀγαλλιάω *agalliaō.*
1 Pe. 4. 13 ye may be glad also with exceeding joy

JOYFUL —
1. *Good,* טוֹב *tob.*
Eccl. 7. 14 In the day of prosperity be joyful, but in
2. *Singing,* רְנָנָה *renanah.*
Psa. 63. 5 my mouth shall praise..with joyful lips
3. *Rejoicing,* שָׂמֵחַ *sameach.*
1 Ki. 8. 66 went unto their tents joyful and glad of
Esth. 5. 9 Then went Haman forth that day joyful
Psa. 113. 9 (and to be) a joyful mother of children
4. *With joy,* χαρᾷ *chara.*
2 Co. 7. 4 I am exceeding joyful in..our tribulation

JOYFUL, to be —
1. *To leap, rejoice, joy, be joyful,* גִּיל ,גּוּל *gul, gil.*
Psa. 35. 9 my soul shall be joyful in the LORD: it
149. 2 let the children of Zion be joyful in their
Isa. 49. 13 Sing, O heavens; and be joyful, O earth
61. 10 my soul shall be joyful in my God; for
2. *To rejoice, exult,* עָלַז *alaz.*
Psa. 96. 12 Let the field be joyful, and all that (is)
149. 5 Let the saints be joyful in glory: let them
3. *To rejoice, exult,* עָלַץ *alats.*
Psa. 5. 11 let them also that love thy name be joyful
4. *To sing, cry aloud,* רָנַן *ranan,* 3.
Psa. 98. 8 let the hills be joyful together

JOYFUL, to make —
To make joyful or glad, שָׂמַח *sameach,* 3.
Ezra 6. 22 the LORD had made them joyful, and tur.
Isa. 56. 7 make them joyful in my house of prayer

JOYFUL noise, to make a —
To shout, רוּעַ *rua,* 5.
Psa. 66. 1 Make a joyful noise unto God, all ye lands
81. 1 make a joyful noise unto the God of Jacob
95. 1 let us make a joyful noise to the rock of
95. 2 and make a joyful noise unto him with
98. 4 Make a joyful noise unto the LORD, all
98. 6 make a joyful noise before the LORD, the
100. 1 Make a joyful noise unto the LORD, all ye

JOYFUL sound —
Shout, shouting, תְּרוּעָה *teruah.*
Psa. 89. 15 Blessed..people that know the joyful sou.

JOYFUL voice —
Singing, רְנָנָה *renanah.*
Job 3. 7 that night..let no joyful voice come there

JOYFULLY —
1. *To see life,* רְאֵה חַיִּים *raah chaiyim.*
Eccl. 9. 9 Live joyfully with the wife whom thou
2. *To rejoice,* χαίρω *chairō.*
Luke 19. 6 and came down, and received him joyful.
3. *With joy,* μετα χαρᾶς *meta charas.*
Heb. 10. 34 took joyfully the spoiling of your goods

JOYFULNESS —
1. *Rejoicing, joy, gladness, mirth,* שִׂמְחָה *simchah.*
Deut 28. 47 servedst not the LORD thy God with joy.
2. *Joy,* χαρά *chara.*
Col. 1. 11 all patience and long suffering with joy.

JOYOUS —
1. *Rejoicing, exulting,* עַלִּיז *alliz.*
Isa. 22. 2 a tumultuous city, a joyous city: thy
23. 7 (Is) this your joyous (city), whose antiqu.
32. 13 all the houses of joy (in) the joyous city
2. *Of joy,* χαρᾶς *charas.*
Heb. 12. 11 no chastening..seemeth to be joyous, but

JO-ZA'-BAD, יוֹזָבָד *Jah endows.*
1. A Gederathite in Judah. He joined David in Ziklag. B.C. 1048. [A.V. Josabad.]
1 Ch. 12. 4 and Johanan, and J. the Gederathite
2. Two men of Manasseh that joined David at Ziklag. B.C. 1048.
1 Ch. 12. 20 J...and Michael, and J., and Elihu, and
3. A Levite overseer of the dedicated things in the days of Hezekiah. B.C. 724.
2 Ch. 31. 13 J., and Eliel, and Ismachiah, and Mahath
4. A chief of the Levites in Josiah's time. B.C. 623.
2 Ch. 35. 9 Jeiel and J., chief of the Levites, gave
5. A son of Jeshua who was employed in weighing the vessels of the sanctuary brought from Babylon. B.C. 445.
Ezra 8. 33 J. the son of Jeshua, and Noadiah the son
6. A priest who had taken a strange wife. B.C. 457.
Ezra 10. 22 Maaseiah, Ishmael, Nethaneel, J., and
7. A Levite who had taken a strange wife. B.C. 457.
Ezra 10. 23 J., and Shimei, and Kelaiah, the same (is)
8. A Levite interpreter of the law read by Ezra. B.C. 445.
Neh. 8. 7 J., Hanan, Pelaiah, and the Levites, cau.
9. A chief Levite in Jerusalem after the exile. B.C. 445.
Neh. 11. 16. and J., of the chief of the Levites, (had)

JO-ZA'-CHAR, יוֹזָכָר *Jah remembers.*
The son of Shimeath (a Moabitess) who slew Joash or Jehoash king of Judah. B.C. 839.
2 Ki. 12. 21 J. the son of Shimeath, and Jehozabad

JO-ZA'-DAK, יוֹצָדָק *Jah is great.*
A priest, the father of Jeshua who returned from exile with Zerubbabel. B.C. 536. He is called *Josedech* in Haggai and Zechariah.
Ezra 3. 2 the son of J., and his brethren the priests
3. 8 the son of J., and the remnant of their
5. 2 son of Shealtiel, and Jeshua the son of J.
10. 18 of the sons of Jeshua the son of J., and
Neh. 12. 26 Joiakim the son of Jeshua, the son of J.

JU'-BAL, יוּבָל *playing, nomad.*
A son of Adah, wife of Lamech, a descendant of Cain. B.C. 3504.
Gen. 4. 21 his brother's name (was) J.: he was the

JUBILEE, or JUBILE—
1. *Jubilee, time of shouting,* יוֹבֵל *yobel.*
Lev. 25. 10 it shall be a jubilee unto you; and ye
25. 11 A jubilee shall that fiftieth year be unto
25. 12 For it (is) the jubilee; it shall be holy
25. 13 In the year of this jubilee ye shall return
25. 15 the number of years after the jubilee thou
25. 28 until the year of jubilee: and in the jubi.
25. 30 the house..shall not go out in the jubilee
25. 31 the houses, they shall go out in the jubilee
25. 33 shall go out in (the year of) jubilee: for
25. 40 shall serve thee unto the year of jubilee
25. 50 from the year..unto the year of jubilee
25. 52 if..but few years unto the year of jubilee
25. 54 then he shall go out in the year of jubilee
27. 17 If he sanctify..field from the year of jub.
27. 18 if he sanctify his field after the jubilee
27. 18 remain, even unto the year of the jubilee
27. 21 the field, when it goeth out in the jubilee
27. 23 unto the year of the jubilee: and he shall
27. 24 In the year of the jubilee the field shall
Num. 36. 4 when the jubilee of the children of Israel
2. *Shouting, shout, blowing,* תְּרוּעָה *teruah.*
Lev. 25. 9 shalt thou cause the trumpet of the jubi.

JU'-CAL, יוּכַל *able.*
A son of Shelemiah and prince of Judah, a deadly enemy of Jeremiah. B.C. 590.
Jer. 38. 1 J. the son of Shelemiah, and Pashur the

JU'-DA, JU'-DAH, JU'-DAS, יְהוּדָה *praise.*
1. The fourth son of Jacob by Leah. B.C. 1740.
Gen. 29. 35 she called his name J.: and left bearing
35. 23 and Levi, and J., and Issachar, and Zeb.
37. 26 J. said unto his brethren, What profit (is
38. 1 J. went down from his brethren, and tur.
38. 2 And J. saw there a daughter of a certain
38. 6 J. took a wife for Er his first born, whose
38. 7 J.'s first born, (was) wicked in the sight of
38. 8 J. said unto Onan, Go in unto thy brother's
38. 11 Then said J. to Tamar his daughter in l.
38. 12 daughter of Shuah, J.'s wife, died; and J.
38. 15 When J. saw her, he thought her (to be)
38. 20 J. sent the kid by the hand of his friend
38. 22 he returned to J., and said, I cannot find
38. 23 J. said, Let her take (it) to her, lest we be
38. 24 it was told J. saying, Tamar thy daughter
38. 24 J. said, Bring her forth, and let her be
38. 26 J. acknowledged (them), and said, She
43. 3 And J. spake unto him, saying, The man
43. 8 J. said unto Israel his father, Send the
44. 14 J. and his brethren came to J.'s house
44. 16 J. said, What shall we say unto my lord?
44. 18 J. came near unto him, and said, Oh my lord
46. 12 the sons of J.; Er and Onan, and Shelah
46. 28 he sent J. before him unto Joseph, to di.
49. 8 J., thou (art he) whom thy brethren shall
49. 9 J. (is) a lion's whelp: from the prey, my
Exod. 1. 2 Reuben, Simeon, Levi, and J.
Num 26. 19 the sons of J. (were) Er and Onan: and Er
Ruth 4. 12 Pharez, whom Tamar bare unto J., of
1 Ch. 2. 1 Simeon, Levi, and J., Issachar, and Zebu.
2. 3 The sons of J.; Er, and Onan, and Shelah
2. 3 the first born of J., was evil in the sight
2. 4 All the sons of J. (were) five
2. 10 begat Nahshon, prince of the children of J.
4. 1 The sons of J.; Pharez, Hezron, and Carmi
4. 21 The sons of Shelah the son of J. (were)
4. 27 family multiply, like to the children of J.
5. 2 J. prevailed above his brethren, and of
9. 4 of the children of Pharez the son of J.
Neh. 11. 24 of the children of Zerah the son of J.
Matt. 1. 2 and Jacob begat J. and his brethren
1. 3 J. begat Phares and Zara of Thamar; and
Luke 3. 33 son) of Phares, which was (the son) of J.
2. The tribe which sprang from Judah, and applied also to the territory occupied by them.
Gen. 49. 10 The sceptre shall not depart from J., nor
Exod 31. 2 of Uri, the son of Hur, of the tribe of J.
35. 30 of Uri, the son of Hur, of the tribe of J.
38. 22 of Uri, the son of Hur, of the tribe of J.
Num. 1. 7 Of J.; Nahshon the son of Amminadab
1. 26 Of the children of J., by their generations
1. 27 numbered of them, (even) of the tribe of J.
2. 3 shall they of the standard..of J. pitch
2. 3 (shall be) captain of the children of J.
2. 9 All that were numbered in the camp of J.
7. 12 the son of Amminadab, of the tribe of J.
10. 14 standard of the camp of the children of J.
13. 6 the tribe of J., Caleb the son of Jephun.
26. 20 the sons of J. after their families were
26. 22 These (are) the families of J. according
34. 19 the tribe of J., Caleb the son of Jephunneh
Deut 27. 12 J., and Issachar, and Joseph, and Benja.
33. 7 And this (is the blessing) of J.: and he
33. 7 Hear, LORD, the voice of J., and bring
34. 2 all the land of J., unto the utmost sea
Josh. 7. 1 Zabdi, the son of Zerah, of the tribe of J.
7. 16 rose up early..and the tribe of J. was taken
7. 17 And he brought the family of J.; and he
7. 18 and Achan..of the tribe of J., was taken
11. 21 and cut off..from all the mountains of J.
14. 6 Then the children of J. came unto Joshua
15. 1 the tribe of the children of J. by their fa.
15. 12 This (is) the coast of the children of J.
15. 13 he gave a part among the children of J.
15. 20 the inheritance..of the children of J.
15. 21 cities of the tribe of the children of J.
15. 63 the children of J. could not drive them
15. 63 Jebusites dwell with the children of J.
18. 5 J. shall abide in their coast on the south

Josh. 18. 11 between the children of J. and the childr.
18. 14 Kirjath-jearim, a city of the children of J.
19. 1 within the inheritance of the children of J.
19. 9 Out of the portion of the children of J.
19. 9 the part of the children of J. was too
19. 34 and to J. upon Jordan toward the sunris.
20. 7 which (is) Hebron, in the mountain of J.
21. 4 had by lot out of the tribe of J., and out
21. 9 gave out of the tribe of the children of J.
21. 11 Hebron, in the hill (country) of J., with
Judg. 1. 2 the LORD said, J. shall go up: behold
1. 3 J. said unto Simeon his brother, Come up
1. 4 J. went up; and the LORD delivered the
1. 8 the children of J. had fought against Jer.
1. 9 afterward the children of J. went down
1. 10 J. went against the Canaanites that dwelt
1. 16 went up..with the children of J. into the
1. 16 wilderness of J., which (lieth) in the south
1. 17 J. went with Simeon his brother, and
1. 18 Also J. took Gaza with the coast thereof
1. 19 the LORD was with J.; and he drave out
10. 9 passed over Jordan to fight also against J.
15. 9 Then the Philistines went up, and pitch.
15. 10 the men of J. said, Why are ye come up
15. 11 three thousand men of J. went to the top
17. 7 there was a young man..of the family of J.
18. 12 they went up, and pitched..in J.: wher.
20. 18 And the LORD said, J. (shall go up) first
Ruth 1. 7 on their way to return into the land of J.
1 Sa. 11. 8 children of Israel..and the men of J.
15. 4 Saul gathered..ten thousand men of J.
17. 1 gathered..at Shochoh..(belongeth) to J.
17. 52 men of Israel and of J. arose, and shout.
18. 16 But all Israel and J. loved David, becau.
22. 5 depart, and get thee into the land of J.
23. 3 men said..Behold, we be afraid here in J.
23. 23 search..throughout all..thousands of J.
27. 6 Ziklag pertaineth unto the kings of J.
27. 10 David said, Against the south of J., and
30. 14 upon (the coast) which (belongeth) to J.
30. 16 that they had taken..out of the land of J.
30. 26 he sent of the spoil unto the elders of J.
2 Sa. 1. 18 he bade them teach the children of J.
2. 1 Shall I go up into any of the cities of J.?
2. 4 And the men of J. came, and there they
2. 4 anointed David king over the house of J.
2. 7 house of J. have anointed me king over
2. 10 But the house of J. followed David
2. 11 was king in Hebron over the house of J.
3. 8 which against J. do show kindness this
3. 10 and to set up the throne of David over..J.
5. 5 he reigned over J. seven years and six
5. 5 reigned thirty and three years over all..J.
6. 2 people..(were) with him from Baale of J.
11. 11 The ark, and Israel, and J., abide in tents
12. 8 gave thee the house of Israel and of J.
19. 11 saying, Speak unto the elders of J., saying
19. 14 he bowed the heart of all the men of J.
19. 15 J. came to Gilgal, to go to meet the king
19. 16 Shimei..came down with the men of J.
19. 40 all the people of J. conducted the king
19. 41 Why have..the men of J. stolen thee
19. 42 all the men of J. answered the men of I.
19. 43 men of Israel answered the men of J.
19. 43 words of the men of J. were fiercer than
20. 2 but the men of J. clave unto their king
20. 4 Assemble me the men of J. within three
20. 5 So Amasa went to assemble (the men of) J.
21. 2 slay them in his zeal to the children of..J.
24. 1 he moved..to say, Go, number Israel..J.
24. 7 they went out to the south of J., (even)
24. 9 the men of J. (were) five hundred thousa.
1 Ki. 1. 9 and all the men of J. the king's servants
1. 35 I have appointed him to be ruler..over J.
2. 32 and Amasa..captain of the host of J.
4. 20 J. and Israel (were) many, as the sand
4. 25 J. and Israel dwelt safely, every man under
1 Ch. 6. 55 they gave them Hebron in the land of J.
6. 57 sons of Aaron they gave the cities of J.
6. 65 gave by lot out of the tribe of..J., and
9. 3 in Jerusalem dwelt of the children of J.
12. 16 there came of the children of..J...unto
12. 24 The children of J. that bare shield and sp.
13. 6 to Kirjath-jearim, which (belonged) to J.
27. 18 Of J., Elihu, (one) of the brethren of Da.
28. 4 J. (to be) the ruler; and of the house of J.
2 Ch. 2. 7 that (are) with me in J. and in Jerusalem
9. 11 none such seen before in the land of J.
Ezra 1. 2 build..house at Jerusalem, which (is) in J.
1. 3 let him go up to Jerusalem, which (is) in J.
1. 5 chief of the fathers of J. and Benjamin
1. 8 numbered them..Sheshbazzar..prince of J.
4. 4 weakened the hands of the people of J.
4. 6 against..inhabitants of J. and Jer. 3. 9.
5. 1 prophesied unto the Jews that (were) in J.
7. 14 to enquire concerning J. and Jerusalem
9. 9 to give us a wall in J. and in Jerusalem
10. 7 they made proclamation throughout J.
10. 9 men of J. and Benjamin gathered them.
Neh. 1. 2 That H...came, he and (certain) men of J.
2. 5 thou wouldest send me unto J., unto the
2. 7 may convey me over till I come into J.
4. 10 J. said, The strength of the bearers of
4. 16 rulers (were) behind all the house of J.
5. 14 to be their governor in the land of J.
6. 7 (There is) a king in J.: and now shall it
6. 17 the nobles of J. sent many letters unto
6. 18 For (there were) many in J. sworn unto
7. 6 came again to Jerusalem and to J., every
11. 3 in the cities of J. dwelt every one in his
11. 4 at Jerusalem dwelt..the children of J.
11. 4 Of the children of J.; Athaiah the son of
Neh. 11. 20 the residue..(were) in all the cities of J.
11. 25 the children of J. dwelt at Kirjath-arba
11. 36 of the Levites (were) divisions (in) J., (and)
12. 31 I brought up the princes of J. upon the
12. 32 Hoshaiah, and half of the princes of J.
12. 44 J. rejoiced for the priests and for the
13. 12 Then brought all J. the tithe of the corn
13. 15 those days saw I in J. (some) treading wine
13. 16 sold on the sabbath unto..children of J.
13. 17 I contended with the nobles of J., and
Esth. 2. 6 been carried away with Jeconiah king of J.
Psa. 48. 11 let the daughters of J. be glad, because
60. 7 strength of mine head; J. (is) my lawgiver
63. *title.* D...when he was in the wilderness of J.
68. 27 the princes of J. (and) their council, the
69. 35 save Zion, and will build the cities of J.
76. 1 In J. (is) God known; his name (is) great
78. 68 chose the tribe of J., the mount Zion wh.
97. 8 the daughters of J. rejoiced because of
108. 8 the strength of mine head; J. (is) my law.
114. 2 J. was his sanctuary..Israel his dominion
Matt. 2. 6 And thou, Bethlehem, (in) the land of J.
2. 6 art not the least among the princes of J.
Luke 1. 39 into the hill country..into a city of J.
Heb. 7. 14 is) evident that our Lord sprang out of J.
8. 8 house of Israel and with the house of J.
Rev. 5. 5 the Lion of the tribe of J., the Root of
7. 5 Of the tribe of J. (were) sealed twelve

3. After the revolt of the ten tribes the kingdom over which Rehoboam reigned was called Judah.

1 Ki. 12. 17 Israel which dwelt in the cities of J.
12. 20 none that followed..but the tribe of J.
12. 21 he assembled all the house of J., with
12. 23 king of J., and unto all the house of J.
12. 27 their lord, (even) unto Rehoboam..of J.
12. 27 shall..go again to Rehoboam king of J.
12. 32 feast..like unto the feast that (is) in J.
13. 1 there came a man of God out of J. by
13. 12 the man of God went which came from J.
13. 14 thou the man of God that camest from J.?
13. 21 unto the man of God that came from J.
14. 21 Rehoboam..son of Solomon reigned in J.
14. 22 J. did evil in the sight of the LORD, and
14. 29 book of the chronicles of the kings of J.?
15. 1 eighteenth year..reigned Abijam over J.
15. 7 book of the chronicles of the kings of J.?
15. 9 in the twentieth year..reigned A...over J.
15. 17 king of Israel went up against J., and
15. 17 to go out or come in to Asa king of J.
15. 22 Asa made a proclama. throughout all J.
15. 23 book of the chronicles of the kings of J.?
15. 25 in the second year of Asa king of J.
15. 28, 33 in the third year of Asa king of J.
16. 8 twenty and sixth year of Asa king of J.
16. 10, 15 and seventh year of Asa king of J.
16. 23 thirty and first year of Asa king of J.
16. 29 thirty and eighth year of Asa king of J.
19. 3 to Beer-sheba, which (belongeth) to J.
22. 2 king of J. came down to the king of Isr.
22. 10 ki. of Israel and Jehoshaphat..king of J.
22. 29 the king of J. went up to Ramoth-gilead
22. 41 the son of Asa began to reign over J. in
22. 45 book of the chronicles of the kings of J.?
22. 51 seventeenth year of Jehosha. king of J.
2 Ki. 1. 17 Jehoram the son of Jehoshaphat ki. of J.
3. 1 eighteenth year of Jehoshaphat king of J.
3. 7 sent to Jehoshaphat the king of J., say.
3. 9 and the king of J., and the king of Edom
3. 14 presence of Jehoshaphat the king of J.
8. 16 Jehoshaphat (being) then king of J., Jeho.
8. 16 son of Jehoshaphat king of J. began to
8. 19 the LORD would not destroy J. for David
8. 20, 22 E. revolted from under the hand of J.
8. 23 book of the chronicles of the kings of J.?
8. 25 Ahaziah the son of Jehoram king of J.
8. 29 the son of Jehoram king of J. went down
9. 16 king of J. was come down to see Joram
9. 21 king of Israel and Ahaziah king of J. went
9. 27 when Ahaziah the king of J. saw (this)
9. 29 began Ahaziah to reign over J.
10. 13 with the brethren of Ahaziah king of J.
12. 18 king of J. took all the hallowed things
12. 18 J., and Ahaziah, his fathers, kings of J.
12. 19 book of the chronicles of the kings of J.?
13. 1 of Joash the son of Ahaziah king of J.
13. 10 thirty..seventh year of Joash king of J.
13. 12 he fought against Amaziah king of J.
14. 1 Amaziah the son of Joash king of J.
14. 9 king of Israel sent to Amaziah king of J.
14. 10 shouldest fall, (even) thou, and J. with
14. 11 he and Amaziah king of J. looked one an.
14. 11 at Beth-shemesh, which (belongeth) to J.
14. 12 J. was put to the worse before Israel; and
14. 13 king of Israel took Amaziah king of J.
14. 15 how he fought with Amaziah king of J.
14. 17 the son of Joash king of J. lived after
14. 18 book of the chronicles of the kings of J.?
14. 21 the people of J. took Azariah, which (was)
14. 22 built Elath, and restored it to J., after
14. 23 of Amaziah the son of Joash king of J.
14. 28 Dama...Hamath, (which belonged) to J.
15. 1 began Azariah son of Amaziah king of J.
15. 6 book of the chronicles of the kings of J.?
15. 8 eighth year of Azariah king of J. did
15. 13 and thirtieth year of Uzziah king of J.
15. 17 and thirtieth year of Azariah king of J.
15. 23 the fiftieth year of Azariah king of J.
15. 27 and fiftieth year of Azariah king of J.
15. 32 began Jotham the son of Uzziah king of J.
15. 36 book of the chronicles of the kings of J.?
15. 37 send against J. Rezin the king of Syria
2 Ki. 16. 1 son of Jotham king of J. began to reign
16. 19 book of the chronicles of the kings of J.?
17. 1 In the twelfth year of Ahaz king of J.
17. 13 Israel and against J. by all the prophets
17. 18 was none left but the tribe of J. only
17. 19 J. kept not the commandments of the L.
18. 1 the son of Ahaz king of J. began to reign
18. 5 none like him among all the kings of J.
18. 13 up against all the fenced cities of J.
18. 14 king of J. sent to the king of Assyria to
18. 14 appointed unto Hezekiah king of J. three
18. 16 which Hezekiah king of J. had overlaid
18. 22 hath said to J. and Jerusalem, Ye shall
19. 10 Thus shall ye speak to Hezekiah king of J.
19. 30 remnant that is escaped of the house of J.
20. 20 book of the chronicles of the kings of J.?
21. 11 king of J. hath done these abominations
21. 11 hath made J. also to sin with his idols
21. 12 bringing (such) evil upon Jerusalem..J.
21. 16 beside his sin wherewith he made J. to
21. 17, 25 book of the chronicles of the ki. of J.?
22. 13 for me, and for the people, and for all J.
22. 16 the book which the king of J hath read
22. 18 the king of J., which sent you to enquire
23. 1 all the elders of J. and of Jerusalem
23. 2 the men of J. and all the inhabitants of
23. 5 kings of J. had ordained to burn incense
23. 5 in the high places in the cities of J., and
23. 8 all the priests out of the cities of J., and
23. 11 that the kings of J. had given to the sun
23. 12 altars..which the kings of J. had made
23. 17 of the man of God, which came from J
23. 22 the kings of Israel, nor of the kings of J.
23. 24 spied in the land of J. and in Jerusalem
23. 26 his anger was kindled against J., because
23. 27 I will remove J. also out of my sight, as
23. 28 book of the chronicles of the kings of J.?
24. 2 sent them against J. to destroy it, accor.
24. 3 the commandment..came (this) upon J.
24. 5 book of the chronicles of the kings of J.?
24. 12 the king of J. went out to the king of
24. 20 came to pass in Jerusalem and J., until
25. 21 So J. was carried away out of their land
25. 22 people that remained in the land of J.
25. 27 the captivity of Jehoiachin king of J.
25. 27 lift up the head of Jehoiachin king of J.
1 Ch. 4. 41 came in the days of Hezekiah king of J.
5. 17 genealogies in..days of Jotham king of J.
6. 15 the LORD carried away J. and Jerusalem
9. 1 in the book of the kings of Israel and J.
21. 5 J. (was) four hundred threescore and ten
2 Ch. 10. 17 of Israel that dwelt in the cities of J.
11. 1 gathered of the house of J. and Benjamin
11. 3 king of J., and to all Israel in J. and Ben.
11. 5 Rehoboam..built cities for defence in J.
11. 10 (are) in J. and in Benjamin fenced cities
11. 12 strong, having J. and Benjamin on his side
11. 14 came to J. and Jerusalem: for Jeroboam
11. 17 they strengthened the kingdom of J., and
11. 23 all the countries of J. and Benjamim, unto
12. 4 the fenced cities which (pertained) to J.
12. 5 (to) the princes of J., that were gathered
12. 12 turned..and also in J. things went well
13. 1 Now..began Abijah to reign over J.
13. 13 they were before J., and the ambushment
13. 14 when J. looked back, behold, the battle
13. 15 of J. gave a shout: and as the men of J.
13. 15 smote..all Israel before Abijah and J.
13. 16 the children of Israel fled before J.: and
13. 18 the children of J. prevailed, because they
14. 4 commanded J. to seek the LORD God of
14. 5 he took away out of all the cities of J.
14. 6 he built fenced cities in J.: for the land
14. 7 he said unto J., Let us build these cities
14. 8 Asa had..out of J. three hundred thous.
14. 12 the Ethiopians before Asa, and before J.
15. 2 Hear ye me, Asa, and all J. and Benjamin
15. 8 out of all the land of J. and Benjamin
15. 9 he gathered all J. and Benjamin, and the
15. 15 J. rejoiced at the oath: for they had sworn
16. 1 king of Israel came up against J., and
16. 1 none go out or come in to Asa king of J.
16. 6 king took all J.; and they carried away
16. 7 the seer came to Asa king of J., and said
16. 11 in the book of the kings of J. and Israel
17. 2 of J., and set garrisons in the land of J.
17. 5 J. brought to Jehoshaphat presents; and
17. 6 took..the high places and groves out of J.
17. 7 to Michaiah, to teach in the cities of J.
17. 9 they taught in J., and (had) the book of
17. 9 went about throughout all the cities of J.
17. 10 of the lands that (were) round about J.
17. 12 he built in J. castles, and cities of store
17. 13 he had much business in the cities of J.
17. 14 Of J., the captains of thousands; Adnah
17. 19 put in the fenced cities throughout..J.
18. 3 king of Israel said unto..king of J., Wilt
18. 9 king of Israel and Jehoshaphat king of J.
18. 28 the king of J. went up to Ramoth-gilead
19. 1 the king of J. returned to his house in
19. 5 throughout all the fenced cities of J.
19. 11 Zebadiah..the ruler of the house of J.
20. 3 and proclaimed a fast throughout all J.
20 4 J. gathered themselves together to ask
20. 4 out of all the cities of J. they came to
20. 5 in the congregation of J. and Jerusalem
20. 13 J. stood before the LORD, with their little
20. 15 Hearken ye, all J., and ye inhabitants of
20. 17 see..salvation of the LORD with you, O J.
20. 18 J. and the inhabitants of Jerusalem fell
20. 20 O J., and ye inhabitants of Jerusalem
20. 22 children of Ammon..were come against J.

2 Ch.20. 24 when J. came toward the watch tower
20. 27 they returned, every man of J. and Jerus.
20. 31 And Jehoshaphat reigned over J.,(He was)
20. 35 after this did Jehoshaphat king of J. join
21. 3 precious things, with fenced cities in J.
21. 8 revolted from under the dominion of J.
21. 10 revolted from under the hand of J. unto
21. 11 made high places in the mountains of J.
21. 11 commit fornication, and compelled J.
21. 12 father, nor in the ways of Asa king of J.
21. 13 made J. and the inhabitants of Jerusalem
21. 17 they came up into J., and brake into it
22. 1 the son of Jehoram king of J. reigned
22. 6 the son of Jehoram king of J. went down
22. 8 found the princes of J., and the sons of
22. 10 all the seed royal of the house of J.
23. 2 they went about in J., and gathered the
23. 2 Levites out of all the cities of J., and
23. 8 all J. did according to all things that
24. 5 Go out unto the cities of J., and gather
24. 6 bring in, out of J. and out of Jerusalem
24. 9 a proclamation through J. and Jerusalem
24. 17 after the death..came the princes of J.
24. 18 wrath came upon J. and Jerusalem for
24. 23 came to J. and Jerusalem, and destroyed
25. 5 Amaziah gathered J. together, and made
25. 5 captains..throughout all J. and Benjamin
25. 10 anger was greatly kindled against J.
25. 12 did the children of J. carry away captive
25. 13 fell upon the cities of J., from Samaria
25. 17 Then Amaziah king of J. took advice, and
25. 18 king of Israel sent to Amaziah king of J.
25. 19 shouldest fall, (even) thou, and J. with
25. 21 J., at Beth-shemesh..(belongeth) to J.
25. 22 J. was put to the worse before Israel, and
25. 23 the king of Israel took Amaziah king of J.
25. 25 the son of Joash king of J. lived after
25. 26 in the book of the kings of J. and Israel?
25. 28 buried..with his fathers in the city of J.
26. 1 people of J. took Uzziah, who (was) sixteen
26. 2 He built Eloth, and restored it to J., after
27. 4 he built cities in the mountains of J., and
27. 7 in the book of the kings of Israel and J.
28. 6 the son of Remaliah slew in J. an hundr.
28. 9 LORD God of your fathers..wroth with J.
28. 10 purpose to keep under the children of J.
28. 17 the Edomites had come and smitten J.
28. 18 of the low country, and of the south of J.
28. 19 the LORD brought J. low because of Ahaz
28. 19 he made J. naked, and transgressed sore
28. 25 in every several city of J. he made high
28. 26 in the book of the kings of J. and Israel
29. 8 wrath of the LORD was upon J. and Jeru.
29. 21 kingdom, and for the sanctuary, and for J.
30. 1 Hezekiah sent to all Israel and J., and
30. 6 his princes throughout all Israel and J.
30. 12 in J. the hand of God was to give them
30. 24 king of J. did give to the congregration a
30. 25 the congregation of J., with the priests
30. 25 the strangers..that dwelt in J., rejoiced
31. 1 Israel..went out to the cities of J., and
31. 1 the altars out of all J. and Benjamin, in
31. 6 Israel and J., that dwelt in the cities of J.
31. 20 thus did Hezekiah throughout all J., and
32. 1 entered into J., and encamped against
32. 8 upon the words of Hezekiah king of J.
32. 9 unto Hezekiah king of J., and unto all J.
32. 12 commanded J. and Jerusalem, saying, Ye
32. 23 brought..presents to Hezekiah king of J.
32. 25 wrath upon him, and upon J. and Jerus.
32. 32 in the book of the kings of J. and Israel
32. 33 J. and the inhabitants of Jerusalem did
33. 9 Manasseh made J. and the inhabitants of
33. 14 captains..in all the fenced cities of J.
33. 16 and commanded J. to serve the LORD God
34. 3 in the twelfth year he began to purge J.
34. 5 And he..cleansed J. and Jerusalem
34. 9 remnant of Israel..of all J. and Benjamin
34. 11 houses which the kings of J. had destroy.
34. 21 them that are left in Israel and in J.
34. 24 they have read before the king of J.
34. 26 the king of J., who sent you to enquire of
34. 29 gathered..all the elders of J. and Jerus.
34. 30 men of J., and the inhabitants of Jerusal.
35. 18 all J. and Israel that were present, and
35. 21 What have I to do with thee..king of J.?
35. 24 all J. and Jerusalem mourned for Josiah
35. 27 in the book of the kings of Israel and J.
36. 4, 10 his brother king over J. and Jerusalem
36. 8 in the book of the kings of Israel and J.
36. 23 an house in Jerusalem, which (is) in J.
Ezra 2. 1 came again unto Jerusalem and J., every
4. 1 the adversaries of J. and Benjamin heard
5. 1 prophesied unto the Jews that (were) in J.
7. 14 to enquire concerning J. and Jerusalem
9. 9 to give us a wall in J. and in Jerusalem
Prov 25. 1 the men of Hezekiah king of J. copied
Isa. 1. 1 which he saw concerning J. and Jerusal.
1. 1 Jotham, Ahaz, (and) Hezekiah, kings of J.
2. 1 Isaiah the son of Amoz saw concerning J.
3. 1 from J. the stay and the staff, the whole
3. 8 For Jerusalem is ruined, and J. is fallen
5. 3 men of J., judge, I pray you, betwixt me
5. 7 and the men of J. his pleasant plant: and
7. 1 son of Jotham..son of Uzziah, king of J.
7. 6 Let us go up against J., and vex it, and
7. 17 the day that Ephraim departed from J.
8. 8 he shall pass through J.; he shall overfl.
9. 21 they together (shall be) against J. For all
11. 12 gather together the dispersed of J. from
11. 13 the adversaries of J. shall be cut off
11. 13 Ephraim shall not envy J., and J. shall

Isa. 19. 17 land of J. shall be a terror unto Egypt
22. 8 he discovered the covering of J., and
22. 21 of Jerusalem, and to the house of J.
26. 1 shall this song be sung in the land of J.
36. 1 up against all the defenced cities of J.
36. 7 and said to J. and to Jerusalem, Ye shall
37. 10 Thus shall ye speak to Hezekiah king of J.
37. 31 remnant that is escaped of the house of J.
38. 9 The writing of Hezekiah king of J., when
40. 9 say unto the cities of J., Behold your God
44. 26 to the cities of J., Ye shall be built, and
48. 1 are come forth out of the waters of J.
65. 9 out of J. an inheritor of my mountains
Jer. 1. 2 days of Josiah the son of Amon king of J.
1. 3 of Jehoiakim the son of Josiah king of J.
1. 3 of Zedekiah the son of Josiah king of J.
1. 15 shall come..against all the cities of J.
1. 18 against the kings of J., against the princes
2. 28 the number of thy cities are thy gods, O J.
3. 7 And her treacherous sister J. saw (it)
3. 8 J. feared not, but went and played the
3. 10 J. hath not turned unto me with her wh.
3. 11 justified herself more than treacherous J.
3. 18 house of J. shall walk with the house of
4. 3 thus saith the LORD to the men of J. and
4. 4 ye men of J. and inhabitants of Jerusalem
4. 5 Declare ye in J., and publish in Jerusalem
4. 16 give out their voice against..cities of J.
5. 11 house of Israel and the house of J. have
5. 20 Declare this..and publish it in J., saying
7. 2 (ye of) J., that enter in at these gates to
7. 17 Seest..not what they do in the cities of J.
7. 30 the children of J. have done evil in my
7. 34 I cause to cease from the cities of J.
8. 1 bring out the bones of the kings of J.
9. 11 and I will make the cities of J. desolate
9. 26 J., and Edom, and the children of Amm.
10. 22 to make the cities of J. desolate, (and) a
11. 2 and speak unto the men of J., and to the
11. 6 Proclaim..these words in the cities of J.
11. 9 conspiracy is found among the men of J.
11. 10 house of Israel and the house of J. have
11. 12 Then shall the cities of J. and inhabitants
11. 13 number of thy cities were thy gods, O J.
11. 17 house of Israel, and of the house of J.
12. 14 pluck out the house of J. from among
13. 9 this manner will I mar the pride of J.
13. 11 house of Israel and the whole house of J.
13. 19 J. shall be carried away captive all of
14. 2 J. mourneth, and the gates thereof lang.
14. 19 Hast thou utterly rejected J.? hath thy
15. 4 Manasseh the son of Hezekiah king of J
17. 1 The sin of J. (is) written with a pen
17. 19 whereby the kings of J. come in, and by
17. 20 ye kings of J., and all J., and all the
17. 25 men of J., and the inhabitants of Jerusa.
17. 26 they shall come from the cities of J., and
18. 11 speak to the men of J...to the inhabit.
19. 3 kings of J., and inhabitants of Jerusalem
19. 4 fathers have known, nor the kings of J.
19. 7 make void the counsel of J. and Jerusalem
19. 13 the houses of the kings of J., shall be
20. 4 I will give all J. into the hand of the
20. 5 the treasures of the kings of J. will I
21. 7 I will deliver Zedekiah king of J., and
21. 11 And touching the house of the king of J.
22. 1 Go down to the house of the king of J.
22. 2 Hear the word of the LORD, O king of J.
22. 6 saith the LORD unto the king's house of J.
22. 11 Shallum the son of Josiah king of J., wh.
22. 18 Jehoiakim the son of Josiah king of J.
22. 24 though Coniah..king of J. were the signet
22. 30 no man..shall pros...ruling any more in J.
23. 6 In his days J. shall be saved, and Israel
24. 1 carried away captive Jeconiah..king of J.
24. 1 princes of J., with the carpenters and sm.
24. 5 them that are carried away captive of J.
24. 8 So will I give Zedekiah the king of J., and
25. 1 that came..concerning all the people of J.
25. 1 Jehoiakim the son of Josiah king of J.
25. 2 Jeremiah..spake unto all the people of J.
25. 3 year of Josiah the son of Amon king of J.
25. 18 Jerusalem, and the cities of J...to make
26. 1 Jehoiakim the son of Josiah king of J.
26. 2 Stand..and speak unto all the cities of J.
26. 10 When the princes of J. heard these things
26. 18 prophesied in the days of..king of J., and
26. 18 spake to all the people of J., saying, Thus
26. 19 Did Hezekiah king of J. and all J. put him
27. 1 Jehoiakim the son of Josiah king of J.
27. 3 which come to Jerusalem unto..king of J.
27. 12 I spake also to Zedekiah king of J. acco.
27. 18 are left in..the house of the king of J.
27. 20 king of J...and all the nobles of J. and
27. 21 remain..(in) the house of the king of J.
28. 1 the beginning of the reign of..king of J.
28. 4 I will bring again..Jeconiah..king of J.
28. 4 all the captives of J., that went into Ba.
29. 2 After..the princes of J...were departed
29. 3 whom Zedekiah king of J. sent unto Bab.
29. 22 a curse by all the captivity of J. which
30. 3 that I will bring again the captivity of..J.
30. 4 words that the LORD spake concerning..J.
31. 23 As yet they shall use this speech in..J.
31. 24 there shall dwell in J. itself..husbandmen
31. 27 that I will sow the house..of J. with the
31. 31 make a new covenant with the house of..J.
32. 1 in the tenth year of Zedekiah king of J.
32. 2 the prison, which (was) in the king of J.'s.
32. 3 For Zedekiah king of J. had shut him up
32. 4 Zedekiah king of J. shall not escape out
32. 30 For the children..of J. have only done

Jer. 32. 32 of all the evil..of the children of J., wh.
32. 32 the men of J., and the inhabitants 32.35.
32. 44 take witnesses..in the cities of J., and in
33. 4 houses of the kings of J., which are thro.
33. 7 I will cause the captivity of J...to return
33. 10 without beast, (even) in the cities of J.
33. 13 in the cities of J., shall the flocks pass
33. 14 which I have promised..to the house of J.
33. 16 In those days shall J. be saved, and Jer.
34. 2 Go and speak to Zedekiah king of J., and
34. 4 Yet hear the word..O Zedekiah king of J.
34. 6 all these words unto Zedekiah king of J. in
34. 7 against all the cities of J. that were left
34. 7 these..cities remained of the cities of J.
34. 19 The princes of J., and the princes of Jer.
34. 21 Zedekiah king of J...will I give into the
34. 22 I will make the cities of J. a desolation
35. 1 Jehoiakim the son of Josiah king of J.
35. 13 Go and tell the men of J., and the inhab.
35. 17 Behold, I will bring upon J...all the evil
36. 1, 9 Jehoiakim the son of Josiah king of J.
36. 2 that I have spoken unto thee..against J.
36. 3 It may be that the house of J. will hear
36. 6 also thou shalt read..in the ears of all J.
36. 9 that came from the cities of J. unto Jeru.
36. 28 which Jehoiakim the king of J. hath bur.
36. 29 And thou shalt say to Jehoiakim king of J.
36. 30 saith the LORD of Jehoiakim king of J.
36. 31 I will bring..upon the men of J., all
36. 32 book which Jehoiakim king of J. had bu.
37. 1 whom..king of Babylon made king in..J.
37. 7 Thus shall ye say to the king of J., that
38. 22 women that are left in the king of J.'s h.
39. 1 In the ninth year of Zedekiah king of J.
39. 4 when Zedekiah the king of J. saw them
39. 6 king of Babylon slew all the nobles of J.
39. 10 which had nothing, in the land of J.
40. 1 all that were carried away captive of..J.
40. 5 hath made governor over the cities of J.
40. 11 king of Babylon had left a remnant of J.
40. 12 Even all the Jews..came to the land of J.
40. 15 that all the Jews..and the remnant in J.
42. 15 hear the word..ye remnant of J.; Thus
42. 19 O ye remnant of J.; Go ye not into Egypt
43. 4 obeyed not..to dwell in the land of J.
43. 5 Johanan..took all the remnant of J.
43. 5 were returned..to dwell in the land of J.
43. 9 Take great stones..in..sight of..men of J.
44. 2 I have brought..upon all the cities of J.
44. 6 my fury..was kindled in the cities of J.
44. 7 cut off from you man and woman..out of J.
44. 9 forgotten..wickedness of the kings of J.
44. 9 they have committed in the land of J., and
44. 11 set my face against you..to cut off all J.
44. 12 I will take the remnant of J., that have
44. 14 none of the remnant of J., which are gone
44. 14 they should return into the land of J.
44. 17, 21 in the cities of J., and in the streets of
44. 24 Hear..all J. that (are) in the land of Eg.
44. 26 all J. that dwell in the land of Egypt
44. 26 be named in the mouth of any man of J.
44. 27 men of J. that (are) in the land of Egypt
44. 28 the land of J., and all the remnant of J.
44. 30 I gave Zedekiah king of J. into the hand
45. 1 of Jehoiakim the son of Josiah king of J.
46. 2 of Jehoiakim the son of Josiah king of J.
49. 34 beginning of..reign of Zedekiah king of J.
50. 4 they and the children of J. together, going
50. 20 the sins of J., and they shall not be found
50. 33 the children of J. (were) oppressed toge.
51. 5 not (been) forsaken, nor J. of his God
51. 59 he went with Zedekiah the king of J. into
52. 3 it came to pass in Jerusalem and J., till
52. 10 slew also all the princes of J. in Riblah
52. 27 J. was carried away captive out of his
52. 31 of the captivity of Jehoiachin king of J.
52. 31 lifted..the head of Jehoiachin king of J.
Lam. 1. 3 J. is gone into captivity because of
1. 15 hath trodden the virgin..daughter of J.
2. 2 the strong holds of the daughter of J.
2. 5 increased in the daughter of J. mourning
5. 11 They ravished..maids in the cities of J.
Eze. 4. 6 bear the iniquity of the house of J. forty
8. 1 the elders of J. sat before me, that the
8. 17 Is it a light thing to the house of J.
9. 9 The iniquity of the house of Israel and J.
21. 20 and to J. in Jerusalem the defenced
25. 3 against the house of J., when they went
25. 8 house of J. (is) like unto all the heathen
25. 12 Edom hath dealt against the house of J.
27. 17 J., and the land of Israel, they (were) thy
37. 16 For J., and for the children of Israel his
37. 19 put them with him..with the stick of J.
48. 7 unto the west side, a (portion for) J.
48. 8 by the border of J., from the east side
48. 22 border of J. and the border of Benjamin
48. 31 of Reuben, one gate of J., one gate of Levi
Dan. 1. 1 year of the reign of Jehoiakim king of J.
1. 2 gave Jehoiakim king of J. into his hand
1. 6 the children of J., Daniel, Hananiah, M.
2. 25 I have found a man of the captives of J
5. 13 of the children of the captivity of J.
6. 13 of the children of the captivity of J.
9. 7 to the men of J., and to the inhabitants
Hos. 1. 1 Uzziah, Jotham, Ahaz..Hezekiah, ks. of J.
1. 7 I will have mercy upon the house of J., and
1. 11 the children of J. and the children of
4. 15 let not J. offend; and come not ye unto
5. 5 therefore..J. also shall fall with them
5. 10 princes of J. were like them that remove
5. 12 moth, and to the house of J. as rottenness
5. 13 saw his sickness, and J. (saw) his wound

Hos. 5. 14 as a young lion to the house of J.: I, (even)
6. 4 O J., what shall I do unto thee? for your
6. 11 O J., he hath set an harvest for thee, when
8. 14 J. hath multiplied fenced cities: but I
10. 11 J. shall plow, (and) Jacob shall break his
11. 12 J. yet ruleth with God, and is faithful
12. 2 The LORD hath also a controversy with J.
Joel 3. 1 shall bring again the captivity of J. and
3. 6 The children also of J...have ye sold unto
3. 8 sell..into the hand of the children of J.
3. 18 the rivers of J. shall flow with waters
3. 19 the violence (against) the children of J.
3. 20 J. shall dwell for ever, and Jerusalem
Amos 1. 1 he saw..in the days of Uzziah king of J.
2. 4 For three transgressions of J., and for
2. 5 I will send a fire upon J., and it shall
7. 12 flee thee away into the land of J., and
Obad. 12 have rejoiced over the children of J. in
Mic. 1. 1 Jotham, Ahaz, (and) Hezekiah, kings of J.
1. 5 what (are) the high places of J.? (are they)
1. 9 it is come unto J.; he is come unto the
5. 2 thou be little among the thousands of J.
Nah. 1. 15 O J., keep thy solemn feasts, perform thy
Zeph. 1. 1 days of Josiah the son of Amon, king of J.
1. 4 I will also stretch out mine hand upon J.
2. 7 be for the remnant of the house of J.
Hag. 1. 1, 14 the son of Shealtiel, governor of J.
2. 2 the son of Shealtiel, governor of J., and
2. 21 Speak to Zerubbabel, governor of J., say.
Zech. 1. 12 mercy on Jerusalem and on the cities of J.
1. 19, 21 (are) the horns which have scattered J.
1. 21 horn over the land of J. to scatter it
2. 12 the LORD shall inherit J. his portion in
8. 13 O house of J., and house of Israel
8. 15 unto Jerusalem, and to the house of J.
8. 19 be to the house of J. joy and gladness
9. 7 he shall be as a governor in J., and Ekron
9. 13 I have bent J. for me, filled the bow with
10. 3 hath visited his flock the house of J.
10. 6 I will strengthen the house of J., and I
11. 14 the brotherhood between J. and Israel
12. 2 both against J. (and) against Jerusalem
12. 4 will open mine eyes upon the house of J.
12. 5 the governors of J. shall say in their
12. 6 that day will I make the governors of J.
12. 7 LORD also shall save the tents of J. first
12. 7 do not magnify (themselves) against J.
14. 5 earthquake in..days of Uzziah king of J.
14. 14 J. also shall fight at Jerusalem: and the
14. 21 every pot in Jerusalem and in J. shall be
Mal. 2. 11 J...dealt treacherously, and an abomin.
2. 11 J. hath profaned the holiness of the LORD
3. 4 shall the offering of J. and Jerusalem

The following localities were in the territory of Judah: Achzib, Adadah, Adar, Adithaim, Adoraim, Adullam, Ain, Amam, Anab, Anim, Aphekah, Arab, Aroer, Aruboth, Ashan, Ashdod, Ashnah, Athach, Azal, Azchah, Azem, Azmaveth, Baalah, Bealoth, Berachah, Beth-anoth, Beth-dagon, Beth-ezel, Beth-gader, Beth-lehem Ephratah, Beth-palet, Beth-shemesh, Beth-tappuah, Beth-zur, Bizjothjah, Boscath, Cabbon, Cain, Caleb-Ephratah, Carmel, Chesalon, Chezib, Dannah, Debir, Dilean, Eder, Eglon, Eltekon, En-gannim, Engedi, Enam, Ephes-dammim, Ephron, Eshean, Eshtemoa, Etam, Gederoth, Gederothaim, Gedor, Gibeah, Giloh, Gimzo, Goshen, Hadashah, Halhul, Hareth, Hazar-addar, Hazar-gaddah, Hazezon-tamar, Hazor, Hadattah, Hebron, Heshmon, Holon, Humtah, Ithnan, Iim, Jabez, Jabneel, Jabneh, Jagur, Janam, Jarmuth, Jattir, Jekabzeel, Jiphtah, Jokdeam,Ioktheel, Jorkeam, Juttah, Karkaa, Kedesh, Keilah, Kerioth, Kinah, Kirjath-arba, Kirjath-jearim, Kirjath-sannah or -sepher, Kithlish, Lachish, Lahmam, Lecah, Libnah, Lod, Maarath, Madmen, Makkedah, Mamre, Maon, Mareshah, Mekonah, Middin, Migdal-gad, Mizpah, Naamah, Nebo, Netophah, Nezib, Nibshan, Rabbah, Rachal, Rechah, Rimmon, Sansannah, Saphir, Secacah, Seir, Senaah, Shaaraim, Shamir, Sheba, Shema, Shieron, Shilhim, Shocho, Sorek, Tappuah, Tekoa, Telaim, Telem, Timnah, Zaanan, Zanoah, Zenan, Zephathah, Ziklag, Zior, Ziph, &c.

4. An ancestor of Kadmiel who helped to rebuild the temple. B.C. 535.
Ezra 3. 9 Kadmiel and his sons, the sons of J., toge.

5. A Levite who had taken a strange wife. B.C. 457.
Ezra 10. 23 same (is) Kelita, Pethahiah, J., and Eliezer

6. A Benjamite, son of Senuah; the second in authority over Jerusalem in the days of Nehemiah. B.C. 446-434.
Neh. 11. 9 J. the son of Senuah (was) second over

7. A Levite who came up with Zerubbabel. B.C. 536.
Neh. 12. 8 J., (and) Mattaniah, (which was) over the

8. A prince of Judah. B.C. 445.
Neh. 12. 34 J., and Benjamin, and Shemaiah, and Jer.

9. A priest and musician. B.C. 445.
Neh. 12. 36 J., Hanani, with the musical instruments

JU'-DAS, JU'-DA, JUDE, Ἰούδας.

1. A disciple, surnamed Iscariot, who betrayed his Master and then hanged himself.
Matt 10. 4 and J. Iscariot, who also betrayed him
26. 14 J. Iscariot, went unto the chief priests
26. 25 J., which betrayed him, answered and
26. 47 J., one of the twelve, came, and with him
27. 3 J., which had betrayed him, when he saw
Mark 3. 19 And J. Iscariot, which also betrayed him
14. 10 J. Iscariot, one of the twelve, went unto
14. 43 cometh J., one of the twelve, and with
Luke 6. 16 J. Iscariot, which also was the traitor
22. 3 entered Satan into J. surnamed Iscariot
Luke 22. 47 J., one of the twelve, went before them
22. 48 J., betrayest thou the Son of man with a
John 6. 71 He spake of J. Iscariot (the son) of Simon
12. 4 J. Iscariot, Simon's (son), which should
13. 2 having..put into the heart of J. Iscariot
13. 26 he gave (it) to J. Iscariot, (the son) of S.
13. 29 because J. had the bag, that Jesus had
18. 2 J. also, which betrayed him, knew the
18. 3 J. then, having received a band (of men)
18. 5 J. also, which betrayed him, stood with
Acts 1. 16 spake before concerning J., which was
1. 25 from which J. by transgression fell, that

2. One of the brothers of Jesus.
Matt 13. 55 brethren, James, and Joses, and..J.
Mark 6. 3 of James, and Joses, and of J., and Simon?

3. The brother of James and writer of an epistle known by his name, "JUDE."
Luke 6. 16 And J. (the brother) of James, and..Is.
Acts 1. 13 Simon Zelotes, and J. (the broth.) of James
Jude 1 J., the servant of Jesus Christ, and brother

4. An apostle (not Iscariot), supposed to be Lebbeus or Thaddeus.
John 14. 22 J. saith unto him, not Iscariot, Lord

5. A Galilean who stirred up sedition shortly after the birth of Jesus.
Acts 5. 37 rose up J. of Galilee in the days of the

6. One with whom Paul lodged in Straight St., Damascus.
Acts 9. 11 enquire in the house of J. for (one) called

7. The prophet surnamed Barsabas, sent with Silas to Antioch by the Apostles, to convey their decree regarding circumcision.
Acts 15. 22 J. surnamed Barsabas, and Silas, chief
15. 27 We have sent therefore J. and Silas, who

JU-DE'-A, JEW'-RY, Ἰουδαία.

Another name or form of the name of the land of Judah, which see.

Ezra 5. 8 we went into the province of J., to the
Dan. 5. 13 whom the king my father brought out of J.?
Matt. 2. 1 Jesus was born in Bethlehem of J., in the
2. 5 In Bethlehem of J.: for thus it is written
2. 22 Archelaus did reign in J. in the room of
3. 1 Baptist, preaching in the wilderness of J.
3. 5 J., and all the region round about Jordan
4. 25 and (from) J., and (from) beyond Jordan
19. 1 came into the coasts of J. beyond Jordan
24. 16 let them..in J. flee into the mountains
Mark 1. 5 there went out unto him all the land of J.
3. 7 great multitude from Galilee..and from J.
10. 1 cometh into the coasts of J. by the farther
13. 14 them that be in J. flee to the mountains
Luke 1. 5 was, in the days of Herod the king of J., a
1. 65 were noised abroad throughout all..J.
2. 4 Joseph also went up from Galilee..into J.
3. 1 Pontius Pilate being governor of J., and
5. 17 which were come out of every town of..J.
6. 17 a great multitude of people out of all J.
7. 17 this rumour..went forth throughout all J.
21. 21 let them which are in J. flee to the moun.
23. 5 He stirreth up..teaching throughout..J.
John 3. 22 came Jesus..into the land of J.; and th.
4. 3 He left J., and departed again into Galilee
4. 47 heard that Jesus was come out of J. into
4. 54 when he was come out of J. into Galilee
7. 1 for he would not walk in J., because the
7. 3 Depart hence, and go into J., that thy dis.
11. 7 after that saith he..Let us go into J. again
Acts 1. 8 shall be witnesses unto me..in all J., and
2. 9 the dwellers in Mesopotamia, and in J.
2. 14 Ye men of J...be this known unto you, and
8. 1 were all scattered abroad throughout..J.
9. 31 had the churches rest throughout all J.
10. 37 which was published throughout all J.
11. 1 apostles and brethren that were in J. heard
11. 29 to send relief unto the brethren..in J.
12. 19 And he went down from J. to Cesarea, and
15. 1 certain men which came down from J.
21. 10 there came down from J. a certain prop.
26. 20 and throughout all the coasts of J., and
28. 21 We neither received letters out of J. con.
Rom 15. 31 That I may be delivered from them..in J.
2 Co. 1. 16 of you to be brought on my way toward J.
Gal. 1. 22 unto the churches of J. which were in Ch.
1 Th. 2. 14 the churches of God which in J. are in Ch.

JUDGE —

1. *A judge, discerner,* דַּיָּן *dayyan.*
1 Sa. 24. 15 LORD therefore be judge, and judge betw.
Ezra. 7. 25 set magistrates and judges, which may ju.
Psa. 68. 5 a judge of the widows, (is) God in his holy

2. *A judge, sifter,* פָּלִיל *palil.*
Exod 21. 22 and he shall pay as the judges (determine)
Deut. 32. 31 even our enemies themselves (being) jud.
Job 31. 11 an iniquity (to be punished by) the judge

3. *Judicial,* פְּלִילִי *pelili.*
Job 31. 28 an iniquity (to be punished by) the judge

4. *To judge, act as a magistrate,* שָׁפַט *shaphat.*
Gen. 18. 25 Shall not the Judge of all the earth do
Exod. 2. 14 Who made thee a prince and a judge over
Num 25. 5 Moses said unto the judges of Israel, Slay
Deut. 1. 16 I charged your judges at that time, saying
16. 18 Judges and officers shalt thou make thee
17. 9 unto the judge that shall be in those days
17. 12 will not hearken..unto the judge, even
19. 17 before the priests and the judges which
19. 18 the judges shall make diligent inquisition
21. 2 thy elders and thy judges shall come fo
Deut 25. 2 that the judge shall cause him to lie do.
Josh. 8. 33 all Israel..and their judges, stood on this
23. 2 for their judges, and for their officers, and
24. 1 for their heads, and for their judges, and
Judg. 2. 16 LORD raised up judges, which delivered
2. 17 yet they would not hearken unto their j
2. 18 And when the LORD raised them up judges
2. 18 then the LORD was with the judge, and de.
2. 18 delivered them..all the days of the judge
2. 19 it came to pass, when the judge was dead
11. 27 LORD the Judge be judge this day between
Ruth 1. 1 it came to pass in the days when the ju.
1 Sa. 8. 1 that he made his sons judges over Israel
8. 2 Joel, and..Abiah..judges in Beer-sheba
2 Sa. 7. 11 I commanded judges..over my people I.
15. 4 Oh that I were made judge in the land
2 Ki. 23. 22 from the days of the judges that judged I.
1 Ch. 17. 6 spake I a word to any of the judges of Is.
17. 10 since the time that I commanded judges
23. 4 six thousand (were) officers and judges
26. 29 Chenaniah and his sons (were)..for..ju.
2 Ch. 1. 2 to the captains..and to the judges, and
19. 5 he set judges in the land, throughout all
19. 6 said to the judges, Take heed what ye do
Ezra 10. 14 the elders of every city, and the judges
Job 9. 24 he covereth the faces of the judges there.
12. 17 away spoiled, and maketh the judges fo.
23. 7 so should I be delivered..from my judge
Psa. 2. 10 be instructed, ye judges of the earth
50. 6 shall declare..for God (is) judge himself
75. 7 God (is) the judge: he putteth down one
94. 2 Lift up thyself, thou judge of the earth
141. 6 When their judges are overthrown in st.
148. 11 Kings..princes, and all judges of the earth
Prov. 8. 16 By me princes rule..all the judges of the
Isa. 1. 26 I will restore thy judges as at the first, and
3. 2 the man of war, the judge, and the prop.
33. 22 the LORD (is) our judge, the LORD (is) our
40. 23 he maketh the judges of the earth as va.
Dan. 9. 12 spake..against our judges that judged us
Hos. 7. 7 and have devoured their judges; all their
13. 10 and thy judges of whom thou saidst, Give
Amos 2. 3 I will cut off the judge from the midst th.
Mic. 5. 1 they shall smite the judge of Israel with
7. 3 the judge (asketh) for a reward; and the
Zeph. 3. 3 her judges (are) evening wolves; they gnaw

5. *A judge, judicial functionary,* δικαστής *dikastēs.*
Luke 12. 14 Man, who made me [a judge] or a divider
Acts 7. 27 Who made thee a ruler and a judge over
7. 35 Who made thee a ruler and a judge? the

6. *A judge, critic,* κριτής *kritēs.*
Matt. 5. 25 deliver thee to the judge, and the judge
12. 27 therefore they shall be your judges
Luke 11. 19 therefore shall they be your judges
12. 58 he hale thee to the judge, and the judge
18. 2 There was in a city a judge, which feared
18. 6 Lord said, Hear what the unjust judge
Acts 10. 42 ordained of God..the Judge of quick and
13. 20 after that he gave..judges about the spa.
18. 15 for I will be no judge of such (matters)
24. 10 thou hast been of many years a judge
2 Ti. 4. 8 which the Lord, the righteous judge, shall
Heb. 12. 23 to God the Judge of all, and to the spirits
Jas. 2. 4 and are become judges of evil thoughts?
4. 11 thou art not a doer of the law, but a jud.
5. 9 behold, the judge standeth before the door

JUDGE, to —

1. *To judge, discern,* דִּין *din.*
Gen. 15. 14 also that nation..will I judge: and after.
30. 6 God hath judged me, and hath also heard
49. 16 Dan shall judge his people, as one of the
Deut 32. 36 LORD shall judge his people and repent
1 Sa. 2. 10 LORD shall judge the ends of the earth
Ezra 7. 25 judges, which may judge all the people
Job 36. 31 For by them judgeth he the poeple; he
Psa. 7. 8 The LORD shall judge the people
9. 8 he shall judge the world in righteousness
50. 4 He shall call..that he may judge his peo.
54. 1 Save me, O God..judge me by thy stren.
72. 2 He shall judge thy people with righteous.
96. 10 the LORD..shall judge the people right.
110. 6 He shall judge among the heathen, he
135. 14 the LORD will judge his people, and he will
Isa. 3. 13 The LORD..standeth to judge the people
Jer. 5. 28 they judge not the cause, the cause of the
22. 16 He judged the cause of the poor and needy
Zech 3. 7 thou shalt also judge my house, and shalt

2. *To make manifest, reason, reprove,* יָכַח *yakach,* 5.
Gen. 31. 37 here..that they may judge betwixt us both

3. *To judge, sift, execute judgment,* פָּלַל *palal,* 3.
1 Sa. 2. 25 If one man sin..the judge shall judge him
Eze. 16. 52 Thou also, which hast judged thy sisters

4. *To judge, act as a magistrate,* שָׁפַט *shaphat.*
Gen. 16. 5 said..the LORD judge between me and thee
31. 53 the God of their father, judge betwixt us
Exod. 5. 21 LORD look upon you, and judge; because
18. 13 Moses sat to judge the people: and the p.
18. 16 I judge between one and another, and I
18. 22 let them judge the people at all seasons
18. 22 but every small matter they shall judge
18. 26 And they judged the people at all seasons
18. 26 every small matter they judged themsel.
Lev. 19. 15 in righteousness shalt thou judge thy nei.
Num. 35. 24 the congregation shall judge between the
Deut. 1. 16 judge righteously between (every) man
16. 18 they shall judge the people with just jud.
25. 1 that (the judges) may judge them; then
Judg. 3. 10 and he judged Israel, and went out to war

Judg. 4. 4 Deborah..she judged Israel at that time
10. 2 And he judged Israel twenty and three
10. 3 and judged Israel twenty and two years
11. 27 LORD the Judge be judge this day between
12. 7 And Jephthah judged Israel six years
12. 8 after him Ibzan of Beth-lehem judged Isr.
12. 9 and he judged Israel seven years
12. 11 a Zebulonite, judged Israel; and he judged
12. 13 after him Abdon..a Pirathonite, judged
12. 14 and he judged Israel eight years
15. 20 he judged Israel in the days of the Philist.
16. 31 and he judged Israel twenty years
1 Sa. 3. 13 I have told him that I will judge his house
4. 18 And he had judged Israel forty years
7. 6 Samuel judged the children of Israel in M.
7. 15 Samuel judged Israel all the days of his
7. 16 went..and judged Israel in all those pla.
7. 17 there he judged Israel; and there he built
8. 5 make us a king to judge us like all the
8. 6 when they said, Give us a king to judge
8. 20 that our king may judge us, and go out
24. 12 LORD judge between me and thee, and
24. 15 judge between me and thee, and see, and
1 Ki. 3. 9 to judge thy people, that I may discern
3. 9 who is able to judge this..so great a peop.?
3. 28 of the judgment which the king had judg.
7. 7 a porch for the throne where he might ju.
8. 32 judge thy servants, condemning the wick.
2 Ki. 15. 5 over the house, judging the people of the
23. 22 from the days of the judges that judged
1 Ch. 16. 33 LORD, because he cometh to judge the
2 Ch. 1. 10 for who can judge this thy people, (that
1. 11 that thou mayest judge my people, over
6. 23 judge thy servants, by requiting the wic.
19. 6 ye judge not for man, but for the LORD
20. 12 O our God, wilt thou not judge them? for
26. 21 over the king's house, judging the people
Job 21. 22 seeing he judgeth those that are high
22. 13 God..can he judge through the dark clo.?
Psa. 7. 8 judge me, O LORD, according to my righ.
7. 11 God judgeth the righteous, and God is
9. 4 thou satest in the throne judging right
9. 8 he shall judge the world in righteousness
10. 18 To judge the fatherless and the oppressed
26. 1 Judge me, O LORD; for I have walked in
35. 24 Judge me, O LORD my God, according to
43. 1 Judge me, O God, and plead my cause
51. 4 thou mightest..be clear when thou judg.
58. 1 do ye judge uprightly, O ye sons of men?
58. 11 verily he is a God that judgeth in the earth
67. 4 for thou shalt judge the people righteou.
72. 4 He shall judge the poor of the people
75. 2 When I shall receive..I will judge uprig.
82. 1 God standeth..he judgeth among the gods
82. 2 How long will ye judge unjustly, and ac.
82. 8 Arise, O God, judge the earth: for thou
96. 13 he cometh to judge the earth: he shall j.
98. 9 to judge..righteousness shall he judge
Prov 29. 14 The king that faithfully judgeth the poor
31. 9 judge righteously, and plead the cause of
Eccl. 3. 17 God shall judge the righteous and the w.
Isa. 1. 17 judge the fatherless, plead for the widow
1. 23 they judge not the fatherless, neither doth
2. 4 he shall judge among the nations, and
5. 3 men of Judah, judge, I pray you, betwixt
11. 3 he shall not judge after the sight of his
11. 4 with righteousness shall he judge the poor
16. 5 sit..in the tabernacle of David, judging
51. 5 mine arms shall judge the people: the
Jer. 5. 28 the right of the needy do they not judge
11. 20 O LORD of hosts, that judgest righteously
Lam. 3. 59 O LORD, thou hast seen my wrong; judge
Eze. 7. 3, 8 will judge thee according to thy ways
7. 27 according to their deserts will I judge
11. 10 will judge you in the border of Israel
11. 11 (but) I will judge you in the border of Is.
16. 38 I will judge thee, as women that break
18. 30 I will judge you, O house of Israel, every
20. 4 Wilt thou judge them..wilt thou judge
21. 30 I will judge thee in the place where thou
22. 2 wilt thou judge, wilt thou judge the blo.
23. 24 they shall judge thee according to their
23. 36 wilt thou judge Aholah and Aholibah?
23. 45 they shall judge them after the manner
24. 14 according to thy doings, shall they judge
33. 20 O ye house of Israel, I will judge you
34. 17 I judge between cattle and cattle, betw.
34. 20 I, will judge between the fat cattle and
34. 22 and I will judge between cattle and cat.
35. 11 make myself known..when I have judg.
36. 19 and according to their doings I judged
44. 24 they shall judge it according to my jud.
Dan. 9. 12 spake..against our judges that judged
Joel 3. 12 there will I sit to judge all the heathen
Obad. 21 shall come up on mount Zion to judge
Mic. 3. 11 The heads thereof judge for reward, and
4. 3 he shall judge among many people, and

5. *To judge strictly, afresh,* ἀνακρίνω *anakrinō.*
1 Co. 2. 15 But he that is spiritual judgeth all things
2. 15 yet he himself is judged of no man
4. 3 that I should be judged of you..I judge
4. 4 but he that judgeth me is the Lord
14. 24 he is convinced of all, he is judged of all

6. *To judge thoroughly,* διακρίνω *diakrinō.*
1 Co. 6. 5 that shall be able to judge between his b.
11. 31 For if we would judge ourselves, we should
14. 29 speak two or three, and let the other jud.

7. *To account, think,* ἡγέομαι *hēgeomai.*
Heb. 11. 11 she judged him faithful who had promised

8. *To judge,* κρίνω *krinō.*
Matt. 7. 1 Judge not, that ye be not judged
7. 2 with what judgment ye judge, ye shall be j.
19. 28 shall sit..judging the twelve tribes of Is.
Luke 6. 37 Judge not, and ye shall not be judged: co.
7. 43 he said unto him, Thou hast rightly jud.
12. 57 even of yourselves judge ye not what is ri.
19. 22 Out of thine own mouth will I judge thee
22. 30 and sit..judging the twelve tribes of Isr.
John 5. 22 For the Father judgeth no man, but hath
5. 30 as I hear, I judge: and my judgment is
7. 24 Judge not accord. to the appearance, but j.
7. 51 Doth our law judge (any) man before it
8. 15 Ye judge after the flesh; I judge no man
8. 16 yet if I judge, my judgment is true; for
8. 26 I have many things to say and to judge
8. 50 there is one that seeketh and judgeth
12. 47 if any man..believe not, I judge him not
12. 47 I came not to judge the world, but to save
12. 48 hath one that judgeth..the same shall ju.
16. 11 because the prince of this world is judged
18. 31 Take ye him, and judge him according to
Acts 4. 19 Whether it be right..to hearken..judge ye
7. 7 And the nation..will I judge, said God
13. 46 judge yourselves unworthy of everlasting
16. 15 If ye have judged me to be faithful to the
17. 31 day, in the which he will judge the world
23. 3 for sittest thou to judge me after the law
24. 6 would have [judged] according to our law
25. 9 there be judged of these things before me?
25. 10 at Cesar's..seat, where I ought to be jud.
25. 20 go..and there be judged of these matters
26. 6 I stand and am judged for the hope of the
Rom. 2. 1 O man, whosoever thou art that judgest
2. 1 wherein thou judgest another, thou con.
2. 1 for thou that judgest doest the same things
2. 3 man, that judgest them which do such
2. 12 as many as..sinned in the law shall be j.
2. 16 when God shall judge the secrets of men
2. 27 shall not uncircumcision..judge thee, who
3. 4 mightest overcome when thou art judged
3. 6 for then how shall God judge the world?
3. 7 more..why yet am I also judged as a si.?
14. 3 let not him which eateth not ju.him that
14. 4 Who art thou that judgest another man's
14. 10 why dost thou judge thy brother? or why
14. 13 Let us not therefore judge one another
14. 13 but judge this rather, that no man put a
1 Co. 4. 5 Therefore judge nothing before the time
5. 3 For I verily..have judged already, as
5. 12 what have I to do to judge them also that
5. 12 do not ye judge them that are within?
5. 13 But them that are without God judgeth
6. 2 Do ye not know that the saints shall judge
6. 2 and if the world shall be judged by you
6. 3 Know ye not that we shall judge angels?
10. 15 I speak as to wise men; judge ye what I
10. 29 why is my liberty judged of another..co.?
11. 13 Judge in yourselves: is it comely that a
11. 31 For if we would..we should not be judg.
11. 32 when we are judged, we are chastened
2 Co. 5. 14 we thus judge, that if one died for all, th.
Col. 2. 16 Let no man therefore judge you in meat
2 Ti. 4. 1 who shall judge the quick and the dead
Heb. 10. 30 And again, The Lord shall judge his peo.
13. 4 whoremongers and adulterers God will j.
Jas. 2. 12 that shall be judged by the law of liberty
4. 11 and judgeth his brother..judgeth the law
4. 11 if thou judge the law, thou art not a doer
4. 12 one law giver..who art thou that judgest
1 Pe. 1. 17 who..judgeth according to every man's
2. 23 committed (himself) to him that judgeth
4. 5 is ready to judge the quick and the dead
4. 6 they might be judged according to men
Rev. 6. 10 dost thou not judge and avenge our blood
11. 18 that they should be judged, and that thou
16. 5 and shalt be, because thou hast judged
18. 8 strong (is) the Lord God who judgeth her
19. 2 he hath judged the great whore, which
19. 11 in righteousness he doth judge and make
20. 12 the dead were judged out of those things
20. 13 they were judged every man according to

9. *Place of judgment,* κριτήριον *kritērion.*
1 Co. 6. 2 unworthy to judge the smallest matters?

JUDGE, to be a —
To judge, act as a magistrate, judge, שָׁפַט *shaphat.*
Gen. 19. 9 came in to sojourn, and he will..be a ju.

JUDGED, to be —
1. *Judgment,* מִשְׁפָּט *mishpat.*
Eze. 16. 38 as women that..shed blood are judged

2. *To be judged,* שָׁפַט *shaphat,* 2.
Psa. 9. 19 Arise..let the heathen be judged in thy
37. 33 LORD will not..condemn him when he is j.
109. 7 When he shall be judged, let him be con.

3. *To fall,* נָפַל *naphal,* 3a [? A.V. *palal,* 2].
Eze. 28. 23 the wounded shall be judged in the midst

JUDGES —
1. *Honourable judges,* אֲדַרְגָּזְרַיָּא *adargazeraiya.*
Dan. 3. 2, 3 the captains, the judges, the treasurers

2. *Gods, those representing God,* אֱלֹהִים *elohim.*
Exod 21. 6 his master shall bring him unto the judges
22. 8 master..shall be brought unto the judges
22. 9 come before the judges..whom the judges

3. *To judge, act as a magistrate,* שָׁפַט *shaphat,* 3a.
Job 9. 15 (but) I would make supplication to my j.

JUDGMENT —
1. *Judgment,* דִּין *dun* [V.L. דִּין].
Job 19. 29 of the sword, that ye may know..a judg.

2. *Judgment,* דִּין *din.*
Ezra 7. 26 let judgment be executed speedily upon
Esth. 1. 13 manner toward all that knew law and ju.
Job 35. 14 judgment (is) before him; therefore trust
36. 17 thou hast fulfilled the judgment of the
36. 17 judgment and justice take hold (on thee)
Psa. 76. 8 Thou didst cause judgment to be heard
Prov 20. 8 A king that sitteth in the throne of judg.
31. 5 pervert the judgment of any of the afflic.
Isa. 10. 2 To turn aside the needy from judgment
Dan. 4. 37 whose works (are) truth, and his ways ju.
7. 10 judgment was set, and the books were
7. 22 judgment was given to the saints of the
7. 26 the judgment shall sit, and they shall

3. *Taste,* טְעֵם *taam.*
Psa. 119. 66 Teach me good judgment and knowledge

4. *Place of judgment,* מִדִּין *middin* [R.V. plur. of *mad*].
Judg. 5. 10 ye that sit in judgment, and walk by the

5. *Judgment,* מִשְׁפָּט *mishpat.*
Gen. 18. 19 they shall..do justice and judgment; that
Exod 21. 1 judgments which thou shalt set before
21. 31 according to this judgment shall it be
23. 6 Thou shalt not wrest the judgment of thy
24. 3 Moses came and told..all the judgments
28. 15 thou shalt make the breastplate of judg.
28. 29 the breastplate of judgment upon his
28. 30 thou shalt put in the breastplate of judg.
28. 30 shall bear the judgment of the children
Lev. 18. 4 Ye shall do my judgments, and keep mine
18. 5, 26 Ye shall..keep my statutes, and my j.
19. 15, 35 Ye shall do no unrighteousness in jud.
19. 37 all my statutes, and all my judgments
20. 22 Ye shall..keep all my statutes..all my ju.
25. 18 ye shall do my statutes, and keep my ju.
26. 15 or if your soul abhor my judgments, so
26. 43 because they despised my judgments, and
26. 46 These (are) the statutes and judgments
Num 27. 11 it shall be unto..Israel a statute of judg.
27. 21 after the judgment of Urim before the L.
35. 12 stand before the congregation in judgment
35. 24 shall judge..according to these judgments
35. 29 shall be for a statute of judgment unto you
36. 13 commandments and the judgments which
Deut. 1. 17 Ye shall not respect persons in judgment
1. 17 the judgment (is) God's: and the cause
4. 1 hearken..unto the statutes and unto..j.
4. 5 I have taught you statutes and judgments
4. 8 what nation..that hath statutes and jud.
4. 14 to teach you statutes and judgments, that
4. 45 judgments, which Moses spake unto the
5. 1 Hear, O Israel, the statutes and judgments
5. 31 the judgments, which thou shalt teach
6. 1, 20 statutes, and the judgments, which
7. 11 statutes, and the judgments, which I
7. 12 if ye hearken to these judgments, and
8. 11 his commandments, and his judgments
10. 18 He doth execute the judgment of the fat.
11. 1 his judgments, and his commandments
11. 32 to do all the statutes and judgments which
12. 1 These (are) the statutes and judgments
16. 18 they shall judge the people with just jud.
16. 19 Thou shalt not wrest judgment; thou
17. 8 arise a matter too hard for thee in judg.
17. 9 they shall show thee the sentence of jud.
17. 11 to the judgment which they shall tell thee
24. 17 Thou shalt not pervert the judgment of
25. 1 a controversy..and they come unto judg.
26. 16 to do these statutes and judgments: thou
26. 17 his commandments, and his judgments
27. 19 Cursed (be) he that perverteth the judg.
30. 16 to keep..his statutes, and his judgments
32. 4 his ways (are) judgment: a God of truth
32. 41 and mine hand take hold on judgment
33. 10 They shall teach Jacob thy judgments
33. 21 justice of the LORD, and his judgments
Josh 20. 6 stand before the congregation for judg.
Judg. 4. 5 children of Israel came up to her for jud.
1 Sa. 8. 3 and took bribes, and perverted judgment
2 Sa. 8. 15 David executed judgment and justice unto
15. 2 when any man..came to the king for jud.
15. 6 to all Israel that came to the king for ju.
22. 23 For all his judgments (were) before me
1 Ki. 2. 3 his commandments, and his judgments
3. 11 asked..understanding to discern judgm.
3. 28 all Israel heard of the judgment which
3. 28 the wisdom of God (was) in him to do j.
6. 12 if thou wilt..execute my judgments, and
7. 7 he made a porch..the porch of judgment
8. 58 his statutes, and his judgments, which
9. 4 wilt keep my statutes and my judgments
10. 9 made he thee king, to do judgment and
11. 33 (to keep) my statutes and my judgments
20. 40 So (shall) thy judgment (be); thyself hast
2 Ki. 25. 6 the king..and they gave judgment upon
1 Ch. 16. 12 his wonders, and the judgments of his
16. 14 our God; his judgments (are) in all the
18. 14 David reigned..and executed judgment
22. 13 to fulfil the statutes and judgments which
28. 7 to do my commandments and my judgm.
2 Ch. 7. 17 shalt observe my statutes and my judgm.
9. 8 made he thee king over them, to do jud.
19. 6 for the LORD, who (is) with you in the ju.
19. 8 for the judgment of the LORD, and for con.
19. 10 law and commandment, statutes and jud.
Ezra 7. 10 to teach in Israel statutes and judgments
Neh. 1. 7 nor the statutes, nor the judgments, which

Neh. 9. 13 right judgments, and true laws, good st.
9. 29 but sinned against thy judgments, which
10. 29 and do all..his judgments and his statutes
Job 8. 3 Doth God pervert judgment? or doth the
9. 19 and if of judgment, who shall set me a
9. 32 (and) we should come together in judgm.
14. 3 and bringest me into judgment with thee?
19. 7 I am not heard: I cry aloud, but..no ju.
22. 4 reprove..will he enter with thee into ju.?
27. 2 God liveth, (who) hath taken away my ju.
29. 14 my judgment (was) as a robe and a diad.
32. 9 neither do the aged understand judgment
34. 4 Let us choose to us judgment: let us kn.
34. 5 Job hath said..God hath taken away my j.
34. 12 neither will the Almighty pervert judgm.
34. 23 that he should enter into judgment with
37. 23 excellent in power, and in judgment, and
40. 8 Wilt thou also disannul my judgment?
Psa. 1. 5 the ungodly shall not stand in the judgm.
7. 6 awake for me (to) the judgment..thou
9. 7 he hath prepared his throne for judgment
9. 16 The LORD is known (by) the judgment
10. 5 thy judgments (are)..above out of his sight
18. 22 all his judgments (were) before me, and
19. 9 the judgments of the LORD (are) true
25. 9 The meek will he guide in judgment
33. 5 He loveth righteousness and judgment
35. 23 Stir up thyself, and awake to my judgment
36. 6 thy judgments (are) a great deep: O LORD
37. 6 bring forth..thy judgment as the noon
37. 28 the LORD loveth judgment, and forsaketh
37. 30 wisdom, and his tongue talketh of judg.
48. 11 let..Judah be glad, because of thy judg.
72. 1 Give the king thy judgments, O God, and
72. 2 He shall judge..thy poor with judgment
76. 9 When God arose to judgment, to save all
89. 14 Justice and judgment (are) the habitation
89. 30 If his children..walk not in my judgments
94. 15 But judgment shall return unto righteou.
97. 2 righteousness and judgment (are) the hab.
97. 8 rejoiced because of thy judgments, O LORD
99. 4 The king's strength also loveth judgment
99. 4 thou executest judgment and righteous.
101. 1 I will sing of mercy and judgment: unto
103. 6 The LORD executeth..judgment for all that
105. 5 his wonders, and the judgments of his
105. 7 our God: his judgments (are) in all the earth
106. 3 Blessed (are) they that keep judgment
111. 7 The works of his hands (are) verity and j.
119. 7 when I shall have learned thy righteous j.
119. 13 With my lips have I declared all the jud.
119. 20 longing..unto thy judgments at all times
119. 30 I have chosen..thy judgments have I laid
119. 39 Turn away..for thy judgments (are) good
119. 43 take not..for I have hoped in thy judgm.
119. 52 I remembered thy judgments of old, O Lo.
119. 62 I will rise..because of thy righteous jud.
119. 75 I know, O LORD, thy judgments (are) right
119. 84 when wilt thou execute judgment on them
119. 102 I have not departed from thy judgments
119. 106 that I will keep thy righteous judgments
119. 108 Accept..O LORD, and teach me thy jud.
119. 120 trembleth..and I am afraid of thy judg.
119. 121 I have done judgment and justice: leave
119. 137 Righteous..and upright (are) thy judgm.
119. 149, 156 quicken me according to thy judg.
119. 160 and every one of thy righteous judgments
119. 164 praise..because of thy righteous judgm.
119. 175 Let my soul live..let thy judgments help
122. 5 there are set thrones of judgment, the
143. 2 enter not into judgment with thy servant
146. 7 Which executeth judgment for the oppr.
147. 19 He showeth..his judgments unto Israel
147. 20 his judgments, they have not known them
149. 9 To execute upon them the judgment wri.
Prov. 1. 3 To receive the instruction of..judgment
2. 8 He keepeth the paths of judgment, and
2. 9 righteousness, and judgment, and equity
8. 20 I lead..in the midst of the paths of jud.
13. 23 there is (that is) destroyed for want of j.
16. 10 his mouth transgresseth not in judgment
17. 23 taketh a gift..to pervert the ways of judg.
18. 5 not good..to overthrow the righteous in j.
19. 28 An ungodly witness scorneth judgment
21. 3 To do justice and judgment (is) more acc.
21. 7 destroy..because they refuse to do judg.
21. 15 (It is) joy to the just to do judgment: but
24. 23 to have respect of persons in judgment
28. 5 Evil men understand not judgment: but
29. 4 The king by judgment establisheth the
29. 26 (every) man's judgment (cometh) from the
Eccl. 3. 16 I saw under the sun the place of judgment
5. 8 violent perverting of judgment and justice
8. 5 man's heart discerneth both time and ju.
8. 6 to every purpose there is time and judg.
11. 9 for all..God will bring thee into judgment
12. 14 God shall bring every work into judgment
Isa. 1. 17 Learn to do well; seek judgment, relieve
1. 21 it was full of judgment; righteousness
1. 27 Zion shall be redeemed with judgment
3. 14 The LORD will enter into judgment with
4. 4 by the spirit of judgment, and by the sp.
5. 7 he looked for judgment, but behold opp.
5. 16 LORD of hosts shall be exalted in judgment
9. 7 to establish it with judgment and with
16. 5 judging, and seeking judgment, and hast.
26. 8 Yea, in the way of thy judgments, O LORD
26. 9 for when thy judgments (are) in the earth
28. 6 of judgment to him that sitteth in judg.
28. 17 Judgment also will I lay to the line, and
30. 18 for the LORD (is) a God of judgment
32. 1 Behold..princes shall rule in judgment

Isa. 32. 16 judgment shall dwell in the wilderness
33. 5 he hath filled Zion with judgment and.
34. 5 upon the people of my curse, to judgment
40. 14 taught him in the path of judgment, and
40. 27 my judgment is passed over from my God?
41. 1 speak: let us come near together to judg.
42. 1 he shall bring forth judgment to the Gen.
42. 3 he shall bring forth judgment unto truth
42. 4 till he have set judgment in the earth
49. 4 my judgment (is) with the LORD, and my
51. 4 I will make my judgment to rest for a
53. 8 He was taken from prison and from jud.
54. 17 tongue (that) shall rise against thee in ju.
56. 1 Keep ye judgment, and do justice: for
59. 8 and (there is) no judgment in their goings
59. 9 Therefore is judgment far from us, neith.
59. 11 we look for judgment, but (there is) none
59. 14 judgment is turned away backward, and
59. 15 it displeased him that (there was) no judg.
61. 8 I the LORD love judgment, I hate robbery
Jer. 1. 16 I will utter my judgments against them
4. 2 The LORD liveth, in truth, in judgment
5. 1 if there be..that executeth judgment
5. 4 they know not..the judgment of their G.
5. 5 they have known..the judgment of their
7. 5 if ye throughly execute judgment between
8. 7 my people know not the judgment of the
9. 24 which exercise loving kindness, judgment
10. 24 O LORD, correct me, but with judgment
12. 1 let me talk with thee of (thy) judgments
21. 12 Execute judgment in the morning, and
22. 3 Execute ye judgment and righteousness
22. 15 Did not thy father..do judgment and ju.
23. 5 execute judgment and justice in the ear.
33. 15 execute judgment and righteousness in
39. 5 Hamath, where he gave judgment upon
48. 21 judgment is come upon the plain country
48. 47 bring again..Thus far (is) the judgment
49. 12 they whose judgment (was) not to drink
51. 9 her judgment reacheth unto heaven, and
52. 9 Hamath; where he gave judgment upon
Eze. 5. 6 she hath changed my judgments into wi.
5. 6 they have refused my judgments and my
5. 7 neither have kept my judgments, neither
5. 7 have done according to the judgments of
5. 8 will execute judgments in the midst of
11. 12 neither executed my judgments, but have
18. 8 hath executed true judgment between
18. 9 Hath walked..and hath kept my judgm.
18. 17 hath executed my judgments, hath walk.
20. 11 and showed them my judgments, which
20. 13 and they despised my judgments, which
20. 16 Because they despised my judgments
20. 18 neither observe their judgments, nor de.
20. 19 and keep my judgments, and do them
20. 21 neither kept my judgments to do them
20. 24 they had not executed my judgments, but
20. 25 judgments whereby they should not live
23. 24 I will set judgment before them, and they
23. 24 shall judge thee according to their judg.
34. 16 I will destroy..I will feed them with ju.
36. 27 and ye shall keep my judgments, and do
37. 24 they shall also walk in my judgments
39. 21 all the heathen shall see my judgment
44. 24 they shall judge it according to my judg.
45. 9 execute judgment and justice, take away
Dan. 9. 5 from thy precepts and from thy judgments
Hos. 2. 19 I will betroth thee unto me..in judgm.
5. 1 judgment (is) toward you, because ye ha.
5. 11 Ephraim (is) oppressed..broken in judg.
6. 5 thy judgments (are as) the light (that)
10. 4 judgment springeth up as hemlock in the
12. 6 keep mercy and judgment, and wait on
Amos 5. 7 Ye who turn judgment to wormwood, and
5. 15 establish judgment in the gate: it may
5. 24 let judgment run down as waters, and
6. 12 ye have turned judgment into gall, and
Mic. 3. 1 Hear..(Is it) not for you to know judgme.?
3. 8 I am full..of judgment, and of might, to
3. 9 that abhor judgment, and pervert all equi.
Hab. 1. 4 judgment doth never go forth..wrong j.
1. 7 their judgment and their dignity shall
1. 12 LORD, thou hast ordained them for judg.
Zeph. 2. 3 ye meek..which have wrought his judg.
3. 5 every morning doth he bring his judgment
3. 15 LORD hath taken away thy judgments, he
Zech. 7. 9 Execute true judgment, and show mercy
8. 16 execute the judgment of truth and peace
Mal. 2. 17 When ye say..Where (is) the God of ju.?
3. 5 I will come near to you to judgment; and
4. 4 Remember ye..the statutes and judgments

6. *Judgment,* פְּלִילָה *pelilah.*
Isa. 16. 3 Take counsel, execute judgment; make

7. *Judicial,* פְּלִילִי *pelili.*
Isa. 28. 7 they err in vision, they stumble (in) judg.

8. *Judgment,* שְׁפוֹט *shephot.*
2 Ch. 20. 9 sword, judgment, or pestilence, or famine
Eze. 23. 10 for they had executed judgment upon her

9. *To judge, act as a magistrate,* שָׁפַט *shaphat.*
Eze. 44. 24 in controversy they shall stand in judg.

10. *Word, matter,* דָּבָר *dabar.*
2 Ch. 19. 6 for the LORD, who (is) with you in the ju.

11. *Perception, sense, intelligence,* αἴσθησις *aisthēsis.*
Phil. 1. 9 more and more in knowledge and..judg.

12. *Mind, opinion, sentence,* γνώμη *gnōmē.*
1 Co. 1. 10 in the same mind and in the same judg.
7. 25 I give my judgment, as one that hath
7. 40 she is happier if she so abide, after my j.

13. *A judicial sentence,* δικαίωμα *dikaiōma.*
Rom. 1. 32 Who knowing the judgment of God, that
Rev. 15. 4 O Lord..thy judgments are made manifest

14. *Justice, vengeance,* δίκη *dikē.*
Acts 25. 15 desiring (to have) [judgment] against him

15. *Day,* ἡμέρα *hēmera.*
1 Co. 4. 3 should be judged of you, or of man's jud.

16. *Judgment,* κρίμα *krima.*
Matt. 7. 2 what judgment ye judge, ye shall be j.
John 9. 39 For judgment I am come into this world
Acts 24. 25 as he reasoned of..temperance, and jud.
Rom. 2. 2 we are sure that the judgment of God is
2. 3 that thou shalt escape the judgment of G.?
5. 16 judgment (was) by one to condemnation
11. 33 how unsearchable (are) his judgments
Gal. 5. 10 he that troubleth you shall bear his jud.
Heb. 6. 2 Of the doctrine of baptisms..and of..jud.
1 Pe. 4. 17 judgment must begin at the house of God
2 Pe. 2. 3 whose judgment now of a long time
Rev. 17. 1 the judgment of the great whore that
20. 4 and judgment was given unto them: and

17. *Judgment,* κρίσις *krisis.*
Matt. 5. 21, 22 shall be in danger of the judgment
10. 15 shall be more tolerable..in the day of ju.
11. 22, 24 be more tolerable..at the day of jud.
12. 18 and he shall show judgment to the Gen.
12. 20 till he send forth judgment unto victory
12. 36 shall give account thereof in the day of j.
12. 41 men of Nineveh shall rise in judgment
12. 42 queen of the south shall rise up in the j.
23. 23 weightier (matters) of the law, judgment
Mark 6. 11 [shall be more tolerable..in the day of j.]
Luke 10. 14 more tolerable for Tyre and Sidon at..ju.
11. 31 queen of the south shall rise up in the judg.
11. 32 men of Nineve shall rise up in the judg.
11. 42 pass over judgment and the love of God
John 5. 22 hath committed all judgment unto the Son
5. 27 hath given him authority to execute jud.
5. 30 my judgment is just; because I seek not
7. 24 Judge not..but judge righteous judgment
8. 16 if I judge, my judgment is true; for I am
12. 31 Now is the judgment of this world: now
16. 8 and of righteousness, and of judgment
16. 11 Of judgment, because the prince of this
Acts 8. 33 his humiliation his judgment was taken
2 Th. 1. 5 a manifest token of the righteous judgment
1 Ti. 5. 24 are open beforehand, going before to ju.
Heb. 9. 27 once to die, but after this the judgment
10. 27 a certain fearful looking for of judgment
Jas. 2. 13 he shall have judgment without mercy
2. 13 and mercy rejoiceth against judgment
2 Pe. 2. 4 delivered..to be reserved unto judgment
2. 9 reserve the unjust unto the day of judg.
3. 7 reserved unto fire against the day of jud
1 Jo. 4. 17 we may have boldness in the day of judg.
Jude 6 reserved..unto the judgment of the great
15 To execute judgment upon all, and to con.
Rev. 14. 7 Fear..for the hour of his judgment is come
16. 7 Lord..true and righteous (are) thy judg.
18. 10 Alas..in one hour is thy judgment come
19. 2 For true and righteous (are) his judgments

18. *Place of judgment,* κριτήριον *kritērion.*
1 Co. 6. 4 If then ye have judgments of things per.

JUDGMENT hall, hall of judgment —
Praetor's hall, πραιτώριον *praitōrion.*
John 18. 28 Then led they Jesus..unto the hall of ju.
18. 28 they..went not into the judgment hall
18. 33 Pilate entered into the judgment hall
19. 9 And went again into the judgment hall
Acts 23. 35 commanded him to be kept in H.'s judg. h.

JUDGMENT seat —
1. *Foot print, tribunal,* βῆμα *bēma.*
Matt 27. 19 When he was set down on the judgment s.
John 19. 13 sat down in the judgment seat in a place
Acts 18. 12 the Jews..brought him to the judgment s.
18. 16 he drave them from the judgment seat
18. 17 and beat (him) before the judgment seat
25. 6 next day, sitting on the judgment seat
25. 10 I stand at Cesar's judgment seat, where I
25. 17 on the morrow I sat on the judgment seat
Rom 14. 10 stand before the judgment seat of Christ
2 Co. 5. 10 must all appear before the judgment seat

2. *Place of judgment,* κριτήριον *kritērion.*
Jas. 2. 6 and draw you before the judgment seats?

JUDGMENT, righteous —
Righteous judgment, δικαιοκρισία *dikaiokrisia.*
Rom. 2. 5 revelation of the righteous judgment of G.

JUDGMENT, to do, execute, or minister —
1. *To judge, plead, strive, decide,* דִּין *din.*
Psa. 9. 8 he shall minister judgment to the people

2. *To judge, adjudge, execute judgment,* פָּלַל *palal,* 3.
Psa. 106. 30 executed judgment: and (so) the plague

3. *To visit, inspect,* פָּקַד *paqad.*
Jer. 51. 47, 52 that I will do judgment upon the gr.

4. *To be judged, do judgment,* שָׁפַט *shaphat,* 2.
2 Ch. 22. 8 when Jehu was executing judgment upon

JUDGMENTS, (judgment) —
Judgments, magisterial decisions, שְׁפָטִים *shephatim.*
Exod. 6. 6 with a stretched out arm..with great ju.
7. 4 out of the land of Egypt by great judgm.

Exod12. 12 against all the gods..I will execute judg.
Num 33. 4 upon their gods..the LORD executed judg.
2 Ch.24. 24 So they executed judgment against Joash
Prov 19. 29 Judgments are prepared for scorners, and
Eze. 5. 10 I will execute judgments in thee, and the
5. 15 when I shall execute judgments in thee
11. 9 I will bring..and will execute judgments
14. 21 when I send my four sore judgments upon
16. 41 execute judgments upon thee in the sight
25. 11 I will execute judgments upon Moab; and
28. 22 when I shall have executed judgments in
28. 26 when I have executed judgments upon all
30. 14 will set fire..and will execute judgments
30. 19 Thus will I execute judgments in Egypt

JU'-DITH, יְהוּדִית *Jewess.*
A daughter of Beeri a Hittite, and wife of Esau. B.C. 1796.
Gen. 26. 34 Esau..took to wife J. the daughter of B.

JUICE —
Juice, עָסִיס *asis.*
Song 8. 2 spiced wine of the juice of my pomegran.

JU-LI-A, Ἰουλία.
A female believer in Rome to whom Paul sent a salutation.
Rom 16. 15 Salute Philologus, and J., Nereus, and his

JU-LI-US, Ἰούλιος.
A centurion in whose charge Paul was sent to Rome.
Acts 27. 1 delivered Paul..unto (one) named J., a
27. 3 J. courteously entreated Paul, and gave

JUMP, to —
To skip, dance, רָקַד *raqad,* 3.
Nah. 3. 2 prancing horses, and of the jumping cha.

JU-NI-A, Ἰουνίας.
This ought to be Junias: a believer and kinsman of Paul.
Rom 16. 7 Salute Andronicus and J., my kinsmen

JUNIPER (tree) —
Juniper, broom, רֹתֶם *rothem.*
1 Ki.19. 4 came and sat down under a juniper tree
19. 5 as he lay and slept under a juniper tree
Job 30. 4 Who cut up..juniper roots (for) their meat
Psa.120. 4 arrows of the mighty, with coals of juni.

JU-PI-TER, Ζεύς (*i.e. Zeus-pater*), *father Jove.*
The chief Greek and Roman deity.
Acts 14. 12 they called Barnabas, J.; and Paul, Mer.
14. 13 Then the priest of J...brought oxen and

JUPITER, which fell down from —
What is fallen from Zeus, διοπετής *diopetēs.*
Acts 19. 35 of the (image) which fell down from Jup.?

JURISDICTION —
Authority, privilege, ἐξουσία *exousia.*
Luke 23. 7 knew that he belonged unto Herod's jur.

JU-SHAB HE'-SED, יוּשַׁב חֶסֶד *kindness is returned.*
A son of Zerubbabel, of the family of David. B.C. 500.
1 Ch. 3. 20 Ohel, and Berechiah, and Hasadiah, J.

JUST —
1. *Right, upright, straight.* יָשָׁר *yashar.*
Prov.29. 10 The bloodthirsty hate..but the just seek

2. *Judgment,* מִשְׁפָּט *mishpat.*
Prov 16. 11 A just weight and balance (are) the LORD'S

3. *Right, righteous, just, rigid,* צַדִּיק *tsaddiq.*
Gen. 6. 9 Noah was a just man (and) perfect in his
Deut.32. 4 and without iniquity, just and right (is) he
2 Sa. 23. 3 He that ruleth over men (must be) just, rul.
Neh. 9. 33 thou (art) just in all that is brought upon
Job 12. 4 the just upright (man is) laughed to scorn
27. 17 He may prepare (it), but the just shall put
34. 17 wilt thou condemn him that is most just?
Psa. 7. 9 establish the just: for the righteous God
37. 12 The wicked plotteth against the just, and
Prov. 3. 33 but he blesseth the habitation of the just
4. 18 the path of the just (is) as the shining light
9. 9 teach a just (man), and he will increase
10. 6 Blessings (are) upon the head of the just
10. 7 The memory of the just (is) blessed: but
10. 20 The tongue of the just (is as) choice silver
10. 31 The mouth of the just bringeth forth wis.
11. 9 through knowledge shall the just be del.
12 13 lips: but the just shall come out of trouble
12. 21 There shall no evil happen to the just
13. 22 wealth of the sinner (is) laid up for the just
17. 15 and he that condemneth the just, even
17. 26 Also to punish the just (is) not good, (nor)
18. 17 first in his own cause (seemeth) just; but
20. 7 The just (man) walketh in his integrity
21. 15 (It is) joy to the just to do judgment: but
24. 16 For a just (man) falleth seven times, and
29. 27 unjust man (is) an abomination to the j.
Eccl. 7. 15 there is a just (man) that perisheth in his
7. 20 not a just man upon earth, that doeth go.
8. 14 there be just (men), unto whom it happen.
Isa. 26. 7 The way of the just..the path of the just
29. 21 turn aside the just for a thing of nought
45. 21 a just God and a Saviour..none beside me
Lam. 4. 13 that have shed the blood of the just in the
Eze. 18. 5 if a man be just, and do that which is law.
18. 9 he (is) just, he shall surely live, saith the
Hos. 14. 9 the just shall walk in them: but the tra.
Amos 5. 12 they afflict the just, they take a bribe, and
Hab. 2. 4 not upright..but the just shall live by his
Zeph. 3. 5 The just LORD (is) in the midst thereof
Zech. 9. 9 he (is) just, and having salvation; lowly

4. *Righteousness,* צֶדֶק *tsedeq.*
Lev. 19 36 Just balances, just weights, a just ephah
19. 36 a just hin, shall ye have: I (am) the LORD
Deut16. 18 they shall judge the people with just jud.
16. 20 That which is altogether just shalt thou
25. 15 thou shalt have a perfect and just weight
25. 15 a perfect and just measure shalt thou have
Eze. 45. 10 just balances, and a just ephah, and a just

5. *Finished, perfect, whole,* שָׁלֵם *shalem.*
Prov. 11. 1 the LORD: but a just weight (is) his delight

6. *Just, righteous,* δίκαιος *dikaios.*
Matt. 1. 19 Joseph her husband, being a just (man)
5. 45 sendeth rain on the just and on the unjust
13. 49 and sever the wicked from among the just
27. 19 Have thou nothing to do with that just
27. 24 I am innocent of the blood of this [just]
Mark 6. 20 knowing that he was a just man and an
Luke 1. 17 the disobedient to the wisdom of the just
2. 25 the same man (was) just and devout, wait.
14. 14 recompensed at the resurrection of the j.
15. 7 more than over ninety and nine just per.
20. 20 which should feign themselves just men
23. 50 Joseph a counsellor..a good man, and a j.
John 5. 30 my judgment is just; because I seek not
Acts 3. 14 ye denied the Holy One and the Just, and
7. 52 showed before of the coming of the Just O.
10. 22 Cornelius the centurion, a just man, and
22. 14 see that Just One, and shouldest hear the
24. 15 of the dead, both of the just and unjust
Rom. 1. 17 as it is written, The just shall live by faith
2. 13 For not the hearers of the law (are) just
3. 26 that he might be just, and the justifier of
7. 12 the commandment holy, and just, and
Gal. 3. 11 evident, for, The just shall live by faith
Phil. 4. 8 whatsoever things (are) just, whatsoever
Col. 4. 1 give..that which is just and equal; know.
Titus 1. 8 a lover of good men..just, holy, temper.
Heb. 10. 38 Now the just shall live by faith: but if
12. 23 and to the spirits of just men made perf.
Jas. 5. 6 Ye have condemned (and) killed the just
1 Pe. 3. 18 suffered for sins, the just for the unjust
2 Pe. 2. 7 delivered just Lot, vexed with the filthy
1 Jo. 1. 9 he is faithful and just to forgive us (our)
Rev. 15. 3 just and true (are) thy ways, thou King

7. *In justice, according to justice,* ἔνδικος *endikos.*
Rom. 3. 8 good may come? whose damnation is just
Heb. 2. 2 disobedience received a just recompence

JUST, to be —
To be right, righteous, just, צָדַק *tsadaq.*
Job 4. 17 Shall mortal man be more just than God?
9. 2 but how should man be just with God?
33. 12 Behold, (in) this thou art not just: I will

JUST, that which is altogether —
Right, rightness, צֶדֶק *tsedeq.*
Deut16. 20 That which is altogether just shalt thou

JUSTICE —
1. *Judgment,* מִשְׁפָּט *mishpat.*
Job 36. 17 judgment and justice take hold (on thee)

2. *Right, rightness,* צֶדֶק *tsedeq.*
Job 8. 3 or doth the Almighty pervert justice?
Psa. 89. 14 Justice and judgment (are) the habitation
119. 121 I have done judgment and justice: leave
Prov. 1. 3 To receive the instruction of wisdom, ju.
8. 15 By me kings reign, and princes decree ju.
Eccl. 5. 8 violent perverting of judgment and just.
Isa. 58. 2 they ask of me the ordinances of justice
59. 4 None calleth for justice, nor..pleadeth
Jer. 31. 23 O habitation of justice..mountain of ho.
50. 7 against the LORD, the habitation of just.

3. *Right, rightness,* צְדָקָה *tsedaqah.*
Gen. 18. 19 to do justice and judgment; that the Lo.
Deut33. 21 he executed the justice of the LORD, and
2 Sa. 8. 15 judgment and justice unto all his people
1 Ki. 10. 9 made he thee king, to do judgment and j.
1 Ch.18. 14 executed judgment and justice among all
2 Ch. 9. 8 king over them, to do judgment and jus.
Job 37. 23 and in judgment, and in plenty of justice
Prov21. 3 To do justice and judgment (is) more acc.
Isa. 9. 7 with justice from henceforth even for ever
56. 1 Keep ye judgment, and do justice: for
59. 9 neither doth justice overtake us: we wait
59. 14 justice standeth afar off: for truth is fal.
Jer. 22. 15 and drink, and do judgment and justice
23. 5 execute judgment and justice in the earth
Eze. 45. 9 execute judgment and justice, take away

JUSTICE, to do —
To declare right or just, צָדַק *tsadaq,* 5.
2 Sa. 15. 4 come unto me, and I would do him justice
Psa. 82. 3 Defend..do justice to the afflicted and

JUSTIFICATION —
1. *Judicial sentence, declaration of right,* δικαίωμα.
Rom. 5. 16 the free gift (is) of many offences unto j.

2. *A setting right,* δικαίωσις *dikaiōsis.*
Rom. 4. 25 and was raised again for our justification
5. 18 (came) upon all men unto justification of

JUSTIFIED, to be —
To be or become right, צָדַק *tsadaq.*
Job 11. 2 and should a man full of talk be justified?
13. 18 Behold now..I know that I shall be jus.
25. 4 How then can man be justified with God?
Psa. 51. 4 that thou mightest be justified when
Psa.143. 2 in thy sight shall no man living be justi.
Isa. 43. 9 that they may be justified: or let them
43. 26 declare thou, that thou mayest be justified
45. 25 shall all the seed of Israel be justified

JUSTIFIER —
To make or declare right, δικαιόω *dikaioō.*
Rom. 3. 26 the justifier of him which believeth in J.

JUSTIFY, to —
1. *To make or declare right,* צָדַק *tsadaq,* 3.
Job 32. 2 because he justified himself rather than
33. 32 answer me: speak, for I desire to justify
Jer. 3. 11 backsliding Israel hath justified herself
Eze. 16. 51 hast justified thy sisters in all thine abo.
16. 52 shame, in that thou hast justified thy sis

2. *To make or declare right,* צָדַק *tsadaq,* 5.
Exod23. 7 slay..not, for I will not justify the wicked
Deut25. 1 they shall justify the righteous, and con.
1 Ki. 8. 32 justifying the righteous, to give him acc.
2 Ch. 6. 23 and by justifying the righteous, by giving
Job 27. 5 God forbid that I should justify you: till
Prov17. 15 He that justifieth the wicked, and he that
Isa. 5. 23 Which justify the wicked for reward, and
50. 8 (He is) near that justifieth me; who will
53. 11 shall my righteous servant justify many

3. *To make or declare right,* δικαιόω *dikaioō.*
Matt 11. 19 But wisdom is justified of her children
12. 37 by thy words thou shalt be justified, and
Luke 7. 29 the publicans, justified God, being bapti.
7. 35 But wisdom is justified of all her children
10. 29 he, willing to justify himself, said unto J.
16. 15 Ye are they which justify yourselves bef.
18. 14 this man went down to his house justified
Acts 13. 39 by him all that believe are justified from
13. 39 from which ye could not be justified by
Rom. 2. 13 but the doers of the law shall be justified
3. 4 That thou mightest be justified in thy s.
3. 20 there shall no flesh be justified in his si.
3. 24 Being justified freely by his grace through
3. 28 we conclude that a man is justified by fa.
3. 30 Seeing (it is) one God which shall justify
4. 2 if Abraham were justified by works, he
4. 5 believeth on him that justifieth the ung.
5. 1 being justified by faith, we have peace
5. 9 being now justified by his blood, we shall
8. 30 whom he called, them he also justified
8. 30 whom he justified, them he also glorified
8. 33 charge of God's elect? (It is) God that ju.
1 Co. 4. 4 am I not hereby justified: but he that j.
6. 11 are justified in the name of the Lord Jesus
Gal. 2. 16 Knowing that a man is not justified by
2. 16 that we might be justified by the faith of
2. 16 by the works of the law shall no flesh be j.
2. 17 if, while we seek to be justified by Christ
3. 8 God would justify the heathen through f.
3. 11 that no man is justified by the law in the
3. 24 schoolmaster..that we might be justified
5. 4 whosoever of you are justified by the law
1 Ti. 3. 16 justified in the spirit, seen of angels, pre.
Titus 3. 7 being justified by his grace, we should be
Jas. 2. 21 Was not Abraham our father justified by
2. 24 how that by works a man is justified, and
2. 25 was not Rahab the harlot justified by wo.

JUSTIFY self, to —
To be or become right, צָדַק *tsadaq.*
Job 9. 20 If I justify myself, mine own mouth shall

JUSTLE one against another, to —
To run to and fro, שָׁקַק *shaqaq,* 7a.
Nah. 2. 4 they shall justle one against another in

JUSTLY —
1. *Judgment,* מִשְׁפָּט *mishpat.*
Mic. 6. 8 but to do justly, and to love mercy, and

2. *Justly,* δικαίως *dikaiōs.*
Luke23. 41 we indeed justly; for we receive the due
1 Th. 2. 10 how holily and justly and unblameably

JUS'-TUS, Ἰοῦστος.
1. A surname of Joseph or Barsabas, a disciple nominated with Matthias to succeed Judas Iscariot.
Acts 1. 23 And they appointed two..J., and Matthias

2. A believer in Corinth with whom Paul lodged.
Acts 18. 7 entered..a certain (man's) house, named J.

3. A believing disciple in Rome from whom Paul sends a salutation to the church at Colosse.
Col. 4. 11 Jesus, which is called J., who are of the

JUT'-TAH, יֻטָּה, יוּטָּה.
A Levitical city in Judah; now called *Jutta.* See *Jotbah.*
Josh 15. 55 Maon, Carmel, and Ziph, and J.
21. 16 Ain with her suburbs, and J. with her su.

K

KAB-ZE'-EL, קַבְצְאֵל *God gathers.*
A city in the S. E. of Judah, now called *Ain-el-arus.* See also *Jekabzeel.*
Josh 15. 21 uttermost cities..southward were K., and
2 Sa. 23. 20 Benaiah..the son of a valiant man, of K.
1 Ch.11. 22 Benaiah..the son of a valiant man of K.

KA-DESH, קָדֵשׁ *holy.*
The same as *En-mishpat* and *Kadesh-barnea;* a place in the wilderness of Paran, between Shur and Edom, or in the N. W. of the Paran desert, or the wilderness of Zin, forming the S. border of Canaan and the W. one of Edom. From this place Moses sent out spies, and began the conquest of the land. It was afterwards called the *Waters of Meribah.* Four or five hours to the S. E. of Beer-lahai-roi, or Hagar's well, between Bered and Kadesh, is a place *Kudes* with a fountain, said to be eleven days from Sinai, Deut. 1. 2.

Gen. 14. 7 came to En-mishpat, which (is) K., and
16. 14 Beer-lahai-roi; behold, (it is) between K.
20. 1 Abraham..dwelled between K. and Shur
Num13. 26 Came..unto the wilderness of Paran, to K.
20. 1 the people abode in K.; and Miriam died
20. 14 Moses sent messengers from K. unto the
20. 16 behold, we (are) in K., a city in the utter.
20. 22 the whole congregation journeyed from K.
27. 14 that (is) the water of Meribah in K. in the
33. 36 pitched in the wilderness..which (is) K.
33. 37 they removed from K., and pitched in m.
Deut. 1. 46 So ye abode in K. many days, according
32. 51 ye trespassed..at the waters of Meribah-K.
Judg11. 16 Israel..walked through..and came to K.
11. 17 he would not..and Israel abode in K.
Psa. 29. 8 The LORD shaketh the wilderness of K.
Eze. 47. 19 to the waters of strife (in) K., the river
48. 28 the waters of strife (in) K...to the river to.

KA-DESH BAR-NE'-EA, קָדֵשׁ בַּרְנֵעַ.
The same as the preceding.

Num32. 8 when I sent them from K. B. to see the
34. 4 border..shall be from the south to K. B.
Deut. 1. 2 eleven days' (journey) from H...unto K.B.
1. 19 when we departed..we came to K. B.
2. 14 the space in which we came from K. B.
9. 23 when the LORD sent you from K. B., saying
Josh.10. 41 Joshua smote them from K.B. even unto
14. 6 Thou knowest..the LORD said..in K.B.
14. 7 when Moses..sent me from K. B. to espy
15. 3 ascended up on the south side unto K. B.

KAD-MI'-EL, קַדְמִיאֵל *God the primeval.*
1. A Levite whose descendants returned from Babylon with Zerubbabel. B.C. 636.

Ezra 2. 40 Levites: the children of Jeshua, and K.
Neh. 7. 43 Levites: the children of Jeshua, of K.

2. One apparently of the tribe of Judah, who assisted in rebuilding the temple. B.C. 545.

Ezra 3. 9 K. and his sons, the sons of Judah, toge.

3. A Levite who led the devotions of the people. B.C. 545.

Neh. 9. 4 Then stood up upon the stairs..K., She.
9. 5 Then the Levites, Jeshua, and K...said
10. 9 the Levites: both Jeshua..Binnui..K.
12. 8 K...(and) Mattaniah..over the thanksgiv.
12. 24 Jeshua the son of K...to praise (and) to

KAD-MON-ITES, קַדְמֹנִי *eastern.*
A Phenician tribe, once a portion of the Hivites, N. of Midian, and E. of the kingdom of Sihon.

Gen. 15. 19 Kenites, and the Kenizzites, and the K.

KAL'-LAI, קַלָּי *Jah is light.*
A priest in the days of Joiakim, grandson of Jozadak. B.C. 500.

Neh. 12. 20 Of Sallai, K.; of Amok, Eber

KAN'-AH, קָנָה *a reed, or possession.*
1. A brook between Ephraim and Manasseh; now called *Wady-Kanah.*

Josh. 16. 8 The border went..unto the river K.; and
17. 9 And the coast descended unto the river K.

2. A city in Asher near Hammon and Rehob, not far from Sidon; now called *Ain Kanah.*

Josh.19. 28 and Hammon, and K., (even) unto great

KA-RE'-AH, CA-RE'-AH, קָרֵחַ *bald.*
The father of Johanan, a captain of the Jews when Gedaliah was made governor by Nebuchadnezzar. B.C. 588.

2 Ki.25. 23 there came..Johanan the son of C., and
Jer. 40. 8 Johanan and Jonathan the sons of K., and
40. 13 Johanan the son of K...came to Gedaliah
40. 15 Johanan the son of K. spake to Gedaliah
40. 16 Gedaliah..said unto Johanan the son of K.
41. 11 When Johanan the son of K..heard of all
41. 13 all the people..saw Johanan the son of K.
41. 14 people..went unto Johanan the son of K.
41. 16 Then took Johanan the son of K., and all
42. 1 and Johanan the son of K...came near
42. 8 Then called he Johanan the son of K., and
43. 2 Then spake..Johanan the son of K., and
43. 4 So Johanan the son of K...obeyed not the
43. 5 But Johanan the son of K...took all the

KAR-KA'-A, קַרְקָעָה, accus. of קַרְקַע, *deep ground.*
A city on the S. border of Judah.

Josh 15. 3 up to Adar, and fetched a compass to K.

KAR'-KOR, קַרְקֹר *deep ground.*
A city in Gad, E. of Jordan; one day's journey from Selah.

Judg. 8. 10 Zeba and Zalmunna (were) in K., and their

KAR'-TAH, קַרְתָּה *city.*
A city of the Levites in Zebulun.

Josh 21. 34 Jokneam with her suburbs, and K. with

KAR'-TAN, קַרְתָּן *double city.*
A Levitical city in Naphtali; called *Kirjathaim* in 1 Ch. 6. 76; now called *Kerkeah.*

Josh 21. 32 and K. with her suburbs; three cities

KAT'-TATH, קַטָּת *little.*
A city in Zebulun, near Nahallal; called *Kitron* in Judg. 1. 30. Now called *Sefurieh.*

Josh 19. 15 K., and Nahallal, and Shimron, and Ida.

KE'-DAR, קֵדָר *powerful.*
1. One of the sons of Ishmael, the son of Abraham by Hagar. B.C. 1840.

Gen. 25. 13 first born of Ishmael Nebajoth; and K.
1 Ch. 1. 29 first born of Ishmael, Nebaioth; then K.

2. The tribe which sprang from him, and their territory in the desert between Arabia Petræa and Babylonia.

Psa.120. 5 Woe is me..I dwell in the tents of K.!
Song 1. 5 as the tents of K., as the curtains of Sol.
Isa. 21. 16 Within a year..all the glory of K. shall
21. 17 the children of K., shall be diminished
42. 11 the villages (that) K. doth inhabit: let the
60. 7 All the flocks of K shall be gathered tog.
Jer. 2. 10 send unto K., and consider diligently, and
49. 28 Concerning K., and concerning the king.
49. 28 Arise ye, go up to K., and spoil the men
Eze. 27. 21 Arabia, and all the princes of K., they oc.

KE-DE'-MAH, קֵדְמָה *eastern.*
Youngest son of Ishmael. B.C. 1820.

Gen. 25. 15 Hadar, and Tema, Jetur, Naphish, and K.
1 Ch. 1. 31 Jetur, Naphish, and K. These are the sons

KE-DE'-MOTH, קְדֵמוֹת *eastern parts.*
1. A wilderness in the E. part of Reuben, near the Arnon.

Deut. 2. 26 sent messengers out of..K. unto Sihon

2. A Levitical city of Reuben, near Jahaza and Mephaath.

Josh.13. 18 And Jahaza, and K., and Mephaath
21. 37 K. with her suburbs, and Mephaath with
1 Ch. 6. 79 K. also with her suburbs, and Mephaath

KE'-DESH, קֶדֶשׁ *holy.*
1. A city of the Canaanites near the N. border, its king being defeated by Joshua, it probably became part of Naphtali.

Josh.12. 22 The king of K., one; the king of Jokneam
19. 37 And K., and Edrei, and En-hazor

2. Sometimes called Kedesh-*Naphtali,* a Levitical city of refuge in Naphtali; now called *Kedes,* W. of the Lake Merom.

Josh 20. 7 They appointed K. in Galilee in mount
21. 32 K. in Galilee with her suburbs..a city of
Judg. 4. 6 she sent and called Barak..out of K. N.
4. 9 Deborah arose, and went with Barak to K.
4. 10 Barak called Zebulun and Naphtali to K.
4. 11 unto the plain of Zaanaim, which (is) by K.
2 Ki. 15. 29 Tiglath-pileser..took..K., and Hazor
1 Ch. 6. 76 K. in Galilee with her suburbs, and Ham.

3. A Levitical city in Issachar, elsewhere called *Kishion* or *Kishon,* now *Kison.*

1 Ch. 6. 72 K. with her suburbs, Daberath with her

4. A city of Judah, near Hazor and Ithnan.

Josh.15. 23 And K., and Hazor, and Ithnan

KEEP, to —

1. *Guard, charge, ward,* מִשְׁמֶרֶת *mishmereth.*

Exod12. 6 ye shall keep it up until the fourteenth

2. *To do, make, serve,* עָבַד *abad.*

Ezra 6. 16 kept the dedication of this house of God

3. *To keep back,* אָצַל *atsal.*

Eccl. 2. 10 whatsoever mine eyes desired I kept not

4. *To darken, keep back, spare, withhold,* חָשַׂךְ *chasak.*

1 Sa. 25. 39 hath kept his servant from evil: for the L.

5. *To shut, restrain,* כָּלָא *kala.*

1 Sa. 25. 33 which hast kept me this day from coming

6. *To withhold, keep back,* מָנַע *mana.*

Job 20. 13 (Though) he..keep it still within his mouth

7. *To keep, watch,* נְטַר *netar.*

Dan. 7. 28 As for me..I kept the matter in my heart

8. *To keep, watch,* נָטַר *natar.*

Psa.103. 9 neither will he keep (his anger) for ever
Song 1. 6 (but) mine own vineyard have I not kept
8. 12 those that keep the fruit thereof two hu.
Jer. 3. 12 I (am) merciful..I will not keep (anger)

9. *To keep, watch, reserve,* נָצַר *natsar.*

Deut32. 10 he kept him as the apple of his eye
33. 9 observed thy word, and kept thy covenant
Psa. 25. 10 mercy and truth unto such as keep his
34. 13 Keep thy tongue from evil, and thy lips
78. 7 not forget the works of God, but keep his
105. 45 might observe his statutes, and keep his
119. 2 Blessed (are) they that keep his testimon.
119. 22 Remove..for I have kept thy testimonies
119. 33 the way..and I shall keep it (unto) the
119. 34 Give me understanding, and I shall keep
119. 56 This I had, because I kept thy precepts
119. 69 I will keep thy precepts with (my) whole
119. 100 I understand..because I keep thy prec.
119. 115 I will keep the commandments of my G.
119. 129 wonderful: therefore doth my soul keep
119. 145 hear me, O LORD: I will keep thy statu.
141. 3 Set a watch, O LORD..keep the door of
Prov. 2. 8 He keepeth the paths of judgment, and
2. 11 preserve thee, understanding shall keep
3. 1 but let thine heart keep my commandm.
3. 21 My son..keep sound wisdom and discre.
Prov. 4. 6 preserve thee: love her, and she shall k.
4. 13 let..not go: keep her; for she (is) thy life
4. 23 Keep thy heart with all diligence; for
5. 2 and (that) thy lips may keep knowledge
6. 20 My son, keep thy father's commandment
13. 3 He that keepeth his mouth keepeth his
13. 6 Righteousness keepeth (him that is) upr
16. 17 he that keepeth his way preserveth his
24. 12 he that keepeth thy soul, doth (not) he
27. 18 Whoso keepeth the fig tree shall eat the
28. 7 Whoso keepeth the law (is) a wise son: but
Isa. 26. 3 Thou wilt keep (him) in perfect peace
27. 3 I the LORD do keep it; I will water it
27. 3 lest (any) hurt it, I will keep it night and
42. 6 will hold thine hand, and will keep thee
Nah. 2. 1 keep the munition, watch the way, make

10. *To do, perform,* עָבַד *abad.*

Exod13. 5 thou shalt keep this service in this month

11. *To do, perform,* עָשָׂה *asah.*

Exod12. 47 All the congregation of Israel shall keep
Num. 9. 2 Let the children of Israel also keep the
9. 3 ye shall keep it in his appointed season
9. 3 all the ceremonies thereof, shall ye keep
9. 4 spake..that they should keep the passover
9. 5 they kept the passover on the fourteenth
9. 6 could not keep the passover on that day
9. 10 he shall keep the passover unto the LORD
9. 11 at even they shall keep it, (and) eat it with
9. 12 ordinances of the passover they shall keep
9. 13 forbeareth to keep the passover, even the
9. 14 and will keep the passover unto the LORD
Deut. 5. 15 commanded thee to keep the sabbath day
16. 1 keep the passover unto the LORD thy God
16. 10 thou shalt keep the feast of weeks unto
Josh. 5. 10 kept the passover on the fourteenth day
2 Ki.23. 21 Keep the passover unto the LORD your
1 Ch. 4. 10 that thou wouldest keep (me) from evil
2 Ch. 7. 8 Solomon kept the feast seven days, and
7. 9 they kept the dedication of the altar seven
30. 1 to keep the passover unto the LORD God
30. 2 to keep the passover in the second month
30. 3 they could not keep it at that time, because
30. 5 that they should come to keep the pass.
30. 13 to keep the feast of unleavened bread in
30. 21 kept the feast of unleavened bread seven
30. 23 whole assembly took counsel to keep other
30. 23 and they kept..seven days with gladness
35. 1 Josiah kept a passover unto the LORD in
35. 16 to keep the passover, and to offer burnt
35. 17 kept the passover at that time, and the
35. 18 did..keep such a passover as Josiah kept
Ezra 3. 4 They kept also the feast of tabernacles, as
6. 19 the children of the captivity kept the pass.
6. 22 kept the feast of unleavened bread seven
Neh. 8. 18 they kept the feast seven days; and on the
9. 34 Neither have..our fathers, kept thy law
12. 27 to keep the dedication with gladness, both
Esth. 3. 8 neither keep they the king's laws: there
9. 21 that they should keep the fourteenth day
9. 27 that they would keep these two days acc.
Eze. 5. 7 neither have kept my judgments, neither

12. *To keep sabbath,* שָׁבַת *shabath.*

Lev. 25. 2 then shall the land keep a sabbath unto

13. *To keep, observe, take heed,* שָׁמַר *shamar.*

Gen. 2. 15 garden of Eden to dress it and to keep it
3. 24 sword..to keep the way of the tree of life
17. 9 Thou shalt keep my covenant therefore
17. 10 This (is) my covenant, which ye shall keep
18. 19 they shall keep the way of the LORD, to do
26. 5 Abraham obeyed my voice, and kept my
28. 15 I (am) with thee, and will keep thee in all
28. 20 will keep me in this way that I go, and will
30. 31 If thou wilt..I will again feed (and) keep
41. 35 let them gather..and let them keep food
Exod12. 25 it shall come to pass..ye shall keep this
13. 10 Thou shalt therefore keep this ordinance
15. 26 If thou wilt..keep all his statutes, I will
16. 28 How long refuse ye to keep my command.
19. 5 if ye will obey my voice..and keep my co
20. 6 that love me, and keep my commandme.
21. 29 testified..and he hath not kept him in, but
21. 36 his owner hath not kept him in; he shall
22. 7 money or stuff to keep and it be stolen out
22. 10 or an ox, or a sheep, or any beast, to keep
23. 15 Thou shalt keep the feast of unleavened
23. 20 I send an Angel before thee, to keep thee
31. 13 Verily my sabbaths ye shall keep: for it (is)
31. 14 Ye shall keep the sabbath therefore; for
31. 16 the children of Israel shall keep the sab.
34. 18 feast of unleavened bread shalt thou keep
Lev. 8. 35 keep the charge of the LORD, that ye die
18. 4 keep mine ordinances, to walk therein
18. 5, 26 Ye shall therefore keep my statutes
18. 30 Therefore shall ye keep mine ordinance
19. 3 keep my sabbaths: I (am) the LORD your G
19. 19 Ye shall keep my statutes. Thou shalt not
19. 30 Ye shall keep my sabbaths, and reverence
20. 8 And ye shall keep my statutes, and do
20. 22 Ye shall therefore keep all my statutes
22. 9 They shall therefore keep mine ordinances
22. 31 Therefore shall ye keep my commandme.
25. 18 keep my judgments, and do them; and ye
26. 2 Ye shall keep my sabbaths, and reverence
26. 3 and keep my commandments, and do them
Num. 1. 53 the Levites shall keep the charge of the
3. 7 they shall keep his charge, and the charge
3. 8 they shall keep all the instruments of the
3. 32 oversight of them that keep the charge
6. 24 The LORD bless thee, and keep thee
8. 26 to keep the charge, and shall do no service

Num. 9. 19 the children of Israel kept the charge of
9. 23 they kept the charge of the LORD, at the
18. 3 they shall keep thy charge, and the charge
18. 4 keep the charge of the tabernacle of the c.
18. 5 ye shall keep the charge of the sanctuary
18. 7 shall keep your priest's office for every
31. 30 keep the charge of the tabernacle of the
31. 47 kept the charge of the tabernacle of the
Deut. 4. 2 that ye may keep the commandments of
4. 6 Keep therefore and do (them): for this (is)
4. 9 keep thy soul diligently, lest thou forget
4. 40 Thou shalt keep therefore his statutes, and
5. 1 may learn them, and keep and do them
5. 10 that love me and keep my commandments
5. 12 Keep the sabbath day to sanctify it, as
5. 29 and keep all my commandments always
6. 2 to keep all his statutes, and his comma.
6. 17 Ye shall diligently keep the commandm.
7. 8 because he would keep the oath which he
7. 9 which keepeth covenant and mercy with
7. 9 that love him and keep his commandm.
7. 11 Thou shalt therefore keep the command.
7. 12 if ye hearken to these judgments, and keep
7. 12 that the LORD thy God shall keep unto
8. 2 whether thou wouldest keep his comma.
8. 6 shalt keep the commandments of the L.
8. 11 in not keeping his commandments, and
10. 13 To keep the commandments of the LORD
11. 1 keep his charge, and his statutes, and his
11. 8 Therefore shall ye keep all the comman.
11. 22 For if ye shall diligently keep all these c.
13. 4 fear him, and keep his commandments, and
13. 18 to keep all his commandments which I co.
17. 19 to keep all the words of this law and these
19. 9 If thou shalt keep all these commandm.
23. 23 gone out..thou shalt keep and perform
26. 16 thou shalt therefore keep and do them
26. 17 to keep his statutes, and his commandm.
26. 18 and..shouldest keep all his commandm.
27. 1 Keep all the commandments which I com.
28. 9 if thou shalt keep the commandments of
28. 45 to keep his commandments and his statu.
29. 9 Keep therefore the words of this covenant
30. 10 to keep his commandments and his statu.
30. 16 to walk in his ways, and to keep his com.
Josh. 6. 18 in any wise keep..from the accursed thing
10. 18 Joshua said..set men by it for to keep
22. 2 Ye have kept all that Moses the servant
22. 3 have kept the charge of the commandm,
22. 5 to keep his commandments, and to cleave
23. 6 Be ye..very courageous to keep and to do
Judg. 2. 22 whether they will keep the way of the L.
2. 22 as their fathers did keep (it), or not
1 Sa. 2. 9 He will keep the feet of his saints, and the
7. 1 sanctified Eleazar his son to keep the ark
13. 13 thou hast not kept the commandment of
13. 14 because thou hast not kept (that) which
25. 21 Surely in vain have I kept all that this (f.)
26. 15 wherefore then hast thou not kept thy lord
26. 16 because ye have not kept your master, the
2 Sa. 15. 16 the king left ten women..to keep the house
16. 21 which he hath left to keep the house
20. 3 whom he had left to keep the house
22. 22 I have kept the ways of the LORD, and have
22. 44 hast kept me (to be) head of the heathen
1 Ki. 2. 3 And keep the charge of the LORD thy God
2. 3 to walk in his ways, to keep his statutes
2. 43 Why then hast thou not kept the oath of
3. 6 thou hast kept for him this great kindness
3. 14 to keep my statutes and my commandm.
6. 12 keep all my commandments to walk in
8. 23 who keepest covenant and mercy with thy
8. 24 Who hast kept with thy servant David
8. 25 keep with thy servant David my father
8. 58 to keep his commandments, and his statu.
8. 61 to keep his commandments, as at this day
9. 4 (and) wilt keep my statutes and my judg.
9. 6 and will not keep my commandments
11. 10 kept not that which the LORD commanded
11. 11 thou hast not kept my covenant, and my s.
11. 34 because he kept my commandments and
11. 38 to keep my statutes and my commandm.
13. 21 hast not kept the commandment which
14. 8 David, who kept my commandments, and
14. 27 which kept the door of the king's house
20. 39 Keep this man: if by any means he be m.
2 Ki. 9. 14 Joram had kept Ramoth-gilead, he and
11. 6 so shall ye keep the watch of the house
11. 7 they shall keep the watch of the house of
12. 9 the priests that kept the door put therein
17. 13 keep my commandments (and) my statut.
17. 19 Also Judah kept not the commandments
18. 6 kept his commandments, which the LORD
23. 3 to keep his commandments and his testi.
1 Ch. 10. 13 the word of the LORD, which he kept not
12. 29 greatest part of them had kept the ward
22. 12 that thou mayest keep the law of the Lo.
23. 32 they should keep the charge of the tab.
28. 8 keep and seek for all the commandments
29. 18 keep this for ever in the imagination of
29. 19 to keep thy commandments, thy testimo.
2 Ch. 6. 14 which keepest covenant, and..mercy unto
6. 15 Thou which hast kept with thy servant D.
6. 16 keep with thy servant David my father
12. 10 that kept the entrance of the king's house
13. 11 we keep the charge of the LORD our God
23. 6 all the people shall keep the watch of the
34. 9 which the Levites that kept the doors had
34. 21 because our fathers have not kept the
34. 31 to keep his commandments, and his test.
Ezra 8. 29 Watch ye, and keep (them), until ye weigh
Neh. 1. 5 that keepeth covenant and mercy for

Neh. 1. 7 have not kept the commandments, nor
1. 9 and keep my commandments, and do them
9. 32 God, who keepest covenant and mercy
11. 19 their brethren that kept the gates..an hu.
12. 45 kept the ward of their God, and the ward
13. 22 they should come..keep the gates, to san.
Esth. 2. 14 chamberlain, which kept the concubines
2. 21 two..of those which kept the door, were
Job 23. 11 his way have I kept, and not declined
Psa. 12. 7 Thou shalt keep them, O LORD, thou shalt
17. 4 by the word of thy lips I have kept (me
17. 8 Keep me as the apple of the eye; hide
18. 21 I have kept the ways of the LORD, and
19. 11 in keeping of them (there is) great reward
25. 20 O keep my soul, and deliver me: let me
34. 20 He keepeth all his bones: not one of them
37. 34 Wait on the LORD, and keep his way, and
39. 1 I will keep my mouth with a bridle, while
78. 10 They kept not the covenant of God, and
78. 56 Yet they tempted..and kept not his tes.
89. 28 My mercy will I keep for him for everm.
89. 31 If they break..and keep not my comma.
91. 11 give his angels charge over thee, to keep
99. 7 they kept his testimonies, and the ordin.
103. 18 To such as keep his covenant, and to those
106. 3 Blessed (are) they that keep judgment
119. 4 Thou hast commanded (us) to keep thy
119. 5 O that my ways were directed to keep
119. 8 I will keep thy statutes: O forsake me
119. 17 with thy servant, (that) I may live, and
119. 44 So shall I keep thy law continually for
119. 55 I have remembered..and have kept thy
119. 57 I have said that I would keep thy words
119. 60 I..delayed not to keep thy commandme.
119. 63 I (am) a companion..of them that keep
119. 67 I went astray; but now have I kept thy
119. 88 so shall I keep the testimony of thy mo.
119. 101 I have refrained..that I might keep thy
119. 106 I have sworn..that I will keep thy righ.
119. 134 Deliver me..so will I keep thy precepts
119. 136 run down..because they keep not thy
119. 146 save me, and I shall keep thy testimonies
119. 158 I..was grieved; because they kept not
119. 167 My soul hath kept thy testimonies; and
119. 168 I have kept thy precepts and thy testim.
121. 3 he that keepeth thee will not slumber
121. 4 Behold, he that keepeth Israel shall neit.
127. 1 except the LORD keep the city, the watch.
132. 12 If thy children will keep my covenant and
140. 4 Keep me, O LORD, from the hands of the
141. 9 Keep me from the snares (which) they have
146. 6 Which made heaven..which keepeth truth
Prov. 2. 20 That thou mayest..keep the paths of the
3. 26 and shall keep thy foot from being taken
4. 4 Let thine heart retain my words: keep my
4. 21 keep them in the midst of thine heart
6. 22 when thou sleepest, it shall keep thee
6. 24 To keep thee from the evil woman, from
7. 1 My son, keep my words, and lay up my
7. 2 Keep my commandments, and live; and
7. 5 That they may keep thee from the strange
8. 32 for blessed (are they that) keep my ways
10. 17 He (is in) the way of life that keepeth in.
13. 3 He that keepeth his mouth keepeth his
19. 8 he that keepeth understanding shall find
19. 16 He that keepeth the commandment keep.
21. 23 Whoso keepeth his mouth and..tongue k.
22. 5 he that doth keep his soul shall be far
22. 18 a pleasant thing if thou keep them within
28. 4 such as keep the law contend with them
29. 18 but he that keepeth the law, happy (is) he
Eccl. 3. 6 a time to keep, and a time to cast away
5. 1 Keep thy foot when thou goest to the
8. 2 to keep the king's commandment, and
8. 5 Whoso keepeth the commandment shall
12. 13 Fear God, and keep his commandments
Isa. 26. 2 that the righteous nation which keepeth
56. 1 Keep ye judgment, and do justice: for
56. 2 that keepeth the sabbath from polluting it
56. 2 and keepeth his hand from doing any evil
56. 4 unto the eunuchs that keep my sabbaths
56. 6 every one that keepeth the sabbath from
Jer. 3. 5 Will he reserve..for ever? will he keep (it)
16. 11 have forsaken me, and have not kept my
31. 10 and keep him, as a shepherd (doth) his
35. 18 kept all his precepts, and done according
Eze. 11. 20 and keep mine ordinances, and do them
17. 14 by keeping of his covenant it might stand
18. 9 and hath kept my judgments, to deal
18. 19 hath kept all my statutes, and hath done
18. 21 keep all my statutes, and do that which
20. 19 and keep my judgments, and do them
20. 21 neither kept my judgments to do them
36. 27 and ye shall keep my judgments, and do
43. 11 that they may keep the whole form there.
44. 8 ye have not kept the charge of mine holy
44. 15 that kept the charge of my sanctuary
44. 16 minister unto me, and they shall keep my
44. 24 they shall keep my laws and my statutes
48. 11 which have kept my charge, which went
Dan. 9. 4 and to them that keep his commandments
Hos. 12. 6 keep mercy and judgment, and wait on
12. 12 Israel served..and for a wife he kept (sh.)
Amos 1. 11 because..he kept his wrath for ever
2. 4 have not kept his commandments, and
Mic. 7. 5 keep the doors of thy mouth from her
Zech. 3. 7 if thou wilt keep my charge, then thou
3. 7 shalt also keep my courts, and I will give
Mal. 2. 7 the priest's lips should keep knowledge
2. 9 according as ye have not kept my ways
3. 7 ye are gone away..and have not kept
3. 14 what profit (is it) that we have kept his

14. *To lead, bring,* ἄγω *agō.*
Matt 14. 6 when Herod's birth day [was kept], the d.

15. *To feed,* βόσκω *boskō.*
Matt. 8. 33 they that kept them fled, and went their

16. *To keep thoroughly,* διατηρέω *diatēreō.*
Luke 2. 51 his mother kept all these sayings in her
Acts 15. 29 from which if ye keep yourselves, ye shall

17. *To guard thoroughly,* διαφυλάσσω *diaphulassō.*
Luke 4. 10 give his angels charge over thee, to keep

18. *To have, hold,* ἔχω *echō.*
Luke 19. 20 thy pound, which I have kept laid up in

19. *To lie down, recline,* κατάκειμαι *katakeimai* ἐπί.
Acts 9. 33 Æneas, which had kept his bed eight ye.

20. *To hold fast,* κατέχω *katechō.*
Luke 8. 15 having heard the word, keep (it), and
1 Co. 11. 2 keep the ordinances, as I delivered..to

21. *To hold firm,* κρατέω *krateō.*
Mark 9. 10 And they kept that saying with themsel.

22. *To hold near, offer,* παρέχω *parechō.*
Acts 22. 2 they kept the more silence: and he saith

23. *To do, make,* ποιέω *poieō.*
Matt 26. 18 I will keep the passover at thy house with
John 7. 19 and (yet) none of you keepeth the law?
Acts 18. 21 I must by all means [keep] this feast that
Heb. 11. 28 Through faith he kept the passover, and

24. *To do, practise,* πράσσω *prassō.*
Rom. 2. 25 circumcision..profiteth, if thou keep the

25. *To keep together,* συντηρέω *suntēreō.*
Luke 2. 19 Mary kept all these things, and pondered

26. *To keep, watch, observe,* τηρέω *tēreō.*
Matt 19. 17 if thou wilt enter into life, keep the com.
Mark 7. 9 reject..that [ye may keep] your own tradi.
John 2. 10 thou hast kept the good wine until now
8. 51 If a man keep my saying, he shall never
8. 52 If a man keep my saying, he shall never
8. 55 but I know him, and keep his saying
9. 16 because he keepeth not the sabbath day
12. 7 against the day of my burying hath she k.
14. 15 If ye love me, keep my commandments
14. 21 He that hath my commandments, and k.
14. 23 If a man love me, he will keep my words
14. 24 He that loveth me not keepeth not my
15. 10 If ye keep my commandments, ye shall
15. 10 as I have kept my Father's commandm.
15. 20 have kept my saying, they will keep yours
17. 6 unto the men..and they have kept thy
17. 11 Holy Father, keep through thine own name
17. 12 I kept them in thy name: those that
17. 15 that thou shouldest keep them from the
Acts 12. 5 Peter therefore was kept in prison: but
12. 6 keepers before the door kept the prison
15. 5 and to command..to keep the law of Mo.
15. 24 [be circumcised, and keep the law; to wh.]
16. 23 charging the jailor to keep them safely
24. 23 he commanded a centurion to keep Paul
25. 4 that Paul should be kept at Cesarea, and
25. 21 to be kept till I might send him to Cesar
1 Co. 7. 37 hath so decreed..that he will keep his
2 Co. 11. 9 I have kept myself..and (so) will I keep
Eph. 4. 3 Endeavouring to keep the unity of the
1 Ti. 5. 22 partaker of other men's sins: keep thy.
6. 14 That thou keep (this) commandment with.
2 Ti. 4. 7 I have finished (my) course, I have kept
Jas. 1. 27 to keep himself unspotted from the world
2. 10 whosoever shall keep the whole law, and
1 Jo. 2. 3 we know him, if we keep his commandm.
2. 4 He that saith, I know him, and keepeth
2. 5 whoso keepeth his word, in him verily is
3. 22 because we keep his commandments, and
3. 24 he that keepeth his commandments dwel.
5. 2 we love God, and [keep] his commandm.
5. 3 that we keep his commandments: and
5. 18 he that is begotten of God keepeth hims.
Jude 6 angels which kept not their first estate
21 Keep yourselves in the love of God, look.
Rev. 1. 3 keep those things which are written there.
2. 26 he that overcometh, and keepeth my wo.
3. 8 hast kept my word, and hast not denied
3. 10 Because thou hast kept..I also will keep
12. 17 which keep the commandments of God
14. 12 they that keep the commandments of God
16. 15 keepeth his garments, lest he walk naked
22. 7 blessed (is) he that keepeth the sayings of
22. 9 them which keep the sayings of this book

27. *To watch, keep ward, guard,* φρουρέω *phroureō.*
Gal. 3. 23 we were kept under the law, shut up unto
Phil. 4. 7 shall keep your hearts and minds through
1 Pe. 1. 5 Who are kept by the power of God through

28. *To keep guard, watch,* φυλάσσω *phulassō.*
Matt 19. 20 All these things have I kept from my youth
Luke 2. 8 keeping watch over their flock by night
8. 29 he was kept bound with chains and in f.
11. 21 When a strong man armed keepeth his
11. 28 they that hear the word of God, and keep
18. 21 All these have I kept from my youth up
John 12. 25 he that hateth his life..shall keep it unto
17. 12 those that thou gavest me I have kept
Acts 7. 53 have received the law..and have not kept
12. 4 to four quaternions of soldiers to keep him
16. 4 they delivered them the decrees for to k.
21. 24 also walkest orderly, and keepest the law
22. 20 kept the raiment of them that slew him
23. 35 he commanded him to be kept in Herod's
28. 16 dwell by himself with a soldier that kept

Rom. 2. 26 Therefore if the uncircumcision keep the
Gal. 6. 13 they..who are circumcised keep the law
2 Th. 3. 3 shall stablish you, and keep (you) from
1 Ti. 6. 20 keep that which is committed to thy trust
2 Ti. 1. 12 am persuaded that he is able to keep that
1. 14 keep by the Holy Ghost which dwelleth
1 Jo. 5. 21 Little children, keep yourselves from idols
Jude 24 Now unto him that is able to keep you

[*See also* Alive, bondage, company with, holy, holy day, rank, remembrance, sabbath, secret, silence, solemn feast, watch.]

KEEP back, to —

1. *To keep back, withhold,* חָשַׂךְ *chasak.*
Gen. 39. 9 neither hath he kept back any thing from
Job 33. 18 He keepeth back his soul from the pit, and
Psa. 19. 13 Keep back thy servant also from presum.

2. *To shut, restrain,* כָּלָא *kala.*
Isa. 43. 6 Give up; and to the south, Keep not back

3. *To withhold, keep back,* מָנַע *mana.*
Num24. 11 the LORD hath kept thee back from hon.
1 Sa. 25. 34 which hath kept me back from hurting
Jer. 42. 4 I will declare (it) unto you I will keep..b.
48. 10 cursed (be) he that keepeth back his sword

4. *To put apart for self, purloin,* νοσφίζομαι *nosphi.*
Acts 5. 2 kept back..of the price, his wife also being
5. 3 and to keep back..of the price of the l.?

5. *To put under, suppress,* ὑποστέλλω *hupostellō.*
Acts 20. 20 how I kept back nothing that was profit.

KEEP bed, to —

To fall on, נָפַל לְ *naphal le.*
Exod21. 18 fist, and he die not, but keepeth (his) bed

KEEP cattle, to teach to —

To acquire, buy, possess, קָנָה *qanah,* 5.
Zech.13. 5 man taught me to keep cattle from my

KEEP close, to —

To be or keep silent, σιγάω *sigaō.*
Luke 9. 36 they kept (it) close, and told no man in

KEEP company, to —

1. *To feed, enjoy, be a friend,* רָעָה *raah*; Prov.29.3.
2. *To mix up self together with,* συναναμίγνυμι.
1 Co. 5. 11 I have written unto you not to keep co.
3. *Adhere to, associate with,* κολλάομαι; Acts 10.28

KEEP, to be delivered to —

To be charged with, committed to, פָּקַד *paqad,* 6.
Lev. 6. 4 or that which was delivered him to keep

KEEP fast, to —

To cleave, adhere to, pursue, דָּבַק *dabeq.*
Ruth 2. 21 Thou shalt keep fast by my young men
2. 23 she kept fast by the maidens of Boaz to

KEEP a (solemn) feast or holy day, to —

To keep a feast or festival, (חַג) חָגַג *chagag* (*chag*).
Exod 12. 14 ye shall keep it a feast..ye shall keep it
23. 14 Three times thou shalt keep a feast unto
Lev. 23. 39 ye shall keep a feast unto the LORD; 23.14.
23. 41 ye shall keep it a feast unto the LORD se.
Num 29. 12 ye shall keep a feast unto the LORD seven
Deut 16. 15 Seven days shalt thou keep a solemn feast
Nah. 1. 15 keep thy solemn feasts, perform thy vows
Zech 14. 16, 18, 19 go up..to keep the feast of taber.
Psa. 42. 4 I went..with a multitude that kept holy d.

KEEP from, to —

To hinder, restrain, κωλύω *kōluō.*
Acts 27. 43 the centurion..kept them from (their)

KEEP house, to make to —

To cause to sit down or still, dwell, יָשַׁב *yashab,* 5.
Psa.113. 9 He maketh the barren woman to keep h.

KEEP in, to —

1. *To restrain,* שָׁבַח *shabach,* 3.
Prov 29. 11 a wise (man) keepeth it in till afterwards
2. *To hold together,* συνέχω *sunechō.*
Luke 19. 43 round, and keep thee in on every side

KEEP in memory, to —

To hold fast, κατέχω *katechō.*
1 Co. 15. 2 if ye keep in memory what I preached

KEEP in store, to —

To treasure up, θησαυρίζω *thēsaurizō.*
2 Pe. 3. 7 by the same word are kept in store, res.

KEEP (one's self) far, to —

To be far off, רָחַק *rachaq.*
Exod23. 7 Keep thee far from a false matter; and

KEEP secret, to —

To be or keep silent, σιγάω *sigaō.*
Rom 16. 25 which was kept secret since the world

KEEP secretly, to —

To hide, lay up, צָפַן *tsaphan.*
Psa. 31. 20 thou shalt keep them secretly in a pavil.

KEEP self, to —

1. *To cleave or adhere to,* דָּבַק *dabeq.*
Num36. 7, 9 every one..shall keep himself to the
2. *To be kept, preserved,* שָׁמַר *shamar,* 2.
Deut 23. 9 then keep thee from every wicked thing
1 Sa. 21. 4 if the young men have kept themselves
3. *To keep or preserve self,* שָׁמַר *shamar,* 7.
2 Sa. 22. 24 and have kept myself from mine iniquity
Psa. 18. 23 upright..and I kept myself from mine in.
4. *To keep guard, watch,* φυλάσσω *phulassō.*
Acts 21. 25 save only that they keep themselves from

KEEP self close, to —

To keep in, restrain, עָצַר *atsar.*
1 Ch.12. 1 while he yet kept himself close because

KEEP (sheep), to —

To feed, keep sheep, רָעָה *raah.*
Gen. 29. 9 came with her father's sheep; for she kept
Exod. 3. 1 Moses kept the flock of Jethro his father.
1 Sa. 16. 11 youngest, and, behold, he keepeth the sh.
17. 34 Thy servant kept his father's sheep, and
25. 16 we were with them keeping the sheep

KEEP silence, to —

1. *To be silent, deaf,* חָרַשׁ *charash.*
Psa. 32. 3 When I kept silence, my bones waxed old
35. 22 thou hast seen, O LORD: keep not silence
50. 3 God shall come, and shall not keep silence
50. 21 These..hast thou done, and I kept silence
Isa. 41. 1 Keep silence before me, O islands: and
2. *To be or keep silence,* σιγάω *sigaō.*
Acts 15. 12 Then all the multitude kept silence, and
1 Co. 14. 28 let him keep silence in the church; and
14. 34 Let your women keep silence in the chur.

KEEP still, to —

To keep in, restrain, עָצַר *atsar.*
2 Ch. 22. 9 house of Ahaziah had no power to keep s.

KEEP, that which was delivered to —

Store, deposit, פִּקָּדוֹן *piqqadon.*
Lev. 6. 2, 4 that which was delivered him to keep

KEEP under, to —

1. *To subdue, force,* כָּבַשׁ *kabash.*
2 Ch.28. 10 ye purpose to keep under the children of
2. *To keep down, press under,* ὑπωπιάζω *hupōpiazō.*
1 Co. 9. 27 I keep under my body, and bring (it) into

KEEP with a garrison, to —

To watch, guard, φρουρέω *phroureō.*
2 Co.11. 32 kept the city of the Damascenes with a gar.

KEEPER —

1. *To keep, watch,* נָטַר *natar.*
Song 1. 6 they made me the keeper of the vineyards
8. 11 Solomon..let out the vineyard unto keep.
2. *To keep, watch, reserve,* נָצַר *natsar.*
Job 27. 18 and as a booth (that) the keeper maketh
3. *To feed sheep,* רָעָה *raah.*
Gen. 4. 2 Abel was a keeper of sheep, but Cain was
4. *Prince, captain, chief,* שַׂר *sar.*
Gen. 39. 21 favour in the sight of the keeper of the
39. 22 the keeper of the prison committed to J.
39. 23 The keeper of the prison looked not to any
5. *To keep, observe, preserve,* שָׁמַר *shamar.*
Gen. 4. 9 said, I know not: (Am) I my brother's kee.?
1 Sa. 17. 20 left the sheep with a keeper, and took, and
17. 22 left his carriage in the hand of the keeper
28. 2 I make thee keeper of mine head for ever
2 Ki.11. 5 shall even be keepers of the watch of the
22. 4 which the keepers of the door have gath.
22. 14 the son of Harhas, keeper of the wardrobe
23. 4 the keepers of the door, to bring forth out
25. 18 the second priest, and the three keepers of
1 Ch. 9. 19 service, keepers of the gates of the taber.
9. 19 their fathers..(were) keepers of the entry
2 Ch.34. 22 the son of Hasrah, keeper of the wardrobe
Neh. 2. 8 unto Asaph the keeper of the king's for.
3. 29 also Shemaiah..the keeper of the east gate
Esth. 2. 3 king's chamberlain, keeper of the women
2. 8 the custody of Hegai, keeper of the women
2. 15 what..the keeper of the women, appoint.
6. 2 keepers of the door, who sought to lay
Psa.121. 5 The LORD (is) thy keeper; the LORD (is)
Eccl.12. 3 In the day when the keepers of the house
Song 5. 7 keepers of the walls took away my veil
Jer. 4. 17 As keepers of a field, are they against her
35. 4 above the chamber of..the keeper of the
52. 24 the second priest, and the three keepers
Eze. 40. 45, 46 priests, the keepers of the charge of the
44. 8 ye have set keepers of my charge in my s.
44. 14 I will make them keepers of the charge of
6. *Watchman, guard,* φύλαξ *phulax.*
Acts 5. 23 keepers standing without before the doors
12. 6 keepers before the door kept the prison
12. 19 he examined the keepers, and commanded
7. *To keep, watch, observe,* τηρέω *tēreō.*
Matt 28. 4 for fear of him the keepers did shake, and

KEEPER at home —

One who keeps his own house, οἰκουρός *oikouros.*
Titus 2. 5 discreet, chaste, keepers at home, good

KEEPER of the prison —

Guard of a prison, δεσμοφύλαξ *desmophulax.*
Acts 16. 27 the keeper of the prison awaking out of
16. 36 the keeper of the prison told this saying

KEEPING —

1. *To keep, watch, reserve,* נָצַר *natsar.*
Exod. 34. 7 Keeping mercy for thousands, forgiving
2. *To keep, observe, preserve,* שָׁמַר *shamar.*
Num. 3. 28, 38 keeping the charge of the sanctuary
Neh. 12. 25 keeping the ward at the thresholds of the
Dan. 9. 4 keeping the covenant and mercy to them
3. *Keeping, observing,* τήρησις *tērēsis.*
1 Co. 7. 19 the keeping of the commandments of God

KE-HE-LA'-THAH, קְהֵלָתָה *place of assembly.*

The 18th encampment of Israel from Egypt, and 7th from Sinai.
Num33. 22 journeyed from Rissah, and pitched in K
33. 23 they went from K. and pitched in mount

KE-I'-LAH, קְעִילָה *inclosed.*

1. A city in the hill country of Judah, towards the Philistines, near Achzib; now *Kila,* eight miles from Eleutheropolis.
Josh.15. 44 K., and Achzib, and Mareshah; nine cities
1 Sa. 23. 1 the Philistines fight against K., and they
23. 2 Go and smite the Philistines, and save K.
23. 3 if we come to K. against the armies of the
23. 4 Arise, go down to K.; for I will deliver
23. 5 David..went to K...So David saved..K.
23. 6 when Abiathar..fled to David to K...he
23. 7 it was told Saul that David was come to K.
23. 8 Saul called all the people..go down to K.
23. 10 Saul seeketh to come to K., to destroy the
23. 11 Will the men of K. deliver me up into his
23. 12 Will the men of K. deliver me and my men
23. 13 David and his men..departed out of K.
23. 13 told Saul that David was escaped from K
Neh. 3. 17, 18 the ruler of the half part of K.

2. A descendant of Caleb, son of Jephunneh. B.C. 1400.
1 Ch. 4. 19 K. the Garmite, and Eshtemoa the Maach.

KE-LA-I'AH, קֵלָיָה *Jah is light.*

A Levite who had taken a strange wife during or after the captivity. B.C. 456. Called also *Kelita.*
Ezra 10. 23 Also of the Levites..K., the same (is) K.

KE-LI'-TA, קְלִיטָא *poverty, littleness.*

1. Same as *Kelaiah.* B.C. 456.
Ezra 10. 23 Kelaiah, the same (is) K., Pethahiah, Ju.
2. A priest who explained the law when read by Ezra. B.C. 456.
Neh. 8. 7 K., Azariah, Jozabad, Hanan, Pelaiah
3. A Levite who sealed the covenant made by Nehemiah. B.C. 456.
Neh. 10. 10 their brethren, Shebaniah, Hodijah, K.

KE-MU'-EL, קְמוּאֵל *God stands, or rises.*

1. The third son of Nahor, Abraham's brother. B.C. 1800.
Gen. 22. 21 Huz his first born..K. the father of Aram
2. A prince or chief of Ephraim, one of those appointed to divide the land. B.C. 1452.
Num34. 24 prince..of Ephraim, K. the son of Shiphtan.
3. A Levite, the father of Hashabiah ruler of the Levites in David's reign. B.C. 1015.
1 Ch.27. 17 Of the Levites; Hashabiah, the son of K.

KE'-NAN, קֵינָן *one acquired or begotten.*

The son of Enosh, the grandson of Adam. B.C. 3679–2794. Called *Cainan* in Gen. 5. 9.
1 Ch. 1. 2 K., Mahalaleel, Jered

KE'-NATH, קְנָת *possession.*

A city of Bashan in Argob, taken from the Amorites by *Nobah,* a Manassite, and called after him. Now called *Kunawat.*
Num32. 42 Nobah went and took K., and the villages
1 Ch. 2. 23 And he took..K., and the towns thereof

KEN'-AZ, KEN'-EZ, קְנַז *side, flank.*

1. The fourth son of Eliphaz the son of Esau. B.C. 1740.
Gen. 36. 11 the sons of Eliphaz were Teman..and K.
36. 15 of the sons of Esau..duke Zepho, duke K.
1 Ch. 1. 36 The sons of Eliphaz; Teman, and..K.
2. A duke of Edom. B.C. 1470. Perhaps the same as No. 1.
Gen. 36. 42 Duke K., duke Teman, duke Mibzar
1 Ch. 1. 53 Duke K., duke Teman, duke Mibzar
3. The brother of Caleb the son of Jephunneh, and father of Othniel, one of the judges. B.C. 1490.
Josh 15. 17 Othniel the son of K., the brother of Caleb
Judg. 1. 13 Othniel the son of K., Caleb's younger b.
3. 9 the LORD raised up..Othniel the son of K.
3. 11 And Othniel the son of K. died
1 Ch. 4. 13 the sons of K.; Othniel, and Seraiah
4. A grandson of Caleb the son of Jephunneh. B.C. 1400.
1 Ch. 4. 15 sons of Caleb..sons of Elah, even K.

KEN-E-ZITE, קְנִזִּי *belonging to Kenez.*

The patronymic of Jephunneh the father (or ancestor) of Caleb. B.C. 1490. See also *Kenizzites.*
Num32. 12 Save Caleb the son of Jephunneh the K.
Josh 14. 6 Caleb the son of Jephunneh the K. said
14. 14 Caleb the son of Jephunneh the K. unto

KE-NITES, קֵינִי *belonging to Ken or Qen.*

One of the ten tribes of Palestine in the time of Abraham: apparently destroyed afterwards by the Amorites, and dispersed among the Amalekites in the S. and the Canaanites in the N. Perhaps also called Midianites.
Gen. 15. 19 The K., and the Kenizzites, and the Kad.
Num24. 21 he looked on the K., and took up his
24. 22 Nevertheless the K. shall be wasted, until
Judg. 1. 16 the children of the K...went up out of
4. 11 Heber the K...severed himself from the K.
4. 17 the tent of Jael the wife of Heber the K.
4. 17 betwen Jabin..and the house of H. the K.
5. 24 Blessed..shall Jael..wife of Heber the K.

1 Sa. 15. 6 Saul said unto the K., Go, depart, get
15. 6 So the K. departed from among the Am.
27. 10 David said, Against the south of..the K.
30. 29 to (them) which (were) in..cities of the K.
1 Ch. 2. 55 These (are) the K. that came of Hemath

KE-NIZ-ZITES, קְנִזִּי *belonging to Kenaz.*
One of the ten tribes of Palestine, named between the Kenites in the S. and the Kadmonites in the N.
Gen. 15 19 The Kenites, and the K., and the Kadmon

KEPT, to be —

1. *To be or remain bound,* אָסַר *asar,* 2.
Gen. 42. 16 ye shall be kept in prison, that your words

2. *Guard, charge, ward,* מִשְׁמֶרֶת *mishmereth.*
Exod. 16. 23 lay up for you to be kept until the morn.
16. 32, 33 an omer..be kept for your generations
16. 34 laid it up before the Testimony, to be kept
Num. 17. 10 to be kept for a token against the rebels
19. 9 it shall be kept for the congregation of

3. *To keep in, restrain,* עָצַר *atsar.*
1 Sa. 21. 5 Of a truth women (have been) kept from

4. *To be done,* עָשָׂה *asah,* 2.
2 Ch. 35. 18 there was no passover like to that kept in
35. 19 the reign of Josiah was this passover kept

5. *To set or be set apart,* קָדַשׁ *qadesh,* 7.
Isa. 30. 29 as in the night..a holy solemnity is kept

6. *To keep, preserve,* שָׁמַר *shamar.*
1 Sa. 9. 24 unto this time hath it been kept for thee
Eccl. 5. 13 riches kept for the owners thereof to their

7. *To be kept, observed,* שָׁמַר *shamar,* 7.
Mic. 6. 16 the statutes of Omri are kept, and all the

8. *To be,* הֲוָה *havah.*
Dan. 5. 19 whom he would he kept alive, and whom

9. *To lead or bring on,* ἄγω *agō.*
Matt. 14. 6 when Herod's birthday [was kept,] the

KEPT back, to be —
To be diminished, withdrawn, גָּרַע *gara,* 2.
Num. 9. 7 wherefore are we kept back, that we may

KEPT close, to be —
To hide, סָתַר *sathar,* 2.
Num. 5. 13 and be kept close, and she be defiled, and
Job 28. 21 and kept close from the fowls of the air

KEPT secret, to be —
To be hidden, γίνομαι ἀπόκρυφος *ginomai apokrup.*
Mark 4. 22 neither was any thing kept secret, but that

KERCHIEFS —
Veils, kerchiefs, מִסְפָּחוֹת *mispachoth.*
Eze. 13. 18 make kerchiefs upon the head of every
13. 21 Your kerchiefs also will I tear, and deliver

KE-REN HAP'-PUCH, קֶרֶן הַפּוּךְ *horn for paint.*
The youngest daughter of Job, born after his trial. B.C. 1520.
Job 42. 14 And he called the name..of the third K.

KE-RI'-OTH, KIRIOTH, קְרִיּוֹת *cities, hamlets.*
1. A city in the E. of Judah, now *Kurietem.*
Josh 15. 25 Hazor, Hadattah, and K., (and) Hezron
2. A city of Moab, now *Kureiat* or *Kuveiyah.*
Jer. 48. 24 And upon K., and upon Bozrah, and upon
48. 41 K. is taken, and the strongholds are sur.
Amos 2. 2 it shall devour the palaces of Kirioth

KERNEL —
Kernels, sour grapes, חַרְצַנִּים *chartsannim.*
Num. 6. 4 nothing..from the kernels even to the husk

KE'-ROS, קֵירֹס *bent.*
One of the Nethinim whose descendants returned to Jerusalem with Zerubbabel. B.C. 636.
Ezra 2. 44 The children of K., the children of Siaha
Neh. 7. 47 The children of K., the children of Sia

KETTLE —
Kettle, basket, דּוּד *dud.*
1 Sa. 2. 14 he struck (it) into the pan, or kettle, or

KE-TU'-RAH, קְטוּרָה *fragrance.*
Wife of Abraham after Sarah's death. B.C. 1853.
Gen. 25. 1 Abrah. took a wife, and her name (was) K.
25. 4 All these (were) the children of K.
1 Ch. 1. 32 Now the sons of K., Abraham's concubine
1. 33 All these (are) the sons of K.

KEY —

1. *Key, opener,* מַפְתֵּחַ *maphteach.*
Judg. 3. 25 therefore they took a key, and opened
Isa. 22. 22 the key of the house of David will I lay

2. *A key,* κλείς *kleis.*
Matt. 16. 19 I will give unto thee the keys of the king.
Luke 11. 52 ye have taken away the key of knowledge
Rev. 1. 18 behold I..have the keys of hell and of death
3. 7 he that hath the key of David, he that op.
9. 1 to him was given the key of the bottomless
20. 1 having the key of the bottomless pit and

KE-ZI'-A, קְצִיעָה *cassia.*
The second daughter of Job, born after his trial. B.C. 1520.
Job 42. 14 And He called the name..of the second, K.

KE'-ZIZ, קְצִיץ *border.*
A valley and city of Benjamin.
Josh 18. 21 and Beth-hoglah, and the valley of K.

KIB-ROTH HAT-TA-A'-VAH, קִבְרוֹת הַתַּאֲוָה.
The 12th encampment of Israel from Egypt, and the 1st from Sinai, so called because of the people lusting for flesh while there.
Num 11. 34 And he called the name of that place K.-h.
11. 35 the people journeyed from K.-h. unto H.
33. 16 they remov. from..Sinai, and pitched at K.
33. 17 And they departed from K.-h., and enca.
Deut. 9. 22 at K.-h., ye provoked the LORD to wrath

KIB-ZA'-IM, קִבְצַיִם *double gathering.*
A Levitical city in Ephraim; *Jokneam?*
Josh 21. 22 K. with her suburbs, and Beth-horon with

KICK, to —

1. *To kick,* בָּעַט *baat.*
Deut. 32 15 Jeshurum waxed fat, and kicked: thou art
1 Sa. 2. 29 Wherefore kick ye at my sacrifice and at

2. *To kick (with the heel),* λακτίζω *laktizō.*
Acts 9. 5 hard for thee to kick against the pricks
26. 14 hard for thee to kick against the pricks

KID —

1. *A kid,* גְּדִי *gedi.*
Gen. 27. 9 fetch me from thence two good kids of the
27. 16 she put the skins of the kids of the goats
38. 23 I sent this kid, and thou hast not found
Exod 23. 19 Thou shalt not seethe a kid in his mother's
34. 26 Thou shalt not seethe a kid in his mother's
Judg 14. 6 he rent him as he would have rent a kid
1 Sa. 10. 3 one carrying three kids, and another car

2. *A kid of the goats,* גְּדִי עִזִּים *gedi izzim.*
Gen. 38. 17 said, I will send (thee) a kid from the flock
38. 20 Judah sent the kid by the hand of his fri.
Judg. 6. 19 Gideon went in, and made ready a kid, and
13. 15 until we shall have made ready a kid for
13. 19 Manoah took a kid with a meat offering
15. 1 that Samson visited his wife with a kid
1 Sa. 16. 20 bread, and a bottle of wine, and a kid, and

3. *A kid,* גְּדִיָּה *gediyyah.*
Song 1. 8 feed thy kids beside the shepherds' tents
Isa 11. 6 the leopard shall lie down with the kid

4. *A goat, strong one,* עֵז *ez.*
Deut. 14. 21 Thou shalt not seethe a kid in his mother's
1 Ki. 20. 27 before them like two little flocks of kids

5. *A kid, hairy one,* שָׂעִיר *sair.*
Gen. 37. 31 killed a kid of the goats, and dipped the
Lev. 4. 23 a kid of the goats, a male without blemish
9. 3 Take ye a kid of the goats for a sin offer.
16. 5 two kids of the goats for a sin offering
23. 19 ye shall sacrifice one kid of the goats for
Num 7. 16 One kid of the goats for sin offering
So in v. 22, 28, 34, 40, 46, 52, 58, 64, 70, 76, 82.
7. 87 the kids of the goats for a sin offering
15. 24 and one kid of the goats for a sin offering
28. 15 one kid of the goats for a sin offering unto
28. 30 one kid of the goats, to make an atonem.
29. 5, 11, 16, 19, 25 one kid of the goats..a sin
Eze. 43. 22 thou shalt offer a kid of the goats without
45. 23 a kid of the goats daily..a sin offering

6. *Hairy one, kid,* שְׂעִירָה *seirah.*
Lev. 4. 28 a kid of the goats, a female without blemish
5. 6 a lamb, or a kid of the goats, for a sin off.

7. *Sons of the goats,* בְּנֵי־עִזִּים *bene izzim.*
2 Ch. 35. 7 gave..of the flocks, lambs and kids, all

8. *A kid,* ἔριφος *eriphos.*
Luke 15. 29 thou never gavest me a kid, that I might

KIDNEYS —
Kidneys, reins, כְּלָיוֹת *kelayoth.*
Exod 29. 13, 22 the two kidneys, and the fat that (is)
Lev. 3. 4, 10, 15 the two kidneys, and the fat that
3. 10, 15 the caul above the liver, with the kid.
4. 9 the two kidneys, and the fat that (is) upon
4. 9 the caul above the liver, with the kidneys
7. 4 the two kidneys, and the fat that (is) on
7. 4 the caul..above the liver, with the kidneys
8. 16, 25 liver, and the two kidneys, and their
9. 10, 19 the kidneys, and the caul above the li.
Deut 32. 14 goats, with the fat of kidneys of wheat
Isa. 34. 6 made fat..with the fat of the kidneys of

KID'-RON, קִדְרוֹן *turbid.*
A brook running through the valley between Jerusalem and the Mount of Olives, and falling into the Dead Sea. Called *Cedron* in John 18. 1.
2 Sa. 15. 23 the king..passed over the brook K., and
[1 K. 2. 37; 15. 13; 2 Ki. 23. 4, 6, 6, 12; 2 Ch. 15. 16; 29. 16; 30. 14; Jer. 31. 40.]

KILL, to —

1. *To slay,* הָרַג *harag.*
Gen. 12. 12 will kill me, but they will save thee alive
26. 7 men of the place should kill me for Reb.
27. 42 comfort himself, (purposing) to kill thee
Exod. 2. 14 Intendest thou to kill me, as thou killedst
22. 24 I will kill you with the sword; and your
Lev. 20. 16 thou shalt kill the woman, and the beast
Num 11. 15 kill me, I pray thee, out of hand, if I have
22. 29 a sword in mine hand..now would I kill
31. 17 Now..kill every male among the little ones
31. 17 kill every woman that hath known man
31. 19 whosoever hath killed any person, and
Deut 13. 9 thou shalt surely kill him; thine hand
Judg. 9. 24 which aided him in the killing of his bre.
16. 2 morning, when it is day, we shall kill him
1 Sa. 16. 2 can I go? if Saul hear (it), he will kill me
24. 10 bade (me) kill thee; but (mine eye) spared
24. 11 and killed thee not, know thou and see
24. 18 dealt well..forasmuch as..thou killedst
1 Ki. 12. 27 they shall kill me, and go again to Reho.
Esth. 3. 13 to kill, and to cause to perish, all Jews
Job 5. 2 wrath killeth the foolish man, and envy
Eccl. 3. 3 A time to kill, and a time to heal; a time

2. *To slaughter,* זָבַח *zabach.*
Deut 12. 15 thou mayest kill and eat flesh in all thy g.
12. 21 thou shalt kill of thy herd and of thy flock
1 Sa. 28. 24 she hasted, and killed it, and took flour
2 Ch. 18. 2 Ahab killed sheep and oxen for him in
Eze. 34. 3 ye kill them that are fed..ye feed not the

3. *To pierce, wound,* חָלַל *chalal.*
Judg 20. 31 kill, as at other times, in the highways
20. 39 Benjamin began to smite (and) kill of the

4. *To slaughter,* טָבַח *tabach.*
Exod 22. 1 an ox, or a sheep, and kill it, or sell it
1 Sa. 25. 11 my flesh that I have killed for my shearers
Prov. 9. 2 She hath killed her beasts; she hath min.
Lam. 2. 21 hast slain..thou hast killed..not pitied

5. *To put to death,* מוּת *muth,* 5.
Exod. 1. 16 if it (be) a son, then ye shall kill him: but
4. 24 the LORD met him, and sought to kill him
16. 3 to kill this whole assembly with hunger
17. 3 to kill us and our children and our cattle
21. 29 that he hath killed a man or a woman
Lev. 20. 4 And if the people of the land..kill him
Num 14. 15 thou shalt kill..this people as one man
16. 13 to kill us in the wilderness, except thou
16. 41 saying, Ye have killed the people of the
Deut 32. 39 I kill, and I make alive; I wound, and I
Judg 13. 23 If the LORD were pleased to kill us, he
15. 13 bind thee fast..but surely we will not kill
1 Sa. 2. 6 LORD killeth, and maketh alive: he brin.
19. 1 to all his servants, that they should kill
19. 2 saying, Saul my father seeketh to kill thee
19. 17 He said..Let me go; why should I kill
30. 15 that thou wilt neither kill me, nor deliver
2 Sa. 13. 28 I say unto you, Smite Ammon; then kill
14. 7 that we may kill him, for the life of his
14. 32 if there be..iniquity in me, let him kill
21. 4 neither for us shalt thou kill any man in
21. 17 and smote the Philistine, and killed him
1 Ki. 11. 40 Solomon sought therefore to kill Jeroboam
16. 10 Zimri went in and smote him, and killed
2 Ki. 5. 7 (Am) I God, to kill and to make alive
7. 4 the Syrians..if they kill us, we shall but
11. 15 him that followeth her kill with the sword
15. 25 Pekah..killed him, and reigned in his
1 Ch. 19. 18 killed Shophach the captain of the host
Psa. 59 *title.* sent, and they watched the house to kill
Prov. 21. 25 The desire of the slothful killeth him; for
Isa 14. 30 I will kill thy root with famine, and he sh.

6. *To smite, cause to smite,* נָכָה *nakah,* 5.
Gen. 4. 15 a mark..lest any finding him should kill
37. 21 Reuben heard..and said, Let us not kill
Lev. 24. 17 he that killeth any man shall surely be put
24. 18 he that killeth a beast shall make it good
24. 21 he that killeth a beast, he shall restore it
24. 21 he that killeth a man, he shall be put to d.
Num 35. 11 slayer..which killeth any person at una.
35. 15 every one that killeth any person unawares
35. 30 Whoso killeth any person, the murderer
Deut. 19. 4 Whoso killeth his neighbour ignorantly
Josh. 20. 3 the slayer that killeth (any) person unaw.
20. 9 whosoever killeth (any) person at unawa.
1 Sa. 17. 9 If he be able to fight with me, and to kill
17. 9 if I prevail against him, and kill him, then
17. 25 the man who killeth him, the king will en.
17. 26 What shall be done to the man that killeth
17. 27 So shall it be done to the man that killeth
2 Sa. 12. 9 Thou hast killed Uriah the Hittite with
1 Ki. 16. 7 house of Jeroboam; and because he killed
2 Ch. 25. 3 servants that had killed the king his fath.

7. *To go round,* נָקַף *naqaph.*
Isa 29. 1 add ye year to year; let them kill sacrifices

8. *To kill,* קָטַל *qatal.*
Job 24. 14 The murderer rising with the light killeth

9. *To murder, pierce,* רָצַח *ratsach.*
Exod 20. 13 Thou shalt not kill
Num 35. 27 and the revenger of blood kill the slayer
Deut. 4. 42 which should kill his neighbour unawares
5. 17 Thou shalt not kill
1 Ki. 21. 19 Hast thou killed, and also taken possess.
Hos. 4. 2 By swearing, and lying, and killing, and

10. *To slaughter, kill,* שָׁחַט *shachat.*
Gen. 37. 31 took Joseph's coat, and killed a kid of the
Exod 12. 6 the congregation of Israel shall kill it in
12. 21 take you a lamb..and kill the passover
29. 11 thou shalt kill the bullock before the LORD
29. 20 Then shalt thou kill the ram, and take of
Lev. 1. 5 he shall kill the bullock before the LORD
1. 11 he shall kill it on the side of the altar no.
3. 2 kill it (at) the door of the tabernacle of the
3. 8, 13 and kill it before the tabernacle of the
4. 4 he shall..kill the bullock before the LORD
4. 24 and kill it in the place where they kill the
4. 33 the place where they kill the burnt offer.
7. 2 where they kill the burnt..shall they kill
8. 19 And he killed (it); and Moses sprinkled
14. 13 in the place where he shall kill the sin off.
14. 19 afterward he shall kill the burnt offering
14. 25 he shall kill the lamb of the tresspass off.
14. 50 he shall kill the one of the birds in an
16. 11 shall kill the bullock of the sin offering
16. 15 Then shall he kill the goat of the sin off
17. 3 that killeth..in the camp, or that killeth
22. 28 ye shall not kill it and her young both in
2 Ch. 29. 22 So they killed the bullocks, and the priests

2 Ch.29. 22 when they had killed the rams..they ki.
29. 24 the priests killed them, and they made
30. 15 Then they killed the passover on the four.
35. 1 they killed the passover on the fourteen.
35. 6 So kill the passover, and sanctify yourse.
35. 11 they killed the passover, and the priests
Ezra 6. 20 killed the passover for all the children
Isa. 66. 3 He that killeth an ox (is as if) he slew a

11. *To take away, kill*, ἀναιρέω *anaireō*.
Luke22. 2 scribes sought how they might kill him
Acts 7. 28 Wilt thou kill me, as thou didst the Egy.
9. 23 And after..the Jews took counsel to kill
9. 24 watched the gates day and night to kill
12. 2 he killed James the brother of John with
16. 27 would have killed himself, supposing that
23. 15 we, or ever he come near, are ready to kill
23. 21 neither eat nor drink till they have killed
23. 27 should have been killed of them: then
25. 3 send..laying wait in the way to kill him

12. *To kill entirely*, ἀποκτείνω *apokteinō*.
Matt10. 28 which kill the body, but are not able to k.
16. 21 killed, and be raised again the third day
17. 23 they shall kill him, and the third day he
21. 35 beat one, and killed another, and stoned
21. 38 This is the heir; come, let us kill him
23. 34 (some) of them ye shall kill and crucify
23. 37 Jerusalem..that killest the prophets, and
24. 9 shall kill you: and ye shall be hated of all
26. 4 they might take Jesus by subtilty, and k.
Mark 3. 4 Is it lawful..to save life, or to kill? But
6. 19 would have killed him; but she could not
8. 31 be killed, and after three days rise again
9. 31 into the hands of men, and they shall kill
9. 31 after that he is killed, he shall rise the
10. 34 and shall spit upon him, and shall kill
12. 5 him they killed, and many others..killing
12. 7 This is the heir; come, let us kill him
12. 8 took him, and killed..and cast..out of
Luke11. 47 for ye build..and your fathers killed them
11. 48 they indeed killed them, and ye build
12. 4 Be not afraid of them that kill the body
12. 5 which after he hath killed hath power to
13. 31 and depart hence: for Herod will kill thee
13. 34 which killest the prophets, and stonest
20. 14 let us kill him, that the inheritance may
20. 15 they cast him out of the vineyard, and k.
John 5. 18 Jews sought the more to kill him, because
7. 1 would not..because the Jews sought to k.
7. 19 Did not Moses..Why go ye about to kill
7. 20 people answered..who goeth about to k.
7. 25 said..is not this he whom they seek to k.?
8. 22 Then said the Jews, Will he kill himself
8. 37 ye seek to kill me, because my word hath
8. 40 But now ye seek to kill me, a man that
16. 2 whosoever killeth you will think that he
Acts 3. 15 killed the prince of life, whom God hath
21. 31 as they went about to kill him, tidings c.
23. 12 neither eat nor drink till they had killed
27. 42 the soldiers' counsel was to kill the pris.
Rom 11. 3 Lord, they have killed thy prophets, and
2 Co. 3. 6 the letter killeth, but the spirit giveth
1 Th. 2. 15 Who both killed the Lord Jesus and their
Rev. 2. 23 I will kill her children with death; and
6. 8 to kill with sword, and with hunger, and
6. 11 their brethren, that should be killed as
9. 5 it was given that they should not kill them
9. 18 was the third part of men killed, by the
9. 20 the rest of the men, which were not killed
11. 5 hurt them, he must in this manner be k.
11. 7 the beast..shall overcome them, and kill
13. 10 he that killeth with the sword must be k.
13. 15 would not worship the image..should be k.

13. *To handle violently*, διαχειρίζομαι *diacheirizomai*.
Acts 26. 21 the Jews caught me..and went about to k.

14. *To slaughter, sacrifice*, θύω *thuō*.
Matt22. 4 my oxen and..fatlings (are) killed, and
Mark14. 12 the first day..when they killed the pass.
Luke15. 23 bring hither the fatted calf, and kill..let
15. 27 thy father hath killed the fatted calf, be.
15. 30 thou hast killed for him the fatted calf
22. 7 the day..when the passover must be killed
John10. 10 but for to steal, and to kill, and to destroy
Acts 10. 13 there came a voice..Rise, Peter; kill, and

15. *To slay, kill, wound*, σφάττω *sphattō*, σφάζω.
Rev. 6. 4 that they should kill one another: and

16. *To murder*, φονεύω *phoneuō*.
Matt. 5. 21 Thou shalt not kill..whosoever shall kill
23. 31 ye are the children of them which killed
Mark10. 19 [Do not kill], Do not steal, Do not bear
Luke18. 20 Do not kill, Do not steal, Do not bear false
Rom 13. 9 Thou shalt not kill, Thou shalt not steal
Jas. 2. 11 said, Do not commit adultery..Do not kill
2. 11 if thou kill thou art become a transgres.
4. 2 ye kill, and desire to have, and cannot
5. 6 Ye have condemned..killed the just..he

KILLED, to be —

1. *To be killed*, הָרַג *harag*, 4.
Psa. 44. 22 for thy sake are we killed all the day long

2. *To slaughter*, שָׁחַט *shachat*.
Lev. 4. 15 the bullock shall be killed before the L.
14. 5 shall command that one of the birds be k.

3. *To be slaughtered*, שָׁחַט *shachat*, 2.
Lev. 6. 25 is killed shall the sin offering be killed be.
14. 6 in the blood of the bird..killed over the

4. *To put to death*, θανατόω *thanatoō*.
Rom. 8. 36 For thy sake we are killed all the day long
2 Co. 6. 9 behold, we live; as chastened, and not k.

KILLING —

1. *To murder*, רָצַח *ratsach*.
Hos. 4. 2 By swearing, and lying, and killing, and

2. *To slaughter*, שָׁחַט *shachat*.
Isa. 22. 13 slaying oxen and killing sheep, eating fl.

3. *A slaughter*, שְׁחִיטָה *shechitah*.
2 Ch. 30. 17 the Levites had the charge of the killing

KIN, near k., near of k., nigh of k. —

1. *Near of flesh*, שְׁאֵר בָּשָׂר *sheer basar*.
Lev. 18. 6 shall approach to any that is near of kin
25. 49 or (any) that is nigh of kin unto him of his

2. *Flesh, relation*, שְׁאֵר *sheer*.
Lev. 20. 19 for he uncovereth his near kin: they 21.2.

2a. *Near kin*, גֹּאֵל קָרוֹב [*gaal*]. Lev. 25. 25.

3. *Of the same race*, συγγενής *suggenēs*.
Mark 6. 4 among his own [kin], and in his own house

KI'-NAH, קִינָה *smithy*.
A city in the S. of Judah, near Dimonah.
Josh.15. 22 And K., and Dimonah, and Adadah

KIND (divers) —

1. *Species, kind*, זַן *zan*.
2 Ch.16. 14 divers kinds..prepared by the apothecar.
Dan. 3. 5 psaltery, dulcimer, and all kinds of mus.
3. 7 sackbut, psaltery, and all kinds of music
3. 10, 15 psaltery, and dulcimer, and all kinds

2. *Kind, species*, מִין *min*.
Gen. 1. 11 the fruit tree yielding fruit after his kind
1. 12 herb yielding seed after his kind, and the
1. 12 whose seed (was) in itself, after his kind
1. 21 after their kind, and..fowl after his kind
1. 24 the living creature after his kind, cattle
1. 24 beast of the earth after his kind: and it
1. 25 made the beast of the earth after his kind
1. 25 cattle after their kind, and every thing
1. 25 creepeth upon the earth after his kind: and
6. 20 Of fowls after their kind
6. 20 and of cattle after their kind, of every
6. 20 creeping thing of the earth after his kind
7. 14 They, and every beast after his kind
7. 14 and all the cattle after their kind
7. 14 and every creeping thing..after his kind
7. 14 and every fowl after his kind, every bird
Lev. 11. 14 the vulture, and the kite after his kind
11. 15 Every raven after his kind
11. 16 the cuckoo, and the hawk after his kind
11. 19 the stork, the heron after her kind, and
11. 22 ye may eat; the locust after his kind, and
11. 22 and the bald locust after his kind
11. 22 and the beetle after his kind
11. 22 and the grasshopper after his kind
11. 29 the mouse, and the tortoise after his kind
Deut 14. 13 the kite, and the vulture after his kind
14. 14 And every raven after his kind
14. 15 the cuckow, and the hawk after his kind
14. 18 the stork, and the heron after her kind
Eze. 47. 10 their fish shall be according to their kinds

3. *Family*, מִשְׁפָּחָה *mishpachah*.
Gen. 8. 19 Every beast..after their kinds, went forth
Jer. 15. 3 I will appoint over them four kinds, saith

4. *Kind, species, race*, γένος *genos*.
Matt 13. 47 into the sea, and gathered of every kind
17. 21 this [kind] goeth not out but by prayer
Mark 9. 29 This kind can come forth by nothing but
1 Co. 12. 10 to another..kinds of tongues; to another
14. 10 There are, it may be, so many kinds of

5. *Nature*, φύσις *phusis*.
Jas. 3. 7 every kind of beasts, and of birds, and of

KIND —

Useful, beneficial, χρηστός *chrēstos*.
Luke 6. 35 he is kind unto the unthankful and..the
Eph. 4. 32 be ye kind one to another, tender hearted

KIND, to be —

To be useful, beneficial, χρηστεύομαι *chrēsteuomai*.
1 Co. 13. 4 Charity suffereth long..is kind; charity

KIND of, a —

A certain, τις *tis*.
Jas. 1. 18 that we should be a kind of firstfruits of

KINDLE, to —

1. *To cause brightness, give light*, אוֹר *or*, 5.
Mal. 1. 10 neither do ye kindle (fire) on mine altar

2. *To burn*, בָּעַר *baar*.
2 Sa. 22. 9 fire..devoured: coals were kindled by it
22. 13 Through the brightness..were coals..kin.
Psa. 2. 12 when his wrath is kindled but a little
18. 8 fire..devoured: coals were kindled by it
106. 18 a fire was kindled in their company; the
Isa. 30. 33 the breath of the LORD..doth kindle it
43. 2 neither shall the flame kindle upon thee
Jer. 44. 6 was kindled in the cities of Judah and in

3. *To make to burn*, בָּעַר *baar*, 3.
Exod35. 3 Ye shall kindle no fire throughout your
Isa. 50. 11 and in the sparks (that) ye have kindled
Jer. 7. 18 the fathers kindle the fire, and the women
Eze. 20. 48 shall see that I the LORD have kindled it

4. *To cause to burn*, בָּעַר *baar*, 5.
Exod22. 6 he that kindled the fire shall surely make

5. *To burn, pursue hotly*, דָּלַק *dalaq*.
Obad. 18 they shall kindle in them, and devour them

6. *To cause to burn, kindle*, דָּלַק *dalaq*, 5.
Eze. 24. 10 Heap on wood, kindle the fire, consume

7. *To cause to burn*, חָרָה *charah*, 5.
Job 19. 11 He hath also kindled his wrath against

8. *To kindle*, חָרַר *charar*, 3a.
Prov 26. 21 so (is) a contentious man to kindle strife

9. *To kindle, burn*, יָצַת *yatsath*.
Isa. 9. 18 shall kindle in the thickets of the forest

10. *To kindle, burn*, יָצַת *yatsath*, 5.
Jer. 11. 16 he hath kindled fire upon it, and the bra.
17. 27 then will I kindle a fire in the gates the.
21. 14 I will kindle a fire in the forest thereof
43. 12 I will kindle a fire in the houses of the g.
49. 27 I will kindle a fire in the wall of Damas.
50. 32 I will kindle a fire in his cities, and it sh.
Lam. 4. 11 hath kindled a fire in Zion, and it hath d.
Eze. 20. 47 I will kindle a fire in thee, and it shall
Amos 1. 14 I will kindle a fire in the wall of Rabbah

11. *To burn, kindle*, יָקַד *yaqad*.
Isa. 10. 16 under his glory he shall kindle a burning

12. *To set on fire, burn*, לָהַט *lahat*, 3.
Job 41. 21 His breath kindleth coals, and a flame

13. *To burn*, נָשַׂק *nasaq*, 5.
Isa. 44. 15 yea, he kindleth (it), and baketh bread

14. *To kindle, be kindled*, קָדַח *qadach*.
Isa. 50. 11 Behold, all ye that kindle a fire, that com.
Jer 17. 4 for ye have kindled a fire in mine anger

15. *To perfume, make or offer perfume*, קָטַר *qatar*, 5.
Jer. 33. 18 to kindle meat offerings, and to do sacri.

16. *To burn, kindle*, שָׂרַף *saraph*.
Lev. 10. 6 the burning which the LORD hath kindled

17. *To light up*, ἀνάπτω *anaptō*.
Luke 12. 49 and what will I, if it be already kindled?
Acts 28. 2 [they kindled] a fire, and received us every
Jas. 3. 5 how great a matter a little fire kindleth!

18. *To light*, ἅπτω *haptō*.
Luke 22. 55 when [they had kindled] a fire in the midst

KINDLED, to be —

1. *To burn*, חָרָה *charah*.
Gen. 30. 2 Jacob's anger was kindled against Rachel
39. 19 it came to pass..that his wrath was kind.
Exod 4. 14 the anger of the LORD was kindled against
Num11. 1 the LORD heard..and his anger was kind.
11. 10 the anger of the LORD was kindled greatly
11. 33 the wrath of the LORD was kindled against
12. 9 the anger of the LORD was kindled against
22. 22 God's anger was kindled because he went
22. 27 Balaam's anger was kindled, and he smote
24. 10 Balak's anger was kindled against Balaam
25. 3 the anger of the LORD was kindled again.
32. 10 the LORD'S anger was kindl. the same time
Deut. 6. 15 the anger of the LORD..be kindled against
7. 4 so will the anger of the LORD be kindled
11. 17 the LORD'S wrath be kindled against you
29. 27 the anger of the LORD was kindled against
31. 17 Then my anger shall be kindled against
Josh. 7. 1 the anger of the LORD was kindled against
23. 16 then shall the anger of the LORD be kind.
Judg. 9. 30 city heard the words..his anger was ki.
14. 19 his anger was kindled, and he went up to
1 Sa. 11. 6 when he heard..his anger was kindled
17. 28 Eliab's anger was kindled against David
20. 30 Then Saul's anger was kindled against J.
2 Sa. 6. 7 the anger of the LORD was kindled against
12. 5 David's anger was greatly kindled against
24. 1 the anger of the LORD was kindled against
2 Ki. 13. 3 the anger of the LORD was kindled against
23. 26 his anger was kindled against Judah, bec.
1 Ch. 13. 10 the anger of the LORD was kindled against
2 Ch. 25. 10 their anger was greatly kindled against J.
25. 15 anger of the LORD was kindled against A.
Job 32. 2 Then was kindled the wrath of Elihu the
32. 2 against Job was his wrath kindled, becau.
32. 3 against his three friends was his wrath ki.
32. 5 When Elihu saw..then his wrath was ki.
42. 7 My wrath is kindled against thee, and
Psa. 106. 40 Therefore was the wrath of the LORD kin.
124. 3 when their wrath was kindled against us
Isa. 5. 25 Therefore is the anger of the LORD kind.
Hos. 8. 5 mine anger is kindled against them: how
Zech. 10. 3 Mine anger was kindled against the shep.

2. *To be kindled, burned*, יָצַת *yatsath*, 2.
2 Ki. 22. 13 the wrath of the LORD that is kindled again.
22. 17 my wrath shall be kindled against this

3. *To be burning, yearning*, כָּמַר *kamar*, 2.
Hos. 11. 8 Mine heart..my repentings are kindled

4. *To be kindled*, נָשַׂק *nasaq*, 2.
Psa. 78. 21 so a fire was kindled against Jacob, and

5. *To be kindled*, קָדַח *qadach*.
Deut 32. 22 a fire is kindled in mine anger, and shall
Jer. 15. 14 a fire is kindled in mine anger. (which)

KINDLY —

1. *Kindness*, חֶסֶד *chesed*.
Gen. 24. 49 if ye will deal kindly and truly with my
47. 29 deal kindly and truly with me; bury me not
Josh. 2. 14 that we will deal kindly and truly with
Ruth 1. 8 LORD deal kindly, with you, as ye have
1 Sa. 20. 8 thou shalt deal kindly with thy servant

2. *Good*, טוֹב *tob*.
2 Ki. 25. 28 he spake kindly to him, and set his throne
Jer. 52. 32 spake kindly unto him, and set his throne

3. *To the heart,* עַל־לֵב *al leb.*
Gen. 34. 3 he loved the damsel, and spake kindly unto
50. 21 he comforted them, and spake kindly unto

KINDLY affectioned —
Loving with natural affection, φιλόστοργος *philo.*
Rom 12. 10 kindly affectioned one to another with

KINDNESS —
1. *Kindness,* חֶסֶד *chesed.*
Gen. 20. 13 This (is) thy kindness which thou shalt
21. 23 according to the kindness that I have done
24. 12 show kindness unto my master Abraham
24. 14 thou hast showed kindness unto my mas.
40. 14 show kindness, I pray thee, unto me, and
Josh. 2. 12 since I have showed you kindness, that ye
2. 12 ye will also show kindness unto my father
Judg. 8. 35 Neither showed they kindness to the hou.
Ruth 2. 20 who hath not left off his kindness to the
3. 10 thou hast showed more kindness in the
1 Sa. 15. 6 ye showed kindness to..the children of I.
20. 14 show me the kindness of the LORD, that I
20. 15 thou shalt not cut off thy kindness from
2 Sa. 2. 5 that ye have showed this kindness unto
2. 6 LORD show kindness and truth unto you
3. 8 which against Judah do show kindness
9. 1 that I may show him kindness for Jonathan
9. 3 that I may show the kindness of God unto
9. 7 I will surely show thee kindness for Jon.
10. 2 I will show kindness unto Hanun the son
10. 2 as his father showed kindness unto me
16. 17 (Is) this thy kindness to thy friend? why
1 Ki. 2. 7 show kindness unto the sons of Barzillai
3. 6 thou hast kept for him this great kindness
1 Ch. 19. 2 I will show kindness unto Hanun the son
19. 2 because his father showed kindness to me
2 Ch. 24. 22 the king remembered not the kindness
Neh. 9. 17 a God..slow to anger, and of great kind.
Esth. 2. 9 pleased him, and she obtained kindness
Psa. 31. 21 he hath showed me his marvellous kind.
141. 5 (it shall be) a kindness; and let him rep.
Prov 19. 22 The desire of a man (is) his kindness: and
31. 26 and in her tongue (is) the law of kindness
Isa. 54. 8 with everlasting kindness will I have m.
54. 10 my kindness shall not depart from thee
Jer. 2. 2 kindness of thy youth, the love of thine
Joel 2. 13 slow to anger, and of great kindness, and
Jon. 4. 2 slow to anger, and of great kindness, and

2. *Good,* טוֹב *tob.*
2 Sa. 2. 6 I also will requite you this kindness, bec.

3. *Love of mankind,* φιλανθρωπία *philanthrōpia.*
Acts 28. 2 barbarous people showed us no little kind.

4. *Usefulness, beneficence,* χρηστότης *chrēstotēs.*
2 Co. 6. 6 by longsuffering, by kindness, by the H. G.
Eph. 2. 7 kindness toward us through Christ Jesus
Col. 3. 12 kindness, humbleness of mind, meekness
Titus 3. 4 the kindness and love of God our Saviour

KINDNESS, brotherly —
Love of the brotherhood, φιλαδελφία *philadelphia.*
2 Pe. 1. 7 godliness brotherly kindness..to br. kind.
[*See also* Loving kindness, merciful.]

KINDRED —
1. *Brother,* אָח *ach.*
1 Ch. 12. 29 of the children of Benjamin, the kindred

2. *Relationship,* גְּאֻלָּה *geullah.*
Eze. 11. 15 thy brethren, the men of thy kindred, and

3. *Acquaintance,* מוֹדַעַת *modaath.*
Ruth 3. 2 And now (is) not Boaz of our kindred

4. *Birth, kindred,* מוֹלֶדֶת *moledeth.*
Gen. 12. 1 out of thy country, and from thy kindred
24. 4 go unto my country, and to my kindred
24. 7 from the land of my kindred, and which
31. 3 Return..to thy kindred; and I will be
31. 13 and return unto the land of thy kindred
32. 9 Return unto thy country, and to thy kin.
43. 7 The man asked us straitly..of our kindred
Num 10. 30 will depart to mine own land and to my k.
Esth. 2. 10 had not showed her people nor her kind.
2. 20 Esther had not..showed her kindred nor
8. 6 can I endure..the destruction of my k.?

5. *Family,* מִשְׁפָּחָה *mishpachah.*
Gen. 24. 38 go unto my father's house, and to my ki.
24. 40 shalt take a wife for my son of my kind.
24. 41 when thou comest to my kindred; and if
Josh. 6. 23 they brought out all her kindred, and left
Ruth 2. 3 Boaz, who (was) of the kindred of Elime.
1 Ch. 16. 28 Give unto the LORD, ye kindreds of the
Job 32. 2 Barachel the Buzite, of the kindred of R.
Psa. 22. 27 all the kindreds of the nations shall wor.
96. 7 Give unto the LORD, O ye kindreds of the

6. *Race,* γένος *genos.*
Acts 4. 6 as many as were of the kindred of the
7. 13 Joseph's kindred was made known unto
7. 19 The same dealt subtilely with our kindred

7. *Family, tribe,* πατριά *patria.*
Acts 3. 25 shall all the kindreds of the earth be ble.

8. *The same race,* συγγένεια *suggeneia.*
Luke 1. 61 There is none of thy kindred that is called
Acts 7. 3 out of thy country, and from thy kindred
7. 14 all his kindred, threescore and fifteen souls

9. *Tribe,* φυλή *phulē.*
Rev. 1. 7 all kindreds of the earth shall wail beca.
5. 9 out of every kindred, and tongue, and pe.
7. 9 of all nations, and kindreds, and people
11. 9 they of the people and kindreds, and ton.
13. 7 over all kindreds, and tongues, and nati.
14. 6 nation, and kindred, and tongue, and pe.

KINE —
1. *Ox, steer,* אֶלֶף *eleph.*
Deut. 7. 13 the increase of thy kine, and the flocks
28. 4, 18 the increase of thy kine, and the flocks
28. 51 the increase of thy kine, or flocks of thy

2. *Herd, horned cattle,* בָּקָר *baqar.*
Deut 32. 14 Butter of kine, and milk of sheep, with
2 Sa. 17. 29 butter, and sheep, and cheese of kine, for

3. *Cow, heifer,* פָּרָה *parah.*
Gen. 32. 15 forty kine, and ten bulls, twenty she asses
41. 2 seven well favoured kine and fat fleshed
41. 3 seven other kine came up after them out
41. 3 stood by the..kine upon the brink of the
41. 4 the ill favoured and lean fleshed kine did
41. 4 eat up the seven well favoured and fat k.
41. 18 came up out of the river seven kine
41. 19 seven other kine came up after them, poor
41. 20 And the lean and the ill favoured kine
41. 20 did eat up the first seven fat kine
41. 26 The seven good kine (are) seven years; and
41. 27 the seven thin and ill favoured kine that
1 Sa. 6. 7 make a new cart, and take two milch kine
6. 7 tie the kine to the cart, and bring their
6. 10 took two milch kine, and tied them to the
6. 12 the kine took the straight way to the way
6. 14 offered the kine a burnt offering unto the
Amos 4. 1 Hear this word, ye kine of Bashan, that

KING —
1. *Prince, king,* מֶלֶךְ *melek* [V.L. מלאך].
2 Sa. 11. 1 it came to pass..at the time when kings

2. *King, counsellor,* מֶלֶךְ *melek.*
Gen. 14. 1 in the days of Amraphel king of Shinar
14. 1 Arioch king of Ellasar, Chedorlaomer
14. 1 king of Elam, and Tidal king of nations
14. 2 made war with Bera king of Sodom, and
14. 2 Birsha king of Gomorrah, Shinab king of
14. 2, 8 king of Zeboiim, and the king of Bela
14. 5 the kings that (were) with him, and smote
14. 8 there went out the king of Sodom, and
14. 8 king of Gomorrah, and the king of Admah
14. 9 the king of Elam, and with Tidal king of
14. 9 and Amraphel king of Shinar, and
14. 9 Arioch king of Ellasar; four kings with
14. 10 the kings of Sodom and Gomorrah fled
14. 17 the king of Sodom went out to meet him
14. 17 and of the kings that (were) with him, at
14. 17 valley of Shaveh, which (is) the king's dale
14. 18 Melchizedek king of Salem brought forth
14. 21 the king of Sodom said unto Abram, Give
14. 22 Abram said to the king of Sodom, I have
17. 6 I will make nations of thee, and kings sh.
17. 16 I will bless her..kings of people shall be
20. 2 Abimelech king of Gerar sent and took S.
26. 1 Isaac went unto Abimelech king of the
26. 8 Abimelech king of the Philistines looked
35. 11 and kings shall come out of thy loins
36. 31 these (are) the kings that reigned in the
36. 31 before there reigned any king over the ch.
39. 20 where the king's prisoners (were) bound
40. 1 (that) the butler of the king of Egypt and
40. 1 had offended their lord the king of Egypt
40. 5 the butler and the baker of the king of E.
41. 46 when he stood before Pharaoh king of E.
Exod. 1. 8 there arose up a new king over Egy., which
1. 15 the king of Egypt spake to the Hebrew
1. 17 not as the king of Egypt commanded
1. 18 the king of Egypt called for the midwives
2. 23 it came to pass..the king of Egypt died
3. 18 thou shalt come..unto the king of Egypt
3. 19 the king of Egypt will not let you go, no
5. 4 king of Egypt said unto them, Wherefore
6. 11 Go in, speak unto Pharaoh king of Egypt
6. 13 gave them a charge..unto Pharaoh king
6. 27 which spake to Pharaoh king of Egypt
6. 29 speak thou unto Pharaoh king of Egypt
14. 5 And it was told the king of Egypt that
14. 8 hardened the heart of Pharaoh king of E.
Num 20. 14 Moses sent messengers..unto the king of
20. 17 we will go by the king's (high) way, we
21. 1 king Arad the Canaanite, which dwelt in
21. 21 Israel sent messengers unto Sihon king of
21. 22 we will go along by the king's (high) way
21. 26 city of Sihon the king of the Amorites
21. 26 who had fought against the former king
21. 29 into captivity unto Sihon king of the Am.
21. 33 Og the king of Bashan went out against
21. 34 do to him as thou didst unto Sihon king
22. 4 Balak the son of Zippor (was) king of the
22. 10 Balak the son of Zippor, king of Moab
23. 7 Balak the king of Moab hath brought me
23. 21 and the shout of a king (is) among them
24. 7 and his king shall be higher than Agag
31. 8 they slew the kings of Midian, besides the
31. 8 five kings of Midian: Balaam also the
32. 33 kingdom of Sihon king of the Amorites
32. 33 and the kingdom of Og king of Bashan
33. 40 king Arad the Canaanite, which dwelt in
Deut. 1. 4 After he had slain Sihon the king of the
1. 4 Og the king of Bashan, which dwelt at A.
2. 24 Sihon the Amorite, king of Heshbon, and
2. 26 unto Sihon king of Heshbon with words
2. 30 Sihon king of Heshbon would not let us
3. 1 Og the king of Bashan came out against
3. 2 as thou didst unto Sihon king of the Am.
3. 3 delivered..Og also, the king of Bashan
3. 6 as we did unto Sihon king of Heshbon
3. 8 out of the hand of the two kings of the A.
Deut. 3. 11 For only Og king of Bashan remained of
3. 21 God hath done unto these two kings: so
4. 46 in the land of Sihon king of the Amorites
4. 47 the land of Og king of Bashan, two kings
7. 8 from the hand of Pharaoh king of Egypt
7. 24 shall deliver their kings into thine hand
11. 3 which he did..unto Pharaoh the king of
17. 14 I will set a king over me, like as all the
17. 15 Thou shalt in any wise set (him) king over
17. 15 among thy brethren shalt thou set king
28. 36 thy king which thou shalt set over thee
29. 7 the king of Heshbon, and Og the king of
31. 4 as he did to Sihon and to Og, kings of the
33. 5 he was king in Jeshurun, when the heads
Josh. 2. 2 And it was told the king of Jericho, say.
2. 3 the king of Jericho sent unto Rahab, say.
2. 10 and what ye did unto the two kings of
5. 1 it came to pass, when all the kings of the
5. 1 all the kings of the Canaanites, which
6. 2 given into thine hand Jericho, and the k.
8. 1 I have given into thine hand the king of
8. 2 And thou shalt do to Ai and her king
8. 2 as thou didst unto Jericho and her king
8. 14 came to pass, when the king of Ai saw
8. 23 And the king of Ai they took alive, and
8. 29 the king of Ai he hanged on a tree until
9. 1 when all the kings which (were) on this
9. 10 all that he did to the two kings of the A.
9. 10 to Sihon king of Heshbon, and to Og king
10. 1 when Adonizedek king of Jerusalem had
10. 1 as he had done to Jericho and her king
10. 1 so he had done to Ai and her king; and
10. 3 king of Jerusalem sent unto Hoham king
10. 3 Piram king of Jarmuth..unto Japhia king
10. 3 and unto Debir king of Eglon, saying
10. 5 Therefore the five kings of the Amorites
10. 5, 23 the king of Jerusalem, the king of H.
10. 5, 23 the king of Jarmuth, the king of Lac.
10. 5, 23 the king of Eglon, gathered themselves
10. 6 for all the kings of the Amorites that dw.
10. 16 these five kings fled, and hid themselves
10. 17 The five kings are found hid in a cave at
10. 22 bring out those five kings unto me out of
10. 23 brought forth those five kings unto him
10. 24 when they brought out those kings unto
10. 24 your feet upon the necks of these kings
10. 28 and the king thereof he utterly destroyed
10. 28 and he did to the king of Makkedah
10. 28 as he did unto the king of Jericho
10. 30 delivered it also, and the king thereof
10. 30 unto the king thereof as he did unto the k.
10. 33 Then Horam king of Gezer came up to
10. 37 and the king thereof, and all the cities
10. 39 he took it, and the king thereof, and all
10. 39 so he did to Debir, and to the king thereof
10. 39 had done also to Libnah, and to her king
10. 40 So Joshua smote all..their kings: he left
10. 42 all these kings and their land did Joshua
11. 1 Jabin ki. of Hazor had heard (those things)
11. 1 that he sent to Jobab king of Madon, and
11. 1 to the king of Shimron, and to the king of
11. 2 to the kings that (were) on the north of the
11. 5 when all these kings were met together
11. 10 and smote the king thereof with the sword
11. 12 cities of those kings, and all the kings of
11. 17 all their kings he took, and smote them
11. 18 made war a long time with all those kings
12. 1 Now these (are) the kings of the land
12. 2 Sihon king of the Amorites, who dwelt in
12. 4 the coa. of Og king of Bashan, (which was)
12. 5 Gilead, the border of Sihon king of Heshb.
12. 7 these (are) the kings of the country which
12. 9 The king of Jericho, one; the king of Ai
12. 10 The king of Jerusalem, one; the king of
12. 11 The king of Jarmuth, one; the king of L.
12. 12 The king of Eglon, one; the king of Gezer
12. 13 The king of Debir, one; the king of Ged.
12. 14 The king of Hormah, one; the king of A.
12. 15 The king of Libnah, one; the king of Ad.
12. 16 The king of Makkedah, one; the king of
12. 17 The king of Tappuah, one; the king of H.
12. 18 The king of Aphek, one; the king of La.
12. 19 The king of Madon, one; the king of Ha.
12. 20 The king of Shimron-meron, one; the k.
12. 21 The king of Taanach, one; the king of M.
12. 22 The king of Kedesh, one; the king of Jo.
12. 23 The king of Dor in the coast of Dor, one
12. 23 the king of the nations of Gilgal, one
12. 24 The king of Tirzah, one: all the kings thi.
13. 10 the cities of Sihon king of the Amorites
13. 21 all the kingdom of Sihon king of the Am.
13. 27 the rest of the kingdom of Sihon king of
13. 30 all the kingdom of Og king of Bashan, and
24. 9 Then Balak the son of Zippor, king of M.
24. 12 (even) the two kings of the Amorites
Judg. 1. 7 Threescore and ten kings, having their
3. 8, 10 Chushan-rishathaim king of Mesopota.
3. 12 strengthened Eglon the king of Moab
3. 14 served Eglon the king of Moab eighteen
3. 15 sent a present unto Eglon the king of M.
3. 17 he brought the present unto Eglon king
3. 19 I have a secret errand unto thee, O king
4. 2 sold them into the hand of Jabin king of
4. 17 for (there was) peace between Jabin the k.
4. 23 God subdued on that day Jabin the king
4. 24 prevailed against Jabin the king of Can.
4. 24 they had destroyed Jabin king of Canaan
5. 3 Hear, O ye kings; give ear, O ye princes
5. 19 The kings came..then fought the kings
8. 5 after Zebah and Zalmunna, kings of Mid.
8. 12 pursued..and took the two kings of Mid.
8. 18 each one resembled the children of a king

Judg. 8. 26 purple raiment that (was) on the kings of
9. 6 and went and made Abimelech king, by
9. 8 went forth (on a time) to anoint a king
9. 15 If in truth ye anoint me king over you
11. 12, 13, 14, 28 the king of the children of A.
11. 17 sent messengers unto the king of Edom
11. 17 but the king of Edom would not hearken
11. 17 in like manner they sent unto the king
11. 19 Israel sent messengers unto Sihon king
11. 19 the king of Heshbon; and Israel said
11. 25 than Balak the son of Zippor, king of M.?
17. 6 In those days (there was) no king in Israel
18. 1 In those days (there was) no king in Israel
19. 1 when (there was) no king in Israel, that
21. 25 In those days (there was) no king in Israel
1 Sa. 2. 10 and he shall give strength unto his king
8. 5 now make us a king to judge us like all
8. 6 they said, Give us a king to judge us
8. 9 show them the manner of the king that
8. 10 unto the people that asked of him a king
8. 11 This will be the manner of the king that
8. 18 cry out in that day because of your king
8. 19 Nay; but we will have a king over us
8. 20 that our king may judge us, and go out
8. 22 LORD said..Hearken..and make them a k.
10. 19 have said unto him, (Nay), but set a king
10. 24 people shouted, and said, God save the k.
12. 1 I have hearkened..and have made a king
12. 2 now, behold, the king walketh before you
12. 9 and into the hand of the king of Moab
12. 12 when ye saw that Nahash the king of the
12. 12 Nay; but a king shall reign over us: when
12. 12 when the LORD your God (was) your king
12. 13 behold the king whom ye have chosen
12. 13 behold, the LORD hath set a king over you
12. 14 then shall both ye and also the king that
12. 17 wickedness (is) great.. in asking you a k.
12. 19 have added..(this) evil, to ask us a king
12. 25 shall be consumed, both ye and your king
14. 47 against the kings of Zobah, and against the
15. 1 sent me to anoint thee (to be) king over
15. 8 he took Agag the king of the Amalekites
15. 11 that I have set up Saul (to be) king: for
15. 17 the LORD anointed thee king over Israel?
15. 20 have brought Agag the king of Amalek
15. 23 he hath also rejected thee from (being) k.
15. 26 hath rejected thee from being king over
15. 32 Bring ye hither to me Agag the king of
16. 1 have provided me a king among his sons
17. 25 king will enrich him with great riches
17. 55 (As) thy soul liveth, O king, I cannot tell
17. 56 the king said, Enquire thou whose son the
18. 6 singing and dancing, to meet king Saul
18. 18 that I should be son in law to the king?
18. 22 Behold, the king hath delight in thee, and
18. 22 now therefore be the king's son in law
18. 23 (a) light (thing) to be a king's son in law
18. 25 The king desireth not any dowry, but an
18. 25 to be avenged of the king's enemies
18. 26 it pleased David well to be the king's son
18. 27 they gave them in full tale to the king
18. 27 that he might be the king's son in law
19. 4 Let not the king sin against his servant
20. 5 I should not fail to sit with the king at
20. 24 the king sat him down to eat meat
20. 25 the king sat upon his seat, as at other
20. 29 therefore he cometh not unto the king's
21. 2 The king hath commanded me a business
21. 8 because the king's business required haste
21. 10 David arose..and went to Achish the king
21. 11 (Is) not this David the king of the land?
21. 12 was sore afraid of Achish the king of Gath
22. 3 said unto the king of Moab, Let my father
22. 4 brought them before the king of Moab
22. 11 king sent..and they came..to the king
22. 14 Ahimelech answered the king, and said
22. 14 as David, which (is) the king's son in law
22. 15 Let not the king impute (any) thing unto
22. 16 the king said, Thou shalt surely die, Ah.
22. 17 the king said unto the footmen that stood
22. 17 the servants of the king would not put
22. 18 the king said to Doeg, Turn thou, and fall
23. 20 Now therefore, O king, come down, acco.
23. 20 (shall be) to deliver him into the king's
24. 8 cried after Saul, saying, My lord the king
24. 14 After whom is the king of Israel come o.?
25. 36 he held a feast..like the feast of a king
26. 14 said, Who (art) thou (that) criest to the k.?
26. 15 hast thou not kept thy lord the king?
26. 15 for there came one..to destroy the king
26. 16 now see where the king's spear (is), and
26. 17 said, (It is) my voice, my lord, O king
26. 19 let my lord the king hear the words of
26. 20 king of Israel is come out to seek a flea
26. 22 answered and said, Behold the king's sp.
27. 2 unto Achish, the son of Maoch, king of G.
27. 6 Ziklag pertaineth unto the kings of Judah
28. 13 the king said unto her, Be not afraid: for
29. 3 the servant of Saul the king of Israel
29. 8 against the enemies of my lord the king?
2 Sa. 2. 4 there they anointed David king over the
2. 7 house of Judah have anointed me king
2. 11 the time that David was king in Hebron
3. 3 the daughter of Talmai, king of Geshur
3. 17 sought for David in times past (to be) king
3. 21 gather all Israel unto my lord the king
3. 23 Abner the son of Ner came to the king
3. 24 Then Joab came to the king, and said
3. 31 And king David (himself) followed the
3. 32 the king lifted up his voice, and wept at
3. 33 the king lamented over Abner, and said
3. 36 as whatsoever the king did pleased all the

2 Sa. 3. 37 that it was not of the king to slay Abner
3. 38 the king said unto his servants, Know
3. 39 I (am) this day weak, though anointed k.
4. 8 said to the king, Behold the head of Ish.
4. 8 hath avenged my lord the king this day of
5. 2 in time past, when Saul was king over us
5. 3 the elders of Israel came to the king to H.
5. 3 king David made a league with them in
5. 3 and they anointed David king over Israel
5. 6 the king and his men went to Jerusalem
5. 11 Hiram king of Tyre sent messengers to D.
5. 12 had established him king over Israel, and
5. 17 they had anointed David king over Israel
6. 12 it was told king David, saying, The LORD
6. 16 saw king David leaping and dancing before
6. 20 How glorious was the king of Israel to day
7. 1 when the king sat in his house, and the L.
7. 2 the king said unto Nathan the prophet, See
7. 3 Nathan said to the king, Go, do all that
7. 18 Then went king David in, and sat before
8. 3 David smote also Hadadezer..king of Z.
8. 5 came to succour Hadadezer king of Zobah
8. 8 king David took exceeding much brass
8. 9 When Toi king of Hamath heard that D.
8. 10 Then Toi sent Joram his son unto king D.
8. 11 Which also king David did dedicate unto
8. 12 Hadadezer, son of Rehob, king of Zobah
9. 2 the king said unto him, (Art) thou Ziba?
9. 3 the king said, (Is) there not yet any of the
9. 3 Ziba said unto the king, Jonathan hath
9. 4 the king said unto him, Where (is) he?
9. 4 Ziba said unto the king, Behold, he (is) in
9. 5 Then king David sent and fetched him out
9. 9 the king called to Ziba, Saul's servant, and
9. 11 Then said Ziba unto the king, According
9. 11 all that my lord the king hath commanded
9. 11 eat at my table, as one of the king's sons
9. 13 he did eat continually at the king's table
10. 1 the king of the children of Ammon died
10. 5 the king said, Tarry at Jericho until your
10. 6 and of king Maacah a thousand men, and
10. 19 all the kings (that were) servants to Had.
11. 1 at the time when kings go forth to (battle)
11. 2 walked upon the roof of the king's house
11. 8 Uriah departed out of the king's house, and
11. 8 followed him a mess (of meat) from the k.
11. 9 Uriah slept at the door of the king's house
11. 19 telling the matters of the war unto the k.
11. 20 And if so be that the king's wrath arise
11. 24 and (some) of the king's servants be dead
12. 7 I anointed thee king over Israel, and I
12. 30 he took their king's crown from off his
13. 4 Why (art) thou, (being) the king's son
13. 6 and when the king was come to see him
13. 6 Ammon said unto the king, I pray thee
13. 13 therefore, I pray thee, speak unto the king
13. 18 for with such robes were the king's daug.
13. 21 when king David heard of all these things
13. 23 and Absalom invited all the king's sons
13. 24 And Absalom came to the king, and said
13. 24 let the king, I beseech thee, and his serv.
13. 25 the king said to Absalom, Nay, my son
13. 26 And the king said unto him, Why should
13. 27 he let Ammon and all the king's sons go
13. 29 all the king's sons arose, and every man
13. 30 Absalom hath slain all the king's sons, and
13. 31 Then the king arose, and tare his garme.
13. 32 slain all the young men the king's sons
13. 33 therefore let not my lord the king take
13. 33 think that all the king's sons are dead
13. 35 said unto the king..the king's sons com.
13. 36 the king's sons came..and the king also
13. 37 Talmai, the son of Ammihud, king of Ge.
13. 39 king David longed to go forth unto Absa.
14. 1 perceived that the king's heart (was) tow.
14. 3 come to the king, and speak on this man.
14. 4 spake to the king..and said, Help, O king!
14. 5 the king said unto her, What aileth thee?
14. 8 the king said unto the woman, Go to thine
14. 9 said unto the king, My lord, O king, the
14. 9 and the king and his throne (be) guiltless
14. 10 the king said, Whosoever saith (ought)
14. 11 let the king remember the LORD thy God
14. 12 speak (one) word unto my lord the king
14. 13 for the king doth speak this thing as one
14. 13 in that the king doth not fetch home again
14. 15 speak of this thing unto my lord the king
14. 15 said, I will now speak unto the king
14. 15 it may be that the king will perform the
14. 16 the king will hear, to deliver his handm.
14. 17 The word of my lord the king shall now
14. 17 as an angel of God, so (is) my lord the king
14. 18 the king answered and said unto the wom.
14. 18 woman said, Let my lord the king now
14. 19 the king said, (Is not) the hand of Joab
14. 19 (As) thy soul liveth, my lord the king, none
14. 19 from ought that my lord the king hath
14. 21 the king said unto Joab, Behold now, I
14. 22 and bowed himself, and thanked the king
14. 22 found grace in thy sight, my lord, O king
14. 22 in that the king hath fulfilled the request
14. 24 the king said, Let him turn to his own
14. 24 Absalom returned..and saw not the king's
14. 26 hundred shekels after the king's weight
14. 28 So Absalom dwelt..and saw not the king's
14. 29 to have sent him to the king; but he
14. 32 that I may send thee to the king, to say
14. 32 now therefore let me see the king's face
14. 33 So Joab came to the king, and told him
14. 33 he came to the king, and bowed himself
14. 33 before the king: and the king kissed Ab.
15. 2 when any man..came to the king for jud.

2 Sa. 15. 3 but (there is) no man (deputed) of the king
15. 6 to all Israel that came to the king for
15. 7 Absalom said unto the king, I pray thee
15. 9 the king said unto him, Go in peace
15. 15 the king's servants said unto the king
15. 15 whatsoever my lord the king shall appoint
15. 16 the king went forth..And the king left
15. 17 the king went forth, and all his people
15. 18 six hundred men..passed..before the king
15. 19 Then said the king to Ittai the Gittite
15. 19 return to thy place, and abide with the king
15. 21 Ittai answered the king, and said, (As) the
15. 21 (as) my lord the king liveth, surely in wh.
15. 21 place my lord the king shall be, whether
15. 23 the king also himself passed over the br.
15. 25 the king said unto Zadok, Carry back the
15. 27 The king said also unto Zadok the priest
15. 34 and say..I will be thy servant, O king
15. 35 thou shalt hear out of the king's house
16. 2 the king said unto Ziba, What meanest
16. 2 The asses (be) for the king's household to
16. 3 the king said, And where (is) thy master's
16. 3 Ziba said unto the king, Behold, he abideth
16. 4 Then said the king to Ziba, Behold, thine
16. 4 find grace in thy sight, my lord, O king
16. 5 when king David came to Bahurim, behold
16. 6 cast stones..at all the servants of king D.
16. 9 Then said Abishai..unto the king, Why
16. 9 should this dead dog curse my lord the k.?
16. 10 the king said, What have I to do with you
16. 14 the king, and all the people that (were)
16. 16 said..God save the king, God save the k.
17. 2 shall flee; and I will smite the king only
17. 16 lest the king be swallowed up, and all the
17. 17 and they went and told king David
17. 21 went and told king David, and said unto
18. 2 the king said unto the people, I will surely
18. 4 the king said unto them, What seemeth
18. 4 the king stood by the gate side, and all
18. 5 the king commanded Joab and Abishai
18. 5 when the king gave all..captains charge
18. 12 forth mine hand against the king's son
18. 12 for in our hearing the king charged thee
18. 13 for there is no matter hid from the king
18. 18 a pillar, which (is) in the king's dale: for
18. 19 Let me now run and bear the king tidings
18. 20 no tidings, because the king's son is dead
18. 21 Go tell the king what thou hast seen
18. 25 told the king. And the king said, If he
18. 26 And the king said, He also bringeth tidings
18. 27 the king said, He (is) a good man, and
18. 28 Ahimaaz called, and said unto the king
18. 28 to the earth upon his face before the king
18. 28 lifted up their hand against my lord the k.
18. 29 the king said, Is the young man Absalom
18. 29 When Joab sent the king's servant, and
18. 30 the king said (unto him), Turn aside, (and)
18. 31 Cushi said, Tidings, my lord the king: for
18. 32 the king said unto Cushi, (Is) the young
18. 32 The enemies of my lord the king, and all
18. 33 the king was much moved, and went up
19. 1 the king weepeth and mourneth for Ab.
19. 2 people heard say that day how the king
19. 4 the king covered his face, and the king
19. 5 Joab came into the house to the king, and
19. 8 Then the king arose, and sat in the gate
19. 8 Behold, the king doth sit in the gate
19. 8 And all the people came before the king
19. 9 The king saved us out of the hand of our
19. 10 not a word of bringing the king back?
19. 11 king David sent to Zadok and to Abiathar
19. 11 Why are ye the last to bring the king back
19. 11 speech of all Israel is come to the king
19. 12 are ye the last to bring back the king?
19. 14 so that they sent (this word) unto the king
19. 15 So the king returned, and came to Jordan
19. 15 go to meet the king, to conduct the king
19. 16 hasted and came down..to meet king D.
19. 17 and they went over Jordan before the k.
19. 18 to carry over the king's household, and
19. 18 fell down before the king, as he was come
19. 19 said unto the king, Let not my lord imp.
19. 19 that my lord the king went out of Jerus.
19. 19 that the king should take it to his heart
19. 20 to go down to meet my lord the king
19. 22 know that I (am) this day king over Israel
19. 23 the king said..And the king sware unto
19. 24 came down to meet the king, and had
19. 24 from the day the king departed until the
19. 25 to meet the king, that the king said unto
19. 26 My lord, O king, my servant deceived me
19. 26 I may ride thereon, and go to the king
19. 27 he hath slandered..unto my lord the king
19. 27 but my lord the king (is) as an angel of G.
19. 28 but dead men before my lord the king
19. 28 have I yet to cry any more unto the king?
19. 29 the king said unto him, Why speakest
19. 30 Mephibosheth said unto the king, Yea, let
19. 30 forasmuch as my lord the king is come
19. 31 went over Jordan with the king, to cond.
19. 32 he had provided the king of sustenance
19. 33 the king said unto Barzillai, Come thou
19. 34 Barzillai said unto the king, How long
19. 34 that I should go up with the king unto J.
19. 35 be yet a burden unto my lord the king?
19. 36 a little way over Jordan with the king
19. 36 why should the king recompense it me
19. 37 let him go over with my lord the king; and
19. 38 the king answered, Chimham shall go over
19. 39 when the king was come over, the king
19. 40 Then the king went on to Gilgal, and Ch.
19. 40 the people of Judah conducted the king

2 Sa. 19. 41 came to the king, and said unto the king
19. 41 have brought the king and his household
19. 42 Because the king (is) near of kin to us
19. 42 have we eaten at all of the king's (cost?)
19. 43 We have ten parts in the king, and we
19. 43 not be first had in bringing back our ki.?
20. 2 the men of Judah clave unto their king
20. 3 and the king took the ten women (his)
20. 4 Then said the king to Amasa, Assemble
20. 21 hath lifted up his hand against the king
20. 22 Joab returned to Jerusalem unto the king
21. 2 the king called the Gibeonites, and said
21. 5 they answered the king, The man that
21. 6 And the king said, I will give (them)
21. 7 the king spared Mephibosheth, the son of
21. 8 the king took the two sons of Rizpah the
21. 14 performed all that the king commanded
22. 51 (He is) the tower of salvation for his king
24. 2 For the king said to Joab the captain of
24. 3 Joab said unto the king, Now the LORD
24. 3 that the eyes of my lord the king may see
24. 3 why doth my lord the king delight in this
24. 4 the king's word prevailed against Joab, and
24. 4 went out from the presence of the king to
24. 9 Joab gave up the sum..unto the king: and
24. 20 saw the king and his servants coming on
24. 20 bowed himself before the king on his face
24. 21 Wherefore is my lord the king come to
24. 22 Let my lord the king take and offer up
24. 23 Araunah, (as) a king, give unto the king
24. 23 Araunah said unto the king, The LORD
24. 24 the king said unto Araunah, Nay; but I
1 Ki. 1. 1 king David was old (and) stricken in years
1. 2 Let there be sought for my lord the king
1. 2 let her stand before the king, and let her
1. 2 that my lord the king may get heat
1. 3 found Abishag..and brought her to the k.
1. 4 cherished the king..but the king knew
1. 9 called all his brethren the king's sons, and
1. 9 all the men of Judah the king's servants
1. 13 Go and get thee in unto king David, and
1. 13 Didst not thou, my lord, O king, swear
1. 14 thou yet talkest there with the king, I
1. 15 Bath-sheba went in unto the king into the
1. 15 the king was very old; and Abishag
1. 15 the Shunammite ministered unto the king
1. 16 did obeisance unto the king. And the k.
1. 18 now, my lord the king, thou knowest (it)
1. 19 and hath called all the sons of the king
1. 20 thou, my lord, O king, the eyes of all Isr.
1. 20, 27 sit on the throne of my lord the king
1. 21 when my lord the king shall sleep with
1. 22 while she yet talked with the king, Nathan
1. 23 they told the king, saying, Behold Nathan
1. 23 when he was come in before the king, he
1. 23 bowed himself before the king with his
1. 24 My lord, O king, hast thou said, Adonijah
1. 25 and hath called all the king's sons, and
1. 25 they eat..and say, God save king Adonijah
1. 27 Is this thing done by my lord the king
1. 28 Then king David answered and said, Call
1. 28 into the king's presence..before the king
1. 29 the king sware, and said, (As) the LORD
1. 31 to the king, and said, Let my lord king D.
1. 32 king David said, Call me Zadok the priest
1. 32 And they came before the king
1. 33 The king also said unto them, Take with
1. 34 let..the prophet anoint him there king
1. 34 blow ye..and say, God save king Solomon
1. 36 the son of Jehoiada answered the king
1. 36 the LORD God of my lord the king say so
1. 37 LORD hath been with my lord the king
1. 37 greater than the throne of my lord king
1. 38 caused Solomon to ride upon king David's
1. 39 all the people said, God save king Solomon
1. 43 Verily our lord king David hath made S.
1. 44 the king hath sent with him Zadok the
1. 44 caused him to ride upon the king's mule
1. 45 have anointed him king in Gihon: and they
1. 47 king's servants came to bless our lord king
1. 47 And the king bowed himself upon the bed
1. 48 thus said the king, Blessed (be) the LORD
1. 51 Behold, Adonijah feareth king Solomon
1. 51 Let king Solomon swear unto me to day
1. 53 So king Solomon sent, and they brought
1. 53 came and bowed himself to king Solomon
2. 17 Speak, I pray thee, unto Solomon the ki.
2. 18 Well; I will speak for thee unto the king
2. 19 Bath-sheba therefore went unto king Sol.
2. 19 the king rose up to meet her, and bowed
2. 19 caused a seat to be set for the king's mo.
2. 20 the king said unto her, Ask on, my mother
2. 22 king Solomon answered and said unto his
2. 23 king Solomon swear by the LORD, saying
2. 25 king Solomon sent by the hand of Benaiah
2. 26 unto Abiathar the priest said the king, G.
2. 29 was told king Solomon that Joab was fled
2. 30 said unto him, Thus saith the king, Come
2. 30 And Benaiah brought the king word again
2. 31 the king said unto him, Do as he hath said
2. 35 the king put Benaiah the son of Jehoiada
2. 35 Zadok the priest did the king put in the
2. 36 the king sent and called for Shimei, and
2. 38 Shimei said unto the king, The saying
2. 38 as my lord the king hath said, so will thy
2. 39 unto Achish son of Maachah king of Gath
2. 42 the king sent and called for Shimei and
2. 44 The king said moreover to Shimei, Thou
2. 45 king Solomon (shall be) blessed, and the
2. 46 So the king commanded Benaiah the son
3. 1 made affinity with Pharaoh king of Egypt
3. 4 the king went to Gibeon to sacrifice there

1 Ki. 3. 13 there shall not be any among the kings
3. 16 came there two women..unto the king
3. 22 Thus they spake before the king
3. 23 Then said the king, The one saith, This
3. 24 And the king said, Bring me a sword
3. 24 And they brought a sword before the king
3. 25 the king said, Divide the living child in
3. 26 Then spake the woman..unto the king,
3. 27 Then the king answered and said, Give
3. 28 judgment which the king had judged
3. 28 they feared the king: for they saw that
4. 1 So king Solomon was king over all Israel
4. 5 Zabud..(was) principal officer, (and) the k.'s
4. 7 which provided victuals for the king and
4. 19 king of the Amorites, and of Og king of
4. 24 over all the kings on this side the river
4. 27 provided victual for king Solomon, and
4. 27 for all that came unto king Solomon's table
4. 34 from all kings of the earth, which had hea.
5. 1 Hiram king of Tyre sent his servants unto
5. 1 heard that they had anointed him king in
5. 13 king Solomon raised a levy out of all Isr.
5. 17 the king commanded, and they brought
6. 2 the house which king Solomon built for
7. 13 king Solomon sent and fetched Hiram out
7. 14 he came to king Solomon, and wrought all
7. 40 that he made king Solomon for the house
7. 45 which Hiram made to king Solomon for
7. 46 In the plain of Jordan did the king cast
7. 51 So was ended all the work that king Sol.
8. 1 unto king Solomon in Jerusalem, that they
8. 2 assembled themselves unto king Solomon
8. 5 king Solomon, and..the congregation of I.
8. 14 the king turned his face about, and blessed
8. 62 the king, and all Israel with him, offered
8. 63 So the king and all the children of Israel
8. 64 The same day did the king hallow the
8. 66 they blessed the king, and went unto their
9. 1 when Solomon had finished..the king's
9. 10 the house of the LORD, and the king's ho.
9. 11 Hiram the king of Tyre had furnished S.
9. 11 then king Solomon gave Hiram twenty
9. 14 sent to the king sixscore talents of gold
9. 15 the reason of the levy which king Solomon
9. 16 Pharaoh king of Egypt had gone up and
9. 26 king Solomon made a navy of ships in E.
9. 28 fetched..gold..and brought (it) to king S.
10. 3 was not (any) thing hid from the king
10. 6 she said to the king, It was a true report
10. 9 therefore made he thee king, to do judg.
10. 10 she gave the king an hundred and twenty
10. 10 the queen of Sheba gave to king Solomon
10. 12 the king made of the almug trees pillars
10. 12 for the king's house, harps also and psal.
10. 13 king Solomon gave unto the queen of S.
10. 15 and of all the kings of Arabia, and of the
10. 16 king Solomon made two hundred targets
10. 17 the king put them in the house of the
10. 18 the king made a great throne of ivory, and
10. 21 all king Solomon's drinking vessels (were
10. 22 the king had at sea a navy of Tharshish
10. 23 So king Solomon exceeded all the kings of
10. 26 and with the king at Jerusalem
10. 27 the king made silver (to be) in Jerusalem
10. 28 king's merchants received the linen yarn
10. 29 kings of the Hittites, and for the kings of
11. 1 king Solomon loved many strange women
11. 14 Hadad the Edomite: he (was) of the king's
11. 18 they came to Egypt, unto Pharoah king of
11. 23 fled from his lord Hadadezer king of Zob.
11. 26, 27 he lifted up (his) hand against the king
11. 37 thou shalt reign..and shalt be king over
11. 40 fled into Egypt, unto Shishak king of Eg
12. 2 fled from the presence of king Solomon
12. 6 king Rehoboam consulted with the old
12. 12 as the king had appointed, saying, Come
12. 13 the king answered the people roughly, and
12. 15 the king hearkened not unto the people
12. 16 all Israel saw that the king hearkened not
12. 16 people answered the king, saying, What
12. 18 Then king Rehoboam sent Adoram, who
12. 18 king Rehoboam made speed to get him up
12. 23 the son of Solomon, king of Judah, and
12. 27 unto Rehoboam king of Judah, and they
12. 28 Whereupon the king took counsel, and
13. 4 when king Jeroboam heard the saying of
13. 6 the king answered and said unto the man
13. 6 the king's hand was restored him again
13. 7 the king said unto the man of God, Come
13. 8 the man of God said unto the king, If thou
13. 11 words which he had spoken unto the king
14. 2 which told me that (I should be) king over
14. 14 the LORD shall raise him up a king over Isr.
14. 19, 29 the book of the Chronicles of the kings
14. 25 in the fifth year of king Rehoboam, (that)
14. 25 Shishak king of Egypt came up against
14. 26 and the treasures of the king's house; he
14. 27 king Rehoboam made in their stead brasen
14. 27 which kept the door of the king's house
14. 28 when the king went into the house of the
15. 1 in the eighteenth year of king Jeroboam
15. 7, 23, 31 the book of the Chronicles of the ki.
15. 9 in the twentieth year of Jeroboam king
15. 16, 32 war between Asa and Baasha king of I.
15. 17 Baasha king of Israel went up against J.
15. 17 to go out or to come in to Asa king of Ju.
15. 18 and the treasures of the king's house, and
15. 18 king Asa sent them to Ben-hadad, the son
15. 18 Hezion, king of Syria, that dwelt at Dama.
15. 19 break thy league with Baasha king of Isr.
15. 20 So Ben-hadad hearkened unto king Asa
15. 22 king Asa made a proclamation throughout

1 Ki. 15. 22 king Asa built with them Geba of Benja.
15. 25 in the second year of Asa king of Judah
15. 28, 33 in the third year of Asa king of Judah
16. 5, 14, 20, 27 book of the Chronicles of the k.
16. 8 In the twenty and sixth year of Asa king
16. 10, 15 the twenty and seventh year of Asa k.
16. 16 conspired, and hath also slain the king
16. 18 went into the palace of the king's house
16. 18 burnt the king's house over him with fire
16. 23 In the thirty and first year of Asa king of
16. 29 in the thirty and eighth year of Asa king
16. 31 daughter of Ethbaal, king of the Zidoni.
16. 33 than all the kings of Israel that were bef.
19. 15 when thou comest, anoint Hazael (to be) k.
19. 16 shalt thou anoint (to be) king over Israel
20. 1 the king of Syria gathered all his host
20. 1 (there were) thirty and two kings with him
20. 2 he sent messengers to Ahab king of Israel
20. 4 And the king of Israel answered and said
20. 4 My lord, O king, according to thy saying
20. 7 the king of Israel called all the elders of
20. 9 Tell my lord the king, All that thou didst
20. 11 the king of Israel answered and said, Tell
20. 12 he and the kings in the pavilions, that he
20. 13 there came a prophet unto Ahab king of
20. 16 the kings, the thirty and two kings that
20. 20 the king of Syria escaped on an horse with
20. 21 the king of Israel went out, and smote
20. 22 the prophet came to the king of Israel
20. 22 the king of Syria will come up against
20. 23 the servants of the king of Syria said unto
20. 24 Take the kings away, every man out of
20. 28 spake unto the king of Israel, and said
20. 31 heard that the kings..(are) merciful kings
20. 31 go out to the king of Israel: peradventure
20. 32 came to the king of Israel, and said, Thy
20. 38 and waited for the king by the way, and
20. 39 the king passed by, he cried unto the king
20. 40 And the king of Israel said unto him, So
20. 41 the king of Israel discerned him that he
20. 43 the king of Israel went to his house heavy
21. 1 hard by the palace of Ahab king of Samaria
21. 10 Thou didst blaspheme God and the king
21. 13 Naboth did blaspheme God and the king
21. 18 Arise, go down to meet Ahab king of Is.
22. 2 the king of Judah came down to the king
22. 3 the king of Israel said unto his servants
22. 3 take it not out of the hand of the king of
22. 4 Jehoshaphat said to the king of Israel, I
22. 5 Jehoshaphat said unto the king of Israel
22. 6 Then the king of Israel gathered the pro.
22. 6 shall deliver (it) into the hand of the king
22. 8 the king of Israel said unto Jehoshaphat
22. 8 Jehoshaphat said, Let not the king say so
22. 9 Then the king of Israel called an officer
22. 10, 29 the king of Israel and..the king of J.
22. 12 LORD shall deliver (it) into the king's hand
22. 13 (declare) good unto the king with one
22. 15 he came to the king. And the king said
22. 15 shall deliver (it) into the hand of the king
22. 16 the king said unto him, How many times
22. 18, 30 the king of Israel said unto Jehosha.
22. 26 the king of Israel said, Take Micaiah, and
22. 26 carry him back..to Joash the king's son
22. 27 Thus saith the king, Put this (fellow) in
22. 30 king of Israel disguised himself, and went
22. 31 the king of Syria commanded his thirty
22. 31 saying, Fight..only with the king of Isr.
22. 32 they said, Surely it (is) the king of Israel
22. 33 perceived that it (was) not the king of I.
22. 34 smote the king of Israel between the joints
22. 35 and the king was stayed up in his chariot
22. 37 the king died..and they buried the king
22. 39, 45 book of the Chronicles of the kings of
22. 41 in the fourth year of Ahab king of Israel
22. 44 Jehoshaphat made peace with the king of
22. 47 then no king in Edom: a deputy (was) k.
22. 51 seventeenth year of Jehoshaphat king of
2 Ki. 1. 3 to meet the messengers of the king of S.
1. 6 turn again unto the king that sent you
1. 9 man of God, the king hath said, Come down
1. 11 thus hath the king said, Come down quic.
1. 15 and went down with him unto the king
1. 17 the son of Jehoshaphat king of Judah
1. 18 the book of the Chronicles of the kings of
3. 1 eighteenth year of Jehoshaphat king of J.
3. 4 Mesha king of Moab was a sheep master
3. 4 rendered unto the king of Israel an hun.
3. 5 king of Moab rebelled against the king of
3. 6 king Jehoram went out of Samaria the
3. 7 sent to Jehoshaphat the king of Judah
3. 7 The king of Moab hath rebelled against
3. 9 king of Israel..king of Judah..king of
3. 10 king of Israel said, Alas! that the LORD
3. 10 hath called these three kings together to
3. 11 one of the king of Israel's servants answ.
3. 12 the king of Israel..and the king of Edom
3. 13 Elisha said unto the king of Israel, What
3. 13 the king of Israel said unto him, Nay: for
3. 13 the LORD hath called these three kings to.
3. 14 the presence of Jehoshaphat the king of
3. 21 when all the Moabites heard that the king
3. 23 This (is) blood: the kings are surely slain
3. 26 when the king of Moab saw that the bat.
3. 26 to break through (even) unto the king of
4. 13 wouldst thou be spoken for to the king, or
5. 1 captain of the host of the king of Syria
5. 5 the king of Syria said, Go to, go, and I
5. 5 will send a letter unto the king of Israel
5. 6 brought the letter to the king of Israel
5. 7 when the king of Israel had read the let.
5. 8 had heard that the king of Israel had rent

2 Ki. 5. 8 sent to the king, saying, Wherefore hast
6. 8 the king of Syria warred against Israel
6. 9 man of God sent unto the king of Israel
6. 10 the king of Israel sent to the place which
6. 11 Therefore the heart of the king of Syria
6. 11 show me which of us(is) for the king of I.?
6. 12 said, None, my lord, O king: but Elisha
6. 12 telleth the king of Israel the words that
6. 21 the king of Israel said unto Elisha, when
6. 24 king of Syria gathered all his host, and
6. 26 as the king of Israel was passing by upon
6. 26 there cried a woman..saying, Help..O k.
6. 28 the king said unto her, What aileth thee?
6. 30 when the king heard the words of the
7. 2 a lord on whose hand the king leaned
7. 6 the king of Israel hath hired..the kings
7. 6 and the kings of the Egyptians, to come
7. 9 we may go and tell the king's household
7. 11 they told (it) to the king's house within
7. 12 the king arose in the night, and said unto
7. 14 the king sent after the host of the Syrians
7. 15 the messengers returned, and told the k.
7. 17 the king appointed the lord on whose hand
7. 17 who spake when the king came down to
7. 18 the man of God had spoken to the king
8. 3 she went forth to cry unto the king for
8. 4 the king talked with Gehazi, the servant
8. 5 as he was telling the king how he had rest.
8. 5 cried to the king for her house and for her
8. 5 My lord, O king, this (is) the woman and
8. 6 when the king asked the woman, she told
8. 6 king appointed unto her a certain officer
8. 7 and Ben-hadad the king of Syria was sick
8. 8 the king said unto Hazael, Take a present
8. 9 Thy son Ben-hadad king of Syria hath
8. 13 hath showed me that thou (shalt be) king
8. 16, 25 of Joram the son of Ahab king of Isr.
8. 16 Jehoshaphat (being) then king of Judah
8. 16 Jehoram the son of Jehoshaphat king of
8. 18 walked in the way of the kings of Israel
8. 20 Edom revolted..and made a king over
8. 23 the book of the chronicles of the kings of
8. 25, 29 Ahaziah the son of Jehoram king of J.
8. 26 Athaliah, the daughter of Omri king of I.
8. 28 to the war against Hazael king of Syria
8. 29 king Joram went back to be healed in J.
8. 29 when he fought against Hazael king of S.
9. 3, 12 I have anointed thee king over Israel
9. 6 I have anointed thee king over the people
9. 14 he and all Israel, because of Hazael king
9. 15 king Joram was returned to be healed in
9. 15 when he fought with Hazael king of Syria
9. 16 Ahaziah king of Judah was come down to
9. 18, 19 Thus saith the king, (Is it) peace? And
9. 21 king of Israel and Ahaziah king of Judah
9. 27 But when Ahaziah the king of Judah saw
9. 34 and bury her; for she (is) a king's daugh.
10. 4 Behold, two kings stood not before him
10. 6 Now the king's sons, (being) seventy per.
10. 7 they took the king's sons, and slew seventy
10. 8 have brought the heads of the king's sons
10. 13 the brethren of Ahaziah king of Judah
10. 13 to salute the children of the king and the
10. 34 the book of the Chronicles of the kings of
11. 2 Jehosheba, the daughter of king Joram
11. 2 and stole him from among the king's sons
11. 4 and showed them the king's son
11. 5 be keepers of the watch of the king's ho.
11. 7 they shall keep the watch..about the king
11. 8 compass the king..be ye with the king
11. 10 did the priest give king David's spears
11. 11 the guard stood..round about the king
11. 12 he brought forth the king's son, and put
11. 12 clapped..hands, and said, God save the k.
11. 14 the king stood by a pillar, as the manner
11. 14 the princes and the trumpeters by the k.
11. 16 came into the king's house: and there
11. 17 between the LORD and the king and the
11. 17 between the king also and the people
11. 19 they brought down the king from the ho.
11. 19 the gate of the guard to the king's house
11. 19 And he sat on the throne of the kings
11. 20 they slew Athaliah..(beside) the king's h.
12. 6 in the three and twentieth year of king
12. 7 king Jehoash called for Jehoiada the pr.
12. 10 the king's scribe and the high priest came
12. 17 Hazael king of Syria went up, and fought
12. 18 And Jehoash king of Judah took all the
12. 18 kings of Judah, had dedicated, and his
12. 18 in the king's house, and sent (it) to..king
12. 19 in the book of the Chronicles of the kings
13. 1 Joash the son of Ahaziah king of Judah
13. 3 into the hand of Hazael king of Syria
13. 4 because the king of Syria oppressed them
13. 7 for the king of Syria had destroyed them
13. 8, 12 the book of the chronicles of the kings
13. 10 the thirty and seventh year of Joash king
13. 12 he fought against Amaziah king of Judah
13. 13 was buried in Samaria with the kings of
13. 14 Joash the king of Israel came down unto
13. 16 he said to the king of Israel, Put thine h.
13. 16 Elisha put his hands upon the king's hand
13. 18 said unto the king of Israel, Smite upon
13. 22 Hazael king of Syria oppressed Israel all
13. 24 Hazael king of Syria died; and Ben-hadad
14. 1 of Joash son of Jehoahaz king of Israel
14. 1 Amaziah the son of Joash king of Judah
14. 5 servants which had slain the king his fat.
14. 8 son of Jehoahaz, son of Jehu, king of Isr.
14. 9 the king of Israel sent to Amaziah king
14. 11 Therefore Jehoash king of Israel went up
14. 11 he and Amaziah king of Judah looked

2 Ki. 14. 13 king of Israel took Amaziah king of Judah
14. 14 and in the treasures of the king's house
14. 15 how he fought with Amaziah king of Ju.
14. 15, 18, 28 book of the chronicles of the kings
14. 16 was buried in Samaria with the kings of
14. 17, 23 Amaziah the son of Joash king of Jud.
14. 17 Jehoash, son of Jehoahaz king of Israel
14. 22 after that the king slept with his fathers
14. 23 Jeroboam the son of Joash king of Israel
14. 29 Jeroboam slept..with the kings of Israel
15. 1 Jeroboam king of Israel..Amaziah king of
15. 5 smote the king, so that he was a leper
15. 5 Jotham the king's son (was) over the ho.
15. 6, 11, 15 book of the chronicles of the kings
15. 8 In the thirty and eighth year of Azariah k.
15. 13 nine and thirtieth year of Uzziah king of
15. 17 In the nine and thirtieth year of Azariah k.
15. 19 Pul the king of Assyria came against the
15. 20 give to the king of Assyria: so the king of
15. 21, 26, 31, 36 book of the chronicles of the k.
15. 23 In the fiftieth year of Azariah king of
15. 25 in the palace of the king's house, with Ar.
15. 27 the two and fiftieth year of Azariah king
15. 29 In the days of Pekah king of Israel came
15. 29 Tiglath-pileser king of Assyria, and took
15. 32 Pekah the son of Remaliah king of Israel
15. 32 began Jotham the son of Uzziah king of J.
15. 37 Rezin the king of Syria, and Pekah the
16. 1 Ahaz the son of Jotham king of Judah
16. 3 walked in the way of the kings of Israel
16. 5 Rezin king of Syria and Pekah son of
16. 5 Remaliah king of Israel came up to Jerus.
16. 6 At that time Rezin king of Syria recovered
16. 7 sent messengers to Tiglath-pileser king of
16. 7, 7 out of the hand of the king of
16. 8 and in the treasures of the king's house
16. 8 sent (it for) a present to the king of A.
16. 9 the king of Assyria hearkened unto him
16. 9 for the king of Assyria went up against D.
16. 10 king Ahaz went..to meet..king of Assyria
16. 10 king Ahaz sent to Urijah the priest the
16. 11 according to all that king Ahaz had sent
16. 11 Urijah the priest made (it) against king A.
16. 12 when the king was come from Damascus
16. 12 the king saw the altar: and the king
16. 15 king Ahaz commanded Urijah the priest
16. 15 Upon the great altar burn..the king's
16. 16 according to all that king Ahaz comman.
16. 17 king Ahaz cut off the borders of the bases
16. 18 the king's entry without, turned he from
16. 18 the house of the LORD for the king of As.
16. 19 the book of the chronicles of the kings of
17. 1 In the twelfth year of Ahaz king of Judah
17. 2 but not as the kings of Israel that were
17. 3 Against him came up Shalmaneser king of
17. 4 the king of Assyria found conspiracy in H.
17. 4 for he had sent messengers to So king of
17. 4 and brought no present to the king of A.
17. 4 therefore the king of Assyria shut him up
17. 5 the king of Assyria came up throughout
17. 6 In the ninth year of Hoshea the king of A.
17. 7 from under the hand of Pharaoh king of E.
17. 8 of the kings of Israel, which they had
17. 24 king of Assyria brought (men) from Bab.
17. 26 Wherefore they spake to the king of Ass.
17. 27 Then the king of Assyria commanded
18. 1 third year of Hoshea son of Elah king of I.
18. 1 Hezekiah the son of Ahaz king of Judah
18. 5 none like him among all the kings of Ju.
18. 7 he rebelled against the king of Assyria
18. 9 it came to pass in the fourth year of king
18. 9 seventh year of Hoshea son of Elah king
18. 9 Shalmaneser king of Assyria came up ag.
18. 10 the ninth year of Hoshea king of Israel
18. 11 the king of Assyria did carry away Israel
18. 13 in the fourteenth year of king Hezekiah
18. 13 did Sennacherib king of Assyria come up
18. 14 Hezekiah king of Judah sent to the king
18. 14 And the king of Assyria appointed unto
18. 14 Hezekiah king of Judah three hundred
18. 15 and in the treasures of the king's house
18. 16 king of Judah..gave it to the king of As.
18. 17 the king of Assyria sent..to king Hezek.
18. 18 when they had called to the king, there
18. 19 saith the great king, the king of Assyria
18. 21 so (is) Pharaoh king of Egypt unto all that
18. 23 give pledges to my lord the king of Assy.
18. 28 Hear the word of the great king, the king
18. 29 Thus saith the king, Let not Hezekiah
18. 30 be delivered into the hand of the king of
18. 31 for thus saith the king of Assyria, Make
18. 33 delivered..of the hand of the king of A.?
18. 36 king's commandment was, saying, Answer
19. 1 when king Hezekiah heard (it), that he
19. 4 whom the king of Assyria his master hath
19. 5 servants of king Hezekiah came to Isaiah
19. 6 with which the servants of the king of A.
19. 8 found the king of Assyria warring against
19. 9 when he heard say of Tirhakah king of Et.
19. 10 Thus shall ye speak to Hezekiah king of J.
19. 10 not be delivered into the hand of the king
19. 11 thou hast heard what the kings of Assyria
19. 13 Where (is) the king of Hamath, and the k.
19. 13 and the king of the city of Sepharvaim, of
19. 17 kings of Assyria have destroyed the nati.
19. 20 prayed to me against Sennacherib king
19. 32 thus saith the LORD concerning the king
19. 36 So Sennacherib king of Assyria departed
20. 6 deliver..out of the hand of the king of A.
20. 12 king of Babylon, sent letters and a present
20. 14 Then came Isaiah the prophet unto king
20. 18 shall be eunuchs in the palace of the king

2 Ki. 20. 20 in the book of the chronicles of the kings
21. 3 made a grove, as did Ahab king of Israel
21. 11 Because Manasseh king of Judah hath
21. 17, 25 in the book of the chronicles of the k.
21. 23 conspired..and slew the king in his own
21. 24 all them that had conspired against king
22. 3 in the eighteenth year of king Josiah
22. 3 the king sent Shaphan the son of Azaliah
22. 9 came to the king and brought the king
22. 10 Shaphan the scribe showed the king, say.
22. 10 And Shaphan read it before the king
22. 11 when the king had heard the words of the
22. 12 the king commanded Hilkiah the priest
22. 12 and Asahiah a servant of the king's, saying
22. 16 all the words of the book which the king
22. 18 But to the king of Judah, which sent you
22. 20 And they brought the king word again
23. 1 the king sent, and they gathered unto him
23. 2 the king went up into the house of the L.
23. 3 the king stood by a pillar, and made a cov.
23. 4 the king commanded Hilkiah the high pr.
23. 5 whom the kings of Judah had ordained to
23. 11 horses that the kings of Judah had given
23. 12 which the kings of Judah had made, and
23. 12 the altars..did the king beat down, and
23. 13 the king of Israel..did the king defile
23. 19 which the kings of Israel had made to pr.
23. 21 the king commanded all the people, say.
23. 22 of the kings of Israel, nor of the kings of
23. 23 But in the eighteenth year of king Josiah
23. 25 like unto him was there no king before
23. 28 the book of the chronicles of the kings of
23. 29 king of Egypt went up against the king
23. 29 king Josiah went against him; and he slew
24. 1, 10, 11 Nebuchadnezzar king of Babylon
24. 5 the book of the chronicles of the kings of
24. 7 king of Egypt came not..for the king of B.
24. 7 all that pertained to the king of Egypt
24. 12 king of Judah went out to the king of B.
24. 12 the king of Babylon took him in the eighth
24. 13 and the treasures of the king's house, and
24. 13 which Solomon king of Israel had made
24. 15 the king's mother, and the king's wives
24. 16 even them the king of Babylon brought
24. 17 And the king of Babylon made Mattaniah
24. 20 Zedekiah rebelled against the king of B.
25. 1 Nebuchadnezzar king of Babylon came, he
25. 2 unto the eleventh year of king Zedekiah
25. 4 two walls, which (is) by the king's garden
25. 5 pursued after the king, and overtook him
25. 6 So they took the king, and brought him up
25. 6 to the king of Babylon to Riblah; and they
25. 8 of king Nebuchadnezzar king of Babylon
25. 8 came..a servant of the king of Babylon
25. 9 he burnt..the king's house, and all the
25. 11 fugitives that fell away to the king of Ba.
25. 19 of them that were in the king's presence
25. 20 brought them to the king of Babylon to
25. 21 the king of Babylon smote them, and slew
25. 22 whom Nebuchadnezzar king of Babylon
25. 23 heard that the king of Babylon had made
25. 24 dwell in the land, and serve the king of B.
25. 27 captivity of Jehoiachin king of Judah, in
25. 27 Evil-merodach king of Babylon..did lift
25. 27 the head of Jehoiachin king of Judah out
25. 28 his throne above the throne of the kings
25. 30 continual allowance given him of the king
1 Ch. 1. 43 kings that reigned in the land of Edom
1. 43 before (any) king reigned over the child.
3. 2 Maachah the daughter of Talmai king of
4. 23 there they dwelt with the king for his wo.
4. 41 came in the days of Hezekiah king of Ju.
5. 6 whom Tilgath-pilneser ki. of Assyria
5. 17 in the days of Jotham king of Judah, and
5. 17 in the days of Jeroboam king of Israel
5. 26 stirred up the spirit of Pul king of Assy.
5. 26 the spirit of Tilgath-pilneser king of As.
9. 1 in the book of the kings of Israel and J.
9. 18 hitherto (waited) in the king's gate east.
11. 2 in time past, even when Saul was ki., thou
11. 3 Therefore came all the elders..to the king
11. 3 and they anointed David king over Israel
14. 1 Hiram king of Tyre sent messengers to D.
14. 2 had confirmed him king over Israel; for
14. 8 heard that David was anointed king over
15. 29 Michal..saw king David dancing and pl.
16. 21 yea, he reproved kings for their sakes
17. 16 David the king came and sat before the
18. 3 David smote Hadarezer king of Zobah
18. 5 came to help Hadarezer king of Zobah
18. 9 Tou king of Hamath heard how David had
18. 9 smitten all the host of Hadarezer king of
18. 10 He sent Hadoram his son to king David
18. 11 Them also king David dedicated unto the
18. 17 sons of David (were) chief about the king
19. 1 Nahash the king of the children of Ammon
19. 5 the king said, Tarry at Jericho until your
19. 7 the king of Maachah and his people; who
19. 9 the kings that were come (were) by them.
20. 1 at the time that kings go out to (battle)
20. 2 took the crown of their king from off his
21. 3 but, my lord the king, (are) they not all
21. 4 the king's word prevailed against Joab
21. 6 for the king's word was abominable to J.
21. 23 let my lord the king do (that which is)
21. 24 king David said to Ornan, Nay; but I
24. 6 Shemaiah..wrote them before the king
24. 31 in the presence of David the king, and
25. 2 prophesied according to the order of the k.
25. 5 the sons of Heman the king's seer in the
25. 6 according to the king's order to Asaph
26. 26 which David the king, and the chief fat.

1 Ch. 26. 30 business..and in the service of the king
26. 32 king D. made rulers..for..affairs of the k.
27. 1 their officers that served the king in any
27. 24 the account of the chronicles of king D.
27. 25 over the king's treasures (was) Azmaveth
27. 31 of the substance which (was) king David's
27. 32 son of Hachmoni (was) with the king's
27. 33 the king's counsellor..the king's compan.
27. 34 the general of the king's army (was) Joab
28. 1 the companies that ministered to the king
28. 1 all the substance and possession of the k.
28. 2 Then David the king stood up upon his
28. 4 chose me..to be king over Israel for ever
29. 1 David the king said unto all the congreg.
29. 6 with the rulers of the king's work, offered
29. 9 David the king also rejoiced with great
29. 20 and worshipped the LORD, and the king
29. 23 Solomon sat..as king instead of David his
29. 24 and all the sons likewise of king David
29. 24 submitted themselves unto Solomon the k.
29. 25 as had not been on any king before him
29. 29 Now the acts of David the king, first and
2 Ch. 1. 12 such as none of the kings have had that
1. 14 which he placed..with the king at Jerus.
1. 15 king made silver and gold at Jerusalem
1. 16 the king's merchants received the linen
1. 17 kings of the Hittites, and for the kings of
2. 3 Solomon sent to Huram the king of Tyre
2. 11 the king..answered..he hath made t. k.
2. 12 hath given to David the king a wise son
4. 11 the work that he was to make for king
4. 16 did Huram his father make to king Solo.
4. 17 In the plain of Jordan did the king cast
5. 3 assembled themselves unto the king in
5. 6 Also king Solomon, and all the congregat.
6. 3 the king turned his face, and blessed the
7. 4 the king and all the people offered sacri.
7. 5 king Solomon offered..So the king and all
7. 6 which David the king had made to praise
7. 11 Thus Solomon finished..the king's house
8. 10 these (were) the chief of king Solomon's
8. 11 not dwell in the house of David king of I.
8. 15 commandment of the king unto the
8. 18 and brought (them) to king Solomon
9. 5 she said to the king, (It was) a true report
9. 8 king for the LORD..therefore made he t. k.
9. 9 gave the king an hundred and twenty ta.
9. 9 spice as the queen of Sheba gave king So.
9. 11 the king made..terraces..to the king's
9. 12 king Solomon gave to the queen of Sheba
9. 12 which she had brought unto the king
9. 14 all the kings of Arabia, and governors of
9. 15 king Solomon made two hundred targets
9. 16 the king put them in the house of the
9. 17 Moreover the king made a great throne of
9. 20 all the drinking vessels of king Solomon
9. 21 For the king's ships went to Tarshish with
9. 22 king Solomon passed all the kings of the
9. 23 the kings of the earth sought the presence
9. 25 whom he bestowed..with the king at Je.
9. 26 he reigned over all the kings from the
9. 27 king made silver in Jerusalem as stones
10. 2 from the presence of Solomon the king
10. 6 king Rehoboam took counsel with the old
10. 12 came to Rehoboam..as the king bade, say.
10. 13 the king answered..and king Rehoboam
10. 15 So the king hearkened not unto the people
10. 16 king would not..answered the king, say.
10. 18 Then king Rehoboam sent..but king Re.
11. 3 Speak unto Rehoboam..king of Judah, and.
12. 2 in the fifth year of king Rehoboam..king
12. 6 the princes of Israel and the king humbled
12. 9 Shishak king of Egypt came up against J
12. 9 took away..the treasures of the king's
12. 10 Instead of which king Rehoboam made
12. 10 that kept the entrance of the king's house
12. 11 when the king entered into the house of
12. 13 So king Rehoboam strengthened..in J.
13. 1 Now in the eighteenth year of king Jer.
15. 16 (concerning)..the mother of Asa the king
16. 1 Baasha king of Israel..Asa king of Judah
16. 2 king's house, and sent to Ben-hadad king
16. 3 break thy league with Baasha king of Is.
16. 4 Ben-hadad hearkened unto king Asa, and
16. 6 Then Asa the king took all Judah; and
16. 7 came to Asa king of Judah, and said unto
16. 7 Because thou hast relied on the king of S.
16. 7 therefore is the host of the king of Syria
16. 11 the book of the kings of Judah and Israel
17. 9 waited on the king..whom the king put
18. 3 king of Israel said unto Jehoshaphat king
18. 4 Jehoshaphat said unto the king of Israel
18. 5 the king of Israel gathered together of
18. 5 for God will deliver (it) into the king's
18. 7 the king of Israel..Let not the king say so
18. 8 the king of Israel called for one (of his)
18. 9, 28 king of Israel and Jehoshaphat king
18. 11 shall deliver (it) into the hand of the king
18. 12 (declare) good to the king with one assent
18. 14 when he was come to the king, the king
18. 15 the king said to him, How many times
18. 17 the king of Israel said to Jehoshaphat
18. 19 Who shall entice Ahab king of Israel, that
18. 25 king of Israel said, Take ye Micaiah, and
18. 25 carry him back..to Joash the king's son
18. 26 Thus saith the king, Put this (fellow) in the
18. 29 the king of Israel said unto Jehoshaphat
18. 29 So the king of Israel disguised himself
18. 30 the king of Syria had commanded the cap.
18. 30 Fight ye not..save only with the king of I.
18. 31 that they said, It (is) the king of Israel
18. 32 perceived that it was not the king of Isr.
2 Ch. 18. 33 smote the king of Israel between the joints
18. 34 howbeit the king of Israel stayed (himself)
19. 1 Jehoshaphat the king of Judah returned
19. 2 said to king Jehoshaphat, Shouldest thou
19. 11 and Zebadiah..for all the king's matters
20. 15 Hearken ye..and thou king Jehoshaphat
20. 34 mentioned in the book of the kings of Is.
20. 35 And after this did Jehoshaphat king of J.
20. 35 join himself with Ahaziah king of Israel
21. 2 all these (were) the sons of Jehoshaphat k.
21. 6, 13 walked in the way of the kings of Israel
21. 8 Edomites revolted..made themselves a k.
21. 12 nor in the ways of Asa king of Judah
21. 17 substance (that was) found in the king's
21. 20 but not in the sepulchres of the kings
22. 1 Ahaziah the son of Jehoram king of Judah
22. 5 Ahab king of Israel..against Hazael king
22. 6 when he fought with Hazael king of Syria
22. 6 Azariah the son of Jehoram king of Judah
22. 11, 11 Jehoshabeath, the daughter of the king
22. 11 stole him from among the king's sons that
23. 3 made a covenant with the king in the ho.
23. 3 the king's son shall reign, as the LORD hath
23. 5 And a third part (shall be) at the king's
23. 7 Levites shall compass the king round ab.
23. 7 but be ye with the king when he cometh
23. 9 and shields, that (had been) king David's
23. 10 along by the altar..by the king round ab.
23. 11 they brought out the king's son, and put
23. 11 anointed him, and said, God save the king
23. 12 the people running and praising the king
23. 13 the king stood at his pillar at the entering
23. 13 the princes and the trumpets by the king
23. 15 entering of the horse gate by the king's
23. 16 all the people, and between the king, that
23. 20 brought down the king..and set the king
23. 20 through the high gate into the king's house
24. 6 king called for Jehoiada..and said unto
24. 8 at the king's commandment they made a
24. 11 chest was brought unto the king's office
24. 11 king's scribe and the high priest's officer
24. 12 the king and Jehoiada gave it to such as
24. 14 the rest of the money before the king and
24. 16 in the city of David among the kings, bec.
24. 17 made obeisance to the king: then the king
24. 21 at the commandment of the king in the
24. 22 the king remembered not the kindness
24. 23 sent all the spoil of them unto the king of
24. 25 but..not in the sepulchres of the kings
24. 27 in the story of the book of the kings
25. 3 slew his servants that had killed the king
25. 7 O king, let not the army of Israel go with
25. 16 Art thou made of the king's counsel? for.
25. 17 Amaziah king of Judah took advice, and
25. 17 to Joash..the son of Jehu, king of Israel
25. 18 king of Israel sent to Amaziah king of J.
25. 21 So Joash the king of Israel went up; and
25. 21 (both) he and Amaziah king of Judah, at
25. 23 king of Israel took Amaziah king of Judah
25. 24 and the treasures of the king's house, the
25. 25 Amaziah the son of Joash king of Judah
25. 25 death of Joash, son of Jehoahaz king of I.
25. 26 in the book of the kings of Judah and I.?
26. 2 after that the king slept with his fathers
26. 11 hand of Hananiah, (one) of the king's cap.
26. 13 army..to help the king against the enemy
26. 18 they withstood Uzziah the king, and said
26. 21 Uzziah the king was a leper unto the day
26. 21 Jotham his son (was) over the king's house
26. 23 in the field..which (belonged) to the kings
27. 5 He fought also with the king of the Am.
27. 7 in the book of the kings of Israel and J.
28. 2 he walked in the ways of the kings of I.
28. 5 delivered him into the hand of the king
28. 5 into the hand of the king of Israel, who
28. 7 Z., a mighty man..slew Maaseiah the k.'s
28. 7 and Elkanah (that was) next to the king
28. 16 did king Ahaz send unto the kings of As.
28. 19 brought Judah low because of Ahaz king
28. 20 Tilgath-pilneser king of Assyria came unto
28. 21 of the house of the king, and of the princes
28. 21 and gave (it) unto the king of Assyria: but
28. 22 trespass yet more..this (is that) king A.
28. 23 Because the gods of the kings of Syria
28. 26 in the book of the kings of Judah and Is.
28. 27 not into the sepulchres of the kings of I.
29. 15 according to the commandment of the k.
29. 18 Then they went in to Hezekiah the king
29. 19 which king Ahaz in his reign did cast
29. 20 Then Hezekiah the king rose early, and
29. 23 before the king and the congregation; and
29. 24 the king commanded (that) the burnt off.
29. 25 Gad the king's seer, and Nathan the pro.
29. 27 instruments (ordained) by David king of
29. 29 the king and all that were present with
29. 30 Hezekiah the king and the princes comm.
30. 2 For the king had taken counsel, and his
30. 4 pleased the king and all the congregation
30. 6 the posts went with the letters from the k.
30. 6 according to the commandment of the k.
30. 6 escaped out of the hand of the kings of A.
30. 12 to do the commandment of the king and
30. 24 For Hezekiah king of Judah did give to
30. 26 of Solomon the son of David king of Isr.
31. 3 also the king's portion of his substance
31. 13 the commandment of Hezekiah the king
32. 1 Sennacherib king of Assyria came, and
32. 4 Why should the kings of Assyria come
32. 7 be not afraid nor dismayed for the king
32. 8 upon the words of Hezekiah king of Judah
32. 9 did S. king of Assyria send..unto Hezek.
32. 10 Thus saith Sennacherib king of Assyria
2 Ch. 32. 11 deliver us out of the hand of the king of
32. 20 Hezekiah the king, and the prophet Isaiah
32. 21 captains in the camp of the king of Assy.
32. 22 from the hand of Sennacherib the king
32. 23 and presents to Hezekiah king of Judah
32. 32 in the book of the kings of Judah and Is.
33. 11 the captains of the host of the king of A.
33. 18 in the book of the kings of Israel
33. 25 that had conspired against king Amon
34. 11 which the kings of Judah had destroyed
34. 16 to the king, and brought the king word
34. 18 Then Shaphan the scribe told the king
34. 18 And Shaphan read it before the king.
34. 19 when the king had heard the words of
34. 20 king commanded..Asaiah a ser. of the k.'s
34. 22 and (they) that the king (had appointed)
34. 24 which they have read before the king of J.
34. 26 as for the king of Judah, who sent you to
34. 28 So they brought the king word again
34. 29 Then the king sent and gathered together
34. 30 the king went up into the house of the L.
34. 31 the king stood in his place, and made a
35. 3 which Solomon the son of David king of
35. 4 according to the writing of David king
35. 7 these (were) of the king's substance
35. 10 according to the king's commandment
35. 15 and Heman, and Jeduthun the king's seer
35. 16 according to the commandment of king J.
35. 18 neither did all the kings of Israel keep
35. 20 Necho king of Egypt came up against Car.
35. 21 What have I to do with thee, thou king of
35. 23 the archers shot at king Josiah: and the k.
35. 27 in the book of the kings of Israel and Ju.
36. 3 the king of Egypt put him down at Jeru.
36. 4 king of Egypt made Eliakim his brother
36. 6 came up Nebuchadnezzar king of Babylon
36. 8 in the book of the kings of Israel and Ju.
36. 10 king Nebuchadnezzar sent and brought
36. 13 he also rebelled against king Nebuchadn.
36. 17 Therefore he brought upon them the king
36. 18 the treasures of the king, and of his prin.
36. 22 in the first year of Cyrus king of Persia
36. 22 stirred up the spirit of Cyrus king of Per.
36. 23 Thus saith Cyrus king of Persia, All the k.
Ezra 1. 1 in the first year of Cyrus king of Persia
1. 1 stirred up the spirit of Cyrus king of Per.
1. 2 Thus saith Cyrus king of Persia, The LORD
1. 7 Cyrus the king brought forth the vessels
1. 8 Even those did Cyrus king of Persia bring
2. 1 whom Nebuchadnezzar the king of Baby.
3. 7 the grant that they had of Cyrus king of
3. 10 after the ordinance of David king of Isr.
4. 2 since the days of Esar-haddon king of As.
4. 3 as king Cyrus the king of Persia hath co.
4. 5 Cyrus king of Persia..Darius king of Persia
4. 7 wrote..unto Artaxerxes king of Persia
6. 22 turned the heart of the king of Assyria
7. 1 in the reign of Artaxerxes king of Persia
7. 6 the king granted him all his request, ac.
7. 7 the seventh year of Artaxerxes the king
7. 8 which (was) in the seventh year of the k
7. 11 copy of the letter that the king Artaxerxes
7. 27 (such a thing) as this in the king's heart
7. 28 before the king..and before all the king's
8. 1 in the reign of Artaxerxes the king
8. 22 For I was ashamed to require of the king
8. 22 because we had spoken unto the king, sa.
8. 25 which the king, and his counsellors, and
8. 36 the king's commissions unto the king's
9. 7 and for our iniquities have we, our kings
9. 7 delivered into the hand of the kings of
9. 9 unto us in the sight of the kings of Persia
Neh. 1. 11 For I was the king's cup bearer
2. 1 the twentieth year of Artaxerxes the king
2. 1 took up the wine, and gave (it) unto the k.
2. 2 Wherefore the king said unto me, Why
2. 3 said unto the king, Let the king live for
2. 4 the king said unto me, For what dost thou
2. 5, 7 I said unto the king, If it please the king
2. 6 the king said unto me..it pleased the king
2. 8 unto Asaph the keeper of the king's forest
2. 8 the king granted me, according to the good
2. 9 gave them the king's letters. Now the king
2. 14 Then I went on..to the king's pool: but
2. 18 as also the king's words that he had spoken
2. 19 that ye do? will ye rebel against the king?
3. 15 of the pool of Siloah by the king's garden
3. 25 which lieth out from the king's high house
5. 4 have borrowed money for the king's trib.
5. 14 thirtieth year of Artaxerxes the king
6. 6 that thou mayest be their king, according
6. 7 (There is) a king in Judah: and now shall
6. 7 it be reported to the king according to
7. 6 whom Nebuchadnezzar the king of Baby.
9. 22 of the king of Heshbon, and..of Og king
9. 24 with their kings, and the people of the
9. 32 on our kings..since the time of the kings
9. 34 Neither have our kings, our princes, our
9. 37 unto the kings whom thou hast set over
11. 23 For (it was) the king's commandment co.
11. 24 at the king's hand in all matters concern.
13. 6 thirtieth year of Artaxerxes king of Bab.
13. 6 unto the king..obtained I leave of the king
13. 26 Did not Solomon king of Israel sin by th.
13. 26 among many nations was there no king
13. 26 and God made him king over all Israel
Esth. 1. 2 the king Ahasuerus sat on the throne of
1. 5 the king made a feast unto all the people
1. 5 the court of the garden of the king's pal.
1. 7 according to the state of the king
1. 8 the king had appointed to all the officers
1. 9 the royal house which (belonged) to king A.

Esth. 1. 10 when the heart of the king was merry
1. 10 served in the presence of Ahasuerus the k.
1. 11 To bring Vashti the queen before the king
1. 12 queen Vashti refused to come at the king's
1. 12 therefore was the king very wroth, and
1. 13 Then the king said to the wise men, which
1. 13 for so (was) the king's manner toward all
1. 14 which saw the king's face, (and) which sat
1. 15 the king Ahasuerus by the chamberlains?
1. 16 Memucan answered before the king and
1. 16 hath not done wrong to the king only, but
1. 16 in all the provinces of the king Ahasuerus
1. 17 The king Ahasuerus commanded Vashti
1. 18 say this day unto all the king's princes
1. 19 If it please the king, let there go a royal
1. 19 That Vashti come no more before king A
1. 19 and let the king give her royal estate unto
1. 20 when the king's decree which he shall
1. 21 the saying pleased the king..and the king
1. 22 he sent letters into all the king's provinces
2. 1 when the wrath of king Ahasuerus was
2. 2 Then said the king's servants that minis.
2. 2 be fair young virgins sought for the king
2. 3 let the king appoint officers in all the pr.
2. 3 custody of Hege the king's chamberlain
2. 4 let the maiden which pleaseth the king
2. 4 the thing pleased the king; and he did
2. 6 carried away with Jeconiah king of Judah
2. 6 whom Nebuchadnezzar the king of Baby.
2. 8 when the king's commandment and his
2. 8 Esther was brought also into the king's
2. 9 meet to be given her, out of the king's
2. 12 turn was come to go in to king Ahasuerus
2. 13 Then..came (every) maiden unto the king
2. 13 house of the women unto the king's hou.
2. 14 custody of Shaashgaz the king's chambe
2. 14 in unto the king no more, except the king
2. 15 was come to go in unto the king, she req.
2. 15 nothing but what Hegai the king's cham.
2. 16 So Esther was taken unto king Ahasuerus
2. 17 the king loved Esther above all the wom.
2. 18 Then the king made a great feast unto all
2. 18 according to the state of the king
2. 19 then Mordecai sat in the king's gate
2. 21 sat in the king's gate, two of the king's
2. 21 sought to lay hand on the king Ahasuerus
2. 22 Esther certified the king (thereof) in Mor.
2. 23 the book of the chronicles before the king
3. 1 After these things did king Ahasuerus
3. 2 king's servants, that (were) in the king's
3. 2 for the king had so commanded concern
3. 3 the king's servants, which (were) in the
3. 3 Why transgressest thou the king's comma.
3. 7 in the twelfth year of king Ahasuerus
3. 8 Haman said unto king Ahasuerus, There
3. 8 neither keep they the king's laws: there.
3. 8 (is) not for the king's profit to suffer them
3. 9 If it please the king, let it be written that
3. 9 to bring (it) into the king's treasuries
3. 10 the king took his ring from his hand, and
3. 11 the king said unto Haman, The silver (is)
3. 12 Then were the king's scribes called on the
3. 12 unto the king's lieutenants, and to the
3. 12 in the name of king Ahasuerus was it
3. 12 written, and sealed with the king's ring
3. 13 sent by posts into all the king's provinces
3. 15 being hastened by the king's commandm.
3. 15 the king and Haman sat down to drink
4. 2 came even before the king's gate: for none
4. 2 enter into the king's gate clothed with sac.
4. 3 whithersoever the king's commandment
4. 5 (one) of the king's chamberlains, whom
4. 6 unto the street..which (was) before the k.
4. 7 promised to pay to the king's treasuries
4. 8 that she should go in unto the king, to
4. 11 king's servants, and the people of the king
4. 11 shall come unto the king into the inner
4. 11 except such to whom the king shall hold
4. 11 not been called to come in unto the king
4. 13 that thou shalt escape in the king's house
4. 16 and so will I go in unto the king, which
5. 1 of the king's house, over against the king's
5. 1 the king sat upon his royal throne in the
5. 2 so, when the king saw Esther the queen
5. 2 the king held out to Esther the golden sc.
5. 3 Then said the king unto her, What wilt
5. 4 If (it seem) good unto the king, let the king
5. 5 the king said..So the king and Haman
5. 6 the king said unto Esther at the banquet
5. 8 found favour in the sight of the king, and
5. 8 if it please the king to grant my petition
5. 8 let the king and Haman come to the ban.
5. 8 I will do to-morrow as the king hath said
5. 9 when Haman saw Mordecai in the king's
5. 11 wherein the king had promoted him, and
5. 11 above the princes and servants of the king
5. 12 did let no man come in with the king
5. 12 am I invited unto her also with the king
5. 13 Mordecai the Jew sitting at the king's g.
5. 14 to morrow speak thou unto the king that
5. 14 then go thou in merrily with the king unto
6. 1 On that night could not the king sleep
6. 1 and they were read before the king
6. 2 two of the king's chamberlains, the keep.
6. 2 who sought to lay hand on the king Aha.
6. 3 the king said, What honour and dignity
6. 3 Then said the king's servants that minis.
6. 4 And the king said, Who (is) in the court?
6. 4 into the outward court of the king's house
6. 4 to speak unto the king to hang Mordecai
6. 5 the king's servants said unto him, Behold
6. 5 And the king said, Let him come in

Esth. 6. 6 the king said unto him, What shall be
6. 6 unto the man whom the king delighteth
6. 6 To whom would the king delight to do ho.
6. 7 Haman answered the king, For the man
6. 7, 9, 9, 11 whom the king delighteth to hon.
6. 8 Let the royal apparel..which the king
6. 8 the horse that the king rideth upon, and
6. 9 to the hand of one of the king's most noble
6. 10 Then the king said to Haman, Make haste
6. 10 the Jew, that sitteth at the king's gate
6. 12 Mordecai came again to the king's gate
6. 14 came the king's chamberlain, and hasted
7. 1 So the king and Haman came to banquet
7. 2 the king said again unto Esther on the
7. 3 thy sight, O king, and if it please the king
7. 4 could not countervail the king's damage
7. 5 the king Ahasuerus answered, and said
7. 6 Haman was afraid before the king and
7. 7 king, arising from the banquet of wine
7. 7 evil determined against him by the king
7. 8 the king returned out of the palace garden
7. 8 Then said the king, Will he force the queen
7. 8 As the word went out of the king's mouth
7. 9 Harbonah..said before the king, Behold
7. 9 Mordecai, who had spoken good for the k.
7. 9 Then the king said, Hang him thereon
7. 10 Then was the king's wrath pacified
8. 1 On that day did the king Ahasuerus give
8. 1 and Mordecai came before the king; for
8. 2 the king took off his ring, which he had
8. 3 Esther spake yet again before the king
8. 4 the king held out the golden sceptre tow.
8. 4 So Esther arose, and stood before the king
8. 5 If it please the king, and if I have found
8. 5 and the thing (seem) right before the king
8. 5 which (are) in all the king's provinces
8. 7 Then the king Ahasuerus said unto Esther
8. 8 as it liketh you, in the king's name, and
8. 8 seal (it) with the king's ring: for the
8. 8 in the king's name..with the king's ring
8. 9 Then were the king's scribes called at
8. 10 he wrote in the king Ahasuerus' name
8. 10 sealed (it) with the king's ring; and sent
8. 11 Wherein the king granted the Jews which
8. 12 in all the provinces of king Ahasuerus
8. 14 pressed on by the king's commandment
8. 15 went out from the presence of the king in
8. 17 whithersoever the king's commandment
9. 1 when the king's commandment and his
9. 2, 20 all the provinces of the king Ahasuerus
9. 3 and officers of the king, helped the Jews
9. 4 Mordecai (was) great in the king's house
9. 11 the number..was brought before the king
9. 12 the king said unto Esther the queen, The
9. 12 done in the rest of the king's provinces?
9. 13 If it please the king, let it be granted
9. 14 the king commanded it so to be done: and
9. 16 other Jews that (were) in the king's prov.
9. 25 But when (Esther) came before the king
10. 1 the king Ahasuerus laid a tribute upon the
10. 2 whereunto the king advanced him, (are)
10. 2 in the book of the chronicles of the kings
10. 3 Mordecai the Jew (was) next unto king A.
Job 3. 14 With kings and counsellors of the earth
12. 18 He looseth the bond of kings, and girdeth
15. 24 prevail against him, as a king ready to the
18. 14 it shall bring him to the king of terrors
29. 25 and dwelt as a king in the army, as one
34. 18 (Is it fit) to say to a king, (Thou art) wicked?
36. 7 but with kings (are they) on the throne
41. 34 he (is) a king over all the children of pride
Psa. 2. 2 The kings of the earth set themselves, and
2. 6 Yet have I set my king upon my holy hill
2. 10 Be wise now therefore, O ye kings; be
5. 2 Hearken unto the voice of my cry, my k.
10. 16 The LORD (is) king for ever and ever: the
18. 50 Great deliverance giveth he to his king
20. 9 Save, LORD: let the king hear us when
21. 1 The king shall joy in thy strength, O LORD
21. 7 For the king trusteth in the LORD; and
24. 7, 9 and the king of glory shall come in
24. 8, 10 Who (is) this king of glory? The LORD
24. 10 The LORD of hosts, he (is) the king of gl.
29. 10 yea, the LORD sitteth king for ever
33. 16 There is no king saved by the multitude
44. 4 Thou art my king, O God: command del.
45. 1 which I have made touching the king; my
45. 5 sharp in the heart of the king's enemies
45. 9 King's daughters (were) among thy hono.
45. 11 So shall the king greatly desire thy beauty
45. 13 The king's daughter (is) all glorious within
45. 14 shall be brought unto the king in raiment
45. 15 they shall enter into the king's palace
47. 2 (he is) a great king over all the earth
47. 6 sing praises unto our king, sing praises
47. 7 For God (is) the king of all the earth: sing
48. 2 (is) mount Zion..the city of the great king
48. 4 the kings were assembled, they passed by
61. 6 Thou wilt prolong the king's life; (and)
63. 11 the king shall rejoice in God; every one
68. 12 Kings of armies did flee apace; and she
68. 14 When the Almighty scattered kings in it
68. 24 the goings of my God, my king, in the
68. 29 because of thy temple..shall kings bring
72. 1 Give the king..and..unto the king's son
72. 10 The kings of Tarshish..the kings of Sheba
72. 11 Yea, all kings shall fall down before him
74. 12 For God (is) my king of old, working sa.
76. 12 (he is) terrible to the kings of the earth
84. 3 O LORD of hosts, my king, and my God
89. 18 and the Holy One of Israel (is) our king
89. 27 higher than the kings of the earth

Psa. 95. 3 For the LORD (is) a great..king above all
98. 6 a joyful noise before the LORD, the king
99. 4 The king's strength also loveth judgment
102. 15 and all the kings of the earth thy glory
105. 14 yea, he reproved kings for their sakes
105. 20 The king sent and loosed him; (even) the
105. 30 frogs..in the chambers of their kings
110. 5 shall strike through kings in the day of
119. 46 speak of thy testimonies also before kings
135. 10 smote great nations, and slew mighty k.
135. 11 Sihon king..and Og king of Baashan, and
136. 17 To him which smote great kings: for his
136. 18 slew famous kings: for his mercy (endu.)
136. 19 Sihon king of the Amorites: for his mercy
136. 20 Og the king of Bashan: for his mercy
138. 4 All the kings of the earth shall praise thee
144. 10 (It is he) that giveth salvation unto kings
145. 1 I will extol thee, my God, O King; and I
148. 11 Kings of the earth, and all people; prin.
149. 2 the children of Zion be joyful in their k.
149. 8 To bind their kings with chains, and their
Prov. 1. 1 Solomon the son of David, king of Israel
8. 15 By me kings reign, and princes decree j.
14. 28 In the multitude of people (is) the king's
14. 35 The king's favour (is) toward a wise serv.
16. 10 A divine sentence (is) in the lips of the k.
16. 12 abomination to kings to commit wicked.
16. 13 Righteous lips (are) the delight of kings
16. 14 The wrath of a king (is as) messengers of
16. 15 In the light of the king's countenance
19. 12 The king's wrath (is) as the roaring of a
20. 2 fear of a king (is) as the roaring of a lion
20. 8 A king that sitteth in the throne of judg.
20. 26 A wise king scattereth the wicked, and
20. 28 Mercy and truth preserve the king; and
21. 1 The king's heart (is) in the hand of the L.
22. 11 (for) the grace of his lips the king (shall
22. 29 he shall stand before kings; he shall not
24. 21 My son, fear thou the LORD and the king
25. 1 which the men of Hezekiah king of Judah
25. 2 the honour of kings (is) to search out a
25. 3 and the heart of kings (is) unsearchable
25. 5 Take away the wicked from before the k.
25. 6 Put not forth..in the presence of the king
29. 4 The king by judgment establisheth the
29. 14 The king that faithfully judgeth the poor
30. 27 The locusts have no king, yet go they for.
30. 28 spider taketh hold..and is in king's pala.
30. 31 a king, against whom (there is) no rising
31. 1 The words of king Lemuel, the prophecy
31. 3 thy ways to that which destroyeth kings
31. 4 for kings, O Lemuel, (it is) not for kings to
Eccl. 1. 1 the Preacher, the son of David, king of J.
1. 12 I the Preacher was king over Israel in J.
2. 8 the peculiar treasure of kings and of the
2. 12 the man (do) that cometh after the king
4. 13 a wise child than an old and foolish king
5. 9 the king (himself) is served by the field
8. 2 I (counsel thee) to keep the king's com.
8. 4 Where the word of a king (is, there is) p.
9. 14 and there came a great king against it, and
10. 16 Woe to thee, O land, when thy king (is) a
10. 17 when thy king (is) the son of nobles, and
10. 20 Curse not the king, no not in thy thought
Song 1. 4 The king hath brought me into his cham.
1. 12 While the king (sitteth) at his table, my
3. 9 King Solomon made himself a chariot of
3. 11 and behold king Solomon with the crown
7. 5 the king (is) held in the galleries
Isa. 1. 1 in the days of Uzziah, Jotham..kings of
6. 1 In the year that king Uzziah died I saw
6. 5 for mine eyes have seen the king, the LORD
7. 1 the days of..Uzziah king of Judah, (that)
7. 1 king of Syria, and..king of Israel, went
7. 6 set a king in the midst of it, (even) the son
7. 16 land..shall be forsaken of both her kings
7. 17 departed from Judah; (even) the king of
7. 20 by the king of Assyria, the head, and the
8. 4 shall be taken away before the king of A.
8. 7 (even) the king of Assyria, and all his glory
8. 21 fret themselves, and curse their king and
10. 8 (Are) not my princes altogether kings?
10. 12 of the stout heart of the king of Assyria
14. 4 take up this proverb against the king of B.
14. 9 it hath raised up..all the kings of the na.
14. 18 All the kings of the nations, (even) all of
14. 28 In the year that king Ahaz died was this
19. 4 a fierce king shall rule over them, saith
19. 11 son of the wise, the son of ancient kings?
20. 1 when Sargon the king of Assyria sent him
20. 4 So shall the king of Assyria lead away the
20. 6 to be delivered from the king of Assyria
23. 15 according to the days of one king: after
24. 21 and the kings of the earth upon the earth
30. 33 yea, for the king it is prepared: he hath
32. 1 a king shall reign in righteousness, and
33. 17 Thine eyes shall see the king in his beauty
33. 22 our lawgiver, the LORD (is) our king; he
36. 1 in the fourteenth year of king Hezekiah
36. 1 Sennacherib king of Assyria came up ag.
36. 2 the king of Assyria sent..unto king Hez.
36. 4 Thus saith the great king, the king of A.
36. 6 so (is) Pharaoh king of Egypt to all that
36. 8 give pledges..to my master the king of A.
36. 13 Hear..the words of the great king, the k.
36. 14 Thus saith the king, Let not Hezekiah
36. 15 delivered into the hand of the king of A.
36. 16 for thus saith the king of Assyria, Make
36. 18 his land out of the hand of the king of A.
36. 21 for the king's commandment was, saying
37. 1 when king Hezekiah heard (it), that he
37. 4 whom the king of Assyria his master hath

Isa. 37. 5 the servants of king Hezekiah came to I.
37. 6 the servants of the king of Assyria have
37. 8 found the king of Assyria warring against
37. 9 heard say concerning Tirhakah king of E.
37. 10 Thus shall ye speak to Hezekiah king of
37. 10 given into the hand of the king of Assyria
37. 11 thou hast heard what the kings of Assyria
37. 13 king of Hamath, and the king of Arphad
37. 13 the king of the city of Sepharvaim, Hena
37. 18 the kings of Assyria have laid waste all
37. 21 prayed to me against Sennacherib king of
37. 33 concerning the king of Assyria, He shall
37. 37 So Sennacherib king of Assyria departed
38. 6 out of the hand of the king of Assyria: and
38. 9 The writing of Hezekiah king of Judah
39. 1 king of Babylon, sent letters and a present
39. 3 came Isaiah the prophet unto king Hezek.
39. 7 be eunuchs in the palace of the king of B.
41. 2 called him..and made (him) rule over k.?
41. 21 bring forth..saith the king of Jacob
43. 15 Holy One, the Creator of Israel, your king
44. 6 Thus saith the LORD the king of Israel
45. 1 I will loose the loins of kings, to open
49. 7 kings shall see and arise, princes also
49. 23 kings shall be thy nursing fathers, and
52. 15 the kings shall shut their mouths at him
57. 9 thou wentest to the king with ointment
60. 3 and kings to the brightness of thy rising
60. 10 and their kings shall minister unto thee
60. 11 thy gates shall be open..(that) their kings
60. 16 shalt suck the breasts of kings: and thou
62. 2 thy righteousness, and all kings thy glory
Jer. 1. 2 of Josiah the son of Amon king of Judah
1. 3, 3 the son of Josiah king of Judah, unto the
1. 18 against the kings of Judah, against the
2. 26 their kings, their princes, and their priests
3. 6 unto me in the days of Josiah the king
4. 9 the heart of the king shall perish, and
8. 1 shall bring out the bones of the kings of
8. 19 (Is) not the LORD in Zion? (is) not her king
10. 7 Who would not fear thee, O king of nat.?
10. 10 the living God, and an everlasting King
13. 13 the kings that sit upon David's throne
13. 18 Say unto the king and to the queen, Hu.
15. 4 Manasseh the son of Hezekiah king of J.
17. 19 whereby the kings of Judah come in, and
17. 20 Hear ye the word of the LORD, ye kings
17. 25 Then shall there enter..kings and princes
19. 3 Hear ye the word of the LORD, O kings
19. 4 nor the kings of Judah, and have filled
19. 13 the houses of the kings of Judah, shall
20. 4 into the hand of the king of Babylon, and
20. 5 all the treasures of the kings of Judah
21. 1 when king Zedekiah sent unto him Pas.
21. 2 king of Babylon maketh war against us
21. 4 wherewith ye fight against the king of B.
21. 7 I will deliver Zedekiah king of Judah
21. 7 into the hand of Nebuchadrezzar king of
21. 10 into the hand of the king of Babylon, and
21. 11 touching the house of the king of Judah
22. 1 Go down to the house of the king of Judah
22. 2 Hear the word of the LORD, O king of Ju.
22. 4 then shall there enter..kings sitting upon
22. 6 thus saith the LORD unto the king's house
22. 11 Shallum the son of Josiah king of Judah
22. 18 Jehoiakim the son of Josiah king of Judah
22. 24 Coniah the son of Jehoiakim king of Judah
22. 25 into the hand of Nebuchadrezzar king of
23. 5 and a King shall reign and prosper, and
24. 1 after that Nebuchadrezzar king of Baby
24. 1 Jeconiah the son of Jehoiakim king of J
24. 8 So will I give Zedekiah the king of Judah
25. 1 Jehoiakim the son of Josiah king of Judah
25. 1 the first year of Nebuchadrezzar king of
25. 3 Josiah the son of Amon king of Judah
25. 9 Nebuchadrezzar the king of Babylon, my
25. 11 these nations shall serve the king of Bab.
25. 12 I will punish the king of Babylon, and
25. 14 many nations and great kings shall serve
25. 18 the kings thereof, and the princes thereof
25. 19 Pharaoh king of Egypt, and his servants
25. 20 all the kings..and all the kings of the land
25. 22 the kings of Tyrus, and all the kings
25. 22 the kings of the isles which (are) beyond
25. 24 the kings of Arabia, and all the kings of
25. 25 And all the kings of Zimri, and all the
25. 25 kings of Elam, and all the kings of the M.
25. 26 all the kings of the north, far and near
25. 26 the king of Sheshach shall drink after them
26. 1 Jehoiakim the son of Josiah king of Judah
26. 10 they came up from the king's house unto
26. 18 prophesied in the days of Hezekiah king
26. 19 Did Hezekiah king of Judah and all Judah
26. 21 when..the king..heard his words, the king
26. 22 Jehoiakim the king sent men into Egypt
26. 23 and brought him unto Jehoiakim the k.
27. 1 Jehoiakim the son of Josiah king of Judah
27. 3 to the king of Edom, and to the king of M.
27. 3 king of the Ammonites, and to the king
27. 3 and to the king of Zidon, by the hand of
27. 3 come to Jerusalem unto Zedekiah king of
27. 6 into the hand of Nebuchadnezzar the king
27. 7 many nations and great kings shall serve
27. 8 which will not serve..the king of Babylon
27. 8, 11, 12 under the yoke of the king of Bab.
27. 9, 14 Ye shall not serve the king of Babylon
27. 12 I spake also to Zedekiah king of Judah
27. 13 that will not serve the king of Babylon?
27. 17 serve the king of Babylon, and live: whe.
27. 18, 21 (in) the house of the king of Judah
27. 20 Which Nebuchadnezzar king of Babylon
27. 20 Jeconiah the son of Jehoiakim king of J

Jer. 28. 1 the reign of Zedekiah king of Judah, in
28. 2 I have broken the yoke of the king of Ba.
28. 3 king of Babylon took away from this place
28. 4 Jeconiah the son of Jehoiakim king of J.
28. 4 will break the yoke of the king of Babylon
28. 11 the yoke of Nebuchadnezzar king of Bab.
28. 14 may serve Nebuchadnezzar king of Baby.
29. 2 After that Jeconiah the king, and the qu.
29. 3 king of Judah sent unto..king of Babylon
29. 16 of the king that sitteth upon the throne
29. 21 into the hand of Nebuchadrezzar king of
29. 22 whom the king of Babylon roasted in the
30. 9 But they shall serve..David their king
32. 1 in the tenth year of Zedekiah king of Ju.
32. 2 then the king of Babylon's army besieged
32. 2 prison, which (was) in the king of Judah's
32. 3 Zedekiah king of Judah had shut him up
32. 3, 4 into the hand of the king of Babylon
32. 4 Zedekiah king of Judah shall not escape
32. 28 into the hand of Nebuchadrezzar king of
32. 32 their kings, their princes, their priests
32. 36 delivered into the hand of the king of
33. 4 concerning the houses of the kings of J.
34. 1 when Nebuchadnezzar king of Babylon
34. 2 Go and speak to Zedekiah king of Judah
34. 2 into the hand of the king of Babylon, and
34. 3 behold the eyes of the king of Babylon
34. 4 hear the word..O Zedekiah king of Judah
34. 5 the former kings which were before thee
34. 6 spake all these words unto Zedekiah king
34. 7 When the king of Babylon's army fought
34. 8 after that the king Zedekiah had made a
34. 21 Zedekiah king of Judah, and his princes
35. 21 into the hand of the king of Babylon's
35. 1 days of Jehoiakim the son of Josiah king
35. 11 when Nebuchadrezzar king of Babylon
36. 1, 9 Jehoiakim the son of Josiah king of
36. 12 Then he went down into the king's house
36. 16 We will surely tell the king of all these
36. 20 they went in to the king into the court
36. 20 told all the words in the ears of the king
36. 21 So the king sent Jehudi to fetch the roll
36. 21 and Jehudi read it in the ears of the king
36. 21 the princes which stood beside the king
36. 22 Now the king sat in the winter house, in
36. 24 the king, nor any of his servants that
36. 25 had made intercession to the king that
36. 26 the king commanded Jerahmeel the son
36. 27 after that the king had burnt the roll, and
36. 28, 32 which Jehoiakim king of Judah hath
36. 29 thou shalt say to Jehoiakim king of Judah
36. 29 The king of Babylon shall certainly come
36. 30 saith the LORD of Jehoiakim king of Jud.
37. 1 king Zedekiah the son of Josiah reigned
37. 1 Coniah..whom Nebuchadrezzar king of
37. 3 Zedekiah the king sent Jehucal the son
37. 7 Thus shall ye say to the king of Judah
37. 17 the king sent..and the king asked him
37. 17 be delivered into the hand of the king of
37. 18 Jeremiah said unto king Zedekiah, What
37. 19 king of Babylon shall not come against
37. 20 hear now, I pray thee, O my lord the king
37. 21 Then Zedekiah the king commanded that
38. 3 be given into the hand of the king of Bab.
38. 4 the princes said unto the king, We beseech
38. 5 Zedekiah the king said, Behold, he (is) in
38. 5 for the king (is) not (he that) can do (any)
38. 7 in the king's house..the king then sitting
38. 8 the king's house, and spake to the king
38. 9 My lord the king, these men have done
38. 10 Then the king commanded Ebed-melech
38. 11 went into the house of the king under the
38. 14 Zedekiah the king sent..and the king said
38. 16 the king sware secretly unto Jeremiah
38. 17 go forth unto the king of Babylon's prin
38. 18 if thou wilt not go forth to the king of B.
38. 19 the king said unto Jeremiah, I am afraid
38. 22 that are left in the king of Judah's house
38. 22 (shall be) brought forth to the king of B.
38. 23 shall be taken by the hand of the king of
38. 25 Declare..what thou hast said unto the k.
38. 25 hide it not..what the king said unto thee
38. 26 presented my supplication before the king
38. 27 these words that the king had commanded
39. 1 In the ninth year of Zedekiah king of Ju.
39. 1 came Nebuchadrezzar king of Babylon and
39. 3 all the princes of the king of Babylon came
39. 3 the residue of the princes of the king of B.
39. 4 when Zedekiah the king of Judah saw them
39. 4 by the way of the king's garden, by the
39. 5 brought him up to Nebuchadnezzar king
39. 6 the king of Babylon slew..also the king of
39. 8 the Chaldeans burnt the king's house, and
39. 11 king of Babylon gave charge concerning
39. 13 and all the king of Babylon's princes
40. 5 whom the king of Babylon hath made go.
40. 7 heard that the king of Babylon had made
40. 9 serve the king of Babylon, and it shall be
40. 11 heard that the king of Babylon had left a
40. 14 certainly know that Baalis the king of the
41. 1 the princes of the king, even ten men with
41. 2 whom the king of Babylon had made gov.
41. 9 the king had made for fear of Baasha king
41. 10 the king's daughters, and all the people
41. 18 whom the king of Babylon made governor
42. 11 Be not afraid of the king of Babylon, of
43. 6 the king's daughters, and every person
43. 10 send and take Nebuchadrezzar the king of
44. 9 and the wickedness of the kings of Judah
44. 17 our kings, and our princes, in the cities of
44. 21 your kings, and your princes, and the pe.
44. 30 give Pharaoh-hophra king of Egypt into

Jer. 44. 30 I gave Zedekiah king of Judah into the
44. 30 hand of Nebuchadrezzar king of Babylon
45. 1 of Jehoiakim the son of Josiah king of J.
46. 2 against the army of Pharaoh-necho king
46. 2 which Nebuchadrezzar king of Babylon
46. 2 of Jehoiakim the son of Josiah king of J.
46. 13 how Nebuchadrezzar king of Babylon
46. 17 Pharaoh king of Egypt (is but) a noise
46. 18 (As) I live, saith the king, whose name
46. 25 I will punish..their kings; even Pharaoh
46. 26 into the hand of Nebuchadrezzar king of
48. 15 saith the King, whose name (is) The LORD
49. 1 why (then) doth their king inherit Gad
49. 3 for their king shall go into captivity, (and)
49. 28 which Nebuchadrezzar king of Babylon
49. 30 Nebuchadrezzar king of Babylon hath
49. 34 beginning of the reign of Zedekiah king
49. 38 will destroy from thence the king and
50. 17 first the king..and last this..king of Ba.
50. 18 I will punish the king of Babylon and
50. 18 as I have punished the king of Assyria
50. 41 many kings shall be raised up from the
50. 43 The king of Babylon hath heard the report
51. 11 hath raised up the spirit of the kings of
51. 28 with the kings of the Medes, the captains
51. 31 to show the king of Babylon that his city
51. 34 the king of Babylon hath devoured me
51. 57 saith the King, whose name (is) The LORD
51. 59 when he went with Zedekiah the king of
52. 3 Zedekiah rebelled against the king of B.
52. 4 Nebuchadrezzar king of Babylon came
52. 5 besieged unto the eleventh year of king
52. 7 walls, which (was) by the king's garden
52. 8 the Chaldeans pursued after the king, and
52. 9 Then they took the king, and carried him
52. 9 up to the king of Babylon to Riblah in
52. 10 the king of Babylon slew the sons of Ze.
52. 11 the king of Babylon bound him in chains
52. 12 year of Nebuchadrezzar king of Babylon
52. 12 served the king of Babylon, into Jerusalem
52. 13 burned..the king's house; and all the ho.
52. 15 that fell to the king of Babylon, and the
52. 20 which king Solomon had made in the ho.
52. 25 of them that were near the king's person
52. 26 brought them to the king of Babylon to
52. 27 the king of Babylon smote them, and put
52. 31 year of the captivity of Jehoiachin king
52. 31 Evil-merodach king of Babylon in the first
52. 31 lifted up the head of Jehoiachin king of
52. 32 set his throne above the throne of the king
52. 34 continual diet given him of the king of
Lam. 2. 6 and hath despised..the king and the pr.
2. 9 her king and her princes (are) among the
4. 12 kings of the earth, and all the inhabitants
Eze. 1. 2 which (was) the fifth year of king Jehoia.
7. 27 The king shall mourn, and the prince shall
17. 12 the king of Babylon..hath taken the king
17. 16 in the place (where) the king (dwelleth)
19. 9 and brought him to the king of Babylon
21. 19 that the sword of the king of Babylon
21. 21 the king of Babylon stood at the parting
24. 2 the king of Babylon set himself against
26. 7 Nebuchadrezzar king of Babylon, a king
27. 33 thou didst enrich the kings of the earth
27. 35 their kings shall be sore afraid, they shall
28. 12 take up a lamentation upon the king of T.
28. 17 I will lay thee before kings, that they may
29. 2 set thy face against Pharaoh king of Eg.
29. 3 I (am) against thee, Pharaoh king of Eg.
29. 18 king of Babylon caused his army to serve
29. 19 unto Nebuchadrezzar king of Babylon
30. 10 by the hand of Nebuchadrezzar king of
30. 21 I have broken the arm of Pharaoh king
30. 22 Behold, I (am) against Pharaoh king of E.
30. 24, 25 I will strengthen the arms of the king
30. 25 into the hand of the king of Babylon, and
31. 2 Speak unto Pharaoh king of Egypt, and
32. 2 take up a lamentation for Pharaoh king
32. 10 their kings shall be horribly afraid
32. 11 The sword of the king of Babylon shall
32. 29 There (is) Edom, her kings, and all her
37. 22 and one king shall be king to them all
37. 24 David my servant (shall be) king over
43. 7 (neither) they, nor their kings, by their
43. 7 nor by the carcases of their kings in their
43. 9 the carcases of their kings far from me
Dan. 1. 1 of the reign of Jehoiakim king of Judah
1. 1 came Nebuchadnezzar king of Babylon
1. 2 the Lord gave Jehoiakim king of Judah
1. 3 the king spake unto Ashpenaz the master
1. 4 ability in them to stand in the king's pal.
1. 5 king appointed..provision of the king's
1. 5 that..they might stand before the king
1. 8 with the portion of the king's meat, nor
1. 10 I fear my lord the king, who hath appoint.
1. 10 ye make (me) endanger my head to the k.
1. 13 that eat of the portion of the king's meat
1. 15 which did eat the portion of the king's
1. 18 at the end of the days that the king had
1. 19 king communed..stood they before the k.
1. 20 in all matters..that the king enquired
1. 21 continued (even) unto the first year of k.
2. 2 the king commanded..to show the king
2. 2 So they came and stood before the king
2. 3 the king said unto them, I have dreamed
2. 4 Then spake the Chaldeans to the king in
8. 1 In the third year of the reign of king Bel.
8. 20 thou sawest having (two) horns (are) the k
8. 21 the rough goat (is) the king of Grecia: and
8. 21 that (is) between his eyes (is) the first king
8. 23 in the latter time..a king of fierce coun.
8. 27 I rose up, and did the king's business; and

Dan. 9. 6 which spake in thy name to our kings, our
9. 8 to our kings, to our princes, and to our
10. 1 In the third year of Cyrus king of Persia
10. 13 I remained there with the kings of Persia
11. 2 there shall stand up yet three kings in Pe.
11. 3 a mighty king shall stand up, that shall
11. 5 the king of the south shall be strong, and
11. 6 for the king's daughter of the south shall
11. 6 to the king of the north to make an agree.
11. 7 shall enter into the fortress of the king
11. 8 shall continue (more) years than the king
11. 9 So the king of the south shall come into
11. 11 the king of the south..(even) with the k.
11. 13 For the king of the north shall return
11. 14 shall many stand up against the king
11. 15 So the king of the north shall come, and
11. 25 against the king of the south with a great
11. 25 the king of the south shall be stirred up
11. 27 these kings' hearts (shall be) to do misch.
11. 36 the king shall do according to his will
11. 40 shall the king of the south push at him
11. 40 the king of the north shall come against
Hos. 1. 1 Jotham, Ahaz, (and) Hezekiah, kings of J.
1. 1 of Jeroboam the son of Joash, king of Is
3. 4 shall abide many days without a king, and
3. 5 return, and seek..David their king; and
5. 1 give ye ear, O house of the king; for jud.
5. 13 sent to king Jareb: yet could he not heal
7. 3 They make the king glad with their wick.
7. 5 In the day of our king the princes have
7. 7 all their kings are fallen: (there is) none
8. 10 sorrow..for the burden of the king of pri.
10. 3 We have no king..what then should a k.
10. 6 unto Assyria (for) a present to king Jareb
10. 7 her king is cut off as the foam upon the
10. 15 in a morning shall the king of Israel utt.
11. 5 the Assyrian shall be his king, because
13. 10 I will be thy king..Give me a king and
13. 11 I gave thee a king in mine anger, and took
Amos 1. 1 in the days of Uzziah king of Judah, and
1. 1 of Jeroboam the son of Joash king of Isr.
1. 15 their king shall go into captivity, he and
2. 1 he burned the bones of the king of Edom
7. 1 latter growth after the king's mowings
7. 10 sent to Jeroboam king of Israel, saying
7. 13 for it (is) the king's chapel, and it (is) the
Jon. 3. 6 For word came unto the king of Nineveh
3. 7 by the decree of the king and his nobles
Mic. 1. 1 Jotham, Ahaz, (and) Hezekiah, kings of J.
1. 14 Achzib (shall be) a lie to the kings of Is.
2. 13 their King shall pass before them, and
4. 9 (is there) no king in thee? is thy counsel.
6. 5 remember now what Balak king of Moab
Nah. 3. 18 Thy shepherds slumber, O king of Assyria
Hab. 1. 10 shall scoff at the kings, and the princes
Zeph. 1. 1 days of Josiah the son of Amon, king of
1. 8 punish the princes, and the king's children
3. 15 the king of Israel, (even) the LORD, (is)
Hag. 1. 1, 15 In the second year of Darius the king
Zech. 7. 1 in the fourth year of king Darius, (that)
9. 5 the king shall perish from Gaza, and As.
9. 9 thy king cometh unto thee: he (is) just
11. 6 I will deliver..into the hand of his king
14. 5 earthquake in the days of Uzziah king of
14. 9 the LORD shall be king over all the earth
14. 10 tower of Hananeel unto the king's wine
14. 16 shall even go up..to worship the king
14. 17 to worship the King, the LORD of hosts, even
Mal. 1. 14 for I (am) a great King, saith the LORD of

A king, counsellor, מֶלֶךְ, מַלְכָּא *melek, malka.*

Ezra 4. 8 wrote a letter..to Artaxerxes the king in
4. 11 that they sent..unto Artaxerxes the king
4. 12 Be it known unto the king, that the Jews
4. 13 Be it known now unto the king, that if
4. 13 shalt endamage the revenue of the kings
4. 14 not meet for us to see the king's dishonour
4. 14 therefore have we sent and certified the k.
4. 15 hurtful unto kings and provinces, and that
4. 16 We certify the king, that if this city be bu.
4. 17 sent the king an answer unto Rehum the
4. 19 hath made insurrection against kings, and
4. 20 There have been mighty kings also over
4. 22 damage grow to the hurt of the kings?
4. 23 when the copy of king Artaxerxes' letter
4. 24 second year of the reign of Darius king of
5. 6 letter that Tatnai..sent unto Darius the k.
5. 7 written thus; Unto Darius the king, all p.
5. 8 Be it known unto the king, that we went
5. 11 which a great king of Israel builded and
5. 12 into the hand of Nebuchadnezzar the k.
5. 13 the first year of Cyrus the king of Babylon
5. 13 king Cyrus made a decree to build this h.
5. 14 those did Cyrus the king take out of the
5. 17 if (it seem) good to the king, let there be
5. 17 search made in the king's treasure house
5. 17 a decree was made of Cyrus the king to
5. 17 the king send his pleasure to us concern.
6. 1 Then Darius the king made a decree, and
6. 3 first year of Cyrus the king..the king
6. 4 the expenses be given out of the king's
6. 8 of the king's goods, (even) of the tribute
6. 10 pray for the life of the king, and of his
6. 12 destroy all kings and people that shall
6. 13 according to that which Darius the king
6. 14 Cyrus, and Darius, and Artaxerxes king
6. 15 the sixth year of the reign of Darius the k
7. 12 Artaxerxes, king of kings, unto Ezra the
7. 14 Forasmuch as thou art sent of the king
7. 15 which the king and his counsellors have
7. 20 bestow (it) out of the king's treasure house
7. 21 I, (even) I Artaxerxes the king, do make
Ezra 7. 23 against the realm of the king and his sons?
7. 26 thy God and the law of the king, let judg.
Dan. 2. 4 O king, live for ever: tell thy servants
2. 5 The king answered and said to the Chal.
2. 7 Let the king tell his servants the dream
2. 8 king answered and said, I know of certa.
2. 10 The Chaldeans answered before the king
2. 10 There is not a man..can show the king's
2. 10 therefore (there is) no king, lord, nor ruler
2. 11 a rare thing that the king requireth; and
2. 11 that can show it before the king, except
2. 12 For this cause the king was angry and
2. 14 to Arioch the captain of the king's guard
2. 15 said to Arioch the king's captain, Why
2. 15 decree (so) hasty from the king? Then A.
2. 16 desired of the king that he would give
2. 16 he would show the king the interpretation
2. 21 he removeth kings, and setteth up kings
2. 23 made known unto us the king's matter
2. 24 whom the king had ordained to destroy
2. 24 before the king, and I will show unto the k.
2. 25 brought in Daniel before the king in haste
2. 25 that will make known unto the king the
2. 26 The king answered and said to Daniel
2. 27 answered in the presence of the king, and
2. 27 secret which the king..show unto the king
2. 28 maketh known to the king..what shall
2. 29 As for thee, O king, thy thoughts came
2. 30 make known the interpretation to the k.
2. 31 Thou, O king, sawest, and, behold, a great
2. 36 tell the interpretation..before the king
2. 37 Thou, O king, (art) a king of kings: for
2. 44 in the days of these kings shall the God
2. 45 God hath made known to the king what
2. 46 the king Nebuchadnezzar fell upon his
2. 47 king answered..Of a truth..a Lord of k.
2. 48 Then the king made Daniel a great man
2. 49 Then Daniel requested of the king, and
2. 49 but Daniel (sat) in the gate of the king
3. 1 king made an image of gold, whose height
3. 2 the king sent to gather together the pri.
3. 2 which Nebuchadnezzar the king had set
3. 3, 7 that Nebuchadnezzar the king had set
3. 5 that Nebuchadnezzar the king hath set
3. 9 said to the king Nebuchadnezzar, O king
3. 10 Thou, O king, hast made a decree, that
3. 12 these men, O king, have not regarded thee
3. 13 Then they brought these men before the k.
3. 16 said to the king, O Nebuchadnezzar, we
3. 17 he will deliver..out of thine hand, O king
3. 18 be it known unto thee, O king, that we
3. 22 the king's commandment was urgent, and
3. 24 the king was astonied, and rose up in haste
3. 24 They answered..unto the king, True, O k.
3. 27 captains, and the king's counsellors, being
3. 28 have changed the king's word, and yielded
3. 30 the king promoted Shadrach, Meshach
4. 1 the king, unto all people, nations, and
4. 18 This dream I king Nebuchadnezzar have
4. 19 The king spake, and said, Belteshazzar
4. 22 It (is) thou, O king, that art grown and
4. 23 the king saw a watcher and an holy one
4. 24 This (is) the interpretation, O king, and
4. 24 decree..which is come upon my lord t. k.
4. 27 O king, let my counsel be acceptable unto
4. 28 this came upon the king Nebuchadnezzar
4. 30 The king spake, and said, Is not this great B.
4. 31 While the word (was) in the king's mouth
4. 31 king Nebuchadnezzar, to thee it is spoken
4. 37 and extol and honour the king of heaven
5. 1 the king made a great feast to a thousand
5. 2, 3 the king, and his princes, his wives, and
5. 5 plaister of the wall of the king's palace
5. 5 king saw the part of the hand that wrote
5. 6 the king's countenance was changed, and
5. 7 The king cried aloud to bring in the astro.
5. 7 the king spake, and said to the wise (men)
5. 8 Then came in all the king's wise (men)
5. 8 nor make known to the king the interpr.
5. 9 Then was king Belshazzar greatly troubled
5. 10 by reason of the words of the king and his
5. 10 O king, live for ever: let not thy thoughts
5. 11 whom the king Nebuchadnezzar..the king
5. 12 Daniel, whom the king named Belteshaz.
5. 13 Then was Daniel brought..before the king
5. 13 the king spake and said unto Daniel, (Art)
5. 13 whom the king my father brought out of
5. 17 Daniel answered and said before the king
5. 17 I will read the writing unto the king, and
5. 18 O thou king, the most high God gave N.
5. 30 In that night was Belshazzar the king
6. 2 and the king should have no damage
6. 3 king thought to set him over the whole
6. 6 to the king, and said thus unto him, King
6. 7, 12 save of thee, O king, he shall be cast
6. 8 O king, establish the decree, and sign the
6. 9 king Darius signed the writing and the
6. 12 spake before the king concerning the king's
6. 12 The king answered and said, The thing (is)
6. 13 Then answered they..before the king, That
6. 13 regardeth not thee, O king, nor the decree
6. 14 the king, when he heard (these) words, was
6. 15 unto the king, and said unto the king
6. 15 Know, O king, that the law of the Medes
6. 15 nor statute which the king establisheth
6. 16 king commanded, and they brought Dan.
6. 16 the king spake and said unto Daniel, Thy
6. 17 the king sealed it with his own signet
6. 18 the king went to his palace, and passed
6. 19 the king arose very early in the morning
6. 20 king spake and said to Daniel, O Daniel
6. 21 said Daniel unto the king, O king, live
Dan. 6. 22 before thee, O king, have I done no hurt
6. 23 Then was the king exceeding glad for him
6. 24 the king commanded, and they brought
6. 25 king Darius wrote unto all people, nations
7. 1 first year of Belshazzar king of Babylon
7. 17 kings, (which) shall arise out of the earth
7. 24 horns out of this kingdom (are) ten kings
7. 24 and another..shall subdue three kings

4. *Kingdom*, מְלוּכָה *melukah.*

Eze. 17. 13 hath taken of the king's seed, and made
Dan. 1. 3 and of the king's seed, and of the princes

5. *Kingdom*, מַמְלָכָה *mamlakah.*

Amos 7. 13 it (is) the..chapel, and it (is) the king's

6. *A king*, βασιλεύς *basileus.*

Matt. 1. 6 begat David the king; and David [the k.]
2. 1 in the days of Herod the king, behold
2. 2 Where is he that is born king of the Jews
2. 3 When Herod the king had heard (these)
2. 9 they had heard the king, they departed
5. 35 for it is the city of the great king
10. 18 before governors and kings for my sake
11. 8 they that wear soft (clothing) are in [k.]
14. 9 the king was sorry: nevertheless, for the
17. 25 do the kings of the earth take custom or
18. 23 likened unto a certain king, which
21. 5 thy king cometh unto thee, meek, and
22. 2 is like unto a certain king, which
22. 7 when the king heard..he was wroth: and
22. 11 when the king came in to see the guests
22. 13 Then said the king to the servants, Bind
25. 34 Then shall the king say unto them on his
25. 40 the king shall answer and say unto them
27. 11 saying, Art thou the King of the Jews?
27. 29 mocked him, saying, Hail, king of the J.
27. 37 written, This is Jesus the king of the J.
27. 42 If he be the king of Israel, let him now
Mark 6. 14 king Herod heard (of him); for his name
6. 22 the king said unto the damsel, Ask of me
6. 25 straightway with haste unto the king
6. 26 the king was exceeding sorry; (yet) for his
6. 27 king sent an executioner, and commanded
13. 9 before rulers and kings for my sake, for
15. 2 asked him, Art thou the king of the Jews?
15. 9 I release unto you the king of the Jews?
15. 12 (him) whom ye call the king of the Jews
15. 18 began to salute him, Hail, King of the J.!
15. 26 was written over, The king of the Jews
15. 32 Let Christ the king of Israel descend
Luke 1. 5 in the days of Herod the king of Judea
10. 24 kings have desired to see those things w.
14. 31 king, going to..war against another king
19. 38 king that cometh in the name of the Lord
21. 12 before kings and rulers for my name's sake
22. 25 kings of the Gentiles exercise lordship
23. 2 saying that he himself is Christ a king?
23. 3 saying, Art thou the king of the Jews?
23. 37 If thou be the king of the Jews, save thy.
23. 38 and Hebrew, This is the king of the Jews?
John 1. 49 Son of God; thou art the king of Israel
6. 15 and take him by force, to make him a k.
12. 13 king of Israel that cometh in the name
12. 15 thy king cometh, sitting on an ass's colt
18. 33 and said..Art thou the king of the Jews?
18. 37 Pilate..said unto him, Art thou a king
18. 37 Thou sayest that I am a King
18. 39 I release unto you the king of the Jews?
19. 3 said, Hail, king of the Jews! and they
19. 12 whosoever maketh himself a king speak.
19. 14 he saith unto the Jews, Behold your k.!
19. 15 Pilate saith..Shall I crucify your king
19. 15 priests answered, We have no king but C.
19. 19 Jesus of Nazareth the king of the Jews
19. 21 The king of the Jews..he said, I am king
Acts 4. 26 The kings of the earth stood up, and the
7. 10 wisdom in the sight of Pharaoh king of E.
7. 18 another king arose, which knew not Jos.
9. 15 Gentiles, and kings, and the children of I.
12. 1 the king stretched forth (his) hands to vex
12. 20 made Blastus the king's chamberlain their
13. 21 they desired a king: and God gave unto
13. 22 raised..unto them David to be their king
17. 7 that there is another king, (one) Jesus
25. 13 king Agrippa and Bernice came unto Ces.
25. 14 Festus declared Paul's cause unto the ki.
25. 24 king Agrippa, and all men which are here
25. 26 specially before thee, O king Agrippa, that
26. 2 I think myself happy, king Agrippa, bec.
26. 7 For which hope's sake, king Agrippa, I am
26. 13 At mid day, O king, I saw in the way a light
26. 19 Whereupon, O king Agrippa, I was not
26. 26 the king knoweth of these things, before
26. 27 King Agrippa, believest thou the prophets
26. 30 the king rose up, and the governor, and
2 Co. 11. 32 governor under Aretas the king kept the
1 Ti. 1. 17 unto the king eternal, immortal, invisible
2. 2 For kings, and (for) all that are in autho.
6. 15 Potentate, the king of kings, and Lord
Heb. 7. 1 king of Salem, priest of the most high G.
7. 1 returning from the slaughter of the kings
7. 2 by interpretation king of righteousness
7. 2 also king of Salem, which is, king of peace
11. 23 were not afraid of the king's commandm.
11. 27 not fearing the wrath of the king: for he
1 Pe. 2. 13 Submit..whether it be to the king, as sup.
2. 17 Love the brotherhood..Honour the king
Rev. 1. 5 and the prince of the kings of the earth
1. 6 [kings] and priests unto God and his Fat.
5. 10 made us unto our God [kings] and priests
6. 15 the kings of the earth, and the great men
9. 11 they had a king over them, (which is) the

Rev. 10 11 peoples, and nations, and tongues, and ki.
15 3 just and true (are) thy ways, thou king of
16. 12 the way of the kings of the east might be
16. 14 go forth unto the kings of the earth and
17. 2 With whom the kings of the earth have
17. 10 there are seven kings: five are fallen, and
17. 12 ten horns which thou sawest, are ten kings
17. 12 receive power as kings one hour with the
17. 14 for he is Lord of lords, and King of kings
17. 18 which reigneth over the kings of the earth
18. 3 and the kings of the earth have committed
18. 9 kings of the earth, who have committed
19. 16 a name..King of kings, and Lord of lords
19. 18 That ye may eat the flesh of kings, and
19. 19 the kings of the earth, and their armies
21. 24 the kings of the earth do bring their glory

7. *To rule as a king*, βασιλεύω *basileuō*.
1 Ti. 6. 15 the King of kings, and Lord of lords

KING, to be —
To reign, be or become king, מָלַךְ *malak*.
1 Sa. 23. 17 shalt be king over Israel, and I shall
24. 20 know well that thou shalt surely be king
1 Ki. 1. 5 exalted himself, saying, I will be king
1. 35 he shall be king in my stead: and I have
2 Ki 9. 13 blew with trumpets, saying, Jehu is king

KING, to be made —
To be caused to reign, be made king, מְלַךְ *malak*, 6.
Dan. 9 1 made king over the realm of the Chaldeans

KING, to make, set, set up a —
To cause to reign, make king, מָלַךְ *malak*, 5.
Judg 9. 6 went and made Abimelech king, by the
9. 16 in that ye have made Abimelech king
9. 18 king over the men of Shechem, because
1 Sa. 8. 22 Hearken unto their voice, and make ..a k.
11. 15 made Saul king before the LORD in Gilgal
12 1 Behold, I have..made a king over you
15 11 that I have set up Saul (to be) king: for
15 35 that he had made Saul king over Israel
2 Sa 2 9 made him king over Gilead, and over the
1 Ki 1 43 our lord..David hath made Solomon king
3. 7 made thy servant king instead of David
12. 1 were come to Shechem to make him king
12. 20 called..and made him king over all Israel
16 16 made Omri, the captain of the host, king
16. 21 Tibni the son of Ginath, to make him king
2 Ki 8. 20 revolted and made a king over themselves
10 5 we will not make any king: do thou (that)
11. 12 and they made him king, and anointed
14 21 and made him king instead of his father
17 21 made Jeroboam the son of Nebat king
21 24 made Josiah his son king in his stead
23. 30 and made him king in his father's stead
23 34 made Eliakim the son of Josiah king in
24 17 made Mattaniah his father's brother king
1 Ch 11 10 to make him king, according to the word
12. 31 by name, to come and make David king
12 38 to make David king over all Israel: and
12 38 (were) of one heart to make David king
23 1 he made Solomon his son king over Israel
28 4 liked me to make (me) king over all Israel
29 22 they made Solomon the son of David king
2 Ch. 1 9 thou hast made me king over a people
1. 11 people, over whom I have made thee king
10. 1 to S were all Israel come to make him k.
11 22 brethren: for (he thought) to make him k
21. 8 Edomites revolted, and made them a k.
22. 1 made Ahaziah his youngest son king in
23 11 (gave him) testimony, and made him k
26 1 made him king in the room of his father
33. 25 people..made Josiah his son king in his
36. 1 made him king in his father's stead in
36. 4 made Eliakim his brother king over Jud
36 10 and made Zedekiah his brother king over
Isa. 7. 6 set a king in the midst of it, (even) the
Jer. 37 1 Nebuchadrezzar..made king in the land
Eze 17. 16 that made him king, whose oath he desp
Hos 8. 4 They have set up kings, but not by me

KINGDOM —

1. *Kingdom*, מְלוּכָה *melukah*.
1 Sa. 10. 16 the matter of the kingdom, whereof Sam.
10. 25 told the people the manner of the king.
11 14 go to Gilgal, and renew the kingdom
14 47 Saul took the kingdom over Israel, and
18 8 and (what) can he have more but the ki.?
2 Sa 16. 8 the LORD hath delivered the kingdom
1 Ki. 1. 46 And..sitteth on the throne of the kingdom
2. 15 Thou knowest that the kingdom was
2. 15 kingdom is turned about, and is become
2. 22 ask for him the kingdom also, for he (is)
11. 35 take the kingdom out of his son's hand
12. 21 to bring the kingdom again to Rehoboam
21. 7 Dost thou now govern the kingdom of Is.
1 Ch. 10. 14 turned the kingdom unto David the son
Psa. 22. 28 the kingdom (is) the LORD'S; and he (is)
Isa. 34. 12 shall call the nobles thereof to the king.
Eze. 16. 13 and thou didst prosper into a kingdom
Obad. 21 judge..the kingdom shall be the LORD'S

2. *Kingdom*, מַלְכוּ *maleku*.
Dan. 2. 37 God of heaven hath given thee a kingdom
2. 39 arise another kingdom inferior to thee
2. 39 another third kingdom of brass, which
2. 40 the fourth kingdom shall be strong as
2. 41 part of iron, the kingdom shall be divided
2. 42 the kingdom shall be partly strong, and
2. 44 shall the God of heaven set up a kingdom
2. 44 kingdom shall not be left to other people
2. 44 break..and consume all these kingdoms
4. 3 his kingdom (is) an everlasting kingdom
Dan. 4. 17, 25, 32 Most High ruleth in the kingdom
4. 18 the wise (men) of my kingdom are not
4. 26 thy kingdom shall be sure unto thee
4. 29 in the palace of the kingdom of Babylon
4. 30 that I have built for the house of the ki.
4. 31 O king..The kingdom is departed from
4. 34 kingdom (is) from generation to generation
4. 36 for the glory of my kingdom, mine honour
4. 36 and I was established in my kingdom, and
5. 7 and shall be the third ruler in the king.
5. 11 There is a man in thy kingdom in whom
5. 16 and shalt be..third ruler in the kingdom
5. 18 gave Nebuchadnezzar thy father a kingd.
5. 21 most high God ruled in the kingdom of
5. 26 God hath numbered thy kingdom, and
5. 28 Thy kingdom is divided, and given to the
5. 29 he should be the third ruler in the king
5. 31 And Darius the Median took the kingdom
6. 1 It pleased Darius to set over the kingdom
6. 1 which should be over the whole kingdom
6. 4 against Daniel concerning the kingdom
6. 7 All the presidents of the kingdom, the
6. 26 every dominion of my kingdom men
6. 26 and his kingdom (that) which shall not be
7. 14 given him dominion ..glory, and a kingd.
7. 14 and his kingdom (that) which shall not be
7. 18 take the kingdom, and possess the kingd.
7. 22 came that the saints possessed the king.
7. 23 shall be the fourth kingdom upon earth
7. 23 which shall be diverse from all kingdoms
7. 24 the ten horns out of this kingdom (are)
7. 27 And the kingdom and dominion, and the
7. 27 greatness of the kingdom under the whole
7. 27 whose kingdom (is) an everlasting kingdom

3. *Kingdom*, מַלְכוּת *malekuth*.
Num 24. 7 higher..and his kingdom shall be exalted
1 Sa. 20. 31 shalt not be established, nor thy kingdom
1 Ki. 2 12 and his kingdom was established greatly
1 Ch. 11 10 who strengthened themselves ..in his ki
12 23 turn the kingdom of Saul to him, accord
14 2 his kingdom was lifted up on high, because
17. 11 thy seed ..and I will establish his kingdom
17. 14 in mine house and in my kingdom for ever
22. 10 establish the throne of his kingdom over I
28. 5 the throne of the kingdom of the LORD
28. 7 I will establish his kingdom for ever, if he
2 Ch. 1 1 Solomon ..was strengthened in his king
2 1 And..to build ..an house for his kingdom
7. 18 Then will I stablish the throne of thy ki
11. 17 So they strengthened the kingdom of Ju.
12 1 when Rehoboam had established the kin.
33 13 brought ..again to Jerusalem into his ki
36. 20 until the reign of the kingdom of Persia
36 22 proclamation throughout all his kingdom
Ezra 1 1 proclamation throughout all his kingdom
Neh 9 35 they have not served thee in their king
Esth 1 2 Ahasuerus sat on the throne of his king.
1. 4 he showed the riches of his glorious king
1 14 (and) which sat the first in the kingdom
2. 3 officers in all the provinces of his king.
3. 6 throughout the whole kingdom of Ahas
3 8 dispersed ..in all the provinces of thy ki
4 14 whether thou art come to the kingdom
5 3 even given thee to the half of the kingdom
5 6 to the half of the kingdom it shall be pe.
7 2 shall be performed..to the half of the k.
9 30 twenty and seven provinces of the kingdom
Psa. 45 6 the sceptre of thy kingdom (is) a right
103. 19 The LORD..his kingdom ruleth over all
145 11 They shall speak of the glory of thy king
145 12 and the glorious majesty of his kingdom
145 13 Thy kingdom (is) an everlasting kingdom
Eccl 4 14 (he that is) born in his kingdom becometh
Jer 10. 7 and in all their kingdoms, ..none like unto
Dan. 8 22 four kingdoms shall stand up out of the
8 23 in the latter time of their kingdom, when
10 13 But the prince of the kingdom of Persia
11 4 his kingdom shall be broken, and shall
11 4 his kingdom shall be plucked up, even
11 9 king of the south..come into (his) kingd.
11. 17 with the strength of his whole kingdom
11 20 shall stand (in) the glory of the kingdom
11. 21 shall not give the honour of the kingdom
11 21 come..and obtain the kingdom by flatter.

4. *Kingdom, reign*, מַמְלָכָה *mamlakah*.
Gen 10 10 the beginning of his kingdom was Babel
20 9 thou hast brought on me and on my kingd.
Exod 19. 6 ye shall be unto me a kingdom of priests
Num 32. 33 the kingdom of Sihon king of the Amori.
32 33 the kingdom of Og king of Bashan, the
Deut. 3. 4 all ..Argob, the kingdom of Og in Bashan
3. 10 cities of the kingdom of Og in Bashan
3. 13 all Bashan ..the kingdom of Og, gave I
3. 21 unto all the kingdoms whither thou pas.
17. 18 when he sitteth upon the throne of his k.
17. 20 that he may prolong (his) days in his king.
28 25 removed into all the kingdoms of the
Josh 11 10 Hazor..was the head of all those kingdoms
1 Sa. 10 18 out of the hand of all kingdoms..of them
13 13 established thy kingdom upon Israel for
13 14 thy kingdom shall not continue: the L.
24. 20 the kingdom of Israel shall be established
28 17 hath rent the kingdom out of thine hand
2 Sa. 3 10 to translate the kingdom from the house
3 28 I and my kingdom (are) guiltless before
5. 12 exalted his kingdom for his people Israel's
7 12 thy seed..and I will establish his kingdom
7 13 stablish the throne of his kingdom for ever
7 16 thy kingdom shall be established for ever
1 Ki. 2. 46 the kingdom was established in the hand
4. 21 Solomon reigned over all kingdoms from
1 Ki. 9. 5 I will establish the throne of thy kingdom
10. 20 there was not the like made in any king
11. 11 I will surely rend the kingdom from thee
11. 13 I will not rend away all the kingdom; (but)
11. 31 will rend the kingdom out of the hand of
11 34 I will not take the whole kingdom out of
12. 26 the kingdom return to the house of David
14. 8 rent the kingdom away from the house of
18. 10 there is no nation or kingdom whither my
18. 10 he took an oath of the kingdom and nat.
2 Ki. 14. 5 as the kingdom was confirmed in his hand
15. 19 with him to confirm the kingdom in his
19. 15 thou art the God..of all the kingdoms of
19. 19 that all the kingdoms of the earth may
1 Ch. 16 20 and from (one) kingdom to another people
29. 11 thine (is) the kingdom, O LORD, and thou
29. 30 and over all the kingdoms of the countr.
2 Ch. 9. 19 there was not the like made in any king.
11. 1 might bring the kingdom again to Rehob.
12. 8 the service of the kingdoms of the countr.
13. 5 gave the kingdom over Israel to David for
13. 8 ye think to withstand the kingdom of the
14 5 took away..the images: and the kingdom
17. 5 LORD stablished the kingdom in his hand
17. 10 fear of the LORD fell upon..the kingdoms
20. 6 rulest (not) thou over all the kingdoms of
20. 29 was on all the kingdoms of (those) count.
21. 3 the kingdom gave he to Jehoram, because
21. 4 was risen up to the kingdom of his father
22. 9 Ahaziah had no power to keep still the k.
23. 20 the king upon the throne of the kingdom
25 3 when the kingdom was established to him
29 21 for a sin offering for the kingdom, and
32. 15 no god of any nation or kingdom was able
36 23 All the kingdoms of the earth hath the L.
Ezra 1. 2 hath given me all the kingdoms of the
Neh. 9 22 thou gavest them kingdoms and nations
Psa. 46. 6 heathen raged, the kingdoms were moved
68 32 Sing unto God, ye kingdoms of the earth
79. 6 the kingdoms that have not called upon
102 22 the people ..and the kingdoms, to serve
105. 13 went..from (one) kingdom to another pe.
135 11 Bashan, and all the kingdoms of Canaan
Isa. 9 7 the throne of David, and upon his king.
10 10 hand hath found the kingdoms of the id.
13. 4 of the kingdoms of nations gathered tog.
13 19 the glory of kingdoms, the beauty of the
14 16 (Is) this the man..that did shake kingd.
17. 3 the kingdom from Damascus, and the
19 2 city against city..kingdom against king.
23 11 stretched out his hand..shook the king.
23 17 commit fornication with all the kingdoms
37. 16 thou (art) the God..of all the kingdoms
37. 20 the kingdoms of the earth may know that
47 5 shalt no more be called The lady of king.
60 12 nation and kingdom that will not serve
Jer. 1. 10 over the nations, and over the kingdoms
1. 15 families of the kingdoms of the north
15. 4 to be removed into all kingdoms of the
18 7 concerning a kingdom, to pluck up, and
18. 9 concerning a kingdom, to build and to pl.
24. 9 to be removed into all the kingdoms of
25 26 the kingdoms of the world, which (are)
27 8 the nation and kingdom which will not
28 8 against great kingdoms, of war, and of evil
29 18 to be removed to all the kingdoms of the
34 1 the kingdoms of the earth of his dominion
34. 17 removed into all the kingdoms of the ea.
49 28 concerning the kingdoms of Hazor, which
51. 20 and with thee will I destroy kingdoms
51 27 call together against her the kingdoms of
Lam. 2. 2 hath polluted the kingdom and the prin.
Eze. 17 14 That the kingdom might be base, that it
29. 14 and they shall be there a base kingdom
29. 15 It shall be the basest of the kingdoms
37 22 divided into two kingdoms any more at
Amos 6 2 (be they) better than these kingdoms? or
9 8 eyes of the Lord..upon the sinful kingdom
Mic 4 8 the kingdom shall come to the daughter
Nah 3 5 nakedness, and the kingdoms thy shame
Zeph. 3. 8 I may assemble the kingdoms, to pour
Hag. 2. 22 I will overthrow the throne of kingdoms
2. 22 strength of the kingdoms of the heathen

5. *Kingdom*, מַמְלָכוּת *mamlakuth*.
Josh. 13. 12 the kingdom of Og in Bashan, which rei.
13. 21 the kingdom of Sihon king of the Amori.
13 27 of the kingdom of Sihon king of Heshbon
13. 30 the kingdom of Og king of Bashan, and
13 31 cities of the kingdom of Og in Bashan
1 Sa. 15 28 LORD hath rent the kingdom of Israel
2 Sa. 16. 3 the house of Israel restore me the kingdom
Hos. 1. 4 will cause to cease the kingdom of the ho.

6. *Kingdom*, βασιλεία *basileia*.
Matt. 3 2 Repent ye: for the kingdom of heaven is
4. 8 showeth him all the kingdoms of the wo.
4 17 Repent: for the kingdom of heaven is at
4. 23 and preaching the gospel of the kingdom
5. 3, 10 for theirs is the kingdom of heaven
5. 19 called the least in the kingdom of heaven
5. 19 shall be called great in the kingdom of hea.
5 20 ye shall in no case enter into the kingd.
6. 10 Thy kingdom come. Thy will be done in
6. 13 [thine is the kingdom, and the power, and]
6. 33 seek ye first the kingdom of God, and his
7. 21 shall enter into the kingdom of heaven
8. 11 Isaac, and Jacob, in the kingdom of hea.
8. 12 the children of the kingdom shall be cast
9. 35 preaching the gospel of the kingdom, and
10. 7 saying, The kingdom of heaven is at hand
11 11 he that is least in the kingdom of heaven
11. 12 the kingdom of heaven suffereth violence

Matt 12. 25 Every kingdom divided against itself is
12. 26 Satan..how shall then his kingdom stand?
12. 28 then the kingdom of God is come unto
13. 11 to know the mysteries of the kingdom of
13. 19 any one heareth the word of the kingdom
13. 24 The kingdom of heaven is likened unto a
13. 31, 33, 44, 45, 47 The kingdom of heaven is
13. 38 good seed are the children of the kingdom
13. 41 they shall gather out of his kingdom all
13. 43 shine forth as the sun in the kingdom of
13. 52 (is) instructed unto the kingdom of heaven
16. 19 I will give unto thee the keys of the king
16. 28 see the Son of man coming in his kingdom
18. 1 Who is the greatest in the kingdom of h.
18. 3 ye shall not enter into the kingdom of h.
18. 4 the same is greatest in the kingdom of
18. 23 Therefore is the kingdom of heaven like.
19. 12 eunuchs for the kingdom of heaven's sake
19. 14 Suffer..for of such is the kingdom of he.
19. 23 shall hardly enter into the kingdom of h.
19. 24 a rich man to enter into the kingdom of
20. 1 the kingdom of heaven is like unto a man
20. 21 and the other on the left, in thy kingdom
21. 31 harlots go into the kingdom of God before
21. 43 The kingdom of God shall be taken from
22. 2 The kingdom of heaven is like unto a cer.
23. 13 shut up the kingdom of heaven against
24. 7 kingdom against kingdom: and there sh.
24. 14 this gospel of the kingdom shall be prea.
25. 1 Then shall the kingdom of heaven be lik
25. 34 inherit the kingdom prepared for you from
26. 29 drink it..with you in my Father's kingdom
Mark 1. 14 preaching the gospel [of the kingdom] of
1. 15 the kingdom of God is at hand: repent ye
3. 24 And if a kingdom be divided ..that king.
4. 11 to know the mystery of the kingdom of
4. 26 So is the kingdom of God, as if a man sh.
4. 30 Whereunto shall we liken the kingdom of
6. 23 give (it) thee, unto the half of my kingdom
9. 1 seen the kingdom of God come with power
9. 47 to enter into the kingdom of God with
10. 14 Suffer..for of such is the kingdom of God
10. 15 Whosoever shall not receive the kingdom
10. 23 that have riches enter into the kingdom
10. 24 that trust in riches to enter into the king
10. 25 rich man to enter into the kingdom of God
11. 10 Blessed (be) the kingdom of our father D
12. 34 Thou art not far from the kingdom of God
13. 8 kingdom against kingdom; and there sh.
14. 25 that I drink it new in the kingdom of God
15. 43 which also waited for the kingdom of God
Luke 1. 33 and of his kingdom there shall be no end
4. 5 showed unto him all the kingdoms of the
4. 43 must preach the kingdom of God to other
6. 20 (ye) poor: for yours is the kingdom of G.
7. 28 he that is least in the kingdom of God is
8. 1 the glad tidings of the kingdom of God
8. 10 know the mysteries of the kingdom of God
9. 2 sent them to preach the kingdom of God
9. 11 spake unto them of the kingdom of God.
9. 27 not taste of death, till they see the king.
9. 60 go thou and preach the kingdom of God
9. 62 No man ..looking ..is fit for the kingdom
10. 9, 11 The kingdom of God is come nigh unto
11. 2 Thy kingdom come. Thy will be done
11. 17 Every kingdom divided against itself is b.
11. 18 how shall his kingdom stand? because ye
11. 20 no doubt the kingdom of God is come upon
12. 31 seek ye the kingdom of God; and all these
12. 32 Father's good pleasure to give you the k.
13. 18 Unto what is the kingdom of God like?
13. 20 Whereunto shall I liken the kingdom of G.
13. 28 all the prophets, in the kingdom of God
13. 29 and shall sit down in the kingdom of God
14. 15 that shall eat bread in the kingdom of G.
16. 16 since that time the kingdom of God is p.
17. 20 when the kingdom of God should come
17. 20 The kingdom of God cometh not with
17. 21 behold, the kingdom of God is within you
18. 16 Suffer..for of such is the kingdom of God
18. 17 Whosoever shall not receive the kingdom
18. 24 they that have riches enter into the king.
18. 25 rich man to enter into the kingdom of G.
18. 29 or children, for the kingdom of God's sake
19. 11 kingdom of God should immediately app.
19. 12 to receive for himself a kingdom, and to
19. 15 having received the kingdom, then he c.
21. 10 nation, and kingdom against kingdom
21. 31 that the kingdom of God is nigh at hand
22. 16 until it be fulfilled in the kingdom of God
22. 18 not drink ..until the kingdom of God shall
22. 29 appoint unto you a kingdom, as my Father
22. 30 eat and drink at my table in my kingdom
23. 42 remember..when thou comest into thy k.
23. 51 also himself waited for the kingdom of G.
John 3. 3 be born again, he cannot see the kingdom
3. 5 he cannot enter into the kingdom of God
18. 36 kingdom is not of this world..my kingdom
18. 36 but now is my kingdom not from hence
Acts 1. 3 things pertaining to the kingdom of God
1. 6 wilt thou..restore again the kingdom to I.
8. 12 preaching the things concerning the kin.
14. 22 much tribulation enter into the kingdom
19. 8 the things concerning the kingdom of G.
20. 25 I have gone preaching the kingdom of G.
28. 23 expounded and testified the kingdom of
28. 31 Preaching the kingdom of God, and teach.
Rom 14. 17 the kingdom of God is not meat and drink
1 Co. 4. 20 the kingdom of God (is) not in word, but
6. 9, 10 shall not inherit the kingdom of God
15. 24 shall have delivered up the kingdom to G.
15. 50 flesh and blood cannot inherit the kingd.

Gal. 5. 21 do such things shall not inherit the king.
Eph. 5. 5 hath any inheritance in the kingdom of C.
Col. 1. 13 translated (us) into the kingdom of his
4. 11 fellow workers unto the kingdom of God
1 Th. 2. 12 hath called you unto his kingdom and gl.
2 Th. 1. 5 ye may be counted worthy of the kingdom
2 Ti. 4. 1 dead at his appearing and his kingdom
4. 18 preserve (me) unto his heavenly kingdom
Heb. 1. 8 of righteousness (is) the sceptre of thy k.
11. 33 through faith subdued kingdoms, wrought
12. 28 receiving a kingdom which cannot be mo.
Jas. 2. 5 rich in faith, and heirs of the kingdom
2 Pe. 1. 11 into the everlasting kingdom of our Lord
Rev. 1. 9 and in the kingdom and patience of Jesus
11. 15 The kingdoms of this world are become
12. 10 the kingdom of our God, and the power
16. 10 and his kingdom was full of darkness
17. 12 kings, which have received no kingdom
17. 17 to agree, and give their kingdom unto the

KING'S (country) —
Kingly dwelling, βασιλικός *basilikos.*
Acts 12. 20 their country was nourished by the k.'s c.

KINGS' COURT —
Kingly, royal, βασίλειον *basileion.*
Luke 7. 25 which..live delicately, are in kings' courts

KING'S DALE, עֵמֶק הַמֶּלֶךְ *emeq ham-melek.*
The valley on the E. of Jerusalem, afterwards called the valley of Jehoshaphat, through which the Kidron passes.
Gen. 14. 17 the valley of Shaveh, which (is) the K. d.
2 Sa. 18. 18 reared up..a pillar, which (is) in the K.d.

KING'S POOL, בְּרֵכַת הַמֶּלֶךְ *berekath ham-melek.*
The large reservoir on the W. side of Jerusalem. Also called the Upper or Old Pool, now called *Birket-el-Mamilla.*
Neh. 2. 14 Then I went on..to the K. P.: but
Isa. 7. 3 at the end of the conduit of the Upper P.
22. 11 made..a ditch..for the water of the O. P.

KINGLY —
Kingdom, מַלְכוּ *maleku.*
Dan. 5. 20 he was deposed from his kingly throne

KINSFOLK —
1. *To free, redeem,* גָּאַל *gaal.*
1 Ki. 16. 11 neither of his kinsfolks, nor of his friends
2. *To be known,* יָדַע *yada,* 4.
2 Ki. 10. 11 his great men, and his kinsfolks, and his
3. *Near,* קָרוֹב *qarob.*
Job 19. 14 My kinsfolk have failed, and my familiar
4. *One of the same race, kinsman,* συγγενής *suggenēs.*
Luke 2. 44 they sought him among ..kinsfolk and ac
21. 16 parents, and brethren, and kinsfolks, and

KINSMAN, (next or near) —
1. *To free, redeem,* גָּאַל *gaal.*
Num. 5. 8 if the man have no kinsman to recompe.
Ruth 2. 20 The man (is) near..one of our next kins.
3. 9 spread therefore ..for thou (art) a near k.
3. 12 now it is true that I (am thy) near kins
3. 12 howbeit there is a kinsman nearer than I
4. 1 the kinsman of whom Boaz spake came by
4. 3 he said unto the kinsman, Naomi, that is
4. 6 the kinsman said, I cannot redeem (it)
4. 8 the kinsman said unto Boaz, Buy (it) for
4. 14 hath not left thee this day without a ki.
2. *Acquaintance,* מוֹדַע *moda* [v. L. מֹדַע].
Ruth 2. 1 Naomi had a kinsman of her husband's
3. *Near,* קָרוֹב *qarob.*
Psa. 38. 11 My lovers..and my kinsmen stand afar
4. *Flesh, relation,* שְׁאֵר *sheer.*
Num 27. 11 unto his kinsman that is next to him of
5. *One of the same race, kinsman,* συγγενής *suggenēs.*
Luke 14. 12 neither thy kinsmen, nor..neighbours
John 18. 26 being (his) kinsman whose ear Peter cut
Acts 10. 24 called together his kinsmen and near
Rom. 9. 3 my brethren, my kinsmen according to
16. 7 Salute Andronicus and Junia, my kinsmen
16. 11 Salute Herodion my kinsman. Greet
16. 21 Lucius, and Jason, and Sosipater, my k.

KINSMAN, to do or perform the part of a —
To free, redeem, גָּאַל *gaal.*
Ruth 3. 13 if he will perform..the part of a kinsman
3. 13 well; let him do the kinsman's part: but
3. 13 if he will not do the part of a kinsman
3. 13 then will I do the part of a kinsman to

KINSWOMAN —
1. *Acquaintance, one known,* מֹדַע *moda.*
Prov. 7. 4 and call understanding (thy) kinswoman
2. *Flesh, relation,* שְׁאֵר *sheer.*
Lev. 18. 12 father's sister: she (is) thy father's near k.
18. 13 for she (is) thy mother's near kinswoman
3. *Flesh, relation,* שַׁאֲרָה *shaarah.*
Lev. 18. 17 they (are) her near kinswomen: it (is) wi.

KIR, קִיר *wall.*
1. An Assyrian district between the Caspian and Black seas, near Elam, on the river *Kur; Gulistan,* or *modern Georgia.*
2 Ki. 16. 9 carried (the people of) it captive to K., and
Amos 1. 5 the people..shall go into captivity unto K.
9. 7 Have not I brought..the Syrians from K.?
2. The inhabitants of the district so called.
Isa. 22. 6 Elam bare the quiver..and K. uncovered

KIR of Moab, קִיר־מוֹאָב. See *Kir-haraseth.*
Isa. 15. 1 K. of Moab is laid waste..brought to sil.

KIR HA-RA'-SETH or HAR-E'-SETH, קִיר־חֲרֶשֶׂת *or* קִיר־חֲרֶשֶׂת.
A fortified city of Moab, probably the same as *Kir-haresh, Kir-heres,* and *Kir of Moab;* now *Kerak,* three hours S.E. of *Ar.*
2 Ki. 3. 25 only in K. left they the stones thereof
Isa. 16. 7 for the foundations of K. shall ye mourn

KIR-HA'-RESH, or HE'-RES, חֶרֶשׂ *or* קִיר־חֶרֶשׂ.
A fortified city of Moab. Same as the preceding.
Isa. 16. 11 For Moab, and mine inward parts for K.
Jer. 48. 31 mourn for the men of Kir Har.; 48. 36.

KIRIOTH. *See* **KERIOTH.**

KIR'-JATH, קִרְיַת *city.*
A contraction for *Kirjath-jearim,*
Josh. 18. 28 K.; fourteen cities with their villages

KIR-JA-THA'-IM, KIR-IA-THA'-IM, קִרְיָתַיִם *double c.*
1. A city of Reuben E. of the Jordan, four miles W. of Medeba, which is S.E. of Heshbon.
Num 32. 37 And the children of Reuben built..K.
Josh. 13. 19 And K., and Sibmah, and Zareth-shahar
Jer 48. 1 K. is confounded (and) taken; Misgab is
48. 23 And upon K., and upon Beth-gamul, and
Eze. 25. 9 I will open..the glory of the country..K.
2. A Levitical city in Naphtali; same as *Kartan;* now *Kerkarah.*
1 Ch. 6. 76 out of..Naphtali..K. with her suburbs

KIR-JATH AR'-BA, קִרְיַת אַרְבַּע *city of Arba.*
A city in the hill country of Judea, S. from Jerusalem, originally the city of Arba, the father of Anak; afterwards called *Hebron.*
Gen. 23. 2 Sarah died in K.-a.; the same (is) Hebron
Josh 14. 15 the name of Hebron before (was) K.-a.
15. 54 Humtah, and K.-a., which (is) Hebron, and
20. 7 K.-a., which (is) Hebron, in the mountain
Judg. 1. 10 the name of Hebron before (was) K.-a.
Neh. 11. 25 (some) of..children of Judah dwelt at K.-a.

KIR-JATH A'-RIM, קִרְיַת עָרִים *city of forests.*
Same as *Kirjath-jearim, Kirjath-baal,* or *Baalah.*
Ezra 2. 25 The children of K.-a., Chephirah, and B.

KIR-JATH BA'-AL, קִרְיַת בַּעַל *city of Baal.*
Same as *Kirjath-jearim,* and *Baalah*
Josh. 15. 60 K.-b., which (is) Kirjath-jearim, and Rab.
18. 14 goings out thereof were at K.-b., which

KIR-JATH HU'-ZOTH, קִרְיַת חֻצוֹת *city of the out-places.*
The residence of Balak, king of Moab, near Bamoth-baal; not far from the Arnon. Taken by Sihon, then by Israel.
Num 22. 39 with Balak, and they came unto K.-h.

KIR-JATH JE-A'-RIM, קִרְיַת יְעָרִים *city of forests.*
1. A city of Judah (formerly of the Hivites) on the confines of Benjamin, near Beeroth and Chephirah; called also *Baalah, Kirjath, Kirjath-baal,* and *Kirjath-arim.* Now called *Kurryet el-Enab,* eight miles W. of Jerusalem.
Josh. 9. 17 Gibeon, and Chephirah ..Beeroth..K.-j.
15. 9 border was drawn to Baalah..(is) K.-j.
15. 60 Kirjath-baal, which (is) K.-j., and Rabbah
18. 14 Kirjath-baal, which (is) K.-j., a city of
18. 15 south quarter (was) from the end of K.-j.
Judg 18. 12 pitched in K.-j., in Judah: wherefore
18. 12 Mahaneh-dan ..behold, (it is) behind K.-j.
1 Sa. 6. 21 sent messengers to the inhabitants..K.-j.
7. 1 the men of K.-j. came, and fetched up
7. 2 while the ark abode in K.-j., that the time
1 Ch. 13. 5 Israel..to bring the ark of God from K.-j
13. 6 (that is), to K.-j., which (belonged) to Ju.
2 Ch. 1. 4 ark of God..David brought up from K.-j.
Neh. 7. 29 The men of K.-j., Chephirah, and Beeroth
Jer. 26. 20 the son of Shemaiah of K.-j., who proph.
2. The name or patronymic appellation of a descendant of Caleb the son of Hur. B.C. 650.
1 Ch. 2. 50 the sons of Caleb..Shobal the father of K.
2. 52 Shobal the father of K. had sons; Haroeh
2. 53 families of K.; the Ithrites, and the Pu.

KIR-JATH SAN'-NAH, קִרְיַת־סַנָּה *city of instruction.*
A city in the hill country of Judah one hour S.W. of Hebron; called also *Debir,* and now *De-wirban.*
Josh. 15. 49 And Dannah, and K., which (is) Debir

KIR-JATH SE'-PHER, קִרְיַת־סֵפֶר *city of books.*
Another name for the preceding, and showing the early rise of literature
Josh. 15. 15 and the name of Debir before (was) K.
15. 16 He that smiteth K., and taketh it, to him
Judg. 1. 11 and the name of Debir before (was) K.
1. 12 He that smiteth K., and taketh it, to him

KISH, קִישׁ *bow, power.*
1. A Benjamite, father of Saul the first king of Israel. B.C. 1120. (Same as *Cis* in Acts 13. 21.)
1 Sa. 9. 1 a man of Benjamin, whose name (was) K.
9. 3 the asses of K...were lost. And K. said
10. 11 this (that) is come unto the son of K.? (Is)
10. 21 Saul the son of K. was taken: and when
14. 51 K. (was) the father of Saul; and Ner the
2 Sa. 21. 14 buried..in the sepulchre of K. his father
1 Ch. 8. 33 Ner begat K., and K. begat Saul, and Saul
9. 39 Ner begat K., and K. begat Saul, and Saul
12. 1 kept..close because of Saul the son of K.
26. 28 all that..Saul the son of K...had dedica.

2. Another Benjamite, son of Abi-Gibeon. B.C. 1180.
1 Ch. 8. 30 his first born son Abdon, and Zur, and K.
9. 36 his first born son Abdon, then Zur, and K.

3. A Levite, grandson of Merari. B.C. 1015.
1 Ch.23. 21 Mushi The sons of Mahli; Eleazar and K.
23. 22 and their brethren the sons of K. took
24. 29 Concerning K.: the son of K. (was) Jerah.

4. Another Levite and Merarite, who assisted in cleansing the temple in Hezekiah's time. B.C. 726.
2 Ch.29.12 K. the son of Abdi, and Azariah the son of J.

5. A Benjamite, ancestor of Mordecai, the cousin of Queen Esther. B.C. 610.
Esth 2. 5 son of Shimei, the son of K., a Benjamite

KI'-SHI, קִישִׁי *bow of Jah.*
A Levite of the Merari family, whose son Ethan was set over the service of song. B.C. 1015. Called *Kushaiah* in 1 Ch. 15. 17.
1 Ch. 6. 44 Ethan the son of K., the son of Abdi, the

KISH'-ION, KISH'-ON, קִשְׁיוֹן *hard.*
A Levitical city in Issachar, near Rabbith and Abez; called *Kadish* in 1 Ch. 6. 72; now *Kison.*
Josh.19. 20 And Rabbith, and K., and Abez
21. 28 K. with her suburbs, Dabareh with her

KISH'-ON, KIS'-ON, קִישׁוֹן *winding, binding.*
A brook rising in Mount Tabor and flowing nearly westward into the Mediterranean, near the northern base of Mount Carmel. Called also *Koheifa*, and now *el-Makutta.*
Judg.4. 7 I will draw unto thee, to the river K., Sis.
4. 13 from Harosheth..unto the river of K.
5. 21 river of K...ancient river, the river K.
1 Ki. 18. 40 Elijah brought them down to the brook K.
Psa. 83. 9 (to) Sisera, as (to) Jabin, at the brook of Kis.

KISS —

1. *A kiss, kissing,* נְשִׁיקָה *neshiqah.*
Prov 27. 6 but the kisses of an enemy (are) deceitful
Song 1. 2 Let him kiss me with the kisses of his m.

2. *A kiss, mark of friendship,* φίλημα *philēma.*
Luke 7. 45 Thou gavest me no kiss: but this woman
22. 48 betrayest thou the Son of man with a k.?
Rom 16. 16 Salute one another with an holy kiss. The
1 Co.16. 20 Greet ye one another with an holy kiss
2 Co.13. 12 Greet one another with an holy kiss
1 Th. 5. 26 Greet all the brethren with an holy kiss
1 Pe. 5. 14 Greet ye one another with a kiss of charity

KISS, to —

1. *To kiss, touch,* נָשַׁק *nashaq.*
Gen. 27. 26 said..Come near now, and kiss me, my
27. 27 he came near, and kissed him: and he
29. 11 Jacob kissed Rachel, and lifted up his
33. 4 fell on his neck, and kissed him: and
48. 10 and he kissed them, and embraced them
50. 1 Joseph fell..and wept upon him, and ki.
Exod 4. 27 he went, and met him..and kissed him
18. 7 Moses went..and did obeisance, and kis.
Ruth 1. 9 she kissed them: and they lifted up their
1. 14 Orpah kissed her mother in law; but Ruth
1 Sa. 10. 1 Samuel..poured (it) upon his head, and k.
20. 41 they kissed one another, and wept one
2 Sa. 14. 33 bowed himself..and the king kissed Ab.
15. 5 put forth his hand, and took him, and k.
19. 39 the king kissed Barzillai, and blessed him
20. 9 Joab took Amasa by the beard..to kiss him
1 Ki. 19. 18 and every mouth which hath not kissed
19. 20 Let me, I pray thee, kiss my father and
Job 31. 27 enticed, or my mouth hath kissed my hand
Psa. 85. 10 righteousness and peace have kissed (each
Prov. 7. 13 So she caught him, and kissed him, (and)
24. 26 shall kiss (his) lips that giveth a right ans.
Song 1. 2 Let him kiss me with the kisses of his m.
8. 1 I would kiss thee; yea, I should not be des.
Hos. 13. 2 Let the men that sacrifice kiss the calves

2. *To kiss, touch,* נָשַׁק *nashaq,* 3.
Gen. 29. 13 kissed him, and brought him to his house
31. 28 hast not suffered me to kiss my sons and my
31. 55 Laban..kissed his sons and his daughters
45. 15 he kissed all his brethren, and wept upon
Psa. 2. 12 Kiss the Son, lest he be angry, and ye per.

3. *To kiss thoroughly, be very friendly,* καταφιλέω.
Matt 26. 49 and said, Hail, master; and kissed him
Mark 14. 45 and saith, Master, master; and kissed him
Luke 7. 38 kissed his feet, and anointed..with the
7. 45 this woman..hath not ceased to kiss my
15. 20 ran, and fell on his neck, and kissed him
Acts 20. 37 wept sore, and fell on Paul's neck, and k.

4. *To kiss, be friendly,* φιλέω *phileō.*
Matt 26. 48 Whomsoever I shall kiss, that same is he
Mark 14. 44 Whomsoever I shall kiss, that same is he
Luke 22. 47 Judas..drew near unto Jesus to kiss him

KITE —

Kite, vulture, אַיָּה *ayyah.*
Lev. 11. 14 the vulture, and the kite after his kind
Deut 14. 13 the glede, and the kite, and the vulture

KITH'-LISH, כִּתְלִישׁ *separation.*
A city of Judah, near Lahmam.
Josh.15. 40 And Cabbon, and Lahmam, and K.

KIT'-RON, קִטְרוֹן *shortened, little.*
A city of Zebulun held by the Canaanites; same as *Kattath* in Josh. 19. 15; now called *Sefurich.*
Judg 1. 30 Neither..drive out the inhabitants of K.

KIT'-TIM, כִּתִּים.
A son of Javan, son of Japheth. B.C. 2200, whose descendants are called *Chittim, i.e.* the people of Cyprus and the adjacent coasts and islands.
Gen. 10. 4 sons of Javan; Elishah, and Tarshish, K.
1 Ch. 1. 7 sons of Javan; Elishah, and Tarshish, K.

KNEAD, to —

To knead, לוּשׁ *lush.*
Gen. 18. 6 knead (it), and make cakes upon the hearth
1 Sa. 28. 24 took flour, and kneaded (it), and did bake
2 Sa. 13. 8 kneaded (it), and made cakes in his sight
Jer. 7. 18 the women knead..dough, to make cakes
Hos. 7. 4 ceaseth from raising after he hath kneaded

KNEADING TROUGH —

Kneading trough, מִשְׁאֶרֶת *mishereth.*
Exod. 8. 3 thine ovens, and into thy kneading trough
12. 34 their kneading troughs being bound up in

KNEE —

1. *The knee,* אַרְכֻּבָה *arkubah.*
Dan. 5. 6 and his knees smote one against another

2. *The knee,* בֶּרֶךְ *berek.*
Gen. 30. 3 she shall bear upon my knees, that I may
48. 12 brought them out from between his knees
50. 23 were brought up upon Joseph's knees
Deut 28. 35 The LORD shall smite thee in the knees
Judg. 7. 5 that boweth down upon his knees to drink
7. 6 bowed down upon their knees to drink
16. 19 she made him sleep upon her knees; and
1 Ki. 8. 54 from kneeling on his knees with his hands
18. 42 Elijah..put his face between his knees
19. 18 all the knees which have not bowed unto
2 Ki. 1. 13 came and fell on his knees before Elijah
4. 20 he sat on her knees till noon, and..died
2 Ch. 6. 13 kneeled down upon his knees before all
Ezra 9. 5 I fell upon my knees, and spread out my
Job 3. 12 Why did the knees prevent me? or why
4. 4 and thou hast strengthened the feeble k.
Psa 109. 24 My knees are weak through fasting; and
Isa. 35. 3 Strengthen ye..confirm the feeble knees
45. 23 unto me every knee shall bow, every tong.
66. 12 ye shall be..dandled upon (her) knees
Eze. 7. 17 and all knees shall be weak (as) water
21. 7 and all knees shall be weak (as) water
47. 4 brought me..the waters (were) to the kn.
Dan. 6. 10 he kneeled upon his knees three times a
10. 10 which set me upon my knees and..the
Nah. 2. 10 the knees smite together, and much pain

3. *The knee,* γόνυ *gonu.*
Mark 15. 19 and bowing (their) knees worshipped him
Luke 5. 8 fell down at Jesus' knees, saying, Depart
Rom 11. 4 men, who have not bowed the knee to..B.
14. 11 every knee shall bow to me, and every
Eph. 3. 14 For this cause I bow my knees unto the F.
Phil 2. 10 at the name of Jesus every knee should
Heb 12. 12 which hang down, and the feeble knees

KNEEL (down), to —

1. *To kneel, bow or bend the knee,* בָּרַךְ *barak.*
2 Ch. 6. 13 kneeled down upon his knees before all
Psa. 95. 6 come..let us kneel before the LORD our

2. *To kneel, bow or bend the knee,* בְּרַךְ *berak.*
Dan. 6. 10 he kneeled upon his knees three times a

3. *To put the knees (down),* τίθημι τὰ γόνατα.
Luke 22. 41 he was withdrawn..kneeled down, and
Acts 7. 60 he kneeled down, and cried with a loud
9. 40 Peter put them all forth, and kneeled do.
20. 36 he kneeled down, and prayed with them
21. 5 kneeled down on the shore, and prayed

4. *To fall down on the knees,* γονυπετέω *gonupeteō.*
Matt 17. 14 man, kneeling down to him, and saying
Mark 1. 40 beseeching him, [and kneeling down] to
10. 17 there came one running, and kneeled to

KNEEL down, to make to —

To cause to kneel, bow or bend the knees, בָּרַךְ *barak,* 5.
Gen. 24. 11 he made his camels to kneel down with.

KNEELING —

To bow or bend the knee, כָּרַע *kara.*
1 Ki. 8. 54 Solomon..arose..from kneeling on his k.

KNIFE —

1. *Sword,* חֶרֶב *chereb.*
Josh. 5. 2 Make thee sharp knives, and circumcise
5. 3 Joshua made him sharp knives, and circ.
1 Ki.18. 28 cut themselves..with knives and lancets
Eze. 5. 1 take thee a sharp knife, take thee a barber's
5. 2 take a third part..smite about it with a k.

2. *Knife (for food),* מַאֲכֶלֶת *maakeleth.*
Gen. 22. 6 and he took the fire in his hand, and a k.
22. 10 Abraham..took the knife to slay his son
Judg.19. 29 he took a knife, and laid hold on his con.
Prov.30. 14 their jaw teeth (as) knives, to devour the

3. *Knife, spear,* שַׂכִּין *sakkin.*
Prov.23. 2 put a knife to thy throat, if thou (be) a man

4. *Knife,* מַחֲלָף *machalaph.*
Ezra 1. 9 chargers of silver, nine and twenty knives

KNIT, to be —

1. *Altogether, alike,* יַחַד *yachad.*
1 Ch.12. 17 mine heart shall be knit unto you: but if

2. *To be bound,* קָשַׁר *qashar,* 2.
1 Sa. 18. 1 soul of Jonathan was knit with the soul

3. *To bind, tie, knit,* δέω *deō.*
Acts 10. 11 a great sheet [knit] at the four corners

KNIT together, to —

1. *A companion, associate,* חָבֵר *chaber.*
Judg 20. 11 So all the men..knit together as one man

2. *To cause to go up together,* συμβιβάζω *sumbibazō.*
Col. 2. 2 be comforted, being knit together in love
2. 19 knit together, increaseth with the increa.

KNOCK, to —

1. *To beat, knock,* דָּפַק *daphaq.*
Song 5. 2 the voice of my beloved that knocketh

2. *To knock (at a door),* κρούω *krouō.*
Matt. 7. 7 knock, and it shall be opened unto you
7. 8 and to him that knocketh it shall be op.
Luke 11. 9 knock, and it shall be opened unto you
11. 10 and to him that knocketh it shall be op.
12. 36 that, when he cometh and knocketh, they
13. 25 to knock at the door, saying, Lord, Lord
Acts 12. 13 as Peter knocked at the door of the gate
12. 16 But Peter continued knocking: and when
Rev. 3. 20 Behold, I stand at the door and knock

KNOP —

1. *Capital or chapiter of a column,* כַּפְתּוֹר *kaphtor.*
Exod 25. 31 his knops, and his flowers, shall be of the
25. 33 a knop and a flower..a knop and a flower
25. 34 almonds..their knops and their flowers
25. 35, 35, 35 a knop under two branches of the
25. 36 Their knops and their branches shall be
37. 17 his bowls, his knops, and his flowers, were
37. 19 a knop and a flower..a knop and a flower
37. 20 four bowls made like almonds, his knops
37. 21, 21, 21 a knop under two branches of the
37. 22 Their knops and their branches were of

2. *Knops, gourds, cucumber,* פְּקָעִים *peqaim.*
1 Ki. 6. 18 carved with knops and open flowers: all
7. 24 knops compassing it, ten in a cubit, com.
7. 24 the knops (were) cast in two rows, when

KNOW (by), to—

1. *To understand,* בִּין *bin,* 1, or 5
Job 38. 20 that thou shouldest know the paths (to)

2. *Knowledge,* דַּעַת *daath.*
Job 10. 7 Thou knowest that I am not wicked; and
13. 2 What ye know, (the same) do I..I (am)
Prov 29. 7 (but) the wicked regardeth not to know
Isa. 48. 4 Because I knew that thou (art) obstinate
58. 2 delight to know my ways, as a nation that
Jer. 22. 16 (was) not this to know me? saith the LORD

3. *To know,* יָדַע *yada.*
Gen. 3. 5 God doth know that in the day ye eat
3. 5 ye shall be as gods, knowing good and
3. 7 they knew that they (were) naked; and
3. 22 become as one of us, to know good and
4. 1 Adam knew Eve his wife; and she concei.
4. 9 said, I know not: (Am) I my brother's
4. 17 Cain knew his wife; and she conceived
4. 25 Adam knew his wife again; and she bare
8. 11 Noah knew that the waters were abated
9. 24 and knew what his younger son had done
12. 11 I know that thou (art) a fair woman to
15. 8 whereby shall I know that I shall inherit
15. 13 Know of a surety that thy seed shall be
18. 19 I know him, that he will command his
18. 21 they have done..and if not, I will know
19. 5 bring them..unto us that we may know
19. 8 I have two daughters which have..known
20. 6 I know that thou didst this in the integr.
20. 7 know thou that thou shalt surely die, thou
22. 12 I know that thou fearest God, seeing thou
24. 14 shall I know that thou hast showed kind.
24. 16 a virgin, neither had any man known her
27. 2 I am old, I know not the day of my death
28. 16 LORD is in this place; and I knew (it) not
29. 5 Know ye Laban..And they said, We know
30. 26 knowest my service which I have done
30. 29 Thou knowest how I have served thee, and
31. 6 ye know that with all my power I have
31. 32 Jacob knew not that Rachel had stolen
33. 13 lord knoweth that the children (are) ten.
38. 9 Onan knew that the seed should not be
38. 16 knew not that she (was) his daughter in l.
38. 26 And he knew her again no more
39. 6 he knew not ought he had, save the bread
42. 23 they knew not that Joseph understood
42. 33 Hereby shall I know that ye (are) true
42. 34 then shall I know that ye (are) no spies
43. 7 could we certainly know that he would
44. 27 Ye know that my wife bare me two (sons)
47. 6 thou knowest (any) men of activity among
48. 19 I know (it), my son, I know (it): he also
Exod. 1. 8 new king over Egypt, which knew not J.
3. 7 heard their cry..for I know their sorrows
4. 14 I know that he can speak well. And also
5. 2 I know not the LORD, neither will I let
6. 7 ye shall know that I (am) the LORD your G.
7. 5 Egyptians shall know that I (am) the LORD
7. 17 In this thou shalt know that I (am) the L
8. 10 thou mayest know that (there is) none like
8. 22 thou mayest know that I (am) the LORD
9. 14 thou mayest know that (there is) none like
9. 29 thou mayest know how that the earth (is)
9. 30 I know that ye will not yet fear the LORD
10. 2 that ye may know how that I (am) the L.
10. 7 knowest thou not yet that Egypt is des.?
10. 26 we know not with what we must serve the
11. 7 ye may know how that the LORD doth put
14. 4 the Egyptians may know that I (am) the
14. 18 Egyptians shall know that I (am) the LORD
16. 6 ye shall know that the LORD hath brought

Exod16. 12 shall know that I (am) the LORD your God
18. 11 I know that the LORD (is) greater than all
23. 9 ye know the heart of a stranger, seeing
29. 46 shall know that I (am) the LORD their God
31. 13 (ye) may know that I (am) the LORD that
32. 22 thou knowest the people, that they (are)
33. 5 that I may know what to do unto thee
33. 12 I know thee by name, and thou hast also
33. 13 I may know thee, that I may find grace
33. 17 grace in my sight..I know thee by name
36. 1 to know how to work all manner of work
Lev. 5. 1 whether he hath seen or known..if he do
5. 3, 4 when he knoweth..then he shall be gu.
23. 43 That your generations may know that I
Num 10. 31 thou knowest how we are to encamp in
11. 16 whom thou knowest to be the elders of
14. 31 they shall know the land which ye have
14. 34 and ye shall know my breach of promise
16. 28 ye shall know that the LORD hath sent me
20. 14 Thou knowest all the travel that hath bef.
22. 19 that I may know what the LORD will say
22. 34 I knew not that thou stoodest in the way
24. 16 knew the knowledge of the most High
31. 17 that hath known man by lying with him
31. 18 have not known a man by lying with him
31. 35 that had not known man by lying with him
Deut. 2. 7 knoweth thy walking through this great
3. 19 your cattle..I know that ye have much
4. 35 that thou mightest know that the LORD
4. 39 Know therefore this day, and consider
7. 9 Know therefore that the LORD thy God
7. 15 evil diseases of Egypt, which thou know.
8. 2 to know what (was) in thine heart, whet.
8. 3 knewest not, neither did thy fathers know
8. 16 with manna, which thy fathers knew not
9. 2 whom thou knowest, and (of whom) thou
9. 24 rebellious..from the day that I knew you
11. 2 And know ye this day: for (I speak) not
11. 2 with your children which have not known
11. 28 after other gods, which ye have not known
13. 2 other gods, which thou hast not known
13. 3 to know whether ye love the LORD your
13. 13 serve..gods, which ye have not known
18. 21 How shall we know the word which the
20. 20 knowest that they (be) not trees for meat
22. 2 or if thou know him not, then thou shalt
28. 33 a nation which thou knowest not eat up
28. 36, 64 neither thou nor thy fathers have kn.
29. 6 might know that I (am) the LORD your G
29. 16 ye know how we have dwelt in the land
29. 26 gods whom they knew not, and (whom)
31. 13 children, which have not known (any th.)
31. 21 I know their imagination which they go
31. 27 I know thy rebellion, and thy stiff neck
31. 29 know that after my death ye will utterly
32. 17 gods whom they knew not, to new (gods
33. 9 his brethren, nor knew his own children
34. 6 man knoweth of his sepulchre unto this
34. 10 Moses, whom the LORD knew face to face
Josh. 2. 9 I know that the LORD hath given you the
3. 4 ye may know the way by which ye must
3. 7 they may know that, as I was with Moses
3. 10 shall know that the living God (is) among
4. 24 people of the earth might know the hand
14. 6 Thou knowest the thing that the LORD said
22. 22 LORD..knoweth, and Israel he shall know
23. 13 Know for a certainty that the LORD your
23. 14 know in all your hearts, and in all your
24. 31 which had known all the works of the L.
Judg. 2. 10 which knew not the LORD, nor yet..works
3. 1 as had not known all the wars of Canaan
3. 2 the generations..of Israel might know to
3. 2 at the least such as before knew nothing
3. 4 to know whether they would hearken unto
6. 37 then shall I know that thou wilt save
11. 39 which he had vowed: and she knew no
13. 16 knew not that he (was) an angel of the L.
13. 21 knew that he (was) an angel of the LORD
14. 4 mother knew not that it (was) of the LORD
15. 11 Knowest thou not that the Philistines (are)
17. 13 Now know I..the LORD will do me good
18. 5 we may know whether our way which we
18. 14 Do ye know that there is in these houses
19. 22 Bring..the man..that we may know him
19. 25 and they knew her, and abused her all the
20. 34 but they knew not that evil (was) near
21. 12 had known no man by lying with any male
Ruth 2. 11 people which thou knowest not heretofore
3. 11 doth know that thou (art) a virtuous wo.
3. 18 until thou know how the matter will fall
4. 4 redeem (it, then) tell me that I may know
1 Sa. 1. 19 Elkanah knew Hannah his wife; and the
2. 12 Now the sons of Eli..knew not the LORD
3. 7 Samuel did not yet know the LORD, neit.
3. 13 judge..for the iniquity which he knoweth
3. 20 Israel from Dan even to Beer-sheba knew
6. 9 we shall know that (it is) not his hand
10. 11 all that knew him beforetime saw that
14. 3 the people knew not that Jonathan was
14. 38 know and see wherein this sin hath been
17. 28 I know thy pride, and the naughtiness of
17. 46 may know that there is a God in Israel
17. 47 assembly shall know that the LORD saveth
18. 28 knew that the LORD (was) with David, and
20. 3 Thy father certainly knoweth that I have
20. 3 Let not Jonathan know this, lest he be g.
20. 9 for if I knew certainly that evil were deter
20. 30 do not I know that thou hast chosen the
20. 33 Jonathan knew that it was determined of
20. 39 knew not..only Jonathan and David knew
21. 2 Let no man know anything of the business
22. 3 with you, till I know what God will do for

1 Sa. 22. 15 thy servant knew nothing of all this, less
22. 17 because they knew when he fled, and did
22. 22 I knew (it) that day, when Doeg the Edo.
23. 9 David knew that Saul secretly practised
23. 17 be king..that also Saul my father knoweth
23. 22 know and see his place where his haunt is
24. 11 know thou and see that (there is) neither
24. 20 know well that thou shalt surely be king
25. 11 unto men whom I know not whence they
25. 17 know and consider what thou wilt do
26. 12 no man saw (it), nor knew (it), neither
28. 1 Know thou assuredly, that thou shalt go
28. 2 thou shalt know what thy servant can do
28. 9 thou knowest what Saul hath done, how
29. 9 I know that thou (art) good in my sight
2 Sa. 1. 5 How knowest thou that Saul and Jonat.
2. 26 knowest thou not that it will be bitterness
3. 25 Thou knowest Abner the son of Ner, that
3. 25 to know thy going out..and to know all
3. 26 brought him again..but David knew (it)
3. 38 Know ye not that there is a prince and a
7. 20 for thou, Lord GOD, knowest thy servant
11. 16 a place where he knew that valiant men
11. 20 knew ye not that they would shoot from
14. 20 to know all (things) that (are) in the earth
14. 22 thy servant knoweth that I have found
15. 11 and they went..and they knew not any
17. 8 thou knowest thy father and his men, that
17. 10 knoweth that thy father (is) a mighty man
18. 29 great tumult, but I knew not what (it was)
19. 20 thy servant doth know that I have sinned
19. 22 know that I (am) this day king over Israel
22. 44 people (which) I knew not shall serve me
24. 2 that I may know the number of the people
1 Ki. 1. 4 ministered to him, but the king knew her
1. 11 reign, and David our lord knoweth (it) not?
1. 18 now, my lord the king, thou knowest (it)
2. 5 thou knowest also what Joab the son of
2. 9 knowest what thou oughtest to do unto
2. 15 Thou knowest that the kingdom was mine
2. 32 slew them..my father David not knowing
2. 37 thou shalt know for certain that thou
2. 42 Know for a certain, on the day thou goest
2. 44 Thou knowest all the wickedness which
3. 7 child..I know not (how) to go out or come
5. 3 Thou knowest how that David my father
5. 6 thou knowest that (there is) not among us
8. 38 which shall know every man the plague
8. 39 to every man..whose heart thou knowest
8. 39 knowest the hearts of all the children of
8. 43 people of the earth may know thy name
8. 43 they may know that this house, which I
8. 60 the people..may know that the LORD (is)
14. 2 that thou be not known to be the wife of
17. 24 I know that thou (art) a man of God, (and)
18. 12 Spirit..shall carry thee whither I know not
18. 37 people may know that thou (art) the LORD
20. 13 and thou shalt know that I (am) the LORD
20. 28 and ye shall know that I (am) the LORD
22. 3 Know ye that Ramoth in Gilead (is) ours
2 Ki. 2. 3, 5 Knowest thou that the LORD will take
2. 3, 5 he said, Yea, I know (it); hold ye your
4. 1 knowest that thy servant did fear the L.
4. 39 and shred (them)..for they knew (them)
5. 8 shall know that there is a prophet in Isr.
5. 15 I know that (there is) no God in all the
7. 12 They know that we (be) hungry; therefore
8. 12 I know the evil that thou wilt do unto the
9. 11 Ye know the man and his communication
10. 10 Know now that there shall fall unto the
17. 26, 26 know not the manner of the God of
19. 19 may know that thou (art) the LORD God
19. 27 I know thy abode, and thy going out, and
1 Ch. 12. 32 understanding..to know what Israel ou.
17. 18 can David (speak) more..thou knowest
21. 2 number of them to me, that I may know
28. 9 know thou the God of thy father, and
29. 17 I know also, my God, that thou triest the
2 Ch. 2. 8 know that thy servants can skill to cut
6. 29 shall know his own sore and his own grief
6. 30 every man..whose heart thou knowest
6. 30 thou only knowest the hearts of the chil.
6. 33 people of the earth, may know thy name
6. 33 may know that this house, which I have
12. 8 they may know my service, and the serv.
13. 5 Ought ye not to know that the LORD God
20. 12 neither know we what to do: but our eyes
25. 16 know that God hath determined to destroy
32. 13 Know ye not what I and my fathers have
32. 31 he might know all (that was) in his heart
33. 13 Manasseh knew that the LORD he (was) G.
Neh. 2. 16 the rulers knew not whither I went, or
4. 11 They shall not know, neither see till we
9. 10 knewest that they dealt proudly against
Esth. 1. 13 said to the wise men, which knew the
1. 13 toward all that knew law and judgment
2. 11 to know how Esther did, and what should
4. 5 and..to know what it (was), and why it
4. 11 the people of the king's provinces, do know
4. 14 who knoweth whether thou art come to
Job 5. 24 know that thy tabernacle (shall be) in
5. 25 know also that thy seed (shall be) great
5. 27 hear it, and know thou (it) for thy good
8. 9 we (are but of) yesterday, and know not
9. 2 I know (it is) so of a truth: but how sho
9. 5 removeth the mountains, and they know
9. 21 (were) perfect, (yet) would I not know my
9. 28 know that thou wilt not hold me innocent
10. 13 hast thou hid..I know that this (is) with
11. 6 Know therefore that God exacteth of thee
11. 8 deeper than hell; what canst thou know?
11. 11 knoweth vain men: he seeth wickedness

Job 12. 9 Who knoweth not in all these that the
13. 2 (the same) do I know also: I (am) not in
13. 18 Behold now..I know that I shall be jus.
14. 21 sons come to honour, and he knoweth (it)
15. 9 What knowest thou, that we know not?
15. 23 he knoweth that the day of darkness is
18. 21 (is) the place (of him that) knoweth not
19. 6 Know now that God hath overthrown me
19. 25 I know (that) my redeemer liveth, and
19. 29 that ye may know (there is) a judg.
20. 4 Knowest thou (not) this of old, since man
21. 19 he rewardeth him, and he shall know (it)
21. 27 Behold, I know your thoughts, and the
22. 13 How doth God know? can he judge thro.
23. 3 Oh that I knew where I might find him!
23. 5 I would know the words (which) he would
23. 10 he knoweth the way that I take: (when)
24. 1 do they that know him not see his days?
24. 16 in the day time: they know not the light
28. 7 (There is) a path which no fowl knoweth
28. 13 Man knoweth not the price thereof; nei.
28. 23 God understandeth..he knoweth..place
29. 16 the cause (which) I knew not I searched
30. 23 I know (that) thou wilt bring me (to) death
31. 6 weighed..that God may know mine integ.
32. 22 For I know not to give flattering titles
34. 4 let us know among ourselves what (is) good
34. 33 not I: therefore speak what thou knowest
35. 15 yet he knoweth (it) not in great extremity
36. 26 we know (him) not, neither can the num.
37. 7 sealeth..that all men may know his work
37. 15 Dost thou know when God disposed them
37. 16 Dost thou know the balancings of the cl.
38. 5 Who..laid the measures..if thou knowest?
38. 18 of the earth? declare if thou knowest it
38. 21 Knowest thou (it), because thou wast then
38. 33 Knowest thou the ordinances of heaven?
39. 1 Knowest thou the time when the wild g.
39. 2 or knowest thou the time when they bring
42. 2 I know that thou canst do every (thing)
42. 3 too wonderful for me, which I knew not
Psa. 1. 6 the LORD knoweth the way of the righ.
4. 3 know that the LORD hath set apart him
9. 10 they that know thy name will put their
9. 20 nations may know themselves (to be but)
18. 43 people (whom) I have not known shall
20. 6 know I that the LORD saveth his anointed
31. 7 thou hast known my soul in adversities
35. 11 laid to my charge (things) that I knew not
35. 15 gathered themselves..and I knew (it) not
36. 10 loving kindness unto them that know thee
37. 18 The LORD knoweth the days of the upright
39. 4 what it (is; that) I may know how frail I
39. 6 and knoweth not who shall gather them
40. 9 not refrained my lips, O LORD, thou know.
41. 11 By this I know that thou favourest me
44. 21 for he knoweth the secrets of the heart
46. 10 Be still, and know that I (am) God: I
50. 11 I know all the fowls of the mountains
56. 9 shall mine enemies turn back: this I k.
59. 13 let them know that God ruleth in Jacob
67. 2 That thy way may be known upon earth
69. 5 thou knowest my foolishness; and my
69. 19 Thou hast known my reproach, and my
71. 15 all the day; for I know not the numbers
73. 11 How doth God know? and is there know.
73. 16 When I thought to know this, it (was) too
74. 9 (is there) among us any that knoweth how
78. 3 Which we have heard and known, and
78. 6 the generation to come might know (them
79. 6 the heathen that have not known thee
82. 5 know not, neither will they understand
83. 18 That (men) may know that thou, whose
87. 4 will make mention..to them that know
89. 15 the people that know the joyful sound
90. 11 Who knoweth the power of thine anger?
91. 14 on high, because he hath known my name
92. 6 A brutish man knoweth not; neither doth
94. 11 The LORD knoweth the thoughts of man
95. 10 a people..they have not known my ways
100. 3 Know ye that the LORD he (is) God: (it is)
101. 4 from me: I will not know a wicked (person)
103. 14 he knoweth our frame; he remembereth
104. 19 for seasons: the sun knoweth his going
109. 27 That they may know that this (is) thy h.
119. 75 know, O LORD, that thy judgments (are)
119. 79 and those that have known thy testimonies
119. 125 give me understanding, that I may know
119. 152 have known of old that thou hast founded
135. 5 I know that the LORD (is) great, and (that)
138. 6 he respect..but the proud he knoweth
139. 1 LORD, thou hast searched me, and known
139. 2 knowest my downsitting and mine upris.
139. 4 (but), lo, O LORD, thou knowest it altoge.
139. 14 and (that) my soul knoweth right well
139. 23 know my heart; try me, and know my
140. 12 I know that the LORD will maintain the
142. 3 was overwhelmed..thou knewest my path
147. 20 his) judgments, they have not known
Prov. 1. 2 know wisdom and instruction; to perceive
4. 1 Hear..and attend to know understanding
4. 19 the wicked..they know not at what they
5. 6 moveable, (that) thou canst not know
7. 23 and knoweth not that it (is) for his life
9. 13 clamorous; (she is) simple, and knoweth
9. 18 he knoweth not that the dead (are) there
10. 32 The lips of the righteous know what is
14. 10 The heart knoweth his own bitterness; and
24. 12 If thou sayest, Behold, we knew it not
24. 12 that keepeth thy soul, doth (not) he know
24. 22 and who knoweth the ruin of them both?
27. 1 thou knowest not what a day may bring

Prov.27. 23 Be thou diligent to know the state of thy
30. 18 wonderful for me, yea, four which I know
Eccl. 1. 17 know wisdom, and to know madness and
2. 19 who knoweth whether he shall be a wise
3. 12 I know that (there is) no good in them
3. 14 know that whatsoever God doeth, it shall
3. 21 Who knoweth the spirit of man that goeth
6. 5 hath not seen the sun, nor known (any th.)
6. 8 the poor, that knoweth to walk before the
6. 12 knoweth what (is) good for man in (this)
7. 22 thine own heart knoweth that thou thys.
7. 25 to know, and to search, and to seek out
7. 25 to know the wickedness of folly, even of
8. 1 who knoweth the interpretation of a thing
8. 7 For he knoweth not that which shall be
8. 12 I know that it shall be well with them
8. 16 When I applied mine heart to know wis.
8. 17 though a wise (man) think to know (it)
9. 1 no man knoweth either love or hatred
9. 5 know that they shall die: but the dead kn.
9. 12 For man also knoweth not his time: as
10. 15 because he knoweth not how to go to the
11. 2 knowest not what evil shall be upon the
11. 5 knowest not what (is) the way of the spirit
11. 5 knowest not the works of God who maketh
11. 6 thou knowest not whether shall prosper
11. 9 know thou that for all these (things) God
Song 1. 8 If thou know not, O thou fairest among
Isa. 1. 3 The ox knoweth his owner, and the ass
1. 3 Israel doth not know, my people doth not
5. 19 draw nigh and come, that we may know
7. 15 know to refuse the evil, and choose the
7. 16 the child shall know to refuse the evil
9. 9 the people shall know, (even) Ephraim
19. 12 let them know what the LORD of hosts
19. 21 Egyptians shall know the LORD in that
29. 15 they say, Who seeth us? and who knoweth
37. 20 kingdoms..may know that thou (art) the
37. 28 I know thy abode, and thy going out, and
40. 21 Have ye not known? have ye not heard?
40. 28 Hast thou not known? hast thou not heard
41. 20 they may see, and know, and consider
41. 22 that we may..know the latter end of them
41. 23 that we may know that ye (are) gods: yea
41. 26 Who hath declared..that we may know?
42. 16 the blind by a way (that) they knew not
42. 16 them in paths (that) they have not known
42. 25 it hath set him on fire..yet he knew not
43. 10 may know and believe me, and understand
43. 19 shall spring forth; shall ye not know it?
44. 8 yea, (there is) no God; I know not (any)
44. 9 they see not, nor know; that they may
44. 18 They have not known nor understood: for
45. 3 mayest know that I the LORD, which
45. 6 they may know from the rising of the sun
45. 4 surnamed thee, though thou hast..known
45. 5 girded thee, though thou hast not known
47. 8 neither shall I know the loss of children
47. 11 thou shalt not know from whence it riseth
47. 11 and desolation..(which) thou shalt not k.
48. 6 hidden things, and thou didst not know
48. 7 thou shouldest say, Behold, I knew them
48. 8 thou knewest not; yea, from that time
48. 8 I knew that thou wouldest deal very tre.
49. 23 and thou shalt know that I (am) the LORD
49. 26 all flesh shall know that I the LORD (am)
50. 4 that I should know how to speak a word
50. 7 and I know that I shall not be ashamed
51. 7 Hearken unto me, ye that know righteous.
52. 6 my people shall know my name: therefore
55. 5 thou knowest not, and nations (that) kn.
59. 8 The way of peace they know not; and
59. 8 whosoever goeth therein shall not know
59. 12 and (as for) our iniquities, we know them
60. 16 thou shalt know that I the LORD (am) thy
Jer. 1. 5 Before I formed thee in the belly I knew
2. 8 and they that handle the law knew me
2. 19 know therefore and see that (it is) an evil
2. 23 in the valley, know what thou hast done
4. 22 people (is) foolish, they have not known
5. 1 know, and seek in the broad places ther.
5. 4 they know not the way of the LORD, (nor)
5. 5 they have known the way of the LORD
5. 15 a nation whose language thou knowest
6. 18 know, O congregation, what (is) among
6. 27 that thou mayest know and try their way
7. 9 walk after other gods whom ye know not
8. 7 the stork..knoweth her appointed times
8. 7 people know not the judgment of the L.
9. 3 and they know not me, saith the LORD
9. 6 through deceit they refuse to know me
9. 16 neither they nor their fathers have known
9. 24 he understandeth and knoweth me, that
10. 23 I know that the way of man (is) not in
10. 25 fury upon the heathen that know thee not
11. 18 LORD hath given me knowledge..and I k.
11. 19 I knew not that they had devised devices
12. 3 thou, O LORD, knowest me; thou hast seen
13. 12 Do we not certainly know that every bo.
14. 18 go about into a land that they know not
15. 14 pass..into a land (which) thou knowest
15. 15 LORD, thou knowest: remember me, and
15. 15 know that for thy sake I have suffered reb.
16. 13 I cast you..into a land that ye know not
16. 21 they shall know that my name (is) The L.
17. 4 enemies in the land which thou knowest
17. 16 thou knowest: that which came out of
17. 9 and desperately wicked: who can know
18. 23 knowest all their counsel against me to
19. 4 neither they nor their fathers have known
22. 28 are cast into a land which they know not
24. 7 I will give them an heart to know me, that

Jer. 26. 15 know ye for certain, that, if ye put me to
29. 11 I know the thoughts that I think toward
29. 23 know, and (am) a witness, saith the LORD
31. 34 Know the LORD: for they shall all know
32. 8 knew that this (was) the word of the LORD
33. 3 and mighty things, which thou knowest
36. 19 Go, hide..and let no man know where ye
38. 24 Let no man know of these words, and thou
40. 14 Dost thou certainly know that Baalis the
40. 15 slay Ishmael..and no man shall know (it)
41. 4 he had slain Gedaliah, and no man knew
42. 19 know certainly that I have admonished
42. 22 know certainly that ye shall die by the
44. 3 to serve other gods, whom they knew not
44. 15 the men which knew that their wives had
44. 28 shall know whose words shall stand, mine
44. 29 ye may know that my words shall surely
48. 17 all ye that know his name, say, How is
48. 30 I know his wrath, saith the LORD: but
Eze. 2. 5 shall know that there hath been a prophet
5. 13 shall know that I the LORD have spoken
6. 7 and ye shall know that I (am) the LORD
6. 10 they shall know that I (am) the LORD, and
6. 13 Then shall ye know that I (am) the LORD
6. 14 and they shall know that I (am) the LORD
7. 4 and ye shall know that I (am) the LORD
7. 9 shall know that I (am) the LORD that sm.
7. 27 and they shall know that I (am) the LORD
10. 20 and I knew that they (were) the cherubim
11. 5 I know the things that come into your
11. 10, 12 and ye shall know that I (am) the LORD
12. 15, 16 they shall know that I (am) the LORD
12. 20 and ye shall know that I (am) the LORD
13. 9, 14, 21, 23 ye shall know that I (am) the
14. 8 and ye shall know that I (am) the LORD
14. 23 shall know that I have not done without
15. 7 ye shall know that I (am) the LORD, when
16. 62 and thou shalt know that I (am) the L.
17. 12 Know ye not what these (things mean)?
17. 21 shall know that I the LORD have spoken
17. 24 all the trees of the field shall know that
19. 7 knew their desolate palaces, and he laid
20. 12 they might know that I (am) the LORD
20. 20 ye may know that I (am) the LORD your
20. 26 that they might know that I (am) the L.
20. 38 and ye shall know that I (am) the LORD
20. 42, 44 ye shall know that I (am) the LORD
21. 5 all flesh may know that I the LORD have
22. 16 and thou shalt know that I (am) the LORD
22. 22 ye shall know that I the LORD have pou.
23. 49 and ye shall know that I (am) the Lord
24. 24, 27 shall know that I (am) the Lord GOD
25. 5 and ye shall know that I (am) the LORD
25. 7 and thou shalt know that I (am) the Lo.
25. 11, 17 they shall know that I (am) the LORD
25. 14 they shall know my vengeance, saith the
26. 6 and they shall know that I (am) the LORD
28. 19 they that know thee among the people
28. 22, 23, 24, 26 shall know that I (am) the LORD
29. 6, 9, 16, 21 shall know that I (am) the LORD
30. 8, 19, 25, 26 shall know that I (am) the Lo.
32. 9 the countries which thou hast not known
32. 15 then shall they know that I (am) the L.
33. 29 Then shall they know that I (am) the L.
33. 33 then shall they know that a prophet hath
34. 27 shall know that I (am) the LORD, when I
34. 30 Thus shall they know that I the LORD
35. 4, 12 thou shalt know that I (am) the LORD
35. 9 and ye shall know that I (am) the LORD
35. 15 and they shall know that I (am) the LORD
36. 11 and ye shall know that I (am) the LORD
36. 23 the heathen shall know that I (am) the L.
36. 36 shall know that I the LORD build the ru.
36. 38 and they shall know that I (am) the LORD
37. 3 And I answered, O Lord GOD, thou know.
37. 6, 13 and ye shall know that I (am) the L.
37. 14 ye know that I the LORD have spoken (it)
37. 28 know that I the LORD do sanctify Israel
38. 14 dwelleth safely, shalt thou not know (it)?
38. 16 the heathen may know me, when I shall
38. 23 and they shall know that I (am) the LORD
39. 6 and they shall know that I (am) the LORD
39. 7 the heathen shall know that I (am) the
39. 22 the house of Israel shall know that I (am)
39. 23 the heathen shall know that the house of
39. 28 they know that I (am) the LORD their God
Dan. 2. 3 my spirit was troubled to know the dream
9. 25 Know therefore and understand, (that)
10. 20 Knowest..wherefore I come unto thee?
11. 32 that do know their God shall be strong
11. 38 a god whom his fathers knew not shall
Hos. 2. 8 she did not know that I gave her corn, and
2. 20 betroth thee..and thou shalt know the L.
5. 3 know Ephraim, and Israel is not hid from
5. 4 whoredoms..they have not known the L.
6. 3 we know, (if) we follow on to know the L.
7. 9 devoured his strength, and he knoweth
7. 9 grey hairs are here..yet he knoweth not
8. 2 shall cry unto me, My God, we know thee
8. 4 they have made princes, and I knew (it)
9. 7 Israel shall know (it): the prophet (is) a
11. 3 Ephraim..they knew not that I healed
13. 4 thou shalt know no god but me; for (there)
13. 5 I did know thee in the wilderness, in the
14. 9 prudent, and he shall know them? for
Joel 2. 14 Who knoweth (if) he will return and rep.
2. 27 ye shall know that I (am) in the midst of
3. 17 shall ye know that I (am) the LORD your
Amos 3. 2 You only have I known of all the families
3. 10 they know not to do right, saith the LORD
5. 12 I know your manifold transgressions and
Jon. 1. 7 know for whose cause this evil (is) upon

Jon. 1. 10 men knew that he fled from the presence
1. 12 know that for my sake this great tempest
4. 2 I knew that thou (art) a gracious God, and
Mic. 3. 1 Hear..(Is it) not for you to know judgm.?
4. 12 But they know not the thoughts of the L.
6. 5 ye may know the righteousness of the L.
Nah. 1. 7 and he knoweth them that trust in him
Zeph. 3. 5 faileth not; but the unjust knoweth no
Zech. 2. 9 know that the LORD of hosts hath sent
2. 11 thou shalt know that the LORD of hosts
4. 5, 13 said..Knowest thou not what these be
4. 9 thou shalt know that the LORD of hosts
6. 15 ye shall know that the LORD of hosts hath
7. 14 among all the nations whom they knew
11. 11 poor of the flock that waited upon me k.
Mal. 2. 4 know that I..sent this commandment

4. *To know*, יְדַע *yeda*.
Ezra 4. 15 know, that this city (is) a rebellious city
7. 25 judge..all such as know the laws of thy
7. 25 and teach ye them that know (them) not
Dan. 2. 8 I know of certainty that ye would gain
2. 9 I shall know that ye can show me the in.
2. 21 knowledge to them that know understa.
2. 22 he knoweth what (is) in the darkness, and
2. 30 mightest know the thoughts of thy heart
4. 9 I know that the spirit of the holy gods (is)
4. 17 the living may know that the most high
4. 25 till thou know that the most high ruleth
4. 26 shalt have known that the heavens do
4. 32 until thou know that the most high ruleth
5. 21 he knew that the most high God ruled in
5. 22 not humbled..though thou knewest all
5. 23 gods..which see not, nor hear, nor know
6. 10 Daniel knew that the writing was signed
6. 15 Know, O king, that the law of the Medes

5. *To know, discern*, נָכַר *nakar*, 3.
Job 21. 29 Have ye not asked..do ye not know their

6. *To discern*, נָכַר *nakar*, 5.
Gen. 37. 32 know now whether it (be) thy son's coat
37. 33 he knew it, and said, (It is) my son's coat
42. 7 he knew them, but made himself strange
42. 8 knew his brethren, but they knew not him
Judg.18. 3 they knew the voice of the young man the
Ruth 3. 14 she rose up before one could know another
1 Sa. 26. 17 Saul knew David's voice, and said, (Is)
1 Ki. 18. 7 knew him, and fell on his face, and said
Job 2. 12 lifted up their eyes..and knew him not
7. 10 neither shall his place know him any more
24. 13 they know not the ways thereof, nor abide
24. 17 if (one) know (them, they are in) the ter.
34. 25 he knoweth their works, and he overtur.
Psa.103. 16 the place thereof shall know it no more
142. 4 but (there was) no man that would know

7. *To know*, γινώσκω *ginōskō*.
Matt. 1. 25 knew her not till she had brought forth
6. 3 left hand know what thy right hand doeth
7. 23 will I profess unto them, I never knew you
9. 30 charged them, saying, See (that) no man k.
10. 26 is nothing..hid, that shall not be known
12. 7 if ye had known what (this) meaneth, I
12. 15 when Jesus knew (it), he withdrew himself
12. 33 corrupt: for the tree is known by (his) fr.
13. 11 it is given unto you to know the mysteries
24. 32 putteth forth leaves, ye know that sum.
24. 33 know that it is near, (even) at the doors
24. 39 knew not until the flood came, and took
24. 43 But know this, that if the good man of the
25. 24 I knew thee that thou art an hard man
Mark 4. 11 to [know] the mystery of the kingdom of
4. 13 and how then will ye know all parables
5. 43 charged them..that no man should know
6. 38 when they knew, they say, Five, and two
7. 24 would have no man know (it): but he could
8. 17 when Jesus knew (it), he saith unto them
9. 30 he would not that any man should know
12. 12 they knew that he had spoken the parable
13. 28 putteth forth leaves, ye know that summer
13. 29 So..know that it is nigh, (even) at the doors
15. 10 For he knew that the chief priests had de.
15. 45 when he knew (it) of the centurion, he gave
Luke 1. 18 Whereby shall I know this? for I am an
1. 34 How shall this be, seeing I know not a
2. 43 Joseph and his mother knew not (of it)
6. 44 For every tree is known by his own fruit
7. 39 would have known who and what manner
8. 10 know the mysteries of the kingdom of G.
8. 17 that shall not be known and come abroad
9. 11 the people, when they knew (it), followed
10. 22 no man knoweth who the Son is, but the
12. 2 For..neither hid, that shall not be known
12. 39 And this know, that if the good man of the
12. 47 servant, which knew his lord's will, and
12. 48 he that knew not, and did commit things
16. 15 God knoweth your hearts: for that which
18. 34 neither knew they the things which were
19. 15 know how much every man had gained by
19. 42 If thou hadst known, even thou, at least
19. 44 thou knewest not the time of thy visitat.
21. 20 know that the desolation thereof is nigh
21. 30 know of your own selves that summer is
21. 31 know ye that the kingdom of God is nigh
24. 18 hast not known the things which are come
24. 35 was known of them in breaking of bread
John 1. 10 made by him, and the world knew him not
1. 48 saith unto him, Whence knowest thou me?
2. 24 commit himself..because he knew all (men)
2. 25 needed not..for he knew what was in man
3. 10 a master..and knowest not these things?
4. 1 the Lord knew how the Pharisees had he.

John 4. 53 father knew that (it was) at the same hour
5. 6 knew that he had been now a long time (in
5. 42 I know you, that ye have not the love of
7. 17 he shall know of the doctrine, whether
7. 26 know indeed that this is the very Christ?
7. 27 when Christ cometh no man knoweth
7. 49 people who knoweth not the law are cur.
7. 51 before it hear him, and know what he d.?
8. 28 then shall ye know that I am (he), and
8. 32 And ye shall know the truth, and the truth
8. 52 said..Now we know that thou hast a devil
8. 55 Yet ye have not known him; but I know
10. 14 and know my (sheep), and am known of
10. 15 knoweth me, even so know I the Father
10. 27 My sheep..I know them, and they follow
10. 38 ye may know, and believe, that the Father
11. 57 if any man knew where he were, he should
12. 9 the Jews therefore knew that he was there
13. 7 not now; but thou shalt know hereafter
13. 12 said..Know ye what I have done to you?
13. 28 knew for what intent he spake this unto
13. 35 By this shall all..know that ye are my
14. 7 If ye had known me, [ye should have kn.]
14. 7 henceforth ye know him, and have seen
14. 9 and yet hast thou not known me, Philip?
14. 17 neither knoweth him: but ye know him
14. 20 ye shall know that I (am) in my Father
14. 31 that the world may know that I love the
15. 18 ye know that it hated me before (it hated)
16. 3 they have not known the Father, nor me
16. 19 Jesus knew that they were desirous to ask
17. 3 they might know thee the only true God
17. 7 they have known that all things whatso.
17. 8 [known] surely that I came out from thee
17. 23 world may know that thou hast sent me
17. 25 not known thee: but I have known thee
17. 25 these have known that thou hast sent me
19. 4 ye may know that I find no fault in him
21. 17 thou knowest all things; thou knowest
Acts 1. 7 for you to know the times or the seasons
2. 36 let all the house of Israel know assuredly
9. 24 But their laying await was known of Saul
17. 19 May we know what this new doctrine
17. 20 would know therefore what these things
19. 15 I know, and Paul I know; but who are ye?
19. 35 what man is there that knoweth not how
20. 34 ye yourselves know, that these hands have
21. 24 all may know that those things, whereof
21. 34 could not know the certainty for the tum.
22. 14 thou shouldest know his will, and see
22. 30 would have known the certainty wheref.
23. 28 [known] the cause wherefore they accused
Rom. 1. 21 when they knew God, they glorified (him)
2. 18 knowest (his) will..approvest the things
3. 17 And the way of peace have they not known
6. 6 Knowing this, that our old man is crucified
7. 1 for I speak to them that know the law
7. 7 I had not known sin, but by the law: for
10. 19 Did not Israel know? First Moses saith
11. 34 who hath known the mind of the Lord?
1 Co. 1. 21 after..the world by wisdom knew not God
2. 8 none of the princes..knew..had they kn.
2. 14 neither can he know (them), because they
2. 16 who hath known the mind of the Lord
3. 20 Lord knoweth the thoughts of the wise
4. 19 will know, not the speech of them which
8. 2 knoweth nothing yet as he ought to know
8. 3 if any man love God, the same is known
13. 9 we know in part, and we prophesy in part
13. 12 I know in part; but then..even as also I
14. 7 shall it be known what is piped or harped?
14. 9 how shall it be known what is spoken?
2 Co. 2. 4 ye might know the love which I have
2. 9 I might know the proof of you, whether
3. 2 in our hearts, known and read of all men
5. 16 though we have known Christ after the
5. 16 now henceforth know we (him) no more
5. 21 made him (to be) sin for us, who knew no
8. 9 ye know the grace of our Lord Jesus Ch.
13. 6 I trust that ye shall know that we are not
Gal. 3. 7 Know ye therefore that they which are
4. 9 ye have known God, or rather are known
Eph. 3. 19 know the love of Christ, which passeth k.
5. 5 ye know, that no whoremonger, nor unc.
6. 22 ye might know our affairs, and (that) he
Phil. 2. 19 may be of good comfort, when I know
2. 22 ye know the proof of him, that, as
3. 10 That I may know him, and the power of his
4. 5 Let your moderation be known unto all
Col. 4. 8 he might know your estate, and comfort
1 Th. 3. 5 I sent to know your faith, lest by some
2 Ti. 1. 18 how..he ministered..thou knowest very
2. 19 seal, The Lord knoweth them that are his
3. 1 know also, that in the last days perilous
Heb. 3. 10 alway err..they have not known my ways
8. 11 every man his brother, saying, Know the
10. 34 knowing in yourselves that ye have in
13. 23 Know ye that (our) brother Timothy is set
Jas. 1. 3 Knowing (this), that the trying of your
2. 20 But wilt thou know, O vain man, that fa.
5. 20 Let him know, that he which converteth
2 Pe. 1. 20 Knowing this first, that no prophecy of
3. 3 Knowing this first, that there shall come
1 Jo. 2. 3 we do know that we know him, if we keep
2. 4 He that saith, I know him, and keepeth
2. 5 perfected: hereby know we that we are in
2. 13, 14 known him (that is) from the beginning
2. 13 I write..because ye have known the Fat.
2. 18 Little children..we know that it is the last
2. 29 If ye know that he is righteous, ye know
3. 1 the world knoweth us not, because it kn.
3. 6 sinneth hath not seen him, neither known

1 Jo. 3. 19 hereby we know that we are of the truth
3. 20 For..God is greater..and knoweth all th.
3. 24 hereby we know that he abideth in us, by
4. 2 Hereby know ye the spirit of God: Every
4. 6 he that knoweth God heareth us; he that
4. 6 Hereby know we the spirit of truth, and
4. 7 that loveth is born of God, and knoweth
4. 8 He that loveth not knoweth not God; for
4. 13 Hereby know we that we dwell in him, and
4. 16 we have known and believed the love that
5. 2 we know that we love the children of God
5. 20 that we may know him that is true; and
2 Jo. 1 but also all they that have known the tr.
Rev. 2. 17 which no man [knoweth] saving he that
2. 23 all the churches shall know that I am he
2. 24 known the depths of Satan, as they speak
3. 3 not know what hour I will come upon thee
3. 9 I will make them..to know that I have

8. *Known*, γνωστός *gnōstos*.

Acts 28. 22 know that every where it is spoken against

9. *To see, have seen, known*, οἶδα *oida*.

Matt. 6. 8 your Father knoweth what things ye have
6. 32 knoweth that ye have need of all these
7. 11 know how to give good gifts unto your
9. 4 Jesus, knowing their thoughts, said, Whe.
9. 6 may know that the Son of man hath power
12. 25 knew their thoughts, and said unto them
15. 12 Knowest thou that the Pharisees were off.
20. 22 Ye know not what ye ask. Are ye able to
20. 25 Ye know that the princes of the Gentiles
22. 16 we know that thou are true, and teachest
22. 29 not knowing the scriptures, nor the power
24. 36 of that day and hour knoweth no (man)
24. 42 know not what hour your Lord doth come
24. 43 if the good man of the house had known
25. 12 said, Verily I say unto you, I know you
25. 13 for ye know neither the day nor the hour
25. 26 thou knewest that I reap where I sowed
26. 2 Ye know that after two days is..the pas.
26. 70 denied..saying, I know not what thou sa.
26. 72 denied with an oath, I do not know the
26. 74 and to swear,(saying), I know not the man
27. 18 knew that for envy they had delivered
28. 5 for I know that ye seek Jesus, which was
Mark 1. 24 I know thee who thou art, the Holy One
1. 34 the devils to speak, because they knew h.
2. 10 may know that the Son of man hath power
4. 13 Know ye not this parable? and how then
4. 27 should spring and grow up, he knoweth
5. 33 knowing what was done in her, came and
6. 20 knowing that he was a just man and an h.
10. 19 Thou knowest the commandments, Do not
10. 38 Ye know not what ye ask: can ye drink
10. 42 Ye know that they which are accounted
12. 14 we know that thou art true, and carest
12. 15 he, [knowing] their hypocrisy, said unto
12. 24 ye know not the scriptures, neither the
13. 32 of that day and..hour knoweth no man
13. 33 and pray: for ye know not when the time
13. 35 ye know not when the master of the house
14. 68 know not, neither understand I what thou
14. 71 I know not this man of whom ye speak
Luke 4. 34 I know thee who thou art; the Holy One of
4. 41 to speak: for they knew that he was Chr.
5. 24 may know that the Son of man hath power
6. 8 he knew their thoughts, and said to the
8. 53 And they laughed..knowing that she was
9. 33 and one for Elias: not knowing what he
9. 55 [know not what manner of spirit ye are of]
11. 13 know how to give good gifts unto your ch.
11. 17 knowing their thoughts, said unto them
12. 30 knoweth that ye have need of these things
12. 39 if the goodman of the house had known w.
13. 25 and say unto you, I know not whence ye
13. 27 I tell you, I know you not whence ye are
18. 20 Thou knowest the commandments, Do not
19. 22 Thou knewest that I was an austere man
20. 21 know that thou sayest and teachest rightly
22. 34 thou shalt thrice deny that thou knowest
22. 57 denied him, saying, Woman, I know him
22. 60 Peter said, Man, I know not what thou
23. 34 [forgive them; for they know not what]
John 1. 26 standeth one among you, whom ye know
1. 31 knew him not: but that he should be m.
1. 33 And I knew him not: but he that sent
2. 9 was made wine, and knew not whence it
2. 9 the servants which drew the water knew
3. 2 we know that thou art a teacher come
3. 11 We speak that we do know, and testify
4. 10 If thou knewest the gift of God, and who
4. 22 Ye worship ye know not what: we know
4. 25 I know that Messias cometh, which is cal.
4. 32 I have meat to eat that ye know not of
4. 42 and know that this is indeed the Christ
5. 32 know that the witness which he witness.
6. 6 for he himself knew what he would do
6. 42 Jesus..whose father and mother we know?
6. 61 Jesus knew in himself that his disciples
6. 64 Jesus knew from the beginning who they
7. 15 How knoweth this man letters, having
7. 27 we know this man whence he is: but when
7. 28 Ye both know me, and ye know whence I
7. 28 he that sent me is true, whom ye know
7. 29 I know him: for I am from him, and he
8. 14 I know whence I came, and whither I go
8. 19 answered, Ye neither know me, nor my
8. 19 if ye had known me, ye should have known
8. 37 I know that ye are Abraham's seed; but
8. 55 I know him: and if I should say, I know
8. 55 a liar..but I know him, and keep his say

John 9. 12 said they..Where is he? He said, I know
9. 20 We know that this is our son, and that he
9. 21 But by what means he now seeth, we know
9. 21 or who hath opened his eyes, we know not
9. 24 and said..we know that this man is a sin.
9. 25 sinner (or no), I know not: one thing I k
9. 29 We know that God spake unto Moses: (as
9. 29 this (fellow), we know not from whence
9. 30 ye know not from whence he is, and (yet)
9. 31 Now we know that God heareth not sinners
10. 4 sheep follow him: for they know his voice
10. 5 for they know not the voice of strangers
11. 22 know, that even now, whatsoever thou
11. 24 I know that he shall rise again in the
11. 42 And I knew that thou hearest me always
11. 49 said unto them, Ye know nothing at all
12. 35 in darkness knoweth not whither he goeth
12. 50 And I know that his commandment is life
13. 1 Jesus knew that his hour was come that
13. 3 Jesus knowing that the Father had given
13. 7 thou knowest not now; but thou shalt
13. 11 he knew who should betray him; theref.
13. 17 If ye know these things, happy are ye if
13. 18 I know whom I have chosen: but that the
14. 4 whither I go ye know, and the way [ye k.]
14. 5 Lord, we know not..how can we know the
15. 15 servant knoweth not what his lord doeth
15. 21 because they know not him that sent me
16. 30 Now are we sure that thou knowest all
18. 2 Judas..which betrayed him, knew the pl.
18. 4 knowing all things that should come upon
18. 21 ask them..behold, they know what I said
19. 10 knowest thou not that I have power to
19. 28 Jesus [knowing] that all things were now
19. 35 he knoweth that he saith true, that ye
20. 2 we know not where they have laid him
20. 9 they knew not the scripture, that he must
20. 13 Because..I know not where they have laid
20. 14 saw Jesus..and knew not that it was Je.
21. 4 but the disciples knew not that it was J.
21. 12 Who art thou? knowing that it was the L.
21. 15 Lord; thou knowest that I love thee
21. 16 Lord; thou knowest that I love thee
21. 17 And he said..Lord, thou knowest all th.
21. 24 and we know that his testimony is true
Acts 2. 22 midst of you, as ye yourselves also know
2. 30 knowing that God had sworn with an oath
3. 16 made this man strong, whom ye see and k.
5. 7 wife, not knowing what was done, came
7. 18 Till another king arose, which knew not J.
10. 37 word, (I say), ye know, which was publish.
12. 11 know of a surety, that the Lord hath sent
16. 3 they knew all that his father was a Greek
19. 32 the more part knew not wherefore they
20. 22 not knowing the things that shall befall
20. 25 I know that ye all, among whom I have
20. 29 I know this, that after my departing shall
26. 27 King Agrippa..I know that thou believest
Rom. 3. 19 we know that what things soever the law
5. 3 knowing that tribulation worketh patience
6. 9 Knowing that Christ being raised from the
6. 16 Know ye not, that to whom ye yield you.
7. 7 I had not known lust, except the law had
7. 14 we know that the law is spiritual: but I
7. 18 For I know that in me that is, in my flesh
8. 22 we know that the whole creation groaneth
8. 26 we know not what we should pray for as
8. 27 knoweth what (is) the mind of the spirit
8. 28 we know that all things work together for
13. 11 knowing the time, that now (it is) high
14. 14 I know, and am persuaded by the Lord J.
1 Co. 1. 16 besides, I know not whether I baptized
2. 2 determined not to know any thing among
2. 11 what man knoweth the things of a man
2. 11 the things of God [knoweth] no man, but
2. 12 that we might know the things that are
3. 16 Know ye not that ye are the temple of God
5. 6 Know ye not that a little leaven leaveneth
6. 2 Do ye not know that the saints shall ju.
6. 3 Know ye not that we shall judge angels?
6. 9 Know ye not that the unrighteous shall
6. 15 Know ye not that your bodies are the me.
6. 16 know ye not that he which is joined to
6. 19 know ye not that your body is the temple
7. 16 what knowest thou, O wife, whether thou
7. 16 how knowest thou, O man, whether thou
8. 1 Now..we know that we all have knowle.
8. 2 if any man think that [he knoweth] any
8. 4 know that an idol (is) nothing in the world
9. 13 Do ye not know that they which minister
9. 24 Know ye not that they which run in a race
11. 3 I would have you know, that the head of
12. 2 Ye know that ye were Gentiles, carried
14. 11 if I know not the meaning of the voice, I
15. 58 ye know that your labour is not in vain
16. 15 ye know the house of Stephanas, that it
2 Co. 1. 7 knowing, that as ye are partakers of the
4. 14 Knowing that he which raised up the Lord
5. 1 know that if our earthly house of (this) tab.
5. 6 knowing that, whilst we are at home in the
5. 11 Knowing therefore the terror of the Lord
5. 16 henceforth know we no man after the flesh
9. 2 I know the forwardness of your mind, for
11. 11 because I love you not? God knoweth
11. 31 The God and Father..knoweth that I lie
12. 2 I knew a man in Christ above fourteen y.
12. 2, 3 out of the body, I cannot tell: God kn.
12. 3 I knew such a man, whether in the body
Gal. 2. 16 Knowing that a man is not justified by the
4. 8 when ye knew not God, ye did service unto
4. 13 Ye know how through infirmity of the fl.
Eph. 1. 18 ye may know what is the hope of his call.

Eph. 6. 8 Knowing that whatsoever good thing any
6. 9 knowing that your Master also is in heaven
6. 21 that ye also may know my affairs,(and) how
Phil. 1. 17 knowing that I am set for the defence of
1. 19 know that this shall turn to my salvation
1. 25 I know that I shall abide and continue with
4. 12 I know both how to be abased, and I know
4. 15 know also, that in the beginning of the g.
Col. 2. 1 that ye knew what great conflict I have
3. 24 Knowing that of the Lord ye shall receive
4. 1 knowing that ye also have a Master in h.
4. 6 may know how ye ought to answer every
1 Th. 1. 4 Knowing, brethren beloved, your election
1. 5 as ye know what manner of men we were
2. 1 yourselves..know our entrance in unto
2. 2 as ye know, at Philippi, we were bold in
2. 5 neither..used ..flattering words, as ye k.
2. 11 As ye know how we exhorted and comfor
3. 3 yourselves know that we are appointed
3. 4 told..even as it came to pass and ye know
4. 2 ye know what commandments we gave
4. 4 every one of you should know how to pos.
4. 5 even as the Gentiles which know not God
5. 2 yourselves know perfectly, that the day of
5. 12 to know them which labour among you
2 Th. 1. 8 taking vengeance on them that know not
2. 6 ye know what withholdeth that he might
3. 7 For yourselves know how ye ought to fol.
1 Ti. 1. 8 we know that the law (is) good, if a man
1. 9 Knowing this, that the law is not made
3. 5 a man know not how to rule his own house
3. 15 that thou mayest know how thou oughtest
2 Ti. 1. 12 for I know whom I have believed, and am
1. 15 This thou knowest, that all they which
2. 23 avoid, knowing that they do gender strifes
3. 14 knowing of whom thou..learned (them)
3. 15 And that from a child thou hast known
Titus 1. 16 They profess that they know God; but in
3. 11 Knowing that he that is such is subverted
Phm. 21 knowing that thou wilt also do more
Heb. 8. 11 for all shall know me, from the least to
10. 30 we know him that hath said, Vengeance
Jas. 3. 1 knowing that we shall receive the greater
4. 4 know ye not that the friendship of the
4. 17 to him that knoweth to do good, and doeth
1 Pe. 1. 18 ye know that ye were not redeemed with
3. 9 [knowing] that ye are thereunto called
5. 9 knowing that the same afflictions are ac.
2 Pe. 1. 12 you always in remembrance..though ye k.
1. 14 Knowing that shortly I must put off (this)
2. 9 The Lord knoweth how to deliver the
1 Jo. 2. 11 knoweth not whither he goeth, because
2. 20 have an unction..and ye know all things
2. 21 ye know not the truth, but because ye k.
2. 29 If ye know that he is righteous..every one
3. 2 we know that, when he shall appear, we
3. 5 ye know that he was manifested to take
3. 14 We know that we have passed from death
3. 15 ye know that no murderer hath eternal
5. 13 ye may know that ye have eternal life
5. 15 we know that he hear us, whatsoever we
5. 15 we know that we have the petitions that
5. 18 We know that whosoever is born of God
5. 19 know that we are of God, and the whole
5. 20 we know that the Son of God is come, and
3 John 12 record; and ye know that our record is
Jude 5 ye once knew this, how that the Lord
10 speak evil of those things which they know
Rev. 2. 2 I know thy works, and thy labour, and
2. 9 I know thy works, and tribulation, and
2. 13 I know thy works, and where thou dwell.
2. 19 I know thy works, and charity, and service
3. 1 I know thy works, and thou hast a name
3. 8 I know thy works: behold, I have set be.
3. 15 I know thy works, that thou art neither
3. 17 knowest not that thou art wretched, and
7. 14 And I said unto him, Sir, thou knowest
12. 12 he knoweth that he hath but a short time
19. 12 he had a name written that no man knew

10. *To know about or fully*, ἐπιγινώσκω *epiginōskō*.
Matt 7. 16 Ye shall know them by their fruits. Do
7. 20 Wherefore by their fruits ye shall know
11. 27 and no man knoweth the Son, but the F.
11. 27 neither knoweth any man the Father, save
17. 12 they knew him not, but have done unto
Mark 5. 30 knowing in himself that virtue had gone
6. 33 many [knew] him, and ran afoot thither out
6. 54 And when they were come out..they knew
Luke 1. 4 thou mightest know the certainty of those
7. 37 when she knew that (Jesus) sat at meat
23. 7 as he knew that he belonged unto Herod's
24. 16 eyes were holden that they should not k.
24. 31 their eyes were opened, and they knew
Acts 3. 10 they knew that it was he which sat for
9. 30 when the brethren knew, they brought
12. 14 when she knew Peter's voice, she opened
19. 34 when they knew that he was a Jew, all
22. 24 know wherefore they cried so against him
22. 29 afraid, after he knew that he was a Roman
25. 10 done no wrong, as thou very well knowest
27. 39 when it was day, they knew not the land
28. 1 knew that the island was called Melita
Rom. 1. 32 Who knowing the judgment of God, that
1 Co. 13. 12 then shall I know even as also I am known
2 Co. 13. 5 Know ye not your own selves, how that
Col. 1. 6 since the day ye..knew the grace of God
1 Ti. 4. 3 of them which believe and know the truth
2 Pe. 2. 21 to have known the way of righteousness
2. 21 after they have known (it), to turn from

11. *To understand*, ἐπίσταμαι *epistamai*.
Acts 10. 28 Ye know how that it is an unlawful thing
15. 7 ye know how that a good while ago God
18. 25 he spake..knowing only the baptism of
19. 15 answered and said..Paul I know; but who
19. 25 know that by this craft we have our we.
20. 18 Ye know, from the first day that I came
22. 19 they know that I imprisoned and beat in
24. 10 I know that thou hast been of many years
26. 26 For the king knoweth of these things, before
1 Ti. 6. 4 He is proud, knowing nothing, but doting
Heb. 11. 8 he went out, not knowing whither he went
Jas. 4. 14 Whereas ye know not what (shall be) on
Jude 10 but what they know naturally, as brute b.

12. *To know*, ἵστημι *isēmi*.
Acts 26. 4 My manner of life from my youth..know
Heb. 12. 17 For ye know how that afterward, when he

13. *To know beforehand or formerly*, προγινώσκω.
Acts 26. 5 Which knew me from the beginning, if

14. *To know together*, σύνοιδα *sunoida*.
1 Co. 4. 4 For I know nothing by myself; yet am I

KNOW, to cause, let, or make to —

1. *To make to know*, יָדַע *yada*, 3.
Job 38. 12 Hast thou..caused the day spring to know

2. *To cause to know*, יָדַע *yada*, 5.
Exod 18. 16 I do make (them) know the statutes of G.
33. 12 thou hast not let me know whom thou
Deut 8. 3 that he might make thee know that man
Josh. 4. 22 Then ye shall let your children know, say.
2 Sa. 7. 21 hast thou done all..to make thy servant k.
Job 13. 23 make me to know my transgression and
Psa. 39. 4 LORD, make me to know mine end, and
51. 6 and..thou shalt make me to know wisdom
143. 8 cause me to know the way wherein I sho.
Prov. 22. 21 That I might make thee know the certai.
Jer. 16. 21 behold, I will this once cause them to know
16. 21 I will cause them to know mine hand and
Eze. 16. 2 cause Jerusalem to know her abominations
20. 4 cause them to know the abominations of
Dan. 8. 19 I will make thee know what shall be in

3. *To know*, יְדַע *yeda*, 5.
Dan. 7. 16 and made me know the interpretation of

KNOW before, to —

To know beforehand, προγινώσκω *proginōskō*.
2 Pe. 3. 17 seeing ye know..before, beware lest ye

KNOW fully, to —

To follow alongside, παρακολουθέω *parakoloutheō*.
2 Ti. 3. 10 But thou hast fully known my doctrine

KNOW not, to —

To be ignorant, not to know, ἀγνοέω *agnoeō*.
Acts 13. 27 because they knew him not, nor yet the
Rom. 2. 4 not knowing that the goodness of God
6. 3 know ye not, that so many of us as were
7. 1 Know ye not, brethren..how that the law

KNOW the uttermost, to —

To know thoroughly, διαγινώσκω *diaginōskō*.
Acts 24. 22 I will know the uttermost of your matter

KNOW well, to —

To know about or fully, ἐπιγινώσκω *epiginōskō*.
2 Co. 6. 9 As unknown, and (yet) well known; as

KNOWLEDGE —

1. *Understanding*, בִּינָה *binah*.
Prov. 2. 3 Yea, if thou criest after knowledge, (and)
Dan. 2. 21 knowledge to them that know understa.

2. *Knowledge*, דֵּעַ *dea*.
Job 36. 3 I will fetch my knowledge from afar, and
37. 16 works of him which is perfect in knowle.?

3. *Knowledge*, דֵּעָה *deah*.
1 Sa. 2. 3 for the LORD (is) a God of knowledge, and
Job 36. 4 he that is perfect in knowledge (is) with
Psa. 73. 11 and is there knowledge in the most High?
Isa. 11. 9 the earth shall be full of the knowledge
28. 9 Whom shall he teach knowledge? and
Jer. 3. 15 which shall feed you with knowledge and

4. *Knowledge*, דַּעַת *daath*.
Gen. 2. 9 the tree of knowledge of good and evil
2. 17 of the tree of the knowledge of good and
Exod 31. 3 in understanding, and in knowledge, and
35. 31 in understanding, and in knowledge, and
Num 24. 16 and knew the knowledge of the most H.
Job 15. 2 Should a wise man utter vain knowledge
21. 14 for we desire not the knowledge of thy
21. 22 Shall (any) teach God knowledge? seeing
33. 3 and my lips shall utter knowledge clearly
34. 35 Job hath spoken without knowledge, and
35. 16 he multiplieth words without knowledge
36. 12 obey not..they shall die without knowle.
38. 2 darkeneth counsel by words without kno.
42. 3 (is) he that hideth counsel without know.
Psa. 19. 2 and night unto night showeth knowledge
94. 10 he that teacheth man knowledge, (shall
119. 66 Teach me good judgment and knowledge
139. 6 (Such) knowledge (is) too wonderful for
Prov. 1. 4 To give..to the young man knowledge
1. 7 fear of the LORD (is) the beginning of kn.
1. 22 delight in..scorning, and fools hate kno.
1. 29 For that they hated knowledge, and did
2. 5 Then shalt thou..find the knowledge of
2. 6 out of his mouth (cometh) knowledge and
2. 10 and knowledge is pleasant unto thy soul
3. 20 By his knowledge the depths are broken
5. 2 and (that) thy lips may keep knowledge
8. 9 (are) all..right to them that find knowle.
8. 10 and knowledge rather than choice gold
8. 12 find out knowledge of witty inventions
9. 10 knowledge of the holy (is) understanding
10. 14 Wise (men) lay up knowledge: but the
11. 9 through knowledge shall the just be del.
12. 1 Whoso loveth instruction loveth knowle.
12. 23 A prudent man concealeth knowledge: but
13. 16 prudent (man) dealeth with knowledge
14. 6 knowledge (is) easy unto him that under.
14. 7 when thou perceivest not..the lips of kn.
14. 18 the prudent are crowned with knowledge
15. 2 The tongue of the wise useth knowledge
15. 7 The lips of the wise disperse knowledge
15. 14 hath understanding seeketh knowledge
17. 27 He that hath knowledge spareth his words
18. 15 heart of the prudent getteth knowledge
18. 15 and the ear of the wise seeketh knowledge
19. 2 Also..the soul..without knowledge..not
19. 25 reprove..(and) he will understand know.
19. 27 instruction..to err from the words of kn.
20. 15 lips of knowledge (are) a precious jewel
21. 11 wise is instructed, he receiveth knowledge
22. 12 The eyes of the LORD preserve knowledge
22. 17 and apply thine heart unto my knowledge
22. 20 excellent things in counsels and knowle.
23. 12 and thine ears to the words of knowledge
24. 4 And by knowledge shall the chambers be
24. 5 yea, a man of knowledge increaseth stre.
30. 3 neither learned..nor have the knowledge
Eccl 1. 16 great experience of wisdom and knowledge
1. 18 he that increaseth knowledge increaseth
2. 21 labour (is) in wisdom, and in knowledge
2. 26 giveth to a man..wisdom, and knowledge
7. 12 but the excellency of knowledge (is, that)
9. 10 no work, nor device, nor knowledge, nor
12. 9 he still taught the people knowledge; yea
Isa. 5. 13 captivity, because (they have) no knowle.
11. 2 the spirit of knowledge and of the fear of
32. 4 of the rash shall understand knowledge
33. 6 wisdom and knowledge shall be the stabi.
40. 14 taught him knowledge, and showed to him
44. 19 neither..knowledge nor understanding
44. 25 wise..and maketh their knowledge fool.
47. 10 Thy wisdom and thy knowledge, it hath
53. 11 by his knowledge shall my righteous serv.
Jer. 10. 14 Every man is brutish in (his) knowledge
51. 17 Every man is brutish by (his) knowledge
Dan. 1. 4 cunning in knowledge, and understanding
12. 4 shall run..and knowledge shall be incre.
Hos. 4. 1 no truth, nor mercy, nor knowledge of God
4. 6 My people are destroyed for lack of kno.
4. 6 because thou hast rejected knowledge, I
6. 6 knowledge of God more than burnt offer.
Mal. 2. 7 For the priest's lips should keep knowle.

5. *To know*, יָדַע *yada*.
Prov. 24. 14 So (shall) the knowledge of wisdom (be)
28. 2 but by a man of understanding (and) kn.
Hab. 2. 14 For the earth shall be filled with the kno.

6. *Knowledge*, מַדָּע *madda*.
2 Ch. 1. 10 Give me now wisdom and knowledge, that
1. 11 but hast asked wisdom and knowledge for
1. 12 Wisdom and knowledge (is) granted unto
Dan. 1. 17 God gave them knowledge and skill in all

7. *Knowledge*, מַנְדַּע *manda*.
Dan. 2. 21 knowledge to them that know understand.
5. 12 an excellent spirit, and knowledge, and

8. *Eyes*, עֵינַיִם [*ayin*].
Num. 15. 24 committed by ignorance without the kn

9. *Understanding*, שֵׂכֶל, שֶׂכֶל *sekel*.
2 Ch. 30. 22 Levites that taught the good knowledge

10. *Knowledge*, γνῶσις *gnōsis*.
Luke 1. 77 To give knowledge of salvation unto his
11. 52 ye have taken away the key of knowledge
Rom. 2. 20 which hast the form of knowledge and of
11. 33 both of the wisdom and knowledge of G.
15. 14 filled with all knowledge, able also to ad.
1 Co. 1. 5 enriched..in all utterance, and (in) all k.
8. 1 Now..we know that we all have knowle.
8. 1 Knowledge puffeth up, but charity edifieth
8. 7 Howbeit (there is) not in..that knowled
8. 10 For if any man see thee which hast know.
8. 11 And through thy knowledge shall the w.
12. 8 to another the word of knowledge by the
13. 2 understand all mysteries, and all knowl.
13. 8 whether..knowledge, it shall vanish away
14. 6 knowledge, or by prophesying, or by doc.
2 Co. 2. 14 maketh manifest the savour of his know.
4. 6 the light of the knowledge of the glory of
6. 6 By pureness, by knowledge, by long suffe.
8. 7 faith, and utterance, and knowledge, and
10. 5 thing that exalteth itself against the kno.
11. 6 though..rude in speech, yet not in know.
Eph. 3. 19 the love of Christ, which passeth knowle.
Phil. 3. 8 the excellency of the knowledge of Christ
Col. 2. 3 are hid all the treasures of wisdom and k.
1 Pe. 3. 7 dwell with (them) according to knowledge
2 Pe. 1. 5 add to your faith virtue; and to virtue k.
1. 6 to knowledge temperance; and to temp.
3. 18 the knowledge of our Lord and Saviour J.

11. *Full knowledge*, ἐπίγνωσις *epignōsis*.
Rom. 1. 28 as they did not like to retain God in..kn.
3. 20 for by the law (is) the knowledge of sin
10. 2 a zeal of God but not according to know.
Eph. 1. 17 and revelation in the knowledge of him
4. 13 and of the knowledge of the Son of God
Phil. 1. 9 abound yet more and more in knowledge
Col. 1. 9 be filled with the knowledge of his will in
1. 10 and increasing in the knowledge of God
3. 10 is renewed in knowledge after the image

1 Ti. 2. 4 to come unto the knowledge of the truth
2 Ti. 3. 7 never able to come to the knowledge of
Heb. 10. 26 after that we have received the knowledge
2 Pe. 1. 2 through the knowledge of God, and of J.
1. 3 through the knowledge of him that hath
1. 8 barren nor unfruitful in the knowledge
2. 20 through the knowledge of the Lord and

12. *Understanding,* σύνεσις *sunesis.*
Eph. 3. 4 ye may understand my knowledge in the

KNOWLEDGE, not —
Ignorance, without knowledge, ἀγνωσία *agnōsia.*
1 Co. 15. 34 for some have not the knowledge of God

KNOWLEDGE, to come to —
To be caused to be known, יָדַע *yada,* 6.
Lev. 4. 23, 28 Or if his sin..come to his knowledge

KNOWLEDGE, to give, have, or take —
1. *To know,* יָדַע *yada.*
Deut. 1. 39 had no knowledge between good and evil
1 Sa. 23. 23 take knowledge of all the lurking places
1 Ki. 9. 27 shipmen that had knowledge of the sea
2 Ch. 8. 18 servants that had knowledge of the sea
Neh. 10. 28 every one having knowledge, and having
Job 34. 2 and give ear unto me, ye that have know
Psa. 14. 4 Have all the workers of iniquity no kno.?
53. 4 Have all the workers of iniquity no kno ?
144. 3 what (is) man, that thou takest knowledge
Prov 17. 27 He that hath knowledge spareth his wo.
30. 3 I neither learned..nor have the knowledge
Isa. 8. 4 For before the child shall have knowledge
45. 20 they have no knowledge that set up the
58. 3 afflicted our soul..and thou takest no kn.?
Jer. 4. 22 but to do good they have no knowledge

2. *To cause to know,* יָדַע *yada,* 5.
Jer. 11. 18 the LORD hath given me knowledge (of it)

3. *To discern,* נָכַר *nakar,* 5.
Ruth 2. 10 that thou shouldest take knowledge of me
2. 19 blessed be he that did take knowledge of

4. *To know,* γινώσκω *ginōskō.*
Acts 17. 13 when the Jews of Thessalonica had kno.

5. *To see, know,* οἶδα *oida.*
Acts 24. 22 having more perfect knowledge of (that)

6. *To know about or fully,* ἐπιγινώσκω *epiginōskō.*
Matt 14. 35 when the men of that place had knowledge
Acts 4. 13 they took knowledge of them, that they
24. 8 thyself mayest take knowledge of all these

KNOWLEDGE, endued with —
Understanding, intelligent, ἐπιστήμων *epistēmōn.*
Jas. 3. 13 Who (is) a wise man and endued with k.

KNOWN —
1. *To know,* יָדַע *yada.*
Deut. 1. 13 Take you wise men..known among your
1. 15 So I took..wise men, and known, and made

2. *To be or become known,* יָדַע *yada,* 6 [V. L. 4].
Isa. 12. 5 he hath done excellent things: this (is) k.

3. *Known,* γνωστός *gnōstos.*
John 18. 15 That disciple was known unto the high p.
18. 16 that other disciple, which was known unto
Acts 1. 19 it was known unto all the dwellers at Je.
2. 14 be this known unto you, and hearken to
4. 10 Be it known unto you all, and to all the
9. 42 it was known throughout all Joppa; and
13. 38 Be it known unto you therefore, men..br.
15. 18 [Known unto God are all his works from]
19. 17 And this was known to all the Jews and
28. 28 Be it known therefore unto you, that the

4. *Apparent, manifest,* φανερός *phaneros.*
Matt 12. 16 charged..they should not make him kn.
Mark 3. 12 charged..they should not make him kn.
Acts. 7. 13 Joseph's kindred was made known unto

KNOWN, to be —
1. *To be known,* יָדַע *yada,* 2.
Gen. 41. 21 it could not be known that they had eaten
41. 31 the plenty shall not be known in the land
Exod. 2. 14 feared, and said, Surely this thing is known
6. 3 by my name JEHOVAH was I not known
21. 36 Or if it be known that the ox hath used to
33. 16 wherein shall it be known here that I and
Lev. 4. 14 When the sin..is known, then the congr
Deut 21. 1 (and) it be not known who hath slain him
Judg 16. 9 brake the withs..his strength was not kn.
Ruth 3. 14 Let it not be known that a woman came
1 Sa. 6. 3 it shall be known to you why his hand is
2 Sa. 17. 19 spread a covering..the thing was not kn
1 Ki. 18. 36 let it be known this day that thou (art)
Neh. 4. 15 when our enemies heard that it was known
Esth. 2. 22 the thing was known to Mordecai, who
Psa. 9. 16 The LORD is known (by) the judgment
48. 3 God is known in her palaces for a refuge
76. 1 In Judah (is) God known; his name (is)
77. 19 Thy way..and thy footsteps are not known
79. 10 let him be known among the heathen in
88. 12 Shall thy wonders be known in the dark?
Prov 10. 9 he that perverteth his ways shall be known
12. 16 A fool's wrath is presently known: but a
14. 33 but..in the midst of fools is made known
31. 23 Her husband is known in the gates, when
Eccl. 6. 10 and it is known that it (is) man: neither
Isa. 19. 21 the LORD shall be known to Egypt, and
61. 9 their seed shall be known among the Ge.
66. 14 the hand of the LORD shall be known to.
Jer. 28. 9 the prophet be known that the LORD hath
Eze. 36. 32 be it known unto you: be ashamed and
Eze 38. 23 I will be known in the eyes of many nat.
Nah. 3. 17 and their place is not known where they
Zech 14. 7 one day which shall be known to the LORD

2. *To know,* יְדַע *yeda.*
Ezra 4. 12 Be it known unto the king, that the Jews
4. 13 Be it known now unto the king, that if
5. 8 Be it known unto the king, that we went
Dan. 3. 18 But if not, be it known unto thee, O king

3. *To be known,* נָכַר *nakar,* 2.
Lam. 4. 8 They are not known in the streets: their

4. *To make self known,* נָכַר *nakar,* 7.
Prov 20. 11 Even a child is known by his doings, whe.

KNOWN, to be fully —
To bear or carry fully, πληροφορέω *plērophoreō.*
2 Ti. 4. 17 by me the preaching might be fully known

KNOWN, to be made —
To make self known again, ἀναγνωρίζομαι *anagnō.*
Acts 7. 13 Joseph was made known to his brethren

KNOWN, to make (to be) —
1. *To cause to know,* יָדַע *yada,* 5.
1 Sa. 28. 15 that thou mayest make known unto me
1 Ch. 16. 8 make known his deeds among the people
17. 19 in making known all (these) great things
Neh. 9. 14 madest known unto them thy holy sabbath
Psa. 78. 5 that they should make them known to
89. 1 with my mouth will I make known thy
98. 2 LORD hath made known his salvation: his
103. 7 He made known his ways unto Moses, his
105. 1 make known his deeds among the people
106. 8 that he might make his..power to be kn.
145. 12 To make known to the sons of men his
Prov. 1. 23 Turn..I will make known my words unto
22. 19 I have made known to thee this day, even
Isa. 38. 19 the father to the children shall make kn.
64. 2 to make thy name known to thine adver.
Eze. 39. 7 So will I make my holy name known in
Hos. 5. 9 among the tribes of Israel have I made kn.
Hab. 3. 2 in the midst of the years make known; in

2. *To cause to know,* יְדַע *yeda,* 5.
Dan. 2. 5, 9 if ye will not make known unto me the
2. 15 Then Arioch made the thing known to D.
2. 17 and made the thing known to Hananiah
2. 23 hast made known unto me now what we
2. 23 thou hast..made known unto us the king's
2. 25 will make known unto the king the inter.
2. 26 Art..able to make known unto me the d.
2. 28 maketh known to the king Nebuchadne.
2. 29 he that revealeth secrets maketh known
2. 30 that shall make known the interpretation
2. 45 the great God hath made known to the k.
4. 6, 7, 18 make known unto me the interpre.
5. 8 nor make known to the king the interpr.
5. 15, 16 make known unto me the interpreta.
5. 17 and make known to him the interpretat.

3. *To make known,* γνωρίζω *gnōrizō.*
Luke 2. 15 which the Lord hath made known unto
John 15. 15 for all things..I have made known unto
Acts 2. 28 Thou hast made known to me the ways of
Rom. 9. 22 if God, willing..to make his power known
9. 23 that he might make known the riches of
16. 26 made known to all the nations for the ob.
Eph. 1. 9 Having made known unto us the mystery
3. 3 How that by revelation he made known
3. 5 Which in other ages was not made known
3. 10 might be known by the church the mani
6. 19 to make known the mystery of the gospel
6. 21 Tychicus..shall make known to you all
Phil. 4. 6 let your requests be made known unto God
Col. 1. 27 To whom God would make known what
4. 9 They..make known unto you all things
2 Pe. 1. 16 when we made known unto you the power

KNOWN abroad, to make —
To make known throughout, thoroughly, διαγνωρίζω.
Luke 2. 17 they made known abroad the saying which

KNOWN, which may be —
That which may be known, τὸ γνωστόν *to gnōston.*
Rom. 1. 19 Because that which may be known of God

KNOWN, to make self —
1. *To be or become known,* יָדַע *yada,* 2.
Ruth 3. 3 make not thyself known unto the man, un.
Eze. 20. 5 made myself known unto them in the land
20. 9 in whose sight I made myself known unto
35. 11 I will make myself known among them

2. *To make self known,* יָדַע *yada,* 7.
Gen. 45. 1 while Joseph made himself known unto
Num 12. 6 LORD will make myself known unto him

KO'-A, קוֹעַ.
A people dwelling between Egypt and Syria, named among others as enemies of Jerusalem.
Eze. 23. 23 the Chaldeans, Pekod, and Shoa, and K.

KO'-HATH, קְהָת קְהָת *assembly.*
The second son of Levi, and ancestor of Moses; died aged 133. B.C. 1700.
Gen. 46. 11 sons of Levi; Gershon, K., and Merari
Exod. 6. 16 sons of Levi..Gershon, and K., and Mer.
6. 18 the sons of K.; Amram, and Izhar, and
6. 18 years of the life of K. (were) an hundred
Num. 3. 17 by their names; Gershon, and K., and M.
3. 19 the sons of K. by their families; Amram
3. 27 of K. (was) the family of the Amramites
3. 29 The families of the sons of K. shall pitch
4. 2 Take the sum of the sons of K. from am
Num. 4. 4 service of the sons of K. in the tabernacle
4. 15 the sons of K. shall come to bear (it): but
4. 15 burden of the sons of K. in the tabernacle
7. 9 unto the sons of K. he gave none; because
16. 1 the son of K., the son of Levi, and Dathan
26. 57 of K., the family of the Kohathites: of M.
26. 58 These (are) the families..And K. begat
Josh. 21. 5 the rest of the children of K. (had) by lot
21. 20 the families of the children of K., the
21. 20 which remained of the children of K.
21. 26 of the children of K. that remained
1 Ch. 6. 1, 16 The sons of Levi; Gershon, K., and Me.
6. 2 the sons of K.; Amram, Izhar, and Heb.
6. 18 the sons of K. (were) Gershom
6. 22 The sons of K.; Amminadab his son, Ko.
6. 38 the son of K., the son of Levi, the son of
6. 61 unto the sons of K., (which were) left of
6. 66 residue) of the families of the sons of K.
6. 70 family of the remnant of the sons of K.
15. 5 Of the sons of K.; Uriel the chief, and his
23. 6 sons of Levi, (namely), Gershon, K., and
23. 12 sons of K.; Amram, Izhar, Hebron, and

KO-HATH-ITES, קְהָתִי, קְהָתִי *belonging to Kohath.*
The descendants of Kohath, son of Levi.
Num. 3. 27 these (are) the families of the K.
3. 30 of the father of the families of the K.
4. 18 the tribe of the families of the K.
4. 34 the sons of the K. after their families
4. 37 were numbered of the families of the K.
10. 21 the K. set forward, bearing the sanctuary
26. 57 Kohath, the family of the K.: of Merari
Josh 21. 4 lot came out for the families of the K.
21. 10 (being) of the families of the K., (who were)
1 Ch. 6. 33 of the sons of the K.; Heman a singer, the
6. 54 sons of Aaron, of the families of the K.
9. 32 of their brethren, of the sons of the K.
2 Ch. 20. 19 the Levites, of the children of the K., and
29. 12 of the sons of the K.: and of the sons of
34. 12 of the sons of the K., to set (it) forward

KO-LA-I'AH, קוֹלָיָה *voice of Jah.*
1. A Benjamite, some of whose descendants dwelt in Jerusalem after the exile. B.C. 550.
Neh. 11. 7 the son of Pedaiah the son of K., the son
2. Father of Ahab who suffered death for falsely prophesying the deliverance of the Jews from Babylon. B.C. 636.
Jer. 29. 21 of Ahab the son of K., and of Zedekiah

KO'-RAH, קֹרַח *baldness.*
1. A son of Esau by Aholibamah. B.C. 1780.
Gen. 36. 5 Aholibamah bare Jeush, and..K.: these
36. 14 bare to Esau Jeush, and Jaalam, and K.
36. 18 duke Jeush, duke Jaalam, duke K.: these
1 Ch. 1. 35 sons of Esau; Eliphaz..Jaalam, and K.
2. A son of Eliphaz the son of Esau. B.C. 1740.
Gen. 36. 16 Duke K., duke Gatam, (and) duke Amalek
3. The son of Izhar the grandson of Levi; he conspired with Dathan and Abiram against Moses and Aaron. B.C. 1471.
Exod. 6. 21 the sons of Izhar; K., and Nepheg, and
6. 24 sons of K.; Assir, and Elkanah, and Abi.
Num 16. 1 Now K., the son of Izhar, the son of Ko.
16. 5 spake unto K., and unto all his company
16. 6 Take you censers, K., and all his company
16. 8 Moses said unto K., Hear, I pray you, ye
16. 16 Moses said unto K., Be thou and all thy
16. 19 K. gathered all the congregation against
16. 24 Get you up from about the tabernacle of K.
16. 27 So they gat up from the tabernacle of K.
16. 32 all the men that (appertained) unto K.
16. 40 that he be not as K., and as his company
16. 49 them that died about the matter of K.
26. 9 and against Aaron in the company of K.
26. 10 and swallowed them up together with K.
26. 11 Notwithstanding the children of K. died
27. 3 against the LORD in the company of K.
1 Ch. 6. 37 of Assir, the son of Ebiasaph, the son of K.
9. 19 of Kore, the son of Ebiasaph, the son of K.
4. A son of Hebron, son of Mareshah, son of Caleb, son of Hezron. B.C. 1560.
1 Ch. 2. 43 the sons of Hebron; K., and Tappuah, and
5. A grandson of Kohath son of Levi; ancestor of some of the sacred musicians. B.C. 1015.
1 Ch. 6. 22. The sons of Kohath..K. his son, Assir his
Psa. 42. 45. *title.* To the chief musician..sons of K.
44. 46. *title.* To the chief musician..sons of K.
47. 49. 84. 85. *title.* Psalm for the sons of K.
48. *title.* A song (and) Psalm for the sons of K.
87. 88. *title.* A Psalm (or) song for the sons of K.

KO'-RE, קוֹרֵא *crier, reader.*
1. A Korahite whose son Shallum was a gate keeper at the tabernacle. B.C. 1015.
1 Ch. 9. 19 Shallum the son of K., the son of Ebiasaph
26. 1 Meshelemiah the son of K., of the sons of
26. 19 of the porters among the sons of K., and
2. A Levite set over the free will offerings in Hezekiah's reign. B.C. 720.
2 Ch. 31. 14 K. the son of Imnah the Levite, the por.

KOR-HITES, KO-RA-THITES, KO-RA-HITES, קָרְחִי.
Descendants of Korah, the grandson of Kohath; eleven Psalms are ascribed to them. B.C. 1475-1000.
Exod 6. 24 Abiasaph: these (are) the families of the K.
Num 26. 58 of the Mushites, the family of the K. And
1 Ch. 9. 19 the K., (were) over the work of the service
9. 31 who (was) the first born of Shallum the K.
12. 6 Azareel..Joezer, and Jashobeam, the K.

1 Ch.26. 1 Of the K. (was) Meshelemiah..son of Ko.
2 Ch.20. 19 of the children of the K., stood up to pr.

KOZ, הַקּוֹץ *the thorn.*

1. A priest whose descendants returned from exile with Zerubbabel, but lost their position through being unable to prove their descent. B.C. 1015.
Ezra 2. 61 children of K., the children of Barzillai
Neh. 7. 63 children of K., the children of Barzillai

2. Ancestor of Meremoth, who repaired portions of the wall of Jerusalem in Nehemiah's time. B.C. 1430.
Neh. 3. 4, 21 Meremoth..son of Urijah..son of K.

KU-SHA-I'AH, קוּשָׁיָהוּ *bow of Jah.*

A Merarite, called *Kishi* in 1 Ch. 4. 44; father of a chief singer in David's reign. B.C. 1015.
1 Ch. 15. 17 the sons of Merari..Ethan the son of K.

L

LA-A'-DAH, לַעְדָּה *set time, festival.*

Son of Shelah, the son of Judah. B.C. 1400.
1 Ch. 4. 21 L., the father of Mareshah, and the fami.

LA-A'-DAN, לַעְדָּן *festive-born.*

1. A descendant of Ephraim through his son Beriah. B.C. 1540.
1 Ch. 7. 26 L. his son, Ammihud his son, Elishama his

2. A descendant of Gershon the son of Levi. B.C. 1015.
1 Ch.23. 7 Of the Gershonites (were) L. and Shimei
23. 8 The sons of L.; the chief (was) Jehiel, and
23. 9 These (were) the chief of the fathers of L.
26. 21 (As concerning) the sons of L.; the sons of
26. 21 Gershonite L., chief fathers, (even) of L.

LA'-BAN, לָבָן *white, glorious.*

1. Son of Bethuel, brother of Rebekah, and father of Rachel and Leah. B.C 1740.
Gen. 24. 29 his name (was) L.: and L. ran out unto
24. 50 L. and Bethuel answered and said, The
25. 20 took Rebekah..the sister to L. the Syrian
27. 43 arise, flee thou to L. my brother to Haran
28. 2 the daughters of L. thy mother's brother
28. 5 went to Padan-aram unto L., son of Bet.
29. 5 said unto them, Know ye L. the son of N.?
29. 10 the daughter of L. his mother's brother
29. 10 the sheep of L. his mother's brother, that
29. 10 watered..flock of L. his mother's brother
29. 13 L. heard the tidings of Jacob his sister's
29. 13 And he told L. all these things
29. 14 L. said to him, Surely thou (art) my bone
29. 15 L. said unto Jacob, Because thou (art) my
29. 16 L. had two daughters: the name of the el.
29. 19 L. said, (It is) better that I give her to
29. 21 Jacob said unto L., Give (me) my wife, for
29. 22 L. gathered together all the men of the
29. 24 L. gave unto his daughter Leah Zilpah his
29. 25 he said to L., What (is) this thou hast done
29. 26 And L. said, It must not be so done in our
29. 29 L. gave to Rachel his daughter Bilhah his
30. 25 Jacob said unto L., Send me away, that I
30. 27 L. said unto him, I pray thee, if I have
30. 34 L. said, Behold, I would it might be acco.
30. 36 and Jacob fed the rest of L.'s flocks
30. 40 toward..all the brown in the flock of L.
30. 40 and he put his own flocks..not unto L.'s
30. 42 so the feebler were L.'s, and the stronger
31. 1 heard the word of L.'s sons, saying, Jacob
31. 2 Jacob beheld the countenance of L., and
31. 12 for I have seen all that L. doeth unto thee
31. 19 L. went to shear his sheep: and Rachel
31. 20 Jacob stole away unawares to L. the Syr.
31. 22 it was told L. on the third day that Jacob
31. 24 God came to L. the Syrian in a dream by
31. 25 Then L. overtook Jacob..and L. with his
31. 26 L. said to Jacob, What hast thou done
31. 31 Jacob answered and said to L., Because I
31. 33 L. went into Jacob's tent, and into Leah's
31. 34 L. searched all the tent, but found (them)
31. 36 chode with L.: and Jacob..said to L., What
31. 43 L. answered and said unto Jacob, (These)
31. 47 L. called it Jegar-saha-dutha: but Jacob
31. 48 L. said, This heap (is) a witness between
31. 51 L. said to Jacob, Behold this heap, and
31. 55 L. rose up..and L. departed, and returned
32. 4 I have sojourned with L., and stayed there
46. 18 sons of Zilpah, whom L. gave to Leah his
46. 25 which L. gave unto Rachel his daughter

2. One of the stations of the Israelites after crossing the Red Sea; perhaps the same as *Libnah.*
Deut. 1. 1 between Paran, and Tophel, and L., and

LABOUR —

1. *Labour, weariness,* יְגִיעַ *yegia.*
Gen. 31. 42 God hath seen mine affliction and the lab.
Deut.28. 33 The fruit of thy land, and all thy labours
Neh. 5. 13 from his house, and from his labour, that
Job 39. 11 Wilt thou trust..wilt thou leave thy lab.
39. 16 hardened..her labour is in vain without
Psa. 78. 46 He gave also..their labour unto the locust
109. 11 catch all..and let the strangers spoil his l.
128. 2 For thou shalt eat the labour of thine h.
Isa. 45. 14 The labour of Egypt, and merchandise of
55. 2 your labour for (that which) satisfieth not?
Jer. 3. 24 shame hath devoured the labour of our
20. 5 all the labours thereof, and all the prec.
Eze. 23. 29 shall take away all thy labour, and shall
Hos. 12. 8 (in) all my labours they shall find none
Hag. 1. 11 I called for a drought..upon all the labour

2. *The hand,* יָד *yad.*
Prov13. 11 he that gathereth by labour shall increase

3. *To bear a child,* יָלַד *yalad.*
Gen. 35. 16 Rachel travailed, and she had hard labour
35. 17 when she was in hard labour, that the

4. *Work,* מְלָאכָה *melakah.*
Neh. 4. 22 may be a guard to us, and labour on the

5. *Doing, deed,* מַעֲשֶׂה *maaseh.*
Exod23. 16 the first fruits of thy labours, which thou
23. 16 when thou hast gathered in thy labours
Hab. 3. 17 the labour of the olive shall fail, and the
Hag. 2. 17 with hail in all the labours of your hands

6. *Service, tillage,* עֲבֹדָה *abodah.*
Psa.104. 23 Man goeth forth..to his labour until the

7. *Labour, perverseness, misery,* עָמָל *amal.*
Deut26. 7 looked on our affliction, and our labour
Psa. 90. 10 yet (is) their strength labour and sorrow
105. 44 and they inherited the labour of the peo.
107. 12 he brought down their heart with labour
Eccl. 1. 3 What profit hath a man of all his labour
2. 10 for my heart rejoiced in all my labour
2. 10 and this was my portion of all my labour
2. 11 on the labour that I had laboured to do
2. 18 I hated all my labour which I had taken
2. 19 yet shall he have rule over all my labour
2. 20 cause my heart to despair of all the labour
2. 21 a man whose labour (is) in wisdom, and in
2. 22 For what hath man of all his labour, and
2. 24 make his soul enjoy good in his labour
3. 13 man should..enjoy the good of all his lab
4. 8 (is there) no end of all his labour; neither
4. 9 they have a good reward for their labour
5. 15 shall take nothing of his labour, which he
5. 19 to rejoice in his labour: this (is) the gift
5. 18 to enjoy the good of all his labour that he
6. 7 All the labour of man (is) for his mouth
8. 15 that shall abide with him of his labour
9. 9 in thy labour which thou takest under the
10. 15 The labour of the foolish wearieth every
Jer. 20. 18 I forth out of the womb to see labour and

8. *Grievous burden, one grieved,* עָצֵב *atseb.*
Isa. 58. 3 find pleasure, and exact all your labours

9. *Grievous burden,* עֶצֶב *etseb.*
Prov. 5. 10 Lest..thy labours (be) in the house of a
14. 23 In all labour there is profit: but the talk

10. *Act, work, doing, deed,* פְּעֻלָּה *peullah.*
Prov 10. 16 The labour of the righteous (tendeth) to
Eze. 29. 20 his labour wherewith he served against it

11. *Work,* ἔργον *ergon.*
Phil. 1. 22 this (is) the fruit of my labour: yet what

12. *A beating, wearying out work,* κόπος *kopos.*
John 4. 38 men..ye are entered into their labours
1 Co. 3. 8 own reward, according to his own labour
15. 58 that your labour is not in vain in the Lord
2 Co. 6. 5 in tumults, in labours, in watchings, in
10. 15 of other men's labours; but having hope
11. 23 in labours more abundant, in stripes
1 Th. 1. 3 labour of love, and patience of hope in
2. 9 For ye remember, brethren, our labour
3. 5 have tempted you, and our labour be in
2 Th. 3. 8 wrought with labour and travail night and
Heb. 6. 10 your work and [labour] of love, which ye
Rev. 2. 2 I know thy works, and thy labour, and
14. 13 they may rest from their labours; and their
[*See also* Companion in.]

LABOUR, to—

1. *To press, hasten,* אוּץ *uts,* 5.
Isa 22. 4 labour not to comfort me, because of the

2. *To labour, be weary, fatigued,* יָגַע *yaga.*
Josh.24. 13 a land for which ye did not labour, and
Job 9. 29 (If) I be wicked, why then labour I in
Prov 23. 4 Labour not to be rich; cease from thine
Isa 47. 12 sorceries, wherein thou hast laboured
47. 15 they be..with whom thou hast laboured
49. 4 I have laboured in vain, I have spent my
62. 8 thy wine, for the which thou hast laboured
65. 23 They shall not labour in vain, nor bring
Jer. 51. 58 the people shall labour in vain, and the
Lam. 5. 5 necks (are) under persecution; we labour
Hab. 2. 13 that the people shall labour in the very

3. *To do, serve,* עָבַד *abad.*
Exod20. 9 Six days shalt thou labour and do all thy
Deut. 5. 13 Six days thou shalt labour, and do all thy

4. *To labour,* עָמַל *amal.*
Psa.127. 1 they labour in vain that build it: except
Prov.16. 26 He that laboureth, laboureth for himself
Eccl. 2. 11 on the labour that I had laboured to do
2. 19 over all my labour wherein I have labou.
2. 21 yet to a man that hath not laboured the.
5. 16 what profit hath he that hath laboured
8. 17 though a man labour to seek (it) out, yet
Jon. 4. 10 the gourd, for the which thou hast not l.

5. *Labouring,* עָמֵל *amel.*
Eccl. 2. 22 wherein he hath laboured under the sun?
4. 8 For whom do I labour, and bereave my

6. *To do, make,* עָשָׂה *asah.*
Exod. 5. 9 more work..that they may labour therein
Neh. 4. 21 So we laboured in the work: and half of
Prov.21. 25 killeth him; for his hands refuse to labour

7. *To endeavour,* שְׁדַר *shedar,* 4.
Dan. 6. 14 he laboured till the going down of the sun

8. *To labour, be wearied out,* κοπιάω *kopiaō.*
Matt11. 28 Come unto me, all (ye) that labour and
John 4. 38 other men laboured, and ye are entered
Acts 20. 35 how that so labouring ye ought to support
Rom.16. 12 Salute Tryphena and Tryphosa, who lab.
16. 12 Persis, which laboured much in the Lord
1 Co. 4. 12 And labour, working with our own hands
15. 10 I laboured more abundantly than they all
16. 16 to every one that helpeth with (us), and lab.
Eph. 4. 28 but rather let him labour, working with
Phil. 2. 16 not run in vain, neither laboured in vain
Col. 1. 29 Whereunto I also labour, striving accord.
1 Th. 5. 12 to know them which labour among you
1 Ti. 4. 10 therefore we both labour and suffer repr.
5. 17 especially they who labour in the word
2 Ti. 2. 6 The husbandman that laboureth must be
Rev. 2. 3 for my name's sake hast laboured, and

9. *To make haste, speed,* σπουδάζω *spoudazō.*
Heb. 4. 11 Let us labour therefore to enter into that

10. *To esteem as an honour,* φιλοτιμέομαι *philotim.*
2 Co. 5. 9 we labour, that, whether present or absent
[*See also* Bring forth.]

LABOUR, to bestow —

To labour, be wearied out, κοπιάω *kopiaō.*
John 4. 38 to reap that whereon ye bestowed no lab.
Rom16. 6 Greet Mary, who bestowed much labour
Gal. 4. 11 lest I have bestowed upon you labour in v.

LABOUR fervently, to —

To agonize, contend, wrestle, ἀγωνίζομαι *agōnizomai.*
Col. 4. 12 always labouring fervently for you in pr.

LABOUR for, labouring, to —

To work, ἐργάζομαι *ergazomai.*
John 6. 27 Labour not for the meat which perisheth
1 Th. 2. 9 labouring night and day, because we wo.

LABOUR with, to —

To strive along with any one, συναθλέω *sunathleō.*
Phil. 4. 3 help those women which laboured with

LABOUR, full of —

Labouring, weary, יָגֵעַ *yagea.*
Eccl. 1. 8 All things (are) full of labour; man can.

LABOUR, to make to —

To weary, make weary, יָגַע *yaga,* 3.
Josh. 7. 3 make not all the people to labour thither

LABOUR, strong to —

To be borne, carried, set up, סָבַל *sabal,* 4.
Psa 144. 14 (That) our oxen (may be) strong to labour

LABOURED for, that which he —

What is got by labour, יְגַע *yaga.*
Job 20. 18 That which he laboured for shall he res.

LABOURER (fellow) —

A worker, ἐργάτης *ergatēs.*
Matt. 9. 37 harvest truly (is) plenteous, but the lab.
9. 38 he will send forth labourers into his har.
20. 1 went out early in the morning to hire lab.
20. 2 when he had agreed with the labourers for
20. 8 Call the labourers, and give them (their)
Luke10. 2 but the labourers (are) few: pray ye the.
10. 2 would send forth labourers into his harv.
10. 7; 1 Ti. 5. 18; Jas. 5. 4.

Joint-worker, συνεργός *sunergos.*
Phil. 4. 3; 1 Th. 3. 2; Phm. 1, 24.

LABOURER together with —

A worker together, συνεργός *sunergos.*
1 Co. 3. 9 we are labourers together with God: ye

LABOURETH, that —

Labouring, עָמֵל *amel.*
Prov 16. 26 He that laboureth, laboureth for himself
Eccl. 3. 9 he that worketh in that wherein he labo.

LABOURING man —

To do, serve, עָבַד *abad.*
Eccl. 5. 12 The sleep of a labouring man (is) sweet

LACE —

Ribbon, thread, wire, פָּתִיל *pathil.*
Exod28. 28 unto the rings of the ephod with a lace of
28. 37 thou shalt put it on a blue lace, that it
39. 21 unto the rings of the ephod with a lace of
39. 31 they tied unto it a lace of blue, to fasten

LA'-CHISH, לָכִישׁ *height.*

The name survived in *Um Lakhis,* and the site of the ancient Amorite city has been securely identified by recent exploration at Tell-el-Hesy near by.
Josh10. 3 king of Jerusalem sent unto..king of L.
10. 5 king of L., the king of Eglon, gathered
10. 23 brought forth..out of the cave..king of L.
10. 31 Joshua passed..unto L., and encamped
10. 32 LORD delivered L. into the hand of Israel
10. 33 Horam king of Gezar came up to help L.
10. 34 from L. Joshua passed unto Eglon, and
10. 35 according to all that he had done to L.
12. 11 king of Jarmuth, one; the king of L., one
15.39 L., and Bozkath, and Eglon
2 Ki.14. 19 fled to L.; but they sent after him to L.
18. 14 sent to the king of Assyria to L., saying, I
18. 17 king of Assyria sent..from L. to king He.
19. 8 had heard that he was departed from L.

2 Ch. 11. 9 And Adoraim, and L., and Azekah
25. 27 he fled to L.: but they sent to L. after him
32. 9 but he (himself laid siege) against L., and
Neh. 11. 30 and (in) their villages, at L., and the fields
Isa. 36. 2 sent Rabshakeh from L. to Jerusalem, unto
37. 8 had heard that he was departed from L.
Jer. 34. 7 king of Babylon's army fought..against L.
Mic. 1. 13 O thou inhabitant of L., bind the chariot

LACK —
1. *Need, want, lack,* מַחְסוֹר *machsor.*
Prov. 28. 27 He that giveth unto..poor shall not lack
2. *The thing lacking,* ὑστέρημα *husterēma.*
Phil. 2. 30 to supply your lack of service toward me
3. *Necessity,* χρεία *chreia.*
1 Th. 4. 12 honestly..and (that) ye may have lack of

LACK, to —
1. *To abate, be lacking,* חָסֵר *chaser.*
Gen. 18. 28 Peradventure there shall lack five of the
Deut. 2. 7 these forty years..thou hast lacked noth.
8. 9 thou shalt not lack any (thing) in it; a
Neh. 9. 21 they lacked nothing; their clothes waxed
Eccl. 9. 8 white: and let thy head lack no ointment
2. *Lacking,* חָסֵר *chaser.*
2 Sa. 3. 29 or that is a leper..or that lacketh bread
1 Ki. 11. 22 But what hast thou lacked with me, that
Prov. 6. 32 whoso committeth adultery..lacketh un.
12. 9 that honoureth himself, and lacketh bread
3. *To be lacking,* עָדַר *adar,* 2.
2 Sa. 17. 22 by the morning light there lacked not one
4. *To let be lacking,* עָדַר *adar,* 3.
1 Ki. 4. 27 officers provided victual..they lacked
5. *To be visited, missed,* פָּקַד *paqad,* 2.
Num 31. 49 men of war..there lacketh not one man
Judg 21. 3 should be to day one tribe lacking in Israel?
2 Sa. 2. 30 there lacked of David's servants nineteen
Jer. 23. 4 neither shall they be lacking, saith the L.
6. *To be poor, impoverished,* רוּשׁ *rush.*
Psa. 34. 10 The young lions do lack, and suffer hun.
7. *In want,* ἐνδεής *endeēs.*
Acts 4. 34 Neither was there any..that lacked: for
8. *Not to have,* μὴ ἔχω *mē echō.*
Luke 8. 6 withered away, because it lacked moisture
9. *To leave,* λείπω *leipō.*
Luke 18. 22 Yet lackest thou one thing: sell all that
Jas. 1. 5 If any of you lack wisdom, let him ask
10. *Not to be near one,* μὴ πάρειμι *mē pareimi.*
2 Pe. 1. 9 But he that lacketh these things is blind
11. *To be last, behind,* ὑστερέω *hustereō.*
Matt 19. 20 have I kept my youth up: what lack I
Mark 10. 21 One thing thou lackest: go thy way, sell
Luke 22. 35 lacked ye anything? And they said, Not.
1 Co. 12. 24 abundant honour to that (part) which la.

LACK, to have —
1. *To suffer lack,* חָסֵר *chaser,* 5.
Exod 16. 18 he that gathered little had no lack: they
2. *To make less,* ἐλαττονέω *elattoneō.*
2 Co. 8. 15 he that (had gathered) little had no lack

LACK of, for —
For or from deficiency of, לִבְלִי, מִבְּלִי *li-beli, mib-beli.*
Job 4. 11 The old lion perisheth for lack of prey
38. 41 young ones..they wander for lack of meat
[*See also* Opportunity.]

LACKING, to be —
1. *To be lacking,* עָדַר *adar,* 2.
1 Sa. 30. 19 there was nothing lacking to them, nei.
2. *The thing lacking,* ὑστέρημα *husterēma.*
1 Co. 16. 17 that which was lacking on your part they
2 Co. 11. 9 that which was lacking to me the brethren
1 Th. 3. 10 might perfect that which is lacking in

LACKING in his parts —
To be contracted, קָלַט *qalat.*
Lev. 22. 23 that hath..superfluous or lacking in his p.

LACKING, to suffer to be —
To cause or suffer to cease, שָׁבַת *shabath,* 5.
Lev. 2. 13 suffer the salt..to be lacking from thy meat

LAD —
1. *A young person, child, lad, servant,* נַעַר *naar.*
Gen. 21. 12 be grievous in thy sight because of the lad
21. 17 And God heard the voice of the lad; and
21. 17 God hath heard the voice of the lad where
21. 18 Arise, lift up the lad, and hold him in
21. 19 and filled the bottle..and gave the lad d.
21. 20 God was with the lad; and he grew, and
22. 5 I and the lad will go yonder and worship
22. 12 Lay not thine hand upon the lad, neither
37. 2 the lad (was) with the sons of Bilhah, and
43. 8 Send the lad with me, and we will arise
44. 22 The lad cannot leave his father: for (if)
44. 30 and the lad (be) not with us; seeing that
44. 31 when he seeth that the lad (is) not (with
44. 32 thy servant became surety for the lad unto
44. 33 let thy servant abide instead of the lad a
44. 33 and let the lad go up with his brethren
44. 34 and the lad (be) not with me? lest pera.
48. 16 The angel..bless the lads; and let my
Judg 16. 26 Samson said unto the lad that held him
1 Sa. 20. 21 And, behold, I will send a lad, (saying)
1 Sa. 20. 21 If I expressly say unto the lad, Behold
20. 35 Jonathan went out..and a little lad with
20. 36 he said unto his lad, Run, find out now
20. 36 as the lad ran, he shot an arrow beyond
20. 37 when the lad was come to the place of the
20. 37 Jonathan cried after the lad, and said, (Is)
20. 38 Jonathan cried after the lad, Make speed
20. 38 Jonathan's lad gathered up the arrows, and
20. 39 the lad knew not anything: only Jona.
20. 40 Jonathan gave his artillery unto his lad
20. 41 as soon as the lad was gone, David arose
2 Sa. 17. 18 Nevertheless a lad saw them, and told A.
2 Ki. 4. 19 he said to a lad, Carry him to his mother
2. *A little boy,* παιδάριον *paidarion.*
John 6. 9 There is a lad here, which hath five barley

LADDER —
A ladder, סֻלָּם *sullam.*
Gen. 28. 12 he dreamed, and behold a ladder set up

LADE, LOAD (with), to —
1. *To load,* טָעַן *taan.*
Gen. 45. 17 This do ye; lade your beasts, and go, get
2. *To make heavy, weighty,* כָּבַד *kabed,* 5.
Hab. 2. 6 to him that ladeth himself with thick clay
3. *To lift up on,* נָשָׂא עַל *nasa al.*
Gen. 42. 26 they laded their asses with the corn, and
4. *To lay on, load,* עָמַס *amas.*
Gen. 44. 13 laded every man his ass, and returned to
Neh. 13. 15 and bringing in sheaves, and lading asses
Psa. 68. 19 Blessed (be) the LORD, (who) daily loadeth
Isa. 46. 1 your carriages (were) heavy loaden..a bur.
5. *To lay on, load,* עָמַס *amas,* 5.
1 Ki. 12. 11 now whereas my father did lade you with
6. *To put on or upon,* ἐπιτίθημι *epitithēmi.*
Acts 28. 10 they laded (us) with such things as were
7. *To burden,* φορτίζω *phortizō.*
Luke 11. 46 ye lade men with burdens grievous to be

LADED —
To load, lay on, עָמַשׂ *amas.*
Neh. 4. 17 that bare burdens, with those that laded

LADEN —
1. *Heavy, weighty,* כָּבֵד *kabed.*
Isa. 1. 4 Ah sinful nation, a people laden with ini.
2. *To lift up, bear,* נָשָׂא *nasa.*
Gen. 45. 23 ten asses laden..ten she asses laden with
3. *To heap up,* σωρεύω *sōreuō.*
2 Ti. 3. 6 lead captive silly women laden with sins

LADEN, to be heavy —
To burden, φορτίζω *phortizō.*
Matt. 11. 28 all (ye) that labour and are heavy laden

LADING —
What is borne, burden, φόρτος *phortos.*
Acts 27. 10 not only of [the lading] and ship, but also

LADY —
1. *Mistress,* גְּבֶרֶת *gebereth.*
Isa. 47. 5 thou shalt no more be called, The lady of
47. 7 And thou saidst, I shall be a lady for ever
2. *Princess,* שָׂרָה *sarah.*
Judg. 5. 29 Her wise ladies answered her, yea, she
Esth. 1. 18 shall the ladies of Persia and Media say
3. *Lady,* κυρία *kuria.*
2 John 1 The Elder unto the elect lady and her ch.
5 now I beseech thee, lady, not as though I

LA'-EL, לָאֵל *God-ward.*
A Levite of the family of Gershon. B.C. 1510.
Num. 3. 24 the chief..(shall be) Eliasaph the son of L.

LA'-HAD, לַהַד *dark coloured.*
Great grandson of Shobal the son of Judah. B.C. 1600.
1 Ch. 4. 2 and Jahath begat Ahumai, and L. These

LA-HAI-RO'I, לַחַי רֹאִי *of the Living one who beholds me.*
A well or fountain in the wilderness of Paran, between Kadesh and Bered. [*See also* Beer-Lahai-roi, Gen. 16. 14.]
Gen. 24. 62 Isaac came from the way of the well L.
25. 11 blessed..and Isaac dwelt by the well L.

LAH'-MAM (לַחְמָם) לַחְמָס *place of light.*
A city of Judah. Most Heb. MSS. have *Lahmas.*
Josh. 15. 40 And Cabbon, and L., and Kithlish

LAH'-MI, לַחְמִי *Bethlehemite.*
A brother of Goliath, slain by Elhanan. B.C. 1020.
1 Ch. 20. 5 Elhanan the son of Jair slew L. the brot.

LAID —
1. *To put, place,* שׂוּם *sum.*
Dan. 6. 17 a stone was brought, and laid upon the
2. *To be caused to be laid down,* שָׁכַב *shakab,* 6.
2 Ki. 4. 32 the child was dead, (and) laid upon his bed
[*See also* Desolate, waste.]

LAID, to be —
1. *To go in,* בּוֹא *bo.*
Psa. 105. 18 they hurt with fetters: he was laid in iron
2. *To lift up, bear,* נָשָׂא *nasa.*
1 Ki. 8. 31 an oath be laid upon him to cause him to
2 Ch. 6. 22 an oath be laid upon him to make him s.
Job 6. 2 were..my calamity laid in the balances
3. *To be given,* נָתַן *nathan,* 2.
Eze. 32. 29 her princes, which with their might are laid
4. *To go up,* עָלָה *alah.*
Psa. 62. 9 to be laid in the balance, they (are) alto.
5. *To put, place,* שׂוּם, שִׂים *sum, sim.*
Judg 9. 24 and their blood be laid upon Abimelech
6. *To be put, placed,* שׂוּם, שִׂים *sum, sim,* 2.
Ezra 5. 8 timber is laid in the walls, and this work
7. *To set, put, place,* שִׁית *shith,* 6.
Exod 21. 30 If there be laid on him a sum of money
21. 30 shall give..whatsoever is laid upon him
8. *To be caused to lie down,* שָׁכַב *shakab,* 6.
Eze. 32. 19 go down, and be thou laid with the unc.
32. 32 he shall be laid in the midst of the uncir.
9. *To be set, put,* שָׁתַת *shathath.*
Psa. 49. 14 Like sheep they are laid in the grave
10. *To be laid, to lie,* κεῖμαι *keimai.*
Matt. 3. 10 now also the ax is laid unto the root of
Luke 3. 9 now also the ax is laid unto the root of
23. 53 sepulchre..wherein never man..was laid
24. 12 [beheld the linen clothes laid by thems.]
John 11. 41 [(from the place) where the dead was laid]
1 Co. 3. 11 foundation can no man lay than that is l.
[*See also* Foundation.]

LAID down, to be —
To lie down, שָׁכַב *shakab.*
1 Sa. 3. 2 when Eli (was) laid down in his place, and
3. 3 And ere..Samuel was laid down (to sleep)
2 Sa. 13. 8 went to her brother..and he was laid down

LAID against, or to—[*See* Crime, charge.]

LAID, more be —
To be heavy, weighty, כָּבַד *kabed.*
Exod. 5. 9 Let there more work be laid upon the men

LAID out, to be —
To go out, יָצָא *yatsa.*
2 Ki. 12. 12 that was laid out for the house to repair

LAID over —
To overlay, catch, capture, תָּפַשׂ *taphas.*
Hab. 2. 19 it (is) laid over with gold and silver, and

LAID strongly —
To be borne, set, סְבַל *sebal,* 3b.
Ezra 6. 3 and let the foundations..be strongly laid

LAID thereon or upon, to be —
To lie or be laid upon, ἐπίκειμαι *epikeimai.*
John 21. 9 they saw a fire..and fish laid thereon, and
1 Co. 9. 16 for necessity is laid upon me; yea, woe is

LAID up (in store), to be —
1. *To become strong or great,* חָסַן *chasan,* 2.
Isa. 23. 18 it shall not be treasured nor laid up; for
2. *To store up,* כָּמַס *kamas.*
Deut 32. 34 (Is) not this laid up in store with me, (and)
3. *To lie or be laid,* κεῖμαι *keimai.*
Luke 12. 19 Soul, thou hast much goods laid up for

LAID up, that which —
A deposit, store, פְּקֻדָּה *pequddah.*
Isa. 15. 7 that which they have laid up, shall

LAID waste, to be —
1. *To be laid waste, stripped, burnt,* נָצָה *natsah.*
Jer. 4. 7 thy cities shall be laid waste, without an
2. *To be spoiled, destroyed,* שָׁדַד *shadad,* 4.
Isa. 15. 1 Because in the night Ar of Moab is laid w.
15. 1 because in the night Kir of Moab is laid w.
23. 1 it is laid waste, so that there is no house
23. 14 Howl..for your strength is laid waste
Nah. 3. 7 Nineveh is laid waste: who will bemoan

LA'-ISH, לַיִשׁ, לָיִשׁ.
1. A Sidonian city at the N. extremity of Palestine; called also *Leshem,* Josh. 19. 47; and afterwards *Dan.*
Judg. 18. 7 five men departed, and came to L., and
18. 14 men that went to spy out the country of L.
18. 27 came unto L., unto a people (that were)
18. 29 howbeit the name of the city (was) L. at
Isa. 10. 30 cause it to be heard unto L., O poor Ana.
2. A Benjamite, whose son became the husband of Michal, David's wife. B.C. 1080.
1 Sa. 25. 44 had given Michal..to Phalti the son of L.
2 Sa. 3. 15 and took her..from Phaltiel the son of L.

LAKE —
Lake, λίμνη *limnē.*
Luke 5. 1 it came to pass..he stood by the lake of G.
5. 2 And saw two ships standing by the lake
8. 22 Let us go..unto the other side of the lake
8. 23 came down a storm of wind on the lake
8. 33 violently down a steep place into the lake
Rev. 19. 20 into a lake of fire burning with brimstone
20. 10; 20. 14; 20. 15; 21. 8.

LAMA, λαμά, λαμμᾶ, λεμά, λημά, λιμά, *Heb.* לָמָה.
Aramaic, לְמָא *why,* Matt. 27. 46; Mark 15. 34.

LA'-KUM, לַקּוּם *fortification.*
A border city in Naphtali; said to be *Capernaum* or the sea of Galilee.
Josh. 19. 33 and Adami, Nekeb, and Jabneel, unto L.

LAMB, (he and ewe) —
1. *A he lamb, tender one,* טָלֶה *taleh.*
1 Sa. 7. 9 Samuel took a sucking lamb, and offered
Isa. 65. 25 The wolf and the lamb shall feed together
2. *A he lamb,* כֶּבֶשׂ *kebes.*
Exod 29. 38 two lambs of the first year day by day
29. 39 The one lamb thou shalt offer in the mo.
29. 39 the other lamb thou shalt offer at even
29. 40 with the one lamb a tenth deal of flour m.
29. 41 the other lamb thou shalt offer at even
Lev. 4. 32 if he bring a lamb for a sin offering, he s.
9. 3 a calf and a lamb..of the first year, with.
12. 6 she shall bring a lamb of the first year for
14. 10 he shall take two he lambs without blem.
14. 12 the priest shall take one he lamb, and off.
14. 13 he shall slay the lamb in the place where
14. 21 take one lamb (for) a trespass offering to
14. 24 the priest shall take the lamb of the tres.
14. 25 he shall kill the lamb of the trespass offe.
23. 12 an he lamb without blemish of the first
23. 18 seven lambs without blemish of the first
23. 19 two lambs of the first year for a sacrifice
23. 20 with the two lambs: they shall be holy to
Num. 6. 12 a lamb of the first year for a trespass offer.
6. 14 one he lamb of the first year without ble.
7. 15 one ram, one lamb of the first year
[So in v. 21, 27, 33, 39, 45, 51, 57, 63, 69, 75, 81.]
7. 17 five he goats, five lambs of the first
[So in v. 23, 29, 35, 41, 47, 53, 59, 65, 71, 77, 83.]
7. 88 he goats sixty, the lambs of the first year
15. 5 burnt offering or sacrifice, for one lamb
28. 3 two lambs of the first year without spot
28. 4 The one lamb shalt thou offer in the mo.
28. 4 and the other lamb shalt thou offer at even
28. 7 the fourth (part) of an hin for the one lamb
28. 8 And the other lamb shalt thou offer at even
28. 9 on the sabbath day two lambs of the first
28. 11 seven lambs of the first year without spot
28. 13 oil (for) a meat offering unto one lamb
28. 14 and a fourth (part) of an hin unto a lamb
28. 19 one ram, and seven lambs of the first year
28. 21 every lamb, throughout the seven lambs
28. 27 offer..one ram, seven lambs of the first
28. 29 one lamb, throughout the seven lambs
29. 2 seven lambs of the first year, without ble.
29. 4, 10 for one lamb, throughout the seven la.
29. 8 seven lambs of the first year; they shall
29. 13, 17, 20, 23, 26, 29, 32 fourteen lambs of
29. 15 tenth deal to each lamb of the fourteen l.
29. 18, 21, 24, 27, 30, 33 the rams, and for the lambs
29. 36 seven lambs of the first year, without bl.
29. 37 the bullock, for the ram, and for the lambs
1 Ch. 29. 21 a thousand rams..a thousand lambs, with
2 Ch. 29. 21 seven rams, and seven lambs, and seven
29. 22 killed also the lambs, and they sprinkled
29. 32 an hundred rams, (and) two hundred la.
35. 7 lambs and kids, all for the passover offeri.
Ezra 8. 35 seventy and seven lambs, twelve he goats
Prov. 27. 26 The lambs (are) for thy clothing, and the
Isa. 1. 11 I delight not in the blood..of lambs, or of
5. 17 Then shall the lambs feed after their ma.
11. 6 The wolf also shall dwell with the lamb
Jer. 11. 19 But I (was) like a lamb (or) an ox (that)
Eze. 46. 4 six lambs without blemish, and a ram wi.
46. 5 the meat offering for the lambs as he shall
46. 6 bullock without blemish, and six lambs
46. 7 for the lambs according as his hands shall
46. 11 to the lambs as he is able to give, and an
46. 13 a lamb of the first year without blemish
46. 15 Thus shall they prepare the lamb, and the
Hos. 4. 16 LORD will feed them as a lamb in a large
3. *A she lamb,* כַּבְשָׂה, כִּבְשָׂה *kabsah, kibsah.*
Gen. 21. 28 Abraham set seven ewe lambs of the flock
21. 29 What..these seven ewe lambs which thou
21. 30 seven ewe lambs shalt thou take of my h.
Lev. 14. 10 one ewe lamb of the first year without b.
Num. 6. 14 one ewe lamb of the first year without b.
2 Sa. 12. 3 had nothing, save one little ewe lamb, w.
12. 4 took the poor man's lamb, and dressed it
12. 6 he shall restore the lamb fourfold, because
4. *A stout he lamb, a ram,* כַּר *kar.*
Deut 32. 14 milk of sheep, with fat of lambs, and rams
1 Sa. 15. 9 and of the fatlings, and the lambs, and all
2 Ki. 3. 4 an hundred thousand lambs, and an hun.
Psa. 37. 20 as the fat of lambs: they shall consume
Isa. 16. 1 Send ye the lamb to the ruler of the land
34. 6 with the blood of lambs and goats, with
Jer. 51. 40 I will bring them down like lambs to the
Eze. 27. 21 they occupied with thee in lambs, and rams
39. 18 of rams, of lambs..of goats, of bullocks
Amos 6. 4 and eat the lambs out of the flock, and the
5. *A he lamb,* כֶּשֶׂב *keseb.*
Gen. 30. 40 Jacob did separate the lambs, and set the
Lev. 3. 7 If he offer a lamb for his offering, then
4. 35 as the fat of the lamb is taken away from
17. 3 that killeth an ox, or lamb, or goat, in the
6. *A she lamb,* כִּשְׂבָּה *kisbah.*
Lev. 5. 6 a female from the flock, a lamb, or a kid of
7. *A sheep,* צֹאן *tson.*
Exod 12. 21 Draw out and take you a lamb according to
8. *A young lamb or kid, a sheep,* שֶׂה *seh.*
Gen. 22. 7 but where (is) the lamb for a burnt off.?
22. 8 God will provide himself a lamb for a b.
Exod 12. 3 take..every man a lamb..a lamb for an
12. 4 the household be too little for the lamb
12. 4 every..shall make your count for the lamb
12. 5 Your lamb shall be without blemish, a m.
13. 13 thou shalt redeem with a lamb; and if
Exod 34. 20 firstling..thou shalt redeem with a lamb
Lev. 5. 7 if he be not able to bring a lamb, then he
12. 8 if she be not able to bring a lamb, then
22. 23 Either a bullock or a lamb that hath any
Num 15. 11 one bullock, or for one ram, or for a lamb
1 Sa. 17. 34 there came a lion..and took a lamb out of
Isa. 53. 7 he is brought as a lamb to the slaughter
66. 3 he that sacrificeth a lamb, (as if) he cut
Eze. 45. 15 one lamb out of the flock, out of two hu.
9. *A son of the flock, a young sheep,* בֶּן־צֹאן *ben tson.*
Psa. 114. 4 like rams, (and) the little hills like lambs
114. 6 like rams; (and) ye little hills, like lambs?
10. *Lambs,* אִמְּרִין *immerin.*
Ezra 6. 9 rams, and lambs, for the burnt offerings
6. 17 two hundred rams, four hundred lambs
7. 17 buy speedily with this money..lambs, with
11. *Young or tender lambs,* טְלָאִים *telaim.*
Isa. 40. 11 he shall gather the lambs with his arm
12. *A lamb,* ἀμνός *amnos.*
John 1. 29 Behold the Lamb of God, which taketh
1. 36 looking..he saith, Behold the Lamb of G.!
Acts 8. 32 and like a lamb dumb before his shearer
1 Pe. 1. 19 as of a lamb without blemish and without
13. *A lamb,* ἀρνός *arnos (gen.)*
Luke 10. 3 Go..I send you forth as lambs among wo.
14. *A little lamb,* ἀρνίον *arnion.*
John 21. 15 I love..He saith unto him, Feed my lambs
Rev. 5. 6 stood a Lamb as it had been slain, having
5. 8 twenty elders fell down before the Lamb
5. 12 Worthy is the Lamb that was slain to rec.
5. 13 Blessing..unto the Lamb, for ever and
6. 1 And I saw when the Lamb opened one of
6. 16 and hide us..from the wrath of the Lamb
7. 9 stood before the throne, and before the L.
7. 10 Salvation to our God..and unto the Lamb
7. 14 made them white in the blood of the Lamb
7. 17 For the Lamb which is in the midst of the
12. 11 they overcame him by the blood of the L.
13. 8 written in the book of life of the Lamb
13. 11 he had two horns like a lamb, and he spake
14. 1 a Lamb stood on the mount Sion, and with
14. 4 These are they which follow the Lamb whi.
14. 4 the first fruits unto God and to the Lamb
14. 10 be tormented..in the presence of the L.
15. 3 they sing..the song of the Lamb, saying
17. 14 shall make war with the Lamb, and the La.
19. 7 the marriage of the Lamb is come, and his
19. 9 called unto the marriage supper of the L.
21. 9 I will show thee the bride, the Lamb's w.
21. 14 names of the twelve apostles of the Lamb
21. 22 God Almighty and the Lamb are the temple
21. 23 And the city..the Lamb (is) the light th.
21. 27 which are written in the Lamb's book of
22. 1 out of the throne of God and of the Lamb
22. 3 the throne of God and of the Lamb shall
[*See also* Ewe.]

LAME (man) —
1. *Smitten,* נָכֶה *nakeh.*
2 Sa. 4. 4 Saul's son, had a son..lame of (his) feet
9. 3 Jonathan hath yet a son..lame on (his)
2. *Limping,* פִּסֵּחַ *pisseach.*
Lev. 21. 18 a blind man, or a lame, or he that hath
Deut 15. 21 lame, or blind..any ill blemish, thou shalt
2 Sa. 5. 6 Except thou take away..the lame, thou
5. 8 the lame and the blind..hated of David's
5. 8 The blind and the lame shall not come into
9. 13 Mephibosheth..was lame on both his feet
19. 26 I may ride..because thy servant (is) lame
Job 29. 15 eyes to the blind, and feet..to the lame
Prov 26. 7 The legs of the lame are not equal; so (is)
Isa. 33. 23 is..spoil divided; the lame take the prey
35. 6 Then shall the lame..leap as an hart, and
Jer. 31. 8 them the blind and the lame, the woman
Mal. 1. 8 ye offer the lame and sick, (is it) not evil?
1. 13 the lame, and the sick; thus ye brought
3. *Lame, crippled,* χωλός *chōlos.*
Matt 11. 5 the lame walk, the lepers are cleansed
15. 30 lame, blind, dumb, maimed, and many
15. 31 saw..the lame to walk, and the blind to
21. 14 the blind and the lame came to him in the
Luke 7. 22 how that the blind see, the lame walk, the
14. 13 call the poor, the maimed, the lame, the
Acts 3. 2 a certain man lame from his mother's w.
8. 7 with palsies, and that were lame, were h.

LAME (man), that which is —
The lame, (τὸ) χωλός *(to) chōlos.*
Acts 3. 11 as [the lame man] which was healed held P.
Heb. 12. 13 lest that which is lame be turned out of

LAME, to become —
To become limping, פָּסַח *pasach,* 2.
2 Sa. 4. 4 haste to flee, that he fell, and became lame

LA'-MECH, לֶמֶךְ *overthrower, wild man.*
1. A descendant of Cain, by Methusael. B.C. 3130–2353.
Gen. 4. 18 begat Methusael: and Methusael begat L.
4. 19 L. took unto him two wives: the name of
4. 23 L. said unto his wives..ye wives of L., he.
4. 24 Cain shall be avenged sevenfold, truly L.
2. The son of Methuselah, and father of Noah. B.C. 3000.
Gen. 5. 25 Methuselah lived an hundr...and begat L.
5. 26 Methuselah lived after he begat L. seven
5. 28 L. lived an hundred eighty and two years
5. 30 L. lived after he begat Noah five hundred
5. 31 all the days of L. were seven hundred se.
1 Ch. 1. 3 Henoch, Methuselah, L.
Luke 3. 36 (the son) of Noe, which was (the son) of L.

LAMENT, to —
1. *To mourn, be moist,* אָבַל *abal.*
Isa. 19. 8 all they that cast angle..shall lament, and
2. *To show self a mourner,* אָבַל *abal,* 7.
1 Sa. 6. 19 the people lamented, because the LORD
3. *To wail,* אָלָה *alah.*
Joel 1. 8 Lament like a virgin girded with sackcl.
4. *To lament, mourn,* אָנָה *anah.*
Isa. 3. 26 her gates shall lament and mourn; and
5. *To wail,* נָהָה *nahah.*
Mic. 2. 4 take up a parable against you, and lament
6. *To become wailing,* נָהָה *nahah,* 2.
1 Sa. 7. 2 all the house of Israel lamented after the
7. *To beat the breast, mourn, lament,* סָפַד *saphad.*
1 Sa. 25. 1 lamented him, and buried him in his ho.
28. 3 lamented him, and buried him in Ramah
Isa. 32. 12 They shall lament for the teats, for the
Jer. 4. 8 For this gird you with sackcloth, lament
16. 5 neither go to lament nor bemoan them
16. 6 neither shall (men) lament for them, nor
22. 18, 18 They shall not lament for him..Ah my
34. 5 they will lament thee..Ah lord! for I
49. 3 lament, and run to and fro by the hedges
Joel 1. 13 Gird yourselves, and lament, ye priests
8. *To con, lament, mourn,* קוּן *qun,* 3a.
2 Sa. 1. 17 David lamented with this lamentation
3. 33 the king lamented over Abner, and said
2 Ch. 35. 25 Jeremiah lamented for Josiah; and all
Eze. 27. 32 lament over thee, (saying), What (city is)
32. 16 lamentation wherewith they shall lament
32. 16 the nations..lament her: they shall lam.
9. *To give (praise),* תָּנָה *tanah,* 3.
Judg 11. 40 went yearly to lament the daughter of Je.
10. *To bewail,* θρηνέω *thrēneō.*
Luke 23. 27 women, which also bewailed and lamented
John 16. 20 ye shall weep and lament, but the world
11. *To beat or strike (the breast),* κόπτομαι *koptomai.*
Matt 11. 17 mourned unto you, and ye have not lam.
Rev. 18. 9 shall bewail her, and lament for her, when

LAMENT, to make to —
To cause to mourn, אָבַל *abal,* 5.
Lam. 2. 8 he made the rampart and the wall to la.

LAMENTABLE —
To be grievous, עֲצַב *atsab.*
Dan. 6. 20 cried with a lamentable voice unto Daniel

LAMENTATION —
1. *Lamentation, mourning,* אֲנִיָּה *aniyyah.*
Lam. 2. 5 and hath increased..mourning and lam.
2. *Beating of the breast,* מִסְפֵּד *misped.*
Gen. 50. 10 mourned with a great and very sore lam.
Jer. 6. 26 make thee mourning..most bitter lament.
48. 38 lamentation generally upon all the house
3. *A wailing,* נְהִי *nehi.*
Jer. 31. 15 A voice was heard in Ramah, lamentation
Amos 5. 16 such as are skilful of lamentation to wail.
Mic. 2. 4 lament with a doleful lamentation, (and)
4. *A conning, lamentation,* קִינָה *qinah.*
2 Sa. 1. 17 David lamented with this lamentation
2 Ch. 35. 25 spake of Josiah in their lamentations to
35. 25 behold, they (are) written in the Lament
Jer. 7. 29 take up a lamentation on high places; for
9. 10 a lamentation, because they are
9. 20 and every one her neighbour lamentation
Eze. 2. 10 written therein lamentations, and mour
19. 1 Moreover take thou up a lamentation
19. 14 a lamentation, and shall be for a lamenta
26. 17 they shall take up a lamentation for thee
27. 2 son of man, take up a lamentation for T
27. 32 they shall take up a lamentation for thee
28. 12 Son of man, take up a lamentation upon
32. 2 Son of man, take up a lamentation for P.
32. 16 This (is) the lamentation wherewith they
Amos 5. 1 Hear ye this word..a lamentation, O house
8. 10 I will turn..all your songs into lamentat.
5. *Wailing,* θρῆνος *thrēnos.*
Matt. 2. 18 In Rama was there a voice heard, [lam.]
6. *Beating or smiting (of the breast),* κοπετός *kopetos.*
Acts 8. 2 devout men..made great lamentation over

LAMENTATION, to make —
To weep, בָּכָה *bakah.*
Psa. 78. 64 and their widows made no lamentation

LAMENTED, to be —
To be beaten for, lamented, סָפַד *saphad,* 2.
Jer. 16. 4 they shall not be lamented, neither shall
25. 33 they shall not be lamented, neither gather

LAMP —
1. *A torch, flame,* לַפִּיד *lappid.*
Gen. 15. 17 a burning lamp that passed between those
Judg. 7. 16 empty pitchers, and lamps within the pi.
7. 20 held the lamps in their left hands, and
Job 12. 5 a lamp despised in the thought of him
41. 19 Out of his mouth go burning lamps..spa.
Isa. 62. 1 the salvation thereof as a lamp (that) bu.
Eze. 1. 13 appearance..like the appearance of lamps
Dan. 10. 6 his eyes as lamps of fire, and his arms and

2. *A light, lamp,* נֵר *ner.*
2 Sa. 22. 29 thou (art) my lamp, O LORD: and..LORD

3. *A light, lamp,* נִיר *nir.*
1 Ki. 15. 4 give him a lamp in Jerusalem, to set up

4. *A light, lamp,* נֵר *ner.*
Exod25. 37 thou shalt make the seven lamps thereof
25. 37 they shall light the lamps thereof, that
27. 20 oil olive..to cause the lamp to burn alw.
30. 7 when he dresseth the lamps, he shall burn
30. 8 when Aaron lighteth the lamps at even
35. 14 and his lamps, with the oil for the light
37. 23 he made his seven lamps, and his snuffers
39. 37 the lamps thereof..the lamps to be set in
40. 4 thou shalt bring in..and light the lamps
40. 25 he lighted the lamps before the LORD; as
Lev. 24. 2 oil..to cause..lamps to burn continually
24. 4 He shall order the lamps upon the pure
Num. 4. 9 candlestick of the light, and his lamps
8. 2 When thou lightest the lamps the seven l.
8. 3 Aaron did so; he lighted the lamps thereof
1 Sa. 3. 3 ere the lamp of God went out in the temple
1 Ki. 7. 49 the flowers, and the lamps, and the tongs
1 Ch.28. 15 and for their lamps of gold, by weight
28. 15 every candlestick, and for the lamps the.
28. 15 for the lamps thereof, according to the
2 Ch. 4. 20 the candlesticks with their lamps, that
4. 21 the flowers, and the lamps, and the tongs
13. 11 the candlestick of gold, with the lamps
29. 7 put out the lamps, and have not burnt
Psa.119. 105 Thy word (is) a lamp unto my feet, and
132. 17 I have ordained a lamp for mine anointed
Prov. 6. 23 the commandment (is) a lamp; and the
13. 9 the lamp of the wicked shall be put out
20. 20 his lamp shall be put out in obscure dar.
Zech. 4. 2 with a bowl..and his seven lamps thereon
4. 2 and seven pipes to the seven lamps, which

5. *A lamp, torch,* λαμπάς *lampas.*
Matt25. 1 ten virgins, which took their lamps, and
25. 3 took their lamps, and took no oil with
25. 4 But the wise took oil..with their lamps
25. 7 those virgins arose, and trimmed their l.
25. 8 Give us of your oil, for our lamps are gone
Rev. 4. 5 seven lamps of fire burning before the
8. 10 fell a great star..burning as it were a lamp
[*See also* Burning.]

LANCE —
Halbert, javelin, כִּידוֹן *kidon.*
Jer. 50. 42 They shall hold the bow and the lance

LANCET —
Dart, javelin, spear, רֹמַח *romach.*
1 Ki. 18. 28 with knives and lancets, till the blood

LAND —
1. *Land, earth, ground, firm soil,* אֲדָמָה *adamah.*
Gen. 28. 15 will bring thee again into this land; for
47. 18 there is not..but our bodies, and our lands
47. 19 Wherefore shall we die..we and our land?
47. 19 buy us and our land for bread, and we
47. 19 and our land will be servants unto Phara.
47. 19 and not die, that the land be not desolate
47. 20 Joseph bought all the land of Egypt for P.
47. 22 Only the land of the priests bought he not
47. 22 wherefore they sold not their lands
47. 23 I have bought you this day and your land
47. 23 lo..seed for you, and ye shall sow the l.
47. 26 Joseph made it a law over the land of E.
47. 26 except the land of the priests only,(which)
Exod20. 12 that thy days may be long upon the land
23. 19 The first of the first fruits of thy land thou
34. 26 The first of the first fruits of thy land thou
Lev. 20. 24 Ye shall inherit their land, and I will give
Num11. 12 the land which thou swarest unto their
32. 11 see the land which I sware unto Abraham
Deut. 5. 16 land which the LORD thy God giveth thee
7. 13 the fruit of thy land, thy corn, and thy w.
7. 13 the land which he sware unto thy fathers
11. 9 that ye may prolong..days in the land, w.
11. 17 and that the land yield not her fruit; and
11. 21 the land which the LORD sware unto your
21. 1 If (one) be found slain in the land which
21. 23 that thy land be not defiled, which the
25. 15 thy days may be lengthened in the land
26. 10 have brought the first fruits of the land
26. 15 the land which thou hast given us, as thou
28. 11 the land which the LORD sware unto thy
28. 18 the fruit of thy land, the increase of thy
28. 21 he have consumed thee from off the land
28. 33 The fruit of thy land, and all thy labours
28. 42 fruit of thy land shall the locust consume
28. 51 eat..of thy cattle, and the fruit of thy land
28. 63 ye shall be plucked from off the land wh.
29. 28 the LORD rooted them out of their land in
30. 9 plenteous..in the fruit of thy land for good
30. 18 shall not prolong (your) days upon the l.
30. 20 that thou mayest dwell in the land which
31. 13 as long as ye live in the land whither ye
31. 20 the land which I sware unto their fathers
32. 43 will be merciful unto his land..to his peo.
32. 47 ye shall prolong (your) days in the land
Josh.23. 13 ye perish from off this good land which
23. 15 have destroyed you from off this good land
2 Sa. 9. 10 shall till the land for him, and thou shalt
1 Ki. 8. 34 bring them again unto the land which thou
8. 40 land which thou gavest unto our fathers
9. 7 out of the land which I have given them
14. 15 shall root up Israel out of this good land
2 Ki.17. 23 Israel carried away out of their own land
21. 8 out of the land which I give their fathers
25. 21 Judah was carried away out of their land
2 Ch. 6. 25 bring them again unto the land which thou
6. 31 land which thou gavest unto our fathers
7. 20 out of my land which I have given them
33. 8 the land which I have appointed for your
Neh. 9. 25 they took strong cities, and a fat land, and
Job 31. 38 If my land cry against me, or that the fur.
Psa. 49. 11 call (their) lands after their own names
137. 4 we sing the LORD'S song in a strange land
Prov.12. 11 that tilleth his land shall be satisfied
28. 19 He that tilleth his land shall have plenty
Isa. 1. 7 your land, strangers devour it in your pre.
6. 11 Until the cities..and the land be utterly
7. 16 the land that thou abhorrest shall be fors.
14. 1 the LORD will..set them in their own land
14. 2 Israel shall possess them in the land of
15. 9 Moab, and upon the remnant of the land
19. 17 the land of Judah shall be a terror unto E.
32. 13 Upon the land of my people shall come up
Jer. 12. 14 I will pluck them out of their land, and
16. 15 I will bring them again into their land
23. 8 Israel..they shall dwell in their own land
24. 10 till they be consumed from off the land
25. 5 and dwell in the land that the LORD hath
27. 10 unto you, to remove you far from your land
27. 11 will I let remain still in their own land
35. 7 ye may live many days in the land where
35. 15 ye shall dwell in the land which I have
42. 12 and cause you to return to your own land
52. 27 carried away captive out of his own land
Eze. 7. 2 saith the Lord GOD unto the land of Israel
11. 17 say..and I will give you the land of Israel
12. 19 Thus saith the Lord GOD..of the land of I.
12. 22 proverb (that) ye have in the land of Israel
13. 9 neither shall they enter into the land of I.
18. 2 this proverb concerning the land of Israel
20. 38 they shall not enter into the land of Israel
20. 42 I shall bring you into the land of Israel
21. 2 and prophesy against the land of Israel
21. 3 say to the land of Israel, Thus saith the L.
25. 3 against the land of Israel, when it was d.
25. 6 all thy despite against the land of Israel
28. 25 land that I have given to my servant Ja.
33. 24 those wastes of the land of Israel speak
34. 13 will bring them to their own land, and
34. 27 they shall be safe in their land, and shall
36. 6 Prophesy therefore concerning the land
36. 17 house of Israel dwelt in their own land
36. 24 take..and will bring you into your own l.
37. 12 I will..bring you into the land of Israel
37. 14 and I shall place you in your own land
37. 21 I will..bring them into their own land
38. 18 when Gog shall come against the land of
38. 19 shall be a great shaking in the land of I.
39. 26 when they dwelt safely in their land, and
39. 28 I have gathered them unto their own land
Dan. 11. 9 the king..shall return into his own land
11. 39 Thus shall he..divide the land for gain
Joel 1. 10 The field is wasted, the land mourneth
2. 21 Fear not, O land; be glad and rejoice: for
Amos 5. 2 she is forsaken upon her land..none to
7. 11 be led away captive out of their own land
7. 17 and thy land shall be divided by line
7. 17 die in a polluted land..forth of his land
9. 15 I will plant them upon their land, and
9. 15 out of their land which I have given them
Zeph. 1. 2 I will..consume all..from off the land
1. 3 I will cut off man from off the land, saith
Zech. 2. 12 inherit Judah his portion in the holy land
9. 16 crown, lifted up as an ensign upon his land

2. *Land, earth, country,* אֶרֶץ *erets.*
Gen. 2. 11 which compasseth the whole land of Ha.
2. 12 And the gold of that land (is) good: there
2. 13 that compasseth the whole land of Ethio.
4. 16 in the land of Nod, on the east of Eden
10. 5 these were the isles..divided in their lands
10. 10 Accad, and Calneh, in the land of Shinar
10. 11 Out of that land went forth Asshur, and
10. 31 These..in their lands, after their nations
11. 2 they found a plain in the land of Shinar
11. 28 Haran died..in the land of his nativity
11. 31 they went..to go into the land of Canaan
12. 1 Get thee..unto a land that I will show
12. 5 and into the land of Canaan they came
12. 5 went forth to go into the land of Canaan
12. 6 through the land unto the place of Sichem
12. 6 And the Canaanite (was) then in the land
12. 7 Unto thy seed will I give this land: and
12. 10 there was a famine in the land: and Abr.
12. 10 for the famine (was) grievous in the land
13. 6 the land was not able to bear them, that
13. 7 and the Perizzite dwelt then in the land
13. 9 (Is) not the whole land before thee? Sep.
13. 10 like the land of Egypt, as thou comest
13. 12 Abram dwelt in the land of Canaan, and
13. 15 the land which thou seest, to thee will I
13. 17 walk through the land, in the length of it
15. 7 brought thee..to give thee this land to
15. 13 be a stranger in a land (that is) not theirs
15. 18 Unto thy seed have I given this land, from
16. 3 had dwelt ten years in the land of Canaan
17. 8 the land wherein thou art a stranger, all
17. 8 all the land of Canaan, for an everlasting
19. 28 toward all the land of the plain, and beh.
20. 15 Behold, my land (is) before thee: dwell
21. 21 took him a wife out of the land of Egypt
21. 23 to the land wherein thou hast sojourned
21. 32 they returned into the land of the Philis.
21. 34 sojourned in the Philistines' land many
22. 2 and get thee into the land of Moriah; and
23. 2 the same (is) Hebron in the land of Can.
23. 7 bowed himself to the people of the land
Gen 23. 12 bowed down..before the people of the land
23. 13 in the audience of the people of the land
23. 15 the land (is worth) four hundred shekels
23. 19 the same (is) Hebron in the land of Can.
24. 5 not be willing to follow me unto this land
24. 5 unto the land from whence thou camest
24. 7 and from the land of my kindred, and
24. 7 saying, Unto thy seed will I give this land
24. 37 of the Canaanites, in whose land I dwell
26. 1 there was a famine in the land, beside
26. 2 in the land which I shall tell thee of
26. 3 Sojourn in this land, and I will be with
26. 12 Isaac sowed in that land, and received
26. 22 For now..we shall be fruitful in the land
27. 46 of the daughters of the land, what good
28. 4 inherit the land wherein thou art a stranger
28. 13 the land whereon thou liest, to thee will
29. 1 came into the land of the people of the east
31. 3 Return unto the land of thy fathers, and
31. 13 from this land, and return unto the land
31. 18 to Isaac his father in the land of Canaan
32. 3 to Esau his brother, unto the land of Seir
33. 18 Shechem, which (is) in the land of Canaan
34. 1 went out to see the daughters of the land
34. 10 the land shall be before you; dwell and
34. 21 the land, and trade therein; for the land
34. 30 stink among the inhabitants of the land
35. 6 to Luz, which (is) in the land of Canaan
35. 12 the land which I gave Abraham and Isaac
35. 12 to thy seed after thee will I give the land
35. 22 came to pass, when Israel dwelt in that l.
36. 5 were born unto him in the land of Canaan
36. 6 which he had got in the land of Canaan
36. 7 the land wherein they were strangers could
36. 16 the dukes..of Eliphaz in the land of Edom
36. 17 the dukes..of Reuel in the land of Edom
36. 20 of Seir the Horite, who inhabited the land
36. 21 the children of Seir in the land of Edom
36. 30 these..among their dukes in the land of
36. 31 kings that reigned in the land of Edom
36. 34 Husham of the land of Temani reigned
36. 43 their habitations in the land of their poss.
37. 1 dwelt in the land..in the land of Canaan
40. 15 stolen away out of the land of the Hebrews
41. 19 I never saw in all the land of Egypt for
41. 29 plenty throughout all the land of Egypt
41. 30 plenty shall be forgotten in the land of E.
41. 30 and the famine shall consume the land
41. 31 plenty shall not be known in the land by
41. 33 let Pharaoh..set him over the land of E.
41. 34 let him appoint officers over the land, and
41. 34 take up the fifth part of the land of Egypt
41. 36 that food shall be for store to the land ag.
41. 36 shall be in the land of Egypt; that the land
41. 41 I have set thee over all the land of Egypt
41. 43 he made him..over all the land of Egypt
41. 44 lift up his hand or foot in all the land of E.
41. 45 And Joseph went out over..the land of E.
41. 46 and went throughout all the land of Egypt
41. 48 which were in the land of Egypt, and laid
41. 52 hath caused me to be fruitful in the land
41. 53 plenteousness that was in the land of Eg.
41. 54 was in all lands; but in all the land of E.
41. 55 when all the land of Egypt was famished
41. 56 the famine waxed sore in the land of Eg.
41. 57 that the famine was (so) sore in all lands
42. 5 for the famine was in the land of Canaan
42. 6 Joseph (was) the governor over the land
42. 6 that sold to all the people of the land: and
42. 7 From the land of Canaan to buy food
42. 9, 12 to see the nakedness of the land ye are
42. 13 the sons of one man in the land of Canaan
42. 29 they came unto Jacob..unto the land of
42. 30 The man, (who is) the lord of the land
42. 32 this day with our father in the land of C.
42. 34 your brother..ye shall traffic in the land
43. 1 And the famine (was) sore in the land
43. 11 take of the best fruits in the land in your
44. 8 brought again unto thee out of the land
45. 6 these two years..the famine..in the land
45. 8 and a ruler throughout all the land of E.
45. 10 thou shalt dwell in the land of Goshen
45. 17 and go, get you unto the land of Canaan
45. 18 will give you the good of the land of Eg.
45. 18 and ye shall eat the fat of the land
45. 19 take you wagons out of the land of Egypt
45. 20 the good of all the land of Egypt (is)
45. 25 came into the land of Canaan unto Jacob
45. 26 he (is) governor over all the land of Egypt
46. 6 they had gotten in the land of Canaan
46. 12 Er and Onan died in the land of Canaan
46. 20 unto Joseph in the land of Egypt were
46. 28 and they came into the land of Goshen
46. 31 brethren..which (were) in the land of C.
46. 34 that ye may dwell in the land of Goshen
47. 1 all..are come out of the land of Canaan
47. 1 and, behold, they (are) in the land of Go.
47. 4 For to sojourn in the land are we come
47. 4 the famine (is) sore in the land of Canaan
47. 4 thy servants dwell in the land of Goshen
47. 6 The land of Egypt (is) before thee
47. 6 in the best of the land make thy father
47. 6 in the land of Goshen let them dwell
47. 11 gave them a possession in the land of Eg.
47. 11 best of the land, in the land of Rameses
47. 13 And (there was) no bread in all the land
47. 13 the land of Egypt, and (all) the land of Ca.
47. 14, 15 in the land of Egypt, and in the land
47. 20 Joseph bought..so the land became Pha.
47. 27 Israel dwelt in the land of Egypt, in the
47. 28 Jacob lived in the land of Egypt seventeen
48. 3 appeared unto me at Luz in the land of

Gen. 48. 4 will give this land to thy seed after thee
48. 5 which were born unto thee in the land of
48. 7 Rachel died by me in the land of Canaan
48. 21 bring you again unto the land of your fa.
49. 15 he saw..the land that (it was) pleasant
49. 30 before Mamre, in the land of Canaan, wh.
50. 5 I have digged for me in the land of Canaan
50. 7 and all the elders of the land of Egypt
50. 8 their herds, they left in the land of Gos.
50. 11 And when the inhabitants of the land, the
50. 13 his sons carried him into the land of Can.
50. 24 out of this land unto the land which he s.
Exod. 1. 7 mighty; and the land was filled with them
1. 10 fight..and (so) get them up out of the land
2. 15 Moses fled..and dwelt in the land of Midian
2. 22 I have been a stranger in a strange land
3. 8 out of that land unto a good land and a
3. 8, 17 unto a land flowing with milk and honey
3. 17 bring you..unto the land of the Canaanites
4. 20 Moses..returned to the land of Egypt: and
5. 5 the people of the land now (are) many, and
5. 12 scattered abroad throughout all the land
6. 1 with..hand shall he drive them out of his l.
6. 4 to give them the land of Canaan, the land
6. 8 I will bring you in unto the land, concern.
6. 11 the children of Israel go out of his land
6. 13 the children of Israel out of the land of E.
6. 26 the children of Israel from the land of E.
6. 28 LORD spake unto Moses in the land of E.
7. 2 send the children of Israel out of his land
7. 3 my signs and my wonders in the land of E.
7. 4 out of the land of Egypt by great judgm.
7. 19, 21 blood throughout all the land of Egypt
8. 5 cause frogs to come up upon the land of E.
8. 6 frogs came up, and covered the land of E.
8. 7 brought up frogs upon the land of Egypt
8. 14 together upon heaps; and the land stank
8. 16 thy rod, and smite the dust of the land
8. 16 it may become lice throughout all the land
8. 17 land became lice throughout all the land
8. 22 will sever in that day the land of Goshen
8. 24 into all the land of Egypt: the land was
8. 25 Go ye, sacrifice to your God in the land
9. 5 saying..LORD shall do this thing in the l.
9. 9 become small dust in all the land of Egypt
9. 9, 22, 25 throughout all the land of Egypt
9. 22 there may be hail in all the land of Egypt
9. 23 LORD rained hail upon the land of Egypt
9. 24 in all the land of Egypt since it became a
9. 26 Only in the land of Goshen, where the ch.
10. 12 Stretch..thine hand over the land of Eg.
10. 12 they may come up upon the land of Egypt
10. 12 and eat every herb of the land..all that
10. 13 stretched forth his rod over the land of E.
10. 13 brought an east wind upon the land all
10. 14 the locusts went up over all the land of E.
10. 15 they covered..so that the land was dark.
10. 15 they did eat every herb of the land, and
10. 15 there remained not..through all the land
10. 21 there may be darkness over the land of E.
10. 22 a thick darkness in all the land of Egypt
11. 3 Moses (was) very great in the land of Eg.
11. 5 all the first born in the land of Egypt shall
11. 6 a great cry throughout all the land of E.
11. 9 wonders may be multiplied in the land of E.
11. 10 let the children of Israel go out of his l.
12. 1 unto Moses and Aaron in the land of E.
12. 12 I will pass through the land of Egypt this
12. 12, 29 all the first born in the land of Egypt
12. 13 destroy (you), when I smite the land of E.
12. 17 brought your armies out of the land of E.
12. 19 whether he be a stranger, or born in the l.
12. 25 when ye be come to the land which the L.
12. 33 might send them out of the land in haste
12. 41 the hosts..went out from the land of E
12. 42 for bringing them out from the land of E.
12. 48 he shall be as one that is born in the land
12. 51 out of the land of Egypt by their armies
13. 5, 11 bring thee into the land of the Cana.
13. 5 a land flowing with milk and honey, that
13. 15 slew all the first born in the land of Egypt
13. 17 not..the way of the land of the Philistines
13. 18 went up harnessed out of the land of E
14. 3 They (are) entangled in the land the wil.
16. 1 after their departing out of the land of E.
16. 3 by the hand of the LORD in the land of E
16. 6 brought you out from the land of Egypt
16. 32 LORD hath brought you forth from the l.
16. 35 eat..until they came to a land inhabited
16. 35 unto the borders of the land of Canaan
18. 3 I have been an alien in a strange land
18. 27 and he went his way into his own land
19. 1 were gone forth out of the land of Egypt
20. 2 which have brought thee out of the land
22. 21 for ye were strangers in the land of Egypt
23. 9 seeing ye were strangers in the land of E.
23. 10 six years thou shalt sow thy land, and sh.
23. 26 shall nothing cast their young..in thy l.
23. 29 lest the land become desolate, and the b.
23. 30 until thou be increased, and inherit the la
23. 31 I will deliver the inhabitants of the land
23. 33 They shall not dwell in thy land, lest they
29. 46 that brought them forth out of the land
32. 1, 23 brought us up out of the land of Egypt
32. 4, 8 brought thee up out of the land of Egypt
32. 7 which thou broughtest out of the land of
32. 11 out of the land of Egypt with great power
32. 13 all this land that I have spoken of will I
33. 1 up out of the land of Egypt, unto the land
33. 3 Unto a land flowing with milk and honey
34. 12, 15 covenant with the inhabitants of the l.
34. 24 neither shall any man desire thy land

Lev. 11. 45 LORD that bringeth you up out of the land
14. 34 When ye be come into the land of Canaan
14. 34 in a house of the land of your possession
16. 22 all their iniquities unto a land not inhabi.
18. 3 After the doings of the land of Egypt
18. 3 and after the doings of the land of Canaan
18. 25 the land is defiled: therefore I do visit
18. 25 the land itself vomiteth out her inhabita.
18. 27 these abominations have the men of the l.
18. 27 (were) before you, and the land is defiled
18. 28 That the land spue not you out also, when
19. 9 when ye reap the harvest of your land
19. 23 And when ye shall come into the land, and
19. 29 lest the land fall to whoredom, and the l.
19. 33 if a stranger sojourn with thee in your l.
19. 34 for ye were strangers in the land of Egypt
19. 36 which brought you out of the land of Eg.
20. 2 the people of the land shall stone him with
20. 4 if the people of the land do any ways hide
20. 22 that the land, whither I bring you to dw.
20. 24 a land that floweth with milk and honey
22. 24 neither shall ye make..(thereof) in your l.
22. 33 That brought you out of the land of Egypt
23. 10 When ye be come into the land which I
23. 22 when ye reap the harvest of your land
23. 39 ye have gathered in the fruit of the land
23. 43 when I brought them out of the land of
25. 2 land which I give you, then shall the land
25. 4 shall be a sabbath of rest unto the land, a
25. 5 not reap..it is a year of rest unto the land
25. 6 the sabbath of the land shall be meat for
25. 7 for the beast that (are) in thy land, shall
25. 9 trumpet sound throughout all your land
25. 10 proclaim liberty throughout..the land
25. 18 and ye shall dwell in the land in safety
25. 19 the land shall yield her fruit, and ye shall
25. 23 The land shall not be sold for ever: for
25. 23 the land (is) mine; for ye (are) strangers
25. 24 And in all the land of your possession ye
25. 24 ye shall grant a redemption for the land
25. 38 of the land of Egypt, to give you the land
25. 42, 55 I brought forth out of the land of E.
25. 45 families..which they begat in your land
26. 1 set up (any) image of stone in your land
26. 4 the land shall yield her increase, and the
26. 5 shall eat..and dwell in your land safely
26. 6 I will give peace in the land, and ye shall
26. 6 and I will rid evil beasts out of the land
26. 6 neither shall the sword go through your l.
26. 13 which brought you forth out of the land
26. 20 your land shall not yield her increase
26. 20 neither shall the trees of the land yield
26. 32 And I will bring the land into desolation
26. 33 your land shall be desolate, and your cities
26. 34 Then shall the land enjoy her sabbaths
26. 34 as long as..ye (be) in your enemies' land
26. 34 then shall the land rest, and enjoy her
26. 36 a faintness into their hearts in the lands
26. 38 the land of your enemies shall eat you up
26. 39 in their iniquity in your enemies' lands
26. 41 have brought them into the land of their
26. 42 my covenant..and I will remember the l.
26. 43 The land also shall be left of them, and
26. 44 when they be in the land of their enemies
26. 45 whom I brought forth out of the land of
27. 24 to him to whom the possession of the land
27. 30 tithe of the land..of the seed of the land
Num. 1. 1 after they were come out of the land of E.
3. 13 that I smote all the first born in the land
8. 17 that I smote every first born in the land
9. 1 after they were come out of the land of E.
9. 14 ordinance..for him that was..in the land
10. 9 if ye go to war in your land against the
10. 30 I will depart to mine own land, and to my
13. 2 that they may search the land of Canaan
13. 16 men which Moses sent to spy out the land
13. 17 Moses sent them to spy out the land of C.
13. 18 see the land, what it (is); and the people
13. 19 what the land (is) that they dwell in wh.
13. 20 what the land (is), whether it (be) fat or
13. 20 courage, and bring of the fruit of the land
13. 21 searched the land from the wilderness of
13. 25 they returned from searching of the land
13. 26 and showed them the fruit of the land
13. 27 We came unto the land whither thou sent.
13. 28 people (be) strong that dwell in the land
13. 29 Amalekites dwell in the land of the south
13. 32 they brought up an evil report of the land
13. 32 The land, through which we have gone to
13. 32 (is) a land that eateth up the inhabitants
14. 2 Would God that we had died in the land
14. 3 hath the LORD brought us unto this land
14. 6 (which were) of them..searched the land
14. 7 The land..(is) an exceeding good land
14. 8 then he will bring us into this land, and
14. 8 a land which floweth with milk and honey
14. 9 neither fear ye the people of the land
14. 14 will tell (it) to the inhabitants of this land
14. 16 into the land which he sware unto them
14. 23 the land which I sware unto their fathers
14. 24 him will I bring into the land whereunto
14. 30 Doubtless ye shall not come into the land
14. 31 they shall know the land which ye have
14. 34 of the days in which ye searched the land
14. 36 men which Moses sent to search the land
14. 36 by bringing up a slander upon the land
14. 37 did bring up the evil report upon the land
14. 38 of the men that went to search the land
15. 2 When ye be come into the land of your
15. 18 When ye come into the land whither I
15. 19 when ye eat of the bread of the land, ye
15. 41 which brought you out of the land of E.

Num. 16. 13 hast brought us up out of a land that
16. 14 thou hast not brought us into a land
18. 13 whatsoever is first ripe in the land, which
18. 20 shalt have no inheritance in their land
20. 12 not bring..into the land which I have given
20. 23 mount Hor, by the coast of the land of E.
20. 24 he shall not enter into the land which I
21. 4 of the Red sea, to compass the land of E.
21. 22 Let me pass through thy land: we will not
21. 24 possessed his land from Arnon unto Jab.
21. 26 taken all his land out of his hand, even
21. 31 Israel dwelt in the land of the Amorites
21. 34 and all his people, and his land; and thou
21 35 none left him..and they possessed his land
22. 5 Pethor, which (is) by the river of the land
22. 6 and (that) I may drive them out of the l.
22. 13 Get you into your land; for the LORD ref.
26. 4 which went forth out of the land of Egypt
26. 19 and Er and Onan died in the land of Can.
26. 53 Unto these the land shall be divided for
26. 55 Notwithstanding the land shall be divided
27. 12 see the land which I have given unto the
32. 1 they saw the land of Jazer, and the land
32. 4 the country..(is) a land for cattle, and
32. 5 let this land be given unto thy servants
32. 7 into the land which the LORD hath given
32. 8 when I sent them from Kadesh..to see the l.
32. 9 For when they went up..and saw the land
32. 9 into the land which the LORD had given
32. 17 because of the inhabitants of the land
32. 22 And the land be subdued before the LORD
32. 22 this land shall be your possession before
32. 29 and the land shall be subdued before you
32. 29 then ye shall give them the land of Gilead
32. 30 have possessions among you in the land
32. 32 before the LORD into the land of Canaan
32. 33 land, with the cities thereof in the coasts
33. 1 which went forth out of the land of Egypt
33. 37 mount Hor, in the edge of the land of E.
33. 38 Israel were come out of the land of Egypt
33. 40 dwelt in the south in the land of Canaan
33. 51 passed over Jordan into the land of Canaan
33. 52 drive out all the inhabitants of the land
33. 53 ye shall dispossess..the land, and dwell
33. 53 for I have given you the land to possess
33. 54 ye shall divide the land by lot for an inh.
33. 55 not drive out the inhabitants of the land
33. 55 shall vex you in the land wherein ye dwell
34. 2 into the land of Canaan, this (is) the land
34. 2 the land of Canaan, with the coasts thereof
34. 12 your land with the coasts thereof round
34. 13 This (is) the land which ye shall inherit
34. 17 men which shall divide the land unto you
34. 18 prince..to divide the land by inheritance
34. 29 unto the children of Israel in the land of
35. 10 When ye be come over Jordan into the l.
35. 14 three cities shall ye give in the land of C.
35. 28 shall return into the land of his possession
35. 32 he should come again to dwell in the land
35. 33 ye shall not pollute the land wherein ye
35. 33 for blood it defileth the land: and the land
35. 34 Defile not therefore the land which ye
36. 2 LORD commanded my lord to give the land
Deut. 1. 5 On this side Jordan, in the land of Moab
1. 7 to the land of the Canaanites, and unto L.
1. 8 Behold, I have set the land before you: go
1. 8 go in and possess the land which the LORD
1. 21 LORD thy God hath set the land before
1. 22 they shall search us out the land, and br.
1. 25 they took of the fruit of the land in their
1. 25 a good land which the LORD our God doth
1. 27 he hath brought us forth out of the land
1. 35 of this evil generation see that good land
1. 36 to him will I give the land that he hath
2. 5 I will not give you of their land, no, not
2. 9 will not give thee of their land..a posses
2. 12 as Israel did unto the land of his posses.
2. 19 I will not give thee of the land of the ch.
2. 20 That also was accounted a land of giants
2. 24 Amorite, king of Heshbon, and his land
2. 27 Let me pass through thy land: I will go
2. 29 into the land which the LORD our God
2. 31 I have begun to give Sihon and his land
2. 31 possess, that thou mayest inherit his land
2. 37 Only unto the land of the children of Am.
3. 2 all his people, and his land, into thy hand
3. 8 the land that (was) on this side Jordan
3. 12 that land, (which) we possessed at that time
3. 13 Bashan, which was called the land of gi.
3. 18 God hath given you this land to possess
3. 20 they also possess the land which the LORD
3. 25 let me go over and see the good land that
3. 28 to inherit the land which thou shalt see
4. 1 go in and possess the land which the Lo.
4. 5 so in the land whither ye go to possess it
4. 14 the land whither ye go over to possess it
4. 21 I should not go in unto that good land
4. 22 I must die in this land, I must not go over
4 22 shall go over, and possess that good land
4. 25 ye shall have remained long in the land
4. 26 shall soon utterly perish from off the land
4. 38 to give thee their land (for) an inheritance
4. 46 the land of Sihon king of the Amorites
4. 47 they possessed his land, and the land of
5. 6 which brought thee out of the land of E.
5. 15 that thou wast a servant in the land of E.
5. 31 in the land which I give them to possess
5. 33 ye may prolong..days in the land which
6. 1 in the land whither ye go to possess it
6. 3 the land that floweth with milk and honey
6. 10 into the land which he sware unto thy f.
6. 12 which brought thee forth out of the land

Deut. 6. 18 the good land which the LORD sware unto
6. 23 the land which he sware unto our fathers
7. 1 into the land whither thou goest to possess
8. 1 possess the land which the LORD sware
8. 7 into a good land; a land of brooks of wa.
8. 8 A land of wheat..a land of oil olive and
8. 9 A land wherein thou shalt eat bread with
8. 9 a land whose stones (are) iron, and out of
8. 10 for the good land which he hath given
8. 14 which brought thee forth out of the land of
9. 4 hath brought me in to possess this land
9. 5 dost thou go to possess their land; but
9. 6 giveth thee not this good land to possess
9. 7 thou didst depart out of the land of Egypt
9. 23 Go up and possess the land which I have
9. 28 Lest the land whence thou broughtest us
9. 28 into the land which he promised them
10. 7 and..to Jotbath, a land of rivers of waters
10. 11 that they may go in and possess the land
10. 19 for ye were strangers in the land of Egypt
11. 3 the king of Egypt, and unto all his land
11. 8 go in and possess the land whither ye go
11. 9 a land that floweth with milk and honey
11. 10 the land, whither thou goest in to possess
11. 10 (is) not as the land of Egypt, from whence
11. 11 But the land, whither ye go to possess it
11. 11 (is) a land of hills and valleys, (and) drink.
11. 12 A land which the LORD thy God careth
11. 14 I will give..the rain of your land in his
11. 17 ye perish quickly from off the good land
11. 25 upon all the land that ye shall tread upon
11. 29 the land whither thou goest to possess it
11. 30 in the land of the Canaanites, which dwell
11. 31 the land which the LORD your God giveth
12. 1 which ye shall observe to do in the land
12. 10 dwell in the land which the LORD your G.
12. 29 succeedest them, and dwellest in their land
13. 5, 10 which brought..out of the land of Egypt
15. 4 LORD shall greatly bless thee in the land
15. 7 land which the LORD thy God giveth thee
15. 11 the poor shall never cease out of the land
15. 11 to thy poor, and to thy needy, in thy land
15. 15 that thou wast a bondman in the land of
16. 3, 3 camest forth out of the land of Egypt
16. 20 inherit the land which the LORD thy God
17. 14 unto the land which the LORD thy God
18. 9 into the land which the LORD thy God
19. 1 whose land the LORD thy God giveth thee
19. 2 cities for thee in the midst of thy land
19. 3 divide the coasts of thy land, which the L.
19. 8 give thee all the land which he promised
19. 10 That innocent blood be not shed in thy l.
19. 14 which thou shalt inherit in the land that
20. 1 brought thee up out of the land of Egypt
23. 7 because thou wast a stranger in his land
23. 20 in the land whither thou goest to possess
24. 4 thou shalt not cause the land to sin, which
24. 14 strangers that (are) in thy land within thy
24. 22 thou wast a bondman in the land of Egypt
25. 19 the land which the LORD thy God giveth
26. 1 when thou (art) come in unto the land
26. 2 thy land that the LORD thy God giveth
26. 9 hath given us this land..a land that flow.
26. 15 a land that floweth with milk and honey
27. 2, 3 unto the land which the LORD thy God
27. 3 a land that floweth with milk and honey
28. 8 the land which the LORD thy God giveth
28. 12 give the rain unto thy land in his season
28. 24 LORD shall make the rain of thy land po.
28. 52, 52 all thy gates..throughout all thy land
29. 1 the children of Israel in the land of Moab
29. 2 did before your eyes in the land of Egypt
29. 2 unto all his servants, and unto all his land
29. 8 we took their land, and gave it for an inh.
29. 16 how we have dwelt in the land of Egypt
29. 22 stranger that shall come from a far land
29. 22 when they see the plagues of that land
29. 23 the whole land thereof (is) brimstone, and
29. 24 hath the LORD done thus unto this land?
29. 25 when he brought them forth out of the l.
29. 27 the anger..was kindled against this land
29. 28 cast them into another land, as..this day
30. 5 into the land which thy fathers possessed
30. 16 God shall bless thee in the land whither
31. 4 unto the land of them, whom he destroyed
31. 7 thou must go with this people unto the l.
31. 16 after the gods of the strangers of the land
31. 21 brought them into the land which I sware
31. 23 bring..into the land which I sware unto
32. 10 He found him in a desert land, and in the
32. 49 mount Nebo, which (is) in the land of M.
32. 49 behold the land of Canaan, which I give
32. 52 Yet thou shalt see the land before (thee)
32. 52 unto the land which I give the children
33. 13 Blessed of the LORD (be) his land, for the
33. 28 fountain of Jacob..upon a land of corn and
34. 1 LORD showed him all the land of Gilead
34. 2 the land of Ephraim, and Manasseh, and
34. 2 the land of Judah, unto the utmost sea
34. 4 This (is) the land which I sware unto A.
34. 5 So Moses..died there in the land of Moab
34. 6 he buried him in a valley in the land of
34. 11 sent him to do in the land of Egypt to P.
34. 11 and to all his servants, and to all his land
Josh. 1. 2 unto the land which I do give to them
1. 4 all the land of the Hittites, and unto the
1. 6 thou divide for an inheritance the land
1. 11 to go in to possess the land, which the L.
1. 13 LORD your God..hath given you this land
1. 14 shall remain in the land which Moses gave
1. 15 possessed the land which the LORD your
1. 15 ye shall return unto the land of your pos.

Josh. 2. 1 Go view the land, even Jericho. And they
2. 9 that the LORD hath given you the land
2. 9 all the inhabitants of the land faint bec.
2. 14 when the LORD hath given us the land
2. 18 we come into the land, thou shalt bind this
2. 24 hath delivered into our hands all the land
5. 6 that he would not show them the land
5. 6 a land that floweth with milk and honey
5. 11 they did eat of the old corn of the land
5. 12 they had eaten of the old corn of the land
5. 12 eat of the fruit of the land of Canaan that
7. 9 all the inhabitants of the land shall hear
8. 1 and his people, and his city, and his land
9. 24 servant Moses to give you all the land
9. 24 destroy all the inhabitants of the land from
10. 42 all these kings and their land did Joshua
11. 3 the Hivite under Hermon in the land of
11. 16 Joshua took all that land, the hills, and
11. 16 all the land of Goshen, and the valley, and
11. 22 none..left in the land of the children of
11. 23 Joshua took the whole land..And the land
12. 1 kings of the land..their land on the other
13. 1 there remaineth yet very much land to be
13. 2 This (is) the land that yet remaineth: all
13. 4 all the land of the Canaanites, and Mearah
13. 5 the land of the Giblites, and all Lebanon
13. 7 divide this land for an inheritance unto
13. 25 half the land of the children of Ammon
14. 1 Israel inherited in the land of Canaan
14. 4 gave no part unto the Levites in the land
14. 5 so..Israel did, and they divided the land
14. 7 from Kadesh-barnea to espy out the land
14. 9 Surely the land whereon thy feet have
14. 15 And the land had rest from war
15. 19 thou hast given me a south land; give me
17. 5 beside the land of Gilead and Bashan
17. 6 Manasseh's sons had the land of Gilead
17. 8 Manasseh had the land of Tappuah: but
17. 12 the Canaanites would dwell in that land
17. 15 in the land of the Perizzites and of the
17. 16 all the Canaanites that dwell in the land
18. 1 And the land was subdued before them
18. 3 long (are) ye slack to..possess the land
18. 4 go through the land, and describe it acc.
18. 6 Ye shall therefore describe the land (into)
18. 8 charged them that went to describe the la.
18. 8 Go and walk through the land, and desc.
18. 9 men went and passed through the land
18. 10 Joshua divided the land unto the children
19. 49 of dividing the land for inheritance by
21. 2 at Shiloh in the land of Canaan, saying
21. 43 LORD gave unto Israel all the land which
22. 4 unto the land of your possession, which
22. 9 out of Shiloh, which (is) in the land of C.
22. 9 to the land of their possession, whereof
22. 10 borders of Jordan, that (are) in the land
22. 11 built an altar over against the land of C.
22. 13, 15 tribe of Manasseh, into the land of G.
22. 19 if the land of your possession (be) unclean
22. 19 pass ye over unto the land of the possess.
22. 32 out of the land of Gilead, unto the land of
23. 13 to destroy the land wherein the children
23. 5 ye shall possess their land, as the LORD
23. 16 the good land which he hath given unto
24. 3 led him throughout all the land of Canaan
24. 8 I brought you into the land of the Amor.
24. 8 I gave..that ye might possess their land
24. 13 I have given you a land for which ye did
24. 15 the gods of the Amorites, in whose land
24. 17 brought..our fathers out of the land of E.
24. 18 even the Amorites which dwelt in the land
Judg. 1. 2 behold, I have delivered the land into his
1. 15 thou hast given me a south land; give me
1. 26 the man went into the land of the Hittites
1. 27 the Canaanites would dwell in that land
1. 32, 33 Canaanites, the inhabitants of the land
2. 1 brought you unto the land which I sware
2. 2 league with the inhabitants of this land
2. 6 unto his inheritance to possess the land
2. 12 which brought them out of the land of E.
3. 11 the land had rest forty years. And Oth.
3. 30 And the land had rest fourscore years
5. 31 And the land had rest forty years
6. 5 they entered into the land to destroy it
6. 9 from before you, and gave you their land
6. 10 the gods of the Amorites, in whose land
9. 37 people down by the middle of the land
10. 4 thirty cities..which (are) in the land of
10. 8 in the land of the Amorites, which (is) in
11. 3 Jephthah fled..and dwelt in the land of
11. 5 to fetch Jephthah out of the land of Tob
11. 12 art come against me to fight in my land
11. 13 Israel took away my land, when they came
11. 15 the land of Moab, nor the land of the ch.
11. 17 Let me, I pray thee, pass through thy land
11. 18 compassed the land of Edom, and the land
11. 18 came by the east side of the land of Moab
11. 19 Let us pass, we pray thee, through thy l.
11. 21 possessed all the land of the Amorites
12. 15 buried in Pirathon in the land of Ephraim
18. 2 sent..to spy out the land, and to search
18. 2 they said unto them, Go, search the land
18. 7 and (there was) no magistrate in the land
18. 9 we have seen the land, and, behold, it (is)
18. 9 to go, (and) to enter to possess the land
18. 10 unto a people secure, and to a large land
18. 17 men that went to spy out the land went
18. 30 until the day of the captivity of the land
19. 30 Israel came up out of the land of Egypt
20. 1 to Beer-sheba, with the land of Gilead
21. 12 to Shiloh, which (is) in the land of Canaan
21. 21 every man..and go to the land of Benjamin

Ruth 1. 1 that there was a famine in the land
1. 7 the way to return unto the land of Judah
2. 11 thy mother, and the land of thy nativity
1 Sa. 6. 5 and images of your mice that mar the land
6. 5 from off your gods, and from off your land
9. 4 passed through the land of Shalisha, but
9. 4 they passed through the land of Shalim
9. 4 passed through the land of the Benjamites
9. 5 when they were come to the land of Zuph
9. 16 send thee a man out of the land of Benja.
12. 6 your fathers up out of the land of Egypt
13. 3 blew the trumpet throughout all the land
13. 7 over Jordan to the land of Gad and Gilead
13. 17 leadeth to) Ophrah, unto the land of S.
13. 19 found throughout all the land of Israel
14. 25 And all (they of) the land came to a wood
14. 29 My father hath troubled the land: see, I
21. 11 (Is) not this David the king of the land?
22. 5 depart, and get..into the land of Judah
23. 23 if he be in the land, that I will search him
23. 27 the Philistines have invaded the land
27. 1 escape into the land of the Philistines
27. 8 for those..of old the inhabitants of the l.
27. 8 goest to Shur, even unto the land of Egypt
27. 9 David smote the land, and left neither
28. 3, 9 spirits, and the wizards, out of the land
29. 11 to return into the land of the Philistines
30. 16 the land of the Philistines and out of the l.
31. 9 the land of the Philistines round about
2 Sa. 3. 12 on his behalf, saying, Whose (is) the land?
5. 6 Jebusites, the inhabitants of the land
7. 23 for thy land, before thy people, which thou
10 2 came into the land of the children of Am.
15. 4 Oh that I were made judge in the land, that
17. 26 and Absalom pitched in the land of Gilead
19. 9 now he is fled out of the land for Absalom
21. 14 after that God was entreated for the land
24. 6 to Gilead, and to the land of Tahtim-ho.
24. 8 when they had gone through all the land
24. 13 shall..famine come unto thee in thy land
24. 13 there be three days' pestilence in thy land
24. 25 the LORD was entreated for the land, and
1 Ki. 4. 10 to him..Sochoh, and all the land of Hepher
4. 19 and..the only officer which (was) in the l.
4. 21 from the river unto the land of the Phil.
6. 1 Israel were come out of the land of Egypt
8. 9 when they came out of the land of Egypt
8. 21 he brought them out of the land of Egypt
8. 36 give rain upon thy land, which thou hast
8. 37 If there be in the land famine, if there be
8. 37 if their enemy besiege them in the land of
8. 46 away captives unto the land of the enemy
8. 47 land whither they were carried captives
8. 47 land of them that carried them captives
8. 48 in the land of their enemies, which led
8. 48 pray unto thee toward their land which
9. 8 hath the LORD done this unto this land
9. 9 brought forth their fathers out of the land
9. 11 gave Hiram twenty cities in the land of
9. 13 called them the land of Cabul unto this
9. 18 and Tadmor in the wilderness, in the land
9. 19 to build..in all the land of his dominion
9. 21 that were left after them in the land, whom
9. 26 shore of the Red sea, in the land of Edom
10. 6 true report that I heard in mine own land
11. 18 appointed him victuals, and gave him land
12. 28 brought thee up out of the land of Egypt
14. 24 And there were also Sodomites in the land
15. 12 took away the Sodomites out of the land
15. 20 Cinneroth, with all the land of Naphtali
17. 7 because there had been no rain in the land
18. 5 Go into the land, unto all fountains of water
18. 6 they divided the land between them, to
20. 7 the king..called all the elders of the land
22. 46 And the remnant...he took out of the l.
2 Ki. 3 27 from him, and returned to (their own) land
4. 38 (there was) a dearth in the land; and the
5. 2 brought..out of the land of Israel a little
5. 4 said the maid that (is) of the land of Israel
6. 23 came no more into the land of Israel
8. 1 shall also come upon the land seven years
8. 2 in the land of the Philistines seven years
8. 3 that the woman returned out of the land
8. 6 since the day that she left the land, even
10. 33 the land of Gilead, the Gadites, and the
11. 3 And Athaliah did reign over the land
11. 14 the people of the land rejoiced, and blew
11. 18 people of the land went into the house of
11. 19 the guard, and all the people of the land
11. 20 all the people of the land rejoiced, and
13. 20 bands of the Moabites invaded the land at
15. 5 king's son..judging the people of the land
15. 19 the king of Assyria came against the land
15. 20 the king..stayed not there in the land
15. 29 and Galilee, all the land of Naphtali, and
16. 15 burnt offering of all the people of the land
17. 5 the king..came up throughout all the land
17. 7 had brought them up out of the land of E.
17. 26, 26 not the manner of the God of the land
17. 27 teach..the manner of the God of the land
17. 36 who brought you up out of the land of E.
18. 25 Go up against this land, and destroy it
18. 32 away to a land like your own land, a land
18. 32 a land of bread..a land of oil olive and of
18. 33 delivered at all his land out of the hand
19. 7 hear..and shall return to his own land
19. 7 cause..to fall by the sword in his own land
19. 11 kings of Assyria have done to all lands by
19. 17 have destroyed the nations and their lands
19. 37 and they escaped into the land of Arme.
21. 24 the people of the land slew all them that
21. 24 the people of the land made Josiah his son

2 Ki. 23. 24 in the land of Judah and in Jerusalem
23. 30 the people of the land took Jehoahaz the
23. 33 at Riblah, in the land of Hamath, that he
23. 33 put the land to a tribute of an hundred
23. 35 but he taxed the land to give the money
23. 35 exacted..the gold of the people of the land
24. 7 came not again any more out of his land
24. 14 the poorest sort of the people of the land
24. 15 the mighty of the land; (those) carried he
25. 3 was no bread for the people of the land
25. 12 left of the poor of the land (to be) vine
25. 19 which mustered the people of the land
25. 19 threescore men of the people of the land
25. 21 slew them at Riblah in the land of Ham.
25. 22 people that remained in the land of Judah
25. 24 dwell in the land, and serve the king of B.
1 Ch. 1. 43 the kings that reigned in the land of Edom
1. 45 Husham of the land of the Temanites rei.
2. 22 three and twenty cities in the land of G.
4. 40 the land (was) wide, and quiet, and peac.
5. 9 their cattle were multiplied in the land of
5. 11 dwelt..in the land of Bashan unto Salcah
5. 23 half tribe of Manasseh dwelt in the land
5. 25 after the gods of the people of the land
6. 55 gave them Hebron in the land of Judah
7. 21 men..(that were) born in (that) land slew
10. 9 sent into the land of the Philistines round
11. 4 Jebusites (were), the inhabitants of the l.
13. 2 (that are) left in all the land of Israel, and
14. 17 the fame of David went out into all lands
16. 18 Unto thee will I give the land of Canaan
19. 2 into the land of the children of Ammon
19. 3 and to overthrow, and to spy out the land
21. 12 the pestilence, in the land, and the angel
22. 2 the strangers that (were) in the land of I.
22. 18 of the land into mine hand; and the land
28. 8 ye may possess this good land, and leave
2 Ch. 2. 17 strangers that (were) in the land of Israel
6. 5 brought forth my people out of the land
6. 27 send rain upon thy land, which thou hast
6. 28 if there be dearth in the land, if there be
6. 28 besiege them in the cities of their land
6. 36 away captives unto a land far off or near
6. 37 in the land whither they are carried cap.
6. 37 pray unto thee in the land of their capti.
6. 38 in the land of their captivity, whither
6. 38 pray toward their land, which thou gavest
7. 13 I command the locusts to devour the land
7. 14 forgive their sin, and will heal their land
7. 21 hath the LORD done thus unto this land
7. 22 brought them forth out of the land of E.
8. 6 and throughout all the land of his domi.
8. 8 who were left after them in the land, whom
8. 17 Eloth, at the sea side in the land of Edom
9. 5 I heard in mine own land of thine acts
9. 11 none such seen before in the land of Jud.
9. 12 went away to her own land, she and her
9. 26 from the river even unto the land of the
9. 28 horses out of Egypt, and out of all lands
13. 9 the manner of the nations of (other) lands?
14. 1 In his days, the land was quiet ten years
14. 6 the land had rest, and he had no war in
14. 7 and bars, (while) the land (is) yet before
15. 8 out of all the land of Judah and Benjamin
17. 2 set garrisons in the land of Judah, and in
17. 10 of the lands that (were) round about Jud.
19. 3 hast taken away the groves out of the l.
19. 5 he set judges in the land, throughout all
20. 7 didst drive out the inhabitants of this land
20. 10 when they came out of the land of Egypt
22. 12 hid..and Athaliah reigned over the land
23. 13 people of the land rejoiced, and sounded
23. 20 governors..and all the people of the land
23. 21 all the people of the land rejoiced: and
26. 21 son (was)..judging the people of the land
30. 9 that they shall come again into this land
30. 25 that came out of the land of Israel, and
32. 4 that ran through the midst of the land
32. 13 done unto all the people of (other) lands
32. 13 lands any ways able to deliver their lands
32. 17 the gods of the nations of (other) lands
32. 21 he returned with shame..to his own land
32. 31 of the wonder that was (done) in the land
33. 25 the people of the land slew all them that
33. 25 the people of the land made Josiah his son
34. 7 throughout all the land of Israel, he return.
34. 8 he had purged the land, and the house
36. 1 the people of the land took Jehoahaz the
36. 3 condemned the land in an hundred talents
36. 21 until the land had enjoyed her sabbaths
Ezra 4. 4 the people of the land weakened the hands
6. 21 the filthiness of the heathen of the land
9. 1 separated..from the people of the lands
9. 2 mingled..with the people of (those) lands
9. 7 into the hand of the kings of the lands, to
9. 11 The land, unto which ye go to possess it
9. 11 is an unclean land with the filthiness of
9. 11 of the people of the lands, with their
9. 12 eat the good of the land, and leave (it)
10. 2 strange wives of the people of the land
10. 11 separate..from the people of the land, and
Neh. 4. 4 give them for a prey in the land of capt.
5. 14 to be their governor in the land of Judah
9. 8 with him, to give the land of the Canaan.
9. 10 servants, and on all the people of his land
9. 15 land which thou hadst sworn to give them
9. 22 possessed the land of Sihon, and the land
9. 22 Heshbon, and the land of Og king of B.
9. 23 broughtest them into the land concern.
9. 24 children went in and possessed the land
9. 24 before them the inhabitants of the land
9. 24 the people of the land, that they might
Neh. 9. 30 into the hand of the people of the lands
9. 35 fat land which thou gavest before them
9. 36 the land that thou gavest unto our fathers
10. 28 separated..from the people of the lands
10. 30 our daughters unto the people of the land
10. 31 (if) the people of the land bring ware or
Esth. 8. 17 many of the people of the land became J.
10. 1 Ahasuerus laid a tribute upon the land
Job 1. 1 There was a man in the land of Uz, whose
1. 10 and his substance is increased in the land
10. 21 land of darkness, and the shadow of death
10. 22 A land of darkness, as darkness (itself
28. 13 neither is it found in the land of the living
37. 13 whether for correction, or for his land, or
42. 15 in all the land were no women found (so)
Psa. 10. 16 the heathen are perished out of his land
27. 13 the goodness of the LORD in the land of
35. 20 against (them that are) quiet in the land
37. 3 shalt thou dwell in the land, and verily
37. 29 The righteous shall inherit the land, and
37. 34 he shall exalt thee to inherit the land
42. 6 I remember thee from the land of Jordan
44. 3 they got not the land in possession by their
52. 5 root thee out of the land of the living
63. 1 longeth for thee in a dry and thirsty land
66. 1 Make a joyful noise unto God, all ye lands
74. 8 burnt..the synagogues of God in the land
78. 12 in the land of Egypt, (in) the field of Zoan
80. 9 to take deep root, and it filled the land
81. 5 when he went out through the land of E.
81. 10 which brought thee out of the land of E
85. 1 thou hast been favourable unto thy land
85. 9 fear him; that glory may dwell in our land
85. 12 and our land shall yield her increase
88. 12 righteousness in the land of forgetfulness
100. 1 a joyful noise unto the LORD, all ye lands
101. 6 (shall be) upon the faithful of the land
101. 8 early destroy all the wicked of the land
105. 11 Unto thee will I give the land of Canaan
105. 16 he called for a famine upon the land: he
105. 23 and Jacob sojourned in the land of Ham
105. 27 They showed..wonders in the land of H.
105. 30 Their land brought forth frogs in abund.
105. 32 He gave them..flaming fire in their land
105. 35 did eat up all the herbs in their land, and
105. 36 smote also all the first born in their land
105. 44 And gave them the lands of the heathen
106. 22 Wondrous works in the land of Ham; (and)
106. 24 Yea, they despised the pleasant land; they
106. 27 To overthrow..to scatter them in the la.
106. 38 and the land was polluted with blood
107. 3 gathered them out of the lands, from the
107. 34 A fruitful land into barrenness, for the
116. 9 before the LORD in the land of the living
135. 12 And gave their land (for) an heritage, an
136. 21 gave their land for an heritage: for his
142. 5 (and) my portion in the land of the living
143. 6 (thirsteth) after thee, as a thirsty land
143. 10 good; lead me into the land of upright.
Prov. 2. 21 the upright shall dwell in the land, and
28. 2 For the transgression of a land many (are)
29. 4 king by judgment establisheth the land
31. 23 he sitteth among the elders of the land
Eccl. 10. 16 Woe to thee, O land, when thy king (is)
10. 17 Blessed (art) thou, O land, when thy king
Song 2. 12 voice of the turtle is heard in our land
Isa. 1. 19 obedient, ye shall eat the good of the land
2. 7 Their land also is full of silver and gold
2. 7 their land is also full of horses, neither
2. 8 Their land also is full of idols; they wor.
5. 30 if (one) look unto the land, behold dark.
6. 12 great forsaking in the midst of the land
7. 18 for the bee that (is) in the land of Assyria
7. 22 shall every one eat that is left in the land
7. 24 the land shall become briers and thorns
8. 8 wings shall fill the breadth of thy land
9. 1 land of Zebulun, and the land of Naphtali
9. 2 dwell in the land of the shadow of death
9. 19 Through the wrath..is the land darkened
10. 23 determined, in the midst of all the land
11. 16 that he came up out of the land of Egypt
13. 5 his indignation, to destroy the whole land
13. 9 and fierce anger, to lay the land desolate
13. 14 turn..and flee every one into his own land
14. 20 thou hast destroyed thy land, (and) slain
14. 21 nor possess the land, nor fill the face of the
14. 25 I will break the Assyrian in my land, and
16. 1 Send ye the lamb to the ruler of the land
16. 4 oppressors are consumed out of the land
18. 1 Woe to the land shadowing with wings
18. 2, 7 a nation..whose land the rivers have sp.
19. 18 shall five cities in the land of Egypt speak
19. 19 altar to the LORD in the midst of the land
19. 20 for a witness unto the LORD..in the land
19. 24 (even) a blessing in the midst of the land
21. 1 cometh from the desert, from a terrible l.
21. 14 The inhabitants of the land of Tema bro.
23. 1 from the land of Chittim it is revealed to
23. 10 Pass through thy land as a river, O daug.
23. 13 Behold the land of the Chaldeans; this
24. 3 The land shall be utterly emptied, and
24. 11 is darkened, the mirth of the land is gone
24. 13 thus it shall be in the midst of the land
26. 1 this song be sung in the land of Judah
26. 10 in the land of uprightness will he deal
27. 13 ready to perish in the land of Assyria
27. 13 outcasts in the land of Egypt, and shall
30. 6 Into the land of trouble and anguish, from
32. 2 shadow of a great rock in a weary land
33. 17 they shall behold the land that is very far
34. 6 a great slaughter in the land of Idumea
34. 7 their land shall be soaked with blood, and
Isa. 34. 9 land thereof shall become burning pitch
36. 10 Am I now come up..against this land to
36. 10 Go up against this land, and destroy it
36. 17 you away to a land like your own land
36. 17 a land of corn and wine, a land of bread
36. 18 gods of the nations delivered his land out
36. 20 lands, that have delivered their land out
37. 7 hear a rumour, and return to his own land
37. 7 him to fall by the sword in his own land
37. 11 to all lands by destroying them utterly
37. 38 and they escaped into the land of Armenia
38. 11 (even) the LORD, in the land of the living
41. 18 will make..the dry land springs of water
49. 12 Behold..these from the land of Sinim
49. 19 the land of thy destruction, shall even
53. 8 he was cut off out of the land of the living
57. 13 putteth his trust..shall possess the land
60. 18 Violence shall no more be..in thy land
60. 21 they shall inherit the land for ever, the
61. 7 their land they shall possess the double
62. 4 thy land any more be termed Desolate
62. 4 be called Hephzi-bah, and thy land Beu.
62. 4 LORD delighteth in thee, and thy land shall
Jer. 1. 1 (were) in Anathoth in the land of Benja
1. 14 upon all the inhabitants of the land
1. 18 and brazen walls against the whole land
1. 18 priests..and against the people of the land
2. 2 wilderness, in a land (that was) not sown
2. 6 that brought us up out of the land of Eg.
2. 6 land of deserts and of pits, through a land
2. 6 through a land that no man passed thro.
2. 7 ye defiled my land, and made mine heri.
2. 15 (and) yelled, and they made his land wa.
2. 31 a wilderness unto Israel? a land of dark.
3. 1 shall not that land be greatly polluted?
3. 2 and thou hast polluted the land with thy
3. 9 that she defiled the land, and committed
3. 16 be multiplied and increased in the land
3. 18 out of the land of the north to the land
3. 19 and give thee a pleasant land, a goodly
4. 5 Blow ye the trumpet in the land: cry, ga.
4. 7 from his place to make thy land desolate
4. 20 the whole land is spoiled: suddenly are
4. 27 The whole land shall be desolate; yet will
5. 19 land, so shall ye serve strangers in a land
5. 30 horrible thing is committed in the land
6. 8 make thee desolate, a land not inhabited
6. 12 my hand upon the inhabitants of the land
7. 7 in the land that I gave to your fathers, for
7. 22 that I brought them out of the land of E.
7. 25 came forth out of the land of Egypt unto
7. 34 cause to cease..for the land shall be des.
8. 16 the whole land trembled at the sound of
8. 16 have devoured the land, and all that is
9. 12 the land perisheth (and) is burnt up like
9. 19 we have forsaken the land, because our
10. 17 Gather up thy wares out of the land, O
10. 18 I will sling out the inhabitants of the land
11. 4 I brought them forth out of the land of E.
11. 5 them a land flowing with milk and honey
11. 7 brought them up out of the land of Egypt
11. 19 let us cut him off from the land of the li.
12. 4 How long shall the land mourn, and the
12. 5 and (if) in the land of peace, (wherein)
12. 11 the whole land is made desolate, because
12. 12 land even to the (other) end of the land
12. 15 to his heritage, and every man to his land
13. 13 I will fill all the inhabitants of this land
14. 8 thou be as a stranger in the land, and as
14. 15 and famine shall not be in this land; By
14. 18 go about into a land that they know not
15. 7 fan them with a fan in the gates of the l.
15. 14 pass..into a land (which) thou knowest
16. 3 their fathers that begat them in this land
16. 6 great and the small shall die in this land
16. 13 out of this land into a land that ye know
16. 14 the children of Israel out of the land of E.
16. 15 land of the north, and from all the lands
16. 18 because they have defiled my land, they
17. 4 to serve thine enemies in the land which
17. 6 wilderness, (in) a salt land and not inhab.
17. 26 from the land of Benjamin, and from the
18. 16 make their land desolate, (and) a perpet.
22. 12 captive, and shall see this land no more
22. 27 the land whereunto they desire to return
22. 28 are cast into a land which they know not
23. 7 the children of Israel out of the land of E.
23. 10 For the land is full of adulterers; for
23. 10 because of swearing the land mourneth
23. 15 is profaneness gone forth into all the land
24. 5 into the land of the Chaldeans for (their)
24. 6 and I will bring them again to this land
24. 8 this land, and them that dwell in the land
25. 9 will bring them against this land, and aga.
25. 11 this whole land shall be a desolation, (and)
25. 12 the land of the Chaldeans, and will make
25. 13 I will bring upon that land all my words
25. 20 land of Uz, and all the kings of the land
25. 38 their land is desolate because of the fierce.
26. 17 rose up certain of the elders of the land
26. 20 against this city and against this land
27. 6 now have I given all these lands into the
27. 7 serve..until the very time of his land
30. 3 to the land that I gave to their fathers
30. 10 thy seed from the land of their captivity
31. 16 shall come again from the land of the
31. 23 use this speech in the land of Judah
31. 32 to bring them out of the land of Egypt
32. 15 shall be possessed again in this land
32. 20 signs and wonders in the land of Egypt
32. 21 out of the land of Egypt with signs, and
32. 22 this land..a land flowing with milk and

Jer. 32. 41 I will plant them in this land assuredly
32. 43 And fields shall be bought in this land
32. 44 take witnesses in the land of Benjamin
33. 11 cause to return the captivity of the land
33. 13 in the land of Benjamin, and in the places
33. 15 judgment and righteousness in the land
34. 13 that I brought them forth out of the land
34. 19 all the people of the land, which passed
35. 11 king of Babylon came up into the land
36. 29 shall certainly come and destroy this land
37. 1 king of Babylon made king in the land of
37. 2 nor the people of the land, did hearken
37. 7 shall return to Egypt into their own land
37. 12 went..to go into the land of Benjamin, to
37. 19 come against you, nor against this land
39. 5 brought..to Riblah in the land of Hamath
39. 10 which had nothing, in the land of Judah
40. 4 the land (is) before thee: whither it seem.
40. 6 among the people that were left in the l.
40. 7 the son of Ahikam governor in the land
40. 7 the poor of the land, of them that were
40. 9 dwell in the land, and serve the king of
40. 12 came to the land of Judah, to Gedaliah
41. 2 the king..had made governor over the l.
41. 18 whom the king..made governor in the l.
42. 10 If ye will still abide in this land, then will
42. 13 We will not dwell in this land, neither
42. 14 we will go into the land of Egypt, where
42. 16 shall overtake you there in the land of E.
43. 4 obeyed not..to dwell in the land of Judah
43. 5 been driven, to dwell in the land of Judah
43. 7 they came into the land of Egypt: for
43. 11 when he cometh he shall smite the land
43. 12 shall array himself with the land of Egypt
43. 13 Beth-shemesh, that (is) in the land of E.
44. 1 all the Jews which dwell in the land of E.
44. 8 burning incense unto other gods in the l.
44. 9 they have committed in the land of Judah
44. 12, 14, 28 the land of Egypt to sojourn there
44. 12 consumed, (and) fall in the land of Egypt
44. 13 I will punish them that dwell in the land
44. 14 they should return into the land of Judah
44. 15 the people that dwelt in the land of Egypt
44. 21 the people of the land, did not the LORD
44. 22 therefore is your land a desolation, and
44. 24, 27 Judah that (are) in the land of Egypt
44. 26 all Judah that dwell in the land of Egypt
44. 26 any man of Judah in all the land of Egypt
44. 28 the land of Egypt into the land of Judah
45. 4 and..I will pluck up, even this whole land
46. 12 and thy cry hath filled the land: for the
46. 13 should come (and) smite the land of Egypt
46. 16 and to the land of our nativity, from the
46. 27 thy seed from the land of their captivity
47. 2 shall overflow the land, and all that is
47. 2 the inhabitants of the land shall howl
48. 24 upon all the cities of the land of Moab
48. 33 plentiful field, and from the land of Moab
50. 1 against the land of the Chaldeans by Jer.
50. 3 which shall make her land desolate, and
50. 8 go forth out of the land of the Chaldeans
50. 16 they shall flee every one to his own land
50. 18 punish the king of Babylon and his land
50. 21 Go up against the land of Merathaim
50. 22 A sound of battle (is) in the land, and of
50. 25 the work..in the land of the Chaldeans
50. 28 that flee and escape out of the land of B.
50. 34 he may give rest to the land, and disquiet
50. 38 it (is) the land of graven images, and they
50. 45 purposed against the land of the Chaldeans
51. 2 shall fan her, and shall empty her land
51. 4 shall fall in the land of the Chaldeans
51. 5 their land was filled with sin against the
51. 27 Set ye up a standard in the land, blow
51. 28 rulers..and all the land of his dominion
51. 29 the land shall tremble and sorrow: for
51. 29 to make the land of Babylon a desolation
51. 43 Her cities are a desolation, a dry land, and
51. 43 a land wherein no man dwelleth, neither
51. 46 rumour that shall be heard in the land
51. 46 and violence in the land, ruler against
51. 47 her whole land shall be confounded, and
51. 52 through all her land the wounded shall
51. 54 destruction from the land of..Chaldeans
52. 6 was no bread for the people of the land
52. 9 carried..to Riblah in the land of Hamath
52. 16 of the poor of the land for vine dressers
52. 25 who mustered the people of the land; and
52. 25 threescore men of the people of the land
52. 27 put them to death in Riblah in the land
Lam. 4. 21 daughter..that dwellest in the land of Uz
Eze. 1. 3 the land of the Chaldeans, by the river
6. 14 hand upon them, and make the land des.
7. 2 is come upon the four corners of the land
7. 7 O thou that dwellest in the land: the time
7. 23 the land is full of bloody crimes, and the
7. 27 hands of the people of the land shall be
8. 17 they have filled the land with violence
9. 9 the land is full of blood, and the city full
11. 15 unto us is this land given in possession
12. 13 to Babylon (to) the land of the Chaldeans
12. 19 say unto the people of the land, Thus saith
12. 19 her land may be desolate from all that
12. 20 laid waste, and the land shall be desolate
14. 13 land sinneth against me by trespassing
14. 15 noisome beasts to pass through the land
14. 16 delivered, but the land shall be desolate
14. 17 land, and say, Sword, go through the land
14. 19 I send a pestilence into that land, and pour
15. 8 I will make the land desolate, because they
16. 3 thy nativity (is) of the land of Canaan
16. 29 in the land of Canaan unto Chaldea; and

Eze. 17. 4 carried it into a land of traffic; he set it
17. 5 He took also of the seed of the land, and
17. 13 he hath also taken the mighty of the land
19. 4 him with chains unto the land of Egypt
19. 7 the land was desolate, and the fulness
20. 5 known unto them in the land of Egypt
20. 6 forth of the land of Egypt into a land that
20. 6, 15 which (is) the glory of all lands
20. 8 anger..in the midst of the land of Egypt
20. 9 bringing them forth out of the land of E.
20. 10 to go forth out of the land of Egypt, and
20. 15 them into the land which I had given
20. 28 I had brought them into the land, (for)
20. 36 in the wilderness of the land of Egypt, so
20. 40 Israel, all of them in the land, serve me
21. 19 twain shall come forth out of one land
21. 30 I will judge thee..in the land of thy nat.
21. 32 thy blood shall be in the midst of the land
22. 24 Thou (art) the land that is not cleansed
22. 29 people of the land have used oppression
22. 30 stand in the gap before me for the land
23. 15 of Chaldea, the land of their nativity
23. 19 played the harlot in the land of Egypt
23. 27 whoredom (brought) from the land of Eg
23. 48 cause lewdness to cease out of the land
26. 20 I shall set glory in the land of the living
27. 17 land of Israel, they (were) thy merchants
27. 29 all the pilots..shall stand upon the land
29. 9 land of Egypt shall be desolate and waste
29. 10 will make the land of Egypt utterly waste
29. 12 I will make the land of Egypt desolate
29. 14 (into) the land of Pathros, into the land
29. 19 Behold, I will give the land of Egypt unto
29. 20 I have given him the land of Egypt (for)
30. 5 the men of the land that is in league
30. 11 He..shall be brought to destroy the land
30. 11 they shall..fill the land with the slain
30. 12 sell the land into the hand of the wicked
30. 12 I will make the land waste, and all that
30. 13 there..be no more a prince of the land of E.
30. 13 I will put a fear in the land of Egypt
30. 25 he shall stretch it out upon the land of E.
31. 12 are broken by all the rivers of the land
32. 4 Then will I leave thee upon the land, I
32. 6 will also water with thy blood the land
32. 8 set darkness upon thy land, saith the LORD
32. 15 I shall make the land of Egypt desolate
32. 23 which caused terror in the land of the liv.
32. 24, 26 their terror in the land of the living
32. 25 terror was caused in the land of the living
32. 27 terror of the mighty in the land of the living
32. 32 caused my terror in the land of the living
33. 2 upon a land, if the people of the land take
33. 3 he seeth the sword come upon the land
33. 24 the land: but we (are) many; the land is
33. 25 shed blood: and shall ye possess the land?
33. 26 ye defile..and shall ye possess the land?
33. 28 I will lay the land most desolate, and
33. 29 when I have laid the land most desolate
34. 25 the evil beasts to cease out of the land
34. 28 shall the beast of the land devour them
34. 29 no more consumed with hunger in the land
36. 5 which have appointed my land into their
36. 18 blood that they had shed upon the land
36. 20 These..are gone forth out of his land
36. 28 in the land that I gave to your fathers
36. 34 the desolate land shall be tilled, whereas
36. 35 This land that was desolate is become like
37. 22 in the land upon the mountains of Israel
37. 25 they shall dwell in the land that I have
38. 2 Gog, the land of Magog, the chief prince
38. 8 land (that is) brought back from the sword
38. 9 shalt be like a cloud to cover the land
38. 11 go up to the land of unwalled villages
38. 12 nations..dwell in the midst of the land
38. 16 shalt come..as a cloud to cover the land
38. 16 I will bring thee against my land, that
39. 12 burying..that they may cleanse the land
39. 13 all the people of the land shall bury (them)
39. 14 passing through the land, to bury with
39. 15 the passengers (that) pass through the l.
39. 16 Thus shall they cleanse the land
39. 27 gathered them out of their enemies' lands
40. 2 brought he me into the land of Israel, and
45. 1 ye shall divide by lot the land for inheri.
45. 1 unto the LORD, an holy portion of the land
45. 4 The holy (portion) of the land shall be for
45. 8 In the land shall be his possession in Is.
45. 8 (the rest of) the land shall they give to the
45. 16 All the people of the land shall give this
45. 22 for all the people of the land a bullock
46. 3 the people of the land shall worship at
46. 9 the people of the land shall come before
47. 13 border whereby ye shall inherit the land
47. 14 land shall fall unto you for inheritance
47. 15 border of the land toward the north side
47. 18 from the land of Israel (by) Jordan, from
47. 21 So shall ye divide this land unto you
48. 12 (this) oblation of the land that is offered
48. 14 nor alienate the first fruits of the land
48. 29 This (is) the land which ye shall divide
Dan. 1. 2 which he carried into the land of Shinar
9. 6 fathers, and to all the people of the land
9. 15 brought thy people forth out of the land
11. 16 he shall stand in the glorious land, which
11. 19 his face toward the fort of his own land
11. 28 he return into his land with great riches
11. 28 do (exploits), and return to his own land
11. 41 He shall enter also into the glorious land
11. 42 and the land of Egypt shall not escape
Hos. 1. 2 the land hath committed great whoredom
1. 11 they shall come up out of the land: for

Hos. 2. 3 set her like a dry land, and slay her with
2. 15 when she came up out of the land of Eg.
4. 1 controversy with..inhabitants of the land
4. 1 mercy, nor knowledge of God in the land
4. 3 Therefore shall the land mourn, and every
7. 16 this (shall be) their derision in the land
9. 3 They shall not dwell in the LORD'S land
10. 1 according to the goodness of his land they
11. 5 shall not return into the land of Egypt
11. 11 and as a dove out of the land of Assyria
12. 9 the LORD thy God from the land of Egypt
13. 4 the LORD thy God from the land of Egypt
13. 5 the wilderness, in the land of great drought
Joel 1. 2 give ear, all ye inhabitants of the land
1. 6 a nation is come up upon my land, strong
1. 14 all the inhabitants of the land (into) the
2. 1 the inhabitants of the land tremble: for
2. 3 land (is) as the garden of Eden before them
2. 18 Then will the LORD be jealous for his land
2. 20 drive him into a land barren and desolate
3. 2 among the nations, and parted my land
3. 19 have shed innocent blood in their land
Amos 2. 10 I brought you up from the land of Egypt
2. 10 led you..to possess the land of the Amo.
3. 1 which I brought up from the land of Eg.
3. 9 Publish..in the palaces in the land of E.
3. 11 (there shall be) even round about the land
7. 2 made an end of eating the grass of the land
7. 10 the land is not able to bear all his words
7. 12 flee thee away into the land of Judah, and
8. 4 even to make the poor of the land to fail
8. 8 Shall not the land tremble for this, and
8. 11 I will send a famine in the land, not a
9. 5 God of hosts (is) he that toucheth the land
9. 7 brought up Israel out of the land of Eg.?
Mic. 5. 5 when the Assyrian shall come into our l.
5. 6 they shall waste the land of Assyria with
5. 6 land of Nimrod in the entrances thereof
5. 6 when he cometh into our land, and when
5. 11 I will cut off the cities of thy land, and th.
6. 4 brought thee up out of the land of Egypt
7. 13 the land shall be desolate because of them
7. 15 of thy coming out of the land of Egypt
Nah. 3. 13 the gates of thy land shall be set wide open
Hab. 1. 6 march through the breadth of the land, to
2. 8, 17 the violence of the land, of the city, and
3. 7 curtains of the land of Midian did tremble
3. 12 Thou didst march through the land in ind.
Zeph. 1. 18 the whole land shall be devoured by the
1. 18 riddance of all them that dwell in the land
2. 5 the land of the Philistines, I will even
3. 19 land where they have been put to shame
Hag. 1. 11 I called for a drought upon the land, and
2. 4 be strong, all ye people of the land, saith
Zech. 1. 21 horn over the land of Judah to scatter it
2. 6 flee from the land of the north, saith the
3. 9 remove the iniquity of that land in one
5. 11 To build it an house in the land of Shinar
7. 5 Speak unto all the people of the land, and
7. 14 the land was desolate after them, that no
7. 14 for they laid the pleasant land desolate
9. 1 word of the LORD in the land of Hadrach
10. 10 I will bring them ..out of the land of E.
10. 10 into the land of Gilead and Lebanon; and
11. 6 no more pity the inhabitants of the land
11. 6 they shall smite the land, and out of their
11. 16 I will raise up a shepherd in the land
12. 12 the land shall mourn, every family apart
13. 2 the names of the idols out of the land, and
13. 2 the unclean spirit to pass out of the land
13. 8 shall come to pass, (that) in all the land
14. 10 the land shall be turned as a plain from
Mal. 3. 12 ye shall be a delightsome land, saith the

Field, country, level place, שָׂדֶה *sadeh.*

Ruth 4. 3 Naomi..selleth a parcel of land, which
1 Sa. 14. 14 within as it were an half acre of land
2 Sa. 9. 7 restore..all the land of Saul thy father
19. 29 have said, Thou and Ziba divide the land
2 Ki. 8. 3, 5 the king for her house and for her land
Neh. 5. 3 We have mortgaged our lands, vineyards
5. 4 (and that upon) our lands and vineyards
5. 5 other men have our lands and vineyards
5. 11 their lands, their vineyards, their olive y.
5. 16 neither bought we any land: and all my

4. *Field,* ἀγρός *agros.*

Matt. 19. 29 or mother, or wife, or children, or lands
Mark 10. 29 mother, or wife, or children, or lands, for
10. 30 sisters..mothers, and children, and lands
Acts 4. 37 Having land, sold (it), and brought the m.

5. *Land, earth,* γῆ *gē.*

Matt. 2. 6 (in) the land of Juda, art not the least am.
2. 20 go into the land of Israel: for they are d.
2. 21 arose..and came into the land of Israel
4. 15 The land of Zabulon, and the land of N.
9. 26 fame..went abroad into all that land
10. 15 be more tolerable for the land of Sodom
11. 24 be more tolerable for the land of Sodom
14. 34 they came into the land of Gennesaret
27. 45 over all the land unto the ninth hour
Mark 4. 1 multitude was by the sea on the land
6. 47 midst of the sea, and he alone on the land
6. 53 they came into the land of Gennesaret, and
15. 33 over the whole land until the ninth hour
Luke 4. 25 great famine was throughout all the land
5. 3 would thrust out a little from the land
5. 11 when they had brought their ships to land
8. 27 when he went forth to land, there met him
14. 35 It is neither fit for the land, nor yet for
21. 23 there shall be great distress in the land
John 3. 22 and his disciples into the land of Judea

John 6. 21 ship was at the land whither they went
21. 8 they were not far from land, but as it were
21. 9 As soon then as they were come to land
21. 11 drew the net to land full of great fishes
Acts 7. 3 into the land which I shall show thee
7. 4 came he out of the land of the Chaldeans
7. 4 he removed him into this land, wherein ye
7. 6 seed should sojourn in a strange land
7. 11 over all [the land of] Egypt and Chanaan
7. 29 and was a stranger in the land of Madian
7. 36 wonders and signs in the land of Egypt
7. 40 which brought us out of the land of Egypt
13. 17 when they dwelt as strangers in the land
13. 19 had destroyed seven nations in the land
13. 19 he divided their land to them by lot
27. 39 when it was day, they knew not the land
27. 43 (themselves)..(into the sea), and get to l.
27. 44 it came to pass..escaped all safe to land
Heb. 8. 9 by the hand to lead them out of the land
11. 9 By faith he sojourned in the land of prom.
Jude 5 having saved the people out of the land

6. *Dry land,* ξηρός *xēros.*
Matt 23. 15 for ye compass sea and land to make one

7. *Place, region,* χώρα *chōra.*
Mark 1. 5 there went out unto him all the land of J.
Luke 15. 14 there arose a mighty famine in that land
Acts 10. 39 in the land of the Jews, and in Jerusalem

8. *A small place, spot,* χωρίον *chōrion.*
Acts 4. 34 for as many as were possessors of lands
5. 3 keep back (part) of the price of the land?
5. 8 Tell me whether ye sold the land for so
[*See also* Barren, dry, piece, thirsty.]

LAND, to —
1. *To lead down, bring to land,* κατάγω *katagō.*
Acts 21. 3 and sailed into Syria, and [landed] at T.
28. 12 landing at Syracuse, we tarried..three

2. *To come down,* κατέρχομαι *katerchomai.*
Acts 18. 22 when he had landed at Cesarea, and gone
[*See also* Bring to.]

LAND, born in the —
Native, aboriginal, indigenous, אֶזְרָח *ezrach.*
Lev. 24. 16 the stranger, as he that is born in the land
Num 15. 30 born in the land, or a stranger, the same

LAND MARK —
1. *Border,* גְּבוּל *gebul.*
Deut 19. 14 shalt not remove thy neighbour's landmark
27. 17 he that removeth his neighbour's landmark
Prov 22. 28 Remove not the ancient landmark, which
23. 10 Remove not the old landmark; and enter

2. *Border,* גְּבוּלָה *gebulah.*
Job 24. 2 remove the landmarks: they violently

LANE —
A narrow passage, ῥύμη *rhumē.*
Luke 14. 21 Go out quickly into the streets and lanes

LANGUAGE —
1. *Word,* דָּבָר *dabar.*
Psa. 19. 3 no speech nor language..their voice is not

2. *Tongue,* לָשׁוֹן *lashon.*
Neh. 13. 24 but according to the language of each
Esth. 1. 22 and to every people after their language
1. 22 published according to the language of
3. 12 and (to) every people after their language
8. 9 unto every people after their language
8. 9 to the Jews..according to their language
Jer. 5. 15 a nation whose language thou knowest
Eze. 3. 5, 6 strange speech and of an hard language
Zech. 8. 23 out of all languages of the nations, even

3. *Tongue,* לִשָּׁן *lishshan.*
Dan. 3. 4 cried aloud..O people, nations, and lan.
3. 7 all the people, the nations, and the lang.
3. 29 That every people, nation, and language
4. 1 unto all people, nations, and languages
5. 19 all people, nations, and languages, trem.
6. 25 wrote unto all people, nations, and lang.
7. 14 that all people, nations, and languages

4. *Lip,* שָׂפָה *saphah.*
Gen. 11. 1 the whole earth was of one language, and
11. 6 they have all one language; and this they
11. 7 go down, and there confound their lang.
11. 9 LORD did there confound the language of
Psa. 81. 5 I heard a language (that) I understood not
Isa. 19. 18 speak the language of Canaan, and swear
Zeph. 3. 9 will I turn to the people a pure language

5. *Dialect, tongue,* διάλεκτος *dialektos.*
Acts 2. 6 heard them speak in his own language

LANGUAGE, strange —
To speak a strange language, לָעַז *laaz.*
Psa. 114. 1 went out..from a people of strange la.

LANGUISH, to —
To become weak, languish, אָמַל *amal,* 4*b*.
Isa. 16. 8 the fields of Heshbon languish..the vine
19. 8 and they that spread nets..shall languish
24. 4 the world languisheth (and) fadeth away
24. 4 haughty people of the earth do languish
24. 7 The new wine mourneth, the vine langui.
33. 9 The earth mourneth..languisheth: Leb.
Jer. 14. 2 the gates thereof languish; they are black
15. 9 She that hath borne seven languisheth
Lam. 2. 8 the rampart and the wall..languished tog.
Hos. 4. 3 every one that dwelleth therein shall la.
Joel 1. 10 new wine is dried up, the oil languisheth
Joel 1. 12 The vine is dried up..the fig tree languis.
Nah. 1. 4 Bashan languisheth..the flower..langui.

LANGUISHING —
Sick, sickness, דְּוַי *devai.*
Psa. 41. 3 will strengthen him upon the bed of lan.

LANTERN —
A light, flambeau, lantern, φανός *phanos.*
John 18. 3 cometh thither with lanterns and torches

LA-O-DI-CE'-A, Λαοδίκεια.
The chief city of Phrygia Pacatiana in Asia Minor, on the river Lycus, a little above its junction with the Meander, and not far to the S. of Colosse and Hierapolis. Its earlier name was Diospolis, and afterwards Rhoas; it was enlarged by Antiochus II., and called by him Laodicea, after his wife. About A.D. 64 it was destroyed as also Colosse and Hierapolis, by an earthquake, but was rebuilt by Marcus Aurelius. Its ruins are called *Eski-hissar.*
Col. 2. 1 (for) them at L., and (for) as many as have
4. 13 them (that are) in L., and them in Hiera.
4. 15 Salute the brethren which are in L., and
4. 16 that ye likewise read the (epistle) from L.
Rev. 1. 11 Sardis, and unto Philadelphia, and unto L.

LA-O-DI-CE-AN, Λαοδικεύς.
An inhabitant of Laodicea.
Col. 4. 16 it be read also in the church of the L.
Rev. 3. 14 unto the angel of the church of the L.

LAP —
1. *Cloak, garment, covering,* בֶּגֶד *beged.*
2 Ki. 4. 39 gathered thereof wild gourds his lap full

2. *Bosom, centre,* חֵיק *cheq.*
Prov 16. 33 The lot is cast into the lap; but the whole

3. *Lap, bosom,* חֹצֶן *chotsen.*
Neh. 5. 13 I shook my lap, and said, So God shake

LAP, to —
1. *To lick, lap,* לָקַק *laqaq.*
Judg. 7. 5 Every one that lappeth..as a dog lappeth

2. *To lick, lap,* לָקַק *laqaq,* 3.
Judg. 7. 6 And the number of them that lapped
7. 7 By the three hundred men that lapped

LAP-I'-DOTH, לַפִּידוֹת *lamps, lightnings.*
The husband of Deborah the prophetess. B.C. 1316.
Judg. 4. 4 the wife of L., she judged Israel at that

LAPWING —
Lapwing, woodcock, דּוּכִיפַת *dukiphath.*
Lev. 11. 19 And the stork..the lapwing, and the bat
Deut 14. 18 And the stork..the lapwing, and the bat

LARGE —
1. *To be airy,* רָוַח *ravach,* 4.
Jer. 22. 14 build me a wide house and large chamb.

2. *To be broad, wide,* רָחַב *rachab,* 2.
Isa. 30. 23 in that day shall thy cattle feed in large

3. *Broad, wide,* רָחָב *rachab.*
Gen. 34. 21 the land, behold, (it is) large enough for
Exod. 3. 8 unto a good land and a large, unto a land
Neh. 4. 19 The work (is) great and large, and we are
9. 35 in the large and fat land which thou gav.
Eze. 23. 32 drink of thy sister's cup deep and large

4. *Broad of hands,* רַחֲבַת יָדַיִם [*rachab*].
Judg 18. 10 unto a people secure, and to a large land
Neh. 7. 4 Now the city (was) large and great; but
Isa. 22. 18 toss thee (like) a ball into a large country

5. *Sufficient,* ἱκανός *hikanos.*
Matt 28. 12 they gave large money unto the soldiers

6. *Great, large,* μέγας *megas.*
Mark 14. 15 And he will show you a large upper room
Luke 22. 12 And he shall show you a large upper room
[*See also* As, how.]

LARGE, to make —
To make broad or wide, רָחַב *rachab,* 5.
Isa. 30. 33 he hath made (it) deep (and) large; the

LARGE place or room —
Broad or wide place, מֶרְחָב *merchab.*
2 Sa. 22. 20 He brought me forth also into a large pl.
Psa. 18. 19 He brought me forth also into a large pl.
31. 8 thou hast set my feet in a large room
118. 5 the LORD answered me..in a large place
Hos. 4. 16 will feed them as a lamb in a large place

LARGENESS —
Breadth, width, רֹחַב *rochab.*
1 Ki. 4. 29 largeness of heart, even as the sand that

LASCIVIOUSNESS —
Excess, licentiousness, ἀσέλγεια *aselgeia.*
Mark 7. 22 lasciviousness, an evil eye, blasphemy
2 Co. 12. 21 lasciviousness..they have committed
Gal. 5. 19 Adultery, fornication, uncleanness, lasci.
Eph. 4. 19 have given themselves over unto lascivi.
1 Pe. 4. 3 when we walked in lasciviousness, lusts
Jude 4 turning the grace of our God into lascivi.

LA-SE'-A, Λασαία.
A city on a promontory at the S.E. extremity of Crete, five miles E. of Fair Havens, and close to Cape Leonda. The name is now given to a small island off the coast.
Acts 27. 8 place..nigh whereunto was the city (of) L.

LA'-SHA, לֶשַׁע *bursting forth.*
A place at the S. extremity of Canaan, E. of the Salt Sea; called also *Callinhoë.*
Gen. 10. 19 as thou goest, unto Sodom..even unto L.

LASH-A'-RON, לַשָּׁרוֹן *the plain of Sharon.*
Josh. 12. 18 The king of Aphek, one; the king of L.

LAST —
1. *Last, latter,* אַחֲרוֹן *acharon.*
2 Sa. 19. 11 Why are ye the last to bring the king back
19. 12 wherefore then are ye the last to bring
23. 1 Now these (be) the last words of David
1 Ch. 23. 27 For by the last words of David the Levites
29. 29 the acts of David the king, first and last
2 Ch. 9. 29 rest of the acts of Solomon, first and last
12. 15 Now the acts of Rehoboam, first and last
16. 11 behold, the acts of Asa, first and last, lo
20. 34 the acts of Jehoshaphat, first and last, be.
25. 26 rest of the acts of Amaziah, first and last
26. 22 rest of the acts of Uzziah, first and last, did
28. 26 the rest of his acts..first and last, behold
35. 27 And his deeds, first and last, behold, they
Ezra 8. 13 the last sons of Adonikam, whose names
Neh. 8. 18 from the first day unto the last day, he
Isa. 41. 4 I the LORD, the first, and with the last
44. 6 I (am) the first, and I (am) the last; and
48. 12 I (am) he; I (am) the first, I also..the last
Jer. 50. 17 last this Nebuchadrezzar king of Babylon
Dan. 8. 3 one (was) higher..the higher came up last

2. *Last or latter end,* אַחֲרִית *acharith.*
Gen. 49. 1 which shall befall you in the last days
Isa. 2. 2 And it shall come to pass in the last days
Jer. 12. 4 because they said..shall not see our last
Amos 9. 1 I will slay the last of them with the sword
Mic. 4. 1 But in the last days it shall come to pass

3. *Last,* ἔσχατος *eschatos.*
Matt 19. 30 first shall be last; and the last (shall be)
20. 8 give..beginning from the last unto the fi.
20. 12 These last have wrought (but) one hour
20. 14 I will give unto this last, even as unto thee
20. 16 the last shall be first, and the first last
27. 64 the last error shall be worse than the first
Mark 9. 35 first..shall be last of all, and servant of all
10. 31 many..first shall be last; and the last first
12. 6 he sent him also last unto them, saying
12. 22 no seed: [last] of all the woman died also
Luke 12. 59 not..till thou hast paid the very last mite
13. 30 behold, there are last which shall be first
13. 30 and there are first which shall be last
John 6. 39 but should raise it up again at the last day
6. 40, 44, 54 I will raise him up at the last day
7. 37 In the last day, that great (day) of the f.
8. 9 [beginning at the eldest..unto the last]
11. 24 again in the resurrection at the last day
12. 48 the same shall judge him in the last day
Acts 2. 17 And it shall come to pass in the last days
1 Co. 4. 9 God hath set forth us the apostles last
15. 8 last of all he was seen of me also, as of
15. 26 last enemy (that) shall be destroyed (is) d.
15. 45 the last Adam (was)..a quickening spirit
15. 52 in the twinkling of an eye, at the last tr.
2 Ti. 3. 1 in the last days perilous times shall come
Heb. 1. 2 Hath in these last days spoken unto us by
Jas. 5. 3 heaped treasure together for the last days
1 Pe. 1. 5 salvation ready to be revealed in the last
1. 20 was manifest in these last times for you
2 Pe. 3. 3 that there shall come in the last days sc.
1 Jo. 2. 18 Little children, it is the last time: and
2. 18 whereby we know that it is the last time
Jude 18 there should be mockers in the last time
Rev. 1. 11 Alpha and Omega, [the first and the last]
1. 17 saying..Fear not; I am the first and the l.
2. 8 These things saith the first and the last
2. 19 I know..the last (to be) more than the fi.
15. 1 seven angels having the seven last plagues
21. 9 seven vials full of the seven last plagues
22. 13 Alpha and Omega..the first and the last

4. *Later than, after,* ὕστερον *husteron.*
Matt 22. 27 And last of all the woman died also
Luke 20. 32 Last of all the woman died also

LAST, to —
To be, הָיָה *hayah.*
Judg 14. 17 the seven days, while their feast lasted

LAST, at the —
1. *At last,* אָחֳרֵין *ochoren.*
Dan. 4. 8 But at the last Daniel came in before me

2. *Last or latter end,* אַחֲרִית *acharith.*
Prov. 5. 11 And thou mourn at the last, when thy
23. 32 At the last it biteth like a serpent, and

3. *Heel, end,* עֵקֶב *aqeb.*
Gen. 49. 19 him: but he shall overcome at the l.

4. *At any time,* ποτέ *pote.*
Phil. 4. 10 that now at the last your care of me hath

5. *At last, after all,* ὕστερον *husteron.*
Matt 26. 60 At the last came two false witnesses

LAST of all —
At last, after all, ὕστερον *husteron.*
Matt 21. 37 But last of all he sent unto them his son

LAST or latter (end or time or state) —
1. *Last or latter end,* אַחֲרִית *acharith.*
Num 23. 10 righteous, and let my last end be like his
Deut. 8. 16 prove..to do thee good at thy latter end
32. 29 (that) they would consider their latter end!

Job 8. 7 yet thy latter end should greatly increase
42. 12 So the LORD blessed the latter end of Job
Prov 19. 20 that thou mayest be wise in thy latter end
Isa. 41. 22 that we may..know the latter end of them
47. 7 neither didst remember the latter end of
Lam. 1. 9 she remembereth not her last end; there.
Dan. 8. 19 what shall be in the last end of the indig.
8. 23 in the latter time of their kingdom, when

2. *Last*, ἔσχατος *eschatos*.
Matt12. 45 the last (state) of that man is worse than
Luke11. 26 the last (state) of that man is worse than
2 Pe. 2. 20 the latter end is worse with them than

LASTING —
Age lasting, עוֹלָם *olam*.
Deut 33. 15 for the precious things of the lasting hills

LATCHET —
1. *Latchet*, שְׂרוֹךְ *serok*.
Gen. 14. 23 from a thread even to a shoe latchet, and
Isa. 5. 27 nor the latchet of their shoes be broken
2. *Latchet, thong, strap*, ἱμάς *himas*.
Mark 1. 7 the latchet of whose shoes I am not worthy
Luke 3. 16 the latchet of whose shoes I am not wor.
John 1. 27 whose shoe's latchet I am not worthy to
[*See also* Shoe-latchet.]

LATE, to be —
To tarry, delay, hinder, אָחַר *achar*, 3.
Psa. 127. 2 to sit up late, to eat the bread of sorrows

LATE, of —
1. *Yesterday*, (אֶתְמוֹל) אֶתְמוּל *ethmul*.
Mic. 2. 8 Even of late my people is risen up as an
2. *Now*, νῦν *nun*.
John11. 8 Master, the Jews of late sought to stone

LATELY —
Recently, προσφάτως *prosphatōs*.
Acts 18. 2 lately come from Italy, with his wife Pr.

LATIN, Ῥωμαϊκός, Ῥωμαϊστί *Romaic, Romaisti*.
The language of the Romans.
Luke23. 38 written over him in letters of..L., and H.
John 19. 20 written in Hebrew, (and) Greek, (and) L.

LATTER —
1. *Last, latter*, אַחֲרוֹן *acharon*.
Exod. 4. 8 they will believe the voice of the latter
Deut 24. 3 And (if) the latter husband hate her, and
24. 3 or if the latter husband die, which took
Ruth 3. 10 showed more kindness in the latter end
2 Sa. 2. 26 that it will be bitterness in the latter end?
Job. 19. 25 he shall stand at the latter (day) upon the
Dan. 11. 29 shall not be as the former, or as the latter
Hag. 2. 9 The glory of this latter house shall be gr.
2. *Last or latter end*, אַחֲרִית *acharith*.
Num 24. 14 shall do to thy people in the latter days
24. 20 but his latter end..that he perish for ever
Deut. 4. 30 in the latter days, if thou turn to the LORD
31. 29 and evil will befall you in the latter days
Jer. 23. 20 in the latter days ye shall consider it per.
30. 24 in the latter days ye shall consider it
48. 47 the captivity of Moab in the latter days
49. 39 But it shall come to pass in the latter d.
Eze. 38. 8 in the latter years thou shalt come into
38. 16 it shall be in the latter days, and I will
Dan. 2. 28 known..what shall be in the latter days
10. 14 shall befall thy people in the latter days
Hos. 3. 5 the LORD and his goodness in the latter
3. *Late, latter*, ὄψιμος *opsimos*.
Jas. 5. 7 until he receive the early and latter rain
4 *Latter*, ὕστερος *husteros*.
1 Ti. 4. 1 that in the latter times some shall depart

LATTER (growth) —
The latter growth, gathering, לֶקֶשׁ *leqesh*.
Amos 7. 1 of the shooting up of the latter growth
7. 1 the latter growth after the king's mowings

LATTER rain —
The latter or gathered rain, מַלְקוֹשׁ *malqosh*.
Deut11. 14 the first rain, and the latter rain, that thou
Job 29. 23 opened their mouth wide..for..latter rain
Prov 16. 15 his favour (is) as a cloud of the latter rain
Jer. 3. 3 Therefore..there hath been no latter rain
5. 24 giveth rain, both the former and the latter
Hos. 6. 3 as the latter (and) former rain unto the e.
Joel 2. 23 the former rain, and the latter rain in the
Zech 10. 1 Ask..rain in the time of the latter rain

LATTICE —
1. *Lattice, casement*, אֶשְׁנָב *eshnab*.
Judg. 5. 28 cried through the lattice, Why is his cha.
2. *Lattices*, חֲרַכִּים *charakkim*.
Song 2. 9 looketh..showing himself through the l.
3. *Net or wreathed work*, שְׂבָכָה *sebakah*.
2 Ki. 1. 2 Ahaziah fell down through a lattice in his

LAUD, to —
To applaud, ἐπαινέω *epaineō*.
Rom 15. 11 Praise the Lord..laud him, all ye people

LAUGH, to —
1. *To scorn*, לָעַג *laag*.
Job 9. 23 he will laugh at the trial of the innocent
Psa. 80. 6 and our enemies laugh among themselves
2. *Laughter*, צְחֹק *tsechoq*.
Gen. 21. 6 God hath made me to laugh ..all that hear

3. *To laugh*, צָחַק *tsachaq*.
Gen. 17. 17 Abraham fell upon his face, and laughed
18. 12 Sarah laughed within herself, saying, Af.
18. 13 Wherefore did Sarah laugh, saying, Shall
18. 15 Sarah denied, saying, I laughed not; for
18. 15 And he said, Nay; but thou didst laugh
21. 6 (so that) all that hear will laugh with me
4. *To laugh*, שָׂחַק *sachaq*.
Job 5. 22 At destruction and famine thou shalt la.
29. 24 (If) I laughed on them, they believed (it)
41. 29 Darts are counted as stubble: he laugheth
Psa. 2. 4 He that sitteth in the heavens shall laugh
37. 13 The LORD shall laugh at him; for he seeth
52. 6 shall see, and fear, and shall laugh at him
59. 8 But thou, O LORD, shalt laugh at them
Prov. 1. 26 I also will laugh at your calamity; I will
Eccl. 3. 4 A time to weep, and a time to laugh; a
5. *To laugh*, γελάω *gelaō*.
Luke 6. 21 Blessed..that weep now: for ye shall la.
6. 25 Woe unto you that laugh now! for ye sh.

LAUGH to scorn, to —
1. *To scorn*, לָעַג *laag*.
2 Ki. 19. 21 daughter of Zion..laughed thee to scorn
Job 22. 19 glad; and the innocent laugh them to sc.
Neh. 2. 19 they laughed us to scorn, and despised
Psa. 22. 7 All they that see me laugh me to scorn
Isa. 37. 22 daughter of Zion..laughed thee to scorn
2. *To laugh, deride*, שָׂחַק *sachaq*, 5.
2 Ch. 30. 10 they laughed them to scorn, and mocked
3. *Laughter*, צְחֹק *tsechoq*.
Eze. 23. 32 thou shalt be laughed to scorn and had in
4. *Laughter, derision, play*, שְׂחוֹק *sechoq*.
Job 12. 4 the just upright (man is) laughed to scorn
5. *To laugh at, or down*, καταγελάω *katagelaō*.
Matt. 9. 24 sleepeth. And they laughed him to scorn
Mark 5. 40 And they laughed him to scorn. But when
Luke 8. 53 And they laughed him to scorn, knowing

LAUGHING or laughter —
1. *Laughter*, שְׂחוֹק *sechoq*.
Job 8. 21 Till he fill thy mouth with laughing, and
Psa. 126. 2 Then was our mouth filled with laughter
Prov. 14. 13 Even in laughter the heart is sorrowful
Eccl. 2. 2 I said of laughter, (It is) mad; and of mi.
7. 3 Sorrow (is) better than laughter: for by
7. 6 under a pot, so (is) the laughter of the fool
10. 19 A feast is made for laughter, and wine
2. *Laughter*, γέλως *gelōs*.
Jas. 4. 9 let your laughter be turned to mourning

LAUNCH (forth or out), to —
1. *To lead up, launch out*, ἀνάγω *anagō*.
Luke 8. 22 side of the lake. And they launched fo.
Acts 21. 1 we were gotten from them, and had lau.
27. 2 we launched, meaning to sail by the co.
27. 4 when we had launched from thence, we
2. *To lead up upon, launch forth*, ἐπανάγω *epanagō*.
Luke 5. 4 Launch out into the deep, and let down

LAVER —
Pan, laver, כִּיּוֹר *kiyyor*.
Exod30. 18 Thou shalt also make a laver (of) brass
30. 28 all his vessels, and the laver and his foot
31. 9 his furniture, and the laver and his foot
35. 16 and all his vessels, the laver and his foot
38. 8 he made the laver (of) brass, and the foot
39. 39 and all his vessels, the laver and his foot
40. 7 thou shalt set the laver between the tent
40. 11 thou shalt anoint the laver and his foot
40. 30 he set the laver between the tent of the
Lev. 8. 11 both the laver and his foot, to sanctify
1 Ki. 7. 30 under the laver (were) undersetters mol.
7. 38 Then made he ten lavers of brass: one la.
7. 38 (and) every laver was four cubits: (and)
7. 38 upon every one of the ten bases one laver
7. 40 Hiram made the lavers, and the shovels
7. 43 the ten bases, and ten lavers on the bases
2 Ki. 16. 17 removed the laver from off them; and
2 Ch. 4. 6 He made also ten lavers, and put five on
4. 14 He made also bases, and lavers made he

LAVISH, to —
To lightly esteem, pour forth, זוּל *zul*.
Isa. 46. 6 They lavish gold out of the bag, and we.

LAW —
1. *Law, sentence*, דָּת *dath*.
Deut33. 2 from his right hand (went) a fiery law for
Ezra 7. 12, 21 a scribe of the law of the God of hea.
7. 14 according to the law of thy God which (is)
7. 25 judge..all such as know the laws of thy G.
7. 26 whosoever will not do the law of thy God
7. 26 and the law of the king, let judgment be
Esth. 1. 8 the drinking (was) according to the law
1. 13 toward all that knew law and judgment
1. 15 unto the queen Vashti according to law
1. 19 let it be written among the laws of the P.
3. 8 and their laws (are) diverse from all peo.
3. 8 neither keep they the king's laws: there.
4. 11 one law of his to put (him) to death, ex.
4. 16 go in..which (is) not according to the law
Dan. 6. 5 except we find (it)..concerning the law of
6. 8, 12 according to the law of the Medes and
6. 15 Know, O king, that the law of the Medes
7. 25 he shall think to change times and laws

2. *Statute, decree*, חֹק *choq*.
Gen. 47. 26 Joseph made it a law over the land of E.
1 Ch. 16. 17 hath confirmed the same to Jacob for a l
Psa. 94. 20 thee, which frameth mischief by a law?
105. 10 confirmed the same unto Jacob for a law
3. *To decree, grave*, חָקַק *chaqaq* 4.
Prov. 31. 5 Lest they drink, and forget the law, and
4. *Command, precept, charge*, מִצְוָה *mitsvah*.
Jer. 32. 11 which was sealed (according) to the law
5. *Judgment*, מִשְׁפָּט *mishpat*.
Psa. 81. 4 this (was) a statute for Israel, (and) a law
6. *Direction, teaching*, תּוֹרָה *torah*.
Gen. 26. 5 Because that Abraham obeyed..my laws
Exod12. 49 One law shall be to him that is home born
13. 9 that the LORD'S law may be in thy mouth
16. 4 whether they will walk in my law, or no
16. 28 How long refuse ye to keep..my laws?
18. 16 know the statutes of God, and his laws
18. 20 shalt teach them ordinances and laws
24. 12 will give thee tables of stone, and a law
Lev. 6. 9 This (is) the law of the burnt offering: It
6. 14 this (is) the law of the meat offering: the
6. 25 This (is) the law of the sin offering: In
7. 1 this (is) the law of the trespass offering
7. 7 one law for them: the priest that maketh
7. 11 this (is) the law of the sacrifice of peace
7. 37 This (is) the law of the burnt offering, of
11. 46 This (is) the law of the beasts, and of the
12. 7 This (is) the law for her that hath born a
13. 59 This (is) the law of the plague of leprosy
14. 2 This shall be the law of the leper in the
14. 32 This (is) the law (of him) in whom (is) the
14. 54 This (is) the law for all manner of plague
14. 57 when (it is) clean: this (is) the law of le.
15. 32 This (is) the law of him that hath an issue
26. 46 These (are) the statutes..and laws which
Num. 5. 29 This (is) the law of jealousies, when a wife
5. 30 priest shall execute upon her all this law
6. 13 this (is) the law of the Nazarite, when the
6. 21 This (is) the law..after the law of his se.
15. 16 One law and one manner shall be for you
15. 29 Ye shall have one law for him that sinneth
19. 2 This (is) the ordinance of the law which
19. 14 This (is) the law, when a man dieth in a
31. 21 This (is) the ordinance of the law which
Deut. 1. 5 began Moses to declare this law, saying
4. 8 righteous as all this law, which I set before
4. 44 this (is) the law which Moses set before
17. 11 According to the sentence of the law which
17. 18 he shall write him a copy of this law in a
17. 19 keep all the words of this law and these
27. 3, 8 thou shalt write..the words of this law
27. 26 confirmeth not (all) the words of this law
28. 58 not observe to do all the words of this law
28. 61 which (is) not written in the book of this l.
29. 21 that are written in this book of the law
29. 29 that (we) may do all the words of this law
30. 10 (which are) written in this book of the law
31. 9 Moses wrote this law, and delivered it unto
31. 11 thou shalt read this law before all Israel
31. 12 and observe to do all the words of this law
31. 24 of writing the words of this law in a book
31. 26 Take this book of the law, and put it in
32. 46 to observe to do, all the words of this law
33. 4 Moses commanded us a law, (even) the
33. 10 They shall teach..Israel thy law: they
Josh. 1. 7 observe to do according to all the law
1. 8 This book of the law shall not depart out of
8. 31 as it is written in the book of the law of M.
8. 32 he wrote there..a copy of the law of M.
8. 34 he read all the words of the law, the bl.
8. 34 all that is written in the book of the law
22. 5 take diligent heed to do..the law, which
23. 6 is written in the book of the law of M.
24. 26 wrote these words in the book of the law
1 Ki. 2. 3 as it is written in the law of Moses, that
2 Ki. 10. 31 Jehu took no heed to walk in the law of
14. 6 is written in the book of the law of M.
17. 13 according to all the law which I comma.
17. 34 neither do they..after the law and com.
17. 37 the law..which he wrote for you, ye shall
21. 8 according to all the law that my servant
22. 8 I have found the book of the law in the
22. 11 heard the words of the book of the law
23. 24 he might perform the words of the law
23. 25 according to all the law of Moses; neither
1 Ch. 16. 40 according to all that is written in the law
22. 12 that thou mayest keep the law of the L.
2 Ch. 6. 16 take heed to their way to walk in my law
12. 1 he forsook the law of the LORD, and all I.
14. 4 and to do the law and the commandment
15. 3 long season Israel (hath been)..without l.
17. 9 the book of the law of the LORD with them
19. 10 between law and commandment, statutes
23. 18 written in the law of Moses, with rejoicing
25. 4 written in the law in the book of Moses
30. 16 according to the law of Moses the man of G.
31. 3 as (it is) written in the law of the LORD
31. 4 they might be encouraged in the law of
31. 21 in the law, and in the commandments, to
33. 8 according to the whole law and the stat.
34. 14 Hilkiah the priest found a book of the law
34. 15 I have found the book of the law in the
34. 19 the king had heard the words of the law
35. 26 according to (that..) written in the law
Ezra 3. 2 written in the law of Moses the man of G.
7. 6 he (was) a ready scribe in the law of Mo.
7. 10 had prepared his heart to seek the law of
10. 3 and let it be done according to the law

Neh. 8. 1 to bring the book of the law of Moses
8. 2 Ezra the priest brought the law before the
8. 3 (were attentive) unto the book of the law
8. 7 caused the people to understand the law
8. 8 So they read in the book, in the law of G.
8. 9 when they heard the words of the law
8. 13 even to understand the words of the law
8. 14 they found written in the law which the
8. 18 he read in the book of the law of God
9. 3 read in the book of the law of the LORD
9. 13 gavest them..true laws, good statutes and
9. 14 commandedst them..laws, by the hand of
9. 26 cast thy law behind their backs, and slew
9. 29 mightest bring them again unto thy law
9. 34 Neither have our kings..kept thy law; nor
10. 28 from the people of the lands unto the law
10. 29 to walk in God's law, which was given by
10. 34 to burn..as (it is) written in the law
10. 36 of our cattle, as (it is) written in the law
12. 44 portions of the law for the priests and L.
13. 3 came to pass, when they had heard the law
Job 22. 22 Receive, I pray thee, the law from his m.
Psa. 1. 2 in the law of the LORD; and in his law
19. 7 The law of the LORD (is) perfect, convert.
37. 31 The law of his God (is) in his heart; none
40. 8 I delight to do thy will..yea, thy law (is)
78. 1 Give ear, O my people, (to) my law: inc.
78. 5 appointed a law in Israel, which he com.
78. 10 kept not..and refused to walk in his law
89. 30 If his children forsake my law, and walk
94. 12 O LORD, and teachest him out of thy law
105. 45 observe his statutes, and keep his laws
119. 1 the undefiled..who walk in the law of the
119. 18 behold wondrous things out of thy law
119. 29 Remove..and grant me thy law graciously
119. 34 I shall keep thy law; yea, I shall observe
119. 44 So shall I keep thy law continually for
119. 51 (yet) have I not declined from thy law
119. 53 because of the wicked that forsake thy law
119. 55 remembered thy name..have kept thy law
119. 61 me: (but) I have not forgotten thy law
119. 70 fat as grease; (but) I delight in thy law
119. 72 The law of thy mouth (is) better unto me
119. 77 that I may live: for thy law (is) my deli.
119. 85 digged pits..which (are) not after thy law
119. 92 Unless thy law (had been) my delights, I
119. 97 O how love I thy law! it (is) my meditat.
119. 109 in my hand: yet do I not forget thy law
119. 113 I hate (vain) thoughts: but thy law do I
119. 126 work; (for) they have made void thy law
119. 136 run down..because they keep not thy law
119. 142 righteousness, and thy law (is) the truth
119. 150 draw nigh..they are far from thy law
119. 153 deliver me; for I do not forget thy law
119. 163 I hate and abhor lying: (but) thy law do
119. 165 Great peace have they which love thy law
119. 174 longed for thy salvation..and thy law
Prov. 1. 8 and forsake not the law of thy mother
3. 1 My son, forget not my law; but let thine
4. 2 good doctrine, forsake ye not my law
6. 20 and forsake not the law of thy mother
6. 23 law (is) light; and reproofs of instruction
7. 2 Keep..my law as the apple of thine eye
13. 14 The law of the wise (is) a fountain of life
28. 4 They that forsake the law praise the wi.
28. 4 such as keep the law contend with them
28. 7 Whoso keepeth the law (is) a wise son: but
28. 9 turneth away his ear from hearing the law
29. 18 but he that keepeth the law, happy (is) he
31. 26 and in her tongue (is) the law of kindness
Isa. 1. 10 give ear unto the law of our God, ye pe.
2. 3 for out of Zion shall go forth the law, and
5. 24 because they have cast away the law of the
8. 16 Bind up the testimony, seal the law am.
8. 20 To the law and to the testimony: if they
24. 5 because they have transgressed the laws
30. 9 children (that) will not hear the law of the
42. 4 earth: and the isles shall wait for his law
42. 21 magnify the law, and make (it) honourable
42. 24 neither were they obedient unto his law
51. 4 a law shall proceed from me, and I will
51. 7 the people in whose heart (is) my law; fear
Jer. 2. 8 they that handle the law knew me not: the
6. 19 not hearkened unto my words, nor to my l.
8. 8 We (are) wise, and the law of the LORD (is)
9. 13 Because they have forsaken my law which
16. 11 forsaken me, and have not kept my law
18. 18 for the law shall not perish from the pri.
26. 4 to walk in my law, which I have set before
31. 33 I will put my law in their inward parts
32. 23 obeyed not..neither walked in thy law
44. 10 neither have they..walked in my law, nor
44. 23 not obeyed..nor walked in his law
Lam. 2. 9 the law (is) no (more); her prophets also
Eze. 7. 26 the law shall perish from the priest, and
22. 26 Her priests have violated my law, and have
43. 11 show them..all the laws thereof: and wr.
43. 12 the law of the house..the law of the house
44. 5 I say unto thee concerning..all the laws
44. 24 they shall keep my laws and my statutes
Dan. 9. 10 to walk in his laws, which he set before
9. 11 Yea, all Israel have transgressed thy law
9. 11 the oath that (is) written in the law of M.
9. 13 written in the law of Moses, all this evil
Hos. 4. 6 thou hast forgotten the law of thy God, I
8. 1 they have..trespassed against my law
8. 12 written to him the great things of my law
Amos 2. 4 they have despised the law of the LORD
Mic. 4. 2 for the law shall go forth of Zion, and the
Hab. 1. 4 Therefore the law is slacked, and judgm.
Zeph. 3. 4 her priests have..done violence to the law
Hag. 2. 11 Ask now the priests (concerning) the law

Zech. 7. 12 they should hear the law, and the words
Mal. 2. 6 The law of truth was in his mouth, and
2. 7 they should seek the law at his mouth: for
2. 8 have caused many to stumble at the law
2. 9 not kept..but have been partial in the law
4. 4 Remember ye the law of Moses my serv.

7. *Belonging to the forum*, ἀγοραῖος *agoraios*.
Acts 19. 38 the law is open, and there are deputies

8. *A law, ordinance, custom*, νόμος *nomos*.
Matt. 5. 17 Think not that I am come to destroy the l.
5. 18 shall in no wise pass from the law, till all
7. 12 do ye even so to them: for this is the law
11. 13 all the prophets and the law prophesied
12. 5 have ye not read in the law, how that on
22. 36 (is) the great commandment in the law?
22. 40 On these two..hang all the law and the
23. 23 omitted the weightier (matters) of the law
Luke 2. 22 when the days..according to the law of M.
2. 23 it is written in the law of the Lord, Every
2. 24 that which is said in the law of the Lord
2. 27 to do for him after the custom of the law
2. 39 performed all things according to the law
10. 26 What is written in the law? how readest
16. 16 The law and the prophets (were) until J.
16. 17 it is easier..than one tittle of the law to
24. 44 which were written in the law of Moses
John 1. 17 For the law was given by Moses, (but) gr.
1. 45 found him of whom Moses in the law, and
7. 19 Did not Moses give you the law, and (yet)
7. 19 none of you keepeth the law? Why go ye
7. 23 the law of Moses should not be broken
7. 49 people..knoweth not the law are cursed
7. 51 Doth our law judge (any) man before it
8. 5 [Moses in the law commanded us, that]
8. 17 It is also written in your law, that the
10. 34 Is it not written in your law, I said, Ye
12. 34 We have heard out of the law that Christ
15. 25 the word..that is written in their law, They
18. 31 and judge him according to your law
19. 7 We have a law, and by our law he ought
Acts 6. 13 blasphemous words against this..law
7. 53 Who have received the law by the dispo.
13. 15 after the reading of the law and the prop.
13. 39 could not be justified by the law of Moses
15. 5 command (them) to keep the law of Moses
15. 24 [(Ye must) be circumcised, and keep the l.]
18. 13 men to worship God contrary to the law
18. 15 But if it be a question of..your law, look
21. 20 believe; and they are all zealous of the law
21. 24 also walkest orderly, and keepest the law
21. 28 This is the man that teacheth..the law
22. 3 perfect manner of the law of the fathers
22. 12 a devout man according to the law, having
23. 3 for sittest thou to judge me after the law
23. 29 to be accused of questions of their law, but
24. 6 [would have judged according to our law]
24. 14 all things which are written in the law
25. 8 Neither against the law of the Jews, neit.
28. 23 both out of the law of Moses, and (out of)
Rom 2. 12 in the law shall be judged by the law
2. 13 For not the hearers of [the] law (are) just
2. 13 but the doers of [the] law shall be justified
2. 14 the Gentiles which have not the law, do
2. 14 by nature the things contained in the law
2. 14 these, having not the law, are a law unto
2. 15 Which show the work of the law written
2. 17 art called a Jew, and restest in [the] law
2. 18 excellent, being instructed out of the law
2. 20 of knowledge and of the truth in the law
2. 23 boast of the law, through breaking the law
2. 25 verily profiteth, if thou keep the law: but
2. 25 if thou be a breaker of the law, thy cir.
2. 26 keep the righteousness of the law, shall
2. 27 which is by nature, if it fulfil the law, ju.
2. 27 by the letter..dost transgress the law?
3. 19 we know that what things soever the law
3. 19 it saith to them who are under the law
3. 20 by the deeds of the law there shall no flesh
3. 20 for by the law (is) the knowledge of sin
3. 21 the righteousness of God without the law
3. 21 witnessed by the law and the prophets
3. 27 what law? of works? Nay; but by the law
3. 28 justified by faith without..deeds of the l.
3. 31 Do we then make void the law through
3. 31 God forbid: yea, we establish the law
4. 13 to his seed, through the law, but through
4. 14 For if they which are of the law (be) heirs
4. 15 the law worketh wrath: for where no law
4. 16 not to that only which is of the law, but
5. 13 For until the law sin was in the world
5. 13 sin is not imputed when there is no law
5. 20 the law entered, that the offence might ab.
6. 14 ye are not under the law, but under grace
6. 15 because we are not under the law, but
7. 1 them that know the law, how that the law
7. 2 which hath an husband is bound by the l.
7. 2 she is loosed from the law of (her) husband
7. 3 husband be dead, she is free from that law
7. 4 ye also are become dead to the law by the
7. 5 the motions of sins, which were by the law
7. 6 we are delivered from the law, that being
7. 7 What shall we say then? (Is) the law sin?
7. 7 Nay, I had not known sin but by the law
7. 7 except the law had said, Thou shalt not
7. 8 For without the law sin (was) dead
7. 9 I was alive without the law once: but
7. 12 the law (is) holy, and the commandment
7. 14 we know that the law is spiritual: but I
7. 16 I consent unto the law that (it is) good
7. 21 I find then a law, that, when I would do

Rom. 7. 22 I delight in the law of God after the inward
7. 23 law in my members, warring aga. the law
7. 23 to the law of sin which is in my members
7. 25 the law of God, but with the flesh the law
8. 2 the law of the spirit of life in Christ Jesus
8. 2 made me free from the law of sin and de.
8. 3 what the law could not do, in that it was
8. 4 That the righteousness of the law might
8. 7 it is not subject to the law of God, neither
9. 31 Israel, which followed after the law of
9. 31 hath not attained to the law of righteous.
9. 32 but as it were by the works [of the law]
10. 4 For Christ (is) the end of the law for right.
10. 5 describeth the righteousness..of the law
13. 8 that loveth another hath fulfilled the law
13. 10 therefore love (is) the fulfilling of the law
1 Co. 7. 39 The wife is bound [by the law] as long as
9. 8 a man? or saith not the law the same also?
9. 9 For it is written in the law of Moses, Thou
9. 20 that are under the law, as under the law
9. 20 I might gain them that are under the law
14. 21 the law it is written, With (men of) other
14. 34 be under obedience, as also saith the law
15. 56 The sting..and..strength of sin (is) the law
Gal. 2. 16 man is not justified by..works of the law
2. 16 not..of the law: for by..works of the law
2. 19 I through the law am dead to the law, that
2. 21 if righteousness (come) by the law, then
3. 2 the spirit by the works of the law, or by the
3. 5 by the works of the law, or by the hearing
3. 10 as many as are of the works of the law are
3. 10 which are written in the book of the law
3. 11 that no man is justified by the law in the
3. 12 the law is not of faith: but, The man that
3. 13 redeemed us from the curse of the law
3. 17 the law, which was four hundred and th.
3. 18 if the inheritance (be) of the law, (it is)
3. 19 Wherefore then (serveth) the law? It was
3. 21 (Is) the law then against the promises of
3. 21 a law given which could have given life
3. 21 righteousness should have been by the law
3. 23 we were kept under the law, shut up unto
3. 24 Wherefore the law was our schoolmaster
4. 4 Son, made of a woman..under the law
4. 5 To redeem them that were under the law
4. 21 be under the law, do ye not hear the law?
5. 3 testify..he is a debtor to do the whole law
5. 4 whosoever of you are justified by the law
5. 14 For all the law is fulfilled in..word, (even)
5. 18 led of the spirit, ye are not under the law
5. 23 temperance: against such there is no law
6. 2 Bear ye..burdens, and so fulfil the law of
6. 13 they..who are circumcised keep the law
Eph. 2. 15 the enmity..the law of commandments
Phil. 3. 5 Hebrew..as touching the law, a Pharisee
3. 6 touching the righteous. which is in the law
3. 9 own righteousness, which is of the law
1 Ti. 1. 8 we know that the law (is) good, if a man
1. 9 the law is not made for a righteous man
Heb. 7. 5 tithes of the people according to the law
7. 12 made of necessity a change also of the law
7. 16 not after the law of a carnal commandm.
7. 19 For the law made nothing perfect; but
7. 28 the law maketh men high priests which
7. 28 word of the oath, which was since the law
8. 4 priests that offer gifts according to the law
8. 10 I will put my laws into their mind, and
9. 19 to all the people according to [the] law
9. 22 almost all things are by the law purged
10. 1 the law having a shadow of good things
10. 8 burnt offerings..are offered by [the] law
10. 16 I will put my laws into their hearts, and
10. 28 He that despised Moses' law died without
Jas. 1. 25 whoso looketh into the perfect law of lib.
2. 8 If ye fulfil the royal law according to the
2. 9 are convinced of the law as transgressors
2. 10 For whosoever shall keep the whole law
2. 11 thou art become a transgressor of the law
2. 12 that shall be judged by the law of liberty
4. 11 evil of the law, and judgeth the law: but
4. 11 judge the law, thou art not a doer of the l.

[*See also* Daughter, doctor, father, mother, sister, son, sue, teacher, transgress.]

LAW, manner of —

Judgment, מִשְׁפָּט *mishpat*.
Lev. 24. 22 Ye shall have one manner of law, as well

LAW, about the —

Legal, belonging to law, νομικός *nomikos*.
Titus 3. 9 But avoid..strivings about the law; for

LAW, contrary to the —

To act aside from law, παρανομέω *paranomeō*.
Acts 23. 3 me to be smitten contrary to the law?

LAW, giving of the —

Lawgiving, νομοθεσία *nomothesia*.
Rom. 9. 4 the covenants, and the giving of the law

LAW, to go to, or sue at the —

1. *To have a lawsuit*, ἔχω κρίμα *echō krima*.
1 Co. 6. 7 because ye go to law one with another

2. *To judge, sift*, κρίνω *krinō*.
Matt. 5. 40 if any man will sue thee at the law, and
1 Co. 6. 1 Dare any of you..go to law before the un.
6. 6 But brother goeth to law with brother, and

LAW, to receive the —

To set, appoint or give a law, νομοθετέω *nomotheteō*.
Heb. 7. 11 for under it the people received the law

LAW, transgression of the —
Lawlessness, ἀνομία anomia.
1 Jo. 3. 4 for sin is the transgression of the law
LAW, under the —
Within law, ἔννομος ennomos.
1 Co. 9. 21 but under the law [to Christ], that I might
LAW, without —
1. *Lawless, ἄνομος anomos.*
1 Co. 9. 21 To them that are without law, as without l.
9. 21 being not without law to God, but under
9. 21 I might gain them that are without law
2. *Lawlessly, ἀνόμως anomōs.*
Rom. 2. 12 without law shall also perish without law
LAWFUL —
1. *Judgment, מִשְׁפָּט mishpat.*
Eze. 18. 5 if a man do..that which is lawful and right
18. 19 When the son hath done that which is l.
18. 21 and do that which is lawful and right, he
18. 27 doeth that which is lawful and right, he
33. 14, 19 and do that which is lawful and right
33. 16 he hath done that which is lawful and ri.
2. *Right, righteous, just, rigid, צַדִּיק tsaddiq.*
Isa. 49. 24 Shall the prey be taken..or the lawful cap.
3. *In conformity to law, ἔννομος ennomos.*
Acts 19. 39 it shall be determined in a lawful assembly
LAWFUL, to be —
1. *A ruler, שַׁלִּיט shallit.*
Ezra 7. 24 it shall not be lawful to impose toll, tribute
2. *It is privileged, authorized, ἔξεστι exesti.*
Matt12. 2 thy disciples do that which is not lawful
12. 4 which was not lawful for him to eat, nei.
12. 10 Is it lawful to heal on the sabbath days?
12. 12 it is lawful to do well on the sabbath days
14. 4 John said..It is not lawful for thee to
19. 3 Is it lawful for a man to put away his w.
20. 15 Is it not lawful for me to do what I will with
22. 17 Is it lawful to give tribute unto Cesar, or
27. 6 It is not lawful for to put them into the
Mark 2. 24 why do they..that which is not lawful?
2. 26 which is not lawful to eat but for the priests
3. 4 Is it lawful to do good on the sabbath
6. 18 It is not lawful for thee to have thy broth.
10. 2 Is it lawful for a man to put away (his) w.?
12. 14 Is it lawful to give tribute to Cesar, or
Luke 6. 2 Why do ye that which is not lawful to do
6. 4 which it is not lawful to eat but for the p.
6. 9 Is it lawful on the sabbath days to do good
14. 3 Is it lawful to heal on the sabbath day?
20. 22 Is it lawful for us to give tribute unto C.
John 5. 10 it is not lawful for thee to carry (thy) bed
18. 31 It is not lawful for us to put any man to
Acts 16. 21 teach customs..not lawful for us to receive
22. 25 Is it lawful for you to scourge a man that
1 Co. 6. 12 All things are lawful..all things are law.
10. 23, 23 All things are lawful for me, but all
2 Co.12. 4 which it is not lawful for a man to utter
LAWFULLY —
Lawfully, according to law, νομίμως nomimōs.
1 Ti. 1. 8 the law (is) good, if a man use it lawfully
2 Ti. 2. 5 is he not crowned, except he strive lawf.
LAWGIVER —
1. *To grave, decree, חָקַק chaqaq, 3a.*
Gen. 49. 10 nor a lawgiver from between his feet, until
Num21. 18 digged it by (the direction of) the lawgiver
Deut 33. 21 there, (in) a portion of the lawgiver, (was
Psa. 60. 7 strength of mine head: Judah (is) my la.
108. 8 strength of mine head: Judah (is) my la.
Isa. 33. 22 LORD (is) our lawgiver, the LORD (is) our
2. *One who gives a law, νομοθέτης nomothetēs.*
Jas. 4. 12 There is one lawgiver, who is able to save
LAWLESS —
Lawless, ἄνομος anomos.
1 Ti. 1. 9 but for the lawless and disobedient, for
LAWYER —
Lawyer, belonging to the law, νομικός nomikos.
Matt22. 35 Then one of them, (which was) a lawyer
Luke 7. 30 the Pharisees and lawyers rejected the
10. 25 a certain lawyer stood up, and tempted
11. 45 Then answered one of the lawyers, and
11. 46 Woe unto you also, (ye) lawyers! for ye
11. 52 Woe unto you, lawyers! for ye have taken
14. 3 Jesus answering spake unto the lawyers
Titus 3. 13 Bring Zenas the lawyer and Apollos on
LAY, to —
1. *To fall, נָפַל naphal.*
Judg. 4. 22 behold, Sisera lay dead, and the nail (was)
2. *To cause to lie down, רָבַץ rabats, 5.*
Isa. 54. 11 I will lay thy stones with fair colours, and
3. *A lying, שְׁכָבָה shekabah.*
Exod16. 13 in the morning the dew lay round about
16. 14 And when the dew that lay was gone up
4. *To send sickness, חָלָה chalah, 3.*
Deut29. 22 sicknesses which the LORD hath laid upon
5. *To give, יְהַב yehab.*
Ezra 5. 16 laid the foundation of the house of God
6. *To cause to rest, place, נוּחַ nuach, 5.*
Judg. 6. 20 lay (them) upon this rock, and pour out
1 Ki. 13. 29 laid it upon the ass, and brought it back
13. 30 And he laid his carcase in his own grave
1 Ki. 13. 31 When I am dead..lay my bones beside his
Eze. 40. 42 whereupon also they laid the instruments
42. 13 there shall they lay the most holy things
42. 14 there they shall lay their garments wher.
44. 19 lay them in the holy chambers, and they
7. *To found, lay a foundation, יָסַד yasad.*
2 Ch.31. 7 they began to lay the foundation of the
Psa.104. 5 (Who) laid the foundations of the earth
8. *To cast, יָרָה yarah.*
Job 38. 6 or who laid the corner stone thereof
9. *To let escape, hatch, מָלַט malat, 3.*
Isa. 34. 15 shall the great owl make her nest, and lay
10. *A sending or stretching forth, מִשְׁלוֹחַ mishloach.*
Isa. 11. 14 they shall lay their hand upon Edom and
11. *To cause to rest, leave, put down, נוּחַ nuach, 5.*
Isa. 30. 32 which the LORD shall lay upon him, (it)
12. *To stretch out, נָטָה natah, 5.*
Hos. 11. 4 I drew them..and I laid meat unto them
13. *To set up, נָצַב natsab, 5.*
2 Sa. 18. 17 laid a very great heap of stones upon him
14. *To lift up, נָשָׂא nasa.*
2 Ki. 9. 25 Ahab..the LORD laid this burden upon
15. *To give, נָתַן nathan.*
Gen. 15. 10 and laid each piece one against another
Exod. 7. 4 that I may lay my hand upon Egypt, and
Deut. 7. 15 will lay them upon all (them) that hate
11. 25 God shall lay the fear of you and the dr.
26. 6 afflicted us, and laid upon us hard bond.
1 Sa. 6. 8 lay it upon the cart; and put the jewels
1 Ki. 18. 23 and lay (it) on wood, and put no fire (un.)
2 Ki. 5. 23 and laid (them) upon two of his servants
2 Ch.31. 6 brought in the tithe..and laid (them) by
Neh. 13. 5 where aforetime they laid the meat offer.
Psa.119. 110 The wicked have laid a snare for me
Eccl. 7. 2 end..and the living will lay (it) to his h.
Isa. 22. 22 the key of the house of David will I lay
Jer. 6. 21 I will lay stumbling blocks before this p.
Eze. 3. 20 and I lay a stumbling block before him
4. 1 lay it before thee, and pourtray upon it
4. 2 lay siege against it, and build a fort aga.
4. 5 For I have laid upon thee the years of
4. 8 I will lay bands upon thee, and thou shalt
6. 5 I will lay the dead carcases of the child.
25. 14 I will lay my vengeance upon Edom by
25. 17 when I shall lay my vengeance upon them
28. 17 I will lay thee before kings, that they may
32. 5 I will lay thy flesh upon the mountains
32. 27 have laid their swords under their heads
33. 28 For I will lay the land most desolate, and
33. 29 when I have laid the land most desolate
36. 29 will increase it, and lay no famine upon
37. 6 I will lay sinews upon you, and will bring
Jon. 1. 14 lay not upon us innocent blood: for thou
Zech. 3. 9 the stone that I have laid before Joshua
16. *To sustain, support, סָמַךְ samak.*
Lev. 3. 2, 8, 13 he shall lay his hand upon the head
4. 4 shall lay his hand upon the bullock's head
4. 15 shall lay their hands upon the head of
4. 24, 29, 33 he shall lay his hand upon the head
8. 14, 18, 22 Aaron and his sons laid their hands
16. 21 Aaron shall lay both his hands upon the
24. 14 let all that heard..lay their hands upon
Num. 8. 12 the Levites shall lay their hands upon the
27. 18 Take thee Joshua..and lay thine hand
27. 23 he laid his hands upon him, and gave him
Deut34. 9 for Moses had laid his hands upon him
2 Ch.29. 23 he goats..and they laid their hands upon
17. *To cause to pass over, put away, עָבַר abar, 5.*
Jon. 3. 6 and he laid his robe from him, and cove.
18. *To cause to meet, פָּגַע paga, 5.*
Isa. 53. 6 LORD hath laid on him the iniquity of us
19. *To put, place, set, שׂוּם, שִׂים sum, sim.*
Gen. 9. 23 laid (it) upon both their shoulders, and
22. 6 laid (it) upon Isaac his son; and he took
22. 9 and laid him on the altar upon the wood
30. 41 Jacob laid the rods before the eyes of the
Exod. 2. 3 she laid (it) in the flags by the river's brink
5. 8 ye shall lay upon them; ye shall not dim.
19. 7 laid before their faces all these words wh.
22. 25 neither shalt thou lay upon him usury
Lev. 2. 15 thou shalt put oil upon it, and lay frank.
Num 11. 11 that thou layest the burden of all this p.
16. 18 put fire in them, and laid incense thereon
Josh. 8. 2 lay thee an ambush for the city behind it
10. 27 and laid great stones in the cave's mouth
Judg. 9. 48 took it, and laid (it) on his shoulder, and
18. 19 Hold thy peace, lay thine hand upon thy
1 Sa. 6. 11 they laid the ark of the LORD upon the cart
11. 2 and lay it (for) a reproach upon all Israel
15. 2 how he laid (wait) for him in the way, when
19. 13 Michal took an image, and laid (it) in the
25. 18 hundred cakes of figs, and laid..on asses
2 Sa. 13. 19 laid her hand on her head, and went on
1 Ki.18. 23 and lay (it) on wood, and put no fire (under)
18. 33 and cut the bullock in pieces, and laid
2 Ki. 4. 29 and lay my staff upon the face of the child
4. 31 laid the staff upon the face of the child
10. 8 Lay ye them in two heaps at the entering
11. 16 they laid hands on her; and she went by
20. 7 they took and laid (it) on the boil, and he
2 Ch.23. 15 So they laid hands on her; and when she
Esth.10. 1 And the king Ahasuerus laid a tribute upon
Job 21. 5 Mark me..lay..hand upon (your) mouth
24. 12 Men groan..yet God layeth not folly (to)
29. 9 princes refrained talking, and laid (their)
Job 34. 23 For he will not lay upon man more (than
38. 5 Who hath laid the measures thereof, if thou
40. 4 Behold..I will lay mine hand upon my
41. 8 Lay thine hand upon him, remember the
Psa. 66. 11 Thou..thou laidst affliction upon our loins
79. 1 O God..they have laid Jerusalem on heaps
Isa. 13. 9 to lay the land desolate: and he shall des.
28. 17 Judgment also will I lay to the line, and
42. 25 it burned him, yet he laid (it) not to heart
47. 7 that thou didst not lay these..to thy heart
51. 23 thou hast laid thy body as the ground, and
57. 1 The righteous perisheth, and no man lay.
57. 11 nor laid (it) to thy heart? have not I held
Jer. 9. 8 peaceably..but in heart he layeth his wait
12. 11 desolate, because no man layeth (it) to he.
Eze. 4. 4 lay the iniquity of the house of Israel upon
11. 7 Your slain, whom ye have laid in the mi.
26. 12 they shall lay thy stones and thy timber
35. 4 I will lay thy cities waste, and thou shalt
39. 21 and my hand that I have laid upon them
Joel 1. 7 He hath laid my vine waste, and barked
Obad. 7 (they that eat) thy bread have laid a wo.
Mic. 1. 7 and all the idols thereof will I lay desol.
5. 1 he hath laid siege against us; they shall
7. 16 they shall lay..hand upon..mouth, their
Zech. 7. 14 for they laid the pleasant land desolate
Mal. 1. 3 I hated Esau, and laid his mountains and
2. 2 if ye will not lay (it) to heart, to give glory
2. 2 cursed..because ye do not lay (it) to heart
20. *To make equal, compare, place, שָׁוָה shavah, 3.*
Psa. 21. 5 honour and majesty hast thou laid upon
89. 19 I have laid help upon (one that is) mighty
119. 30 the way of truth; thy judgments have I la.
21. *To set, שִׁית shith.*
Gen. 48. 14 and laid (it) upon Ephraim's head, who
48. 17 when Joseph saw that his father laid his
Exod21. 22 as the woman's husband will lay upon him
Num12. 11 lay not the sin upon us, wherein we have
Ruth 3. 15 laid (it) on her: and she went into the
4. 16 Naomi took the child, and laid it in her
Job 9. 33 daysman..might lay his hand upon us
Psa. 84. 3 for herself, where she may lay her young
88. 6 Thou hast laid me in the lowest pit, in
139. 5 Thou hast beset..and laid thine hand upon
Isa. 5. 6 I will lay it waste: it shall not be pruned
22. *To cause to lie down, שָׁכַב shakab, 5.*
1 Ki. 3. 20 laid it in her bosom, and laid her dead
17. 19 carried him..and laid him upon his own
2 Ki. 4. 21 she went up, and laid him on the bed of
2 Ch.16. 14 laid him in the bed which was filled with
23. *To cause to tabernacle, שָׁכַן shaken, 5.*
Psa. 7. 5 and lay mine honour in the dust. Selah
24. *To send forth, שָׁלַח shalach.*
Gen. 22. 12 Lay not thine hand upon the lad, neither
37. 22 Shed no blood..and lay no hand upon him
Exod24. 11 And upon the nobles..he laid not his hand
Esth. 2. 21 sought to lay hand on the king Ahasuerus
3. 6 he thought scorn to lay hands on Morde.
6. 2 sought to lay hand on the king Ahasuerus
8. 7 because he laid his hand upon the Jews
9. 2 to lay hand on such as sought their hurt
9. 10 on the spoil laid they not their hand
9. 15 but on the prey they laid not their hand
9. 16 but they laid not their hands on the prey
Neh.13. 21 if ye do (so) again, I will lay hands on you
Obad. 13 nor have laid (hands) on their substance
25. *To send forth, שָׁלַח shalach, 3.*
Prov31. 19 She layeth her hands to the spindle, and
26. *To lay back or up, ἀνακλίνω anaklinō.*
Luke 2. 7 laid him in a manger; because there was
27. *To cast, throw, βάλλω ballō.*
Matt. 8. 14 he saw his wife's mother laid, and sick of
Mark 7. 30 she found..her daughter laid upon the bed
Luke16. 20 which was laid at his gate, full of sores
28. *To cast down, καταβάλλω kataballō.*
Heb. 6. 1 not laying again the foundation of repen.
29. *To put down, κατατίθημι katatithēmi.*
Mark15. 46 [laid] him in a sepulchre which was hewn
30. *To lie, be laid, κεῖμαι keimai.*
Matt28. 6 Come, see the place where the Lord lay
31. *To lay, incline, κλίνω klinō.*
Matt. 8. 20 Son of man hath not where to lay (his) h.
Luke 9. 58 Son of man hath not where to lay (his) h.
32. *To put, place, τίθημι tithēmi.*
Matt27. 60 And laid it in his own new tomb, which
Mark 6. 29 took up his corpse, and laid it in a tomb
6. 56 laid the sick in the streets, and besought
15. 47 Mary Magdalene..beheld where he was l.
16. 6 Jesus..behold the place where they laid
Luke 5. 18 to bring him in, and to lay (him) before
6. 48 digged deep, and laid the foundation on
14. 29 Lest haply, after he hath laid the founda.
23. 53 laid it in a sepulchre that was hewn in
23. 55 women..beheld..how his body was laid
John11. 34 Where have ye laid him? They said unto
19. 41 sepulchre, wherein was never man yet l.
19. 42 There laid they Jesus therefore, because of
20. 2 and we know not where they have laid him
20. 13 and I know not where they have laid him
20. 15 tell me where thou hast laid him, and I
Acts 3. 2 whom they laid daily at the gate of the t.
4. 37 the money, and laid (it) at the apostles' f.
5. 2 certain part and laid (it) at the apostles' f.
5. 15 laid (them) on beds and couches, that at
7. 16 laid in the sepulchre that Abraham bought

Acts 9. 37 washed, they laid (her) in an upper cham.
13. 29 from the tree, and laid (him) in a sepulchre
Rom. 9. 33 I lay in Sion a stumbling stone and rock
1 Co. 3. 10 I have laid the foundation, and another
3. 11 For other foundation can no man lay than
1 Pe. 2. 6 I lay in Sion a chief corner stone, elect

33. *To bear, carry, φέρω pherō.*
Acts 25. 7 laid many and grievous complaints agai.

[*See also* Beams, dying, foundation, hands, heavily, hold, low, plaster, pledge, siege, snare, wait, waste.]

LAY along, to —
To fall, נָפַל naphal.
Judg. 7. 12 all the children of the east lay along in
7. 13 and overturned it, that the tent lay along

LAY apart or aside, to —
1. *To put away, ἀποτίθεμαι apotithemai.*
Heb. 12. 1 let us lay aside every weight, and the sin
Jas. 1. 21 Wherefore lay apart all filthiness and su.
1 Pe. 2. 1 Wherefore laying aside all malice, and all
2. *To send away, ἀφίημι aphiēmi.*
Mark 7. 8 For, laying aside the commandment of G.
3. *To put, place, τίθημι tithēmi.*
John 13. 4 laid aside his garments; and took a towel

LAY at, to —
To attain, overtake, cause to reach, נָשַׂג nasag, 5.
Job 41. 26 The sword of him that layeth at him can.

LAY away or by, to —
To turn aside, סוּר sur, 5.
Gen. 38. 19 laid by her veil from her, and put on the
Eze. 26. 16 lay away their robes, and put off their

LAY down, to —
1. *To cause to rest, place, נוּחַ nuach, 5.*
Josh. 4. 8 where they lodged, and laid them down
2. *To (cause to) stretch out, נָטָה natah, 5.*
Amos 2. 8 And they lay (themselves) down upon cl.
3. *To put, place, שׂוּם, שִׂים sim, sum.*
Job 17 3 Lay down now, put me in a surety with
4. *To put away or off, ἀποτίθεμαι apotithemai.*
Acts 7. 58 the witnesses laid down their clothes at
5. *To put, place, τίθημι tithēmi.*
Luke 19. 21 thou takest up that thou layedst not down
19. 22 taking up that I laid not down and reap.
John 10. 15 know I..and I lay down my life for the
10. 17 because I lay down my life, that I might
10. 18 I lay it down..I have power to lay it down
13. 37 Lord..I will lay down my life for thy sake
13. 38 Wilt thou lay down thy life for my sake?
15. 13 that a man lay down his life for his friends
Acts 4. 35 And laid (them) down at the apostles' feet
1 Jo. 3. 16 because he laid down his life for us: and
3. 16 we ought to lay down..lives for the bret.
6. *To put or place under, ὑποτίθημι hupotithēmi.*
Rom. 16. 4 Who have for my life laid down their own

LAY for; to —[*See* Foundation.]

LAY even with the ground, to —
To rase to the ground, ἐδαφίζω edaphizō.
Luke 19. 44 And shall lay thee even with the ground

LAY hold (of, on or upon), to —
1. *To lay or keep hold on, אָחַז achaz.*
2 Sa. 2. 21 lay thee hold on one of the young men, and
Eccl. 2. 3 to lay hold on folly, till I might see what
Isa. 5. 29 they shall roar, and lay hold of the prey
2. *To catch, capture, keep hold, תָּפַשׂ taphas.*
Deut 21. 19 shall his father and his mother lay hold on
22. 28 lay hold on her, and lie with her, and they
1 Ki. 13. 4 saying, Lay hold on him. And his hand

LAY in —[*See* Order.]

LAY meat, to —
To give to eat, אָכַל akal, 5.
Hos. 11 4 I drew them..and I laid meat unto them

LAY on or upon, to —
1. *To cast or throw upon, ἐπιβάλλω epiballō.*
Matt 26. 50 Then came they, and laid hands on Jesus
Mark 14. 46 they laid their hands on him, and took him
Luke 20. 19 the same hour sought to lay hands on him
21. 12 shall lay their hands on you, and persec.
John 7. 30 no man laid hands on him, because his
7. 44 taken him; but no man laid hands on him
Acts 4. 3 they laid hands on them, and put..in hold
5. 18 laid their hands on the apostles, and put
21. 27 the Jews..when they saw..laid hands on
2. *To lie or be laid upon, ἐπίκειμαι epikeimai.*
John 11. 38 It was a cave, and a stone lay upon it
21. 9 they saw a fire of coals there, and fish laid
Acts 27. 20 And when..no small tempest lay on (us)
3. *To put or place upon, ἐπιτίθημι epitithēmi.*
Matt. 9. 18 come and lay thy hand upon her, and she
19. 15 he laid (his) hands on them, and departed
23. 4 lay..on men's shoulders; but they..will
Mark 5. 23 come and lay thy hands on her, that she
6. 5 save that he laid his hands upon a few
16. 18 they shall lay hands on the sick, and they
Luke 4. 40 he laid his hands on every one of them, and
13. 13 he laid (his) hands on her: and immediately
15. 5 And..he layeth (it) on his shoulders, rej.
23. 26 on him they laid the cross, that he might
Acts 6. 6 they had prayed, they laid (their) hands on
8. 17 Then laid they (their) hands on them, and
Acts 8. 19 that on whomsoever I lay hands, he may
13. 3 laid (their) hands on them; they sent (them)
15. 28 to lay upon you no greater burden than
16. 23 when they had laid many stripes upon
19. 6 when Paul had laid (his) hands upon them
28. 3 had gathered a bundle of sticks, and laid
28. 8 and laid his hands on him, and healed him
1 Ti. 5. 22 Lay hands suddenly on no man, neither
Rev. 1. 17 he laid his right hand upon me, saying unto

LAY open, to —
To spread forth or abroad, פָּרַשׂ paras.
Prov. 13. 16 knowledge: but a fool layeth open (his) folly

LAY out, to —
1. *To cause to go out, expend, יָצָא yatsa, 5.*
2 Ki. 12. 11 laid it out to the carpenters and builders
2. *To pour out, יָצַק yatsaq, 5.*
Josh. 7. 23 brought..and laid them out before the L.

LAY privily, to —
To hide, secrete, טָמַן taman.
Psa. 31. 4 the net that they had laid privily for me
64. 5 they commune of lay..snares privily; they
142. 3 In the way .have they privily laid a snare

LAY self down, to —
To lie down, שָׁכַב shakab.
Ruth 3. 4 and uncover his feet, and lay thee down
3. 7 and uncovered his feet, and laid her down
2 Sa. 13. 5 Lay thee down on thy bed, and make th.
1 Ki. 19. 6 did eat and drink, and laid him down ag.
21. 4 he laid him down upon his bed, and tur.
Psa. 3. 5 I laid me down and slept; I awaked; for
4. 8 I will both lay me down in peace, and sl.

LAY sick of —
To hold or press together, συνέχω sunechō.
Acts 28. 8 that the father of Publius lay sick of a fe.

LAY to the charge of, to —
1. *To set, place, ἵστημι histēmi.*
Acts 7. 60 cried..Lord, lay not this sin to their ch.
2. *To count, reckon, λογίζομαι logizomai.*
2 Ti. 4. 16 that it may not be laid to their charge

LAY snare, to —
To lay a snare, יָקַשׁ yaqash.
Psa. 141. 9 Keep me from the snares..they have laid
Jer. 50. 24 I have laid a snare for thee, and thou art

LAY to—[*See* Charge.]

LAY unto, to —
To put toward, add to, προστίθημι prostithēmi.
Acts 13. 36 was laid unto his fathers, and saw corr.

LAY unto charge, to —
To give, נָתַן nathan.
Deut 21. 8 lay not..unto thy people of Israel's cha.

LAY up, to —
1. *To cause to rest, place, נוּחַ nuach, 5.*
Gen. 39. 16 she laid up his garment by her until his l.
Exod 16. 23 that which remaineth over lay up for you
16. 24 they laid it up till the morning, as Moses
16. 33 lay it up before the LORD, to be kept for
16. 34 so Aaron laid it up before the Testimony
Num 17. 4 thou shalt lay them up in the tabernacle
17. 7 Moses laid up the rods before the LORD in
19. 9 lay..up without the camp in a clean place
Deut 14. 28 bring forth..and shalt lay (it) up within
1 Sa. 10. 25 wrote..in a book, and laid (it) up before
2. *To put down, נָחַת nechath, 5.*
Ezra 6. 1 where the treasures were laid up in Baby.
3. *To give, נָתַן nathan.*
Gen. 41. 48 laid up the food..the food..laid he up in
4. *To number, appoint, charge, lay up, פָּקַד paqad, 5.*
Isa. 10. 28 at Michmash he hath laid up his carriages
5. *To heap up, צָבַר tsabar.*
Gen. 41. 35 and lay up corn unto the hand of Pharaoh
6. *To hide, lay up, צָפַן tsaphan.*
Job 21. 19 God layeth up his iniquity for his children
Psa. 31. 19 which thou hast laid up for them that fear
Prov. 2. 7 He layeth up sound wisdom for the righ.
7. 1 My son..lay up my commandments with
10. 14 Wise (men) lay up knowledge: but the
13. 22 the wealth of the sinner (is) laid up for
Song 7. 13 I have laid up for thee, O my beloved
7. *To put, place, שׂוּם, שִׂים sim, sum.*
1 Sa. 21. 12 David laid up these words in his heart
Job 22. 22 Receive..lay up his words in thine heart
8. *To set, שִׁית shith.*
Job 22. 24 Then shalt thou lay up gold as dust, and
Prov 26. 24 He that hateth..layeth up deceit within
9. *To lie or be laid away, ἀπόκειμαι apokeimai.*
Luke 19. 20 thy pound, which I have kept laid up in
Col. 1. 5 For the hope which is laid up for you in h.
2 Ti. 4. 8 Henceforth there is laid up for me a crown
10. *To treasure up, θησαυρίζω thēsaurizō.*
Matt. 6. 19 Lay not up for yourselves treasures upon
6. 20 But lay up for yourselves treasures in h.
2 Co. 12. 14 children ought not to lay up for the par.
11. *To put, place, τίθημι tithēmi.*
Luke 1. 66 they that heard..laid (them) up in their h.

LAY up in store, to —
1. *To treasure up, אָצַר atsar.*
2 Ki. 20. 17 which thy fathers have laid up in store
Isa. 39. 6 which thy fathers have laid up in store
2. *To treasure off or away, ἀποθησαυρίζω apothēsau.*
1 Ti. 6. 19 Laying up in store for themselves a good

LAY up treasure, by or in store, to —
To treasure up, θησαυρίζω thēsaurizō.
Luke 12. 21 So (is) he that layeth up treasure for him.
1 Co. 16. 2 let every one of you lay by him in store

LAY wait (for), to —
1. *To lie in wait, אָרַב arab.*
Judg. 9. 34 laid wait against Shechem in four comp.
9. 43 and laid wait in the field, and looked, and
16. 2 laid wait for him all night in the gate of
Ezra 8. 31 and of such as lay in wait by the way
Job 31. 9 I have laid wait at my neighbour's door
Prov. 1. 11 Come with us, let us lay wait for blood
1. 18 they lay wait for their (own) blood; they
24. 15 Lay not wait, O wicked (man), against the
Lam. 4. 19 Our persecutors..laid wait for us in the w.
2. *To lay wait, אָרַב arab, 5.*
1 Sa. 15. 5 And Saul came..and laid wait in the val.
3. *To behold, look, שׁוּר shur.*
Jer. 5. 26 lay wait, as he that setteth snares; they
4. *To make a snare, ποιέω ἐνέδραν poieō enedran.*
Acts 25. 3 would send..laying wait in the way to kill
5. *To lie in wait, ἐνεδρεύω enedreuō.*
Luke 11. 54 [Laying wait for] him, and seeking to catch
6. *To be counsel against (one), ἐπιβουλή γίνεσθαι.*
Acts 20. 3 when the Jews laid wait for him, as he was
7. *A plot to be about to be, ἐπιβουλή μέλλειν εἶναι.*
Acts 23. 30 how that the [Jews laid wait] for the man

LAY, where each —
A crouching place, רֵבֶץ rebets.
Isa. 35. 7 the habitation of dragons, where each lay

LAY, while he—
Dwelling, שִׁיבָה shibah.
2 Sa. 19. 32 the king of sustenance while he lay at M.

LAYING of wait, laying await —
1. *A hunting, lying in wait, צְדִיָּה tsediyyah.*
Num 35. 20 or hurl at him by laying of wait, that he
35. 22 upon him any thing without laying of wait
2. *Counsel against (one), plot, ἐπιβουλή epiboulē.*
Acts 9. 24 But their laying await was known 20. 19.

LAYING on —
A putting upon, ἐπίθεσις epithesis.
Acts 8. 18 when Simon saw that through laying on
1 Ti. 4. 14 with the laying on of the hands of the pres.
Heb. 6. 2 the doctrine of baptisms, and of laying on

LAZ-AR'-US, Λάζαρος *without help.*
1. A symbolic name in one of the parables.
Luke 16. 20 there was a certain beggar named L., wh.
16. 23 seeth Abraham afar off, and L. in his bo.
16. 24 Abraham, have mercy on me, and send L.
16. 25 good things, and likewise L. evil things
2. A man of Bethany whom Jesus raised from the dead, brother of Martha and Mary.
John 11. 1 Now a certain (man) was sick, (named) L.
11. 2 It was (that) Mary..whose brother L. was
11. 5 Jesus loved Martha, and her sister, and L.
11. 11 Our friend L. sleepeth; but I go, that I
11. 14 Then said Jesus unto them plainly, L. is
11. 43 he cried with a loud voice, L., come forth
12. 1 where L. was which had been dead, whom
12. 2 but L. was one of them that sat at the ta.
12. 9 but that they might see L. also, whom he
12. 10 consulted that they might put L. also to
12. 17 that was with him when he called L. out

LEACH—[*See* Horse leach.]

LEAD —
Lead, עֹפֶרֶת ophereth.
Exod 15. 10 they sank as lead in the mighty waters
Num 31. 22 the brass, the iron, the tin, and the lead
Job 19. 24 were graven with an iron pen and lead in
Jer. 6. 29 the bellows are burnt, the lead is consu.
Eze. 22. 18 iron, and lead, in the midst of the furnace
22. 20 they gather silver, and brass..and lead
27. 12 with silver..and lead, they traded in thy
Zech. 5. 7 there was lifted up a talent of lead: and
5. 8 he cast the weight of lead upon the mouth

LEAD (a life), to —
1. *To declare happy, אָשַׁר ashar, 3.*
Isa. 3. 12 they which lead thee cause (thee) to err
2. *To cause to come or bring in, בּוֹא bo, 5.*
Jer. 23. 8 which led the seed of the house of Israel
Eze. 17. 12 taken..and led them with him to Babylon
3. *To cause to tread, דָּרַךְ darak, 5.*
Psa. 25. 5 Lead me in thy truth, and teach me: for
Prov. 4. 11 I have taught..I have led thee in right p.
Isa. 42. 16 I will lead them in paths..they have not
48. 17 leadeth thee by the way..thou shouldest
4. *To make to go on, הָלַךְ halak, 3.*
Prov. 8. 20 I lead in the way of righteousness, in the
5. *To cause to flow or move on, יָבַל yabal, 5.*
Jer. 31. 9 and with supplications will I lead them
6. *To cause to go on, יָלַךְ yalak, 5.*
Deut. 8. 2 all the way which the LORD thy God led

Deut. 8. 15 Who led thee through that great and ter.
29. 5 I have led you forty years in the wildern.
Jos. 24. 3 led him throughout all the land of Canaan
2 Ki. 6. 19 I will bring you..But he led them to Sam.
Job 12. 17 He leadeth counsellors away spoiled, and
12. 19 He leadeth princes away spoiled, and
Psa.106. 9 so he led them through the depths, as th.
136. 16 To him which led his people through the
Prov 16. 29 and leadeth him into the way (that is) not
Isa. 48. 21 they thirsted not (when) he led them thr.
63. 12 That led..by the right hand of Moses
63. 13 That led them through the deep, as an h.
Jer. 2. 6 led us through the wilderness, through
2. 17 thy God, when he led thee by the way?
32. 5 he shall lead Zedekiah to Babylon, and
Amos 2. 10 Also I..led you forty years through the

7. *To lead, drive,* נָהַג *nahag.*
Exod. 3. 1 he led the flock to the backside of the de.
Psa. 80. 1 thou that leadest Joseph like a flock; thou
Song 8. 2 I would lead thee..bring thee into my m.
Isa. 11. 6 together; and a little child shall lead them
Lam 3. 2 He hath led me, and brought..darkness

8. *To lead, drive,* נָהַג *nahag,* 3.
Deut. 4. 27 the heathen, whither the LORD shall lead
28. 37 all nations whither the LORD shall lead
Isa. 49. 10 he that hath mercy on them shall lead
63. 14 so didst thou lead thy people, to make thy.
Nah. 2. 7 her maids shall lead (her) as with the vo.

9. *To lead, tend, feed,* נָהַל *nahal,* 3.
Psa. 23. 2 to lie down..he leadeth me beside the still

10. *To lead forth,* נָחָה *nachah.*
Gen. 24. 27 LORD led me to the house of my master's
Exod 13. 17 God led them not..the way of the land of
32. 34 Therefore now go, lead the people unto
Psa. 5. 8 Lead me, O LORD, in thy righteousness
27. 11 lead me in a plain path, because of mine
60. 9 Who will bring..who will lead me into E.?
77. 20 Thou leddest thy people like a flock by the
108. 10 Who will bring..who will lead me into E.?
139. 24 And see..and lead me in the way everla.

11. *To lead forth, put,* נָחָה *nachah,* 5.
Gen. 24. 48 which had led me in the right way to take
Exod 13. 21 in a pillar of a cloud, to lead them the way
Deut 32. 12 the LORD alone did lead him, and..no st.
Neh. 9. 12 thou leddest them in the day by a cloudy
9. 19 from them by day, to lead them in the way
Psa. 23. 3 He restoreth my soul: he leadeth me in
31. 3 for thy name's sake lead me, and guide
43. 3 thy light and thy truth: let them lead me
61. 2 lead me to the rock (that) is higher than I
78. 14 In the day time also he led them with a cl.
78. 53 he led them on safely, so that they feared
139. 10 Even there shall thy hand lead me, and
143. 10 Teach..lead me into the land of upright.
Prov. 6. 22 When thou goest, it shall lead thee; when
Isa. 57. 18 I will lead him also, and restore comforts

12. *Head,* רֹאשׁ *rosh.*
Deut 20. 9 shall make captains..to lead the people

13. *To lead,* ἄγω *agō.*
Mark 13. 11 when they shall lead..and deliver you
Luke 4. 1 was led by the Spirit into the wilderness
4. 29 led him unto the brow of the hill whereon
22. 54 Then took they him, and led..and brought
23. 1 the whole..arose, and led him unto Pilate
23. 32 two other...led with him to be put to d.
John 18. 28 Then led they Jesus from Caiaphas unto
Acts 8. 32 He was led as a sheep to the slaughter
Rom. 2. 4 knowing that the goodness of God leadeth
8. 14 as many as are led by the the Spirit of God
1 Co. 12. 2 Gentiles, carried away..as ye were led
Gal. 5. 18 if ye be led by the Spirit, ye are not under

14. *To lead up or back,* ἀνάγω *anagō.*
Luke 22. 66 came together, and [led] him into their c.

15. *To lead away,* ἀπάγω *apagō.*
Matt. 7. 13 broad (is) the way, that leadeth to destr.
7. 14 narrow (is) the way, which leadeth unto l.

16. *To lead throughout,* διάγω *diagō.*
1 Ti. 2. 2 that we may lead a quiet and peaceable l.

17. *To lead the way,* ὁδηγέω *hodēgeō.*
Matt. 15. 14 if the blind lead the blind, both shall fall
Luke 6. 39 Can the blind lead the blind? shall they
Rev. 7. 17 shall lead them unto living fountains of w.

18. *To bear, carry,* φέρω *pherō.*
Acts 12. 10 the iron gate that leadeth unto the city
[*See also* Captive, hand.]

LEAD about, to —
1. *To turn or bring round about,* סָבַב *sabab,* 3*a*.
Deut 32. 10 he led him about, he instructed him, he
2. *To turn or bring round about,* סָבַב *sabab,* 5.
Exod 13. 18 God led the people about..the way of the
Eze. 47. 2 led me about the way without unto the
3. *To lead around about,* περιάγω *periagō.*
1 Co. 9. 5 Have we not power to lead about a sister

LEAD away, to —
1. *To lead, drive,* נָהַג *nahag.*
1 Sa. 30. 22 that they may lead (them) away, and de.
Isa. 20. 4 So shall the king of Assyria lead away the
2. *To lead away,* ἀπάγω *apagō.*
Matt. 26. 57 led (him) away to Caiaphas the high priest
27. 2 they led (him) away, and delivered him to
27. 31 they took..and led him away to crucify
Mark 14. 44 is he; take him, and lead..away safely
14. 53 they led Jesus away to the high priest
15. 16 the soldiers led him away into the hall
Luke 13. 15 loose..and lead (him) away to watering?
23. 26 as they led him away, they laid hold upon
John 18. 13 And [led him away] to Annas first: for he
19. 16 And they took Jesus, and [led (him) away]

LEAD captive, to —
To cause to remove, exile, גָּלָה *galah,* 5.
Jer. 22. 12 place whither they have led him captive

LEAD forth, to —
1. *To cause to tread,* דָּרַךְ *darak,* 5.
Psa. 107. 7 he led them forth by the right way, that
2. *To cause to go on,* יָלַךְ *yalak,* 5.
Psa. 125. 5 LORD shall lead them forth with the wor.
3. *To lead, drive,* נָהַג *nahag.*
1 Ch. 20. 1 Joab led forth the power of the army, and
2 Ch. 25. 11 Amaziah..led forth his people, and went
4. *To lead forth,* נָחָה *nachah.*
Exod 15. 13 Thou in thy mercy hast led forth the peo.

LEAD on, gently, to —
1. *To lead, tend, feed,* נָהַל *nahal,* 3.
Isa. 40. 11 shall gently lead those that are with young
2. *To lead self on,* נָהַל *nahal,* 7.
Gen. 33. 14 I will lead on softly, according as the cat.

LEAD into, to —
1. *To lead into,* εἰσάγω *eisagō.*
Acts 21. 37 as Paul was to be led into the castle, he
2. *To bear or carry into,* εἰσφέρω *eispherō.*
Matt. 6. 13 lead us not into temptation, but deliver
Luke 11. 4 lead us not into temptation; but deliver
3. *To lead together,* συνάγω *sunagō.*
Rev. 13. 10 [He that leadeth into] captivity shall go

LEAD out, to —
1. *To cause to go out or forth,* יָצָא *yatsa,* 5.
Num 27. 17 which may lead them out, and which may
2 Sa. 5. 2 Also..thou wast he that leddest out..I.
1 Ch. 11. 2 he that leddest out and broughtest in I.
2. *To lead out or forth,* ἐξάγω *exagō.*
Mark 8. 23 [led him out] of the town; and when he
15. 20 they took..and [led him out] to crucify
Luke 24. 50 And he led them out as far as to Bethany
John 10. 3 own sheep by name, and leadeth them out
Acts 21. 38 and leddest out into the wilderness four
Heb. 8. 9 took..to lead them out of the land of E.

LEAD up, to —
1. *To lead up,* ἀνάγω *anagō.*
Matt. 4. 1 Then was Jesus led up of the spirit into
2. *To bear or carry up,* ἀναφέρω *anapherō.*
Mark 9. 2 leadeth them up into an high mountain

LEADER —
1. *To declare happy, cause to step,* אָשַׁר *ashar,* 3.
Isa. 9. 16 the leaders of this people cause..to err
2. *Leader, one who goes before,* נָגִיד *nagid.*
1 Ch. 12. 27 Jehoiada (was) the leader of the Aaronites
13. 1 David consulted with the captains..leader
2 Ch. 32. 21 the leaders and captains in the camp of
Isa. 55. 4 I have given him..a leader and comman.
3. *Leader of the way,* ὁδηγός *hodēgos.*
Matt 15. 14 Let them alone: they be blind leaders of

LEAF —
1. *Any thing torn away, a leaf,* טֶרֶף *tereph.*
Eze. 17. 9 it shall wither in all the leaves of her sp.
2. *What go up, a leaf,* עָלֶה *aleh.*
Gen. 3. 7 they sewed fig leaves together, and made
8. 11 in her mouth (was) an olive leaf pluckt off
Lev. 26. 36 sound of a shaken leaf shall chase them
Job 13. 25 Wilt thou break a leaf driven to and fro?
Psa. 1. 3 his leaf also shall not wither; and what.
Isa. 1. 30 ye shall be as an oak whose leaf fadeth
34. 4 as the leaf falleth off from the vine, and
64. 6 we all do fade as a leaf; and our iniquit.
Jer. 8. 13 nor figs on the fig tree, and the leaf shall
17. 8 when heat cometh, but her leaf shall be
Eze. 47. 12 whose leaf shall not fade, neither shall the
47. 12 for meat, and the leaf thereof for medic.
3. *A rib, side,* צֶלַע *tsela.*
1 Ki. 6. 34 two leaves of the one door (were) folding
4. *A leaf,* φύλλον *phullon.*
Matt 21. 19 found nothing thereon, but leaves only
24. 32 is yet tender, and putteth forth leaves, ye
Mark 11. 13 seeing a fig tree, afar off having leaves, he
11. 13 he found nothing but leaves; for the time
13. 28 is yet tender, and putteth forth leaves
Rev. 22. 2 the leaves of the tree (were) for the healing

LEAGUE —
1. *An eating, covenant, league,* בְּרִית *berith.*
Josh. 9. 6, 11 now therefore make ye a league with
9. 7 and how shall we make a league with you?
9. 15 made a league with them, to let them live
9. 16 three days after they had made a league
Judg. 2. 2 ye shall make no league with the inhabit.
2 Sa. 3. 12 Make thy league with me, and, behold, my
3. 13 Well; I will make a league with thee: but
3. 21 that they may make a league with thee
5. 3 king David made a league with them in H.
1 Ki. 5. 12 peace..and they two made a league tog.
15. 19 (There is) a league between me and thee
1 Ki. 15. 19 come and break thy league with Baasha
2 Ch. 16. 3 (There is) a league between me and thee
16. 3 break thy league with Baasha king of Is.
2. *To join selves together,* חָבַר *chabar,* 7.
Dan. 11. 23 And after the league..with him he shall

LEAGUE, to be in or make a —
1. *An eating, covenant, league,* בְּרִית *berith.*
Job 5. 23 thou shalt be in league with the stones of
Eze. 30. 5 and the men of the land that is in league
2. *To cut, prepare, make,* כָּרַת *karath.*
1 Sa. 22. 8 that my son hath made a league with the

LE'-AH, לֵאָה *weary.*
The elder daughter of Laban and first wife of Jacob. B.C. 1730.
Gen. 29. 16 name of the elder (was) L., and the name
29. 17 L. (was) tender eyed; but Rachel was be.
29. 23 he took L. his daughter, and brought her
29. 24 Laban gave unto his daughter L. Zilpah
29. 25 in the morning, behold, it (was) L.: and he
29. 30 he loved also Rachel more than L., and
29. 31 When the LORD saw that L. (was) hated, he
29. 32 L. conceived, and bare a son, and she cal.
30. 9 When L. saw that she had left bearing
30. 10, 12 And Zilpah, L.'s maid, bare Jacob a
30. 11 L. said, A troop cometh: and she called
30. 13 L. said, Happy am I, for the daughters
30. 14 brought them unto his mother L. Then
30. 14 Rachel said to L., Give me, I pray thee, of
30. 16 and L. went out to meet him, and said
30. 17 God hearkened unto L., and she conceived
30. 18 L. said, God hath given me my hire, bec.
30. 19 L. conceived again, and bare Jacob the
30. 20 L. said, God hath endued me (with) a good
31. 4 Jacob sent and called Rachel and L. to the
31. 14 Rachel and L. answered and said unto him
31. 33 Laban went..into L.'s tent, and into the
31. 33 Then went he out of L.'s tent, and entered
33. 1 he divided the children unto L., and unto
33. 2 L. and her children after, and Rachel and
33. 7 L. also with her children came near, and
34. 1 Dinah the daughter of L., which she bare
35. 23 The sons of L.; Reuben, Jacob's first born
35. 26 sons of Zilpah, L.'s handmaid; Gad and
46. 15 These (be) the sons of L., which she bare
46. 18 whom Laban gave to L. his daughter; and
49. 31 buried Abraham..and there I buried L.
Ruth 4. 11 LORD make the woman..like L., which

LEAN —
1. *Weak, poor, lean,* דַּל *dal.*
2 Sa. 13. 4 Why (art) thou..lean from day to day?
2. *Lean,* רָזֶה *razeh.*
Num 13. 20 whether it (be) fat or lean, whether there
Eze. 34. 20 the fat cattle and between the lean cattle
3. *Thin, lean,* רַק *raq.*
Gen. 41. 20 the lean and the ill favoured kine did eat

LEAN, to —
1. *To take hold on,* חָזַק *chazaq,* 5.
2 Sa. 3. 29 that is a leper, or that leaneth on a staff
2. *To support,* סָמַךְ *samak.*
Amos 5. 19 or went into the house, and leaned his
3. *To be supported,* סָמַךְ *samak,* 2.
2 Ki. 18. 21 on which if a man lean, it will go into
Isa. 36. 6 whereon if a man lean, it will go into his
4. *To strengthen or rest self,* רָפַק *raphaq,* 7.
Song 8. 5 that cometh up..leaning upon her beloved?
5. *To be supported, lean on,* שָׁעַן *shaan,* 2.
Judg 16. 26 feel the pillars..I may lean upon them
2 Sa. 1. 6 Saul leaned upon his spear; and lo, the
2 Ki. 5. 18 he leaneth on my hand, and I bow myself
7. 2 Then a lord on whose hand the king leaned
7. 17 the lord on whose hand he leaned to have
Job 8. 15 He shall lean upon his house, but it shall
Prov. 3. 5 and lean not unto thine own understand.
Eze. 29. 7 when they leaned upon thee, thou brak.
Mic. 3. 11 yet will they lean upon the LORD, and say
6. *To lie or be laid up or back,* ἀνάκειμαι *anakeimai.*
John 13. 23 Now there was leaning on Jesus' bosom
7. *To fall up or back,* ἀναπίπτω *anapiptō.*
John 21. 20 which also leaned on his breast at supper

LEAN, to wax —
To become lean, רָזָה *razah,* 2.
Isa. 17. 4 and the fatness of his flesh shall wax lean

LEAN fleshed —
Thin of flesh, דַּק בָּשָׂר (רַק), *(raq) daq basar.*
Gen. 41. 3 other kine..ill favoured and lean fleshed
41. 4 the ill favoured and lean fleshed; 41. 19

LEANNESS —
1. *Failure, lie, feigning,* כַּחַשׁ *kachash.*
Job 16. 8 my leanness rising up in me beareth wit.
2. *Leanness,* רָזוֹן *razon.*
Psa. 106. 15 He gave..but sent leanness into their soul
Isa. 10. 16 shall..send among his fat ones leanness
3. *Leanness, secret,* רָזִי *razi.*
Isa. 24. 16 My leanness, my leanness, woe unto me!

LE-AN'-NOTH, לְעַנּוֹת. *See* **MAHALATH.**

LEAP —
1. *To leap, skip,* דָּלַג *dalag.*
Zeph. 1. 9 punish all those that leap on the thresh.

2. *To leap, skip,* דָּלַג *dalag*, 3.
2 Sa. 22. 30 For..by my God have I leaped over a w.
Psa. 18. 29 For..by my God have I leaped over a w.
Song 2. 8 he cometh leaping upon the mountains
Isa. 35. 6 Then shall the lame..leap as an hart, and

3. *To leap with violence,* זָנַק *zanaq*, 3.
Deut33. 22 a lion's whelp: he shall leap from Bashan

4. *To move, leap,* נָתַר *nathar*, 3.
Lev. 11. 21 have legs..to leap withal upon the earth

5. *To go up,* עָלָה *alah.*
Gen. 31. 10 the rams which leaped upon the cattle
31. 12 all the rams which leap upon the cattle

6. *To pass over, leap,* פָּסַח *pasach*, 3.
1 Ki.18. 26 they leaped upon the altar which was m.

7. *To leap, watch enviously,* רָצַד *ratsad*, 3.
Psa. 68. 16 Why leap ye, ye..hills? (this is) the hill

8. *To dance, skip, bound,* רָקַד *raqad*, 3.
Joel 2. 5 shall they leap, like the noise of a flame

9. *To leap,* ἅλλομαι *hallomai.*
Acts 3. 8 walking, and leaping, and praising God
14. 10 Said..Stand upright..And he leaped and

10. *To bound, spring,* σκιρτάω *skirtaō.*
Luke 1. 41 the babe leaped in her womb; and Elisa.
1. 44 the babe leaped in my womb for joy

LEAP for joy, to —
To bound, spring, σκιρτάω *skirtaō.*
Luke 6. 23 Rejoice ye in that day, and leap for joy

LEAP on, to —
To leap upon, ἐφάλλομαι *ephallomai.*
Acts 19. 16 leaped on them, and overcame them, and

LEAP out, to —
To escape, deliver self, slip away, מָלַט *malat*, 7.
Job 41. 19 Out of his mouth..sparks of fire leap out

LEAP up, to —
To leap forth or out of, ἐξάλλομαι *exallomai.*
Acts 3. 8 he leaping up stood, and walked, and en.

LEAPING —
To move, leap, פָּזַז *pazaz*, 3.
2 Sa. 6. 16 saw king David leaping and dancing bef.

LEARN, to —
1. *To learn,* אָלַף *alaph.*
Prov.22. 25 Lest thou learn his ways, and get a snare

2. *To learn, accustom self,* לָמַד *lamad.*
Deut. 4. 10 that they may learn to fear me all the days
5. 1 ye may learn them, and keep and do them
14. 23 mayest learn to fear the LORD thy God al.
17. 19 that he may learn to fear the LORD his G.
18. 9 thou shalt not learn to do after the abom.
31. 12 may learn, and fear the LORD your God
31. 13 may hear, and learn to fear the LORD your
Psa.106. 35 among the heathen, and learned their w.
119. 7 when I shall have learned thy righteous j.
119. 71 good for me..that I might learn thy stat.
119. 73 give me understanding, that I may learn
Prov 30. 3 I neither learned wisdom, nor have the k.
Isa. 1. 17 Learn to do well; seek judgment, relieve
2. 4 And..neither shall they learn war any m.
26. 9 inhabitants of the world will learn right.
26. 10 (yet) will he not learn righteousness: and
29. 24 they that murmured shall learn doctrine
Jer. 10 2 Learn not the way of the heathen, and be
12. 16 if they will diligently learn the ways of my
Eze. 19. 3 it learned to catch the prey; it devoured
19. 6 learned to catch the prey, (and) devoured
Mic. 4. 3 And..neither shall they learn war any m.

3. *To learn,* μανθάνω *manthanō.*
Matt. 9. 13 go ye and learn what (that) meaneth, I
11. 29 Take my yoke upon you, and learn of me
24. 32 Now learn a parable of the fig tree: When
Mark13. 28 Now learn a parable of the fig tree; When
John 6. 45 that hath heard, and hath learned of the
7. 15 How knoweth this man..having never le.
Rom16. 17 contrary to the doctrine which ye have l.
1 Co. 4. 6 that ye might learn in us not to think (of)
14. 31 that all may learn, and all may be comf.
14. 35 if they will learn any thing, let them ask
Gal. 3. 2 This only would I learn of you, Received
Eph. 4. 20 But ye have not so learned Christ
Phil. 4. 9 which ye have both learned, and received
4. 11 for I have learned, in whatsoever state I
Col. 1. 7 As ye also learned of Epaphras our dear
1 Ti. 2. 11 Let the woman learn in silence with all
5. 4 let them learn first to show piety at home
5. 13 And withal they learn (to be) idle, wand.
2 Ti. 3. 7 Ever learning, and never able to come to
3. 14 in the things which thou hast learned and
3. 14 knowing of whom thou hast learned (them)
Titus 3. 14 let ours also learn to maintain good works
Heb. 5. 8 Though he were a Son, yet learned he ob.
Rev. 14. 3 and no man could learn that song but the

4. *To instruct, train up,* παιδεύω *paideuō.*
1 Ti. 1. 20 delivered..that they may learn not to

LEARN by experience, to —
To observe diligently, נָחַשׁ *nachash*, 3.
Gen. 30. 27 I have learned by experience that the L.

LEARNED, to be —
1. *To know a book,* יָדַע סֵפֶר *yada sepher.*
Isa. 29. 11 (men) deliver to one that is learned, saying
29. 12 him that is not learned..I am not learned

2. *Who is taught, learned,* לִמּוּד *limmud.*
Isa. 50. 4 hath given me the tongue of the learned
50. 4 wakeneth mine ear to hear as the learned

3. *To instruct,* παιδεύω *paideuō.*
Acts 7. 22 Moses was learned in all the wisdom of

LEARNING —
1. *Reception, a taking in,* לֶקַח *leqach.*
Prov. 1. 5 A wise (man)..will increase learning; and
9. 9 teach..and he will increase in learning
16. 21 the sweetness of the lips increaseth lear.
16. 23 The heart of the wise..addeth learning

2. *A book, literature,* סֵפֶר *sepher.*
Dan. 1. 4 whom they might teach the learning and
1. 17 knowledge and skill in all learning and

3. *A letter, something written, learning,* γράμμα.
Acts 26. 24 Paul..much learning doth make thee mad

4. *Teaching, instruction,* διδασκαλία *didaskalia.*
Rom.15. 4 were written for our learning; that we

LEASING —
A lie, deceit, כָּזָב *kazab.*
Psa. 4. 2 will ye love vanity, (and) seek after leas.?
5. 6 Thou shalt destroy them that speak leas.

LEAST (that thing which is)—
1. *Small, little, young,* צָעִיר *tsair.*
Judg. 6. 15 and I (am) the least in my father's house
1 Sa. 9. 21 my family the least of all the families of
Jer. 49. 20 Surely the least of the flock shall draw
50. 45 Surely the least of the flock shall draw

2. *Little, small,* קָטָן *qatan.*
2 Ki.18. 24 face..of the least of my master's servants
1 Ch.12. 14 one of the least (was) over an hundred
Isa. 36. 9 face..of the least of my master's servants
Jer. 6. 13 For from the least of them even unto the
31. 34 from the least of them unto the greatest
Jon. 3. 5 greatest of them even to the least of them

3. *Little, small, young,* קָטֹן *qaton.*
Jer. 8. 10 from the least even unto the greatest is g.
42. 1, 8 all..from the least even unto the greatest
44. 12 die, from the least even unto the greatest

4. *The least,* ἐλάχιστος *elachistos.*
Matt. 2. 6 art not the least among the princes of J.
5. 19 shall break one of these least commandme.
5. 19 he shall be called the least in the kingdom
25. 40 unto one of the least of these my brethren
25. 45 ye did (it) not to one of the least of these
Luke12. 26 not able to do that thing which is least
16. 10 He that is faithful in that which is least
16. 10 he that is unjust in the least is unjust also
1 Co. 15. 9 I am the least of the apostles, that am

5. *Little, small,* μικρός *mikros.*
Acts 8. 10 To whom they all gave heed, from the le.
Heb. 8. 11 shall know me, from the least to the gre.

6. *Lesser, smaller,* μικρότερος *mikroteros.*
Matt11. 11 he that is least in the kingdom of heaven
13. 32 Which indeed is the least of all seeds; but
Luke 7. 28 he that is least in the kingdom of God is g.
9. 48 he that is least among you all, the same
[*See* At, esteemed, less.]

LEAST, at (the) —
1. *Or, it may be,* אוֹ *o.*
Gen. 24. 55 let..abide with us..days, at the least ten

2. *Only,* רַק *raq.*
Judg. 3. 2 at the least such as before knew nothing

3. *Even indeed,* καί γε *kai ge.*
Luke19. 42 known, even thou, [at least] in this thy

4. *Even if,* κἄν *kan.*
Acts 5. 15 at the least the shadow of Peter passing

LEAST, to gather —
To make few or little, מָעַט *maat*, 5.
Num 11. 32 he that gathered least gathered ten ho.

LEATHER, LEATHERN —
1. *Skin,* עוֹר *or.*
2 Ki. 1. 8 with a girdle of leather about his loins

2. *Made of skin,* δερμάτινος *dermatinos.*
Matt. 3. 4 John had..a leathern girdle about his l.

LEAVE, to —
1. *To cease,* חָדַל *chadal.*
Gen. 41. 49 very much, until he left numbering; for
Judg. 9. 9 Should I leave my fatness, wherewith by
9. 13 Should I leave my wine, which cheereth
Ruth 1. 18 minded to go..she left speaking unto her
1 Sa. 9. 5 lest my father leave (caring) for the asses

2. *To cause to rest, place,* נוּחַ *nuach*, 5.
Gen. 42. 33 leave one of your brethren..with me, and
Lev. 7. 15 shall not leave any of it until the morning
16. 23 shall put off..and shall leave them there
Num 32. 15 he will yet again leave them in the wild.
Josh. 4. 3 leave them in the lodging place where ye
6. 23 and left them without the camp of Israel
Judg. 2. 23 Therefore the LORD left those nations
3. 1 these (are) the nations which the LORD left
2 Sa. 16. 21 concubines, which he hath left to keep
20. 3 concubines, whom he had left to keep the
1 Ki. 7. 47 Solomon left all the vessels..because they
19. 3 And..he arose..and left his servant there
Psa. 17. 14 leave the rest of their (substance) to their
119. 121 I have done..leave me not to mine opp.
Eccl. 2. 18 because I should leave it unto the man
10. 4 leave not thy place; for yielding pacifieth
Isa. 65. 15 ye shall leave your name for a curse unto
Jer. 14. 9 we are called by thy name; leave us not
43. 6 the captain of the guard had left with G.
Eze. 16. 39 they shall strip..and leave thee naked and
22. 20 and I will leave (you there), and melt you

3. *To set up, place,* יָצַג *yatsag*, 5.
Gen. 33. 15 Let me now leave with thee..of the folk

4. *To leave, let remain over,* יָתַר *yathar*, 5.
Exod 10. 15 fruit of the trees which the hail had left
16. 19 said, Let no man leave of it till the
16. 20 some of them left of it until the morning
Lev. 22. 30 ye shall leave none of it until the morrow
Deut28. 54 remnant of his children which he shall l.
Ruth 2. 14 and she did eat, and was sufficed, and left
2 Ki. 4. 43 They shall eat, and shall leave (thereof)
4. 44 they did eat, and left..according to the
2 Ch.31. 10 we have had enough to eat, and have left
Isa. 1. 9 Except the LORD of hosts had left unto us
Jer. 44. 7 out of Judah, to leave you none to remain
Eze. 12. 16 I will leave a few men of them from the
39. 28 and have left none of them any more there

5. *To finish,* כָּלָה *kalah*, 3.
Gen. 18. 33 as soon as he had left communing with A.
44. 12 at the eldest, and left at the youngest

6. *To leave, spread out,* נָטַשׁ *natash.*
1 Sa. 10. 2 thy father hath left the care of the asses
17. 20 left the sheep with a keeper, and took
17. 22 David left his carriage in the hand of the
17. 28 with whom hast thou left those few sheep
Neh. 10. 31 we would leave the seventh year, and the
Psa. 27. 9 leave me not, neither forsake me, O God
Jer. 12. 7 I have left mine heritage; I have given
Eze. 29. 5 I will leave thee..into the wilderness, thee
31. 12 strangers..have cut him off, and have l.
31. 12 all the people of the earth..have left him
32. 4 Then will I leave thee upon the land, I
Hos. 12. 14 therefore shall he leave his blood upon h.

7. *To give,* נָתַן *nathan.*
Eccl. 2. 21 to a man..shall he leave it (for) his port.
Jer. 40. 11 the king of Babylon had left a remnant of

8. *To forsake, leave, abandon,* עָזַב *azab.*
Gen. 2. 24 Therefore shall a man leave his father and
24. 27 who hath not left destitute my master of
28. 15 I will not leave thee, until I have done
39. 6 he left all that he had in Joseph's hand
39. 12 left his garment in her hand, and fled, and
39. 13 when she saw that he had left his garment
39. 15, 18 he left his garment with me, and fled
44. 22 cannot leave..for (if) he should leave his
50. 8 their herds, they left in the land of Goshen
Exod. 2. 20 why (is) it..ye have left the man? call him
9. 21 left his servants and his cattle in the field
Lev. 19. 10 thou shalt leave them for the poor and st.
23. 22 thou shalt leave them unto the poor, and
Num10. 31 And he said, Leave us not, I pray thee
Josh. 8. 17 they left the city open, and pursued after
22. 3 Ye have not left your brethren these many
Judg. 2. 21 nations which Joshua left when he died
Ruth 1. 16 Entreat me not to leave thee from follow.
2. 11 thou hast left thy father and thy mother
2. 16 and leave..that she may glean..and reb.
1 Sa. 30. 13 my master left me, because three days
2 Sa. 5. 21 there they left their images, and David
15. 16 the king left ten women..concubines
1 Ki. 8. 57 God..let him not leave us, nor forsake us
19. 20 he left the oxen, and ran after Elijah, and
2 Ki. 2. 2, 4, 6 thy soul liveth, I will not leave thee
4. 30 (as) thy soul liveth, I will not leave thee
7. 7 left their tents, and their horses, and their
8. 6 since the day that she left the land, even
17. 16 they left all the commandments of the L.
1 Ch.14. 12 when they had left their gods there, David
16. 37 So he left there, before the ark of the co.
2 Ch.11. 14 For the Levites left their suburbs, and their
12. 5 therefore have I also left you in the hand
24. 18 they left the house of the LORD God of
24. 25 for they left him in great diseases, his own
28. 14 So the armed men left the captives and
32. 31 God left him, to try him, that he might
Neh. 9. 28 therefore leftest thou them in the hand of
Job 10. 1 I will leave my complaint upon myself
39. 11 Wilt thou trust..wilt thou leave thy lab.
39. 14 Which leaveth her eggs in the earth, and
Psa. 16. 10 For thou wilt not leave my soul in hell
37. 33 The LORD will not leave him in his hand
49. 10 wise men die..and leave their wealth to
Prov. 2. 13 Who leave the paths of uprightness, to
Isa. 10. 3 help? and where will ye leave your glory?
17. 9 which they left because of the children of
Jer. 9. 2 that I might leave my people, and go from
17. 11 shall leave them in the midst of his days
18. 14 Will (a man) leave the snow of Lebanon
48. 28 leave the cities, and dwell in the rock, and
49. 11 Leave thy fatherless children, I will pres.
Eze. 23. 8 Neither left she her whoredoms..from E.
23. 29 shall leave thee naked and bare; and the
24. 21 your daughters whom ye have left shall
Zech11. 17 Woe to the idol shepherd that leaveth the
Mal. 4. 1 it shall leave them neither root nor branch

9. *To stand, stand still,* עָמַד *amad.*
Gen. 29. 35 she called his name Judah: and left bearing
30. 9 When Leah saw that she had left bearing

10. *To let fall,* רָפָה *raphah*, 5.
Neh. 6. 3 whilst I leave it, and come down to you?

11. *To put, place,* שׂוּם שִׂים *sum, sim.*
2 Sa. 14. 7 shall not leave to my husband..name nor

12. *To leave, let remain,* שָׁאַר *shaar,* 5.
Exod10. 12 eat every herb..all that the hail hath left
Num. 9. 12 They shall leave none of it unto the mo.
21. 35 until there was none left him alive: and
Deut. 2. 34 And..of every city, we left none to remain
3. 3 we smote him until none was left to him
28. 51 shall not leave thee..corn, wine, or oil
28. 55 because he hath nothing left him in the
Josh.10. 33 smote..until he had left him none rema.
10. 37 he left none remaining, according to all
10. 39 he left none remaining: as he had done
10. 40 he left none remaining, but utterly dest.
11. 8 smote..until they left them none remain.
11. 14 they smote..neither left they any to bre
Judg. 6. 4 left no sustenance for Israel, neither sheep
1 Sa. 14. 36 Saul said..let us not leave a man of them
25. 22 if I leave of all that (pertain) to him, by
1 Ki. 15. 29 he left not to Jeroboam any that breathed
16. 11 he left him not one that pisseth against
19. 18 I have left..seven thousand in Israel, all
2 Ki. 3. 25 only in Kir-haraseth left they the stones
10. 11 slew all..until he left him none remain.
10. 14 and slew them..neither left he any of them
13. 7 Neither did he leave of the people to Je.
25. 12 the captain of the guard left of the poor
25. 22 whom Nebuchadnezzar..had left, even
Ezra 9. 8 to leave us a remnant to escape, and to
Jer. 39. 10 captain..left of the poor of the people
49. 9 would they not leave..gleaning grapes?
52. 16 left..of the poor of the land for vine dre.
Joel 2. 14 leave a blessing behind him..a meat off.
Amos 5. 3 The city that went out..shall leave an h.
5. 3 that which went forth..shall leave ten
Obad. 5 to thee, would they not leave (some) gr.?
Zeph. 3. 12 I will also leave in the midst of thee an

13. *To leave, let alone,* שְׁבַק *shebaq.*
Dan. 4. 15 leave the stump of his roots in the earth
4. 23 leave the stump of the roots thereof in
4. 26 And..to leave the stump of the tree roots

14. *To cause or suffer to cease,* שָׁבַת *shabath,* 5.
Ruth 4. 14 LORD, which hath not left thee this day

15. *To send up or back,* ἀνίημι *aniēmi.*
Heb. 13. 5 I will never leave thee, nor forsake thee

16. *To leave behind or off,* ἀπολείπω *apoleipō.*
2 Ti. 4. 13 The cloak that I left at Troas with Car
4. 20 Trophimus have I left at Miletum sick
Jude 6 left their own habitation, he hath reserved

17. *To send away, let go,* ἀφίημι *aphiēmi.*
Matt. 4. 11 Then the devil leaveth him; and, behold
4. 20 they straightway left (their) nets, and fo.
4. 22 they immediately left the ship and their
5. 24 Leave there thy gift before the altar, and
8. 15 he touched her hand, and the fever left
18. 12 doth he not leave the ninety and nine, and
22. 22 marvelled, and left him, and went their
22. 25 having no issue, left his wife unto his br.
23. 23 done, and not to leave the other undone
23. 38 Behold, your house is left unto you deso.
24. 2 There shall not be left here one stone upon
24. 40, 41 the one shall be taken, and the other l.
26. 44 he left them, and went away again, and
Mark 1. 20 they left their father Zebedee in the ship
1. 31 immediately the fever left her, and she
8. 13 he left them, and, entering into the ship
10. 28 we have left all, and have followed thee
10. 29 There is no man that hath left house, or
12. 12 feared..and they left him, and went their
12. 19 and leave no children, that his brother sh.
12. 20 first took a wife, and dying left no seed
12. 21 [neither left he any seed: and the third]
12. 22 And the seven had her, and left no seed
13. 2 there shall not be left one stone upon
13. 34 who left his house, and gave authority to
Luke 4. 39 stood..and rebuked the fever; and it left
10. 30 wounded..and departed, leaving..half
11. 42 to have done, and not to leave the other
13. 35 Behold, your house is left unto you deso.
17. 34 shall be taken, and the other shall be left
17. 35 the one shall be taken, and the other left
17. 36 [the one shall be taken, and the other left]
18. 28 said, Lo, we have left all, and followed
18. 29 There is no man that hath left house, or
19. 44 they shall not leave in thee one stone upon
21. 6 there shall not be left one stone upon an.
John 4. 3 He left Judea, and departed again into G.
4. 28 The woman then left her water pot, and
4. 52 Yesterday at the seventh hour the fever l.
8. 29 the Father hath not left me alone; for I
10. 12 seeth the wolf coming, and leaveth the
14. 18 I will not leave you comfortless: I will
14. 27 Peace I leave with you, my peace I give
16. 28 I leave the world, and go to the Father
16. 32 shall leave me alone: and yet I am not a.
Acts 14. 17 he left not himself without witness, in
Rom. 1. 27 men, leaving the natural use of the woman
1 Co. 7. 13 pleased to dwell with her, let her not le.
Heb. 2. 8 he left nothing (that is) not put under him
6. 1 Therefore leaving the principles of the
Rev. 2. 4 I have..against thee..thou hast left thy

18. *To let, suffer,* ἐάω *eaō.*
Acts 23. 32 On the morrow they left the horsemen to

19. *To leave down in,* ἐγκαταλείπω *egkataleipō.*
Acts 2. 27 [thou wilt not leave] my soul in hell
Rom. 9. 29 Except the Lord of Sabaoth had left us a

20. *To cast out, or forth,* ἐκβάλλω *ekballō.*
Rev. 11. 2 But the court..leave out, and measure it

21. *To leave down, behind, utterly,* καταλείπω.
Matt. 4. 13 leaving Nazareth, he came and dwelt in C.
16. 4 no sign..And he left them, and departed
19. 5 For this cause shall a man leave father
21. 17 he left them, and went out of the city into
Mark10. 7 For this cause shall a man leave his father
12. 19 If a man's brother die, and leave (his) wife
14. 52 he left the linen cloth, and fled from them
Luke 5. 28 And he left all, rose up, and followed him
10. 40 that my sister hath left me to serve alone?
15. 4 doth not leave the ninety and nine in the
20. 31 the seven..and they left no children, and
John 8. 9 [Jesus was left alone, and the woman]
Acts 2. 31 that his soul was not left in hell, neither
6. 2 It is not reason that we should leave the
18. 19 he came to Ephesus, and left them there
21. 3 we left it on the left hand, and sailed into
24. 27 to show the Jews a pleasure, left Paul bo.
25. 14 There is a certain man left in bonds by F.
Eph. 5. 31 For this cause shall a man leave his father
1 Th. 3. 1 we thought it good to be left at Athens
Titus 1. 5 For this cause [left I] thee in Crete, that
Heb. 4. 1 a promise being left (us) of entering into

22. *To cease,* παύομαι *pauomai.*
Luke 5. 4 Now when he had left speaking, he said
Acts 21. 32 when they saw..they left beating of Paul

23. *To leave behind,* ὑπολιμπάνω *hupolimpanō.*
1 Pe. 2. 21 also suffered for us, leaving us an example

LEAVE destitute, to —
To forsake, leave, עָזַב *azab.*
Gen. 24. 27 who hath not left destitute my master of
[*See also* Alive, sixth part, unpunished.]

LEAVE, to give —
1. *To give, suffer,* נָתַן *nathan.*
Num22. 13 LORD refuseth to give me leave to go with
2. *To turn over upon one, permit,* ἐπιτρέπω *epitrepō.*
Mark 5. 13 And forthwith Jesus gave them leave
John 19. 38 Pilate gave..leave. He came therefore

LEAVE, to obtain —
To ask for oneself, שָׁאַל *shaal,* 2.
Neh. 13. 6 after certain days obtained I leave of the

LEAVE for, to—[*See* Inheritance.]

LEAVE off, to —
1. *To cease, leave off, forbear,* חָדַל *chadal.*
Gen. 11. 8 LORD scattered..and they left off to build
1 Ki.15. 21 he left off building of Ramah, and dwelt
2 Ch.16. 5 he left off building of Ramah, and let his
Psa. 36. 3 he hath left off to be wise, (and) to do good
Jer. 44. 18 But since we left off to burn incense to the
2. *To cause to rest, place,* נוּחַ *nuach,* 5.
Amos 5. 7 and leave off righteousness in the earth
3. *To finish,* כָּלָה *kalah,* 3.
Gen. 17. 22 he left off talking with him, and God went
4. *To leave, spread out,* נָטַשׁ *natash.*
Prov.17. 14 leave off contention, before it be meddled
5. *To forsake, abandon,* עָזַב *azab.*
Ruth 2. 20 who hath not left off his kindness to the
Neh. 5. 10 I pray you, let us leave off this usury
Job 9. 27 I will leave off my heaviness, and comfort
Hos. 4. 10 they have left off to take heed to the LORD
6. *To remove, leave off,* עָתַק *athaq,* 5.
Job 32. 15 They were amazed..they left off speaking

LEAVE of, to take —
1. *To arrange oneself off from any one,* ἀποτάσσομαι.
Acts 18. 18 took his leave of the brethren, and sailed
2 Co. 2. 13 taking my leave of them, I went from th.
2. *To salute,* ἀσπάζομαι *aspazomai.*
Acts 21. 6 when [we had taken our leave] one of an.

LEAVE off speaking, to —
To keep or remain silent, חָרַשׁ *charash,* 5.
Jer. 38. 27 So they left off speaking with him; for

LEAVE a remnant, to —
To let remain, יָתַר *yathar,* 5.
Eze. 6. 8 Yet will I leave a remnant, that ye may

LEAVE undone, to —
To turn aside, סוּר *sur,* 5.
Josh 11. 15 he left nothing undone of all that the L.

LEAVE, what they —
What remains over, יֶתֶר *yether.*
Exod23. 11 what they leave the beasts of the field

LEAVED—[*See* Gates.]

LEAVEN, leavened bread —
1. *Anything leavened or fermented,* חָמֵץ *chamets.*
Exod12. 15 whosoever eateth leavened bread from
13. 3 there shall no leavened bread be eaten
13. 7 there shall no leavened bread be seen with
23. 18 Blood of my sacrifice with leavened bread
34. 25 offer the blood of my sacrifice with leaven
Lev. 2. 11 No meat offering..shall be made with l.
6. 17 It shall not be baken with leaven. I have
7. 13 leavened bread with the sacrifice of thanks
23. 17 wave loaves..they shall be baken with l.
Deut16. 3 Thou shalt eat no leavened bread with it
Amos 4. 5 offer a sacrifice of thanks giving with lea.
2. *Leaven,* שְׂאֹר *seor.*
Exod12. 15 ye shall put away leaven out of your hou
12. 19 Seven days shall there be no leaven found
Exod13. 7 neither shall there be leaven seen with
Lev. 2. 11 ye shall burn no leaven, nor any honey
Deut16. 4 there shall be no leavened bread seen with
3. *Leaven,* ζύμη *zumē.*
Matt13. 33 The kingdom of heaven is like unto leaven
16. 6, 11 beware of the leaven of the Pharisees
16. 12 not beware of the leaven of bread, but of
Mark 8. 15 the leaven of the Pharisees, and..the le.
Luke 12. 1 Beware ye of the leaven of the Pharisees
13. 21 It is like leaven, which a woman took and
1 Co. 5. 6 a little leaven leaveneth the whole lump?
5. 7 Purge out therefore the old leaven, that
5. 8 not with old leaven, neither with the le.
Gal. 5. 9 A little leaven leaveneth the whole lump

LEAVEN, to —
To leaven, ζυμόω *zumoō.*
Matt13. 33 took and hid..till the whole was leavened
Luke13. 21 took and hid..till the whole was leavened
1 Co. 5. 6 a little leaven [leaveneth] the whole lump?
Gal. 5. 9 A little leaven leaveneth the whole lump

LEAVEN, without —
Unleavened, pressed, מַצָּה *matstsah.*
Lev. 10. 12 and eat it without leaven beside the altar

LEAVENED, to be —
1. *To be or become leavened,* חָמֵץ *chamets.*
Exod12. 34 took their dough before it was leavened
12. 39 it was not leavened; because they were
Hos. 7. 4 kneaded the dough, until it be leavened
2. *To leaven,* חָמֵץ *chamets,* 5.
Exod12. 19 whosoever eateth that which is leavened
12. 20 Ye shall eat nothing leavened; in all your

LEAVES, (two leaved gates) —
1. *Leaf (of a door or gate),* דֶּלֶת *deleth.*
Isa. 45. 1 to open before him the two leaved gates
Jer. 36. 23 when Jehudi had read three or four leaves
Eze. 41. 24 doors had two leaves..two turning leaves
41. 24 two..for the one door, and two leaves for
2. *Leaf (of a tree or flower),* עֳפִי *ophi.*
Dan. 4. 12 The trees thereof (were) fair, and the fr.
4. 14 shake of his leaves, and scatter his fruit
4. 21 Whose leaves (were) fair, and the fruit
Rev. 22. 2 leaves of the tree (were) for the healing
3. *Hangings,* קְלָעִים *qelaim.*
1 Ki 6. 34 two leaves of the other door (were) fold.

LE-BA'-NAH, LE-BA'-NA, לְבָנָה, לְבָנָא *whiteness.*
One of the Nethinim whose descendants accompanied Zerubbabel. B.C. 636.
Ezra 2. 45 The children of L., the childr. of Hagabah
Neh. 7. 48 The children of L., the childr. of Hagaba

LE-BA'-NON, לְבָנוֹן *white, snowy.*
The mountain range which, commencing near Tyre, runs N.E. through Syria, nearly parallel to the sea-coast, sometimes as high as 9000 feet above the sea.
Deut. 1. 7 take your journey..unto L., unto the gr.
3. 25 me go over and see the good land..and L.
11. 24 from the wilderness and L., from the river
Josh. 1. 4 From the wilderness and this L., even unto
9. 1 coasts of the great sea over against L., the
11. 17 even unto Baal-gad in the valley of L.
12. 7 from Baal-gad in the valley of L. even unto
13. 5 the land of the Giblites, and all L., toward
13. 6 All the inhabitants..from L. unto Misre.
Judg. 3. 3 Hivites that dwelt in mount L., from m.
9. 15 fire come out..and devour the cedars of L.
1 Ki. 4. 33 from the cedar tree that (is) in L. even
5. 6 that they hew me cedar trees out of L.
5. 9 My servants shall bring them down from L.
5. 14 sent them to L...a month they were in L.
7. 2 built also the house of the forest of L.; the
9. 19 which Solomon desired to build in..L., and
10. 17 put them in the house of the forest of L.
10. 21 vessels of the house of the forest of L.
2 Ki.14. 9 The thistle that (was) in L. sent to the ce.
14. 9 that (was) in L., saying, Give thy daughter
14. 9 passed by a wild beast that (was) in L.
19. 23 I am come up..to the sides of L., and will
2 Ch. 2. 8 Send me also cedar trees..out of L.; for
2. 8 thy servants can skill to cut timber in L.
2. 16 we will cut wood out of L., as much as
8. 6 Solomon desired to build..in L., and th.
9. 20 vessels of the house of the forest of L. v. 16.
25. 18 The thistle that (was) in L. sent to the
25. 18 that (was) in L., saying, Give thy daughter
25. 18 passed by a wild beast that (was) in L., and
Ezra 3. 7 to bring cedar trees from L. to the sea of
Psa. 29. 5 yea, the LORD breaketh the cedars of L.
29. 6 L. and Sirion like a young unicorn
72. 16 fruit thereof shall shake like L.: and (they)
92. 12 righteous..shall grow like a cedar in L.
104. 16 the cedars of L., which he hath planted
Song 3. 9 made himself a chariot of the wood of L.
4. 8 come with me from L...from L.: look from
4. 11 and the smell..(is) like the smell of L.
4. 15 fountain of gardens..and streams from L.
5. 15 his countenance (is) as L., excellent as the
7. 4 thy nose (is) as the tower of L. which lo.
Isa. 2. 13 upon all the cedars of L., (that are) high
10. 34 shall cut down the thickets..and L. shall
14. 8 trees rejoice at thee, (and) the cedars of L.
29. 17 L. shall be turned into a fruitful field, and
33. 9 L. is ashamed (and) hewn down; Sharon
35. 2 glory of L. shall be given unto it, the ex.
37. 24 I come up..to the sides of L.; and I will
40. 16 L. (is) not sufficient to burn, nor the beasts
60. 13 The glory of L. shall come unto thee, the
Jer. 18. 14 Will (a man) leave the snow of L. (which
22. 6 Thou (art)..the head of L.: (yet) surely I

Jer. 22. 20 Go up to L., and cry; and lift up thy voice
22. 23 O inhabitant of L., that makest thy nest
Eze. 17. 3 A great eagle..came unto L., and took the
27. 5 they have taken cedars from L. to make
31. 3 (was) a cedar in L. with fair branches
31. 15 I caused L. to mourn for him, and all the
31. 16 the choice and best of L., all that drink
Hos. 14. 5 he shall..cast forth his roots as L.
14. 6 be as the olive tree, and his smell as L.
14. 7 scent thereof (shall be) as the wine of L.
Nah. 1. 4 Bashan..and the flower of L. languisheth
Hab. 2. 17 the violence of L. shall cover thee, and
Zech. 10. 10 bring them into the land of Gilead and L.
11. 1 Open thy doors, O L., that the fire may

LE-BA'-OTH, לְבָאוֹת *place of lionesses.*
A city of Simeon, in the S. of Judah near Shilhim; the same as *Beth-lebaoth* in Jos. 19. 6. It is also called *Beth-birei,* "place of stout ones," in 1 Ch. 4. 31.
Josh. 15. 32 L., and Shilhim, and Ain, and Rimmon

LEB-BE'-US, Λεββαῖος *man of heart.*
An apostle surnamed Thaddeus; supposed to be the same as Jude, the brother of James.
Matt 10. 3 Alpheus, and L., whose surname was Th.

LE-BO'-NAH, לְבוֹנָה *frankincense.*
A city of Ephraim, a little N. of Shiloh; now called *Lubban.*
Judg 21. 19 Beth-el to Shechem, and on the south of L.

LE'-CAH, לֵכָה *addition, attached place.*
Son of Er, the son of Shelah, the son of Judah, B.C. 1660; or the place where Er dwelt.
1 Ch. 4. 21 the father of L., and Laadah, the father

LED, to be —
To be caused to step, declared happy, אָשַׁר *ashar,* 4.
Isa. 9. 16 (they that are) led of them (are) destroyed

LED away, to be —
To lead, ἄγω *agō.*
2 Ti. 3. 6 laden with sins, led away with divers lu.

LED away captive, to be —
To be removed, exiled, גָּלָה *galah,* 4.
Nah. 2. 7 Huzzab shall be led away captive, she

LED away with, to be —
To lead away with, συναπάγω *sunapagō.*
2 Pe. 3. 17 beware lest ye also, being led away with

LED forth, to be —
To be caused to flow or go forth, יָבַל *yabal,* 6.
Isa. 55. 12 ye shall go out with joy, and be led forth

LED into, to be —
To lead into, εἰσάγω *eisagō.*
Acts 21. 37 as Paul was to be led into the castle, he

LED into captivity, to cause to be —
To cause to remove, exile, גָּלָה *galah,* 5.
Eze. 39. 28 which caused them to be led into captivity

LEDGE —
1. *Hand, spoke,* יָד *yad.*
1 Ki. 7. 35 on the top of the base the ledges thereof
7. 36 on the plates of the ledges thereof, and
2. *Joints, joinings,* שְׁלַבִּים *shelabbim.*
1 Ki. 7. 28 and the borders (were) between the ledges
7. 29 between the ledges (were) lions, oxen, and
7. 29 upon the ledges (there was) a base above

LEEK —
Herb, leek, חָצִיר *chatsir.*
Num 11. 5 melons, and the leeks, and the onions,

LEES —
Preserves, שְׁמָרִים *shemarim.*
Isa. 25. 6 a feast of wines on the lees, of fat things
25. 6 marrow, of wines on the lees well refined
Jer. 48. 11 he hath settled on his lees, and hath not
Zeph. 1. 12 punish..men that are settled on their lees
[*See also* Wines].

LEFT (hand, side) —
1. *The left hand, side,* שְׂמֹאל, שְׂמֹאול *semol.*
Gen. 13. 9 if..the left hand, then I will go to the ri.
14. 15 Hobah, which (is) on the left hand of Da.
24. 49 to the right hand or to the left
[So in Num. 20. 17; 22. 26; Deut. 2. 27; 5. 32; 17. 11, 20; 28. 14; Josh. 1. 7; 23. 6; 1 Sa. 6. 12; 2 Sa. 2. 19; 2 Ki. 22. 2; 2 Ch. 34. 2; Prov. 4. 27].
Gen. 48. 13 took..Ephraim..toward Israel's left hand
48. 13 and Manasseh in his left hand toward I.
48. 14 and his left hand upon Manasseh's head
Exod 14. 22, 29 on their right hand, and on their left
Josh 19. 27 and goeth out to Cabul on the left hand
Judg. 3. 21 Ehud put forth his left hand, and took
7. 20 and held the lamps in their left hands
16. 29 Samson took hold..of the other with his l.
2 Sa. 2. 21 Turn..aside to thy right hand or to thy l.
16. 6 men..on his right hand and on his left
1 Ki. 7. 39 five on the left side of the house: and he
7. 49 five on the left, before the oracle, with the
22. 19 by him on his right hand and on his left
2 Ki. 23. 8 on a man's left hand at the gate of the city
1 Ch. 6. 44 the sons of Merari (stood) on the left hand
2 Ch. 3. 17 the right hand, and the other on the left
4. 6, 7, 8 the right hand, and five on the left
18. 18 standing on his right hand and (on) his left
Neh. 8. 4 on his left hand, Pedaiah, and Mishael
Job 23. 9 On the left hand, where he doth work
Prov. 3. 16 (and) in her left hand riches and honour
Eccl. 10. 2 right hand; but a fool's heart at his left
Song. 2. 6 His left hand (is) under my head, and his
8. 3 His left hand (should be) under my head
Isa. 9. 20 he shall eat on the left hand, and they
54. 3 break forth on the right hand and on the l.
Eze. 1. 10 four had the face of an ox on the left side
16. 46 her daughters that dwell on thy left hand
39. 3 I will smite thy bow out of thy left hand
Dan. 12. 7 held up his right hand and his left hand
Jon. 4. 11 between their right hand and their left h.
Zech. 4. 3 and the other upon the left (side) thereof
4. 11 upon the right..and upon..left..thereof?
12. 6 devour..on the right hand and on the left

2. *To turn to the left,* שָׂמַאל *samal,* 5.
2 Sa. 14. 19 or to the left from ought that my lord the
1 Ch. 12. 2 could use both the right hand and the left
Eze. 21. 16 Go thee..on the right hand, (or) on the left

3. *The left hand, side,* שְׂמָאלִי *semali.*
Lev. 14. 15, 26 into the palm of his own left hand
14. 16, 27 the oil that (is) in his left hand
1 Ki. 7. 21 he set up the left pillar, and called the
2 Ki. 11. 11 to the left corner of the temple..by the
2 Ch. 3. 17 and the name of that on the left Boaz
23. 10 to the left side of the temple, along by
Eze. 4. 4 Lie thou also upon thy left side, and lay

4. *Remnant, residue,* שְׁאֵרִית *sheerith.*
Jer. 50. 26 destroy her..let nothing of her be left

5. *To be sent forth,* שָׁלַח *shalach,* 4.
Prov 29. 15 a child left (to himself) bringeth his mot.

6. *Having a good name, the left,* εὐώνυμος *euōnumos.*
Matt 20. 21 and the other on the left, in thy kingdom
20. 23 to sit on my right hand, and on my left
25. 33 on his right hand, but the goats on the l.
25. 41 shall he say also unto them on the left h.
27. 38 on the right hand, and another on the left
Mark 10. 37 the other on thy [left hand], in thy glory
10. 40 to sit on my right hand and on my left h.
15. 27 his right hand, and the other on his left
Acts 21. 3 we left it on the left hand, and sailed into
Rev. 10. 2 and he set..(his) left (foot) on the earth

LEFT, to be —
1. *To be made to rest, placed,* נוּחַ *nuach,* 6.
Eze. 41. 9 (that) which (was) left (was) the place of
41. 11 doors..(were) towa. (the place that was) l.
41. 11 and the breadth of the place that was left

2. *To be left, remain over,* יָתַר *yathar,* 2.
Gen. 32. 24 Jacob was left alone; and there wrestled
44. 20 he alone is left of his mother, and his fa.
Lev. 2. 10 And that which is left of the meat offering
10. 12 unto Aaron, and..his sons that were left
10. 16 with..the sons of Aaron (which were) left
Num 26. 65 there was not left a man of them, save C.
Josh 11. 11 there was not any left to breathe: and he
11. 22 There was none of the Anakims left in the
Judg. 8. 10 all that were left of all the hosts of the c.
9. 5 yet..the youngest son of Jerubbaal was l.
1 Sa. 2. 36 every one that is left in thine house shall
25. 34 surely there had not been any left unto N.
2 Sa. 9. 1 Is there yet any that is left of the house
13. 30 king's..and there is not one of them left
17. 12 all..there shall not be left so much as one
1 Ki. 9. 20 all the people..left of the Amorites, Hit.
9. 21 Their children that were left after them
15. 18 left in the treasures of the house of the L.
17. 17 sore, that there was no breath left in him
19. 10 I only, am left; and they seek my life, to
19. 14 I, (even) I only, am left; and they seek
20. 30 seven thousand of the men (that were) left
2 Ki. 20. 17 shall be carried..nothing shall be left
1 Ch. 6. 61 left of the family of that tribe..out of the
2 Ch. 8. 7 all the people..left of the Hittites, and
8. 8 were left after them in the land, whom
31. 10 we have had enough to eat, and have left
31. 10 and that which is left (is) this great store
Neh. 6. 1 (that) there was no breach left therein
Psa. 106. 11 enemies; there was not one of them left
Isa. 1. 8 the daughter of Zion is left as a cottage
7. 22 shall every one eat (that is) left in the land
30. 17 till ye be left as a beacon upon the top of
39. 6 shall be carried..nothing shall be left
Jer. 27. 18 that the vessels which are left in the ho.
34. 7 against..the cities of Judah that were left
Eze. 14. 22 therein shall be left a remnant that shall
48. 15 the five thousand..left in the breadth over
Zech 13. 8 shall come to pass..the third shall be left
14. 16 every one that is left of all the nations

3. *To lodge, pass the night,* לוּן, לִין *lun, lin.*
Exod 34. 25 neither shall the sacrifice..be left unto

4. *To be found,* מָצָא *matsa,* 2.
2 Ki. 19. 4 lift up..prayer for the remnant that are l.
Isa. 37. 4 lift up..prayer for the remnant that is left

5. *To be forsaken, left, abandoned,* עָזַב *azab,* 2.
Lev. 26. 43 The land also shall be left of them, and
Isa. 18. 6 They shall be left together unto the fowls
27. 10 the habitation forsaken, and left like a

6. *To be forsaken, left, abandoned,* עָזַב *azab,* 4.
Isa. 32. 14 the multitude of the city shall be left; the
Jer. 49. 25 How is the city of praise not left, the city

7. *Remnant, remaining one,* שָׂרִיד *sarid.*
Job 20. 21 There shall none of his meat be left
20. 26 it shall go ill with him that is left in his
Jer. 31. 2 The people..left of the sword found grace

8. *To remain, be left,* שָׁאַר *shaar,* 2.
Gen. 32. 8 other company which is left shall escape
42. 38 his brother is dead, and he is left alone
47. 18 there is not ought left in the sight of my
Exod 10. 26 there shall not an hoof be left behind
Lev. 26. 36 upon them that are left..of you I will send
26. 39 they that are left of you shall pine away
Deut. 4. 27 ye shall be left few in number among the
7. 20 until they that are left..be destroyed
28. 62 ye shall be left few in number, whereas
Josh. 8. 17 there was not a man left in Ai or Bethel
Judg. 4. 16 all the host..fell..there was not a man
Ruth 1. 3 Elimelech..died; and she was left, and
1. 5 the woman was left of her two sons and
1 Sa. 5. 4 only (the stump of) Dagon was left to him
9. 24 Behold that which is left! set (it) before
11. 11 so that two of them were not left together
2 Sa. 14. 7 so they shall quench my coal which is left
2 Ki. 7. 13 of the horses that remain, which are left
7. 13 as all the multitude of Israel that are left
10. 21 that there was not a man left that came
17. 18 was none left but the tribe of Judah only
25. 11 the rest of the people..left in the city, and
1 Ch. 13. 2 our brethren..left in all the land of Israel
2 Ch. 21. 17 so that there was never a son left him
34. 21 for them that are left in Israel and in J.
Neh. 1. 2 the Jews..which were left of the captivity
1. 3 The remnant that are left of the captivity
Isa. 4. 3 he that is) left in Zion, and (he that) rem.
11. 11, 16 remnant of his people which shall be l.
17. 6 Yet gleaning grapes shall be left in it, as
24. 6 curse devoured the earth..and few men l.
24. 12 In the city is left desolation, and the gate
49. 21 I was left alone; these, where (had) they
Jer. 21. 7 (such as are) left in this city from the pe.
38. 22 all the women that are left in the king of
40. 6 among the people that were left in the l.
42. 2 we are left..a few of many, as thine
Eze. 9. 8 they were slaying them, and I was left
36. 36 Then the heathen that are left round ab.
Dan. 10. 8 Therefore I was left alone, and saw this
10. 17 no strength..neither is there breath left
Hag. 2. 3 Who (is) left among you that saw this h.

9. *To let remain, be left,* שָׁאַר *shaar,* 5.
Num 21. 35 smote..until there was none left him alive
Deut. 3. 3 we smote him until none was left to him
28. 55 he hath nothing left him in the siege, and

10. *To be left,* שְׁבַק *shebaq,* 4.
Dan. 2. 44 the kingdom shall not be left to other p.

11. *To be over and above,* περισσεύω *perisseuō.*
Matt 15. 37 took up of the broken (meat) that was l.

12. *To be left behind,* ὑπολείπομαι *hupoleipomai.*
Rom 11. 3 I am left alone, and they seek my life

LEFT behind, to be —
To be left, remain over, יָתַר *yathar,* 2.
1 Sa. 30. 9 where those that were left behind stayed

LEFT, to go or turn to the —
To go to the left, שָׂמַאל *samal,* 5.
Gen. 13. 9 the right hand then will I go to the left
Isa. 30. 21 right hand, and when ye turn to the left

LEFT hand —
The left, ἀριστερός *aristeros.*
Matt. 6. 3 let not thy left hand know what thy right
Luke 23. 33 the right hand, and the other on the left
2 Co. 6. 7 armour..on the right hand and on the l.

LEFT, that was —
What is left over and above, περίσσευμα *perisseuma.*
Mark 8. 8 took up of the broken (meat) that was left

LEFT, that hath —
What remains or is left over, יֶתֶר *yether.*
Joel 1. 4 That which the palmerworm hath left
1. 4 that which the locust hath left hath the
1. 4 that which the cankerworm hath left

LEFT HANDED —
Bound of the right hand, אִטֵּר יַד־יְמִין *itter yad yamin.*
Judg. 3. 15 son of Gera, a Benjamite, a man left han.
20. 16 seven hundred chosen men left handed

LEG —
1. *Two legs,* כְּרָעַיִם *keraayim.*
Exod 12. 9 his head with his legs, and with
29. 17 wash the inwards of him, and his legs
Lev. 1. 9 his inwards and his legs shall he wash in
1. 13 he shall wash the inwards and the legs
4. 11 with his head, and with his legs, and his
8. 21 he washed the inwards and the legs in w.
9. 14 he did wash the inwards and the legs, and
11. 21 which have legs above their feet, to leap
Amos 3. 12 taketh out of the mouth of..lion two legs
2. *Foot,* רֶגֶל *regel.*
1 Sa. 17. 6 And..greaves of brass upon his legs, and
3. *Leg,* שׁוֹק *shoq.*
Deut 28. 35 and in the legs, with a sore botch that
Psa. 147. 10 taketh not pleasure in the legs of a man
Prov 26. 7 The legs of the lame are not equal; so (is)
Song 5. 15 His legs (are as) pillars of marble set upon
4. *Leg,* שָׁק *shaq.*
Dan. 2. 33 His legs of iron, his feet part of iron and
5. *Skirt, train,* שֹׁבֶל *shobel.*
Isa. 47. 2 uncover thy locks, make bare the leg, unc.
6. *Leg,* σκέλος *skelos.*
John 19. 31 besought Pilate that their legs might be

John19. 32 brake the legs of the first, and of the other
19. 33 saw..he was dead..they brake not his legs
[See also Ornament.]

LEGION —
A legion, λεγεών *legeōn (from Lat. legio).*
Matt26. 53 give me more than twelve legions of angels?
Mark 5. 9 saying, my name (is) Legion: for we are
5. 15 and see him that..had the legion, sitting
Luke 8. 30 What is thy name? And he said, Legion

LE-HA'-BIM, לְהָבִים *flame-coloured, red.*
The third son of Mizraim, supposed to be the ancestor of the Egyptian Lybians.
Gen. 10. 13 Ludim, and Anamim, and L., and Naph.
1 Ch. 1. 11 L., and Anamim, and L., and Naphtuhim

LE'-HI, לֶחִי, לְחִי *jaw-bone.*
A district in the hill country of Judah near Philistia, and not far from Jerusalem.
Judg15. 9 pitched in Judah..spread themselves in L.
15. 14 he came unto L., the Philistines shouted
15. 19 En-hakkore, which (is) in L. unto this day

LEISURE, to have —
To have a favourable opportunity, εὐκαιρέω *eukaireō.*
Mark 6. 31 and they had no leisure so much as to eat

LE-MU'-EL, לְמוּאֵל, לְמוֹאֵל *Godward, God is bright.*
A king, generally supposed to be Solomon. B.C. 1000.
Prov.31. 1 The words of king L., the prophecy that
31. 4 O L., (it is) not for kings to drink wine

LEND, to —
1. *To cause to join, lend,* לָוָה *lavah,* 5.
Exod22. 25 If thou lend money to (any of) my people
Deut 28. 12 thou shalt lend unto many nations, and
28. 44 He shall lend..and thou shalt not lend to
Psa. 37. 26 (He is) ever merciful, and lendeth; and
112. 5 A good man showeth favour, and lendeth
Prov19. 17 He that hath pity upon the poor lendeth
2. *To bite, lend on usury,* נָשָׁה *nashah.*
Deut24. 11 the man to whom thou dost lend shall bring
Jer. 15. 10 I have neither lent..nor men have lent to
3. *To cause to bite, lend on usury,* נָשָׁה *nashah,* 5.
Deut15. 2 Every creditor that lendeth..unto his ne.
24. 10 When thou dost lend thy brother any thing
4. *To give,* נָתַן *nathan.*
Lev. 25. 37 Thou shalt not..lend him thy victuals for
5. *To suffer to borrow, lend,* עָבַט *abat,* 5.
Deut15. 6 thou shalt lend unto many nations, but
15. 8 shalt surely lend him sufficient for his
6. *To suffer to ask,* שָׁאַל *shaal,* 5.
Exod12. 36 so that they lent unto them (such things
1 Sa. 1. 28 Therefore..I have lent him to the LORD
7. *To lend, make a loan,* δανείζω *daneizō.*
Luke 6. 34 if ye lend (to them) of whom ye hope to rec.
6. 34 for sinners also lend to sinners, to receive
6. 35 do good, and lend, hoping for nothing
8. *To give as a piece of business,* κίχρημι *kichrēmi.*
Luke11. 5 and say..Friend, lend me three loaves
[See Usury.]

LENDER —
To cause to be bound, lend, לָוָה *lavah,* 5.
Prov 22. 7 and the borrower (is) servant to the lender
Isa. 24. 2 as with the lender, so with the borrower

LENGTH, (at) —
1. *Latter end, furthest part,* אַחֲרִית *acharith.*
Prov 29. 21 shall have him become (his) son at the le.
2. *Length,* אֹרֶךְ *orek.*
Gen. 6. 15 The length of the ark..three hundred cu.
13. 17 walk through the land, in the length of it
Exod25. 10, 17 two cubits and a half..the length the.
25. 23 two cubits..the length thereof, and a cu.
26. 2, 8 The length of one curtain (shall be)
26. 13 in the length of the curtains of the tent
26. 16 Ten cubits..the length of a board, and a
27. 11 And likewise for the north side in length
27. 18 The length of the court..an hundred cu.
28. 16 a span..the length thereof, and a span
30. 2 A cubit..the length thereof, and a cubit
36. 9, 15 The length of one curtain (was)
36. 21 The length of a board..ten cubits, and
37. 1, 6 two cubits and a half (was) the length
37. 10 two cubits..the length thereof, and a cu.
37. 25 the length of it..a cubit, and the breadth
38. 1 five cubits..the length thereof, and five c.
38. 18 twenty cubits..the length, and the height
39. 9 a span..the length thereof, and a span
Deut. 3. 11 nine cubits..the length thereof, and four
30. 20 he (is) thy life, and the length of thy days
Judg. 3. 16 Ehud made him a dagger..of a cubit len.
1 Ki. 6. 2 the length thereof..threescore cubits, and
6. 3 twenty cubits..the length thereof, accor.
6. 20 twenty cubits in length, and twenty cub.
7. 2 the length thereof..an hundred cubits, and
7. 6 the length thereof..fifty cubits, and the
7. 27 four cubits..the length of one base, and
2 Ch. 3. 3 The length by cubits after the first meas.
3. 4 the length (of it was) according to the br.
3. 8 the length whereof (was) according to the
4. 1 twenty cubits the length thereof, and tw.
Job 12. 12 and in length of days understanding
Psa. 21. 4 thou gavest..length of days for ever and
Prov. 3. 2 length of days, and long life, and peace
3. 16 Length of days (is) in her right hand
Eze. 31. 7 in the length of his branches: for his root
Eze. 40. 11 the length of the gate, thirteen cubits
40. 18 over against the length of the gates, (was)
40. 20 he measured the length thereof, and the
40. 21 the length thereof..fifty cubits, and the
40. 25, 36 the length..fifty cubits; and the bre.
40. 49 The length of the porch..twenty cubits
41. 2 he measured the length thereof, forty cu.
41. 4 So he measured the length thereof, twenty
41. 12 the building..the length thereof ninety
41. 15 he measured the length of the building
41. 22 The altar of wood..the length thereof two
41. 22 the corners thereof, and the length there.
42. 2 Before the length of an hundred cubits
42. 7 the wall..the length thereof..fifty cubits
42. 8 For the length of the chambers that (were)
45. 1 the length..the length of five and twenty
45. 3 the length of five and twenty thousand
45. 5 the five and twenty thousand of length
45. 7 the length (shall be) over against one of
48. 8 and (in) length as one of the (other) parts
48. 9, 10, 13 five and twenty thousand in length
48. 13 all the length..five and twenty thousand
48. 18 the residue in length over against the obl.
Zech. 2. 2 he said..to see..what (is) the length the.
5. 2 the length thereof (is) twenty cubits, and
3. *Length,* μῆκος *mēkos.*
Eph. 3. 18 what (is) the breadth, and length, and de.
Rev. 21. 16 and the length is as large as the breadth
21. 16 The length, and the breadth, and..height
4. *At any time,* ποτέ *pote.*
Rom. 1. 10 if by any means now at length I might

LENGTHEN, be lengthened, to —
To lengthen, make long, אָרַךְ *arak,* 5.
Deut25. 15 that thy days may be lengthened in the
1 Ki. 3. 14 if thou wilt walk..then will I lengthen
Isa. 54. 2 lengthen thy cords, and strengthen thy

LENGTHENING —
Lengthening, אֲרֻכָה *arekah.*
Dan. 4. 27 if it may be a lengthening of thy tranquil.

LENT, to be —
To ask, שָׁאַל *shaal.*
1 Sa. 2. 20 seed..for the loan which is lent to the L.

LENTILES —
Lentiles, עֲדָשִׁים *adashim.*
Gen. 25. 34 Jacob gave Esau bread and pottage of l.
2 Sa. 17. 28 and beans, and lentiles, and parched
23. 11 where was a piece of ground full of lenti.
Eze. 4. 9 beans, and lentiles, and millet, and fitches

LEOPARD —
1. *Leopard,* נָמֵר *namer.*
Song 4. 8 look..from the mountains of the leopards
Isa. 11. 6 the leopard shall lie down with the kid
Jer. 5. 6 a leopard shall watch over their cities
13. 23 Can the Ethiopian change..skin, or the leo.
Hos. 13. 7 as a leopard by the way will I observe
Hab. 1. 8 Their horses also are swifter than the le.
2. *Leopard,* נְמַר *nemar.*
Dan. 7. 6 another, like a leopard, which had upon
3. *Leopard, panther,* πάρδαλις *pardalis.*
Rev. 13. 2 the beast which I saw was like unto a le.

LEPER, LEPROUS —
1. *To be leprous,* צָרַע *tsara.*
Lev. 13. 44 He is a leprous man, he (is) unclean: the
13. 45 the leper in whom the plague (is), his clo.
14. 3 plague of leprosy be healed in the leper
22. 4 What man soever..(is) a leper, or hath a
Num. 5. 2 that they put out of the camp every leper
2. *To be or become leprous,* צָרַע *tsara,* 4.
Exod 4. 6 And..behold, his hand (was) leprous as
Lev. 14. 2 This shall be the law of the leper in the
Num 12. 10 behold, Miriam..leprous..as snow..lepr.
2 Sa. 3. 29 one that hath an issue, or that is a leper
2 Ki. 5. 1 was also a mighty man in valour..a leper
5. 11 hand over the place, and recover the le.
5. 27 And he went out from his presence a le.
7. 3 there were four leprous men at the ente.
7. 8 when these lepers came to the uttermost
15. 5 so that he was a leper unto the day of his
2 Chr.26. 20 he (was) leprous in his forehead, and they
26. 21 Uzziah the king was a leper unto the day
26. 21 and dwelt in a several house..a leper
26. 23 for they said, He (is) a leper: and Jotham
3. *Scabbed, scaly, a leper,* λεπρός *lepros.*
Matt. 8. 2 there came a leper and worshipped him
10. 8 Heal the sick, cleanse the lepers, raise the
11. 5 the lepers are cleansed, and the deaf hear
26. 6 Jesus was..in the house of Simon the le.
Mark 1. 40 there came a leper to him, beseeching him
14. 3 in Bethany, in the house of Simon the le.
Luke 4. 27 many lepers were in Israel in the time of
7. 22 the lepers are cleansed, the deaf hear, the
17. 12 there met him ten men that were lepers

LEPROSY —
1. *Leprosy,* צָרַעַת *tsaraath.*
Lev. 13. 2 in the skin of his flesh..the plague of le.
13. 3 it (is) a plague of leprosy: and the priest
13. 8 shall pronounce him unclean: it (is) a le.
13. 9 When the plague of leprosy is in a man
13. 11 It (is) an old leprosy in the skin of his flesh
13. 12 if a leprosy break out abroad in the skin
13. 12 and the leprosy cover all the skin of (him
13. 13 (if) the leprosy have covered all his flesh
13. 15 (for) the raw flesh (is) unclean: it (is) a l.
Lev. 13. 20 a plague of leprosy broken out of the boil
13. 25 it (is) a leprosy broken out of the burning
13. 25, 27 him unclean: it (is) the plague of lep.
13. 30 dry scall..a leprosy upon the head or be.
13. 42 it (is) a leprosy sprung up in his bald head
13. 43 as the leprosy appeareth in the skin of the
13. 47 The garment also that the plague of lepr.
13. 49 it (is) a plague of leprosy, and shall be
13. 51 the plague (is) a fretting leprosy; it (is)
13. 52 it (is) a fretting leprosy; it shall be burnt
13. 59 This (is) the law of the plague of leprosy
14. 3 (if) the plague of leprosy be healed in the
14. 7 him that is to be cleansed from the leprosy
14. 32 in whom (is) the plague of leprosy, whose
14. 34 I put the plague of leprosy in a house of
14. 44 it (is) a fretting leprosy in the house: it
14. 54 the law for all manner of plague of leprosy
14. 55 for the leprosy of a garment, and of a house
14. 57 when (it is) clean: this (is) the law of lepr.
Deut24. 8 Take heed in the plague of leprosy, that
2 Ki. 5. 3 for he would recover him of his leprosy
5. 6 that thou mayest recover him of his lep.
5. 7 unto me to recover a man of his leprosy?
5. 27 The leprosy therefore of Naaman shall
2 Ch. 26. 19 the leprosy even rose up in his forehead
2. *Leprosy,* λέπρα *lepra.*
Matt 8. 3 And immediately his leprosy was cleansed
Mark 1. 42 immediately the leprosy departed from
Luke 5. 12 behold a man full of leprosy; who seeing
5. 13 immediately the leprosy departed from

LE'-SHEM, לֶשֶׁם *fortress.*
A city on the W. of Mount Hermon, between Naphtali and Manasseh; called also *Laish* and *Dan.*
Josh.19. 47 children of Dan went up to fight against L.
19. 47 called L., Dan, after the name of Dan their

LESS, LESSER —
1. *Beneath, below,* מַטָּה *mattah.*
Ezra 9. 13 hast punished us less than our iniquities
2. *To make little, few, less,* מָעַט *maat,* 5.
Exod16. 17 did so, and gathered, some more, some l.
3. *Little, small, young,* קָטָן *qatan.*
Num22. 18 I cannot go beyond..to do less or more
Eze. 43. 14 from the lesser settle..to the greater set.
4. *Little, small, young,* קָטֹן *qaton.*
Gen. 1. 16 God made..the lesser light to rule the ni.
1 Sa. 22. 15 thy servant..knew nothing of all this, less
25. 36 she told him nothing, less or more, until
5. *Less,* ἐλάσσων *elassōn.*
Heb. 7. 7 without all contradiction the less is bles.
6. *Worse, inferior, less,* ἥττων *hēttōn.*
2 Co. 12. 15 the more abundantly I love you, the less
7. *Little, small, short,* μικρός *mikros.*
Mark15. 40 Mary the mother of James the less and of
8. *Less, smaller, shorter,* μικρότερος *mikroteros.*
Mark 4. 31 less than all the seeds that be in the earth
[See also Honourable, how much, sorrowful.]

LESS than the least —
Less than the least, ἐλαχιστότερος *elachistoteros.*
Eph. 3. 8 Unto me, who am less than the least of

LESS than nothing —
End, cessation, אֶפֶס *ephes.*
Isa. 40. 17 they are counted to him less than nothing

LESS, to give (the) —
To make little, or few, מָעַט *maat,* 5.
Exod30. 15 the poor shall not give less, than half a
Num26. 54 to few thou shalt give the less inheritance
33. 54 to the fewer ye shall give the less inheri.

LESSER — [See Cattle.]

LEST —
1. *Not,* בַּל *bal.*
Psa. 32. 9 must be held in..lest they come near unto
2. *Not, that not,* לְבִלְתִּי *le-bilti.*
Gen. 4. 15 a mark..lest any finding him should kill
38. 9 lest that he should give seed to his brother
3. *That not,* לְמַעַן לֹא *le-maan lo.*
Psa.125. 3 lest the righteous put forth their hands
4. *Facing, fronting, lest,* פֶּן *pen.*
Gen. 3. 3 said..neither shall ye touch it, lest ye die
5. *That not,* ἵνα μή *hina mē.*
Matt 17. 27 lest we should offend them, go thou to
26. 5 lest there be an uproar among the people
Mark 3. 9 because of the multitude, lest they should
14. 38 Watch ye and pray, lest ye enter into te.
Luke 8. 12 taketh away the word..lest they should
14. 29 Lest haply, after he hath laid the founda.
16. 28 lest they also come into this place of tor.
18. 5 lest by her continual coming she weary
22. 46 rise and pray, lest ye enter into temptat.
John 3. 20 neither cometh..lest his deeds should be
5. 14 sin no more, lest a worse thing come unto
12. 35 Walk while ye have the light, lest darkn.
12. 42 they did not confess (him), lest they sho.
18. 28 lest they should be defiled, but that they
Acts 5. 26 feared..[lest] they should have been sto.
Rom 11. 25 lest ye should be wise in your own conce.
15. 20 lest I should build upon another man's
1 Co. 1. 15 Lest any should say that I had baptized in
1. 17 not with wisdom of words, lest the cross
8. 13 no flesh..lest I make my brother to offend
9. 12 suffer all things, lest we should hinder

2 Co. 2. 3 I wrote this same unto you, lest, when I
2. 11 Lest Satan should get an advantage of us
9. 3 lest our boasting of you should be in vain
12. 7 lest I should be exalted above measure
12. 7 [lest I should be exalted above measure]
13. 10 lest being present I should use sharpness
Gal. 6. 12 lest they should suffer persecution for the
Eph. 2. 9 Not of works, lest any man should boast
Phil 2. 27 lest I should have sorrow upon sorrow
Col. 2. 4 this I say, lest any man should beguile
3. 21 provoke not your children..lest they be
1 Ti. 3. 6 Not a novice, lest being lifted up with
3. 7 lest he fall into reproach and the snare of
Heb. 3. 13 lest any of you be hardened through the
4. 11 lest any man fall after the same example
11. 28 lest he that destroyed the first born should
12. 3 lest ye be wearied and faint in your minds
12. 13 make straight paths for your feet, lest that
Jas. 5. 9 Grudge not..brethren, lest ye be condem.
5. 12 nay, nay; lest ye fall into condemnation
2 Pe. 3. 17 beware lest ye also, being led away with
Rev. 16. 15 keepeth his garments, lest he walk naked

6. *Not*, μή *mē*.
Mark 13. 5 say, Take heed lest any (man) deceive you
13. 36 Lest, coming suddenly, he find you sleeping
Acts 13. 40 Beware therefore, lest that come upon you
23. 10 fearing lest Paul should have been pulled
27. 17 fearing lest they should fall into the qui.
27. 42 kill the prisoners, lest any of them should
1 Co. 10. 12 let him that..standeth take heed lest he
2 Co. 12. 6 lest any man should think of me above
12. 21 lest, when I come again, my God will hum.
Gal. 6. 1 considering thyself, lest thou also be temp.
Col. 2. 8 Beware lest any man spoil you through
Heb. 12. 15 Looking diligently lest any man fail of the
12. 15 lest any root of bitterness springing v. 16.

7. *In order that not*, εἰς τὸ μή, 2 Co. 4. 4.

8. *Lest at any time, that at no time*, μήποτε *mēpote*.
Matt. 7. 6 lest they trample them under their feet
13. 29 Nay; lest, while ye gather up the tares, ye
15. 32 I will not send them away fasting, lest they
25. 9 lest there be not enough for us and you
27. 64 lest his disciples come by night, and steal
Mark 14. 2 Not on the feast..lest there be an uproar
Luke 12. 58 lest he hale thee to the judge, and the j.
14. 8 lest a more honourable man than thou be
14. 12 lest they also bid thee again, and a reco.
Acts 28. 27 their eyes have they closed; lest they sh.
Heb. 3. 12 Take heed, brethren, lest there be in any
4. 1 Let us therefore fear, lest, a promise be.

9. *Lest in any way, that in no way*, μήπως *mēpōs*.
Acts 27. 29 Then fearing [lest] we should have fallen
Rom. 11. 21 (take heed) [lest] he also spare not thee
2 Co. 12. 20 For I fear, lest, when I come..lest (there be)
Gal. 4. 11 I am afraid of you, lest I have bestowed

LEST at any time, or by any or some means —

1. *Lest at any time, that at no time*, μήποτε *mēpote*.
Matt. 4. 6 lest at any time thou dash thy foot against
5. 25 lest at any time the adversary deliver thee
13. 15 lest at any time they should see with (th.)
Mark 4. 12 lest at any time they should be converted
Luke 4. 11 lest at any time thou dash thy foot agai.
21. 34 lest at any time your hearts be overchar.
Heb. 2. 1 lest at any time we should let (them) slip

2. *Lest in any way, that in no way*, μήπως *mēpōs*.
1 Co. 8. 9 lest by any means this liberty of yours
9. 27 lest that by any means, when I have pre.
2 Co. 11. 3 lest by any means, as the serpent beguiled
Gal. 2. 2 lest by any means I should run, or had run
1 Th. 3. 5 lest by some means the tempter have te.

LEST haply, perhaps, peradventure —

1. *Facing, fronting, lest*, פֶּן *pen*.
Gen. 42. 4 Lest peradventure mischief befall him

2. *Lest at any time, that at no time*, μήποτε *mēpote*.
Luke 14. 29 Lest haply, after he hath laid the found.
Acts 5. 39 lest haply ye be found even to fight agai.

3. *Lest in any way, that in no way*, μήπως *mēpōs*.
2 Co. 2. 7 lest perhaps such a one should be swall.
9. 4 Lest haply if they of Macedonia come with

LET, to —

1. *To give, let, suffer, permit*, נָתַן *nathan*.
Exod. 3. 19 that the king of Egypt will not let you go
Lev. 18. 21 thou shalt not let any of thy seed pass
1 Sa. 18. 2 would let him go no more home to his f.
2 Ch. 16. 1 that he might let none go out or come in
2 Ch. 20. 10 whom thou wouldest not let Israel invade

2. *To make free*, פָּרַע *para*, 5.
Exod. 5. 4 do ye..let the people from their works?

3. *To cause or suffer to remain*, שָׁאַר *shaar*, 5.
Josh. 8. 22 so that they let none of them remain or
10. 28 he let none remain: and he did to the k.
10. 30 he let none remain in it; but did unto the

4. *To cause to turn back*, שׁוּב *shub*, 5.
Isa. 43. 13 none..I will work, and who shall let it?

5. *To send away, let go away*, ἀφίημι *aphiēmi*.
Matt. 7. 4 Let me pull out the mote out of thine eye
8. 22 Follow me; and let the dead bury their d.
13. 30 Let both grow together until the harvest
Mark 7. 27 Let the children first be filled: for it is
Luke 6. 42 let me pull out the mote that is in thine
9. 60 Let the dead bury their dead: but go thou
John 11. 44 Jesus saith..Loose him, and let him go
18. 8 If therefore ye seek me, let these go their

6. *To permit, suffer, let go*, ἐάω *eaō*.
Acts 27. 32 cut off the ropes..and let her fall off

7. *It is privileged, authorized*, ἔξεστι *exesti*.
Acts 2. 29 brethren, let me freely speak unto you of

8. *To turn over upon, permit*, ἐπιτρέπω *epitrepō*.
Luke 9. 61 let me first go bid them farewell which

9. *To hold down or fast*, κατέχω *katechō*.
2 Th. 2. 7 only he who now letteth (will let), until

10. *To hinder, restrain, forbid*, κωλύω *kōluō*.
Rom. 1. 13 purposed to come unto you, but was let

[*See also* Cease, come, conversation, depart, down, drink drive, fail, fall, gender, go, go out, hear, heard, know, live, loose, redeemed, remain, rest, run down, see, slip, wander.]

LET alone, to —

1. *To cease*, חָדַל *chadal*.
Exod 14. 12 Let us alone, that we may serve the Eg.
Job 7. 16 I would not live alway: let me alone; for

2. *To cause to rest, place*, נוּחַ *nuach*, 5.
Exod 32. 10 Now therefore let me alone, that my wrath
2 Sa. 16. 11 Let..alone, and let him curse; for the L.
2 Ki. 23. 18 And he said, Let him alone; let no man
Hos. 4. 17 Ephraim (is) joined to idols: let him alone

3. *To let escape*, מָלַט *malat*, 3.
2 Ki. 23. 18 So they let his bones alone, with the bones

4. *To cause or suffer to fall, let go*, רָפָה *raphah*, 5.
Deut. 9. 14 Let me alone, that I may destroy them
Judg 11. 37 let me alone two months, that I may go
2 Ki. 4. 27 And the man of God said, Let her alone
Job 7. 19 let me alone till I swallow down my spittle

5. *To leave, let alone*, שְׁבַק *shebaq*.
Ezra. 6. 7 Let the work of this house of God alone

6. *To set, place*, שִׁית *shith*.
Job 10. 20 let me alone, that I may take comfort a

7. *To send away, let go*, ἀφίημι *aphiēmi*.
Matt 15. 14 Let them alone: they be blind leaders of
Mark 14. 6 Let her alone; why trouble ye her? she
15. 36 and gave him to drink, saying, Let alone
Luke 13. 8 Lord, let it alone this year also, till I shall
John 11. 48 If we let him thus alone, all..will believe
12. 7 Then said Jesus, Let her alone: against

8. *To permit, suffer, let go*, ἐάω *eaō*.
Mark 1. 24 [Let..alone;] what have..to do with thee
Luke 4. 34 Let..alone; what have we to do with thee
Acts 5. 38 now I say unto you..[let them alone]: for

LET down, to —

1. *To cause to go down, let down*, יָרַד *yarad*, 5.
Gen. 24. 18 she hasted, and let down her pitcher upon
24. 46 she made haste, and let down her pitcher
Josh. 2. 15 Then she let them down by a cord through
2. 18 window which thou didst let us down by
1 Sa. 19. 12 Michal let David down through a window

2. *To cause to rest, put down*, נוּחַ *nuach*, 5.
Exod 17. 11 when he let down his hand, Amalek prev.

3. *To cause to stretch out*, נָטָה *natah*, 5.
Gen. 24. 14 Let down thy pitcher, I pray thee, that

4. *To let fall, be feeble*, רָפָה *raphah*, 3.
Eze. 1. 24 when they stood, they let down their wi.
1. 25 when they stood, (and) had let down their

5. *To send*, שָׁלַח *shalach*, 3.
Jer. 38. 6 and they let down Jeremiah with cords
38. 11 let them down by cords into the dungeon

6. *To cause to sink, let sink*, שָׁקַע *shaqa*, 5.
Job 41. 1 tongue with a cord..thou lettest down?

7. *To send down*, καθίημι *kathiēmi*.
Luke 5. 19 and let him down through the tiling with
Acts 9. 25 and let (him) down by the wall in a basket
10. 11 a great sheet knit..and let down to the
11. 5 sheet, let down from heaven by four cor.

8. *To loose, let loose, let down*, χαλάω *chalaō*.
Mark 2. 4 they let down the bed wherein the sick
Luke 5. 4 Launch out into the deep, and let down
5. 5 nevertheless at thy word I will let down
Acts 9. 25 and let (him) down by the wall in a basket
27. 30 when they had let down the boat into the
2 Co. 11. 33 through a window in a basket was I let d.

LET down, to be —

To go on, יָלַךְ *yalak*.
2 Ki. 13. 21 when the man was let down, and touched

LET go or get away, to —

1. *To escape, let off*, מָלַט *malat*, 2.
1 Sa. 20. 29 Let me get away, I pray thee, and see my br.

2. *To let fall, desist*, רָפָה *raphah*.
Exod. 4. 26 So he let him go: then she said, A bloody

3. *To cause to fall, let fall*, רָפָה *raphah*, 5.
Job 27. 6 I hold fast, and will not let it go: my h.
Prov. 4. 13 let..not go: keep her; for she (is) thy life
Song 3. 4 I held him, and would not let him go

4. *To send*, שָׁלַח *shalach*.
2 Sa. 13. 27 that he let..the king's sons go with him

5. *To send*, שָׁלַח *shalach*, 3.
Gen. 32. 26 Let me go..I will not let thee go, except
Exod. 3. 20 smite..and after that he will let you go
4. 21 Pharaoh..he shall not let the people go
4. 23 Let my son go, that he may serve me: and
4. 23 if thou refuse to let him go, behold, I will
Exod. 5. 1 Let my people go, that they may hold a f.
5. 2 that I should obey his voice to let Israel go
5. 2 I know not..neither will I let Israel go
6. 1 with a strong hand shall he let them go
6. 11 that he let the children of Israel go out
7. 14 Pharaoh..he refuseth to let the people go
7. 16 Let my people go, that they may serve me
8. 1 Let my people go, that they may serve me
8. 2 if thou refuse to let..go, behold, I will
8. 8 I will let the people go, that they may do
8. 20 Let my people go, that they may serve me
8. 21 if thou wilt not let my people go, behold
8. 28 I will let you go, that ye may sacrifice to
8. 29 in not letting the people go to sacrifice to
8. 32 this time..neither would he let the peo. go
9. 1 Let my people go, that they may serve me
9. 2 thou refuse to let..go, and wilt hold them
9. 7 hardened, and he did not let the people go
9. 13 Let my people go, that they may serve me
9. 17 exaltest..that thou wilt not let them go?
9. 28 I will let you go, and ye shall stay no lo.
9. 35 neither would he let the children..go
10. 3 let my people go, that they may serve me
10. 4 if thou refuse to let my people go, behold
10. 7 let the men go, that they may serve the
10. 10 as I will let you go, and your little ones
10. 20 would not let the children of Israel go
10. 27 hardened..and he would not let them go
11. 1 yet..afterwards he will let you go hence
11. 1 when he shall let (you) go, he shall surely
11. 10 would not let the children of Israel go
13. 15 when Pharaoh would hardly let us go
13. 17 when Pharaoh had let the people go, that
14. 5 we have let Israel go from serving us?
21. 26, 27 he shall let him go free for his..sake
Lev. 14. 53 he shall let go the living bird out of the
16. 10 to let him go for a scape goat into the wild.
16. 22 he shall let go the goat in the wilderness
16. 26 he that let go the goat for the scape goat
Deut 15. 12 then..thou shalt let him go free from thee
15. 13 And..thou shalt not let him go away em.
21. 14 then thou shalt let her go whither she
22. 7 thou shalt in any wise let the dam go, and
Judg 1. 25 but they let go the man and all his family
2. 6 when Joshua had let the people go, the
7. 5 he let..go into the standing corn of the
19. 25 and when the day began..they let her go
1 Sa. 6. 6 did they not let the people go, and they
9. 19 to morrow I will let thee go, and will tell
19. 17 said..Let me go; why should I kill thee?
20. 5 let me go, that I may hide myself in the
20. 29 And he said, Let me go, I pray thee; for
24. 19 will he let him go well away? wherefore
1 Ki. 11. 22 Nothing: howbeit let me go in any wise
20. 42 Because thou hast let go out of (thy) hand
2 Ki. 5. 24 and he let the men go, and they departed
Isa. 45. 13 he shall let go my captives, not for price
58. 6 to let the oppressed go free, and that ye b.
Jer. 34. 9, 10 should let his man servant..go free
34. 10 heard..then they obeyed, and let (them) go
34. 11 the handmaids, whom they had let go free
34. 14 let ye go every man his brother an Hebrew
34. 14 thou shalt let him go free from thee: but
40. 1 the captain of the guard had let him go
40. 5 gave..victuals and a reward, and let him go
50. 33 held them fast; they refused to let them go
Eze. 13. 20 will let the souls go..the souls that ye h.

6. *To loose away*, ἀπολύω *apoluō*.
Luke 22. 68 if I also ask..ye will not..let (me) go

7. *To send away*, ἀφίημι *aphiēmi*.
Mark 11. 6 they said unto them..and they let them go
[*See also* Free.]

LET forth, to —

To give forth or out, ἐκδίδωμι *ekdidōmi*.
Luke 20. 9 man planted a vineyard, and let it forth

LET out, to —

1. *To give*, נָתַן *nathan*.
Song 8. 11 let out the vineyard unto keepers; every

2. *To open, free*, פָּטַר *patar*.
Prov 17. 14 one letteth out water; therefore leave

3. *To give out or forth*, ἐκδίδωμι *ekdidōmi*.
Matt 21. 33 let it out to husbandmen, and went into
21. 41 and will let out (his) vineyard unto other
Mark 12. 1 let it out to husbandmen, and went into

LET be or have, to —

To send away, let go, ἀφίημι *aphiēmi*.
Matt. 5. 40 take..thy coat, let him have (thy) 27. 49.

To be, εἰμί *eimi*.
Matt. 5. 37; 18. 17; 20. 26, 27; Luke 12. 35; Gal. 1. 8, 9; 1 Ti. 3. 12; Jas. 1. 19; 1 Pe. 3. 3.

LET remain, to —

To cause to rest, place, נוּחַ *nuach*, 5.
Jer. 27. 11 those will I let remain still in their own

LETTER —

1. *A letter*, אִגְּרָא *iggera*.
Ezra 4. 8 wrote a letter against Jerusalem to Arta.
4. 11 This (is) the copy of the letter that they
5. 6 The copy of the letter that Tatnai, gover.

2. *A letter*, אִגֶּרֶת *iggereth*.
2 Ch. 30. 1 wrote letters also to Ephraim and Manas.
30. 6 the posts went with the letters from the
Neh. 2. 7 let letters be given me to the governors
2. 8 And a letter unto Asaph the keeper of the
2. 9 I came..and gave them the king's letters
6. 5 Then sent..with an open letter in v. 17. 19.

Esth. 9. 26 Therefore for all the words of this letter
9. 29 wrote..to confirm this second letter of P.

3. *Epistle, letter,* נִשְׁתְּוָן *nishtevan.*

Ezra 4. 7 the writing of the letter (was) written in
4. 18 The letter which ye sent unto us hath been
4. 23 when the copy of king Artaxerxes' letter
5. 5 they returned answer by letter concerning
7. 11 this (is) the copy of the letter that the king

4. *A book, account,* סְפַר *sepher.*

2 Sa. 11. 14 that David wrote a letter to Joab, and
11. 15 he wrote in the letter, saying, Set ye Ur.
1 Ki. 21. 8 she wrote letters in Ahab's name, and s.
21. 8 and sent the letters unto the elders, and
21. 9 she wrote in the letters, saying, Proclaim
21. 11 as it (was) written in the letters which she
2 Ki. 5. 5 I will send a letter unto the king of Israel
5. 6 he brought the letter to the king of Israel
5. 6 Now when this letter is come unto thee
5. 7 when the king of Israel had read the let.
10. 1 Jehu wrote letters, and sent to Samaria
10. 2 Now as soon as this letter cometh to you
10. 6 Then he wrote a letter the second time to
10. 7 it came to pass, when the letter came to
19. 14 Hezekiah received the letter of the hand
20. 12 sent letters and a present unto Hezekiah
2 Ch. 32. 17 He wrote also letters to rail on the LORD
Esth. 1. 22 For he sent letters into all the king's
3. 13 the letters were sent by posts into all the
8. 5 to reverse the letters devised by Haman
8. 10 and sent letters by posts on horse back
9. 20 and sent letters unto all the Jews that
9. 25 he commanded by letters, that his wicked
9. 30 he sent the letters unto all the Jews, to
Isa. 37. 14 Hezekiah received the letter from the hand
39. 1 sent letters and a present to Hezekiah
Jer. 29. 1 these (are) the words of the letter that J.
29. 25 Because thou hast sent letters in thy name
29. 29 Zephaniah the priest read this letter in

5. *Matter, word, sentence,* פִּתְגָם *pithgam.*

Ezra 5. 7 They sent a letter unto him, wherein was

6. *A letter, anything written,* γράμμα *gramma.*

Luke 23. 38 [written over him in letters of Greek]
John 7. 15 How knoweth this man letters, having
Acts 28. 21 We neither received letters out of Judea
Rom. 2. 27 who by the letter and circumcision dost
2. 29 in the spirit, (and) not in the letter
7. 6 serve..not (in) the oldness of the letter
2 Co. 3. 6 the letter, but of the spirit: for the letter
Gal. 6. 11 Ye see how large a letter I have written

7. *An epistle, any thing sent,* ἐπιστολή *epistolē.*

Acts 9. 2 desired of him letters to Damascus to the
22. 5 from whom also I received letters unto
23. 25 And he wrote a letter after this manner
1 Co. 16. 3 whomsoever ye shall approve by (your) l.
2 Co. 7. 8 For though I made you sorry with a letter
10. 9 not seem as if I would terrify you by let.
10. 10 For (his) letters, say they, (are) weighty
10. 11 such as we are in word by letters when
2 Th. 2. 2 nor by word, nor by letter as from us, as

LETTER —[*See* Write.]

LE-TU'-SHIM, לְטוּשִׁם *oppressed, struck.*

Son of Dedan, who was grandson of Abraham by Keturah. B.C. 1800.

Gen. 25. 3 the sons..were Asshurim, and L., and Le.

LE-UM'-MIM, לְאֻמִּים.

Son of Dedan, who was grandson of Abraham by Keturah. B.C. 1800. Also the name of the tribe that sprung from him, called *Beni Lam*, in Asyrland, S. of Hedgaz, in the province of Shira, five stations from Mecca, on the mountain between Tubuk and Akhdar; also in Babylonia and Mesopotamia.

Gen. 25. 3 sons..were Asshurim..Letushim, and L.

LE'-VI, לֵוִי *joined,* Λευΐ.

1. The third son of Jacob by Leah. B.C. 1756–1619.

Gen. 29. 34 therefore was his name called L.
34. 25 Simeon and L., Dinah's brethren, took each
34. 30 And Jacob said to Simeon and L., Ye have
35. 23 and L., and Judah, and Issachar, and Ze
46. 11 the sons of L.; Gershon, Kohath, and M.
49. 5 Simeon and L. (are) brethren; instruments
Exod. 1. 2 Reuben, Simeon, L., and Judah
6. 16 sons of L. according to their generations
6. 16 years of the life of L. (were) an hundred
Num. 3. 17 these were the sons of L. by their names
16. 1 the son of L., and Dathan and Abiram the
26. 59 daughter of L., whom (her m.) bare to L.
1 Ch. 2. 1 Simeon, L., and Judah, Issachar, and Ze.
6. 1, 16 sons of L.; Gershon, Kohath, and M.
6. 38 Kohath, the son of L., the son of Israel
6. 43 Jahath, the son of Gershom, the son of L.
6. 47 of Mushi, the son of Merari, the son of L.
Ezra 8. 18 of Mahli, the son of L., the son of Israel

2. The tribe descended from Levi.

Exod. 2. 1 of L., and took (to wife) a daughter of L.
6. 19 these (are) the families of L. according to
32. 26 sons of L. gathered themselves together
32. 28 the children of L. did according to the
Num. 1. 49 Only thou shalt not number the tribe of L.
3. 6 Bring the tribe of L. near, and present
3. 15 Number the children of L. after the house
4. 2 sons of Kohath from among the sons of L.
16. 7 (ye take) too much upon you, ye sons of L.
16. 8 Moses said..Hear, I pray you, ye sons of L.
16. 10 all thy brethren the sons of L. with thee
17. 3 shalt write Aaron's name upon the rod of L.
17. 8 rod of Aaron for..house of L. was budded
Num 18. 2 thy brethren also of the tribe of L., the
18. 21 I have given the children of L. all the
Deut 10. 8 the LORD separated the tribe of L., to bear
10. 9 L. hath no part nor inheritance with his
18. 1 the tribe of L., shall have no part nor
21. 5 the sons of L. shall come near; for them
27. 12 L., and Judah, and Issachar, and Joseph
31. 9 delivered it unto..priests the sons of L.
33. 8 of L. he said, (Let) thy Thummim and thy
Josh 13. 14 the tribe of L. he gave none inheritance
13. 33 tribe of L. Moses gave not (any) inherita.
21. 10 Kohath., (who were) of the children of L.
1 Ki. 12. 31 people, which were not of the sons of L.
1 Ch. 9. 18 in the companies of the children of L.
12. 26 the children of L., four thousand and six
21. 6 L. and Benjamin counted he not among
23. 6 divided..into courses among the sons of L.
23. 14 his sons were named of the tribe of L.
23. 24 These (were) the sons of L. after the house
24. 20 And the rest of the sons of Levi (were th.)
Ezra 8. 15 and found there none of the sons of L.
Neh. 10. 39 children of L. shall bring the offering
12. 23 The sons of L., the chief of the fathers
Psa. 135. 20 Bless the LORD, O house of L.: ye that fear
Eze. 40. 46 the sons of Zadok among the sons of L.
48. 31 Reuben, one gate of Judah, one gate of L.
Zech 12. 13 The family of the house of L. apart, and
Mal. 2. 4 my covenant might be with L., saith the
2. 8 ye have corrupted the covenant of L., saith
3. 3 he shall purify the sons of L., and purge
Heb. 7. 5 verily they that are of the sons of L.
7. 9 L. also, who receiveth tithes, payed tithes
Rev. 7. 7 tribe of L. (were) sealed twelve thousand

3. An apostle, called also Matthew, formerly a publican or Roman tax-gatherer.

Mark 2. 14 saw L. the (son) of Alpheus sitting at the
Luke 5. 27 named L., sitting at the receipt of custom
5. 29 L. made him a great feast in his own house

4. An ancestor of Jesus.

Luke 3. 24 which was (the son) of L., which was (the

5. Another ancestor of Jesus.

Luke 3. 29 (son) of Matthat, which was (the son) of L.

LEVIATHAN —

Leviathan, great water animal, לִוְיָתָן *livyathan.*

Job 41. 1 Canst thou draw out leviathan with an
Psa. 74. 14 Thou brakest the heads of leviathan in
104. 26 that leviathan..thou hast made to play
Isa. 27. 1 leviathan the piercing serpent..leviathan

LE-VITE, לֵוִי, הַלְוִיִּם, Λευΐτης.

An appellation of the descendants of Levi.

Exod 4. 14 (Is) not Aaron the L. thy brother? I know
6. 25 (are) the heads of the fathers of the L.
38. 21 (for) the service of the L., by the hand of
Lev. 25. 32 the cities of the L., (and) the houses of
25. 32 the houses..may the L. redeem at any
25. 33 if a man purchase of the L., then the house
25. 33 the houses of the cities of the L. (are)
Num. 1. 47 the L. after the tribe of their fathers
1. 50 shalt appoint the L. over the tabernacle
1. 51 setteth forward, the L. shall take it down
1. 51 the tabernacle..the L. shall set it up
1. 53 L. shall pitch round about the tabernacle
1. 53 L. shall keep the charge of the tabernacle
2. 17 camp of the L. in the midst of the camp
2. 33 L. were not numbered among the children
3. 9 thou shalt give the L. unto Aaron and to
3. 12 have taken the L. from among the children
3. 12 therefore the L. shall be mine
3. 20 These (are) the families of the L. according
3. 32 (shall be) chief over the chief of the L.
3. 39 All that were numbered of the L., which
3. 41 thou shalt take the L. for me..instead
3. 41 the cattle of the L. instead of all the
3. 45 Take the L. instead of all the first born
3. 45 the L. instead of their cattle; and the L.
3. 46 of Israel, which are more than the L.
3. 49 above them that were redeemed by the L.
4. 18 families of..Kohathites from among the L.
4. 46 those that were numbered of the L., whom
7. 5 thou shalt give them unto the L., to every
7. 6 and the oxen, and gave them unto the L.
8. 6 Take the L. from among the children of
8. 9 shalt bring the L. before the tabernacle
8. 10 thou shalt bring the L. before the LORD
8. 10 Israel shall put their hands upon the L.
8. 11 Aaron shall offer the L. before the LORD
8. 12 L. shall lay their hands upon the heads
8. 12 offering..to make an atonement for the L.
8. 13 thou shalt set the L. before Aaron, and
8. 14 Thus shalt thou separate the L. from amo.
8. 14 the children of Israel: and the L. shall be
8. 15 after that shall the L. go in to do the serv.
8. 18 I have taken the L. for all the first born
8. 19 I have given the L. (as) a gift to Aaron
8. 20 did to the L. according unto all that the
8. 20 LORD commanded Moses concerning the L.
8. 21 the L. were purified, and they washed their
8. 22 after that went the L...concerning the L.
8. 24 This (is it) that (belongeth) unto the L.
8. 26 Thus shalt thou do unto the L. touching
18. 6 I have taken your brethren the L. from
18. 23 L. shall do the service of the tabernacle
18. 24 I have given to the L. to inherit: therefore
18. 26 speak unto the L., and say unto them, When
18. 30 it shall be counted unto the L. as the
26. 57 they that were numbered of the L. after
26. 58 These (are) the families of the L.: the family
31. 30 give them unto the L., which keep the
31. 47 gave them unto the L., which kept the ch.
Num 35. 2 they give unto the L., of the inheritance
35. 2 ye shall give (also) unto the L. suburbs
35. 4, 6, 7 cities which ye shall give unto the L.
35. 8 every one..give of his cities unto the L.
Deut 12. 12, 18 and the L. that (is) within your gates
12. 19 thou forsake not the L. as long as thou
14. 27 the L. that (is) within thy gates; thou shalt
14. 29 L., because he hath no part nor inheritance
16. 11 the L. that (is) within thy gates, and the
16. 14 thou shalt rejoice..and the L., the stran.
17. 9 thou shalt come unto the priests the L.
17. 18 of (that which is) before the priests the L.
18. 1 The priests the L., (and) all the tribe of L.
18. 6 if a L. come from any of thy gates out of
18. 7 minister..as all his brethren the L. (do)
24. 8 according to all that the priests the L.
26. 11 thou shalt rejoice..and the L., and the
26. 12 given (it) unto the L., the stranger, the
26. 13 and also have given them unto the L., and
27. 9 Moses and the priests the L. spake unto
27. 14 the L. shall speak, and say unto all the
31. 25 Moses commanded the L., which bare the
Josh. 3. 3 the priests the L. bearing it, then ye shall
8. 33 on that side before the priests the L., wh.
14. 3 but unto the L. he gave none inheritance
14. 4 therefore they gave no part unto the L. in
18. 7 the L. have no part among you; for the
21. 1 heads of the fathers of the L. unto Eleazar
21. 3 children of Israel gave unto the L. out of
21. 4 children of Aaron..(which were) of the L.
21. 8 children of Israel gave by lot unto the L.
21. 20 the L. which remained of the children of
21. 27 of the families of the L., out of the (other)
21. 34 the rest of the L., out of the tribe of Zeb.
21. 40 were remaining of the families of the L.
21. 41 All the cities of the L. within the posses.
Judg 17. 7 there was a young man..who (was) a L.
17. 9 he said unto him, I (am) a L. of Beth-lehem
17. 10 said..Dwell with me..So the L. went in
17. 11 the L. was content to dwell with the man
17. 12 Micah consecrated the L.; and the young
17. 13 LORD will do me good, seeing I have a L.
18. 3 knew the voice of the young man the L.
18. 15 came to the house of the young man the L.
19. 1 there was a certain L. sojourning on the
20. 4 the L., the husband of the woman that
1 Sa. 6. 15 the L. took down the ark of the LORD, and
2 Sa. 15. 24 lo Zadok also, and all the L. (were) with
1 Ki. 8. 4 even those did the priests and the L. bring
1 Ch. 6. 19 these (are) the families of the L. according
6. 48 Their brethren also the L. (were) appoin.
6. 64 children of Israel gave to the L. (these)
9. 2 first inhabitants..(were)..the priests, L.
9. 14 of the L.; Shemaiah the son of Hasshub
9. 26 For these L., the four chief porters, were
9. 31 Mattithiah, (one) of the L., who (was) the
9. 33 the singers, chief of the fathers of the L.
9. 34 These chief fathers of the L. (were) chief
13. 2 and L. (which are) in their cities (and)
15. 2 None ought to carry the ark..but the L.
15. 4 David assembled the children of..the L.
15. 11 David called for Zadok and..for the L.
15. 12 Ye (are) the chief of the fathers of the L.
15. 14 So the priests and the L. sanctified them.
15. 15 children of the L. bare the ark of God
15. 16 David spake to the chief of the L. to app.
15. 17 So the L. appointed Heman the son of J.
15. 22 Chenaniah, chief of the L., (was) for song
15. 26 when God helped the L. that bare the ark
15. 27 and all the L. that bare the ark, and the
16. 4 he appointed (certain) of the L. to minister
23. 2 gathered together..the priests and the L.
23. 3 Now the L. were numbered from the age
23. 26 unto the L.: they shall no (more) carry
23. 27 For by the last words of David the L.
24. 6 Shemaiah..(one) of the L., wrote them
24. 6, 31 chief of the fathers of the priests..L.
24. 30 These (were) the sons of the L. after the
26. 17 Eastward (were) six L., northward four a
26. 20 of the L., Ahijah (was) over the treasures
27. 17 Of the L.; Hashabiah the son of Kemuel
28. 13 for the courses of the priests and the L.
28. 21 the courses of the priests and the L., (even
2 Ch. 5. 4 all the elders of Israel came; and the L.
5. 5 these did the priest (and) the L. bring up
5. 12 Also the L. (which were) the singers, all
7. 6 L. also with instruments of music of the
8. 14 he appointed..the L. to their charges, to
8. 15 commandment of the king unto the L.
11. 13 priests and the L. that (were) in all Israel
11. 14 For the L. left their suburbs, and their
13. 9 Have ye not cast out..the L., and have
13. 10 priests, which minister..and the L. (wait)
17. 8 with them (he sent) L., (even) Shemaiah
17. 8 Asahel..and Tobijah, and Tob-adonijah, L.
19. 8 did Jehoshaphat set of the L., and (of)
19. 11 also the L. (shall be) officers before you
20. 14 Then upon Jahaziel..a L. of the sons of A.
20. 19 the L., of the children of the Kohathites
23. 2 gathered the L. out of all the cities of J.
23. 4 of the L., (shall be) porters of the doors
23. 6 none..save..they that minister of the L.
23. 7 the L. shall compass the king round about
23. 8 So the L. and all Judah did according
23. 18 by the hand of the priests the L., whom
24. 5 gathered together the priests and the L.
24. 5 Howbeit the L. hastened (it) not
24. 6 Why hast thou not required of the L. to
24. 11 was brought..by the hand of the L.
29. 4 he brought in the priests and the L., and
29. 5 Hear me, ye L.; sanctify now yourselves
29. 12 the L. arose, Mahath the son of Amasai

2 Ch.29. 16 the L. took (it), to carry (it) out abroad into
29. 25 he set the L. in the house of the LORD
29. 26 the L. stood with the instruments of David
29. 30 princes commanded the L. to sing praise
29. 34 their brethren the L. did help them, till
29. 34 L. (were) more upright in heart to sanctify
30. 15 L. were ashamed, and sanctified themsel.
30. 16 (which they received) of the hand of the L.
30. 17 the L. had the charge of the killing of
30. 21 the L. and the priests praised the
30. 22 the L. that taught the good knowledge of
30. 25 the L., and all the congregation that came
30. 27 the L. arose and blessed the people : and
31. 2 the priest and the L. after their courses
31. 2 and L. for burnt offerings and for peace
31. 4 give the portion of the priests and the L.
31. 9 questioned with the priests and the L.
31. 12 Cononiah the L. (was) ruler, and Shimei
31. 14 the son of Imnah the L., the porter towa.
31. 17 the L. from twenty years old and upward
31. 19 reckoned by genealogies among the L.
34. 9 the L. that kept the doors had gathered
34. 12 Jahath and Obadiah, the L., of the sons of
34. 12 the L., all that could skill of instruments
34. 13 of the L. (there were) scribes, and officers
34. 30 the L., and all the people, great and small
35. 3 said unto the L. that taught all Israel
35. 5 the division of the families of the L.
35. 8 the people, to the priests, and to the L.
35. 9 Jozabad, chief of the L., gave unto the L.
35. 10 the L. in their courses, according to the
35. 11 killed the passover..and the L. flayed
35. 14 the L. prepared for themselves, and for
35. 15 their brethren the L. prepared for them
35. 18 the L., and all Judah and Israel that were
Ezra 1. 5 the L., with all (them) whose spirit God
2. 40 The L. : the children of Jeshua, and Kad.
2. 70 L., and (some) of the people, and the sin.
3. 8 of their brethren the priests and the L.
3. 8 appointed the L., from twenty years old
3. 9 (with) their sons and their brethren the L.
3. 10 the L., the sons of Asaph, with cymbals
3. 12 many of the priests and L., and chief of
6. 16 the L., and the rest of the children of
6. 18 the L. in their courses, for the service
6. 20 priests and the L. were purified together
7. 7 the L., and the singers, and the porters
7. 13 people of Israel, and (of) his priests and L.
7. 24 touching any of the priests and L., singers
8. 20 had appointed for the service of the L.
8. 29 before the chief of the priests and the L.
8. 30 So took the priests and the L. the weight
8. 33 J., and Noadiah the son of Binnui, L.
9. 1 the L., have not separated themselves from
10. 5 and made the chief priests, the L., and all
10. 15 and Shabbethai the L. helped them
10. 23 of the L. ; Jozabad, and Shimei, and Ke.
Neh. 3. 17 after him repaired the L., Rehum the son
7. 1 the singers and the L. were appointed
7. 43 The L. : the children of Jeshua, of Kad.
7. 73 the L., and the porters, and the singers
8. 7 the L., caused the people to understand
8. 9 the L. that taught the people, said unto
8. 11 the L. stilled all the people, saying, Hold
8. 13 were gathered..the priests, and the L.
9. 4, 5 the L., Jeshua, and Kadmiel, Bani, Sh.
9. 38 our princes, L., (and) priests, seal (unto
10. 9 the L.: both Jeshua the son of Azaniah
10. 28 L., the porters, the singers, the Nethinims
10. 34 we cast the lots among the priests, the L.
10. 37 of our ground unto the L., that the sa. L.
10. 38 the L., when the L. take tithes: and the L.
11. 3 the L., and the Nethinims, and the child.
11. 15 of the L.: Shemaiah the son of Hashub, the
11. 16 Jozabad, of the chief of the L., (had) the
11. 18 the L. in the holy city (were) two hundred
11. 20 residue of Israel, of the priests..the L.
11. 22 The overseer also of the L. at Jerusalem
11. 36 of the L. (were) divisions in Judah, (and)
12. 1 the L. that went up with Zerubbabel the
12. 8 the L.: Jeshua, Binnui, Kadmiel, Sherebiah
12. 22 The L., in the days of Eliashib, Joiada
12. 24 the chief of the L.: Hashabiah, Sherebiah
12. 27 they sought the L. out of all their places
12. 30 the L. purified themselves, and purified
12. 44 portions of the law for the priests and L.
12. 44 for the priests and for the L. that waited
12. 47 (holy things) unto the L.; and the L.
13. 5 was commanded (to be given) to the L.
13. 10 L. had not been given (them): for the L.
13. 13 of the L., Pedaiah : and next to them (was)
13. 22 commanded the L. that they should cleanse
13. 29 covenant of the priesthood, and of the L.
13. 30 appointed the wards..and the L., every
Isa. 66. 21 I will also take of them..for L., saith the
Jer. 33. 18 Neither shall the priests the L. want a
33. 21 and with the L. the priests, my ministers
33. 22 so will I multiply..the L. that minister
Eze. 43. 19 thou shalt give to the priests the L. that
44. 10 the L. that are gone away far from me
44. 15 the priests the L., the sons of Zadok, that
45. 5 shall also the L...have for themselves, for
48. 11 went not astray..as the L. went astray
48. 12 a thing most holy by the border of the L.
48. 13 against the border of the priests the L.
48. 22 Moreover from the possession of the L.
Luke10. 32 likewise a L., when he was at the place
John 1. 19 when the Jews sent priests and L. from
Acts 4. 36 Joses..a L., (and) of the country of Cyp.

LEVITICAL, Λευϊτικός *belonging to the Levites*
Heb. 7. 11 If therefore perfection were by the L. pr.

LEVY —
A burden, tribute, מַס *mas*.
1 Ki. 5. 13 Solomon raised a levy out of all Israel
5. 13 and the levy was thirty thousand men
5. 14 and Adoniram (was) over the levy
9. 15 this (is) the reason of the levy which king

LEVY, to —
1. *To cause to go up*, עָלָה *alah*, 5.
1 Ki. 9. 21 upon those did Solomon levy a tribute of
2. *To cause to be high, lift up*, רוּם *rum*, 5.
Num31. 28 levy a tribute unto the LORD of the men

LEWD, LEWDLY —
1. *Wicked thought or device*, זִמָּה *zimmah*.
Eze. 16. 27 that hate..which are ashamed of thy lewd
22. 11 another hath lewdly defiled his daughter
23. 44 Aholah and..Aholibah, the lewd women
2. *Causing or having labour, bad, evil*, πονηρός.
Acts 17. 5 certain lewd fellows of the baser sort, and

LEWDNESS —
1. *Wicked thought or device*, זִמָּה *zimmah*.
Judg20. 6 they have committed lewdness and folly
Jer. 13. 27 thy neighings, the lewdness of thy whore.
Eze. 16. 43 thou shalt not commit this lewdness above
16. 58 Thou hast borne thy lewdness and thine
22. 9 in the midst of thee they commit lewdness
23. 21 thou calledst to remembrance the lewdn.
23. 27 Thus will I make thy lewdness to cease
23. 29 both thy lewdness and thy whoredoms
23. 35 therefore bear thou also thy lewdness and
23. 48 Thus will I cause lewdness to cease out
23. 48 may be taught not to do after your lewd.
23. 49 they shall recompense your lewdness upon
24. 13 In thy filthiness (is) lewdness : because I
Hos. 6. 9 the company of priests..they commit le.
2. *Wicked thought or device*, מְזִמָּה *mezimmah*.
Jer. 11. 15 she hath wrought lewdness with many
3. *Emptiness, folly, dishonour*, נַבְלוּת *nabluth*.
Hos. 2. 10 now will I discover her lewdness in the
4. *Work of levity, recklessness*, ῥᾳδιούργημα *rhadi*.
Acts 18. 14 If it were a matter of wrong or wicked l.

LIAR —
1. *Lying, failing*, אַכְזָב *akzab*.
Jer. 15. 18 wilt thou be altogether unto me as a liar
2. *A device*, בַּד *bad*.
Isa. 44. 25 That frustrateth the tokens of the liars
Jer. 50. 36 A sword (is) upon the liars; and they
3. *To be a liar, deceiver*, כָּזַב *kazab*.
Psa.116. 11 I said in my haste, All men (are) liars
4. *A lie, falsehood*, שֶׁקֶר *sheqer*.
Prov.17. 4 (and) a liar giveth ear to a naughty tongue
5. *A man of lies*, אִישׁ כָּזָב *ish kazab*.
Prov.19. 22 and a poor man (is) better than a liar
6. *Lying*, ψευδής *pseudēs*.
Rev. 2. 2 and are not, and hast found them liars
21. 8 all [liars], shall have their part in the lake
7. *A liar*, ψεύστης *pseustēs*.
John 8. 44 the devil..he is a liar, and the father of
8. 55 I shall be a liar like unto you : but I know
Rom. 3. 4 let God be true, but every man a liar ; as
1 Ti. 1. 10 for liars, for perjured persons, and if there
Titus 1. 12 The Cretians (are) alway liars, evil beasts
1 Jo. 1. 10 we make him a liar, and his word is not
2. 4 He..is a liar, and the truth is not in him
2. 22 Who is a liar but he that denieth that J.
4. 20 and hateth his brother, he is a liar : for
5. 10 believeth not God hath made him a liar

LIAR, to be found or make a —
1. *To become or prove a liar*, כָּזַב *kazab*, 2.
Prov.30. 6 he reprove thee, and thou be found a liar
2. *To cause to lie, prove a liar*, כָּזַב *kazab*, 5.
Job 24. 25 who will make me a liar, and make my s.
3. *To feign*, כָּחַשׁ *kachash*, 2.
Deut33. 29 thine enemies shall be found liars unto thee

LIBERAL, liberal things —
1. *A blessing*, בְּרָכָה *berakah*.
Prov.11. 25 The liberal soul shall be made fat ; and he
2. *Free, willing, noble*, נָדִיב *nadib*.
Isa. 32. 5 vile person shall be no more called liberal
32. 8 liberal deviseth liberal things; and by l.
3. *Simplicity, unaffectedness*, ἁπλότης *haplotēs*.
2 Co. 9. 13 for..liberal distribution unto them, and

LIBERALITY —
1. *Unaffectedness, simplicity*, ἁπλότης *haplotēs*.
2 Co. 8. 2 abounded unto the riches of their libera.
2. *A gracious act, benevolence*, χάρις *charis*.
1 Co. 16. 3 send to bring your liberality unto Jerus.

LIBERALLY —
1. *To encircle*, עָנַק *anaq*, 5.
Deut15. 14 Thou shalt furnish him liberally out of
2. *Simply, in simplicity*, ἁπλῶς *haplōs*.
Jas. 1. 5 ask of God, that giveth to all..liberally

LIBERTINES, Λιβερτῖνοι (*Lat. Libertini*), *freedmen.*
Jews who had been captives at Rome, but being freed had returned to Jerusalem, where they had a synagogue.
Acts 6. 9 which is called (the synagogue) of the L.

LIBERTY —
1. *Freedom*, דְּרוֹר *deror*.
Lev. 25. 10 proclaim liberty throughout..the land
Isa. 61. 1 to proclaim liberty to the captives, and
Jer. 34. 8 all the people..to proclaim liberty unto
34. 15 in proclaiming liberty every man to his
34. 17 in proclaiming liberty, every one to his
34. 17 behold, I proclaim a liberty for you, saith
Eze. 46. 17 then it shall be his to the year of liberty
2. *Free*, חָפְשִׁי *chophshi*.
Jer. 34. 16 whom he had set at liberty at their plea.
3. *A sending back, letting loose*, ἄνεσις *anesis*.
Acts 24. 23 to keep Paul, and to let (him) have liberty
4. *A sending away, remission*, ἄφεσις *aphesis*.
Luke 4. 18 sent me..to set at liberty them that are
5. *Freedom, liberty*, ἐλευθερία *eleutheria*.
Rom. 8. 21 the glorious liberty of the children of God
1 Co.10. 29 for why is my liberty judged of another
2 Co. 3. 17 the spirit of the Lord (is), there (is) liberty
Gal. 2. 4 came in privily to spy out our liberty wh
5. 1 Stand fast therefore in the liberty where.
5. 13 brethren, ye have been called unto liberty
5. 13 (use) not liberty for an occasion to the fl.
Jas. 1. 25 looketh into the perfect law of liberty, and
2. 12 that shall be judged by the law of liberty
1 Pe. 2. 16 As free, and not using (your) liberty for a
2 Pe. 2. 19 While they promise them liberty, they
6. *Authority, privilege*, ἐξουσία *exousia*.
1 Co. 8. 9 lest by any means this liberty of yours

LIBERTY, at —
1. *Broad, wide*, רָחָב *rachab*.
Psa.119. 45 I will walk at liberty : for I seek thy pre
2. *Free*, ἐλεύθερος *eleutheros*.
1 Co. 7. 39 she is at liberty to be married to whom

LIBERTY, to give —
To turn over upon, permit, ἐπιτρέπω *epitrepō*.
Acts 27. 3 gave (him) liberty to go unto his friends

LIBERTY, to set at —
To loose away, ἀπολύω *apoluō*.
Acts 26. 32 This man might have been set at liberty
Heb.13. 23 Know ye that..Timothy is set at liberty

LIB'-NAH, לִבְנָה *whiteness*.
1. The 16th station of Israel from Egypt and 5th from Sinai. See *Laban*.
Num33. 20 And they departed..and pitched in L.
33. 21 they removed from L., and pitched at R.
2. A Levitical city in Judah, S. from Jerusalem ; now *Tel-el-safieh*, a mile from *Eleutheropolis*.
Josh.10. 29 Joshua passed..unto L...fought aga. L.
10. 31 Joshua passed from L., and all Israel with
10. 32 according to all that he had done to L.
10. 39 as he had done also to L., and to her king
12. 15 The king of L., one ; the king of Adullam
15. 42 L., and Ether, and Ashan
21. 13 they gave to the children..L. with her su.
2 Ki. 8. 22 Yet Edom revolted..Then L. revolted at
19. 8 found the king..warring against L.: for
23. 31 Hamutal, the daughter of Jeremiah of L.
24. 18 Hamutal, the daughter of Jeremiah of L.
1 Ch. 6. 57 they gave..L. with her suburbs, and Ja.
2 Ch.21. 10 The same time (also) did L. revolt from
Isa. 37. 8 found the king..warring against L.: for
Jer. 52. 1 Hamutal the daughter of Jeremiah of L.

LIB'-NI, לִבְנִי *white, distinguished.*
1. Son of Gershon, the son of Levi. B.C. 1491.
Exod. 6. 17 sons of Gershon ; L. and Shimi, according
Num. 3. 18 sons of Gershon by their families ; L., and
1 Ch. 6. 17 names of the sons of Gershom ; L., and
6. 20 Of Gershom ; L. his son, Jahath his son
2. Grandson of Merari, the son of Levi. B.C. 1491.
1 Ch. 6. 29 The sons of Merari ; Mahli, L. his son, S.

LIB-NITES, הַלִּבְנִי *the Libnite.*
Descendants of Libni the son of Gershon. B.C. 1491.
Num. 3. 21 Of Gershon (was) the family of the L., and
26. 58 These (are)..the family of the L., the fam.

LIB'-YA, פּוּט *Put.*
The *Greek* name for the region W. from Egypt along the African coast. The Hebrew name is *Phut.*
Eze. 30. 5 Ethiopia, and L., and Lydia, and all the
38. 5 Persia, Ethiopia, and L. with them ; all
Acts 2. 10 and in the parts of L. about Cyrene, and

LIB'-YANS, פּוּט *put*, לֻבִים *lubbim, bowmen.*
The inhabitants of Libya, supposed to have sprung from Phut, the son of Ham. B.C. 2300. (See *Lubim*).
Jer 46. 9 Ethiopians and the L., that handle the
Dan. 11. 43 the L. and the Ethiopians (shall be) at his

LICE —
1. *Gnat, louse*, כֵּן *ken*.
Exod. 8. 16 that it may become lice throughout all the
8. 17 the dust of the land became lice through.
8. 18 did so..to bring forth lice, but they could
Psa.105. 31 He spake, and there came..lice in all their
2. *Gnats, lice*, כִּנָּם *kinnam*.
Exod.8. 17 and it became lice in man and in beast
8. 18 so there were lice upon man and upon

LICENCE —
Place, τόπος *topos.*
Acts 25. 16 and have licence to answer for himself
LICENCE, to give —
To turn over upon, permit, ἐπιτρέπω *epitrepō.*
Acts 21. 40 when he had given him licence, Paul stood
LICK (up), to —
1. *To lick up,* לָחַךְ *lachak.*
Num 22. 4 as the ox licketh up the grass of the field
2. *To lick up,* לָחַךְ *lachak,* 3.
Num 22. 4 Now shall this company lick up all..round
1 Ki. 18. 38 licked up the water that (was) in the tre.
Psa. 72. 9 that dwell..and his enemies shall lick
Isa. 49. 23 bow..and lick up the dust of thy feet
Mic. 7. 17 They shall lick the dust like a serpent
3. *To lick, lap,* לָקַק *laqaq.*
1 Ki. 21. 19 where dogs licked ..shall dogs lick thy bl.
22. 38 the dogs licked up his blood; and they
4. *To lick off or away,* ἀπολείχω *apoleichō.*
Luke 16. 21 moreover the dogs came and [licked] his
LID —
Leaf, lid, door, דֶּלֶת *deleth.*
2 Ki 12. 9 bored a hole in the lid of it, and set it bes.
LIE —
1. *Lying, failing,* אַכְזָב *akzab.*
Mic. 1. 14 Achzib (shall be) a lie to the kings of Is.
2. *Device,* בַּד *bad.*
Job 11. 3 Should thy lies make men hold their peace?
Isa. 16. 6 Moab..very proud..his lies (shall) not (be)
Jer. 48. 30 but..not..so; his lies shall not so effect (it)
3. *A lie, deceit,* כָּזָב *kazab.*
Judg 16. 10, 13 thou hast mocked me, and told me lies
Psa. 40. 4 respecteth not..such as turn aside to lies
58. 3 astray as soon as they be born, speaking l.
62. 4 they delight in lies: they bless with their
62. 9 men of high degree (are) a lie: to be laid
Prov. 6. 19 A false witness (that) speaketh lies, and
14. 5 not lie: but a false witness will utter lies
14. 25 delivereth..but a deceitful..speaketh lies
19. 5 and (he that) speaketh lies shall not esca.
19. 9 and (he that) speaketh lies shall perish
30. 8 Remove far from me vanity and lies; give
Isa. 28. 15 we have made lies our refuge, and under
28. 17 the hail shall sweep away the refuge of l.
Eze. 13. 8 ye have spoken vanity, and seen lies, th.
13. 9 that see vanity, and that divine lies: they
13. 19 by your lying to my people that hear..lies?
21. 29 whiles they divine a lie unto thee, to bring
22. 28 seeing vanity, and divining lies unto them
Dan. 11. 27 they shall speak lies at one table; but it
Hos. 7. 13 redeemed them, yet they have spoken lies
12. 1 he daily increaseth lies and desolation
Amos 2. 4 their lies caused them to err, after the
Zeph. 3. 13 Israel shall not do iniquity, nor speak lies
4. *Feigning,* כַּחַשׁ *kachash.*
Hos. 7. 3 wickedness, and the princes with their lies
10. 13 ye have eaten the fruit of lies: because
11. 12 Ephraim compasseth me about with lies
Nah. 3. 1 it (is) all full of lies (and) robbery; the
5. *Vain thing,* שָׁוְא *shav.*
Isa. 59. 4 they trust in vanity, and speak lies; they
6. *A lie, falsehood,* שֶׁקֶר *sheqer.*
Job 13. 4 ye (are) forgers of lies, ye (are) all physic.
Psa. 63. 11 the mouth of them that speak lies shall
101. 7 he that telleth lies shall not tarry in my
119. 69 The proud have forged a lie against me
Isa. 9. 15 and the prophet that teacheth lies, he (is)
44. 20 nor say, (Is there) not a lie in my right h.?
59. 3 your lips have spoken lies, your tongue
Jer. 9. 3 bend their tongues (like) their bow (for) l.
9. 5 they have taught their tongue to speak l.
14. 14 The prophets prophesy lies in my name
16. 19 Surely our fathers have inherited lies, va.
20. 6 friends, to whom thou hast prophesied l.
23. 14 they commit adultery, and walk in lies
23. 25 that prophesy lies in my name, saying, I
23. 26 heart of the prophets that prophesy lies?
23. 32 cause my people to err by their lies, and
27. 10, 14, 16 For they prophesy a lie unto you
27. 15 yet they prophesy a lie in my name; that
28. 15 makest this people to trust in a lie
29. 21 which prophesy a lie unto you in my name
29. 31 Shemaiah..he caused you to trust in a lie
Eze. 13. 22 Because with lies ye have made the heart
Mic. 6. 12 the inhabitants thereof have spoken lies
Hab. 2. 18 the molten image, and a teacher of lies
Zech. 10. 2 the diviners have seen a lie, and have told
13. 3 thou speakest lies in the name of the L.
7. *A word of falsehood,* דְּבַר שֶׁקֶר [*dabar*].
Prov. 29. 12 If a ruler hearken to lies, all his servants
8. *Sorrows,* תְּאֻנִים *teunnim.*
Eze. 24. 12 She hath wearied (herself) with lies, and
9. *A lie, lying, falsehood,* ψεῦδος *pseudos.*
John 8. 44 When he speaketh a lie, he speaketh of
Rom. 1. 25 Who changed the truth of God into a lie
2 Th. 2. 11 send..delusion, that they sh. believe a lie
1 Jo. 2. 21 because ye know it, and that no lie is of
2. 27 is truth, and is no lie, and even as it hath
Rev. 21. 27 worketh abomination or (maketh) a lie
22. 15 and whosoever loveth and maketh a lie
10. *What is false,* ψεῦσμα *pseusma.*
Rom. 3. 7 hath more abounded through my lie unto
LIE, to —
1. *To lie, act as a liar,* כָּזַב *kazab,* 3.
Num 23. 19 God (is) not a man, that he should lie
2 Ki. 4. 16 man of God, do not lie unto thine hand.
Job 6. 28 look..for (it is) evident unto you if I lie
34. 6 Should I lie against my right? my wound
Psa. 78. 36 and they lied unto him with their tongues
89. 35 Once have I sworn..I will not lie unto D.
Prov 14. 5 A faithful witness will not lie: but a false
Isa. 57. 11 that thou hast lied, and hast not remem.
Mic. 2. 11 If a man walking in the spirit..do lie..I
Hab. 2. 3 but at the end it shall speak, and not lie
2. *To feign,* כָּחַשׁ *kachash,* 3.
Lev. 6. 2 and lie unto his neighbour in that which
6. 3 and lieth concerning it, and sweareth fal.
1 Ki. 13. 18 an angel spake..(But) he lied unto him
3. *To lie, deal falsely,* שָׁקַר *shaqar,* 3.
Lev. 19. 11 neither deal falsely, neither lie one to ano.
1 Sa. 15. 29 the Strength of Israel will not lie nor rep.
Isa. 63. 8 my people, children (that) will not lie: so
4. *To face, front,* פָּנָה *panah,* 6.
Eze. 9. 2 higher gate, which lieth toward the north
5. *To crouch,* רָבַץ *rabats.*
Gen. 4. 7 thou doest not well, sin lieth at the door
29. 2 three flocks of sheep lying by it; for out
49. 25 with..blessings of the deep that lieth un.
Exod 23. 5 lying under his burden, and wouldest
Deut 29. 20 all the curses..shall lie upon him, and
Isa. 13. 21 wild beasts of the desert shall lie there
Eze. 29. 3 the great dragon that lieth in the midst
34. 14 there shall they lie in a good fold, and
6 *To lie down,* שָׁכַב *shakab.*
Gen. 19. 32 we will lie with him, that we may preserve
19. 33 first born went in, and lay with her father
19. 34 I lay yesternight with my father: let us
19. 34 go thou in..lie with him, that we may p.
19. 35 the younger arose, and lay with him; and
26. 10 might lightly have lien with thy wife, and
28. 13 the land whereon thou liest, to thee will
30. 15 he shall lie with thee to night for thy son's
30. 16 mandrakes. And he lay with her that ni.
34. 2 he took her, and lay with her, and defiled
35. 22 that Reuben went and lay with Bilhah his
39. 7 his master's wife..she said, Lie with me
39. 10 he hearkened not unto her, to lie by her
39. 12 she caught him..saying, Lie with me: and
39. 14 he came in unto me to lie with me, and I
47. 30 I will lie with my fathers; and thou shalt
Exod 22. 16 if a man entice a maid..and lie with her
22. 19 Whosoever lieth with a beast shall surely
Lev. 14. 47 he that lieth in the house shall wash his c.
15. 4 Every bed whereon he lieth that hath the
15. 18 The woman also with whom man shall lie
15. 20 every thing that she lieth upon in her se.
15. 24 if any man lie with her at all, and her
15. 24 all the bed whereon he lieth shall be un.
15. 26 Every bed whereon she lieth all the days
15. 33 of him that lieth with her that is unclean
18. 22 Thou shalt not lie with mankind as with
19. 20 whosoever lieth carnally with a woman
20. 11 the man that lieth with his father's wife
20. 12 a man lie with his daughter in law, both
20. 13 If a man also lie with mankind, as he
20. 18 if a man shall lie with a woman having her
20. 20 if a man shall lie with his uncle's wife, he
Num. 5. 13 And a man lie with her carnally, and it be
5. 19 If no man have lain with thee, and if thou
Deut 11. 19 when thou liest down, and when thou ri.
22. 22 If a man be found lying with a woman
22. 22 the man that lay with the woman, and the
22. 23 man find her in the city, and lie with her
22. 25 and the man force her, and lie with her
22. 25 the man only that lay with her shall die
22. 28 lay hold on her, and lie with her, and they
22. 29 the man that lay with her shall give unto
27. 20, 21, 22, 23 Cursed (be) he that lieth with
28. 30 betroth..and another man shall lie with
Judg 16. 3 Samson lay till midnight, and arose at m.
Ruth 3. 4 shalt mark the place where he shall lie
3. 8 turned..and, behold, a woman lay at his
3. 14 she lay at his feet until the morning
1 Sa. 2. 22 how they lay with the women that assem.
3. 15 Samuel lay until the morning, and opened
26. 5 David beheld the place where Saul lay
26. 5 Saul lay in the trench, and the people pi.
26. 7 Saul lay sleeping within the trench, and
26. 7 Abner and the people lay round about him
2 Sa. 4. 5 of Ish-bosheth, who lay on a bed at noon
4. 7 he lay on his bed in his bed chamber, and
11. 4 she came in unto him, and he lay with her
11. 11 eat and to drink, and to lie with my wife?
11. 13 at even he went out to lie on his bed with
12. 3 lay in his bosom, and was unto him as a d.
12. 11 he shall lie with thy wives in the sight of
12. 16 went in, and lay all night upon the earth
12. 24 went in unto her, and lay with her; and
13. 11 said unto her, Come lie with me, my sister
13. 14 stronger than she, forced her, and lay with
13. 31 tare his garments, and lay on the earth
1 Ki. 1. 2 let her lie in thy bosom, that my lord the
19. 5 as he lay and slept under a juniper tree
21. 27 Ahab..lay in sackcloth, and went softly
2 Ki 4. 11 he turned into the chamber, and lay there
4. 34 he went up, and lay upon the child, and
9. 16 and went to Jezreel; for Joram lay there
Job 40. 21 He lieth under the shady trees, in the co
Psa. 3. 5 I laid me down and slept; I waked; for
41. 8 (now) that he lieth he shall rise up no
57. 4 I lie (even among) them that are set on
68. 13 Though ye have lien among the pots, (yet
88. 5 like the slain that lie in the grave, whom
Prov 23. 34 or as he that lieth upon the top of a mast
Eccl. 4. 11 if two lie together, then they have heat
Isa. 14. 18 all of them, lie in glory, every one in his
51. 20 they lie at the head of all the streets, as
Lam. 2. 21 The young and the old lie on the ground
Eze. 4. 4 Lie thou also upon thy left side, and lay
4. 4, 9 number of the days that thou shalt lie
4. 6 lie again on thy right side, and thou shalt
23. 8 in her youth they lay with her, and they
31. 18 thou shalt lie in the midst of the uncirc.
32. 21 they lie uncircumcised, slain by the sword
32. 27 And they shall not lie with the mighty
32. 28 and shalt lie with..slain with the sword
32. 29 they shall lie with the uncircumcised, and
32. 30 they lie uncircumcised with..slain by the
Amos 6. 4 That lie upon beds of ivory, and stretch
Jon. 1. 5 gone down..and he lay, and was fast asl.
Mic. 7. 5 keep the doors..from her that lieth in thy
7. *To be supported,* שָׁעַן *shaan,* 2.
Num 21. 15 Ar, and lieth upon the border of Moab
8. *To be caused to spread out,* יָצַע *yatsa,* 6.
Esth. 4. 3 wailing; and many lay in sackcloth and
9. *To give an effusion,* נָתַן שְׁכֹבֶת *nathan shekobeth.*
Lev. 18. 20 Moreover thou shalt not lie carnally with
18. 23 Neither shalt thou lie with any beast to
20. 15 if a man lie with a beast, he shall surely
Num. 5. 20 some man have lain with thee besides thine
10. *To be laid up,* ἀνάκειμαι *anakeimai.*
Mark 5. 40 entereth in where the damsel was [lying]
11. *To cast, throw,* βάλλω *ballō.*
Matt. 8. 6 my servant lieth at home sick of the pa.
9. 2 a man sick of the palsy, lying on a bed
12. *To have,* ἔχω *echō.*
Mark 5. 23 My little daughter lieth at the point of d
13. *To be laid upon,* ἐπίκειμαι *epikeimai.*
John 11. 38 It was a cave, and a stone lay upon it
Acts 27. 20 no small tempest lay on (us), all hope that
14. *To be laid down,* κατάκειμαι *katakeimai.*
Mark 1. 30 Simon's wife's mother lay sick of a fever
2. 4 the bed wherein the sick of the palsy lay
Luke 5. 25 took up that whereon he lay, and departed
John 5. 3 In these lay a great multitude of impotent
5. 6 When Jesus saw him lie, and knew that he
Acts 28. 8 the father of Publius lay sick of a fever
15. *To lie, be laid,* κεῖμαι *keimai.*
Matt 28. 6 Come, see the place where the Lord lay
Luke 2. 12 Ye shall find the babe..lying in a manger
2. 16 found Mary and Joseph, and the babe lying
John 20. 5 saw the linen clothes lying; yet went he
20. 6 Simon Peter..seeth the linen clothes lie
20. 7 not lying with the linen clothes, but wrap.
20. 12 sitting..where the body of Jesus had lain
1 Jo. 5. 19 and the whole world lieth in wickedness
Rev. 21. 16 the city lieth four square, and the length
16. *To lie, speak falsely,* ψεύδομαι *pseudomai.*
Acts 5. 3 why hath Satan filled thine heart to lie
5. 4 thou hast not lied unto men, but unto G.
Rom. 9. 1 I say the truth in Christ, I lie not, my
2 Co. 11. 31 The God and Father..knoweth that I lie
Gal. 1. 20 the things which I write..before God, I lie
Col. 3. 9 Lie not one to another, seeing that ye have
1 Ti. 2. 7 I speak the truth in Christ, (and) lie not
Heb. 6. 18 in which (it was) impossible for God to lie
Jas. 3. 14 But..glory not, and lie not against the
1 Jo. 1. 6 walk in darkness, we lie, and do not the
Rev. 3. 9 say they are Jews, and are not, but do lie
LIE, that cannot —
That cannot lie, ἀψευδής *apseudēs.*
Titus 1. 2 God, that cannot lie, promised before the
LIE (towards the north), to —
To look, βλέπω *blepō.*
Acts 27. 12 lieth toward the south west and north west
LIE all night, to —
To pass the night, לִין ,לוּן *lun, lin.*
2 Sa. 12. 16 went in, and lay all night upon the earth
Job 29. 19 and the dew lay all night upon my branch
Song 1. 13 he shall lie all night betwixt my breasts
Joel 1. 13 come, lie all night in sackcloth, ye mini
LIE by man, to —
Know the lying of, יָדַע מִשְׁכָּב *yada mishkab.*
Judg 21. 11 destroy..every woman that hath lain by m
LIE down, to —
1. *To fall,* נָפַל *naphal.*
1 Sa. 19. 24 lay down naked all that day and all that
2. *To crouch,* רָבַץ *rabats.*
Job 11. 19 thou shalt lie down, and none shall make
Psa. 104. 22 they gather..and lay them down in their
Isa. 11. 6 the leopard shall lie down with the kid
11. 7 their young ones shall lie down together
14. 30 the needy shall lie down in safety: and I
17. 2 shall be for flocks, which shall lie down
27. 10 there shall he lie down, and consume the
Eze. 19. 2 she lay down among lions, she nourished
Zeph. 2. 7 shall they lie down in the evening: for
2. 14 flocks shall lie down in the midst of her
3. 13 they shall feed and lie down, and none

3. *To lie down,* שָׁכַב *shakab.*
Gen. 19. 4 before they lay down, the men of the city
19. 33, 35 he perceived not when she lay down
Lev.26. 6 ye shall lie down, and none shall make
Num23. 24 he shall not lie down until he eat..the p.
24. 9 He couched, he lay down as a lion, and
Deut. 6. 7 when thou liest down, and when thou ri.
Josh. 2. 8 before they were laid down, she came up
Judg. 5. 27 At her feet he bowed, he fell, he lay down
Ruth 3. 4 it shall be, when he lieth down, that thou
3. 7 he went to lie down at the end of the heap
3. 13 Tarry this night..lie down until the mor.
1 Sa. 3. 5 lie down again. And he went and lay down
3. 6 I called not, my son; lie down again
3. 9 lie down: So Samuel went and lay down
2 Sa. 13. 5 Lay thee down on thy bed, and make th.
13. 6 Amnon lay down, and made himself sick
1 Ki. 19. 6 did eat and drink, and laid him down ag.
21. 4 he laid him down upon his bed, and tur.
Job 3. 13 For now should I have lain still and been
7. 4 When I lie down, I say, When shall I arise
14. 12 So man lieth down, and riseth not: till
20. 11 which shall lie down with him in the dust
21. 26 They shall lie down alike in the dust, and
27. 19 The rich man shall lie down, but he shall
Prov. 3. 24 When thou liest down, thou shalt not be
3. 24 thou shalt lie down, and thy sleep shall
23. 34 thou shalt be as he that lieth down in the
Isa. 14. 8 Since thou art laid down, no feller is come
43. 17 they shall lie down together, they shall
50. 11 This shall ye have..ye shall lie down in
56. 10 all..sleeping, lying down, loving to slum.
Jer. 3. 25 We lie down in our shame, and our con.

LIE down, to cause or make to —

1. *To cause to fall,* נָפַל *naphal,* 5.
Deut25. 2 that the judge shall cause him to lie down

2. *To cause to crouch,* רָבַץ *rabats,* 5.
Psa. 23. 2 He maketh me to lie down in green pas.
Jer. 33. 12 of shepherds causing..flocks to lie down
Eze. 34. 15 I will cause them to lie down, saith the

3. *To cause to lie down,* שָׁכַב *shakab,* 5.
Hos. 2. 18 In that day will I..make them to lie down

LIE down in, to —

A crouching, רֵבֶץ *rebets.*
Isa. 65. 10 a place for the herds to lie down in, for

LIE down, place to —

A place of crouching, מַרְבֵּץ *marbets.*
Zeph. 2. 15 a place for beasts to lie down in! every

LIE down to, to —

To lie down, רָבַע *raba.*
Lev. 18. 23 stand before a beast to lie down thereto
20. 16 approach unto any beast..lie down thereto

LIE down to sleep, to —

To lie down, שָׁכַב *shakab.*
Gen. 28. 11 lighted..and lay down in that place to s.

LIE hard, to —

To lean, סָמַךְ *samak.*
Psa. 88. 7 Thy wrath lieth hard upon me, and thou

LIE in ambush or in wait, to —

1. *To lie in wait,* אָרַב *arab.*
Deut.19. 11 lie in wait for him, and rise up against
Josh. 8. 4 Behold, ye shall lie in wait against the
8. 12 set them to lie in ambush between Beth-el
Judg. 9. 32 up by night..and lie in wait in the field
21. 20 saying, Go and lie in wait in the vineyards
1 Sa.22. 8 against me, to lie in wait, as at this day?
22. 13 he should rise against me, to lie in wait
Ezra 8. 31 hand..of such as lay in wait by the way
Psa. 10. 9 He lieth in wait secretly as a lion in his
10. 9 he lieth in wait to catch the poor: he doth
59. 3 For, lo, they lie in wait for my soul: the
Prov. 7. 12 now in the streets, and lieth in wait at
12. 6; 23. 28; Hos. 7. 6; Mic. 7. 2.

2. *Toward the methodizing,* πρὸς τὴν μεθοδείαν.
Eph. 4. 14 whereby they lie in wait to deceive

3. *A lying in wait,* אֶרֶב *ereb.*
Job 38. 40 When they..abide in the covert to lie in

4. *To hunt, ensnare,* צָדָה *tsadah.*
Exod21. 13 if a man lie not in wait, but God deliver

LIE on, to —

To fall upon, ἐπιπίπτω *epipiptō.*
John13. 25 He then [lying on] Jesus' breast saith unto

LIE out, to —

To go forth or out, יָצָא *yatsa.*
Neh. 3. 25 the tower which lieth out from the king's
3. 26 unto..over against..tower that lieth out
3. 27 over against the..tower that lieth out

LIE sore, to —

To press, צוּק *tsuq,* 5.
Judg 14. 17 told her, because she lay sore upon him

LIE still, to —

1. *To spread out, leave,* נָטַשׁ *natash.*
Exod23. 11 thou shalt let it rest and lie still; that

2. *To lie down,* שָׁכַב *shakab.*
Job 3. 13 For now should I have lain still and been

LIE, that —

To incline, חָנָה *chanah.*
Num10. 5, 6 then the camps that lie on the east parts

LIE or be lien with, to —

1. *To lie with,* שָׁגַל *shagal* [V.L. שָׁכַב].
Deut28. 30 and another man shall lie with her: thou

2. *To lie down* or *with,* שָׁגַל [V.L. שָׁכַב, 4] *shagal,* 4.
Jer. 3. 2 see where thou hast not been lien with

LIER in ambush or in wait —

1. *To lie in wait,* אָרַב *arab.*
Josh. 8. 14 liers in ambush against him behind the c.
Judg.16. 12 And..liers in wait abiding in the chamber
20. 29 Israel set liers in wait round about Gibeah
20. 33 the liers in wait of Israel came forth out
20. 36 they trusted unto the liers in wait which
20. 37 the liers in wait hasted and rushed upon
20. 37 the liers in wait drew..along, and smote
20. 38 between..Israel and the liers in wait, that

2. *To lie in wait,* אָרַב *arab,* 3.
Judg. 9. 25 the men of Shechem set liers in wait for

3. *The rear, hinder part,* עָקֵב *aqeb.*
Josh. 8. 13 set..their liers in wait on the west of the

LIES, to speak —

One speaking a falsehood, ψευδολόγος *pseudologos.*
1 Ti. 4. 2 Speaking lies in hypocrisy; having their c.

LIETH with —

A lying, מִשְׁכָּב *mishkab.*
Lev. 20. 13 as he lieth with a woman, both of them

LIEUTENANTS —

Satraps, אֲחַשְׁדַּרְפְּנִים *achashdarpenim.*
Ezra 8. 36 delivered..commissions unto the king's l.
Esth 3. 12 unto the king's lieutenants, and to the
8. 9 to the lieutenants, and the deputies, and
9. 3 the lieutenants, and the deputies, and offi.

LIFE, lives —

1. *Life,* חַיִּים *chaiyim.*
Gen. 2. 7 breathed into his nostrils..breath of life
2. 9 the tree of life also in the midst of the
3. 14 dust shalt thou eat all the days of thy life
3. 17 shalt thou eat..it all the days of thy life
3. 22 take also of the tree of life, and eat, and
3. 24 sword..to keep the way of the tree of life
6. 17 all flesh, wherein (is) the breath of life
7. 11 In the six hundredth year of Noah's life
7. 15 of all flesh, wherein (is) the breath of life
7. 22 in whose nostrils (was) the breath of life
18. 10, 14 unto thee according to the time of life
23. 1 (these were) the years of the life of Sarah
25. 7 the years of Abraham's life which he lived
25. 17 these (are) the years of the life of Ishmael
27. 46 I am weary of my life because of the d.
27. 46 if Jacob take..what good shall my life do
† 42. 15 By the life of Pharaoh ye shall not go forth
† 42. 16 by the life of Pharaoh surely ye (are) spies
47. 9 have the days of the years of my life been
47. 9 unto the days of the years of the life of my
Exod. 1. 14 they made their lives bitter with hard
6. 16 the years of the life of Levi (were) an hu.
6. 18 the years of the life of Kohath (were) an
6. 20 the years of the life of Amram (were) an
Lev. 18. 18 to uncover..besides the other in her life
Deut. 4. 9 from thy heart all the days of thy life; but
6. 2 and thy son's son, all the days of thy life
16. 3 mayest remember..all the days of thy life
17. 19 shall read therein all the days of his life
28. 66 thy life shall hang in doubt before thee
28. 66 and shalt have none assurance of thy life
30. 15 I have set before thee this day life and
30. 19 I have set before you life and death, ble.
30. 19 therefore choose life, that both thou and
30. 20 he (is) thy life, and the length of thy days
32. 47 because it (is) your life: and through this
Josh. 1. 5 stand before thee all the days of thy life
4. 14 they feared him..all the days of his life
Judg16. 30 more than (they) which he slew in his life
1 Sa. 1. 11 unto the LORD all the days of his life and
7. 15 Samuel judged Is. all the days of his life
18. 18 Who (am) I? and what (is) my life, (or) my
25. 29 shall be bound in the bundle of life with
2 Sa. 1. 23 lovely and pleasant in their lives, and in
15. 21 whether in death or life, even there also
1 Ki. 4. 21 served Solomon all the days of his life
11. 34 make him prince all the days of his life
15. 5 all the days of his life, save only in the m.
15. 6 there was war..all the days of his life
2 Ki. 4. 16 according to the time of life, thou shalt
† 4. 17 bare a son..according to the time of life
25. 29 did eat..before him all the days of his life
25. 30 a daily rate..all the days of his life
Ezra 6. 10 pray for the life of the king, and of his
Job 3. 20 Wherefore is..life unto the bitter (in) soul
7. 7 O remember that my life (is) wind: mine
9. 21 not know my soul: I would despise my l.
10. 1 My soul is weary of my life: I will leave
10. 12 Thou hast granted me life and favour, and
24. 22 he riseth up, and no (man) is sure of life
* 33. 18 and his life from perishing by the sword
33. 20 So that his life abhorreth bread, and his
33. 22 unto the grave, and his life to the destro.
33. 28 into the pit, and his life shall see the light
36. 14 They die in youth, and their life (is) among
Psa 7. 5 let him tread down my life upon the earth
16. 11 Thou wilt shew me the path of life: in
17. 14 (which have) their portion in (this) life
21. 4 He asked life of thee..thou gavest (it) him
23. 6 mercy shall follow me all..days of my life
26. 9 Gather not my soul..nor my life with bl.
27. 1 the LORD (is) the strength of my life; 27.4.

† Heb. *chai.* * Heb. *chaiyah.*

Psa. 30. 5 in his favour (is) life: weeping may endure
31. 10 my life is spent with grief, and my years
34. 12 What man (is he that) desireth life, (and)
36. 9 with thee (is) the fountain of life: in thy
42. 8 (and) my prayer unto the God of my life
63. 3 thy loving kindness (is) better than life
64. 1 preserve my life from fear of the enemy
66. 9 Which holdeth our soul in life, and suff.
78. 50 but gave their life over to the pestilence
88. 3 and my life draweth nigh unto the grave
103. 4 Who redeemeth thy life from destruction
128. 5 shalt see the good..all the days of thy life
133. 3 commanded the blessing..life for everm.
* 143. 3 he hath smitten my life down to the ground
Prov. 2. 19 neither take they hold of the paths of life
3. 2 long life, and peace, shall they add to thee
3. 18 She (is) a tree of life to them that lay hold
3. 22 So shall they be life unto thy soul, and g.
4. 10 and the years of thy life shall be many
4. 13 let..not go: keep her; for she (is) thy life
4. 22 they (are) life unto those that find them
4. 23 thy heart..out of it (are) the issues of life
5. 6 Lest thou..ponder the path of life, her
6. 23 reproofs of instruction (are)..way of life
8. 35 whoso findeth me findeth life, and shall
9. 11 and the years of thy life shall be increased
10. 11 a well of life: but violence covereth the m.
10. 16 The labour of the righteous (tendeth) to l.
10. 17 He (is in) the way of life that keepeth ins.
11. 19 As righteousness (tendeth) to life; so he
11. 30 the fruit of the righteous..a tree of life
12. 28 In the way of righteousness (is) life; and
13. 12 (when) the desire cometh, (it is) a tree of l.
13. 14 The law of the wise (is) a fountain of life
14. 27 fear of the LORD (is) a fountain of life, to
14. 30 A sound heart (is) the life of the flesh: but
15. 4 A wholesome tongue (is) a tree of life: but
15. 24 The way of life (is) above to the wise, that
15. 31 The ear that heareth the reproof of life
16. 15 In the light of the king's countenance..l.
16. 22 Understanding (is) a well spring of life
18. 21 Death and life (are) in the power of the t.
19. 23 The fear of the LORD (tendeth) to life: and
21. 21 He..findeth life, righteousness, and hon.
22. 4 humility..(are) riches, and honour, and l.
31. 12 good and not evil all the days of her life
Eccl. 2. 3 they should do..all the days of their life
2. 17 Therefore I hated life; because the work
3. 12 for..to rejoice, and to do good in his life
5. 18 all the days of his life, which God giveth
5. 20 not much remember the days of his life
6. 12 in (this) life, all the days of his vain life
8. 15 the days of his life, which God giveth him
9. 9 all the days of the life of thy vanity, which
9. 9 for that (is) thy portion in (this) life, and
Isa. 38. 12 I have cut off like a weaver my life; he
38. 16 in all these..(is) the life of my spirit: so
38. 20 we will sing..all the days of our life in
* 57. 10 thou hast found the life of thine hand
Jer. 8. 3 death shall be chosen rather than life by
21. 8 I set before you the way of life, and the
52. 33 did..eat..before him all the days of his l.
52. 34 given..every day..all the days of his life
Lam. 3. 53 They have cut off my life in the dungeon
3. 58 O Lord, thou..thou hast redeemed my life
Eze. 7. 13 strengthen himself in..iniquity of his life
33. 15 walk in the statutes of life, without com.
Dan. 7. 12 their lives were prolonged for a season
12. 2 some to everlasting life, and some to sh.
Jon. 2. 6 hast thou brought up my life; Mal. 2. 5

* Heb. *chaiyah.*

2. *Days,* יוֹמִים [*yom*].
1 Ki. 3. 11 and hast not asked for thyself long life
2 Ch. 1. 11 neither yet hast asked long life; but hast
Psa. 61. 6 Thou wilt prolong the king's life..his ye.
91. 16 With long life will I satisfy him, and show

3. *Breath,* נֶפֶשׁ *nephesh.*
Gen. 9. 4 flesh with the life thereof..the blood the.
9. 5 blood of your lives..will I require the life
19. 17 Escape for thy life; look not behind thee
19. 19 hast showed unto me in saving my life
32. 30 I have seen God face to face, and my life
44. 30 that his life is bound up in the lad's life
Exod. 4. 19 all the men are dead which sought thy life
21. 23 mischief follow, thou shalt give life for life
21. 30 he shall give for the ransom of his life
Lev. 17. 14 For the life of the flesh (is) in the blood
17. 11 For (it is) the life of all flesh; the blood
17. 14 the life of all flesh (is) the blood thereof
17. 14 For..the blood of it (is) for the life ther.
Num35. 31 take no satisfaction for the life of a mur
Deut12. 23 eat not the blood..the blood (is) the life
12. 23 thou mayest not eat the life with the fl.
19. 21 life..for life, eye for eye, tooth for tooth
24. 6 for he taketh (a man's) life to pledge
Josh. 2. 13 save alive..and deliver our lives from de.
2. 14 Our life for your's, if ye utter not this our
9. 24 were sore afraid of our lives because of
Judg. 5. 18 jeoparded their lives unto the death in
9. 17 my father..adventured his life far, and
12. 3 I put my life in my hands, and passed
18. 25 run upon thee, and..lose thy life, with
Ruth 4. 15 he shall be unto thee a restorer of..life
1 Sa. 19. 5 he did put his life in his hand, and slew
19. 11 If thou save not thy life to night, to mor.
20. 1 before thy father, that he seeketh my life?
22. 23 he that seeketh my life seeketh thy life
23. 15 saw that Saul was come out to seek his l.
26. 24 as thy life..so let my life be much set by
28. 9 layest thou a snare for my life, to cause
28. 21 I have put my life in my hand, and have

2 Sa. 1. 9 slay me..because my life (is) yet whole
4. 8 Saul thine enemy, which sought thy life
14. 7 for the life of his brother whom he slew
16. 11 Behold, my son..seeketh my life: how
18. 13 wrought falsehood against mine own life
19. 5 have saved thy live, and the lives of thy
19. 5 the lives of thy wives, and the lives of thy
1 Ki. 1. 12 mayest save thine own life, and the life of
2. 23 not spoken this word against his own life
3. 11 nor hast asked the life of thine enemies
19. 2 if I make not thy life as the life of one of
19. 3 he arose, and went for his life, and came
19. 4 now, O LORD, take away my life; for I (am)
19. 14 and they seek my life, to take it away
20. 31 the king..peradventure he will save thy
20. 39 then shall thy life be for his life, or else
20. 42 therefore thy life shall go for his life, and
2 Ki. 1. 13 let my life, and the life of these fifty thy
1. 14 let my life now be precious in thy sight
7. 7 Wherefore they arose..and fled for their l.
10. 24 (If) any..escape..his life (shall be) for the
1 Ch. 11. 19 God forbid..for with..their lives they br.
2 Ch. 1. 11 nor the life of thine enemies, neither yet
Esth. 7. 3 let my life be given me at my petition
7. 7 to make request for his life to Esther
8. 11 to stand for their life, to destroy, to slay
9. 16 stood for their lives, and had rest from
Job 2. 4 all..a man hath will he give for his life
2. 6 he (is) in thine hand; but save his life
6. 11 mine end, that I should prolong my life?
13. 14 Wherefore do I..put my life in mine hand?
31. 39 caused the owners thereof to lose their l.
Psa. 31. 13 while..they devised to take away my life
38. 12 They also that seek after my life lay snares
Prov. 1. 18 And..they lurk privily for their (own) lives
1. 19 taketh away the life of the owners thereof
6. 26 adulteress will hunt for..precious life
7. 23 and knoweth not that it (is) for his life
12. 10 A righteous (man) regardeth the life of
13. 3 He that keepeth his mouth keepeth his l.
13. 8 The ransom of a man's life (are) his riches
Isa. 15. 4 Moab..his life shall be grievous unto him
43. 4 give men for thee, and people for thy l.
Jer. 4. 30 lovers will despise thee..will seek thy l.
11. 21 the men of Anathoth, that seek thy life
19. 7 by the hands of them that seek their lives
19. 9 their enemies, and they that seek their li.
21. 7 into the hand of those that seek their life
21. 9 and his life shall be unto him for a prey
22. 25 into the hand of them that seek thy life
34. 20, 21 into the hand of them that seek their l
38. 2 shall have his life for a prey, and shall l.
38. 16 the hand of these men that seek thy life
39. 18 but thy life shall be for a prey unto thee
44. 30 into the hand of them that seek his life
44. 30 king..his enemy, and that sought his life
45. 5 thy life will I give unto thee for a prey in
46. 26 into the hand of those that seek their li.
48. 6 Flee, save your lives, and be like the heath
49. 37 and before them that seek their life
Lam. 2. 19 for the life of thy young children, that
5. 9 we gat our bread with the peril of our l.
Eze. 32. 10 every man for his own life, in the day of
Jon. 1. 14 let us not perish for this man's life, and l.
4. 3 take, I beseech thee, my life from me; for

4. *Living* (or *life*) *breath*, נֶפֶשׁ חַיָּה [*nephesh*].
Gen. 1. 20 the moving creature that hath life, and
1. 30 and to every thing..wherein (there is) l

5. *Bone*, עֶצֶם *etsem*.
Job 7. 15 my soul chooseth..death rather than my l.

6. *Manner, means or period of life*, βίος *bios*.
Luke 8. 14 with cares and riches and pleasures of..l.
1 Ti. 2. 2 we may lead a quiet and peaceable life in
2 Ti. 2. 4 entangleth himself with the affairs of..l.
1 Pe. 4. 3 the time past [of..life] may suffice us to
1 Jo. 2. 16 the pride of life, is not of the Father, but

7. *Life, motion, activity*, ζωή *zōē*.
Matt. 7. 14 narrow (is) the way, which leadeth unto l.
18. 8, 9 it is better for thee to enter into life
19. 16 shall I do, that I may have eternal life?
19. 17 if thou wilt enter into life, keep the com.
19. 29 every one..shall inherit everlasting life
25. 46 go away..but the righteous into life eternal
Mark 9. 43, 45 it is better for thee to enter into life
10. 17 shall I do that I may inherit eternal life?
10. 30 receive..in the world to come eternal life
Luke 1. 75 In..righteousness..all the days [of our life]
10. 25 what shall I do to inherit eternal life?
12. 15 man's life consisteth not in the abundance
18. 18 what shall I do to inherit eternal life?
18. 30 and in the world to come life everlasting
John 1. 4 In him was life; and the life was the light
3. 15, 16 should not perish, but have eternal l.
3. 36 He that believeth..hath everlasting life
3. 36 believeth not the Son shall not see life
4. 14 of water springing up into everlasting life
4. 36 reapeth..gathereth fruit to life eternal
5. 24 hath everlasting life, and shall not come
5. 24 believeth..is passed from death unto life
5. 26 For as the Father hath life in himself
5. 26 so hath he given to the Son to have life in
5. 29 done good, unto the resurrection of life
5. 39 for in them ye think ye have eternal life
5. 40 will not come to me, that ye might have l.
6. 27 meat which endureth unto everlasting life
6. 33 cometh down from heaven, and giveth life
6. 35 I am the bread of life: he that cometh to
6. 40 believeth on him, may have everlasting l.
6. 47 He that believeth..hath everlasting life
6. 48 I am that bread of life
John 6. 51 which I will give for the life of the world
6. 53 and drink his blood, ye have no life in you
6. 54 Whoso..drinketh my blood, hath eternal l.
6. 63 words that I speak unto you..(they) are life
6. 68 Lord..thou hast the words of eternal life
8. 12 followeth me..shall have the light of life
10. 10 I am come that they might have life, and
10. 28 I give unto them eternal life; and they
11. 25 I am the resurrection, and the life: he
12. 25 that hateth..shall keep it unto life eternal
12. 50 I know..his commandment is life everlas.
14. 6 I am the way, the truth, and the life
17. 2 that he should give eternal life to as many
17. 3 This is life eternal, that they might know
20. 31 believing ye might have life through his
Acts 2. 28 Thou hast made known to me the ways of l.
3. 15 killed the Prince of life, whom God hath
5. 20 speak..to the people all the words of..l.
8. 33 declare..for his life is taken from the ea.
11. 18 Then hath God..granted repenta. unto life
13. 46 yourselves unworthy of everlasting life
13. 48 as many as were ordained to eternal life
17. 25 seeing he giveth to all life, and breath
Rom. 2. 7 who..seek for..immortality, eternal life
5. 10 reconciled, we shall be saved by his life
5. 17 shall reign in life by one, Jesus Christ
5. 18 upon all men unto justification of life
5. 21 through righteousness unto eternal life
6. 4 so we also should walk in newness of life
6. 22 unto holiness, and the end everlasting life
6. 23 eternal life through Jesus Christ our L.
7. 10 commandment, which (was ordained) to life
8. 2 the law of the spirit of life in Christ Jesus
8. 6 to be spiritually minded (is) life and peace
8. 10 the spirit (is) life because of righteousness
8. 38 neither death, nor life, nor angels, nor p.
11. 15 what..the receiving..but life from the d.?
1 Co. 3. 22 or life, or death, or things present, or th.
15. 19 If in this life only we have hope in Christ
2 Co. 2. 16 to the other the savour of life unto life
4. 10, 11 that the life also of Jesus might be
4. 12 So then death worketh in us, but life in
5. 4 mortality might be swallowed up of life
Gal. 6. 8 he..shall of the spirit reap life everlasting
Eph. 4. 18 being alienated from the life of God thro.
Phil. 1. 20 magnified..whether (it be) by life, or by d.
2. 16 Holding forth the word of life; that I may
4. 3 other..whose names..in the book of life
Col. 3. 3 and your life is hid with Christ in God
3. 4 When Christ..our life, shall appear, then
1 Ti. 1. 16 should hereafter believe on him to life
4. 8 having promise of the life that now is
6. 12 lay hold on eternal life, whereunto thou
6. 19 that they may lay hold on [eternal] life
2 Ti. 1. 1 according to the promise of life which is
1. 10 hath brought life and immortality to light
Titus 1. 2 In hope of eternal life, which God, that c.
3. 7 heirs according to the hope of eternal life
Heb. 7. 3 neither beginning of days, nor end of life
7. 16 made..after the power of an endless life
Jas. 1. 12 he shall receive the crown of life, which
4. 14 what (is) your life? It is even a vapour
1 Pe. 3. 7 being heirs together of the grace of life
3. 10 he that will love life, and see good days
2 Pe. 1. 3 (pertain) unto life and godliness, through
1 Jo. 1. 1 hands have handled, of the word of life
1. 2 the life was manifested..that eternal life
2. 25 And this is the promise..eternal life
3. 14 that we have passed from death unto life
3. 15 no murderer hath eternal life abiding in
5. 11 hath given to us eternal life, and this life
5. 12 He that hath the Son hath life; (and) he
5. 12 that hath not the Son of God hath not life
5. 13 that ye may know that ye have eternal life
5. 16 he shall give him life for them that sin
5. 20 This is the true God, and eternal life
Jude 21 of our Lord Jesus Christ unto eternal life
Rev. 2. 7 will I give to eat of the tree of life, which
2. 10 behold..I will give thee a crown of life
3. 5 not blot..his name out of the book of life
11. 11 the spirit of life from God entered into
13. 8 not written in the book of life of the Lamb
17. 8 were not written in the book of life from
20. 12 another book was opened, which is..of l.
20. 15 not found written in the book of life was
21. 6 of the fountain of the water of life freely
21. 27 are written in the Lamb's book of life
22. 1 a pure river of water of life, clear as c.
22. 2 the tree of life, which bare twelve..fruits
22. 14 that they may have right to the tree of l.
22. 17 whosoever..let him take the water of life
22. 19 take away his part out of the book of life

8. *Spirit*, πνεῦμα *pneuma*.
Rev. 13. 15 to give life unto the image of the beast

9. *Animal life, breath*, ψυχή *psuchē*.
Matt. 2. 20 dead which sought the young child's life
6. 25 Take no thought for your life, what ye
6. 25 Is not the life more than meat, and the
10. 39 He that findeth his life shall lose it: and
10. 39 he that loseth his life for my sake shall
16. 25 whosoever will save his life shall lose it
16. 25 whosoever will lose his life for my sake
20. 28 and to give his life a ransom for many
Mark 3. 4 lawful..to do evil? to save life, or to kill?
8. 35 whosoever will save his life shall lose it
8. 35 whosoever shall lose his life for my sake
10. 45 and to give his life a ransom for many
Luke 6. 9 Is it lawful..to save life, or to destroy (it)?
9. 24 whosoever will save his life shall lose it
9. 24 whosoever will lose his life for my sake
9. 56 is not come to destroy men's lives, but to
Luke 12. 22 Take no thought for your life, what ye
12. 23 The life is more than meat, and the body
14. 26 and sisters, yea, and his own life also, he
17. 33 Whosoever shall seek to save his life shall
17. 33 whosoever shall lose his life shall preserve
John 10. 11 the good shepherd giveth his life for the
10. 15 so know I..and I lay down my life for the
10. 17 I lay down my life, that I might take it
12. 25 He that loveth his life shall lose it; and
12. 25 he that hateth his life in this world shall
13. 37 Lord..I will lay down my life for thy sake
13. 38 Wilt thou lay down thy life for my sake?
15. 13 that a man lay down his life for his friends
Acts 15. 26 Men that have hazarded their lives for the
20. 10 Trouble not yourselves; for his life is in
20. 24 neither count I my life dear unto myself
27. 10 with hurt and much damage..of our lives
27. 22 there shall be no loss of..life among you
Rom. 11. 3 I am left alone, and they seek my life
16. 4 Who have for my life laid down their own
Phil. 2. 30 nigh unto death, not regarding his life, to
1 Jo. 3. 16 because he laid down his life for us: and
3. 16 we ought to lay down (our) lives for the br.
Rev. 8. 9 which were in the sea, and had life, died
12. 11 they loved not their lives unto the death

10. *To live, move*, ζάω *zaō*.
2 Co. 1. 8 insomuch that we despaired even of life
[*See also* Jeopardy, lead, preserve, promise, restore, save.]

LIFE again—[*See* Raise to.]

LIFE, of this, things pertaining to —
Belonging or pertaining to life, βιωτικός *biōtikos*.
Luke 21. 34 drunkenness, and cares of this life, and
1 Co. 6. 3 much more things that pertain to this l.?
6. 4 judgment of things pertaining to this life

LIFE, things without —
The things without breath, τὰ ἄψυχα *ta apsucha*.
1 Co. 14. 7 even things without life giving sound

LIFE, manner of —
1. *Course of life*, ἀγωγή *agōgē*.
2 Ti. 3. 10 thou hast fully known my..manner of life
2. *Manner of life*, βίωσις *biōsis*.
Acts 26. 4 My manner of life from my youth, which

LIFE, to give or preserve —
1. *To give, preserve, or revive life*, חָיָה *chayah*, 3.
Job 33. 4 breath of the Almighty hath given me l.
36. 6 He preserveth not the life of the wicked
Eccl. 7. 12 wisdom giveth life to them that have it
2. *To make alive, or living*, ζωοποιέω *zōopoieō*.
2 Co. 3. 6 the letter killeth, but the spirit giveth life
Gal. 3. 21 a law given which could have given life

LIFE TIME —
1. *Life, alive, living*, חַי *chai*.
2 Sa. 18. 18 Absalom in his lifetime had taken and r.
2. *Life, motion, activity*, ζωή *zōē*.
Luke 16. 25 thou in thy lifetime receivedst thy good
3. *To live, be alive*, ζάω *zaō*.
Heb. 2. 15 were all their lifetime subject to bondage

LIFT up or out, to —
1. *To make great, magnify*, גָּדַל *gadal*, 5.
Psa. 41. 9 friend..hath lifted up (his) heel against
2. *To draw up*, דָּלָה *dalah*, 3.
Psa. 30. 1 thou hast lifted me up, and hast not made
3. *To wave*, נוּף *nuph*, 5.
Exod 20. 25 for if thou lift up thy tool upon it, thou
Deut 27. 5 thou shalt not lift up..iron..upon them
Josh. 8. 31 over which no man hath lift up..iron
Job 31. 21 If I have lifted up my hand against the
4. *To lift up*, נְטַל *netal*.
Dan. 4 34 I Nebuchadnezzar lifted up mine eyes
5. *To lift up, bear, carry away*, נָשָׂא *nasa*.
Gen. 13. 10 Lot lifted up his eyes, and beheld all the
13. 14 Lift up now thine eyes, and look from the
18. 2 he lift up his eyes and looked, and, lo, th.
21. 16 she sat over against..and lift up her voice
21. 18 Arise, lift up the lad, and hold him in thine
22. 4 Abraham lifted up his eyes, and saw the
22. 13 Abraham lifted up his eyes, and looked
24. 63 he lifted up his eyes, and saw, and, behold
24. 64 Rebekah lifted up her eyes, and when she
27. 38 And Esau lifted up his voice, and wept
29. 11 Jacob kissed Rachel, and lifted up his v.
31. 10 I lifted up mine eyes, and saw in a dream
31. 12 Lift up now thine eyes, and see, all the
33. 1 Jacob lifted up his eyes, and looked, and
33. 5 he lifted up his eyes, and saw the women
37. 25 they lifted up their eyes and looked, and
40. 13, 19 within three days shall Pharaoh lift up
40. 20 he lifted up the head of the chief butler
43. 29 he lifted up his eyes, and saw his brother
Exod 14. 10 the children of Israel lifted up their eyes
Lev. 9. 22 Aaron lifted up his hand toward the peo.
Num. 6. 26 The LORD lift up his countenance upon
14. 1 all the congregation lifted up their voice
24. 2 Balaam lifted up his eyes, and he saw Is.
Deut. 3. 27 lift up thine eyes westward, and north.
4. 19 lest thou lift up thine eyes unto heaven
32. 40 I lift up my hand to heaven, and say, I
Josh. 5. 13 that he lifted up his eyes and looked, and
Judg. 2. 4 the people lifted up their voice, and wept
8. 28 that they lifted up their heads no more
9. 7 lifted up his voice and cried, and said

Judg19. 17 when he had lifted up his eyes, he saw a
21. 2 and lifted up their voices, and wept sore
Ruth 1. 9, 14 they lifted up their voice, and wept
1 Sa. 6. 13 they lifted up their eyes, and saw the ark
11. 4 the people lifted up their voices, and wept
24. 16 And Saul lifted up his voice, and wept
30. 4 lifted up their voice and wept, until they
2 Sa. 3. 32 the king lifted up his voice, and wept at
13. 34 the young man..lifted up his eyes and l.
13. 36 came, and lifted up their voice and wept
18. 24 lifted up his eyes, and looked, and behold
18. 28 lifted up their hand against my lord the
20. 21 hath lifted up his hand against the king
2 Ki. 9. 32 he lifted up his face to the window, and
14. 10 and thine heart hath lifted thee up: glory
19. 4 lift up..prayer for the remnant that are
19. 22 lifted up thine eyes on high?..against the
25. 27 did lift up the head of Jehoiachin king of
1 Ch. 21. 16 David lifted up his eyes, and saw the an.
2 Ch.25. 19 and thine heart lifted thee up to boast
Job 2. 12 when they lifted up their eyes afar off, and
2. 12 they lifted up their voice, and wept; and
10. 15 (if) I be righteous, (yet) will I not lift up
11. 15 then shalt thou lift up thy face without
22. 26 For then..shalt lift up thy face unto God
30. 22 Thou liftest me up to the wind; thou ca.
Psa. 4. 6 lift thou up the light of thy countenance
10. 12 lift up thine hand: forget not the humble
24. 4 who hath not lifted up his soul unto van.
24. 7 Lift up your heads, O ye gates; and be ye
24. 9 Lift up your heads, O ye gates..lift..up
25. 1 Unto thee, O LORD, do I lift up my soul
28. 2 when I lift up my hands toward thy holy
63. 4 I will lift up my hands in thy name
83. 2 they that hate thee have lifted up the h.
86. 4 unto thee, O LORD, do I lift up my soul
93. 3 The floods have lifted up..have lifted up
93. 3 O LORD..the floods lift up their waves
102. 10 for thou hast lifted me up, and cast me
106. 26 he lifted up his hand against them, to over.
119. 48 My hands also will I lift up unto thy com.
121. 1 I will lift up mine eyes unto the hills
123. 1 Unto thee lift I up mine eyes, O thou that
134. 2 Lift up your hands (in) the sanctuary, and
143. 8 cause me to know..for I lift up my soul
Isa. 2. 4 nation shall not lift up sword against na.
5. 26 he will lift up an ensign to the nations
10. 24 shall lift up his staff against thee, after
10. 26 so shall he lift it up after the manner of
13. 2 Lift ye up a banner upon the high mount.
18. 3 he lifteth up an ensign on the mountains
24. 14 They shall lift up their voice, they shall
37. 4 lift up..prayer for the remnant that is l.
37. 23 exalted (thy) voice, and lifted up thine
40. 26 Lift up your eyes on high, and behold who
42. 2 He shall not cry nor lift up, nor cause his
42. 11 Let the wilderness and the cities..lift up
49. 18 Lift up thine eyes round about, and beh.
49. 22 I will lift up mine hand to the Gentiles
51. 6 Lift up your eyes to the heavens, and look
52. 8 Thy watchmen shall lift up the voice; with
60. 4 Lift up thine eyes round about, and see
Jer. 3. 2 Lift up thine eyes unto the high places
7. 16 neither lift up cry nor prayer for them
11. 14 neither lift up a cry or prayer for them
13. 20 Lift up your eyes, and behold them that
52. 31 lifted up the head of Jehoiachin king of J
Lam. 2. 19 lift up thy hands toward him for the life
3. 41 Let us lift up our heart with..hands unto
Eze. 3. 14 So the spirit lifted me up, and took me
8. 3 the spirit lifted me up between the earth
8. 5 lift up thine eyes now the way toward the
8. 5 So I lifted up mine eyes the way toward
10. 16 when the cherubim lifted up their wings
10. 19 the cherubim lifted up their wings, and
11. 1 the spirit lifted me up, and brought me
11. 22 Then did the cherubim lift up their wings
18. 6, 15 neither hath lifted up his eyes to the
18. 12 hath lifted up his eyes to the idols, hath
20. 5, 5, 6, 15, 23 I lifted up mine hand unto them
20. 28, 42 I lifted up mine hand to give it to them
23. 27 thou shalt not lift up thine eyes unto them
33. 25 and lift up your eyes toward your idols
36. 7 I have lifted up mine hand, Surely the h.
44. 12 therefore have I lifted up mine hand ag.
47. 14 I lifted up mine hand to give it unto your
Dan. 8. 3 Then I lifted up mine eyes, and saw, and
10. 5 Then I lifted up mine eyes, and looked
Mic. 4. 3 nation shall not lift up a sword against n.
Hab. 3. 10 the deep..lifted up his hands on high
Zech. 1. 18 Then lifted I up mine eyes, and saw, and
1. 21 so that no man did lift up his head: but
1. 21 which lifted up (their) horn over the land
2. 1 I lifted up mine eyes again, and looked
5. 1 Then I turned, and lifted up mine eyes
5. 5 Lift up now thine eyes, and see what (is)
5. 9 Then lifted I up mine eyes, and looked
5. 9 they lifted up the ephah between the earth
6. 1 And I turned, and lifted up mine eyes, and

6. *To lift up, bear, carry away,* נָשָׂא *nasa,* 3.
Psa. 28. 9 feed them also, and lift them up for ever

7. *To give,* נָתַן *nathan.*
Prov. 2. 3 liftest up thy voice for understanding
Jer. 22. 20 lift up thy voice in Bashan, and cry from

8. *To cause to stand,* עוּד *ud,* 3*a.*
Psa.147. 6 The LORD lifteth up the meek: he casteth

9. *To stir up,* עוּר *ur,* 3*a.*
2 Sa. 23. 18 lifted up his spear against three hundred
1 Ch.11. 11 lifted up his spear against three hundred

10. *To cause to come up, draw up,* עָלָה *alah,* 5.
Gen. 37. 28 drew and lifted up Joseph out of the pit
Nah. 3. 3 The horseman lifteth up both the bright

11. *To answer, respond,* עָנָה *anah.*
Jer. 51. 14 and they shall lift up a shout against thee

12. *To cry aloud, rejoice, neigh,* צָהַל *tsahal,* 3.
Isa. 10. 30 Lift up thy voice, O daughter of Gallim

13. *To cause to rise up,* קוּם *qum,* 5.
Eccl. 4. 10 if they fall, the one will lift up his fellow
Eze. 26. 8 He shall..lift up the buckler against thee

14. *To make high,* רוּם *rum,* 3*a.*
1 Sa. 2. 7 The LORD..bringeth low, and lifteth up
2 Sa. 22. 49 thou also hast lifted me up on high above
Psa. 9. 13 that liftest me up from the gates of death
18. 48 thou liftest me up above those that rise
107. 25 wind, which lifteth up the waves thereof

15. *To make high,* רוּם *rum,* 5.
Gen. 14. 22 I have lift up mine hand unto the LORD
39. 15 when he heard that I lifted up my voice
39. 18 it came to pass, as I lifted up my voice
41. 44 without thee shall no man lift up his hand
Exod. 7. 20 he lifted up the rod, and smote the waters
14. 16 lift thou up thy rod, and stretch out thine
Num20. 11 Moses lifted up his hand, and with his rod
1 Sa. 2. 8 lifteth up the beggar from the dunghill
1 Ki.11. 26, 27 he lifted up (his) hand against the king
1 Ch.25. 5 All..the sons of Heman..to lift up the h.
2 Ch. 5. 13 when they lifted up (their) voice with the
Ezra 9. 6 blush to lift up my face to thee, my God
Job 38. 34 Canst thou lift up thy voice to the clouds
Psa. 74. 3 Lift up thy feet unto the perpetual deso.
75. 4 I said..to the wicked, Lift not up the horn
75. 5 Lift not up your horn on high: speak (not)
110. 7 He shall drink..therefore shall he lift up
113. 7 He..lifteth the needy out of the dunghill
Isa. 10. 15 shake (itself) against them that lift it up
10. 15 as if the staff should lift up (itself), as if
40. 9 lift up thy voice with strength; lift (it) up
58. 1 lift up thy voice like a trumpet, and show
62. 10 Go through..lift up a standard for the p.
Eze. 21. 22 to lift up the voice with shouting, to ap.

16. *To cause to enter upward,* בּוֹא לְמַעְלָה *bo* (5) *le-malah*
Psa. 74. 5 he had lifted up axes upon the thick trees

17. *To lift up,* αἴρω *airō.*
Luke17. 13 they lifted up (their) voices, and said, J.
John11. 41 Jesus lifted up (his) eyes, and said, Father
Acts 4. 24 they lifted up their voice to God with one
Rev. 10. 5 the angel..lifted up his hand to heaven

18. *To cause to stand up,* ἀνίστημι *anistēmi.*
Acts 9. 41 he gave her (his) hand, and lifted her up

19. *To set upright again,* ἀνορθόω *anorthoō.*
Heb. 12. 12 lift up the hands which hang down, and

20. *To lift out,* ἐγείρω *egeirō.*
Matt 12. 11 will he not lay hold on it and lift (it) out?
Mark 1. 31 took her by the hand, and lifted her up
9. 27 took him by the hand, and lifted him up
Acts 3. 7 took him by the right hand, and lifted..up

21. *To lift up, raise upon,* ἐπαίρω *epairō.*
Matt17. 8 when they had lifted up their eyes, they
Luke 6. 20 he lifted up his eyes on his disciples, and
11. 27 a certain woman..lifted up her voice, and
16. 23 in hell he lift up his eyes, being in torm.
18. 13 would not lift up so much as (his) eyes unto
21. 28 then look up, and lift up your heads; for
24. 50 he lifted up his hands, and blessed them
John 4. 35 Lift up your eyes, and look on the fields
6. 5 When Jesus then lifted up (his) eyes, and
13. 18 that eateth bread with me hath lifted up
17. 1 lifted up his eyes to heaven, and said, F.
Acts 2. 14 lifted up his voice, and said unto them
14. 11 lifted up their voices, saying in the speech
22. 22 lifted up their voices, and said, Away with
1 Ti. 2. 8 lifting up holy hands, without wrath and

22. *To exalt, elevate, set on high,* ὑψόω *hupsoō.*
John 3. 14 as Moses lifted up the serpent in the wil.
3. 14 even so must the Son of man [be lifted up]
8. 28 When ye have lifted up the Son of man
12. 32 I, if I be lifted up from the earth, will d.
12. 34 The Son of man must be lifted up? who is
Jas. 4. 10 Humble yourselves..he shall lift you up

LIFT up again, to help to —
To cause to rise up, קוּם *qum,* 5.
Deut22. 4 thou shalt surely help him to lift..up ag.

LIFT up as or on—[*See* Ensign, high.]

LIFT up self, to —
1. *To be or become high or haughty,* גָּבַהּ *gabah.*
Eze. 31. 10 thou hast lifted up thyself in height, and

2. *To lift self on high,* מָרָא *mara,* 5.
Job 39. 18 What time she lifteth up herself on high

3. *To be lifted up,* נָשָׂא *nasa,* 2.
Psa. 7. 6 lift up thyself, because of the rage of mine
94. 2 Lift up thyself, thou judge of the earth
Isa. 33. 10 Now will I rise..now will I lift up myself

4. *To lift up self,* נָשָׂא *nasa,* 7.
Num16. 3 wherefore then lift ye up yourselves above
23. 24 and lift up himself as a young lion: he shall
Prov.30. 32 hast done foolishly in lifting up thyself
Eze. 17. 14 that it might not lift itself up..that by k.

5. *To stir up self,* עוּר *ur,* 7*a.*
Job 31. 29 or lifted up myself when evil found him

6. *To lift up self, go up high,* עָלָה *alah,* 7.
Jer. 51. 3 against (him that) lifteth himself up in

7. *To lift up or exalt self,* רוּם *rum,* 7*a.*
Dan. 5. 23 hast lifted up thyself against the Lord of

8. *To be lifted up,* רָמַם *ramam,* 2.
Eze. 10. 17 (these) lifted up themselves..for the spirit

9. *To lift self up again,* ἀνακύπτω *anakuptō.*
Luke13. 11 a woman..could in no wise lift up (hers.)
John 8. 7 [lifted up himself, and said unto them]
8. 10 [When Jesus had lifted up himself, and]

LIFT up standard or ensign, to —
1. *To cause to flee, lift up an ensign,* נוּס *nus,* 3*a.*
Isa. 59. 19 LORD shall lift up a standard against him

2. *To lift up self, display self,* נָסַס *nasas,* 7*a.*
Zech. 9. 16 lifted up as an ensign upon his land

LIFTED up, to be —
1. *To be or become high or haughty,* גָּבַהּ *gabah.*
2 Ch. 17. 6 his heart was lifted up in the ways of the
26. 16 his heart was lifted up to (his) destruction
32. 25 his heart was lifted up: therefore there was
Eze. 28. 2 Because thine heart (is) lifted up, and thou
28. 5 thine heart is lifted up because of thy ri.
28. 17 Thine heart was lifted up because of thy

2. *To be lifted up,* נָטַל *netal.*
Dan. 7. 4 it was lifted up from the earth, and made

3. *To be lifted up,* נָשָׂא *nasa,* 2.
1 Ch.14. 2 for his kingdom was lifted up on high be.
Psa. 24. 7 and be ye lift up, ye everlasting doors; and
Prov 30. 13 their eyes! and their eyelids are lifted up
Isa. 2. 12 and upon every (one that is) lifted up, and
2. 13 all the cedars..(that are)..lifted up, and
2. 14 and upon all the hills (that are) lifted up
6. 1 upon a throne, high and lifted up, and
Jer. 51. 9 her judgment..is lifted up..to the skies
Eze. 1. 19 when the living creatures were lifted up
1. 19 from the earth, the wheels were lifted up
1. 20 the wheels were lifted up over against
1. 21 when those were lifted up from the earth
1. 21 the wheels were lifted up over against

4. *To be drawn away,* נָתַק *nathaq,* 2.
Josh. 4. 18 the priests' feet were lifted up unto the

5. *To be lifted up, presumptuous,* עָפַל *aphal,* 4.
Hab. 2. 4 Behold, his soul (which) is lifted up is not

6. *To be high,* רָאַם *raam.*
Zech.14. 10 it shall be lifted up, and inhabited in her

7. *To be high,* רוּם *rum.*
Gen. 7. 17 the ark, and it was lift up above the earth
Deut. 8. 14 Then thine heart be lifted up, and thou
17. 20 That his heart be not lifted up above his
Psa. 27. 6 now shall mine head be lifted up above
Isa. 26. 11 LORD..thy hand is lifted up, they will not
Eze. 10. 17 stood; and when they were lifted up, (th.)
31. 10 and his heart is lifted up in his height
Dan. 5. 20 when his heart was lifted up, and his mind
11. 12 his heart shall be lifted up; and he shall
Mic. 5. 9 Thine hand shall be lifted up upon thine

8. *To be lifted up,* רָמַם *ramam,* 2.
Eze. 10. 15 And the cherubims were lifted up. This

LIFTED up with pride, to be —
To be puffed up, τυφόομαι *tuphoomai.*
1 Ti. 3. 6 lest being lifted up with pride he fall into

LIFTER up —
To make high, רוּם *rum,* 5.
Psa. 3. 3 my glory, and the lifter up of mine head

LIFTING up —
1. *Rising, lifting up,* גֵּאוּת *geuth.*
Isa. 9. 18 shall mount up (like) the lifting up of sm.

2. *Rising, lifting up,* גֵּוָה *gevah.*
Job 22. 29 thou shalt say, (There is) lifting up; and

3. *Lifting up,* מֹעַל *moal.*
Neh. 8. 6 Amen, Amen, with lifting up their hands

4. *Lifting up,* מַשְׂאֵת *maseth.*
Psa.141. 2 the lifting up of my hands (as) the evening

5. *To stir up,* עוּר *ur,* 3*a.*
1 Ch. 11. 20 for lifting up his spear against three hun.

6. *To make high,* רוּם *rum,* 5.
1 Ch.15. 16 sounding, by lifting up the voice with joy

LIFTING up of self —
Lifting up, רוֹמֵמוּת *romemuth.*
Isa. 33. 3 at the lifting up of thyself the nations

LIGHT —
1. *Light,* אוֹר *or.*
Gen. 1. 3 Let there be light: and there was light
1. 4 God saw the light, that (it was) good; and
1. 4 God divided the light from the darkness
1. 5 God called the light Day, and the darkness
1. 18 and to divide the light from the darkness
Exod10. 23 all the children of Israel had light in their
Judg19. 26 fell down at the door..till it was light
1 Sa. 14. 36 spoil them until the morning light, and
25. 22 that (pertain) to him, by the morning light
25. 34 left unto Nabal by the morning light any
25. 36 told him nothing..until the morning light
2 Sa. 17. 22 by the morning light there lacked not one
23. 4 as the light of the morning (when) the sun
2 Ki. 7. 9 if we tarry till the morning light, some

Job 3. 9 let it look for light, but (have) none; nei.
3. 16 not been; as infants (which) never saw li.
3. 20 Wherefore is light given to him that is in
12. 22 bringeth out to light the shadow of death
12. 25 They grope in the dark without light, and
17. 12 the light (is) short because of darkness
18. 5 the light of the wicked shall be put out
18. 6 The light shall be dark in his tabernacle
18. 18 He shall be driven from light into dark.
22. 28 and the light shall shine upon thy ways
24. 13 They are..those that rebel against the l.
24. 14 The murderer rising with the light killeth
24. 16 in the day time: they know not the light
25. 3 and upon whom doth not his light arise?
28. 11 thing that is) hid bringeth he forth to li.
29. 3 by his light I walked (through) darkness
29. 24 the light of my countenance they cast not
30. 26 I waited for light, there came darkness
33. 28 into the pit, and his life shall see the light
33. 30 to be enlightened with the light of the liv.
36. 30 he spreadeth his light upon it, and cover.
36. 32 With clouds he covereth the light; and c.
37. 15 and caused the light of his cloud to shine?
37. 21 And now (men) see not the bright light
38. 15 from the wicked their light is withholden
38. 19 Where (is) the way..light dwelleth? and
38. 24 By what way is the light parted, (which)
41. 18 By his neesings a light doth shine, and his
Psa. 4. 6 lift thou up the light of thy countenance
27. 1 The LORD (is) my light and my salvation
36. 9 with thee..in thy light shall we see light
37. 6 bring forth thy righteousness as the light
38. 10 light of mine eyes, it also is gone from me
43. 3 O send out thy light and thy truth: let
44. 3 and the light of thy countenance, because
49. 19 of his fathers; they shall never see light
56. 13 that I may walk before God in the light
78. 14 he led them..all the night with a light
89. 15 they shall walk, O LORD, in the light of
97. 11 Light is sown for the righteous, and gla.
104. 2 Who coverest..with light as..a garment
112. 4 Unto the upright there ariseth light in
119. 105 a lamp unto my feet, and a light unto
136. 7 To him that made great lights: for his
139. 11 even the night shall be light about me
148. 3 Praise ye..praise him, all ye stars of light
Prov. 4. 18 as the shining light, that shineth more
6. 23 the law (is) light; and reproofs of instru.
13. 9 The light of the righteous rejoiceth: but
16. 15 In the light of the king's countenance (is)
Eccl. 2. 13 excelleth..as far as light excelleth dark.
11. 7 Truly the light (is) sweet, and a pleasant
12. 2 or the light, or the moon, or the stars, be
Isa. 2. 5 and let us walk in the light of the LORD
5. 20 that put darkness for light, and light for
5. 30 light is darkened in the heavens thereof
9. 2 The people..have seen a great light: they
9. 2 that dwell..upon them hath the light sh.
10. 17 the light of Israel shall be for a fire, and
13. 10 For the stars..shall not give their light
13. 10 moon shall not cause her light to shine
30. 26 light of the moon shall be as the light
30. 26 light of the sun shall be..as the light of
42. 6 I..give thee..for a light of the Gentiles
42. 16 I will make darkness light before them
45. 7 I form the light, and create darkness; I
49. 6 I will also give thee for a light to the G.
51. 4 I will make my judgment to rest for a li.
58. 8 Then shall thy light break forth as the mo.
58. 10 then shall thy light rise in obscurity, and
59. 9 we wait for light, but behold obscurity
60. 1 Arise, shine; for thy light is come, and
60. 3 the Gentiles shall come to thy light, and
60. 19 The sun shall be no more thy light by day
60. 19 shall be unto thee an everlasting light, and
60. 20 the LORD shall be thine everlasting light
Jer. 4. 23 and the heavens, and they (had) no light
13. 16 while ye look for light, he turn it into the
25. 10 of the millstones, and the light of the c.
31. 35 LORD, which giveth the sun for a light by
31. 35 and of the stars for a light by night
Lam. 3. 2 and brought..darkness, but not..light
Eze. 32. 7 and the moon shall not give her light
Hos. 6. 5 thy judgments..the light (that) goeth
Amos 5. 18 the day of the LORD (is) darkness..not li.
5. 20 the day of the LORD (be) darkness..not li.
Mic. 2. 1 when the morning is light, they practise
7. 8 when I sit in darkness, the LORD..a light
7. 9 he will bring me forth to the light..I shall
Hab. 3. 4 And (his) brightness was as the light; he
3. 11 at the light of thine arrows they went
Zeph. 3. 5 doth he bring his judgment to light, he f.
Zech. 14. 6 the light shall not be clear, (nor) dark
14. 7 pass, (that) at evening time it shall be l.

2. *Light*, אוּר *ur.*
Isa. 50. 11 walk in the light of your fire, and in the

3. *Light*, אוֹרָה *orah.*
Esth. 8. 16 The Jews had light, and gladness, and joy
Psa. 139. 12 the darkness and the light (are) both alike

4. *Light giver*, מָאוֹר *maor.*
Gen. 1. 14 Let there be lights in the firmament of the
1. 15 let them be for lights in the firmament of
1. 16 And God made two great lights; the
1. 16 greater light to rule..the lesser light to
Exod 25. 6 Oil for the light, spices for anointing oil
27. 20 pure oil olive beaten for the light, to ca.
35. 8 oil for the light, and spices for anointing
35. 14 The candlestick also for the light, and his
35. 14 and his lamps, with the oil for the light
35. 28 spice, and oil for the light, and for the
Exod 39. 37 all the vessels thereof, and the oil for light
Lev. 24. 2 pure oil olive beaten for the light, to cause
Num. 4. 9 and cover the candlestick of the light, and
4. 16 the oil for the light, and the sweet incense
Psa. 74. 16 thou hast prepared the light and the sun
90. 8 our secret (sins) in the light of thy count.
Prov 15. 30 The light of the eyes rejoiceth the heart

5. *Place of sight, vision, window*, מֶחֱזָה *mechezah.*
1 Ki. 7. 4, 5 light (was) against light (in) three ranks

6. *Shining*, נֹגַהּ *nogah.*
Isa. 50. 10 walketh (in) darkness, and hath no light?

7. *Light*, נְהוֹר, [V.L. נְהִיר] *nehor.*
Dan. 2. 22 knoweth..and the light dwelleth with him

8. *Light*, נַהִירוּ *nahiru.*
Dan. 5. 11 light and understanding and wisdom, like
5. 14 light and understanding and excellent w.

9. *Light*, נְהָרָה *neharah.*
Job 3. 4 darkness..neither let the light shine upon

10. *Light*, נִיר *nir.*
1 Ki. 11. 36 David my servant may have a light alway
2 Ki. 8. 19 he promised him to give him..a light
2 Ch. 21. 7 as he promised to give a light to him and

11. *Light*, נֵר *ner.*
2 Sa. 21. 17 that thou quench not the light of Israel

12. *Dawning*, שַׁחַר *shachar.*
Isa. 8. 20 (it is) because (there is) no light in them

13. *Light, not heavy*, ἐλαφρός *elaphros.*
Matt 11. 30 my yoke (is) easy, and my burden is light
2 Co. 4. 17 our light affliction, which is but for a m.

14. *A torch*, λαμπάς *lampas.*
Acts 20. 8 there were many lights in the upper cha.

15. *A lamp*, λύχνος *luchnos.*
Matt 6. 22 The light of the body is the eye: if ther.
Luke 11. 34 The light of the body is the eye: therefore
12. 35 Let your loins be girded about, and..lights
John 5. 35 He was a burning and a shining light: and
2 Pe. 1. 19 as unto a light that shineth in a dark place
Rev. 21. 23 And the city..the Lamb (is) the light th.

16. *Splendour, brightness, a shining light*, φέγγος.
Matt 24. 29 the moon shall not give her light, and the
Mark 13. 24 after that..the moon shall not give her l.
Luke 11. 33 that they which come in may see [the li.]

17. *Light, radiance*, φῶς *phōs.*
Matt. 4. 16 The people..saw great light; and to them
4. 16 in the..shadow of death light is sprung up
5. 14 Ye are the light of the world. A city that
5. 16 Let your light so shine before men, that
6. 23 If therefore the light that is in thee be
10. 27 What I tell you..speak ye in light: and
17. 2 and his raiment was white as the light
Luke 2. 32 A light to lighten the Gentiles, and the
8. 16 that they which enter in may see the light
11. 35 the light which is in thee be not darkness
12. 3 shall be heard in the light; and that which
16. 8 generation wiser than the children of light
John 1. 4 In him was life, and the life was the light
1. 5 the light shineth in darkness; and the dar.
1. 7 came..to bear witness of the Light, that
1. 8 not that Light, but..witness of that Light
1. 9 the true Light, which lighteth every man
3. 19 that light is come into the world, and men
3. 19 loved darkness rather than light, because
3. 20 every one that doeth evil hateth the light
3. 20 neither cometh to the light, lest his deeds
3. 21 cometh to the light, that his deed may be
5. 35 willing for a season to rejoice in his light
8. 12 I am the light of the world: he that foll.
8. 12 not walk..but shall have the light of life
9. 5 As long as I am in the world, I am the li.
11. 9 because he seeth the light of this world
11. 10 stumbleth, because there is no light in him
12. 35 Yet a little while is the light with you
12. 35 Walk while ye have the light, lest darkness
12. 36 While ye have light, believe in the light
12. 36 that ye may be the children of light. These
12. 46 I am come a light into the world, that who.
Acts 9. 3 there shined round about him a light from
12. 7 came upon..and a light sh..ed in the pr.
13. 47 I have set thee to be a light of the Gent.
16. 29 he called for a light, and sprang in, and
22. 6 there shone from heaven a great light ro.
22. 9 they that were with me saw indeed the l.
22. 11 And when I could not see for..that light
26. 13 I saw in the way a light from heaven, ab.
26. 18 to turn..from darkness to light, and (from)
26. 23 should show light unto the people, and
Rom. 2. 19 art..a light of them which are in darkness
13. 12 let us therefore..put on the armour of li.
2 Co. 4. 6 God, who commanded the light to shine
6. 14 what communion hath light with dark.?
11. 14 Satan..is transformed into an angel of l.
Eph. 5. 8 light in the Lord: walk as children of li.
5. 13 all things..are made manifest by the light
5. 13 whatsoever doth make manifest is light
Col. 1. 12 of the inheritance of the saints in light
1 Th. 5. 5 Ye are all the children of light, and the
1 Ti. 6. 16 the light which no man can approach
Jas. 1. 17 cometh down from the Father of lights
1 Pe. 2. 9 hath called you..into his marvellous light
1 Jo. 1. 5 declare unto you, that God is light, and
1. 7 if we walk in the light, as he is in the li.
2. 8 is past, and the true light now shineth
2. 9 He that saith he is in the light, and hateth
2. 10 He that loveth..abideth in the light, and
Rev. 18. 23 the light of a candle shall shine no more
21. 24 the nations..shall walk in the light of it
22. 5 they need no candle, neither light of the

18. *Light giver*, φωστήρ *phōstēr.*
Phil. 2. 15 among whom ye shine as lights in the w.
Rev. 21. 11 her light..like unto a stone most precious

19. *Light, illumination*, φωτισμός *phōtismos.*
2 Co. 4. 4 lest the light of the glorious gospel of C.
4. 6 the light of the knowledge of the glory of
[See Give, set, show.]

LIGHT —
1. *To be unstable*, פָּחַז *pachaz.*
Judg. 9. 4 Abimelech hired vain and light persons
Zeph. 3. 4 Her prophets (are) light (and) treacher.

2. *Light, not heavy*, קַל *qal.*
2 Sa. 2. 18 Asahel (was as) light of foot as a wild roe

3. *Very light*, קְלֹקֵל *qeloqel.*
Num 21. 5 spake..our soul loatheth this light bread

LIGHT, to —
1. *To light, kindle*, אוֹר *or*, 5.
Psa. 18. 28 thou wilt light my candle: the LORD my

2. *To come down*, יָרַד *yarad.*
1 Sa. 25. 23 she hasted, and lighted off the ass, and

3. *To fall*, נָפַל *naphal.*
Gen. 24. 64 when she saw Isaac, she lighted off the c.
Isa. 9. 8 The LORD sent..and it hath lighted upon

4. *To cause to go up*, עָלָה *alah*, 5.
Exod 25. 37 they shall light the lamps thereof, that
30. 8 when Aaron lighteth the lamps at even
40. 4 bring in the candlestick, and light the l.
40. 25 he lighted the lamps before the LORD; as
Num. 8. 2 When thou lightest the lamps, the seven
8. 3 Aaron did so; he lighted the lamps ther.

5. *To light, kindle*, ἅπτω *haptō.*
Luke 8. 16 No man, when he hath lighted a candle
11. 33 No man, when he hath lighted a candle
15. 8 doth not light a candle, and sweep the

6. *To burn, cause to burn*, καίω *kaiō.*
Matt. 5. 15 Neither do men light a candle, and put

7. *To fall, fall upon*, πίπτω *piptō.*
Rev. 7. 16 neither shall the sun light on them, nor

8. *To enlighten*, φωτίζω *phōtizō.*
John 1. 9 which lighteth every man that cometh

9. *To come*, ἔρχομαι *erchomai.*
Matt. 3. 16 descending like a dove, and lighting upon

LIGHT, to be —
1. *To be or become light*, אוֹר *or.*
Gen. 44. 3 As soon as the morning was light, the men
1 Sa. 29. 10 as soon as ye be up..and have light, dep.

2. *To (cause to) shine*, יָפַע *yapha*, 5.
Job 10. 22 without any order, and..the light (is) as

LIGHT down, to —
1. *To come down*, יָרַד *yarad.*
Judg. 4. 15 Sisera lighted down off (his) chariot, and

2. *To fall*, נָפַל *naphal.*
2 Ki. 5. 21 he lighted down from the chariot to meet

LIGHT (from off), to —
To alight, sink down, צָנַח *tsanach.*
Josh 15. 18 she lighted off (her) ass; and Caleb said
Judg. 1. 14 she lighted from off (her) ass; and Caleb

LIGHT, to bring to —
To enlighten, bring to light, φωτίζω *phōtizō.*
1 Co. 4. 5 will bring to light the hidden things of d.
2 Ti. 1. 10 hath brought life and immortality to light

LIGHT, full of —
Full of light, shining, bright, φωτεινός *phōteinos.*
Matt. 6. 22 single, thy whole body shall be full of li.
Luke 11. 34 single, thy whole body also is full of light
11. 36 If thy whole body..(be) full of light, hav.
11. 36 the whole shall be full of light, as when

LIGHT, to give or show —
1. *To cause or give light*, אוֹר *or*, 5.
Gen. 1. 15 to give light upon the earth: and it was
1. 17 God set them..to give light upon the ea.
Exod 13. 21 in a pillar of fire, to give them light; to
14. 20 it gave light by night..so that the one came
25. 37 that they may give light over against it
Num. 8. 2 shall give light over against the candles.
Neh. 9. 12 to give them light in the way wherein they
9. 19 pillar of fire by night, to show them light
Psa. 105. 39 He spread..fire to give light in the night
118. 27 LORD, which hath showed us light: bind
119. 130 The entrance of thy words giveth light
Isa. 60. 19 for brightness shall the moon give light

2. *To cause to appear or shine upon*, ἐπιφαίνω.
Luke 1. 79 To give light to them that sit in darkness

3. *To appear or shine upon*, ἐπιφαύω *epiphauō.*
Eph. 5. 14 Awake..and Christ shall give thee light

4. *To give the light of a torch*, λάμπω *lampō.*
Matt. 5. 15 it giveth light unto all that are in the ho.

5. *To enlighten*, φωτίζω *phōtizō.*
Luke 11. 36 shining of a candle doth give thee light
Rev. 22. 5 the Lord God giveth them light: and they

LIGHT of, to make —
To be careless, disregard, ἀμελέω *ameleō.*
Matt22. 5 they made light of (it), and went their w.
LIGHT on, or upon, to —
1. *To find,* מָצָא *matsa.*
Deut19. 5 lighteth upon his neighbour, that he die
2 Ki. 10. 15 he lighted on Jehonadab the son of Rec.
2. *To come or strike upon,* פָּגַע *paga* ; Gen. 28. 11.
3. *Encounter,* קָרָה *qarah* ; Ruth 2. 3.
LIGHT thing, to be or seem a —
To be or become light, קָלַל *qalal,* 2.
1 Sa. 18. 23 Seemeth it to you (a) light (thing) to be a
1 Ki. 16. 31 as if it had been a light thing for him to
2 Ki. 3. 18 this is..a light thing in the sight of the
20. 10 It is a light thing for the shadow to go
Isa. 49. 6 It is a light thing that thou shouldest be
Eze. 8. 17 Is it a light thing to the house of Judah
LIGHTS, of—*Latticed* (?), שְׁקֻפִים *shequphim,* 1 Ki. 6. 4.
LIGHTEN, to —
1. *To cause or give light,* אוֹר *or,* 5.
Ezra 9. 8 that our God may lighten our eyes, and
Psa. 13. 3 O LORD my God: lighten mine eyes, lest
77. 18 the lightnings lightened the world: the
Prov 29. 13 meet..the LORD lighteneth both their
2. *To cause to shine,* נָגַהּ *nagah,* 5.
2 Sa. 22. 29 and the LORD will lighten my darkness
3. *To make light, lighten,* קָלַל *qalal,* 5.
1 Sa. 6. 5 he will lighten his hand from off you, and
Jon. 1. 5 cast forth the wares..to lighten (it) of
4. *To lighten as lightning,* ἀστράπτω *astraptō.*
Luke17. 24 as the lightning, that lighteneth out of
5. *To lighten, make light,* κουφίζω *kouphizō.*
Acts 27. 38 they lightened the ship, and cast out the
6. *To make a clearance or casting out,* ἐκβολὴν ποιέ.
Acts 27. 18 And..the next (day) they lightened the
7. *To enlighten, give light,* φωτίζω *phōtizō.*
Rev. 18. 1 and the earth was lightened with his glory
21. 23 the glory of God did lighten it, and the L.
8. *Uncovering,* εἰς ἀποκάλυψιν *eis apokalupsin.*
Luke 2. 32 A light to lighten the Gentiles, and the
LIGHTENED, to be —
To become bright, נָהַר *nahar.*
Psa. 34. 5 They looked unto him, and were lightened
LIGHTER, to make (somewhat) —
To make light, קָלַל *qalal,* 5.
1 Ki.12. 4 make thou the grievous service..lighter
12. 9 Make the yoke..thy father..put upon us l.
12. 10 make thou (it) lighter unto us; thus shalt
2 Ch.10. 10 make thou (it) somewhat lighter for us
LIGHTING down —
Coming down, נַחַת *nachath.*
Isa. 30. 30 shall show the lighting down of his arm
LIGHTLY —
1. *As a little thing,* כִּמְעַט *ki-meat.*
Gen. 26. 10 one of the people might lightly have lien
2. *Quickly, hastily,* ταχύ *tachu.*
Mark 9. 39 no man..that can lightly speak evil of me
[*See also* Afflict, move.]
LIGHTLY esteem, to —
To dishonour, נָבֵל *nabel,* 3.
Deut32. 15 lightly esteemed the Rock of his salvation
LIGHTNESS —
1. *Instability,* פַּחֲזוּת *pachazuth.*
Jer. 23. 32 to err by their lies, and by their lightness
2. *Lightness,* קֹל *qol.*
Jer. 3. 9 came to pass through the lightness of her
3. *Lightness,* ἐλαφρία *elaphria.*
2 Co. 1. 17 did I use lightness? or the things that I
LIGHTNING —
1. *Light,* אוֹר *or.*
Job 37. 3 his lightning unto the ends of the earth
2. *Lightning,* בָּרָק *baraq.*
Exod19. 16 that there were thunders and lightnings
2 Sa. 22. 15 he sent out..lightning, and discomfited
Job 38. 35 Canst thou send lightnings, that they may
Psa. 18. 14 he shot out lightnings, and discomfited
77. 18 the lightnings lightened the world: the
97. 4 His lightnings enlightened the world: the
135. 7 he maketh lightnings for the rain: he b.
144. 6 Cast forth lightning, and scatter them
Jer. 10. 13 he maketh lightnings with rain, and brin.
51. 16 he maketh lightnings with rain, and brin.
Eze. 1. 13 and out of the fire went forth lightning
Dan. 10. 6 his face as the appearance of lightning
Nah. 2. 4 The chariots..shall run like the lightnings
Zech. 9. 14 his arrow shall go forth as the lightning
3. *Brightness, lightning,* חֲזִיז *chaziz.*
Job 28. 26 and a way for the lightning of the thunder
38. 25 or a way for the lightning of thunder
4. *Flame,* לַפִּיד *lappid.*
Exod20. 18 the thunderings, and the lightnings, and
5. *Lightning,* ἀστραπή *astrapē.*
Matt.24. 27 as the lightning cometh out of the east
28. 3 His countenance was like lightning, and
Luke10. 18 I beheld Satan as lightning fall from he.
17. 24 as the lightning, that lighteneth out of
Rev. 4. 5 lightnings and thunderings and voices
8. 5 voices, and thunderings, and lightnings
11. 19 there were lightnings, and voices, and th.
16. 18 were voices, and thunders, and light.
LIGHTNING, flash of —
Lightning, בָּזָק *bazaq.*
Eze. 1. 14 as the appearance of a flash of lightning
LIGN aloes. *See* **TREES.**
LIGURE —
Opal, jacinth, לֶשֶׁם *leshem.*
Exod28. 19 third row a ligure, an agate, and an am.
39. 12 third row, a ligure, an agate, and an am.
LIKE (things, occupation) —
1. *A brother,* אָח *ach.*
Eze. 18. 10 (that) doeth the like to (any) one of these
2. *Likeness,* דְּמוּת *demuth.*
Psa. 58. 4 Their poison (is) like the poison of a serp.
3. *Thus,* כֹּה *koh.*
Jer. 23. 29 (Is) not my word like as a fire? saith the
4. *Like,* כְּמוֹ *kemo.*
2 Ch. 35. 18 there was no passover like to that kept in
Isa. 46. 9 I (am) God, and (there is) none like me
51. 6 they that dwell therein shall die in like
Lam. 1. 21 hast called, and they shall be like unto me
5. *Simile, similitude,* מָשָׁל *mashal.*
Job 13. 12 Your remembrances (are) like unto ashes
6. *Similitude,* מֹשֶׁל *moshel.*
Job 41. 33 Upon earth there is not his like, who is
7. *With,* עִם *im.*
Psa. 73. 5 neither are they plagued like (other) men
Dan. 5. 21 his heart was made like the beasts, and
8. *Likeness,* דִּמְיוֹן *dimyon.*
Psa. 17. 12 Like as a lion..is greedy of his prey, and
9. *As these, like these,* כָּהֵמָּה *ka-hemah.*
Jer. 36. 32 there were added besides..many like w.
10. *Like, equal,* ἴσος *isos.*
Acts 11. 17 God gave them the like gift as..unto us
11. *Like, resembling,* ὅμοιος *homoios.*
Matt 11. 16 It is like unto children sitting in the ma.
13. 31 The kingdom of heaven is like to a grain
13. 33 The kingdom of heaven is like unto leaven
13. 44 the kingdom of heaven is like unto treas.
13. 45 the kingdom of heaven is like unto a m.
13. 47 the kingdom of heaven is like unto a net
13. 52 is like unto a man..an householder which
20. 1 the kingdom of heaven is like unto a man
22. 39 the second (is) like unto it, Thou shalt love
Mark12. 31 the second (is) [like]..this, Thou shalt love
Luke 6. 47 I will show you to whom he is like
6. 48 He is like a man which built an house
6. 49 is like a man that..built an house upon
7. 31 And the Lord said..to what are they like?
7. 32 They are like unto children sitting in the
12. 36 like unto men that wait for their lord
13. 18 Unto what is the kingdom of God like?
13. 19 It is like a grain of mustard seed, which
13. 21 It is like leaven, which a woman took
John 8. 55 I shall be a liar like unto you: but I know
9. 9 others (said), He is like him..he said, I am
Acts 17. 29 that the Godhead is like unto gold, or
Gal. 5. 21 drunkenness, revellings, and such like: of
1 Jo. 3. 2 we shall be like him; for we shall see him
Jude 7 the cities about them, in like manner giv.
Rev. 1. 13 like unto the Son of man, clothed with
1. 15 his feet like unto fine brass, as if they
2. 18 the Son of God..his feet (are) like fine b.
4. 3 he that sat was to look upon like a jasper
4. 3 a rainbow..in sight [like] unto an emerald
4. 6 a sea of glass like unto crystal: and in the
4. 7 like a lion, and the second beast like a
4. 7 and the fourth beast..like a flying eagle
9. 7 locusts..like unto horses prepared unto
9. 7 as it were crowns [like] gold, and their
9. 10 they had tails like unto scorpions, and
9. 19 their tails..like unto serpents, and had
11. 1 there was given me a reed like unto a rod
13. 2 the beast which I saw was like unto a
13. 4 Who (is) like unto the beast? who is able
13. 11 he had two horns like a lamb, and he spake
14. 14 (one) sat like unto the Son of man, having
16. 13 I saw three unclean spirits [like] frogs
18. 18 saying, What (city is) like unto this great
21. 11 her light (was) like unto a stone most pr.
21. 18 the city..pure gold, like unto clear glass
12. *Thus as,* οὕτως ὡς *houtōs hōs.*
John 7. 46 [Never man spake like this man]
13. *Nearly like, similar,* παρόμοιος *paromoios.*
Mark 7. 8 [and many other such like things ye do]
7. 13 and many such like things
14. *These,* ταῦτα *tauta.*
1 Th. 2. 14 ye also have suffered like things of your
15. *Such as these,* τοιαῦτα *toiauta.*
Acts 19. 25 with the workmen of like occupation, and
16. *As, so as,* ὡς *hōs.*
Matt. 6. 29 Solomon..was not arrayed like one of th.
28. 3 His countenance was like lightning, and
Mark 4. 31 (It is) like a grain of mustard seed, which
Luke12. 27 Solomon..was not arrayed like one Jo. 7. 46.
Acts 8. 32 like a lamb dumb before his shearer, so
Rev. 18. 21 took up a stone like a great millstone, and
17. *As if,* ὡσεί *hōsei.*
Matt. 3. 16 saw the spirit of God descending like a d.
Mark 1. 10 spirit [like] a dove descending upon him
Luke 3. 22 descended in a bodily shape [like] a dove
John 1. 32 spirit descending from heaven [like] a dove
Rev. 1. 14 His head and..hairs..white [like] wool
[*See also* Come, each, even, figure, manner, men, occupation, passions, precious, such, tires.]
LIKE, to —
1. *To love,* אָהַב *aheb.*
Amos 4. 5 for this liketh you, O ye children of Israel
2. *To delight,* חָפֵץ *chaphets.*
Deut25. 7 if the man like not to take his brother's
25. 8 (if) he stand..and say, I like not to take
3. *To be pleased,* רָצָה *ratsah.*
1 Ch.28. 4 he liked me to make (me) king over all I.
4. *To make trial, proof,* δοκιμάζω *dokimazō.*
Rom. 1. 28 even as they did not like to retain God in
LIKE, to be —
1. *To be like,* דָּמָה *damah.*
Psa.102. 6 I am like a pelican of the wilderness; I
144. 4 Man is like to vanity: his days (are) as a
Song 2. 9 My beloved is like a roe or a young hart
2. 17 be thou like a roe or a young hart upon
7. 7 This thy stature is like to a palm tree, and
8. 14 be thou like to a roe or to a young hart
Isa. 1. 9 we should have been like unto Gomorrah
46. 5 equal..compare me, that we may be like?
Jer. 6. 2 I have likened the daughter of Zion to a
Eze. 31. 2 speak..Whom art thou like in thy great.?
31. 8 the fir trees were not like his boughs, and
31. 8 nor any tree..was like unto him in his b.
31. 18 To whom art thou thus like in glory and
2. *To be or become like,* דָּמָה *damah,* 2.
Eze. 32. 2 Thou art like a young lion of the nations
3. *To liken self,* דָּמָה *damah,* 7.
Isa. 14. 14 I will ascend..I will be like the most H.
4. *To be like,* דְּמָה *demah.*
Dan. 3. 25 form of the fourth is like the Son of God
7. 5 behold another beast, a second, like to a
5. *To be, become,* הָיָה *hayah.*
Jer. 48. 6 Flee..be like the heath in the wilderness
6. *To think, reckon,* חָשַׁב *chashab,* 3.
Jon. 1. 4 sea, so that the ship was like to be broken
7. *To be or become like,* מָשַׁל *mashal,* 2.
Psa. 49. 12 Nevertheless..he is like the beasts (that)
49. 20 Man (that is)..is like the beasts (that) pe.
143. 7 like unto them that go down into the pit
8. *To be equal, compared,* שָׁוָה *shavah.*
Prov.26. 4 Answer not..lest thou also be like unto
9. *To be like, in the image of,* ἔοικα *eoika,* εἴκω *eikō.*
Jas. 1. 6 he that wavereth is like a wave of the sea
1. 23 he is like unto a man beholding his natural
10. *To make like,* ὁμοιόω *homoioō.*
Matt 6. 8 Be not ye therefore like unto them: for
22. 2 The kingdom of heaven is like unto a cer.
LIKE, to become —
1. *To be or become like,* מָשַׁל *mashal,* 2.
Psa. 28. 1 I become like them that go down into the
Isa. 14. 10 Art thou also..art thou become like unto
2. *To be or become like,* מָשַׁל *mashal,* 7.
Job 30. 19 and I am become like dust and ashes
LIKE, to be made —
1. *To make equal,* שְׁוָה *shevah,* 3.
Dan. 5. 21 his heart was made like the beasts, and
2. *To liken off,* ἀφομοιόω *aphomoioō.*
Heb. 7. 3 made like unto the Son of God; abideth
LIKE, to make —
1. *To make equal, compare,* שָׁוָה *shavah,* 3.
2 Sa. 22. 34 He maketh my feet like hind's (feet); and
Psa. 18. 33 He maketh my feet like hind's (feet), and
2. *To make like,* ὁμοιόω *homoioō.*
Rom. 9. 29 Sodoma, and been made like unto Gom.
Heb. 2. 17 it behoved him to be made like unto (his)
LIKE manner, in —
1. *So,* כֵּן *ken.*
Exod. 7. 11 did in like manner with their enchantm.
Deut 22. 3 In like manner shalt thou do with his ass
2. *And,* καί *kai.*
Mark13. 29 So ye in like manner, when ye shall see
3. *According to these,* κατὰ ταῦτα *kata tauta.*
Luke 6. 23 in the like manner did their fathers unto
4. *In the same way,* ὡσαύτως *hōsautōs.*
Luke20. 31 in like manner the seven also: and they
1 Ti. 2. 9 In like manner also, that women adorn
LIKE as —
1. *Likeness,* דְּמוּת *demuth.*
Isa. 13. 4 The noise..like as of a great people; a tu.
2. *As, even as,* כְּמוֹ *kemo.*
Isa. 26. 17 Like as a woman with child, (that) draw.

3. *According to the likeness*, καθ' ὁμοιότητα *kath ho.*
Heb. 4. 15 but was in all points tempted like as (we
4. *As, so as*, ὡς *hōs.*
Matt12. 13 it was restored whole, like as the other
5. *As if*, ὡσεί *hōsei.*
Acts 2. 3 appeared unto them cloven tongues, like as
6. *Just as*, ὥσπερ *hōsper.*
Rom. 6 4 that like as Christ was raised up from the
LIKE, the —
So, thus, כֵּן *ken.*
1 Ki. 10. 20 there was not the like made in any king.
LIKE to, made —
A likeness, something made like, ὁμοίωμα *homoiōma.*
Rom. 1. 23 into an image made like to corruptible
LIKE unto, (to be)—
To be or act nearly like, παρομοιάζω *paromoiazō.*
Matt23. 27 [ye are like unto] whited sepulchres, which
As, ὡς *hōs*, Acts 3. 22; 7. 37; Rev. 2. 18.
LIKE MINDED, to be —
1. *To mind the same thing*, τὸ αὐτὸ φρονέω [*phroneō*]
Rom.15. 5 grant you to be like minded one toward
Phil. 2. 2 Fulfil ye my joy, that ye be like minded
2. *One of a like or equal soul*, ἰσόψυχος *isopsuchos.*
Phil. 2. 20 I have no man like minded, who will na.
3. *Joint-souled*, σύμψυχος *sumpsuchos*, Phil. 2. 2
LIKEN, or be likened to —
1. *To liken*, דָּמָה *damah*, 3.
Isa. 40. 18 To whom then will ye liken God? or what
40. 25 To whom then will ye liken me, or shall
46. 5 To whom will ye liken me, and make (me)
Lam. 2. 13 what thing shall I liken to thee, O daug.
2. *To liken, compare*, דָּמָה *damah.*
Psa. 89. 6 (who) among..sons..can be likened unto
Jer. 6. 2 I have likened the daughter of Zion to a
3. *To make like*, ὁμοιόω *homoioō.*
Matt. 7. 24 I will liken him unto a wise man, which
7. 26 shall be likened unto a foolish man, which
11. 16 But whereunto shall I liken this genera.?
13. 24 The kingdom of heaven is likened unto a
18. 23 Therefore is the kingdom of heaven like
25. 1; Mark 4. 30; Luke 7. 31; 13. 20.
LIKENESS —
1. *Likeness*, דְּמוּת *demuth.*
Gen. 1. 26 Let us make man..after our likeness: and
5. 1 day that God created man, in the likeness
5. 3 Adam..begat (a son) in his own likeness
Isa. 40. 18 or what likeness will ye compare unto him?
Eze. 1. 5 out of the midst..(came) the likeness of
1. 5 And this..they had the likeness of a man
1. 10 As for the likeness of their faces, they four
1. 13 As for the likeness of the living creatures
1. 16 they four had one likeness: and their
1. 22 the likeness of the firmament upon the h.
1. 26 above the firmament..(was) the likeness
1. 26 upon the likeness of the throne..the like
1. 28 This (was) the appearance of the likeness
8. 2 a likeness as the appearance of fire: from
10. 1 the appearance of the likeness of a throne
10. 10 they four had one likeness, as if a wheel
10. 21 the likeness of the hands of a man ..under
10. 22 the likeness of their faces (was) the same
2. *Pattern, form, building*, תַּבְנִית *tabnith*
Deut. 4. 16 any figure, the likeness of male or female
4. 17 likeness of any beast..likeness of any wi.
4. 18 likeness of any thing..likeness of any fish
3. *Form, similitude, likeness*, תְּמוּנָה *temunah.*
Exod20. 4 or any likeness (of any thing) that (is) in
Deut. 4. 23 the likeness of any (thing), which the L.
4. 25 make a graven image, (or) the likeness of
5. 8 Thou shalt not make thee..any likeness
Psa. 17. 15 satisfied, when I awake, with thy likeness
4. *A likeness, something made like*, ὁμοίωμα *homoiōma.*
Rom. 6. 5 if we have been planted..in the likeness
8. 3 God, sending his own Son in the likeness
Phil. 2. 7 took..and was made in the likeness of men
5. *To make like*, ὁμοιόω *homoioō.*
Acts 14. 11 gods are come down to us in the likeness
LIKETH (best) —
Is good to (or *in the eyes of*), (בְּעֵינֵי) טוֹב לְ *tob le (be-ene)*
Deut23. 16 He shall dwell..where it liketh him best
Esth. 8. 8 Write ye also for the Jews, as it liketh you
LIKEWISE —
1. *Also*, גַּם *gam.*
Deut12. 30 How did these..even so will I do likewise
2. *Thus, according to this*, כָּזֹאת *ka-zoth.*
Judg. 8. 8 to Penuel, and spake unto them likewise
3. *Together, alike, at once*, יַחַד, יַחְדָּו, יַחְדָּיו *yachad.*
Job 31. 38 or that the furrows likewise thereof com.
4. *So, thus*, כֵּן *ken.*
Exod 22. 30 Likewise shalt thou do with thine oxen
5. *And*, καί *kai.*
Matt.18. 35; 20. 10; 24. 33; Lu. 3. 14; 17. 10; 19. 19;
21. 31; Acts 3. 24; 1 Co. 14. 9; Col. 4. 16; 1 Pe. 4. 1.
6. *In like manner, likewise*, ὁμοίως *homoiōs.*
Matt.22. 26 Likewise the second also, and the third
26. 35; 27. 41; Mark 4. 16; 15. 31.
Luke 3. 11 and he that hath meat, let him do likewise
5. 33 and likewise (the disciples) of the Phari.
6. 31 should do to you, do ye also to them like.
10. 32 likewise a Levite, when he was at the pl.
10. 37 Then said Jesus unto him, Go..do thou l.
13. 5 except ye repent, ye shall all [likewise]
16. 25 likewise Lazarus evil things: but now he
17. 28 Likewise also as it was in the days of Lot
17. 31 the field, let him likewise not return back
22. 36 let him take (it), and likewise (his) scrip
John 5. 19 what..doeth, these..doeth the Son like.
6. 11 likewise of the fishes as much as they wo.
21. 13 Jesus then..taketh bread..and fish like.
Rom. 1. 27 likewise also the men, leaving the natural
1 Co. 7. 3 likewise also the wife unto the husband
7. 4 likewise also the husband hath not power
7. 22 likewise also he that is called, (being) free
Jas. 2. 25 Likewise also, was not Rahab the harlot j.
1 Pe. 3. 1 Likewise, ye wives, (be) in subjection to
3. 7 Likewise, ye husbands, dwell with (them)
5. 5 Likewise, ye younger, submit yourselves
Jude 8 Likewise also these..dreamers defile the
Rev. 8. 12 the day shone not..and the night likewise
7. *Thus, so*, οὕτω *houtō.*
Matt17. 12 Likewise shall also the Son of man suffer
Luke15. 7 likewise joy shall be in heaven over one
15. 10 Likewise, I say unto you, There is joy in
Rom. 6. 11 Likewise reckon ye also yourselves to be
8. *Very near to*, παραπλησίως *paraplēsiōs.*
Heb. 2. 14 he also himself likewise took part of the
9. *So, in the same manner*, ὡσαύτως *hōsautōs.*
Matt20. 5 went out about the sixth..and did likew.
21. 30 And he came to the second, and said like.
21. 36 other servants..and they did unto them l.
25. 17 likewise he that (had received) two, he
Mark12. 21 the second took her..and the third like.
14. 31 I will not deny thee..Likewise also said
Luke13. 3 except ye repent, ye shall all [likewise]
22. 20 Likewise also the cup after supper, saying
Rom. 8. 26 Likewise the spirit also helpeth our infi.
1 Ti. 3. 8 Likewise..the deacons (be) grave, not d.
5. 25 Likewise also the good works..are mani.
Titus 2. 3 aged women likewise, that..in behaviour
2. 6 Young men likewise exhort to be sober mi.
LIK'-HI, לִקְחִי *Jah is doctrine.*
Son of Shemidah, a Benjamite B.C. 1400.
1 Ch. 7. 19 the sons of Shemidah were..L. and Aniam
LIKING, in good —
To be safe, sound, חָלַם *chalam.*
Job 39. 4 Their young ones are in good liking, they
LILY —
1. *A lily*, שׁוֹשַׁן *shoshan.*
1 Ki. 7. 22 upon the top of the pillars (was) lily work
7. 26 the brim of a cup, with flowers of lilies
Song 2. 16 and I (am) his: he feedeth among the lil.
4. 5 that are twins, which feed among the lil.
5. 13 his lips.. lilies, dropping sweet smelling
6. 2 to feed in the gardens, and to gather lilies
6. 3 beloved (is) mine, he feedeth among the l.
7. 2 an heap of wheat set about with lilies
2. *A lily*, שׁוּשַׁן *shushan.*
1 Ki. 7. 19 the chapiters..of lily work in the porch
3. *A lily*, שׁוֹשַׁנָּה *shoshannah.*
2 Ch. 4. 5 the brim of a cup, with flowers of lilies
Song 2. 1 I (am) the rose of Sharon..the lily of the
2. 2 As the lily among thorns, so (is) my love
Hos. 14. 5 he shall grow as the lily, and cast forth
4. *A lily*, κρίνον *krinon.*
Matt. 6. 28 Consider the lilies of the field, how they
Luke12. 27 Consider the lilies how they grow: they
LIME —
Plaster, lime, שִׂיד *sid.*
Isa. 33. 12 people shall be (as) the burnings of lime
Amos 2. 1 he burned the bones of the king..into lime
LIMIT —
A border, גְּבוּל *gebul.*
Eze. 43. 12 the whole limit thereof round about (sh.
LIMIT, to —
1. *To mark off, limit*, תָּוָה *tavah*, 5.
Psa. 78. 41 Yea, they..limited the Holy One of
2. *To mark off*, ὁρίζω *horizō.*
Heb. 4. 7 Again, he limiteth a certain day, saying
LINE —
1. *Cord, line, rope*, חֶבֶל *chebel.*
2 Sa. 8. 2 with a line..with two lines..one full line
Psa. 16. 6 The lines are fallen unto me in pleasant
78. 55 He..divided them an inheritance by line
Amos 7. 17 thy land shall be divided by line; and thou
Zech. 2. 1 behold, a man with a measuring line in
2. *A thread, cord*, חוּט *chut.*
1 Ki. 7. 15 a line of twelve cubits did compass either
3. *Ribbon, thread*, פָּתִיל *pathil.*
Eze. 40. 3 a man..with a line of flax in his hand, and
4. *A line, rule*, קַו, קָו, קְוֵה *qav, qeveh.*
1 Ki. 7. 23 a line of thirty cubits did compass it ro.
2 Ki. 21. 13 I will stretch over Jerusalem the line of S.
2 Ch. 4. 2 a line of thirty cubits did compass it round
Job 38. 5 or who hath stretched the line upon it?
Psa. 19. 4 Their line is gone out through all the ea.
Isa. 28. 10, 13 line upon line, line upon line; here a
28. 17 judgment also will I lay to the line, and
Isa. 34. 11 he shall stretch out upon it the line of con.
34. 17 his hand hath divided it unto them by line
Jer. 31. 39 the measuring line shall yet go forth over
Lam. 2. 8 he hath stretched out a line, he hath not
Eze. 47. 3 when the man that had the line in his h.
Zech. 1. 16 a line shall be stretched forth upon Jeru.
5. *A cutting instrument, red ochre*, שֶׂרֶד *sered.*
Isa. 44. 13 he marketh it out with a line, he fitteth
6. *Line*, תִּקְוָה *tiqvah.*
Josh. 2. 18 thou shalt bind this line of scarlet thread
2. 21 she bound the scarlet line in the window
7. *A canon, reed, rule*, κανών *kanōn.*
2 Co. 10. 16 not to boast in another man's line of things
LINEAGE —
Paternal descent, πατριά *patria.*
Luke 2. 4 he was of the house and lineage of David
LINEN —
1. *Fine linen*, בַּד *bad.*
Exod28. 42 thou shalt make them linen breeches to c.
39. 28 and linen breeches (of) fine twined linen
Lev. 6. 10 the priest shall put on his linen garment
6. 10 his linen breeches shall he put upon his
16. 4 He shall put on the holy linen coat, and
16. 4 he shall have the linen breeches upon his
16. 4 a linen girdle, and with the linen mitre
16. 23 shall put off the linen garments which he
16. 32 shall put on the linen clothes..the holy
1 Sa. 2. 18 (being) a child, girded with a linen ephod
22. 18 slew..persons that did wear a linen ephod
2 Sa. 6. 14 David (was) girded with a linen ephod
1 Ch.15. 27 David..(had) upon him an ephod of linen
Eze. 9. 2 one man among them..clothed with linen
9. 3 and he called to the man clothed with li.
9. 11 behold, the man clothed with linen, which
10. 2 he spake unto the man clothed with linen
10. 6 had commanded the man clothed with li.
10. 7 hands of (him that was) clothed with linen
Dan. 10. 5 a certain man clothed in linen, whose lo.
12. 6 And..said to the man clothed in linen
12. 7 I heard the man clothed in linen, which
2. *Linen, flax*, פִּשְׁתֶּה *pishteh.*
Lev. 13. 47 a woollen garment, or a linen garment
13. 48 of linen, or of woollen, whether in a skin
13. 52 whether warp or woof, in woollen or in l.
13. 59 in a garment of woollen or linen, either
Deut22. 11 of divers sorts, (as) of woollen and linen
Jer. 13. 1 Go and get thee a linen girdle, and put it
Eze. 44. 17 they shall be clothed with linen garments
44. 18 They shall have linen bonnets upon their
44. 18 shall have linen breeches upon their loins
3. *Flax, linen*, λίνον *linon.*
Rev.15. 6 angels..clothed in pure and white [linen]
4. *Muslin, fine linen*, σινδών *sindōn.*
Mark15. 46 fine linen..and wrapped him in the linen
Luke23. 53 wrapped it in linen, and laid it in a sepul.
LINEN and woollen —
Mixed cloth, שַׁעַטְנֵז *shaatnez.*
Lev. 19. 19 shall a garment mingled of linen and wo.
LINEN, fine —
1. *Linen garment*, סָדִין *sadin.*
Prov.31. 24 She maketh fine linen, and selleth (it)
Isa. 3. 23 The glasses, and the fine linen, and the
2. *Fine linen*, שֵׁשׁ, שְׁשִׁי *sheshi, shesh.*
Gen. 41. 42 arrayed him in vestures of fine linen, and
Exod25. 4 purple, and scarlet, and fine linen, and
26. 1 ten curtains (of) fine twined linen, and
26. 31 and fine twined linen, of cunning work
26. 36 fine twined linen, wrought with needlewo.
27. 9 hangings for the court (of) fine twined l.
27. 16 fine twined linen, wrought with needlewo.
27. 18 the height five cubits (of) fine twined linen
28. 5 they shall take gold..and fine linen
28. 6 shall make the ephod (of)..fine twined l.
28. 8 girdle..shall be of..fine twined linen
28. 15 (of) fine twined linen, shalt thou make it
28. 39 shalt embroider the coat of fine linen
28. 39 thou shalt make the mitre (of) fine linen
35. 6, 23 purple, and scarlet, and fine linen, and
35. 25 that which they had spun..of fine linen
35. 35 the embroiderer..in fine linen, and of the
36. 8 made ten curtains (of) fine twined linen
36. 35 And he made a veil (of)..fine twined linen
36. 37 he made..fine twined linen, of needlewo.
38. 9, 16 the hangings..(were of) fine twined l.
38. 18 needlework, (of) blue..and fine twined l.
38. 23 and an embroiderer in blue..and fine li.
39. 2, 5, 8 purple, and scarlet..fine twined linen
39. 3 and in the fine linen, (with) cunning work
39. 27 they made coats (of) fine linen, (of) woven
39. 28 mitre (of) fine linen..bonnets (of) fine li.
39. 28 and linen breeches (of) fine twined linen
39. 29 a girdle (of) fine twined linen, and blue
Eze. 16. 10 I girded thee about with fine linen, and
16. 13 thy raiment (was of) fine linen, and silk
27. 7 Fine linen with broidered work from E.
3. *Made of fine linen*, βύσσινος *bussinos.*
Rev. 18. 16 that great city, that was clothed in fine l.
19. 8 that she should be arrayed in fine linen
19. 8 the fine linen is the righteousness of saints
19. 14 the armies..followed..clothed in fine linen
4. *Fine flax or linen*, βύσσος *bussos.*
Luke16. 19 which was clothed in purple and fine linen
Rev. 18. 12 merchandise of gold..and [fine linen], and

LINEN cloth, clothes —

1.*A piece of fine linen,* ὀθόνιον *othonion.*

Luke 24. 12 [beheld the linen clothes laid by thems.]
John 19. 40 wound it in linen clothes with the spices
20. 5 saw the linen clothes lying ; yet went he
20. 6 cometh Simon..and seeth the linen clot.
20. 7 napkin..not lying with the linen clothes

2.*Muslin, fine linen,* σινδών *sindōn.*

Matt 27. 59 Joseph..wrapped it in a clean linen cloth
Mar. 14. 51 having a linen cloth cast about (his) naked
14. 52 left the linen cloth, and fled from them

LINEN yarn —

Linen yarn, מִקְוֶה *miqveh,* מִקְוֵא *miqve.*

1 Ki. 10. 28 Solomon had horses..and linen yarn : the
10. 28 merchants received the linen yarn at a p.
2 Ch. 1. 16 And Solomon had horses..and linen yarn
1. 16 merchants received the linen yarn at a p.

LINGER, to —

1. *To tarry, linger, delay,* מָהַהּ *mahah,* 7a.

Gen. 19. 16 while he lingered, the men laid hold upon
43. 10 except we had lingered, surely now we

2. *To be inactive,* ἀργέω *argeō.*

2 Pe. 2. 3 whose judgment..lingereth not, and their

LINTEL (upper) —

1.*A ram, post,* אַיִל *ayil.*

1 Ki. 6. 31 the lintel (and) side posts (were) a fifth

2.*Capital of a column,* כַּפְתּוֹר *kaphtor.*

Amos 9. 1 Smite the lintel of the door, that the posts
Zeph. 2. 14 the bittern shall lodge in the upper lintels

3. *Lintel, upper door post,* מַשְׁקוֹף *mashqoph.*

Exod 12. 22 strike the lintel and the two side posts
12. 23 when he seeth the blood upon the lintel

LI'-NUS, Λῖνος.

A Christian at Rome.

2 Ti. 4. 21 Eubulus greeteth thee L., and Claudia

LION —

1.*A lion,* אֲרִי, אַרְיֵה *ari, aryeh.*

Gen. 49. 9 Judah (is) a lion's whelp : from the prey
49. 9 he stooped down, he couched as a lion
Num 24. 9 he lay down as a lion, and as a great lion
Deut 33. 22 Dan (is) a lion's whelp : he shall leap from
Judg 14. 8 he turned aside to see the carcase of the l.
14. 8 bees and honey in the carcase of the lion
14. 9 taken the honey out of the carcase of the l.
14. 18 what (is) stronger than a lion? And he said
1 Sa 17. 34 there came a lion and a bear, and took a
17. 36 Thy servant slew both the lion and the b.
17. 37 delivered me out of the paw of the lion, and
2 Sa. 1. 23 swifter than eagles..stronger than lions
17. 10 whose heart (is) as the heart of a lion, sh.
23. 20 a lion in the midst of a pit in time of snow
1 Ki. 7. 29 the borders..lions, oxen, and cherubim
7. 29 beneath the lions and oxen (were) certain
7. 36 he graved cherubim, lions, and palm trees
10. 19 seat, and two lions stood beside the stays
10. 20 twelve lions stood there on the one side
13. 24 a lion met him..the lion also stood by the
13. 25 men..saw..the lion standing by the carc.
13. 26 the LORD hath delivered him unto the lion
13. 28 found..the lion standing by the carcase
13. 28 the lion had not eaten the carcase, nor
20. 36 as soon as thou art departed..a lion shall
20. 36 as soon as he was departed..a lion found
2 Ki. 17. 25 therefore the LORD sent lions among them
17. 26 therefore he hath sent lions among them
1 Ch. 11. 22 also he went down and slew a lion in a pit
12. 8 whose faces (were like) the faces of lions
2 Ch. 9. 18 stays..and two lions standing by the sta.
9. 19 twelve lions stood there on the one side
Job 4. 10 The roaring of the lion, and the voice of
Psa. 7. 2 Lest he tear my soul like a lion, rending
10. 9 He lieth in wait secretly as a lion in his
17. 12 like as a lion (that) is greedy of his prey
22. 13 gaped..(as) a ravening and a roaring lion
22. 21 Save me from the lion's mouth : for thou.
Prov 22. 13 a lion without, I shall be slain in the str.
26. 13 saith..a lion (is) in the streets
28. 15 (As) a roaring lion, and a ranging bear
Eccl. 9. 4 a living dog is better than a dead lion
Song. 4. 8 from the lion's dens, from the mountains
Isa. 11. 7 and the lion shall eat straw like the ox
15. 9 I will bring..lions upon him that escapeth
21. 8 he cried, A lion : My lord, I stand conti.
31. 4 Like as the lion..roaring on his prey
35. 9 no lion shall be there, nor (any) ravenous
38. 13 as a lion, so will he break all my bones
65. 25 the lion shall eat straw like the bullock
Jer 2. 30 hath devoured..like a destroying lion
4. 7 The lion is come up from his thicket, and
5. 6 a lion out of the forest shall slay them
12. 8 Mine heritage is unto me as a lion in the
49. 19 shall come up like a lion from the swell.
50. 17 the lions have driven (him) away : first
50. 44 he shall come up like a lion from the
51. 38 shall roar..they shall yell as lions' whelps
Lam. 3. 10 He (was) unto me..a lion in secret places
Eze. 1. 10 the face of a lion on the right side ; and
10. 14 and the third the face of a lion, and the
19. 2 she lay down among lions, she nourished
19. 6 he went up and down among the lions, he
22. 25 like a roaring lion ravening the prey : they
Dan 6. 7, 12, shall be cast into the den of lions
6. 16 brought..and cast (him) into the den of l.
6. 19 and went in haste unto the den of lions
Dan. 6. 20 is thy God..able to deliver..from the l.?
6. 22 My God..hath shut the lions' mouths, that
6. 24 they cast..into the den of lions, them
6. 24 the lions had the mastery of them, and
6. 27 delivered D. from the power of the lions
7. 4 The first..like a lion, and had eagle's wi.
Hos. 11. 10 he shall roar like a lion : when he shall
Joel 1. 6 whose teeth (are) the teeth of a lion, and
Amos 3. 4 Will a lion roar in the forest when he
3. 8 The lion hath roared, who will not fear?
3. 12 taketh out of the mouth of the lion two
5. 19 As if a man did flee from a lion, and a bear
Mic. 5. 8 as a lion among the beasts of the forest
Nah. 2. 11 Where (is) the dwelling of the lions, and
2. 11 where the lion..walked..the lions' whelp
2. 12 The lion did tear in pieces enough for his
Zeph. 3. 3 Her princes within her (are) roaring lions

2.*A young lion, whelp,* כְּפִיר *kephir.*

Judg 14. 5 behold, a young lion roared ; Psa. 35. 17.
Prov 19. 12 The king's wrath (is) as the roaring of a l.
20. 2 The fear of a king (is) as the roaring of a l.
28. 1 flee..but the righteous are bold as a lion
Jer. 25. 38 He hath forsaken his covert, as the lion
51. 38 They shall roar together like lions ; they

3.*Lions,* לְבָאִים *lebaim.*

Psa. 57. 4 My soul (is) among lions..I lie (..among)

4.*A bold lion,* לָבִיא *labi.*

Deut 33. 20 he dwelleth as a lion, and teareth the
Job 38. 39 Wilt thou hunt the prey for the lion, or
Isa. 5. 29 Their roaring (shall be) like a lion, they
Hos. 13. 8 there will I devour them like a lion : the

5.*An old lion,* לַיִשׁ *layish.*

Prov 30. 30 A lion, (which is) strongest among beasts

6.*A roaring lion,* שַׁחַל *shachal.*

Psa. 91. 13 Thou shalt tread upon the lion and adder
Prov 26. 13 The slothful..saith, (There is) a lion in
Hos. 5. 14 For I (will be) unto Ephraim as a lion, and
13. 7 Therefore I will be unto them as a lion

7.*Pride,* שַׁחַץ *shachats.*

Job 28. 8 The lions' whelps have not trodden it ; nor

8.*A lion,* λέων *leōn.*

2 Ti. 4. 17 I was delivered out of the mouth of the lion
Heb. 11. 33 through faith..stopped the mouths of l.
1 Pe. 5. 8 as a roaring lion, walketh about, seeking
Rev 4. 7 And the first beast (was) like a lion, and
5. 5 behold, the Lion of the tribe of Juda, the
9. 8 and their teeth were as (the teeth) of lions
9. 17 the heads..(were) as the heads of lions
10. 3 with a loud voice, as (when) a lion roar.
13. 2 and his mouth as the mouth of a lion

LION, fierce —

A roaring lion, שַׁחַל *shachal.*

Job 4. 10 the voice of the fierce lion, and the teeth
10. 16 Thou huntest me as a fierce lion ; and aga.
28. 8 trodden it ; nor the fierce lion passed by

LION, great, old, stout —

1.*A bold lion,* לָבִיא *labi.*

Gen. 49. 9 he couched..as an old lion ; who shall
Num 23. 24 the people shall rise up as a great lion
24. 9 he lay down..as a great lion : who shall
Job 4. 11 and the stout lion's whelps are scattered
Joel 1. 6 and he hath the cheek teeth of a great l.
Nah. 2. 11 where..the old lion, walked..and none

2.*An old lion,* לַיִשׁ *layish.*

Job 4. 11 The old lion perisheth for lack of prey, and
Isa 30. 6 from whence (come) the young and old l.

LION, young —

1.*A lion,* אֲרִי, אַרְיֵה *ari, aryeh.*

Num 23. 24 lift up himself as a young lion : he shall

2.*A bold lion,* לָבִיא *labi.*

Isa. 30. 6 from whence come the young and old lion

3.*A young lion, whelp,* כְּפִיר *kephir.*

Job 4. 10 and the teeth of the young lions, are bro.
38. 39 or fill the appetite of the young lions
Psa. 17. 12 and as it were a young lion lurking in se.
34. 10 The young lions do lack, and suffer hunger
58. 6 break out the..teeth of the young lions
91. 13 the young lion and the dragon shalt thou
104. 21 The young lions roar after their prey, and
Isa. 5. 29 they shall roar like young lions ; yea, they
11. 6 the calf and the young lion and the fatl.
31. 4 the young lion roaring on his prey, when
Jer. 2. 15 The young lions roared upon him, (and) y.
Eze. 19. 2 she nourished her whelps among young l.
19. 3. 6 became a young lion, and it learned to
19. 5 she took another .. made him a young l.
32. 2 Thou art like a young lion of the nations
38. 13 Sheba..with all the young lions thereof
41. 19 the face of a young lion toward the palm
Hos. 5. 14 and as a young lion to the house of Judah
Amos 3. 4 will a young lion cry out of his den if he
Mic. 5. 8 as a young lion among the flocks of sheep
Nah. 2. 11 and the feeding place of the young lions
2. 13 and the sword shall devour thy young l.
Zech 11. 3 a voice of the roaring of young lions ; for

LIONESS —

1.*A bold lioness,* לְבִיָּא *lebiya.*

Eze. 19. 2 say, What (is) thy mother? A lioness : she

2. *Bold lionesses,* לְבָאוֹת *lebaoth.*

Nah. 2. 12 strangled for his lionesses, and filled his

LION LIKE men —

Lion of God, אֲרִאֵל, אֲרִיאֵל *ariel.*

2 Sa. 23. 20 Benaiah..slew two lion like men of Moab
1 Ch. 11. 22 Benaiah..slew two lion like men of Moab

LIP —

1.*Lip, ledge,* שָׂפָה *saphah.*

Exod. 6. 12 hear me, who (am) of uncircumcised lips?
6. 30 I (am) of uncircumcised lips, and how
Lev. 5. 4 pronouncing with (his) lips to do evil, or
Num 30. 6 vowed, or uttered ought out of her lips
30. 8 that which she uttered with her lips, w
30. 12 whatsoever proceeded out of her lips co.
Deut 23. 23 That which is gone out of thy lips thou
1 Sa. 1. 13 only her lips moved, but her voice was not
2 Ki. 19. 28 I will put..my bridle in thy lips, and I
Job 2. 10 In all this did not Job sin with his lips
8. 21 Till he fill..thy lips with rejoicing
11. 5 oh that God would..open his lips against
13. 6 and hearken to the pleadings of my lips
15. 6 yea, thine own lips testify against thee
16. 5 the moving of my lips should asswage
23. 12 back from the commandment of his lips
27. 4 My lips shall not speak wickedness, nor
32. 20 I will speak..I will open my lips and
33. 3 and my lips shall utter knowledge clearly
Psa. 12. 2 flattering lips..with a double heart, do they
12. 3 LORD shall cut off all flattering lips..the
12. 4 our lips (are) our own : who (is) lord over
16. 4 nor take up their names into my lips
17. 1 prayer, (that goeth) not out of feigned lips
17. 4 by the word of thy lips I have kept (me
21. 2 hast not withholden the request of his lips
22. 7 they shoot out the lip, they shake the h.
31. 18 Let the lying lips be put to silence ; which
34. 13 Keep thy tongue from evil, and thy lips
40. 9 I have not refrained my lips, O LORD, thou
45. 2 grace is poured into thy lips : therefore G.
51. 15 O LORD, open thou my lips ; and my mo.
59. 7 swords (are) in their lips : for who..doth
59. 12 the words of their lips let them even be
63. 3 Because thy loving kindness..my lips sh.
63. 5 my mouth shall praise..with joyful lips
66. 14 Which my lips have uttered, and my mo.
71. 23 My lips shall greatly rejoice when I sing
89. 34 nor alter the thing..gone out of my lips
106. 33 that he spake unadvisedly with his lips
119. 13 With my lips have I declared all the ju.
119. 171 My lips shall utter praise, when thou
120. 2 Deliver my soul, O LORD, from lying lips
140. 3 adders' poison (is) under their lips. Selah
140. 9 let the mischief of their own lips cover
141. 3 Set a watch..keep the door of my lips
Prov 4. 24 froward..and perverse lips put far from
5. 2 and (that) thy lips may keep knowledge
5. 3 For the lips of a strange woman drop (as)
7. 21 with the flattering of her lips she forced
8. 6 the opening of my lips (shall be) right th.
8. 7 wickedness (is) an abomination to my lips
10. 13 In the lips of him that hath understand.
10. 18 He that hideth hatred (with) lying lips
10. 19 sin : but he that refraineth his lips (is) wise
10. 21 The lips of the righteous feed many : but
10. 32 The lips of the righteous know what is ac.
12. 13 The wicked is snared by..(his) lips : but
12. 19 The lip of truth shall be established for
12. 22 Lying lips (are) abomination to the LORD
13. 3 he that openeth wide his lips shall have
14. 3 but the lips of the wise shall preserve them
14. 7 when thou perceivest not..the lips of k.
14. 23 but the talk of the lips..only to penury
15. 7 The lips of the wise disperse knowledge
16. 10 A divine sentence (is) in the lips of the
16. 13 Righteous lips (are) the delight of kings
16. 21 the sweetness of the lips increaseth lear.
16. 23 heart of the wise..addeth learning to..l.
16. 27 and in his lips (there is) as a burning fire
16. 30 moving his lips he bringeth evil to pass
17. 4 A wicked doer giveth heed to false lips
17. 7 becometh not a fool ; much less do lying l.
17. 28 he that shutteth his lips (is esteemed) a
18. 6 A fool's lips enter into contention, and his
18. 7 A fool's mouth..and his lips (are) the sn.
18. 20 with the increase of his lips shall he be
19. 1 than (he that is) perverse in his lips, and
20. 15 lips of knowledge (are) a precious jewel
20. 19 not with him that flattereth with his lips
22. 11 (for) the grace of his lips the king (shall be)
22. 18 For..they shall withal be fitted in thy lips
23. 16 my reins shall rejoice when thy lips speak
24. 2 their heart..and their lips talk of misch.
24. 26 (Every man) shall kiss (his) lips that giveth
24. 28 cause ; and deceive (not) with thy lips
26. 23 Burning lips and a wicked heart (are like)
26. 24 He that hateth dissembleth with his lips
27. 2 another man praise..not thine own lips
Eccl. 10. 12 but the lips of a fool will swallow up him.
Song 4. 3 Thy lips (are) like a thread of scarlet, and
4. 11 Thy lips, O (my) spouse, drop (as) the hon.
5. 13 his lips (like) lilies, dropping sweet smell.
7. 9 causing the lips of those that are asleep
Isa. 6. 5 I (am) a man of unclean lips, and I dwell
6. 5 in the midst of a people of unclean lips
6. 7 Lo, this hath touched thy lips ; and thine
11. 4 with the breath of his lips shall he slay
28. 11 with stammering lips..will he speak to
29. 13 this people..with their lips do honour me
30. 27 his lips are full of indignation, and his to.
37. 29 therefore will I put..my bridle in thy lips
57. 19 I create the fruit of the lips ; Peace, peace
59. 3 your lips have spoken lies, your tongue

Jer. 17. 16 that which came out of my lips was (right)
Lam. 3. 62 The lips of those that rose up against me
Eze. 36. 3 ye are taken up in the lips of talkers, and
Dan. 10. 16 (one) like..sons of men touched my lips
Hos. 14. 2 so will we render the calves of our lips
Hab. 3. 16 When I heard..my lips quivered at the
Mal. 2. 6 and iniquity was not found in his lips: he
2. 7 For the priest's lips should keep knowle.

2. *Upper lip,* שָׂפָם *sapham.*
Eze. 24. 17 cover not (thy) lips, and eat not the bread
24. 22 ye shall not cover (your) lips, nor eat the
Mic. 3. 7 yea, they shall all cover their lips: for

3. *A lip,* χεῖλος *cheilos.*
Matt.15. 8 people..honoureth me with (their) lips
Mark 7. 6 people honoureth me with (their) lips
Rom. 3. 13 the poison of asps (is) under their lips
1 Co. 14. 21 With (men of)..other lips will I speak unto
Heb. 13. 15 the fruit of (our) lips giving thanks to his
1 Pe. 3. 10 let him refrain..his lips that they speak

LIP, upper —
Upper lip, שָׂפָם *sapham.*
Lev. 13. 45 shall put a covering upon his upper lip

LIQUOR —
1. *A tear, liquid,* דֶּמַע *dema.*
Exod22. 29 Thou shalt not delay..the first..of thy l.
2. *A mixture,* מֶזֶג *mezeg.*
Song 7. 2 a round goblet, (which) wanteth not liquor
3. *Liquor,* מִשְׁרָה *mishrah.*
Num. 6. 3 neither shall he drink any liquor of grapes

LIST, to —
1. *To wish,* βούλομαι *boulomai.*
Jas. 3. 4 turned..whithersoever the governor liste.
2. *To will, wish,* θέλω *thelō.*
Matt17. 12 have done unto him whatsoever they list.
Mark 9. 13 have done unto him whatsoever they list.
John 3. 8 The wind bloweth where it listeth, and

LISTEN, to —
To hear, שָׁמַע *shamea.*
Isa. 49. 1 Listen, O isles, unto me; and hearken, ye

LITTER —
Litter, covered coach, צָב *tsab.*
Isa. 66. 20 upon horses, and in chariots, and in litters

LITTLE, (for a, farther, one, time) —
1. *Small, little, young,* זְעֵיר *zeer.*
Job 36. 2 Suffer me a little, and I will show thee that
Isa. 28. 10, 13 here a little, (and) there a little
Dan. 7. 8 came up among them another little horn

2. *A little, few,* מְעַט *meat.*
Gen. 18. 4 Let a little water, I pray you, be fetched
24. 17 Let me, I pray thee, drink a little water
24. 43 Give me, I pray thee, a little water of thy
30. 30 For (it was) little which thou hadst before
43. 2 their father said, Go..buy us a little food
43. 11 a present, a little balm and a little honey
44. 25 father said..Go again, buy us a little food
Exod23. 30 By little and little I will drive them out
Deut. 7. 22 God will put out those..by little and little
28. 38 shalt gather..little in; for the locust shall
Josh.22. 17 (Is) the iniquity of Peor too little for us
Judg 4. 19 Give me, I pray thee, a little water to dr.
Ruth 2. 7 until now, that she tarried a little in the
1 Sa. 14. 29 enlightened, because I tasted a little of
14. 43 I did but taste a little honey with the end
2 Sa. 12. 8 and if (that had been) too little, I would
16. 1 And when David was a little past the top
19. 36 Thy servant will go a little way over Jor.
1 Ki.17. 10 Fetch me, I pray thee, a little water in a
17. 12 I have not a cake, but..a little oil in a c.
2 Ki.10. 18 Ahab served Baal a little..Jehu shall serve
Ezra 9. 8 And now for a little space grace hath been
9. 8 and give us a little reviving in our bond.
Job 10. 20 let me alone, that I may take comfort a li.
Psa. 2. 12 when his wrath is kindled but a little
8. 5 thou hast made him a little lower than the
37. 16 A little that a righteous man hath (is) b
Prov. 6. 10 a little sleep, a little slumber, a little fo.
10. 20 the heart of the wicked (is) little worth
15. 16 Better (is) little with the fear of the LORD
16. 8 Better (is) a little with righteousness than
24. 33 a little sleep, a little slumber, a little fol.
Eccl. 5. 12 (is) sweet, whether he eat little or much
10. 1 a little folly him that is in reputation for
Song 3. 4 but a little that I passed from them, but
Isa. 10. 25 a very little while, and the indignation
Jer. 51. 33 yet a little while, and the time of her har.
Eze. 11. 16 yet will I be to them as a little sanctuary
16. 47 but, as (if that were) a very little (thing)
Dan. 11. 34 they shall be holpen with a little help: but
Hos. 1. 4 yet a little..and I will avenge the blood
8. 10 they shall sorrow a little for the burden
Hag. 1. 6 Ye have sown much, and bring in little
1. 9 looked for much, and, lo, (it came) to little
Zech. 1. 15 for I was but a little displeased and they
3. *Little, small,* מִצְּעִירָה (A.V. translates צעירה) [*tsair*].
Dan. 8. 9 out of one of them came forth a little horn
4. *Little, small,* צָעִיר *tsair.*
Psa. 68. 27 There (is) little Benjamin (with) their ruler
Mic. 5. 2 (though) thou be little among the thous.
5. *Little, small,* קָטָן *qatan.*
2 Sa. 12. 3 the poor (man) had nothing, save one little
1 Ki.11. 17 Hadad fled..Hadad (being) yet a little c.
17. 13 make me thereof a little cake first, and
1 Ki.18. 44 there ariseth a little cloud out of the sea
2 Ki. 2. 23 there came forth little children out of the
4. 10 Let us make a little chamber, I pray thee
5. 2 had brought away captive..a little maid
Prov 30. 24 There be four things..little upon the ea.
Eccl. 9. 14 a little city, and few men within it; and
Song 2. 15 Take us..the little foxes, that spoil the
8. 8 We have a little sister, and she hath no

6. *Little, small,* קָטֹן *qaton.*
1 Sa. 2. 19 his mother made him a little coat, and b.
15. 17 When thou (wast) little in thine own sight
20. 35 Jonathan went out..and a little lad with
1 Ki. 3. 7 and..a little child: I know not..to go out
8. 64 the brasen altar..(was) too little to rece.
12. 10 My little (finger) shall be thicker than my
2 Ki. 5. 14 his flesh came again like..a little child
2 Ch.10. 10 My little (finger) shall be thicker than my
Isa. 11. 6 together; and a little child shall lead them
60. 22 A little one shall become a thousand, and
Amos 6. 11 he will smite..the little house with clefts
7. *A little way,* כִּבְרָה *kibrah.*
Gen. 35. 16 there was but a little way to come to Ep.
48. 7 yet..but a little way to come unto Ephr.
2 Ki. 5. 19 Go..So he departed from him a little way
8. *A little thing, sound,* שֶׁמֶץ *shemets.*
Job 4. 12 a thing..mine ear received a little thereof
26. 14 but how little a portion is heard of him?
9. *Outpouring,* שֶׁצֶף *shetseph.*
Isa. 54. 8 In a little wrath I hid my face from thee
10. *Short, small,* βραχύ τι *brachu ti.*
John 6. 7 that every one of them may take a little
Acts 27. 28 when they had gone a little further, they
Heb. 2. 7 Thou madest him a little lower than the
2. 9 who was made a little lower than the an.
11. *In a measure,* μετρίως *metriōs.*
Acts 20. 12 man alive, and were not a little comforted
12. *Small, little, short,* μικρόν *mikron.*
Matt26. 39 went a little farther, and fell on his face
Mark14. 35 he went forward a little, and fell on the
14. 70 a little after, they that stood by said again
2 Co. 11. 1 ye could bear with me a little in (my) fo.
11. 16 receive me, that I may boast myself a lit.
Heb.10. 37 yet a little while, and he that shall come
13. *Small, little,* μικρός *mikros.*
Matt10. 42 unto one of these little ones a cup of cold
18. 6 whoso shall offend one of these little ones
18. 10 that ye despise not one of these little ones
18. 14 that one of these little ones should perish
Mark 9. 42 shall offend one of (these) little ones that
Luke12. 32 Fear not, little flock; for it is your Father's
17. 2 he should offend one of these little ones
19. 3 could not..because he was little of stature
John 7. 33 Yet a little while am I with you, and (then)
12. 35 Yet a little while is the light with you
1 Co. 5. 6 Know ye not that a little leaven leaveneth
Gal. 5. 9 A little leaven leaveneth the whole lump
Jas. 3. 5 Even so the tongue is a little member, and
Rev. 3. 8 thou hast a little strength and hast kept
6. 11 they should rest yet for a [little] season
20. 3 after that he must be loosed a little sea.
14. *Little,* ὀλίγος *oligos, -ov.*
Mark 1. 19 when he had gone a little further thence
Luke 5. 3 he would thrust out a little from the land
7. 47 but to whom little is forgiven..loveth li.
2 Co. 8. 15 and he that (had gathered) little had no
1 Ti. 4. 8 bodily exercise profiteth little; but godl.
5. 23 use a little wine for thy stomach's sake
Jas. 3. 5 how great a matter [a little] fire kindleth!
4. 14 a vapour, that appeareth for a little time
15. *To happen, occur,* τυγχάνω *tugchanō.*
Acts 28. 2 the barbarous people showed us no little
[*See also* Book, chamber, child, children, daughter, faith, fish, flock, river, ship, while].

LITTLE, as it were for a —
As a little, כִּמְעַט *ki-meat.*
Isa. 26. 20 hide thyself as it were for a little moment

LITTLE, to be, gather, or seem —
1. *To be or become few or little,* מָעַט *maat.*
Exod12. 4 if the household be too little for the lamb
Neh. 9. 32 let not all the trouble seem little before
2. *To make few or little,* מָעַט *maat,* 5.
Exod16. 18 he that gathered little had no lack: they

LITTLE, a very —
Least, smallest, ἐλάχιστος *elachistos.*
Luke19. 17 thou hast been faithful in a very little

LITTLE hill —
A height or hill, גִּבְעָה *gibah.*
Psa. 65. 12 and the little hills rejoice on every side
72. 3 people, and the little hills, by righteousn.
114. 4, 6 skipped like rams..little hills, like la.

LITTLE one —
1. *Little, small,* מִצְעָר *mitsar.*
Gen. 19. 20 a little one..(is) it not a little one?
2. *A suckling,* עֲוִיל *avil.*
Job 21. 11 They send forth their little ones like a fl.
3. *A suckling,* עוֹלֵל *olal.*
Psa.137. 9 that taketh and dasheth thy little ones
4. *Little, small,* צָעִיר [V.L. צעור] *tsair.*
Jer. 14. 3 their nobles have sent their little ones to
48. 4 her little ones have caused a cry to be h.
5. *To be little or small,* צָעַר *tsaar.*
Zech 13. 7 will turn mine hand upon the little ones
6. *Little, small,* קָטָן *qatan.*
Gen. 44. 20 a child of his old age, a little one; and his
7. *Infant, heap, mass,* טַף *taph.*
Gen. 34. 29 all their little ones..took they captive, and
43. 8 that we may live..also our little ones
45. 19 take you wagons..for your little ones, and
46. 5 sons of Israel carried..their little ones
47. 24 four parts shall be..for your little ones
50. 8 little ones..they left in the land of Goshen
50. 21 I will nourish you, and your little ones
Exod10. 10 as I will let you go, and your little ones
10. 24 Go ye..let your little ones also go with you
Num14. 31 your little ones, which ye said should be
31. 9 took (all) the women..and their little ones
31. 17 kill every male among the little ones, and
32. 16 We will build..cities for our little ones
32. 17 our little ones shall dwell in the fenced
32. 24 Build you cities for your little ones, and
32. 26 Our little ones..shall be there in the
Deut. 1. 39 your little ones, which ye said should be
2. 34 we..destroyed..the little ones, of every
3. 19 your little ones..shall abide in your cities
20. 14 the little ones..shalt thou take unto thy.
29. 11 Your little ones, your wives, and thy str.
Josh. 1. 14 your little ones..shall remain in the land
8. 35 with the women, and the little ones, and
Judg18. 21 So they..put the little ones..before them
2 Sa. 15. 22 all the little ones that (were) with him
2 Ch.20. 13 Judah stood before..with their little ones
31. 18 to the genealogy of all their little ones
Ezra. 8. 21 to seek..a right way..for our little ones
Esth. 8. 11 to cause to perish..little ones and women

LITTLE owl —
A little owl, pelican, כּוֹס *kos.*
Lev. 11. 17 the little owl, and the cormorant, and the
Deut14. 16 The little owl, and the great owl, and the

LITTLE thing, very —
Lean, thin, small, dwarfish, דַּק *daq.*
Isa 40. 15 taketh up the isles as a very little thing

LITTLE while or space —
1. *Little, small,* מְעַט *meat.*
Job 24. 24 They are exalted for a little while, but
Psa. 37. 10 For yet a little while, and the wicked (sh.)
Hag. 2. 6 a little while, and I will shake the heav.
2. *Little, small,* מִצְעָר *mitsar.*
Isa. 63. 18 people..have possessed (it) but a little wh.
3. *Short, small,* βραχύς *brachus,* βραχύ *brachu.*
Luke22. 58 after a little while, another saw him, and
Acts 5. 34 and..to put the apostles forth a little space
4. *Small, little,* μικρόν *mikron.*
John13. 33 Little children, yet a little while I am with
14. 19 Yet a little while, and the world seeth me
16. 16, 17, 19 A little while..again, a little while
16. 18 What is this that he saith, A little while?

LIVE coal —
Burning coal, hot stone, רִצְפָּה *ritspah.*
Isa. 6. 6 having a live coal in his hand. he had ta.

LIVE, to —
1. *Living, alive,* חַי *chai.*
Gen. 9. 3 Every moving thing that liveth shall be m.
25. 6 while he yet lived, eastward, unto the east
45. 3 I (am) Joseph: doth my father yet live?
Lev. 25. 35 or a sojourner; that he may live with thee
25. 36 God; that thy brother may live with thee
Num14. 21 I live, all the earth shall be filled with the
14. 28 I live, saith the LORD, as ye have spoken
Deut. 4. 10 to fear me all the days that they shall live
12. 1 do..all the days that ye live upon the ea.
30. 6 and with all thy soul, that thou mayest l.
31. 13 as long as ye live in the land whither ye
32. 40 I lift up my hand..and say, I live for ever
Judg 8. 19 LORD liveth, if ye had saved them alive, I
Ruth 3. 13 LORD liveth: lie down till the morning
1 Sa. 1. 26 thy soul liveth, my lord, I (am) the woman
14. 39 LORD liveth, which saveth Israel, though
14. 45 LORD liveth, there shall not one hair of
17. 55 (As) thy soul liveth, O king, I cannot tell
19. 6 (As) the LORD liveth, he shall not be slain
20. 3 LORD liveth, and..thy soul liveth..but a
20. 14 thou shalt not only while yet I live show
20. 21 peace to thee, and no hurt, (as) the LORD l.
25. 6 And thus shall ye say to him that liveth (i.
25. 26 LORD liveth, and..thy soul liveth, seeing
25. 34 LORD God of Israel liveth, which hath k.
26. 10 LORD liveth, the LORD shall smite him
26. 16 LORD liveth, ye (are) worthy to die, beca.
28. 10 LORD liveth, there shall no punishment
29. 6 LORD liveth, thou hast been upright, and
2 Sa. 2. 27 God liveth, unless thou hadst spoken, sure.
4. 9 LORD liveth, who hath redeemed my soul
11. 11 thou livest, and..thy soul liveth, I will
12. 5 LORD liveth, the man that hath done this
12. 22 be gracious to me, that the child may live?
14. 11 LORD liveth, there shall not one hair of thy
14. 19 thy soul liveth, my lord the king, none can
15. 21 LORD liveth, and..my lord the king liveth
19. 6 if Absalom had lived, and all we had died
19. 34 How long have I to live, that I should go
22. 47 LORD liveth; and blessed (be) my rock; and
Ki. 1. 29 LORD liveth, that hath redeemed my soul
2. 24 LORD liveth, which hath established me
3. 23 The one saith, This (is) my son that liveth
8. 40 may fear thee all the days that they live

1 Ki. 12. 6 Solomon his father while he yet lived, and
17. 1 LORD God of Israel liveth, before whom
17. 12 LORD thy God liveth, I have not a cake
17. 23 Elijah took..and..said, See, thy son liveth
18. 10 LORD thy God liveth, there is no nation
18. 15 LORD of hosts liveth, before whom I stand
22. 14 LORD liveth, what the LORD saith unto me
2 Ki. 2. 2, 4, 6 LORD liveth, and (as) thy soul liveth
3. 14 LORD of hosts liveth, before whom I stand
4. 30 LORD liveth, and (as) thy soul liveth, I
5. 16 LORD liveth, before whom I stand, I will
5. 20 LORD liveth, I will run after him, and
2 Ch. 6. 31 so long as they live in the land which
10. 6 Solomon his father while he yet lived
18. 13 LORD liveth, even what my God saith, that
Job 19. 25 For I know..my redeemer liveth, and..he
27. 2 God liveth, (who) hath taken away my j.
Psa. 18. 46 LORD liveth; and blessed (be) my rock
49. 18 Though while he lived he blessed his soul
63. 4 Thus will I bless thee while I live: I will
104. 33 I will sing unto the LORD as long as I live
146. 2 While I live will I praise the LORD; I will
Eccl. 9. 3 madness (is) in their heart while they live
9. 9 Live joyfully with the wife whom thou lo.
Isa. 49. 18 live, saith the LORD, thou shalt surely cl.
Jer. 4. 2 LORD liveth, in truth, in judgment, and in
5. 2 The LORD liveth; surely they swear falsely
12. 16 The LORD liveth; as they taught my peo.
16. 14, 15 The LORD liveth, that brought up the
22. 24 I live, saith the LORD, though Coniah the
23. 7, 8 The LORD liveth, which brought up the
38. 16 LORD liveth, that made us this soul, I will
44. 26 be named..saying, The Lord GOD liveth
46. 18 I live, saith the king, whose name (is) The
Eze. 5. 11 (As) I live, saith the Lord GOD
[So in 14. 16, 18, 20; 16. 48; 17. 16, 19; 18. 3; 20. 3, 31; 33. 11; 34. 8; 35. 6, 11.]
Eze. 33. 27 I live, surely they that (are) in the wastes
47. 9 And..every thing that liveth, which mo.
Dan. 4. 34 I praised and honoured him that liveth
12. 7 and sware by him that liveth for ever, that
Hos. 4. 15 neither go ye..nor swear, The LORD liveth
Amos 8. 14 They that swear..say, Thy God, O Dan, l.
8. 14 and, The manner of Beer-sheba liveth; even
Jon. 4. 3, 8 for..better for me to die than to live
Zeph. 2. 9 I live, saith the LORD of hosts, the God

2. *To live, be alive,* חָיָה *chayah.*

Gen. 5. 3 Adam lived an hundred and thirty years
5. 6 Seth lived an hundred and five years, and
5. 7 Seth lived after he begat Enos eight hu.
5. 9 Enos lived ninety years, and begat Cainan
5. 10 Enos lived after he begat Cainan eight h.
5. 12 Cainan lived seventy years, and begat M.
5. 13 Cainan lived after he begat Mahalaleel e.
5. 15 Mahalaleel lived sixty and five years, and
5. 16 Mahalaleel lived after he begat Jared eight
5. 18 Jared lived an hundred sixty and two ye.
5. 19 Jared lived after he begat Enoch eight h.
5. 21 Enoch lived sixty and five years, and be.
5. 25 Methuselah lived an hundred eight and
5. 26 Methuselah lived after he begat Lamech
5. 28 Lamech lived an hundred eighty and two
5. 30 Lamech lived after he begat Noah five h.
9. 28 Noah lived after the flood three hundred
11. 11 Shem lived after he begat Arphaxad five
11. 13 Arphaxad lived after he begat Salah four
11. 15 Salah lived after he begat Eber four hun.
11. 16 Eber lived four and thirty years, and be.
11. 17 Eber lived after he begat Peleg four hun.
11. 18 And Peleg lived thirty years, and begat R.
11. 19 Peleg lived after he begat Reu two hund.
11. 20 Reu lived two and thirty years, and begat
11. 21 Reu lived after he begat Serug two hund.
11. 22 Serug lived thirty years, and begat Nahor
11. 23 Serug lived after he begat Nahor two hu.
11. 24 Nahor lived nine and twenty years, and
11. 25 Nahor lived after he begat Terah an hun.
11. 26 Terah lived seventy years, and begat Ab
12. 13 sister..and my soul shall live because of
17. 18 O that Ishmael might live before thee!
19. 20 Oh, let me escape..and my soul shall live
20. 7 shall pray for thee, and thou shalt live
27. 40 by thy sword shalt thou live, and shalt
31. 32 whomsoever thou findest..let him not live
42. 2 get you down..that we may live, and not
42. 18 Joseph said..This do, and live..I fear God
43. 8 that we may live, and not die, both we
47. 19 give (us) seed, that we may live, and not
47. 28 Jacob lived in the land of Egypt seventeen
50. 22 and Joseph lived an hundred and ten ye.
Exod 19. 13 whether..beast or man, it shall not live
Num. 4. 19 that they may live, and not die, when they
14. 38 Joshua the son of Nun, and Caleb..lived
24. 23 Alas, who shall live when God doeth this?
Deut 4. 1 that ye may live, and go in and possess
4. 33 Did (ever) people hear the voice..and live?
5. 26 who..hath heard the voice..and lived?
5. 33 Ye shall walk..that ye may live, and (that)
8. 1 shall ye observe to do, that ye may live
8. 3 man doth not live by bread only, but by
8. 3 by every (word)..of the LORD doth man l.
16. 20 that thou mayest live, and inherit the land
30. 16 love..that thou mayest live and multiply
30. 19 that both thou and thy seed may live
33. 6 Let Reuben live, and not die; and let (not)
Josh. 6. 17 only Rahab the harlot shall live, she and
9. 21 Let them live; but let them be hewers of
2 Sa. 1. 10 I was sure that he could not live after he
1 Ki. 1. 31 Let my lord king David live for ever
20. 32 Benhadad saith, I pray thee, let me live
2 Ki. 4. 7 live thou and thy children of the rest
2 Ki. 7. 4 if they save us alive, we shall live; and
10. 19 whosoever shall be wanting..shall not l.
14. 17 Amaziah..lived after the death of Jeho.
18. 32 that ye may live, and not die: and hear.
20. 1 in order; for thou shalt die, and not live
2 Ch. 25. 25 Amaziah..lived after the death of Joash
Neh. 2. 3 Let the king live for ever: why should
5. 2 we take up corn..that we may eat, and l.
9. 29 which if a man do, he shall live in them
Esth. 4. 11 out the golden sceptre, that he may live
Job 7. 16 I loathe (it); I would not live alway: let
14. 14 If a man die, shall he live (again)? All the
21. 7 Wherefore do the wicked live, become old
42. 16 After this lived Job an hundred and forty
Psa. 22. 26 seek him: your heart shall live for ever
49. 9 he should still live for ever, (and) not see
69. 32 and your heart shall live that seek God
72. 15 he shall live, and to him shall be given
89. 48 What man..liveth, and shall not see de.
118. 17 I shall not die, but live, and declare the
119. 17 Deal bountifully..(that) I may live, and
119. 77 Let thy tender mercies..that I may live
119. 116 Uphold..unto thy word, that I may live
119. 144 give me understanding, and I shall live
119. 175 Let my soul live, and it shall praise thee
Prov. 4. 4 said..keep my commandments, and live
7. 2 Keep my commandments, and live; and
9. 6 Forsake the foolish, and live; and go in
15. 27 but he that hateth gifts shall live
Eccl. 6. 3 If a man..live many years, so that the d.
6. 6 Yea, though he live a thousand years
11. 8 if a man live many years, (and) rejoice
Isa. 26. 14 (They are) dead, they shall not live; (they)
26. 19 Thy dead (men) shall live, (together with)
38. 1 in order: for thou shalt die, and not live
38. 16 by these (things men) live, and in all these
55. 3 hear, and your soul shall live; and I
Jer. 21. 9 he shall live, and his life shall be unto
27. 12 and serve him and his people, and live
27. 17 serve the king of Babylon, and live: wh.
35. 7 ye may live many days in the land where
38. 2 he that goeth..to the Chaldeans shall live
38. 17 thy soul shall live, and this city shall
38. 17 go..and thou shalt live, and thine house
38. 20 be well unto thee, and thy soul shall live
Lam. 4. 20 Under his shadow we shall live among
Eze. 3. 21 he shall surely live, because he is warned
13. 19 save the souls alive that should not live
16. 6, 6 I said unto thee..in thy blood, Live
18. 9 he shall surely live, saith the Lord GOD
18. 13 he shall not live: he
18. 17 he shall not die..he shall surely live
18. 19 and hath done them, he shall surely live
18. 21 But..he shall surely live, he shall not die
18. 22 in his righteousness..done he shall live
18. 23 he should return from his ways, and live
18. 28 he shall surely live, he shall not die
18. 32 no pleasure..wherefore turn..and live ye
20. 25 judgments whereby they should not live
33. 10 pine away in them, how should we..live?
33. 11 the wicked turn from his way and live
33. 12 neither shall the righteous be able to live
33. 13 When I shall say..he shall surely live; if
33. 15 walk..he shall surely live, he shall not die
33. 16 he hath done that..he shall surely live
33. 19 if the wicked turn..he shall live thereby
37. 3 Son of man, can these bones live? And I
37. 5 I will cause breath..and ye shall live
37. 6 put breath in you, and ye shall live; and
37. 9 breathe upon these slain..they may live
37. 10 the breath came into them, and they lived
37. 14 put my Spirit in you, and ye shall live
47. 9 whithersoever the rivers..come, shall live
Hos. 6. 2 he will raise us up, and we shall live in
Amos 5. 4 the LORD..Seek ye me, and ye shall live
5. 6 Seek the LORD, and ye shall live; lest he
5. 14 Seek good, and not evil, that ye may live
Hab. 2. 4 but the just shall live by his faith
Zech. 1. 5 and the prophets, do they live for ever?
10. 9 they shall live with their children, and
13. 3 Thou shalt not live; for thou speakest lies

3. *To live,* חָיָא, חָיָה *chayah, chaya.*

Dan. 2. 4 O king, live for ever: tell thy servants the
3. 9 They spake and said..O king, live for e.
5. 10 O king, live for ever: let not thy thoughts
6. 6 said thus..king Darius, live for ever
6. 21 Then said Daniel. O king, live for ever

4. *To live,* חַי *chayai.*

Gen. 3. 22 take also of the tree..and live for ever
5. 5 all the days that Adam lived were nine
11. 12 Arphaxad lived five and thirty years, and
11. 14 Salah lived thirty years, and begat Eber
25. 7 the years of Abraham's life which he lived
Exod. 1. 16 if it (be) a daughter, then she shall live
33. 20 for there shall no man see me, and live
Lev. 18. 5 which if a man do, he shall live in them
Num 21. 8 when he looketh upon it, shall live
21. 9 he beheld the serpent of brass, he lived
Deut. 4. 42 fleeing unto one of these cities he might l.
5. 24 that God doth talk with man, and he liv.
19. 4 which shall flee thither, that he may live
19. 5 shall flee unto one of those cities, and live
1 Sa. 20. 31 as long as the son of Jesse liveth upon
Jer. 38. 2 shall have his life for a prey, and shall live
Eze. 18. 13 hath taken increase: shall he then live?
18. 24 that the wicked (man) doeth, shall he live?
20. 11, 13, 21 which (if) a man do, he shall even l.
47. 9 every thing shall live whither the river

5. *To turn, conduct self,* ἀναστρέφομαι *anastrephomai*

Heb. 13. 18 trust..in all things willing to live honestly

2 Pe. 2. 18 clean escaped from them who live in error

6. *To live,* βιόω *bioō.*

1 Pe. 4. 2 That he no longer should live the rest of

7. *To eat, consume, devour,* ἐσθίω *esthiō.*

1 Co. 9. 13 they which minister about holy things l.

8. *To live, have life,* ζάω *zaō.*

Matt. 4. 4 Man shall not live by bread alone, but by
9. 18 lay thy hand upon her, and she shall live
Mark 5. 23 lay thy hands on her..and she shall live
Luke 2. 36 she was of a great age, and had lived with
4. 4 man shall not live by bread alone, but by
10. 28 answered right: this do, and thou shalt l.
20. 38 a God..of the living: for all live unto him
John 4. 50 Go thy way; thy son liveth. And the man
4. 51 servants..told (him), saying, Thy son liveth
4. 53 which Jesus said unto him Thy son liveth
5. 25 shall hear..and they that hear shall live
6. 51 If any man eat of this bread, he shall live
6. 57 Father hath sent me, and I live by the F.
6. 57 he that eateth me..he shall live by me
6. 58 he that eateth of this bread shall live for
11. 25 though he were dead, yet shall he live
11. 26 whosoever liveth and believeth in me sh.
14. 19 ye see me: because I live, ye shall live
Acts 17. 28 For in him we live, and move, and have
22. 22 Away..for it is not fit that he should live
25. 24 crying that he ought not to live any longer
26. 5 after the most straitest sect..I lived a P
28. 4 whom..yet vengeance suffereth not to l.
Rom. 1. 17 it is written, The just shall live by faith
6. 2 How shall we..live any longer therein?
6. 10 but in that he liveth, he liveth unto God
7. 1 dominion over a man as long as he liveth
7. 2 bound..to (her) husband so long as he liv.
7. 3 if, while (her) husband liveth, she be ma.
8. 12 not to the flesh, to live after the flesh
8. 13 For if ye live after the flesh, ye shall die
8. 13 but if ye..mortify the deeds..ye shall l.
10. 5 man which doeth those things shall live
14. 7 none of us liveth to himself, and no man
14. 8 whether we live, we live unto the Lord
14. 8 whether we live therefore, or die, we are
14. 11 I live, saith the Lord, every knee shall b.
1 Co. 7. 39 by the law as long as her husband liveth
9. 14 they which preach the Gospel should live
2 Co. 4. 11 we which live are alway delivered unto
5. 15 they which live should not henceforth l.
6. 9 as dying, and, behold, we live; as chast.
13. 4 crucified..yet he liveth by the power of
13. 4 but we shall live with him by the power
Gal. 2. 14 If thou, being a Jew, livest after the ma.
2. 19 I..am dead to the law, that I might live
2. 20 yet not I, but Christ liveth in me
2. 20 life which I now live in the flesh I live by
3. 11 evident: for, The just shall live by faith
3. 12 The man that doeth them shall live in
5. 25 If we live in the Spirit, let us also walk
Phil. 1. 21 For to me to live (is) Christ, and to die (is)
1. 22 if I live in the flesh, this (is) the fruit of
Col. 3. 7 ye also walked sometime, when ye lived
1 Th. 3. 8 For now we live, if ye stand fast in the L.
5. 10 whether we wake or sleep, we should live
1 Ti. 5. 6 But she..in pleasure is dead while she l.
2 Ti. 3. 12 Yea, and all that will live godly in Christ
Titus 2. 12 we should live soberly, righteously, and
Heb. 7. 8 he..of whom it is witnessed that he liveth
7. 25 seeing he ever liveth to make intercession
9. 17 of no strength at all while the testator li.
10. 38 Now the just shall live by faith: but if
12. 9 much rather be in subjection..and live?
Jas. 4. 15 If the Lord will, we shall live, and do this
1 Pe. 1. 23 by the word of God, which liveth and ab
2. 24 that we, being dead to sins, should live
4. 6 but live according to God in the spirit
1 Jo. 4. 9 God sent..that we might live through him
Rev 1. 18 (I am) he that liveth, and was dead; and
3. 1 that thou hast a name that thou livest
4. 9 to him that sat on the throne, who liveth
4. 10 worship him that liveth for ever and ever
5. 14 worshipped him that liveth for ever and e.
10. 6 sware by him that liveth for ever and ever
13. 14 had the wound by a sword, and did live
15. 7 vials full of the wrath of God, who liveth
20. 4 they lived and reigned with Christ a tho

9. *To preserve life,* ζωογονέω *zōogoneō.*

Acts 7. 19 cast out..to the end they might not live

10. *To be a citizen,* πολιτεύομαι *politeuomai.*

Acts 23. 1 I have lived in all good conscience before

11. *To begin to be,* ὑπάρχω *huparchō.*

Luke 7. 25 apparelled, and live delicately, are in ki.
[*See also* Jews, peace, pleasure, ungodly.]

LIVE again, to —

To live again, ἀναζάω *anazaō.*

Rev. 20. 5 rest of the dead [lived not again] until the

LIVE deliciously, to —

To be luxuriant, στρηνιάω *strēniaō.*

Rev. 18. 7 she hath glorified herself, and lived deli.
18. 9 And the kings..lived deliciously with her

LIVE long, to —

To be long timed, long lived, εἰμὶ μακροχρόνιος.

Eph. 6. 3 and thou mayest live long on the earth

LIVE peaceably, or in peace, to —

To be peaceable, εἰρηνεύω *eirēneuō.*

Rom. 12. 18 If it be possible..live peaceably with all
2 Co. 13. 11 be of one mind, live in peace; and the G.

LIVE with, to —
To live with, συζάω *suzaō.*
Rom. 6. 8 we believe that we shall also live with him
2 Co. 7. 3 ye are in our hearts to die and live with
2 Ti. 2. 11 if we be dead with..we shall also live with

LIVE, to let, or suffer, or make to —
1. *To live, keep living or alive, revive,* חָיָה *chayah,* 3.
Exod22. 18 Thou shalt not suffer a witch to live
Josh. 9. 15 made a league with them, to let them live

2. *To cause to live, let live,* חָיָה *chayah,* 5.
Josh. 9. 20 we will even let them live, lest wrath be
Isa. 38. 16 so wilt thou recover me..make me to live

LIVE, so long as I. *See* **LONG.**
LIVE, have to, to —
Are the days of the years of my life; 2 Sam. 19. 34
LIVE, LIVELY, LIVING —
1. *Living, alive, lively,* חַי *chai.*
Gen. 1. 21 God created..every living creature that
1. 24 Let the earth bring forth the living crea.
2. 7 breathed..and man became a living soul
2. 19 whatsoever Adam called every living cre.
3. 20 because she was the mother of all living
9. 12, 15 between me and you and every living
9. 16 between God and every living creature of
Exod21. 35 they shall sell the live ox, and divide the
Lev. 11. 10 any living thing which (is) in the waters
11. 46 This (is) the law of..every living creature
14. 6 As for the living bird, he shall take it
14. 6 shall dip..the living bird in the blood
14. 7 shall let the living bird loose into the open
14. 51 he shall take..the living bird, and dip
14. 52 with the living bird, and with the cedar
14. 53 he shall let go the living bird out of the
16. 20 he shall bring the live goat
16. 21 his hands upon the head of the live goat
Num 16. 48 he stood between the dead and the living
Deut. 5. 26 hath heard the voice of the living God
Josh. 3. 10 ye shall know that the living God (is) am.
Ruth 2. 20 not left off his kindness to the living and
1 Sa. 17. 26, 36 should defy the armies of the living G?
1 Ki. 3. 22 Nay; but the living (is) my son, and the d.
3. 22 dead (is) thy son, and the living (is) my son
3. 23 thy son (is) the dead..my son (is) the liv.
3. 25 Divide the living child in two, and give
3. 26 the woman whose the living child (was)
3. 26, 27 give her the living child, and in no w.
2 Ki. 19. 4, 16 hath sent to reproach the living God
Job [12. 10 In whose hand (is) the soul of every living]
28. 13 neither is it found in the land of the liv.
28. 21 Seeing it is hid from the eyes of all living
30. 23 and (to) the house appointed for all living
33. 30 enlightened with the light of the living
Psa. 27. 13 see the goodness..in the land of the living
38. 19 But mine enemies (are) lively..they are
42. 2 My soul thirsteth..for the living God
52. 5 and root thee out of the land of the living
56. 13 that I may walk..in the light of the living
58. 9 he shall take them away..both living
69. 28 be blotted out of the book of the living
84. 2 and my flesh crieth out for the living God
116. 9 before the LORD in the land of the living
142. 5 (and) my portion in the land of the living
143. 2 for in thy sight shall no man living be just.
(*Note*: *chai* is rendered by man living.)
Eccl. 4. 2 I praised the dead..more than the living
4. 15 I considered all the living which walk
6. 8 poor, that knoweth to walk before the li.
7. 2 men; and the living will lay (it) to his he.
9. 4 to him that is joined to all the living there
9. 4 for a living dog is better than a dead lion
9. 5 the living know that they shall die: but
Song 4. 15 a well of living waters, and streams from
Isa. 4. 3 every one..written among the living in J.
8. 19 people seek unto their God? for the living
37. 4, 17 hath sent to reproach the living God
38. 11 see the LORD..in the land of the living
38. 19 The living, the living, he shall praise thee
53. 8 he was cut off out of the land of the living
Jer. 2. 13 forsaken me, the fountain of living waters
10. 10 he (is) the living God, and an everlasting
11. 19 let us cut him off from the land of the li.
17. 13 forsaken the LORD, the fountain of living
23. 36 have perverted the words of the living G.
Lam. 3. 39 Wherefore doth a living man complain, a
Eze. 26. 20 I shall set glory in the land of the living
32. 23, 24, 25, 26, 27, 32 in the land of the living
Dan. 2. 30 wisdom that I have more than any living
4. 17 that the living may know that the most
6. 20 O Daniel, servant of the living God, is thy
6. 26 he (is) the living God, and stedfast for ever
Hos. 1. 10 be said..(Ye are) the sons of the living G.
Zech. 14. 8 living waters shall go out from Jerusalem

2. *Life, lively,* חָיֶה *chayeh.*
Exod. 1. 19 they (are) lively, and are delivered ere the

3. [*In widowhood*] *of life,* חַיּוּת *chayyuth.*
2 Sa. 20. 3 So they were shut up..living in widowh.

4. *Means of life,* βίος *bios.*
Mark12. 44 did cast in all that she had..all her living
Luke 8. 43 had spent all her living upon physicians
15. 12 give..And he divided unto them (his) liv.
15. 30 which hath devoured thy living with har.
21. 4 she..hath cast in all the living that she

5. *To lead or go through,* διάγω *diagō.*
Titus 3. 3 living in malice and envy, hateful..hating

6. *To live,* ζάω *zaō.*
Matt 16. 16 Thou art the Christ, the Son of the living
22. 32 not the God of the dead, but of the living
26. 63 I adjure thee by the living God, that thou
Mark12. 27 not the God of the dead, but..of the living
Luke15. 13 wasted his substance with riotous living
20. 38 is not a God of the dead, but of the living
24. 5 Why seek ye the living among the dead?
John 4. 10 and he would have given thee living water
4. 11 whence then hast thou that living water?
6. 51 I am the living bread which came down
6. 57 As the living Father hath sent me, and I
6. 69 thou art that Christ, the Son of the living
7. 38 out of his belly shall flow rivers of living
Acts 7. 38 received the lively oracles to give unto us
14. 15 that ye should turn..unto the living God
Rom. 9. 26 they be called the children of the living G.
12. 1 ye present your bodies a living sacrifice
14. 9 might be Lord both of the dead and living
1 Co. 15. 45 The first man Adam was made a living s.
2 Co. 3. 3 written..with the Spirit of the living God
6. 16 for ye are the temple of the living God; as
Col. 2. 20 why, as though living in the world, are
1 Th. 1. 9 how ye turned..to serve the living and
1 Ti. 3. 15 which is the church of the living God, the
4. 10 because we trust in the living God, who is
6. 17 in [the living] God, who giveth us richly
Heb. 3. 12 unbelief, in departing from the living G.
9. 14 from dead works to serve the living God
10. 20 By a new and living way, which he hath
10. 31 to fall into the hands of the living God
12. 22 the city of the living God, the heavenly J.
1 Pe. 1. 3 hath begotten us again unto a lively hope
2. 4 To whom coming, (as unto) a living stone
2. 5 Ye also, as lively stones, are built up a sp.
Rev. 7. 2 angel..having the seal of the living God
7. 17 shall lead them unto [living] fountains of
16. 3 blood..and every [living] soul died in the

LIVER —
Liver, כָּבֵד *kabed.*
Exod29. 13, 22 the caul..above the liver, and the two
Lev. 3. 4, 10, 15 caul above the liver, with the kid.
4. 9 the caul above the liver, with the kidneys
7. 4 the caul..above the liver, with the kidn.
8. 16, 25 caul (above) the liver, and the two ki.
9. 10, 19 the kidneys, and the caul (above) the
Prov. 7. 23 Till a dart strike through his liver; as a
Lam. 2. 11 my liver is poured upon the earth, for the
Eze. 21. 21 the king of Babylon..looked in the liver

LIVING creature —
A living being, חַיָּה *chaiyah.*
Eze. 1. 5 Also..the likeness of four living creatures
1. 13 As for the likeness of the living creatures
1. 13 it went up and down among the living c.
1. 14 the living creatures ran and returned as
1. 15 Now as I beheld the living creatures, be.
1. 15 one wheel upon the earth by the living c.
1. 19 when the living creatures went, the whe.
1. 19 when the living creatures were lifted up
1. 20, 21 for the spirit of the living creature
1. 22 upon the heads of..living creature (was)
3. 13 also the noise of the wings of the living c.
10. 15, 20 This (is) the living creature that I saw
10. 17 for the spirit of the living creature..in

LIVING thing —
1. *Living (being),* חַי *chai.*
Gen. 6. 19, 8. 1, 8. 21; Job 12. 10; Psa. 145. 16.
2. *Living being,* חַיָּה *chaiyah.*
Gen. 1. 28, 8. 17.

LIVING substance —
Living substance, יְקוּם *yequm.*
Gen. 7. 4 every living substance that I have made
7. 23 every living substance was destroyed wh.

LIZARD —
A lizard, לְטָאָה *letaah.*
Lev. 11. 30 and the lizard, and the snail, and the m.

LO —
1. *Lo, see,* אֲרוּ *aru.*
Dan. 7. 6 After this I beheld..lo another, like a l.
2. *Lo, ha!* הָא *ha.*
Dan. 3. 25 He answered and said, Lo, I see four men
3. *Lo, he!* הֵא *he.*
Gen. 47. 23 lo..seed for you, and ye shall sow the l.
4. *Lo, see, behold,* הֵן *hen.*
Gen. 29. 7 Lo..yet high day, neither..time that the
Exod. 8. 26 lo, shall we sacrifice the abomination of
5. *Lo, see, behold,* הִנֵּה *hinneh.*
Gen. 42. 28 My money is restored; and, lo..even in
50. 5 My father made me swear, saying, Lo, I
6. *To see,* רָאָה *raah.*
1 Ch. 21. 23 lo, I give..the oxen..for burnt offerings
Eccl. 7. 29 Lo, this only have I found, that God hath
Eze. 4. 15 Lo, I have given thee cow's dung for ma.
7. *See, behold,* ἴδε *ide.*
Matt. 25. 25 and hid thy talent..lo..thou hast..thine
John 7. 26 lo, he speaketh boldly, and they say not.
16. 29 Lo, now speakest thou plainly, and speak.
8. *See, behold,* ἰδού *idou.*
Matt. 2. 9 lo, the star, which they saw in the east
3. 16 lo, the heavens were opened unto him
3. 17 lo a voice from heaven, saying, This is my
24. 23 Lo, here (is) Christ, or there; believe (it)
26. 47 lo, Judas, one of the twelve, came, and

Matt28. 7 there shall ye see him: lo, I have told
28. 20 lo, I am with you alway..unto the end
Mark10. 28 Lo, we have left all, and have followed
13. 21 [Lo,] here (is) Christ; or, [lo,] (he is) there
14. 42 let us go; lo, he that betrayeth me is at
Luke 1. 44 lo, as soon as the voice of thy salutation
2. 9 lo, the angel of the Lord came upon them
9. 39 lo, a spirit taketh him, and he suddenly
13. 16 Satan hath bound, lo, these eighteen ye.
15. 29 Lo, these many years do I serve thee, ne.
17. 21 Neither shall they say, Lo here! or, [lo]
18. 28 said, Lo, we have left all, and followed
23. 15 lo, nothing worthy of death is done unto
Acts 13. 46 ye put it from you..lo, we turn to the G.
27. 24 lo, God hath given thee all them that sail
Heb. 10. 7 said I, Lo, I come..to do thy will, O God
10. 9 Then said he, Lo, I come to do thy will
Rev. 5. 6 [lo,] in the midst of the throne and of the
6. 5 lo a black horse: and he that sat on him
6. 12 [lo,] there was a great earthquake; and
7. 9 [lo,] a great multitude, which no man
14. 1 lo, a Lamb stood on the mount Sion, and

LO AM-'MI, לֹא עַמִּי *not my people.*
A symbolic name given by Hosea to his son. B.C. 765.
Hos. 1. 9 Then said (God), Call his name L.: for
[In v. 9, 10; 2. 23 the name is translated.]

LO DE'-BAR, לוֹ דְבָר *or* לֹא *no pasture.*
A city in Manasseh beyond Jordan in Gilead, near Mahanaim. Here Mephibosheth resided with Machir the Ammonite.
2 Sa. 9. 4 house of Machir, the son of Ammiel, in L.
9. 5 of Machir, the son of Ammiel, from L.
17. 27 the son of Ammiel of L., and Barzillai

LOAD, to —(*See also* Lade.)
1. *To lay on, load,* עָמַס *amas.*
Psa. 68. 19 Blessed (be) the Lord, (who) daily loadeth
2. *To heap up, load,* σωρεύω *sōreuō.*
2 Ti. 3. 6 lead captive silly women laden with sins

LOAF —
1 *Cake,* כִּכָּר *kikkar.*
Exod29. 23 one loaf of bread, and one cake of oiled
Judg. 8. 5 Give, I pray you, loaves of bread unto
1 Sa. 10. 3 another carrying three loaves of bread
1 Ch. 16. 3 to every one a loaf of bread, and a good
2. *Bread, food,* לֶחֶם *lechem.*
Lev. 23. 17 bring..two wave loaves of two tenth de.
1 Sa. 17. 17 Take..these ten loaves, and run to the
25. 18 Abigail..took two hundred loaves, and
1 Ki. 14. 3 take with thee ten loaves, and cracknels
2 Ki. 4. 42 twenty loaves of barley, and full ears of
3. *Bread, a loaf,* ἄρτος *artos.*
Matt 14. 17 We have here but five loaves, and two fi.
14. 19 took the five loaves..and gave the loaves
15. 34 How many loaves have ye? And they said
15. 36 he took the seven loaves and the fishes, and
16. 9 neither remember the five loaves of the
16. 10 Neither the seven loaves of the four tho.
Mark 6. 38 saith..How many loaves have ye? go and
6. 41 when he had taken the five loaves and the
6. 41 and blessed, and brake the loaves, and g.
6. 44 they that did eat of the loaves were about
6. 52 For they considered not..of the loaves
8. 5 he asked them, How many loaves have ye?
8. 6 he took the seven loaves, and gave thanks
8. 14 had they..with them more than one loaf
8. 19 When I brake the five loaves among five
Luke 9. 13 have no more but five loaves and two fish.
9. 16 he took the five loaves and the two fishes
11. 5 say unto him, Friend, lend me three loaves
John 6. 9 a lad here, which hath five barley loaves
6. 11 Jesus took the loaves; and when he had
6. 13 with the fragments of the five barley loa.
6. 26 because ye did eat of the loaves, and were f.

LOAN —
Asking, request, שְׁאֵלָה *sheelah.*
1 Sa. 2. 20 give..for the loan which is lent to the L.

LOATHE, to —
1. *To tread down,* בּוּס *bus.*
Prov. 27. 7 The full soul loatheth an honeycomb: but
2. *To despise, reject,* מָאַס *maas.*
Job 7. 16 I loathe (it); I would not live alway: let
3. *To be vexed, weary,* קוּץ *quts.*
Num. 21. 5 no bread..our soul loatheth this light br.
[*See also* Lothe.]

LOATHSOME —
1. *A strange abomination,* זָרָא *zara.*
Num. 11. 20 until..it be loathsome unto you: because
2. *To be burning or loathsome,* קָלָה *qalah,* 2.
Psa. 38. 7 For my loins are filled with a loathsome

LOATHSOME, to be or become —
1. *To cause a stink, abhorrence,* בָּאַשׁ *baash,* 5.
Prov. 13. 5 a wicked (man) is loathsome, and cometh
2. *To be despised, rejected,* מָאַס *maas,* 2.
Job 7. 5 my skin is broken, and become loathsome

LOCK —
1. *A lock of door,* מַנְעוּל *manul.*
Neh. 3. 3, 6, 13, 14, 15 locks thereof, and the bars
Song 5. 5 dropped..myrrh, upon the handles of the L.
2. *A fringe or lock of hair,* צִיצִת *tsitsith.*
Eze. 8. 3 took me by a lock of mine head; and the

3.*Braided locks of hair,* מַחְלָפוֹת *machlaphoth.*
Judg 16. 13 If thou weavest the seven locks of my h.
16. 19 caused him to shave off the seven locks

4.*Locks or other part of the hair of the head,* פֶּרַע *pera.*
Num. 6. 5 shall let the locks of the hair of his head
Eze. 44. 20 Neither..suffer their locks to grow long

5.*A lock of hair, veil,* צַמָּה *tsammah.*
Song 4. 1 thou (hast) doves' eyes within thy locks
4. 3 a piece of a pomegranate within thy locks
6. 7 a piece of a pomegranate..within thy lo.
Isa. 47. 2 uncover thy locks, make bare the leg, un.

6.*Ends or locks of hair,* קְוֻצּוֹת *qevutstsoth.*
Song 5. 2 dew..my locks with the drops of the ni.
5. 11 his locks (are) bushy, (and) black as a ra.

LOCK, to —
To bolt, nail, נָעַל *naal.*
Judg. 3. 23 shut the doors..upon him, and locked th.
3. 24 behold, the doors of the parlour (were) l.

LOCUST —
1.*A locust,* אַרְבֶּה *arbeh.*
Exod10. 4 to morrow will I bring the locusts into thy
10. 12 for the locusts, that they may come up
10. 13 morning, the east wind brought the loc.
10. 14 the locusts went up over all the land of
10. 14 there were no such locusts as they, neit.
10. 19 west wind, which took away the locusts
10. 19 there remained not one locust in all the
Lev. 11. 22 these of them ye may eat; the locust after
Deut28. 38 little in; for the locust shall consume it
1 Ki. 8. 37 if there be..blasting, mildew, locust, (or)
2 Ch. 6. 28 If there be..mildew, locusts, or catterpil.
Psa. 78. 46 He gave also..their labour unto the locust
105. 34 He spake, and the locusts came, and cat.
109. 23 I am gone..tossed up and down as the l.
Prov 30. 27 The locusts have no king, yet go they fo.
Joel 1. 4 palmerworm hath left hath the locust
1. 4 that which the locust hath left hath the
2. 25 restore..the years that the locust hath
Nah. 3. 15 many as the cankerworm..as the locusts
3. 17 Thy crowned (are) as the locusts, and thy

2.*A locust, grasshopper,* גֵּב *geb.*
Isa. 33. 4 as the running to and fro of locusts shall

3.*A grasshopper,* חָגָב *chagab.*
2 Ch. 7. 13 if I command the locusts to devour the

4.*A locust, cymbal, shadow,* צְלָצַל *tselatsal.*
Deut28. 42 All thy trees..shall the locusts consume

5.*A locust,* ἀκρίς *akris.*
Matt. 3. 4 and his meat was locusts and wild honey
Mark 1. 6 And John..did eat locusts and wild honey
Rev 9. 3 there came out of the smoke locusts upon
9. 7 the shapes of the locusts..like unto horses

LOCUST, bald —
Bald or devouring locust, סָלְעָם *solam.*
Lev. 11. 22 bald locust after his kind, and the beetle

LOD, לֹד *fissure.*
A city in Benjamin, near Joppa, on the road from Jerusalem to Cesarea. Under the Syrian supremacy it belonged to Samaria, then to Judah, and was left to Jonathan for a possession. It was destroyed during the Jewish war by Cestius the Roman general, but being afterwards restored, it became the seat of an academy. The Greeks called it Lydda, Lydde, and others Diospolis. Now called *Liddi.*
1 Ch. 8. 12 built Ono and L., with the towns thereof
Ezra 2. 33 The children of L., Hadid, and Ono, seven
Neh. 7. 37 The children of L., Hadid, and Ono, seven
11. 35 L., and Ono, the valley of craftsmen

LODGE —
Place for passing the night, מְלוּנָה *melunah.*
Isa. 1. 8 as a lodge in a garden of cucumbers, as a

LODGE (all night, or all this night), to —
1. *To pass the night, lodge,* לִין, לוּן *lun, lin.*
Gen. 24. 23 is there room (in) thy father's..to lodge in?
24. 25 and provender enough, and room to lodge
32. 13 he lodged there that same night; and took
32. 21 himself lodged that night in the company
Num22. 8 Lodge here this night, and I will bring you
Josh. 3. 1 and lodged there before they passed over
4. 3 lodging place where ye shall lodge this
6. 11 they came into the camp, and lodged in
8. 9 Joshua lodged that night among the peo.
Judg18. 2 to the house of Micah, they lodged there
19. 4 they did eat and drink, and lodged there
19. 7 urged him: therefore he lodged there ag.
19. 9 the day groweth to an end; lodge here
19. 11 let us turn in into this city..and lodge in
19. 13 to lodge all night, in Gibeah, or in Ramah
19. 15 to go in (and) to lodge in Gibeah: and
19. 20 Peace (be) with thee..only lodge not in
20. 4 said, I came..I and my concubine, to lo.
Ruth 1. 16 where thou lodgest, I will lodge: thy pe.
2 Sa. 17. 8 thy father..will not lodge with the people
17. 16 Lodge not this night in the plains of the
1 Ki.19. 9 And he came..unto a cave, and lodged
1 Ch. 9. 27 they lodged round about the house of God
Neh. 4. 22 Let every one with his servant lodge with
13. 20 sellers of all kind of ware, lodged without
13. 21 Why lodge ye about the wall? if ye do (so)
Job. 31. 32 The stranger did not lodge in the street
Song 7. 11 Come, my beloved..let us lodge in the vi.
Isa. 1. 21 righteousness lodged in it; but now mur.
21. 13 In the forest in Arabia shall ye lodge, O ye
65. 4 Which..lodge in the monuments; which
Zeph. 2. 14 the bittern shall lodge in the upper lintels

2. *To pass the night,* לִין, לוּן *lun, lin.*
Jer. 4. 14 How long shall thy vain thoughts lodge

3. *To lie down,* שָׁכַב *shakab.*
Josh. 2. 1 into a harlot's house..and lodged there

4. *To lie in a fold,* αὐλίζομαι *aulizomai.*
Matt21. 17 went out..into Bethany; and he lodged

5. *To loose down, ungird,* καταλύω *kataluō.*
Luke 9. 12 that they may go..lodge, and get victuals

6.*To rest as in a tent,* κατασκηνόω *kataskēnoō.*
Matt 13. 32 birds of the air come and lodge in the br.
Mark 4. 32 fowls of the air may lodge under the sha.
Luke13. 19 fowls of the air lodged in the branches of

7.*To receive a stranger,* ξενίζω *xenizō.*
Acts10. 6 He lodgeth with one Simon a tanner, wh.
10. 18 and asked whether Simon..were lodged
10. 23 Then called he them in, and lodged (them)
10. 32 he is lodged in the house of..Simon a ta.
21. 16 an old disciple, with whom we should lo.
28. 7 Publius..lodged us three days courteous.

LODGE, to cause to —
To cause to pass the night, לִין, לוּן *lin, lun,* 5.
Job 24. 7 They cause the naked to lodge without c.

LODGE, lodging place, place where to, lodging —
1.*Place for passing the night,* מָלוֹן *malon.*
Josh 4. 3 in the lodging place, where ye shall lodge
4. 8 unto the place where they lodged, and l.
2 Ki.19. 23 I will enter into the lodgings of his bord.
Isa. 10. 29 they have taken up their lodging at Geba
Jer. 9. 2 a lodging place of wayfaring men, that I

2.*A place for strangers,* ξενία *xenia.*
Acts 28. 23 there came many to him into (his) lodging
Phm. 22 But withal prepare me also a lodging: for

3.*Lodging,* לִין [*lin* infin.], Judg. 19. 15.

LOFT —
Upper chamber, עֲלִיָּה *aliyyah.*
1 Ki.17. 19 carried him up into a loft, where he abode

LOFTILY —
High thing, place or person, מָרוֹם *marom.*
Psa. 73. 8 They are corrupt, and..they speak loftily

LOFTINESS —
1.*Height, loftiness, haughtiness,* גֹּבַהּ *gobah.*
Jer. 48. 29 the pride of Moab..his loftiness, and his

2.*Loftiness, haughtiness, height,* גַּבְהוּת *gabhuth.*
Isa. 2. 17 the loftiness of man shall be bowed down

LOFTY —
1.*High, lofty, haughty,* גָּבֹהַּ *gaboah.*
Isa. 5. 15 and the eyes of the lofty shall be humbled
57. 7 Upon a lofty and high mountain hast thou

2.*Height, loftiness, haughtiness,* גַּבְהוּת *gabhuth.*
Isa. 2. 11 The lofty looks of man shall be humbled

3.*To be lifted up,* נָשָׂא *nasa,* 2.
Isa. 57. 15 For thus saith the high and lofty One that

4.*To be or become high,* רוּם *rum.*
Isa. 2. 12 upon every (one that is) proud and lofty

5.*To be or become high or strong,* שָׂגַב *sagab,* 2.
Isa. 26. 5 the lofty city, he layeth it low; he layeth

LOFTY, to be —
To be high, רוּם *rum.*
Psa.131. 1 heart is not haughty, nor mine eyes lofty
Prov.30. 13 a generation, O how lofty are their eyes!

LOG —
A log, a liquid measure, ⅝ of an imperial pint, לֹג *log.*
Lev. 14. 10 meat..mingled with oil, and one log of oil
14. 12 for a trespass offering, and the log of oil
14. 15 the priest shall take..of the log of oil, and
14. 21 flour..for a meat offering, and a log of oil
14. 24 of the trespass offering, and the log of oil

LOIN —
1.*Loin,* חָרָץ *charats.*
Dan. 5. 6 so that the joints of his loins were loosed

2.*Loins,* חֲלָצַיִם *chalatsayim.*
Gen. 35. 11 a nation..kings shall come out of thy loins
1 Ki. 8. 19 son, that shall come forth out of thy loins
2 Ch. 6. 9 son, which shall come forth out of thy lo.
Job 31. 20 If his loins have not blessed me, and (if)
38. 3 Gird up now thy loins like a man; for I
40. 7 Gird up thy loins now like a man: I will
Isa. 5. 27 neither shall the girdle of their loins be l.
32. 11 make you bare, and gird..upon (your) l.
Jer. 30. 6 see every man with his hands on his loins

3.*Thigh,* יָרֵךְ *yarek.*
Gen. 46. 26 souls..which came out of his loins, besides
Exod 1. 5 all the souls that came out of the loins of J.

4.*Flank,* כֶּסֶל *kesel.*
Psa. 38. 7 For my loins are filled with a loathsome

5.*Loins,* מָתְנַיִם *mothnayim.*
Gen. 37. 34 put sackcloth upon his loins, and mourned
Exod12. 11 your loins girded, your shoes on your feet
28. 42 from the loins even unto the thighs they
Deut33. 11 smite through the loins of them that rise
2 Sa. 20. 8 a sword fastened upon his loins in the sh.
1 Ki. 2. 5 about his loins, and in his shoes that (w.)
12. 10 little..shall be thicker than my father's l.
18. 46 he girded up his loins, and ran before Ahab
20. 31 let us..put sackcloth on our loins and
1 Ki. 20. 32 So they girded sackcloth on their loins
2 Ki. 1. 8 with a girdle of leather about his loins
4. 29 Gird up thy loins, and take my staff in
9. 1 Gird up thy loins, and take this box of oil
2 Ch.10. 10 little..shall be thicker than my father's l.
Job 12. 18 looseth..and girdeth their loins with a g.
40. 16 Lo now, his strength (is) in his loins, and
Psa. 66. 11 Thou..thou laidst affliction upon our loins
69. 23 and make their loins continually to shake
Prov.31. 17 She girdeth her loins with strength, and
Isa. 11. 5 shall be the girdle of his loins, and faith.
20. 2 loose the sackcloth from off thy loins, and
21. 3 Therefore are my loins filled with pain
45. 1 I will loose the loins of kings, to open
Jer. 1. 17 Thou therefore gird up thy loins, and ar.
13. 1 linen girdle, and put it upon thy loins, and
13. 2 I got a girdle..and put (it) on my loins
13. 4 which (is) upon thy loins, and arise, go to
13. 11 as the girdle cleaveth to the loins of a m.
48. 37 be) cuttings, and upon the loins sackcloth
Eze. 1. 27, 27 from the appearance of his loins even
8. 2 from the appearance of his loins even d.
8. 2 from his loins even upward, as the appe.
21. 6 with the breaking of..loins; and with bi
23. 15 Girded with girdles upon their loins, ex.
29. 7 madest all their loins to be at a stand
44. 18 shall have linen breeches upon their loins
47. 4 he measured..the waters (were) to the lo.
Dan. 10. 5 whose loins..girded with fine gold of Up
Amos 8. 10 I will bring up sackcloth upon all loins
Nah. 2. 1 watch the way, make..loins strong, for.
2. 10 much pain (is) in all loins, and the faces

6.*The loins, lower part of the back,* ὀσφύς *osphus.*
Matt. 3. 4 a leathern girdle about his loins; and his
Mark 1. 6 and with a girdle of a skin about his loins
Luke12. 35 Let your loins be girded about, and..lights
Acts 2. 30 that of the fruit of his loins, according
Eph. 6. 14 having your loins girt about with truth
Heb. 7. 5 though they come out of the loins of Abr.
7. 10 he was yet in the loins of his father when
1 Pe. 1. 13 Wherefore gird up the loins of your mind

LO'-IS, Λωΐς.
The grandmother of Timothy, commended by Paul for her faith.
2 Ti. 1. 5 which dwelt first in thy grandmother L.

LONG —
1.*Length,* אֹרֶךְ *orek.*
Exod27. 1 altar..five cubits long, and five cubits br.
27. 9 of an hundred cubits long for one side
27. 11 hangings of an hundred..long, and his
2 Ch. 3. 11 wings of the cherubim..twenty cubits long
6. 13 brasen scaffold, of five cubits long, and
Psa. 91. 16 With long life will I satisfy him, and show
Prov25. 15 By long forbearing is a prince persuaded
Lam. 5. 20 forget us for ever..forsake us so long t.?
Eze. 40. 7 little chamber..one reed long, and one
40. 29 fifty cubits long, and five and twenty cu.
40. 30 five and twenty cubits long, and five cu.
40. 33 fifty cubits long, and five and twenty cu.
40. 42 tables..of a cubit and an half long, and a
40. 47 the court, an hundred cubits long, and
41. 13 measured the house, an hundred cubits l.
41. 13 and the building..an hundred cubits long
42. 11 as long as they..as broad as they: and all
43. 16 altar..twelve (cubits) long, twelve broad
43. 17 the settle..fourteen (cubits) long and fo.
45. 6 five and twenty thousand long, over aga.
46. 22 courts joined of forty (cubits) long, and

2.*Length,* אֲרֻכָּה *arukkah.*
2 Sa. 3. 1 Now there was long war between the ho.
Jer. 29. 28 This (captivity is) long: build ye houses

3.*Great,* גָּדוֹל *gadol.*
Dan. 10. 1 but the time appointed (was) long: and

4.*When?* מָתַי *mathai.*
Exod10. 3 How long wilt thou refuse to humble thy

5.*Age lasting, indefinite (time),* עוֹלָם *olam.*
Psa.143. 3 dwell..as those that have been long dead
Eccl.12. 5 because man goeth to his long home; and

6.*Time,* עֵת *eth.*
Esth. 5. 13 so long as I see Mordecai the Jew sitting
Hos. 13. 13 he should not stay long in..the breaking

7.*Abundance, multitude,* רֹב *rob.*
Josh. 9. 13 become old by reason of the very long jo.
2 Ch.30. 5 for they had not done (it) of a long (time

8.*Many, much,* רַב *rab.*
Num20. 15 and we have dwelt in Egypt a long time
Deut20. 19 When thou shalt besiege a city a long time
Josh11. 18 Joshua made war a long time with all th.
23. 1 it came to pass, a long time after that the
24. 7 ye dwelt in the wilderness a long season
2 Sa.14. 2 as a woman that had a long time mourned
1 Ki. 3 11 hast not asked for thyself long life; neit.
2 Ch 1. 11 neither yet hast asked long life; but hast
15. 3 Now for a long season Israel (hath been)
Psa.120. 6 My soul hath long dwelt with him that

9.*Far off,* רָחוֹק *rachoq.*
Prov. 7. 19 For the good man..is gone a long journ.

10.*A year,* שָׁנָה *shanah.*
Prov. 3. 2 length of days, and long life, and peace

11.*Not a little,* οὐκ ὀλίγον *ouk oligon.*
Acts 14. 28 there they abode long time with the dis.

12.*More, additional,* ἐπὶ πλεῖον *epi pleion.*
Acts 20. 9 as Paul was long preaching, he sunk down

13. *Sufficient*, ἱκανός *hikanos*.
Luke 8. 27 certain man, which had devils long time
20. 9 went into a far country for a long time
Acts 8. 11 of long time he had bewitched them with
14. 3 Long time therefore abode they speaking

14. *Long*, μακρός *makros*.
Matt 23. 14 for a pretence make long prayer: theref.
Mark 12. 40 for a pretence make long prayers: these
Luke 20. 47 for a show make long prayers: the same

15. *Much, many*, πολύς *polus*.
Matt 25. 19 After a long time the lord of those serv.
John 5. 6 knew that he had been now a long time
Acts 27. 14 But not long after there arose against it
27. 21 after long abstinence Paul stood forth in

[*See also* All life, bear, clothing, enjoy, garment, grow, hair, how, live, remain, patience, robe, sew, span, suffer, tarry, time.]

LONG, to —

1. *To desire*, אָוָה *avah*, 3.
Deut. 12. 20 because thy soul longeth to eat flesh, thou

2. *To desire for oneself*, אָוָה *avah*, 7.
2 Sa. 23. 15 David longed, and said, Oh that one wou.
1 Ch. 11. 17 David longed, and said, Oh that one wou.

3. *To wait*, חָכָה *chakah*, 3.
Job 3. 21 Which long for death, but it (cometh)

4. *To join to, be filletted*, חָשַׁק *chashaq*.
Gen. 34. 8 The soul of my son Shechem longeth for

5. *To desire, incline to*, יָאַב *yaab*.
Psa. 119. 131 I opened..I longed for thy commandm

6. *To consume, make an end*, כָּלָה *kalah*, 3.
2 Sa. 13. 39 king David longed to go forth unto Abs.

7. *To long for, pine, be weary*, כָּמַהּ *kamah*.
Psa. 63. 1 my flesh longeth for thee in a dry and th.

8. *To have a desire*, כָּסַף *kasaph*, 2.
Gen. 31. 30 because thou sore longedst after thy fat.
Psa. 84. 2 My soul longeth, yea, even fainteth for

9. *To run to and fro*, שָׁקַק *shaqaq*.
Psa. 107. 9 he satisfieth the longing soul, and filleth

10. *To desire, incline to*, תָּאַב *taab*.
Psa. 119. 40 I have longed after thy precepts: quicken
119. 174 I have longed for thy salvation, O LORD

11. *To desire much or upon*, ἐπιποθέω *epipotheō*.
Rom. 1. 11 I long to see you, that I may impart unto

LONG, to be —

1. *To be or become long*, אָרַךְ *arak*.
Gen. 26. 8 when he had been there a long time, that

2. *To make long, prolong, lengthen*, אָרַךְ *arak*, 5.
Exod 20. 12 that thy days may be long upon the land w.

3. *To delay, be long*, בּוֹשׁ *bosh*, 3a.
Judg 5. 28 Why is his chariot (so) long in coming? why

4. *To be many, much, great*, רָבָה *rabah*.
Deut 14. 24 if the way be too long for thee, so that
19. 6 overtake him, because the way is long, and
1 Sa. 7. 2 the time was long; for it was twenty years

LONG after (greatly), to —

To desire much or upon, ἐπιποθέω *epipotheō*.
2 Co. 9. 14 which long after you for the exceeding g.
Phil. 1. 8 how greatly I long after you in the bowels
2. 26 he longed after you all, and was full of h.

LONG, to become, make, or sound —

1. *To be or become long*, אָרַךְ *arak*.
Eze. 31. 5 his branches became long, because of the

2. *To make long, lengthen, prolong*, אָרַךְ *arak*, 5.
Psa. 129. 3 plowers plowed..they made long their f.

3. *To draw (along or out)*, מָשַׁךְ *mashak*.
Exod 19. 13 when the trumpet soundeth long, they
Josh. 6. 5 when they make a long (blast) with the

LONG, to bear, suffer, or live —

1. *To be long suffering*, μακροθυμέω *makrothumeō*.
Luke 18. 7 God avenge..though he bear long with
1 Co. 13. 4 Charity suffereth long, (and) is kind; ch.

2. *Long timed*, μακροχρόνιος *makrochronios*.
Eph. 6. 3 and thou mayest live long on the earth

LONG continuance (to be) of —

To be steady, אָמַן *aman*, 2.
Deut 28. 59 great plagues, and of long continuance
28. 59 sore sicknesses, and of long continuance

LONG ago —

1. *Far off*, רָחוֹק *rachoq*.
2 Ki. 19. 25 Hast thou not heard long ago..I have d.
Isa. 22. 11 respect unto him that fashioned it long a.
37. 26 Hast thou not heard long ago..I have d.

2. *Long ago, formerly, anciently*, πάλαι *palai*.
Matt 11. 21 they would have repented long ago in s.

LONG as, so long as, as —

1. *A day*, יוֹם *yom*.
Lev. 26. 34 as long as it lieth desolate, and ye (be) in
26. 35 As long as it lieth desolate it shall rest
Num. 9. 18 as long as the cloud abode upon the tab.
Deut 12. 19 forsake not the Levite as long as thou liv.
31. 13 as long as ye live in the land whither ye
1 Sa. 1. 28 as long as he liveth he shall be lent to the
20. 31 as long as the son of Jesse liveth upon the
25. 15 as long as we were conversant with them
29. 8 so long as I have been with thee unto this
2 Ch. 6. 31 so long as they live in the land which thou
26. 5 as long as he sought the LORD, God made
36. 21 as long as she lay desolate, she kept sabb.

2. *At the face of*, לִפְנֵי *li-phene*.
Psa. 72. 17 his name shall be continued as long as the

3. *As much time as*, ὅσον χρόνον, *hoson chronon*.
Mark 2. 19 as long as they have the bridegroom with
Rom. 7. 1 law hath dominion over a man as long as
1 Co. 7. 39 The wife is bound by the law as long as her
Gal. 4. 1 the heir, as long as he is a child, differeth

LONG as I live, so —

During my days, מִיָּמָי [*yom*].
Job 27. 6 heart shall not reproach..so long as I l.

LONG, all my life —

From my being, מֵעוֹדִי *me-od-i*.
Gen. 48. 15 the God which fed me all my life long unto

LONG enough —

Much, many, abundant, רַב *rab*.
Deut 1. 6 Ye have dwelt long enough in this mount
2. 3 compassed this mountain long enough

LONG for, (thing that I) —

1. *Hope, expectation*, תִּקְוָה *tiqvah*.
Job 6. 8 would grant (me) the thing that I long for

2. *One much desired*, ἐπιπόθητος *epipothētos*.
Phil. 4. 1 my brethren dearly beloved and longed for

LONG (season or) while —

1. *Many, much*, רַב *rab*.
Josh 24. 7 ye dwelt in the wilderness a long season
2 Ch. 15. 3 Now for a long season Israel (hath been)

2. *Out of sufficiency*, ἐξ ἱκανοῦ, ἐφ' ἱκανόν.
Luke 23. 8 for he was desirous to see him [of a long s.]
Acts 20. 11 talked a long while, even till break of day

LONG time —

From indefinite time, מֵעוֹלָם *me-olam*.
Isa. 42. 14 I have long time holden my peace; I have

LONGER, (any) —

1. *Length*, אֲרֻכָּה *arukkah*.
Job 11. 9 The measure thereof (is) longer than the

2. *Yet, still, any more, again*, עוֹד *od*.
Exod. 2. 3 when she could not longer hide him, she
Judg. 2. 14 so that they could not any longer stand

3. *Yet, still*, ἔτι *eti*.
Luke 16. 2 account..for thou mayst be no longer
Rom. 6. 2 are dead to sin, live any longer therein?

4. *More*, πλείων *pleiōn*.
Acts 18. 20 When they desired (him) to tarry longer

5. *To add*, יָסַף *yasaph*, 5.
Exod 9. 28 will let you go, and ye shall stay no longer

LONGING —

A desire, inclination, longing, תַּאֲוָה *taabah*.
Psa. 119. 20 My soul breaketh for the longing (that

LONG SUFFERING —

1. *Long of face or anger*, אֶרֶךְ אַף *erek aph*.
Exod 34. 6 merciful and gracious, longsuffering and
Num 14. 18 The LORD (is) long suffering, and of great
Psa. 86. 15 long suffering, and plenteous in mercy and
Jer. 15. 15 take me not away in thy long suffering

2. *Long suffering*, μακροθυμία *makrothumia*.
Rom. 2. 4 goodness and forbearance and long suffer.
9. 22 endured with much long suffering the ves.
2 Co. 6. 6 by long suffering, by kindness, by the H.
Gal 5. 22 the fruit of the spirit is..long suffering
Eph. 4. 2 with long suffering, forbearing one anot.
Col. 1. 11 unto all patience and long suffering with
3. 12 humbleness of mind, meekness, long suff.
1 Ti. 1. 16; 2 Ti. 3. 10; 4. 2; 1 Pe. 3. 20; 2. Pe. 3. 15.

LONGED for —

Much desired, ἐπιπόθητος *epipothētos*.
Phil. 4. 1 brethren, dearly beloved and longed for

LONG SUFFERING, to be —

To be long suffering, μακροθυμέω *makrothumeō*.
2 Pet. 3. 9 is long suffering to us ward, not willing

LONG WINGED —

Long of wing, אֶרֶךְ אֵבֶר *erek eber*.
Eze. 17. 3 great eagle with great wings, long winged

LOOK —

1. *Vision, sight*, חֵזֵו *chezev*.
Dan. 7. 20 whose look..more stout than his fellows

2. *Eyes*, עֵינַיִם [*ayin*].
Psa. 18. 27 thou wilt save..wilt bring down high looks
101. 5 that hath an high look and a proud heart
Prov. 6. 17 A proud look, a lying tongue, and hands
21. 4 An high look, and a proud heart..the plo.
Isa. 2. 11 The lofty looks of man shall be humbled
10. 12 I will punish..the glory of his high looks

LOOK, to —

1. *To be pained, stay*, חוּל, חִיל *chul, chil*.
Job 20. 21 therefore shall no man look for his goods

2. *To see, behold, look*, חָזָה *chazah*.
Song 6. 13 return, return, that we may look upon thee
Isa. 33. 20 Look upon Zion, the city of our solemnities
Mic. 4. 11 nations..that say..let our eye look upon

3. *To look attentively*, נָבַט *nabat*, 3.
Isa. 5. 30 if (one) look unto the land, behold dark.

4. *To look attentively*, נָבַט *nabat*, 5.
Gen. 15. 5 Look now toward heaven, and tell the st.
19. 17 look not behind thee, neither stay thou
19. 26 his wife looked back from behind him
Exod. 3. 6 Moses hid his face; for he was afraid to l.
33. 8 the people..looked after Moses, until he
1 Sa. 16. 7 Look not on his countenance, or on the h.
17. 42 when the Philistine looked about, and saw
24. 8 And when Saul looked behind him, David
1 Ki. 18. 43 look toward the sea..And he..looked
19. 6 he looked, and, behold..a cake baken on
2 Ki. 3. 14 I would not look toward thee, nor see thee
1 Ch. 21. 21 as David came to Ornan, Ornan looked
Job 6. 19 The troops of Tema looked, the companies
28. 24 For he looketh to the ends of the earth
35. 5 Look unto the heavens, and see; and beh.
Psa. 22. 17 I may tell all my bones: they look (and)
33. 13 The LORD looketh from heaven; he beho.
34. 5 They looked unto him, and were lightened
84. 9 and look upon the face of thine anointed
104. 32 He looketh on the earth, and it trembleth
142. 4 I looked on (my) right hand, and beheld
Prov. 4. 25 Let thine eyes look right on, and let thine
Isa. 8. 22 they shall look unto the earth; and beh.
22. 8 thou didst look in that day to the armour
22. 11 ye have not looked unto the maker there.
42. 18 Hear, ye deaf; and look, ye blind, that ye
51. 1 look unto the rock (whence) ye are hewn
51. 2 Look unto Abraham your father, and unto
51. 6 look upon the earth beneath; for the he.
63. 5 I looked, and (there was) none to help; and
63. 15 Look down from heaven, and behold from
66. 2 but to this (man) will I look, (even) to (him
Jon. 2. 4 I will look again toward thy holy temple
Hab. 1. 13 to behold evil, and canst not look on ini.
1. 13 wherefore lookest thou upon them that
2. 15 that thou mayest look on their nakedness
Zech. 12. 10 they shall look upon me whom they have

5. *Sight of the eyes*, מַרְאֵה עֵינַיִם [*mareh*].
Lev. 13. 12 cover all..wheresoever the priest looketh

6. *To turn the face*, פָּנָה *panah*.
Exod. 2. 12 he looked this way and that way, and w
16. 10 that they looked toward the wilderness
Num 12. 10 Aaron looked upon Miriam, and, behold
16. 42 that they looked toward the tabernacle
Deut. 9. 27 look not unto the stubbornness of this p.
Josh. 8. 20 when the men of Ai looked behind them
15. 2 sea, from the bay that looketh southward
15. 7 and so northward, looking toward Gilgal
Judg. 6. 14 the LORD looked upon him, and said, Go
20. 40 the Benjamites looked behind them, and
2 Sa. 1. 7 when he looked behind him, he saw me
2. 20 Then Abner looked behind him, and said
9. 8 that thou shouldest look upon such a dead
1 Ki. 7. 25, 25, 25, 25 three looking toward the
2 Ch. 4. 4, 4, 4, 4 three looking toward the
13. 14 when Judah looked back, behold, the ba.
20. 24 they looked unto the multitude, and, beh
26. 20 all the priests, looked upon him, and, be.
Job 6. 28 Now therefore be content; look upon me
Psa. 119. 132 Look thou upon me, and be merciful unto
Eccl. 2. 11 I looked on all the works that my hands
Isa. 8. 21 curse their king and their God, and look
45. 22 Look unto me, and be ye saved, all the e.
56. 11 they all look to their own way, every one
Eze. 8. 3 inner gate that looketh toward the north
10. 11 to the place whither the head looked they
11. 1 unto the east gate..which looketh eastw.
29. 16 when they shall look after them: but they
43. 1 gate..the gate that looketh toward the e.
43. 17 and his stairs shall look toward the east
44. 1 of the gate..which looketh toward the e.
46. 1 The gate of the inner court that looketh
46. 12 open..the gate that looketh toward the
46. 19 of the gate..which looked toward the n.
47. 2 utter gate by the way that looketh east.
Hos. 3. 1 who look to other gods, and love flagons
Hag. 1. 9 Ye looked for much, and, lo..little: and

7. *To inspect*, פָּקַד *paqad*.
1 Sa. 17. 18 look how thy brethren fare, and take th.

8. *To wait, expect*, קָוָה *qavah*, 3.
Job 3. 9 let it look for light, but (have) none; ne.
7. 2 and as an hireling looketh for..his work
30. 26 When I looked for good, then evil came
Psa. 69. 20 I looked (for some) to take pity, but..n.
Isa. 5. 2, 4 looked that it should bring forth grapes
5. 7 he looked for judgment, but behold opp.
8. 17 I will wait upon the LORD..will look for
59. 11 we look for judgment, but..none; for sa.
64. 3 didst terrible things..we looked not for
Jer. 8. 15 We looked for peace, but no good..for a
13. 16 while ye look for light, he turn it into the
14. 19 we looked for peace, and..no good; and
Lam. 2. 16 certainly this (is) the day that we looked

9. *To see, look, behold*, רָאָה *raah*.
Gen. 6. 12 God looked upon the earth, and, behold
8. 13 Noah..looked, and, behold, the face of
13. 14 Lift up now thine eyes, and look from the
16. 13 Have I also here looked after him that
18. 2 he lift up his eyes and looked, and, lo
22. 13 Abraham lifted up his eyes, and looked
29. 2 he looked, and behold a well in the field
29. 32 the LORD hath looked upon my affliction
33. 1 Jacob lifted up his eyes, and looked, and
37. 25 they lifted up their eyes and looked, and
39. 23 The keeper of the prison looked not to any
40. 6 Joseph..looked upon them, and, behold
Exod. 2. 11 looked on their burdens: and he spied an
2. 25 God looked upon the children of Israel

Exod. 3. 2 he looked, and, behold, the bush burned
4. 31 that he had looked upon their affliction
5. 21 LORD look upon you, and judge; because
10. 10 And he said..look..for evil (is) before you
25. 40 look that thou make (them) after their pa.
39. 43 Moses did look upon all the work, and
Lev. 13. 3, 50 And the priest shall look on the plague
13. 25, 43 the priest shall look upon it: and, be.
13. 31 if the priest look on the plague of the s.
13. 32, 34 in the seventh day the priest shall lo.
13. 39 Then the priest shall look: and, behold
13. 51 he shall look on the plague on the seventh
13. 53, 56 if the priest look, and, behold, the p.
13. 55 the priest shall look on the plague, after
14. 3 the priest shall look, and, behold..the p.
14. 37 he shall look on the plague: and, behold
14. 39 come again the seventh day, and shall look
14. 44 the priest shall come and look, and behold
14. 48 if the priest shall come in, and look..and
Num 15. 39 that ye may look upon it, and remember
17. 9 they looked, and took every man his rod
21. 8 every one..when he looketh upon it, shall
24. 20 when he looked on Amalek, he took up
24. 21 he looked on the Kenites, and took up his
Deut. 9. 16 I looked, and, behold, ye had sinned ag.
26. 7 LORD heard our voice, and looked on our
28. 32 thine eyes shall look, and fail..for them
Josh. 5. 13 that he lifted up his eyes and looked, and
Judg. 7. 17 Look on me, and do likewise: and, behold
9. 43 laid wait in the field, and looked, and be.
13. 19, 20 and Manoah and his wife looked on
1 Sa. 1. 11 O LORD of hosts, if thou wilt..look on the
6. 19 because they had looked into the ark of
9. 16 I have looked upon my people, because
14. 16 the watchmen of Saul in Gibeah..looked
16. 6 he looked on Eliab, and said, Surely the
16. 7 man looketh on the outward..LORD look.
2 Sa. 13. 34 looked, and, behold, there came much
16. 12 It may be that the LORD will look on m.
18. 24 looked, and behold a man running alone
2 Ki. 6. 30 he passed by..and the people looked, and
6. 32 Look, when the messenger cometh, shut
9. 2 when thou comest thither, look out there
10. 3 Look even out the best and meetest of yo.
10. 23 look that there be here with you none of
11. 14 when she looked, behold, the king stood
1 Ch. 12. 17 the God of our fathers look..and rebuke
2 Ch. 23. 13 she looked, and, behold, the king stood
24. 22 The LORD look upon (it), and require (it)
Neh. 4. 14 I looked, and rose up, and said unto the
Esth. 1. 11 her beauty: for she (was) fair to look on
Job 40. 12 Look on every one..proud, (and) bring
Psa. 25. 18 Look upon mine affliction and my pain
109. 25 they looked upon me they shaked their
Prov. 23. 31 Look not thou upon the wine when it is
24. 32 I looked upon (it, and) received instruct.
Eccl. 12. 3 those that look out of the windows be d.
Song 1. 6 Look not upon me, because I (am) black
Isa. 28. 4 which (when) he that looketh upon it
66. 24 and look upon the carcases of the men
Eze. 1. 4 I looked, and, behold, a whirlwind came
2. 9 when I looked, behold, an hand..sent
8. 7 when I looked, behold, a hole in the wall
10. 1 I looked, and, behold, in the firmament
10. 9 when I looked, behold, the four wheels
16. 8 when I passed by thee, and looked upon
21. 21 the king of Babylon..looked in the liver
44. 4 I looked, and, behold, the glory of the L.
Dan. 10. 5 I lifted up mine eyes, and looked, and be.
12. 5 I Daniel looked, and, behold, there stood
Obad. 12, 13 thou shouldest not have looked on the
Nah. 3. 7 all they that look upon thee shall flee from
Zech. 2. 1 I lifted up mine eyes again, and looked
4. 2 I have looked, and, behold, a candlestick
5. 1 I turned..looked, and, behold, a flying roll
5. 9 Then lifted I up mine eyes, and looked
6. 1 I..looked, and, behold, there came four

10. *To look,* שָׁגַח *shagach,* 5.
Psa. 33. 14 he looketh upon all the inhabitants of the
Song 2. 9 he looketh forth at the windows, showing

11. *To behold, look,* שׁוּר *shur.*
Job 33. 27 He looketh upon men; and (if any) say
Song 4. 8 look from the top of Amana, from the top

12. *To look, glance,* שָׁעָה *shaah.*
2 Sa. 22. 42 They looked, but..none to save..unto the
Isa. 17. 7 At that day shall a man look to his Maker
17. 8 he shall not look to the altars, the work
31. 1 they look not unto the Holy One of Israel

13. *To look, be seen,* שָׁקַף *shaqaph,* 2.
Num 21. 20 Pisgah, which looketh toward Jeshimon
23. 28 top of Peor, that looketh toward Jeshimon
Judg. 5. 28 The mother of Sisera looked out at a win.
1 Sa. 13. 18 the way of the border that looketh to the
2 Sa. 6. 16 Saul's daughter looked through a window
1 Ch. 15. 29 daughter of Saul looking out at a window
Prov. 7. 6 For at the window .I looked through my

14. *To look,* שָׁקַף *shaqaph,* 5.
Gen. 18. 16 the men rose up..and looked toward So.
19. 28 he looked toward Sodom and Gomorrah
Exod 14. 24 in the morning watch the LORD looked
2 Sa. 24. 20 Araunah looked, and saw the king and

15. *To set the heart,* שִׁית לֵב *shith leb.*
Prov 27. 23 Be thou diligent..look well to thy herds

16. *To look up or again,* ἀναβλέπω *anablepō.*
Mark 16. 4 when they looked, they saw that the stone

17. *To be intent,* ἀτενίζω *atenizō.*
Acts 10. 4 when he looked on him, he was afraid

18. *To look away,* ἀφοράω *aphoraō.*
Heb. 12. 2 Looking unto Jesus, the author and finis.

19. *To look,* βλέπω *blepō.*
Luke 9. 62 No man..looking back, is fit for the kin.
John 13. 22 the disciples looked one on another, dou.
Acts 3. 4 And Peter..with John, said, Look on us

20. *To see, perceive,* εἴδω *eidō.*
John 7. 52 Search, and look: for out of Galilee ariseth
Rev. 4. 1 After this I looked, and, behold, a door
6. 8; 14. 1; 14. 14; 15. 5.

21. *See!* ἴδε *ide.*
John 7. 52 Search and look; for out of Galilee

22. *To see, behold, look after,* ὄπτομαι *optomai.*
John 19. 37 They shall look on him whom they pierced
Acts 18. 15 look ye (to it); for I will be no judge of

23. *To stoop alongside of,* παρακύπτω *parakuptō.*
Jas. 1. 25 whoso looketh into the perfect law of li.
1 Pe. 1. 12 which things the angels desire to look into

24. *To look or watch toward,* προσδοκάω *prosdokaō.*
Acts 28. 6 they looked when he should have swollen
28. 6 but after they had looked a great while, and

LOOK round about (on), to —

To look around, περιβλέπω *periblepō.*
Mark 3. 5 when he had looked round about on them
3. 34 he looked round about on them which sat
5. 32 he looked round about to see her that had
9. 8 when they had looked round about, they
10. 23 Jesus looked round about, and saith unto
11. 11 when he had looked round about upon all
Luke 6. 10 looking round about upon them all, he said

LOOK at or on, to —

To view, inspect, σκοπέω *skopeō.*
2 Co. 4. 18 While we look not at the things which
Phil. 2. 4 Look not every man on his own things

LOOK away, to —

To look, שָׁעָה *shaah.*
Isa. 22. 4 Look away from me; I will weep bitterly

LOOK back, to —

To turn the face, פָּנָה *panah,* 5.
Jer. 46. 5 are fled apace, and look not back..fear
47. 3 fathers shall not look back to..children
Nah. 2. 8 Stand, stand..but none shall look back

LOOK diligently —

To view or inspect, ἐπισκοπέω *episkopeō.*
Heb. 12. 15 Looking diligently lest any man fail of

LOOK down, to —

1. *To look attentively, regard,* נָבַט *nabat,* 5.
Psa. 80. 14 look down from heaven, and behold, and

2. *To look,* שָׁקַף *shaqaph,* 2.
Psa. 85. 11 righteousness shall look down from hea.

3. *To look,* שָׁקַף *shaqaph,* 5.
Deut 26. 15 Look down from thy holy habitation
Psa. 14. 2 LORD looked down from heaven upon the
53. 2 God looked down from heaven upon the
102. 19 he hath looked down from the height of
Lam. 3. 50 Till the LORD look down, and behold from

LOOK earnestly on or upon, to —

To be intent, ἀτενίζω *atenizō.*
Luke 22. 56 earnestly looked upon him, and said, This
Acts. 3. 12 or why look ye so earnestly on us, as tho.

LOOK for, to —

1. *To receive out from, wait long for,* ἀπεκδέχομαι.
Phil. 3. 20 from whence also we look for the Saviour
Heb. 9. 28 unto them that look for him shall he ap.

2. *To receive out, wait for,* ἐκδέχομαι *ekdechomai.*
1 Co. 16. 11 may come..for I look for him with the
Heb. 11. 10 he looked for a city which hath foundation

3. *To receive toward, wait,* προσδέχομαι *prosdecho.*
Luke 2. 38 to all them that looked for redemption
Acts 23. 21 are..ready, looking for a promise from
Titus 2. 13 Looking for that blessed hope, and the
Jude 21 looking for the mercy of our Lord Jesus

4. *To look or watch toward,* προσδοκάω *prosdokaō.*
Matt 11. 3 Art thou he..or do we look for another?
24. 50 come in a day when he looketh not for
Luke 7. 19, 20 Art thou he..or look we for another?
12. 46 come in a day when he looketh not for (h.)
2 Pe. 3. 12 Looking for and hasting unto the coming
3. 13 look for new heavens and a new earth
3. 14 seeing that ye look for such things, be d.

LOOK forth, to —

To look, look out, שָׁקַף *shaqaph,* 2.
Song 6. 10 Who (is) she (that) looketh forth as the

LOOK, to narrowly —

To look, שָׁגַח *shagach,* 5.
Isa. 14. 16 They that see thee shall narrowly look

LOOK on or upon, to —

1. *Appearance, sight,* מַרְאֶה *mareh.*
Gen. 12. 11 that thou (art) a fair woman to look upon
24. 16 damsel..very fair to look upon, a virgin
26. 7 kill me..because she (was) fair to look u.
2 Sa. 11. 2 woman (was) very beautiful to look upon
Esth. 1. 11 Vashti the queen..(was) fair to look on

2. *To see,* רָאָה *raah.*
Gen. 9. 16 I will look upon it, that I may remember
Lev. 13. 3, 5, 6, 27 And the priest shall look on him
Lev. 13. 21, 26 if the priest look on it, and, behold
13. 36 Then the priest shall look on him: and
2 Ki. 2. 24 he turned back, and looked on them, and
Psa. 35. 17 LORD, how long wilt thou look on? rescue
Esth. 2. 15 in the sight of all them that looked upon

3. *To be seen,* רָאָה *raah,* 2.
Dan. 1. 13 Then let our countenances be looked upon

4. *To see, behold, scorch,* שָׁזַף *shazaph.*
Song 1. 6 because the sun hath looked upon me

5. *To look,* βλέπω *blepō.*
Matt. 5. 28 whosoever looketh on a woman to lust
2 Co. 10. 7 Do ye look on things after the outward
Rev. 5. 3, 4 open the book, neither to look thereon

6. *To see, perceive,* εἴδω *eidō.*
Mark 8. 33 when he had turned about, and looked on
Luke 10. 32 and looked..and passed by on the other s.

7. *To look in,* ἐμβλέπω *emblepō.*
Mark 10. 27 Jesus, looking upon them, saith, With men
14. 67 she looked upon him, and said, And thou
Luke 22. 61 And the Lord turned, and looked upon P.
John 1. 36 looking upon Jesus as he walked, he saith

8. *To look upon,* ἐπιβλέπω *epiblepō.*
Luke 9. 38 Master, I beseech thee, look upon my son

9. *To look upon,* ἐπεῖδον *epeidon.*
Luke 1. 25 in the days wherein he looked on (me)

10. *To view,* θεωρέω *theōreō.*
Mark 15. 40 There were also women looking on afar off

11. *To view, contemplate,* θεάομαι *theaomai.*
John 4. 35 Lift up your eyes, and look on the fields
1 Jo. 1. 1 which we have looked upon, and our hands

12. *The sight, aspect,* ὅρασις *horasis.*
Rev. 4. 3 he that sat was to look upon like a jasper

LOOK one (upon) another, to —

To see or look on one another, רָאָה *raah,* 7.
Gen. 42. 1 said..Why do ye look one upon another?
2 Ki. 14. 8 Come, let us look one another in the face
14. 11 he and Amaziah..looked one another in

LOOK out —

1. *To see, provide,* רָאָה *raah.*
Gen. 41. 33 let Pharaoh look out a man discreet and

2. *To look,* שָׁקַף *shaqaph,* 5.
Gen. 26. 8 Abimelech..looked out at a window, and
2 Ki. 9. 30 tired her head, and looked out at a window
9. 32 there looked out to him two..three eun.

3. *To look out for,* ἐπισκέπτομαι *episkeptomai.*
Acts 6. 3 look ye out among you seven men of honest

LOOK stedfastly, to —

To be intent, ἀτενίζω *atenizō.*
Acts 1. 10 while they looked stedfastly toward he.
6. 15 looking stedfastly on him, saw his face
7. 55 looked up stedfastly into heaven, and s.
2 Cor. 3. 13 could not stedfastly look to the end of

LOOK to or toward, to —

1. *Appearance, sight,* מַרְאֶה *mareh.*
Lev. 13. 12 cover all..wheresoever the priest looketh
Eze. 23. 15 all of them princes to look to, after the

2. *To look out, watch,* צָפָה *tsaphah,* 3.
Song 7. 4 tower..which looketh toward Damascus
Mic. 7. 7 I will look unto the LORD; I will wait for

3. *A spectacle, sight, appearance,* רֳאִי *roi.*
1 Sa. 16. 12 beautiful countenance..goodly to look to

4. *To look,* βλέπω *blepō.*
2 John 8 Look to yourselves, that we lose not those

LOOK up, to —

1. *To look out, watch,* צָפָה *tsaphah,* 3.
Psa. 5. 3 will I direct..unto thee, and will look up

2. *To see,* רָאָה *raah.*
Psa. 40. 12 so that I am not able to look up: they

3. *To look up,* ἀναβλέπω *anablepō.*
Matt 14. 19 looking up to heaven, he blessed, and br.
Mark 6. 41 he looked up to heaven, and blessed, and
7. 34 looking up to heaven, he sighed, and said
8. 24 he looked up, and said, I see men as trees
8. 25 [made him look up]: and he was restored
Luke 9. 16 looking up to heaven, he blessed them
19. 5 he looked up, and saw him, and said unto
21. 1 he looked up, and saw the rich men cast.
Acts 22. 13 And the same hour I looked up upon him

4. *To bend up or back again,* ἀνακύπτω *anakuptō.*
Luke 21. 28 look up, and lift up your heads; for your

LOOK well, to —

1. *To understand, consider, discover, attend,* בִּין *bin*
Prov. 14. 15 the prudent..looketh well to his going

2. *To look out, watch,* צָפָה *tsaphah.*
Prov. 31. 27 She looketh well to the ways of her househ

3. *To set the eye,* שׂוּם עַיִן *sum ayin.*
Jer. 39. 12 look well to him, and do him no harm; but
40. 4 come, and I will look well unto thee; but

LOOKETH, looked —

Face, פָּנִים *panim.*
Eze. 40. 6, 22 gate which looketh toward the east
40. 20 the gate..that looked toward the north

LOOKING after or for —

1. *To look or watch toward,* προσδοκάω *prosdokaō*
Luke 21. 26 for looking after those things which are

2. *A reception, waiting for,* ἐκδοχή *ekdochē.*
Heb. 10. 27 a certain fearful looking for of judgment

LOOKING GLASS —

1. *Appearance,* מַרְאָה *marah.*
Exod38. 8 of the looking glasses of (the women) asse.

2. *Looking glass,* רְאִי *rei.*
Job 37. 18 the sky . . as a molten looking glass

LOOKS, to look —

Face, פָּנִים *panim.*
Gen. 40. 7 saying, Wherefore look ye (so) sadly to d.?
Eze. 2. 6 nor be dismayed at their looks, though
3. 9 neither be dismayed at their looks, tho.

LOOPS —

Loops, לֻלָאֹת *lulaoth.*
Exod26. 4 thou shalt make loops of blue upon the
26. 5, 5 Fifty loops shalt thou make in the
26. 5 that the loops may take hold one of ano.
26. 10, 10 fifty loops on the edge of the . . curtain
26. 11 put the taches into the loops, and couple
36. 11 he made loops of blue on the edge of one
36. 12 Fifty loops made he in one curtain, and
36. 12 fifty loops made he in the edge of the cu.
36. 12 the loops held one (curtain) to another
36. 17 he made fifty loops upon the uttermost
36. 17 fifty loops made he upon the edge of the

LOOSE, to —

1. *To draw off,* חָלַץ *chalats.*
Deut25. 9 loose his shoe from off his foot, and spit
25. 10 The house of him that hath his shoe loo.

2. *To cast off,* נָשַׁל *nashal.*
Josh 5. 15 Loose thy shoe from off thy foot; for

3. *To loose, shake off,* נָתַר *nathar,* 5.
Psa.105. 20 The king sent and loosed him . . the ruler
146. 7 hungry. The LORD looseth the prisoners

4. *To open,* פָּתַח *pathach,* 3.
Job 12. 18 He looseth the bond of kings, and girdeth
30. 11 Because he hath loosed my cord, and affl.
38. 31 Canst thou . . loose the bands of Orion?
39. 5 who hath loosed the bands of the wild ass?
Psa.102. 20 to loose those that are appointed to death
116. 16 O LORD, truly . . thou hast loosed my bonds
Isa. 20. 2 Go and loose the sackcloth from off thy l.
45. 1 I will loose the loins of kings, to open
58. 6 to loose the bands of wickedness, to undo
Jer. 40. 4 I loose thee this day from the chains wh.

5. *To loose off or away,* ἀπολύω *apoluō.*
Matt 18. 27 and loosed him, and forgave him the debt
Luke13. 12 Woman, thou art loosed from thine infir.

6. *To make inactive,* καταργέω *katargeō.*
Rom. 7. 2 she is loosed from the law of (her) husb.

7. *To loose,* λύω *luō.*
Matt 16. 19 whatsoever thou shalt loose . . shall be lo.
18. 18 whatsoever ye shall loose . . shall be loosed
21. 2 and a colt . . loose . . and bring . . unto me
Mark 7. 35 the string of his tongue was loosed, and
11. 2 ye shall find a colt . . loose him, and bring
11. 4 found the colt tied . . and they loose him
11. 5 certain . . said . . What do ye, loosing the c.?
Luke13. 15 on the sabbath loose his ox or . . ass from
13. 16 be loosed from this bond on the sabbath
19. 30 ye shall find a colt . . loose him, and bring
19. 31 And if any man ask you, Why do ye loose
19. 33 And as they were loosing the colt, the
19. 33 owners . . said unto them, Why loose ye the
John11. 44 Jesus saith unto them, Loose him, and let
Acts 2. 24 having loosed the pains of death: because
13. 25 one . . whose shoes . . I am not worthy to l.
22. 30 loosed him from . . bands, and commanded
24. 26 [that he might loose him: wherefore he]
1 Co. 7. 27 Art thou loosed from a wife? seek not a
Rev. 5. 2 is worthy to open the book, and to loose
5. 5 and [to loose] the seven seals thereof
9. 14 Loose the four angels which are bound in
9. 15 the four angels were loosed, which were
20. 3 after that he must be loosed a little sea.
20. 7 And . . Satan shall be loosed out of his pr.

8. *To send again or up, let go,* ἀνίημι *aniēmi.*
Acts 16. 26 opened, and every one's bands were loosed
27. 40 loosed the rudder bands, and hoised up

9. *To lift up,* αἴρω *airō.*
Acts 27. 13 loosing (thence), they sailed close by Cre.

10. *To lead forth,* ἀνάγω *anagō.*
Acts 13. 13 when Paul and his company loosed from
16. 11 loosing from Troas, we came with a stra.
27. 21 not have loosed from Crete, and to have

LOOSE, to let —

1. *To loose, shake off,* נָתַר *nathar,* 5.
Job 6. 9 that he would let loose his hand, and cut

2. *To send forth or away,* שָׁלַח *shalach.*
Gen. 49. 21 Naphtali (is) a hind let loose: he giveth

3. *To send forth or away,* שָׁלַח *shalach,* 3.
Lev. 14. 7 shall let the living bird loose into the open
Job 30. 11 they have also let loose the bridle before

LOOSE self, to —

To open for one's self, פָּתַח *pathach,* 7.
Isa. 52. 2 loose thyself from the bands of thy neck

LOOSED, to be —

1. *To be loosed,* זָחַח *zachach,* 2.
Exod28. 28 that the breastplate be not loosed from the
39. 21 that the breast plate might not be loosed

2. *To be melted,* מָסַס *masas,* 2.
Judg15. 14 and his bands loosed from off his hands

3. *To be spread out,* נָטַשׁ *natash,* 2.
Isa. 33. 23 Thy tacklings are loosed; they could not

4. *To be opened,* פָּתַח *pathach,* 2.
Isa. 5. 27 neither shall the girdle of their loins be l.
51. 14 exile hasteneth that he may be loosed, and

5. *To be bound (?),* רָתַק *rathaq* [V.L. רָחַק *rachaq*].
Eccl.12. 6 Or ever the silver cord be loosed, or the

6. *To loose,* שְׁרָא *shere.*
Dan. 3. 25 Lo, I see four men loose, walking in the

7. *To be loosed,* שְׁרָא *shere,* 4.
Dan. 5. 6 so that the joints of his loins were loosed

8. *A loosening,* λύσις *lusis.*
1 Co. 7. 27 Art thou bound unto . . seek not to be lo.

LOP, to —

To lop, cast off, סָעַף *saaph,* 3.
Isa. 10. 33 LORD of hosts shall lop the bough with

LORD —

1. *Lord, sir, master,* אָדוֹן *adon.*
Gen. 18. 12 shall I have pleasure, my lord being old
19. 2 now, my lords, turn in, I pray you, into
19. 18 Lot said unto them, Oh! not so, my lord
23. 6 Hear us, my lord: Thou (art) a mighty p.
23. 11 Nay, my lord, hear me: the field give I
23. 15 My lord, hearken unto me: the land (is w.)
24. 18 she said, Drink, my lord: and she hasted
31. 35 Let it not displease my lord that I cannot
32. 4 Thus shall ye speak unto my lord Esau
32. 5 I have sent to tell my lord, that I may find
32. 18 it (is) a present sent unto my lord Esau
33. 8 (are) to find grace in the sight of my lord
33. 13 My lord knoweth that the children (are)
33. 14 Let my lord, I pray thee, pass over before
33. 14 lead on . . until I come unto my lord unto
33. 15 let me find grace in the sight of my lord
39. 16 she laid up his garment . . until his lord
40. 1 had offended their lord the king of Egypt
40. 7 with him in the ward of his lord's house
42. 10 Nay, my lord, but to buy food are thy se.
42. 30 The man, (who is) the lord of the land, s.
42. 33 the lord of the country, said unto us, He.
44. 5 (Is) not this (it) in which my lord drink.
44. 7 Wherefore saith my lord these words? G.
44. 8 how then should we steal out of thy lord's
44. 9 and we also will be my lord's bond men
44. 16 say unto my lord? . . we (are) my lord's se.
44. 18 Oh my lord, let thy servant, I pray thee
44. 18 speak a word in my lord's ears, and let not
44. 19 My lord asked his servants, saying, Have
44. 20 we said unto my lord, We have a father
44. 22 we said unto my lord, The lad cannot le.
44. 24 came . . we told him the words of my lord
44. 33 abide instead . . a bond man to my lord
45. 8 lord of all his house, and a ruler through
45. 9 God hath made me lord of all Egypt: come
47. 18 We will not hide (it) from my lord, how
47. 18 my lord also hath our herds of cattle: th.
47. 18 is not ought left in the sight of my lord
47. 25 let us find grace in the sight of my lord
Exod23. 17 thy males shall appear before the Lord GOD
32. 22 Let not the anger of my lord wax hot
34. 23 men children appear before the Lord GOD
Num11. 28 answered and said, My lord Moses, forbid
12. 11 Aaron said unto Moses, Alas! my lord, I
32. 25 servants will do as my lord commandeth
32. 27 every man armed for war . . as my lord sa.
36. 2 commanded my lord to give the land for
36. 2 my lord was commanded . . to give the in.
Deut10. 17 Lord of lords, a great God, a mighty, and
Josh. 3. 11 ark of the covenant of the Lord of all the
3. 13 ark of . . the Lord of all the earth, shall
5. 14 What saith my lord unto his servant?
Judg. 3. 25 their lord (was) fallen down dead on the
4. 18 Turn in, my lord, turn in to me; fear not
6. 13 Gideon said unto him, Oh my Lord, if the
19. 26 of the man's house where her lord (was)
19. 27 her lord rose up in the morning, and ope.
Ruth 2. 13 Let me find favour in thy sight, my lord
1 Sa. 1. 15 No, my lord; I (am) a woman of a sorrow.
1. 26 Oh my lord, (as) thy soul liveth, my lord, I
16. 16 Let our lord now command thy servants
22. 12 And he answered, Here I (am), my lord
24. 8 cried after Saul, saying, My lord the king
24. 10 not put forth mine hand against my lord
25. 24 Upon me, my lord, (upon) me (let this)
25. 25 Let not my lord, I pray thee, regard this
25. 25 saw not the young men of my lord, whom
25. 26 Now therefore, my lord . . (as) thy soul li.
25. 26 they that seek evil to my lord, be as Na.
25. 27 thine handmaid hath brought unto my l.
25. 27 unto the young men that follow my lord
25. 28 will certainly make my lord a sure house
25. 28 because my lord fighteth the battles of the
25. 29 but the soul of my lord shall be bound in
25. 30 shall have done to my lord according to
25. 31 no grief . . nor offence of heart unto my l.
25. 31 or that my lord hath avenged himself
25. 31 shall have dealt well with my lord, then
25. 41 to wash the feet of the servants of my lord
26. 15 hast thou not kept thy lord the king?
26. 15 came one . . to destroy the king thy lord
1 Sa. 26. 17 David said, (It is) my voice, my lord, O king
26. 18 Wherefore doth my lord thus pursue after
26. 19 let my lord the king hear the words of his
29. 8 go fight against the enemies of my lord the
2 Sa. 1. 10 have brought them hither unto my lord
2. 5 showed this kindness unto your lord,
3. 21 gather all Israel unto my lord the king
4. 8 hath avenged my lord the king this day of
9. 11 According to all that my lord the king hath
10. 3 said unto Hanun their lord, Thinkest thou
11. 9 slept . . with all the servants of his lord, and
11. 11 my lord Joab, and the servants of my l.
11. 13 lie . . with the servants of his lord, but went
13. 32 Let not my lord suppose (that) they have
13. 33 Now therefore let not my lord the king
14. 9 My lord, O king, the iniquity (be) on me
14. 12 speak (one) word unto my lord the king
14. 15 to speak of this thing unto my lord the k.
14. 17 The word of my lord the king shall now be
14. 17 as an angel of God, so (is) my lord the k.
14. 18 woman said, Let my lord the king now sp.
14. 19 my lord the king, none can turn to the ri·
14. 19 ought that my lord the king hath spoken
14. 20 my lord (is) wise, according to the wisdom
14. 22 I have found grace in thy sight, my lord
15. 15 whatsoever my lord the king shall appoi.
15. 21 (As) the LORD liveth, and (as) my lord the
15. 21 in what place my lord the king shall be
16. 4 I may find grace in thy sight, my lord, O
16. 9 Why should this dead dog curse my lord
18. 28 lifted up their hand against my lord the
18. 31 Cushi said, Tidings, my lord the king: for
18. 32 The enemies of my lord the king, and all
19. 19 Let not my lord impute iniquity unto me
19. 19 my lord the king went out of Jerusalem
19. 20 first . . to go down to meet my lord the king
19. 26 My lord, O king, my servant deceived me
19. 27 unto my lord the king; but my lord the
19. 28 but dead men before my lord the king; yet
19. 30 my lord the king is come again in peace
19. 35 be yet a burden unto my lord the king?
19. 37 let him go over with my lord the king
20. 6 take thou thy lord's servants, and pursue
24. 3 the eyes of my lord the king may see (it)
24. 3 why doth my lord the king delight in this
24. 21 is my lord the king come to his servant?
24. 22 Let my lord the king take and offer up
1 Ki. 1. 2 sought for my lord the king a young
1. 2 that my lord the king may get heat
1. 11 reign, and David our lord knoweth (it)
1. 13 Didst not thou, my lord, O king, swear
1. 17 said unto him, My lord, thou swarest by
1. 18 now, my lord the king, thou knowest (it)
1. 20 my lord, O king, the eyes of all Israel (are)
1. 20, 27 throne of my lord the king after him
1. 21 my lord the king shall sleep with his
1. 24 My lord, O king, hast thou said, Adonijah
1. 27 Is this thing done by my lord the king, and
1. 31 said, Let my lord king David live for ever
1. 33 Take with you the servants of your lord
1. 36 the . . God of my lord the king say so (too)
1. 37 hath been with my lord the king, even so
1. 37 than the throne of my lord king David
1. 43 lord king David hath made Solomon king
1. 47 servants came to bless our lord king David
2. 38 as my lord the king hath said, so will thy
3. 17 O my lord, I and this woman dwell in one
3. 26 O my lord, give her the living child, and
11. 23 from his lord Hadadezer king of Zobah
12. 27 of this people turn again unto their lord
18. 7 and said, (Art) thou that my lord Elijah?
18. 8, 11, 14 tell thy lord, Behold, Elijah (is here)
18. 10 whither my lord hath not sent to seek thee
18. 13 Was it not told my lord what I did when
20. 4 My lord, O king, according to thy saying
20. 9 Tell my lord the king, All that thou didst
2 Ki. 2. 19 the situation . . (is) pleasant, as my lord
4. 16 my lord, (thou) man of God, do not lie
4. 28 Did I desire a son of my lord? did I not
5. 3 Would God my lord (were) with the pro.
5. 4 (one) went in, and told his lord, saying
6. 12 None, my lord, O king: but Elisha, the
6. 26 cried a woman . . saying, Help, my lord, O
8. 5 My lord, O king, this (is) the woman, and
8. 12 Hazael said, Why weepeth my lord? And
9. 11 Jehu came forth to the servants of his l.
18. 23 pledges to my lord the king of Assyria
1 Ch.21. 3 lord the king, (are) they not all my lord's
21. 3 why then doth my lord require this thing?
21. 23 let my lord . . king do (that which is) good
2 Ch. 2. 14 cunning men of my lord David thy father
2. 15 the wine, which my lord hath spoken of
13. 6 and hath rebelled against his lord
Neh. 3. 5 their necks to the work of their Lord
8. 10 (this) day (is) holy unto our Lord: neither
10. 29 do all the commandments of . . our Lord
Psa. 8. 1, 9 Lord, how excellent (is) thy name in all
12. 4 our lips (are) our own: who (is) lord over
45. 11 for he (is) thy Lord; and worship thou
97. 5 presence of the Lord of the whole earth
105. 21 He made him lord of his house, and ruler
110. 1 said unto my Lord, Sit thou at my right
114. 7 the presence of the Lord, at the presence
135. 5 I know . . (that) our Lord (is) above all gods
136. 3 give thanks to the Lord of lords: for his
147. 5 Great (is) our Lord, and of great power
Isa. 1. 24 Therefore saith the Lord . . the mighty One
3. 1 the Lord . . doth take away from Jerusalem
10. 16 Therefore shall the Lord . . send among his
10. 33 the Lord . . shall lop the bough with terror
19. 4 I give over into the hand of a cruel lord
19. 4 king shall rule over them, saith the Lord

Isa. 22. 18 (shall be) the shame of thy lord's house
26. 13 lords besides thee have had dominion over
51. 22 Thus saith thy Lord..and thy God (that)
Jer. 22. 18 for him, (saying), Ah lord! or, Ah his glory
34. 5 they will lament thee, (saying), Ah lord!
37. 20 hear now, I pray thee, O my lord the king
38. 9 My lord the king, these men have done
Dan. 1. 10 fear my lord the king, who hath appoint
10. 16 O my lord, by the vision my sorrows are
10. 17 of this my lord talk with this my lord? for
10. 19 my lord speak; for thou hast strengthened
12. 8 O my lord, what (shall be) the end of these
Hos. 12. 14 reproach shall his Lord return unto him
Mic. 4. 13 substance unto the Lord of the whole ea.
Zech. 1. 9 Then said I, O my lord, what (are) these?
4. 4 with me, saying, What (are) these, my lo.?
4. 5, 13 knowest thou not..And I said, No, my l.
4. 14 that stand by the Lord of the whole earth
6. 4 I answered..What (are) these, my lord?
6. 5 standing before the Lord of all the earth
Mal. 3. 1 the Lord, whom ye seek, shall suddenly

2. *My lords*, אֲדֹנָי *adonai.*

Gen. 15. 2 Lord GOD, what wilt thou give me, seeing
15. 8 Lord GOD, whereby shall I know that I sh.
18. 3 My Lord, if now I have found favour in
18. 27, 31 taken upon me to speak unto the Lord
18. 30, 32 let not the Lord be angry, and I will
20. 4 Lord, wilt thou slay also a righteous nat.
Exod. 4. 10 O my Lord, I (am) not eloquent, neither h.
4. 13 O my Lord, send, I pray thee, by the hand
5. 22 Lord, wherefore hast thou (so) evil 15. 17.
34. 9 O Lord, let my Lord, I pray thee, go am.
Num 14. 17 let the power of my Lord be great, accor.
Deut. 3. 24 O Lord GOD, thou hast begun to show thy
9. 26 O Lord GOD, destroy not thy people and
Josh. 7. 7 O Lord GOD, wherefore hast thou at all b.
7. 8 Lord, what shall I say, when Israel turn.
Judg. 6. 15 Oh my Lord, wherewith shall I save Isr.
6. 22 O Lord GOD! for because I have seen an
13. 8 O my Lord, let the man of God which
16. 28 O Lord GOD, remember me, I pray thee
2 Sa. 7. 18 Who (am) I, O Lord GOD? and what (is)
7. 19 yet a small thing in thy sight, O Lord GOD
7. 19 And (is) this the manner of man, O Lord
7. 20 for thou, Lord GOD, knowest thy servant
7. 28 O Lord GOD, thou (art) that God, and thy
7. 29 for thou, O Lord GOD, hast spoken (it)
1 Ki. 2. 26 thou barest the ark of the Lord GOD be.
3. 10; 8. 53; 22. 6; 2 Ki. 7. 6; 19. 23; Ezra
10. 3; Neh. 1. 11; 4. 14; Job 28. 28; Psa. 2. 4; 16. 2;
22. 30; 35. 17, 22; 44. 23; 57. 9; 66. 18; 68. 11, 26;
77. 2; 89. 9; 90. 1; 130. 6.
Psa. 35. 23 (even) unto my cause, my God and my L.
37. 13 The Lord shall laugh at him; for he se.
38. 9 Lord, all my desire (is) before thee; and
38. 15 do I hope: thou wilt hear, O Lord my G.
38. 22 Make haste to help me, O Lord my salva.
39. 7 Lord, what wait I for? my hope (is) in
40. 17 the Lord thinketh upon me: thou (art)
51. 15 O Lord, open thou my lips; and my mo.
54. 4 the Lord (is) with them that uphold my
55. 9 Destroy, O Lord, (and) divide their tong.
59. 11 and bring them down, O Lord our shield
62. 12 Also unto thee, O Lord, (belongeth) me.
68. 17 the Lord (is) among them, (as) in Sinai
68. 19 Blessed (be) the Lord, (who) daily load.
68. 20 unto GOD the Lord (belong) the issues
68. 22 The Lord said, I will bring again from B.
68. 32 Sing unto God..O sing praises unto the L.
69. 6 Let not them that wait on thee, O Lord GOD
71. 5 For thou (art) my hope, O Lord GOD..my
71. 16 I will go in the strength of the Lord GOD
73. 20 O Lord, when thou awakest, thou shalt
73. 28 I have put my trust in the Lord GOD, that
77. 7 Will the Lord cast off for ever? and will
78. 65 Then the Lord awaked as one out of sleep
79. 12 wherewith they have reproached .O Lord
86. 3 Be merciful unto me, O Lord: for I cry
86. 4 for unto thee, O Lord, do I lift up my soul
86. 5 thou, Lord, (art) good, and ready to forg.
86. 8 none like unto thee, O Lord; neither (are
86. 12 I will praise thee, O Lord my God, with
86. 15 But thou, O Lord, (art) a God full of com.
89. 49 Lord, where (are) thy former loving kin.
89. 50 Remember, Lord, the reproach of thy se.
109. 21 do thou for me, O GOD the Lord, for thy
110. 5 The Lord at thy right hand shall strike
130. 2 Lord, hear my voice; let thine ears be
130. 3 If thou..shouldest mark..O Lord, who
140. 7 O GOD the Lord, the strength of my salv.
141. 8 mine eyes (are) unto thee, O GOD the Lord
Isa 3. 15 What mean ye..saith the Lord GOD of h.
3. 17 the Lord will smite with a scab the crown
3. 18 In that day the Lord will take away the
4. 4 When the Lord shall have washed away
6. 11 Then said I, Lord, how long? And 6. 1 8.
7. 7 saith the Lord GOD, It shall not v. 14, 20.
7. 7 the Lord bringeth up upon them the wa.
9. 8 the Lord sent a word into Jacob, and it
9. 17 the Lord shall have no joy in their young
10. 12 when the Lord hath performed his whole
10. 16 shall..the Lord of hosts, send among his
10. 23 For the Lord GOD of hosts shall make a
10. 24 saith the Lord GOD of hosts, O my people
11. 11 Lord shall set his hand again the second
21. 6 thus hath the Lord said unto me, Go, set
21. 8 he cried, A lion: My lord, I stand contin.
21. 16 thus hath the Lord said unto me, Within
22. 5 by the Lord GOD of hosts in the valley of
22. 12 in that day did the Lord GOD of hosts call
22. 14 till ye die, saith the Lord GOD of hosts

Isa. 22. 15 Thus saith the Lord GOD of hosts, Go, get
25. 8 Lord GOD will wipe away tears from off all
28. 2 the Lord hath a mighty and a strong one
28. 16 saith the Lord GOD, Behold, I lay in Zion
28. 22 I have heard from the Lord GOD of hosts
29. 13 the Lord said, Forasmuch as this people
30. 15 saith the Lord GOD, the Holy One of Israel
30. 20 the Lord give you the bread of adversity
37. 24 reproached the Lord, and hast said, By the
38. 16 O Lord, by these (things men) live, and in
40. 10 the Lord GOD will come with strong (hand)
48. 16 the Lord GOD, and his spirit, hath sent me
49. 14 But Zion said..my Lord hath forgotten me
49. 22 Thus saith the Lord GOD, Behold, I will
50. 4 Lord GOD hath given me the tongue of the
50. 5 Lord GOD hath opened mine ear, and I
50. 7 For the Lord GOD will help me; therefore
50. 9 Behold, the Lord GOD will help me; who
52. 4 saith the Lord GOD, My people went down
56. 8 The Lord GOD which gathereth the out c.
61. 1 spirit of the Lord GOD (is) upon me; bec.
61. 11 the Lord GOD will cause righteousness and
65. 13 saith the Lord GOD, Behold, my servants
65. 15 for the Lord GOD shall slay thee, and call
Jer. 1. 6 Then said I, Ah, Lord GOD! behold, I can.
2. 19 my fear (is) not in thee, saith the Lord G.
2. 22 thine iniquity is marked..saith the Lord
4. 10 Then said I, Ah, Lord GOD! surely thou
7. 20 saith the Lord GOD; Behold, mine anger
14. 13 Then said I, Ah, Lord GOD! behold, the
32. 17 Ah Lord GOD! behold, thou hast made
32. 25 thou hast said unto me, O Lord GOD, Buy
44. 26 in all the land of Egypt, saying, The Lord
46. 10 day of the Lord..for the Lord GOD of h.
49. 5 bring a fear upon thee, saith the Lord G.
50. 25 this (is) the work of the Lord GOD of hosts
50. 31 I (am) against thee..saith the Lord GOD of
Lam. 2. 1 How hath the Lord covered, 1. 14, 15, 15.
2. 2 Lord hath swallowed up all the habitations
2. 5 Lord was as an enemy: he hath swallowed
2. 7 The Lord hath cast off his altar, he hath
2. 18 Their heart cried unto the Lord, O wall of
2. 19 like water before the face of the Lord v. 20
3. 31 For the Lord will not cast off for ever
3. 36 To subvert a man..the Lord approveth
3. 37 it cometh to pass, (when) the Lord c.
3. 58 O Lord, thou hast pleaded the causes of
Eze. 2. 4 Thus saith the Lord GOD
[So in 3. 11, 27; 5. 5, 7, 8; 6. 3, 11; 7. 2, 5; 11. 7, 16, 17;
12. 10, 19, 23, 28; 13. 3, 8, 13, 18, 20; 14. 4, 6, 21; 15. 6;
16. 3, 36, 59; 17. 3, 9, 19, 22; 18. 3, 9, 23, 30, 32; 20. 3, 5,
27, 30, 39, 47; 21. 24, 26, 28; 22. 3, 19, 28; 23. 22, 28, 32,
35, 46; 24. 3, 6, 9, 21; 25. 3, 6, 8, 12, 13, 15, 16; 26. 3, 7,
15, 19; 27. 3; 28. 2, 6, 12, 22, 25; 29. 3, 8, 13, 19; 30. 2,
10, 13, 22; 31. 10, 15; 32. 3, 11; 33. 25, 27; 34. 2, 10, 11,
17, 20; 35. 3, 14; 36. 2, 3, 4, 5, 6, 7, 13, 22, 33, 37; 37. 5,
9, 12, 19, 21; 38. 3, 10, 14, 17; 39. 1, 17, 25; 43. 18; 44.
6, 9; 45. 9, 18; 46. 1, 16; 47. 13.]
Eze. 4. 14 Then said I, Ah Lord GOD! behold, my
5. 11 saith the Lord GOD
[So in 11. 8, 21; 12. 25, 28; 13. 8, 16; 14. 11, 14, 16, 18,
20, 23; 15. 8; 16. 8, 14, 19, 23, 30, 43, 48, 63; 17. 16; 18.
3, 9, 23, 30, 32; 20. 3, 31, 33, 36, 40, 44; 21. 7, 13; 22. 12,
31; 23. 34; 24. 14; 25. 14; 26. 5, 14, 21; 28. 10; 30. 6;
31. 18; 32. 8, 14, 16, 31, 32; 33. 11; 34. 8, 15, 30, 31; 35.
6; 36. 14, 15, 23, 32; 38. 18, 21; 39. 5, 8, 10, 13, 20, 29;
43. 19, 27; 44. 12, 15, 27; 45. 9, 15; 47. 23; 48. 29.]
Eze. 6. 3 hear the word of the Lord GOD; Thus saith
8. 1 hand of the Lord GOD fell there upon me
9. 8 Ah Lord God! wilt thou destroy all the
11. 13 Ah Lord God! wilt thou make a full end
13. 9 ye shall know that I (am) the Lord GOD
18. 25, 29 The way of the Lord is not equal
20. 49 Ah Lord GOD! they say of me, Doth he
23. 49 ye shall know that I (am) the Lord GOD
24. 24 ye shall know that I (am) the Lord GOD
25. 3 Hear the word of the Lord GOD; Thus
28. 24 they shall know that I (am) the Lord GOD
29. 16 they shall know that I (am) the Lord GOD
29. 20 they wrought for me, saith the Lord GOD
33. 17, 20 The way of the Lord is not equal
36. 4 hear the word of the Lord GOD; Thus saith
37. 3 I answered, O Lord GOD, thou knowest
Dan. 1. 2 Lord gave Jehoiakim king of Judah into
9. 3 I set my face unto the Lord God, to seek
9. 4 I prayed..and said, O Lord, the great and
9. 7 O Lord, righteousness (belongeth) unto
9. 8 O Lord, to us (belongeth) confusion of face
9. 9 To the Lord our God (belong) mercies and
9. 15 O Lord our God, that hast brought thy p.
9. 16 O Lord, according to all thy righteousness
9. 17 O our God, hear the prayer..for the Lo.
9. 19 O Lord, hear; O Lord, forgive; O Lord
Amos 1. 8 the remnant..shall perish, saith the Lord
3. 7 Surely the Lord GOD will do nothing, but
3. 8 the Lord GOD hath spoken, who can but
3. 11 thus saith the Lord GOD; An adversary
3. 13 Hear ye, and testify..saith the Lord GOD
4. 2 The Lord GOD hath sworn by his holiness
4. 5 ye children of Israel, saith the Lord GOD
5. 3 For thus saith the Lord God; The city that
5. 16 the Lord, saith thus; Wailing (shall be) in
6. 8 The Lord GOD hath sworn by himself, saith
7. 1, 4 Thus hath the Lord GOD showed unto
7. 2 said O Lord GOD, forgive, I beseech thee
7. 4 the Lord GOD called to contend by fire
7. 5 said I, O Lord GOD, cease, I beseech thee
7. 6 This also shall not be, saith the Lord GOD
7. 7 the Lord stood upon a wall (made) by a
7. 8 said the Lord, Behold, I will set a plum.
8. 1 Thus hath the Lord GOD showed unto me
8. 3 howlings in that day, saith the Lord GOD

Amos 8. 9 it shall come to pass..saith the Lord GOD
8. 11 days come, saith the Lord GOD, that I will
9. 1 I saw the Lord standing upon the altar
9. 5 Lord GOD of hosts (is) he that toucheth the
9. 8 eyes of the Lord GOD (are) upon the sinful
Obad. 1 saith the Lord GOD concerning Edom; We
Mic. 1. 2 let the Lord GOD..the Lord from; Hab. 3. 19
Zeph. 1. 7 Hold thy peace at the presence of the L.
Zech. 9. 4 Behold, the Lord will cast her out, and he
9. 14 the Lord GOD shall blow the trumpet, and
Mal. 1. 14 sacrificeth unto the Lord a corrupt thing

3. *Lord, master, owner*, בַּעַל *baal.*

Num 21. 28 the lords of the high places of Arnon
Isa. 16. 8 lords of the heathen have broken down

4. *A mighty or strong one*, גְּבִיר *gebir.*

Gen. 27. 29 be lord over thy brethren, and let thy
27. 37 I have made him thy lord, and all his br.

5. *He (who) is*, יְהוָֹה *yahweh* (read *adonai*).

Gen. 2. 4 LORD God made the earth and the heavens
2. 5 the LORD God had not caused it to rain
2. 7 the LORD God formed man (of) the dust of
2. 8 the LORD God planted a garden eastward
2. 9 out of the ground made the LORD God to
2. 15 the LORD God took the man, and put him
2. 16 the LORD God commanded the man, saying
2. 18 the LORD God said, (It is) not good that
2. 21 the LORD God caused a deep sleep to fall
2. 22 which the LORD God had taken from man
3. 1 any beast..which the LORD God had made
3. 8 And they heard the voice of the LORD God
3. 8 from the presence of the LORD God amon.
3. 9 the LORD God called unto Adam, and said
3. 13, 14, 21, 22, 23; 4. 1, 3, 4, 6, 9, 13, 15, 15,
16, 26; 5. 29; 6. 3, 5, 6, 7, 8; 7. 1, 5, 16; 8. 20, 21, 21;
9. 26; 10. 9, 9; 11. 5, 6, 8, 9, 9; 12. 1, 4, 7, 7, 8, 8, 17;
13. 4, 10, 10, 13, 14, 18; 14. 22; 15. 1, 4, 6, 7, 18; 16. 2,
5, 7, 9, 10, 11, 11, 13; 17. 1; 18. 1, 13, 14, 17, 19, 19, 20,
22, 26, 33; 19. 13, 13, 14, 16, 24, 24, 27; 20. 18; 21. 1, 1,
33; 22. 11, 14, 15, 16; 24. 1, 3, 7, 12, 21, 26, 27, 27, 31, 35,
40, 42. 44, 48, 48, 50, 51, 52, 56; 25. 21, 21, 22, 23; 26. 2,
12, 22, 24, 25, 28, 29; 27. 7, 20, 27; 28. 13, 13, 16, 21; 29.
31, 32, 33, 35; 30. 24, 27, 30; 31. 3, 49; 32. 9; 38. 7, 7,
10; 39. 2, 3, 3, 5, 5, 21, 23, 23; 49. 18.
Exod. 3. 2, 4, 7, 15, 16, 18, 18; 4. 1, 2, 4, 5, 6, 10, 11,
11, 14, 19, 21, 22, 24, 27, 28, 30, 31; 5. 1, 2, 2, 3, 17, 21,
22; 6. 1, 2, 3, 6, 7, 8, 10, 12, 13, 26, 28, 29, 29, 30; 7. 1,
5, 6, 8, 10, 13, 14, 16, 17, 17, 19, 20, 22, 25; 8. 1, 1, 5, 8,
8, 10, 12, 13, 15, 16, 19, 20, 20, 22, 24, 26, 27, 28, 29, 29,
30, 31; 9. 1, 1, 3, 4, 5, 5, 6, 8, 12, 12, 13, 13, 20, 21, 22,
23, 23, 27, 28, 29, 29, 30, 33, 35; 10. 1, 2, 3, 7, 8, 9,
10, 11, 12, 13, 16, 17, 18, 19, 20, 21, 24, 25, 26, 26, 27; 11.
1, 3, 4, 7, 9, 10; 12. 1, 11, 12, 14, 23, 23, 25, 27, 28, 29, 31,
36, 41, 42, 42, 43, 48, 50, 51; 13. 1, 3, 5, 6, 8, 9, 9, 11, 12,
12, 14, 15, 15, 16, 21; 14. 1, 4, 8, 10, 13, 14, 15, 18, 21, 24,
25, 26, 27, 30, 31, 31, 31; 15. 1, 1, 3, 3, 6, 6, 11, 16, 17,
18, 19, 21, 25, 25, 26, 26; 16. 3, 4, 6, 7, 7, 8, 8, 8, 9, 10,
11, 12, 15, 16, 23, 23, 25, 28, 29, 32, 33, 34; 17. 1, 2, 4, 5,
7, 7, 14, 16; 18. 1, 8, 8, 9, 10, 11; 19. 3, 7, 8, 8, 9, 9,
10, 11, 18, 20, 20, 21, 21, 22, 22, 23, 24, 24; 20. 2, 5, 7, 7,
10, 11, 11, 12, 22; 22. 11, 20; 23. 17, 19, 25; 24. 1, 2, 3, 3,
4, 5, 7, 8, 12, 16, 17; 25. 1; 27. 21; 28. 12, 29, 30, 30, 35,
36, 38; 29. 11, 18, 18, 23, 24, 25, 25, 26, 28, 41, 42, 46, 46;
30. 8, 10, 11, 12, 13, 14, 15, 16, 17, 20, 22, 34, 37; 31. 1, 12,
13, 15, 17; 32. 5, 7, 9, 11, 11, 14, 26, 27, 29, 30, 31, 33, 35;
33. 1, 5, 7, 11, 12, 17, 19, 21; 34. 1, 4, 5, 5, 6, 6, 6, 10, 14,
23, 24, 26, 27, 28, 32, 34; 35. 1, 2, 4, 5, 5, 10, 21, 22, 24,
29, 29, 30; 36. 1, 1, 2, 5; 38. 22; 39. 1, 5, 7, 21, 26, 29,
30, 31, 32, 42, 43; 40. 1, 16, 19, 21, 23, 23, 25, 25, 27, 29,
32, 34, 35, 38.
Lev. 1. 1, 2, 3, 5, 9, 11, 13, 14, 17; 2. 1, 2, 3, 8, 9, 10,
11, 11, 12, 14, 16; 3. 1, 3, 5, 6, 7, 9, 11, 12, 14, 16; 4. 1,
2, 3, 4, 4, 6, 7, 13, 15, 15, 17, 18, 22, 24, 27, 31, 35; 5. 6,
7, 12, 14, 15, 15, 17, 19; 6. 1, 2, 6, 7, 8, 14, 15, 18, 19, 20,
21, 22, 24, 25; 7. 5, 11, 14, 20, 21, 22, 25, 28, 29, 29, 30,
30, 35, 35, 36, 38, 38; 8. 1, 4, 5, 9, 13, 17, 21, 21, 26,
27, 28, 29, 29, 34, 35, 36; 9. 2, 4, 4, 5, 6, 6, 7, 10, 21, 23,
24; 10. 1, 2, 2, 3, 6, 7, 8, 11, 12, 13, 15, 15, 17, 19, 19; 11.
1, 44, 45; 12. 1, 7; 13. 1; 14. 1, 11, 12, 16, 18, 23, 24, 27,
29, 31, 33; 15. 1, 14, 15, 30; 16. 1, 1, 2, 7, 8, 9, 10, 12, 13,
18, 30, 34; 17. 1, 2, 4, 4, 5, 5, 6, 6, 9; 18. 1, 2, 4, 5, 6, 21,
30; 19. 1, 2, 3, 4, 5, 8, 10, 12, 14, 16, 18, 21, 22, 24, 25,
28, 30, 31, 32, 34, 36, 37; 20. 1, 7, 8, 24, 26; 21. 1, 6, 8,
12, 15, 16, 21, 23; 22. 1, 2, 3, 3, 8, 9, 15, 16, 17, 18, 21, 22,
22, 24, 26, 27, 29, 30, 31, 32, 33; 23. 1, 2, 3, 4, 5, 6, 8, 9,
11, 12, 13, 16, 17, 18, 18, 20, 20, 22, 23, 25, 26, 27, 28, 33,
34, 36, 36, 37, 37, 38, 38, 39, 40, 41, 43, 44; 24. 1, 3, 4, 6,
7, 8, 9, 12, 13, 16, 22, 23; 25. 1, 2, 4, 17, 38, 55; 26.
1, 2, 13, 44, 45, 46; 27. 1, 2, 9, 9, 11, 14, 16, 21, 22, 23,
26, 26, 28, 28, 30, 30, 32, 34.
Num. 1. 1, 19, 48, 54; 2. 1, 33, 34; 3. 1, 4, 4, 5, 11, 13,
14, 16, 39, 40, 41, 42, 44. 45, 51, 51; 4. 1, 17, 21, 37, 41,
45, 49, 49; 5. 1, 4, 5, 6, 8, 11, 16, 18, 21, 21, 25, 30; 6. 1, 2,
5, 6, 8, 12, 14, 16, 17, 20, 21, 22, 24, 25, 26; 7. 3, 4, 11; 8
1, 3, 4, 5, 10, 11, 11, 12, 13, 20, 21, 22, 23; 9. 1, 5, 7, 8, 9,
10, 13, 14, 18, 18, 19, 20, 20, 23, 23, 23, 23; 10. 1, 9, 10, 13,
29, 29, 32, 33, 33, 34, 35, 36; 11. 1, 1, 1, 2, 3, 10, 11, 16,
18, 18, 20, 23, 23, 24, 25, 29, 29, 31, 33, 33; 12. 2, 2, 4, 5, 6, 8,
9, 13, 14; 13. 1, 3; 14. 3, 8, 9, 9, 10, 11, 13, 14, 14, 16, 18,
20, 21, 26, 28, 35, 37, 40, 41, 42, 43, 43, 44; 15. 1, 3, 3, 4,
7, 8, 10, 13, 14, 15, 17, 19, 21, 22, 23, 23, 24, 25, 25, 28, 30,
31, 35, 36, 37, 39, 41, 41; 16. 3, 3, 5, 7, 7, 9, 11, 15, 16, 17, 19,
20, 23, 28, 29, 30, 30, 35, 36, 38, 40, 40, 41, 42, 44, 46; 17.
1, 7, 9, 10, 11, 13; 18. 1, 6, 8, 12, 13, 15, 17, 19, 19, 20,
24, 25, 26, 28, 28, 29; 19. 1, 2, 13, 20; 20. 3, 4, 6, 7, 9, 12,
13, 16, 23, 27; 21. 2, 3, 6, 7, 7, 8, 14, 16, 34; 22. 8, 13, 18,
19, 22, 23, 24, 25, 26, 27, 28, 31, 31, 32, 34, 35; 23. 3, 5, 8,
12, 16, 17, 21, 26; 24. 1, 6, 11, 13, 13; 25. 3, 4, 4, 4, 10, 16;
26. 1, 4, 9, 52, 61, 65; 27. 3, 5, 6. 11, 12, 15, 16, 17, 18, 21,
22, 23; 28. 1, 3, 6, 7, 8, 11, 13, 15, 16, 19, 24, 26, 27; 29.
2, 6, 8, 12, 13, 36, 39, 40; 30. 1, 2, 3, 5, 8, 12, 16; 31. 1,

Nah. 1. 2, 2, 2, 3, 3, 7, 9, 11, 12, 14; 2. 2, 13; 3. 5.
Hab. 1. 2, 12; 2. 2, 13, 14, 16, 20; 3. 2, 2, 8, 18.
Zeph. 1. 1, 2, 3, 5, 6, 6, 7, 7, 8, 10, 12, 14, 14, 17, 18; 2. 1, 2, 3, 3, 5, 7, 9, 10, 11; 3. 2, 5, 8, 9, 12, 15, 15, 17, 20.
Hag. 1. 1, 2, 2, 3, 5, 7, 8, 9, 12, 12, 13, 13, 13, 14, 14; 2. 1, 4, 4, 4, 6, 7, 8, 9, 9, 10, 11, 14, 15, 17, 18, 20, 23, 23, 23.
Zech. 1. 1, 2, 3, 3, 3, 4, 4, 6, 7, 10, 11, 12, 12, 13, 14, 16, 16, 17, 17, 20; 2. 6, 6, 8, 9, 10, 11, 11, 12, 13; 3. 1, 2, 2, 2, 5, 6, 7, 9, 10; 4 6, 6, 8, 9, 10; 5. 4; 6. 9, 12, 12, 13, 14, 15, 15, 15; 7. 1, 2, 3, 4, 7, 8, 9, 12, 12, 13; 8. 1, 2, 3, 3, 4, 6, 6, 7, 9, 9, 11, 14, 14, 17, 18, 19, 20, 21, 21, 22, 22, 23; 9. 1, 1, 14, 15, 16; 10. 1, 1, 3, 5, 6, 7, 12, 12; 11. 4, 5, 6, 11, 13, 13, 15; 12. 1, 1, 4, 5, 7, 8, 8; 13. 2, 3, 7, 8, 9; 14. 1, 3, 5, 7, 9, 9, 12, 13, 16, 17, 18, 20, 20, 21, 21.
Mal. 1. 1, 2, 2, 4, 4, 5, 6, 7, 8, 9, 10, 11, 12, 13, 13, 14; 2. 2, 4, 7, 8, 11, 12, 12, 13, 14, 16, 16, 17, 17; 3. 1, 3, 4, 5, 6, 7, 10, 11, 12, 13, 14, 16, 16, 16, 17; 4. 1, 3, 5.

6. *One high or exalted,* מָרֵא *mare.*

Dan. 2. 47 a Lord of kings, and a revealer of secrets
4. 19 My lord, the dream (be) to them that hate
4. 24 decree..which is come upon my lord the
5. 23 hast lifted up thyself against the Lord of

7. *Jah, (a contraction of Jehovah),* יָהּ *yah.*

Exod 15. 2 LORD (is) my strength and song, and he is
17. 16 For he said, Because the LORD hath sworn
Psa. 77. 11 I will remember the works of the LORD
89. 8 who (is) a strong LORD like unto thee? or
94. 7 The LORD shall not see, neither shall the
94. 12 the man whom thou chastenest, O LORD
102. 18 and the people..shall praise the LORD
104. 35 Bless thou the LORD, O my soul. Praise
105. 45 and keep his laws. Praise ye the LORD
106. 1 give thanks unto the LORD; for (he is)
106. 48 the people say, Amen. Praise ye the LORD
111. 1 Praise ye the LORD. I will praise..in the
112. 1 Praise ye the LORD. Blessed (is) the man
113. 1 Praise ye the LORD. Praise, O ye servants
113. 9 (be) a joyful mother..Praise ye the LORD
115. 17 The dead praise not the LORD, neither any
115. 18 we will bless the LORD..Praise the LORD
116. 1 I love the LORD, because he hath heard
116. 19 In the courts of the LORD'S house, in the
118. 5 called upon the LORD in distress: the LORD
118. 14 The LORD (is) my strength and song, and
118. 17 live, and declare the works of the LORD
118. 18 The LORD hath chastened me sore: but
118. 19 go in to them, (and) I will praise the LORD
122. 4 the tribes go up, the tribes of the LORD
130. 3 If thou, LORD, shouldest mark iniquities
135. 1 Praise ye the LORD. Praise ye the name
135. 3 Praise the LORD..sing praises unto his na.
135. 4 the LORD hath chosen Jacob unto himself
135. 21 dwelleth at Jerusalem. Praise ye the LORD
146. 1 Praise ye the LORD..O my soul
146. 10 unto all generations. Praise ye the LORD
147. 1 Praise ye the LORD: for (it is) good to sing
147. 20 have not known them. Praise ye the LORD
148. 1 Praise ye the LORD..from the heavens
148. 14 people near unto him. Praise ye the LORD
149. 1 Praise ye the LORD. Sing..a new song
149. 9 this honour have all..Praise ye the LORD
150. 1 Praise ye the LORD. Praise God in his sa.
150. 6 breath praise the LORD. Praise ye the L.
Isa. 12. 2 LORD Jehovah (is) my strength and (my)
26. 4 LORD Jehovah (is) everlasting strength
38. 11 I shall not see the LORD, (even) the LORD

8. *A prince, axle,* סֶרֶן *seren.*

Josh. 13. 3 five lords of the Philistines; the Gazath.
Judg. 3. 3 five lords of the Philistines, and all the C.
16. 5 the lords of the Philistines came up unto
16. 8 the lords of the Philistines brought up to
16. 18 called for the lords of the Philistines, say.
16. 18 lords of the Philistines came up unto her
16. 27 all the lords of the Philistines (were) there
16. 30 the house fell upon the lords, and upon
1 Sa. 5. 8 gathered all the lords of the Philistines
5. 11 together all the lords of the Philistines
6. 4 the number of the lords of the Philistines
6. 4 one plague..on you all, and on your lords
6. 12 the lords of the Philistines went after them
6. 16 the five lords of the Philistines had seen
6. 18 the cities..(belonging) to the five lords
7. 7 lords of the Philistines went up against
29. 2 the lords of the Philistines passed on by
29. 6 nevertheless the lords favour thee not
29. 7 that thou displease not the lords of the P.
1 Ch. 12. 19 the lords of the Philistines upon advise.

9. *A great one,* רַב *rab.*

Dan. 2. 10 no king, lord, nor ruler..asked such thi.

10. *Prince, head, chief, captain,* שַׂר *sar.*

Ezra 8. 25 his lords, and all Israel (there) present

11. *One of or over three,* שָׁלִישׁ *shalish.*

2 Ki. 7. 2 Then a lord on whose hand the king lea.
7. 17 the king appointed the lord on whose h.
7. 19 that lord answered the man of God, and
Eze. 23. 23 great lords and renowned, all of them rid.

12. *Great ones,* רַבְרְבָן *rabreban.*

Dan. 4. 36 counsellors and my lords sought unto me
5. 1 a great feast to a thousand of his lords
5. 9 greatly troubled..and his lords were ast.
5. 10 of the words of the king and his lords
5. 23 thy lords, thy wives, and thy concubines
6. 17 king sealed it..with the signet of his lords

13. *A despot, master,* δεσπότης *despotēs.*

Luke 2. 29 Lord, now lettest thou thy servant depart
Acts 4. 24 Lord, thou (art) God, which hast made
2 Pe. 2. 1 denying the Lord that bought them, and
Jude 4 and denying the only Lord God, and our
Rev. 6. 10 How long, O Lord, holy and true, dost thou

14. *Lord, sir, master,* κύριος *kurios.*

Matt. 1. 20 the angel of the Lord appeared unto him
1. 22 which was spoken of the Lord by the pro.
1. 24 did as the angel of the Lord had bidden
2. 13 the angel of the Lord appeareth to Joseph
2. 15 which was spoken of the Lord by the pr.
2. 19 an angel of the Lord appeareth in a dream
3. 3 Prepare ye the way of the Lord, make his
4. 7 Thou shalt not tempt the Lord thy God
4. 10 Thou shalt worship the Lord thy God, and
5. 33 shalt perform unto the Lord thine oaths
7. 21 every one that saith unto me, Lord, Lord
7. 22 Lord, Lord, have we not prophesied in thy
8. 2 Lord, if thou wilt, thou canst make me
8. 6 Lord, my servant lieth at home sick of the
8. 8 Lord, I am not worthy that thou should.
8. 21 Lord, suffer me first to go and bury my f.
8. 25 awoke him, saying, Lord, save us: we pe.
9. 28 Believe ye..They said unto him, Yea, L.
9. 38 Pray ye therefore the Lord of the harvest
10. 24 (his) master, nor the servant above his l.
10. 25 as his master, and the servant as his lord
11. 25 O Father, Lord of heaven and earth, bec.
12. 8 Son of man is Lord even of the sabbath
13. 51 Have ye understood..They say..Yea, [L.]
14. 28 Lord, if it be thou, bid me come unto thee
14. 30 beginning to sink..cried..Lord, save me
15. 22 Have mercy on me, O Lord, (thou) son of
15. 25 and worshipped him, saying, Lord, help
15. 27 Truth, Lord: yet the dogs eat of the cru.
16. 22 Be it far from thee, Lord: this shall not
17. 4 Lord, it is good for us to be here: if thou
17. 15 Lord, have mercy on my son: for he is l.
18. 21 Lord, how oft shall my brother sin against
18. 25 his lord commanded him to be sold, and
18. 26 [Lord,] have patience with me, and I will
18. 27 the lord of that servant was moved with
18. 31 came and told unto their lord all that was
18. 32 his lord, after that he had called him, said
18. 34 his lord was wroth, and delivered him to
20. 8 lord of the vineyard saith unto his steward
20. 30, 31 Have mercy on us, O Lord..son of D.
20. 33 They say..Lord, that our eyes may be op.
21. 3 ye shall say, The Lord hath need of them
21. 9 he that cometh in the name of the Lord
21. 40 the Lord therefore of the vineyard v. 42
21. 42 is the Lord's doing, and it is marvellous
22. 37 Thou shalt love the Lord thy God with all
22. 43 then doth David in spirit call him Lord
22. 44 The Lord said unto my Lord, Sit thou on
22. 45 If David then call him Lord, how is he his
23. 39 (is) he that cometh in the name of the L.
24. 42 know not what hour your Lord doth come
24. 45 his lord hath made ruler over his house.
24. 46 lord when he cometh shall find so doing
24. 48 say in his heart, My lord delayeth his co.
24. 50 The lord of that servant shall come in a
25. 11 other virgins, saying, Lord, Lord, open to
25. 18 digged in the earth, and hid his lord's m.
25. 19 the lord of those servants cometh, and r.
25. 20 Lord, thou deliveredst unto me five talo.
25. 21 His lord said unto him, Well done, (thou)
25. 21, 23 enter thou into the joy of thy lord
25. 22 Lord, thou deliveredst unto me two tale
25. 23 His lord said unto him, Well done, good
25. 24 Lord, I knew thee that thou art an hard
25. 26 His lord answered..said unto him, (Thou)
25. 37 Lord, when saw we thee an hungered, and
25. 44 Lord, when saw we thee an hungered, or
26. 22 one of them to say unto him, Lord, is it
27. 10 potter's field, as the Lord appointed me
28. 2 angel of the Lord descended from heaven
28. 6 Come, see the place where [the Lord] lay
Mark 1. 3 Prepare ye the way of the Lord, make his
2. 28 Son of man is Lord also of the sabbath
5. 19 great things the Lord hath done for thee
7. 28 Yes, Lord: yet the dogs under the table
9. 24 [Lord,] I believe; help thou mine unbelief
11. 3 say ye that the Lord hath need of him
11. 9 that cometh in the name of the Lord
11. 10 [that cometh in the name of the Lord]
12. 9 What shall therefore the lord of the vin.
12. 11 was the Lord's doing, and it is marvellous
12. 29 O Israel; The Lord our God is one Lord
12. 30 love the Lord thy God with all thy heart
12. 36 The Lord said to my Lord, Sit thou on my
12. 37 David therefore himself calleth him Lord
13. 20 except that the Lord had shortened those
16. 19 [after the Lord had spoken unto them]
16. 20 [the Lord working with (them), and con.]
Luke 1. 6 commandments and ordinances of the L.
1. 9 when he went into the temple of the Lord
1. 11 appeared unto him an angel of the Lord
1. 15 he shall be great in the sight of the Lord
1. 16 many..shall he turn to the Lord their God
1. 17 make ready a people prepared for the L.
1. 25 Thus hath the Lord dealt with me in the
1. 28 highly favoured, the Lord (is) with thee
1. 32 the Lord God shall give unto him the
1. 38 Behold the handmaid of the Lord; be it
1. 43 the mother of my Lord should come to
1. 45 things which were told her from the L.
1. 46 Mary said, My soul doth magnify the L.
1. 58 the Lord had showed great mercy upon
1. 66 And the hand of the Lord was with him
1. 68 Blessed (be) the Lord God of Israel; for he
1. 76 thou shalt go before the face of the Lord
2. 9 the angel of the Lord came upon them, and
2. 9 glory [of the Lord] shone round about them
Luke 2. 11 born..a Saviour, which is Christ the L.
2. 15 which the Lord hath made known unto
2. 22 to Jerusalem, to present (him) to the L.
2. 23 As it is written in the law of the Lord, Ev.
2. 23 male..shall be called holy to the Lord
2. 24 that which is said in the law of the Lord
2. 26 not..before he had seen the Lord's Christ
2. 38 she..gave thanks likewise unto [the Lord]
2. 39 all things according to the law of the L.
3. 4 Prepare ye the way of the Lord, make
4. 8 Thou shalt worship the Lord thy God, and
4. 12 Thou shalt not tempt the Lord thy God
4. 18 The Spirit of the Lord (is) upon me, be.
4. 19 To preach the acceptable year of the L.
5. 8 from me; for I am a sinful man, O Lord
5. 12 Lord, if thou wilt, thou canst make me
5. 17 power of the Lord was (present) to heal
6. 5 Son of man is Lord also of the sabbath
6. 46 why call ye me, Lord, Lord, and do not
7. 6 Lord, trouble not thyself; for I am not
7. 13 when the Lord saw her, he had compassion
7. 31 [Lord said, Whereunto then shall I liken]
9. 54 Lord, wilt thou that we command fire to
9. 57 [Lord,] I will follow thee whithersoever
9. 59 Lord, suffer me first to go and bury my
9. 61 Lord, I will follow thee; but let me first
10. 1 the Lord appointed other seventy also, and
10. 2 pray ye therefore the Lord of the harvest
10. 17 Lord, even the devils are subject unto us
10. 21 Father, Lord of heaven and earth, that
10. 27 love the Lord thy God with all thy heart
10. 40 Lord, dost thou not care that my sister
11. 1 Lord, teach us to pray, as John also tau.
11. 39 Lord said unto him, Now do ye Pharisees
12. 36 ye..like unto men that wait for their lord
12. 37 lord when he cometh shall find watching
12. 41 Lord, speakest thou this parable unto us
12. 42 the Lord said, Who then is that faithful
12. 42 lord shall make ruler over his household
12. 43 his lord when he cometh shall find so do.
12. 45 say in his heart, My lord delayeth his co.
12. 46 The lord of that servant will come in a
12. 47 that servant, which knew his lord's will
13. 8 Lord, let it alone this year also, till I
13. 15 The Lord then answered him, and said
13. 23 said..Lord, are there few that be saved?
13. 25 the door, saying, Lord, [Lord,] open unto
13. 35 he that cometh in the name of the Lord
14. 22 Lord, it is done as thou hast commanded
14. 23 the lord said unto the servant, Go out
16. 3 lord taketh away from me the stewardship
16. 5 So he called every one of his lord's debt.
16. 5 said..How much owest thou unto my l.?
16. 8 the lord commended the unjust steward
17. 5 the apostles said unto the Lord, Increase
17. 6 the Lord said, If ye had faith as a grain
17. 37 they answered and said.. Where, Lord
18. 6 the Lord said, Hear what the unjust judge
18. 41 he said, Lord, that I may receive my sight
19. 8 said unto the Lord; Behold, Lord, the half
19. 16 Lord, thy pound hath gained ten pounds
19. 18 Lord, thy pound hath gained five pounds
19. 20 Lord, behold, (here is) thy pound, which
19. 25 they said unto him, Lord, he hath ten po.
19. 31 say..Because the Lord hath need of him
19. 34 And they said, The Lord hath need of him
19. 38 King that cometh in the name of the L.
20. 13 Then said the lord of the vineyard, What
20. 15 shall the lord of the vineyard do unto them
20. 37 he calleth the Lord the God of Abraham
20. 42 The Lord said unto my Lord, Sit thou on
20. 44 David therefore calleth him Lord, how is
22. 31 [the Lord said, Simon, Simon, behold, S.]
22. 33 Lord, I am ready to go with thee, both
22. 38 they said, Lord, behold, here (are) two s.
22. 49 Lord, shall we smite with the sword?
22. 61 And the Lord turned, and looked upon
22. 61 Peter remembered the word of the Lord
23. 42 [Lord,] remember me when thou comest
24. 3 and found not the body of [the Lord] Je.
24. 34 Lord is risen indeed, and hath appeared
John 1. 23 Make straight the way of the Lord, as
4. 1 Lord knew how the Pharisees had heard
6. 23 eat..after that [the Lord] had given thanks
6. 34 said they..Lord, evermore give us this b.
6. 68 Lord, to whom shall we go? thou hast the
8. 11 [She said, No man, Lord. And Jesus said]
9. 36 Who is he, Lord, that I might believe on
9. 38 he said, Lord, I believe. And he worship.
11. 2 which anointed the Lord with ointment
11. 3 Lord, behold, he whom thou lovest is sick
11. 12 said his disciples, Lord, if he sleep, he shall
11. 21, 32 Lord, if thou hadst been here, my br.
11. 27 Lord: I believe that thou art the Christ
11. 34 They said unto him, Lord, come and see
11. 39 Lord, by this time he stinketh: for he hath
12. 13 king..that cometh in the name of the L.
12. 38 Lord, who hath believed our report? and
12. 38 hath the arm of the Lord been revealed?
13. 6 Peter saith..Lord, dost thou wash my feet?
13. 9 Lord, not my feet only, but also (my) hands
13. 13 Ye call me Master and Lord: and ye say
13. 14 I then, (your) Lord and Master, have wa.
13. 16 The servant is not greater than his lord
13. 25 He then..saith unto him, Lord, who is it?
13. 36 said unto him, Lord, whither goest thou?
13. 37 Lord, why cannot I follow thee now? I will
14. 5 Lord, we know not whither thou goest
14. 8 Lord, show us the Father, and it sufficeth
14. 22 Lord, how is it that thou wilt manifest
15. 15 servant knoweth not what his lord doeth
15. 20 The servant is not greater than his lord

John 20. 2 taken away the Lord out of the sepulchre
20. 13 they have taken away my Lord, and I kn.
20. 18 and told..that she had seen the Lord
20. 20 the disciples glad when they saw the Lord
20. 25 said unto him, We have seen the Lord
20. 28 and said unto him, My Lord and my God
21. 7 disciple..saith unto Peter, It is the Lord
21. 7 Simon Peter heard that it was the Lord
21. 12 durst ask..knowing that it was the Lord
21. 15, 16 Yea, Lord; thou knowest that I love
21. 17 Lord, thou knowest all things; thou kno.
21. 20 said, Lord, which is he that betrayeth thee
21. 21 saith..Lord, and what (shall) this man (do)
Acts 1. 6 Lord, wilt thou at this time restore again
1. 21 the Lord Jesus went in and out among us
1. 24 Thou, Lord, which knowest the hearts of
2. 20 great and notable day of the Lord come
2. 21 on the name of the Lord shall be saved
2. 25 I foresaw the Lord always before my face
2. 34 The LORD said unto my Lord, Sit thou on
2. 36 whom ye have crucified, both Lord and C.
2. 39 as many as the Lord our God shall call
2. 47 the Lord added to the church daily such
3. 19 shall come from the presence of the Lord
3. 22 A Prophet shall the Lord your God raise
4. 26 were gathered together against the Lord
4. 29 Lord, behold their threatenings: and grant
4. 33 witness of the resurrection of the Lord J.
5. 9 together to tempt the spirit of the Lord?
5. 14 believers were the more added to the Lord
5. 19 the angel of the Lord by night opened the
7. 30 Angel of the Lord in a flame of fire in a b.
7. 31 and..the voice [of the Lord] came unto h.
7. 33 Then said the Lord to him, Put off thy s.
7. 37 A Prophet shall [the Lord] your God raise
7. 49 what house will ye build..saith the Lord
7. 59 and saying, Lord Jesus, receive my spirit
7. 60 Lord, lay not this sin to their charge
8. 16 baptized in the name of the Lord Jesus
8. 24 Pray ye to the Lord for me, that none of
8. 25 and preached the word of the Lord
8. 26 the angel of the Lord spake unto Philip
8. 39 the spirit of the Lord caught away Philip
9. 1 slaughter against the disciples of the Lord
9. 5 said, Who art thou, Lord? And [the Lord]
9. 6 [said, Lord, what wilt thou have me to do?]
9. 6 [the Lord (said) unto him, Arise, and go]
9. 10 to him said the Lord in a vision, Ananias
9. 10 And he said, Behold, I (am here), Lord
9. 11 the Lord (said) unto him, Arise, and go
9. 13 Lord, I have heard by many of this man
9. 15 the Lord said unto him, Go thy way: for
9. 17 the Lord, (even) Jesus, that appeared unto
9. 27 how he had seen the Lord in the way, and
9. 29 spake boldly in the name of the Lord Je.
9. 31 walking in the fear of the Lord, and in the
9. 35 and Saron saw him, and turned to the L.
9. 42 all Joppa; and many believed in the Lord
10. 4 he was afraid, and said, What is it, Lord?
10. 14 Not so, Lord; for I have never eaten any
10. 36 peace by Jesus Christ: he is Lord of all
10. 48 to be baptized in the name of [the Lord]
11. 8 Not so, Lord: for nothing common or un
11. 16 Then remembered I the word of the Lord
11. 17 who believed on the Lord Jesus Christ
11. 20 unto the Grecians, preaching the Lord J.
11. 21 the hand of the Lord was with them: and
11. 21 number believed, and turned unto the L.
11. 23 that..they would cleave unto the Lord
11. 24 and much people was added unto the L.
12. 7 the angel of the Lord came upon (him)
12. 11 the Lord hath sent his angel, and hath
12. 17 Lord had brought him out of the prison
12. 23 the angel of the Lord smote him, because
13. 2 they ministered to the Lord, and fasted
13. 10 cease to pervert the right ways of the L.
13. 11 the hand of the Lord (is) upon thee, and
13. 12 astonished at the doctrine of the Lord
13. 47 so hath the Lord commanded us, (saying)
13. 48 glorified the word of the Lord: and as m.
13. 49 word of the Lord was published throughout
14. 3 abode they speaking boldly in the Lord
14. 23 they commended them to the Lord, on w.
15. 11 through the grace of the Lord Jesus Christ
15. 17 residue of men might seek after the Lord
15. 17 saith the Lord, who doeth all these things
15. 26 lives for the name of our Lord Jesus Christ
15. 35 preaching the word of the Lord, with many
15. 36 we have preached the word of the Lord
16. 10 [the Lord] had called us for to preach the
16. 14 whose heart the Lord opened, that she
16. 15 have judged me to be faithful to the Lord
16. 31 Believe on the Lord Jesus Christ, and thou
16. 32 they spake unto him the word of the Lord
17. 24 seeing that he is Lord of heaven and earth
17. 27 they should seek [the Lord], if haply they
18. 8 believed on the Lord with all his house
18. 9 spake the Lord to Paul in the night by a
18. 25 man was instructed in the way of the L.
18. 25 taught diligently the things of [the Lord]
19. 5 baptized in the name of the Lord Jesus
19. 10 they..heard the word of the Lord Jesus
19. 13 to call over..the name of the Lord Jesus
19. 17 the name of the Lord Jesus was magnified
19. 20 So mightily grew the word of God and p.
20. 19 Serving the Lord with all humility of m.
20. 21 and faith toward our Lord Jesus Christ
20. 24 which I have received of the Lord Jesus
20. 35 to remember the words of the Lord Jesus
21. 13 to die..for the name of the Lord Jesus
21. 14 ceased, saying, The will of the Lord be d.
21. 20 they glorified [the Lord], and said unto him

Acts 22. 8 I answered, Who art thou, Lord? v.10,10.
22. 16 baptized..calling on the name [of the L.]
22. 19 Lord, they know that I imprisoned and b.
23. 11 Lord stood by him, and said, Be of good
25. 26 no certain thing to write unto my lord
26. 15 I said, Who art thou, Lord? And he said
28. 31 things which concern the Lord Jesus Chr.
Rom. 1. 3 Concerning his Son Jesus Christ our Lord
1. 7 God our Father, and the Lord Jesus Christ
4. 8 man to whom the Lord will not impute
4. 24 raised up Jesus our Lord from the dead
5. 1 with God through our Lord Jesus Christ
5. 11 joy in God through our Lord Jesus Christ
5. 21 unto eternal life by Jesus Christ our Lord
6. 11 unto God through Jesus Christ [our Lord]
6. 23 eternal life through Jesus Christ our Lord
7. 25 thank God through Jesus Christ our Lord
8. 39 love..which is in Christ Jesus our Lord
9. 28 work will the Lord make upon the earth
9. 29 the Lord of Sabaoth had left us a seed
10. 9 confess with thy mouth the Lord Jesus
10. 12 the same Lord over all is rich unto all
10. 13 shall call upon the name of the Lord
10. 16 saith, Lord, who hath believed our report?
11. 3 Lord, they have killed thy prophets, and
11. 34 who hath known the mind of the Lord? or
12. 11 Not slothful in business..serving the [L.]
12. 19 is written..I will repay, saith the Lord
13. 14 put ye on the Lord Jesus Christ, and make
14. 6 the day, regardeth (it) unto the Lord; and
14. 6 [to the Lord he doth not regard (it)]
14. 6 He that eateth, eateth to the Lord, for he
14. 6 that eateth not, to the Lord he eateth not
14. 8 For whether we live, we live unto the Lord
14. 8 and whether we die, we die unto the Lord
14. 8 we live therefore, or die, we are the Lord's
14. 11 (As) I live, saith the Lord, every knee shall
14. 14 I know, and am persuaded by the Lord J.
15. 6 even the Father of our Lord Jesus Christ
15. 11 Praise the Lord, all ye Gentiles; and laud
15. 30 for the Lord Jesus Christ's sake, and for
16. 2 ye receive her in the Lord, as becometh
16. 8 Greet Amplias my beloved in the Lord
16. 11 them..of Narcissus, which are in the Lord
16. 12 and Tryphosa, who labour in the Lord
16. 12 [Persis, which laboured much in the Lord]
16. 13 Salute Rufus chosen in the Lord, and his
16. 18 such serve not our Lord Jesus Christ, but
16. 20 grace of our Lord Jesus Christ (be) with
16. 22 I Tertius..salute you in the Lord
16. 24 [The grace of our Lord Jesus Christ]
1 Co. 1. 2 upon the name of Jesus Christ our Lord
1. 3 our Father, and (from) the Lord Jesus C.
1. 7 for the coming of our Lord Jesus Christ
1. 8 blameless in the day of our Lord Jesus C.
1. 9 the fellowship of his Son Jesus..our Lord
1. 10 by the name of our Lord Jesus Christ, that
1. 31 He that glorieth, let him glory in the Lord
2. 8 would not have crucified the Lord of glory
2. 16 who hath known the mind of the Lord, that
3. 5 ministers..as the Lord gave to every man
3. 20 The Lord knoweth the thoughts of the wise
4. 4 nothing..but he that judgeth me is the L.
4. 5 until the Lord come, who both will bring
4. 17 my beloved son, and faithful in the Lord
4. 19 will come to you shortly, if the Lord will
5. 4 In the name of our Lord Jesus Christ, when
5. 4 with the power of our Lord Jesus Christ
5. 5 may be saved in the day of the Lord Jesus
6. 11 justified in the name of the Lord Jesus
6. 13 for the Lord, and the Lord for the body
6. 14 God hath both raised up the Lord, and
6. 17 he that is joined unto the Lord is one sp.
7. 10 I command, (yet) not I, but the Lord, Let
7. 12 to the rest speak I, not the Lord: If any
7. 17 as [the Lord] hath called every one, so let
7. 22 in the Lord, (being) a servant, is the Lord's
7. 25 I have no commandment of the Lord: yet
7. 25 obtained mercy of the Lord to be faithful
7. 32 to the Lord, how he may please the Lord
7. 34 woman careth for the things of the Lord
7. 35 attend upon the Lord without distraction
7. 39 married to whom she will; only in the L
8. 5 as there be gods many, and lords many
8. 6 and one Lord Jesus Christ, by whom (are)
9. 1 our Lord? are not ye my work in the Lord
9. 2 the seal of mine apostleship..in the Lord
9. 5 (as) the brethren of the Lord, and Cephas
9. 14 the Lord ordained that they which preach
10. 21 Ye cannot drink the cup of the Lord, and
10. 21 ye cannot be partakers of the Lord's table
10. 22 Do we provoke the Lord to jealousy? are
10. 26 the earth (is) the Lord's, and the fulness
10. 28 [the earth (is) the Lord's, and the fulness]
11. 11 the woman without the man, in the Lord
11. 23 I have received of the Lord that which
11. 23 the Lord Jesus the (same) night in which
11. 26 ye do show the Lord's death till he come
11. 27 and drink (this) cup of the Lord, unworth.
11. 27 guilty of the body and blood of the Lord
11. 29 damnation..not discerning the [Lord's]
11. 32 we are chastened of the Lord, that we
12. 3 no man can say that Jesus is the Lord, but
12. 5 there are differences..but the same Lord
14. 21 that will they not hear me, saith the Lord
14. 37 unto you are..commandments of the Lord
15. 31 which I have in Christ Jesus our Lord
15. 47 the second man (is) [the Lord] from hea.
15. 57 the victory through our Lord Jesus Christ
15. 58 always abounding in the work of the Lord
15. 58 your labour is not in vain in the Lord
16. 7 tarry a while with you, if the Lord permit

1 Co. 16. 10 he worketh the work of the Lord, as I also
16. 19 and Priscilla salute you much in the Lord
16. 22 If any man love not the Lord Jesus Christ
16. 23 grace of our Lord Jesus Christ (be) with
2 Co. 1. 2 our Father, and (from) the Lord Jesus C.
1. 3 the Father of our Lord Jesus Christ, the
1. 14 also (are) ours in the day of the Lord Je.
2. 12 and a door was opened unto me of the L.
3. 16 it shall turn to the Lord, the veil shall
3. 17 Now the Lord is that spirit: and where
3. 17 the spirit of the Lord (is), there (is) liberty
3. 18 as in a glass the glory of the Lord, are ch.
3. 18 to glory, (even) as by the spirit of the L.
4. 5 not ourselves, but Christ Jesus the Lord
4. 10 in the body the dying of [the Lord] Jesus
4. 14 he which raised up the Lord Jesus shall
5. 6 in the body, we are absent from the Lord
5. 8 absent..and to be present with the Lord
5. 11 Knowing therefore the terror of the Lord
6. 17 be ye separate, saith the Lord, and touch
6. 18 and daughters, saith the Lord Almighty
8. 5 but first gave their own selves to the Lord
8. 9 ye know the grace of our Lord Jesus Chr.
8. 19 by us to the glory of the same Lord, and
8. 21 not only in the sight of the Lord, but also
10. 8 the Lord hath given us for edification
10. 17 that glorieth, let him glory in the Lord
10. 18 is approved, but whom the Lord commen.
11. 17 I speak (it) not after the Lord, but as it
12. 1 come to visions and revelations of the L.
12. 8 I besought the Lord thrice, that it might
13. 10 the Lord hath given me to edification
13. 14 The grace of the Lord Jesus Christ, and
Gal. 1. 3 the Father, and (from) our Lord Jesus C.
1. 19 saw I none, save James the Lord's brother
4. 1 from a servant, though he be lord of all
5. 10 have confidence in you through the Lord
6. 14 in the cross of our Lord Jesus Christ
6. 17 in my body the marks of [the Lord] Jesus
6. 18 the grace of our Lord Jesus Christ (be)
Eph. 1. 2 our Father, and (from) the Lord Jesus C.
1. 3 God and Father of our Lord Jesus Christ
1. 15 I heard of your faith in the Lord Jesus
1. 17 That the God of our Lord Jesus Christ, the
2. 21 groweth unto an holy temple in the Lord
3. 11 which he purposed in Christ Jesus our L.
3. 14 [the Father of our Lord Jesus Christ]
4. 1 I therefore, the prisoner of the Lord, be.
4. 5 One Lord, one faith, one baptism
4. 17 testify in the Lord, that ye henceforth w.
5. 8 but now..light in the Lord: walk as ch.
5. 10 Proving what is acceptable unto the Lord
5. 17 understanding what the will of [the Lo.]
5. 19 making melody in your heart to the Lord
5. 20 in the name of our Lord Jesus Christ
5. 22 unto your own husbands, as unto the Lord
5. 29 cherisheth it, even as [the Lord] the church
6. 1 obey your parents [in the Lord]: for this is
6. 4 the nurture and admonition of the Lord
6. 7 service, as to the Lord, and not to men
6. 8 the same shall he receive of the Lord
6. 10 be strong in the Lord, and in the power
6. 21 brother and faithful minister in the Lord
6. 23 God the Father and the Lord Jesus Christ
6. 24 love our Lord Jesus Christ in sincerity
Phil. 1. 2 our Father, and (from) the Lord Jesus C.
1. 14 many of the brethren in the Lord, waxing
2. 11 should confess that Jesus Christ (is) Lord
2. 19 trust in [the Lord] Jesus to send Timoth.
2. 24 I trust in the Lord that I also myself
2. 29 Receive him therefore in the Lord with
3. 1 Finally, my brethren, rejoice in the Lord
3. 8 of the knowledge of Christ Jesus my Lord
3. 20 for the Saviour, the Lord Jesus Christ
4. 1 stand fast in the Lord, (my) dearly belo.
4. 2 that they be of the same mind in the Lord
4. 4 Rejoice in the Lord alway: (and) again I
4. 5 known unto all men. The Lord (is) at hand
4. 10 I rejoiced in the Lord greatly, that now at
4. 23 grace of our Lord Jesus Christ (be) with
Col. 1. 2 [God our Father and the Lord Jesus Ch.]
1. 3 and the Father of our Lord Jesus Christ
1. 10 walk worthy of the Lord unto all pleasing
2. 6 therefore received Christ Jesus the Lord
3. 16 with grace in your hearts to [the Lord]
3. 17 (do) all in the name of [the Lord] Jesus
3. 18 your own husbands, as it is fit in the Lord
3. 20 for this is well pleasing unto the Lord
3. 23 heartily, as to the Lord, and not unto men
3. 24 that of the Lord..for ye serve the Lord C.
4. 7 minister and fellow servant in the Lord
4. 17 which thou hast received in the Lord
1 Th. 1. 1 the Father and (in) the Lord Jesus Christ
1. 1 [God our Father, and the Lord Jesus C.]
1. 3 patience of hope in our Lord Jesus Christ
1. 6 became followers of us, and of the Lord
1. 8 from you sounded out the word of the L.
2. 15 the Lord Jesus and their own prophets
2. 19 presence of our Lord Jesus Christ at his
3. 8 now we live, if ye stand fast in the Lord
3. 11 our Lord Jesus Christ, direct our way unto
3. 12 [the Lord] make you to increase and abo.
3. 13 at the coming of our Lord Jesus Christ
4. 1 exhort (you) by the Lord Jesus, that as ye
4. 2 commandments we gave you by the Lord
4. 6 the Lord (is) the avenger of all such, as
4. 15 we say unto you by the word of the Lord
4. 15 (and) remain unto the coming of the Lord
4. 16 Lord himself shall descend from heaven
4. 17 the clouds, to meet the Lord in the air
4. 17 and so shall we ever be with the Lord
5. 2 the day of the Lord so cometh as a thief

1 Th. 5. 9 obtain salvation by our Lord Jesus Christ
5. 12 are over you in the Lord, and admonish
5. 23 unto the coming of our Lord Jesus Christ
5. 27 charge you by the Lord that this epistle
5. 28 grace of our Lord Jesus Christ (be) with
2 Th. 1. 1, 2 our Father and the Lord Jesus Christ
1. 7 Lord Jesus shall be revealed from heaven
1. 8 obey not the gospel of our Lord Jesus C.
1. 9 destruction from the presence of the Lord
1. 12 That the name of our Lord Jesus Christ
1. 12 grace of our God and the Lord Jesus Ch.
2. 1 by the coming of our Lord Jesus Christ
2. 8 the Lord shall consume with the spirit
2. 13 brethren beloved of the Lord, because God
2. 14 obtaining of the glory of our Lord Jesus
2. 16 our Lord Jesus Christ himself, and God
3. 1 word of the Lord may have (free) course
3. 3 [the Lord] is faithful, who shall stablish
3. 4 have confidence in the Lord touching you
3. 5 the Lord direct your hearts into the love
3. 6 in the name of our Lord Jesus Christ, that
3. 12 exhort by our Lord Jesus Christ, that with
3. 16 the Lord of peace himself give you peace
3. 16 by all means. The Lord (be) with you all
3. 18 grace of our Lord Jesus Christ (be) with
1 Ti. 1. 1 [Lord] Jesus Christ, (which is) our hope
1. 2 God our Father and Jesus Christ our L.
1. 12 I thank Christ Jesus our Lord, who hath
1. 14 grace of our Lord was exceeding abundant
5. 21 [Lord] Jesus Christ, and the elect angels
6. 3 the words of our Lord Jesus Christ, and
6. 14 until the appearing of our Lord Jesus C.
6. 15 only Potentate, the King of kings, and L.
2 Ti. 1. 2 God the Father and Christ Jesus our Lord
1. 8 ashamed of the testimony of our Lord
1. 16 The Lord give mercy unto the house of
1. 18 The Lord grant unto him that he may find
1. 18 mercy of the Lord in that day: and in how
2. 7 Lord give thee understanding in all things
2. 14 charging (them) before [the Lord] that they
2. 19 seal, The Lord knoweth them that are his
2. 22 that call on the Lord out of a pure heart
2. 24 the servant of the Lord must not strive
3. 11 but out of (them) all the Lord delivered
4. 1 [the Lord] Jesus Christ, who shall judge
4. 8 which the Lord, the righteous judge, sh.
4. 14 Lord reward him according to his works
4. 17 the Lord stood with me, and strengthened
4. 18 the Lord shall deliver me from every evil
4. 22 The Lord Jesus Christ (be) with thy spirit
Titus 1. 4 and [the Lord] Jesus Christ our Saviour
Phil. 3 God our Father and the Lord Jesus Christ
5 which thou hast toward the Lord Jesus
16 more..both in the flesh, and in the Lord
20 the Lord: refresh my bowels in [the Lord]
25 grace of our Lord Jesus Christ (be) with
Heb. 1. 10 Thou, Lord, in the beginning hast laid
2. 3 the first began to be spoken by the Lord
7. 14 evident that our Lord sprang out of Juda
7. 21 The Lord sware and will not repent, Thou
8. 2 tabernacle, which the Lord pitched, and
8. 8 the days come, saith the Lord, when I will
8. 9 and I regarded them not, saith the Lord
8. 10 of Israel after those days, saith the Lord
8. 11 shall not teach..saying, Know the Lord
10. 16 with them after those days, saith the Lord
10. 30 saith [the Lord]. And again, The Lord sh.
12. 5 despise not thou the chastening of the L.
12. 6 whom the Lord loveth he chasteneth, and
12. 14 without which no man shall see the Lord
13. 6 The Lord (is) my helper, and I will not
13. 20 brought again from the dead our Lord J.
Jas. 1. 1 a servant of God and of the Lord Jesus C.
1. 7 that he shall receive any thing of the L.
1. 12 [Lord] hath promised to them that love
2. 1 have not the faith of our Lord Jesus Ch.
4. 10 Humble yourselves in the sight of the L.
4. 15 If the Lord will, we shall live, and do this
5. 4 entered into the ears of the Lord of sab.
5. 7 Be patient..unto the coming of the Lord
5. 8 for the coming of the Lord draweth nigh
5. 10 who have spoken in the name of the Lord
5. 11 seen the end of the Lord; that [the Lord]
5. 14 him with oil in the name of the Lord
5. 15 the sick, and the Lord shall raise him up
1 Pe. 1. 3 God and Father of our Lord Jesus Christ
1. 25 the word of the Lord endureth for ever
2. 3 ye have tasted that the Lord (is) gracious
2. 13 every ordinance of man for the Lord's sake
3. 6 as Sara obeyed Abraham, calling him lord
3. 12 the eyes of the Lord (are) over the righte.
3. 12 face of the Lord (is) against them that do
3. 15 sanctify the Lord God in your hearts: and
2 Pe. 1. 2 knowledge of God, and of Jesus our Lord
1. 8 in the knowledge of our Lord Jesus Christ
1. 11 kingdom of our Lord and Saviour Jesus C.
1. 14 as our Lord Jesus Christ hath showed me
1. 16 power and coming of our Lord Jesus Ch.
2. 9 The Lord knoweth how to deliver the go.
2. 11 accusation against them before [the Lord]
2. 20 knowledge of the Lord and Saviour Jesus
3. 2 us the apostles of the Lord and Saviour
3. 8 day (is) with the Lord as a thousand years
3. 9 Lord is not slack concerning his promise
3. 10 the day of the Lord will come as a thief
3. 15 long suffering of our Lord (is) salvation
3. 18 knowledge of our Lord and Saviour Jesus
2 John 3 from [the Lord] Jesus Christ, the Son of
Jude 4 the only..God, and our Lord Jesus Christ
5 how that [the Lord], having saved the pe.
9 durst not..but said, The Lord rebuke thee
14 the Lord cometh with ten thousand of his
Jude 17 of the apostles of our Lord Jesus Christ
21 for the mercy of our Lord Jesus Christ unto
Rev. 1. 8 beginning and the ending, saith the Lord
4. 8 Holy, holy, holy, Lord God Almighty, w.
4. 11 Thou art worthy, O Lord, to receive glory
11. 8 city..where also our Lord was crucified
11. 15 are become (the kingdoms) of our Lord, and
11. 17 O Lord God Almighty, which art, and wast
14. 13 dead which die in the Lord from hencefo.
15. 3 marvellous (are) thy works, Lord God Al.
15. 4 Who shall not fear thee, [O Lord], and gl.
16. 5 Thou art righteous [O Lord], which art
16. 7 Lord God Almighty, true and righteous
17. 14 Lamb shall overcome them: for he is L.
18. 8 strong (is) [the Lord] God who judgeth her
19. 1 honour, and power, unto [the Lord] our
19. 6 for the Lord God omnipotent reigneth
19. 16 written, King of kings, and Lord of lords
21. 22 the Lord God Almighty and the Lamb are
22. 5 the Lord God giveth them light: and they
22. 6 the Lord God of the holy prophets sent
22. 20 come quickly. Amen. Even so, come, L.
22. 21 grace of our Lord Jesus Christ (be) with

15. *My master, my rabbi, (from Heb.* רַבּוּנִי), *ῥαββονί.*
Mark10. 51 said..Lord, that I might receive my sight

16. *To be lord, κυριεύω kurieuō.*
1 Ti. 6. 15 only Potentate..King of kings, and..of l.

17. *Great men, μεγιστᾶνες megistanes.*
Mark 6. 21 made a supper to his lords, high captains

LORD, to be —

1. *To rule, רוד rud.*
Jer. 2. 31 We are lords; we will come no more unto

2. *To be lord, κυριεύω kurieuō.*
Rom.14. 9 might be Lord both of the dead and living

LORD over, to be —

To lord it over one, κατακυριεύω katakurieuō.
1 Pe. 5. 3 Neither as being lords over (God's) heri.

LORD'S, the —

Belonging to the Lord, κυριακός kuriakos.
1 Co. 11. 20 ye come..(this) is not to eat the Lord's
Rev. 1. 10 I was in the spirit on the Lord's day, and

LORDLY —

Honourable, אַדִּיר addir.
Judg. 5. 25 brought forth butter in a lordly dish

LORDSHIP over, to exercise —

1. *To be a very lord, κατακυριεύω katakurieuō.*
Mark10. 42 accounted to rule..exercise lordship over

2. *To be lord, κυριεύω kurieuō.*
Luke22. 25 The kings..exercise lordship over them

LO RU-HA'-MAH, לֹא רֻחָמָה *not pitied.*
A symbolic name given to Hosea's daughter, indicating God's rejection of Israel. B.C. 783.
Hos. 1. 6 Call her name L.: for I will no more have
1. 8 when she had weaned L., she conceived
[In Hos. 2. 23 the name is translated.]

LOSE, to —

1. *To be lost from, אָבַד מִן abad min.*
Deut22. 3 which he hath lost, and thou hast found

2. *To lose, אָבַד abad, 3.*
Eccl. 3. 6 A time to get, and a time to lose; a time

3. *To gather, אָסַף asaph.*
Judg.18. 25 and thou lose thy life, with the lives of

4. *To fall, from, נָפַל מִן naphal min.*
1 Ki. 20. 25 an army like the army that thou hast lost

5. *To corrupt, mar, שָׁחַת shachath, 3.*
Prov.23. 8 shalt thou vomit up, and lose thy sweet

6. *To cut, cut off, כָּרַת karath, 5.*
1 Ki. 18. 5 find grass..that we lose not all the beasts

7. *To lose ἀπόλλυμι apollumi.*
Matt 10. 39 shall lose it: and he that loseth his life
10. 42 verily..he shall in no wise lose his reward
16. 25 shall lose it: and whosoever will lose his
Mark 8. 35 shall lose it; but whosoever shall lose his
9. 41 verily I say..he shall not lose his reward
Luke 9. 24 shall lose it: but whosoever will lose his
9. 25 if he gain the whole world, and lose him.
15. 4 if he lose one of them, doth not leave the
15. 8 if she lose one piece, doth not light a ca.
15. 9 I have found the piece which I had lost
17. 33 shall lose it; and whosoever shall lose
John 6. 39 I should lose nothing, but should raise it
12. 25 He that loveth his life shall lose it; and he
18. 9 Of them which thou gavest me have I lost
2 John 8 that we lose not those things which we

8. *To cause loss, ζημιόω zēmioō.*
Matt16. 26 if he shall gain the whole world, and lose
Mark 8. 36 if he shall gain the whole world, and lose

LOSE children, to —

To be bereaved, שָׁכֹל shakol.
Isa. 49. 21 seeing I have lost my children, and am de.

LOSE, to cause to —

To cause to breathe out, נָפַח naphach, 5.
Job 31. 39 caused the owners thereof to lose their l.

LOSS —

1. *A casting away, ἀποβολή apobolē.*
Acts 27. 22 there shall be no loss of..life among you

2. *Loss, ζημία zēmia.*
Acts 27. 21 and to have gained this harm and loss
Phil. 3. 7 what things were gain..those I counted l.
3. 8 I count all things..loss for the excellency

LOSS, to bear the —

To atone for, make good, חָטָא chata, 3.
Gen. 31. 39 I bare the loss of it; of my hand didst

LOSS of (children or) others, to have after the —

1. *Bereavement, שְׁכוֹל shekol.*
Isa. 47. 8 neither shall I know the loss of children
47. 9 the loss of children, and widowhood: they

2. *Bereaved, שִׁכֻּלִים shikkulim.*
Isa. 49. 20 shalt have, after thou hast lost the other

LOSS, to suffer —

To cause loss, ζημιόω zēmioō.
1 Co. 3. 15 he shall suffer loss: but he himself shall
Phil. 3. 8 for whom I have suffered the loss of all

LOST, to be —

1. *To perish, be lost, אָבַד abad.*
1 Sa. 9. 3 the asses of Kish, Saul's father, were lost
9. 20 as for thine asses that were lost three days
Psa.119. 176 I have gone astray like a lost sheep: seek
Jer. 50. 6 My people hath been lost sheep; their sh.
Eze. 19. 5 when she saw that..her hope was lost
34. 4 neither have ye sought that which was lost
34. 16 I will seek that which was lost, and bring
37. 11 our hope is lost: we are cut off for our pa.

2. *To fall, נָפַל naphal.*
Num. 6. 12 the days that were before shall be lost, be.

3. *To lose away, destroy, waste, ἀπόλλυμι apollu.*
Matt 10. 6 go rather to the lost sheep of the house
15. 24 I am not sent but unto the lost sheep of
18. 11 [Son..is come to save that which was lost]
Luke15. 4 go after that which is lost, until he find
15. 6 for I have found my sheep which was lost
15. 24 For this my son was..lost, and is found
15. 32 this thy brother..was lost, and is found
19. 10 to seek and to save that which was lost
John 6. 12 Gather..fragments..that nothing be lost
17. 12 none of them is lost, but the son of perdi.
2 Co. 4. 3 gospel be hid, it is hid to them that are l.

LOST (thing), that which was —

Lost thing, אֲבֵדָה abedah.
Exod22. 9 (or) for any manner of lost thing, which
Lev. 6. 3 Or have found that which was lost, and
6. 4 shall restore..the lost thing which he fo.
Deut22. 3 with all lost thing of thy brother's, which

LOT —

1. *A lot, גּוֹרָל goral.*
Lev. 16. 8 Aaron shall cast lots upon the two goats
16. 8 one lot for the LORD, and the other lot for
16. 9 bring the goat upon which the LORD'S lot
16. 10 But the goat, on which the lot fell to be
Num26. 55 the land shall be divided by lot: accord.
26. 56 According to..lot shall the possession th.
33. 54 ye shall divide the land by lot for an inh.
33. 54 shall be in the place where his lot falleth
34. 13 the land which ye shall inherit by lot, wh.
36. 2 to give the land for an inheritance by lot
36. 3 so shall it be taken from the lot of our in.
Josh.14. 2 By lot (was) their inheritance, as the LORD
15. 1 (This) then was the lot of the tribe of the
16. 1 the lot of the children of Joseph fell from
17. 1 There was also a lot for the tribe of Man.
17. 14 Why hast thou given me..one lot and one
17. 17 great power: thou shalt not have one lot
18. 6, 8 that I may cast lots for you here before
18. 10 Joshua cast lots for them in Shiloh before
18. 11 the lot of the tribe of the children of B.
18. 11 the coast of their lot came forth between
19. 1 the second lot came forth to Simeon..for
19. 10 the third lot came up for the children of
19. 17 the fourth lot came out to Issachar, for
19. 24 the fifth lot came out for the tribe of the
19. 32 The sixth lot came out to the children of N.
19. 40 the seventh lot came out for the tribe of
19. 51 divided for an inheritance by lot in Shiloh
21. 4 lot came out for the families of the Koh.
21. 4 had by lot out of the tribe of Judah, and
21. 5 lot out of the families of the tribe of Ep.
21. 6 the children of Gershon (had) by lot out
21. 8 gave by lot unto the Levites these cities
21. 10 Kohathites; for theirs was the first lot
21. 20 they had the cities of their lot out of the
21. 40 all the cities..were (by) their lot twelve
Judg. 1. 3 Come up with me into my lot, that we may
1. 3 I likewise will go with thee into thy lot
20. 9 the thing which we will do..by lot against
1 Ch. 6. 54 of the Kohathites; for theirs was the lot
6. 61 (out of) the half..of Manasseh, by lot, ten
6. 63 Unto the sons of Merari..by lot..twelve
6. 65 they gave by lot out of the tribe of the c
24. 5 Thus were they divided by lot, one sort
24. 7 Now the first lot came forth to Jehoiarib
24. 31 These likewise cast lots over against their
25. 8 they cast lots, ward against (ward), as well
25. 9 Now the first lot came forth for Asaph to
26. 13 they cast lots, as well the small as the g.
26. 14 And the lot eastward fell to Shelemiah
26. 14 they cast lots; and his lot came out nor.
Neh. 10. 34 we cast the lots among the priests, the Lev.
11. 1 the rest of the people also cast lots, to br.
Esth. 3. 7 they cast Pur, that (is), the lot, before H.
9. 24 had cast Pur, that (is), the lot, to consume
Psa. 16. 5 and of my cup: thou maintainest my lot

Psa. 22. 18 They part..and cast lots upon my vesture
125. 3 shall not rest upon the lot of the righteous
Prov. 1. 14 Cast in thy lot among us; let us all have
16. 33 The lot is cast into the lap; but the whole
18. 18 The lot causeth contentions to cease, and
Isa. 17. 14 the portion..and the lot of them that rob
34. 17 he hath cast the lot for them, and his hand
57. 6 they, they (are) thy lot: even to them hast
Jer. 13. 25 thy lot, the portion of thy measures from
Eze. 24. 6 Woe to the bloody city..let no lot fall upon
Dan. 12. 13 thou shalt rest, and stand in thy lot at
Joel 3. 3 they have cast lots for my people; and
Obad. 11 and cast lots upon Jerusalem, even thou
Jon. 1. 7 Come, and let us cast lots, that we may
1. 7 they cast lots, and the lot fell upon Jon.
Mic. 2. 5 that shall cast a cord by lot in the cong.
Nah. 3. 10 they cast lots for her honourable men, and

2. *A cord, portion, snare,* חֶבֶל, חֶבֶל *chebel.*
Deut 32. 9 For..Jacob (is) the lot of his inheritance
1 Ch. 16. 18 land of Canaan, the lot of your inheritance
Psa. 105. 11 land of Canaan, the lot of your inherita.

3. *A lot,* κλῆρος *klēros.*
Matt 27. 35 [and parted his garments, casting lots]
27. 35 [and upon my vesture did they cast lots]
Mark 15. 24 they parted his garments, casting lots upon
Luke 23. 34 And they parted his raiment, and cast lots
John 19. 24 and for my vesture they did cast lots
Acts 1. 26 they gave forth their lots; and the lot fell
8. 21 Thou hast neither part nor lot in this m.

LOT, לוֹט *concealed, dark coloured.*
Abraham's brother's son, father of Moab and Ben-ammi. B.C. 1898.
Gen. 11. 27 Nahor, and Haran; and Haran begat L.
11. 31 L. the son of Haran his son's son, and S.
12. 4 Abram departed..and L. went with him
12. 5 And Abram took Sarai his wife, and L.
13. 1 wife and all that he had, and L. with him
13. 5 L. also, which went with Abram, had flo.
13. 7 strife between..the herdmen of L.'s cattle
13. 8 Abram said unto L., Let there be no strife
13. 10 L. lifted up his eyes, and beheld all the
13. 11 L. chose him..the plain of Jordan; and L.
13. 12 L. dwelt in the cities of the plain, and
13. 14 Abram, after that L. was separated from
14. 12 they took L., Abram's brother's son, who
14. 16 brought again his brother L., and his goods
19. 1 L. sat in the gate of Sodom: and L. see.
19. 5 And they called unto L., and said unto
19. 6 L. went out at the door unto them, and
19. 9 they pressed sore upon the man, (even) L.
19. 10 pulled L. into the house to them, and shut
19. 12 the men said unto L., Hast thou here any
19. 14 L. went out, and spake unto his sons in
19. 15 the angels hastened L., saying, Arise, take
19. 18 And L. said unto them, Oh! not so, my
19. 23 The sun was risen upon the earth when L.
19. 29 sent L. out of the midst of the overthrow
19. 29 overthrew the cities in the which L. dwelt
19. 30 L. went up out of Zoar, and dwelt in the
19. 36 Thus were both the daughters of L. with
Deut. 2. 9, 19 the children of L. (for) a possession
Psa. 83. 8 they have holpen the children of L. Selah
Luke 17. 28 as it was in the days of L.; they did eat
17. 29 the same day that L. went out of Sodom
17. 32 Remember L.'s wife.
2 Pe. 2. 7 delivered just L., vexed with the filthy

LOT, to be one's, to cast —
To cast a lot, obtain by lot, λαγχάνω *lagchanō.*
Luke 1. 9 his lot was to burn incense when he went
John 19. 24 Let us not rend it, but cast lots for it, wh.

LO'-TAN, לוֹטָן *a covering.*
Son of Seir the Horite. B.C. 1800.
Gen. 36. 20 L., and Shobal, and Zibeon, and Anah
36. 22 children of L..Hori and Heman; and L.'s
36. 29 duke L., duke Shobal, duke Zibeon, duke
1 Ch. 1. 38 L., and Shobal, and Zibeon, and Anah, and
1. 39 L.; Hori, and Homam: and Timna (was) L.'s

LOTHE, to —
1. *To loathe, cast away,* גָּעַל *gaal.*
Jer. 14. 19 hath thy soul lothed Zion? why hast thou
Eze. 16. 45 that lotheth her husband and her children
16. 45 which lothed their husbands and their ch.

2. *To be or become weary,* לָאָה *laah,* 2.
Exod 7. 18 Egyptians shall lothe to drink of the wa.

3. *To be short, grieved,* קָצַר *qatsar.*
Zech. 11. 8 my soul lothed them, and their soul also
[*See also* Loathe.]

LOTHE selves, to —
To be cut off, loathed, קוּט *qut,* 2.
Eze. 6. 9 they shall lothe themselves for the evils
20. 43 shall lothe yourselves in your own sight
36. 31 shall lothe yourselves in your own sight

LOTHING —
Casting away, גֹּעַל *goal.*
Eze. 16. 5 to the lothing of thy person, in the day

LOUD —
1. *Great, (old, high, loud),* גָּדוֹל *gadol.*
Gen. 39. 14 he came in..and I cried with a loud voice
1 Sa. 28. 12 she cried with a loud voice: and the wo.
2 Sa. 15. 23 all the country wept with a loud voice, and
19. 4 the king cried with a loud voice, O my son
1 Ki. 8. 55 and blessed all..with a loud voice, saying
2 Ki. 18. 28 with a loud voice in the Jews' language
2 Ch. 15. 14 sware unto the LORD with a loud voice, and
20. 19 to praise the LORD..with a loud voice on
32. 18 Then they cried with a loud voice in the
Ezra 3. 12 wept with a loud voice; and many shou.
3. 13 the people shouted with a loud shout, and
10. 12 congregation..said with a loud voice, As
Neh. 9. 4 cried with a loud voice unto the LORD
Esth. 4. 1 Mordecai..cried with a loud and a bitter
Prov. 27. 14 He that blesseth his friend with a loud vo.
Isa. 36. 13 with a loud voice in the Jews' language
Eze. 8. 18 though they cry in mine ears with a loud
9. 1 He cried also in mine ears with a loud v.
11. 13 cried with a loud voice, and said, Ah Lord

2. *To roar, move, sound, make a noise,* הָמָה *hamah.*
Prov. 7. 11 She (is) loud and stubborn; her feet abide

3. *Strong, hard, severe,* חָזָק *chazaq.*
Exod 19. 16 the voice of the trumpet exceeding loud

4. *Strength, might, hardness,* עֹז *oz.*
2 Ch. 30. 21 with loud instruments unto the LORD

5. *To be high,* רוּם *rum.*
Deut 27. 14 the Levites shall speak..with a loud voice

6. *Hearing,* שֶׁמַע *shema.*
Psa. 150. 5 Praise him upon the loud cymbals: praise

7. *Great,* μέγας *megas.*
Matt 27. 46 Jesus cried with a loud voice, saying, Eli!
27. 50 when he had cried again with a loud voice
Mark 1. 26 had torn him, and cried with a loud voice
5. 7 cried with a loud voice, and said, What
15. 34 Jesus cried with a loud voice, saying, Eloi!
15. 37 Jesus cried with a loud voice, and gave up
Luke 1. 42 she spake out with a loud voice, and said
4. 33 unclean devil, and cried out with a loud
8. 28 with a loud voice said, What have I to do
17. 15 turned back, and with a loud voice glori.
19. 37 began to..praise God with a loud voice
23. 23 they were instant with loud voices, req.
23. 46 when Jesus had cried with a loud voice
John 11. 43 he cried with a loud voice, Lazarus, come
Acts 7. 57 Then they cried out with a loud voice, and
7. 60 cried with a loud voice, Lord, lay not this
8. 7 unclean spirits, crying with loud voice
14. 10 Said with a loud voice, Stand upright on
16. 28 Paul cried with a loud voice, saying, Do
26. 24 Festus said with a loud voice, Paul, thou
Rev. 5. 2 strong angel proclaiming with a loud voice
5. 12 Saying with a loud voice, Worthy is the
6. 10 they cried with a loud voice, saying, How
7. 2 he cried with a loud voice to the four an.
7. 10 cried with a loud voice, saying, Salvation
8. 13 saying with a loud voice Woe, woe, woe
10. 3 cried with a loud voice, as..a lion roareth
12. 10 I heard a loud voice saying in heaven
14. 7 Saying with a loud voice, Fear God, and
14. 9 saying with a loud voice, If any man wo.
14. 15 crying with a loud voice to him that sat
14. 18 cried with a loud cry to him that had
19. 17 he cried with a loud voice, saying to all

LOUD, to sing —
To cause to be heard, שָׁמַע *shamea,* 5.
Neh. 12. 42 And the singers sang loud, with Jezrah.

LOUDER and louder —
Much in strength, חָזֵק מְאֹד *chazeq meod.*
Exod 19. 19 sounded long, and waxed louder and lou.

LOVE —
1. *Love,* אַהֲבָה *ahabah.*
Gen. 29. 20 (but) a few days, for the love he had to her
2 Sa. 1. 26 thy love to me was..passing the love of
13. 15 than the love wherewith he; 1 Ki. 11. 2.
Psa. 109. 4 For my love they are my adversaries
109. 5 they have rewarded me..hatred for my love
Prov. 5. 19 and be thou ravished always with her love
10. 12 Hatred stirreth up strifes: but love cover.
15. 17 Better (is) a dinner of herbs where love is
17. 9 that covereth a transgression seeketh love
27. 5 Open rebuke (is) better than secret love
Eccl. 9. 1 no man knoweth either love or hatred (by)
9. 6 Also their love, and their hatred, and their
Song 2. 4 house, and his banner over me (was) love
2. 5 comfort me with apples: I (am) sick of love
2. 7 that ye stir not up, nor awake (my) love
3. 5 that ye stir not up, nor awake (my) love
3. 10 the midst thereof being paved (with) love
5. 8 ye tell him, that I (am) sick of love
7. 6 how pleasant art thou, O love, for delights
8. 4 that ye stir not up, nor awake (my) love
8. 6 love (is) strong as death; jealousy (is) cruel
8. 7 Many waters cannot quench love, neither
8. 7 if a man would give all..for love, it would
Isa. 63. 9 in his love and in his pity he redeemed
Jer. 2. 2 the love of thine espousals, when thou w.
2. 33 Why trimmest thou thy way to seek love?
31. 3 have loved thee with an everlasting love
Hos. 3. 1 according to the love of the LORD toward
11. 4 with cords of a man, with bands of love
Zeph. 3. 17 he will rest in his love; he will joy over

2. *Acts of love,* אֲהָבִים *ohabim.*
Prov. 7. 18 Come..let us solace ourselves with loves

3. *Offices of love,* דּוֹד *dod.*
Prov. 7. 18 let us take our fill of love until the morn.
Song 1. 2 his mouth..thy love (is) better than wine
1. 4 we will remember thy love more than wine
4. 10 How fair is thy love, my sister..spouse
4. 10 how much better is thy love than wine!
7. 12 the vineyards..there will I give thee my l.
Eze. 16. 8 behold, thy time (was) the time of love
23. 17 came to her into the bed of love, and they

4. *A female friend,* רַעְיָה *rayah.*
Song 1. 9 I have compared thee, O my love, to a co.
1. 15 Behold, thou (art) fair, my love; behold
2. 2 As the lily among thorns, so (is) my love
2. 10 Rise up, my love, my fair one, and come
2. 13 Arise, my love, my fair one, and come away
4. 1 Behold, thou (art) fair, my love; behold
4. 7 Thou (art) all fair, my love..no spot in
5. 2 Open to me, my sister, my love, my dove
6. 4 Thou (art) beautiful, O my love, as Tirzah

5. *Love,* ἀγάπη *agapē.*
Matt 24. 12 because iniquity shall abound, the love of
Luke 11. 42 pass over judgment and the love of God
John 5. 42 that ye have not the love of God in you
13. 35 my disciples, if ye have love one to anot.
15. 9 so have I loved..continue ye in my love
15. 10 abide in my love..as I..abide in his love
15. 13 Greater love hath no man than this, that
17. 26 that the love wherewith thou hast loved
Rom. 5. 5 because the love of God is shed abroad in
5. 8 But God commendeth his love toward us
8. 35 Who shall separate us from the love of C.?
8. 39 able to separate us from the love of God
12. 9 (Let) love be without dissimulation. Ab.
13. 10 Love worketh no ill to his neighbour..love
15. 30 for the love of the spirit, that ye strive
1 Co. 4. 21 shall I come unto you..in love, and (in)
16. 24 My love (be) with you all in Christ Jesus
2 Co. 2. 4 that ye might know the love which I have
2. 8 that ye would confirm..love toward him
5. 14 For the love of Christ constraineth us; be.
6. 6 by the Holy Ghost, by love unfeigned
8. 7 and (in) all diligence, and (in) your love
8. 8 and to prove the sincerity of your love
8. 24 show ye..the proof of your love, and of our
13. 11 God of love and peace shall be with you
13. 14 the love of God, and the communion of
Gal. 5. 6 uncircumcision; but faith..worketh by lo.
5. 13 to the flesh, but by love serve one another
5. 22 the fruit of the spirit is love, joy, peace
Eph. 1. 4 and without blame before him in love
1. 15 of your faith..and [love] unto all the sai.
2. 4 for his great love wherewith he loved us
3. 17 that ye, being rooted and grounded in love
3. 19 And to know the love of Christ, which
4. 2 meekness..forbearing one another in love
4. 15 speaking the truth in love, may grow up
4. 16 the body unto the edifying of itself in l.
5. 2 walk in love, as Christ also hath loved us
6. 23 and love with faith, from God the Father
Phil. 1. 9 this I pray, that your love may abound
1. 17 the other of love, knowing that I am set
2. 1 if any comfort of love, if any fellowship
2. 2 ye be like minded, having the same love
Col. 1. 4 of the love (which ye have) to all the sa.
1. 8 Who also declared unto us your love in
2. 2 be comforted, being knit together in love
1 Th. 1. 3 your work of faith, and labour of love
3. 12 and abound in love one toward another
5. 8 putting on..breast plate of faith and love
5. 13 to esteem them very highly in love for
2 Th. 2. 10 because they received not the love of the
3. 5 direct your hearts into the love of God
1 Ti. 1. 14 with faith and love which is in Christ
6. 11 follow after..faith, love, patience, meek.
2 Ti. 1. 7 of power, and of love, and of a sound m.
1. 13 in faith and love which is in Christ Jesus
Phil. 5 Hearing of thy love and faith, which thou
7 have great joy and consolation in thy love
9 Yet for love's sake I rather beseech..b.
Heb. 6. 10 your work and labour of love, which ye
10. 24 to provoke unto love and to good works
1 Jo. 2. 5 in him verily is the love of God perfected
2. 15 world, the love of the Father is not in
3. 1 Behold what manner of love the Father
3. 16 Hereby perceive we the love (of God), be.
3. 17 But..how dwelleth the love of God in him?
4. 7 for love is of God; and every one that l.
4. 8 loveth not knoweth not God..God is love
4. 9 In this was manifested the love of God to.
4. 10 Herein is love, not that we loved God, but
4. 12 dwelleth..and his love is perfected in us
4. 16 and believed the love that God hath to us
4. 16 God is love; and he that dwelleth in love
4. 17 Herein is our love made perfect, that we
4. 18 There is no fear in love; but perfect love
4. 18 He that feareth is not made perfect in love
5. 3 For this is the love of God, that we keep
2 John 3 Grace be with you..in truth and love
6 this is love, that we walk after his com.
Jude 2 Mercy unto you, and peace, and love, be
21 Keep yourselves in the love of God, look.
Rev. 2. 4 have..because thou hast left thy first love

LOVE, to —
1. *To love,* אָהֵב *aheb.*
Gen. 22. 2 thine only (son) Isaac, whom thou lovest
24. 67 and she became his wife; and he loved her
25. 28 And Isaac loved Esau..but Rebekah loved
27. 4 make me savoury meat, such as I love
27. 9 make..meat for thy father, such as he l.
27. 14 made savoury meat, such as his father lo
29. 18 Jacob loved Rachel; and said, I will serve
29. 30 and he loved also Rachel more than Leah
29. 32 now therefore my husband will love me
34. 3 he loved the damsel, and spake kindly
37. 3 Israel loved Joseph more than all his ch.
37. 4 when his brethren saw..their father l.
44. 20 he alone is left..and his father loveth him
Exod 20. 6 that love me, and keep my commandme.
21. 5 I love my master, my wife, and my child.
Lev. 19. 18 thou shalt love thy neighbour as thyself
19. 34 thou shalt love him as thyself; for ye w.

Deut. 4. 37 because he loved thy fathers, therefore he
5. 10 unto thousands of them that love me and
6. 5 thou shalt love the LORD thy God with all
7. 9 mercy with them that love him and keep
7. 13 he will love thee, and bless thee, and mu.
10. 12 to walk in all his ways, and to love him
10. 15 had a delight in thy fathers to love them
10. 18 loveth the stranger, in giving him food
10. 19 Love ye therefore the stranger: for ye w.
11. 1 thou shalt love the LORD thy God, and
11. 13 to love the LORD your God, and to serve
11. 22 to love the LORD your God, to walk in all
13. 3 know whether ye love the LORD your God
15. 16 because he loveth thee and thine house
19. 9 to love the LORD thy God, and to walk
23. 5 turned..because the LORD thy God loved
30. 6 to love the LORD thy God with all thine
30. 16 In that I command thee this day to love
30. 20 That thou mayest love the LORD thy God
Josh. 22. 5 charged you, to love the LORD your God
23. 11 Take good heed..that ye love the LORD
Judg. 5. 31 (let) them that love him (be) as the sun
14. 16 Thou dost but hate me, and lovest me not
16. 4 he loved a woman in the valley of Sorek
16. 15 How canst thou say, I love thee, when
Ruth 4. 15 for thy daughter in law, which loveth thee
1 Sa. 1. 5 he loved Hannah: but the LORD had shut
16. 21 he loved him greatly; and he became his
18. 1 and Jonathan loved him as his own soul
18. 16 But all Israel and Judah loved David
18. 20 And Michal, Saul's daughter, loved David
18. 22 all his servants love thee: now therefore
18. 28 (that) Michal, Saul's daughter, loved him
20. 17 for he loved him as..his own soul
2 Sa. 12. 24 bare a son..Solomon..and the LORD loved
13. 1 and Ammon the son of David loved her
13. 4 Amnon said unto him, I love Tamar, my
13. 15 than the love wherewith he had loved her
19. 6 In that thou lovest thine enemies, and ha.
1 Ki. 3. 3 Solomon loved the LORD, walking in the
11. 1 king Solomon loved many strange women
2 Ch. 11. 21 Rehoboam loved Maachah the daughter of
19. 2 Shouldest thou..love them that hate the
26. 10 and in Carmel: for he loved husbandry
Neh. 1. 5 mercy for them that love him and observe
Esth. 2. 17 the king loved Esther above all the women
Job 19. 19 they whom I loved are turned against me
Psa. 4. 2 will ye love vanity, (and) seek after leas.?
5. 11 let them also that love thy name be joyful
11. 5 and him that loveth violence his soul ha.
11. 7 For the righteous LORD loveth righteous.
26. 8 LORD, I have loved the habitation of thy
31. 23 O love the LORD, all ye his saints..the L.
33. 5 He loveth righteousness and judgment
34. 12 loveth (many) days, that he may see good?
37. 28 the LORD loveth judgment, and forsaketh
40. 16 such as love thy salvation say continually
45. 7 Thou lovest righteousness, and hatest wi.
47. 4 the excellency of Jacob whom he loved
52. 3 Thou lovest evil more than good..lying
52. 4 Thou lovest all devouring words, O..dece.
69. 36 they that love his name shall dwell ther.
70. 4 let such as love thy salvation say contin.
78. 68 But chose..the mount Zion which he loved
87. 2 The LORD loveth the gates of Zion more
97. 10 Ye that love the LORD, hate evil: he pr.
99. 4 The king's strength also loveth judgment
109. 17 As he loved cursing, so let it come unto
116. 1 I love the LORD, because he hath heard
119. 47, 48 thy commandments, which I have loved
119. 97 O how I love thy law! it (is) my meditat.
119. 113 I hate..thoughts: but thy law do I love
119. 119 Thou puttest away..therefore I love thy
119. 127 I love thy commandments above gold
119. 132 usest to do unto those that love thy name
119. 140 very pure: therefore thy servant loveth
119. 159 Consider how I love thy precepts: qui.
119. 163 I hate and abhor lying..thy law do I love
119. 165 Great peace have they which love thy law
119. 167 thy testimonies..I love them exceedingly
122. 6 Jerusalem: they shall prosper that love
145. 20 LORD preserveth all them that love him
146. 8 bowed down: the LORD loveth the righ.
Prov. 1. 22 How long, ye simple ones, will ye love si.?
3. 12 For whom the LORD loveth he correcteth
4. 6 preserve thee: love her, and she shall keep
8. 17 I love them that love me; and those that
8. 21 That I may cause those that love me to
8. 36 own soul: all they that hate me love de.
9. 8 rebuke a wise man, and he will love thee
12. 1 Whoso loveth instruction loveth knowle.
13. 24 he that loveth him chasteneth him betimes
15. 9 he loveth him that followeth after right.
15. 12 A scorner loveth not one that reproveth
16. 13 and they love him that speaketh right
17. 17 A friend loveth at all times, and a brother
17. 19 He loveth transgression that loveth strife
18. 21 they that love it shall eat the fruit thereof
19. 8 He that getteth wisdom loveth his own
20. 13 Love not sleep, lest thou come to poverty
21. 17 He that loveth pleasure (shall be) a poor
21. 17 he that loveth wine and oil shall not be
22. 11 He that loveth pureness of heart, (for) the
29. 3 Whoso loveth wisdom rejoiceth his father
Eccl. 3. 8 A time to love, and a time to hate; a time
5. 10 He that loveth silver shall not be satisfied
5. 10 nor he that loveth abundance with increase
9. 9 Live joyfully with the wife whom thou lo.
Song 1. 3 ointment..therefore do the virgins love
1. 7 Tell me, O thou whom my soul loveth, wh.
1. 4 we will run after thee..the upright love
3. 1 I sought him whom my soul loveth: I so.
Song 3. 2 I will seek him whom my soul loveth: I
3. 3 watchmen..Saw ye him whom my soul lo.?
3. 4 but I found him whom my soul loveth: I
Isa. 1. 23 every one loveth gifts, and followeth after
43. 4 I have loved thee: therefore will I give
48. 14 The LORD hath loved him: he will do his
56. 6 and to love the name of the LORD, to be
56. 10 sleeping, lying down, loving to slumber
57. 8 thou lovedst their bed where thou sawest
61. 8 I the LORD love judgment, I hate robbery
66. 10 and be glad with her, all ye that love her
Jer. 2. 25 I have loved strangers, and after them will
5. 31 my people love (to have it) so: and what
8. 2 whom they have loved, and whom they
14. 10 Thus have they loved to wander, they have
31. 3 I have loved thee with an everlasting love
Eze. 16. 37 and all (them) that thou hast loved, with
Dan. 9. 4 covenant and mercy to them that love him
Hos. 3. 1 love a woman beloved of (her) friend, yet
3. 1 who took to other gods, and love flagons
4. 18 her rulers (with) shame do love, Give ye
9. 1 thou hast loved a reward upon every corn.
9. 10 abominations were according as they loved
10. 11 Ephraim..an heifer..taught..loveth to
11. 1 then I loved him, and called my son out
12. 7 (He is) a merchant..he loveth to oppress
14. 4 I will love them freely: for mine anger is
Amos 5. 15 Hate the evil, and love the good, and est.
Mic. 3. 2 Who hate the good, and love the evil; who
Zech. 8. 17 love no false oath: for all these..that I
8. 19 feasts; therefore love the truth and peace
Mal. 1. 2 have loved you..Wherein hast thou loved
1. 2 not Esau Jacob's brother?..yet I loved J.
2. 11 the holiness of the LORD which he loved

2. *Love*, אַהֲבָה *ahabah.*
Deut. 7. 8 because the LORD loved you, and because
1 Sa. 18. 3 made..because he loved him as his own s.
20. 17 because he loved him..as he loved his own
1 Ki. 10. 9 because the LORD loved Israel for ever
2 Ch. 2. 11 Because the LORD hath loved his people
9. 8 because thy God loved Israel, to establish
Hos. 9. 15 I will love them no more: all their princes
Mic. 6. 8 but to do justly, and to love mercy, and

3. *To love, have in the bosom*, חָבַב *chabab.*
Deut. 33. 3 Yea, he loved the people; all his saints

4. *To love, pity, be merciful*, רָחַם *racham.*
Psa. 18. 1 I will love thee, O LORD, my strength

5. *To love*, ἀγαπάω *agapaō.*
Matt. 5. 43 Thou shalt love thy neighbour, and hate
5. 44 I say unto you, Love your enemies, bless
5. 46 For if ye love them which love you, what
6. 24 either he will hate the one, and love the
19. 19 Thou shalt love thy neighbour as thyself
22. 37 Thou shalt love the Lord thy God with all
22. 39 Thou shalt love thy neighbour as thyself
Mark 10. 21 Then Jesus, beholding him, loved him, and
12. 30 thou shalt love the Lord thy God with all
12. 31 Thou shalt love thy neighbour as thyself
12. 33 to love him with all the heart, and with
12. 33 to love (his) neighbour as himself, is more
Luke 6. 27 Love your enemies, do good to them which
6. 32 if ye love them which love you, what th.
6. 32 for sinners also love those that love them
6. 35 love ye your enemies, and do good, and l.
7. 5 he loveth our nation, and he hath built us
7. 42 Tell me..which of them will love him m.?
7. 47 she loved much; but..(the same) loveth li.
10. 27 Thou shalt love the Lord thy God with all
11. 43 ye love the uppermost seats in the synag.
16. 13 either he will hate the one, and love the
John 3. 16 God so loved the world, that he gave his
3. 19 and men loved darkness rather than light
3. 35 The Father loveth the Son, and hath given
8. 42 If God were your Father, ye would love
10. 17 Therefore doth my Father love me, bec.
11. 5 Jesus loved Martha, and her sister and L.
12. 43 they loved the praise of men more than
13. 1 having loved his own..he loved them unto
13. 23 Now..one of his disciples, whom Jesus l.
13. 34 A new commandment..That ye love one
13. 34 as I have loved you, that ye also love me
14. 15 If ye love me, keep my commandments
14. 21 and keepeth them, he it is that loveth me
14. 21 he that loveth me shall be loved of my F.
14. 21 I will love him, and will manifest myself
14. 23 If a man love me, he will keep my words
14. 23 my Father will love him, and we will come
14. 24 He that loveth me not keepeth not my
14. 28 If ye loved me, ye would rejoice, because
14. 31 that the world may know that I love the F.
15. 9 As the Father hath loved me, so have I l.
15. 12 That ye love one another, as I have loved
15. 17 I command you, that ye love one another
17. 23 and hast loved them, as thou hast loved
17. 24 thou lovedst me before the foundation of
17. 26 that the love wherewith thou hast loved
19. 26 and the disciple standing by whom he l.
21. 7 that disciple whom Jesus loved saith unto
21. 15 Simon..lovest thou me more than these?
21. 16 again..Simon, (son) of Jonas, lovest thou
21. 20 seeth the disciple whom Jesus loved fol.
Rom. 8. 28 work..for good to them that love God
8. 37 than conquerors, through him that loved
9. 13 As it is written, Jacob have I loved, but
13. 8 Owe no man anything, but to love one an.
13. 8 he that loveth another hath fulfilled the
13. 9 Thou shalt love thy neighbour as thyself
1 Co. 2. 9 God hath prepared for them that love him
8. 3 if any man love God, the same is known of
2 Co. 9. 7 or of necessity: for God loveth a cheerful
11. 11 Wherefore? because I love you not? God
12. 15 abundantly I love you, the less I be loved
Gal. 2. 20 the Son of God, who loved me, and gave
5. 14 Thou shalt love thy neighbour as thyself
Eph. 2. 4 for his great love wherewith he loved us
5. 2 walk in love, as Christ also hath loved us
5. 25 love your wives, even as Christ..loved
5. 28 So ought men to love their wives as their
5. 28 He that loveth his wife loveth himself
5. 33 let every one..so love his wife even as h.
6. 24 Grace (be) with all them that love our L.
Col. 3. 19 Husbands, love (your) wives, and be not
1 Th. 4. 9 ye yourselves are taught of God to love
2 Th. 2. 16 even our Father, which hath loved us, and
2 Ti. 4. 8 unto all them also that love his appearing
4. 10 Demas..having loved this present world
Heb. 1. 9 Thou hast loved righteousness, and hated
12. 6 For whom the Lord loveth he chasteneth
Jas. 1. 12 Lord hath promised to them that love him
2. 5 he hath promised to them that love him?
2. 8 Thou shalt love thy neighbour as thyself
1 Pe. 1. 8 Whom having not seen, ye love; in whom
1. 22 love one another with a pure heart ferven.
2. 17 Honour all (men). Love the brotherhood
3. 10 he that will love life, and see good days
2 Pe. 2. 15 who loved the wages of unrighteousness
1 Jo. 2. 10 He that loveth his brother abideth in the
2. 15 Love not the world, neither the things
2. 15 If any man love the world, the love of the
3. 10 neither he that loveth not his brother
3. 11 the message..that we should love one an.
3. 14 We know that..because we love the bre.
3. 14 He that loveth not (his) brother abideth
3. 18 My little children, let us not love in word
3. 23 and love one another, as he gave us com.
4. 7 let us love one another..every one that l.
4. 8 He that loveth not knoweth not God; for
4. 10 not that we loved God, but that he loved
4. 11 if God so loved us, we ought also to love
4. 12 If we love one another, God dwelleth in
4. 19 We love him, because he first loved us
4. 20 If a man say, I love God, and hateth his
4. 20 that loveth not his brother..how can he l.
4. 21 That he who loveth God love his brother
5. 1 every one that loveth him that begat lov.
5. 2 By this we know that we love the children
5. 2 when we love God, and keep his comma.
2 John 1 whom I love in the truth; and not I only
5 new commandment..that we love one a.
3 John 1 well beloved Gaius, whom I love in the
Rev. 1. 5 Unto him that loved us, and washed us
3. 9 make them..to know that I have loved
12. 11 they loved not their lives unto the death

6. *To will or wish*, θέλω *thelō.*
Mark 12. 38 scribes, which love to go in long clothing

7. *To be a friend*, φιλέω *phileō.*
Matt. 6. 5 for they love to pray standing in the syn.
10. 37 He that loveth father or mother more
10. 37 he that loveth son or daughter more than
23. 6 love the uppermost rooms at feasts, and
Luke 20. 46 love greetings in the markets, and the
John 5. 20 the Father [loveth] the Son, and showeth
11. 3 Lord, behold, he whom thou lovest is sick
11. 36 Then said the Jews, Behold, how he loved
12. 25 He that loveth his life shall lose it; and
15. 19 the world would love his own: but beca.
16. 27 Father..loveth you, because ye have loved
20. 2 to the other disciple whom Jesus loved
21. 15, 16, 17 Lord, thou knowest that I love thee
21. 17 lovest thou me?..Lovest thou me?
1 Co. 16. 22 If any man love not the Lord Jesus Christ
Titus 3. 15 Greet them that love us in the faith. Grace
Rev. 3. 19 As many as I love, I rebuke and chasten
22. 15 and whosoever loveth and maketh a lie

LOVE, in —

1. *To love*, אָהֵב *aheb.*
1 Ki. 11. 2 the nations..Solomon clave unto these in l.

2. *To cleave to*, חָשַׁק *chashaq.*
Isa. 38. 17 thou hast in love to my soul (delivered

LOVE, inordinate or much —

1. *Doting love*, עֲגָבָה *agabah.*
Eze. 23. 11 she was more corrupt in her inordinate l.

2. *Doting loves*, עֲגָבִים *agabim.*
Eze. 33. 31 for with their mouth they show much love

LOVE to have the pre-eminence, to —

To love to be first, φιλοπρωτεύω *philoprōteuō.*
3 John 9 Diotrephes, who loveth to have the pre-e.

LOVE, to set —

To cleave to, חָשַׁק *chashaq.*
Deut 7. 7 The LORD did not set his love upon you
Psa. 91. 14 Because he hath set his love upon me

LOVE, tender —

Pity, mercy, רַחֲמִים *rachamim.*
Dan. 1. 9 into favour and tender love with the pri.

LOVE as brethren —

Loving one's brethren, φιλάδελφος *philadelphos.*
1 Pe. 3. 8 love as brethren, (be) pitiful, (be) court.

LOVE of the brethren, or brotherly love —

Love of the brethren, φιλαδελφία *philadelphia.*
Rom. 12. 10 one to another with brotherly love; in hon.
1 Th. 4. 9 as touching brotherly love ye need not
Heb. 13. 1 Let brotherly love continue
1 Pe. 1. 22 purified..unto unfeigned love of the bre.

LOVE of money —
Love of silver, φιλαργυρία *philarguria.*
1 Ti. 6. 10 For the love of money is the root of all e.

LOVE one's children or husband —
1. *Lover of children,* φιλότεκνος *philoteknos.*
Titus 2. 4 teach the young women..to love their ch.
2. *Lover of husband,* φίλανδρος *philandros.*
Titus 2. 4 women to be sober, to love their husbands

LOVE toward man —
Love of mankind, φιλανθρωπία *philanthrōpia.*
Titus 3. 4 and love of God our Saviour toward man

LOVELY —
1. *To be loved,* אָהֵב *aheb,* 2.
2 Sa. 1. 23 Saul and Jonathan (were) lovely and ple.
2. *Desire, a desirable thing,* מַחְמָד *machmad.*
Song 5. 16 yea, he (is) altogether lovely. This (is) my
3. *Very lovely, or lovable,* προσφιλής *prosphilēs.*
Phil. 4. 8 whatsoever things (are) lovely..think on

LOVELY, very —
Doting acts of love, עֲגָבִים *agabim.*
Eze. 33. 32 as a very lovely song of one that hath a pl.

LOVER —
1. *To love,* אָהֵב *aheb.*
1 Ki. 5. 1 for Hiram was ever a lover of David
Psa. 38. 11 My lovers and my friends stand aloof from
88. 18 Lover and friend hast thou put far from
Lam. 1. 2 among all her lovers she hath none to co.
2. *To love,* אָהֵב *aheb,* 3.
Jer. 22. 20 and cry..for all thy lovers are destroyed
22. 22 thy lovers shall go into captivity: surely
30. 14 All thy lovers have forgotten thee; they
Lam. 1. 19 I called for my lovers..they deceived me
Eze. 16. 33 thou givest thy gifts to all thy lovers, and
16. 36 with thy lovers, and with all the idols of
16. 37 I will gather all thy lovers, with whom
23. 5 she doted on her lovers, on the Assyrians
23. 9 delivered her into the hand of her lovers
23. 22 I will raise up thy lovers against thee, from
Hos. 2. 5 I will go after my lovers, that gave (me)
2. 7 she shall follow after her lovers, but she
2. 10 her lewdness in the sight of her lovers
2. 12 my rewards that my lovers have given me
2. 13 she went after her lovers, and forgat me
3. *To dote on, love,* עָגַב *agab.*
Jer. 4. 30 lovers will despise thee, they will seek thy
4. *A friend, companion,* רֵעַ *rea.*
Jer. 3. 1 hast played the harlot with many lovers
5. *Loves,* אֳהָבִים *ahabim.*
Hos. 8. 9 alone by himself: Ephraim hath hired lo.

LOVER of God —
Lover of God, φιλόθεος *philotheos.*
2 Ti. 3. 4 of pleasures more than lovers of God

LOVER of good men —
Lover of the good, φιλάγαθος *philagathos.*
Titus 1. 8 a lover of good men, sober, just, holy, tem.

LOVER of hospitality —
Lover of strangers or of hospitality, φιλόξενος.
Titus 1. 8 But a lover of hospitality..sober, just, h.

LOVER of own self —
Lover of self, φίλαυτος *philautos.*
2 Ti. 3. 2 men shall be lovers of their own selves

LOVER of pleasures —
Lover of pleasure, φιλήδονος *philēdonos.*
2 Ti. 3. 4 lovers of pleasures more than..of God

LOVES —
Beloved, יָדִיד *yadid.*
Psa. 45. *title.* sons of Korah. Maschil, A song of loves

LOVING —
1. *Loves,* אֳהָבִים *ahabim.*
Prov. 5. 19 the loving hind and pleasant roe; let her
2. *Good,* טוֹב *tob.*
Prov 22. 1 loving favour rather than silver and gold

LOVING kindness —
Kindness, חֶסֶד *chesed.*
Psa. 17. 7 Show thy marvellous loving kindness, O
25. 6 tender mercies and thy loving kindnesses
26. 3 thy loving kindness (is) before mine eyes
36. 7 How excellent (is) thy loving kindness, O
36. 10 O continue thy loving kindness unto them
40. 10 I have not concealed thy loving kindness
40. 11 let thy loving kindness and thy truth co.
42. 8 LORD will command his loving kindness
48. 9 We have thought of thy loving kindness
51. 1 O God, according to thy loving kindness
63. 3 thy loving kindness (is) better than life
69. 16 Hear me, O LORD; for thy loving kindn.
88. 11 Shall thy loving kindness be declared in
89. 33 my loving kindness will I not utterly take
89. 49 where (are) thy former loving kindnesses
92. 2 To show forth thy loving kindness in the
103. 4 who crowneth thee with loving kindness
107. 43 they shall understand the loving kindness
119. 88 Quicken me after thy loving kindness; so
119. 149 Hear..according unto thy loving kind.
119. 159 O LORD, according to thy loving kindness
138. 2 praise thy name for thy loving kindness
Psa. 143. 8 Cause me to hear thy loving kindness in
Isa. 63. 7 I will mention the loving kindnesses of
63. 7 to the multitude of his loving kindnesses
Jer. 9. 24 I (am) the LORD which exercise loving ki.
16. 5 my peace..loving kindness and mercies
31. 3 with loving kindness have I drawn thee
32. 18 showest loving kindness unto thousands
Hos. 2. 19 betroth..in loving kindness, and in mer.

LOW —
1. *A (common) man,* אָדָם *adam.*
Psa. 49. 2 Both low and high, rich and poor, toget.
2. *Low, humble,* שָׁפָל *shaphal.*
Job 5. 11 To set up on high those that be low; that
Eccl. 12. 4 when the sound of the grinding is low, and
Eze. 17. 6 became a spreading vine of low stature
17. 24 I the LORD..have exalted the low tree
21. 26 exalt (him that is) low, and abase (him that
3. *Lower, under,* תַּחְתִּי *tachti.*
Lam. 3. 55 I called..O LORD, out of the low dungeon
[*See also* Bring, brought, degree, man.]

LOW, to —
To low, גָּעָה *gaah.*
1 Sa. 6. 12 along the highway, lowing as they went
Job 6. 5 grass? or loweth the ox over his fodder?

LOW, to be —
1. *To be bowed down,* שָׁחַח *shachach,* 2.
Isa. 29. 4 thy speech shall be low out of the dust
2. *To be low, humble,* שָׁפֵל *shaphel.*
Isa. 32. 19 and the city shall be low in a low place

LOW, to be made —
1. *To be low, humble,* שָׁפֵל *shaphel.*
Isa. 2. 17 the haughtiness of man shall be made low
40. 4 every mountain and hill shall be made low
2. *Humiliation, lowliness,* ταπείνωσις *tapeinōsis.*
Jas. 1. 10 But the rich, in that he is made low: be.

LOW, to bring or lay —
To make low or humble, שָׁפֵל *shaphel,* 5.
1 Sa. 2. 7 The LORD..he bringeth low, and lifteth
Prov 29. 23 A man's pride shall bring him low: but h.
Isa. 13. 11 will lay low the haughtiness of the terrible
25. 12 of thy walls shall he bring down, lay low
26. 5 lofty city, he layeth it low..layeth it low

LOW, to be brought —
1. *To be low,* מָכַךְ *makak.*
Psa. 106. 43 and were brought low for their iniquity
2. *To be made low,* מָכַךְ *makak,* 6.
Job 24. 24 but are gone and brought low; they are
3. *Become low, dependent,* דָּלַל *dalal.*
Psa. 79. 8, 116. 6, 142. 6
4. *To be bowed down,* שָׁחַח *shachach,* 1 and 2.
Psa. 107. 39 are..b. low; Eccl. 12. 4
5. *To be low, humble,* שָׁפֵל *shaphel.*
Isa. 2. 12 and..lifted up..he shall be brought low
6. *To make low,* ταπεινόω *tapeinoō.*
Luke 3. 5 every mount. and hill shall be brought low

LOW country or plain —
Low country, low land, שְׁפֵלָה *shephelah.*
1 Ch. 27. 28 sycamore trees that (were) in the low pl.
2 Ch. 9. 27 that (are) in the low plains in abundance
26. 10 had much cattle, both in the low country
28. 18 had invaded the cities of the low country

LOW estate, or place, or degree —
1. *Low, humble place,* שֵׁפֶל *shephel.*
Psa. 136. 23 Who remembered us in our low estate
Eccl. 10. 6 great dignity, and the rich sit in low pl.
2. *Lowness, low place,* שִׁפְלָה *shiphlah.*
Isa. 32. 19 and the city shall be low in a low place
3. *Low, humble,* ταπεινός *tapeinos.*
Luke 1. 52 put down..and exalted them of low deg.
Rom 12. 16 condescend to men of low estate. Be not
Jas. 1. 9 Let the brother of low degree rejoice in
4. *Lowliness, low estate,* ταπείνωσις *tapeinōsis.*
Luke 1. 48 For he hath regarded the low estate of

LOW, lower or lowest parts —
Lower, under, תַּחְתִּי *tachti.*
Psa. 63. 9 shall go into the lower parts of the earth
139. 15 wrought in the lowest parts of the earth
Isa. 44. 23 shout, ye lower parts of the earth: break
Eze. 26. 20 shall set thee in the low parts of the earth

LOW, very —
Beneath, low, מַטָּה *mattah.*
Deut 28. 43 high, and thou shalt come down very low

LOWER, lowest —
1. *End, extremity,* קָצָה *qatsah.*
1 Ki. 12. 31 made priests of the lowest of the people
13. 33 made..of the lowest of the people priests
2 Ki. 17. 32 and made unto themselves of the lowest
2. *Low, humble,* שָׁפָל *shaphal.*
Lev. 13. 20 behold, it (be) in sight lower than the skin
13. 21 and (if) it (be) not lower than the skin, but
13. 26 and it (be) no lower than the (other) skin
14. 37 which in sight (are) lower than the wall
3. *Lower, under,* תַּחְתּוֹן *tachton.*
Isa. 22. 9 gathered together the waters of the lower
Eze. 40. 18 And the pavement..(was) the lower pav.
40. 19 from the forefront of the lower gate unto
41. 7 and so increased (from) the lowest..to the
42. 5 than the lower, and than the middlemost
42. 6 straitened more than the lowest and the
43. 14 to the lower settle (shall be) two cubits
4. *Lower, under,* תַּחְתִּי *tachti.*
Gen. 6. 16 lower, second, and third..shalt thou make
Deut 32. 22 shall burn unto the lowest hell, and shall
Neh. 4. 13 Therefore set I in the lower places behind
Psa. 86. 13 thou hast delivered my soul from the lo.
88. 6 Thou hast laid me in the lowest pit, in da.
5. *Last, most extreme, distant,* ἔσχατος *eschatos.*
Luke 14. 9 begin with shame to take the lowest room
14. 10 But..go and sit down in the lowest room
6. *Lower down,* κατώτερος *katōteros.*
Eph. 4. 9 descended first into the lower parts of the

LOWER or LOUR, to —
To lour, be dark, gloomy, στυγνάζω *stugnazō.*
Matt 16. 3 for the sky is red and lowering..hypocrites

LOWER, to make —
1. *To let or make to lack,* חָסֵר *chaser,* 3.
Psa. 8. 5 thou hast made him a little lower than the
2. *To make low, less,* ἐλαττόω *elattoō.*
Heb. 2. 7 madest him a little lower than the ang.
2. 9 who was made a little lower than the an.

LOWER, to be put —
To make low, humble, שָׁפֵל *shaphel,* 5.
Prov 25. 7 than that thou shouldest be put lower in

LOWING —
A voice, קוֹל *qol.*
1 Sa. 15. 14 and the lowing of the oxen which I hear?

LOWLINESS (of mind) —
Lowliness of mind, ταπεινοφροσύνη *tapeinophrosunē.*
Eph. 4. 2 With all lowliness and meekness, with
Phil. 2. 3 in lowliness of mind let each esteem other

LOWLY —
1. *Low, afflicted,* עָנָו [v.L. עָנִי] *anav* or עָנִי *ani.*
Prov. 3. 34 scorneth..but he giveth grace unto the l.
16. 19 of..with the l.; Zech. 9. 9, lowly and riding
2. *To be lowly,* צָנַע *tsana.*
Prov 11. 2 cometh shame: but with the lowly (is) w.
3. *Low, humble,* שָׁפָל *shaphal.*
Psa. 138. 6 yet hath he respect unto the lowly: but
4. *Low, humble,* ταπεινός *tapeinos.*
Matt 11. 29 I am meek and lowly in heart: and ye

LU-'BIMS, לוּבִים.
The inhabitants of N. Africa, W. from Egypt. (See *Libyans*).
2 Ch. 12. 3 the L., the Sukkiims, and the Ethiopians
16. 8 Were not..Ethiopians and..L. a huge
Nah. 3. 9 Put and Lubim were thy helpers

LUC'-AS, LUKE, Λουκᾶς *light-giving.*
A physician who travelled much with the apostle Paul, and is understood to have written the third gospel and the Acts of the Apostles.
Col. 4. 14 L., the beloved physician, and Demas
2 Ti. 4. 11 Only L. is with me. Take Mark, and bring
Phm. 24 Marcus, Aristarchus, Demas, L., my fell.

LU-CI-FER, הֵילֵל *shining one.*
A translation of *helel* applied to the king of Babylon by Isaiah, in reference to his glory and pomp. B.C. 720.
Isa. 14. 12 O L., son of the morning! (how) art thou

LU-CI'-US, Λούκιος *of light.*
1. A Christian from Cyrene, ministering at Antioch.
Acts 13. 1 L. of Cyrene, and Manaen, which had been
2. A kinsman of Paul; perhaps the same as No 1.
Rom. 16. 21 Timotheus my work fellow, and L., and

LUCRE —
1. *Dishonest gain,* בֶּצַע *betsa.*
1 Sa. 8. 3 turned aside after lucre, and took bribes
2. *Gain, profit,* κέρδος *kerdos.*
Titus 1. 11 teaching things..for filthy lucre's sake

LUCRE, given to or greedy of filthy —
A shameful gainer, αἰσχροκερδής *aischrokerdēs.*
Titus 1. 7 must be..no striker, not given to filthy l.
1 Ti. 3. 3, 8 not double tongued..not greedy of filthy l.

LUCRE, for filthy —
Shamefully gaining, αἰσχροκερδῶς *aischrokerdōs.*
1 Pe. 5. 2 not for filthy lucre, but of a ready mind

LUCRE, not greedy of filthy —
Not loving silver, ἀφιλάργυρος *aphilarguros.*
1 Ti. 3. 3 no striker, not greedy of filthy lucre; but

LUD, לוּד.
1. Son of Shem, B.C. 2280; supposed to have founded the kingdom of Lydia in Asia Minor.
Gen. 10. 22 The children of Shem..Arphaxad, and L.
1 Ch. 1. 17 The sons of Shem..Arphaxad, and L., and
2. Descendants of Lud in N. Africa, Asia Minor, Assyria, &c.
Isa. 66. 19 I will send those that escape..(to) Lud.
Eze 27. 10 They of Persia and of L. and of Phut were

LU'-DIM, לוּדִים.
Son of Mizraim; the African *Lewatah* in Mauritania.
Gen. 10. 13 Mizraim begat L., and Anamim, and Leh.
1 Ch. 1. 11 Mizraim begat L., and Anamim, and Leh.

LU'-HITH, לוּחִית, לֻחִית *table.*
A city of Moab between Ar and Zoar, at the S. extremity of the Salt Sea.
Isa. 15. 5 for by the mounting up of L. with weep.
Jer. 48. 5 For in the going up of L. continual weep.

LUKEWARM —
Somewhat warm, χλιαρός *chliaros.*
Rev. 3. 16 So then because thou art lukewarm, and

LUMP (of figs) —
1. *Bunch of dried figs,* דְּבֵלָה *debelah.*
2 Ki. 20. 7 And Isaiah said, Take a lump of figs. And
Isa. 38. 21 Let them take a lump of figs, and lay (it)
2. *Mass of things mixed,* φύραμα *phurama.*
Rom. 9. 21 of the same lump to make one vessel unto
11. 16 if the first fruit (be) holy, the lump (is) also
1 Co. 5. 6 a little leaven leaveneth the whole lump?
5. 7 that ye may be a new lump, as ye are unl.
Gal. 5. 9 A little leaven leaveneth the whole lump

LUNATICK, to be —
To be moon-struck, σεληνιάζομαι *seleniazomai.*
Matt. 4. 24 those which were lunatick, and those that
17. 15 he is lunatick, and sore vexed: for oft

LURK privily, to —.
To hide, watch secretly, צָפַן *tsaphan.*
Prov. 1. 11 let us lurk privily for the innocent witho.
1. 18 And..they lurk privily for their (own) lives

LURKING —
To sit still or down, יָשַׁב *yashab.*
Psa. 17. 12 as it were a young lion lurking in secret

LURKING place —
1. *Place of lying in wait,* מַאְרָב *maarab.*
Psa. 10. 8 He sitteth in the lurking places of the vill.
2. *Hiding place,* מַחֲבֹאִים *machaboim.*
1 Sa. 23. 23 take knowledge of all the lurking places

LUST —
1. *Soul, breath, desire,* נֶפֶשׁ *nephesh.*
Exod 15. 9 my lust shall be satisfied upon them; I
Psa. 78. 18 they tempted..by asking meat for their l.
2. *Stubbornness, enmity, imagination,* שְׁרִירוּת *sheriruth*
Psa. 81. 12 gave them up unto their own hearts' lust
3. *Object of desire,* תַּאֲוָה *taavah.*
Psa. 78. 30 They were not estranged from their lust
4. *Desire, over desire,* ἐπιθυμία *epithumia.*
Mark 4. 19 the lusts of other things entering in, choke
John 8. 44 the lusts of your father ye will do. He w.
Rom. 1. 24 through the lusts of their own hearts, to
6. 12 [that ye should obey it in the lusts thereof]
7. 7 for I had not known lust, except the law
13. 14 provision for the flesh, to (fulfil) the lusts
Gal. 5. 16 and ye shall not fulfil the lust of the flesh
5. 24 have crucified the flesh with the..lusts
Eph. 2. 3 conversation in times past in the lusts of
4. 22 corrupt according to the deceitful lusts
1 Ti. 6. 9 many foolish and hurtful lusts, which dr.
2 Ti. 2. 22 Flee also youthful lusts: but follow righ.
3. 6 silly women..led away with divers lusts
4. 3 after their own lusts shall they heap to
Titus 2. 12 denying ungodliness and worldly lusts
3. 3 serving divers lusts and pleasures, living
Jas. 1. 14 when he is drawn away of his own lust
1. 15 when lust hath conceived, it bringeth fo.
1 Pe. 1. 14 according to the former lusts in your ig.
2. 11 abstain from fleshly lusts, which war ag.
4. 2 in the flesh to the lusts of men, but to the
4. 3 when we walked in lasciviousness, lusts
2 Pe. 1. 4 the corruption..in the world through lust
2. 10 that walk after the flesh in the lust of un.
2. 18 they allure through the lusts of the flesh
3. 3 come..scoffers, walking after their own l.
1 Jo. 2. 16 lust of the flesh, and the lust of the eyes
2. 17 the world passeth away, and the lust the.
Jude 16 complainers, walking after their own lusts
18 should walk after their own ungodly lusts
5. *Pleasure, sweetness,* ἡδονή *hēdonē.*
Jas. 4. 1 of your lusts that war in your members?
4. 3 ask..that ye may consume (it) upon your l.
6. *Eager desire,* ὄρεξις *orexis.*
Rom. 1. 27 burned in their lust one towards another
7. *Suffering, affection,* πάθος *pathos.*
1 Th. 4. 5 Not in the lust of concupiscence even as

LUST (after), to —
1. *To desire, incline to,* אָוָה *avah,* 7.
Num 11. 34 there they buried the people that lusted
Psa. 106. 14 But lusted exceedingly in the wilderness
2. *To desire,* אָוָה *avah,* 3.
Deut 14. 26 for whatsoever thy soul lusted after, for
3. *Desire,* אַוָּה *avvah.*
Deut 12. 15, 20, 21 whatsoever thy soul lusteth after
4. *To desire,* חָמַד *chamad.*
Prov. 6. 25 Lust not after her beauty in thine heart
5. *To desire greatly,* ἐπιθυμέω *epithumeō.*
Matt. 5. 28 whosoever looketh on a woman to lust af.
1 Co. 10. 6 not..after evil things, as they also lusted
Gal. 5. 17 the flesh lusteth against the spirit, and
Jas. 4. 2 Ye lust, and have not: ye kill, and desire
6. *To be desiring,* εἶναι ἐπιθυμητής *einai epithumētēs.*
1 Co. 10. 6 we should not lust after evil things, as they
7. *Desire, over desire,* ἐπιθυμία *epithumia.*
Rev. 18. 14 the fruits that thy soul lusted after are d.
8. *To desire upon or eagerly,* ἐπιποθέω *epipotheō.*
Jas. 4. 5 The spirit that dwelleth in us lusteth to

LUSTING—
Desire, תַּאֲוָה *taavah.*
Num 11. 4 the mixed multitude..fell a lusting: and

LUSTY—
Fat, lusty, שָׁמֵן *shamen.*
Judg. 3. 29 about ten thousand men, all lusty, and

LUZ, לוּז *bending, curve.*
1. A city of the Canaanites, afterwards called Beth-el; in the lot of Benjamin. Now called *Beitin.*
Gen. 28. 19 the name of that city (was called) L. at the
35. 6 So Jacob came to L., which (is) in the land
48. 3 God Almighty appeared unto me at L. in
Josh. 16. 2 goeth out from Beth-el to L., and passeth
18. 13 toward L., to the side of L., which (is) B.
Judg. 1. 23 now the name of the city before (was) L.
2. A city in the land of the Hittites; built by the man who showed the entrance of Luz or Bethel to the spics of Israel. B.C. 1425.
Judg. 1. 26 called the name thereof L.: which (is) the

LY-CA-O-NI'-A, Λυκαονία.
A province of Asia Minor N. from Cilicia, W. from Cappadocia, and S. from Galatia. Its chief cities were Derbe, Lystra, and Iconium.
Acts 14. 6 fled unto Lystra and Derbe, cities of L.
14. 11 saying in the speech of L., The gods are

LY-CI'-A, Λυκία.
A province in the extreme S. of Asia Minor.
Acts 27. 5 Pamphylia, we came to Myra, (a city) of L.

LYD'-DA, Λύδδα.
A city of Dan, ten miles E. from Joppa; once called *Lod* and *Diospolis;* now *Ludd.*
Acts 9. 32 down also to the saints which dwelt at L.
9. 35 all that dwelt in L. and Saron saw him
9. 38 forasmuch as L. was nigh to Joppa, and

LY-DI'-A, לוּד Λυδία.
1. *Lud.* A country and people in the N. of Africa, W. from Egypt.
Eze. 30. 5 Ethiopia, and Libya, and L., and all the
2. A devout woman of Thyatira, converted by Paul's preaching at Philippi.
Acts 16. 14 certain woman named L., a seller of pur.
16. 40 entered into (the house of) L.: and when

LYDIANS, לוּדִים.
A people of Africa. See *Lud, Ludim.*
Jer. 46. 9 the L., that handle (and) bend the bow

LYING —
1. *A lying, deceitful one,* כְּדַב *kedab.*
Dan. 2. 9 ye have prepared lying and corrupt words
2. *To lie, deceive, fail,* כָּזַב *kazab,* 3.
Eze. 13. 19 your lying to my people that hear (your) l.?
3. *A lie, deceit,* כָּזָב *kazab.*
Eze. 13. 6 They have seen vanity and lying divination
13. 7 and have ye not spoken a lying divination
4. *To fail, feign, lie, deceive,* כָּחַשׁ *kachash,* 3.
Isa. 59. 13 In transgressing and lying against the L.
Hos. 4. 2 By swearing, and lying, and killing, and
5. *A lie, failure, feigning,* כַּחַשׁ *kachash.*
Psa. 59. 12 and for cursing and lying (which) they s.
6. *Lying,* כֶּחָשִׁים *kechashim.*
Isa. 30. 9 lying children, children (that) will not
7. *To fall,* נָפַל *naphal.*
Deut 21. 1 If (one) be found slain..lying in the field
8. *Vanity, falsehood,* שָׁוְא *shav.*
Psa. 31. 6 I have hated them that regard lying va.
Jon. 2. 8 They that observe lying vanities forsake
9. *Falsehood, lie,* שֶׁקֶר *sheqer.*
1 Ki. 22. 22 I will be a lying spirit in the mouth of
22. 23 LORD hath put a lying spirit in the mouth
2 Ch. 18. 21 lying spirit in the mouth of all his proph.
18. 22 LORD hath put a lying spirit in the mouth
Psa. 31. 18 Let the lying lips be put to silence; which
109. 2 they have spoken against me with a lying
119. 29 Remove from me the way of lying; and
119. 163 I hate and abhor lying: (but) thy law do
120. 2 Deliver my soul, O LORD, from lying lips
Prov. 6. 17 A proud look, a lying tongue, and hands
10. 18 He that hideth hatred (with) lying lips
12. 19 but a lying tongue (is) but for a moment
12. 22 Lying lips (are) abomination to the LORD
17. 7 becometh not a fool; much less do lying l.
21. 6 The getting of treasures by a lying tongue
26. 28 A lying tongue hateth (those that are) affl.
Isa. 32. 7 devices to destroy the poor with lying wo.
Jer. 7. 4 Trust ye not in lying words, saying, The
7. 8 ye trust in lying words, that cannot profit
29. 23 have spoken lying words in my name, wh.
10. *A word of falsehood,* דְּבַר שֶׁקֶר [*dabar*].
Prov. 13. 5 A righteous (man) hateth lying: but a wicked
11. *A lie, falsehood,* ψεῦδος *pseudos.*
Eph. 4. 25 Wherefore putting away lying, speak ev.
2 Th. 2. 9 with all power and signs and lying won.

LYING down —
1. *A couch, lying down,* רֶבַע *reba.*
Psa. 139. 3 compassest my path and my lying down
2. *To lie, lie down,* שָׁכַב *shakab.*
Isa. 56. 10 sleeping, lying down, loving to slumber

LYING in wait —
1. *Place of lying in wait,* ἔνεδρον *enedron.*
Acts 23. 16 heard of their lying in wait, he went and
2. *Counsel against one,* ἐπιβουλή *epiboulē.*
Acts 20. 19 befell me by the lying in wait of the Jews

LYING in wait, (men) —
1. *To lie in wait,* אָרַב *arab.*
Judg 16. 9 men lying in wait, abiding with her in the
2. *Place of lying in wait,* מַאְרָב *maarab.*
Judg. 9. 35 Abimelech rose up..from lying in wait

LYING with —
1. *A place of lying down,* מִשְׁכָּב *mishkab.*
Num 31. 17 woman that hath known man by lying w.
31. 18 that hath not known a man by lying with
31. 35 that had not known man by lying with him
Judg 21. 12 that had known no man by lying with any
2. *To lie, lie down,* שָׁכַב *shakab.*
Gen. 34. 7 folly..in lying with Jacob's daughter; w.
Deut 22. 22 If a man be found lying with a woman m.

LY-SA-NI'-AS, Λυσανίας.
A tetrarch of Abilene. A.D. 26.
Luke 3. 1 Herod being tetrarch of Galilee..and L.

LY-SI'-AS, Λυσίας.
Chief captain of the Roman garrison at Jerusalem.
Acts 23. 26 Claudias L. unto the most excellent gov.
24. 7 [chief captain L. came (upon us), and with]
24. 22 When L. the chief captain..come down

LYS'-TRA, Λύστρα.
A city of Lycaonia, in Asia Minor, forty miles W of Iconium. Now called *Latik.*
Acts 14. 6 They were ware of (it), and fled unto L.
14. 8 there sat a certain man at L., impotent in
14. 21 they returned again to L., and (to) Icon.
16. 1 Then came he to Derbe and L.: and, beh.
16. 2 by the brethren that were at L. and Ico.
2 Ti. 3. 11 afflictions, which came unto me..at L.

M

MA-A'-CHAH, (**MA-A'-CAH**, 2 Sam 3. 3), מַעֲכָה *depression*
1. Son of Nahor, Abraham's brother, by Reumah a concubine. B.C. 1860.
Gen. 22. 24 his concubine..bare also Tebah..and M.
2. One of David's wives, and mother of Absalom. B.C. 1060.
2 Sa. 3. 3 Absalom, the son of M. the daughter of T.
1 Ch. 3. 2 Absalom the son of M. the daughter of T.
3. A district and city of Syria, in Manasseh, E. of Jordan.
2 Sa. 10. 8 Ish-tob, and M., (were) by themselves in
1 Ch. 19. 6 to hire them chariots..out of Syria-M.
19. 7 So they hired..the king of M. and his pe.
4. A king of Maachah. B.C. 1060.
2 Sa. 10. 6 sent and hired..of king M. a thousand
5. The father of Achish king of Gath in Solomon's time. B.C. 1038.
1 Ki. 2. 39 ran away unto Achish son of M. king of G.
6. The wife of Rehoboam and mother of Abijah king of Judah. B.C. 1000.
1 Ki. 15. 2 his mother's name (was) M., the daughter
2 Ch. 11. 20 after her he took M. the daughter of Ab.
11. 21 Rehoboam loved M. the daughter of Abs.
11. 22 Rehoboam made Abijah the son of M. the
7. The mother of Asa king of Judah. B.C. 960.
1 Ki. 15. 10 his mother's name (was) M., the daughter
15. 13 also M. his mother, even her he removed
2 Ch. 15. 16 (concerning) M. the mother of Asa the king
8. Concubine of Caleb the son of Hezron. B.C. 1500.
1 Ch. 2. 48 M., Caleb's concubine, bare Sheber, and
9. A woman of Benjamin, married to Machir, son of Manasseh. B.C. 1630.
1 Ch. 7. 15 whose sister's name (was) M.; and the name
7. 16 M. the wife of Machir bare a son, and she
10. Wife of Jehiel the father or founder of Gibeon. B.C. 1250.
1 Ch 8. 29 father of Gibeon; whose wife's name..M.
9. 35 dwelt..Jehiel, whose wife's name..M.
11. The father of Hanun, one of David's warriors. B.C. 1048.
1 Ch. 11. 43 Hanun, the son of M., and Joshaphat the
12. The father of Shephatiah, who ruled the Simeonites in David's time. B.C. 1038.
1 Ch. 27. 16 the Simeonites; Shephatiah the son of M.

MA-A-CHA-THITES, מַעֲכָתִי, מַעֲכָת.
Patronymic of the inhabitants of Maachah or Maachath, near Mount Hermon, at the W. slope of South Anti-lebanus. *Maachathi* in Deut. 3. 14.
Deut. 3. 14 Argob unto the coasts of Geshuri and M.
Josh.12. 5 the border of the Geshurites, and the M.
13. 11 and the border of the Geshurites and M.
13. 13 expelled not..the M.; but..the M. dwell
2 Sa. 23. 34 Ahasbai, the son of the M., Eliam the son
2 Ki.25. 23 Jaazaniah the son of a M., they and their
1 Ch. 4. 19 Naham, the father of..Eshtemoa the M.
Jer. 40. 8 Jezaniah the son of a M., they and their

MA-A'-DAI, מַעֲדַי *Jah is ornament.*
One who had taken a strange wife. B.C. 456.
Ezra 10. 34 Of the sons of Bani; M., Amram, and Uel

MA-AD-I'AH, מַעַדְיָה *Jah is ornament.*
A priest who returned from Babylon with Zerubbabel. B.C. 538.
Neh. 12. 5 Miamim, M., Bilgah

MA'-AI, מָעַי *Jah is compassionate.*
One of the priests who purified the people after their return from Babylon. B.C. 445.
Neh. 12. 36 his brethren..Milalai, Gilalai, M., Neth.

MA-A'-LEH AC-RAB'-BIM, מַעֲלֵה עַקְרַבִּים.
An acclivity on the S. border of Judah, between Kedish and the Salt Sea, with a bend toward the East.
Josh 15. 3 it went out to the south side to M.-A., and

MA-A'-RATH, מַעֲרָת *bare place.*
A city in the hill country of Judah near Beth-anon; now *Umman.*
Josh.15. 59 M., and Beth-anoth, and Eltekon ; six

MA-A-SE'-IAH, מַעֲשֵׂיָהוּ, מַעֲשֵׂיָה *work of Jah.*
1. A Levite appointed for the service of praise. B.C. 1015.
1 Ch.15. 18 with them their brethren..M., and Matt.
15. 20 Eliab, and M., and Benaiah, with psalter.
2. One of the captains who assisted in setting Joash on the throne of Judah. B.C. 878.
2 Ch.23. 1 M. the son of Adaiah, and Elishaphat the
3. An officer of king Uzziah. B.C. 810.
2 Ch.26. 11 hand of Jeiel the scribe, and M. the ruler
4. Son of Ahaz, king of Judah. B.C. 741.
2 Ch.28. 7 slew M. the king's son, and Azrikam the
5. The governor of Jerusalem in Josiah's reign. B.C. 640.
2 Ch.34. 8 M. the governor of the city, and Joah the
6. A priest who had taken a strange wife. B.C. 456.
Ezra 10. 18 M., and Eliezer, and Jarib, and Gedaliah
7. A priest of the family of Harim, who had taken a strange wife. B.C. 456.
Ezra 10. 21 M., and Elijah, and Shemaiah, and Jehiel
8. A priest, family of Pashur, who had taken a strange wife. B.C. 456.
Ezra 10. 22 M., Ishmael, Nethanel, Jozabad, and El.
9. One who had taken a strange wife of the family of Pahath-Moab. B.C. 486.
Ezra 10. 30 M., Mattaniah, Bezaleel, and Binnui, and
10. Father of Azariah who repaired part of the wall of Jerusalem. B.C. 470.
Neh. 3. 23 After him repaired Azariah the son of M.
11. A priest who stood beside Ezra while he read the law. B.C. 445.
Neh. 8. 4 M., on his right hand; and on his left hand
12. A priest who explained the law read by Ezra. Perhaps the same with No. 11.
Neh. 8. 7 M., Kelita, Azariah, Jozabad, Hanan, Pe.
13. One who sealed the covenant made by Nehemiah. B.C. 445.
Neh. 10. 25 Rehum, Hashabnah, M.
14. A descendant of Pharez, dwelling in Jerusalem after the captivity. B.C. 445.
Neh. 11. 5 M. the son of Baruch, the son of Col-hozeh
15. A Benjamite whose descendants dwelt in Jerusalem after the captivity. B.C. 445.
Neh. 11. 7 the son of M., the son of Ithiel, the son of
16. A priest who assisted at the purification of the wall. Perhaps the same with No. 11.
Neh. 12. 41 M., Miniamin, Michaiah, Elioenai, Zech.
17. Another priest who took part in the above ceremony. B.C. 445.
Neh. 12. 42 M., and Shemaiah, and Eleazar, and Uzzi
18. A priest whose son was sent by king Zedekiah to inquire of the Lord. B.C. 680.
Jer. 21. 1 and Zephaniah the son of M. the priest
29. 25 Zephaniah the son of M. the priest, and
37. 3 and Zephaniah the son of M. the priest
19. The father of a false prophet during the Babylonish captivity. B.C. 638.
Jer. 29. 21 of Ahab..and of Zedekiah the son of M.
20. An officer of the temple in Jehoiakim's reign. B.C. 601.
Jer. 35. 4 above the chamber of M. the son of Shal.

MAA-SE'-IAH, מַחְסֵיָה *Jah is a refuge.*
The grandfather of Baruch, Jeremiah's amanuensis and messenger. B.C. 650.
Jer. 32. 12 Baruch the son of Neriah, the son of M.
51. 59 Seraiah the son of Neriah, the son of M.

MA-A-SI'-AI, מַעְשַׂי *work of Jah.*
An Aaronite whose family dwelt in Jerusalem after the captivity. B.C. 445.
1 Ch. 9. 12 M. the son of Adiel, the son of Jahzerah

MA'-ATH, Μαάθ.
An ancestor of Jesus, through Mary.
Luke 3. 26 Which was (the son) of M., which was (the

MA'-AZ, מַעַץ *counsellor.*
A son of Ram, the eldest son of Jerahmeel, great grand-son of Judah. B.C. 1470.
1 Ch. 2. 27 the sons of Ram..were M., and Jamin, and

MA-AZ-I'AH, מַעַזְיָהוּ, מַעַזְיָה *strength of Jah.*
1. A priest to whom the charges of the sanctuary were assigned by lot in the days of David. B.C. 1015.
1 Ch.24. 18 to Delaiah, the four and twentieth to M.
2. A priest or family of priests that sealed the covenant made by Nehemiah. B.C. 445.
Neh. 10. 8 M., Bilgai, Shemaiah: these (were) the p.

MA-CE-DO-NI-A, *Macedonian,* Μακεδονία, Μακεδών.
A region N. of Greece proper, having Thessaly and Epirus on the S., Thrace and the Ægean Sea on the E., the Adriatic and Illyria on the W., and Dardania and Mœsia on the N. The towns were Amphipolis, Apollonia, Berea, Philippi, and Thessalonica. The Romans divided the whole country S. of the valley of the Danube into Illyricum, Achaia, and Macedonia, which included Thessaly. In Macedonia proper are Amphipolis, Beræa, Philippi, Thessalonica, and Apollonia.
Acts 16. 9 M., and prayed him..Come over into M.
16. 10 we endeavoured to go into M., assuredly
16. 12 which is the chief city of that part of M.
18. 5 Silas and Timotheus were come from M.
19. 21 when he had passed through M. and Ac.
19 22 sent into M. two of them that ministered
19. 29 caught Gaius and Aristarchus, men of M.
20. 1 and departed for to go into M.
20. 3 he purposed to return through M.
27. 2 a M. of Thessalonica, being with us
Rom 15. 26 it hath pleased them of M. and Achaia
1 Co. 16. 5 pass through M.: for I do pass through M.
2 Co. 1. 16 by you into M...to come again out of M.
2. 13 leave of them, I went from thence into M.
7. 5 when we were come into M., our flesh had
8. 1 grace of God bestowed on..churches of M.
9. 2 I boast of you to them of M., that Achaia
9. 4 if they of M. come with me, and find you
11. 9 the brethren which came from M. supplied
Phil. 4. 15 I departed from M., no churches commu.
1 Th. 1. 7 to all that believe in M. and Achaia
1. 8 word of the Lord not only in M. and Ach.
4. 10 all the brethren which are in all M.: but
1 Ti. 1. 3 abide still at Ephesus, when I went into M.

MACH-BAN'-AI, מַכְבַּנַּי *thick.*
A Gadite warrior who joined David in Ziklag. B.C. 1058.
1 Ch 12. 13 Jeremiah the tenth, M. the eleventh

MACH-BE'-NAH, מַכְבֵּנָא *knob, lump.*
Patronymic of a descendant of Caleb the son of Jephunneh; comp. *Cabbon,* Josh. 15. 40.
1 Ch. 2. 49 the father of M., and the father of Gibea

MA'-CHI, מָכִי.
A Gadite, the father of Geuel whom Moses sent to spy out the land. B.C. 1520.
Num 13. 15 Of the tribe of Gad Geuel the son of M.

MA'-CHIR, מָכִיר *salesman.*
1. Son of Manasseh. B.C. 1635.
Gen. 50. 23 children also of M. the son of Manasseh
Num26. 29 M., the family of the Machirites: and M.
27. 1 the son of M., the son of Manasseh, of the
32. 39 the children of M. the son of Manasseh
32. 40 gave Gilead unto M. the son of Manasseh
36. 1 the son of M., the son of Manasseh, of the
Deut. 3. 15 And I gave Gilead unto M.
Josh.13. 31 the children of M. the son of Manasseh
13. 31 of the children of M. by their families
17. 1 M., the first born of Manasseh, the father
17. 3 Gilead, the son of M., the son of Manasseh
Judg. 5. 14 out of M. came down governors, and out
1 Ch. 2. 21 the daughter of M. the father of Gilead
2. 23 to) the sons of M., the father of Gilead
7. 14 the Aramitess bare M. the father of Gilead
7. 15 M. took to wife (the sister) of Huppim and
7. 16 the wife of M. bare a son, and she called
7. 17 Gilead, the son of M., the son of Manasseh
2. A Manassite, living near Mahanaim in the days of David. B.C. 1040.
2 Sa. 9. 4, 5 the house of M., the son of Ammiel
17. 27 and M. the son of Ammiel of Lo-debar, and

MA-CHIR-ITES, מָכִירִי *Descendants of the preceding.*
Num26. 29 of Machir, the family of the M.: and M.

MACH-NAD-E'-BAI, מַכְנַדְבַי *gift of the noble one.*
A Jew who had taken a strange wife during or after the captivity. B.C. 445.
Ezra 10. 40 M., Shashai, Sharai

MACH-PE'-LAH, מַכְפֵּלָה *winding, spiral form.*
A field before Mamre in Hebron with a cave bought for a burying place by Abraham from Ephron the Hittite.
Gen.23. 9 he may give me the cave of M., which he
23. 17 the field of Ephron, which (was) in M.
23. 19 the cave of the field of M. before Mamre
25. 9 Ishmael buried him in the cave of M., in
49. 30 In the cave that (is) in the field of M.
50. 13 buried him in the cave of the field of M.

MAD —
1. *To pretend to be feeble,* לָהַהּ *lahah,* 7
Prov.26. 18 As a mad (man), who casteth fire brands
2. *To be mad, erring,* שָׁגַע *shaga,* 4.
Deut28. 34 So that thou shalt be mad for the sight
2 Ki. 9. 11 wherefore came this mad (fellow) to thee?
Jer. 29. 26 for every man (that is) mad, and maketh
Hos. 9. 7 the spiritual man (is) mad, for the mult.
3. *Madness,* μανία *mania.*
Acts 26. 25 I am not mad, most noble Festus; but sp.

MAD, to be or feign self —
1. *To be foolish, to shine,* הָלַל *halal.*
Eccl. 2. 2 I said of laughter, (It is) mad; and of m.
2. *To show self foolish,* הָלַל *halal,* 7*a.*
1 Sa. 21. 13 feigned himself mad in their hands, and
Jer. 25. 16 shall drink, and be moved, and be mad
50. 38 images, and they are mad upon (their) id.
51. 7 drunken..therefore the nations are mad
3. *To show self mad or erring,* שָׁגַע *shaga,* 7.
1 Sa. 21. 14 Lo, ye see the man is mad: wherefore
4. *To be furious, raving, mad,* μαίνομαι *mainomai.*
John10. 20 He hath a devil, and is mad; why hear ye
Acts 12. 15 And they said unto her, Thou art mad. B.
26. 25 I am not mad, most noble Festus; but sp.
1 Co. 14. 23 come in..will they not say that ye are m.?

MAD against, to be —
1. *To act foolishly,* הָלַל *halal,* 3*a.*
Psa.102. 8 they that are mad against me are sworn
2. *To be furious or mad with any one,* ἐμμαίνομαι.
Acts 26. 11 being exceedingly mad against them, I.

MAD, to make —
1. *To act foolishly, make foolish,* הָלַל *halal,* 3*a.*
Eccl. 7. 7 Surely oppression maketh a wise man m.
Isa. 44. 25 maketh diviners mad; that turneth wise
2. *To turn round into madness,* περιτρέπω εἰς μανίαν.
Acts 26. 24 Paul..much learning doth make thee mad

MA'-DAI, מָדַי *middle.*
A son of Japheth, B.C. 2320, whose descendants (Medes) lived in *Media,* the region S. of the Caspian Sea, having Hyrcania and Parthia on the E., Persia and Susiana on the S., Assyria and Armenia on the W.
Gen. 10. 2 M., and Javan, and Tubal, and Meshech
1 Ch. 1. 5 M., and Javan, and Tubal, and Meshech

MADE —
Make, עָשָׂה *asah* [V.L. עָשַׂר *asar*].
1 Ki. 22 48 Jehoshaphat made ships of Tharshish to

MADE, to be —
1. *To be borne, brought forth,* חִיל, חוּל *chul, chil,* 4*b.*
Job 15. 7 (Art) thou the first..or wast thou made
2. *To be given,* נָתַן *nathan,* 2.
Isa. 51. 12 son of man (which) shall be made (as) gr.
3. *To be destroyed,* אָבַד *abad,* 2.
Ezra 4. 19 rebellion and sedition have been made
6. 11 let his house be made a dunghill for this
4. *To be made,* עָשָׂה *asah,* 2.
Exod25. 31 beaten work shall the candlestick be made
Lev. 2. 7 oblation..shall be made (of) fine flour with
2. 8 bring the meat offering that is made of
2. 11 No meat offering..shall be made with le.
6. 21 In a pan it shall be made with oil..baken
13. 51 spread..in any work that is made of skin
Num. 4. 26 all that is made for them: so shall they
6. 4 shall he eat nothing that is made of the
1 Ki. 10. 20 there was not the like made in any king.
2 Ki. 12. 13 there was not made for the house of the L.
2 Ch. 9. 19 there was not the like made in any king.
Psa. 33. 6 were the heavens made; and all the host
5. *To be made,* עָשָׂה *asah,* 4.
Psa.139. 15 when I was made in secret..curiously w.
6. *To set,* שִׂים, שׂוּם *sum, sim.*
2 Sa. 15. 4 O that I were made judge in the land, that
Ezra 5. 17 that a decree was made of Cyrus the king
7. *To be set,* שׂוּם *sum,* 2.
Dan. 2. 5 and your houses shall be made a dunghill
8. *To be made like, appointed,* שְׁוָה *shevah,* 4.
Dan. 3. 29 their houses shall be made a dunghill
9. *To beget, bring forth,* γεννάω *gennaō.*
2 Pe. 2. 12 But these..[made] to be taken and destr.
10. *To become, begin to be,* γίνομαι *ginomai.*
Matt. 4. 3 command that these stones be made bread
9. 16 taketh from the garment, and the rent is
23. 15 when he is made, ye make him twofold
25. 6 And at midnight there was a cry made
27. 24 but..rather a tumult was made, he took
Mark 2. 21 away from the old, and the rent is made
2. 27 The sabbath was made for man, and not
14. 4 Why was this waste of the ointment made?
Luke 4. 3 command this stone that it be made bread
8. 17 nothing is secret that shall not be made
14. 12 bid thee again, and a recompence be made
23. 12 Pilate and Herod were made friends tog.
23. 19 Who for a certain sedition made in the city
John 1. 3 All things were made by him; and with.
1. 3 was not any thing made that was made
1 10 the world was made by him, and the wo.
1. 14 the Word was made flesh, and dwelt am.
2. 9 had tasted the water that was made wine
5. 4 [was made whole of whatsoever disease]

John 5. 6 saith unto him, Wilt thou be made whole?
5. 9 immediately the man was made whole, and
5. 14 Behold, thou art made whole: sin no more
8. 33 how sayest thou, Ye shall be made free?
9. 39 that they which see might be made blind
Acts 7. 13 Joseph's kindred was made known unto
12. 5 prayer was made without ceasing of the
13. 32 how that the promise which was made
14. 5 when there was an assault made both of
19. 26 they be no gods which are made with ha.
21. 40 when there was made a great silence, he
26. 6 the promise made of God unto our fathers
Rom. 1. 3 which was made of the seed of David acc.
2. 25 thy circumcision is made uncircumcision
7. 13 Was then that which is good made death
10. 20 I was made manifest unto them that asked
11. 9 Let their table be made a snare, and a t.
1 Co. 1. 30 who of God is made unto us wisdom, and
3. 13 Every man's work shall be made manifest
4. 9 we are made a spectacle unto the world
4. 13 we are made as the filth of the world, (and)
7. 21 if thou mayest be made free, use (it) ra.
9. 22 I am made all things to all (men), that I
11. 19 approved may be made manifest among
14. 25 thus are the secrets of his heart made m.
15. 45 The first man Adam was made a living
2 Co. 5. 21 that we might be made the righteousness
Gal. 3. 13 Christ hath redeemed us..being made a
4. 4 Son, made of a woman, made under the
Eph. 2. 13 ye..are made nigh by the blood of Christ
3. 7 Whereof I was made a minister, according
Phil. 2. 7 took..and was made in the likeness of men
Col. 1. 23 gospel..whereof I Paul am made a min.
1. 25 Whereof I am made a minister, according
Titus 3. 7 we should be made heirs according to the
Heb. 1. 4 Being made so much better than the an.
3. 14 For we are made partakers of Christ, if
5. 5 Christ glorified not himself to be made
6. 4 and were made partakers of the Holy G
6. 20 made an high priest for ever, after the
7. 12 there is made of necessity a change also
7. 16 Who is made, not after the law of a car.
7. 21 For those priests were made without an
7. 22 By so much was Jesus made a surety of
7. 26 an high priest..made higher than the h.
11. 3 were not made of things which do appear
Jas. 3. 9 which are made after the similitude of G.
1 Pe. 2. 7 the same is made the head of the corner

11. *To be*, εἶναι *einai.*
Acts 16. 13 where prayer was wont to be made; and

12. *To lay, be laid*, κεῖμαι *keimai.*
1 Ti. 1. 9 the law is not made for a righteous man

[*See also* Almonds, appear, atonement, bald, better, breach, bring forth, broad, cedars, clean, confession, conformable, desolate, drunk, fat, gazingstock, glorious, inquisition, king, like, low, mention, naked, partition, plain, possess, reckoning, red, search, serve, slaughter, straight, strong, sure, sweet, thin, unclean, white, whole].

MADE of, that is —
Vessel, instrument, כְּלִי *keli.*
Num 31. 20 all that is made of skins, and all work of

MADE, thing —
1. *Work*, מְלָאכָה *melakah.*
Lev. 13. 48 in a skin, or in any thing made of skin

2. *Deed, work*, מַעֲשֶׂה *maaseh.*
1 Ch. 9. 31 the things that were made in the pans
Psa. 45. 1 I speak of the things which I have made

3. *Anything made*, ποίημα *poiēma.*
Rom. 1. 20 being understood by the things that are m.

MADE ready to hand —
Ready, prepared, ἕτοιμος *hetoimos.*
2 Co. 10. 16 line of things made ready to our hand

MADE with or without hands, not —
Not made with hands, ἀχειροποίητος *acheiropoiētos.*
Mark 14. 58 I will build another made without hands
2 Co. 5. 1 an house not made with hands, eternal
Col. 2. 11 with the circumcision made without ha.

MADE up, to be —
A healing (scar) went up on, עָלְתָה אֲרֻכָה [*arukah*].
Neh 4 7 that the walls of Jerusalem were made up

MADIAN, Μαδιάμ.—See *Midian.*
Acts 7. 29 was a stranger in the land of M., where he

MAD MAN, (to play the) —
1. *To be mad or erring*, שָׁגַע *shaga*, 4.
1 Sa. 21. 15 Have I need of mad men, that ye have

2. *To show self mad or erring*, שָׁגַע *shaga*, 7.
1 Sa. 21. 15 to play the mad man in my presence?

MAD-MAN'-NAH, מַדְמַנָּה *heap.*
1. A city of Judah, near Ziklag. Same as *El-Minyay*, fifteen miles from Gaza.
Josh. 15. 31 And Ziklag, and M., and Sansannah
2. Patronymic of a son of Caleb the son of Jephunneh.
1 Ch. 2. 49 She bare also Shaaph the father of M.

MAD'-MEN, מַדְמֵן *heap.*
A city of Moab, whose destruction was foretold by Jeremiah. B.C. 628–586.
Jer. 48. 2 thou shalt be cut down, O M.; the sword

MAD-ME'-NAH, מַדְמֵנָה *heap.*
A city of Benjamin, near Jerusalem.
Isa. 10. 31 M. is removed; the inhabitants of Gebim

MADNESS —
1. *Foolishness, madness, boasting*, הוֹלֵלָה *holelah.*
Eccl. 1. 17 I gave my heart to know..madness and
2. 12 to behold wisdom, and madness, and folly
7. 25 of folly, even of foolishness (and) madness
9. 3 madness (is) in their heart while they live

2. *Foolishness, madness, boasting*, הוֹלֵלוּת *holeluth.*
Eccl. 10. 13 the end of his talk (is) mischievous mad.

3. *Madness, erring*, שִׁגָּעוֹן *shiggaon.*
Deut 28. 28 LORD shall smite thee with madness, and
Zech 12. 4 I will smite..his rider with madness; and

4. *Want of thought or sense*, ἄνοια *anoia.*
Luke 6. 11 they were filled with madness; and com.

5. *Wrong mindedness*, παραφρονία *paraphronia.*
2 Pe. 2. 16 dumb ass..forbade the madness of the pr.

MA'-DON, מָדוֹן *district of the dan.*
A Canaanitish city in the N. of the Holy Land.
Josh 11. 1 he sent to Jobab king of M., and to the
12. 19 The king of M., one; the king of Hazor

MAG'-BISH, מַגְבִּישׁ *a fortress.*
A place named with Bethel, Ai, &c.
Ezra 2. 30 children of M., an hundred fifty and six

MAG-DA'-LA, Μαγδαλά, Μαγαδάν *a tower, greatness.*
A city of Galilee, S.W. of the Sea of Tiberias; the same with *Dalmanutha*, or near it; comp. Mark 8. 10. Now a small village called *Mejdel*, three miles N. of Tiberias.
Matt 15 39 took ship, and came into the coasts of [M.]

MAG-DA-LE'-NE, Μαγδαληνή.
A woman of Magdala, called Mary.
Matt 27. 56 Among which was Mary M., and Mary the
27. 61 And there was Mary M., and the other M.
28. 1 the first (day) of the week, came Mary M.
Mark 15. 40 among whom..Mary M., and Mary the m.
15. 47 And Mary M. and Mary (the mother) of J.
16. 1 Mary M., and Mary the (mother) of James
16. 9 [he appeared first to Mary M., out of w.]
Luke 8. 2 Mary called M., out of whom went seven
24. 10 It was Mary M., and Joanna, and Mary
John 19. 25 Mary the (wife) of Cleophas, and Mary M.
20. 1 first (day) of the week cometh Mary M.
20. 18 Mary M. came and told the disciples that

MAG-DI'-EL, מַגְדִּיאֵל *God is renowned.*
A duke of Edom. B.C. 1450.
Gen. 36. 43 Duke M., duke Iram: these (be) the dukes
1 Ch. 1. 54 Duke M., duke Iram. These (are) the dukes

MAGICIAN —
1. *Scribes, magicians*, חַרְטֻמִּים *chartummim.*
Gen. 41. 8 sent and called for all the magicians of E.
41. 24 And I told (this) unto the magicians; but
Exod. 7. 11 the magicians of Egypt, they also did in
7. 22 the magicians of Egypt did so with their
8. 7, 18 the magicians did so with their ench.
8. 19 the magicians said unto Pharaoh, This (is)
9. 11 the magicians could not stand before M.
9. 11 the boil was upon the magicians, and upon
Dan. 1. 20 ten times better than all the magicians
2. 2 the king commanded to call the magicians

2. *Scribe, magician*, חַרְטֹם *chartom.*
Dan. 2. 10 asked such things at any magician, or as.
2. 27 the astrologers, the magicians, the sooth.
4. 7 the magicians, the astrologers, the Chal.
4. 9 O Belteshazzar, master of the magicians
5. 11 of the magicians astrologers, Chaldeans

MAGISTRATE —
1. *A judge, magistrate*, שֹׁפֵט *shaphet.*
Ezra 7. 25 set magistrates and judges, which may j.

2. *To possess restraint*, יָרַשׁ עֶצֶר *yarash etser.*
Judg 18. 7 no magistrate in the land, that might put

3. *Ruler, the first, foremost*, ἀρχή *archē.*
Luke 12. 11 when they bring you unto..magistrates

4. *A ruler*, ἄρχων *archōn.*
Luke 12. 58 thou goest with..adversary to the magi.

5. *Leader of a host*, στρατηγός *stratēgos.*
Acts 16. 20 brought them to the magistrates, saying
16. 22 the magistrates rent off their clothes, and
16. 35 the magistrates sent the serjeants, saying
16. 36 The magistrates have sent to let you go
16. 38 serjeants told these words unto the mag.

MAGISTRATES, to obey —
To be obedient to rulers, πειθαρχέω *peitharcheō.*
Titus 3. 1 to obey magistrates, to be ready to every

MAGNIFICAL —
To make great, גָּדַל *gadal*, 5.
1 Ch. 22. 5 house..(must be) exceeding magnifical

MAGNIFICENCE —
Greatness, μεγαλειότης *megaleiotēs.*
Acts 19. 27 and her magnificence should be destroyed

MAGNIFIED, to be —
1. *To be or become great*, גָּדַל *gadal.*
2 Sa. 7. 26 let thy name be magnified for ever, say.
1 Ch. 17. 24 that thy name may be magnified for ever
Psa. 35. 27 Let the LORD be magnified, which hath
40. 16 let such..say continually, The LORD be
70. 4 let such..say continually, Let God be ma.
Zech 12. 7 do not magnify (themselves) against Ju.
Mal. 1. 5 The LORD will be magnified from the bor.

2. *To be lifted up*, נָשָׂא *nasa*, 2.
2 Ch. 32. 23 so that he was magnified in the sight of

MAGNIFY, to —
1. *To magnify*, גָּדַל *gadal*, 3.
Josh. 3. 7 This day will I begin to magnify thee in
4. 14 On that day the LORD magnified Joshua
1 Ch. 29. 25 the LORD magnified Solomon exceedingly
2 Ch. 1. 1 his God (was) with him, and magnified him
Job 7. 17 What (is) man, that thou shouldest mag.
Psa. 34. 3 O magnify the LORD with me, and let us
69. 30 and will magnify him with thanksgiving

2. *To make great*, גָּדַל *gadal*, 5.
Gen. 19. 19 thou hast magnified thy mercy, which thou
Job 19. 5 If indeed ye will magnify..against me, and
Psa. 35. 26 clothed with shame and dishonour that m.
38. 16 when my foot slippeth, they magnify..ag.
55. 12 neither..he that hated me..did magnify
138. 2 thou hast magnified thy word above all
Isa. 42. 21 he will magnify the law, and make (it) h.
Jer. 48. 26 Make ye him drunken; for he magnified (h.)
48. 42 because he hath magnified..against the L.
Lam. 1. 9 O LORD, behold..for the enemy hath ma.
Dan. 8. 11 Yea, he magnified..even to the prince of
8. 25 he shall magnify..in his heart, and by pe.
Zeph. 2. 8, 10 have reproached..and magnified..aga.

3. *To make great, magnify, increase*, שָׂגָא *saga*, 5.
Job 36. 24 Remember that thou magnify his work, w.

4. *To make honourable or glorious*, δοξάζω *doxazō.*
Rom 11. 13 apostle of the Gentiles, I magnify mine

5. *To make great*, μεγαλύνω *megalunō.*
Luke 1. 46 Mary said, My soul doth magnify the L.
Acts 5. 13 durst no man..but the people magnified
10. 46 them speak with tongues, and magnify G.
19. 17 the name of the Lord Jesus was magnified
Phil. 1. 20 also Christ shall be magnified in my body

MAGNIFY self, to —
To make self great, גָּדַל *gadal*, 7.
Isa. 10. 15 shall the saw magnify itself against him
Eze. 38. 23 Thus will I magnify myself, and sanctify
Dan. 11. 36 magnify himself above every god, and sh.
11. 37 for he shall magnify himself above all

MA'-GOG, מָגוֹג, Μαγώγ.
1. The second son of Japheth. B.C. 2340.
Gen. 10. 2 M., and Madai, and Javan, and Tubal, and
1 Ch. 1. 5 M., and Madai, and Javan, and Tubal, and
2. The descendants of Magog and their land, called Scythia, in the N. of Asia and Europe.
Eze. 38. 2 set thy face against Gog, the land of M.
39. 6 I will send a fire on M., and among them
Rev. 20. 8 Gog and M., to gather them together to

MA-GOR MIS-SA'-BIB, מָגוֹר מִסָּבִיב *terror is about.*
A symbolic name of Pashur. B.C. 600.
Jer. 20. 3 hath not called thy name Pashur, but M.

MAG-PI'-ASH, מַגְפִּיעָשׁ *collector of a cluster of stars.*
A person or family in the time of Nehemiah. B.C. 445.
Neh. 10 20 M., Meshullam, Hezir.

MAGUS, Μάγος, *magian.* Acts 13. 6, 8.

MA-HA'-LAH, מַחְלָה *tenderness, mildness.*
Great grandson of Manasseh, through Hammoleketh B.C. 1400.
1 Ch. 7. 18 sister Hammoleketh bare..Abiezer, and M.

MA-HA-LAL'-EEL, מַהֲלַלְאֵל *God is splendour.*
1. Son of Cainan the grandson of Seth. B. C. 3609–2714.
Gen 5. 12 Cainan lived seventy years, and begat M.
5. 13 Cainan lived after he begat M. eight hun.
5. 15 M. lived sixty and five years, and begat J.
5. 16 M. lived after he begat Jared eight hund.
5. 17 all the days of M. were eight hundred ni.
1 Ch. 1. 2 Kenan, M., Jered
2. One whose descendants dwelt in Jerusalem after the captivity. B.C. 566.
Neh. 11. 4 Shephatiah, the son of M., of the children

MA-HA'-LATH, מַחֲלַת *mild.*
1. A daughter of Ishmael, and one of Esau's wives. B.C. 1760.
Gen. 28. 9 took unto the wives which he had M. the
2. A grand-daughter of David, and wife of Rehoboam.
2 Ch. 11. 18 Rehoboam took him M. the daughter of J.
3. A musical choir. (*See* Leannoth.)
Psa. 53. *title.* To the chief musician upon M., Maschil
88. .. to the chief musician upon M. Leannoth

MAHALI. *See* **MAHLI.**

MA-HA-NA'-IM, מַחֲנַיִם *two camps.*
A town E. of Jordan S. of the Jabbok, so named by Jacob; afterwards a Levitical city of Gad. On the upper course of the *Wady-Jabes*, N. of *Tibni*, are rivers called Mahaneh.
Gen. 32. 2 and he called the name of that place M.
Josh 13. 26 and from M. unto the border of Debir
13. 30 their coast was from M., all Bashan, all
21. 38 city of refuge for the slayer; and M. with
2 Sa. 2. 8 Abner..son of Ner..brought him..to M.
2. 12 Abner the son of Ner..went out from M.
2. 29 through all Bithron, and they came to M.
17. 24 Then David came to M. And Absalom pa.
17. 27 came to pass, when David was come to M.
19. 32 provided..sustenance while he lay at M.
1 Ki. 2. 8 cursed me..in the day when I went to M.
4. 14 Ahinadab the son of Iddo (had) M.
1 Ch. 6. 80 Ramoth in Gilead..and M. with her sub.

MA-HA'-NEH DAN, מַחֲנֵה־דָן *camp of Dan.*
A place in Judah, W. of Kirjath-jearim.
Judg.18. 12 they called that place M.D. unto this day

MA-HA'-RAI, מַהֲרַי *hasty.*
One of David's warriors. B.C. 1048.
2 Sa.23. 28 Zalmon the Ahohite, M. the Netophathite
1 Ch.11. 30 M. the Netophathite, Heled the son of B.
27. 13 The tenth (captain)..(was) M. the Netop.

MA'-HATH, מַחַת *dissolution.*
1. A descendant of Kohath the son of Levi. B.C. 1380.
1 Ch. 6. 35 the son of Elkanah, the son of M., the son
2 Ch.29. 12 Then the Levites arose, M. the son of Am.
2. A Levite, overseer of the dedicated things in Hezekiah's reign. B.C. 726; or perhaps the same as No 1.
2 Ch.31. 13 M., and Benaiah, (were) overseers under

MA-HA-VITE, מַחֲוִים.
Patronymic of Eliel, one of David's warriors. Locality unknown.
1 Ch.11. 46 Eliel the M., and Jeribai and Joshaviah

MA-HA-ZI'-OTH, מַחֲזִיאוֹת *visions.*
One of the sons of Heman, set over the service of song in David's reign. B.C. 1015.
1 Ch.25. 4 Of Heman..Mallothi, Hothir, (and) M.
25. 30 The three and twentieth to M., (he), his

MA'-HER SHA'-LAL HASH BAZ, מַהֵר שָׁלָל חָשׁ בַּז.
Symbolical name given to a son of Isaiah, signifying "hasten the spoil, rush on the prey." B.C. 741.
Isa. 8. 1 Take..and write in it..concerning M.
8. 3 Then said the LORD to me, Call his name M.

MAH'-LAH, מַחְלָה *mildness.*
The eldest daughter of Zelophehad, descended from Manasseh, and allowed a portion in the land because her father left no male issue. B.C. 1452.
Num26. 33 the names..(were) M., and Noah, Hoglah
27. 1 these (are) the names of his daughters; M.
36. 11 For M., Tirzah, and Hoglah, and Milcah
Josh.17. 3 these (are) the names of his daughters, M.

MAH'-LI, מַחְלִי *mild.* (In Ex.6.19 some editions *Mahali.*)
1. Son of Merari, son of Levi. B.C. 1490.
Exod.6. 19 sons of Merari; M. and Mushi: these (are)
Num. 3. 20 sons of Merari by their families; M., and
1 Ch. 6. 19 sons of Merari; M., and Mushi. And these
6. 29 sons of Merari; M., Libni his son, Shimei
23. 21 M. and Mushi. The sons of M.; Eleazar
24. 26 sons of Merari (were) M. and Mushi: the
24. 28 Of M. (came) Eleazar, who had no sons
Ezra 8. 18 of the sons of M., the son of Levi, the son
2. Son of Mushi the son of Merari. B.C. 1015.
1 Ch. 6. 47 The son of M., the son of Mushi, the son
23. 23 sons of Mushi; M., and Eder, and Jerem.
24. 30 sons also of Mushi; M., and Eder, and J.

MAH-LITES, מַחְלִי.
Descendants of Mahli the son of Merari.
Num. 3. 33 Of Merari (was) the family of the M., and
26. 58 family of the M., the family of the Mus.

MAH'-LON, מַחְלוֹן *mild.*
Elder son of Naomi, and first husband of Ruth. B.C. 1312.
Ruth 1. 2 the name of his two sons M. and Chilion
1. 5 M. and Chilion died also both of them
4. 9 bought..all that (was) Chilion's and M.'s
4. 10 Ruth the Moabitess, the wife of M., have

MA'-HOL, מָחוֹל *dancer.*
The father of certain men renowned for wisdom in Solomon's time. B.C. 1000
1 Ki. 4. 31 For he was wiser than..the sons of M.: and

MAID, MAIDEN —
1. *Handmaid,* אָמָה *amah.*
Gen. 30. 3 Behold my maid Bilhah, go in unto her
Exod. 2. 5 when she saw..she sent her maid to fetch
21. 20 if a man smite..his maid, with a rod, and
21. 26 if a man smite..the eye of his maid, that
Lev. 25. 6 for thy servant, and for thy maid, and for
Ezra 2. 65 Besides their servants and their maids, of
Job 19. 15 my maids, count me for a stranger: I am
Nah. 2. 7 her maids shall lead..as with the voice of
2. *A virgin,* בְּתוּלָה *bethulah.*
Exod22. 16 if a man entice a maid that is not betro.
Judg19. 24 Behold..my daughter, a maiden, and his
2 Ch.36. 17 no compassion upon young man or maiden
Job 31. 1 eyes; why then should I think upon a m.?
Psa. 78. 63 their maidens were not given to marriage
148. 12 Both young men and maidens; old men
Jer. 2. 32 Can a maid forget her ornaments, (or) a
51. 22 will I break..the young man and the m.
Lam. 5. 11 They ravished..the maids in the cities of
Eze. 9. 6 both maids, and little children, and wo.
44. 22 they shall take maidens of the seed of
Zech. 9. 17 make..cheerful, and new wine the maids
3. *Marks of virginity,* בְּתוּלִים *bethulim.*
Deut22. 14 when I came to her I found her not a m.
22. 17 saying, I found not thy daughter a maid
4. *A maid, maiden,* נַעֲרָה *naarah.*
Exod. 2. 5 and her maidens walked along by the
Ruth 2. 8 Go not..but abide here fast by my maid.
2. 22 that thou go out with his maidens, that
2. 23 So she kept fast by the maidens of Boaz
3. 2 (is) not Boaz..with whose maidens thou
1 Sa. 9. 11 they found young maidens going out to
2 Ki 5. 2 had brought away captive..a little maid
2 Ki. 5. 4 said the maid that (is) of the land of Isr.
Esth. 2. 4 let the maiden which pleaseth the king
2. 7 Esther..the maid (was) fair and beautiful
2. 8 when many maidens were gathered toge.
2. 9 the maiden pleased him, and she obtained
2. 9 and seven maidens..meet to be given her
2. 9 he preferred her and her maids unto the
2. 12 when every maid's turn was come to go
2. 13 Then thus came (every) maiden unto the
4. 4 Esther's maids and her chamberlains came
4. 16 I also and my maidens will fast likewise
Job 41. 5 or wilt thou bind him for thy maidens?
Prov. 9. 3 She hath sent forth her maidens: she cri.
27. 27 and..the maintenance for thy maidens
31. 15 She riseth..and giveth..a portion to her m.
Amos 2. 7 will go in unto the..maid, to profane
5. *A young woman, virgin,* עַלְמָה *almah.*
Exod 2. 8 the maid went and called the child's mo.
Prov.30. 19 the sea, and the way of a man with a m.
6. *A maid, servant,* שִׁפְחָה *shiphchah.*
Gen. 16. 2 I pray thee, go in unto my maid; it may
16. 3 Sarai, Abram's wife, took Hagar her maid
16. 5 I have given my maid into thy bosom
16. 6 Behold, thy maid (is) in thy hand; do to
16. 8 Hagar, Sarai's maid, whence camest thou?
29. 24 gave..Zilpah his maid (for) an handmaid
29. 29 gave..Bilhah his handmaid to be her m.
30. 7 Bilhah, Rachel's maid, conceived again
30. 9 she took Zilpah her maid, and gave her J.
30. 10 And Zilpah, Leah's maid, bare Jacob a son
30. 12 Zilpah, Leah's maid, bare Jacob a second
30. 18 I have given my maiden to my husband
Psa 123. 2 as the eyes of a maiden unto the hand of
Eccl. 2. 7 I got..servants and maidens, and had ser.
Isa. 24. 2 as with the maid, so with her mistress; as
7. *A damsel,* κοράσιον *korasion.*
Matt. 9. 24 Give place..the maid is not dead, but sle.
9. 25 took her by the hand, and the maid arose
8. *A little maid,* παιδίσκη *paidiskē.*
Mark14. 66 there cometh one of the maids of the high
14. 69 a maid saw him again, and began to say
Luke12. 45 to beat the men servants and maidens, and
22. 56 a certain maid beheld him as he sat by the
9. *A maid, maiden, child,* παῖς *pais.*
Luke 8. 51 the father and the mother of the maiden
8. 54 took her by the hand, and called..Maid

MAID CHILD —
A female, נְקֵבָה *neqebah.*
Lev. 12. 5 if she bear a maid child, then she shall be

MAID SERVANT—
1. *Handmaid,* אָמָה *amah.*
Gen. 20. 17 God healed..his wife, and his maid serv.
31. 33 into the two maid servants' tents; but he
Exod20. 10 thy man servant, nor thy maid servant, nor
20. 17 nor his man servant, nor his maid servant
21. 7 if a man sell his daughter to be a maid s.
21. 27 if he smite out..his maid servant's tooth
21. 32 shall push a man servant or maid servant
Deut. 5. 14 nor thy man servant, nor thy maid servant
5. 14 thy maid servant may rest as well as thou
5. 21 or his man servant, or his maid servant
12. 12 your men servants, and your maid serv.
12. 18 thy man servant, and thy maid servant
15. 17 unto thy maid servant thou shalt do like.
16. 11, 14 thy man servant, and thy maid servant
Judg. 9. 18 made Abimelech, the son of his maid se.
2 Sa. 6. 22 the maid servants which thou hast spoken
Neh. 7. 67 their man servants and..maid servants
Job 31. 13 If I did des. the cause..of my maid serv.
2. *Maid servant,* שִׁפְחָה *shiphchah.*
Gen. 12. 16 men servants, and maid servants, and
24. 35 and men servants, and maid servants, and
30. 43 maid servants, and men servants, and ca.
Exod11. 5 unto the first born of the maid servant that
2 Ki. 5. 26 oxen, and men servants, and maid servants?
Jer. 34. 9 That every man should let his..maid ser.
34. 10 every one should let his..maid servant

MAIL —
Scales, fins, armour, קַשְׂקֶשֶׂת *qasqeseth.*
1 Sa. 17. 5 and he (was) armed with a coat of mail
[*See also* Coat.]

MAIMED —
1. *To cut off,* חָרַץ *charats.*
Lev. 22. 22 Blind, or broken, or maimed, or having a
2. *Maimed, deprived of a limb,* ἀνάπηρος *anapēros.*
Luke 14. 13 call the poor, the maimed, the lame, the
14. 21 the poor, and the maimed, and the halt
3. *Distorted, crooked,* κυλλός *kullos.*
Matt 15. 30 lame, blind, dumb, maimed, and many
15. 31 the maimed to be whole, the lame to walk
18. 8 for thee to enter into life halt or maimed
Mark 9. 43 it is better for thee to enter into life mai.

MAINSAIL —
Main sail, jib, dolon, ἀρτέμων *artemōn.*
Acts 27. 40 hoised up the mainsail to the wind, and

MAINTAIN, to —
1. *To make or keep strong,* חָזַק *chazaq,* 3.
1 Ch.26. 27 Out of the spoils..to maintain the house
2. *To reason, make prominent,* יָכַח *yakach,* 5.
Job 13. 15 I will maintain mine own ways before him
3. *To do,* עָשָׂה *asah.*
1 Ki. 8. 45, 49 Then hear thou..and maintain their
8. 59 that he maintain the cause of his servant
2 Ch. 6. 35, 39 Then hear thou..and maintain their
Psa. 9. 4 thou hast maintained my right and my c.
140. 12 I know that the LORD will maintain the c.
4. *To hold, uphold, retain,* תָּמַךְ *tamak.*
Psa. 16. 5 The LORD..thou maintainest my lot
5. *To cause to stand before or forward,* προΐστημι.
Titus 3. 8 might be careful to maintain good works
3. 14 let ours also learn to maintain good works

MAINTENANCE, (to have)
1. *Life,* חַיִּים *chayim.*
Prov.27. 27 and (for) the maintenance for thy maidens
2. *To salt salt,* מְלַח מְלַח *melach melach.*
Ezra 4. 14 Now because we have maintenance from

MAJESTY —
1. *Excellency,* גָּאוֹן *gaon.*
Job 40. 10 Deck thyself now (with) majesty and ex.
Isa. 2. 10, 19, 21 and for the glory of his majesty
24. 14 they shall sing for the majesty of the L.
Eze. 7. 20 he set it in majesty; but they made the
Mic. 5. 4 in the majesty of the name of the LORD
2. *Excellency,* גֵּאוּת *geuth.*
Psa. 93. 1 The LORD reigneth; he is clothed with m.
Isa. 26. 10 and will not behold the majesty of the L.
3. *Greatness,* גְּדוּלָּה *gedulah.*
Esth. 1. 4 showed..the honour of his excellent ma.
4. *Honour, majesty, beauty,* הָדָר *hadar.*
Psa. 21. 5 honour and majesty hast thou laid upon
29. 4 the voice of the LORD (is) full of majesty
45. 3 Gird thy sword..with thy glory and thy m.
45. 4 in thy majesty ride prosperously, because
96. 6 Honour and majesty (are) before him: s
104. 1 thou art clothed with honour and majesty
145. 12 and the glorious majesty of his kingdom
5. *Honour, majesty, beauty,* הֲדַר *hadar.*
Dan. 4. 30 I have built..for the honour of my maj.?
6. *Honour, beauty, majesty,* הוֹד *hod.*
1 Ch.29. 11 the glory, and the victory, and the maj.
29. 25 bestowed upon him..royal majesty as had
Job 37. 22 Fair weather..with God (is) terrible ma.
Psa.145. 5 I will speak of..glorious honour of thy m.
7. *Greatness,* רְבוּ *rebu.*
Dan. 4. 36 and excellent majesty was added unto me
5. 18 a kingdom, and majesty, and glory, and
5. 19 for the majesty that he gave him, all pe.
8. *Greatness,* μεγαλειότης *megaleiotēs.*
2 Pe. 1. 16 fables..but were eye witnesses of his ma.
9. *Greatness,* μεγαλωσύνη *megalōsunē.*
Heb. 1. 3 on the right hand of the majesty on high
8. 1 on the right hand of the throne of the m.
Jude 25 glory and majesty, dominion and power

MA'-KAZ, מָקַץ *end.*
A town or district in the N.W. of Judah. See *Michmash.*
1 Ki. 4. 9 son of Dekar, in M., and in Shaalbim, and

MAKE (ruler), to—
1. *To build, build up,* בָּנָה *banah.*
Gen. 2. 22 the rib..made he a woman, and brought
1 Ki.22. 39 the ivory house which he made, and all
Eze. 27. 5 They have made all thy..boards of fir
2. *To build, build up,* בְּנָא *bena.*
Ezra 5. 4 What are the names of the men that m.
3. *To prepare,* בָּרָא *bara.*
Num16. 30 if the LORD make a new thing, and the
Psa. 89. 47 wherefore hast thou made all men in v.?
4. *To hew, dig,* חָצַב *chatseb.*
Isa. 5. 2 and also made a wine press therein: and
5. *To set up, place,* יָצַג *yatsag,* 5.
Job 17. 6 He hath made me also a byword of the p.
Jer. 51. 34 he hath made me an empty vessel, he hath
6. *To form, constitute, fashion, frame,* יָצַר *yatsar.*
Psa. 74. 17 thou hast made summer and winter
104. 26 leviathan..thou hast made to play therein.
Isa. 44. 9 They that make a graven image (are) all of
7. *To give,* נָתַן *nathan.*
Gen. 9. 12 the token of the covenant which I make
17. 2 I will make my covenant between me and
17. 5 a father of many nations have I made thee
17. 6 I will make nations of thee, and kings shall
17. 20 Ishmael..I will make him a great nation
41. 43 he made him..over all the land of Egypt
48. 4 I will make of thee a multitude of people
Exod. 7. 1 See, I have made thee a god to Pharaoh
18. 16 I do make (them) know the statutes of God
18. 25 made them heads over the people, rulers
23. 27 I will make all thine enemies turn their
Lev. 19. 28 Ye shall not make any cuttings in your fl.
22. 22 nor make an offering by fire of them upon
26. 19 I will make your heaven as iron, and your
26. 31 I will make your cities waste, and bring
26. 46 laws which the LORD made between him
Num. 5. 21 LORD make thee a curse and an oath am.
5. 21 when the LORD doth make thy thigh to rot
14. 4 Let us make a captain, and let us return
Deut. 1. 15 wise men, and known, and made them h.
16. 18 Judges and officers shalt thou make thee

Deut.28. 13 LORD shall make thee the head, and not
28. 24 LORD shall make the rain of thy land po.
Josh. 7. 19 make confession unto him; and tell me
9. 27 Joshua made them that day hewers of w.
22. 25 LORD hath made Jordan a border between
Ruth 4. 11 LORD make the woman that is come into
1 Sa. 9. 22 made them sit in the chiefest place among
1 Ki. 6. 6 he made narrowed rests round about, that
9. 22 of Israel did Solomon make no bondmen
10. 27 the king made silver (to be) in Jerusalem
10. 27 cedars made he..as the sycamore trees
14. 7 and made thee prince over my people I.
16. 2 and made thee prince over my people I.
16. 3 will make thy house like the house of J.
21. 22 will make thine house like the house of
2 Ki. 9. 9 I will make the house of Ahab like the
1 Ch.12. 18 David received them, and made them ca.
17. 22 thy people Israel didst thou make thine
2 Ch. 1. 15 the king made silver and gold at Jerusalem
1. 15 cedar trees made he as the sycamore trees
2. 11 the LORD..hath made thee king over them
7. 20 and will make it..a proverb and a byword
8. 9 of Israel did Solomon make no servants
9. 8 therefore made he thee king over them
9. 27 the king made silver in Jerusalem as
9. 27 cedar trees made he as the sycamore trees
24. 9 they made a proclamation through Judah
25. 16 Art thou made of the king's counsel? for.
35. 25 and made them an ordinance in Israel: and
Ezra 10. 11 make confession unto the LORD God of
Neh. 13. 26 and God made him king over all Israel
Psa. 18. 32 (It is) God that..maketh my way perfect
39. 5 Behold, thou hast made my days (as) an h.
69. 11 I made sackcloth also my garment; and I
89. 27 Also I will make him..first born, higher
106. 46 He made them also to be pitied of all those
148. 6 he hath made a decree which shall not p.
Isa. 43. 16 Thus saith the LORD, which maketh a way
53. 9 he made his grave with the wicked, and
Jer. 1. 18 I have made thee this day a defenced city
5. 14 I will make my words in thy mouth fire
9. 11 And I will make Jerusalem heaps..a den
9. 11 I will make the cities of Judah desolate
12. 10 they have made my pleasant portion a d.
15. 20 I will make thee unto this people a fenced
19. 12 Thus will I do..make this city as Tophet
20. 4 I will make thee a terror to thyself, and
25. 18 to make them a desolation, an astonishm.
26. 6 Then will I make this house like Shiloh
26. 6 and will make this city a curse to all the
29. 17 will make them like vile figs, that cannot
29. 26 LORD hath made thee priest in the stead of
34. 17 I will make you to be removed into all
34. 22 I will make the cities of Judah a desola.
49. 15 I will make thee small among the heathen
51. 25 Behold, I..will make thee a burnt mount.
Lam. 1. 13 he hath made me desolate..faint all the
2. 7 they have made a noise in the house of the
Eze. 3. 8 I have made thy face strong against their
3. 9 an adamant harder than flint have I made
3. 17 I have made thee a watchman unto the h.
5. 14 I will make thee waste, and a reproach
6. 14 and make the land desolate, yea, more d.
15. 8 I will make the land desolate, because they
22. 4 therefore have I made thee a reproach
25. 4 and make their dwellings in thee: they
25. 5 I will make Rabbah a stable for camels
25. 13 and I will make it desolate from Teman
26. 4 scrape..and make her like the top of a r.
26. 8 he shall make a fort against thee, and cast
26. 19 When I shall make thee a desolate city
26. 21 I will make thee a terror, and thou (shalt
29. 10, 12 I will make the land of Egypt
30. 12 I will make the rivers dry, and sell the
32. 15 When I shall make the land of Egypt de.
34. 26 I will make them and the places round
35. 3 Behold..I will make thee most desolate
35. 7 Thus will I make mount Seir most desol.
35. 9 I will make thee perpetual desolations
44. 14 I will make them keepers of the charge
Hos. 11. 8 how shall I make thee as Admah?..shall
Joel 2. 19 I will no more make you a reproach am.
Obad. 2 I have made thee small among the heat.
Mic. 6. 16 that I should make thee a desolation, and
Zeph. 3. 20 I will make you a name and a praise am.
Mal. 2. 9 have I also made you contemptible and

8. *To make, do,* עֲבַד *abad.*
Jer. 10. 11 the gods that have not made the heavens
Dan. 3. 1 Nebuchadnezzar the king made an image
3. 15 and worship the image which I have made
5. 1 Belshazzar the king made a great feast to
7. 21 the same horn made war with the saints

9. *To cause to stand, set up,* עָמַד *amad,* 5.
2 Ch.11. 22 Rehoboam made Abijah the son of Maac.
25. 5 made them captains over thousands, and
Neh. 10. 32 Also we made ordinances for us, to charge

10. *To take pains, labour,* עָצַב *atsab,* 3.
Job 10. 8 Thine hands have made me, and fashione.

11. *To do, make,* עָשָׂה *asah.*
Gen. 1. 7 God made the firmament, and divided the
1. 16 God made two great lights; the greater l.
1. 25 God made the beast of the earth after his
1. 26 Let us make man in our image, after our
1. 31 God saw every thing that he had made
2. 2 God ended his work which he had made
2. 2 day from all his work which he had made
2. 3 all his work which God created and made
2. 4 LORD God made the earth and the heav.
2. 18 I will make him an help meet for him
3. 1 any beast..which the LORD God had made
Gen. 3. 7 fig leaves together, and made themselves
3. 21 God make coats of skins, and clothed them
5. 1 man, in the likeness of God made he him
6. 6 that he had made man on the earth, and
6. 7 for it repenteth me that I have made them
6. 14 Make thee an ark..rooms shalt thou make
6. 15 And this..which thou shalt make it..The
6. 16 A window shalt thou make to the ark, and
6. 16 lower, second, and third..shalt thou make
7. 4 every living substance that I have made
8. 6 the window of the ark which he had made
9. 6 man..for in the image of God made he man
11. 4 let us make us a name, lest we be scatt.
12. 2 I will make of thee a great nation, and I
13. 4 altar, which he had made there at the fi.
14. 2 made war with Bera king of Sodom, and
18. 6 knead..and make cakes upon the hearth
19. 3 made them a feast, and did bake unleav.
21. 6 God hath made me to laugh..all that hear
21. 8 Abraham made a great feast the..day that
26. 30 he made them a feast, and they did eat
27. 4 make me savoury meat, such as I love, and
27. 7 make me savoury meat, that I may eat, and
27. 9 I will make them savoury meat for thy f.
27. 14 his mother made savoury meat, such as his
27. 31 And he also had made savoury meat, and
29. 22 Laban gathered..the men..and made a
31. 46 they took stones, and made an heap: and
33. 17 built him an house, and made booths for
35. 1 make there an altar unto God, that appe.
35. 3 I will make there an altar unto God, who
37. 3 and he made him a coat of (many) colours
40. 20 that he made a feast unto all his servants
50. 10 made a mourning for his father seven days
Exod. 1. 21 it came to pass..that he made them houses
5. 8 the tale of the bricks, which they did make
5. 16 they say to us, Make brick: and, behold
20. 4 Thou shalt not make unto thee any graven
20. 11 six days the LORD made heaven and earth
20. 23 Ye shall not make with me gods of silver
20. 23 neither shall ye make unto you gods of g.
20. 24 An altar of earth shalt thou make unto
20. 25 if thou wilt make me an altar of stone
25. 8 let them make me a sanctuary; that I may
25. 9 and the pattern..even so shall ye make (it)
25. 10 they shall make an ark (of) shittim wood
25. 11 make upon it a crown of gold round about
25. 13 thou shalt make staves (of) shittim wood
25. 17 thou shalt make a mercy seat (of) pure g.
25. 18 thou shalt make two cherubim (of) gold
25. 18 beaten work shalt thou make them, in the
25. 19 make one cherub on the one end, and the
25. 19 shall ye make the cherubim on the two
25. 23 Thou shalt also make a table (of) shittim
25. 24 make thereto a crown of gold round about
25. 25 thou shalt make unto it a border of an h.
25. 25 thou shalt make a golden crown to the b.
25. 26 thou shalt make for it four rings of gold
25. 28 thou shalt make the staves (of) shittim w.
25. 29 to cover withal..pure gold shalt thou ma.
25. 31 thou shalt make a candlestick (of) pure g
25. 37 thou shalt make the seven lamps thereof
25. 39 a talent of pure gold shall he make it, with
25. 40 look that thou make..after their pattern
26. 1 thou shalt make the tabernacle..ten cu.
26. 1 cherubim of cunning work shalt thou make
26. 4 thou shalt make loops of blue upon the
26. 4 likewise shalt thou make in the uttermost
26. 5, 5 Fifty loops shalt thou make in the
26. 6 thou shalt make fifty taches of gold, and
26. 7 And thou shalt make curtains (of) goat's
26. 7 tabernacle; eleven curtains shalt thou m.
26. 10 thou shalt make fifty loops on the edge
26. 11 thou shalt make fifty taches of brass, and
26. 14 thou shalt make a covering for the tent
26. 15 thou shalt make boards for the tabernacle
26. 17 thus shalt thou make for all the boards of
26. 18 thou shalt make the boards for the taber.
26. 19 thou shalt make forty sockets of silver un.
26. 22 for the sides..thou shalt make six boards
26. 23 two boards shalt thou make for the corner
26. 26 thou shalt make bars (of) shittim wood
26. 29 make their rings (of) gold..places for the
26. 31 thou shalt make a veil (of) blue, and pur.
26. 37 thou shalt make for the hanging five pill.
27. 1 thou shalt make an altar (of) shittim wood
27. 2 thou shalt make the horns of it upon the
27. 3 thou shalt make his pans to receive his as.
27. 3 all the vessels thereof thou shalt make (of)
27. 4 thou shalt make for it a grate of net work
27. 4 upon the net shalt thou make four brazen
27. 6 Thou shalt make staves for the altar, sta.
27. 8 Hollow with boards shalt thou make it
27. 8 as it was showed..so shall they make (it)
27. 9 thou shalt make the court of the taberna.
28. 2, 4 make holy garments for Aaron thy
28. 3 that they may make Aaron's garments to
28. 4 these..the garments which they shall m.
28. 6 they shall make the ephod (of) gold, (of)
28. 11 thou shalt make them to be set in ouches
28. 13 And thou shalt make ouches (of) gold
28. 14 (of) wreathen work shalt thou make them
28. 15 thou shalt make the breast plate of judg.
28. 15 after the work of the ephod thou shalt m.
28. 15 (of) fine twined linen, shalt thou make it
28. 22, 23 thou shalt make upon the breast plate
28. 26 thou shalt make two rings of gold, and
28. 27 two..rings of gold thou shalt make, and
28. 31 thou shalt make the robe of the ephod all
28. 33 thou shalt make pomegranates (of) blue
28. 36 thou shalt make a plate (of) pure gold, and
28. 39 thou shalt make the mitre (of) fine linen
Exod.28. 39 thou shalt make the girdle (of) needlework
28. 40 for Aaron's sons thou shalt make coats
28. 40 and thou shalt make for them girdles, and
28. 40 bonnets shalt thou make for them, for
28. 42 thou shalt make them linen breeches to
29. 2 (of) wheaten flour shalt thou make them
30. 1 thou shalt make an altar to burn incense
30. 1 (of) shittim wood shalt thou make it
30. 3 thou shalt make unto it a crown of gold
30. 4 two golden rings shalt thou make to it un.
30. 4 upon the two sides of it shalt thou make
30. 5 thou shalt make the staves (of) shittim w
30. 18 Thou shalt also make a laver (of) brass
30. 25 thou shalt make it an oil of holy ointment
30. 32 neither shall ye make..like it, after the
30. 35 thou shalt make it a perfume, a confection
30. 37 And..the perfume which thou shalt make
30. 37 ye shall not make to yourselves according
30. 38 Whosoever shall make like unto that, to
31. 6 that they may make all that I have com.
31. 17 six days the LORD made heaven and earth
32. 1 make us gods, which shall go before us
32. 4 tool, after he had made it a molten calf
32. 8 they have made them a molten calf, and
32. 10 and I will make of thee a great nation
32. 20 he took the calf which they had made, and
32. 23 Make us gods which shall go before us
32. 31 this people..have made them gods of gold
32. 35 because they made the calf which Aaron m.
34. 17 Thou shalt make thee no molten gods
35. 10 and make all that the LORD hath comm.
35. 33 And..to make any manner of cunning w.
36. 3 And they received of Moses all..to make it
36. 4 every man from the work which they made
36. 5 work which the LORD commanded to make
36. 6 Let neither man nor woman make anymore
36. 7 was sufficient for all the work to make it
36. 8 made ten curtains (of) fine twined linen, and
36. 8 cherubim of cunning work made he them
36. 11 he made loops of blue on the edge of one
36. 11 likewise he made in the uttermost side of
36. 12 Fifty loops made he in one curtain, and
36. 12 fifty loops made he in the edge of the
36. 13 he made fifty taches of gold, and coupled
36. 14 made curtains..eleven curtains he made
36. 17 made fifty loops upon the uttermost edge
36. 17 fifty loops made he upon the edge of the
36. 18 he made fifty taches (of) brass to couple
36. 19 he made a covering for the tent (of) ram's
36. 20 he made boards for the tabernacle (of) s.
36. 22 thus did he make for all the boards of
36. 23 he made boards for the tabernacle; twenty
36. 24 forty sockets of silver he made under the t.
36. 25 for the other side..he made twenty boards
36. 27 for the sides..westward he made six bo.
36. 28 two boards made he for the corners of the
36. 31 he made bars of shittim wood; five for the
36. 33 he made the middle bar to shoot through
36. 34 made their rings (of) gold..places for the
36. 35 he made a veil (of) blue, and purple, and
36. 35 (with) cherubim made he it of cunning
36. 36 And he made thereunto four pillars (of)
36. 37 he made an hanging for the tabernacle
37. 1 Bezaleel made the ark (of) shittim wood
37. 2 and made a crown of gold to it round ab.
37. 4 he made staves (of) shittim wood, and
37. 6 he made the mercy seat (of) pure gold
37. 7 And he made two cherubim (of) gold
37. 7 beaten out of one piece made he them
37. 8 out of the mercy seat made he the cher.
37. 10 he made the table (of) shittim wood: two
37. 11 made thereunto a crown of gold round
37. 12 Also he made thereunto a border of an
37. 12 and made a crown of gold for the border
37. 15, 28 he made the staves (of) shittim wood
37. 16 he made the vessels which (were) upon
37. 17 he made the candlestick (of) pure gold
37. 17 (of) beaten work made he the candlestick
37. 23 he made his seven lamps, and his snuffers
37. 24 (Of) a talent of pure gold made he it, and
37. 25 made the incense altar (of) shittim wood
37. 26 he made unto it a crown of gold round
37. 27 he made two rings of gold for it under
37. 29 he made the holy anointing oil, and the
38. 1 he made the altar of burnt offering (of)
38. 2 he made the horns thereof on the four
38. 3 he made all the vessels of the altar, the
38. 3 all the vessels thereof made he (of) brass
38. 4 he made for the altar a brazen grate of
38. 6 he made the staves (of) shittim wood, and
38. 7 And..he made the altar hollow with bo.
38. 8 he made the laver (of) brass, and the foot
38. 9 he made the court: on the south side so.
38. 22 made all that the LORD commanded M.
38. 28 he made hooks for the pillars, and over.
38. 30 he made the sockets to the door of the
39. 1 they made cloths of service, to do service
39. 1 and made the holy garments for Aaron
39. 2 he made the ephod (of) gold, blue, and
39. 4 They made shoulder pieces for it, to cou.
39. 8 he made the breast plate (of) cunning w.
39. 9 they made the breast plate double: a s.
39. 15 they made upon the breast plate chains
39. 16 they made two ouches (of) gold, and two
39. 19 they made two rings of gold, and put (th.)
39. 20 they made two..golden rings, and put
39. 22 he made the robe of the ephod (of) woven
39. 24 they made upon the hems of the robe po.
39. 25 they made bells (of) pure gold, and put
39. 27 they made coats (of) fine linen, (of) woven
39. 30 they made the plate of the holy crown (of)
39. 42 so the children of Israel made all the w.

Lev. 19. 4 nor make to yourselves molten gods: I
22. 24 cut; neither shall ye make..in your land
26. 1 Ye shall make you no idols nor graven i.
Num. 8. 4 the pattern..so he made the candlestick
10. 2 Make..of a whole piece shalt thou make
11. 8 baked (it) in pans, and made cakes of it
14. 12 will make of thee a greater nation and
15. 3 will make an offering by fire unto the L.
15. 3 to make a sweet savour unto the LORD, of
15. 38 bid them that they make them fringes in
16. 38 let them make them broad plates..a cov.
21. 8 Make thee a fiery serpent, and set it upon
21. 9 Moses made a serpent of brass, and put
Deut. 4. 16 Lest ye corrupt..and make you a graven
4. 23 lest ye..make you a graven image, (or) the
4. 25 When thou shalt..make a graven image
5. 8 Thou shalt not make thee (any) graven i.
9. 12 for..they have made them a molten image
9. 14 I will make of thee a nation mightier and
9. 16 had made you a molten calf: ye had tur
9. 21 I took your sin, the calf which ye had m.
10. 1 and come. and make thee an ark of wood
10. 3 I made an ark (of) shittim wood, and he
10. 5 put the tables in the ark which I had made
15. 1 At the end of..seven years thou shalt make
16. 21 unto the altar..which thou shalt make
20. 12 but will make war against thee, then thou
20. 20 build bulwarks against the city that ma.
22. 8 thou shalt make a battlement for thy roof
22. 12 Thou shalt make thee fringes upon the four
26. 19 high above all nations which he hath m.
27. 15 Cursed (be) the man that maketh (any) g.
32. 6 hath he not made thee, and established
32. 15 then he forsook God (which) made him
Josh. 5. 2 Make thee sharp knives, and circumcise
5. 3 Joshua made him sharp knives, and cir.
9. 15 Joshua made peace with them, and made
11. 18 Joshua made war a long time with all those
22. 28 which our fathers made, not for burnt off.
Judg. 3. 16 Ehud made him a dagger which had two
6. 2 the children of Israel made them the dens
6. 19 Gideon went in, and made ready a kid, and
8. 27 Gideon made an ephod thereof, and put
9. 27 and trode (the grapes), and made merry
13. 15 until we shall have made ready a kid for
14. 10 Samson made there a feast; for so used
17. 3 to make a graven image, and a molten i.
17. 4 who made thereof a graven image and a m.
17. 5 made an ephod, and teraphim and con.
18. 3 Who brought thee hither? and what ma.
18. 24 Ye have taken away my gods which I ma.
18. 27 they took (the things) which Micah had m.
18. 31 set..up Micah's graven image, which he
21. 15 had made a breach in the tribes of Israel
1 Sa. 2. 19 his mother made him a little coat, and b.
6. 5 ye shall make images of your emerods, and
6. 7 make a new cart, and take two milch k.
8. 12 to make his instruments of war, and ins.
12. 22 pleased the LORD to make you his people
13. 19 Lest the Hebrews make..swords or spears
17. 25 and make his father's house free in Israel
25. 28 will certainly make my lord a sure house
2 Sa. 3. 20 David made Abner, and the men..a feast
7. 9 have made thee a great name, like unto
7. 11 telleth..that he will make thee an house
13. 10 Tamar took the cakes which she had made
1 Ki. 2. 24 who hath made me an house, as he prom.
3. 15 Solomon..made a feast to all his servants
6. 4 for the house he made windows of narrow
6. 5 oracle: and he made chambers round about
6. 23 within the oracle he made two cherubim
6. 31 for the entering of the oracle he made d.
6. 33 So also made he for the door of the tem.
7. 6 he made a porch of pillars; the length th.
7. 7 he made a porch for the throne where he
7. 8 Solomon made also an house for Pharaoh's
7. 16 he made two chapiters (of) molten brass
7. 18 he made the pillars, and two rows round
7. 23 he made a molten sea, ten cubits from the
7. 27 he made ten bases of brass; four cubits
7. 37 After this..he made the ten bases: all of
7. 38 Then made he ten lavers of brass: one
7. 40 Hiram made the lavers, and the shovels
7. 40 all the work that he made king Solomon
7. 45 all these vessels, which Hiram made to
7. 48 And Solomon made all the vessels that
7. 51 all the work that king Solomon made for
9. 26 king Solomon made a navy of ships in E
10. 12 the king made of the almug trees pillars
10. 16 king Solomon made two hundred targets
10. 18 the king made a great throne of ivory, and
12. 28 king took counsel, and made two calves
12. 31 he made an house of high places, and m.
12. 32 sacrificing unto the calves that he had m.
12. 32 priests of the high places which he had m.
12. 33 upon the altar which he had made in B.
13. 33 made again of the lowest of the people
14. 9 thou hast gone and made thee other gods
14. 15 because they have made their groves, p.
14. 16 who did sin, and who made Israel to sin
14. 26 the shields of gold which Solomon had m.
14. 27 made in their stead brasen shields, and
15. 12 removed..the idols that his fathers had m.
15. 13 because she had made an idol in a grove
16. 33 Ahab make a grove; and Ahab did more
17. 13 make me thereof a little cake first, and
17. 13 and after make for thee and for thy son
18. 26 they leaped upon the altar which was m.
18. 32 he made a trench about the altar, as great
22. 11 Zedekiah the son of Chenaanah made him
22. 48 Jehoshaphat made ships of Tharshish to
2 Ki. 3. 2 the image of Baal that his father had m.
2 Ki. 3. 16 And he said..Make this valley full of di.
4. 10 Let us make a little chamber, I pray thee
6. 2 let us make us a place there, where we may
7. 2, 19 (if) the LORD would make windows in
16. 11 made (it) against king Ahaz came from D.
17. 8 walked in the statutes..which they had m.
17. 16 made them molten images..two calves
17. 19 in the statutes of Israel which they made
17. 30 the men of Babylon made Succoth-benoth
17. 30 made Nergal..men of Hamath made Ash.
17. 31 Avites made Nibhaz and Tartak, and the
17. 29 every nation made gods of their own, and
17. 29 high places which the Samaritans had m.
17. 32 made unto themselves of the lowest of
18. 4 the brazen serpent that Moses had made
18. 31 Make..with me by a present, and come
19. 15 O LORD..thou hast made heaven and earth
20. 20 how he made a pool, and a conduit, and
21. 3 made a grove, as did Ahab king of Israel
21. 7 the grove that he had made in the house
23. 12 altars..which the kings of Judah had made
23. 12 the altars which Manasseh had made in
23. 15 high place which Jeroboam..had made
23. 19 which the kings of Israel had made to pro.
24. 13 which Solomon king of Israel had made
25. 16 the bases which Solomon had made for
1 Ch. 5. 10 in the days of Saul they made war with
5. 19 they made war with the Hagarites, with
15. 1 made him houses in the city of David, and
16. 26 the gods..(are) idols: but the LORD made
17. 8 have made thee a name like the name of
18. 8 wherewith Solomon made the brasen sea
21. 29 the tabernacle of the LORD, which M. made
22. 8 Thou hast shed blood..and hast made
23. 5 LORD with the instruments which I made
2 Ch. 1. 3 Moses the servant of the LORD had made
1 5 Bezaleel the son of Uri,..had made
2. 12 LORD God of Israel, that made heaven and
3. 8 he made the most holy house, the length
3. 10 he made two cherubim of image work, and
3. 14 he made the veil (of) blue, and purple, and
3. 15 he made before the house two pillars of
3. 16 he made chains, (as) in the oracle. and m.
4. 1 he made an altar of brass twenty cubits
4. 2 he made a molten sea of ten cubits from
4. 6 He made also ten lavers, and put five on
4. 7 he made ten candlesticks of gold accord.
4. 8 He made also ten tables, and placed..in
4. 8 And he made an hundred basons of gold
4. 9 he made the court of the priests, and the
4. 11 Huram made the pots, and the shovels
4. 11 finished the work that he was to make for
4. 14 He made also bases, and lavers made he
4. 16 did Huram his father make to king Solo.
4. 18 Solomon made all these vessels in great
4. 19 Solomon made all the vessels that (were
5. 1 all the work that Solomon made for the h.
6. 13 Solomon had made a brasen scaffold, of five
7. 6 which David the king had made to praise
7. 7 the brasen altar which Solomon had made
7. 9 in the eighth day they made a solemn as.
7. 11 all that came into Solomon's heart to m.
9. 11 the king made (of) the algum trees, terraces
9. 15 king Solomon made two hundred targets
9. 17 the king made a great throne of ivory, and
11. 15 priests..for the calves which he had made
12. 9 the shields of gold which Solomon had m.
12. 10 king Rehoboam made shields of brass, and
13. 8 calves, which Jeroboam made you for gods
13. 9 have made you priests after the manner
15. 16 because she had made an idol in a grove
18. 10 Zedekiah the son of Chenaanah had made
20. 36 make ships to go to Tarshish: and they m.
21. 11 he made high places in the mountains of
21. 19 his people made no burning for him, like
24. 8 they made a chest, and set it without at
24. 14 whereof were made vessels for the house
26. 13 that made war with mighty power, to help
26. 15 he made in Jerusalem engines, invented
28. 2 and made also molten images for Baalim
28. 24 he made him altars in every corner of J.
28. 25 he made high places to burn incense unto
32. 5 and made darts and shields in abundance
32. 27 he made himself treasuries for silver, and
33. 3 he reared up altars for Baalim and made
33. 7 a carved image, the idol which he had m
33. 22 images which Manasseh his father had m
Neh. 8. 4 pulpit of wood, which they had made for
8. 12 to make great mirth, because they had
8. 15 branches of thick trees, to make booths
8. 16 made themselves booths, every one upon
8. 17 made booths, and sat under the booths
9. 6 thou hast made heaven, the heaven of h.
9. 18 when they had made them a molten calf
Esth. 1. 3 he made a feast unto all his princes and
1. 5 the king made a feast unto all the people
1. 9 Vashti the queen made a feast for the w.
1. 20 the king's decree which he shall make
2. 18 the king made a great feast unto all his
2. 18 he made a release to the provinces, and
5. 14 Let a gallows be made of fifty cubits high
5. 14 and he caused the gallows to be made
7. 9 gallows..which Haman had made for M.
9. 17, 18 made it a day of feasting and gladness
9. 19 made the fourteenth day of the month A.
9. 22 they should make them days of feasting
Job 9. 9 maketh Arcturus, Orion, and Pleiades, and
10. 9 Remember..thou hast made me as the c.
15. 27 and maketh collops of fat on (his) flanks
25. 2 he maketh peace in his high places
27. 18 and as a booth..the keeper maketh
28. 25 To make the weight for the winds; and
Job 28. 26 When he made a decree for the rain, and
31. 15 did not he that made me in the womb..m.
33. 4 The spirit of God hath made me, and the
40. 15 behemoth, which I made with thee; he
40. 19 he that made him can make his sword to
Psa. 9. 15 heathen are sunk down in the pit..they m.
86. 9 All nations whom thou hast made shall
95. 5 The sea (is) his, and he made it; and his
96. 5 the gods..(are) idols: but the LORD made
100. 3 he (that) hath made us, and not we ours.
104. 4 Who maketh his angels spirits; his mini.
104. 24 in wisdom hast thou made them all: the
106. 19 They made a calf in Horeb, and worship.
111. 4 He hath made his wonderful works to be
115. 8 They that make them are like unto them
115. 15 Ye (are) blessed of the LORD which made
118. 24 This (is) the day (which) the LORD hath m.
119. 73 Thy hands have made me and fashioned
121. 2 My help..from the LORD, which made h.
124. 8 of the LORD, who made heaven and earth
134. 3 The LORD that made heaven and earth b.
135. 7 he maketh lightnings for the rain: he br.
135. 18 They that make them are like unto them
136. 5 To him that by wisdom made the heavens
136. 7 To him that made great lights: for his m.
146. 6 Which made heaven and earth, the sea
149. 2 Let Israel rejoice in him that made him
Prov. 8. 26 While as yet he had not made the earth
20. 12 the LORD hath made even both of them
20. 18 counsel; and with good advice make war
23. 5 for (riches) certainly make themselves w.
24. 6 by wise counsel thou shalt make thy war
31. 22 She maketh herself coverings of tapestry
31. 24 She maketh fine linen, and selleth (it); and
Eccl. 2. 5 I made me gardens and orchards, and I p.
2. 6 I made me pools of water, to water there.
3. 11 He hath made every (thing) beautiful in
3. 11 can find out the work that God maketh
7. 29 God hath made man upright; but they
10. 19 A feast is made for laughter, and wine
11. 5 knowest not..works of God who maketh
12. 12 of making many books (there is) no end
Song 1. 11 We will make thee borders of gold, with
3. 9 King Solomon made himself a chariot of
3. 10 He made the pillars thereof (of) silver, the
Isa. 2. 8 that which their own fingers have made
2. 20 which they made..for himself to worship
10. 23 Lord GOD of hosts shall make a consump.
17. 8 which his fingers have made, either the
19. 10 all that make sluices (and) ponds for fish
22. 11 Ye made also a ditch between the two
25. 6 make unto all people a feast of fat things
27. 5 he may make peace with me..he shall m.
27. 11 he that made them will not have mercy on
29. 16 for shall the work say of him that made it
29. 16 He made me not? or shall the thing fra.
31. 7 which your own hands have made unto you
36. 16 Make (an agreement) with me (by) a pre.
37. 16 O LORD..thou hast made heaven and earth
40. 23 he maketh the judges of the earth as va.
43. 7 I have formed him; yea, I have made him
44. 2 Thus saith the LORD that made thee, and
44. 13 and maketh it after the figure of a man
44. 15 he maketh it a graven image, and falleth
44. 17 the residue thereof he maketh a god..his
44. 19 shall I make the residue thereof an abo.?
44. 24 I (am) the LORD that maketh all (things)
45. 7 I make peace, and create evil: I the L.
45. 9 Shall the clay say..What makest thou?
45. 12 I have made the earth, and created man
45. 18 God himself that formed the earth, and m.
46. 4 I have made, and I will bear; even I will
46. 6 hire a goldsmith; and he maketh it a god
57. 16 the spirit..the souls (which) I have made
63. 12 led..to make himself an everlasting name?
63. 14 thou lead..to make thyself a glorious n.
66. 2 all those..hath mine hand made, and all
66. 22 and the new earth, which I will make
Jer. 2. 28 where..thy gods which thou hast made
4. 27 land shall be desolate; yet will I not make
5. 10 and destroy; but make not a full end: take
5. 18 saith the LORD, I will not make a full end
6. 26 make thee mourning, (as for) an only son
7. 18 to make cakes to the queen of heaven, and
8. 8 Lo, certainly in vain made he (it); the pen
10. 12 He hath made the earth by his power, he
10. 13 he maketh lightnings with rain, and bri.
14. 22 O LORD our God..thou hast made all these
16. 20 Shall a man make gods unto himself, and
18. 4 vessel that he made of clay was marred
18. 4 so he made it..as seemed good..to make
27. 2 Make thee bonds and yokes, and put them
27. 5 I have made the earth, the man and the b.
28. 13 but thou shalt make for them yokes of i.
30. 11 though I make a full end of all nations
30. 11 yet will I not make a full end of thee; but
32. 17 thou hast made the heaven and the earth
32. 20 and hast made thee a name, as at this day
37. 15 the house..for they had made that the pr.
38. 16 LORD liveth, that made us this soul, I will
41. 9 which Asa the king had made for fear of
44. 19 did we make her cakes to worship her
46. 28 I will make a full end of all the nations
46. 28 I will not make a full end of thee, but co.
51. 15 He hath made the earth by his power, he
51. 16 he maketh lightnings with rain, and bri.
52. 20 which king Solomon had made in the h.
Eze. 4. 9 make thee bread thereof..to the number
7. 20 made the images of their abominations
7. 23 Make a chain; for the land is full of blo.
11. 13 wilt thou make a full end of the remnant
13. 18 Woe to the (women) that..make kerchiefs

Eze. 16. 17 madest to thyself images of men, and di.
16. 24 hast made thee an high place in every
16. 31 and makest thine high place in every st.
17. 17 make for him in the war, by casting up
18. 31 make you a new heart and a new spirit
20. 17 make an end of them in the wilderness
22. 3 maketh idols against herself to defile her.
22. 4 defiled..in thine idols which thou hast m.
22. 13 thy dishonest gain which thou hast made
24. 17 Forbear to cry, make no mourning for the
27. 5 taken cedars from Lebanon to make masts
27. 6 (Of) the oaks of Bashan have they made
27. 6 Ashurites have made thy benches(of)ivory
29. 3 My river (is) mine own, and I have made
29. 9 The river (is) mine, and I have made (it)
31. 9 I have made him fair by the multitude of
35. 14 When the whole earth rejoiceth, I will m.
37. 19 make them one stick, and they shall be
37. 22 I will make them one nation in the land
40. 14 He made also posts of threescore cubits
43. 27 the priests shall make your burnt offerings
Dan. 11. 6 shall come to the king..to make an agre.
Hos. 8. 4 their gold have they made them idols
8. 6 the workman made it; therefore it (is) not
13. 2 have made them molten images of their
Amos 4. 13 that maketh the morning darkness, and
5. 8 that maketh the seven stars and Orion
5. 26 the star of your god, which ye made to
9. 14 they shall also make gardens, and eat the
Jon. 1. 9 God..which hath made the sea and the
4. 5 made him a booth, and sat under it in the
Mic. 1. 8 I will make a wailing like the dragons
Nah. 1. 8 he will make an utter end of the place
1. 9 he will make an utter end: affliction sh.
Hab. 1. 14 makest men as the fishes of the sea, as the
2. 18 that..trusteth therein, to make dumb id.?
Zeph. 1. 18 he shall make even a speedy riddance of
Zech. 6. 11 take silver and gold, and make crowns
10. 1 LORD shall make bright clouds, and give
Mal. 2. 15 And did not he make one? Yet had he
3. 17 in that day when I make up my jewels

12. *To ponder*, פָּלַס *palas*, 3.
Psa. 78. 50 He made a way to his anger; he spared

13. *To work, make*, פָּעַל *paal.*
Exod 15. 17 thou hast made for thee to dwell in; (in)
Psa. 7. 15 and is fallen into the ditch (which) he m.
Prov 16. 4 The LORD hath made all (things) for
Isa. 44. 15 he maketh a god, and worshippeth (it)

14. *To give a charge*, פָּקַד *paqad.*
Deut 20. 9 they shall make captains of the armies

15. *To give a charge*, פָּקַד *paqad*, 5
1 Ki. 11. 28 he made him ruler over all the charge of
2 Ki. 25. 23 that the king..had made Gedaliah gove.
Jer. 40. 5 whom the king hath made governor over
40. 7 had made Gedaliah..governor in the land
41. 2 whom the king..had made governor, 41.18
[*See* ruler *and* governor]

16. *To cause to rise or stand still*, קוּם *qum*, 5.
Psa. 107. 29 He maketh the storm a calm, so that the
Dan. 5. 11 made master of the magicians, astrologers

17. *To set, put, lay*, שׂוּם שִׂים *sum, sim.*
Gen. 13. 16 I will make thy seed as the dust of the e.
21. 13 of the son of the bond woman will I make
21. 18 lift up the lad..I will make him a great
27. 37 I have made him thy lord, and all his br.
32. 12 make thy seed as the sand of the sea, w.
45. 8 he hath made me a father to Pharaoh, and
45. 9 God hath made me lord of all Egypt: come
46. 3 I will there make of thee a great nation
47. 6 then make them rulers over my cattle
47. 26 Joseph made it a law over the land of E.
48. 20 God make thee as Ephraim, and as Man.
Exod. 2. 14 Who made thee a prince and a judge over
4. 11 Who hath made man's mouth? or who m.
14. 21 LORD..made the sea dry..and the waters
15. 25 there he made for them a statute and an
Deut. 1. 13 Take..and I will make them rulers over
10. 22 hath made thee as the stars of heaven for
14. 1 nor make any baldness between your eyes
Josh. 6. 18 make the camp of Israel a curse, and tro.
8. 28 Joshua burnt Ai, and made it an heap for
Judg. 8. 33 Israel turned..and made Baal-berith their
11. 11 the people made him head and captain
1 Sa. 8. 1 that he made his sons judges over Israel
8. 5 make us a king to judge us like all the na.
18. 13 and made him his captain over a thousand
22. 7 make you all captains of thousands, and
28. 2 I make thee keeper of mine head for ever
30. 25 he made it a statute and an ordinance for
2 Sa. 7. 23 to make him a name, and to do for you
15. 4 Oh that I were made judge in the land
17. 25 Absalom made Amasa captain of the host
23. 5 he hath made with me an everlasting co.
1 Ki. 10. 9 therefore made he thee king, to do judg.
19. 2 if I make not thy life as the life of one of
20. 34 and thou shalt make streets for thee in D
20. 34 in Damascus as my father made in Sam.
2 Ki. 10. 27 and made it a draught house unto this day
13. 7 had made them like the dust by threshing
1 Ch. 17. 21 to make thee a name of greatness and te.
26. 10 Simri..yet his father made him the chief
Job 1. 17 The Chaldeans made out three bands, and
18. 2 How long (will it be ere) ye make an end
24. 25 who will make me a liar, and make my
31. 24 If I have made gold my hope, or have said
38. 9 When I made the cloud the garment the.
39. 6 Whose house I have made the wilderness
41. 31 he maketh the sea like a pot of ointment
Psa. 18. 43 thou hast made me the head of the hea.

Psa. 39. 8 make me not the reproach of the foolish
40. 4 Blessed (is) that man that maketh the L.
44. 13 Thou makest us a reproach to our neigh.
44. 14 Thou makest us a byword among the h.
46. 8 what desolations he hath made in the ea.
52. 7 Lo..the man (that) made not God his st.
66. 2 Sing forth the honour of his name; make
80. 6 Thou makest us a strife unto our neigh.
89. 29 His seed also will I make..for ever, and
91. 9 Because thou hast made the LORD..thy
104. 3 who maketh the clouds his chariot; who
105. 21 He made him lord of his house, and ruler
107. 41 and maketh (him) families like a flock
147. 14 He maketh peace (in) thy borders..filleth
Prov. 30. 26 yet make they their houses in the rocks
Song 1. 6 they made me the keeper of the vineyards
6. 12 my soul made me (like) the chariots of A.
Isa. 3. 7 saying..make me not a ruler of the peo.
14. 17 made the world as a wilderness, and des.
14. 23 I will also make it a possession for the
25. 2 For thou hast made of a city an heap; (of)
27. 9 when he maketh all the stones of the a.
28. 15 we have made lies our refuge, and under
41. 15 I will make thee a new sharp threshing
41. 15 small, and shalt make the hills as chaff
41. 18 I will make the wilderness a pool of wa.
42. 15 I will make the rivers islands, and I will
42. 16 I will make darkness light before them
43. 19 I will even make a way in the wilderness
49. 2 he hath made my mouth like a sharp sw.
49. 2 he hid me, and made me a polished shaft
49. 11 I will make all my mountains a way, and
50. 2 I make the rivers a wilderness: their fish
50. 3 heavens..I make sackcloth their covering
51. 3 he will make her wilderness like Eden, and
51. 10 hath made the depths of the sea a way for
53. 10 when thou shalt make his soul an offering
54. 12 I will make thy windows of agates, and thy
60. 15 I will make thee an eternal excellency, a
60. 17 I will also make thy officers peace, and
62. 7 till he make Jerusalem a praise in the e.
Jer. 2. 7 and made mine heritage an abomination
4. 7 he is gone forth from his place to make
6. 8 lest I make thee desolate, a land not in.
10. 22 to make the cities of Judah desolate..a
12. 11 They have made it desolate..desolate it
17. 5 Cursed (be) the man that..maketh flesh
18. 16 To make their land desolate..a perpetual
19. 8 I will make this city desolate, and an hi.
25. 9 and make them an astonishment, and an
25. 12 and will make it perpetual desolations
29. 22 LORD make thee like Zedekiah, and like A.
31. 21 make thee high heaps: set thine heart to.
51. 29 to make the land of Babylon a desolation
Lam. 3. 11 pulled me in pieces: he hath made me d.
3. 45 Thou hast made us..the offscouring and
Eze. 19. 5 took another of her whelps..made him
20. 28 there also they made their sweet savour
Hos. 2. 3 make her as a wilderness, and set her like
2. 12 I will make them a forest, and the beasts
Amos 8. 10 I will make it as the mourning of an only
Mic. 1. 6 I will make Samaria as an heap of the fi.
4. 7 I will make her that halted a remnant
4. 13 I will make thine horn iron, and I will m.
Nah. 1. 14 I will make thy grave; for thou art vile
Hab. 3. 19 he will make my feet like hinds' (feet)
Zeph. 2. 13 And he..will make Nineveh a desolation
Hag. 2. 23 will make thee as a signet: for I have ch
Zech. 7. 12 they made their hearts..an adamant stone
9. 13 made thee as the sword of a mighty man
10. 3 hath made them as his goodly horse in the
12. 2 I will make Jerusalem a cup of trembling
12. 3 in that day will I make Jerusalem a bur.
12. 6 In that day will I make the governors of

18. *To set, place*, שׂוּם *sum.*
Ezra 5. 13 made a decree to build this house of God
5. 14 Sheshbazzar, whom he had made governor
6. 1 Then Darius the king made a decree, and
6. 3 Cyrus the king made a decree (concerning)
6. 8 I make a decree what ye shall do to the
6. 11 I have made a decree, that whosoever s.
6. 12 I Darius have made a decree; let it be d.
7. 13 I make a decree, that all they of the peo.
7. 21 I..do make a decree to all the treasurers
Dan. 3. 10 Thou, O king, hast made a decree, that
3. 29 I make a decree, That every people, nat.
4. 6 Therefore made I a decree to bring in all
6. 26 I make a decree, That in every dominion

19. *To set, put, lay*, שִׁית *shith.*
2 Sa. 22. 12 he made darkness pavilions round about
1 Ki. 11. 34 I will make him prince all the days of his
Psa. 18. 11 He made darkness his secret place; his
21. 6 thou hast made him most blessed for ever
21. 9 Thou shalt make them as a fiery oven in
21. 12 Therefore shalt thou make them turn th.
45. 16 whom thou mayest make princes in all
83. 11 Make their nobles like Oreb and like Z.
83. 13 O my God, make them like a wheel; as the
84. 6 make it a well; the rain also filleth the
88. 8 thou hast made me an abomination unto
104. 20 Thou makest darkness, and it is night: w.
110. 1 until I make thine enemies thy foot stool
Isa. 16. 3 make thy shadow as the night in the midst
Jer. 2. 15 they made his land waste: his cities are
13. 16 he turn it..(and) make (it) gross darkness
22. 6 surely I will make thee a wilderness..ci.
50. 3 which shall make her land desolate, and
51. 39 In their heat I will make their feasts, and

20. *To dig, prepare*, כָּרָה *karah.*
2 Ch. 16. 14 in his own sepulchres, which he had made

Psa. 7. 15 He made a pit, and digged it, and is fallen

21. *To loose, unloose*, נָתַר *nathar*, 5.
2 Sa. 22. 33 God (is) my strength..he maketh my way

22. *To put, set, or lay out throughout*, διατίθεμαι.
Acts 3. 25 of the covenant which God made with our
Heb. 8. 10 this (is) the covenant that I will make 10; 16

23. *To give*, δίδωμι *didomi*, 2 Th. 3. 9; Rev. 3. 9.

24. *To make an end of*, ἐπιτελέω *epiteleō.*
Heb. 8. 5 when he was about to make the tabern.

25. *To be*, εἰμί *eimi.*
Mark 12. 42 threw in two mites, which make a farthing

26. *To set down*, καθίστημι *kathistēmi.*
Matt 24. 45 whom his lord hath made ruler over his
24. 47 he shall make him ruler over all his goods
25. 21, 23 I will make thee ruler over many things
Luke 12. 14 Man, who made me a judge or a divider
12. 42 lord shall make ruler over his household
12. 44 he will make him ruler over all that he
Acts 7. 10 he made him governor over Egypt and all
7. 27, 35 Who made thee a ruler and a judge?
Rom. 5. 19 For as by one..many were made sinners
5. 19 by the obedience of one shall many be m.
Heb. 7. 28 the law maketh men high priests which
2 Pe. 1. 8 they make..neither..barren nor unfruit.

27. *To prepare thoroughly*, κατασκευάζω *kataskeuazō.*
Heb. 9. 2 For there was a tabernacle made; the first

28. *To make, found*, κτίζω *ktizō.*
Eph. 2. 15 to make in himself of twain one new man

29. *To do, make*, ποιέω *poieō.*
Matt. 3. 3 the way of the Lord, make his paths str.
4. 19 Follow me..I will make you fishers of men
5. 36 thou canst not make one hair white or b.
12. 16 charged..they should not make him kn.
12. 33 make the tree good..or..make the tree c.
17. 4 let us make here three tabernacles; one
19. 4 he which [made]..at the beginning made
20. 12 thou hast made them equal unto us, which
21. 13 My house..ye have made it a den of thi.
22. 2 a certain king, which made a marriage for
23. 15 to make one proselyte; and when he is m.
23. 15 ye make him twofold more the child of h.
25. 16 with the same, and [made]..other five ta.
Mark 1. 3 Prepare ye the way of the Lord, make his
1. 17 I will make you to become fishers of men
3. 12 charged..they should not make him known
6. 21 Herod, on his birthday made a supper to
7. 37 he maketh both the deaf to hear, and the
8. 25 [made him look up]: and he was restored
9. 5 let us make three tabernacles; one for thee
10. 6 from the beginning..God made them male
11. 17 My house..ye have made it a den of thieves
Luke 3. 4 Prepare ye the way of the Lord, make his
5. 29 Levi made him a great feast in his own h.
5. 33 fast often, and make prayers, and likewise
5. 34 Can ye make the children of the bride ch.
9. 33 let us make three tabernacles; one for
11. 40 did not he that made that..without make
14. 12 When thou makest a dinner or a supper
14. 13 when thou makest a feast, call the poor
14. 16 A certain man made a great supper, and
15. 19 no more..make me as one of thy hired se.
16. 9 Make to yourselves friends of the mammon
19. 46 My house..ye have made it a den of thieves
John 2. 15 when he had made a scourge of small cords
2. 16 make not my Father's house an house of
4. 1 that Jesus made and baptized more disc.
4. 46 Cana of Galilee, where he made the water
5. 11 He that made me whole, the same said
5. 15 it was Jesus which had made him whole
5. 18 God was his Father, making himself equal
6. 10 And Jesus said, Make the men sit down
6. 15 come and take him by force, to make him
7. 23 I have made a man every whit whole on
8. 53 the prophets are dead: whom makest thou
9. 6 he spat on the ground, and made clay of
9. 11 Jesus made clay, and anointed mine eyes
9. 14 Jesus made the clay, and opened his eyes
10. 33 that thou, being a man, makest thyself G.
12. 2 There they made him a supper; and Ma.
14. 23 we will come unto him, and make our ab.
18. 18 had made a fire of coals; for it was cold
19. 7 because he made himself the Son of God
19. 12 whosoever maketh himself a king speak.
19. 23 took his garments, and made four parts
Acts 1. 1 The former treatise have I made, O The.
2. 36 God hath made that same Jesus, whom ye
3. 12 or holiness we had made this man to w.?
4. 24 Lord, thou (art) God, which hast made h.
7. 40 Saying unto Aaron, Make us gods to go be.
7. 43 figures which ye made to worship them
7. 44 should make it according to the fashion
7. 50 Hath not my hand made all these things?
8. 2 devout men..made great lamentation over
9. 39 the coats and garments which Dorcas m.
14. 15 unto the living God, which made heaven
17. 24 God that made the world and all things
17. 26 hath made of one blood all nations of men
19. 24 which made silver shrines for Diana, br.
23. 13 they were more than forty which had m.
Rom. 1. 9 that without ceasing I make mention of
9. 20 say to him..Why hast thou made me thus?
9. 21 to make one vessel unto honour, and an.
9. 28 a short work will the Lord make upon the
13. 14 make not provision for the flesh, to..the
15. 26 to make a certain contribution for the p.
1 Co. 6. 15 and make (them) the members of an har.
10. 13 make a way to escape, that ye may be able

2 Co. 5. 21 he hath made him..sin for us, who knew
Eph. 1. 16 thanks..making mention of you in my pr.
2. 14 he is our peace, who hath made both one
2. 15 of twain one new man, (so) making peace
4. 16 maketh increase of the body unto the edi.
Phil. 1. 4 Always..for you all making request with
1 Th. 1. 2 always..making mention of you in our p.
1 Ti. 2. 1 prayers, intercessions..be made for all m.
Phil. 4 making mention of thee always in my pr.
Heb. 1. 2 heir of all things, by whom also he made
1. 7 Who maketh his angels spirits, and his
8. 5 thou make all things according to the pa.
8. 9 the covenant that I made with their fat.
12. 13 make straight paths for your feet, lest that
12. 27 that are shaken, as of things that are m.
Jas. 3. 18 is sown in peace of them that make peace
2 Pe. 1. 10 to make your calling and election sure: for
1 Jo. 1. 10 we make him a liar, and his word is not
5. 10 he that believeth not God hath made him
Rev. 1. 6 hath made us kings and priests unto God
3. 9 I will make them to come and worship be.
3. 12 Him that overcometh will I make a pillar
5. 10 hast made us unto our God kings and pr.
11. 7 the beast..shall make war against them
12. 17 went to make war with the remnant of
13. 7 [it was given unto him to make war with]
13. 13 [he maketh] fire come down from heaven
13. 14 they should make an image to the beast
14. 7 worship him that made heaven, and earth
17. 16 shall make her desolate and naked, and
19. 19 gathered together to make war against h.
21. 5 Behold, I make all things new. And he
22. 15 and whosoever loveth and maketh a lie

30. *To hand forth*, προχειρίζομαι *procheirizomai.*
Acts 26. 16 to make thee a minister and a witness

31. *To speak, utter*, ἐρῶ *erō.*
Gal. 3. 16 Now to Abraham..were the promises m.

32. *To place together, set*, συνίστημι *sunistēmi.*
Gal. 2. 18 if I build..I make myself a transgressor

33. *To end with, accomplish*, συντελέω *sunteleō.*
Heb. 8. 8 when I will make a new covenant with

34. *To set, put, lay*, τίθημι *tithēmi.*
Matt22. 44 Sit..till I make thine enemies thy foots.?
Mark12. 36 Sit..till I make thine enemies thy footst.
Luke20. 43 Till I make thine enemies thy footstool
Acts 2. 35 Until I make thy foes thy footstool
20. 28 the Holy Ghost hath made you overseers
Rom. 4. 17 I have made thee a father of many nati.
1 Co. 9. 18 I may make the gospel of Christ without
Heb. 1. 13; 10. 13; 2 Pe 2. 6.

35 *To cast or put together*, συμβάλλω εἰς, Lu. 14. 31

[*See also* Abhorred, abide, abominable, about, account of, accursed, ado, affected, afraid, alive, ashamed, astonished, amazed, amends, appointment, approach, atonement, bald, banquet, bear, beams, bed, better, bitter, boast, boil, brick, bright, bring forth, broad, cakes, calf, cease, cheerful, childless, clean, cleave, come up, confession, conspiracy, consume, count, crooked, cry, dark, deep, defence, desolate, differ, difference, distribution, doubt, drink, drunk, drunken, dry, dust, dwell, eat, empty, end, endanger, enjoy, enquiry, equal, err, eunuch, excuse, fail, fall, fast, fat, few, firm, first born, fit, flee, flourish, fly, fold, foolish, fools, forget, free, fret, friend, friendship with, fruitful, full, gain, glad, glorious, go, go forth, go over, go up, good, goodly, great, great man, grievous, grow, hard, haste, hear, heard, heavy, hedge, high, honourable, hope, howl, increase, inhabited, inherit, inquisition, intercession, invasion, journey, joyful, joyful noise, keep (house), king, kneel down, know, known, labour, lament, large, league, liar, lie down, light, lighter, like, long, lower, many, marriages, matter, meet, melody, melt, mention, mention of, merchandise, merry, mirth, mock, more, move, multiply, murmur, naked, nest, noise, obedient, obeisance, obstinate, odious, offend, offender, oil, old, oration, overflow, overseer, pass, pass by, pay, payment, peace, perfect, perish, plain, plenteous, poor, possess, prayer, precious, preparation, princes, proclamation, promise, prosper, prosperous, provision, queen, ready, reconciliation, refuge, reign, rejoice, remembered, rent, request, rest, restitution, return, rich, ride, rise up, rode, room, rot, rule, ruler, run away, rushing, sad, search, see, separation, serve, servants, shake, show, shine, shipwreck, signs, sin, singular, skip, slaughter, sleep, sit down, sit together, small, soft, sore, sorry, sound, speed, spoil, sport, stagger, stand, stiff, stink, stoop, straight, strange, strong, stronger, suck, subject, suddenly, suit, supplication, sure, swear, sweet, swell, swim, tinkling, transgress, treasurer, tremble, trouble, trust, tumult, turn, understand, uproar, vain, vile, void, walk, wander, war, waste, weak, weary, which, white, whole, wide, willing, wise, wiser, wonderful, wonderfully.]

MAKE as though, to —
To make toward, προσποιέομαι *prospoieomai.*
Luke24. 28 he made as though he would have gone

MAKE away, utterly to —
To devote (to God by destruction), חָרַם *charam*, 5.
Dan. 11. 44 to destroy, and utterly to make away m.

MAKE (baldness), to —
To make bald, קָרַח *qarach.*
Lev 21. 5 They shall not make baldness upon their

MAKE (bed), to —
1. *To turn over, change*, הָפַךְ *haphak.*
Psa. 41. 3 thou wilt make all his bed in his sickness

2. *To spread out*, רָפַד *raphad*, 3.
Job 17. 13 If I wait..I have made my bed in the da.

MAKE (breach), to —
To break forth, פָּרַץ *parats.*
2 Sa. 6. 8 the LORD had made a breach upon Uzzah
1 Ch.13. 11 the LORD had made a breach upon Uzza
15. 13 LORD our God made a breach upon us, for

MAKE (brick), to
To make brick, לָבַן *laben.*
Gen. 11. 3 let us make brick, and burn them thro.
Exod. 5. 7 no more..give straw to make brick, as

MAKE(burning)to —
To make a burning, שָׂרַף *saraph.*
2 Ch.16. 14 and they made a very great burning for

MAKE cakes, to —
To make cakes לָבַב *labab*, 3.
2 Sa. 13. 6 make me a couple of cakes in my sight
13. 8 made cakes in his sight, and did bake the

MAKE choice, to —
To lay or choose out, ἐκλέγομαι *eklegomai.*
Acts 15. 7 how that a good while ago God made ch.

MAKE (conspiracy), to —
To conspire, bind together, קָשַׁר *qashar.*
2 Ki.12. 20 his servants arose, and made a conspiracy
14 19 they made a conspiracy against him in J.
15. 15 Shallum, and his conspiracy which he m.
15. 30 Hoshea..made a conspiracy against Pek.
2 Ch 25. 27 they made a conspiracy against him in J.

MAKE (covenant or league), to —
To cut or prepare, כָּרַת *karath.*
Gen. 15. 18 the LORD made a covenant with Abram
21. 27 gave..and both of them made a covenant
21. 32 Thus they made a covenant at Beer-sheba
26. 28 said..let us make a covenant with thee
31. 44 let us make a covenant, I and thou; and
Exod23. 32 Thou shalt make no covenant with them
24. 8 of the covenant, which the LORD hath m.
34. 10 I make a covenant: before all thy people
34. 12, 15 lest thou make a covenant with the in.
34. 27 I have made a covenant with thee and
Deut. 4. 23 lest ye forget the covenant of the LORD
5. 2 LORD our God made a covenant with us
5. 3 LORD made not this covenant with our
7. 2 thou shalt make no covenant with them
9. 9 of the covenant which the LORD made
29. 1 covenant..LORD commanded Moses to m.
29. 1 the covenant which he made with them
29. 12 covenant..which the LORD..maketh with
29. 14 Neither with you only do I make this co.
29. 25 have forsaken the covenant..he made
31. 16 break my covenant which I have made
Josh. 9. 6, 11 now therefore make ye a league with
9. 7 and how shall we make a league with you?
9. 15 made a league with them, to let them live
9. 16 after they had made a league with them
24. 25 Joshua made a covenant with the people
Judg 2. 2 ye shall make no league with the inhabi.
1 Sa. 11. 1 Make a covenant with us, and we will se.
11. 2 On this..will I make (a covenant) with you
18. 3 Then Jonathan and David made a coven.
20. 16 So Jonathan made (a covenant) with the
23. 18 they two made a covenant before the LORD
2 Sa. 3. 12 Make thy league with me, and, behold, my
3. 13 I will make a league with thee: but one
3. 21 that they may make a league with thee
5. 3 David made a league with them in Heb.
1 Ki. 5. 12 and they two made a league together
8. 9 when the LORD made (a covenant) with
8. 21 the ark, wherein (is) the covenant..he ma.
20. 34 he made a covenant with him, and sent
2 Ki. 11. 4 made a covenant with them, and took an
11. 17 Jehoiada made a covenant between the L.
17. 15 they rejected..his covenant that he made
17. 35 With whom the LORD had made a coven.
17. 38 the covenant that I have made with you
23. 3 made a covenant before the LORD, to walk
1 Ch.11 3 David made a covenant with them in Heb.
16. 16 (Even of the covenant) which he made
2 Ch. 5. 10 when the LORD made (a covenant) with
6. 11 covenant of the LORD, that he made with
21. 7 because of the covenant that he had made
23 3 all the congregation made a covenant with
23. 16 Jehoiada made a covenant between him
29. 10 to make a covenant with the LORD God
34. 31 made a covenant before the LORD, to walk
Ezra 10. 3 let us make a covenant with our God to
Neh. 9. 8 madest a covenant with him, to give the
9. 38 because of all this we make a sure (coven)
Job 31. 1 I made a covenant with mine eyes; why
41. 4 Will he make a covenant with thee? wilt
Psa. 50 5 that have made a covenant with me by sa.
89. 3 I have made a covenant with my chosen
105. 9 Which (covenant) he made with Abraham
Isa. 28. 15 We have made a covenant with death, and
55. 3 I will make an everlasting covenant with
57. 8 and made thee (a covenant) with them
61. 8 I will make an everlasting covenant with
Jer. 11. 10 have broken my covenant which I made
31. 31 I will make a new covenant with the ho.
31. 32 Not according to the covenant that I made
31. 33 the covenant that I will make with the
32. 40 I will make an everlasting covenant with
34. 8 Zedekiah had made a covenant with all
34. 13 I made a covenant with your fathers in
34. 15 ye had made a covenant before me in the
34. 18 words of the covenant which they had m.

Eze. 17. 13 made a covenant with him, and hath ta.
34. 25 I will make with them a covenant of peace
37. 26 I will make a covenant of peace with them
Hos. 2. 18 in that day will I make a covenant for
10. 4 swearing falsely in making a covenant
12. 1 they do make a covenant with the Assy.
Zech.11. 10 I might break my covenant which I..m.

MAKE (cuttings), to —
To cut in, make an incision, שָׂרַט *sarat.*
Lev. 21. 5 They shall not..make any cuttings in their

MAKE (ensample), to —
To give, δίδωμι *didōmi.*
2 Th. 3. 9 to make ourselves an ensample unto you
Rev. 3. 9 I will make them of the synagogue of Sa.

MAKE for, things which —
The things, τά *ta.*
Rom.14. 19 follow after the things which make for p.

MAKE full (proof) of, to —
To bear on fully, πληροφορέω *plērophoreō.*
2 Ti. 4. 5 watch thou..make full proof of thy min.

MAKE glorious, to —
To make honourable or glorious, δοξάζω *doxazō.*
2 Co. 3. 10 even that which was made glorious had

MAKE (go) up and down, to —
To move, shake, stagger, wander, נוּעַ *nua.*
2 Sa. 15. 20 should I..make thee go up and down with

MAKE (interpretations), to —
To interpret, פְּשַׁר *peshar.*
Dan. 5. 16 thou canst make interpretations, and dis.

MAKE (a king), to —
To make a king, cause to reign, מָלַךְ *malak*, 5.
1 Sa. 8. 22 LORD said. Hearken..and make them a ki.
12. 1 I have hearkened..and have made a king

MAKE mad, to —
To turn round to raving, περιτρέπω εἰς μανίαν.
Acts 26. 24 Paul..much learning doth make thee m.

MAKE merchandise, to —
To travel, traffic, cheat, ἐμπορεύομαι *emporeuomai.*
2 Pe. 2. 3 with feigned words make merchandise of

MAKE (noise), to —
To cause to hear or be heard, שָׁמַע *shamea*, 5.
Josh. 6. 10 ye shall not..make any noise with your

MAKE (ointment), to —
To mix, compound, רָקַח *raqach.*
1 Ch. 9. 30 the priests made the ointment of the sp

MAKE out, to —
To set, place, lay, שִׂים, שׂוּם *sum, sim.*
Job 1. 17 The Chaldeans made out three bands, and

MAKE peace, to —
To make peace, εἰρηνοποιέω *eirēnopoieō.*
Col. 1. 20 having made peace through the blood of

MAKE perfect, to —
To make an end of, perfect, ἐπιτελέω *epiteleō.*
Gal. 3. 3 Are ye so foolish?..are ye now made per.

MAKE (petition), to —
To request, pray, seek, בְּעָא *bea.*
Dan. 6. 13 but maketh his petition three times a day

MAKE (prayer or supplication), to —
1. *To entreat grace or favour*, חָנַן *chanan*, 7.
1 Ki. 9. 3 and thy supplication that thou hast made

2. *To judge for oneself*, פָּלַל *palal*, 7.
1 Ki. 8 29 the prayer which thy servant shall make
2 Ch. 6. 21 supplications..which they shall make to.

MAKE ready, to —
1. *Finished, perfect, whole*, שָׁלֵם *shalem.*
1 Ki. 6. 7 of stone made ready before it was brou.

2. *To make ready*, ἑτοιμάζω *hetoimazō.*
Matt26. 19 And the disciples..made ready the pass.
Mark14. 15 large upper room..there make ready for
14. 16 And his disciples..made ready the pass.
Luke 1. 17 to make ready a people prepared for the
9. 52 they went..into a village..to make ready
17. 8; 22. 12; 22. 13; Acts 23. 23; Rev. 19. 7.

MAKE up beforehand —
To make fully ready beforehand, προκαταρτίζω.
2 Co. 9. 5 and make up beforehand your bounty

MAKE self —
[*See* Fair, known, many, poor, prey, prince, prophet, rich, sick, strong, unclean, wise.]

MAKE (slaughter), to —
To smite, נָכָה *nakah*, 5.
1 Sa. 14. 14 that first slaughter which Jonathan..ma.

MAKE to rise, to —
To rise or spring up, raise, ἀνατέλλω *anatellō.*
Matt. 5. 45 he maketh his sun to rise on the evil and

MAKE toward, to —
To hold down, κατέχω *katechō.*
Acts 27. 40 unto the sea..and made toward shore

MAKE up, to —
1. *To hedge about, make a hedge,* גָּדַר *gadar.*
Eze. 13. 5 neither made up the hedge for the house
22. 30 for a man..that should make up the he.
2. *To perfect, finish, complete,* כְּלַל *kelal,* 5a.
Ezra 5. 3 Who hath commanded..to make up this
5. 9 Who commanded you..to make up these
MAKE (vow), to —
To vow, נָדַר *nadar.*
Jon. 1. 16 a sacrifice unto the LORD, and made vows
MAKE (wall), to —
To hedge, hedge about, גָּדַר *gadar.*
Hos. 2. 6 I will..make a wall, that she shall not find
MAKE (war), to —
To cast or throw together with, συμβάλλω *sumba.*
Luke 14. 31 Or what king, going to make war against
MAKER —
1. *Graver,* חָרָשׁ *charash.*
Isa. 45. 16 go to confusion together (that are) makers
2. *To form,* יָצַר *yatsar.*
Isa. 45. 9 Woe unto him that striveth with his mak.!
45. 11 LORD, the Holy One of Israel, and his Ma.
Hab. 2. 18 that the maker thereof hath graven it; the
2. 18 that the maker of his work trusteth ther.
3. *To do, make,* עָשָׂה *asah.*
Job 4. 17 shall a man be more pure than his maker?
32. 22 For..my maker would soon take me away
35. 10 But none saith, Where (is) God my maker
Psa. 95. 6 let us kneel before the LORD our maker
Prov 14. 31 oppresseth the poor reproacheth his Ma.
17. 5 mocketh the poor reproacheth his Maker
22. 2 rich and poor..the LORD (is) the maker of
Isa. 17. 7 At that day shall a man look to his Maker
22. 11 ye have not looked unto the maker the.
51. 13 forgettest the LORD thy maker, that hath
54. 5 For thy Maker (is) thine husband; The
Jer. 33. 2 Thus saith the LORD, the maker thereof
Hos. 8. 14 For Israel hath forgotten his Maker, and
4. *To work, make,* פָּעַל *paal.*
Job 36. 3 and will ascribe righteousness to my M.
5. *Worker, doer,* פֹּעַל [*paal*]; otherwise פֹּעַל *poal.*
Isa. 1. 31 and the maker of it as a spark, and they
6. *A public worker,* δημιουργός *dēmiourgos.*
Heb 11. 10 a city..whose builder and maker (is) God
MAK-HE'-LOTH, מַקְהֵלֹת *assemblies.*
The twenty-first station of Israel from Egypt. Locality uncertain.
Num 33. 25 removed from Haradah, and pitched in M.
33. 26 they removed from M., and encamped at
MAK-KE'-DAH, מַקֵּדָה *place of shepherds.*
A city twelve miles S.W. of Jerusalem, in the plain country of Judah, near Naamah; now called *Mughar.*
Josh. 10. 10 and smote them to Azekah, and unto M.
10. 16 fled, and hid themselves in a cave at M.
10. 17 The five kings..found hid in a cave at M.
10. 21 returned to the camp to Joshua at M. in
10. 28 that day Joshua took M., and smote it
10. 28 he did to the king of M. as he did unto
10. 29 Then Joshua passed from M., and all Isr.
12. 16 The king of M., one; the king of Beth-el
15. 41 Beth-dagon, and Naamah, and M.; sixt.
MAKING —
To do, make, עָשָׂה *asah.*
Eccl. 12. 12 of making many books (there is) no end
MAKING, wares of —
Work, deed, doing, מַעֲשֶׂה *maaseh.*
Eze 27. 16, 18 the multitude of the wares of thy m.
MAK'-TESH, מַכְתֵּשׁ *depression.*
A district in or near Jerusalem where merchants traded.
Zeph. 1. 11 Howl, ye inhabitants of M., for all the m.
MAL-A'-CHI, מַלְאָכִי *messenger of Jah.*
The last of the O. T. prophets. B.C. 400–300.
Mal. 1. 1 The burden of the word..to Israel by M.
MAL'-CHAM, מַלְכָּם *thinking.*
1. Son of Shaharaim, a Benjamite. B.C. 1350.
1 Ch. 8. 9 begat of Hodesh his wife..Mesha, and M.
2. An idol of the Ammonites. Supposed the same with *Molech* and *Milcom.* (Amos 1. 15.)
Zeph 1. 5 swear by the LORD, and that swear by M.
MAL-CHI'-AH, MAL-CHI'-JAH, מַלְכִּיָּה *Jah is king.*
1. A Gershonite, ancestor of Asaph, a leader of the singing in David's reign. B.C. 1015.
1 Ch. 6. 40 Michael, the son of Baaseiah..son of M.
2. An Aaronite (B.C. 630) whose descendants dwelt in Jerusalem after the captivity. B.C. 445.
1 Ch. 9. 12 the son of Pashur, the son of M., and M.
Neh. 11. 12 Zechariah, the son of Pashur..son of M.
3. The head of a family of priests when the charges of the sanctuary were assigned by lot. B.C. 1015. Perhaps the same as No. 2.
1 Ch. 24. 9 The fifth to M., the sixth to Mijamin
4. One who had taken a strange wife during or after the captivity. B.C. 456.
Ezra 10. 25 of the sons of Parosh; Ramiah..M., and
5. Another who had done the same.
Ezra 10. 25 Miamin, and Eleazar, and M., and Bena.
6. Another who had done the same.
Ezra 10. 31 Eliezer, Ishijah, M., Shemaiah, Shimeon
7. One who assisted in reparing the wall after the captivity. B.C. 456. May be the same as No 6.
Neh. 3. 11 M...son of Harim, and Hashub..son of P.
8. One of the Rechab family, who did the same.
Neh. 3. 14 But the dung gate repaired M. the son of
9. Another who did the same. May be the same as No. 7 or 8.
Neh. 3. 31 After him repaired M. the goldsmith's son
10. A prince or Levite who stood beside Ezra while he read the law. B.C. 445.
Neh. 8. 4 on his left hand..M., and Hashum, and
11. A priest who assisted in purifying the wall of Jerusalem. B.C. 445.
Neh. 10. 3 Pashur, Amariah, M.
12. 42 Jehohanan, and M., and Elam, and Ezer
12. Father of Pashur whom Zedekiah sent to Jeremiah to consult the Lord B.C. 630.
Jer. 21. 1 Pashur the son of Melchiah, and
38. 1 Pashur the son of M., heard the words
MAL-CHI'-EL, מַלְכִּיאֵל *God is a king.*
A son of Beriah, son of Asher. B.C. 1660.
Gen. 46. 17 and the sons of Beriah; Heber and M.
Num 26. 45 Of the sons of Beriah..of M., the family
1 Ch. 7. 31 sons of Beriah; Heber, and M., who (is)
MAL-CHI-EL-ITES, מַלְכִּיאֵלִי.
The descendants of the preceding.
Num 26. 45 the sons of..Malchiel, the family of the M.
MAL-CHI'-RAM, מַלְכִּירָם *my king is exalted.*
Son or grandson of Jeconiah, son of Jehoiakim king of Judah. B.C. 580.
1 Ch. 3. 18 M. also, and Pedaiah, and Shenazar, Jec.
MAL-CHI'-SHUA—See *Melchi-shua.*
MAL'-CHUS, Μάλχος *counsellor.*
A servant of the high priest whose ear Peter cut off, but who was healed by Jesus.
John 18. 10 the high priest's..servant's name was M.
MALE —
1. *A male,* זָכוּר *zakur.*
Exod 23. 17 Three times in the year all thy males sh.
Deut 16. 16 Three times in a year shall all thy males
20. 13 thou shalt smite every male thereof with
2. *A man, individual,* אִישׁ *ish.*
Gen. 7. 2 the male and his female..the male and
3. *Male,* זָכָר *zakar.*
Gen. 1. 27 God..male and female created he them
5. 2 Male and female created he them; and
6. 19 with thee; they shall be male and female
7. 3 the male and the female; to keep seed
7. 9 went in two and two..the male and the
7. 16 went in male and female of all flesh, as
17. 23 every male among the men of Abraham's
34. 15 If ye will be as we..that every male of
34. 22 if every male among us be circumcised
34. 24 every male was circumcised, all that w.
34. 25 came upon the city..and slew all the m.
Exod 12. 5 a male of the first year: ye shall take (it)
12. 48 let all his males be circumcised, and then
13. 12 every firstling..the males (shall be) the L.
13. 15 all that openeth the matrix, being males
Lev. 1. 3 let him offer a male without blemish: he
1. 10 he shall bring it a male without blemish
3. 1 whether (it be) a male or female, he shall
3. 6 male or female, he shall offer it without
4. 23 he shall bring..a kid..a male without ble.
6. 18 All the males among the children of Aaron
6. 29 All the males among the priests shall eat
7. 6 Every male among the priests shall eat
12. 7 for her that hath born a male or a female
22. 19 at your own will a male without blemish
27. 3 the male from twenty years old even unto
27. 5, 6 then thy estimation shall be of the male
27. 7 if (it be) a male, then thy estimation shall
Num. 1. 2 Take ye the sum..every male by their p.
1. 20, 22 every male from twenty years old and
3. 15 every male from a month old and upward
3. 22 according to the number of all the males
3. 28, 34, 39 all the males, from a month old and
3. 40 Number all the first born of the males of
3. 43 all the first born males by the number of
5. 3 Both male and female shall ye put out
18. 10 every male shall eat it: it shall be holy
26. 62 all males from a month old and upward
31. 7 they warred..and they slew all the males
31. 17 kill every male among the little ones, and
Deut. 4. 16 any figure, the likeness of male or female
15. 19 All the firstling males that come of thy h.
Josh. 5. 4 males, (even) all the men of war, died in
17. 2 the male children of Manasseh the son of
Judg 21. 11 Ye shall utterly destroy every male, and
21. 12 had known no man by lying with any m.
1 Ki. 11. 15 after he had smitten every male in Edom
11. 16 until he had cut off every male in Edom
2 Ch. 31. 16 Besides their genealogy of males, from thr.
31. 19 to give portions to all the males among
Ezra 8. 3 were reckoned by genealogy of the males
8. 4, 5, 6, 7, 8, 9, 10, 11, 12 and with him..m.
8. 13 last sons..and with them threescore m.
8. 14 the sons also..and with them seventy m.
Mal. 1. 14 which hath in his flock a male, and voweth
4. *A male,* ἄρσην *arsēn.*
Matt 19. 4 at the beginning made them male and fe.
Mark 10. 6 But..God made them male and female
Luke 2. 23 Every male that openeth the womb shall
Gal. 3. 28 there is neither male nor female: for ye
MALEFACTOR —
1. *Evil doer,* κακοποιός *kakopoios.*
John 18. 30 If he were not a malefactor, we would not
2. *Evil worker,* κακοῦργος *kakourgos.*
Luke 23. 32 there were also two others, malefactors
23. 33 there they crucified him, and the malefa.
23. 39 one of the malefactors which were hanged
MA-LE-LE'-EL, Μαλελεήλ—See *Mahalaleel.*
Luke 3. 37 Jared, which was (the son) of M., which
MALICE, MALICIOUSNESS —
Evil, badness, κακία *kakia.*
Rom. 1. 29 Being filled with all..maliciousness; full
1 Co. 5. 8 neither with the leaven of malice and w.
14. 20 in malice be ye children, but in underst.
Eph. 4. 31 all..be put away from you, with all mal.
Col. 3. 8 also put off all these; anger, wrath, mal.
Titus 3. 3 living in malice and envy, hateful..hating
1 Pe. 2. 1 laying aside all malice, and all guile, and
2. 16 for a cloke of maliciousness, but as the
MALICIOUS —
Laborious, evil, πονηρός *ponēros.*
3 John 10 prating against us with malicious words
MALIGNITY —
Evil disposition, κακοήθεια *kakoētheia.*
Rom. 1. 29 full of envy..deceit, malignity; whisperers
MAL-LO'-THI, מַלּוֹתִי *Jah is speaking, or splendid.*
One of the sons of Heman, set over the service of song. B.C. 1015.
1 Ch. 25. 4 the sons of Heman, Joshbekashah, M.
25. 26 The nineteenth to M., (he), his sons, and
MAL'-LUCH, מַלּוּךְ *counsellor.*
1. A Merarite whose descendant Ethan was set over the service of song by David. B.C. 1015.
1 Ch. 6. 44 son of Kishi, the son of Abdi, the son of M.
2. A son of Bani who had taken a strange wife. B.C. 456.
Ezra 10. 29 the sons of Bani; Meshullam, M., and A.
3. One of the family of Harim that had done the same.
Ezra 10. 32 Benjamin, M., (and) Shemariah
4. A priest who, with Nehemiah, sealed the covenant. B.C. 445.
Neh. 10. 4 Hattush, Shebaniah, M.
12. 2 Amariah, M., Hattush
5. A chief of the people that did the same.
Neh. 10. 27 M., Harim, Baanah
MALLOWS —
Salt plant מַלּוּחַ *malluach.*
Job 30. 4 Who cut up mallows by the bushes, and
MAMMON —
Wealth, riches, μαμμωνᾶς *mammōnas* (Aram. מָמוֹן).
Matt. 6. 24 No man..Ye cannot serve God and mam.
Luke 16. 9 Make to yourselves friends of the mam.
16. 11 not been faithful in the unrighteous ma.
16. 13 No..Ye cannot serve God and mammon
MAM'-RE, מַמְרֵא *firmness, vigour.*
1. A place, two miles N. of Hebron, with oaks; now *Rameh* or *Ramel*
Gen. 13. 18 Abram..came and dwelt in the plain of M.
18. 1 the LORD appeared..in the plains of M.
23. 17 Machpelah, which (was) before M., the fi.
23. 19 cave of the field of Machpelah before M.
25. 9 cave of Machpelah..which (is) before M.
35. 27 Jacob came..unto M., unto the city of A.
49. 30 field of Machpelah, which (is) before M.
50. 13 cave of the field of Machpelah..before M.
2. An Amorite, confederate with Abraham.
Gen. 14. 13 he dwelt in the plain of M. the Amorite
14. 24 Save only..the portion of..Eschol, and M.
MAN, (man's, of) —
1. *A man, human being,* אָדָם *adam.*
Gen. 1. 26 Let us make man in our image, after our
1. 27 So God created man in his (own) image
2. 5 and (there was) not a man to till the gro.
2. 7 God formed man (of) the dust of the gro.
2. 7 breathed..and man became a living soul
2. 8 there he put the man whom he had formed
2. 15 God took the man, and put him into the
2. 16 the LORD God commanded the man, saying
2. 18 not good that the man should be alone
2. 22 which the LORD God had taken from man
2. 22 woman, and brought her unto the man
2. 25 were both naked, the man and his wife
3. 12 man said, The woman whom thou gavest
3. 22 Behold, the man is become as one of us, to
3. 24 So he drove out the man; and he placed
5. 1 In the day that God created man, in the
6. 1 when men began to multiply on the face
6. 2 sons of God saw the daughters of men that
6. 3 My spirit shall not always strive with m.
6. 4 came in unto the daughters of men, and
6. 5 saw that the wickedness of man (was) gr.
6. 6 repented the LORD that he had made man
6. 7 I will destroy man..both man, and beast
7. 21 creepeth upon the earth, and every man

Gen. 7. 23 both man, and cattle, and the creeping
8. 21 curse the ground any more for man's sake
8. 21 for the imagination of man's heart (is) evil
9. 5 will I require it, and at the hand of man
9. 5 at the hand..will I require the life of man
9. 6 Whoso sheddeth man's blood, by man shall
9. 6 for in the image of God made he man
11. 5 tower, which the children of men builded
16. 12 he will be a wild man; his hand (will be)
Exod 4. 11 Who hath made man's mouth? or who m.
8. 17 it became lice in man and in beast; all the
8. 18 there were lice upon man and upon beast
9. 9, 10 breaking forth (with) blains upon man
9. 19 every man and beast which shall be found
9. 22 that there may be hail..upon man, and
9. 25 the hail smote..both man and beast; and
12. 12 will smite all..both man and beast; and
13. 2 whatsoever..(both) of man and of beast
13. 13 the first born of man among thy children
13. 15 both the first born of man, and the first
30. 32 Upon man's flesh shall it not be poured
33. 20 for there shall no man see me, and live
Lev. 1. 2 If any man of you bring an offering unto
5. 3 whatsoever uncleanness (it be) that a man
5. 4 that a man shall pronounce with an oath
6. 3 in any of all these that a man doeth, sin.
7. 21 the uncleanness of man, or (any) unclean
13. 2 When a man shall have in the skin of his
13. 9 When the plague of leprosy is in a man
16. 17 there shall be no man in the tabernacle
18. 5 which if a man do, he shall live in them
22. 5 a man of whom he may take uncleanness
24. 17 he that killeth any man shall surely be
24. 20 as he hath caused a blemish in a man, so
24. 21 he that killeth a man, he shall be put to
27. 28 no devoted thing that a man shall devote
27. 29 devoted, which shall be devoted of men, s.
Num. 3. 13 I hallowed..both man and beast; mine
5. 6 or woman shall commit any sin that men
8. 17 all the first born..man and beast: on
9. 6, 7 defiled by the dead body of a man
12. 3 above all the men which (were) upon the
16. 29 die the common death of all men, or if
16. 29 be visited after the visitation of all men
16. 32 the men that (appertained) unto Korah
18. 15 of men..nevertheless the first born of man
19. 11, 13 toucheth the dead body of any man
19. 14 This (is) the law, when a man dieth in a
19. 16 whosoever toucheth..a bone of a man, or
23. 19 that he should lie; neither the son of man
31. 11 they took all the spoil..of men and of b.
31. 26 Take the sum of the prey..of man and of
31. 47 Moses took one portion of fifty..of man
Deut. 4. 28 serve gods, the work of men's hands, wood
4. 32 since the day that God created man upon
5. 24 seen this day that God doth talk with man
8. 3 that man doth not live by bread only
8. 3 but by every (word)..doth man live
20. 19 for the tree of the field (is) man's (life)
Josh. 11. 14 every man they smote with the edge of
14. 15 (which Arba was) a great man among the
Judg. 16. 7, 11 shall I be weak, and be as another man
16. 17 become weak, and be like any (other) man
18. 7, 28 had no business with (any) man
1 Sa. 15. 29 for he (is) not a man, that he should repent
16. 7 not as man seeth; for man looketh on
17. 32 Let no man's heart fail because of him
24. 9 Wherefore hearest thou men's words, say.
25. 29 Yet a man is risen to pursue thee, and
26. 19 but if (they be) the children of men, cur.
2 Sa. 7. 14 with the stripes of the children of men
7. 19 (is) this the manner of man, O Lord GOD?
23. 3 He that ruleth over men (must be) just
24. 14 and let me not fall into the hand of man
1 Ki. 4. 31 For he was wiser than all men; than E.
8. 38 supplication soever be (made) by any man
8. 39 give to every man according to his ways
8. 46 for (there is) no man that sinneth not, and
13. 2 and men's bones shall be burnt upon thee
2 Ki. 7. 10 neither voice of man, but horses tied, and
19. 18 no gods, but the work of men's hands, wood
23. 14 filled their places with the bones of men
23. 20 and burned men's bones upon them, and
1 Ch. 5. 21 two thousand, and of men an hundred th.
17. 17 according to the estate of a man of high
21. 13 but let me not fall into the hand of man
29. 1 for the palace (is) not for man, but for the
2 Ch. 6. 18 will God in very deed dwell with men on
6. 29 what prayer..shall be made of any man
6. 30 render unto every man according unto all
6. 36 for (there is) no man which sinneth not
19. 6 ye judge not for man, but for the LORD
32. 19 (which were) the work of the hands of m.
Neh. 2. 10 there was come a man to seek the welfare
2. 12 neither told I (any) man what my God had
9. 29 which if a man do, he shall live in them
Job 5. 7 Yet man is born unto trouble, as the spa.
7. 20 do unto thee, O thou preserver of men?
11. 12 though man be born (like) a wild ass's colt
14. 1 Man (that is) born of a woman (is) of few
14. 10 man giveth up the ghost, and where (is)
15. 7 (Art) thou the first man (that) was born?
16. 21 Oh that one might plead..as a man..for
20. 4 Knowest thou (not) this of old, since man
20. 29 This (is) the portion of a wicked man from
21. 4 As for me, (is) my complaint to man? and
21. 33 every man shall draw after him, as (these
25. 6 How much less..the son of man, (which
27. 13 This (is) the portion of a wicked man with
28. 28 unto man he said, Behold, the fear of the
32. 21 neither..give flattering titles unto man
33. 17 That he may withdraw man (from his) p.

Job 33. 23 a messenger..to show unto man his upr.
34. 11 For the work of a man shall he render
34. 15 All flesh shall perish together, and man
34. 29 whether (it be done)..against a man only
35. 8 righteousness (may profit) the son of man
36. 25 Every man may..behold (it) afar off
36. 28 clouds do drop (and) distil upon man ab.
37. 7 He sealeth up the hand of every man; th.
38. 26 the wilderness, wherein (there is) no man
Psa. 8. 4 and the son of man, that thou visitest h.?
11. 4 behold, his eyelids try, the children of m.
12. 1 the faithful fail from..the children of m.
12. 8 The wicked walk..when the vilest men
14. 2 looked down..upon the children of men
17. 4 Concerning the works of men, by the word
21. 10 their seed from among the children of m.
22. 6 reproach of men, and despised of the pe.
31. 19 that trust in thee before the sons of men!
32. 2 Blessed (is) the man unto whom the LORD
33. 13 The LORD..beholdeth all the sons of men
36. 6 O LORD, thou preservest man and beast
36. 7 the children of men put their trust under
39. 5 man at his best state (is) altogether vanity
39. 11 like a moth: surely every man (is) vanity
45. 2 Thou art fairer than the children of men
49. 12 man (being) in honour abideth not: he is
49. 20 Man (that is) in honour, and understand.
53. 2 looked down..upon the children of men
56. 11 I will not be afraid what man can do unto
57. 4 sons of men, whose teeth (are) spears and
58. 1 do ye judge uprightly, O ye sons of men?
58. 11 So that a man shall say, Verily (there is)
60. 11 Give us help..for vain (is) the help of m.
64. 9 all men shall fear, and shall declare the
66. 5 (he is) terrible..toward..children of men
68. 18 thou hast received gifts for men; yea
73. 5 neither are they plagued like (other) men
76. 10 Surely the wrath of man shall praise thee
78. 60 forsook..tent (which) he placed among m.
80. 17 upon the son of man (whom) thou madest
82. 7 ye shall die like men, and fall like one of
84. 5 Blessed (is) the man whose strength (is)
84. 12 blessed (is) the man that trusteth in thee
89. 47 wherefore hast thou made all men in v.?
90. 3 Thou..sayest, Return, ye children of men
94. 10 he that teacheth man knowledge, (shall
94. 11 LORD knoweth the thoughts of man, that
104. 14 herb for the service of man: that he may
104. 23 Man goeth forth unto his work and to his
105. 14 He suffered no man to do them wrong; yea
107. 8, 15, 21, 31 wonderful..to..children of men!
108. 12 Give us help..for vain (is) the help of man
115. 4 silver and gold, the work of men's hands
115. 16 earth hath he given to the children of men
116. 11 I said in my haste, All men (are) liars
118. 6 I will not fear: what can man do unto
118. 8 to trust..than to put confidence in man
119. 134 Deliver me from the oppression of man
124. 2 on our side, when men rose up against us
135. 8 Who smote the first born..both of man
135. 15 silver and gold, the work of men's hands
140. 1 Deliver me, O LORD, from the evil man
144. 3 what (is) man, that thou takest knowle.
144. 4 Man is like to vanity: his days (are) as a
145. 12 To make known to the sons of men his
146. 3 Put not your trust..in the son of man, in
Prov. 3. 4 find favour..in the sight of God and man
3. 13 Happy (is) the man..and the man (that)
3. 30 Strive not with a man without cause, if he
8. 4 I call; and my voice..to the sons of man
8. 31 and my delights (were) with..sons of men
8. 34 Blessed (is) the man that heareth me, w.
11. 7 When a wicked man dieth, (his) expect.
12. 3 man shall not be established by wicked.
12. 14 the recompence of a man's hands shall be
12. 23 A prudent man concealeth knowledge
12. 27 the substance of a diligent man (is) pre.
15. 11 much more..hearts of the children of men?
15. 20 but a foolish man despiseth his mother
16. 1 The preparations of the heart in man, and
16. 9 A man's heart deviseth his way: but the
17. 18 A man void of understanding striketh
18. 16 A man's gift maketh room for him, and
19. 3 foolishness of man perverteth his way
19. 11 discretion of a man deferreth his anger
19. 22 desire of a man (is) his kindness: and a
20. 6 Most men will proclaim every one his own
20. 24 how can a man then understand his own
20. 25 (It is) a snare to the man (who) devoureth
20. 27 The spirit of man (is) the candle of the L.
21. 16 The man that wandereth out of the way
21. 20 treasure..but a foolish man spendeth it
23. 28 and increaseth the transgressors among m.
24. 9 and the scorner (is) an abomination to m.
24. 12 shall (not) he render to (every) man acco.
24. 30 vineyard of the man void of understand.
27. 19 As in water..so the heart of man to man
27. 20 so the eyes of man are never satisfied
28. 2 by a man of understanding (and) knowl.
28. 12 but when the wicked rise, a man is hidden
28. 14 Happy (is)..man that feareth alway: but
28. 17 A man that doeth violence to the blood
28. 23 He that rebuketh a man, afterwards shall
28. 28 When the wicked rise, men hide themse.
29. 23 A man's pride shall bring him low: but
29. 25 fear of man bringeth a snare: but whoso
30. 2 and have not the understanding of a man
30. 14 to devour..the needy from (among) men
Eccl. 1. 3 What profit hath a man of all his labour
1. 13 travail hath God given to the sons of man
2. 3 what (was) that good for the sons of men
2. 8 the delights of the sons of men, (as) mus.

Eccl. 2. 12 what (can) the man (do) that cometh after
2. 18 because I should leave it unto the man
2. 21 there is a man..yet to a man that hath
2. 22 For what hath man of all his labour, and
2. 24 nothing better for a man, (than) that he
2. 26 giveth to a man that (is) good in his sight
3. 10 God hath given to the sons of men to be
3. 11 so that no man can find out the work that
3. 13 also that every man should eat and drink
3. 18 concerning the estate of the sons of men
3. 19 For that which befalleth the sons of men
3. 19 man hath no pre-eminence above a beast
3. 21 Who knoweth the spirit of man that goeth
3. 22 that a man should rejoice in his own works
5. 19 Every man also to whom God hath given
6. 1 There is an evil..it (is) common among m.
6. 7 All the labour of man (is) for his mouth
6. 10 it is known that it (is) man: neither may
6. 11 there be many things..(is) man the better?
6. 12 who knoweth what (is) good for man in
6. 12 who can tell a man what shall be after him
7. 2 for that (is) the end of all men; and the
7. 14 to the end that man should find nothing
7. 20 For (there is) not a just man upon earth
7. 28 one man among a thousand have I found
7. 29 God hath made man upright; but they
8. 1 a man's wisdom maketh his face to shine
8. 6 the misery of man (is) great upon him
8. 8 (There is) no man that hath power over
8. 11 the heart of the sons of men is fully set
8. 15 a man hath no better thing under the sun
8. 17 a man cannot find out the work that is
8. 17 though a man labour to seek (it) out, yet
9. 1 no man knoweth either love or hatred (by)
9. 3 heart of the sons of men is full of evil
9. 12 For man also knoweth not his time: as
9. 12 so (are) the sons of men snared in an evil
9. 15 yet no man remembered that same poor
10. 14 man cannot tell what shall be; and what
11. 8 if a man live many years, (and) rejoice in
12. 5 man goeth to his long home: and the m.
12. 13 Fear God..this (is) the whole (duty) of man
Isa 2. 11 The lofty looks of man shall be humbled
2. 17 the loftiness of man shall be bowed down
2. 20 a man shall cast his idols of silver, and
2. 22 Cease ye from man, whose breath (is) in
6. 11 the houses without man, and the land be
6. 12 the LORD have removed men far away, and
13. 12 even a man than the golden wedge of O.
17. 7 that day shall a man look to his Maker
22. 6 bare the quiver with chariots of men (and)
29. 19 the poor among men shall rejoice in the
29. 21 That make a man an offender for a word
31. 3 the Egyptians (are) men, and not God; and
37. 19 the work of men's hands, wood and stone
38. 11 I shall behold man no more with the
43. 4 therefore will I give men for thee, and
44. 11 they (are) of men: let them all be gathe.
44. 13 according to the beauty of a man; that
44. 15 Then shall it be for man to burn: for he
45. 12 made the earth, and created man upon it
47. 3 and I will not meet (thee as) a man
51. 12 son of man (which) shall be made (as) grass
52. 14 and his form more than the sons of men
56. 2 and the son of man (that) layeth hold on
58. 5 Is it..a day for a man to afflict his soul?
Jer. 2. 6 through a land..where no man dwelt?
4. 25 (there was) no man, and all the birds of the
7. 20 upon man, and upon beast, and upon the
9. 22 the carcases of men shall fall as dung
10. 14 Every man is brutish in (his) knowledge
10. 23 I know that the way of man (is) not in h.
16. 20 Shall a man make gods unto himself, and
17. 5 that trusteth in man, and maketh flesh
21. 6 inhabitants of this city..man and beast
27. 5 the man and beast that (are) upon the g.
31. 27 sow..house of Judah with the seed of man
31. 30 every man that eateth the sour grape, his
32. 19 open upon all the ways of the sons of men
32. 20 set signs..in Israel, and among (other) men
32. 43 (It is) desolate without man or beast: it
33. 5 to fill them with the dead bodies of men
33. 10, 12 desolate without man and without b.
33. 10 without man, and without inhabitant, and
36. 29 cause to cease from thence man and beast
47. 2 the men shall cry, and all the inhabitants
49. 15 lo, I will make thee..despised among men
49. 18 neither shall a son of man dwell in it
49. 33 abide there, nor (any) son of man dwell in
50. 3 they shall depart, both man and beast
50. 40 neither shall any son of man dwell therein
51. 14 fill thee with men, as with caterpillars
51. 17 Every man is brutish by (his) knowledge
51. 43 neither doth (any) son of man pass thereby
51. 62 shall remain in it, neither man nor beast
Lam. 3. 36 To subvert a man in his cause, the Lord
3. 39 Wherefore doth a living man complain, a
Eze. 1. 5 appearance; they had the likeness of a man
1. 8 (they had) the hands of a man under their
1. 10 they four had the face of a man, and the
1. 26 as the appearance of a man above upon
2. 1, 3 And he said unto me, Son of man
2. 6 son of man, be not afraid of them, neither
2. 8 son of man, hear what I say unto thee; Le
3. 1, 3, 4, 10 he said unto me, Son of man
3. 17 Son of man, I have made thee a watchman
3. 25 son of man, behold, they shall put bands
4. 1 son of man, take thee a tile, and lay it
4. 12 bake it with dung that cometh out of man
4. 15 I have given thee cow's dung for man's d.
4. 16 Son of man, behold, I will break the staff
5. 1 son of man, take thee a sharp knife, take

Eze. 6. 2 Son of man, set thy face toward the mo.
7. 2 son of man, thus saith the Lord GOD unto
8. 5, 8 Then said he unto me, Son of man
8. 6 Son of man, seest thou what they do?
8. 12 Son of man, hast thou seen what the an.
8. 15, 17 said..Hast thou seen (this), O son of man
10. 8 the form of a man's hand under their w.
10. 14 the second face (was) the face of a man, and
10. 21 the likeness of the hands of a man (was)
11. 2 said he unto me, Son of man, these (are)
11. 4 prophesy against them..O son of man
11. 15 Son of man, thy brethren, (even) thy bre.
12. 2 Son of man, thou dwellest in the midst of
12. 3 son of man, prepare thee stuff for remov.
12. 9 Son of man, hath not the house of Israel
12. 18 Son of man, eat thy bread with quaking
12. 22 Son of man, what (is) that proverb (that) ye
12. 27 Son of man, behold, (they of) the house
13. 2 Son of man, prophesy against the proph.
13. 17 thou son of man, set thy face against the
14. 3 Son of man, these men have set up their
14. 13 Son of man, when the land sinneth agai.
14 13, 17, 19, 21 cut off man and beast from it
15. 2 Son of man, What is the vine tree more
16. 2 Son of man, cause Jerusalem to know her
17. 2 Son of man, put forth a riddle, and speak
19. 3, 6 learned to catch the prey; it devoured m.
20. 3 Son of man, speak unto the elders of Isr.
20. 4 Wilt thou judge them, son of man? wilt
20. 11, 13, 21 which (if) a man do, he shall even
20. 27 son of man, speak unto the house of Israel
20. 46 Son of man, set thy face toward the south
21. 2 Son of man, set thy face toward Jerusalem
21. 6 Sigh therefore, thou son of man, with the
21. 9 Son of man, prophesy, and say, Thus saith
21. 12 howl, son of man; for it shall be upon my
21. 14 son of man, prophesy, and smite (thine)
21. 19 son of man, appoint thee two ways, that
21. 28 son of man, prophesy, and say, Thus saith
22. 2 son of man, wilt thou judge, wilt thou
22. 18 Son of man, the house of Israel is to me
22. 24 Son of man, say unto her, Thou (art) the
23. 2 Son of man, there were two women, the
23. 36 Son of man, wilt thou judge Aholah and
24. 2 Son of man, Write thee the name of the
24. 16 Son of man, behold, I take away from thee
24. 25 son of man, (shall it) not (be), in the day
25. 2 Son of man, set thy face against the
25. 13 will cut off man and beast from it; and I
26. 2 Son of man, because that Tyrus hath said
29. 8 and cut off man and beast out of thee
29. 11 No foot of man shall pass through it
29. 18 Son of man, Nebuchadrezzar king of Ba.
30. 2 Son of man, prophesy and say, Thus saith
30. 21 Son of man, I have broken the arm of
31. 2 Son of man, speak unto Pharaoh king of
31. 14 in the midst of the children of men, with
32. 2 Son of man, take up a lamentation for
33. 7 son of man, I have set thee a watchman
33. 10 son of man, speak unto the house of Isr.
33. 24 Son of man, they that inhabit those wa.
33. 30 son of man, the children of thy people
34. 2 Son of man, prophesy against the sheph.
34. 31 the flock of my pasture, (are) men, (and)
35. 2 Son of man, set thy face against mount
36. 1 son of man, prophesy unto the mountains
36. 10 will multiply men upon you, all the house
36. 11 I will multiply upon you man and beast
36. 12 I will cause men to walk upon you, (even)
36. 13 Thou (land) devourest up men, and hast
36. 14 thou shalt devour men no more, neither
36. 17 Son of man, when the house of Israel d.
36. 37 will increase them with men like a flock
36. 38 waste cities be filled with flocks of men
37. 3 he said..Son of man, can these bones live?
37. 9 prophesy, son of man, and say to the wind
37. 11 Son of man, these bones are the whole h.
37. 16 son of man, take thee one stick, and write
38. 2 Son of man, set thy face against Gog, the
38. 14 son of man, prophesy and say unto Gog
38. 20 men that (are) upon the face of the earth
39. 1 son of man, prophesy against Gog, and say
39. 15 when (any) seeth a man's bone, then shall
39. 17 son of man, thus saith the Lord GOD; Sp.
40. 4 Son of man, behold with thine eyes, and
41. 19 the face of a man (was) toward the palm
43. 7 Son of man, the place of my throne, and
43. 10 son of man, show the house to the house
43. 18 Son of man, thus saith the Lord GOD; These
44. 5 Son of man, mark well, and behold with
47. 6 he said..Son of man, hast thou seen (this)
Dan. 8. 16 I heard a man's voice between (the banks
8. 17 Understand, O son of man; for at the time
10. 16 (one) like the similitude of the sons of men
10. 18 (one) like the appearance of a man, and
Hos. 6. 7 they, like men..transgressed the covenant
9. 12 (there shall) not (be) a man (left): yea, woe
11. 4 drew them with cords of a man, with bands
13. 2 the men that sacrifice kiss the calves
Joel 1. 12 joy is withered away from the sons of men
Amos 4. 13 declareth unto man what (is) his thought
Jon. 3. 7 Let neither man nor beast, herd nor flock
3. 8 But let man and beast be covered with
Mic. 2. 12 noise by reason of (the multitude of) men
5. 5 seven shepherds, and eight principal men
5. 7 tarrieth..nor waiteth for the sons of men
6. 8 He hath showed thee, O man, what (is) good
7. 2 (there is) none upright among men: they
Hab. 1. 14 makest men as the fishes of the sea, as
2. 8, 17 because of men's blood, and (for) the
Zeph. 1. 3 will consume man and beast; I will con.
1. 3 I will cut off man from off the land, saith
Zeph. 1. 17 I will bring distress upon men, that they
Hag. 1. 11 upon men, and upon cattle, and upon all
Zech. 2. 4 speak to this young man, saying, Jerusa.
8. 10 there was no hire for man, nor any hire
8. 10 set all men every one against his neighb.
9. 1 the eyes of man, as of all the tribes of
11. 6 I will deliver the men every one into
12. 1 and formeth the spirit of man within him
13. 5 man taught me to keep cattle from my
Mal. 3. 8 Will a man rob God? Yet ye have robbed

2. *A man, husband, individual,* אִישׁ *ish.*

Gen. 2. 23 Woman, because she was taken out of m.
2. 24 Therefore shall a man leave his father
4. 1 said, I have gotten a man from the LORD
4. 23 I have slain a man to my wounding, and
6. 9 Noah was a just man (and) perfect in his
13. 16 if a man can number the dust of the earth
19. 8 two daughters which have not known man
19. 9 they pressed sore upon the man, (even) L.
19. 31 (there is) not a man in the earth to come
20. 7 restore the man (his) wife; for he (is) a p.
24. 21 the man wondering at her held his peace
24. 22 the man took a golden ear ring of half a
24. 26 man bowed down his head, and worship.
24. 29 Laban ran out unto the man, unto the w.
24. 30 saying, Thus spake the man unto me
24. 30 he came unto the man; and, behold, he
24. 32 man came into the house: and he ungir.
24. 58 said unto her, Wilt thou go with this m.?
24. 61 rode upon..camels, and followed the man
24. 65 What man (is) this that walketh in the fi.
25. 27 was a cunning hunter, a man of the field
26. 11 He that toucheth this man or his wife
26. 13 the man waxed great, and went forward
27. 11 (is) a hairy man, and I (am) a smooth man
29. 19 that I should give her to another man
30. 43 the man increased exceedingly, and had
31. 50 If thou shalt afflict..no man (is) with us
32. 6 he cometh..and four hundred men with
32. 24 there wrestled a man with him until the
33. 1 Esau came, and with him four hundred men
37. 15 a certain man found him, and, behold, he
37. 15 man asked him, saying, What seekest thou?
37. 17 the man said, They are departed hence
38. 25 the man whose these (are am) I with child
39. 2 he was a prosperous man; and he was in
41. 33 let Pharaoh look out a man discreet and
41. 38 a man in whom the spirit of God (is)
41. 44 without thee shall no man lift up his
42. 11 We (are) all one man's sons: we (are) true
42. 13 the sons of one man in the land of Canaan
42. 30 The man, (who is) the lord of the land, sp.
42. 33 the man, the lord of the country, said unto
42. 35 every man's bundle of money (was) in his
43. 3 The man did solemnly protest unto us, s.
43. 5 the man said unto us, Ye shall not see my
43. 6 to tell the man whether ye had..a brother
43. 7 The man asked us straitly of our state
43. 11 carry down the man a present, a little b.
43. 13 Take..your brother..go again unto the m.
43. 14 Almighty give you mercy before the man
43. 17 the man did as Joseph bade; and the man
43. 21 (every) man's money (was) in the mouth of
43. 24 the man..gave (them) water, and they wa.
44. 1 put every man's money in his sack's mouth
44. 11 took down every man his sack to the gro.
44. 11 Then they..opened every man his sack
44. 13 laded every man his ass, and returned to
44. 15 that such a man as I can certainly divine
44. 17 the man in whose hand the cup is found
44. 26 we may not see the man's face, except our
45. 1 cried, Cause every man to go out from me
45. 1 there stood no man with him while Joseph
49 6 for in their anger they slew a man, and in
Exod. 2. 1 there went a man of the house of Levi, and
2. 20 why (is) it (that) ye have left the man?
2. 21 Moses was content to dwell with the man
11. 2 let every man borrow of his neighbour, and
11. 3 the man Moses (was) very great in the land
11. 7 not a dog move his tongue, against man
12. 44 But every man's servant that is bought
15. 3 The LORD (is) a man of war: the LORD (is)
16. 19 Let no man leave of it till the morning
16. 29 abide ye every man in his place; let no m.
19. 13 whether (it be) beast or man, it shall not
21. 7 if a man sell his daughter to be a maid
21. 12 He that smiteth a man so that he die, shall
21. 14 if a man come presumptuously upon his
21. 16 he that stealeth a man, and selleth him
21. 20 if a man smite his servant, or his maid
21. 26 if a man smite the eye of his servant, or
21. 28 If an ox gore a man or a woman, that they
21. 29 but that he hath killed a man or a woman
21. 33 if a man shall open a pit, or if a man
21. 35 if one man's ox hurt another's, that he die
22. 1 If a man shall steal an ox, or a sheep, and
22. 5 If a man shall cause a field or vineyard
22. 7 If a man shall deliver unto his neighbour
22. 7 and it be stolen out of the man's house
22. 10 If a man deliver unto his neighbour an
22. 14 if a man borrow (ought) of his neighbour
22. 16 And if a man entice a maid that is not
32. 1, 23 the man that brought us up out of the
32. 28 and there fell..about three thousand men
33. 4 and no man did put on him his ornaments
33. 11 spake..as a man speaketh unto his friend
34. 3 no man shall come up with thee, neither
35. 22 every man that offered (offered) an offering
35. 23 every man with whom was found blue, and
35. 29 every man and woman, whose heart made
36. 1, 2 every wise hearted man, in whom the
Exod. 36. 6 Let neither man nor woman make any m.
Lev. 13. 29 If a man or woman have a plague upon
13. 38 If a man also or a woman have in the skin
13. 40 the man whose hair is fallen off his head
13. 44 He is a leprous man, he (is) unclean: the
14. 11 present the man that is to be made clean
15. 18 The woman also with whom man shall lie
16. 21 send (him) away by the hand of a fit man
17. 3, 8, 10, 13 What man soever (there be) of
17. 4 that man; he hath shed blood; and that m.
17. 9 that man shall be cut off from among his
20. 3, 5 I will set my face against that man, and
20. 4 do any ways hide their eyes from the man
20. 10 man that committeth with..(another) man's
20. 11 the man that lieth with his father's wife
20. 12 if a man lie with his daughter in law, both
20. 13 If a man also lie with mankind, as he lieth
20. 14 if a man take a wife and her mother, it (is)
20. 15 if a man lie with a beast, he shall surely
20. 17 a man shall take his sister, his father's
20. 18 if a man shall lie with a woman having
20. 20 if a man shall lie with his uncle's wife
20. 21 if a man shall take his brother's wife, it
20. 27 A man also or woman that hath a familiar
21. 18 whatsoever man (he be) that hath a ble.
21. 18 a blind man, or a lame, or he that hath a
21. 19 Or a man that is broken footed, or broken
21. 21 No man that hath a blemish of the seed
22. 4 What man soever of the seed of Aaron (is)
22. 4 or a man whose seed goeth from him
22. 14 a man eat (of) the holy thing unwittingly
24. 10 son of the Israelitish (woman) and a man
24. 17 he that killeth any man shall surely be
24. 19 if a man cause a blemish in his neighbour
25. 26 if the man have none to redeem it, and
25. 27 restore the overplus unto the man to whom
25. 29 if a man sell a dwelling house in a walled
27. 2 When a man shall make a singular vow
27. 14 when a man shall sanctify his house (to
27. 16 if a man shall sanctify unto the LORD
27. 20 if he have sold the field to another man
27. 26 firstling of the beasts..no man shall san.
27. 28 no devoted thing that a man shall devote
27. 31 if a man will at all redeem (ought) of his
Num. 1. 4 with you there shall be a man of every tr.
1. 44 princes of Israel, (being) twelve men: each
5. 6 When a man or woman shall commit any
5. 8 if the man have no kinsman to recompense
5. 13 a man lie with her carnally, and it be hid
5. 15 Then shall the man bring his wife unto
5. 19 If no man have lain with thee, and if thou
5. 20 some man have lain with thee besides
5. 31 Then shall the man be guiltless from ini.
6. 2 When either man or woman shall separate
9. 13 man that (is) clean..that man shall bear
11. 16 Gather unto me seventy men of the elders
11. 24 gathered the seventy men of the elders
12. 3 Now the man Moses (was) very meek
13. 2 of every tribe..shall ye send a man, every
14. 15 thou shalt kill (all) this people as one man
15. 32 they found a man that gathered sticks
15. 35 The man shall be surely put to death: all
16. 7 it shall be (that) the man whom the LORD
16. 22 shall one man sin, and wilt thou be wroth
16. 35 consumed the two hundred and fifty men
17. 5 the man's rod, whom I shall choose, shall
19. 9 man (that is) clean shall gather up the
19. 20 man that shall be unclean, and shall not
23. 19 God (is) not a man, that he should lie
25. 8 went after the man..the man of Israel
26. 10 fire devoured two hundred and fifty men
26. 64 among these there was not a man of them
26. 65 there was not left a man of them, save
27. 8 If a man die, and have no son, then ye
27. 16 Let the LORD..set a man over the congre.
27. 18 Take thee Joshua..a man in whom (is)
30. 2 If a man vow a vow..or swear an oath to
30. 16 statutes..between a man and his wife
31. 17 kill every woman that hath known man
31. 49 and there lacketh not one man of us
Deut. 1. 16 judge righteously between (every) man
1. 17 ye shall not be afraid of the face of man
1. 31 bare thee, as a man doth bear his son, in
3. 11 the breadth of it, after the cubit of a man
4. 3 for all the men that followed Baal-peor
7. 24 there shall no man be able to stand before
8. 5 as a man chasteneth his son, (so) the LORD
11. 25 There shall no man be able to stand bef.
17. 2 man or woman, that hath wrought wick.
17. 5 bring forth that man..(even) that man or
17. 12 man that will do..even that man shall die
19. 11 if any man hate his neighbour, and lie in
19. 15 One witness shall not rise up against a m
19. 16 a false witness rise up against any man
20. 5 What man (is there) that hath built a new
20. 5, 6, 7 die in the battle, and another man
20. 6 what man (is he) that hath planted a vin
20. 7 what man (is there) that hath betrothed a
20. 8 What man (is there that is) fearful and fa.
21. 15 If a man have two wives, one beloved, and
21. 18 If a man have a stubborn and rebellious
21. 22 if a man have committed a sin worthy of
22. 16 gave my daughter unto this man to wife
22. 18 elders of that city shall take that man and
22. 22 If a man be found lying with a woman m.
22. 22 man that lay with the woman, and the w.
22. 23 man find her in the city, and lie with her
22. 24 the man, because he hath humbled his ne.
22. 25 if a man find..and the man force her, and
22. 25 then the man only that lay with her shall
22. 26 for as when a man riseth against his nei.
22. 28 If a man find a damsel (that is) a virgin

Deut 22. 29 Then the man that lay with her shall give
22. 30 A man shall not take his father's wife, nor
24. 1 When a man hath taken a wife, and mar.
24. 2 she may go and be another man's (wife)
24. 5 When a man hath taken a new wife, he
24. 7 If a man be found stealing any of his br.
24. 11 man to whom thou dost lend shall bring
24. 12 if the man (be) poor, thou shalt not sleep
25. 7 if the man like not to take his brother's
25. 9 So shall it be done unto that man that
27. 14 say unto all the men of Israel with a loud
27. 15 Cursed (be) the man that maketh (any) g.
28. 30 shalt betroth a wife, and another man sh.
28. 54 (So that) the man (that is) tender among
29. 10 and your officers, (with) all the men of I.
29. 18 Lest there should be among you man, or
29. 20 his jealousy shall smoke against that man
32. 25 sword..shall destroy both the young man
33. 1 Moses the man of God blessed the children
34. 6 no man knoweth of his sepulchre unto this
Josh 3. 12 twelve men..out of every tribe a man
4. 2 Take you twelve..out of every tribe a man
4. 4 Joshua called the twelve men, whom he
4. 4 children of Israel, out of every tribe a man
5. 13 there stood a man over against him with
6. 21 utterly destroyed..both man and woman
6. 26 Cursed (be) the man before the LORD that
7. 3 let about two or three thousand men go
7. 4 there went up..about three thousand men
7. 5 smote of them about thirty and six men
8. 3 chose out thirty thousand mighty men of
8. 12 took about five thousand men, and set
8. 17 there was not a man left in Ai or Beth-el
8. 25 all that fell that day, both of men and wo.
9. 6 said unto him, and to the men of Israel
9. 7 men of Israel said unto the Hivites, Per.
10. 8 there shall not a man of them stand before
10. 14 LORD hearkened unto the voice of a man
10. 24 Joshua called for all the men of Israel
14. 6 said unto Moses the man of God concern.
17. 1 because he was a man of war, therefore
21. 44 there stood not a man of all their enemies
22. 20 that man perished not alone in his iniqu.
23. 9 no man hath been able to stand before
23. 10 One man of you shall chase a thousand
Judg. 1. 4 slew of them in Bezek ten thousand men
1. 24 spies saw a man come forth out of the city
1. 25 but they let go the man and all his family
1. 26 the man went into the land of the Hittites
3. 15 a Benjamite, a man left handed: and
3. 17 unto Eglon..and Eglon (was) a very fat m.
3. 28 took the fords..and suffered not a man to
3. 29 about ten thousand men..all men of va.
3. 29 they slew..and there escaped not a man
3. 31 slew of the Philistines six hundred men
4. 6 take with thee ten thousand men of the
4. 10 went up with ten thousand men at his
4. 14 Barak went down..and ten thousand men
4. 22 will show thee the man whom thou seek.
6. 16 thou shalt smite the Midianites as one man
7. 6 number of them..were three hundred men
7. 7 By the three hundred men that lapped
7. 8 he sent..every man unto his tent, and
7. 13 a man that told a dream unto his fellow
7. 14 Gideon the son of Joash, a man of Israel
7. 16 divided the three hundred men (into) three
7. 19 So Gideon, and the hundred men that
7. 23 men of Israel gathered themselves toge.
7. 24 the men of Ephraim gathered themselves
8. 1 the men of Ephraim said unto him, Why
8. 4 the three hundred men that (were) with
8. 10 and twenty thousand men that drew sw.
8. 14 described..threescore and seventeen men
8. 21 for as the man (is, so is) his strength
8. 22 the men of Israel said unto Gideon, Rule
9. 49 likewise cut down every man his bough
9. 49 died also, about a thousand men and w.
9. 55 men of Israel saw that Abimelech was d.
9. 55 they departed every man unto his place
10. 1 Puah, the son of Dodo, a man of Issachar
10. 18 What man (is he) that will begin to fight
11. 39 that she returned..and she knew no man
12. 1 the men of Ephraim gathered themselves
13. 2 there was a certain man of Zorah, of the
13. 6 man of God came unto me, and his coun.
13. 8 let the man of God which thou didst send
13. 10 the man hath appeared unto me, that came
13. 11 and came to the man, and said unto him
13. 11 (Art) thou the man that spakest unto the
14. 19 slew thirty men of them, and took their
15. 10 the men of Judah said, Why are ye come
15. 11 three thousand men of Judah went to the
15. 15 took it, and slew a thousand men there.
15. 16 with the jaw..have I slain a thousand m.
16. 19 she called for a man, and she caused him
16. 27 three thousand men and women, that be.
17. 1 there was a man of mount Ephraim, whose
17. 5 the man Micah had an house of gods, and
17. 8 And the man departed out of the city from
17. 11 Levite was content to dwell with the man
18. 11, 16 hundred men appointed with weapons
18. 17 six hundred men (that were) appointed
18. 19 to be a priest unto the house of one man
19. 6 the damsel's father had said unto the man
19. 7, 9 And when the man rose up to depart
19. 10 the man would not tarry that night, but
19. 15 (there was) no man that took them into
19. 16 there came an old man from his work out
19. 17 a wayfaring man in the street of the city
19. 17 the old man said, Whither goest thou? and
19. 18 there (is) no man that receiveth me to house
19. 20 And the old man said, Peace (be) with thee
Judg 19. 22 Bring forth the man that came into thine
19. 23 the man, the master of the house, went
19. 23 this man is come into mine house, do not
19. 24 but unto this man do not so vile a thing
19. 26 fell down at the door of the man's house
19. 28 the man took her (up) upon an ass, and
20. 1 was gathered together as one man, from
20. 8 the people arose as one man, saying, We
20. 11 So all the men of Israel were gathered
20. 11 against the city, knit together as one man
20. 15 and six thousand men that drew sword
20. 15 were numbered seven hundred chosen m.
20. 16 (were) seven hundred chosen men left h.
20. 17 the men of Israel, besides Benjamin, were
20. 17 men that drew sword: all these (were) men
20. 20 men of Israel went out to battle against
20. 20 the men of Israel put themselves in array
20. 21 destroyed..twenty and two thousand men
20. 22 the men of Israel, encouraged themselves
20. 25 destroyed..again eighteen thousand men
20. 31 began to smite..about thirty men of Israel
20. 33 the men of Israel rose up out of their
20. 34 ten thousand chosen men out of all Israel
20. 35 and five thousand and an hundred men
20. 36 men of Israel gave place to the Benjamites
20. 38 the men of Israel and the liers in wait
20. 39 the men of Israel retired in the battle
20. 39 kill of the men of Israel about thirty
20. 41 the men of Israel turned again, the men
20. 42 turned (their backs) before the men of I
20. 44 fell of Benjamin eighteen thousand men
20. 45 gleaned..in..highways five thousand men
20. 45 pursued..and slew two thousand men of
20. 46 and five thousand men that drew the s.
20. 47 six hundred men turned and fled to the
20. 48 the men of Israel turned again upon the
21. 1 Now the men of Israel had sworn in Mi.
21. 10 twelve thousand men of the valiantest
21. 12 had known no man by lying with any male
Ruth 1. 1 a certain man of Beth-lehem-judah went
1. 2 the name of the man (was) Elimelech, and
2. 1 a mighty man of wealth, of the family of
2. 19 The man's name with whom I wrought to
2. 20 The man (is) near of kin unto us, one of
3. 3 make not thyself known unto the m., until
3. 8 the man was afraid, and turned himself
3. 16 told her all that the man had done to her
3. 18 the man will not be in rest until he have
4. 7 a man plucked off his shoe, and gave (it)
1 Sa 1. 1 Now there was a certain man of Ramath.
1. 3 this man went up out of his city yearly
1. 21 the man Elkanah, and all his house
2. 9 for by strength shall no man prevail
2. 15 said to the man that sacrificed, Give
2. 23 If one man sin against another, the judge
2. 25 if a man sin against the LORD, who shall
2. 27 there came a man of God unto Eli, and
2. 33 the man of thine, (whom) I shall not cut
4. 2 slew of the army..about four thousand m.
4. 12 there ran a man of Benjamin out of the
4. 13 the man came into the city, and told (it)
4. 14 And the man came in hastily, and told E.
4. 16 the man said unto Eli, I (am) he that came
4. 18 he died; for he was an old man, and heavy
6. 19 fifty thousand and threescore and ten men
9. 1 there was a man of Benjamin, whose name
9. 6 a man of God, and (he is) an honourable m.
9. 7 what shall we bring the man? for the b.
9. 7 not a present to bring to the man of God
9. 8 give to the man of God to tell us our way
9. 9 when a man went to enquire of God, thus
9. 10 unto the city where the man of God (was)
9. 16 send..a man out of the land of Benjamin
9. 17 Behold the man whom I spake to thee of
10. 6 and shalt be turned into another man
10. 22 if the man should yet come thither
11. 8 and the men of Judah thirty thousand
11. 9 Thus shall ye say unto the men of Jabesh
11. 13 There shall not a man be put to death
13. 6 the men of Israel saw that they were in
13. 14 hath sought him a man after his own he.
13. 15 present with him, about six hundred men
14. 2 the people..(were) about six hundred m.
14. 14 was about twenty men, within as it were
14. 22 men of Israel which had hid themselves
14. 24 men of Israel were distressed that day
14. 24, 28 Cursed (be) the man that eateth (any)
14. 36 spoil..and let us not leave a man of them
14. 52 Saul saw any strong man, or any valiant
15. 3 slay both man and woman, infant and s.
15. 4 numbered them..ten thousand men of J
16. 16 to seek out a man, (who is) a cunning pl.
16. 17 Provide me now a man that can play well
16. 18 a man of war, and prudent in matters, and
17. 2 the men of Israel were gathered together
17. 8 choose you a man for you, and let him
17. 10 give me a man, that we may fight together
17. 12 had eight sons: and the man went among
17. 19 the men of Israel, (were) in the valley of
17. 24 the men of Israel, when they saw the man
17. 25 men of Israel said, Have ye seen this man
17. 25 the man who killeth him, the king will
17. 26 What shall be done to the man that killeth
17. 27 So shall it be done to the man that killeth
17. 33 and he a man of war from his youth
17. 41 man that bare the shield (went) before him
18. 23 that I (am) a poor man, and lightly estee.
18. 27 David arose and went, he and his men
21. 1 Why (art) thou alone, and no man with
21. 2 Let no man know any thing of the business
21. 7 Now a certain man of the servants of Saul
21. 14 ye see the man is mad: wherefore (then)
1 Sa. 22. 2 were with him about four hundred men
22. 19 smote he..both men and women, children
24. 2 Saul took three thousand chosen men out
24. 19 For if a man find his enemy, will he let
25. 2 a man in Maon, whose possessions (were)
25. 2 the man (was) very great, and he had th.
25. 3 name of the man..but the man (was) ch.
25. 13 there went up..about four hundred men
25. 25 Let not my lord..regard this man of Belial
26. 2 having three thousand chosen men of Isr.
26. 15 (Art) not thou a (valiant) man? and who
27. 2 passed over with the six hundred men that
27. 9 left neither man nor woman alive, and
27. 11 David saved neither man nor woman alive
28. 14 An old man cometh up; and he (is) cover.
30. 9 he and the six hundred men that (were)
30. 10 pursued, he and four hundred men: for
30. 17 there escaped not a man of them, save
30. 17 young men, which rode upon camels, and
30. 22 Then answered all the wicked men..of
31. 12 All the valiant men arose, and went all
2 Sa. 1. 2 a man came out of the camp from Saul
2. 30 lacked of David's servants nineteen men
2. 31 three hundred and three score men died
6. 19 as well to the women as men, to every one
8. 5 David slew..two and twenty thousand m.
10. 6 and of king Maacah a thousand men, and
12. 4 came a traveller unto the rich man; and
12. 4 poor man's lamb..dressed it for the man
12. 5 anger was greatly kindled against the m.
12. 5 man that hath done this (thing) shall surely
12. 7 Nathan said to David, Thou (art) the man
13. 3 and Jonadab (was) a very subtil man
13. 9 Ammon said, Have out all men from me
14. 16 out of the hand of the man (that would)
15. 1 and horses, and fifty men to run before
15. 11 with Absalom went two hundred men out
15. 13 hearts of the men of Israel are after Abs.
15. 18 six hundred men..passed on before the
16. 5 thence came out a man of the family of
16. 7 thou bloody man, and thou man of Belial
16. 8 mischief, because thou (art) a bloody man
16. 15 men of Israel, came to Jerusalem, and A.
16. 18 Nay; but whom..men of Israel, choose
16. 23 as if a man had enquired at the oracle of
17. 1 Let me..choose out twelve thousand men
17. 3 man whom thou seekest (is) as if all retu.
17. 8 father (is) a man of war, and will not lo.
17. 14 all the men of Israel said, The counsel of
17. 18 came to a man's house in Bahurim, which
17. 24 passed over Jordan, he and all the men
17. 25 which Amasa (was) a man's son whose n.
18. 10 a certain man saw (it), and told Joab, and
18. 11 Joab said unto the man that told him, And
18. 12 man said unto Joab, Though I should re.
18. 24 looked, and behold a man running alone
18. 26 the watchman saw another man running
18. 26 said, Behold (another) man running alone
18. 27 He (is) a good man, and cometh with good
19. 16 came down with the men of Judah to m.
19. 17 a thousand men of Benjamin with him
19. 32 provided..for he (was) a very great man
19. 41 all the men of Israel..said unto the king
19. 41 Why have our brethren the men of Judah
19. 42 men of Judah answered the men of Israel
19. 43 men of Israel answered the men of Judah
19. 43 And the words of the men of Judah were
19. 43 fiercer than the words of the men of Israel
20. 1 there happened to be there a man of B.
20. 2 but the men of Judah clave unto their
20. 4 Assemble me the men of Judah within
20. 12 when the man saw that all the people
20. 21 man of mount Ephraim, Sheba the son of
21. 5 man that consumed us, and that devised
21. 20 where was a man of (great) stature, that
22. 49 hast delivered me from the violent man
23. 7 the man (that) shall touch them must be
23. 9 and the men of Israel were gone away
23. 20 the son of a valiant man, of Kabzeel, who
23. 21 he slew an Egyptian, a goodly man: and
24. 9 eight hundred thousand valiant men that
24. 9 men..(were) five hundred thousand men
24. 15 died of the people..seventy thousand men
1 Ki 1. 5 he prepared..fifty men to run before him
1. 42 Come in; for thou (art) a valiant man, and
1. 49 and rose up, and went every man his way
2. 2 be thou strong..and show thyself a man
2. 4 there shall not fail thee..a man on the
2. 9 for thou (art) a wise man, and knowest
5. 13 and the levy was thirty thousand men
7. 14 his father (was) a man of Tyre, a worker
8. 2 all the men of Israel assembled themsel.
8. 25 There shall not fail thee a man in my sight
9. 5 There shall not fail thee a man upon the
11. 28 the man Jeroboam (was) a mighty..and
12. 22 came unto Shemaiah the man of God, say.
13. 1 there came a man of God out of Judah by
13. 4 Jeroboam heard the saying of the man of
13. 5 according to the sign which the man of G.
13. 6 king answered and said unto the man of
13. 6 man of God besought the LORD, and the
13. 7 king said unto the man of God, Come h.
13. 8 man of God said unto the king, If thou
13. 11 told him all the works that the man of G.
13. 12 had seen what way the man of God went
13. 14 went after the man of God, and found him
13. 14 (Art) thou the man of God that camest
13. 21 he cried unto the man of God that came
13. 26 It (is) the man of God, who was disobed.
13. 29 prophet took up the carcase of the man
13. 31 sepulchre wherein the man of God (is) b.
17. 18 What have I to do with thee, O thou man

1 Ki. 17. 24 by this I know that thou (art) a man of G.
18. 13 how I hid an hundred men of the LORD'S
18. 22 prophets (are) four hundred and fifty men
18. 44 cloud out of the sea, like a man's hand
20. 20 they slew every one his man: and the Sy.
20. 28 there came a man of God, and spake unto
20. 30 twenty and seven thousand of the men (th.
20. 35 certain man..said..And the man refused
20. 37 found another man..And the man smote
20. 39 man turned aside, and brought a man unto
20. 39 Keep this man: if by any means he be m.
20. 42 thou hast let go out of (thy) hand a man
22. 6 gathered..about four hundred men, and
22. 8 (There is) yet one man, Micaiah the son
22. 17 let them return every man to his house
22. 34 man drew a bow at a venture, and smote
2 Ki. 1. 6 There came a man up to meet us, and said
1. 7 What manner of man (was he) which came
1. 8 (He was) an hairy man, and girt with a g.
1. 9 Thou man of God, the king hath said, Come
1. 10, 12 Elijah answered..If I (be) a man of G.
1. 11 O man of God, thus hath the king said, C.
1. 13 man of God, I pray thee, let my life, and
2. 7 fifty men of the sons of the prophets went
2. 17 They sent therefore fifty men; and they
3. 26 he took with him seven hundred men that
4. 7 Then she came and told the man of God
4. 9 I perceive that this (is) an holy man of God
4. 16 man of God, do not lie unto thine hand.
4. 21 laid him on the bed of the man of God
4. 22 that I may run to the man of God, and c.
4. 25 came unto the man..when the man of G.
4. 27 when she came to the man..the man of
4. 40 man of God, (there is) death in the pot
4. 42 came a man..and brought the man of
4. 43 should I set this before an hundred men?
5. 1 great man..he was also a mighty man in
5. 7 doth send unto me to recover a man of
5. 8 when Elisha the man of God had heard
5. 14 according to the saying of the man of G.
5. 15 returned to the man of God, he and all
5. 20 Gehazi, the servant of the man of God
5. 26 when the man turned again from his ch.
6. 6 man of God said, Where fell it? And he
6. 9 man of God sent unto the king of Israel
6. 10 which the man of God told him and war.
6. 15 when the servant of the man of God was
6. 19 will bring you to the man whom ye seek
6. 32 sent a man from before him: but ere the
7. 2 answered the man of God, and said, Beh.
7. 5 when they were come..(there was) no man
7. 10 no man there, neither voice..but horses
7. 17 died, as the man of God had said, who sp.
7. 18 as the man of God had spoken to the king
7. 19 lord answered the man of God, and said
8. 2 did after the saying of the man of God
8. 4 with Gehazi, the servant of the man of G.
8. 7 saying, The man of God is come hither
8. 8 meet the man of God, and enquire of the
8. 11 settled his countenance..and the man of
9. 11 Ye know the man, and his communication
10. 14 slew..two and forty men; neither left he
10. 21 so that there was not a man left that came
10. 24 Jehu appointed fourscore men without
12. 4 money that cometh into any man's heart
13. 19 man of God was wroth with him, and said
13. 21 as they were burying a man..they spied
13. 21 cast the man..and when the man was let
15. 20 exacted..of each man fifty shekels of sil.
15. 25 and with him fifty men of the Gileadites
18. 21 staff..on which if a man lean, it will go
22. 15 Thus saith the LORD..Tell the man that
23. 2 all the men of Judah and all the inhabit.
23. 8 on a man's left hand at the gate of the c.
23. 10 no man might make his son or his daugh.
23. 16 word of the LORD, which the man of God
23. 17 (It is) the sepulchre of the man of God
23. 18 Let him alone; let no man move his bones
25. 19 and threescore men of the people of the
1 Ch. 10. 1 men of Israel fled from before the Philis.
10. 7 when all the men..saw that they fled, and
10. 12 They arose, all the valiant men, and took
11. 22 son of a valiant man of Kabzeel, who had
11. 23 slew an Egyptian, a man of (great) stature
16. 21 suffered no man to do them wrong; yea
18. 5 David slew..two and twenty thousand m.
20. 6 at Gath, where was a man of (great) stat.
21. 5 an hundred thousand men that drew sw.
21. 5 threescore and ten thousand men that dr.
21. 14 there fell of Israel seventy thousand men
22. 9 son shall be born..who shall be a man of
23. 14 Now (concerning) Moses the man of God
27. 32 was a counsellor, a wise man, and a scribe
28. 3 because thou (hast been) a man of war
2 Ch. 2. 2 told out threescore and ten thousand men
2. 7 Send me now therefore a man cunning to
2. 13 I have sent a cunning man, endued with
2. 14 his father (was) a man of Tyre, skilful to
5. 3 all the men of Israel assembled themselves
6. 5 neither chose I any man to be a ruler over
6. 16 There shall not fail thee a man in my sight
6. 22 If a man sin against his neighbour, and
7. 18 There shall not fail thee a man (to be) ru.
8. 14 so had David the man of God commanded
11. 2 came to Shemaiah the man of God, saying
13. 3 with an army of valiant men of war, (even)
13. 3 with eight hundred thousand chosen men
13. 15 Then the men..as the men of Judah sho.
13. 17 fell down..five hundred thousand men
15. 13 whether small or great, whether man or
18. 5 gathered..four hundred men, and said
18. 7 (There is) yet one man, by whom we may

2 Ch. 18. 33 a..man drew a bow at a venture, and sm.
20. 27 Then they returned, every man of Judah
25. 7 there came a man of God to him, saying
25. 9 said to the man..And the man of God
30. 16 according to the law of Moses the man of
34. 23 answered..Tell ye the man that sent you
34. 30 king went up..and all the men of Judah
Ezra 3. 1 gathered themselves together as one man
3. 2 (it is) written in the law of Moses..man
8. 18 they brought us a man of understanding
Neh. 1. 11 grant him mercy in the sight of this man
6. 11 Should such a man as I flee? and who (is
7. 2 for he (was) a faithful man, and feared God
8. 1 gathered themselves together as one man
8. 2 both of men and women, and all that co.
12. 24 commandment of David the man of God
12. 36 musical instruments of David..man of G.
Esth. 1. 22 every man should bear rule in his own h.
4. 11 that whosoever, whether man or woman
6. 6, 7, 9, 9, 11 man whom the king delighteth
9. 2 no man could withstand them; for the
9. 4 this man Mordecai waxed greater and gr.
9. 6 Jews slew and destroyed five hundred m.
9. 12 slain and destroyed five hundred men in
9. 15 slew three hundred men at Shushan: but
Job 1. 1 There was a man..and that man was per.
1. 3 so that this man was the greatest of all the
1. 8 perfect and an upright man, one that fe.
2. 3 perfect and an upright man, one that fe.
2. 4 all that a man hath will he give for his
9. 32 For (he is) not a man, as I (am, that) I sh.
11. 2 and should a man full of talk be justified?
11. 12 For vain man would be wise, though..born
12. 14 he shutteth up a man, and there can be
14. 12 So man lieth down, and riseth not: till
15. 16 much more abominable and filthy (is) m.
22. 8 But (as for) the mighty man, he had the
32. 13 say..God thrusteth him down, not man
32. 21 Let me not..accept any man's person
34. 21 For his eyes (are) upon the ways of man
34. 23 For he will not lay upon man more (than
35. 8 Thy wickedness (may hurt) a man as thou
37. 20 If a man speak, surely he shall be swall.
38. 26 to rain on the earth, (where) no man (is
Psa. 1. 1 Blessed (is) the man that walketh not in
4. 2 O ye sons of men, how long (will ye turn)
5. 6 LORD will abhor..bloody and deceitful m.
18. 48 hast delivered me from the violent man?
22. 6 But I (am) a worm, and no man; a repr.
25. 12 What man (is) he that feareth the LORD?
31. 20 shalt hide them..from the pride of man
34. 12 What man (is he that) desireth life, (and)
37. 7 because of the man who bringeth wicked
37. 37 behold the upright: for the end of (that) m.
38. 14 Thus I was as a man that heareth not, and
39. 11 When thou with rebukes dost correct man
43. 1 O deliver me from the deceitful..man
62. 3 will ye imagine mischief against a man?
78. 25 Man did eat angels food: he sent them
80. 17 Let thy hand be upon the man of thy ri.
87. 5 This and that man was born in her: and
90. *title.* A prayer of Moses the man of God
92. 6 A brutish man knoweth not; neither doth
105. 17 He sent a man before them, (even) Joseph
109. 16 but persecuted the poor and needy man
112. 1 Blessed (is) the man (that) feareth the L.
112. 5 A good man showeth favour, and lendeth
140. 1 O LORD..preserve me from the violent m.
140. 11 evil shall hunt the violent man to overt.
141. 4 to practise wicked works with men that
147. 10 taketh not pleasure in the legs of a man
Prov. 2. 12 To deliver thee..from the man that spea.
5. 21 For the ways of man (are) before the eyes
6. 11 poverty..and thy want as an armed man
6. 12 a wicked man, walketh with a froward m.
6. 27 Can a man take fire in his bosom, and his
8. 4 Unto you, O men, I call; and my voice
10. 23 but a man of understanding hath wisdom
11. 12 man of understanding holdeth his peace
11. 17 merciful man doeth good to his own soul
12. 2 a man of wicked devices will he condemn
12. 8 man shall be commended according to
12. 14 man shall be satisfied with good by the f.
12. 25 Heaviness in the heart of man maketh it
13. 2 man shall eat good by the fruit of (his) m.
13. 8 The ransom of a man's life (are) his riches
14. 7 Go from the presence of a foolish man
14. 12 is a way which seemeth right unto a man
14. 14 a good man (shall be satisfied) from him.
14. 17 and a man of wicked devices is hated
15. 18 A wrathful man stirreth up strife: but (he
15. 21 man of understanding walketh uprightly
15. 23 man hath joy by the answer of his mouth
16. 2 All the ways of a man (are) clean in his own
16. 7 When a man's ways please the LORD, he
16. 14 messengers of death: but a wise man will
16. 25 way that seemeth right unto a man; but
16. 27 An ungodly man diggeth up evil; and in
16. 28 A froward man soweth strife; and a wh.
16. 29 A violent man enticeth his neighbour, and
17. 12 bear robbed of her whelps meet a man
17. 27 man of understanding is of an excellent
18. 4 words of a man's mouth (are as) deep wa.
18. 12 Before destruction the heart of man is h.
18. 14 spirit of a man will sustain his infirmity
18. 20 A man's belly shall be satisfied with the
18. 24 man (that hath) friends must show hims.
19. 21 (There are) many devices in a man's heart
20. 3 (It is) an honour for a man to cease from
20. 5 Counsel in the heart of man (is like) deep
20. 5 a man of understanding will draw it out
20. 6 his own goodness: but a faithful man

Prov 20. 17 Bread of deceit (is) sweet to a man; but
21. 2 Every way of a man (is) right in his own
21. 8 The way of man (is) froward and strange
21. 17 He that loveth pleasure (shall be) a poor
21. 28 the man that heareth speaketh constantly
21. 29 A wicked man hardeneth his face: but (as
22. 24 and with a furious man thou shalt not go
22. 29 Seest thou a man diligent in his business
24. 5 a man of knowledge increaseth strength
24. 29 I will render to the man according to his
24. 34 poverty..and thy want as an armed man
25. 18 man that beareth false witness against his
26. 16 than seven men that can render a reason
26. 19 So (is) the man (that) deceiveth his neigh.
26. 21 so (is) a contentious man to kindle strife
27. 8 so (is) a man that wandereth from his pl.
27. 17 as a man sharpeneth the countenance of
27. 21 the furnace for gold; so (is) a man to his
28. 11 The rich man (is) wise in his own conceit
28. 20 A faithful man shall abound with blessings
29. 6 In the transgression of an evil man (there
29. 9 a wise man contendeth with a foolish man
29. 13 poor and the deceitful man meet together
29. 20 Seest thou a man (that is) hasty in his w.?
29. 22 An angry man stirreth up strife, and a fu.
29. 26 but..man's judgment (cometh) from the
29. 27 An unjust man (is) an abomination to the
30. 2 Surely I (am) more brutish than (any) man
Eccl. 1. 8 All things (are) full of labour; man can.
4. 4 for this a man is envied of his neighbour
6. 2 A man to whom God hath given riches
6. 3 If a man beget an hundred (children), and
7. 5 than for a man to hear the song of fools
9. 15 Now there was found in it a poor wise man
9. 15 yet no..remembered that same poor man
Song 3. 8 every man (hath) his sword upon his thigh
8. 7 if a man would give all the substance of
Isa. 2. 9 the great man humbleth himself: theref.
3. 2 man of war, the judge, and the prophet
3. 6 When a man shall take hold of his brother
4. 1 seven women shall take hold of one man
5. 3 men of Judah, judge, I pray thee, betwixt
5. 7 and the men of Judah his pleasant plant
6. 5 because I (am) a man of unclean lips, and
7. 21 a man shall nourish a young cow and two
9. 19 as the fuel of the fire: no man shall spare
14. 16 (Is) this the man that made the earth to
21. 9 there cometh a chariot of men, (with) a co.
32. 2 man shall be as an hiding place from the
36. 6 whereon if a man lean, it will go into his
41. 28 I beheld, and (there was) no man; even
42. 13 he shall stir up jealousy like a man of war
44. 13 and maketh it after the figure of a man
46. 11 man that executeth my counsel from a far
50. 2 Wherefore, when I came, (was there) no m.?
52. 14 visage was so marred more than any man
53. 3 He is despised and rejected of men; a man
55. 7 and the unrighteous man his thoughts: and
57. 1 perisheth, and no man layeth (it) to heart
59. 16 saw that (there was) no man, and wonder.
66. 3 that killeth an ox (is as if) he slew a man
Jer. 2. 6 a land that no man passed through, and
3. 1 They say, If a man put away his wife, and
3. 1 she go from him, and become another ma.
4. 3 thus saith the LORD to the men of Judah
4. 4 men of Judah and inhabitants of Jerusa.
4. 29 be) forsaken, and not a man dwell therein
5. 1 if ye can find a man, if there be (any) that
6. 23 set in array as men for war, against thee
7. 5 judgment between a man and his neigh.
8. 6 no man repented him of his wickedness
9. 12 Who (is) the wise man, that may unders.
10. 23 (it is) not in man that walketh to direct
11. 2 speak unto the men of Judah, and to the
11. 3 the man that obeyeth not the words of
11. 9 A conspiracy is found among the men of
12. 11 desolate, because no man layeth (it) to h.
13. 11 the girdle cleaveth to the loins of a man
14. 9 Why shouldest thou be as a man astonied
15. 10 hast born me a man of strife and a man
17. 25 the men of Judah, and the inhabitants of
18. 11 go..speak to the men of Judah, and to the
20. 15 Cursed (be) the man who brought tidings
20. 16 let that man be as the cities which the
22. 30 saith the LORD, Write ye this man child
22. 30 no man of his seed shall prosper, sitting
23. 9 like a man whom wine hath overcome, be.
23. 34 I will even punish that man and his house
26. 11 This man (is) worthy to die; for he hath
26. 16 This man (is) not worthy to die: for he
26. 20 there was also a man that prophesied in
29. 32 not have a man to dwell among this peop.
32. 32 the men of Judah, and the inhabitants of
33. 17 David shall never want a man to sit upon
33. 18 shall the priests the Levites want a man
35. 4 Hanan, the son of Igdaliah, a man of God
35. 13 tell the men of Judah, and the inhabita.
35. 19 want a man to stand before me for ever
36. 31 upon the men of Judah, all the evil that
38. 4 let this man be put to death; for thus he
38. 4 this man seeketh not the welfare of this
38. 24 Let no man know of these words, and thou
40. 15 no man shall know (it): wherefore should
41. 4 he had slain Gedaliah, and no man knew
41. 5 fourscore men, having their beards shaven
44. 7 to cut off from you man and woman, child
44. 26 named in the mouth of any man of Judah
44. 27 the men of Judah that (are) in the land of
49. 18 no man shall abide there, neither shall a
49. 33 there shall no man abide there, nor (any)
50. 40 (so) shall no man abide there, neither shall
50. 42 like a man to the battle, against thee, O

Jer. 51. 22 also will I break in pieces man and wom.
51. 43 a land wherein no man dwelleth, neither
52. 25 threescore men of the people of the land
Lam. 3. 33 he doth not..grieve the children of men
Eze. 8. 11 seventy men of the ancients of the house
8. 11 with every man his censer in his hand; and
8. 16 five and twenty men, with their backs
9. 2 every man a slaughter weapon in his hand
9. 2 one man among them (was) clothed with
9. 3 he called to the man clothed with linen
9. 6 come not near any man upon whom (is) the
9. 11 the man clothed with linen, which (had)
10. 2 he spake unto the man clothed with linen
10. 3 stood on the right..when the man went
10. 6 had commanded the man clothed with li.
11. 1 at..door of the gate five and twenty men
14. 8 I will set my face against that man, and
18. 5 if a man be just, and do that which is
18. 8 executed true judgment between man and
22. 30 I sought for a man among them, that sho.
33. 2 people of the land take a man of their
39. 20 filled at my table..with all men of war
40. 3 (there was) a man, whose appearance (was)
40. 4 the man said unto me..behold with thine
40. 5 in the man's hand a measuring reed of six
43. 6 heard (him) speaking..and the man stood
44. 2 no man shall enter in by it; because the
47. 3 the man that had the line in his hand
Dan. 9. 7 the men of Judah, and to the inhabitants
9. 21 the man Gabriel, whom I had seen in the
10. 5 behold a certain man clothed in linen
10. 11 O Daniel, a man greatly beloved, under.
10. 19 O man greatly beloved, fear not: peace
12. 6 (one) said to the man clothed in linen
12. 7 I heard the man clothed in linen, which
Hos. 3. 3 thou shalt not be for (another) man: so
4. 4 let no man strive, nor reprove another
6. 9 as troops of robbers wait for a man, (so)
9. 7 spiritual man (is) mad, for the multitude
11. 9 I (am) God, and not man; the Holy One
Amos 2. 7 a man and his father will go in unto the
5. 19 man did flee from a lion, and a bear met
Jon. 1. 14 let us not perish for this man's life, and
Mic. 2. 2 so they oppress..a man and his heritage
2. 11 If a man walking in the spirit and falseho.
5. 7 tarrieth not for man, nor waiteth for the
7. 6 a man's enemies (are)..of his own house
Zeph. 3. 6 that there is no man, that there is none
Zech. 1. 8 behold a man riding upon a red horse
1. 10 the man that stood among the myrtle trees
1. 21 no man did lift up his head: but these
2. 1 a man with a measuring line in his hand
4. 1 a man that is wakened out of his sleep
6. 12 Behold the man whose name (is) The Bran.
Mal. 2. 12 The LORD will cut off the man that doeth

3. *A man, a mortal*, אֱנוֹשׁ *enosh.* (plur. *anashim*).
Gen. 6. 4 the same (became) mighty..men of reno.
12. 20 Pharaoh commanded (his) men concerning
13. 13 the men of Sodom (were) wicked and sin.
14. 24 the men which went with me, Aner, Esh.
17. 23 every male among the men of Abraham's
17. 27 the men of his house, born in the house
18. 2 three men stood by him: and, when he
18. 16 the men rose up from thence, and looked
18. 22 the men turned their faces from thence
19. 4 the men of the city, (even) the men of S.
19. 5 Where (are) the men which came in to thee
19. 8 unto these men do nothing, for therefore
19. 10 But the men put forth their hand, and p.
19. 11 they smote the men that (were) at the d.
19. 12 And the men said unto Lot, Hast thou h.
19. 16 the men laid hold upon his hand, and
20. 8 called all his servants..and the men were
24. 13 the daughters of the men of the city come
24. 32 and the men's feet that (were) with him
24. 54 he and the men that (were) with him, and
24. 59 they sent..Abraham's servant, and his m.
26. 7 men of the place asked (him) of his wife
26. 7 the men of the place should kill me for
29. 22 Laban gathered together all the men of
32. 28 hast thou power with God and with men
34. 7 the men were grieved, and they were very
34. 20 and communed with the men of their city
34. 21 These men (are) peaceable with us; ther.
34. 22 Only herein will the men consent unto us
38. 21 Then he asked the men of that place, sa.
38. 22 also the men of the place said, (that) these
39. 11 (there was) none of the men of the house
39. 14 she called unto the men of the house, and
43. 15 And the men took that present, and they
43. 16 Bring (these) men home, and slay, and m.
43. 16 for (these) men shall dine with me at noon
43. 17, 24 brought the men into Joseph's house
43. 18 And the men were afraid, because they
43. 33 and the men marvelled one at another
44. 1 Fill the men's sacks (with) food, as much
44. 3 the men were sent away, they and their
44. 4 Up, follow after the men; and when thou
46. 32 the men (are) shepherds, for their trade
47. 2 And he took..five men, and presented
47. 6 if thou knowest (any) men of activity am
Exod. 2. 13 behold, two men of the Hebrews strove
4. 19 for all the men are dead which sought
5. 9 Let there more work be laid upon the men
10. 7 let the men go, that they may serve the
17. 9 Choose us out men, and go out, fight with
18. 21 provide..able men, such as fear God, men
18. 25 Moses chose able men out of all Israel
21. 18 And if men strive together, and one smite
21. 22 If men strive, and hurt a woman with c.
22. 31 ye shall be holy men unto me: neither shall

Exod. 35. 22 men and women, as many as were willing
Lev. 18. 27 these abominations have the men of the
Num. 1. 5 these (are) the names of the men that shall
1. 17 Aaron took these men which are expressed
9. 7 those men said unto him, We (are) defiled
11. 26 there remained two (of the) men in the
13. 2 Send thou men, that they may search the
13. 3 those men (were) heads of the children of
13. 16 These (are) the names of the men which M
13. 31 the men that went up with him said, We
13. 32 the people that we saw in it (are) men of
14. 22 those men which have seen my glory, and
14. 36 men which Moses sent to search the land
14. 37 Even those men that did bring up the evil
14. 38 of the men that went to search the land
16. 2 famous in the congregation, men of ren.
16. 14 wilt thou put out the eyes of these men?
16. 26 Depart..from the tents of..wicked men
16. 30 that these men have provoked the LORD
22. 9 and said, What men (are) these with thee?
22. 20 If the men come to call thee, rise up, (and)
22. 35 Go with the men: but only the word that
25. 5 Slay ye every one his men that were joined
31. 21 the priest said unto the men of war which
31. 28 the men of war which went out to battle
31. 42 which Moses divided from the men that
31. 49 the men of war which (are) under our ch.
31. 53 For the men of war had taken spoil, every
32. 11 none of the men that came up out of E.
32. 14 an increase of sinful men, to augment yet
34. 17 These (are) the names of the men which
34. 19 And the names of the men (are) these: Of
Deut. 1. 13 Take you wise men, and understanding
1. 15 I took the chief of your tribes, wise men
1. 22 We will send men before us, and they shall
1. 23 I took twelve men of you, one of a tribe
1. 35 there shall not one of these men of this
2. 14 generation of the men of war were wasted
2. 16 the men of war were consumed and dead
13. 13 (Certain) men, the children of Belial, are
19. 17 the men, between whom the controversy
21. 21 the men of his city shall stone him with
22. 21 the men of the city shall stone her with
25. 1 If there be a controversy between men, and
25. 11 When men strive together one with ano.
31. 12 men, women, and children, and thy str.
32. 26 remembrance of them to cease..among m.
Josh. 2. 1 son of Nun sent out of Shittim two men
2. 2 there came men in hither to night of the
2. 3 Bring forth the men that are come to thee
2. 4 the woman took the two men, and hid
2. 4 There came men unto me, but I wist not
2. 5 the men went out: whither the men went
2. 7 men pursued after them the way to Jordan
2. 9 she said unto the men, I know that the L.
2. 14 the men answered her, Our life for yours
2. 17 the men said unto her, We (will be) bla.
2. 23 the two men returned, and descended from
4. 2 Take you twelve men out of the people
5. 4 the men of war, died in the wilderness
5. 6 the people (that were) men of war, which
6. 3 shall compass the city, all (ye) men of war
6. 22 Joshua had said unto the two men that
7. 2 Joshua sent men from Jericho to Ai, which
7. 2 And the men went up and viewed Ai
7. 4 and they fled before the men of Ai
7. 5 the men of Ai smote of them about thirty
8. 14 men of the city went out against Israel
8. 20 when the men of Ai looked behind them
8. 21 they turned again, and slew the men of
9. 14 the men took of their victuals, and asked
10. 2 and all the men thereof (were) mighty
10. 6 the men of Gibeon sent unto Joshua to
10. 18 cave, and set men by it for to keep them
18. 4 Give out from among you three men for
18. 8 the men arose, and went away: and Jos.
18. 9 the men went and passed through the land
Judg. 6. 27 Gideon took ten men of his servants, and
6. 27 father's household, and the men of the city
6. 28 the men of the city arose early in the
6. 30 the men of the city said unto Joash, Bring
8. 5 he said unto the men of Succoth, Give, I
8. 8 the men of Penuel answered him as the men
8. 9 spake also unto the men of Penuel, saying
8. 14 And caught..of the men of Succoth, and
8. 15 came unto the men of Succoth, and said
8. 15 give bread unto thy men (that are) weary
8. 16 with them he taught the men of Succoth
8. 17 beat down the tower..and slew the men
8. 18 What manner of men (were they) whom
9. 9 wherewith by me they honour God and m.
9. 13 leave my wine, which cheereth God and m.
9. 28 Serve the men of Hamor the father of
9. 36 seest the shadow..as (if they were) men
9. 49 the men of the tower of Shechem died also
9. 51 thither fled all the men and women, and
9. 57 the evil of the men of Shechem did God
11. 3 there were gathered vain men to Jephthah
12. 4 gathered together all the men of Gilead
12. 4 the men of Gilead smote Ephraim, because
12. 5 the men of Gilead said unto him, (Art) thou
14. 18 the men of the city said unto him on the
16. 27 the house was full of men and women; and
18. 2 five men from their coasts, men of valour
18. 7 the five men departed, and came to Laish
18. 14 Then answered the five men that went to
18. 17 the five men that went to spy out the
18. 22 the men that (were) in the houses near to
19. 16 but the men of the place (were) Benjamites
19. 22 the men of the city, certain sons of Belial
19. 25 the men would not hearken to him; so the
20. 10 will take ten men of an hundred throug.

Judg. 20. 12 the tribes of Israel sent men through all
20. 13 deliver (us) the men, the children of Belial
20. 44, 46 all these (were) men of valour
Ruth 4. 2 he took ten men of the elders of the city
1 Sa. 1. 11 wilt give unto thine handmaid a man child
2. 17 for men abhorred the offering of the LORD
2. 26 favour..with the LORD, and also with m.
4. 9 quit yourselves like men, O ye Philistines
4. 9 quit yourselves like men, and fight
5. 7 when the men of Ashdod saw that (it was)
5. 9 he smote the men of the city, both small
5. 12 the men that died not were smitten with
6. 10 the men did so; and took two milch kine
6. 15 and the men of Beth-shemesh offered bu.
6. 19 he smote the men of Beth-shemesh beca
6. 20 the men of Beth-shemesh said, Who is able
7. 1 men of Kirjath-jearim came, and fetched
7. 11 the men of Israel went out of Mizpeh, and
8. 22 Samuel said unto the men of Israel, Go ye
10. 2 shalt find two men by Rachel's sepulchre
10. 3 there shall meet thee three men going up
11. 1 the men of Jabesh said unto Nahash, M.
11. 5 told him the tidings of the men of Jabesh
11. 9 came and showed (it) to the men of Jabesh
11. 10 the men of Jabesh said, To morrow we will
11. 12 bring the men, that we may put them to
11. 15 and all the men of Israel rejoiced greatly
14. 8 we will pass over unto (these) men, and
14. 12 the men of the garrison answered Jonat.
17. 12 went among men..in the days of Saul
17. 26 David spake to the men that stood by him
17. 28 brother heard when he spake unto the men
17. 52 the men of Israel and of Judah arose, and
18. 5 Saul set him over the men of war; and he
18. 27 and went, he and his men, and slew of the
22. 6 discovered, and the men that (were) with
23. 3 David's men said unto him, Behold; we
23. 5 his men went to Keilah, and fought with
23. 8 to Keilah, to besiege David and his men
23. 12 deliver me and my men into the hand of
23. 13 his men, (which were) about six hundred
23. 24 his men (were) in the wilderness of Maon
23. 25 his men went to seek (him). And they told
23. 26 and his men on that side of the mountain
23. 26 his men compassed David and his men
24. 2 went to seek David and his men upon the
24. 3 his men remained in the sides of the cave
24. 4 the men of David said unto him, Behold
24. 6 he said unto his men The LORD forbid that
24. 22 and his men gat them up unto the hold
25. 11 unto men whom I know not whence they
25. 13 David said unto his men, Gird ye on every
25. 15 the men (were) very good unto us, and we
25. 20 his men came down against her; and she
27. 3 dwelt with Achish at Gath, he and his men
27. 8 men went up, and invaded the Geshurites
28. 1 out with me to battle, thou and thy men
28. 8 he went, and two men with him, and they
29. 2 his men passed on in the rereward with
29. 4 (should it) not (be)..heads of these men
29. 11 his men rose up early to depart in the
30. 1 his men were come to Ziklag on the third
30. 3 his men came to the city, and, behold, (it)
30. 21 David came to the two hundred men which
30. 31 himself and his men were wont to haunt
31. 1 the men of Israel fled from before the
31. 6 his armour bearer, and all his men, that
31. 7 the men of Israel that (were) on the other
31. 7 saw that the men of Israel fled, and that
2 Sa. 1. 11 likewise all the men that (were) with him
2. 3 men that (were) with him did David bring
2. 4 the men of Judah came, and there they
2. 4 the men of Jabesh-gilead (were they) that
2. 5 messengers unto the men of Jabesh-gilead
2. 17 Abner was beaten, and the men of Israel
2. 29 his men walked all that night through the
2. 31 smitten of Benjamin, and of Abner's men
2. 32 his men went all night, and they came to
3. 20 So Abner came..and twenty men with him
3. 20 Abner, and the men that (were) with him
3. 39 these men the sons of Zeruiah (be) too h.
4. 2 had two men (that were) captains of bands
4. 11 when wicked men have slain a righteous
5. 6 men went to Jerusalem unto the Jebusites
5. 21 images, and David and his men burnt them
7. 14 I will chasten him with the rod of men
10. 5 the men were greatly ashamed: and the
11. 16 place where he knew that valiant men
11. 17 the men of the city went out and fought
11. 23 the men prevailed against us, and came
12. 1 There were two men in one city; the one
15. 6 stole the hearts of the men of Israel
15. 22 his men, and all the little ones that (w.)
16. 13 as David and his men went by the way, S.
17. 8 thou knowest thy father and his men, that
17. 12 of all the men that (are) with him there
18. 28 the men that lifted up their hand against
19. 28 all (of) my father's house were..dead men
19. 41 and all David's men with him, over Jordan
20. 7 there went out after him Joab's men, and
21. 6 Let seven men of his sons be delivered unto
21. 17 the men of David sware unto him, saying
23. 17 the men that went in jeopardy of their
1 Ki. 1. 9 all the men of Judah the king's servants
2. 32 two men more righteous and better than
9. 22 they (were) men of war, and his servants
10. 8 Happy (are) thy men, happy (are) these thy
11. 18 they took men with them out of Paran, and
11. 24 gathered men unto him, and became ca.
13. 25 men passed by, and saw the carcase cast
20. 17 saying, There are men come out of Sam.
20. 33 the men did diligently observe whether

1 Ki.21. 10 set two men, sons of Belial, before him
21. 11 the men of his city, (even) the elders and
21. 13 there came in two men, children of Belial
21. 13 the men of Belial witnessed against him
2 Ki. 2. 16 there be with..servants fifty strong men
2. 19 men of the city said unto Elisha, Behold
4. 40 they poured out for the men to eat: and
5. 24 and he let the men go, and they departed
7. 3 were four leprous men at the entering
10. 6 the heads of the men your master's sons
10. 24 of the men whom I have brought into your
11. 9 men that were to come in on the sabbath
12. 15 they reckoned not with the men into wh.
17. 30 the men of Babylon made Succoth-benoth
17. 30 the men of Cuth made Nergal, and the m.
18. 27 (sent me) to the men which sit on the w.
20. 14 What said these men? and from whence
23. 17 And the men of the city told him, (It is)
24. 16 the men of might, (even) seven thousand
25. 4 the men (of war) fled by night by the way
25. 19 was set over the men of war, and five m.
25. 23 their men, heard that the king of Babylon
25. 23 there came to Gedaliah..they and their m.
25. 24 Gedaliah sware to them, and to their men
25. 25 Ishmael..came, and ten men with him, and
1 Ch. 4. 12 Paseah, and Tehinnah..These (are) the m.
4. 22 the men of Chozeba, and Joash, and Sa.
4. 42 five hundred men, went to mount Seir, h.
5. 18 men able to bear buckler and sword, and
5. 24 men of valour, famous men, (and) heads
7. 21 the men of Gath (that were) born in (that)
7. 40 number..(was) twenty and six thousand m.
8. 40 sons of Ulam were mighty men of valour
9. 9 these men (were) chief of the fathers in
11. 19 shall I drink the blood of these men that
12. 8 men of war (fit) for the battle, that could
12. 38 these men of war, that could keep rank
19. 5 told David how the men were served: and
19. 5 he sent..the men were greatly ashamed
2 Ch. 8. 9 they (were) men of war, and chief of his
9. 7 Happy (are) thy men, and happy (are) these
13. 7 there are gathered unto him vain men, the
14. 11 our God; let not man prevail against thee
17. 13 and the men of war..(were) in Jerusalem
23. 8 men that were to come in on the sabbath
24. 24 Syrians came with a small company of men
28. 15 men which were expressed by name rose
31. 19 the men that were expressed by name, to
34. 12 the men did the work faithfully: and the
Ezra 1. 4 let the men of his place help him with
2. 2 number of the men of the people of Israel
2. 22 The men of Netophah, fifty and six
2. 23 The men of Anathoth, an hundred twenty
2. 27 men of Michmas, an hundred twenty and
2. 28 men of Beth-el and Ai, two hundred tw.
10. 1 congregation of men and women and ch.
10. 9 the men of Judah and Benjamin gathered
10. 17 the men that had taken strange wives by
Neh. 1. 2 he and (certain) men of Judah; and I as.
2. 12 in the night, I and some few men with me
3. 2 next unto him builded the men of Jericho
3. 7 the men of Gibeon and of Mizpah, unto
3. 22 repaired the priests, the men of the plain
4. 23 the men of the guard which followed me
7. 7 The number, (I say), of the men of the pe.
7. 26 men of Beth-lehem and Netophah, an hu.
7. 27 The men of Anathoth, an hundred twenty
7. 28 The men of Beth-azmaveth, forty and two
7. 29 The men of Kirjath-jearim, Chephirah, and
7. 30 men of Ramah and Gaba, six hundred tw.
7. 31 The men of Michmas, an hundred and tw.
7. 32 men of Beth-el and Ai, an hundred twenty
7. 33 The men of the other Nebo, fifty and two
8. 3 before the men and the women, and those
11. 2 the men that willingly offered themselves
11. 6 hundred three score and eight valiant men
Job 4. 13 the night, when deep sleep falleth on men
5. 17 happy (is) the man whom God correcteth
7. 1 not an appointed time to man upon earth?
7. 17 What (is) man, that thou shouldest magn
9. 2 but how should man be just with God?
10. 4 eyes of flesh? or seest thou as man seeth?
10. 5 (Are) thy days as the days of man? (are)
14. 19 and thou destroyest the hope of man
15. 14 What (is) man, that he should be clean?
25. 4 How then can man be justified with God?
25. 6 How much less man, (that is) a worm; and
28. 4 are dried up, they are gone away from m.
28. 13 Man knoweth not the price thereof; neit.
32. 1 So these three men ceased to answer Job
32. 5 no answer in the mouth of (these) three m.
32. 8 But (there is) a spirit in man: and the
33. 12 answer thee, that God is greater than man
33. 15 night, when deep sleep falleth upon men
33. 16 he openeth the ears of men, and sealeth
33. 26 will render unto man his righteousness
33. 27 He looketh upon men; and (if any) say, I
34. 8 goeth..and walketh with wicked men
34. 10 hearken unto me, ye men of understanding
34. 34 Let men of understanding tell me, and
34. 36 because of (his) answers for wicked men
36. 24 thou magnify his work, which men beh.
36. 25 may see it; man may behold (it) afar off
37. 7 sealeth..that all men may know his work
37. 24 Men do therefore fear him; he respecteth
Psa. 8. 4 What is man, that thou art mindful of him?
9. 19 let not man prevail; let the heathen be
9. 20 nations know themselves (to be but) men
10. 18 the man of the earth may no more oppr
26. 9 Gather not..my life with bloody men
55. 13 thou, a man mine equal, my guide, and m.
55. 23 deceitful men shall not live out half their
Psa. 56. 1 man would swallow me up: he fighting
59. 2 Deliver me..and save me from bloody m.
66. 12 hast caused men to ride over our heads
73. 5 They (are) not in trouble (as other) men
76. 5 none of the men of might have found th.
90. 3 Thou turnest man to destruction; and say.
103. 15 (As for) man, his days (are) as grass; as a
104. 15 wine (that) maketh glad the heart of man
104. 15 and bread (which) strengtheneth man's h.
139. 19 depart from me therefore, ye bloody men
144. 3 son of man, that thou makest account of
Prov. 24. 1 Be not thou envious against evil men
25. 1 men of Hezekiah king of Judah copied out
28. 5 Evil men understand not judgment: but
29. 8 Scornful men bring a city into a snare
Eccl. 9. 14 (was) a little city, and few men within it
12. 3 the strong men shall bow themselves, and
Isa. 2. 11 haughtiness of men shall be bowed down
2. 17 the haughtiness of men shall be made low
5. 22 men of strength to mingle strong drink
7. 13 (Is it) a small thing for you to weary men
8. 1 write in it with a man's pen concerning
13. 7 be faint, and every man's heart shall melt
13. 12 make a man more precious than fine gold
24. 6 inhabitants..are burned, and few men left
28. 14 ye scornful men, that rule this people
29. 13 their fear..taught by the precept of men
33. 8 despised the cities, he regardeth no man
36. 12 (sent me) to the men that sit upon the w.
39. 3 What said these men? and from whence
45. 14 merchandise..of the Sabeans, men of st.
51. 7 fear ye not the reproach of men neither
51. 12 shouldest be afraid of..man (that) shall d.
56. 2 Blessed (is) the man (that) doeth this, and
57. 1 merciful men (are) taken away, none con.
66. 24 men that have transgressed against me
Jer. 5. 26 lay wait..they set a trap, they catch men
11. 21 saith the LORD of the men of Anathoth
11. 23 will bring evil upon the men of Anathoth
18. 21 let their men be put to death; (let) their
19. 10 in the sight of the men that go with thee
26. 22 king sent men into Egypt, (namely), Eln.
26. 22 and (certain) men with him into Egypt
34. 18 will give the men that have transgressed
37. 10 there remained (but) wounded men among
38. 4 the men of war that remain in this city
38. 9 these men have done evil in all that they
38. 10 Take from hence thirty men with thee, and
38. 11 Ebed melech took the men with him, and
38. 16 the hand of these men that seek thy life
39. 4 king of Judah saw them, and..men of war
39. 17 hand of the men of whom thou (art) afraid
40. 7 their men, heard that the king of Babylon
40. 7 had committed unto him men, and women
40. 8 the sons of Ephai..they and their men
40. 9 sware unto them, and to their men, saying
41. 1 ten men with him, came unto Gedaliah
41. 2 and the ten men that were with him, and
41. 3 and the Chaldeans..(and) the men of war
41. 7 he, and the men that (were) with him
41. 8 ten men were found among them that said
41. 9 had cast all the dead bodies of the men
41. 12 they took all the men, and went to fight
41. 15 escaped from Johanan with eight men, and
41. 16 men of war, and the women, and the ch
42. 17 the men that set their faces to go into
43. 2 the son of Kareah, and all the proud men
43. 9 hide..in the sight of the men of Judah
44. 15 the men which knew that their wives had
44. 19 drink offerings unto her, without our m?
48. 14 We (are) mighty and strong men for the war
48. 31 shall mourn for the men of Kir-heres
48. 36 shall sound..for the men of Kir-heres
49. 26 the men of war shall be cut off in that day
50. 30 her man of war shall be cut off in that
51. 32 burned..and the men of war are affrigh.
52. 7 the men of war fled, and went forth out
52. 25 charge of the men of war; and seven men
Eze. 9. 2 men came from the way of the higher gate
9. 4 the men that sigh and that cry for all
9. 6 ancient men which (were) before the ho.
11. 2 these (are) the men that devise mischief
11. 15 the men of thy kindred, and all the house
12. 16 leave a few men of them from the sword
14. 3 these men have set up their idols in their
14. 14 these three men, Noah, Daniel, and Job
14. 16, 18 (Though) these three men (were) in it
21. 31 deliver thee into the hand of brutish men
22. 9 are men that carry tales to shed blood
23. 14 she saw men pourtrayed upon the wall
23. 40 ye have sent for men to come from far
23. 42 the men of the common sort (were) brou.
23. 45 the righteous men, they shall judge them
24. 17 cover not..and eat not the bread of men
24. 22 cover (your) lips, nor eat the bread of men
27. 10 They..were in thine army, thy men of war
27. 27 thy men of war, that (are) in thee, and in
39. 14 sever out men of continual employment
Dan. 10. 7 men that were with me saw not the vision
Joel 2. 7 they shall climb the wall like men of war
3. 9 let all the men of war draw near; let them
Amos 6. 9 if there remain ten men in one house, that
Obad. 7 the men of thy confederacy have brought
7 the men that were at peace with thee have
Jon. 1. 10 Then were the men exceedingly afraid, and
1. 10 men knew that he fled from the presence
1. 13 men rowed hard to bring (it) to the land
1. 16 the men feared the LORD exceedingly, and
Mic. 7. 6 enemies (are) the men of his own house
Nah. 2. 3 the valiant men (are) in scarlet: the char
Zeph. 1. 12 punish the men that are settled on their
Zech. 3. 8 they (are) men wondered at: for, behold
Zech. 7. 2 Sherezer and Regem-melech, and their m.
8. 23 men shall take hold out of all languages

4. *A man, mortal*, אֱנָשׁ *enash.*

Ezra 4. 11 men on this side the river, and at such
Dan. 2. 10 There is not a man upon the earth that
2. 38 wheresoever the children of men dwell
2. 43 mingle themselves with the seed of men
3. 10 every man that shall hear the sound of
4. 16 Let his heart be changed from man's, and
4. 17, 25, 32 Most High ruleth in..kingdom of m.
4. 17 and setteth up over it the basest of men
4. 25, 32 they shall drive thee from men, and
4. 33 he was driven from men, and did eat grass
5. 5 came forth fingers of a man's hand, and
5. 21 he was driven from the sons of men; and
5. 21 most high God ruled in the kingdom of men
6. 7 shall ask a petition of any god or man
6. 12 not signed a decree, that every man that
6. 12 shall ask (a petition) of any god or man
7. 4 stand upon the feet as a man, and a man's
7. 8 in this horn (were) eyes like..eyes of man
7. 13 (one) like the Son of man came with the

5. *One connected with or possessing, a son*, בֵּן *ben.*

1 Ki. 1. 52 If he will show himself a worthy man
2 Ki. 2. 16 there be with thy servants fifty strong m.
Judg 18. 2 men of valour, from Zorah, and from Esh.
Eze. 23. 7 chosen men of Assyria, and with all on
27. 11 The men of Arvad with thine army (were)
27. 15 The men of Dedan (were) thy merchants
1 Sa. 14. 52 when Saul saw..any valiant man, he took
2 Sa. 3. 34 as a man falleth before wicked men, (so)
17. 10 (they) which (be) with him (are) valiant m.
1 Ch. 26. 7 whose brethren (were) strong men, Elihu
26. 9 had sons and brethren, strong men, eight
26. 30 men of valour, a thousand and seven hu.
26. 32 And his brethren, men of valour, (were)
2 Ch. 26. 17 priests of the LORD, (that were) valiant men
28. 6 hundred and twenty thousand..valiant m.
Job 1. 3 the greatest of all the men of the east
Jer. 49. 28 Arise ye..and spoil the men of the east
Eze. 25. 4 I will deliver thee to the men of the
25. 10 the men of the east with the Ammonites
30. 5 the men of the land that is in league

6. *A son of man, a human being*, בֶּן־אָדָם *ben adam.*

Job 16. 21 as a man (pleadeth) for his neighbour
Psa. 12. 8 walk on every side, when the vilest men
89. 47 wherefore hast thou made all men in vain
Eccl. 3. 21 Who knoweth the spirit of man that goeth

7. *Owner, master, lord*, בַּעַל *baal.*

Gen. 20. 3 the woman which thou hast..(is) a man's
Exod 24. 14 if any man have any matters to do, let
Judg. 9. 2, 3 in the ears of all the men of Shechem
9. 6 the men of Shechem gathered together
9. 7 Hearken unto me, ye men of Shechem
9. 18 king over the men of Shechem, because he
9. 20 devour the men of Shechem, and the house
9. 20 let fire come out from the men of Shechem
9. 23 the men of Shechem; and the men of S.
9. 24 upon the men of Shechem, which aided
9. 25 the men of Shechem set liers in wait for
9. 26 men of Shechem put their confidence in
9. 39 Gaal went out before the men of Shechem
9. 46 men of the tower of Shechem heard (that)
9. 47 men of the tower of Shechem were gath.
20. 5 the men of Gibeah rose against me, and
1 Sa. 23. 11 Will the men of Keilah deliver me up into
23. 12 Will the men of Keilah deliver me and my
2 Sa. 21. 12 from the men of Jabesh-gilead, which had
Prov 22. 24 Make no friendship with an angry man
23. 2 if thou (be) a man given to appetite
29. 22 a furious man aboundeth in transgression

8. *A (mighty) man*, גִּבּוֹר *gibbor.*

2 Sa. 22. 26 with the upright man thou wilt show
1 Ch 12. 8 there separated..unto David..men of mi.
28. 1 and with all the valiant men
2 Ch 13. 3 an army of valiant men of war, (even) four

9. *A (mighty) man*, גְּבַר *gebar.*

Ezra 4. 21 commandment to cause these men to ce.
5. 4 What are the names of the men that make
5. 10 the names of the men that (were) the chief
6. 8 forthwith expences..given unto these men
Dan. 2. 25 have found a man of the captives of Judah
3. 12 these men, O king, have not regarded thee
3. 13 they brought these men before the king
3. 20 most mighty men that (were) in his army
3. 21 these men were bound in their coats, their
3. 22 flame..slew those men that took up Sha.
3. 23 And these three men, Shadrach, Meshach
3. 24 Did not we cast three men bound into the
3. 25 I see four men loose, walking in the midst
3. 27 saw these men, upon whose bodies the fire
5. 11 There is a man in thy kingdom in whom
6. 5 Then said these men, We shall not find
6. 15 these men assembled unto the king, and
6. 24 brought those men which had accused D.

10. *A (mighty) man*, גֶּבֶר *geber.*

Exod 10. 11 go now ye (that are) men, and serve the
12. 37 hundred thousand on foot (that were) men
Num 24. 3, 15 the man whose eyes are open hath said
Deut 22. 5 pertaineth unto a man, neither shall a m.
Josh. 7. 14 and the household..shall come man by m.
7. 17 the family of the Zarhites man by man
7. 18 he brought his household man by man; and
Judg 5. 30 to every man a damsel (or) two; to Sisera
2 Sa 23. 1 the man (who was) raised up on high, the
1 Ch. 23. 3 their number by their polls, man by man

1 Ch. 24. 4 there were more chief men found of the
26. 12 (even)among the chief men,(having) wards
Job 3. 3 was said, There is a man child conceived
3. 23 (Why is light given) to a man whose way
4. 17 shall a man be more pure than his Maker
10. 5 (Are) thy days..thy years as man's days
14. 10 But man dieth, and wasteth away; yea
14. 14 If a man die, shall he live (again)? All the
16. 21 Oh that one might plead for a man with
22. 2 Can a man be profitable unto God, as he
33. 17 may withdraw..and hide pride from man
33. 29 these..worketh God oftentimes with m.
34. 7 What man (is) like Job, (who) drinketh up
34. 9 It profiteth a man nothing that he should
34. 34 and let a wise man hearken unto me
38. 3 Gird up now thy loins like a man; for I
40. 7 Gird up thy loins now like a man: I will
Psa. 34. 8 blessed (is) the man (that) trusteth in him
37. 23 steps of a (good) man are ordered by the
40. 4 Blessed (is) that man that maketh the L.
52. 7 the man (that) made not God his strength
88. 4 I am counted..I am as a man (that hath)
89. 48 What man (is he that) liveth, and shall
94. 12 Blessed (is) the man whom thou chasten.
127. 5 Happy (is) the man that hath his quiver
128. 4 thus shall the man be blessed that feareth
Prov. 6. 34 jealousy (is) the rage of a man; therefore
20. 24 Man's goings (are) of the LORD; how can
24. 5 A wise man (is) strong; yea..of knowle.
28. 3 A poor man that oppresseth the poor (is
28. 21 for a piece of bread (that) man will trans.
29. 5 man that flattereth his neighbour sprea.
30. 1 man spake unto Ithiel, even unto Ithiel
30. 19 and the way of a man with a maid
Jer. 17. 5 Thus saith the LORD, Cursed (be) the man
17. 7 Blessed (is) the man that trusteth in the
22. 30 a man (that) shall not prosper in his days
23. 9 and like a man whom wine hath overcome
30. 6 wherefore do I see every man with his
31. 22 new thing..A woman shall compass a m.
43. 6 men, and women, and children..the king's
44. 20 Then Jeremiah said..to the men, and to
Lam. 3. 1 I (am) the man (that) hath seen affliction
3. 27 (It is) good for a man that he bear the
3. 35 To turn aside the right of a man before
3. 39 a man for the punishment of his sins?
Dan. 8. 15 there stood before..the appearance of a m.
Mic. 2. 2 so they oppress a man and his house, even
Hab. 2. 5 a proud man, neither keepeth at home
Zech. 13. 7 Awake, O sword..against the man (that

11. *A (mighty) man,* גְּבַר *gebar.*

Psa. 18. 25 with an upright man thou wilt show thy.

12. *A male,* זָכָר *zakar.*

Lev. 15. 33 of the man, and of the woman, and of him
Num 31. 17 kill every woman that hath known man by
31. 18 have not known a man by lying with him
31. 35 women that had not known man by lying
Judg 21. 11 and every woman that hath lain by man
Jer. 20. 15 A man child is born unto thee, making
30. 6 see whether a man doth travail with child
Eze. 16. 17 madest to thyself images of men, and didst

13. *A soul, breathing creature,* נֶפֶשׁ *nephesh.*

2 Ki. 12. 4 money that every man is set at, (and) all
1 Ch. 5. 21 they took..of men an hundred; Ex. 12. 16.

14. *One,* אֶחָד *echad.*

Judg. 4. 16 Barak pursued..(and) there was not a man

15. *A man, husband,* ἀνήρ *anēr.*

Matt. 7. 24 I will liken him unto a wise man, which
7. 26 shall be likened unto a foolish man, which
12. 41 men of Nineve shall rise in judgment with
14. 21 they..were about five thousand men, bes.
14. 35 when the men of that place had knowledge
15. 38 they that did eat were four thousand men
Mark 6. 20 knowing that he was a just man and an
6. 44 And they..were about five thousand men
10. 2 Is it lawful for a man to put away (his) w.?
Luke 1. 27 To a virgin espoused to a man whose name
1. 34 How shall this be, seeing I know not a m.?
5. 8 Depart from me; for I am a sinful man
5. 12 a man full of leprosy; who, seeing Jesus
5. 18 men brought in a bed..and they sought
7. 20 When the men were come unto him, they
8. 27 there met him out of the city a certain man
8. 38 Now the man out of whom the devils were
8. 41 there came a man named Jairus, and he
9. 14 For they were about five thousand men
9. 30 there talked with him two men, which were
9. 32 they saw his glory, and the two men that
9. 38 man of the company cried out, saying, M.
11. 31 rise up in the judgment with the men of
11. 32 men of Nineve shall rise up in the judgm.
14. 24 none of those men which were bidden shall
17. 12 there met him ten men that were lepers
19. 2 man named Zaccheus, which was the chief
19. 7 he was gone to be guest with a man that
22. 63 men that held Jesus mocked him, and sm.
23. 50 a man named Joseph..a good man, and a
24. 4 two men stood by them in shining garm.
John 1. 13 not of blood..nor of the will of man, but
1. 30 After me cometh a man which is preferred
6. 10 So the men sat down, in number about five
Acts 1. 10 two men stood by them in white apparel
1. 11 Ye men of Galilee, why stand ye gazing
1. 16 Men (and) brethren, this scripture must
1. 21 Wherefore of these men which have com.
2. 5 devout men, out of every nation under h.
2. 14 Ye men of Judea, and all (ye) that dwell
2. 22 Ye men of Israel..a man approved of God
2. 29 Men (and) brethren, let me freely speak

Acts 2. 37 said..Men (and) brethren, what shall we
3. 2 certain man lame from his mother's womb
3. 12 Ye men of Israel, why marvel ye at this?
4. 4 number of the men was about five thou.
5. 1 certain man named Ananias, with Sapph.
5. 14 multitudes both of men and women
5. 25 men whom ye put in prison are standing
5. 35 Ye men of Israel, take heed to yourselves
5. 36 to whom a number of men..joined them.
6. 3 look ye out among you seven men of ho.
6. 5 they chose Stephen, a man full of faith and
6. 11 Then they suborned men, which said, We
7. 2 Men, brethren, and fathers, hearken; The
8. 2 devout men carried Stephen (to his burial)
8. 3 haling men and women, committed (them)
8. 9 there..a certain man called Simon, which
8. 12 they were baptized, both men and women
8. 27 man of Ethiopia, an eunuch of great aut.
9. 2 whether they were men or women, he might
9. 7 men which journeyed with him stood sp.
9. 12 hath seen in a vision a man named Anan.
9. 13 I have heard by many of this man, how
9. 38 they sent unto him two [men], desiring
10. 1 There was a certain man in Cesarea called
10. 5 send men to Joppa, and call for (one) Simon
10. 17 men which were sent from Cornelius had
10. 19 spirit said unto him, Behold, three men
10. 21 Then Peter went down to the men which
10. 22 Cornelius the centurion, a just man, and
10. 28 unlawful thing for a man that is a Jew to
10. 30 a man stood before me in bright clothing
11. 3 Thou wentest in to men uncircumcised
11. 11 three men already come unto the house
11. 12 and we entered into the man's house
11. 13 Send [men] to Joppa, and call for Simon
11. 20 some of them were men of Cyprus and C.
11. 24 For he was a good man, and full of the
13. 7 Sergius Paulus, a prudent man; who ca.
13. 15 men (and) brethren, if ye have any word
13. 16 Men of Israel, and ye that fear God, give
13. 21 gave..a man of the tribe of Benjamin, by
13. 22 I have found David..[a man] after mine own
13. 26 Men (and) brethren..to you is the word
13. 38 Be it known unto you therefore, men (and)
14. 8 there sat a certain man at Lystra, impo.
15. 7 Men (and) brethren, ye know how that a
15. 13 James answered, saying, Men (and) bre.
15. 22 send chosen men..chief men among the
15. 25 send chosen men unto you with our bel.
16. 9 There stood a man of Macedonia, and pr.
17. 12 many of them believed..of men, not a few
17. 22 men of Athens, I perceive that in all th.
17. 31 (that) man whom he hath ordained..he
17. 34 certain men clave unto him, and believed
18. 24 an eloquent man, (and) mighty in the Scr.
19. 7 And all the men were about twelve
19. 35 what man is there that knoweth not how
19. 37 For ye have brought hither these men
20. 30 Also of your own selves shall men arise
21. 11 So shall the Jews..bind the man that ow.
21. 23 We have four men which have a vow on
21. 26 Then Paul took the men, and the next day
21. 28 Crying out, Men of Israel, help: This is
21. 38 four thousand men that were murderers?
22. 1 Men, brethren, and fathers, hear ye my
22. 3 I am verily a man (which am) a Jew, born
22. 4 delivering into prisons both men and wo
22. 12 devout man according to the law, having
23. 1 Men (and) brethren, I have lived in all
23. 6 Men (and) brethren, I am a Pharisee, the
23. 21 lie in wait..more than forty men, which
23. 27 This man was taken of the Jews, and sh.
23. 30 how that the Jews laid wait for the man
24. 5 For we have found this man (a) pestilent
25. 5 go down with (me), and accuse this man
25. 14 There is a certain man left in bonds by F.
25. 17 commanded the man to be brought forth
25. 23 with the chief captains and principal m.
25. 24 all men which are here present with us
28. 17 Men (and) brethren, though I have com.
Rom. 4. 8 Blessed (is) the man to whom the Lord
7. 3, 3 she be married to another man
11. 4 reserved to myself seven thousand men
1 Co. 7. 16 how knowest thou, O man, whether thou
11. 3 know, that the head of every man is Christ
11. 3 and the head of the woman (is) the man
11. 4 Every man praying or prophesying, having
11. 7 For a man indeed ought not to cover (his)
11. 7 but the woman is the glory of the man
11. 8 man is not..but the woman of the man
11. 9 Neither was the man created for the wo.
11. 9 but the woman for the man
11. 11 neither is the man without the woman
11. 11 neither the woman without the man, in
11. 12 woman (is) of the man, even so (is) the m.
11. 14 if a man have long hair, it is a shame unto
13. 11 when I became a man, I put away childish
Eph. 4. 13 unto a perfect man, unto the measure of
5. 28 So ought men to love their wives as their
1 Ti. 2. 8 I will therefore that men pray every where
2. 12 nor to usurp authority over the man, but
5. 9 widow..having been the wife of one man
Jas. 1. 8 A double minded man (is) unstable in all
1. 12 Blessed (is) the man that endureth temp.
1. 20 wrath of man worketh not the righteous.
1. 23 he is like unto a man beholding his natu.
2. 2 For if there come..a man with a gold ring
3. 2 the same (is) a perfect man, (and) able also

16. *Belonging to man or humanity,* ἀνθρώπινος.

1 Co. 2. 4 not with enticing words of [man's] wisdom
2. 13 not in the words which man's wisdom te.
1 Co. 4. 3 be judged of you, or of man's judgment
1 Pe. 2. 13 Submit..to every ordinance of man for

17. *A man, a human being,* ἄνθρωπος *anthrōpos.*

Matt. 4. 4 Man shall not live by bread alone, but
4. 19 Follow..and I will make you fishers of m.
5. 13 and to be trodden under foot of men
5. 16 Let your light so shine before men, that
5. 19 Whosoever therefore..shall teach men so
6. 1 do not your alms before men, to be seen
6. 2 that they may have glory of men. Verily
6. 5 standing..that they may be seen of men
6. 14 For if ye forgive men their trespasses, your
6. 15 ye forgive not men their trespasses, neither
6. 16 that they may appear unto men to fast
6. 18 That thou appear not unto men to fast
7. 9 Or what man is there of you, whom if his
7. 12 whatsoever ye would that men should do
8. 9 For I am a man under authority, having
8. 20 but the Son of man hath not where to lay
8. 27 the men marvelled saying, What manner
9. 6 the Son of man hath power on earth to for.
9. 8 God, which had given such power unto m.
9. 9 saw a man, named Matthew, sitting at the
9. 32 brought to him a dumb [man] possessed
10. 17 But beware of men; for they will deliver
10. 23 not have gone..till the Son of man be come
10. 32 Whosoever..shall confess me before men
10. 33 whosoever shall deny me before men, him
10. 35 For I am come to set a man at variance
10. 36 man's foes (shall be) they of his own hou.
11. 8 man clothed in soft raiment? Behold, they
11. 19 The Son of man came eating and drinking
11. 19 say, Behold a man gluttonous, and a wine
12. 8 For the Son of man is lord even of the
12. 10 there was a man which had (his) hand w
12. 11 What man shall there be among you that
12. 12 How much then is a man better than a
12. 13 Then saith he to the man, Stretch forth
12. 31 and blasphemy shall be forgiven [unto m.]
12. 31 blasphemy..shall not be forgiven unto m.
12. 32 speaketh a word against the Son of man
12. 35 A good man..and an evil man, out of the
12. 36 every idle word that men shall speak
12. 40 so shall the Son of man be three days and
12. 43 When the unclean spirit is gone out of a
12. 45 last (state) of that man is worse than the
13. 24 kingdom of heaven is likened unto a man
13. 25 while men slept, his enemy came and so.
13. 31 grain of mustard seed, which a man took
13. 37 He that soweth the..seed is the Son of man
13. 41 The Son of man shall send forth his ang.
13. 44 which when a man hath found, he hideth
13. 45 like unto a merchant man seeking goodly
13. 52 like unto a man (that is) an householder
15. 9 worship..teaching..commandments of m.
15. 11 defileth a man; but..this defileth a man
15. 18 forth from the heart; and they defile the m.
15. 20 These are (the things) which defile a man
15. 20 eat with unwashen hands defileth not a m.
16. 13 Whom do men say that I the Son of man
16. 23 not the things..but those that be of men
16. 26 what is a man..or what shall a man give
16. 27 For the Son of man shall come in the gl.
16. 28 till they see the Son of man coming in his
17. 9 until the Son of man be risen again from
17. 12 Likewise shall also the Son of man suffer
17. 14 there came to him a (certain) man, kneel.
17. 22 The Son of man shall be betrayed into
17. 22 shall be betrayed into the hands of men
18. 7 woe to that man by whom the offence co.
18. 11 [For the Son of man is come to save that]
18. 12 If a man have an hundred sheep, and one
19. 3 Is it lawful for [a man] to put away his w.
19. 5 For this cause shall a man leave father and
19. 6 What..God hath joined..let not man put
19. 10 If the case of the man be so with (his) w.
19. 12 eunuchs, which were made eunuchs of m.
19. 26 With men this is impossible; but with G.
19. 28 when the Son of man shall sit in the thr.
20. 1 kingdom of heaven is like unto a man (that
20. 18 the Son of man shall be betrayed unto the
20. 28 Even as the Son of man came not to be m.
21. 25 whence was it? from heaven, or of men?
21. 26 But if we shall say, Of men; we fear the
21. 28 A (certain) man had two sons; and he c.
22. 11 a man which had not on a wedding garm.
22. 16 for thou regardest not the person of men
23. 4 bind heavy burdens..and lay (them) on m.
23. 5 their works they do for to be seen of men
23. 7 greetings..to be called of men, Rabbi, R.
23. 13 for ye shut up the kingdom..against men
23. 28 outwardly appear righteous unto men, but
24. 27 so shall also the coming of the Son of man
24. 30 sign of the Son of man..see the Son of man
24. 37, 39 shall also the coming of the Son of man
24. 44 an hour as ye think not the Son of man
25. 13 day nor the hour wherein the Son of man
25. 14 For (the kingdom of heaven is) as a man
25. 24 I knew thee that thou art an hard man
25. 31 When the Son of man shall come in his
26. 24 The Son of man goeth..the Son of man is
26. 45 the Son of man is betrayed into the hands
26. 64 Hereafter shall ye see the Son of man sit.
26. 72 again he denied..I do not know the man
26. 74 I know not the man. And immediately the
27. 32 they found a man of Cyrene, Simon by name
27. 57 there came a rich man of Arimathea, na.
Mark 1. 17 I will make you to become fishers of men
1. 23 there was..a man with an unclean spirit
2. 10 that the Son of man hath power on earth
2. 27 sabbath was made for man, and not man

Mark 2. 28 the Son of man is Lord also of the sabbath
3. 1 there was a man which had a withered
3. 3 he saith unto the man which had the wi.
3. 5 saith unto the man, Stretch forth thine
3. 28 sins shall be forgiven unto the sons of men
4. 26 a man should cast seed into the ground
5. 2 there met him out of the tombs a man w.
5. 8 Come out of the man, (thou) unclean sp.
7. 7 (for) doctrines the commandments of men
7. 8 ye hold the tradition of men, (as) the w.
7. 11 if a man shall say to his father or mother
7. 15 There is nothing from without a man, that
7. 15 but..those are they that defile the man
7. 18 thing from without entereth into the man
7. 20 cometh out of the man..defileth the man
7. 21 For from within, out of the heart of men
7. 23 All these evil things..defile the man
8. 24 looked up, and said, I see men as trees
8. 27 saying unto them, Whom do men say that
8. 33 thou savourest..the things..be of men
8. 36 For what shall it profit a man, if he shall
8. 37 what shall [a man] give in exchange for
8. 38 of him also shall the Son of man be asha.
9. 9 till the Son of man were risen from the
9. 12 how it is written of the Son of man, that
9. 31 Son of man is delivered..the hands of men
10. 7 For this cause shall a man leave his father
10. 9 What..God hath joined..let not man put
10. 27 With men (it is) impossible, but not with
10. 33 the Son of man shall be delivered unto the
10. 45 the Son of man came not to be ministered
11. 2 find a colt tied, whereon never man sat
11. 30 The baptism of John, was (it)..of men?
11. 32 if we shall say, Of men; they feared the
12. 1 man planted a vineyard, and set an hedge
12. 14 thou art true, and carest for no man; for
13. 26 then shall they see the Son of man coming
13. 34 the Son..is) as a man taking a far journey
14. 13 there shall meet you a man bearing a pit.
14. 21 The Son of man indeed goeth, as it is wr.
14. 21 woe to that man by whom the Son of man
14. 21 for that man if he had never been born
14. 41 the Son of man is betrayed into the hands
14. 62 ye shall see the Son of man sitting on
14. 71 I know not this man of whom ye speak
15. 39 said, Truly this man was the Son of God
Luke 1. 25 to take away my reproach among men
2. 14 and on earth peace, good will toward men
2. 25 there was a man..the same man (was) just
2. 52 Jesus increased..favour with God and m.
4. 4 That man shall not live by bread alone
4. 33 in the synagogue there was a man which
5. 10 from henceforth thou shalt catch men
5. 18 a man which was taken with a palsy: and
5. 20 said unto him, Man, thy sins are forgiven
5. 24 that the Son of man hath power upon e.
6. 5 the Son of man is Lord also of the sabb.
6. 6 there was a man whose right hand was
6. 8 said to the [man] which had the withered
6. 10 said unto [the man], Stretch forth thy h.
6. 22 Blessed are ye when men shall hate you
6. 22 cast out..as evil, for the Son of man's s.
6. 26 Woe unto you when all men shall speak
6. 31 as ye would that men should do to you, do
6. 45 A good man..and an evil [man] out of the
6. 48 He is like a man which built an house, and
6. 49 like a man that without a foundation built
7. 8 For I also am a man set under authority
7. 25 what went ye out for to see? A man cloth.
7. 31 Whereunto then shall I liken the men of
7. 34 The Son of man is come eating and drin.
7. 34 Behold a gluttonous man, and a wine bib.
8. 29 the unclean spirit to come out of the man
8. 33 Then went the devils out of the man, and
8. 35 found the man out of whom the devils were
9. 22 The Son of man must suffer many things
9. 25 what is a man advantaged, if he gain the
9. 26 of him shall the Son of man be ashamed
9. 44 the Son of man shall be delivered into..m.
9. 56 [Son of man is not come to destroy men's]
9. 58 but the Son of man hath not where to lay
11. 24 the unclean spirit is gone out of a man, he
11. 26 last (state) of that man (is) worse than the
11. 30 so shall also the Son of man be to this
11. 44 the men that walk over (them) are not a.
11. 46 for ye lade men with burdens grievous to
12. 8 Whosoever shall confess me before men
12. 8 shall the Son of man also confess before
12. 9 he that denieth me before men shall be
12. 10 shall speak a word against the Son of man
12. 14 Man, who made me a judge or a divider
12. 16 ground of a certain rich man brought forth
12. 36 like unto men that wait for their lord, w.
12. 40 the Son of man cometh at an hour when
13. 4 sinners above all men that dwelt at Jeru.
13. 19 grain of mustard seed, which a man took
14. 2 there was a certain man before him which
14. 16 A certain man made a great supper, and
14. 30 This man began to build, and was not able
15. 4 What man of you, having an hundred sh.
15. 11 And he said, A certain man had two sons
16. 1 There was a certain rich man which had
16. 15 which justify yourselves before men; but
16. 15 which is highly esteemed among men is
16. 19 There was a certain rich man, which was
17. 22 to see one of the days of the Son of man
17. 24 so shall also the Son of man be in his day
17. 26 it be also in the days of the Son of man
17. 30 it be in the day when the Son of man is
18. 2 which feared not God, neither regarded m.
18. 4 Though I fear not God, nor regard man
18. 8 when the Son of man cometh, shall he find

Luke 18. 10 Two men went up into the temple to pray
18. 11 I thank thee, that I am not as other men
18. 27 things which are impossible with men are
18. 31 concerning the Son of man shall be acco.
19. 10 For the Son of man is come to seek and
19. 21 feared..because thou art an austere man
19. 22 Thou knewest that I was an austere man
19. 30 colt tied, whereon yet never man sat: loose
20. 4 The baptism of John, was it..of men?
20. 6 if we say, Of men; all the people will stone
20. 9 certain man planted a vineyard, and let
21. 26 Men's hearts failing them for fear, and
21. 27 then shall they see the Son of man coming
21. 36 worthy..to stand before the Son of man
22. 10 there shall a man meet you, bearing a p.
22. 22 truly the Son of man goeth, as it was det.
22. 22 woe unto that man by whom he is betrayed
22. 48 betrayest thou the Son of man with a kiss?
22. 58 also of them. And Peter said, Man, I am
22. 60 Peter said, Man, I know not what thou
22. 69 Hereafter shall the Son of man sit on the
23. 4 Then said Pilate..I find no fault in this m.
23. 6 he asked whether the man were a Galilean
23. 14 Ye have brought this man unto me, as one
23. 14 have found no fault in this man touching
23. 47 saying, Certainly this was a righteous m.
24. 7 The Son of man must be delivered into the
24. 7 hands of sinful men, and be crucified
John 1. 4 was life; and the life was the light of men
1. 6 There was a man sent from God, whose
1. 9 lighteth every man that cometh into the
1. 51 angels..descending upon the Son of man
2. 10 Every man at the beginning doth set forth
2. 25 testify of man..he knew what was in man
3. 1 There was a man of the Pharisees, named
3. 4 How can a man be born when he is old?
3. 13 but he..the Son of man which is in heav
3. 14 even so must the Son of man be lifted up
3. 19 men loved darkness rather than light, b.
3. 27 man can receive nothing, except it be gi.
4. 28 woman..went..and saith to the men
4. 29 see a man which told me all things that
4. 50 man believed the word that Jesus had sp.
5. 5 certain man was there, which had an inf.
5. 7 I have no man, when the water is troub.
5. 9 immediately the man was made whole
5. 12 What man is that which said unto thee
5. 15 man departed, and told the Jews that it
5. 27 authority..because he is the Son of man
5. 34 I receive not testimony from man: but
5. 41 I receive not honour from men
6. 10 Jesus said, Make the men sit down. Now
6. 14 men, when they had seen the miracle that
6. 27 which the Son of man shall give unto you
6. 53 Except ye eat the flesh of the Son of man
6. 62 and if ye shall see the Son of man ascend
7. 22 ye on the sabbath day circumcise a man
7. 23 If a man on the sabbath day receive circ.
7. 23 I have made a man every whit whole on
7. 46 answered, Never man spake like this [m.]
7. 51 Doth our law judge (any) man before it h.
8. 17 written..that the testimony of two men
8. 28 When ye have lifted up the Son of man
8. 40 man that hath told you the truth, which
9. 1 he saw a man which was blind from (his)
9. 11 man that is called Jesus made clay, and
9. 16 This man is not of God, because he keep.
9. 16 How can a man that is a sinner do such
9. 24 Then again called they the man that was
9. 24 Give God the praise: we know that this m.
9. 30 man answered..Why herein is a marvel.
10. 33 because that thou, being a man, makest
11. 47 What do we? for this man doeth many
11. 50 that one man should die for the people
12. 23 The hour is come, that the Son of man sh.
12. 34 The Son of man..who is this Son of man?
12. 43 loved the praise of men more than the p.
13. 31 Now is the Son of man glorified, and God
16. 21 for joy that a man is born into the world
17. 6 have manifested thy name unto the men
18. 14 expedient that one man should die for the
18. 17 Art not thou also (one) of this man's dis.
18. 29 What accusation bring ye against this m.?
19. 5 (Pilate) saith unto them, Behold the man!
Acts 4. 9 the good deed done to the impotent man
4. 12 name under heaven given among men w.
4. 13 that they were unlearned and ignorant m.
4. 14 the man which was healed standing with
4. 16 What shall we do to these men? for that
4. 17 speak henceforth to no man in this name
4. 22 For the man was above forty years old on
5. 4 thou hast not lied unto men, but unto G.
5. 28 intend to bring this man's blood upon us
5. 29 We ought to obey God rather than men
5. 35 what ye intend to do as touching these men
5. 38 Refrain from these men, and let them al.
5. 38 for if this counsel or this work be of men
6. 13 This man ceaseth not to speak blasphem.
7. 56 I see..the Son of man standing on the right
9. 33 there he found a certain man named Eneas
10. 26 saying, Stand up; I myself also am a man
10. 28 should not call any man common or unc.
12. 22 It is) the voice of a god, and not of a man
14. 11 come down to us in the likeness of men
14. 15 We also are men of like passions with you
15. 17 residue of men might seek after the Lord
15. 26 Men that have hazarded their lives for the
16. 17 These men are the servants of the most
16. 20 These men, being Jews, do exceedingly
16. 35 magistrates sent..saying, Let those men
17. 25 Neither is worshipped with [men's] hands
17. 26 made of one blood all nations of men for

Acts 17. 29 silver, or stone, graven by art and man's
17. 30 commandeth all men every where to repent
18. 13 persuadeth men to worship God contrary
19. 16 man in whom the evil spirit was leaped on
19. 35 what man is there that knoweth not how
21. 28 This is the man that teacheth all (men) ev.
21. 39 I am a man (which am) a Jew of Tarsus
22. 15 thou shalt be his witness unto all men of
22. 25 Is it lawful for you to scourge a man that
22. 26 Take heed what thou doest: for this man
23. 9 We find no evil in this man: but if a spirit
24. 16 a conscience void of offence toward..men
25. 16 deliver any man to die, before that he w.
25. 22 Agrippa said..I would also hear the man
26. 31 This man doeth nothing worthy of death
26. 32 This man might have been set at liberty
28. 4 No doubt this man is a murderer, whom
Rom. 1. 18 against all..unrighteousness of men, wh
1. 23 an image made like to corruptible man
2. 1 O man, whosoever thou art that judgest
2. 3 O man, that judgest them which do such
2. 9 upon every soul of man that doeth evil, of
2. 16 when God shall judge the secrets of men
2. 29 a Jew..whose praise (is) not of men, but
3. 4 let God be true, but every man a liar; v. 5
3. 28 man is justified by faith without the deeds
4. 6 describeth the blessedness of the man, unto
5. 12 by one man..so death passed upon all men
5. 15 if through the offence of one many be dead
5. 18 (judgment came) upon all men to condem.
5. 18 (the free gift came) upon all men unto j.
5. 19 For as by one man's disobedience many
6. 6 our old man is crucified with (him), that
7. 1 the law hath dominion over a man as long
7. 22 delight in the law of God after the in. m.
7. 24 O wretched man that I am! who shall de.
9. 20 Nay but, O man, who art thou that repli.
10. 5 man which doeth those things shall live
12. 17 things honest in the sight of all men
12. 18 If it be possible..live peaceably with all m.
14. 18 he that..serveth Christ (is)..approved of m.
14. 20 evil for that man who eateth with offence
1 Co. 1. 25 the foolishness of God is wiser than men
1. 25 the weakness of God is stronger than men
2. 5 should not stand in the wisdom of men
2. 9 have entered into the heart of man, the
2. 11 For what man knoweth the things of a m.
2. 11 save the spirit of man which is in him
2. 14 natural man receiveth not the th.; 3. 3.
4. 1 Let a man so account of us as of the min.
4. 9 a spectacle unto the world..and to men
6. 18 Every sin that a man doeth is without the
7. 1 (It is) good for a man not to touch a wo.
7. 7 would that all men were even as I myself
7. 23 Ye are bought..be not ye the servants of m.
7. 26 (I say), that (it is) good for a man so to be
11. 28 let a man examine himself, and so let him
13. 1 Though I speak with the tongues of men
14. 2 speaketh not unto men, but unto God: for
14. 3 But he that prophesieth speaketh unto m.
15. 19 in Christ, we are of all men most; v. 32.
15. 21 For since by man (came) death, by man
15. 39 but (there is) one (kind of) flesh of men
15. 45 The first [man] Adam was made a living s.
15. 47 The first man..the second man (is) the L.
2 Co. 3. 2 are our epistle..known and read of all m.
4. 2 to every man's conscience in the sight of
4. 16 though our outward man perish, yet the
5. 11 we persuade men: but we are made mani.
8. 21 not only..but also in the sight of men
12. 2 I knew a man in Christ above four.; 9. 8.
12. 3 I knew such a man, whether in the body
12. 4 which it is not lawful for a man to utter
Gal. 1. 1 not of men, neither by man, but by Jesus
1. 10 men, or God? or do I seek to please men?
1. 10 if I yet pleased men, I should not v. 11.
1. 12 I neither received it [of man], neither was
2. 6 God accepteth no man's person: for they
2. 16 a man is not justified by the works of
3. 12 man that doeth them shall live in them
3. 15 Though (it be) but a man's cov...no man
5. 3 again to every man that is circumcised
6. 1 if a man be overtaken in a fault, ye which
6. 7 whatsoever a man soweth, that shall he
Eph. 2. 15 to make in himself of twain one new man
3. 5 was not made known unto the sons of m.
3. 16 with might by his spirit in the inner man
4. 8 captivity captive, and gave gifts unto men
4. 14 the sleight of men, (and) cunning craftiness
4. 22 the old man, which is corrupt according
4. 24 that ye put on the new man, which after
5. 31 shall a man leave his father and mother
6. 7 service, as to the Lord, and not to men
Phil. 2. 7 and was made in the likeness of men
2. 8 being found in fashion as a man, he hum.
4. 5 Let your moderation be known unto all m.
Col. 1. 28 warning every man, and teaching every [m.]
1. 28 we may present every man perfect in Ch.
2. 8 after the tradition of men, after the rudi.
2. 22 the commandments and doctrines of men
3. 9 have put off the old man with his deeds
3. 23 heartily, as to the Lord, and not unto men
1 Th. 2. 4 not as pleasing men, but God, which trieth
2. 6 Nor of men sought we glory, neither of you
2. 13 ye received (it) not (as) the word of men
2. 15 please not God, and are contrary to all men
4. 8 despiseth not man, but God, who hath also
2 Th. 2. 3 that man of sin be revealed, the son of
3. 2 from unreasonable and wicked men
1 Ti. 2. 1 (and) giving of thanks, be made for all men
2. 4 Who will have all men to be saved, and to
2. 5 one mediator between God and men, the

1 Ti. 4. 10 who is the saviour of all men, specially
5. 24 men's sins are open beforehand, going be.
6. 5 Perverse disputings of men of corrupt m.
6. 9 drown men in destruction and perdition
6. 11 O man of God, flee these things..follow
6. 16 whom no man hath seen, nor can see: to
2 Ti. 2. 2 the same commit thou to faithful men, who
3. 2 men shall be lovers of their own selves
3. 8 men of corrupt minds, reprobate concer.
3. 13 evil men and seducers shall wax worse and
3. 17 the man of God may be perfect, throughly
Titus 1. 14 commandments of men, that turn from
2. 11 grace of God..hath appeared to all men
3. 2 speak evil of no man, to be no brawlers
3. 8 things are good and profitable unto men
3. 10 A man that is an heretic after the first
Heb. 2. 6 What is man, that thou art mindful of
2. 6 or the son of man, that thou visitest him
5. 1 taken from among men is ordained for m.
6. 16 men verily swear by the greater; and an
7. 8 here men that die receive tithes; but there
7. 28 the law maketh men high priests which
8. 2 which the Lord pitched, and not man
9. 27 it is appointed unto men once to die, but
13. 6 will not fear what man shall do unto me
Jas. 1. 7 For let not that man think that he shall
1. 19 let every man be swift to hear, slow to
2. 20 But wilt thou know, O vain man, that faith
2. 24 by works a man is justified, and not by
3. 8 tongue can no man tame; (it is) an unruly
3. 9 therewith curse we men, which are made
5. 17 Elias was a man subject to like passions
1 Pe. 1. 24 the glory [of man] as the flower of grass
2. 4 disallowed indeed of men, but chosen of G.
2. 15 to silence the ignorance of foolish men
3. 4 (let it be) the hidden man of the heart, in
4. 2 live..in the flesh to the lusts of men, but
4. 6 be judged according to men in the flesh
2 Pe. 1. 21 old time by the will of man; but holy men
2. 16 the dumb ass speaking with man's voice
3. 7 judgment and perdition of ungodly men
1 Jo. 5. 9 If we receive the witness of men, the
Jude 4 there are certain men crept in unawares
Rev. 4. 7 the third beast had a face as a man, and
8. 11 men died of the waters, because they were
9. 4 those men which have not the seal of God
9. 5 of a scorpion, when he striketh a man
9. 6 in those days shall men seek death, and
9. 7 and their faces (were) as the faces of men
9. 10 their power (was) to hurt men five months
9. 15 loosed..for to slay the third part of men
9. 18 By these three was the third part of men
9. 20 the rest of the men, which were not killed
11. 13 in the earthquake were slain men of seven
13. 13 maketh fire come down..in the sight of m.
13. 18 it is the number of a man; and his number
14. 4 These were redeemed from among men
16. 2 the men which had the mark of the beast
16. 8 given unto him to scorch men with fire
16. 9 And men were scorched with great heat
16. 18 as was not since men were upon the earth
16. 21 fell upon men a great hail out of heaven
16. 21 men blasphemed God because of the pla.
18. 13 and chariots, and slaves, and souls of men
21. 3 the tabernacle of God (is) with men, and he
21. 17 (according to) the measure of a man, that

18. *A male*, ἄῤῥην *arrhēn*.
Rom. 1. 27 also the men, leaving the natural use of
Rev. 12. 5 she brought forth a man child, who was

19. *A male*, ἄρσην *arsēn*.
Rom. 1. 27 men with men working that which is un.

20. *Some one, a certain one*, τις *tis*.
Matt. 8. 28 so that no man might pass by that way
18. 12 If a man have an hundred sheep, and one
22. 24 If a man die, having no children, his br.
Mark 8. 4 From whence can a man satisfy these (m.)
12. 19 If a man's brother die, and leave (his) w.
Luke 12. 15 for a man's life consisteth not in the ab.
John 3. 3 Except a man be born again, he cannot
3. 5 Except a man be born of water and (of)
6. 50 that a man may eat thereof, and not die
8. 51 If a man keep my saying, he shall never
8. 52 thou sayest, If a man keep my saying, he
11. 10 But if a man walk in the night, he stumb.
14. 23 If a man love me, he will keep my words
15. 6 If a man abide not in me, he is cast forth
15. 13 a man lay down his life for his friends
Acts 13. 41 not..believe, though a man declare it unto
Rom. 8. 24 what a man seeth, why doth he yet hope
1 Co. 4. 2 it is required..that a man be found faith.
2 Co. 8. 12 accepted according to that [a man] hath
11. 20 if a man..a man..a man..a man..a man
Gal. 6. 3 For if a man think himself to be someth.
1 Ti. 1. 8 the law (is) good, if a man use it lawfully
3. 1 If a man desire the office of a bishop, he
3. 5 For if a man know not how to rule his own
2 Ti. 2. 5 And if a man also strive for masteries
2. 21 If a man..purge himself from; Heb. 5. 4.
Jas. 2. 14 though a man say he hath faith, and have
2. 18; 1 Pe. 2. 19; 2 Pe. 2. 19; 1 Jo. 4. 20.

21. *Perfect*, τέλειος *teleios*.
1 Co. 14. 20 Brethren..in understanding be men

[*See also* Aged, another, any, every, free, heathen, impotent, no, old, wise, young, &c.]

MAN appointed, to —
The man of, אִישׁ *ish*, 1 Ki. 20. 42.

MAN, common to —
Human, belonging to man, ἀνθρώπινος *anthrōpinos*.
1 Co. 10. 13 temptation..but such as is common to m.

MAN CHILD —
A male, זָכָר *zakar*.
Gen. 17. 10 Every man child among you shall be cir.
17. 12 every man child in your generations, he
17. 14 the uncircumcised man child, whose flesh
Lev. 12. 2 have conceived seed, and born a man child
Isa. 66. 7 Before..she was delivered of a man child

MAN, every —
A skull, poll, גֻּלְגֹּלֶת *gulgoleth*.
Exod 16. 16 an omer for every man..the number of
38. 26 A bekah for every man..half a shekel

MAN of great —
1. *Great*, גָּדוֹל *gadol*.
Prov. 19. 19 A man of great wrath shall suffer punish.

MAN of war —
Army, military force, στράτευμα *strateuma*.
Luke 23. 11 Herod with his men of war set him at no.

MAN, strong —
Strong, ἰσχυρός *ischuros*.
Matt 12. 29 how can one enter into a strong man's ho.
12. 29 except he first bind the strong man? and
Mark 3. 27 No man can enter into a strong man's ho.
3. 27 except he will first bind the strong man
Luke 11. 21 When a strong man armed keepeth his p.

MAN, young —
1. *Youth, young man*, עֶלֶם *elem*.
1 Sa. 20. 22 But if I say thus unto the young man

2. *Youth, young man*, νεανίας *neanias*.
Acts 7. 58 their clothes at a young man's feet, whose
20. 9 certain young man named Eutychus, being
23. 17 Bring this young man unto the chief cap.
23. 18 prayed me to bring this [young man] unto
23. 22 let [the young man] depart, and charged

3. *Youth, youngster*, νεανίσκος *neaniskos*.
Matt 19. 20 The young man saith unto him, All these
19. 22 when the young man heard that saying
Mark 14. 51 a certain young man..and [the young men]
16. 5 they saw a young man sitting on the right
Luke 7. 14 said, Young man, I say unto thee, Arise
Acts 2. 17 your young men shall see visions, and y.
5. 10 the young men came in, and found her
1 Jo. 2. 13 I write unto you, young men, because ye
2. 14 I have written unto you, young men, be.

MA-NA'-EN, Μαναήν *comforter*.
An early associate of Herod the tetrarch, and one of the five prophets or teachers in Antioch.
Acts 13. 1 M., which had been brought up with H.

MA-NA'-HATH, מָנַחַת, מָנָחַת *resting place, rest*.
1. A son of Shobal, son of Seir the Horite. B.C. 1760.
Gen. 36. 23 the children of Shobal (were) these..M.
1 Ch. 1. 40 The sons of Shobal; Alian, and M., and E.
2. A city in Benjamin, over against Gibeah.
1 Ch. 8. 6 inhabitants of Geba..removed them to M.

MA-NA-HETH-ITES, מְנֻחוֹת, מָנַחְתִּי.
The families of Shobal and Salma, two sons of Caleb son of Hur.
1 Ch. 2. 52 Shobal..had sons; Haroeh..half of the M.
2. 54 The sons of Salma..half of the M., the. Z.

MA-NAS'-SEH, מְנַשֶּׁה, מְנַשִּׁי, *causing forgetfulness*.
1. Elder son of Joseph. B.C. 1700.
Gen. 41. 51 Joseph called..the first born M.: For God
46. 20 unto Joseph..were born M. and Ephraim
48. 1 and he took with him..M. and Ephraim
48. 5 thy two sons, Ephraim and M...(are) mi.
48. 13 Joseph took..M. in his left hand toward
48. 14 Israel..laid..his left hand upon M's head
48. 14 guiding his hand wittingly; for M. (was)
48. 17 to remove it from Ephraim's..unto M.'s
48. 20 God make thee as Ephraim, and as M.: and
48. 20 blessed them..he set Ephraim before M.
50. 23 the children also of Machir the son of M.
Num 26. 28 The sons of Joseph..(were) M. and Eph.
26. 29 Of the sons of M.: of Machir, the family
27. 1 Gilead, the son of Machir, the son of M.
27. 1 the families of M. the son of Joseph: and
32. 39 children of Machir the son of M. went to
32. 40 Moses gave Gilead unto..the son of M.; and
32. 41 Jair the son of M. went and took the sm.
36. 1 Gilead, the son of Machir, the son of M.
Deut. 3. 14 Jair the son of M. took all the country
Josh 13. 31 the children of Machir the son of M., (even)
17. 1 for Machir, the first born of M., the father
17. 2 There was (a lot) for..the children of M.
17. 2 these (were) the male children of M. the
17. 3 Gilead, the son of Machir, the son of M.
1 Ki. 4. 13 the towns of Jair the son of M., which
1 Ch. 7. 14 The sons of M.; Ashriel, whom she bare
7. 17 Gilead, the son of Machir, the son of M.

2. His posterity.
Num. 1. 10 Of the children..of M.; Gamaliel the son
1. 34 Of the children of M., by their generations
1. 35 Those..of the tribe of M., (were) thirty and
2. 20 And by him (shall be) the tribe of M.
2. 20 the captain of the children of M. (shall
7. 54 Gamaliel..prince of the children of M.
10. 23 over..the children of M. (was) Gamaliel
13. 11 of the tribe of M., Gaddi the son of Susi
26. 34 These (are) the families of M., and those
32. 33 Moses gave..unto half the tribe of M.
34. 14 half the tribe of M. have received their
34. 23 for the tribe of the children of M., Han.
36. 12 the families of the sons of M. the son of
Deut 3. 13 gave I unto the half tribe of M.; all the
29. 8 an inheritance..to the half tribe of M.
33. 17 ten thousands of Ephraim..thous. of M.
34. 2 all Naphtali..and M., and all the land
Josh. 1. 12 to half the tribe of M., spake Joshua
4. 12 half the tribe of M., passed over armed
12. 6 a possession unto..the half tribe of M.
13. 7 an inheritance unto..the half tribe of M.
13. 29 (inheritance) unto the half tribe of M.
13. 29 (the possession)..of the children of M. by
14. 4 children of Joseph were two tribes, M. and
16. 4 the children of Joseph, M. and Ephraim
16. 9 among the inheritance of..M., all the
17. 1 There was also a lot for the tribe of M.
17. 5 There fell ten portions to M., besides the
17. 6 Because the daughters of M. had an inh.
17. 6 the rest of M.'s sons had the land of Gilead
17. 7 the coast of M. was from Asher to Michme.
17. 8 (Now) M. had the land of Tappuah: but
17. 8 Tappuah on the border of M. (belonged)
17. 9 these cities..(are) among the cities of M.
17. 9 the coast of M. also (was) on the north side
17. 10 northward (it was) M.'s, and the sea is his
17. 11 M. had in Issachar and in Asher, Beth-sh.
17. 12 Yet the children of M. could not drive out
17. 17 Joshua spake unto..M., saying, Thou (art)
18. 7 half the tribe of M., have received their
20. 8 assigned..Golan..out of the tribe of M.
21. 5 and out of the half tribe of M., ten cities
21. 6 out of the half tribe of M...thirteen cities
21. 25 out of the half tribe of M., Taanach with
21. 27 out of the (other) half tribe of M., (they g.)
22. 1 Then Joshua called..the half tribe of M.
22. 7 Now to the (one) half of the tribe of M.
22. 9, 10, 11, 21 and the half tribe of M.
22. 13 sent..to the half tribe of M., into the land
22. 15 they came unto..the half tribe of M., unto
22. 30 heard the words that the..children of M.
22. 31 Phinehas..said..to the children of M.
Judg. 1. 27 Neither did M. drive out (the inhabitants
6. 15 my family (is) poor in M., and I (am) the
6. 35 he sent messengers throughout all M., who
7. 23 gathered themselves..out of all M., and
11. 29 he passed over Gilead and M., and passed
1 Ch. 5. 18 and half the tribe of M., of valiant men
5. 23 children of the half tribe of M. dwelt in
5. 26 carried..away, even..the half tribe of M.
6. 61 (out of) the half (tribe) of M., by lot, ten
6. 62 out of the tribe of M. in Bashan, thirteen
6. 70 out of the half tribe of M.; Aner with her
6. 71 given) out of the..half tribe of M., Golan
7. 29 by the borders of the children of M., Be.
9. 3 and of the children of Ephraim, and M.
12. 19 there fell (some) of M. to David, when he
12. 20 there fell to him of M., Adnah, and Joz.
12. 20 captains of the thousands that (were) of M.
12. 31 of the half tribe of M. eighteen thousand
12. 37 of the half tribe of M., with all manner
26. 32 rulers over..the half tribe of M., for every
27. 20 of the half tribe of M.; Joel the son of P.
27. 21 Of the half (tribe) of M. in Gilead; Iddo
2 Ch. 15. 9 strangers..out of Ephraim and M., and
30. 1 wrote letters also to Ephraim and M., that
30. 10 passed..through the country of..M. even
30. 11 divers of Asher and M. and of Zebulun h.
30. 18 many of Ephraim, and M., Issachar, and
31. 1 the high places..in Ephraim also and M.
34. 6 (so did he) in the cities of M., and Ephraim
34. 9 gathered of the hand of M. and Ephraim
Psa. 60. 7 Gilead (is) mine, and M. (is) mine; Ephr.
80. 2 Before Ephraim and Benjamin and M. stir
108. 8 Gilead (is) mine; M. (is) mine; Ephraim
Isa. 9. 21 M., Ephraim; and Ephraim, M.: (and) they
Eze. 48. 4 border of Naphtali..a (portion for) M.
48. 5 by the border of M...a (portion for) Eph.

The following localities were in the territory of Manasseh: Abel, Abel-beth-maachah, Abel-maim, Adam, Aner, Ashtaroth, Beeshterah, Beth-shean, Beth-shittah, Bilcam, Dor, Edrei, Endor, Gath-rimmon, Gilead, Golan, Gur, Ibleam, Megiddo, Michmethah, Nophah, Ophrah, Taanach, Tappuah, Zarthan, Zereda, &c.

3. The grandfather of Jonathan who, with his sons, became priests to the tribe of Dan when they set up a graven image in Laish; but perhaps *Manasseh* should be read *Moses* in this passage. B.C. 1450.
Judg 18. 30 Gershom, the son of M., he and his sons

4. The son of Hezekiah, and father of Amon king of Judah. B.C. 680.
2 Ki. 20. 21 Hezekiah slept..and M. his son reigned in
21. 1 M. (was) twelve years old when he began
21. 9 M. seduced them to do more evil than did
21. 11 Because M. king of Judah hath done these
21. 16 Moreover M. shed innocent blood very mu.
21. 17 the rest of the acts of M., and all that he
21. 18 M. slept with his fathers, and was buried
21. 20 And he did..evil..as his father M. did
23. 12 the altars which M. had made in the two
23. 26 the provocations that M. had provoked
24. 3 to remove (them)..for the sins of M., ac.
1 Ch. 3. 13 Ahaz his son, Hezekiah his son, M. his son
2 Ch. 32. 33 Hezekiah slept..And M. his son reigned in
33. 1 M. (was) twelve years old when he began
33. 9 So M. made Judah and the inhabitants of
33. 10 the LORD spake to M., and to his people
33. 11 the captains..took M. among the thorns
33. 13 M. knew that the LORD he (was) God
33. 18 the rest of the acts of M., and his prayer
33. 20 So M. slept with his fathers, and they bu.
33. 22 he did..evil..as did M. his father: for A.
33. 22 carved images which M. his father had m.

2 Ch 33. 23 humbled not himself..as M. his father had
Jer. 15. 4 M. the son of Hezekiah king of Judah, for

5. One of the family of Pahath-moab who had taken a strange wife. B.C. 456.

Ezra 10. 30 the sons of Pahath-moab; Adna..and M.

6. One of the family of Hashum, who had done the same.

Ezra 10. 33 the sons of Hashum; Mattenai..M., (and)

MA-NAS'-SES, Μανασσῆς—See *Manasseh.*

1. A king of Judah. B.C. 680.

Matt. 1. 10 Ezekias begat M.; and M. begat Amon

2. The descendants of Joseph's elder son.

Rev. 7. 6 Of the tribe of M. (were) sealed twelve

MA-NAS-SITES, מְנַשִּׁי.

The descendants of Manasseh, elder son of Joseph.

Deut.4. 43 (Namely)..Golan in Bashan, of the M.
Judg12. 4 among the Ephraimites,(and)among the M.
2 Ki.10. 33 the Reubenites, and the M., from Aroer

MANDRAKES —

Love apples, דּוּדַי *dudai.*

Gen. 30. 14 found mandrakes in the field, and brought
30. 14 Give me, I pray thee, of thy son's mandra.
30. 15 wouldest thou take away my son's mand.
30. 15 lie with thee to night for thy son's mand.
30. 16 have hired thee with my son's mandrakes
Song 7. 13 The mandrakes give a smell, and at our

MANEH —

A weight, $\frac{1}{60}$ *of a talent,* מָנֶה *maneh.*

Eze. 45. 12 And..fifteen shekels, shall be your maneh

MANGER —

Manger, crib, φάτνη *phatnē.*

Luke 2. 7 laid him in a manger; because there was
2. 12 Ye shall find the babe..lying in a manger
2. 16 found Mary..and the babe lying in a ma.

MANIFEST —

1. *Evident,* δῆλος *dēlos.*

1 Co. 15. 27 (it is) manifest that he is excepted which

2. *Very evident,* ἔκδηλος *ekdēlos.*

2 Ti. 3. 9 for their folly shall be manifest unto all

3. *Fully manifest, apparent,* ἐμφανής *emphanēs.*

Rom.10. 20 I was made manifest unto them that ask.

4. *Manifest, apparent,* φανερός *phaneros.*

Luke 8. 17 is secret that shall not be made manifest
Acts 4. 16 manifest to all them that dwell in Jerus.
Rom. 1. 19 is manifest in them; for God hath showed
1 Co. 3. 13 Every man's work shall be made manifest
11. 19 that they..may be made manifest among
14. 25 are the secrets of his heart made manifest
Gal. 5. 19 Now the works of the flesh are manifest
Phil. 1. 13 So that my bonds in Christ are manifest
1 Jo. 3. 10 In this the children of God are manifest

MANIFEST, to —

1. *To purify, clear,* בָּרַר *barar.*

Eccl. 3. 18 that God might manifest them, and that

2. *To manifest,* φανερόω *phaneroō.*

Mark 4. 22 is nothing hid, which shall not be mani.
John17. 6 I have manifested thy name unto the men
Rom. 3. 21 without the law is manifested, being w.
1 Ti. 3. 16 God was manifest in the flesh, justified
Titus 1. 3 But hath in due times manifested his word
1 Pe. 1. 20 but was manifest in these last times for
1 Jo. 1. 2 the life was manifested, and we have seen
1. 2 that eternal life which..was manifested
3. 5 ye know that he was manifested to take
3. 8 the Son of God was manifested, that he
4. 9 In this was manifested the love of God to.

3. *To make fully manifest,* ἐμφανίζω *emphanizō.*

John14. 21 love him, and will manifest myself to him
14. 22 how is it that thou wilt manifest thyself

MANIFEST beforehand —

Evident beforehand, πρόδηλος *prodēlos.*

1 Ti. 5. 25 the good works..are manifest beforehand

MANIFEST forth, to —

To make manifest, φανερόω *phaneroō.*

John 2. 11 and manifested forth his glory: and his

MANIFEST, to make or be —

To make manifest, φανερόω *phaneroō.*

John 1. 31 that he should be made manifest to Israel
3. 21 that his deeds may be made manifest, that
9. 3 the works..should be made manifest in
Rom.16. 26 But now is made manifest, and by the sc.
1 Co. 4. 5 make manifest the counsels of the hearts
2 Co. 2. 14 maketh manifest the savour of his know.
4. 10,11 life also of Jesus might be made manifest
5. 11 we are made manifest unto God; and I trust
5. 11 I trust also are made manifest in your c.
11. 6 but we have been throughly made manif.
Eph. 5. 13 all things..are made manifest by the light
5. 13 whatsoever doth make manifest is light
Col. 1. 26 but now is made manifest to his saints
4. 4 That I may make it manifest, as I ought
2 Ti. 1. 10 But is now made manifest by the appear.
Heb. 9. 8 was not yet made manifest, while as the
1 Jo. 2. 19 that they might be made manifest that they
Rev.15. 4 O Lord..thy judgments are made manifest

MANIFEST, not —

Not manifest, ἀφανής *aphanēs.*

Heb. 4. 13 Neither is there any..that is not manifest

MANIFESTATION —

1. *Uncovering,* ἀποκάλυψις *apokalupsis.*

Rom. 8. 19 waiteth for the manifestation of the sons

2. *Manifestation,* φανέρωσις *phanerōsis.*

1 Co.12. 7 But the manifestation of the spirit is gi.
2 Co. 4. 2 by manifestation of the truth commending

MANIFOLD —

1. *Many, abundant,* רַב *rab.*

Neh. 9. 19 Yet thou in thy manifold mercies forsook
9. 27 according to thy manifold mercies thou
Amos 5. 12 For I know your manifold transgressions

2. *To be many, multiplied,* רָבַב *rabab.*

Psa.104. 24 O LORD, how manifold are thy works! in

3. *Manifold,* ποικίλος *poikilos.*

1 Pe. 1. 6 in heaviness through manifold temptations
4. 10 as good stewards of the manifold grace of

4. *Very manifold,* πολυποίκιλος *polupoikilos.*

Eph. 3. 10 by the church the manifold wisdom of God

MANIFOLD more —

Manifold more, πολλαπλασίων *pollaplasiōn.*

Luke18. 30 Who shall not receive manifold more in

MANKIND —

1. *A male,* זָכָר *zakar.*

Lev. 18. 22 Thou shalt not lie with mankind as with
20. 13 If a man also lie with mankind, as he

2. *Flesh of man,* בְּשַׂר־אִישׁ [*basar*].

Job 12. 10 the soul..and the breath of all mankind

3. *Human nature,* φύσις ἀνθρωπίνη *phusis anthrō.*

Jas. 3. 7 is tamed, and hath been tamed of mank.

MANNA —

1. *Man, a sweet gum or resin,* מָן *man.*

Exod16. 15 they said one to another, It (is) manna
16. 31 And..Israel called the name thereof M.
16. 33 put an omer full of manna therein, and
16. 35 the children of Israel did eat manna forty
16. 35 they did eat manna until they came unto
Num 11. 6 nothing at all, besides this manna,(before)
11. 7 And the manna (was) as coriander seed
11. 9 And..in the night, the manna fell upon
Deut. 8. 3 fed thee with manna, which thou knewest
8. 16 Who fed thee in the wilderness with ma.
Josh. 5. 12 the manna ceased on the morrow after they
5. 12 had the children of Israel manna any
Neh. 9. 20 withheldest not thy manna from their
Psa. 78. 24 had rained down manna upon them to eat

2. *A sweet resin or gum, (from Heb.)* μάννα *manna.*

John 6. 31 Our fathers did eat manna in the desert
6. 49 Your fathers did eat manna in the wilde.
6. 58 not as your fathers did eat [manna], and
Heb. 9. 4 the golden pot that had manna, and A.'s
Rev. 2. 17 will I give to eat of the hidden manna

MANNER —

1. *Path, custom,* אֹרַח *orach.*

Gen. 18. 11 to be with Sarah after the manner of w.

2. *Word, thing, matter,* דָּבָר *dabar.*

Gen. 18. 25 That be far from thee to do after this m.
32. 19 On this manner shall ye speak unto Esau
39. 19 After this manner did thy servant to me
Exod22. 9 For all manner of trespass..for ox, for
Deut 15. 2 And this (is) the manner of the release
1 Sa. 17. 27 people answered him after this manner
17. 30 he turned..and spake after the same man.
17. 30 answered him again after the former ma.
18. 24 saying, On this manner spake David
2 Sa. 14. 3 come..and speak on this manner unto him
15. 6 on this manner did Absalom to all Israel
17. 6 Ahithophel hath spoken after this manner
Neh. 6. 4 I answered them after the same manner
6. 5 in like manner the fifth time with an open
Esth. 1. 13 for so (was) the king's manner toward all

3. *Leading, pasture,* דֹּבֶר *dober.*

Isa. 5. 17 Then shall the lambs feed after their ma.

4. *Likeness,* דְּמוּת *demuth.*

Eze. 23. 15 after the manner of the Babylonians of

5. *Way,* דֶּרֶךְ *derek.*

Gen. 19. 31 unto us after the manner of all the earth
1 Sa. 21. 5 and (the bread is) in a manner common
Isa. 10. 24 against thee, after the manner of Egypt
10. 26 shall he lift it up after the manner of Egypt
Jer. 22. 21 this..thy manner from thy youth, that
Eze. 20. 30 Are ye polluted after the manner of your
Amos 4. 10 the pestilence after the manner of Egypt
8. 14 The manner of Beer-sheba liveth; even

6. *Law, sentence,* דָּת *dath.*

Esth. 2. 12 according to the manner of the women

7. *Statute, custom,* חֻקָּה *chuqqah.*

Lev. 20. 23 ye shall not walk in the manners of the n.

8. *Judgment,* מִשְׁפָּט *mishpat.*

Gen. 40. 13 after the former manner when thou wast
Exod21. 9 he shall deal with her after the manner
Lev. 5. 10 a burnt offering, according to the manner
9. 16 and offered it according to the manner
24. 22 Ye shall have one manner of law, as well
Num. 9. 14 according to the manner thereof, so shall
15. 16 One law and one manner shall be for you
15. 24 his drink offering, according to the man.
29. 6 drink offerings, according unto their ma.
29. 18, 21, 24, 27, 30, 33, 37 number, after the m.
Josh. 6. 15 compassed the city after the same manner
Judg18. 7 after the manner of the Zidonians, quiet
1 Sa. 8. 9 show them the manner of the king that
8. 11 This will be the manner of the king that
10. 25 the manner of the kingdom, and wrote
27. 11 his manner all the while he dwelleth in
1 Ki.18. 28 cut themselves, after their manner, with
2 Ki. 1. 7 What manner of man (was he) which came
11. 14 the king stood by a pillar, as the manner
17. 26, 26 know not the manner of the God of the
17. 27 let him teach them the manner of the God
17. 33 after the manner of the nations whom they
17. 34 they do after the former manners: they
17. 40 but they did after their former manner
1 Ch.24. 19 according to their manner, under Aaron
2 Ch. 4. 20 burn after the manner before the oracle
30. 16 they stood in their place after their man.
Neh. 8. 18 solemn assembly, according unto the m.
Jer. 30. 18 the palace shall remain after the manner
Eze. 11. 12 have done after the manners of the heathen
23. 45 they shall judge them after the manner of
23. 45 after the manner of women that shed bl.

9. *Instruction, direction,* תּוֹרָה *torah.*

2 Sa. 7. 19 (is) this the manner of man, O Lord GOD?

10. *Custom, habit, manner,* ἔθος *ethos.*

John19. 40 spices, as the manner of the Jews is to b.
Acts 15. 1 Except ye be circumcised after the man.
25. 16 It is not the manner of the Romans to d.
Heb. 10. 25 Not forsaking..as the manner of some (is)

11. *A mark, impression, type,* τύπος *tupos.*

Acts 23. 25 And he wrote a letter after this manner

[*See also* After, all, any, like, know, perfect, that, this, what, workmanship.]

MANNER, after this, or in this, or in like —

1. *Also,* גַּם *gam.*

1 Sa. 19. 24 prophesied before Samuel in like manner

2. *In which manner, or turn,* ὃν τρόπον *hon tropon.*

Acts 1. 11 shall so come in like manner as ye have

3. *Thus, so, accordingly,* οὕτω *houtō.*

Matt 6. 9 After this manner therefore pray ye
Mark13. 29 So ye, in like manner, when ye shall see
1 Co. 7. 7 one after this manner, and another after
1 Pe. 3. 5 For after this manner in the old time the
Rev. 11. 5 hurt them, he must in this manner be k.

4. *These things, thus,* τάδε *tade.*

Acts 15. 23 they wrote..by them [after this manner]

5. *In like manner, turn,* τὸν ὅμοιον τρόπον *ton homoi.*

Jude 7 in like manner giving themselves over

MANNER, after what —

How? πῶς *pōs.*

Acts 20. 18 after what manner I have been with you

MANNER of, such —

Concerning this, εἰς τὴν περὶ τούτου *eis tēn peri toutou.*

Acts 25. 20 because I doubted of such manner of q.

MANNER of life —

1. *Course of life,* ἀγωγή *agōgē.*

2 Ti. 3. 10 thou hast fully known my..manner of life

2. *Act of living, mode of life,* βίωσις *biōsis.*

Acts 26. 4 My manner of life from my youth, which

MANNER of store, all —

From (one) kind to (another) kind, מִזַּן אֶל־זַן [*zan*].

Psa.144. 13 affording all manner of store; (that) our

MANNER was —

According to habit, κατὰ τὸ εἰωθός *kata to eiōthos.*

Acts 17. 2 Paul, as his manner was, went in unto

MANNERS —

Habit, manner, ἦθος *ēthos.*

1 Co. 15. 33 evil communications corrupt good man.

MANNERS, to suffer the —

To bear with the manners of others, τροποφορέω.

Acts 13. 18 forty years [suffered he their manners] in

MA-NO'-AH, מָנוֹחַ *rest.*

A man of Zorah in Dan, and father of Samson. B.C. 1150.

Judg13. 2 a certain man..whose name (was) M.; and
13. 8 Then M. entreated the LORD, and said, O
13. 9 God hearkened to the voice of M.; and the
13. 9 but M. her husband (was) not with her
13. 11 And M. arose, and went after his wife, and
13. 12 And M. said, Now let thy words come to
13. 13, 16 And the angel of the LORD said unto M.
13. 15, 17 And M. said unto the angel of the L.
13. 16 For M. knew not that he (was) an angel
13. 19 So M. took a kid with a meat offering, and
13. 19 (the angel) did wondrously; and M. and
13. 20 And M. and his wife looked on (it), and fell
13. 21 the angel..did no more appear to M. and
13. 21 Then M. knew that he (was) an angel of the
13. 22 M. said unto his wife, We shall surely die
16. 31 in the burying place of M. his father: and

MAN SERVANT —

1. *Servant,* עֶבֶד *ebed.*

Gen. 12. 16 he asses, and men servants, and maid se.
20. 14 oxen, and men servants, and women ser.
24. 35 silver, and gold, and men servants, and
30. 43 and men servants, and camels, and asses
32. 5 oxen, and asses, flocks, and men servants
Exod20. 10 thy man servant, nor thy maid servant
20. 17 nor his man servant, nor his maid servant
21. 7 she shall not go out as the men servants
21. 27 if he smite out his man servant's tooth, or

Exod21. 32 If the ox shall push a man servant or maid
Deut. 5. 14 nor thy man servant, nor thy maid servant
5. 14 that thy man servant..may rest as well as
5. 21 or his man servant, or his maid servant
12. 12 your men servants, and your maid servants
12. 18 and thy man servant, and thy maid serv.
16. 11, 14 and thy man servant, and thy maid se.
1 Sa. 8. 16 will take your men servants, and your m.
2 Ki. 5. 26 oxen, and men servants, and maid serv.?
Neh. 7. 67 Besides their man servants and their ma.
Job 31. 13 If I did despise the cause of my man ser.
Jer. 34. 9 That every man should let his man servant
34. 10 should let his man servant..go free, that

2. *Child, boy, servant,* παῖς *pais.*
Luke 12. 45 to beat the men servants and maidens, and

MANSION —
Mansion, abode, μονή *monē.*
John14. 2 In my Father's house are many mansions

MAN SLAYER —
1. *To murder,* רָצַח *ratsach.*
Num 35. 6 which ye shall appoint for the man slayer
35. 12 that the man slayer die not, until he stand

2. *Man-murderer,* ἀνδροφόνος *androphonos.*
1 Ti. 1. 9 and murderers of mothers, for man slayers

MANTLE —
1. *Ornamental mantle,* אַדֶּרֶת *addereth.*
1 Ki. 19. 13 that he wrapped his face in his mantle
19. 19 Elijah passed by him, and cast his mantle
2 Ki. 2. 8 Elijah took his mantle, and wrapped (it)
2. 13 He took up also the mantle of Elijah that
2. 14 he took the mantle of Elijah that fell from

2. *Coverings, mantles, wrappers,* מַעֲטָפוֹת *maataphoth.*
Isa. 3. 22 suits of apparel, and the mantles, and the

3. *Upper robe,* מְעִיל *meil.*
1 Sa. 15. 27 he laid hold upon the skirt of his mantle
28. 14 And she said..he (is) covered with a man.
Ezra 9. 3 I rent my garment and my mantle, and
9. 5 having rent my garment and my mantle
Job 1. 20 Then Job arose, and rent his mantle, and
2. 12 rent every one his mantle, and sprinkled
Psa.109. 29 with their own confusion, as with a man.

4. *A coverlet,* שְׂמִיכָה *semikah.*
Judg. 4. 18 turned in..she covered him with a man.

MANY (things, of) —
1. *Multitude,* הָמוֹן *hamon.*
Gen. 17. 4 and thou shalt be a father of many nations
17. 5 father of many nations have I made thee
2 Ch. 11. 23 And he desired many wives

2. *Many,* רַב *rab.*
Gen. 21. 34 sojourned in the Philistines' land many
37. 34 Jacob..mourned for his son many days
Exod. 5. 5 the people of the land now (are) many
19. 21 lest they..gaze, and many of them perish
23. 2 to decline after many to wrest (judgm.)
Lev. 15. 25 have an issue of her blood many days out
25. 51 If..yet many years..according unto them
Num. 9. 19 when the cloud tarried many days, then
13. 18 whether they..strong or weak, few or m.
22. 3 of the people, because they (were) many
24. 7 and his seed..in many waters, and his k.
26. 54 To many thou shalt give the more inheri.
26. 56 possession..be divided between many and
35. 8 from (them that have) many ye shall give
Deut. 1. 46 So ye abode in Kadesh many days, accor.
2. 1 and we compassed mount Seir many days
2. 10, 21 a people great, and many, and tall, as
7. 1 hath cast out many nations before thee
15. 6 thou shalt lend unto many nations, but
15. 6 thou shalt reign over many nations, but
25. 3 and beat him above these with many stri.
28. 12 thou shalt lend unto many nations, and
31. 17 many evils and troubles shall befall them
31. 21 many evils and troubles are befallen them
Josh.11. 4 went out..with horses and chariots..m.
22. 3 Ye have not left your brethren these many
Judg. 7. 2 The people..with thee (are) too many for
7. 4 The people (are) yet (too) many; bring
8. 30 threescore and ten sons..for he had many
9. 40 many were overthrown (and) wounded
1 Sa.14. 6 no restraint to the LORD to save by many
2 Sa. 22. 17 he took me; he drew me out of many w.
1 Ki. 2. 38 And Shimei dwelt in Jerusalem many d.
4. 20 Judah and Israel (were) many, as the sand
11. 1 But king Solomon loved many strange w.
18. 1 came to pass, (after) many days, that the
18. 25 ye (are) many; and call on the name of
2 Ki. 9. 22 whoredoms..her witchcrafts (are so) m.?
1 Ch. 4. 27 but his brethren had not many children
5. 22 For there fell down many slain, because
7. 22 Ephraim their father mourned many days
28. 5 for the LORD hath given me many sons
2 Ch.14. 11 whether with many, or with them that
30. 17 For (there were) many in the congregation
30. 18 multitude of the people, (even) many of E.
32. 23 many brought gifts unto the LORD to Jer.
Ezra 3. 12 many..wept..and many shouted aloud
10. 13 people (are) many, and (it is) a time of
Neh. 5. 2 our daughters, (are) many: therefore we
6. 18 For (there were) many in Judah sworn
7. 2 faithful man, and feared God above many
9. 28 many times didst thou deliver them acc.
9. 30 Yet many years didst thou forbear them
13. 26 yet among many nations was there no k.
Esth. 1. 4 many days, (even) an hundred and fours.
2. 8 when many maidens were gathered toge.
Esth. 4. 3 wailing; and many lay in sackcloth and
8. 17 many of the people of the land became J
Job 4. 3 Behold, thou hast instructed many, and
11. 19 thou shalt lie down..yea, many shall make
16. 2 have heard many such things: miserable
23. 14 performeth..and many such (things are)
Psa. 3. 1 LORD..many (are) they that rise up against
3. 2 Many (there be) which say of my soul, (Th.
4. 6 many that say, Who will show us (any) g.
18. 16 he took me, he drew me out of many wa.
22. 12 Many bulls have compassed me: strong
29. 3 thundereth: the LORD (is) upon many w.
31. 13 For I have heard the slander of many: f.
32. 10 Many sorrows (shall be) to the wicked: but
34. 19 Many (are) the afflictions of the righteous
37. 16 (is) better than the riches of many wicked
40. 3 many shall see (it), and fear, and shall
40. 5 Many..(are) thy wonderful works (which)
55. 18 hath delivered..for there were many with
56. 2 for (they be) many that fight against me
71. 7 I am as a wonder unto many: but thou
93. 4 (is) mightier than the noise of many wat.
106. 43 Many times did he deliver them; but they
110. 6 shall wound the heads over many count.
119. 157 Many (are) my persecutors and mine e.
Prov. 7. 26 For she hath cast down many wounded
10. 21 lips of the righteous feed many: but fools
14. 20 poor is hated..but the rich (hath) many
19. 4 Wealth maketh many friends: but the
19. 6 Many will entreat the favour of the prince
19. 21 many devices in a man's heart; neverthe.
28. 2 For the transgression of a land many (are)
28. 27 he that hideth his eyes shall have many
29. 26 Many seek the ruler's favour: but (every)
31. 29 Many daughters have done virtuously, but
Ecc. 6. 3 If a man..live many years, so that the
6. 3 days of his years be many, and his soul be
7. 29 but they have sought out many inventions
Song 8. 7 Many waters cannot quench love, neither
Isa. 2. 3 many people shall go and say, Come ye
2. 4 shall rebuke many people; and they shall
5. 9 Of a truth many houses shall be desolate
8. 7 the waters of the river, strong and many
8. 15 many among them shall stumble, and fall
17. 12 Woe to the multitude of many people
17. 13 shall rush like the rushing of many waters
31. 1 and trust in chariots, because (they are)
52. 14 and his form more than the sons of men
52. 15 So shall he sprinkle many nations; the
53. 11 shall my righteous servant justify many
53. 12 bare the sin of many, and made interces.
Jer. 3. 1 but thou hast played the harlot with m.
11. 15 she hath wrought lewdness with many
12. 10 Many pastors have destroyed my vineyard
13. 6 came to pass after many days, that the
16. 16 send for many fishers..many hunters, and
20. 10 For I heard the defaming of many, fear
22. 8 many nations shall pass by this city, and
25. 14 For many nations and great kings shall
27. 7 many nations and great kings shall serve
28. 8 prophesied both against many countries
32. 14 put them..that they may continue many
35. 7 that ye may live many days in the land
36. 32 were added besides unto them many like
37. 16 and Jeremiah had remained there many
50. 41 many kings shall be raised up from the
51. 13 O thou that dwellest upon many waters
Lam. 1. 22 for my sighs (are) many, and my heart
Eze. 3. 6 Not to many people of a strange speech
12. 27 The vision that he seeth (is) for many days
16. 41 execute judgments..in the sight of many
17. 7 eagle with great wings and many feathers
17. 9 without great power or many people to
17. 17 and building forts, to cut off many persons
19. 10 full of branches by reason of many waters
26. 3 will cause many nations to come up aga.
27. 3 a merchant of the people for many isles
27. 15 many isles (were) the merchandise of th.
27. 33 thou filledst many people; thou didst
32. 3 over thee with a company of many people
32. 9 I will also vex the hearts of many people
32. 10 I will make many people amazed at thee
33. 24 but we (are) many; the land is given us
37. 2 (there were) very many in the open valley
38. 6 all his bands; (and) many people with thee
38. 8 After many days thou shalt be visited: in
38. 8 (is) gathered out of many people, against
38. 9 all thy bands, and many people with thee
38. 15 many people with thee, all of them riding
38. 22 upon the many people that (are) with him
38. 23 will be known in the eyes of many nations
39. 27 sanctified..in the sight of many nations
43. 2 his voice (was) like a noise of many wate.
47. 7 many trees on the one side and on the
47. 10 the fish of the great sea, exceeding many
Dan. 8. 25 by peace shall destroy many: he shall also
8. 26 the vision; for it (shall be) for many days
9. 27 he shall confirm the covenant with many
11. 14 there shall many stand up against the
11. 18 face unto the isles, and shall take many
11. 26 overflow; and many shall fall down slain
11. 33 they that understand..shall instruct ma.
11. 34 many shall cleave to them with flatteries
11. 39 he shall cause them to rule over many, and
11. 40 and with horsemen, and with many ships
11. 41 many (countries) shall be overthrown: but
11. 44 to destroy, and utterly to make away ma.
12. 2 many of them that sleep in the dust of
12. 3 they that turn many to righteousness as
12. 4 many shall run to and fro, and knowledge
12. 10 Many shall be purified, and made white
Hos. 3. 3 Thou shalt abide for me many days; thou
Hos. 3. 4 shall abide many days without a king
Amos 8. 3 (shall be) many dead bodies in every place
Mic. 4. 2 many nations shall come, and say, Come
4. 3 And he shall judge among many people
4. 11 many nations are gathered against thee
4. 13 thou shalt beat in pieces many people: and
5. 7 shall be in the midst of many people as
5. 8 the Gentiles in the midst of many people
Nah. 1. 12 Though (they be) quiet, and likewise m.
Hab. 2. 8 thou hast spoiled many nations, all the
2. 10 hast consulted shame..by cutting off m.
Zech. 2. 11 many nations shall be joined to the LORD
8. 20 people, and the inhabitants of many cities
8. 22 many people and strong nations shall co.
Mal. 2. 6 and did turn many away from iniquity
2. 8 have caused many to stumble at the law

3. *Abundance,* רֹב *rob.*
1 Ki. 7. 47 they were exceeding many: neither was
Isa. 24. 22 and after many days shall they be

4. *Myriad,* רְבָבָה *rebabah.*
Num. 10. 36 Return..unto the many thousands of I.

5. *Great,* שַׂגִּיא *saggi.*
Ezra 5. 11 that was builded these many years ago
Dan. 2. 48 gave him many great gifts, and made him

6. *Sufficient,* ἱκανός *hikanos.*
Luke 7. 11 many of his disciples went with him, and
8. 32 an herd of many swine feeding on the
23. 9 he questioned with him in many words
Acts 9. 23 after that many days were fulfilled, the
9. 43 he tarried many days in Joppa with one
12. 12 where many were gathered together pra.
14. 21 when they..had taught many, they retu.
19. 19 Many of them also which used curious arts
20. 8 were many lights in the upper chamber
27. 7 we had sailed slowly many days, and sca.
1 Co.11. 30 many (are) weak and sickly among you

7. *More, greater,* πλείων *pleiōn.*
Luke11. 53 to provoke him to speak of many things
Acts 2. 40 with many other words did he testify and
13. 31 he was seen many days of them which c.
21. 10 as we tarried (there) many days, there c.
24. 17 after many years I came to bring alms to
25. 14 when they had been there many days, F.
27. 20 sun nor stars in many days appeared
28. 23 there came many to him into (his) lodging
1 Co.10. 5 with many of them God was not well ple.
2 Co. 2. 6 punishment, which (was inflicted) of ma.
4. 15 might through the thanksgiving of many
Phil. 1. 14 many of the brethren in the Lord, waxing
Heb. 7. 23 they truly were many priests, because they

8. *Much, many,* πολύς *polus.*
Matt. 3. 7 But when he saw many of the Pharisees
7. 13 broad..and many there be which go in
7. 22 Many will say to me in that day, Lord, L.
7. 22 and in thy name done many wonderful
8. 11 many shall come from the east and west
8. 16 many that were possessed with devils: and
8. 30 there was..an herd of many swine feeding
9. 10 many publicans and sinners came and sat
10. 31 ye are of more value than many sparrows
13. 3 he spake many things unto them in par.
13. 17 many prophets and righteous (men) have
13. 58 he did not many mighty works there, be.
15. 30 blind, dumb, maimed, and many others
16. 21 and suffer many things of the elders and
19. 30 But many (that are) first shall be last; and
20. 16 first last: [for many be called, but few c.]
20. 28 and to give his life a ransom for many
22. 14 For many are called, but few (are) chosen
24. 5 many shall come..and shall deceive many
24. 10 then shall many be offended, and shall
24. 11 many false prophets shall..deceive many
24. 12 iniquity shall abound, the love of many
25. 21, 23 I will make thee ruler over many th.
26. 28 is shed for many for the remission of sins
26. 60 [yea, though many false witnesses came]
27. 19 I have suffered many things this day in a
27. 52 many bodies of the saints which slept arose
27. 53 into the holy city, and appeared unto many
27. 55 many women were there beholding afar
Mark 1. 34 healed many..and cast out many devils
2. 2 straightway many were gathered together
2. 15 many publicans and sinners sat also tog.
2. 15 for there were many, and they followed
3. 10 For he had healed many; insomuch that
4. 2 he taught them many things by parables
4. 33 with [many] such parables spake he the
5. 9 saying, My name (is) Legion: for we are m
5. 26 suffered many things of many physicians
6. 2 [many] hearing (him) were astonished, sa.
6. 13 many devils, and anointed with oil many
6. 20 he did many things, and heard him gladly
6. 31 for there were many coming and going, and
6. 33 many knew him, and ran afoot thither out
6. 34 and he began to teach them many things
7. 4 many other things there be which they
7. 8 [and many other such like things ye do]
7. 13 delivered: and many such like things do
8. 31 Son of man must suffer many things, and
9. 12 he must suffer many things, and be set at
9. 26 was as one dead; insomuch that many said
10. 31 But many (that are) first shall be last; and
10. 45 and to give his life a ransom for many
10. 48 many charged him that he should hold his
11. 8 many spread their garments in the way
12. 5 him they killed, and many others; beating
12. 41 and many that were rich cast in much
13. 6 many shall come..and shall deceive many

Mark 14. 24 This is my blood..which is shed for many
14. 56 many bare false witness against him, but
15. 3 the chief priests accused him of many th.
15. 41 many other women which came up with
Luke 1. 1 many have taken in hand to set forth in
1. 14 gladness; and many shall rejoice at his
1. 16 many of the children of Israel shall he turn
2. 34 for the fall and rising again of many in I.
2. 35 the thoughts of many hearts may be re.
3. 18 many other things in his exhortation pr.
4. 25 many widows were in Israel in the days
4. 27 many lepers were in Israel in the time of
4. 41 devils also came out of many, crying out
7. 21 he cured many of (their) infirmities and pl.
7. 21 and unto many (that were) blind he gave
7. 47 Her sins, which are many, are forgiven; for
8. 3 Susanna, and many others, which minis.
8. 30 because many devils..entered into him
9. 22 Son of man must suffer many things, and
10. 24 For I tell you, that many prophets and k.
10. 41 thou art careful and troubled about many
12. 7 ye are of more value than many sparrows
12. 19 hast much goods laid up for many years
12. 47 that servant..shall be beaten with many
13. 24 for many, I say unto you, will seek to enter
14. 16 A..man made a great supper, and bade m.
15. 13 And not many days after, the younger son
17. 25 But first must he suffer many things, and
21. 8 for many shall come in my name, saying
22. 65 many other things blasphemously spake
23. 8 because he had heard many things of him
John 2. 12 and they continued there not many days
2. 23 many believed in his name, when they saw
4. 39 many of the Samaritans of that city beli.
4. 41 many more believed because of his own
6. 60 Many therefore of his disciples, when they
6. 66 From..(time) many..disciples went back
7. 31 many of the people believed on him, and
7. 40 [Many] of the people therefore, when they
8. 26 I have many things to say and to judge of
8. 30 As he spake these words many believed on
10. 20 many of them said, He hath a devil, and is
10. 32 Many good works have I showed you from
10. 41 many resorted unto him, and said, John
10. 42 And many believed on him there
11. 19 many of the Jews came to Martha and M.
11. 45 Then many of the Jews which came to M.
11. 47 What do we? for this man doeth many
11. 55 many went out of the country up to Jeru.
12. 11 Because that by reason of him many of the
12. 42 among the chief rulers also many believed
14. 2 In my Father's house are many mansions
16. 12 I have yet many things to say unto you
19. 20 This title then read many of the Jews; for
20. 30 many other signs truly did Jesus in the p.
21. 25 there are also many other things which J.
Acts 1. 3 by many infallible proofs, being seen of t.
1. 5 baptized with the Holy Ghost not many
2. 43 many wonders and signs were done by the
4. 4 Howbeit many of them which heard the
5. 12 by the hands of the apostles were many s.
8. 7 came out of many..and many taken with
8. 25 preached the gospel in many villages of
9. 13 Lord, I have heard by many of this man
9. 42 known..and many believed in the Lord
10. 27 and found many that were come together
13. 43 many of the Jews and religious proselytes
15. 32 exhorted the brethren with many words
15. 35 the word of the Lord, with many others
16. 18 this did she many days. But Paul, being
16. 23 when they had laid many stripes upon them
17. 12 Therefore many of them believed; also
18. 8 many of the Corinthians hearing believed
19. 18 many that believed came, and confessed
20. 19 with [many] tears, and temptations, which
24. 10 know that thou hast been for many years
25. 7 laid many and grievous complaints agai.
26. 9 that I ought to do many things contrary
26. 10 many of the saints did I shut up in prison
28. 10 Who also honoured us with many honours
Rom. 4. 17 have made thee a father of many nations
4. 18 might become the father of many nations
5. 15 if through the offence of one many be dead
5. 15 grace of God..hath abounded unto many
5. 16 but the free gift (is) of many offences unto
5. 19 by one man's disobedience many were m.
5. 19 the obedience of one shall many be made
8. 29 that he might be the first born among
12. 4 For as we have many members in one b.
12. 5 So we, (being) many, are one body in Ch.
15. 23 having a great desire these many years
16. 2 for she hath been a succourer of many
1 Co. 1. 26 many wise..not many mighty, not many
4. 15 yet (have ye) not many fathers: for in C.
8. 5 earth, as there be gods many... lords m.
10. 17 For we (being) many are one bread, (and)
10. 33 mine own profit, but the (profit) of many
11. 30 For this cause many (are) weak and sickly
12. 12 For as the body is one, and hath many m.
12. 12 members of that one body, being many
12. 14 For the body is not one member, but m.
12. 20 But now (are they) many members, yet
16. 9 opened unto me, and (there are) many ad.
2 Co. 1. 11 upon us by the means of many persons
1. 11 thanks may be given by many on our be.
2. 4 I wrote unto you with many tears; not
2. 17 For we are not as [many], which corrupt
6. 10 as poor, yet making many rich; as having
8. 22 proved diligent in many things, but now
9. 12 is abundant also by many thanksgivings
11. 18 Seeing that many glory after the flesh, I
12. 21 I shall bewail many which have sinned
Gal. 1. 14 above many my equals in mine own nat.
3. 16 He saith not, And to seeds, as of many
4. 27 for the desolate hath many more children
Phil. 3. 18 For many walk, of whom I have told you
1 Ti. 6. 9 and (into) many foolish and hurtful lusts
6. 10 pierced themselves through with many
6. 12 a good profession before many witnesses
2 Ti. 2. 2 hast heard of me among many witnesses
Titus 1. 10 For there are many unruly and vain talk.
Heb. 2. 10 in bringing many sons unto glory, to make
5. 11 Of whom we have many things to say
9. 28 was once offered to bear the sins of many
12. 15 trouble (you), and thereby [many] be defi.
Jas. 3. 1 My brethren, be not many masters, kno.
3. 2 For in many things we offend all. If any m.
2 Pe. 2. 2 many shall follow their pernicious ways
1 Jo. 2. 18 even now are there many antichrists; wh.
4. 1 because many false prophets are gone out
2 John 7 For many deceivers are entered into the
12 Having many things to write unto you, I
3 John 13 I had many things to write, but I will not
Rev. 1. 15 and his voice as the sound of many waters
5. 11 heard the voice of many angels round ab.
8. 11 many men died of the waters, because they
9. 9 as the sound of chariots of many horses
10. 11 must prophesy again before many peoples
14. 2 as the voice of many waters, and as the v.
17. 1 great whore that sitteth upon many waters
19. 6 as the voice of many waters, and as the
19. 12 on his head (were) many crowns; and he
[*See also* How, so, these very.]

MANY thousands —
A myriad, רְבָבָה *rebabah.*
Num 10. 36 Return..unto the many thousands of Is.

MANY, to be, do, give, have, make, use —
1. *To be many, multiplied*, רָבַב *rabab.*
1 Sa. 25. 10 There be many servants now a days that
Psa. 25. 19 Consider mine enemies, for they are many
Isa. 22. 9 of the city of David, that they are many
66. 16 and the slain of the LORD shall be many
Jer. 5. 6 because their transgressions are many
14. 7 for our backslidings are many; we have
2. *To be many*, רָבָה *rabah.*
1 Ch. 23. 17 but the sons of Rehabiah were very many
Prov. 4. 10 and the years of thy life shall be many
3. *To make many*, רָבָה *rabah*, 5.
Num 35. 8 from (them that have)..ye shall give many
1 Ch. 7. 4 for war..for they had many wives and
8. 40 had many sons, and sons' sons, an hund.
23. 11 but Jeush and Beriah had not many sons
Ezra 10. 13 we are many that have transgressed in
Job 41. 3 Will he make many supplications unto
Prov. 6. 35 rest content, though thou givest many
Isa. 1. 15 yea, when ye make many prayers, I will
Jer. 46. 11 in vain shalt thou use many medicines
46. 16 He made many to fall, yea, one fell upon
Eze. 22. 25 they have made her many widows in the
Hos. 8. 11 Because Ephraim hath made many altars
4. *Many, abundant*, רַב *rab.*
1 Sa. 2. 5 that hath many children is waxed feeble
2 Sa. 23. 20 of Kabzeel, who had done many acts, he
1 Ch. 11. 22 man of Kabzeel, who had done many acts
5. *Abundance*, רֹב *rob.*
1 Ki. 7. 47 because they were exceeding many: nei.

MANY a time —
1. *Many, abundant*, רַב *rab.*
Psa. 129. 1, 2 Many a time have they afflicted me from
2. *To make many*, רָבָה *rabah*, 5.
Psa. 78. 38 many a time turned he his anger away, and

MANY, to make self —
To make self heavy, כָּבֵד *kabed*, 7.
Nah. 3. 15 make thyself many..make thyself many

MANY things —
Many, abundant, רַב *rab.*
Isa. 42. 20 Seeing many things, but thou observest

MA'-OCH, מָעוֹךְ *poor.*
Father of Achish king of Gath, to whom David fled when persecuted by Saul. B.C. 1060.
1 Sa. 27. 2 unto Achish, the son of M., king of Gath

MA'-ON, מָעוֹן *habitation.*
1. A city and wilderness in Judah, near Ziph and Carmel; now called *Main*, seven miles S.E. of Hebron.
Josh 15. 55 M., Carmel, and Ziph, and Juttah
1 Sa. 25. 2 (there was) a man in M., whose possessions
2. A descendant of Caleb, son of Hezron, *or* his abode. B.C. 1400.
1 Ch. 2. 45 And the son of Shammai (was) M.: and M.

MA-ON-ITES, מָעוֹן.
A tribe (near Amalek) that oppressed Israel. See *Mehunim.*
Judg 10. 12 the M., did oppress you; and ye cried to

MAR, to —
1. *To give pain, mar*, כָּאַב *kaab*, 5.
2 Ki. 3. 19 and mar every good piece of land with s.
2. *To break down, mar*, נָתַס *nathas.*
Job 30. 13 They mar my path, they set forward my
3. *To corrupt*, שָׁחַת *shachath*, 3.
Nah. 2. 2 emptied them out, and marred their vine
4. *To corrupt*, שָׁחַת *shachath*, 5.
Lev. 19. 27 neither shalt thou mar the corners of thy
Ruth 4. 6 lest I mar mine own inheritance: redeem
1 Sa. 6. 5 images of your mice that mar the land; and
Jer. 13. 9 After this manner will I mar the pride of

MA'-RA, מָרָא *bitter.*
An appellation assumed by Naomi, B.C. 1320, instead of her former one which signified "pleasant."
Ruth 1. 20 Call me not Naomi, call me M.: for the

MA'-RAH, מָרָה *bitter.*
The first station of Israel on the E. of the Red Sea, in the peninsula of Sinai.
Exod 15. 23 when they came to M., they could not d.
15. 23 drink of the waters of M., for they (were) b.
15. 23 therefore the name of it was called M.
Num 33. 8 And they departed..and pitched in M.
33. 9 and they removed from M., and came unto

MAR-A'-LAH, מַרְעֲלָה *declivity.*
A city in Zebulun, now called *Arrabeh.*
Josh 19. 11 border went up toward the sea, and M.

MAR-AN-A'-THA, Μαρὰν ἀθά, Aramaic מָרַן אֲתָא.
An emphatic assertion of the apostle Paul, in Aramaic or Syriac, meaning "*Our Lord has come*" (or "*will come*").
1 Co. 16. 22 love not..let him be anathema maranatha

MARBLE —
1. *White marble*, שַׁיִשׁ, שֵׁשׁ *shesh, shayish.*
1 Ch. 29. 2 stones, and marble stones in abundance
Esth. 1. 6 silver rings and pillars of marble: the b.
Song 5. 15 His legs (are as) pillars of marble set upon
2. *Shining marble*, μάρμαρος *marmaros.*
Rev. 18. 12 wood, and of brass, and iron, and marble

MARCH (through), to —
1. *To go on*, הָלַךְ *halak.*
Hab. 1. 6 which shall march through the breadth
2. *To go on*, יָלַךְ *yalak.*
Jer. 46. 22 for they shall march with an army, and
Joel 2. 7 they shall march every one on his ways
3. *To remove, journey*, נָסַע *nasa.*
Exod 14. 10 Egyptians marched after them; and they
4. *To step forward*, צָעַד *tsaad.*
Judg. 5. 4 when thou marchedst out of the field of
Psa. 68. 7 thou didst march through the wilderness
Hab. 3. 12 Thou didst march through the land in in.

MA-RE'-SHAH, מָרֵאשָׁה, מָרֵשָׁה *possession.*
1. A fortified city in the plain of Judah, one and a half miles S. of Eleutheropolis.
Josh. 15. 44 Keilah, and Achzib, and M., nine cities
2 Ch. 11. 8 And Gath, and M., and Ziph
14. 9 And there came out against them..unto M.
14. 10 and they set the battle in array..at M.
20. 37 Then Eliezer the son of Dodavah of M. p.
Mic. 1. 15 an heir unto thee, O inhabitant of M.: he
2. The father of Hebron. B.C. 1400.
1 Ch. 2. 42 and the sons of M. the father of Hebron
3. The son of Laadah. B.C. 1400.
1 Ch. 4. 21 Laadah, the father of M., and the families

MARINER —
1. *Mariner*, מַלָּח *mallach.*
Eze. 27. 9 the ships of the sea with their mariners
27. 27 thy mariners, and thy pilots, thy calkers
27. 29 the mariners, (and) all the pilots of the
Jon. 1. 5 Then the mariners were afraid, and cried
2. *To go to and fro, row*, שׁוּט *shut.*
Eze. 27. 8 inhabitants of Zidon..were thy mariners

MARISH —
Ditch, marshy place, גֶּבֶא *gebe.*
Eze. 47. 11 marishes thereof shall not be healed; t.

MARK, MAR-CUS, Μάρκος.
1. The surname of John, cousin (or nephew) of Barnabas, the companion of Paul.
Acts 12. 12 John, whose surname was M.; where m.
12. 25 took with..John, whose surname was M.
15. 37 with them John, whose surname was M.
15. 39 Barnabas took M., and sailed unto Cyprus
Col. 4. 10 M., sister's son to Barnabas, touching whom
2 Ti. 4. 11 Take M., and bring him with thee: for he
Phm. 24 M., Aristarchus, Demas, Lucas, my fellow
2. A son or disciple of Peter, said to have written the second Gospel.
1 Pe. 5. 13 The (church)..saluteth you; and..M. my son

MARK —
1. *A sign*, אוֹת *oth.*
Gen. 4. 15 LORD set a mark upon Cain, lest any find
2. *A butt, mark*, מַטָּרָא, מַטָּרָה *mattarah, mattara.*
1 Sa. 20. 20 I will shoot..as though I shot at a mark
Job 16. 12 shaken me..and set me up for his mark
Lam. 3. 12 bent his bow, and set me as a mark for the
3. *A butt, mark*, מִפְגָּע *miphga.*
Job 7. 20 why hast thou set me as a mark against
4. *A mark*, תָּו *tav.*
Eze. 9. 4 set a mark upon the foreheads of the men
9. 6 not near any man upon whom (is) the m.
5. *A cross mark*, קַעֲקַע *qaaqa.*
Lev. 19. 28 Ye shall not..print any marks upon you

6. *Mark, goal, aim,* σκοπός *skopos.*
Phil. 3. 14 I press towards the mark for the prize of

7. *A point, puncture,* στίγμα *stigma.*
Gal. 6. 17 for I bear in my body the marks of the

8. *Impressed mark, engraving,* χάραγμα *charagma.*
Rev. 13. 16 to receive a mark in their right hand, or
13. 17 save he that had the mark, or the name
14. 9 receive (his) mark in his forehead, or in
14. 11 whosoever receiveth the mark of his name
15. 2 [and over his image, and over his mark]
16. 2 the men which had the mark of the beast
19. 20 that had received the mark of the beast
20. 4 neither had received (his) mark upon th.

MARK, to —

1. *To understand,* בִּין *bin.*
Job 18. 2 mark, and afterwards we will speak

2. *To seal, shut up,* חָתַם *chatham,* 3.
Job 24. 16 (which) they had marked for themselves

3. *To know,* יָדַע *yada.*
Ruth 3. 4 that thou shalt mark the place where he
1 Ki. 20. 7 Mark, I pray you, and see how this (man)
20. 22 Go, strengthen thyself, and mark, and s.

4. *To face, front,* פָּנָה *panah.*
Job 21. 5 Mark me, and be astonished, and lay (your)

5. *To give attention,* קָשַׁב *qashab,* 5.
Jer. 23. 18 who hath marked his word, and heard (it)

6. *To see,* רָאָה *raah.*
2 Sa. 13. 28 Mark ye now when Amnon's heart is m.

7. *To observe, watch,* שָׁמַר *shamar.*
1 Sa. 1. 12 it came to pass..that Eli marked her m.
Job 10. 14 If I sin, then thou markest me, and thou
22. 15 Hast thou marked the old way which w.
33. 11 in the stocks, he marketh all my paths
39. 1 canst thou mark when the hinds do calve?
Psa. 37. 37 Mark the perfect (man), and behold the
56. 6 they hide themselves, they mark my steps
130. 3 If thou, LORD, shouldest mark iniquities

8. *To hold on or upon,* ἐπέχω *epechō.*
Luke 14. 7 when he marked how they chose out the

9. *To look at, watch,* σκοπέω *skopeō.*
Rom 16. 17 mark them which cause divisions and off.
Phil. 3. 17 mark them which walk so as ye have us

MARK out, to —

To mark out, תָּאַר *taar,* 3.
Isa. 44. 13 he marketh it out with a line, he fitteth
44. 13 he marketh it out with the compass, and

MARK well, to —

1. *To give attention,* קָשַׁב *qashab,* 5.
Job 33. 31 Mark well, O Job; hearken unto me: hold

2. *To set heart (to),* (ל) שִׂים לֵב *sim leb (le).*
Eze. 44. 5 Son of man, mark well, and behold with
44. 5 mark well the entering in of the house

3. *To set heart to,* שִׁית לֵב לְ *shith leb le.*
Psa. 48. 13 Mark ye well her bulwarks, consider her

MARKED, to be —

To be treasured up, marked, spotted, כָּתַם *katham,* 2.
Jer. 2. 22 (yet) thine iniquity is marked before me

MARKET (place) —

1. *Merchandise,* מַעֲרָב *maarab.*
Eze. 27. 13 of men and vessels of brass in thy market
27. 17 they traded in thy market wheat of Min.
27. 19 cassia, and calamus, were in thy market
27. 25 Tarshish did sing of thee in thy market

2. *Market place, place of assembly,* ἀγορά *agora.*
Matt 11. 16 unto children sitting in the markets, and
20. 3 others standing idle in the market place
23. 7 greetings in the markets, and to be called
Mark 7. 4 (when they come) from the market, except
12. 38 and (love) salutations in the market places
Luke 7. 32 unto children sitting in the market place
11. 43 for ye love..greetings in the markets
20. 46 love greetings in the markets, and the hi
Acts 16. 19 drew (them) into the market place unto
17. 17 in the market daily with them that met

MA'-ROTH, מָרוֹת *lordship.*
A city in the N.W. of Judah; perhaps the same as *Jarmuth.*
Mic. 1. 12 the inhabitant of M. waited carefully for

MARRED, to be —

1. *Corruption, marring,* מִשְׁחָת *mishchath.*
Isa. 52. 14 his visage was so marred more than any

2. *To corrupt, mar,* שָׁחַת *shachath,* 2.
Jer. 13. 7 and, behold, the girdle was marred, it
18. 4 vessel that he made of clay was marred

3. *To lose, destroy,* ἀπόλλυμι *apollumi.*
Mark 2. 22 is spilled, and the bottles will be marred

MARRIAGE —

Marriage or wedding feast, γάμος *gamos.*
Matt 22. 2 king, which made a marriage for his son
22. 4 things (are) ready: come unto the marri.
22. 9 many as ye shall find, bid to the marriage
25. 10 went in with him to the marriage: and
John 2. 1 the third day there was a marriage in C.
2. 2 called, and his disciples, to the marriage
Heb. 13. 4 Marriage (is) honourable in all, and the
Rev. 19. 7 for the marriage of the Lamb is come, and
19. 9 they which are called unto the marriage

MARRIAGE, duty of —

Cohabitation, עוֹנָה *onah.*
Exod 21. 10 her raiment, and her duty of marriage

MARRIAGE, to give, be given in or to —

1. *To be praised,* הָלַל *halal,* 4.
Psa. 78. 63 their maidens were not given to marriage

2. *To be given in marriage,* γαμίσκομαι *gamiskomai.*
Mark 12. 25 neither marry, nor [are given in marriage]

3. *To give out in marriage,* ἐκγαμίζω *ekgamizō.*
Matt 22. 30 nor [are given in marriage], but are as the
24. 38 marrying and [giving in marriage],
Luke 17. 27 [they were given in marriage], until the
1 Co. 7. 38 So then [he that giveth (her) in marriage]
7. 38 but [he that giveth (her) not in marriage]

4. *To be given out in marriage,* ἐκγαμίσκομαι.
Luke 20. 34 children..marry, and [are given in mar.]
20. 35 neither marry, nor [are given in marriage]

MARRIAGES, to make —

To intermarry, חָתַן *chathan,* 7.
Gen. 34. 9 make ye marriages with us, (and) give your
Deut. 7. 3 Neither shalt thou make marriages with
Josh 23. 12 and shall make marriages with them, and

MARRIED, to be —

1. *Lord, master, owner,* בָּעַל *baal.*
Deut 22. 22 with a woman married to an husband, then
Jer. 3. 14 for I am married unto you: and I will take

2. *To be lord, master, owner,* בָּעַל *baal,* 2.
Prov 30. 23 For an odious (woman) when she is marr.
Isa. 62. 4 in thee, and thy land shall be married

3. *Owner of a wife,* בַּעַל אִשָּׁה *baal ishshah.*
Exod 21. 3 if he were married, then his wife shall go

4. *Wives,* נָשִׁים *nashim.*
Num 36. 3 if they be married to any of the sons of
36. 11 married unto their father's brother's sons
36. 12 they were married into the families of the

5. *To marry,* γαμέω *gameō.*
Mark 10. 12 if a woman..be married to another, she
1 Co. 7. 10 unto the married I command, (yet) not
7. 33 But he that is married careth for the th.
7. 34 but she that is married careth for the th.
7. 39 she is at liberty to be married to whom

6. *To become,* γίνομαι *ginomai.*
Rom. 7. 3 she be married to another man, she shall
7. 3 no adulteress, though she be married to
7. 4 that ye should be married to another, (even)

MARRIED wife —

To be master, owner, בָּעַל *baal.*
Isa. 54. 1 more..than the children of the married w.

MARROW, (full of) —

1. *Fat,* חֵלֶב *cheleb.*
Psa. 63. 5 soul shall be satisfied as (with) marrow and

2. *Marrow,* מֹחַ *moach.*
Job 21. 24 and his bones are moistened with marrow

3. *To be full of marrow,* מָחָה *machah,* 4.
Isa. 25. 6 of fat things full of marrow, of wines on

4. *Juice, marrow,* שִׁקּוּי *shiqqui.*
Prov. 3. 8 health to thy navel, and marrow to thy b.

5. *Marrow,* μυελός *muelos.*
Heb. 4. 12 and spirit, and of the joints and marrow

MARRY (a wife), to —

1. *To be master, owner,* בָּעַל *baal.*
Deut 24. 1 hath taken a wife, and married her, and
Isa. 62. 5 For (as) a young man marrieth a virgin
62. 5 shall thy sons marry thee: and (as) the b.
Mal. 2. 11 hath married the daughter of a strange

2. *To marry a brother's widow,* יָבַם *yabam,* 3.
Gen. 38. 8 unto thy brother's wife, and marry her

3. *To cause to sit down or still,* יָשַׁב *yashab,* 5.
Neh. 13. 23 Jews (that) had married wives of Ashdod
13. 27 transgress against our God in marrying s.

4. *To take,* לָקַח *laqach.*
Gen. 19. 14 sons in law, which married his daughters
Num 12. 1 the Ethiopian woman whom he had mar.
12. 1 for he had married an Ethiopian woman
1 Ch. 2. 21 whom he married when he (was) threesc.

5. *To lift up,* נָשָׂא *nasa.*
2 Ch. 13. 21 waxed mighty, and married fourteen wi.

6. *Become wives,* הָיָה לְנָשִׁים *[hayah].*
Num 36. 6 Let them marry to whom they think best
36. 6 only to the family..shall they marry

To marry, γαμέω *gameō.*
Matt. 5. 32 whosoever shall marry her that is divor.
19. 9 Whosoever..shall marry another, comm.
19. 9 whoso marrieth her which is put away a.
19. 10 be so with (his) wife, it is not good to m.
22. 25 first, when he had married a wife, decea.
22. 30 neither marry, nor are given in marriage
24. 38 marrying and given in marriage, until
Mark 6. 17 Philip's wife; for he had married her
10. 11 shall put away his wife, and marry anot.
12. 25 neither marry, nor are given in marriage
Luke 14. 20 And another said, I have married a wife
16. 18 putteth away his wife, and marrieth an.
16. 18 whosoever marrieth her that is put away
17. 27 they drank, they married wives, they were
20. 34 children of this world marry, and are gi.
20. 35 neither marry, nor are given in marriage
1 Co. 7. 9 But if they cannot contain, let them marry
7. 9 for it is better to marry than to burn
7. 28 But and if thou marry, thou hast not sin.
7. 28 and if a virgin marry, she hath not sinned
7. 36 what he will, he sinneth not: let them m.
1 Ti. 4. 3 Forbidding to marry, (and commanding)
5. 11 wax wanton against Christ, they will ma.
5. 14 therefore that the younger women marry

8. *To marry a brother's widow,* ἐπιγαμβρεύω.
Matt 22. 24 his brother shall marry his wife, and raise

MAR-SE'-NA, מַרְסְנָא *worthy.*
One of the seven princes of Media and Persia which saw the king's face at pleasure. B.C. 519.
Esth. 1. 14 next unto him (was) Carshena..Meres, M.

MARS' HILL, Ἄρειος πάγος *areios pagos.* See *Areopagus.*
A hill in Athens with an open space, where sat the court of the Areopagus, the supreme tribunal of justice modified by Solon.
Acts 17. 22 Paul stood in the midst of M. H., and said

MART —

A mart, merchandise, סָחַר *sachar.*
Isa. 23. 3 her revenue; and she is a mart of nations

MAR'-THA, Μάρθα, *from Ch.* מָרְתָא *lady.*
The elder sister of Mary and Lazarus in Bethany.
Luke 10. 38 a certain woman named M. received him
10. 40 But M. was cumbered about much serving
10. 41 Jesus..said unto her, M., M., thou are c.
John 11. 1 (named) Lazarus, of Bethany..town of..M.
11. 5 Now Jesus loved M., and her sister, and
11. 19 many of the Jews came to M. and Mary
11. 20 Then M., as soon as she heard that Jesus
11. 21 Then said M. unto Jesus, Lord, if thou h.
11. 24 M. saith unto him, I know that he shall r.
11. 30 Jesus..was in that place where M. met him
11. 39 M., the sister of him that was dead, saith
12. 2 they made him a supper; and M. served

MARTYR —

A witness, martyr, μάρτυς, μάρτυρ *martus, martur.*
Acts 22. 20 the blood of thy martyr Stephen was shed
Rev. 2. 13 Antipas (was) my faithful martyr, who was
17. 6 with the blood of the martyrs of Jesus

MARVEL —

Admirable, wonderful, θαυμαστός *thaumastos.*
2 Co. 11. 14 And no [marvel]; for Satan himself is

MARVEL (at), to —

1. *To wonder, marvel,* תָּמַהּ *tamah.*
Gen. 43. 33 and the men marvelled one at another
Psa. 48. 5 they marvelled; they were troubled, (and)
Eccl. 5. 8 marvel not at the matter: for (he that is)

2. *To admire, wonder,* θαυμάζω *thaumazō.*
Matt. 8. 10 marvelled, and said to them that followed
8. 27 the men marvelled, saying, What manner
9. 8 [they marvelled], and glorified God, which
9. 33 the multitudes marvelled, saying, It was
21. 20 they marvelled, saying, How soon is the
22. 22 they marvelled, and left him, and went
27. 14 that the governor marvelled greatly
Mark 5. 20 great things..and all (men) did marvel
6. 6 he marvelled because of their unbelief
12. 17 And they marvelled at him
15. 5 answered nothing; so that Pilate marvel.
15. 44 Pilate marvelled if he were already dead
Luke 1. 21 and marvelled that he tarried so long in
1. 63 His name is John. And they marvelled
2. 33 his mother marvelled at those things which
7. 9 he marvelled at him, and turned him about
11. 38 marvelled that he had not first washed
20. 26 they marvelled at his answer, and held
John 3. 7 Marvel not that I said unto thee, Ye must
4. 27 marvelled that he talked with the woman
5. 20 greater works..that ye may marvel
5. 28 Marvel not at this: for the hour is coming
7. 15 the Jews marvelled, saying, How knoweth
7. 21 I have done one work, and ye all marvel
Acts 2. 7 marvelled, saying one to another, Behold
3. 12 why marvel ye at this? or why look ye
4. 13 they marvelled; and they took knowledge
Gal. 1. 6 I marvel that ye are so soon removed from
1 Jo. 3. 13 Marvel not, my brethren, if the world h.
Rev. 17. 7 Wherefore didst thou marvel? I will tell

MARVELLOUS (thing or work) —

1. *To be wonderful, singular,* פָּלָא *pala,* 2.
1 Ch. 16. 12 his marvellous works that he hath done
16. 24 his marvellous works among all nations
Job 5. 9 doeth..marvellous things without num.
Psa. 9. 1 will show forth all thy marvellous works
98. 1 he hath done marvellous things: his right
105. 5 his marvellous works that he hath done
139. 14 marvellous (are) thy works; and (that)
Dan. 11. 36 shall speak marvellous things against the
Mic. 7. 15 will I show unto him marvellous (things)

2. *A wonder,* פֶּלֶא *pele.*
Psa. 78. 12 Marvellous things did he in the sight of

3. *Admirable, wonderful,* θαυμαστός *thaumastos.*
Matt 21. 42 doing, and it is marvellous in our eyes?
Mark 12. 11 doing, and it is marvellous in our eyes?
John 9. 30 herein is a marvellous thing, that ye
1 Pe. 2. 9 out of darkness into his marvellous light
Rev. 15. 1 saw another sign..great and marvellous
15. 3 Great and marvellous (are) thy works, L.

MARVELLOUS, to be or show self —

1. *To be wonderful, singular,* פָּלָא *pala,* 2.
Psa. 118. 23 LORD'S doing; it (is) marvellous in our e.

Zech. 8. 6 If it be marvellous in the eyes of the
8. 6 should it also be marvellous in mine eyes

2. *To make wonderful,* פָּלָא *pala,* 5.
Psa. 31. 21 his marvellous kindness in a strong city

3. *To show self wonderful,* פָּלָא *pala,* 7.
Job 10. 16 thou shewest thyself marvellous upon me

4. *To make wonderful,* פָּלָה *palah,* 5.
Psa. 17. 7 Show thy marvellous loving kindness, O

MARVELLOUS work, to do a —
To make wonderful, do singularly, פָּלָא *pala,* 5.
Isa. 29. 14 to do a marvellous work among this peo.

MARVELLOUSLY, to be —
1. *To be wonderful,* פָּלָא *pala,* 2.
Job 37. 5 God thundereth marvellously with his v.

2. *To make wonderful,* פָּלָא *pala,* 5.
2 Ch. 26. 15 he was marvellously helped, till he was

3. *To wonder, marvel,* תָּמַה *tamah.*
Hab. 1. 5 wonder marvellously: for (I) will work a

MARVELS —
To be wonderful, פָּלָא *pala,* 2.
Exod 34. 10 I will do marvels, such as have not been

MARY, Μαρία, Μαριάμ, *from Heb.* מִרְיָם *bitter.*
1. The mother of Jesus, and wife of Joseph.
Matt. 1. 16 Joseph the husband of M., of whom was
1. 18 When as his mother M. was espoused to J.
1. 20 fear not to take unto thee M. thy wife; for
2. 11 they saw the young child with M. his m.
13. 55 is not his mother called M.? and his bret.
Mark 6. 3 the son of M., the brother of James, and
Luke 1. 27 virgin espoused..virgin's name (was) M.
1. 30 Fear not, M.; for thou hast found favour
1. 34 Then said M. unto the angel, How shall
1. 38 And M. said, Behold the handmaid of the
1. 39 And M. arose in those days and went into
1. 41 when Elisabeth heard the salutation of M.
1. 46 And M. said, My soul doth magnify the
1. 56 And M. abode with her about three mon.
2. 5 To be taxed with M. his espoused wife, be.
2. 16 they came with haste, and found M. and
2. 19 But M. kept all these things, and pondered
2. 34 Simeon..said unto M. his mother, Behold
Acts 1. 14 and M. the mother of Jesus, and with his

2. A woman of Magdala, in Galilee.
Matt 27. 56 Among which was M. Magdalene and..the
27. 61 there was M. Magdalene..sitting over ag.
28. 1 In the end of the sabbath..came M. Ma.
Mark 15. 40 among whom was M. Magdalene, and..the
15. 47 And M. Magdalene..beheld where he was
16. 1 when the sabbath was past, M. Magdalene
16. 9 he appeared first to M. Magdalene, out of
Luke 8. 2 M. called Magdalene, out of whom went
24. 10 It was M. Magdalene, and Joanna, and
John 19. 25 Now there stood by the cross..M. Magd.
20. 1 The first (day) of the week cometh M. M.
20. 11 But M. stood without at the sepulchre
20. 16 Jesus saith unto her, M.! She turned he.
20. 18 M. Magdalene came and told the disciples

3. Mother of James and Joses, the apostles.
Matt 27. 56 Among which was..M. the mother of J.
27. 61 And there was..the other M., sitting over
28. 1 as it began to dawn..came..the other M.
Mark 15. 40 among whom was..M. the mother of J.
15. 47 M. (the mother) of Joses beheld where he
16. 1 when the sabbath was past..M. the (mot.)
Luke 24. 10 It was..M. (the mother) of James, and

4. Wife of Cleophas.
John 19. 25 there stood by the cross..M. the (wife) of

5. Sister of Lazarus and Martha in Bethany.
Luke 10. 39 she had a sister called M., which also sat
10. 42 M. hath chosen that good part, which shall
John 11. 1 Bethany, the town of M. and her sister
11. 2 It was (that) M. which anointed the Lord
11. 19 many of the Jews came to Martha and M.
11. 20 Martha..went and met him: but M. sat
11. 28 called M. her sister secretly, saying, The
11. 31 when they saw M., that she rose up hastily
11. 32 Then when M. was come where Jesus was
11. 45 many of the Jews which came to M., and
12. 3 Then took M. a pound of ointment of sp.

6. Mother of John Mark, nephew of Barnabas.
Acts 12. 12 he came to the house of M. the mother of

7. A female believer in Rome who had helped Paul.
Rom 16. 6 Greet [M.], who bestowed much labour on

MASCHIL —
Didactic poem (?), מַשְׂכִּיל *maschil.*
Psa. 32. *title.* (A psalm) of David, Maschil
42. ,, To the chief Musician, Maschil, for the
44. ,, for the sons of Korah, Maschil
45. ,, for the sons of Korah, Maschil, A Song of
52. ,, To the chief Musician, Maschil, (A)
53. ,, chief Musician upon Mahalath, Maschil
54. ,, chief Musician upon Neginoth, Maschil
55. ,, To the chief Musician on Neginoth, Mas.
74. ,, Maschil of Asaph
78. ,, Maschil of Asaph
88. ,, Maschil of Heman the Ezrahite
89. ,, Maschil of Ethan the Ezrahite
142. ,, Maschil of David; A prayer when he

MASH, מַשׁ.
A son of Aram, son of Shem, the same as *Meshech,* in 1 Ch. 1. 17.
Gen. 10. 23 children of Aram; Uz, and Hul..and M.

MA'-SHAL, מָשָׁל *depressed.*
A Levitical city in Asher. See *Misheal.*
1 Ch. 6. 74 of the tribe of Asher; M. with her subu.

MASON —
1. *Hewer of stone wall,* חָרָשׁ אֶבֶן קִיר *charash eben qir.*
2 Sa. 5. 11 and masons: and they built David an ho.

2. *To make a hedge or wall,* גָּדַר *gadar.*
2 Ki. 12. 12 to masons, and hewers of stone, and to
22. 6 carpenters, and builders, and masons, and

3. *To hew, dig,* חָצַב *chatsab.*
1 Ch. 22. 2 he set masons to hew wrought stones to
2 Ch. 24. 12 hired masons and carpenters to repair the
Ezra 3. 7 They gave money also unto the masons

4. *Hewer of a wall,* חָרָשׁ קִיר *charash qir.*
1 Ch. 14. 1 masons and carpenters, to build him an

MAS-RE'-KAH, מַשְׂרֵקָה *place of rivers.*
A place in Edom, between Petra and Shobek, the place of Samlah, the fifth king of Edom.
Gen. 36. 36 Hadad died, and Samlah of M. reigned in
1 Ch. 1. 47 when Hadad was dead, Samlah of M. rei.

MAS'-SA, מַשָּׂא *burden.*
A son of Ishmael, son of Hagar, and his land near Dumah, in Mount Seir. B.C. 1880.
Gen. 25. 14 And Mishma, and Dumah, and M.
1 Ch. 1. 30 Mishma, and Dumah, M., Hadad, and T.

MAS'-SAH, מַסָּה *trial, temptation.*
A place also called *Meribah,* in the wilderness, where the people murmured for want of water. B.C. 1492.
Exod 17. 7 he called the name of the place M., and
Deut. 6. 16 Ye shall not tempt the LORD..as..in M.
9. 22 and at M...ye provoked the LORD to wr.
33. 8 thy holy one, whom thou didst prove at M.

MAST —
1. *Mast, cable, rope,* חִבֵּל *chibbel.*
Prov 23. 34 as he that lieth upon the top of a mast

2. *A pole, mast,* תֹּרֶן *toren.*
Isa. 33. 23 they could not well strengthen their mast
Eze. 27. 5 have taken cedars..to make masts for thee

MASTER, (ship) —
1. *Lord, sir,* אָדוֹן *adon.*
Gen. 24. 9 under the thigh of Abraham his master
24. 10 ten camels of the camels of his master
24. 10 the goods of his master (were) in his hand
24. 12, 27, 42, 48 LORD God of my master Abra.
24. 12 and show kindness unto my master Abra.
24. 14 thou hast showed kindness unto my master
24. 27 who hath not left destitute my master of
24. 27 led..to the house of my master's brethren
24. 35 the LORD hath blessed my master greatly
24. 36 my master's wife bare a son to my master
24. 37 my master made me swear, saying, Thou
24. 39 I said unto my master, Peradventure the
24. 44 hath appointed out for my master's son
24. 48 take my master's brother's daughter unto
24. 49 will deal kindly and truly with my master
24. 51 let her be thy master's son's wife, as the
24. 54 and he said, Send me away unto my master
24. 56 send me away that I may go to my master
24. 65 And the servant (had) said, It (is) my ma.
39. 2 in the house of his master the Egyptian
39. 3 his master saw that the LORD (was) with
39. 7 master's wife cast her eyes upon Joseph
39. 8 unto his master's wife, Behold, my master
39. 19 his master heard the words of his wife
39. 20 Joseph's master took him, and put him
Exod 21. 4 If his master have given him a wife, and
21. 4 her children shall be her master's, and he
21. 5 I love my master, my wife, and my chil.
21. 6 master shall bring him unto the judges
21. 6 his master shall bore his ear through
21. 8 If she please not her master, who hath
21. 32 unto their master thirty shekels of silver
Deut 23. 15 Thou shalt not deliver unto his master
23. 15 which is escaped from his master unto
Judg 19. 11 the servant said unto his master, Come, I
19. 12 master said unto him, We will not turn
1 Sa. 20. 38 And Jonathan's lad..came to his master
24. 6 I should do this thing unto my master
25. 10 that break away every man from his ma.
25. 14 salute our master; and he railed on them
25. 17 evil is determined against our master, and
26. 16 ye have not kept your master, the LORD's
29. 4 he reconcile himself unto his master?
29. 10 master's servants that are come with thee
30. 13 and my master left me, because three d.
30. 15 deliver me into the hands of my master
2 Sa. 2. 7 your master Saul is dead, and also the
9. 9 I have given unto thy master's son all
9. 10 thy master's son may have food to eat
9. 10 thy master's son shall eat bread alway
12. 8 thy master's house, and thy master's wi.
16. 3 king said, And where (is) thy master's son?
1 Ki. 22. 17 These have no master; let them return
2 Ki. 2. 3, 5 the LORD will take away thy master
2. 16 seek thy master: lest peradventure the
5. 1 Naaman..was a great man with his master
5. 18 when my master goeth into the house of
5. 20 Behold, my master hath spared Naaman
5. 22 My master hath sent me, saying, Behold
5. 25 he went in, and stood before his master
6. 5 and he cried, and said, Alas, master!
6. 15 Alas, my master! how shall we do?
6. 22 may eat and drink, and go to their master
6. 23 and they went to their master. So the bands
2 Ki. 6. 32 sound of his master's feet behind him?
8. 14 came to his master; who said to him
9. 7 shalt smite the house of Ahab thy master
9. 31 (Had) Zimri peace, who slew his master?
10. 2 seeing your master's sons (are) with you
10. 3 best and meetest of your master's sons
10. 3 Look..out and fight for your master's house
10. 6 the heads of the men your master's sons
10. 9 I conspired against my master, and slew
18. 24 of the least of my master's servants, and
18. 27 Hath my master sent me to thy master
19. 4 whom..his master hath sent to reproach
19. 6 Thus shall ye say to your master, Thus saith
1 Ch. 12. 19 saying, He will fall to his master Saul to
2 Ch. 18. 16 and the LORD said, These have no master
Job 3. 19 the servant (is) free from his master
Psa. 123. 2 (look) unto the hand of their masters
Prov 25. 13 for he refresheth the soul of his masters
27. 18 he that waiteth on his master shall be
30. 10 Accuse not a servant unto his master, lest
Isa. 24. 2 as with the servant, so with his master
36. 8 to my master the king of Assyria, and
36. 9 of the least of my master's servants, and
36. 12 Hath my master sent me to thy master
37. 4 his master hath sent to reproach the
37. 6 Thus shall ye say unto your master, Thus
Jer. 27. 4 command them to say unto their masters
27. 4 Thus shall ye say unto your masters
Amos 4. 1 which say to their masters, Bring, and
Zeph. 1. 9 which fill their masters' houses with viol.
Mal. 1. 6 a servant his master: if then I (be) a father
1. 6 if I (be) a master, where (is) my fear? saith

2. *Master, owner,* בַּעַל *baal.*
Exod 22. 8 the master of the house shall be brought
Judg 19. 22 spake to the master of the house, the old
19. 23 the master of the house, went out unto
Eccl. 12. 11 fastened (by) the masters of assemblies
Isa. 1. 3 the ass his master's crib: (but) Israel doth

3. *Great, mighty, elder,* רַב *rab.*
Dan. 1. 3 unto Ashpenaz the master of his eunuchs
4. 9 O Belteshazzar, master of the magicians
5. 11 made master of the magicians, astrologers
Jon. 1. 6 the ship master came to him, and said unto

4. *Prince, head, chief, captain,* שַׂר *sar.*
Exod. 1. 11 they did set over them task masters to
1 Ch. 15. 27 the master of the song with the singers

5. *To awake, stir up,* עוּר *ur.*
Mal. 2. 12 the master and the scholar, out of the

6. *A despot, sovereign master,* δεσπότης *despotēs.*
1 Ti. 6. 1 count their own masters worthy of all
6. 2 they that have believing masters, let them
2 Ti. 2. 21 and meet for the master's use, (and) pre.
Titus 2. 9 to be obedient unto their own masters
1 Pe. 2. 18 (be) subject to (your) masters with all fear

7. *Teacher,* διδάσκαλος *didaskalos.*
Matt. 8. 19 Master, I will follow thee whithersoever
9. 11 Why eateth your Master with publicans
10. 24 The disciple is not above (his) master, nor
10. 25 It is enough..that he be as his master
12. 38 Master, we would see a sign from thee
17. 24 and said, Doth not your master pay tribute
19. 16 Master, what good thing shall I do, that
22. 16 Master, we know that thou art true, and
22. 24 Master, Moses said, If a man die, having
22. 36 Master, which (is) the great commandm.
26. 18 The Master saith, My time is at hand; I
Mark 4. 38 Master, carest thou not that we perish?
5. 35 why troublest thou the Master any further
9. 17 Master, I have brought unto thee my son
9. 38 Master, we saw one casting out devils in
10. 17 Good Master, what shall I do that I may
10. 20 Master, all these have I observed from my
10. 35 Master, we would that thou shouldest do
12. 14 Master, we know that thou art true, and
12. 19 Master, Moses wrote unto us, If a man's
12. 32 Master, thou hast said the truth: for there
13. 1 Master, see what manner of stones and
14. 14 Master saith, Where is the guest chamber
Luke 3. 12 and said unto him, Master, what shall we
6. 40 The disciple is not above his master: but
6. 40 that is perfect shall be as his master
7. 40 say unto thee. And he saith, Master, say
8. 49 daughter is dead; trouble not the Master
9. 38 Master, I beseech thee, look upon my son
10. 25 Master, what shall I do to inherit eternal
11. 45 Master, thus saying thou reproachest us
12. 13 Master, speak to my brother, that he di.
18. 18 Master, what shall I do to inherit eternal
19. 39 said unto him, Master, rebuke thy disciples
20. 21 saying, Master, we know that thou sayest
20. 28 Master, Moses wrote unto us, If any man's
20. 39 answering said, Master, thou hast well said
21. 7 Master, but when shall these things be?
22. 11 The Master saith unto thee, Where is the
John 1. 38 which is to say, being interpreted, Master
3. 10 Art thou a master of Israel, and knowest
8. 4 [They say unto him, Master, this woman]
11. 28 The Master is come, and calleth for thee
13. 13 Ye call me Master and Lord: and ye say
13. 14 If I then, (your) Lord and Master, have
20. 16 saith..Rabboni! which is to say, Master
Jas. 3. 1 My brethren, be not many masters, kno.

8. *Superintendent, one who stands over,* ἐπιστάτης.
Luke 5. 5 Master, we have toiled all the night, and
8. 24 awoke him, saying, Master, master, we
8. 45 Master, the multitude throng thee and
9. 33 Peter said unto Jesus, Master, it is good

Luke 9. 49 Master, we saw one casting out devils in
17. 13 and said, Jesus, Master, have mercy on us

9. *A leader*, καθηγητής *kathēgētēs*.
Matt. 23. 8, 10 for one is your [Master], (even) Christ
23. 10 Neither be ye called masters: for one is

10. *Master, lord, sir*, κύριος *kurios*.
Matt. 6. 24 No man can serve two masters: for either
15. 27 crumbs which fall from their masters' ta.
Mark 13. 35 not when the master of the house cometh
Luke 14. 21 the master of the house, being angry, said
16. 13 No servant can serve two masters: for
Acts 16. 16 which brought her masters much gain by
16. 19 her masters saw that the hope of their
Rom 14. 4 to his own master he standeth or falleth
Eph. 6. 5 are (your) masters according to the flesh
6. 9 ye masters, do the same things unto them
6. 9 knowing that your Master..is in heaven
Col. 3. 22 (your) masters according to the flesh
4. 1 Masters, give unto (your) servants that wh.
4. 1 knowing that ye also have a Master in he.

11. *Rabbi, my teacher*, (*Heb.* רַבִּי) ῥαββί *rhabbi*.
Matt 26. 25 Then Judas..said, Master, is it I? He said
26. 49 and said, Hail, Master! and kissed him
Mark 9. 5 Master, it is good for us to be here: and
11. 21 saith unto him, Master, behold, the fig tree
14. 45 and saith, Master, [master]; and kissed
John 4. 31 his disciples prayed him, saying, Master
9. 2 Master, who did sin, this man, or his
11. 8 disciples say unto him, Master, the Jews

12. *Pilot, steersman, governor*, κυβερνήτης *kubernētēs*.
Acts 27. 11 centurion believed the master and the
Rev. 18. 17 And every ship master, and all the com.

MASTER BUILDER —
Chief architect, ἀρχιτέκτων *architektōn*.
1 Co. 3. 10 as a wise master builder, I have laid the
[*See also* Sheep master, task master, ship master.]

MASTERY, (to have) —
1. *Might*, גְּבוּרָה *geburah*.
Exod 32. 18 the voice of (them that) shout for mastery

2. *To rule, have power*, שְׁלֵט *shelet*.
Dan. 6. 24 and the lions had the mastery of them

MATE —
Friend, companion, neighbour, רְעוּת *reuth*.
Isa. 34. 15 also be gathered, every one with her mate
34. 16 none shall want her mate: for my mouth

MA-THU-SA'-LA, Μαθουσάλα—See *Methuselah*.
Luke 3. 37 M., which was (the son) of Enoch, which

MAT'-RED, מַטְרֵד *God is pursuer*.
Mother of Mehetabel, wife of Hadar, last of the old kings of Edom. B.C. 1500.
Gen. 36. 39 Mehetabel, the daughter of M., the dau.
1 Ch. 1. 50 Mehetabel, the daughter of M., the daug.

MAT'-RI, מַטְרִי *Jah is watching*.
Head of a Benjamite family from which Saul came. B.C. 1096.
1 Sa. 10. 21 the family of M. was taken, and Saul the

MATRIX —
Womb, רֶחֶם *rechem*.
Exod 13. 12 set apart..all that openeth the matrix, and
13. 15 all that openeth the matrix, being males
34. 19 All that openeth the matrix (is) mine; and
Num. 3. 12 the first born that openeth the matrix
18. 15 Every thing that openeth the matrix in all

MAT'-TAN, מַתָּן *gift*.
1. A priest of Baal in Jerusalem in the days of Athaliah, and slain along with her. B.C. 878.
2 Ki. 11. 18 slew M. the priest of Baal before the alt.
2 Ch. 23. 17 slew M. the priest of Baal before the alt.
2. The father of Shephatiah, a prince of Judah in the time of Zedekiah. B.C. 630.
Jer. 38. 1 Shephatiah the son of M., and Gedaliah

MAT-TA'-NAH, מַתָּנָה *gift*.
A station of Israel, N. of the Arnon, and W. of the wilderness of Kedemoth.
Num 21. 18 And from the wilderness (they went) to M.
21. 19 And from M. to Nahaliel: and from Na.

MAT-TAN'-IAH, מַתַּנְיָה, מַתַּנְיָהוּ *gift of Jah*.
1. A brother of Jehoiakim, made king instead of his nephew Jehoiakim, also called *Zedekiah*. B.C. 590. The last king of Judah.
2 Ki. 24. 17 made M. his father's brother king in his
2. A Levite, descendant of Asaph, whose family dwelt in Jerusalem. B.C. 1015.
1 Ch. 9. 15 Heresh, and Galal, and M. the son of Mi.
2 Ch. 20. 14 the son of M., a Levite of the sons of As.
Neh. 11. 17 And M. the son of Micha, the son of Za.
11. 22 Hashabiah, the son of M., the son of Mi.
12. 8 M., (which was) over the thanksgiving, he
12. 25 M., and Bakbukiah, Obadiah, Meshullam
12. 35 Shemaiah, the son of M., the son of Mic.
3. A son of Heman the singer. B.C. 1015.
1 Ch. 25. 4 sons of Heman; Bukkiah, M., Uzziel
25. 16 The ninth to M., (he), his sons, and his br.
4. A descendant of Asaph who helped to cleanse the temple in the days of king Hezekiah. B.C. 726.
2 Ch. 29. 13 of the sons of Asaph; Zechariah and M.
5. A descendant of Elam that had taken a strange wife. B.C. 436.
Ezra 10. 26 of the sons of Elam; M., Zechariah, and
6. A son of Zattu that had done the same.
Ezra 10. 27 the sons of Zattu; Elioenai, Eliashib, M.
7. One of the family of Pahath-Moab who had done the same.
Ezra 10. 30 the sons of Pahath-moab; Adna, and..M.
8. A son of Bani that had done the same.
Ezra 10. 37 M., Mattenai, and Jaasau
9. A Levite whose descendant Hanan was one of the treasurers appointed by Nehemiah. B.C. 536.
Neh. 13. 13 Hanan the son of Zaccur, the son of M.

MAT-TA'-THA, Ματταθά *gift*.
An ancestor of Jesus.
Luke 3. 31 Menan, which was (the son) of M., which

MAT-TA'-THAH, מַתַּתָּה.
One of the family of Hashum that had taken a strange wife. B.C. 456.
Ezra 10. 33 Of the sons of Hashum; Mattenai, M., Z.

MAT-TA-THI'-AS, Ματταθίας.
1. An ancestor of Jesus.
Luke 3. 25 M., which was (the son) of Amos, which
2. An ancestor of the former in the sixth remove.
Luke 3. 26 Maath, which was (the son) of M., which

MAT-TE-NA'-I, מַתְּנַי *gift of Jah*.
1. One of the family of Hashum that had taken a strange wife. B.C. 456.
Ezra 10. 33 of the sons of Hashum; M., Mattathah
2. One of the family of Bani that had done the same.
Ezra 10. 37 Mattaniah, M., and Jaasau
3. A priest of the family of Joiarib. B.C. 500.
Neh. 12. 19 And of Joiarib, M.; of Jedaiah, Uzzi

MATTER —
1. *Word, matter, thing*, דָּבָר *dabar*.
Gen. 24 9 and sware to him concerning that matter
Exod 18. 16 When they have a matter, they come unto
18. 22 every great matter they shall bring unto
18. 22 but every small matter they shall judge
18. 26 every small matter they judged themsel.
23. 7 Keep thee far from a false matter; and
24. 14 if any man have any matters to do, let him
Num. 16. 49 them that died about the matter of Kor.
25. 18 in the matter of Peor, and in the matter
31. 16 commit trespass..in the matter of Peor
Deut. 3. 26 speak no more unto me of this matter
17. 8 If there arise a matter too hard for thee
17. 8 matters of controversy, within thy gates
19. 15 witnesses, shall the matter be established
22. 26 and slayeth him, even so (is) this matter
Ruth 3. 18 how the matter will fall: for the man will
1 Sa. 10. 16 But of the matter of the kingdom, whereof
16. 18 a man of war, and prudent in matters
20. 23 (as touching) the matter which thou and
20. 39 only Jonathan and David knew the matt.
30. 24 who will hearken unto you in this matter?
2 Sa. 1. 4 How went the matter? I pray thee, tell
11. 19 made an end of telling the matters of the
15. 3 See, thy matters (are) good and right; but
18. 13 for there is no matter hid from the king
19. 29 speakest thou any more of thy matters?
19. 42 wherefore then be ye angry for this ma.?
20. 21 The matter (is) not so: but a man of m.
1 Ki. 8. 59 at all times, as the matter shall require
15. 5 save only in the matter of Uriah the Hit.
1 Ch. 26. 32 for every matter pertaining to God, and
27. 1 that served the king in any matter of the
2 Ch. 8. 15 concerning any matter, or concerning the
19. 11 priest (is) over you in all matters of the L.
19. 11 for all the king's matters: also the Levites
24. 5 see that ye hasten the matter. Howbeit
Ezra 10. 4 Arise; for (this) matter (belongeth) unto
10. 9 because of (this) matter, and for the great
10. 14 wrath of our God for this matter be turned
10. 16 and sat down..to examine the matter
Neh. 11. 24 at the king's hand in all matters concer.
Esth. 2. 23 when inquisition was made of the matter
3. 4 to see whether Mordecai's matters would
9. 31 the matters of the fastings and their cry
9. 32 confirmed these matters of Purim; and
Job 19. 28 seeing the root of the matter is found in
33. 13 giveth not account of any of his matters
Psa. 35. 20 devise deceitful matters against (them)
45. 1 My heart is inditing a good matter: I sp.
64. 5 encourage themselves (in) an evil matter
Prov. 11. 13 of a faithful spirit concealeth the matter
16. 20 He that handleth a matter wisely shall
17. 9 but he that repeateth a matter separateth
18. 13 He that answereth a matter before he he.
25. 2 honour of kings (is) to search out a matter
Eccl. 10. 20 that which hath wings shall tell the mat.
12. 13 hear the conclusion of the whole matter
Jer. 38. 27 left off..for the matter was not perceived
Eze. 9. 11 reported the matter, saying, I have done
Dan. 1. 14 So he consented to them in this matter
1. 20 in all matters of wisdom (and) understan.
9. 23 therefore understand the matter, and co.

2. *Business, matter, pleasure*, חֵפֶץ *chephets*.
Eccl. 5. 8 marvel not at the matter: for (he that

3. *Reason, behaviour, decree*, טְעֵם *taam*.
Ezra 5. 5 to cease, till the matter came to Darius

4. *Word, speech, matter*, מִלָּה *millah*.
Job 32. 18 For I am full of matter; the spirit within
Dan. 2. 10 that can show the king's matter: theref
2. 23 made known unto us the king's matter
7. 1 wrote..(and) told the sum of the matters
7. 28 Hitherto (is) the end of the matter. As
7. 28 troubled..but I kept the matter in my

5. *Sentence, matter, letter*, פִּתְגָם *pithgam*.
Dan. 3. 16 not careful to answer thee in this matter
4. 17 This matter (is) by the decree of the wa.

6. *Word, thing, matter*, λόγος *logos*.
Mark 1. 45 to blaze abroad the matter, insomuch
Acts 8. 21 hast neither part nor lot in this matter
15. 6 came together for to consider of this mat.
19. 38 if Demetrius..have a matter against any

7. *Anything done, affair, matter*, πρᾶγμα *pragma*.
1 Co. 6. 1 Dare any of you, having a matter against
2 Co. 7. 11 approved yourselves..in this m., 1 Th. 4. 6

8. *Against*, κατά *kata*, Acts 24. 22.

9. *Matter*, ὕλη *hulē*.
Jas. 3. 5 Behold how great a matter a little fire
[*See also* Great, small, this, wrong.]

MATTER, to make —
To bear or carry diversely, διαφέρω *diapherō*.
Gal. 2. 6 it maketh no matter to me: God accept.

MAT'-THAN, Ματθάν, Μαθθάν.
An ancestor of Jesus, through Joseph.
Matt. 1. 15 and Eleazar begat M.; and M. begat Jacob

MAT'-THAT, Ματθάτ, Μαθθάτ.
1. The grandfather of Joseph, the husband of Mary.
Luke 3. 24 (the son) of M., which was (the son) of L.
2. A more remote ancestor still.
Luke 3. 29 Jorim, which was (the son) of M., which

MAT'-THEW, Ματθαῖος, Μαθθαῖος.
A tax gatherer (called also *Levi*, the son of Alpheus) who became an apostle of Christ, and is generally reckoned to have written the first gospel. A.D. 40.
Matt. 9. 9 Jesus..saw a man, named M., sitting at
10. 3 Thomas, and M. the publican; James (the
Mark 3. 18 Bartholomew, and M., and Thomas, and
Luke 6. 15 M. and Thomas, James the (son) of Alph.
Acts 1. 13 Bartholomew, and M., James (the son) of

MAT-THI'-AS, Ματθίας, Μαθθίας.
A disciple surnamed *Justus*, chosen by lot to succeed Judas Iscariot as an apostle.
Acts 1. 23 And they appointed two, Joseph..and M.
1. 26 the lot fell upon M.; and he was numbered

MAT-TITH'-IAH, מַתִּתְיָה, מַתִּתְיָהוּ *gift of Jah*.
1. A Korahite who had the charge of "things made in the pans." B.C. 500.
1 Ch. 9. 31 And M., (one) of the Levites, who (was)
2. A Levite, singer and gate keeper in the days of David. B.C. 1015.
1 Ch. 15. 18 And with them..Maaseiah, and M., and E.
15. 21 And M., and Elipheleh, and Mikneiah
16. 5 next to him..M., and Eliab, and Benaiah
3. Son of Jeduthun, in the days of David. B.C. 1015.
1 Ch. 25. 3 sons of Jeduthun; Gedaliah..and M. six
25. 21 The fourteenth to M., (he), his sons, and
4. One of the family of Nebo that had taken a strange wife. B.C. 456.
Ezra 10. 43 the sons of Nebo; Jeiel, M., Zabad, Zeb.
5. A prince, priest, or Levite that stood beside Ezra when he read the law of the people. B.C. 445.
Neh. 8. 4 beside him stood M., and Shema, and A.

MAY, mayest, might —
1. *To be able*, יָכֹל *yakol*.
Gen. 43. 32 because the Egyptians might not eat bread
44. 26 for we may not see the man's face, except
Deut 7. 22 thou mayest not consume them at once
12. 17 Thou mayest not eat within thy gates the
16. 5 Thou mayest not sacrifice the passover
17. 15 thou mayest not set a stranger over thee
21. 16 he may not make the son of the beloved
22. 3 do likewise: thou mayest not hide thyself
22. 19, 29 he may not put her away all his days
24. 4 may not take her again to be his wife, after
Josh. 9. 19 now therefore we may not touch them
Judg 21. 18 Howbeit we may not give them wives of
2 Sa. 17. 17 for they might not be seen to come into
1 Ki. 13. 16 I may not return with thee, nor go in with
20. 9 I will do: but this thing I may not do. And
Eccl. 6. 10 neither may he contend with him that is
Jer. 13. 23 may ye also do good, that are accustomed

2. *To be able*, δύναμαι *dunamai*.
Matt 26. 9 this ointment might have been sold for
26. 42 if this cup may not pass away from me
Mark 4. 32 fowls of the air may lodge under the sha.
14. 5 it might have been sold for more than th.
14. 7 whensoever ye will ye may do them good
Luke 16. 2 for thou mayest be no longer steward
Acts 17. 19 May we know what this new doctrine, w.
19. 40 no cause whereby we may give an account
24. 8 by examining of whom thyself mayest take
24. 11 Because that thou mayest understand, that
25. 11 no man may deliver me unto them. I ap.
26. 32 This man might have been set at liberty
27. 12 if by any means they might attain to Ph.
1 Co. 7. 21 but if thou mayest be made free, use (it)
14. 31 For ye may all prophesy one by one, that
Eph. 3. 4 Whereby, when ye read, ye may unders.
1 Th. 2. 6 when we might have been burdensome
Rev. 13. 17 that no man might buy or sell, save he that

3. *It is allowed, privileged, possible,* ἔξεστι *exesti.*
Acts 8. 37 If thou believest..thou mayest. And he
21. 37 May I speak unto thee? Who said, Canst
4. *To be strong, have strength,* ἰσχύω *ischuō.*
Matt. 8. 28 so that no man might pass by that way

MAY be, it —
1. *If so be, it may be, unless,* אוּלַי, אֻלַי *ulai.*
Gen. 16. 2 it may be that I may obtain children by
2 Ki. 19. 4 It may be the LORD thy God will hear all
Job 1. 5 It may be that my sons have sin. Zeph. 2. 3
2. *If perhaps,* εἰ τύχοι *ei tuchoi,* 1 Co. 14. 10; 16. 6.
3. *Perhaps,* ἴσως *isōs.*
Luke 20. 13 it may be they will reverence (him) when

MATTOCK —
1. *Sword, weapon, axe, tool,* חֶרֶב *chereb.*
2 Ch. 34. 6 even unto Naphtali, with their mattocks
2. *Mattock,* מַחֲרֵשָׁה *machareshah.*
1 Sa. 13. 20 his coulter, and his ax, and his mattock
13. 21 Yet they had a file for the mattocks, and
3. *A rake,* מַעְדֵּר *mader.*
Isa. 7. 25 that shall be digged with the mattock

MAUL —
A maul, axe, מֵפִיץ *mephits.*
Prov. 25. 18 (is) a maul, and a sword, and a sharp ar.

MAW —
Maw, stomach, קֵבָה *qebah.*
Deut 18. 3 shoulder, and the two cheeks, and the maw

MAZ-ZA'-ROTH, מַזָּרוֹת.
The (twelve) constellations of the Zodiac.
Job. 38. 32 Canst thou bring forth M. in his season?

ME —
1. *I, I myself,* אֲנִי *ani.*
1 Sa. 25. 24 my lord, (upon) me (let this) iniquity (be)
2. *Soul, breath,* נֶפֶשׁ *nephesh.*
Num 23. 10 Let me die the death of the righteous, and
Judg 16. 30 Let me die with the Philistines. And he b.
1 Ki. 20. 32 saith, I pray thee, let me live. And he said
3. *I, I myself,* ἐγώ *egō.*
Phm. 20 Yea, brother, let me have joy of thee in
4. *Of myself,* ἐμαυτοῦ *emautou.*
Matt. 8. 9 authority, having soldiers under me: and
Luke 7. 8 authority, having under me soldiers; and
John 12. 32 And I..will draw all (men) unto me
Phm. 13 Whom I would have retained with me
5. *Me,* ἐμέ (*acc.*) *eme.*
Matt 10. 37, 37 more than me, is not worthy of me
10. 40 receiveth me; and he that receiveth me
18. 5 little child in my name receiveth me
18. 6 these little ones which believe in me, it
18. 21 how oft shall my brother sin against me
26. 10 for she hath wrought a good work upon me
26. 11 always with you; but me ye have not al.
[This particle occurs so translated 72 times.]
6. *To me,* ἐμοί (*dat.*) *emoi.*
Matt 10. 32 Whosoever therefore shall confess me be.
11. 6 whosoever shall not be offended in me
18. 26, 29 have patience [with me], and I will p.
25. 40 my brethren, ye have done (it) unto me
25. 45 of the least of these, ye did (it) not to me
26. 31 All ye shall be offended because of me this
[This particle occurs so translated 34 times.]
7. *Of me,* ἐμοῦ (*gen.*) *emou.*
Matt. 7. 23 never knew you: depart from me, ye that
11. 29 Take my yoke upon you, and learn of me
12. 30 He that is not with me is against me; and
12. 30 he that gathereth not with me scattereth
15. 5 by..thou mightest be profited by me
15. 8 honoureth..but their heart is far from me
17. 27 that take, and give unto them for me and
25. 41 Depart from me, ye cursed, into everlast.
26. 23 He that dippeth (his) hand with me in the
26. 38 saith..tarry ye here, and watch with me
26. 39 it be possible, let this cup pass from me
26. 40 What! could ye not watch with me one
26. 42 if this cup may not pass away [from me]
[This particle occurs so translated 82 times]
8. *Me,* μέ (*acc.*) *me.*
Matt. 3. 14 I have need..and comest thou to me?
8. 2 Lord, if thou wilt, thou canst make me
10. 33 But whosoever shall deny me before men
10. 40 receiveth..receiveth him that sent me
11. 28 Come unto me, all (ye) that labour and
14. 28 if it be thou, bid me come unto thee on
14. 30 to sink, he cried, saying, Lord, save me
15. 8 and honoureth me with (their) lips; but
15. 9 But in vain they do worship me, teaching
15. 22 Have mercy on me, O Lord, (thou) son of
18. 32 all that debt, because thou desiredst me
19. 14 and forbid them not, to come unto me; for
19. 17 Why callest thou me good? (there is) none
22. 18 said, Why tempt ye me, (ye) hypocrites?
23. 39 Ye shall not see me henceforth, till ye sh.
25. 35 I was thirsty, and ye gave me drink: I
25. 35 I was a stranger, and ye took me in
25. 36 and ye clothed me..and ye visited me
25. 36 I was in prison, and ye came unto me
25. 42 I was thirsty, and ye gave me no drink
25. 43 took me not in: naked, and ye clothed me
25. 43 sick, and in prison, and ye visited me not
26. 21 unto you, That one of you shall betray me
26. 23 He that dippeth..the same shall betray me
26. 34 this night ..thou shalt deny me thrice
Matt 26. 46 behold, he is at hand that doth betray me
26. 55 with swords and staves for to take me? I
26. 55 in the temple, and ye laid no hold on me
26. 75 Before the cock crow, thou shalt deny me
27. 46 my God! why hast thou forsaken me?
28. 10 go into Galilee, and there shall they see me
Mark 1. 40; 5. 7; 6. 22, [23]; 7. 6, 7; 8. 38; 9. 19, 37,
39; 14. 10, 18, 47, 48; 12. 15; 14. 18, 30, 42, 48, 49, 72;
15. 34; Luke 1. 43, 48; 2. 49; 4. 18, 18; 5. 12; 6. 46, 47;
8. 28; 9. 26, 48; 10. 16, 40; 11. 6; 12. 9, 14; 13. 35; 14.
18, 19, 26; 15. 19; 16. 4, 24; 18. 3, 5, 16, 19, 38, 39; 20.
[23]; 22. 21, 34, 61; 24. 39; John 1. 33, 48; 2. 17; 4. 34;
5. 7, 11, 24, 30, 36, 37, 40, 43; 6. 26, [35, 36,] 37, 39, [40,
44], 44, [45], 57, 57, 65; 7. 16, 19, 28, 29, 33, 34, 36, 37; 8.
16, 18, 21, 26, 38, 29, 29, 37, 40, 42, 46, 49, 54; 9. 4; 10.
15, 17, [32]; 11. 42; 12. 27, 44, 45, 49; 13. 13, 20, 21, 33,
38; 14. 7, 9, 15, 19, 19, 21, 21, 23, 24, 24, 28; 15. 9, 16, 21,
25; 16. 5, 5, 10, 16, 16, 17, 17, 19, 19; 17. 5, 8, 21, 23, 24,
25, 26; 18. 21, 23; 19. 11, 20, 21, 29; 21. 15, 16, 17, 17;
Acts 2. 28; 7. 28; 8. 31, 36; 9. 4, [6], 17; 10. 29; 11. 11;
12. 11; 16. 25; 20. 23; 22. 7, [8], 10, [13], 21; 23. 3, 3, 18,
22; 24. 12, 18, [19]; 25. 11; 26. 5, 13, 14, 14, 21, 28; 28.
18; Rom. 7. 11, 23, 24; 8. [2]; 9. 20; 1 Co. 1. 17; 4. 4;
16. 6, [11]; 2 Co. 2. 2; 11. 16, 16, 32; 12. 6, 7, 11, [21];
Gal. 1. 15; 2. 20; 4. 12, 14; Phil. 2. 30; 4. 13; 1 Ti. 1.
12, 12; 2 Ti. 1. 15, 16, 17; 3. 11; 4. 9, 16, 17, 18; Titus
3. 12; Heb. 3. [9, 9]; 8. 11; 11. 32; Rev. 17. 3; 21. [9], 10.
9. *To me,* μοί (*dat.*) *moi.*
Matt. 2. 8 bring me word again, that I may come
4. 9 if thou wilt fall down and worship me
7. 21 Not every one that saith unto me, Lord
7. 22 Many will say to me in that day, Lord, L.
8. 21 Lord, suffer me first to go and bury my f.
8. 22 But Jesus said unto him, Follow me; and
9. 9 and he saith unto him, Follow me. And he
11. 27 All things are delivered unto me of my
14. 8 Give me here John Baptist's head in a ch.
14. 18 He said, Bring them hither to me
15. 8 This people draweth nigh unto me with
15. 25 and worshipped him, saying, Lord, help
15. 32 because they continue with me now three
16. 24 and take up his cross, and follow me
17. 17 Jesus answered..Bring him hither to me
18. 28 the throat, saying, Pay [me] that thou ow.
19. 21 and thou shalt have treasure..follow me
19. 28 That ye which have followed me, in the
20. 13 didst not thou agree with me for a penny?
20. 15 Is it not lawful for me to do what I will
21. 2 her: loose..and bring (them) unto me
21. 24 which if ye tell me, I in likewise will
22. 19 Show me the tribute money. And they
25. 20 Lord, thou deliveredst unto me five tale.
25. 22 Lord, thou deliveredst unto me two tale.
25. 35 I was an hungered, and ye gave me meat
25. 42 I was an hungered, and ye gave me no m.
26. 15 What will ye give me, and I will deliver
26. 53 he shall presently give me more than tw.
27. 10 potter's field, as the Lord appointed me
28. 18 All power is given unto me in heaven and
Mark 2. 14; 6. 25; [8. 2], 34; 10. 21; 11. 29, 30; 12.
15; Luke 1. 25, 38, 43, 49; 4. 23; 5. 27; 7. 45; 9. 23, 59,
61; 10. 22, 40; 11. 5, 7; 15. 6, 9, 12; 17. 8; 18. 5, 13, 22;
20. 3, 24; 22. 29, [68]; 23. 14; John 1. 33, 43; 3. 28; 4. 7,
10, 15, 21, 29, 39; 5. 11, 36; 6. 37, 39; 8. 45, 46; 9. 11; 10.
27, 29, 37; 12. 49, 50; 13. 36, [36]; 14. 11, [11], 31; 17. 4,
6, 7, 8, 9, 11, 12, 22, 24, 24; 18. 9, 11; 20. 15; 21. 19, 22;
Acts 1. 8; 2. 28; 5. 8; 3. 6; 5. 8; 7. 7, 42, 49, 49; 9. 15;
11. 7, [9], 12; 12. 8; 13. 2; 20. 19, 22; 21. 39; 22. 5, 7, 9,
11, 13, 18, 27; 23. 19, 30; 25. 24, 27; 27. 21, 23, 25; Rom.
7. 13, 18; 9. 1, 19; 12. 3; 15. 15, 30; 1 Co. 1. 11; 3. 10;
6. 12, 12; 7. 1; 9. 15, 16, 16; 10. 23, 23; 15. 32; 16. 9; 2
Co. 9. 1; 12. 1, 7, 9, 13; 13. 10; Gal. 2. 6, 9; 4. 15, 21; 6.
17; Eph. 3. 2, 3, 7; 6. 19; Phil. 2. 18; 3. 7; 4. 3, 15; Col.
1. 25; 4. 11; 2 Ti. 3. 11; 4. 8, 8, 11, 14, 16, 17; Phm. 13.
19, 22; Heb. 1. 5; 2. 13; 8. 10; 10. 5; 13. 6; Jas. 2. 18;
2 Pe. 1. 14; Rev. 1. 17; 5. 5; 7. 13, 14; 10. 4, 9, 9, 11;
11. 1; 14. 13; 17. 1, 7, 15; 19. 9, 10; 21. 5, 6, 10; 22. 1,
6, 8, 9, 10.
10. *Of me,* μοῦ (*gen.*) *mou.*
Matt. 3. 11 he that cometh after me is mightier than
4. 19 And he saith unto them, Follow me, and
10. 37 more than me, is not worthy of me; and
10. 38 followeth after me, is not worthy of me
16. 23 said unto Peter, Get thee behind me, Sa.
16. 23 thou art an offence unto me; for thou sa.
16. 24 If any (man) will come after me, let him
[This particle occurs so translated 39 times.]
11. *Me,* ִ◌י, ◌ַי. (a suffix of various forms, *i, ai,* &c.).
Gen. 3. 12 The woman whom thou gavest..with me
19. 19 mercy, which thou hast showed unto me
20. 9 thou hast done deeds unto me that ought
21. 23 thou shalt do unto me, and to the land
29. 19 And Laban said..abide with me
29. 27 thou shalt serve with me yet seven other
31. 5 but the God of my father hath been w. me
31. 7 your father..God suffered..not to hurt me
Deut. 1. 23 and the saying pleased me well; and I
Judg 14. 3 said unto his father..she pleaseth me well
Jer. 27. 5 it unto whom it seemed meet unto me
[Very frequent]
12. *Mine eyes,* עֵינַי [*ayin*].
Psa. 73. 16 to know this, it (was) too painful for me
Jer. 32. 30 Judah have only done evil before me from
13. *My face,* פָּנַי [*panim*].
Gen. 24. 12 I pray thee, send me good speed this day
27. 20 said..the LORD thy God brought (it) to me
32. 20 that goeth before me..will accept of me
44. 29 if ye take this also from me, and mischief
Exod 20. 3 Thou shalt have no other gods before me
Num 22. 33 turned from me..turned from me, surely
1 Ki. 2. 16 now I ask one petition of thee, deny me
[*Note.*—Sometimes, e.g., 1 Ki. 2. 16, partly rendered by [Eng. verb.]
14. *Before me,* קֳדָמַי *qodamai.*
Dan. 2. 6 ye shall receive of me gifts and rewards

ME also (to)
And I, to me also, κἀγώ, κἀμοί *kagō, kamoi.*
Luke 1. 3 It seemed good to me also, having had
Acts 8. 19 Give me also this power, that on whom.
1 Co. 15. 8 last of all he was seen of me also, as of one

ME, as for —
1. *I, I myself,* אֲנָה, אֲנָא *ana, anah.*
Dan. 2. 30 But as for me, this secret is not revealed
7. 28 As for me Daniel, my cogitations much
2. *I, I myself,* אֲנִי *ani.*
Gen. 17. 4 As for me, behold, my covenant (is) with
3. *I, I myself,* אָנֹכִי *anoki.*
1 Sa. 12. 23 as for me, God forbid that I should sin

ME, of —
Of me, my, ἐμός (*gen.*) *emos.*
Luke 22. 19 saying..this do in remembrance of me
1 Co. 11. 24 and said..this do in remembrance of me
11. 25 this do ye..in remembrance of me, Col. 4. 18
Of me, my, μοῦ (*gen.*) Matt. 10. 37.

MEADOW —
1. *Reed, meadow,* אָחוּ *achu.*
Gen. 41. 2, 18 and they fed in a meadow
2. *Cave, forest,* מַעֲרֵה *maareh.*
Judg 20. 33 came forth..out of the meadows of Gibeah

ME'-AH, מֵאָה *hundred.*
A tower near the sheep gate of Jerusalem.
Neh. 3. 1 even unto the tower of M. they sanctified
12. 39 from..the tower of M., even unto the sh.

MEAL (fine) —
1. *Meal, fine meal,* קֶמַח סֹלֶת *qemach soleth.*
Gen. 18. 6 quickly three measures of fine meal, knead
2. *Meal,* קֶמַח *qemach.*
Num. 5. 15 the tenth (part) of an ephah of barley meal
1 Ki. 4. 22 fine flour, and threescore measures of meal
17. 12 but an handful of meal in a barrel, and a
17. 14 The barrel of meal shall not waste, neither
17. 16 the barrel of meal wasted not, neither did
2 Ki. 4. 41 But he said, Then bring meal: and he cast
1 Ch. 12. 40 meat, meal, cakes of figs, and bunches of
Isa. 47. 2 Take the millstones, and grind meal: un.
Hos. 8. 7 the bud shall yield no meal: if so be it
3. *Ground flour, meal,* ἄλευρον *aleuron.*
Matt 13. 33 took and hid in three measures of meal
Luke 13. 21 took and hid in three measures of meal

MEAL TIME
Time of eating, עֵת אֹכֶל *eth okel.*
Ruth 2. 14 At meal time come thou hither, and eat

MEAN (man)
1. *A man, human being,* אָדָם *adam.*
Isa. 2. 9 the mean man boweth down, and the gr.
5. 15 the mean man shall be brought down, and
31. 8 sword, not of a mean man, shall devour
2. *Obscure,* חָשֹׁךְ *chashok.*
Prov 22. 29 he shall not stand before mean (men)
3. *Unmarked, obscure,* ἄσημος *asēmos.*
Acts 21. 39 a citizen of no mean city: and, I beseech

MEAN, (should), to —
1. *To think, devise,* דָּמָה *damah,* 3.
Isa. 10. 7 he meaneth not so, neither doth his heart
2. *To think, devise, reckon, esteem,* חָשַׁב *chashab.*
Gen. 50. 20 God meant it unto good, to bring to pass
3. *He, she or it is,* ἐστί *esti.*
Matt. 9. 13 learn what (that) meaneth, I will have m
12. 7 if ye had known what (this) meaneth, I
Mark 9. 10 what the rising from the dead should m
4. *It would be,* εἴη *eiē.*
Luke 15. 26 called..and asked what these things meant
18. 36 multitude pass by, he asked what it meant
Acts 10. 17 this vision which he had seen should mean
5. *To will or wish to be,* θέλω εἶναι *thelō einai.*
Acts 2. 12 saying one to another, What meaneth this?
17. 20 know therefore what these things mean
6. *To be about,* μέλλω *mellō.*
Acts 27. 2 meaning to sail by the coasts of Asia
7. *To do,* ποιέω *poieō.*
Acts 21. 13 mean ye to weep and to break mine heart?

MEANING —
1. *Understanding,* בִּינָה *binah.*
Dan. 8. 15 sought for the meaning, then, behold, th
2. *Power,* δύναμις *dunamis.*
1 Co. 14. 11 if I know not the meaning of the voice, I

MEANS
1. *Hand, power,* יָד *yad.*
1 Ki. 10. 29 did they bring (them) out by their means
2 Ch. 1. 17 for the kings of Syria, by their means
Jer. 5. 31 the priests bear rule by their means; and
Mal. 1. 9 this hath been by your means: will he
2. *Thought, device,* מַחֲשֶׁבֶת *machashebeth.*
2 Sa. 14. 14 yet doth he devise means, that his banish

MEANS, by all —
1. *By all means, altogether, entirely,* πάντως *pantōs.*
Acts 18. 21 I must by all means keep this feast that
1 Co. 9. 22 that I might by all means save some
2. *In every way,* ἐν παντὶ τρόπῳ *en panti tropō.*
2 Th. 3. 16 Lord..give you peace always by all [means]

MEANS, by any, some, no —
1. *Any how,* πως, *pōs*
Acts 27. 12 if by any means they might attain to Ph.
Rom. 1. 10; 11. 14; 1 Co. 8. 9, 9. 27; 2 Co. 11. 3; Gal. 2. 2; Phil. 3. 11; 1 Th. 3. 5.
2. *Not at all,* οὐ μή *ou mē.*
Matt. 5. 26 Thou shalt by no means come out
3. *Through any turn,* κατὰ μηδένα τρόπον *kata.*
2 Th. 2. 3 Let no man deceive you by any means

MEANS, by this —
Over against this, לָקֳבֵל דְּנָה *lo-qobel denah.*
Ezra 4. 16 by this means thou shalt have no portion

MEANS, by what —
How, πῶς *pōs.*
Luke 8. 36 by what means he that was possessed of
John 9. 21 by what means he now seeth. we know not
By what, ἐν τίνι *en tini,* Acts 4. 9.

MEANS of, by —
1. *Through,* בְּעַד *bead.*
Prov. 6. 26 For by means of a whorish woman (a man
2. *Out of,* ἐκ *ek,* 2 Co. 1. 11.
3. *To become,* γίνομαι *ginomai,* Heb. 9. 15.

MEAN WHILE, in the —
1. *Unto thus,* עַד כֹּה *ad koh.*
1 Ki. 18. 45 it came to pass in the mean while, that
2. *After, between, mean while,* μεταξύ *metaxu.*
John 4. 31 In the mean while his disciples prayed
Rom. 2. 15 (their) thoughts the mean while accusing

ME-A'-RAH, מְעָרָה *cave.*
A place in the N of Canaan, near Sidon; now *Adlan.*
Josh. 13. 4 M. that (is) beside the Sidonians, unto A.

MEASURE —
1. *An ephah, measure* (3 *seahs*), אֵיפָה *ephah.*
Deut 25. 14 Thou shalt not have..divers measures
25. 15 just measure shalt thou have: that thy
Prov 20. 10 Divers weights, (and) divers measures
Mic. 6. 10 and the scant measure (that is) abomin.
2. *A fore arm, cubit, measure,* אַמָּה *ammah.*
Jer. 51. 13 (and) the measure of thy covetousness
3. *Statute, limit,* חֹק *choq.*
Isa. 5. 14 and opened her mouth without measure
4. *A cor, measure* (10 *ephahs*), כֹּר *kor.*
1 Ki. 4. 22 for one day was thirty measures of fine
4. 22 fine flour, and threescore measures of meal
5. 11 twenty thousand measures of wheat (for)
5. 11 and twenty measures of pure oil: thus
2 Ch. 2. 10 twenty thousand measures of beaten wheat
2. 10 twenty thousand measures of barley, and
27. 5 ten thousand measures of wheat, and ten
5. *Cors, measures* (10 *ephahs each*), כּוֹרִין *korin.*
Ezra 7. 22 to an hundred measures of wheat, and to
6. *A measure, long robe,* מַד *mad.*
Job 11. 9 The measure thereof (is) longer than the
Jer. 13. 25 the portion of thy measures from me
7. *Measure, long robe,* מִדָּה *middah.*
Exod 26 2 of the curtains shall have one measure
26 8 curtains (shall be all) of one measure
Josh. 3 4 about two thousand cubits by measure
1 Ki. 6. 25 the cherubim (were) of one measure and
7. 9 according to the measures of hewed stones
7. 11 after the measures of hewed stones, and
7. 37 had one casting, one measure, (and) one size
2 Ch. 3. 3 length by cubits after the first measure
Job 28. 25 and he weigheth the waters by measure
Psa. 39. 4 know mine end, and the measure of my
Eze. 40. 10 one measure: and the posts had one me.
40. 21 were after the measure of the first gate
40. 22 measure of the gate that looketh toward
40. 24, 28, 29, 32, 33, 35 according to these mea.
41. 17 about, within and without, by measure
43. 13 measures of the altar after the cubits
45. 3 of this measure shalt thou measure the
46. 22 these four corners (were) of one measure
48. 16 these (shall be) the measures thereof: the
48. 30, 33 four thousand and five hundred mea.
8. *Measures,* מְמַדִּים *memaddim.*
Job 38. 5 Who hath laid the measures thereof, if
9. *A liquid measure,* מְשׂוּרָה *mesurah.*
Lev. 19. 35 in mete yard, in weight, or in measure
1 Ch. 23. 29 and for all manner of measure and size
Eze. 4. 11 Thou shalt drink also water by measure
4. 16 they shall drink water by measure, and
10. *Judgment,* מִשְׁפָּט *mishpat.*
Jer. 30. 11 I will correct thee in measure, and will
46. 28 end of thee, but correct thee in measure
11. *Measure, proper quantity,* מַתְכֹּנֶת *mathkoneth.*
Eze. 45. 11 measure thereof shall be after the homer
12. *A seah, measure* (*third of an ephah*), סְאָה *seah.*
Gen. 18. 6 Make ready quickly three measures of fine
1 Sa. 25. 18 and five measures of parched (corn), and
1 Ki. 18. 32 as would contain two measures of seed
2 Ki. 7. 1 measure of fine flour (be sold) for a shekel
7. 1, 16, 18 two measures of barley for a shekel
7. 16 So a measure of fine flour was (sold) for a
7. 18 and a measure of fine flour for a shekel
13. [*Meaning uncertain*], סַאסְּאָה *sasseah.*
Isa. 27. 8 In measure, when it shooteth forth, thou
14. *A threefold measure,* שָׁלִישׁ *shalish.*
Psa. 80. 5 givest them tears to drink in great mea.
Isa. 40. 12 the dust of the earth in a measure, and
15. *Weight or measure,* תֹּכֶן *token.*
Eze 45. 11 the bath shall be of one measure, that the
16. *Bath* (7½ *gallons, Heb.* בַּת), βάτος *batos.*
Luke 16. 6 And he said, An hundred measures of oil
17. *A cor* (75½ *gallons*), *Heb.* כֹּר, κόρος *koros.*
Luke 16. 7 And he said, An hundred measures of w.
18. *A measure* (*of length or capacity*), μέτρον *metron.*
Matt. 7. 2 what measure ye mete, it shall be measu.
23. 32 Fill ye up then the measure of your fath.
Mark 4. 24 what measure ye mete, it shall be measu.
Luke 6. 38 good measure, pressed down, and shaken
6. 38 the same measure that ye mete withal
John 3. 34 giveth not the spirit by measure (unto him)
Rom. 12. 3 dealt to every man the measure of faith
2 Co. 10. 13 the measure of the rule which God hath
10. 13 to us, a measure to reach even unto you
Eph. 4. 7 accor to the measure of the gift of Christ
4. 13 the measure of the stature of the fulness
4. 16 working in the measure of every part
Rev. 21. 17 the measure of a man, that (is), of the an.
19. *A seat* (2½ *gallons, Heb.* סְאָה), σάτον *saton.*
Matt 13 33 took and hid in three measures of meal
Luke 13. 21 took and hid in three measures of meal
20. *A choinix* (1½ *pints*), χοῖνιξ *choinix.*
Rev. 6 6 A measure of wheat..and three measures

MEASURE, to —
1. *To measure, stretch out,* מָדַד *madad.*
Num 35. 5 ye shall measure from without the city
Deut 21. 2 they shall measure unto the cities which
Ruth 3. 15 he measured six (measures) of barley, and
Isa. 40 12 Who hath measured the waters in the ha.
65. 7 therefore will I measure their former wo.
Eze 40. 5 he measured the breadth of the building
40 6 measured the threshold of the gate, (wh.
40. 8 He measured also the porch of the gate
40 9 Then measured he the porch of the gate
40 11 he measured the breadth of the entry of
40 13 He measured then the gate from the roof
40 19 he measured the breadth, from the fore
40. 20 he measured the length thereof, and the
40. 23, 27 and he measured from gate to gate
40. 24 he measured the posts thereof, and the
40 28 he measured the south gate according to
40. 32 he measured the gate according to these
40. 35 measured (it) according to these measures
40 47 he measured the court, an hundred cubits
40. 48 and measured (each) post of the porch, five
41. 1 measured the posts, six cubits broad on
41. 2 and he measured the length thereof, forty
41. 3 measured the post of the door two cubits
41. 4 So he measured the length thereof, twen.
41. 5 he measured the wall of the house six
41. 13 he measured the house, an hundred cub.
41. 15 he measured the length of the building
42. 15 toward the east, and measured it round
42. 16 measured the east side with the measur.
42. 17 He measured the north side, five hundred
42. 18 He measured the south side, five hundred
42. 19 measured five hundred reeds, with the m.
42. 20 He measured it by the four sides: it had
43. 10 iniquities; and let them measure the pa.
45. 3 And of this measure shalt thou measure
47. 3 measured a thousand cubits, and he bro
47. 4, 4 Again he measured a thousand
47. 5 Afterward he measured a thousand; (and
47. 18 the east side ye shall measure from Hau
Zech. 2. 2 he said unto me, To measure Jerusalem
2. *To measure,* מָדַד *madad,* 3.
2 Sa. 8. 2 measured them with a line, casting them
8. 2 even with two lines measured he to put
3. *To stretch out self, to measure,* מָדַד *madad,* 3a.
Hab. 3. 6 He stood, and measured the earth: he
4 *To measure,* μετρέω *metreō.*
2 Co. 10. 12 measuring themselves by themselves, and
Rev 11. 1 Rise, and measure the temple of God, and
11. 2 the temple leave out, and measure it not
21. 15 had a golden reed to measure the city, and
21. 16 he measured the city with the reed, twe.
21 17 he measured the wall thereof, an hundred

MEASURE, above —
Above measure, ὑπερβαλλόντως *huperballontōs.*
2 Co. 11. 23 in stripes above measure, in prisons more

MEASURE again, to —
To measure in return, correspondingly, ἀντιμετρέω.
Matt. 7. 2 mete, it shall be measured to you [again]
Luke 6. 38 withal it shall be measured to you [again]

MEASURE, beyond or out of —
1. *Abundantly, excessively,* ἐκ περισσοῦ *ek perissou.*
Mark 6. 51 amazed in themselves [beyond measure]
2. *Beyond measure,* καθ' ὑπερβολὴν *kath' huperbolēn.*
2 Co. 1. 8 that we were pressed out of measure, ab.
Gal. 1. 13 how that beyond measure I persecuted
3. *Most abundantly or excessively,* ὑπερπερισσῶς.
Mark 7. 37 And were beyond measure astonished, s.
4. *Abundantly, excessively,* περισσῶς *perissōs.*
Mark 10. 26 they were astonished out of measure, sa.

MEASURE, thing without —
Unmeasured, without measure, ἄμετρος *ametros.*
2 Co. 10. 13 boast of things without (our) measure, but
10. 15 Not boasting of things without (our) me.

MEASURED, to be —
1. *To be measured,* מָדַד *madad,* 2.
Jer. 31. 37 If heaven above can be measured, and the
33. 22 neither the sand of the sea measured; so
Hos. 1. 10 which cannot be measured nor numbered
2. *To measure,* μετρέω *metreō.*
Mark 4. 24 it shall be measured to you; and unto you

MEASURING —
Measure, מִדָּה *middah.*
Jer. 31. 39 And the measuring line shall yet go forth
Eze. 40. 3 flax in his hand, and a measuring reed
40. 5 in the man's hand a measuring reed of six
42. 15 when he had made an end of measuring
42. 16, 16, 17, 18, 19 with the measuring reed
Zech. 2. 1 and, behold, a man with a measuring line

MEAT —
1. *What is eaten, food,* אֲכִילָה *akilah.*
1 Ki. 19. 8 went in the strength of that meat forty days
2. *To eat,* אָכַל *akal.*
Lev. 25. 7 shall all the increase thereof be meat
1 Sa. 20. 5 not fail to sit with the king at meat: but
Job 34. 3 trieth words, as the mouth tasteth meat
Psa. 59. 15 Let them wander up and down for meat
3. *What is eaten, food,* אֹכֶל *okel.*
Lev. 11. 34 Of all meat which may be eaten, (that) on
Deut. 2. 6 Ye shall buy meat of them for money, that
2. 28 Thou shalt sell me meat for money, that
Job 12. 11 try words? and the mouth taste his meat?
20. 21 There shall none of his meat be left; the.
36. 31 judgeth he the people; he giveth meat
38. 41 cry unto God, they wander for lack of m.
Psa. 78. 18 tempted God..by asking meat for their
78. 30 while their meat (was) yet in their mouths
104. 21 The young lions..seek their meat from G.
104. 27 mayest give (them) their meat in due sea.
107. 18 Their soul abhorreth all manner of meat
145. 15 thou givest them their meat in due season
Lam. 1. 11 have given their pleasant things for meat
1. 19 they sought their meat to relieve their so.
Joel 1. 16 Is not the meat cut off before our eyes
Hab. 3. 17 the fields shall yield no meat; the flock
Mal. 1. 12 fruit thereof, (even) his meat, (is) con.
4. *What is eaten, food,* אָכְלָה *oklah.*
Gen. 1. 29 yielding seed; to you it shall be for meat
1. 30 (I have given) every green herb for meat
9. 3 thing that liveth shall be meat for you
Lev. 25. 6 the sabbath of the land shall be meat for
Eze. 29. 5 I have given thee for meat to the beasts
34. 5 and they became meat to all the beasts
34. 8 my flock became meat to every beast of
34. 10 their mouth that they may not be meat
5 *To eat,* בָּרָה *barah,* 3.
Lam. 4. 10 they were their meat in the destruction
6. *Food, eating,* בָּרוּת *baruth.*
Psa. 69. 21 They gave me also gall for my meat; and
7. *Food, eating,* בִּרְיָה *biryah.*
2 Sa. 13. 5 dress the meat in my sight, that I may see
13. 7 now to..Amnon's house, and dress him m.
13. 10 Bring the meat into the chamber, that I
8 *Torn food,* טֶרֶף *tereph.*
Psa. 111. 5 He hath given meat unto them that fear
Prov 31. 15 and giveth meat to her household, and
Mal. 3. 10 that there may be meat in mine house, and
9. *Bread, food, flesh,* לֶחֶם *lechem.*
Lev. 22. 11 in his house: they shall eat of his meat
22. 13 she shall eat of her father's meat; but
Num 28. 24 the meat of the sacrifice made by fire
1 Sa. 20. 24 and..the king sat him down to eat meat
20. 27 cometh not the son of Jesse to meat, nei.
20. 34 did eat no meat the second day of the m.
2 Sa. 3. 35 people came to cause David to eat meat
13. 5 Tamar come and give me meat, and dress
Job 6. 7 The things..(are) as my sorrowful meat
20. 14 his meat in his bowels is turned, (it is) the
30. 4 who cut up..juniper roots (for) their meat
Psa. 42. 3 My tears have been my meat day and night
Prov. 6. 8 Provideth her meat in the summer, (and)
23. 3 his dainties; for they (are) deceitful meat
30. 22 and a fool when he is filled with meat
30. 25 they prepare their meat in the summer
Isa. 65. 25 dust (shall be) the serpent's meat. They
Eze. 16. 19 My meat also which I gave thee, fine flour
10. *What is eaten, food,* מַאֲכָל *maakal.*
Gen. 40. 17 (there was) of all manner of bake meats
Deut 20. 20 knowest that they (be) not trees for meat
28. 26 thy carcase shall be meat unto all fowls
Judg 14. 14 Out of the eater came forth meat, and out
1 Ki. 10. 5 the meat of his table, and the sitting of
1 Ch. 12. 40 on mules, and on oxen, (and) meat, meal
2 Ch. 9. 4 the meat of his table, and the sitting of
Ezra 3. 7 meat, and drink, and oil, unto them of Z.
Job 33. 20 abhorreth bread, and his soul dainty meat
Psa. 44. 11 given us like sheep (appointed) for meat

Psa. 74. 14 gavest him (to be) meat to the people in.
79. 2 dead bodies..have they given (to be) meat
Isa. 62. 8 give thy corn (to be) meat for thine enemies
Jer. 7. 33 shall be meat for the fowls of the heaven
16. 4 shall be meat for the fowls of heaven, and
19. 7 will I give to be meat for the fowls of the
34. 20 their dead bodies shall be for meat unto
Eze. 4. 10 thy meat which thou shalt eat (shall be)
47. 12 shall grow all trees for meat, whose leaf
47. 12 and the fruit thereof shall be for meat, and
Dan. 1. 10 who hath appointed your meat and your
Hab. 1. 16 portion (is) fat, and their meat plenteous
Hag. 2. 12 or wine, or oil, or any meat, shall it be h.?

11. *Food*, מָזוֹן *mazon.*
Gen. 45. 23 corn and bread and meat for his father by
Dan. 4. 12, 21 and in it (was) meat for all

12. *Morsel*, פַּת *path.*
2 Sa. 12. 3 it did eat of his own meat, and drank of

13. *Hunting, venison, provision*, צֵידָה *tsedah.*
Psa. 78. 25 eat angels' food: he sent them meat to the

14. *Food, meat*, βρῶμα *brōma.*
Mark 7. 19 out into the draught, purging all meats?
Luke 3. 11 and he that hath meat, let him do likewise
9. 13 except we should go and buy meat for all
John 4. 34 My meat is to do the will of him that sent
Rom 14. 15 if thy brother be grieved with (thy) meat
14. 15 Destroy not him with thy meat for whom
14. 20 For meat destroy not the work of God. All
1 Co. 3. 2 fed you with milk, and not with meat
6. 13 Meats for the belly, and the belly for meats
8. 8 But meat commendeth us not to God: for
8. 13 if meat make my brother to offend, I will
10. 3 And did all eat the same spiritual meat
1 Ti. 4. 3 (and commanding) to abstain from meats
Heb. 9. 10 (Which stood) only in meats and drinks
13. 9 not with meats, which have not profited

15. *Eatable, what may be eaten*, βρώσιμος *brōsimos.*
Luke 24. 41 he said unto them, Have ye here any m.?

16. *Act of eating, food*, βρῶσις *brōsis.*
John 4. 32 I have meat to eat that ye know not of
6. 27 Labour not for the meat which perisheth
6. 27 but for that meat which endureth unto
6. 55 For my flesh is meat indeed, and my blood
Rom 14. 17 For the kingdom of God is not meat and
Col. 2. 16 Let no man therefore judge you in meat

17. *Any thing to eat*, προσφάγιον *prosphagion.*
John 21. 5 Children, have ye any meat? They answ.

18. *Table*, τράπεζα *trapeza.*
Acts 16. 34 he set meat before them, and rejoiced, b.

19. *Nourishment*, τροφή *trophē.*
Matt. 3. 4 and his meat was locusts and wild honey
6. 25 Is not the life more than meat, and the b.
10. 10 for the workman is worthy of his meat
24. 45 made ruler..to give them meat in due se.
Luke 12. 23 The life is more than meat, and the body
John 4. 8 were gone away unto the city to buy meat
Acts 2. 46 did eat their meat with gladness and sin.
9. 19 when he had received meat, he was stren.
27. 33 Paul besought (them) all to take meat, sa.
27. 34 Wherefore I pray you to take (some) meat
27. 36 good cheer, and they also took (some) meat
Heb. 5. 12 have need of milk, and not of strong meat
5. 14 But strong meat belongeth to them that

20. *To eat, feed on, consume, corrode*, φάγω *phagō.*
Matt 25. 35 I was an hungered, and ye gave me meat
25. 42 I was an hungered, and ye gave me no m.
Luke 8. 55 and he commanded to give her meat

MEAT offering —

An offering, present, מִנְחָה *minchah.*
Exod 29. 41 shalt do thereto according to the meat off.
30. 9 Ye shall offer no..meat offering; neither
40. 29 and offered upon it..the meat offering; as
Lev. 2. 1 when any will offer a meat offering unto
2. 3 And the remnant of the meat offering (shall
2. 4 if thou bring an oblation of a meat offer.
2. 5, 7 if thy oblation (be) a meat offering..in
2. 6 pour oil thereon: it (is) a meat offering
2. 8 thou shalt bring the meat offering that is
2. 9 the priest shall take from the meat offer.
2. 10 And that which is left of the meat offering
2. 11 No meat offering, which ye shall bring
2. 13 every oblation of thy meat offering shalt
2. 13 suffer..to be lacking from thy meat offer.
2. 14 if thou offer a meat offering of thy first
2. 14 offer for the meat offering of thy first fru.
2. 15 lay frankincense thereon: it (is) a meat o.
5. 13 and..shall be the priest's, as a meat offer
6. 14 And this (is) the law of the meat offering
6. 15 of the flour of the meat offering, and of
6. 15 frankincense which (is) upon the meat off.
6. 20 of an ephah of fine flour for a meat offer.
6. 21 the baken pieces of the meat offering shalt
6. 23 For every meat offering for the priest shall
7. 9 all the meat offering that is baken in the
7. 10 every meat offering mingled with oil, and
7. 37 This (is) the law..of the meat offering, and
9. 4 and a meat offering mingled with oil: for
9. 17 And he brought the meat offering, and took
10. 12 Take the meat offering that remaineth of
14. 10 he shall take..(for) a meat offering, min.
14. 20 the priest shall offer..the meat offering
14. 21 fine flour mingled with oil for a meat off.
14. 31 a burnt offering, with the meat offering
23. 13 the meat offering thereof..two tenth deals
23. 16 ye shall offer a new meat offering unto the
Lev. 23. 18 with their meat offering and their drink
23. 37 a burnt offering, and a meat offering, a
Num. 4. 16 the daily meat offering, and the anointing
6. 15 their meat offering, and their drink offer.
6. 17 the priest shall offer also his meat offering
7. 13 flour mingled with oil, for a meat offering
[So in v. 19, 25, 31, 37, 43, 49, 55, 61, 67, 73, 79.]
7. 87 All the oxen..with their meat offering
8. 8 take a young bullock with his meat offer.
15. 4, 9 Then shall he..bring a meat offering of
15. 6 thou shalt prepare (for) a meat offering
15. 24 with his meat offering, and his drink off.
18. 9 every meat offering of theirs, and every
28. 5 And .of an ephah of flour for a meat off.
28. 8 as the meat offering of the morning, and
28. 9, 12, 12 two tenth deals of flour (for) a m. o.
28. 13 flour mingled with oil (for) a meat offering
28. 20 their meat offering..flour mingled with
28. 26 when ye bring a new meat offering unto
28. 28 their meat offering of flour mingled with
28. 31 continual burnt offering, and his meat o.
29. 3, 9, 14 their meat offering..flour mingled
29. 6 offering of the month, and his meat offer.
29. 6 the daily burnt offering, and his meat off.
29. 11 continual burnt offering, and the meat off.
29. 16, 22, 25, 28, 31, 34, 38 his meat offering, and
29. 18, 21, 24, 27, 30, 33, 37 their meat offering
29. 19 the meat offering thereof, and their drink
29. 39 for your meat offerings, and for your dr. o.
Josh. 22. 23 or if to offer thereon..meat offering, or if
22. 29 to build an altar..for meat offerings, or
Judg 13. 19 Manoah took a kid with a meat offering
13. 23 would not have received..a meat offering
1 Ki. 8. 64 for there he offered..meat offerings, and
8. 64 too little to receive the..meat offerings
2 Ki. 3. 20 when the meat offering was offered, that
16. 13 And he burnt..his meat offering, and po.
16. 15 burn..the evening meat offering, and the
16. 15 their meat offering, and their drink offer.
1 Ch. 21. 23 the wheat for the meat offering; I give it
23. 29 for the fine flour for meat offering, and for
2 Ch. 7. 7 the burnt offerings, and the meat offerings
Ezra 7. 17 lambs, with their meat offerings and their
Neh. 10. 33 for the continual meat offering, and for
13. 5 where aforetime they laid the meat offer.
13. 9 with the meat offering and the frankinc.
Isa. 57. 6 to them..thou hast offered a meat offer.
Jer. 17. 26 bringing..meat offerings and incense, and
33. 18 to kindle meat offerings, and to do sacri.
Eze. 42. 13 there shall they lay..the meat offering
44. 29 They shall eat the meat offering, and the
45. 15 one lamb..for a meat offering, and for a
45. 17 meat offerings, and drink offerings, in the
45. 17 he shall prepare..the meat offering, and
45. 24 he shall prepare a meat offering of an ep.
45. 25 according to the meat offering, and acco.
46. 5 And the meat offering..an ephah for a
46. 5 and the meat offering for the lambs as he
46. 7 he shall prepare a meat offering, an ephah
46. 11 the meat offering shall be an ephah to a
46. 14 thou shalt prepare a meat offering for it
46. 14 a meat offering continually by a perpet.
46. 15 Thus shall they prepare..the meat offer.
46. 20 where they shall bake the meat offering
Joel 1. 9, 13 The meat offering and the drink offer.
2. 14 a meat offering and a drink offering unto
Amos 5. 22 Though ye offer me..your meat offerings

MEAT, morsel of —

Act of eating, food, βρῶσις *brōsis.*
Heb. 12. 16 who for one morsel of meat sold his birth.

MEAT, portion or provision of —

Morsel or portion of food, פַּתְבַּג *pathbag.*
Dan. 1. 5 them a daily provision of the king's meat
1. 8 with the portion of the king's meat, nor
1. 13 that eat of the portion of the king's meat
1. 15 which did eat the portion of the king's m.
1. 16 took away the portion of their meat, and
11. 26 they that feed of the portion of his meat

[*See also* Broken, dainty, lay, offered to idols, portion, sit, savoury.]

ME-BUN'-NAI, מְבֻנַּי *built up.*

One of David's valiant men of the family of Hushah and tribe of Judah. B.C. 1048. In Ch. 11 29; 2 Sa. 23. 27, it is Sibbecai, Abiezer the Anethothite, M. the Hushathite.

2 Sa. 23. 27 Abiezer the Anethothite M. the Hushath.

MECH-ER-A-THITE, מְכֵרָתִי.

Patronymic of Hepher, one of David's valiant men; place unknown. B.C. 1048.

1 Ch. 11 36 Hepher the M., Ahijah the Pelonite

ME'-DAD, מֵידָד *love.*

An elder on whom the spirit fell when remaining in the camp with Eldad. B.C. 1492.

Num 11. 26 But there remained..Eldad, and..M.: and
11. 27 said, Eldad and M. do prophesy in the c.

ME'-DAN, מְדָן *judgment.*

A son of Abraham by Keturah, brother of *Midian.* B.C. 1844.

Gen. 25. 2 she bare him Zimran, and..M., and Mid.
1 Ch. 1. 32 she bare Zimran, and Jokshan, and M

MEDDLE (with), to —

1. *To stir self up*, גָּרָה *garah*, 7.
Deut. 2. 5 Meddle not with them; for I will not give
2. 19 distress them not, nor meddle with them
2 Ki. 14. 10 why shouldest thou meddle to (thy) hurt
2 Ch. 25. 19 why shouldest thou meddle to (thine) h

2. *To cause self to pass over*, עָבַר *abar*, 7.
Prov 26. 17 meddleth with strife (belonging) not to h

3. *To mix self up with*, עָרַב *arab*, 7.
Prov 20. 19 meddle not with him that flattereth with
24. 21 meddle not with them that are given to

MEDDLING, meddled with, to be —

To intermeddle with, גָּלַע *gala*, 7.
Prov 17. 14 leave off contention, before it be meddled w.
20. 3 cease from strife..every fool will be me.

ME-DE'-BA, מֵידְבָא *full waters.*

A plain and city in Reuben, S.E. of Heshbon on the right side of the Arnon; taken from Moab by Sihon, but finally retaken. Now called *Madizabeh.*

Num 21. 30 unto Nophah, which (reacheth) unto M.
Josh. 13. 9 the city..and all the plain of M. unto Di.
13. 16 city..in the..river, and all the plain by M.
1 Ch. 19. 7 and the king..came and pitched before M.
Isa. 15. 2 Moab shall howl over Nebo, and over M.

MEDES, מָדַי, מָדָי, Μῆδοι, *the middle, midst.*

The inhabitants of Media, a rude and uncultivated race.

2 Ki. 17. 6 and placed them..in the cities of the M.
18. 11 and put them..in the cities of the M.
Ezra 6. 2 palace that (is) in the province of the M.
Esth. 1. 19 the laws of the Persians and the M., that
Isa. 13. 17 I will stir up the M. against them, which
Jer. 25. 25 kings of Elam, and all the kings of the M.
51. 11 the spirit of the kings of the M.: for his
51. 28 Prepare against her..the kings of the M.
Dan. 5. 28 Thy kingdom is divided, and given to..M.
6. 8, 12 the law of the M. and Persians, which
6. 15 the law of the M. and Persians (is), That
9. 1 Ahasuerus, of the seed of the M., which was
11. 1 first year of Darius the M., (even) I, stood
Acts 2. 9 Parthians, and M., and Elamites, and the

ME'-DIA, מָדַי *middle land.*

A country having the Caspian Sea on the N., Hyrcania and Parthia on the E., Persia and Susiana on the S., and Assyria and Armenia Major on the W. It separated from Assyria B.C. 711, and became a republic; in 709 Deioces became king; in 656 it was invaded, and Deioces was defeated and slain; in 634 its king Phraortes, with his army, perished before Babylon; in 632 it is invaded by the Scythians; in 609 they are expelled; in 603 the Lydian war commences; in 593 Cyrus was born; in 584 the Lydian war closes by the battle of Halys; in 560 Cyrus deposes Astyages, and raises Cyaxares II. or Darius the Mede, to the throne; in 551 Cyrus becomes its king; in 547 Larissa and Mespila, cities of Media, revolt but are subdued; in 538 Cyrus takes Babylon, and marries the daughter of his uncle Cyaxares, thereby uniting Persia and Media.

Esth. 1. 3 the power of Persia and M., the nobles
1. 14 the seven princes of Persia and M., which
1. 18 (Likewise) shall the ladies of Persia and M.
10. 2 Chronicles of the kings of M. and Persia?
Isa. 21. 2 Go up, O Elam: besiege, O M.: all the
Dan. 8. 20 (two) horns (are) the kings of M. and Pe.

ME-DI-AN, מָדָיא.

A native of Media. B.C. 538.

Dan. 5. 31 Darius the M. took the kingdom, (being)

MEDIATOR —

Middle man, mediator, μεσίτης *mesitēs.*
Gal. 3. 19 ordained by angels in the hand of a med.
3. 20 Now a mediator is not..of one; but God
1 Ti. 2. 5 and one mediator between God and men
Heb. 8. 6 he is the mediator of a better covenant
9. 15 for this cause he is the mediator of the
12. 24 to Jesus the mediator of the new covenant

MEDICINE —

1. *Medicine*, גֵּהָה *gehah.*
Prov 17. 22 A merry heart doeth good (like) a medicine

2. *Curatives, medicine*, רְפֻאוֹת *rephuoth.*
Jer. 30. 13 none to plead..thou hast no healing me.
46. 11 in vain shalt thou use many medicines

3. *Healing remedy, medicine*, תְּרוּפָה *teruphah.*
Eze. 47. 12 fruit..for meat, and the leaf..for medi.

MEDITATE, (upon), to —

1. *To meditate, mutter*, הָגָה *hagah.*
Josh. 1. 8 thou shalt meditate therein day and night
Psa. 1. 2 in his law doth he meditate day and
63. 6 meditate on thee in the (night) watches
77. 12 I will meditate also of all thy work, and
143. 5 I meditate on all thy works; I muse on
Isa. 33. 18 Thine heart shall meditate terror. Where

2. *To bow down, muse, meditate* שׂוּחַ, שִׂיחַ *siach, suach.*
Gen. 24. 63 Isaac went out to meditate in the field at
Psa. 119. 15 I will meditate in thy precepts, and have
119. 23 thy servant did meditate in thy statutes
119. 48 and I will meditate in thy statutes
119. 78 (but) I will meditate in thy precepts
119. 148 watches, that I might meditate in thy w

3. *To be careful, take care*, μελετάω *meletaō.*
1 Ti. 4. 15 Meditate upon these things; give thyself

MEDITATE before, to —

To take care beforehand, προμελετάω *promeletaō.*
Luke 21. 14 to meditate before what ye shall answer

MEDITATION —

1. *Meditation*, הָגוּת *haguth.*
Psa. 49. 3 the meditation of my heart (shall be) of

2. *Earnest meditation,* הָגִיג *hagig.*
Psa. 5. 1 Give ear..O LORD; consider my medita.

3. *Meditation,* הִגָּיוֹן *higgayon.*
Psa. 19. 14 Let ..the meditation of my heart, be ac.

4. *Meditation,* שִׂיחַ *siach.*
Psa.104. 34 My meditation of him shall be sweet : I

5. *A bowing down, musing,* שִׂיחָה *sichah.*
Psa.119. 97 thy law ! it (is) my meditation all the day
119. 99 for thy testimonies (are) my meditation

MEEK —

1. *Humble,* עָנָו *anav.*
Psa. 22. 26 The meek shall eat and be satisfied : they
25. 9 The meek will he guide in judgment; and
25. 9 and the meek will he teach his way
37. 11 the meek shall inherit the earth; and sh.
76. 9 When God arose ..to save all the meek of
147. 6 The LORD lifteth up the meek : he casteth
149. 4 he will beautify the meek with salvation
Isa. 11. 4 and reprove with equity for the meek of
29. 19 The meek also shall increase..joy in the
61. 1 me to preach good tidings unto the meek
Amos 2. 7 pant..and turn aside the way of the meek
Zeph. 2. 3 all ye meek of the earth, which have wr.

2. *Humble,* עָנָיו [V.L. עָנָו] *anav.*
Num12. 3 Now the man Moses (was) very meek, ab.

3. *Meek, easy, mild,* πρᾶος *praos.*
Matt11. 29 I am [meek] and lowly in heart : and ye

4. *Meek, easy, mild,* πραΰς *praus.*
Matt. 5. 5 Blessed (are) the meek : for they shall inh.
21 5 Behold, thy king cometh unto thee, meek
1 Pe. 3. 4 of a meek and quiet spirit, which is in the

MEEKNESS —

1. *Humility,* עֲנָוָה *anvah.*
Psa. 45. 4 because of truth, and meekness (and) rig.

2. *Humility,* עֲנָוָה *anavah.*
Zeph. 2. 3 seek righteousness, seek meekness : it

3. *Meekness, mildness,* πραότης *praotēs.*
1 Co. 4. 21 or in love, and (in) the spirit of [meekness]
2 Co. 10. 1 by the [meekness] and gentleness of Chri.
Gal. 5. 23 [Meekness], temperance : against such
6. 1 restore such an one in the spirit of [me.]
Eph. 4. 2 With all lowliness and [meekness], will
Col. 3. 12 Put on therefore..[meekness], long suffe.
1 Ti. 6. 11 follow after..love, patience, [meekness]
2 Ti. 2. 25 In [meekness] instructing those that opp.
Titus 3. 2 gentle,showing all [meekness] unto all m.

4. *Meekness, mildness,* πραΰτης *prautēs.*
Jas. 1. 21 receive with meekness the ingrafted word
3. 13 let him show..his works with meekness
1 Pe. 3. 15 hope that is in you with meekness and f.

MEET, (more than is) —

1. *Sons of,* בְּנֵי [*ben*].
Deut. 3. 18 shall pass over..all (that are) meet for the

2. *Upright, right,* יָשָׁר *yashar.*
Jer. 26. 14 do with me as seemeth good and meet unto

3. *Uprightness,* יֹשֶׁר *yosher.*
Prov11. 24 that withholdeth more than is meet, but

4. *Chosen,* רָאָה *raah* (partic.).
Esth. 2. 9 meet to be given her, out of the king's h.

5. *Worthy,* ἄξιος *axios.*
Matt. 3. 8 Bring forth therefore fruits meet for rep.
Acts 26. 20 they should..do works meet for repentan.
1 Co. 16. 4 if it be meet that I go also, they shall go
2 Th. 1. 3 We are bound to thank God..as it is meet

6. *Just, right,* δίκαιος *dikaios.*
Phil. 1. 7 Even as it is meet for me to think this of
2 Pe. 1. 13 Yea, I think it meet, as long as I am in

7. *Well set,* εὔθετος *euthetos.*
Heb. 6. 7 bringeth forth herbs meet for them by

8. *Sufficient,* ἱκανός *hikanos.*
1 Co. 15. 9 that am not meet to be called an apostle

9. *Honest, beautiful,* καλός *kalos.*
Matt15. 26 It is not [meet] to take the children's br.
Mark 7. 27 it is not meet to take the children's bread

MEET, (together or with), be met, to —

1. *To meet together by appointment,* יָעַד *yaad,* 2.
Exod25. 22 And there I will meet with thee, and I
29. 42 where I will meet you, to speak there unto
29. 43 there I will meet with the children of Is.
30. 6, 36 testimony, where I will meet with thee
Num17. 4 testimony, where I will meet with you
Josh.11. 5 when all these kings were met together
Neh. 6. 2 Come, let us meet together in..the villa.
6. 10 Let us meet together in the house of God

2. *To find,* מָצָא *matsa.*
1 Sa. 10. 3 there shall meet thee three men going up
1 Ki. 13. 24 a lion met him by the way, and slew him
2 Ki. 4. 29 if thou meet any man, salute him not; and
9. 21 they went out against Jehu, and met him
10. 13 Jehu met with the brethren of Ahaziah k.

3. *To come or fall upon,* פָּגַע *paga.*
Gen. 32. 1 went..and the angels of God met him
Exod. 5. 20 they met Moses and Aaron, who stood in
23. 4 If thou meet thine enemy's ox or his ass
Num35. 19 when he meeteth him, he shall slay him
35. 21 shall slay the murderer when he meeteth
Josh. 2. 16 Get you to..lest the pursuers meet you
Josh.17. 10 they met together in Asher on the north
Ruth 2. 22 that they meet thee not in any other field
1 Sa. 10. 5 thou shalt meet a company of prophets
Isa. 47. 3 I will take vengeance, and I will not meet
64. 5 Thou meetest him that rejoiceth and w.
Amos 5. 19 did flee from a lion, and a bear met him

4. *To meet,* פָּגַשׁ *pagash.*
Gen. 32. 17 When Esau my brother meeteth thee, and
33. 8 What..thou by all this drove which I met
Exod. 4. 24 the LORD met him, and sought to kill him
4. 27 met him in the mount of God, and kissed
1 Sa. 25. 20 men came down against her; and she met
2 Sa. 2. 13 went out, and met together by the pool
Prov.17. 12 Let a bear robbed of her whelps meet a m.
Isa. 34. 14 wild beasts of the desert shall also meet
Jer. 41. 6 as he met them, he said unto them, Come
Hos. 13. 8 I will meet them as a bear (that is) bere.

5. *To be met,* פָּגַשׁ *pagash,* 2.
Psa. 85. 10 Mercy and truth are met together; right.
Prov.22. 2 The rich and poor meet together : the L.
29. 13 The poor and the deceitful man meet to.

6. *To meet,* פָּגַשׁ *pagash,* 3.
Job 5. 14 They meet with darkness in the day time

7. *To go or come before,* קָדַם *qadam,* 3.
Deut23. 4 Because they met you not with bread and
Neh. 13. 2 Because they met not the children of I.

8. *To meet, happen, come,* קָרָא *qara.*
Gen. 14. 17 the king of Sodom went out to meet him
18. 2 when he saw..he ran to meet them from
19. 1 Lot seeing..rose up to meet them ; and
24. 17 the servant ran to meet her, and said, Let
24. 65 this that walketh in the field to meet us
29. 13 he ran to meet him, and embraced him
30. 16 Leah went out to meet him, and said, Thou
32. 6 he cometh to meet thee, and four hundred
33. 4 Esau ran to meet him, and embraced him
46. 29 went up to meet Israel his father, to Gos.
Exod. 4. 14 he cometh forth to meet thee : and when
4. 27 said..Go into the wilderness to meet M.
18. 7 Moses went out to meet his father in law
19. 17 people out of the camp to meet with God
Num22. 36 he went out to meet him unto a city of M.
23. 3 peradventure the LORD will come to meet
31. 13 went forth to meet them without the ca.
Josh. 9. 11 go to meet them, and say unto them, We
Judg. 4. 18 Jael went out to meet Sisera, and said
4. 22 Jael came out to meet him, and said unto
6. 35 And he sent..and they came up to meet
11. 31 forth of the doors of my house to meet me
11. 34 his daughter came out to meet him with
19. 3 the father..saw him, he rejoiced to meet
1 Sa. 10. 10 behold, a company of prophets met him
13. 10 Saul went out to meet him, that he might
15. 12 when Samuel rose early to meet Saul in
17. 48 and came and drew nigh to meet David
17. 48 ran toward the army to meet the Philistine
18. 6 the women came out..to meet king Saul
25. 32 God..which sent thee this day to meet
25. 34 thou hadst hasted and come to meet me
30. 21 they went forth to meet David, and to meet
2 Sa. 6. 20 Michal..came out to meet David, and said
10 5 he sent to meet them, because the men
15. 32 Hushai the Archite came to meet him w.
16. 1 Ziba..servant of Mephibosheth met him
19. 15 Judah came to Gilgal, to go to meet the
19. 16 came down with the men of Judah to m.
19. 20 I am come the first..to meet my lord the
19. 24 the son of Saul came down to meet the k.
19. 25 when he was come to Jerusalem to meet
1 Ki. 2. 8 he came down to meet me at Jordan, and
2. 19 the king rose up to meet her, and bowed
18. 7 as Obadiah was in the way..Elijah met
18. 16 went to meet Ahab...And Ahab went to m.
21. 18 Arise, go down to meet Ahab king of Isr.
2 Ki. 1. 3 Arise, go up to meet the messengers of the
1. 6 There came a man up to meet us, and said
1 7 which came up to meet you, and told you
2. 15 they came to meet him, and bowed them.
4. 26 Run now, I pray thee, to meet her, and
4. 31 wherefore he went again to meet him. and
5. 21 he lighted down from the chariot to meet
5. 26 turned again from his chariot to meet thee?
8. 8 meet the man of God, and enquire of the
8. 9 So Hazael went to meet him, and took a p.
9. 17 Take an horseman, and send to meet them
9. 18 So there went one on horseback to meet
10. 15 the son of Rechab (coming) to meet him
16. 10 king Ahaz went to Damascus to meet Ti.
1 Ch.19. 5 and he sent to meet them : for the men
Job 39. 21 He paweth..he goeth on to meet the armed
Prov. 7. 10 there met him a woman (with) the attire
7. 15 therefore came I forth to meet thee, dili.
Isa. 7. 3 Go forth now to meet Ahaz, thou, and Sh.
14. 9 Hell..is moved for thee to meet (thee) at
Jer. 41. 6 And..went..from Mizpah to meet them
51. 31 One post shall run to meet another
51. 31 and one messenger to meet another, to s.
Amos 4. 12 Therefore..prepare to meet thy God, O
Zech. 2. 3 and another angel went out to meet him

9. *To meet, come (to view),* (לִפְנֵי) קָרָא *qara,* 2 (*li-phene*).
Exod. 5. 3 The God of the Hebrews hath met with us
2 Sa.18. 9 And Absalom met the servants of David

10. *To meet, happen, come,* קָרָה *qarah.*
Deut25. 18 How he met thee by the way, and smote

11. *To meet, happen, come,* קָרָה *qarah,* 2.
Exod 3. 18 The LORD God of the Hebrews hath met
Num23. 4 God met Balaam : and he said unto him
23. 15 Stand..by thy burnt offering, while I meet
23. 16 LORD met Balaam, and put a word in his

12. *To the face of,* לִפְנֵי or אֶל־פְּנֵי [*panim*].
1 Ch. 12. 17 David went out to meet them, and answ.
2 Ch. 15. 2 he went out to meet Asa, and said unto h.
19. 2 son of Hanani the seer went..to meet him

13. *To meet,* ἀπαντάω *apantaō.*
Matt28. 9 behold, Jesus [met] them, saying, All hail
Mark 5. 2 there [met] him out of the tombs a man
14. 13 there shall meet you a man bearing a pi.
Luke14. 31 he be able with ten thousand [to meet]
17. 12 there met him ten men that were lepers
John 4. 51 his servants [met] him, and told..saying
Acts 16. 16 a certain damsel possessed..[met] us, w.

14. *For a meeting,* εἰς ἀπάντησιν *eis apantēsin.*
Matt25. 1 virgins, which..went forth [to meet] the
25. 6 the bridegroom cometh; go ye out to meet
Acts 28. 15 they came to meet us as far as Appii Fo.
1 Th. 4. 17 shall be caught up..to meet the Lord in

15. *To happen to be near,* παρατυγχάνω *paratugchanō.*
Acts 17. 17 disputed..daily with them that met with

16. *To cast together, come up with,* συμβάλλω *sum.*
Acts 20. 14 when he met with us at Assos, we took

17. *To meet together,* συναντάω *sunantaō.*
Luke 9. 37 it came to pass, that..much people met
22. 10 there shall a man meet you, bearing a p.
Acts 10. 25 Cornelius met him, and fell down at his
Heb. 7. 1 who met Abraham returning from the s.
7. 10 loins of his father when Melchisedec met

18. *For a meeting with,* εἰς συνάντησιν *eis sunantēsin.*
Matt. 8. 34 the whole city came out [to meet] Jesus

19. *To come to meet,* ὑπαντάω *hupantaō.*
Matt. 8. 28 there met him two possessed with devils
Luke 8. 27 there met him out of the city a certain man
John11. 30 was in that place where Martha met him
12. 18 For this cause the people also met him

20. *In order to a meeting,* εἰς ὑπάντησιν *eis hupant.*
John 12. 13 went forth to meet him, and cried, Hos.

MEET, go and —

To come to meet, ὑπαντάω *hupantaō.*
John11. 20 Then Martha..went and met him : but

MEET, to be —

1. *To have patience,* אֲרַךְ *arak.*
Ezra 4. 14 it was not meet for us to see the king's

2. *To be right, prepared,* כּוּן *kun,* 2.
Exod. 8. 26 It is not meet so to do; for we shall sac.

3. *To be made, used,* עָשָׂה *asah,* 2.
Eze. 15. 5 when it was whole, it was meet for no work
15. 5 shall it be meet yet for (any) work, when

4. *To prosper,* צָלַח *tsaleach.*
Eze. 15. 4 cast into the fire. .Is it meet for (any) w.?

5. *It behoveth,* δεῖ *dei.*
Luke15. 32 It was meet that we should make merry
Rom. 1. 27 recompence of their error which was meet

MEET for use —

Very useful, εὔχρηστος *euchrēstos.*
2 Ti. 2. 21 sanctified, and meet for the master's use

MEET, to make —

To make sufficient, ἱκανόω *hikanoō.*
Col. 1. 12 which hath made us meet to be partaker

MEET, to seem —

To be or seem right, יָשָׁר *yashar.*
Jer. 27. 5 have given it unto whom it seemed meet

MEETEST —

Right, upright, יָשָׁר *yashar.*
2 Ki.10. 3 Look even out the best and meetest of your

MEETING —

To meet, happen, come, קָרָא *qara.*
1 Sa. 21. 1 Ahimelech was afraid at the meeting of

MEETING (two ways) —

Double way, crossway, ἄμφοδον *amphodon.*
Mark11. 4 without in a place where two ways met

ME-GID'-DO, ME-GID'-DON, מְגִדּוֹ, מְגִדּוֹן *place of God.*
A city in Issachar or Manasseh, W. of Jordan, in the plain of Jezreel, at the N.E. of Mount Carmel, near Taanach and Ibleam; once *Legio,* now *Leggun.*
Josh 12. 21 The king of Taanach, one; the king of M.
17. 11 the inhabitants of M. and her towns, (even)
Judg. 1. 27 nor the inhabitants of M. and her towns
5. 19 Taanach by the waters of M.; they took
1 Ki. 4. 12 (to him pertained) Taanach and M., and
9. 15 to build the house of the LORD..and M.
2 Ki. 9. 27 Ahaziah the king..fled to M., and died
23. 29 he slew him at M., when he had seen him
23. 30 carried him in a chariot dead from M., and
1 Ch. 7. 29 M. and her towns, Dor and her towns. In
2 Ch.35. 22 Josiah..came to fight in the valley of M.
Zech 12. 11 as the mourning of H. in the valley of M.

ME-HE-TAB'-EL, מְהֵיטַבְאֵל *God is doing good.*
1. Wife of Hadar, eighth king of Edom. B.C. 1500.
Gen. 36. 39 M., the daughter of Matred, the daughter
1 Ch. 1. 50 M., the daughter of Matred, the daughter

2. A person whose grandson tried to intimidate Nehemiah when threatened by Sanballat and Tobiah. B.C. 490.
Neh. 6. 10 Delaiah the son of Mehetabeel, who (was)

ME-HI'-DA, מְחִידָא *famous.*
A Nethinim whose descendants returned with Zerubbabel from exile. B.C. 536.
Ezra 2. 52 the children of M., the children of Hars.
Neh. 7. 54 the children of M., the children of Hars.

ME'-HIR, מְחִיר *dexterity.*
A son of Chelub, through Caleb son of Hur. B.C. 1420.
1 Ch. 4. 11 Chelub the brother of Shuah begat M.

ME-HO-LA-THITE, מְחֹלָתִי.
An inhabitant of a city in Issachar, also called *Abel-meholah.*
1 Sa. 18. 19 she was given unto Adriel the M. to wife
2 Sa. 21. 8 for Adriel the son of Barzillai the M.

ME-HU-JA'-EL, מְחוּיָאֵל *God is combating.*
Son of Irad, a descendant of Cain, and father of Methusael. B.C. 3700.
Gen. 4. 18 Irad begat M.: and M. begat Methusael

ME-HU'-MAN, מְהוּמָן.
One of the seven chamberlains that served in the presence of Ahasuerus king of Persia. B.C. 500.
Esth. 1. 10 the king..commanded M., Biztha, Harb.

ME-HU'-NIM, ME-U'-NIM, מְעוּנִים.
One of the Nethinim whose descendants returned with Zerubbabel. B.C. 536.
Ezra 2. 50 the children of M., the children of Neph.
Neh. 7. 52 the children of M., the children of Neph.

ME-HU'-NIMS, מְעוּנִים.
An Arab tribe at the S. of the Salt Sea, and towards Petra.
2 Ch. 26. 7 And God helped him against..the M.

ME JAR'-KON, מֵי הַיַּרְקוֹן.
A city in Dan, near Rakkon; now called *Oyun Kara.*
Josh. 19. 46 And M., and Rakkon, with the border b.

ME-KO'-NAH, מְכֹנָה *foundation.*
A city in Judah, near Ziklag.
Neh. 11. 28 And at Ziklag, and at M., and in the vill.

ME-LAT'-IAH, מְלַטְיָה *Jah delivers.*
A Gibeonite who helped to repair the wall after Nehemiah came from Shushan. B.C. 445.
Neh. 3. 7 next unto them repaired M. the Gibeonite

MEL'-CHI, Μελχί, Μελχεί, *from Heb.* מַלְכִּי *my king.*
1. An ancestor of Jesus through Mary.
Luke 3. 24 Levi which was (the son) of M., which was
2. A still more remote ancestor. Luke 3. 28.

MELCHIAH. *See* MALCHIAH, No. 12.

MEL-CHI-SE'-DEC, Μελχισεδέκ. See *Melchizedek.*
Heb. 5. 6 a Priest for ever, after the order of M.
5. 10 Called..a..Priest after the order of M.
6. 20 High Priest for ever, after the order of M.
7. 1 For this M., king of Salem, priest of the
7. 10 in the loins of his father when M. met
7. 11 priest should rise after the order of M.
7. 15 after the similitude of M. there ariseth
7. 17, 21 [a Priest for ever, after the order of M.]

MEL-CHI-SHU'-A, MAL-CHI-SHU'-A, מַלְכִּישׁוּעַ.
The third son of king Saul. B.C. 1056.
1 Sa. 14. 49 the sons of Saul were Jonathan..and M.
31. 2 the Philistines slew Jonathan..and Mel.
1 Ch. 8. 33 Saul begat Jonathan, and M., and Abina.
9. 39 Saul begat Jonathan, and M., and Abin.
10. 2 the Philistines slew Jonathan..and M.

MEL-CHI-ZE'-DEK, מַלְכִּי־צֶדֶק *my king is righteous.*
The priest and king of Salem, who met Abraham and blessed him. B.C. 1917.
Gen. 14. 18 And M. king of Salem brought forth bread
Psa. 110. 4 (art) a priest for ever after the order of M.

ME-LE'-A, Μελεᾶς.
An ancestor of Jesus, through Mary.
Luke 3. 31 Which was (the son) of M., which was (the

ME'-LECH, מֶלֶךְ *king.*
A son of Micah, grandson of Jonathan son of king Saul. B.C. 970.
1 Ch. 8. 35 the sons of Micah (were) Pithon, and M.
9. 41 the sons of Micah (were) Pithon, and M.

ME-LI'-CU, מְלִיכוּ *counsellor* [V.L. מלוכי].
A priest in Jerusalem in the days of Joiakim, grandson of Jozadak; called also *Malluch.* B.C. 536.
Neh. 12. 14 Of M., Jonathan; of Shebaniah, Joseph

ME-LI'-TA, Μελίτη.
An island in the Adriatic, where Paul was shipwrecked; now called *Malta,* which is twenty miles long by twelve broad; or it may have been *Meleda* or *Melita,* a small isle near Dalmatia.
Acts 28. 1 they knew that the island was called M.

MELODY —
1. *Song or instrument of praise,* זִמְרָה *zimrah.*
Isa. 51. 3 joy..thanksgiving, and the voice of melody
Amos 5. 23 for I will not hear the melody of thy viols
2. *To play on a stringed instrument,* נָגַן *nagan,* 3.
Isa. 23. 16 make sweet melody, sing many songs, that

MELODY, to make —
To play on a stringed instrument, ψάλλω *psallō.*
Eph. 5. 19 making melody in your heart to the Lord

MELONS —
Melons, אֲבַטִּחִים *abaltichim.*
Num 11. 5 the cucumbers, and the melons, and the

MELT (away), to
1. *To drop,* דָּלַף *dalaph.*
Psa. 119. 28 My soul melteth for heaviness: strengthen
2. *To melt, waste,* מָסָה *masah,* 5.
Psa. 147. 18 He sendeth out his word and melteth them
3. *To be loathed, despised, rejected,* מָאַס *maas,* 2.
Psa. 58. 7 Let them melt away as waters (which) run
4. *To melt, dissolve,* מוּג *mug.*
Psa. 46. 6 he uttered his voice, the earth melted
Amos 9. 5 it shall melt, and all that dwell therein
5. *To be melted, dissolved,* מוּג *mug,* 2.
Exod 15. 15 the inhabitants of Canaan shall melt away
1 Sa. 14. 16 the multitude melted away, and they went
6. *To be melted,* מוּג *mug,* 7a.
Amos 9. 13 sweet wine, and all the hills shall melt
Nah. 1. 5 the hills melt, and the earth is burned at
7. *To be melted, wasted,* מָסַס *masas,* 2.
Exod 16. 21 and when the sun waxed hot, it melted
Josh. 2. 11 our hearts did melt, neither did there re.
5. 1 their heart melted, neither was their spi.
7. 5 the hearts of the people melted, and be.
2 Sa. 17. 10 And he also..shall utterly melt: for all I.
Psa. 68. 2 as wax melteth before the fire, (so) let the
97. 5 The hills melted like wax at the presence
112. 10 he shall gnash with his teeth, and melt away
Isa. 13. 7 Therefore..every man's heart shall melt
19. 1 the heart of Egypt shall melt in the midst
Eze. 21. 7 every heart shall melt, and all hands shall
Mic. 1. 4 the mountains shall be molten under him
Nah. 2. 10 the heart melteth, and the knees smite
8. *To flow,* נָזַל *nazal.*
Judg. 5. 5 The mountains melted from before the
9. *To pour out,* נָסַךְ *nasak.*
Isa. 40. 19 The workman melteth a graven image, and
44. 10 Who hath formed a god, or molten a gra
10. *To pour out,* נָתַךְ *nathak,* 5.
Eze. 22. 20 to blow the fire upon it, to melt (it); so
22. 20 and I will leave (you there), and melt you
11. *To refine, purify,* צָרַף *tsaraph.*
Jer. 6. 29 the founder melteth in vain; for the wi.
9. 7 Behold, I will melt them, and try them
12. *A melting or wasting away,* תֶּמֶס *temes.*
Psa. 58. 8 As a snail (which) melteth, let (every one
13. *To loose,* λύω *luō.*
2 Pe. 3. 10 the elements shall melt with fervent heat
14. *To be dissolved, melted, liquified,* τήκομαι *tēkomai.*
2 Pe. 3. 12 the elements shall melt with fervent heat?

MELT, to make —
To melt, waste, מָסָה *masah,* 5.
Josh. 14. 8 brethren..made the heart of the people m.

MELTED, to be —
1. *Melting,* הִתּוּךְ *hittuk.*
Eze. 22. 22 As silver is melted in the midst of the fu.
2. *To be melted,* מוּג *mug,* 7a.
Psa. 107. 26 their soul is melted because of trouble
3. *To be melted,* מָסַס *masas,* 2.
Psa. 22. 14 it is melted in the midst of my bowels
Isa. 34. 3 the mountains shall be melted with their
4. *To be poured out,* נָתַךְ *nathak,* 2.
Eze. 22. 21 ye shall be melted in the midst thereof
5. *To be poured out,* נָתַךְ *nathak,* 6.
Eze. 22. 22 so shall ye be melted in the midst thereof

MELTING —
Stubble, meltings, refuse, הֲמָסִים *hamasim.*
Isa. 64. 2 As (when) the melting fire burneth, the

MEL'-ZAR, הַמֶּלְצַר *the overseer.*
One to whose care Daniel and his companions were committed by the chief of the eunuchs of Nebuchadnezzar. B.C. 530.
Dan. 1. 11 Then said Daniel to M., whom the prince
1. 16 Thus M. took away the portion of their m.

MEMBER —
1. *Things formed,* יְצֻרִים *yetsurim.*
Job 17. 7 and all my members (are) as a shadow
2. *A member, limb, part of the body,* μέλος *melos.*
Matt 5. 29, 30 that one of thy members should perish
Rom. 6. 13 Neither yield ye your members (as) inst.
6. 13 your members (as) instruments of right.
6. 19 as ye have yielded your members servants
6. 19 yield your members servants to righteous.
7. 5 did work in our members to bring forth
7. 23 I see another law in my members, warring
7. 23 to the law of sin which is in my members
12. 4 For as we have many members in one body
12. 4 and all members have not the same office
12. 5 and every one members one of another
1 Co. 6. 15 that your bodies are the members of Ch.
6. 15 shall I then take the members of Christ
1 Co. 6. 15 and make (them) the members of an har.?
12. 12 as the body is one, and hath many mem.
12. 12 all the members of that one body, being
12. 14 For the body is not one member, but many
12. 18 But now hath God set the members every
12. 19 And if they were all one member, where
12. 20 But now (are they) many members, yet
12. 22 Nay, much more those members of the
12. 25 the members should have the same care
12. 26 whether one member suffer, all the mem.
12. 26 one member be honoured, all the members
12. 27 ye are the body of Christ, and members
Eph. 4. 25 for we are members one of another
5. 30 For we are members of his body, of his
Col. 3. 5 Mortify therefore your members which
Jas. 3. 5 Even so the tongue is a little member, and
3. 6 so is the tongue among our members, that
4. 1 of your lusts that war in your members?

MEMORIAL —
1. *Memorial,* אַזְכָּרָה *azkarah.*
Lev. 2. 2 the priest shall burn the memorial of it
2. 9 shall take from the meat offering a mem.
2. 16 the priest shall burn the memorial of it
5. 12 a memorial thereof, and burn (it) on the
6. 15 shall burn..the memorial of it, unto the
24. 7 that it may be on the bread for a memor.
Num. 5. 26 the memorial thereof, and burn (it) upon
2. *Remembrance, memorial,* זֵכֶר, זֶכֶר *zeker.*
Exod. 3. 15 this (is) my memorial unto all generations
Esth. 9. 28 nor the memorial of them perish from
Psa. 9. 6 their memorial is perished with them
135. 13 thy memorial, O LORD, throughout all g
Hos. 12. 5 LORD God of hosts; the LORD (is) his me
3. *Memorial, remembrance,* זִכָּרוֹן *zikkaron.*
Exod 12. 14 this day shall be unto you for a memorial
13. 9 for a memorial between thine eyes, that
17. 14 Write this (for) a memorial in a book, and
28. 12 stones of memorial unto the children of
28. 12 upon his two shoulders, for a memorial
28. 29 for a memorial before the LORD continu.
30. 16 it may be a memorial unto the children
39. 7 stones for a memorial to the children of
Lev. 23. 24 a memorial of blowing of trumpets, an
Num. 5. 15 an offering of memorial, bringing iniquity
5. 18 put the offering of memorial in her hands
10. 10 that they may be to you for a memorial
16. 40 (To be) a memorial unto the children of I
31. 54 a memorial for the children of Israel before
Josh. 4. 7 these stones shall be for a memorial unto
Neh. 2. 20 ye have no portion, nor right, nor memorial
Zech. 6. 14 for a memorial in the temple of the LORD
4. *A memorial, token of remembrance,* μνημόσυνον.
Matt 26. 13 shall also this..be told for a memorial of
Mark 14. 9 shall be spoken of for a memorial of her
Acts 10. 4 are come up for a memorial before God

MEMORY —
Memory, remembrance, memorial, זֵכֶר, זֶכֶר *zeker.*
Psa. 109. 15 that he may cut off the memory of them
145. 7 They shall abundantly utter the memory
Prov 10. 7 The memory of the just (is) blessed: but
Eccl. 9. 5 for the memory of them is forgotten
Isa. 26. 14 hast thou..made all their memory to pe

MEM'-PHIS, מֹף *moph.*
A city in Central Egypt, on the W. of the Nile, the seat of the 3rd, 4th, 7th, and 8th dynasty of Manetho; after Psammetichus the royal residence; also called *Noph.*
Hos. 9. 6 M. shall bury them: the pleasant (places)

ME-MU'-CAN, מְמוּכָן.
One of the seven princes of Persia and Media that saw the king's face at pleasure. B.C. 519.
Esth. 1. 14 next unto him (was) Carshena..(and) M.
1. 16 M. answered before the king and the prin.
1. 21 The king did according to the word of M.

MEN — [See also Man.]
1. *Men, tall ones,* מְתִים *methim.*
Deut. 2. 34 utterly destroyed the men, and the women
3. 6 utterly destroying the men, women, and
33. 6 Let Reuben live..let (not) his men be few
Job 11. 3 Should thy lies make men hold their p.?
11. 11 For he knoweth vain men: he seeth wic.
22. 15 old way which wicked men have trodden?
24. 12 Men groan from out of the city, and the
31. 31 If the men of my tabernacle said not, Oh
Psa. 17. 14 From men (which are) thy hand, O LORD
17. 14 from men of the world, (which have) their
105. 12 When they were (but) a few men in number
Isa. 3. 25 Thy men shall fall by the sword, and thy
5. 13 their honourable men (are) famished, and
41. 14 Fear not, thou worm Jacob..ye men of I.
2. *Wholeness,* מְתֹם *methom* [prob. error: A.V. translates as if = No. 1]. Judg. 20. 48
3. *People,* עַם *am.*
Num 31. 32 the prey which the men of war had caught
4. *Male,* ἄρσην *arsēn.*
Rom. 1. 27 men with men working that which is un

MEN, certain —
Men, אֲנָשִׁים *anashim.*
Num. 9. 6 there were certain men, who were defiled

MEN of low degree —
Sons of Adam or of man, בְּנֵי־אָדָם *beneadam.*
Psa. 62. 9 Surely men of low degree (are) vanity, (and)

MEN, after the manner of —
Human, belonging to man, ἀνθρώπινος *anthrōpinos.*
Rom. 6. 19 I speak after the manner of men because

MEN'S persons —
Face, πρόσωπον *prosōpon.*
Jude 16 having men's persons in admiration beca.

MEN, to play or quit like —
1. *To strengthen self,* חָזַק *chazaq,* 7.
2 Sa. 10. 12 let us play the men for our people, and
2. *To act as men,* ἀνδρίζομαι *andrizomai.*
1 Co. 16. 13 Watch ye..quit you like men, be strong

MEN, to show selves —
To show self a man, אִישׁ *ish,* 7a.
Isa. 46. 8 Remember this, and show yourselves men

ME-NA'-HEM, מְנַחֵם *comforter.*
The son of Gadi who slew Shallum, and was succeeded by his son Pekahiah. B.C. 761.
2 Ki. 15. 14 M. the son of Gadi went up from Tirzah
15. 16 Then M. smote Tiphsah, and all that (were)
15. 17 began M. the son of Gadi to reign over I.
15. 19; 15. 20; 15. 21; 15. 22; 15. 23.

MENE —
To Number, מְנָא, מְנֵה *mena, menah.*
Dan. 5. 26 MENE, God hath numbered thy kingd. v. 25

ME'-NAN, Μαϊνάν, *or* Μεννᾶ.
An ancestor of Jesus, through Mary.
Luke 3. 31 Melea, which was (the son) of [M.,] which

MEN CHILDREN —
A male, זָכוּר *zakur.*
Exod 34. 23 Thrice in the year shall all your men ch.

MEND, to —
1. *To strengthen,* חָזַק *chazaq,* 3.
2 Ch. 24. 12 and brass to mend the house of the LORD
2. *To make thoroughly fit,* καταρτίζω *katartizō.*
Matt 4. 21 he saw other two brethren. mending their
Mark 1. 19 who also were in the ship mending their

MEN PLEASERS —
Pleasing men, ἀνθρωπάρεσκος *anthrōpareskos.*
Eph. 6. 6 Not with eye service, as men pleasers; but
Col. 3. 22 not with eye service, as men pleasers; but

MEN STEALER —
Men enslaver, ἀνδραποδιστής *andrapodistēs.*
1 Ti. 1. 10 for men stealers, for liars, for perjured p.

MENSTRUOUS woman or cloth —
1. *One separated,* נִדָּה *niddah.*
Lam. 1. 17 Jerusalem is as a menstruous woman am.
Eze. 18. 6 neither..come near to a menstruous wo
2. *Sick, menstruous,* דָּוֶה *daveh.*
Isa. 30. 22 shalt cast them away as a menstruous cl.

MENTION —
Mention, μνεία *mneia.*
Rom. 1. 9 I make mention of you always in my pra.
Eph. 1. 16 making mention of you in my prayers
1 Th. 1. 2 making mention of you in our prayers
Phm. 4 making mention of thee always in my pr.

MENTION (of, to make), to —
1. *To remember, be mindful of,* זָכַר *zakar.*
Jer. 20. 9 I will not make mention of him, nor sp
23. 36 the burden of the LORD shall ye mention
2. *To make mention,* זָכַר *zakar,* 5.
Gen. 40. 14 make mention of me unto Pharaoh, and
Exod 23. 13 make no mention of the name of other g.
Josh. 23. 7 neither make mention of the name of their
1 Sa. 4. 18 when he made mention of the ark of God
Psa. 71. 16 I will make mention of thy righteousness
87. 4 I will make mention of Rahab and Babylon
Isa. 12. 4 make mention that his name is exalted
19. 17 every one that maketh mention thereof
26. 13 by thee only will we make mention of thy
48. 1 which..make mention of the God of Isr.
49. 1 mother hath he made mention of my name
62. 6 ye that make mention of the LORD, keep
63. 7 I will mention the lovingkindnesses of the
Jer. 4. 16 Make ye mention to the nations; behold
Amos 6. 10 we may not make mention of the name of
3. *To mention, remember,* μνημονεύω *mnēmoneuō.*
Heb. 11. 22 made mention of the departing of the ch.

MENTION of, to be made —
To be remembered, mentioned, זָכַר *zakar,* 2.
Job 28. 18 No mention shall be made of coral, or of

MENTIONED —
What is heard, report, tidings, שְׁמוּעָה *shemuah.*
Eze. 16. 56 thy sister Sodom was not mentioned by

MENTIONED, to be —
1. *To go or come in,* בּוֹא *bo.*
1 Ch. 4. 38 these mentioned by..names..princes in
2. *To be remembered, mentioned,* זָכַר *zakar,* 2.
Eze. 18. 22 they shall not be mentioned unto him
18. 24 that he hath done shall not be mentioned
33. 16 hath committed shall be mentioned unto
3. *To be caused to come up,* עָלָה *alah,* 6.
2 Ch. 20. 34 who (is) mentioned in the book of the ki.
4. *To call, read,* קָרָא *qara.*
Josh 21. 9 cities which are (here) mentioned by name

ME-O-NE'-NIM, מְעוֹנְנִים.
A place in Ephraim, near Shechem.
Judg. 9. 37 company come along by the plain of M.

ME-O-NO'-THAI, מְעוֹנֹתַי *Jah's dwellings.*
Father of Ophrah, and descendant of Judah through Caleb son of Hur. B.C. 1450.
1 Ch. 4. 14 M. begat Ophrah: and Seraiah begat Joab

ME-PHA'-ATH, מֵיפַעַת, מֵפַעַת *height.*
A Levitical city in Reuben, near Kedemoth or Kirjathaim. In Jer. 48. 21, V.L. מוֹפַעַת.
Josh. 13. 18 And Jahaza, and Kedemoth, and M.
21. 37 Kedemoth with her suburbs, M. with her
1 Ch. 6. 79 Kedemoth also with her suburbs, and M.
Jer. 48. 21 judgment is come upon Jahazah, and..M.

ME-PHI-BO'-SHETH, מְפִיבֹשֶׁת *utterance of Baal.*
1. Son of Jonathan, son of Saul. B.C. 1068.
2 Sa. 4. 4 was five years old..And his name (was) M.
9. 6 Now when M., the son of Jonathan, the
9. 6 David said, M. And he answered, Behold
9. 10 but M. thy master's son shall eat bread
9. 11 As for M (said the king,) he shall eat at
9. 12 And M. had a young son, whose name (was)
9. 12 the house of Ziba (were) servants unto M.
9. 13 So M. dwelt in Jerusalem; for he did eat
16. 1 Ziba the servant of M. met him, with a
16. 4 thine (are) all that (pertained) unto M. And
19. 24 And M. the son of Saul came down to meet
19. 25 Wherefore wentest not thou with me, M.?
19. 30 And M. said unto the king, Yea, let him
21. 7 the king spared M., the son of Jonathan

2. A son of Rizpah, Saul's concubine, whom David gave up to the Gibeonites.
2 Sa. 21. 8 the king took..Armoni and M.; and the

ME'-RAB, מֵרַב *increase.*
Elder daughter of king Saul, promised to David, but given to Adriel the Meholathite. B.C. 1060.
1 Sa. 14. 49 the name of the first born M., and the name
18. 17 Behold my elder daughter M., her will I
18. 19 when M., Saul's daughter, should have

ME-RA'-IAH, מְרָיָה *revelation of Jah.*
A priest in Jerusalem in the days of Joiakim, grandson of Jozadak. B.C. 600.
Neh. 12. 12 of Seraiah, M.: of Jeremiah, Hananiah

ME-RA'-IOTH, מְרָיוֹת *revelations.*
1. An Aaronite, and ancestor of Azariah the priest in the days of Solomon. B.C. 1100
1 Ch. 6. 6 Uzzi begat Zerahiah, and Zerahiah..M.
6. 7 M. begat Amariah, and Amariah begat A.
6. 52 M. his son, Amariah his son, Ahitub his
Ezra 7. 3 Amariah, the son of Azariah, the son of M.

2 Another priest of the same line. B.C. 800.
1 Ch. 9. 11 Zadok, the son of M., the son of Ahitub
Neh. 11. 11 Zadok, the son of M., the son of Ahitub

3. A priest at the close of the exile. B.C. 536.
Neh. 12. 15 Of Harim, Adnah; of M. Helkai

ME-RA'-RI, מְרָרִי *bitter, excited.*
The third and youngest son of Levi, ancestor of the Merarites. B.C. 1700.
Gen. 46. 11 sons of Levi; Gershon, Kohath, and M.
Exod. 6. 16 sons of Levi..Gershon..Kohath, and M.
6. 19 the sons of M.; Mahli and Mushi: these
Num. 3. 17 sons of Levi .Gershon, and Kohath..M.
3. 20 sons of M. by their families; Mahli; and M
3. 33 of M. (was) the family of the Mahlites, and
3. 33 the Mushites: these (are) the family of M.
3. 35 the chief..of the families of M. (was) Zu
3. 36 (under) the..charge of the sons of M. shall
4. 29 As for the sons of M, thou shalt number
4. 33 the families of the sons of M., according
4. 42 the families of the sons of M., throughout
4. 45 the families of the sons of M., whom Mo.
7. 8 he gave unto the sons of M., according unto
10. 17 the sons of M. set forward, bearing the t.
26. 57 they that were numbered of .M, the fa.
Josh. 21. 7 The children of M. by their families (had)
21. 34 the families of the children of M., the rest
21. 40 the children of M., by their families, wh.
1 Ch. 6. 1 sons of Levi; Gershon, Kohath, and M.
6. 16 The sons of Levi; Gershon, Kohath, and M.
6. 19 The sons of M.; Mahli, and Mushi. And
6. 29 sons of M.; Mahli, Libni his son, Shimei
6. 44 the sons of M., (stood) on the left hand: E.
6. 47 of Mushi, the son of M., the son of Levi
6. 63 Unto the sons of M. (were given) by lot
6. 77 Unto the rest of the children of M. (were
9. 14 the son of Hashabiah, of the sons of M.
15. 6 Of the sons of M.; Asaiah the chief, and
15. 17 of the sons of M. their brethren, Ethan
23. 6 the sons of Levi..Gershon, Kohath, and M.
23. 21 The sons of M.; Mahli and Mushi. The
24. 26 The sons of M. (were) M. and Mushi: the
24. 27 The sons of M. by Jaaziah; Beno, and Sh.
26. 10 Hosah, of the children of M., had sons
26. 19 among the sons of Kore, and..sons of M.
2 Ch. 29. 12 of the sons of M.; Kish the son of Abdi
34. 12 Levites, of the sons of M.; snd Zechariah
Ezra 8. 19 Jeshaiah of the sons of M., his brethren

ME-RA-RITES, הַמְּרָרִי *the Merari.*
The descendants of Merari.
Num 26. 57 Levites..of Merari, the family of the M.

ME-RA-THA'-IM, מְרָתַיִם *double bitterness.*
A symbolic name for Babylon. B.C. 628—586.
Jer. 50. 21 Go up against the land of M., (even) against

MERCHANDISE —
1. *Merchandise, barter, traffic,* מַעֲרָב *maarab.*
Eze. 27. 9 all..were in thee to occupy thy merchan.
27. 27 thy merchandise, thy mariners, and thy p.
27. 27 and the occupiers of thy merchandise, and
27. 33 multitude of thy riches, and of thy merc.
27. 34 thy merchandise, and all thy company in
2. *Merchandise, traffic,* מַרְכֹּלֶת *markoleth.*
Eze. 27. 24 made of cedar, among thy merchandise
3. *Gain of merchandise,* סָחַר *sachar.*
Prov. 3. 14 better than the merchandise of silver, and
Isa. 45. 14 merchandise of Ethiopia, and of the Sa.
4. *Gain of merchandise,* סָחַר *sachar.*
Prov. 3. 14 the merchandise of it (is) better than the
31. 18 She perceiveth that her merchandise (is) g.
Isa. 23. 18 her merchandise and her hire shall be h.
23. 18 for her merchandise shall be for them that
5. *Merchandise, trade or gain,* סְחֹרָה *sechorah.*
Eze. 27. 15 many isles (were) the merchandise of thine
6. *Merchandise, traffic, trade, ware,* רְכֻלָּה *rekullah.*
Eze. 26. 12 and make a prey of thy merchandise
28. 16 By the multitude of thy merchandise they
7. *Merchandise, the lading of a ship,* γόμος *gomos.*
Rev. 18. 11 no man buyeth their merchandise any m.
18. 12 The merchandise of gold, and silver, and
8. *Trade, merchandise, traffic,* ἐμπορία *emporia.*
Matt 22. 5 one to his farm, and another to his mer.
9. *A place of trade or traffic,* ἐμπόριον *emporion.*
John 2. 16 not my Father's house an house of merc.

MERCHANDISE, to make —
1. *To show self a tyrant,* עָמַר *amar,* 7.
Deut 21. 14 thou shalt not make merchandise of her
24. 7 maketh merchandise of him, or selleth
2. *To traffic, make a trade of,* ἐμπορεύομαι *empore.*
2 Pe. 2. 3 shall they with feigned word make merc.

MERCHANT (man) —
1. *Canaanite, merchant,* כְּנַעַן *kenaan.*
Isa. 23. 11 given a commandment against the merc.
Hos. 12. 7 (He is) a merchant, the balances of deceit
Zeph. 1. 11 for all the merchant people are cut down
2. *Canaanite, merchant,* כְּנַעֲנִי *kenaani.*
Job 41. 6 shall they part him among the merchants
Prov 31. 24 and delivereth girdles unto the merchant
3. *To go about, trade,* סָחַר *sachar.*
Gen. 23. 16 shekels of silver, current..with the mer.
37. 28 there passed by Midianites, merchant m.
1 Ki. 10. 28 the king's merchants received the linen
2 Ch. 1. 16 the king's merchants received the linen
9. 14 (that which) chapmen and merchants br.
Prov 31. 14 She is like the merchants' ship; she brin.
Isa. 23. 2 thou whom the merchants of Zidon, that
23. 8 whose merchants (are) princes, whose tr.
47. 15 thy merchants, from thy youth; they sh.
Eze. 27. 12 Tarshish (was) thy merchant by reason of
27. 16 Syria (was) thy merchant by reason of the
27. 18 Damascus (was) thy merchant in the mu.
27. 21 goats: in these (were they) thy merchants
27. 36 The merchants among the people shall h.
38. 13 Sheba, and Dedan, and the merchants of
4. *To go to and fro, be a merchant,* רָכַל *rakal.*
Neh. 3. 31 unto the place..of the merchants, over
3. 32 repaired the goldsmiths and the merchants
13. 20 So the merchants, and sellers of all kind
Song 3. 6 perfumed..with all powders of the mer.
Eze. 17. 4 He cropped off..he set it in a city of me.
27. 3 a merchant of the people for many isles
27. 13 Tubal, and Meshech, they (were) thy me.
27. 15 The men of Dedan (were) thy merchants
27. 17 the land of Israel, they (were) thy merc.
27. 20 Dedan (was) thy merchant in precious c.
27. 22 The merchants of Sheba and Raamah
27. 22 they (were) thy merchants: they occupied
27. 23 the merchants of Sheba..(were) thy mer.
27. 24 These (were) thy merchants in all sorts (of
Nah. 3. 16 Thou hast multiplied thy merchants above
5. *To go about, trade, search,* תּוּר *tur.*
1 Ki. 10. 15 Besides..of the merchant men, and of the
6. *A traveller, trader,* ἔμπορος *emporos.*
Matt 13. 45 like unto a merchant man seeking goodly
Rev. 18. 3 the merchants of the earth are waxed rich
18. 11 the merchants of the earth shall weep and
18. 15 The merchants of these things, which were
18. 23 thy merchants were the great men of the

MERCHANT, spice —
To go to and fro, be a merchant, רָכַל *rakal.*
1 Ki. 10. 15 of the traffic of the spice merchants and

MERCIES, (great or tender) —
1. *Bowels, mercies,* רַחֲמִין *rachamin.*
Dan. 2. 18 That they would desire mercies of the God
2. *Bowels, mercies,* רַחֲמִים *rachamim.*
2 Sa. 24. 14 his mercies (are) great: and let me not fall
1 Ch. 21. 13 very great (are) his mercies: but let me not
Neh. 9. 19 Yet thou in thy manifold mercies forsook
9. 27 according to thy manifold mercies thou g.
9. 28 didst..deliver them according to thy m.
9. 31 for thy great mercies' sake thou didst not

Psa. 25. 6 Remember, O LORD, thy tender mercies
40. 11 Withhold not thou thy tender mercies fr.
51. 1 acc. unto the multitude of thy tender merc.
69. 16 acc. to the multitude of thy tender mercies
77. 9 hath he in anger shut up his tender mer.
79. 8 let thy tender mercies speedily prevent us
103. 4 with loving kindness and tender mercies
119. 77 Let thy tender mercies come unto me, that
119. 156 Great (are) thy tender mercies, O LORD
145. 9 his tender mercies (are) over all his works
Prov. 12. 10 the tender mercies of the wicked (are) cruel
Isa. 54. 7 but with great mercies will I gather thee
63. 7 according to his mercies, and according
63. 15 the sounding..of thy mercies toward me?
Jer. 16. 5 my peace..loving kindness and mercies
42. 12 I will show mercies unto you, that he may
Dan 9. 9 To the Lord our God (belong) mercies and
9. 18 our righteousnesses, but for thy great m.
Hos. 2. 19 unto me..in loving kindness, and in mer.
Zech. 1. 16 I am returned to Jerusalem with mercies

3. *The kindnesses, judgments,* τὰ ὅσια *ta hosia.*
Acts 13. 34 I will give you the sure mercies of David

MERCIFUL (kindness) —

1. *Pity,* חֶמְלָה *chemlah.*
Gen. 19. 16 the LORD being merciful unto him: and

2. *Kindness,* חֶסֶד *chesed.*
1 Ki. 20. 31 the kings of the house of Israel (are) me.
Psa. 117. 2 his merciful kindness is great toward us
119. 76 Let, I pray thee, thy merciful kindness be
Prov 11. 17 The merciful man doeth good to his own
Isa. 57. 1 merciful men (are) taken away, none con.

3. *Kind,* חָסִיד *chasid.*
2 Sa. 22. 26 With the merciful..wilt show thyself m.
Psa. 18. 25 With the merciful..wilt show thyself m.
Jer. 3. 12 I (am) merciful, saith the LORD..I will not

4. *Pitiful, merciful,* רַחוּם *rachum.*
Exod 34. 6 The LORD God, merciful and gracious, lo.
Deut. 4. 31 For the LORD thy God (is) a merciful God
2 Ch. 30. 9 LORD your God (is) gracious and merciful
Neh. 9. 17 a God ready to pardon, gracious and me.
9. 31 for thou (art) a gracious and merciful God
Psa. 103. 8 The LORD (is) merciful and gracious, slow
Joel 2. 13 he (is) gracious and merciful, slow to anger
Jon. 4. 2 thou (art) a gracious God, and merciful

5. *To love, pity, be merciful,* רָחַם *racham,* 3.
Psa. 116. 5 and righteous; yea, our God (is) merciful

6. *Kind, compassionate,* ἐλεήμων *eleēmōn.*
Matt. 5. 7 Blessed (are) the merciful: for they shall
Heb. 2. 17 that he might be a merciful and faithful

7. *Kind, propitious,* ἵλεως *hileōs.*
Heb. 8. 12 I will be merciful to their unrighteousness

8. *Pitiful,* οἰκτίρμων *oiktirmōn.*
Luke 6. 36 Be ye..merciful, as your Father..is mer

MERCIFUL, to be (or show self) —

1. *To be gracious, inclined to,* חָנַן *chanan.*
Psa. 26. 11 redeem me, and be merciful unto me
37. 26 (He is) ever merciful, and lendeth; and
41. 4 be merciful unto me: heal my soul; for I
41. 10 be merciful unto me, and raise me up, that
56. 1 Be merciful unto me, O God; for man w.
57. 1 Be merciful unto me, O God, be merciful
59. 5 be not merciful to any wicked transgress.
67. 1 God be merciful unto us, and bless us; (and)
86. 3 Be merciful unto me, O Lord: for I cry
119. 58 be merciful unto me according to thy word
119. 132 be merciful unto me, as thou usest to do

2. *To cover, pardon,* כָּפַר *kaphar,* 3.
Deut 21. 8 Be merciful, O LORD, unto thy people I.
32. 43 will be merciful unto his land..to his p.

3. *To show self kind,* חָסַד *chasad,* 7.
2 Sa. 22. 26 thou wilt show thyself merciful..with the
Psa. 18. 25 thou wilt show thyself merciful; with an

4. *To be propitious, appeased,* ἱλάσκομαι *hilaskomai.*
Luke 18. 13 saying, God be merciful to me a sinner

MER-CU-RI'-US, Ἑρμῆς *Hermēs.*
One of the false gods of Greece and Rome, their messenger, and patron of eloquence and trade.
Acts 14. 12 they called..Paul, M., because he was the

MERCY —

1. *Kindness, loving kindness,* חֶסֶד *chesed.*
Gen. 19. 19 thou hast magnified thy mercy, which thou
24. 27 not left destitute my master of his mercy
32. 10 not worthy of the least of all the mercies
39. 21 showed him mercy, and gave him favour
Exod 15. 13 Thou in thy mercy hast led forth the peo.
20. 6 showing mercy unto thousands of them
34. 7 Keeping mercy for thousands, forgiving
Num 14. 18 The LORD (is)..of great mercy, forgiving
14. 19 according unto the greatness of thy mercy
Deut. 5. 10 showing mercy unto thousands of them
7. 9 which keepeth covenant and mercy with
7. 12 thy God shall keep unto thee..the mercy
Judg. 1. 24 into the city, and we will show thee mercy
2 Sa. 7. 15 But my mercy shall not depart away from
15. 20 return thou..mercy and truth (be) with
22. 51 showeth mercy to his anointed, unto D.
1 Ki. 3. 6 Thou hast showed..great mercy, accord.
8. 23 who keepest covenant and mercy with thy
1 Ch. 16. 34 give thanks..for his mercy (endureth)
16. 41 thanks..because his mercy (endureth)
17. 13 I will not take my mercy away from him
2 Ch. 1. 8 Thou hast showed great mercy unto David
5. 13 (he is) good; for his mercy (endureth) for
2 Ch. 6. 14 mercy unto thy servants that walk before
6. 42 remember the mercies of David thy serv.
7. 3 (he is) good; for his mercy (endureth) for
7. 6 because his mer. (endureth) for ever, when
20. 21 Praise the LORD; for his mercy (endureth)
Ezra 3. 11 his mercy (endureth) for ever toward Is.
7. 28 hath extended mercy unto me before the
9. 9 hath extended mercy unto us in the sight
Neh. 1. 5 that keepeth covenant and mercy for them
9. 32 God, who keepest covenant and mercy, let
13. 22 according to the greatness of thy mercy
Job 37. 13 for correction, or for his land, or for mercy
Psa. 5. 7 thy house in the multitude of thy mercy
6. 4 Return..oh save me for thy mercies' sake
13. 5 I have trusted in thy mercy; my heart
18. 50 showeth mercy to his anointed, to David
21. 7 through the mercy of the most High he
23. 6 Surely goodness and mercy shall follow
25. 7 according to thy mercy remember thou
25. 10 All the paths of the LORD (are) mercy and
31. 7 I will be glad and rejoice in thy mercy
31. 16 thy servant: save me for thy mercies' sake
32. 10 he that trusteth..mercy shall compass
33. 18 fear him, upon them that hope in his m.
33. 22 Let thy mercy, O LORD, be upon us, acc.
36. 5 Thy mercy, O LORD, (is) in the heavens
44. 26 Arise..and redeem us for thy mercies' s.
52. 8 I trust in the mercy of God for ever and
57. 3 God shall send forth his mercy and his t.
57. 10 For thy mercy (is) great unto the heavens
59. 10 The God of my mercy shall prevent me
59. 16 I will sing aloud of thy mercy in the mo.
59. 17 God (is) my defence..the God of my me.
61. 7 O prepare mercy and truth, (which) may
62. 12 Also unto thee, O Lord, (belongeth) me.
66. 20 God..hath not turned..his mercy from
69. 13 in the multitude of thy mercy hear me, in
77. 8 Is his mercy clean gone for ever? doth (his)
85. 7 Show us thy mercy, O LORD, and grant us
85. 10 Mercy and truth are met together; right.
86. 5 plenteous in mercy unto all them that c.
86. 13 great (is) thy mercy toward me; and thou
86. 15 thou..a God..plenteous in mercy and
89. 1 I will sing of the mercies of the LORD for
89. 2 Mercy shall be built up for ever: thy fai.
89. 14 mercy and truth shall go before thy face
89. 24 my faithfulness and my mercy (shall be)
89. 28 My mercy will I keep for him for everm.
90. 14 O satisfy us early with thy mercy; that
94. 18 My foot slippeth; thy mercy, O LORD, h.
98. 3 He hath remembered his mercy and his
100. 5 the LORD (is) good; his mercy (is) everla.
101. 1 I will sing of mercy and judgment: unto
103. 8 LORD..slow to anger, and plenteous in m.
103. 11 great is his mercy toward them that fear
103. 17 the mercy of the LORD (is) from everlast.
106. 1 (he is) good: for his mercy (endureth) for
106. 7 remembered not the multitude of thy m.
106. 45 according to the multitude of his mercies
107. 1 (he is) good; for his mercy (endureth) for
108. 4 thy mercy (is) great above the heavens, and
109. 12 Let there be none to extend mercy unto
109. 16 he remembered not to show mercy, but
109. 21 because thy mercy (is) good, deliver thou
109. 26 Help.. save me according to thy mercy
115. 1 glory, for thy mercy..for thy truth's sake
118. 1, 2, 3, 4, 29 his mercy (endureth) for ever
119. 41 Let thy mercies come also unto me, O L.
119. 64 The earth, O LORD, is full of thy mercy
119. 124 Deal with thy servant acc. unto thy me.
130. 7 for with the LORD (there is) mercy, and
136. 1, 2, 3, 4, 5, 6, 7 for his mercy (endureth) for
[So in v. 8, 9, 10, 11, 12, 13, 14, 15, 16, 17, 18, 19, 20, 21, 22, 23, 24, 25, 26.]
138. 8 thy mercy, O LORD, (endureth) for ever
143. 12 of thy mercy cut off mine enemies, and
145. 8 The LORD..slow to anger, and of great m.
147. 11 pleasure..in those that hope in his mercy
Prov. 3. 3 Let not mercy and truth forsake thee
14. 22 mercy and truth (shall be) to them that
16. 6 By mercy and truth iniquity is purged; and
20. 28 Mercy and truth preserve the king
20. 28 and his throne is upholden by mercy
21. 21 He that followeth after..mercy findeth
Isa. 16. 5 in mercy shall the throne be established
55. 3 covenant with you..the sure mercies of
Jer. 33. 11 for the LORD (is) good; for his mercy
Lam. 3. 22 (It is of) the LORD'S mercies that we are
3. 32 according to the multitude of his mercies
Dan. 9. 4 keeping the covenant and mercy to them
Hos. 4. 1 no truth, nor mercy, nor knowledge of God
6. 6 I desired mercy, and not sacrifice; and the
10. 12 Sow..in righteousness, reap in mercy; br.
12. 6 keep mercy and judgment, and wait on
Jon. 2. 8 They that observe..forsake their own m.
Mic. 6. 8 to do justly, and to love mercy, and to walk
7. 18 he retaineth not..he delighteth (in) mercy
7. 20 Thou wilt perform..the mercy to Abraham
Zech. 7. 9 show mercy and compassions every man

2. *To love, pity, be merciful,* רָחַם *racham,* 3.
Hab. 3. 2 make known; in wrath remember mercy

3. *Bowels, mercies,* רַחֲמִים *rachamim.*
Gen. 43. 14 God Almighty give..mercy before the m.
Deut 13. 17 the LORD may turn..and show thee mercy
Neh. 1. 11 grant him mercy in the sight of this man
Isa. 47. 6 thou didst show them no mercy; upon the

4. *Kindness, beneficence,* ἔλεος *eleos.*
Matt. 9. 13 I will have [mercy], and not sacrifice: for
12. 7 I will have [mercy], and not sacrifice, ye
23. 23 (matters) of the law, judgment, [mercy]
Luke 1. 50 his mercy (is) on them that fear him from
1. 54 He hath holpen..in remembrance of (his)
1. 58 the Lord had showed great mercy upon
1. 72 To perform the mercy (promised) to our
1. 78 Through the tender mercy of our God, w.
10. 37 And he said, He that showed mercy on him
Rom. 9. 23 on the vessels of mercy, which he had afore
11. 31 through your mercy they also may obtain
15. 9 the Gentiles might glorify God for (his) m.
Gal. 6. 16 peace (be) on them, and mercy, and upon
Eph. 2. 4 God, who is rich in mercy, for his great love
1 Ti. 1. 2 Grace, mercy, (and) peace, from God our
2 Ti. 1. 2 Grace, mercy, (and) peace from God the
1. 16 The Lord give mercy unto the house of
1. 18 that he may find mercy of the Lord in that
Titus 1. 4 Grace, mercy, (and) peace, from God the F.
3. 5 according to his [mercy] he saved us, by
Heb. 4. 16 that we may obtain [mercy], and find grace
Jas. 2. 13 have judgment..that hath showed no m.
2. 13 and mercy rejoiceth against judgment
3. 17 full of mercy and good fruits, without p.
1 Pe. 1. 3 which according to his abundant mercy
2 Jo. 3 Grace be with you, mercy, (and) peace
Jude 2 Mercy unto you, and peace, and love, be
21 looking for the mercy of our Lord Jesus

5. *Pity, merciful compassion,* οἰκτιρμός *oiktirmos.*
Rom 12. 1 I beseech you..by the mercies of God, that
2 Co. 1. 3 the Father of mercies, and the God of all
Phil. 2. 1 if any fellowship..if any bowels and me.
Col. 3. 12 Put on therefore..bowels of mercies, kind.
Heb. 10. 28 died without mercy under two or three

MERCY on or upon, to find, have, obtain, receive, show —

1. *To be gracious, inclined to,* חָנַן *chanan.*
Deut. 7. 2 no covenant with them, nor show mercy
Psa. 4. 1 have mercy upon me, and hear my prayer
6. 2 Have mercy upon me, O LORD; for I (am)
9. 13 Have mercy upon me, O LORD; consider
25. 16 Turn thee unto me, and have mercy upon
27. 7 have mercy also upon me, and answer me
30. 10 Hear, O LORD, and have mercy upon me
31. 9 Have mercy upon me, O LORD, for I am
37. 21 the righteous showeth mercy, and giveth
51. 1 Have mercy upon me, O God, according
86. 16 O turn unto me, and have mercy upon me
123. 2 God, until that he have mercy upon us
123. 3 Have mercy upon us, O LORD, have mercy u.
Prov 14. 31 he that honoureth him hath mercy on the

2. *To be gracious, inclined to,* חָנַן *chanan,* 3a.
Prov 14. 21 he that hath mercy on the poor, happy (is)

3. *To be gracious, inclined to,* חָנַן *chanan.*
Dan. 4. 27 break off..thine iniquities by showing m.

4. *To love, pity, be merciful,* רָחַם *racham,* 3.
Exod 33. 19 will show mercy on whom I will show m.
Psa. 102. 13 Thou shalt arise, (and) have mercy upon
Isa. 9. 17 neither shall have mercy on their father.
14. 1 the LORD will have mercy on Jacob, and
27. 11 he that made them will not have mercy on
30. 18 exalted, that he may have mercy upon
49. 10 he that hath mercy on them shall lead
49. 13 LORD..will have mercy upon his afflicted
54. 8 with everlasting kindness will I have m. o.
54. 10 saith the LORD that hath mercy on thee
55. 7 return..and he will have mercy upon him
60. 10 in my favour have I had mercy on thee
Jer. 6. 23 they (are) cruel, and have no mercy; their
13. 14 I will not pity, nor spare, nor have mercy
21. 7 he shall not..have pity, nor have mercy
30. 18 and have mercy on his dwelling places
31. 20 I will surely have mercy upon him, saith
33. 26 I will cause..to return, and have mercy on
42. 12 I will show mercies unto you, that he
42. 12 that he may have mercy upon you, and
50. 42 they (are) cruel, and will not show mercy
Eze. 39. 25 have mercy upon the whole house of Isr.
Hos. 1. 6 I will no more have mercy upon the house
1. 7 I will have mercy upon the house of Judah
2. 4 I will not have mercy upon her children
2. 23 I will have mercy upon her that had not
Zech. 1. 12 how long wilt thou not have mercy on J.
10. 6 for I have mercy upon them: and they s.

5. *To be loved, pitied, find pity,* רָחַם *racham,* 4.
Prov 28. 13 confesseth and forsaketh..shall have me.
Hos. 2. 23 upon her that had not obtained mercy
14. 3 for in thee the fatherless findeth mercy

6. *To be kind, beneficent,* ἐλεέω *eleeō.*
Matt. 5. 7 the merciful: for they shall obtain mercy
9. 27 saying, (Thou) son of David, have mercy on
15. 22 Have mercy on me, O Lord (thou) son
17. 15 Lord, have mercy on my son: for he is l.
20. 30, 31 Have mercy on us, O Lord, (thou) son
Mark 10. 47, 48 (Thou) son of David, have mercy on me
Luke 16. 24 Father Abraham, have mercy on me, and
17. 13 and said, Jesus, Master, have mercy on us
18. 38, 39 (thou) son of David, have mercy on me
Rom. 9. 15 I will have mercy on whom I will have m.
9. 16 nor of him..but of God that showeth me.
9. 18 Therefore hath he mercy on whom he will
11. 30 yet have now obtained mercy through th.
11. 31 Even so..that..they also may obtain m.
11. 32 concluded..that he might have mercy upon
12. 8 he that showeth mercy, with cheerfulness
1 Co. 7. 25 as one that hath obtained mercy of the
2 Co. 4. 1 as we have received mercy, we faint not
Phil. 2. 27 God had mercy on him; and not on him
1 Ti. 1. 13 I obtained mercy, because I did (it) igno.
1. 16 for this cause I obtained mercy, that in
1 Pe. 2. 10 had not obt. mercy, but now have obt. m.

MERCY, of tender —
Tender, pitiful, οἰκτίρμων *oiktirmōn.*
Jas. 5. 11 the Lord is very pitiful, and of tender m.

MERCY, without —
Without kindness, ἀνίλεως *anileōs.*
Jas. 2. 13 he shall have judgment [without mercy]

MERCY SEAT —
1. *A lid, place of covering (sin),* כַּפֹּרֶת *kapporeth.*
Exod 25. 17 thou shalt make a mercy seat (of) pure g.
25. 18 cherubim..in the two ends of the mercy s.
25. 19 of the mercy seat shall ye make the che.
25. 20 covering the mercy seat..toward the m. s.
25. 21 thou shalt put the mercy seat above upon
25. 22 commune with thee from above the m. s.
26. 34 thou shalt put the mercy seat upon the
30. 6 before the mercy seat that (is) over the
31. 7 the mercy seat that (is) thereupon, and
35. 12 (with) the mercy seat, and the veil of the
37. 6 And he made the mercy seat (of) pure g.
37. 7 cherubim..on the two ends of the mercy s.
37. 8 out of the mercy seat made he the cher.
37. 9 over the mercy seat..to the mercy seat
39. 35 and the staves thereof, and the mercy seat
40. 20 and put the mercy seat above upon the
Lev. 16. 2 within the veil before the mercy seat, wh.
16. 2 I will appear in the cloud upon the m. s.
16. 13 cloud of the incense may cover the m. s.
16. 14 upon the mercy seat..before the mercy s.
16. 15 upon the mercy seat, and before the m. s.
Num. 7. 89 from off the mercy seat that (was) upon
1 Ch.28. 11 the pattern..of the place of the mercy s.
2. *Place of propitiation, or appeasement,* ἱλαστήριον.
Heb. 9. 5 cherubim of glory shadowing the mercy s.

ME'-RED, מֶרֶד, מָרֶד *bold, rebellious.*
A son of Ezra, a descendant of Judah, through Caleb son of Jephunneh. B.C. 1400.
1 Ch. 4. 17 the sons of Ezra (were) Jether, and M., and
4. 18 these (are) the sons of Bithiah..which M.

ME-RE'-MOTH, מְרֵמוֹת *strong, firm.*
1 The son of Uriah the priest who weighed the gold and silver vessels he had brought. B.C. 457.
Ezra 8. 33 M. the son of Uriah the priest; and with
Neh. 3. 4 next unto them repaired M. the son of U.
3. 21 After him repaired M. the son of Urijah the
2. One of the family of Bani that had taken a strange wife. B.C. 456.
Ezra 10. 36 Vaniah, M., Eliashib
3. A priest who, with Nehemiah, sealed the covenant. B.C. 457.
Neh. 10. 5 Harim, M Obadiah
12. 3 Shechaniah, Rehum, M.

ME'-RES, מֶרֶס *worthy.*
One of the seven princes of Persia and Media that saw the king's face at pleasure. B C 520.
Esth. 1. 14 M., Marsena, (and) Memucan, the seven

ME-RI'-BAH, מְרִיבָה, (מְרִיבַת קָדֵשׁ) *strife, contention.*
A place in Rephidim between Sin and Sinai, at Kadesh-barnea, where Moses struck the rock and water flowed out. B C. 1491.
Exod.17. 7 he called the name of the place..M , be
Num 20. 13 This (is) the water of M ; because the c.
20. 24 because ye rebelled..at the water of M
27. 14 that (is) the water of M. in Kadesh in the
Deut 32. 51 the waters of M.-Kadesh, in the wilderness
33. 8 thou didst strive at the waters of M.
Psa. 81. 7 I proved thee at the waters of M. Selah.

ME-RIB BA'-AL, מְרִי בַעַל, מְרִיב בַּעַל, מְרִי בְּבַעַל.
Son of Jonathan son of Saul, and father of Micah. B.C. 1020.
1 Ch. 8. 34 the son of Jonathan (was) M. ; and M. be.
9. 40 the son of Jonathan (was) M. : and M. be.

ME-RO'-DACH, מְרֹדַךְ *bold.*
A Babylonian idol, the god of war Compare *Evil-Merodach* and also *Merodach-baladan*
Jer. 50. 2 Bel is confounded, M. is broken in pieces

ME-RO-DACH BA-LA'-DAN, מְראֹדַךְ בַּלְאֲדָן.
The king of Babylon in the days of Hezekiah. B.C. 712. See *Berodach-baladan.*
Isa. 39. 1 At that time M., the son of Baladan, king

ME'-ROM, מֵרוֹם *high place.*
The district in which lies a small lake N. of Cinneroth, nearer the springs of Jordan.
Josh. 11. 5 pitched together at the waters of M., to
11. 7 J. came..against them by the waters of M.

ME-RO-NO-THITE, מֵרֹנֹתִי.
An inhabitant of a district in Zebulun. Compare *Shimron-meron.*
1 Ch.27. 30 and over the asses (was) Jehdeiah the M.
Neh. 3. 7 next unto them repaired..Jadon the M.

ME'-ROZ, מֵרוֹז.
A place N. of Mount Tabor, near the lake of Merom.
Judg. 5. 23 Curse ye M., said the angel of the LORD

MERRILY, MERRY —
1. *Praised things,* הִלּוּלִים *hillulim.*
Judg. 9. 27 made merry, and went into the house of
2. *Good,* טוֹב *tob.*
Judg 16. 25 when their hearts were merry, that they
1 Sa. 25. 36 and Nabal's heart (was) merry within him
2 Sa. 13. 28 when Amnon's heart is merry with wine
2 Ch. 7. 10 glad and merry in heart for the goodness
Esth. 1. 10 when the heart of the king was merry with
Prov.15. 15 he that is of a merry heart (hath) a contin.
Eccl. 9. 7 drink thy wine with a merry heart; for G.
3. *Rejoicing,* שָׂמֵחַ *sameach.*
Esth. 5. 14 then go thou in merrily with the king unto
Prov 15. 13 A merry heart maketh a cheerful counte.
17. 22 A merry heart doeth good (like) a medicine

MERRY, to be —
1. *To be or become good, glad,* יָטַב *yatab.*
Judg 19. 6 Be content..and let thine heart be merry
19. 9 lodge here, that thine heart may be merry
Ruth 3. 7 And when..his heart was merry, he went
1 Ki.21. 7 eat bread, and let thine heart be merry
2. *To rejoice,* שָׂמַח *sameach.*
Eccl. 8. 15 than to eat, and to drink, and to be merry
3. *To be cheerful, merry,* שָׁכַר *shakar.*
Gen. 43. 34 And they drank, and were merry with him
4. *To be of good courage,* εὐθυμέω *euthumeō.*
Jas. 5. 13 let him pray. Is any merry? let him sing
5. *To have an easy mind, be merry,* εὐφραίνομαι.
Luke12. 19 take thine ease, eat, drink, (and) be merry
15. 23 and kill (it); and let us eat, and be merry
15. 24 is found. And they began to be merry

MERRY, to make —
1. *To do good, make glad,* יָטַב *yatab,* 5.
Judg19. 22 as they were making their hearts merry
2. *To gladden, life,* שָׂמַח חַיִּים *sameach* (3) *chayim.*
Eccl.10. 19 wine maketh merry: but money answereth
3. *To have an easy mind, be merry,* εὐφραίνομαι.
Luke15. 29 that I might make merry with my friends
15. 32 It was meet that we should make merry
Rev. 11. 10 shall rejoice over them, and make merry

MERRY, (making) —
Becoming glad, rejoicing, שָׂמֵחַ *sameach.*
1 Ki. 4. 20 eating and drinking, and making merry

MERRY, that make —
To laugh, deride, play, rejoice, שָׂחַק *sachaq,* 3.
Jer. 30. 19 and the voice of them that make merry
31. 4 in the dances of them that make merry

MERRY HEARTED —
Rejoicing of heart, שְׂמֵחַ לֵב [*sameach*].
Isa. 24. 7 the vine languisheth, all the merry hear.

ME'-SHA, מֵישַׁע, מֵישָׁע *freedom.*
1. A king of Moab in the days of Ahab, Ahaziah, and Jehoram, kings of Israel, who rebelled against Ahaziah. B.C. 896.
2 Ki. 3. 4 And M. king of Moab was a sheep master
2. Eldest son of Caleb, brother of Jerahmeel, and grand-son of Pharez. B.C. 1540.
1 Ch. 2. 42 the sons of Caleb..(were) M. his first born

ME'-SHA, מֵשָׁא, מֵישָׁא.
1. A place in Yemen, or S.E. Arabia.
Gen. 10. 30 their dwelling was from M., as thou goest
2. A Benjamite. B.C. 1350.
1 Ch. 8. 9 And he begat..Zibia, and M., and Malcham

ME'-SHACH, מֵישַׁךְ.
The name given to Michael, one of Daniel's companions, by the chief of Nebuchadnezzar's eunuchs. B.C. 600.
Dan. 1. 7 he gave..(the name)..of M.; and to Azariah
2. 49 he set Shadrach, M., and Abed-nego, over
3. 12 Shadrach, M., and Abed-nego; these men
3. 13 commanded to bring Shadrach, M., and
3. 14 (Is it) true, O Shadrach, M., and Abed-nego
3. 16 Shadrach, M., and Abed-nego, answered
3. 19 visage was changed against Shadrach, M.
3. 20 he commanded..to bind Shadrach, M., and
3. 22 those men that took up Shadrach, M., and
3. 23 Shadrach, M., and Abed-nego, fell down
3. 26 said, Shadrach, M., and Abed-nego, ye se.
3. 26 Shadrach, M., and Abed-nego, came forth
3. 28 Blessed (be) the God of Shadrach, M., and
3. 29 the God of Shadrach, M., and Abed-nego
3. 30 the king promoted Shadrach, M., and A.

ME'-SHECH, ME'-SECH, מֶשֶׁךְ.
1. A son of Japheth. B C. 2320.
Gen. 10. 2 The sons of Japheth; Gomer..and M., and
1 Ch. 1. 5 The sons of Japheth; Gomer..and M., and
2. A son of Shem. B.C. 2320.
1 Ch. 1. 17 sons of Shem; Elam..and Gether, and M.
3. A tribe joined with Kedar.
Psa.120. 5 Woe is me, that I sojourn in M., (that)
4. The descendants of the son of Japheth, the Moschi or *Mosochi.*
Eze. 27. 13 Javan, Tubal, and M., they (were) thy m.
32. 26 There (is) M., Tubal, and all her multitude
38. 2 set thy face against..M. and Tubal, and
38. 3 Gog, the chief prince of M. and 39. 1

ME-SHE-LEM'-IAH, מְשֶׁלֶמְיָהוּ, מְשֶׁלֶמְיָה *Jah recompenses.*
A Kohathite whose son Zechariah was a gate keeper of the tabernacle. B.C. 470.
1 Ch. 9. 21 Zechariah the son of M. (was) porter of
26. 1 Of the Korhites (was) M. the son of Kore
26. 2 And the sons of M. (were) Zechariah the
26. 9 And M. had sons and brethren, strong men

ME-SHE-ZAB'-EEL, מְשֵׁיזַבְאֵל *God is deliverer.*
1. One whose descendant, Meshullam, helped to repair the wall. B.C. 506.
Neh. 3. 4 the son of Berechiah, the son of M. And
2. A person or family that, with Nehemiah, sealed the covenant. B.C. 445.
Neh. 10. 21 M., Zadok, Jaddua
11. 24 Pethahiah the son of M., of the children

ME-SHIL-LE'-MITH, מְשִׁלֵּמִית *recompense.*
A priest whose descendants dwelt in Jerusalem. B.C. 500.
1 Ch. 9. 12 Meshullam, the son of M., the son of Im.

ME-SHIL-LE'-MOTH, מְשִׁלֵּמוֹת *recompenses.*
1. An Ephraimite whose son Berechiah opposed making slaves of the Jewish captives. B.C. 770.
2 Ch.28. 12 Berechiah the son of M., and Jehizkiah
2. A priest of the family of Immer, whose descendant Amashai dwelt in Jerusalem. B.C. 500.
Neh. 11. 13 the son of Ahasai, the son of M., the son of

ME-SHO'-BAB, מְשׁוֹבָב *returned, delivered.*
A Simeonite. B.C. 800.
1 Ch. 4. 34 And M., and Jamlech, and Joshah the son

ME-SHUL'-LAM, מְשֻׁלָּם *associate, friend.*
1. Grandfather of Shaphan, a scribe in the days of king Josiah. B.C. 700.
2 Ki.22. 3 the son of Azaliah, the son of M., the scr.
2. A descendant of Jeconiah, son of Jehoiakim king of Judah. B.C. 520.
1 Ch. 3. 19 the sons of Zerubbabel; M., and Hananiah
3. The head of a Gadite family. B.C. 1070.
1 Ch. 5. 13 And their brethren..(were) Michael, and M.
4. A Benjamite of the family of Elpaal. B.C. 1300.
1 Ch. 8. 17 And Zebadiah, and M., and Hezeki, and
5. A Benjamite of the family of Hasenuah, whose son dwelt in Jerusalem. B.C. 470.
1 Ch. 9. 7 Sallu the son of M., the son of Hodaviah
6. A Benjamite of the family of Shephatiah who dwelt in Jerusalem. B.C. 510.
1 Ch. 9. 8 and M. the son of Shephathiah, the son
7. An Aaronite of the family of Zadok, whose descendants dwelt in Jerusalem. B.C. 500.
1 Ch. 9. 11 Hilkiah, the son of M., the son of Zadok
Neh. 11. 11 Hilkiah, the son of M., the son of Zadok
8. A priest, ancestor of a family that dwelt in Jerusalem. B.C. 470.
1 Ch. 9. 12 Jahzerah, the son of M., the son of Mesh.
9. A Kohathite appointed to oversee the repairs of the temple by Josiah. B.C. 640.
2 Ch.34. 12 Zechariah and M., of the sons of the Koh.
10. A chief man who returned with Ezra. B.C. 457.
Ezra 8. 16 Then sent I for Eliezer..and for M., chief
11. One who assisted in taking account of those who had taken strange wives. B.C. 457.
Ezra 10. 15 M. and Shabbethai the Levite helped them
12. A son of Bani who had taken a strange wife. B.C. 456.
Ezra 10. 29 of the sons of Bani; M., Malluch, and
13. A person who rebuilt two portions of the wall. B.C. 445.
Neh. 3. 4 next unto them repaired M. the son of
3. 30 After him repaired M. the son of Berech.
6. 18 Johanan had taken the daughter of M.
14. Another who repaired a portion. B.C. 445.
Neh. 3. 6 and M. the son of Besodeiah; they laid
15. A prince, priest, or Levite who stood beside Ezra. B.C. 457.
Neh. 8. 4 on his left hand..Zechariah, (and) M.
16. A priest who sealed the covenant with Nehemiah. B.C. 445.
Neh.10. 7 M., Abijah, Mijamin.
17. A chief man who sealed the covenant with Nehemiah. B.C. 445.
Neh. 10. 20 Magpiash, M., Hezir.
18. A Benjamite whose descendants dwelt in Jerusalem. B.C. 470.
Neh. 11. 7 Sallu the son of M., the son of Joed
19. A priest of the family of Ezra who assisted in the dedication of the wall. B.C. 470.
Neh. 12. 13 Of Ezra, M.; of Amariah, Jehohanan
12. 33 And Azariah, Ezra, and M.
20. One of the family of Ginnethon in the days of Joiakim the priest. B.C. 445.
Neh. 12. 16 Of Iddo, Zechariah; of Ginnethon, M.
21. A Levite and gate keeper for the sanctuary after the exile. B.C. 445.
Neh. 12. 25 M., Talmon, Akkub, (were) porters, keep

ME-SHUL-LE'-METH, מְשֻׁלֶּמֶת.
Wife of Manasseh, and mother of Amon, kings of Judah, and daughter of Haruz of Jotbah. B.C. 670.
2 Ki. 21. 19 And his mother's name (was) M., the da.

ME-SO-BA-ITE, מְצֹבָיָה.
The patronymic of Jasiel, one of David's valiant men; place unknown. B.C. 1048.
1 Ch.11. 47 Eliel, and Obed, and Jasiel the M.

ME-SO-PO-TAM'-IA, אֲרַם נַהֲרַיִם Μεσοποταμία.
The country between the Tigris and Euphrates, on the N.W. of Babylonia and S.W. of Assyria. See *Aram-Naharaim.* It passed successively under the Babylonians, the Medes, and the Persians; after the battle of Issus, B.C. 333, it came under the Macedonians; in A.D. 165 under the Romans; in 363 under the Persians; in 902 under the Carmathians; and in 1514 under the Turks, who still possess it.

Gen. 24. 10 he arose, and went to M., unto the city of
Deut 23. 4 Balaam the son of Beor of Pethor of M.
Judg. 3. 8 the hand of Chushanrishathaim king of M.
3. 10 the LORD delivered..king of M. into his
1 Ch.19. 6 chariots and horsemen out of M., and out
Acts 2. 9 dwellers in M., and in Judea, and Cappa.
7. 2 Abraham, when he was in M., before he

MESS —
Lifting, burden, gift, מַשְׂאֵת *maseth.*
Gen. 43. 34 he took (and sent) messes unto them from
43. 34 Benjamin's mess was five times so much
2 Sa. 11. 8 and there followed him a mess (of meat)

MESSAGE —
1. *Word, thing, matter,* דָּבָר *dabar.*
Judg. 3. 20 I have a message from God unto thee
1 Ki. 20. 12 when (Ben-hadad) heard this message, as
Prov 26. 6 He that sendeth a message by the hand of

2. *Message,* מַלְאֲכוּת *malakuth.*
Hag. 1. 13 spake..in the LORD'S message unto the p.

3. *Message,* ἀγγελία *aggelia.*
1 Jo. 3. 11 this is the message that ye heard from the

4. *Message, promise,* ἐπαγγελία *epaggelia.*
1 Jo. 1. 5 This then is [the message] which we have

5. *Embassy,* πρεσβεία *presbeia.*
Luke 19. 14 sent a message after him, saying, We w.

MESSENGER —
1. *To tell (good) news,* בָּשַׂר *basar,* 3.
1 Sa. 4. 17 the messenger answered and said, Israel is

2. *Messenger,* מַלְאָךְ *malak.*
Gen. 32. 3 Jacob sent messengers before him to Esau
32. 6 the messengers returned to Jacob, saying
Num20. 14 And Moses sent messengers from Kadesh
21. 21 And Israel sent messengers unto Sihon
22. 5 He sent messengers therefore unto Balaam
24. 12 Spake I not also to thy messengers which
Deut. 2. 26 And I sent messengers out of the wilderne.
Josh. 6. 17 because she hid the messengers that we
6. 25 because she hid the messengers which
7. 22 So Joshua sent messengers, and they ran
Judg. 6. 35 And he sent messengers throughout all
6. 35 and he sent messengers unto Asher, and
7. 24 And Gideon sent messengers throughout
9. 31 And he sent messengers unto Abimelech
11. 12 And Jephthah sent messengers unto the
11. 13 answered unto the messengers of Jepht.
11. 14 And Jephthah sent messengers again unto
11. 17 Then Israel sent messengers unto the king
11. 19 And Israel sent messengers unto Sihon
1 Sa. 6. 21 And they sent messengers to the inhabita.
11. 3 that we may send messengers unto all the
11. 4 Then came the messengers to Gibeah of
11. 7 by the hands of messengers, saying, Whoso
11. 9 And they said unto the messengers that
11. 9 And the messengers came and showed (it)
16. 19 Wherefore Saul sent messengers unto
19. 11 Saul also sent messengers unto David's
19. 14 And when Saul sent messengers to take
19. 15 And Saul sent the messengers (again) to
19. 16 And when the messengers were come in
19. 20 And Saul sent messengers to take David
19. 20 the spirit of God was upon the messengers
19. 21 he sent other messengers, and they prop.
19. 21 Saul sent messengers again the third time
23. 27 there came a messenger unto Saul, saying
25. 14 David sent messengers out of the wilder.
25. 42 she went after the messengers of David
2 Sa. 2. 5 David sent messengers unto the men of Ja.
3. 12 Abner sent messengers to David on his
3. 14 David sent messengers to Ishbosheth, S.
3. 26 he sent messengers after Abner, which
5. 11 Hiram king of Tyre sent messengers to D.
11. 4 And David sent messengers, and took her
11. 19 charged the messenger, saying, When thou
11. 22 So the messenger went, and came and sh.
11. 23 the messenger said unto David, Surely the
11. 25 Then David said unto the messenger, Thus
12. 27 Joab sent messengers to David, and said
1 Ki.19. 2 Then Jezebel sent a messenger unto Elijah
20. 2 he sent messengers to Ahab king of Israel
20. 5 the messengers came again, and said, Thus
20. 9 Wherefore he said unto the messengers of
20. 9 the messengers departed, and brought him
22. 13 the messenger that was gone to call M.
2 Ki. 1. 2 he sent messengers, and said unto them
1. 3 Arise, go up to meet the messengers of the
1. 5 when the messengers turned back unto him
1. 16 Forasmuch as thou hast sent messengers
5. 10 Elisha sent a messenger unto him, saying
6. 32 ere the messenger came to him, he said
6. 32 when the messenger cometh, shut the door
6. 33 the messenger came down unto him: and
7. 15 the messengers returned, and told the king
9. 18 The messenger came to them, but he co.
10. 8 there came a messenger, and told him
14. 8 Then Amaziah sent messengers to Jehoash
16. 7 So Ahaz sent messengers to Tiglath-Pileser
17. 4 he had sent messengers to So king of Eg.
2 Ki. 19. 9 he sent messengers again unto Hezekiah
19. 14 received the letter of the hand of the m.
19. 23 By thy messengers thou hast reproached
1 Ch.14. 1 Now Hiram king of Tyre sent messengers
19. 2 David sent messengers to comfort him
19. 16 they sent messengers, and drew forth the
2 Ch.18. 12 the messenger that went to call Micaiah
36. 15 sent to them by his messengers, rising up
36. 16 they mocked the messengers of God, and
Neh. 6. 3 I sent messengers unto them, saying, I (am)
Job 1. 14 there came a messenger unto Job, and
33. 23 If there be a messenger with him, an int.
Prov 13. 17 A wicked messenger falleth into mischief
16. 14 The wrath of a king (is as) messengers of
17. 11 a cruel messenger shall be sent against
Isa. 14. 32 What shall (one) then answer the messe.
18. 2 Go, ye swift messengers, to a nation sca.
37. 9 he sent messengers to Hezekiah, saying
37. 14 letter from the hand of the messengers
42. 19 or deaf, as my messenger (that) I sent?
44. 26 performeth the counsel of his messengers
Jer. 27. 3 by the hand of the messengers which come.
Eze. 23. 16 sent messengers unto them into Chaldea
23. 40 unto whom a messenger (was) sent; and
30. 9 In that day shall messengers go forth from
Nah. 2. 13 the voice of thy messengers shall no more
Hag. 1. 13 Then spake Haggai the LORD'S messenger
Mal. 2. 7 he (is) the messenger of the LORD of hosts
3. 1 I will send my messenger, and he shall
3. 1 even the messenger of the covenant, whom

3. *To cause to go before, tell, declare,* נָגַד *nagad,* 5.
2 Sa. 15. 13 there came a messenger to David, saying
Jer. 51. 31 one messenger to meet another, to show

4. *Ambassador,* צִיר *tsir.*
Prov.25. 13 a faithful messenger to them that send
Isa. 57. 9 didst send thy messengers far off, and

5. *Messenger,* ἄγγελος *aggelos.*
Matt11. 10 I send my messenger before thy face, wh.
Mark 1. 2 I send my messenger before thy face, w.
Luke 7. 24 when the messengers of John were dep.
7. 27 I send my messenger before thy face, w.
9. 52 sent messengers before his face: and they
2 Co.12. 7 the messenger of Satan to buffet me, lest
Jas. 2. 25 when she had received the messengers

6. *Apostle, one sent off,* ἀπόστολος *apostolos.*
2 Co. 8. 23 the messengers of the churches..the
Phil. 2. 25 your messenger, and he that ministered

MESSENGER, to send a —
To lay a charge, command, צָוָה *tsavah,* 3.
Gen. 50. 16 they sent a messenger unto Joseph, saying

MES-SI'-AH, מָשִׁיחַ *anointed.*
The prince who was to come as Leader.
Dan. 9. 25 unto the M. the Prince (shall be) seven
9. 26 after threescore and two weeks shall M.

MES-SI'-AS, Μεσσίας Μεσίας *Gr. form of preceding.*
John 1. 41 We have found the M., which is, being in.
4. 25 I know that M. cometh, which is called C.

METE (out), to —
1. *To measure,* מָדַד *madad.*
Exod16. 18 when they did mete (it) with an omer, he

2. *To measure,* מָדַד *madad,* 3.
Psa. 60. 6 I will divide Shechem, and mete out the
108. 7 I will divide Shechem, and mete out the

3. *To weigh, measure,* תָּכַן *takan,* 3.
Isa. 40. 12 Who hath..meted out heaven with the spa.

4. *To measure,* μετρέω *metreō.*
Matt. 7. 2 with what measure ye mete, it shall be m.
Mark 4. 24 with what measure ye mete, it shall be m.
Luke 6. 38 with the same measure that ye mete wit.

METED out —
A line, rule, קַו, קָו *qav.*
Isa. 18. 2, 7 a nation meted out and trodden

METE YARD —
A measure, mete yard, מִדָּה *middah.*
Lev. 19. 35 in judgment, in mete yard, in weight, or

ME-THEG AM'-MAH, מֶתֶג הָאַמָּה *bridle of metropolis.*
A place in Philistia not known.
2 Sa. 8. 1 David took M. out of the hand of the P.

ME-THU-SA'-EL, מְתוּשָׁאֵל.
Son of Mehujael, a descendant of Cain, and father of Lamech. B.C. 3800.
Gen. 4. 18 Mehujael begat M.: and M. begat Lamech

ME-THU-SE'-LAH, מְתוּשֶׁלַח.
Son of Enoch, and grandfather of Noah. B.C. 3317–2348.
Gen. 5. 21 Enoch lived sixty..years, and begat M.
5. 22 Enoch walked with God after he begat M.
5. 25 M. lived an hundred and eighty and seven
5. 26 M. lived after he begat Lamech seven hu.
5. 27 all the days of M. were nine hun.; 1 Ch. 1. 3.

MEUNIM. *See* **MEHUNIM.**

ME ZA'-HAB, מֵי זָהָב *offspring of the shining one.*
Grandfather of Mehetabel, wife of Hadar the eighth king of Edom. B.C. 1500.
Gen.36. 39 the daughter of Matred, the daughter of M.
1 Ch. 1. 50 the daughter of Matred, the daughter of M.

MI-A'-MIN, מִיָּמִן *fortunate.*
1. One of the family of Parosh who had taken a strange wife. B.C. 450.
Ezra 10. 25 of the sons of Parosh; Ramiah..and M.

2. A priest who returned with Zerubbabel. B.C. 536. See *Mijamin.*
Neh.12. 5 M., Maadiah, Bilgah

MIB'-HAR, מִבְחָר *choice, youth.*
A son of Haggeri, and one of David's valiant men. B.C. 1048.
1 Ch.11. 38 Joel the brother of Nathan, M. the son of

MIB'-SAM, מִבְשָׂם *sweet odour.*
1. A son of Ishmael son of Hagar. B.C. 1840.
Gen. 25. 13 the sons of Ishmael..Adbeel, and M.
1 Ch. 1. 29 Nebaioth; then Kedar, and Adbeel, and M.
2. A son of Simeon. B.C. 1200.
1 Ch. 4. 25 Shallum his son, M. his son, Mishma his

MIB'-ZAR, מִבְצָר *fortified.*
A chief of Edom, descendant from Esau. B.C. 1470.
Gen. 36. 42 Duke Kenaz, duke Teman, duke M.
1 Ch. 1. 53 Duke Kenaz, duke Teman, duke M.

MI'-CAH, (MI'-CHAH), מִיכָה.
1. An Ephraimite who hired a Levite to be priest to his image. B.C. 1406.
Judg17. 1 there was a man..whose name (was) M.
17. 4 made..a graven image..in the house of M.
17. 5 the man M. had an house of gods, and
17. 8 he came..to the house of M., as he journ.
17. 9 M. said unto him, Whence comest thou?
17. 10 M. said unto him, Dwell with me, and
17. 12 And M. consecrated the Levite; and the
17. 12 and the young man..was in the house of M.
17. 13 Then said M., Now know I that the LORD
18. 2 when they came to..the house of M., they
18. 3 When they (were) by the house of M., they
18. 4 Thus and thus dealeth M. with me, and
18. 13 And they passed..unto the house of M.
18. 15 and came to the house of..M., and saluted
18. 18 these went into M.'s house, and fetched
18. 22 a good way from the house of M., the men
18. 22 the men..in the houses near to M.'s house
18. 23 they turned their faces, and said unto M.
18. 26 when M. saw that they (were) too strong
18. 27 they took (the things) which M. had made
18. 31 they set them up M.'s graven image, which
2. Head of a family of Reuben. B.C. 1470.
1 Ch. 5. 5 M. his son, Reaia his son, Baal his son
3. The son of Merib-baal the grandson of Saul. B.C. 1020.
1 Ch. 8. 34 And the son of Jonathan..begat M.
8. 35 the sons of M. (were) Pithon, and Melech
9. 40 And the son of Jonathan..begat M.
9. 41 the sons of M. (were) Pithon, and Melech
4. A Levite of the family of Asaph, whose descendants dwelt in Jerusalem. B.C. 480. The Hebrew is מִיכָא, Micha. *See* Micha, No. 3.
1 Ch. 9. 15 Mattaniah the son of M., the son of Zichri
5. A Kohathite. B.C. 1015.
1 Ch. 23. 20 Of the sons of Uzziel; M. the first, and J.
24. 24 of Uzziel; Michah: of the sons of Michah
24. 25 The brother of Michah (was) Isshiah:
6. Father of Abdon whom Josiah sent to inquire of the Lord when the Book of the Law was found. B.C. 642.
2 Ch. 34. 20 the king commanded..Abdon the son of M.
7. A prophet surnamed the Morasthite (from Moresheth Gath), he was nearly contemporary with Hosea and Amos. B.C. 750–700. In Jer. 26. 18, V.L. Michaiah.
Jer. 26. 18 M. the Morasthite prophesied in the days
Mic. 1. 1 came to M. the Morasthite in the days of

MI-CA-I'-AH, מִיכָיְהוּ *who is like Jah?*
A prophet, the son of Imlah, who foretold the fall of Ahab at Ramoth Gilead. B.C. 897.
1 Ki. 22. 8 (There is) yet one man, M. the son of Im.
22. 9 Then the king..said, Hasten (hither) M.
22. 13 the messenger that was gone to call M.
22. 14 And M. said, (As) the LORD liveth, what
22. 15 the king said unto him, M., shall we go
22. 24 But Zedekiah..smote M. on the cheek, and
22. 25 And M. said, Behold, thou shalt see in that
22. 26 Take M., and carry him back unto Amon
22. 28 And M. said, If thou return at all in peace
2 Ch.18. 7 (There is) yet one man..the same (is) M.
18. 8 the king..said, Fetch quickly M. the son
18. 12 the messenger that went to call M. spake
18. 13 And M. said, (As) the LORD liveth, even
18. 14 the king said unto him, M., shall we go to
18. 23 Then Zedekiah..smote M. upon the cheek
18. 24 And M. said, Behold, thou shalt see on
18. 25 Take ye M., and carry him back to Amon
18. 27 And M. said, If thou certainly return in

MI'-CHA, מִיכָא.
1. Son of Mephibosheth, son of Jonathan. B.C. 1020.
2 Sa. 9. 12 a young son, whose name (was) M. And
2. A Levite who sealed the covenant with Nehemiah.
Neh. 10. 11 M., Rehob, Hashabiah
3. A Levite. Neh. 11. 17, 22. *See* Micah, No. 4.

MI-CHA'-EL, מִיכָאֵל Μιχαήλ *who is like God?*
1. An Asherite, father of Sethur whom Moses sent to spy the land. B.C. 1520.
Num13. 13 the tribe of Asher, Sethur the son of M.
2. A Gadite who settled in Bashan. B.C. 1070
1 Ch. 5. 13 And their brethren..(were) M., and Mes.
3. A Gadite. B.C. 1070.
1 Ch. 5. 14 Gilead, the son of M., the son of Jeshishai

4. A Gershonite whose great-grandson Asaph was a chief singer in the temple. B.C. 1100.
1 Ch. 6. 40 M., the son of Baaseiah, the son of Malc.

5. A chief man of Issachar. B.C. 1500.
1 Ch. 7. 3 the sons of Izrahiah; M., and Obadiah

6. A Benjamite, in Jerusalem. B.C. 1350.
1 Ch. 8. 16 And M., and Ispah, and Joha, the sons of

7. A Manassite, who joined David in Ziklag. B.C. 1048.
1 Ch. 12. 20 of Manasseh, Adnah..and M., and Jozabad

8. The father of Omri prince of Issachar. B.C. 1040.
1 Ch. 27. 18 of David: of Issachar; Omri the son of M.

9. A son of Jehoshaphat. B.C. 890.
2 Ch. 21. 2 the sons of Jehoshaphat..M., and Shep.

10. The father of Zebadiah who returned with Ezra. B.C. 470.
Ezra 8. 8 Zebadiah the son of M., and with him four.

11. The messenger of God who came to Daniel, and is called by him prince of the people of Israel. B.C. 530.
Dan. 10. 13 but, lo, M., one of the chief princes, came
10. 21 and (there is) none..but M. your prince
12. 1 at that time shall M. stand up, the great
Jude 9 Yet M. the archangel, when contending
Rev. 12. 7 M. and his angels fought against the dragon

MI-CHA'-IAH, מִיכָיָה, מִיכָיְהוּ, מִכָיְהוּ, מִיכָיהוּ, מִיכָה *who is like J.?*
1. Father of Achbor, a chief officer of king Josiah. B.C. 620.
2 Ki. 22. 12 the king commanded..Achbor the son of M.

2. Daughter of Uriel of Gibeah, wife of Rehoboam, and mother of Abijah. B.C. 960. In 1 Ki. 15. 2 she is called Maachah, daughter of Abishalom, and in 2 Ch. 11. 20 Maachah, daughter of Absalom.
2 Ch. 13. 2 His mother's name also (was) M. the dau.

3. A prince of Judah ordered by Jehoshaphat to teach the people. B.C. 913.
2 Ch. 17. 7 he sent to his princes..to M., to teach

4. A priest of the family of Asaph, one of whose descendants took part in the purification of the wall. B.C. 445.
Neh. 12. 35 Mattaniah, the son of M., the son of Zac.
12. 41 And the priests; Eliakim..M., Elioenai

5. The son of Gemariah, one of the princes of Judah in the days of Jehoiakim. B.C. 606.
Jer. 36. 11 When M., the son of Gemariah, the son
36. 13 Then M. declared unto them all the words

MI'-CHAL, מִיכַל *who is like God?*
The younger daughter of king Saul who became David's wife, saved him in his distress, and mocked him in his triumph. B.C. 1050.
1 Sa. 14. 49 names of his two daughters..Merab..M.
18. 20 And M., Saul's daughter, loved David: and
18. 27 And Saul gave him M. his daughter to w.
18. 28 Saul saw..(that) M., Saul's daughter, loved
19. 11 M., David's wife, told him, saying, If thou
19. 12 So M. let David down through a window
19. 13 And M. took an image, and laid (it) in the
19. 17 And Saul said unto M., Why hast thou
19. 17 And M. answered S., He said unto me, Let
25. 44 But Saul had given M. his daughter, Da.
2 Sa. 3. 13 except thou first bring M., Saul's daughter
3. 14 Deliver (me) my wife M., which I espous.
6. 16 M., Saul's daughter, looked through a w.
6. 20 And M. the daughter of Saul came out to
6. 21 David said unto M., (It was) before the L.
6. 23 Therefore M. the daughter of Saul had no
21. 8 the five sons of M. the daughter of Saul
1 Ch. 15. 29 M. the daughter of Saul, looking out at a

MICH'-MAS, מִכְמָס *place of Chemosh.*
A place to which some belonged who returned with Zerubbabel: the same as *Michmash.*
Ezra 2. 27 The men of M., an hundred twenty and
Neh. 7. 31 The men of M., an hundred and twenty

MICH'-MASH, מִכְמָשׁ, מִכְמָשׂ.
A city in Benjamin; *Mukhmas*, seven miles N. of Jerusalem, and E. of *Beth-aven.*
1 Sa. 13. 2 two thousand were with Saul in M. and in
13. 5 And the Philistines..pitched in M., east.
13. 11 the Philistines gathered..together at M.
13. 16 but the Philistines encamped in M.
13. 23 the Philistines went..to the passage of M.
14. 5 the fore front..(was)..over against M., and
14. 31 they smote the Philistines..from M. to A.
Neh. 11. 31 Benjamin from Geba (dwelt) at M., and
Isa. 10. 28 He is come to Aiath..at M. he hath laid

MICH-ME'-THAH, מִכְמְתָת *lurking place.*
A city between Ephraim and Manasseh.
Josh 16. 6 And the border went out..to M. on the
17. 7 And the coast..was from Asher to M., that

MICH'-RI, מִכְרִי *Jah possesses.*
A Benjamite, ancestor of the head of a family in Jerusalem. B.C. 480.
1 Ch. 9. 8 Uzzi, the son of M., and Meshullam the

MICH'-TAM, מִכְתָּם.
The name of a particular kind of Psalm; perhaps "golden."
Psa. 16. *title.* M. of David
56. ,, M. of David, when the Philistines took
57. ,, M. of David, when he fled from Saul in
58. ,, To the chief Musician..M. of David
59. ,, M. of David, when Saul sent, and they
60. ,, To the chief Musician..M. of David, to

MID DAY —
1. *Double brightness*, צָהֳרַיִם *tsohorayim.*
1 Ki. 18. 29 when mid day was past, and they proph.

2. *Mid day*, מַחֲצִית הַיּוֹם *machatsith hay-yom.*
Neh. 8 3 from the morning until mid day, before

3. *Middle of the day*, ἡμέρας μέσης *hēmeras mesēs.*
Acts 26. 13 At mid day O king, I saw in the way a l.

MID'-DIN, מִדִּין *extension.*
A city in the desert, S. of Judah.
Josh 15. 61 In the wilderness, Beth-arabah, M., and

MIDDLE, MIDST —
1. *Half, middle, midst*, חֲצִי, חֵצִי *chatsi, chetsi.*
Exod 27. 5 that the net may be even to the midst of
38. 4 a brasen grate..beneath unto the midst
Josh. 10. 13 the sun stood still in the midst of heaven
2 Sa. 10. 4 and cut off their garments in the middle
1 Ch. 19. 4 cut off their garments in the midst hard
Psa. 102. 24 take me not away in the midst of my days
Jer. 17. 11 shall leave them in the midst of his days
Dan. 9. 27 in the midst of the week he shall cause
Zech 14. 4 shall cleave in the midst thereof toward

2. *Back, body, midst*, גַּו *gav.*
Dan. 3. 6, 11, 15 be cast into the midst of a burning
3. 21, 23 into the midst of the burning fiery fur.
3. 24 Did not we cast..into the midst of the fire?
3. 25 walking in the midst of the fire, and they
3. 26 Shadrach..came forth of the midst of
4. 10 behold a tree in the midst of the earth
7. 15 was grieved in my spirit in the midst of

3. *Bosom, centre*, חֵיק *cheq.*
1 Ki. 22. 35 blood ran out of the wound into the midst

4. *Middle, navel, high part*, טַבּוּר *tabbur.*
Judg. 9. 37 See there come people down by the midd.
Eze. 38. 12 people..that dwell in the midst of the land

5. *Palm*, כַּף *kaph.*
1 Sa. 25. 29 them shall he sling out..of the middle of

6. *Heart*, לֵב *leb.*
Deut 4. 11 burned with fire unto the midst of heaven
2 Sa. 18. 14 while (he) was yet alive in the midst of the
Psa. 46. 2 the mountains be carried into the midst of
Prov 23. 34 as he that lieth down in the midst of the
30. 19 the way of a ship in the midst of the sea
Jer. 51. 1 against them that dwell in the midst of
Eze. 27. 4 Thy borders are in the midst of the seas
27. 25 made very glorious in the midst of the s.
27. 26 hath broken thee in the midst of the seas
27. 27 shall fall into the midst of the seas in the
28. 2 I (am) a god, I sit..in the midst of the s.
28. 8 (them that are) slain in the midst of the s.

7. *Heart*, לֵבָב *lebab.*
Jon. 2. 3 hadst cast me into..the midst of the seas

8. *Inward part*, קֶרֶב *qereb.*
Gen. 48. 16 into a multitude in the midst of the earth
Exod. 3. 20 wonders which I will do in the midst the.
8. 22 I (am) the LORD in the midst of the earth
23. 25 take sickness away from the midst of thee
33. 3 for I will not go up in the midst of thee
33. 5 I will come up into the midst of thee in
34. 12 lest it be for a snare in the midst of thee
Deut. 4. 34 (and) take him a nation from the midst of
11. 6 And what he did..in the midst of all Isr.
13. 5 put the evil away from the midst of thee
17. 20 he, and his children, in the midst of Isr.
18. 15 a Prophet from the midst of thee, of thy
23. 14 LORD thy God walketh in the midst of thy
Josh. 7. 13 an accursed thing in the midst of thee, O
Judg 18. 20 took..and went in the midst of the peop.
1 Sa. 16 13 anointed him in the midst of his brethren
1 Ki 20. 39 Thy servant went out into the midst of the
Psa. 46. 5 God (is) in the midst of her; she shall not
48. 9 We have thought..in the midst of thy te.
55. 10 mischief also and sorrow (are) in the mi.
55. 11 Wickedness (is) in the midst thereof; de.
74. 4 Thine enemies roar in the midst of thy c.
74. 12 working salvation in the midst of the ea.
78. 28 he let (it) fall in the midst of their camp
110. 2 rule thou in the midst of thine enemies
138. 7 Though I walk in the midst of trouble
Prov 14. 33 (that which is) in the midst of fools is m.
Isa. 4. 4 the blood of Jerusalem from the midst
5. 8 be placed alone in the midst of the earth
5. 25 their carcases. .torn in the midst of the
6. 12 a great forsaking in the midst of the land
10. 23 a consumption..in the midst of all the la.
12. 6 the Holy One of Israel in the midst of thee
19. 1 the heart of Egypt shall melt in the midst
19. 3 spirit of Egypt shall fail in the midst
19. 14 hath mingled a perverse spirit in the mi.
19. 24 (even) a blessing in the midst of the land
24. 13 When thus it shall be in the midst of the
25. 11 shall spread forth his hands in the midst
29. 23 the work of mine hands, in the midst of
Jer. 6. 1 to flee out of the midst of Jerusalem, and
6. 6 she (is) wholly oppression in the midst of
14. 9 yet thou, O LORD, (art) in the midst of us
29. 8 diviners, that (be) in the midst of you, de.
30. 21 their governor shall proceed from the m.
46. 21 her hired men (are) in the midst of her
Lam. 1. 15 all my mighty (men) in the midst of me
3. 45 Thou hast made us..refuse in the midst
4. 13 shed the blood of the just in the midst of
Eze. 22. 27 Her princes in the midst thereof (are) like
Hos. 5. 4 spirit of whoredoms (is) in the midst of
11. 9 the Holy One in the midst of thee: and I
Joel 2. 27 ye shall know that I (am) in the midst of I.
Amos 2. 3 will cut off the judge from the midst the.
3. 9 behold the great tumults in the midst the.
7. 8 I will set a plumb line in the midst of my
7. 10 hath conspired against thee in the midst
Mic. 5. 7, 8 shall be in the midst of many people
5. 10 I will cut off thy horses out of the midst
5. 13 thy standing images out of the midst of
5. 14 I will pluck up thy groves out of the midst
6. 14 thy casting down (shall be) in the midst
Nah. 3. 13 thy people in the midst of thee (are) wo.
Hab. 2. 19 and..no breath at all in the midst of it
3. 2 revive thy work in the midst of the years
3. 2 in the midst of the years make known
Zeph. 3. 5 The just LORD (is) in the midst thereof; he
3. 11 I will take away out of the midst of thee
3. 12 I will also leave in the midst of thee an
3. 15 the LORD, (is) in the midst of thee: thou
3. 17 The LORD thy God in the midst of thee (is)
Zech. 14. 1 spoil shall be divided in the midst of thee

9. *Middle, midst*, תָּוֶךְ *tavek.*
Gen. 1. 6 Let there be a firmament in the midst of
2. 9 the tree of life also in the midst of the ga.
3. 3 the fruit of the tree which (is) in the midst
15. 10 divided them in the midst, and laid each
19. 29 sent Lot out of the midst of the overthrow
Exod. 3. 2 in a flame of fire out of the midst of a bush
3. 4 God called unto him out of the midst of
11. 4 About midnight will I go out into the m.
14. 16 dry (ground) through the midst of the sea
14. 22 went into the midst of the sea upon the
14. 23 went in after them to the midst of the sea
14. 27 overthrew the Egyptians in the midst of
14. 29 walked upon dry (land) in the midst of the
15. 19 went on dry (land) in the midst of the sea
24. 16 he called unto Moses out of the midst of
24. 18 Moses went into the midst of the cloud
26. 28 the middle bar in the midst of the boards
28. 32 an hole in the top of it, in the midst ther.
39. 23 And..an hole in the midst of the robe, as
Lev. 16. 16 among them in the midst of their unclean.
Num. 2. 17 with the camp of the Levites in the midst
5. 3 their camps, in the midst whereof I dwell
16. 47 and ran into the midst of the congregation
19. 6 into the midst of the burning of the heifer
33. 8 passed through the midst of the sea into
35. 5 the city (shall be) in the midst: this shall
Deut. 4. 12 LORD spake unto you out of the midst of
4. 15 spake unto you in Horeb out of the midst
4. 33 the voice of God speaking out of the midst
4. 36 thou heardest his words out of the midst
5. 4 in the mount, out of the midst of the fire
5. 22 in the mount, out of the midst of the fire
5. 23 when ye heard the voice out of the midst
5. 24 we have heard his voice out of the midst
5. 26 God speaking out of the midst of the fire
9. 10 in the mount, out of the midst of the fire
10. 4 in the mount, out of the midst of the fire
11. 3 which he did in the midst of Egypt unto
13. 16 gather all the spoil of it into the midst of
19. 2 separate three cities for thee in the midst
32. 51 ye sanctified me not in the midst of the c.
Josh. 3. 17 stood firm on dry ground in the midst of
4. 3 Take you hence out of the midst of Jordan
4. 5 into the midst of Jordan, and take you up
4. 8 took up twelve stones out of the midst of
4. 9 Joshua set up twelve stones in the midst
4. 10 stood in the midst of Jordan, until every
4. 18 were come up out of the midst of Jordan
7. 21 hid in the earth in the midst of my tent
7. 23 they took them out of the midst of the tent
8. 13 Joshua went that night into the midst of
8. 22 so they were in the midst of Israel, some
12. 2 from the middle of the river, and from h.
13. 9, 16 the city that (is) in the midst of the r.
Judg 15. 4 put a fire brand in the midst between two
16. 29 Samson took hold of the two middle pill.
20. 42 them..they destroyed in the midst of them
1 Sa. 11. 11 they came into the midst of the host in the
18. 10 prophesied in the midst of the house: and
25. 29 them shall he sling out..of the middle of
2 Sa. 1. 25 How are the mighty fallen in the midst of
4. 6 they came thither into the midst of the
6. 17 in the midst of the tabernacle that David
20. 12 Amasa wallowed in blood in the midst of
23. 12 he stood in the midst of the ground, and
23. 20 slew a lion in the midst of a pit in time
24. 5 side of the city that [lieth] in the midst
1 Ki. 3. 8 thy servant (is) in the midst of thy people
6. 27 touched one another in the midst of the
8. 51 out of Egypt, from the midst of the furn.
8. 64 did the king hallow the middle of the court
2 Ki. 6. 20 and behold..in the midst of Samaria
1 Ch. 11. 14 they set themselves in the midst of (that)
16. 1 set it in the midst of the tent that David
2 Ch. 6. 13 and had set it in the midst of the court
7. 7 Solomon hallowed the middle of the court
20. 14 the LORD in the midst of the congregation
32. 4 the brook that ran through the midst of
Neh. 4. 11 till we come in the midst among them
9. 11 so that they went through the midst of
Esth. 4. 1 went out into the midst of the city, and
Psa. 22. 14 it is melted in the midst of my bowels
22. 22 in the midst of the congregation will I p.
57. 6 into the midst whereof they are fallen
116. 19 in the midst of thee, O Jerusalem. Praise
135. 9 sent tokens and wonders into the midst
136. 14 made Israel to pass through the midst of
137. 2 our harps upon the willows in the midst
Prov. 4. 21 keep them in the midst of thine heart
5. 14 I was almost in all evil in the midst of the
8. 20 I lead..in the midst of the paths of judg.

Song 3. 10 the midst thereof being paved (with) love
Isa. 5. 2 built a tower in the midst of it, and also
6. 5 I dwell in the midst of a people of unclean
7. 6 set a king in the midst of it..the son of T.
16. 3 as the night in the midst of the noon day
19. 19 an altar to the LORD in the midst of the l.
24. 18 he that cometh up out of the midst of the
41. 18 and fountains in the midst of the valleys
52. 11 go ye out of the midst of her; be ye clean
58. 9 If thou take away from the midst of thee
66. 17 in the gardens behind one (tree) in the m.
Jer. 9. 6 Thine habitation (is) in the midst of dec.
12. 16 then shall they be built in the midst of my
21. 4 I will assemble them into the midst of
37. 12 to separate himself thence in the midst of
39. 3 princes..came in, and sat in the middle g.
41. 7 when they came into the midst of the city
41. 7 into the midst of the pit, he, and the men
50. 8 Remove out of the midst of Babylon, and
50. 37 mingled people that (are) in the midst of
51. 6 Flee out of the midst of Babylon, and de.
51. 45 My people, go ye out of the midst of her
51. 47 all her slain shall fall in the midst of her
51. 63 and cast it into the midst of Euphrates
52. 25 (that were) found in the midst of the city
Eze. 1. 4 out of the midst thereof..out of the midst
1. 5 Also out of the midst thereof (came) the
1. 16 as it were a wheel in the middle of a wh.
5. 2 burn with fire a third part in the midst of
5. 4 cast them into the midst of the fire, and
5. 5 I have set it in the midst of the nations
5. 8 execute judgments in the midst of thee in
5. 10 fathers shall eat the sons in the midst of
5. 12 shall they be consumed in the midst of thee
6. 7 And the slain shall fall in the midst of you
7. 4 thine abominations shall be in the midst
7. 9 thine abominations (that) are in the midst
8. 11 in the midst of them stood Jaazaniah the
9. 4 LORD said..Go through the midst of the
9. 4 through the midst of Jerusalem, and set
9. 4 abominations that be done in the midst
10. 10 as if a wheel had been in the midst of a
11. 7 whom ye have laid in the midst of it, they
11. 7 I will bring you forth out of the midst of
11. 9 I will bring you out of the midst thereof
11. 11 neither shall ye be the flesh in the midst
11. 23 glory..went up from the midst of the city
12. 2 thou dwellest in the midst of a rebellious
13. 14 ye shall be consumed in the midst thereof
14. 8 I will cut him off from the midst of my p.
14. 9 will destroy him from the midst of my p.
15. 4 fire devoureth..the midst of it is burnt
16. 53 the captivity of thy captives in the midst
17. 16 with him in the midst of Babylon he shall
20. 8 them in the midst of the land of Egypt
21. 32 thy blood shall be in the midst of the land
22. 3 The city sheddeth blood in the midst of it
22. 7 in the midst of thee have they dealt by
22. 9 in the midst of thee they commit lewdness
22. 13 thy blood which hath been in the midst of
22. 18 iron. and lead, in the midst of the furnace
22. 19 I will gather you into the midst of Jeru.
22. 20 lead, and tin, into the midst of the furnace
22. 21 ye shall be melted in the midst thereof
22. 22 As silver is melted in the midst of the fu.
22. 22 so shall ye be melted in the midst thereof
22. 25 a conspiracy of her prophets in the midst
22. 25 have made her many widows in the midst
23. 39 thus have they done in the midst of mine
24. 7 For her blood is in the midst of her; she
26. 5 the spreading of nets in the midst of the
26. 12 shall lay..thy dust in the midst of the w.
26. 15 when the slaughter is made in the midst
27. 27 company which (is) in the midst of thee
27. 32 like the destroyed in the midst of the sea
27. 34 thy company in the midst of thee, shall
28. 14 thou hast walked up and down in the m.
28. 16 they have filled the midst of thee with
28. 16 destroy..from the midst of the stones of
28. 18 will I bring forth a fire from the midst of
28. 22 I will be glorified in the midst of thee
28. 23 the wounded shall be judged in the midst
29. 3 the great dragon that lieth in the midst
29. 4 I will bring thee up out of the midst of thy
29. 12 make..desolate in the midst of the coun.
29. 21 opening of the mouth in the midst of them
30. 7 they shall be desolate in the midst of the
30. 7 her cities shall be in the midst of the cit.
31. 14 in the midst of the children of men, with
31. 17 dwelt under his shadow in the midst of the
31. 18 thou shalt lie in the midst of the uncircu.
32. 20 They shall fall in the midst of (them that)
32. 21 shall speak to him out of the midst of hell
32. 25 They have set her a bed in the midst of the
32. 25 he is put in the midst of (them that be)
32. 28 thou..be broken in the midst of the unc.
32. 32 he shall be laid in the midst of the uncir.
36. 23 which ye have profaned in the midst of
37. 1 set me down in the midst of the valley w.
37. 26 will set my sanctuary in the midst of them
37. 28 when my sanctuary shall be in the midst
39. 7 will I make my holy name known in the m.
43. 7 where I will dwell in the midst of the ch.
43. 9 I will dwell in the midst of them for ever
46. 10 the prince in the midst of them, when they
48. 8 the sanctuary shall be in the midst of it
48. 10 the sanctuary..shall be in the midst the.
48. 15 and the city shall be in the midst thereof
48. 21 and the sanctuary..in the midst thereof
48. 22 in the midst (of that) which is the prince's
Amos 3. 9 behold the great tumults in the midst th.
6. 4 the calves out of the midst of the stall
Mic. 2. 12 as the flock in the midst of their fold
7. 14 dwell solitarily (in) the wood, in the midst
Zeph. 2. 14 flocks shall lie down in the midst of her
Zech. 2. 5 and will be the glory in the midst of her
2. 10, 11 and I will dwell in the midst of thee
5. 4 it shall remain in the midst of his house
5. 7 this (is) a woman that sitteth in the midst
5. 8 And he cast it into the midst of the ephah
8. 3 and will dwell in the midst of Jerusalem
8. 8 they shall dwell in the midst of Jerusalem

10. *Middle*, תִּיכוֹן *tikon.*
Exod26. 28 the middle bar in..the boards shall reach
36. 33 he made the middle bar to shoot through
Judg. 7. 19 came..in the beginning of the middle w.
1 Ki. 6. 6 the middle (was) six cubits broad, and the
6. 8 The door for the middle chamber (was) in
6. 8 went up with winding stairs into the m.
6. 8 went up..out of the middle into the third
2 Ki. 20. 4 afore Isaiah was gone out into the middle
Eze. 41. 7 lowest (chamber) to the highest by the m.

11. *Middle, midst*, μέσος *mesos, -ον.*
Matt 10. 16 I send you forth as sheep in the midst of
14. 24 [the ship was now in the midst of the sea]
18. 2 And Jesus..set him in the midst of them
18. 20 two or three..there am I in the midst of
Mark 6. 47 the ship was in the midst of the sea, and
7. 31 through the midst of the coasts of Decap.
9. 36 he took a child, and set him in the midst
14. 60 the high priest stood up in the midst, and
Luke 2 46 sitting in the midst of the doctors, both
4. 30 he passing through the midst of them w.
4. 35 when the devil had thrown him in the m.
5. 19 with (his) couch into the midst before J.
6. 8 Rise up, and stand forth in the midst
17. 11 he passed through the midst of Samaria
21. 21 let them which are in the midst of it de.
22. 55 when they had kindled a fire in the midst
23. 45 the veil of the temple was rent in the m.
24. 36 Jesus himself stood in the midst of them
John 8. 3 [when they had set her in the midst]
8. 9 [and the woman standing in the midst]
8. 59 going through the midst of them, and so
19. 18 on either side one, and Jesus in the midst
20. 19 came Jesus and stood in the midst, and
20. 26 came Jesus..and stood in the midst, and
Acts 1. 15 in those days Peter stood up in the midst
1. 18 he burst asunder in the midst, and all his
2. 22 which God did by him in the midst of you
4. 7 when they had set them in the midst, they
17. 22 Then Paul stood in the midst of Mars' hill
27. 21 Paul stood forth in the midst of them, and
Phil. 2. 15 in the [midst] of a crooked and perverse
Heb. 2. 12 in the midst of the church will I sing pr.
Rev. 1. 13 in [the midst] of the seven candlesticks (one)
2. 1 who walketh in the midst of the seven g.
2. 7 which is in [the midst] of the paradise of
4. 6 in the midst of the throne, and round about
5. 6 in the midst of the throne and of the four
5. 6 in the midst of the elders, stood a Lamb
6. 6 I heard a voice in the midst of the four b.
7. 17 the Lamb which is [in the midst] of the
22. 2 In the midst of the street of it, and on

MIDDLE wall between —
Middle wall, μεσότοιχον *mesotoichon.*
Eph. 2. 14 hath broken down the middle wall.. bet.

MIDDLEMOST —
Middle, midst, תִּיכוֹן *tikon.*
Eze. 42. 5 and than the middlemost of the building
42. 6 more than the lowest and the middlemost

MID'-IAN, מִדְיָן *contention.*
1. A son of Abraham by Keturah. B.C. 1840.
Gen. 25. 2 And she bare him Zimran. .and M., and
25. 4 And the sons of M., Ephah, and Epher
1 Ch. 1. 32 she bare Zimran. .and M., and Ishbak, and
1. 33 the sons of M.; Ephah, and Epher, and H.
2. His descendants and their land beyond the Jordan, in Edom, the Sinai peninsula, and Arabia Petræa.
Gen. 36. 35 Hadad the son of Bedad, who smote M. in
Exod. 2. 15 Moses fled. .and dwelt in the land of M.
2. 16 Now the priest of M. had seven daughters
3. 1 Jethro his father in law, the priest of M.
4. 19 the LORD said unto Moses in M., Go, ret.
18. 1 Jethro, the priest of M., Moses' father in l.
Num22. 4 Moab said unto the elders of M., Now sh.
22. 7 the elders of M. departed with the rewards
25. 15 he (was) head..of a chief house in M.
25. 18 the daughter of a prince of M., their sister
31. 3 Moses spake..saying..avenge the LORD of M.
31. 8 they slew the kings of M., besides the rest
31. 8 Zur, and Hur, and Rĕba, five kings of M.
31. 9 took (all) the women of M. captives, and
Josh 13. 21 Moses smote with the princes of M., Evi
Judg. 6. 1 delivered them into the hand of M. seven
6. 2 the hand of M. prevailed against Israel
7. 8 the host of M. was beneath him in the v.
7. 13 a cake..tumbled into the host of M., and
7. 14 into his hand hath God delivered M., and
7. 15 delivered into your hand the host of M.
7. 25 And they..pursued M., and brought the
8. 3 princes of M., Oreb and Zeeb: and what
8. 5 and I am pursuing after..kings of M.
8. 12 took the two kings of M., Zebah and Zal.
8. 22 thou hast delivered us from the hand of M.
8. 26 raiment that (was) on the kings of M., and
8. 28 Thus was M. subdued before the children
9. 17 and delivered you out of the hand of M.
1 Ki. 11. 18 they arose out of M., and came to Paran
1 Ch. 1. 46 which smote M. in the field of Moab, reig.
Isa. 9. 4 hast broken the yoke..as in the day of M.
10. 26 according to the slaughter of M. at the r.
60. 6 the dromedaries of M. and Ephah; all the
Hab. 3. 7 the curtains of the land of M. did tremble

MID-IAN-ITES, מִדְיָן, מִדְיָנִים.
They are distinguished (but not always) from the *Ishmaelites*, as in Judg. 6. 33 and 7. 12.
Gen. 37. 28 Then there passed by M., merchant men
37. 36 And the M. sold him into Egypt unto Po.
Num10. 29 Hobab, the son of Raguel the M., Moses'
25. 17 Vex the M., and smite them
31. 2 Avenge the children of Israel of the M.
31. 3 let them go against the M., and avenge
31. 7 they warred against the M., as the LORD
Judg. 6. 2 because of the M. the children of Israel
6. 3 the M. came up, and the Amalekites
6. 6 Israel was..impoverished because of the M.
6. 7 Israel cried unto the L. because of the M.
6. 11 threshed wheat..to hide (it) from the M.
6. 13 and delivered us into the hands of the M.
6. 14 shalt save Israel from the hand of the M.
6. 16 and thou shalt smite the M. as one man
6. 33 Then all the M. and the Amalekites and
7. 1 the host of the M. were on the north side
7. 2 to give the M. into their hands, lest Israel
7. 7 and deliver the M. into thine hand: and
7. 12 the M. and the Amalekites and all the
7. 23 the men of Israel..pursued after the M.
7. 24 Come down against the M., and take before
7. 25 they took two princes of the M., Oreb and
8. 1 when thou wentest to fight with the M.?
Psa. 83. 9 Do unto them as (unto) the M.; as (to) S.

MID-IAN-IT-ISH, מִדְיָנִית *fem. of* מִדְיָנִי.
Belonging to Midian.
Num25. 6 brought unto his brethren a M. woman in
25. 14 that was slain with the M. woman, (was)
25. 15 the name of the M. woman that was slain

MID NIGHT, (at)—
1. *Mid night*, חֲצוֹת לַיְלָה *chatsoth layelah.*
Exod11. 4 About mid night will I go out into them.
Job 34. 20 the people shall be troubled at mid night
Psa 119. 62 At mid night I will rise to give thanks unto
2. *Mid night*, חֲצִי הַלַּיְלָה *chatsi hal-layelah.*
Exod12. 29 at mid night the LORD smote all the first
Judg16. 3 Samson lay till mid night, and arose at mid.
Ruth 3. 8 it came to pass at mid night, that the man
3. *Mid night*, תּוֹךְ הַלַּיְלָה *tok hal-layelah.*
1 Ki. 3. 20 she arose at mid night, and took my son
4. *Middle of the night*, μέσης (*or* μέσον τῆς) νυκτός.
Matt25. 6 at mid night there was a cry made, Behold
Acts 27. 27 about mid night the shipmen deemed that
5. *Mid night*, μεσονύκτιον *mesonuktion.*
Mark13. 35 cometh, at even, or at mid night, or at the
Luke11. 5 shall go unto him at mid night, and say unto
Acts 16. 25 at mid night Paul and Silas prayed, and
20. 7 and continued his speech until mid night

MIDST of heaven —
Mid heaven, μεσουράνημα *mesouranēma.*
Rev. 8. 13 an angel flying through the midst of he.
14. 6 another angel fly in the midst of heaven
19. 17 all the fowls that fly in the midst of hea.

MIDST, about the —
To be or reach the middle, μεσόω *mesoō.*
John 7. 14 about the midst of the feast, Jesus went

MIDST, to be cut off in the —
To be halved, חָצַץ *chatsats*, 4.
Job 21. 21 number of his months is cut off in the m.

MIDST, to reach to the —
To halve, come to the middle, חָצָה *chatsah.*
Isa. 30. 28 shall reach to the midst of the neck, to

MIDWIFE, (to do the office of a) —
To help to bear, be a midwife, יָלַד *yalad*, 3.
Gen. 35. 17 the midwife said unto her, Fear not; thou
38. 28 the midwife took and bound upon his hand
Exod. 1. 15 king of Egypt spake to the Hebrew midw.
1. 16 When ye do the office of a midwife to the
1. 17 the midwives feared God, and did not as
1. 18 the king of Egypt called for the midwives
1. 19 the midwives said unto Pharaoh, Because
1. 19 are delivered ere the midwives come in un.
1. 20 Therefore God dealt well with the midw.
1. 21 it came to pass, because the midwives fe.

MIG'-DAL EL, מִגְדַּל־אֵל *tower of God.*
A fortified city in Naphtali, near Iron and Horem, supposed by some to be the Magdala of the New Testament, on the W. of the sea of Galilee, but the latter is in Zebulon, S. of Capernaum, and one and a half hours from Tiberias.
Josh. 19. 38 Iron, and M., Horem, and Beth-anath

MIG'-DAL GAD, מִגְדַּל־גָּד *tower of Gad.*
A city in the plain of Judah, now *Mejdal.*
Josh. 15. 37 Zenan, and Hadashah, and M.

MIG'-DOL, מִגְדֹּל, מִגְדּוֹל *tower.*
1. A place W. of the Red Sea.
Exod14. 2 Pi-hahiroth, between Migdol and the sea
Num33. 7 they removed..and they pitched before M.
2. A city in the N.E. of Egypt from Palestine, as Syene was in the south.
Jer. 44. 1 all the Jews which dwell..at M., and at
46. 14 Declare ye in Egypt, and publish in M.

MIGHT —
1. *Strength,* אוֹן *on.*
Isa. 40. 26 by names by the greatness of his might
40. 29 to (them that have) no might he increas.
2. *Might,* אֵל *el.*
Deut28. 32 and (there shall be) no might in thine hand
3. *Might,* גְּבוּרָה *geburah.*
Deut. 3. 24 God..that can do..according to thy might
Judg. 5. 31 as the sun when he goeth forth in his m
1 Ki.15. 23 all his might, and all that he did, and the
16. 5 what he did, and his might, (are) they not
16. 27 which he did, and his might that he sho
22. 45 his might that he showed, and how he w
2 Ki.10. 34 all that he did, and all his might, (are)
13. 8 all that he did, and his might, (are) they
13. 12 his might wherewith he fought against A.
14. 15 his might, and how he fought with Ama
14. 28 all that he did, and his might, how he
20. 20 all his might, and how he made a pool
1 Ch.29. 12 in thine hand (is) power and might; and
29. 30 With all his reign and his might, and the
2 Ch.20. 6 power and might, so that none is able to
Esth.10. 2 all the acts of his power, and of his might
Isa. 11. 2 the spirit of counsel and might, the spirit
33. 13 ye (that are) near, acknowledge my might
Jer. 9. 23 neither let the mighty..glory in his might
10. 6 Forasmuch as..thy name (is) great in m
16. 21 cause..to know mine hand and my might
49. 35 the bow of Elam, the chief of their might
51. 30 their might hath failed; they became as
Eze. 32. 29 princes, which with their might are laid
32. 30 their terror they are ashamed of their m.
Dan. 2. 20 and ever: for wisdom and might are his
2. 23 who hast given me wisdom and might, and
Mic. 3. 8 I am full..of judgment, and of might, to
7. 16 see, and be confounded at all their might
4. *Force, army, strength,* חַיִל *chayil.*
2 Ki.24. 16 all the men of might..seven thousand
1 Ch. 7. 2 valiant men of might in their generations
7. 5 valiant men of might, reckoned in all by
12. 8 men of might..men of war..for the battle
Psa. 76. 5 none of the men of might have found their
Zech. 4. 6 Not by might, nor by power, but by my s.
5. *To be able,* יָכֹל *yakol.*
Gen. 43. 32 the Egyptians might not eat bread with
6. *Power,* כֹּחַ *koach.*
Gen. 49. 3 Reuben, thou (art) my first born, my might
Num 14. 13 thou broughtest up this people in thy m.
Judg. 6. 14 Go in this thy might, and thou shalt save
16. 30 he bowed himself with (all his) might
1 Ch.29. 2 I have prepared with all my might for the
2 Ch.20. 12 we have no might against this great com.
Eccl. 9. 10 hand findeth to do, do (it) with thy m.
7. *Might,* מְאֹד *meod.*
Deut. 6. 5 with all thy soul, and with all thy might
2 Ki.23. 25 with all his might, according to all the law
8. *Strength, might, vigour,* עֹז *oz.*
2 Sa. 6. 14 danced before the LORD with all (his) m.
1 Ch.13. 8 played before God with all (their) might
9. *Strength, vigour,* עֱזוּז *ezuz.*
Psa.145. 6 shall speak of the might of thy terrible
10. *Substance, bone,* עֹצֶם *otsem.*
Deut. 8. 17 My power and the might of (mine) hand
11. *Strength, might,* תְּקֹף *teqoph.*
Dan. 4. 30 by the might of my power, and for the
12. *Power,* δύναμις *dunamis.*
Eph. 1. 21 all principality, and power, and might
3. 16 to be strengthened with might by his spirit
Col. 1. 11 Strengthened with all might, according
2 Pe 2. 11 angels, which are greater in power and m.
13. *Strength,* ἰσχύς *ischus.*
Eph. 6. 10 in the Lord, and in the power of his might
Rev. 7. 12 honour, and power, and might, (be) unto
14. *To be strong, have strength,* ἰσχύω *ischuō.*
Matt 8. 28 so that no man might pass by that way

MIGHTIER, MIGHTILY, MIGHTY, (that is) —
1. *Mighty,* אַבִּיר *abbir.*
Job 24. 22 He draweth also the mighty with his po.
34. 20 the mighty shall be taken away without
Lam. 1. 15 all my mighty (men) in the midst of me
2. *Mighty,* אָבִיר *abir.*
Gen. 49. 24 by the hands of the mighty (God) of Jacob
Psa.132. 2 vowed unto the mighty (God) of Jacob
132. 5 habitation for the mighty (God) of Jacob
Isa. 1. 24 LORD of hosts, the mighty One of Israel
49. 26 thy Redeemer, the mighty One of Jacob
60. 16 thy Redeemer, the mighty One of Jacob
3. *Honourable, shining,* אַדִּיר *addir.*
Exod 15. 10 they sank as lead in the mighty waters
1 Sa. 4. 8 us out of the hand of these mighty Gods
Psa. 93. 4 mightier than..the mighty waves of the
Zech.11. 2 because the mighty are spoiled: howl, O
4. *Mighty one,* אוּל *ul.*
2 Ki.24. 15 his officers, and the mighty of the land
5. *Mighty ones,* אֵילִים *elim.*
Job 41. 25 When he raiseth up himself, the mighty
Eze. 17. 13 he hath also taken the mighty of the land
6. *Strong, firm, perennial,* אֵיתָן, אֵתָן *ethan.*
Job 12. 19 He leadeth..and overthroweth the migh.
Psa. 74. 15 Thou didst cleave..thou driedst up mig.
Jer. 5. 15 a mighty nation, it (is) an ancient nation
Amos 5. 24 as waters, and righteousness as a mighty
7. *Mighty one,* אֵל *el.*
Psa. 29. 1 Give unto the LORD, O ye mighty, give
50. 1 The mighty God..the LORD, hath spoken
82. 1 standeth in the congregation of the mig.
89. 6 (who) among the sons of the mighty can
8. *Strong, courageous,* אַמִּיץ, אַמִּץ *ammits.*
Job 9. 4 (He is) wise in heart, and mighty in stre.
9. *Force,* אָפִיק *aphiq.*
Job 12. 21 and weakeneth the strength of the mighty
10. *Mighty one,* גִּבּוֹר *gibbor.*
Gen. 10. 9 He was a mighty hunter before the LORD
10. 9 as Nimrod the mighty hunter before the
Deut10. 17 a great God, a mighty, and a terrible, which
Josh.10. 2 Gibeon..all the men thereof (were) migh.
Judg. 5. 13 made me have dominion over the mighty
5. 23 to the help of the LORD against the mighty
Ruth 2. 1 a mighty man of wealth, of the family of E.
1 Sa.16. 18 a mighty valiant man, and a man of war
2 Sa. 1. 19, 25, 27 How are the mighty fallen
1. 21 there the shield of the mighty is vilely c.
1. 22 from the fat of the mighty, the bow of J.
2 Ki. 5. 1 Naaman..was also a mighty man in valour
1 Ch. 1. 10 he began to be mighty upon the earth
5. 24 mighty men of valour, famous men..heads
11. 12 the Ahohite, who (was one) of the three m.
11. 19 These things did these three mightiest
11. 24 and had the name among the three mighti.
12. 28 Zadok, a young man mighty of valour, and
27. 6 Benaiah..mighty (among) the thirty, and
Ezra 7. 28 and before all the king's mighty princes
Neh. 3. 16 over against..unto the house of the mighty
9. 32 the great, the mighty, and the terrible God
Psa. 24. 8 LORD strong and mighty, the LORD mighty
45. 3 Gird thy sword upon (thy) thigh, O..mig.
89. 19 I have laid help upon (one that is) mighty
112. 2 His seed shall be mighty upon earth: the
120. 4 Sharp arrows of the mighty, with coals of
Prov.16. 32 slow to anger (is) better than the mighty
21. 22 A wise (man) scaleth the city of the mighty
Isa. 5. 22 Woe unto (them that are) mighty to drink
9. 6 Wonderful, Counsellor, The mighty God
10. 21 the remnant of Jacob, unto the mighty G.
49. 24 Shall the prey be taken from the mighty
49. 25 Even the captives of the mighty shall be
Jer. 20. 11 But the LORD (is) with me as a mighty te.
32. 18 The Great, the Mighty God, the LORD of
46. 12 hath stumbled against the mighty, (and)
48. 14 We (are) mighty and strong men for the
Eze. 32. 12 By the swords of the mighty will I cause
32. 21 The strong among the mighty shall speak
32. 27 And they shall not lie with the mighty
32. 27 the terror of the mighty in the land of
39. 18 Ye shall eat the flesh of the mighty, and
Dan. 11. 3 a mighty king shall stand up, that shall
Amos 2. 14 neither shall the mighty deliver himself
2. 16 courageous among the mighty shall flee aw.
Obad. 9 mighty (men), O Teman, shall be dismayed
Zeph. 3. 17 LORD thy God in the midst of thee (is) mi.
Zech.10. 5 they shall be as mighty (men), which tread
10. 7 Ephraim shall be like a mighty (man), and
11. *Might,* גְּבוּרָה *geburah.*
Psa. 89. 13 Thou hast a mighty arm: strong is thy h.
Isa. 3. 25 Thy men shall fall..and thy mighty in the
12. *Mighty,* גִּבָּר *gibbar.*
Dan. 3. 20 he commanded the most mighty men that
13. *Great,* גָּדוֹל *gadol.*
Lev. 19. 15 nor honour the person of the mighty: (but)
Deut. 4. 37 brought thee..with his mighty power out
7. 21 God (is) among you, a mighty God and t.
7. 23 shall destroy them with a mighty destru.
9. 29 thou broughtest out by thy mighty power
Eze. 17. 17 Neither shall Pharaoh with (his) mighty
Jon. 1. 4 and there was a mighty tempest in the sea
14. *Arm,* זְרוֹעַ *zeroa.*
Job 22. 8 But..the mighty man, he had the earth
15. *Strong, hard,* חָזָק *chazaq.*
Exod. 3. 19 not let you go, no, not by a mighty hand
32. 11 with great power, and with a mighty hand
Deut. 3. 24 to show..thy greatness, and thy mighty
4. 34 by war, and by a mighty hand, and by a
5. 15 brought thee out thence through a mighty
6. 21 brought us out of Egypt with a mighty h.
7. 8 LORD brought you out with a mighty hand
7. 19 the wonders, and the mighty hand, and
9. 26 brought forth out of Egypt with a mighty
11. 2 his greatness, his mighty hand, and his s.
26. 8 brought us forth out of Egypt with a mi.
34. 12 in all that mighty hand, and in all the g.
Josh. 4. 24 the hand of the LORD, that it (is) mighty
2 Ch. 6. 32 thy mighty hand, and thy stretched out
Job 5. 15 But he saveth..from the hand of the mi.
Prov23. 11 their Redeemer (is) mighty; he shall plead
Isa. 28. 2 the LORD hath a mighty and strong one
Eze. 20. 33,34 with a mighty hand, and with a stret.
Dan. 9. 15 out of the land of Egypt with a mighty
16. *Strength, hardness,* חֶזְקָה *chezqah.*
Judg. 4. 3 twenty years he mightily oppressed the
Jon. 3. 8 cry mightily unto God; yea, let them turn
17. *Force, might,* חַיִל *chayil.*
2 Ch.26. 13 that made war with mighty power to help
18. *Heavy,* כַּבִּיר *kabbir.*
Job 34. 24 He shall break in pieces mighty men wi.
36. 5 God (is) mighty..mighty in strength (and)
Isa. 17. 12 make a rushing like the rushing of mig.
28. 2 as a flood of mighty waters overflowing
19. *Might,* מְאֹד *meod.*
Exod10. 19 LORD turned a mighty strong west wind
Deut. 6. 3 that ye may increase mightily, as the L.
Nah. 2. 1 make..loins strong, fortify..power migh.
20. *Strong,* עַז *az.*
Neh. 9. 11 threwest..as a stone into the mighty wa.
Psa. 59. 3 the mighty are gathered against me; not
Isa. 43. 16 which maketh..a path in the mighty wa.
21. *Terror,* עַיָם *ayam.*
Isa. 11. 15 with his mighty wind shall he shake his
22. *Bony, substantial,* עָצוּם *atsum.*
Gen. 18. 18 shall surely become a great and mighty
Exod. 1. 9 of Israel (are) more and mightier than we
Num 14. 12 a greater nation and mightier than they
22. 6 for they (are) too mighty for me: peradv.
Deut. 4. 38 greater and mightier than thou..to bring
7. 1 seven nations greater and mightier than
9. 1 nations greater and mightier than thyself
9. 14 a nation mightier and greater than they
11. 23 greater nations and mightier than yourse.
26. 5 there a nation, great, mighty, and popul.
Psa. 135. 10 Who smote great nations, and slew mig.
Prov.18. 18 The lot..parteth between the mighty
Dan. 8. 24 shall destroy the mighty and the holy p.
11. 25 to battle with a very great and mighty a.
Amos 5. 12 manifold transgressions and your mighty
23. *Terrible,* עָרִיץ *arits.*
Job 6. 23 Redeem me from the hand of the mighty
24. *Great, mighty,* רַב *rab.*
Job 35. 9 cry out by reason of the arm of the mighty
25. *Ruler, ruling,* שַׁלִּיט *shallit.*
Eccl. 7. 19 more than ten mighty..which are in the
26. *Strong,* תַּקִּיף *taqqiph.*
Ezra 4. 20 There have been mighty kings also over
Eccl. 6. 10 may he contend with him that is mightier
Dan. 4. 3 how mighty (are) his wonders! his kingdom
27. *God, godlike, mighty,* אֱלֹהִים *elohim.*
Gen. 23. 6 Thou (art) a mighty prince among us: in the
28. *Might,* גֶּבֶר *geber.*
Isa. 22. 17 carry thee away with a mighty captivity
Jer. 41. 16 mighty men of war, and the women, and
29. *Sons of the mighty,* בְּנֵי אֵלִים *bene elim.*
Psa. 29. 1 Give unto the LORD, O ye mighty, give unto
30. *Forcible, violent,* βίαιος *biaios.*
Acts 2. 2 as of a rushing mighty wind, and it filled
31. *Power,* δύναμις *dunamis.*
Rom 15. 19 Through mighty signs and wonders, by
Col. 1. 29 working, which worketh in me mightily
2 Th. 1. 7 be revealed from heaven with his mighty
32. *Able, powerful one,* δυνάστης *dunastēs.*
Luke 1. 52 He hath put down the mighty from (their)
33. *Able, powerful,* δυνατός *dunatos.*
Luke 1. 49 he that is mighty hath done to me great
24. 19 which was a prophet mighty in deed and w.
Acts 7. 22 Moses..was mighty in words and in deeds
18. 24 mighty in the scriptures, came to Ephesus
1 Co. 1. 26 how that..not many mighty, not many
2 Co.10. 4 but mighty through God to the pulling d.
34. *Intently, intensely,* εὐτόνως *eutonōs.*
Acts 18. 28 he mightily convinced the Jews..publicly
35. *Of might, in strength,* ἰσχύος *or* ἐν ἰσχύϊ.
Eph. 1. 19 acc. to the working of his mighty power
Rev. 18. 2 [And he cried mightily with a strong voice]
36. *Strong,* ἰσχυρός *ischuros.*
Matt. 3. 11 he that cometh after me is mightier than
Mark 1. 7 There cometh one mightier than I after
Luke 3. 16 one mightier than I cometh, the latchet
15. 14 there arose a mighty famine in that land
1 Co. 1. 27 to confound the things which are mighty
Rev. 10. 1 I saw another mighty angel come down
18. 10 that great city Babylon, that mighty city
18. 21 a mighty angel took up a stone like a gr.
19. 6 as the voice of mighty thunderings, saying
19. 18 the flesh of mighty men, and the flesh of
37. *According to or in strength,* κατὰ κράτος *kata.*
Acts 19. 20 So mightily grew the word of God and p.
38. *Strong,* κραταιός *krataios.*
1 Pe. 5. 6 Humble yourselves therefore under the m.
39. *Great,* μέγας *megas.*
Rev. 6. 13 tree..when she is shaken of a mighty wind
[*See also* Deed, powers, works.]

MIGHTY, mightier, to be —
1. *To be or become mighty,* גָּבַר *gabar.*
Job 21. 7 the wicked..become old, yea, are mighty
2. *To be or become bony, substantial,* עָצַם *atsam.*
Gen. 26. 16 Go from us; for thou art much mightier
Psa. 69. 4 they..mine enemies wrongfully, are migh.
Dan. 8. 24 his power shall be mighty, but not by his
3. *To be able, have power,* δυνατέω *dunateō.*
2 Co. 13. 3 which to you ward is not weak, but is m.
4. *To work in,* ἐνεργέω *energeō.*
Gal. 2. 8 the same was mighty in me toward the G.

MIGHTY act or power —
Might, mighty deed, גְּבוּרָה *geburah.*
Psa.106. 2 Who can utter the mighty acts of the L.?

Psa.106. 8 might make his mighty power to be kno.
145. 4 One generation..shall declare thy mighty
145. 12 To make known..his mighty acts, 150. 2.

2. *Greatness*, μεγαλειότης *megaleiotēs*, Luke 9. 43.

MIGHTY, to become or wax —

1. *To strengthen self*, חָזַק *chazaq*, 7.
2 Ch.13. 21 Abijah waxed mighty, and married four.
27. 6 So Jotham became mighty, because he p.

2. *To be or become bony, substantial*, עָצַם *atsam*.
Exod. 1. 7 multiplied, and waxed exceeding mighty
1. 20 people multiplied, and waxed very mighty

MIGHTY deed or work —

Power, δύναμις *dunamis*.
Matt11. 20 wherein most of his mighty works were
11. 21 if the mighty works which were done in
11. 23 if the mighty works, which have been d.
13. 54 Whence..thiswisdom,and(these)mightyw.
13. 58 he did not many mighty works there, be.
14. 2 therefore mighty works do show forth th.
Mark 6. 2 that even such mighty works are wrought
6. 5 he could there do no mighty work, save
6. 14 therefore mighty works do show forth th.
Luke10. 13 if the mighty works had been done in Tyre
19. 37 all the mighty works that they had seen
2 Co.12. 12 in signs, and wonders, and mighty deeds

MIGHTY God —

A rock, firm one, צוּר *tsur*.
Hab. 1. 12 O mighty God, thou hast established them

MIGHTY man —

1. *A man, male*, אִישׁ *ish*.
Isa. 5. 15 the mighty man shall be humbled, and
31. 8 fall with the sword, not of a mighty man

2. *Mighty*, גִּבּוֹר *gibbor*.
Gen. 6. 4 the same(became)mighty men which(we.)
Josh. 1. 14 the mighty men of valour, and help them
6. 2 I have given into thine hand..mighty men
8. 3 thirty thousand mighty men of valour
10. 7 with him,and all the mighty men of valour
Judg. 6. 12 LORD (is) with thee, thou mighty man of
11. 1 Jephthah..was a mighty man of valour
1 Sa. 2. 4 The bows of the mighty men (are) broken
9. 1 Kish..a Benjamite, a mighty man of po.
2 Sa. 10. 7 Joab, and all the host of the mighty men
16. 6 and all the people and all the mighty m.
17. 8 his men, that they (be) mighty men, and
17. 10 knoweth that thy father (is) a mighty man
20. 7 and the Pelethites, and all the mighty m.
23. 8 These (be) the names of the mighty men
23. 9 (one) of the three mighty men with David
23. 16 the three mighty men brake through the
23. 17 These things did these three mighty men
23. 22 and had the name among three mighty m.
1 Ki. 1. 8 Shimei, and Rei, and the mighty men w.
1. 10 and Benaiah, and the mighty men, and S.
11. 28 the man Jeroboam (was) a mighty man of
2 Ki. 15. 20 of all the mighty men of wealth, of each
24. 14 princes, and all the mighty men of valour
1 Ch. 7. 7 mighty men of valour; and were reckoned
7. 9 of their fathers, mighty men of valour
7. 11 of their fathers, mighty men of valour
7. 40 choice..mighty men of valour, chief of the
8. 40 the sons of Ulam were mighty men of va.
11. 10 the chief of the mighty men whom David
11. 11 number of the mighty men whom David
12. 1 among the mighty men, helpers of the w.
12. 4 a mighty man among the thirty, and over
12. 21 for they (were) all mighty men of valour
12. 25 of Simeon, mighty men of valour for the
12. 30 mighty men of valour, famous throughout
19. 8 Joab, and all the host of the mighty men
26. 6 for they (were) mighty men of valour
26. 31 found among them mighty men of valour
28. 1 with the mighty men, and with all the
29. 24 all the princes, and the mighty men, and
2 Ch.13. 3 chosen men, (being) mighty men of valour
14. 8 And..all these (were) mighty men of valour
17. 13 and the men of war, mighty men of valour
17. 14 and with him mighty men of valour three
17. 16 two hundred thousand mighty men of va.
17. 17 Eliada a mighty man of valour, and with
25. 6 an hundred thousand mighty men of val.
26. 12 chief of the fathers of the mighty men of
28. 7 Zichri, a mighty man of Ephraim, slew M.
32. 3 with his princes and his mighty men to
32. 21 which cut off all the mighty men of valour
Neh.11. 14 their brethren, mighty men of valour, an
Psa. 33. 16 a mighty man is not delivered by much
52. 1 Why boastest thou..O mighty man? the
78. 65 like a mighty man that shouteth by reason
127. 4 As arrows (are) in the hand of a mighty m.
Song 4. 4 thousand bucklers, all shields of mighty m.
Isa. 3. 2 The mighty man, and the man of war, the
21. 17 the mighty men of the children of Kedar
42. 13 The LORD shall go forth as a mighty man
Jer. 5. 16 open sepulchre, they (are) all mighty men
9. 23 neither..the mighty (man) glory in his m.
14. 9 as a mighty man (that) cannot save? yet
26. 21 Jehoiakim the king, with all his mighty m.
46. 6 Let not the swift..nor the mighty man
46. 9 let the mighty men come forth; the
46. 12 the mighty man hath stumbled against the
48. 41 the mighty men's hearts in Moab at that
49. 22 shall the heart of the mighty men of
50. 9 their arrows..as of a mighty expert man
50. 36 a sword (is) upon her mighty men; and
51. 30 The mighty men of Babylon have
51. 56 upon Babylon, and her mighty men are
Jer. 51. 57 make drunk..her rulers, and her mighty m.
Eze. 39. 20 with mighty men, and with all men of war
Hos. 10. 13 trust..in the multitude of thy mighty men
Joel. 2. 7 They shall run like mighty men; they sh.
3. 9 Prepare war, wake up the mighty men, let
Nah. 2. 3 The shield of his mighty men is made red
Zeph. 1. 14 the mighty man shall cry there bitterly
Zech. 9. 13 made thee as the sword of a mighty man

3. *Mighty or strong ones*, אֵילִים *elim*.
Exod15. 15 the mighty men of Moab, trembling shall

4. *Powerful*, δυνατός *dunatos*.
Rev. 6. 15 the chief captains, and the [mighty men]

MIGHTY one —

1. *Mighty*, אַבִּיר *abbir*.
Judg. 5. 22 by..the prancings of their mighty ones

2. *Honourable, shining*, אַדִּיר *addir*.
Isa. 10. 34 and Lebanon shall fall by a mighty one

3. *Mighty one, god*, אֵל *el*.
Eze. 31. 11 into the hand of the mighty one of the h.

4. *Mighty one*, גִּבּוֹר *gibbor*.
Gen. 10. 8 he began to be a mighty one in the earth
Isa. 13. 3 I have also called my mighty ones for m.
Jer. 46. 5 their mighty ones are beaten down, and
Joel 3. 11 thither cause thy mighty ones to come d.

5. *A rock, firm one*, צוּר *tsur*.
Isa. 30. 29 mountain of the LORD, to the mighty One

MIGHTY things —

To cut off, fence, בָּצַר *batsar*.
Jer. 33. 3 show thee great and mighty things, which

MIGHTY, so —

Such, so much, τηλικοῦτος *tēlikoutos*.
Rev. 16. 18 so mighty an earthquake, (and) so great

MIG'-RON, מִגְרוֹן *land-slip*.

A city in Benjamin near Gibeah, where the main road from Aiath to Michmash passed, Isa. 10. 28. Now called *Makrun*.
1 Sa. 14. 2 a pomegranate tree which (is) in M.: and
Isa. 10. 28 He is come to Aiath, he is passed to M.; at

MI-JA'-MIN, מִיָּמִן *fortunate*.

1. A priest in the time of David. B.C. 1040.
1 Ch.24. 9 The fifth to Malchijah, the sixth to M.

2. A priest that, with Nehemiah, sealed the covenant. (See *Mi-amin*). B.C. 450.
Neh. 10. 7 Meshullam, Abijah, M.

MIK'-LOTH, מִקְלוֹת *twigs, sticks*.

1. A Benjamite in Jerusalem. B.C. 1160.
1 Ch. 8. 32 And M. begat Shimeah. And these also
9. 37 Gedor, and Ahio, and Zechariah, and M.
9. 38 And M. begat Shimeam. And they also

2. A ruler in the second division of the guard appointed by David. B.C. 1020.
1 Ch. 27. 4 of his course (was) M. also the ruler: in

MIK-NE'-IAH, מִקְנֵיָהוּ *Jah is zealous*.

A Levite musician. B.C. 1015.
1 Ch.15. 18 brethren of the second (degree), Zech...M.
15. 21 M., and Obed-edom, and Jeiel, and Azaziah

MI-LA'-LAI, מִלֲלַי *Jah is elevated*.

A priest that took part in the purification of the wall. B.C. 445.
Neh. 12. 36 And his brethren..M., Gilalai, Maai, Ne.

MIL'-CAH, מִלְכָּה *counsel*.

1. Daughter of Haran Abraham's brother, wife of Nahor, and mother of Bethuel. B.C. 1996.
Gen. 11. 29 and the name of Nahor's wife, M., the d.
11. 29 Haran, the father of M., and the father
22. 20 Behold, M., she hath also born children
22. 23 these eight M. did bear to Nahor, Abra.
24. 15 who was born to Bethuel, son of M., the
24. 24 (am) the daughter of Bethuel the son of M.
24. 47 The daughter of Bethuel..whom M. bare

2. A daughter of Zelophehad, a Manassehite.
Num26. 33 the daughters of Zelophehad (were)..M.
27. 1 these (are) the names of his daughters..M.
36. 11 For Mahlah..and M., and Noah, the dau.
Josh.17. 3 these (are) the names of his daughters..M.

MILCH —

1. *To suckle, give suck*, יָנַק *yanaq*, 5.
Gen. 32. 15 Thirty milch camels with their colts, forty

2. *To suckle*, עוּל *ul*.
1 Sa. 6. 7 take two milch kine, on which there hath
6. 10 took two milch kine, and tied them to the

MIL'-COM, מִלְכֹּם.

The national deity of the Ammonites, the same as *Molech, Malcham*, or *Malchan*.
1 Ki. 11. 5 Solomon went after..M. the abomination
11. 33 and have worshipped..M. the god of the
2 Ki. 23. 13 had builded for..M. the abomination of

MILDEW —

Mildew, greenness, paleness, יֵרָקוֹן *yeraqon*.
Deut28. 22 smite thee..with blasting, and with mil.
1 Ki. 8. 37 if there be pestilence, blasting, mildew, l.
2 Ch. 6. 28 if there be blasting, or mildew, locusts, or
Amos 4. 9 I have smitten you with blasting and mil.
Hag. 2. 17 I smote you with blasting and with mild.

MILE —

A mile, μίλιον (*from Lat. miliarium*) *milion*.
Matt. 5. 41 whosoever shall compel thee to go a mile

MI-LE'-TUS, MI-LE'-TUM, Μίλητος.

A city and seaport in the province of Caria, at the S. of Ionia, on the confines of Caria, forty miles S. of Ephesus; it is now ten miles inland, and its ruins are called *Melas*. It had a temple of Apollo, and was the birthplace of Thales and Anaximander.
Acts 20. 15 And we sailed thence, and..we came to M.
20. 17 And from M. he sent to Ephesus, and ca.
2 Ti. 4. 20 but Trophimus have I left at M. sick

MILK —

1. *Milk, fat*, חָלָב *chalab*.
Gen. 18. 8 he took butter, and milk, and the calf w.
49. 12 with wine, and his teeth white with milk
Exod. 3. 8, 17 unto a land flowing with milk and hon.
[So in 13. 5; 33. 3; Lev. 20. 24; Num. 14. 8; 16. 13, 14; Deut. 6. 3; 11. 9; 26. 9, 15; 27. 3; Josh. 5. 6; Jer. 11. 5; 32. 22; Eze. 20. 6, 15.]
Exod23. 19 shalt not seethe a kid in his mother's milk
34. 26 shalt not seethe a kid in his mother's milk
Num13. 27 and surely it floweth with milk and honey
Deut14. 21 shalt not seethe a kid in his mother's milk
31. 20 land..that floweth with milk and honey
32. 14 Butter of kine, and milk of sheep, with fat
Judg. 4. 19 she opened a bottle of milk, and gave him
5. 25 He asked water..she gave..milk; she br.
Job 10. 10 Hast thou not poured me out as milk, and
21. 24 His breasts are full of milk, and his bones
Prov 27. 27 goats' milk..for thy food, for the food
30. 33 Surely the churning of milk bringeth forth
Song 4. 11 honey and milk (are) under thy tongue
5. 1 I have drunk my wine with my milk: eat
5. 12 His eyes..washed with milk..(and) fitly set
Isa. 7. 22 for the abundance of milk (that) they shall
28. 9 weaned from the milk..drawn from the
55. 1 come, buy wine and milk without money
60. 16 Thou shalt also suck the milk of the Ge.
Lam. 4. 7 they were whiter than milk, they were m.
Eze. 25. 4 eat thy fruit, and they shall drink thy m.
Joel 3. 18 the hills shall flow with milk, and all the

2. *Milk*, γάλα *gala*.
1 Co. 3. 2 I have fed you with milk, and not with m.
9. 7 or who..eateth not of the milk of the flo
Heb. 5. 12 are become such as have need of milk, and
5. 13 every one that useth milk (is) unskilful in
1 Pe. 2. 2 As new born babes, desire the sincere m.

MILK out, to —

To wring, suck, or milk out, מָצַץ *matsats*.
Isa. 66. 11 that ye may milk out, and be delighted

MILL (stone, nether or upper) —

1. *Mill stones*, רֵחַיִם *rechayim*.
Exod11. 5 the maid servant that (is) behind the mill
Num11. 8 ground (it) in mills, or beat (it) in a mor.
Deut24. 6 No man shall take the nether..millstone
Isa. 47. 2 Take the millstones, and grind meal: un.
Jer. 25. 10 the sound of the millstones, and the light

2. *A rider, upper mill stone*, רֶכֶב *rekeb*.
Deut24. 6 no man shall take the..upper millstone
Judg. 9. 53 cast a piece of a millstone, 2 Sa. 11. 21.

3. *A millstone*, λίθος μυλικός *lithos mulik.*, Mr. 9. 42.

4. *A mill*, μύλων *mulōn*.
Matt24. 41 Two (women shall be) grinding [at the m.]

5. *A millstone turned by an ass*, μύλος ὀνικός [*mulos*].
Matt18. 6 that [a millstone] were hanged about his
Luke17. 2 that [a millstone] were hanged about his
Rev. 18. 21 took up a stone like a great [millstone]
18. 22 the sound of a millstone shall be heard no

MILLET —

Millet, corn, דֹּחַן *dochan*.
Eze. 4. 9 beans, and lentiles, and millet, and fitches

MILLIONS —

A myriad, ten thousand, רְבָבָה *rebabah*.
Gen. 24. 60 be thou (the mother) of thousands of m

MIL'-LO, מִלּוֹא, מִלֹּא *fulness*.

1. A fortification near Shechem.
Judg. 9. 6 men of Shechem..and all the house of M
9. 20 and devour..the house of M.; and let fire
9. 20 men of Shechem..from the house of M

2. One near Jerusalem, enlarged by David and Solomon and wherein Joash was slain.
2 Sa. 5. 9 David built round about from M. and in.
1 Ki. 9. 15 to build..his own house, and M., and the
9. 24 had built for her: then did he build M.
11. 27 Solomon built M., (and) repaired the bre.
2 Ki.12. 20 slew Joash in the house of M., which
1 Ch.11. 8 he built the city..even from M. round
2 Ch.32. 5 and repaired M. (in) the city of David, and

MINCE, to —

To mince, trip nicely, טָפַף *taphaph*.
Isa. 3. 16 walking and mincing (as) they go, and mak.

MIND —

1. *Imagination, frame, formation*, יֵצֶר *yetser*.
Isa. 26. 3 in perfect peace, (whose) mind (is) stayed

2. *Heart*, לֵב *leb*.
Num16. 28 (I have) not (done them) of mine own mind
24. 13 go..to do..good or bad of mine own mind
1 Sa. 9. 20 set not thy mind on them; for they are
Neh. 4. 6 was joined..for the people had a mind to

Psa. 31. 12 I am forgotten as a dead man out of mind
Isa. 46. 8 bring (it) again to mind, O ye transgress.
65. 17 not be remembered, nor come into mind
Jer. 3. 16 neither shall it come to mind, neither sh.
19. 5 spake (it), neither came (it) into my mind
32. 35 neither came it into my mind, that they
44. 21 remember..and came it (not) into his m.
Lam. 3. 21 This I recall to my mind, therefore have

3. *Heart*, לְבַב *lebab*.
Deut 30. 1 thou shalt call (them) to mind among all
1 Ch.22. 7 it was in my mind to build an house unto
Jer. 51. 50 and let Jerusalem come into your mind
Eze. 38. 10 same time shall things come into thy mind

4. *Soul, breath*, נֶפֶשׁ *nephesh*.
Gen. 23. 8 If it be your mind that I should bury my
Deut 18. 6 come with all the desire of his mind unto
28. 65 give thee..failing of eyes, and sorrow of m.
1 Sa. 2. 35 which (is) in mine heart and in my mind
2 Sa. 17. 8 they (be) chafed in their minds, as a bear
2 Ki. 9. 15 If it be your minds..let none go forth (nor)
1 Ch.28. 9 a perfect heart and with a willing mind
Jer. 15. 1 my mind (could) not (be) toward this pe.
Eze. 23. 17 and her mind was alienated from them
23. 18 then my mind was alienated from her
23. 18 like as my mind was alienated from her
23. 22 from whom thy mind is alienated, and I
23. 28 into the hand (of them) from whom thy m.
24. 25 that whereupon they set their minds, th.
36. 5 with despiteful minds, to cast it out for

5. *Mouth*, פֶּה *peh*.
Lev. 24. 12 that the mind of the LORD might be sho.

6. *Spirit*, רוּחַ *ruach*.
Gen. 26. 35 Which were a grief of mind unto Isaac
Prov.29. 11 A fool uttereth all his mind: but a wise
Eze. 11. 5 know the things that come into your m.
20. 32 that which cometh into your mind shall
Dan. 5. 20 and his mind hardened in pride, he was d.
Hab. 1. 11 Then shall (his) mind change, and he sh.

7. *Knowledge, opinion, decision*, γνώμη *gnōmē*.
Phm. 14 But without thy mind would I do nothing
Rev. 17. 13 These have one mind, and shall give their

8. *Intellect, full or thorough mind*, διάνοια *dianoia*.
Matt22. 37 with all thy soul, and with all thy mind
Mark12. 30 with all thy soul, and with all thy mind
Luke10. 27 with all thy strength, and with all thy m.
Eph. 2. 3 the desires of the flesh and of the mind
Col. 1. 21 enemies in (your) mind by wicked works
Heb. 8. 10 I will put my laws into their mind, and
10. 16 my laws..in their minds will I write them
1 Pe. 1. 13 Wherefore gird up the loins of your mind
2 Pe. 3. 1 I stir up your pure minds by way of rem.

9. *Inner mind, purpose*, ἔννοια *ennoia*.
1 Pe. 4. 1 arm yourselves likewise with the same m.

10. *Thought*, νόημα *noēma*.
2 Co. 3. 14 their minds were blinded; for until this day
4. 4 hath blinded the minds of them which bel.
11. 3 so your minds should be corrupted from
Phil. 4. 7 shall keep your hearts and minds through

11. *Mind, will*, νοῦς *nous*.
Rom. 1. 28 God gave them over to a reprobate mind
7. 23 warring against the law of my mind, and
7. 25 So then with the mind I myself serve the
11. 34 For who hath known the mind of the L.?
12. 2 transformed by the renewing of your mi.
14. 5 man be fully persuaded in his own mind
1 Co. 1. 10 joined together in the same mind and in
2. 16 For who hath known the mind of the Lord
2. 16 But we have the mind of Christ
Eph. 4. 17 ye..walk not..in the vanity of their mind
4. 23 be renewed in the spirit of your mind
Col. 2. 18 not..vainly puffed up by his fleshly mind
2 Th. 2. 2 That ye be not soon shaken in mind, or
1 Ti. 6. 5 disputings of men of corrupt minds, and
2 Ti. 3. 8 men of corrupt minds, reprobate concern.
Titus 1. 15 even their mind and conscience is defiled
Rev. 17. 9 And here (is) the mind which hath wisdom

12. *Mind, inclination*, φρόνημα *phronēma*.
Rom. 8. 7 Because the carnal mind (is) enmity aga.
8. 27 knoweth what (is) the mind of the Spirit

13. *Soul, animal life*, ψυχή *psuchē*.
Acts 14. 2 made their minds evil affected against the
Phil. 1. 27 with one mind striving together for the f.
Heb. 12. 3 lest ye be wearied and faint in your minds

MIND, to —

1. *To be about*, μέλλω *mellō*.
Acts 20. 13 he appointed, minding himself to go afoot

2. *To mind, will*, φρονέω *phroneō*.
Rom. 8. 5 they that are after the flesh do m; 12. 16.
Phil. 3. 16 [same rule, let us mind the same thing]
3. 19 glory is in their shame, who mind earthly t.

[*See also* Cast, change, doubtful, fervent, forwardness, humbleness, humility, lowliness, put in readiness, ready, sound, wicked, willing.]

MIND, to be in a right —

To have a sound mind, σωφρονέω *sōphroneō*.
Mark 5. 15 see him..clothed, and in his right mind
Luke 8. 35 feet of Jesus, clothed, and in his right m.

MIND, let this —

To mind this, φρονέω τοῦτο *phroneō touto*.
Phil. 2. 5 Let this [mind] be in you, which was also

MIND, to be of one or the same —

To mind the same thing, τὸ αὐτὸ φρονέω [*phroneō*].
Rom.12. 16 (Be) of the same mind; 2 Co.13. 11, Phil. 4. 2.

MIND, be according to —

[*Be*] *from with*, מֵעִם. Job 34. 33.

MIND, to call to —

To remind, put in mind, ἀναμιμνήσκω *anamimnēs*.
Mark14. 72 Peter called to mind the word that Jesus

MIND, of one —

1. *Of a like mind*, ὁμόφρων *homophrōn*.
1 Pe. 3. 8 Finally..all of one mind, having compas.

2. *To mind the same thing*, φρονέω τὸ ἕν [*phroneō*].
Phil. 2. 2 the same love..of one accord, of one mind

MIND, to put in —

To remind quietly, ὑπομιμνήσκω *hupomimnēskō*.
Titus 3. 1 Put them in mind to be subject to princ.

MIND, with one —

With the like mind, ὁμοθυμαδόν *homothumadon*.
Rom 15. 6 That ye may with one mind..one mouth

MINDED, to be —

1. *To be with the heart*, הָיָה עִם לֵב *hayah im leb*.
2 Ch.24. 4 Joash was minded to repair the house of

2. *To wish, will, determine*, βούλομαι, βουλεύομαι.
Matt. 1. 19 Joseph..was minded to put her away pr.
Acts 27. 39 a shore, into the which they were minded
2 Co. 1. 15 I was minded to come unto you before
1. 17 When I therefore was thus [minded], did

3. *To mind, set the mind on*, φρονέω *phroneō*.
Gal. 5. 10 that ye will be none otherwise minded
Phil. 3. 15 Let..be thus minded..be otherwise minded

MINDED, to be carnally —

The mind of the flesh, φρόνημα τῆς σαρκός *phron*.
Rom. 8. 6 For to be carnally minded (is) death; but

MINDED, to be sober —

To be of a sound mind, σωφρονέω *sōphroneō*.
Titus 2. 6 men likewise exhort to be sober minded

MINDED, to be spiritually —

The mind of the spirit, φρόνημα τοῦ πνεύματος.
Rom. 8. 6 to be spiritually minded (is) life and peace

MINDED, to be high —

To be raised or puffed up, τυφόομαι *tuphoomai*.
2 Ti. 3. 4 Traitors, heady, high minded, lovers of pl.

MINDFUL (of), to be —

1. *To remember, be mindful of*, זָכַר *zakar*.
1 Ch.16. 15 Be ye mindful always of his covenant, the
Neh. 9. 17 neither were mindful of thy wonders that
Psa. 8. 4 What is man, that thou art mindful of
111. 5 he will ever be mindful of his covenant
115. 12 The LORD hath been mindful of us: he
Isa. 17. 10 hast not been mindful of the Rock of thy

2. *To remember, be mindful of*, μιμνήσκομαι *mimn*.
2 Ti. 1. 4 being mindful of thy tears, that I may be
Heb. 2. 6 What is man, that thou art mindful of him
2 Pe. 3. 2 That ye may be mindful of the words wh.

3. *To remember, recollect*, μνημονεύω *mnēmoneuō*.
Heb.11. 15 truly, if they had been mindful of that

MINE —

1. *I, I myself*, אֲנִי *ani*.
Prov 23. 15 be wise, my heart shall rejoice, even mine

2. *To me*, לִי [*le*].
Gen. 31. 43, 48. 5; Exod 13. 2, 19. 5, 34. 19, *&c., &c.*

3. *With me*, עִמָּדִי [*immad*].
Psa. 50. 11 and the wild beasts of the field (are) mine

4. *To me, my, mine*, ἐμοί (*dat.*) *emoi*.
Rom 12. 19 Vengeance (is) mine; I will repay, saith

5. *Of me, my, mine*, ἐμός (*gen.*) *emos*.
Matt20. 23 is not mine to give, but..for whom it is
John 7. 16 My doctrine is not mine, but his that sent
10. 14 and know my (sheep), and am known of m.
14. 24 the word which ye hear is not mine, but
16. 14 he shall receive of mine, and shall show (it)
16. 15 All things that the Father hath are mine
16. 15 therefore said I, that he shall take of m.
17. 10 And all mine are thine, and thine are m.
1 Co. 9. 2 seal of mine apostleship are ye in the L.
9. 3 Mine answer to them that do examine me

6. *Of me, my, mine*, ἐμοῦ (*gen.*) *emou*.
Rom 16. 13 Salute Rufus..and his mother and mine

7. *To me, my, mine*, μοί (*dat.*) *moi*.
Luke 9. 38 look upon my son; for he is mine only c.

8. *Of me, mine, my*, μου (*gen.*) *mou*.
Matt. 7. 24 whosoever heareth these sayings of mine
7. 26 every one that heareth these sayings of m.
Luke 1. 44 the voice of thy salutation sounded in mine
11. 6 For a friend of mine in his journey is come
18. 3 came..saying, Avenge me of mine adver.
19. 27 But those mine enemies, which would not
John 9. 11 Jesus made clay, and anointed mine eyes
9. 15 He put clay upon mine eyes, and I washed
9. 30 a marvellous thing..he hath opened mine
Rom. 11. 13 apostle of the Gentiles, I magnify mine of.
2 Co.11. 30 I will glory of..things which concern m.
12. 5 of myself I will not glory, but in [mine] in.
Phil. 1. 4; Rev. 22. 16; Mark 9. 24; Luke 2. 30; John 2. 4; Acts 21. 13; Rom. 16. 23.

MINE own (self) —

1. *He, it*, αὐτός *autos*.
Luke19. 23 I might have required mine own with us.?

2. *Of myself*, ἐμαυτοῦ (*gen.*) *emautou*.
John 5. 30 I can of mine own self do nothing: as I
1 Co. 4. 3 small thing..yea, I judge not mine own s.
10. 33 not seeking mine own profit, but the (profit)

3. *To me, my, mine*, ἐμός (*dat.*) *emos*.
Matt25. 27 I should have received mine own; 20. 15.
John 5. 30 I seek not mine own will, but the will of
6. 38 not to do mine own will, but the will of
1 Co. 1. 15 say that I had baptized in mine own name
16. 21 The salutation of (me) Paul with mine own
Gal. 6. 11 I have written unto you with mine own
Phil. 3. 9 not having mine own righteousness, wh.
2 Th. 3. 17 The salutation of Paul with mine own h.
Phm. 12 therefore receive him that is mine own bo.
19 I Paul have written (it) with mine own h.

4. *Of me, my, mine*, μου (*gen.*) *mou*.
John 8. 50 I seek not mine own glory: there is one
Acts 13. 22 a man after mine own heart, which shall
26. 4 which was at the first among mine own na.
Gal. 1. 14 above many my equals in mine own nation

MINGLE, to —

1. *To mix*, בָּלַל *balal*.
Exod29. 40 tenth deal of flour mingled with the fou.
Lev. 2. 4 unleavened cakes of fine flour mingled w.
2. 5 fine flour unleavened, mingled with oil
7. 10 every meat offering mingled with oil, and
7. 12 unleavened cakes mingled with oil, and
7. 12 cakes mingled with oil, of fine flour, fried
9. 4 a meat offering mingled with oil: for to day
14. 10 a meat offering, mingled with oil, and one
14. 21 one tenth deal of fine flour mingled with
23. 13 two tenth deals of fine flour mingled with
Num. 6. 15 cakes of fine flour mingled with oil, and wa.
7. 13 full of fine flour mingled with oil, for
[So in v. 19, 25, 31, 37, 43, 49, 55, 61, 67, 73, 79.]
8. 8 fine flour mingled with oil, and another
15. 4, 6, 9 of a tenth deal of flour mingled with
28. 5 mingled with the fourth (part) of an hin
28. 9, 12, 12 a meat offering, mingled with oil
28. 13 a several tenth deal of flour mingled with
28. 20, 28 their meat offering..of flour mingled
29. 3, 9, 14 their meat offering..flour mingled

2. *To mix, mingle*, מָסַךְ *masak*.
Psa.102. 9 I have..mingled my drink with weeping
Prov. 9. 2 she hath mingled her wine; she hath also
9. 5 drink of the wine (which) I have mingled
Isa. 5. 22 men of strength to mingle strong drink
19. 14 The LORD hath mingled a perverse spirit

3. *To mix, mingle*, μίγνυμι *mignumi*.
Matt27. 34 They gave him vinegar to drink mingled
Luke13. 1 whose blood Pilate had mingled with their
Rev. 8. 7 followed hail and fire mingled with blood
15. 2 I saw as it were a sea of glass mingled with

MINGLE selves, be mingled, to —

1. *To mingle self*, עָרַב *arab*, 7.
Ezra 9. 2 the holy seed have mingled themselves
Psa.106. 35 But were mingled among the heathen, and

2. *To be mingled*, עֲרַב *arab*, 4.
Dan. 2. 43 they shall mingle themselves with the seed

MINGLED people —

The mixture, Arab, הָעֶרֶב *ha-ereb*.
Jer. 25. 20 all the mingled people, and all the kings
25. 24 all the kings of the mingled people that
Eze. 30. 5 Lydia, and all the mingled people, and Ch.

MINGLED (seed)—

1. *Two divers kinds*, כִּלְאַיִם *kilayim*.
Lev. 19. 19 shalt not sow thy field with mingled seed
19. 19 neither shall a garment mingled of linen

2. *To take or catch self*, לָקַח *laqach*, 7.
Exod. 9. 24 So there was hail, and fire mingled with

MIN-IA'-MIN, מִנְיָמִן *fortunate*.

1. A Levite in the days of Hezekiah who distributed the tithes and oblations. B.C. 724.
2 Ch.31. 15 next him (were) Eden, and M., and Jeshua

2. A priest who returned with Zerubbabel, called also *Miamin*. B.C. 450.
Neh. 12. 17 Of Abijah, Zichri; of M., of Moadiah, Piltai
12. 41 the priests; Eliakim, Maaseiah, M., Michaiah

MINISH, be minished, to —

1. *To diminish, withdraw*, גָּרַע *gara*.
Exod. 5. 19 Ye shall not minish..from your bricks of

2. *To be or become little, few*, מָעַט *maat*.
Psa. 107. 39 are minished and brought low through

MINISTER — [*See* PRIEST'S OFFICE.]

1. *To split, till, serve*, פְּלַח *pelach*.
Ezra 7. 24 or ministers of this house of God, it shall

2. *To minister, serve*, שָׁרַת *sharath*, 3.
Exod24. 13 Moses rose up, and his minister Joshua
Josh. 1. 1 Joshua the son of Nun, Moses' minister
1 Ki.10. 5 the attendance of his ministers, and their
2 Ch. 9. 4 the attendance of his ministers, and their
Ezra 8. 17 they should bring unto us ministers for the
Psa.103. 21 (ye) ministers of his, that do his pleasure
104. 4 Who maketh..his ministers a flaming fire
Isa. 61. 6 (men) shall call you the ministers of our
Jer. 33. 21 the Levites the priests, my ministers
Eze 44. 11 Yet they shall be ministers in my sanct.
45. 4 the priests the ministers of the sanctuary
45. 5 the Levites, the ministers of the house
46. 24 where the ministers of the house shall b.
Joel 1. 9 the priests, the LORD'S ministers, mourn
1. 13 ye ministers of the altar..ye ministers of
2. 17 Let the priests, the ministers of the LORD

3. *Deacon, labourer, ministrant,* διάκονος *diakonos.*
Matt 20. 26 great among you, let him be your minister
Mark 10. 43 be great among you, shall be your minis.
Rom. 13. 4 For he is the minister of God to thee for
13. 4 for he is the minister of God, a revenger
15. 8 Christ was a minister of the circumcision
1 Co. 3. 5 but minister by whom ye believed, even
2 Co. 3. 6 Who also hath made us able ministers of
6. 4 approving ourselves as the ministers of G.
11. 15 (it is) no great thing if his ministers also
11. 15 transformed as the ministers of
11. 23 Are they ministers of Christ? I speak as
Gal. 2. 17 (is) therefore Christ the minister of sin?
Eph. 3. 7 Whereof I was made a minister, according
6. 21 a beloved brother and faithful minister
Col. 1. 7 who is for you a faithful minister of Chr.
1. 23 gospel..whereof I Paul am made a mini.
1. 25 Whereof I am made a minister, according
4. 7 a beloved brother, and a faithful minister
1 Th. 3. 2 [our brother, and minister of God, and]
1 Ti. 4. 6 thou shalt be a good minister of Jesus C.

4. *Public worker, or labourer,* λειτουργός *leitourgos.*
Rom 13. 6 they are God's ministers, attending cont.
15. 16 That I should be the minister of Jesus C.
Heb. 1. 7 Who maketh..his ministers a flame of fire
8. 2 A minister of the sanctuary, and of the true

5. *An under rower, assistant,* ὑπηρέτης *hupēretēs.*
Luke 1. 2 eye witnesses, and ministers of the word
4. 20 gave (it) again to the minister, and sat d.
Acts 13. 5 and they had also John to (their) minister
26. 16 make thee a minister and a witness both
1 Co. 4. 1 so account of us as of the ministers of C.

MINISTER (to or unto), to —

1. *To minister,* שְׁמַשׁ *shemash,* 3.
Dan. 7. 10 thousand thousands ministered unto him

2. *To minister, serve,* שָׁרַת *sharath,* 3.
Exod 28. 35 And it shall be upon Aaron to minister
28. 43 they come near unto the altar to minister
29. 30 when he cometh..to minister in the holy
30. 20 when they come near to the altar to min.
35. 19 The cloths..to minister in the priest's offi.
39. 26 round about the hem of the robe to mini.
39. 41 The cloths..to minister in the priest's offi.
Num 1. 50 they shall minister unto it, and shall
3. 6 priest, that they may minister unto him
3. 31 wherewith they minister, and the hanging
4. 9 oil vessels..wherewith they minister unto
4. 12 wherewith they minister in the sanctuary
4. 14 wherewith they minister about it..censers
8. 26 But shall minister with their brethren in
16. 9 the congregation to minister unto them
18. 2 may be joined unto thee, and minister unto
Deut 10. 8 to stand before the LORD to minister unto
17. 12 the priest that standeth to minister there
18. 5 to stand to minister in the name of the L.
18. 7 Then..shall minister in the name of the L.
21. 5 LORD thy God hath chosen to minister unto
1 Sa. 2. 11 the child did minister unto the LORD be.
2. 18 But Samuel ministered before the LORD
3. 1 the child Samuel ministered unto the LORD
2 Sa. 13. 17 he called his servant that ministered unto
1 Ki. 1. 4 cherished the king, and ministered to him
1. 15 Abishag the Shunammite ministered unto
8. 11 the priests could not stand to minister bec.
19. 21 went after Elijah, and ministered unto
2 Ki. 25. 14 the vessels of brass wherewith they mi.
1 Ch. 6. 32 they ministered before the dwelling place
15. 2 to carry the ark of God, and to minister
16. 4 to minister before the ark of the LORD
16. 37 to minister before the ark continually, as
23. 13 to minister unto him, and to bless in his
26. 12 men..to minister in the house of the LORD
28. 1 captains of the companies that ministered
2 Ch. 5. 14 the priests could not stand to minister by
8. 14 to praise and minister before the priests
13. 10 the priests, which minister unto the LORD
22. 8 the brethren of Ahaziah, that ministered
23. 6 and they that minister of the Levites
29. 11 that ye should minister unto him, and burn
31. 2 to minister, and to give thanks, and to p.
Neh. 10. 36 priests that minister in the house of our
10. 39 the priests that minister, and the porters
Esth. 2. 2 said the king's servants that ministered u.
6. 3 said the king's servants that ministered u.
Isa. 60. 7 rams of Nebaioth shall minister unto thee
60. 10 their kings shall minister unto thee; for
Jer. 33. 22 David..and the Levites that minister unto
52. 18 vessels of brass wherewith they ministered
Eze. 40. 46 which come near to the LORD to minister u.
42. 14 shall lay their garments wherein they m.
43. 19 to minister unto me, saith the Lord GOD
44. 11 ministering to the house..to minister unto
44. 12 Because they ministered unto them before
44. 15 they shall come near to me to minister unto
44. 16 shall come near to my table, to minister
44. 17 whiles they minister in the gates of the
44. 19 off their garments wherein they ministered
44. 27 to minister in the sanctuary, he shall offer
45. 4 which shall come near to minister unto

3. *Ministry,* שָׁרֵת *shareth.*
2 Ch. 24. 14 were made..vessels to minister, and to

4. *To act as a deacon, serve,* διακονέω *diakoneō.*
Matt. 4. 11 angels came and ministered unto him
8. 15 and she arose, and ministered unto them
20. 28 not to be ministered unto, but to minister
25. 44 in prison, and did not minister unto thee?
27. 55 which followed Jesus..ministering unto
Mark 1. 13 tempted..and the angels ministered unto
Mark 1. 31 fever left her, and she ministered unto th.
10. 45 not to be ministered unto, but to minister
15. 41 followed him, and ministered unto him
Luke 4. 39 immediately she arose and ministered unto
8. 3 which ministered unto him of their subs.
Acts 19. 22 sent..two of them that ministered unto
Rom 15. 25 I go unto Jerusalem to minister unto the
2 Co. 3. 3 to be the epistle of Christ ministered by
2 Ti. 1. 18 in how many things he ministered unto
Phm. 13 he might have ministered unto me in the
Heb. 6. 10 ye have ministered to the saints, and do m.
1 Pe. 1. 12 they did minister the things which are
4. 10 minister the same one to another, as good
4. 11 if any man minister, (let him do it) as of

5. *Unto ministration,* εἰς διακονίαν *eis diakonian.*
Heb. 1. 14 spirits, sent forth to minister for them who

6. *To give,* δίδωμι *didōmi.*
Eph. 4. 29 that it may minister grace unto the hea.

7. *To supply,* ἐπιχορηγέω *epichorēgeō.*
2 Co. 9. 10 Now he that ministereth seed to the sower
Gal. 3. 5 He therefore that ministereth to you the
2 Pe. 1. 11 For so an entrance shall be ministered unto

8. *To work as a priest,* ἱερουργέω *hierourgeō.*
Rom 15. 16 ministering the gospel of God, that the

9. *To work publicly,* λειτουργέω *leitourgeō.*
Acts 13. 2 As they ministered to the Lord, and fas.
Rom. 15. 27 their duty is also to minister unto them
Heb. 10. 11 every priest standeth daily ministering

10. *To hold alongside,* παρέχω *parechō.*
1 Ti. 1. 4 endless genealogies, which minister que.

11. *To act as an under rower, assist,* ὑπηρετέω.
Acts 20. 34 these hands have ministered unto my nec.
24. 23 forbid none of his acquaintance to minis.

12. *To supply, (lead the chorus),* χορηγέω *chorēgeō.*
2 Co. 9. 10 both minister bread for (your) food, and m.

MINISTER about, to —
To work, ἐργάζομαι *ergazomai.*
1 Co. 9. 13 that they which minister about holy things

MINISTER judgment, to —
To judge, plead, strive, decide, דִּין *din.*
Psa. 9. 8 he shall minister judgment to the people

MINISTERED (nourishment) —

1. *Public worker or servant,* λειτουργός *leitourgos.*
Phil. 2. 25 your messenger, and he that ministered

2. *To supply, (lead the chorus),* ἐπιχορηγέω *epichor.*
Col. 2. 19 having nourishment ministered, and knit

MINISTERING —

1. *Service,* עֲבוֹדָה *abodah.*
1 Ch. 9. 28 had the charge of the ministering vessels

2. *Ministration,* διακονία *diakonia.*
Rom 12. 7 (let us wait) on (our) ministering; or he
2 Co. 8. 4 the fellowship of the ministering to the s.
9. 1 For as touching the ministering to the sa.

3. *Liturgical, working publicly,* λειτουργικός.
Heb. 1. 14 Are they not all ministering spirits, sent

MINISTRATION —

1. *Ministration,* διακονία *diakonia.*
Acts 6. 1 were neglected in the daily ministration
2 Co. 3. 7 But if the ministration of death, written
3. 8 How shall not the ministration of the sp.
3. 9 For if the ministration of condemnation
3. 9 much more doth the ministration of righ.
9. 13 Whiles by the experiment of this ministra.

2. *Public work,* λειτουργία *leitourgia.*
Luke 1. 23 as soon as the days of his ministration

MINISTRY —

1. *Hand,* יָד *yad.*
2 Ch. 7. 6 when David praised by their ministry; and
Hos. 12. 10 I have also spoken..by the ministry of the

2. *Ministry,* שָׁרֵת *shareth.*
Num. 4. 12 shall take all the instruments of ministry

3. *Ministration,* διακονία *diakonia.*
Acts 1. 17 and had obtained part of this ministry
1. 25 That he may take part of this ministry
6. 4 to prayer, and to the ministry of the word
12. 25 when they had fulfilled (their) ministry
20. 24 finish my course with joy, and the minis.
21. 19 wrought among the Gentiles by his min.
Rom 12. 7 Or ministry, (let us wait)..or he that tea.
1 Co. 16. 15 have addicted themselves to the ministry
2 Co. 4. 1 seeing we have this ministry, as we have
5. 18 hath given to us the ministry of reconcil.
6. 3 no offence..that the ministry be not bla.
Eph. 4. 12 for the work of the ministry, for the edi.
Col. 4. 17 Take heed to the ministry which thou
1 Ti. 1. 12 counted..faithful, putting me into the m.
2 Ti. 4. 5 watch thou..make full proof of thy mini.
4. 11 for he is profitable to me for the ministry

4. *Public work,* λειτουργία *leitourgia.*
Heb. 8. 6 hath he obtained a more excellent minis.
9. 21 sprinkled..all the vessels of the ministry

MINISTRY, service of the —
Service, עֲבוֹדָה *abodah.*
Num. 4. 47 that came to do the service of the ministry

MIN'-NI, מִנִּי.
The district of Manavas in the centre of later Armenia, near Ararat.
Jer. 51. 27 the kingdoms of Ararat, M., and Ashche.

MIN'-NITH, מִנִּית *distribution.*
A city in the E. of Ammon, four miles from Heshbon, on the way to Philadelphia, whence grain was taken by merchants to Tyre.
Judg 11. 33 till thou come to M., (even) twenty cities
Eze. 27. 17 they traded in thy market wheat of M.

MINSTREL —

1. *To play on a stringed instrument,* נָגַן *nagan,* 3.
2 Ki. 3. 15 bring me a minstrel..when the minstrel

2. *Piper,* αὐλητής *aulētēs.*
Matt. 9. 23 saw the minstrels and the people making

MINT —
Mint, a fragrant herb, ἡδύοσμον *hēduosmon.*
Matt 23. 23 ye pay tithe of mint and anise and cummin
Luke 11. 42 ye tithe mint and rue, and all manner of

MIPH'-KAD, מִפְקָד *appointed place.*
Gate of Jerusalem or of the temple, near the S.E. corner.
Neh. 3. 31 over against the gate M., and to the going

MIRACLE —

1. *A sign,* אוֹת *oth.*
Num 14. 22 my miracles which I did in Egypt and in
Deut 11. 3 his miracles, and his acts, which he did

2. *Miracle, wonder, sign, type,* מוֹפֵת *mopheth.*
Exod. 7. 9 Show a miracle for you: then thou shalt
Deut 29. 3 temptations..the signs, and those great m.

3. *To be wonderful,* פָּלָא *pala,* 2.
Judg. 6. 13 where (be) all his miracles which our fa.

4. *Act of power,* δύναμις *dunamis.*
Mark 9. 39 no man, which shall do a miracle in my
Acts 2. 22 approved of God among you by miracles
8. 13 beholding the miracles and signs which
19. 11 God wrought special miracles by the ha.
1 Co. 12. 10 To another the working of miracles; to
12. 28 thirdly, teachers, after that miracles, then
Gal. 3. 5 therefore that..worketh miracles among
Heb. 2. 4 with divers miracles, and gifts of the Holy

5. *A sign,* σημεῖον *sēmeion.*
Luke 23. 8 he hoped to have seen some miracle done
John 2. 11 This beginning of miracles did Jesus in Ca.
2. 23 when they saw the miracles which he did
3. 2 no man can do these miracles that thou
4. 54 This (is) again the second miracle..Jesus
6. 2 they saw his miracles which he did on
6. 14 when they had seen the miracle that Jesus
6. 26 not because ye saw the miracles, but be.
7. 31 will he do more miracles than these which
9. 16 can a man that is a sinner do such miracles
10. 41 unto him, and said, John did no miracle?
11. 47 What do we? for this man doeth many m.
12. 18 that they heard that he had done this m.
12. 37 though he had done so many miracles be.
Acts 4. 16 for that indeed a notable miracle hath
4. 22 on whom this miracle of healing was sh.
6. 8 did great wonders and miracles among
8. 6 hearing and seeing the miracles which he
15. 12 declaring what miracles and wonders God
Rev. 13. 14 by..those miracles which he had power
16. 14 they are the spirits of devils, working m.
19. 20 the false prophet that wrought miracles

MIRACLES, workers of —
Power; (pl.) powers, δύναμις *dunamis.*
1 Co. 12. 29 (are) all teachers? (are) all workers of m.?

MIRE —

1. *Mire,* בֹּץ *bots.*
Jer. 38. 22 thy feet are sunk in the mire..they are

2. *Mire,* בִּצָּה *bitstsah.*
Job 8. 11 Can the rush grow up without mire? can

3. *Heap, clay,* חֹמֶר *chomer.*
Job 30. 19 He hath cast me into the mire, and I am
Isa. 10. 6 to tread them down like the mire of the

4. *Mud, mire,* טִיט *tit.*
2 Sa. 22. 43 I did stamp them as the mire of the street
Job 41. 30 spreadeth sharp pointed things on the m.
Psa. 69. 14 Deliver me out of the mire, and let me not
Jer. 38. 6 but mire, so Jeremiah sunk in the mire
Mic. 7. 10 shall she be trodden down as the mire of
Zech. 9. 3 and fine gold as the mire of the streets
10. 5 tread down (their enemies) in the mire of

5. *Mire,* יָוֵן *yaven.*
Psa. 69. 2 I sink in deep mire, where..no standing

6. *Filth, mire,* רֶפֶשׁ *rephes.*
Isa. 57. 20 sea..whose waters cast up mire and dirt

7. *Mire, filth,* βόρβορος *borboros.*
2 Pe. 2. 22 was washed to her wallowing in the mire

MI-RI'-AM, מִרְיָם *fat, thick, strong.*
1. The elder sister of Aaron and Moses; she watched over Moses, sang at the Red Sea, murmured against Moses, and was smitten with leprosy. B.C. 1578–1460.
Exod 15. 20 And M. the prophetess, the sister of Aaron
15. 21 And M. answered them, Sing ye to the L.
Num 12. 1 And M. and Aaron spake against Moses
12. 4 And the LORD spake..unto M., Come out
12. 5 called Aaron and M: and they both came
12. 10 behold, M. (became) leprous, (white) as s.
12. 10 Aaron looked upon M., and behold, (she

Num12. 15 And M. was shut out from the camp seven
12. 15 the people journeyed not till M. was bro.
20. 1 the people abode in Kadesh; and M. died
26. 59 she bare unto Amram..M. their sister
Deut 24. 9 Remember what the LORD..did unto M.
1 Ch. 6. 3 the children of Amram; Aaron..and M.
Mic. 6. 4 I sent before thee Moses, Aaron, and M.

2. A daughter of Ezra of the tribe of Judah.
1 Ch. 4. 17 she bare M., and Shammai, and Ishbah

MIR'-MA, מִרְמָה *height*,
A son of Shaharaim, a Benjamite. B.C. 1350.
1 Ch. 8. 10 Jeuz, and Shachia, and M. These (were)

MIRTH —
1. *Joy, rejoicing*, מָשׂוֹשׂ *masos.*
Isa. 24. 8 The mirth of tabrets ceaseth, the noise of
24. 11 all joy is darkened, the mirth of the land
Hos. 2. 11 I will also cause all her mirth to cease, her
2. *Rejoicing, joy, gladness, mirth*, שִׂמְחָה *simchah.*
Gen. 31. 27 that I might have sent thee away with m.
Neh. 8. 12 to send portions, and to make great mirth
Psa. 137. 3 they that wasted us (required of us) mirth
Prov 14. 13 and the end of that mirth (is) heaviness
Eccl. 2. 1 Go to now, I will prove thee with mirth
2. 2 I said of laughter..and of mirth, What d.
7. 4 the heart of fools (is) in the house of m.
8. 15 Then I commended mirth, because a man
3. *Joy, rejoicing, gladness*, שָׂשׂוֹן *sason.*
Jer. 7. 34 voice of mirth, and the voice of gladness
16. 9 voice of mirth, and the voice of gladness
25. 10 voice of mirth, and the voice of gladness

MIRTH, to make —
To enjoy, rejoice, שׂוּשׂ, שִׂישׂ, *sis, sus.*
Eze. 21. 10 it is furbished..should we then make m.?

MIRY (place) —
1. *Mire*, בִּצָּה *bitstsah.*
Eze. 47. 11 the miry places thereof, and the marishes
2. *Mire, mud*, טִין *tin.*
Dan. 2. 41, 43 thou sawest the iron mixed with miry
3. *Mire*, יָוֵן *yaven.*
Psa. 40. 2 He brought me up..out of the miry clay

MISCARRY, to —
To bereave, cause to miscarry, שָׁכֹל *shakol*, 5.
Hos. 9. 14 give them a miscarrying womb and dry b.

MISCHIEF —
1. *Iniquity, vanity*, אָוֶן *aven.*
Psa. 36. 4 He deviseth mischief upon his bed: he s.
55. 10 mischief also and sorrow (are) in the midst
Eze. 11. 2 these (are) the men that devise mischief
2. *Mischief, injury*, אָסוֹן *ason.*
Gen. 42. 4 Lest peradventure mischief befall him
42. 38 if mischief befall him by the way in the
44. 29 and mischief befall him, ye shall bring d.
Exod 21. 22 so that her fruit depart..yet no mischief
21. 23 if..mischief follow, then thou shalt give
3. *Mischief, calamity*, הַוָּה *havvah.*
Psa. 52. 2 thy tongue deviseth mischiefs; like a sh.
4. *Mischief, accident*, הֹוָה *hovah.*
Isa. 47. 11 mischief shall fall upon thee; thou shalt
Eze. 7. 26 Mischief shall come upon mischief, and
5. *Wicked thought or device*, זִמָּה *zimmah.*
Psa. 26. 10 In whose hands (is) mischief, and their ri.
119. 150 They draw nigh that follow after mischi.
Prov. 10. 23 (It is) as sport to a fool to do mischief: but
6. *Perversity, punishment for iniquity*, עָוֹן *avon.*
2 Ki. 7. 9 some mischief will come upon us: now
7. *Labour, perverseness, misery*, עָמָל *amal.*
Job 15. 35 They conceive mischief, and bring forth
Psa. 7. 14 conceived mischief, and brought forth fa.
7. 16 His mischief shall return upon his own h.
10. 7 under his tongue (is) mischief and vanity
10. 14 for thou beholdest mischief and spite, to
94. 20 throne..which frameth mischief by a law
140. 9 let the mischief of their own lips cover the.
Prov 24. 2 studieth..and their lips talk of mischief.
Isa. 59. 4 they conceive mischief, and bring forth in.
8. *Evil, wrong*, רַע *ra.*
Exod 32. 12 For mischief did he bring them out, to
32. 22 the people, that they (are set) on mischief
Deut 32. 23 I will heap mischiefs upon them; I will
1 Sa. 23. 9 knew that Saul secretly practised mischief
2 Sa. 16. 8 thou (art taken) in thy mischief, because
1 Ki. 11. 25 besides the mischief that Hadad (did): and
20. 7 and see how this (man) seeketh mischief
Neh. 6. 2 But they thought to do me mischief
Esth. 8. 3 to put away the mischief of Haman the A.
Psa. 28. 3 speak peace..mischief (is) in their hearts
52. 1 Why boastest thou thyself in mischief, O
140. 2 Which imagine mischiefs in (their) heart
Prov. 6. 14 he deviseth mischief continually; he so.
6. 18 feet that be swift in running to mischief
11. 27 he that seeketh mischief, it shall come
12. 21 but the wicked shall be filled with misch.
13. 17 A wicked messenger falleth into mischief
17. 20 a perverse tongue falleth into mischief
24. 16 but the wicked shall fall into mischief
28. 14 hardeneth his heart shall fall into misch.
Dan. 11. 27 these king's hearts (shall be) to do misch.
Hos. 7. 15 yet do they imagine mischief against me
9. *Easy work, craftiness*, ῥαδιουργία *rhadiourgia.*
Acts 13. 10 O full of all subtilty and all mischief

MISCHIEF, to do or imagine —
1. *To do evil*, רָעַע *raa*, 5.
Prov. 4. 16 sleep not, except they have done mischief
2. *To devise mischief*, הָתַת *hathath*, 3*a*.
Psa. 62. 3 How long will ye imagine mischief against

MISCHIEVOUS (device or thing) —
1. *Mischief, calamity*, הַוָּה *havvah.*
Psa. 38. 12 that seek my hurt speak mischievous th.
Mic. 7. 3 uttereth his mischievous desire: so they
2. *Wicked device*, מְזִמָּה *mezimmah.*
Psa. 21. 11 For..they imagined a mischievous device
Prov 24. 8 to do evil shall be called a mischievous
3. *Evil, bad, sad, wrong*, רַע *ra.*
Eccl. 10. 13 the end of his talk (is) mischievous mad.

MISERABLE, that is in misery, most —
1. *Laborious, perverse, miserable*, עָמָל *amal.*
Job 16. 2 I have heard..miserable comforters (are)
2. *Labouring, perverse, miserable*, עָמֵל *amel.*
Job 3. 20 is light given to him that is in misery
3. *An object for kindness*, ἐλεεινός *eleeinos.*
1 Co. 15. 19 in this life..we are of all men most mis.
Rev. 3. 17 thou art wretched, and miserable, and

MISERABLY —
Evilly, κακῶς *kakōs.*
Matt 21. 41 He will miserably destroy those wicked

MISERY —
1. *Miserable, mourning*, מָרוּד *marud.*
Lam. 1. 7 remembered in the days..of her miseries
3. 19 Remembering..my misery, the wormwood
2. *Labour, perverseness, misery*, עָמָל *amal.*
Judg 10. 16 his soul was grieved for the misery of Is.
Job 11. 16 Because thou shalt forget (thy) misery
Prov 31. 7 forget his poverty, and remember his m.
3. *Evil*, רַע *ra.*
Eccl. 8. 6 therefore the misery of man (is) great upon
4. *Grievous misery*, ταλαιπωρία *talaipōria.*
Rom. 3. 16 Destruction and misery (are) in their ways
Jas. 5. 1 howl for your miseries that shall come

MIS'-GAB, הַמִּשְׂגָּב *the high land.*
The mountainous country of Moab.
Jer. 48. 1 thus saith the LORD..M. is confounded

MI-SHA'-EL, מִישָׁאֵל *who is what God is?*
1. A son of Uzziel, son of Kohath. B.C. 1452.
Exod. 6. 22 the sons of Uzziel; M., and Elzaphan, and
Lev. 10. 4 Moses called M. and Elzaphan, the sons
2. One who stood beside Ezra when he read the law. B.C. 445.
Neh. 8. 4 on his left hand, Pedaiah, and M., and M.
3. A companion of Daniel, also called Meshek. B.C. 607.
Dan. 1. 6 among these were..Hananiah, M., and
1. 7 he gave..(the name)..to M., of Meshach
1. 11 had set over Daniel, Hananiah, M., and
1. 19 none like Daniel, Hananiah, M., and Az.
2. 17 Daniel..made the thing known to..M.

MISH'-AM, מִשְׁעָם *impetuous, haste, fame.*
A Benjamite, son of Elpaal. B.C. 1400.
1 Ch. 8. 12 The sons of Elpaal; Eber, and M., and S.

MISH-E'-AL, MISH'-AL, מִשְׁאָל *depression.*
A Levitical city in Asher, near Amad.
Josh 19. 26 Alammelech, and Amad, and M.; and
21. 30 of the tribe of Asher, M. with her suburbs

MISH'-MA, מִשְׁמָע *fame.*
A son of Ishmael, son of Hagar. B.C. 1846.
Gen. 25. 14 And M., and Dumah, and Massa
1 Ch. 1. 30 M., and Dumah, Massa, Hadad, and Tema
4. 25 Shallum his son, Mibsam his son, M. his
4. 26 sons of M.; Hamuel his son, Zacchur his

MISH-MAN'-NAH, מִשְׁמַנָּה *strength, vigour.*
A Gadite that joined David in Ziklag. B.C. 1058.
1 Ch. 12. 10 M. the fourth, Jeremiah the fifth

MISH-RA-ITES, מִשְׁרָעִי.
A family of Kirjath-jearim.
1 Ch. 2. 53 the Shumathites, and the M.: of them c.

MIS-PE'-RETH, מִסְפֶּרֶת *writing.*
The person called Mispar in Ezra 2. 2, who returned with Zerubbabel. B.C. 538.
Neh 7. 7 Who came with Zerubbabel, Jeshua..M.

MIS-RE-PHOTH MA'-IM, מִשְׂרְפוֹת מַיִם *burning waters.*
A city E. of Sidon; same as *Zarephath.*
Josh 11. 8 chased them unto..M., and unto the va.
13. 6 the hill country from Lebanon unto M.

MISS, to —
1. *To err, sin, miss*, חָטָא *chata*, 5.
Judg 20. 16 sling stones at an hair..and not miss
2. *To inspect, look after*, פָּקַד *paqad.*
1 Sa. 20. 6 If thy father at all miss me, then say, D.
25. 15 neither missed we anything, as long as we

MISSED, MISSING, to be —
To inspect, look after, פָּקַד *paqad*, 2.
1 Sa. 20. 18 thou shalt be missed, because thy seat will
25. 7 neither was there ought missing unto them
25. 21 so that nothing was missed of all that
1 Ki. 20. 39 if by any means he be missing, then shall

MIST —
1. *Mist, vapour*, אֵד *ed.*
Gen. 2. 6 there went up a mist from the earth, and
2. *Thick mist, fog*, ἀχλύς *achlus.*
Acts 13. 11 immediately there fell on him a mist and
3. *Thick darkness, blackness*, ζόφος *zophos.*
2 Pe. 2. 17 to whom the mist of darkness is reserved

MISTRESS —
1. *Lady, owner*, בַּעֲלָה *baalah.*
1 Ki. 17. 17 the son of..the mistress of the house, fell
Nah. 3. 4 the mistress of witchcrafts, that selleth
2. *Mistress, mighty one*, גְּבֶרֶת *gebereth.*
Gen. 16. 4 her mistress was despised in her eyes
16. 8 I flee from the face of my mistress Sarai
16. 9 Return to thy mistress, and submit thy.
2 Ki. 5. 3 she said unto her mistress, Would God my
Psa. 123. 2 eyes of a maiden unto the hand of her m.
Prov 30. 23 an handmaid that is heir to her mistress
Isa. 24. 2 as with the maid, so with her mistress

MISUSE, to —
To show self a deceiver, תָּעַע *taa*, 7*a*.
2 Ch. 36. 16 misused his prophets, until the wrath of

MITE —
A lepton, (tenth of a penny), λεπτόν *lepton.*
Mark 12. 42 she threw in two mites, which make a f.
Luke 12. 59 not..till thou hast paid the very last mite
21. 2 poor widow casting in thither two mites

MITH'-CAH, מִתְקָה *sweet place.*
The 24th station of Israel from Egypt, and the 13th from Sinai, in Arabia the rocky.
Num 33. 28 removed from Tarah, and pitched in M.
33. 29 they went from M., and pitched in Hash.

MITH-NITE, מִתְנִי.
Patronymic of Joshaphat, one of David's valiant men. B.C. 1048.
1 Ch. 11. 43 son of Maachah, and Joshaphat the M.

MITH-RE'-DATH, מִתְרְדָת *given by Mithra*, i.e. *sun.*
1. The treasurer of Cyrus king of Persia. B.C. 536.
Ezra 1. 8 by the hand of M. the treasurer, and nu.
2. An enemy of the Jews in the days of Artaxerxes king of Persia. B.C. 522.
Ezra 4. 7 in the days of Artaxerxes wrote..M., Tab.

MITRE —
1. *A mitre*, מִצְנֶפֶת *mitsnepheth.*
Exod 28. 4 a broidered coat, a mitre, and a girdle
28. 37 blue lace, that it may be upon the mitre
28. 37 upon the forefront of the mitre it shall be
28. 39 thou shalt make the mitre (of) fine linen
29. 6 And thou shalt put the mitre upon his h.
29. 6 and put the holy crown upon the mitre
39. 28 a mitre (of) fine linen, and goodly bonnets
39. 31 lace to fasten (it) on high upon the mitre
Lev. 8. 9 And he put the mitre upon his head; also
8. 9 also upon the mitre..upon his fore front
16. 4 with the linen mitre shall he be attired
2. *Diadem, hood*, צָנִיף *tsaniph.*
Zech. 3. 5 Let them set a fair mitre upon his head
3. 5 So they set a fair mitre upon his head, and

MI-TY-LE'-NE, Μιτυλήνη.
The capital city of Lesbos, in the Ægean Sea, birthplace of Sappho, Alcæus, Pittacus, &c.; now *Castro* and *Mitylen.*
Acts 20. 14 at Assos, we took him in, and came to M.

MIX self, to —
To mix self, בָּלַל *balal*, 7*a*.
Hos. 7. 8 Ephraim, he hath mixed himself among

MIXED (with), to be —
1. *To mix*, מָהַל *mahal.*
Isa. 1. 22 Thy silver is..dross, thy wine mixed with
2. *To mingle*, עָרַב *arab*, 3.
Dan. 2. 41 thou sawest the iron mixed with miry c.
2. 43 whereas thou sawest iron mixed with miry
3. *To mingle self*, עָרַב *arab*, 4.
Dan. 2. 43 not cleave..even as iron is not mixed with
4. *Mingled crowd*, עֶרֶב *ereb.*
Exod 12. 38 a mixed multitude went up also with them
Neh. 13. 3 separated from Israel all the mixed mul.
5. *To mix, mingle with*, συγκεράννυμι *sugkerannumi.*
Heb. 4. 2 not being mixed with faith in them that

MIXTURE —
1. *Mixture*, מֶסֶךְ *mesek.*
Psa. 75. 8 it is full of mixture; and he poureth out
2. *Mixture*, μίγμα *migma.*
John 19. 39 brought a mixture of myrrh and aloes, ab.

MIXTURE, without —
Unmixed, ἄκρατος *akratos.*
Rev. 14. 10 which is poured out without mixture into

MIZ'-AR, מִצְעָר *little, small.*
A hill near Hermon.
Psa. 42. 6 therefore will I remember..the hill M.

MIZ'-PAH, MIZ'-PEH, מִצְפָּה, מִצְפֶּה, *watch-tower.*
1. A city of Gad in Gilead, called also *Galeed* and *Jegar-sahadutha.*
Gen. 31. 49 And M.; for he said, The LORD watch be.
Judg 10. 17 the children of Israel..encamped in M.
11. 11 and Jephthah uttered all his words..in M.
11. 29 Jephthath..passed over M. of Gilead, and
11. 29 from M. of Gilead he passed over (unto)
11. 34 Jephthah came to M. unto his house, and
2. A valley in Manasseh, at Mount Hermon.
Josh. 11. 3 Hivite under Hermon in the land of M.
11. 8 and chased them..unto the valley of M.
3. A city in the plain of Judah, near Dilean and Gilgal, and Geba.
Josh 15. 38 And Dilean, and M., and Joktheel
Judg 20. 1 the children of Israel went out..unto..M.
20. 3 the children of Israel were gone up to M.
21. 1 the men of Israel had sworn in M., saying
21. 5 him that came not up to the LORD to M.
21. 8 came not up to M. to the LORD? And, be.
1 Sa. 7. 5 Samuel said, Gather all Israel to M., and
7. 6 they gathered together to M., and drew
7. 6 Samuel judged the children of Israel in M.
7. 7 children of Israel were gathered..to M.
7. 11 the men of Israel went out of M., and p.
7. 12 Samuel..set(it) between M. and Shen, and
7. 16 he went..in circuit to Bethel..and M., and
10. 17 Samuel called the people together..to M.
2 Ki. 25. 23 there came to Gedaliah to M., even Ishm.
25. 25 the Chaldees that were with him at M.
2 Ch. 16. 6 and he built therewith Geba and M.
Jer. 40. 6 Then went Jeremiah..to M., and dwelt
40. 8 Then they came to Gedaliah to M., even
40. 10 As for me, behold, I will dwell at M., to
40. 12 all the Jews returned..unto M., and gat.
40. 13 Moreover Johan...came to Gedaliah to M.
40. 15 Then Johanan..spake to Gedaliah in M.
41. 1 Ishmael..came..to M., and there they did
41. 1 and there they did eat bread together in M.
41. 3 Ishmael also slew..Gedaliah, at M., and
41. 6 And Ishmael..went forth from M. to meet
41. 10 the residue of the people that (were) in M.
41. 10 and all the people that remained in M.
41. 14 Ishmael had carried away captive from M.
41. 16 all the remnant of the people..from M.
Hos. 5. 1 ye have been a snare on M., and a net spr.
4. A city in Benjamin, near Chephirah, on- hour from *Rama*, and now called *Neby Samuil.*
Josh. 18. 26 And M., and Chephirah, and Mozah
1 Ki. 15. 22 king Asa built with them Geba..and M.
Neh. 3. 7 the men of Gibeon and of M., unto the th.
5. A city in Moab.
1 Sa. 22. 3 David went thence to M. of Moab: and he
6. A city or district of part of which Shallum was ruler.
Neh. 3. 15 repaired Shallun...the ruler of part of M.
7. A place of which Ezer son of Jeshua was ruler.
Neh. 3. 19 Ezer the son of Jeshua, the ruler of M.

MIZ'-PAR, מִסְפָּר *writing.*
A chief man who returned with Zerubbabel, B.C. 538; called in Neh. 7. 7 *Mispereth.*
Ezra 2. 2 Which came with Zerubbabel..M., Bigvai

MIZ-RA'-IM, מִצְרַיִם.
The second son of Ham, and father of Ludim, &c.; his descendants in *Egypt.* B.C. 2300.
Gen. 10. 6 the sons of Ham; Cush, and M., and Phut
10. 13 And M. begat Ludim, and Anamim, and
1 Ch. 1. 8 The sons of Ham; Cush, and M., Put, and
1. 11 And M. begat Ludim, and Anamim, and

MIZ'-ZAH, מִזָּה *terror, joy.*
Son of Reuel son of Esau, one of the dukes of Edom. B.C. 1700.
Gen. 36. 13 these (are) the sons of Reuel; Nahath..M.
36. 17 these (are) the sons of Reuel..duke M.
1 Ch. 1. 37 The sons of Reuel; Nahath, Zerah..and M.

MNA'-SON, Μνάσων.
A native of Cyprus, an aged disciple with whom Paul lodged on his last visit to Jerusalem.
Acts 21. 16 brought with them one M. of Cyprus, an

MO'-AB, מוֹאָב *water of a father.*
1. Son of Lot and his elder daughter. B.C. 1897.
Gen. 19. 37 And the first born..called his name M.
2. His place and race, in the S.E. of Judah, and E. of the Salt Sea, and S. of Reuben. Its chief places are Ar, the Arnon, Bamoth Baal, Beer, Elim, Beth-Diblathaim, Dibon or Dimon, Eglaim, Eglath-shelishiya, Horonaim, Kirjathaim, Kirjath-huzoth, Kir-haraseth, -haresh, -heres, Kir-Moab, Luhith, Medeba, Nimrim or Nimrah, Nobah or Nophah, Hap-Pisgah, Hap-Peor Shaveh-Keriathaim, Zophim, Zoar, &c.
Gen. 36. 35 Bedad, who smote Midian in the field of M.
Exod 15. 15 the mighty men of M., trembling shall
Num 21. 11 the wilderness which (is) before M., tow.
21. 13 Arnon (is) the border of M., between M.
21. 15 And at the stream..upon the border of M.
21. 20 the valley, that (is) in the country of M.
21. 26 had fought against the former king of M.
21. 28 it hath consumed Ar of M., (and) the lords
21. 29 Woe to thee, M.! thou art undone, O peo.
22. 1 pitched in the plains of M. on this side J.
22. 3 And M. was sore afraid of the people, be.
22. 3 and M. was distressed because of the chil.
22. 4 And M. said unto the elders of Midian
22. 7 the elders of M. and the elders of Midian
22. 8 and the princes of M. abode with Balaam
Num 22. 10 Balak the son of Zippor, king of M., hath
22. 14 the princes of M. rose up, and they went
22. 21 And Balaam..went with the princes of M.
22. 36 he went out to meet him unto a city of M.
23. 6 he stood..he, and all the princes of M.
23. 7 Balak the king of M. hath brought me from
23. 17 he stood..and the princes of M. with him
24. 17 shall smite the corners of M., and destroy
25. 1 commit whoredom..the daughters of M.
26. 3 the priest spake with them in..M., by Jo.
26. 63 the plains of M. by Jordan (near) Jericho
31. 12 the plains of M., which (are) by Jordan
33. 44 pitched in Ije-abarim, in the border of M.
33. 48 and pitched in the plains of M., by Jordan
33. 49 they pitched by Jordan..in the plains of M.
33. 50 the plains of M., by Jordan (near) Jericho
35. 1 the plains of M. by Jordan (near) Jericho
36. 13 the plains of M. by Jordan (near) Jericho
Deut. 1. 5 On this side Jordan, in the land of M., be.
2. 8 passed by the way of the wilderness of M.
2. 18 Thou art to pass over..the coast of M.
29. 1 the children of Israel in the land of M.
32. 49 mount Nebo, which (is) in the land of M.
34. 1 Moses went up from the plains of M. unto
34. 5 So Moses..died there in the land of M.
34. 6 buried him in a valley in the land of M.
34. 8 Israel wept for Moses in..M. thirty days
Josh. 13. 32 inheritance in the plains of M., on the
24. 9 Balak the son of Zippor, king of M., arose
Judg. 3. 12 LORD strengthened Eglon the king of M.
3. 14 children of Israel served..the king of M.
3. 15 sent a present unto Eglon the king of M.
3. 17 brought the present unto Eglon king of M.
3. 28 and took the fords of Jordan toward M.
3. 29 they slew of M. at that time about ten th.
3. 30 So M. was subdued that day under the h.
10. 6 gods of M., and the gods of the children
11. 15 I. took not away the land of M., nor the l.
11. 17 in like manner..unto the king of M.: but
11. 18 compassed the land..of M., and came by
11. 18 east side of the land of M., and pitched on
11. 18 border of M.: for Arnon..the border of M.
11. 25 (art)..anything better than..king of M.?
Ruth 1. 1 went to sojourn in the country of M., he
1. 2 came into the country of M., and continued
1. 4 they took them wives of the women of M.
1. 6 she might return from the country of M.
1. 6 she had heard in the country of M. how
1. 22 which returned out of the country of M.
2. 6 back with Naomi out of the country of M.
4. 3 is come again out of the country of M., se.
1 Sa. 12. 9 sold them..into the hand of the king of M.
14. 47 So Saul..fought..against M., and against
22. 3 David went thence to Mizpeh of M.; and
22. 3 said unto the king of M., Let my father
22. 4 brought them before the king of M.; and
2 Sa. 8. 2 he smote M., and measured them with a
8. 12 Of Syria, and of M., and of the children of
23. 20 he slew two lion like men of M.: he went
1 Ki. 11. 7 the abomination of M., in the hill that (is)
2 Ki. 1. 1 Then M. rebelled against Israel after the
3. 4 Mesha king of M. was a sheep master, and
3. 5 king of M. rebelled against the king of I.
3. 7 The king of M. hath rebelled against me
3. 7 wilt thou go with me against M. to battle?
3. 10, 13 to deliver them into the hand of M.
3. 23 And they said..now therefore, M., to the
3. 26 when the king of M. saw that the battle
1 Ch. 1. 46 which smote Midian in the field of M., r.
4. 22 Saraph, who had the dominion in M., and
8. 8 begat (children) in the country of M., after
11. 22 he slew two lion like men of M.: also he
18. 2 he smote M.; and the Moabites became
18. 11 gold that he brought..from M., and from
2 Ch. 20. 1 children of M...came against Jehoshaphat
20. 10 children of Ammon and M. and mount S.
20. 22 against the children of Ammon, M., and
20. 23 For the children of Ammon and M. stood
Neh. 13. 23 saw I Jews (that)..married wives..of M.
Psa. 60. 8 M. (is) my wash pot; over Edom will I cast
83. 6 The tabernacle of Edom..of M., and the
108. 9 M. (is) my wash pot; over Edom will I c.
Isa. 11. 14 shall lay their hand upon Edom and M.
15. 1 burden of M...Ar of M. is laid waste, (and)
15. 1 Kir of M. is laid waste, (and) brought to
15. 2 M. shall howl over Nebo, and over Med.
15. 4 therefore the armed soldiers of M. shall
15. 5 My heart shall cry out for M.; his fugitives
15. 8 cry is gone round about the borders of M.
15. 9 lions upon him that escapeth of M., and
16. 2 daughters of M. shall be at the fords of A.
16. 4 Let mine outcasts dwell with thee, M.; be
16. 6 We have heard of the pride of M.; he (is)
16. 7 Therefore shall M. howl for M., every one
16. 11 my bowels shall sound like an harp for M.
16. 12 when it is seen that M. is weary on the
16. 13 LORD hath spoken concerning M. since
16. 14 glory of M. shall be contemned, with all
25. 10 M. shall be trodden down under him, even
Jer. 9. 26 children of Ammon, and M., and all (that
25. 21 Edom, and M., and the children of Am.
27. 3 send them..to the king of M., and to the
40. 11 when all the Jews that (were) in M., and
48. 1 Against M. thus saith the LORD of hosts
48. 2 (There shall be) no more praise of M.: in
48. 4 M. is destroyed; her little ones have
48. 9 Give wings unto M., that it may flee and
48. 11 M. hath been at ease from his youth, and
48. 13 M. shall be ashamed of Chemosh, as the
48. 15 M. is spoiled, and gone up (out of) her c.
48. 16 calamity of M. (is) near to come, and his
48. 18 for the spoiler of M. shall come upon thee
Jer. 48. 20 M. is confounded..tell ye it..that M. is
48. 24 upon all the cities of the land of M., far
48. 25 horn of M. is cut off, and his arm is broken
48. 26 M. also shall wallow in his vomit, and he
48. 28 O ye that dwell in M., leave the cities, and
48. 29 We have heard the pride of M., he is ex.
48. 31 howl for M., and I will cry out for all M.
48. 33 gladness is taken..from the land of M.
48. 35 Moreover I will cause to cease in M., saith
48. 36 mine heart shall sound for M. like pipes
48. 38 all the house tops of M...I have broken M.
48. 39 how hath M. turned..so shall M. be a d.
48. 40 Behold, he..shall spread his wings over M.
48. 41 mighty men's hearts in M. at that day s.
48. 42 M. shall be destroyed from (being) a pe.
48. 43 Fear..(shall be) upon thee, O inhabi. of M.
48. 44 for I will bring upon it, (even) upon M.
48. 45 a flame..shall devour the corner of M., and
48. 46 Woe be unto thee, O M.! the people of Ch.
48. 47 Yet will I bring again the captivity of M.
48. 47 Thus far (is) the judgment of M.
Eze. 25. 8 Because that M. and Seir do say, Behold
25. 9 I will open the side of M. from the cities
25. 11 I will execute judgments upon M.; and
Dan. 11. 41 these shall escape..(even) Edom, and M.
Amos 2. 1 For three transgressions of M., and for
2. 2 I will send a fire upon M...and M. shall
Mic. 6. 5 remember now what Balak king of M. co.
Zeph. 2. 8 I have heard the reproach of M., and the
2. 9 Surely M. shall be as Sodom, and the chi.

MO-AB-ITES, מֹאָבִי, מוֹאָבִי, מוֹאָבִים, מוֹאָב.
The posterity of the preceding; they were not to be received into Israel; were conquered by David; rebel after Ahab's death; again defeated, when their king offers his son a sacrifice.
Gen. 19. 37 the same (is) the father of the M. unto this
Num 22. 4 Balak the son of Zippor (was) king of the M.
Deut. 2. 9 Distress not the M., neither contend with
2. 11 accounted giants..but the M. call them E.
2. 29 As the..M. which dwell in Ar, did unto
23. 3 An Ammonite or M. shall not enter into
Judg. 3. 28 delivered your enemies the M. into your
2 Sa. 8. 2 the M. became David's servants, (and) b.
1 Ki. 11. 33 worshipped..Chemosh the god of the M.
2 Ki. 3. 18 he will deliver the M. also into your hand
3. 21 when all the M. heard that the kings were
3. 22 the M. saw the water on the other side (as)
3. 24 smote the M...smiting the M., even in
13. 20 bands of the M. invaded the land at the
23. 13 for Chemosh the abomination of the M.
24. 2 LORD sent against him..bands of the M.
1 Ch. 11. 46 the sons of Elnaam, and Ithmah the M.
18. 2 the M. became David's servants, (and) br.
Ezra 9. 1 abominations, (even) of the..M., the Eg.
Neh. 13. 1 that the Ammonite and the M. should not

MO-AB-ITESS, MO-AB-IT-ISH, מוֹאֲבִיָּה, מוֹאֲבִית.
1. Patronymic of Ruth, the wife of Boaz. B.C. 1312.
Ruth 1. 22 So Naomi returned, and Ruth the M., her
2. 2 Ruth the M. said unto Naomi, Let me now
2. 6 It (is) the M. damsel that came back with
2. 21 Ruth the M. said, He said unto me also
4. 5 thou must buy (it) also of Ruth the M., the
4. 10 Moreover Ruth the M., the wife of Mahlon
2. Some of Solomon's wives. B.C. 1015.
1 Ki. 11. 1 women of the M., Ammonites, Edomites
3. Shimrith, who slew king Joash. B.C. 835.
2 Ch. 24. 26 and Jehozabad the son of Shimrith a M.

MO-AD-I'AH, מוֹעַדְיָה *festival of Jah.*
A priest in the days of Joiakim, grandson of Jozadak; also called *Maadiah (which see).* B.C. 536.
Neh. 12. 17 Of Abijah, Zichri; of Miniamin, of M.

MOCK (on), to —
1. *To play upon, deceive, mock,* הָתַל *hathal,* 3.
Judg 16. 10 Behold, thou hast mocked me, and told
16. 13 Hitherto thou hast mocked me, and told
16. 15 thou hast mocked me these three times
1 Ki. 18. 27 Elijah mocked them, and said, Cry aloud
Job 13. 9 as one man mocketh..do ye (so) mock him
2. *To mock,* לָעַב *laab,* 5.
2 Ch. 36. 16 they mocked the messengers of God, and
3. *To scorn,* לָעַג *laag.*
Job 11. 3 when thou mockest, shall no man make
Prov. 1. 26 I also..I will mock when your fear cometh
17. 5 Whoso mocketh the poor reproacheth his
30. 17 The eye (that) mocketh at (his) father, and
Jer. 20. 7 I am in derision daily, every one mocketh
4. *To scorn,* לָעַג *laag,* 5.
2 Ch. 30. 10 laughed them to scorn, and mocked them
Neh. 4. 1 took great indignation, and mocked the J.
Job 21. 3 and after that I have spoken, mock on
5. *To roll self, abuse, insult,* עָלַל *alal,* 7.
Num 22. 29 Because thou hast mocked me: I would
Jer. 38. 19 deliver me into their hand, and they mock
6. *To mock, play with,* צָחַק *tsachaq,* 3.
Gen. 19. 14 he seemed as one that mocked unto his s.
21. 9 Sarah saw the son of Hagar..mocking
39. 14 brought in an Hebrew unto us to mock us
39. 17 Hebrew servant..came in unto me to mock
7. *To show self a derider, scoffer,* קָלַס *qalas,* 7.
2 Ki. 2. 23 mocked him, and said unto him, Go up
Eze. 22. 5 (those that be) far from thee, shall mock
8. *To laugh, deride, play,* שָׂחַק *sachaq.*
Job 39. 22 He mocketh at fear, and is not affrighted
Lam. 1. 7 saw her, (and) did mock at her sabbaths

9. *To treat as a child, mock,* ἐμπαίζω *empaizō.*
Matt. 2. 16 Herod, when he saw that he was mocked
20. 19 to mock, and to scourge, and to crucify
27. 29 mocked him, saying, Hail, King of the J.
27. 31 And after that they had mocked him, they
27. 41 Likewise also the chief priests, mocking
Mark10. 34 they shall mock him, and shall scourge him
15. 20 when they had mocked him, they took off
15. 31 Likewise also the chief priests mocking
Luke14. 29 all that behold (it) begin to mock him
18. 32 shall be mocked, and spitefully entreated
22. 63 the men that held Jesus mocked him, and
23. 11 set him at nought, and mocked..and arr.
23. 36 the soldiers also mocked him, coming to

10. *To mock, scoff, deride, laugh,* χλευάζω *chleuazō.*
Acts 2. 13 Others [mocking], said, These men are full
17. 32 of the resurrection of the dead, some mo.

MOCK, to make a —
To scorn, לוּץ *luts,* 5.
Prov14. 9 Fools make a mock at sin: but among the

MOCKED, to be —
1. *Laughter, derision, play,* שְׂחוֹק *sechoq.*
Job 12. 4 I am (as) one mocked of his neighbour, who
2. *To sneer, mock,* μυκτηρίζομαι *muktērizomai.*
Gal. 6. 7 Be not deceived; God is not mocked: for

MOCKER —
1. *Deceivers, mockers,* הֲתֻלִים *hathulim.*
Job 17. 2 (Are there) not mockers with me? and doth
2. *To scorn,* לוּץ *luts.*
Prov 20. 1 Wine (is) a mocker, strong drink (is) rag.
3. *To show self a scorner,* לוּץ *luts,* 7a.
Isa. 28. 22 Now therefore be ye not mockers, lest your
4. *Mocking, stammering,* לָעֵג *laeg.*
Psa. 35. 16 With hypocritical mockers in feasts, they
5. *To laugh, deride, play,* שָׂחַק *sachaq,* 3.
Jer. 15. 17 I sat not in the assembly of the mockers
6. *Sporting as children,* ἐμπαίκτης *empaiktēs.*
Jude 18 they told you there should be mockers in

MOCKING —
1. *Derision, scoffing,* קַלָּסָה *qallasah.*
Eze. 22. 4 have I made thee..a mocking to all coun.
2. *Sporting,* ἐμπαιγμός *empaigmos.*
Heb. 11. 36 others had trial of..mockings and scour.

MODERATELY —
To rightness, לִצְדָקָה *litsedaqah.*
Joel 2. 23 hath given you the former rain moderat.

MODERATION —
Yieldingness, pliability, τὸ ἐπιεικές *to epieikes.*
Phil. 4. 5 Let your moderation be known unto all

MODEST —
Orderly, becoming, κόσμιος *kosmios.*
1 Ti. 2. 9 that women adorn themselves in modest

MOIST —
Moist, fresh, לַח *lach.*
Num. 6. 3 neither shall he..eat moist grapes, or dr.

MOISTENED, to be —
To be watered, moistened, שָׁקָה *shuqah,* 4.
Job 21. 24 and his bones are moistened with marrow

MOISTURE —
1. *Moisture, freshness,* לְשַׁד *leshad.*
Psa. 32. 4 my moisture is turned into the drought
2. *Moisture, humour,* ἰκμάς *ikmas.*
Luke 8. 6 it withered away, because it lacked mois.

MOLE —
1. *Chamelion, owl,* תִּנְשֶׁמֶת *tinshemeth.*
Lev. 11. 30 the lizard, and the snail, and the mole
2. *A mole,* חֲפַרְפֵּרָה *chapharperah* [conjec. reading].
Isa. 2. 20 shall cast his idols..to the moles

MO-LA'-DAH, מוֹלָדָה, מֹלָדָה *birth.*
A city in the S.W. of Judah, near Shema, Sheba, or Jeshua.
Josh. 15. 26 Amam, and Shema, and M.
19. 2 had in their inheritance..Sheba, and M.
1 Ch. 4. 28 they dwelt at Beer-sheba, and M., and H.
Neh. 11. 26 at Jeshua, and at M., and at Beth-phelet

MO'-LECH, MO'-LOCH, מֹלֶךְ Μολόχ *counsellor, king.*
A god of the Ammonites; called also *Milcom, Malcam,* and *Malcan.*
Lev. 18. 21 shalt not let..pass through (the fire) to M.
20. 2 Whosoever..giveth..seed unto Molech
20. 3 because he hath given of his seed unto M.
20. 4 when he giveth of his seed unto M., and
20. 5 to commit whoredom with M., from among
1 Ki. 11. 7 for M., the abomination of the children
2 Ki. 23. 10 his daughter to pass through the fire to M.
Jer. 32. 35 daughters to pass through (the fire) unto M.
Amos 5. 26 ye have borne the tabernacle of your M.
Acts 7. 43 ye took up the tabernacle of M., and the

MO'-LID, מוֹלִיד *begetter.*
A descendant of Jerahmeel, grandson of Pharez son of Judah. B.C. 1400.
1 Ch. 2. 29 Abihail, and she bare him Ahban, and M.

MOLLIFIED, to be —
To be made tender, soft, רָכַךְ *rakak,* 4.
Isa. 1. 6 bound up, neither mollified with ointment

MOLTEN (image) —
1. *To cast, melt, pour, be firm,* יָצַק *yatsaq.*
1 Ki. 7. 30 under the laver (were) undersetters molten
2. *To be poured out, cast firm,* יָצַק *yatsaq,* 6.
1 Ki. 7. 16 he made two chapiters (of) molten brass, to
7. 23 he made a molten sea, ten cubits from the
7. 33 their felloes, and their spokes..all molten
2 Ch. 4. 2 he made a molten sea of ten cubits from
Job 37. 18 strong, (and) as a molten looking-glass
3. *A molten image,* מַסֵּכָה *massekah.*
Exod32. 4 And..after he had made it a molten calf
32. 8 they have made them a molten calf, and
34. 17 Thou shalt make thee no molten gods
Lev. 19. 4 nor make to yourselves molten gods: I (am)
Num33. 52 destroy all their molten images, and quite
Deut. 9. 12 they have made them a molten image
9. 16 had made you a molten calf: ye had turned
27. 15 that maketh (any) graven or molten image
Judg17. 3, 4 a graven image, and a molten image
18. 14 and a graven image and a molten image
18. 17, 18 and the teraphim, and the molten im.
1 Ki. 14. 9 made thee other gods, and molten images
2 Ki. 17. 16 and made them molten images..two cal.
2 Ch. 28. 2 and made also molten images for Baalim
34. 3, 4 carved images, and the molten images
Neh. 9. 18 when they had made them a molten calf
Psa. 106. 19 made..and worshipped the molten image
Isa. 30. 22 the ornament of thy molten images of g.
42. 17 that say to the molten images, Ye (are) our
Hos. 13. 2 have made them molten images of their
Nah. 1. 14 the graven image and the molten image
Hab. 2. 18 the molten image, and a teacher of lies
4. *A pouring out, molten image,* נֶסֶךְ, נָסֶךְ *nesek.*
Isa. 41. 29 their molten images (are) wind and con.
48. 5 my molten image, hath commanded them
Jer. 10. 14 for his molten image (is) falsehood, and
51. 17 for his molten image (is) falsehood, and

MOLTEN, to be —
1. *To be poured out, melted,* נָתַךְ *nathak,* 2.
Eze. 24. 11 the filthiness of it may be molten in it
2. *To pour out,* צוּק *tsuq.*
Job 28. 2 and brass (is) molten (out of) the stone

MOMENT —
1. *A moment,* רֶגַע *rega.*
Exod33. 5 come up into the midst of thee in a mom.
Num16. 21 that I may consume them in a moment
16. 45 that I may consume them as in a moment
Job 7. 18 visit him every morning..try him every m.
20. 5 the joy of the hypocrite (but) for a mom.
21. 13 and in a moment go down to the grave
34. 20 In a moment shall they die, and the peo.
Psa. 30. 5 For his anger (endureth but) a moment
73. 19 How are they..unto desolation, as in a m.
Isa. 26. 20 hide thyself as it were for a little moment
27. 3 I will water it every moment: lest (any)
47. 9 shall come to thee in a moment in one d.
54. 7 For a small moment have I forsaken thee
54. 8 I hid my face from thee for a moment
Jer. 4. 20 my tents spoiled..my curtains in a mom.
Lam. 4. 6 overthrown as in a moment, and no hands
Eze. 26. 16 shall tremble at (every) moment, and be
32. 10 they shall tremble at (every) moment, ev.
2. *In a moment,* ἐν ἀτόμῳ *(dat.) en atomō.*
1 Co. 15. 52 In a moment, in the twinkling of an eye
3. *Point, puncture,* στιγμή *stigmē.*
Luke 4. 5 kingdoms of the world in a moment of t.

MOMENT, but for a —
Instant(ly), momentary, παραυτίκα *parautika.*
2 Co. 4. 17 our light affliction, which is but for a m.

MOMENT, to be a —
To cause to rest, רָגַע *raga,* 5.
Prov 12. 19 but a lying tongue (is) but for a moment

MONEY —
1. *Silver, money,* כֶּסֶף *keseph.*
Gen. 17. 12 or bought with money of any stranger
17. 13 he that is bought with thy money, must
17. 23 all that were bought with his money, ev.
17. 27 bought with money of the stranger, were
23. 9 for as much money as it is worth he shall
23. 13 I will give thee money for the field; take
31. 15 and hath quite devoured also our money
42. 25 to restore every man's money into his sack
42. 27 he espied his money; for, behold, it (was)
42. 28 My money is restored; and, lo, (it is) even
42. 35 every man's bundle of money (was) in his
42. 35 and their father saw the bundles of money
43. 12 And take double money in your hand
43. 12 and the money that was brought again in
43. 15 they took double money in their hand, and
43. 18 Because of the money that was returned
43. 21 (every) man's money (was) in the mouth
43. 21 of his sack, our money in full weight: and
43. 22 other money have we brought down in our
43. 22 we cannot tell who put our money in our
43. 23 I had your money. And he brought Sim.
44. 1 put every man's money in his sack's mouth
44. 2 and his corn money. And he did accord.
44. 8 the money which we found in our sack's
47. 14 Joseph gathered up all the money that
47. 14 Joseph brought the money into Pharaoh's
Gen. 47. 15 when money failed in the land of Egypt
47. 15 why should we die..for the money faileth
47. 16 I will give you for your cattle, if money
47. 18 We will not hide..how that our money
Exod12. 44 every man's servant..bought for money
21. 11 then shall she go out free without money
21. 21 he shall not be punished: for he (is) his m.
21. 34 (and) give money unto the owner of them
21. 35 sell the live ox, and divide the money of
22. 7 shall deliver unto his neighbour money or
22. 17 he shall pay money according to the dowry
22. 25 If thou lend money to..my people (that is)
30. 16 thou shalt take the atonement money of
Lev. 22. 11 if the priest buy (any) soul with his money
25. 37 Thou shalt not give him thy money upon
25. 51 out of the money that he was bought for
27. 15, 19 shall add the fifth..of the money of thy
27. 18 the priest shall reckon unto him the money
Num. 3. 48 thou shalt give the money, wherewith the
3. 49 Moses took the redemption money of them
3. 50 of the children of Israel took he the money
3. 51 Moses gave the money of them that were
18. 16 for the money of five shekels, after the s.
Deut. 2. 6 Ye shall buy meat of them for money, that
2. 6 ye shall also buy water of them for money
2. 28 Thou shalt sell me meat for money, that
2. 28 give me water for money, that I may drink
14. 25 turn (it) into money, and bind up the m.
14. 26 thou shalt bestow that money for whats.
21. 14 thou shalt not sell her at all for money
23. 19 usury of money, usury of victuals, usury
Judg. 5. 19 The kings came..they took no gain of m.
16. 18 came..and brought money in their hand
17. 4 Yet he restored the money unto his mother
1 Ki. 21. 2 I will give thee the worth of it in money
21. 6 Give me thy vineyard for money; or else
21. 15 which he refused to give thee for money
2 Ki. 5. 26 (Is it) a time to receive money, and to r.
12. 4 All the money of the dedicated things that
12. 4 the money of every one that passeth (the
12. 4 the money that every man is set at, (and)
12. 4 all the money that cometh into any man's
12. 7 receive no (more) money of your acquain.
12. 8 consented to receive no (more) money of
12. 9 put therein all the money..brought into
12. 10 when they saw that..much money in the
12. 10 told the money..found in the house of the
12. 11 they gave the money, being told, into the
12. 13 of the money..brought into the house of
12. 15 into whose hand they delivered the money
12. 16 The trespass money and sin money was
15. 20 Menahem exacted the money of Israel
22. 7 no reckoning made with them of the mo.
22. 9 Thy servants have gathered the money
23. 35 but he taxed the land to give the money
2 Ch. 24. 5 gather of all Israel money to repair the
24. 11 when they saw that..much money, the
24. 11 Thus they did..and gathered money in
24. 14 they brought the rest of the money before
34. 9 they delivered the money that was brought
34. 14 when they brought out the money that was
34. 17 they have gathered together the money
Ezra 3. 7 They gave money also unto the masons
Neh. 5. 4 We have borrowed money for the king's
5. 10 I..might exact of them money and corn
5. 11 also the hundredth (part) of the money
Esth. 4. 7 of the sum of the money that Haman had
Job 31. 39 If I have eaten the fruits..without money
Psa. 15. 5 putteth not out his money to usury, nor
Prov. 7. 20 He hath taken a bag of money with him
Eccl. 7. 12 wisdom (is) a defence..money (is) a defe.
10. 19 wine maketh merry: but money answereth
Isa. 43. 24 bought me no sweet cane with money
52. 3 and ye shall be redeemed without money
55. 1 and he that hath no money; come ye, buy
55. 1 come, buy wine and milk without money
55. 2 Wherefore do ye spend money for (that
Jer. 32. 9 weighed him the money..seventeen shek.
32. 10 and weighed..the money in the balances
32. 25 Buy thee the field for money, and take w.
32. 44 Men shall buy fields for money, and sub.
Lam. 5. 4 We have drunken our water for money
Mic. 3. 11 and the prophets thereof divine for money

2. *Silver, money,* כְּסַף *kesaph.*
Ezra 7. 17 thou mayest buy speedily with this money
3. *Silver, money,* ἀργύριον *argurion.*
Matt25. 18 digged in the earth, and hid his lord's m.
25. 27 oughtest therefore to have put my money
28. 12 they gave large money unto the soldiers
28. 15 So they took the money, and did as they
Mark14. 11 were glad, and promised to give him money
Luke 9. 3 nor scrip, neither bread, neither money
19. 15 to whom he had given the money, that he
19. 23 gavest thou not my money into the bank
22. 5 were glad, and covenanted to give him m.
Acts 7. 16 that Abraham bought for a sum of money
8. 20 Thy money perish with thee, because thou
4. *Small coin, clipped money,* κέρμα *kerma.*
John 2. 15 poured out the changers' money, and over.
5. *Legal or lawful coin,* νόμισμα *nomisma.*
Matt22. 19 Show me the tribute money. And they br.
6. *Copper, copper coin,* χαλκός *chalkos.*
Mark 6. 8 no scrip, no bread, no money in (their) p.
12. 41 beheld how the people cast money into
7. *A thing, possession, money,* χρῆμα *chrēma.*
Acts 4. 37 Having land, sold (it), and brought the m.
8. 18 Holy Ghost was given, he offered them m

Acts 8. 20 gift of God may be purchased with money
24. 26 He hoped..that money should have been

MONEY, piece of —
1. *A qesitah, (a silver coin),* קְשִׂיטָה *qesitah.*
Gen. 33. 19 he bought..for an hundred pieces of mo.
Job 42. 11 every man also gave him a piece of money

2. *A stater (24 drachmas),* στατήρ *statēr.*
Matt 17. 27 thou shalt find a piece of money : that

MONEY, with —
Acquisition, substance, קִנְיָן *qinyan.*
Lev. 22. 11 if the priest buy (any) soul with his money

MONEY CHANGER —
A changer of small coin, κολλυβιστής *kollubistēs.*
Matt 21. 12 overthrew the tables of the money chan.
Mark 11. 15 overthrew the tables of the money chan.

MONSTER, sea —
Dragons, תַּנִּין *tannin.*
Lam. 4. 3 Even the sea monsters draw out the bre.

MONTH, —
1. *New moon, month,* חֹדֶשׁ *chodesh.*
Gen. 7. 11 second month, the seventeenth..of the m.
8. 4 month, on the seventeenth..of the month
8. 5 the tenth month..on the first..of the m.
8. 13 first (month), the first (day) of the month
8. 14 And in the second month, on the seven
8. 14 and twentieth day of the month, was the
29. 14 he abode with him the space of a month
38. 24 it came to pass, about three months after
Exod 12. 2 This month..unto you the beginning of m.
12. 2 it (shall be) the first month of the year to
12. 3 In the tenth..of this month they shall take
12. 6 until the fourteenth day of the same mo.
12. 18 on the fourteenth day of the month at even
12. 18 the one and twentieth day of the month
13. 4 This day came ye out, in the month Abib
13. 5 thou shalt keep this service in this month
16. 1 on the fifteenth day of the second month
19. 1 In the third month, when the children of
23. 15 in the time appointed of the month Abib
34. 18 unleavened..in the time of the month A
34. 18 for in the month Abib thou camest out
40. 2 On the first day of the first month shalt
40. 17 the first month..on the first..of the month
Lev. 16. 29 the seventh mon., on the tenth..of the m.
23. 5 In the fourteenth..of the first month at
23. 6 on the fifteenth day of the same month (is)
23. 24 seventh month, in the first..of the month
23. 27 on the tenth (day) of this seventh month
23. 32 in the ninth (day) of the month at even
23. 34, 39 The fifteenth day of this seventh month
23. 41 ye shall celebrate it in the seventh month
25. 9 on the tenth (day) of the seventh month
27. 6 if (it be) from a month old even unto five
Num. 1. 1, 18 on the first (day) of the second month
3. 15, 22, 28, 34, 39, 40, 43 from a month old and
9. 1 in the first month of the second year after
9. 3 In the fourteenth day of this month, at
9. 5 on the fourteenth day of the first month
9. 11 The fourteenth day of the second month
9. 22 two days, or a month, or a year, that the
10. 10 in the beginnings of your months, ye shall
10. 11 on the twentieth..of the second month
11. 20 even a whole month, until it come out
11. 21 flesh, that they may eat a whole month
18. 16 from a month old shalt thou redeem, ac.
20. 1 into the desert of Zin in the first month
26. 62 all males from a month old and upward
28. 11 in the beginnings of your months ye shall
28. 14 of every month throughout the months of
28. 16 in the fourteenth day of the first month
28. 17 in the fifteenth day of this month (is) the
29. 1 seventh month, on the first..of the month
29. 6 Beside the burnt offering of the month, and
29. 7 on the tenth..of this seventh month an
29. 12 on the fifteenth day of the seventh month
33. 3 departed from Rameses in the first month
33. 3 on the fifteenth day of the first month
33. 38 and died..in the first (day) of the fifth mon.
Deut. 1. 3 eleventh month, on the first..of the mo.
16. 1 Observe the month of Abib, and keep the
16. 1 for in the month of Abib the LORD thy God
Josh. 4. 19 came up..on the tenth..of the first month
5. 10 on the fourteenth day of the month at even
Judg 11. 37 let me alone two months, that I may go
11. 38 And he sent her away..two months : and
11. 39 it came to pass, at the end of two months
19. 2 went away..and was there four whole m.
20. 47 abode in the rock Rimmon four months
1 Sa. 6. 1 the country of the Philistines seven months
20. 27 on the morrow..the second..of the month
20. 34 eat no meat the second day of the month
27. 7 the time..was a full year and four months
2 Sa. 2. 11 of Judah was seven years and six months
5. 5 over Judah seven years and six months
6. 11 continued in the house three..months: and
24. 8 at the end of nine months and twenty days
24. 13 or wilt thou flee three months before thine
1 Ki. 4. 7 each man his month in a year made pro.
4. 27 every man in his month : they lacked no.
5. 14 sent them..ten thousand a month by co.
5. 14 a month they were in Lebanon..two mo.
6. 1 the month Zif, which (is) the second mo.
6. 38 in..Bul, which (is) the eighth month, was
8. 2 Ethanim, which (is) the seventh month
11. 16 six months did Joab remain there with all
12. 32 month, on the fifteenth day of the month
1 Ki. 12. 33 the fifteenth day of the eighth month
12. 33 in the month which he had devised of his
2 Ki. 15. 8 reign over Israel in Samaria six months
23. 31 and he reigned three months in Jerusalem
24. 8 he reigned in Jerusalem three months
25. 1 ninth year of his reign, in the tenth mo.
25. 1 in the tenth..of the month..Nebuchad.
25. 3 on the ninth..of the..month the famine
25. 8 fifth month, on the seventh..of the month
25. 25 it came to pass in the seventh month, that
25. 27 twelfth month, on the..(day) of the month
1 Ch. 3. 4 there he reigned seven years and six mo.
12. 15 that went over Jordan in the first month
13. 14 family of Obed-edom in his house three m.
21. 12 or three months to be destroyed before thy
27. 1 came in and went out month by month
27. 1 throughout all the months of the year, of
27. 2 Over the first course for the first month
27. 3 the chief..of the host for the first month
27. 4 And over the course of the second month
27. 5 third captain of the host for the third mo.
27. 7 The fourth..for the fourth month (was)
27. 8 The fifth..for the fifth month (was) Sha.
27. 9 The sixth..for the sixth month (was) Ira
27. 10 The seventh..for the seventh month (was)
27. 11 The eighth..for the eighth month (was) S.
27. 12 The ninth..for the ninth month (was) A.
27. 13 The tenth..for the tenth month (was) M.
27. 14 The eleventh..for the eleventh mon. (was)
27. 15 The twelfth..for the twelfth month (was)
2 Ch. 3. 2 in the second (day) of the second month
5. 3 in the feast which (was) in the seventh m.
7. 10 day of the seventh month he sent the pe.
15. 10 at Jerusalem in the third month, in the
29. 3 in the first month, opened the doors of the
29. 17 they began on the first..of the first month
29. 17 on the eighth day of the month came they
27. 17 in the sixteenth day of the first month they
30. 2 to keep the passover in the second month
30. 13 to keep the feast..in the second month, a
30. 15 on the fourteenth..of the second month
31. 7 In the third month they began to lay the
31. 7 and finished (them) in the seventh month
35. 1 on the fourteenth (day) of the first month
36. 2 and he reigned three months in Jerusalem
36. 9 he reigned three months and ten days
Ezra 3. 1 when the seventh month was come, and
3. 6 From the first day of the seventh month
3. 8 in the second month, began Zerubbabel
6. 19 upon the fourteenth (day) of the first m.
7. 8 he came to Jerusalem in the fifth month
7. 9 For upon the first (day) of the first month
7. 9 on the first (day) of the fifth month came he
8. 31 departed..on the twelfth..of the first m.
10. 9 ninth month, on the twentieth..of the m.
10. 16 sat down in the first day of the tenth m.
10. 17 an end..by the first day of the first month
Neh. 1. 1 it came to pass in the month Chisleu, in
2. 1 it came to pass in the month Nisan, in the
7. 73 when the seventh month came, the chil.
8. 2 upon the first day of the seventh month
8. 14 in booths in the feast of the seventh mo.
9. 1 in the twenty and fourth day of this mo.
Esth. 2. 12 after that she had been twelve months, ac.
2. 12 six months with oil of myrrh, and six mo.
2. 16 in the tenth month, which (is) the month
3. 7 In the first month, that (is), the month N.
3. 7 from day to day, and from month to mo.
3. 7 the twelfth (month), that (is), the month
3. 12 on the thirteenth day of the first month
3. 13 upon the thirteenth..of the twelfth month
3. 13 which (is) the month Adar, and (to take)
8. 9 in the third month, that (is), the month
8. 12 twelfth month, which (is) the month Adar
9. 1 the twelfth month, that (is), the month A.
9. 15 on the fourteenth day also of the month
9. 17 On the thirteenth day of the month Adar
9. 19 made the fourteenth day of the month A.
9. 21 keep the fourteenth day of the month A.
9. 22 the month which was turned unto them
Job 14. 5 the number of his months (are) with thee
21. 21 when the number of his months is cut off
Jer. 1. 3 away of Jerusalem captive in the fifth m.
2. 24 wild ass..in her month they shall find her
28. 1 in the fourth year, (and) in the fifth month
28. 17 died the same year, in the seventh month
36. 9 in the ninth month..they proclaimed a
36. 22 in the winter house, in the ninth month
39. 1 In the ninth year..in the tenth month, c.
39. 2 in the fourth month, the ninth..of the m.
41. 1 Now it came to pass in the seventh month
52. 4 tenth month, in the tenth..of the month
52. 6 the fourth month, in the ninth..of the m.
52. 12 the fifth month, in the tenth..of the mo.
52. 31 month, in the five and twentieth..of the m.
Eze. 1. 1, 2 In the fifth (day) of the month
8. 1 in the fifth (day) of the month, (as) I sat in
20. 1 the tenth (day) of the month..certain of the
24. 1 in the tenth month, in the tenth..of the m.
26. 1 in the first..of the month..the word of the
29. 1 in the twelfth..of the month, the word of
29. 17 in the first..of the month, the word of the
30. 20 in the seventh..of the month..the word
31. 1 in the first..of the month..the word of the
32. 1 the twelfth month, in the first..of the mo.
32. 17 in the fifteenth..of the month..the word
33. 21 in the fifth..of the month..one that had
39. 12 seven months shall the house of Israel be
39. 14 after the end of seven months shall they
40. 1 in the tenth..of the month, in the fourte.
45. 18 in the first..of the month, thou shalt take
45. 20 so thou shalt do the seventh..of the month
Eze. 45. 21 in the fourteenth day of the month, ye
45. 25 in the fifteenth day of the month, shall he
47. 12 bring forth new fruit according to his m.
Dan. 10. 4 four and twentieth day of the first month
Hos. 5. 7 now shall a month devour them with th.
Amos 4. 7 when..yet three months to the harvest
Hag. 1. 1 sixth month, in the first day of the month
1. 15 four and twentieth day of the sixth month
2. 1 in the one and twentieth..of the month
2. 20 in the four and twentieth..of the month
Zech. 1. 1 In the eighth month, in the second year
1. 7 eleventh month, which (is) the month Seb.
7. 1 in the fourth..of the ninth month..in Ch.
7. 3 Should I weep in the fifth month, separ.

2. *Moon, month,* יֶרַח *yerach.*
Exod. 2. 2 (a) goodly (child), she hid him three months
Deut 21. 13 her father and her mother a full month
1 Ki. 6. 37 In the fourth year..in the month Zif
6. 38 in the month Bul, which (is) the eighth
8. 2 the month Ethanim, which (is) the seventh
2 Ki. 15. 13 and he reigned a full month in Samaria
Job 3. 6 let it not come in to the number of the m.
7. 3 So am I made to possess months of vanity
29. 2 Oh that I were as (in) months past, as (in)
39. 2 Canst thou number the months..they fu.
Zech. 11. 8 Three shepherds also I cut off in one mo.

3. *Moon, month,* יְרַח *yerach.*
Ezra 6. 15 on the third day of the month Adar, which
Dan. 4. 29 At the end of twelve months he walked in

4. *A month,* μήν *mēn.*
Luke 1. 24 conceived, and hid herself five months
1. 26 in the sixth month the angel Gabriel was
1. 36 this is the sixth month with her, who was
1. 56 Mary abode with her about three months
4. 25 was shut up three years and six months
Acts 7. 20 nourished..in his father's house three m.
18. 11 he continued..a year and six months, te.
19. 8 spake boldly for the space of three months
20. 3 And..abode three months. And when the
28. 11 after three months we departed in a ship
Gal. 4. 10 Ye observe days, and months, and times
Jas. 5. 17 by the space of three years and six months
Rev. 9. 5 that they should be tormented five months
9. 10 their power (was) to hurt men five months
9. 15 for an hour, and a day, and a month, and
11. 2 they tread under foot forty..two months
13. 5 unto him to continue forty (and) two mon.
22. 2 yielded her fruit every month : and the l.
[*See also* Four, three.]

MONTHLY —
New moon, month, חֹדֶשׁ *chodesh.*
Isa. 47. 13 Let now..the monthly prognosticators

MONUMENTS —
To keep, watch, preserve, נָצַר *natsar.*
Isa. 65. 4 and lodge in the monuments; which eat

MOON —
1. *Moon, wandering,* יָרֵחַ *yareach.*
Gen. 37. 9 the sun, and the moon, and the eleven stars
Deut. 4. 19 when thou seest the sun, and the moon
17. 3 either the sun, or moon, or any of the host
Josh. 10. 12 and thou, moon, in the valley of Ajalon
10. 13 and the moon stayed, until the people had
2 Ki. 23. 5 to the sun, and to the moon, and to the pl.
Job 25. 5 Behold even to the moon, and it shineth
31. 26 If I beheld..the moon walking (in) bright.
Psa. 8. 3 the moon and the stars, which thou hast
72. 5 shall fear thee as long as the sun and m.
72. 7 abundance of peace so long as the moon
89. 37 It shall be established for ever as the m.
104. 19 He appointed the moon for seasons : the
121. 6 shall not smite thee by day, nor the moon
136. 9 The moon and stars to rule by night : for
148. 3 Praise ye him, sun and moon : praise him
Eccl. 12. 2 While the sun, or the light, or the moon
Isa. 13. 10 the moon shall not cause her light to shine
60. 19 neither for brightness shall the moon give
Jer. 8. 2 the moon, and all the host of heaven
31. 35 the ordinances of the moon and of the stars
Eze. 32. 7 and the moon shall not give her light
Joel 2. 10 the sun and the moon shall be dark, and
2. 31 and the moon into blood, before the great
3. 15 The sun and the moon shall be darkened
Hab. 3. 11 sun (and) moon stood still in their habit.

2. *The moon,* יְרַח *yerach.*
Deut 33. 14 the precious things put forth by the moon
Isa. 60. 20 neither shall thy moon withdraw itself

3. *The moon (from its whiteness),* לְבָנָה *lebanah.*
Song 6. 10 fair as the moon, clear as the sun..terrible
Isa. 24. 23 Then the moon shall be confounded, and
30. 26 the light of the moon shall be as the light

4. *The moon,* σελήνη *selēnē.*
Matt 24. 29 the moon shall not give her light, and the
Mark 13. 24 and the moon shall not give her light
Luke 21. 25 shall be signs in the sun, and in the moon
Acts 2. 20 the moon into blood, before that great
1 Co. 15. 41 another glory of the moon, and another
Rev. 6. 12 became black..and the moon became as
8. 12 the third part of the moon, and the third
12. 1 the moon under her feet, and upon her
21. 23 the city had no need..of the moon, to shine

MOON, new —
1. *New moon,* חֹדֶשׁ *chodesh.*
1 Sa. 20. 5 to morrow (is) the new moon, and I should
20. 18 to David, To morrow (is) the new moon: and
20. 24 when the new moon was come, the king
2 Ki. 4. 23 said..(it is) neither new moon nor sabbath

1 Ch.23. 31 in the sabbaths, in the new moons, and on
2 Ch. 2. 4 on the sabbaths, and on the new moons
8. 13 on the sabbaths, and on the new moons
31. 3 for the sabbaths, and for the new moons
Ezra 3. 5 burnt offering, both of the new moons, and
Neh. 10. 33 of the sabbaths, of the new moons, for the
Psa. 81. 3 Blow up the trumpet in the new moon, in
Isa. 1. 13 the new moons and sabbaths, the calling
1. 14 Your new moons and your appointed fea.
66. 23 from one new moon to another, and from
Eze. 45. 17 in the feasts, and in the new moons, and
46. 1 in the day of the new moon it shall be
46. 3 worship..in the sabbaths and in the new m.
46. 6 in the day of the new moon..a young bu.
Hos. 2. 11 her feast days, her new moons, and her
Amos 8. 5 When will the new moon be gone, that

2. *New moon*, νουμηνία *noumēnia*, νεομηνία.
Col. 2. 16 of an holy day, or of the new moon, or of

MOR-AS-THITE, מֹרַשְׁתִּי.
Patronymic of Micah the prophet from Moresheth Gath.
B.C. 750—721.
Jer. 26. 18 Micah the M. prophesied in the days of
Mic. 1. 1 word..that came to Micah the M. in the

MOR-DE-CA'I, מָרְדֳּכַי *dedicated to Mars.*
1. A chief man that returned with Zerubbabel. B.C. 536.
Ezra 2. 2 M., Bilshan, Mizpar, Bigvai, Rehum, Ba.
Neh. 7. 7 Who came with Zerubbabel, Jeshua..M.

2. A Benjamite, cousin of Esther the queen of Ahasuerus.
B.C. 520.
Esth. 2. 5 there was a..Jew, whose name (was) M.
2. 7 whom M...took for his own daughter
2. 10 M. had charged her that she should not
2. 11 M. walked every day before the court of
2. 15 M., who had taken her for his daughter
2. 19 when the virgins were gathered..M. sat
2. 20 had not (yet) showed..as M. had charged
2. 20 Esther did the commandment of M., like
2. 21 while M. sat in the king's gate, two of the
2. 22 the thing was known to M., who told (it)
2. 22 certified the king (thereof) in M.'s name
3. 2 but M. bowed not, nor did (him) reverence
3. 3 Then the king's servants..said unto M.
3. 4 to see whether M.'s matters would stand
3. 5 Haman saw that M. bowed not, nor did
3. 6 he thought scorn to lay hands on M. alone
3. 6 for they had showed him the people of M.
3. 6 Haman sought to destroy..people of M.
4. 1 When M. perceived all that was done, M.
4. 4 she sent raiment to clothe M., and to take
4. 5 gave him a commandment to M., to know
4. 6 Hatach went forth to M. unto the street
4. 7 M. told him of all that had happened unto
4. 9 Hatach came and told E...words of M.
4. 10 Esther spake..gave him command. unto M.
4. 12 And they told to M. Esther's words
4. 13 M. commanded to answer Esther, Think
4. 15 Esther bade (them) return M. (this answer)
4. 17 M. went his way, and did according to all
5. 9 Haman saw M. in the king's gate, that he
5. 9 he was full of indignation against M.
5. 13 so long as I see M. the Jew sitting at the
5. 14 speak thou..that M. may be hanged the
6. 2 M. had told of Bigthana and Teresh, two
6. 3 What honour..hath been done to M. for
6. 4 to hang M. on the gallows that he had
6. 10 do even so to M. the Jew, that sitteth at
6. 11 arrayed M., and brought him on horseback
6. 12 M. came again to the king's gate. but H.
6. 13 If M. (be) of the seed of the Jews, before
7. 9 the gallows..which Haman..made for M.
7. 10 the gallows that he had prepared for M.
8. 1 M. came before the king; for Esther had
8. 2 and gave it unto M. And Esther set M.
8. 7 unto Esther the queen, and to M. the Jew
8. 9 written according to all that M. comman.
8. 15 M. went out from the presence of the king
9. 3 because the fear of M. fell upon them
9. 4 M. (was) great in the king's house, and his
9. 4 for this man M. waxed greater and grea.
9. 20 M. wrote these things, and sent letters
9. 23 to do..as M. had written unto them
9. 29 M. the Jew, wrote with all authority, to
9. 31 as M. the Jew and Esther the queen had
10. 2 the declaration of the greatness of M.
10. 3 M. the Jew (was) next unto king Ahasue

MORE, (the)—
1. *Great*, גָּדוֹל *gadol.*
Num22. 18 the word of the LORD..to do less or more
1 Sa. 22. 15 for thy servant knew nothing..less or m
25. 36 she told him nothing, less or more, until
Isa. 56. 12 shall be as this day..much more abund.

2. *Outside of*, חוּץ *chuts.*
Eccl. 2. 25 or who else can hasten..more than I?

3. *Advantage, farther*, יוֹתֵר *yother.*
Esth. 6. 6 the king delight to do honour more than
Eccl. 2. 15 why was I then more wise? Then I said
6. 8 For what hath the wise more than the f.

4. *Again, yet, any more*, עוֹד *od.*
Gen. 9. 15 the waters shall no more become a flood to

5. *Abundant, much, many*, רַב *rab.*
Gen. 36. 7 For their riches were more than that they
Exod. 1. 9 the children of Israel (are) more and mi.
Num22. 15 And Balak sent yet again princes, more
33. 54 to the more ye shall give the..inheritance
Deut. 7. 17 These nations (are) more than I; how can
20. 1 a people more than thou, be not afraid of
Judg 16. 30 were more than (they) which he slew in
2 Ki. 6. 16 they that (be) with us (are) more than they
1 Ch.24. 4 there were more chief men found of the
2 Ch.32. 7 for (there be) more with us than with him
Isa. 54. 1 for more (are) the children of the desolate

6. *Second, other, again*, שֵׁנִית *shenith.*
Lev. 13. 5 priest shall shut him up seven days more
13. 33 up (him that hath) the scall seven days m.
13. 54 and he shall shut it up seven days more

7. *Other*, ἄλλος *allos.*
Matt25. 20 I have gained beside them five talents m.

8. *Yet, still*, ἔτι *eti.*
Matt18. 16 take with thee one or two more, Lu. 20.36.
John11. 54 Jesus therefore walked no more openly
14. 19 little while, and the world seeth me no m.
16. 10 I go to my Father, and ye see me no more
16. 21 she remembereth no more the anguish
16. 25 when I shall no more speak unto you in
17. 11 now I am no more in the world, but these
Rom. 6. 9 Christ..dieth no more; death hath no m.
7. 17, 20 it is no more I that do it, but sin that
11. 6 more of works; otherwise grace is no m.
11. 6 no more grace; otherwise work is no more
2 Co. 5. 16 yet now henceforth know we..no more
Gal. 3. 18 (it is) no more of promise: but God gave
4. 7 thou art no more a servant, but a son; and
Heb. 8. 12 their iniquities will I remember no more
10. 2 should have had no more conscience of
10. 17 sins and iniquities will I remember no m.
10. 18 remission of these (is, there is) no more
10. 26 there remaineth no more sacrifice for sins
11. 32 what shall I more say? for the time wou.
Rev. 3. 12 he shall go no more out: and I will write
7. 16 They shall hunger no more, neither thirst
9. 12 behold, there come two woes more 12. 8,
18. 21 thrown down, and shall be found no more
18. 22, 22 shall be heard no more at all in thee
18. 23 shall shine no more at all in thee; and the
18. 23 shall be heard no more at all in thee
20. 3 that he should deceive the nations no m.
21. 1 And I saw..and there was no more sea
21. 4 there shall be no more death, neither so.
22. 3 there shall be no [more] curse: but the th.

9. *More, rather*, μᾶλλον *mallon.*
Matt. 6. 30 not much more (clothe) you, O ye of little
7. 11 how much more shall your Father which
10. 25 how much more..them of his household?
18. 13 he rejoiceth more of that..than of the n.
Luke11. 13 how much more shall (your) heavenly F.
12. 24 how much more are ye better than the f.
12. 28 how much more..you, O ye of little faith
John12. 43 they loved the praise of men more than
Acts 4. 19 to hearken unto you more than unto God
20. 35 It is more blessed to give than to receive
27. 11 more than those things which were spok.
Rom. 5. 9 Much more then, being now justified by
5. 10 much more, being reconciled, we shall be
5. 15 much more the grace of God, and the gr.
5. 17 much more they which receive abundance
11. 12 the fall of them..how much more their
11. 24 how much more shall these, which be the
1 Co 12. 22 Nay, much more those members of the b
14. 18 I speak with tongues more than ye all
2 Co. 3. 9 much more doth the ministration of righ.
3. 11 much more that which remaineth (is) glo
Gal. 4. 27 the desolate hath many more children than
Phil. 2. 12 now much more in my absence; 1. 9, 9.
3. 4 whereof he might trust in the flesh, I m.
2 Ti. 3. 4 lovers of pleasure more than lovers of G.
Phm. 16 how much more unto thee, both in the fl.
Heb. 9. 14 How much more shall the blood of Christ
12. 25 much more (shall not) we..if we turn away

10. *Greater, more*, μείζων *meizōn.*
Jas. 4. 6 But he giveth more grace Wherefore he

11. *Abundant, exceeding*, περισσός *perissos.*
Matt. 5. 37 whatsoever is more than these cometh of
5. 47 what do ye more..do not even the publi.

12. *More abundant*, περισσότερον *perissoteron.*
Matt11. 9 yea, I say unto you, and more than a pr
Luke12. 4 after that have no more that they can do
12. 48 to whom..of him they will ask the more
2 Co. 10. 8 I should boast somewhat more of our au.

13. *More*, πλείων *pleiōn*, πλεῖον, πλέον.
Matt6. 25 Is not the life more than meat. and the
20. 10 that they should have received more; and
21. 36 he sent other servants more than the first
26. 53 give me more than twelve legions of an.?
Mark12. 33 is [more] than all whole burnt offerings
12. 43 That this poor widow hath cast more in
Luke 3. 13 Exact no more than that which is appoi.
9. 13 We have no more but five loaves and two
12. 23 The life is more than meat, and the body
21. 3 that this poor widow hath cast in more
John 4. 1 made and baptized more disciples than J
4. 41 many more believed because of his own
7. 31 will he do more miracles than these which
15. 2 purgeth it, that it may bring forth more
21. 15 lovest thou me more than these? He saith
Acts 23. 13 they were more than forty which had made
23. 21 there lie in wait for him of them more than
25. 6 when he had tarried among them more
1 Co. 9. 19 servant unto all, that I might gain the m.
2 Ti. 2. 16 they will increase unto more ungodliness
Heb. 3. 3 was counted worthy of more glory than M.
3. 3 he who hath builded the house hath more
Rev. 2. 19 I know..the last (to be) more than the first

14. *Above, beyond, more than*, ὑπέρ *huper.*
2 Co. 11. 23 Are they ministers of Christ..I (am) more
[*See also* Abominable, afflict, any, carefully, cheerfully, come, enough, excellent, get, give, honourable, how much, laid, much, not, put to, ready, show, so many, so much, spend, surely, twofold, value, vile.]

15. *To weep*, בָּכָה *bakah.*
Isa. 30. 19 thou shalt weep no more: he will be very

16. *To add*, יָסַף *yasaph.*
Lev. 26. 18 I will punish you seven times more for your
Judg. 8. 28 so that they lifted up their heads no more
1 Sa. 27. 4 and he sought no more again for him
2 Sa. 2. 28 stood still..neither fought they any more
2 Ki. 6. 23 So the bands of Syria came no more into

17. *To be added*, יָסַף *yasaph*, 2.
Isa. 15. 9 I will bring more upon Dimon, lions upon

18. *On, above*, עַל *al.*
Dan. 3. 19 heat the furnace one seven times more

19. *To cause to multiply, make many*, רָבָה *rabah*, 5.
1 Sa. 2. 3 Talk no more so exceeding proudly; let
2 Sa. 18. 8 the wood devoured more people that day

MORE, to be —
1. *To be over and above*, עָדַף *adaph.*
Num. 3. 46 of Israel, which are more than the Levites

2. *To be bony, substantial*, עָצַם *atsam.*
Psa. 40. 5 they are more than can be numbered
40. 12 they are more than the hairs of mine head

3. *To be many, multiplied*, רָבַב *rabab.*
Psa. 69. 4 They..are more than the hairs of mine h.

MORE and more —
1. *To go on*, הָלַךְ *halak.*
Prov. 4. 18 that shineth more and more unto the pe.

2. *To cause to add*, יָסַף *yasaph*, 5.
Psa. 71. 14 and will yet praise thee more and more
115. 14 The LORD shall increase you more and m.
Isa. 1. 5 Why..ye will revolt more and more
Hos. 13. 2 now they sin more and more, and have m.

3. *To cause to multiply, make many*, רָבָה *rabah*, 5.
2 Ch.33. 23 but Amon trespassed more and more

4. *More, rather*, μᾶλλον *mallon.*
1 Th.4. 1 God, (so) ye would abound more and more
4. 10 brethren, that ye increase more and more

MORE excellent —
Thoroughly excelling, καθ' ὑπερβολήν *kath' huper.*
1 Co. 12. 31 yet show I unto you a more excellent way

MORE, far or much —
1. *To cause to multiply, make many*, רָבָה *rabah*, 5.
2 Ch.25. 9 LORD is able to give thee much more than

2. *To cause to add*, יָסַף *yasaph*, 5.
1 Sa. 20. 13 The LORD do so and much more to Jona.

3. *More abundantly*, περισσότερον *perissoteron.*
Luke 7. 26 I say unto you..much more than a prop.
Heb. 7. 15 it is yet far more evident: for that after

4. *More abundantly*, περισσοτέρως *perissoterōs.*
Phil. 1. 14 are much more bold to speak the word

MORE, can no —
Thus neither, οὕτως οὐδέ *houtōs oude.*
John15. 4 no more can ye, except ye abide in me

MORE part —
More, greater, πλείων *pleiōn.*
Acts 19. 32 the more part knew not wherefore they
27. 12 the more part advised to depart thence

MORE than —
1. *From, out of, above*, מִן *min.*
Dan. 2. 30 wisdom that I have more than any living

2. *With*, עִם *im.*
Eccl. 2. 16 no remembrance of the wise more than of

3. *Except*, כִּי אִם *ki im.*
2 Ki. 9. 35 they found no more of her than the skull

4. *Before*, לִפְנֵי *li-phene.*
Job 34. 19 nor regardeth the rich more than the poor

5. *Except*, εἰ μή *ei mē.*
Mark 8. 14 had they in the ship with them more than

6. *Above, upon, over, more than*, ἐπάνω *epanō.*
Mark14. 5 For it might have been sold for more than

7. *Beyond, alongside of, more than*, παρά (acc.) *para.*
Rom. 1. 25 served the creature more than the; 12. 3.

8. *Than*, ἤ *ē*, Luke 15. 7.

.*Over, above, beyond, more than*, ὑπέρ (acc.) *huper.*
Matt 10. 37 He that loveth father or mother more than
10. 37 he that loveth son or daughter more than
Phm. 21 knowing that thou wilt also do more than

MORE, any —
To cause to multiply, make abundant, רָבָה *rabah*, 5.
2 Sa. 14. 11 the revengers of blood to destroy any m.

MORE, to add, be, bring, do, make or put —
1. *To add*, יָסַף *yasaph.*
Lev. 26. 21 I will bring seven times more plagues upon
Deut. 5. 22 he added no more: and he wrote them in
Judg 13. 21 the angel of the LORD did no more appear

2. *To cause to add*, יָסַף *yasaph*, 5.
1 Ch.21. 3 make..an hundred times so many more

2 Ch. 10. 11 I will put more to your yoke: my father
28. 22 did he trespass yet more against the LORD
Job 34. 32 I have done iniquity, I will do no more
41. 8 Lay..remember the battle, do no more
Isa. 1. 13 Bring no more vain oblations; incense is
Neh. 13. 18 yet ye bring more wrath upon Israel by

MORE, to give or have (the) —
1. *To pass over,* עָבַר *abar.*
Psa. 73. 7 they have more than heart could wish
2. *To cause to multiply, make many,* רָבָה *rabah,* 5.
Exod 30. 15 The rich shall not give more, and the poor
Lev. 11. 42 or whatsoever hath more feet among all
Num 26. 54 To many thou shalt give the more inher.
33. 54 to the more ye shall give the more inher.

MORE in number, to be —
1. *Abundance,* רֹב *rob.*
Deut. 7. 7 because ye were more in number than any
2. *To be many,* רָבָה *rabah.*
Psa. 139. 18 they are more in number than the sand

MORE, to (see) —
To turn back, שׁוּב *shub.*
Job 7. 7 remember..mine eye shall no more see

MORE, (so much) the —
1. *To cause to add,* יָסַף *yasaph,* 5.
Gen. 37. 5, 8 And they hated him yet the more
1 Sa. 18. 29 Saul was yet the more afraid of David
2. *So,* כֵּן *ken.*
Exod. 1. 12 the more they multiplied and grew
3. *Rather, more,* μᾶλλον *mallon.*
Mark 7. 36 so much the more a great deal they pub.
10. 48 he cried the more a great deal, (Thou) son
14. 31 he spake [the more] vehemently, If I should
Luke 5. 15 so much the more went there a fame abr.
18. 39 cried so much the more, (thou) son of D.
John 5. 18 Therefore the Jews sought the more to
19. 8 heard that saying, he was the more afraid
Acts 5. 14 believers were the more added to the L.
9. 22 Saul increased the more in strength, and
22. 2; 2 Co. 7. 7; 7. 13; Heb. 10. 25.
4. *Greater,* μεῖζον *meizon.*
Matt 20. 31 they cried the more, saying, Have mercy
5. *As much as,* ὅσος *hosos.*
Mark 7. 36 but the more he charged them, so much
6. *Abundantly,* περισσῶς *perissōs.*
Matt 27. 23 they cried out the more, saying, Let him

MORE, whatsoever —
Remnant, residue, שְׁאָר *shear.*
Ezra 7. 20 whatsoever more shall be needful for the

MORE, to be yet the —
To cause to add, יָסַף *yasaph,* 5.
Exod. 9. 34 he sinned yet more, and hardened his he.
1 Sa. 18. 29 Saul was yet the more afraid of David

MO'-REH, מוֹרֶה, מֹרֶה *teacher.*
1. A place in Ephraim, near Gilgal and Mount Gerizim.
Gen. 12. 6 the place of Sichem, unto the plain of M.
Deut 11. 30 against Gilgal, beside the plains of M.
2. A hill in Issachar, at the E. end of Jezreel.
Judg 7. 1 the north side of them, by the hill of M.

MOREOVER —
1. *Also, even, but, yea, although,* אַף *aph.*
Num 16. 14 Moreover thou hast not brought us into
2. *Also, even, yea, yet, truly,* גַּם *gam.*
Gen. 32. 20 say ye moreover, Behold, thy servant Ja.
1 Ch. 11. 2 moreover in time past, even when Saul
3. *Advantage, more,* יֹתֵר *yother.*
Eccl. 12. 9 And moreover, because the Preacher was
4. *Again, yet, while, any more,* עוֹד *od.*
Exod. 3. 15 God said moreover unto Moses, Thus sh.
5. *But even,* ἀλλὰ καί *alla kai.*
Luke 16. 21 moreover the dogs came and licked his s.
6. *Yet, still,* ἔτι *eti.*
Acts 2. 26 moreover also my flesh shall rest in hope
Heb. 11. 36 yea, moreover of bonds and imprisonment
7. *But what is left over,* ὃ δὲ λοιπόν *ho de loipon.*
1 Co. 4. 2 Moreover it is required in stewards, that
8. *And,* καί, *and also* δὲ καί, 1 Ti. 3. 7.
9. *And likewise,* καὶ ὁμοίως *kai homoiōs,* He. 9. 21.

MOREOVER if —
And if, וְאִם *veim.*
2 Sa. 17. 13 Moreover if he be gotten into a city, then

MO-RE'-SHETH GATH, מוֹרֶשֶׁת גַּת *possession of Gath.*
A city in the W. of Judah, birthplace of Micah the prophet.
Mic. 1. 14 Therefore shalt thou give presents to M.

MO-RI'-AH, מֹרִיָּה, מוֹרִיָּה *Jah provides.*
The hill on the N.W. of Jebus (afterwards called the city of David), on which Solomon's temple was built.
Gen. 22. 2 get thee into the land of M.; and offer
2 Ch. 3. 1 house of the LORD at Jerus. in mount M.

MORNING, (in the)—
1. *Light,* אוֹר *or.*
Neh. 8. 3 from the morning until mid day, before
2. *Morning,* בֹּקֶר *boqer.*
Gen. 1. 5, 8, 13, 19, 23, 31 the evening and the mo.
19. 27 Abraham gat up early in the morning to
20. 8 Abimelech rose early in the morning, and
21. 14 Abraham rose up early in the morning
22. 3 Abraham rose up early in the morning
24. 54 they rose up in the morning; and he said
26. 31 they rose up betimes in the morning, and
28. 18 Jacob rose up early in the morning, and
29. 25 that in the morning, behold, it (was) Leah
31. 55 early in the morning Laban rose up, and
40. 6 Joseph came in unto them in the morning
41. 8 it came to pass in the morning, that his
44. 3 As soon as the morning was light, the men
49. 27 in the morning he shall devour the prey
Exod. 7. 15 Get thee unto Pharaoh in the morning
8. 20 Rise up early in the morning, and stand
9. 13 Rise up early in the morning, and stand
10. 13 when it was morning, the east wind bro.
12. 10 let nothing of it remain until the morning
12. 10 that which remaineth of it until the m.
12. 22 none of you shall go out..until the mor.
14. 24 in the morning watch the LORD looked
14. 27 returned to his strength when the morn.
16. 7 in the morning, then shall ye see the gl.
16. 8 in the morning bread to the full; for that
16. 12 in the morning ye shall be filled with b.
16. 13 in the morning the dew lay round about
16. 19 Let no man leave of it till the morning
16. 20 some of them left of it until the morning
16. 21 they gathered it every morning, every man
16. 23 lay up for you to be kept until the morn.
16. 24 they laid it up till the morning, as Moses
18. 13 the people stood by Moses from the mor.
18. 14 all the people stand by thee from morning
19. 16 it came to pass..the morning, that there
23. 18 shall the fat..remain until the morning
24. 4 Moses..rose up early in the morning, and
27. 21 shall order it from evening to morning be.
29. 34 if ought..remain unto the morning, then
29. 39 one lamb thou shalt offer in the morning
29. 41 according to the meat offering of the m.
30. 7 burn thereon sweet incense every morn.
34. 2 ready in the morning..come up in the m.
34. 4 Moses rose up early in the morning, and
34. 25 the sacrifice..be left unto the morning
36. 3 they brought yet unto him..every morn.
Lev. 6. 9 the burning..all night unto the morning
6. 12 priest shall burn wood on it every morn.
6. 20 half of it in the morning, and half thereof
7. 15 he shall not leave any of it until the mo.
9. 17 beside the burnt sacrifice of the morning
19. 13 shall not abide with thee..until the mor.
24. 3 shall Aaron order it..unto the morning
Num 9. 12 They shall leave none of it unto the mor.
9. 15 the appearance of fire, until the morning
9. 21 when the cloud abode..unto the morning
9. 21 the cloud was taken up in the morning
14. 40 they rose up early in the morning, and gat
22. 13 Balaam rose up early in the morning, and
22. 21 Balaam rose up in the morning, and sad.
28. 4 The one lamb shalt thou offer in the mo.
28. 8 as the meat offering of the morning, and
28. 23 beside the burnt offering in the morning
Deut 16. 4 neither..remain all night until the morn.
16. 7 thou shalt turn in the morning, and go
28. 67 In the morning thou shalt say, Would God
28. 67 thou shalt say, Would God it were morn.
Josh. 3. 1 Joshua rose early in the morning; and
6. 12 Joshua rose early in the morning, and
7. 14 In the morning therefore ye shall be bro.
7. 16 So Joshua rose up early in the morning
8. 10 Joshua rose up early in the morning, and
Judg. 6. 28 when the men..arose early in the morn.
6. 31 let him be put to death whilst..morning
9. 33 it shall be..in the morning, as soon as
16. 2 In the morning, when it is day, we shall
19. 5 when they arose early in the morning
19. 8 he arose early in the morning, on the fifth
19. 25 abused her all the night unto the morning
19. 27 her lord rose up in the morning, and op.
20. 19 the children of Israel rose up in the mo.
Ruth 2. 7 hath continued even from the morning
3. 13 Tarry..and it shall be in the morning
3. 13 LORD liveth: lie down until the morning
3. 14 she lay at his feet until the morning; and
1 Sa. 1. 19 they rose up in the morning early, and
3. 15 Samuel lay until the morning, and opened
5. 4 when they arose early on the morrow m.
11. 11 midst of the host in the morning watch
14. 36 and spoil them until the morning light
15. 12 Samuel rose early to meet Saul in the m.
17. 20 David rose up early in the morning, and
19. 2 take heed to thyself until the morning
19. 11 to watch him, and to slay him in the mo.
20. 35 it came to pass in the morning, that Jon.
25. 22 if I leave of all..by the morning light, any
25. 34 had not been left..by the morning light
25. 36 told him nothing..until the morning light
25. 37 it came to pass in the morning, when the
29. 10 now rise up early in the morning with thy
29. 10 as soon as ye be up early in the morning
29. 11 rose up early to depart in the morning, to
2 Sa. 2. 27 surely then in the morning the people had
11. 14 it came to pass in the morning, that Da.
17. 22 by the morning light there lacked not one
23. 4 as the light of the morning..a morning
24. 11 when David was up in the morning, the
24. 15 from the morning even to the time appo.
1 Ki. 3. 21 when I rose in the morning to give my
3. 21 when I had considered it in the morning
17. 6 brought him bread and flesh in the morn.
1 Ki. 18. 26 called on the name of Baal from morning
2 Ki. 3. 20 it came to pass in the morning, when the
3. 22 they rose up early in the morning, and the
7. 9 if we tarry till the morning light, some
10. 8 Lay ye them in two heaps..until the mor.
10. 9 it came to pass in the morning, that he
16. 15 Upon the great altar burn the morning
19. 35 when they arose early in the morning, b.
1 Ch. 9. 27 the opening thereof every morning..to
16. 40 To offer..continually morning and even.
23. 30 to stand every morning to thank and pr
2 Ch. 2. 4 for the burnt offerings morning and eve.
13. 11 they burn unto the LORD every morning
20. 20 they rose early in the morning, and went
31. 3 for the morning and evening burnt offer.
Ezra 3. 3 offered..burnt offerings morning and eve.
Job 1. 5 rose up early in the morning, and offered
4. 20 They are destroyed from morning to eve.
7. 18 shouldest visit him every morning..try
11. 17 shine forth, thou shalt be as the morning
24. 17 the morning (is) to them even as the sh.
38. 7 When the morning stars sang together, and
38. 12 Hast thou commanded the morning since
Psa. 5. 3 My voice shalt thou hear in the morning
5. 3 in the morning will I direct..unto thee
30. 5 endure for a night, but joy..in the morn.
49. 14 shall have dominion over them in the m.
55. 17 Evening, and morning, and at noon, will
59. 16 I will sing aloud of thy mercy in the mo.
65. 8 thou makest the outgoings of the morning
73. 14 been plagued, and chastened every morn.
88. 13 in the morning shall my prayer prevent
90. 5 in the morning..like grass (which) grow.
90. 6 In the morning it flourisheth, and grow.
92. 2 To show forth..in the morning, and thy
130. 6, 6 they that watch for the morning
143. 8 Cause me to hear..in the morning; for in
Prov. 7. 18 let us take our fill of love until the mor.
27. 14 with a loud voice, rising early in the mo.
Eccl. 10. 16 Woe to thee..thy princes eat in the mo.
11. 6 In the morning sow thy seed, and in the
Isa. 5. 11 Woe unto them that rise up..in the mo.
17. 11 in the morning shalt thou make thy seed
17. 14 And behold..before the morning he (is)
21. 12 The watchmen said, The morning cometh
28. 19 for morning by morning shall it pass over
33. 2 be thou their arm every morning, our sa.
37. 36 when they arose early in the morning, b.
38. 13 I reckoned till morning..as a lion, so will
50. 4 he wakeneth morning by morning, he w.
Jer. 20. 16 let him hear the cry in the morning, and
21. 12 Execute judgment in the morning, and d.
Lam. 3. 23 new every morning: great (is) thy faithful.
Eze. 12. 8 in the morning came the word of the LORD
24. 18 So I spake unto the people in the morning
24. 18 I did in the morning as I was commanded
33. 22 until he came to me in the morning; and
46. 13 lamb..thou shalt prepare it every morn.
46. 14 prepare a meat offering for it every mor.
46. 15 shall they prepare the lamb..every mor.
Dan. 8. 26 the vision of the evening and the morning
Hos. 6. 4 for your goodness (is) as a morning cloud
7. 6 in the morning it burneth as a flaming fire
13. 3 they shall be as the morning cloud, and as
Amos 4. 4 and bring your sacrifices every morning
5. 8 the shadow of death into the morning
Mic. 2. 1 when the morning is light, they practise
Zeph. 3. 5 every morning doth he bring his judgment
3. *Dawn,* מִשְׁחָר *mishchar.*
Psa. 110. 3 of holiness from the womb of the morning
4. *Shining, brightness,* נֹגַהּ *nogah.*
Dan. 6. 19 Then the king arose very early in the m.
5. *An awakening, warning, mishap,* צְפִירָה *tsephirah.*
Eze. 7. 7 The morning is come unto thee, O thou
7. 10 the morning is gone forth; the rod hath
6. *Dawn,* שַׁחַר *shachar.*
Gen. 19. 15 when the morning arose, then the angels
Neh. 4. 21 from the rising of the morning till the
Job 41. 18 his eyes..like the eyelids of the morning
Psa. 139. 9 I take the wings of the morning..dwell in
Song 6. 10 looketh forth as..morning, fair as the m.
Isa. 14. 12 O Lucifer, son of the morning! (how) art
58. 8 shall thy light break forth as the morning
Hos. 6. 3 his going forth is prepared as the morn.
10. 15 in a morning shall the king of Israel utt.
Joel 2. 2 the morning spread upon the mountains
Amos 4. 13 that maketh the morning darkness, and
Jon. 4. 7 God prepared a worm when the morning
7. *To rise or go early,* שָׁכַם *shakam,* 5.
1 Sa. 17. 16 the Philistine drew near morning and ev.
8. *To wander,* שָׁכָה *shakah,* 5.
Jer. 5. 8 They were (as) fed horses in the morning
9. *Of the early dawn,* ὀρθρινός *orthrinos.*
Rev. 22. 16 I am the root..the bright and [morning] s.
10. *Early, former,* πρωϊνός *prōinos.*
Rev. 2. 28 And I will give him the morning star
11. *Early,* πρωΐ *prōi.*
Matt 16. 3 in the morning..foul weather to day
Mark 1. 35 in the morning, rising up a great while
11. 20 in the morning, as they passed by, they
13. 35 master..cometh, at even..or in the m.
15. 1 straightway in the morning the chief pr.
Acts 28. 23 persuading them..from morning till eve.
12. *Early dawn,* πρωΐα *prōia.*
Matt 21. 18 Now [in the morning], as he returned into
27. 1 When the morning was come, all the chief
John 21. 4 when the morning was now come, Jesus

MORNING, to come early in the —

To be early in dawn or morning, ὀρθρίζω *orthrizō.*

Luke 21. 38 all the people came early in the morning

MORNING, early in the —

1. *Early dawn or morning,* ὄρθρος *orthros.*

John 8. 2 [early in the morning he came again into]
Acts 5. 21 entered into the temple early in the mor.

2. (*When it was*) *early,* (ἅμα) πρωΐ (*hama*) *prōi.*

Matt 20. 1 which went out early in the morning to
Mark 16. 2 very early in the morning, the

MORROW (after) —

1. *Morning,* בֹּקֶר *boqer.*

Lev. 22. 30 ye shall leave none of it until the morrow
Num 16. 5 Even to morrow the LORD will show who
22. 41 it came to pass on the morrow, that Balak
1 Sa. 9. 19 to morrow I will let thee go, and will tell
Esth. 2. 14 on the morrow she returned into the se.
5. 14 to morrow speak thou unto the king that
Zeph. 3. 3 they gnaw not the bones till the morrow

2. *Morrow,* מָחֳרָת *mochorath.*

Gen. 19. 34 it came to pass on the morrow, that the
Exod 9. 6 the LORD did that thing on the morrow
18. 13 it came to pass on the morrow, that Moses
32. 6 they rose up early on the morrow, and
32. 30 it came to pass on the morrow, that Moses
Lev. 7. 16 the morrow also the remainder of it shall
19. 6 the same day ye offer it, and on the mor.
23. 11 on the morrow after the sabbath the priest
23. 15 ye shall count unto you from the morrow
23. 16 Even unto the morrow after the seventh
Num 16. 41 on the morrow all the congregation of the
17. 8 it came to pass, that on the morrow Moses
33. 3 on the morrow after the passover the ch.
Josh. 5. 11 they did eat of the old corn..on the mor.
5. 12 the manna ceased on the morrow after they
Judg. 6. 38 he rose up early on the morrow, and th.
9. 42 it came to pass on the morrow, that the p.
21. 4 it came to pass on the morrow, that the p.
1 Sa. 5. 3 when they..arose early on the morrow, be.
5. 4 when they arose early on the morrow m.
11. 11 it was (so) on the morrow, that Saul put
18. 10 it came to pass on the morrow, that the
20. 27 it came to pass on the morrow..the second
31. 8 it came to pass on the morrow, when the
2 Sa. 11. 12 Tarry..and to morrow I will let thee de.
2 Ki. 8. 15 it came to pass on the morrow, that he
1 Ch. 10. 8 it came to pass on the morrow, when the
29. 21 on the morrow after that day..a thousand
Jer. 20. 3 it came to pass on the morrow, that Pa.

3. *The dawn, to morrow,* αὔριον *aurion.*

Matt. 6. 34 Take therefore no thought for the morrow
6. 34 for the morrow shall take thought for the
Luke 10. 35 on the morrow, when he departed, he took
Acts 4. 5 it came to pass on the morrow, that their
Jas. 4. 14 Whereas ye know not what..on the mor.

4. *Succeeding* (*day*), ἑξῆς *hexēs.*

Acts 25. 17 without any delay on the morrow I sat on

5. *The morrow,* ἐπαύριον *epaurion.*

Mark 11. 12 on the morrow, when they were come from
Acts 10. 9 On the morrow, as they went on their
10. 23 on the morrow Peter went away with them
10. 24 the morrow after they entered into Cesarea
20. 7 preached..ready to depart on the morrow
22. 30 On the morrow, because he would have k.
23. 32 On the morrow they left the horsemen to
25. 23 on the morrow, when Agrippa was come

MORROW, to — [See *To morrow.*]

MORSEL (of meat) —

1. *A cake,* כִּכָּר *kikkar.*

1 Sa. 2. 36 shall..crouch to him for..a morsel of br.

2. *Morsel,* פַּת *path.*

Gen. 18. 5 I will fetch a morsel of bread, and comf.
Judg 19. 5 Comfort thine heart with a morsel of br.
Ruth. 2. 14 come thou..and dip thy morsel in the vi.
1 Sa. 28. 22 let me set a morsel of bread before thee
1 Ki. 17. 11 Bring me, I pray thee, a morsel of bread
Job 31. 17 Or have eaten my morsel myself alone
Psa. 147. 17 He casteth forth his ice like morsels: who
Prov 17. 1 Better (is) a dry morsel, and quietness
23. 8 The morsel..thou hast eaten shalt thou

3. *Act of eating, food,* βρῶσις *brōsis.*

Heb. 12. 16 who for one morsel of meat sold his birth.

MORTAL (man) —

1. *A man,* אֱנוֹשׁ *enosh.*

Job 4. 17 Shall mortal man be more just than God?

2. *Mortal, dying,* θνητός *thnētos.*

Rom. 6. 12 Let not sin therefore reign in your mortal
8. 11 shall also quicken your mortal bodies by
1 Co. 15. 53 and this mortal (must) put on immortality
15. 54 this mortal shall have put on immortality
2 Co. 4. 11 might be made manifest in our mortal flesh

MORTALITY —

Dying, mortal, θνητόν *thnēton.*

2 Co. 5. 4 that mortality might be swallowed up of

MORTALLY —

Soul, breath, נֶפֶשׁ *nephesh.*

Deut 19. 11 smite him mortally that he die, and flee.

MORTAR, MORTER —

1. *Clay, heap,* חֹמֶר *chomer.*

Gen. 11. 3 for stone, and slime had they for mortar
Exod. 1. 14 hard bondage, in mortar, and in brick, and
Isa. 41. 25 he shall come upon princes as..mortar
Nah. 3. 14 go into clay, and tread the mortar, make

2. *A mortar,* מְדֹכָה *medokah.*

Num 11. 8 or beat (it) in a mortar, and baked (it) in

3. *A mortar, hollow place,* מַכְתֵּשׁ *maktesh.*

Prov 27. 22 Though thou shouldest bray a fool in a m.

4. *Dust,* עָפָר *aphar.*

Lev. 14. 42 he shall take other morter, and shall pl.
14. 45 all the morter of the house: and he shall

MORTGAGE, to —

To mingle, traffic, negotiate, pledge, עָרַב *arab.*

Neh. 5. 3 We have mortgaged our lands, vineyards

MORTIFY, to —

1. *To put to death, kill,* θανατόω *thanatoō.*

Rom. 8. 13 if ye through the Spirit do mortify the d.

2. *To put to death, deaden,* νεκρόω *nekroō.*

Col. 3. 5 Mortify therefore your members which are

MO-SE'-RA, מוֹסֵרָה *chastisement.*

The place where Aaron died and was buried; between Bereth Bene-jaaken and Gudgodah.

Deut 10. 6 Beeroth of the children of Jaakan to M.

MO-SE'-ROTH, מֹסֵרוֹת, מוֹסֵרוֹת.

The 26th station of Israel in the wilderness, and 15th from Sinai, between Hashmanah and Bene-jaaken.

Num 33. 30 departed from Hash., and encamped at M.
33. 31 they departed from M., and pitched in B.

MO'-SES, מֹשֶׁה, Μωσῆς, Μωϋσῆς, Μωυσῆς *drawer out.*

The youngest son of Amram and Jochebed, born B.C. 1571, just at the time when the king of Egypt had resolved on the destruction of every newly born male child among the Israelites. Being saved by Pharaoh's daughter, she gave him her own title, the "drawer out," from the water, and brought him up as an adopted son, so that he was skilled in all the wisdom of the Egyptians. His patriotic desire for his brethren at last compelled him to leave Egypt when forty years of age, to which he returned after an interval of forty years' sojourn in Midian only at the repeated command of God. His successive interviews with his brethren, and with the king of Egypt, his wonderful miracles, and the admirable patience, faith, and skill he evinced throughout his whole career, are graphically depicted in his works that remain. He is traditionally supposed to have written the introductory chapters of the Book of Job, and the conclusion of the whole. His authorship of Exodus, Leviticus, Numbers, and Deuteronomy are attested by every possible mark of an internal and of an external kind. These books bear incontestable evidence that they were composed in a wilderness state, yet with an express view to a speedy settlement in a fruitful land. Repeatedly in these Moses is directed to write in *a* book (or more properly, in *the* Book), Exod. 17. 14; 34. 27, and he is represented as writing in Exod. 24. 4-7; 34. 28. These passages refer to the wars, the ten commandments, the treatment of the Canaanites, and the various festivals. In Num. 33. 2 it is said he "wrote their goings out according to their journeys by the commandment of the Lord," that is, apparently, a kind of "Daily Journal." Deuteronomy is, if possible, even more express on the point, in such passages as 31. 9, 22, 24, enjoining, "the book—the song—the law," to be read and rehearsed and preserved. Accordingly the Book of Joshua makes express mention of "the Book of the Law of Moses," in 1. 7, 8; 8. 32, 34; 23. 3, 6, 16; 24. 26, and all the succeeding books of Scripture support the same view. The ten tribes who revolted after the death of Solomon, held fast to the Pentateuch, which they certainly would not have done had it been composed after that event. The Book which Hilkiah found in the temple was probably the Book of Leviticus—a book so strictly appropriate for the priests alone, that it is not wonderful it was left very much in their hands—the threatenings of which in chapter xxvi. are so well fitted to have stirred the heart of the pious king Josiah. As a historian, an orator, a leader, a statesman, a legislator, a patriot, and a man, Moses stands pre-eminent. But no mere genius could have made him the originator of sound jurisprudence—the great teacher of monotheism and sound morality—except he had also been a prophet of the Most High, supernaturally guided and aided in his work. He died in the plains of Moab, over against Beth-peor, B.C. 1451, at the ripe age of 120 years, while yet "his eye was not dim, nor his natural force abated."

Exod. 2. 10 she called his name M.: and she said, Be.
2. 11 when M. was grown, that he went out
2. 14 M. feared, and said, Surely this thing is
2. 15 he sought to slay M. but M. fled from the
2. 17 M. stood up and helped them, and wate.
2. 21 And M. was content to dwell with the man
2. 21 and he gave M. Zipporah his daughter
3. 1 M. kept the flock of Jethro his father in
3. 3 M. said, I will now turn aside, and see
3. 4 God called unto him..and said, M., M.
3. 6 M. hid his face; for he was afraid to look
3. 11 M. said unto God, Who (am) I, that I sho.
3. 13 M. said unto God, Behold, (when) I come
3. 14 God said unto M., I am that I am: and he
3. 15 God said moreover unto M., Thus shalt
4. 1 M. answered and said, But, behold, they
4. 3 became a serpent; and M. fled from bef.
4. 4 And the LORD said unto M.

So in 4. 19, 21; 6. 1; 7. 1, 14; 8. 16, 20; 9. 1, 8, 13, 22; 10. 1, 12, 21; 11. 1, 9; 12. 43; 14. 15, 26; 16. 28; 17. 5, 14; 19. 9, 10, 21; 20. 22; 24. 12; 30. 34; 32. 9, 33; 33. 17; 34. 1, 27. Lev. 10. 3; 21. 1. Num. 3. 40; 7. 11; 11. 16, 23; 12. 14; 14. 11; 15. 35; 17. 10; 21. 8, 34; 25. 4; 27. 12, 18. Deut. 31. 14, 16.

Exod. 4. 10 M. said unto the LORD, O my Lord, I (am)
4. 14 anger of the LORD was kindled against M.
4. 18 M. went and returned to Jethro his father
4. 18 And Jethro said to M., Go in peace
4. 20 M. took his wife and his sons, and set
4. 20 and M. took the rod of God in his hand
4. 27 said..Go into the wilderness to meet M.
4. 28 M. told Aaron all the words of the LORD
4. 29 M. and Aaron went and gathered together
4. 30 words which the LORD had spoken unto M.
5. 1 M. and Aaron went in, and told Pharaoh
5. 4 Wherefore do ye, M. and Aaron, let the
5. 20 they met M. and Aaron, who stood in the
5. 22 M. returned unto the LORD, and said, L.
6. 2 God spake unto M., and said unto him, I
6. 9 M. spake so unto the children of Israel
6. 9 they hearkened not unto M. for anguish
6. 10 And the LORD spake unto M., saying
6. 12 M. spake before the LORD, saying, Behold
6. 13 the LORD spake unto M. and unto Aaron
6. 20 she bare him Aaron and M.; and the years
6. 26 These (are) that Aaron and M., to whom
6. 27 these (are) that M. and Aaron
6. 28 LORD spake unto M. in the land of Egypt
6. 29 the LORD spake unto M., saying, I (am)
7. 6 M. and Aaron did as the LORD comman.
7. 7 And M. (was) fourscore years old, and A.
7. 8 LORD spake unto M. and unto Aaron,
7. 10 M. and Aaron went in unto Pharaoh, and
7. 19 The LORD spake unto M., Say unto Aaron
7. 20 M. and Aaron did so, as the LORD comm.
8. 1 The LORD spake unto M., Go unto Pharaoh
8. 5 the LORD spake unto M., Say unto Aaron
8. 8 Pharaoh called for M. and Aaron, and said
8. 9 M. said unto Pharaoh, Glory over me: w.
8. 12 M. and Aaron went out from Pharaoh..M.
8. 13, 31 LORD did according to the word of M.
8. 25 Pharaoh called for M. and for Aaron, and
8. 26 M. said, It is not meet so to do; for we
8. 29 M. said, Behold, I go out from thee, and
8. 30 M. went out from Pharaoh, and entreated
9. 8 let M. sprinkle it toward the heaven in
9. 10 M. sprinkled it up toward heaven; and it
9. 11 magicians could not stand before M.
9. 12 as the LORD had spoken unto M.
9. 23 M. stretched forth his rod toward heaven
9. 27 called for M. and Aaron, and said unto
9. 29 M. said unto him, As soon as I am gone
9. 33 M. went out of the city from Pharaoh, and
9. 35 hardened..as the LORD had spoken by M.
10. 3 M. and Aaron came in unto Pharaoh, and
10. 8 And M. and Aaron were brought again
10. 9 M. said, We will go with our young and
10. 13 M. stretched forth his rod over the land
10. 16 Pharaoh called for M. and Aaron in haste
10. 22 M. stretched forth his hand toward heaven
10. 24 And Pharaoh called unto M., and said, Go
10. 25 M. said, Thou must give us also sacrifices
10. 29 M. said, Thou hast spoken well, I will see
11. 3 M. (was) very great in the land of Egypt
11. 4 M. said, Thus saith the LORD, About mid.
11. 10 M. and Aaron did all these wonders before
12. 1 the LORD spake unto M. and Aaron in the
12. 21 M. called for all the elders of Israel, and
12. 28 did as the LORD had commanded M., and A.
12. 31 he called for M. and Aaron by night, and
12. 35 did according to the word of M.; and they
12. 50 as the LORD commanded M. and Aaron
13. 1 And the LORD spake unto M., saying

So in 14. 1; 16. 11; 25. 1; 30. 11, 17, 22; 31. 1, 12; 40. 1. Lev. 4. 1; 5. 14; 6. 1, 8, 19, 24; 7. 22, 28; 8. 1; 12. 1; 14. 1; 17. 1; 18. 1; 19. 1; 20. 1; 21. 16; 22. 1, 17, 26; 23. 1, 9, 23, 33; 24. 1, 13; 27. 1. Num. 3. 5, 11, 14, 44; 5. 1, 5, 11; 6. 1; 7. 4; 8. 1, 5, 23; 9. 9; 10. 1; 13. 1; 15. 1, 17, 37; 16. 20, 23, 36, 44; 17. 1; 18. 25; 19. 1; 20. 7; 25. 10, 16; 26. 52; 27. 6; 28. 1; 31. 1, 25; 34. 1, 16; 35. 9.

Exod 13. 3 M. said unto the people, Remember this
13. 19 M. took the bones of Joseph with him: for
14. 11 they said unto M., Because (there were)
14. 13 M. said unto the people, Fear ye not, stand
14. 21 M. stretched out his hand over the sea
14. 27 M. stretched forth his hand over the sea
14. 31 and believed the LORD, and his servant M.
15. 1 Then sang M. and the children of Israel
15. 22 So M. brought Israel from the Red Sea
15. 24 people murmured against M., saying, W.
16. 2 murmured against M. and Aaron in the
16. 4 Then said the LORD unto M., Behold, I
16. 6 M. and Aaron said unto all the children
16. 8 M. said, (This shall be), when the LORD
16. 9 M. spake unto Aaron, Say unto all the
16. 15 M. said unto them, This (is) the bread
16. 19 M. said, Let no man leave of it till the m.
16. 20 hearkened not unto M...and M. was wroth
16. 22 and all the rulers..came and told M.
16. 24 they laid it up till the morning, as M. bade
16. 25 M. said, Eat that to day, for to day (is) a
16. 32 M. said, This (is) the thing which the L.
16. 33 M. said unto Aaron, Take a pot, and put
16. 34 As the LORD commanded M., so Aaron
17. 2 people did chide with M...And M. said
17. 3 people murmured against M., and said
17. 4 M. cried unto the LORD, saying, What
17. 6 M. did so in the sight of the elders of Is.
17. 9 M. said unto Joshua, Choose us out men

Exod17. 10 Joshua did as M. had said..and M., Aaron
17. 11 when M. held up his hand, that Israel p.
17. 12 M.' hands (were) heavy; and they took
17. 15 M. built an altar, and called the name of
18. 1 When Jethro..M.' father in law, heard
18. 1 that God had done for M., and for Israel
18. 2 M.' father in law, took Zipporah, M.' wife
18. 5 M.' father in law, came with his sons and
18. 5 came..unto M. into the wilderness, where
18. 6 he said unto M., I thy father in law Jethro
18. 7 M. went out to meet his father in law, and
18. 8 M. told his father in law all that the
18. 12 M.' father in law, took a burnt offering
18. 12 eat bread with M.' father in law before God
18. 13 that M. sat to judge the people: and the
18. 13 people stood by M. from the morning unto
18. 14 M.' father in law saw all that he did to
18. 15 M. said unto his father in law, Because
18. 17 M.' father in law said unto him, The thing
18. 24 M. hearkened to the voice of his father
18. 25 M. chose able men out of all Israel, and
18. 26 the hard causes they brought unto M.
18. 27 M. let his father in law depart; and he
19. 3 M. went up unto God, and the LORD call.
19. 7 M. came and called for the elders of the
19. 8 M. returned the words of the people unto
19. 9 M. told the words of the people unto the
19. 14 M. went down from the mount unto the
19. 17 And M. brought forth the people out of
19. 19 M. spake, and God answered him by a voice
19. 20 called M. (up) to the top of the mount
19. 23 M. said unto the LORD, The people cannot
19. 25 M. went down unto the people, and spake
20. 19 they said unto M., Speak thou with us
20. 20 M. said unto the people, Fear not: for God
20. 21 M. drew near unto the thick darkness w.
24. 1 he said unto M., Come up unto the LORD
24. 2 M. alone shall come near the LORD; but
24. 3 M. came and told the people all the words
24. 4 M. wrote all the words of the LORD, and
24. 6 M. took half of the blood, and put (it) in
24. 8 M. took the blood, and sprinkled (it) on
24. 9 Then went up M., and Aaron, Nadab, and
24. 13 M. rose up, and his minister Joshua: and
24. 13, 15 And M. went up into the mount
24. 16 he called unto M. out of the midst of the
24. 18 M. went into the midst of the cloud, and
24. 18 M. was in the mount forty days and forty
31. 18 he gave unto M., when he had made an
32. 1 M. delayed to come down out of the mo.
32. 1 (as for) this M., the man that brought us
32. 7 the LORD said unto M., Go, get thee down
32. 11 M. besought the LORD his God, and said
32. 15 M. turned, and went down from the mo.
32. 17 he said unto M., (There is) a noise of war
32. 19 M.' anger waxed hot, and he cast the ta.
32. 21 M. said unto Aaron, What did this people
32. 25 M. saw that the people (were) naked, for
32. 26 M. stood in the gate of the camp, and said
32. 28 Levi did according to the word of M.: and
32. 29 M. had said, Consecrate yourselves to day
32. 30 M. said unto the people, Ye have sinned
32. 31 M. returned unto the LORD, and said, Oh
33. 1 LORD said unto M., Depart, (and) go up hence.
33. 5 the LORD had said unto M., Say unto the
33. 7 And M. took the tabernacle, and pitched
33. 8 M. went out unto the tabernacle, (that) all
33. 8 looked after M., until he was gone into the
33. 9 as M. entered into the tabernacle, the
33. 9 descended..and (the LORD) talked with M.
33. 11 the LORD spake unto M. face to face, as a
33. 12 M. said unto the LORD, See, thou sayest
34. 4 M. rose up early in the morning, and went
34. 8 M. made haste, and bowed his head tow.
34. 29 when M. came down from mount Sinai
34. 29 the two tables of testimony in M.' hand
34. 29 M. wist not that the skin of his face shone
34. 30 Aaron and..the children of Israel saw M.
34. 31 M. called unto them; and Aaron and all
34. 31 returned unto him: and M. talked with
34. 33 (till) M. had done speaking with them, he
34. 34 M. went in before the LORD to speak with
34. 35 M., that the skin of M.' face shone: and M.
35. 1 M. gathered all the congregation of the
35. 4 M. spake unto all the congregation of the
35. 20 Israel departed from the presence of M.
35. 29 commanded to be made by the hand of M.
35. 30 M. said unto the children of Israel, See
36. 2 M. called Bezaleel and Aholiab, and every
36. 3 they received of M. all the offering which
36. 5 they spake unto M., saying, The people
36. 6 M. gave commandment, and they caused
38. 21 according to the commandment of M.
38. 22 made all that the LORD commanded M.
39. 1, 5, 7, 21, 26, 29, 31 as the LORD com. M.
39. 32 all that the LORD commanded M., so did
39. 33 they brought the tabernacle unto M., the
39. 42 all that the LORD commanded M., so the
39. 43 M. did look upon all the work..and M.
40. 16 Thus did M.: according to all that the
40. 18 M. reared up the tabernacle, and fastened
40. 19, 21, 23, 25, 27, 29, 32 as the LORD com. M.
40. 31 M. and Aaron and his sons washed their
40. 33 he reared up the court..So M. finished
40. 35 M. was not able to enter into the tent of
Lev. 1. 1 LORD called unto M., and spake unto him
7. 38 Which the LORD commanded M. in mount
8. 4 M. did as the LORD commanded him; and
8. 5 M. said unto the congregation, This (is)
8. 6 M. brought Aaron and his sons, and wa.
8. 9, 13, 17, 21, 29 as the LORD commanded M.
8. 10 M. took the anointing oil, and anointed

Lev. 8. 13 M. brought Aaron's sons, and put coats
8. 15 M. took the blood, and put (it) upon the
8. 16 he took..their fat, and M. burned (it) upon
8. 19 M. sprinkled the blood upon the altar ro.
8. 20 M. burnt the head, and the pieces, and
8. 21 M. burnt the whole ram upon the altar
8. 23 M. took of the blood of it, and put (it) upon
8. 24 M. put of the blood..and M. sprinkled the
8. 28 M. took them from off their hands, and
8. 29 M. took the breast..it was M.' part; as
8. 30 M. took of the anointing oil, and of the b.
8. 31 M. said unto Aaron and to his sons, Boil
8. 36 the LORD commanded by the hand of M.
9. 1 M. called Aaron and his sons, and the el.
9. 5 they brought (that) which M. commanded
9. 6 M. said, This (is) the thing which the L.
9. 7 M. said unto Aaron, Go unto the altar, and
9. 10 he burnt..as the LORD commanded M.
9. 21 wave offering before the LORD; as M. co.
9. 23 M. and Aaron went into the tabernacle
10. 3 M. said unto Aaron, This (is it) that the
10. 4 M. called Mishael and Elzaphan, the sons
10. 5 went near, and carried them..as M. had
10. 6 M. said unto Aaron, and unto Eleazar and
10. 7 And they did according to the word of M.
10. 11 hath spoken unto them by the hand of M.
10. 12 M. spake unto Aaron, and unto Eleazar
10. 16 M. diligently sought the goat of the sin o.
10. 19 A. said unto M., Behold, this day have
10. 20 And when M. heard (that), he was content
11. 1 LORD spake unto M. and to Aaron, saying
13. 1 And the LORD spake unto M. and Aaron
14. 33 LORD spake unto M. and unto Aaron, sa.
15. 1 And the LORD spake unto M. and to Aaron
16. 1 LORD spake unto M., after the death of
16. 34 And he did as the LORD commanded M.
21. 24 M. told (it) unto Aaron, and to his sons
23. 44 M. declared unto the children of Israel
24. 11 brought him unto M.: and his mother's
24. 23 M. spake unto the children of Israel, that
24. 23 Israel did as the LORD commanded M.
25. 1 LORD spake unto M. in mount Sinai, say.
26. 46 which the LORD made..by the hand of M.
27. 34 which the LORD commanded M. for the
Num. 1. 1 the LORD spake unto M. in the wilderness
1. 17 And M. and Aaron took these men which
1. 19 As the LORD commanded M., so he num.
1. 44 which M. and Aaron numbered, and the
1. 48 For the LORD had spoken unto M., saying
1. 54 accord. to all that..LORD commanded M.
2. 1 LORD spake unto M. and unto Aaron, say.
2. 33 numbered..as the LORD commanded M.
2. 34 accord. to all that..LORD commanded M.
3. 1 M., in the day (that) the LORD spake with M.
3. 16 M. numbered them, according to the word
3. 38 those that encamp before..(shall be) M.
3. 39 M. and Aaron numbered at the comman.
3. 42 M. numbered, as the LORD commanded
3. 49 M. took the redemption money of them
3. 51 M. gave the money of them that were re.
3. 51 word of the LORD, as the LORD comma. M.
4. 1, 17, 21 And the LORD spake unto M. and
4. 34 And M. and Aaron and the chief of the
4. 37 which M. and Aaron did number, accor.
4. 37 command. of the LORD by the hand of M.
4. 41 M. and Aaron did number according to the
4. 45 whom M. and Aaron numbered, according
4. 45 that were numbered..by the hand of M.
4. 46 whom M. and Aaron and the chief of Isr.
4. 49 they were numbered by the hand of M.
4. 49 numbered of him..the LORD command. M.
5. 4 as the LORD spake unto M., so did the ch.
7. 1 M. had fully set up the tabernacle, and
7. 6 M. took the wagons and the oxen, and
7. 89 M. was gone into the tabernacle of the
8. 3 lighted the lamps..as the LORD comma. M.
8. 4 pattern which the LORD had showed M.
8. 20 M., and Aaron, and all the congregation
8. 20, 22 commanded M. concerning the Levites
9. 1 the LORD spake unto M. in the wilderness
9. 4 M. spake unto the children of Israel, that
9. 5 all that the LORD commanded M., so did
9. 6 they came before M. and before Aaron on
9. 8 M. said unto them, Stand still, and I will
9. 23 command. of the LORD by the hand of M.
10. 13 command. of the LORD by the hand of M.
10. 29 M. said unto Hobab, the son of..M.' father
10. 35 M. said, Rise up, LORD, and let thine en.
11. 2 the people cried unto M.; and when M. pr.
11. 10 M. heard the people weep throughout th.
11. 10 anger of the LORD..M. also was displeased
11. 11 M. said unto the LORD, Wherefore hast
11. 21 M. said, The people, among whom I (am)
11. 24 M. went out, and told the people the wo.
11. 27 and told M., and said, Eldad and Medad
11. 28 the servant of M., (one) of his young men
11. 28 answered and said, My lord M., forbid
11. 29 M. said unto him, Enviest thou for my s.?
11. 30 M. gat him into the camp, he and the el.
12. 1 and Aaron spake against M. because of
12. 2 Hath the LORD indeed spoken only by M.
12. 3 M. (was) very meek, above all the men w.
12. 4 the LORD spake suddenly unto M., and
12. 7 M. (is) not so, who (is) faithful in all mine
12. 8 not afraid to speak against my servant M.
12. 11 Aaron said unto M., Alas! my lord, I be.
12. 13 M. cried unto the LORD, saying, Heal her
13. 3 M. by the commandment of the LORD sent
13. 16 which M. sent to spy out the land. And M.
13. 17 M. sent them to spy out the land of Can.
13. 26 and came to M., and to Aaron, and to all
13. 30 Caleb stilled the people before M., and

Num 14. 2 murmured against M. and against Aaron
14. 5 M. and Aaron fell on their faces before
14. 13 M. said unto the LORD, Then the Egypt.
14. 26 LORD spake unto M. and unto Aaron, say.
14. 36 the men which M. sent to search the land
14. 39 M. told these sayings unto all the children
14. 41 M. said, Wherefore now do ye transgress
14. 44 ark of the covenant of the LORD, and M.
15. 22 which the LORD hath spoken unto M.
15. 23 hath commanded you by the hand of M.
15. 33 they that..brought him unto M. and Aa.
15. 36 and he died; as the LORD commanded M.
16. 2 they rose up before M., with certain of
16. 3 gathered themselves together against M.
16. 4 And when M. heard (it), he fell upon his
16. 8 M. said unto Korah, Hear, I pray you, ye
16. 12 M. sent to call Dathan and Abiram, the
16. 15 M. was very wroth, and said unto the L.
16. 16 M. said unto Korah, Be thou and all thy
16. 18 and stood in the door..with M. and Aaron
16. 25 M. rose up, and went unto Dathan and Ab.
16. 28 M. said, Hereby ye shall know that the L.
16. 40 the LORD said to him by the hand of M.
16. 41 murmured against M. and against Aaron
16. 42 was gathered against M. and against Aa.
16. 43 M. and Aaron came before the tabernacle
16. 46 M. said unto Aaron, Take a censer, and
16. 47 Aaron took as M. commanded, and ran
16. 50 Aaron returned unto M. unto the door of
17. 6 M. spake unto the children of Israel, and
17. 7 M. laid up the rods before the LORD in
17. 8 M. went into the tabernacle of witness
17. 9 M. brought out all the rods from before
17. 11 M. did (so): as the LORD commanded him
17. 12 children of Israel spake unto M., saying
20. 2 gathered themselves together against M.
20. 3 the people chode with M., and spake, sa.
20. 6 M. and Aaron went from the presence of
20. 9 M. took the rod from before the LORD, as
20. 10 And M. and Aaron gathered the congre.
20. 11 M. lifted up his hand, and with his rod
20. 12 LORD spake unto M. and Aaron, Because
20. 14 M. sent messengers from Kadesh unto the
20. 23 LORD spake unto M. and Aaron in mount
20. 27 M. did as the LORD commanded: and
20. 28 M. stripped Aaron of his garments, and
20. 28 M. and Eleazar came down from the m.
21. 5 people spake against God, and against M.
21. 7 the people came to M...And M. prayed
21. 9 M. made a serpent of brass, and put it
21. 16 the well whereof the LORD spake unto M.
21. 32 M. sent to spy out Jaazer, and they took
25. 5 M. said unto the judges of Israel, Slay ye
25. 6 a Midianitish woman in the sight of M.
26. 1 LORD spake unto M. and unto Eleazar the
26. 3 M. and Eleazar the priest spake with them
26. 4 the LORD commanded M. and the children
26. 9 who strove against M. and against Aaron
26. 59 she bare unto Amram Aaron and M., and
26. 63 were numbered by M. and Eleazar the pr.
26. 64 them whom M. and Aaron the priest nu.
27. 2 they stood before M., and before Eleazar
27. 5 And M. brought their cause before the L.
27. 11 a statute..as the LORD commanded M.
27. 15 And M. spake unto the LORD, saying
27. 22 M. did as the LORD commanded him: and
27. 23 as the LORD commanded by the hand of M.
29. 40 M. told the children of Israel according
29. 40 according to all..the LORD commanded M.
30. 1 And M. spake unto the heads of the tribes
30. 16 statutes which the LORD commanded M.
31. 3 M. spake unto the people, saying, Arm
31. 6 M. sent them to the war, a thousand of
31. 7 they warred..as the LORD commanded M.
31. 12 unto M., and Eleazar the priest, and unto
31. 13 And M., and Eleazar the priest, and all
31. 14 M. was wroth with the officers of the host
31. 15 M. said unto them, Have ye saved all the
31. 21 of the law which the LORD commanded M.
31. 31 M. and Eleazar..did as the LORD com. M.
31. 41 M. gave the tribute, (which was) the L.
31. 41 unto Eleazar..as the LORD command. M.
31. 42 which M. divided from the men that wa.
31. 47 M. took one portion of fifty, (both) of man
31. 47 gave them..as the LORD commanded M.
31. 48 captains of hundreds, came near unto M.
31. 49 they said unto M., Thy servants have taken
31. 54 M. and Eleazar the priest took the gold
32. 2 spake unto M., and to Eleazar the priest
32. 6 M. said unto the children of Gad and to
32. 20 M. said unto them, If ye will do this thing
32. 25 children of Reuben spake unto M., saying
32. 28 M. commanded Eleazar the priest, and J.
32. 29 M. said unto them, If the children of Gad
32. 33 M. gave unto them, (even) to the children
32. 40 And M. gave Gilead unto Machir the son
33. 1 armies under the hand of M. and Aaron
33. 2 M. wrote their goings out according to
33. 50 the LORD spake unto M. in the plains of
34. 13 M. commanded the children of Israel, s.
36. 1 spake before M., and before the princes
36. 5 And M. commanded the children of Israel
36. 10 Even as the LORD commanded M., so did
36. 13 which the LORD comma. by the hand of M.
Deut. 1. 1 M. spake unto all Israel on this side
1. 3 (that) M. spake unto the children of I.
1. 5 land of Moab, began M. to declare this law
4. 41 M. severed three cities on this side Jordan
4. 44 which M. set before the children of Israel
4. 45 M. spake unto the children of Israel, after
4. 46 whom M. and the children of Israel smote
5. 1 M. called all Israel, and said unto them

Deut 27. 1 M. with the elders of Israel commanded
27. 9 M. and the priests the Levites spake unto
27. 11 M. charged the people the same day, say.
29. 1 covenant which the LORD commanded M.
29. 2 M. called unto all Israel, and said unto
31. 1 M. went and spake these words unto all
31. 7 M. called unto Joshua, and said unto him
31. 9 M. wrote this law, and delivered it unto
31. 10 M. commanded them, saying, At the end
31. 14 M. and Joshua went, and presented the.
31. 22 M. therefore wrote this song the same day
31. 24 M. had made an end of writing the words
31. 25 M. commanded the Levites, which bare
31. 30 M. spake in the ears of..the congregation
32. 44 M. came and spake all the words of this
32. 45 M. made an end of speaking all these w.
32. 48 the LORD spake unto M. that self same day
33. 1 M. the man of God blessed the children
33. 4 M. commanded us a law, (even) the inhe.
34. 1 M. went up from the plains of Moab unto
34. 5 M. the servant of the LORD died there in
34. 7 M. (was) an hundred and twenty years old
34. 8 the children of Israel wept for M. in the
34. 8 weeping (and) mourning for M. were ended
34. 9 for M. had laid his hands upon him: and
34. 9 hearkened..and did as..LORD comman. M.
34. 10 a prophet since in Israel like unto M.
34. 12 which M. showed in the sight of all Israel
Josh. 1. 1 the death of M. the servant of the LORD
1. 1 unto Joshua the son of Nun, M.' minister
1. 2 M. my servant is dead; now therefore arise
1. 3 have I given unto you, as I said unto M.
1. 5 as I was with M., (so) I will be with thee
1. 7 the law which M. my servant commanded
1. 13 M. the servant of the LORD commanded
1. 14 land which M. gave you on this side Jor.
1. 15 M. the LORD'S servant gave you on this
1. 17 as we hearkened unto M. in all things, so
1. 17 thy God be with thee, as he was with M.
3. 7 as I was with M., (so) I will be with thee
4. 10 according to all that M. commanded Jo.
4. 12 passed over armed..as M. spake unto them
4. 14 as they feared M., all the days of his life
8. 31 M. the servant of the LORD commanded
8. 31 is written in the book of the law of M.
8. 32 upon the stones a copy of the law of M.
8. 33 M. the servant of the LORD had comman.
8. 35 was not a word of all that M. commanded
9. 24 God commanded his servant M. to give
11. 12 as M. the servant of the LORD commanded
11. 15 the LORD commanded M. his servant, so
11. 15 undone of all that the LORD comman. M.
11. 20 destroy them, as the LORD commanded M.
11. 23 according to all that..LORD said unto M.
12. 6 M. the servant of the LORD and the chil.
12. 6 M. the servant of the LORD gave it (for) a
13. 8 which M. gave them, beyond Jordan east.
13. 8 as M. the servant of the LORD gave them
13. 12 for these did M. smite, and cast them out
13. 15 M. gave unto the tribe of the children of
13. 21 whom M. smote with the princes of Mid.
13. 24 M. gave (inheritance) unto the tribe of Gad
13. 29 M. gave (inheritance) unto the half tribe
13. 32 (are the countries) which M. did distribute
13. 33 tribe of Levi M. gave not (any) inheritance
14. 2 as the LORD commanded by the hand of M.
14. 3 M. had given the inheritance of two tribes
14. 5 As the LORD commanded M., so the chil.
14. 6 that the LORD said unto M. the man of God
14. 7 M. the servant of the LORD sent me from
14. 9 M. sware on that day, saying, Surely the
14. 10 the LORD spake this word unto M., while
14. 11 strong..(I was) in the day that M. sent me
17. 4 LORD commanded M. to give us an inherit.
18. 7 which M. the servant of the LORD gave them
20. 2 whereof I spake unto..by the hand of M.
21. 2, 8 LORD commanded by the hand of M.
22. 2 Ye have kept all that M. the servant of
22. 4 which M. the servant of the LORD gave you
22. 5 which M. the servant of the LORD charged
22. 7 (one) half of the tribe of Manasseh M. had
22. 9 to the word of the LORD by the hand of M.
23. 6 is written in the book of the law of M.
24. 5 I sent M. also and Aaron, and I plagued
Judg. 1. 16 the children of the Kenite, M.' father in
1. 20 they gave Hebron unto Caleb, as M. said
3. 4 commanded their fathers by..hand of M.
4. 11 Heber the Kenite..the father in law of M.
1 Sa. 12. 6 (It is) the LORD that advanced M. and A.
12. 8 then the LORD sent M. and Aaron, which
1 Ki. 2. 3 as it is written in the law of M., that thou
8. 9 two tables of stone, which M. put there
8. 53 as thou spakest by the hand of M. thy s.
8. 56 which he promised by the hand of M. his
2 Ki. 14. 6 is written in the book of the law of M.
18. 4 brake in pieces the brasen serpent that M.
18. 6 but kept..which the LORD commanded M.
18. 12 transgressed..all that M. the servant of
21. 8 all the law that my servant M. commanded
23. 25 turned..according to all the law of M.
1 Ch. 6. 3 children of Amram; Aaron, and M., and
6. 49 according to all that M. the servant of G.
15. 15 as M. commanded according to the word
21. 29 tabernacle of the LORD, which M. made in
22. 13 judgments which the LORD charged M.
23. 13 sons of Amram; Aaron and M.: and Aa.
23. 14 Now (concerning) M. the man of God, his
23. 15 The sons of M. (were) Gershom and Elie.
26. 24 Shebuel the son of Gershom, the son of M.
2 Ch. 1. 3 which M. the servant of the LORD had m.
5. 10 the two tables which M. put (therein) at H.
8. 13 according to the commandment of M., on
2 Ch. 23. 18 as (it is) written in the law of M., with
24. 6 (according to the commandment) of M.
24. 9 bring in to the LORD the collection..M.
25. 4 written in the law in the book of M., where
30. 16 according to the law of M. the man of G.
33. 8 law and the statutes..by the hand of M.
34. 14 a book of the law of the LORD (given) by M.
35. 6 to the word of the LORD by the hand of M.
35. 12 as (it is) written in the book of M.: and
Ezra 3. 2 as (it is) written in the law of M. the man
6. 18 set..as it is written in the book of M.
7. 6 he (was) a ready scribe in the law of M.
Neh. 1. 7 which thou commandedst thy servant M.
1. 8 that thou commandedst thy servant M.
8. 1 bring the book of the law of M., which
8. 14 the LORD had commanded by M., that the
9. 14 statutes, and laws, by the hand of M. thy
10. 29 which was given by M. the servant of G.
13. 1 On that day they read in the book of M.
Psa. 77. 20 leddest thy people..by the hand of M. and
90. *title.* A prayer of M. the man of God
99. 6 M. and Aaron among his priests, and Sa.
103. 7 He made known his ways unto M., his a.
105. 26 He sent M. his servant, (and) Aaron whom
106. 16 They envied M. also in the camp, (and) A.
106. 23 had not M. his chosen stood before him in
106. 32 so that it went ill for M. for their sakes
Isa. 63. 11 Then he remembered the days of old, M.
63. 12 That led (them) by the right hand of M.
Jer. 15. 1 Though M. and Samuel stood before me
Dan. 9. 11 oath that (is) written in the law of M. the
9. 13 As (it is) written in the law of M., all this
Mic. 6. 4 and I sent before thee M., Aaron, and M.
Mal. 4. 4 Remember ye the law of M. my servant
Matt. 8. 4 offer the gift that M. commanded, for a
17. 3 there appeared unto them M. and Elias
17. 4 one for thee, and one for M., and one for
19. 7 Why did M. then command to give a wr.
19. 8 M. because of the hardness of your hearts
22. 24 Master, M. said, If a man die, having no
23. 2 scribes and the Pharisees sit in M.'s seat
Mark 1. 44 offer..those things which M. commanded
7. 10 For M. said, Honour thy father and thy m.
9. 4 there appeared unto them Elias with M.
9. 5 one for thee, and one for M., and one for
10. 3 he answered..What did M. command you?
10. 4 M. suffered to write a bill of divorcement
12. 19 M. wrote unto us, If a man's brother die
12. 26 have ye not read in the book of M., how
Luke 2. 22 purification according to the law of M.
5. 14 offer..according as M. commanded, for a
9. 30 talked with him two men, which were M.
9. 33 one for thee, and one for M., and one for
16. 29 They have M. and the prophets; let them
16. 31 If they hear not M. and the prophets, ne.
20. 28 M. wrote unto us, If any man's brother
20. 37 even M. showed at the bush, when he ca.
24. 27 beginning at M. and all the prophets, he
24. 44 which were written in the law of M., and
John 1. 17 For the law was given by M., (but) grace
1. 45 We have found him of whom M. in the law
3. 14 as M. lifted up the serpent in the wilder.
5. 45 there is (one) that accuseth you, (even) M.
5. 46 For had ye believed M., ye would have b.
6. 32 M. gave you not that bread from heaven
7. 19 Did not M. give you the law, and (yet)
7. 22 M. therefore gave..not because it is of M.
7. 23 that the law of M. should not be broken
8. 5 [Now M. in the law commanded us, that]
9. 28 Thou art his disciple; but we are M.'s dis.
9. 29 We know that God spake unto M.: (as for)
Acts 3. 22 For M. truly said unto the fathers, A pr.
6. 11 speak blasphemous words against M., and
6. 14 shall change the customs which M. deli.
7. 20 M. was born, and was exceeding fair, and
7. 22 M. was learned in all the wisdom of the
7. 29 Then fled M. at this saying, and was a
7. 31 When M. saw (it), he wondered at the si.
7. 32 Then M. trembled, and durst not behold
7. 35 M. whom they refused, saying, Who made
7. 37 M. which said unto the children of Israel
7. 40 M., which brought us out of the land of
7. 44 speaking unto M., that he should make
13. 39 could not be justified by the law of M.
15. 1 ye be circumcised after the manner of M.
15. 5 to command (them) to keep the law of M.
15. 21 M. of old time hath in every city them that
21. 21 thou teachest all the Jews..to forsake M.
26. 22 the prophets and M. did say should come
28. 23 of the law of M., and (out of) the prophets
Rom. 5. 14 death reigned from Adam to M., even over
9. 15 he saith to M., I will have mercy on whom
10. 5 M. describeth the righteousness which is
10. 19 M. saith, I will provoke you to jealousy
1 Co. 9. 9 it is written in the law of M., Thou shalt
10. 2 were all baptized unto M. in the cloud and
2 Co. 3. 7 could not stedfastly behold the face of M.
3. 13 M., (which) put a veil over his face, that
3. 15 when M. is read, the veil is upon their
2 Ti. 3. 8 as Jannes and Jambres withstood M., so do
Heb. 3. 2 as also M. (was faithful) in all his house
3. 3 was counted worthy of more glory than M.
3. 5 M. verily (was) faithful in all his house
3. 16 not all that came out of Egypt by M.
7. 14 M. spake nothing concerning priesthood
8. 5 M. was admonished of God when he was
9. 19 M. had spoken every precept to all the
10. 28 He that despised M.' law died without m.
11. 23 M., when he was born, was hid three mo.
11. 24 M., when he was come to years, refused
12. 21 (that) M. said, I exceedingly fear and qu.
Jude 9 when..he disputed about the body of M.
Rev. 15. 3 they sing the song of M. the servant of

MOST —

1. *Abundant, great, mighty,* כַּבִּיר *kabbir.*
Job 34. 17 wilt thou condemn him that is most just?
2. *Abundance,* רֹב *rob.*
Prov 20. 6 Most men will proclaim every one his own
3. *Good,* טוֹב *tob.*
Lam. 4. 1 How..is the most fine gold changed! tho
4. *More,* πλείων *pleiōn.*
Luke 7. 42 Tell me..which of them will love him m.
7. 43 I suppose that..to whom he forgave most
5. *Most,* πλεῖστος *pleistos*
Matt 11. 20 wherein most of his mighty works were
1 Co. 14. 27 by two, or at the most..three, and..by

[*See also* Believed, bitter, bitterly, holy, noble, rebellious, upright.]

MOST desolate —

Waste and desolation, שְׁמָמָה וּשְׁמָמָה [*shimamah*].
Eze. 35. 7 Thus will I make mount Seir most deso!

MOST fine gold —

Pure gold, כֶּתֶם *kethem.*
Song 5. 11 His head..the most fine gold; his locks

MOST high —

High, most high, ὕψιστος *hupsistos.*
Mark 5. 7 Jesus, (thou) Son of the most high God
Luke 8. 28 Jesus, (thou) Son of God most high
Acts 7. 48 Howbeit the most High dwelleth not in t.
16. 17 These men are the servants of the most h.
Heb. 7. 1 Melchisedec..priest of the most high God

MOST (mighty) —

Strength, might, power, חַיִל *chayil.*
Dan. 3. 20 he commanded the most mighty men that

MOST strong —

Strong place or hold, מָעוֹז *maoz.*
Dan. 11. 39 Thus shall he do in the most strong holds

MOST of all —

Most of all, chiefly, μάλιστα *malista.*
Acts 20. 38 Sorrowing most of all for the words which

MOTE —

Chaff, stubble, splinter, κάρφος *karphos.*
Matt 7. 3 why beholdest thou the mote that is in
7. 4 Let me pull out the mote out of thine eye
7. 5 to cast out the mote out of thy brother's
Luke 6. 41 why beholdest thou the mote that is in
6. 42 let me pull out the mote that is in thine
6. 42 to pull out the mote that is in thy broth.

MOTH —

1. *Moth, worm,* עָשׁ *ash.*
Job 4. 19 houses..(which) are crushed before the m.
13. 28 consumeth, as a garment that is moth eat.
27. 18 He buildeth his house as a moth, and as
Psa. 39. 11 his beauty to consume away like a moth
Isa. 50. 9 Behold..the moth shall eat them up
51. 8 For the moth shall eat them up like a ga.
Hos. 5. 12 unto Ephraim as a moth, and to the house
2. *Moth,* σής *sēs.*
Matt. 6. 19 where moth and rust doth corrupt, and
6. 20 where neither moth nor rust doth corrupt
Luke 12. 33 where no thief approacheth, neither moth

MOTH EATEN —

Moth eaten, σητόβρωτος *sētobrōtos.*
Jas. 5. 2 corrupted, and your garments are moth e.

MOTHER —

1. *Mother, dam, ancestress,* אֵם *em.*
Gen. 2. 24 shall a man leave his father and his mot.
3. 20 because she was the mother of all living
20. 12 not the daughter of my mother; and she
21. 21 his mother took him a wife out of the l.
24. 28 and told..her mother's house these things
24. 53 he gave also..to her mother precious thi.
24. 55 her brother and her mother said, Let the
24. 67 Isaac brought her into his mother Sarah's
24. 67 Isaac was comforted after his mother's (d.)
27. 11 Jacob said to Rebekah his mother, Behold
27. 13 his mother said unto him, Upon me..thy
27. 14 and fetched, and brought..to his mother
27. 14 his mother made savoury meat, such as
27. 29 let thy mother's sons bow down to thee
28. 2 the house of Bethuel thy mother's father
28. 2 daughters of Laban thy mother's brother
28. 5 brother of Rebekah, Jacob's and Esau's m.
28. 7 that Jacob obeyed his father and his mo.
29. 10 the daughter of Laban his mother's brot.
29. 10 the sheep of Laban his mother's brother
29. 10 watered the flock of Laban his mother's
30. 14 brought them unto his mother Leah
32. 11 will come and smite..the mother with the
37. 10 Shall I and thy mother and thy brethren
43. 29 saw his brother Benjamin, his mother's
44. 20 he alone is left of his mother, and his father
Exod. 2. 8 the maid went and called the child's mo.
20. 12 Honour thy father and thy mother: that
21. 15 he that smiteth his father or his mother
21. 17 he that curseth his father or his mother
23. 19 shalt not seethe a kid in his mother's m.
34. 26 shalt not seethe a kid in his mother's m.
Lev. 18. 7 or the nakedness of thy mother, shalt
18. 7 she (is) thy mother; thou shalt not unc.
18. 9 or daughter of thy mother..born at home
18. 13 uncover the nakedness of thy mother's

Lev. 18. 13 for she (is) thy mother's near kinswoman
19. 3 Ye shall fear every man his mother and
20. 9 For every one that curseth..his mother
20. 9 he hath cursed his father or his mother
20. 14 if a man take a wife and her mother, it
20. 17 if a man shall take..his mother's daughter
20. 19 not uncover the nakedness of thy mother's
21. 2 for his mother, and for his father, and for
21. 11 defile himself for his father, or for his m.
24. 11 his mother's name (was) Shelomith, the d.
Num. 6. 7 for his father or for his mother, for his
12. 12 when he cometh out of his mother's womb
Deut. 5. 16 Honour thy father and thy mother, as the
13. 6 If thy brother, the son of thy mother, or
14. 21 shalt not seethe a kid in his mother's milk
21. 13 bewail her father and her mother a full m.
21. 18 will not obey..the voice of his mother, and
21. 19 Then shall his father and his mother lay
22. 15 the father of the damsel, and her mother
27. 16 that setteth light by his father or his mo.
27. 22 with his sister..the daughter of his mot.
33. 9 Who said unto his father and to his mot.
Josh. 2. 13 ye will save alive my father, and my mot.
2. 18 thou shalt bring thy father, and thy mo.
6. 23 Rahab, and her father, and her mother
Judg. 5. 7 that I Deborah arose, that I arose a m.
5. 28 The mother of Sisera looked out at a wi.
8. 19 They..my brethren..the sons of my mo.
9. 1 went to Shechem unto his mother's bret.
9. 1 all the family of the house of his mother's
9. 3 his mother's brethren spake of him in the
14. 2 told his father and his mother, and said
14. 3 Then his father and his mother said unto
14. 4 his father and his mother knew not that
14. 5 Then went Samson down..and his mother
14. 6 he told not his father or his mother what
14. 9 came to his father and mother, and he
14. 16 I have not told..my father nor my mother
16. 17 a Nazarite unto God from my mother's
17. 2 he said unto his mother, The eleven hun.
17. 2 his mother said, Blessed..of the LORD, my
17. 3 to his mother, his mother said, I had wh.
17. 4 unto his mother; and his mother took two
Ruth 1. 8 Go, return each to her mother's house
2. 11 thou hast left thy father and thy mother
1 Sa. 2. 19 his mother made him a little coat, and
15. 33 so shall thy mother be childless among w.
20. 30 unto the confusion of thy mother's nake.
22. 3 Let my father and my mother, I pray thee
2 Sa. 17. 25 Nahash, sister to Zeruiah, Joab's mother
19. 37 by the grave of my father and of my mo.
20. 19 to destroy a city and a mother in Israel
1 Ki. 1. 11 Nathan spake unto Bath-sheba the mother
2. 13 came to Bath-sheba the mother of Solomon
2. 19 caused a seat to be set for the king's mo.
2. 20 the king said unto her, Ask on, my moth.
2. 22 Solomon answered and said unto his mo.
3. 27 in no wise slay it: she (is) the mother
11. 26 Jeroboam..whose mother's name (was)
14. 21, 31 his mother's name (was) Naamah an
15. 2, 10 his mother's name (was) Maachah, the
15. 13 also Maachah his mother, even her he re.
17. 23 delivered him unto his mother: and Elij
19. 20 Let me..kiss my father and my mother
22. 42 his mother's name (was) Azubah the dau.
22. 52 walked..in the way of his mother, and in
2 Ki. 3. 2 but not like his father, and like his moth.
3. 13 get thee..to the prophets of thy mother
4. 19 he said to a lad, Carry him to his mother
4. 20 brought him to his mother, he sat on her
4. 30 the mother of the child said..the LORD
8. 26 And his mother's name (was) Athaliah
9. 22 so long as the whoredoms of thy mother
11. 1 when Athaliah the mother of Ahaziah saw
12. 1 his mother's name (was) Zibiah of Beer-s
14. 2 his mother's name (was) Jehoaddan of J.
15. 2 his mother's name (was) Jecholiah of Je.
15. 33 his mother's name (was) Jerusha, the da.
18. 2 his mother's name also (was) Abi, the da.
21. 1 And his mother's name (was) Hephzi-bah
21. 19 his mother's name (was) Meshullemeth
22. 1 his mother's name (was) Jedidah, the da.
23. 31 his mother's name (was) Hamutal, the d.
23. 36 his mother's name (was) Zebudah, the da
24. 8 his mother's name (was) Nehushta, the d.
24. 12 he, and his mother, and his servants, and
24. 15 he carried away..the king's mother, and
24. 18 his mother's name (was) Hamutal, the d.
1 Ch. 2. 26 Atarah: she (was) the mother of Onam
4. 9 his mother called his name Jabez, saying
2 Ch. 12. 13 his mother's name (was) Naamah an Am.
13. 2 His mother's name also (was) Michaiah
15. 16 Maachah the mother of Asa the king, he
20. 31 his mother's name (was) Azubah the da.
22. 2 His mother's name also (was) Athaliah
22. 3 his mother was his counsellor to do wick.
22. 10 when Athaliah the mother of Ahaziah saw
24. 1 His mother's name also (was) Zibiah of B.
25. 1 his mother's name (was) Jehoaddan of J.
26. 3 His mother's name also (was) Jecoliah
27. 1 His mother's name also (was) Jerushah
29. 1 his mother's name was Abijah, the daug.
Esth. 2. 7 she had neither father nor mother, and
2. 7 when her father and mother were dead
Job 1. 21 Naked came I out of my mother's womb
17. 14 I have said..to the worm..my mother
31. 18 I have guided her from my mother's wo.
Psa. 22. 9 make me hope..upon my mother's breasts
22. 10 thou (art) my God from my mother's belly
27. 10 When my father and my mother forsake
35. 14 bowed..as one that mourneth (for his) m.
50. 20 thou slanderest thine own mother's son
Psa. 51. 5 Behold..in sin did my mother conceive me
69. 8 and an alien unto my mother's children
71. 6 that took me out of my mother's bowels
109. 14 let not the sin of his mother be blotted
113. 9 He maketh..a joyful mother of children
131. 2 as a child that is weaned of his mother
139. 13 thou hast covered me in my mother's wo.
Prov. 1. 8 and forsake not the law of thy mother
4. 3 and only (beloved) in the sight of my mo.
6. 20 My son..forsake not the law of thy mother
10. 1 a foolish son (is) the heaviness of his mot.
15. 20 but a foolish man despiseth his mother
19. 26 He that..chaseth away (his) mother, (is) a
20. 20 Whoso curseth his father or his mother
23. 22 and despise not thy mother when she is
23. 25 Thy father and thy mother shall be glad
28. 24 Whoso robbeth his father or his mother
29. 15 but a child..bringeth his mother to shame
30. 11 a generation..doth not bless their mother
30. 17 despiseth to obey (his) mother, the ravens
31. 1 the prophecy that his mother taught him
Eccl. 5. 15 As he came forth of his mother's womb
Song 1. 6 my mother's children were angry with me
3. 4 had brought him into my mother's house
3. 11 with the crown wherewith his mother cr.
6. 9 she (is) the (only) one of her mother, she
8. 1 that sucked the breasts of my mother
8. 2 I would..bring thee into my mother's ho.
8. 5 there thy mother brought thee forth; th.
Isa. 8. 4 shall have knowledge to cry..my mother
49. 1 from the bowels of my mother hath he m.
50. 1 Where (is) the bill of your mother's divorc.
50. 1 for your transgressions is your mother put
66. 13 As one whom his mother comforteth, so
Jer. 15. 8 against the mother of the young men a s.
15. 10 Woe is me, my mother, that thou hast b.
16. 3 concerning their mothers that bare them
16. 7 cup of consolation to drink..for their moth.
20. 14 let not the day wherein my mother bare me
20. 17 that my mother might have been my grave
22. 26 I will cast thee out, and thy mother that
50. 12 Your mother shall be sore confounded
52. 1 his mother's name (was) Hamutal the da.
Lam. 2. 12 They say to their mothers, Where (is) corn
2. 12 was poured out into their mother's bosom
5. 3 We are orphans..our mothers (are) as wid.
Eze. 16. 3 thy father..an Amorite..thy mother an H.
16. 44 saying, As (is) the mother, (so is) her dau.
16. 45 Thou (art) thy mother's daughter, that l.
16. 45 your mother (was) an Hittite, and your fa.
19. 2 What (is) thy mother? A lioness: she lay
19. 10 Thy mother (is) like a vine in thy blood
22. 7 In thee..they set light by father and mo
23. 2 two women, the daughters of one mother
44. 25 or for mother..they may defile themsel.
Hos. 2. 2 Plead with your mother, plead; for she
2. 5 For their mother hath played the harlot
4. 5 prophet also..and I will destroy thy mo.
10. 14 the mother was dashed in pieces upon
Mic. 7. 6 the daughter riseth up against her mother
Zech. 13. 3, 3, his father and his mother that begat

2. *Mother*, μητηρ *mētēr*.
Matt. 1. 18 When as his mother Mary was espoused
2. 11 saw the young child with Mary his mother
2. 13 take the young child and his mother, and
2. 14 he took the young child and his mother by
2. 20 take the young child and his mother, and
2. 21 and took the young child and his mother
10. 35 the daughter against her mother, and the
10. 37 He that loveth father or mother more than
12. 46 mother and his brethren stood without
12. 47 thy mother and thy brethren stand with
12. 48 Who is my mother? and who are my breth.
12. 49 said, Behold my mother and my brethren
12. 50 same is my brother, and sister, and mother
13. 55 is not his mother called Mary? and his
14. 8 she, being before instructed of her mother
14. 11 damsel, and she brought (it) to her mot.
15. 4 saying, Honour thy father and mother
15. 4 He that curseth father or mother, let him
15. 5 Whosoever shall say to..father or..mot
15. 6 And honour not his father or his mother
19. 5 shall a man leave father and mother, and
19. 12 which were so born from..mother's womb
19. 19 Honour thy father and (thy) mother: and
19. 29 [every one that hath forsaken..mother, or]
20. 20 Then came to him the mother of Zebedee's
27. 56 mother of James and Joses, and the mo.
Mark 3. 31 There came then his brethren and his m.
3. 32 thy mother and thy brethren without seek
3. 33 saying, Who is my mother, or my breth?
3. 34 Behold my mother and my brethren!
3. 35 is my brother, and my sister, and mother
5. 40 he taketh the father and the mother of the
6. 24 she went forth, and said unto her mother
6. 28 head..and the damsel gave it to her mo
7. 10 Honour thy father and thy mother; and
7. 10 Whoso curseth father or mother, let him
7. 11 If a man shall say to his father or mother
7. 12 to do ought for his father or his mother
10. 7 shall a man leave his father and mother
10. 19 Defraud not, Honour thy father and mo.
10. 29 There is no man that hath left..mother
10. 30 he shall receive..sisters, and mothers, and
15. 40 among whom was..Mary the mother of
Luke 1. 15 shall be great..even from his mother's
1. 43 that the mother of my Lord should come
1. 60 And his mother answered and said, Not
2. 33 Joseph and his mother marvelled at those
2. 34 Simeon..said unto Mary his mother, Be.
2. 43 [and Joseph and his mother knew not]
Luke 2. 48 his mother said unto him, Son, why hast
2. 51 his mother kept all these sayings in her
7. 12 only son of his mother, and she was a w.
7. 15 And he delivered him to his mother
8. 19 Then came to him (his) mother and his
8. 20 Thy mother and thy brethren stand with.
8. 21 My mother and my brethren are
8. 51 the father and the mother of the maiden
12. 53 the mother against the daughter, and the
12. 53 and the daughter against the mother
14. 26 hate not his father, and mother, and wife
18. 20 Honour thy father and thy mother
John 2. 1 Cana..and the mother of Jesus was there
2. 3 the mother of Jesus saith unto him, They
2. 5 His mother saith unto the servants, Wh.
2. 12 went down to Capernaum, he, and his m.
3. 4 can he enter..into his mother's womb, and
6. 42 Jesus..whose father and mother we know?
19. 25 there stood by the cross of Jesus his mo.
19. 25 his mother's sister, Mary the (wife) of C.
19. 26 When Jesus therefore saw his mother, and
19. 26 he saith unto his mother, Woman, behold
19. 27 Then saith he..Behold thy mother! And
Acts 1. 14 with the women, and Mary the mother of
3. 2 a certain man lame from his mother's wo.
12. 12 to the house of Mary the mother of John
14. 8 being a cripple from his mother's womb
Rom 16. 13 Salute Rufus..and his mother and mine
Gal. 1. 15 who separated me from my mother's w.
4. 26 Jerusalem..which is the mother of us all
Eph. 5. 31 For this cause shall a man leave his..m.
6. 2 Honour thy father and mother; which
1 Ti. 5. 2 The elder women as mothers; the younger
2 Ti. 1. 5 which dwelt first in..thy mother Eunice
Rev. 17. 5 The mother of harlots and abominations

MOTHER IN LAW —

1. *Husband's mother*, חָמוֹת *chamoth*.
Ruth 1. 14 Orpah kissed her mother in law; but R.
2. 11 that thou hast done unto thy mother in l.
2. 18 her mother in law saw what she had gle.
2. 19 her mother in law said unto her, Where
2. 19 she showed her mother in law with whom
2. 23 So she..dwelt with her mother in law
3. 1 Then Naomi her mother in law said unto
3. 6 did..all that her mother in law bade her
3. 16 when she came to her mother in law, she
3. 17 said..Go not empty unto thy mother in law
Mic. 7. 6 daughter in law against her mother in law

2. *To be a father or mother in law*, חָתַן *chathan*.
Deut 27. 23 Cursed (be) he that lieth with his m. in l.

3. *A husband's mother*, πενθερά *penthera*.
Matt 10. 35 daughter in law against her mother in law
Luke 12. 53 mother in law against her daughter in law
12. 53 daughter in law against her mother in law

MOTHER, wife's —

A wife's mother, πενθερά *penthera*.
Matt. 8. 14 he saw his wife's mother laid, and sick of
Mark 1. 30 Simon's wife's mother lay sick of a fever
Luke 4. 38 Simon's wife's mother was taken with a

MOTHER, without —

Motherless, without mother, ἀμήτωρ *amētōr*.
Heb. 7. 3 Without father, without mother, without

MOTHER, murderer of a —

One who beats a mother, μητραλῴας, μητρολῴας.
1 Ti. 1. 9 murderers of fathers and murderers of m.

MOTION —

Suffering, affection, πάθημα *pathēma*.
Rom. 7. 5 motions of sins, which were by the law

MOULDY —

Small round cakes, נִקֻּדִים *niqqudim*.
Josh. 9. 5 bread of their provision was dry..mouldy
9. 12 but now, behold, it is dry, and it is mouldy

MOUNT, MOUNTAIN —

1. *Mount, hill*, הַר *har*.
Gen. 7. 20 Fifteen cubits..and the mountains were
8. 4 the ark rested..upon the mountains of A.
8. 5 were the tops of the mountains seen
10. 30 as thou goest, unto Sephar, a mount of the
12. 8 he removed from thence unto a mountain
14. 10 they that remained fled to the mountain
19. 17 escape to the mountain, lest thou be con.
19. 19 I cannot escape to the mountain, lest some
19. 30 Lot went up..and dwelt in the mountain
22. 2 upon one of the mountains which I will
22. 14 In the mount of the LORD it shall be
31. 21 and set his face (toward) the mount Gilead
31. 23 they overtook him in the mount Gilead
31. 25 Jacob had pitched his tent in the mount
31. 25 brethren pitched in the mount of Gilead
31. 54 Jacob offered sacrifice upon the mount, and
31. 54 and they..tarried all night in the mount
36. 8 Thus dwelt Esau in mount Seir: Esau (is)
36. 9 the father of the Edomites in mount Seir
Exod. 3. 1 and came to the mountain of God..to H.
3. 12 ye shall serve God upon this mountain
4. 27 he went, and met him in the mount of God
15. 17 plant them in the mountain of thine inh.
18. 5 where he encamped at the mount of God
19. 2 and there Israel camped before the mount
19. 3 LORD called unto him out of the mountain
19. 11 in the sight of all the people upon mount
19. 12 go (not) up into the mount, or touch the
19. 12 whosoever toucheth the mount shall be
19. 13 soundeth..they shall come up to the mo.
19. 14 Moses went down from the mount unto

Exod.19. 16 a thick cloud upon the mount, and the
19. 17 they stood at the nether part of the mount
19. 18 mount Sinai was altogether on a smoke
19. 18 and the whole mount quaked greatly
19. 20 upon mount Sinai, on the top of the mount
19. 20 LORD called Moses..to the top of the mo.
19. 23 The people cannot come up to mount S.
19. 23 Set bounds about the mount, and sanctify
20. 18 all the people saw..the mountain smoking
24. 12 Come up to me into..mount, and be there
24. 13 and Moses went up into the mount of G.
24. 15 the mount, and a cloud covered the mount
24. 16 the glory of the LORD abode upon mount
24. 17 like devouring fire on the top of the mount
24. 18 And Moses..gat him up into the mount: and
24. 18 Moses was in the mount forty days and fo.
25. 40 pattern, which was showed thee in the m.
26. 30 fashion..which was showed thee in the m.
27. 8 as it was showed thee in the mount, so
31. 18 an end of communing with him upon mo.
32. 1 Moses delayed to come down out of the m.
32. 12 to slay them in the mountains, and to c.
32. 15 Moses turned, and went down from the m.
32. 19 cast ..and break them beneath the mount
33. 6 stripped..of their ornaments by the mo.
34. 2 come up in the morning unto mount Sinai
34. 2 present thyself..to me in the top of the m.
34. 3 neither let any..throughout all the mount
34. 3 neither let..herds feed before that mount
34. 4 went up unto mount Sinai, as the LORD
34. 29 when Moses came down from mount Sinai
34. 29 when he came down from the mount, that
34. 32 LORD had spoken with him in mount Sinai
Lev. 7. 38 the LORD commanded Moses in mount S.
25. 1 the LORD spake unto Moses in mount Si.
26. 46 which the LORD made..in mount Sinai by
27. 34 the LORD commanded Moses..in mount S.
Num. 3. 1 the LORD spake with Moses in mount Si.
10. 33 they departed from the mount of the L.
13. 17 southward, and go up into the mountain
13. 29 and the Amorites, dwell in the mountains
14. 40 gat them up into the top of the mountain
20. 22 from Kadesh, and came unto mount Hor
20. 23 spake unto Moses and Aaron in mount H.
20. 25 Take..and bring them up unto mount H.
20. 27 they went up into mount Hor in the sight
20. 28 Aaron died there in the top of the mount
20. 28 and Eleazar came down from the mount
21. 4 journeyed from mount Hor by the way
27. 12 Get thee up into this mount Abarim, and
28. 6 which was ordained in mount Sinai for a
33. 23 they went..and pitched in mount Shapher
33. 24 they removed from mount Shapher, and
33. 37 pitched in mount Hor, in the edge of the
33. 38 Aaron the priest went up into mount Hor
33. 39 Aaron (was)..old when he died in mount
33. 41 they departed from mount Hor, and pit.
33. 47 pitched in the mountains of Abarim, bef.
33. 48 they departed from the mountains of Ab.
34. 7 great sea ye shall point out for you mount
34. 8 From mount Hor ye shall point out (your
Deut. 1. 2 from Horeb by the way of mount Seir unto
1. 6 Ye have dwelt long enough in this mount
1. 7 go to the mount of the Amorites, and unto
1. 19 which ye saw by the way of the mountain
1. 20 Ye are come unto the mountain of the A.
1. 24 they turned and went up into the mount.
1. 44 the Amorites, which dwelt in that moun.
2. 1 and we compassed mount Seir many days
2. 3 Ye have compassed this mountain long
2. 5 because I have given mount Seir unto E.
2. 37 unto the cities in the mountains, nor unto
3. 8 from the river of Arnon unto mount Her
3. 12 and half mount Gilead, and the cities th.
3. 25 land..that goodly mountain, and Lebanon
4. 11 ye came near and stood under the mount.
4. 11 the mountain burned with fire unto the
4. 48 even unto mount Sion, which (is) Hermon
5. 4 talked with you face to face in the mount
5. 5 of the fire, and went not up into the mo.
5. 22 spake unto all your assembly in the mount
5. 23 for the mountain did burn with fire
9. 9 When I was gone up into the mount to r.
9. 9 then I abode in the mount forty days and
9. 10 which the LORD spake with you in the m.
9. 15 came down from the mount, and the mo.
9. 21 the brook that descended out of the mo
10. 1 come up unto me into the mount, and m.
10. 3 went up into the mount, having the two
10. 4 the LORD spake unto you in the mount
10. 5 I turned..and came down from the mount
10. 10 I stayed in the mount, according to the
11. 29 upon mount Gerizim..the curse upon m.
12. 2 upon the high mountains, and upon the
27. 4 ye shall set up these stones..in mount E.
27. 12 These shall stand upon mount Gerizim to
27. 13 these shall stand upon mount Ebal to c.
32. 22 set on fire the foundations of the mount.
32. 49 Get thee up into this mountain Abarim
32. 49 mount Nebo, which (is) in the land of M.
32. 50 die in the mount whither thou goest up
32. 50 as Aaron thy brother died in mount Hor
33. 2 he shined forth from mount Paran, and he
33. 19 They shall call the people unto the mou.
34. 1 from the plains of Moab unto the moun.
Josh. 2. 16 Get you to the mountain, lest the pursu.
2. 22 they went, and came unto the mountain
2. 23 descended from the mountain, and passed
8. 30 Then Joshua built an altar..in mount E.
8. 33 half of them over against mount Gerizim
8. 33 and half of them over against mount Ebal
10. 6 the Amorites that dwell in the mountains

Josh. 11. 2 kings that (were) on the north of the m.
11. 3 the Jebusite in the mountains, and (to)
11. 16 the mountain of Israel, and the valley of
11. 17 from the mount Halak, that goeth up to S.
11. 17 in the valley of Lebanon, under mount H.
11. 21 cut off the Anakims from the mountains
11. 21 mountains of Judah, and from all the m.
12. 1 from the river Arnon unto mount Hermon
12. 5 reigned in mount Hermon, and in Salcah
12. 7 unto the mount Halak, that goeth up to
12. 8 In the mountains, and in the valleys, and
13. 5 from Baal-gad under mount Hermon unto
13. 11 all mount Hermon, and all Bashan unto S.
13. 19 Zareth-shahar in the mount of the valley
14. 12 Now therefore give me this mountain, w.
15. 8 went up to the top of the mountain that
15. 9 went out to the cities of mount Ephron
15. 10 from Baalah westward unto mount Seir
15. 10 the side of mount Jearim, which (is) Che.
15. 11 passed along to mount Baalah, and went
15. 48 in the mountains, Shamir, and Jattir, and
16. 1 up from Jericho, throughout mount Be.
17. 15 if mount Ephraim be too narrow for thee
17. 18 the mountain shall be thine; for it (is) a
18. 12 went up through the mountains westward
18. 16 border came down to the end of the mou.
19. 50 he asked..Timnath-serah in mount Ephr.
20. 7 And..Kedesh in Galilee in mount Naph.
20. 7 and Shechem in mount Ephraim, and
20. 7 Kirjath-arba..in the mountain of Judah
21. 21 Shechem with her suburbs in mount Eph.
24. 4 I gave unto Esau mount Seir, to possess
24. 30 which (is) in mount Ephraim, on the north
24. 33 which was given him in mount Ephraim
Judg. 1. 9 Canaanites, that dwelt in the mountain
1. 19 he drave out (the inhabitants) of the mo.
1. 34 forced the children of Dan into the mou.
1. 35 the Amorites would dwell in mount Heres
2. 9 in the mount of Ephraim, on the north s.
3. 3 the Hivites that dwelt in mount Lebanon
3. 3 from mount Baal-hermon unto the enter.
3. 27 he blew a trumpet in the mountain of E.
3. 27 went down with him from the mount, and
4. 5 between Ramah and Beth-el in mount E.
4. 6 Go and draw toward mount Tabor, and
4. 12 son of Abinoam was gone up to mount T.
4. 14 So Barak went down from mount Tabor
5. 5 The mountains melted from before the L.
6. 2 made..the dens which (are) in the moun.
7. 3 return and depart early from mount Gilea.
7. 24 sent messengers throughout all mount E.
9. 7 he went and stood in the top of mount G.
9. 25 liers in wait for him in the top of the m.
9. 36 come people down from the top of the m.
9. 36 Thou seest the shadow of the mountains
9. 48 Abimelech gat him up to mount Zalmon
10. 1 and he dwelt in Shamir in mount Ephraim
11. 37 that I may go up and down upon the m.
11. 38 bewailed her virginity upon the mountains
12. 15 of Ephraim, in the mount of the Amalek.
17. 1 there was a man of mount Ephraim, whose
17. 8 he came to mount Ephraim, to the house
18. 2 who when they came to mount Ephraim
18. 13 they passed thence unto mount Ephraim
19. 1 sojourning on the side of mount Ephraim
19. 16 an old man..which (was) also of mount E
19. 18 passing..toward the side of mount Ephr.
1 Sa. 1. 1 man of Ramathaim-Zophim of mount Ep.
9. 4 he passed through mount Ephraim, and
13. 2 were with Saul in Michmash and in mount
14. 22 which had hid themselves in mount Eph.
17. 3 the Philistines stood on a mountain on the
17. 3 Israel stood on a mountain on the other
23. 14 remained in a mountain in the wilderness
23. 26 Saul went on this side of the mountain
23. 26 David and his men on that side of the m.
26. 20 doth hunt a partridge in the mountains
31. 1 fled..and fell down slain in mount Gilboa
31. 8 Saul and his three sons fallen in mount G
2 Sa. 1. 6 As I happened by chance upon mount G.
1. 21 Ye mountains of Gilboa, no dew, neither
20. 21 a man of mount Ephraim, Sheba the son
1 Ki. 4. 8 And these..The son of Hur, in mount E.
5. 15 fourscore thousand hewers in the mount.
12. 25 Jeroboam built Shechem in mount Ephr.
18. 19 gather to me all Israel unto mount Carmel
18. 20 the prophets together unto mount Carmel
19. 8 and went..unto Horeb the mount of God
19. 11 Go forth, and stand upon the mount bef.
19. 11 a great and strong wind rent the mount.
2 Ki. 2. 16 cast him upon some mountain, or into
2. 25 And he went from thence to mount Car.
4. 25 came unto the man of God unto mount C.
5. 22 even now there be come to me from mount
6. 17 the mountain (was) full of horses and cha.
19. 23 I am come up to the height of the moun.
19. 31 and they that escape out of mount Zion
23. 13 on the right hand of the mount of corru.
23. 16 sepulchres that (were) there in the mount
1 Ch. 4. 42 went to mount Seir, having for their cap.
5. 23 Baal-hermon and Senir, and unto mount
6. 67 Shechem in mount Ephraim with her su.
10. 1 fled..and fell down slain in mount Gilboa
10. 8 found Saul and his sons fallen in mount G.
12. 8 as swift as the roes upon the mountains
2 Ch. 2. 2 fourscore thousand to hew in the mount.
2. 18 fourscore thousand..hewers in the moun.
3. 1 to build..at Jerusalem in mount Moriah
13. 4 Abijah stood up upon mount Zemaraim
13. 4 which (is) in mount Ephraim, and said
15. 8 which he had taken from mount Ephraim
18. 16 I did see..Israel scattered upon the mo.

2 Ch. 19. 4 went out..from Beer-sheba to mount Ep.
20. 10 children of Ammon and Moab and mount
20. 22 children of Ammon, Moab, and mount S.
20. 23 stood up against the inhabitants of mount
21. 11 he made high places in the mountains of
26. 10 vine dressers in the mountains, and in C.
27. 4 he built cities in the mountains of Judah
33. 15 all the altars that he had built in the mo.
Neh. 8. 15 Go forth unto the mount, and fetch olive
9. 13 Thou camest down also upon mount Sinai
Job 9. 5 Which removeth the mountains, and they
14. 18 surely the mountain falling cometh to n.
24. 8 They are wet with the showers of the mo.
28. 9 he overturneth the mountains by the roots
39. 8 The range of the mountains (is) his pasture
40. 20 Surely the mountains bring him forth food
Psa. 11. 1 how say ye..Flee (as) a bird to your mou.
46. 2 though the mountains be carried into the
46. 3 mountains shake with the swelling thereof
48. 1 in the city of our God..the mountain of
48. 2 the joy of the whole earth, (is) mount Zion
48. 11 Let mount Zion rejoice, let the daughters
50. 11 I know all the fowls of the mountains: and
65. 6 Which by his strength setteth fast the m.
72. 3 The mountains shall bring peace to the p.
72. 16 corn in the earth upon the top of the mo.
74. 2 this mount Zion, wherein thou hast dwelt
78. 54 this mountain..his right hand had purc.
78. 68 chose the tribe of Judah, the mount Zion
83. 14 as the flame setteth the mountains on fire
90. 2 Before the mountains were brought forth
104. 6 the waters stood above the mountains
104. 8 They go up by the mountains; they go d.
114. 4 The mountains skipped like rams..little
114. 6 Ye mountains..ye skipped like rams..ye
125. 1 They that trust in the LORD..as mount Z.
125. 2 the mountains (are) round about Jerusa.
144. 5 touch the mountains, and they shall sm.
147. 8 who maketh grass to grow upon the mou.
148. 9 Mountains, and all hills; fruitful trees
Prov. 8. 25 Before the mountains were settled, before
27. 25 and herbs of the mountains are gathered
Song 2. 8 he cometh leaping upon the mountains
2. 17 a young hart upon the mountains of Be.
4. 1 a flock of goats, that appear from mount
4. 6 I will get me to the mountain of myrrh
8. 14 a young hart upon the mountains of spi.
Isa. 2. 2 the mountain of the LORD'S house shall be
2. 2 be established in the top of the mountains
2. 3 Come ye, and let us go up to the mount.
2. 14 upon all the high mountains, and upon
4. 5 create upon every dwelling place of mou.
8. 18 LORD of hosts, which dwelleth in mount
10. 12 whole work upon mount Zion and on Je.
10. 32 the mount of the daughter of Zion, the
11. 9 not hurt nor destroy in all my holy mou.
13. 2 Lift ye up a banner upon the high moun.
13. 4 The noise of a multitude in the mountains
14. 13 I will sit also upon the mount of the con.
14. 25 upon my mountains tread him under foot
16. 1 unto the mount of the daughter of Zion
17. 13 shall be chased as the chaff of the moun.
18. 3 when he lifteth up an ensign on the mou.
18. 6 left..unto the fowls of the mountains, and
18. 7 the name of the LORD of hosts, the mount
22. 5 the walls, and of crying to the mountains
24. 23 LORD of hosts shall reign in mount Zion
25. 6 in this mountain shall the LORD of hosts
25. 7 he will destroy in this mountain the face
25. 10 in this mountain shall the hand of the L.
27. 13 worship the LORD in the holy mount at J.
28. 21 the LORD shall rise up as (in) mount Per.
29. 8 nations be that fight against mount Zion
30. 17 as a beacon upon the top of a mountain
30. 25 there shall be upon every high mountain
30. 29 to come into the mountain of the LORD
31. 4 come down to fight for mount Zion, and
34. 3 mountains shall be melted with their bl.
37. 24 I come up to the height of the mountains
37. 32 and they that escape out of mount Zion
40. 4 every mountain and hill shall be made l.
40. 9 O Zion..get thee up into the high mount.
40. 12 weighed the mountains in scales, and the
41. 15 thou shalt thresh the mountains, and beat
42. 11 let them shout from the top of the moun.
42. 15 I will make waste mountains and hills, and
44. 23 break forth into singing, ye mountains, O
49. 11 I will make all my mountains a way, and
49. 13 break forth into singing, O mountains: for
52. 7 How beautiful upon the mountains are the
54. 10 For the mountains shall depart, and the
55. 12 the mountains and the hills shall break
56. 7 Even them will I bring to my holy moun.
57. 7 Upon a lofty and high mountain hast thou
57. 13 but he..shall inherit my holy mountain
64. 1 that the mountains might flow down at
64. 3 the mountains flowed down at thy prese.
65. 7 which have burnt incense upon the mou.
65. 9 out of Judah an inheritor of my mounta.
65. 11 that forget my holy mountain, that pre.
65. 25 not hurt nor destroy in all my holy mou.
66. 20 to my holy mountain Jerusalem, saith the
Jer. 3. 6 she is gone up upon every high mountain
3. 23 from the hills..the multitude of mount.
4. 15 publisheth affliction from mount Ephraim
4. 24 I beheld the mountains, and, lo, they tr.
9. 10 For the mountains will I take up a weep.
13. 16 your feet stumble upon the dark mount.
16. 16 they shall hunt them from every mountain
17. 26 from the mountains, and from the south
26. 18 the mountain of the house as the high p.
31. 5 Thou shalt yet plant vines upon the mo.

Jer. 31. 6 watchmen upon the mount Ephraim shall
31. 23 O habitation of justice..mountain of ho.
32. 44 in the cities of the mountains, and in the
33. 13 In the cities of the mountains, in the cit
46. 18 Surely as Tabor (is) among the mountains
50. 6 they have turned them away (on) the m.
50. 6 they have gone from mountain to hill, they
50. 19 his soul shall be satisfied upon mount E.
51. 25 I (am) against thee, O destroying mount.
51. 25 and will make thee a burnt mountain
Lam. 4. 19 they pursued us upon the mountains, they
5. 18 Because of the mountain of Zion, which is
Eze. 6. 2 set thy face toward the mountains of Israel
6. 3 Ye mountains of Israel, hear the word of
6. 3 Thus saith the Lord GOD to the mountains
6. 13 in all the tops of the mountains, and under
7. 7 not the sounding again of the mountains
7. 16 shall be on the mountains like doves of
11. 23 stood upon the mountain which (is) on the
17. 22 will plant (it) upon an high mountain and
17. 23 In the mountain of the height of Israel
18. 6, 15 hath not eaten upon the mountains
18. 11 but even hath eaten upon the mountains
19. 9 voice should no more be heard upon the m.
20. 40 in mine holy mountain, in the mountain
22. 9 and in thee they eat upon the mountains
28. 14 thou wast upon the holy mountain of God
28. 16 I will cast thee as profane out of the m.
31. 12 upon the mountains and in all the valleys
32. 5 I will lay thy flesh upon the mountains
32. 6 I will also water..the land..to the mou.
33. 28 the mountains of Israel shall be desolate
34. 6 My sheep wandered through all the mo.
34. 13 and feed them upon the mountains of I
34. 14 upon the high mountains of Israel shall
34. 14 shall they feed upon the mountains of I
35. 2 Son of man, set thy face against mount S.
35. 3 Behold, O mount Seir, I (am) against thee
35. 7 Thus will I make mount Seir most desol
35. 8 And I will fill his mountains with his sl.
35. 12 which thou hast spoken against the mou.
35. 15 thou shalt be desolate, O mount Seir, and
36. 1 prophesy unto the mountains of Israel, and
36. 1, 4 ye mountains of Israel, hear the word
36. 4 Thus saith the Lord GOD to the mountains
36. 6 say unto the mountains, and to the hills
36. 8 But ye, O mountains of Israel, ye shall
37. 22 in the land upon the mountains of Israel
38. 8 against the mountains of Israel, which
38. 20 the mountains shall be thrown down, and
38. 21 call..against him throughout all my mo.
39. 2 will bring thee upon the mountains of I.
39. 4 Thou shalt fall upon the mountains of Is.
39. 17 a great sacrifice upon the mountains of I.
40. 2 set me upon a very high mountain, by w
43. 12 Upon the top of the mountain the whole
Dan 9. 16 from thy city Jerusalem, thy holy moun.
9. 20 before the LORD my God for the holy m.
11. 45 between the seas in the glorious holy m.
Hos. 4. 13 They sacrifice upon the tops of the mou.
10. 8 they shall say to the mountains, Cover us
Joel 2. 1 and sound an alarm in my holy mountain
2. 2 as the morning spread upon the mountains
2. 5 Like..noise of chariots on the tops of m.
2. 32 in mount Zion and in Jerusalem shall be
3. 17 your God dwelling in Zion, my holy mou.
3. 18 the mountains shall drop down new wine
Amos 3. 9 Assemble yourselves upon the mountains
4. 1 that (are) in the mountain of Samaria
4. 13 For, lo, he that formeth the mountains
6. 1 and trust in the mountain of Samaria
9. 13 and the mountains shall drop sweet wine
Obad. 8 understanding out of the mount of Esau?
9 that every one of the mount of Esau may
16 For as ye have drunk upon my holy mou:
17 But upon mount Zion shall be deliverance
19 the south shall possess the mount of Esau
21 come up on mount Zion to judge the mo
Jon. 2. 6 I went down to the bottoms of the moun.
Mic. 1. 4 the mountains shall be molten under him
3. 12 the mountain of the house as the high p.
4. 1 the mountain of the house of the LORD
4. 1 be established in the top of the mountains
4. 2 Come, and let us go up to the mountain
4. 7 LORD shall reign over them in mount Z
6. 1 Arise, contend thou before the mountains
6. 2 Hear ye, O mountains, the LORD'S contro.
7. 12 from sea to sea, and: .mountain to mou.
Nah. 1. 5 The mountains quake at him, and the h.
1. 15 Behold upon the mountains the feet of
3. 18 thy people is scattered upon the mount.
Hab. 3. 3 the holy one from mount Paran. Selah
3. 10 The mountains saw thee, they trembled
Zeph. 3. 11 be haughty because of my holy mountain
Hag. 1. 8 Go up to the mountain, and bring wood
1. 11 upon the land, and upon the mountains
Zech. 4. 7 Who (art) thou O great mountain? before
6. 1 four chariots out from between two mo
6. 1 the mountains (were) mountains of brass
8. 3 be called..the mountain..The holy mou.
14. 4 feet shall stand in that day upon the m.
14. 4 the mount of Olives shall cleave in the
14. 4 half of the mountain shall remove toward
14. 5 ye shall flee (to) the valley of the mount.
14. 5 the valley of the mountains shall reach
Mal. 1. 3 I hated Esau, and laid his mountains and

2. *Mountain, hill,* הַרְרָר הֲרָר *herer, harar.*
Gen. 14. 6 the Horites in their mount Seir, unto E.
Num 23. 7 brought me from Aram, out of the mou.
Deut 33. 15 for the chief things of the ancient moun.
Psa. 30. 7 thou hast made my mountain to stand
Psa. 36. 6 Thy righteousness (is) like the great mo.
76. 4 more glorious..than the mountains of p.
87. 1 His foundation (is) in the holy mountains
133. 3 that descended upon the mountains of Z.
Song 4. 8 look..from the mountains of the leopards
Jer. 17. 3 O my mountain in the field, I will give thy
Hab. 3. 6 the everlasting mountains were scattered

3. *Something set up, station,* מֻצָּב *mutstsab.*
Isa. 29. 3 will lay siege against thee with a mount

4. *What is raised up, mount,* סֹלְלָה *solelah.*
Jer. 6. 6 Hew ye down trees, and cast a mount a.
32. 24 Behold the mounts, they are come unto
33. 4 which are thrown down by the mounts
Eze. 4. 2 build a fort against it, and cast a mount
17. 17 by casting up mounts, and building forts
21. 22 against the gates, to cast a mount..to b.
26. 8 cast a mount against thee, and lift up the
Dan. 11. 15 of the north shall come, and cast up a m.

5. *Round tower, height,* טוּר *tur.*
Dan. 2. 35 became a great mountain, and filled the
2. 45 that the stone was cut out of the mount.

6. *Mount, mountain, hill,* ὄρος *oros.*
Matt. 4. 8 taketh him up into an exceeding high m.
5. 1 he went up into a mountain: and when
8. 1 When he was come down from the moun.
14. 23 he went up into a mountain apart to pray
15. 29 went up into a mountain, and sat down
17. 1 bringeth them up into an high mountain
17. 9 as they came down from the mountain, J.
17. 20 ye shall say unto this mountain, Remove
18. 12 goeth into the mountains, and seeketh that
21. 1 were come. unto the mount of Olives
21. 21 if ye shall say unto this mountain, Be thou
24. 3 as he sat upon the mount of Olives, the d.
24. 16 let them which be in Judea flee into the m.
26. 30 they went out into the mount of Olives
28. 16 went away into Galilee, into a mountain
Mark 3. 13 he goeth up into a mountain, and calleth
5. 5 night and day, he was in the mountains
5. 11 there was there, nigh [unto the mountains]
6. 46 And..he departed into a mountain to p.
9. 2 leadeth them up into an high mountain
9. 9 as they came down from the mountain
11. 1 at the mount of Olives, he sendeth forth
11. 23 whosoever shall say unto this mountain
13. 3 as he sat upon the mount of Olives, over
13. 14 let them that be in Judea flee to the mo.
14. 26 And..they went out into the mount of O
Luke 3. 5 every mountain and hill shall be brought
4. 5 [the devil, taking him up into an high m.]
6. 12 that he went out into a mountain to pray
8. 32 an herd of many swine feeding on the m.
9. 28 and went up into a mountain to pray
19. 29 at the mount called (the mount) of Olives
19. 37 now at the descent of the mount of Olives
21. 21 let them which are in Judea flee to the m.
21. 37 abode in the mount that is called..of Ol
22. 39 went, as he was wont, to the mount of O
23. 30 Then shall they begin to say to the mou
John 4. 20 Our fathers worshipped in this mountain
4. 21 when ye shall neither in this mountain
6. 3 Jesus went up into a mountain, and there
6. 15 departed again into a mountain himself
8. 1 [Jesus went unto the mount of Olives]
Acts 1. 12 from the mount called Olivet, which is
7. 30 appeared to him in the wilderness of m.
7. 38 angel which spake to him in the mount
1 Co. 13. 2 so that I could remove mountains, and
Gal. 4. 24 one from the mount Sinai, which gender
4. 25 For this Agar is mount Sinai in Arabia
Heb. 8. 5 the pattern showed to thee in the mount
11. 38 they wandered in deserts, and mountains
12. 18 For ye are not come unto the [mount] that
12. 20 if so much as a beast touch the mountain
12. 22 ye are come unto mount Sion, and unto
2 Pe. 1. 18 when we were with him in the holy mount
Rev. 6. 14 every mountain and island were moved
6. 15 in the dens and in the rocks of the moun
6. 16 said to the mountains and rocks, Fall on
8. 8 as it were a great mountain burning with
14. 1 a Lamb stood on the mount Sion, and with
16. 20 fled away, and the mountains were not
17. 9 The seven heads are seven mountains, on
21. 10 in the spirit to a great and high mountain

[*See also* Abarim, Ararat, Baalah, Baal hermon, Beth-el, Bether, Carmel, Ebal, Ephraim, Ephron, Gerizim, Gilboa, Gilead, Halak, Heres, Hermon, Hor, Horeb, Jearim, Lebanon, Moriah, Naphtali, Nebo, Olivet, Paran, Perazim, Samaria, Seir, Shaphar, Sion, Sinai, Tabor, Zalmon, Zemaraim Zion, &c.]

MOUNT up, to —

1. *To raise self up,* אָבַךְ *abak,* 7.
Isa. 9. 18 they shall mount up..the lifting up of

2. *To go up high,* גָּבַהּ *gabah,* 5.
Job 39. 27 Doth the eagle mount up at thy command

3. *To go up,* עָלָה *alah.*
Job 20. 6 Though his excellency mount up to the
Psa. 107. 26 They mount up to the heaven, they go down
Isa. 40. 31 they shall mount up with wings as eagles
Jer. 51. 53 Though Babylon should mount up to he.

4. *To be high,* רוּם *rum.*
Eze. 10. 16 lifted up their wings to mount up from

5. *To be high, lifted up,* רָמַם *ramam,* 2.
Eze. 10. 19 lifted up their wings, and mounted up

MOUNTING up —
Going up, ascent, step, מַעֲלָה *maaleh.*
Isa. 15. 5 by the mounting up of Luhith with we.

MOURN, to —

1. *To mourn,* אָבַל *abal.*
Job 14. 22 and his soul within him shall mourn
Isa. 3. 26 her gates shall lament and mourn; and
24. 4 The earth mourneth..fadeth away, the
24. 7 The new wine mourneth, the vine langu.
33. 9 The earth mourneth (and) languisheth
Jer. 4. 28 For this shall the earth mourn, and the
12. 4 How long shall the land mourn, and the
12. 11 desolate it mourneth unto me; the whole
14. 2 Judah mourneth, and the gates thereof
23. 10 for because of swearing the land mourneth.
Hos. 4. 3 Therefore shall the land mourn, and every
10. 5 the people thereof shall mourn over it
Joel 1. 9 the priests, the LORD'S ministers, mourn
1. 10 The field is wasted, the land mourneth
Amos 1. 2 the habitations of the shepherds shall m.
8. 8 and every one mourn that dwelleth the.
9. 5 and all that dwell therein shall mourn

2. *Mourning,* אָבֵל *abel.*
Psa. 35. 14 I bowed down heavily, as one that mou.
Isa. 61. 2 day..of our God; to comfort all that mo.
61. 3 To appoint unto them that mourn in Zion
Lam. 1. 4 The ways of Zion do mourn, because none

3. *To show self a mourner,* אָבַל *abal,* 7.
Gen. 37. 34 loins, and mourned for his son many days
Exod 33. 4 heard these evil tidings, they mourned
Num 14. 39 Moses told..and the people mourned gr.
1 Sa. 15. 35 Samuel mourned for Saul: and the LORD
16. 1 How long wilt thou mourn for Saul, seeing
2 Sa. 13. 37 And (David) mourned for his son every day
14. 2 that had a long time mourned for the dead
19. 1 the king weepeth and mourneth for Abs.
1 Ch. 7. 22 Ephraim their father mourned many days
2 Ch. 35. 24 Judah and Jerusalem mourned for Josiah
Ezra 10. 6 he mourned because of the transgression of
Neh. 1. 4 wept, and mourned (certain) days, and f.
8. 9 holy unto the LORD your God; mourn not
Isa. 66. 10 Rejoice..with her, all ye that mourn for
Eze. 7. 12 let not..buyer rejoice, nor..seller mourn
7. 27 The king shall mourn, and the prince sh.
Dan. 10. 2 In those days I Daniel was mourning th.

4. *To lament, mourn,* אָנָה *anah.*
Isa. 19. 8 The fishers also shall mourn, and all they

5. *To be sighing, to sigh,* אָנַח *anach,* 2.
Prov 29. 2 the wicked beareth rule, the people mo.

6. *To weep,* בָּכָה *bakah.*
Gen. 50. 3 Egyptians mourned for him three score
Num 20. 29 saw..they mourned for Aaron thirty days

7. *To be grieved, pained,* דָּאַב *daab.*
Psa. 88. 9 Mine eye mourneth by reason of affliction

8. *To meditate, mutter,* הָגָה *hagah.*
Isa. 16. 7 foundations of Kir-hareseth shall ye mou.
38. 14 I did mourn as a dove: mine eyes fail
59. 11 We roar all like bears, and mourn sore
Jer. 48. 31 and..shall mourn for the men of Kir-he.

9. *To sound, make a noise,* הָמָה *hamah.*
Eze. 7. 16 all of them mourning, every one for his i.

10. *To howl, groan,* נָהַם *naham.*
Prov. 5. 11 thou mourn at the last, when thy flesh and
Eze. 24. 23 ye shall pine away..and mourn one tow.

11. *To move, bemoan,* נוּד *nud.*
Job 2. 11 to come to mourn with him and to comf.

12. *To beat (the breast), mourn, lament,* סָפַד *saphad.*
Gen. 23. 2 Abraham came to mourn for Sarah, and
50. 10 there they mourned with a great and very
2 Sa. 1. 12 they mourned and wept, and fasted until
3. 31 gird you with sackcloth, and mourn before
11. 26 was dead, she mourned for her husband
1 Ki. 13. 29 the old prophet came to the city, to mo.
13. 30 they mourned over him..Alas, my broth.
14. 13 all Israel shall mourn for him, and bury
14. 18 all Israel mourned for him, according to
Eccl. 3. 4 a time to mourn, and a time to dance
Eze. 24. 16 yet neither shalt thou mourn nor weep
24. 23 ye shall not mourn nor weep; but ye shall
Zech. 7. 5 When ye fasted and mourned in the fifth
12. 10 they shall mourn for him, as one mourn.
12. 12 the land shall mourn, every family apart

13. *To be black, to mourn,* קָדַר *qadar.*
Job 5. 11 that those which mourn may be exalted to
30. 28 I went mourning without the sun: I stood
Psa. 38. 6 I am troubled..I go mourning all the day
42. 9 why go I mourning because of the oppre.
43. 2 why go I mourning because of the oppr.

14. *To rule, mourn,* רוּד *rud,* 5.
Psa. 55. 2 I mourn in my complaint, and make a

15. *To bewail, lament,* θρηνέω *thrēneō.*
Matt 11. 17 we have mourned unto you, and ye have
Luke 7. 32 we have mourned to you, and ye have not

16. *To beat (the breast),* κόπτομαι *koptomai.*
Matt 24. 30 then shall all the tribes of the earth mo.

17. *To mourn, grieve, sorrow,* πενθέω *pentheō.*
Matt. 5. 4 Blessed (are) they that mourn: for they
9. 15 Can the children of the bridechamber m.
Mark 16. 10 [that had been with him, as they mourned]
Luke 6. 25 Woe unto you that laugh..for ye shall m.
1 Co. 5. 2 ye are puffed up, and have not rather m.

Jas. 4. 9 Be afflicted, and mourn, and weep: let
Rev. 18. 11 merchants of the earth shall weep and m.

MOURN, to cause to —
To make black, cause to mourn, קָדַר *qadar,* 5.
Eze. 31. 15 I caused Lebanon to mourn for him, and

MOURNER, MOURNING —
1. *Mourning one,* אָבֵל *abel.*
Gen. 37. 35 go down into the grave unto my son mo.
Esth. 6. 12 Haman hasted to his house mourning
Job 29. 25 sat..as one (that) comforteth the mourn.
Isa. 57. 18 restore comforts unto him, and to his m.

2. *Mourning,* אֵבֶל *ebel.*
Gen. 27. 41 The days of mourning for my father are
50. 10 he made a mourning for his father seven
50. 11 saw the mourning in the floor of Atad, they
50. 11 This (is) a grievous mourning to the Egy.
Deut 34. 8 so the days of weeping..mourning for M.
2 Sa. 11. 27 when the mourning was past, David sent
14. 2 put on now mourning apparel, and anoint
19. 2 the victory that day was..into mourning
Esth. 4. 3 great mourning among the Jews, and fa.
9. 22 was turned..from mourning into a good
Job 30. 31 My harp also is..to mourning, and my o.
Eccl. 7. 2 better to go to the house of mourning than
7. 4 heart of the wise (is) in the house of mo.
Isa. 60. 20 the days of thy mourning shall be ended
61. 3 the oil of joy for mourning, the garment
Jer. 6. 26 make thee mourning, (as for) an only son
16. 7 neither..tear (themselves) for them in m.
31. 13 I will turn their mourning into joy, and
Lam. 5. 15 ceased; our dance is turned into mourning
Eze. 24. 17 Forbear to cry, make no mourning for the
Amos 5. 16 they shall call the husbandman to mour
8. 10 I will turn your feasts into mourning, and
8. 10 I will make it as the mourning of an only
Mic. 1. 8 like the dragons, and mourning as the o.

3. *Vanity, iniquity,* אָוֶן *aven.*
Deut 26. 14 I have not eaten thereof in my mourning
Hos. 9. 4 as the bread of mourners; all that eat the

4. *A sigh, sighing,* אֲנָחָה *anachah.*
Isa. 51. 11 (and) sorrow and mourning shall flee away

5. *Weeping,* בְּכִית *bekith.*
Gen. 50. 4 when the days of his mourning were past

6. *Meditation, muttering,* הֶגֶה *hegeh.*
Eze. 2. 10 lamentations, and mourning, and

7. *Beating the breast, mourning,* מִסְפֵּד *misped.*
Psa. 30. 11 Thou hast turned for me my mourning into
Isa. 22. 12 call to weeping, and to mourning, and to
Joel 2. 12 Turn ye..with weeping, and with mour.
Mic. 1. 11 came not forth in the mourning of Beth.
Zech. 12. 11 In that day shall there be a great mourn.
12. 11 as the mourning of Hadadrimmon in the

8. *A mourning feast,* מַרְזֵחַ *marzeach.*
Jer. 16. 5 Enter not into the house of mourning, ne.

9 *To beat the breast, mourn,* סָפַד *saphad.*
Eccl. 12. 5 because..the mourners go about the stre.

10. *Lamentation, mourning,* תַּאֲנִיָּה *taaniyyah.*
Lam. 2. 5 in the daughter of Judah mourning and

11. *Leviathan,* לִוְיָתָן *livyathan.*
Job 3. 8 who are ready to raise up their mourning

12. *Lamentation, wailing,* ὀδυρμός *odurmos.*
Matt. 2. 18 lamentation, and weeping, and great mo
2 Co. 7. 7 your mourning, your fervent mind toward

13. *Sorrow, grief, mourning,* πένθος *penthos.*
Jas. 4. 9 let your laughter be turned to mourning
Rev. 18. 8 come in one day, death, and mourning, and

MOURNER, to feign self to be a —
To feign self to be a mourner, אָבַל *abal,* 7.
2 Sa. 14. 2 I pray thee, feign thyself to be a mourner

MOURNFULLY —
In blackness, קְדֹרַנִּית *qedorannith.*
Mal. 3. 14 that we have walked mournfully before the

MOURNING, to cause a —
To cause to mourn, אָבַל *abal,* 5.
Eze. 31. 15 he went down to the grave I caused a m.

MOURNING woman —
To cone, mourn, lament, קִין *qun,* 3a.
Jer. 9. 17 call for the mourning women, that they

MOUSE —
A mouse, עַכְבָּר *akbar.*
Lev. 11. 29 weasel, and the mouse, and the tortoise
1 Sa. 6. 4 Five golden emerods, and five golden mice
6. 5 and images of your mice that mar the land
6. 11 the coffer with the mice of gold, and the
6. 18 the golden mice..the number of all the c.
Isa. 66. 17 eating..the abomination, and the mouse

MOUTH —
1. *Throat,* גָּרוֹן *garon.*
Psa. 149. 6 the high (praises) of God (be) in their mo.

2. *Palate,* חֵךְ *chek.*
Job 12. 11 Doth not the ear try words?..the mouth
20. 13 it not, but keep it still within his mouth
31. 30 Neither have I suffered my mouth to sin
33. 2 Behold..my tongue hath spoken in my m.
34. 3 the ear trieth words, as the mouth tasteth
Prov. 5. 3 a strange woman..her mouth (is) smooth.
8. 7 For my mouth shall speak truth; and w.
Song 5. 16 His mouth (is) most sweet; yea, he (is) al.
Hos. 8. 1 (Set) the trumpet to thy mouth. (He shall

3. *Cheek,* עֲדִי *adi.*
Psa. 32. 9 whose mouth must be held in with bit and
103. 5 Who satisfieth thy mouth with good (thi.)

4. *Mouth,* פֶּה *peh.*
Gen. 4. 11 which hath opened her mouth to receive
8. 11 in her mouth (was) an olive leaf pluckt off
24. 57 call the damsel, and enquire at her mou.
29. 2 a great stone (was) upon the well's mouth
29. 3 they rolled the stone from the well's mo.
29. 3 put the stone again upon the well's mouth
29. 8 they roll the stone from the well's mouth
29. 10 and rolled the stone from the well's mou.
42. 27 money..behold, it (was) in his sack's mo.
43. 12 brought again in the mouth of your sacks
43. 21 man's money (was) in the mouth of his s.
44. 1 put every man's money in his sack's mouth
44. 2 in the sack's mouth of the youngest, and
44. 8 money which we found in our sacks' mo.
45. 12 (it is) my mouth that speaketh unto you
Exod. 4. 11 Who hath made man's mouth? or who m.
4. 12 therefore go, and I will be with thy mouth
4. 15 speak unto him, and put words in his m.
4. 15 will be with thy mouth and with his mo.
4. 16 he shall be to thee instead of a mouth, and
13. 9 that the LORD'S law may be in thy mouth
23. 13 neither let it be heard out of thy mouth
Num. 12. 8 With him will I speak mouth to mouth
16. 30 the earth open her mouth, and swallow
16. 32 the earth opened her mouth, and swallo.
22. 28 the LORD opened the mouth of the ass; and
22. 38 the word that God putteth in my mouth
23. 5 the LORD put a word in Balaam's mouth
23. 12 that which the LORD hath put in my mo.?
23. 16 put a word in his mouth, and said, Go
26. 10 the earth opened her mouth, and swallo.
30. 2 to all that proceedeth out of his mouth
32. 24 which hath proceeded out of your mouth
35. 30 be put to death by the mouth of witnesses
Deut. 8. 3 that proceedeth out of the mouth of the L.
11. 6 how the earth opened her mouth, and s.
17. 6 At the mouth of two..at the mouth of one
18. 18 and will put my words in his mouth; and
19. 15 at the mouth of two..or at the mouth of
23. 23 which thou hast promised with thy mouth
30. 14 word (is) very nigh unto thee, in thy mo.
31. 19 put it in their mouths, that this song may
31. 21 shall not be forgotten out of the mouths
32. 1 and hear, O earth, the words of my mouth
Josh. 1. 8 the law shall not depart out of thy mouth
6. 10 shall (any) word proceed out of your mo.
9. 14 and asked not..at the mouth of the LORD
10. 18 Roll great stones upon the mouth of the
10. 22 Open the mouth of the cave, and bring
10. 27 and laid great stones in the cave's mouth
Judg. 7. 6 lapped, (putting) their hand to their mo.
9. 38 Where (is) now thy mouth, wherewith thou
11. 35 for I have opened my mouth unto the L.
11. 36 thou hast opened thy mouth unto the L.
11. 36 that which hath proceeded out of thy m.
18. 19 Hold thy peace, lay..hand upon thy mo.
1 Sa. 1. 12 it came to pass..that Eli marked her m.
2. 1 my mouth is enlarged over mine enemies
2. 3 let (not) arrogancy come out of your mo.
14. 26 but no man put his hand to his mouth: for
14. 27 put his hand to his mouth; and his eyes
17. 35 and delivered (it) out of his mouth: and
2 Sa. 1. 16 for thy mouth hath testified against thee
14. 3 So Joab put the words in her mouth
14. 19 put all these words in the mouth of thine
18. 25 If he (be) alone, (there is) tidings in his m.
22. 9 fire out of his mouth devoured: coals were
1 Ki. 7. 31 the mouth of it within the chapiter and
7. 31 but the mouth thereof (was) round..the
7. 31 also upon the mouth of it (were) gravings
8. 15 which spake with his mouth unto David
8. 24 thou spakest also with thy mouth, and
13. 21 Forasmuch as thou hast disobeyed the m.
17. 24 the word of the LORD in thy mouth (is)
19. 18 and every mouth which hath not kissed
22. 13 (declare) good unto the king with one m.
22. 22 I will be a lying spirit in the mouth of all
22. 23 LORD hath put a lying spirit in the mouth
2 Ki. 4. 34 put his mouth upon his mouth, and his e.
1 Ch. 16. 12 his wonders, and the judgments of his m.
2 Ch. 6. 4 which he spake with his mouth to my fa.
6. 15 spakest with thy mouth, and hast fulfilled
18. 21 and be a lying spirit in the mouth of all
18. 22 LORD hath put a lying spirit in the mouth
35. 22 unto the words of Necho from the mouth
36. 12 (speaking) from the mouth of the LORD
36. 21 To fulfil the word of the LORD by the m.
36. 22 that the word of the LORD..by the mouth
Ezra 1. 1 that the word of the LORD by the mouth
Neh. 9. 20 withheldest not thy manna from their m.
Esth. 7. 8 As the word went out of the king's mouth
Job 3. 1 After this opened Job his mouth, and cur.
5. 15 from their mouth, and from the hand of
5. 16 hath hope, and iniquity stoppeth her m.
7. 11 Therefore I will not refrain my mouth; I
8. 2 the words of thy mouth..a strong wind
8. 21 Till he fill thy mouth with laughing, and
9. 20 If I justify myself, mine own mouth shall
15. 5 For thy mouth uttereth thine iniquity, and
15. 6 Thine own mouth condemneth thee, and
15. 13 and lettest..words go out of thy mouth
15. 30 by the breath of his mouth shall he go
16. 5 I would strengthen you with my mouth
16. 10 They have gaped upon me with their m.
19. 16 my servant..I entreated him with my m.
Job 20. 12 Though wickedness be sweet in his mouth
21. 5 Mark me..and lay..hand upon..mouth
22. 22 Receive, I pray thee, the law from his m.
23. 4 I would..fill my mouth with arguments
23. 12 I have esteemed the words of his mouth
29. 9 The princes..laid (their) hand on their m.
29. 23 they opened their mouth wide (as) for the
31. 27 heart..or my mouth hath kissed my hand
32. 5 no answer in the mouth of (these) three
33. 2 Behold, now I have opened my mouth, my
35. 16 Therefore doth Job open his mouth in v.
37. 2 and the sound (that) goeth out of his mo.
40. 4 what..I will lay mine hand upon my mo.
40. 23 that he can draw up Jordan into his mo.
41. 19 Out of his mouth go burning lamps, (and)
41. 21 coals, and a flame goeth out of his mouth
Psa. 5. 9 For..no faithfulness in their mouth; their
8. 2 Out of the mouth of babes and sucklings
10. 7 His mouth is full of cursing and deceit
17. 3 I am purposed..my mouth shall not tran.
17. 10 fat: with their mouth they speak proudly
18. 8 fire out of his mouth devoured: coals w.
19. 14 Let the words of my mouth, and the me.
22. 13 They gaped upon me (with) their mouths
22. 21 Save me from the lion's mouth: for thou
33. 6 host of them by the breath of his mouth
34. 1 his praise (shall) continually (be) in my m.
35. 21 they opened their mouth wide against me
36. 3 The words of his mouth (are) iniquity and
37. 30 The mouth of the righteous speaketh wi.
38. 13 as a dumb man (that) openeth not his m.
38. 14 as a man..in whose mouth (are) no repr.
39. 1 I will keep my mouth with a bridle, wh.
39. 9 I was dumb, I opened not my mouth
40. 3 And he hath put a new song in my mouth
49. 3 My mouth shall speak of wisdom; and the
50. 16 shouldest take my covenant in thy mou.?
50. 19 Thou givest thy mouth to evil, and thy
51. 15 and my mouth shall show forth thy praise
54. 2 O God; give ear to the words of my mouth
55. 21 (The words) of his mouth were smoother
58. 6 Break their teeth, O God, in their mouth
59. 7 Behold, they belch out with their mouth
59. 12 (For) the sin of their mouth..the words
62. 4 they bless with their mouth, but they cur.
63. 5 my mouth shall praise..with joyful lips
63. 11 the mouth of them that speak lies shall
66. 14 my lips have uttered, and my mouth hath
66. 17 I cried unto him with my mouth, and he
69. 15 let not the pit shut her mouth upon me
71. 8 Let my mouth be filled (with) thy praise
71. 15 My mouth shall show forth thy righteou.
73. 9 They set their mouth against the heavens
78. 1 incline your ears to the words of my mo.
78. 2 I will open my mouth in a parable: I w.
78. 30 while their meat (was) yet in their mouths
78. 36 they did flatter him with their mouth, and
81. 10 open thy mouth wide, and I will fill it
89. 1 with my mouth will I make known thy
105. 5 his wonders, and the judgments of his m
107. 42 and all iniquity shall stop her mouth
109. 2 the mouth of the wicked and the mouth
109. 30 I will greatly praise..LORD with my mo.
115. 5 They have mouths, but they speak not
119. 13 I declared all the judgments of thy mouth
119. 43 take not the word of truth..out of my m.
119. 72 The law of thy mouth (is) better unto me
119. 88 so shall I keep the testimony of thy mo.
119. 103 (yea, sweeter) than honey to my mouth!
119. 108 Accept the free will offerings of my mo.
119. 131 I opened my mouth, and panted: for I l.
126. 2 Then was our mouth filled with laughter
135. 16 They have mouths, but they speak not
135. 17 neither is there..breath in their mouths
138. 4 when they hear the words of thy mouth
141. 3 Set a watch, O LORD, before my mouth
141. 7 Our bones are scattered at the grave's m.
144. 8, 11 Whose mouth speaketh vanity, and
145. 21 My mouth shall speak the praise of the L.
Prov. 2. 6 out of his mouth..knowledge and under.
4. 5 decline from the words of my mouth
4. 24 Put away from thee a froward mouth, and
5. 7 and depart not from the words of my m.
6. 2 Thou art snared with the words of thy m.
6. 2 thou art taken with the words of thy m.
6. 12 wicked man, walketh with a froward m.
7. 24 Hearken..attend to the words of my m.
8. 8 All the words of my mouth (are) in righ.
8. 13 the evil way, and..froward mouth, do I
10. 6, 11 violence covereth the mouth of the w.
10. 11 The mouth of a righteous (man is) a well
10. 14 the mouth of the foolish (is) near destru.
10. 31 The mouth of the just bringeth forth wis.
10. 32 but the mouth of the wicked..frowardness
11. 9 An hypocrite with (his) mouth destroyeth
11. 11 overthrown by the mouth of the wicked
12. 6 the mouth of the upright shall deliver
12. 14 shall be satisfied..by the fruit of (his) m.
13. 2 man shall eat good by the fruit of (his) m.
13. 3 He that keepeth his mouth keepeth his
14. 3 In the mouth of the foolish (is) a rod of
15. 2 the mouth of fools poureth out foolishness
15. 14 the mouth of fools feedeth on foolishness
15. 23 A man hath joy by the answer of his mo.
15. 28 the mouth of the wicked poureth out evil
16. 10 his mouth transgresseth not in judgment
16. 23 The heart of the wise teacheth his mouth
16. 26 laboureth..for his mouth craveth it of him
18. 4 The words of a man's mouth (are as) deep
18. 6 A fool's..mouth calleth for strokes
18. 7 A fool's mouth (is) his destruction, and
18. 20 shall be satisfied with the fruit of his m.

Prov 19. 24 will not so much as bring it to his mouth
19. 28 the mouth of the wicked devoureth iniq.
20. 17 but..his mouth shall be filled with gravel
21. 23 Whoso keepeth his mouth and his tongue
22. 14 The mouth of strange women (is) a deep
24. 7 a fool..openeth not his mouth in the gate
26. 7, 9 so (is) a parable in the mouth of fools
26. 15 it grieveth him to bring it..to his mouth
26. 28 and a flattering mouth worketh ruin
27. 2 Let..man praise thee..not thine own m.
30. 20 she eateth, and wipeth her mouth, and
30. 32 thought evil, (lay) thine hand upon thy m.
31. 8 Open thy mouth for the dumb in the cause
31. 9 Open thy mouth, judge righteously, and
31. 26 She openeth her mouth with wisdom; and
Eccl. 5. 2 Be not rash with thy mouth, and let not
5. 6 Suffer not thy mouth to cause thy flesh
6. 7 All the labour of man (is) for his mouth
10. 12 The words of a wise man's mouth (are)
10. 13 The beginning of the words of his mouth
Song 1. 2 Let him kiss me with the kisses of his m.
Isa. 1. 20 for the mouth of the LORD hath spoken
5. 14 and opened her mouth without measure
6. 7 he laid (it) upon my mouth, and said, Lo
9. 12 they shall devour Israel with open mouth
9. 17 evil doer, and every mouth speaketh folly
10. 14 that moved the wing, or opened the mo.
11. 4 smite the earth with the rod of his mouth
19. 7 by the brooks, by the mouth of the brooks
29. 13 as this people draw near..with their mo.
30. 2 That walk..and have not asked at my m.
34. 16 for my mouth it hath commanded, and
40. 5 for the mouth of the LORD hath spoken
45. 23 the word is gone out of my mouth (in) ri.
48. 3 they went forth out of my mouth, and I
49. 2 he hath made my mouth like a sharp sw.
51. 16 I have put my words in thy mouth, and
52. 15 the kings shall shut their mouths at him
53. 7 he was afflicted; yet he opened not his m.
53. 7 as a sheep..so he openeth not his mouth
53. 9 neither (was any) deceit in his mouth
55. 11 word be that goeth forth out of my mou.
57. 4 against whom make ye a wide mouth..dra.
58. 14 for the mouth of the LORD hath spoken (it)
59. 21 my words which I have put in thy mouth
59. 21 out of thy mouth, nor out of the mouth of
59. 21 nor out of the mouth of thy seed's seed
62. 2 which the mouth of the LORD shall name
Jer. 1. 9 put forth his hand, and touched my mouth
1. 9 Behold, I have put my words in thy mo.
5. 14 I will make my words in thy mouth fire
7. 28 is perished, and is cut off from their mou.
9. 8 with his mouth, but in heart he layeth his
9. 12 to whom the mouth of the LORD hath sp.
9. 20 let your ear receive the word of his mouth
12. 2 thou (art) near in their mouth, and far fr.
15. 19 from the vile, thou shalt be as my mouth
23. 16 they speak..not out of the mouth of the
32. 4 and shall speak with him mouth to mouth
34. 3 he shall speak with thee mouth to mouth
36. 4 Baruch wrote from the mouth of Jeremi.
36. 6 which thou hast written from my mouth
36. 17 How didst thou write all these..at his m.?
36. 18 all these words unto me with his mouth
36. 27 Baruch wrote at the mouth of Jeremiah
36. 32 who wrote therein, from the mouth of J.
44. 17 thing goeth forth out of our own mouth
44. 25 wives have both spoken with your mouths
44. 26 shall no more be named in the mouth of
45. 1 written these words in a book at the mo.
48. 28 her nest in the sides of the hole's mouth
51. 44 I will bring forth out of his mouth that
Lam. 2. 16 All thine enemies have opened their mo.
3. 29 He putteth his mouth in the dust, if so be
3. 38 Out of the mouth of the most High proc.
3. 46 All our enemies have opened their mouths
Eze. 2. 8 open thy mouth, and eat that I give thee
3. 2 So I opened my mouth, and he caused me
3. 3 it was in my mouth as honey for sweetness
3. 17 therefore hear the word at my mouth, and
3. 27 I will open thy mouth, and thou shalt say
4. 14 came there abominable flesh into my mo.
16. 56 Sodom was not mentioned by thy mouth
16. 63 never open thy mouth any more because
21. 22 to open the mouth in the slaughter, to lift
24. 27 In that day shall thy mouth be opened to
29. 21 I will give thee the opening of the mouth
33. 7 thou shalt hear the word at my mouth, and
33. 22 came and had opened my mouth, until he
33. 22 my mouth was opened, and I was no more
33. 31 for with their mouth they show much love
34. 10 I will deliver my flock from their mouth
35. 13 Thus with your mouth ye have boasted
Dan. 10. 3 neither came flesh nor wine in my mouth
10. 16 then I opened my mouth, and spake, and
Hos. 2. 17 the names of Baalim out of her mouth, and
6. 5 I have slain them by the words of my m.
Joel 1. 5 new wine; for it is cut off from your m.
Amos 3. 12 As the shepherd taketh out of the mouth
Mic. 3. 5 he that putteth not into their mouths, they
4. 4 for the mouth of the LORD of hosts hath
6. 12 their tongue (is) deceitful in their mouth
7. 5 keep the doors of thy mouth from her that
7. 16 they shall lay (their) hand upon (their) m.
Nah. 3. 12 they shall even fall into the mouth of the
Zeph. 3. 13 a deceitful tongue be found in their mouth
Zech. 5. 8 he cast the weight of lead upon the mouth
8. 9 these words by the mouth of the prophets
9. 7 I will take away his blood out of his m.
14. 12 tongue shall consume away in their mouth
Mal. 2. 6 The law of truth was in his mouth, and
2. 7 and they should seek the law at his mouth

5. *Mouth,* פּוּם *pum.*
Dan. 4. 31 While the word (was) in the king's mouth
6. 17 stone was brought, and laid upon the m.
6. 22 hath shut the lions' mouths, that they have
7. 5 three ribs in the mouth of it between the
7. 8 eyes..and a mouth speaking great things
7. 20 and a mouth that spake very great things

6. *Face,* פָּנִים *panim.*
Prov 15. 14 the mouth of fools feedeth on foolishness

7. *Gate,* תְּרַע *tera.*
Dan. 3. 26 Nebuchadnezzar came near to the mouth

8. *Word,* λόγος *logos.*
Acts 15. 27 shall also tell..the same things by mouth

9. *Mouth,* στόμα *stoma.*
Matt. 4. 4 that proceedeth out of the mouth of God
5. 2 he opened his mouth, and taught them
12. 34 out of the abundance of the heart the m.
13. 35 saying, I will open my mouth in parables
15. 8 [draweth nigh unto me with their mouth]
15. 11 Not that which goeth into the mouth de.
15. 11 but that which cometh out of the mouth
15. 17 that whatsoever entereth in at the mouth
15. 18 those things which proceed out of the m.
17. 27 when thou hast opened his mouth, thou
18. 16 that in the mouth of two or three witne.
21. 16 Out of the mouth of babes and sucklings
Luke 1. 64 his mouth was opened immediately, and
1. 70 As he spake by the mouth of his holy pr.
4. 22 words which proceeded out of his mouth
6. 45 for of the abundance of the heart his m.
11. 54 seeking to catch something out of his m.
19. 22 Out of thine own mouth will I judge thee
21. 15 I will give you a mouth and wisdom, which
22. 71 for we ourselves have heard of his own m.
John 19. 29 put (it) upon hyssop, and put (it) to his m.
Acts 1. 16 the Holy Ghost, by the mouth of David
3. 18 which God before had showed by the m.
3. 21 which God hath spoken by the mouth of
4. 25 Who by the mouth of thy servant David
8. 32 before his shearer..opened he not his m.
8. 35 Philip opened his mouth, and began at the
10. 34 Peter opened (his) mouth, and said, Of a
11. 8 hath at any time entered into my mouth
15. 7 the Gentiles by my mouth should hear
18. 14 when Paul was now about to open (his) m.
22. 14 and shouldest hear the voice of his mouth
23. 2 that stood by him to smite him on the m.
Rom. 3. 14 Whose mouth (is) full of cursing and bit.
3. 19 that every mouth may be stopped, and all
10. 8 The word is nigh thee..in thy mouth, and
10. 9 thou shalt confess with thy mouth the L.
10. 10 with the mouth confession is made unto
15. 6 That ye may with one mind..one mouth
2 Co. 6. 11 our mouth is open unto you, our heart is
13. 1 In the mouth of two or three witnesses
Eph. 4. 29 communication proceed out of your mouth
6. 19 that I may open my mouth boldly, to make
Col. 3. 8 filthy communication out of your mouth
2 Th. 2. 8 shall consume with the spirit of his mouth
2 Ti. 4. 17 I was delivered out of the mouth of the
Heb. 11. 33 obtained promises, stopped the mouths of
Jas. 3. 3 we put bits in the horses' mouths, that
3. 10 Out of the same mouth proceedeth bless.
1 Pe. 2. 22 no sin, neither was guile found in his m.
Jude 16 and their mouth speaketh great swelling
Rev. 1. 16 out of his mouth went a sharp two edged
2. 16 against them with the sword of my mouth
3. 16 nor hot, I will spue thee out of my mouth
9. 17 out of their mouths issued fire and smoke
9. 18 brimstone, which issued out of their mo.
9. 19 their power is in their mouth, and in their
10. 9 it shall be in thy mouth sweet as honey
10. 10 and it was in my mouth sweet as honey
11. 5 fire proceedeth out of their mouth, and
12. 15 And the serpent cast out of his mouth wa.
12. 16 the earth opened her mouth, and swallowed
12. 16 flood which the dragon cast out his mouth
13. 2 bear, and his mouth as the mouth of a lion
13. 5 there was given unto him a mouth speak.
13. 6 he opened his mouth in blasphemy against
14. 5 in their mouth was found no guile: for
16. 13 like frogs..out of the mouth of the dragon
16. 13 the mouth of the beast, and out of the m.
19. 15 out of his mouth goeth a sharp sword, that
19. 21 which (sword) proceeded out of his mouth

MOUTH, roof of the —
Palate, חֵךְ *chek.*
Job 29. 10 tongue cleaved to the roof of their mouth
Psa. 137. 6 let my tongue cleave to the roof of my m.
Song 7. 9 the roof of thy mouth like the best wine
Lam. 4. 4 cleaveth to the roof of his mouth for th.
Eze. 3. 26 thy tongue cleave to the roof of thy mouth

MOUTH, to stop the —
To stop the mouth, ἐπιστομίζω *epistomizō.*
Titus 1. 11 Whose mouths must be stopped, who su.

MOVE, to —
1. *To move, tremble,* זוּעַ *zua.*
Esth. 5. 9 that he stood not up, nor moved for him

2. *To bend,* חָפֵץ *chaphets.*
Job 40. 17 He moveth his tail like a cedar: the sin.

3. *To move sharply,* חָרַץ *charats.*
Exod 11. 7 shall not a dog move his tongue, against
Josh 10. 21 none moved his tongue against any of the

4. *To move, flee, wander away,* נָדַד *nadad.*
Isa. 10. 14 and there was none that moved the wing

5. *To move,* נוּעַ *nua.*
1 Sa. 1. 13 only her lips moved, but her voice was not
Isa. 6. 4 the posts of the door moved at the voice

6. *To cause to move,* נוּעַ *nua,* 5.
2 Ki. 23. 18 Let him alone; let no man move his bones

7. *To cause to wave,* נוּף *nuph,* 5.
Deut 23. 25 thou shalt not move a sickle unto thy

8. *To move, persuade, remove,* סוּת *suth,* 5.
Josh 15. 18 she moved him to ask of her father a field
Judg. 1. 14 she moved him to ask of her father a field
2 Sa. 24. 1 he moved David against them to say, Go
2 Ch. 18. 31 and God moved them (to depart) from him
Job 2. 3 although thou movedst me against him

9. *To make, do,* עֲבַד *abad.*
Ezra 4. 15 that they have moved sedition within the

10. *To cause to fall, stumble,* פּוּק *puq,* 5.
Jer. 10. 4 they fasten it with nails..that it move not

11. *To move, cause to step,* פָּעַם *paam.*
Judg 13. 25 spirit of the LORD began to move him at

12. *To move, wink,* קָרַץ *qarats.*
Prov 16. 30 moving his lips he bringeth evil to pass

13. *To be angry, to trouble, tremble,* רָגַז *ragaz.*
2 Sa. 7. 10 dwell in a place of their own, and move
22. 8 the foundations of heaven moved and sh.
Psa. 18. 7 foundations also of the hills moved and
Mic. 7. 17 they shall move out of their holes like w.

14. *To move, shake,* רָחַף *rachaph,* 3.
Gen. 1. 2 spirit of God moved upon the face of the

15. *To teem, bring forth abundantly,* שָׁרַץ *sharats.*
Eze. 47. 9 every thing that liveth, which moveth

16. *A teeming creature,* שֶׁרֶץ *sherets.*
Lev. 11. 10 of all that move in the waters, and of

17. *To stir up, excite,* ἀνασείω *anaseiō.*
Mark 15. 11 the chief priests moved the people, that

18. *To move, agitate, shake, excite,* κινέω *kineō.*
Matt 23. 4 will not move them with one of their fin.
Acts 17. 28 in him we live, and move, and have our

MOVE lightly, to —
To move self lightly, קָלַל *qalal,* 7a.
Jer. 4. 24 they trembled, and all the hills moved l.

MOVE me, none of these things —
To make account of not even one thing, οὐδενὸς λόγον ποιέω *oudenos logon poieō.*
Acts 20. 24 none of these things move me, neither c.

MOVE, to make —
To cause to move, נוּד *nud,* 5.
2 Ki. 21. 8 Neither will I make the feet of Israel m.

MOVE self, to —
To go up and down, הָלַךְ *halak,* 7.
Prov. 23. 31 colour in the cup..it moveth itself aright

MOVABLE or moved, to be —
1. *To shake self, be shaken,* גָּעַשׁ *gaash,* 7, 7a.
Jer. 25. 16 they shall drink, and be moved, and be.
46. 7 flood, whose waters are moved as the riv.?
46. 8 and (his) waters are moved like the rivers

2. *To be moved,* הוּם *hum,* 2.
Ruth 1. 19 all the city was moved about them, and

3. *To move, sound, make a noise,* הָמָה *hamah.*
Song 5. 4 My beloved..my bowels were moved for

4. *To move, slip, fail,* מוֹט *mot.*
Psa. 46. 6 The heathen raged, the kingdoms were m.
55. 22 shall never suffer the righteous to be m.

5. *To be moved,* מוֹט *mot,* 2.
1 Ch. 16. 30 also shall be stable, that it be not moved
Job 41. 23 firm in themselves; they cannot be moved
Psa. 10. 6 hath said in his heart, I shall not be mo.
13. 4 that trouble me rejoice when I am moved
15. 5 He that doeth these..shall never be mo.
16. 8 is) at my right hand, I shall not be moved
21. 7 mercy of the most High he shall not be m.
30. 6 my prosperity I said, I shall never be m.
46. 5 she shall not be moved: God shall help
62. 2 my defence; I shall not be greatly moved
62. 6 He only..my defence; I shall not be mo.
93. 1 also is established, that it cannot be moved
96. 10 shall be established that it shall not be m.
112. 6 Surely he shall not be moved for ever
Prov 12. 3 the root of the righteous shall not be m.
Isa. 40. 20 a graven image, (that) shall not be moved
41. 7 it with nails, (that) it should not be moved

6. *A moving, tottering,* מוֹט *mot.*
Psa. 66. 9 and suffereth not our feet to be moved
121. 3 He will not suffer thy foot to be moved

7. *To move self, be moved,* מוֹט *mot,* 7.
Isa. 24. 19 is clean dissolved, the earth is moved exc.

8. *To shake, be moved, turned,* נוּט *nut.*
Psa. 99. 1 The LORD reigneth..let the earth be mov.

9. *To move, shake, wander,* נוּעַ *nua.*
Prov. 5. 6 her ways are moveable..thou canst not
Isa. 7. 2 his heart was moved, and the heart of
7. 2 as the trees of the wood are moved with
19. 1 idols of Egypt shall be moved at his pres.

10. *To be moved,* נָתַר *nathar.*
Job 37. 1 my heart trembleth, and is moved out of

11. *To tremble, be troubled, angry,* רָגַז *ragaz.*
2 Sa. 18. 33 the king was much moved, and went up
1 Ch. 17. 9 shall dwell in their place, and shall be m.
Isa. 14. 9 Hell from beneath is moved for thee to

12. *To shake, tremble,* רָעַשׁ *raash.*
Jer. 49. 21 The earth is moved at the noise of their

13. *To be shaken,* רָעַשׁ *raash,* 2.
Jer. 50. 46 earth is moved, and the cry is heard am.

14. *To move, agitate, shake, excite,* κινέω *kineō.*
Acts 21. 30 all the city was moved, and the people
Rev. 6. 14 every mountain and island were moved

15. *To fawn upon, cajole,* σαίνω *sainō.*
1 Th. 3. 3 That no man should be moved by these affl.

16. *To shake, agitate, toss,* σαλεύω *saleuō.*
Acts 2. 25 my right hand, that I should not be mo.

17. *To shake, trouble, disturb,* σείω *seiō.*
Matt 21. 10 all the city was moved, saying, Who is t.?

18. *To bear, carry,* φέρω *pherō.*
2 Pe 1. 21 men of God spake..moved by the Holy G.

MOVED away, be —
To move away, or over, μετακινέω *metakineō.*
Col. 1. 23 not moved away from the hope of the g.

MOVED, which cannot be —
Unshaken, ἀσάλευτος *asaleutos.*
Heb. 12. 28 receiving a kingdom which cannot be m.

MOVED with fear, to be —
To be careful, devout, εὐλαβέομαι *eulabeomai.*
Heb. 11. 7 moved with fear, prepared an ark to the

MOVER of —
To move, κινέω *kineō.*
Acts 24. 5 a mover of sedition among all the Jews

MOVING (creature or thing) —
1. *Moving,* נִיד *nid.*
Job 16. 5 and the moving of my lips should asswage
2. *A creeping thing,* רֶמֶשׂ *remes.*
Gen. 9. 3 Every moving thing that liveth shall be
3. *A teeming thing,* שֶׁרֶץ *sherets.*
Gen. 1. 20 the moving creature that hath life, and
4. *Movement, commotion,* κίνησις *kinēsis.*
John 5. 3 folk..[waiting for the moving of the water]

MOWER —
To shorten, reap, קָצַר *qatsar.*
Psa. 129. 7 Wherewith the mower filleth not his hand

MOWING, MOWN grass —
A shearing, mowing, cut grass, גֵּז *gez.*
Psa. 72. 6 come down like rain upon the mown grass
Amos 7. 1 the latter growth after the king's mowings

MO'-ZA, מוֹצָא *origin, offspring.*
1. A son of Caleb, son of Jephunneh. B.C. 1470.
1 Ch. 2. 46 Ephah..begat Haran, and M., and Gazez
2. A Benjamite, descendant of Saul. B.C. 1890.
1 Ch. 8. 36 Azmaveth, and Zimri; and Zimri begat M.
8. 37 M. begat Binea: Rapha (was) his son, Ele.
9. 42 Azmaveth, and Zimri; and Zimri begat M.
9. 43 And M. begat Binea; and Rephaiah his

MO'-ZAH, הַמֹּצָה.
A city in Benjamin, near Rosh, now *Kulonish* or *Mizzeh*
Josh. 18. 26 And Mizpeh, and Chephirah, and M.

MUCH —
1. *Heavy, weighty,* כָּבֵד *kabed.*
Exod. 12. 38 and flocks and herds, (even) very much c.
Num 20. 20 Edom came out against him with much
2. *Abundant, great, mighty,* כַּבִּיר *kabbir.*
Job 15. 10 very aged men, much elder than thy fat
31. 25 and because mine hand had gotten much
3. *Might,* מְאֹד *meod.*
Gen. 26. 16 Go from us; for thou art much mightier
34. 12 Ask me never so much dowry and gift, and
Ruth 1. 13 grieveth me much for your sakes, that
1 Sa. 18. 30 more wisely..so that his name was much
19. 2 Jonathan, Saul's son, delighted much in
2 Sa. 14. 25 there was none to be so much praised as
Neh. 6. 16 they were much cast down in their own
Psa. 119. 107 I am afflicted very much: quicken me, O
Isa. 56. 12 as this day and much more abundant
Jer. 2. 36 Why gaddest thou about so much to cha
4. *Abundance, increase,* מִרְבָּה *mirbah.*
Eze. 23. 32 and had in derision; it containeth much
5. *Bony, substantial,* עָצוּם *atsum.*
Psa. 35. 18 I will praise thee among much people
6. *To spread,* פָּשָׂה *pasah.*
Lev. 13. 35 if the scall spread much in the skin after
7. *Many, much,* רַב *rab.*
Gen. 30. 43 had much cattle, and maid servants, and
50. 20 as (it is) this day, to save much people a.
Num 21. 6 bit the people; and much people of Israel
Deut. 3. 19 your cattle..I know that ye have much
28. 38 Thou shalt carry much seed out into the
Josh 22. 8 Return with much riches unto your tents
22. 8 and with very much cattle, with silver
2 Sa. 13. 34 there came much people by the way of the
1 Ki. 10. 2 and very much gold, and precious stones
2 Ki. 12. 10 when they saw..much money in the chest
1 Ch. 18. 8 very much brass, wherewith Solomon m.
22. 8 because thou hast shed much blood upon
2 Ch. 17. 13 he had much business in the cities of J.
20. 25 in gathering of the spoil, it was so much
24. 11 when they saw that..much money, the
25. 13 three thousand of them, and took much
26. 10 he had much cattle, both in the low cou.
28. 8 and took also away much spoil from them
30. 13 there assembled at Jerusalem much peo.
32. 4 there was gathered much people together
32. 4 kings of Assyria come, and find much w.?
Psa. 19. 10 than gold, yea, than much fine gold; sw.
Prov 15. 6 In the house of the righteous (is) much
Isa. 21. 7 and he hearkened diligently with much he.
Eze. 17. 15 that they might give him horses and m.
22. 5 shall mock thee..infamous..much vexed
26. 7 horsemen, and companies, and much pe.
Jon. 4. 11 and their left hand; and..much cattle
8. *Abundance,* רֹב *rob.*
2 Ch. 27. 3 gate..and on the wall of Ophel he built m.
Psa. 33. 16 a mighty man is not delivered by much
Prov. 7. 21 With her much fair speech she caused him
13. 23 Much food (is in) the tillage of the poor
14. 4 much increase (is) by the strength of the
Eccl. 1. 18 in much wisdom (is) much grief; and he
9. *To cause to multiply, make abundant,* רָבָה *rabah,* 5.
Gen. 41. 49 Joseph gathered corn..very much, until
Josh 13. 1 there remaineth yet very much land to be
22. 8 with iron, and very much raiment: divide
2 Sa. 8. 8 And..king David took exceeding much
1 Ki. 4. 29 God gave Solomon wisdom..exceeding m.
2 Ki. 10. 18 Baal a little..Jehu shall serve him much
21. 6 wrought much wickedness in the sight of
21. 16 Manasseh shed innocent blood very much
1 Ch. 20. 2 he brought also exceeding much spoil out
2 Ch. 14. 13 and they carried away very much spoil
32. 27 Hezekiah had exceeding much riches and
33. 6 wrought much evil in the sight of the L.
Neh. 4. 10 is decayed, and (there is) much rubbish
Prov 25. 27 not good to eat much honey: so..to search
Eccl. 5. 12 (is) sweet, whether he eat little or much
5. 17 much sorrow and wrath with his sickness
5. 20 he shall not much remember the days of
9. 18 war: but one sinner destroyeth much g.
12. 12 and much study (is) a weariness of the fl.
Isa. 30. 33 the pile thereof (is) fire and much wood
Jer. 40. 12 gathered wine and summer fruits very m.
Hag. 1. 6 Ye have sown much, and bring in little
1. 9 Ye looked for much, and, lo, (it came) to
10. *Much, many, great,* שַׂגִּיא *saggi.*
Dan. 4. 12 the fruit thereof much, and in it (was) m.
7. 5 they said thus unto it, Arise, devour m.
7. 28 my cogitations much troubled me, and my
11. *Sufficient,* ἱκανός *hikanos.*
Luke 7. 12 and much people of the city was with her
Acts 5. 37 Judas..drew away [much] people after him
11. 24 and much people was added unto the L.
11. 26 with the church, and taught much people
19. 26 hath persuaded and turned away much p.
27. 9 Now, when much time was spent, and
12. *More, rather,* μᾶλλον *mallon.*
Matt. 6. 26 the fowls..Are ye not much better than
13. *Much, many,* πολύς *polus.*
Matt 6. 30 not much more..you, O ye of little faith
13. 5 stony places, where they had not much
26. 9 this ointment might have been sold for m.
Mark 1. 45 he went out, and began to publish (it) m.
4. 5 stony ground, where it had not much ea.
5. 10 he besought him much that he would not
5. 21 other side, much people gathered unto him
5. 24 much people followed him, and thronged
6. 34 Jesus, when he came out, saw much pe.
Luke 7. 47 Her sins..are forgiven; for she loved mu
8. 4 when much people were gathered tog. 7. 11.
9. 37 down from the hill, much people met him
10. 40 Martha was cumbered about much serving
12. 19 Soul, thou hast much goods laid up for m.
12. 48 much is given, of him shall be much req.
12. 48 to whom men have committed much, of
16. 10 that which is least is faithful also in mu.
16. 10 is unjust in the least is unjust also in much
John 3. 23 because there was much water there: and
6. 10 Now there was much grass in the place
7. 12 there was much murmuring among the p.
12. 9 Much people of the Jews therefore knew
12. 12 On the next day much people that were
12. 24 but if it die, it bringeth forth much fruit
14. 30 Hereafter I will not talk much with you
15. 5 the same bringeth forth much fruit: for
15. 8 is my Father glorified, that ye bear much
Acts 10. 2 which gave much alms to the people, and
14. 22 that we must through much tribulation
15. 7 when there had been much disputing, Pe.
16. 16 which brought her masters much gain by
18. 10 to hurt thee: for I have much people in
18. 27 helped them much which had believed
20. 2 and had given them much exhortation, he
26. 24 Paul..much learning doth make thee mad
27. 10 this voyage will be with hurt and much
Rom. 3. 2 Much every way: chiefly, because that
5. 9 Much more then, being now justified by his
5. 10 much more, being reconciled, we shall be
5. 15 much more the grace of God, and the gift
5. 17 much more they which receive abundance
9. 22 endured with much long suffering the v.
15. 22 I have been [much] hindered from coming
16. 6 Greet Mary, who bestowed much labour
16. 12 [Persis, which laboured much in the Lord]
1 Co. 2. 3 in weakness, and in fear, and in much tr.
12. 22 much more those members of the body
16. 19 Aquila and Priscila salute you much in
2 Co. 2. 4 For out of much affliction and anguish of
3. 9 much more doth the ministration of rig.
3. 11 much more that which remaineth (is) gl.
6. 4 as the ministers of God, in much patience
8. 4 Praying us with much entreaty that we
8. 15 He that (had gathered) much had nothing
8. 22 now much more diligent, upon the great
Phil. 2. 12 but now much more in my absence, work
1 Th. 1. 5 in the Holy Ghost, and in much assurance
1. 6 having received the word in much afflict.
2. 2 the gospel of God with much contention
1 Ti. 3. 8 not given to much wine, not greedy of fi.
2 Ti. 4. 14 Alexander the coppersmith did me much
Titus 2. 3 not given to much wine, teachers of good
Phm. 8 though I might be much bold in Christ to
Heb. 12. 9 shall we not much rather be in subjection
12. 25 much more (shall not) we (escape) if we
Jas. 5. 16 prayer of a righteous man availeth much
1 Pe. 1. 7 being much more precious than of gold
Rev. 5. 4 I wept [much], because no man was found
8. 3 there was given unto him much incense
19. 1 I heard a great voice of much people in
[*See also* And, as, discouraged, displeased, half so, heed, how, love, more, observed, perplexed, over, pain, pained, so, speaking, sufficient, too, twice as, very, work.]

MUCH, to ask, gather, take, or yield —
To cause to multiply, make abundant, רָבָה *rabah,* 5.
Gen. 34. 12 Ask me never so much dowry and gift, and
Exod 16. 18 he that gathered much had nothing over
Neh. 9. 37 it yieldeth much increase unto the kings
Jer. 2. 22 For though thou..take thee much soap

MUCH abroad —
To spread, be spread, פָּשָׂה *pasah.*
Lev. 13. 7 if the scab spread much abroad in the s.
13. 22 if it spread much abroad in the skin, then
13. 27 if it be spread much abroad in the skin

MUCH less, how —
How much less, אַף כִּי לֹא *aph ki lo.*
2 Ch. 32. 15 how much less shall your God deliver you

MUCH more —
1. *To cause to multiply, make abundant,* רָבָה *rabah,* 5.
Exod 36. 5 The people bring much more than enough
2 Ch. 25. 9 The LORD is able to give thee much more
2. *To (cause to) add,* יָסַף *yasaph,* 5.
1 Sa. 20. 13 The LORD do so and much more to Jona.

MUCH perplexed, to be —
To be in doubt or perplexity, διαπορέω *diaporeō.*
Luke 24. 4 as they were much perplexed thereabout

MUCH set by, to be —
To be great, גָּדַל *gadal,*
1 Sa. 26. 24 so let my life be much set by in the eyes

MUCH, to be so —
To be many, abundant, רָבָה *rabah.*
Gen. 43. 34 Benjamin's mess was five times so much

MUCH, too —
1. *To cause to or let remain over,* יָתַר *yathar,* 5.
Exod 36. 7 for all the work to make it, and too much
2. *Many, much, abundant,* רַב *rab.*
Num 16. 3, 7 (Ye take) too much upon you
Josh. 19. 9 the part of..Judah was too much for them
1 Ki. 12. 28 It is too much for you to go up to Jerus.

MUCH, very —
Much, many, abundant, רַב *rab.*
2 Ch. 32. 29 for God had given him substance very m.

MUFFLERS —
A veil, muffler, רַעַל *raal.*
Isa. 3. 19 the chains, and the bracelets, and the m.

MULBERRY TREE —
Baka tree, mulberry, בָּכָא *baka.*
2 Sa. 5. 23 upon them over against the mulberry trees
5. 24 a going in the tops of the mulberry trees
1 Ch. 14. 14 upon them over against the mulberry trees.
14. 15 going in the tops of the mulberry trees

MULE —
1. *A mule, separate one,* פֶּרֶד *pered.*
2 Sa. 13. 29 every man gat him up upon his mule, and
18. 9 Absalom rode upon a mule, and the mule
18. 9 the mule that (was) under him went away
1 Ki. 10. 25 spices, horses, and mules, a rate year by
18. 5 find grass to save the horses and mules al.
2 Ki. 5. 17 be given to thy servant two mules' burden
1 Ch. 12. 40 bread on asses, and on camels, and on m.
2 Ch. 9. 24 spices, horses and mules, a rate year by
Ezra 2. 66 their mules, two hundred forty and five
Neh. 7. 68 their mules, two hundred forty and five
Psa. 32. 9 Be ye not as the horse, (or) as the mule
Isa. 66. 20 in litters, and upon mules, and upon sw.
Eze. 27. 14 traded..with horses..horsemen and mu.
Zech. 14. 15 so shall be the plague of the..mule, of
2. *A female mule,* פִּרְדָּה *pirdah.*
1 Ki. 1. 33 to ride upon mine own mule, and bring
1. 38 Solomon to ride upon king David's mule
1. 44 have caused him to ride upon the king's m.
3. *A swift beast, courser,* רֶכֶשׁ *rekesh.*
Esth. 8. 10 riders on mules, camels, (and) young dro.
8. 14 the posts that rode upon mules (and) ca.

4. *Warm springs,* יֵמִם *yemim.*
Gen. 36. 24 that found the mules in the wilderness

MULTIPLIED, to be —

1. *To be many, multiply,* רָבַב *rabab.*
Gen. 6. 1 when men began to multiply on the face
Job 35. 6 or (if) thy transgressions be multiplied
Psa. 38. 19 they that hate me wrongfully are multip.
Isa. 59. 12 our transgressions are multiplied before

2. *To be many, more, abundant,* רָבָה *rabah.*
Exod 11. 9 that my wonders may be multiplied in the
Deut. 8. 13 is multiplied, and all that thou hast is m.
11. 21 That your days may be multiplied, and
1 Ch. 5. 9 because their cattle were multiplied in
Job 27. 14 If his children be multiplied, (it is) for
Psa. 16. 4 Their sorrows shall be multiplied (that)
107. 38 so that they are multiplied greatly, and
Prov. 9. 11 by me thy days shall be multiplied, and
29. 16 When the wicked are multiplied, transg.
Jer. 3. 16 when ye be multiplied and increased in
Eze. 31. 5 his boughs were multiplied, and his bran.

3. *To cause to multiply, make abundant,* רָבָה *rabah,* 5.
Eze. 21. 15 heart may faint, and (their) ruins be mul

4. *To become great or many,* שְׂגָא *sega.*
Dan. 4. 1 unto all people..Peace be multiplied unto
6. 25 unto all people..Peace be multiplied unto

5. *To multiply, increase,* πληθύνω *plēthunō.*
Acts 6. 1 when the number of the disciples was m.

MULTIPLY —

1. *Abundant,* רַב *rab.*
Exod 23. 29 beast of the field multiply against thee

2. *A myriad, ten thousand,* רְבָבָה *rebabah.*
Eze. 16. 7 I have caused thee to multiply as the bud

MULTIPLY, to —

1. *To multiply (?),* הָמַן *haman* [perhaps error].
Eze. 5. 7 Because ye multiplied more than the na.

2. *To multiply, heap up,* כָּבַר *kabar,* 5.
Job 35. 16 he multiplieth words without knowledge

3. *To multiply, make abundant,* עָתַר *athar,* 5.
Eze. 35. 13 have multiplied your words against me

4. *To be many, abundant,* רָבָה *rabah*
Gen. 1. 22 Be fruitful, and multiply, and fill the w.
1. 22 and let fowl multiply in the earth
1. 28 Be fruitful, and multiply, and replenish
8. 17 be fruitful, and multiply upon the earth
9. 1 Be fruitful, and multiply, and replenish
9. 7 And you, be ye fruitful, and multiply; bring
9. 7 forth abundantly in the earth, and multi.
35. 11 I (am) God Almighty; be fruitful and m.
47. 27 Israel..grew. and multiplied exceedingly
Exod. 1. 7 increased abundantly, and multiplied, and
1. 10 lest they multiply, and it come to pass, that
1. 12 But..the more they multiplied and grew
1. 20 the people multiplied, and waxed very m.
Deut. 8. 1 that ye may live, and multiply, and go in
8. 13 And..thy herds and thy flocks multiply
30. 16 that thou mayest live and multiply: and

5. *To cause to multiply, make abundant,* רָבָה *rabah,* 5.
Gen. 3. 16 I will greatly multiply thy sorrow and thy
16. 10 I will multiply thy seed exceedingly, that
17. 2 covenant..and will multiply thee exceed.
17. 20 will multiply him exceedingly; twelve p.
22. 17 in multiplying I will multiply thy seed as
26. 24 will bless thee, and multiply thy seed, for
28. 3 make thee fruitful, and multiply thee, that
48. 4 I will make thee fruitful, and multiply
Exod. 7. 3 multiply my signs and my wonders in the l.
32. 13 I will multiply your seed as the stars of
Lev. 26. 9 make you fruitful. and multiply you, and
Deut. 1. 10 The LORD your God hath multiplied you
7. 13 he will love thee, and bless thee, and m.
13. 17 multiply thee, as he hath sworn unto thy
17. 16 he shall not multiply horses to himself
17. 16 to the end that he should multiply horses
17. 17 Neither shall he multiply wives to himself
17. 17 neither shall he greatly multiply to him.
28. 63 to do you good, and to multiply you; so
30. 5 he will do thee good and multiply thee
Josh. 24. 3 and multiplied his seed, and gave him I.
1 Ch. 4. 27 neither did all their family multiply, like
Neh. 9. 23 Their children also multipliedst thou as
Job 9. 17 and multiplieth my wounds without cause
29. 18 and I shall multiply (my) days as the sand
34. 37 and multiplieth his words against God
Isa. 9. 3 Thou hast multiplied the nation, (and)
Jer. 30. 19 I will multiply them, and they shall not
33. 22 so will I multiply the seed of David my
Eze. 11. 6 Ye have multiplied your slain in this city
16. 25 to every one that passed by, and multip.
16. 29 Thou hast moreover multiplied thy forn.
16. 51 thou hast multiplied thine abominations
23. 19 Yet she multiplied her whoredoms, in ca.
36. 10 I will multiply men upon you, all the ho.
36. 11 I will multiply upon you man and beast
36. 30 I will multiply the fruit of the tree, and
37. 26 I will place them, and multiply them, and
Hos. 2. 8 wine, and oil, and multiplied her silver
8. 14 and Judah hath multiplied fenced cities
12. 10 I have multiplied visions, and used sim.
Amos 4. 4 at Gilgal multiply transgression; and b.
Nah. 3. 16 Thou hast multiplied thy merchants above

6. *To multiply, increase,* πληθύνω *plēthunō.*
Acts 6. 7 the number of the disciples multiplied in
7. 17 the people grew and multiplied in Egypt
Acts 9. 31 the comfort of the Holy Ghost, were mu.
12. 24 But the word of God grew and multiplied
2 Co. 9. 10 multiply your seed sown, and increase the
Heb. 6. 14 Surely..multiplying I will multiply thee
1 Pe. 1. 2 Grace unto you, and peace, be multiplied
2 Pe. 1. 2 Grace and peace be multiplied unto you
Jude 2 Mercy unto you, and peace, and love, be m.

MULTIPLYING, to make to multiply —

To cause to multiply, make numerous, רָבָה *rabah,* 5.
Gen. 22. 17 in multiplying I will multiply thy seed
26. 4 I will make thy seed to multiply as the

MULTITUDE —

1. *A multitude,* אָמוֹן *amon.*
Jer. 46. 25 Behold, I will punish the multitude of
52. 15 carried away..the rest of the multitude

2. *A multitude, noise, store,* הָמוֹן *hamon.*
Judg. 4. 7 with his chariots, and his multitude; and
1 Sa. 14. 16 and, behold, the multitude melted away
2 Sa. 6. 19 among the whole multitude of Israel, as
1 Ki. 20. 13 Hast thou seen all this great multitude?
20. 28 will I deliver all this great multitude into
2 Ki. 7. 13 as all the multitude of Israel that are left
7. 13 as all the multitude of the Israelites that
25. 11 with the remnant of the multitude, did N.
2 Ch. 13. 8 ye (be) a great multitude, and..with you
14. 11 in thy name we go against this multitude
20. 2 There cometh a great multitude against
20. 15 nor dismayed by reason of this great mu.
20. 24 they looked unto the multitude, and, be.
32. 7 nor for all the multitude that (is) with him
Job 31. 34 Did I fear a great multitude, or did the
39. 7 He scorneth the multitude of the city, n.
Psa. 42. 4 for I had gone with the multitude; I went
Isa. 5. 13 and their multitude dried up with thirst
5. 14 their glory, and their multitude, and their
13. 4 The noise of a multitude in the mountains
16. 14 be contemned, with all that great multi.
17. 12 Woe to the multitude of many people
29. 5 Moreover the multitude of thy strangers
29. 5 the multitude of the terrible ones..as ch.
29. 7 the multitude of all the nations
29. 8 so shall the multitude of all the nations
32. 14 the multitude of the city shall be left; the
Jer. 3. 23 from the hills..the multitude of mount.
10. 13 a multitude of waters in the heavens, and
49. 32 and the multitude of their cattle a spoil
51. 16 (is) a multitude of waters in the heavens
51. 42 she is covered with the multitude of the
Eze. 7. 11 nor of their multitude, nor any of theirs
7. 12 for wrath (is) upon all the multitude th.
7. 13 vision (is) touching the whole multitude
7. 14 my wrath (is) upon all the multitude th.
23. 42 a voice of a multitude being at ease (was)
29. 19 he shall take her multitude, and take her
30. 4 they shall take away her multitude, and
30. 10 I will also make the multitude of Egypt
30. 15 and I will cut off the multitude of No.
31. 2 Pharaoh king of Egypt, and to his multi.
31. 18 This (is) Pharaoh and all his multitude
32. 12 will I cause thy multitude to fall, the ter.
32. 12 and all the multitude thereof shall be destro.
32. 16 for Egypt, and for all her multitude, saith
32. 18 Son of man, wail for the multitude of E.
32. 20 to the sword: draw her and all her multi
32. 24 There (is) Elam and all her multitude ro.
32. 25 in the midst of the slain with all her mu.
32. 26 Meshech, Tubal, and all her multitude
32. 31 shall be comforted over all his multitude
32. 32 Pharaoh and all his multitude, saith the
39. 11 there shall they bury Gog, and all his m
Dan. 10. 6 voice of his words like the voice of a mu.
11. 10 shall assemble a multitude of great forces
11. 11 he shall set forth a great multitude; but
11. 11 the multitude shall be given into his hand
11. 12 when he hath taken away the multitude
11. 13 shall set forth a multitude greater than
Joel 3. 14 Multitudes, multitudes in the valley of de.

3. *Captivity,* שִׁבְיָה *shibyah.*
2 Ch. 28. 5 carried away a great m. of them captives

4. *Full,* מָלֵא *male.*
Jer. 12. 6 they have called a multitude after thee

5. *Fulness,* מְלֹא *melo.*
Gen. 48. 19 his seed shall become a multitude of na.
Isa. 31. 4 when a multitude of shepherds is called

6. *Abundance, increase,* מַרְבִּית *marbith.*
2 Ch. 30. 18 a multitude of the people..many of Eph.

7. *A thick mass, crowd,* סָךְ *sak.*
Psa. 42. 4 for I had gone with the multitude; I went

8. *Company, swarm,* עֵדָה *edah.*
Psa. 68. 30 the multitude of the bulls, with the calves

9. *A congregation, convention,* קָהָל *qahal.*
Gen. 28. 3 that thou mayest be a multitude of people
48. 4 I will make of thee a multitude of people
Jer. 44. 15 a great multitude, even all the people that

10. *Abundant,* רַב *rab.*
Exod 12. 38 a mixed multitude went up also with them
23. 2 Thou shalt not follow a multitude to..evil
Num 32. 1 Gad had a very great multitude of cattle
2 Ch. 1. 9 a people like the dust of the earth in mu.
Psa. 97. 1 let the multitude of isles be glad (thereof)
109. 30 yea, I will praise him among the multit.
Eze. 31. 5 because of the multitude of waters, when

11. *Abundance,* רֹב *rob.*
Gen. 16. 10 that it shall not be numbered for multi.
Gen. 30. 30 and it is (now) increased unto a multitude
32. 12 which cannot be numbered for multitude
48. 16 let them grow into a multitude in the mi.
Lev. 25. 16 According to the multitude of years thou
Deut. 1. 10 this day as the stars of heaven for multi.
10. 22 made thee as the stars of heaven for mu.
28. 62 ye were as the stars of heaven for multi.
Josh. 11. 4 the sand that (is) upon the sea shore in mu.
Judg. 6. 5 and they came as grasshoppers for multi.
7. 12 in the valley like grasshoppers for multit.
7. 12 as the sand by the sea side for multitude
1 Sa. 13. 5 the sand which (is) on the sea shore in m.
2 Sa. 17. 11 as the sand that (is) by the sea for multi.
1 Ki. 3. 8 cannot be numbered nor counted for mu.
4. 20 as the sand which (is) by the sea in mult.
8. 5 could not be told nor numbered for mul.
2 Ch. 5. 6 could not be told nor numbered for mul.
Esth. 5. 11 multitude of his children, and all..where.
10. 3 accepted of the multitude of his brethren
Job 11. 2 Should not the multitude of words be an.
32. 7 multitude of years should teach wisdom
35. 9 By reason of the multitude of oppressions
Psa. 5. 7 thy house in the multitude of thy mercy
5. 10 cast them out in the multitude of their
33. 16 There is no king saved by the multitude
49. 6 boast themselves in the multitude of their
51. 1 according unto the multitude of thy ten.
69. 13 O God, in the multitude of thy mercy hear
69. 16 acc. to the multitude of thy tender merc.
94. 19 In the multitude of my thoughts within
106. 7 they remembered not the multitude of thy
106. 45 repented according to the multitude of
Prov 10. 19 In the multitude of words there wanteth
11. 14 but in the multitude of counsellors..saf.
14. 28 In the multitude of people (is) the king's
15. 22 in the multitude of counsellors they are
20. 15 There is gold, and a multitude of rubies
24. 6 and in multitude of counsellors..safety
Eccl. 5. 3 a dream cometh through the multitude of
5. 3 and a fool's voice..by multitude of words
5. 7 in the multitude of dreams and many w.
Isa. 1. 11 To what purpose (is) the multitude of your
37. 24 By the multitude of my chariots am I come
47. 9 in their perfection for the multitude of thy
47. 12 with the multitude of thy sorceries, wh.
47. 13 Thou art wearied in the multitude of thy
63. 7 according to the multitude of his loving
Jer. 30. 14, 15 for the multitude of thine iniquity
Lam. 1. 5 afflicted her for the multitude of her tra.
3. 32 according to the multitude of his mercies
Eze. 14. 4 according to the multitude of his idols
19. 11 in her height with the multitude of her b.
27. 12 by reason of the multitude of all..riches
27. 16 by reason of the multitude of the wares of
27. 18 in the multitude of the wares of thy ma.
27. 18 for the multitude of all riches; in the wine
27. 33 with the multitude of thy riches, and of
28. 16 By the multitude of thy merchandise they
28. 18 by the multitude of thine iniquities, by
31. 9 I have made him fair by the multitude of
Hos. 9. 7 for the multitude of thine iniquity, and
10. 1 according to the multitude of his fruit he
10. 13 trust..in the multitude of thy mighty men
Nah. 3. 3 a multitude of slain, and a great number
3. 4 Because of the multitude of the whored.
Zech. 2. 4 for the multitude of men and cattle ther.

12. *Strife, pleading,* רִיב *rib.*
Job 33. 19 and the multitude of his bones with strong

13. *A waggon, rider, driver,* רֶכֶב *rekeb.*
2 Ki. 19. 23 With the multitude of my chariots I am

14. *Abundance, company,* שִׁפְעָה *shiphah.*
Isa. 60. 6 The multitude of camels shall cover thee

15. *Crowd,* ὄχλος *ochlos.*
Matt. 4. 25 there followed him great multitudes of pe.
5. 1 And seeing the multitudes he went up into
8. 1 When he was come down..great multitudes
8. 18 when Jesus saw great multitudes about
9. 8 when the multitude saw (it), they marv.
9. 33 the multitudes marvelled, saying, It was
9. 36 when he saw the multitudes, he was mo.
11. 7 Jesus began to say unto the multitudes
12. 15 great [multitudes] followed him, and he
13. 2 great multitudes were gathered together
13. 2 the whole multitude stood on the shore
13. 34 All these things spake Jesus unto the m.
13. 36 Jesus sent the multitude away, and went
14. 5 he feared the multitude, because they c.
14. 14 Jesus went forth, and saw a great multit.
14. 15 send the multitude away, that they may
14. 19 he commanded the multitude to sit down
14. 19 disciples, and the disciples to the multit.
14. 22 other side, while he sent the multitudes
14. 23 when he had sent the multitudes away
15. 10 he called the multitude, and said unto
15. 30 great multitudes came unto him, having
15. 31 Insomuch that the multitude wondered
15. 32 I have compassion on the multitude, bec.
15. 33 so much bread..as to fill so great a mult.
15. 35 he commanded the multitude to sit down
15. 36 disciples, and the disciples to the multitu.
15. 39 he sent away the multitude, and took ship
17. 14 when they were come to the multitude
19. 2 great multitudes followed him; and he
20. 29 as they departed from Jericho, a great m.
20. 31 the multitude rebuked them, because they
21. 8 a very great multitude spread their garm.
21. 9 the multitudes that went before, and that
21. 11 the multitude said, This is Jesus the pro.
21. 46 they feared the multitude, because they

Matt 22. 33 when the multitude heard..they were as.
23. 1 Then spake Jesus to the multitude, and
26. 47 with him a great multitude with swords
26. 55 In that same hour said Jesus to the mul.
27. 20 persuaded the multitude that they should
27. 24 washed..hands before the multitude, say.
Mark 2. 13 all the multitude resorted unto him, and
3. 9 should wait on him because of the multi.
3. 20 the multitude cometh together again, so
3. 32 the multitude sat about him; and they
4. 1 there was gathered unto him a great mu.
4. 1 the whole multitude was by the sea on the
4. 36 when they had sent away the multitude
5. 31 Thou seest the multitude thronging thee
7. 33 he took him aside from the multitude, and
8. 1 In those days the multitude being very g.
8. 2 I have compassion on the multitude, be.
9. 14 he saw a great multitude about them, and
9. 17 one of the multitude answered and said
14. 43 with him a great multitude with swords
15. 8 the multitude, crying aloud, began to d.
Luke 3. 7 Then said he to the multitude that came
5. 15 great multitudes came together to hear
5. 19 might bring him in because of the mult.
6. 19 the whole multitude sought to touch him
8. 45 Master, the multitude throng thee and
9. 12 Send the multitude away, that they may
9. 16 gave to the disciples to set before the m.
14. 25 there went great multitudes with him: and
18. 36 hearing the multitude pass by, he asked
19. 39 some of the Pharisees from among the m.
22. 6 unto them in the absence of the multitude
22. 47 while he yet spake, behold a multitude
John 5. 13 Jesus had conveyed himself away, a mu.
6. 2 a great multitude followed him, because
Acts 13. 45 when the Jews saw the multitudes, they
16. 22 the multitude rose up together against
19. 33 they drew Alexander out of the multitude
21. 34 one thing, some another, among the mu.
24. 18 found me..neither with multitude, nor
Rev. 7. 9 a great multitude, which no man could
17. 15 and multitudes, and nations, and tongues
19. 6 I heard as it were the voice of a great m.

16. *Multitude, fulness,* πλῆθος *plēthos.*
Mark 3. 7 a great multitude from Galilee followed
3. 8 a great multitude, when they had heard
Luke 1. 10 the whole multitude of the people were
2. 13 a multitude of the heavenly host praising
5. 6 they inclosed a great multitude of fishes
6. 17 great multitude of people out of all Judea
8. 37 Then the whole multitude of the country
19. 37 the whole multitude of the disciples began
23. 1 the whole multitude of them arose, and
John 5. 3 In these lay a great multitude of impotent
21. 6 not able to draw it for the multitude of
Acts 2. 6 the multitude came together, and were
4. 32 the multitude of them that believed were
5. 14 added..multitudes both of men and wo.
5. 16 There came also a multitude (out) of the
6. 2 Then the twelve called the multitude of
6. 5 the saying pleased the whole multitude
14. 1 that a great multitude both of the Jews
14. 4 the multitude of the city was divided: and
15. 12 Then all the multitude kept silence, and
15. 30 when they had gathered the multitude to.
17. 4 of the devout Greeks a great multitude
19. 9 spake evil of that way before the multit.
21. 22 the multitude must needs come together
21. 36 the multitude of the people followed after
23. 7 arose a dissension..and the multitude was
25. 24 about whom all the multitude of the Jews
Heb. 11. 12 as the stars of the sky in multitude, and
Jas. 5. 20 from death, and shall hide a multitude of
1 Pe. 4. 8 charity shall cover the multitude of sins

MULTITUDE, innumerable —
Myriad, large number, μυριάς *murias.*
Luke 12. 1 were..an innumerable multitude of peo.

MULTITUDE, mixed or mixt —
1. *Gathered crowd, riff-raff,* אֲסַפְסֻף *asaphsuph.*
Num 11. 4 the mixed multitude that (was) among
2. *Mixture, rabble,* עֵרֶב *ereb.* Neh. 13. 3.

MULTITUDE [of the wicked] —
Life, wild beast, חַיָּה *chaiyah.* Ps. 74. 19.

MUNITION —
1. *Stronghold,* מְצָד *metsad.* Isa. 33. 16.
2. *Stronghold,* מְצוּדָה *metsodah.* Isa. 29. 7.
3. *Siege, bulwark,* מְצוּרָה *metsurah.*
Nah. 2. 1 keep the munition, watch the way, make

MUP'-PIM, מֻפִּים *obscurities.*
A son of Benjamin, Jacob's youngest son. B.C. 1680.
Gen. 46. 21 sons of Benjamin (were)..M., and Huppim

MURDER —
Murder, φόνος *phonos.*
Matt 15. 19 out of the heart proceed evil thoughts, m.
Mark 7. 21 evil thoughts, adulteries, fornications, m.
15. 7 who had committed murder in the insur.
Luke 23. 19 Who..for murder, was cast into prison
23. 25 him that for sedition and murder was c.
Rom. 1. 29 full of envy, murder, debate, deceit, mal.
Gal. 5. 21 Envyings, [murders], drunkenness, revel.
Rev. 9. 21 Neither repented they of their murders

MURDER, to (do) —
1. *To kill,* הָרַג *harag.*
Psa. 10. 8 in the secret places doth he murder the

2. *To do murder,* רָצַח *ratsach.*
Jer. 7. 9 Will ye steal, murder, and commit adul.
3. *To do murder,* רָצַח *ratsach,* 3.
Psa. 94. 6 the stranger, and murder the fatherless
Hos. 6. 9 the company of priests murder in the way
4. *To do murder,* φονεύω *phoneuō.*
Matt 19. 18 Jesus said, Thou shalt do no murder

MURDERER —
1. *To kill,* הָרַג *harag.*
Jer. 4. 31 for my soul is wearied because of murd.
Hos. 9. 13 shall bring forth his children to the mur.
2. *To (cause to) smite,* נָכָה *nakah,* 5.
2 Ki. 14. 6 the children of the murderers he slew not
3. *To murder,* רָצַח *ratsach.*
Num 35. 16, 17, 18 he (is) a murderer: the murderer
35. 19 The revenger..himself shall slay the mu.
35. 21 shall..be put to death..he (is) a murderer
35. 21 the revenger of blood shall slay the mur.
35. 30 the murderer shall be put to death by the
35. 31 take no satisfaction for the life of a mur.
Job 24. 14 The murderer rising with the light killeth
4. *To do murder,* רָצַח *ratsach,* 3.
2 Ki. 6. 32 See ye how this son of a murderer hath
Isa. 1. 21 righteousness lodged in it; but now mu.
5. *Man killer,* ἀνθρωποκτόνος *anthrōpoktonos.*
John 8. 44 He was a murderer from the beginning
1 Jo. 3. 15 Whosoever hateth his brother is a murd.
3. 15 ye know that no murderer hath eternal l.
6. *Assassin,* σικάριος, *Lat. sicarius, from sica.*
Acts 21. 38 four thousand men that were murderers?
7. *Homicide, murderer,* φονεύς *phoneus.*
Matt 22. 7 destroyed those murderers, and burned
Acts 3. 14 desired a murderer to be granted unto
7. 52 ye have been now the betrayers and mu.
28. 4 No doubt this man is a murderer, whom
1 Pe. 4. 15 But let none of you suffer as a murderer
Rev. 21. 8 the abominable, and murderers, and wh.
22. 15 murderers, and idolaters, and whosoever

MURMUR, (to make to) —
1. *To murmur,* לוּן לִין *lun, lin,* 2.
Exod 15. 24 the people murmured against Moses, say.
16. 2 children of Israel murmured against M.
* 16. 7 what (are) we, that ye murmur against us?
Num 14. 2 all the children of Israel murmured agai.
* 16. 11 what (is) Aaron, that ye murmur against
16. 41 children of Israel murmured against M.
Josh. 9. 18 all the congregation murmured against
[* V.L. as No. 2.]
2. *To (cause to) murmur,* לוּן לִין *lun, lin,* 5.
Exod 16. 8 your murmurings which ye murmur aga.
17. 3 the people murmured against Moses, and
Num 14. 27 evil congregation, which murmur against
14. 27 of Israel, which they murmur against me
* 14. 29 numbered..which have murmured against
* 14. 36 all the congregation to murmur; 17. 5.
[* V.L. as No. 1.]
3. *To murmur, be discontented,* רָגַן *ragan.*
Isa. 29. 24 they that murmured shall learn doctrine
4. *To be discontented, murmur,* רָגַן *ragan,* 2.
Deut. 1. 27 And ye murmured in your tents, and said
Psa. 106. 25 murmured in their tents, (and) hearkened
5. *To mutter, murmur, grumble,* γογγύζω *goggyzō.*
Matt 20. 11 they murmured against the good man of
Luke 5. 30 their scribes and Pharisees murmured ag.
John 6. 41 The Jews then murmured at him, because
6. 43 said unto them, Murmur not among your.
6. 61 knew in himself that his disciples murm.
7. 32 Pharisees heard that the people murmu.
1 Co. 10. 10 Neither murmur..as some of them also m.
6. *To murmur throughout,* διαγογγύζω *diagoggyzō.*
Luke 15. 2 Pharisees and scribes murmured, saying
19. 7 when they saw (it), they all murmured, s.

MURMUR against, to —
To groan, censure, chide, ἐμβριμάομαι *embrimaomai.*
Mark 14. 5 been sold..And they murmured against

MURMURER —
Murmurer, γογγυστής *goggustēs.*
Jude 16 These are murmurers, complainers wal.

MURMURING —
1. *Murmuring,* תְּלֻנּוֹת *telunnoth.*
Exod 16. 7 for that he heareth your murmurings aga.
16. 8 the LORD heareth your murmurings which
16. 8 your murmurings (are) not against us, but
16. 9 LORD: for he hath heard your murmurings
16. 12 I have heard the murmurings of the chi.
Num 14. 27 I have heard the murmurings of the chil.
17. 5 I will make to cease from me the murm.
17. 10 thou shalt quite take away their murmu.
2. *Murmuring,* γογγυσμός *goggusmos.*
John 7. 12 there was much murmuring among the p.
Acts 6. 1 there arose a murmuring of the Grecians
Phil. 2. 14 Do all things without murmurings and d.

MURRAIN —
Pestilence, plague, דֶּבֶר *deber.*
Exod. 9. 3 (there shall be) a very grievous murrain

MUSE, to —
1. *To meditate,* שִׂיחַ *siach,* 3a.
Psa. 143. 5 I meditate..I muse on the work of thy h.

2. *To reason diversely,* διαλογίζομαι *dialogizomai.*
Luke 3. 15 and all men mused in their hearts of John

MU'-SHI, מוּשִׁי, מֻשִׁי *drawn out.*
A son of Merari, son of Levi. B.C. 1660.
Exod. 6. 19 sons of Merari; Mahali and M.: these (are)
Num. 3. 20 of Merari by their families; Mahli, and M.
1 Ch. 6. 19 The sons of Merari; Mahli, and M. And
6. 47 The son of Mahli, the son of M., the son
23. 21 The sons of Merari; Mahli and M. The
23. 23 The sons M.; Mahli, and Eder, and Jere.
24. 26 The sons of Merari (were) Mahli and M.
24. 30 The sons also of M.; Mahli, and Eder, and

MU-SHITES, הַמּוּשִׁי.
The family of Mushi son of Merari.
Num. 3. 33 Of Merari (was)..the family of the M.
26. 58 (are) the families..the family of the M.

MUSIC —
1. *Singing of praise, music,* זְמָר *zemar.*
Dan. 3. 5 all kinds of music, ye fall down and wor.
3. 7 all kinds of music, all the people, the nat.
3. 10 all kinds of music, shall fall down and w.
3. 15 all kinds of music, ye fall down and wor.
2. *Music, song with instrument,* מַנְגִּינָה *manginah.*
Lam. 3. 63 Behold..their rising up; I (am) their mu.
3. *Stringed instrumental music,* נְגִינָה *neginah.*
Lam. 5. 14 the gate, the young men from their music
4. *Song,* שִׁיר *shir.*
1 Ch. 15. 16 the singers with instruments of music, ps.
2 Ch. 5. 13 cymbals, and instruments of music, and
7. 6 Levites also with instruments of music of
23. 13 the singers with instruments of music, and
34. 12 all that could skill of instruments of music
Neh. 12. 36 with the musical instruments of David
Eccl. 12. 4 all the daughters of music shall be brou.
Amos 6. 5 invent to themselves instruments of mu.
5. *Symphony, harmony,* συμφωνία *sumphōnia.*
Luke 15. 25 drew nigh to the house, he heard music

MUSICAL —
A song, שִׁיר *shir.*
1 Ch. 16. 42 cymbals..with musical instruments of G.
Neh. 12. 36 with the musical instruments of David the

MUSICAL instrument —
Mistress, breast, שִׁדָּה *shiddah.*
Eccl. 2. 8 musical instruments, and that of all sorts

MUSICIAN, (chief) —
1. *To be pre-eminent, prominent,* נָצַח *natsach,* 3.
Psa. 4. *title.* To the chief Musician
[*So* Ps. 5, 6, 9, 11, 12, 13, 14, 18, 19, 20, 21, 22, 31, 36, 39, 40, 41, 42, 44, 45, 46, 47, 49, 51, 52, 53, 54, 55, 56, 57, 58, 59, 60, 61, 62, 64, 65, 66, 67, 68, 69, 70, 75, 76, 77, 80, 81, 84, 85, 88, 109, 139, 140.] *Also* Psa. 8.
2. *Musician,* μουσικός *mousikos.*
Rev. 18. 22 the voice of harpers, and musicians, and

MUSING —
Earnest meditation, הָגִיג *hagig.*
Psa. 39. 3 while I was musing the fire burned: (then)

MUST —
It behoveth, δεῖ *dei.*
Matt 16. 21 how that he must go unto Jerusalem, and
17. 10 Why then say the scribes that Elias must
24. 6 for all..must come to pass, but the end is
26. 54 Scriptures be fulfilled, that thus it must be?
Mark 8. 31 that the Son of man must suffer many th.
9. 11 Why say the scribes that Elias must first
13. 10 the Gospel must first be published among
Luke 2. 49 that I must be about my Father's business
4. 43 he said unto them, I must preach the king.
9. 22 The Son of man must suffer many things
13. 33 Nevertheless I must walk to day, and to
17. 25 But first must he suffer many things, and
19. 5 come down; for to day I must abide at thy
21. 9 for these things must first come to pass; but
22. 7 bread, when the passover must be killed
22. 37 that is written must yet be accomplished
24. 7 The Son of man must be delivered into
24. 44 that all things must be fulfilled which w.
John 3. 7 Marvel not that I said..Ye must be born
3. 14 even so [must] the Son of man be lifted up
3. 30 He must increase, but I (must) decrease
4. 24 they that worship him must worship..in
9. 4 I must work the works of him that sent
10. 16 them also I must bring, and they shall
12. 34 thou, The Son of man must be lifted up
20. 9 not..that he must rise again from the dead
Acts 1. 22 must one be ordained to be a witness with
3. 21 Whom the heaven must receive until the
4. 12 given among men whereby we must be sav
9. 6 it shall be told thee what thou must do
9. 16 I will show him how great things he must
14. 22 that we must through much tribulation
16. 30 and said, Sirs, what must I do to be saved
18. 21 I [must] by all means keep this feast that
19. 21 After I have been there, I must also see
23. 11 so must thou bear witness also at Rome
27. 24 Fear not, Paul; thou must be brought bef.
27. 26 Howbeit we must be cast upon a certain
1 Co. 11. 19 there must be also heresies among you
15. 25 he must reign, till he hath put all enem.
15. 53 this corruptible must put on incorrupt.
2 Co. 5. 10 we must all appear before the judgment
1 Ti. 3. 2 A bishop then must be blameless, the hus.
3. 7 Moreover he must have a good report of

2 Ti. 2. 6 The husbandman that laboureth must be
2. 24 the servant of the Lord must not strive
Titus 1. 7 a bishop must be blameless, as the steward
1. 11 Whose mouths must be stopped, who sub.
Heb. 9. 26 For then must he often have suffered since
11. 6 he that cometh to God must believe that
Rev. 1. 1 things which must shortly come to pass
4. 1 show thee things which must be hereafter
10. 11 Thou must prophesy again before many p.
11. 5 if any man will hurt them, he must in this
13. 10 he that killeth with the sword, must be
17. 10 when he cometh, he must continue a short
20. 3 after that he must be loosed a little 22. 6.

2. *In order that,* ἵνα *hina,* Mark 14. 49.

MUST needs, of necessity —

1. *It behoveth,* δεῖ *dei.*
Mark 13. 7 must needs be; but the end (shall) not (be)
John 4. 4 And he must needs go through Samaria
Acts 1. 16 this scripture must needs have been fulfi.
17. 3 that Christ must needs have suffered, and
21. 22 the multitude must needs come together
2 Co. 11. 30 If I must needs glory, I will glory of the

2. *To have a necessity,* ἔχω ἀνάγκην *echō anagkēn.*
Luke 14. 18 bought a piece of ground, and I must ne

3. *A necessity,* ἀνάγκη *anagkē.*
Matt 18. 7 for it must needs be that offences come
Luke 23. 17 For of necessity he must release one unto
Rom 13. 5 Wherefore (ye) must needs be sub. He. 9. 16.

4. *To be indebted,* ὀφείλω *opheilō,* 1 Co. 5. 10.

MUSTARD seed —

Mustard tree or seed, σίναπι *sinapi*
Matt 13. 31 kingdom..is like to a grain of mustard s
17. 20 If ye have faith as a grain of mustard seed
Mark 4. 31 (It is) like a grain of mustard seed, which
Luke 13. 19 It is like a grain of mustard seed, which
17. 6 If ye had faith as a grain of mustard seed

MUSTER, to —

1. *To inspect,* פָּקַד *paqad,* 3.
Isa. 13. 4 LORD of hosts mustereth the host of the

2. *To cause to assemble,* צָבָא *tsaba,* 5.
2 Ki. 25. 19 which mustered the people of the land
Jer. 52. 25 who mustered the people of the land; and

MUTH LABBEN —

Death of Ben, or of the son, מוּת לַבֵּן *muth labben.*
Psa. 9. *title.* To the chief musician upon Muth labben

MUTTER, to —

1. *To mutter, meditate,* הָגָה *hagah.*
Isa. 59. 3 your tongue hath muttered perverseness

2. *To (cause to) mutter,* הָגָה *hagah,* 5.
Isa. 8. 19 unto wizards that peep and that mutter

MUTUAL —

In each other, ἐν ἀλλήλοις *en allēlois.*
Rom. 1. 12 by the mutual faith both of you and me

MUZZLE —

1. *To muzzle, stop,* חָסַם *chasam.*
Deut 25. 4 Thou shalt not muzzle the ox when he t

2. *To muzzle, gag,* φιμόω *phimoō.*
1 Co. 9. 9 Thou shalt not muzzle the mouth of the
1 Ti. 5. 18 saith, Thou shalt not muzzle the ox that

MY —

1. *Relating to me,* κατ' ἐμέ *kat' eme.*
Eph. 6. 21 that ye also may know my affairs..how
Col. 4. 7 All my state shall Tychicus declare unto

2. *To me,* ἐμοί *emoi.*
Heb. 13. 6 The Lord (is) my helper, and I will not f.

3. *My, mine,* ἐμός *emos.*
Matt 18. 20 two or three are gathered together in my
Mark 8. 38 shall be ashamed of me and of my words
Luke 9. 26 shall be ashamed of me and of my words
John 3. 29 voice. This my joy therefore is fulfilled
4. 34 My meat is to do the will of him that sent
5. 30 as I hear, I judge: and my judgment is
5. 47 his writings, how shall ye believe my w.?
7. 6 My time is not yet come: but your time is
7. 8 this feast; for my time is not yet full come
8. 16 And yet if I judge, my judgment is true
8. 31 If ye continue in my word (then) are ye
8. 37 but..because my word hath no place in
8. 43 Why do ye not understand my speech?
8. 43 (even) because ye cannot hear my word
8. 51 If a man keep my saying, he shall never
8. 56 Your father Abraham rejoiced to see my
10. 14 and know my (sheep), and am known of m.
10. 26 ye are not of my sheep, as I said unto you
10. 27 My sheep hear my voice, and I know them
12. 26 where I am, there shall also my servant be
13. 35 By this shall all..know that ye are my d.
14. 15 If ye love me, keep my commandments
14. 27 Peace I leave with you, my peace I give
15. 8 that ye bear much fruit; so shall ye be my
15. 9 have I loved you: continue ye in my love
15. 11 that my joy might remain in you, and (that)
15. 12 This is my commandment, That ye love one
17. 13 they might have my joy fulfilled in them.
17. 24 that they may behold my glory, which thou
18. 36 Jesus answered, My kingdom is not of this
18. 36 If my kingdom were of this world, then
18. 36 would my servants fight, that I should not
18. 36 but now is my kingdom not from hence
Rom. 3. 7 hath more abounded through my lie unto
10. 1 Brethren, my heart's desire and prayer to
1 Co. 5. 4 and my spirit, with the power of our Lord

1 Co. 7. 40 she is happier if she so abide after my j.
11. 25 This cup is the new testament is my blood
16. 18 For they have refreshed my spirit and y.
2 Co. 1. 23 I call God for a record upon my soul, that
2. 3 in you all, that my joy is..of you all
8. 23 my partner and fellow helper concerning
Gal. 1. 13 For ye have heard of my conversation in
Phil. 1. 26 abundant..for me by my coming to you
2 Ti. 4. 6 and the time of [my] departure is at hand
Phm. 10 I beseech thee for my son Onesimus
2 Pe. 1. 15 that ye may be able after my decease to
3 Jo. 4 than to hear that my children walk in tr.
Rev. 2. 20 to teach and to seduce my servants to com.

4. *Of me, my, mine,* (παρ') ἐμοῦ *(par') emou.*
Matt 5. 11 all..evil against you falsely, for my sake
10. 18 before governors and kings for my sake
10. 39 he that loseth his life for my sake shall
16. 25 whosoever will lose his life for my sake
Mark 8. 35 whosoever shall lose his life for my sake
10. 29 left..lands, for my sake, and the gospel's
13. 9 brought before rulers and kings for my
Luke 9. 24 whosoever will lose his life for my sake
John 13. 38 Wilt thou lay down thy life for my sake?
Rom 11. 27 this (is) my covenant unto them, when I

5. *Me,* μέ *me.*
Matt 26. 12 ointment on my body, she did (it) for my

6. *To me,* μοί *moi.*
Mark 5. 9 My name (is) Legion: for we are many
Acts 7. 49 Heaven (is) my throne, and earth (is)
1 Co. 9. 18 What is [my] reward then?..that, when
2 Co. 6. 16 their God, and they shall be [my] people
6. 18 ye shall be my sons and daughters, saith
7. 4 Great (is) my boldness of speech toward
7. 4 great (is) my glorying of you: I am filled
Phil. 1. 19 For I know that this shall turn to my sal.
1. 22 in the flesh, this (is) the fruit of my labour
4. 16 ye sent once and again unto my necessity
Rev. 21. 7 I will be his God, and he shall be my son

7. *Of me, my, mine,* μοῦ *mou.*
Matt. 2. 6 Governor, that shall rule my people Israel
2. 15 saying, Out of Egypt have I called my son
3. 17 This is my beloved son, in whom I am w.
7. 21 but he that doeth the will of my Father w.
8. 6 Lord, my servant lieth at home sick of the
8. 8 that thou shouldest come under my roof
8. 8 word only, and my servant shall be heal.
8. 9 to my servant, Do this, and he doeth (it)
8. 21 suffer me first to go and bury my father
9. 18 My daughter is even now dead: but come
10. 22 ye shall be hated of all..for my name's sake
10. 32 also before my Father which is in heaven
10. 33 deny before my Father which is in heaven
11. 10 I send my messenger before thy face, w.
11. 27 All things are delivered unto me of my F.
11. 29 Take my yoke upon you, and learn of me
11. 30 my yoke (is) easy, and my burden is light
12. 18 Behold my servant, whom I have chosen
12. 18 my beloved, in whom my soul is well ple.
12. 18 I will put my Spirit upon him, and he sh.
12. 44 I will return into my house from whence
12. 48 Who is my mother? and who are my bre.
12. 49 said, Behold my mother and my brethren!
12. 50 shall do the will of my Father which is in
12. 50 the same is my brother, and sister, and m.
13. 30 to burn..but gather the wheat into my b.
13. 35 I will open my mouth in parables; I will
15. 13 Every plant, which my heavenly Father
15. 22 my daughter is grievously vexed with a d.
16. 17 hath not revealed (it) unto thee, but my
16. 18 and upon this rock I will build my church
17. 5 This is my beloved son, in whom I am well
17. 15 Lord, have mercy on my son: for he is lu.
18. 5 shall receive one such little child in my
18. 10 do always behold the face of my Father
18. 19 it shall be done for them of my Father which
18. 21 how oft shall my brother sin against me
18. 35 So likewise shall my heavenly Father do
19. 20 All these things have I kept from [my] y.
19. 29 for my name's sake, shall receive an hun.
20. 21 Grant that these my two sons may sit, the
20. 23 Ye shall drink indeed of my cup, and be
20. 23 to sit on my right hand, and on my left, is
20. 23 for whom it is prepared of [my] Father
21. 13 My house shall be called the house of pr.
21. 28 said, Son, go work to day in [my] vineyard
21. 37 son, saying, They will reverence my son
22. 4 I have prepared my dinner: my oxen and
22. 44 unto my Lord, Sit thou on my right hand
24. 5 many shall come in my name, saying, I am
24. 9 ye shall be hated of all nations for my n.
24. 35 Heaven and earth shall pass away, but my
24. 36 not the angels of heaven, but [my] Father
24. 48 say in his heart, My lord delayeth his co.
25. 27 to have put my money to the exchangers
25. 34 Come, ye blessed of my Father, inherit the
25. 40 unto one of the least of these [my] breth.
26. 12 she hath poured this ointment on my body
26. 18 The Master saith, My time is at hand; I
26. 18 the passover at thy house with my discip.
26. 26 gave..and said, Take, eat; this is my body
26. 28 this is my blood of the new testament, w.
26. 38 My soul is exceeding sorrowful, even unto
26. 39 O [my] Father, if it be possible, let this
26. 42 O my Father, if this cup may not pass a.
26. 53 that I cannot now pray to my Father, and
27. 35 [They parted my garments among them]
27. 35 [and upon my vesture did they cast lots]
27. 46 My God! my God! why hast thou forsaken
28. 10 go tell my brethren that they go into G.

Mark 1. 2, 11; 3. 33, [33], 34, 34, 35, [35]; 5. 23, 30; 6.
23; 9. 7, 17, 37, 39, [41]; 10. 20, 40, [40]; 11. 17; 12. 6, 36,
36; 13. 6, 13, 31; 14. 8, 14, 22, 24, 34; 15. 34, 34; 16. [17].
Luke 1. 18, 20, 25, 43, 44, 46, 47, 47; 2. 49; 3. 22; 6.
47; 7. 6, 7, 8, 27, [44], 44, 45, 46, [46]; 8. 21, 21; 9. 35,
38, 48, 59, 61; 10. 22, 29, 40; 11. 7, 24; 12. 4, 13, 17, 18,
[18], 18, 19, 45; 14. 23, 24, 26, 27, 33; 15. 6, 17, 18, 24,
29; 16. 3, 5, 24, 27; 18. [21]; 19. 8, 23, 46; 20. 13, 42, 42;
21. 8, 12, 17, 33; 22. 11, 19, 20, 28, 29, 30, 30, 42; 23. 46;
24. 39, 39, 49.
John 2. 16; 4. 49; 5. 17, 24, 31, 43; 6. 32, 51, 54, 54,
55, 55, 56, 56, [65]; 8. 14, 19, 19, [28], 31, [38], 49, 52, 54,
54; 10. 15, 16, 17, 18, 25, 27, 28, 29, [29, 32], 37; 11. 21,
32; 12. 7, 27, 47, 48; 13. 6, 8, 9, 37; 14. 2, 7, [12], 13, 14,
20, 21, 21, 23, 23, 24, 26, [28]; 15. 1, 7, 8, 10, 10, [10], 14,
15, 16, 20, 21, 23, 24; 16. [10], 23, 24, 26; 18. 37; 19. 24,
24; 20. 13, [17], 17, 17, 17, 25, 25, 27, 27, 28, 28; 21. 15
16, 17.
Acts 2. 14, 17, 18, 18, 18, 25, 25, 26, 26, 26, 27, 34, 34; 7.
34, 49, 49, 50, 59; 9. 15, 16; 10. 30; 11. 8; 13. 22, 33; 15.
7, 17; 16 15; 20. [24], 24, 25, 29, 34; 22. 1; 24. 17; 26.
4; 28. 19.
Rom. 1. 8, 9, 9, 9; 2. 15; 7. 4, 18, 23, 23, 23; 9. 1, 2,
3, 3, 17, 17, 25, 25, 26; 10. 21; 11. 3, 14; 15. 14, 31; 16.
3, 4, 5, 7, 7, 8, 9, 11, 21, 21, 25.
1 Co. 1. 4, 11; 2. 4, 4; 4. 14, 17, 17; 8. 13, 13; 9. 1,
15, 18, 27; 10. 14, 29; 11. 24, 33; 13. 3, 3; 14. 14, 14, [18],
19; 15. 58; 16. 24.
2 Co. 2. 13, 13; 12. 9, [9], 9, 21; Gal. 1. 14, 15; 4. [14],
14, 19, 20; 6. 17.
Eph. 1. 16; 3. 4, 13, 14; 6. [10], 19; Phil. 1. 3, 7, 7, 8,
13, 14, 16, 20, 20; 2. 2, 12, 12, 12, 25, 25; 3. 1, [8]; 4. 1,
1, 3, 14, 19; Col. 1. [24], 24; 2. 1; 4. 10, 18.
2 Ti. 1. 3, 6, 16; 2. 1, 8; 3. 10; 4. 16; Phm. 4, 4, [10],
20, 23, 24.
Heb. 1. 5, 13; 2. 12; 3. 9, 10, 11, 11; 4. 3, 3, 5; 5. 5;
8. 9, 10; 10. 16, [34], 38; 12. 5; Jas. 1. 2, 16, 19; 2. 1, 3,
5, 14, [18]; 3. 1, 10, 12; 5. [10], 12; 1 Pe. 5. 13; 2 Pe. 1.
14, 17; 1 Jo. 2. 1; 3. 13, [18]; Rev 1. 20; 2. 3, 13, 13, 13,
16, 26, 27; 3. 5, 8, 8, 10, 12, 12, 12, 12, 12, 16, 20, 21, 21;
10. 10, 10; 11. 3; 18. 4; 22. 12.

MY'-RA, Μύρα, Μύρρα.

One of the chief cities of Lycia, a province on the S.W. of Asia Minor, between Caria and Pamphylia; forty miles E. of Patara; now called *Dembra.*
Acts 27. 5 when we had sailed..we came to M..of Lycia

MYRRH —

1. *Gum of the cistus, ladanum,* לֹט *lot.*
Gen. 37. 25 bearing spicery and balm and myrrh, go.
43. 11 honey, spices, and myrrh, nuts, and alm.

2. *Myrrh,* מֹר *mor.*
Exod 30. 23 of pure myrrh five hundred (shekels), and
Esth. 2. 12 six months with oil of myrrh, and six m.
Psa. 45. 8 All thy garments (smell) of myrrh, and al.
Prov. 7. 17 I have perfumed my bed with myrrh, aloes
Song 1. 13 A bundle of myrrh (is) my well beloved
3. 6 perfumed with myrrh and frankincense
4. 6 I will get me to the mountain of myrrh
4. 14 myrrh and aloes, with all the chief spices
5. 1 I have gathered my myrrh with my spice
5. 5 my hands dropped (with) myrrh, and
5. 5 my fingers (with) sweet smelling myrrh
5. 13 (like) lilies, dropping sweet smelling my.

3. *Myrrh,* σμύρνα *smurna.*
Matt 2. 11 presented..gold, and frankincense, and m.
John 19. 39 brought a mixture of myrrh and aloes, ab.

MYRRH, to be mingled with —

To mix or mingle with myrrh, σμυρνίζω *smurnizō.*
Mark 15. 23 gave him to drink wine mingled with m

MYRTLE (tree) —

Myrtle tree, הֲדַס *hadas.*
Neh. 8. 15 pine branches, and myrtle branches, and
Isa. 41. 19 the cedar, the shittah tree, and the myr.
55. 13 of the brier shall come up the myrtle tree
Zech. 1. 8 and he stood among the myrtle trees that
1. 10 the man that stood among the myrtle tr.
1. 11 angel..that stood among the myrtle trees

MYSELF —

1. *I, I myself,* אֲנִי *ani.*
2 Sa. 18. 2 I will surely go forth with you myself also

2. *My life (soul),* נֶפֶשׁ *nephesh.* Psa. 131. 2.

2a. *My flesh,* בְּשָׂרִי *[basar].* Eccl. 2. 3.

3. *Of myself,* ἐμαυτοῦ *emautou.*
Luke 7. 7 Wherefore neither thought I myself wor.
John 5. 31 If I bear witness of myself, my witness is
7. 17 be of God, or (whether) I speak of myself
7. 28 I am not come of myself, but he that sent
8. 14 Though I bear record of myself..my record
8. 18 I am one that bear witness of myself, and
8. 28 I do nothing of myself; but as my Father
8. 42 neither came I of myself, but he sent me
8. 54 Jesus answered, If I honour myself, my
10. 18 taketh it from me, but I lay it down of m.
12. 49 I have not spoken of myself; but the Fa.
14. 3 I will come again, and receive..unto my.
14. 10 that I speak unto you I speak not of my.
14. 21 love him, and will manifest myself to him
17. 19 for their sakes I sanctify myself, that they
Acts 20. 24 neither count I my life dear unto myself
24. 10 I do the more cheerfully answer for my.
26. 2 I think myself happy, king Agrippa, bec.
26. 9 I verily thought with myself, that I ought
Rom 11. 4 I have reserved to myself seven thousand
1 Co. 4. 4 For I know nothing by myself; yet am I
4. 6 I have in a figure transferred to myself and

1 Co. 9. 19 yet have I made myself servant unto 7. 7.
2 Co. 2. 1 I determined this with myself, that I would
11. 7 Have I committed an offence in abasing m.
11. 9 I have kept myself from being burdensome
12. 5 yet of myself I will not glory, but in mine
Gal. 2. 18 I destroyed, I make myself a tr. Phil. 3. 13.

4. *He, himself*, αὐτός *autos*, Ro. 9. 3 ; 16. 2.

5. *Me*, ἐμέ *eme*.
Phm. 17 If thou count me..receive him as myself

MY'-SIA, Μυσία.
A province in the N.W. of Asia Minor, having Lydia on the S., Bithynia on the E., and the Propontis on the N.; Assos, Pergamos, and Troas were its chief cities.
Acts 16. 7 After they were come to M., they assayed
16. 8 And they passing by M. came down to T.

MYSTERY —
What is known only to the initiated, μυστήριον.
Matt 13. 11 it is given unto you to know the mysteries
Mark 4. 11 Unto you it is given to know the mystery
Luke 8. 10 Unto you it is given to know the mysteries
Rom 11. 25 that ye should be ignorant of this mystery
16. 25 according to the revelation of the mystery
1 Co. 2. 7 we speak the wisdom of God in a mystery
4. 1 and stewards of the mysteries of God
13. 2 and understand all mysteries, and all kn.
14. 2 howbeit in the spirit he speaketh myste.
15. 51 Behold, I show you a mystery ; We shall
Eph. 1. 9 Having made known unto us the mystery
3. 3 How..he made known unto me the mys.
3. 4 may understand my knowledge in the m.
3. 9 see what(is)the fellowship of the mystery
5. 32 This is a great mystery: but I speak conce.
6. 19 to make known the mystery of the gospel
Col. 1. 26 the mystery which hath been hid from ages
1. 27 what (is) the riches of the glory of this m.
2. 2 to the acknowledgment of the mystery of
4. 3 to speak the mystery of Christ, for which
2 Th. 2. 7 the mystery of iniquity doth already work
1 Ti. 3. 9 Holding the mystery of the faith in a pure
3. 16 without controversy great is the mystery
Rev. 1. 20 The mystery of the seven stars which thou
10. 7 the mystery of God should be finished, as
17. 5 Mystery, Babylon the great, the mother of
17. 7 I will tell thee the mystery of the woman

N

NA'-AM, נַעַם *pleasantness.*
A son of Caleb, son of Jephunneh. B.C. 1450.
1 Ch. 4. 15 the sons of Caleb..Iru, Elah, and N.: and

NA-A'-MAH, נַעֲמָה.
1. Sister of Tubal-cain, and daughter of Zillah wife of Lamech, of the race of Cain. B.C. 3874.
Gen. 4. 22 and the sister of Tubal-cain (was) N.
2. An Ammonitess, mother of Rehoboam. B.C. 998.
1 Ki. 14. 21, 31 his mother's name (was) N. an Amm.
2 Ch. 12. 13 his mother's name (was) N. an Ammonit.
3. A city in the S.W. of Judah, near Beth-dagon.
Josh 15. 41 Gederoth, Beth-dagon, and N., and Mak.

NA-A' MAN, נַעֲמָן, Νεεμάν, Ναιμάν, *pleasant.*
1. A son of Benjamin. B.C. 1700.
Gen. 46. 21 N., Ehi, and Rosh, Muppim, and Huppim
2. A son of Bela, son of Benjamin. B.C. 1600.
Num 26. 40 the sons of Bela were Ard and N.: (of Ard)
26. 40 (and) of N., the family of the Naamites
1 Ch. 8. 4 And Abishua, and N., and Ahoah
3. A son of Ehud or Abihud, grandson of Benjamin. B.C. 1600.
1 Ch. 8. 7 N., and Ahiah, and Gera, he removed them
4. A Syrian captain in the days of Joram son of Ahab, who was cured of leprosy by Elisha the prophet. B.C. 894.
2 Ki. 5. 1 N., captain of the host of the king of Sy.
5. 2 a little maid ; and she waited on N.'s wife
5. 6 I have (therewith) sent N. my servant to
5. 9 N. came with his horses and with his ch.
5. 11 N. was wroth, and went away, and said
5. 17 N. said, Shall there not then, I pray thee
5. 20 my master hath spared N. this Syrian, in
5. 21 Gehazi followed after N. And when N. saw
5. 23 And N. said, Be content, take two talents
5. 27 The leprosy therefore of N. shall cleave
Luke 4. 27 and none..was cleansed, saving [N.] the

NA-A-MA-THITE, נַעֲמָתִי, *Naamathi.*
Patronymic of Zophar, one of Job's friends; probably from Edom.
Job 2. 11 Bildad the Shuhite, and Zophar the N.
11. 1 Then answered Zophar the N., and said
20. 1 Then answered Zophar the N., and said
42. 9 the N. went and did according as the L.

NA-A-MITES, הַנַּעֲמִי *the Naami.*
The family of Naaman, grandson of Benjamin youngest son of Jacob.
Num 26. 40 (and) of Naaman, the family of the N.

NA-A'-RAH, נַעֲרָה *shoot, posterity.*
A wife of Ashur, descended from Judah through Caleb son of Hur. B.C. 1560.
1 Ch. 4. 5 father of Tekoa had..wives, Helah and N.
4. 6 N. bare him Ahuzam, and Hepher, and
4. 6 These (were) the sons of N.

NA-A'-RAI, נַעֲרַי *pleasantness of Jah.*
One of David's valiant men, and son of Ezbai; in 2 Sa. 23. 35 called *Paarai* the Arbite. B.C. 1048.
1 Ch. 11. 37 Hezro the Carmelite, N. the son of Ezbai

NA-A'-RAN, נַעֲרָן *waterfall.*
A city in Ephraim ; the same as the succeeding.
1 Ch. 7. 28 the towns thereof, and eastward N., and

NA-A'-RATH, נַעֲרָתָה *waterfall.*
A city in Ephraim or Benjamin, near Jericho.
Josh. 16. 7 it went down from Janohah..to N., and

NA-A'-SHON, נַחְשׁוֹן *oracle.*
Brother of Elisheba, Aaron's wife ; perhaps the same as Nahshon son of Amminadab. B.C. 1492.
Exod. 6. 23 Aaron took Elisheba..sister of N. to wife

NA-AS'-SON, Ναασσών. *An ancestor of Jesus.*
Matt. 1. 4 Aminadab begat N.; and N. begat Salmon
Luke 3. 32 (the son) of Salmon..was (the son) of N.

NA'-BAL, נָבָל *fool, projecting.*
A rich man in Maon who insulted David and died of fright, husband of Abigail whom David afterwards married. B.C. 1060.
1 Sa. 25. 3 Now the name of the man (was) N., and
25. 4 David heard in the wilderness that N. did
25. 5 Get you up to Carmel, and go to N., and
25. 9 they spake to N. according to all those w.
25. 10 N. answered David's servants, and said
25. 14 told Abigail, N.'s wife, saying, Behold, D.
25. 19 But she told not her husband N.
25. 25 N.: for as his name (is), so (is) he ; N. (is)
25. 26 and they that seek evil to my lord, be as N.
25. 34 surely there had not been left unto N. by
25. 36 Abigail came to N...and N.'s heart (was)
25. 37 when the wine was gone out of N., and
25. 38 came to pass..that the LORD smote N.
25. 39 when David heard that N. was dead, he
25. 39 cause of my reproach from the hand of N.
25. 39 hath returned the wickedness of N. upon
27. 3 David..and Abigail the Carmelitess, N.'s
30. 5 Ahinoam..and Abigail the wife of N. the
2 Sa. 2. 2 Ahinoam..and Abigail, N.'s wife, 3. 3.

NA'-BOTH, נָבוֹת *prominence.*
A Jezreelite of the tribe of Issachar, whom Jezebel, wife of Ahab, caused to be put to death to obtain his vineyard. B.C. 899.
1 Ki. 21. 1 N. the Jezreelite had a vineyard, which
21. 2 Ahab spake unto N., saying, Give me thy
21. 3 N. said to Ahab, The LORD forbid it me
21. 4 displeased because of the word which N.
21. 6 Because I spake unto N. the Jezreelite
21. 7 I will give thee the vineyard of N. the J.
21. 8 the nobles..in his city dwelling with N.
21. 9 Proclaim a fast, and set N. on high among
21. 12 They proclaimed a fast, and set N. on high
21. 13 against N...saying, N. did blaspheme God
21. 14 Then they sent to Jezebel, saying, N. is
21. 15 when Jezebel heard that N. was stoned
21. 15 possession of the vineyard of N...for N.
21. 16 when Ahab heard that N. was dead, that
21. 16 rose up to go down to the vineyard of N.
21. 18 in the vineyard of N., whither he
21. 19 the place where dogs licked the blood of N.
2 Ki. 9. 21 met him in the portion of N. the Jezreel.
9. 25 cast him in the portion of the field of N.
9. 26 I have seen yesterday the blood of N., and

NA'-CHON, נָכוֹן *stroke.*
A Benjamite at whose thrashing floor Uzzah was smitten for touching the ark. B.C. 1042. In 1 Ch. 13. 9 called also *Chidon* (*which see*).
2 Sa. 6. 6 when they came to N.'s threshing floor

NA'-CHOR, Ναχώρ. *An ancestor of Jesus.*
Luke 3. 34 (son) of Thara, which was (the son) of N.

NA'-DAB, נָדָב *liberal, willing.*
1. Elder son of Aaron, slain by fire for offering strange fire. B.C. 1490.
Exod. 6. 23 she bare him N., and Abihu, Eleazar, and
24. 1 Come up..thou, and Aaron, N., and Ab.
24. 9 Then went up Moses, and Aaron, N., and
28. 1 Aaron, N. and Abihu, Eleazar and Itham.
Lev. 10. 1 N. and Abihu, the sons of Aaron, took eit.
Num. 3. 2 N. the first born, and Abihu, Eleazar, and
3. 4 N. and Abihu died before the LORD, when
26. 60 unto Aaron was born N. and Abihu, Ele.
26. 61 N. and Abihu died, when they offered
1 Ch. 6. 3 The sons also of Aaron ; N., and Abihu
24. 1 of Aaron ; N., and Abihu, Eleazar, and I.
24. 2 N. and Abihu died before their father, and
2. Son of Jeroboam I. king of Israel, and slain by Baasha. B.C. 954.
1 Ki. 14. 20 and N. his son reigned in his stead
15. 25 N. the son of Jeroboam began to reign o.
15. 27 N. and all Israel laid siege to Gibbethon
15. 31 the acts of N., and all that he did, (are)
3. Great grandson of Jerahmeel, son of Hezron. B.C. 1410.
1 Ch. 2. 28 And the sons of Shammai; N., and Abis.
2. 30 the sons of N., Seled and Appaim: but S.
4. A Benjamite of the kindred of king Saul. B.C. 1180.
1 Ch. 8. 30 Abdon..Zur, and Kish, and Baal, and N.
9. 36 Zur, and Kish, and Baal, and Ner, and N.

NAG'-GE, Ναγγαί. *An ancestor of Jesus.*
Luke 3. 25 (the son) of Esli, which was (the son) of N.

NA-HA-LI'-EL, נַחֲלִיאֵל *inheritance of God.*
A station of the Israelites in the wilderness, between Mattanah and Bamoth, N. of Moab, near the wilderness of Kedemoth, and watered by a tributary of the Arnon.
Num 21. 19 from Mattanah to N.: and from N. to B.

NA-HAL'-LAL, NA-HA'-LAL, NA-HA'-LOL, נַהֲלָל, נַהֲלֹל.
A Levitical city in Zebulun, retained by the Canaanites, near Kattath and Dimnah. Now called *Mahlul.*
Josh. 19. 15 N., and Shimron, and Idalah, and Beth-le.
21. 35 Dimnah..N. with her suburbs ; four cit.
Judg. 1. 30 of Kitron, nor the inhabitants of N.

NAH'-AM, נַחַם *consolation.*
Brother of Hodiah wife of Ezra, descendant of Caleb son of Jephunneh. B.C. 1400.
1 Ch. 4. 19 the sister of N., the father of Keilah the

NA-HA-MA'-NI, נַחֲמָנִי *comforter.*
A chief man who returned with Zerubbabel from exile. B.C. 536.
Neh. 7. 7 N., Mordecai, Bilshan, Mispereth, Bigvai

NA-HA-RA'-I, NA-HA-RI, נַחְרַי, נַחֲרַי *snorting one.*
One of David's valiant men, from Beeroth in Benjamin. B.C. 1048.
2 Sa. 23. 37 N. the Beerothite, armour bearer to Joab
1 Ch. 11. 39 N. the Berothite, the armour bearer to Joab

NA'-HASH, נָחָשׁ *oracle.*
1. An Ammonite king who besieged Jabesh-gilead, and was defeated by Saul. B.C. 1090.
1 Sa. 11. 1 Then N. the Ammonite came up, and enc.
11. 1 all the men of Jabesh said unto N., Make
11. 2 N. the Ammonite answered them, On this
12. 12 N. the king of the children of Ammon c.
2. Another king of Ammon and father of Shobi and Hanan. B.C. 1050.
2 Sa. 10. 2 show kindness unto Hanun the son of N.
17. 27 the son of N. of Rabbah of the children
1 Ch. 19. 1 N. the king of the children of Ammon d.
19. 2 show kindness unto Hanun the son of N.
3. Mother of Abigail the mother of Amasa, Absalom's general, and sister of Zeruiah Joab's mother. B.C. 1090.
2 Sa. 17. 25 that went in to Abigail the daughter of N.

NA'-HATH, נַחַת *lowness.*
1. A son of Reuel, son of Esau. B.C. 1700.
Gen. 36. 13 N., and Zerah, Shammah, and Mizzah
36. 17 duke N., duke Zerah, duke Shammah, d.
1 Ch. 1. 37 sons of Reuel ; N., Zerah, Shammah, and
2. A Kohathite, son of Zophai ; perhaps the same as *Toah* in 1 Ch. 6. 34. B.C. 1170.
1 Ch. 6. 26 of Elkanah ; Zophai his son, and N. his s.
3. A Levite, overseer of the offerings in the days of Hezekiah. B.C. 726.
2 Ch. 31. 13 N., and Asahel, and Jerimoth, and Joza.

NAH'-BI, נַחְבִּי *Jah is protection, consolation.*
A prince of Naphtali whom Moses sent out to spy the land. B.C. 1490.
Num 13. 14 the tribe of Naphtali, N. the son of Vop.

NA'-HOR, נָחוֹר *piercer, slayer.*
1. Grandfather of Abraham, and great grandson of Peleg, fourth from Shem. B.C. 2140.
Gen. 11. 22 And Serug lived thirty years, and begat N.
11. 23 Serug lived after he begat N. two hundred
11. 24 N. lived nine and twenty years, and begat
11. 25 N. lived after he begat Terah an hundred
1 Ch. 1. 26 Serug, N., Terah
2. Son of Terah, brother of Abraham, husband of Milcah, who bore him eight children. B.C. 1950.
Gen. 11. 26 Terah lived..and begat Abram, N., and
11. 27 Terah begat Abram, N., and Haran; and
11. 29 Abram and N. took them wives : the name
11. 29 the name of N.'s wife, Milcah, the daugh.
22. 20 also born children unto thy brother N.
22. 23 these eight Milcah did bear to N., Abra.
24. 10 went to Mesopotamia, unto the city of N.
24. 15 Milcah, the wife of N., Abraham's brother
24. 24 the son of Milcah, which she bare unto N.
24. 47 Bethuel, N.'s son, whom Milcah bare unto
29. 5 unto them, Know ye Laban the son of N.
31. 53 and the God of N., the God of their father
Josh. 24. 2 father of Abraham, and the father of N.

NAH'-SHON, נַחְשׁוֹן *oracle.*
Son of Aminadab, and prince of Judah in the days of Moses. See *Naashon.* B.C. 1492.
Num. 1. 7 Of Judah ; N. the son of Amminadab
2. 3 N. the son of Amminadab (shall be) capt.
7. 12 he that offered..was N. the son of Amm.
7. 17 the offering of N. the son of Amminadab
10. 14 over his host (was) N. the son of Ammin.
Ruth 4. 20 And Amminadab begat N., and N. begat
1 Ch. 2. 10 Amminadab begat N., prince of the chil.
2. 11 And N. begat Salma, and Salma begat B.

NA'-HUM, נַחוּם *comforter.*
One of the later prophets, a native of Elkosh in Galilee, who prophesied against Nineveh. B.C. 713.
Nah. 1. 1 The book of the vision of N. the Elkoshite

NAIL —
1. *Nail, claw*, צִפֹּרֶן *tsipporen* [printed: טְפַר *tephar*].
Dan. 4. 33 like eagles' (feathers), and his nails like
7. 19 (were of) iron, and his nails (of) brass

2. *A pin, nail,* יָתֵד *yathed.*
Judg. 4. 21 took a nail of the tent, and took an ham.
4. 21 smote the nail into his temples, and fast.
4. 22 lay dead, and the nail (was) in his temples
5. 26 She put her hand to the nail, and her ri.
Ezra 9. 8 and to give us a nail in his holy place, that
Isa. 22. 23 And I will fasten him (as) a nail in a sure
22. 25 shall the nail that is fastened in the sure
Zech. 10. 4 came forth the corner, out of him the na.

3. *A nail or pin,* מַסְמֵר *masmer.*
1 Ch. 22. 3 prepared iron in abundance for the nails
2 Ch. 3. 9 the weight of the nails (was) fifty shekels
Isa. 41. 7 he fastened it with nails, (that) it should
Jer. 10. 4 fasten it with nails and with hammers, that

4. *Nails, or pins,* מַשְׂמְרוֹת *masmeroth.*
Eccl. 12. 11 and as nails fastened (by) the masters of

5. *Nail, print,* צִפֹּרֶן *tsipporen.*
Deut 21. 12 shall shave her head, and pare her nails

6. *Nail,* ἧλος *hēlos.*
John 20. 25 see in his hands the print of the nails, and
20. 25 my finger into the print of the nails, and

NAIL, to —
To nail, προσηλόω *prosēloō.*
Col. 2. 14 took it out of the way, nailing it to his c.

NA'-IN, Ναΐν.
A city in Galilee, two miles S. of Mount Tabor, a little S.W. of the sea of Galilee, where Jesus restored a widow's son to life; now called *Nain.*
Luke 7. 11 he went into a city called N.; and many

NA'-IOTH, נָיוֹת [V. L. נוית] *dwelling.*
A place in Ramah where Samuel dwelt.
1 Sa. 19. 18 And he and Samuel went and dwelt in N.
19. 19, 23, 23 Behold, David (is) at N. in Ramah
19. 22 And (one) said, Behold, (they be) at N. in
20. 1 David fled from N. in Ramah, and came

NAKED —
1. *Naked ones,* מַעֲרֻמִּים *maarummim.*
2 Ch. 28. 15 clothed all that were naked among them

2. *Naked,* עֵירֹם *erom.*
Gen. 3. 7 and they knew that they (were) naked; and
3. 10 and I was afraid, because I (was) naked
3. 11 Who told thee that thou (wast) naked?
Eze. 16. 7 grown, whereas thou (wast) naked and
16. 22 when thou wast naked and bare, (and)
16. 39 fair jewels, and leave thee naked and ba.
18. 7, 16 hath covered the naked with a garment
23. 29 and shall leave thee naked and bare; and

3. *Naked,* עָרוֹם *arom.*
Gen. 2. 25 they were both naked, the man and his
1 Sa. 19. 24 and lay down naked all that day and all
Job 1. 21 Naked came I out of my mother's womb
1. 21 naked shall I return thither: the LORD
22. 6 and stripped the naked of their clothing
24. 7 They cause the naked to lodge without cl.
24. 10 They cause (him) to go naked without c.
26. 6 Hell (is) naked before him, and destruct.
Eccl. 5. 15 naked shall he return to go as he came
Isa. 20. 2 And he did so, walking naked and baref.
20. 3 Isaiah hath walked naked and barefoot
20. 4 young and old, naked and barefoot, even
58. 7 when thou seest the naked, that thou cover
Hos. 2. 3 Lest I strip her naked, and set her as in
Amos 2. 16 shall flee away naked in that day, saith
Mic. 1. 8 I will go stripped and naked: I will make

4. *Nakedness,* עֶרְיָה *eryah.*
Mic. 1. 11 of Saphir, having thy shame naked: the

5. *To free, expose,* פָּרַע *para.*
Exod 32. 25 when Moses saw that the people (were) n.

6. *Naked,* γυμνός *gumnos.*
Matt 25. 36 Naked, and ye clothed me: I was sick, and
25. 38 took (thee) in? or naked, and clothed (thee)?
25. 43 naked, and ye clothed me not: sick, and
25. 44 or athirst, or a stranger, or naked, or sick
Mark 14. 51 a linen cloth cast about (his) naked (body)
14. 52 the linen cloth, and fled from them naked
John 21. 7 for he was naked, and did cast himself
Acts 19. 16 so that they fled out of that house naked
2 Co. 5. 3 being clothed we shall not be found nak.
Heb. 4. 13 but all things (are) naked and opened unto
Jas. 2. 15 If a brother or sister be naked, and dest.
Rev. 3. 17 miserable, and poor, and blind, and nak.
16. 15 he walk naked, and they see his shame
17. 16 and shall make her desolate and naked, and

NAKED, to be (made) —
1. *To be naked,* עוּר *ur,* 2.
Hab. 3. 9 Thy bow was made quite naked, (accor.)

2. *To be naked, destitute,* γυμνητεύω *gumnēteuō.*
1 Co. 4. 11 thirst, and are naked, and are buffeted

NAKED, to make (self) —
1. *To make or show self naked,* עָרָה *arah,* 7.
Lam. 4. 21 be drunken, and shalt make thyself naked

2. *To free, expose,* פָּרַע *para.*
Exod 32. 25 Aaron had made them naked unto (their)

3. *To make free, expose,* פָּרַע *para,* 5.
2 Ch. 28. 19 he made Judah naked, and transgressed

NAKEDNESS —
1. *Nakedness,* מָעוֹר *maor.*
Hab. 2. 15 that thou mayest look on their nakedness

2. *Nakedness, void space,* מַעַר *maar.*
Nah. 3. 5 I will show the nations thy nakedness, and

3. *Naked,* עֵירֹם *erom.*
Deut 28. 48 and in thirst, and in nakedness, and in

4. *Nakedness,* עֶרְוָה *ervah.*
Gen. 9. 22 saw the nakedness of his father, and told
9. 23 and covered the nakedness of their father
9. 23 and they saw not their father's nakedness
42. 9 see the nakedness of the land ye are come
42. 12 Nay, but to see the nakedness of the land
Exod 20. 26 that thy nakedness be not discovered th.
Lev. 18. 6 shall approach..to uncover (their) naked.
18. 7 nakedness of thy father, or the nakedness
18. 7, 11, 15 thou shalt not uncover her naked.
18. 8 The nakedness of thy father's wife shalt
18. 8 not uncover: it (is) thy father's nakedness
18. 9 The nakedness of thy sister, the daughter
18. 9 (even) their nakedness thou shalt not un.
18. 10 The nakedness of thy son's daughter, or
18. 10 their nakedness thou shalt not uncover
18. 10 for theirs (is) thine own nakedness
18. 11 The nakedness of thy father's wife's dau.
18. 12, 13, 14, 15, 16, 17 shalt not uncover the n.
18. 16 brother's wife: it (is) thy brother's nake.
18. 17 to uncover her nakedness; (for) they (are)
18. 18 to vex (her), to uncover her nakedness, be.
18. 19 to uncover her nakedness as long as she
20. 11 hath uncovered his father's nakedness: b.
20. 17 see her nakedness, and she see his naked.
20. 17 he hath uncovered his sister's nakedness
20. 18 shall uncover her nakedness, he hath dis.
20. 19 And thou shalt not uncover the nakedness
20. 20 he hath uncovered his uncle's nakedness
20. 21 he hath uncovered his brother's nakedness
1 Sa. 20. 30 the confusion of thy mother's nakedness
Isa. 47. 3 Thy nakedness shall be uncovered, yea, thy
Lam. 1. 8 because they have seen her nakedness; yea
Eze. 16. 8 over thee, and covered thy nakedness
16. 36 and thy nakedness discovered through thy
16. 37 and will discover thy nakedness unto them
16. 37 that they may see all thy nakedness
22. 10 they discovered their father's nakedness
23. 10 These discovered her nakedness: they t.
23. 18 discovered her nakedness: then my mind
23. 29 and the nakedness of thy whoredoms shall
Hos. 2. 9 and my flax (given) to cover her nakedness

5. *Flesh of nakedness,* בְּשַׂר עֶרְוָה [*basar*].
Exod 28. 42 linen breeches to cover their nakedness

6. *Nakedness,* γυμνότης *gumnotēs.*
Rom. 8. 35 famine, or nakedness, or peril, or sword
2 Co. 11. 27 in fastings often, in cold and nakedness
Rev. 3. 18 the shame of thy nakedness do not appear

NAME —
1. *Name, renown,* שֵׁם *shem.*
Gen. 2. 11 name of the first (is) Pison: that (is) it wh.
2. 13 And the name of the second river (is) Gi.
2. 14 And the name of the third river (is) Hid.
2. 19 living creature, that (was) the name ther.
2. 20 Adam gave names to all cattle, and to the
3. 20 Adam called his wife's name Eve; because
4. 17 called the name of the city, after the name
4. 19 name of the one (was) Adah, and the name
4. 21 his brother's name (was) Jubal: he was the
4. 25 she bare a son, and called his name Seth
4. 26 born a son; and he called his name Enos
4. 26 began men to call upon the name of the L.
5. 2 blessed them, and called their name Adam
5. 3 after his image; and called his name Seth
5. 29 And he called his name Noah, saying, This
10. 25 the name of one (was) Peleg; for in his d.
10. 25 divided; and his brother's name (was) Jo.
11. 4 let us make us a name, lest we be scattered
11. 9 Therefore is the name of it called Babel
11. 29 the name of Abram's wife (was) Sarai
11. 29 name of Nahor's wife, Milcah..daughter
12. 2 will bless thee, and make thy name great
12. 8 and called upon the name of the LORD
13. 4 there Abram called on the name of the L.
16. 1 had..an Egyptian, whose name (was) H.
16. 11 a son, and shalt call his name Ishmael
16. 13 she called the name of the LORD that sp.
16. 15 Abram called his son's name, which Hag.
17. 5 Neither shall thy name any more be called
17. 5 but thy name shall be Abraham; for a f.
17. 15 name Sarai, but Sarah (shall) her name (be)
17. 19 and thou shalt call his name Isaac: and
19. 22 Therefore the name of the city was called
19. 37 bare a son, and called his name Moab: the
19. 38 bare a son, and called his name Ben-ammi
21. 3 Abraham called the name of his son that
21. 33 and called there on the name of the LORD
22. 14 Abraham called the name of that place J.
22. 24 his concubine, whose name (was) Reumah
24. 29 had a brother, and his name (was) Laban
25. 1 took a wife, and her name (was) Keturah
25. 13 these (are) the names of the sons of Ishm.
25. 13 by their names, according to their gener.
25. 16 of Ishmael, and these (are) their names
25. 25 garment; and they called his name Esau
25. 26 and his name was called Jacob: and Isaac
25. 30 faint; therefore was his name called Edom
26. 18 he called their names after the names by
26. 20 and he called the name of the well Esek
26. 21 also: and he called the name of it Sitnah
26. 22 and he called the name of it Rehoboth
26. 25 and called upon the name of the LORD
26. 33 the name of the city (is) Beer-sheba unto
28. 19 he called the name of that place Beth-el

Gen. 28. 19 the name of that city (was called) Luz at
29. 16 name of the elder (was) Leah, and the n.
29. 32 she called his name Reuben: for she said
29. 33 (son) also: and she called his name Sime.
29. 34 sons: therefore was his name called Levi
29. 35 therefore she called his name Judah: and
30. 6 a son: therefore called she his name Dan
30. 8, 11, 13, 18, 20 and she called his name
30. 21 a daughter, and called her name Dinah
30. 24 And she called his name Joseph; and said
31. 48 Therefore was the name of it called Gale.
32. 2 he called the name of that place Mahan.
32. 27 he said unto him, What (is) thy name?
32. 28 Thy name shall be called no more Jacob
32. 29 said, Tell (me), I pray thee, thy name. And
32. 29 (is) it (that) thou dost ask after my name?
32. 30 Jacob called the name of the place Peniel
33. 17 therefore the name of the place is called
35. 8 the name of it was called Allon-bachuth
35. 10 God said unto him, Thy name (is) Jacob
35. 10 thy name shall not be called any more J.
35. 10 shall be thy name; and he called his name
35. 15 Jacob called the name of the place where
35. 18 that she called his name Ben-oni: but his
36. 10 These (are) the names of Esau's sons; E.
36. 32, 35, 39 and the name of his city (was)
36. 39 his wife's name (was) Mehetabel, the da.
36. 40 these (are) the names..by their names
38. 1 certain Adullamite, whose name (was) H.
38. 2 certain Canaanite, whose name (was) Sh.
38. 3 and bare a son; and he called his name Er
38. 4 bare a son; and she called his name Onan
38. 5 bare a son; and called his name Shelah
38. 6 Judah took a wife..whose name (was) T.
38. 29 therefore his name was called Pharez
38. 30 his hand: and his name was called Zarah
41. 45 Pharaoh called Joseph's name Zaphnath.
41. 51 Joseph called the name of the first born
41. 52 the name of the second called he Ephraim
46. 8 these (are) the names of the children of I.
48. 6 called after the name of their brethren in
48. 16 my name be named on them, and the name
50. 11 the name of it was called Abel-mizraim
Exod. 1. 1 Now these (are) the names of the children
1. 15 name of the one (was) Shiphrah..the name
2. 10 And she called his name Moses: and she
2. 22 a son, and he called his name Gershom
3. 13 they shall say to me, What (is) his name?
3. 15 this (is) my name for ever, and this (is)
5. 23 I came to Pharaoh to speak in thy name
6. 3 but by my name Jehovah was I not known
6. 16 And these (are) the names of the sons of
9. 16 that my name may be declared throughout
15. 3 (is) a man of war: the LORD (is) his name
15. 23 therefore the name of it was called Marah
16. 31 the house of Israel called the name thereof
17. 7 he called the name of the place Massah
17. 15 and called the name of it Jehovah-nissi
18. 3 of which the name of the one (was) Gers.
18. 4 And the name of the other (was) Eliezer
20. 7 Thou shalt not take the name of the LORD
20. 7 hold him guiltless that taketh his name
20. 24 In all places where I record my name I
23. 13 make no mention of the name of other g.
23. 21 will not pardon..for my name (is) in him
28. 9 grave on them the names of the children
28. 10 Six of their names on one stone, and (the
28. 10 six names of the rest on the other stone
28. 11 with the names of the children of Israel
28. 12 Aaron shall bear their names before the
28. 21 be with the names of the children of Isr.
28. 21 twelve, according to their names, (like)
28. 21 every one with his name shall they be ac
28. 29 Aaron shall bear the names of the child.
31. 2 See, I have called by name Bezaleel the
33. 12 yet thou hast said, I know thee by name
33. 17 grace in my sight, and I know thee by n.
33. 19 and I will proclaim the name of the LORD
34. 5 and proclaimed the name of the LORD
34. 14 for the LORD, whose name (is) Jealous, (is)
35. 30 LORD hath called by name Bezaleel the sor
39. 6, 14 the names of the children of Israel
39. 14 twelve, according to their names, (like) th
39. 14 every one with his name, according to th
Lev. 18. 21 neither shalt thou profane the name of
19. 12 And ye shall not swear by my name falsely
19. 12 neither shalt thou profane the name of thy
20. 3 sanctuary, and to profane my holy name
21. 6 and not profane the name of their God
22. 2 that they profane not my holy name (in
22. 32 Neither shall ye profane my holy name
24. 11 Israelitish woman's son blasphemed the n.
24. 11 and his mother's name (was) Shelomith
24. 16 he that blasphemeth the name of the L.
24. 16 when he blasphemeth the name..shall be
Num. 1. 2 with the number of (their) names, every
1. 5 these (are) the names of the men that shall
1. 17 men which are expressed by (their) names
1. 18 according to the number of the names
So in v. 20, 22, 24, 26, 28, 30, 32, 34, 36, 38, 40, 42.
3. 2, 3 these (are) the names of the sons of A.
3. 17 these were the sons of Levi by their names
3. 18 these (are) the names of the sons of Gers.
3. 40 and take the number of their names
4. 32 by the number of names, from a month old
4. 32 by name ye shall reckon the instruments
6. 27 And they shall put my name upon the c.
11. 3 he called the name of the place Taberah
11. 26 the camp, the name of the one (was) Eld.
11. 26 and the name of the other Medad: and
11. 34 he called the name of that place Kibroth.
13. 4 these (were) their names: of the tribe of

Num 13. 16 These (are) the names of the men which M.
17. 2 write thou every man's name upon his rod
17. 3 thou shalt write Aaron's name upon the
21. 3 and he called the name of the place Hor.
25. 14 Now the name of the Israelite that was
25. 15 the name of the Midianitish woman that
26. 33 the names of the daughters of Zelophehad
26. 46 And the name of the daughter of Asher
26. 53 shall be..according to the number of na.
26. 55 according to the names of the tribes of
26. 59 the name of Amram's wife (was) Jochebed
27. 1 these (are) the names of his daughters; M.
27. 4 Why should the name of our father be
32. 38 Baal-meon, their names being changed
32. 38 and gave other names unto the cities wh.
32. 42 and called it Nobah, after his own name
34. 17 These (are) the names of the men which
34. 19 the names of the men (are) these: Of the
Deut. 3. 14 called them after his own name, Bashan.
5. 11 Thou shalt not take the name of the LORD
5. 11 hold (him) guiltless that taketh his name in
6. 13 and serve him, and shalt swear by his n.
7. 24 and thou shalt destroy their name from
9. 14 blot out their name from under heaven
10. 8 and to bless in his name, unto this day
10. 20 shalt thou cleave, and swear by his name
12. 3 destroy the names of them out of that p.
12. 5 out of all your tribes to put his name th.
12. 11 choose to cause his name to dwell there
12. 21 thy God hath chosen to put his name th.
14. 23 he shall choose to place his name there
14. 24 God shall choose to set his name there
16. 2 LORD shall choose to place his name there
16. 6 thy God shall choose to place his name in
16. 11 God hath chosen to place his name there
18. 5, 7 minister in the name of the LORD
18. 19 words which he shall speak in my name
18. 20 shall presume to speak a word in my name
18. 20 that shall speak in the name of other gods
18. 22 When a prophet speaketh in the name of
21. 5 and to bless in the name of the LORD; and
22. 14 bring up an evil name upon her, and say
22. 19 because he hath brought up an evil name
25. 6 shall succeed in the name of his brother
25. 6 that his name be not put out of Israel
25. 7 raise up unto his brother a name in Israel
25. 10 his name shall be called in Israel, The h.
26. 2 God shall choose to place his name there
26. 19 in praise, and in name, and in honour; and
28. 10 see that thou art called by the name of
28. 58 fear this glorious and fearful name, The
29. 20 LORD shall blot out his name from under
32. 3 Because I will publish the name of the L.
Josh. 5. 9 Wherefore the name of the place is called
7. 9 and cut off our name from the earth: and
7. 9 what wilt thou do unto thy great name?
7. 26 the name of that place was called, The v.
9. 9 because of the name of the LORD thy God
14. 15 the name of Hebron before (was) Kirjath.
15. 15 and the name of Debir before (was) Kir.
17. 3 and these (are) the names of his daughters
19. 47 Dan, after the name of Dan their father
21. 9 cities which are (here) mentioned by name
23. 7 make mention of the name of their gods
Judg. 1. 10 the name of Hebron before (was) Kirjath.
1. 11 the name of Debir before (was) Kirjath-s.
1. 17 the name of the city was called Hormah
1. 23 now the name of the city before (was) Luz
1. 26 a city, and called the name thereof Luz
1. 26 which (is) the name thereof unto this day
2. 5 they called the name of that place Bochim
8. 31 a son, whose name he called Abimelech
13. 2 the Danites, whose name (was) Manoah
13. 6 whence he (was), neither told he me his n.
13. 17 What (is) thy name, that when thy sayings
13. 18 him, Why askest thou thus after my name
13. 24 bare a son, and called his name Samson
15. 19 he called the name thereof En-hakkore
16. 4 loved a woman..whose name (was) Del.
17. 1 man of mount Ephraim, whose name (was)
18. 29 And they called the name of the city Dan
18. 29 after the name of Dan their father, who
18. 29 the name of the city (was) Laish at the fi.
Ruth 1. 2 And the name of the man (was) Elimelech
1. 2 name of his wife Naomi, and the name
1. 4 of Moab; the name of the one (was) Or.
1. 4 name of the other Ruth: and they dwelt
2. 1 of Elimelech; and his name (was) Boaz
2. 19 The man's name with whom I wrought
4. 5, 10 to raise up the name of the dead upon
4. 10 that the name of the dead be not cut off
4. 14 that his name may be famous in Israel
4. 17 the women her neighbours gave it a name
4. 17 and they called his name Obed: he (is) the
1 Sa. 1. 1 and his name (was) Elkanah, the son of J.
1. 2 name of the one (was) Hannah, and the n.
1. 20 bare a son, and called his name Samuel
7. 12 and called the name of it Eben-ezer, say.
8. 2 Now the name of his first born was Joel
8. 2 the name of his second, Abiah: (they were)
9. 1 whose name (was) Kish, the son of Abiel
9. 2 And he had a son, whose name (was) Saul
12. 22 not forsake his people for his great name's
14. 4 the name of the one (was) Bozez, and the n.
14. 49 the names of his two daughters (were th.
14. 49 name of the first born Merab, and the na.
14. 50 the name of Saul's wife (was) Ahinoam, the
14. 50 name of the captain of his host (was) Ab.
17. 12 of that Ephrathite..whose name (was) J.
17. 13 the names of his three sons that went to
17. 23 the Philistine of Gath, Goliath by name
17. 45 I come to thee in the name of the LORD

1 Sa. 18. 30 wisely..so that his name was much set by
20. 42 sworn both of us in the name of the LORD
21. 7 his name (was) Doeg, an Edomite, the ch.
24. 21 destroy my name out of my father's house
25. 3 name of the man (was) Nabal, and the n.
25. 5 and go to Nabal, and greet him in my n.
25. 9 they spake to Nabal..in the name of Da.
25. 25 his name (is), so (is) he; Nabal (is) his n.
2 Sa. 3. 7 a concubine, whose name (was) Rizpah, the
4. 2 name of the one (was) Baanah, and the n.
4. 4 became lame. And his name (was) Mep.
5. 14 the names of those that were born unto
5. 20 called the name of that place Baal-pera.
6. 2 whose name is called by the name of
6. 18 he blessed the people in the name of the
7. 9 made thee a great name, like unto the n.
7. 13 He shall build an house for my name; and
7. 23 to make him a name, and to do for you
7. 26 let thy name be magnified for ever, saying
8. 13 David gat (him) a name when he returned
9. 2 (there was)..a servant, whose name (was)
9. 12 had a young son, whose name (was) Micah
12. 24 he called his name Solomon: and the L.
12. 25 he called his name Jedidiah, because of
12. 28 the city, and it be called after my name
13. 1 had a fair sister, whose name (was) Tamar
13. 3 a friend, whose name (was) Jonadab, the
14. 7 (neither) name nor remainder upon the
14. 27 and one daughter, whose name (was) T.
16. 5 whose name (was) Shimei, the son of Gera
17. 25 (was) a man's son whose name (was) Ithra
18. 18 no son to keep my name in remembrance
18. 18 he called the pillar after his own name
20. 1 a man of Belial, whose name (was) Sheba
20. 21 Sheba the son of Bichri by name, hath
22. 50 and I will sing praises unto thy name
23. 8 the names of the mighty men whom Da.
23. 18 (and) slew (them), and had the name am.
23. 22 and had the name among three mighty m.
1 Ki. 1. 47 the name of Solomon better than thy n.
3. 2 no house built unto the name of the L.
4. 8 these (are) their names: The son of Hur
5. 3, 5 build an house unto the name of the L.
5. 5 he shall build an house unto my name
7. 21 pillar, and called the name thereof Jachin
7. 21 pillar, and called the name thereof Boaz
8. 16 an house, that my name might be therein
8. 17, 20 an house for the name of the LORD God
8. 18 was in thine heart to build..unto my name
8. 19 he shall build the house unto my name
8. 29 thou hast said, My name shall be there
8. 33 and confess thy name, and pray, and make
8. 35 confess thy name, and turn from their sin
8. 41 out of a far country for thy name's sake
8. 42 they shall hear of thy great name, and of
8. 43 people of the earth may know thy name
8. 43 that this house..is called by thy name
8. 44, 48 house that I have built for thy name
9. 3 hast built, to put my name there for ever
9. 7 house, which I have hallowed for my name
10. 1 concerning the name of the LORD, she
11. 26 whose mother's name (was) Zeruah, a w.
11. 36 I have chosen me to put my name there
13. 2 a child shall be born..Josiah by name
14. 21 LORD did choose..to put his name there
14. 21, 31 mother's name (was) Naamah an A.
15. 2, 10 mother's name (was) Maachah, the d.
16. 24 called the name of the city which he built
16. 24 after the name of Shemer, owner of the
18. 24 And call ye on the name of your gods, and
18. 24 I will call on the name of the LORD; and
18. 25 call on the name of your gods, but put no
18. 26 called on the name of Baal from morning
18. 31 came, saying, Israel shall be thy name
18. 32 built an altar in the name of the LORD
21. 8 she wrote letters in Ahab's name, and s.
22. 16 (which is) true in the name of the LORD
22. 42 his mother's name (was) Azubah the dau.
2 Ki. 2. 24 and cursed them in the name of the LORD
5. 11 call on the name of the LORD his God, and
8. 26 his mother's name (was) Athaliah, the d.
12. 1 his mother's name (was) Zibiah of Beer-s.
14. 2 mother's name (was) Jehoaddan of Jeru.
14. 7 called the name of it Joktheel unto this
14. 27 he would blot out the name of Israel from
15. 2 and his mother's name (was) Jecoliah of
15. 33 his mother's name (was) Jerusha, the da.
18. 2 mother's name also (was) Abi, the daug.
21. 1 And his mother's name (was) Hephzi-bah
21. 4 said, In Jerusalem will I put my name
21. 7 In this house..I put my name for ever
21. 19 his mother's name (was) Meshullemeth
22. 1 his mother's name (was) Jedidah, the da.
23. 27 of which I said, My name shall be there
23. 31 his mother's name (was) Hamutal, the d.
23. 34 and turned his name to Jehoiakim, and to.
23. 36 his mother's name (was) Zebudah, the d.
24. 8 And his mother's name (was)
24. 17 the king..changed his name to Zedekiah
24. 18 his mother's name (was) Hamutal, the
1 Ch. 1. 19 the name of the one (was) Peleg, because
1. 19 and his brother's name (was) Joktan
1. 43 and the name of his city (was) Dinhabah
1. 46 and the name of his city (was) Avith
1. 50 and the name of his city (was) Pai; and
1. 50 wife's name (was) Mehetabel, the daughter
2. 26 also another wife, whose name (was) Atar.
2. 29 name of the wife of Abishur (was) Abiha.
2. 34 servant, an Egyptian, whose name (was)
4. 3 the name of their sister (was) Hazelelponi
4. 9 his mother called his name Jabez, saying
4. 38 These mentioned by (their) names (were)

1 Ch. 4. 41 these written by name came in the days
6. 17 these (be) the names of the sons of Gers.
6. 65 cities which are called by (their) names
7. 15 sister's name (was) Maachah; and the name
7. 16 she called his name Peresh: and the name
7. 23 and he called his name Beriah, because
8. 29 father of Gibeon; whose wife's name (was)
8. 38 had six sons, whose names (are) these
9. 35 Jehiel, whose wife's name (was) Maachah
9. 44 Azel had six sons, whose names (are) these
11. 20 slew (them), and had a name among the
11. 24 and had the name among the three mighti.
12. 31 which were expressed by name, to come
13. 6 cherubim, whose name is called (on it)
14. 4 these (are) the names of (his) children wh.
14. 11 called the name of that place Baal-perazim
16. 2 blessed the people in the name of the L.
16. 8 call upon his name, make known his deeds
16. 10 Glory ye in his holy name: let the heart
16. 29 Give..the LORD the glory..unto his name
16. 35 we may give thanks to thy holy name, (and)
16. 41 were chosen, who were expressed by name
17. 8 have made thee a name like the name of
17. 21 to make thee a name of greatness and
17. 24 thy name may be magnified for ever, saying
21. 19 which he spake in the name of the LORD
22. 7 house unto the name of the LORD my God
22. 8 shalt not build an house unto my name
22. 9 his name shall be Solomon, and I will g.
22. 10 He shall build an house for my name
22. 19 is to be built to the name of the LORD
23. 13 to minister..and to bless in his name for
23. 24 counted by number of names by their
28. 3 shalt not build an house for my name
29. 13 thank thee, and praise thy glorious name
29. 16 build thee an house for thine holy name
2 Ch. 2. 1 build an house for the name of the LORD
2. 4 I build an house to the name of the LORD
3. 17 called the name of that on the right hand
3. 17 and the name of that on the left Boaz
6. 5 an house in, that my name might be there
6. 6 Jerusalem, that my name might be there
6. 7, 10 for the name of the LORD God of Israel
6. 8 in thine heart to build an house for my n.
6. 9 he shall build the house for my name
6. 20 that thou wouldest put thy name there
6. 24 confess thy name, and pray, and make
6. 26 confess thy name, and turn from their sin
6. 32 a far country for thy great name's sake
6. 33 all people of the earth may know thy na.
6. 33 house..I have built, is called by thy na.
6. 34, 38 house which I have built for thy name
7. 14 If my people, which are called by my na.
7. 16 that my name may be there for ever; and
7. 20 house, which I have sanctified for my na.
12. 13 LORD had chosen..to put his name there
12. 13 mother's name (was) Naamah an Ammon.
13. 2 His mother's name also (was) Michaiah the
14. 11 in thy name we go against this multitude
18. 15 the truth to me in the name of the LORD
20. 8 built..a sanctuary therein for thy name
20. 9 presence, for thy name (is) in this house
20. 26 the name of the same place was called
20. 31 his mother's name (was) Azubah the da.
22. 2 His mother's name also (was) Athaliah the
24. 1 mother's name also (was) Zibiah of Beer.
25. 1 mother's name (was) Jehoaddan of Jeru.
26. 3 his mother's name also (was) Jecoliah of
26. 8 name spread abroad (even) to the entering
26. 15 his name spread far abroad; for he was
27. 1 His mother's name also (was) Jerushah
28. 9 prophet of the LORD..whose name (was)
28. 15 men which were expressed by name rose
29. 1 his mother's name (was) Abijah, the da.
31. 19 the men that were expressed by name, to
33. 4 In Jerusalem shall my name be for ever
33. 7 In this house..I put my name for ever
33. 18 in the name of the LORD God of Israel
36. 4 and turned his name to Jehoiakim. And
Ezra 2. 61 Gileadite, and was called after their name
8. 13 whose names (are) these, Eliphelet, Jeiel
8. 20 all of them were expressed by name
10. 16 all of them by (their) names, were separ.
Neh. 1. 9 that I have chosen to set my name there
1. 11 thy servants, who desire to fear thy name
7. 63 to wife, and was called after their name
9. 5 and blessed be thy glorious name, which is
9. 7 and gavest him the name of Abraham
9. 10 so didst thou get thee a name, as (it is)
Esth. 2. 5 certain Jew, whose name (was) Mordecai
2. 14 in her, and that she were called by name
2. 22 certified the king..in Mordecai's name
3. 12 in the name of king Ahasuerus was it w.
8. 8 as it liketh you, in the king's name, and
8. 8 which is written in the king's name, and
8. 10 And he wrote in the king Ahasuerus' na.
9. 26 these days Purim, after the name of Pur
Job 1. 1 whose name (was) Job; and that man was
1. 21 away; blessed be the name of the LORD
18. 17 and he shall have no name in the street
42. 14 he called the name of the first, Jemima
42. 14 the name of the second, Kezia; and the n.
Psa. 5. 11 them also that love thy name be joyful in
7. 17 will sing praise to the name of the LORD
8. 1 excellent (is) thy name in all the earth!
9. 2 I will sing praise to thy name, O thou M.
9. 5 hast put out their name for ever and ever
9. 10 they that know thy name will put their
16. 4 offer, nor take up their names into my l.
18. 49 heathen, and sing praises unto thy name
20. 1 the name of the God of Jacob defend thee
20. 5 in the name of our God we will set up (our)

Psa. 20. 7 we will remember the name of the LORD
22. 22 I will declare thy name unto my brethren
23. 3 paths of righteousness for his name's sake
25. 11 For thy name's sake, O LORD, pardon m.
29. 2 the LORD the glory due unto his name; w.
31. 3 therefore for thy name's sake lead me
33. 21 because we have trusted in his holy name
34. 3 magnify..and let us exalt his name toget.
41. 5 When shall he die, and his name perish?
44. 5 through thy name will we tread them un.
44. 8 the day long, and praise thy name for ever
44. 20 If we have forgotten the name of our God
45. 17 I will make thy name to be remembered
48. 10 According to thy name, O God, so (is) thy
49. 11 they call (their) lands after their own na.
52. 9 I will wait on thy name; for (it is) good
54. 1 Save me, O God, by thy name, and judge
54. 6 I will praise thy name, O LORD, for (it is)
61. 5 the heritage of those that fear thy name
61. 8 So will I sing praise unto thy name for ever
63. 4 live: I will lift up my hands in thy name
66. 2 Sing forth the honour of his name; make
66. 4 sing unto thee; they shall sing (to) thy n.
68. 4 Sing unto God, sing praises to his name
68. 4 rideth upon the heavens by his name Jah
69. 30 I will praise the name of God with a song
69. 36 and they that love his name shall dwell
72. 17 His name shall endure for ever: his name
72. 19 And blessed (be) his glorious name for ever
74. 7 dwelling place of thy name to the ground
74. 10 the enemy blaspheme thy name for ever?
74. 18 foolish people have blasphemed thy name
74. 21 let the poor and needy praise thy name
75. 1 for (that) thy name (is) near thy wondrous
76. 1 God known; his name (is) great in Israel
79. 6 kingdoms that have not called upon thy n.
79. 9 our salvation, for the glory of thy name
79. 9 purge away our sins, for thy name's sake
80. 18 quicken us, and we will call upon thy na.
83. 4 that the name of Israel may be no more
83. 16 that they may seek thy name, O LORD
83. 18 that thou, whose name alone (is) Jehovah
86. 9 thee, O LORD; and shall glorify thy name
86. 11 truth: unite my heart to fear my name
86. 12 and I will glorify thy name for evermore
89. 12 Tabor and Hermon shall rejoice in thy n.
89. 16 In thy name shall they rejoice all the
89. 24 and in my name shall his horn be exalted
91. 14 on high, because he hath known my name
92. 1 sing praises unto thy name, O most High
96. 2 Sing unto the LORD, bless his name; show
96. 8 Give..the glory (due unto) his name: br.
99. 3 Let them praise thy..terrible name, (for)
99. 6 among them that call upon his name; and
100. 4 thankful unto him, (and) bless his name
102. 15 So the heathen shall fear the name of the
102. 21 To declare the name of the LORD in Zion
103. 1 all that is within me, (bless) his holy name
105. 1 call upon his name: make known his
105. 3 Glory ye in his holy name: let the heart
106. 8 he saved them for his name's sake, that he
106. 47 to give thanks unto thy holy name, (and)
109. 13 generation following let their name be
109. 21 do thou for me..for thy name's sake: be.
111. 9 for ever: holy and reverend (is) his name
113. 1 of the LORD, praise the name of the LORD
113. 2 Blessed be the name of the LORD from this
113. 3 From the rising of the sun. the LORD'S n.
115. 1 but unto thy name give glory, for thy m.
116. 4 Then called I upon the name of the LORD
116. 13, 17 call upon the name of the LORD
118. 10 in the name of the LORD will I destroy
118. 11, 12 in the name of the LORD I will destroy
118. 26 Blessed (be) he that cometh in the name
119. 55 I have remembered thy name, O LORD, in
119. 132 usest to do unto those that love thy name
122. 4 to give thanks unto the name of the LORD
124. 8 Our help (is) in the name of the LORD, who
129. 8 you: we bless you in the name of the Lo
135. 1 Praise ye the name of the LORD; praise
135. 3 sing praises unto his name; for (it is) pl
135. 13 Thy name, O LORD, (endureth) for ever
138. 2 praise thy name for thy loving kindness
138. 2 magnified thy word above all thy name
140. 13 righteous shall give thanks unto thy name
142. 7 of prison, that I may praise thy name: the
143. 11 Quicken me, O LORD, for thy name's sake
145. 1 I will bless thy name for ever and ever
145. 2 I will praise thy name for ever and ever
145. 21 let all flesh bless his holy name for ever
147. 4 stars; he calleth them all by (their) names
148. 5, 13 Let them praise the name of the LORD
148. 13 for his name alone is excellent; his glory
149. 3 Let them praise his name in the dance
Prov 10. 7 blessed: but the name of the wicked shall
18. 10 The name of the LORD (is) a strong tower
21. 24 (is) his name who dealeth in proud wrath
22. 1 A (good) name (is) rather to be chosen than
30. 4 his name, and what (is) his son's name, if
30. 9 lest I..steal, and take the name of my God
Eccl. 6. 4 his name shall be covered with darkness
7. 1 A (good) name (is) better than precious o.
Song 1. 3 thy name (is as) ointment poured forth
Isa. 4. 1 only let us be called by thy name, to take
7. 14 a son, and shall call his name Immanuel
8. 3 Call his name Maher-shalal-hash-baz
9. 6 and his name shall be called Wonderful
12. 4 say, Praise the LORD, call upon his name
12. 4 make mention that his name is exalted
14. 22 cut off from Babylon the name, and rem.
18. 7 to the place of the name of the LORD of h.
24. 15 (even) the name of the LORD God of Israel

Isa. 25. 1 I will exalt thee, I will praise thy name
26. 8 desire of (our) soul (is) to thy name, and
26. 13 only will we make mention of thy name
29. 23 of him, they shall sanctify my name, and
30. 27 the name of the LORD cometh from far
40. 26 calleth them all by names by the greatn.
41. 25 shall he call upon my name; and he shall
42. 8 I (am) the LORD: that (is) my name: and
43. 1 I have called (thee) by thy name; thou
43. 7 every one that is called by my name: for
44. 5 shall call (himself) by the name of Jacob
44. 5 surname (himself) by the name of Israel
45. 3 I the LORD, which call (thee) by thy name
45. 4 I have even called thee by thy name: I
47. 4 LORD of hosts (is) his name, the Holy One
48. 1 which are called by the name of Israel
48. 1 which swear by the name of the LORD, and
48. 2 Israel: The LORD of hosts (is) his name
48. 9 For my name's sake will I defer mine ang.
48. 19 his name should not have been cut off
49. 1 hath he made mention of my name
50. 10 let him trust in the name of the LORD, and
51. 15 waves roared: The LORD of hosts (is) his n.
52. 5 name continually every day (is) blasphe.
52. 6 Therefore my people shall know my name
54. 5 The LORD of hosts (is) his name; and thy
55. 13 and it shall be to the LORD for a name, for
56. 5 a place and a name better than of sons
56. 5 I will give them an everlasting name, that
56. 6 and to love the name of the LORD, to be
57. 15 high and lofty One..whose name (is) Holy
59. 19 So shall they fear the name of the LORD
60. 9 unto the name of the LORD thy God, and
62. 2 and thou shalt be called by a new name
63. 12 to make himself an everlasting name?
63. 14 people, to make thyself a glorious name
63. 16 Redeemer; thy name (is) from everlasting
63. 19 them; they were not called by thy name
64. 2 make thy name known to thine adversar.
64. 7 (there is) none that calleth upon thy name
65. 1 nation (that) was not called by my name
65. 15 ye shall leave your name for a curse unto
65. 15 and call his servants by another name
66. 5 that cast you out for my name's sake, said
66. 22 so shall your seed and your name remain
Jer. 3. 17 to the name of the LORD, to Jerusalem
7. 10, 11, 14, 30 house, which is called by my n.
7. 12 Shiloh, where I set my name at the first
10. 6 great, and thy name (is) great in might
10. 16 inheritance. The LORD of hosts (is) his n.
10. 25 the families that call not on thy name: for
11. 16 The LORD called thy name, A green olive
11. 19 that his name may be no more remembe.
11. 21 Prophesy not in the name of the LORD
12. 16 ways of my people, to swear by my name
13. 11 for a name, and for a praise, and for a gl.
14. 7 do thou (it) for thy name's sake: for our
14. 9 we are called by thy name; leave us not
14. 14 The prophets prophesy lies in my name
14. 15 the prophets that prophesy in my name
14. 21 Do not abhor (us), for thy name's sake, do
15. 16 for I am called by thy name, O LORD God
16. 21 shall know that my name (is) The LORD
20. 3 The LORD hath not called thy name Pas.
20. 9 of him, nor speak any more in his name
23. 6 (is) his name whereby he shall be called
23. 25 that prophesy lies in my name, saying, I
23. 27 to cause my people to forget my name by
23. 27 their fathers have forgotten my name
25. 29 on the city which is called by my name
26. 9 Why hast thou prophesied in the name of
26. 16 for he hath spoken to us in the name of
26. 20 that prophesied in the name of the LORD
27. 15 yet they prophesy a lie in my name; that
29. 9 prophesy falsely unto you in my name: I
29. 21 which prophesy a lie unto you in my name
29. 23 and have spoken lying words in my name
29. 25 thou hast sent letters in thy name unto all
31. 35 thereof roar; The LORD of hosts (is) his n.
32. 18 Mighty God, the LORD of hosts (is) his n.
32. 20 hast made thee a name, as at this day
32. 34 in the house which is called by my name
33. 2 to establish it; The LORD (is) his name
33. 9 it shall be to me a name of joy, a praise
34. 15 in the house which is called by my name
34. 16 But ye turned, and polluted my name, and
37. 13 name (was) Irijah, the son of Shelemiah
44. 16 spoken unto us in the name of the LORD
44. 26 Behold, I have sworn by my great name
44. 26 that my name shall no more be named in
46. 18 king, whose name (is) The LORD of hosts
48. 15 king, whose name (is) The LORD of hosts
48. 17 and all ye that know his name, say, How
50. 34 strong; The LORD of hosts (is) his name
51. 19 inheritance: The LORD of hosts (is) his n.
51. 57 King, whose name (is) The Lord of hosts
52. 1 his mother's name (was) Hamutal the da.
Lam. 3. 55 I called upon thy name, O LORD, out of the
Eze. 20. 9, 14, 22 wrought for my name's sake, that it
20. 29 And the name thereof is called Bamah
20. 39 but pollute ye my holy name no more with
20. 44 have wrought with you for my name's sake
23. 4 And the names of them (were) Aholah the
23. 4 Thus (were) their names; Samaria (is) Ah.
24. 2 Write thee the name of the day, (even) of
36. 20 they profaned my holy name, when they
36. 21 But I had pity for mine holy name, which
36. 22 but for mine holy name's sake, which ye
36. 23 And I will sanctify my great name, which
39. 7 So will I make my holy name known in the
39. 7 will not (let them) pollute my holy name
39. 16 also the name of the city (shall be) Ham.

Eze. 39. 25 and will be jealous for my holy name
43. 7 my holy name, shall the house of Israel
43. 8 they have even defiled my holy name by
48. 1 Now these (are) the names of the tribes
48. 31 after the names of the tribes of Israel: t.
48. 35 and the name of the city from (that) day
Dan. 1. 7 the prince of the eunuchs gave names: for
9. 6 the prophets, which spake in thy name to
9. 18 and the city which is called by thy name
9. 19 city and thy people are called by thy name
10. 1 whose name was called Belteshazzar; and
Hos. 1. 4 said unto him, Call his name Jezreel; for
1. 6 said unto him, Call her name Lo-ruhamah
1. 9 Then said (God), Call his name Lo-ammi
2. 17 For I will take away the names of Baalim
2. 17 no more be remembered by their name
Joel 2. 26 and praise the name of the LORD your G.
2. 32 whosoever shall call on the name of the L.
Amos 2. 7 the (same) maid, to profane my holy name
4. 13 The LORD, The God of hosts, (is) his name
5. 8 face of the earth; The LORD (is) his name
5. 27 LORD, whose name (is) The God of hosts
6. 10 not make mention of the name of the Lo.
9. 6 face of the earth; The LORD (is) his name
9. 12 which are called by my name, saith the L.
Mic. 4. 5 walk every one in the name of his god
4. 5 we will walk in the name of the LORD our
5. 4 in the majesty of the name of the LORD his
6. 9 (the man of) wisdom shall see thy name
Nah. 1. 14 thee, (that) no more of thy name be sown
Zeph. 1. 4 (and) the name of the Chemarims with the
3. 9 may all call upon the name of the LORD
3. 12 they shall trust in the name of the LORD
3. 20 for I will make you a name and a praise
Zech. 5. 4 of him that sweareth falsely by my name
6. 12 the man whose name (is) The Branch; and
10. 12 they shall walk up and down in his name
13. 2 I will cut off the names of the idols out of
13. 3 speakest lies in the name of the LORD
13. 9 they shall call on my name, and I will hear
14. 9 there be one LORD, and his name one
Mal 1. 6 you, O priests, that despise my name. And
1. 6 ye say, Wherein have we despised thy na.?
1. 11, 11 my name (shall be) great among the
1. 11 incense (shall be) offered unto my name
1. 14 my name (is) dreadful among the heathen
2. 2 to heart, to give glory unto my name, saith
2. 5 feared me, and was afraid before my name
3. 16 that feared..and that thought upon his n.
4. 2 But unto you that fear my name shall the

2. *Name, renown,* שֵׁם *shum.*
Ezra 5. 1 in the name of the God of Israel, (even)
5. 4 What are the names of the men that make
5. 10 We asked them names also, to certify
5. 10 the names of the men that (were) the chief
5. 14 unto (one), whose name (was) Sheshbazzar
6. 12 God that hath caused his name to dwell
Dan. 2. 20 Blessed be the name of God for ever and
2. 26 to Daniel, whose name (was) Belteshazzar
4. 8 Daniel came..whose name (was) Beltesh.
4. 8 according to the name of my god, and in
4. 19 Daniel, whose name (was) Belteshazzar

3. *To call,* καλέω *kaleō.*
Acts 7. 58 at a young man's feet, whose name was S.

4. *Name,* ὄνομα *onoma.*
Matt. 1. 21 thou shalt call his name Jesus; for he
1. 23 they shall call his name Emmanuel, which
1. 25 first born son: and he called his name Je.
6. 9 pray ye: Our Father..Hallowed be thy n.
7. 22 prophesied in thy name? and in thy name
7. 22 in thy name done many wonderful works?
10. 2 the names of the twelve apostles are these
10. 22 be hated of all (men) for my name's sake
10. 41 He that receiveth a prophet in the name
10. 41 receiveth a righteous man in the name of
10. 42 cold (water) only in the name of a disciple
12. 21 And in his name shall the Gentiles trust
18. 5 such little child in my name receiveth me
18. 20 three are gathered together in my name
19. 29 or children, or lands, for my name's sake
21. 9 he that cometh in the name of the Lord
23. 39 he that cometh in the name of the Lord
24. 5 many shall come in my name, saying, I am
24. 9 hated of all nations for my name's sake
27. 32 they found a man of Cyrene, Simon by n.
28. 19 baptizing them in the name of the Father
Mark 5. 9 thy name? And he answered, saying, My n.
5. 22 cometh one of the rulers..Jairus [by name]
6. 14 for his name was spread abroad: and he
9. 37 receive one of such children in my name
9. 38 saw one casting out devils in thy name
9. 39 man which shall do a miracle in my name
9. 41 give..a cup of water to drink in my name
11. 9 that cometh in the name of the Lord
11. 10 [that cometh in the name of the Lord]
13. 6 many shall come in my name, saying, I am
13. 13 be hated of all (men) for my name's sake
16. 17 [In my name shall they cast out devils]
Luke 1. 5 and his wife..her name (was) Elisabeth
1. 13 a son, and thou shalt call his name John
1. 27 espoused to a man whose name was Joseph
1. 27 a virgin..and the virgin's name (was) M.
1. 31 bring..a son, and shalt call his name Jesus
1. 49 For he that is mighty..holy (is) his name
1. 59 Zacharias, after the name of his father
1. 61 none of thy kindred..called by this name
1. 63 saying, His name is John. And they ma.
2. 21 his name was called Jesus, which was so
2. 25 man in Jerusalem, whose name (was) Si.

Luke 6. 22 cast out your name as evil, for the Son
8. 30 Jesus asked him, saying, What is thy n.
9. 48 shall receive this child in my name receiv.
9. 49 saw one casting out devils in thy name
10. 17 are subject unto us through thy name
10. 20 because your names are written in heaven
11. 2 say, Our Father..Hallowed be thy name
13. 35 he that cometh in the name of the Lord
19. 38 King that cometh in the name of the Lord
21. 8 many shall come in my name, saying, I
21. 12 before kings and rulers for my name's sa.
21. 17 be hated of all (men) for my name's sake
24. 18 the one of them, whose name was Cleopas
24. 47 be preached in his name among all nations
John 1. 6 man sent from God, whose name (was) J.
1. 12 (even) to them that believe on his name
2. 23 many believed in his name, when they saw
3. 18 he hath not believed in the name of the
5. 43 I am come in my Father's name, and ye
5. 43 another shall come in his own name, him
10. 3 and he calleth his own sheep by name, and
10. 25 the works that I do in my Father's name
12. 13 that cometh in the name of the Lord
12. 28 Father, glorify thy name. Then came there
14. 13 whatsoever ye shall ask in my name, that
14. 14 If ye shall ask anything in my name, I
14. 26 whom the Father will send in my name
15. 16 ye shall ask of the Father in my name, he
15. 21 will they do unto you for my name's sake
16. 23 Whatsoever ye shall ask..in my name, he
16. 24 ye asked nothing in my name: ask, and
16. 26 that day ye shall ask in my name: and I
17. 6 I have manifested thy name unto the men
17. 11 keep through thine own name those whom
17. 12 I kept them in thy name: those that thou
17. 26 I have declared unto them thy name, and
18. 10 The servant's name was Malchus
20. 31 But..ye might have life through his name
Acts 1. 15 the number of the names together were
2. 21 whosoever shall call on the name of the
2. 38 be baptized every one of you in the name
3. 6 In the name of Jesus Christ of Nazareth
3. 16 his name through faith in his name hath
4. 7 or by what name, have ye done this?
4. 10 the name of Jesus Christ of Nazareth, w.
4. 12 there is none other name under heaven
4. 17 speak henceforth to no man in this name
4. 18 to speak..nor teach in the name of Jesus
4. 30 done by the name of thy holy child Jesus
5. 28 that ye should not teach in this name?
5. 40 should not speak in the name of Jesus
5. 41 worthy to suffer shame for his name
8. 12 concerning..the name of Jesus Christ
8. 16 baptized in the name of the Lord Jesus
9. 14 priests to bind all that call on thy name
9. 15 to bear my name before the Gentiles, and
9. 16 things he must suffer for my names sake
9. 21 which called on this name in Jerusalem
9. 27 boldly at Damascus in the name of Jesus
9. 29 spake boldly in the name of the Lord Je.
10. 43 through his name whosoever believeth in
10. 48 to be baptized in the name of the Lord
13. 6 prophet, a Jew, whose name (was) Bar-J.
13. 8 for so is his name by interpretation
15. 14 take out of them a people for his name
15. 17 the Gentiles, upon whom my name is cal.
15. 26 for the name of our Lord Jesus Christ
16. 18 command thee in the name of Jesus Christ
18. 15 if it be a question of words and names
19. 5 baptized in the name of the Lord Jesus
19. 13 call over them..the name of the Lord Jesus
19. 17 the name of the Lord Jesus was magnified
21. 13 to die at Jerusalem for the name of the
22. 16 baptized..calling on the name of the Lord
26. 9 contrary to the name of Jesus of Nazareth
28. 7 of the chief man..whose name was Publ.
Rom. 1. 5 the faith among all nations, for his name
2. 24 the name of God is blasphemed among the
9. 17 that my name might be declared through.
10. 13 whosoever shall call upon the name of the
15. 9 I will confess..and sing unto thy name
1 Co. 1. 2 upon the name of Jesus Christ our Lord
1. 10 by the name of our Lord Jesus Christ
1. 13 or were ye baptized in the name of Paul?
1. 15 say that I had baptized in mine own name
5. 4 In the name of our Lord Jesus Christ
6. 11 justified in the name of the Lord Jesus
Eph. 1. 21 every name that is named, not only in
5. 20 in the name of our Lord Jesus Christ
Phil. 2. 9 given him a name which is above every n.
2. 10 That at the name of Jesus every knee
4. 3 and..whose names (are) in the book of life
Col. 3. 17 (do) all in the name of the Lord Jesus
2 Th. 1. 12 That the name of our Lord Jesus Christ
3. 6 in the name of our Lord Jesus Christ
1 Ti. 6. 1 that the name of God and (his) doctrine
2 Ti. 2. 19 every one that nameth the name of Christ
Heb. 1. 4 obtained a more excellent name than they
2. 12 will declare thy name unto my brethren
6. 10 love, which ye have showed toward his n.
13. 15 the fruit of (our) lips..thanks to his name
Jas. 2. 7 Do not they blaspheme that worthy name
5. 10 who have spoken in the name of the Lord
5. 14 anointing him with oil in the name of the
1 Pe. 4. 14 ye be reproached for the name of Christ
1 Jo. 2. 12 sins are forgiven you for his name's sake
3. 23 we should believe on the name of his Son
5. 13 [believe on the name of the Son of God]
5. 13 believe on the name of the Son of God
3 John 7 for his name's sake they went forth, tak.
14 salute thee. Greet the friends by name
Rev. 2. 3 for my name's sake hast laboured, and

Rev. 2. 13 thou holdest fast my name, and hast not
2. 17 in the stone a new name written, which
3. 1 thou hast a name that thou livest, and art
3. 4 Thou hast a few names even in Sardis
3. 5 blot out his name out of the book of life
3. 5 will confess his name before my Father
3. 8 kept my word, and hast not denied my n.
3. 12 upon him the name of my God, and the n.
3. 12 and (I will write upon him) my new name
6. 8 his name that sat on him was Death, and
8. 11 the name of the star is called Wormwood
9. 11 whose name in the Hebrew tongue (is) A.
9. 11 in the Greek tongue hath (his) name Ap.
11. 18 them that fear thy name, small and great
13. 1 and upon his heads the name of blasphemy
13. 6 to blaspheme his name, and his tabernacle
13. 8 whose names are not written in the book
13. 17 name of the beast, or the number of his n.
14. 1 Father's name written in their foreheads
14. 11 whosoever receiveth the mark of his name
15. 2 the victory..over the number of his name
15. 4 not fear thee, O Lord, and glorify thy na.
16. 9 blasphemed the name of God, which hath
17. 3 coloured beast, full of names of blasphemy
17. 5 upon her forehead (was) a name written
17. 8 whose names were not written in the book
19. 12 he had a name written that no man knew
19. 13 and his name is called The Word of God
19. 16 he hath on his thigh a name written, King
21. 12 and names written thereon, which are
21. 14 name of the twelve apostles of the Lamb
22. 4 and his name (shall be) in their foreheads

NAME, to —

1. *To say*, אָמַר *amar*.
1 Sa. 16. 3 anoint unto me (him) whom I name unto
28. 8 me (him) up whom I shall name unto
Mic. 2. 7 O (thou that art) named The house of Ja.

2. *To speak*, דָּבַר *dabar*, 3.
Gen. 23. 16 which he had named in the audience of

3. *To mark out, define*, נָקַב *naqab*.
Isa. 62. 2 which the mouth of the LORD shall name
Amos 6. 1 (which are) named chief of the nations, to

4. *To call*, קָרָא *qara*.
1 Sa. 4. 21 And she named the child I-chabod, saying

5. *To place (give) name as*, שִׂים שֵׁם *sim shum*.
Dan. 5. 12 Daniel, whom the king named Belteshaz.

6. *To place (give) name as*, שִׂים שֵׁם *sim shem*.
2 Ki. 17. 34 children of Jacob, whom he named Israel

7. *To say, call*, λέγω *legō*.
Matt. 9. 9 he saw a man, named Matthew, sitting at
Mark 15. 7 And there was (one) named Barabbas, (wh.

8. *To name, give a name*, ὀνομάζω *onomazō*.
Luke 6. 13 twelve, whom also he named apostles
6. 14 Simon, whom he also named Peter, and
Rom 15. 20 the gospel, not where Christ was named
1 Co. 5. 1 as is not [so much as named] among the
Eph. 1. 21 and every name that is named, not only
3. 15 whole family in heaven and earth is named
5. 3 let it not be once named among you, as
2 Ti. 2. 19 every one that nameth the name of Christ

NAMED —

1. *(And) his (her) name was*, שֵׁם *shem*.
Josh. 2. 1 came into an harlot's house, named Rah.
1 Sa. 17. 4 named Goliath, of Gath, whose height
22. 20 the son of Ahitab, named Abiathar, esca.

2. *Name*, ὄνομα *onoma*.
Matt 27. 57 a rich man of Arimathea, named Joseph
Mark 14. 32 to a place which was named Gethsemane
Luke 1. 5 a certain priest named Zacharias, of the
1. 26 unto a city of Galilee, named Nazareth
5. 27 saw a publican, named Levi, sitting at the
8. 41 behold, there came a man named Jairus
10. 38 a certain woman named Martha received
16. 20 there was a certain beggar named 19. 2.
23. 50 behold, (there was) a man named Joseph
John 3. 1 a man of the Pharisees, named Nicodemus
Acts 5. 1 But a certain man named Ananias, with
5. 34 a Pharisee, named Gamaliel, a doctor of
9. 10 disciple at Damascus, named Ananias; and
9. 12 seen in a vision a man named Ananias
9. 33 there he found a certain man named Eneas
9. 36 at Joppa, a certain disciple named Tabitha
11. 28 there stood up one of them named Agabus
12. 13 a damsel came to hearken, named Rhoda
16. 1 disciple was there, named Timotheus, the
16. 14 certain woman named Lydia, a seller of
17. 34 woman named Damaris, and others with
18. 2 found a certain Jew named Aquila, born
18. 7 a certain (man's) house, named Justus
18. 24 And a certain Jew named Apollos, born
19. 24 For a certain (man) named Demetrius, a
20. 9 a certain young man named Eutychus
21. 10 from Judea a certain prophet, named A.
27. 1 unto (one) named Julius, a centurion of A.

NAMED, to be —

1. *To call a name*, קָרָא שֵׁם *qara shem*.
Gen. 27. 36 he said, Is not he rightly named Jacob?

2. *To be called*, קָרָא *qara*, 2.
Gen. 48. 16 and let my name be named on them, and
1 Ch. 23. 14 his sons were named of the tribe of Levi
Eccl. 6. 10 is named already [Heb., its name is called]
Isa. 61. 6 ye shall be named the priests of the LORD
Jer. 44. 26 that my name shall no more be named in

3. *To call*, καλέω (ὄνομα) *kaleō (onoma)*.
Luke 2. 21 which was so named of the angel before he
19. 2 behold, (there was) a man named Zaccheus

NAMELY —

In the, in this, ἐν τῷ *en tō*.
Rom 13. 9 comprehended in this saying, [namely]

NA-O'-MI, נָעֳמִי *pleasant*.
Wife of Elimelech, mother of Mahlon and Chilion, and mother in law of Ruth the Moabitess. B.C. 1312.
Ruth 1. 2 the name of his wife N., and the name of
1. 3 N.'s husband died; and she was left, and
1. 8 N. said unto her two daughters in law, Go
1. 11 N. said, Turn again, my daughters; why
1. 19 moved about them..they said, (Is) this N.
1. 20 Call me not N., call me Mara: for the Alm.
1. 21 why (then) call ye me N., seeing the LORD
1. 22 N. returned, and Ruth the Moabitess, her
2. 1 N. had a kinsman of her husband's, a mi.
2. 2 the Moabitess said unto N., Let me now
2. 6 Moabitish damsel that came back with N.
2. 20 N. said unto her daughter in law, Blessed
2. 20 N. said unto her, The man (is) near of kin
2. 22 N. said unto Ruth her daughter in law
3. 1 Then N. her mother in law said unto her
4. 3 N., that is come again out of the country
4. 5 thou buyest the field of the hand of N.
4. 9 that I have bought all..of the hand of N.
4. 14 the women said unto N., Blessed (be) the
4. 16 N. took the child, and laid it in her bosom
4. 17 a name, saying, There is a son born to N.

NA'-PHISH, NE'-PHISH, נָפִישׁ *numerous*.
1. A son of Ishmael, son of Abraham and Hagar. B.C. 1840.
Gen. 25. 15 Hadar, and Tema, Jetur, N., and Kedemah
1 Ch. 1. 31 Jetur, N., and Kedemah. These are the son
2. His descendants, W. of Jordan, subdued along with the Hagarites and Jeter and Nodah by the two and a half tribes.
1 Ch. 5. 19 the Hagarites, with Jetur, and N., and N.

NAPH-TA'-LI, נַפְתָּלִי *wrestling*.
1. Sixth son of Jacob, and second of Bilhah Rachel's maid. B.C. 1747.
Gen. 30. 8 have prevailed: and she called his name N.
35. 25 Bilhah, Rachel's handmaid; Dan and N.
46. 24 the sons of N.; Jahzeel, and Guni, and J.
49. 21 N. (is) a hind let loose: he giveth goodly
Exod. 1. 4 Dan, and N., Gad, and Asher
1 Ch. 2. 2 Dan, Joseph, and Benjamin, N., Gad, and
7. 13 The sons of N.; Jahziel, and Guni, and Ge.
2. His descendants and their territory which lay in Galilee, E. of Asher and N. of Zebulun. See *Nephthalim*.
Num. 1. 15 Of N.; Ahira the son of Enan
1. 42 Of the children of N., throughout their
1. 43 numbered of them, (even) of the tribe of N.
2. 29 N.: and the captain of the children of N.
7. 78 son of Enan, prince of the children of N.
10. 27 host of the tribe of the children of N.
13. 14 Of the tribe of N., Nahbi the son of Vop.
26. 48 (Of) the sons of N. after their families: of
26. 50 families of N. according to their families
34. 28 prince of the tribe of the children of N.
Deut 27. 13 Gad, and Asher, and Zebulun, Dan, and N.
33. 23 of N. he said, O N., satisfied with favour
34. 2 N., and the land of Ephraim, and Manas.
Josh 19. 32 children of N. (even) for the children of N.
19. 39 tribe of the children of N. according to
20. 7 appointed Kedesh in Galilee in mount N.
21. 6 out of the tribe of N., and out of the half
21. 32 out of the tribe of N., Kedesh in Galilee
Judg. 1. 33 Neither did N. drive out the inhabitants
4. 6 ten thousand men of the children of N.
4. 10 Barak called Zebulun and N. to Kedesh
5. 18 Zebulun and N. (were) a people (that) jeop.
6. 35 unto Asher, and unto Zebulun, and unto N.
7. 23 gathered themselves together out of N.
1 Ki. 4. 15 Ahimaaz (was) in N.; he also took Basm.
7. 14 He (was) a widow's son of the tribe of N.
15. 20 and all Cinneroth, with all the land of N.
2 Ki. 15. 29 and Gilead, and Galilee, all the land of N.
1 Ch. 6. 62 out of the tribe of N., and out of the tribe
6. 76 out of the tribe of N.; Kedesh in Galilee
12. 34 of N. a thousand captains, and with them
12. 40 (even) unto Issachar and Zebulun and N.
27. 19 of N.; Jerimoth the son of Azriel
2 Ch. 16. 4 Abel-maim, and all the store cities of N.
34. 6 and Ephraim, and Simeon, even unto N.
Psa. 68. 27 princes of Zebulun, (and) the princes of N.
Isa. 9. 1 the land of Zebulun, and the land of N.
Eze. 48. 3 even unto the west side, a (portion for) N.
48. 4 by the border of N., from the east side
48. 34 of Gad, one gate of Asher, one gate of N.
The following localities were in the territory of Naphtali: Adamah, Adami, Allon, Aznoth-tabor, Beth-anath, Beth-shemesh, En-hazor, Hammath, Hammon, Hazor, Heleph, Horem, Hukkok, Ijon, Iron, Jabneel, Kartan, Kedesh, Kirjathaim, Lakum, Migdal-el, Neker, Rakkath, Ramah, Tishb, Zaanannim, Zer, &c.

NAPH-TU'-HIM, נַפְתֻּחִים.
The inhabitants of Central Egypt, as the Pathrusim are of Upper Egypt.
Gen. 10. 13 begat Ludim..Anamim, and Lehabim..N.
1 Ch. 1. 11 begat Ludim..Anamim, and Lehabim..N.

NAPKIN—
Napkin, handkerchief, σουδάριον (*Lat. sudarium*)
Luke 19. 20 which I have kept laid up in a napkin
John 11. 44 and his face was bound about with a na.
20. 7 the napkin, that was about his head, not

NAR-CIS'-SUS, Νάρκισσος *flower causing lethargy.*
A believer at Rome, whose household Paul salutes; perhaps the favourite freedman of Claudius the emperor.
Rom 16. 11 Greet them that be of..N., which are in the

NARROW, (to be) —
1. *To be narrow, shut, stopped,* אָטַם *atam.*
Eze. 40. 16 narrow windows to the little chambers
41. 16 The door posts, and the narrow windows
41. 26 narrow windows and palm trees on the
2. *To be narrow, pressed,* אוּץ *uts.*
Josh 17. 15 if mount Ephraim be too narrow for thee
3. *To be straitened, distressed,* יָצַר *yatsar.*
Isa. 49. 19 shall even now be too narrow by reason of
4. *Strait,* צַר *tsar.*
Num 22. 26 went further, and stood in a narrow place
Prov 23. 27 and a strange woman (is) a narrow pit
5. *To be straitened,* צָרַר *tsarar.*
Isa. 28. 20 covering narrower than that he can wrap
6. *Compressed,* θλίβω *thlibō* (pass. partic.).
Matt. 7. 14 narrow (is) the way, which leadeth unto

NARROW—
Closed, latticed, אֲטֻמִים [*atam* (pass. partic.)].
1 Ki. 6. 4 for the house he made windows of narrow l.

NARROWED rests —
Ledges, rests, מִגְרָעוֹת *migraoth.*
1 Ki. 6. 6 he made narrowed rests round about, that

NARROWLY, to look —
To observe, watch, take heed, שָׁמַר *shamar.*
Job 13. 27 and lookest narrowly unto all my paths

NA'-THAN, נָתָן *giver.*
1. A son of David, born after he came to reign over Israel. B.C. 1030.
2 Sa. 5. 14 Shammuah, and Shobab..N...Solomon
1 Ch. 3. 5 N., and Solomon, four, of Bathshua the d.
14. 4 Shammua, and Shobab, N., and Solomon
2. One of David's prophets. B.C. 1040.
2 Sa. 7. 2 the king said unto N. the prophet, See now
7. 3 N. said to the king, Go, do all that (is) in
7. 4 the word of the LORD came unto N., say.
7. 17 According to all..so did N. speak unto D.
12. 1 the LORD sent N. unto David. And he c
12. 5 he said to N.,(As) the LORD liveth, the m
12. 7 And N. said to David, Thou (art) the man
12. 13 David said unto N., I have sinned against
12. 13 N. said unto David, The LORD also hath put
12. 15 N. departed unto his house And the L.
12. 25 he sent by the hand of N. the prophet; and
1 Ki. 1. 8 N. the prophet, and Shimei, and Rei, and
1. 10 N. the prophet, and Benaiah, and the mi.
1. 11 N. spake unto Bath-sheba the mother of
1. 22 And, lo..N. the prophet also came in
1. 23 told the king, saying, Behold N. the prop.
1. 24 And N. said, My lord, O king, hast thou
1. 32, 38, 44 N the prophet, and Benaiah the
1. 34 let Zadok the priest and N. the prophet
1. 45 priest and N. the prophet have anointed
1 Ch. 17. 1 David said to N. the prophet, Lo, I dwell
17. 2 N. said unto David, Do all that (is) in thine
17. 3 that the word of God came to N., saying
17. 15 According to all..so did N. speak unto D.
29. 29 in the book of N. the prophet, and in the
2 Ch. 9. 29 not written in the book of N. the prophet
29. 25 of Gad the king's seer, and N. the prophet
Psa. 51. *title.* N. the prophet came unto him, after he
3. From Zobah in Syria, and father of Igal, one of David's valiant men. B.C. 1070.
2 Sa. 23. 36 Igal the son of N. of Zobah, Bani the Ga.
4. Father of Azariah who was over Solomon's officers. B.C. 1060.
1 Ki. 4. 5 the son of N. (was) over the officers; and
5. Father of Solomon's chief officer. B.C. 1060.
1 Ki. 4. 5 the son of N. (was) principal officer, (and)
6. Son of Attai, and father of Zabad, of the family of Jerahmeel. B.C. 1400.
1 Ch. 2. 36 And Attai begat N., and N. begat Zabad
7. Brother of Joel, one of David's valiant men. B.C. 1048.
1 Ch. 11. 38 the brother of N., Mibhar the son of Hag.
8. A chief man who returned from exile with Ezra. B.C. 457.
Ezra 8. 16 for N., and for Zechariah, and for Mesh.
9. One of the family of Banni who had taken a strange wife. B.C. 456.
Ezra 10. 39 And Shelemiah, and N., and Adaiah
10. A chief man in Israel. B.C. 1030.
Zech. 12. 12 the family of the house of N. apart, and
11. An ancestor of Jesus.
Luke 3. 31 (the son) of N., which was (the son) of D.

NA-THAN ME'-LECH, נְתַן־מֶלֶךְ *the king is giver.*
A eunuch or chamberlain of king Josiah. B.C. 640.
2 Ki 23. 11 the chamber of N. the chamberlain, which

NA-THA-NA'-EL, Ναθαναήλ *gift of God.*
A native of Cana in Galilee; supposed to be the same as *Bartholomew* the apostle.
John 1. 45 Philip findeth N., and saith unto him, We
1. 46 N. said unto him, Can there any good th.
1. 47 Jesus saw N. coming to him, and saith of
1. 48 N. saith unto him, Whence knowest thou
1. 49 N. answered and saith unto him, Rabbi
21. 2 and N. of Cana in Galilee, and the (sons)

NATION —
1. *A nation,* אֻמָּה *ummah.*
Ezra 4. 10 the rest of the nations whom the great and
Dan. 3. 4 To you it is commanded, O people, nations
3. 7 people, the nations, and the languages, fell
3. 29 That every people, nation, and language
4. 1 unto all people, nations, and languages
5. 19 nations, and languages, trembled and fe.
6. 25 Darius wrote unto all people, nations, and
7. 14 that all people, nations, and languages
2. *A nation, corporate body,* גּוֹי *goi.*
Gen. 10. 5 after their families, in their nations
10. 20 in their countries, (and) in their nations
10. 31 tongues, in their lands, after their nations
10. 32 after their generations, in their nations
10. 32 and by these were the nations divided in
12. 2 I will make of thee a great nation, and
14. 1 king of Elam, and Tidal king of nations
14. 9 of Elam, and with Tidal king of nations
15. 14 And also that nation, whom they shall
17. 4 and thou shalt be a father of many nations
17. 5 a father of many nations have I made thee
17. 6 I will make nations of thee, and kings shall
17. 16 she shall be (a mother) of nations; kings
17. 20 beget, and I will make him a great nation
18. 18 surely become a great and mighty nation
18. 18 all the nations of the earth shall be blessed
20. 4 Lord, wilt thou slay..a righteous nation?
21. 13 of the bond woman will I make a nation
21. 18 hand; for I will make him a great nation
22. 18 And in thy seed shall all the nations of
25. 23 Two nations (are) in thy womb, and two
26. 4 shall all the nations of the earth be bles.
35. 11 a nation, and a company of nations
46. 3 I will there make of thee a great nation
48. 19 seed shall become a multitude of nations
Exod. 9. 24 land of Egypt since it became a nation
19. 6 a kingdom of priests, and an holy nation
32. 10 and I will make of thee a great nation
33. 13 and consider that this nation (is) thy pe.
34. 10 done in all the earth, nor in any nation
34. 24 I will cast out the nations before thee
Lev. 18. 24 for in all these the nations are defiled w.
18. 28 as it spued out the nations that (were)
20. 23 not walk in the manners of the nations
Num 14. 12 and will make of thee a greater nation and
14. 15 then the nations which have heard the f.
23. 9 not be reckoned among the nations
24. 8 he shall eat up the nations his enemies
24. 20 said, Amalek (was) the first of the nations
Deut. 4. 6 the nations, which shall hear all these st.
4. 7, 8 what nation (is there so) great
4. 27 LORD shall scatter you among the nations
4. 34 take him a nation from the midst of (ano.)
4. 34 nation, by temptations, by signs, and by
4. 38 To drive out nations from before thee gre.
7. 1 hath cast out many nations before thee
7. 1 nations greater and mightier than thou
7. 17 These nations (are) more than I; how can
7. 22 LORD thy God will put out those nations
8. 20 As the nations which the LORD destroyeth
9. 1 to go in to possess nations greater and
9. 4, 5 but for the wickedness of these nations
9. 14 I will make of thee a nation mightier and
11. 23 will the LORD drive out all these nations
11. 23 and ye shall possess greater nations and
12. 2 all the places wherein the nations which
12. 29 shall cut off the nations from before thee
12. 30 How did these nations serve their gods?
15. 6 and thou shalt lend unto many nations
15. 6 and thou shalt reign over many nations
17. 14 like as all the nations that (are) about me
18. 9 after the abominations of those nations
18. 14 For these nations, which thou shalt pos.
19. 1 LORD thy God hath cut off the nations
20. 15 which (are) not of the cities of these nat.
26. 5 became there a nation, great, mighty, and
26. 19 And to make thee high above all nations
28. 1 will set thee on high above all nations of
28. 12 and thou shalt lend unto many nations
28. 36 unto a nation which neither thou nor thy
28. 49 The LORD shall bring a nation against thee
28. 49 a nation whose tongue thou shalt not un.
28. 50 A nation of fierce countenance, which sh.
28. 65 among these nations shalt thou find no
29. 16 how we came through the nations which
29. 18 go (and) serve the gods of these nations
29. 24 Even all nations shall say, Wherefore hath
30. 1 call (them) to mind among all the nations
31. 3 he will destroy these nations from before
32. 8 divided to the nations their inheritance
32. 21 provoke them to anger with a foolish na.
32. 28 For they (are) a nation void of counsel.
32. 43 Rejoice, O ye nations, (with) his people
Josh 23. 3 your God hath done unto all these nations
23. 4 have divided unto you by lot these nations
23. 4 with all the nations that I have cut off
23. 7 That ye come not among these nations
23. 9 from before you great nations and strong
23. 12 cleave unto the remnant of these nations
23. 13 drive out (any of) these nations from bef.
Judg. 2. 21 the nations which Joshua left when he d.
2. 23 Therefore the LORD left those nations, wi.
3. 1 Now these (are) the nations which the L.
1 Sa. 8. 5 make us a king to judge us like all the n.
8. 20 That we also may be like all the nations
2 Sa. 7. 23 And what one nation in the earth (is) like
7. 23 Egypt, (from) the nations and their gods?
8. 11 he had dedicated of all nations which he
1 Ki. 4. 31 his fame was in all nations round about
11. 2 Of the nations (concerning) which the L.
14. 24 to all the abominations of the nations wh.
18. 10 there is no nation or kingdom whither my
18. 10 took an oath of the kingdom and nation
2 Ki. 17. 26 The nations which thou hast removed, and
17. 29 Howbeit every nation made gods of their
17. 29 every nation in their cities wherein they
17. 33 after the manner of the nations whom they
17. 41 So these nations feared the LORD, and se.
18. 33 Hath any of the gods of the nations deli.
19. 12 Have the gods of the nations delivered
19. 17 have destroyed the nations and their lands
21. 9 did the nations whom the LORD destroyed
1 Ch. 14. 17 brought the fear of him upon all nations
16. 20 (when) they went from nation to nation
16. 31 and let (men) say among the nations, The
17. 21 And what one nation in the earth (is) like
17. 21 by driving out nations from before thy p.
18. 11 that he brought from all (these) nations
2 Ch. 15. 6 And nation was destroyed of nation, and
32. 13 were the gods of the nations of those lands
32. 14 among all the gods of those nations that
32. 15 for no god of any nation or kingdom was
32. 17 As the gods of the nations of (other) lands
32. 23 was magnified in the sight of all nations
Neh. 13. 26 yet among many nations was there no king
Job 12. 23 increaseth the nations, and destroyeth
12. 23 enlargeth the nations, and straiteneth them
34. 29 whether (it be done) against a nation, or
Psa. 9. 17 into hell, (and) all the nations that forget
9. 20 (that) the nations may know themselves
22. 27 kindreds of the nations shall worship be.
22. 28 and he (is) the governor among the nat.
33. 12 Blessed (is) the nation whose God (is) the
43. 1 plead my cause against an ungodly nation
66. 7 his eyes behold the nations: let not the
67. 2 thy saving health among all nations
72. 11 fall down before him; all nations shall
72. 17 in him: all nations shall call him blessed
82. 8 the earth: for thou shalt inherit all nat.
83. 4 let us cut them off from (being) a nation
86. 9 All nations whom thou hast made shall
105. 13 they went from one nation to another, from
106. 5 may rejoice in the gladness of thy nation
106. 27 overthrow their seed also among the na.
113. 4 The LORD (is) high above all nations, (and)
117. 1 O praise the LORD, all ye nations: praise
118. 10 All nations compassed me about: but in
135. 10 Who smote great nations, and slew mig.
147. 20 He hath not dealt so with any nation: and
Prov 14. 34 Righteousness exalteth a nation: but sin
Isa. 1. 4 Ah sinful nation, a people laden with in.
2. 2 the hills; and all nations shall flow unto
2. 4 And he shall judge among the nations
2. 4 nation shall not lift up sword against n.
5. 26 he will lift up an ensign to the nations
9. 1 beyond Jordan, in Galilee of the nations
9. 3 Thou hast multiplied the nation, (and)
10. 6 send him against an hypocritical nation
10. 7 to destroy and cut off nations not a few
11. 12 he shall set up an ensign for the nations
13. 4 kingdoms of nations gathered together
14. 6 he that ruled the nations in anger, is p.
14. 9 hath raised up..all the kings of the nat.
14. 12 ground, which didst weaken the nations!
14. 18 All the kings of the nations, (even) all of
14. 26 that is stretched out upon all the nat.
14. 32 then answer the messengers of the nation?
18. 2 Go, ye swift messengers, to a nation sca.
18. 2, 7 hitherto; a nation meted out and trod.
23. 3 her revenue; and she is a mart of nations
25. 3 the city of the terrible nations shall fear
25. 7 and the veil that is spread over all nations
26. 2 that the righteous nation which keepeth
26. 15, 15 Thou hast increased the nation
29. 7, 8 the multitude of all the nations
30. 28 to sift the nations with the sieve of vanity
33. 3 at the lifting up of thyself the nations
34. 1 Come near, ye nations, to hear; and he.
34. 2 indignation of the LORD (is) upon all nat.
36. 18 Hath any of the gods of the nations del.
37. 12 Have the gods of the nations delivered
40. 15 Behold, the nations (are) as a drop of a b.
40. 17 nations before him (are) as nothing; and
41. 2 gave..nations before him, and made (him)
43. 9 Let all the nations be gathered together
45. 1 holden, to subdue nations before him; and
45. 20 ye (that are) escaped of the nations: they
49. 7 to him whom the nation abhorreth, to a
52. 10 his holy arm in the eyes of all the nations
52. 15 So shall he sprinkle many nations: the
55. 5 thou shalt call a nation..and nations (that)
58. 2 as a nation that did righteousness, and
60. 12 For the nation and kingdom that will not
60. 12 yea, (those) nations shall be utterly wasted
60. 22 and a small one a strong nation: I the L.
61. 11 praise to spring forth before all the nations
64. 2 the nations may tremble at thy presence
65. 1 unto a nation (that) was not called by my
66. 8 shall a nation be born at once? for as soon
66. 18 I will gather all nations and tongues; and
66. 19 that escape of them unto the nations, (to)
66. 20 out of all nations, upon horses, and in c.

Jer. 1. 5 ordained thee a prophet unto the nations
1. 10 I have this day set thee over the nations
2. 11 Hath a nation changed (their) gods, which
3. 17 all the nations shall be gathered unto it
3. 19 a goodly heritage of the hosts of nations
4. 2 the nations shall bless themselves in him
4. 16 Make ye mention to the nations; behold
5. 9, 29 soul be avenged on such a nation as
5. 15 I will bring a nation..a mighty nation, it
5. 15 an ancient nation, a nation whose language
6. 18 Therefore hear, ye nations, and know, O
6. 22 great nation shall be raised from the sides
7. 28 This (is) a nation that obeyeth not the voice
9. 9 soul be avenged on such a nation as this?
9. 26 for all (these) nations (are) uncircumcised
10. 7 Who would not fear thee, O king of nat.?
10. 7 as among all the wise (men) of the nations
10. 10 the nations shall not be able to abide his
12. 17 utterly pluck up and destroy that nation
18. 7, 9 I shall speak concerning a nation, and
18. 8 If that nation, against whom I have pro.
22. 8 And many nations shall pass by this city
25. 9 against all these nations round about, and
25. 11 these nations shall serve the king of Ba
25. 12 punish the king of Babylon, and that na.
25. 13 hath prophesied against all the nations
25. 14 For many nations and great kings shall
25. 15 and cause all the nations, to whom I send
25. 17 made all the nations to drink, unto whom
25. 31 LORD hath a controversy with the nations
25. 32 evil shall go forth from nation to nation
26. 6 make this city a curse to all the nations of
27. 7 And all nations shall serve him, and his
27. 7 many nations and great kings shall serve
27. 8 the nation and kingdom which will
27. 8 that nation will I punish, saith the LORD
27. 11 But the nations that bring their neck u.
27. 13 LORD hath spoken against the nation that
28. 11 from the neck of all nations within the s.
28. 14 iron upon the neck of all these nations
29. 14 and I will gather you from all the nations
29. 18 reproach, among all the nations whither
30. 11 though I make a full end of all nations
31. 7 and shout among the chief of the nations
31. 10 Hear the word of the LORD, O ye nations
31. 36 also shall cease from being a nation bef.
33. 9 and an honour before all the nations of
33. 24 should be no more a nation before them
36. 2 against all the nations, from the day I s.
43. 5 that were returned from all nations whi.
44. 8 reproach among all the nations of the ea.
46. 12 nations have heard of thy shame, and thy
46. 28 will make a full end of all the nations w
48. 2 let us cut it off from (being) a nation
49. 31 get you up unto the wealthy nation that
49. 36 shall be no nation whither the outcasts
50. 2 Declare ye among the nations, and publ
50. 3 there cometh up a nation against her w
50. 9 an assembly of great nations from the n
50. 12 behold, the hindermost of the nations
50. 23 become a desolation among the nations
50. 41 and a great nation, and many kings shall
50. 46 and the cry is heard among the nations
51. 7 nations have drunken..therefore the na
51. 20 with thee will I break in pieces the nations
51. 27 among the nations, prepare the nations
51. 28 Prepare against her the nations with the
51. 41 become an astonishment among the nat.
51. 44 nations shall not flow together any more
Lam. 1. 1 she (that was) great among the nations
4. 17 we have watched for a nation (that) could
Eze. 2. 3 a rebellious nation that hath rebelled ag
5. 5 I have set it in the midst of the nations
5. 6 into wickedness more than the nations
5. 7, 7, 14, 15 the nations that (are) round ab
5. 8 midst of thee in the sight of the nations
6. 8 shall escape the sword among the nations
6. 9 shall remember me among the nations w
12. 15 when I shall scatter them among the nati
19. 4 The nations also heard of him; he was ta.
19. 8 Then the nations set against him on every
25. 10 may not be remembered among the nati.
26. 3 will cause many nations to come up aga.
26. 5 and it shall become a spoil to the nations
28. 7 upon thee, the terrible of the nations and
29. 12 scatter the Egyptians among the nations
29. 15 exalt itself any more above the nations
29. 15 they shall no more rule over the nations
30. 11 the terrible of the nations, shall be brought
30. 23, 26 scatter the Egyptians among the nat
31. 6 under his shadow dwelt all great nations
31. 12 strangers, the terrible of the nations, have
31. 16 I made the nations to shake at the sound
32. 2 Thou art like a young lion of the nations
32. 9 bring thy destruction among the nations
32. 12 terrible of the nations, all of them; and
32. 16 the daughters of the nations shall lament
32. 18 and the daughters of the famous nations
35. 10 two nations and these two countries shall
36. 13 devourest..men, and hast bereaved thy n.
36. 14 neither bereave thy nations any more, sa.
36. 15 neither shalt thou cause thy nations to
37. 22 I will make them one nation in the land
37. 22 they shall be no more two nations, neither
38. 12 people (that are) gathered out of the nat.
38. 23 be known in the eyes of many nations
39. 27 in them in the sight of many nations
Dan. 8. 22 shall stand up out of the nation, but not
12. 1 such as never was since there was a nation
Hos. 8. 10 though they have hired among the nations
9. 17 they shall be wanderers among the nations
Joel 1. 6 For a nation is come up upon my land, str.
Joel 3. 2 I will also gather all nations, and will br.
3. 2 they have scattered among the nations
Amos 6. 1 (which are) named chief of the nations, to
6. 14 I will raise up against you a nation, O h.
9. 9 sift the house of Israel among all nations
Mic. 4. 2 And many nations shall come, and say
4. 3 and rebuke strong nations afar off; and
4. 3 nation shall not lift up..against nation
4. 7 her that was cast far off a strong nation
4. 11 Now also many nations are gathered agai.
7. 16 The nations shall see, and be confounded
Nah. 3. 4 that selleth nations through her whored.
3. 5 I will show the nations thy nakedness
Hab. 1. 6 (that) bitter and hasty nation, which sh.
1. 17 not spare continually to slay the nations?
2. 5 but gathereth unto him all nations, and
2. 8 Because thou hast spoiled many nations
3. 6 he beheld, and drove asunder the nations
Zeph. 2. 1 yea, gather together, O nation not desired
2. 5 Woe unto..the nation of the Cherethites!
2. 14 all the beasts of the nations: both the
3. 6 I have cut off the nations: their towers
3. 8 my determination (is) to gather the nati.
Hag. 2. 7 all nations, and the desire of all nations
2. 14 so (is) this nation before me, saith the
Zech. 2. 8 sent me unto the nations which spoiled
2. 11 many nations shall be joined to the LORD
7. 14 among all the nations whom they knew
8. 22 strong nations shall come to seek the L.
8. 23 hold out of all languages of the nations
12. 9 the nations that come against Jerusalem
14. 2 will gather all nations against Jerusalem
14. 3 forth, and fight against those nations, as
14. 16 the nations which came against Jerusalem
14. 19 all nations that come not up to keep the
Mal. 3. 9 ye have robbed me, (even) this whole nat.
3. 12 all nations shall call you blessed: for ye

3. *A nation, people,* לְאֹם *leom.*
Gen. 27. 29 people serve thee, and nations bow down
Psa. 47. 3 shall subdue..the nations under our feet
57. 9 I will sing unto thee among the nations
67. 4 let the nations be glad, and sing for joy
67. 4 thou shalt..govern the nations upon earth
108. 3 sing praises unto thee among the nations
Prov 24. 24 the people curse, nations shall abhor him
Isa. 17. 12 the rushing of nations, (that) make a rush.
17. 13 The nations shall rush like the rushing
51. 4 give ear unto me, O my nation: for a law

4. *A people,* עַם *am.*
Exod 21. 8 to sell her unto a strange nation he shall
Deut. 2. 25 nations (that are) under the whole heaven
4. 6 understanding in the sight of the nations
4. 19 unto all nations under the whole heaven
4. 27 LORD shall scatter you among the nations
14. 2 all the nations that (are) upon the earth
28. 33 shall a nation which thou knowest not eat
28. 37 among all nations whither the LORD shall
30. 3 gather thee from all the nations, whither
1 Ch. 16. 24 his marvellous works among all nations
2 Ch. 7. 20 proverb and a by word among all nations
13. 9 the manner of the nations of (other) lands
Neh. 1. 8 will scatter you abroad among the nations
9. 22 thou gavest them kingdoms and nations
Psa. 96. 5 the gods of the nations (are) idols: but
106. 34 did not destroy the nations, concerning
Eze. 38. 8 it is brought forth out of the nations, and

5. *Generation, race,* γενεά *genea.*
Phil. 2. 15 midst of a crooked and perverse nation

6. *Generation, race,* γένος *genos.*
Mark 7. 26 was a Greek, a Syrophenician by nation
Gal. 1. 14 above many my equals in mine own nat.

7. *A nation,* ἔθνος *ethnos.*
Matt 21. 43 and given to a nation bringing forth the
24. 7 For nation shall rise against nation, and
24. 9 ye shall be hated of all nations for my
24. 14 preached. for a witness unto all nations
25. 32 before him shall be gathered all nations
28. 19 teach all nations, baptizing them in the
Mark 11. 17 My house shall be called of all nations
13. 8 For nation shall rise against nation, and
13. 10 must first be published among all nations
Luke 7. 5 he loveth our nation, and he hath built us
12. 30 these things do the nations of the world
21. 10 Nation shall rise against nation, and king.
21. 24 shall be led away captive into all nations
21. 25 upon the earth distress of nations, with
23. 2 found this (fellow) perverting the nation
24. 47 preached in his name among all nations
John 11. 48 and take away both our place and nation
11. 50 die..and that the whole nation perish not
11. 51 that Jesus should die for that nation
11. 52 not for that nation only, but that also
18. 35 Thine own nation and the chief priests
Acts 2. 5 men, out of every nation under heaven
7. 7 nation to whom they shall be in bondage
10. 22 good report among all the nation of the
10. 35 in every nation he that feareth him, and
13. 19 he had destroyed seven nations in the
14. 16 Who in times past suffered all nations to
17. 26 hath made of one blood all nations of men
24. 2 worthy deeds are done unto this nation
24. 10 of many years a judge unto this nation
24. 17 I came to bring alms to my nation, and
26. 4 first among mine own nation at Jerusalem
28. 19 that I had ought to accuse my nation of
Rom. 1. 5 obedience to the faith among all nations
4. 17 have made thee a father of many nations
4. 18 might become the father of many nations
10. 19 (and) by a foolish nation I will anger you
Rom 16. 26 made known to all nations for the obedience
Gal. 3. 8 preached..In thee shall all nations be bless.
1 Pe. 2. 9 ye (are)..an holy nation, a peculiar people
Rev. 2. 26 him will I give power over the nations
5. 9 kindred, and tongue, and people, and na.
7. 9 all nations, and kindreds, and people, and
10. 11 many peoples, and nations, and tongues
11. 9 kindreds, and tongues, and nations, shall
11. 18 the nations were angry, and thy wrath is
12. 5 was to rule all nations with a rod of iron
13. 7 all kindreds, and tongues, and nations
14. 6 every nation, and kindred, and tongue, and
14. 8 she made all nations drink of the wine of
15. 4 all [nations] shall come and worship before
16. 19 the cities of the nations fell: and great
17. 15 and multitudes, and nations, and tongues
18. 3 all nations have drunk of the wine of the
18. 23 by thy sorceries were..nations deceived
19. 15 that with it he should smite the nations
20. 3 he should deceive the nations no more, till
20. 8 shall go out to deceive the nations which
21. 24 the nations of them which are saved shall
21. 26 bring the glory and honour of the nations
22. 2 leaves..(were) for the healing of the nations

8. *Nations, peoples,* אֻמּוֹת *ummoth.*
Gen. 25. 16 twelve princes according to their nations

9. *Land, country,* אֶרֶץ *erets.*
Isa. 37. 18 the kings..have laid waste all the nations

NATION, of one's own —
Aboriginal, native, indigenous, אֶזְרָח *ezrach.*
Lev. 18. 26 (neither) any of your own nation, nor any

NATIVE, NATIVITY —
1. *Birth, kindred,* מוֹלֶדֶת *moledeth.*
Gen. 11. 28 Haran died..in the land of his nativity
Ruth 2. 11 thy mother, and the land of thy nativity
Jer. 22. 10 return no more, nor see his native country
46. 16 and let us go..to the land of our nativity
Eze. 16. 3 and thy nativity (is) the land of Canaan
16. 4 (as for) thy nativity, in the day thou wast
23. 15 of Chaldea, the land of their nativity

2. *A cutting out, birth,* מְכוּרָה *mekurah.*
Eze. 21. 30 wast created, in the land of thy nativity

NATURAL (force), nature —
1. *Origin, birth,* γένεσις *genesis.*
Jas. 1. 23 man beholding his natural face in a glass
3. 6 setteth on fire the course of nature; and

2. *According to nature,* κατὰ φύσιν *kata phusin.*
Rom 11. 21 if God spared not the natural branches
11. 24 these, which be the natural (branches), be

3. *Natural, belonging to nature,* φυσικός *phusikos.*
Rom. 1. 26 women did change the natural use into
1. 27 men, leaving the natural use of the woman
2 Pe. 2. 12 as natural brute beasts, made to be taken

4. *Nature,* φύσις *phusis.*
Rom. 1. 26 the..use into that which is against nature
2. 14 do by nature the things contained in the
2. 27 not uncircumcision which is by nature
11. 24 the olive tree, which is wild by nature
11. 24 wert graffed contrary to nature into a
1 Co. 11. 14 Doth not even nature itself teach you, that
Gal. 2. 15 We (who are) Jews by nature, and not si.
4. 8 unto them which by nature are no gods
Eph. 2. 3 and were by nature the children of wrath
2 Pe. 1. 4 ye might be partakers of the divine nature

5. *Animal, sensuous,* ψυχικός *psuchikos.*
1 Co. 2. 14 But the natural man receiveth not the th.
15. 44 It is sown a natural body; it is raised a
15. 44 There is a natural body, and there is a
15. 46 which is spiritual, but that which is natural

6. *Moistness, freshness, greenness,* לֵחַ *leach.*
Deut 34. 7 was not dim, nor his natural force abated

NATURALLY —
1. *Genuinely, sincerely,* γνησίως *gnēsiōs.*
Phil. 2. 20 who will naturally care for your state

2. *Naturally,* φυσικῶς *phusikōs.*
Jude 10 but what they know naturally, as brute b.

NAUGHT, NAUGHTINESS, NAUGHTY —
1. *Without profit, worthless,* בְּלִיַּעַל *beliyyaal.*
Prov. 6. 12 A naughty person, a wicked man, walketh

2. *Mischief, calamity,* הַוָּה *havvah.*
Prov 11. 6 shall be taken in (their own) naughtiness
17. 4 (and) a liar giveth ear to a naughty tongue

3. *Evil, bad,* רַע *ra.*
2 Ki. 2. 19 the water (is) naught, and the ground b.
Prov. 20. 14 (It is) naught, (it is) naught, saith the b.
Jer. 24. 2 other basket (had) very naughty figs, wh.

4. *Evil, badness,* רֹעַ *roa.*
1 Sa. 17. 28 pride, and the naughtiness of thine heart

5. *Badness, evil, wickedness,* κακία *kakia.*
Jas. 1. 21 superfluity of naughtiness, and receive

NA'-UM, Ναούμ, *from Heb.* נחום *comfort.*
An ancestor of Jesus, through Mary.
Luke 3. 25 which was (the son) of N., which was (the

NAVE —
Nave, back, ring, גַּב *gab.*
1 Ki. 7. 33 their axletrees, and their naves, and their

NAVEL —

1. *Navel, nerve, sinew,* שֹׁר *shor.*
Prov. 3. 8 it shall be health to thy navel, and marrow
Eze. 16. 4 day thou wast born thy navel was not cut

2. *Muscle or sinew,* שָׁרִיר *sharir.*
Job 40. 16 and his force (is) in the navel of his belly

3. *Navel,* שֹׁרֶר *shorer.*
Song 7. 2 Thy navel (is like) a round goblet, (which)

NAVY (of ships) —

A ship, navy, אֳנִי *oni.*
1 Ki. 9. 26 And king Solomon made a navy of ships
9. 27 And Hiram sent in the navy his servants
10. 11 And the navy also of Hiram, that brought
10. 22 For the king had at sea a navy of Tharsh.
10. 22 with the navy of Hiram..came the navy

NAY —

1. *Not,* אַל *al.*
Judg19. 23 Nay, my brethren, (nay), I pray you, do

2. *No,* לֹא *lo.*
Gen. 18. 15 And he said, Nay; but thou didst laugh
23. 11 Nay, my lord, hear me: the field give I

3. *But, except, unless,* ἀλλά *alla.*
Rom. 7. 7 Nay, I had not known sin but by the law
8. 37 Nay, in all these things we are more than
1 Co. 6. 8 Nay, ye do wrong, and defraud, and that
12. 22 Nay, much more those members of the b.

4. *No, not,* οὐ *ou.*
Matt. 5. 37 your communication be, Yea, yea; Nay; nay
13. 29 Nay; lest, while ye gather up the tares, ye
John 7. 12 said, Nay; but he deceiveth the people
Acts 16. 37 nay verily; but let them come themselves
2 Co. 1. 17 there should be yea yea, and nay nay?
1. 18 our word toward you was not yea and nay
1. 19 was not yea and nay, but in him was yea
Jas. 5. 12 let your yea be yea; and (your) nay, nay

5. *No, not,* οὐχί *ouchi.*
Luke12. 51 I tell you, Nay; but rather division
13. 3, 5 Nay: but, except ye repent, ye shall
16. 30 Nay, father Abraham: but if one went
Rom. 3. 27 of works? Nay; but by the law of faith

NAY but —

Therefore indeed, yea verily, μενοῦνγε *menounge.*
Rom. 9. 20[Nay but,] O man, who art thou that repli.

NAY...NEITHER —

Also...also, גַּם...גַּם *gam ..gam.*
Jer. 6. 15 nay, they were not at all ashamed, neither

NAZ-AR-ENE, Ναζωραῖος. *A native of Nazareth.*
Matt. 2. 23 which was spoken..He shall be called a N
Acts 24. 5 man..a ringleader of the sect of the N.

NAZ-AR'-ETH, Ναζαρέθ, -έτ, -άθ, -ά.
A city in Zebulun, in Lower Galilee, seventy miles N. of Jerusalem, six miles W. of Mount Tabor, and twenty-four S.E. of Accho or Acre. It is not mentioned in the Old Testament, but still exists under the name of *el-Nazirah.*
Matt. 2. 23 he came and dwelt in a city called N.: th.
4. 13 leaving N., he came and dwelt in Capern
21. 11 This is Jesus the prophet of N. of Galilee
26. 71 This (fellow) was also with Jesus of N.
Mark 1. 9 Jesus came from N. of Galilee, and was
1. 24 what have we to do with thee..J. of N
10. 47 when he heard that it was Jesus of N. he
14. 67 And thou also wast with Jesus of N.
16. 6 Ye seek Jesus of N., which was crucified
Luke 1. 26 was sent..unto a city of Galilee, named N
2. 4 out of the city of N., into Judea, unto the
2. 39 returned into Galilee, to their own city N
2. 51 came to N., and was subject unto them
4. 16 he came to N., where he had been brought
4. 34 what have we to do with thee..Jesus of N
18. 37 they told him, that Jesus of N. passeth by
24. 19 Concerning Jesus of N., which was a pro.
John 1. 45 have found..Jesus of N. the son of Joseph
1. 46 Can there any good thing come out of N.?
18. 5 They answered him, Jesus of N. Jesus
18. 7 Whom seek ye? And they said, Jesus of N.
19. 19 writing was, Jesus of N. the king of the J.
Acts 2. 22 Jesus of N., a man approved of God among
3. 6 In the name of Jesus Christ of N. rise up
4. 10 by the name of Jesus Christ of N., whom
6. 14 Jesus of N. shall destroy this place, and
10. 38 How God anointed Jesus of N. with the
22. 8 I am Jesus of N., whom thou persecutest
26. 9 thing contrary to the name of Jesus of N.

NAZ-AR-ITE, נָזִיר *separated.*
The appellation of one who by a vow refrains from certain things for a longer or shorter time.
Num. 6. 2 separate (themselves) to vow a vow of a N.
6. 13 this (is) the law of the N., when the days
6. 18 N. shall shave the head of his separation
6. 19 shall put (them) upon the hands of the N.
6. 20 and after that the N. may drink wine
6. 21 This (is) the law of the N. who hath vowed
Judg 13. 5, 7 the child shall be a N. unto God from
16. 17 I (have been) a N. unto God from my mo.
Lam. 4. 7 Her N. were purer than snow, they were
Amos 2. 11 And I raised up..of your young men for N.
2. 12 ye gave the N. wine to drink; and comm.

NE'-AH, הַנֵּעָה *the settlement.*
A city in Zebulun.
Josh 19. 13 and goeth out to Remmon-methoar, to N.

NE-A-PO'-LIS, Νεάπολις.
A seaport on the E. of Macedonia, ten miles S.E. of Philippi, on the Sinus Strymonicus; now called *Kavalla.*
Acts 16. 11 to Samothracia, and the next (day) to N.

NEAR, NEARER, (unto or to) —

1. *To the hand of,* אֶל־יַד *el yad.*
2 Sa. 14. 30 Joab's field is near mine, and he hath bar.

2. *Near,* אֵצֶל *etsel.*
Deut16. 21 a grove of any trees near unto the altar
Prov. 7. 8 Passing through the street near her corner
Dan. 8. 17 he came near where I stood; and when he

3. *By the hand,* עַל־יַד *al yad.*
Josh.15. 46 all that (lay) near Ashdod, with their
2 Ch.21. 16 Arabians, that (were) near the Ethiopians

4. *To touch, come upon, strike,* נָגַע *naga.*
Judg.20. 34 but they knew not that evil (was) near

5. *Near,* קָרוֹב *qarob.*
Gen. 19. 20 this city (is) near to flee unto, and it (is)
45. 10 thou shalt be near unto me, thou, and thy
Exod13. 17 land of the Philistines..that (was) near
Lev. 21. 2 his kin that is near unto him, (that is)
Ruth 3. 12 howbeit there is a kinsman nearer than
1 Ki. 8. 46 unto the land of the enemy, far or near
21. 2 it (is) near unto my house: and I will give
2 Ch. 6. 36 captives unto a land far off or near
Psa. 22. 11 for trouble (is) near; for (there is) none
75. 1 (that) thy name (is) near thy wondrous w.
119. 151 Thou (art) near, O LORD; and all thy
148. 14 children of Israel, a people near unto him
Prov 10. 14 mouth of the foolish (is) near destruction
27. 10 better (is) a neighbour (that is) near, than
Isa. 13. 22 her time (is) near to come, and her days
33. 13 and ye (that are) near, acknowledge my
50. 8 (He is) near that justifieth me; who will
51. 5 My righteousness (is) near; my salvation
55. 6 Seek..call ye upon him while he is near
56. 1 for my salvation (is) near to come, and my
57. 19 Peace..to (him that is) near, saith the L.
Jer. 12. 2 thou (art) near in their mouth, and far
25. 26 the kings of the north, far and near, one
48. 16 The calamity of Moab (is) near to come
48. 24 the cities of the land of Moab, far or near
Eze. 6. 12 he that is near shall fall by the sword
7. 7 the day of trouble (is) near, and not
11. 3 (It is) not near; let us build houses: this
22. 5 (Those that be) near, and (those that be)
30. 3 (is) near, even the day of the LORD (is) near
Dan. 9. 7 all Israel, (that are) near, and (that are)
Joel 3. 14 day of the LORD (is) near in the valley
Obad. 15 the day of the LORD (is) near upon all the
Zeph. 1. 14 great day of the LORD (is) near, (it is) near

6. *Necessary, closely connected,* ἀναγκαῖος *anagkaios.*
Acts 10. 24 called..his kinsmen and near friends

7. *Nigh,* ἐγγύς *eggus.*
Matt24. 33 know that it is near, (even) at the doors
Mark13. 28 leaves, ye know that summer is near
John 3. 23 also was baptizing in Aenon near to Salim
11. 54 unto a country near to the wilderness

8. *Nigher, nearer,* ἐγγύτερον *egguteron.*
Rom 13. 11 now (is) our salvation nearer than when

9. *Close to, near,* πλησίον *plēsion.*
John 4. 5 near to the parcel of ground that Jacob

[*See also* Bring, come, draw, go, kin, kinsman, kinswoman.]

NEAR, to be —

1. *To be nigh,* נָגַשׁ *nagash.*
Job 41 16 One is so near to another, that no air

2. *To be near,* קָרַב *qarab.*
Lam. 4. 18 our end is near, our days are fulfilled; for

3. *To see,* רָאָה *raah.*
Jer. 52. 25 of them that were near the king's person

NE-AR-I'AH, נְעַרְיָה *Jah drives away.*
1. Grandson of Shechaniah, descended from David. B.C. 456.
1 Ch. 3. 22 and Igeal and Bariah, and N., and Shap.
3. 23 the sons of N.; Elioenai, and Hezekiah

2. A Simeonite captain who smote the remnant of the Amalekites in Mount Seir B.C. 722
1 Ch. 4. 42 N., and Rephaiah, and Uzziel, the sons

NE'-BAI, נֵיבַי *marrowy, projecting* [V.L. נוֹבַי].
A person or family that with Nehemiah sealed the covenant. B.C. 445.
Neh. 10. 19 Hariph, Anathoth, N.

NE-BA'-JOTH, NE-BA'-IOTH, נְבָיֹת, נְבָיוֹת *husbandry.*
1. Eldest son of Ishmael son of Hagar B.C. 1840.
Gen. 25. 13 the first born of Ishmael, N.; and Kedar
28. 9 the daughter of Ishmael..the sister of N.
36. 3 Bashem, Ishmael's daughter, sister of N.
1 Ch. 1. 29 The first born of Ishmael, N.; then Kedar

2. His descendants, the Nabatheans, in Arabia Petraea and Arabia Felix.
Isa. 60. 7 the rams of N. shall minister unto thee

NE-BAL'-LAT, נְבַלָּט *hard, firm.*
A city in Judah or Benjamin, now called *Bir Nebala.*
Neh. 11. 34 Hadid, Zeboim, N.

NE'-BAT, נְבָט *look, cultivation.*
Father of Jeroboam who rebelled against Rehoboam, and became the first king of the ten tribes of Israel, and set up the two golden calves at Bethel and Dan. B.C. 1010.
1 Ki. 11. 26 the son of N., an Ephrathite of Zereda
12. 2 the son of N., who was yet in Egypt, heard
12. 15 LORD spake..unto Jeroboam the son of N.
15. 1 the..year of king Jeroboam the son of N.
16. 3 like the house of Jeroboam the son of N.
16. 26 in all the way of Jeroboam the son of N.
16. 31 walk in the sins of Jeroboam the son of N.
21. 22 like the house of Jeroboam the son of N.
22. 52 in the way of Jeroboam the son of N., who
2 Ki. 3. 3 unto the sins of Jeroboam the son of N.
9. 9 like the house of Jeroboam the son of N.
10. 29 (from) the sins of Jeroboam the son of N.
13. 2 followed the sins of Jeroboam..son of N.
13. 11 all the sins of Jeroboam the son of N., who
14. 24 all the sins of Jeroboam the son of N.
15. 9, 18, 24, 28 sins of Jeroboam the son of N.
17. 21 they made Jeroboam the son of N. king
23. 15 high place which Jeroboam the son of N.
2 Ch. 9. 29 visions..against Jeroboam the son of N.?
10. 2 when Jeroboam the son of N...heard (it)
10. 15 which he spake..to Jeroboam the son of N.
13. 6 Yet Jeroboam the son of N...is risen up

NE'-BO, נְבוֹ *height.*
1. A city in Reuben, E. of Jordan
Num32. 3 Elealeh, and Shebam, and N., and Beon
32. 38 N., and Baal-meon, their names being c.
33. 47 and pitched in the mountains..before N.
1 Ch. 5. 8 Bela the son of Azaz..even unto N. and
Isa. 15. 2 Moab shall howl over N., and over Med.
Jer. 48. 1 Woe unto N.! for it is spoiled; Kiriathaim
48. 22 upon Dibon, and upon N., and upon Beth.

2. A mount E. of Jordan over against Jericho, in Moab, part of the Abarim range, with a top called *Pisgah,* six miles W. of Heshbon.
Deut 32. 49 Get thee up..(unto) mount N., which (is)
34. 1 went up..unto the mountain of N., to the

3. A twofold city in Judah; perhaps *Beith-Nube,* near Lydda.
Ezra 2. 29 The children of N., fifty and two
Neh. 7. 33 The men of the other N., fifty and two

4. The name of a Chaldean idol.
Isa. 46. 1 Bel boweth down, N. stoopeth; their idols

5. The ancestor of certain Jews who had taken strange wives during or after the captivity.
Ezra 10. 43 Of the sons of N., Jeiel, Mattithiah, Zab.

NE-BU-CHAD-NEZ'-ZAR, or **REZ'-ZAR,** נְבֻכַדְנֶאצַּר, נְבֻכַדְנֶצַּר, נְבוּכַדְנֶאצַּר, נְבוּכַדְרֶאצַּר, נְבֻכַדְרֶאצַּר.
Son of Nabopolassar, and king of Babylon who invaded Judah, captured Jerusalem, destroyed it and the temple, carried the inhabitants to Babylon, set up a golden image in the plain of Dura, put three young men into the fiery furnace, became proud, had a dream which Daniel explained, was driven for a time from men, but restored and praised God. B.C. 600.
2 Ki.24. 1 In his days N. king of Babylon came up
24. 10 At that time the servants of N. king of B.
24. 11 N. king of Babylon came against the city
25. 1 N. king of Babylon came, he, and all his
25. 8 which (is) the nineteenth year of king N.
25. 22 people..whom N. king of Babylon had left
1 Ch. 6. 15 carried away Judah..by the hand of N.
2 Ch.36. 6 Against him came up N. king of Babylon
36. 7 N. also carried of the vessels of the house
36. 10 when the year was expired king N. sent
36. 13 he also rebelled against king N., who had
Ezra 1. 7 which N. had brought forth out of Jerus.
2. 1 whom N. the king of Babylon had carried
5. 12 he gave them into the hand of N. the ki.
5. 14 which N. took out of the temple that (was)
6. 5 which N. took forth out of the temple w.
Neh. 7. 6 whom N. the king of Babylon had carried
Esth. 2. 6 whom N. the king of Babylon had carried
Jer. 21. 2 for N. king of Babylon maketh war again.
21. 7 into the hand of N. king of Babylon, and
22. 25 even into the hand of N. king of Babylon
24. 1 after that N. king of Babylon had carried
25. 1 that (was) the first year of N. king of B.
25. 9 take..N. the king of Babylon, my servant
27. 6 given all these lands into the hand of N.
27. 8 which will not serve the same N. the king
27. 20 Which N. king of Babylon took not, when
28. 3 that N. king of Babylon took away from
28. 11 Even so will I break the yoke of N. king
28. 14 that they may serve N. king of Babylon
29. 1 all the people whom N. had carried away
29. 3 whom Zedekiah..sent unto Babylon to N.
29. 21 I will deliver them into the hand of N.
32. 1 year..which (was) the eighteenth ..of N.
32. 28 into the hand of N. king of Babylon, and
34. 1 when N. king of Babylon..fought against
35. 11 when N. king of Babylon came up into the
37. 1 whom N. king of Babylon made king..of J.
39. 1 came N. king of Babylon and all his army
39. 5 they brought him up to N. king of Baby.
39. 11 Now N. king of Babylon gave charge co.
43. 10 I will send and take N. the king of Bab.
44. 30 gave Zedekiah..into the hand of N. king
46. 2 which N. king of Babylon smote in the
46. 13 how N. king of Babylon should come (and)
46. 26 into the hand of N. king of Babylon, and
49. 28 which N. king of Babylon shall smite, thus
49. 30 for N. king of Babylon hath taken counsel

Jer. 50. 17 N. king of Babylon hath broken his bones
51. 34 N. the king of Babylon hath devoured me
52. 4 N. king of Babylon came, he and all his a.
52. 12 the nineteenth year of N. king of Babylon
52. 28 the people whom N. carried away captive
52. 29 In the eighteenth year of N. he carried
52. 30 In the three and twentieth year of N.
Eze. 26. 7 will bring upon Tyrus N. king of Babylon
29. 18 N. king of Babylon caused his army to s.
29. 19 I will give the land of Egypt unto N. king
30. 10 cease by the hand of N. king of Babylon
Dan. 1. 1 came N. king of Babylon unto Jerusalem
1. 18 then the prince..brought them in before N.
2. 1 in the second year of the reign of N., N.
2. 28 maketh known to the king N. what shall
2. 46 N. fell upon his face, and worshipped D.
3. 1 N. the king made an image of gold, whose
3. 2 N. the king sent to gather together the
3. 2, 3, 3, 5, 7 image which N. the king had set
3. 9 said to the king N., O king, live for ever
3. 13 N. in (his) rage and fury commanded to br.
3. 14 N. spake and said unto them, (Is it) true
3. 16 O N., we (are) not careful to answer thee in
3. 19 Then was N. full of fury, and the form of
3. 24 N. the king was astonied, and rose up in
3. 26 N. came near to the mouth of the burning
3. 28 N. spake, and said, Blessed (be) the God of
4. 1 N. the king, unto all people, nations, and
4. 4 I N. was at rest in mine house, and flour.
4. 18 This dream I king N. have seen. Now thou
4. 28 All this came upon the king N.
4. 31 (saying), O king N., to thee it is spoken
4. 33 same hour was the thing fulfilled upon N.
4. 34 I N. lifted up mine eyes unto heaven, and
4. 37 I N. praise and extol and honour the King
5. 2 N. had taken out of the temple which (was)
5. 11 N. thy father, the king, I (say), thy father
5. 18 God gave N. thy father a kingdom, and

NE-BU-SHAS'-BAN, נְבוּשַׁזְבָּן.
A prince of Nebuchadnezzar king of Babylon. B.C. 600.
Jer. 39. 13 N., Rabsaris, and Nergal-sharezer, Rab.

NE-BU-ZAR-A'-DAN, נְבוּזַרְאֲדָן.
The captain of the guard whom Nebuchadnezzar left behind him in Jerusalem for a time. B.C. 600.
2 Ki. 25. 8 came N., captain of the guard, a servant
25. 11 did N., the captain of the guard, carry a.
25. 20 And N., captain of the guard, took these
Jer. 39. 9 N. the captain of the guard carried away
39. 10 N. the captain of the guard left of the
39. 11 to N. the captain of the guard, saying
39. 13 So N. the captain of the guard sent, and
40. 1 N. the captain of the guard had let him
41. 10 N. the captain of the guard had commit.
43. 6 N. the captain of the guard had left with
52. 12 came N., captain of the guard, (which) s.
52. 15, 30 N. the captain of the guard carried a.
52. 16 N. the captain of the guard had left (ce.)
52. 26 N. the captain of the guard took them, and

NECESSARY, NECESSITY, (must of) —
1. *Statute,* חֹק *choq.*
Job 23. 12 esteemed the words..more than my nec.
2. *Necessary,* ἀναγκαῖος *anagkaios.*
Acts 13. 46 It was necessary that the word of God
1 Co. 12. 22 members..which seem..feeble, are nece.
2 Co. 9. 5 I thought it necessary to exhort the
Phil. 2. 25 Yet I supposed it necessary to send to you
Titus 3. 14 maintain good works for necessary uses
3. *Necessity,* ἀνάγκη *anagkē.*
1 Co. 7. 37 having no necessity, but hath power over
9. 16 for necessity is laid upon me; yea, woe is
2 Co. 6. 4 in afflictions, in necessities, in distresses
9. 7 not grudgingly, or of necessity: for God
12. 10 I take pleasure..in necessities, in perse.
Phm. 14 should not be as it were of necessity, but
Heb. 7. 12 there is made of necessity a change also
9. 16 must also of necessity be the death of the
9. 23 (It was) therefore necessary that the pat.
4. *The things necessary,* τὰ ἐπάναγκες *ta epanagkes.*
Acts 15. 28 greater burden than these necessary things
5. *Use, need, necessity,* χρεία *chreia.*
Acts 20. 34 have ministered unto my necessities, and
28. 10 laded (us) with such things as were [nec.]
Rom 12. 13 Distributing to the necessity of saints
Phil. 4. 16 ye sent once and again unto my necessity

NECESSITY, of —
1. *To have necessity,* ἔχω ἀνάγκην *echō anagkēn.*
Luke 23. 17 [For of necessity he must release one unto]
2. *Necessary,* ἀναγκαῖος *anagkaios.*
Heb. 8. 3 (it is) of necessity that this man have so.

NE'-CHO, נְכוֹ.
An appellation given to the king of Egypt who succeeded Psammetichus and fought against Nabopolassar in the days of king Josiah, and after making Eliakim (or Jehoiakim) king, carried off Jehoahaz his brother to Egypt. B.C. 610. *See also* Pharaoh.
2 Ch. 35. 20 N. king of Egypt came up to fight against
35. 22 hearkened not unto the words of N. from
36. 4 N. took Jehoahaz his brother, and carried

NECK —
1. *Throat, neck,* גַּרְגְּרוֹת *gargeroth.*
Prov. 1. 9 unto thy head, and chains about thy neck
3. 3 bind them about thy neck; write them
3. 22 life unto thy soul, and grace to thy neck
6. 21 thine heart, (and) tie them about thy neck
2. *Throat,* גָּרוֹן *garon.*
Isa. 3. 16 walk with stretched forth necks, and wa.
Eze. 16. 11 upon thy hands, and a chain on thy neck
3. *Bone or vertebrae,* מַפְרֶקֶת *maphreqeth.*
1 Sa. 4. 18 the gate, and his neck brake, and he died
4. *Neck, back,* עֹרֶף *oreph.*
Gen. 49. 8 (shall be) in the neck of thine enemies; thy
Lev. 5. 8 and wring off his head from his neck, but
Deut 31. 27 I know thy rebellion, and thy stiff neck: b.
2 Sa. 22. 41 Thou hast also given me the necks of mine
2 Ki. 17. 14 would not hear, but hardened their necks
17. 14 like to the neck of their fathers, that did
2 Ch. 36. 13 but he stiffened his neck, and hardened
Neh. 9. 16 hardened their necks, and hearkened not
9. 17 but hardened their necks, and in their re.
9. 29 hardened their neck, and would not hear
Job 16. 12 he hath also taken (me) by my neck, and
Psa. 18. 40 Thou hast also given me the necks of mine
Prov 29. 1 being often reproved, hardeneth (his) neck
Isa. 48. 4 and thy neck (is) an iron sinew, and thy
Jer. 7. 26 their ear, but hardened their neck: they
17. 23 made their neck stiff, that they might not
19. 15 because they have hardened their necks
5. *Neck, nape,* צַוָּאר *tsavvar.*
Gen. 27. 16 hands, and upon the smooth of his neck
27. 40 shalt break his yoke from off thy neck
33. 4 fell on his neck, and kissed him: and they
41. 42 and put a gold chain about his neck
45. 14 he fell upon his brother Benjamin's neck
45. 14 wept; and Benjamin wept upon his neck
46. 29 he fell on his neck, and wept on his neck
Deut 28. 48 he shall put a yoke of iron upon thy neck
Josh. 10. 24 put your feet upon the necks of these ki.
10. 24 and put their feet upon the necks of them
Judg. 5. 30 for the necks of (them that take) the sp.?
8. 21 ornaments that (were) on their camel's n.
8. 26 chains that (were) about their camel's ne.
Neh. 3. 5 but their nobles put not their necks to
Job 15. 26 runneth upon him, (even) on (his) neck
39. 19 hast thou clothed his neck with thunder?
41. 22 In his neck remaineth strength, and sor.
Psa. 75. 5 horn on high: speak (not) with a stiff n.
Song 1. 10 rows (of jewels), thy neck with chains (of
4. 4 Thy neck (is) like the tower of David bu.
7. 4 Thy neck (is) as a tower of ivory; thine
Isa 8. 8 he shall reach (even) to the neck: and the
10. 27 his yoke from off thy neck, and the yoke
30. 28 shall reach to the midst of the neck, to
52. 2 loose thyself from the bands of thy neck
Jer. 27. 2 Make..yokes, and put them upon thy neck
27. 8 that will not put their neck under the
27. 11 the nations that bring their neck under
27. 12 Bring your necks under the yoke of the
28. 10 yoke from off the prophet Jeremiah's neck
28. 11 from the neck of all nations within the
28. 12 had broken the yoke from off the neck of
28. 14 iron upon the neck of all these nations
30. 8 I will break his yoke from off thy neck
Lam. 1. 14 are wreathed, (and) come up upon my n.
5. 5 Our necks (are) under persecution: we la.
Eze. 21. 29 upon the necks of (them that are) slain
Dan. 5. 7, 29 a chain of gold about his neck, and
5. 16 (have) a chain of gold about thy neck, and
Hos. 10. 11 I passed over upon her fair neck: I will
Mic. 2. 3 from which ye shall not remove your ne.
Hab. 3. 13 discovering the foundation unto the neck
6. *Neck,* צַוְּרֹנִים *tsavveronim.*
Song 4. 9 of thine eyes, with one chain of thy neck
7. *Neck,* τράχηλος *trachēlos.*
Matt 18. 6 a millstone were hanged about his neck
Mark 9. 42 a millstone were hanged about his neck
Luke 15. 20 ran, and fell on his neck, and kissed him
17. 2 a millstone were hanged about his neck
Acts 15. 10 a yoke upon the neck of the disciples
20. 37 and fell on Paul's neck, and kissed him
Rom. 16. 4 for my life laid down their own necks

NECK, to break, cut or strike off the —
To break the neck, behead, cause to drop, עָרַף *araph.*
Exod 13. 13 thou shalt break his neck: and all the
34. 20 if thou redeem (him) not..break his neck
Deut 21. 4 shall strike off the heifer's neck there
Isa. 66. 3 a lamb, (as if) he cut off a dog's neck

NECROMANCER —
To enquire at the dead, דֹּרֵשׁ אֶל הַמֵּתִים מֵתִים [*darash*].
Deut 18. 11 a charmer..or a wizard, or a necromancer

NE-DAB-I'AH, נְדַבְיָה *Jah is willing, liberal.*
Son of Jeconiah, son of Jehoiakim king of Judah. B.C. 590.
1 Ch. 3. 18 Shenazar, Jecamiah, Hoshama, and N.

NEED, needs, needful, to need —
1. *Needful things, necessaries,* חַשְׁחוּת *chashchuth.*
Ezra 7. 20 whatsoever more shall be needful for the
2. *Need, want, lack,* מַחְסוֹר *machsor.*
Deut 15. 8 surely lend him sufficient for his need
3. *Necessity, need,* צֹרֶךְ *tsorek.*
2 Ch. 2. 16 will cut wood..as much as thou shalt n.
4. *Necessity,* ἀνάγκη *anagkē.*
Heb. 7. 27 Who needeth not daily, as those high
Jude 3 it was needful for me to write unto you
5. *It behoveth,* δεῖ *dei.*
Acts 15. 5 it was needful to circumcise them, and
1 Pe. 1. 6 if need be, ye are in heaviness through
6. *To owe, be under obligation,* ὀφείλω *opheilō.*
1 Co. 7. 36 need so require. let him do what he will
7. *To want besides, need more,* προσδέομαι *prosdeomai*
Acts 17. 25 as though he needed any thing, seeing he
8. *Use, need, necessity,* χρεία *chreia.*
Matt. 3. 14 I have need to be baptized of thee, and c.
6. 8 Father knoweth what things ye have need
9. 12 They that be whole need not a physician
14. 16 They need not depart; give ye them to eat
21. 3 ye shall say, The Lord hath need of them
26. 65 what further need have we of witnesses?
Mark 2. 17 They that are whole have no need of the
2. 25 read what David did, when he had need
11. 3 say ye that the Lord hath need of him
14. 63 saith, What need we any further witnes.?
Luke 5. 31 They that are whole need not a physician
9. 11 and healed them that had need of healing
10. 42 But one thing is needful: and Mary hath
15. 7 nine just persons, which need no repen.
19. 31 say unto him, Because the Lord hath need
19. 34 And they said, The Lord hath need of him
22. 71 they said, What need we any further wi.?
John 2. 25 needed not that any should testify of man
13. 10 He that is washed needeth not save to w.
13. 29 Buy..that we have need of against the f.
16. 30 needest not that any man should ask thee
Acts 2. 45 parted them to all..as every man had need
4. 35 unto every man according as he had need
1 Co. 12. 21 eye cannot say unto the hand, I have no n.
12. 21 the head to the feet, I have no need of you
12. 24 For our comely (parts) have no need: but
Eph. 4. 28 that he may have to give to him that ne.
Phil. 4. 19 But my God shall supply all your need ac.
1 Th. 1. 8 so that we need not to speak anything
4. 9 ye need not that I write unto you; for ye
5. 1 But..ye have no need that I write unto
Heb. 5. 12 ye have need that one teach you again w.
5. 12 are become such as have need of milk, and
7. 11 what further need..that another priest s.
10. 36 have need of patience, that, after ye have
1 Jo. 2. 27 and ye need not that any man teach you
3. 17 seeth his brother have need, and shutteth
Rev. 3. 17 increased with goods and have need of n.
21. 23 the city had no need of the sun, neither
22. 5 they need no candle, neither light of the
9. *To want, need,* χρήζω *chrēzō.*
Luke 11. 8 and give him as many as he ne.; 2 Co. 3. 1.
10. *Necessary,* ἀναγκαῖος *anagkaios.* Phil. 1. 24.

NEED of, to have —
1. *To abate, lack,* חָסֵר *chaser.*
Prov 31. 11 trust..so that he shall have no need of sp.
2. *Lacking,* חָסֵר *chaser.*
1 Sa. 21. 15 Have I need of mad men, that ye have br.
3. *To have need,* חֲשַׁח *chashach.*
Ezra 6. 9 that which they have need of, both young
4. *To want, need,* χρήζω *chrēzō.*
Matt 6. 32 Father knoweth that ye have need of all
Luke 12. 30 Father knoweth that ye have need of these
Rom 16. 2 in whatsoever business she hath need of

NEEDFUL, things which are —
The things suitable, convenient, τὰ ἐπιτήδεια *epitēdeia*
Jas. 2. 16 those things which are needful to the body

NEEDLE —
A needle, ῥαφίς *rhaphis.*
Matt 19. 24 for a camel to go through the eye of a ne.
Mark 10. 25 for a camel to go through the eye of a ne.
Luke 18. 25 for a camel to go through a [needle's] eye

NEEDLE WORK (wrought with) —
1. *Work of the embroiderer,* מַעֲשֵׂה רֹקֵם [*maaseh*].
Exod 26. 36 fine twined linen, wrought with needle w.
27. 16 fine twined linen, wrought with needle w.
28. 39 thou shalt make the girdle (of) needle wo.
36. 37 scarlet, and fine twined linen, of needle w.
38. 18 hanging for the gate of the court..n. w.
39. 29 blue, and purple, and scarlet, of needle w.
2. *Embroidered work,* רִקְמָה *riqmah.*
Judg. 5. 30 a prey of divers colours of needle work, of
5. 30 of divers colours of needle work on both s.
Psa. 45. 14 shall be brought..in raiment of needle w.

NEEDS, must —
1. *To be necessary,* ἔχω ἀνάγκην, ἀνάγκη ἐστιν.
Matt 18. 7 for [it] must needs be that offences come
Luke 14. 18 ground, and I must needs go and see it
Rom 13. 5 must needs be subject, not only for wrath
2. *It behoveth,* δεῖ *dei.*
Mark 13. 7 must needs be; but the end (shall) not (be)
John 4. 4 And he must needs go through Samaria
Acts 1. 16 this scripture must needs have been ful.
17. 3 that Christ must needs have suff. 21. 22.
2 Co. 11. 30 If I must needs glory, I will glory of the
3. *By all means it behoves,* πάντως δεῖ *pantōs dei.*
Acts 21. 22 [the multitude must needs come together]

NEEDY —
1. *Needy, desiring,* אֶבְיוֹן *ebyon.*
Deut 15. 11 to thy poor, and to thy needy, in thy land
24. 14 oppress an hired servant..poor and needy
Job 24. 4 They turn the needy out of the way: the
24. 14 killeth the poor and needy, and in the ni.
Psa. 9. 18 For the needy shall not alway be forgotten
12. 5 for the sighing of the needy, now will I
35. 10 poor and the needy from him that spoileth
37. 14 to cast down the poor and needy..to slay
40. 17 But I..poor and needy..the Lord thinketh
70. 5 But I (am) poor and needy; make haste
72. 4 he shall save the children of the needy, and
72. 12 he shall deliver the needy when he crieth

Psa. 72. 13 He shall spare the poor and needy
72. 13 and shall save the souls of the needy
74. 21 let the poor and needy praise thy name
82. 4 Deliver the poor and needy: rid..out of
86. 1 LORD, hear me; for I (am) poor and needy
109. 16 persecuted the poor and needy man, that
109. 22 I (am) poor and needy, and my heart is
113. 7 He..lifteth the needy out of the dung hill
Prov 30. 14 to devour the poor..and the needy from
31. 9 and plead the cause of the poor and needy
31. 20 she reacheth forth her hands to the needy
Isa. 14. 30 the needy shall lie down in safety: and
25. 4 a strength to the needy in his distress, a
32. 7 to destroy..even when the needy speaketh
41. 17 (When) the poor and needy seek water
Jer. 5. 28 the right of the needy do they not judge
22. 16 He judged the cause of the poor and needy
Eze. 16. 49 strengthen the hand of the poor and ne.
18. 12 Hath oppressed the poor and needy, hath
22. 29 have vexed the poor and needy; yea, they
Amos 4. 1 which oppress the poor..crush the needy
8. 4 Hear this, O ye that swallow up the needy
8. 6 That we may buy..the needy for a pair of

2. *Lean, thin, weak,* דַּל *dal.*
Isa. 10. 2 To turn aside the needy from judgment
26. 6 the feet of the poor..the steps of the ne.

[3. *Afflicted, humble, poor,* עָנִי *ani.*
Prov 31. 20 she reacheth forth..hands to the needy]

4. *To be poor, lacking,* רוּשׁ *rush.*
Psa. 82. 3 do justice to the afflicted and needy

NEESING —
A sneesing, עֲטִישָׁה *atishah.*
Job 41. 18 By his neesings a light doth shine, and his

NE-GI'-NAH, NE-GI'-NOTH, נְגִינָה, נְגִינוֹת.
A kind of stringed instrument.
Psa. 4. *title.* To the chief musician on Neginoth
[So in Psa. 6. 54. 55. 61. 67. 76.]

NEGLECT, (to hear) to —
1. *To be careless, not to care,* ἀμελέω *ameleō.*
1 Ti. 4. 14 Neglect not the gift that is in thee, which
Heb. 2. 3 How shall we escape, if we neglect so gr.
2. *To view amiss, overlook, neglect,* παραθεωρέω.
Acts 6. 1 because their widows were neglected in
3. *To hear amiss, disregard,* παρακούω *parakouō.*
Matt 18. 17 if he shall neglect to hear them, tell (it)
18. 17 if he neglect to hear the church, let him

NEGLECTING —
Unsparing severity, ἀφειδία *apheidia.*
Col. 2. 23 and humility, and neglecting of the body

NEGLIGENT, to be —
1. *To be deceived, at rest,* שָׁלָה *shalah,* 2.
2 Ch. 29. 11 My sons, be not now negligent; for the
2. *To be careless, not to care,* ἀμελέω *ameleō.*
2 Pe. 1. 12 Wherefore [I will not be negligent] to put

NE-HE-LA'-MITE, נֶחֱלָמִי, נְחֶלָמִי.
Patronymic of Shemaiah, a presumptuous person whom God reproved by the mouth of Jeremiah.
Jer. 29. 24 thou also speak to Shemaiah the N., say.
29. 31 saith..LORD concerning Shemaiah the N.
29. 32 I will punish Shemaiah the N., and his

NE-HEM-I'AH, נְחֶמְיָה *Jah is comfort.*
1. A chief man who returned from exile. B.C. 536.
Ezra 2. 2 N., Seraiah, Reelaiah, Mordecai, Bilshan
Neh. 7. 7 N., Azariah, Raamiah, Nahamani, Mord.
2. The son of Hachaliah, who being cup bearer to Artaxerxes, was sent by him to Jerusalem where he became governor for many years. B.C. 445.
Neh. 1. 1 The words of N. the son of Hachaliah
8. 9 N., which (is) the Tirshatha, and Ezra the
10. 1 Now those that sealed (were) N., the Tir.
12. 26 and in the days of N. the governor, and
12. 47 all Israel..in the days of N., gave the por.
3. A person who repaired a portion of the wall. B.C. 445.
Neh. 3. 16 After him repaired N. the son of Azbuk

NE-HI'-LOTH, נְחִילוֹת.
Name of a music choir, inheritance.
Psa. 5. *title.* To the chief musician upon Nehiloth

NE'-HUM, נְחוּם *comfort.*
A chief man that returned from the exile with Zerubbabel; called *Rehum* in Ezra 2. 2. B.C. 536.
Neh. 7. 7 Who came with Zerubbabel..M., Baanah

NE-HUSH'-TA, נְחֻשְׁתָּא *basis, ground, support.*
Wife of Jehoiakim and mother of Jehoiachin. B.C. 600.
2 Ki. 24. 8 his mother's name (was) N., the daughter

NE-HUSH'-TAN, נְחֻשְׁתָּן *brazen serpent.*
The contemptuous appellation given by Hezekiah to the brazen serpent made by Moses in the wilderness, when men began to worship it.
2 Ki. 18. 4 brake the images..and he called it N.

NE-I'-EL, נְעִיאֵל *dwelling of God.*
A city in Asher (or Naphtali), near Beth-emek; now *Mi'ar.*
Josh. 19. 27 toward the north side of..N., and goeth

NEIGH, to —
To cry aloud, neigh, צָהַל *tsahal.*
Jer. 5. 8 every one neighed after his neighbour's w.

NEIGHBOUR —
1. *Neighbour, equal, fellow,* עָמִית *amith.*
Lev. 6. 2 lie unto his neighbour in that which was
Lev. 6. 2 by violence, or hath deceived his neighb.
18. 20 thou shalt not lie carnally with thy neig.
19. 15 in righteousness shalt thou judge thy ne.
19. 17 thou shalt in any wise rebuke thy neighb.
24. 19 if a man cause a blemish in his neighbour
25. 14 if thou sell..ought unto thy neighbour, or
25. 14 buyest..of thy neighbour's hand, ye shall
25. 15 after the jubilee thou shalt buy of thy n.

2. *Near one,* קָרוֹב *qarob.*
Exod 32. 27 his companion, and every man his neigh.
Josh. 9. 16 they heard that they (were) their neighb.
Psa. 15. 3 nor taketh up a reproach against his nei.
Eze. 23. 5 on her lovers, on the Assyrians (her) nei.
23. 12 She doted upon the Assyrians (her) neigh.

3. *Friend, companion, neighbour,* רֵעַ *rea.*
Exod 11. 2 let every man borrow of his neighbour
20. 16 shalt not bear false witness against thy n.
20. 17 Thou shalt not covet thy neighbour's ho.
20. 17 thou shalt not covet thy neighbour's wife
20. 17 nor his ass, nor any thing that (is) thy ne.
21. 14 if a man come presumptuously upon his n.
22. 7 If a man shall deliver unto his neighbour
22. 8 he have put his hand unto his neighbour's
22. 9 he shall pay double unto his neighbour
22. 10 If a man deliver unto his neighbour an ass
22. 11 that he hath not put his hand unto his n.
22. 14 if a man borrow..of his neighbour, and it
22. 26 If thou at all take thy neighbour's raime.
Lev. 19. 13 Thou shalt not defraud thy neighbour, n.
19. 16 thou stand against the blood of thy neig.
19. 18 thou shalt love thy neighbour as thyself
20. 10 that committeth adultery with his neigh.
Deut. 4. 42 which should kill his neighbour unawares
5. 20 Neither..bear false witness against thy n.
5. 21 Neither shalt thou desire thy neighbour's
5. 21 neither shalt thou covet thy neighbour's
5. 21 his ass, or any (thing) that (is) thy neighb.
15. 2 Every creditor that lendeth..unto his ne.
15. 2 he shall not exact (it) of his neighbour, or
19. 4 Whoso killeth his neighbour ignorantly
19. 5 a man goeth into the wood with his neig.
19. 5 lighteth upon his neighbour, that he die
19. 11 if any man hate his neighbour, and lie in
19. 14 Thou shalt not remove thy neighbour's l.
22. 24 because he hath humbled his neighbour's
22. 26 for as when a man riseth against his nei.
23. 24 When thou comest into thy neighbour's
23. 25 comest into the standing corn of thy nei.
23. 25 thou shalt not move a sickle unto thy ne.
27. 17 he that removeth his neighbour's land m.
27. 24 Cursed (be) he that smiteth his neighbour
Josh. 20. 5 because he smote his neighbour unwitti.
Ruth 4. 7 plucked off his shoe, and gave..to his ne.
1 Sa. 15. 28 given it to a neighbour of thine..better
28. 17 and given it to thy neighbour..to David
2 Sa. 12. 11 and give..unto thy neighbour, and he sh.
1 Ki. 8. 31 If any man trespass against his neighbour
20. 35 unto his neighbour in the word of the L.
2 Ch. 6. 22 If a man sin against his neighbour, and
Job 12. 4 I am (as) one mocked of his neighbour
16. 21 might plead..as a man..for his neighbour
31. 9 I have laid wait at my neighbour's door
Psa. 12. 2 They speak vanity every one with his ne.
15. 3 with his tongue, nor doeth evil to his ne.
28. 3 which speak peace to their neighbours, but
101. 5 Whoso privily slandereth his neighbour
Prov. 3. 28 Say not unto thy neighbour, Go, and come
3. 29 Devise not evil against thy neighbour, se.
6. 29 So he that goeth in to his neighbour's w.
11. 9 An hypocrite..destroyeth his neighbour
11. 12 He that is void of wisdom despiseth his n.
12. 26 The righteous..more excellent than his n.
14. 20 The poor is hated even of his own neigh.
14. 21 He that despiseth his neighbour sinneth
16. 29 A violent man enticeth his neighbour
18. 17 his neighbour cometh and searcheth him
19. 4 but the poor is separated from his neigh.
21. 10 his neighbour findeth no favour in his eyes
24. 28 Be not a witness against thy neighbour
25. 8 when thy neighbour hath put thee to sh.
25. 9 Debate thy cause with thy neighbour(him.)
25. 17 Withdraw thy foot from thy neighbour's
25. 18 that beareth false witness against his ne.
26. 19 So (is) the man (that) deceiveth his neig.
29. 5 A man that flattereth his neighbour spr.
Eccl. 4. 4 that for this a man is envied of his neig.
Isa. 3. 5 one by another, and every one by his ne.
19. 2 every one against his neighbour; city ag.
41. 6 They helped every one his neighbour; and
Jer. 5. 8 every one neighed after his neighbour's
7. 5 judgment between a man and his neigh.
9. 4 Take ye heed every one of his neighbour
9. 4 and every neighbour will walk with slan.
9. 5 they will deceive every one his neighbour
9. 8 speaketh peaceably to his neighbour with
22. 8 they shall say every man to his neighbour
22. 13 useth his neighbour's service without w.
23. 27 which they tell every man to his neighb.
23. 30 steal my words every one from his neigh.
23. 35 Thus shall ye say every one to his neighbour
29. 23 have committed adultery with their nei.
31. 34 shall teach no more every man his neigh.
34. 15 proclaiming liberty every man to his nei.
34. 17 to his brother, and every man to his nei.
Eze. 18. 6 neither hath defiled his neighbour's wife
18. 11 but even hath..defiled his neighbour's w.
18. 15 hath not defiled his neighbour's wife
22. 11 hath committed abomination with his n.
22. 12 thou hast greedily gained of thy neighb.
33. 26 and ye defile every one his neighbour's w.
Hab 2. 15 Woe unto him that giveth his neighbour
Zech. 3. 10 shall ye call every man his neighbour un.
8. 10 for I set all men every one against his n.
8. 16 Speak ye every man the truth to his nei.
8. 17 imagine evil in your hearts against your n.
11. 6 men every one into his neighbour's hand
14. 13 lay hold every one on the hand of his ne
14. 13 shall rise up against the hand of his neig.

4. *Female friend, companion, neighbour,* רְעוּת *reuth.*
Exod 11. 2 every woman of her neighbour, jewels
Jer. 9. 20 and every one her neighbour lamentation

5. *Dweller, neighbour, inhabitant,* שָׁכֵן *shaken.*
Exod. 3. 22 But every woman shall borrow of her ne.
12. 4 let him and his neighbour next unto his
Ruth 4. 17 the women her neighbours gave it a name
2 Ki. 4. 3 borrow thee vessels abroad of all thy ne.
Psa. 31. 11 especially among my neighbours, and a fear
44. 13 Thou makest us a reproach to our neigh.
79. 4 We are become a reproach to our neighb.
79. 12 render unto our neighbours seven fold in.
80. 6 Thou makest us a strife unto our neighb.
89. 41 spoil him: he is a reproach to his neighb.
Prov. 27. 10 better (is) a neighbour..near, than a bro.
Jer. 6. 21 the neighbour and his friend shall perish
12. 14 saith the LORD against all mine evil neig.
49. 10 his brethren, and his neighbours, and he
49. 18 Sodom and Gomorrah, and the neighbour
50. 40 Sodom and Gomorrah and the neighbour
Eze 16. 26 with the Egyptians thy neighbours, great

6. *Fellow countryman,* γείτων *geitōn.*
Luke 14. 12 call not thy..rich neighbours; lest they
15. 6 he calleth together (his) friends and nei.
15. 9 she calleth (her) friends and (her) neigh.
John 9. 8 The neighbours therefore, and they which

7. *One dwelling around about,* περίοικος *perioikos.*
Luke 1. 58 her neighbours and her cousins heard how

8. *The one near or close to,* ὁ πλησίον *ho plēsion.*
Matt. 5. 43 Thou shalt love thy neighbour, and hate
19. 19 Thou shalt love thy neighbour as thyself
22. 39 Thou shalt love thy neighbour as thyself
Mark 12. 31 Thou shalt love thy neighbour as thyself
12. 33 and to love (his) neighbour as himself
Luke 10. 27 all thy mind; and thy neighbour as thys.
10. 29 said unto Jesus, And who is my neighbour?
10. 36 was neighbour unto him that fell among
Acts 7. 27 he that did his neighbour wrong thrust
Rom 13. 9 Thou shalt love thy neighbour as thyself
13. 10 Love worketh no ill to his neighbour
15. 2 Let every one of us please (his) neighbour
Gal. 5. 14 Thou shalt love thy neighbour as thyself
Eph. 4. 25 speak every man truth with his neighbour
Heb. 8. 11 they shall not teach every man his [nei.]
Jas. 2. 8 Thou shalt love thy neighbour as thyself

NEIGHING —
Loud cryings, neighings, מִצְהָלוֹת *mitshaloth.*
Jer. 8. 16 at the sound of the neighing of his strong
13. 27 I have seen thine adulteries, and thy ne.

NEITHER —
1. *There is not, there are not,* אַיִן *ayin.*
Gen. 45. 6 (there shall) neither (be) earing nor harv.
2. *Also...not,* גַּם...אַל *gam...al.*
Exod 34. 3 neither let the flocks nor herds feed before
3. *Or,* אִם *im.*
Eze. 14. 20 they shall deliver neither son nor daught.
4. *And not,* וּבַל *u-bal.*
Isa. 26. 18 neither have the inhabitants of the world
5. *In order not,* לְבִלְתִּי *le-bilti.*
2 Ki. 12. 8 neither to repair the breaches of the ho.
6. *And...not,* וְ...לָא *ve...la.*
Dan. 3. 27 neither were their coats changed, nor the
6. 18 neither were instruments of music brou.
7. *And (also) not,* וְ(גַם) לֹא *ve(-gam) lo.*
Gen. 21. 26 neither didst thou tell me, neither yet h.
2 Sa. 19. 24 had neither dressed his feet, nor trimmed
8. *From,* מִן *min.*
1 Sa. 30. 19 there was nothing lacking to them, neither
9. *Either, or,* ἤ *ē.*
Acts 24. 12 disputing..neither raising up the people
Rom. 1. 21 they glorified (him) not as God, neither
Jas. 1. 17 no variableness, neither shadow of turning
10. *Not,* μή *mē.*
Matt 10. 9 Provide neither gold, nor silver, nor brass
24. 18 Neither let him which is in the field ret.
Luke 10. 4 Carry neither purse, nor scrip, nor shoes
12. 29 shall drink, neither be ye of doubtful m.
18. 2 which feared not God, neither regarded
Rom 14. 21 (It is) good neither to eat flesh, nor to d.
2 John 10 receive him not..neither bid him God s.
11. *Not even, nor, neither,* μηδέ *mēde.*
Matt. 7. 6 neither cast ye your pearls before swine
10. 10 neither two coats, neither shoes, nor yet
23. 10 Neither be ye called masters: for one is
24. 20 be not in the winter, neither on the sab.
Mark 8. 26 Neither go into the town, nor tell (it) to
12. 24 not the Scriptures, neither the power of
13. 11 ye shall speak, [neither do ye premeditate]
13. 15 neither enter..to take any thing out of his
Luke 3. 14 Do violence to no man, neither accuse
12. 22 neither for the body, what ye shall put on
12. 47 neither did according to his will, shall be
14. 12 [nor thy brethren, neither thy kinsmen]
16. 26 neither can they pass to us..from thence
John 4. 15 I thirst not, neither come hither to draw
14. 27 Let not your heart be troubled, neither

Acts 21. 21 to circumcise..neither to walk after the
23. 8 there is no resurrection, [neither] angel
Rom. 6. 13 Neither yield ye your members..instrum.
9. 11 neither having done any good or evil, that
1 Co. 5. 8 neither with the leaven of malice and wi.
10. 7 Neither be ye idolaters, as..some of them
10. 8 Neither let us commit fornication, as some
10. 9 Neither let us tempt Christ, as some of
10. 10 Neither murmur ye, as some of them also
2 Th. 3. 10 if any would not work, neither should he
1 Ti. 1. 4 Neither give heed to fables and endless
5. 22 neither be partaker of other men's sins
1 Pe. 3. 14 be not afraid of their terror, neither be
5. 3 [Neither] as being lords over (God's) her.
1 Jo. 2. 15 Love not the world, neither the things
3. 18 let us not love in word, neither in tongue

12. *Not even*, μήτε *mēte*.
Matt. 5. 34 neither by heaven; for it is God's throne
5. 35 neither by Jerusalem; for it is the city of
5. 36 Neither shalt thou swear by thy head, be.
11. 18 John came neither eating nor drinking
Luke 7. 33 John the Baptist came neither eating br
9. 3 Take nothing for (your) journey, neither
9. 3 neither bread, neither money; neither
Acts 23. 12, 21 they would neither eat nor drink till
27. 20 when neither sun nor stars in many days
Eph. 4. 27 [Neither] give place to the devil
2 Th. 2. 2 neither by spirit, nor by word, nor by le.
1 Ti. 1. 7 understanding neither what they say, nor
Heb. 7. 3 having neither beginning of days, nor end
Jas. 5. 12 neither by heaven, neither by the earth
5. 12 neither by any other oath: but let your
Rev. 7. 3 Hurt not the earth, neither the sea, nor

13. *Assuredly not, not at all*, οὐ μή *ou mē*.
Mark 13. 19 God created unto this time, neither shall
Luke 1. 15 shall drink neither wine nor strong drink

14. *No, not*, οὐ *ou*.
Matt 23. 13 for ye neither go in..neither suffer ye them
25. 13 for ye know neither the day nor the hour
Luke 8. 43 spent all..upon physicians, neither could
12. 24 they [neither] sow nor reap; which neith.
John 17. 20 Neither pray I for these alone, but for them
Acts 8. 21 Thou hast neither part nor lot in this m.
9. 9; 24. 18; Gal. 3. 28; Col. 3. 11; 2 Pe. 1. 8.

15. *And not*, καὶ οὐ *kai ou* or οὐκ δέ *ouk de*.
Matt. 22. 16; Mark 8. 14; 14. 40; Luke 8. 27; 18. 34;
20. 21; Jo. 3. 20; 10. 28; Acts 4. 12; 1 Co. 2. 9, 14;
11. 9; Eph. 5. 4; 6. 9; Heb. 4. 13; Rev. 9. 21; 20. 4.

16. *Not even, neither*, οὐδέ *oude*.
Matt. 5. 15 Neither do men light a candle, and put it
6. 15 neither will your Father forgive your tre.
6. 26 for they sow not, neither do they reap, nor
6. 28 the lilies..they toil not, neither do they
7. 18 neither..a corrupt tree bring forth good
9. 17 Neither do men put new wine into old bo
11. 27 neither knoweth any man the Father, save
12. 4 neither for them which were with him, but
12. 19 neither shall any man hear his voice in the
13. 13 they hear not; neither do they understand
16. 9 Do ye not yet understand, neither reme
16. 10 Neither the seven loaves of the four tho
21. 27 Neither tell I you by what authority I do
22. 46 neither durst any..from that day forth
23. 13 neither suffer ye them that are entering
Mark 4. 22 neither was any thing kept secret, but that
8. 17 perceive ye not yet, neither understand?
11. 26 [neither will your Father which is in he.]
11. 33 Neither do I tell you by what authority
12. 21 the second took her, and died, neither left
13. 32 not the angels..neither the Son, but the
14. 59 neither so did their witness agree together
14. 68 [neither] understand I what thou sayest
16. 13 [told..the residue: neither believed they]
Luke 6. 43 neither doth a corrupt tree bring forth g
7. 7 neither thought I myself worthy to come
8. 17 neither..hid that shall not be known and
11. 33 neither under a bushel, but on a candles.
12. 33 where no thief approacheth, neither moth
16. 31 neither will they be persuaded though one
17. 21 Neither shall they say, Lo here! or, lo there
20. 8 Neither tell I you by what authority I do
John 6. 24 saw that Jesus was not there, neither his
7. 5 neither did his brethren believe in him
8. 11 [Neither do I condemn thee: go, and sin]
8. 42 neither came I of myself, but he sent me
13. 16 neither he that is sent greater than he that
14. 17 it seeth him not, neither knoweth him
Acts 2. 27 neither wilt thou suffer thine Holy One to
2. 31 that..[neither] his flesh did see corruption
4. 32 neither said any..that ought of the things
4. 34 Neither was there any among them that
16. 21 not lawful for us to receive, neither to o.
17. 25 Neither is worshipped with men's hands
20. 24 [neither] count I my life dear unto myself
Rom. 2. 28 neither (is that) circumcision which is out.
9. 7 Neither, because they are the seed of A.
1 Co. 11. 16 we have no such custom, neither the ch.
15. 50 neither doth corruption inherit incorru.
Gal. 1. 1 not of men, neither by man, but by Jesus
1. 12 I neither received it of man..but by the
1. 17 Neither went I up to Jerusalem to them
2. 3 But neither Titus, who was with me, being
6. 13 For neither they themselves who are cir.
Phil. 2. 16 not run in vain, neither laboured in vain
2 Th. 3. 8 Neither did we eat any man's bread for n.
Heb. 9. 12 Neither by the blood of goats and calves
9. 18 Whereupon neither the first..dedicated
10. 8 for sin thou wouldest not, neither hadst
1 Pe. 2. 22 Who did no sin, neither was guile found
1 Jo. 3. 6 sinneth hath not seen him, neither known
Rev. 5. 3 in heaven, nor in earth, neither under the
5. 3 to open the book, neither to look thereon
7. 16 They shall hunger no more, neither thirst
7. 16 neither shall the sun light on them, nor
9. 4 neither any green thing, neither any tree
21. 23 the city had no need of the sun, neither of

17. *Not even, neither*, οὔτε *oute*.
Luke 20. 36 Neither can they die any more: for they
Acts 24. 12 they neither found me in the temple dis.
24. 12 neither in the synagogues, nor in the city
24. 13 Neither can they prove the things whereof
25. 8 Neither against the law of the Jews, nei.
Rom. 8. 38 For I am persuaded, that neither death
1 Co. 3. 7 neither is he that planteth..neither he
6. 9 neither fornicators, nor idolaters, nor ad.
Gal. 1. 12 neither was I taught (it), but by the revel.
1 Th. 2. 6 Nor of men sought we glory, neither of you
3 John 10 neither doth he himself receive the breth.
Rev. 5. 4 to read the book, neither to look thereon
9. 20 which neither can see, nor hear, nor walk
12. 8 [neither] was their place found any more
20. 4 not worshipped the beast, neither his im.
21. 4 neither sorrow, nor crying, neither shall

18. *But not even*, ἀλλ' οὔτε *all' oute*.
1 Co. 3. 2 hitherto ye were not able..neither yet now

NEITHER...NEITHER —
Not even...not even, οὔτε...οὔτε *oute...oute*.
Matt 12. 32 neither in this world, neither in the (wo.)
Act 28. 21 We neither received letters..neither any
1 Co. 3. 7 neither is he that planteth..neither he
8. 8 neither, if we eat..neither, if we eat not
11. 11 neither is the man without..neither the

NEITHER...NOR (yet) —
Not even...not even, οὔτε..οὔτε *oute...oute*.
Matt. 6. 20 where neither moth nor rust doth corrupt
22. 30 neither marry, nor are given in marriage
Mark 12. 25 neither marry, nor are given in marriage
Luke 14. 35 It is neither fit for the land, nor yet for
20. 35 neither marry, nor are given in marriage
John 4. 21 ye shall neither in this mountain, nor yet
5. 37 neither heard his voice at any time, nor
8. 19 Ye neither know me, nor my Father: if
9. 3 Neither hath this man sinned, nor his pa.
Acts 15. 10 which neither our fathers nor we were able
19. 37 are neither robbers of churches, nor yet
Gal. 5. 6 neither circumcision availeth..nor uncir.
6. 15 neither circumcision availeth..nor uncir.
1 Th. 2. 5 neither..used we flattering words..nor a
Rev. 3. 15 I know..that thou art neither cold nor
3. 16 thou art lukewarm, and neither cold nor

NEITHER...any (man or thing) —
Not even one, καὶ οὐδείς *kai oudeis*.
Mark 5. 4 in pieces: neither could any..tame him
16. 8 neither said they any thing to any..for
Jas. 1. 13 God cannot..neither tempteth he any man

NEITHER at any time —
Not even at any time, οὐδέποτε *oudepotē*.
Luke 15. 29 neither transgressed I at any time thy co.

NEITHER indeed —
Not even, οὐδέ *oude*.
Rom. 8. 7 to the law of God, neither indeed can be

NE'-KEB, הַנֶּקֶב *the hollow*.
A city in Naphtali, between Adami and Jabneel; now called *Huzethi*.
Josh. 19. 33 their coast was from Heleph..N., and J.

NE-KO'-DA, נְקוֹדָא *herdsman*.
1. One of the Nethinim whose descendants returned from exile with Zerubbabel. B.C. 536.
Ezra 2. 48 the children of N., the children of Gazzam
Neh. 7. 50 the children of Rezin, the children of N.
2. A person whose descendants did the same, but could not show their genealogy. B.C. 536.
Ezra 2. 60 the children of Tobiah, the children of N.
Neh. 7. 62 the children of Tobiah, the children of N.

NE-MU'-EL, נְמוּאֵל *God is spreading*.
1 A Reubenite, son of Eliab, and brother of Dathan and Abiram who strove against Moses. B.C. 1490.
Num 26. 9 the sons of Eliab; N., and Dathan, and
2 A son of Simeon, second son of Jacob and Leah. B.C. 1700.
Num 26. 12 of N., the family of the Nemuelites: of
1 Ch. 4. 24 The sons of Simeon (were) N., and Jamin

NE-MUE-LI-TES, נְמוּאֵלִי.
The family of Nemuel son of Simeon.
Num 26. 12 of Nemuel, the family of the N.: of Jamin

NE'-PHEG, נֶפֶג *sprout*.
1. A son of Izhar, son of Kohath. B.C. 1491.
Exod 6. 21 the sons of Izhar; Korah, and N., and Z.
2. A son born to David after he became king of Israel. B.C. 1028.
2 Sa. 5. 15 Ibhar also, and Elishua, and N., and Japhia
1 Ch. 3. 7 And Nogah, and N., and Japhia
14. 6 And Nogah, and N., and Japhia

NEPHEW —
1. *Sons of sons, grandchildren*, בְּנֵי בָנִים *bene banim*.
Judg 12. 14 he had forty sons and thirty nephews, that
2. *Successor, progeny*, נֶכֶד *neked*.
Job 18. 19 He shall neither have son nor nephew am.
Isa. 14. 22 name, and remnant, and son, and nephew
3. *Offspring, descendants*, ἔκγονα *ekgona*.
1 Ti. 5. 4 if any widow have children or nephews

NEPHISH. *See* **NAPHISH.**

NE-PHI-SHE'-SIM, נְפִישְׁסִים *expansions* [V.L. נפושסים].
A family of the Nephinim who returned with Zerubbabel. B.C. 536. In Ezra 2. 50, Nephushim.
Neh. 7. 52 children of Meunim, the children of N.

NEPH-THA'-LIM, Νεφθαλείμ.
The country and tribe of *Naphtali*. (*which see*).
Matt. 4. 13 in Capernaum..in the borders of..N.
4. 15 the land of N., (by) the way of the sea
Rev. 7. 6 Of the tribe of N. (were) sealed twelve th.

NEPH-TO'-AH, נֶפְתּוֹחַ.
A small stream on the W. or N.W. of Jerusalem.
Josh. 15. 9 unto the fountain of the water of N., and
18. 15 and went out to the well of waters of N.

NE-PHU'-SIM, נְפוּסִים *expansions* [V.L. נפישים].
A family of the Nethinim whose descendants returned with Zerubbabel. B.C. 536. (See *Nephishesim*.)
Ezra 2. 50 children of Mehunim, the children of N.

NER, נֵר *light*.
A Benjamite, grandfather of Saul the first king of Israel, and father of Abner his chief captain. B.C. 1112.
1 Sa. 14. 50 name..(was) Abner, the son of N., Saul's
14. 51 N. the father of Abner (was) the son of A.
26. 5 Abner the son of N., the captain of his h.
26. 14 David cried..to Abner the son of N., sa.
2 Sa. 2. 8 Abner the son of N...took Ish-bosheth
2. 12 Abner the son of N...went out from Ma.
3. 23 Abner the son of N. came to the king, and
3. 25 Thou knowest Abner the son of N., that
3. 28 from the blood of Abner the son of N.
3. 37 not of the king to slay Abner..son of N.
1 Ki. 2. 5 what he did..unto Abner the son of N.
2. 32 Abner the son of N., captain of the host
1 Ch. 8. 33 N. begat Kish, and Kish begat Saul, and
9. 36 first born son Abdon, then Zur..N.
9. 39 N. begat Kish, and Kish begat Saul, and
26. 28 all that..Abner the son of N...had dedi.

NE-RE'-US, Νηρεύς.
A believer at Rome to whom Paul sends a salutation.
Rom 16. 15 Salute Philologus, and Julia, N., and his

NER'-GAL, נֵרְגַל.
The war god of the men of Cuth whom Shalmaneser placed in the cities of Israel in place of the ten tribes.
2 Ki. 17. 30 men of Cuth made N., and the men of H.

NER-GAL SHAR-E'-ZER, נֵרְגַל שַׂרְאֶצֶר.
1. A prince of Nebuchadnezzar. B.C. 600.
Jer. 39. 3 all the princes..came in..(even) N., Sam.
2. Another of the same name, at the same time.
Jer. 39. 3 N., Rab-mag, with all the residue of the
39. 13 N., Rab-mag, and all the king of Babylon's

NE'-RI, Νηρί. *An ancestor of Jesus.*
Luke 3. 27 (son) of Salathiel, which was (the son) of N.

NE-RI'-AH, נֵרִיָּה, נֵרִיָּהוּ *Jah is light*.
Father of Baruch the amanuensis and messenger of Jeremiah. B.C. 630.
Jer. 32. 12 gave..unto Baruch the son of N., the son
32. 16 had delivered..unto Baruch the son of N.
36. 4 Jeremiah called Baruch the son of N.: and
36. 8 Baruch the son of N. did according to all
36. 14 So Baruch the son of N. took the roll in
36. 32 it to Baruch..the son of N.; who wrote
43. 3 Baruch the son of N. setteth thee on ag.
43. 6 the prophet, and Baruch the son of N.
45. 1 prophet spake unto Baruch the son of N.
51. 59 commanded Seraiah the son of N., the son

NEST —
1. *A nest, cell*, קֵן *qen*.
Num 24. 21 Strong..and thou puttest thy nest in a rock
Deut 22. 6 If a bird's nest chance to be before thee
32. 11 As an eagle stirreth up her nest, flutter.
Job 29. 18 Then I said, I shall die in my nest, and
39. 27 thy command, and make her nest on high?
Psa. 84. 3 the swallow a nest for herself, where she
Prov 27. 8 As a bird that wandereth from her nest
Isa. 10. 14 my hand hath found as a nest the riches
16. 2 as a wandering bird cast out of the nest
Jer. 49. 16 though thou shouldest make thy nest as
Obad. 4 though thou set thy nest among the stars
Hab. 2. 9 that he may set his nest on high, that he
2. *Place for roosting in*, κατασκήνωσις *kataskēnōsis*.
Matt 8. 20 birds of the air (have) nests; but the Son
Luke 9. 58 birds of the air (have) nests; but the Son

NEST, to make a —
1. *To nestle, make a nest*, קָנַן *qanan*, 3.
Psa. 104. 17 Where the birds make their nests..the st.
Isa. 34. 15 There shall the great owl make her nest
Jer. 48. 28 be like the dove (that) maketh her nest in
Eze. 31. 6 All the fowls of heaven made their nests
2. *To be nestled*, קָנַן *qanan*, 4.
Jer. 22. 23 that makest thy nest in the cedars, how

NET —
1. *A net, snare, harm*, חֵרֶם *cherem*.
Eccl. 7. 26 the woman whose heart (is) snares and n.
Eze. 26. 5 the spreading of nets in the midst of the
26. 14 thou shalt be (a place) to spread nets upon
32. 3 and they shall bring thee up in my net
47. 10 they shall be a (place) to spread forth n.

Mic. 7. 2 they hunt every man his brother with a n.
Hab. 1. 15 they catch them in their net, and gather
1. 16 Therefore they sacrifice unto their net, and
1. 17 Shall they therefore empty their net, and

2. *A drag or net*, מִכְמָר, מַכְמֹר *makmor, mikmar.*
Psa. 141. 10 Let the wicked fall into their own nets
Isa. 51. 20 of all the streets, as a wild bull in a net

3. *A drag or net*, מִכְמֹרֶת *mikmoreth.*
Isa. 19. 8 they that spread nets upon the waters sh

4. *A fortress, net*, מְצוּד, מָצוֹד *matsod, matsud.*
Job 19. 6 that God..hath compassed me with his n.
Prov 12. 12 The wicked desireth the net of evil (men)

5. *A fortress, net*, מְצוּדָה, מְצוֹדָה *metsodah, metsudah.*
Psa. 66. 11 Thou broughtest us into the net; thou l.
Eccl. 9. 12 as the fishes that are taken in an evil net

6. *A net, what takes possession*, רֶשֶׁת *resheth.*
Exod 27. 4 upon the net shalt thou make four brasen
27. 5 that the net may be even to the midst of
Job 18. 8 For he is cast into a net by his own feet
Psa. 9. 15 in the net which they hid is their own f.
10. 9 the poor, when he draweth him into his n.
25. 15 for he shall pluck my feet out of the net
31. 4 Pull me out of the net that they have laid
35. 7 without cause..they hid for me their net
35. 8 let his net that he hath hid catch himself
57. 6 They have prepared a net for my steps; my
140. 5 they have spread a net by the way side
Prov. 1. 17 Surely in vain the net is spread in the si.
29. 5 flattereth..spreadeth a net for his feet
Lam. 1. 13 he hath spread a net for my feet; he hath
Eze. 12. 13 My net also will I spread upon him, and
17. 20 I will spread my net upon him, and he
19. 8 spread their net over him: he was taken
32. 3 I will therefore spread out my net over
Hos. 5. 1 a snare on Mizpah, and a net spread upon
7. 12 When they shall go, I will spread my net

7. *A net*, שְׂבָכָה *sabak.*
1 Ki. 7. 17 nets of checker work, and wreaths of chain

8. *A large fishing net*, ἀμφίβληστρον *amphiblēstron.*
Matt 4. 18 Andrew his brother, casting a net into the
Mark 1. 16 Andrew his brother casting [a net] into

9. *A fishing net*, δίκτυον *diktuon.*
Matt 4. 20 they straightway left (their) nets, and fo.
4. 21 Zebedee their father, mending their nets
Mark 1. 18 straightway they forsook their nets, and
1. 19 also were in the ship mending their nets
Luke 5. 2 gone out of them, and were washing..nets
5. 4 Launch out..and let down your nets for
5. 5 said..at thy word I will let down the net
5. 6 great multitude of fishes: and their net
John 21. 6 Cast the net on the right side of the ship
21. 8 little ship..dragging the net with fishes
21. 11 drew the net to land full of great fishes
21. 11 there were so many, yet was not the net

10. *A drag net*, σαγήνη *sagēnē.*
Matt 13. 47 the kingdom of heaven is like unto a net

NE-THAN'-EEL, נְתַנְאֵל *God gives.*
1. The prince of Issachar, and son of Zuar, whom Moses sent to spy out the land. B.C. 1490.
Num. 1. 8 Of Issachar; N. the son of Zuar
2. 5 N. the son of Zuar (shall be) captain of
7. 18 On the second day N. the son of Zuar, pr.
7. 23 this (was) the offering of N. the son of Z.
10. 15 And over the host..(was) N. the son of Z.
2. One of David's brothers. B.C. 1060.
1 Ch. 2. 14 N. the fourth, Raddai the fifth
3. A priest who helped to bring up the ark from the house of Obed-edom. B.C. 1042.
1 Ch. 15. 24 Shebaniah, and Jehoshaphat, and N., and
4. A Levite whose son Shemaiah was employed by David to write down the distribution of the Levites in the service of the sanctuary. B.C. 1070.
1 Ch. 24. 6 Shemaiah the son of N. the scribe, (one)
5. A son of Obed-edom appointed by David as gate keeper for the tabernacle. B.C. 1042.
1 Ch. 26. 4 sons of Obed-edom (were)..N. the fifth
6. A prince of Judah whom king Jehoshaphat sent to teach the people. B.C. 912.
2 Ch. 17. 7 he sent to his princes..to N., and to Mi.
7. A chief Levite in the days of Josiah. B.C. 623.
2 Ch. 35. 9 Conaniah also, and Shemaiah, and N., his
8. A person who returned with Ezra, and had taken a strange wife. B.C. 456.
Ezra 10. 22 of the sons of Pashur..N., Jozabad, and
9. A priest of the family of Jedaiah, who lived in the days of Joiakim grandson of Jozadak. B.C. 500.
Neh. 12. 21 of Hilkiah, Hashabiah; of Jedaiah, N.
10. An Aaronite musician who helped in the ceremony of purification. B.C. 445.
Neh. 12. 36 his brethren, Shemaiah..N., and Judah

NE-THAN-I'AH, נְתַנְיָה, נְתַנְיָהוּ *Jah gives.*
1. Father of Ishmael who slew Gedaliah, whom Nebuchadnezzar had left governor in the land. B.C. 625.
2 Ki. 25. 23 there came..even Ishmael the son of N.
25. 25 Ishmael the son of N...came, and ten men
Jer. 40. 8 they came..even Ishmael the son of N.
40. 14 sent Ishmael the son of N. to slay thee?
40. 15 I will slay Ishmael the son of N., and no
41. 1 the son of N. the son of Elishama, of the
41. 2 Then arose Ishmael the son of N., and the
41. 6 the son of N. went forth from Mizpah to
Jer. 41. 7 the son of N. slew them, (and cast them)
41. 9 the son of N. filled it with (them that
41. 10 the son of N. carried them away captive
41. 11 evil that Ishmael the son of N. had done
41. 12 went to fight with Ishmael the son of N.
41 15 the son of N. escaped from Johanan with
41. 16 had recovered from Ishmael the son of N.
41. 18 the son of N. had slain Gedaliah the son
2. A chief singer in the days of David.
1 Ch. 25. 2 N., and Asarelah, the sons of Asaph, under
25. 12 fifth to N., (he), his sons, and his brethren
3. A Levite whom Jehoshaphat sent to teach in the cities of Judah. B.C. 912.
2 Ch. 17. 8 N., and Zebadiah, and Asahel, and Shem.
4. Father of Jehudi whom the princes of Judah sent to bring Baruch. B.C. 625.
Jer. 36. 14 the princes sent Jehudi the son of N., the

NETHER (part), nethermost —

1. *Lower, under*, תַּחְתּוֹן *tachton.*
Josh. 16. 3 unto the coast of Beth-horon the nether
18. 13 on the south side of the nether Beth-hor.
1 Ki. 6. 6 The nethermost chamber (was) five cub.
9. 17 built Gezer, and Beth-horon the nether
1 Ch. 7. 24 Sherah, who built Beth horon the nether
2 Ch. 8. 5 Also he built..Beth-horon the nether, fen.

2. *Lower, under*, תַּחְתִּי *tachti.*
Exod 19. 17 they stood at the nether part of..mount
Josh. 15. 19 the upper springs, and the nether springs
Judg. 1. 15 the upper springs and the nether springs
Job 41. 24 as hard as a piece of the nether (millstone)
Eze. 31. 14 to the nether parts of the earth, in the
31. 16 shall be comforted in the nether parts of
31. 18 Eden unto the nether parts of the earth
32. 18 unto the nether parts of the earth, with
32. 24 are gone down..into the nether parts of

NETHER and upper millstone —
The two millstones, רֵחַיִם *rechayim.*
Deut 24. 6 No man shall take the nether..millstone

NE-THIN'-IMS, נְתִינִים *dedicated.*
A class of persons employed as servants or assistants to the Levites; probably the Gibeonites and others reduced to servitude.
1 Ch. 9. 2 Israelites, the priests, Levites, and the N.
Ezra 2. 43 The N.: the children of Ziha, the children
2. 58 N., and the children of Solomon's servants
2. 70 N., dwelt in their cities, and all Israel
7. 7 the singers, and the porters, and the N.
7. 24 N., or ministers of this house of God
8. 17 and to his brethren the N., at the place
8. 20 of the N., whom David and the prince had
8. 20 two hundred and twenty N.: all of them
Neh. 3. 26 the N. dwelt in Ophel, unto (the place)
3. 31 goldsmith's son unto the place of the N.
7. 46 the N.: the children of Ziha, the children
7. 60 N., and the children of Solomon's servants
7. 73 N., and all Israel, dwelt in their cities
10. 28 the N., and all they that had separated
11. 3 N., and the children of Solomon's servants
11. 21 But the N. dwelt in Ophel
11. 21 and Ziha and Gispa (were) over the N.

NE-TO'-PHAH, נְטֹפָה *resin-dropping.*
A city in Judah, S. of Jerusalem, near Bethlehem; now called *Beit-Netiph.*
Ezra 2. 22 The men of N., fifty and six
Neh. 7. 26 The men of Beth-lehem and N., an hund.

NE-TO-PHA'-THI, נְטֹפָתִי *Inhabitant of Netophah.*
Neh. 12. 28 plain country..and from the villages of N.

NE-TO-PHA-THITE, נְטֹפָתִי *same as preceding.*
2 Sa. 23. 28 Zalmon the Ahohite, Maharai the N.
23. 29 the son of Baanah, a N., Ittai the son of
2 Ki. 25. 23 the son of Tanhumeth the N., and Jaaza.
1 Ch. 2. 54 the N., Ataroth, the house of Joab, and
9. 16 that dwelt in the villages of the N.
11. 30 the N., Heled the son of Baanah the N.
27. 13 The tenth (captain)..(was) Maharai the N.
27. 15 The twelfth (captain)..(was) Heldai the N.
Jer. 40. 8 the sons of Ephai the N., and Jezaniah the

NETTLE —

1. *Nettle, thorn, shrub*, חָרוּל *charul.*
Job 30. 7 under the nettles they were gathered toge.
Prov 24. 31 nettles had covered the face thereof, and
Zeph. 2. 9 the breeding of nettles, and salt pits, and

2. *Thorn, nettle*, קִימוֹשׁ, קִמּוֹשׁ *qimmosh, qimosh.*
Isa. 34. 13 nettles and brambles in the fortresses th.
Hos. 9. 6 for their silver, nettles shall possess them

NET WORK —

1. *Net or white work*, חוֹר *chor.*
Isa. 19. 9 they that weave net works, shall be conf.

2. *Net or wreathed work, lattice*, שְׂבָכָה *sebakah.*
1 Ki. 7. 18 rows round about upon the one net work
7. 20 the belly which (was) by the net work: and
7. 41 the two net works, to cover the two bowls
7. 42 for the two net works..for one net work
Jer. 52. 22 with net work and pomegranates upon the
52. 23 all the pomegranates upon the net work

3. *Work of net*, מַעֲשֵׂה רֶשֶׁת *maaseh resheth.*
Exod 27. 4 thou shalt make for it a grate of net work
38. 4 he made..a brasen grate of net work un.

NEVER —

1. *There is not, there are not*, אַיִן *ayin.*
Judg 14. 3 (Is there) never a woman among the dau.
Eze. 28. 19 thou shalt be a terror, and never (shalt)

2. *No*, לֹא *lo.*
Gen. 41. 19 such as I never saw in all the land of Eg.
Num 19. 2 a red heifer..upon which never came yo.
Prov 27. 20 Hell and destruction are never full; so
Jer. 33. 17 David shall never want a man to sit upon

3. *For generations not*, לְדֹר וָדֹר לֹא *le-dor va-dor lo.*
Psa. 10. 6 for (I shall) never (be) in adversity

4. *Not to the age*, לֹא לְעוֹלָם *lo le-olam.*
Judg. 2. 1 I will never break my covenant with you
2 Sa. 12. 10 Now therefore the sword shall never de.
Psa. 15. 5 He that doeth these..shall never be mo.
30. 6 in my prosperity I said, I shall never be
31. 1 let me never be ashamed: deliver me in
55. 22 he shall never suffer the righteous to be
71. 1 LORD..let me never be put to confusion
119. 93 I will never forget thy precepts: for with
Prov 10. 30 The righteous shall never be removed: but
Isa. 14. 20 seed of evil doers shall never be renowned
25. 2 palace..to be no city; it shall never be bu.
63. 19 We are (thine); thou never barest rule
Eze. 26. 21 yet shalt thou never be found again, saith
Joel. 2. 26, 27 and my people shall never be ashamed

5. *Not to the ages*, לָא לְעָלְמִין *la le-alemin.*
Dan. 2. 44 kingdom, which shall never be destroyed

6. *Not continual*, תָּמִיד לֹא *tamid lo.*
Isa. 62. 6 shall never hold their peace day nor night

7. *Not to the age*, אַל לְעוֹלָם *al le-olam.*
Psa. 31. 1 let me never be ashamed: deliver me in
71. 1 LORD..let me never be put to confusion

8. *Not to perpetuity*, לֹא לָנֶצַח *lo la-netsach.*
Psa. 10. 11 he hideth his face; he will never see (it)
49. 19 his fathers; they shall never see light
Isa. 13. 20 It shall never be inhabited, neither shall
Amos 8. 7 Surely I will never forget any of their w.
Hab. 1. 4 and judgment doth never go forth: for

9. *Not*, μή *mē.*
John 7. 15 How knoweth this man letters, having ne.

10. *Not at any time*, μηδέποτε *mēdepote.*
2 Ti. 3. 7 Ever learning, and never able to come to

11. *Assuredly not, not at all*, οὐ μή *ou mē.*
John 6. 35 he that cometh to me shall never hunger
Heb. 13. 5 I will never leave thee, nor forsake thee

12. *Not at all to the age*, οὐ μὴ εἰς τὸν αἰῶνα *ou mē.*
John 4. 14 [that I shall give him, shall never thirst]
8. 51 If a man keep my saying, he shall never see
8. 52 If a man keep my saying, he shall [never]
10. 28 they shall never perish, neither shall any
11. 26 whosoever..believeth in me shall never
13. 8 Peter saith unto him, Thou shalt never wa.

13. *Not to the age*, οὐκ εἰς αἰῶνα *ouk eis aiōna.*
Mark 3. 29 hath [never] forgiveness, but is in danger

14. *Not at all at any time*, οὐ μὴ πώποτε *ou mē pōpo.*
John 6. 35 he that believeth on me shall never thirst

15. *No, not*, οὐ *ou.*
Mark 14. 21 good were it for that man if he had never
Luke 23. 29 that never bare, and the paps which never

16. *Not even*, οὐδέ *oude.*
Matt 27. 14 And he answered him to never a word

17. *Not even one*, οὐδεὶς πώποτε *oudeis pōpote.*
Mark 11. 2 shall find a colt tied, whereon never man
Luke 19. 30 find a colt tied, whereon yet never man sat

18. *Not even at any time*, οὐδέποτε *oudepote.*
Matt. 7. 23 will I profess unto them, I never knew you
9. 33 saying, It was never so seen in Israel
21. 16 have ye never read, Out of the mouth of
21. 42 Did ye never read in the Scriptures, The
26. 33 Though all..(yet) will I never be offended
Mark 2. 12 God, saying, We never saw it on this fas.
2. 25 Have ye never read what David did, when
Luke 15. 29 thou never gavest me a kid, that I might
John 7. 46 answered, Never man spake like this man
Acts 10. 14 for I have never eaten anything that is
14. 8 cripple from his mother's womb, who never
1 Co. 13. 8 Charity never faileth..whether (there be)
Heb. 10. 1 can never with those sacrifices which they
10. 11 sacrifices, which can never take away sins

19. *Not at all at any time*, οὐ μή ποτε *ou mē pote.*
2 Pe. 1. 10 for if ye do these things, ye shall never

NEVER before or yet —
Not even yet, οὐδέπω *oudepō.*
Luke 23. 53 stone, wherein never man before was laid
John 19. 41 sepulchre, wherein was never man yet laid

NEVER so —
With cleanness, purity, בְּבֹר *be-bor.*
Job 9. 30 If I wash ..make my hands never so clean

NEVER...any man —
Not even at any time, οὐδεὶς πώποτε *oudeis pōpote.*
John 8. 33 We..were never in bondage to any man

NEVERTHELESS —

1. *But, verily*, אֲבָל *abal.*
2 Ch. 19. 3 Nevertheless there are good things found
33. 17 Nevertheless the people did sacrifice still

2. *Only*, אַךְ *ak.*
Lev. 11. 4 Nevertheless these shall ye not eat of th.

3. *Surely, but, yet*, אָכֵן *aken.*
Psa. 31. 22 nevertheless thou heardest the voice of

4.*End, cessation, only,* אֶפֶס *ephes.*
Num 13. 28 Nevertheless the people (be) strong that
5.*But,* בְּרַם *beram.*
Dan. 4. 15 Nevertheless, leave the stump of his roots
6.*Because, when,* כִּי *ki.*
1 Sa.15. 35 nevertheless Samuel mourned for Saul: and
7.*Only, surely, nevertheless,* רַק *raq.*
1 Ki. 8. 19 Nevertheless thou shalt not build the h.
8.*But, but surely,* כִּי אִם *ki im.*
Num 24. 22 Nevertheless the Kenite shall be wasted
9.*But,* ἀλλά *alla.*
Mark14. 36 nevertheless not what I will, but what
John11. 15 I am glad..nevertheless, let us go unto
16. 7 Nevertheless I tell you the truth; It is
Rom. 5. 14 Nevertheless death reigned from Adam
1 Co. 9. 12 Nevertheless we have not used this power
2 Co. 7. 6 Nevertheless God, that comforteth those
12. 16 nevertheless, being crafty, I caught you
Gal. 4. 30 Nevertheless what saith the scripture?
2 Ti. 1. 12 nevertheless I am not ashamed; for I k.
Rev. 2. 4 Nevertheless I have..against thee, beca.
10.*And consequently indeed,* καί τοι γε *kai toi ge.*
Acts 14. 17 Nevertheless he left not himself without
11.*At the same time indeed,* ὅμως μέντοι *homōs.*
John12. 42 Nevertheless among the chief rulers also
12.*But yet, nevertheless,* πλήν *plēn.*
Matt 26. 39 nevertheless not as I will, but as thou
26. 64 nevertheless, I say unto you, Hereafter
Luke13. 33 Nevertheless I must walk to day, and to
18. 8 Nevertheless when the Son of man cometh
22. 42 nevertheless not my will, but thine, be
1 Co.11. 11 Nevertheless neither is the man without
Eph. 5. 33 Nevertheless let every one Ph. 3. 16.
13.*But,* δέ *de,* Gal. 4. 20.
14.*Nevertheless, yet indeed,* ὁ μέν τοι *ho men toi.*
2 Ti. 2. 19 Nevertheless the foundation of God stan.

NEW (man, moon, thing) —
1.*New,* חָדָשׁ *chadash.*
Exod.1. 8 Now there arose up a new king over E.
Lev. 23. 16 ye shall offer a new meat offering unto
26. 10 and bring forth the old because of the new
Num28. 26 when ye bring a new meat offering unto
Deut20. 5 What man..that hath built a new house
22. 8 When thou buildest a new house, then
24. 5 When a man hath taken a new wife, he
32. 17 to gods whom they knew not, to new (gods
Josh. 9. 13 these bottles of wine..(were) new; and
Judg. 5. 8 They chose new gods; then (was) war in
15. 13 they bound him with two new cords, and
16. 11 If they bind me fast with new ropes that
16. 12 Delilah therefore took new ropes, and bo.
1 Sa. 6. 7 Now therefore make a new cart, and take
2 Sa. 6. 3 they set the ark of God upon a new cart
6. 3 the sons of Abinadab, drave the new cart
21. 16 he, being girded with a new (sword), tho.
1 Ki.11. 29 he had clad himself with a new garment
11. 30 And Ahijah caught the new garment that
2 Ki. 2. 20 Bring me a new cruse, and put salt ther.
1 Ch.13. 7 they carried the ark of God in a new cart
2 Ch.20. 5 in the house of the LORD, before the new
Job 32. 19 my belly..is ready to burst like new bot.
Psa. 33. 3 Sing unto him a new song; play skilfully
40. 3 And he hath put a new song in my mouth
96. 1 O sing unto the LORD a new song; sing
98. 1 O sing unto the LORD a new song; for he
144. 9 I will sing a new song unto thee, O God
Eccl. 1. 9 (there is) no new (thing) under the sun
1. 10 whereof it may be said, See, this (is) new?
Song 7. 13 all manner of pleasant (fruits), new and
Isa. 41. 15 I will make thee a new sharp threshing
42. 9 are come to pass, and new things do I d.
42. 10 Sing unto the LORD a new song..his praise
43. 19 I will do a new thing: now it shall spring
48. 6 I have showed thee new things from this
62. 2 thou shalt be called by a new name, wh.
65. 17 I create new heavens, and a new earth
66. 22 as the new heavens, and the new earth
Jer. 26. 10 sat down in the entry of the new gate of
31. 22 the LORD hath created a new thing in the
31. 31 that I will make a new covenant with the
36. 10 at the entry of the new gate of the LORD'S
Lam. 3. 23 new every morning: great (is) thy faithful.
Eze. 11. 19 I will put a new spirit within you; and I
18. 31 make you a new heart and a new spirit
36. 26 A new heart..will I give you, and a new
2.*New,* חֲדַת *chadath.*
Ezra 6. 4 rows of great stones, and a row of new ti.
3.*Fresh, raw,* טְרִי *tari.*
Judg15. 15 he found a new jaw bone of an ass, and
4.*A creation,* בְּרִיאָה *beriah.*
Num16. 30 if the LORD make a new thing, and the
5.*Unsmoothed, unfinished,* ἄγναφος *agnaphos.*
Matt. 9. 16 No man putteth a piece of new cloth unto
Mark 2. 21 No man also soweth a piece of new cloth
6.*New, fresh, recent, newly made,* καινός *kainos.*
Matt. 9. 17 into new bottles, and both are preserved
13. 52 out of his treasure (things) new and old
26. 28 For this is my blood of the [new] testam.
26. 29 until that day when I drink it new with
27. 60 laid it in his own new tomb, which he
Mark 1. 27 what new doctrine (is) this? for with au.
2. 21 else the new piece that filled it up taketh
2. 22 [but..wine must be put into new bottles]
14. 24 This is my blood of the [new] testament
14. 25 until that day that I drink it new in the
16. 17 [In my name..they shall speak with new]
Luke 5. 36 a piece of a new garment upon an old
5. 36 then both the new maketh a rent, and the
5. 36 piece that was (taken) out of the new agr.
5. 38 wine must be put into new bottles; and
22. 20 This cup (is) the new testament in my bl.
John13. 34 A new commandment I give unto you, T.
19. 41 in the garden a new sepulchre, wherein
Acts 17. 19 May we know what this new doctrine, w.
17. 21 either to tell, or to hear some new thing
1 Co. 11. 25 This cup is the new testament in my bl.
2 Co. 3. 6 hath made us able ministers of the new
5. 17 if any man (be) in Christ, (he is) a new c.
5. 17 away; behold, all things are become new
Gal. 6. 15 nor uncircumcision, but a new creature
Eph. 2. 15 to make in himself of twain one new
4. 24 that ye put on the new man, which after
Heb. 8. 8 when I will make a new covenant, with
8. 13 In that he saith, A new..he hath made the
9. 15 he is the mediator of the new testament
2 Pe. 3. 13 look for new heavens and a new earth, w.
1 Jo. 2. 7 I write no new commandment unto you
2. 8 a new commandment I write unto you
2 Jo. 5 not as though I wrote a new commandm.
Rev. 2. 17 in the stone a new name written, which
3. 12 the name of the city of my God..new Jeru.
3. 12 and (I will write upon him) my new name
5. 9 they sung a new song, saying, Thou art w.
14. 3 they sung as it were a new song before the
21. 1 And I saw a new heaven and a new earth
21. 2 I John saw the holy city, new Jerusalem
21. 5 he..said, Behold, I make all things new
7.*New, young,* νέος *neos.*
Matt. 9. 17 Neither do men put new wine into old b.
9. 17 they put new wine into..bottles, and both
Mark 2. 22 no man putteth new wine into old bottles
2. 22 else the [new] wine doth burst the bottles
2. 22 [but new wine must be put into..bottles]
Luke 5. 37 new wine into old bottles; else the new
5. 38 new wine must be put into..bottles; and
5. 39 straightway desireth new; for he saith, The
1 Co. 5. 7 the old leaven, that ye may be a new lump
Col. 3. 10 have put on the new (man), which is rene.
Heb.12. 24 to Jesus the mediator of the new covena
8.*Newly slain, recent,* πρόσφατος *prosphatos.*
Heb. 10. 20 By a new and living way, which he hath

NEW fruit, to bring —
To bring forth first fruit, בָּכַר *bakar,* 3.
Eze. 47. 12 it shall bring forth new fruit according to

NEW moon —
New moon, month, חֹדֶשׁ *chodesh.*
1 Sa. 20. 5 Behold, to morrow (is) the new moon, and
20. 18 To morrow (is) the new moon: and thou
20. 24 when the new moon was come, the king
2 Ki. 4. 23 said..(it is) neither new moon nor sabbath
1 Ch.23. 31 in the sabbaths, in the new moons, and
2 Ch. 2. 4 on the sabbaths, and on the new moons
8. 13 on the sabbaths, and on the new moons
31. 3 for the sabbaths, and for the new moons
Ezra 3. 5 both of the new moons, and of all the set
Neh. 10. 33 of the sabbaths, of the new moons, for the
Psa. 81. 3 Blow up the trumpet in the new moon
Isa. 66. 23 from one new moon to another, and from
Eze. 45. 17 in the feasts, and in the new moons, and
46. 3 in the sabbaths, and in the new moons
46. 6 in the day of the new moon..a young bu.
Hos. 2. 11 her feast days, her new moons, and her s.
Amos 8. 5 When will the new moon be gone, that we

NEW wine —
1.*New sweet wine, or juice of grapes,* תִּירוֹשׁ *tirosh.*
Neh. 10. 39 the offering of the corn, of the new wine
13. 5 the tithes of the corn, the new wine, and
13. 12 the tithe of the corn, and the new wine
Prov. 3. 10 thy presses shall burst out with new wine
Isa. 24. 7 The new wine mourneth, the vine langui.
65. 8 As the new wine is found in the cluster
Hos. 4. 11 Whoredom and wine and new wine take
9. 2 The floor..and the new wine shall fail in
Joel 1. 10 the corn is wasted: the new wine is dried
Hag. 1. 11 upon the new wine, and upon the oil, and
Zech. 9. 17 young men cheerful, and new wine the m.
2.*Must, sweet new wine,* γλεῦκος *gleukos.*
Acts 2. 13 Others..said, These men are full of new w.

NEW born —
Now born, lately born, ἀρτιγέννητος *artigennētos.*
1 Pe. 2. 2 As new born babes, desire the sincere mi.

NEWLY, (but) —
1.*Setting,* קוּם *qum,* 5 (adv. inf.).
Judg. 7. 19 and they had but newly set the watch
2.*Recently,* מִקָּרוֹב *miq-qarob.*
Deut32. 17 to new (gods that) came newly up, whom

NEWNESS —
Newness, freshness, καινότης *kainotēs.*
Rom. 6. 4 so we also should walk in newness of life
7. 6 that we should serve in newness of spirit

NEWS —
Report, tidings, שְׁמוּעָה *shemuah.*
Prov 25. 25 so (is) good news from a far country

NEXT, (that is) —
1.*After, later, next,* אַחַר *acher.*
Gen. 17. 21 bear..at this set time in the next year
2 Ki. 6. 29 I said unto her on the next day, Give thy
2.*The second,* מִשְׁנֶה *mishneh.*
1 Sa. 17. 13 and next unto him, Abinadab; and the
23. 17 I shall be next unto thee; and that also
1 Ch. 5. 12 Shapham the next, and Jaanai, and Sha.
16. 5 next to him Zechariah, Jeiel, and Shem.
2 Ch.28. 7 and Elkanah (that was) next to the king
31. 12 ruler, and Shimei his brother..the next
Esth 10. 3 the Jew (was) next unto king Ahasuerus
3.*Near,* קָרוֹב *qarob.*
Exod12. 4 him and his neighbour next unto his house
Num27. 11 his kinsman that is next to him of his
Deut21. 3 the city (which is) next unto the slain man
21. 6 elders..(that are) next unto the slain (man)
Esth. 1. 14 the next unto his (was) Carshena, Shethar
4.*In succession,* ἑξῆς *hexēs.*
Luke 9. 37 the next day, when they were come down
5.*Coming on,* ἐπιοῦσα *epiousa.*
Acts 7. 26 the next day he showed himself unto them
6.*To come,* ἔρχομαι *erchomai.*
Acts 13. 44 And the [next] sabbath day came almost
7.*After, between,* μεταξύ *metaxu.*
Acts 13. 42 be preached to them the next sabbath
8.*To have, hold, adhere to, adjoin,* ἔχω *echō.*
Mark 1. 38 Let us go into the next towns, that I may
Acts 21. 26 the next day purifying himself with them

NEXT day (after)—
1.*At noon,* מָחֳרָת *mochorath.*
Num11. 32 all (that) night, and all the next day, and
1 Sa. 30. 17 even unto the evening of the next day
Jon. 4. 7 when the morning rose the next day, and
2.*In succession,* ἑξῆς *hexēs.*
Acts 27. 18 the next (day) they lightened the Lu. 7. 11.
3.*The morrow,* αὔριον *aurion.*
Acts 4. 3 put (them) in hold unto the next day: for
4.*Belonging to the second day,* δευτεραῖος *deuteraios.*
Acts 28. 13 and we came the next day to Puteoli
5.*Coming on,* ἐπιοῦσα *epiousa.*
Acts 16. 11 we came..the next (day) to Neapolis
20. 15 came the next day over against Chios; and
6.*To morrow,* ἐπαύριον *epaurion.*
Matt27. 62 the next day, that followed the day of
John 1. 29 The next day John seeth Jesus coming
1. 35 the next day after, John stood, and two
12. 12 the next day much people that were come
Acts 14. 20 the next day he departed with Barnabas
21. 8 next (day) we that were of Paul's company
25. 6 the next day, sitting on the judgment seat
7.*Other, the other, different from,* ἕτερος *heteros.*
Acts 20. 15 and the next (day) we arrived at Samos
27. 3 next (day) we touched at Sidon. And Ju.
8.*To have, hold, adhere to, adjoin,* ἔχω *echō.*
Acts 20. 15 and the next (day) we came to Miletus

NE-ZI'-AH, נְצִיחַ *pre-eminent.*
One of the Nethinim whose descendants returned with Zerubbabel. B.C. 536.
Ezra 2. 54 The children of N., the children of Hatipha
Neh. 7. 56 The children of N., the children of Hatipha

NE'-ZIB, נְצִיב *plantation.*
A city in Judah; now called *Beit Nasib,* near Ashna.
Josh.15. 43 And Jiphtah, and Ashnah, and N.

NIB'-HAZ, נִבְחַז.
An idol of the Avites (in the form of a dog) brought to Samaria along with *Tartak,* etc.
2 Ki.17. 31 And the Avites made N. and Tartak, and

NIB'-SHAN, הַנִּבְשָׁן *the furnace.*
A city in the S.E. of Judah, near the city of Salt, and En-gedi, supposed to be the same as *Ashan* and *Chor-Ashan;* but these were rather in the tribe of Simeon to the S.W.
Josh.15. 62 N., and the city of Salt, and En-gedi; six

NI-CA'-NOR, Νικάνωρ *conqueror.*
One of the seven disciples chosen to serve tables in the church at Jerusalem.
Acts 6. 5 N., and Timon, and Parmenas, and Nicolas

NI-CO-DE'-MUS, Νικόδημος *innocent blood.*
A rabbi who came to Jesus by night; who vindicated him, and who at last embalmed him.
John 3. 1 was a man of the Pharisees, named N.
3. 4 N. saith unto him, How can a man be born
3. 9 N. answered and said unto him, How can
7. 50 N. saith unto them, he that came to Jesus
19. 39 there came also N., which at the first came

NI-CO-LAI-TANES, Νικολαΐται.
The followers of one Nicolas, whose deeds are condemned without being mentioned. B.C. 70.
Rev. 2. 6 thou hatest the deeds of the N., which I
2. 15 also them that hold the doctrine of the N.

NI-CO'-LAS, Νικόλαος *conqueror of the people.*
A proselyte of Antioch, and one of the seven disciples chosen to serve tables.
Acts 6. 5 and Parmenas, and N. a proselyte of An.

NI-CO-PO'-LIS, Νικόπολις *city of victory.*
A city of Thrace, now called *Nikopi*, on the river Nessus (Karasu), the boundary between Thrace and Macedonia.
Titus 3. 12 be diligent to come unto me to N: for I

NI'-GER, Νίγερ.
Surname of Simeon, one of the prophets and teachers at Antioch when Paul and Barnabas returned thither after carrying the contributions of the brethren to the poor saints at Jerusalem.
Acts 13. 1 Simeon that was called N., and Lucius of

NIGH (at hand, to or unto)—
1. *Near*, קָרוֹב *qarob.*
Lev. 10. 3 be sanctified in them that come nigh me
21. 3 a virgin, that is nigh unto him, which h.
Num 24. 17 I shall behold him, but not nigh: there
Deut. 4. 7 who (hath) God (so) nigh unto them, as
13. 7 which (are) round about you, nigh unto
22. 2 if thy brother (be) not nigh unto thee, or
30. 14 the word (is) very nigh unto thee, in thy
1 Ki. 8. 59 nigh unto the LORD our God day and night
1 Ch. 12. 40 Moreover they that were nigh them, (ev.)
Esth. 9. 20 in all the provinces..(both) nigh and far
Psa. 34. 18 The LORD (is) nigh unto them that are of
85. 9 his salvation (is) nigh them that fear him
145. 18 The LORD (is) nigh unto all them that call
Joel 2. 1 for the day of the LORD..(is) nigh at hand
2. *Flesh, relation*, שְׁאֵר *sheer.*
Lev. 25. 49 (any) that is nigh of kin unto him of his
3. *Neighbour*, שָׁכֵן *shaken.*
Deut. 1. 7 (the places) nigh thereunto, in the plain
4. *Nigh*, ἐγγύς *eggus.*
Matt 24. 32 leaves, ye know that summer (is) nigh
Mark 13. 29 know that it is nigh, (even) at the doors
Luke 19. 11 because he was nigh to Jerusalem, and
21. 30 and know..that summer is now nigh at
21. 31 that the kingdom of God is nigh at hand
John 6. 4 the passover, a feast of the Jews, was ni.
6. 19 see Jesus..drawing nigh unto the ship
6. 23 nigh unto the place where they did eat
11. 18 Now Bethany was nigh unto Jerusalem
11. 55 the Jews' passover was nigh at hand: and
19. 20 place where Jesus was crucified was nigh
19. 42 for the sepulchre was nigh at hand
Acts 9. 38 Lydda was nigh to Joppa, and the discip.
27. 8 nigh whereunto was the city (of) Lasea
Rom. 10. 8; Eph. 2. 13; 2. 17; Heb. 6. 8.
5. *To be or come nigh*, ἐγγίζω *eggizō.*
Luke 21. 20 that the desolation..is nigh, Phil. 2. 30
6. *Alongside of*, παρά (acc.) *para.*
Matt 15. 29 and came nigh unto the sea of Galilee
Mark 5. 21 passed over..he was nigh unto the sea
7. *Very near or nigh to*, παραπλήσιον *paraplēsion.*
Phil. 2. 27 he was sick nigh unto death: but God had
8. *Toward*, πρός (acc.) *pros.*
Mark 5. 11 there was there, [nigh unto] the mount.

NIGHT, (by or in the)—
1. *Darkness*, חֹשֶׁךְ *choshek.*
Job 26. 10 until the day and night come to an end
2. *Night*, לַיִל, לַיְלָה *layelah, layil.*
Gen. 1. 5 and the darkness he called night. And
1. 14 lights..to divide the day from the night
1. 16 and the lesser light to rule the night: (he
1. 18 to rule over the day and over the night
7. 4, 12 upon the earth forty days and forty n.
8. 22 winter, and day and night shall not cease
14. 15 he and his servants, by night, and smote
19. 5 the men which came in to thee this night?
19. 33 made their father drink wine that night
19. 34 let us make him drink wine this night also
19. 35 their father drink wine that night also
20. 3 came to Abimelech in a dream by night
26. 24 LORD appeared unto him the same night
30. 16 mandrakes. And he lay with her that n.
31. 24 to Laban the Syrian in a dream by night
31. 39 (whether) stolen by day, or stolen by night
31. 40 consumed me, and the frost by night; and
32. 13 And he lodged there that same night; and
32. 21 himself lodged that night in the company
32. 22 And he rose up that night, and took his
40. 5 each man his dream in one night, each
41. 11 And we dreamed a dream in one night, I
46. 2 unto Israel in the visions of the night, and
Exod 10. 13 the land all that day, and all (that) night
12. 8 they shall eat the flesh in that night, ro.
12. 12 pass through the land of Egypt this night
12. 30 And Pharaoh rose up in the night, he, and
12. 31 he called for Moses and Aaron by night
12. 42 It (is) a night to be much observed unto
12. 42 this (is) that night of the LORD to be obs.
13. 21 and by night in a pillar of fire
13. 21 to give them light; to go by day and night
13. 22 nor the pillar of fire by night, (from) before
14. 20 but it gave light by night (to these): so
14. 20 one came not near the other all the night
14. 21 by a strong east wind all that night, and
24. 18 in the mount forty days and forty nights
34. 28 with the LORD forty days and forty nights
40. 38 and fire was on it by night, in the sight of
Lev. 6. 9 burning upon the altar all night unto the
8. 35 Therefore shall ye abide..day and night
Num. 9. 16 and the appearance of fire by night
9. 21 whether (it was) by day or by night that the
11. 9 the dew fell upon the camp in the night
Num 11. 32 stood up all that day, and all (that) night
14. 1 and cried; and the people wept that night
14. 14 cloud, and in a pillar of fire by night
22. 8 said unto them, Lodge here this night, and
22. 19 I pray you, tarry ye also here this night
22. 20 And God came unto Balaam at night, and
Deut. 1. 33 in fire by night, to show you by what way
9. 9, 11, 18, 25 forty days and forty nights
10. 10 first time, forty days and forty nights; and
16. 1 brought thee forth out of Egypt by night
23. 10 uncleanness that chanceth him by night
28. 66 thou shalt fear day and night, and shalt
Josh. 1. 8 shalt meditate therein day and night, that
4. 3 lodging place where ye shall lodge this n.
8. 3 of valour, and sent them away by night
8. 9 but Joshua lodged that night among the
8. 13 Joshua went that night into the midst of
10. 9 Joshua..went up from Gilgal all night
Judg. 6. 25 came to pass the same night, that the L.
6. 27 not do (it) by day, that he did (it) by night
6. 40 And God did so that night: for it was dry
7. 9 And it came to pass the same night, that
9. 32 Now therefore up by night, thou and the
9. 34 people that (were) with him, by night, and
16. 2 laid wait for him all night in the gate of
16. 2 and were quiet all the night, saying, In the
19. 25 knew her, and abused her all the night
20. 5 beset the house round about..by night
Ruth 3. 13 Tarry this night, and it shall be in the m.
1 Sa. 14. 34 every man his ox with him that night, and
14. 36 go down after the Philistines by night, and
15. 11 and he cried unto the LORD all night
15. 16 what the LORD hath said to me this night
19. 10 and David fled, and escaped that night
19. 24 naked all that day and all that night
25. 16 They were a wall unto us, both by night
26. 7 and Abishai came to the people by night
28. 8 and they came to the woman by night: and
28. 20 no bread all the day, nor all the night
28. 25 they rose up, and went away that night
30. 12 (any) water, three days and three nights
31. 12 valiant men arose, and went all night, and
2 Sa. 2. 29 Abner and his men walked all that night
2. 32 Joab and his men went all night, and they
4. 7 gat them away through the plain all night
7. 4 And it came to pass that night, that the
17. 1 arise and pursue after David this night
17. 16 Lodge not this night in the plains of the
19. 7 will not tarry one with thee this night: and
21. 10 by day, nor the beasts of the field by nig.
1 Ki. 3. 5 appeared to Solomon in a dream by night
3. 19 this woman's child died in the night; be.
8. 29 may be open toward this house night and
8. 59 nigh unto the LORD our God day and night
19. 8 forty days and forty nights unto Horeb
2 Ki. 6. 14 they came by night, and compassed the c.
7. 12 the king arose in the night, and said unto
8. 21 he rose by night, and smote the Edomites
19. 35 it came to pass that night, that the angel
25. 4 all the men..fled by night by the way of
1 Ch. 9. 33 they were employed in..work day and n.
17. 3 it came to pass the same night, that the
2 Ch. 1. 7 In that night did God appear unto Solo.
6. 20 may be open upon this house day and ni.
7. 12 LORD appeared to Solomon by night, and
21. 9 rose up by night, and smote the Edomites
35. 14 of burnt offerings and the fat until night
Neh. 1. 6 which I pray before thee now, day and n.
2. 12 I arose in the night, I and some few men
2. 13 I went out by night by the gate of the v.
2. 15 Then went I up in the night by the brook
4. 9 set a watch against them day and night
4. 22 that in the night they may be a guard to
6. 10 in the night will they come to slay thee
9. 12 in the night by a pillar of fire, to give
9. 19 neither the pillar of fire by night, to show
Esth. 4. 16 neither eat nor drink three days, night or
6. 1 On that night could not the king sleep
Job 2. 13 they sat down..seven days and seven ni.
3. 3 and the night..it was said, There is a man
3. 6 that night, let darkness seize upon it; let
3. 7 Lo, let that night be solitary; let no joy.
4. 13 In thoughts from the visions of the night
5. 14 and grope in the noon day as in the night
7. 3 and wearisome nights are appointed to me
17. 12 They change the night into day: the lig.
20. 8 be chased away as a vision of the night
24. 14 and needy, and in the night is as a thief
27. 20 a tempest stealeth him away in the night
33. 15 In a dream, in a vision of the night, when
34. 25 he overturneth..in the night, so that they
35. 10 my maker, who giveth songs in the night
36. 20 Desire not the night, when people are cut
Psa. 1. 2 in his law doth he meditate day and night
6. 6 all the night make I my bed to swim; I
17. 3 thou hast visited..in the night; thou ha.
19. 2 and night unto night showeth knowledge
22. 2 and in the night season, and am not silent
32. 4 day and night thy hand was heavy upon
42. 3 My tears have been my meat day and ni.
42. 8 in the night his song (shall be) with me
55. 10 Day and night they go about it upon the
74. 16 The day (is) thine, the night also (is) thine
77. 2 my sore ran in the night, and ceased not
77. 6 call to remembrance my song in the night
78. 14 led them..all the night with a light of f.
88. 1 I have cried day (and) night before thee
90. 4 when it is past, and (as) a watch in the n.
91. 5 Thou shalt not be afraid for..terror by n.
92. 2 To show forth..thy faithfulness every n.
104. 20 Thou makest darkness, and it is night
105. 39 covering; and fire to give light in the ni.
Psa. 119. 55 remembered..in the night, and have kept
121. 6 not smite thee by day, nor the moon by n.
134. 1 which by night stand in the house of the
136. 9 The moon and stars to rule by night: for
139. 11 even the night shall be light about me
139. 12 the night shineth as the day: the darkn.
Prov. 7. 9 in the evening, in the black and dark ni.
31. 15 She riseth also while it is yet night, and
31. 18 good: her candle goeth not out by night
Eccl. 2. 23 yea, his heart taketh not rest in the night
8. 16 neither day nor night seeth sleep with his
Song 3. 1 By night on my bed I sought him whom
3. 8 upon his thigh, because of fear in the ni.
5. 2 (and) my locks with the drops of the night
Isa. 4. 5 the shining of a flaming fire by night: for
15. 1, 1 Because in the night..of Moab is laid w.
16. 3 make thy shadow as the night in the mid.
21. 8 and I am set in my ward whole nights
21. 11 what of the night?..what of the night?
21. 12 The morning cometh, and also the night
26. 9 my soul have I desired thee in the night
27. 3 lest (any) hurt it, I will keep it night and
28. 19 shall it pass over, by day and by night; and
29. 7 all..shall be as a dream of a night vision
30. 29 Ye shall have a song, as in the night, (w.)
34. 10 It shall not be quenched night nor day
38. 12, 13 from day..to night wilt thou make an
60. 11 thy gates..shall not be shut day nor night
62. 6 shall never hold their peace day nor night
Jer. 6. 5 Arise, and let us go by night, and let us
9. 1 that I might weep day and night for the
14. 17 Let mine eyes run down with tears night
16. 13 shall ye serve other gods day and night
31. 35 ordinances..of the stars for a light by ni.
33. 20 of the day, and my covenant of the night
33. 20 that there should not be day and night
33. 25 If my covenant (be) not with day and ni.
36. 30 cast out in..to the heat, and in the night
39. 4 went forth out of the city by night, by
49. 9 if thieves by night, they will destroy till
52. 7 went forth out of the city by night, by the
Lam. 1. 2 She weepeth sore in the night, and her
2. 18 run down like a river day and night: give
2. 19 Arise, cry out in the night; in the begin.
Hos. 4. 5 also shall fall with thee in the night, and
7. 6 wait: their baker sleepeth all the night
Amos 5. 8 and maketh the day dark with night: that
Obad. 5 thieves came to thee, if robbers by night
Jon. 1. 17 belly of the fish three days and three ni.
4. 10 came up in a night, and perished in a ni.
Mic. 3. 6 Therefore night (shall be) unto you, that
Zech. 1. 8 I saw by night, and behold a man riding
14. 7 known to the LORD, not day, nor night: but
3. *Night*, לֵילְיָא *lelya.*
Dan. 2. 19 revealed unto Daniel..night vision. Then
5. 30 In that night was Belshazzar the king of
7. 2 and said, I saw in my vision by night, and
7. 7 After this I saw in the night visions, and
7. 13 I saw in..night visions, and, behold, (one)
4. *The twilight*, נֶשֶׁף *nesheph.*
Isa. 5. 11 that continue until night, (till) wine in.
21. 4 the night of my pleasure hath he turned
59. 10 we stumble at noon day as in the night
5. *Evening*, עֶרֶב *ereb.*
Gen. 49. 27 and at night he shall divide the spoil
Lev. 6. 20 in the morning, and half thereof at night
Job 7. 4 When shall I arise, and the night be gone?
Psa. 30. 5 weeping may endure for a night, but joy
6. *Night*, νύξ *nux.*
Matt. 2. 14 the young child and his mother by night
4. 2 he had fasted forty days and forty nights
12. 40 as Jonas was three days and three nights
12. 40 the Son of man be three days and three n.
14. 25 in the fourth watch of the night Jesus w.
26. 31 shall be offended because of me this night
26. 34 That this night, before the cock crow, thou
27. 64 lest his disciples come [by night], and steal
28. 13 His disciples came by night, and stole him
Mark 4. 27 should sleep, and rise night and day, and
5. 5 And always, night and day, he was in the
6. 48 about the fourth watch of the night he
14. 27 shall be offended because of me [this ni.]
14. 30 That this day, (even) in this night, before
Luke 2. 8 keeping watch over their flock by night
2. 37 with fastings and prayers night and day
5. 5 Master, we have toiled all the night, and
12. 20 fool, this night thy soul shall be required
17. 34 I tell you, in that night there shall be two
18. 7 elect, which cry day and night unto him
21. 37 at night he went out, and abode in the
John 3. 2 The same came to Jesus by night, and said
7. 50 he that came to Jesus [by night], being one
9. 4 the night cometh, when no man can work
11. 10 But if a man walk in the night, he stum.
13. 30 went immediately out: and it was night
19. 39 which at the first came to Jesus by night
21. 3 and that night they caught nothing
Acts 5. 19 But the angel of the Lord by night opened
9. 24 they watched the gates day and night to
9. 25 Then the disciples took him by night, and
12. 6 same night Peter was sleeping between
16. 9 a vision appeared to Paul in the night
16. 33 he took them the same hour of the night
17. 10 sent away Paul and Silas by night unto B.
18. 9 spake the Lord to Paul in the night by a
20. 31 I ceased not to warn every one night and
23. 11 night following, the Lord stood by him
23. 23 hundred, at the third hour of the night
23. 31 and brought (him) by night to Antipatris
26. 7 instantly serving (God) day and night, ho.

Acts 27. 23 For there stood by me this night the angel
27. 27 But when the fourteenth night was come
Rom 13. 12 The night is far spent, the day is at hand
1 Co. 11. 23 That the Lord Jesus the (same) night in
1 Th. 2. 9 for labouring night and day, because we
3. 10 Night and day praying exceedingly that
5. 2 the day..so cometh as a thief in the night
5. 5 we are not of the night, nor of darkness
5. 7 For they that sleep sleep in the night; and
5. 7 that be drunken are drunken in the night
2 Th. 3. 8 wrought with labour and travail night and
1 Ti. 5. 5 supplications and prayers night and day
2 Ti. 1. 3 remembrance of thee in my prayers night
2 Pe. 3. 10 will come as a thief [in the night]; in the
Rev. 4. 8 they rest not day and night, saying, Holy
7. 15 serve him day and night in his temple: and
8. 12 third part of it, and the night likewise
12. 10 accused them before our God day and n.
14. 11 and they have no rest day nor night, who
20. 10 shall be tormented day and night for ever
21. 25 day: for there shall be no night there
22. 5 there shall be no night there; and they

NIGHT and a day, a —

A night and a day, νυχθήμερον *nuchthēmeron.*

2 Co. 11. 25 a night and a day I have been in the deep

NIGHT, to pass the —

To pass the night, בּוּת *buth.*

Dan. 6. 18 Then the king..passed the night fasting

NIGHT HAWK —

Owl, swallow, cuckoo, תַּחְמָס *tachmas.*

Lev. 11. 16 the night hawk, and the cuckoo, and the
Deut 14. 15 the night hawk, and the cuckoo, and the

NIGHT season —

Night, לַיִל *layil.*

Job 30. 17 are pierced in me in the night season
Psa. 16. 7 my reins..instruct me in the night seasons

NIM'-RAH, נִמְרָה *flowing water.*

A city in Gad in Gilead, bordering on Moab, between Jazer and Heshbon, or in the valley near Beth-aram. See *Beth-nimrah.*

Num 32. 3 N., and Heshbon, and Elealeh, and Shebam

NIM'-RIM, נִמְרִים *flowing streams.*

Waters on the borders of Gad and Moab; the ruins of a city *Nimrin* still remain near Ramoth (*el-Salt*).

Isa. 15. 6 the waters of N. shall be desolate: for the
Jer. 48. 34 the waters also of N. shall be desolate

NIM'-ROD, נִמְרֹד, נִמְרוֹד *valiant, strong.*

1. Son of Cush, son of Ham. B.C. 2218.

Gen. 10. 8 Cush begat N.: he began to be a mighty
10. 9 as N. the mighty hunter before the LORD
1 Ch. 1. 10 Cush begat N.: he began to be mighty upon

2. His land, *i.e.* Babylonia.

Mic. 5. 6 the land of N. in the entrances thereof

NIM'-SHI, נִמְשִׁי *Jah reveals.*

Grandfather or father of Jehu, who smote Joram son of Ahab, and reigned in his stead over Israel. B.C. 950.

1 Ki. 19. 16 the son of N. shalt thou anoint (to be) k.
2 Ki. 9. 2, 14 Jehu..son of Jehoshaphat, the son of N.
9. 20 (is) like the driving of J. the son of N.
2 Ch. 22. 7 he went out..against Jehu the son of N.

NINE —

1. *Nine,* תִּשְׁעָה, תֵּשַׁע *tesha, tishah.*

Gen. 5. 5 days..were nine hundred and thirty ye.
5. 8 the days of Seth were nine hundred and
5. 11 the days of Enos were nine hundred and
5. 14 the days of Cainan were nine hundred and
5. 20 the days of Jared were nine hundred sixty
5. 27 were nine hundred sixty and nine years
9. 29 the days of Noah were nine hundred and
11. 19 Peleg lived..two hundred and nine years
11. 24 Nahor lived nine and twenty years, and
17. 1, 24 Abram was ninety years old and nine
Exod 38. 24 the gold..was twenty and nine talents, and
Lev. 25. 8 shall be unto thee forty and nine years
Num. 1. 23 fifty and nine thousand and three hundr.
2. 13 fifty and nine thousand and three hundred
29. 26 on the fifth day nine bullocks, two rams
34. 13 commanded to give unto the nine tribes
Deut. 3. 11 nine cubits (was) the length thereof, and
Josh 13. 7 for an inheritance unto the nine tribes
14. 2 the nine tribes, and (for) the half tribe
15. 32 the cities (are) twenty and nine, with th.
15. 44, 54 nine cities with their villages
21. 16 nine cities out of those two tribes
Judg. 4. 3 he had nine hundred chariots of iron: and
4. 13 nine hundred chariots of iron, and all
2 Sa. 24. 8 the end of nine months and twenty days
2 Ki. 14. 2 reigned twenty and nine years in Jerus.
15. 13 the nine and thirtieth year of Uzziah
15. 17 the nine and thirtieth year of Azariah
17. 1 reign in Samaria over Israel nine years
18. 2 reigned twenty and nine years in Jerusa.
1 Ch. 3. 8 Elishama, and Eliada, and Eliphelet, nine
9. 9 brethren..nine hundred and fifty and six
2 Ch. 25. 1 reigned twenty and nine years in Jerusa.
29. 1 reigned nine and twenty years in Jerusa.
Ezra 1. 9 thousand chargers..nine and twenty kn.
2. 8 The children of Zattu, nine hundred forty
2. 36 children..nine hundred seventy and three
2. 42 (in) all an hundred thirty and nine
Neh. 7. 38 three thousand nine hundred and thirty
7. 39 children..nine hundred seventy and three
11. 1 and nine parts (to dwell) in (other) cities
11. 8 Sallai, nine hundred twenty and eight

2. *Nine,* ἐννέα *ennea.*

Luke 17. 17 not ten cleansed? but where (are) the nine?

NINETEEN —

Nine-ten, תְּשַׁע־עֶשְׂרֵה, תִּשְׁעָה־עָשָׂר *tesha esre, tishah asar.*

Gen. 11. 25 Nahor lived..an hundred and nineteen
Josh 19. 38 nineteen cities with their villages
2 Sa. 2. 30 lacked of David's servants nineteen men

NINETEENTH —

Nine-ten, תִּשְׁעָה־עָשָׂר, תְּשַׁע־עֶשְׂרֵה *tesha esre, tisha asar.*

2 Ki. 25. 8 which (is) the nineteenth year of king N.
1 Ch. 24. 16 The nineteenth to Pethahiah, the twenti.
25. 26 The nineteenth to Mallothi, (he), his sons
Jer. 52. 12 which (was) the nineteenth year of Nebu.

NINETY —

Ninety, תִּשְׁעִים *tishim.*

Gen. 5. 9 And Enos lived ninety years, and begat C.
5. 17 were eight hundred ninety and five years
5. 30 Lamech lived..five hundred ninety and
17. 1 And when Abram was ninety years old
17. 17 shall Sarah, that is ninety years old, bear?
17. 24 And Abram (was) ninety years old and n.
1 Sa. 4. 15 Now Eli was ninety and eight years old
1 Ch. 9. 6 their brethren, six hundred and ninety
Ezra 2. 16 children of Ater of Hezekiah, ninety and
2. 20 The children of Gibbar, ninety and five
2. 58 servants, (were) three hundred ninety and
8. 35 ninety and six rams, seventy and seven
Neh. 7. 21 of Ater of Hezekiah, ninety and eight
7. 25 The children of Gibeon, ninety and five
7. 60 (were) three hundred ninety and two
Jer. 52. 23 there were ninety and six pomegranates on
Eze. 4. 5 the days, three hundred and ninety days
4. 9 three hundred and ninety days shalt thou
41. 12 and the length thereof ninety cubits
Dan. 12. 11 a thousand two hundred and ninety days

NINETY and nine —

Ninety nine, ἐννενηκονταεννέα *ennenēkontaennea.*

Matt 18. 12 doth he not leave the ninety and nine
18. 13 than of the ninety and nine which went
Luke 15. 4 doth not leave the ninety and nine in the
15. 7 more than over ninety and nine just per.

NIN-E'-VE, Νινευΐ. *Same as succeeding.*

Luke 11. 32 men [of N.] shall rise up in the judgment

NI-NE'-VEH, נִינְוֵה, Νινευή.

A city on a tract above the confluence of the Zabatus or Lycus (great Zab) with the Tigris; now called *Kouyanjak.* It was greater than Babylon, being in circumference 480 stadia, or twenty-four hours (three days') journey, Jonah 3. 3; was the capital of Assyria; had more than 120,000 infants in it at one time; it was taken by Arbaces the Mede, B.C. 876; warned by Jonah in 852; conquered and destroyed by Cyaxares and Nebuchadnezzar in 606; Heraclius and Rhazates fought a great battle on its site, A.D. 627; it was explored by Layard in 1840-1853.

Gen. 10. 11 builded N., and the city Rehoboth, and
10. 12 Resen between N. and Calah: the same
2 Ki. 19. 36 and went and returned, and dwelt at N.
Isa. 37. 37 and went and returned, and dwelt at N.
Jon. 1. 2 go to N., that great city, and cry against
3. 2 go unto N., that great city, and preach
3. 3 Jonah arose, and went unto N., according
3. 3 N. was an exceeding great city of three
3. 4 yet forty days, and N. shall be overthro.
3. 5 the people of N. believed God, and proclai.
3. 6 word came unto the king of N., and he arose
3. 7 published through N. by the decree of the
4. 11 And should not I spare N., that great city
Nah. 1. 1 The burden of Nineveh. The book of the
2. 8 N. (is) of old like a pool of water; yet
3. 7 N. is laid waste: who will bemoan her? w.
Zeph. 2. 13 will make N. a desolation, (and) dry like
Matt 12. 41 The men of N. shall rise in judgment with

NI-NE-VITES, Νινευῖται. *Inhabitants of Nineveh.*

Luke 11. 30 as Jonas was a sign unto the N., so shall

NINTH —

1. *Ninth,* תְּשִׁיעִי *teshii.*

Lev. 25. 22 eat (yet) of old fruit until the ninth year
Num 7. 60 On the ninth day Abidan the son of Gid.
2 Ki. 17. 6 In the ninth year of Hoshea the king of
25. 1 And it came to pass in the ninth year of
1 Ch. 12. 12 Johanan the eighth, Elzabad the ninth
24. 11 The ninth to Jeshuah, the tenth to Shec.
25. 16 The ninth to Mattaniah, (he), his sons
27. 12 The ninth (captain) for the ninth month
Ezra 10. 9 It (was) the ninth month, and the twentieth
Jer. 36. 9 it came to pass..in the ninth month, (that)
36. 22 in the winter house, in the ninth month
39. 1 In the ninth year of Zedekiah king of Ju.
52. 4 it came to pass in the ninth year of his
Eze. 24. 1 Again in the ninth year, in the tenth m.
Hag. 2. 10, 18 four and twentieth (day) of..ninth (m.)
Zech. 7. 1 in the fourth (day) of the ninth month

2. *Nine,* תִּשְׁעָה, תֵּשַׁע *tesha, tishah.*

Lev. 23. 32 in the ninth (day) of the month at even
2 Ki. 18. 10 that (is) the ninth year of Hoshea king of
25. 3 And on the ninth (day) of the (fourth) m.
2 Ch. 16. 12 in the thirty and ninth year of his reign
Jer. 39. 2 in the fourth month, the ninth (day) of the
52. 6 in the fourth month, in the ninth (day) of

3. *Ninth,* ἔννατος *ennatos,* ἔνατος *enatos.*

Matt 20. 5 went out about the sixth and ninth hour
27. 45 over all the land unto the ninth hour
27. 46 about the ninth hour Jesus cried with a
Mark 15. 33 over the whole land until the ninth hour
Mark 15. 34 at the ninth hour Jesus cried with a loud
Luke 23. 44 over all the earth until the ninth hour
Acts 3. 1 the hour of prayer, (being) the ninth (ho.)
10. 3 He saw..about the ninth hour of the day
10. 30 at the ninth hour I prayed in my house
Rev. 21. 20 the eighth, beryl; the ninth, a topaz; the

NI'-SAN, נִיסָן.

The first month of the year (called *Abib* in the Books of Moses), beginning with the new moon at the end of March. It is the name of the Babylonian god of "spring."

Neh. 2. 1 And it came to pass in the month N., in the
Esth. 3. 7 the first month, that (is), the month N.

NIS'-ROCH, נִסְרֹךְ *eagle, hawk.*

An Assyrian idol with a temple in Nineveh, in which Sennacherib was slain, B.C. 698: it had a human form with an eagle's head, according to Philo, as quoted by Eusebius.

2 Ki. 19. 37 worshipping in the house of N. his god
Isa. 37. 38 worshipping in the house of N. his god

NITRE —

Nitre, נֶתֶר *nether.*

Prov 25. 20 vinegar upon nitre, so (is) he that singeth
Jer. 2. 22 though thou wash thee with nitre, and

NO, נֹא.

A city on both sides of the Nile; the capital of Upper Egypt, called also *Thebes* and *Diospolis;* the chief seat of the worship of Amon, with a famous temple. It was destroyed. B.C. 81.

Jer. 46. 25 I will punish the multitude of N., and
Eze. 30. 14 in Zoan, and will execute judgments in N
30. 15 and I will cut off the multitude of N.
30. 16 N. shall be rent asunder, and Noph (shall)
Nah. 3. 8 Art thou better than populous N., that was

NO —

1. *There is not, there are not,* אַיִן *ayin.*

1 Ki. 18. 26 But (there was) no voice, nor any that
Jer. 7. 32 shall bury in Tophet, till there be no place

2. *Not (anything),* (מְאוּמָה) אַל *al (meumah).*

Gen. 13. 8 Abram said unto Lot, Let there be no
Jer. 39. 12 look well to him, and do him no harm

3. *End, cessation, only,* אֶפֶס *ephes.*

Isa. 5. 8 lay field to field, till..no place, that they
Prov 26. 20 Where no wood is..the fire goeth out; so
Amos 6. 10 he shall say, No. Then shall he say, Hold

4. *Not,* בַּל *bal.*

Isa. 33. 21 wherein shall go no galley with oars, neither

5. *Not any,* כֹּל לָא *kol la.*

Ezra 4. 16 by this means thou shalt have no portion
Dan. 2. 10 therefore..no king, lord, nor ruler..asked
2. 35 no place was found for them: and the st.
3. 25 the midst of..fire, and they have no hurt
3. 27 upon whose bodies the fire had no power
3. 29 because there is no other God that can de.
4. 9 no secret troubleth thee, tell me the visi.
6. 2 accounts..and the king should have no
6. 15 That no decree nor statute which the king
6. 22 before thee, O king, have I done no hurt

6. *No,* לֹא *lo.*

Gen. 15. 3 Behold, to me thou hast given no seed: and
16. 1 Sarai, Abram's wife, bare him no children

7. *Without,* בְּלֹא, לְלֹא *le-lo, be lo.*

1 Ch. 12. 17 seeing..no wrong in mine hands, the God
2 Ch. 13. 9 may be a priest of (them that are) no gods
Job 26. 3 hast thou counselled (him that hath) no w.?

8. *But,* ἀλλά *alla.*

Luke 23. 15 No, nor yet Herod: for I sent you to him

9. *No, not,* μή *mē.*

Matt 6. 31 Therefore take no thought, saying, What
6. 34 Take therefore no thought for the morrow
9. 36 were scattered abroad, as sheep having no
10. 19 take no thought how or what ye shall sp.
13. 5 sprung up, because they had no deepness
13 6 because they had no root, they withered
22. 23 which say that there is no resurrection, and
22. 24 If a man die, having no children, his bro.
22. 25 having no issue, left his wife unto his br.
23. 9 call no (man) your father upon the earth
Mark 4. 5 sprang up, because it had no depth of ea.
4. 6 and because it had no root, it withered a.
6. 8 save a staff only; no scrip, no bread, no
12. 18 Sadducees, which say there is no resurre.
12. 19 leave no children, that his brother should
13. 11 take no thought beforehand what ye shall
Luke 12. 11 take ye no thought how or what thing ye
12. 22 Take no thought for your life, what ye
13. 11 was bowed together, and could in no wise
22. 36 he that hath no sword, let him sell his g.
Acts 1. 20 be desolate, and let no man dwell therein
23. 8 For the Sadducees say that there is no r.
Rom. 5. 13 but sin is not imputed when there is no l.
7. 3 so that she is no adulteress, though she
1 Co. 1. 10 and (that) there be no divisions among you
7. 37 standeth stedfast in his heart, having no
2 Co. 5. 21 made him..sin for us, who knew no sin
13. 7 Now I pray to God that ye do no evil; not
Gal. 4. 8 service unto them which by nature are no
Eph. 2. 12 having no hope, and without God in the w.
5. 11 have no fellowship with the unfruitful w.
1 Th. 4. 6 That no (man) go beyond and defraud his
4. 13 not, even as others which have no hope
2 Th. 3. 14 have no company with him, that he may
1 Ti. 1. 3 charge some that they teach no other do.
3. 3 Not given to wine, no striker, not greedy

Titus 1. 7 not given to wine, no striker, not given to
Jas. 2. 13 without mercy that hath showed no me.
1 Pe. 3. 10 refrain..his lips that they speak no guile

10. *Not any, μή τι mē ti.*
Luke 11. 36 full of light, having no part dark, 12. 4.

11. *Not even one, μηδείς mēdeis.*
Luke 3. 13 Exact no more than that which is appoin.
Acts 4. 17 speak henceforth to no man in this name
13. 28 And though they found no cause of death
15. 28 to lay upon you no greater burden than
16. 28 Do thyself no harm; for we are all here
19. 40 there being no cause whereby we may give
21. 25 [concluded that they observe no such thing]
28. 6 had looked a great while, and saw no harm
28. 18 because there was no cause of death in me
1 Co. 1. 7 So that ye come behind in no gift; wait.
10. 25, 27 asking no question for conscience' sake
2 Co. 6. 3 Giving no offence in any thing, that the m.
13. 7 Now I pray to God that ye do no evil; not
Heb. 10. 2 should have had no more conscience of

12. *Assuredly not, not at all, οὐ μή ou mē.*
1 Co. 8. 13 I will eat no flesh while the world stand.
Rev. 18. 7 I sit a queen..and shall see no sorrow

13. *Not, no, οὐ ou.*
Matt. 6. 1 otherwise ye have no reward of your Fat.
12. 39 there shall no sign be given to it, but the
16. 4 there shall no sign be given unto it, but
16. 7 (It is) because we have taken no bread
16. 8 why..because ye have brought no bread?
19. 18 Thou shalt do no murder, Thou shalt
20. 13 Friend, I do thee no wrong: didst not thou
25. 3 took their lamps, and took no oil with them
25. 42 was an hungered, and ye gave me no meat
25. 42 I was thirsty, and ye gave me no drink
26. 55 teaching in the temple, and ye laid no hold
Mark 2. 17 They that are whole have no need of the
4. 7 thorns..choked it, and it yielded no fruit
4. 17 have no root in themselves, and so endure
4. 40 [so fearful? how is it that ye have no fa.?]
8. 16 they reasoned..(It is) because we have no
8. 17 Why reason ye because ye have no bread?
9. 3 so as no fuller on earth can white them
12. 20 first took a wife, and dying left no seed
12. 22 And the seven had her, and left no seed
Luke 1. 7 they had no child, because that Elisabeth
1. 33 and of his kingdom there shall be no end
2. 7 because there was no room for them in the
7. 44 thou gavest me no water for my feet: but
7. 45 Thou gavest me no kiss: but this woman
8. 13 these have no root, which for a while be.
8. 14 of..life, and bring no fruit to perfection
8. 27 had devils long time, and ware no clothes
9. 13 We have no more but five loaves and two
11. 29 there shall no sign be given it, but the sign
12. 17 What shall I do, because I have no room
12. 33 where no thief approacheth, neither moth
15. 7 just persons, which need no repentance
16. 2 account..for thou mayest be no longer
20. 22 Is it lawful for us to give tribute..or no?
20. 31 the seven..they left no children, and died
22. 53 ye stretched forth no hands against me
John 1. 21 thou that prophet? And he answered, No
1. 47 an Israelite indeed, in whom is no guile!
2. 3 mother..saith unto him, They have no w.
4. 9 for the Jews have no dealings with the S.
4. 17 woman answered and said, I have no hu.
4. 17 Thou hast well said, I have no husband
4. 38 to reap that whereon ye bestowed no la.
4. 44 a prophet hath no honour in his own co.
5. 7 Sir, I have no man, when the water is tr.
6. 53 and drink his blood, ye have no life in you
7. 18 is true, and no unrighteousness is in him
7. 52 look: for out of Galilee ariseth no prophet
8. 37 to kill me, because my word hath no place
8. 44 in the truth, because there is no truth in
9. 41 If ye were blind, ye should have no sin: but
11. 10 he stumbleth, because there is no light in
13. 8 If I wash thee not, thou hast no part with
15. 22 but now they have no cloak for their sin
19. 6 and crucify..for I find no fault in him
19. 9 Whence art thou? But Jesus gave him no
19. 15 answered, We have no king but Cesar
21. 5 have ye any meat? They answered him, No
Acts 7. 5 his seed after him, when..he had no chi.
7. 11 dearth..and our fathers found no sustena.
10. 34 I perceive that God is no respecter of pe.
12. 18 there was no small stir among the soldi.
13. 37 whom God raised again, saw no corrupt.
15. 2 had no small dissension and disput. v. 24.
18. 15 for I will be no judge of such (matters)
19. 23 the same time there arose no small stir
19. 24 brought no small gain unto the craftsmen
19. 26 saying that they be no gods which are
21. 39 Tarsus..in Cilicia, a citizen of no mean c.
25. 26 Of whom I have no certain thing to write
27. 20 and no small tempest lay on..all hope that
28. 2 the barbarous people showed us no little
Rom. 2. 11 For there is no respect of persons with G.
3. 9 No, in no wise: for we have before proved
3. 18 There is no fear of God before their eyes
3. 22 all them that believe; for there is no diff.
4. 15 for where no law is..no transgression
7. 18 in my flesh, dwelleth no good thing: for
10. 12 For there is no difference between the Jew
10. 19 you to jealousy by (them that are) no pe.
13. 1 there is no power but of God: the powers
13. 10 Love worketh no ill to his neighbour: th.
1 Co. 7. 25 I have no commandment of the Lord: yet
10. 13 There hath no temptation taken you but
11. 16 we have no such custom, neither the ch.
12. 21 eye cannot say unto the hand, I have no
12. 21 nor again the head to the feet, I have no
12. 24 our comely (parts) have no need: but God
13. 5 is not easily provoked, thinketh no evil
15. 12 that there is no resurrection of the dead?
15. 13 But if there be no resurrection of the dead
2 Co. 2. 13 I had no rest in my spirit, because I found
8. 15 that (had gathered) little had no lack
11. 14 no marvel; for Satan himself is transfor.
11. 15 Therefore..no great thing if his ministers
Gal. 2. 6 God accepteth no man's person: for they
5. 23 temperance: against such there is no law
Phil. 3. 3 For we..have no confidence in the flesh
Col. 3. 25 receive..and there is no respect of persons
1 Th. 5. 1 But..ye have no need that I write unto
2 Ti. 3. 9 But they shall proceed no further, for
Heb. 8. 7 then should no place have been sought for
9. 22 without shedding of blood is no remission
10. 6 offerings..for sin thou hast had no plea.
10. 38 but..my soul shall have no pleasure in him
12. 17 he found no place of repentance, though
13. 10 whereof they have no right to eat which
13. 14 here have we no continuing city, but we
Jas. 1. 17 with whom is no variableness, neither s.
2. 11 Now if thou commit no adultery, yet if
1 Pe. 2. 22 Who did no sin, neither was guile found
1 Jo. 1. 8 If we say that we have no sin, we deceive
2. 7 I write no new commandment unto you
2. 27 is truth, and is no lie, and even as it hath
3. 5 to take away our sins; and in him is no
4. 18 There is no fear in love; but perfect love
3 John 4 I have no greater joy than to hear that my
Rev. 7. 16 They shall hunger no more, neither thirst
10. 6 sware..that there should be time no lon.
14. 5 in their mouth was found no guile: for
14. 11 they have no rest day nor night, who wor.
18. 7 I sit a queen, and am no widow, and
20. 6 on such the second death hath no power
20. 11 and there was found no place for them
21. 1 passed away; and there was no more sea
21. 4 there shall be no more death, neither so.
21. 22 I saw no temple therein: for the Lord God
21. 23 the city had no need of the sun, neither
21. 25 not be shut..for there shall be no night
22. 3 there shall be no more curse: but the th.
22. 5 shall be no night there..they need no c.

14. *Not any by any means, οὐ (μή) πᾶς ou (mē) pas.*
Matt 24. 22 there should no flesh be saved: but for
Mark 13. 20 no flesh should be saved: but for the el.
Rom. 3. 20 there shall no flesh be justified in his sight
1 Co. 1. 29 That no flesh should glory in his presence
Gal. 2. 16 by the works of the law shall no flesh be
Eph. 4. 29 Let no corrupt communication proceed
5. 5 For this ye know, that no whoremonger
Heb. 12. 11 no chastening for the present seemeth
2 Pe. 1. 20 Knowing this first, that no prophecy of
1 Jo. 2. 21 because ye know it, and that no lie is of
3. 15 ye know that no murderer hath eternal
Rev. 18. 22 shall be heard no more at all in thee

15. *Not even, οὐδέ oude.*
Rom. 4. 15 for where..law is..no trans. Matt. 24. 21.
2 Co. 3. 10 had [no] glory in this respect, by reason

16. *Not even one, οὐδείς oudeis.*
Mark 6. 5 he could there do no mighty work, save
Luke 4. 24 No prophet is accepted in his own country
16. 13 No servant can serve two masters: for e.
23. 4 (to) the people, I find no fault in this man
23. 14 have found no fault in this man touching
23. 22 I have found no cause of death in him: I
John 10. 41 John did no miracle: but all things 18. 38.
16. 29 speakest thou plainly, and speakest no p.
19. 4 ye may know that I find no fault in v. 11
Acts 15. 9 put no difference between us and them
23. 9 We find no evil in this man: but if a spi.
25. 10 to the Jews have I done no wrong, as thou
27. 22 there shall be no loss of..life among you
28. 5 he shook off the beast..and felt no harm
Rom. 8. 1 therefore now no condemnation to them
2 Co. 7. 5; 2 Ti. 2. 14; Ph. 4. 15; He. 6. 13; Ja. 3. 12.

17. *If, εἰ ei*, Mark 8. 12.

18. *No more, μηκέτι mēketi*, Mark 2. 2.

19. *No not, οὐ μή ou mē*, 1 Co. 8. 13; Rev. 18. 7.
[*See also* Doubt, hope, means, purpose, rising.]

NO...as yet —
Not yet, οὔπω oupō.
Rev. 17. 12 which have received no kingdom as yet

NO...at all —
1. *Not at any time, μή ποτε mē pote*
Heb. 9. 17 otherwise it is of no strength at all while
2. *No, not even one, οὐ...οὐδείς ou...oudeis.*
1 Jo. 1. 5 is light, and in him is no darkness at all

NO ..is, where —
Without, בְּלִי *beli.*
Psa. 63. 1 a dry and thirsty land, where no water is

NO case, in —
Assuredly not, not at all, οὐ μή ou mē.
Matt 5. 20 ye shall in no case enter into the kingdom

NO doubt —
1. *In truth, indeed, ἄρα ara.*
Luke 11. 20 no doubt the kingdom of God is come upon
2. *For, wherefore, truly, γάρ gar.*
1 Co. 9. 10 For our sakes no doubt, (this) is written

NO...henceforward —
Not any more, μηκέτι mēketi.
Matt 21. 19 Let no fruit grow on thee henceforward

NO longer —
1. *Not any more, μηκέτι mēketi.*
1 Th. 3. 1 when we could no longer forbear, we th.
3. 5 when I could no longer forbear, I sent to
1 Ti. 5. 23 Drink no longer water, but use a little w
1 Pe. 4. 2 That he no longer should live the rest of
2. *Not any more, not again, οὐκέτι ouketi.*
Gal. 3. 25 we are no longer under a; Rev. 10. 6.

NO man —
1. *Not even one, μηδείς mēdeis.*
Matt 8. 4 saith unto him, See thou tell no man; but
9. 30 saying, See (that) no man know (it)
16. 20 tell no man that he was Jesus the Christ
17. 9 Tell the vision to no man, until the Son of
Mark 5. 43 straitly that no man should know it; and
7. 36 charged them that they should tell no m.
8. 30 charged them that they should tell no m.
9. 9 charged them that they should tell no m.
11. 14 No man eat fruit of thee hereafter for ever
Luke 3. 14 violence to no man, neither accuse (any)
5. 14 he charged him to tell no man: but go, and
8. 56 charged them that they should tell no m.
9. 21 commanded (them) to tell no man that
10. 4 nor shoes: and salute no man by the way
Acts 9. 7 hearing a voice, but seeing no man
23. 22 (See thou) tell no man that thou hast sh.
Rom 12. 17 Recompense to no man evil for evil. Pro.
13. 8 Owe no man anything, but to love one an.
1 Co. 3. 18 Let no man deceive himself. If any man
3. 21 Therefore let no man glory in men. For
10. 24 Let no man seek his own, but every man
Gal. 6. 17 From henceforth let no man trouble me
Eph. 5. 6 Let no man deceive you with vain words
Col. 2. 18 Let no man beguile you of your reward in
1 Th. 3. 3 That no man should be moved by these
1 Ti. 4. 12 Let no man despise thy youth; but be thou
5. 22 Lay hands suddenly on no man, neither be
Titus 2. 15 with all authority. Let no man despise
3. 2; Jas. 1. 13; 1 Jo. 3. 7; Rev. 3. 11.
2. *No, no one, μή, μή τις mē, mē tis*, Matt. 8. 28.
Rom. 14. 13; 1 Co. 16. 11; 2 Co. 11. 16; Col. 2. 16;
2 Th. 2. 3.
3. *Not, no, οὐ ou.*
2 Co. 11. 10 no man shall stop me of this boasting in
4. *Not even one, οὐδείς oudeis.*
Matt 6. 24 No man can serve two masters: for either
9. 16 No man putteth a piece of new cloth unto
11. 27 no man knoweth the Son, but the Father
17. 8 eyes, they saw no man, save Jesus only
20. 7 unto him, Because no man hath hired us
22. 46 And no man was able to answer him a w.
24. 36 of that day and hour knoweth no (man)
Mark 2. 21 No man also seweth a piece of new cloth
2. 22 And no man putteth new wine into old
3. 27 No man can enter into a strong man's h.
5. 3 and no man could bind him, no, not with
5. 37 And he suffered no man to follow him, s.
7. 24 house, and would have no man know (it)
9. 8 they saw no man any more, save Jesus
9. 39 there is no man which shall do a miracle
10. 29 There is no man that hath left house, or
12. 14 thou art true, and carest for no man
12. 34 And no man after that durst ask him (any
13. 32 knoweth no man, no, not the angels which
Luke 5. 36 No man putteth a piece of a new garment
5. 37 And no man putteth new wine into old
5. 39 No man also having drunk old (wine) st.
8. 16 No man, when he hath lighted a candle
8. 51 [he suffered no man to go in, save Peter]
9. 36 told no man in those days any of those
9. 62 No man, having put his hand to the plo.
10. 22 no man knoweth who the Son is, but the
11. 33 No man, when he hath lighted a candle
15. 16 swine did eat: and no man gave unto him
18. 29 There is no man that hath left house, or
John 1. 18 No man hath seen God at any time; the
3. 2 for no man can do these miracles that t.
3. 13 And no man hath ascended up to heaven
3. 32 and no man receiveth his testimony
4. 27 yet no man said, What seekest thou? or
5. 22 For the Father judgeth no man, but hath
6. 44 No man can come to me, except the Father
6. 65 that no man can come unto me, except it w.
7. 4 For (there is) no man (that) doeth any t.
7. 13 Howbeit no man spake openly of him for
7. 27 cometh, no man knoweth whence he is
7. 30 but no man laid hands on him, because
7. 44 taken him; but no man laid hands on him
8. 10 [accusers? hath no man condemned thee?]
8. 11 [She said, No man, Lord. And Jesus said]
8. 15 Ye judge after the flesh; I judge no man
8. 20 and no man laid hands on him; for his h.
9. 4 the night cometh, when no man can work
10. 18 No man taketh it from me, but I lay it d.
13. 28 Now no man at the table knew for what
14. 6 no man cometh unto the Father, but by
15. 13 Greater love hath no man than this, that
16. 22 and your joy no man taketh from you
Acts 5. 13 of the rest durst no man join himself to
5. 23 when we had opened, we found no man
9. 8 when his eyes were opened, he saw [no m.]
18. 10 and no man shall set on thee to hurt thee
20. 33 I have coveted no man's silver, or gold, or
25. 11 no man may deliver me unto them. I app.
Rom 14. 7 to himself, and no man dieth to himself

1 Co. 2. 11 so the things of God knoweth no man, but
2. 15 yet he himself is judged of no man
3. 11 For other foundation can no man lay than
12. 3 that no man speaking by the spirit of God
12. 3 no man can say that Jesus is the Lord, but
14. 2 unto God: for no man understandeth (him)
2 Co. 5. 16 Wherefore henceforth know we no man
7. 2 Receive us; we have wronged no man, we
7. 2 corrupted no man, we have defrauded no m.
11. 9 I was chargeable [to no man]: for that w.
Gal. 3. 11 But that no man is justified by the law in
3. 15 no man disannulleth, or addeth thereto
Eph. 5. 29 For no man ever yet hated his own flesh
Phil. 2. 20 For I have no man like minded, who will
1 Ti. 6. 16 whom no man hath seen, nor can see: to
2 Ti. 2. 4 No man that warreth entangleth himself
4. 16 At my first answer no man stood with me
Heb. 7. 13 of which no man gave attendance at the
12. 14 without which no man shall see the Lord
Jas. 3. 8 But the tongue can no man tame; (it is) an
1 Jo. 4. 12 No man hath seen God at any time. If we
Rev. 2. 17 which no man knoweth saving he that re.
3. 7 he that openeth, and no man shutteth
3. 7 and shutteth, and no man openeth
3. 8 an open door, and no man can shut it: for
5. 3 no man in heaven, nor in earth, neither
5. 4 because no man was found worthy to open
7. 9 multitude, which no man could number
14. 3 and no man could learn that song but the
15. 8 no man was able to enter into the temple
18. 11 for no man buyeth their merchandise any
19. 12 written that no man knew but he himself

NO manner —

Not any, כֹּל לֹא *kol la.*

Dan. 6. 23 and no manner of hurt was found upon

NO more —

1. *Without, save, not,* בִּלְתִּי *bilti.*

Job 14. 12 till the heavens (be) no more, they shall

2. *Not any more,* μηκέτι *mēketi.*

Mark 1. 45 insomuch that Jesus could no more openly
9. 25 out of him, and enter no more into him
John 5. 14 sin no more, lest a worse thing come unto
8. 11 [do I condemn thee: go, and sin no more]
Acts 13. 34 no more to return to corruption, he said
Rom 15. 23 But now having no more place in these
Eph. 4. 28 Let him that stole steal no more; but ra.

3. *So not even,* οὕτως οὐδέ *houtōs oude.*

John 15. 4 no more can ye, except ye abide in me

4. *Not any more, not again,* οὐκέτι *ouketi.*

Matt 19. 6 Wherefore they are no more twain, but
Mark 7. 12 And ye suffer him no more to do ought
10. 8 so then they are no more twain, but one
14. 25 I will drink no more of the fruit of the v.
Luke 15. 19, 21 am no more worthy to be called thy
John 6. 66 went back, and walked no more with him
11. 54 Jesus therefore walked no more openly
14. 19 while, and the world seeth me no more
16. 10 I go to my Father, and ye see me no more
16. 21 she remembereth no more the anguish, for
16. 25 time cometh, when I shall no more speak
17. 11 And now I am no more in the world, but
Acts 8. 39 that the eunuch saw him no more: and he
20. 25 kingdom of God, shall see my face no m.
20. 38 that they should see his face no more
Rom. 6. 9 being raised from the dead dieth no more
6. 9 death hath no more dominion over him
7. 17, 20 it is no more I that do it, but sin that
11. 6 And if by grace, then (is it) no more of w.
11. 6 otherwise grace is no more grace. But if
11. 6 [no more grace, otherwise work is no more]
2 Co. 5. 16 yet now henceforth know we (him) no more
Gal. 3. 18 (be) of the law, (it is) no more of promise
4. 7; Eph. 2. 19; Heb. 10. 18; 10. 26; Re. 18. 14

5. *No more at all,* οὐ μὴ ἔτι, Heb. 8. 12; 10. 21.

6. *No more at all,* πᾶς οὐ μὴ ἔτι, Rev. 18. 22.

NO, nor yet —

But not even, ἀλλ' οὐδέ *all' oude.*

Luke 23. 15 No, nor yet Herod: for I sent you to him

NO not (one) —

1. *Not even,* μηδέ *mēde.*

1 Co. 5. 11 extortioner; with such an one no not to

2. *Not even,* οὐδέ *oude.*

Matt. 8. 10 not found so great faith, [no, not] in Isr.
24. 36 knoweth no (man), no, not the angels of
Mark 13. 32 hour knoweth no man, no, not the angels
Luke 7. 9 not found so great faith, no, not in Israel
Acts 7. 5 no, not (so much as) to set his foot on: yet
Rom. 3. 10 There is none righteous, no, not one
1 Co. 6. 5 [no, not] one that shall be able to, Gal. 2. 5

3. *Unto, up to,* ἕως *heōs,* Rom. 3. 12.

4. *Not even,* οὔτε *oute.*

Mark 5. 3 man could bind him, [no, not] with chains

NO room —

Not any more, μηκέτι *mēketi.*

Mark 2. 2 that there was no room to receive (them)

NO ... so much as —

Not even, οὐδέ *oude.*

Mark 6. 31 they had no leisure so much as to eat

NO value —

Nought, אֱלִיל *elil.*

Job 13. 4 ye (are) all physicians of no value

NO where —

There is not, there are not, אַיִן *ayin.*

1 Sa. 10. 14 we saw that (they were) no where, we

NO whither —

No whither, לֹא אָנֶה וָאָנָה *lo aneh va-anah.*

2 Ki. 5. 25 And he said, Thy servant went no whither

NO wise, in —

Assuredly not, not at all, οὐ μή *ou mē.*

Matt. 5. 18 one tittle shall in no wise pass from the
10. 42 I say unto you, he shall in no wise lose
Luke 18. 17 as a little child shall in no wise enter
John 6. 37 him that cometh to me I will in no wise
Acts 13. 41 a work which ye shall in no wise believe
Rev. 21. 27 there shall in no wise enter into it any

NO-AD-I'AH, נוֹעַדְיָה *Jah assembles.*

1. A Levite who weighed the vessels of the sanctuary. B.C. 457.

Ezra 8. 33 Jozabad..and N. the son of Binnui, Lev.

2. A female partisan of Sanballat and Tobiah, called a prophetess, who tried to terrify Nehemiah. B.C. 445.

Neh. 6. 14 on the prophetess N., and the rest of the

NO'-AH, NO'-E, נֹחַ *rest.* Νῶε.

Son of Lamech, and father of Shem, Ham, and Japheth; born B.C. 2948, died 1998, aged 950 years; he was the tenth from Adam through Seth, and was born 126 years after the death of Adam, and 14 after that of Seth; he was contemporary with Enos for 84 years, with Terah for 128 years, and with Abram for about 50 years. The Babylonians called him *Xisuthrus,* son of Oliartes; the Chinese, *Yao* or *Fo-Hi;* others Prometheus, Deucalion, Atlas, Theuth, Inachus, Osiris, Dagon, &c.

Gen. 5. 29 he called his name N., saying, This (sa.)
5. 30 Lamech lived after he begat N. five hun.
5. 32 N. was five hundred years old: and N. b.
6. 8 But N. found grace in the eyes of the Lo.
6. 9 These (are) the generations of N.: N. was
6. 9 just man..(and) N. walked with God
6. 10 N. begat three sons, Shem, Ham, and J.
6. 13 God said unto N., The end of all flesh is
6. 22 Thus did N.; according to all that God
7. 1 the LORD said unto N., Come thou and all
7. 5 N. did according unto all that the LORD
7. 6 And N. (was) six hundred years old when
7. 7 N. went in, and his sons, and his wife, and
7. 9 two and two unto N...God..comman. N.
7. 11 In the sixth hundredth year of N.'s life, in
7. 13 the selfsame day entered N., and Shem
7. 13 the sons of N., and N.'s wife, and the th.
7. 15 they went in unto N. into the ark, two
7. 23 N. only remained (alive), and they that
8. 1 God remembered N., and every living th.
8. 6 N. opened the window of the ark which
8. 11 N. knew that the waters were abated from
8. 13 N. removed the covering of the ark, and
8. 15 And God spake unto N., saying
8. 18 N. went forth, and his sons, and his wife
8. 20 N. builded an altar unto the LORD; and
9. 1 God blessed N. and his sons, and said unto
9. 8 God spake unto N., and to his sons with
9. 17 God said unto N., This (is) the token of
9. 18 the sons of N., that went forth of the ark
9. 19 These (are) the three sons of N.: and of
9. 20 N. began (to be) an husbandman, and he
9. 24 N. awoke from his wine, and knew what
9. 28 N. lived after the flood three hundred and
9. 29 the days of N. were nine hundred and fifty
10. 1 (are) the generations of the sons of N.
10. 32 These (are) the families of the sons of N.
1 Ch. 1. 4 N., Shem, Ham, and Japheth
Isa. 54. 9 For this (is as) the waters of N. unto me
54. 9 have sworn that the waters of N. should
Eze. 14. 14 Though these three men, N., Daniel, and
14. 20 Though N., Daniel, and Job, (were) in it
Matt 24. 37 But as the days of N. (were), so shall also
24. 38 until the day that N. entered into the ark
Luke 3. 36 which was (the son) of N., which was (the
17. 26 as it was in the days of N., so shall it be
17. 27 until the day that N. entered into the ark
Heb. 11. 7 By faith N., being warned of God of things
1 Pe. 3. 20 waited in the days of N., while the ark was
2 Pe. 2. 5 spared not the old world, but saved N.

NO'-AH, נֹעָה *flattery.*

A daughter of Zelophehad, the grandson of Gilead, the grandson of Manasseh, the elder son of Joseph. B.C. 1470.

Num 26. 33 names of the daughters..(were)..N., Hog.
27. 1 Mahlah, N., and Hoglah, and Milcah, and
36. 11 For Mahlah..and N., the daughters of Zel.
Josh. 17. 3 names of his daughters, Mahlah, and N.

NOB, נֹב *height.*

A Levitical city in Benjamin, two miles N. of Jerusalem, where eighty-five priests and their families were slain by Doeg.

1 Sa. 21. 1 Then came David to N. to Ahimelech the
22. 9 I saw the son of Jesse coming to N., to
22. 11 king sent to call..priests that (were) in N.
22. 19 N...smote he with the edge of the sword
Neh. 11. 32 (And) at Anathoth, N., Ananiah
Isa. 10. 32 As yet shall he remain at N. that day

NO'-BAH, נֹבַח *prominent.*

1. A Manassite who took *Kenath,* an Amorite city in mount Gilead. B.C. 1452.

Num 32. 42 N. went and took Kenath, and the villag.

2. The city *Kenath* in Trachonitis at Bostra (Argob in Bashan); now called *Kanuat;* it is called *Nophah.* E. of Moab, or of the kingdom of Sihon, near Medeba.

Num 32. 42 took Kenath..and called it N., after his
Judg. 8. 11 that dwelt in tents on the east of N. and

NOBLE —

1. *Honourable,* אַדִּיר *addir.*

Judg. 5. 13 dominion over the nobles among the peo.
2 Ch. 23. 20 nobles, and the governors of the people
Neh. 3. 5 their nobles put not their necks to the
10. 29 They clave to their brethren, their nobles
Jer. 14. 3 their nobles have sent their little ones
30. 21 their nobles shall be of themselves, and
Nah. 3. 18 thy nobles shall dwell (in the dust): thy

2. *Great,* גָּדוֹל *gadol.*

Jon. 3. 7 by the decree of the king and his nobles

3. *Freemen, nobles,* חוֹרִים *chorim.*

1 Ki. 21. 8 the nobles that (were) in his city dwelling
21. 11 the nobles who were the inhabitants in
Neh. 2. 16 nor to the nobles, nor to the rulers, nor
4. 14, 19 said unto the nobles, and to the rulers
5. 7 I rebuked the nobles, and the rulers, and
6. 17 nobles of Judah sent many letters unto
7. 5 the nobles, and the rulers, and the people
13. 17 I contended with the nobles of Judah, and
Eccl. 10. 17 thy king (is) the son of nobles, and thy
Isa. 34. 12 call the nobles thereof to the kingdom
Jer 27. 20 all the nobles of Judah and Jerusalem
39. 6 the king of Babylon slew all the nobles

4. *Rare, precious, prized,* יַקִּיר *yaqqir.*

Ezra 4. 10 the great and noble Asnapper brought over

5. *A leader,* נָגִיד *nagid.*

Job 29. 10 The nobles held their peace, and their

6. *Willing hearted, liberal,* נָדִיב *nadib.*

Num 21. 18 the nobles of the people digged it, by
Psa. 83. 11 Make their nobles like Oreb and like Zeeb
Prov. 8. 16 By me princes rule, and nobles, (even) all
Isa. 13. 2 they may go into the gates of the nobles

7. *Well born, of good birth,* εὐγενής *eugenēs.*

Acts 17. 11 These were more noble than those in Th.
1 Co. 1. 26 not many mighty, not many noble, (are c.)

NOBLE, most —

1. *Foremost ones,* פַּרְתְּמִים *partemim.*

Esth. 6. 9 of one of the king's most noble princes

2. *Strongest, most powerful,* κράτιστος *kratistos.*

Acts 24. 3 always, and in all places, most noble Felix
26. 25 I am not mad, most noble Festus; but speak

NOBLEMAN —

1. *Kingly, belonging to a king,* βασιλικός *basilikos.*

John 4. 46 there was a certain nobleman, whose son
4. 49 The nobleman saith unto him, Sir, come

2. *A man well born,* εὐγενὴς ἄνθρωπος *eugenēs anthrō.*

Luke 19. 12 certain nobleman went into a far country

NOBLES —

1. *Those near, nobles,* אֲצִילִים *atsilim.*

Exod 24. 11 the nobles of the children of Israel he

2. *Fugitive (?),* בָּרִיחַ *bariach.*

Isa. 43. 14 have brought down all their nobles, and

3. *To be heavy, weighty, honoured,* כָּבֵד *kabed,* 2.

Psa. 149. 8 and their nobles with fetters of iron

4. *Foremost ones,* פַּרְתְּמִים *partemim.*

Esth. 1. 3 the nobles and princes of the provinces

NOD, נוֹד *wandering.*

A land E. of Eden, supposed by some to be China or Tartary.

Gen. 4. 16 dwelt in the land of N. on the E. of Eden

NO'-DAB, נוֹדָב *liberal, willing.*

Patronymic of a tribe E. of Jordan, conquered along with Jetur, Nephish, and the Hagarites, by the two and a half tribes.

1 Ch. 5. 19 Hagarites..Jetur, and Nephish, and N.

NO'-GAH, נֹגַהּ *shining.*

A son born to David after he became king of Israel. B.C. 1030.

1 Ch. 3. 7 And N., and Nepheg, and Japhia
14. 6 And N., and Nepheg, and Japhia

NO'-HAH, נוֹחָה *rest.*

Fourth son of Benjamin. B.C. 1700.

1 Ch. 8. 2 N. the fourth, and Rapha the fifth

NOISE —

1. *To roar, move, sound,* הָמָה *hamah.*

Isa. 17. 12 like the noise of the seas; and to the

2. *Noise, multitude,* הָמוֹן *hamon.*

1 Sa. 14. 19 the noise that (was) in the host of the
Isa. 31. 4 nor abase himself for the noise of them
Eze. 26. 13 I will cause the noise of thy songs to
Amos 5. 23 Take thou away from me the noise of thy

3. *Noise, multitude,* הֶמְיָה *hemyah.*

Isa. 14. 11 Thy pomp is brought down..(and) the no.

4. *Voice,* קוֹל *qol.*

Exod 20. 18 the noise of the trumpet, and the moun.
32. 17 Joshua heard the noise of the people as
32. 17 said..(There is) a noise of war in the camp
32. 18 (but) the noise of (them that) sing do I
Judg. 5. 11 (They that are delivered) from the noise
1 Sa. 4. 6 Philistines heard the noise of the shout

1 Sa. 4. 6 the noise of this great shout in the camp
4. 14 when Eli heard the noise of the crying
4. 14 What (meaneth) the noise of this tumult?
1 Ki. 1. 41 Wherefore (is this) noise of the city being
1. 45 This (is) the noise that ye have heard
2 Ki. 7. 6 the Syrians to hear a noise of chariots
7. 6 a noise of horses, (even) the noise of a
11. 13 Athaliah heard the noise of the guard
2 Ch. 23. 12 Athaliah heard the noise of the people
Ezra 3. 13 noise of the shout of joy from the noise
3. 13 shout, and the noise was heard afar off
Psa. 42. 7 Deep calleth unto deep at the noise of
93. 4 mightier than the noise of many waters
Isa. 13. 4 The noise of a multitude in the mountains
13. 4 a tumultuous noise of the kingdoms of
24. 18 he who fleeth from the noise of the fear
29. 6 great noise, with storm and tempest, and
33. 3 At the noise of the tumult the people
Jer. 4. 29 The whole city shall flee for the noise of
10. 22 the noise of the bruit is come, and a great
11. 16 with the noise of a great tumult he hath
47. 3 At the noise of the stamping of the hoofs
49. 21 earth is moved at the noise of their fall
49. 21 noise thereof was heard in the Red sea
50. 46 At the noise of the taking of Babylon the
Lam. 2. 7 they have made a noise in the house of the
Eze. 1. 24 the noise of their wings, like the noise of
1. 24 the voice of speech, as the noise of an host
3. 13 noise of the wings..the noise..a noise of
19. 7 the land was desolate..by the noise of his
26. 10 thy walls shall shake at the noise of the
37. 7 as I prohesied, there was a noise, and be.
43. 2 his voice (was) like a noise of many wat.
Joel 2. 5 Like the noise of chariots on the tops of m.
2. 5 like the noise of a flame of fire that devo.
Nah. 3. 2 The noise of a whip, and the noise of the
Zeph. 1. 10 the noise of a cry from the fish gate, and

5. *Trembling, trouble, anger, rage,* רֹגֶז *rogez.*
Job 37. 2 Hear attentively the noise of his voice, and

6. *Outcry, shouting,* רֵעַ *rea.*
Job 36. 33 The noise thereof showeth concerning it

7. *Wasting, desolation, noise,* שָׁאוֹן *shaon.*
Psa. 65. 7 stilleth the noise of the seas, the noise of
Isa. 24. 8 the noise of them that rejoice endeth
25. 5 Thou shalt bring down the noise of stra.
66. 6 A voice of noise from the city, a voice from
Jer. 25. 31 A noise shall come..to the ends of the e.
46. 17 Pharaoh king of Egypt (is but) a noise; he
51. 55 do roar..a noise of their voice is uttered

8. *Cry, crying, noise,* תְּשֻׁאוֹת *teshuoth.*
Job 36. 29 the clouds, (or) the noise of his tabernacle?

9. *Sound, voice, tone,* φωνή *phōnē.*
Rev. 6. 1 I heard, as it were the noise of thunder

NOISE, loud —
Shout, shouting, blowing, תְּרוּעָה *teruah.*
Psa. 33. 3 new song, play skilfully with a loud noise

NOISE, to make a (loud) —
1. *To (cause to) make a noise,* הוּם *hum,* 5.
Psa. 55. 2 I mourn in my complaint, and make a n.
Mic. 2. 12 they shall make great noise by reason of

2. *To roar, move, sound,* הָמָה *hamah.*
Psa. 59. 6 they make a noise like a dog, and go round
59. 14 let them make a noise like a dog, and go
Isa. 17. 12 of many people (which) make a noise like
Jer. 4. 19 my heart maketh a noise in me, Zec. 9. 15

3. *To break forth,* פָּצַח *patsach.*
Psa. 98. 4 Make a loud noise and rejoice, and sing p.

4. *To cause to hear or be heard,* שָׁמַע *shamea,* 5.
Josh. 6. 10 Ye shall not shout, nor make any noise.
1 Ch. 15. 28 making a noise with psalteries and harps

5. *To disturb, cause a tumult,* θορυβέω *thorubeō.*
Matt. 9. 23 minstrels and the people making a noise

NOISE, with great —
With a hissing noise, ῥοιζηδόν *rhoizēdon.*
2 Pe. 3. 10 shall pass away with a great noise, and the

NOISED (abroad), to be —
1. *To bear,* ἀκούω *akouō.*
Mark 2. 1 it was noised that he was in the house

2. *To talk or speak throughout,* διαλαλέω *dialaleō.*
Luke 1. 65 and all these sayings were noised abroad

3. *There came a voice,* γίνομαι φωνή, Acts 2. 6.

NOISOME —
1. *Mischief, calamity,* הַוָּה *havvah.*
Psa. 91 3 deliver thee..from the noisome pestilence

2. *Evil,* רַע *ra.*
Eze. 14. 15 If I cause noisome beasts to pass through
14. 21 the famine, and the noisome beast, and the

3. *Evil, bad,* κακός *kakos.*
Rev. 16. 2 there fell a noisome and grievous sore u.

NON, נוֹן *continuation.*
An Ephraimite through Beriah, who was born to Ephraim after the men of Gath had slain some of his sons; supposed by some to be the same as *Nun* the father of Joshua. B.C. 1492.
1 Ch. 7. 27 N. his son, Jehoshuah his son

NONE —
1. *There is not,* אַיִן *ayin.*
Isa. 45. 21 and a Saviour; (there is) none besides me
Jer. 30. 7 great, so that none (is) like; 2 Ch. 20. 24.

2. *Not,* אַל *al.*
2 Ki. 9. 15 (then) let none go forth (nor) escape out

3. *End, cessation, except, only,* אֶפֶס *ephes.*
Deut 32. 36 is gone, and (there is) none shut up, or left
Isa. 46. 9 (I am) God, and (there is) none like me

4. *Not,* בַּל *bal.*
Psa. 10. 15 seek out his wickedness (till) thou find n.

5. *Nothingness, not,* בְּלִי *beli.*
Job 18. 15 his tabernacle, because (it is) none of his
Isa. 14. 6 he..is persecuted, (and) none hindereth

6. *Without,* בִּלְתִּי *bilti.*
Num 21. 35 until there was none left him alive: and

7. *No,* לָא *la.*
Dan. 2. 11 and there is none other that can show it
4. 35 none can stay his hand, or say unto him
6. 4 they could find none occasion nor fault

8. *No,* לֹא *lo.*
Exod. 9. 24 was none like it in all the land of Egypt
Num. 7. 9 But unto the sons of Kohath he gave none

9. *Not a man,* אִישׁ לֹא *ish lo.*
Gen. 23. 6; Psa. 49. 7; Jer. 23. 14; Zech. 8. 17, &c.

10. *Not any,* כֹּל לֹא *kol lo.*
Lev. 27. 29 None devoted, which shall be devoted of

11. *Not a woman,* אִשָּׁה לֹא *ishshah lo.*
Isa. 34. 16 these shall fail, none shall want her mate

12. *Not any,* לָא כָּל־ *la kol.*
Dan. 6. 4 but they could find none occasion nor fa.

13. *Not,* μή *mē.*
Luke 3. 11 let him impart to him that hath none
11. 24 finding none, he saith, I will return unto
1 Co. 7. 29 that have wives be as though they had n.

14. *Not even one,* μηδείς *mēdeis.*
John 8. 10 [saw none but the woman, he said unto h.]
Acts 8. 24 Pray..that none of these things which ye
11. 19 preaching the word to none but unto the
24. 23 that he should forbid none of his acquai.
1 Ti. 5. 14 give none occasion to the adversary to sp.
Rev. 2. 10 Fear [none of] those things which thou sh.

15. *No, not,* οὐ *ou.*
Matt 12. 43 dry places, seeking rest, and findeth none
26. 60 But found none: yea, though many false
26. 60 witnesses came, [(yet) found they none]
Mark 12. 31 There is none other commandment grea.
12. 32 there is one God; and there is none other
14. 55 sought..to put..to death; and found none
Luke 13. 6 and sought fruit thereon, and found none
13. 7 seeking fruit on this fig tree, and find none
John 6. 22 saw that there was none other boat there
Acts 3. 6 Silver and gold have I none; but such as
7. 5 he gave him none inheritance in it, no, not
Rom. 3. 10 As it is written, There is none righteous
3. 11 none that understandeth, there is none
3. 12 there is none that doeth good, no, not one
8. 9 not the spirit of Christ, he is none of his
2 Co. 1. 13 we write none other things unto you than
Gal. 1. 19 other of the apostles saw I none, save Ja.
1 Jo. 2. 10 there is none occasion of stumbling in him
Rev. 2. 24 But..I will put upon you none other bur.

16. *Not even one,* οὐδείς *oudeis.*
Matt 19. 17 [(there is) none good but one, (that is)]
Luke 1. 61 There is none of thy kindred that is ca.
4. 26 unto none of them was Elias sent, save
4. 27 none of them was cleansed, saving Naa.
14. 24 that none of these men which were bid.
18. 19 good? none (is) good, save one, (that is)
18. 34 And they understood none of these things
John 7. 19 none of you keepeth the law? Why go ye
15. 24 done..the works which none other man
16. 5 none of you asketh me, Whither goest
17. 12 none of them is lost, but the son of perd.
18. 9 them which thou gavest me..I lost none
21. 12 none of the disciples durst ask him, Who
Acts 8. 16 as yet he was fallen upon none of them
18. 17 And Gallio cared for none of those; 20. 24.
25. 11 if there be none of these things whereof
25. 18 they brought none accusation of such t.
26. 22 saying none other things than those v. 26.
Rom. 14. 7 none of us liveth to himself, and no man
1 Co. 1. 14 I thank God that I baptized none of you
2. 8 Which none of the princes of this world
8. 4 we know..that..none other God but one
9. 15 I have used none of these things: neither
14. 10 and none of them (is) without signification
Gal. 5. 10 that ye will be none otherwise minded

17. *Not even,* οὔτε *oute.*
Acts 4. 12 there is [none] other name under heaven

18. *Not any,* μή τις *mē tis.*
1 Pe. 4. 15 But let none of you suffer as a murderer

19. *Not any,* οὔ τις *ou tis.*
Acts 26. 26 I am persuaded that [none] of these thi.

20. *Not any,* בְּלִי אִישׁ *beli ish.*
Jer. 9. 10 so that none can pass through (them)

NONE (else) besides me —
1. *None except me,* אֶפֶס בִּלְעָדַי [*ephes bilade*].
Isa. 45. 6 they may know..that..none besides me

2. [*There is*] *none still,* אַפְסִי עוֹד *aphsi od.*
Isa. 47. 8, 10 heart, I (am), and none else besides me
Zeph. 2. 15 in her heart, I (am), and..none besides me

NOON (day or tide) —
1. *Brightness, bright thing, noon,* צֹהַר *tsohar.*
Gen. 43. 16 for (these) men shall dine with me at noon
43. 25 the present against Joseph came at noon
Deut 28. 29 thou shalt grope at noon day, as the blind
2 Sa. 4. 5 Ishbosheth, who lay on a bed at noon
1 Ki. 18. 26 name of Baal from morning even until n.
18. 27 it came to pass at noon, that Elijah moc.
20. 16 they went out at noon: but Benhadad
2 Ki. 4. 20 he sat on her knees till noon, and..died
Job 5. 14 and grope in the noon day as in the night
11. 17 age shall be clearer than the noon day
Psa. 37. 6 bring forth..thy judgment as the noon d.
55. 17 Evening, and morning, and at noon, will
91. 6 the destruction (that) wasteth at noon d.
Song 1. 7 where thou makest (thy flock) to rest at n.
Isa. 16. 3 as the night in the midst of the noon day
58. 10 and thy darkness (be) as the noon day
59. 10 we stumble at noon day as in the night
Jer. 6. 4 Prepare ye war..arise..let us go up at n.
15. 8 brought upon them..a spoiler at noon d.
Amos 8. 9 I will cause the sun to go down at noon
Zeph. 2. 4 shall drive out Ashdod at the noon day

2. *Even time,* עֵת צָהֳרַיִם *eth tsohorayim.*
Jer. 20. 16 the morning, and the shouting at noon t.

3. *Mid day,* μεσημβρία *mesēmbria.*
Acts 22. 6 was come nigh unto Damascus about noon

NOPH, נֹף.
A city in Egypt, the same as Memphis (or Moph), on the W. bank of the Nile, S. of Cairo or *Kahira.*
Isa. 19. 13 the princes of N. are deceived; they have
Jer. 2. 16 Also the children of N. and Tahapanes h.
44. 1 and at N., and in the country of Pathros
46. 14 and publish in N. and in Tahpanhes: say
46. 19 N. shall be waste and desolate without
Eze. 30. 13 will cause (their) images to cease out of N.
30. 16 and N. (shall have) distresses daily

NO'-PHAH, נֹפַח *height.*
A city in the E. of the kingdom of Sihon, near Medeba. See *Nobah.*
Num 21. 30 we have laid them waste unto N., which

NOR —
1. *Or,* אוֹ *o.*
Judg 11. 34 beside her he had neither son nor daugh.

2. *And is (was) not,* וְאֵין *ve-ayin.*
1 Ki. 18. 26 But (there was) no voice nor any that
Isa. 40. 16 Lebanon (is) not sufficient to burn, nor the

3. *And not,* וְ...אַל *ve...al.*
Josh 22. 19 rebel not against the LORD, nor rebel ag.

4. *Or,* אִם *im.*
1 Sa. 30. 15 that thou wilt neither kill me, nor deliver
Eze. 14. 20 they shall deliver neither son nor daughter

5. *And not,* וּבַל *u-bal.*
Psa. 16. 4 will I not offer, nor take up their names

6. *And not,* וְ...לָא *ve...la.*
Dan. 3. 12 they serve not thy gods, nor worship the
3. 27 the fire had no power, nor was an hair of
3. 27 were their coats changed, nor the smell
5. 23 the gods..which see not, nor hear, nor k.
6. 4 but they could find none occasion nor fa.

7. *And not,* וְלֹא *ve-lo.*
Exod 11. 6 such as there was none like it, nor shall
2 Sa. 19. 24 nor trimmed his beard, nor washed his c.

8. *Or, either,* ἤ *ē.*
Luke 22. 68 if I also ask..ye will not answer me, [nor]
1 Co. 12. 21 nor again the head to the feet, I have no
Eph. 5. 4 foolish talking, nor jesting, which are not
5. 5 no whoremonger, nor unclean person, nor

9. *Not,* μή *mē.*
Matt 10. 10 Nor scrip for..journey, neither two coats
Luke 10. 4 Carry neither purse, nor scrip..and salute

10. *Not even,* μηδέ *mēde.*
Matt 10. 9 Provide neither gold, [nor] silver, nor br.
10. 14 shall not receive you, nor hear your words
22. 29 not knowing the Scriptures, nor the power
Mark 6. 11 shall not receive you, nor hear you, when
8. 26 Neither go into the town, nor tell..to any
Luke 10. 4 Carry neither purse..nor shoes: and salu.
14. 12 nor thy brethren, neither thy kinsman, nor
17. 23 or, see there! go not after..nor follow (th.)
Acts 4. 18 commanded them not to speak at all nor
Rom 14. 21 neither to eat flesh, nor to drink wine nor
2 Co. 4. 2 not walking in craftiness, nor handling the
1 Ti. 6. 17 that they be not high minded, nor trust
2 Ti. 1. 8 ashamed of the testimony of our Lord, nor
Heb. 12. 5 nor faint when thou art rebuked of him

11. *Not even, nor,* μήτε *mēte.*
Matt. 5. 35 Nor by the earth; for it is his foot stool
11. 18 John came neither eating nor drinking
Luke 7. 33 came neither eating bread nor drinking
9. 3 neither staves, nor scrip, neither bread
Acts 23. 8 is no resurrection, neither angel, nor spi.
23. 21 that they will neither eat nor drink till
27. 20 when neither sun nor stars in many days
2 Th 2. 2 nor by word, nor by letter as from us, as
1 Ti. 1. 7 understanding neither what they say, nor
Heb. 7. 3 having neither beginning of days, nor end
Rev. 7. 1 not blow on the earth, nor on the sea, nor
7. 3 Hurt not the earth, neither the sea, nor

12. *No, not,* οὐ *ou,* οὐχί *ouchi.*
Luke 18. 4 Though I fear not God, [nor] regard man

1 Co. 2. 9 Eye hath not seen, nor ear heard, neither
6. 10 nor revilers, nor extortioners, shall inhe.

13. *Not even,* οὐδέ *oude.*

Matt. 6. 20 where thieves do not break through nor
6. 26 neither do they reap, nor gather into barns
10. 24 (his) master; nor the servant above his l.
12. 19 He shall not strive, nor cry; neither shall
24. 21 was not..to this time, no, nor ever shall
25. 13 for ye know neither the day nor the hour
Luke 6. 44 nor of a bramble bush gather they grapes
12. 24 the ravens: for they neither sow [nor] r.
12. 24 which neither have store house nor barn
21. 15 shall not be able to gainsay [nor] resist
John 1. 13 nor of the will of the flesh, nor of the will
11. 50 Nor consider that it is expedient for us
16. 3 they have not known the Father, nor me
Acts 8. 21 Thou hast neither part nor lot in this m.
9. 9 three days..and neither did eat nor drink
24. 18 neither with multitude, nor with tumult
Rom. 9. 16 not of him that willeth, nor of him that
1 Co. 2. 6 yet not the wisdom of this world, nor of
2 Co. 7. 12 nor for his cause that suffered wrong, but
Gal. 3. 28 Jew nor Greek..bond nor free..male nor
4. 14 in my flesh ye despised not, nor rejected
1 Th. 2. 3 our exhortation (was) not of deceit, nor
5. 5 we are not of the night, nor of darkness
1 Ti. 2. 12 nor to usurp authority over the man, but
6. 16 whom no man hath seen, nor can see: to
Heb. 13. 5 I will never leave thee, nor forsake thee
2 Pe. 1. 8 neither (be) barren nor unfruitful in the
Rev. 5. 3 no man in heaven, nor in earth, neither
7. 16 neither shall the sun light on them, nor

14. *Not even, nor,* οὔτε *oute.*

Matt. 6. 20 where neither moth nor rust doth corrupt
22. 30 neither marry, nor are given in marriage
Mark 12. 25 neither marry, nor are given in marriage
Luke 20. 35 neither marry, nor are given in marriage
John 1. 25 if thou be not that Christ, [nor] Elias, nei.
5. 37 neither heard his voice at any time, nor
8. 19 Ye neither know me, nor my Father: if
9. 3 Neither hath this man sinned, nor his p.
Acts 15. 10 which neither our fathers nor we were
24. 12 neither in the synagogues, nor in the city
Rom. 8. 38 death, nor life, nor angels, nor principal.
8. 38 nor powers, nor things present, nor things
8. 39 Nor height, nor depth, nor any other cr.
1 Co 6. 9 nor idolaters, nor adulterers, nor effemi.
6. 9 nor abusers of themselves with mankind
6. 10 Nor thieves, nor covetous, [nor] drunkards
Gal. 5. 6 nor uncircumcision; but faith which wo.
6. 15 nor uncircumcision, but a new creature
1 Th. 2. 3 not of deceit..of uncleanness, nor in guile
2. 5 nor a cloak of covetousness; God (is) wit.
2. 6 Nor of men..nor (yet) of others, when we
Rev. 3. 15 that thou art neither cold nor hot: I wo.
3. 16 thou art lukewarm, and neither cold nor
9. 20 which neither can see, nor hear, nor v. 21.

15. *And,* καί *kai.*

Gal. 3. 28 there is neither male nor female; Jo. 12. 40

NOR any thing —

There is not, אַיִן *ayin.*

Ecc. 3. 14 nothing can be put to it, nor any thing

NOR ever —

Assuredly not, not at all, οὐ μή *ou mē.*

Matt 24. 21 was not..to this time, no, nor ever shall

NOR yet —

1. *Not even,* μηδέ *mēde.*

Matt. 6. 25 nor yet for your body, what ye shall put
10. 10 neither two coats, neither shoes, nor yet

2. *Not even,* οὐδέ *oude.*

Heb. 9. 25 Nor yet that he should offer himself often

3. *Not even, nor,* οὔτε *oute.*

Acts 25. 8 nor yet against Cesar, have I offended any

NORTH, Northern, side, wind, ward —

1. *Scattering winds,* מְזָרִים *mezarim.*

Job 37. 9 the whirlwind; and cold out of the north

2. *North,* צָפוֹן *tsaphon.*

Gen. 13. 14 look from the place where thou art north.
28. 14 to the east, and to the north, and to the
Exod 26. 20 side of the tabernacle, on the north side
26. 35 thou shalt put the table on the north side
27. 11 And likewise for the north side in length
36. 25 toward the north corner, he made twenty
38. 11 for the north side..an hundred cubits, t.
40. 22 upon the side of the tabernacle northward
Lev. 1. 11 shall kill it on the side of the altar north.
Num. 2. 25 standard of the camp of Dan..on the n. s.
3. 35 pitch on the side of the tabernacle north.
34. 7 this shall be your north border: from the
34. 9 Hazar-enan: this shall be your north bo.
35. 5 and on the north side two thousand cub.
Deut. 2. 3 compassed..long enough: turn you north.
3. 27 lift up thine eyes westward, and northw.
Josh. 8. 11 before the city, and pitched on the north s.
8. 13 all the host that (was) on the north of the
11. 2 to the kings that (were) on the north of
13. 3 even unto the borders of Ekron northward
15. 5 border in the north quarter (was) from the
15. 6 passed along by the north of Beth-arabah
15. 7 from the valley of Achor, and so northw.
15. 8 at the end of the valley of the giants n w.
15. 10 side of mount Jearim..on the north side
15. 11 went out unto the side of Ekron northw.
16. 6 toward the sea to Michmethah on the n. s.
Josh. 17. 9 the north side of the river, and the out.
17. 10 northward (it was) Manasseh's, and the
17. 10 they met together in Asher on the north
18. 5 shall abide in their coasts on the north
18. 12 their border on the north side was from
18. 12 went up to the side of Jericho on the no.
18. 16 in the valley of the giants on the north
18. 17 was drawn from the north, and went forth
18. 18 toward the side over against Arabah, n. w.
18. 19 along to the side of Beth-hoglah northw.
18. 19 out goings of the border were at the no.
19. 14 the border compasseth it on the north s.
19. 27 toward the north side of Beth-emek, and
24. 30 Timnath-serah..on the north side of the
Judg. 2. 9 Timnath-heres..on the north side of the
7. 1 host of the Midianites were on the north
12. 1 went northward, and said unto Jephthah
21. 19 which (is) on the north side of Bethel, on
1 Sa 14. 5 situate northward over against Michmash
1 Ki. 7. 25 twelve oxen, three looking towards the n.
2 Ki. 16. 14 and put it on the north side of the altar
1 Ch. 9. 24 were..toward the east, west, north, and
26. 14 Zechariah..and his lot came out northw.
26. 17 Levites, northward four a day, southward
2 Ch. 4. 4 twelve oxen, three looking towards the n.
Job 26. 7 He stretcheth out the north over the em.
37. 22 Fair weather cometh out of the north: w.
Psa. 48. 2 mount Zion, (on) the sides of the north
89. 12 The north and the south thou hast created
107. 3 west, from the north, and from the south
Prov 25. 23 The north wind driveth away rain; so (d.)
Eccl. 1. 6 the south, and turneth about unto the n.
11. 3 or toward the north, in the place where
Song 4. 16 Awake, O north wind; and come, thou s.
Isa. 14. 13 the congregation, in the sides of the north
14. 31 there shall come from the north a smoke
41. 25 I have raised up (one) from the north, and
43. 6 I will say to the north, Give up; and to
49. 12 lo, these from the north and from the w.
Jer. 1. 13 and the face thereof (is) towards the north
1. 14 Out of the north an evil shall break forth
1. 15 the families of the kingdoms of the north
3. 12 proclaim these words toward the north
3. 18 come together out of the land of the north
4. 6 I will bring evil from the north, and a g.
6. 1 evil appeareth out of the north, and great
6. 22 a people cometh from the north country
10. 22 a great commotion out of the north coun.
13. 20 behold them that come from the north
15. 12 Shall iron break the northern iron and the
16. 15 from the land of the north, and from all
23. 8 house of Israel out of the north country
25. 9 send and take all the families of the north
25. 26 all the kings of the north, far and near
31. 8 I will bring them from the north country
46. 6 fall toward the north by the river Euphr.
46. 10 the north country by the river Euphrates
46. 20 destruction cometh..cometh out of the n.
46. 24 into the hand of the people of the north
47. 2 waters rise up out of the north, and shall
50. 3 out of the north there cometh up a nation
50. 9 assembly of great nations from the north
50. 41 Behold, a people shall come from the north
51. 48 spoilers shall come unto her from the n.
Eze. 1. 4 a whirlwind came out of the north, a great
8. 3 inner gate that looketh toward the north
8. 5 lift up thine eyes..the way toward the n.
8. 5 lifted..mine eyes the way toward the no.
8. 5 northward at the gate of the altar this
8. 14 door of the gate..which (was) toward the n.
9. 2 higher gate, which lieth toward the north
20. 47 all faces from the south to the north shall
21. 4 against all flesh from the south to the no.
26. 7 king of kings, from the north, with horses
32. 30 There (be) the princes of the north, all of
38. 6 the house of Togarmah of the north qua.
38. 15 shalt come from thy place out of the north
39. 2 will cause thee to come up from the north
40. 19 an hundred cubits eastward and north w.
40. 20 outward court that looked toward the no.
40. 23 over against the gate toward the north
40. 35 he brought me to the north gate, and m.
40. 40 as one goeth up to the entry of the north
40. 44 which (was) at the side of the north gate
40. 44 gate (having) the prospect toward the nor.
40. 46 chamber whose prospect (is) toward the n.
41. 11 one door toward the north, and another
42. 1 the outer court, the way toward the north
42. 1 (was) before the building toward the nor.
42. 2 of an hundred cubits (was) the north door
42. 4 one cubit; and their doors toward the n.
42. 11 the chambers which (were) toward the n.
42. 13 The north chambers (and) the south cham.
42. 17 He measured the north side, five hundred
44. 4 the way of the north gate before the ho.
46. 9 he that entereth in by the way of the north
46. 9 shall go forth by the way of the north gate
46. 19 the priests, which looked toward the no.
47. 2 brought..me out of the way of the gate n. w.
47. 15 border of the land toward the north side
47. 17 north northward..(this is) the north side
48. 1 From the north end to the coast of the way
48. 1 the border of Damascus northward, to the
48. 10 toward the north five and twenty thous.
48. 16 the north side four thousand and five hu.
48. 17 suburbs of the city shall be toward the n.
48. 30 the goings out of the city on the north side
48. 31 three gates northward; one gate of Reu.
Dan. 8. 4 I saw the ram pushing westward, and n. w.
11. 6 shall come to the king of the north to m.
11. 7 into the fortress of the king of the north
11. 8 (more) years than the king of the north
Dan. 11. 11 fight with him..with the king of the north
11. 13 king of the north shall return, and shall
11. 15 So the king of the north shall come, and
11. 40 the king of the north shall come against
11. 44 tidings out of the east and out of the no.
Amos 8. 12 from the north even to the east, they shall
Zeph. 2. 13 he will stretch out his hand against the n.
Zech. 2. 6 flee from the land of the north, saith the
6. 6 therein go forth into the north country
6. 8 these that go toward the north country
6. 8 quieted my spirit in the north country
14. 4 mountain shall remove toward the north

3. *Northern,* צְפוֹנִי *tsephoni.*

Joel 2. 20 I will remove far off from you the north.

4. *North wind, north,* βοῤῥᾶς *borrhas.*

Luke 13. 29 from the north, and..the south, and shall
Rev. 21. 13 on the north, three gates; on the south

NORTH WEST —

North west wind, north west, (Lat. corus) χῶρος.

Acts 27. 12 toward the south west and north west

NOSE, NOSTRILS —

1. *Nose,* אַף *aph.*

Gen. 2. 7 breathed into his nostrils the breath of life
7. 22 All in whose nostrils (was) the breath of
Exod 15. 8 with the blast of thy nostrils the waters
Num 11. 20 until it come out at your nostrils, and it
2 Sa. 22. 9 There went up a smoke out of his nostrils
22. 16 at the blast of the breath of his nostrils
2 Ki. 19. 28 I will put my hook in thy nose, and my
Job 4. 9 by the breath of his nostrils are they con.
27. 3 and the spirit of God (is) in my nostrils
40. 24 He taketh it with his eyes; (his) nose
41. 2 Canst thou put an hook into his nose? or
Psa. 18. 8 There went up a smoke out of his nostrils
18. 15 at the blast of the breath of thy nostrils
115. 6 ears..noses have they, but they smell not
Prov 30. 33 wringing of the nose bringeth forth blood
Song 7. 4 thy nose (is) as the tower of Lebanon wh.
7. 8 and the smell of thy nose like apples
Isa. 2. 22 from man, whose breath (is) in his nostr.
3. 21 The rings, and nose jewels
37. 29 therefore will I put my hook in thy nose
65. 5 These (are) a smoke in my nose, a fire that
Lam. 4. 20 The breath of our nostrils, the anointed
Eze. 8. 17 and, lo, they put the branch to their nose
23. 25 they shall take away thy nose and thine
Amos 4. 10 of your camps to come up unto your nos.

2. *Snorting,* נַחַר *nachar.*

Job 39. 20 afraid..the glory of his nostrils (is) terr.

3. *Nostrils,* נְחִירַיִם *nechirim.*

Job 41. 20 Out of his nostrils goeth smoke, as..of a

NOSE, to have a flat —

To have a flat nose, חָרַם *charam.*

Lev. 21. 18 or a lame, or he that hath a flat nose, or

NOT —

1. *There is not,* אַיִן *ayin.*

Gen. 2. 5 and (there was) not a man to till the gro.
Lam. 5. 7 Our fathers have sinned, (and are) not

2. *There is not,* אִין *in.*

1 Sa. 21. 8 is there not here under thine hand spear

3. *Not,* אַל *al.*

Dan. 2. 24 Destroy not the wise (men) of Babylon
4. 19 let not the dream, or the interpretation
5. 10 let not thy thoughts trouble thee, nor let
9. 19 defer not, for thine own sake, O my God

4. *If,* אִם *im.*

1 Sa. 19. 6 (As) the LORD liveth, he shall not be slain

5. *End, cessation,* אֶפֶס *ephes.*

2 Sa. 9. 3 (Is) there not yet any of the house of Saul
Isa. 54. 15 they shall surely gather together..not by

6. *Not,* בַּל *bal.*

Isa. 26. 10 (yet) will he not learn righteousness
26. 10 and will not behold the majesty of the L.

7. *Without,* בְּלִי *beli.*

Gen. 31. 20 unawares..in that he told him not that he

8. *Without, save, besides,* בִּלְעֲדֵי *bilade.*

Job 34. 32 (That which) I see not, teach thou me; if

9. *Without,* בִּלְתִּי *bilti.*

Gen. 3. 11 commanded thee that thou shouldest not
Exod 8. 29 in not letting the people go to sacrifice
Lev. 20. 4 of his seed unto Molech, and kill him not
Num 14. 16 Because the LORD was not able to bring
Ruth 3. 10 inasmuch as thou followedst not young
1 Sa. 20. 26 Something hath befallen him, he is not c.

10. *No, not,* לָא *la.*

Ezra 4. 13 will they not pay toll, tribute, and custom
4. 14 it was not meet for us to see the king's
4. 21 to cease, and that this city be not builded
5. 5 that they could not cause them to cease
5. 16 hath it been in building, and..it is not finis
6. 8 given unto these men, that they be not h.
7. 24 it shall not be lawful to impose toll, tribute
7. 25 and teach ye them that know (them) not
7. 26 whosoever will not do the law of thy God
Jer. 10. 11 The gods that have not made the heavens
Dan. 2. 5, 9 if ye will not make known unto me the
2. 10 There is not a man upon the earth that
2. 11 the gods, whose dwelling is not with flesh
2. 18 that Daniel and his fellows should not p.
2. 30 this secret is not revealed to me for (any)
2. 43 not cleave one to another..as iron is not

Dan. 2. 44 kingdom shall not be left to other people
3. 6, 11 whoso falleth not down and worship.
3. 12 these men, O king, have not regarded thee
3. 12 they serve not thy gods, nor worship the
3. 14 do not ye serve my gods, nor worship the
3. 15 if ye worship not, ye shall be cast the sa.
3. 16 we (are) not careful to answer thee in this
3. 18 But if not, be it known unto thee, O king
3. 18 that we will not serve thy gods, nor wor.
3. 24 Did not we cast three men bound into the
3. 28 that they might not serve nor worship any
4. 7 but they did not make known unto me the
4. 18 are not able to make known unto me the
4. 30 Is not this great Babylon, that I have bu.
5. 8 but they could not read the writing, nor
5. 15 they could not show the interpretation of
5. 22 thou his son, O Belshazzar, hast not hu.
5. 23 which see not, nor hear, nor know: and
6. 5 We shall not find any occasion against t.
6. 8 sign the writing, that it be not changed
6. 8 Medes and Persians, which altereth not
6. 12 Hast thou not signed a decree, that every
6. 12 the Medes and Persians, which altereth not
6. 13 regardeth not thee, O king, nor the decr.
6. 17 that the purpose might not be changed
6. 22 the lions' mouths, that they have not h.
6. 26 kingdom..which shall not be destroyed
7. 14 shall not pass away..which shall not be

11. *No, not,* לֹא *lo.*

Gen. 2. 5 the Lord God had not caused it to rain

12. *Without, not,* בְּלֹא *be-lo.*

Num35. 23 seeing (him) not, and cast (it) upon him
Deut 32. 21 me to jealousy with (that which is) not
32. 21 to jealousy with (those that are) not a p.

13. *No, not,* לֹה *loh.*

Deut. 3. 11 (is) it not in Rabbath of the children of A.

14. *From,* מִן *min.*

Deut 33. 11 them that hate him, that they rise not

15. *Not,* μή *mē.*

Matt. 1. 19 not willing to make her a public example
1. 20 fear not to take unto thee Mary thy wife
2. 12 that they should not return to Herod, they
3. 9 think not to say within yourselves, We h.
3. 10 which bringeth not forth good fruit is h.
5. 17 Think not that I am come to destroy the
5. 29, 30 not (that) thy whole body should be c.
5. 34 Swear not at all: neither by heaven; for
5. 39 That ye resist not evil; but whosoever
5. 42 that would borrow of thee turn not thou
6. 1 Take heed that ye do not your alms before
6. 2 do not sound a trumpet before thee, as the
6. 3 let not thy left hand know what thy right
6. 7 when ye pray, use not vain repetitions, as
6. 8 Be not ye therefore like unto them: for
6. 13 lead us not into temptation, but deliver
6. 16 Moreover, when ye fast, be not, as the hy.
6. 18 That thou appear not unto men to fast
6. 19 Lay not up for yourselves treasures upon
7. 1 Judge not, that ye be..judged
7. 6 Give not that which is holy unto the dogs
7. 19 Every tree that bringeth not forth good
7. 26 and doeth them not, shall be likened unto
10. 5 Go not into the way of the Gentiles, and
10. 5 into..city of the Samaritans enter ye not
10. 26 Fear them not therefore: for there is not.
10. 28 And fear not them which kill the body.
10. 28 but are not able to kill the soul: but rat.
10. 31 Fear ye not therefore, ye are of more va.
10. 34 Think not that I am come to send peace
12. 30 He that is not with me is against me
12. 30 he that gathereth not with me scattereth
13. 19 of the kingdom, and understandeth..not
14. 27 Be of good cheer: It is I; be not afraid
17. 7 touched..and said, Arise, and be not afr.
18. 13 the ninety and nine which went not ast.
18. 25 But forasmuch as he had not to pay, his
19. 6 God hath joined together, let not man put
19. 14 and forbid them not, to come unto me
21. 21 If ye have faith, and doubt not, ye shall
22. 12 how camest thou in hither not having a
22. 29 Ye do err, not knowing the Scriptures, n.
23. 3 but do not ye after their works: for they
23. 8 But be not ye called Rabbi: for one is
23. 23 to have done, and not to leave the other
24. 17 Let him which is on the house top not c.
24. 23 here (is) Christ, or there; believe (it) not
24. 26 Behold, he is in the desert; go not forth
24. 26 in the secret chambers; believe (it) not
25. 29 from him that hath not shall be taken
26. 5 But they said, Not on the feast..lest there
28. 5 Fear not ye; for I know that ye seek Je.
28. 10 Be not afraid: go tell my brethren that

Mark 2. 4; 3. 20; 4. 12, 12; 5. 36; 6. 9, 11, 34, 50; 9. 39;
10. 9, 14, 19, [19,] 19, 19, 19; 11. 23; 12. 15, 24; 13. 7, 15,
16, 21; 14. 2; 16. 6.

Luke 1. 13, 20, 30; 2. 10, 26, 45; 3. 8, 9; 4. 42; 5. 10,
19; 6. 29, 30, 37, 37, 49; 7. 6, 13, 30; 8. 10, 10, 18, 28, [49],
50, 52; 9. 5, 33, 50; 10. 7, 10, 20; 11. 4, 7, 23, 23, 35, 42;
12. 4, 7, 21, 29, 32, 33, 47, 48; 13. 14; 14. 8, 12, 29; 16. 26;
17. 23, 31, 31, 31, 31; 18. 1, 2, 16, 20, 20, 20, 20; 19. 26, 27;
20. 7; 21. 8, 9, 14, 21; 22. 40, 42; 23. 28; 24. 16, 23.

John 2. 16; 3. 7, [16], 18, 18; 5. 23, 28, 45; 6. 20, 27,
43, 64; 7. 24, 49; 8. [6]; 9. 39; 10. 1, 37, 38; 11. 37, 50; 12.
15, [47], 48; 13. 9; 14. 1, 24, 27; 15. 2; 18. 17, 25, 40; 19.
21, 24; 20. 17, 27, 29.

Acts 1. 4; 3. 23; 4. 18; 5. 7, 28, 40; 7. 19, 60; 9. 26,
38; 10. 15, 47; 11. 9; 12. 19; 13. 11; 14. 18; 15. 19, 38, 38;
17. 6; 18. 9, 9; 19. 31; 20. 10, 16, 22, 29; 21. 4, 12, 14, 21,
34; 23. [9], 21; 25. 24, 27; 27. 7, 15, 21, 24.

Rom. 1. 28; 2. 14, 14, 21, 22; 3. 8; 4. 5, 17, 19; 5. [14];
6. 12; 8. [1], 4; 9. 30; 10. 6, 20, 20; 11. 8, 8, 10, 18, 20; 12.
2, 3, 11, 14, 16, 16, 19, 21; 13. 3, 13, 13, 13, 14; 14. 1, 3,
3, 3, [6], 6, 15, 16, 20, 22; 15. 1.

1 Co. 1. 28; 4. 7, 18; 5. 8, 9, 11; 6. 9; 7. 1, 5, 10, 11, 12,
13, 18, 18, 21, 23, 27, 27, 30, 30, 30, 31, 38; 9. 18, 21; 10.
6, 28, 33; 11. [22], 29; 13. 1, 2, 3; 14. 20, 39; 15. 33, 34;
2 Co. 2. 1, 13; 3. 7, 13; 4. 2, 7, 18, 18, 18; 5. 19; 6. 1, 9,
14, 17; 9. 5, 7; 10. 2, 14; 12. 21.

Gal. 3. [1]; 4. 18; 5. 1, 7, 13, 26; 6. 7, 9, 9; Eph. 3. 13;
4. 26, 26, 30; 5. 7, 15, 17, 18, 27; 6. 4, 6; Phil. 2. 4, 12; 3.
9; Col. 1. 23; 2. [18], 21; 3. 2, 9, 19, 21, 22; 1 Th. 1. 8; 2. 9,
15; 4. 5, 5; 5. 6, 19, 20; 2 Th. 1. 8, 8; 2. 2, 12; 3. 6, 8, 13,
15; 1 Ti. 1. 20; 2. 9; 3. 3, [3], 6, 8, 8, 8, 11; 4. 14; 5. 1,
9, 13, 16, 19; 6. 2, 3, 17; 2 Ti. 1. 8; 2. 14; Titus 1. 6, 7, 7,
7, 7, 11, 14; 2. 3, 3, 9, 10.

Heb. 3. 8, 15, 18; 4. 2, 7, 15; 6. 1; 7. 6; 9. 9; 10. 25,
25; 11. 3, 5, 8, 13, 27; 12. 5, 19, 27; 13. 2, 9, 16, 17; Jas.
1. 5, 7, 16, 22, 26; 2. 1, 11, 11, 14, 16; 3. 1, 14; 4. 2, 11,
17; 5. 9, 12, 17.

1 Pe. 1. 8, 14; 2. 16; 3. 6, 7, 9, 14; 4. 4, 12, 16; 5. 2;
2 Pe. 2. 21; 3. 8, 9; 1 John 2. 4, 15, 28; 3. 10, 10, 13, 14,
18, 21; 4. 1, 3, 8, 20; 5. 10, 12, 16, 16; 2 John 7, 9, 10;
3 John 10, 11; Jude 5, 6, 19; Rev. 1. 17; 3. 18; 5. 5; 6. 6;
7. 3; 8. 12; 10. 4; 11. 2; 13. 15; 19. 10; 22. 9, 10.

16. *If not, except,* ἐὰν μή *ean mē.*

Mark 4. 22 there is nothing hid, which shall not be

17. *Not even,* μηδέ *mēde.*

Col. 2. 21 taste not, handle not
1 Pe. 5. 2 not for filthy lucre, but of a ready mind

18. *Not even one,* μηδείς *mēdeis.*

Luke 4. 35 came out..and hurt him not, Acts 10. 28.

19. *No not, yes verily,* μὴ οὐκ *mē ouk.*

Rom 10. 18 Have they not heard? Yes verily, their
10. 19 Did not Israel know? First Moses saith
1 Co. 9. 4 Have we not power to eat and to drink?
9. 5 Have we not power to lead about a sister
11. 22 have ye not houses to eat and to drink in?

20. *What?* μήτι *mēti.*

Matt 12. 23 And all..said, Is not this the son of Da.?
John 4. 29 things that ever I did: is not this the C.?

21. *Assuredly not,* οὐ μή *ou mē.*

Matt 10. 23 Ye shall not have gone over the cities of
13. 14 By hearing ye shall hear, and shall not un
13. 14 seeing ye shall see, and shall not perceive
15. 6 And honour not his father or his mother
16. 22 from thee, Lord: this shall not be unto
16. 28 which shall not taste of death, till they
18. 3 ye shall not enter into the kingdom of h.
23. 39 Ye shall not see me henceforth, till ye s.
24. 2 There shall [not] be left here one stone
24. 2 that shall [not] be thrown down
24. 34 This generation shall not pass, till all
24. 35 pass away, but my words shall not pass
26. 29 I will not drink henceforth of this fruit of
26. 35 should die with thee, yet will I not deny
Mark 9. 1 which shall not taste of death, till they
9. 41 say unto you, he shall not lose his reward
10. 15 he shall not enter therein
13. 2 there shall not be left..that shall not be
13. 30 this generation shall not pass, till all th.
13. 31 pass away; but my words shall not pass
16. 18 [they drink any deadly thing, it shall not]
Luke 6. 37 shall [not] be judged..shall not be con.
9. 27 which shall not taste of death, till they
12. 59 thou shalt not depart thence, till thou
13. 35 Ye shall not see me, until (the time) come
18. 7 And shall not God avenge his own
18. 30 Who shall not receive manifold more in
21. 18 But there shall not an hair of your head
21. 32 This generation shall not pass away till
21. 33 pass away; but my words shall not pass
22. 16 I will not any more eat thereof, until it
22. 18 I will not drink of the fruit of the vine
22. 34 Peter, the cock shall [not] crow this day
22. 67 he said..If I tell you, ye will not believe
22. 68 if I also ask..ye will not answer me, nor
John 4. 48 Except ye see signs..ye will not believe
8. 12 he that followeth me shall not walk in d.
10. 5 a stranger will they not follow, but will
11. 56 What think ye, that he will not come to
13. 38 The cock shall not crow, till thou hast d.
20. 25 my hand into his side, I will not believe
Acts 28. 26 Hearing ye shall hear, and shall not und.
28. 26 and seeing ye shall see, and not perceive
Rom. 4. 8 man to whom the Lord will not impute
Gal. 4. 30 the son of the bond woman shall not be h.
5. 16 ye shall not fulfil the lust of the flesh
1 Th. 4. 15 shall not prevent them which are asleep
5. 3 woman with child; and they shall not es.
Heb. 8. 11 they shall not teach every man his neigh.
1 Pe. 2. 6 he that believeth on him shall not be con.
Rev. 2. 11 He that overcometh shall not be hurt of
3. 3 thou shalt not know what hour
3. 5 and I will not blot out his name out of
15. 4 Who shall not fear thee, O Lord, and gl.

22. *Not,* οὐ, οὐκ *ou, ouk.*

Matt. 1. 25 knew her not till she had brought forth
2. 18 would not be comforted, because they are
3. 11 whose shoes I am not worthy to bear: he
4. 4 Man shall not live by bread alone, but by
4. 7 Thou shalt not tempt the Lord thy God
5. 17 I am not come to destroy, but to fulfil
5. 21 Thou shalt not kill; and whosoever shall
5. 27 heard..Thou shalt not commit adultery
5. 33 Thou shalt not forswear thyself, but shalt
6. 5 thou shalt not be as the hypocrites (are)
6. 20 and where thieves do not break through

Matt. 6. 26 for they sow not, neither do they reap
6. 26 Behold. Are ye not much better than they?
6. 28 lilies..they toil not, neither do they spin
6. 30 (shall he) not much more (clothe) you, O
7. 3 but considerest not the beam that is in th.
7. 21 Not every one that saith unto me, Lord
7. 22 Lord, have we not prophesied in thy name
7. 25 it fell not: for it was founded upon a rock
7. 29 having authority, and not as the scribes
8. 8 I am not worthy that thou shouldest come
8. 20 but the Son of man hath not where to lay
9. 12 They that be whole need not a physician
9. 13 mercy, and not sacrifice: for I am not
9. 14 we..fast oft, but thy disciples fast not?
9. 24 for the maid is not dead, but sleepeth
10. 20 For it is not ye that speak, but the spirit
10. 24 The disciple is not above (his) master, nor
10. 26 there is nothing covered, that shall not be
10. 26 is nothing..hid, that shall not be known
10. 29 one of them shall not fall on the ground w.
10. 34 I came not to send peace, but a sword
10. 37, 37 more than me, is not worthy of me
10. 38 taketh [not] his cross..is not worthy of me
11. 11 there hath not risen a greater than John
11. 17 ye have not danced..ye have not lamen.
11. 20 to upbraid..because they repented not
12. 2 thy disciples do that which is not lawful
12. 3 Have ye not read what David did, when
12. 4 did eat the showbread, which was not la.
12. 5 Or have ye not read in the Law, how that
12. 7 what..I will have mercy, and not sacrifice
12. 7 ye would not have condemned the guiltl.
12. 19 He shall not strive, nor cry; neither shall
12. 20 A bruised reed shall he not break, and
12. 20 smoking flax shall he not quench, till he
12. 24 This (fellow) doth not cast out devils, but
12. 25 every city or house divided..shall not st.
12. 31 blasphemy..shall not be forgiven unto m.
12. 32 it shall not be forgiven him, neither in
13. 5 upon stony places, where they had not m.
13. 11 it is given unto you..but to them it is not
13. 12 whosoever hath not, from him shall be
13. 13 they seeing, see not; and hearing, they
13. 17 and have not seen..and have not heard
13. 21 Yet hath he not root in himself, but dur.
13. 34 without a parable spake he [not] unto them
13. 55 Is not this the carpenter's son? is not his
13. 57 A prophet is not without honour, save in
13. 58 he did not many mighty works there, be.
14. 4 said..It is not lawful for thee to have her
14. 16 They need not depart; give ye them to eat
15. 2 wash not their hands when they eat bread
15. 11 Not that which goeth into the mouth de.
15. 13 which my heavenly Father hath not pla.
15. 20 to eat with unwashen hands defileth not
15. 23 he answered her not a word. And his dis.
15. 24 I am not sent but unto the lost sheep of
15. 26 It is not meet to take the children's bread
15. 32 will not send them away fasting, lest they
16. 11 How is it that ye do not understand that
16. 11 I spake..not to you concerning bread, that
16. 12 he bade..not beware of the leaven of br.
16. 17 flesh and blood hath not revealed (it) unto
16. 18 the gates of hell shall not prevail against
16. 23 savourest not the things that be of God
17. 12 they knew him not, but have done unto
17. 21 [this kind goeth not out but by prayer and]
17. 24 said, Doth not your master pay tribute?
18. 14 Even so it is not the will of your Father
18. 22 I say not unto thee, Until seven times; but
18. 30 he would not; but went and cast him into
18. 33 Shouldest not thou also have had compa.
19. 4 Have ye not read, that he which made
19. 8 He saith..from the beginning it was not
19. 10 His disciples say..it is not good to marry
19. 11 All..cannot receive this saying, save..to
19. 18 Jesus said..Thou shalt not commit adul.
19. 18 Thou shalt not steal, Thou shalt not bear
20. 15 Is it not lawful for me to do what I will
20. 22 Jesus answered and said, Ye know not w.
20. 23 to sit on my right hand..is not mine to
20. 26 it shall not be so among you: but whoso.
20. 28 Even as the Son of man came not to be
21. 21 ye shall not only do this..to the fig tree
21. 25 say..Why did ye not then believe him?
21. 29 He answered and said, I will not: but a.
21. 30 answered and said, I (go), sir; and went not
21. 32 ye believed him not..repented [not] aft.
22. 3 sent..to call them..and they would not
22. 8 but they which were bidden were not w.
22. 11 he saw there a man which had not on a w.
22. 16 for thou regardest not the person of men
22. 17 Is it lawful to give tribute unto C., or not?
22. 31 have ye not read that which was spoken
22. 32 God is not the God of the dead, but of the
23. 3 do..ye after..for they say, and do not
23. 4 but they..will not move them with one of
23. 30 we would not have been partakers with
23. 37 would I have gathered..and ye would not
24. 2 See ye [not] all these things? Verily I say
24. 21 such as was not since the beginning of the
24. 29 the moon shall not give her light, and the
24. 39 knew not until the flood came, and took
24. 42 know not what hour your Lord doth come
24. 43 would not have suffered his house to be b.
24. 44 in such an hour as ye think not the Son of
24. 50 shall come in a day when he looketh not
24. 50 and in an hour that he is not aware of
25. 9 lest there be [not] enough for us and you
25. 12 Verily I say unto you, I know you not
25. 24 thou hast not sown, and..thou hast not
25. 26 I sowed not, and gather where I have not

Matt25. 43 ye took me not in..ye clothed me not
25. 43 sick, and in prison, and ye visited me not
25. 44 in prison, and did not minister unto thee?
25. 45 Inasmuch as ye did (it) not to one of the
26. 11 ye have the poor..but me ye have not al.
26. 24 had been good for that man if he had not
26. 39 nevertheless not as I will, but as thou (wilt)
26. 40 What! could ye not watch with me one h.?
26. 42 if this cup may not pass away from me
26. 70 denied..saying, I know not what thou say.
26. 72 again he denied with an oath, I do not k.
26. 74 curse and to swear..I know not the man
27. 6 It is not lawful for to put them into the
27. 13 Hearest thou not how many things they
27. 34 and when he had tasted..he would not dr.
28. 6 He is not here; for he is risen, as he said
[This particle occurs in all about 1270 times.]

23. *By no means, in no wise,* οὐδαμῶς *oudamōs.*
Matt. 2. 6 art not the least among the princes of J.

24. *Not even,* οὐδέ *oude.*
Matt25. 45 Inasmuch as ye did..ye did (it) not to me
Mark12. 10 have ye not read this scripture; The stone
Luke12. 27 [they toil not, they spin not]; and yet I say
12. 27 Solomon in all his glory was not arrayed
23. 40 Dost not thou fear God, seeing thou art in
John 1. 3 without him was not any thing made that
1 Co. 4. 3 judged..yea, I judge not mine own self
14. 21 for all that will they not hear me, saith
Heb. 8. 4 if he were on earth he should not be a p.
1 Jo. 2. 23 denieth the Son, the same hath not the F.

25. *Not even one,* οὐδείς *oudeis.*
Luke 7. 28 there is not a greater prophet than John

26. *Not even,* οὔτε *oute.*
Luke12. 26 If ye then be not able to do that thing w.

27. *No, not,* οὐχί *ouchi.*
Matt. 5. 46 if ye love them which love you .do not ev.
5. 47 if ye salute your brethren..do not even
6. 25 Is not the life more than meat, and the bo.
10. 29 Are not two sparrows sold for a farthing?
12. 11 will he not lay hold on it, and lift (it) out?
13. 27 didst not thou sow good seed in thy field?
13. 55 is [not] his mother called Mary? and his
13. 56 And his sisters, are they not all with us?
18. 12 doth he not leave the ninety and nine, and
20. 13 didst not thou agree with me for a penny?
Luke 6. 39 shall they not both fall into the 1. 60.
12. 6 not one of them is forgotten before God
14. 28 which of you..sitteth not down first, and
14. 31 Or what king..sitteth not down first, and
15. 8 what woman..doth not light a candle, and
17. 8 will not rather say unto him, Make ready
17. 17 Were there [not] ten cleansed? but where
22. 27 (is) not he that sitteth at meat? but I am
24. 26 Ought not Christ to have suffered these t.
24. 32 Did not our heart burn within us, while
John 7. 42 Hath [not] the scripture said, That Christ
11. 9 Are there not twelve hours in the day? If
13. 10 Jesus saith..and ye are clean, but not all
13. 11 knew..therefore said he, Ye are not all cl.
14. 22 thou wilt manifest thyself unto us, and not
Acts 5. 4 Whiles it remained, was it not thine own?
7. 50 Hath not my hand made all these things
Rom. 2. 26 shall [not] his uncircumcision be counted
3. 29 (is he) not also of the Gentiles? Yes, of the
8. 32 how shall he not with him also freely give
1 Co. 1. 20 hath not God made foolish the wisdom of
3. 3 divisions, are ye [not] carnal, and walk as
3. 4 and another, I (am) of Apollos; are ye [not]
5. 2 ye are puffed up, and have not rather mo.
5. 12 For..do not ye judge them that are wit.?
6. 1 before the unjust, and not before the sa.?
6. 7 do ye not rather take wrong..why do ye n.
8. 10 shall not the conscience of him which is
9. 1 have I not seen Jesus Christ our Lord?
9. 8 Say I these things..saith [not] the law the
10. 16, 16 is it not the communion of the...Christ
10. 18 are [not] they which eat of the sacrifices
10. 29 Conscience, I say, not thine own, but of
2 Co. 3. 8 How shall not the ministration of the sp.
10. 13; 1 Th. 2. 19; Heb. 1. 14; 3. 17.

28. *If,* εἰ *ei,* Heb. 3. 11.

[*See also* And, after that, agreeing, albeit, also, appearing, as, ashamed, believe, believing, brawler, circumcised, commodious, doubtless, equal, even, failing, hereafter, hitherto, if, inhabited, know, knowledge, no, now, obey, please, possible, put under, regard, speak, suffer, surely, tempted, than, that, then, understand, whither, worthy.]

NOT any (man) —

1. *End, cessation, none,* אֶפֶס *ephes.*
2 Ki. 14. 26 not any shut up, nor any left, nor any h.

2. *Not,* בַּל *bal.*
Isa. 26. 18 we have not wrought any deliverance in

3. *Not even one,* μηδείς *mēdeis.*
Acts 10. 28 that I should not call any man common

4. *Not even one,* οὐδείς *oudeis,* Lu. 20. 40; Ac. 27. 34

NOT a whit —

Not even one, μηδείς *mēdeis.*
2 Co. 11. 5 I suppose I was not a whit behind the very

NOT...any more —

1. *Not any more,* μηκέτι *mēketi.*
Rom 14. 13 Let us not..judge one another any more

2. *Not any more, no more,* οὐκέτι *ouketi.*
Luke22. 16 I will [not any more] eat thereof, until it

NOT, for —

Without, בְּלֹא *be-lo.*
Isa. 55. 2 ye spend money for (that which is) not b.
55. 2 your labour for (that which) satisfieth not

NOT, of —

Of (or by) not, לְלֹא *le-lo.*
Isa. 65. 1 I am sought of (them that) asked not (for
65. 1 I am found of (them that) sought me not

NOT as yet —

Not any more, no more, οὐκέτι *ouketi* 2 Co. 1. 23
Not yet, μηδέπω *mēdepō,* Heb. 11. 7.

NOT at all —

1. *Not even one,* μηδείς *mēdeis.*
2 Th. 3. 11 working not at all, but are busy bodies

2. *Assuredly not, not at all,* οὐ μή *ou mē.*
Rev. 21. 25 the gates of it shall not be shut at all by

3. *Not even one,* οὐδείς *oudeis.*
Gal. 4. 12 Brethren..ye have not injured me at all

NOT (can) —

1. *Not to be able, to be unable,* οὐ δύναμαι *ou duna.*
Matt. 5. 14 city that is set on an hill cannot be hid
5. 36 thou canst not make one hair white or bl.
6. 24 Ye cannot serve God and mammon
7. 18 A good tree cannot bring forth evil fruit
16. 3 but can ye not..the signs of the times?
17. 16 thy disciples, and they could not cure him
17. 19 and said, Why could not we cast him out?
26. 53 Thinkest thou that I cannot now pray to
27. 42 He saved others; himself he cannot save
Mark 2. 19 as long as they have..with them, they can.
3. 24, 25 divided against itself, that..cannot st.
3. 26 divided, he cannot stand, but hath an end
6. 19 would have killed him; but she could not
7. 18 thing from without..(it) cannot defile him
7. 24 would have no man know..but he could not
9. 28 asked..Why could not we cast him out?
15. 31 He saved others; himself he cannot save
Luke 1. 22 when he came out, he could not speak unto
8. 19 and could not come at him for the press
9. 40 I besought thy disciples..they could not
11. 7 he from within shall answer..I cannot r.
14. 20 married a wife, and therefore I cannot c.
14. 26 hate not his father..he cannot be my di.
14. 27 doth not bear his cross..cannot be my d.
14. 33 that forsaketh not all..he cannot be my d.
16. 13 Ye cannot serve God and mammon
19. 3 could not for the press, because he was
John 3. 3 Except a man be born again, he cannot see
3. 5 he cannot enter into the kingdom of God
7. 7 The world cannot hate you; but me it h.
7. 34, 36 and where I am..ye cannot come
8. 21 Then said Jesus..whither I go, ye cannot
8. 22 because he saith, Whither I go, ye cannot
8. 43 do ye not..because ye cannot hear my w.
10. 35 called..and the Scripture cannot be bro.
12. 39 Therefore they could not believe, because
13. 33 Whither I go, ye cannot come; so now I
13. 36 Whither I go, thou canst not follow me
13. 37 Lord, why cannot I follow thee now? I w.
14. 17 the spirit of truth; whom the world can.
15. 4 As the branch cannot bear fruit of itself
16. 12 have yet many things..but ye cannot bear
Acts 4. 16 (is) manifest to all..and we cannot deny
4. 20 we cannot but speak the things which we
5. 39 if it be of God, ye cannot overthrow it
13. 39 from which ye could not be justified by
15. 1 Except ye be circumcised..ye cannot be
27. 31 Except these abide in the ship, ye cannot
Rom. 8. 8 So then they that are in the flesh cannot
1 Co. 3. 1 I, brethren, could not speak unto you as
10. 21 Ye cannot drink the cup of the Lord, and
10. 21 ye cannot be partakers of the Lord's table
12. 21 the eye cannot say unto the hand, I have
2 Co. 3. 7 so that the children of Israel could not s.
1 Ti. 5. 25 and they that are otherwise cannot be hid
2 Ti. 2. 13 he abideth faithful: he cannot deny him.
Heb. 3. 19 So we see that they could not enter in b.
Jas. 4. 2 ye kill, and desire to have, and cannot ob.
1 Jo. 3. 9 he cannot sin, because he is born of God
Rev. 2. 2 thou canst not bear them which are evil

2. *Not to be able,* μὴ δύναμαι *mē dunamai.*
Mark 2. 4 when they could not come nigh unto him
3. 20 so that they could not so much as eat br.
Luke 5. 19 when they could not find by what (way)
16. 26 so that they which would pass..cannot
20. 7 they answered, That they could not tell
Acts 21. 34 when he could not know the certainty for
27. 15 ship..could not bear up into the wind, we
Heb. 4. 15 we have not an high priest which cannot
9. 9 that could not make him that did the se.

3. *It is not,* οὐκ ἔστι *ouk esti.*
Heb. 9. 5 of which we cannot now speak particula.

4. *Not to have strength,* οὐκ ἰσχύω *ouk ischuō.*
Luke16. 3 What shall I do?..I cannot dig; to beg I

NOT be, (can) —

It is not receivable, οὐκ ἐνδέχεται *ouk endechetai.*
Luke13. 33 cannot be that a prophet perish out of J.

NOT contain, can —

Not to have inward strength, οὐκ ἐγκρατεύομαι.
1 Co. 7. 9 But if they cannot contain, let them ma.

NOT tell, can —

Not to know, οὐκ οἶδα *ouk oida.*
Matt21. 27 And they answered Jesus..We cannot tell
Mark11. 33 And they..said unto Jesus, We cannot t.
Luke20. 7 they answered, That they could not tell w.
John 3. 8 but canst not tell whence it cometh, and
8. 14 ye cannot tell whence I come, and whit.
16. 18 They said..we cannot tell what he saith
2 Co. 12. 2 a man..whether in the body, I cannot tell
12. 2 or whether out of the body, I cannot tell
12. 3 whether..out of the body, I cannot tell

NOT even, even...not —

Not even, οὐδέ *oude.*
Matt 6. 29 That even Solomon in all his glory was not
1 Co. 11. 14 Doth not even nature itself teach you, that

NOT henceforth, henceforth...not —

Not any more, μηκέτι *mēketi.*
Rom. 6. 6 that henceforth we should not serve sin
2 Co. 5. 15 they which live should not henceforth live
Eph. 4. 17 that ye henceforth walk not as other Ge.

NOT in me —

Without, save, besides me, בִּלְעָדַי *[bilade].*
Gen. 41. 16 Joseph answered Pharaoh..(It is) not in me

NOT...in any wise —

Assuredly not, not at all, οὐ μή *ou mē.*
Mark14. 31 he spake..I will not deny thee in any wise

NOT now, now...not —

Not any more, no more, οὐκέτι *ouketi.*
John 4. 42 Now we believe, not because of thy saying
21. 6 now they were not able to draw it for the
Rom 14. 15 grieved..now walkest thou not charitably
Phm. 16 Not now as a servant, but above a servant

NOT...once —

Not even, μηδέ *mēde.*
Eph. 5. 3 let it not be once named among you, as b.

NOT out of —

Without, in not, not in, בְּלֹא *be-lo.*
Psa. 17. 1 prayer, (that goeth) not out of feigned lips

NOT so —

By no means, in no wise, μηδαμῶς *mēdamōs.*
Acts 10. 14 Not so, Lord; for I have never eaten any
11. 8 Not so, Lord: for nothing common or un.

NOT so much as, no —

1. *Not even,* μηδέ *mēde.*
Mark 2. 2 no room..no, not so much as about the

2. *Not even,* ἀλλ' οὐδέ *all' oude.*
Luke 6. 3 Have ye not read so much as this, what
Acts 19. 2 We have not so much as heard whether
1 Co. 5. 1 as is not so much as named among the G.

NOT...yet —

1. *Not yet, before,* טֶרֶם *terem.*
Exod10. 7 knowest thou not yet that Egypt is dest.?
1 Sa. 3. 7 Now Samuel did not yet know the LORD

2. *Not even yet,* μηδέπω *mēdepō.*
Heb. 11. 7 warned of God of things not seen as yet

3. *Not yet,* μήπω *mēpō.*
Rom. 9. 11 For (the children) being not yet born, ne.
Heb. 9. 8 way into the holiest of all was not yet m.

4. *Not even yet,* οὐδέπω *oudepō.*
John 7. 39 because that Jesus was [not yet] glorified

5. *Not yet,* οὔπω *oupō.*
Matt 15. 17 Do not ye [yet] understand, that whatsoev.
16. 9 Do ye not yet understand, neither reme.
24. 6 must come to pass, but the end is not yet
Mark 8. 17 perceive ye not yet, neither understand?
13. 7 needs be; but the end (shall) not (be) yet
John 2. 4 Jesus saith..mine hour is not yet come
3. 24 For John was not yet cast into prison
7. 6 My time is not yet come: but your time is
7. 8 I go not up [yet]..for my time is not yet
7. 30 laid hands..because his hour was not yet
7. 39 the Holy Ghost was not yet..because that
8. 20 laid hands..for his hour was not yet come
8. 57 Thou art not yet fifty years old, and hast
11. 30 Now Jesus was not yet come into the town
20. 17 Touch me not; for I am not yet ascended
Heb. 2. 8 now we see not yet all things put under
12. 4 Ye have not yet resisted unto blood, str.
1 Jo. 3. 2 it doth not yet appear what we shall be
Rev. 17. 10 one is..the other is [not yet] come; and

NOT to be —

[*See* Approached, condemned, repented of, spoken against.]

NOTABLE (one), of note —

1. *Vision, sight,* חָזוּת *chazuth.*
Dan. 8. 5 the goat (had) a notable horn between his
8. 8 for it came up four notable ones, toward

2. *Known, knowable,* γνωστός *gnōstos.*
Acts 4. 16 for that indeed a notable miracle hath b.

3. *Noted, notable,* ἐπίσημος *episēmos.*
Matt27. 16 they had then a notable prisoner, called
Rom 16. 7 who are of note among the apostles, who

4. *Very manifest,* ἐπιφανής *epiphanēs.*
Acts 2. 20 before that great and notable day of the

NOTE, be noted, to —

1. *To grave, decree, write,* חָקַק *chaqaq.*
Isa. 30. 8 note it in a book, that it may be for the

2. *To note down, note, sign,* רָשַׁם *rasham.*
Dan. 10. 21 I will show thee that which is noted in

3. *To put a sign on,* σημειόω *sēmeioō.*
2 Th. 3. 14 note that man, and have no company with

NOTHING, no thing —

1. *There is not, there are not,* אַיִן *ayin.*
Eccl. 3. 14 nothing can be put to it, nor ; Isa. 41. 24.

2. *End, cessation, nothing,* אֶפֶס *ephes.*
Isa. 34. 12 They shall call..her princes shall be noth.
41. 29 their works (are) nothing : their molten

3. *Without any thing,* בְּלִימָה *belimah.*
Job 26. 7 stretcheth..hangeth the earth upon noth.

4. *Without, save, not,* בִּלְתִּי *bilti.*
Isa. 44. 10 or molten a graven image..profitable for n.
Amos 3. 4 cry out of his den if he hath taken noth.?

5. *Ruin, vacancy,* תֹּהוּ *tohu.*
Job 6. 18 The paths..are turned aside; they go to n.

6. *Not a thing,* לֹא דָבָר *lo dabar.*
Gen. 19. 8 do ye to them..only unto these men do n.
1 Sa. 20. 2 my father will do nothing, either great or

7. *Not any (thing),* לֹא כֹּל *lo kol.*
Gen. 11. 6 now nothing will be restrained from them
Prov. 13. 7 There is that maketh himself rich, yet..n.

8. *Not any thing,* לֹא מְאוּמָה *lo meumah.*
Gen. 40. 15 here also have I done nothing that they
Judg 14. 6 he rent him..and..nothing in his hand
1 Sa. 25. 21 so that nothing was missed of all that
1 Ki. 10. 21 it was nothing accounted of in the days of
18. 43 and looked, and said, (There is) nothing
Eccl. 5. 14 begetteth a son, and (there is) nothing
5. 15 shall take nothing of his labour, which he
7. 14 that man should find nothing after him
Jer. 39. 10 of the poor of the people which had noth.

9. *Not any thing,* בַּל מָה *bal mah.*
Prov. 9. 13 A foolish woman..knoweth nothing

10. *Not,* μή *mē.*
Luke 7. 42 when they had nothing to pay, he frankly

11. *Not anything,* μή τι *mē ti.*
Mark 8. 1 being very great, and having nothing to
1 Co. 4. 5 Therefore judge nothing before the time

12. *Not any one,* μηδείς *mēdeis.*
Matt 27. 19 Have thou nothing to do with that just m.
Mark 1. 44 See thou say nothing to any man : but go
5. 26 was nothing bettered, but rather grew w.
6. 8 that they should take nothing for..journey
Luke 6. 35 do good, and lend, hoping for nothing ag
9. 3 Take nothing for (your) journey, neither
Acts 4. 21 finding nothing how they might punish th.
10. 20 Arise..and go with them, doubting noth
11. 12 spirit bade me go with them, nothing do.
19. 36 ought to be quiet, and to do nothing ras.
23. 14 will eat nothing until we have slain Paul
23. 29 to have nothing laid to his charge worthy
25. 25 had committed nothing worthy of death
27. 33 continued fasting, having taken nothing
2 Co. 6. 10 as having nothing, and ..possessing all t.
7. 9 ye might receive damage by us in nothing
Gal. 6. 3 think..to be something, when he is not.
Phil. 1. 28 in nothing terrified by your adversaries
2. 3 (Let) nothing (be done) through strife or
4. 6 Be careful for nothing ; but in every thing
1 Th. 4. 12 honestly..and..ye may have lack of not.
1 Ti. 5. 21 observe these..doing nothing by partial.
6. 4 He is proud, knowing nothing, but doting
Titus 2. 8 ashamed, having no evil thing to say of
3. 13 Bring..that nothing be wanting unto t
Jas. 1. 4 may be perfect and entire, wanting not.
1. 6 But let him ask in faith, nothing waveri.
3 John 7 went forth, taking nothing of the Gentiles

13. *No, not,* οὐ *ou.*
Luke 8. 17 For nothing is secret that shall not be
11. 6 come..and I have nothing to set before him
1 Co. 9. 16 though I preach..I have nothing to glory

14. *Not any,* οὔ τις *ou tis.*
Matt 15. 32 they continue..and have nothing to eat
Mark 6. 36 buy..bread: [for they have nothing to eat]
8. 2 with me three days, and have nothing to

15. *Not any word,* οὐ πᾶν ῥῆμα *ou pan rhēma.*
Luke 1. 37 For with God nothing shall be impossible

16. *Not even any,* οὐ δέ τις *ou de tis.*
1 Ti. 6. 7 it is) certain we can carry nothing out

17. *Not even one,* οὐδείς *oudeis.*
Matt. 5. 13 it is thenceforth good for nothing, but to
10. 26 there is nothing covered that shall not be
17. 20 and nothing shall be impossible unto you
21. 19 found nothing thereon, but leaves only
23. 16 shall swear by the temple, it is nothing
23. 18 shall swear by the altar, it is nothing ; but
26. 62 said unto him, Answerest thou nothing?
27. 12 when he was accused..he answered not.
27. 24 When Pilate saw that he could prevail n.
Mark 7. 15 There is nothing from without a man, t.
9. 29 This kind can come forth by nothing but
11. 13 when he came to it, he found nothing but
14. 60 asked Jesus, saying, Answerest thou not.?
14. 61 But he held his peace, and answered no.
15. 3 accused him..[but he answered nothing]
15. 4 Pilate asked him..Answerest thou noth.?
15. 5 Jesus yet answered nothing; so that Pilate
Luke 4. 2 in those days he did eat nothing : and w.
5. 5 we have toiled..and have taken nothing
10. 19 and nothing shall by any means hurt you
Luke 12. 2 there is nothing covered, that shall not be
22. 35 lacked ye any thing? And they said, No.
23. 9 he questioned..but he answered him no.
23. 15 nothing worthy of death is done unto him
23. 41 but this man hath done nothing amiss
John 3. 27 A man can receive nothing, except it be
5. 19 The Son can do nothing of himself, but w.
5. 30 I can of mine own self do nothing : as I h.
6. 63 the flesh profiteth nothing : the words that
7. 26 he speaketh boldly, and they say nothing
8. 28 shall ye know..(that) I do nothing of mys.
8. 54 If I honour myself, my honour is nothing
9. 33 this man were not of God, he could do n.
12. 19 Perceive ye how ye prevail nothing? beh.
14. 30 prince..cometh, and hath nothing in me
15. 5 branches..without me ye can do nothing
16. 23 And in that day ye shall ask me nothing
16. 24 Hitherto have ye asked nothing in my n.
18. 20 Jesus answered..in secret have I said n.
21. 3 They went..and that night they caught n.
Acts 4. 14 beholding the man..they could say noth.
17. 21 spent their time in nothing else, but eit.
20. 20 how I kept back nothing that was profit.
21. 24 all may know that those things..are noth.
26. 31 This man doeth nothing worthy of death
28. 17 though I have committed nothing against
Rom 14. 14 that (there is) nothing unclean of itself
1 Co. 4. 4 For I know nothing by myself ; yet am I
7. 19 Circumcision is n...uncircumcision is no
8. 2 he knoweth [nothing] yet as he ought to
8. 4 we know that an idol (is) nothing in the
13. 3 have not charity, it profiteth me nothing
2 Co. 12. 11 in nothing am I behind..though I be no.
Gal. 2. 6 for they who seemed..added nothing to
4. 1 differeth nothing from a servant, though
5. 2 if..circumcised, Christ shall profit you n.
Phil. 1. 20 hope, that in nothing I shall be ashamed
1 Ti. 4. 4 nothing to be refused, if it be received w
6. 7 For we brought nothing into (this) world
Titus 1. 15 unto them that are defiled..(is) nothing
Phm. 14 But without thy mind would I do nothing
Heb. 2. 8; 7. 14; 7. 19; Rev. 3. 17.

18. *Nothing,* οὐθέν *outhen,* 1 Co. 13. 2.

19. *Not even,* οὔτε *oute.*
John 4. 11 Sir, thou hast nothing to draw with, and

NOTHING...at any time, at all —

Any thing not even at any time, πᾶν...οὐδέποτε.
Acts 11. 8 [nothing] common or unclean hath at any t.

Not a thing, οὐκ οὐθέν *ouk outhen,* Jo. 11. 49.

NOTHING, as —

No, nothing, לָה *lah.*
Dan. 4. 35 all the inhabitants..(are) reputed as not.

NOTHING, to bring to —

1. *To make few, little,* מָעַט *maat,* 5.
Jer. 10. 24 in thine anger, lest thou bring me to no.

2. *To put away or aside,* ἀθετέω *atheteō.*
1 Co. 1. 19 will bring to nothing the understanding

NOTHING but —

Only, רַק *raq.*
Gen. 26. 29 we have done unto thee nothing but good

NOTHING, (for) —

Gratis, free, for nought, חִנָּם *chinnam.*
Exod 21. 2 the seventh he shall go out free for noth.
2 Sa. 24. 24 offer..that which doth cost me nothing

NOTHING worth —

For nothing, לְאַל *le-al.*
Job 24. 25 who will..make my speech nothing wo.?

NOTICE, to take —

To discern, נָכַר *nakar,* 5.
2 Sa. 3. 36 all the people took notice..and it pleased

NOTICE before, to have —

To tell or announce beforehand, προκαταγγέλλω.
2 Co. 9. 5 your bounty whereof [ye had notice bef.]

NOTWITHSTANDING —

1. *Only,* אַךְ *ak.*
Exod 21. 21 Notwithstanding, if he continue a day or

2. *And only,* וְאַךְ *ve-ak.*
Josh 22. 19 Notwithstanding, if the land of your po.

3. *End, cessation, nothing,* אֶפֶס *ephes.*
Judg. 4. 9 notwithstanding the journey that thou

4. *Only,* רַק *raq.*
2 Ch. 6 9 Notwithstanding thou shalt not build the

5. *But,* ἀλλά *alla.*
Rev. 2. 20 Notwithstanding I have a few things ag.

6. *But yet,* πλήν *plēn.*
Luke 10. 11 notwithstanding, be ye sure of this, that
10. 20 Notwithstanding in this rejoice not, that
Phil. 1. 18 notwithstanding, every way, whether in
4. 14 Notwithstanding ye have done well that

NOUGHT —

1. *Vanity,* אָוֶן *aven.*
Amos 5. 5 seek not Beth-el..Beth-el shall come to n.

2. *Ruin, vacancy,* תֹּהוּ *tohu.*
Isa. 49. 4 I have spent my strength for nought, and

3. *Not anything,* לֹא מְאוּמָה *lo meumah.*
Deut 13. 17 there shall cleave nought of the cursed

4. *Confutation, full conviction,* ἀπελεγμός *apelegmos.*
Acts 19. 27 our craft is in danger to be set at nought

5. *Not even one,* οὐδείς *oudeis.*
Acts 5. 36 all..were scattered, and brought to noug.

NOUGHT, for —

1. *Gratis, for nought,* חִנָּם *chinnam.*
Gen. 29. 15 shouldest thou therefore serve me for n.?
Job 1. 9 and said, Doth Job fear God for nought?
22. 6 taken a pledge from thy brother for nou.
Isa. 52. 3 Ye have sold yourselves for nought ; and
52. 5 that my people is taken away for nought?
Mal. 1. 10 do ye kindle (fire) on mine altar for nou.

2. *Without wealth or substance,* בְּלֹא הוֹן *be-lo hon.*
Psa. 44. 12 Thou sellest thy people for nought, and

3. *Freely, without payment,* δωρεάν *dōrean.*
2 Th. 3. 8 Neither did we eat any man's bread for n.

NOUGHT, (thing) of —

1. *Nought, nothing,* אֶפַע *epha.*
Isa. 41. 24 ye (are) of nothing, and your work of no.

2. *End, cessation, nothing,* אֶפֶס *ephes.*
Isa. 41. 12 shall be as nothing, and as a thing of no.

3. *Not a thing,* לֹא דָבָר *lo dabar.*
Amos 6. 13 Ye which rejoice in a thing of nought, w.

4. *Ruin, vacancy,* תֹּהוּ *tohu.*
Isa. 29. 21 turn aside the just for a thing of nought

NOUGHT, to bring or come to —

1. *To fade or wear away,* נָבֵל *nabel.*
Job 14. 18 surely the mountain falling cometh to n

2. *To make void,* פּוּר *pur,* 5.
Psa. 33. 10 bringeth the counsel of the heathen to n.

3. *To break off, make void,* פָּרַר *parar,* 5.
Neh. 4. 15 God had brought their counsel to nought

4. *To be broken, made void,* פָּרַר *parar,* 6.
Isa. 8. 10 Take counsel..and it shall come to nought

5. *To cut off, lay waste, destroy,* שָׁמַד *shamad,* 5.
Deut 28. 63 destroy you, and to bring you to nought

6. *To desolate, lay waste,* ἐρημόω *erēmoō.*
Rev. 18. 17 in one hour so great riches is come to n.

7. *To make useless, without effect,* καταργέω *katar.*
1 Co. 1. 28 things which are not, to bring to nought
2. 6 princes of this world, that come to nought

8. *To loose down,* καταλύω *kataluō.*
Acts 5. 38 if..this work be of men, it will come to no.

NOUGHT, to be brought to —

To cease, fail, have an end, אָפֵס *aphes.*
Isa. 29. 20 For the terrible one is brought to nought

NOUGHT, to set at —

To free, make void, refuse, פָּרַע *para.*
Prov. 1. 25 But ye have set at nought all my counsel

NOUGHT, to come to —

It is not, אַיִן *ayin.*
Job 8. 22 place of the wicked shall come to nought

NOURISH (up in), to —

1. *To make great, magnify, bring up,* גָּדַל *gadal,* 3.
Isa. 1. 2 I have nourished and brought up children
23. 4 neither do I nourish up young men, (nor)
44. 14 planteth an ash, and the rain doth nour.
Dan. 1. 5 so nourishing them three years, that at the

2. *To keep living or alive,* חָיָה *chayah,* 3.
2 Sa. 12. 3 which he had bought and nourished up
Isa. 7. 21 shall nourish a young cow and two sheep

3. *To provide, nourish, sustain,* כּוּל *kul,* 3a.
Gen. 45. 11 And there will I nourish thee ; for yet
47. 12 Joseph nourished his father, and his bre.
50. 21 I will nourish you, and your little ones
Ruth 4. 15 he shall be..a nourisher of thine old age

4. *To multiply, nourish,* רָבָה *rabah,* 3.
Eze. 19. 2 she nourished her whelps among young

5. *To nourish or bring up,* ἀνατρέφω *anatrephō.*
Acts 7. 20 nourished up in his father's house three
7. 21 took him up, and nourished him for her

6. *To nourish much,* ἐκτρέφω *ektrephō.*
Eph. 5. 29 nourisheth and cherisheth it, even as the

7. *To be nourished in,* ἐντρέφομαι *entrephomai.*
1 Ti. 4. 6 nourished up in the words of faith and of

8. *To nourish,* τρέφω *trephō.*
Acts 12. 20 because their country was nourished by
Jas. 5. 5 ye have nourished your hearts, as in a day
Rev. 12. 14 where she is nourished for a time, and t.

NOURISHMENT ministered, to have —

To supply besides, ἐπιχορηγέω *epichorēgeō.*
Col. 2. 19 having nourishment ministered, and knit

NOVICE —

One newly planted, νεόφυτος *neophutos.*
1 Ti. 3. 6 Not a novice, lest being lifted up with p.

NOW —

1. *Then,* אֱדַיִן *edayin.*
Ezra 4. 23 Now when the copy of king Artaxerxes'

2. *Then,* אָז *az.*
Josh. 22. 31 now ye have delivered the children of I.

3. *Here, now,* אֵפוֹא, אֵפוֹ *ephō.*
Gen. 27. 37 what shall I do now unto thee, my son?
43. 11 father Israel said unto them, If..so now
Judg. 9. 38 Where (is) now thy mouth, wherewith thou
2 Ki. 10. 10 Know now that there shall fall unto the
Job 17. 15 where (is) now my hope? as for my hope

Job. 19. 6 Know now that God hath overthrown me
19. 23 Oh that my words were now written! Oh
24. 25 And if..not (so) now, who will make me
Prov. 6. 3 Do this now, my son, and deliver thyself
Isa. 22. 1 What aileth thee now, that thou art wh.

4. *Here, hither, then,* הֵנָּה *henah.*
Num14. 19 hast forgiven this people..even until now

5. *This,* זֶה *zeh.*
2 Ki. 1. 5 said unto them, Why are ye now turned

6. *To day,* הַיּוֹם *hay-yom.*
Deut31. 21 even now, before I have brought them into
1 Sa. 9. 9 for (he that is) now (called) a prophet was
Neh. 1. 6 I pray before thee now, day and night
Jer. 34. 15 ye were now turned, and had done right

7. *Already, now,* כְּבָר *kebar.*
Eccl. 3. 15 That which hath been is now; and that
9. 6 their hatred, and their envy, is now per.
9. 7 Go thy way..God now accepteth thy works

8. *Because,* כִּי *ki.*
Josh. 5. 5 Now all the people that came out were

9. *Now,* כְּעַן *kean.*
Ezra 4. 13 Be it known now unto the king, that if
4. 14 Now because we have maintenance from
4. 21 Give ye now commandment to cause these
5. 16 since that time even until now hath it
6. 6 Now..Tatnai, governor beyond the river
Dan. 2. 23 hast made known unto me now what we
3. 15 Now if ye be ready that at what time ye
4. 37 Now I Nebuchadnezzar praise and extol
5. 12 now let Daniel be called, and he will show
5. 15 now the wise (men), the astrologers, have
5. 16 now if thou canst read the writing, and
6. 8 Now, O king, establish the decree, and si.

10. *Pray, please now,* נָא *na.*
Gen. 12. 11 Behold now, I know that thou (art) a fair

11. *Now,* עַתָּה *attah.*
Gen. 22. 12 now I know that thou fearest God, seeing
26. 22 now the LORD hath made room for us, and
26. 29 thou (art) now the blessed of the LORD

12. *A step, time,* פַּעַם *paam.*
Gen. 2. 23 This (is) now bone of my bones, and flesh
29. 35 and she said, Now will I praise the LORD
30. 20 now will my husband dwell with me, bec.
46. 30 Now let me die, since I have seen thy face
Prov. 7. 12 Now (is she) without, now in the streets

13. *Now, at present,* ἄρτι *arti.*
Matt. 3. 15 Jesus answering..unto him, Suffer..now
11. 12 from the days of J. the Baptist until now
26. 53 Thinkest thou that I cannot now pray to
John 2. 10 thou hast kept the good wine until now
9. 19 born blind? how then doth he now see?
9. 25 I know, that, whereas I was blind, now I
13. 7 What I do thou knowest not now; but
13. 19 Now I tell you before it come, that, when
13. 33 as I said unto the Jews..so now I say to
13. 37 Why cannot I follow thee now? I will
16. 12 things to say..ye cannot bear them now
16. 31 Jesus answered them, Do ye now believe?
1 Co.13. 12 For now we see through a glass, darkly
13. 12 now I know in part; but then shall I know
16. 7 For I will not see you now by the way; but
Gal. 1. 9 As we said before, so say I now again, If
1. 10 For do I now persuade men, or God? or
4. 20 I desire to be present with you now, and
1 Th. 3. 6 But now when Timotheus came from you
2 Th. 2. 7 only he who now letteth (will let), until he
1 Pe. 1. 6 though now for a season, if need be, ye are
1. 8 in whom, though now ye see (him) not, yet
1 Jo. 2. 9 He that..hateth..is in darkness..until now
Rev. 12. 10 Now is come salvation, and strength, and

14. *But, now, and, further* δέ *de.*
Matt 1. 22 Now all this was done that it might be
[*See also* John 5. 25; 6. 10; 19. 23; Acts 27. 9; Rom. 15. 8; 1 Cor. 10. 11; 15. 50; Gal. 1. 20; 4. 1, &c.]

15. *Truly, certainly, therefore,* δή *dē.*
Luke 2. 15 Let us now go even unto Bethlehem, and

16. *Still, yet, hitherto,* ἔτι *eti.*
John21. 6 now they were not able to draw it for the
Rom 14. 15 if thy brother be grieved..now walkest

17. *Now, already,* ἤδη *ēdē.*
Matt. 3. 10 now also the ax is laid unto the root of
14. 15 This is a desert place, and the time is now
14. 24 the ship was now in the midst of the sea
15. 32 because they continue with me now three
Mark 4. 37 beat into the ship, so that it was now full
6. 35 And when the day was now far spent, his
6. 35 This is a desert place, and now the time
8. 2 because they have now been with me three
11. 11 now the eventide was come, he went out
15. 42 now when the even was come, because it
Luke 3. 9 now also the ax is laid unto the root of
7. 6 when he was now not far from the house
11. 7 Trouble me not: the door is now shut, and
14. 17 to say..Come; for all things are now ready
21. 30 When they now shoot forth, ye see and
21. 30 and know..that summer is now nigh at h.
John 4. 51 as he was now going down, his servants
5. 6 knew that he had been now a long time
6. 17 it was now dark, and Jesus was not come
7. 14 Now about the midst of the feast, Jesus
13. 2 the devil having now put into the heart of
15. 3 Now ye are clean through the word which
19. 28 Jesus knowing that all things were now
21. 4 when the morning was now come, Jesus
21. 14 This is now the third time that Jesus show.

Acts 4. 3 and put..in hold..for it was now eventide
27. 9 when sailing was now dangerous, because
Rom. 1. 10 if by any means now at length I might h.
4. 19 he considered not his own body [now] d.
13. 11 now (it is) high time to awake out of sleep
1 Co. 4. 8 Now ye are full, now ye are rich, ye have
6. 7 Now therefore there is utterly a fault am.
Phil. 4. 10 that now at the last your care of me hath
2 Ti. 4. 6 I am now ready to be offered, and the time
2 Pe. 3. 1 This second epistle, beloved, I now write
1 Jo. 2. 8 darkness is past, and the true light now s.

18. *As to the rest, henceforth,* τὸ λοιπόν *to loipon.*
Matt26. 45 Sleep on now, and take..rest, behold, the
Mark14. 41 Sleep on now, and take..rest: it is enough

19. *Now,* νῦν *nun.*
Matt26. 65 behold, now ye have heard his blasphemy
27. 42 let him now come down from the cross, and
27. 43 let him deliver him now, if he will have
Mark10. 30 he shall receive an hundred fold now in
15. 32 Let Christ the king of Israel descend now
Luke 2. 29 now lettest thou thy servant depart in p.
6. 21 Blessed (are ye) that hunger now: for ye
6. 21 Blessed (are ye) that weep now: for ye sh.
6. 25 Woe unto you that laugh now! for ye sh.
11. 39 Now do ye Pharisees make clean the out.
16. 25 now he is comforted, and thou art torm.
19. 42 If thou hadst known..but now they are
22. 36 But now, he that hath a purse, let him t.
John 2. 8 Draw out now, and bear unto the governor
4. 18 he whom thou now hast is not thy husband
4. 23 the hour cometh, and now is, when the
5. 25 The hour is coming, and now is, when the
8. 40 But now ye seek to kill me, a man that
8. 52 said..Now we know that thou hast a de.
9. 21 by what means he now seeth, we know not
9. 41 now ye say, We see; therefore your sin re.
11. 22 But I know, that even now, whatsoever
12. 27 Now is my soul troubled; and what shall
12. 31 Now is the judgment of this world: now
13. 31 Now is the Son of man glorified, and God
13. 36 Whither I go, thou canst not follow me n
14. 29 now I have told you before it come to p.
15. 22 but now they have no cloak for their sin
15. 24 now have they both seen and hated both
16. 5 But now I go my way to him that sent me
16. 22 ye now therefore have sorrow; but I will
16. 29 now speakest thou plainly, and speakest
16. 30 Now are we sure that thou knowest all
16. 32 Behold, the hour cometh, yea, is [now] c.
17. 5 now, O Father, glorify thou me with th.
17. 7 Now they have known that all things w.
17. 13 now come I to thee; and these things I
18. 36 but now is my kingdom not from hence
21. 10 Bring of the fish which ye have now cau.
Acts 2. 33 he hath shed forth this, which ye [now]
3. 17 now, brethren, I wot that through igno.
7. 4 removed him into this land, wherein ye n.
7. 34 And now come, I will send thee into E.
7. 52 of whom ye have been now the betrayers
10. 5 And now send men to Joppa, and call for
10. 33 Now therefore are we all here present b.
12. 11 Now I know of a surety, that the Lord
13. 11 now, behold, the hand of the Lord (is) u.
15. 10 Now therefore why tempt ye God, to put
16. 36 sent..now therefore depart, and go in p.
16. 37 now do they thrust us out privily? nay
20. 22 now, behold, I go bound in the spirit unto
20. 25 now, behold, I know that ye all, among
22. 1 fathers, hear ye my defence..now unto you
22. 16 now why tarriest thou? arise, and be bap.
23. 15 Now therefore ye with the council signi.
23. 21 now are they ready, looking for a promise
24. 13 can they prove the things whereof they [n.]
26. 6 now I stand and am judged for the hope
26. 17 the Gentiles, unto whom [now] I send thee
Rom. 3. 21 But now the righteousness of God without
5. 9 being now justified by his blood, we shall
5. 11 by whom we have now received the aton.
6. 19 now yield your members servants to right.
6. 21 those things whereof ye are now ashamed?
8. 1 therefore now no condemnation to them
8. 22 and travaileth in pain together until now
11. 30 have now obtained mercy through their
11. 31 Even so have these also now not believed
13. 11 now (is) our salvation nearer than when we
16. 26 But now is made manifest, and by the Sc.
1 Co. 3. 2 ye were not able..neither yet now are ye
7. 14 else were your children unclean; but now
12. 20 But now..many members, yet but one b.
2 Co. 5. 16 yet now henceforth know we (him) no m.
6. 2 now (is) the accepted time..now (is) the d.
7. 9 Now I rejoice, not that ye were made so.
13. 2 being absent now I write to them which
Gal. 1. 23 now preacheth the faith which once he d.
2. 20 the life which I now live in the flesh I l.
3. 3 having begun in the Spirit, are ye now
4. 9 But now, after that ye have known God
4. 25 answereth to Jerusalem which now is, and
4. 29 as then he..persecuted him..so..now
Eph. 2. 2 the spirit that now worketh in the child.
3. 5 as it is now revealed unto his holy apost.
3. 10 To the intent that now, unto the princi.
5. 8 For ye were sometimes darkness, but now
Phil. 1. 5 in the gospel from the first day until now
1. 20 now also Christ shall be magnified in my
1. 30 ye saw in me, (and) now hear (to be) in
2. 12 but now much more in my absence, work
3. 18 I have told you often, and now tell you even
Col. 1. 24 Who now rejoice in my sufferings for you
1 Th. 3. 8 now we live, if ye stand fast in the Lord
2 Th. 2. 6 now ye know what withholdeth, that he
1 Ti. 4. 8 having promise of the life that now is, and
2 Ti. 1. 10 But is now made manifest by the appear.
Heb. 2. 8 But now we see not yet all things put un.
9. 5 of which we cannot now speak particula.
9. 24 now to appear in the presence of God for
9. 26 but [now] once, in the end of the world
12. 26 but now he hath promised, saying, Yet
Jas. 4. 13 Go to now, ye that say, To day, or to mo.
4. 16 But now ye rejoice in your boastings: all
5. 1 Go to now..rich men, weep and howl for
1 Pe. 1. 12 they did minister the things which are now
2. 10 (are) now the people of God..but now h.
2. 25 but are now returned unto the shepherd
3. 21 whereunto..baptism doth also now save
2 Pe. 3. 7 the heavens and the earth which are now
3. 18 To him (be) glory both now and for ever
1 Jo. 2. 18 even now are there many antichrists, wh.
2. 28 And now, little children, abide in him
3. 2 Beloved, now are we the sons of God; and
4. 3 and even now already is it in the world
2 John 5 And now I beseech thee, lady, not as th.
Jude 25 (be) glory and majesty..both now and ever

20. *The now, the present things,* τὰ νῦν *ta nun.*
Acts 4. 29 And now, Lord, behold their threatenings
5. 38 And now I say unto you, Refrain from th.
20. 32 And now, brethren, I commend you to G.
27. 22 And now I exhort you to be of good che.

21. *Now, at this moment,* νυνί *nuni.*
Rom. 6. 22 But now being made free from sin, and
7. 6 But now we are delivered from the law
7. 17 Now then it is no more I that do it, but
15. 23 But now having no more place in these
15. 25 But now I go unto Jerusalem to minister
1 Co. 5. 11 But now I have written unto you not to
12. 18 But now hath God set the members every
13. 13 And now abideth faith, hope, charity, th.
14. 6 Now, brethren, if I come unto you spea.
15. 20 But now is Christ risen from the dead
2 Co. 8. 11 Now therefore perform the doing..that
8. 22 but now much more diligent, upon the
Eph. 2. 13 But now in Christ Jesus ye who someti.
Col. 1. 21 you, that were..alienated..now hath he
1. 26 the mystery which..now is made manifest
3. 8 But now ye also put off all these; anger
Phm. 9 and now also a prisoner of Jesus Christ
11 but now profitable to thee and to me
Heb. 8. 6 But now hath he obtained a more excell.
11. 16 But [now] they desire a better..that is, an

22. *Therefore, then, now,* οὖν *oun.*
Mark12. 20 [Now] there were seven brethren: and the
Luke10. 36 Which [now] of these three, thinkest thou
John16. 19 [Now] Jesus knew that they were desirous
19. 29 [Now] there was set a vessel full of vine.
21. 7 Now when Simon Peter heard that it was
Acts 1. 18 Now this man purchased a field with the
11. 19 Now they which were scattered abroad
25. 1 Now when Festus was come, 1 Co. 9. 25.

23. *And,* καί *kai,* 1 Co. 4. 7.

NOW already —
Even now or already, καὶ ἤδη *kai ēdē.*
Acts 27. 9 because the fast was now already past, F.

NOW...not, or no more —
Not any more, no more, οὐκέτι *ouketi.*
John 4. 42 Now we believe, not because of thy say.
17. 11 And now I am no more in the world, but
21. 6 now they were not able to draw it for the
Rom 14. 15 be grieved..now walkest thou not charit.
Phm. 16 Not now as a servant, but above a servant

NOW then, or henceforth —
Therefore, then, now, οὖν *oun.*
2 Co. 5. 20 Now then we are ambassadors 2 Co. 5. 16.

NOW, seeing that which —
Already, now, כְּבָר *kebar.*
Eccl. 2. 16 seeing that which now (is), in the days to

NUMBER —

1. *Search, searching,* חֵקֶר *cheqer.*
Job 34. 24 break in pieces mighty men without num.

2. *Number, amount,* מִכְסָה *miksah.*
Exod12. 4 take..according to the number of the souls

3. *Meni, goddess of fate,* מְנִי *meni.*
Isa. 65. 11 furnish the drink offering unto that num.

4. *Number,* מִנְיָן *minyan.*
Ezra 6. 17 according to the number of the tribes of

5. *Number, narration, reckoning,* מִסְפָּר *mispar.*
Gen. 34. 30 few in number, they shall gather thems.
41. 49 he left numbering; for (it was) without n.
Exod16. 16 an omer for every man..the number of y.
23. 26 barren..the number of thy days I will ful
Lev. 25. 15, 15 According to the number of years
25. 16 to the number..of the fruits doth he sell
25. 50 shall be according unto the number of y.
Num. 1. 2 with the number of..names, every male
1. 18 according to the number of the names
So in v. 20, 22, 24, 26, 28, 30, 32, 34, 36, 38, 40, 42.
3. 22, 34 according to the number of all the m.
3. 28 In the number of all the males, from a m.
3. 40 LORD said..take the number of their na.
3. 43 all the first born males by the number of
14. 29 according to your whole number, from t.
14. 34 After the number of the days in which ye
15. 12 According to the number that ye shall pr.
15. 12 do to every one according to their number
23. 10 and the number of the fourth..of Israel
26. 53 divided..according to the number of na

Num29. 18, 21, 24, 27, 30, 33, 37 according to their n.
31. 36 the half..was in number three hundred
Deut. 4. 27 ye shall be left few in number among the
32. 8 according to the number of the children
Josh 4. 5, 8 according unto the number of the tribes
Judg. 6. 5 they and their camels were without num.
7. 6 the number of them that lapped, (putting)
7. 12 their camels (were) without number, as
21. 23 and took..wives, according to their num.
1 Sa. 6. 4 the number of the lords of the Philistines
6. 18 the number of all the cities of the Philis.
2 Sa. 2. 15 Then there arose and went over by numb.
21. 20 every foot six toes, four and twenty in n.
24. 2 that I may know the number of the peo.
1 Ki.18. 31 according to the number of the tribes of
1 Ch. 7. 2 whose number (was) in the days of David
7. 40 the number throughout the genealogy of
11. 11 this (is) the number of the mighty men
12. 23 these (are) the numbers of the bands..rea.
21. 2 bring the number of them to me that I
21. 5 Joab gave the sum of the number of the
22. 16 Of the gold..and the iron..no number
23. 3 their number by their polls, man by man
23. 24 as they were counted by number of names
23. 31 by number, according to the order com.
25. 1 the number of the workmen according to
25. 7 So the number of them, with their breth.
27. 1 Now the children of Israel after their n.
27. 23 David took not the number of them from
27. 24 neither was the number put in the acco
2 Ch.12. 3 the people (were) without number that c
26. 11 according to the number of their account
26. 12 The whole number of the chief of the fa
29. 32 the number of the burnt offerings, which
35. 7 to the number of thirty thousand, and th.
Ezra 1. 9 this (is) the number of them: thirty cha.
2. 2 The number of the men of the people of
3. 4 the daily burnt offerings by number. ac.
8. 34 By number (and) by weight of every one
Neh. 7. 7 the number..of the men of the people of
Esth. 9. 11 On that day the number of those that w.
Job 1. 5 burnt offerings..to the number of them
3. 6 let it not come in to the number of the m.
5. 9 doeth..marvellous things without numb.
9. 10 doeth great things wonders without nu.
14. 5 the number of his months (are) with thee
15. 20 the number of years is hidden to the op
21. 21 when the number of his months is cut off
25. 3 Is there any number of his armies? and
31. 37 I would declare unto him the number of
36. 26 neither can the number of his years be s.
38. 21 because..the number of thy days (is) gr.
Psa.105. 12 When they were..a few men in number
105. 34 and caterpillars, and that without number
147. 4 He telleth the number of the stars; he
Song 6. 8 There are. queens..virgins without num.
Isa. 21. 17 the residue of the number of archers, the
40. 26 that bringeth out their host by number
Jer. 2. 28 the number of thy cities are thy gods, O J
2. 32 people have forgotten me days without n
11. 13 the number of thy cities were thy gods, O
11. 13 the number of the streets of Jerusalem
44. 28 Yet a small number that escape the sword
Eze. 4. 4, 9 to the number of the days that thou s.
4. 5 according to the number of the days, th.
5. 3 Thou shalt also take thereof a few in nu
Dan. 9. 2 I, Daniel understood by books the num.
Hos. 1. 10 Yet the number of the children of Israel
Joel 1. 6 For a nation..strong, and without number

6. *Number, inspection,* מִפְקָד *miphqad.*
2 Sa. 24. 9 Joab gave up the sum of the number of
1 Ch.21. 5 Joab gave the sum of the number of the

7. *Number,* סְפֹרָה *sephorah.*
Psa. 71. 15 all the day; for I know not the numbers

8. *Number,* ἀριθμός *arithmos.*
Luke22. 3 Judas..being of the number of the twelve
John 6. 10 sat down, in number about five thousand
Acts 4. 4 the number of the men was about five th.
5. 36 to whom a number of men, about four h.
6. 7 the number of the disciples multiplied in
11. 21 a great number believed, and turned unto
16. 5 the churches..increased in number daily
Rom. 9. 27 Though the number of the children of Is.
Rev. 5. 11 [the number of them was ten thousand]
7. 4 I heard the number of them which were
9. 16 the number of the army..I heard the nu
13. 17 of the beast, or the number of his name
13. 18 Let him..count the number..for it is the n.
13. 18 his number (is) Six hundred threescore
15. 2 victory..over the number of his name
20. 8 the number of whom..as the sand of the

NUMBER (of people) —
Crowd, ὄχλος *ochlos.*
Mark10. 46 his disciples and a great number of peo.
Acts 1. 15 the number of names together were

NUMBER, to make of the —
To judge in, reckon among, ἐγκρίνω *egkrinō.*
2 Co.10. 12 we dare not make ourselves of the num.

NUMBER, to —
1. *To number, count, appoint,* מָנָה *manah.*
Gen. 13. 16 so that if a man can number the dust of
2 Sa. 24. 1 moved David..to say, Go, number Israel
1 Ki.20. 25 number thee an army like the army that
1 Ch.21. 1 Satan..provoked David to number Israel
27. 24 Joab the son of Zeruiah began to number
Psa. 90. 12 So teach (us) to number our days, that
Isa. 65. 12 Therefore will I number you to the sword

2. *To number, count, appoint,* מְנָא *mena.*
Dan. 5. 26 God hath numbered thy kingdom, and fi.

3. *To write, cypher, number,* סָפַר *saphar.*
Gen. 15. 5 tell the stars, if thou be able to number
Lev. 15. 13 he shall number to himself seven days for
15. 28 then she shall number to herself seven d.
23. 16 Even unto the morrow..shall ye number
25. 8 thou shalt number seven sabbaths of years
Deut16. 9 Seven weeks shalt thou number unto thee
16. 9 begin to number the seven weeks from
2 Sa. 24. 10 heart smote him after that he had numb.
1 Ch.21. 2 number Israel from Beer-sheba even to D.
2 Ch. 2. 17 Solomon numbered all the strangers that
2. 17 wherewith David his father had numbered
Ezra 1. 8 numbered them unto Sheshbazzar, the p.
Job 14. 16 For now thou numberest my steps: dost
39. 2 Canst thou number the months..they fu.
Isa. 22. 10 ye have numbered the houses of Jerusal.

4. *To number, recount,* סְפַר *saphar,* 3.
Job 38. 37 Who can number the clouds in wisdom?

5. *To inspect,* פָּקַד *paqad.*
Exod30. 12 when thou numberest..when (thou) nu.
Num. 1. 3 thou and Aaron shall number them by
1. 19 so he numbered them in the wilderness
1. 44 which Moses and Aaron numbered, and
3. 15 Number the children of Levi after the ho.
3. 15 from a month. and upward shalt thou n.
3. 16 Moses numbered them, according to the
3. 39 which Moses and Aaron numbered at the
3. 40 Number all the first born of the males
3. 42 Moses numbered, as the LORD commanded
4. 23 From thirty years old..shalt thou number
4. 29 thou shalt number them after..their fami.
4. 30 shalt thou number them, every one that
4. 34 Moses and Aaron..numbered the sons of
4. 37, 41, 45 whom Moses and Aaron did num.
4. 46 whom..the chief of Israel numbered
26. 63 who numbered the children of Israel in
26. 64 numbered, when they numbered the ch.
Josh. 8. 10 Joshua rose up..and numbered the people
1 Sa. 11. 8 when he numbered them in Bezek, the c.
13. 15 Saul numbered the people..present with
14. 17 Number now, and see who is gone from
14. 17 And when they had numbered, behold, J.
15. 4 Saul..numbered them in Telaim, two h.
2 Sa. 18. 1 David numbered the people that (were)
24. 2 number ye the people, that I may know
24. 4 went out..to number the people of Israel
1 Ki. 20. 15 Then he numbered the young men of the
20. 15 after them he numbered all the people
20. 26 Ben-hadad numbered the Syrians, and w.
2 Ki. 3. 6 Jehoram went out..and numbered all I.
2 Ch.25. 5 he numbered them from twenty years old

6. *To number,* ἀριθμέω *arithmeō.*
Rev. 7. 9 great multitude, which no man could nu.

7. *To reckon,* λογίζομαι *logizomai.*
Mark15 28 [he was numbered with the transgressors]

NUMBER, to take into the —
To be laid or put down, καταλέγομαι *katalegomai.*
1 Ti. 5. 9 Let not a widow be taken into the number

NUMBER after or throughout the genealogy, to —
To reckon self by genealogy, יָחַשׂ *yachas,* 7.
1 Ch. 7. 9 the number of them, after their genealogy
7. 40 the number throughout the genealogy of

NUMBER, certain —
Number, reckoning, מִסְפָּר *mispar.*
Deut25. 2 according to his fault, by a certain number

NUMBER, odd —
To be over and above, superfluous, עָדַף *adaph.*
Num. 3. 48 wherewith the odd number of them is to

NUMBERED —
Number, reckoning, מִסְפָּר *mispar.*
1 Ch.23. 27 the Levites (were) numbered from twenty

NUMBERED, to be —
1. *To number,* מָנָה *manah.*
1 Ch.21. 17 (that) commanded the people to be num.?

2. *To be numbered,* מָנָה *manah,* 2.
Gen. 13. 16 (then) shall thy seed also be numbered
1 Ki. 3. 8 that cannot be numbered nor counted for
8. 5 that could not be told nor numbered for
2 Ch. 5. 6 which could not be told nor numbered for
Eccl. 1. 15 that which is wanting cannot be numbered
Isa. 53. 12 and he was numbered with the transgres.

3. *To be written, cyphered, numbered,* סָפַר *saphar,* 2.
Gen. 16. 10 that it shall not be numbered for multit.
32. 12 which cannot be numbered for multitude
1 Ch 23. 3 the Levites were numbered from the age
Jer. 33. 22 As the host of heaven cannot be numbered
Hos. 1. 10 which cannot be measured nor numbered

4. *To number, recount,* סָפַר *saphar,* 3.
Psa. 40. 5 works..they are more than can be numb.

5. *To inspect,* פָּקַד *paqad.* (pass. partic.).
Exod30. 13, 14 that passeth among them that are nu.
38. 25 the silver of them that were numbered of
38. 26 for every one that went to be numbered
Num. 1. 21 Those that were numbered of them
So in v. 22, 23, 25, 27, 29, 31, 33, 35, 37, 39, 41, 43.
1. 44 These (are) those that were numbered, w.
1. 45 So were all those that were numbered of
1. 46 Even all they that were numbered, were
2. 4 his host, and those that were numbered
So in v. 6, 8, 11, 13, 15, 19, 21, 23, 26, 28, 30.

Num. 2. 9, 16 All that were numbered in the camp
2. 24 All that were numbered of the camp of E.
2. 31 All they that were numbered in the camp
2. 32 These (are) those which were numbered o
2. 32 all those that were numbered of the camps
3. 22, 22, 34, 43 Those that were numbered of
3. 39 All that were numbered of the Levites
4. 36, 38, 40, 42, 44, 45, 46, 48 those that were n
4. 37, 41 they that were numbered of the fami.
7. 2 and were over them that were numbered
14. 29 all that were numbered of you, according
26. 7 they that were numbered of them were fo.
26. 18 according to those that were numbered of
So in v. 22, 25, 27, 37, 43, 47.
26. 34, 62 and those that were numbered of them
26. 41, 50 and they that were numbered of them
26. 51 These..the numbered of the children of
26. 54 according to those that were numbered of
26. 57, 63 And these..they that were numbered

5a. *He inspected, counted,* פָּקַד *paqad*; Num. 4. 49.

6. *To inspect self, charge self,* פָּקַד *paqad,* 7.
Judg20. 15 the children of Benjamin were numbered
20. 15 which were numbered seven hundred ch.
20. 17 were numbered four hundred thousand
21. 9 For the people were numbered, and, beh.

7. *To inspect or charge self,* פָּקַד *paqad,* 7a.
Num. 1. 47 the Levites..were not numbered among
2. 33 But the Levites were not numbered amo.
26. 62 they were not numbered among the chil.
1 Ki.20. 27 the children of Israel were numbered, and

8. *To number,* ἀριθμέω *arithmeō.*
Matt10. 30 the very hairs of your head are all numb.
Luke12. 7 the very hairs of your head are all numb.

NUMBERED with, to be —
1. *To be numbered down,* καταριθμέομαι *katarithm.*
Acts 1. 17 he was numbered with us, and had obta.

2. *To be voted down with,* συγκαταψηφίζομαι *sugk.*
Acts 1. 26 and he was numbered with the eleven a.

NUMBERING —
1. *To write, cypher, number,* סָפַר *saphar.*
Gen. 41. 49 gathered corn..until he left numbering

2. *Numbering,* סְפָר *sephar.*
2 Ch. 2. 17 after the numbering wherewith David his

NUMBERS —
Inspection, charge, number, פְּקֻדָּה *pequddah.*
2 Ch.17. 14 these (are) the numbers of them accord.

NUN, נוּן *continuation.*
An Ephraimite, father of Joshua, the servant of Moses, and leader of Israel over Jordan, born B.C. 1536, died B.C. 1426, aged 110 years.
Exod33. 11 the son of N. a young man, departed not
Num11. 28 the son of N., the servant of Moses, (one)
13. 8 the tribe of Ephraim, Oshea the son of N.
13. 16 Moses called Oshea the son of N., Jehosh.
14. 6, 38 son of N., and Caleb the son of Jephu.
14. 30 son of Jephunneh..Joshua the son of N.
26. 65 son of Jephunneh..Joshua the son of N.
27. 18 the son of N., a man in whom (is) the sp.
32. 12 son of Jephunneh..Joshua the son of N.
32. 28 the son of N., and the chief fathers of
34. 17 Eleazar the priest, and Joshua..son of N.
Deut. 1. 38 the son of N., which standeth before thee
31. 23 he gave Joshua the son of N. a charge, and
32. 44 and spake..he and Hoshea the son of N.
34. 9 son of N. was full of the spirit of wisdom
Josh. 1. 1 the LORD spake unto Joshua the son of N.
2. 1 the son of N. sent out of Shittim two men
2. 23 came to Joshua the son of N., and told
6. 6 the son of N. called the priests, and said
14. 1 the son of N., and the heads of the fathers
17. 4 before Joshua the son of N., and before the
19. 49 an inheritance to Joshua the son of N.
19. 51 the son of N., and the heads of the fathers
21. 1 unto Joshua the son of N., and unto the
24. 29 the son of N., the servant of the LORD d
Judg. 2. 8 the son of N., the servant of the LORD d
1 Ki 16. 34 which he spake by Joshua the son of N.
Neh. 8. 17 since the days of Jeshua the son of N.

NURSE, (nursing mother or father) —
1. *To nurse, be faithful, be a support,* אָמַן *aman.*
Num11. 12 as a nursing father beareth the sucking
Ruth 4. 16 laid it in her bosom, and became nurse
2 Sa. 4. 4 his nurse took him up, and fled: and it
Isa. 49. 23 kings shall be thy nursing fathers, and

2. *To suckle, give suck,* יָנַק *yanaq,* 5.
Gen. 24. 59 they sent away Rebekah..and her nurse
35. 8 Deborah, Rebekah's nurse, died, and she
Exod. 2. 7 Shall I go and call to thee a nurse of the
2 Ki. 11. 2 they hid him..him and his nurse, in the
2 Ch.22. 11 put him and his nurse in a bed chamber
Isa. 49. 23 and their queens thy nursing mothers

3. *A nurse, nourisher,* τροφός *trophos.*
1 Th. 2. 7 even as a nurse cherisheth her children

NURSE, be nursed, to —
1. *To be nursed, supported,* אָמַן *aman,* 2.
Isa. 60. 4 thy daughters shall be nursed at (thy) side

2. *To suckle, give suck,* יָנַק *yanaq,* 5.
Exod. 2. 7 that she may nurse the child for thee?
2. 9 Take this child away, and nurse it for me

3. *To suckle, give suck,* נוק *nuq,* 5.
Exod. 2. 9 the woman took the child, and nursed it

NURTURE —
Nurture, instruction, chastening, παιδεία *paideia.*
Eph. 6. 4 bring them up in the nurture and admo.

NUT —
1. *A nut, nut tree,* אֱגוֹז *egoz.*
Song 6. 11 I went down into the garden of nuts to
2. *Pistacia nuts,* בָּטְנִים *botnim.*
Gen. 43. 11 honey,spices,and myrrh,nuts,and almonds

NYMPH'-AS, Νυμφᾶς.
A believer at Colosse or Laodicea, to whom Paul sends a salutation.
Col. 4. 15 N., and the church which is in his house

O, OH! —
1. *I pray thee! O! Oh!* אָנָּא, אָנָּה *ana, anah.*
Exod 32. 31 Oh, this people have sinned a great sin,and
Psa. 116. 16 O LORD, truly I (am) thy servant; I (am)
Dan. 9. 4 O Lord, the great and dreadful God, keep.
2. *O! Oh!* בִּי *bi.*
Gen. 43. 20 O sir, we came indeed down at the first
44. 18 Oh my lord, let thy servant, I pray thee
Exod 4. 10 O my Lord, I (am) not eloquent, neither
4. 13 O my Lord, send, I pray thee, by the hand
Josh. 7. 8 O Lord, what shall I say, when Israel tur.
Judg. 6. 13 O my Lord, if the LORD be with us, why
6. 15 Oh my Lord, wherewith shall I serve Isr.?
13. 8 O my Lord, let the man of God which th.
1 Sa. 1. 26 Oh my lord, (as) thy soul liveth, my lord
1 Ki. 3. 17 O my lord, I and this woman dwell in one
3. 26 O my lord, give her the living child, and
3. *Ho!* הוֹי *hoi.*
Isa. 10. 5 O Assyrian, the rod of mine anger, and
Jer. 47. 6 O thou sword of the LORD, how long..ere
4. *Pray, please now,* נָא *na.*
Gen. 18. 30 Oh let not the Lord be angry, and I will
5. *Oh!* ὦ *ō.*
Matt 15. 28 O woman, great (is) thy faith: be it unto
17. 17 O faithless and perverse generation, how
Mark 9. 19 O faithless generation, how long shall I
Luke 9. 41 O faithless and perverse generation! how
24. 25 O fools, and slow of heart to believe all
Acts 1. 1 The former treatise have I made, O Theo.
13. 10 O full of all subtility and all mischief
18. 14 O (ye) Jews, reason would that I should
Rom. 2. 1 Therefore thou art inexcusable, O man
2. 3 thinkest thou this, O man, that judgest
9. 20 Nay but, O man, who art thou that repl.
11. 33 O the depth of the riches both of the wis.
Gal. 3. 1 O foolish Galatians, who hath bewitched
1 Ti. 6. 20 O Timothy, keep that which is committed
Jas. 2. 20 But wilt thou know, O vain man, that fa.

O that, oh that —
1. *Would that, O that,* אַחֲלֵי, אַחֲלַי *achalai.*
Psa. 119. 5 O that my ways were directed to keep thy
2. *If,* אִם *im.*
1 Ch. 4. 10 Oh that thou wouldest bless me indeed,and
3. *If, O that,* לוּ, לוּא *lu.*
Gen. 17. 18 said..O that Ishmael might live before
Deut 32. 29 Oh that they were wise, (that) they under.
Job 6. 2 Oh that my grief were throughly weighed
Psa. 81. 13 Oh that my people had hearkened unto
Isa. 48. 18 O that thou hadst hearkened to my com.
64. 1 Oh that thou wouldest rend the heavens
4. *Who will give?* מִי יִתֵּן *mi yitten.*
Deut. 5. 29 O that there were such an heart in them
Job 6. 8 O that I might have my request; 11. 5.
13. 5 O that ye would altogether hold your pe.
14. 13 O that thou wouldest hide me in the gra.
19. 23 Oh that my words were now written! oh
23. 3 Oh that I knew where I might find him
29. 2 Oh that I were as (in) months past, as(in)
31. 31 Oh that we had of his flesh! we cannot be
31. 35 Oh that one would hear me! behold, my
Psa. 14. 7 Oh that the salvation of Israel (were co.)
53. 6 Oh that the salvation of Israel (were co.)
55. 6 I said, Oh that I had wings like a dove!
Song 8. 1 Oh that thou..as my brother, that sucked
Jer. 9. 1 Oh that my head were waters, and mine
9. 2 Oh that I had in the wilderness a lodging

OAK —
1. *An oak, terebinth,* אֵלָה *elah.*
Gen. 35. 4 Jacob hid them under the oak which (was)
Judg 6. 11 sat under an oak which (was) in Ophrah
6. 19 brought (it) out unto him under the oak
2 Sa. 18. 9 went under the thick boughs of a great oak
18. 9 his head caught hold of the oak, and he
18. 10 Behold, I saw Absalom hanged in an oak
18. 14 he (was) yet alive in the midst of the oak
1 Ki 13. 14 went..and found him sitting under an oak
1 Ch. 10. 12 buried their bones under the oak in Jabe.
Isa. 1. 30 ye shall be as an oak whose leaf fadeth
Eze. 6. 13 every green tree..under every thick oak
2. *Oak, terebinth,* אַלָּה *allah.*
Josh. 24. 26 and set it up there under an oak that (was)
3. *An oak,* אַלּוֹן *allon.*
Gen. 35. 8 was buried beneath Beth-el under an oak
Isa. 2. 13 upon all the cedars..and upon all the oaks
6. 13 as a teil tree, and as an oak, whose subs.
44. 14 taketh the cypress and the oak, which he
Eze. 27. 6 (Of) the oaks of Bashan have they made
Hos. 4. 13 burn incense upon the hills, under oaks
Amos 2. 9 he (was) strong as the oaks; yet I destro.
Zech 11. 2 howl, O ye oaks of Bashan; for the forest
4. *Oaks,* אֵילִים *elim.*
Isa. 1. 29 they shall be ashamed of the oaks which

OAR —
1. *An oar, rudder,* מָשׁוֹט *mashot.*
Eze. 27. 29 And all that handle the oar, the mariners
2. *An oar, rudder,* מִשׁוֹט *mishshot.*
Eze. 27. 6 oaks of Bashan have they made thine oars
3. *An oar, rudder,* שַׁיִט *shayit.*
Isa. 33. 21 wherein shall go no galley with oars, nei.

OATH —
1. *Execration, curse, oath,* אָלָה *alah.*
Gen. 24. 41 Then shalt thou be clear from..my oath
24. 41 give not..thou shalt be clear from my oath
26. 28 said, Let there be now an oath betwixt us
Deut 29. 12 and into his oath, which the LORD thy God
29. 14 only do I make this covenant and this oath
1 Ki. 8. 31 and an oath be laid upon him to cause him
8. 31 oath come before thine altar in this house
2 Ch. 6. 22 and an oath be laid upon him to make him
6. 22 oath come before thine altar in this house
Eze. 16. 59 which hast despised the oath in breaking
17. 13 made a covenant..and hath taken an oath
17. 16 whose oath he despised, and whose cove.
17. 18 Seeing he despised the oath by breaking
17. 19 surely mine oath that he hath despised
2. *Swearing,* שְׁבוּעָה *shebuah.*
Gen. 24. 8 then thou shalt be clear from this my oath
26. 3 I will perform the oath which I sware
Exod 22. 11 (Then) shall an oath of the LORD be bet.
Lev. 5. 4 that a man shall pronounce with an oath
Num. 5. 21 priests shall charge the woman with an o.
5. 21 The LORD make thee a curse and an oath
30. 2 or swear an oath to bind his soul with a
30. 10 or bound her soul by a bond with an oath
30. 13 Every vow, and every binding oath to affl.
Deut. 7. 8 because he would keep the oath which he
Josh. 2. 17 We (will be) blameless of this thine oath
2. 20 then we will be quit of thine oath which
9. 20 because of the oath which we sware unto
Judg 21. 5 For they had made a great oath concern
1 Sa. 14. 26 no man put..for the pe ple feared the o.
2 Sa. 21. 7 because of the LORD'S oath that (was) be.
1 Ki. 2. 43 Why then hast thou not kept the oath of
1 Ch. 16. 16 he made with Abraham, and of his oath
2 Ch. 15. 15 all Judah rejoiced at the oath: for they
Neh. 10. 29 entered into a curse, and into an oath
Psa. 105. 9 he made with Abraham, and his oath unto
Eccl. 8. 2 and (that) in regard of the oath of God
9. 2 that sweareth, as (he) that feareth an oath
Jer. 11. 5 That I may perform the oath which I have
Eze. 21. 23 divination..to them that have sworn oaths
Dan. 9. 11 the oath that (is) written in the law of M.
Hab. 3. 9 to the oaths of the tribes, (even thy) wo.
Zech. 8. 17 and love no false oath: for all these (are
3. *Oath, promise,* ὅρκος *horkos.*
Matt. 5. 33 shalt perform unto the Lord thine oaths
14. 7 Whereupon he promised with an oath to
14. 9 for the oath's sake, and them which sat
26. 72 again he denied with an oath, I do not k.
Mark 6. 26 for his oath's sake, and for their sakes w.
Luke 1. 73 The oath which he sware to our father A.
Acts 2. 30 knowing that God had sworn with an oath
Heb. 6. 16 an oath for confirmation (is) to them an
6. 17 Wherein God..confirmed (it) by an oath
Jas. 5. 12 by the earth, neither by any other oath
4. *The swearing of an oath,* ὁρκωμοσία *horkōmosia.*
Heb. 7. 20 And inasmuch as not without an oath(he
7. 21 For those priests were made without an o.
7. 21 this with an oath by him that said unto
7. 28 but the word of the oath, which was since

OATH, to bind with an —
To anathematize, ἀναθεματίζω *anathematizō.*
Acts 23. 21 which have bound themselves with an o.

OATH, to take or charge by or with an —
To cause to swear, שָׁבַע *shaba,* 5.
Gen. 50. 25 Joseph took an oath of the children of I.
Num. 5. 19 And the priest shall charge her by an oath
1 Sa. 14. 28 straitly charged the people with an oath
1 Ki. 18. 10 he took an oath of the kingdom and nat.
2 Ki. 11. 4 took an oath of them in..house of the L.
Neh. 5. 12 took an oath of them, that they should

O-BAD-I'AH, עֹבַדְיָה, עֹבַדְיָהוּ *servant of Jah.*
1. The pious governor of Ahab's house. B.C. 916.
1 Ki. 18. 3 Ahab called O., which (was) the governor
18. 3 Now O. feared the LORD greatly
18. 4 O. took an hundred prophets, and hid th.
18. 5 Ahab said unto O., Go into the land, unto
18. 6 and O. went another way by himself
18. 7 as O. was in the way, behold, Elijah met
18. 16 O. went to meet Ahab, and told him: and
2. Head of a family from David. B.C. 500.
1 Ch. 3. 21 the sons of O., the sons of Shechaniah
3. A descendant of Tola son of Issachar. B.C. 1500.
1 Ch. 7. 3 Michael, and O., and Joel, Ishiah, five: all
4. Son of Azel, a Benjamite of the family of Saul. B.C. 860.
1 Ch. 8. 38 and Ishmael, and Sheariah, and O., and
9. 44 and Ishmael, and Sheariah, and O., and H.
5. Son of Shemaiah a Levite, from Netophah near Jerusalem. B.C. 445.
1 Ch. 9. 16 O. the son of Shemaiah, the son of Galal
6. A Gadite who joined David in Ziklag. B.C. 1058.
1 Ch. 12. 9 the first, O. the second, Eliab the third
7. Father of Ishmaiah, prince of Zebulun in the days of David. B.C. 1040.
1 Ch. 27. 19 Of Zebulun; Ishmaiah the son of O.: of
8. A prince of Judah whom Jehoshaphat sent to teach in the cities of Judah. B.C. 916.
2 Ch. 17. 7 to O., and to Zechariah, and to Nethaneel
9. A Levite, overseer of the repairs of the temple in the days of Josiah. B.C. 634.
2 Ch. 34. 12 overseers of them (were) Jahath and O.
10. Son of Jehiel, and chief man that returned with Ezra. B.C. 457.
Ezra 8. 9 O. the son of Jehiel, and with him two
11. A priest that sealed, with Nehemiah, the covenant. B.C. 445.
Neh. 10. 5 Harim, Meremoth, O.
12. A gate keeper for the sanctuary. B.C. 445.
Neh. 12. 25 O., Meshullam, Talmon, Akkub, (were)
13. A prophet who is reckoned to have lived about B.C. 587.
Obadiah 1 The vision of O. Thus saith the Lord GOD

O'-BAL, עוֹבָל *bare.*
A son of Joktan, of the family of Shem, B.C. 2190; in 1 Ch. 1. 22 he is called *Ebal* (*which see*).
Gen. 10. 28 And O., and Abimael, and Sheba

O'-BED, עוֹבֵד, 'Ωβήδ, 'Ιωβήδ, *serving.*
1. Son of Boaz by Ruth, and father of Jesse. B.C. 1300.
Ruth 4. 17 they called his name O: he (is) the father
4. 21 And Salmon begat Boaz, and Boaz begat O.
4. 22 And O. begat Jesse, and Jesse begat David
1 Ch. 2. 12 And Boaz begat O., and O. begat Jesse
Matt. 1. 5 Booz begat O. of Ruth; and O. begat J.
Luke 3. 32 which was (the son) of O., which was (the
2. Son of Ephlal, descendant of Judah. B.C. 1380.
1 Ch. 2. 37 Zabad begat Ephlal, and Ephlal begat O.
2. 38 And O. begat Jehu, and Jehu begat Azar.
3. One of David's valiant men. B.C. 1048.
1 Ch. 11. 47 Eliel, and O., and Jasiel, the Mesobaite
4. A son of Shemaiah, a Kohathite, a gate keeper of the tabernacle in the days of David. B.C. 1015.
1 Ch. 26. 7 O., Elzabad, whose brethren (were) strong
5. Father of Azariah, a captain who helped Jehoiada the priest in making Joash king of Judah. B.C. 878.
2 Ch. 23. 1 and Azariah the son of O., and Maaseiah

O-BED E'-DOM, עֹבֵד אֱדוֹם *servant of Edom.*
1. A Levite in whose house the ark lay three months B.C. 1050.
2 Sa. 6. 10 carried it aside into the house of O., the
6. 11 in the house of O...and the LORD blessed O.
6. 12 LORD hath blessed the house of O., and
6. 12 from the house of O. into the city of Dav.
1 Ch. 13. 13 carried it aside into the house of O. the G.
13. 14 remained with the family of O. in his ho.
13. 14 LORD blessed the house of O., and all that
15. 25 bring up the ark..out of the house of O.
2. A gate keeper of the tabernacle, appointed to bring up the ark.
1 Ch. 15. 18 Mikneiah, and O., and Jeiel, the porters
15. 21 O., and Jeiel, and Azaziah, with harps on
15. 24 O. and Jehiah (were) door keepers for the
26. 4 Moreover the sons of O. (were) Shemaiah
26. 8 sons of O...(were) threescore and two of O.
26. 15 To O. southward; and to his sons the ho.
3. A Levite appointed to minister before the ark.
1 Ch. 16. 5 next to him..Eliab, and Benaiah, and O.
16. 38 O. with their brethren, threescore and e.
4. A Levite, son of Jeduthun, a gate keeper of the tabernacle.
1 Ch. 16. 38 O. also the son of Jeduthun, and Hosah
5. An Aaronite, having charge of the vessels of the sanctuary in the days of Amaziah king of Judah. B.C. 839–810.
2 Ch. 25. 24 were found in the house of God with O.

OBEDIENCE —
Hearkening submissively, ὑπακοή *hupakoē.*
Rom. 1. 5 for obedience to the faith among all nat.
5. 19 so by the obedience of one shall many be
6. 16 death, or of obedience unto righteousness?
16. 19 For your obedience is come abroad unto
16. 26 made known to all nations for the obed.
2 Co. 7. 15 he remembereth the obedience of you all
10. 5 every thought to the obedience of Christ
10. 6 to revenge..when your obedience is fulfi.
Phm. 21 Having confidence in thy obedience I wro.
Heb. 5. 8 learned he obedience by the things which
1 Pe. 1. 2 unto obedience and sprinkling of the blo.

OBEDIENCE, to be under —
To set in array under, ὑποτάσσω *hupotassō.*
1 Co. 14. 34 but..to be under obedience, as also saith

OBEDIENT, (to be or make) —

1. *To hear, hearken,* שָׁמַע *shamea.*

Exod 24. 7 LORD hath said will we do, and be obed.
Num 27. 20 that all the congregation..may be obedi.
Deut 4. 30 if thou..shalt be obedient unto his voice
8. 20 because ye would not be obedient unto the
Prov. 25. 12 (is) a wise reprover upon an obedient ear
Isa. 1. 19 If ye be willing and obedient, ye shall eat
42. 24 neither were they obedient unto his law

2. *To be heard, hearkened to,* שָׁמַע *shamea,* 2.

2 Sa. 22. 45 as soon as they hear, they shall be obed.

3. *Towards obedience, of obedience,* ὑπακοή *hupakoē.*

Rom 15. 18 to make the Gentiles obedient, by word
1 Pe. 1. 14 As obedient children, not fashioning yo.

4. *To hearken submissively, obey,* ὑπακούω *hupakouō.*

Acts 6. 7 a great company of the priests were obed.
Eph. 6. 5 Servants, be obedient to them that are

5. *Hearkening submissively,* ὑπήκοος *hupēkoos.*

2 Co. 2. 9 know..whether ye be obedient in all thi.
Phil. 2. 8 he humbled himself, and became obedient

6. *To set in order under,* ὑποτάσσω *hupotassō.*

Titus 2. 5 good, obedient to their own husbands, t.
2. 9 servants to be obedient unto their own m.

OBEISANCE, to do or make —

To bow self down, שָׁחָה *shachah, 7a.*

Gen. 37. 7 stood round about, and made obeisance
37. 9 and the eleven stars, made obeisance to
43. 28 bowed down their heads, and made obei.
Exod 18. 7 Moses went..and did obeisance, and kis.
2 Sa. 1. 2 that he fell to the earth, and did obeisance
14. 4 fell on her face to the ground. and did o.
15. 5 when any man came nigh..to do him ob.
1 Ki. 1. 16 Bath-sheba bowed and did obeisance unto
2 Ch. 24. 17 came the princes of Judah, and made ob.

OBEY, to —

1. *Obedience, expectation,* יְקָהָה *yiqqehah.*

Prov 30. 17 The eye (that) despiseth to obey (his) mo.

2. *Hearing, hearkening,* מִשְׁמַעַת *mishmaath.*

Isa. 11. 14 the children of Ammon shall obey them

3. *To hear, hearken,* שָׁמַע *shamea.*

Gen. 22. 18 blessed; because thou hast obeyed my v.
26. 5 Because that Abraham obeyed my voice
27. 8 Now therefore, my son, obey my voice
27. 13 only obey my voice, and go fetch me (t.)
27. 43 Now therefore, my son, obey my voice
28. 7 that Jacob obeyed his father and his mo.
Exod. 5. 2 Who (is) the LORD, that I should obey his
19. 5 Now therefore, if ye will obey my voice
23. 21 Beware of him, and obey his voice, prov.
23. 22 But if thou shalt indeed obey his voice
Deut 11. 27 A blessing, if ye obey the commandments
11. 28 And a curse, if ye will not obey the com.
13. 4 keep his commandments, and obey his v.
21. 18 which will not obey the voice of his fath.
21. 20 stubborn and rebellious, he will not obey
27. 10 Thou shalt therefore obey the voice of the
28. 62 because thou wouldest not obey the voice
30. 2 and shalt obey his voice, according to all
30. 8 thou shalt return, and obey the voice of
30. 20 that thou mayest obey his voice, and that
Josh. 5. 6 because they obeyed not the voice of the
22. 2 have obeyed my voice in all that I comm.
24. 24 will we serve, and his voice will we obey
Judg. 2. 2 ye have not obeyed my voice: why have
2. 17 obeying the commandments of the LORD
6. 10 I said..but ye have not obeyed my voice
1 Sa. 8. 19 Nevertheless the people refused to obey
12. 14 fear the LORD, and serve him, and obey
12. 15 if ye will not obey the voice of the LORD
15. 19 Wherefore then didst thou not obey the
15. 20 Yea, I have obeyed the voice of the LORD
15. 22 delight..as in obeying the voice of the L.?
15. 22 Behold, to obey (is) better than sacrifice
15. 24 I feared the people, and obeyed their vo
28. 18 Because thou obeyedst not the voice of the
28. 21 thine handmaid hath obeyed thy voice, and
1 Ki. 20. 36 Because thou hast not obeyed the voice of
2 Ki. 18. 12 Because they obeyed not the voice of the
1 Ch. 29. 23 and prospered; and all Israel obeyed him
2 Ch. 11. 4 they obeyed the words of the LORD, and
Neh. 9. 17 refused to obey, neither were mindful of
Job 36. 11 If they obey and serve..they shall spend
36. 12 But if they obey not, they shall perish by
Prov. 5. 13 have not obeyed the voice of my teachers
Isa. 50. 10 that obeyeth the voice of his servant, that
Jer. 3. 13 ye have not obeyed my voice, saith the L.
3. 25 have not obeyed the voice of the LORD our
7. 23 Obey my voice, and I will be your God
7. 28 This (is) a nation that obeyeth not the voice
9. 13 have not obeyed my voice, neither walked
11. 3 Cursed (be) the man that obeyeth not the
11. 4 Obey my voice, and do them, according to
11. 7 rising early and protesting, saying, Obey
11. 8 Yet they obeyed not, nor inclined their
12. 17 But if they will not obey, I will utterly p.
17. 23 But they obeyed not, neither inclined th.
18. 10 If it do evil in my sight, that it obey not
22. 21 thy manner from thy youth..thou obeye.
26. 13 obey the voice of the LORD your God
32. 23 but they obeyed not thy voice, neither w.
34. 10 when all the princes..heard..then they o.
35. 8 Thus have we obeyed the voice of Jonadab
35. 10 have obeyed, and done according to all
35. 14 they..obey their father's commandment
35. 18 Because ye have obeyed the commandm.
38. 20 Obey, I beseech thee, the voice of the L.
Jer. 40. 3 because ye..have not obeyed his voice
42. 6 we will obey the voice of the LORD our God
42. 6 when we obey the voice of the LORD our
42. 13 neither obey the voice of the LORD your G.
42. 21 ye have not obeyed the voice of the LORD
43. 4 obeyed not the voice of the LORD, to dwell
43. 7 for they obeyed not the voice of the LORD
44. 23 have not obeyed the voice of the LORD, nor
Dan. 9. 10 Neither have we obeyed the voice of the
9. 11 by departing, that they might not obey thy
9. 14 God (is) righteous..for we obeyed not his
Zeph. 3. 2 She obeyed not the voice; she received not
Hag. 1. 12 obeyed the voice of the LORD their God
Zech. 6. 15 if ye will diligently obey the voice of the

4. *To be hearing, hearkening,* שָׁמַע *shamea,* 2.

Psa. 18. 44 As soon as they hear of me, they shall ob.

5. *To be hearing, hearkening,* שְׁמַע *shema,* 4.

Dan. 7. 27 and all dominions shall serve and obey

6. *To obey a chief or ruler,* πειθαρχέω *peitharcheō.*

Acts 5. 29 said, We ought to obey God rather than
5. 32 whom God hath given to them that obey

7. *To persuade,* πείθω *peithō.*

Acts 5. 36 as many as obeyed him, were scattered
5. 37 as many as obeyed him, were dispersed
Rom. 2. 8 the truth, but obey unright., indignation
Gal. 3. 1 [bewitched you, that ye should not obey]
5. 7 who did hinder you that ye should not o.
Heb. 13. 17 Obey them that have the rule over you
Jas. 3. 3 bits in..horses' mouths, that they may o.

8. *A hearkening submissively,* ὑπακοή *hupakoē.*

Rom 6. 16 to whom ye yield yourselves servants to o.

9. *To hearken submissively, obey,* ὑπακούω *hupakouō.*

Matt. 8. 27 that even the winds and the sea obey him
Mark 1. 27 even the unclean spirits, and they do obey
4. 41 that even the wind and the sea obey him?
Luke 8. 25 even the winds and water, and they obey
17. 6 be..planted in the sea, and it should obey
Rom 6. 12 that ye should obey it in the lusts thereof
6. 16 his servants ye are to whom ye obey; w.
6. 17 ye have obeyed from the heart that form
10. 16 But they have not all obeyed the gospel
Eph. 6. 1 Children, obey your parents in the Lord
Phil. 2. 12 as ye have always obeyed, not as in my pres.
Col. 3. 20 Children, obey (your) parents in all things
3. 22 Servants, obey in all things (your) masters
2 Th. 1. 8 that obey not the gospel of our Lord Jesus
3. 14 if any man obey not our word by this epi.
Heb. 5. 9 eternal salvation unto all them that obey h.
11. 8 Abraham, when he was called to go..ob.
1 Pe. 3. 6 Even as Sara obeyed Abraham, calling

10. *Become submissive,* ὑπήκοος γίνομαι *[ginomai].*

Acts 7. 39 To whom our fathers would not obey, but

OBEY magistrates, to —

To obey a chief or ruler, πειθαρχέω *peitharcheō.*

Titus 3. 1 Put them in mind..to obey magistrates

OBEY not, to —

To be unpersuaded, disobedient, ἀπειθέω *apeitheō.*

Rom. 2. 8 But unto them that..do not obey the tr.
1 Pe. 3. 1 that, if any obey not the word, they also
4. 17 shall the end (be) of them that obey not

OBEYING —

1. *To hear, hearken,* שָׁמַע *shamea.*

Judg. 2. 17 out of the way..their fathers walked in, o.
1 Sa. 15. 22 delight..as in obeying the voice of the L.

2. *A submissive hearkening,* ὑπακοή *hupakoē.*

1 Pe. 1. 22 in obeying the truth through the Spirit

O'-BIL, אוֹבִיל *driver, leader.*

An Ishmaelite camel driver in the days of David. B.C. 1015.

1 Ch. 27. 30 Over the camels also (was) O. the Ishma.

OBJECT, to —

To speak against or down, κατηγορέω *katēgoreō.*

Acts 24. 19 and object, if they had ought against me

OBLATION —

1. *Offering, present,* מִנְחָה *minchah.*

Isa. 1. 13 Bring no more vain oblations; incense is
19. 21 Egyptians..shall do sacrifice and oblation
66. 3 he that offereth an oblation..swine's blood
Jer. 14. 12 when they offer burnt offering and an obl.
Dan. 2. 46 commanded that they should offer an obl.
9. 21 me about the time of the evening oblation
9. 27 he shall cause the sacrifice and the oblat.

2. *Lifting up, burden, gift,* מַשְׂאֵת *maseth.*

Eze. 20. 40 I require..the first fruits of your oblations

3. *Thing brought near,* קָרְבָּן *qorban.*

Lev. 2. 4 if thou bring an oblation of a meat offeri.
2. 5, 7 And if thy oblation (be) a meat offering
2. 12 As for the oblation of the first fruits, ye
2. 13 every oblation of thy meat offering shalt
3. 1 if his oblation (be) a sacrifice of peace of.
7. 14 of it he shall offer one out of the whole o.
7. 29 shall bring his oblation unto the LORD of
7. 38 to offer their oblations to the LORD, in
22. 18 that will offer his oblation for all his vo.
Num 18. 9 every oblation of theirs, every meat off.
31. 50 We have therefore brought an oblation

4. *Heave offering,* תְּרוּמָה *terumah.*

2 Ch. 31. 14 to distribute the oblations of the LORD
Isa. 40. 20 (is) so impoverished that he hath no ob.
Eze. 44. 30 every oblation of all..of your oblations
45. 1 ye shall offer an oblation unto the LORD
Eze. 45. 6 over against the oblation of the holy (p.)
45. 7 the other side of the oblation of the holy
45. 7 the city, before the oblation of the holy
45. 13 This (is) the oblation that ye shall offer
45. 16 the people of the land shall give this ob.
48. 9 The oblation that ye shall offer unto the
48. 10 them..for the priests, shall be..holy obl.
48. 18, 18 over against the oblation of the holy
48. 20 All the oblation..five and twenty thous.
48. 20 ye shall offer the holy oblation four squ.
48. 21 of the holy oblation..of the oblation to.
48. 21 it shall be the holy oblation; and the sa.

5. *Heave offering,* תְּרוּמִיָּה *terumiyyah.*

Eze. 48. 12 (this) oblation of the land that is offered

O'-BOTH, אֹבֹת *hollows.*

A station of Israel, E. of Edom, between Punon and *Ije-abarim.*

Num 21. 10 children..set forward, and pitched in O
21. 11 they journeyed from O., and pitched at I.
33. 43 departed from Punon, and pitched in O.
33. 44 they departed from O., and pitched in I.

OBSCURE, Obscurity —

1. *Blackness,* אֱשׁוּן, [V.L. אִישׁוֹן *ishon*], *eshun.*

Prov 20. 20 his lamp shall be put out in obscure dar.

2. *Thick darkness,* אֹפֶל *ophel.*

Isa. 29. 18 the eyes of the blind shall see out of obs.

3. *Darkness,* חֹשֶׁךְ *choshek.*

Isa. 58. 10 then shall thy light rise in obscurity, and
59. 9 wait for light, but behold obscurity; for

OBSERVATION —

An intense watching, παρατήρησις *paratērēsis.*

Luke 17. 20 The kingdom of God cometh not with ob.

OBSERVE, to —

1. *To keep, watch,* נָצַר *natsar.*

Prov 23. 26 give me thine heart, and let thine eyes o

2. *To do, make,* עָשָׂה *asah.*

Exod 31. 16 to observe the sabbath throughout their
34. 22 thou shalt observe the feast of weeks, of
Num 15. 22 if ye have erred, and not observed all these
Deut 16. 13 Thou shalt observe the feast of tabernac.

3. *To behold, look,* שׁוּר *shur.*

Hos. 13. 7 a leopard by the way will I observe (them)
14. 8 I have heard (him), and observed him: I

4. *To observe, keep, take heed,* שָׁמַר *shamar.*

Gen. 37. 11 his brethren envied him; but his father o.
Exod 12. 17 ye shall observe (the feast of) unleavened
12. 17 therefore shall ye observe this day in your
12. 24 ye shall observe this thing for an ordina.
34. 11 Observe thou that which I command thee
Lev. 19. 37 Therefore shall ye observe all my statutes
Num 28. 2 shall ye observe to offer unto me in their
Deut. 5. 32 Ye shall observe to do therefore as the L.
6. 3 Hear therefore, O Israel, and observe to
6. 25 if we observe to do all these commandm.
8. 1 shall ye observe to do, that ye may live
11. 32 ye shall observe to do all the statutes and
12. 1 which ye shall observe to do in the land
12. 28 Observe and hear all these words which I
12. 32 What thing soever I command you, obse.
15. 5 to observe to do all these commandments
16. 1 Observe the month of Abib, and keep the
16. 12 thou shalt observe and do these statutes
17. 10 thou shalt observe to do according to all
24. 8 Take heed..that thou observe diligently
24. 8 as I commanded them..ye shall observe
28. 1 to observe..to do all his commandments
28. 13 which I command thee this day, to obse.
28. 15 to observe to do all his commandments
28. 58 If thou wilt not observe to do all the wo.
31. 12 and observe to do all the words of this law
32. 46 shall command your children to observe
33. 9 they have observed thy word, and kept
Josh. 1. 7, 8 that thou mayest observe to do accord.
Judg 13. 14 all that I commanded her let her observe
2 Sa. 11. 16 it came to pass, when Joab observed the
2 Ki. 17. 37 law..ye shall observe to do for evermore
21. 8 only if they will observe to do according
2 Ch. 7. 17 shalt observe my statutes and my judgm.
Neh. 1. 5 mercy for them that love him and observe
10. 29 to observe and do all the commandments
Psa. 105. 45 That they might observe his statutes, and
107. 43 Whoso (is) wise, and will observe these
119. 34 yea, I shall observe it with (my) whole h.
Eccl. 11. 4 He that observeth the wind shall not sow
Isa. 42. 20 Seeing many things, but thou observest
Jer. 8. 7 the crane and the swallow observe the t.
Eze. 20. 18 neither observe their judgments, nor de.
37. 24 they shall..observe my statutes, and do

5. *To observe, keep, take heed,* שָׁמַר *shamar,* 3.

Jon. 2. 8 They that observe lying vanities forsake

6. *To watch intensely or amiss,* παρατηρέω *paratēreō.*

Gal. 4. 10 Ye observe days, and months, and times

7. *To do, make,* ποιέω *poieō.*

Acts 16. 21 not lawful for us to receive, neither to o.

8. *To watch with,* συντηρέω *suntēreō.*

Mark 6. 20 For Herod feared John..and observed him

9. *To watch,* τηρέω *tēreō.*

Matt 23. 3 whatsoever they bid you [observe]..obse.
28. 20 Teaching them to observe all things whi.
Acts 21. 25 [concluded that they observe no such th.]

10. *To guard, keep watch,* φυλάσσω *phulassō.*

Mark 10. 20 all these have I observed from my youth
1 Ti. 5. 21 that thou observe these things without

OBSERVE diligently, to —
To observe diligently, divine, נָחַשׁ *nachash,* 3.
1 Ki.20. 33 the men did diligently observe whether
OBSERVE times, to —
To observe the clouds, עָנַן *anan,* 3a.
Lev. 19. 26 shall ye use enchantment, nor observe t.
Deut 18. 10 shall not be found..an observer of times
18. 14 hearkened unto observers of times, and
2 Ki.21. 6 observed times, and used enchantments
2 Ch.33. 6 he observed times, and used enchantme.
OBSERVED, to be (much) —
Of observances, שִׁמֻּרִים *shimmurim.*
Exod12. 42 It (is) a night to be much observed unto
12. 42 this (is) that night of the LORD to be obs.
OBSTINATE —
Hard, sharp, קָשֶׁה *qasheh.*
Isa. 48. 4 Because I knew that thou (art) obstinate
OBSTINATE, to make —
To strengthen, harden, אָמֵץ *amats,* 3.
Deut. 2. 30 made his heart obstinate, that he might
OBTAIN, to —
1. *To take or keep fast hold,* חָזַק *chazaq,* 5.
Dan. 11. 21 he shall come in peaceably, and obtain
2. *To lift up,* נָשָׂא *nasa.*
Esth. 2. 9 the maiden pleased him, and she obtained
2. 15 Esther obtained favour in the sight of all
2. 17 she obtained grace and favour in his sight
5. 2 when the king saw Esther..she obtained
3. *To cause to reach, attain, overtake,* נָשַׂג *nasag,* 5.
Isa. 35. 10 they shall obtain joy and gladness, and
51. 11 they shall obtain gladness and joy
4. *To bring out, cause to come forth,* פּוּק *puq,* 5.
Prov. 8. 35 findeth life, and shall obtain favour of the
12. 2 A good (man) obtaineth favour of the Lo.
18. 22 findeth a good (thing), and obtaineth fa.
5. *To happen or come upon,* ἐπιτυγχάνω *epitugchanō.*
Rom11. 7 Israel hath not obtained that which he se.
11. 7 the election hath obtained it, and the rest
Heb. 6. 15 so, after he had patiently endured, he ob.
11. 33 wrought righteousness, obtained promises
Jas. 4. 2 ye kill, and desire to have, and cannot o.
6. *To find,* εὑρίσκω *heuriskō.*
Heb. 9. 12 entered..having obtained eternal redem.
7. *To take or receive thoroughly,* καταλαμβάνω *kat.*
1 Co. 9. 24 one receiveth..So run, that ye may obtain
8. *To hold fast, obtain, attain,* κρατέω *krateō.*
Acts 27. 13 supposing that they had obtained (their)
9. *To acquire, possess,* κτάομαι *ktaomai.*
Acts 22. 28 With a great sum obtained I this freedom
10. *To obtain by lot,* λαγχάνω *lagchanō.*
Acts 1. 17 was numbered with us, and had obtained
2 Pe. 1. 1 to them that have obtained like precious
11. *To take, receive,* λαμβάνω *lambanō.*
1 Co. 9. 25 they (do it) to obtain a corruptible crown
Heb. 4. 16 that we may obtain mercy, and find grace
12. *Towards a laying up, acquiring,* εἰς περιποίησιν.
1 Th. 5. 9 to obtain salvation by our Lord Jesus C.
13. *To happen, come upon,* τυγχάνω *tugchanō.*
Luke20. 35 which shall be accounted worthy to obt.
Acts 26. 22 Having therefore obtained help of God
2 Ti. 2. 10 that they may also obtain the salvation
Heb 8. 6 But now hath he obtained a more excellent
11. 35 that they might obtain a better resurrec.
[*See also* Children, leave, mercy, witness, good report.]
OBTAIN by inheritance, to —
To obtain by lot, κληρονομέω *klēronomeō.*
Heb. 1. 4 as he hath by inheritance obtained a more
OBTAIN an inheritance, to —
To choose by lot, κληρόω *klēroō.*
Eph. 1. 11 In whom also we have obtained an inhe.
OBTAINING —
To a laying up, acquiring, εἰς περιποίησιν.
2 Th. 2. 14 to the obtaining of the glory of our Lord
OCCASION —
1. *A rolling, occasion, opportunity,* עִלָּה *illah.*
Dan. 6. 4 sought to find occasion against Daniel co.
6. 4 but they could find none occasion nor fa.
6. 5 We shall not find any occasion against
3. *A rolling, opportunity, occasion,* עֲלִילָה *alilah.*
Deut22. 14 And give occasions of speech against her
22. 17 And, lo, he hath given occasions of speech
4. *A meeting,* תַּאֲנָה *taanah.*
Jer. 2. 24 in her occasion who can turn her away?
5. *A meeting,* תֹּאֲנָה *toanah.*
Judg14. 4 that he sought an occasion against the P.
6. *A quarrel, removal,* תְּנוּאָה *tenuah.*
Job 33. 10 Behold, he findeth occasions against me
7. *Occasion, excitement, impulse,* ἀφορμή *aphormē.*
Rom. 7. 8, 11 sin, taking occasion by the command.
2 Co. 5. 12 give you occasion to glory on our behalf
11. 12 cut off occasion from them which desire o.
Gal. 5. 13 only (use) not liberty for an occasion to the
1 Ti. 5. 14 give none occasion to the adversary to speak

OCCASION of, by —
Through, by means of, διά (*gen.*) *dia.*
2 Co. 8. 8 but by occasion of the forwardness of ot.
OCCASION (of stumbling), to fall —
A stumbling block, σκάνδαλον *skandalon.*
Rom 14. 13 or an occasion to fall, in..brother's way
1 Jo. 2. 10 there is none occasion of stumbling in him
OCCASION, to (have) —
1. *To fall,* נָפַל *nephal.*
Ezra 7. 20 which thou shalt have occasion to bestow
2. *To bring round about,* סָבַב *sabab.*
1 Sa. 22. 22 I have occasioned (the death) of all the p.
OCCASION serves, to find occasion, as —
Thy hand finds, תִּמְצָא יָדְךָ [*yad*].
Judg. 9. 33 then mayest thou..as thou shalt find oc.
1 Sa. 10. 7 do as occasion serve thee; for God (is) with
OCCUPATION —
1. *Work,* מְלָאכָה *melakah.*
Jon. 1. 8 What (is) thine occupation? and whence
2. *Doing, work,* מַעֲשֶׂה *maaseh.*
Gen. 46. 33 Pharaoh..shall say, What (is) your occu.?
47. 3 said unto his brethren, What (is) your oc.
3. *Art, trade, profession,* τέχνη *technē.*
Acts 18. 3 by their occupation they were tent makers
OCCUPIED, to be —
1. *To do work,* עָשָׂה מְלָאכָה *asah melakah,* 2.
Judg 16. 11 with new ropes that never were occupied
2. *To do, use,* עָשָׂה *asah.*
Exod38. 24 All the gold that was occupied for the w.
3. *To walk round about,* περιπατέω *peripateō.*
Heb. 13. 9 not profited them that have been occupied
OCCUPY, to —
1. *To give,* נָתַן *nathan.*
Eze. 27. 16 they occupied in thy fairs with emeralds
27. 19 Dan also and Javan going to and fro occ.
27. 22 they occupied in thy fairs with chief of all
2. *To mingle, traffic,* עָרַב *arab.*
Eze. 27. 9 all the ships..were in thee to occupy thy
27. 27 the occupiers of thy merchandise, and all
3. *To fill up or again,* ἀναπληρόω *anaplēroō.*
1 Co.14. 16 how shall he that occupieth the room of
4. *To do business,* πραγματεύομαι *pragmateuomai.*
Luke19. 13 called..and said unto them, Occupy till
OCCUPY with, to —
To go about, trade, סָחַר *sachar.*
Eze. 27. 21 they occupied with thee in lambs, and r.
OCCURRENT —
A coming or falling upon, occurrence, פֶּגַע *pega.*
1 Ki. 5. 4 (is) neither adversary nor evil occurrent
OC'-RAN, עָכְרָן *troubler.*
Father of Pagiel, an Asherite whom Moses chose to number the people. B.C. 1490.
Num. 1. 13 Of Asher; Pagiel the son of O.
2. 27 the captain..(shall be) Pagiel the son of O.
7. 72 On the eleventh day Pagiel the son of O.
7. 77 (was) the offering of Pagiel the son of O.
10. 26 over the host..(was) Pagiel the son of O.
O'-DED, עֹדֵד, עוֹדֵד *aiding.*
1. Father of the prophet Azariah who encouraged Asa king of Judah. B.C. 941.
2 Ch.15. 1 spirit..came upon Azariah the son of O.
15. 8 when Asa heard..the prophecy of O. the
2. A prophet in Samaria who obtained the release of the captives of Judah. B.C. 741.
2 Ch.28. 9 prophet..was there, whose name (was) O.
ODIOUS —
To hate, שָׂנֵא *sane.*
Prov30. 23 For an odious (woman) when she is mar.
ODIOUS, to make selves —
To cause self to stink or be abhorred, בָּאַשׁ *baash,* 7.
1 Ch.19. 6 saw that they had made themselves odi.
ODOUR, (sweet) —
1. *Rest, sweetness, sweet thing,* נִיחוֹחַ *nichoach.*
Lev. 26. 31 will not smell the savour of your sweet o.
Dan. 2. 46 should offer an oblation and sweet odours
2. *Smell, odour, savour,* ὀσμή *osmē.*
John12. 3 was filled with the odour of the ointment
Phil. 4. 18 an odour of a sweet smell, a sacrifice ac.
3. *Incense, perfume,* θυμίαμα *thumiama.*
Rev. 5. 8 golden vials full of odours, which are the
18. 13 cinnamon, and odours, and ointments, and
OF —
1. *Unto, concerning,* אֶל *el.*
Gen. 20. 2 A. said of Sarah his wife, She (is) my sis.
2. *With,* אֵת *eth.*
1 Ch. 2. 18 Caleb..begat..of Azubah (his) wife, and
3. *Of,* דִּי *di.*
Ezra 5. 14 vessels also of gold and silver of the house
4. *From, out of,* מִן *min.*
Gen. 2. 7 LORD God formed man (of) the dust of the
5. *From before,* מִן קֳדָם *min qodam.*
Ezra 4. 15 moved sedition within the same of old t.

Ezra 4. 19 it is found that this city of old time hath
5. 17 that a decree was made of Cyrus the king
7. 14 Forasmuch as thou art sent of the king
Dan. 2. 6 ye shall receive of me gifts and rewards
2. 8 I know of certainty that ye would gain
2. 16 desired of the king that he would give him
2. 18 they would desire mercies of the God
2. 25 I have found a man of the captives of J.
2. 35 became like the chaff of the summer thr.
2. 41 but there shall be in it of the strength
2. 47 Of a truth..your God (is) a God of gods, and
2. 49 Daniel requested of the king, and he set S.
3. 26 Then..came forth of the midst of the fire
4. 12 the fruit thereof..all flesh was fed of it
5. 13 which (art) of the children of the captivity
6. 7, 12 of any god or man..save of thee, O ki.
6. 13 That Daniel, which (is) of the children
7. 16 I came near unto one of them that stood
6. *Concerning, upon, over,* עַל *al.*
2 Sa. 21. 4 We will have no silver..of Saul, nor of his
Jer. 8. 6 no man repented him of his wickedness
Dan. 5. 14 I have even heard of thee, that the spirit
5. 16 I have heard of thee, that thou canst make
7. 19 I would know the truth of the fourth be.
7. 20 of the ten horns that (were) in his head
7. *From with,* מֵעִם *me-im.*
Exod22. 14 if a man borrow (ought) of his neighbour
8. *From with me,* מֵעִמָּדִי *me-immad-i.*
1 Sa. 20. 28 David earnestly asked..of me..to Beth.
9. *From the face of,* מִלִּפְנֵי *mil-li-phene.*
Exod23. 21 Beware of him, and obey his voice, provoke
36. 3 they received of Moses all the offering w.
10. *From the hand of,* מִיַּד *miy-yad.*
2 Sa.18. 31 LORD hath avenged thee this day of; 18.19
11. *From, of,* ἀπό *apo.*
Matt. 3. 4 the same John had his raiment of camel's
5. 42 from him that would borrow of thee turn
7. 15 Beware of false prophets, which come to
7. 16 Do men gather grapes of..or figs of thistles
10. 17 But beware of men; for they will deliver
11. 19 But wisdom is justified of her children
11. 29 Take my yoke upon you, and learn of me
15. 1 scribes and Pharisees, which were of Jer.
15. 27 the dogs eat of the crumbs which fall from
16. 6 11 beware of the leaven of the Pharisees
16. 12 not beware of the leaven of bread, but of
16. 21 suffer many things of the elders and chief
17. 25 of whom do the kings..take custom or t.
17. 25 of their own children, or of strangers?
17. 26 Peter saith..Of strangers. Jesus saith
21. 11 said, This is Jesus the prophet of Nazareth
24. 32 Now learn a parable of the fig tree: 27. 9.
27. 21 Whether of the twain will ye that I release
27. 24 saying, I am innocent of the blood..see
27. 57 there came a rich man of Arimathea, na.
Mark 5. 29, 34; 6. 43; 7. 28; 8. 15, [31]; 12. 2, 38; 13.
28; 15. 43, 45; Luke 5. 15; 6. 13, 17, 30; 7. 21, 35; 8. 2,
[3]; 9. 22, 38; 11. 50, 51; 12. 1, 4, 15, 20, 57; 17. 25; 18.
3; 20. 10, 46; 21. 30; 22. 18, 71; 23. 51; 24. [42]; John
1. 44, 45; 5. 19, 30; 7. 17, 18, 28; 8. 28, 42; 10. 18; 11.
1, 51; 12. 21; 14. 10; 15. 4; 16. 13; 18. 34; 19. 38; 21.
2, 10; Acts 2. 17, 18, 22; 5. 2, 3; 6. 9; 8. 22; 10. 38; 12.
1; 13. 23; 15. 5; 17. 13; 19. [13]; 21. 16, 27; 23. 34; 27.
44; Rom. 13. [1]; 1 Co. 1. 30; 4. 5; 6. 19; 11. 23; 2 Co.
2. 3; 3. 5; 10. 7; Gal. 1. 1; 2. 6; 3. 2; Phil. 1. 28; Col.
1. 7; 3. 24; 1 Th. 2. 6, 6; 1 Ti. 3. 7; Heb. 7. 2, 13; 11.
13; 12. 15; 13. 24; Jas. 1. 13; 5. 4; 1 Jo. 1. 5; 2. 27; 3
Jo. 7; Rev. 2. [17]; 12. 6; 16. 12.
12. *Through, by means of,* διά (*gen.*) *dia.*
Rom 14. 14 (there is) nothing unclean of itself; but to
13. *Through, because of,* διά (*acc.*) *dia.*
Phil. 1. 15 preach Christ even of envy..some also of
14. *In regard to,* εἰς *eis.*
Matt. 5. 22 Thou fool! shall be in danger of hell fire
Acts 25. 20 because I doubted of such manner of qu.
2 Co.10. 13 But we will not boast of things without
10. 15 Not boasting of things without (our) me.
10. 16 not to boast in another man's line of th.
12. 6 lest any man should think of me above
Heb. 7. 14 of which tribe Moses spake nothing con.
1 Pe. 1. 11 testified beforehand the sufferings of Ch.
15. *Out of,* ἐκ *ek,* ἐξ *ex.*
Matt. 1. 3 And Judas begat Pharez and Zara of
1. 5 And Salmon begat Booz of Rachab; and
1. 5 Booz begat Obed of Ruth; and Obed be.
1. 6 And David the king begat Solomon of her
1. 16 of whom was born Jesus who is called C.
1. 18 she was found with child of the Holy Gh.
1. 20 that which is conceived in her is of the
3. 9 God is able of these stones to raise up c.
5. 37 whatsoever is more than these cometh of
6. 27 Which of you, by taking thought, can add
7. 9 Or what man is there of you, whom if his
10. 29 one of them shall not fall on the ground
13. 47 was cast into the sea, and gathered of eve.
18. 12 and one of them be gone astray, doth he
21. 25 whence was it? from heaven, or of men?
21. 26 if we shall say, Of men; we fear the peo.
21. 31 Whether of them twain did the will of
22. 35 one of them..a lawyer, asked..tempting
23. 25 within they are full [of] extortion and ex.
25. 2 five of them were wise, and five..foolish
25. 8 Give us of your oil; for our lamps are g.
26. 21 I say unto you, That one of you shall bet.
26. 27 gave (it) to them, saying, Drink ye all of
26. 29 I will not drink henceforth of this fruit

Matt27. 29 when they had platted a crown of thorns
27. 48 straightway one of them ran, and took a
Mark 9. 17; 11. 14, 30, 32; 12. 44, 44; 14. 18, [20], 23, 25; 16. [12]; Luke 1. 5, 5, 27, [35]; 2. 4, 35, 36; 3. 8; 6. 44, 44, 45; 10. 11; 11. 5, 15, 27, 49; 12. 6. 13, 25; 14. 28, 33; 15. 4, 4; 16. 9; 17. [7], 15; 20. 4, 6; 21. 4, 4, 18; 22. 3, 23, 50, 58; 24. 13, [18], 22; John 1. 13, 13, 13, 13, 16, 24, 35, 40; 2. 15; 3. 1, 5, 6, 6, 8, 31, 31; 4. 7, 13, 14, 22, 39; 6. 8, 11, 13, 26, 51, 60, 64, 65, 70, 71; 7. 17, 19, 22, 22, 25, 31, 40, 42, 44, 48, 48, 50, 52; 8. 23, 23, 41, 44, 44, 46, 47, 47; 9. 6, 16; 10. 16, 20, 26; 11. 19, 37, 45, 46, 49; 12. [4], 9, 49; 13. 21; 15. 19, 19; 16. 5, 14, 15; 17. 12, 14, 14, 16, 16; 18. 9, 26, 36, 36, 37; 19. 2; 20. 24; 21. 2.
Acts 1. 24; 2. 30; 3. 22; 4. 6; 5. 38, 39; 6. 9; 7. 37; 10. 1, 45; 11. 2. 20, 28; 13. 21; 15. 2, 21, 22, 23; 17. 4; 12. 26; 20. 30; 22. 14; 23. 21, 34; 24. 10.
Rom. 1. 3; 2. 29, 29; 4. 12, 14, 16, 16, 16; 5. 16; 9. 5, 6, 11, 11, 21, 24, 24, 30; 10. 5, 6; 11. 1, 6, [6], 14, 36; 13. 3; 14. 23, 23; 16. 10, 11; 1 Co. 1. 30; 2. 12; 7. 7; 8. 6; 9. [7], 7, 13, 14; 10. 4, 17; 11. 8, 8, 12, 12, 28, 28; 12. 15, 15, 16, 16; 15. 6, 47; 2 Co. 2. 17, 17; 3. 5, 5; 4. 7; 5. 1, 18; 9. 7; 12. 6; Gal. 2. 12, 15; 3. 7, 9, 10, 12, 18, 18; 4. 4, 23, 23; 5. 8; 6. 8, 8; Eph. 2. 8, 9; 3. 15; 5. [30, 30]; Phil. 1. 16, 17; 3. 5, 5, 9, 9; 4. 22; Col. 4. 11; 1 Th. 2. 3, 3, 6; 2 Ti. 2. 8; 3. 6; Titus 1. 10, 12; 2. 8.
Heb. 2. 11; 3. 13; 4. 1; 7. 4, 5, 12; 11. 3; Jas. 2. 16; 4. 1; 1. Pe. 1. 23; 4. 11; 1 Jo. 2. 16, 16, 19, 19, 19, 21, 29; 3. 8, 9, 9, 10, 12, 19; 4. 1, 2, 3, 4, 5, 5, 6, 6, 7, 7, 13; 5. 1, 1, 4, 18, 18, 19; 2 Jo. 4; 3 Jo. 11; Rev. 1. [5]; 2. 7, 10, 11, 17, 21, 22; 5. 5, 5; 6. 1, 1; 7. 4, 5, 5, 5, 6, 6, 6, 7, 7, 7, 8, 8, 8, 9, 13; 8. 11; 9. 20, 21, 21, 21, 21; 14. 8, 10; 15. 7; 16. 11; 17. 1, 11; 18. 3, 4, 12; 21. 6, 21.

16.*In, by, with,* ἐν *en.*
Luke 1. 61 There is none [of] thy kindred that is ca.
Acts26. 20 But showed first unto them of Damascus
Rom. 2. 17 called a Jew . . and makest thy boast of
2. 23 Thou that makest thy boast of the law
11. 2 Wot ye not what the scripture saith of E.?
2 Co. 2. 12 and a door was opened unto me of the L.
10. 15 Not boasting..of other men's labours; but
Gal. 4. 20 change my voice; for I stand in doubt of
Eph. 4. 1 I therefore, the prisoner of the Lord, be.
Titus 3. 5 Not by works of righteousness which we
Jas. 5. 19 if any of you do err from the truth, and
2 Pe. 2. 12 speak evil of the things that they under.

17.*On, upon, over,* ἐπί *(gen.) epi.*
Luke 4. 25 But I tell you of a truth, many widows
22. 59 of a truth this (fellow) also was with him
Acts 4. 27 For of a truth against thy holy child Jes.
10. 34 Of a truth I perceive that God is no resp.
Gal. 3. 16 not, And to seeds, as of many; but as of
Rev. 8. 13 woe, woe to the inhabiters of the earth

18.*In regard to, upon, over,* ἐπί *(dat.) epi.*
Matt 18. 13 He rejoiceth more of that (sheep), than of
Mark 6. 52 For they considered not (the miracle) of
John12. 16 that these things were written of him, and
Acts 4. 9 If we this day be examined of the good de.
1 Co.16. 17 I am glad of the coming of Stephanas and
2 Co. 12. 21 have not repented of the uncleanness,and
Heb. 8. 1 Now of the things which we have spoken
11. 4 he obtained witness..God testifying of his

19.*On, upon, over,* ἐπί *(acc.) epi.*
Mark 9. 12 how it is written of the Son of man, that
9. 13 and they have done..as it is written of
Heb. 7. 13 For he of whom these things are spoken

20.*Down against,* κατά *(gen.) kata.*
1 Co.15. 15 because we have testified of God that he

21.*Over against,* κατά *(acc.) kata.*
Acts 27. 2 launched, meaning to sail by the coasts of
27. 5 when we had sailed over the sea of Silicia
Rom. 4. 4 reward not reckoned of grace, but of debt
1 Co. 7. 6 I speak this by permission..not of com.
Phm. 14 should not be as it were of necessity, but

22.*With,* μετά *(gen.) meta.*
Matt18. 23 which would take account of his servants

23.*From,* παρά *(gen.) para.*
Matt. 2. 4 he demanded of them where Christ should
2. 7 enquired of them diligently what time the
2. 16 had diligently enquired of the wise men
18. 19 it shall be done for them of my Father w.
20. 20 came to him..desiring a certain thing [of]
Mark 8. 11 seeking of him a sign from heaven, temp.
Luke 6. 34 if ye lend (to them) of whom ye hope to r.
11. 16 others, tempting..sought of him a sign from
12. 48 unto whomsoever much is given, of him
John 1. 14 glory as of the only begotten of the Father
4. 9 How is it that thou..askest drink of me
4. 52 Then enquired he of them the hour when
5. 44 which receive honour one of another, and
6. 45 that hath heard, and hath learned of the
6. 46 save he which is of God, he hath seen the
8. 26 speak..those things which I have heard of
8. 40 told you the truth, which I have heard of
9. 16 This man is not of God, because he keepeth
9. 33 If this man were not of God, he could do
10. 18 This commandment have I received of my
15. 15 all things that I have heard of my Father
17. 7 have known that all things..are of thee
Acts 2. 33 having received of the Father the promise
3. 2 to ask alms of them that entered into the
3. 5 expecting to receive something of them
7. 16 sepulchre that Abraham bought..of the so.
9. 2 desired of him letters to Damascus to the
10. 22 to send for thee..to hear words of thee
17. 9 when they had taken security of Jason, and
20. 24 ministry which I have received of the Lord
Acts 22. 30 certainty wherefore he was accused[of] the
24. 8 by examining of whom thyself mayest take
26. 22 Having therefore obtained help [of] God
28. 22 we desire to hear of thee what thou thin.
Gal. 1. 12 I neither received it of man, neither was
Eph. 6. 8 the same shall he receive of the Lord, wh.
Phil. 4. 18 having received of Epaphroditus the thi.
1 Th. 2. 13 ye received the word..which ye heard of
4. 1 as ye have received of us how ye ought to
2 Th. 3. 6 after the tradition which he received of us
2 Ti. 1. 13 sound words, which thou hast heard of me
1. 18 that he may find mercy of the Lord in th. b.
2. 2 the things that thou hast heard of me a.
3. 14 knowing of whom thou hast learned (them)
Jas. 1. 5 any of you lack wisdom, let him ask of God
1. 7 that he shall receive anything of the Lord
1 Jo. 3. 22 whatsoever we ask, we receive [of] him, b.
5. 15 have the petitions that we desired [of] him
Rev. 2. 27 shall rule..even as I received of my Fat.
3. 18 I counsel thee to buy of me gold tried in

24.*By the side of,* παρά *(dat.) para.*
Matt. 6. 1 ye have no reward of your Father which
1 Pe. 2. 4 disallowed indeed of men..chosen of God

25.*About, concerning,* περί *(gen.) peri.*
Matt 11. 10 For this is (he), of whom it is written, B.
15. 7 hypocrites, well did Esaias prophesy of
17. 13 understood that he spake unto them of J.
22. 42 What think ye of Christ? whose son is he?
24. 36 But of that day and hour knoweth no (m.)
26. 24 Son of man goeth as it is written of him
Mark 1. 30 lay sick..and anon they tell him of her
5. 27 When she had heard of Jesus, came in the
7. 6 Well hath Esaias prophesied of you hyp.
7. 25 heard of him, and came and fell at his f.
8. 30 charged..that they should tell no man of
10. 10 his disciples asked him again of the same
13. 32 But of that day and..hour knoweth no m.
14. 21 Son..indeed goeth, as it is written of him
Luke 1. 1 a declaration of those things which are
2. 33 at those things which were spoken of him
2. 38 spake of him to all them that looked for
3. 15 and all men mused in their hearts of John
4. 14 there went out a fame of him through all
4. 37 the fame of him went out into every place
5. 15 the more went there a fame abroad of him
7. 3 when he heard of Jesus, he sent unto him
7. 17 this rumour of him went forth throughout
7. 18 the disciples of John showed him of all
7. 27 This is (he) of whom it is written, Behold
9. 9 but who is this of whom I hear such th.?
9. 11 spake unto them of the kingdom of God
9. 45 and they feared to ask him of that saying
11. 53 to provoke him to speak of many things
13. 1 told him of the Galileans, whose blood
16. 2 How is it that I hear this of thee? give
21. 5 as some spake of the temple, how it was
23. 8 because he had heard many things of him
24. 14 they talked together of all these things
John 1. 7, 8, 15, 22, [30], 47; 2. 21, 25; 5. 31, 32, 32, 36, 37, 39, 46; 7. 7, 13, 17, 39; 8. 13, 14, 18, 18, 26, 46; 9. 17; 10. 25, 41; 11. 13, 13; 12. 41; 13. 18, 22, 24; 15. 26; 16. 8, 8, 8, 9, 10, 11, 19, 25; 18. 19, 19, 23, 34; 21. 24; Acts 1. 1; 2. 29, 31; 5. 24; 7. 52; 8. 34, 34, 34; 9. 13; 11. 22; 13. 29; 15. 6; 17. 32; 18. 15, 25; 21. 21; 22. 10; 23. 6, 11, 20, 29; 24. 8, 22, 25; 25. 9, 19, 19, 20, 26; 26. 26; 28. 21; Rom. 14. 12; 15. 14, 21; 1 Co. 1. 11; 2 Co. 10. 8; 1 Th. 1. 9; 4. 6; 5. 1; 2 Ti. 1. 3; Titus 2. 8; Heb. 4. 4, 8; 5. 11; 6. 9; 9. 5; 10. 7; 11. 7, [22], 32; 1 Pe. 1. 10, 10; 3. 15; 2 Pe. 1. 12; 3. 16; 1 Jo. 1. 1; 2. 27; 5. 9, 10; Jude 3, 15, 15.

26.*About, around, concerning,* περί *(acc.) peri.*
Mark 4. 19 the lusts of other things entering in, cho.

27.*Towards, to, unto,* πρός *(acc.) pros.*
Heb. 1. 7 of the angels he saith, Who maketh his a.
11. 18 Of whom it was said, That in Isaac shall

28.*In behalf of, for,* ὑπέρ *(gen.) huper.*
2 Co. 1. 7 our hope of you (is) stedfast, knowing, t.
1. 8 not..have you ignorant [of] our trouble
7. 4 great (is) my glorying of you: I am filled
7. 14 if I have boasted any thing to him of you
8. 23 Whether..of Titus..my partner and fello.
9. 2 for which I boast of you to them of Mac.
9. 3 lest our boasting of you should be in vain
12. 5 Of such an one will I glory: yet of myself
Phil. 2. 13 both to will and to do of (his) good 4. 10.

29.*In the presence of, before,* ἔμπροσθεν Mat. 18.14

30.*By, under,* ὑπό *(gen.) hupo.*
Matt. 1. 22 which was spoken of the Lord by the pr.
2. 15 which was spoken of the Lord by the pr.
2. 16 when he saw that he was mocked of the
3. 6 were baptized of him in Jordan, confess.
3. 13 cometh..unto John, to be baptized of him
3. 14 I have need to be baptized of thee, and
4. 1 Then was Jesus led up of the Spirit into
4. 1 the wilderness to be tempted of the devil
5. 13 cast out, and to be trodden under foot of
6. 2 that they may have glory of men. Verily
10. 22 ye shall be hated of all (men) for my name
11. 27 All things are delivered unto me of my F.
14. 8 she, being before instructed of her moth.
17. 12 Likewise shall..the Son of man suffer of
19. 12 eunuchs, which were made eunuchs of m.
20. 23 but..for whom it is prepared of my Fath.
23. 7 in the markets, and to be called of men
24. 9 ye shall be hated of all nations for my n.
27. 12 when he was accused of the chief priests
Mark 1. 5, 9, 13; 2. 3, 5, 26; 13. 13; 16. [11]; Luke 2. 21; 3. 7; 4. 2, 15; 7. 30; 8. 29, [43]; 9. 7, 8, 10, 22; 14. 8, 8; 17. 20; 21. 17, 24; John 10. [14]; 14. 21; Acts 2. 24; 4. 11; 10. [33], 38, 41, 42; 12. 5; 15. [4]; 16. 4, 6, 14; 17. 13; 21. 35; 22. 11, 12; 23. 10, 27, 27; 24. 26; 26. 2, 6, 7; Rom. 12. 21; 13. 1; 15. 15; 1 Co. 2. 12, 15; 4. 3, 3; 6. 12; 7. 25; 8. 3; 10. 9, 10, 29; 11. 32; 14. 24, 24; 2 Co. 1. 4, 16; 2. 6; 3. 2; 5. 4; 8. 19; 11. 24; 12. 11; Gal. 1. 14; 3. 17; 4. 9; 5. 15; Eph. 5. 12; Phil. 3. 12; 1 Th. 1. 4; 2. 4, 14, 14; 2 Th. 2. 13; Heb. 5. 4, 10; 7. 7; 11. 23; 12. 3, 5; Jas. 1. 14; 2. 9; 3. 4, 6; 1 Pe 2. 4; 3 Jo. 12. 12; Jude 12, 17; Rev. 6. 13.

OF fire —
Fiery, of fire, πύρινος *purinos.*
Rev. 9. 17 sat on them, having breast plates of fire

OF him, or of himself —
Of him or himself, αὑτοῦ, αὐτοῦ *hautou, autou.*
Eph. 1. 17 and revelation in the knowledge of him
Heb. 9. 26 to put away sin by the sacrifice of himself

OF, there —
Concerning it, περὶ αὐτοῦ *peri autou.*
Matt12. 36 they shall give account thereof in the day

OF, where —
1.*Concerning which,* περὶ ἧς *peri hēs.*
Heb. 2. 5 put in subjection the world..whereof we

2.*Concerning certain things,* περὶ τίνων *peri tinōn.*
1 Ti. 1. 7 neither what they say, nor whereof they
[*See also* Full, plenty, speak, weary.]

OFF —
1.*From off,* מֵעַל *me-al.*
Gen. 24. 64 when she saw Isaac, she lighted off the

2.*The face,* פָּנִים *panim.*
Zeph. 1. 2 I will utterly consume all..from off the
1. 3 I will cut..man from off the land, saith the

3.*From, off, away,* ἀπό *apo.*
Matt26. 58 Peter followed him afar off unto the high
27. 55 many women were there beholding afar off
Mark 5. 6 when he saw Jesus afar off, he ran and w.
14. 54 Peter followed him afar off, even into the
15. 40 There were also women looking on afar off
Luke16. 23 seeth Abraham afar off, and Lazarus in his
John 11. 18 Bethany was..about fifteen furlongs off
Rev. 18. 10 Standing afar off for the fear of her torm.
18. 15 shall stand afar off for the fear of her to.
18. 17 and as many as trade by sea, stood afar off

4.*Out off,* ἐκ *ek.*
Mark11. 8 others cut down branches off the trees, and
[*See also* Afar, beat, branch, break, broken, cast, cast far, crop, cut, cutting, draw, fall, fallen, far, from, good way, leave, neck, pluck, pluckt, pull, put, putting, rend, remove, ring, scrape, shake, shave, smite, strip, take, taken, wipe.]

OFFENCE —
1.*Sin,* חֵטְא *chet.*
Eccl.10. 4 leave not..yielding pacifieth great offen.

2.*A stumbling,* מִכְשׁוֹל *mikshol.*
1 Sa. 25. 31 this shall be no..offence of heart unto my
Isa. 8. 14 stone of stumbling and for a rock of offe.

3.*Sin, error,* ἁμαρτία *hamartia.*
2 Co. 11. 7 Have I committed an offence in abasing m.

4.*A falling aside or away,* παράπτωμα *paraptōma.*
Rom. 4. 25 Who was delivered for our offences, and
5. 15 But not as the offence, so also (is) the free
5. 15 For if through the offence of one many be
5. 16 the free gift (is) of many offences unto ju.
5. 17 if by one man's offence death reigned by
5. 18 Therefore as by the offence of one (judg.
5. 20 Moreover the law entered, that the offen.

5.*A stumbling block,* πρόσκομμα *proskomma.*
Rom 14. 20 (is) evil for that man who eateth with off.

6.*A stumbling block,* προσκοπή *proskopē.*
2 Co. 6. 3 Giving no offence in any thing, that the

7.*A stumbling block,* σκάνδαλον *skandalon.*
Matt16. 23 thou art an offence unto me; for thou sa.
18. 7 Woe unto the world because of offences!
18. 7 for it must needs be that offences come
18. 7 but woe to that man by whom the offence
Luke17. 1 It is impossible but that offences will co.
Rom. 9. 33 Behold, I lay in Sion a..rock of offence
16. 17 mark them which cause divisions and off.
Gal. 5. 11 then is the offence of the cross ceased
1 Pe. 2. 8 a stone of stumbling, and a rock of offence

OFFENCE, none, void of, without —
Not causing to stumble, ἀπρόσκοπος *aproskopos.*
Acts 24. 16 to have always a conscience void of offe.
1 Co.10. 32 Give none offence, neither to the Jews, nor
Phil. 1. 10 that ye may be sincere and without offen.

OFFENCE, to acknowledge —
To be guilty, confess guilt, אָשֵׁם *ashem.*
Hos. 5. 15 till they acknowledge their offence, and

OFFEND, to (make to) —
1.*To be guilty,* אָשֵׁם *ashem.*
Jer. 2. 3 all that devour him shall offend; evil sh.
50. 7 We offend not, because they have sinned
Eze. 25. 12 hath greatly offended, and revenged him.
Hos. 4. 15 let not Judah offend: and come not ye u.
13. 1 but when he offended in Baal, he died
Hab. 1. 11 offend, (imputing) this his power unto his

2.*Guilt is upon us,* אַשְׁמָה עַל *ashmah al.*
2 Ch. 28. 13 whereas we have offended against the Lo.

3. *To deal treacherously,* בָּגַד *bagad.*
Psa. 73. 15 I should offend (against) the generation

4. *To act wickedly,* חָבַל *chabal.*
Job 34. 31 meet to be said unto God..I will not off.

5. *To sin, err, miss the mark,* חָטָא *chata.*
Gen. 20. 9 what have I offended thee, that thou hast
40. 1 had offended their lord the king of Egypt
2 Ki.18. 14 saying, I have offended; return from me
Jer. 37. 18 What have I offended against thee, or a.

6. *To sin, err, miss the mark,* ἁμαρτάνω *hamartanō.*
Acts 25. 8 nor yet against Cesar, have I offended any

7. *To stumble, fall,* πταίω *ptaiō.*
Jas. 2. 10 shall keep the whole law, and yet offend
3. 2 in many things we offend all. If any..o.

8. *To cause to stumble,* σκανδαλίζω *skandalizō.*
Matt. 5. 29 if thy right eye offend thee, pluck it out
5. 30 if thy right hand offend thee, cut it off
11. 6 blessed is (he), whosoever shall not be o.
13. 21 when..persecution ariseth..he is offended
13. 57 they were offended in him. But Jesus said
15. 12 Knowest thou that the Pharisees were of.
17. 27 lest we should offend them, go thou to
18. 6 But whoso shall offend one of these little
18. 8 if thy hand or thy foot offend thee, cut th.
18. 9 if thine eye offend thee, pluck it out, and
24. 10 then shall many be offended, and shall b.
26. 31 All ye shall be offended because of me t.
26. 33 Though all..be offended..will I never be o.
Mark 4. 17 when..persecution ariseth..they are off.
6. 3 the carpenter..And they were offended at
9. 42 whosoever shall offend one of (these) little
9. 43 if thy hand offend thee, cut it off: it is b.
9. 45 if thy foot offend thee, cut it off: it is be.
9. 47 if thine eye offend thee, pluck it out: it is
14. 27 All ye shall be offended because of me t.
14. 29 Although all shall be offended, yet (will)
Luke 7. 23 blessed is (he), whosoever shall not be o.
17. 2 than that he should offend one of these l.
John 6. 61 he said unto them, Doth this offend you?
16. 1 spoken unto you, that ye should not be o.
Rom 14. 21 stumbleth, [or is offended], or is made w.
1 Co. 8. 13 if meat make my brother to offend, I will
8. 13 eat no flesh..lest I make my brother to o.
2 Co.11. 29 Who is weak..who is offended, and I burn

OFFEND, (no) thing —
A stumbling, stumbling block, מִכְשׁוֹל *mikshol.*
Psa.119. 165 which love thy law..nothing shall offend

OFFENDED —
To step over, transgress, פָּשַׁע *pasha,* 2.
Prov 18. 19 A brother offended (is harder to be won)

OFFENDER, (to be or make an) —

1. *Sinful or erring one,* חַטָּא *chatta.*
1 Ki. 1. 21 I and my son Solomon shall be counted of.

2. *To cause to sin or err,* חָטָא *chata,* 5.
Isa. 29. 21 That make a man an offender for a word

3. *To be unrighteous, unjust,* ἀδικέω *adikeō.*
Acts 25. 11 For if I be an offender, or have committed

OFFENDS, thing that —
A stumbling block, σκάνδαλον *skandalon.*
Matt13. 41 they shall gather..all things that offend

OFFER, to —

1. *To slaughter, offer sacrifice,* זָבַח *zabach.*
Gen. 31. 54 Then Jacob offered sacrifice upon the m.
46. 1 offered sacrifices unto the God of his fat.
Exod23. 18 Thou shalt not offer the blood of my sac.
Lev. 17. 5 sacrifices, which they offer..and offer th.
17. 7 they shall no more offer their sacrifices
19. 5 if ye offer a sacrifice..ye shall offer it at
22. 29 when ye will offer a sacrifice..offer (it)
Num22. 40 Balak offered oxen and sheep, and sent
Deut18. 3 priests' due..from them that offer a sacr.
27. 7 thou shalt offer peace offerings, and shalt
33. 19 there they shall offer sacrifices of righte.
Judg16. 23 gathered them together for to offer a
1 Sa. 1. 4 when the time was that Elkanah offered
1. 21 went up to offer unto the LORD the yearly
2. 13 when any man offered sacrifice, the priests'
2. 19 when she came up with her husband to o.
2 Sa. 15. 12 A. sent for A...while he offered sacrifices
1 Ki. 8. 62 all Israel with him, offered sacrifice before
8. 63 Solomon offered a sacrifice..which he off.
13. 2 upon thee shall he offer the priests of the
1 Ch.15. 26 they offered seven bullocks and seven ra.
2 Ch. 7. 4 the king and all the people offered sacri.
7. 5 king Solomon offered a sacrifice of twenty
15. 11 they offered unto the LORD the same time
Neh.12. 43 Also that day they offered great sacrifices
Psa. 4. 5 Offer the sacrifices of righteousness, and
27. 6 therefore will I offer in his tabernacle s.
50. 14 Offer unto God thanksgiving; and pay thy
50. 23 Whoso offereth praise glorifieth me; and
116. 17 I will offer to thee the sacrifice of thank.
Isa. 57. 7 thither wentest thou up to offer sacrifice
Eze. 20. 28 they offered there their sacrifices, and th.
Jon. 1. 16 offered a sacrifice unto the LORD, and m.

2. *To slaughter, offer sacrifice,* זָבַח *zabach,* 3.
1 Ki.22. 43 the people offered and burnt incense yet

3. *Slaughter, sacrifice,* זֶבַח *zebach.*
Lev. 19. 6 It shall be eaten the same day ye offer it

4. *To cause to draw nigh, bring nigh,* נָגַשׁ *nagash,* 5.
Amos 5. 25 Have ye offered unto me sacrifices and off.
Mal. 1. 7 Ye offer polluted bread upon mine altar
Mal. 1. 8 if ye offer the blind..if ye offer the lame
2. 12 him that offereth an offering unto the L.
3. 3 they may offer unto the LORD an offering

5. *To (cause to) wave, offer,* נוּף *nuph,* 5.
Exod35. 22 every man that offered, (offered) an offer.
Num. 8. 11 Aaron shall offer the Levites before the
8. 13 offer them (for) an offering unto the LORD
8. 15 cleanse them, and offer them (for) an off.
8. 21 Aaron offered them (as) an offering before

6. *To stretch out to,* נָטָה עַל *natah al.*
1 Ch.21. 10 Thus saith the LORD, I offer thee three

7. *To lift up to,* נָטַל עַל *natal al.*
2 Sa. 24. 12 Thus saith the LORD, I offer thee three

8. *To pour out,* נָסַךְ *nasak.*
Hos. 9. 4 They shall not offer wine (offerings) to the

9. *To cause to pour out,* נָסַךְ *nasak,* 5.
Psa. 16. 4 drink offerings of blood will I not offer

10. *To pour out,* נְסַךְ *nesak,* 3.
Dan. 2. 46 commanded that they should offer an ob.

11. *To lift up,* נָשָׂא *nasa.*
Eze. 20. 31 For when ye offer your gifts, when ye m.

12. *To give,* נָתַן *nathan.*
Num18. 12 first fruits of them which they shall offe.
Eze. 6. 13 the place where they did offer sweet savour

13. *To ascend,* עָלָה *alah.*
1 Sa. 2. 28 to offer upon mine altar, to burn incense

14. *To cause to go up,* עָלָה *alah,* 5.
Gen. 8. 20 and offered burnt offerings on the altar
22. 2 offer him there for a burnt offering upon
22. 13 offered him up for a burnt offering in the
Exod24. 5 he sent young men..which offered burnt
30. 9 Ye shall offer no strange incense thereon
32. 6 rose up..and offered burnt offerings, and
40. 29 offered upon it the burnt offering, and the
Lev. 14. 20 the priest shall offer the burnt offering
17. 8 that offereth a burnt offering or sacrifice
Num23. 2, 4 offered on (every) altar a bullock and a ram
23. 14, 30 offered a bullock and a ram on (every)
Deut 12. 13 offer not thy burnt offerings in every pla.
12. 14 there thou shalt offer thy burnt offerings
27. 6 thou shalt offer burnt offerings thereon
Josh. 8. 31 they offered thereon burnt offerings unto
22. 23 to offer thereon burnt offering or meat of.
Judg. 6. 26 offer a burnt sacrifice with the wood of
11. 31 and I will offer it up for a burnt offering
13. 16 if thou wilt offer..thou must offer it unto
13. 19 and offered (it) upon a rock unto the LORD
20. 26 offered burnt offerings and peace offerings
21. 4 offered burnt offerings and peace offerings
1 Sa. 6. 14 offered the kine a burnt offering unto the
6. 15 offered burnt offerings and sacrificed sa.
7. 9 Samuel took a sucking lamb, and offered
7. 10 as Samuel was offering up the burnt offe.
10. 8 I will come down unto thee, to offer burnt
13. 9 And Saul..offered the burnt offering
13. 10 as soon as he had made an end of offering
13. 12 I forced myself therefore, and offered a b.
2 Sa. 6. 17 David offered burnt offerings and peace o.
6. 18 as soon as David had made an end of off.
24. 22 Let my lord the king take and offer up
24. 24 neither will I offer burnt offerings unto
24. 25 offered burnt offerings and peace offerings
1 Ki. 3. 4 a thousand burnt offerings did S. offer upon
3. 15 offered up burnt offerings, and offered p.
9. 25 three times in a year did Solomon offer b.
12. 32 ordained a feast..he offered upon the al.
12. 33 So he offered upon the altar which he had
12. 33 offered upon the altar, and burnt incense
2 Ki. 3. 27 and offered him..a burnt offering upon
16. 12 the king approached to the altar, and off.
1 Ch.16. 2 when David had made an end of offering
16. 40 To offer burnt offerings unto the LORD up
21. 24 I will not..offer burnt offerings without
21. 26 offered burnt offerings and peace offerings
23. 31 to offer all burnt sacrifices unto the LORD
29. 21 and offered burnt offerings unto the LORD
2 Ch. 1. 6 offered a thousand burnt offerings upon
4. 6 such things as they offered for the burnt.
8. 12 Then Solomon offered burnt offerings unto
8. 13 offering according to the commandment
23. 18 to offer the burnt offering of the LORD, as
24. 14 vessels..to offer.. and they offered burnt
29. 7 have not..offered burnt offerings in the
29. 21 commanded..to offer..on the altar of the
29. 27 Hezekiah commanded to offer the burnt o.
29. 29 when they had made an end of offering, the
35. 14 the sons of Aaron (were busied) in offering
35. 16 to offer burnt offerings upon the altar of
Ezra 3. 2 to offer burnt offerings thereon, as..writ.
3. 3 they offered burnt offering thereon unto
3. 6 to offer burnt offerings unto the LORD
Job 1. 5 and offered burnt offerings..to the num.
42. 8 and offer up for yourselves a burnt offer.
Psa. 51. 19 then shall they offer bullocks upon thine
66. 15 I will offer unto thee..I will offer bullocks
Isa. 57. 6 to them..thou hast offered a meat offering
66. 3 he that offereth an oblation..swine's
Jer. 14. 12 when they offer burnt offering and an
33. 18 want a man before me to offer burnt off.
48. 35 him that offereth in the high places, and
Eze. 43. 18 to offer burnt offerings thereon, and to
43. 24 they shall offer them up..a burnt offering
Amos 5. 22 Though ye offer me burnt offerings and

15. *To do, make,* עָשָׂה *asah.*
Exod29. 36 And thou shalt offer every day a bullock
29. 38 Now this (is that) which thou shalt offer
Exod29. 39 The one lamb thou shalt offer in the mor.
29. 39, 41 and the other lamb thou shalt offer at
Lev. 5. 10 he shall offer the second..a burnt offering
6. 22 the priest..that is anointed..shall offer it
9. 7 offer thy sin offering..offer the offering of
9. 16 and offered it according to the manner
14. 19 the priest shall offer the sin offering, and
14. 30 he shall offer the one of the turtle doves
15. 15 priest shall offer them, the one..a sin of.
15. 30 the priest shall offer the one..a sin offer.
16. 9 Aaron shall bring the goat..and offer him
16. 24 come forth, and offer his burnt offering
17. 9 bringeth it not..to offer it unto the LORD
22. 23 that mayest thou offer..a free will offer.
23. 12 ye shall offer that day when ye wave the
Num. 6. 11 the priest shall offer the one for a sin off.
6. 16 the priest..shall offer his sin offering, and
6. 17 shall offer the ram..shall offer also his m.
Josh.22. 23 or if to offer peace offerings thereon, let the
Judg 13. 16 if thou wilt offer a burnt offering, thou
1 Ki. 3. 15 offered up burnt offerings, and offered p.
8. 64 there he offered burnt offerings, and meat
2 Ki. 5. 17 thy servant will henceforth offer neither
10. 24 when they went in to offer sacrifices and
2 Ch. 7. 7 there he offered burnt offerings, and the
Psa. 66. 15 I will offer bullocks with goats. Selah

16. *To make perfume, offer incense,* קָטַר *qatar,* 5.
Num16. 40 that no stranger..come near to offer inc.
1 Ch. 6. 49 Aaron and his sons offered upon the altar

17. *To be or bring near,* קָרַב *qarab.*
Lev. 16. 1 when they offered before the LORD, and

18. *To cause to come near,* קָרַב *qarab,* 5.
Lev. 1. 3 let him offer a male..he shall offer it of
2. 1 when any will offer a meat offering unto
2. 12 ye shall offer them unto the LORD: but
2. 13 with all thine offerings thou shalt offer s.
2. 14 if thou offer a meat offering..thou shalt o
3. 1 if he offer (it) of the herd..he shall offer
3. 3, 9 he shall offer of the sacrifice of the pe.
3. 6 male or female, he shall offer it without
3. 7 If he offer a lamb..then shall he offer it
3. 12 goat, then he shall offer it before the Lo.
3. 14 And he shall offer thereof his offering
4. 14 shall offer a young bullock for the sin, and
5. 8 shall offer (that) which (is) for the sin ot
6. 14 the sons of Aaron shall offer it before the
6. 20 which they shall offer unto the LORD in
6. 21 baken pieces..shalt thou offer..a sweet
7. 3 And he shall offer of it all the fat thereof
7. 8 the priest that offereth any man's burnt
7. 8 the burnt offering which he hath offered
7. 9 all..shall be the priest's that offereth it
7. 11 of the sacrifice..which he shall offer unto
7. 12 If he offer it for a thanksgiving, then
7. 12 he shall offer with the sacrifice of thank.
7. 13 he shall offer..his offering unleavened b.
7. 14 of it he shall offer one out of the whole
7. 16 the same day that he offereth his sacrifice
7. 18 shall it be imputed unto him that offereth
7. 25 men offer an offering made by fire unto the
7. 29 He that offereth the sacrifice of his peace
7. 33 that offereth the blood of the peace offer
7. 38 commanded the children of Israel to offer
9. 2 Take thee..and offer (them) before the L.
10. 1 offered strange fire before the LORD, which
10. 19 this day have they offered their sin offer.
12. 7 Who shall offer it before the LORD, and
14. 12 the priest shall take one he lamb, and of.
16. 6 Aaron shall offer his bullock of the sin o.
17. 4 to offer an offering unto the LORD before
21. 6 (and) the bread of their God, they do offer
21. 8 for he offereth the bread of thy God: he
21. 17 let him not approach to offer the bread of
21. 21 shall come nigh to offer the offerings of the
21. 21 he shall not come nigh to offer the bread
22. 18 that will offer his oblation for all his vows
22. 18 which they will offer unto the LORD for a
22. 20 hath a blemish, (that) shall ye not offer; for
22. 21 whosoever offereth a sacrifice of peace off.
22. 22 ye shall not offer these unto the LORD, nor
22. 24 ye shall not offer unto the LORD that wh.
22. 25 shall ye offer the bread of your God of any
23. 8, 25, 27, 36, 36, 37 offer an offering made by
23. 16 ye shall offer a new meat offering unto
23. 18 ye shall offer with the bread seven lambs
27. 11 of which they do not offer a sacrifice unto
Num. 3. 4 when they offered strange fire before the
5. 25 and shall wave..and offer it upon the al.
6. 14 he shall offer his offering unto the LORD
7. 2 That the princes of Israel, heads..offered
7. 10 the princes offered for dedication of the
7. 10 the princes offered their offering before
7. 11 They shall offer their offering, each prince
7. 12 he that offered his offering the first day
7. 18 On the second day Nethaneel..did offer
7. 19 He offered (for) his offering one silver c.
9. 7 that we may not offer an offering of the
15. 4 Then shall he that offereth his offering
15. 7 for a drink offering thou shalt offer the
16. 35 and consumed the..men that offered in.
16. 38 they offered them before the LORD, ther
16. 39 wherewith they that were burnt had off.
26. 61 when they offered strange fire before the
28. 2 shall ye observe to offer unto me in their
28. 3 the offering..which ye shall offer unto the
28. 11 ye shall offer a burnt offering unto the L.
28. 19 But ye shall offer a sacrifice made by fire
28. 27 But ye shall offer the burnt offering for a
29. 8 But ye shall offer a burnt offering unto the
29. 13, 36 ye shall offer a burnt offering, a sacr.

Judg. 3. 18 when he had made an end to offer the p.
1 Ch.16. 1 they offered burnt sacrifices and peace o.
2 Ch.35. 12 to offer unto the LORD, as (it is) written
Ezra 8. 35 offered burnt offerings unto the God of
Psa. 72. 10 kings of Sheba and Seba shall offer gifts
Eze. 43. 22 on the second day thou shalt offer a kid
43. 23 thou shalt offer a young bullock without
43. 24 thou shalt offer them before the LORD
44. 7 when ye offer my bread, the fat and the
44. 15 they shall stand before me to offer unto
44. 27 he shall offer his sin offering, saith the L.
46. 4 the burnt offering that the prince shall o.
Hag. 2. 14 and that which they offer there (is) uncl.
Mal. 1. 8 offer it now unto thy governor; will he

19. *To bring near,* קְרֵב *qereb,* 3.
Ezra 7. 17 offer them upon the altar of the house of

20. *To cause to come near,* קְרֵב *qereb,* 5.
Ezra 6. 10 That they may offer sacrifices of sweet sa.
6. 17 offered at the dedication of this house of

21. *To cause to lift up,* רוּם *rum,* 5.
Exod35. 24 Every one that did offer an offering of sil.
Lev. 22. 15 the holy things..which they offer unto the
Num18. 19 which..children of Israel offer unto the L.
18. 24 which they offer (as) an heave offering
18. 28 Thus ye also shall offer an heave offering
18. 29 all your gifts ye shall offer every heave off.
Ezra 8. 25 the offering..which the king..had offered
Eze. 45. 1 ye shall offer an oblation unto the LORD
45. 13 This (is) the oblation that ye shall offer
48. 8 shall be the offering which ye shall offer
48. 9 The oblation that ye shall offer unto the
48. 20 ye shall offer the holy oblation four squa.

22. *To slaughter,* שָׁחַט *shachat.*
Exod34. 25 Thou shalt not offer the blood of my sac.

23. *To lead up,* ἀνάγω *anagō.*
Acts 7. 41 offered sacrifice unto the idol, and rejoiced

24. *To bear up,* ἀναφέρω *anapherō.*
Heb.13. 15 By him therefore let us offer the sacrifice
Jas. 2. 21 when he had offered Isaac his son upon the

25. *To give,* δίδωμι *didōmi.*
Luke 2. 24 to offer a sacrifice according to that wh.
Rev. 8. 3 that he should offer (it) with the prayers

26. *To bear toward,* προσφέρω *prospherō.*
Matt. 5. 24 be reconciled..then come and offer thy g.
8. 4 offer the gift that Moses commanded, for
Mark 1. 44 offer for thy cleansing those things which
Luke 5. 14 offer for thy cleansing, according as Moses
23. 36 coming to him, and offering him vinegar
Acts 7. 42 have ye offered to me slain beasts and sa.
8. 18 And when Simon saw..he offered them
Heb. 5. 1 that he may offer both gifts and sacrifices
5. 3 he ought..also for himself, to offer for sins
8. 3 every high priest is ordained to offer gifts
8. 3 that this man have somewhat also to offer
8. 4 that there are priests that offer gifts
9. 7 which he offered for himself, and..v. 9.
9. 14 who..offered himself without spot to God
9. 25 Nor yet that he should offer himself often
10. 1 with those sacrifices which they offered
10. 11 offering oftentimes the same sacrifices, w.
10. 12 after he had offered one sacrifice for sins
11. 4 By faith Abel offered unto God a more ex.

27. *To give upon or besides,* ἐπιδίδωμι *epididōmi.*
Luke11. 12 Or if he shall ask an egg, will he offer him

28. *To hold near,* παρέχω *parechō.*
Luke 6. 29 unto him that smiteth..offer also the ot.

OFFER up, to, unto, to —

1. *To cause to be high or lifted up,* רוּם *rum,* 5.
Num15. 19 ye shall offer up an heave offering unto
15. 20 Ye shall offer up a cake of the first of your
18. 26 ye shall offer up an heave offering of it
31. 52 gold of the offering that they offered up to

2. *To bear up or again,* ἀναφέρω *anapherō.*
Heb. 7. 27 Who needeth not..to offer up sacrifice
7. 27 for this he did once, when he offered up
1 Pe. 2. 5 to offer up spiritual sacrifices, acceptable

3. *To bear toward,* προσφέρω *prospherō.*
Heb. 5. 7 when he had offered up prayers and sup.
11. 17 offered up Isaac..offered up his only be.

OFFER for sin, to —

To offer a sin offering, חָטָא *chata,* 3.
Lev. 6. 26 The priest that offereth it for sin shall eat
9. 15 slew it, and offered it for sin, as the first

OFFER (selves) freely or willingly, to —

1. *To show self willing hearted,* נָדַב *nadab,* 7.
Judg. 5. 2 when the people willingly offered thems.
5. 9 that offered themselves willingly among
1 Ch.29. 6 the chief of the fathers..offered willingly
29. 9 rejoiced, for that they offered willingly
29. 9 because..they offered willingly to the L.
29. 14 that we should be able to offer so willingly
29. 17 I have willingly offered all these things
29. 17 seen with joy thy people..to offer willin.
2 Ch.17. 16 who willingly offered himself unto the L.
Ezra 1. 6 And..besides all (that) was willingly off.
2. 68 offered freely for the house of God to set
3. 5 every one that willingly offered a free will
Neh. 11. 2 the men that willingly offered themselves

2. *To be offered willingly,* נָדַב *nedab,* 4.
Ezra 7. 15 have freely offered unto the God of Israel
7. 16 offering willingly for the house of their G.

OFFER incense or sacrifice, to —

1. *To make perfume, offer incense,* קָטַר *qatar,* 3.
Jer. 11. 17 to provoke me to anger, in offering ince.
32. 29 upon whose roofs they have offered ince.
Amos 4. 5 offer a sacrifice of thanksgiving with lea.

2. *To slaughter, offer sacrifice,* דְּבַח *debach.*
Ezra 6. 3 the place where they offered sacrifices, and

OFFERED, to be (ready to be) —

1. *To be brought or caused to come nigh,* נָגַשׁ *nagash,* 6.
Mal. 1. 11 in every place incense (shall be) offered

2. *To go up,* עָלָה *alah.*
2 Ki. 3. 20 when the meat offering was offered, that

3. *To be brought or caused to go up,* עָלָה *alah,* 6.
Judg. 6. 28 second bullock was offered upon the altar

4. *To be made, done,* עָשָׂה *asah,* 2.
Num28. 24 After this manner ye shall offer daily

5. *A heave offering,* תְּרוּמָה *terumah.*
Eze. 48. 12 (this) oblation of the land that is offered

6. *What is brought near,* קָרְבָּן *qorban.*
Lev. 7. 15 be eaten the same day that it is offered

7. *To bear toward,* προσφέρω *prospherō.*
Acts 21. 26 offering should be offered for every one
Heb. 9. 28 So Christ was once offered to bear the s.
10. 2 would they not have ceased to be offered?
10. 8 burnt offerings..which are offered by the

8. *To be poured out,* σπένδομαι *spendomai.*
Phil. 2. 17 Yea, and if I be offered upon the sacrifice
2 Ti. 4. 6 For I am now ready to be offered, and the

OFFERED (in sacrifice) to idols, meats or things —

Any thing sacrificed to an idol, εἰδωλόθυτον *eidō.*
Acts 15. 29 That ye abstain from meats offered to id.
21. 25 keep themselves from (things) offered to i.
1 Co. 8. 1 Now as touching things offered unto idols
8. 4 things that are offered in sacrifice unto i.
8. 7 eat (it) as a thing offered unto an idol; and
8. 10 eat those things which are offered to idols
10. 19 or that which is offered in sacrifice to id.
10. 28 This is offered in sacrifice unto idols, eat
Rev. 2. 14 to eat things sacrificed unto idols, and to
2. 20 seduce..to eat things sacrificed unto idols

OFFERED things —

Work, deed, מַעֲשֶׂה *maaseh.*
2 Ch. 4. 6 such things as they offered for the burnt

OFFERING —

1. *Slaughter, sacrifice,* זֶבַח *zebach.*
Exod24. 5 sacrificed peace offerings of oxen unto the
Lev. 17. 5 offer them (for) peace offerings unto the L.
Josh.22. 23 or if to offer peace offerings thereon, let
2 Ch.30. 22 offering peace offerings, and making con.
33. 16 sacrificed thereon peace offerings and th.
Prov. 7. 14 (I have) peace offerings with me; this day

2. *Offering, present,* מִנְחָה *minchah.*
Gen. 4. 3 that Cain brought..an offering unto the
4. 4 had respect unto Abel and to his offering
4. 5 unto Cain and to his offering he had not
Num. 5. 15 an offering of jealousy, an offering of m.
5. 18 put the offering of memorial in her hands
5. 18 which (is) the jealousy offering: and the
5. 25 the priest shall take the jealousy offering
5. 25 shall wave the offering before the LORD
5. 26 the priest shall take an handful of the o.
16. 15 Respect not thou their offering: I have
1 Sa. 2. 17 for men abhorred the offering of the LORD
2. 29 Wherefore kick ye..at mine offering, wh.
2. 29 the chiefest of all the offerings of Israel
3. 14 not be purged with sacrifice nor offering
26. 19 let him accept an offering: but if (they be)
1 Ch.16 29 bring an offering, and come before him
Psa. 20. 3 Remember all thy offerings, and accept
40. 6 Sacrifice and offering thou didst not des.
96. 8 bring an offering, and come into his courts
Isa. 43. 23 not caused thee to serve with an offering
66. 20 they shall bring all your brethren..an of.
66. 20 bring an offering in a clean vessel into the
Jer. 41. 5 with offerings and incense in their hand
Amos 5. 25 Have ye offered unto me sacrifices and o.
Zeph. 3. 10 the daughter..shall bring mine offering
Mal. 1. 10 neither will I accept an offering at your
1. 11 (shall be) offered..and a pure offering: for
1. 13 thus ye brought an offering: should I ac.
2. 12 him that offereth an offering unto the L.
2. 13 insomuch that he regardeth not the offer.
3. 3 that they may offer unto the LORD an off.
3. 4 Then shall the offering of Judah and Jer.

3. *Going up,* עָלָה *alah* (infin.).
1 Ki. 18. 29 prophesied until the (time) of the offering
18. 36 it came to pass at..the offering of the..s.

4. *To cause to go up,* עָלָה *alah,* 5 (infin.).
1 Sa. 13. 10 as soon as he had made an end of offering
2 Sa. 6. 18 as soon as David had made an end of off.
1 Ch. 16. 2 when David had made an end of offering
2 Ch. 8. 13 offering according to the commandment
29 29 when they had made an end of offering, the
35. 14 the sons of Aaron (were busied) in offering

5. *To do, make,* עָשָׂה *asah* (infin.).
Lev. 9 22 and came down from offering of the sin o.
2 Ki 10. 25 as soon as he had made an end of offering

6. *To bring or cause to come near,* קָרַב *qarab,* 5 (infin.).
Num15 13 do these things after this manner in off.

7. *What is brought near,* קָרְבָּן *qorban.*
Lev. 1. 2 If any man of you bring an offering unto
1. 2 ye shall bring your offering of the cattle
1. 3 If his offering (be) a burnt sacrifice of the
1. 10 if his offering (be) of the flocks, (namely)
1. 14 the burnt sacrifice for his offering to the
1. 14 he shall bring his offering of turtle doves
2. 1 when any will offer a meat offering unto
2. 1 his offering shall be (of) fine flour; and he
2. 13 with all thine offerings thou shalt offer
3. 2, 8 lay his hand upon the head of his offer.
3. 6 And if his offering for a sacrifice of peace
3. 7 If he offer a lamb for his offering, then
3. 12 if his offering (be) a goat, then he shall of.
3. 14 he shall offer thereof his offering, (even)
4. 23, 28 he shall bring his offering, a kid of
4. 32 if he bring a lamb for a sin offering, he
5. 11 he that sinned shall bring for his offering
6. 20 This (is) the offering of Aaron, and of his
7. 13 he shall offer..his offering leavened bread
7. 16 if the sacrifice of his offering (be) a vow
9. 7 offer the offering of the people, and make
9. 15 he brought the people's offering, and took
17. 4 to offer an offering unto the LORD before
22. 27 it shall be accepted for an offering made
23. 14 that ye have brought an offering unto your
27. 9 whereof men bring an offering unto the L.
Num. 5. 15 he shall bring her offering for her, the t.
6. 14 he shall offer his offering unto the LORD
6. 21 his offering unto the LORD for his separa.
7. 3 they brought their offering before the L.
7. 10 the princes offered their offering before
7. 11 They shall offer their offering, each prince
7. 12 he that offered his offering the first day
7. 13 his offering (was) one silver charger, the
7. 17 this (was) the offering of Nahshon the son
7. 19 He offered..his offering one silver charger
7. 23 this (was) the offering of Nethaneel the
7. 25 His offering..one silver charger, the wei.
[So in v. 31, 37, 43, 49, 55, 61, 67, 73, 79.]
7. 29 this (was) the offering of..the son of
[So in v. 35, 41, 47, 53, 59, 65, 71, 77, 83.]
9. 7 that we may not offer an offering of the
9. 13 because he brought not the offering of the
15. 4 Then shall he that offereth his offering
15. 25 they shall bring their offering, a sacrifice
28. 2 My offering..my bread for my sacrifices
Eze. 20. 28 presented the provocation of their offering
40. 43 upon the tables (was) the flesh of the off.

8. *What is brought near,* קֻרְבָּן *qurban.*
Neh. 10. 34 we cast the lots..for the wood offering
13. 31 for the wood offering, at times appointed

9. *A wave offering,* תְּנוּפָה *tenuphah.*
Exod35. 22 offered..an offering of gold unto the LORD
38. 24 the gold of the offering, was twenty and
38. 29 the brass of the offering (was) seventy tal.
Num. 8. 11 an offering of the children of Israel, that
8. 13 and offer them..an offering unto the LORD
8. 15 cleanse them, and offer them..an offering
8. 21 Aaron offered them..an offering before the

10. *A heave offering,* תְּרוּמָה *terumah.*
Exod25. 2 Speak..that they bring me an offering
25. 2 of every man..ye shall take my offering
25. 3 this (is) the offering which ye shall take
30. 13 an half shekel (shall be) the offering of the
30. 14 Every one..shall give an offering unto the
30. 15 when (they) give an offering unto the Lo.
35. 5 Take ye from among you an offering unto
35. 5 let him bring it, an offering of the LORD
35. 21 they brought the LORD'S offering to the w.
35. 24 Every one that did offer an offering of sil.
35. 24 and brass, brought the LORD'S offering: and
36. 3 they received of Moses all the offering wh.
36. 6 make any more work for the offering of
Lev. 22. 12 she may not eat of an offering of the holy
Num. 5. 9 every offering of all the holy things of the
31. 52 all the gold of the offering that they offe.
2 Sa. 1. 21 rain upon you, nor fields of offerings: for
2 Ch.31. 10 began to bring the offerings into the house
31. 12 brought in the offerings and the tithes
31. 14 (was) over the free will offerings of God
Ezra 8. 25 the offering of the house of our God, which
Neh. 10. 37 our offerings, and the fruit of all manner
10. 39 children of Levi shall bring the offering
12. 44 were some appointed..for the offerings
13. 5 the tithes..and the offerings of the priests
Eze. 20. 40 there will I require your offerings, and
48. 8 shall be the offering which ye shall offer
Mal. 3. 8 Wherein have we robbed thee? In..offer.

11. *A gift,* δῶρον *dōron.*
Luke21. 4 all these have..cast in unto the offerings

12. *What is borne forward or toward,* προσφορά.
Acts 21. 26 until that an offering should be offered
24. 17 came to bring alms to my nation, and off.
Eph. 5. 2 hath given himself for us an offering and
Heb. 10. 5 Sacrifice and offering thou wouldest not
10. 8 Sacrifice and offering and burnt offerings
10. 10 through the offering of the body of Jesus
10. 14 For by one offering he hath perfected for
10. 18 Now..(there is) no more offering for sin

[*See also* Burnt, drink, free, freewill, heave, meat, passover, peace, sin, thank, trespass, voluntary, wave, whole, willing.]

OFFERING up —

1. *To cause to go up,* עָלָה *alah,* 5.
1 Sa. 7. 10 as Samuel was offering up the burnt offe.

2. *What is borne forward or toward,* προσφορά.
Rom.15. 16 that the offering up of the Gentiles might

OFFERING (or sacrifice) made by fire —
A fire offering, אִשֶּׁה *ishsheh.*
Exod29. 18, 25, 41 offering made by fire unto the LORD
[So in v. 30. 20; Lev. 2 16; 3. 3, 9, 14; 7. 5, 25; 8. 21, 28; 22. 27; 23. 8, 13, 25, 27, 36, 36, 37; 24. 7; Num. 29. 6.]
Lev. 1. 9 an offering made by fire, of a sweet savour
[So in v. 13, 17; 2. 2, 9; 3. 5; Num. 15. 10, 13, 14; 18. 17; 28. 8, 24; 29. 13, 36.]
Lev. 2. 3, 10 of the offerings of the LORD made by fire
2. 11 in any offering of the LORD made by fire
3. 11, 16 (it is) the food of the offering made by
4. 35 according to the offerings made by fire u.
5. 12 according to the offerings made by fire u.
6. 17 their portion of my offerings made by fire
6. 18 the offerings of the LORD made by fire
7. 30, 35 the offerings of the LORD made by fire
10. 12 the offerings of the LORD made by fire
10. 13 of the sacrifices of the LORD made by fire
10. 15 with the offerings made by fire of the fat
21. 6, 21 the offerings of the LORD made by fire
22. 22 nor make an offering by fire of them upon
23. 18 an offering made by fire, of sweet savour
24. 9 of the offerings of the LORD made by fire
Num15. 3 will make an offering by fire unto the Lo.
15. 25 a sacrifice made by fire unto the LORD
28. 2 my bread for my sacrifices made by fire
28. 3 This (is) the offering made by fire which ye
28. 6, 13 a sacrifice made by fire unto the LORD
28. 19 ye shall offer a sacrifice made by fire
Deut 18. 1 eat the offerings of the LORD made by fire
Josh 13. 14 the sacrifices..made by fire (are) their inh.
1 Sa. 2. 28 did I give..all the offerings made by fire

OFFERING for sin —
A guilt offering, אָשָׁם *asham.*
Isa. 53. 10 thou shalt make his soul an offering for s.

OFFERING incense —
To make perfume, offer incense, קָטַר *qatar,* 3.
Jer. 11. 17 to provoke me..in offering incense unto

OFFERINGS —
Givings, gifts, הַבְהָבִים *habhabim.*
Hos. 8. 13 They sacrifice..the sacrifices of mine off.

OFFICE —
1. *Base, station,* כֵּן *ken.*
Gen. 41. 13 me he restored unto mine office, and him
2. *Standing, station,* מַעֲמָד *maamad.*
1 Ch. 23. 28 their office (was) to wait on the sons of A.
3. *Watch, guard,* מִשְׁמָר *mishmar.*
Neh. 13. 14 deeds that I have done..for the offices th.
4. *Watch, guard,* מִשְׁמֶרֶת *mishmereth.*
2 Ch. 7. 6 the priests waited on their offices; the L.
5. *Service,* עֲבוֹדָה *abodah.*
1 Ch. 6. 32 they waited on their office according to
6. *Inspection, charge,* פְּקֻדָּה *pequddah.*
Num. 4. 16 to the office of Eleazar the son of Aaron
1 Ch. 24. 3 according to their offices in their service
2 Ch. 23. 18 Jehoiada appointed the offices of the ho.
24. 11 the chest was brought unto the king's office
Psa. 109. 8 Let..be few..let another take his office
7. *Ministration,* διακονία *diakonia.*
Rom 11. 13 apostle of the Gentiles, I magnify mine o.
8. *Work, action, office, use,* πρᾶξις *praxis.*
Rom 12. 4 and all members have not the same office

OFFICE of a bishop —
Oversight, superintendence, ἐπισκοπή *episkopē.*
1 Ti. 3. 1 If a man desire the office of a bishop, he

OFFICE of the priesthood, priest's office —
Priesthood, ἱερατεία *hierateia.*
Luke 1. 9 According to..custom of the priest's office
Heb. 7. 5 they..who receive the office of the priest.

OFFICE, to do, execute, or minister in the priest's —
1. *To act as a priest,* כָּהַן *kahan,* 3.
Exod28. 1, 3, 4, 41 minister unto me in the priest's office
29. 1, 44 minister unto me in the priest's office
30. 30 minister unto me in the priest's office
31. 10 his sons, to minister in the priest's office
35. 19 his sons, to minister in the priest's office
39. 41 garments, to minister in the priest's office
40. 13, 15 minister unto me in the priest's office
Lev. 7. 35 minister unto the LORD in the priest's of.
16. 32 consecrate to minister in the priest's office
Num. 3. 3 consecrated to minister in the priest's of.
3. 4 Ithamar ministered in the priest's office
Deut 10. 6 ministered in the priest's office in his ste.
1 Ch. 6. 10 that executed the priest's office in the te.
24. 2 and Ithamar executed the priest's office
2 Ch. 11. 14 from executing the priest's office unto the
Eze. 44. 13 to do the office of a priest unto me, nor
2. *To act as a priest,* ἱερατεύω *hierateuō.*
Luke 1. 8 while he executed the priest's office before

OFFICER —
1. *To be set up,* נָצַב *natsab,* 2.
1 Ki. 4. 5 Azariah..(was) over the officers; and Zab.
4. 7 Solomon had twelve officers over all Isr.
4. 27 those officers provided victual for king S.
5. 16 Besides the chief of Solomon's officers w.
9. 23 These (were) the chief of the officers that
2 Ch. 8. 10 these..the chief of king Solomon's officers
2. *One set up,* נְצִיב *netsib.*
1 Ki. 4. 19 (was) the only officer which (was) in the
3. *A eunuch, officer,* סָרִיס *saris.*
Gen. 37. 36 an officer of Pharaoh's..captain of the g.
39. 1 an officer of Pharaoh, captain of the gua.
40. 2 P. was wroth against two (of) his officers
40. 7 he asked Pharaoh's officers, that (were)
1 Sa. 8. 15 give to his officers, and to his servants
1 Ki. 22. 9 Then the king of Israel called an officer
2 Ki. 8. 6 the king appointed unto her a certain of.
24. 12 he, and his mother..and his officers: and
24. 15 his officers, and the mighty of the land
25. 19 out of the city he took an officer that was
1 Ch. 28. 1 with the officers, and with the mighty men
2 Ch. 18. 8 king..called for one (of his) officers, and s.
4. *Men appointed,* פָּקַד *paqad* (partic.).
Num 31. 14 Moses was wroth with the officers of the
31. 48 the officers which (were) over thousands
2 Ki. 11. 15 the priest commanded..the officers of the
5. *Inspection, charge,* פְּקֻדָּה *pequddah.*
2 Ki. 11. 18 the priest appointed officers over the ho.
1 Ch. 26. 30 officers among them of Israel on this side
Isa. 60. 17 I will also make thy officers peace, and t.
6. *Inspector,* פָּקִיד *paqid.*
Gen. 41. 34 let him appoint officers over the land, and
Judg. 9. 28 the son of Jerubbaal? and Zebul his offi.?
2 Ch. 24. 11 high priest's officer came and emptied the
Esth 2. 3 let the king appoint officers in all the
Jer. 29. 26 that ye should be officers in the house of
7. *Great one,* רַב *rab.*
Esth. 1. 8 the king had appointed to all the officers
8. *Doers of work,* עֹשֵׂה מְלָאכָה *asah melakah.*
Esth. 9. 3 and officers of the king, helped the Jews
9. *Writer,* שֹׁטֵר *shatar* (partic.).
Exod. 5. 6 task masters of the people, and their offi.
5. 10 task masters of the people..and their of.
5. 14, 15, 19 the officers of the children of Israel
Num 11. 16 elders of the people, and officers over them
Deut. 1. 15 captains over tens, and officers among
16. 18 Judges and officers shalt thou make thee
20. 5 the officers shall speak unto the people
20. 8 officers shall speak further unto the peo.
20. 9 when the officers have made an end of s.
29. 10 and your officers, (with) all the men of I.
31. 28 the elders of your tribes, and your officers
Josh. 1. 10 Then Joshua commanded the officers of
3. 2 it came to pass..that the officers went
8. 33 all Israel, and their elders, and officers
23. 2 called..for their judges, and for their o.
24. 1 called..for their judges, and for their o.
1 Ch. 23. 4 six thousand (were) officers and judges
26. 29 business over Israel, for officers and ju.
27. 1 their officers that served the king in any
2 Ch. 19. 11 also the Levites (shall be) officers before
34. 13 of the Levites..scribes, and officers, and
10. *Police officer, bailiff,* πράκτωρ *praktōr.*
Luke 12. 58 deliver thee to the officer, and the officer
11. *An under rower, assistant,* ὑπηρέτης *hupēretēs.*
Matt. 5. 25 the judge deliver thee to the officer, and
John 7. 32 the chief priests sent officers to take him
7. 45 Then came the officers to the chief priests
7. 46 The officers answered, Never man spake
18. 3 having received a band (of men) and offi.
18. 12 officers of the Jews took Jesus, and bound
18. 18 the servants and officers stood there, who
18. 22 one of the officers which stood by struck
19. 6 When the chief priests..and officers saw
Acts 5. 22 when the officers came, and found them
5. 26 Then went the captain with the officers

OFFSCOURING —
1. *Scrapings, offscouring,* סְחִי *sechi.*
Lam. 3. 45 Thou hast made us (as) the offscouring
2. *Offscouring, scrapings round about,* περίψημα.
1 Co. 4. 13 the offscouring of all things unto this

OFFSPRING —
1. *Outcomers, issue, produce,* צֶאֱצָאִים *tseetsaim.*
Job 5. 25 thine offspring as the grass of the earth
21. 8 Their seed is established..their offspring
27. 14 his offspring shall not be satisfied with b.
31. 8 eat; yea, let my offspring be rooted out
Isa. 22. 24 they shall hang upon him..the offspring
44. 3 will pour..my blessing upon thine offsp.
48. 19 the offspring of thy bowels like the gravel
61. 9 their seed shall be known..and their off.
65. 23 they (are) the seed..and their offspring
2. *Race, kind,* γένος *genos.*
Acts 17. 28 certain..said, For we are also his offspring
17. 29 Forasmuch then as we are the offspring of
Rev. 22. 16 I am the root and the offspring of David

OFT, OFTEN, OFTENER —
1. *Many a time, often,* πολλάκις *pollakis.*
Matt 17. 15 falleth into the fire, and oft into the water
Mark 5. 4 Because that he had been often bound
Acts 26. 11 I punished them oft in every synagogue
2 Co. 11. 23 in prisons more frequent, in deaths oft
11. 26 (In) journeyings often, (in) perils of waters
11. 27 in watchings often..in fastings often, in
Phil. 3. 18 many walk, of whom I have told you oft.
2 Ti. 1. 16 he oft refreshed me, and was not ashamed
Heb. 6. 7 drinketh in the rain that cometh oft upon
9. 25 Nor yet that he should offer himself often
9. 26 For then must he often have suffered since
2. *Much,* πολλά *polla.*
Matt. 9. 14 Why do we and the Pharisees fast [oft], but
3. *With the fist,* πυγμῇ *pugmē.*
Mark 7. 3 except they wash..hands oft, eat not, ho.
4. *Thick, close, frequently,* πυκνός *puknos.*
Luke 5. 33 Why do the disciples of John fast often
Acts 24. 26 wherefore he sent for him the oftener, and
1 Ti. 5. 23 use a little wine for..thine often infirmi.

OFT TIMES, OFTEN TIMES —
1. *Two steps (or) three,* פַּעֲמַיִם שָׁלוֹשׁ *paamayim shalosh*
Job 33. 29 Lo, all these..worketh God often times
2. *Many steps, times,* פְּעָמִים רַבּוֹת *peamim rabboth.*
Eccl. 7. 22 often times also thine own heart knoweth
3. *Many times,* πολλοῖς χρόνοις *pollois chronois.*
Luke 8. 29 often times it had caught him: and he was
4. *Many a time, often,* πολλάκις *pollakis.*
Matt 17. 15 for ofttimes he falleth into the fire, and
Mark 9. 22 oft times it hath cast him into the fire, and
John 18. 2 Jesus ofttimes resorted thither with his d.
Rom. 1. 13 oftentimes I purposed to come unto you
2 Co. 8. 22 whom we have often times proved diligent
Heb. 10. 11 offering oftentimes the same sacrifices, w.

OG, עוֹג *long-necked, giant.*
The king of Bashan defeated at Edrei, whose land was assigned to the half tribe of Manasseh, beyond Jordan. B.C. 1452.
Num 21. 33 O. the king of Bashan went out against
32. 33 the kingdom of O. king of Bashan, the la.
Deut. 1. 4 After he had slain..O. the king of Bashan
3. 1 O. the king of Bashan came out against us
3. 3 our God delivered into our hands O. also
3. 4 the region of Argob, the kingdom of O. in
3. 10 and Edrei, cities of the kingdom of O. in
3. 11 For only O. king of Bashan remained of
3. 13 all Bashan, (being) the kingdom of O., gave
4. 47 possessed his land, and the land of O. king
29. 7 O. the king of Bashan, came out against
31. 4 shall do..as he did to Sihon and to O., ki.
Josh. 2. 10 Sihon and O., whom ye utterly destroyed
9. 10 to O. king of Bashan, which (was) at Asht.
12. 4 coast of O. king of Bashan, (which was) of
13. 12 All the kingdom of O. in Bashan, which
13. 30 all the kingdom of O. king of Bashan, and
13. 31 and Edrei, cities of the kingdom of O. in
1 Ki. 4. 19 of O. king of Bashan; and (he was) the only
Neh. 9. 22 so they possessed..the land of O. king of
Psa. 135. 11 O. king of Bashan, and all the kingdoms
136. 20 O. the king of Bashan: for his mercy (en.

O'-HAD, אֹהַד *powerful.*
The third son of Simeon. B.C. 1700.
Gen. 46. 10 Jemuel, and Jamin, and O., and Jachin
Exod. 6. 15 Jemuel, and Jamin, and O., and Jachin

O'-HEL, אֹהֶל *family, race, tent.*
A son of Zerubbabel, descended from Jehoiakim king of Judah. B.C. 500.
1 Ch. 3. 20 Hashubah, and O., and Berechiah, and

OIL —
1. *Shining, oil,* יִצְהָר *yitshar.*
Num 18. 12 All the best of the oil, and all the best of
Deut. 7. 13 he will also bless..thine oil, the increase
11. 14 mayest gather in thy corn..and thine oil
12. 17 mayest not eat..the tithe..of thy oil, or
14. 23 shalt eat..the tithe..of thine oil, and the
18. 4 The first fruit..of thine oil, and the first
28. 51 shall not leave thee..corn, wine, or oil, (or)
2 Ki. 18. 32 a land of oil olive and of honey, that ye
2 Ch. 31. 5 children of Israel brought..oil, and honey
32. 28 for the increase of corn, and wine, and oil
Neh. 5. 11 the wine, and the oil, that ye exact of them
10. 37 of all manner of trees, of wine, and of oil
10. 39 shall bring the offering of..the oil, unto
13. 5 they laid the meat offerings..and the oil
13. 12 brought all Judah the tithe of..the oil
Jer. 31. 12 for oil, and for the young of the flock
Hos. 2. 8 that I gave her corn, and wine, and oil
2. 22 hear the corn, and the wine, and the oil
Joel 1. 10 new wine is dried up, the oil languisheth
2. 19 I will send you corn, and wine, and oil
2. 24 the fats shall overflow with wine and oil
Hag. 1. 11 upon the new wine, and upon the oil, and
2. *Oil,* מְשַׁח *meshach.*
Ezra 6. 9 wheat, salt, wine, and oil, according to
7. 22 to an hundred baths of oil, and salt with.
3. *Oil, ointment, fatness,* שֶׁמֶן *shemen.*
Gen. 28. 18 set it up..a pillar, and poured oil upon the
35. 14 drink offering thereon, and he poured oil
Exod25. 6 Oil for the light, spices for anointing oil
27. 20 that they bring thee pure oil olive beaten
29. 2 tempered with oil..wafers..anointed..o.
29. 7 Then shalt thou take the anointing oil
29. 21 thou shalt take..of the anointing oil, and
29. 40 with the fourth part of an hin of beaten oil
30. 24 And of cassia..and of oil olive an hin
30. 25 thou shalt make it an oil of holy ointment
30. 25 ointment..it shall be an holy anointing oil
30. 31 This shall be an holy anointing oil unto me
31. 11 the anointing oil, and sweet incense for the
35. 8 oil for the light..spices for anointing oil
35. 14 The candlestick..with the oil for the light
35. 15 the anointing oil, and the sweet incense
35. 28 oil for the light, and for the anointing oil
37. 29 he made the holy anointing oil, and the
39. 37 The pure candlestick..and the oil for lig.
39. 38 the anointing oil, and the sweet incense
40. 9 thou shalt take the anointing oil, and an.
Lev. 2. 1 he shall pour oil upon it, and put frank.

Lev. 2. 2 of the oil thereof, with all the frankince.
2. 4 mingled with oil, or..anointed with oil
2. 5 fine flour unleavened, mingled with oil
2. 6 pour oil thereon: it (is) a meat offering
2. 7 it shall be made (of) fine flour with oil
2. 15 thou shalt put oil upon it, and lay frank.
2. 16 of the oil thereof, with all the frankince.
5. 11 he shall put no oil upon it, neither shall
6. 15 of the oil thereof, and all the frankincen.
6. 21 In a pan it shall be made with oil..baken
7. 10 every meat offering mingled with oil, and
7. 12 cakes mingled with oil..anointed with oil
7. 12 cakes mingled with oil, of fine flour, fried
8. 2 the anointing oil, and a bullock for the s.
8. 10 Moses took the anointing oil, and anointed
8. 12 poured of the anointing oil upon Aaron's
8. 30 Moses took of the anointing oil, and of the
9. 4 a meat offering mingled with oil: for to
10. 7 for the anointing oil of the LORD (is) upon
14. 10 offering, mingled with oil..one log of oil
14. 12 the priest shall take..the log of oil, and
14. 15 the priest shall take..of the log of oil, and
14. 16 shall dip his right finger in the oil that
14. 16 shall sprinkle of the oil with his finger
14. 17 of the rest of the oil that (is) in his hand
14. 18 the remnant of the oil that (is) in the pr.
14. 21 oil for a meat offering, and a log of oil
14. 24 the priest shall take..the log of oil, and
14. 26 the priest shall pour of the oil into the
14. 27 of the oil that (is) in his left hand seven
14. 28 the priest shall put of the oil that (is) in
14. 29 the rest of the oil that (is) in the priest's
21. 10 upon whose head the anointing oil was p.
21. 12 the crown of the anointing oil of his God
23. 13 of fine flour mingled with oil, an offering
24. 2 that they bring unto thee pure oil olive
Num. 4. 9 all the oil vessels thereof, wherewith they
4. 16 the oil for..light..and the anointing oil
5. 15 he shall pour no oil upon it, nor put fran.
6. 15 cakes of fine flour mingled with oil, and
6. 15 of unleavened bread anointed with oil, and
7. 13 full of fine flour mingled with oil, for
So in v. 19, 25, 31, 37, 43, 49, 55, 61, 67, 73, 79.
8. 8 fine flour mingled with oil, and another
11. 8 taste of it was as the taste of fresh oil
15. 4 flour..with the fourth..of an hin of oil
15. 6 flour..with the third..of an hin of oil
15. 9 of flour mingled with half an hin of oil
28. 5 with the fourth..of an hin of beaten oil
28. 9, 12, 12 a meat offering, mingled with oil
28. 13 a several tenth deal..mingled with oil
28. 20 (shall be of) flour mingled with oil: three
28. 28 meat offering of flour mingled with oil
29. 3, 9, 14 meat offering..flour mingled with oil
35. 25 which was anointed with the holy oil
Deut. 8. 8 A land of wheat..a land of oil olive and
28. 40 thou shalt not anoint..with the oil
32. 13 made him to suck..oil out of the flinty r.
33. 24 Asher he said..let him dip his foot in oil
1 Sa. 10. 1 Samuel took a vial of oil, and poured (it)
16. 1 Fill thine horn with oil, and go, I will s.
16. 13 Samuel took the horn of oil, and anointed
2 Sa. 1. 21 shield of Saul..not..anointed with oil
14. 2 anoint not thyself with oil, but be as a
1 Ki. 1. 39 took an horn of oil out of the tabernacle
5. 11 gave Hiram..twenty measures of pure oil
17. 12 I have not a cake, but..a little oil in a c.
17. 14 neither shall the cruse of oil fail, until
17. 16 neither did the cruse of oil fail, according
2 Ki. 4. 2 any thing in the house, save a pot of oil
4. 6 (is) not a vessel more. And the oil stayed
4. 7 Go, sell the oil, and pay thy debt, and live
9. 1 take this box of oil in thine hand, and go
9. 3 Then take the box of oil, and pour (it) on
9. 6 he poured the oil on his head, and said unto
1 Ch. 9. 29 appointed to oversee..the oil, and the fra.
12. 40 brought bread on asses..and oil, and oxen
27. 28 and over the cellars of oil (was) Joash
2 Ch. 2. 10 I will give..twenty thousand baths of oil
2. 15 the oil..let him send unto his servants
11. 11 and store of victual, and of oil and wine
Ezra 3. 7 They gave..drink, and oil, unto them of
Esth. 2. 12 six months with oil of myrrh, and six m.
Job 29. 6 and the rock poured me out rivers of oil
Psa. 23. 5 thou anointest my head with oil; my cup
45. 7 hath anointed thee with the oil of gladness
55. 21 his words were softer than oil, yet (were)
89. 20 David..with my holy oil have I anointed
92. 10 (horn)..I shall be anointed with fresh oil
109. 18 let it come..like water, and like oil into
141. 5 (it shall be) an excellent oil, (which) shall
Prov. 5. 3 woman..her mouth (is) smoother than oil
21. 17 he that loveth wine and oil shall not be
21. 20 (There is) treasure to be desired and oil in
Isa. 41. 19 I will plant in the wilderness..the oil tree
61. 3 to give unto them..the oil of joy for mo.
Jer. 40. 10 gather ye wine..and oil, and put (them)
41. 8 we have treasures in the field..of oil, and
Eze. 16. 9 washed I thee..and I anointed thee with oil
16. 13 didst eat fine flour, and honey, and oil
16. 18 thou hast set mine oil and mine incense
16. 19 which I gave thee, fine flour, and oil, and
23. 41 thou hast set mine incense and mine oil
27. 17 they traded in thy market..oil, and balm
32. 14 will I..cause their rivers to run like oil
45. 14 the ordinance of oil, the bath of oil..the
45. 24 he shall prepare..an hin of oil for an ep.
45. 25 shall he do the like..according to the oil
46. 5, 7, 11 and an hin of oil to an ephah
46. 14 the third part of an hin of oil, to temper
46. 15 Thus shall they prepare..the oil, every m.
Hos. 2. 5 that give..my flax, mine oil and my drink
Hos. 12. 1 they do make a covenant..and oil is car.
Mic. 6. 7 the LORD be pleased with..rivers of oil?
6. 15 but thou shalt not anoint thee with oil
Hag. 2. 12 touch bread, or pottage, or wine, or oil, or

4. *Olive oil*, ἔλαιον *elaion.*
Matt 25. 3 foolish took their lamps, and took no oil
25. 4 But the wise took oil in their vessels with
25. 8 Give us of your oil; for our lamps are gone
Mark 6. 13 anointed with oil many that were sick, and
Luke 7. 46 My head with oil thou didst not anoint
10. 34 bound up his wounds, pouring in oil and
16. 6 And he said, An hundred measures of oil
Heb. 1. 9 hath anointed thee with the oil of gladn.
Jas. 5. 14 anointing him with oil in the name of the
Rev. 6. 6 and (see) thou hurt not the oil and the w.
18. 13 wine, and oil, and fine flour, and wheat

OIL, oiled, to make —
1. *To cause to be bright*, צָהַר *tsahar*, 5.
Job 24. 11 make oil within their walls..tread..wine
2. *Of oil*, שֶׁמֶן *shemen.*
Exod 29. 23 one cake of oiled bread, and one wafer
Lev. 8. 26 a cake of oiled bread and one wafer

OINTMENT, (pot of) —
1. *Pot of perfumes*, מֶרְקָחָה *merqachah.*
Job 41. 31 he maketh the sea like a pot of ointment
2. *Perfume*, מִרְקַחַת *mirqachath.*
1 Ch. 9. 30 the priests made the ointment of the spi.
Exod 30. 25 an ointment compound after the art of
3. *Oil*, שֶׁמֶן *shemen.*
2 Ki. 20. 13 Hezekiah..showed them..the precious o.
Psa. 133. 2 like the precious ointment upon the head
Prov 27. 9 Ointment and perfume rejoice the heart
27. 16 the ointment of his right hand..betrayeth
Eccl. 7. 1 name (is) better than precious ointment
9. 8 always white; and let thy head lack no o.
10. 1 Dead flies cause the ointment of the apo.
Song 1. 3 Because of the savour of thy good ointm.
1. 3 thy name (is as) ointment poured forth
4. 10 smell of thine ointments than all spices
Isa. 1. 6 bound up, neither mollified with ointme.
39. 2 the spices, and the precious ointment, and
57. 9 thou wentest to the king with ointment
Amos 6. 6 anoint themselves with the chief ointme.
4. *Myrrh, ointment, aromatic balm*, μύρον *muron.*
Matt 26. 7 alabaster box of very precious ointment
26. 9 this [ointment] might have been sold for
26. 12 in that she hath poured this ointment on
Mark 14. 3 having an alabaster box of ointment of
14. 4 Why was this waste of the ointment made?
Luke 7. 37 she..brought an alabaster box of ointme.
7. 38 his feet, and anointed..with the ointment
7. 46 this woman hath anointed my feet with oi.
23. 56 they returned, and prepared spices and o.
John 11. 2 Mary which anointed the Lord with oint
12. 3 Then took Mary a pound of ointment of
12. 3 was filled with the odour of the ointment
12. 5 Why was not this ointment sold for three
Rev. 18. 13 cinnamon, and odours, and ointments, and

OLD (man, men, women, things) —
1. *Worn out*, בָּלֶה *baleh.*
Josh. 9. 4 took old sacks..and wine bottles, old, and
9. 5 And old shoes and..old garments upon
Eze. 23. 43 said I unto (her that was) old in adulteries
2. *Worn out*, בְּלוֹא *belo.*
Jer. 38. 11 took thence old cast clouts and old rotten
38. 12 Put now (these) old cast clouts and rotten
3. *A son of*, בֵּן *ben.*
Gen. 5. 32 Noah was five hundred years old: and N.
7. 6 Noah (was) six hundred years old when
11. 10 Shem (was) an hundred years old, and be.
12. 4 Abram (was) seventy and five years old
16. 16 Abram (was) fourscore and six years old
17. 1 when Abram was ninety years old and n.
17. 12 he that is eight days old shall be circum.
17. 17 born unto him that is an hundred years o.
17. 24 Abraham (was) ninety years old and nine
17. 25 Ishmael his son (was) thirteen years old
21. 4 Isaac being eight days old, as God had c.
21. 5 Abraham was an hundred years old when
25. 20 Isaac was forty years old when he took R.
25. 26 Isaac (was) threescore years old when she
26. 34 Esau was forty years old when he took to
37. 2 Joseph..seventeen years old, was feeding
41. 46 Joseph (was) thirty years old when he st.
50. 26 Joseph died..an hundred and ten years o.
Exod. 7. 7 fourscore years old..fourscore and t.y's o.
30. 14 Every one..from twenty years old and ab.
38. 26 every one..from twenty years old and u.
Lev. 27. 3 twenty years old even unto sixty years old
27. 5 five years old even unto twenty years old
27. 6 from a month old even unto five years old
27. 7 And if..from sixty years old and above
Num. 1. 3 From twenty years old and upward, all
1. 18 from twenty years old and upward, by th.
1. 20 every male from twenty years old and u.
So in v. 22, 24, 26, 28, 30, 32, 34, 36, 38, 40, 42, 45.
3. 15 male from a month old and upward
So in v. 22, 28, 34, 39, 40, 43.
4. 3 From thirty years old..until fifty years o.
So in v. 23, 30, 35, 39, 43, 47.
8. 24 from twenty and five years old and upw.
14. 29 all..from twenty years old and upward
18. 16 And..from a month old shalt thou redeem
26. 2, 4 Take..from twenty years old and upw.
26. 62 all males from a month old and upward
Num 32. 11 men..from twenty years old and upward
33. 39 hundred and twenty and three years old
Deut 31. 2 I (am) an hundred and twenty years old
34. 7 Moses (was) an hundred..twenty years o.
Josh 14. 7 Forty years old (was) I when Moses the
14. 10 I (am) this day fourscore and five years o.
24. 29 died, (being) an hundred and ten years o.
Judg. 2. 8 died, (being) an hundred and ten years o.
1 Sa. 4. 15 Now Eli was ninety and eight years old
2 Sa. 2. 10 forty years old when he began to reign
4. 4 He was five years old when the tidings c.
5. 4 David (was) thirty years old when he be.
19. 32 a very aged man, (even) fourscore years o.
19. 35 I (am) this day fourscore years old..can I
1 Ki. 14. 21 forty and one years old when he
22. 42 J. (was) thirty and five years old when he
2 Ki. 8. 17 Thirty and two years old was he when he
8. 26 Two and twenty years old (was) Ahaziah
11. 21 Seven years old (was) J. when he began to
14. 2 He was twenty and five years old when he
14. 21 Azariah, which (was) sixteen years old, and
15. 2 Sixteen years old was he when he began
15. 33 Five and twenty years old was he when he
16. 2 Twenty years old (was) A. when he began
18. 2 Twenty and five years old was he when he
21. 1 Manasseh (was) twelve years old when he
21. 19 Amon (was) twenty and two years old w.
22. 1 Josiah (was) eight years old when he beg.
23. 31 Jehoahaz (was) twenty and three years o.
23. 36 Jehoiakim (was) twenty and five years old
24. 8 Jehoiachin (was) eighteen years old when
24. 18 Zedekiah (was) twenty and one years old
1 Ch. 2. 21 married when he (was) threescore years o.
23. 27 numbered from twenty years old and ab.
27. 23 not the number..from twenty years old
2 Ch. 12. 13 Rehoboam (was) one and forty years old
20. 31 (He was) thirty and five years old when he
21. 5 Jehoram (was) thirty and two years old
21. 20 Thirty and two years old was he when he
22. 2 Forty and two years old (was) Ahaziah w.
24. 1 Joash (was) seven years old when he beg.
24. 15 an hundred and thirty years old..when
25. 1 Amaziah (was) twenty and five years old
25. 5 he numbered them from twenty years old
26. 1 took Uzziah, who (was) sixteen years old
26. 3 Sixteen years old (was) Uzziah when he
27. 1 Jotham (was) twenty and five years old
27. 8 He was five and twenty years old when he
28. 1 Ahaz (was) twenty years old when he beg.
29. 1 began to reign..five and twenty years old
31. 16 of males, from three years old and upward
31. 17 Levites from twenty years old and upward
33. 1 Manasseh (was) twelve years old when he
33. 21 Amon (was) two and twenty years old w.
34. 1 Josiah (was) eight years old when he beg
36. 2 Jehoahaz (was) twenty and three years o.
36. 5 Jehoiakim (was) twenty and five years old
36. 9 Jehoiachin (was) eight years old when he
36. 11 Zedekiah (was) one and twenty years old
Ezra 3. 8 Levites, from twenty years old and upw.
Isa. 65. 20 the child shall die an hundred years old
65. 20 the sinner..an hundred years old, shall be
Jer. 52. 1 Zedekiah (was) one and twenty years old
Mic. 6. 6 shall I come..with calves of a year old?
4. *A son of*, בַּר *bar.*
Dan. 5. 31 (being) about threescore and two years old
5. *A daughter of*, בַּת *bath.*
Gen. 17. 17 shall Sarah, that is ninety years old, bear?
6. *Aged*, זָקֵן *zaqen.*
Gen. 18. 11 Abraham and Sarah (were) old..well str.
19. 4 compassed the house..both old and young
25. 8 died in a good..age, an old man, and full
35. 29 and died..old and full of days: and his s.
43. 27 (Is) your father well, the old man of whom
44. 20 We have a father, an old man, and a child
Exod 10. 9 We will go with our young..with our old
Lev. 19. 32 honour the face of the old man, and fear
Deut 28. 50 shall not regard the person of the old, nor
Judg 19. 16 there came an old man from his work out
19. 17 the old man said, Whither goest thou? and
19. 20 the old man said, Peace (be) with thee
19. 22 to the master of the house, the old man
1 Sa. 2. 31, 32 there shall not be an old man in thine
28. 14 An old man cometh up; and he (is) cove.
1 Ki. 12. 6 king Rehoboam consulted with the old m.
12. 8 But he forsook the counsel of the old men
12. 13 forsook the old men's counsel that they g.
13. 11 Now there dwelt an old prophet in Beth.
13. 25 in the city where the old prophet dwelt
13. 29 the old prophet came to the city, to mou.
2 Ch. 10. 6 Rehoboam took counsel with the old men
10. 8 he forsook the counsel which the old men
10. 13 Rehoboam forsook the counsel of the old
36. 17 had no compassion upon..old man, or h.
Esth. 3. 13 destroy..all Jews, both young and old
Job 42. 17 So Job died, (being) old, and full of days
Psa. 148. 12 Both young men and maidens; old men
Prov 17. 6 Children's children (are) the crown of old m.
20. 29 the beauty of old men (is) the grey head
Eccl. 4. 13 Better..than an old and foolish king, wh.
Isa. 20. 4 the Ethiopians captives, young and old
65. 20 nor an old man that hath not filled his
Jer. 31. 13 rejoice..both young men and old together
51. 22 with thee will I break in pieces old and
Lam. 2. 21 The young and the old lie on the ground
Eze. 9. 6 Slay utterly old (and) young, both maids
Joel 1. 2 Hear this, ye old men, and give ear, all ye
2. 28 your old men shall dream dreams, your
Zech. 8. 4 There shall yet old men and old women

7. *To be aged,* זָקֵן *zaqen.*
Gen. 19. 31 Our father (is) old, and..not a man in the
1 Sa. 17. 12 the man went among men..an old man
8. *Life,* חַיִּים *chayyim.*
Gen. 23. 1 hundred and seven and twenty years old
9. *Days,* יָמִים *yamim.*
Nah. 2. 8 Nineveh (is) of old like a pool of water
10. *Days of the years of life,* יְמֵי שְׁנֵי חַיִּים [*yom.*]
Gen. 47. 8 P. said unto Jacob, How old (art thou?
11. *To be old, aged,* יָשֵׁן *yashan,* 2.
Lev. 13. 11 It(is)an old leprosy in the skin of his flesh
12. *Old, aged,* יָשָׁן *yashan.*
Lev. 25. 22 eat..of old fruit until..ye..eat..the old
26. 10 eat old store, and bring forth the old
Neh. 3. 6 the old gate repaired Jehoiada the son of
12. 39 above the old gate, and above the fish gate
Song 7. 13 manner of pleasant (fruits), new and old
Isa. 22. 11 Ye made..a ditch..for the water of the old
13. *Perpetuity, antiquity,* עַד *ad.*
Job 20. 4 Knowest thou (not) this of old, since man
14. *An age, indefinite time,* עוֹלָם *olam.*
Deut 32. 7 Remember the days of old, consider the
Job 22. 15 Hast thou marked the old way which w.
Prov 23. 10 Remove not the old landmark; and enter
Isa. 61. 4 they shall build the old wastes, 58. 12, 63. 9.
63. 11 Then he remembered the days of old, M.
Jer. 6. 16 ask for the old paths, where (is) the good
Lam. 3. 6 He..set me in dark places as..dead of old
Eze. 25. 15 with..heart, to destroy (it) for the old h.
26. 20 into the pit with the people of old time
Mic. 7. 14 flock..let them feed..as in the days of old
Mal. 3. 4 as in the days of old, and as in former ye.
15. *An age, indefinite time,* עָלַם *alam.*
Ezra 4. 15 moved sedition within the same of old ti.
4. 19 it is found that this city of old time hath
16. *Before, before time,* קֶדֶם *qedem.*
Neh. 12. 46 in the days of David and Asaph of old
Psa. 44. 1 didst in their days, in the times of old
55. 19 God shall hear..he that abideth of old
68. 33 heavens of heavens, (which were) of old
74. 2 (which) thou hast purchased of old; the
77. 5 I have considered the days of old, the y.
77. 11 surely I will remember thy wonders of old
78. 2 I will..I will utter dark sayings of old
119. 152 I have known of old that thou hast fou.
143. 5 I remember the days of old; I meditate
Jer. 46. 26 shall be inhabited, as in the days of old
Lam. 1. 7 things that she had in the days of old, w.
2. 17 that he had commanded in the days of old
5. 21 Turn thou us..renew our days as of old
Mic. 5. 2 whose goings forth (have been) from of old
7. 20 which..hast sworn..from the days of old
17. *Before, former,* קַדְמוֹנִי *qadmoni.*
Eze. 38. 17 he of whom I have spoken in old time by
18. *Primeval, old, ancient,* ἀρχαῖος *archaios.*
Luke 9. 8 that one of the old prophets was risen ag.
9. 19 that one of the old prophets is risen again
Acts 21. 16 Mnason of Cyprus, an old disciple, 15. 21.
2 Pe. 2. 5 spared not the old world, but saved Noah
Rev. 12. 9 the great dragon was cast out, that old s.
20. 2 he laid hold on the dragon, that old ser.
19. *Old,* γέρων *gerōn.*
John 3. 4 How can a man be born when he is old?
20. *Old, ancient, worn out,* παλαιός *palaios.*
Matt. 9. 16 putteth a piece of new cloth unto an old
9. 17 Neither do men put new wine into old b.
13. 52 out of his treasure (things) new and old
Mark 2. 21 seweth a piece of new cloth on an old ga.
2. 21 that filled it up taketh away from the old
2. 22 no man putteth new wine into old bottles
Luke 5. 36 man putteth a piece of a new..upon an o.
5. 36 out of the new agreeth not with the old
5. 37 no man putteth new wine into old bottles
5. 39 No man also having drunk old (wine) str.
5. 39 desireth new; for he saith, The old is bet.
Rom. 6. 6 Knowing this, that our old man is crucified
1 Co. 5. 7 Purge out therefore the old leaven, that
5. 8 let us keep the feast, not with old leaven
2 Co. 3. 14 untaken away in the reading of the Old T.
Eph. 4. 22 That ye put off..the old man, which is
Col. 3. 9 seeing that ye have put off the old man
1 Jo. 2. 7 I write no new commandment..but an old
2. 7 The old commandment is the word which
21. *Long ago, formerly, anciently,* πάλαι *palai.*
2 Pe. 1. 9 forgotten that he was purged from his old
Jude 4 were before of old ordained to this conde.
22. *Elder, aged,* πρεσβύτερος *presbuteros.*
Acts 2. 17 shall see visions, and your old men shall
23. *Old, aged,* πρεσβύτης *presbutēs.*
Luke 1. 18 I am an old man, and my wife well stric.
24. *Time,* χρόνος *chronos.*
Acts 7. 23 when he was full forty years old, it came
[*See also* Age, corn, ever, lion, store, three years.]

OLD, to be, become, make, wax —
1. *To wear out,* בָּלָה *balah.*
Gen. 18. 12 After I am waxed old shall I have pleasu.
Deut. 8. 4 Thy raiment waxed not old upon thee
29. 5 your clothes are not waxen old upon you
29. 5 thy shoe is not waxen old upon thy foot
Josh. 9. 13 are become old by reason of the very long
Neh. 9. 21 their clothes waxed not old, and their feet
Psa. 32. 3 When I kept silence, my bones waxed old
102. 26 all of them shall wax old like a garment
Isa. 50. 9 they all shall wax old as a garment; the
51. 6 the earth shall wax old like a garment
2. *To wear out,* בָּלָה *balah,* 3.
Lam. 3. 4 My flesh and my skin hath he made old
3. *To be or become aged,* זָקֵן *zaqen.*
Gen. 18. 12 Sarah laughed..saying..my lord being old
18. 13 I of a surety bear a child, which am old?
24. 1 Abraham was old, (and) well stricken in
27. 1 it came to pass, that when Isaac was old
27. 2 Behold now, I am old, I know not the day
Josh. 13. 1 Joshua was old..stricken in years; and
13. 1 Thou art old..stricken in years, and there
23. 1 that Joshua waxed old..stricken in age
23. 2 said unto them, I am old..stricken in age
Ruth 1. 12 Turn..for I am too old to have an husb.
1 Sa. 2. 22 Now Eli was very old, and heard all that
4. 18 he died; for he was an old man, and heavy
8. 1 it came to pass, when Samuel was old, that
8. 5 Behold, thou art old, and thy sons walk
12. 2 I am old and grey headed; and, behold
1 Ki. 1. 1 Now king David was old..stricken in ye.
1. 15 Bath-sheba went..the king was very old
2 Ki. 4. 14 she hath no child, and her husband is old
1 Ch. 23. 1 So when David was old and full of days
2 Ch. 24. 15 Jehoiada waxed old, and was full of days
Psa. 37. 25 I have been young, and (now) am old; yet
Prov. 23. 22 despise not thy mother when she is old
4. *To make or become aged,* זָקֵן *zaqen,* 5.
Job 14. 8 Though the root thereof wax old in the e.
Prov 22. 6 when he is old, he will not depart from
5. *Age,* זִקְנָה *ziqnah.*
Gen. 24. 36 bare a son to my master when she was old
1 Ki. 11. 4 For it came to pass, when Solomon was old
Psa. 71. 18 Now also when I am old and grey headed
6. *To be removed, aged,* עָתַק *athaq.*
Job 21. 7 Wherefore do the wicked live, become old
Psa. 6. 7 it waxeth old because of all mine enemies
7. *To become old,* γηράσκω *gēraskō.*
John 21. 18 when thou shalt be old, thou shalt stre.
Heb. 8. 13 Now that which decayeth and waxeth old
8. *To make old,* παλαιόω *palaioō.*
Luke 12. 33 provide yourselves bags which wax not old
Heb. 1. 11 they all shall wax old as doth a garment
8. 13 that he saith..he hath made the first old

OLD age —
1. *Age,* זִקְנָה *ziqnah.*
1 Ki. 15. 23 in the time of his old age he was diseased
Psa. 71. 9 Cast me not off in the time of old age; for
Isa. 46. 4 And (even) to..old age I (am) he; and
2. *Age, old age,* זְקֻנִים *zequnim.*
Gen. 21. 2 bare Abraham a son in his old age, at the
21. 7 for I have born (him) a son in his old age
37. 3 because he (was) the son of his old age
44. 20 a child of his old age, a little one; and
3. *Old age, grey hairs,* שֵׂיבָה *sebah.*
Gen. 15. 15 thou shalt be buried in a good old age
25. 8 up the ghost, and died in a good old age
Judg. 8. 32 the son of Joash died in a good old age
Ruth 4. 15 he shall be..a nourisher of thine old age
1 Ch. 29. 28 he died in a good old age, full of days
Psa. 92. 14 shall still bring forth fruit in old age
4. *Old age,* γῆρας *gēras.*
Luke 1. 36 she hath..conceived a son in her old age

OLD estate —
Former state, קַדְמָה *qadmah.*
Eze. 36. 11 I will settle you after your old estates, and

OLD (time) of, in (the) —
1. *From then, that time,* מֵאָז *me-az.*
Psa. 93. 2 Thy throne (is) established of old: thou(art)
2. *From yesterday, former time,* מֵאֶתְמוֹל *me-ethmol.*
Isa. 30. 33 For Tophet (is) ordained of old; yea, for
3. *From indefinite time,* מֵעוֹלָם *me-olam.*
Gen. 6. 4 mighty men which (were) of old, men of
1 Sa. 27. 8 for those..of old the inhabitants of the l.
Psa. 119. 52 I remembered thy judgments of old, O L.
Isa. 46. 9 Remember the former things of old: 57. 11
Jer. 2. 20 For of old time I have broken; Eze. 26. 20.
4. *In (the) ages,* לְעֹלָמִים *le-olamim.*
Eccl. 1. 10 it hath been already of old time, which
5. *Of (the) ages, antiquity,* עוֹלָמִים *olamim.*
Isa. 51. 9 the ancient days, in the generations of old
6. *From antiquity,* מִן־הָעוֹלָם *min ha-olam*
Jer. 28. 8 before me and before thee of old proph.
7. *Previously,* לְפָנִים *le-phanim.*
Deut. 2. 20 giants dwelt therein in old time; and the
1 Ch. 4. 40 for (they) of Ham had dwelt there of old
Psa. 102. 25 Of old hast thou laid the foundation of
8. *First, former,* רִאשׁוֹן *rishon.*
2 Sa 20. 18 They were wont to speak in old time, say.
9. *Far off,* רָחוֹק *rachoq.*
Isa. 25. 1 (thy) counsels of old (are) faithfulness..t.
Jer. 31. 3 The LORD hath appeared of old unto me
10. *From old time,* ἔκπαλαι *ekpalai.*
2 Pe. 3. 5 the heavens were of old, and the earth st.
11. *Once, at some time or other,* ποτέ *pote.*
1 Pe. 3. 5 For after this manner in the old time the
2 Pe. 1. 21 For the prophecy came not in old time by

OLD time, (them) of —
Primeval, old, ancient, ἀρχαῖος *archaios.*
Matt. 5. 21 heard that it was said by them of old time
5. 27 heard that it was said [by them of old t.]
5. 33 it hath been said by them of old time
Acts 15. 21 For Moses of old time hath in every city

OLD things, things of old —
1. *Ancient things,* τὰ ἀρχαῖα [*archaios*]; 2 Co. 5. 17.
2. *Former things,* קַדְמֹנִי *qadmoni* · Isa. 43. 18.

OLD, very —
One very aged, יָשִׁישׁ *yashish.*
Job 32. 6 I (am) young, and ye (are) very old..I was

OLDNESS —
Oldness, antiquity, παλαιότης *palaiotēs.*
Rom. 7. 6 should serve..not (in) the oldness of the

OLIVE, (berries or trees, yard) —
1. *Olive (berry, tree, yard),* זַיִת *zayith.*
Gen. 8. 11 in her mouth (was) an olive leaf pluckt off
Exod 23. 11 with thy vine yard, (and) with thy olive yard
27. 20 that they bring thee pure oil olive beaten
30. 24 And of cassia..and of oil olive an hin
Lev. 24. 2 that they bring unto thee pure oil olive b.
Deut. 6. 11 and olive trees, which thou plantedst not
8. 8 A land of wheat..a land of oil olive and
24. 20 When thou beatest thine olive tree, thou
28. 40 Thou shalt have olive trees throughout all
28. 40 not anoint..for thine olive shall cast
Josh 24. 13 of the vine yards and olive yards which ye
Judg. 9. 8 they said unto the olive tree, Reign thou
9. 9 But the olive tree said unto them, Should
15. 5 and burnt up..the vine yards (and) olives
1 Sa. 8. 14 take..your vine yards, and your olive yards
2 Ki. 5. 26 (Is it) a time to receive..olive yards, and
18. 32 take you away to..a land of oil olive and
1 Ch. 27. 28 over the olive trees and the sycomore tre.
Neh. 5. 11 Restore..their olive yards, and their ho.
8. 15 Go forth..and fetch olive branches, and
9. 25 possessed..olive yards, and fruit trees in
Job 15. 33 and shall cast off his flower as the olive
Psa. 52. 8 I (am) like a green olive tree in the house
128. 3 thy children like olive plants round about
Isa. 17. 6 left in it, as the shaking of an olive tree
24. 13 (shall be) as the shaking of an olive tree
Jer. 11. 16 LORD called thy name, A green olive tree
Hos. 14. 6 his beauty shall be as the olive tree, and
Amos 4. 9 when..your olive trees increased, the pal.
Mic. 6. 15 thou shalt tread the olives, but thou shalt
Hab. 3. 17 the labour of the olive shall fail, and the
Hag. 2. 19 the pomegranate, and the olive tree, hath
Zech. 4. 3 two olive trees by it, one upon the right
4. 11 What (are) these two olive trees upon the
4. 12 What (be these) two olive branches which
2. *Oil, oil tree,* שֶׁמֶן *shemen.*
1 Ki. 6. 23 And..he made two cherubim (of) olive tr.
6. 31 he made doors (of) olive tree: the lintel
6. 32 The two doors also (were of) olive tree
6. 33 So also made he..posts (of) olive tree, a
3. *Olive, tree or berry,* ἐλαία *elaia.*
Rom 11. 17 of the root and fatness of the olive tree
11. 24 these..be graffed into their own olive tree
Jas. 3. 12 Can the fig tree..bear olive berries? either
Rev. 11. 4 These are the two olive trees, and the two

OLIVE tree, good —
A good olive tree, καλλιέλαιος *kallielaios.*
Rom 11. 24 and wert graffed..into a good olive tree

OLIVE tree, wild —
A field or wild olive tree, ἀγριέλαιος *agrielaios.*
Rom 11. 17 thou, being a wild olive tree, wert graffed
11. 24 cut out of the olive tree, which is wild by

OLIVES —
Mount of Olives, τὸ ὄρος τῶν ἐλαιῶν. See *Olivet.*
Matt 21. 1 come to Bethphage, unto the mount of O.
24. 3 as he sat upon the mount of O., the disc.
26. 30 sung..they went out into the mount of O.
Mark 11. 1 at the mount of O., he sendeth forth two
13. 3 he sat upon the mount of O., over against
14. 26 sung..they went out into the mount of O.
Luke 19. 29 at the mount called..of O., he sent two of
19. 37 even now at the descent of the mount of O.
21. 37 abode in the mount that is called..of O.
22. 39 went, as he was wont, to the mount of O
John 8. 1 [Jesus went unto the mount of O.]

O-LI'-VET, Ἐλαιών *olives.*
A ridge of hills on the E. of Jerusalem, about a mile from N. to S., and 200 feet above the site of the temple; named in the O. T., in 2 Sam. 15. 30, and Zech. 14. 4; called also the Mount of Corruption, 2 Ki. 23. 13.
Acts 1. 12 unto Jerusalem from the mount called O.

O-LYM'-PAS, Ὀλυμπᾶς.
A believer at Rome whom Paul salutes.
Rom 16. 15 O., and all the saints which are with them

O'-MAR, אוֹמָר *mountaineer.*
A son of Eliphaz son of Esau. B.C. 1670.
Gen. 36. 11 were Teman, O., Zepho, and Gatam, and
36. 15 duke Teman, duke O., duke Zepho, duke
1 Ch. 1. 36 and O., Zephi, and Gatam, Kenaz, and T.

OM-E'-GA, Ὠμέγα.
An appellation of the Lord Jesus Christ, signifying "the last," as *Alpha* does "the first."
Rev. 1. 8 I am Alpha and O., the beginning and the

Rev. 1. 11 [I am Alpha and O., the first and the last]
21. 6 I am Alpha and O., the beginning and the
22. 13 I am Alpha and O., the beginning and the

OMER —
An omer, (tenth of an ephah), עֹמֶר *omer.*
Exod16. 16 an omer for every man..the number of
16. 18 when they did mete (it) with an omer, he
16. 22 they gathered..two omers for one (man)
16. 32 Fill an omer of it to be kept for your gen.
16. 33 put an omer full of manna therein, and
16. 36 Now an omer (is) the tenth (part) of an ep.

OMIT, to —
To send away, let go, ἀφίημι *aphiēmi.*
Matt23. 23 have omitted the weightier (matters) of

OMNIPOTENT —
All powerful, παντοκράτωρ *pantokratōr.*
Rev. 19. 6 Alleluia..the Lord God omnipotent reign.

OM'-RI, עָמְרִי *Jah apportions.*
1. Father of Ahab, and captain of the host, afterwards made king instead of Zimri who had slain Elah. B.C. 929–907.
1 Ki.16. 16 Israel made O., the captain of the host
16. 17 O. went up from Gibbethon, and all Israel
16. 21 to make him king; and half followed O.
16. 22 But the people that followed O. prevailed
16. 22 prevailed..so Tibni died, and O. reigned
16. 23 began O. to reign over Israel, twelve ye.
16. 25 O. wrought evil in the eyes of the LORD
16. 27 the acts of O. which he did, and his mi.
16. 28 O. slept with his fathers, and was buried
16. 29 began Ahab the son of O. to reign over
16. 29 son of O. reigned over Israel in Samaria
16. 30 the son of O. did evil in the sight of the
2 Ki. 8. 26 Athaliah, the daughter of O. king of Isr.
2 Ch.22. 2 name..(was) Athaliah the daughter of O.
Mic. 6. 16 the statutes of O. are kept, and all the
2. A son of Becher son of Benjamin. B.C. 1600.
1 Ch. 7. 8 O., and Jerimoth, and Abiah, and Anath.
3. A descendant of Pharez son of Judah. B.C. 640.
1 Ch. 9. 4 the son of O., the son of Imri, the son of
4. Son of Michael, and ruler of Issachar in the days of David. B.C. 1015.
1 Ch.27. 18 of the brethren of David: of Issachar; O.

ON, אוֹן *sun.*
1. Capital of Lower Egypt, E. of the Nile, and a little N. of Memphis; it is called also Heliopolis, as well as Beth-shemesh, *i.e.* "house of the sun."
Gen. 41. 45, 50 daughter of Potipherah priest of O.
46. 20 the daughter of Potipherah priest of O.
2. A Reubenite, son of Peleth, who joined with Korah, Dathan, and Abiram in murmuring against Moses and Aaron. B.C. 1472.
Num.16. 1 O. the son of Peleth, sons of Reuben, took

ON —
1. *Unto,* אֶל *el.*
Exod19. 20 the LORD came down..on the top of the
2. *Going,* הָלַךְ *halak* (adv. infin.).
Judg14. 9 And he took thereof..and went on Jos.6.13.
1 Sa. 14. 19 that the noise..went on and increased
19. 23 he went on and prophesied, until he came
2 Sa. 5. 10 And David went on, and grew great, and
13. 19 and rent her garment..and went on crying
3. *Up to,* עַד *ad.*
Ezra 6. 15 this house was finished on the third day
4. *On, upon, over,* עַל *al.*
Gen. 6. 1 men began to multiply on the face of the
Dan. 6. 14 set (his) heart on Daniel to deliver him
5. *At the face of,* לִפְנֵי *li-phene.*
2 Ki. 5. 2 little maid; and she waited on Naaman's
6. *To set, place, put,* שׂוּם, שִׂים *sum, sim,* 5.
Eze. 21. 16 on the right hand, (or) on the left, whither.
7. *From,* ἀπό *apo.*
Rev. 6. 10 judge and avenge our blood [on] them that
21. 13 On the east..on the north..on the s..on
8. *Toward, to, into,* εἰς *eis.*
Matt27. 30 took the reed, and smote him on the head
Mark 4. 8 other fell on good ground, and did yield
8. 23 when he had spit on his eyes, and put his
14. 6 said..she hath wrought a good work [on]
Luke 6. 20 he lifted up his eyes on his disciples, and
8. 23 there came down a storm of wind on the
12. 49 I am come to send fire [on] the earth; and
15. 22 put a ring on his hand, and shoes on (his)
John 1. 12 power..to them that believe on his name
2. 11 did Jesus..and his disciples believed on
3. 18 He that believeth on him is not condem.
3. 36 He that believeth on the Son hath everl.
4. 39 many..believed on him for the saying of
6. 29 that ye believe on him whom he hath sent
6. 35 he that believeth on me shall never thirst
6. 40 which seeth the Son, and believeth on him
6. 47 He that believeth [on] me hath everlasting
7. 31 many of the people believed on him, and
7. 38 He that believeth on me, as the scripture
7. 39 which they that believe on him should r.
7. 48 Have any of the rulers..believed on him?
8. 6 [with (his) finger wrote on the ground]
8. 8 [stooped down, and wrote on the ground]
8. 30 As he spake these..many believed on him
9. 35 said..Dost thou believe on the Son of God?
9. 36 Who is he..that I might believe on him?
John10. 42 And many believed on him there
11. 45 Then many of the Jews..believed on him
11. 48 If we let..alone, all..will believe on him
12. 11 the Jews went away, and believed on Je.
12. 37 though he had done..they believed not
12. 42 the chief rulers..many believed on him
12. 44 Jesus cried and said, He that believeth on
12. 44 believeth not on me, but on him that sent
12. 46 that whosoever believeth on me should
13. 22 Then the disciples looked one on another
14. 12 He that believeth on me, the works that
16. 9 Of sin, because they believe not on me
17. 20 which shall believe on me through their
19. 37 They shall look on him whom they pierced
21. 4 when..morning was..come, J. stood [on]
21. 6 Cast the net on the right side of the ship
Acts 6. 15 looking stedfastly on him, saw his face as
13. 9 filled with the Holy Ghost, set his eyes on
14. 23 they commended them to the Lord, on
19. 4 that they should believe on him which
19. 4 should come after him, that is, on Christ
Rom16. 6 Greet Mary, who bestowed much labour on
2 Co.11. 20 ye suffer..if a man smite you on the face
Gal. 3. 14 might come on the Gentiles through Jesus
Phil. 1. 29 not only to believe on him, but also to s.
1 Jo. 5. 10 He that believeth on the Son of God hath
5. 13 unto you that believe [on] the name of the
5. 13 that ye may believe on the name of the
Rev. 13. 13 maketh fire come down from heaven on
9. *Out of,* ἐκ *ek.* [*See* left (on)].
Matt21. 19 Let no fruit grow on thee henceforward
Rev. 18. 20 Rejoice..for God hath avenged you on
10. *In, among, during,* ἐν *en.*
Matt22. 40 On these two commandments hang all the
24. 20 that your flight be not..[on] the sabbath
26. 5 they said, Not on the feast..lest there be
Mark 2. 23 he went through the corn fields on the s.
2. 24 why do they [on] the sabbath day that w.
14. 2 they said, Not on the feast..lest there be
16. 5 they saw a young man sitting on the right
Luke 1. 59 it came to pass, that on the eighth day
4. 16 he went into the synagogue on the sabbath
4. 31 came..and taught them on the sabbath
5. 17 it came to pass on a certain day, as he was
6. 1 it came to pass, on the second sabbath
6. 2 which is not lawful to do [on] the sabbath
6. 6 it came to pass also on another sabbath
6. 7 whether he would heal on the sabbath d.
8. 15 that on the good ground are they, which
8. 22 it came to pass on a certain day, that he
8. 32 an herd of many swine feeding on the m.
9. 37 it came to pass, that [on] the next day, w.
12. 51 that I am come to give peace on earth?
13. 7 I come seeking fruit on this fig tree, and
13. 10 teaching in one of the synagogues on the
14. 5 straightway pull him out [on] the sabbath
20. 1 on one of those days, as he taught the pe.
John 5. 9 walked: and on the same day was the sa.
5. 16 he had done these things on the sabbath
7. 22 ye [on] the sabbath day circumcise a man
7. 23 If a man on the sabbath day receive cir.
7. 23 I have made a man..whole on the sabbath
13. 23 there was leaning on Jesus' bosom one of
19. 31 not remain upon the cross on the sabbath
Rom12. 7 on..ministering: or he that teacheth on
12. 8 Or he that exhorteth, on exhortation: he
2 Co. 4. 8 troubled on every side, yet not distressed
7. 5 had no rest, but we were troubled on every
8. 1 of the grace of God bestowed on the chu.
Heb. 1. 3 on the right hand of the majesty on high
8. 1 who is set on the right hand of the throne
10. 12 for ever, sat down on the right hand of God
1 Pe. 3. 22 who is gone into heaven, and is on the r.
4. 16 ashamed; but let him glorify God on this
Rev. 1. 10 I was in the spirit on the Lord's day, and
5. 13 every creature which is in heaven, and [on]
11. *Above, upon,* ἐπάνω *epanō.*
Matt. 5. 14 city that is set on an hill cannot be hid
21. 7 put on them their clothes, and..set..the.
Luke10. 19 give unto you power to tread on serpents
Rev. 6. 8 his name that sat on him was Death, and
12. *On, upon,* ἐπί (gen.) *epi.*
Matt. 9. 2 a man sick of the palsy, lying on a bed
9. 6 Son of man hath power on earth to forgi.
14. 25 Jesus went unto them, walking [on] the sea
16. 19 shalt bind on earth..shalt loose on earth
18. 18 shall bind on earth..shall loose on earth
18. 19 That if two of you shall agree on earth
24. 17 Let him which is on the house top not c.
26. 12 she hath poured this ointment on my body
27. 19 When he was set down on the judgment
Mark 2. 10 Son of man hath power on earth to forgive
4. 1 whole multitude was by the sea on the l.
6. 47 midst of the sea, and he alone on the land
8. 6 commanded the people to sit down on the
9. 3 so as no fuller on earth can white them
9. 20 fell on the ground, and wallowed foaming
13. 15 let him that is on the house top not go
14. 35 forward a little, and fell [on] the ground
Luke 2. 14 and on earth peace, good will toward men
8. 13 They on the rock (are they), which, when
8. 16 setteth (it) on a candlestick, that they
18. 8 cometh, shall he find faith on the earth?
22. 21 that betrayeth me (is) with me on the ta.
22. 30 sit on thrones judging the twelve tribes
John 6. 2 they saw his miracles which he did on t.
6. 19 they see Jesus walking on the sea, and d.
17. 4 I have glorified thee on the earth: I have
19. 19 Pilate wrote a title, and put (it) on the c.
Acts 2. 30 [would raise up Christ to sit on his throne]
5. 15 laid..on beds and couches, that at the l.
5. 30 Jesus, whom ye slew, and hanged on a t.
10. 39 he..whom they slew, and hanged on a t.
21. 23 We have four men which have a vow on
21. 40 Paul stood on the stairs, and beckoned w.
25. 6 the next day, sitting on the judgment seat
25. 17 on the morrow I sat on the judgment seat
27. 44 some..and some on (broken pieces) of the
1 Co.11. 10 ought the woman to have power on (her)
Gal. 3. 13 Cursed (is) every one that hangeth on a
Eph. 1. 10 which are in heaven, and which are on
6. 3 That..thou mayest live long on the earth
Col. 3. 2 things above, not..things on the earth
Heb. 8. 4 For if he were on earth he should not be
11. 13 were strangers and pilgrims on the earth
12. 25 not who refused him that spake on earth
Jas. 5. 5 Ye have lived in pleasure on the earth, and
5. 17 it rained not on the earth by the space of
Rev. 4. 2 set in heaven, and (one) sat on the throne
4. 9 and thanks to him that sat on the throne
4. 10 fall down before him that sat on the thr.
5. 1 I saw in the right hand of him that sat on
5. 10 made us..priests: and we shall reign on the
6. 10 avenge our blood..them that dwell on the
6. 16 from the face of him that sitteth on the
7. 1 standing on the four corners of the earth
7. 1 not blow on the earth, nor on the sea, nor
7. 15 he that sitteth on the throne shall dwell
9. 17 I saw..horses..and them that sat on them
11. 10 prophets tormented them that dwelt on
13. 14 deceiveth them that dwell on the earth
13. 14 saying to them that dwell on the earth
14. 6 to preach unto them that dwell on the e.
14. 14 having on his head a golden crown, and
14. 15 And..crying..to him that sat on the clo.
17. 8 they that dwell on the earth shall wonder
17. 9 mountains, on which the woman sitteth
19. 4 worshipped God that sat on the throne
19. 18 of them that sit on them, and the flesh of
19. 19 to make war against him that sat on the
20. 6 on such the second death hath no power
20. 11 I saw a..throne, and him that sat on it
13. *On, upon,* ἐπί (dat.) *epi.*
Mark 2. 21 No man..seweth a piece of new cloth on
Luke 7. 13 had compassion on her, and said unto her
John 4. 6 Jesus..being wearied..sat thus on the w.
Acts 27. 44 And the rest, some on boards, and some
Rom. 9. 33 whosoever believeth on him shall not be
10. 11 Whosoever believeth on him shall not be
1 Ti. 1. 16 which should hereafter believe on him to
1 Pe. 2. 6 he that believeth on him shall not be co.
Rev. 6. 2 he that sat on him had a bow; and a cro.
6. 5 he that sat on him had a pair of balances
14. *On, upon,* ἐπί (acc.) *epi.*
Matt. 4. 5 setteth him on a pinnacle of the temple
5. 15 put it under a bushel, but on a candlest.
5. 39 whosoever shall smite thee [on] thy right
5. 45 maketh his sun to rise on the evil and
5. 45 sendeth rain on the just and..the unjust
10. 29 one of them shall not fall [on] the ground
10. 34 Think not that I am come to send peace o.
13. 2 the whole multitude stood on the shore
14. 19 commanded the multitude to sit down on
14. 26 when the disciples saw him walking on the
14. 28 Lord..bid me come unto thee on v. 29.
15. 32 I have compassion on the multitude, be.
15. 35 commanded the multitude to sit down on
17. 6 they fell on their face, and were sore afr.
21. 44 whosoever shall fall on this stone shall be
21. 44 [but on whomsoever it shall fall, it will]
23. 4 bind heavy burdens..and lay (them) on
26. 7 ointment, and poured (it) on his head, as
26. 39 he went a little farther, and fell on his f.
26. 50 Then came they, and laid hands on Jesus
27. 25 His blood (be) on us, and on our children
Mark 4. 5 some fell on stony ground, where it had
4. 16 these are they likewise which are sown on
4. 20 these are they which are sown on good g.
4. 21 put under..and not to be set on a candl.
4. 38 he was in the hinder part..asleep on a p.
8. 2 I have compassion on the multitude, be.
9. 22 but..have compassion on us, and help us
14. 46 they laid their hands [on] him, and took
16. 18 [they shall lay hands on the sick..they]
Luke 1. 65 fear came on all that dwelt round about
4. 9 and set him on a pinnacle of the temple
5. 12 who) seeing Jesus, fell on (his) face, and be.
6. 29 unto him that smiteth thee on the..cheek
6. 48 digged deep, and laid the foundation on
8. 8 other fell [on] good ground, and sprang
10. 34 set him on his own beast, and brought him
10. 35 on the morrow, when he departed, he took
11. 33 on a candlestick, that they which come in
15. 5 he layeth (it) on his shoulders, rejoicing
15. 20 ran, and fell on his neck, and kissed him
17. 16 fell down on (his) face at his feet, giving
20. 18 on whomsoever it shall fall, it will grind
20. 19 the same hour sought to lay hands on him
21. 12 they shall lay their hands on you, and p.
21. 35 shall it come on all them that dwell on
23. 30 begin to say to the mountains, Fall on us
John 1. 33 spirit descending, and remaining on him
3. 36 believeth not..wrath of God abideth on
7. 30 no man laid hands on him, because his h.
7. 44 have taken him; but no man laid hands on
12. 15 thy king cometh, sitting on an ass's colt
13. 25 He then lying on Jesus' breast saith unto
21. 20 which also leaned on his breast at supper
Acts 2. 18 on my servants and on my hand maidens
4. 5 it came to pass on the morrow, that their

Acts 4. 22 the man was above forty years old on w.
5. 5 great fear came on all them that heard t.
5. 18 laid their hands on the apostles, and put
7. 54 and they gnashed on him with (their) teeth
8. 17 Then laid they..hands on them, and they
9. 17 putting his hands on him, said, Brother
10. 44 Holy Ghost fell on all them which heard
10. 45 because that on the Gentiles also was po.
11. 15 Holy Ghost fell on them, as on us at the
11. 17 as..unto us, who believed on the Lord Je.
13. 11 there fell on him a mist and a darkness
14. 10 Said with a loud voice, Stand upright on
16. 31 Believe on the Lord Jesus Christ, and th.
17. 26 to dwell on all the face of the earth, and
19. 6 the Holy Ghost came on them; and they
19. 16 leaped on them, and overcame them, and
19. 17 fear fell on them all, and the name of the
20. 37 and fell on Paul's neck, and kissed him
21. 5 we kneeled down on the shore, and prayed
21. 27 stirred up..the people, and laid hands on
22. 19 I imprisoned..them that believed on thee
28. 3 laid (them) on the fire, there came a viper
Rom. 4. 5 believeth on him that justifieth the ungo.
4. 24 if we believe on him that raised up Jesus
9. 23 the riches of his glory on the vessels of m.
11. 22 on them which fell, severity; but toward
12. 20 thou shalt heap coals of fire on his head
15. 3 reproaches..that reproached thee fell on
1 Co. 14. 25 so falling down on (his) face he will wor.
Gal. 6. 16 peace (be) on them, and mercy, and upon
Col. 3. 6 [the wrath of God cometh on the children]
1 Ti. 1. 18 the prophecies which went before on thee
Titus 3. 6 Which he shed on us abundantly through
1 Pe. 2. 24 bare our sins in his own body on the tree
Rev. 3. 3 I will come [on] thee as a thief, and thou
4. 4 they had on their heads crowns of gold
6. 16 Fall on us, and hide us from the face of
7. 1 standing on the four corners of the earth
7. 1 that the wind should not blow..on any
7. 11 fell before the throne on their faces, and
7. 16 neither shall the sun light on them, nor
9. 7 on their heads..as it were crowns like
10. 2 right foot upon the sea, and (his) left..on
11. 16 elders which sat before God on their seats
14. 1 a Lamb stood on the mount Sion, and w.
14. 16 sat on the cloud thrust in his sickle on the
15. 2 stand on the sea of glass, having the harps
18. 19 they cast dust on their heads, and cried
19. 12 on his head (were) many crowns; and he
19. 16 he hath on (his) vesture and on his thigh
20. 9 they went up on the breadth of the earth

15. *Down upon,* κατά *(gen.) kata.*
Mark 14. 3 brake the box, and poured (it) [on] his h.

16. *Down through, over against,* κατά *(acc.) kata.*
Acts 8. 36 as they went on (their) way, they came u.

17. *Among, with,* μετά *(gen.) meta.*
Luke 10. 37 And he said, He that showed mercy on him

18. *About, round about,* περί *(gen.) peri.*
Matt 9. 36 he was moved with compassion on them
Acts 10. 19 While Peter thought on the vision, the

[*See also* About, affection, ask, behalf, bestow, bind, breathe, bring, call, come, coming, compassion, draw, driven, edge, fasten, follow, foot, go, have, high, hold, horseback, lay, lead, leap, light, look, mercy, pass, pressed, put, putting, ride, right, say, set, seize, smoke, take, take hold, wait, walk, way, write.]

ON behalf —

1. *On, upon,* ἐπί *(dat.) epi.*
Rom 16. 19 I am glad therefore on your behalf: but

2. *About, round about,* περί *(gen.) peri.*
1 Co. 1. 4 I thank my God always on your behalf, for

ON continually —

Going, הָלֹךְ *halak* (adv. infin.).
Josh. 6. 13 And seven priests..went on continually

ON either side —

From hence, ἐντεῦθεν *enteuthen.*
John 19. 18 on either side one, and Jesus in the midst
Rev. 22. 2 [on either side] of the river..the tree of

ON...part —

Down through, throughout, κατά *(acc.) kata.*
1 Pe. 4. 14 [on their part he is evil..on your part he]

ON the part —

For, in behalf of, ὑπέρ *(gen.) huper.*
Mark 9. 40 he that is not against us is on our part

ON this side...on that side —

Hither...thither, לְהֵנָּה...לְהֵנָּה *la-henah...la-henah.*
Eze. 1. 23 covered on this side..covered on that s.

O'-NAM, אוֹנָם *strength.*

1. Second son of Shobal son of Seir. B.C. 1700.
Gen. 36. 23 and Manahath, and Ebal, Shepho, and O.
1 Ch. 1. 40 and Manahath, and Ebal, Shephi, and O.

2. A son of Jerameel son of Hezron son of Pharez son of Judah. B.C. 1490.
1 Ch. 2. 26 name (was) Atarah..(was) the mother of O.
2. 28 And the sons of O. were Shammai, and J.

O'-NAN, אוֹנָן *strength.*

Second son of Judah, by the daughter of Shua the Canaanite. B.C. 1700.
Gen. 38. 4 bare a son; and she called his name O.
38. 8 Judah said unto O., Go in unto thy brot.
38. 9 O. knew that the seed should not be his
46. 12 sons of Judah; Er, and O...but Er and O.
Num. 26. 19 of Judah (were) Er and O.: and Er and O.
1 Ch. 2. 3 The sons of Judah; Er and O., and Shel.

ONCE, at once, this once, for all, when —

1. *From then or that (time),* מֵאָז *me-az.*
Psa. 76. 7 who may stand..when once thou art an.?

2. *One,* אֶחָד *echad.*
Exod 30. 10 upon the horns of it once in a year with
30. 10 once in the year shall he make atonement
Lev. 16. 34 to make an atonement for..sins, once a
1 Ki. 10. 22 once in three years came the navy of
2 Ki. 6. 10 saved himself there, not once nor twice
2 Ch. 9. 21 every three years once came the ships or
Job 33. 14 For God speaketh once, yea, twice,
40. 5 Once have I spoken, but I will not answer
Psa. 62. 11 God hath spoken once; twice; Hag. 2. 6.

2a. *At once,* (בְּאַחַת) בְּאַחַת *be-achath.*
Prov 28. 18 is) perverse (in his) ways shall fall at once

3. *Hasting, hastily,* מַהֵר *maher.*
Deut. 7. 22 thou mayest not consume them at once

3a. *In one vengeance,* נָקָם אֶחָד *naqam echad.*
Judg 16. 28 that I may be at once avenged of the P.

4. *Yet, still, any more,* עוֹד *od.*
Jer. 13. 27 Woe unto thee..when (shall it) once (be)?

5. *Step, beat, time,* פַּעַם *paam.*
Gen. 18. 32 And he said..I will speak yet but this o.
Exod 10. 17 forgive..my sin only this once, and intr.
Judg. 6. 39 I will speak but this once..but this once
16. 18 Come up this once, for he hath showed
16. 28 strengthen me, I pray thee, only this on.
Neh. 13. 20 without Jerusalem once or; Jer. 16. 21.

5a. *One beat, one time,* פַּעַם אַחַת *paam achath.*
Josh. 6. 3 And ye shall..go round about the city o.
6. 11 compassed the city, going about (it) once
6. 14 the second day they compassed the city o.
1 Sa. 26. 8 with the spear even to the earth at once
Isa. 66. 8 shall a nation be born at once? for as soon

5b. *At [this] time,* [בַּפַּעַם [הַזֹּאת *[be-paam].*
Jer. 10. 18 sling out the inhabitants..at this once, and

6. *Once, once for all,* ἅπαξ *hapax.*
2 Co. 11. 25 once was I stoned, thrice I suffered shipw.
Phil. 4. 16 For even in Thessalonica ye sent once and
1 Th. 2. 18 we would have come unto you..once and
Heb. 6. 4 impossible for those who were once enli.
9. 7 (went) the high priest alone once every
9. 26 now once in the end of the world hath
9. 27 as it is appointed unto men once to die
9. 28 So Christ was once offered to bear the sins
10. 2 the worshippers once purged should have
12. 26 Yet once more I shake not the earth only
12. 27 Yet once more, signifieth the removing of
1 Pe. 3. 18 For Christ also hath once suffered for sins
3. 20 when [once] the long suffering of God w.
Jude 3 which was once delivered unto the saints
5 though ye once knew this, how that the L.

7. *From,* ἀφ' οὗ ἂν *aph' hou an.*
Luke 13. 25 When once the master of the house is risen

8. *At once, once for all,* ἐφάπαξ *ephapax.*
Rom. 6. 10 For in that he died, he died unto sin once
1 Co. 15. 6 seen of above five hundred brethren at o.
Heb. 7. 27 this he did once, when he offered up him.
9. 12 he entered in once into the holy place
10. 10 offering of the body of Jesus..once

9. *Once, at some time,* ποτέ *pote.*
Rom. 7. 9 For I was alive without the law once: but
Gal. 1. 23 preacheth the faith which once he destro.

ONE —

1. *One,* אֶחָד *echad.*
Gen. 1. 9 be gathered together unto one place, and
2. 21 he took one of his ribs, and closed up the
2. 24 unto his wife; and they shall be one flesh
3. 22 the man is become as one of us, to know
4. 19 the name of the one (was) Adah, and the
10. 25 were born two sons: the name of one (was)
11. 1 was of one language, and of one speech
11. 6 the people (is) one, and they have all one
19. 9 This one..came in to sojourn, and he will
21. 15 she cast the child under one of the shrubs
22. 2 upon one of the mountains which I will t.
26. 10 one of the people might lightly have lien
27. 38 Hast thou but one blessing, my father? b.
27. 45 I be deprived also of you both in one day?
32. 8 If Esau come to the one company, and s.
33. 13 if men should overdrive them one day, all
34. 16 dwell with you, and we will become one
34. 22 to be one people, if every male among us
40. 5 each man his dream in one night, each m.
41. 5 seven ears of corn came up upon one stalk
41. 11 we dreamed a dream in one night, I and
41. 22 seven ears came up in one stalk, full and g.
41. 25 The dream of Pharaoh (is) one: God hath
41. 26 good ears (are) seven years: the dream (is)
42. 11 We (are) all one man's sons: we (are) true
42. 13 the sons of one man in the land..and one
42. 16 Send one of you, and let him fetch your b.
42. 19 let one of your brethren be bound in the
42. 27 as one of them opened his sack, to give his
42. 32 sons of our father; one (is) not, and the yo.
42. 33 leave one of your brethren (here) with me
44. 28 And the one went out from me, and I said
48. 22 I have given to thee one portion above thy
49. 16 Dan shall judge his people, as one of the
Exod. 1. 15 of which the name of the one (was) Ship.
8. 31 removed the swarms..remained not one
9. 6 but of the cattle of..Israel died not one
Exod. 9. 7 there was not one of the cattle of the Is.
10. 19 there remained not one locust in all the
11. 1 Yet will I bring one plague..upon Phar.
12. 18 until the one and twentieth day of the
12. 46 In one house shall it be eaten: thou sha.
12. 49 One law shall be to him that is home born
14. 28 there remained not so much as one of them
16. 22 they gathered twice..two omers for one
17. 12 the one on the one side, and the other on
18. 3 of which the name of the one (was) Gers.
23. 29 not drive them out from before thee in o.
24. 3 all the people answered with one voice
25. 12 two rings..in the one side of it, and two
25. 19 make one cherub on the one end, and the
25. 32 three branches..out of the one side, and
25. 33 (with) a knop and a flower in one branch
25. 36 all of it..one beaten work (of) pure gold
26. 2, 8 The length of one..the breadth of one
26. 2 and..the curtains shall have one measure
26. 4 make loops..upon the edge of the one c.
26. 5 Fifty loops shalt thou make in the one c.
26. 6 and couple..and it shall be one taberna.
26. 8 and the eleven curtains..of one measure
26. 10 make fifty loops on the edge of the one c.
26. 11 couple the tent together, that it..be one
26. 16 a cubit and a half..the breadth of one b.
26. 17 Two tenons..in one board, set in order
26. 19, 21, 25 two sockets under one board
26. 24 coupled..above the head of it unto one r.
26. 26 five for the boards of the one side of the
27. 9 of an hundred cubits long for one side
28. 10 Six of their names on one stone, and..six
29. 1 Take one young bullock, and two rams
29. 3 thou shalt put them into one basket, and
29. 15 Thou shalt also take one ram; and Aaron
29. 23 one loaf of bread, and one cake..and one
29. 39 The one lamb thou shalt offer in the mor.
29. 40 with the one lamb a tenth deal of flour
36. 9 length of one curtain..the breadth of one
36. 9 four cubits: the curtains (were) all of one s.
36. 10 coupled the five..one unto another..one
36. 11 he made loops of blue on the edge of one
36. 12 Fifty loops made he in one curtain, and
36. 12 the loops held one (curtain) to another
36. 13 coupled..one unto another..it became o
36. 15 of one curtain..of one curtain..of one s
36. 18 to couple the tent..that it might be one
36. 22 One board..two tenons, equally distant o.
36. 24, 26 two sockets under one board
36. 29 coupled together at the head..to one ring
36. 31 five for the boards of the one side of the
37. 3 two rings upon the one side of it, and two
37. 8 One cherub on the end on this side, and
37. 19 made after the fashion of almonds in o.
37. 22 all of it..one beaten work (of) pure gold
Lev. 5. 4, 5 he shall be guilty in one of these
5. 7 one for a sin offering, and the other for a
5. 13 sin that he hath sinned in one of these
7. 7 one law for them: the priest that maketh
7. 14 of it he shall offer one out of the whole
8. 26 he took one unleavened cake, and..one
12. 8 one for the burnt offering, and the other
13. 2 unto Aaron the priest, or unto one of his
14. 5 the priest shall command that one of the
14. 10 one ewe lamb of the first year..and one
14. 12 the priest shall take one he lamb, and offer
14. 21 he shall take one lamb..and one tenth
14. 22 the one shall be a sin offering, and the o.
14. 30 he shall offer the one of the turtle doves
14. 31 the one (for) a sin offering, and the other
14. 50 he shall kill the one of the birds in an e.
15. 15, 30 the one..a sin offering, and the other
16. 5 he shall take..one ram for a burnt offer.
16. 8 one lot for the LORD, and the other lot
22. 28 not kill it and her young both in one day
23. 18 ye shall offer..one young bullock, and
23. 19 ye shall sacrifice one kid of the goats for
24. 5 And..two tenth deals shall be in one cake
24. 22 Ye shall have one manner of law, as well
25. 48 he may be redeemed..one of his brethren
26. 26 ten women shall bake your bread in one
Num. 1. 41 forty and one thousand and five hundred
1. 44 each one was for the house of his fathers
2. 16 fifty and one thousand and four hundred
2. 28 forty and one thousand and five hundred
6. 11 the priest shall offer the one for a sin off.
6. 14 one he lamb..and one ewe lamb..and one
6. 19 one unleavened cake..one unleavened w.
7. 13 one silver charger..one silver bowl
So in v. 19, 25, 31, 37, 43, 49, 55, 61, 67, 73, 79.
7. 14, 20 one spoon of ten (shekels) of gold, full
7. 15 One young bullock, one ram, one lamb
So in v. 21, 27, 33, 39, 45, 51, 57, 63, 69, 75, 81.
7. 16, 22, 28, 34, 40, 46 One kid of the goats
7. 52, 58, 64, 70, 76, 82 One kid of the goats
7. 26 One golden spoon of ten (shekels)
So in v. 32, 38, 44, 50, 56, 62, 68, 74, 80.
8. 12 thou shalt offer the one..a sin offering, and
9. 14 ye shall have one ordinance, both for the
10. 4 if they blow..with one..then the princes
11. 19 Ye shall not eat one day, nor two days
11. 26 the name of the one..Eldad, and the name
13. 23 cut down from thence a branch with one
14. 15 thou shalt kill..this people as one man
15. 5 drink offering shalt thou prepare..for one
15. 11 shall it be done for one bullock..for one
15. 15 One ordinance..for you of the congregat.
15. 16 One law and one manner shall be for you
15. 24 offer one young bullock..and one kid of
15. 29 Ye shall have one law for him that sinneth
16. 15 have not taken one ass..neither..hurt o.
16. 22 shall one man sin, and wilt thou be wroth

Num 17. 3 one rod..for the head of the house of their
17. 6 for each prince one, according to their f.
28. 4 one lamb shalt thou offer in the morning
28. 7 the fourth (part) of an hin for the one la.
28. 11, 19 offer..two young bullocks, and one ram
28. 12 three tenth deals of flour..for one bullock
28. 12 two tenth deals of flour..for one ram
28. 13 with oil (for) a meat offering unto one la.
28. 15 one kid of the goats for a sin offering unto
28. 22 one goat..a sin offering, to make an ato.
28. 27 two young bullocks, one ram, seven lambs
28. 28 unto one bullock, two tenth deals unto o.
28. 29 A several tenth deal unto one lamb, thro.
28. 30 one kid of the goats, to make an atonem.
29. 2, 8 one young bullock, one ram..seven lambs
29. 4 one tenth deal for one lamb, throughout
29. 5 one kid of the goats..a sin offering, to
29. 9 mingled with oil..two tenth deals to one
29. 10 A several tenth deal for one lamb, throu.
29. 11, 16, 19, 25 one kid of the goats (for) a sin
29. 22, 28, 31, 34, 38 one goat (for) a sin offering
29. 36 one bullock, one ram, seven lambs of the
31. 28 one soul of five hundred..of the persons
31. 30 thou shalt take one portion of fifty, of the
31. 34 And threescore and one thousand asses
31. 39 the LORD'S tribute (was) threescore and
31. 47 Moses took one portion of fifty..of man
34. 18 ye shall take one prince of every tribe, to
35. 30 one witness shall not testify against any
36. 8 shall be wife unto one of the family of the
Deut. 1. 23 I took twelve men of you, one of a tribe
4. 42 that fleeing unto one of these cities he
6. 4 Hear..The LORD our God (is) one LORD
12. 14 which the LORD shall choose in one of thy
13. 12 If thou shalt hear..in one of thy cities
15. 7 If there be among you a poor man of one
17. 6 at the mouth of one witness he shall not
19. 5 shall flee unto one of those cities, and live
19. 11 if any man..fleeth into one of these cities
19. 15 One witness shall not rise up against a m.
21. 15 If a man have two wives, one beloved, and
23. 16 which he shall choose in one of thy gates
24. 5 he shall be free at home one year, and sh.
25. 5 If brethren dwell together, and one of th.
25. 11 the wife of the one draweth near for to
28. 7 they shall come out against thee one way
28. 25 thou shalt go out one way against them
32. 30 How should one chase a thousand, and two
Josh. 9. 2 to fight with Joshua and..Israel, with one
10. 2 Gibeon (was) a great city, as one of the ro.
10. 42 all these kings..did J. take at one time
12. 9 The king of..one; the king of..one
So in v. 10, 11, 12, 13, 14, 15, 16, 17, 18, 19, 20, 21, 22, 23.
12. 24 king of Tirzah, one: all..thirty and one
17. 14 Why hast thou given me..one lot and one
17. 17 saying..thou shalt not have one lot (only)
20. 4 when he that doth flee unto one of those
23. 10 One man of you shall chase a thousand
23. 14 not one thing..not one thing hath failed
Judg. 6. 16 thou shalt smite the Midianites as one m.
8. 18 each one resembled the children of a king
9. 2 Whether (is) better..that all..or that one
9. 5, 18 threescore and ten persons, upon one
16. 29 Samson took hold..of the one with his ri.
17. 5 consecrated one of his sons, who became
17. 11 the young man was unto him as one of his
18. 19 to be a priest unto the house of one man
19. 13 let us draw near to one of these places to
20. 1 was gathered together as one man, from
20. 8 And all the people arose as one man, say.
20. 11 were gathered..knit together as one man
20. 31 of which one goeth up to the house of G.
21. 3 that there should be to day one tribe lac.
21. 6 There is one tribe cut off from Israel this
21. 8 What one (is there) of the tribes of Israel
Ruth 1. 4 the name of the one..Orpah, and the na.
2. 13 though I be not like unto one of thine h
1 Sa. 1. 2 the name of the one..Hannah, and the na.
1. 24 one ephah of flour, and a bottle of wine
2. 34 in one day they shall die both of them
2. 36 Put me, I pray thee, into one of the pri.
6. 4 one plague (was) on you all, and on your
6. 17 for Ashdod one, for Gaza one, for Askelon
6. 17 one, for Gath one, for Ekron one
9. 3 Take now one of the servants with thee
10. 3 one carrying three kids, and another ca.
11. 7 the people..came out with one consent
13. 17 one company turned unto the way (that)
14. 4 the name of the one (was) Bozez, and the
14. 5 The fore front of the one (was) situate n.
14. 40 said he unto all Israel, Be ye on one side
16. 18 Then answered one of the servants, and
17. 36 this..Philistine shall be as one of them
22. 20 one of the sons of Ahimelech the son of A.
25. 14 But one of the young men told Abigal, N.
26. 15 there came one of the people in to destroy
26. 22 let one of the young men come over and
27. 1 I shall now perish one day by the hand of
2 Sa. 1. 15 David called one of the young men, and s.
2. 21 lay thee hold on one of the young men, and
2. 25 became one troop, and stood on the top
3. 13 but one thing I require of thee, that is
4. 2 the name of the one..Baanah, and the n.
6. 20 as one of the vain fellows shamelessly u.
7. 23 what one nation in the earth (is) like thy
9. 11 he shall eat at my table, as one of the ki.
12. 1 There were two men in one city; the one
12. 3 poor (man) had nothing, save one little
13. 13 thou shalt be as one of the fools in Israel
13. 30 slain all the king's sons, and there is not
14. 6 but the one smote the other, and slew h.
14. 27 were born three sons, and one daughter

2 Sa. 15. 2 Thy servant..of one of the tribes of Israel
17. 12 and of all..shall not be left so much as o.
17. 22 by the morning light there lacked not one
19. 14 he bowed..even as (the heart of) one man
23. 8 against eight hundred, whom he slew at o.
24. 12 choose thee one of them, that I may (do)
1 Ki. 2. 16 now I ask one petition of thee, deny me
2. 20 Then she said, I desire one small petition
3. 17 And the one woman said, O my lord, I and
3. 17 this woman dwell in one house; and I was
4. 22 Solomon's provision for one day was thirty
6. 24 five cubits..the one wing of the cherub
6. 25 the cherubim..of one measure and one
6. 26 The height of the one cherub (was) ten c.
6. 27 so that the wing of the one touched the
6. 34 the two leaves of the one door (were) fol.
7. 16 the height of the one chapiter..five cubits
7. 17 seven for the one chapiter, and seven for
7. 18 rows round about upon the one net work
7. 27 four cubits..the length of one base, and
7. 34 undersetters to the four corners of one
7. 37 had one casting, one measure..one size
7. 38 one laver contained forty baths..every la.
7. 38 upon every one of the ten bases one laver
7. 42 rows of pomegranates for one net work, to
7. 44 one sea, and twelve oxen under the sea
8. 56 there hath not failed one word of all his
10. 14 of gold that came to Solomon in one year
10. 16 six hundred..of gold went to one target
10. 17 three pound of gold went to one shield
11. 13 will give one tribe to thy son for David
11. 32 he shall have one tribe for my servant D.
11. 36 unto his son will I give one tribe, that D.
12. 29 he set the one in Beth-el, and the other
12. 30 the people went..before the one..unto D.
14. 21 Rehoboam (was) forty and one years old
15. 10 forty and one years reigned he in Jerusa.
18. 6 Ahab went one way by himself, and Oba.
18. 23 let them choose one bullock for themsel.
18. 25 Choose you one bullock for yourselves, and
19. 2 if I make not thy life as the life of one of
20. 29 an hundred thousand footmen in one day
22. 8 yet one man, Micaiah the son of Imlah, by
22. 13 (declare) good unto the king with one m.
22. 13 let thy word..be like the word of one of
2 Ki. 3. 11 And one of the king of Israel's servants
4. 22 Send me..one of the young men, and one
4. 39 one went out into the field to gather herbs
6. 3 one said, Be content, I pray thee, and go
6. 5 as one was felling a beam, the axe head
6. 12 one of his servants said, None, my lord, O
7. 8 they went into one tent, and did eat and
7. 13 And one of his servants answered and said
8. 26 and he reigned one year in Jerusalem
9. 1 Elisha the prophet called one of the child.
14. 23 Jeroboam..(reigned) forty and one years
17. 27 Carry thither one of the priests whom ye
17. 28 Then one of the priests, whom they had
18. 24 wilt thou turn away the face of one capt.
22. 1 he reigned thirty and one years in Jerusa.
24. 18 Zedekiah (was) twenty and one years old
25. 16 The two pillars, one sea, and the bases wh.
25. 17 The height of the one pillar (was) eighteen
1 Ch. 1. 19 the name of the one (was) Peleg, because
11. 11 against three hundred, slain..at one time
12. 14 one of the least (was) over an hundred, and
12. 38 (were) of one heart to make David king
17. 21 what one nation in the earth (is) like thy
21. 10 choose thee one of them, that I may do (it)
23. 11 therefore they were in one reckoning, ac.
24. 6 one principal household being taken for E.
24. 17 The one and twentieth to Jachin, the two
25. 28 The one and twentieth to Hothir..his sons
2 Ch. 3. 11 one wing..(was) five cubits, reaching to the
3. 17 he reared up..one on the right hand, and
4. 15 One sea, and twelve oxen under it
5. 13 singers (were) as one, to make one sound
9. 13 of gold that came to Solomon in one year
9. 15 (shekels) of beaten gold went to one target
9. 16 hundred (shekels) of gold went to one sh.
12. 13 Rehoboam (was) one and forty years old
16. 13 in the one and fortieth year of his reign
18. 7 yet one man, by whom we may enquire of
18. 8 the king of Israel called for one (of his) of
18. 12 (declare) good to the king with one assent
18. 12 let thy word..be like one of theirs, and s.
22. 2 and he reigned one year in Jerusalem
28. 6 an hundred and twenty thousand in one
30. 12 hand of God was to give them one heart
32. 12 Ye shall worship before one altar, and b.
34. 1 reigned in Jerusalem one and thirty years
36. 11 Zedekiah (was) one and twenty years old
Ezra 2. 26 The children..six hundred twenty and one
3. 1 gathered themselves together as one man
10. 13 neither (is this) a work of one day or two
Neh. 1. 2 Hanani, one of my brethren, came, he and
4. 17 with one of his hands wrought in the work
5. 18 which was prepared..daily (was) one ox
7. 30 men of..Gaba, six hundred twenty and one
7. 37 children..seven hundred twenty and one
8. 1 gathered themselves together as one man
11. 1 to bring one of ten to dwell in Jerusalem
Esth. 3. 13 to cause to perish, all Jews..in one day
4. 11 one law of his to put (him) to death, exc.
7. 9 Harbonah, one of the chamberlains, said
8. 12 Upon one day, in all the provinces of king
Job 2. 10 Thou speakest as one of the foolish women
9. 3 he cannot answer him one of a thousand
9. 22 This (is) one (thing), therefore I said (it)
14. 4 Who can bring a clean (thing) out..not one
23. 13 But he (is) in one (mind), and who can t
31. 15 and did not one fashion us in the womb?

Job 33. 23 If there be..one among a thousand, to s.
41. 16 One is so near to another, that no air can
Psa. 14. 3 (there is) none that doeth good, no, not o.
27. 4 One (thing) have I desired of the LORD
34. 20 He keepeth all his bones: not one of them
53. 3 (is) none that doeth good, no, not one
82. 7 ye shall die like men, and fall like one of
106. 11 enemies; there was not one of them left
Prov. 1. 14 Cast in thy lot..let us all have one purse
Eccl. 2. 14 I myself perceived also that one event h.
3. 19 one thing befalleth them..they have all o.
3. 20 All go unto one place; all are of the dust
4. 8 There is one..and..not a second; yea, he
4. 9 Two (are) better than one; because they
4. 10 if they fall, the one will lift up his fellow
4. 11 they have heat: but how can one be warm
4. 12 if one prevail against him, two shall with.
6. 6 seen no good: do not all go to one place?
7. 27 (counting) one by one, to find out the ac.
7. 28 one man among a thousand have I found
9. 2 one event to the righteous, and to the w.
9. 3 This (is) an evil..that (there is) one event
9. 18 but one sinner destroyeth much good
12. 11 assemblies, (which) are given from one s.
Song 4. 9 with one of thine eyes, with one chain of
6. 9 my undefiled is..one..the (only) one of
Isa. 4. 1 seven women shall take hold of one man
5. 10 ten acres of vineyard shall yield one bath
6. 6 Then flew one of the seraphim unto me
9. 14 LORD will cut off from Israel..in one day
10. 17 devour his thorns and his briers in one
19. 18 one shall be called, The city of destruct.
23. 15 years, according to the days of one king
27. 12 ye shall be gathered one by one, O ye ch.
30. 17 One thousand..at the rebuke of one; at
34. 16 no one of these shall fail, none shall want
36. 9 wilt thou turn away the face of one capt.
47. 9 shall come to thee in a moment in one day
66. 8 earth be made to bring forth in one day?
66. 17 in the gardens behind one (tree) in the
Jer. 3. 14 I will take you one of a city, and two of
24. 2 One basket (had) very good figs..like the
32. 39 I will give them one heart, and one way
35. 2 bring them..into one of the chambers, and
52. 1 Zedekiah (was) one and twenty years old
52. 20 two pillars, one sea, and twelve brasen b.
52. 21 the height of one pillar (was) eighteen c.
52. 22 the height of one chapiter (was) five cub.
Eze. 1. 15 behold one wheel upon the earth by the
1. 16 they four had one likeness: and their ap.
4. 9 put them in one vessel, and make thee b.
9. 2 one man among them (was) clothed with
10. 9 one wheel by one cherub, and another w.
10. 10 they four had one likeness, as if a wheel
11. 19 I will give them one heart, and I will put
18. 10 and..doeth the like to (any) one of these
19. 3 she brought up one of her whelps: it be.
21. 19 both twain shall come forth out of one l.
23. 2 two women, the daughters of one mother
23. 13 then I saw...they (took) both one way
33. 24 Abraham was one, and he inherited the l.
34. 23 I will set up one shepherd over them, and
37. 16 take thee one stick, and write upon it, For
37. 17 join them one to another into one stick
37. 17 and they shall become one in thine hand
37. 19 make them one stick..they shall be one
37. 22 I will make them one nation in the land
37. 22 one king shall be king to them all: and t.
37. 24 they all shall have one shepherd: they s.
40. 5 the breadth..one reed; and the height, one
40. 6 one reed broad, and the other..one reed b.
40. 7 (was) one reed long, and one reed broad
40. 7 and the threshhold of the gate..one reed
40. 8 also the porch of the gate within, one reed
40. 10 chambers..they three (were) of one mea.
40. 10 the posts had one measure on this side
40. 12 one cubit..the space (was) one cubit on
40. 26, 49 one on this side, and another on that
40. 42 And the four tables (were)..one cubit h.
40. 44 one at the side of the east gate (having)
41. 11 one door toward the north, and another
41. 24 two..for the one door, and two leaves for
42. 4 And before the chambers..a way of one
43. 14 two cubits, and the breadth one cubit; and
45. 7 over against one of the portions, from the
45. 11 The ephah and the bath shall be of one m.
45. 15 one lamb out of the flock, out of two hu.
46. 17 But if he give..to one of his servants, then
46. 22 these four corners (were) of one measure
48. 8 and (in) length as one of the (other) parts
48. 31 one gate of Reuben, one gate of J., one g.
48. 32 one gate of Joseph, one gate of Benj., one
48. 33 one gate of Simeon, one gate of Issa., one
48. 34 one gate of Gad, one gate of Asher, one g.
Dan. 8. 3 one..higher than the other, and the hig.
8. 9 out of one of them came forth a little ho.
8. 13 Then I heard one saint speaking, and an.
9. 27 he shall confirm the covenant..for one w.
10. 13 withstood me one and twenty days: but
10. 13 Michael, one of the chief princes, came to
11. 27 they shall speak lies at one table; but it
12. 5 one on this side of the bank of the river
Hos. 1. 11 appoint themselves one head, and they s.
Amos 4. 7 I caused it to rain upon one city, and ca.
4. 7 one piece was rained upon, and the piece
4. 8 So two (or) three cities wandered unto one
6. 9 if there remain ten men in one house, t.
Obad. 11 In the day..even thou (wast) as one of t.
Zeph. 3. 9 may all call..to serve him with one con.
Hag. 2. 1 in the one and twentieth (day) of the mo.
Zech. 3. 9 behold..upon one stone (shall be) seven
3. 9 remove the iniquity of that land in one

Zech. 4. 3 two olive trees by it, one upon the right
8. 21 the inhabitants of one..shall go to anot.
11. 7 one I called beauty, and the other I called
11. 8 Three shepherds also I cut off in one mo.
14. 7 it shall be one day which shall be known
14. 9 shall there be one LORD, and his name one
Mal. 2. 10 Have we not all one father? hath not one
2. 15 did not he make one?..And wherefore one?

2. *A man,* אִישׁ *ish.*
Gen. 11. 3 they said one to another, Go to, let us m
11. 7 that they may not understand one anoth.
13. 11 separated themselves the one from the o.
26. 31 And they rose up..and sware one to ano.
31. 49 watch..when we are absent one from an.
34. 14 to give our sister to one that is uncircu.
37. 19 they said one to another Behold, this d.
42. 21 they said one to another, We (are) verily
42. 28 they were afraid, saying one to another
43. 33 they sat..and the men marvelled one at
Exod 10. 23 They saw not one another, neither rose any
16. 15 they said one to another, It (is) manna: for
18. 16 I judge between one and another, and I
37. 9 covered..with their faces one to another
Lev. 7. 10 shall all the sons of Aaron have, one (as
19. 11 Ye shall not steal..neither lie one to an.
25. 46 ye shall not rule one over another with ri.
26. 37 they shall fall one upon another, as it were
Num 14. 4 they said one to another, Let us make a
Deut. 1. 35 Surely there shall not one of these men
Judg. 6. 29 they said one to another, Who hath done
10 18 princes of Gilead said one to another, W
1 Sa. 10. 11 the people said one to another, What (is)
10. 12 one of the same place answered and said
20. 41 they kissed one another, and wept one w.
22. 2 every one in distress..every one..every o
2 Sa. 19. 7 there will not tarry one with thee this n.
1 Ki. 18. 40 Take the prophets..let not one of them e
2 Ki. 3. 23 they have smitten one another: now there
7. 3 they said one to another, Why sit we here
7. 6 they said one to another, Lo, the king of
7. 9 they said one to another, We do not well
12. 9 on the right side as one cometh into the
Esth. 6. 9 horse be delivered to the hand of one of
9. 19, 22 and of sending portions one to another
Job 41. 17 They are joined one to another, they stick
Psa. 49. 16 Be not thou afraid when one is made rich
Prov. 6. 28 Can one go upon hot coals, and his feet
Isa. 13. 8 they shall be amazed one at another; their
40. 26 that (he is) strong in power; not one fail.
66. 13 As one whom his mother comforteth, so
Jer. 13. 14 I will dash them one against another, even
25. 26 the kings..far and near, one with another
Eze. 4. 17 astonied one with another, and consume
24. 23 but ye shall pine..and mourn one toward
47. 14 ye shall inherit it, one as well as another
Joel 2. 8 Neither shall one thrust another; they
Mal. 3. 16 Then they..spake often one to another

3. *Such an one,* פְּלֹנִי אַלְמֹנִי *peloni almoni.*
Ruth 4. 1 Ho, such a one! turn aside, sit down here

4. *A woman,* אִשָּׁה *ishshah.*
Exod 26. 3 coupled..one to another. coupled one to
26. 5 that the loops may take hold one of anot
26. 17 Two tenons..set in order one against an.
Eze. 1. 9 Their wings (were) joined one to another
1. 23 their wings straight the one toward the o.
3. 13 the living creatures that touched one an.

5. *Also, even,* גַּם *gam.*
2 Sa. 17. 13 until there be not one small stone found

6. *One,* חַד *chad.*
Eze. 33. 30 thy people..speak one to another, every
Dan. 2. 9 one decree for you; for ye have prepared
3. 19 one seven times more than it was wont to
4. 19 Then Daniel..was astonied for one hour
7. 5 it raised up itself on one side, and (it had)
7. 16 I came near unto one of them that stood

7. *Soul, breathing creature,* נֶפֶשׁ *nephesh.*
Lev. 4. 27 And if any one of the common people sin

8. *Another,* ἄλλος *allos.*
John 4. 37 herein is that saying true, One soweth, and
Acts 2. 12 were in doubt, saying one to another, W.
1 Co. 15. 39 one..flesh of men, another flesh of beasts
15. 41 one glory of the sun, and another glory

9. *One,* εἷς *heis.*
Matt. 5. 18 one jot or..tittle shall in no wise pass from
5. 29, 30 one of thy members should perish, and
6. 24 he will hate the one, and love the other
6. 24 or else he will hold to the one, and despi.
6. 27 Which of you..can add one cubit unto his
6. 29 Solomon..was not arrayed like one of these
10. 29 one of them shall not fall on the ground
10. 42 whosoever shall give to drink unto one of
12. 11 that shall have one sheep, and if it fall into
13. 46 Who, when he had found one pearl of g.
16. 14 said..others, Jeremias, or one of the pro.
18. 5 whoso shall receive one such little child
18. 6 whoso shall offend one of these little ones
18. 10 Take heed that ye despise not one of these
18. 12 If..one of them be gone astray, doth he
18. 14 that one of these little ones should perish
18. 16 take with thee one or two more, that in
18. 24 one was brought unto him, which owed
18. 28 found one of his fellow servants, which
19. 16 one came and said unto him, Good Master
19. 17 none good but one, (that is), God: but if
20. 13 he answered one of them, and said, Friend
20. 21 the one on thy right hand, and the other
21. 24 I also will ask you one thing, which if ye
Matt 22. 35 Then one of them..a lawyer, asked..tem.
23. 8 for one is your Master..Christ; and all ye
23. 9 for one is your Father, which is in heaven
23. 10 Neither be ye called masters: for [one] is
23. 15 ye compass sea and land to make one pro.
24. 40 the one shall be taken, and the other left
25. 15 gave..to another two, and to another one
25. 18 he that had received one went and digged
25. 24 he which had received the one talent came
25. 40 Inasmuch as ye have done (it) unto one of
25. 45 Inasmuch as ye did (it) not to one of the
26. 14 one of the twelve, called Judas Iscariot
26. 21 I say unto you, That one of you shall be.
26. 47 Judas, one of the twelve, came, and with
26. 51 one of them which were with Jesus stret.
27. 48 straightway one of them ran, and took a
Mark 5. 22 there cometh one of the rulers of the sy.
6. 15 it is a prophet, or as one of the prophets
8. 14 neither had they..with them more than one
8. 28 but some (say) Elias; and others, One of the
9. 17 one of the multitude answered and said
9. 37 Whosoever shall receive one of such chi.
9. 42 whosoever shall offend one of (these) little
10. 17 there came one running, and kneeled to
10. 18 (there is) none good but one, (that is), God
10. 21 One thing thou lackest: go thy way, sell
10. 37 one on thy right hand, and the other on
11. 29 I will also ask of you one question, and
12. 6 Having yet therefore one son, his well bel.
12. 28 one of the scribes came, and having hea.
12. 29 Hear, O Israel; The Lord our God is one
12. 32 there is one God; and there is none other
13. 1 one of his disciples saith unto him, Mas.
14. 10 one of the twelve, went unto the chief p.
14. 18 One of you which eateth with me shall b.
14. 20 one of the twelve, that dippeth with me
14. 43 cometh Judas, one of the twelve, and with
14. 47 one of them that stood by drew a sword
15. 6 at (that) feast he released unto them one
15. 27 the one on his right hand, and the other
15. 36 [one] ran and filled a sponge full of vine.
Luke 4. 40 he laid his hands on every one of them
5. 3 he entered into one of the ships, which
7. 41 the one owed five hundred pence, and the
9. 8 that [one] of the old prophets was risen
11. 46 touch not the burdens with one of your
12. 6 not one of them is forgotten before God
12. 25 which of you..can add to his stature [one]
12. 27 Solomon..was not arrayed like one of th.
12. 52 there shall be five in one house divided
15. 4 if he lose one of them, doth not leave the
15. 7 joy shall be in heaven over one sinner that
15. 10 There is joy..over one sinner that repen.
15. 19 And am no more worthy..make me as one
15. 26 he called one of the servants, and asked w.
16. 5 So he called every one of his lord's debtors
16. 13 he will hate the one, and love the other
16. 13 he will hold to the one, and despise the o.
17. 2 that he should offend one of these little
17. 15 one of them, when he saw that he was h.
17. 34, 36 [the one shall be taken, and the other]
18. 10 one a Pharisee, and the other a publican
18. 19 said. none (is) good, save one, (that is), G.
20. 3 I will also ask you [one] thing; and ans.
22. 3 he that was called Judas, one of the tw.
22. 47 he that was called Judas, one of the tw.
22. 50 one of them smote a servant of the high
23. 17 [must release one unto them at the feast]
23. 39 one of the malefactors which were hanged
24. 18 the one of them, whose name was Cleopas
John 1. 40 One of the two which heard John..and f.
6. 8 One of his disciples, Andrew..saith unto
6. 22 save that one whereinto his disciples were
6. 70 Have not I chosen you twelve, and one of
6. 71 that should betray him, being one of the
7. 21 I have done one work, and ye all marvel
7. 50 came to Jesus by night, being one of them
8. 41 Then said they..we have one Father..God
10. 16 and there shall be..fold, and one shepherd
10. 30 I and (my) Father are one
11. 49 one of them..Caiaphas, being the high p.
11. 50 that it is expedient..that one man should
11. 52 he should gather together in one the ch.
12. 2 Lazarus was one of them that sat at the
12. 4 Then saith one of his disciples, Judas Isc.
13. 21 I say unto you..one of you shall betray me
13. 23 there was leaning on Jesus' bosom one of
17. 11 Holy Father, keep..that they may be one
17. 21 That they all may be one; as thou, Father
17. 21 that they also may be [one] in us: that the
17. 22 that they may be one, even as we are one
17. 23 that they may be made perfect in one
18. 14 that it was expedient that one man shou.
18. 22 one of the officers which stood by struck
18. 26 One of the servants of the high priest, b.
18. 39 that I should release unto you one at the
19. 34 one of the soldiers with a spear pierced
20. 12 the one at the head, and the other at the
20. 24 Thomas, one of the twelve, called Didy.
21. 25 which, if they should be written every o.
Acts 1. 22 must one be ordained to be a witness w.
11. 28 there stood up one of them named Agabus
17. 26 hath made of one blood all nations of m.
17. 27 though he be not far from every one of us
20. 31 to warn every one night and day with te.
21. 26 should be offered for every one of them
23. 6 when Paul perceived that the one part we.
23. 17 Then Paul called one of the centurions
28. 25 after that Paul had spoken one word, Well
Rom. 3. 10 it is written..none righteous, no, not one
3. 12 there is none that doeth good, no, not one
3. 30 Seeing (it is) one God which shall justify
5. 12 as by one man sin entered into the world
Rom. 5. 15 if through the offence of one many be de.
5. 15 by one man, Jesus Christ, hath abounded
5. 16 not as..by one that sinned, (so is) the g.
5. 16 for the judgment (was) by one to condem.
5. 17 by one man's offence death reigned by one
5. 17 much more they..shall reign in life by o.
5. 18 as by the offence of one (judgment came)
5. 18 so by the righteousness of one (the free)
5. 19 as by one man's disobedience many were
5. 19 so by the obedience of one shall many be
9. 10 when Rebecca also had conceived by one
12. 4 For as we have many members in one bo.
12. 5 we, (being) many, are one body in Christ
15. 6 That ye may with..one mouth glorify G.
1 Co. 3. 8 he that planteth..he that watereth are one
4. 6 that no one of you be puffed up for one
6. 16 which is joined to an harlot is one body?
6. 17 he that is joined unto the Lord is one sp.
8. 4 and that (there is) none other God but o.
8. 6 to us..one God, the Father..one Lord J.
9. 24 they..run all, but one receiveth the prize?
10. 17 For we..many are one bread..one body
10. 17 we are all partakers of that one bread
11. 5 that is even all one as if she were shaven
12. 11 all these worketh that one and the self
12. 12 For as the body is one, and hath many
12. 12 all the members of that [one] body..are one
12. 13 by one Spirit are we all baptized into one
12. 13 have been all made to drink into one Sp.
12. 14 For the body is not one member, but m.
12. 18 hath God set the members every one of
12. 19 if they were all one member, where..the
12. 20 But now..many members, yet but one b.
12. 26 whether one member suffer, all the mem.
12. 26 or one member be honoured, all the me.
14. 27 If any man speak in a..tongue..let one in.
2 Co. 5. 14 because we thus judge, that if one died for
11. 2 I have espoused you to one husband, that
Gal. 3. 16 but as of one, And to thy seed, which is
3. 20 a mediator is not..of one; but God is one
3. 28 neither..for ye are all one in Christ Jesus
4. 22 the one by a bondmaid, the other by a free
5. 14 For all the law is fulfilled in one word, (e.)
Eph. 2. 14 who hath made both one, and hath broken
2. 15 to make in himself of twain one new man
2. 16 he might reconcile both unto God in one
2. 18 through him we both have access by one sp.
4. 4 one body, and one spirit, even as ye are c.
4. 5 One Lord..one baptism
4. 6 One God and Father of all, who (is) above
4. 7 But unto every one of us is given grace a.
Phil. 1. 27 that ye stand fast in one spirit, with one
2. 2 that ye be..of one accord, of one mind
Col. 3. 15 to the which also ye are called in one body
1 Th. 2. 11 comforted and charged every one of you
2 Th. 1. 3 the charity of every one of you all toward
1 Ti. 2. 5 For..one God, and one mediator between
5. 9 not a widow..having been the wife of one
Heb. 2. 11 and they who are sanctified (are) all of one
11. 12 Therefore sprang there even of one, and
Jas. 2. 10 keep the whole law, and yet offend in one
2. 19 Thou believest that there is one God; thou
4. 12 There is one lawgiver, who is able to save
1 Jo. 5. 7 [there are three..and these three are one]
5. 8 there are three..these three agree in one
Rev. 5. 5 one of the elders saith unto me, Weep not
6. 1 I heard..one of the four beasts saying, C.
7. 13 one of the elders answered, saying unto
15. 7 one of the four beasts gave unto the seven
17. 1 there came one of the seven angels which
17. 10 five are fallen, and one..the other is not
21. 9 there came unto me one of the seven an.
21. 21 every several gate was of one pearl: and

10. *Other, different,* ἕτερος *heteros.*
1 Co. 15. 40 but the glory of the celestial (is) one, and

11. *One, (fem.)* μία *mia.*
Matt. 5. 18 one tittle shall in no wise pass from the
5. 19 shall break one of these least commandm.
5. 36 thou canst not make one hair white or b.
17. 4 one for thee, and one for Moses, and one
19. 5 cleave..and they twain shall be one flesh
19. 6 Wherefore they are no more twain, but o
20. 12 These last have wrought..one hour, and
24. 41 the one shall be taken, and the other left
26. 40 What! could ye not watch with me one h.?
Mark 9. 5 one for thee..one for Moses, and one for E.
10. 8 one flesh..they are no more twain, but one
14. 37 saith..couldest not thou watch one hour?
14. 66 there cometh one of the maids of the high
Luke 9. 33 one for thee, and one for Moses, and one
13. 10 he was teaching in one of the synagogues
14. 18 they all with one (consent) began to make
15. 8 if she lose one piece, doth not light a ca.
16. 17 easier..than one tittle of the law to fail
17. 22 ye shall desire to see one of the days of the
17. 34 there shall be two (men) in [one] bed; the
20. 1 on one of those days, as he taught the pe.
22. 59 about the space of one hour after, another
John 10. 16 and there shall be one fold (and)..shepherd
Acts 4. 32 multitude..were of one heart and of one
12. 10 went out, and passed on through one str.
19. 34 all with one voice about the space of two
21. 7 the brethren, and abode with them one day
24. 21 Except it be for this one voice, that I cried
28. 13 after one day the south wind blew, and we
1 Co. 6. 16 body? for two, saith he, shall be one flesh
10. 8 fell in one day three and twenty thousand
2 Co. 11. 24 five times received I forty..save one
Gal. 4. 24 one from the mount Sinai, which gendereth
Eph. 4. 4 as ye are called in one hope of your calling
4. 5 Lord, one faith. baptism

Eph. 5. 31 be joined..and they two shall be one flesh
Phil. 1. 27 with one mind striving together for the f.
1 Ti. 3. 2 husband of one wife, vigilant, sober, of g.
Titus 1. 6 If any be blameless, the husband of one
Heb. 10. 12 this man, after he had offered one sacrifice
10. 14 For by one offering he hath perfected for
12. 16 who for one morsel of meat sold his birth.
2 Pe. 3. 8 that one day (is) with the Lord as a thou.
3. 8 years and a thousand years as one day
Rev. 6. 1 I saw when the Lamb opened one of the
9. 12 One woe is past..behold, there come two
13. 3 I saw one of his heads as it were wounded
17. 12 receive power as kings one hour with the
17. 13 These have one mind, and shall give their
18. 8 Therefore shall her plagues come in one
18. 10 saying..in one hour is thy judgment come
18. 17 in one hour so great riches is come to no.
18. 19 saying..in one hour is she made desolate

12. *A certain one*, τις, τι *tis, ti.*
Matt 12. 29 Or else how can one enter into a strong
12. 47 Then one said unto him, Behold, thy mo.
Luke 11. 45 Then answered one of the lawyers, and s.
12. 13 one of the company said unto him, Master
13. 23 Then said one unto him, Lord, are there
14. 1 as he went into the house of one of the c.
14. 15 when one of them that sat at meat with
16. 30 but if one went unto them from the dead
16. 31 neither will they be persuaded though one
23 26 they laid hold upon one Simon, a Cyrenian
Acts 5. 34 Then stood there up one in the council
7. 24 seeing one..suffer wrong, he defended
9. 43 he tarried many days in Joppa with one
10. 6 He lodgeth with one Simon a tanner, wh.
19. 9 disputing daily in the school of [one] Ty.
25. 19 and of one Jesus, which was dead, whom
Rom. 5. 7 scarcely for a righteous man will one die
1 Co. 3. 4 For while one saith, I am of Paul; and a.
5. 1 such..that one should have his father's
14. 24 and there come in one that believeth not
Titus 1. 12 One of themselves..a prophet of their o.
Heb. 2. 6; Jas. 2. 16; 5. 19; Mr. 9. 38; 15. 21; Lu.
7. 36; 8. 49; 9. 19, 49; 11. 1; Ac. 5. 25; 21. 16; 22. 12.

13. *This one*, οὗτος (*dat.*) *houtos.*
Luke 7. 8 I say unto one, Go, and he goeth; and to

14. *Peace*, εἰρήνη *eirēnē.*
Acts 7. 26 would have set them at one again, saying

[*See also* Accord, any, each, every, holy, look, mind, see, side, such.]

ONE ..(from)...**another** —

1. *This*, דָּא *da.*
Dan. 5. 6 and his knees smote one against another
7. 3 four great beasts. diverse one from anot.

2. *This*, דֵּן *den.*
Dan. 2. 43 but they shall not cleave one to another

3. *A vessel*, כְּלִי *keli.*
Esth. 1. 7 the vessels being diverse one from another

4. *A wing*, כָּנָף *kanaph.*
1 Ki. 6. 27 their wings touched one another in the

5. *Each other*, ἀλλήλων *allēlōn.*
Matt 24. 10 betray one another, and shall hate one a.
25. 32 he shall separate them one from another
Mark 4. 41 said one to another, What manner of man
9. 50 Have salt..and have peace one with ano.
Luke 2. 15 the shepherds said one to another, Let us
6. 11 communed one with another what they m.
7. 32 calling one to another, and saying, We h
8. 25 saying one to another, What manner of
12. 1 insomuch that they trode one upon anot.
24. 17 these that ye have one to another, as ye
24. 32 they said one to another, Did not our he.
John 4. 33 Therefore said the disciples one to anot.
5. 44 which receive honour one of another, and
13. 14 ye also ought to wash one another's feet
13. 22 Then the disciples looked one on another
13. 34 That ye love one another .also love one a.
13. 35 my disciples, if ye have love one to anot
15. 12 That ye love one another, as I have loved
15. 17 I command you, that ye love one another
Acts 2. 7 saying [one to another,] Behold, are not
7. 26 brethren; why do ye wrong one to anoth.
19. 38 Wherefore..let them implead one another
21. 6 when we had taken our leave one of ano.
Rom. 1. 27 burned in their lust one toward another
2. 15 and..accusing or else excusing one anot.
12. 5 and every one members one of another
12. 10 one to another..in honour preferring one a.
12. 16 (Be) of the same mind one toward anoth.
13. 8 Owe no man anything, but to love one an.
14. 13 Let us not therefore judge one another any
14. 19 and things wherewith one may edify ano.
15. 5 grant you to be like minded one toward a.
15. 7 Wherefore receive ye one another, as Chr.
15. 14 are..able also to admonish [one another]
16. 16 Salute one another with an holy kiss. The
1 Co. 11. 33 when ye come together..tarry one for an.
12. 25 should have the same care one for anoth.
16. 20 Greet ye one another with an holy kiss
2 Co. 13. 12 Greet one another with an holy kiss
Gal. 5. 13 For, brethren..by love serve one another
5. 15 if ye bite and devour one another, take
5. 15 that ye be not consumed one of another
5. 26 provoking one another, envying one ano.
6. 2 Bear ye one another's burdens, and so f.
Eph. 4. 2 With all lowliness..forbearing one anoth.
4. 25 speak..for we are members one of another
4. 32 be ye kind one to another, tender hearted
5. 21 Submitting yourselves one to another in
Col. 3. 9 Lie not one to another, seeing that ye have
3. 13 Forbearing one another..and forgiving
1 Th. 3. 12 and abound in love one toward another
4. 9 ye..are taught of God to love one another
4. 18 Wherefore comfort one another with these
Titus 3. 3 ourselves were..hateful..hating one ano.
Heb. 10. 24 let us consider one another to provoke
Jas. 4. 11 Speak not evil one of another, brethren
5. 9 Grudge not one against another, brethren
5. 16 Confess..faults one to another..pray one
1 Pe. 1. 22 love one another with a pure heart ferv.
4. 9 Use hospitality one to another without g.
5 5 Yea, all..be subject one to another, and
5. 14 Greet ye one another with a kiss of char.
1 Jo. 1. 7 we have fellowship one with another, and
3. 11 ye heard..that we should love one another
3. 23 love one another, as he gave us command.
4. 7 let us love one another: for love is of God
4. 11 Beloved..we ought also to love one ano.
4. 12 If we love one another, God dwelleth in
2 John 5 I beseech thee..that we love one another
Rev 6. 4 given..that they should kill one another
11. 10 And they..shall send gifts one to another

6. *Of himself, herself, itself*, ἑαυτοῦ *heautou.*
1 Co. 6. 7 fault..because ye go to law one with an.
Eph. 4. 32 forgiving one another, even as God for C.
Col. 3. 13 forgiving one another, if any man have a
3. 16 teaching and admonishing one another in
Heb. 3. 13 But exhort one another daily, while it is
1 Pe. 4. 10 minister the same one to another, as good

7. *Other*, ἄλλος, Jo 4. 37; Ac. 2. 12; 1 Co. 15. 39, 40

8. *One...one*, εἷς...εἷς *heis...heis.*
Matt. 27. 38 one on the right hand, and another on

9. *One the other*, εἷς τὸν ἕνα *heis ton hena.*
1 Th. 5. 11 and edify one another, even as also ye do

ONE by one —

1. *One by one*, εἷς καθ' εἷς *heis kath heis.*
Mark 14. 19 they began..to say unto him one by one
John 8. 9 went out one by one, beginning at the e.

2. *One by one*, καθ' ἕνα *kath hena.*
1 Co. 14. 31 ye may all prophesy one by one, that all

ONE sort with another —

These with these, אֵלֶּה עִם־אֵלֶּה *eleh im eleh.*
1 Ch. 24. 5 were they divided by lot, one sort with a.

ONE, the —

This, זֹאת *zoth.*
1 Ki. 3. 23 The one saith, This (is) my son that liveth

ONE...the other, the —

1. *This*, זֶה...זֶה *zeh...zeh.*
Exod. 14. 20 so that the one came not near the other
Ecc. 3. 19 as the one dieth, so dieth the other; yea

2. *Each other*, ἀλλήλων *allēlōn.*
Acts 15. 39 they departed asunder one from the other
1 Co. 7. 5 Defraud ye not one the other, except (it
Gal. 5. 17 and these are contrary the one to the other

ONE thing —

1. *One thing*, ἕν *hen.*
Luke 10. 42 one thing is needful: and Mary hath ch.
18. 22 yet lackest thou one thing: sell all that
John 9. 25 one thing I know, that, whereas I was bl,
Phil. 3. 13 one thing..forgetting those things which
2 Pe. 3. 8 be not ignorant of this one thing, that one

2. *A certain thing*, τι *ti.*
Luke 6. 9 said..unto them, I will ask you [one thi.]

ONE, tumultuous —

Sons of tumult, בְּנֵי שָׁאוֹן [*ben*].
Jer. 48. 45 crown of the head of the tumultuous ones

O-NE-SI'-MUS, Ὀνήσιμος *profitable.*
A native of Colosse, and a slave of Philemon, from whom he had escaped, but to whom he was sent back as a Christian brother by Paul, who had converted him in Rome.
Col. 4. 9 With O., a faithful and beloved brother
Phm. 10 I beseech thee for my son O., whom I h.

O-NE-SI-PHO'-RUS, Ὀνησίφορος *bringing profit.*
A disciple in Ephesus who when in Rome had sought out and befriended Paul.
2 Ti. 1. 16 Lord give mercy unto the house of O.; for
4. 19 Salute Prisca..and the household of O.

ONION —

Onion, בָּצָל *betsel.*
Num. 11. 5 the melons, and the leeks, and the onions

ONLY —

1. *One*, אֶחָד *echad.*
1 Ki. 4. 19 and..the only officer which (was) in the
Eze. 7. 5 saith..An evil, an only evil, behold, is c.

2. *Only*, אַךְ *ak.*
Gen. 7. 23 Noah only remained..and they that (were)

3. *Alone*, לְבַד *le-bad.*
Eccl. 7. 29 Lo, this only have I found, that God hath

4. *Alone by itself*, לְבַדּוֹ [*le-bad*].
Deut. 8. 3 know that man doth not live by bread o.

5. *Alone, solitary*, לְבָדָד *le-badad.*
Psa. 4. 8 thou, LORD, only makest me dwell in sa.

6. *Save, except, besides*, זוּלָה *zulah.*
Deut. 4. 12 saw no similitude; only (ye heard) a voice

7. *Together, at once*, יַחַד *yachad.*
Job 34. 29 whether (it be done)..against a man only

8. *Singly, lonely, only*, יָחִיד *yachid.*
Gen. 22. 2 Take now thy son, thine only (son) Isaac
22. 16 not withheld thy son, thine only (son)
Prov. 4. 3 only (beloved) in the sight of my mother
Amos 8. 10 I will make it as the mourning of an only
Zech. 12. 10 mourn..as one mourneth for (his) only

9. *Cutting short*, קָסַם *kasam* (adv. infin.).
Eze. 44. 20 they shall only poll their heads

10. *Only, surely*, רַק *raq.*
Gen. 6. 5, 14. 28, 19. 8, 24. 8, &c., &c.

11. *One*, εἷς *heis.*
Mark 2. 7 Why..who can forgive sins but God only?

12. *Alone*, μόνον *monon.*
Matt. 5. 47 if ye salute your brethren only, what do
8. 8 speak the word only, and my servant sh.
10. 42 a cup of cold (water) only in the name of a
14. 36 might only touch the hem of his garment
21. 19 and found nothing thereon, but leaves o.
21. 21 ye shall not only do this..to the fig tree
Mark 5. 36 saith unto the ruler..Be not afraid, only
6. 8 they should take nothing..save a staff o.
Luke 8. 50 believe only, and she shall be made whole
John 5. 18 because he not only had broken the sabb.
11. 52 not for that nation only, but that also he
12. 9 they came not for Jesus' sake only, but
13. 9 Lord, not my feet only, but also (my) ha.
Acts 8. 16 only they were baptized in the name of the
11. 19 preaching..to none but unto the Jews o.
18. 25 taught..knowing only the baptism of Jo.
19. 27 So that not only this our craft is in dan.
21. 13 I am ready not to be bound only, but also
26. 29 I would to God, that not only thou, but
27. 10 not only of the lading and ship, but also
Rom. 1. 32 not only do the same, but have pleasure
3. 29 (Is he) the God of the Jews only?..not a.
4. 12 them who are not of the circumcision on.
4. 16 not to that only which is of the law, but
5. 3 not only (so), but we glory in tribulations
5. 11 not only (so), but we also joy in God thro.
8. 23 not only (they), but ourselves also, which
9. 10 not only (this); but when Rebecca also had
9. 24 not of the Jews only, but also of the Gen.?
13. 5 must needs be subject, not only for wrath
1 Co. 7. 39 married to whom she will; only in the Lo.
15. 19 If in this life only we have hope in Christ
2 Co. 7. 7 not by his coming only, but by the consol.
8. 10 begun before, not only to do, but also to
8. 19 not (that) only, but who was also chosen
8. 21 Providing for honest things, not only in
9. 12 not only supplieth the want of the saints
Gal. 1. 23 they had heard only, that he which pers.
2. 10 Only..that we should remember the poor
3. 2 This only would I learn of you, Received
4. 18 and not only when I am present with you
5. 13 only (use) not liberty for an occasion to
6. 12 only lest they should suffer persecution
Eph. 1. 21 named, not only in this world, but also
Phil. 1. 27 Only let your conversation be as it beco.
1. 29 not only to believe on him, but also to
2. 12 not as in my presence only but now much
2. 27 not on him only, but on me also, lest I
1 Th. 1. 5 our gospel came not unto you in word only
1. 8 sounded out the word..not only in Mac.
2. 8 not the gospel of God only, but also our
2 Th. 2. 7 only he who now letteth (will let), until
1 Ti. 5. 13 they learn (to be) idle..and not only idle
2 Ti. 2. 20 there are not only vessels of gold and of
4. 8 not to me only, but unto all them also that
Heb. 9. 10 only in meats and drinks, and divers wa.
12. 26 Yet once more I shake not the earth only
Jas. 1. 22 ye doers of the word, and not hearers only
2. 24 a man is justified, and not by faith only
1 Pe. 2. 18 not only to the good and gentle, but
1 Jo. 2. 2 not for ours only, but also for..the whole
5. 6 not by water only, but by water and blood

13. *Alone*, μόνος *monos.*
Matt. 4. 10 worship the Lord thy God, and him only
12. 4 not lawful..to eat..but only for the pri.
17. 8 lifted up their eyes, they saw..Jesus only
24. 36 knoweth..not..angels..but my Father o.
Mark 9. 8 they saw no man any more, save Jesus o.
Luke 4. 8 worship..God, and him only shalt thou
24. 18 Art thou only a stranger in Jerusalem, and
John 5. 44 and seek not the honour..from God only?
17. 3 they might know thee the only true God
Rom. 16. 4 unto whom not only I give thanks, but
16. 27 To God only wise, (be) glory through J.
1 Co. 9. 6 Or I only and Barnabas, have not we po.
14. 36 out from you? or came it unto you only?
Phil. 4. 15 no church communicated...but ye only
Col. 4. 11 These only..fellow workers unto the ki.
1 Ti. 1. 17 unto..the only wise God, (be) honour and
6. 15 the blessed and only Potentate, the king
6. 16 Who only hath immortality, dwelling in
2 Ti. 4. 11 Only Luke is with me. Take Mark, and
2 John 1 I only, but also all they that have known
Jude 4 denying the only Lord God, and our Lord
25 To the only wise God our Saviour, (be) g.
Rev. 9. 4 [only] those men which have not the seal
15. 4 for (thou) only (art) holy: for all nations

ONLY (child) —

Only begotten, μονογενής *monogenēs.*
Luke 7. 12 the only son of his mother, and she was
8. 42 he had one only daughter, about twelve
9. 38 look upon my son: for he is mine only c.

O'-NO, אוֹנוֹ *strong*.

1. A city in Benjamin, near Lod and Hadad; now called *Auna*.

1 Ch. 8. 12 Shamed, who built O. and Lod, with the
Ezra 2. 33 The children of Lod, Hadid, and O., seven
Neh. 7. 37 The children of Lod, Hadid, and O., seven
11. 35 Lod, and O., the valley of craftsmen

2. The plain or valley in which the above city was, near Jerusalem.

Neh. 6. 2 let us meet together..in the plain of O.

ONYCHA —

Onyx or perfume crab, שְׁחֵלֶת *shecheleth*.

Exod 30. 34 Take unto thee..stacte, and onycha, and

ONYX —

The leek green beryl, שֹׁהַם *shoham*.

Gen. 2. 12 And..there (is) bdellium and the onyx s.
Exod 25. 7 Onyx stones, and stones to be set in the
28. 9 thou shalt take two onyx stones, and gr.
28. 20 the fourth row a beryl, and an onyx, and
35. 9 onyx stones, and stones to be set for the
35. 27 the rulers brought onyx stones, and stones
39. 6 they wrought onyx stones inclosed in ou.
39. 13 the fourth row, a beryl, an onyx, and a j.
1 Ch. 29. 2 onyx stones, and (stones) to be set, glist.
Job 28. 16 valued..with the precious onyx, or the s.
Eze. 28. 13 the onyx, and the jasper, the sapphire, and

OPEN (place, sight of others) —

1. *To be uncovered, revealed*, גָּלָה *galah*, 4.

Prov 27. 5 Open rebuke (is) better than secret love

2. *Entrance to Enayim* (?), פֶּתַח עֵינַיִם *pethach enayim*.

Gen. 38. 14 sat in an open place, which (is) by the way

3. *To free, let away*, פָּטַר *patar*.

1 Ki. 6. 18 (was) carved with knops and open flowers
6. 29 he carved all the walls..with..open flowers
6. 32 carved upon them carvings of..open flo.
6. 35 he carved (thereon) cherubim..and open

4. *Face of*, פְּנֵי *pene*.

Gen. 1. 20 may fly above the earth in the open firm.
Lev. 14. 7 let the living bird loose into the open fi.
14. 53 let go..out of the city into the open
17. 5 sacrifices, which they offer in the open fi.
Num 19. 16 that is slain with a sword in the open fi.
2 Sa. 11. 11 servants..are encamped in the open fields
Jer. 9. 22 carcases..shall fall as dung upon the open
Eze. 16. 5 thou wast cast out in the open field, to the
29. 5 thou shalt fall upon the open fields; thou
32. 4 I will cast thee forth upon the open field
33. 27 him that (is) in the open field will I give
37. 2 very many in the open valley; and, lo
39. 5 Thou shalt fall upon the open field; for

5. *To be broken forth*, פָּרַץ *parats*, 2.

1 Sa. 3. 1 And the word..was precious..no open v.

6. *To open*, פָּתַח *pathach*.

Num 19. 15 every open vessel which hath no covering
Josh. 8. 17 left the city open, and pursued after Isr.
1 Ki. 8. 29, 52 That thine eyes may be open
2 Ch. 6. 20 That thine eyes may be open upon this ho.
6. 40 let, I beseech thee, thine eyes be open, and
7. 15 Now mine eyes shall be open, and mine
Neh. 1. 6 and thine eyes open, that thou mayest h.
6. 5 Then sent...with an open letter in his hand
Psa. 5. 9 Their throat (is) an open sepulchre; they
Jer. 5. 16 their quiver (is) as an open sepulchre, t.

7. *To open*, פָּתַח *pathach*, 3.

Job 41. 14 Who can open the doors of his face? his
Isa. 28. 24 doth he open and break the clods of his g.

8. *To open up*, ἀνοίγω *anoigō*.

John 1. 51 ye shall see heaven open, and the angels
Acts 16. 27 seeing the prison doors open, he drew out
Rom. 3. 13 Their throat (is) an open sepulchre: with
Rev. 3. 8 I have set before thee an open door, and
10. 2 had in his hand a little book open, 10. 8

9. *To open up*, ἀνακαλύπτω *anakaluptō*, 2 Co. 3. 18

10. *Opening*, פִּתְחוֹן *pithechon*.

Eze. 16. 63 never open thy mouth any more because

11. *Place of beholders*, מְקוֹם רֹאִים [*maqom*].

Job 34. 26 He striketh them..in the open sight of ot.

OPEN, to —

1. *To remove, uncover*, גָּלָה *galah*.

Num 24. 4, 16 saw the vision..but having his eyes o.
Job 33. 16 he openeth the ears of men, and sealeth
36. 10 He openeth also their ear to discipline
36. 15 He delivereth the poor..and openeth th.
Jer. 32. 11 that which was sealed..that which was o.
32. 14 is sealed and this evidence which is open

2. *To remove, uncover*, גָּלָה *galah*, 3.

Num 22. 31 the LORD opened the eyes of Balaam, and
Psa. 119. 18 Open thou mine eyes, that I may behold
Jer. 20. 12 O Lord..unto thee have I opened my ca.

3. *To prepare, pierce*, כָּרָה *karah*.

Psa. 40. 6 mine ears hast thou opened: burnt offer.

4. *To open, gape*, פָּעַר *paar*.

Psa 119. 131 I opened my mouth, and panted: for I
Isa. 5. 14 and opened her mouth without measure

5. *To open, gape*, פָּצָה *patsah*.

Gen. 4. 11 the earth which hath opened her mouth
Num 16. 30 the earth open her mouth, and swallow
Deut 11. 6 how the earth opened her mouth, and sw.
Judg 11. 35 for I have opened my mouth unto the L.
Judg 11. 36 thou hast opened thy mouth unto the L.
Job 35. 16 Therefore doth Job open his mouth in vain
Isa. 10. 14 none that moved the wing, or opened the
Lam. 2. 16 All thine enemies have opened their mo.
3. 46 All our enemies have opened their mouths
Eze. 2. 8 open thy mouth, and eat that I give thee

6. *To open, open up*, פָּקַח *paqach*.

Gen. 21. 19 God opened her eyes, and she saw a well
2 Ki. 4. 35 sneezed seven times, and the child opened
6. 17 I pray thee, open his eyes, that he may s.
6. 17 LORD opened the eyes of the young man
6. 20 open the eyes of these..that they may see
6. 20 LORD opened their eyes, and they saw; and
19. 16 open, LORD, thine eyes, and see; and hear
Job 14. 3 dost thou open thine eyes upon such an o.
27. 19 The rich..openeth his eyes, and he (is) not
Psa. 146. 8 LORD openeth (the eyes of) the blind: the
Prov 20. 13 open thine eyes..thou shalt be satisfied
Isa. 37. 17 open thine eyes, O LORD, and see; and h.
42. 7 To open the blind eyes, to bring out the
42. 20 observest not; opening the ears, but
Jer. 32. 19 thine eyes (are) open upon all the ways of
Dan. 9. 18 open thine eyes, and behold our desolat.
Zech 12. 4 I will open mine eyes upon the house of

7. *To open wide*, פָּשַׂק *pasaq*.

Eze. 16. 25 hast opened thy feet to every one that p.

8. *To open*, פָּתַח *pathach*.

Gen. 8. 6 opened the window of the ark which he
29. 31 he opened her womb: but Rachel (was)
30. 22 God hearkened to her, and opened her w.
41. 56 Joseph opened all the store houses, and
42. 27 as one of them opened his sack, to give
43. 21 we opened our sacks, and, behold, (every)
44. 11 took down..and opened every man his
Exod. 2. 6 when she had opened..she saw the child
21. 33 if a man shall open a pit, or if a man shall
Num 16. 32 the earth opened her mouth, and swallo.
22. 28 And the LORD opened the mouth of the
26. 10 the earth opened her mouth, and swallo.
Deut 20. 11 if it make..answer of peace, and open
28. 12 LORD shall open unto thee his good trea.
Josh. 10. 22 Open the mouth of the cave, and bring
Judg 3. 25 opened not the doors..therefore they..o.
4. 19 she opened a bottle of milk, and gave him
19. 27 opened the doors of the house, and went
1 Sa. 3. 15 opened the doors of the house of the Lo.
2 Ki. 9. 3 Then open the door and flee, and tarry not
9. 10 none to bury..And he opened the door, and
13. 17 Open the window eastward: and he open.
15. 16 because they opened not..therefore he
2 Ch. 29. 3 opened the doors of the house of the LORD
Neh. 8. 5 Ezra opened the book in the sight of all.
8. 5 when he opened it, all the people stood up
Job 3. 1 After this opened Job his mouth, and cu.
11. 5 oh that God would speak, and open his l.
31. 32 did not lodge in the street..I opened my
32. 20 I will speak..I will open my lips and an.
33. 2 now I have opened my mouth, my tongue
Psa. 38. 13 as a dumb man (that) openeth not his m.
39. 9 I was dumb, I opened not my mouth; be.
49. 4 I will open my dark saying upon the harp
51. 15 open thou my lips; and my mouth shall
78. 2 I will open my mouth in a parable: I will
78. 23 Though he had..opened the doors of he.
104. 28 thou openest thine hand, they are filled
105. 41 He opened the rock, and the waters gushed
106. 17 The earth opened and swallowed up Dath.
118. 19 Open to me the gates of righteousness: I
145. 16 Thou openest thine hand, and satisfiest
Prov. 24. 7 a fool..openeth not his mouth in the gate
31. 8 Open thy mouth for the dumb in the cause
31. 9 Open thy mouth, judge righteously, and
31. 26 She openeth her mouth with wisdom; and
Song 5. 2 Open to me, my sister, my love, my dove
5. 5 I rose up to open to my beloved; and my
5. 6 I opened to my beloved; but my beloved
Isa. 14. 17 (that) opened not the house of his prison.
22. 22 And..so he shall open, and none shall shut
22. 22 and he shall shut, and none shall open
26. 2 Open ye the gates, that the righteous na.
41. 18 I will open rivers in high places, and fo.
45. 1 to open before him the two leaved gates
45. 8 let the earth open, and let him bring forth
50. 5 Lord GOD hath opened mine ear, and I was
53. 7 he opened not his mouth..so he openeth
Jer. 13. 19 shall be shut up, and none shall open (t.)
50. 25 LORD hath opened his armoury, and hath
50. 26 Come against her..open her storehouses
Eze. 3. 2 So I opened my mouth, and he caused me
3. 27 I will open thy mouth, and thou shalt say
21. 22 to open the mouth in the slaughter, to lift
25. 9 I will open the side of Moab from the ci.
33. 22 the hand of the LORD..had opened my m.
37. 12 I will open your graves, and cause you to
37. 13 when I have opened your graves, O my peo.
46. 12 shall then open him the gate that looketh
Dan. 10. 16 I opened my mouth, and spake, and said
Zech. 11. 1 Open thy doors, O Lebanon, that the fire
Mal. 3. 10 if I will not open you the windows of h.

9. *To unfold, unroll*, ἀναπτύσσω *anaptussō*.

Luke 4. 17 when [he had opened] the book, he found

10. *To open up or again*, ἀνοίγω *anoigō*.

Matt. 2. 11 when they had opened their treasures, th.
3. 16 the heavens were opened unto him, and
5. 2 he opened his mouth, and taught them
7. 7 knock, and it shall be opened unto you
7. 8 to him that knocketh it shall be opened
9. 30 their eyes were opened: and Jesus stra.
Matt 13. 35 I will open my mouth in parables; I will
17. 27 when thou hast opened his mouth, thou
20. 33 say..Lord, that our eyes may be open.
25. 11 came also..saying, Lord, Lord, open to
27. 52 the graves were opened; and many bod.
Luke 1. 64 his mouth was opened immediately, and
3. 21 it came to pass, that..the heaven was op.
11. 9 knock, and it shall be opened unto you
11. 10 to him that knocketh it shall be opened
12. 36 that..they may open unto him immedia.
13. 25 knock at the door, saying, Lord, Lord, o.
John 9. 10 said they..How were thine eyes opened?
9. 14 Jesus made the clay, and opened his ey.
9. 17 What sayest thou of him, that he hath o.
9. 21 or who hath opened his eyes, we know
9. 26 What did he to thee? how opened he th.
9. 30 ye know not..and..he hath opened mine
9. 32 was it not heard that any man opened the
10. 3 To him the porter openeth; and the sh.
10. 21 Can a devil open the eyes of the blind?
11. 37 Could not this man, which opened the e.
Acts 5. 19 opened the prison doors, and brought t.
5. 23 when [we had opened], we found no man
7. 56 I see the heavens [opened], and the Son of
8. 32 like a lamb dumb..so opened he not his
8. 35 Then Philip opened his mouth, and beg.
9. 8 when his eyes were opened, he saw no m.
9. 40 she opened her eyes: and when she saw
10. 11 saw heaven opened, and a certain vessel
10. 34 Then Peter opened (his) mouth, and said
12. 10 which opened to them of his own accord
12. 14 she opened not the gate for gladness, but
12. 16 when they had opened..and saw him, they
14. 27 how he had opened the door of faith un.
16. 26 all the doors were opened, and every one's
18. 14 when Paul was now about to open (his) m.
26. 18 To open their eyes..to turn..from dark.
1 Co. 16. 9 a great door and effectual is opened unto
2 Co. 2. 12 and a door was opened unto me of the L.
6. 11 our mouth is open unto you, our heart is
Col. 4. 3 that God would open unto us a door of ut.
Rev. 3. 7 he that openeth, and no man shutteth
3. 7 he that..shutteth, and no man openeth
3. 20 if any man hear my voice, and open the
4. 1 a door (was) opened in heaven: and the
5. 2, 5 to open the book, and to loose the seals
5. 3 was able to open the book, neither to look
5. 4 because no man was found worthy to open
5. 9 to take the book, and to open the seals
6. 1 I saw when the Lamb opened one of the
6. 3, 5, 7, 9, 12 when he had opened the..seal
8. 1 when he had opened the seventh seal, there
9. 2 [he opened the bottomless pit; and there]
11. 19 the temple of God was opened in heaven
12. 16 the earth opened her mouth, and swallo.
13. 6 he opened his mouth in blasphemy against
15. 5 the temple of the tabernacle..was opened
19. 11 I saw heaven opened, and behold a white
20. 12 I saw the dead..and the books were ope.
20. 12 another book was opened, which is..of l.

11. *In the opening*, ἐν ἀνοίξει *en anoixei*.

Eph. 6. 19 that I may open my mouth boldly, to m.

12. *To open up thoroughly*, διανοίγω *dianoigō*.

Mark 7. 34 saith unto him, Ephphatha, that is, Be o.
7. 35 straightway his ears [were opened], and
Luke 2. 23 Every male that openeth the womb shall
24. 31 their eyes were opened, and they knew
24. 32 and while he opened to us the scriptures?
24. 45 Then opened he their understanding, that
Acts 16. 14 whose heart the Lord opened, that she a.
17. 3 Opening and alleging that Christ must n.

13. *To rend, tear*, σχίζω *schizō*.

Mark 1. 10 he saw the heavens opened, and the spi.

OPEN, opened, to be (set) —

1. *To be removed*, גָּלָה *galah*, 2.

Job 38. 17 Have the gates of death been opened unto

2. *To be opened*, פָּקַח *paqach*, 2.

Gen. 3. 5 know that..then your eyes shall be ope.
3. 7 the eyes of them both were opened, and
Isa. 35. 5 Then the eyes of the blind shall be opened

3. *To open*, פָּתַח *pathach*.

Neh. 13. 19 should not be opened till after the sabbath
Psa. 109. 2 the mouth of the deceitful are opened

4. *To be opened*, פָּתַח *pathach*, 2.

Gen. 7. 11 and the windows of heaven were opened
Neh. 7. 3 Let not the gates of Jerusalem be opened
Isa. 24. 18 the windows from on high are open, and
Eze. 1. 1 the heavens were opened, and I saw visi.
24. 27 In that day shall thy mouth be opened to
33. 22 my mouth was opened, and I was no more
44. 2 gate shall be shut, it shall not be opened
46. 1 on the sabbath it shall be opened, and in
46. 1 the day of the new moon, it shall be opened
Nah. 2. 6 The gates of the rivers shall be opened
3. 13 gates of thy land shall be set wide open
Zech 13. 1 there shall be a fountain opened to the

5. *To open*, פָּתַח *pathach*, 3.

Isa. 48. 8 from that time (that) thine ear was not o.
60. 11 Therefore thy gates shall be open contin.

6. *To open*, פְּתַח *pethach*.

Dan. 6. 10 his windows being open in his chamber
7. 10 judgment was set, and the books were o.

7. *To lead on*, ἄγω *agō*.

Acts 19. 38 have a matter against any..the law is op.

8. *To have the neck bent back,* τραχηλίζομαι.
Heb. 4. 13 all things (are) naked and opened unto the

OPEN wide, to —

1. *To open, gape,* פָּעַר *paar.*
Job 29. 23 they opened their mouth wide (as) for the

2. *To open wide,* פָּשַׂק *pasaq.*
Prov 13. 3 he that openeth wide his lips shall have

3. *To open,* פָּתַח *pathach.*
Deut 15. 8, 11 thou shalt open thine hand wide unto

OPEN beforehand —

Evident or manifest before, πρόδηλος *prodēlos.*
1 Ti. 5. 24 Some men's sins are open beforehand, going

OPEN, OPENETH, (such as) —

1. *Opening,* פִּטְרָה *pitrah.*
Num. 8. 16 given..instead of such as open every wo.

2. *Opening,* פֶּטֶר *peter.*
Exod 13. 2 whatsoever openeth the womb among the
13. 12 all that openeth the matrix, and every fi.
13. 15 all that openeth the matrix, being males
34. 19 All that openeth the matrix (is) mine; and
Num. 3. 12 all the first born that openeth the matrix
18. 15 Every thing that openeth the matrix in all
Eze. 20. 26 all that openeth the womb, that I might

3. *To open (? shut),* שָׁתַם *shatham.*
Num 24. 3, 15 the man whose eyes are open hath said

OPENING, (to be) —

1. *Opening,* מַפְתֵּחַ *maphteach.*
1 Ch. 9. 27 and the opening thereof every morning

2. *Opening,* מִפְתָּח *miphtach.*
Prov. 8. 6 and the opening of my lips..right things

3. *To open,* פָּקַח *paqach.*
Isa. 42. 20 observest not; opening the ears, but he

4. *Opening,* פֶּתַח *pethach.*
Prov. 1. 21 She crieth..in the openings of the gates

5. *To open,* פָּתַח *pathach,* 2.
Job 12. 14 he shutteth..and there can be no opening

6. *Opening,* פִּתְחוֹן *pithechon.*
Eze. 29. 21 I will give thee the opening of the mouth

OPENING of the prison —

Opening of the prison, פְּקַח־קוֹחַ *peqach-qoach.*
Isa. 61. 1 to proclaim..the opening of the prison to

OPENLY —

1. *In the eyes, openly,* בָּעֵינַיִם *ba-enayim.*
Gen. 38. 21 Where (is) the harlot that (was) openly by

2. *Manifestly,* ἐν τῷ φανερῷ *en tō phanerō.*
Matt. 6. 4, 6, 18, thy Father..shall reward thee [o.]

3. *In public,* δημοσίᾳ *dēmosia.*
Acts 16. 37 They have beaten us openly uncondemned

4. *Manifest,* ἐμφανής *emphanēs.*
Acts 10. 40 him God raised up..and showed him op.

5. *Freely, openly,* παῤῥησίᾳ *parrhēsia.*
Mark 8. 32 he spake that saying openly. And Peter
John 7. 4 and he himself seeketh to be known openly
7. 13 Howbeit no man spake openly of him for f.
11. 54 Jesus therefore walked no more openly
18. 20 I spake openly to the world; Col. 2. 15.

6. *Manifestly,* φανερῶς *phanerōs.*
Mark 1. 45 that Jesus could no more openly enter into
John 7. 10 went he also up into the feast, not openly

OPERATION —

1. *Work,* מַעֲשֶׂה *maaseh.*
Psa. 28. 5 they regard not..the operation of his ha.
Isa. 5. 12 they regard not..the operation of his ha.

2. *Energy, inworking,* ἐνέργεια *energeia.*
Col. 2. 12 through the faith of the operation of God

3. *Energy, inworking,* ἐνέργημα *energēma.*
1 Co. 12. 6 there are diversities of operations, but it

O'-PHEL, הָעֹפֶל *the high place.*

A part of Jerusalem, on the E. of Zion; perhaps the same as Millo; in 2 Ki. 5. 24 it is translated "tower;" and was perhaps a fortified place near Samaria.
2 Ch. 27. 3 and on the wall of O he built much
33. 14 compassed about O., and raised it up a
Neh. 3. 26 Moreover the Nethinims dwelt in O., unto
3. 27 that lieth out, even unto the wall of O.
11. 21 But the Nethinims dwelt in O.: and Ziha

O'-PHIR, אוֹפִר, אוֹפִיר *fat, rich.*

1. A son of Joktan, a descendant of Shem. B.C. 2200.
Gen. 10. 29 O., and Havilah, and Jobab: all these (w.)
1 Ch. 1. 23 O., and Havilah, and Jobab. All these

2. A place in S. Arabia, from whence the products of India were brought to the West.
1 Ki. 9. 28 they came to O., and fetched from thence
10. 11 brought gold from O., brought in from O.
22. 48 made ships of Tharshish to go to O. for gold
1 Ch. 29. 4 thousand talents of gold, of the gold of O.
2 Ch. 8. 18 they went with the servants..to O., and
9. 10 servants..which brought gold from O., br.
Job 22. 24 the (gold) of O. as the stones of the brooks
28. 16 It cannot be valued with the gold of O.
Psa. 45. 9 on thy right..stand the queen in gold of O.
Isa. 13. 12 even a man than the golden wedge of O.

OPH'-NI, הָעָפְנִי *the high place.*

A place in Benjamin, between Chephar-haammonai and Gaba, five Roman miles from the latter, and also not far from Gibeah of Saul; now called *Jifneh.*
Josh. 18. 24 Chephar-haammonai, and O., and Gaba

OPH'-RAH, עָפְרָה *hamlet.*

1. A city in Benjamin, near Parah. (See *Aphrah*). Now called *Taiyebeh.*
Josh 18. 23 And Avim, and Parah, and O.
1 Sa. 13. 17 turned unto the way (that leadeth to) O.

2. A city in Manasseh; now called *Arrabeh.*
Judg. 6. 11 sat under an oak which (was) in O., that
6. 24 unto this day it (is) yet in O. of the Abi.
8. 27 put it in his city, (even) in O.: and all Is.
8. 32 sepulchre of Joash his father, in O. of the
9. 5 And he went unto his father's house at O.

3. Son of Meonothai, head of a family in Judah. B.C. 1450.
1 Ch. 4. 14 Meonothai begat O.: and Seraiah begat

OPINION —

1. *Knowledge, opinion,* דֵּעַ *dea.*
Job 32. 6 afraid, and durst not show you mine op.
32. 10 Hearken to me; I also will show mine o.
32. 17 I will answer..I also will show mine op.

2. *Branches, opinions,* סְעִפִּים *seippim.*
1 Ki. 18. 21 How long halt ye between two opinions?

OPPORTUNITY —

1. *A fit season or opportunity,* εὐκαιρία *eukairia.*
Matt 26. 16 from that time he sought opportunity to
Luke 22. 6 he promised, and sought opportunity to

2. *A season, opportunity,* καιρός *kairos.*
Gal. 6. 10 As we have therefore opportunity, let us
Heb. 11. 15 they might have had opportunity to have

OPPORTUNITY, to lack —

To be without an opportunity, ἀκαιρέομαι *akaireo.*
Phil. 4. 10 ye were also careful, but ye lacked oppo.

OPPOSE, to —

To be laid (lie) opposite, ἀντίκειμαι *antikeimai.*
2 Th. 2. 4 Who opposeth and exalteth himself abo.

OPPOSE self (against), to —

1. *To hate, oppose,* שָׂטַם *satam.*
Job 30. 21 with..hand thou opposest thyself against

2. *To be placed over against,* ἀντιδιατίθεμαι *antid.*
2 Ti. 2. 25 instructing those that oppose themselves

3. *To be arranged over against,* ἀντιτάσσομαι *ant.*
Acts 18. 6 when they opposed themselves, and bla.

OPPOSITION —

A placing over against, ἀντίθεσις *antithesis.*
1 Ti. 6. 20 and oppositions of science falsely so cal.

OPPRESS to —

1. *To bruise,* דָּכָא *daka,* 3.
Prov 22. 22 neither oppress the afflicted in the gate

2. *To put down,* יָנָה *yanah,* 5.
Lev. 25. 14 And..ye shall not oppress one another
25. 17 Ye shall not therefore oppress one anot.
Deut 23. 16 dwell with thee..thou shalt not oppress
Isa. 49. 26 I will feed them that oppress thee with
Eze. 18. 7 hath not oppressed any..hath restored
18. 12 Hath oppressed the poor and needy, hath
18. 16 Neither hath oppressed any, hath not with.
45. 8 my princes shall no more oppress my p.

3. *To press, oppress, crush,* לָחַץ *lachats.*
Exod. 3. 9 wherewith the Egyptians oppress them
22. 21 Thou shalt neither vex a stranger, nor o.
23. 9 Also thou shalt not oppress a stranger; for
Judg. 2. 18 by reason of them that oppressed them
4. 3 he mightily oppressed the children of Isr.
6. 9 out of the hand of all that oppressed you
10. 12 The Zidonians also..did oppress you; and
1 Sa. 10. 18 out of the hand..of them that oppressed
2 Ki. 13. 4 because the king of Syria oppressed them
13. 22 Hazael king of Syria oppressed Israel all
Psa. 56. 1 for man..he fighting daily oppresseth me
106. 42 Their enemies also oppressed them, and
Jer. 30. 20 and I will punish all that oppress them

4. *To terrify,* עָרַץ *arats.*
Psa. 10. 18 the man of the earth may no more oppr.

5. *To oppress,* עָשַׁק *ashaq.*
Deut 24. 14 Thou shalt not oppress an hired servant
Job 10. 3 good unto thee that thou shouldest opp.
Psa. 119. 122 Be surety..let not the proud oppress me
Prov 14. 31 He that oppresseth the poor reproacheth
22. 16 He that oppresseth the poor to increase
28. 3 A poor man that oppresseth the poor (is
Isa. 52. 4 Assyrian oppressed them without cause
Jer. 7. 6 (If) ye oppress not the stranger, the fath.
Eze. 18. 18 because he cruelly oppressed, spoiled hi.
22. 29 they have oppressed the stranger wrong.
Hos. 12. 7 (He is) a merchant..he loveth to oppress
Amos 4. 1 which oppress the poor, which crush the
Mic. 2. 2 so they oppress a man and his house, even
Zech. 7. 10 oppress not the widow, nor the fatherless
Mal. 3. 5 against those that oppress the hireling in

6. *To distress, be an adversary,* צָרַר *tsarar.*
Num 10. 9 against the enemy that oppresseth you

7. *To break, oppress, bruise,* רָצַץ *ratsats.*
1 Sa. 12. 3 whom have I oppressed? or of whose ha.
12. 4 Thou hast not defrauded us, nor oppressed

8. *To break, oppress, bruise,* רָצַץ *ratsats,* 3a.
Judg 10. 8 that year they vexed and oppressed the
2 Ch. 16. 10 Asa oppressed (some) of the people the
Job 20. 19 Because he hath oppressed..hath forsak.

9. *To spoil, destroy,* שָׁדַד *shadad.*
Psa. 17. 9 From the wicked that oppress me, (from)

10. *Be overpowered,* καταδυναστεύω *katadunasteuō.*
Acts 10. 38 healing all that were oppressed of the d.
Jas. 2. 6 Do not rich men oppress you, and draw you

OPPRESSED —

1. *Bruised, oppressed,* דַּךְ *dak.*
Psa. 9. 9 Lord also will be a refuge for the oppres.
10. 18 To judge the fatherless and the oppressed
74. 21 O let not the oppressed return ashamed

2. *Oppressed one,* חָמוֹץ *chamots.*
Isa. 1. 17 relieve the oppressed, judge the fatherl.

3. *Oppressed ones,* עֲשׁוּקִים *ashuqim.*
Amos 3. 9 behold..the oppressed in the midst the.

4. *To be oppressed,* עָשַׁק *ashaq,* 4.
Isa. 23. 12 O thou oppressed virgin, daughter of Z.

5. *To oppress,* עָשַׁק *ashaq.*
Deut 28. 29 thou shalt be only oppressed and spoiled
28. 33 thou shalt be only oppressed and crushed
Psa. 103. 6 and judgment for all that are oppressed
146. 7 Which executeth judgment for the oppr.
Eccl. 4. 1 and behold the tears of (such as were) op.
Jer. 50. 33 the children of Judah (were) oppressed
Hos. 5. 11 Ephraim (is) oppressed..broken in judg.

6. *Oppression is to me,* עָשְׁקָה לִּי [*oshqah*].
Isa. 38. 14 O LORD, I am oppressed; undertake for

7. *To break, oppress, bruise,* רָצַץ *ratsats.*
Isa. 58. 6 to let the oppressed go free, and that ye

OPPRESSED, to be —

1. *To be exacted,* נָגַשׂ *nagas,* 2.
Isa. 3. 5 the people shall be oppressed, every one
53. 7 He was oppressed, and he was afflicted

2. *To be worn down,* καταπονέομαι *kataponeomai.*
Acts 7. 24 avenged him that was oppressed, and sm.

OPPRESSING —

To oppress, break, יָנָה *yanah.*
Jer. 46. 16 and let us go..from the oppressing sword
50. 16 for fear of the oppressing sword they shall
Zeph. 3. 1 Woe to her that is filthy..the oppressing

OPPRESSION —

1. *Oppression,* לַחַץ *lachats.*
Exod. 3. 9 I have also seen the oppression wherewi.
Deut 26. 7 LORD..looked on our..labour, and our o.
2 Ki. 13. 4 he saw the oppression of Israel, because
Job 36. 15 He delivereth the poor..in oppression
Psa. 42. 9 why go I mourning because of the oppre.
43. 2 why go I mourning because of the oppre.
44. 24 forgettest our affliction and..oppression?

2. *Oppression, scabbing,* מִשְׂפָּח *mispach.*
Isa. 5. 7 he looked for judgment, but behold opp.

3. *Restraint,* עֹצֶר *otser.*
Psa. 107. 39 brought low through oppression, affliction

4. *Oppression,* עָקָה *aqah.*
Psa. 55. 3 because of the oppression of the wicked

5. *Oppression,* עֹשֶׁק *osheq.*
Psa. 62. 10 Trust not in oppression, and become not
73. 8 and speak wickedly (concerning) oppres.
119. 134 Deliver me from the oppression of man
Eccl. 5. 8 If thou seest the oppression of the poor
7. 7 Surely oppression maketh a wise man mad
Isa. 30. 12 and trust in oppression and perverseness
54. 14 thou shalt be far from oppression; for thou
59. 13 speaking oppression and revolt, conceivi.
Jer. 6. 6 she (is) wholly oppression in the midst of
22. 17 for to shed innocent blood, and for oppr.
Eze. 22. 7 have they dealt by oppression with the st.
22. 29 The people of the land have used oppres

6. *Spoiling,* שֹׁד *shod.*
Psa. 12. 5 For the oppression of the poor, for the s.

7. *Oppressions,* מַעֲשַׁקּוֹת *maashaqqoth.*
Isa. 33. 15 he that despiseth the gain of oppressions

8. *Oppressed ones or things,* עֲשׁוּקִים *ashuqim.*
Job 35. 9 By reason of the multitude of oppressions
Eccl. 4. 1 considered all the oppressions that are d.

OPPRESSION, to thrust out by —

To thrust out or away, יָנָה *yanah,* 5.
Eze. 46. 18 not take..by oppression, to thrust them out

OPPRESSOR —

1. *A man of violence,* אִישׁ חָמָס *ish chamas.*
Prov. 3. 31 Envy thou not the oppressor, and choose

2. *To oppress, thrust out,* יָנָה *yanah.*
Jer. 25. 38 because of the fierceness of the oppressor

3. *To press,* לָחַץ *lachats.*
Isa. 19. 20 they shall cry..because of the oppressors

4. *To exact,* נָגַשׂ *nagas.*
Job 3. 18 prisoners..hear not the voice of the opp
Isa. 3. 12 children (are) their oppressors, and women
9. 4 thou hast broken..the rod of his oppres.
14. 2 and they shall rule over their oppressors
14. 4 How hath the oppressor ceased! the gol.
Zech. 9. 8 no oppressor shall pass through them any
10. 4 Out of him came forth..every oppressor

5. *Terrible one,* עָרִיץ *arits.*
Job 15. 20 the number of years is hidden to the op.
27. 13 This (is)..the heritage of oppressors..th.
Psa. 54. 3 oppressors seek after my soul: they have

6. *Oppressions,* מַעֲשַׁקּוֹת *maashaqqoth.*
Prov.28. 16 prince..(is)also a great oppressor: (but)

7. *Oppressor,* עָשׁוֹק *ashoq.*
Jer. 22. 3 deliver..out of the hand of the oppressor

8. *To oppress,* עָשַׁק *ashaq.*
Psa. 72. 4 He..shall break in pieces the oppressor
119. 121 I have done..leave me not to mine opp.
Eccl. 4. 1 and on the side of their oppressors..pow.
Jer. 21. 12 deliver..out of the hand of the oppressor

9. *To distress, oppress, straiten,* צוּק *tsuq,* 5.
Isa. 51. 13 fury of the oppressor..fury of the oppr.?

10. *To tread, trample down,* רָמַס *ramas.*
Isa. 16. 4 oppressors are consumed out of the land

OR, or else, or ever —

1. *Or,* אוֹ *o.*
Gen. 24. 49 that I may turn to the right hand or to
24. 50 we cannot speak unto thee bad or good
31. 43 or unto their children which they have
Exod19. 13 he shall surely be stoned or shot through
21. 18 one smite another with a stone, or with
Lev. 20. 17 his father's daughter, or his mother's da.

2. *If,* אִם *im.*
Gen. 24. 21 had made his journey prosperous or not
Joel 1. 2 Hath this been in your days, or even in

3. *Lo, if, though, whether, or,* הֵן *hen.*
Ezra 7. 26 unto death, or to banishment, or to con.

4. *Up to,* עַד *ad.*
Gen. 31. 24 thou speak not to Jacob either good or b.

5. *Not,* לָא *la.*
Dan. 6. 24 or ever they came at the bottom of the d.

6. *Whether, or,* εἴτε *eite.*
Rom.12. 7 Or ministry..on (our) ministering; or he
12. 8 [Or]he that exhorteth, on exhortation: he
1 Co. 3. 22 Paul, or Apollos, or Cephas, or the world
3. 22 or life or death, or things present, or th.
8. 5 called gods, whether in heaven or in earth
10. 31 Whether therefore ye eat, or drink, or w.
12. 13 whether..Jews or Gentiles, whether..bo.
12. 26 [or] one member be honoured, all he m.
14. 7 whether pipe or harp, except they give a
15. 11 whether..I or they, so we preach and so
2 Co. 5. 9 whether present or absent, we may be a.
5. 10 that he hath done, whether..good or bad
8. 23 or our brethren..the messengers
12. 3 whether in the body, or out of the body
Eph. 6. 8 receive of the Lord, whether..bond or f.
Phil. 1. 18 whether in pretence, or in truth, Christ is
1. 20 magnified..whether (it be) by life, or by
1. 27 whether I come and see you, or else be a.
Col. 1. 16 or dominions, or principalities, or powers
1. 20 be) things in earth, or things in heaven
1 Th. 5. 10 whether we wake or sleep, we should live
2 Th. 2. 15 taught, whether by word, or, 1 Pe. 2. 14.

7. *If not,* εἰ μή *ei mē,* 2 Co. 3. 1.

8. *Or, either,* ἤ *ē.*
Matt. 5. 17 that I am come to destroy the law, or the
5. 18 one jot or one tittle shall in no wise pass
5. 36 thou canst not make one hair white or b.
6. 24, 31; 7. 4, 9, 16; 9. 5; 10. 11, 14, 19, 37, 37; 11. 3; 12. 5, 25, 29, 33; 13. 21; 15. 4, 5, [6]; 16. 14, 26; 17. 25, 25; 18. 8, 8, 16, 16, 20; 19. 29, 29, [29, 29, 29,] 29, 29; 24. 23, 23; 25. 37, 38, 39, 44, 44, 44, 44; 27. 17. Mark 2. 9; 3. 4, 4, 33; 4. 21, 30; 6. [15], 56, 56; 7. 10, 11, 12; 8. 37; 10. 29, 29, 29, 29, [29], 29, 29; 11. 30; 12. 14, 15; 13. [21], 35, 35, 35; Luke 2. 24; 8. 16, 19, 27; 12. 14; 13. 15; 14. 5, 12; 17. 7, 21, [23]; 18. 11, 29, 29, 29, 29; John 2. 6; 6. 19; 7. 48; 9. 21; 13. 29; Acts 1. 7; 3. 12; 4. 7, 34; 5. 38; 10. [14], 28, 28; 11. 8; 17. 29, 29; 18. 14; 19. 12; 20. 33, 33; 23. 9, 29; 24. 20, [23]; 26. 31; 28. 6, 17, 21; Rom. 2. 15; 4. 13; 9. 11; 10. 7; 14. 4, 10, 13, 21, [21]; 1 Co. 2. 1; 4. 3; 5. 10, [10], 10, 11, 11, 11, 11, 11; 7. 11. 15; 11. 4, 5, 6; 13. 1; 14. 7, 23, 24, 27, 29, 37; 15. 37; 2 Co. 1. 13; 9. 7; 10. 12; 11. 4, 4; 12. 6; Gal. 1. 8; 2. 2; 3. 15; Eph. 3. 20; 5. 3, 27, 27; Phil. 2. [3]; Col. 2. 16, 16, 16, 16; 3. 17; 2 Th 2. 4; 1 Ti. 2. [9], 9, 9; 5. 4, [16], 19; Titus 1. 6; 3. 12; Phm. 18; Heb. 2. 6; 10. 28; 12. 16, [20]; Jas. 2. 3, 15; 4. 15; 1 Pe. 1. 11; 3. 3, 9; 14. 15, 15, 15; Rev. 3. 15; 13. 16, 17, [17], 17; 14. 9.
Interrogative:—Matt. 6. 31, 31; 7. 4, 9, 16; 9. 5; 11. 3; 12. 5; 16. 26; 17. 25; 21. 25; 22. 17; 23. 17, 19; 25; 37, 38; 27. 17; Mark 2. 9; 3. 4, 4, [33]; 4. 21, 30; 8. [37]; 11. 30; 12. 14, 15; Luke 5. 23; 6. 9, 9; 7. 19, 20; 11. 12; 12. [11], 11, [29], 41; 13. 4; 14. 31; 20. 2, 4, 22; 22. 27; John 4. 27; 7. 11; 9. 2; 18. 34; Acts 3. 12; 7. 49; 8. 34; Rom. 2. 4; 3. 1; 4. 9, 10; 8. 35, 35, 35, 35, 35, 35; 11. 34, 35; 1 Co. 1. 13; 4. 21; 7. 16; 9. 6, [7], 8, 10; 10. [19]; 11. 22; 14. 36; 2 Co. 1. 17; 3. [1], 1; 6. 16; Gal. 1. 10, 12; 3. 2, 5; 1 Th. 2. 19, 19.

9. *And not, neither, nor,* μήτε *mēte.*
2 Th. 2. 2 That ye be not soon shaken in mind, [or]

ORACLE —

1. *Word,* דָּבָר *dabar.*
2 Sa. 16. 23 as if a man had enquired at the oracle of

2. *Oracle, speaking place, hinder part,* דְּבִיר *debir.*
1 Ki. 6. 5 the walls..of the temple and of the oracle
6. 16 built..for the oracle..for the most holy (p.)
6. 19 the oracle he prepared in the house within
6. 20 the oracle in the fore part (was) twenty c.
1 Ki. 6. 21 made..by the chains of gold before the or.
6. 22 the whole altar that (was) by the oracle
6. 23 within the oracle he made two cherubim
6. 31 for the entering of the oracle he made do.
7. 49 before the oracle, with the flowers, and the
8. 6 into the oracle of the house, to the most
8. 8 were seen out in the holy..before the or.
2 Ch. 3. 16 he made chains, (as) in the oracle, and put
4. 20 burn after the manner before the oracle
5. 7 brought in the ark..to the oracle of the h.
5. 9 were seen from the ark before the oracle
Psa. 28. 2 I lift up my hands toward thy holy oracle

3. *Oracle,* λόγιον *logion.*
Acts 7. 38 who received the lively oracles to give unto
Rom. 3. 2 unto them were committed the oracles of
Heb. 5. 12 the first principles of the oracles of God
1 Pe. 4. 11 If any man speak..as the oracles of God

ORATION, to make an —

To address the people, δημηγορέω *dēmēgoreō.*
Acts 12. 21 sat upon his throne, and made an oration

ORATOR —

1. *Whisper, charm,* לַחַשׁ *lachash.*
Isa. 3. 3 cunning artificer, and the eloquent orat.

2. *A speaker, orator,* ῥήτωρ *rhētōr.*
Acts 24. 1 a certain orator..Tertullus, who informed

ORCHARD —

Park, garden ground, fruitful land, פַּרְדֵּס *pardes.*
Eccl. 2. 5 I made me gardens and orchards, and I
Song 4. 13 Thy plants (are) an orchard of pomegra.

ORDAIN, to —

1. *To lay a foundation, appoint, settle,* יָסַד *yasad,* 3.
1 Ch. 9. 22 whom David and Samuel the seer did or.
Psa. 8. 2 hast thou ordained strength because of

2. *To form, prepare, establish,* כּוּן *kun,* 3a.
Psa. 8. 3 moon and the stars, which thou hast or.

3. *To number, appoint,* מְנָא, מָנָה *mena, menah,* 3.
Dan. 2. 24 whom the king had ordained to destroy

4. *To give,* נָתַן *nathan.*
2 Ki. 23. 5 whom the kings of Judah had ordained
Jer. 1. 5 I ordained thee a prophet unto the nati.

5. *To cause to stand,* עָמַד *amad,* 5.
2 Ch. 11. 15 he ordained him priests for the high pla.

6. *To arrange, set in array,* עָרַךְ *arak.*
Psa. 132. 17 I have ordained a lamp for mine anoint.

7. *To work, do, use,* פָּעַל *paal.*
Psa. 7. 13 he ordaineth his arrows against the per.

8. *To raise up, establish,* קוּם *qum,* 3.
Esth. 9. 27 The Jews ordained, and took upon them

9. *To set, place, put,* שׂוּם ,שִׂים *sum, sim.*
1 Ch. 17. 9 Also I will ordain a place for my people
Psa. 81 5 This he ordained in Joseph..a testimony
Hab. 1. 12 O LORD, thou hast ordained them for ju.

10. *To set on, appoint,* שָׁפַת *shaphath.*
Isa. 26. 12 LORD, thou wilt ordain peace for us: for

11. *To arrange throughout,* διατάσσω *diatassō.*
1 Co. 7. 17 so let him walk. And so ordain I in all
9. 14 Even so hath the Lord ordained, that th.
Gal. 3. 19 ordained by angels in the hand of a med.

12. *To place or set down,* καθίστημι *kathistēmi.*
Titus 1. 5 that thou shouldest..ordain elders in every
Heb. 5. 1 every high priest..is ordained for men in
8. 3 every high priest is ordained to offer gifts

13. *To prepare fully,* κατασκευάζω *kataskeuazō.*
Heb. 9. 6 Now when these things were thus orda.

14. *To judge, decide,* κρίνω *krinō.*
Acts 16. 4 that were ordained of the apostles and e.

15. *To mark out or off,* ὁρίζω *horizō.*
Acts 10. 42 to testify that it is he which was ordained
17. 31 judge..by (that) man whom he hath ord.

16. *To do, make,* ποιέω *poieō.*
Mark 3. 14 he ordained twelve, that they should be

17. *To mark out publicly or before,* προορίζω *proorizō.*
1 Co. 2. 7 which God ordained before the world unto

18. *To arrange, set in array,* τάσσω *tassō.*
Acts 13. 48 as many as were ordained to eternal life
Rom 13. 1 the powers that be are ordained of God

19. *To put, place, set,* τίθημι *tithēmi.*
John 15. 16 but I have chosen you, and ordained you
1 Ti. 2. 7 Whereunto I am ordained a preacher, and

20. *To elect by stretching out the hand,* χειροτονέω.
Acts 14. 23 when they had ordained them elders in

ORDAIN before, to —

1. *To write or describe before,* προγράφω *prographō.*
Jude 4 who were before of old ordained to this

2. *To make ready before,* προετοιμάζω *proetoimazō.*
Eph. 2. 10 which God hath before ordained that we

ORDAINED (to be), to be —

1. *To set in array,* עָרַךְ *arak.*
Isa. 30. 33 For Tophet (is) ordained of old; yea, for

2. *To become,* γίνομαι *ginomai.*
Acts 1. 22 must one be ordained to be a witness with

ORDER —

1. *Leading, manner,* דִּבְרָה *dibrah.*
Psa. 110. 4 Thou (art) a priest for ever after the order

2. *Hand,* יַד *yad.*
1 Ch. 25. 2 which prophesied according to the order
25. 6 according to the king's order to Asaph, J.

3. *Judgment,* מִשְׁפָּט *mishpat.*
Judg 13. 12 how shall we order the child, and (how)
1 Ch. 6. 32 waited on their office accord. to their or.
23. 31 according to the order commanded unto
2 Ch. 8. 14 according to the order of David his father

4. *Order, arrangements,* סְדָרִים *sedarim.*
Job 10. 22 A land of darkness..without any order

5. *Step, beat,* פַּעַם *paam.*
Eze. 41. 6 one over another, and thirty in order; and

6. *Arrangement, order,* τάγμα *tagma.*
1 Co. 15. 23 every man in his own order; Christ the

7. *Arrangement, order,* τάξις *taxis.*
Luke 1. 8 while he executed..in the order of his c.
1 Co. 14. 40 Let all things be done decently and in or.
Col. 2. 5 joying and beholding your order, and the
Heb. 5. 6 Thou (art) a priest for ever, after the order
5. 10 called of God an high priest after the or.
6. 20 made an high priest for ever, after the or.
7. 11 that another priest should rise after the or.
7. 11 and not be called after the order of Aaron?
7. 17 Thou (art) a priest for ever, after the order
7. 21 [Thou (art) a priest for ever after the order]

ORDER, by or in —

In succession, consecutively, καθεξῆς *kathexēs.*
Luke 1. 3 to write unto thee in order, most excellent
Acts 11. 4 Peter..expounded (it) by order unto them
18. 23 departed, and went over..country..in or.

ORDER, due —

Judgment, מִשְׁפָּט *mishpat.*
1 Ch. 15. 13 that we sought him not after the due order

ORDER, to (give) —

1. *To bind, direct,* אָסַר *asar.*
1 Ki. 20. 14 Then he said, Who shall order the battle?

2. *To prepare, establish,* כּוּן *kun,* 5.
Psa. 119. 133 Order my steps in thy word: and let not
Isa. 9. 7 to order it, and to establish it with judg.

3. *To array,* עָרַךְ *arak.*
Exod27. 21 Aaron and his sons shall order it from ev.
Lev. 24. 3 shall Aaron order it from the evening unto
24. 4 He shall order the lamps upon the pure
Job 13. 18 Behold now, I have ordered (my) cause; I
23. 4 I would order (my) cause before him, and
37. 19 Teach us..we cannot order..by reason of
Jer. 46. 3 Order ye the buckler and shield, and draw

4. *To set, place, put,* שׂוּם ,שִׂים *sum, sim.*
Psa. 50. 23 and to him that ordereth (his) conversa.

5. *To arrange throughout,* διατάσσω *diatassō.*
1 Co. 16. 1 as I have given order to the churches of

ORDER, to lay, put or set in —

1. *To array,* עָרַךְ *arak.*
Gen. 22. 9 laid the wood in order, and bound Isaac
Exod. 40. 4 thou shalt bring in..and set in order the
40. 23 he set the bread in order upon it before
Lev. 1. 7 and lay the wood in order upon the fire
1. 8 shall lay the parts..in order upon the w.
1. 12 shall lay them in order upon the wood that
6. 12 and lay the burnt offering in order upon
24. 8 Every sabbath he shall set it in order be.
Josh. 2. 6 which she had laid in order upon the ro.
1 Ki. 18. 33 he put the wood in order, and cut the b.
Job 33. 5 If thou canst answer me, set..in order b.
Psa. 50. 21 I will reprove thee, and set..in order be.
Isa. 44. 7 who..shall declare it, and set in order for

2. *To set up, command, charge,* צָוָה *tsavah,* 3.
2 Sa. 17. 23 put his household in order, and hanged
2 Ki. 20. 1 Set thine house in order; for thou shalt
Isa. 38. 1 Set thine house in order: for thou shalt

3. *To make straight or right,* תָּקַן *taqan,* 3.
Eccl. 12. 9 sought out, (and) set in order many pro.

4. *To arrange thoroughly,* διατάσσω *diatassō.*
1 Co. 11. 34 the rest will I set in order when I come

ORDER, set or reckoned up in —

1. *To be formed, prepared, established,* כּוּן *kun,* 2.
2 Ch. 29. 35 the service of the house..was set in order

2. *Arrangement, array, order,* מַעֲרָכָה *maarakah.*
Exod. 39. 37 the lamps to be set in order, and all the

3. *To set in array, arrange,* עָרַךְ *arak.*
Psa. 40. 5 they cannot be reckoned up in order un.

4. *To be joined,* שָׁלַב *shalab,* 4.
Exod. 26. 17 Two tenons..set in order one against an.

ORDER, things that are to be set in —

Array, עֵרֶךְ *erek.*
Exod. 40. 4 the things that are to be set in order up.

ORDERED, to be —

1. *To be formed, prepared, established,* כּוּן *kun,* 4.
Psa. 37. 23 The steps of a (good) man are ordered by

2. *To set in array, arrange,* עָרַךְ *arak.*
2 Sa. 23. 5 everlasting covenant, ordered in all..and

ORDERED place —

Arrangement, מַעֲרָכָה *maarakah.*
Judg. 6. 26 build an altar..in the ordered place, and

ORDERING —
Inspection, visitation, פְּקֻדָּה *pequddah.*
1 Ch.24. 19 These..the orderings of them in their se.

ORDINANCE —
1. *Statute, decree,* חֹק *choq.*
Exod12. 24 ye shall observe this thing for an ordina.
18. 20 thou shalt teach them ordinances and laws
Num 18. 8 have I given them..by an ordinance for
2 Ch.35. 25 lamentations..and made them an ordin.
Psa. 99. 7 they kept his testimonies, and the ordin.
Isa. 24. 5 changed the ordinance, broken the ever.
Jer. 31. 36 If those ordinances depart from before me
Eze. 45. 14 Concerning the ordinance of oil, the bath
Mal. 3. 7 ye are gone away from mine ordinances

2. *Statute, decree,* חֻקָּה *chuqqah.*
Exod12. 14 ye shall keep it a feast by an ordinance
12. 17 shall ye observe this day..by an ordina.
12. 43 This (is) the ordinance of the passover : T.
13. 10 Thou shalt therefore keep this ordinance
Lev. 18. 3 neither shall ye walk in their ordinances
18. 4 keep mine ordinances, to walk therein
Num 9. 12 according to all the ordinances of the pa.
9. 14 according to the ordinance of the passover
9. 14 ye shall have one ordinance, both for the
10. 8 they shall be to you for an ordinance for
15. 15 One ordinance..an ordinance for ever in
19. 2 This (is) the ordinance of the law which
31. 21 This (is) the ordinance of the law which
Job 38. 33 Knowest thou the ordinances of heaven?
Jer. 31. 35 the ordinances of the moon and of the st.
33. 25 I have not appointed the ordinances of h.
Eze. 43. 11 show..all the ordinances..keep..all the o.
43. 18 These (are) the ordinances of the altar in
44. 5 concerning all the ordinances of the hou.
46. 14 continually by a perpetual ordinance unto

3. *Hand,* יָד *yad.*
Ezra 3. 10 after the ordinance of David king of Isr

4. *Command, charge, precept,* מִצְוָה *mitsvah.*
Neh. 10. 32 we made ordinances for us, to charge ou.

5. *Watch, ward, guard,* מִשְׁמֶרֶת *mishmereth.*
Lev. 18. 30 Therefore shall ye keep mine ordinance, t.
22. 9 They shall therefore keep mine ordinance
Mal. 3. 14 what profit..that we have kept his ordina.

6. *Judgment,* מִשְׁפָּט *mishpat.*
Exod15. 25 he made for them a statute and an ordin.
Josh 24. 25 set them a statute and an ordinance in S.
1 Sa. 30. 25 that he made it a statute and an ordinance
2 Ki.17. 34 after their ordinances, or after the law and
17. 37 the statutes, and the ordinances, and the
2 Ch.33. 8 whole law and the statutes and the ordin.
35. 13 roasted..with fire according to the ordin.
Psa.119. 91 They continue..according to thine ordin.
Isa. 58. 2 and forsook not the ordinance of their G.
58. 2 they ask of me the ordinances of justice
Eze. 11. 20 That they may..keep mine ordinances, and

7. *Thorough arrangement,* διαταγή *diatagē.*
Rom.13. 2 Whosoever therefore..resisteth the ordi.

8. *A judicial appointment,* δικαίωμα *dikaiōma.*
Luke 1. 6 walking in all the..ordinances of the Lord
Heb. 9. 1 had also ordinances of divine service, and
9. 10 carnal ordinances, imposed..until the ti.

9. *Dogma, determination, decree,* δόγμα *dogma.*
Eph. 2. 15 the law of commandments..in ordinances
Col. 2. 14 Blotting out the hand writing of ordinan.

10. *Any made thing,* κτίσις *ktisis.*
1 Pe. 2. 13 Submit yourselves to every ordinance of

11. *A giving over,* παράδοσις *paradosis.*
1 Co.11. 2 keep the ordinances as I delivered..to you

ORDINANCES, to be subject to —
To be under a decree, δογματίζομαι *dogmatizomai.*
Col. 2. 20 Wherefore..are ye subject to ordinances

ORDINARY —
Statute, decree, חֹק *choq.*
Eze. 16. 27 have diminished thine ordinary (food), and

O'-REB, עוֹרֵב, עֹרֵב *raven, bustard.*
1. A prince of Midian defeated by Gibeon, and slain by the Ephramites at the Jordan. B.C. 1249.
Judg. 7. 25 took..O...and they slew O. upon the rock
7. 25 brought the heads of O. and Zeeb to Gid.
8. 3 God hath delivered..O. and Zeeb: and w.
Psa. 83. 11 Make their nobles like O. and like Zeeb

2. A rock E. of the Jordan, near Beth-bareh, whereon Oreb and Zeeb were slain. Now called *Ash-el-Ghorab.*
Judg. 7. 25 they slew..upon the rock O., and Zeeb they
Isa. 10. 26 the slaughter of Midian at the rock of O.

O'-REN, אֹרֶן *strength.*
Third son of Jerahmeel, grandson of Pharez son of Judah. B.C. 1510.
1 Ch. 2. 25 and Bunah, and O., and Ozem, (and) Ah.

ORGAN —
Lute, flute, עוּגָב, עֻגָב *uggab, ugab.*
Gen. 4. 21 of all such as handle the harp and organ
Job 21. 12 They..rejoice at the sound of the organ
30. 31 my organ into the voice of them that w.
Psa.150. 4 praise..with stringed instruments and o.

O-RI'-ON, כְּסִיל *strong.*
The southern constellation seen in November; called in Hebrew *Ke-sil.*
Job 9. 9 Which maketh Arcturus, O., and Pleiades
Job 38. 31 Canst thou bind..or loose the bands of O.?
Amos 5. 8 that maketh the seven stars and O., and

ORNAMENT —
1. *Ephod,* אֲפֻדָּה *aphuddah.*
Isa. 30. 22 the ornament of thy molten images of g.

2. *Ornament, trinket,* חֲלִי *chali.*
Prov 25. 12 (As) an ear ring of gold, and an ornament

3. *Wreath, addition,* לִוְיָה *livyah.*
Prov. 1. 9 they..an ornament of grace unto thy he.
4. 9 She shall give to thine head an ornament

4. *Ornament, desirable thing,* עֲדִי *adi.*
Exod33. 4 and no man did put on him his ornaments
33. 5 now put off thy ornaments from thee, that
33. 6 stripped themselves of their ornaments by
2 Sa. 1. 24 who put on ornaments of gold upon your
Isa. 49. 18 clothe thee with them all, as with an or.
Jer. 2. 32 Can a maid forget her ornaments..a bride
4. 30 though thou deckest thee with ornaments
Eze. 7. 20 As for the beauty of his ornament, he set
16. 7 and thou art come to excellent ornaments
16. 11 I decked thee also with ornaments and I
23. 40 for whom thou..deckedst thyself with o.

5. *A moon shaped ornament,* שַׂהֲרֹנִים *saharonim.*
Judg. 8. 21 and took away the ornaments that (were)
8. 26 besides ornaments, and collars, and pur.

6 *Beauty, ornament, head dress,* פְּאֵר *peer.*
Isa. 61. 10 as a bridegroom decketh (himself) with o.

ORNAMENT of the legs —
Bracelet for arm or ankle, צְעָדָה *tseadah.*
Isa. 3. 20 The bonnets, and the ornaments of the l.

ORNAMENTS, tinkling —
A tinkling clasp, עֶכֶס *ekes.*
Isa. 3. 18 take away the bravery of..tinkling orna.

OR'-NAN, אָרְנָן *strong.*
A Jebusite prince whose thrashing-floor was purchased by David for an altar, called Araunah in 2 Sa. 24. 16. B.C. 1017.
1 Ch.21. 15 LORD stood by the threshing floor of O.
21. 18, 28 in the threshing floor of O. the Jebus.
21. 20 O. turned back..Now O. was threshing
21. 21 as David came to O., O. looked, and saw D.
21. 22 David said to O., Grant me the place of
21. 23 O. said unto David, Take (it) to thee, and
21. 24 David said to O., Nay; but I will verily
21. 25 So David gave to O. for the place six hu.
2 Ch. 3. 1 had prepared in the threshing floor of O.

OR'-PAH, עָרְפָּה *youthful freshness.*
A daughter in law of Naomi, and wife of Chilion, who returned to her own people. B.C. 1312.
Ruth 1. 4 the name of the one (was) O., and the name
1. 14 O. kissed her mother in law; but Ruth

ORPHAN —
Fatherless child, orphan, יָתוֹם *yathom.*
Lam. 5. 3 We are orphans and fatherless, our mo.

O'-SEE, 'Ωσηέ. *Greek name of the prophet Hosea.*
Rom. 9. 25 As he saith also in O., I will call them my

O-SHE'-A, הוֹשֵׁעַ *God saves.*
Same as *Joshua* son of Nun, servant of Moses.
Num13. 8 Of the tribe of Ephraim, O. the son of Nun
13. 16 Moses called O. the son of Nun, Jehoshua

OSPRAY —
Ospray, עָזְנִיָּה *ozniyyah.*
Lev. 11. 13 the eagle, and the ossifrage, and the ospr
Deut14. 12 the eagle, and the ossifrage, and the ospr.

OSSIFRAGE —
Ossifrage, bone breaker, פֶּרֶס *peres.*
Lev. 11. 13 the eagle, and the ossifrage, and the ospr.
Deut14. 12 the eagle, and the ossifrage, and the ospr.

OSTRICH —
1. *Ostriches, screamers,* יְעֵנִים *yeenim.*
Lam. 4. 3 cruel, like the ostriches in the wilderness

2. *Stork,* חֲסִידָה *chasidah.*
Job 39. 13 or wings and feathers unto the ostrich?

OTHER (things, matters, of), OTHERS —
1. *A brother,* אָח *ach.*
Gen. 13. 11 separated themselves the one from the o.

2. *One,* אֶחָד *echad.*
Exod17. 12 the one on the one side, and the other on
18. 4 And the name of the other (was) Eliezer
25. 19 And make..the other cherub on the other
25. 33 three bowls made like almonds in the ot.
Lev. 5. 7 one for a sin offering, and the other for
12. 8 the one for the burnt offering, and the o.
14. 22 one shall be a sin offering, and the other
14. 31 the one (for) a sin offering, and the other
15. 15, 30 the one (for) a sin offering, and the other
16. 8 one lot for the LORD, and the other lot for
Num. 6. 11 the one for a sin offering, and the other
8. 12 the one (for) a sin offering, and the other
Judg20. 31 and the other to Gibeah in the field, about
1 Sa. 14. 4 Bozez, and the name of the other Seneh
14. 5 the other southward over against Gibeah
14. 40 Jonathan my son will be on the other side
2 Sa. 12. 1 two men..the one rich, and the other po.
14. 6 but the one smote the other, and slew him
1 Ki. 3. 25 give half to the one, and half to the other
12. 29 he set the one in Beth-el, and the other
18. 23 I will dress the other bullock, and lay (it)
2 Ch. 3. 12 (one) wing of the other cherub (was) five
3. 17 one on the right hand, and the other on
Neh. 4. 17 and with the other (hand) held a weapon
Jer. 24. 2 the other basket (had) very naughty figs
Eze. 40. 6 and the other threshold..one reed broad
Dan. 12. 5 the other on that side of the bank of the
Zech. 4. 3 the other upon the left (side) thereof
11. 7 the one I called Beauty, and the other I

3. *A sister,* אָחוֹת *achoth.*
Eze. 1. 23 wings straight, the one toward the other

4. *Other, another, next,* אַחֵר *acher.*
Gen. 8. 10 he stayed yet other seven days; and again
8. 12 he stayed yet other seven days; and sent
29. 27 shalt serve with me yet seven other years
29. 30 and served with him yet seven other ye.
41. 3, 19 seven other kine came up after them
43. 14 that he may send away your other broth.
43. 22 other money have we brought down in our
Exod20. 3 Thou shalt have no other gods before me
23. 13 make no mention of the name of other g.
34. 14 For thou shalt worship no other god: for
Lev. 6. 11 put on other garments, and carry forth
14. 42 And they shall take other stones, and put
14. 42 he shall take other mortar, and shall pl.
Deut. 5. 7 Thou shalt have none other gods before
6. 14 Ye shall not go after other gods, of the g.
7. 4 turn away..that they may serve other g.
8. 19 walk after other gods, and serve them, and
11. 16 and serve other gods, and worship them
11. 28 to go after other gods, which ye have not
13. 2 Let us go after other gods, which thou h.
13. 6, 13 Let us go and serve other gods, which
17. 3 hath gone and served other gods, and w.
18. 20 that shall speak in the name of other gods
28. 14 not go aside..to go after other gods to s.
28. 36 there shalt thou serve other gods, wood
28. 64 and there thou shalt serve other gods, w.
29. 26 they went and served other gods, and w.
30. 17 and worship other gods, and serve them
31. 18 in that they are turned unto other gods
31. 20 then will they turn unto other gods, and
Josh 23. 16 have gone and served other gods, and bo.
24. 2 Your fathers dwelt..they served other gods
24. 16 should forsake the LORD, to serve other g.
Judg. 2. 12 followed other gods, of the gods of the p.
2. 17 but they went a whoring after other gods
2. 19 in following other gods to serve them, and
10. 13 ye have forsaken me, and served other g.
Ruth 2. 22 that they meet thee not in any other field
1 Sa. 8. 8 have forsaken me, and served other gods
19. 21 sent other messengers, and they prophesi.
21. 9 take (it); for (there is) no other save that
26. 19 driven me out..saying, Go, serve other g.
28. 8 disguised himself, and put on other raim
2 Sa. 13. 16 greater than the other that thou didst unto
1 Ki. 3. 22 the other woman said, Nay; but the living
9. 6 go and serve other gods, and worship them
9. 9 have taken hold upon other gods, and h.
11. 4 wives turned away his heart after other g.
11. 10 that he should not go after other gods.
14. 9 for thou hast gone and made thee other
2 Ki. 5. 17 offer neither..sacrifice unto other gods
17. 7 children of Israel..had feared other gods
17. 35 Ye shall not fear other gods, nor bow yo.
17. 37 observe..and ye shall not fear other gods
17. 38 not forget; neither shall ye fear other gods
22. 17 burnt incense unto other gods, that they
1 Ch.23. 17 Eliezer had none other sons; but the sons
2 Ch. 3. 11 and the other wing (was likewise) five cu.
3. 11 reaching to the wing of the other cherub
3. 12 wing of the other cherub (was) five cubits
3. 12 other wing (was) five cubits (also) joining
7. 19 shall go and serve other gods, and worsh.
7. 22 laid hold on other gods, and worshipped
28. 25 burn incense unto other gods, and provo.
30. 23 assembly took counsel to keep other seven
34. 25 burned incense unto other gods, that they
Ezra 1. 10 Thirty basins of gold..(and) other vessels
2. 31 children of the other Elam, a thousand two
Neh. 5. 5 for other men have our lands and vineya.
7. 33 The men of the other Nebo, fifty and two
7. 34 children of the other Elam, a thousand two
Job 8. 19 Behold..out of the earth shall others grow
31. 10 let my wife grind..and let others bow do.
34. 24 break in pieces..and set others in thei.
Psa. 49. 10 men die..and leave their wealth to others
Prov. 5. 9 Lest thou give thine honour unto others
Eccl. 7. 22 thou thyself likewise hast cursed others
Jer. 1. 16 have burnt incense unto other gods, and
6. 12 their houses shall be turned unto others
7. 6 neither walk after other gods to your hurt
7. 9 walk after other gods whom ye know not
7. 18 pour out drink offerings unto other gods
8. 10 Therefore will I give their wives unto ot.
11. 10 they went after other gods to serve them
13. 10 walk after other gods, to serve them, and
16. 11 walked after other gods, and have served
16. 13 there shall ye serve other gods day and ni.
19. 4 have burnt incense in it unto other gods
19. 13 poured out drink offerings unto other go.
22. 9 and worshipped other gods, and served
25. 6 go not after other gods to serve them, and
32. 29 poured out drink offerings unto other gods
35. 15 and go not after other gods to serve them
44. 3 to serve other gods, whom they knew not
44. 5 to burn no incense unto other gods
44. 8 burning incense unto other gods in the l.
44. 15 wives had burnt incense unto other gods
Eze. 40. 40 on the other side, which (was) at the po.
41. 24 one door, and two leaves for the other (d.)
42. 14 put on other garments, and shall approach

Eze.44. 19 they shall put on other garments; and they
Dan. 11. 4 plucked up, even for others besides those
12. 5 there stood other two, the one on this side
Hos. 3. 1 look to other gods, and love flagons of w.

5. *Other, another,* אָחֳרִי *ochori.*
Dan. 7. 20 and (of) the other which came up, and b.

6. *Other, another,* אָחֳרָן *ochoran.*
Dan. 2. 11 there is none other that can show it be.
2. 44 kingdom shall not be left to other people
3. 29 no other god that can deliver after this so.

7. *Rest, remnant,* שְׁאָר *shear.*
Esth. 9. 16 But the other Jews that (were) in the ki.

8. *Second, other,* שֵׁנִי, שֵׁנִית *shenith, sheni.*
Gen. 4. 19 Adah, and the name of the other Zillah
Exod 1. 15 Shiphrah, and the name of the other Puah
25. 12 one side of it, and two rings in the other
25. 32 and three branches..out of the other side
26. 27 five bars for the boards of the other side
27. 15 on the other side (shall be) hangings fifteen
28. 10 six names of the rest on the other stone
29. 19 thou shalt take the other ram; and Aaron
29. 39, 41 the other lamb thou shalt offer at even
36. 25, 32 the other side of the tabernacle
37. 3 and two rings upon the other side of it
37. 18 three branches..out of the other side th.
38. 15 for the other side of the court gate, on this
Lev. 8. 22 brought the other ram, the ram of conse.
Num 11. 26 name of the other Medad: and the spirit
28. 4, 8 the other lamb shalt thou offer at even
Ruth 1. 4 name of the other Ruth: and they dwelt
1 Sa. 1. 2 name of the other Peninnah: and Penin.
2 Sa. 4. 2 name of the other Rechab, the sons of R.
1 Ki. 6. 24 and five cubits the other wing of the ch.
6. 25 the other cherub (was) ten cubits: both
6. 26 ten cubits, and so (was it) of the other c.
6. 27 wing of the other cherub touched the ot.
6. 34 two leaves of the other door (were) folding
7. 16 height of the other chapiter (was) five c.
7. 17 one chapiter, and seven for the other ch.
7. 18 pomegranates: and so did he for the oth.
7. 20 in rows round about upon the other cha.
Neh. 3. 11 repaired the other piece, and the tower
3. 20 earnestly repaired the other piece, from
12. 38 other (company of them that gave) thanks
Dan. 8. 3 but one (was) higher than the other, and
Zech. 11. 14 Then I cut asunder mine other staff, (even)

9. *Wing,* כָּנָף *kanaph.*
1 Ki. 6. 24 unto the uttermost part of the other (were)

10. *A friend, companion,* רֵעַ *rea.*
Exod 18. 7 they asked each other of (their) welfare
Jer. 36. 16 they were afraid, both one and other, and

11. *Other, another,* ἄλλος *allos.*
Matt. 4. 21 he saw other two brethren, James (the son)
5. 39 thy right cheek, turn to him the other also
12. 13 and it was restored whole, like as the other
13. 8 other fell into good ground, and brought
20. 3 saw others standing idle in the market p
20. 6 found others standing idle, and saith unto
21. 8 others cut down branches from the trees
21. 36 he sent other servants more than the first
21. 41 let out (his) vineyard unto other husband.
22. 4 sent forth other servants, saying, Tell them
25. 16 traded with the same, and made (them) o.
25. 17 And likewise..he also gained other two
25. 20 came and brought other five talents, say.
25. 22 have gained two other talents besides them
27. 42 He saved others; himself he cannot save
27. 61 other Mary, sitting over against the sep
28. 1 Mary Magdalene and the other Mary to
Mark 3. 5 his hand was restored [whole as the other]
4. 8 other fell on good ground, and did yield
4. 36 there were also with him other little ships
6. 15 Others said, That it is Elias. And others
7. 4 many other things there be which they h
7. 8 [and many other such like things ye do]
8. 28 some (say), Elias; and others, One of the
11. 8 others cut down branches off the trees, and
12. 5 him they killed, and many others; beating
12. 9 and will give the vineyard unto others
12. 31 There is none other commandment greater
12. 32 is one God; and there is none other but
15. 31 He saved others; himself he cannot save
15. 41 many other women which came up with
Luke 5. 29 and of others that sat down with them
6. 10 [his hand was restored whole as the other]
6. 29 offer also the other; and him that taketh
9. 8 of others, that one of the old prophets was
9. 19 others (say), that one of the old prophets
20. 16 shall give the vineyard to others. And
23. 35 He saved others; let him save himself if
John 4. 38 other men laboured, and ye are entered
6. 22 saw that there was none other boat there
6. 23 Howbeit there came other boats from Ti
7. 12 others said, Nay; but he deceiveth the p.
7. 41 Others said, This is the Christ. But some
9. 9 others (said), He is like him: (but) he said
9. 16 Others said, How can a man that is a sin.
10. 16 other sheep I have, which are not of this
10. 21 Others said, These are not the words of him
12. 29 said that it thundered: others said, An a.
15. 24 the works which none other man did, they
18. 16 Then went out that other disciple, which
18. 34 Sayest thou..or did others tell it thee of
19. 18 crucified him, and two other with him
19. 32 brake the legs..of the other which was c.
20. 2 to the other disciple whom Jesus loved
20. 3 went forth, and that other disciple, and
20. 4 other disciple did outrun Peter, and came
John 20. 8 Then went in also that other disciple wh.
20. 25 The other disciples therefore said unto him
20. 30 many other signs truly did Jesus in the p.
21. 2 of Zebedee, and two other of his disciples
21. 8 other disciples came in a little ship; for
21. 25 there are also many other things which J.
Acts 4. 12 [Neither is there salvation in any other]
15. 2 certain other of them, should go up to J.
1 Co. 1. 16 I know not whether I baptized any other
3. 11 For other foundation can no man lay than
9. 2 If I be not an apostle unto others, yet d.
9. 12 If others be partakers of (this) power over
9. 27 when I have preached to others, I myself
14. 19 that (by my voice) I might teach others also
14. 29 speak two or three, and let the other judge
2 Co. 1. 13 For we write none other things unto you
8. 13 For (I mean) not that other men be eased
11. 8 I robbed other churches, taking wages (of
Phil. 3. 4 If any other man thinketh that he hath
1 Th. 2. 6 nor (yet) of others, when we might have
Heb. 11. 35 others were tortured, not accepting deli.
Jas. 5. 12 neither by any other oath: but let your yea
Rev. 2. 24 I will put upon you none other burden
17. 10 and one is, (and) the other is not yet come

12. *Belonging to another,* ἀλλότριος *allotrios.*
Heb. 9. 25 holy place every year with blood of others

13. *He,* αὐτός *autos.*
Luke 14. 32 while the other is yet a great way off, he

14. *One,* εἷς *heis.*
Matt 20. 21 one on thy right hand, and the other on
24. 40 the one shall be taken, and the other left
Mark 10. 37 one on thy right hand, and the other on
15. 27 one on his right hand, and the other on
John 20. 12 one at the head, and the other at the feet
Gal. 4. 22 one by a bond maid, the other by a free w.

15. *That, that one,* ἐκεῖνος *ekeinos.*
Luke 18. 14 justified (rather) than the other: for every

16. *Even that,* κἀκεῖνος *kai ekeinos.*
Matt 23. 23 done, and not to leave the other undone
Luke 11. 42 done, and not to leave the other undone

17. *Other, different,* ἕτερος *heteros.*
Matt. 6. 24 he will hate the one, and love the other
6. 24 will hold to the one, and despise the other
12. 45 taketh with himself seven other spirits
15. 30 blind, dumb, maimed, and many others
16. 14 some, Elias; and others, Jeremias, or one
Luke 3. 18 many other things in his exhortation pre.
4. 43 must preach the kingdom of God to other
5. 7 partners, which were in the other ship, that
7. 41 owed five hundred pence, and the other
8. 3 many others, which ministered
8. 8 other fell on good ground, and sprang up
10. 1 Lord appointed other seventy also, and
11. 16 others, tempting (him), sought of him a s.
11. 26 taketh (to him) seven other spirits more
16. 13 he will hate the one, and love the other
16. 13 will hold to the one, and despise the other
17. 34 one shall be taken, and the other shall be
17. 35, 36 [one shall be taken, and the other left]
18. 10 the one a Pharisee, and the other a publ.
22. 65 many other things blasphemously spake
23. 32 there were also two others, malefactors, led
23. 40 But the other answering rebuked him, say.
Acts 2. 4 began to speak with other tongues, as the
2. 13 others mocking said, These men are full
2. 40 with many other words did he testify and
4. 12 for there is none other name under heaven
8. 34 this? of himself, or of some other man?
15. 35 teaching and preaching..with many oth.
17. 34 woman named Damaris, and others with
19. 39 if ye enquire any thing [concerning other]
23. 6 one part were Sadducees, and the other
27. 1 delivered Paul and certain other prison.
Rom. 8. 39 Nor height, nor depth, nor any other cre.
13. 9 if (there be) any other commandment, it
1 Co. 8. 4 and that (there is) none [other] God but
10. 29 not thine own, but of the other: for why
14. 17 givest thanks well, but the other is not
14. 21 With (men of)..other lips will I speak u.
2 Co. 8. 8 by occasion of the frowardness of others
Gal 1. 19 other of the apostles saw I none, save Ja.
Eph. 3. 5 Which in other ages was not made known
Phil 2. 4 but every man also on the things of others
1 Ti 1. 10 if there be any other thing that is contr.
2 Ti. 2 2 men, who shall be able to teach others also
Heb 11. 36 others had trial of (cruel) mockings and

18 *Rest, remaining,* λοιπός *loipos.*
Matt 25. 11 Afterward came also the other virgins
Mark 4. 19 lusts of other things entering in, choke
Luke 8. 10 to others in parables; that seeing they m.
18. 9 that they were righteous, and despised o.
18. 11 I thank thee, that I am not as other men
24. 10 other (women that were) with them, wh.
Acts 17. 9 taken security of Jason, and of the other
28. 9 others also, which had diseases in the is.
Rom. 1. 13 among you also, even as among other Ge.
1 Co. 9. 5 as well as other apostles, and (as) the br.
15. 37 it may chance of wheat, or of some other
2 Co. 12. 13 wherein ye were inferior to other churches
13. 2 heretofore have sinned, and to all other
Gal. 2. 13 other Jews dissembled likewise with him
Eph. 2. 3 were..the children of wrath, even as oth.
4. 17 henceforth walk not as [other] Gentiles w.
Phil. 1. 13 manifest in all the palace, and in all other
4. 3 other my fellow labourers, whose names
1 Th. 4. 13 sorrow not, even as others which have no
5. 6 Therefore let us not sleep, as (do) others
1 Ti. 5. 20 rebuke before all, that others also may f.
2 Pe. 3. 16 as (they do) also the other scriptures, unto
Rev. 8. 13 by reason of the other voices of the trum.

19. *One, (fem.)* μία *mia.*
Matt 24. 41 the one shall be taken, and the other left

OTHER side, on, to or unto the —

1. *Thus, so, here, there,* כֹּה *koh.*
Num 11. 31 as it were a day's journey on the other s.

2. *Beyond, over, other side,* πέραν *peran.*
Matt. 8. 18 command. to depart unto the other side
8. 28 when he was come to the other side, into
14. 22 to go before him unto the other side, w.
16. 5 his disciples were come to the other side
Mark 4. 35 saith..Let us pass over unto the other s.
5. 1 they came over unto the other side of the
5. 21 passed over..unto the other side, much
6. 45 to go to the other side before unto Beth.
8. 13 left them, and..departed to the other s.
Luke 8. 22 Let us go over unto the other side of the
John 6. 22 people which stood on the other side of
6. 25 when they had found him on the other s.

OTHER, the —

1. *These,* אֵלֶּה *eleh.*
1 Ki. 20. 29 pitched one over against the other seven
Eze. 9. 5 to the others he said in mine hearing

2. *This, (fem.)* זֹאת *zoth.*
1 Ki. 3. 23 the other saith, Nay; but thy son (is) the

3. *This, (mas.)* זֶה *zeh.*
Exod 14. 20 so that the one came not near the other

OTHER, each —

Each other, ἀλλήλων *allēlōn.*
Phil. 2. 3 let each esteem other better than thems.
2 Th. 1. 3 charity of every one..toward each other

OTHER man —

Other, ἄλλος *allos.*
John 4. 38 other men laboured, and ye are entered
15. 24 done..the works which none other man
2 Co. 8. 13 not that other men be eased, and ye bu.
Phil. 3. 4 If any other man thinketh that he hath

OTHER men's —

Belonging to another, ἀλλότριος *allotrios.*
2 Co. 10. 15 without (our) measure, (that is), of other m.
1 Ti. 5. 22 neither be partaker of other men's sins: k.

OTHER than —

Outside, ἐκτός *ektos.*
Acts 26. 22 none other things than those which the

OTHER way, some —

From some other place, ἀλλαχόθεν *allachothen.*
John 10. 1 climbeth up some other way, the same is

OTHERWISE, (if) —

1. *Or, otherwise,* אוֹ *o.*
2 Sa. 18. 13 Otherwise I should have wrought falseh.

2. *Without,* בְּלֹא *belo.*
2 Ch. 30. 18 yet did they eat the passover otherwise

3. *And,* וְ *ve.*
1 Ki. 1. 21 Otherwise it shall come to pass, when my

4. *Another, other,* ἄλλος *allos.*
Gal. 5. 10 that ye will be none otherwise minded

5. *Otherwise,* ἄλλως *allōs.*
1 Ti. 5. 25 and they that are otherwise cannot be hid

6. *But if not,* εἰ δὲ μήγε *ei de mēge.*
Matt. 6. 1 otherwise ye have no reward of your Fat.
Luke 5. 36 if otherwise, then both the new maketh
2 Co. 11. 16 if otherwise, yet as a fool receive me, that

7. *For then, otherwise,* ἐπεί *epei.*
Rom 11. 6 otherwise grace is no more grace. But if
11. 6 [grace; otherwise work is no more work]
11. 22 but..otherwise thou also shalt be cut off
Heb. 9. 17 otherwise it is of no strength at all while

8. *Otherwise, differently,* ἑτέρως *heterōs.*
Phil. 3. 15 if in any thing ye be otherwise minded, God

OTH'-NI, עָתְנִי *Jah is force.*

A son of Shemaiah, gatekeeper of the tabernacle in the days of David. B.C. 1015.
1 Ch. 26. 7 The sons of Shemaiah; O., and Rephael

OTH-NI'-EL, עָתְנִיאֵל *God is force.*

1. A Son of Kenaz, younger brother of Caleb, who, after death of Joshua, became judge for forty years, from 1394-1354 B.C.
Josh. 15. 17 O. the son of Kenaz, the brother of Caleb
Judg. 1. 13 O. the son of Kenaz, Caleb's younger bro.
3. 9 who delivered them, (even) O. the son of
3. 11 land had rest forty years. And O. the son
1 Ch. 4. 13 And the sons of Kenaz; O., and Seraiah: and
4. 13 and the sons of O.; Hathah

2. Perhaps the same as the preceding.
1 Ch. 27. 15 (was) Heldai the Netophathite, of O.: and

OUCHES —

Settings, textures, brocades, מִשְׁבְּצוֹת *mishbetsoth.*
Exod 28. 11 shalt make them to be set in ouches of g.
28. 13 And thou shalt make ouches (of) gold
28. 14 fasten the wreathen chains to the ouches
28. 25 thou shalt fasten in the two ouches, and
39. 6 onyx stones inclosed in ouches of gold
39. 13 inclosed in ouches of gold in their inclos.
39. 16 they made two ouches (of) gold, and two
39. 18 they fastened in the two ouches, and put

OUGHT, AUGHT —

1. *A thing, matter,* דָּבָר *dabar.*

Exod. 5. 11 not ought of your work shall be diminis.
Josh. 21. 45 There failed not ought of any good thing

2. *Any thing,* כֹּל מְאוּמָה *kol meumah.*

Gen. 39. 6 he knew not ought he had, save the bread
1 Sa. 12. 4 hast thou taken ought of any man's hand
12. 5 that ye have not found ought in my hand
25. 7 neither was there ought missing unto
2 Sa. 3. 35 if I taste bread, or ought else, till the

3. *Thing sold, ware,* מִמְכָּר *mimkar.*

Lev. 25. 14 if thou sell ought unto thy neighbour, or

4. *Not one thing,* οὐδέν *ouden.*

Mark 7. 12 suffer him no more to do ought for his

5. *Any thing,* τις *tis.*

Matt. 5. 23 that thy brother hath ought against thee
21. 3 if any (man) say ought unto you, ye shall
Mark 11. 25 forgive, if ye have ought against any; that
Acts 4. 32 neither said any (of them) that ought of
28. 19 that I had ought to accuse my nation of
Phm. 18 oweth (thee) ought, put that on mine acc.

6. *It behoveth,* δεῖ *dei.*

Matt 23. 23 these ought ye to have done, and not to
25. 27 Thou oughtest therefore to have put my
Mark 13. 14 standing where it ought not, let him that
Luke 11. 42 these ought ye to have done, and not to
12. 12 in the same hour what ye ought to say
13. 14 are six days in which men ought to work
13. 16 ought not this woman, being a daughter
18. 1 men ought always to pray, and not to f.
24. 26 Ought not Christ to have suffered these
John 4. 20 is the place where men ought to worship
Acts 5. 29 said, We ought to obey God rather than m.
10. 6 [shall tell thee what thou oughtest to do]
19. 36 ye ought to be quiet, and to do nothing r.
20. 35 how..ye ought to support the weak, and
24. 19 Who ought to have been here before thee
25. 10 judgment seat, where I ought to be judg.
25. 24 crying that he ought not to live any long.
26. 9 I ought to do many things contrary to the
Rom. 8. 26 know not what we should pray..as we o.
12. 3 not to think..more highly than he ought
1 Co. 8. 2 knoweth nothing yet as he ought to know
2 Co. 2. 3 sorrow from them of whom I ought to re.
Eph. 6. 20 I may speak boldly, as I ought to speak
Col. 4. 4 may make it manifest, as I ought to speak
4. 6 may know how ye ought to answer every
1 Th. 4. 1 ye ought to walk and to please God, (so)
2 Th. 3. 7 yourselves know how ye ought to follow
1 Ti. 3. 15 thou oughtest to behave thyself in the h.
5. 13 speaking things which they ought not
Titus 1. 11 teaching things which they ought not, for
Heb. 2. 1 we ought to give the more earnest heed
2 Pe. 3. 11 what manner (of persons) ought ye to be

7. *To owe, be obliged, indebted,* ὀφείλω *opheilō.*

John 13. 14 ye also ought to wash one another's feet
19. 7 he ought to die, because he made himself
Acts 17. 29 we ought not to think that the Godhead
Rom 15. 1 ought to bear the infirmities of the weak
1 Co. 11. 7 a man indeed ought not to cover (his) he.
11. 10 ought the woman to have power on (her)
2 Co. 12. 11 I ought to have been commended of you
12. 14 the children ought not to lay up for the
Eph. 5. 28 So ought men to love their wives as their
Heb. 5. 3 he ought, as for the people, so also for him.
5. 12 when for the time ye ought to be teachers
1 Jo. 2. 6 ought himself also so to walk, even as he
3. 16 we ought to lay down (our) lives for the
4. 11 Beloved..we ought also to love one anot.
3 John 8 We therefore ought to receive such, that

8. *It needs, it is necessary,* χρή *chrē.*

Jas. 3. 10 brethren, these things ought not so to be

OUR, OURS —

1. *Our,* נוּ (suff. of various forms), Gen. 37. 26, *&c., &c.*

1a. *To us,* לָנוּ *la-nu,* Gen. 26. 20, 31. 16, *&c.*

2. *For our sake,* δι᾽ ἡμᾶς *di' hēmas.*

1 Co. 9. 10 altogether for our sakes? For our sakes

3. *Our own,* ἡμέτερος *hēmeteros.*

Acts 2. 11 we do hear them speak in our tongues the
24. 6 would have judged according to our law
26. 5 the most straitest sect of our religion
Rom 15. 4 aforetime were written for our learning
2 Ti. 4. 15 for he hath greatly withstood our words
Titus 3. 14 let ours also learn to maintain good words
1 Jo. 1. 3 our fellowship (is) with the Father, and w.
2. 2 not for ours only, but also for (the sins of)

4. *To us,* ἡμῖν *hēmin.*

Luke 17. 5 said unto the Lord, Increase o. Ac. 19. 27.

5. *Of us, our,* ἡμῶν *hēmōn.*

Matt. 6. 9 Our Father which art in heaven, Hallow.
6. 11 Give us this day our daily bread
6. 12 forgive us our debts, as we forgive our d.
8. 17 Himself took our infirmities, and bare
20. 33 They say..Lord, that our eyes may be o.
21. 42 Lord's doing, and it is marvellous in our
23. 30 we had been in the days of our fathers
25. 8 Give us of your oil; for our lamps are gone
27. 25 His blood (be) on us, and on our children

Mark 9. [40]; 11. 10; 12. 7, 11, 29; Luke 1. 55, 71, 72, 73, [74], 75, 78, 79; 7. 5; 11. [2], 3, 4; 13. 26; 20. 14; 24. 20, 32; John 3. 11; 4. 12, 20; 6. 31; 7. 51; 8. 39, 53; 9. 20; 11. 11, 48; 12. 38; [19. 7]. Acts 2. 8, 39; 3. 13, 25; 5. 30; 7. 2, 11, 12, 15, 19, [19], 38, 39, 44, 45-45; 13. 17; 14. [17]; 15. 10, 26, 26, [36]; 16. 20; 17. 20; 19. [25]; 20. 21; 22. 14; 24. [7]; 26. 7; 27. 10; 28. [25]; Rom. 1. 3, 7; 3. 5; 4. 1, 12, 24, 25, 25; 5. 1, 5, 11, 21; 6. 6, [11], 23; 7. 5, 25; 8. 16, 23, 26, 39; 9. 10; 10. 16; 13. 11; 15. 6; 16. [1], 9, 18, 20, 24; 1 Co. 1. 2, 2, 3, 7, 8, 9, 10; 2. 7; 5. [4, 4], 7; 6. 11; 9. 1; 10. 1, 6, 11; 12. 23, 24; 15. 3, 14, 31, 57; 2 Co. 1. 2, 3, 4, 5, 7, 8, [11], 12, 12, 14, 18, 22; 3. 2, 5; 4. 3, 6, 10, 11, 16, 17; 5. 1, 2, [12]; 6. 11, 11; 7. 4, 5, [12, 14]; 8. 9, 22, 23, 24; 9. 3; 10. 4, 8, 15; 11. [31]; Gal. 1. 3, 4, 4; 2. 4; 3. 24; 6. 14, 18; Eph. 1. 2, 3, 14, 17; 2. 3, 14; 3. 11, [14]; 5. 20; 6. 22, 24; Phil. 1. 2; 3. 20, 21; 4. 20, [23]; Col. 1. 2, 3, 7; 3. [4]; 1 Th. 1. [1], 2, 3, 3, 5; 2. 1, 2, 3, 4, 9, 19, 19, 20; 3. 2, [2], 5, 7, 9, 11, 11, 11, 13, 13; 5. 9, 23, 28; 2 Th. 1. 1, [2], 8, 10, 11, 12, 12; 2. 1, 1, 14, 14, 15, 16, 16; 3. [6, 12], 14, 18; 1 Ti. 1. 1, 1, [2], 12, 14; 6. 3, 14; 2 Ti. 1. 2, 8, 9, 10; Titus 1. 3, 4; 2. [10], 13; 3. 4, 6; Phm. 1, 2, 3, 25; Heb. 1. [3]; 3. 1; 4. 15; 7. 14; 12. 9, 29; 13. 20; Jas. 2. 1, 21; 3. 6; 1 Pe. 1. 3; 2. 24; 2 Pe. 1. [1], 2, 8, 11, 14, 16; 3. 15, 15, 18; 1 Jo. 1. 1, 1, 9; 2. 2; 3. [5], 19, 20, [21]; 4. 10; 5. 4; 2 Jo. [12]; 3 Jo. 12; Jude 4, 4, 17, 21, 25; Rev. 1. 5; 5. [10]; 6. 10; 7. 3, [10], 12; 11. [8], 15; 12. 10, 10, 10; 19. 1, 5; 22. [21].

6. *With us,* μεθ' ἡμῶν *meth hēmōn.*

1 Jo. 4. 17 Herein is our love made perfect, that we

OUR company, of —

Of us, ἐκ ἡμῶν *ek hēmōn.*

Luke 24. 22 certain women also of our company made

OUR own —

1. *Of selves,* ἑαυτῶν *heautōn.*

1 Th. 2. 8 our own souls, because ye were dear unto

2. *One's own, proper,* ἴδιος *idios.*

Acts 3. 12 by our own power or holiness we had made
1 Co. 4. 12 labour, working with our own hands: be.

OURSELVES —

1. *We, we ourselves,* אֲנַחְנוּ *anachnu.*

Num 32. 17 we ourselves will go ready armed before

2. *Selves,* ἑαυτούς, *&c.,* [*heautou*].

Acts 23. 14 have bound ourselves under a great curse
Rom. 8. 23 even we ourselves groan within o. Rom. 15. 1
1 Co. 11. 31 if we would judge ourselves, we should not
2 Co. 1. 9 had the sentence of death in ourselves
1. 9 we should not trust in ourselves, but in
3. 1 Do we begin again to commend ourselves
3. 5 sufficient of ourselves to think..[ourselv.]
4. 2 commending ourselves to every..conscien.
4. 5 we preach not ourselves, but Christ Jesus
4. 5 and ourselves your servants for Jesus' sa.
5. 12 we commend not ourselves again unto you
6. 4 approving ourselves as the ministers of G.
7. 1 let us cleanse ourselves from..filthiness
10. 12 compare ourselves with some that comm.
10. 14 For we stretch not ourselves beyond (our
2 Th. 3. 9 to make ourselves an ensample unto you
Heb 10. 25 Not forsaking the assembling of ourselves
Rom. 15. 1 ought to bear..and not to please ourselv.
1 Jo. 1. 8 we deceive ourselves, and the truth is not

OUT, (from) —

1. *Outside, without,* חוּץ *chuts.*

Gen. 24. 29 Laban ran out unto the man, unto the w.
39. 12, 15 left his garment..fled, and got him out
39. 18 he left his garment with me, and fled out
Num 12. 14 be shut out from the camp seven days
12. 15 was shut out from the camp seven days
2 Sa. 13. 17 Put now this (woman) out from me, and b.
13. 18 his servant brought her out, and bolted
[*See also* Bear, beat, beaten, belch, blot.]

2. *Without, outside,* ἔξω *exō.*

Matt. 5. 13 to be cast out, and to be trodden under
26. 75 And Peter..went out, and wept bitterly
Mark 14. 68 went out into the porch; and the cock c
Luke 13. 28 in the kingdom of God, and you..th. 8. 54
14. 35 nor..for the dunghill; (but) men cast it out
22. 62 And Peter went out, and wept bitterly
24. 50 he led them [out] as far as to Bethany; and
John 6. 37 cometh to me I will in no wise cast out
9. 34 dost thou teach us? And they cast him out
9. 35 Jesus heard that they had cast him out; and
12. 31 shall the prince of this world be cast out
Acts 16. 30 brought them out, and said, Sirs, what m.
1 Jo. 4. 18 perfect love casteth out fear: because fear
Rev 3. 12 he shall go no more out: and I will write
11. 2 court which is without..temple leave [out]

OUT of, that goeth —

With, בְּ *be.*

Psa. 17. 1 prayer (that goeth) not out of feigned lips

OUT of —

1. *As to,* אֵת *eth.*

Gen. 37. 23 they stripped Joseph out of his coat, (his)

2. *From within,* מִבֵּין *mib-ben.*

Num 16. 37 take up the censers out of the burning

3. *In not, otherwise than in,* בְּלֹא *be-lo.*

Lev. 15. 25 out of the time of her separation

4. *Outside, without,* חוּץ *chuts.*

Lev. 10. 4 from before the sanctuary out of the camp
10. 5 carried them in their coats out of the ca.
14. 3 the priest shall go forth out of the camp
14. 45 he shall carry (them) forth out of the city
14. 53 he shall let go the living bird out of the
17. 3 What man..that killeth (it) out of the c.
24. 23 bring forth him that had cursed out of the
1 Ki. 21. 13 they carried him forth out of the city, and
2 Ch. 33. 15 And he took..and cast (them) out of the
Neh. 13. 8 cast..household stuff..out of the chamber

5. *From, out of,* מִן *min.*

Gen. 2. 9 out of the ground made the LORD God to
Ezra 5. 14 out of the temple that (was) in Jerusalem
5. 14 king take out of the temple of Babylon
6. 4 expences be given out of the king's house
6. 5 out of the temple which (is) at Jerusalem
Dan. 3. 15 that shall deliver you out of my hands
3. 17 will deliver (us) out of thine hand, O king
5. 2 out of the temple which (was) in Jerusa.
5. 3 vessels that were taken out of the temple
5. 13 whom the king my father brought out of
6. 23 they should take Daniel up out of the den
6. 23 Daniel was taken up out of the den, and
7. 17 kings, (which) shall arise out of the earth

6. *From on,* מֵעַל *me-al.*

Exod 23. 13 neither let it be heard out of thy mouth
Deut. 9. 17 cast them out of my two hands, and brake
2 Ch. 33. 8 out of the land which I have appointed

7. *Heart, midst, centre,* קֶרֶב *qereb.*

Num 14. 44 and Moses, departed not out of the camp
Psa. 74. 11 thy right hand? pluck (it) out of thy bos.

8. *Out of the midst of,* מִתּוֹךְ *mit-tok.*

Exod 33. 11 Joshua..departed not out of the tabern.
Prov. 5. 15 and running waters out of thine own well
Jer. 44. 7 child and suckling out of Judah, to leave

9. *From, away from,* ἀπό *apo.*

Matt. 3. 16 went up straightway out of the water: and
7. 4 Let me pull out the mote [out of] thine eye
8. 34 that he would depart out of their coasts
12. 43 the unclean spirit is gone out of a man
13. 1 The same day went Jesus [out of] the ho.
14. 13 they followed him on foot out of the cities
14. 29 when Peter was come down out of the ship
15. 22 a woman of Canaan came out of the same
17. 18 he departed out of him: and the child was
24. 27 the lightning cometh out of the east, and
Mark 1. 10 coming up [out of] the water, he saw the
5. 17 to pray him to depart out of their coasts
6. 33 ran a foot thither out of all cities, and out
7. 15 the things which come [out of] him, those
10. 46 he went [out of] Jericho with his disciples
15. 21 who passed by, coming out of the country
16. 9 [out of whom he had cast seven devils]
Luke 4. 35 he came out of him, and hurt him not
4. 41 And devils also came out of many, crying
5. 2 the fishermen were gone out of them, and
5. 36 the piece that was (taken) out of the new
6. 17 of people out of all Judea and Jerusalem
8. 2 Magdalene, out of whom went seven dev.
8. 12 taketh away the word out of their hearts
8. 29 the unclean spirit to come out of the man
8. 33 Then went the devils out of the man, and
8. 35, 38 out of whom the devils were departed
8. 46 for I perceive that virtue is gone out of me
9. 5 when ye go out of that city, shake off the
11. 24 When the unclean spirit is gone out of a
12. 54 When ye see a cloud rise out of the west
17. 29 the same day that Lot went out of Sodom
23. 26 a Cyrenian, coming out of the country, and
John 7. 42 out of the town of Bethlehem, where Da.
Acts 1. 9 a cloud received him out of their sight
2. 5 men, out of every nation under heaven
13. 50 and expelled them out of their coasts
16. 18 and said..I command thee..to come out of
17. 2 reasoned with them out of the Scriptures
19. 12 So that..the evil spirits went [out of] them
28. 21 letters out of Judea concerning thee
28. 23 out of the law of Moses, and..the prophets
2 Co. 1. 16 to come again out of Macedonia unto you
Heb. 11. 34 out of weakness were made strong, waxed
Rev. 16. 17 a great voice [out of] the temple of, 22. 19

10. *Through,* διά (*gen.*) *dia,* Matt. 4. 4.

11. *Out of,* ἐκ *ek,* ἐξ *ex.*

Matt. 2. 6 out of thee shall come a Governor, that
2. 15 saying, Out of Egypt have I called my son
7. 5 first cast out the beam out of thine own
7. 5 cast out the mote out of thy brother's eye
8. 28 coming out of the tombs, exceeding fierce
12. 34 out of the abundance of the heart the m.
12. 35 out of the good treasure..out of the evil
13. 41 they shall gather out of his kingdom all
13. 52 bringeth forth out of his treasure (things)
15. 11 that which cometh out of the mouth, this
15. 18 those things which proceed out of the m.
15. 19 For out of the heart proceed evil thoughts
17. 5 a voice out of the cloud, which said, This
21. 16 Out of the mouth of babes and sucklings
24. 17 come..to take any thing out of his house
27. 53 And came out of the graves after his

Mark 1. 25, [26], 29; 5. 2, 2, [8], 30; 6. 54; 7. 20, 21, [26], 29; 9. 7, [25]; 13. 1, 15; 15. 46; Luke 1. 74; 2. 4; 4. 22, [35], [38]; 5. 3, 17; 6. 42, 45, 45; 8. 27; 9. 35; 11. 54; 17. 24; 19. 22; John 1. 46; 2. 15; 4. 30, 47, 54; 7. 38, 41, 52; 8. 59; 10. 28, 29, 39; 11. 55; 12. 17, 34; 13. 1; 15. 19; 17. 6, 15; 20. 2; Acts 7. 3, 4, 10, 40; 8. 39; 12. 11, 17; 13. 17, [42]; 15. 14; 16. 40; 19. 16, 33; 22. 18; 24. [7]; 27 29, 30, 30; 28. [3]; Rom. 2. 18; 11. 24, 26; 13. 11; 1 Co. 5. 10; 2 Co. 2. 4; 4. 6; 8. 11; Eph. 4. 29; Col. 2. 14; 3. 8; 2 Th. 2. 7; 1 Ti. 1. 5; 2 Ti. 2. 22, 26; 3. 11; 4. 17; Heb. 3. 16; 7. 5, 14; 8. 9; Jas. 3. 10, 13; 1 Pe. 2. 9; 2 Pe. 2. 9; 3. 5; 3 Jo. 10; Jude 5, 23; Rev. 1. 16; 2. 5; 3. 5, 12, 16; 4. 5; 5. 7, 9; 6. 14; 7. [14]; 8. 4; 9. 2, 3, 17, 18; 10. 10; 11. 5, 7; 12. 15, 16; 13. 1, 11; 14. [15], 17, 20; 15. [6]; 16. [1], [7]; 3. 13, 13, 21; 17. 8; 18. 4; 19. [5], 15, 21; 20. 7, 9, 12; 21. 2, 3, 10; 22. 1, [19].

12. *Outside, without,* ἐκτός *ektos.*

2 Co. 12. 2, 3 [out of] the body, I cannot tell, God k.

13. *Without, outside,* ἔξω *exō.*

Matt 21. 17 went out of the city into Bethany; and he

Matt 21. 39 cast (him) out of the vineyard, and slew
Mark 5. 10 that he would not send them away out of
8. 23 led him out of the town; and when he had
11. 19 when even was come, he went out of the
12. 8 killed..and cast (him) out of the vineyard
Luke 4. 29 thrust him out of the city, and led him
13. 33 it cannot be that a prophet perish out of
20. 15 they cast him out of the vineyard, and k.
Acts 4. 15 commanded them to go aside out of the
7. 58 And cast (him) out of the city, and stoned
14. 19 drew (him) out of the city, supposing he
16. 13 we went out of the city by a river side
21. 5 till (we were) out of the city: and we kn.
21. 30 drew him out of the temple: and forew.

14. *From the side of, from,* παρά *(gen.) para.*
Luke 6. 19 for there went virtue out of him, and he.
[*See also* Come, course, hand, joint, measure, not, season, sleep, synagogue, uttered, way.]

OUT, to seek —
To search, investigate, חָקַר *chaqar,* 3.
Eccl. 12. 9 sought out, (and) set in order many pro.

OUTCAST —
1. *To be driven away or down,* דָּחָה *dachah,* 2.
Psa. 147. 2 he gathereth together the outcasts of Is.
Isa. 11. 12 shall assemble the outcasts of Israel, and
56. 8 GOD which gathereth the outcasts of Israel
2. *To be driven or forced away,* נָדַח *nadach,* 2.
Isa. 16. 3 hide the outcasts; bewray not him that
16. 4 Let mine outcasts dwell with thee, Moab
27. 13 and the outcasts in the land of Egypt, and
Jer. 30. 17 they called thee an outcast, (saying,) This
49. 36 whither the outcasts of Elam shall not

OUTER or UTTER —
1. *Outward, without, outer,* חִיצוֹן *chitson.*
Eze. 10. 5 sound..was heard (even) to the outer court
40. 31 arches thereof (were) toward the outer c.
40. 37 posts thereof (were) toward the outer court
42. 1 he brought me forth into the outer court
42. 3 the pavement which (was) for the outer c.
42. 7 the outer court on the fore part of the
42. 8 the chambers that (were) in the outer c.
42. 9 one goeth into them from the outer court
42. 14 shall they not go..into the outer court, but
44. 19 the outer court, (even) into the outer cou.
46. 20 bear (them) not out into the outer court
46. 21 he brought me forth into the outer court
2. *Outer, exterior,* ἐξώτερος *exōteros.*
Matt. 8. 12 But..shall be cast out into outer darkness
22. 13 cast (him) into outer darkness; there shall
25. 30 cast ye the..servant into outer darkness

OUTGO, to —
To come or go before, προέρχομαι *proerchomai.*
Mark 6. 33 [outwent them, and came together unto]

OUTGOING —
1. *Outgoing, place of outgoing,* מוֹצָא *motsa.*
Psa. 65. 8 thou makest the outgoings of the morn.
2. *Outgoings,* תּוֹצָאוֹת *totsaoth.*
Josh 17. 9 and the outgoings of it were at the sea
17. 18 the outgoings of it shall be thine: for thou
18. 19 the outgoings of the border were at the
19. 14 the outgoings thereof are in the valley of
19. 22 outgoings of their border were at Jordan
19. 29 outgoings thereof are at the sea from the
19. 33 and the outgoings thereof were at Jordan

OUTLANDISH —
Strange, unknown person, נָכְרִי *nokri.*
Neh. 13. 26 nevertheless even him did outlandish w.

OUTLIVE, OVERLIVE, to —
To prolong days after, הֶאֱרִיךְ יָמִים אַחַר *[arak, 5].*
Josh 24. 31 that overlived Joshua, and which had
Judg. 2. 7 all the days of the elders that outlived J.

OUTMOST (coast) —
1. *Outward,* קִיצוֹן *qitson.*
Exod 26. 10 edge of the one curtain (that is) outmost
2. *End, extremity,* קָצֶה *qatseh.*
Num 34. 3 border shall be the outmost coast of the

OUTRAGEOUS —
An overflowing, flood, שֶׁטֶף *sheteph.*
Prov 27. 4 Wrath (is) cruel, and anger (is) outrageo.

OUTRUN, to —
To run before quickly, προτρέχω τάχιον *protrechō.*
John 20. 4 other disciple did outrun Peter, and came

OUTSIDE —
1. *Outside, without,* חוּץ *chuts.*
1 Ki. 7. 9 (so) on the outside toward the great court
Eze. 40. 5 behold a wall on the outside of the house
2. *End, extremity,* קָצֶה *qatseh.*
Judg. 7. 11 unto the outside of the armed men that
7. 17 when I come to the outside of the camp
7. 19 came unto the outside of the camp in the
3. *Outside, without,* ἐκτός *ektos.*
Matt 23. 26 that the outside of them may be clean also
4. *From without, externally,* ἔξωθεν *exōthen.*
Matt 23. 25 for ye make clean the outside of the cup
Luke 11. 39 make clean the outside of the cup and the

OUTSTRETCHED —
To stretch out, נָטָה *natah.*
Deut 26. 8 a mighty hand, and with an outstretched
Jer. 21. 5 fight against you with an outstretched h.
27. 5 have made the earth..by my outstretched

OUTWARD —
1. *Outside, without,* חוּץ *chuts.*
Num 35. 4 and outward a thousand cubits round ab.
2. *Outward, without,* חִיצוֹן *chitson.*
1 Ch 26. 29 for the outward business over Israel, for
Neh. 11. 16 oversight of the outward business of the
Esth. 6. 4 Now Haman was come into the outward
Eze. 40. 17 Then brought he me into the outward co.
40. 20 gate of the outward court that looked to.
44. 1 way of the gate of the outward sanctuary
3. *Outside, without,* ἔξω *exō.*
2 Co. 4. 16 but though our outward man perish, yet
4. *From without, exterior,* ἔξωθεν *exōthen.*
Matt 23. 27 which indeed appear beautiful outward
1 Pe. 3. 3 Whose adorning let it not be that outward
5. *Manifestly,* ἐν τῷ φανερῷ *en tō phanerō.*
Rom. 2. 28 circumcision which is outward in the fle.

OUTWARD appearance—[*See* Appearance].

OUTWARDLY —
1. *Manifestly,* ἐν τῷ φανερῷ *en tō phanerō.*
Rom. 2. 28 For he is not a Jew which is one outwardly
2. *From without,* ἔξωθεν *exōthen.*
Matt 23. 28 Even so ye also outwardly appear right.

OVEN —
1. *Furnace, oven,* תַּנּוּר *tannur.*
Exod. 8. 3 into thine ovens, and into thy kneading
Lev. 2. 4 bring an oblation..baken in the oven, (it
7. 9 meat offering that is baken in the oven
11. 35 oven, or ranges for pots, they shall be b.
26. 26 women shall bake your bread in one oven
Psa. 21. 9 Thou shalt make them as a fiery oven in
Lam. 5. 10 Our skin was black like an oven because
Hos. 7. 4 adulterers, as an oven heated by the baker
7. 6 have made ready their heart like an oven
7. 7 They are all hot as an oven, and have de.
Mal. 4. 1 day cometh that shall burn as an oven; and
2. *Oven, furnace,* κλίβανος *klibanos.*
Matt. 6. 30 and to morrow is cast into the oven, (shall
Luke 12. 28 and to morrow is cast into the oven; how

OVER —
1. *In,* בְּ *be.*
2 Sa. 3. 21 that thou mayest reign over all that thine
2. *Through, over, behind,* בְּעַד *bead.*
2 Sa. 20. 21 head shall be thrown to thee over the w.
3. *More, farther,* יוֹתֵר *yother.*
Eccl. 7. 16 neither make thyself over wise: why sh.
4. *From, than, above,* מִן *min.*
1 Sa. 17. 50 So David prevailed over the Philistine
5. *Above, over,* לְמַעְלָה, מִלְמַעְלָה, מַעַל *maal, le-malah.*
Num. 4. 6 shall spread over (it) a cloth wholly of
1 Ch. 29. 3 over and above all that I have prepared
Ezra. 9. 6 our iniquities are increased over (our) h.
6. *At the front, before,* לְנֶגֶד *le-neged.*
Neh. 11. 22 singers (were) over the business of the h.
7. *Over, beyond,* עֵבֶר *eber.*
Deut 30. 13 Who shall go over the sea for us, and b.
8. *On, upon, over, above,* עַל *al.*
Gen. 8. 1 God made a wind to pass over the earth
Ezra 4. 20 There have been mighty kings also over
Dan. 2. 48 ruler over..and chief of the governors over
2. 49 over the affairs of the province of Babylon
3. 12 Jews whom thou hast set over the affairs
4. 16 changed..and let seven times pass over
4. 17 and setteth up over it the basest of men
4. 23 let it be wet..till seven times pass over
4. 25, 32 and seven times shall pass over thee
5. 21 he appointeth over it whomsoever he will
6. 1 It pleased Darius to set over the kingdom
6. 3 thought to set him over the whole realm
9. *Over above,* עֵלָּא מִן *ela min.*
Dan. 6. 2 over these three presidents, of whom D.
10. *Out of,* ἐκ *ek.*
Rev. 15. 2 victory over the beast, and over his image
15. 2 [over his mark, (and) over the number of]
11. *In, among,* ἐν *en.*
Acts 20. 28 to all the flock over the which the Holy G.
12. *Above, upon, over,* ἐπάνω *epanō.*
Matt. 2. 9 till it came and stood over where the yo.
27. 37 set up over his head his accusation writ.
Luke 4. 39 stood over her, and rebuked the fever; and
11. 44 the men that walk over (them) are not a.
19. 17 said unto him..have thou authority over
19. 19 said likewise to him, Be thou also over five
13. *On, upon, over,* ἐπί *(gen.) epi.*
Matt 24. 45 whom his lord hath made ruler over his
25. 21, 23 I will make thee ruler over many thi.
Luke 12. 42 whom (his) lord shall make ruler over his
Acts 6. 3 whom we may appoint over this business
Rom. 9. 5 Christ (came), who is over all, God blessed
Rev. 2. 26 to him will I give power over the nations
9. 11 had a king over them, (which is) the angel
11. 6 have power over waters to turn them to
14. 18 angel..which had power over fire; and c.
17. 18 which reigneth over the kings of the earth
14. *On, upon, over,* ἐπί *(dat.) epi.*
Matt 24. 47 he shall make him ruler over all his goods
Luke 12. 44 will make him ruler over all that he hath
15. 7 over one sinner..more than over ninety
15. 10 There is joy..over one sinner that repen.
19. 41 near, he beheld the city, and wept over it
23. 38 was written over him in letters of Greek
Acts 8. 2 and made great lamentation over him
1 Th. 3. 7 we were comforted over you in all our a.
Rev. 11. 10 shall rejoice over them, and make merry
18. 11 merchants..shall weep and mourn over
15. *On, upon, over, about,* ἐπί *(acc.) epi.*
Matt 25. 21, 23 thou hast been faithful over a few th.
27. 45 darkness over all the land unto the ninth
Mark 15. 33 darkness over the whole land until the n.
Luke 1. 33 shall reign over the house of Jacob for e.
2. 8 keeping watch over their flock by night
9. 1 gave them power and authority over all
10. 19 over all the power of the enemy: and no.
12. 14 who made me a judge or a divider over
19. 14 We will not have this (man) to reign over
19. 27 would not that I should reign over them
23. 44 darkness over all the earth until the ninth
Acts 7. 10 make him governor over Egypt and all his
7. 11 Now there came a dearth over all the land
7. 27 Who made thee a ruler and a judge over
19. 13 took upon them to call over them which
Rom. 5. 14 even over them that had not sinned after
2 Co. 3. 13 not as Moses, (which) put a veil over his
Heb. 2. 7 [didst set him over the works of thy hands]
3. 6 But Christ as a Son over his own house
10. 21 (having) an high priest over the house of G.
Jas. 5. 14 let them pray over him, anointing him w
1 Pet. 3. 12 For the eyes of the Lord (are) over the ri.
Rev. 6. 8 power was given unto them over the fourth
13. 7 power..given him over all kindreds, and
16. 9 which hath power over these plagues: and
18. 20 Rejoice over her, (thou) heaven, and (ye)
16. *Beyond, over, on the other side,* πέραν *peran.*
John 6. 1 Jesus went over the sea of Galilee, which
6. 17 and went over the sea toward Capernaum
18. 1 went forth with his disciples over the br.
17. *Concerning,* περί *(gen.) peri.*
Luke 4. 10 He shall give his angels charge over thee
1 Co. 7. 37 but hath power over his own will, and h.
18. *Above, beyond,* ὑπέρ *(acc.) huper.*
Eph. 1. 22 gave him (to be) the head over all (things)
19. *To be far above,* ὑπεράνω *huperanō.*
Heb. 9. 5 over it the cherubim of glory shadowing
[*See also* Against, boughs, bring, carry, come, conduct, convey, covered, dominion, get, give, go, going, grown, have, be lord, laid, pass, passed, passing, rule, run, running, sail, send, set, spread, stand, triumph, write.]

OVER, to be —
1. *To change, pass on, away, through,* חָלַף *chalaph.*
Song 2. 11 the winter is past, the rain is over (and)
2. *To stand over,* עָמַד עַל *amad al.*
Num. 7. 2 and were over them that were numbered
3. *To set before,* προΐστημι *proistēmi.*
1 Th. 5. 12 are over you in the Lord, and admonish

OVER (and above), to have or be —
1. *To be over and above, superfluous,* עָדַף *adaph.*
Num. 3. 49 them that were over and above them that
2. *To have superfluity,* עָדַף *adaph,* 5, Exod. 16. 18.
3. *Have more than enough,* πλεονάζω, 2 Cor. 8. 15.

OVER against —
1. *In front of,* אֶל מוּל *el mul.* Josh. 8. 33.
1a. *Straight opposite,* נֹכַח *nekach.* Eze. 46. 9.
2. *On the face of,* עַל־פְּנֵי *al pene.*
Num. 8. 2 seven lamps shall give light over against
8. 3 he lighted the lamps thereof over against
Deut 32. 49 land of Moab, that (is) over against, 34. 1.
1 Sa. 15. 7 comest to Shur, that (is) over against Egy.
Eze. 48. 15, 48. 21 over against the five and twenty
3. *Over against, before,* קֳבֵל, קְבֵל *qobel, qebel.*
Dan. 5. 5 wrote over against the candlestick upon
4. *Over against, opposite to,* ἀντικρύ *antikru.*
Acts 20. 15 and came the next (day) over against Ch.
5. *Over against, on the opposite side,* ἀντιπέραν.
Luke 8. 26 Gadarenes, which is over against Galilee
6. *Over against, in opposition to,* ἀπέναντι *apenanti.*
Matt. 21. 2 Go into the village [over against] you, and
27. 61 other Mary, sitting over against the sep.
7. *Of the opposite side,* ἐξ ἐναντίας *ex enantias.*
Mark 15. 39 centurion, which stood over against him
8. *Down to, over against,* κατά *(acc.) kata.*
Acts 27. 7 scarce were come over against Cnidus, the
27. 7 we sailed under Crete, over against Salm.
9. *Over against,* κατέναντι *katenanti.*
Mark 11. 2 Go your way into the village over against
12. 41 Jesus sat [over against] the treasury, and
13. 3 the mount of Olives, over against the te.
Luke 19. 30 Go ye into the village over against (you)

OVERCHARGE, be overcharged, to —
1. *To be loaded, burdened,* βαρύνομαι *barunomai.*
Luke 21. 34 at any time your hearts be overcharged
2. *To overload, over burden,* ἐπιβαρέω *epibareō.*
2 Co. 2. 5 in part; that I may not overcharge you

OVERCOME, to —
1. *To assault,* גּוּד *gud.*
Gen. 49. 19 overcome him: but he shall overcome at

2. *To be able, prevail,* יָכֹל *yakol.*
Num 13. 30 possess it; for we are well able to overco.

3. *To consume,* לָחַם *lacham,* 2.
Num22. 11 peradventure I shall be able to overcome
2 Ki. 16. 5 besieged Ahaz, but could not overcome

4. *To pass over,* עָבַר *abar.*
Jer. 23. 9 like a man whom wine hath overcome, be.

5. *To enlarge, puff up,* רָהַב *rahab,* 5.
Song 6. 5 for they have overcome me: thy hair (is)

6. *To be or become inferior,* ἡττάομαι *hettaomai.*
2 Pe. 2. 19 for of whom a man is overcome, of the sa.
2. 20 For if..they are again..overcome, the

7. *To domineer, have full power,* κατακυριεύω, *kat.*
Acts 19. 16 overcame them, and prevailed against th.

8. *To gain the victory,* νικάω *nikaō.*
Luke 11. 22 when a stronger than he shall..overcome
John16. 33 be of good cheer; I have overcome the w.
Rom. 3. 4 mightest overcome when thou art judged
12. 21 of evil, but overcome evil with good
1 Jo. 2. 13, 14 ye have overcome the wicked one
4. 4 have overcome them; because greater is
5. 4 whatsoever is born of God overcometh the
5. 4 the victory that overcometh the world,(ev.)
5. 5 Who is he that overcometh the world, but
Rev. 2. 7, 17 To him that overcometh will I give to
2. 11 He that overcometh shall not be hurt of
2. 26 he that overcometh, and keepeth my works
3. 5 He that overcometh, the same shall be cl.
3. 12 Him that overcometh will I make a pillar
3. 21 To him that overcometh..as I also overc.
11. 7 and shall overcome them, and kill them
12. 11 overcame him by the blood of the Lamb, and
13. 7 [it was given unto him..to overcome them]
17. 14 Lamb shall overcome them: for he is Lord
21. 7 He that overcometh shall inherit all things

OVERCOME (with), to be —

1. *Weakness,* חֲלוּשָׁה *chalushah.*
Exod32. 18 voice of (them that) cry for being overcome

2. *To beat, beat down,* הָלַם *halam.*
Isa. 28. 1 valleys of them that are overcome with w.

3. *To gain victory,* νικάω *nikaō.*
Rom.12. 21 Be not overcome of evil, but..evil with

OVERDRIVE, to —

To beat, knock, דָּפַק *daphaq.*
Gen. 33. 13 if men should overdrive them one day, all

OVERFLOW, to —

1. *To run over,* שׁוּק *shuq,* 5.
Joel 2. 24 the fats shall overflow with wine and oil
3. 13 fats overflow: for their wickedness (is)

2. *To overflow,* שָׁטַף *shataph.*
Psa. 69. 2 deep waters, where the floods overflow me
69. 15 Let not the water flood overflow me, nei.
78. 20 streams overflowed; can he give bread
Isa. 8. 8 he shall overflow and go over; he shall
10. 22 the consumption decreed shall overflow
28. 17 the waters shall overflow the hiding place
43. 2 they shall not overflow thee: when thou
Jer. 47. 2 waters rise up..and shall overflow the la.
Dan. 11. 10 shall certainly come, and overflow, and
11. 26 his army shall overflow; and many shall
11. 40 countries, and shall overflow and pass

3. *To be full over,* מָלֵא עַל *male al.*
Josh. 3. 15 for Jordan overfloweth all his banks all

4. *To fill over,* מָלֵא עַל *male* (3) *al.*
1 Ch.12. 15 when it had overflown all his banks; and

OVERFLOW, to make to —

To cause to flow, צוּף *tsuph,* 5.
Deut11. 4 made the water..to overflow them, as they

OVERFLOWED or OVERFLOWN, to be —

1. *To be poured out,* יָצַק *yatsaq,* 6.
Job 22 16 whose foundation was overflown with a

2. *To be overflown,* שָׁטַף *shataph,* 2.
Dan. 11. 22 shall they be overflown from before him

3. *To be overflowed, thoroughly washed,* κατακλύζω.
2 Pe. 3. 6 world that then was, being overflowed

OVERFLOWING —

1. *Weeping,* בְּכִי *beki.*
Job 28. 11 He bindeth the floods from overflowing

2. *Inundation,* זֶרֶם *zerem.*
Hab. 3. 10 the overflowing of the water passed by

3. *To overflow,* שָׁטַף *shataph.*
Isa. 28. 2 as a flood of mighty waters overflowing
28. 15, 18 when the overflowing scourge shall p.
30. 28 his breath, as an overflowing stream, shall
Jer. 47. 2 shall be an overflowing flood, and shall
Eze. 13. 11, 13 there shall be an overflowing shower
38. 22 an overflowing rain, and great hailstones

4. *Overflowing,* שֶׁטֶף *sheteph.*
Job 38. 25 divided a watercourse for the overflowing

OVERLAID, to be —

1. *To be covered, wrapped up,* עָלַף *alaph,* 4.
Song 5. 14 belly (is as) bright ivory overlaid (with)

2. *To be overlaid, covered, spread out,* צָפָה *tsaphah,* 4.
Exod26. 32 pillars of shittim (wood) overlaid with g.

3. *To cover round about,* περικαλύπτω *perikaluptō.*
Heb. 9. 4 ark of the covenant overlaid round about

OVERLAY, to —

1. *To cover, ceil,* חָפָה *chaphah,* 3.
2 Ch. 3. 5 which he overlaid with fine gold, and set
3. 7 He overlaid also the house, the beams, the
3. 8 overlaid it with fine gold, (amounting) to
3. 9 he overlaid the upper chambers with gold

2. *To plaister, daub, overlay,* טוּחַ *tuach.*
1 Ch.29. 4 to overlay the walls of the houses (with.)

3. *To cover, overlay,* צָפָה *tsaphah,* 3.
Exod25. 11 And thou shalt overlay it with pure gold
25. 11 within and without shalt thou overlay it
25. 13 make staves..and overlay them with gold
25. 24 thou shalt overlay it with pure gold, and
25. 28 overlay them with gold, that the table may
26. 29, 29 And thou shalt overlay..with gold
26. 37 overlay them with gold, (and) their hooks
27. 2 and thou shalt overlay it with brass
27. 6 shalt make staves..and overlay them with
30. 3 thou shalt overlay it with pure gold, the
30. 5 shalt make the staves. and overlay them
36. 34 overlaid the boards..and overlaid the bars
36. 36 overlaid them with gold: their hooks (we.
36. 38 he overlaid their chapiters and their fillets
37. 2, 11, 26 And he overlaid it with pure gold
37. 4, 15, 28 and overlaid them with gold
38. 2 made the horns..and he overlaid it with
38. 6 made the staves..and overlaid them with
38. 28 overlaid their chapiters, and filleted them
1 Ki. 6. 20 overlaid it with pure gold; and (so) cove.
6. 21 overlaid the house..and he overlaid it w.
6. 22 the whole house he overlaid with gold
6. 22 that (was) by the oracle he overlaid with
6. 28 And he overlaid the cherubim with gold
6. 30 floor of the house he overlaid with gold
6. 32 overlaid (them) with gold, and spread gold
10. 18 made a great throne of ivory, and overlaid
2 Ki.18. 16 which Hezekiah king of Judah had overl.
2 Ch. 3. 4 And he overlaid it within with pure gold
3. 10 made two cherubim..and overlaid them
4. 9 and overlaid the doors of them with brass
9. 17 made a great throne of ivory, and overlaid

4. *To lie upon,* שָׁכַב עַל *shakab al.*
1 Ki. 3. 19 died in the night; because she overlaid it

OVERLAYING —

Overlaying, covering, צִפּוּי *tsippui.*
Exod38. 17 the overlaying of their chapiters (of) silver
38. 19 overlaying of their chapiters and their fi.

OVER MUCH, (to be) —

1. *To cause to multiply, make abundant,* רָבָה *rabah,* 5.
Eccl. 7. 16 Be not righteous over much
7. 17 Be not over much wicked, neither be thou

2. *Over abundantly,* περισσότερος *perissoteros.*
2 Co. 2. 7 be swallowed up with over much sorrow

OVERPASS, be overpast, to —

To go or pass over, עָבַר *abar.*
Psa. 57. 1 refuge, until (these) calamities be overp.
Isa. 26. 20 hide..until the indignation be overpast
Jer. 5. 28 yea, they overpass the deeds of the wicked

OVERPLUS —

To be over and above, superfluous, עָדַף *adaph.*
Lev. 25. 27 restore the overplus unto the man to wh.

OVERRUN, to —

To go or pass over, עָבַר *abar.*
2 Sa.18. 23 ran by the way of the plain, and overran
Nah. 1. 8 But with an overrunning flood he will m.

OVERSEE, to —

To overlook, be pre-eminent, נָצַח *natsach,* 3.
2 Ch. 2. 2 three thousand and six hundred to overs.

OVERSEER, (to make) —

1. *To overlook, be pre-eminent,* נָצַח *natsach,* 3.
2 Ch. 2. 18 three thousand and six hundred overseers
34. 13 overseers of all that wrought the work in

2. *To be overlooked, inspected,* פָּקַד *paqad,* 6.
2 Ch.34. 12 overseers of them (were) Jahath and Ob.
34. 17 delivered it into the hand of the overse.

3. *To make inspector,* פָּקַד *paqad,* 5.
Gen. 39. 4 made him overseer over his house, and
39. 5 from the time (that) he had made him o.

4. *Inspector,* פָּקִיד *paqid.*
2 Ch. 31. 13 overseers under the hand of Cononiah and
Neh. 11. 9 Joel the son of Zichri (was) their overseer
11. 14 their overseer (was) Zabdiel, the son of
11. 22 The overseer also of the Levites at Jerus.
12. 42 singers sang loud, with Jezrahiah (their) o.

5. *To administrate,* שָׁטַר *shatar.*
Prov. 6. 7 Which having no guide, overseer, or ruler

6. *Overseer, inspector,* ἐπίσκοπος *episkopos.*
Acts 20. 28 the Holy Ghost hath made you overseers

OVERSHADOW, to —

To overshadow, ἐπισκιάζω *episkiazō.*
Matt17. 5 bright cloud overshadowed them: and b.
Mark 9. 7 there was a cloud that overshadowed them
Luke 1. 35 power of the Highest shall overshadow t.
9. 34 there came a cloud and overshadowed t.
Acts 5. 15 passing by might overshadow some of them

OVERSIGHT —

1. *Oversight, error,* מִשְׁגֶּה *mishgeh.*
Gen. 43. 12 hand; peradventure it (was) an oversight

2. *Oversight, charge, inspection,* פְּקֻדָּה *pequddah.*
Num. 3. 32 oversight of them that keep the charge of
4. 16 oversight of all the tabernacle, and of all

OVERSIGHT, to have or take the — [*paqad,* 1].

1. *Be put in charge,* פָּקַד *paqad,* 6 [2 Ki. 12. 11, V.L. p.p.
2 Ki. 12. 11 that had the oversight of the house of the
22. 5, 9 that have the oversight of; 2 Ch. 34. 10.

2. *Entrusted with,* נָתוּן בְּ [*nathan*]. Neh. 13. 4.

3. *To look over, inspect,* ἐπισκοπέω *episkopeō.*
1 Pe. 5. 2 taking the oversight (thereof), not by con.

OVERSPREAD, overspreading, to be —

1. *A wing,* כָּנָף *kanaph.*
Dan. 9. 27 for the overspreading of abominations he

2. *To spread out,* נָפַץ *naphats.*
Gen. 9. 19 of them was the whole earth overspread

OVERTAKE, be overtaken, to —

1. *To cleave or adhere to,* דָּבַק *dabeq,* 5.
Gen. 31. 23 and they overtook him in the mount Gilead
Judg18. 22 gathered together, and overtook the chil.
20. 42 but the battle overtook them; and them

2. *To come or draw nigh,* נָגַשׁ *nagash,* 2.
Amos 9. 13 the plowman shall overtake the reaper

3. *To cause to come nigh, approach,* נָגַשׁ *nagash,* 5.
Amos 9. 10 The evil shall not overtake nor prevent us

4. *To cause to reach, attain, overtake,* נָשַׂג *nasag,* 5.
Gen. 31. 25 Then Laban overtook Jacob. Now Jacob
44. 4 when thou dost overtake them, say unto
44. 6 overtook them, and he spake unto them
Exod14. 9 overtook them encamping by the sea, be.
15. 9 enemy said, I will pursue, I will overtake
Deut19. 6 overtake him, because the way is long, and
28. 2 overtake thee, if thou shalt hearken unto
28. 15 curses shall come upon thee, and overtake
28. 45 and overtake thee, till thou be destroyed
Josh. 2. 5 pursue after them..for ye shall overtake
1 Sa. 30. 8 shall I overtake..thou shalt surely overt.
2 Sa. 15. 14 depart, lest he overtake us suddenly, and
2 Ki. 25. 5 overtook him in the plains of Jericho: and
1 Ch.21. 12 that the sword of thine enemies overtak.
Psa. 18. 37 pursued mine enemies..overtaken them
Isa. 59. 9 neither doth justice overtake us: we wait
Jer. 39. 5 overtook Zedekiah in the plains of Jericho
42. 16 which ye feared, shall overtake you there
52. 8 overtook Zedekiah in the plains of Jericho
Lam. 1. 3 persecutors overtook her between the st.
Hos. 2. 7 shall not overtake them; and she shall seek
10. 9 children of iniquity did not overtake them

5. *To take thoroughly,* καταλαμβάνω *katalambanō.*
1 Th. 5. 4 that that day should overtake you as a t.

6. *To take publicly,* προλαμβάνω *prolambanō.*
Gal. 6. 1 if a man be overtaken in a fault, ye which

OVERTHROW —

1. *Overthrow,* הֲפֵכָה *haphekah.*
Gen. 19. 29 sent Lot out of the midst of the overthrow

2. *Overthrow,* מַהְפֵּכָה *mahpekah.*
Deut29. 23 like the overthrow of Sodom, and Gomo.
Jer. 49. 18 As in the overthrow of Sodom and Gom.

3. *Catastrophe, overthrow,* καταστροφή *katastrophē.*
2 Pe. 2. 6 condemned (them) with an overthrow, m.

OVERTHROW, to —

1. *To thrust away or down,* דָּחָה *dachah.*
Psa.140. 4 who have purposed to overthrow my go.

2. *To turn, overturn,* הָפַךְ *haphak.*
Gen. 19. 21 not overthrow this city, for the which t.
19. 25 overthrew those cities, and all the plain
19. 29 overthrew the cities in the which Lot d.
Deut 29. 23 Zeboim, which the LORD overthrew in h.
2 Sa. 10. 3 and to spy it out, and to overthrow (it)?
1 Ch.19. 3 for to search, and to overthrow, and to s.
Jer. 20. 16 be as the cities which the LORD overthrew
Lam. 4. 6 overthrown as in a moment, and no hands
Amos 4. 11 I have overthrown (some) of you, as God
Hag. 2. 22 overthrow the throne..and I will overth

3. *To break, throw down,* הָרַס *haras.*
Exod15. 7 thou hast overthrown them that rose up
2 Sa. 11. 25 make thy battle more strong..and overt.
Prov 29. 4 but he that receiveth gifts overthroweth

4. *To break, throw down,* הָרַס *haras,* 3.
Exod23. 24 thou shalt utterly overthrow them, and

5. *Pressings, overthrowings,* מַדְחֵפֹת *madchephoth.*
Psa.140. 11 evil shall hunt the violent man to overt.

6. *Overthrow, overturn,* מַהְפֵּכָה *mahpekah.*
Isa. 13. 19 shall be as when God overthrew Sodom
Jer. 50. 40 As God overthrew Sodom and Gomorrah
Amos 4. 11 as God overthrew Sodom and Gomorrah

7. *To stretch out, incline,* נָטָה *natah,* 5.
Prov 18. 5 to overthrow the righteous in judgment

8. *To shake off,* נָעַר *naar,* 3.
Exod14. 27 overthrew the Egyptians in the midst of
Psa.136. 15 overthrew Pharaoh and his host in the Red

9. *To cause to fall,* נָפַל *naphal,* 5.
Psa.106. 26 lifted up his hand .to overthrow them in
106. 27 To overthrow their seed also among the

10. *To break down,* נָתַץ *nathats,* 3.
Deut12. 3 ye shall overthrow their altars, and break

11. *To overthrow, pervert,* סָלַף *salaph,* 3.
Job 12. 19 leadeth princes away spoiled, and overth.

Prov 13. 6 but wickedness overthroweth the sinner
21. 12 overthroweth the wicked for (their) wic.
22. 12 overthroweth the words of the transgres.
12. *To turn upside down*, עָוַת *avath*, 3.
Job 19. 6 Know now that God hath overthrown me
13. *To turn up or over*, ἀναστρέφω *anastrephō.*
John 2. 15 drove them all out..and overthrew the t.
14. *To turn up or over*, ἀνατρέπω *anatrepō.*
2 Ti. 2. 18 have erred..and overthrow the faith of some
15. *To loose down, dissolve*, καταλύω *kataluō.*
Acts 5. 39 But if it be of God, ye cannot overthrow
16. *To turn down*, καταστρέφω *katastrephō.*
Matt 21. 12 overthrew the tables of the money chan.
Mark 11. 15 overthrew the tables of the money chan.

OVERTHROWN, to be —
1. *To turn, overturn*, הָפַךְ *haphak.*
Prov 12. 7 The wicked are overthrown, and (are) not
Lam. 4. 6 (that was) overthrown as in a moment
2. *To be turned, overturned*, הָפַךְ *haphak*, 2.
Jon. 3. 4 Yet forty days, and Nineveh shall be ov.
3. *To break or throw down*, הָרַס *haras*, 2.
Prov 11. 11 is overthrown by the mouth of the wicked
4. *To be feeble, stumbled*, כָּשַׁל *kashal*, 2.
Dan. 11. 41 and many (countries) shall be overthrown
5. *To be caused to stumble*, כָּשַׁל *kashal*, 6.
Jer. 18. 23 but let them be overthrown before thee
6. *Overturn, overthrow*, מַהְפֵּכָה *mahpekah.*
Isa. 1. 7 (it is) desolate, as overthrown by strangers
7. *To fall*, נָפַל *naphal.*
Judg. 9. 40 and many were overthrown (and) wounded
2 Sa. 17. 9 when some of them be overthrown at the
8. *To be destroyed, cut off, laid waste*, שָׁמַד *shamad*, 2.
Prov 14. 11 The house of the wicked shall be overth.
9. *To be let go, thrown down*, שָׁמַט *shamat*, 2.
Psa. 141. 6 When their judges are overthrown in st.
10. *To strew down*, καταστρώννυμι *katastrōnnumi.*
1 Co. 10. 5 for they were overthrown in the wildern.

OVERTURN, to —
1. *To overturn (upwards)* הָפַךְ (לְמַעְלָה) *haphak (le-malah)*
Judg. 7. 13 and overturned it, that the tent lay along
Job 9. 5 which overturneth them in his anger
12. 15 sendeth them out, and they overturn the
28. 9 overturneth the mountains by the roots
34. 25 he overturneth (them) in the night, so that
2. *To make an overturn*, שׂוּם עַוָּה *sum avvah.*
Eze. 21. 27 I will overturn, overturn, overturn it: and

OVERWHELM, to —
1. *To cover*, כָּסָה *kasah*, 3.
Psa. 55. 5 come upon me, and horror hath overwhe.
78. 53 but the sea overwhelmed their enemies
2. *To cause to fall*, נָפַל *naphal*, 5.
Job 6. 27 ye overwhelm the fatherless, and ye dig (a
3. *To overflow*, שָׁטַף *shataph.*
Psa. 124. 4 Then the waters had overwhelmed us, the

OVERWHELMED, to be —
1. *To be feeble*, עָטַף *ataph.*
Psa. 61. 2 when my heart is overwhelmed: lead me
102. title. prayer of the afflicted, when he is over.
2. *To show self feeble*, עָטַף *ataph*, 7.
Psa. 77. 3 complained, and my spirit was overwhel.
142. 3 When my spirit was overwhelmed within
143. 4 Therefore is my spirit overwhelmed within

OWE (besides), to —
1. *To owe, be obliged, indebted*, ὀφείλω *opheilō.*
Matt 18. 28 found one..which owed him an hundred
18. 28 laid hands..saying, Pay me that thou o.
Luke 7. 41 one owed five hundred pence, and the ot.
16. 5 said..How much owest thou unto my l.?
16. 7 said he to another, And how much owest
Rom 13. 8 Owe no man any thing, but to love one a.
Phm. 18 If he hath wronged thee, or oweth (thee)
2. *To owe besides*, προσοφείλω *prosopheilō.*
Phm. 19 I do not say to thee how thou owest..besid.

OWED, which —
A debtor, one who is owing, ὀφειλέτης *opheiletēs.*
Matt 18. 24 one was brought unto him, which owed

OWL (great, little, or screech) —
1. *Night owl, ibis*, יַנְשׁוּף *yanshuph.*
Lev. 11. 17 and the cormorant, and the great owl
Deut 14. 16 The little..and the great owl, and the s.
Isa. 34. 11 the owl also and the raven shall dwell in
2. *Pelican, little owl*, כּוֹס *kos.*
Lev. 11. 17 And the little owl, and the cormorant, and
Deut 14. 16 The little owl, and the great..and the s.
Psa. 102. 6 wilderness; I am like an owl of the desert
3. *Daughter of howling, ostrich*, בַּת יַעֲנָה *bath yaanah.*
Lev. 11. 16 the owl, and the night hawk, and the cu.
Deut 14. 15 the owl, and the night hawk, and the cu.
Job 30. 29 brother to dragons, and a companion to o.
Isa. 13. 21 owls shall dwell there, and satyrs shall d.
34. 13 habitation of dragons..a court for owls
43. 20 shall honour me, the dragons and the owls
Jer. 50. 39 owls shall dwell therein: and it shall be
Mic. 1. 8 I will make a..mourning as the owls
4. *Night owl*, לִילִית *lilith.*
Isa. 34. 14 screech owl also shall rest there, and find
5. *Bittern, arrow snake*, קִפּוֹז *qippoz.*
Isa. 34. 15 There shall the great owl make her nest

OWN —
1. *Soul, breath*, נֶפֶשׁ *nephesh.*
Prov 14. 10 heart knoweth his own bitterness; and a
2. *Priest*, כֹּהֵן *kohen.*
Lev. 14. 26 pour..into the palm of his own left hand
3. *He, it*, αὐτός *autos.*
Luke 2. 35 sword shall pierce through thy own soul
Acts 21. 11 bound his own hands and feet, and said
4. *Genuine*, γνήσιος *gnēsios*
1 Ti. 1. 2 Unto Timothy, (my) own son in the faith
Titus 1. 4 To Titus, (mine) own son after the comm.
5. *One's own*, ἴδιος *idios.*
John 1. 11 He came unto..and his own received him n.
10. 12 whose own the sheep are not, seeth the wolf
19. 27 that disciple took her unto his own (ho.)
Acts 2. 6 every man heard them speak in his own
2. 8 how hear we every man in our own tong.
2 Pe. 3. 3 scoffers, walking after their own lusts
3. 16 wrest..unto their own destruction
Titus 1. 12 One of themselves..a prophet of their own

OWN, to —
Whose is, οὗ ἐστιν *hou estin.*
Acts 21. 11 bind the man that owneth this girdle, and
[*See also* Accord, conceits, country, freewill, hands, her, his, mine, nation, our, their, thine.]

OWN (voluntary) will —
Good pleasure, or will, רָצוֹן *ratson.*
Lev. 1. 3 shall offer it of his own voluntary will at
19. 5 the LORD, ye shall offer it at your own w.
22. 19 (Ye shall offer) at your own will a male
22. 29 will offer a sacrifice..at your own will
Dan. 11. 16 shall do according to his own will, and

OWN (poets) —
Down among, κατά (acc.) *kata.*
Acts 17. 28 your own poets have said, For we are also

OWNER —
1. *Lord, master*, אָדוֹן *adon.*
1 Ki. 16. 24 after the name of Shemer, owner of the
2. *Owner*, בַּעַל *baal.*
Exod 21. 28 but the owner of the ox (shall be) quit
21. 29 testified to his owner..his owner also shall
21. 34 owner..shall..give money unto the owner
21. 36 his owner hath not kept him in; he shall
22. 11 owner of it shall accept (thereof), and he
22. 12 shall make restitution unto the owner
22. 14 owner thereof (being) not with it; he sh.
22. 15 owner thereof (be) with it, he shall not
Job 31. 39 have caused the owners thereof to lose
Prov. 1. 19 taketh away the life of the owners thereof
Eccl. 5. 11 and what good (is there) to the owners
5. 13 riches kept for the owners thereof to their
3. *To acquire, purchase*, קָנָה *qanah* (partic.).
Isa. 1. 3 The ox knoweth his owner, and the ass
4. *Lord, master, sir*, κύριος *kurios.*
Luke 19. 33 owners thereof said unto them, Why loose

OX, OXEN —
1. *Ox or cow*, אַלּוּף, אֶלֶף *alluph.*
Psa. 144. 14 our oxen (may be) strong to labour; (that
Jer. 11. 19 But I (was) like a lamb (or) an ox (that) is
2. *Oxen, herd, cattle*, בָּקָר *baqar.*
Gen. 12. 16 he had sheep, and oxen, and he asses, and
20. 14 Abimelech took sheep, and oxen, and men
21. 27 Abraham took sheep and oxen, and gave
34. 28 They took their sheep, and their oxen, and
Exod. 9. 3 upon the camels, upon the oxen, and upon
20. 24 peace offerings, thy sheep, and thine oxen
22. 1 he shall restore five oxen..and four sheep
Num. 7. 3 covered wagons, and twelve oxen
7. 6 Moses took the wagons and the oxen, and
7. 7 Two wagons and four oxen he gave unto
7. 8 four wagons and eight oxen he gave unto
7. 17, 23, 29, 35, 41, 47, 53, 59, 65, 71, 77, 83 oxen
7. 87 All the oxen for the burnt offering (were)
7. 88 all the oxen, for the sacrifice of the peace
22. 40 offered oxen and sheep, and sent to Bal.
Deut 14. 26 for oxen, or for sheep, or for wine, or for
Judg. 3. 31 slew..six hundred men with an ox goad
1 Sa. 11. 7 took a yoke of oxen, and hewed them in
11. 7 so shall it be done unto his oxen. And the
14. 32 took sheep, and oxen, and calves, and s.
15. 9, 15 the best of the sheep, and of the oxen
15. 14 and the lowing of the oxen which I hear?
15. 21 people took of the spoil, sheep and oxen
27. 9 took away the sheep, and the oxen, and
2 Sa. 6. 6 and took hold of it; for the oxen shook
24. 22 oxen for burnt sacrifice, and threshing i.
24. 22 and (other) instruments of the oxen for
24. 24 bought the threshing floor and the oxen
1 Ki. 1. 9 Adonijah slew sheep and oxen and fat c..
4. 23 Ten fat oxen, and twenty oxen out of the
7. 25 It stood upon twelve oxen, three looking
7. 29 between the ledges (were) lions, oxen, and
7. 29 beneath the lions and oxen (were) certain
7. 44 one sea, and twelve oxen under the sea
8. 5 sacrificing sheep and oxen, that could not
8. 63 two and twenty thousand oxen, and an h.
19. 20 left the oxen, and ran after Elijah, and s.
19. 21 took a yoke of oxen, and slew them, and
1 Ki. 19. 21 boiled..with the instruments of the oxen
2 Ki. 5. 26 vineyards, and sheep, and oxen, and men
16. 17 took down the sea from off the brasen o.
1 Ch. 12. 40 brought bread..on oxen..and oil, and ox.
13. 9 put forth his hand..for the oxen stumbled
21. 23 I give (thee) the oxen (also) for burnt off.
2 Ch. 4. 3 under it (was) the similitude of oxen, wh.
4. 3 Two rows of oxen (were) cast, when it was
4. 4 It stood upon twelve oxen, three looking
4. 15 One sea, and twelve oxen under it
5. 6 sacrificed sheep and oxen, which could not
7. 5 sacrifice of twenty and two thousand oxen
15. 11 seven hundred oxen and seven thousand
18. 2 killed sheep and oxen for him in abund.
29. 33 consecrated things (were) six hundred o.
31. 6 also brought in the tithe of oxen and sh.
35. 8 gave unto the priests..three hundred oxen
35. 9 gave unto the Levites..five hundred oxen
35. 12 they removed..and so (did they) with the o.
Job 1. 3 five hundred yoke of oxen, and five hund.
1. 14 oxen were plowing, and the asses feeding
40. 15 Behold now..he eateth grass as an ox
42. 12 for he had..a thousand yoke of oxen, and
Isa. 11. 7 and the lion shall eat straw like the ox
22. 13 slaying oxen and killing sheep, eating fl.
Amos 6. 12 will (one) plow (there) with oxen? for ye
3. *A bullock, calf*, פַּר *par.*
Exod 24. 5 sacrificed peace offerings of oxen unto the
Num 23. 1 prepare me here seven oxen and seven r.
4. *Ox, bull*, שׁוֹר *shor.*
Gen. 32. 5 I have oxen, and asses, flocks, and men s.
Exod 20. 17 shalt not covet..his ox, nor his ass, nor
21. 28 If an ox gore a man..then the ox shall be
21. 28 not be eaten; but the owner of the ox
21. 29 But if the ox were wont to push with his
21. 29 ox shall be stoned, and his owner also s.
21. 32 If the ox shall push..the ox shall be sto.
21. 33 not cover it, and an ox or an ass fall the.
21. 35 if one man's ox hurt another's, that he die
21. 35 shall sell the live ox, and divide the mo.
21. 36 Or if it be known that the ox hath used
21. 36 he shall surely pay ox for ox; and the d.
22. 1 If a man shall steal an ox, or a sheep, and
22. 1 restore five..for an ox, and four sheep for
22. 4 whether it be ox, or ass, or sheep, he shall
22. 9 for ox, for ass, for sheep, for raiment, (or)
22. 10 If a man deliver..an ox, or a sheep, or any
22. 30 Likewise shalt thou do with thine oxen
23. 4 If thou meet thine enemy's ox or his ass
23. 12 that thine ox and thine ass may rest, and
34. 19 every firstling..ox or sheep, (that is male)
Lev. 7. 23 Ye shall eat no manner of fat, of ox, or of
17. 3 What man soever..killeth an ox, or lamb
27. 26 whether (it be) ox or sheep, it (is) the L.
Num. 7. 3 for each one an ox: and they brought th.
22. 4 as the ox licketh up the grass of the field
Deut. 5. 14 thou shalt not do any work..nor thine ox
5. 21 neither shalt thou covet..his ox, or his
14. 4 beasts which ye shall eat: The ox, the s.
18. 3 whether (it be) ox or sheep; and they sh.
22. 1 Thou shalt not see thy brother's ox or his
22. 4 not see thy brother's..ox fall down by the
22. 10 Thou shalt not plow with an ox and an ass
25. 4 Thou shalt not muzzle the ox when he tre.
28. 31 Thine ox (shall be) slain before thine eyes
Josh. 6. 21 utterly destroyed..ox, and sheep, and ass
7. 24 his daughters, and his oxen, and his asses
Judg. 6. 4 left no sustenance..neither sheep, nor ox
1 Sa. 12. 3 whose ox have I taken? or whose ass ha.
14. 34 Bring me hither every man his ox, and e.
14. 34 brought every man his ox with him that
15. 3 slay both..ox and sheep, camel and ass
22. 19 sucklings, and oxen, and asses, and sheep
2 Sa. 6. 13 it was (so), that..he sacrificed oxen and
1 Ki. 1. 19 he hath slain oxen and fat cattle and sh.
1. 25 hath slain oxen and fat cattle and sheep
Neh. 5. 18 one ox, (and) six choice sheep; also fowls
Job 6. 5 Doth the wild ass bray..or loweth the ox
24. 3 they take the widow's ox for a pledge
Psa. 69. 31 shall please the LORD better than an ox
106. 20 into the similitude of an ox that eateth g.
Prov. 7. 22 as an ox goeth to the slaughter, or as a fool
14. 4 increase (is) by the strength of the ox
15. 17 than a stalled ox and hatred therewith
Isa. 1. 3 ox knoweth his owner, and the ass his m.
7. 25 it shall be for the sending forth of oxen
32. 20 send forth (thither) the feet of the ox
66. 3 He that killeth an ox (is as if) he slew a
Eze. 1. 10 they four had the face of an ox on the left
5. *Ox, bull*, תּוֹר *tor.*
Dan. 4. 25, 32 they shall make thee to eat grass as o.
4. 33 did eat grass as oxen, and his body was
5. 21 they fed him with grass like oxen, and
6. *A beeve, bull, cow*, βοῦς *bous.*
Luke 13. 15 doth not each one..loose his ox or (his) ass
14. 5 Which of you shall have an ass or an ox fal.
14. 19 said, I have bought five yoke of oxen, and
John 2. 14 found in the temple those that sold oxen
2. 15 he drove them all out..and the oxen; and
1 Co. 9. 9 shalt not muzzle the mouth of the ox that
9. 9 it is written..Doth God take care for oxen?
1 Ti. 5. 18 Thou shalt not muzzle the ox that tread.
7. *A bull, beeve*, ταῦρος *tauros.*
Matt 22. 4 my oxen and (my) fatlings (are) killed, and
Acts 14. 13 brought oxen and garlands unto the gates
8. *Ox, cow*, אֶלֶף *eleph.*
Psa. 8. 7 All sheep and oxen, yea, and the beasts
Isa. 30. 24 oxen likewise and the young asses that ear

OX, wild —
Antelope, goat, תְּאוֹ *teo.*
Deut14. 5 pygarg, and the wild ox, and the chamois

O'-ZEM, אֹצֶם *strength.*
1. Sixth son of Jesse the Bethlehemite. B.C. 1090.
1 Ch. 2. 15 O. the sixth, David the seventh
2. A son of Jerahmeel, son of Hezron. B.C. 1500.
1 Ch. 2. 25 and Bunah, and Oren, and O., (and) Ahi.

O-ZI'-AS, Ὀζίας.
An ancestor of Jesus. See *Uzziah.*
Matt. 1. 8 Josaphat begat Joram; and Joram begat O.
1. 9 O. begat Joatham; and Joatham begat A.

OZ'-NI, אָזְנִי *Jah hears.*
A son of Gad, the seventh son of Jacob. B.C. 1700.
Num26. 16 Of O., the family of the Oznites: of Eri

OZ-NITES, הָאָזְנִי *the Ozni.*
Descendants of the preceding.
Num26. 16 Of Ozni, the family of the O.: of Eri, the

P

PA-A'-RAI, פַּעֲרַי *revelation of Jah.*
One of David's valiant men, from Aruboth in Judah B.C. 1058; called *Naarai* in 1 Ch. 11. 37.
2 Sa. 23. 35 Hezrai the Carmelite, P. the Arbite

PACE —
A step, pace, צַעַד *tsaad.*
2 Sa. 6. 13 when they..had gone six paces, he sacri.

PACIFIED, to be —
1. *To cover, pacify,* כָּפַר *kaphar,* 3.
Eze. 16. 63 when I am pacified toward thee for all t.
2. *To sink down, cease,* שָׁכַךְ *shakak.*
Esth. 7. 10 Then was the king's wrath pacified

PACIFY, to —
1. *To cause to rest,* נוּחַ, 5.
Eccl.10. 4 leave not thy place; for yielding pacifieth
2. *To avert, extinguish,* כָּפָה *kaphah.*
Prov.21. 14 A gift in secret pacifieth anger, and a rew
3. *To cover, pacify,* כָּפַר *kaphar,* 3.
Prov 16. 14 wrath of a king..wise man will pacify it

PAD'-AN, פַּדָּן *a plain. Same as the succeeding.*
Gen. 48. 7 when I came from P., Rachel died by me

PAD-AN A'-RAM, פַּדַּן אֲרָם *the plain of Aram.*
The plains of Mesopotamia, or the land between the Tigris and the Euphrates, in opposition to the hilly country of Palestine and the Lebanon ranges.
Gen. 25. 20 the daughter of Bethuel the Syrian of P.
28. 2 Arise, go to P., to the house of Bethuel
28. 5 he went to P. unto Laban, son of Bethuel
28. 6 sent him away to P., to take him a wife
28. 7 obeyed his father..and was gone to P.
31. 18 of his getting, which he had gotten in P.
33. 18 J. came to Shalem..when he came from P.
35. 9 appeared unto Jacob..he came out of P.
35. 26 sons of Jacob, which were born to him in P
46. 15 which she bare unto Jacob in P, with his

PADDLE —
Pin, nail, יָתֵד *yathed.*
Deut23. 13 thou shalt have a paddle upon thy weapon

PA'-DON, פָּדוֹן *deliverance.*
One of the Nethinim whose descendants returned with Zerubbabel. B.C. 538.
Ezra 2. 44 the children of Siaha, the children of P.
Neh. 7. 47 the children of Sia, the children of P.

PAG-I'-EL, פַּגְעִיאֵל *God meets.*
A son of Ocran and head of the tribe of Asher, chosen to number the people. B.C. 1451.
Num. 1. 13 Of Asher; P. the son of Ocran
2. 27 the captain..(shall be) P. the son of Ocran
7. 72 P. the son of Ocran, prince of the children
7. 77 (was) the offering of P. the son of Ocran
10. 26 And over the host..(was) P. the son of O.

PA-HATH MO'-AB, פַּחַת מוֹאָב *prefect of Moab.*
1. A person, part of whose posterity returned with Zerubbabel. B.C. 538.
Ezra 2. 6 children of P., of the children of Jeshua
10. 30 of the sons of P.; Adna, and Chelal, Ben.
Neh. 3. 11 the son of P., repaired the other piece, and
7. 11 children of P., of the children of Jeshua
2. Another, part of whose posterity returned with Ezra. B.C. 447.
Ezra 8. 4 Of the sons of P.; Elihoenai the son of
3. A family that, with Nehemiah, sealed the covenant. B.C. 445.
Neh. 10. 14 of the people; Parosh, P., Elam, Zatthu

PA'-I, פָּעִי *yawning deep.*
A city in Edom, where Hadad the last of the early kings was born or reigned; called *Pau* in Gen. 36. 39.
1 Ch. 1. 50 the name of his city (was) P.; and his wi.

PAID, to be —
To be given, יְהַב *yehab,* 2.
Ezra 4. 20 toll, tribute, and custom, was paid unto

PAIN, (great or much) —
1. *Pang, cord,* חֶבֶל *chebel.*
Isa. 66. 7 before her pain came, she was delivered
2. *Pain, writhing,* חִיל *chil.*
Psa. 48. 6 Fear took hold upon them there,(and) pain
Jer. 6. 24 anguish hath taken hold of us, (and) pain
22. 23 when pangs come upon thee, the pain as
3. *Great pain,* חַלְחָלָה *chalchalah.*
Isa. 21. 3 Therefore are my loins filled with pain: p.
Eze. 30. 4 great pain shall be in Ethiopia, when the
30. 9 great pain shall come upon them, as in the
Nah. 2. 10 much pain (is) in all loins, and the faces
4. *Pain,* כְּאֵב *keeb.*
Jer. 15. 18 Why is my pain perpetual, and my wound
5. *Pain, sorrow,* מַכְאוֹב *makob.*
Job 33. 19 He is chastened also with pain upon his
Jer. 51. 8 take balm for her pain, if so be she may
6. *Straitness, distress,* מֵצַר *metsar.*
Psa.116. 3 pains of hell gat hold upon me: I found t.
7. *Labour,* עָמָל *amal.*
Psa. 25. 18 Look upon mine affliction and my pain; and
8. *Pain, pang,* צִיר *tsir.*
1 Sa. 4. 19 bowed herself and travailed; for her pains
9. *Labour,* πόνος *ponos.*
Rev. 16. 10 and they gnawed their tongues for pain
16. 11 blasphemed..because of their pains and
21. 4 neither shall there be any more pain: for
10. *Pang,* ὠδίν *ōdin.*
Acts 2. 24 raised up, having loosed the pains of death

PAIN, to be in or have, fall with —
1. *To be pained, writhe,* חִיל, חוּל *chul, chil.*
Isa. 13. 8 they shall be in pain as a woman that tr.
26. 17 is in pain, (and) crieth out in her pangs
26. 18 we have been in pain, we have as it were
Jer. 30. 23 shall fall with pain upon the head of the
Eze. 30. 16 Sin shall have great pain, and No shall be
Mic. 4. 10 Be in pain, and labour to bring forth, O
2. *To be pained,* כָּאַב *kaab.*
Job 14. 22 his flesh upon him shall have pain, and his

PAIN, to put selves to —
To become sick, grieved, pained, חָלָה *chalah,* 2.
Jer. 12. 13 have put themselves to pain, (but) shall

PAINED, to be (much or sore) —
1. *To be pained, writhe,* חִיל, חוּל *chul, chil.*
Psa. 55. 4 My heart is sore pained within me; and
Isa. 23. 5 shall they be sorely pained at the report
Joel 2. 6 people shall be much pained; all faces
2. *To be pained, writhe,* יָחַל *yachal,* 5.
Jer. 4. 19 I am pained at my very heart; my heart
3. *To try, torture,* βασανίζω *basanizō.*
Rev. 12. 2 travailing in birth, and pained to be del.

PAINFUL, PAINFULNESS —
1. *Labour, misery,* עָמָל *amal.*
Psa. 73. 16 thought to know this, it (was) too painful
2. *Labour, toil,* μόχθος *mochthos.*
2 Co. 11. 27 In weariness and painfulness, in watchful

PAINT, to —
1. *To paint, colour,* כָּחַל *kachal.*
Eze. 23. 40 paintedst thine eyes, and deckedst thyself
2. *To anoint, smear,* מָשַׁח *mashach.*
Jer. 22. 14 ceiled with cedar, and painted with ver
3. *To put in paint,* שׂוּם בַּפּוּךְ *sum bap-puk.*
2 Ki. 9. 30 she painted her face, and tired her head

PAINTING —
Paint, painting, פּוּךְ *puk.*
Jer. 4. 30 though thou rentest thy face with painting

PAIR —
A pair, a yoke, ζεῦγος *zeugos.*
Luke 2. 24 A pair of turtle doves, or two young pig.

PAIR of balances —
A yoke, beam of a balance, ζυγός *zugos.*
Rev. 6. 5 he that sat on him had a pair of balances

PALACE —
1. *Palace, ornament, idol,* אַפֶּדֶן *appeden.*
Dan. 11. 45 plant the tabernacles of his palace between
2. *High place,* אַרְמוֹן *armon.*
1 Ki.16. 18 went into the palace of the king's house
2 Ki. 15. 25 smote him in Samaria, in the palace of the
2 Ch.36. 19 burnt all the palaces thereof with fire, and
Psa. 48. 3 God is known in her palaces for a refuge
48. 13 consider her palaces; that ye may tell (it)
122. 7 Peace..(and) prosperity within thy palaces
Isa. 23. 13 they raised up the palaces thereof; (and)
25. 2 palace of strangers to be no city; it shall
32. 14 Because the palaces shall be forsaken; the
34. 13 thorns shall come up in her palaces, net.
Jer. 6. 5 go by night, and let us destroy her palaces
9. 21 is entered into our palaces, to cut off the
17. 27 it shall devour the palaces of Jerusalem
30. 18 palace shall remain after the manner the.
49. 27 it shall consume the palaces of Ben-hadad
Lam. 2. 5 he hath swallowed up all her palaces: he
2. 7 hand of the enemy the walls of her palaces
Hos. 8. 14 and it shall devour the palaces thereof
Amos 1. 4 which shall devour the palaces of Ben-h.
Amos 1. 7, 10, 14 shall devour the palaces thereof
1. 12 which shall devour the palaces of Bozrah
2. 2, 5 and it shall devour the palaces of
3. 9 Publish in the palaces..and in the palaces
3. 10 store up violence and robbery in their pal.
3. 11 bring down thy strength..and thy palaces
6. 8 hate his palaces: therefore will I deliver
Mic. 5. 5 when he shall tread in our palaces, then
3. *Palace, castle, temple,* בִּירָה *birah.*
1 Ch. 29. 1 for the palace (is) not for man, but for
29. 19 do all (these things), and to build the pal.
Ezra 6. 2 there was found at Achmetha, in the pal.
Neh. 1. 1 came to pass..as I was in Shushan the p.
2. 8 to make beams for the gates of the palace
7. 2 I gave..Hananiah the ruler of the palace
Esth. 1. 2 kingdom, which (was) in Shushan the pa.
1. 5 that were present in Shushan the palace
2. 3 fair young virgins unto Shushan the pal.
2. 5 in Shushan the palace there was a certain
2. 8 gathered together unto Shushan the pal.
3. 15 the decree was given in Shushan the pal.
8. 14 the decree was given at Shushan the pal.
9. 6 in Shushan the palace the Jews slew and
9. 11 that were slain in Shushan the palace was
9. 12 five hundred men in Shushan the palace
Dan. 8. 2 I (was) at Shushan (in) the palace, which
4. *House,* בַּיִת *bayith.*
2 Ch. 9. 11 made..terraces..to the king's palace, and
5. *House,* בִּיתָן *bithan.*
Esth. 1. 5 the court of the garden of the king's pala.
7. 7 king..(went) into the palace garden: and
7. 8 Then the king returned out of the palace
6. *Temple, palace,* הֵיכָל *hekal.*
1 Ki. 21. 1 which (was) in Jezreel, hard by the palace
2 Ki.20. 18 they shall be eunuchs in the palace of the
Ezra 4. 14 have maintenance from (the king's) palace
Psa. 45. 8 out of the ivory palaces, whereby they h.
45. 15 they shall enter into the king's palace
144. 12 polished (after) the similitude of a palace
Prov 30. 28 taketh hold..and is in king's palaces
Isa. 13. 22 dragons in (their) pleasant palaces: and
39. 7 eunuchs in the palace of the king of Baby.
Dan. 1. 4 ability in them to stand in the king's pal.
4. 4 was at rest..and flourishing in my palace
4. 29 in the palace of the kingdom of Babylon
5. 5 the plaster of the wall of the king's pala.
6. 18 the king went to his palace, and passed
Nah. 2. 6 opened, and the palace shall be dissolve.
7. *High place,* הַרְמוֹן *harmon.*
Amos 4. 3 ye shall cast (them) into the palace, saith
8. *Tower,* טִירָה *tirah.*
Song 8. 9 we will build upon her a palace of silver
Eze. 25. 4 they shall set their palaces in thee, and
9. *Court,* αὐλή *aulē.*
Matt26. 3 unto the palace of the high priest, who
26. 58 followed..unto the high priest's palace
26. 69 Peter sat without in the palace: and a da.
Mark14. 54 followed..into the palace of the high pr.
14. 66 as Peter was beneath in the palace, there
Luke11. 21 When a strong man armed keepeth his p.
John18. 15 went in..into the palace of the high priest
10. *Praetor's court,* πραιτώριον *praitōrion (from Lat.)*
Phil. 1. 13 my bonds..are manifest in all the palace

PA'-LAL, פָּלָל *a judge.*
A son of Uzzai, who helped to repair the wall of Jerusalem after Nehemiah came from Shushan. B.C. 445.
Neh. 3. 25 P. the son of Uzai, over against the turn.

PALE —
Green, pale, sallow, χλωρός *chlōros.*
Rev. 6. 8 I looked, and behold a pale horse: and his

PALE, to wax —
To become pale or white, חָוַר *chavar.*
Isa. 29. 22 Jacob..neither shall his face now wax pale

PALENESS —
Greenness, mildew, יֵרָקוֹן *yeraqon.*
Jer. 30. 6 do I see..all faces are turned into pale.?

PA-LES-TI-NA, PA-LES-TINE, פְּלֶשֶׁת,פְּלֶשֶׁת *emigration.*
The W. coast of Canaan, from the river of Egypt or the brook Besor (a little S. of Gaza) to Joppa; see Isa. 14. 29, 31; Joel 3. 4.
Exod15. 14 shall take hold on the inhabitants of P.
Isa. 14. 29 Rejoice not thou, whole P., because the
14. 31 cry..thou whole P., (art) dissolved: for
Joel 3. 4 Tyre, and Zidon, and all the coasts of P.

PAL'-LU, PHAL'-LU, פַּלּוּא *distinguished, wonderful.*
The second son of Reuben. B.C. 1700.
Gen. 46. 9 Reuben, Hanoch, and P., and Hezron and
Exod. 6. 14 and P., Hezron, and Carmi: these (be) the
Num 26. 5 of P., the family of the Palluites
26. 8 And the sons of P.; Eliab
1 Ch. 5. 3 sons..were Hanoch, and P., Hezron, and

PAL-LU-ITES, הַפַּלֻּאִי *the Pallui.*
The descendants of the preceding.
Num 26. 5 of Pallu the family of the P.

PALM, PALM TREE —
1. *Palm (of hand), sole (of foot),* כַּף *kaph.*
Lev. 14. 15 pour (it) into the palm of his own left h.
14. 26 the oil into the palm of his own left hand
1 Sa. 5. 4 the palms of his hands (were) cut off up.
2 Ki. 9. 35 and the feet, and the palms of (her) hand

Isa. 49. 16 graven thee upon the palms of (my) han.
Dan. 10. 10 my knees and (upon) the palms of my ha.

2. *A palm tree,* תָּמָר *tamar.*
Exod 15. 27 three score and ten palm trees: and they
Lev. 23. 40 branches of palm trees, and the boughs of
Num 33. 9 three score and ten palm trees; and they
Deut 34. 3 valley of Jericho, the city of palm trees
Judg. 1. 16 went up out of the city of palm trees with
3. 13 went..and possessed the city of palm trees
2 Ch. 28. 15 to Jericho, the city of palm trees, to their
Neh. 8. 15 palm branches, and branches of thick tr.
Psa. 92. 12 righteous shall flourish like the palm tree
Song. 7. 7 This thy stature is like to a palm tree, and
7. 8 I will go up to the palm tree, I will take
Joel 1. 12 tree, the palm tree also, and the apple t.

3. *A palm tree,* תֹּמֶר *tomer.*
Judg. 4. 5 she dwelt under the palm tree of Deborah
Jer. 10. 5 They (are) upright as the palm tree, but

4. *A palm tree, (artificial),* תִּמֹּרָה *timmorah.*
1 Ki. 6. 29, 32, 35 and palm trees and open flowers
6. 32 upon the cherubim, and upon the palm tr.
7. 36 he graved cherubim, lions, and palm trees
2 Ch. 3. 5 and set thereon palm trees and chains
Eze. 40. 16 and upon (each) post (were) palm trees
40. 22 their palm trees (were) after the measure
40. 26 it had palm trees, one on this side, and
40. 31, 34, 37 and palm trees (were) upon the po.
41. 18 cherubim and palm trees, so that a palm tr.
41. 19 (was) toward the palm tree on the one s.
41. 19 face..toward the palm tree on the other
41. 20 (were) cherubim and palm trees made, and
41. 25 palm trees, like as (were) made upon the
41. 26 palm trees on the one side and on the ot.

5. *A palm tree or branch,* φοίνιξ *phoinix.*
John 12. 13 Took branches of palm trees, and went
Rev. 7. 9 clothed with white robes, and palms in

PALM of the hand, to strike with —
To give slaps, δίδωμι ῥάπισμα *didōmi rhapisma.*
Mark 14. 65 strike him with the palms of their hands
John 18. 22 one..struck Jesus with the palm of his h.

PALMER WORM —
Palmer worm, caterpillar, creeping locust, גָּזָם *gazam.*
Joel 1. 4 That which the palmer worm hath left h.
2. 25 and the caterpillar, and the palmer worm
Amos 4. 9 the palmer worm devoured (them): yet

PALSY, one that has, or is sick of, or taken with the —
1. *To be paralytic, paralyzed,* παραλύομαι *paraluom.*
Luke 5. 18 behold..a man which was taken with a p.
5. 24 he said unto [the sick of the palsy], I say
Acts 8. 7 many taken with palsies, and that were l.
9. 33 named Eneas, which..was sick of the pa.

2. *Paralytic, paralyzed,* παραλυτικός *paralutikos.*
Matt. 4. 24 those that had the palsy; and he healed
8. 6 my servant lieth at home sick of the pal.
9. 2 a man sick of the palsy, lying on a bed
9. 2 said unto the sick of the palsy, Son, be of
9. 6 then saith he to the sick of the palsy, Ar
Mark 2. 3 bringing one sick of the palsy, which was
2. 4 the bed wherein the sick of the palsy lay
2. 5 he said unto the sick of the palsy, Son be
2. 9 is it easier to say to the sick of the palsy
2. 10 may know..he saith to the sick of the p.

PAL'-TI, פַּלְטִי *Jah delivers.*
A chief Benjamite, son of Raphu, and chosen to spy out the land. B.C. 1490.
Num 13. 9 the tribe of Benjamin, P. the son of Raphu

PAL-TI'-EL, PHAL-TI'-EL, פַּלְטִיאֵל *God delivers.*
1. A chief of Issachar, son of Azzan, and chosen to divide the land W. of Jordan. B.C. 1452.
Num 34. 26 prince of the tribe..P. the son of Azzan
2. A Benjamite, son of Laish, called also *Phalti*, to whom Michal, David's wife, was given. B.C. 1060.
2 Sa. 3. 15 (her) husband, (even) from P. the son of

PAL-TITE, הַפַּלְטִי *the Palti.*
A Patronymic of Helez, from *Beth-Palet* in the S. of Judah.
2 Sa. 23. 26 Helez the P. Ira the son of Ikkesh the T

PAM-PHY-LI-A, Παμφυλία.
A province in the S. of Asia Minor, having Cilicia on the E., Pisidia on the N., Lycia on the W., and the Mediterranean on the S. Perga is the only one of its cities named in the New Testament.
Acts 2. 10 P., in Egypt, and in the parts of Lybia
13. 13 they came to Perga in P.: and John dep.
14. 24 passed throughout Pisidia, they came to P.
15. 38 who departed from them from P., and
27. 5 had sailed over the sea of Cilicia and P.

PAN —
1. *Pans,* חֲבִתִּים *chabittim.*
1 Ch. 9. 31 over the things that were made in the pan

2. *Pan, laver,* כִּיּוֹר *kiyyor.*
1 Sa. 2. 14 he struck (it) into the pan, or kettle, or c.

3. *Thin plate,* מַחֲבַת *machabath.*
Lev. 2. 5 if thy oblation (be)..(baken) in a pan, it s.
6. 21 In a pan it shall be made with oil; (and
7. 9 all that is dressed..in the pan, shall be
1 Ch. 23. 29 for (that which is baked in) the pan, and
Eze. 4. 3 take thou unto thee an iron pan, and set

4. *Frying pan,* מַשְׂרֵת *masreth.*
2 Sa. 13. 9 she took a pan, and poured (them) out b.

5. *A pot,* סִיר *sir.*
Exod 27. 3 thou shalt make his pans to receive his

6. *A pan, pot,* פָּרוּר *parur.*
Num 11. 8 baked (it) in pans, and made cakes of it

7. *Dish, pan, cruise,* צְלָחָה *tselachah.*
2 Ch. 35. 13 in pots, and in caldrons, and in pans, and

PANG —
1. *Pang, cord,* חֵבֶל *chebel.*
Isa. 26. 17 Like as a woman..crieth out in her pangs
Jer. 22. 23 shalt thou be when pangs come upon thee

2. *Pain, writhing,* חִיל *chil.*
Jer. 50. 43 anguish..pangs as of a woman in travail
Mic. 4. 9 for pangs have taken thee as a woman in

3. *Pain, pang,* צִיר *tsir.*
Isa. 13. 8 pangs and sorrows shall take hold of them
21. 3 pangs have taken hold upon me, as the p.

4. *To straiten, distress,* צָרַר *tsarar,* 5.
Jer. 48. 41 be as the heart of a woman in her pangs
49. 22 be as the heart of a woman in her pangs

PAN'-NAG, פַּנַּג *sweet.*
A place on the road from Damascus to Baalbeck, also called *Piggi.*
Eze. 27. 17 in thy market wheat of Minnith, and P.

PANT, to —
1. *To go about, pant,* סָחַר *sachar,* 3a.
Psa. 38. 10 My heart panteth, my strength faileth me

2. *To long for, pant,* עָרַג *arag.*
Psa. 42. 1 panteth after the water brooks, so pant.

3. *To swallow up, pant,* שָׁאַף *shaaph.*
Psa. 119. 131 I opened my mouth, and panted: for I
Amos 2. 7 That pant after the dust of the earth on

4. *To err, wander, go astray,* תָּעָה *taah.*
Isa. 21. 4 My heart panted, fearfulness affrighted

PAP —
1. *Breast,* שַׁד *shad.*
Eze. 23. 21 in bruising thy teats..for the paps of thy

2. *Breast, pap,* μαστός *mastos.*
Luke 11. 27 Blessed..the paps which thou hast sucked
23. 29 Blessed (are)..the paps which never gave
Rev. 1. 13 [girt about the paps] with a golden girdle

PAPER (REEDS) —
1. *Green bushy meadows,* עָרוֹת *aroth.*
Isa. 19. 7 The paper reeds by the brooks, by the m.

2. *Paper,* χάρτης *chartēs.*
2 John 12 I would not (write) with paper and ink

PA'-PHOS, Πάφος.
A city on the W. of Cyprus (now *Baffe*), the station of a Roman pro-consul; about sixty stadia off was a temple of Venus.
Acts 13. 6 they had gone through the isle unto P.
13. 13 when Paul and his company loosed from P.

PARABLE —
1. *Similitude, parable, proverb,* מָשָׁל *mashal.*
Num 23. 7, 18 And he took up his parable, and said
24. 3, 15, 20, 21, 23 took up his parable, and
Job 27. 1 Job continued his parable, and said
29. 1 Job continued his parable, and said
Psa. 49. 4 I will incline mine ear to a parable; I w.
78. 2 I will open my mouth in a parable: I will
Prov 26. 7, 9 so (is) a parable in the mouth of fools
Eze. 17. 2 speak a parable unto the house of Israel
20. 49 they say of me, Doth he not speak parab
24. 3 utter a parable unto the rebellious house
Mic. 2. 4 shall (one) take up a parable against you
Hab. 2. 6 all these take up a parable against him

2. *A parable, similitude,* παραβολή *parabolē.*
Matt 13. 3 spake many things unto them in parables
13. 10 Why speakest thou unto them in parables?
13. 13 Therefore speak I to them in parables: be.
13. 18 Hear ye therefore the parable of the sower
13. 24, 31 Another parable put he forth unto th.
13. 33 Another parable spake he unto them; The
13. 34 in parables; and without a parable spake
13. 35 I will open my mouth in parables; I will
13. 36 Declare unto us the parable of the tares
13. 53 when Jesus had finished these parables
15. 15 said unto him, Declare unto us this par.
21. 33 Hear another parable: There was a cert.
21. 45 when the..Pharisees had heard his para.
22. 1 spake unto them again by parables, and
24. 32 learn a parable of the fig tree: When his
Mark 3. 23 said unto them in parables, How can Sa.
4. 2 he taught them many things by parables
4. 10 with the twelve asked of him the parable
4. 11 but..all (these) things are done in parabl.
4. 13 said unto them, Know ye..this parable?
4. 13 and how then will ye know all parables?
4. 33 with many such parables spake he the w.
4. 34 without a parable spake he not unto them
7. 17 disciples asked him concerning the para.
12. 1 he began to speak unto them by parables
12. 12 he had spoken the parable against them
13. 28 learn a parable of the fig tree; When her
Luke 5. 36 he spake also a parable unto them: No man
6. 39 he spake a parable unto them: Can the
8. 4 were come to him..he spake by a parable
8. 9 asked..saying..What might this parable
8. 10 but to others in parables; that seeing th.
8. 11 the parable is this: The seed is the word
12. 16 he spake a parable unto them, saying, The
Luke 12. 41 speakest thou this parable unto us, or even
13. 6 He spake also this parable, A certain (man)
14. 7 he put forth a parable to those which w.
15. 3 he spake this parable unto them, saying
18. 1 he spake a parable unto them (to this end)
18. 9 he spake this parable unto certain which
19. 11 spake a parable, because he was nigh to
20. 9 began he to speak to the people this par.
20. 19 he had spoken this parable against them
21. 29 he spake to them a parable; Behold the

3. *Adage, dark saying,* παροιμία *paroimia.*
John 10. 6 This parable spake Jesus unto them: but

PARADISE —
Park, garden ground, παράδεισος (*from Heb.* פַּרְדֵּס).
Luke 23. 43 To day shalt thou be with me in paradise
2 Co. 12. 4 he was caught up into paradise, and hea.
Rev. 2. 7 which is in the midst of the paradise of

PA'-RAH, הַפָּרָה *the wild place.*
A city in Benjamin, near Avim and Ophrah.
Josh. 18. 23 And Avim, and P., and Ophrah

PARAMOUR —
A concubine, (male or female), פִּלֶגֶשׁ *pillegesh.*
Eze. 23. 20 she doted upon their paramours, whose

PA'-RAN, פָּארָן *full of caverns.*
A wilderness at S. and S.W. of Canaan, and W. of Edom, reaching westward to Shur, and S. to the Elanitic gulf, also called *Mount* Paran, and *el-Paran.*
Gen. 21. 21 he dwelt in the wilderness of P.: and his
Num 10. 12 the cloud rested in the wilderness of P.
12. 16 people..pitched in the wilderness of P.
13. 3 Moses..sent them from..wilderness of P.
13. 26 unto the wilderness of P., to Kadesh; and
Deut. 1. 1 between P., and Tophel, and Laban, and
33. 2 he shined forth from mount P., and he
1 Sa. 25. 1 and went down to the wilderness of P.
1 Ki. 11. 18 P.: and they took men with them out of P.
Hab. 3. 3 from Teman, the Holy One from mount P.

PAR'-BAR, פַּרְבָּר *open summer house.*
A place W. of the temple and surrounded by a wall. Comp. "*suburb,*" in 2 Ki. 23. 11.
1 Ch. 26. 18 P. westward, four at the...and two at P.

PARCEL (of ground) —
1. *A portion,* חֶלְקָה *chelqah.*
Gen. 33. 19 he bought a parcel of a field, where he
Josh. 24. 32 a parcel of ground which Jacob bought
Ruth 4. 3 Naomi..selleth a parcel of land, which
1 Ch. 11. 13 where was a parcel of ground full of bar.
11. 14 set themselves in the midst of (that) par.

2. *Field, place,* χωρίον *chōrion.*
John 4. 5 the parcel of ground that Jacob gave to

PARCHED (corn, ground or places) —
1. *Burnt or parched places,* חֲרֵרִים *chărerim.*
Jer. 17. 6 parched places in the wilderness, (in) a

2. *To roast,* קָלָה *qalah.*
Josh. 5. 11 did eat..parched (corn) in the self same

3. *Roasted corn or grain,* קָלִי, קָלִיא *qali.*
Lev. 23. 14 shall eat neither bread, nor parched corn
Ruth 2. 14 he reached her parched (corn) and she did
1 Sa. 17. 17 Take..an ephah of this parched (corn), and
25. 18 five measures of parched (corn), and an
2 Sa. 17. 28 parched (corn)..beans, and lentiles, and

4. *Heat, mirage,* שָׁרָב *sharab.*
Isa. 35. 7 the parched ground shall become a pool

PARCHMENT —
A thin skin of parchment, μεμβράνα (*from Lat.*).
2 Ti. 4. 13 the books, (but) especially the parchments

PARDON —
A passing over, forgiveness, סְלִיחָה *selichah.*
Neh. 9. 17 thou (art) a God ready to pardon, gracious

PARDON, to —
1. *To cover, pacify,* כָּפַר *kaphar,* 3.
2 Ch. 30. 18 saying, The good LORD pardon every one

2. *To lift up,* נָשָׂא *nasa.*
Exod 23. 21 for he will not pardon your transgressions
1 Sa. 15. 25 pardon my sin, and turn again with me
Job 7. 21 why dost thou not pardon my transgres.
Mic. 7. 18 that pardoneth iniquity, and passeth by

3. *To pass over, forgive,* סָלַח *salach.*
Exod 34. 9 pardon our iniquity, and our sin, and take
Num 14. 19 Pardon, I beseech thee, the iniquity of this
14. 20 I have pardoned, according to thy word
2 Ki. 5. 18, 18 the LORD pardon thy servant
24. 4 blood that he shed..LORD would not pa.
Psa. 25. 11 LORD, pardon mine iniquity; for it (is) g.
Isa. 55. 7 to our God, for he will abundantly pardon
Jer. 5. 1 seeketh the truth; and I will pardon it
5. 7 How shall I pardon thee for this? thy c.
33. 8 will pardon all their iniquities, whereby
50. 20 for I will pardon them whom I reserve
Lam. 3. 42 and have rebelled: thou hast not pardoned

PARDONED, to be —
To be pleasing, accepted, רָצָה *ratsah,* 2.
Isa. 40. 2 that her iniquity is pardoned: for she hath

PARE, to —
To make, do, prepare, עָשָׂה *asah.*
Deut 21. 12 shall shave her head, and pare her nails

PARENT —

1. *Parent, begetter,* γονεύς *goneus.*

Matt 10. 21 children shall rise..against (their) parents
Mark 13. 12 children shall rise..against (their) parents
Luke 2. 27 the parents brought in the child Jesus, to
2. 41 his parents went to Jerusalem every year
8. 56 her parents were astonished: but he ch.
18. 29 or parents, or brethren, or wife, or child.
21. 16 ye shall be betrayed both by parents, and
John 9. 2 who did sin, this man, or his parents, that
9. 3 Neither..this man sinned, nor his parents
9. 18 the parents of him that had received his
9. 20 His parents answered them, and said, We
9. 22 These (words) spake his parents, because
9. 23 Therefore said his parents, He is of age
Rom. 1. 30 inventors of evil..disobedient to parents
2 Co. 12. 14 lay up for the parents, but the parents
Eph. 6. 1 obey your parents in the Lord: for this is
Col. 3. 20 obey (your) parents in all things: for this
2 Ti. 3. 2 disobedient to parents, unthankful, unho.

2. *Father,* πατήρ *patēr.*

Heb. 11. 23 was hid three months of his parents

3. *Progenitor,* πρόγονος *progonos.*

1 Ti. 5. 4 to requite their parents: for that is good

PARLOUR —

1. *Inner or secret place,* חֶדֶר *cheder.*

1 Ch. 28. 11 and of the inner parlours thereof, and of

2. *A chamber, parlour,* לִשְׁכָּה *lishkah.*

1 Sa. 9. 22 Samuel..brought them into the parlour

3. *Upper place,* עֲלִיָּה *aliyyah.*

Judg. 3. 20 and he was sitting in a summer parlour
3. 23 and shut the doors of the parlour upon
3. 24 that..the doors of the parlour (were) lo.
3. 25 and..he opened not the doors of the par.

PAR-MASH'-TA, פַּרְמַשְׁתָּא.

A son of Haman the Agagite, in the days of Ahasuerus and Esther. B.C. 510.

Esth. 9. 9 And P., and Arisai, and Aridai, and Vaje.

PAR-ME'-NAS, Παρμενᾶς.

One of the seven disciples chosen to serve tables.

Acts 6. 5 and P., and Nicolas a proselyte of Antioch

PAR'-NACH, פַּרְנָךְ.

The father of Elizaphan a chief of Zebulun, chosen to divide the land W. of the Jordan. B.C. 1490.

Num 34. 25 And the prince..Elizaphan the son of P.

PAR'-OSH, PHAR'-OSH, פַּרְעֹשׁ *fleeing, fugitive.*

1. One whose descendants returned with Zerubbabel. B.C. 536.

Ezra 2. 3 The children of P., two thousand an hun.
Neh. 7. 8 The children of P., two thousand an hun.

2. One whose descendants returned with Ezra. B.C. 447.

Ezra 8. 3 the sons of P.; Zechariah: and with him

3. One whose descendants had taken strange wives. B.C. 447.

Ezra 10. 25 of the sons of P.; Ramiah, and Jeziah, and

4. The father of Pedaiah who helped to repair the wall. B.C. 447.

Neh. 3. 25 After him Pedaiah the son of P.

5. A family that, with Nehemiah, sealed the covenant. B.C. 445.

Neh. 10. 14 The chief..P., Pahath-moab, Elam, Zatthu

PAR-SHAN-DA'-THA, פַּרְשַׁנְדָּתָא.

A son of Haman the Agagite. B.C. 510.

Esth. 9. 7 And P., and Dalphon, and Aspatha

PART (in)—

1. *Part,* בַּד *bad.*

Job 41. 12 I will not conceal his parts, nor his power

2. *Piece,* בֶּתֶר *bether.*

Jer. 34. 18 when they..passed between the parts th.
34. 19 which passed between the parts of the c.

3. *Section,* גֶּזֶר *gezer.*

Psa. 136. 13 him which divided the Red sea into parts

4. *Word, matter,* דָּבָר *dabar.*

1 Ki. 6. 38 finished throughout all the parts thereof

5. *Portion,* חֵלֶק *cheleq.*

Num 18. 20 have any part among them: I (am) thy p.
Deut 10. 9 Levi hath no part nor inheritance with
12. 12 he hath no part nor inheritance with you
14. 27, 29 hath no part nor inheritance with thee
18. 1 have no part nor inheritance with Israel
Josh. 14. 4 gave no part unto the Levites in the land
15. 13 gave a part among the children of Judah
18. 5 And they shall divide it into seven parts
18. 6 describe the land (into) seven parts, and
18. 7 the Levites have no part among you; for
18. 9 described it by cities into seven parts in a
19. 9 the part of the children of Judah was too
22. 25 ye have no part in the LORD: so shall yo.
22. 27 may not say..Ye have no part in the Lo.
1 Sa. 30. 24 as his part (is) that goeth down to the ba.
30. 24 so (shall) his part (be) that tarrieth by the
2 Sa. 20. 1 We have no part in David, neither have
Job 32. 17 I will answer also my part; I also will s.
Eze. 48. 8 (in) length as one of the (other) parts, from
Amos 7. 4 devoured the great deep, and..eat up a p.

6. *Portion,* חֶלְקָה *chelqah.*

Ruth 2. 3 on a part of the field (belonging) unto B.

7. *Half,* חֲצִי, חֵצִי *chetsi, chatsi.*

1 Ki. 16. 21 the people of Israel divided into two pa.
Isa. 44. 16 burneth part thereof in the fire; with p.
44. 19 I have burnt part of it in the fire; yea

8. *From, out of, some of,* מִן *min.*

Dan. 2. 33 legs of iron, his feet part of iron and part
2. 41 part of potter's clay, and part of iron, the
2. 42 the toes..part of iron, and part of clay

9. *Portion, allotment,* מָנָה *manah.*

Exod 29. 26 take the breast..and it shall be thy part
Lev. 7. 33 shall have the right shoulder for (his) pa.
8. 29 (for) of the ram..it was Moses' part; as

10. *Mouth,* פֶּה *peh.*

Zech 13. 8 two parts therein shall be cut off (and) die

11. *Circuit,* פֶּלֶךְ *pelek.*

Neh. 3. 9, 12 the ruler of the half part of Jerusalem
3. 14 Malchiah..ruler of part of Beth-haccerem
3. 15 Shallum..the ruler of part of Mizpah; he
3. 16 the ruler of the half part of Beth-zur, unto
3. 17 ruler of the half part of Keilah, in his part
3. 18 Bavai..the ruler of the half part of Keilah

12. *End, extremity,* פַּס *pas.*

Dan. 5. 5 king saw the part of the hand that wrote
5. 24 was the part of the hand sent from him

13. *End, extremity, fraction,* קָצָה *qatsah.*

Job 26. 14 these (are) parts of his ways; but how li.

14. *End, extremity, fraction,* קְצָת *qetsath.*

Dan. 1. 2 with part of the vessels of the house of G.

15. *Lot, portion,* κλῆρος *klēros.*

Acts 1. 17 and had obtained part of this ministry
1. 25 take [part] of this ministry and apostleship

16. *Climate, region, district,* κλίμα *klima.*

Rom 15. 23 having no more place in these parts, and

17. *Division, part,* μερίς *meris.*

Luke 10. 42 Mary hath chosen that good part, which
Acts 8. 21 Thou hast neither part nor lot in this ma.
16. 12 the chief city of that [part] of Macedonia
2 Co. 6. 15 what part hath he that believeth with an

18. *Division, part,* μέρος *meros.*

Matt. 2. 22 he turned aside into the parts of Galilee
Mark 8. 10 and came into the parts of Dalmanutha
Luke 11. 36 (be) full of light, having no part dark, the
John 13. 8 wash thee not, thou hast no part with me
19. 23 and made four parts, to every soldier a p.
Acts 2. 10 in the parts of Libya about Cyrene, and
5. 2 brought a certain part, and laid (it) at the
20. 2 he had gone over those parts, and had gi.
23. 6 the one part were Sadducees, and the ot.
23. 9 [scribes (that were) of the Pharisees' part]
Rom 11. 25 blindness in part is happened to Israel
1 Co. 13. 9 we know in part, and we prophesy in part
13. 10 that which is in part shall be done away
13. 12 now I know in part; but then shall I know
2 Co. 1. 14 ye have acknowledged us in part, that we
2. 5 he hath not grieved me, but in part; that
Eph. 4. 9 also descended first into the lower [parts]
4. 16 the..working in the measure of every [p.]
Rev. 16. 19 the great city was divided into three parts
20. 6 Blessed and holy (is) he that hath part in
21. 8 But..shall have their part in the 22. 19

19. *The one...the other,* οἱ μὲν...οἱ δέ, Acts 14. 4.

20. *Hand,* יָד *yad.*

Gen. 47. 24 four parts shall be your own, for seed of
2 Ki. 11. 7 two parts of all you that go forth on the
Neh. 11. 1 and nine parts (to dwell) in (other) cities

21. *Extremities,* יַרְכָתַיִם [*yarekah*].

Eze. 38. 15 come from thy place out of the north parts
39. 2 cause thee to come up from the north pa.

22. *A cut piece,* נֵתַח *nethach.*

Lev. 1. 8 shall lay the parts, the head, and the fat

[*See also* Back, east, fifth, first, forth, greater, greatest, habitable, hallowed, highest, hinder, inner, innermost, inward, kinsman, lacking, low, more, neither, secret, sixth, tenth third, two, utmost.]

PART, on (one's)—

1. *Down through,* κατά (*acc.*) *kata.*

1 Pe. 4. 14 [on their part he is evil..on your part he]

2. *In behalf of,* ὑπέρ (*gen.*) *huper.*

Mark 9. 40 For he that is not against us is on our part

PART, to have, give, or take a —

1. *To have a portion,* חָלַק *chalaq.*

1 Sa. 30. 24 that tarrieth by the stuff: they shall part
Prov 17. 2 shall have part of the inheritance among

2. *To give a portion, apportion,* חָלַק *chalaq,* 3.

Psa. 22. 18 They part my garments among them, and
Joel 3. 2 whom they have scattered..and parted my

3. *To halve, divide,* חָצָה *chatsah.*

Job 41. 6 shall they part him among the merchants?

4. *To be halved, divided,* חָצָה *chatsah,* 2.

2 Ki. 2. 14 they parted hither and thither: and Elis.

5. *To snatch or take away,* נָצַל *natsal,* 5.

2 Sa. 14. 6 (there was) none to part them, but the one

6. *To part, separate,* פָּרַד *parad,* 5.

Ruth 1. 17 do so..(if ought) but death part thee and
2 Ki. 2. 11 parted them both asunder; and Elijah
Prov. 18. 18 The lot..parteth between the mighty

7. *To divide, part,* פָּרַס *paras,* 5.

Lev. 11. 3 Whatsoever parteth the hoof, and is cloven
Deut 14. 6 every beast that parteth the hoof, and cl.

8. *To divide,* פָּתַת *pathath.*

Lev. 2. 6 Thou shalt part it in pieces, and pour oil

9. *To divide throughout,* διαμερίζω *diamerizō.*

Matt 27. 35 parted his garments, casting lots: that it
27. 35 They parted my garments among them, and
Mark 15. 24 they parted his garments, casting lots upon
Luke 23. 34 And they parted his raiment, and cast lots
John 19. 24 They parted my raiment among them, and
Acts 2. 45 parted them to all (men), as every man had

10. *To divide,* μερίζω *merizō.*

Heb. 7. 2 Abraham gave a tenth part of all; first be.

11. *To hold along with,* μετέχω *metechō.*

Heb. 2. 14 also himself likewise took part of the same

PARTAKE, PARTAKER (with)—

1. *Portion,* חֵלֶק *cheleq.*

Psa. 50. 18 and hast been partaker with adulterers

2. *To receive in return,* ἀντιλαμβάνομαι *antilambano.*

1 Ti. 6. 2 faithful and beloved, partakers of the be.

3. *To become a joint partaker,* συγκοινωνὸς γίνομαι.

Rom 11. 17 partakest of the root and fatness of the
1 Co. 9. 23 that I might be partaker thereof with (you)
Phil. 1. 7 inasmuch as..ye all are partakers of my

4. *Holding along with,* μέτοχος *metochos.*

Heb. 3. 1 partakers of the heavenly calling, consi.
3. 14 we are made partakers of Christ, if we hold
6. 4 and were made partakers of the Holy Gh.
12. 8 without chastisement, where of all are p.

5. *One having in common,* κοινωνός *koinōnos.*

Matt 23. 30 we would not have been partakers with
1 Co. 10. 18 are not they which eat of the sacrifices p.
2 Co. 1. 7 that as ye are partakers of the sufferings
1 Pe. 5. 1 a partaker of the glory that shall be rev
2 Pe. 1. 4 ye might be partakers of the divine nature

6. *Division, portion,* μερίς *meris.*

Col. 1. 12 meet to be partakers of the inheritance

7. *A joint holder,* συμμέτοχος *summetochos.*

Eph. 3. 6 partakers of his promise in Christ by the
5. 7 Be not ye therefore partakers with them

PARTAKER of or with, (afflictions), to be—

1. *To give or have in common,* κοινωνέω *koinōneō.*

Rom. 15. 27 have been made partakers of their spirit.
1 Ti. 5. 22 neither be partaker of other men's sins
Heb. 2. 14 as the children are partakers of flesh and
1 Pe. 4. 13 as ye are partakers of Christ's sufferings
2 Jo. 11 he that biddeth him God speed is partak. of

2. *To take, receive, with,* μεταλαμβάνω *metalambanō.*

2 Ti. 2. 6 The husbandman..must be first partak. of
Heb. 12. 10 that (we) might be partakers of his holi.

3. *To hold with,* μετέχω *metechō.*

1 Co. 9. 10 and that he..should be partaker of his ho-
9. 12 If others be partakers of (this) power over
10. 17 for we are all partakers of that one bread
10. 21 ye cannot be partakers of the Lord's table
10. 30 if I by grace be a partaker, why am I evil

4. *To suffer evil with,* συγκακοπαθέω *sugkakopatheō.*

2 Ti. 1. 8 be thou partaker of the afflictions of the

5. *Have in common with,* συγκοινωνέω *sugkoinōneō.*

Rev. 18. 4 that ye be not partakers of her sins, and

6. *To have a part with,* συμμερίζομαι *summerizomai.*

1 Co. 9. 13 which wait..are partakers with the altar?

PARTED, to be —

1. *To be portioned, apportioned,* חָלַק *chalaq,* 2.

Job 38. 24 By what way is the light parted, (which)

2. *To be parted, separated,* פָּרַד *parad,* 2.

Gen. 2. 10 it was parted, and became into four heads

3. *To set or place apart,* διΐστημι *diistēmi.*

Luke 24. 51 he was parted from them, and carried up

PAR-THI-ANS, Πάρθοι.

The inhabitants of Parthia proper, which is N.W. of Persia, and about 600 miles long; having Hyrcania on the N.W., Media on the S., Asia on the E., and Carmania Deserta on the S.; it is wholly surrounded by mountains; it was early subject to Media, then to Persia, and also to Alexander and his successors; it became independent in B.C. 256; at the death of Mithridates, B.C. 130, it extended from the Euphrates to the Jordan, and from the Oxus to the Persian Gulf; in B.C. 53 it was invaded by Crassus, who was defeated and slain; in A.D. 226 it became subject to Persia.

Acts 2. 9 P., and Medes, and Elamites, and the dwe.

PARTIAL, to be —

1. *To lift up the face,* נָשָׂא פָּנִים *nasa phanim.*

Mal. 2. 9 have not kept my ways, but have been p.

2. *To judge diversely,* διακρίνω *diakrinō.*

Jas. 2. 4 Are ye not then partial in yourselves, and

PARTIALITY (without) —

1. *Not judging diversely, impartial,* ἀδιάκριτος.

Jas. 3. 17 without partiality, and without hypocrisy

2. *A bearing toward, partiality,* πρόσκλισις *prosk.*

1 Ti. 5. 21 before another, doing nothing by [part.]

PARTICULAR (in)—
Individually, imperfectly, ἐκ μέρους *ek merous.*
1 Co. 12. 27 body of Christ, and members in particular

PARTICULARLY —
1. *Down to or in parts,* κατὰ μέρος *kata meros.*
Heb. 9. 5 of which we cannot now speak particular.
2. *Down to each one,* καθ' ἓν ἕκαστον *kath hen hek.*
Acts 21. 19 he declared particularly what things God

PARTING —
The mother, אֵם *em.*
Eze. 21. 21 the king of Babylon stood at the parting

PARTITION —
Fence, hedge, φραγμός *phragmos.*
Eph. 2. 14 broken down the middle wall of partition

PARTITION, to make a —
To make to pass over, עָבַר *abar,* 3.
1 Ki. 6. 21 made a partition by the chains of gold be.

PARTLY —
1. *End, extremity,* קְצָת *qetsath.*
Dan. 2. 42 shall be partly strong, and partly broken
2. *Some part,* μέρος τι *meros ti.*
1 Co. 11. 18 divisions among you; and I partly believe
3. *This (indeed),* τοῦτο (μὲν) *touto (men).*
Heb. 10. 33 Partly, whilst ye were..partly, whilst ye

PARTNER —
1. *To have a portion, apportion,* חָלַק *chalaq.*
Prov. 29. 24 Whoso is partner with a thief hateth his
2. *One having in common,* κοινωνός *koinōnos.*
Luke 5. 10 sons of Zebedee, which were partners w.
2 Co. 8. 23 my partner and fellow helper concerning
Phm. 17 If thou count me therefore a partner, re.
3. *One holding along with,* μέτοχος *metochos.*
Luke 5. 7 they beckoned unto (their) partners, wh.

PARTRIDGE —
A partridge, caller, קֹרֵא *qore.*
1 Sa. 26. 20 as when one doth hunt a partridge in the
Jer. 17. 11 partridge sitteth (on eggs), and hatcheth

PA-RU'-AH, פָּרוּחַ *increase.*
Father of Jehoshaphat, one of Solomon's purveyors. B.C. 1040.
1 Ki. 4. 17 Jehoshaphat the son of P. in Issachar

PAR-VA'-IM, פַּרְוַיִם.
An unknown gold region.
2 Ch. 3. 6 precious stones..the gold (was) gold of P.

PA'-SACH, פָּסַךְ *limping.*
A son of Japhlet, great-grandson of Asher. B.C. 1590.
1 Ch. 7. 33 P., and Bimhal, and Ashvath. These (are)

PAS-DAM-MIM, פַּס דַּמִּים *extremity of the flowings.*
A place in the W. of Judah, between Shocho and Azekah; in 1 Sa. 17. 1 it is Ephes-dammim.
1 Ch. 11. 13 He was with David at P., and there the

PA-SE'-AH, PHA-SE'-AH, פָּסֵחַ *limping.*
1. A son of Eshton, grandson of Chelub, descendant of Caleb son of Hur. B.C. 1420.
1 Ch. 4. 12 and P., and Tehinnah the father of Irn.
2. One whose descendants were reckoned among the Nethinim.
Ezra 2. 49 the children of P., the children of Besai
Neh. 7. 51 the children of Uzza, the children of P.
3. Father of Jehoiada who helped to repair the wall. B.C. 445.
Neh. 3. 6 old gate repaired Jehoiada the son of P.

PASH'-UR, פַּשְׁחוּר *free.*
1. Head of a priestly family in Jerusalem. B.C. 589.
1 Ch. 9. 12 son of P., the son of Malchijah, and
Ezra 2. 38 The children of P., a thousand two hund.
10. 22 And of the sons of P.; Elioenai, Maaseiah
Neh. 7. 41 The children of P., a thousand two hund.
11. 12 Zechariah, the son of P., the son of Mal.
2. A priest who sealed with Nehemiah the covenant. B.C. 445.
Neh. 10. 3 P., Amariah, Malchijah
3. A son of Immer the priest, and chief governor of the house of the Lord in the days of Jeremiah. B.C. 605.
Jer. 20. 1 Now P. the son of Immer the priest, who
20. 2 Then P. smote Jeremiah the prophet, and
20. 3 P. brought forth Jeremiah out of the sto.
20. 3 The LORD hath not called thy name P., but
20. 6 And thou, P., and all that dwell in thine
38. 1 Then..Gedaliah the son of P., and Jucal
4. Son of Melchiah, a prince of Judah in the days of Jeremiah. B.C. 605.
Jer. 21. 1 P. the son of Melchiah, and Zephaniah
38. 1 P. the son of Malchiah, heard the words

PASS, (along, away, beyond, by, forth, on, out, over, through, throughout), to —
1. *To be greater than,* גָּדַל מִן *gadal min.*
2 Ch. 9. 22 king Solomon passed all the kings of the
2. *To go on,* הָלַךְ *halak.*
Job 14. 20 Thou prevailest..and he passeth: thou
Psa. 58. 8 let (every one of them) pass away; (like)
78. 39 wind that passeth away, and cometh not
Eccl. 1. 4 generation passeth away, and (another)
Hos. 13. 3 and as the early dew that passeth away
3. *To pass on,* חָלַף *chalaph.*
Job 4. 15 Then a spirit passed before my face; the
9. 11 he passeth on also, but I perceive him not
9. 26 They are passed away as the swift ships
Isa. 8. 8 shall pass through Judah; he shall overf.
21. 1 As whirlwinds in the south pass through
4. *To pass on,* חֲלַף *chalaph.*
Dan. 4. 16, 23 and let..seven times pass over him
4. 25, 32 and seven times shall pass over thee
5. *To go or pass over,* עָבַר *abar.* [Josh. 5. 1.]
Gen. 12. 6 Abram passed through the land unto the
15. 17 burning lamp that passed between those
18. 3 pass not away, I pray thee, from thy ser.
18. 5 after that ye shall pass on: for therefore
30. 32 will pass through all thy flock to day, rem.
31. 21 passed over the river, and set his face (to.)
31. 52 not pass over..thou shalt not pass over
32. 10 for with my staff I passed over this Jordan
32. 16 Pass over before me, and put a space bet.
32. 22 took his two wives..and passed over the
32. 31 as he passed over Penuel the sun rose upon
33. 3 passed over before them, and bowed hims.
33. 14 Let my lord..pass over before his servant
37. 28 there passed by Midianites, merchant m.
Exod 12. 12 pass through the land of Egypt this night
12. 23 will pass through to smite the Egyptians
15. 16 till thy people pass over, O LORD, till the
15. 16 people pass over, (which) thou hast purc.
30. 13 passeth among them that are numbered
30. 14 Every one that passeth among them that
33. 22 while my glory passeth by, that I will put
33. 22 cover thee with my hand while I pass by
34. 6 LORD passed by before him, and proclaim.
Lev. 27. 32 (even) of whatsoever passeth under the
Num 14. 7 land, which we passed through to search
20. 17 Let us pass..through thy country: we
20. 17 not pass through the fields, or through the
20. 17 not turn..until we have passed thy bord.
20. 18 Thou shalt not pass by me, lest I come out
21. 22 Let me pass through thy land: we will
21. 23 would not suffer Israel to pass through
32. 27 servants will pass over, every man armed
32. 29 If the children..will pass with you over
32. 30 if they will not pass over with you armed
32. 32 We will pass over armed before the LORD
33. 8 passed through the midst of the sea into
34. 4 pass on to Zin..and pass on to Azmon
Deut. 2. 4 Ye (are) to pass through the coast of your
2. 8 when we passed by..and passed by the
2. 18 Thou art to pass over through Ar, the co.
2. 24 Rise ye up..and pass over the river Arnon
2. 27 Let me pass through thy land: I will go
2. 28 only I will pass through on my feet
2. 29 until I shall pass over Jordan, into the la.
3. 18 ye shall pass over armed before your bre.
3. 21 all the kingdoms whither thou passest
9. 1 Thou (art) to pass over Jordan this day
11. 31 For ye shall pass over Jordan to go in to
27. 2 on the day when ye shall pass over Jordan
29. 16 through the nations which ye passed by
30. 18 land whither thou passest over Jordan to
Josh. 1. 11 Pass through the host, and command the
1. 11 for within three days ye shall pass over
1. 14 but ye shall pass before your brethren ar.
2. 23 passed over, and came to Joshua the son
3. 1 and lodged there before they passed over
3. 4 for ye have not passed (this) way hereto.
3. 6 Take up the ark..and pass over before the
3. 11 ark of the covenant..passeth over before
3. 14 removed from their tents, to pass over J.
3. 16 the people passed over right against Jer.
3. 17 Israelites passed over on dry ground, 4. 1.
4. 5 Pass over before the ark of the LORD your
4. 7 when it passed over Jordan the waters of
4. 10 and the people hasted and passed over
4. 11 that the ark of the LORD passed over, and
4. 12 passed over armed before the children of
4. 13 passed over before the LORD unto battle
6. 7 Pass on..let him that is armed pass on
6. 8 passed on before the LORD, and blew with
10. 29 Then Joshua passed from Makkedah, and
10. 31 Joshua passed from Libnah, and all Israel
10. 34 from Lachish Joshua passed unto Eglon
15. 3 passed along to Zin..and passed along to
15. 4 it passed toward Azmon, and went out
15. 6 passed along by the north of Beth-arabah
15. 7 passed toward the waters of En-shemesh
15. 10 passed along..and passed on to Timnah
15. 11 passed along to mount Baalah, and went
16. 2 passeth along unto the borders of Archi
16. 6 and passed by it on the east to Janohah
18. 9 men went and passed through the land
18. 18 passed along toward the side over against
18. 19 passed along to the side of Beth-hoglah
19. 13 from thence passeth on along on the east
22. 19 pass ye over unto the land of the posses.
24. 17 all the people through whom we passed
Judg. 3. 26 passed beyond the quarries, and escaped
3. 28 went..and suffered not a man to pass over
8. 4 Gideon..passed over, he, and the three
10. 9 passed over Jordan to fight also against
11. 17 Let me, I pray thee, pass through thy land
11. 19 Let us pass..through thy land into my p.
11. 20 trusted not Israel to pass through his co.
11. 29 passed over Gilead..and passed over Mi.
11. 29, 32 passed over (unto) the children of A.
12. 1 Wherefore passedst thou over to fight a.
12. 3 passed over against the children of Am.
18. 13 they passed thence unto mount Ephraim
19. 12 not turn aside..we will pass over to Gib.
Judg 19. 14 they passed on and went their way; and
1 Sa. 9. 4 he passed through mount Ephraim, and
9. 4 they passed through..and he passed thr.
9. 27 pass on before us, and he passed on, but
14. 8 Behold, we will pass over unto (these) men
14. 23 and the battle passed over unto Beth-aven
15. 12 is gone about, and passed on, and gone d.
27. 2 he passed over with the six hundred men
29. 2 lords of the Philistines passed on by hun.
29. 2 David and his men passed on in the rere.
2 Sa. 2. 29 passed over Jordan, and went through all
10. 17 and passed over Jordan, and came to H.
15. 18 all his servants passed on beside him; and
15. 18 six hundred men..passed on before the
15. 22 pass over. And Ittai the Gittite passed o.
15. 23 passed over: the king..passed over the b.
15. 23 people passed over, toward the way of the
15. 33 If thou passest on with me, then thou sh.
17. 16 speedily pass over; lest the king be swa.
17. 21 pass quickly over the water: for thus ha.
17. 22 passed over Jordan: by the morning light
17. 24 Absalom passed over Jordan, he and all
24. 5 passed over Jordan, and pitched in Aroer
1 Ki. 2. 37 on the day thou..passest over the brook
9. 8 every one that passeth by it shall be ast.
13. 25 men passed by, and saw the carcase cast
18. 6 divided the land..to pass throughout it
19. 11 LORD passed by, and a great and strong
19. 19 passed by him, and cast his mantle upon
20. 39 as the king passed by, he cried unto the
2 Ki. 4. 8 passed to Shunem..And..as he passed by
4. 9 holy man of God which passeth by us con.
4. 31 passed on before them, and laid the staff
6. 9 Beware that thou pass not such a place
6. 30 passed by upon the wall, and the people
12. 4 money of every one that passeth (the ac.)
14. 9 there passed by a wild beast that (was) in
1 Ch. 19. 17 passed over Jordan, and came upon them
2 Ch. 7. 21 astonishment to every one that passeth by
25. 18 there passed by a wild beast that (was) in
30. 10 passed from city to city through the co.
Neh. 2. 14 (there was) no place for the beast..to pass
Job 6. 15 as the stream of brooks they pass away
11. 16 remember (it) as waters (that) pass away
14. 5 appointed his bounds that he cannot pass
15. 19 given, and no stranger passed among them
19. 8 fenced up my way that I cannot pass, and
30. 15 and my welfare passeth away as a cloud
34. 20 be troubled at midnight, and pass away
37. 21 but the wind passeth, and cleanseth them
Psa. 8. 8 passeth through the paths of the seas
18. 12 thick clouds passed, hail (stones) and coals
37. 36 Yet he passed away, and, lo, he (was) not
48. 4 kings were assembled, they passed by to.
80. 12 so that all they which pass by the way do
84. 6 passing through the valley of Baca make
89. 41 All that pass by the way spoil him: he is
103. 16 For the wind passeth over it, and it is gone
104. 9 set a bound that they may not pass over
144. 4 his days (are) as a shadow that passeth away
148. 6 hath made a decree which shall not pass
Prov. 4. 15 pass not by it, turn from it, and pass away
8. 29 waters should not pass his commandment
10. 25 As the whirlwind passeth, so (is) the wick.
19. 11 (it is) his glory to pass over a transgression
22. 3 but the simple pass on, and are punished
26. 17 He that passeth by, (and) meddleth with
27. 12 (but) the simple pass on, (and) are punis.
Song 3. 4 (It was) but a little that I passed from them
Isa. 8. 21 they shall pass through it hardly bestead
23. 2 merchants of Zidon, that pass over the sea
23. 6 Pass ye over to Tarshish; howl, ye inha.
23. 10 Pass through thy land as a river, O daug.
23. 12 pass over to Chittim; there also shalt thou
28. 15, 18 the overflowing scourge shall pass th.
28. 19 for morning by morning shall it pass over
29. 5 as chaff that passeth away; yea, it shall
31. 9 he shall pass over to his strong hold for
33. 21 neither shall gallant ship pass thereby
34. 10 none shall pass through it for ever and e.
35. 8 unclean shall not pass over it; but it (shall
40. 27 my judgment is passed over from my God
41. 3 pursued them, (and) passed safely; (even)
43. 2 When thou passest through the waters, I
47. 2 uncover the thigh, pass over the rivers
51. 10 the sea a way for the ransomed to pass o.?
Jer. 2. 6 a land that no man passed through, and
2. 10 For pass over the isles of Chittim, and see
5. 22 a perpetual decree, that it cannot pass it
5. 22 they roar, yet can they not pass over it?
8. 13 have given them shall pass away from them
9. 10 so that none can pass through (them); n.
9. 12 like a wilderness, that none passeth th.?
13. 24 passeth away by the wind of the wilder.
18. 16 every one that passeth thereby shall be
19. 8 every one that passeth thereby shall be
22. 8 many nations shall pass by this city, and
33. 13 shall the flocks pass again under the hands
34. 18 and passed between the parts thereof
34. 19 which passed between the parts of the c.
51. 43 neither doth (any) son of man pass thereby
Lam. 1. 12 (Is it) nothing to you, all ye that pass by?
2. 15 All that pass by clap (their) hands at thee
3. 44 that (our) prayer should not pass through
4. 21 the cup also shall pass through unto thee
Eze. 5. 14 a reproach..in the sight of all that pass by
5. 17 pestilence and blood shall pass through
14. 15 that no man may pass through because of
16. 6 when I passed by thee, and saw thee pol.
16. 8 when I passed by thee, and looked upon
16. 15 on every one that passed by; his it was
16. 25 hast opened..to every one that passed by

Eze. 29. 11 No foot of man shall pass through it, nor
29. 11 foot of beast shall pass through it, neither
33. 28 be desolate, that none shall pass through
35. 7 cut off from it him that passeth out and
36. 34 desolate in the sight of all that passed by
39. 15 the passengers (that) pass through the land
47. 5 river that I could not pass over: for the
Dan. 11. 10 certainly come, and overflow, and pass t.
11. 40 enter..and shall overflow and pass over
Hos. 10. 11 but I passed over upon her fair neck: I
Joel 3. 17 no strangers pass through her any more
Amos 5. 5 pass not to Beer-sheba: for Gilgal shall
5. 17 for I will pass through thee, saith the L.
6. 2 Pass ye unto Calneh, and see; and from
7. 8 I will not again pass by them any more
8. 2 I will not again pass by them any more
Jon. 2. 3 thy billows and thy waves passed over me
Mic. 1. 11 Pass ye away, thou inhabitant of Saphir
2. 8 from them that pass by securely as men
2. 13 have broken up, and have passed through
2. 13 their king shall pass before them, and the
7. 18 passeth by the transgression of the rem.
Nah. 1. 12 be cut down, when he shall pass through
1. 15 wicked shall no more pass through thee
3. 19 upon whom hath not thy wickedness pa.
Hab. 1. 11 he shall pass over, and offend, (imputing)
3. 10 the overflowing of the water passed by
Zeph. 2. 2 the day pass as the chaff, before the fierce
2. 15 every one that passeth by her shall hiss
3. 6 their streets waste, that none passeth by
Zech. 7. 14 that no man passed through nor returned
9. 8 because of him that passeth by, and be.
9. 8 no oppressor shall pass through them any
10. 11 shall pass through the sea with affliction

6. *To cause to pass over,* עָבַר *abar,* 5.
Lev. 18. 21 not let..pass through (the fire) to Molech
Jer. 46. 17 Pharaoh..hath passed the time appointed

7. *To pass by or on,* עָדָה *adah.*
Job 28. 8 trodden it; nor the fierce lion passed by

8. *To pass by or on,* עֲדָה *adah.*
Dan. 3. 27 nor the smell of fire had passed on them
7. 14 dominion, which shall not pass away

9. *To leap or pass over,* פָּסַח *pasach.*
Exod 12. 13 when I see the blood, I will pass over you
12. 23 LORD will pass over the door, and will not
12. 27 who passed over the houses of the childr.

10. *To turn up, behave,* ἀναστρέφω *anastrephō.*
1 Pe. 1. 17 pass the time of your sojourning (here)

11. *To go up through,* διαβαίνω *diabainō.*
Luke 16. 26 so that they which would pass from hence
Heb. 11. 29 By faith they passed through the Red sea

12. *To pass over through,* διαπεράω *diaperaō.*
Matt. 9. 1 passed over, and came into his own city
Mark 5. 21 when Jesus was passed over again by ship
6. 53 when they had passed over, they came

13. *To pass on through,* διαπορεύομαι *diaporeuomai.*
Luke 18. 36 hearing the multitude pass by, he asked

14. *To come or go through,* διέρχομαι *dierchomai.*
Mark 4. 35 saith..Let us pass over unto the other si.
Luke 4. 30 passing through the midst of them went
17. 11 passed through the midst of Samaria and
19. 1 (Jesus) entered and passed through Jer.
19. 4 climbed up..for he was to pass that (way)
Acts 8. 40 passing through he preached in all the c.
9. 32 came to pass, as Peter passed throughout
14. 24 after they had passed throughout Pisid.
15. 3 they passed through Phenice and Samaria
17. 23 For as I passed by, and beheld your dev.
18. 27 he was disposed to pass into Achaia, the
19. 1 Paul having passed through the upper c.
19. 21 when he had passed through Macedonia
Rom. 5. 12 death passed upon all men, for that all
1 Co. 10. 1 under the cloud, and all passed through
16. 5 come unto you, when I shall pass through
16. 5 Macedonia: for I do pass through Mace.
2 Co. 1. 16 [to pass] by you into Macedonia, and to

15. *To travel through,* διοδεύω *diodeuō.*
Acts 17. 1 when they had passed through Amphip.

16. *To come,* ἔρχομαι *erchomai.*
Acts 5. 15 shadow of Peter passing by might oversh.

17. *To go up over,* μεταβαίνω *metabainō.*
1 Jo. 3. 14 We know that we have passed from death

18. *To lead along by,* παράγω *paragō.*
Matt. 9. 9 as Jesus passed forth from thence, he saw
20. 30 when they heard that Jesus passed by, c.
Mark 2. 14 as he passed by, he saw Levi the (son) of
15. 21 who passed by, coming out of the country
John 8. 59 [Jesus hid himself..and so passed by]
9. 1 as (Jesus) passed by, he saw a man which
1 Co. 7. 31 for the fashion of this world passeth aw.
1 Jo. 2. 17 world passeth away, and the lust there.

19. *To lie along by,* παραλέγομαι *paralegomai.*
Acts 27. 8 hardly passing it, came unto a place wh.

20. *To pass on along,* παραπορεύομαι *paraporeuomai.*
Matt 27. 39 they that passed by reviled him, wagging
Mark 9. 30 departed thence, and [passed] through
11. 20 as they passed by, they saw the fig tree
15 29 they that passed by railed on him, wagging

21. *To come or go along,* παρέρχομαι *parerchomai.*
Matt 5. 18 Till heaven and earth pass, one jot or one
5. 18 tittle shall in no wise pass from the law
8. 28 so that no man might pass by that way
24. 34 This generation shall not pass, till all t.
Matt 24. 35 pass away, but my words shall not pass a.
26. 39 if it be possible, let this cup pass from
26. 42 if this cup may not pass away from me
Mark 6. 48 saw them toiling..would have passed by
13. 30 generation shall not pass, till all these t.
13. 31 pass away, but my words shall not pass a.
14. 35 if it were possible, the hour might pass
Luke 11. 42 pass over judgment and the love of God
16. 17 it is easier for heaven and earth to pass
18. 37 told him, that Jesus of Nazareth passeth by
21. 32 generation shall not pass away till all be
21. 33 pass away; but my words shall not pass a.
Acts 16. 8 they passing by Mysia came down to Tr.
2 Co. 5. 17 old things are passed away; behold, all
Jas. 1. 10 because as the flower..he shall pass away
2 Pe. 3. 10 heavens shall pass away with a great no.
Rev. 21. 1 heaven and the first earth [were passed]

22. *To cast over, surpass,* ὑπερβάλλω *huperballō.*
Eph. 3. 19 love of Christ, which passeth knowledge

23. *To hold over, excel,* ὑπερέχω *huperechō.*
Phil. 4. 7 peace of God, which passeth all underst.

PASS, to bring to —
1. *To cause to go in,* בּוֹא *bo,* 5.
2 Ki. 19. 25 now have I brought it to pass, that thou sh.
Isa. 46. 11 I will also bring it to pass; I have purpo.

2. *To finish, determine,* כָּלָה *kalah,* 3.
Prov 16. 30 moving his lips he bringeth evil to pass

3. *To do, make,* עָבַד *abad.*
Isa. 28. 21 and bring to pass his act, his strange act

PASS, to be brought to —
To become, γίνομαι *ginomai.*
1 Co. 15. 54 then shall be brought to pass the saying

PASS, can —
To pass through, διαπεράω *diaperaō.*
Luke 16. 26 neither can they pass to us, that (would

PASS, to come to —
To be done, made, עָשָׂה *asah,* 2.
Eze. 12. 25 word that I shall speak shall come to pass
[*See under* Come to pass.]

PASS (by or through), to make (cause, let) to —
To cause to pass over, עָבַר *abar,* 5.
Gen. 8. 1 God made a wind to pass over the earth
Exod 33. 19 will make all my goodness pass before
Num 27. 7 cause the inheritance..to pass unto them
27. 8 cause his inheritance to pass unto his da.
Deut. 2. 30 would not let us pass by him: for the L.
18. 10 maketh his son..to pass through the fire
1 Sa. 16. 8 called Abinadab, and made him pass bef.
16. 9 Then Jesse made Shammah to pass by
16. 10 Jesse made seven of his sons to pass bef.
2 Sa. 12. 31 made them pass through the brick kiln
2 Ki. 16. 3 made his son to pass through the fire, a.
17. 17 they caused their sons..to pass through
21. 6 he made his son pass through the fire, and
23. 10 no man might make his son..pass through
2 Ch. 33. 6 caused his children to pass through the
Psa. 78. 13 caused them to pass through; and he made
136. 14 made Israel to pass through the midst of
Jer. 15. 14 I will make (thee) to pass with thine ene.
32. 35 cause their sons..to pass through (the fi.)
Eze. 5. 1 cause (it) to pass upon thine head and up.
14. 15 If I cause noisome beasts to pass through
16. 21 cause them to pass through (the fire) for
20. 26 caused to pass through (the fire) all that
20. 31 when ye make your sons to pass through
20. 37 I will cause you to pass under the rod, and
23. 37 caused their sons..to pass for them throu.
37. 2 And caused me to pass by them round ab.
46. 21 caused me to pass by the four corners of
Zech. 3. 4 caused thine iniquity to pass from thee
13. 2 will cause the prophets..to pass out of the

PASS by on the other side, to —
To come along over against, ἀντιπαρέρχομαι *anti.*
Luke 10. 31 saw him, he passed by on the other side
10. 32 looked..and passed by on the other side

PASS the flower of one's age, to —
Beyond the point (of age), ὑπέρακμος *huperakmos.*
1 Co. 7. 36 if she pass the flower of (her) age, and n.

PASS, place where it shall —
Passage, ford, מַעֲבָר *maabar.*
Isa. 30. 32 place where the grounded staff shall pass

PASS on through —
To come before, προέρχομαι *proerchomai.*
Acts 12. 10 went out, and passed on through one st.

PASSAGE —
1. *Passage, ford,* מַעֲבָר *maabar.*
1 Sa. 13. 23 garrison..went out to the passage of Mi.

2. *Passage, ford,* מַעְבָּרָה *mabarah.*
Judg 12. 5 Gileadites took the passages of Jordan be.
12. 6 took him, and slew him at the passages of
1 Sa. 14. 4 between the passages, by which Jonathan
Isa. 10. 29 They are gone over the passage: they have
Jer. 51. 32 passages are stopped, and the reeds they

3. *Passage,* עֵבֶר *eber.*
Jer. 22. 20 cry from the passages: for all thy lovers

PASSAGE, to give —
To pass over, עָבַר *abar.*
Num 20. 21 refused to give Israel passage through his

PASSED (away or over), to be —
1. *To front, turn the face,* פָּנָה *panah.*
Psa. 90. 9 For all our days are passed away in thy w.

2. *To pass over,* עָבַר *abar.*
Num 33. 51 When ye are passed over Jordan into the
Deut 27. 3 when thou art passed over, that thou m.
Josh. 3. 17 until all the people were passed clean over
4. 1, 11 when all the people were clean passed o.
4. 23 until ye were passed over, as the LORD your
Isa. 10. 28 He is come to Aiath, he is passed to Mig.
Jer. 11. 15 holy flesh is passed from thee? when thou

3. *To be passed over,* עָבַר *abar,* 2.
Eze. 47. 5 a river that could not be passed over

4. *To come or go away or off,* ἀπέρχομαι *aperchomai.*
Rev. 21. 4 for the former things are passed away

5. *To come or go through,* διέρχομαι *dierchomai.*
Heb. 4. 14 high priest, that is passed into the heavens

6. *To go up over,* μεταβαίνω *metabainō.*
John 5. 24 not come..but is passed from death unto

PASSENGER —
1. *To pass over the way,* עָבַר דֶּרֶךְ *abar* (partic.) *derek.*
Prov. 9. 15 To call passengers who go right on their

2. *To pass over,* עָבַר *abar* (partic.).
Eze. 39. 11 valley of the passengers on the east of the
39. 11 it shall stop the (noses) of the passengers
39. 14 bury with the passengers those that rem.
39. 15 passengers (that) pass through the land

PASSING (over) —
1. *To pass over,* עָבַר *abar.*
Judg 19. 18 We (are) passing from Beth-lehem-judah
2 Sa. 15. 24 until all the people had done passing out
2 Ki. 6. 26 as the king of Israel was passing by upon
Prov. 7. 8 Passing through the street near her corner
Eze. 39. 14 passing through the land, to bury with the

2. *To leap or pass over,* פָּסַח *pasach.*
Isa. 31. 5 As birds flying..passing over he will pre.

PASSION —
To suffer, πάσχω *paschō.*
Acts 1. 3 he showed himself alive after his passion

PASSIONS, of or subject to like—
Suffering like things, ὁμοιοπαθής *homoiopathēs.*
Acts 14. 15 We also are men of like passions with you
Jas. 5. 17 Elias was a man subject to like passions

PASSOVER (offering) —
1. *A passing over, the passover festival,* פֶּסַח *pesach.*
Exod 12. 11 eat it in haste: it (is) the LORD'S passover
12. 21 take you a lamb..and kill the passover
12. 27 It (is) the sacrifice of the LORD'S passover
12. 43 This (is) the ordinance of the passover
12. 48 will keep the passover to the LORD, let all
34. 25 sacrifice of the feast of the passover be
Lev. 23. 5 first month at even (is) the LORD'S passov.
Num. 9. 2 Let the children..also keep the passover
9. 4 spake..that they should keep the passov.
9. 5 they kept the passover on the fourteenth
9. 6 that they could not keep the passover on
9. 10 yet he shall keep the passover unto the L.
9. 12 according to all the ordinances of the pa.
9. 13 forbeareth to keep the passover, even the
9. 14 and will keep the passover unto the LORD
9. 14 according to the ordinance of the passov.
28. 16 the first month (is) the passover of the L.
33. 3 on the morrow after the passover the ch.
Deut 16. 1 keep the passover unto the LORD thy G.
16. 2 Thou shalt therefore sacrifice the passover
16. 5 Thou mayest not sacrifice the passover w
16. 6 there thou shalt sacrifice the passover at
Josh. 5. 10 kept the passover on the fourteenth day
5. 11 did eat..on the morrow after the passo.
2 Ki. 23. 21 Keep the passover unto the LORD your G.
23. 22 there was not holden such a passover from
23. 23 passover was holden to the LORD in Jerus.
2 Ch. 30. 1, 5 keep the passover unto the LORD God
30. 2 keep the passover in the second month
30. 15 killed the passover on the fourteenth (day)
30. 17 charge of the killing of the passovers for
30. 18 yet did they eat the passover otherwise
35. 1 kept a passover..and they killed the pas.
35. 6 So kill the passover, and sanctify yoursel.
35. 7 all for the passover offerings, for all that
35. 8 gave unto the priests for the passover off.
35. 9 gave unto the Levites for passover offer.
35. 11 killed the passover, and the priests spri.
35. 13 roasted the passover with fire according
35. 16 keep the passover, and to offer burnt off.
35. 17 kept the passover at that time, and the
35. 18 there was no passover like to that kept in
35. 18 keep such a passover as Josiah kept, and
35. 19 In the eighteenth year..was this passover
Ezra 6. 19 kept the passover upon the fourteenth
6. 20 killed the passover for all the children of
Eze. 45. 21 ye shall have the passover, a feast of seven

2. *Passover,* (*from Heb.* פֶּסַח) πάσχα *pascha.*
Matt 26. 2 after two days is (the feast of) the passo.
26. 17 we prepare for thee to eat the passover
26. 18 will keep the passover at thy house with
26. 19 appointed..and they made ready the pas.
Mark 14. 1 After two days was (the feast of) the pas.
14. 12 when they killed the passover, his discip.
14. 12 prepare that thou mayest eat the passov.
14. 14 where I shall eat the passover with my d.
14. 16 them: and they made ready the passover
Luke 2. 41 went..every year at the feast of the pass.

Luke 22. 1 feast..drew nigh, which is called the pas.
22. 7 Then came the day..when the passover
22. 8 Go and prepare us the passover, that we
22. 11 where I shall eat the passover with my d.
22. 13 them: and they made ready the passover
22. 15 have desired to eat this passover with you
John 2. 13 passover was at hand; and Jesus went up
2. 23 when he was in Jerusalem at the passover
6. 4 the passover, a feast of the Jews, was nigh
11. 55 Jews' passover was nigh at hand: and m.
11. 55 went..up to Jerusalem before the passo.
12. 1 six days before the passover, came to Be.
13. 1 Now before the feast of the passover, wh.
18. 28 but that they might eat the passover
18. 39 release unto you one at the passover: wi.
19. 14 it was the preparation of the passover, and
1 Co. 5. 7 For even Christ our passover is sacrificed
Heb 11. 28 Through faith he kept the passover, and

PAST —

1. *Till there is not,* עַד־אַיִן *ad en.*
Job 9. 10 Which doeth great things past finding out

2. *Before,* קֶדֶם *qedem.*
Job 29. 2 Oh that I were as (in) months past, as (in)

3. *First,* רִאשׁוֹן *rishon.*
Deut. 4. 32 For ask now of the days that are past, w.

4. *Beyond, παρά (acc.) para.*
Heb. 11. 11 was delivered of a child when she was p.

5. *To pass away, παρέρχομαι parerchomai.*
1 Pe. 4. 3 For the time past of (our) life may suffice

6. *To pass or go along, παροίχομαι paroichomai.*
Acts 14. 16 Who in times past suffered all nations to

PAST, to be —

1. *To turn aside,* סוּר *sur.*
1 Sa. 15. 32 said, Surely the bitterness of death is past

2. *To pass over,* עָבַר *abar.*
Gen. 50. 4 when the days of his mourning were past
Num 21. 22 will go along..until we be past thy border
2 Sa. 11. 27 when the mourning was past, David sent
16. 1 when David was a little past the top (of
1 Ki. 18. 29 when midday was past, and they prophe.
Job 17. 11 My days are past, my purposes are broken
Psa. 90. 4 as yesterday when it is past, and (as) a w.
Song 2. 11 the winter is past, the rain is over (and)
Jer. 8. 20 The harvest is past, the summer is ended

3. *To be pursued,* רָדַף *radaph,* 2.
Eccl. 3. 15 and God requireth that which is past

4. *To turn back,* שׁוּב *shub.*
Job 14. 13 keep me secret, until thy wrath be past

5. *To come away or off, ἀπέρχομαι aperchomai.*
Rev. 9. 12 One woe is past; (and) behold, there come
11. 14 The second woe is past; (and), behold, the

6. *To become, γίνομαι ginomai.*
Luke 9. 36 when the voice was past, Jesus was found
2 Ti. 2. 18 saying that the resurrection is past alrea.

7. *To become through or past, διαγίνομαι diaginomai.*
Mark 16. 1 when the sabbath was past, Mary Magda.

8. *To come through, διέρχομαι dierchomai.*
Acts 12. 10 When they were past the first and the se.

9. *To lead alongside, παράγω paragō.*
1 Jo. 2. 8 because the darkness is past, and the true

10. *To come alongside, παρέρχομαι parerchomai.*
Matt 14. 15 time is now past; send the multitude away
Acts 27. 9 because the fast was now already past, P.

11. *To become before, προγίνομαι proginomai.*
Rom. 3. 25 for the remission of sins that are past, th.

PAST finding out —

Not to be traced out, ἀνεξιχνίαστος anexichniastos.
Rom 11. 33 unsearchable..his ways past finding out

PAST, in time —

1. *Long ago, formerly, anciently, πάλαι palai.*
Heb. 1. 1 spake in time past unto the fathers by the

2. *Once, at some time or other, ποτέ pote.*
Rom 11. 30 For as ye in times past have not believed
Gal. 1. 13 For ye have heard..in times past in the
1. 23 he which persecuted us in times past now
Eph. 2. 2 Wherein in time past ye walked according
2. 3 had our conversation in time past in the
2. 11 ye (being) in time past Gentiles in the fle.
Phm. 11 in time past was to thee unprofitable, but
1 Pe. 2. 10 Which in time past (were) not a people

PASTOR —

1. *To feed,* רָעָה *raah* (partic.).
Jer. 2. 8 the pastors also transgressed against me
3. 15 I will give you pastors according to mine
10. 21 the pastors are become brutish, and have
12. 10 Many pastors have destroyed my vineyard
17. 16 I have not hastened from (being) a pastor
22. 22 The wind shall eat up all thy pastors, and
23. 1 Woe be unto the pastors that destroy and
23. 2 saith..against the pastors that feed my pe.

2. *Shepherd, feeder, ποιμήν poimēn.*
Eph. 4. 11 evangelists; and some, pastors and teac.

PASTURE, (fat or large) —

1. *Fat pasture,* כַּר *kar.*
Psa. 65. 13 The pastures are clothed with flocks; the
Isa. 30. 23 day shall thy cattle feed in large pastures

2. *Pasture, feeding,* מִרְעֶה *mireh.*
Gen. 47. 4 thy servants have no pasture for their flo.
1 Ch. 4. 39 they went..to seek pasture for their flocks
4. 40 they found fat pasture and good, and the
4. 41 (there was) pasture there for their flocks
Job 39. 8 The range of the mountains (is) his past.
Isa. 32. 14 dens..a joy of wild asses, a pasture of flo.
Lam. 1. 6 are become like harts (that) find no pas.
Eze. 34. 14 I will feed them in a good pasture, and
34. 14 (in) a fat pasture shall they feed upon the
34. 18 to have eaten up the good pasture, but ye
34. 18 tread down..the residue of your pastures?
Joel 1. 18 they have no pasture; yea, the flocks of

3. *Pasture, feeding,* מַרְעִית *marith.*
Psa. 74. 1 smoke against the sheep of thy pasture?
79. 13 So we thy people, and sheep of thy past.
95. 7 we (are) the people of his pasture, and the
100. 3 his people, and the sheep of his pasture
Isa. 49. 9 their pastures (shall be) in all high places
Jer. 23. 1 destroy and scatter the sheep of my past.
25. 36 for the LORD hath spoiled their pasture
Eze. 34. 31 And ye my flock, the flock of my pasture
Hos. 13. 6 According to their pasture, so were they

4. *A watered country or place,* מַשְׁקֶה *mashqeh.*
Eze. 45. 15 out of the fat pastures of Israel, for a meat.

5. *Comely place, habitation, pasture,* נָאָה *naah.*
Psa. 23. 2 He maketh me to lie down in green past.
65. 12 They drop (upon) the pastures of the wil.
Joel 1. 19, 20 devoured the pastures of the wilderness
2. 22 the pastures of the wilderness do spring

6. *Pasture, feeding place,* רְעִי *rei.*
1 Ki. 4. 23 twenty oxen out of the pastures, and an

7. *Pasture, food, νομή nomē.*
John 10. 9 and shall go in and out, and find pasture

PA-TA'-RA, Πάταρα.

A city on the coast of Lycia in Asia Minor, nearly opposite to Rhodes, with a famous oracle of Apollo, about forty miles W. of Myra; it is now in ruins.
Acts 21. 1 we came..unto Rhodes..thence unto P.

PATE —

Pate, crown of the head, קָדְקֹד *qodqod.*
Psa. 7. 16 dealing shall come down upon his own p.

PATH, PATHWAY —

1. *Path, customary road,* אֹרַח *orach.*
Gen. 49. 17 an adder in the path, that biteth the horse
Job 6. 18 The paths of their way are turned aside
8. 13 So (are) the paths of all that forget God
13. 27 and lookest narrowly unto all my paths
33. 11 feet in the stocks, he marketh all my paths
Psa. 8. 8 fish..passeth through the paths of the seas
16. 11 Thou wilt show me the path of life: in
17. 4 I have kept (me from) the paths of the d.
25. 4 Show me thy ways, O LORD, teach me thy p.
25. 10 All the paths of the LORD (are) mercy and
27. 11 lead me in a plain path, because of mine
139. 3 Thou compassest my path and my lying
Prov. 2. 8 He keepeth the paths of judgment, and p.
2. 13 Who leave the paths of uprightness, to
2. 19 neither take they hold of the paths of life
2. 20 That thou mayest..keep the paths of the
3. 6 acknowledge him..he shall direct thy pa.
4. 18 the path of the just (is) as the shining l.
5. 6 Lest thou shouldest ponder the path of l.
Isa. 2. 3 we will walk in his paths: for out of Zion
3. 12 to err, and destroy the way of thy paths
40. 14 taught him in the path of judgment and
Mic. 4. 2 and we will walk in his paths: for the law

2. *Highway,* מְסִלָּה *mesillah.*
Isa. 59. 7 wasting and destruction (are) in their p.
Joel 2. 8 they shall walk every one in his path: and

3. *A path for waggons, broad path,* מַעְגָּל *magal.*
Psa. 23. 3 leadeth me in the paths of righteousness
65. 11 Thou crownest..and thy paths drop fatn.
Prov. 2. 9 judgment, and equity; (yea), every good p.
4. 11 I have taught..I have led thee in right p.
4. 26 Ponder the path of thy feet, and let all thy
Isa. 26. 7 thou..dost weigh the path of the just

4. *A path for waggons, broad path,* מַעְגָּלָה *magalah.*
Psa. 17. 5 Hold up my goings in thy paths, (that) my
Prov. 2. 15 crooked, and (they) froward in their paths
2. 18 house inclineth unto death, and her paths

5. *A narrow path,* מִשְׁעוֹל *mishol.*
Num 22. 24 the angel of the LORD stood in a path of

6. *A trodden path,* נָתִיב *nathib.*
Job 28. 7 a path which no fowl knoweth, and which
41. 32 He maketh a path to shine after him; (one)
Psa. 119. 35 to go in the path of thy commandments

7. *A trodden path,* נְתִיבָה *nethibah.*
Job 19. 8 and he hath set darkness in my paths
24. 13 know not..nor abide in the paths thereof
30. 13 They mar my path, they set forward my
38. 20 shouldest know the paths (to) the house
Psa 119. 105 word (is) a lamp..and a light unto my p.
142. 3 thou knewest my path. In the way wher.
Prov. 1. 15 son..refrain thy foot from their path
3. 17 pleasantness, and all her paths (are) pe.
7. 25 to her ways, go not astray in her paths
8. 2 by the way in the places of the paths
8. 20 I lead..in the midst of the paths of judg.
Isa. 42. 16 I will lead them in paths (that) they have
43. 16 which maketh..a path in the mighty wat.
58. 12 called..The restorer of the paths to dwell
59. 8 have made them crooked paths; whoso.

Jer. 6. 16 ask for the old paths, where (is) the good
18. 15 to walk in paths, (in) a way not cast up
Lam. 3. 9 inclosed my ways..he hath made my path
Hos. 2. 6 make a wall..she shall not find her paths

8. *A going on, path,* שְׁבִיל *shebil* [Jer. 18. 15, V.L. שבול].
Psa. 77 19 thy path in the great waters, and thy fo.
Jer. 18. 15 them to stumble..(from) the ancient paths

9. *A rubbed or trodden path, τρίβος tribos.*
Matt. 3. 3 Prepare ye the way..make his paths str.
Mark 1. 3 Prepare ye the way..make his paths str.
Luke 3. 4 Prepare ye the way..make his paths str.

10. *A track, τροχιά trochia.*
Heb. 12. 13 make straight paths for your feet, lest th.

11. *A path way,* דֶּרֶךְ נְתִיבָה *derek nethibah.*
Prov 12. 28 (in) the pathway (thereof there is) no death

PATH'-ROS, פַּתְרוֹס.

Upper Egypt or Thebaid, as distinguished from Mazor, Lower Egypt, and *Mizraim,* including both. See Jer. 44. 1; 44. 15; Eze. 29. 14 and 30. 14.
Isa. 11. 11 his people, which shall be left, from..P.
Jer. 44. 1 at Noph, and in the country of P., saying
44. 15 all the people that dwelt..in P., answered
Eze. 29. 14 cause them to return (into) the land of P.
30. 14 And I will make P. desolate, and will set

PATH-RU'-SIM, פַּתְרֻסִים.

A descendant of the fifth son of Mizraim son of Ham.
Gen. 10. 14 P., and Casluhim, out of whom came Ph.
1 Ch. 1. 12 P., and Casluhim, of whom came the Ph.

PATIENCE —

1. *Forbearance, long suffering, μακροθυμία makroth.*
Heb. 6. 12 who through faith and patience inherit
Jas. 5. 10 example of suffering affliction, and of pa.

2. *Endurance, continuance, ὑπομονή hupomonē.*
Luke 8. 15 keep (it), and bring forth fruit with pat.
21. 19 In your patience possess ye your souls
Rom. 5. 3 knowing that tribulation worketh patien.
5. 4 patience, experience; and experience, h.
8. 25 (then) do we with patience wait for (it)
15. 4 we through patience and comfort of the
15. 5 the God of patience and consolation gra.
2 Co. 6. 4 much patience, in afflictions, in necessities
12. 12 were wrought among you in all patience
Col. 1. 11 unto all patience and long suffering with
1 Th. 1. 3 patience of hope in our Lord Jesus Christ
2 Th. 1. 4 for your patience and faith in all your
1 Ti. 6. 11 godliness, faith, love, patience, meekness
2 Ti. 3. 10 my..faith, long suffering, charity, pat.
Titus 2. 2 be..sound in faith, in charity, in patience
Heb. 10. 36 ye have need of patience, that, after ye
12. 1 let us run with patience the race that is
Jas. 1. 3 the trying of your faith worketh patience
1. 4 let patience have (her) perfect work, that
5. 11 Ye have heard of the patience of Job, and
2 Pe. 1. 6 to temperance patience; and to patience
Rev. 1. 9 in the kingdom and patience of Jesus Ch.
2. 2 thy works, and thy labour, and thy patie.
2. 3 hast borne, and hast patience, and for my
2. 19; 3. 10; 13. 10; 14. 12

PATIENT waiting —

Endurance, ὑπομονή hupomonē, 2 Th. 3. 5.

PATIENCE, to have (long) —

To forbear, bear long, μακροθυμέω makrothumeō.
Matt 18. 26, 29 have patience with me, and I will pay
Jas 5. 7 hath long patience for it, until he receive

PATIENT —

1. *Long,* אָרֵךְ *arek.*
Eccl. 7. 8 the patient in spirit (is) better than the p.

2. *Holding up under evil, ἀνεξίκακος anexikakos.*
2 Ti. 2. 24 gentle unto all (men), apt to teach, pati.

3. *Yielding, lenient, ἐπιεικής epieikēs.*
1 Ti. 3. 3 but patient, not a brawler, not covetous

4. *To remain under, ὑπομένω hupomenō.*
Rom 12. 12 patient in tribulation; continuing instant

PATIENT, to be —

To forbear, suffer long, μακροθυμέω makrothumeō.
1 Th. 5. 14 support the weak, be patient toward all
Jas. 5. 7 Be patient therefore, brethren, unto the
5. 8 Be ye also patient; stablish your hearts

PATIENTLY, (to take) —

1. *To wait, expect,* קָוָה *qavah,* 3.
Psa. 40. 1 I waited patiently for the LORD; and he

2. *Forbearingly, with long suffering, μακροθύμως.*
Acts 26. 3 wherefore I beseech thee to hear me pat.

3. *To remain under, ὑπομένω hupomenō.*
1 Pe. 2. 20 ye shall take is patiently?..ye take it pat.
[*See also* Continuance, endure, wait, waiting.]

PAT'-MOS, Πάτμος.

A sterile island about thirty miles in circumference, in the Ægean Sea, S. W. of Samos, and forty-five miles W. of Miletus; now called Patino, or Patimo, or Patmosa, and reckoned among the Sporades, with an excellent harbour.
Rev. 1. 9 was in the isle that is called P., for the

PATRIARCH —

Head of a father's house, πατριάρχης patriarchēs.
Acts 2. 29 let me freely speak unto you of the patr.
7. 8 and so..Jacob (begat) the twelve patria.

Acts 7. 9 the patriarchs, moved with envy, sold Jo.
Heb. 7. 4 the patriarch Abraham gave the tenth of

PATRIMONY, of his —
Upon (concerning) the fathers (clans), עַל־הָאָבוֹת [*al*].
Deut 18. 8 that which cometh of the sale of his pat.

PA-TRO'-BAS, Πατρόβας.
A believer in Rome to whom Paul sends a salutation.
Rom.16. 14 Salute Asyncritus..P., Hermes..and the

PATTERN —
1. *Sight, appearance*, מַרְאֶה *mareh*.
Num. 8. 4 pattern which the LORD had showed Mo
2. *Building, form, pattern*, תַּבְנִית *tabnith*.
Josh 22. 28 the pattern of the altar of the LORD, wh.
Exod 25. 9 the pattern of the tabernacle, and the p.
25. 40 look that thou make (them) after their p.
2 Ki. 16. 10 the pattern of it, according to all the
1 Ch. 28. 11 the pattern of the porch, and of the houses
28. 12 the pattern of all that he had by the spirit
28. 18 pattern of the chariot of the cherubim
28. 19 understand..all the works of this pattern
3. *Standard, measurement*, תָּכְנִית *toknith*.
Eze. 43. 10 show..and let them measure the pattern
4. *A type, model*, τύπος *tupos*.
Titus 2. 7 showing thyself a pattern of good works
Heb. 8. 5 according to the pattern showed to thee
5. *An exhibition, pattern*, ὑπόδειγμα *hupodeigma*.
Heb. 9. 23 that the patterns of things in the heavens
6. *An under or lesser type*, ὑποτύπωσις *hupotupōsis*.
1 Ti. 1. 16 a pattern to them which should hereafter

PA'-U, פָּעוּ, *a yawning deep*.
The city of Hadar, the last of the early kings of Edom.
Gen. 36. 39 the name of his city (was) P.; and his w.
[*See* PAI.]

PAUL, PAULUS, Παῦλος *little*.
1. The surname of the Roman deputy at Paphos who believed the gospel when Elymas the sorcerer was struck blind.
Acts 13. 7 Sergius P., a prudent man: who called

2. The apostle of the Gentiles, whose original name was Saul. He was of the tribe of Benjamin, a Hebrew of the Hebrews, born in Tarsus, the chief city of Cilicia, in Asia Minor. He was brought up a Pharisee, and educated at Jerusalem, at the feet of Gamaliel, a celebrated Rabbi. His vernacular tongue was Greek, but his residence in Palestine gave him a knowledge of the Syro-chaldaic of that day, which is called in the New Testament "Hebrew." He was acquainted with several of the ancient Greek poets, whom he occasionally quotes. Like all Jews, he was brought up to a trade, which, in his case, was that of a tent maker. His residence at Jerusalem augmented his natural regard for Judaism, and led him, while yet a young man, to bear his testimony against Christianity, by consenting to the martyrdom of Stephen, and watching over the clothes of those who stoned him.
Soon the great landmarks of his life began to appear. Foremost of all was his conversion, A.D. 38, which became the main root of his after life Then his evangelistic labours at Antioch, A.D 42; his missionary journey in the eastern part of Asia Minor. in which he first assumed the character of an apostle to the Gentiles; his visit to Jerusalem, A.D. 50, to settle the question of the relation of the Gentiles to the law of Moses; his second missionary journey when he introduced the gospel into Europe, with his visit to Phillipi, Athens, and Corinth. Then comes his third great missionary journey which was chiefly marked by a long stay at Ephesus, and interesting in connection with the writing of his four leading Epistles. Then followed his visit to Jerusalem, A.D. 58, and his apprehension there, with his long confinement at Cesarea, and his eventual imprisonment at Rome, A.D. 61, whence he wrote most of his other epistles. Of his later history we know nothing. As to his temperament and character, Paul is himself the best painter. His humility induced him to abandon the grand title of "Saul," and assume the humble one of "Paul," *i.e.*, the "little one," appropriate, perhaps, from his bodily size, but adopted, no doubt, from that humility which makes him count himself to be "less than the least of all saints, and not worthy to be called an apostle." His speeches and epistles convey to us the truest impression of him. In these we perceive the warmth and ardour of his nature, his affectionate disposition, the tenderness of his sense of honour, the courtesy and personal dignity of his bearing, and his perfect frankness. We see also the rare combination of subtility, tenacity, and versatility existing in his intellect, with a practical wisdom generally associated with a cooler temperament than his, and a forbearance and tolerance seldom united with such impetuous convictions as he entertained.

Acts 13. 9 Then Saul who also (is called) P., filled with
13. 13 Now when P. and his company loosed from
13. 16 Then P. stood up, and beckoning with
13. 43 many of the Jews..followed P. and Barn.
13. 45 against..things which were spoken by P.
13. 46 Then P. and Barnabas waxed bold, and
13. 50 and raised persecution against P. and B.
14. 9 The same heard P. speak: who stedfastly
14. 11 And when the people saw what P. had
14. 12 And they called..P., Mercurius, because
14. 14 when the apostles, Barnabas and P., heard
14. 19 and, having stoned P., drew (him) out of
15. 2 When therefore P. and Barnabas had no
Acts 15. 2 they determined that P. and Barnabas
15. 12 gave audience to Barnabas and P., decla.
15. 22 to send..to Antioch with P. and Barnab.
15. 25 to send..with our beloved Barnabas..P.
15. 35 P. also and Barnabas continued in Antioch
15. 36 And some days after, P. said unto Barna.
15. 38 But P. thought not good to take him with
15. 40 And P. chose Silas, and departed, being re.
16. 3 Him would P. have to go forth with him
16. 9 And a vision appeared to P. in the night
16. 14 unto the things which were spoken of P.
16. 17 The same followed P. and us, and cried
16. 18 But P., being grieved, turned and said to
16. 19 they caught P. and Silas, and drew (them)
16. 25 And at midnight P. and Silas prayed, and
16. 28 But P. cried with a loud voice, saying, Do
16. 29 and fell down before P. and Silas
16. 36 And the keeper..told this saying to P.
16. 37 But Paul said unto them, They have bea.
17. 2 And P., as his manner was, went in unto
17. 4 and consorted with P. and Silas; and of
17. 10 the brethren immediately sent away P.
17. 13 the word of God was preached of P. at B.
17. 14 immediately the brethren sent away P.
17. 15 And they that conducted P. brought him
17. 16 Now while P. waited for them at Athens
17. 22 Then P. stood in the midst of Mars' hill
17. 33 So P. departed from among them
18. 1 After these things [P.] departed from Ath.
18. 5 P. was pressed in the spirit, and testified
18. 9 Then spake the Lord to P. in the night by
18. 12 the Jews made insurrection..against P.
18. 14 And when P. was now about to open (his)
18. 18 And P. (after this) tarried (there) yet a
19. 1 P. having passed through the upper coa.
19. 4 Then said P., John verily baptized with
19. 6 And when P. had laid (his) hands upon the.
19. 11 And God wrought..by the hands of P.
19. 13 We adjure you by Jesus whom P. preach.
19. 15 Jesus I know, and P. I know; but who are
19. 21 P. purposed in the spirit, when he had p.
19. 26 this P. hath persuaded and turned away
19. 29 men of Macedonia, P.'s companions in tr.
19. 30 And when P. would have entered in unto
20. 1 P. called unto (him) the disciples, and em.
20. 7 P. preached unto them, ready to depart
20. 9 and as P. was long preaching, he sunk
20. 10 And P. went down, and fell on him, and
20. 13 there intending to take in P.: for so had
20. 16 For P. had determined to sail by Ephesus
20. 37 and fell on P.'s neck, and kissed him
21. 4 who said to P. through the spirit, that he
21. 8 we that were of P.'s company departed, and
21. 11 he took P.'s girdle, and bound his own han.
21. 13 Then P. answered, What mean ye to weep
21. 18 And the (day) following P. went in with
21. 26 Then P. took the men, and the next day
21. 29 whom they supposed that P. had brought
21. 30 and they took P., and drew him out of the
21. 32 and when they saw..they left beating of P.
21. 37 And as P. was to be led into the castle, he
21. 39 But P. said, I am a man (which am) a Jew
21. 40 P. stood on the stairs, and beckoned with
22. 25 P. said unto the centurion that stood by
22. 28 With a great sum..And P. said, But I was
22. 30 and brought P. down, and set him before
23. 1 And P., earnestly beholding the council
23. 3 Then said P. unto him, God shall smite
23. 5 Then said P., I wist not, brethren, that
23. 6 But when P. perceived that the one part
23. 10 fearing lest P. should have been pulled
23. 11 Be of good cheer, [P.]: for as thou hast
23. 12 eat nor drink till they had killed P.
23. 14 will eat nothing until we have slain P.
23. 16 when P.'s sister's son heard of their lying
23. 16 and entered into the castle, and told P.
23. 17 Then P. called one of the centurions
23. 18 P. the prisoner called me unto (him), and
23. 20 bring down P to morrow into the council
23. 24 that they may set P. on, and bring (him)
23. 31 Then the soldiers..took P., and brought
23. 33 when they came to Cesarea..presented P.
24. 1 who informed the governor against P.
24. 10 Then P, after that the governor had bec.
24. 23 he commanded a centurion to keep [P.]
24. 24 he sent for P., and heard him concerning
24. 26 money should have been given him of P.
24. 27 to show the Jews a pleasure, left P. bound
25. 2 chief of the Jews informed him against P.
25. 4 P. should be kept at Cesarea, and that
25. 6 the next day..commanded P. to be brou.
25. 7 [many and grievous complaints against P.]
25. 9 answered P., and said, Wilt thou go up to
25. 10 Then said P., I stand at Cesar's judgment
25. 14 Festus declared P.'s cause unto the king
25. 19 which was dead, whom P. affirmed to be
25. 21 P. had appealed to be reserved unto the
25. 23 at Festus' commandment P. was brought
26. 1 Agrippa said unto P., Thou art permitted
26. 1 P. stretched forth the hand, and answered
26. 24 P., thou art beside thyself; much learning
26. 28 Agrippa said unto P., Almost thou pers.
26. 29 P. said, I would to God, that not only thou
27. 1 delivered P. and certain other prisoners
27. 3 Julius courteously entreated P., and gave
27. 9 the fast was now..past, P. admonished
27. 11 than those things which were spoken by P.
27. 21 P. stood forth in the midst of them, and
27. 24 Fear not, P.; thou must be brought bef.
27. 31 P. said to the centurion and to the soldi.
27. 33 P. besought (them) all to take meat, say.
27. 43 the centurion, willing to save P., kept th.
Acts 28 3 P. had gathered a bundle of sticks, and
28. 8 P. entered in, and prayed, and laid his h.
28. 15 when P. saw, he thanked God, and took
28. 16 P. was suffered to dwell by himself with
28. 17 [P.] called the chief of the Jews together
28. 25 after that P. had spoken one word, Well
28. 30 [P.] dwelt two whole years in his own hi.
Rom. 1. 1 P., a servant of Jesus Christ, called (to be)
1 Co. 1. 1 P., called (to be) an apostle of Jesus Chr.
1. 12 I am of P.; and I of Apollos; and I of Ce.
1. 13 Is Christ divided? was P. crucified for you?
1. 13 or were ye baptized in the name of P.?
3. 4 I am of P.; and another, I (am) of Apollos
3. 5 Who then is P., and who (is) Apollos, but
3. 22 Whether P., or Apollos, or Cephas, or the
16. 21 The salutation of (me) P. with mine own
2 Co. 1. 1 P., an apostle of Jesus Christ by the will
10. 1 I P. myself beseech you by the meekness
Gal. 1. 1 P., an apostle, not of men, neither by man
5. 2 I P. say unto you, that if ye be circumcised
Eph. 1. 1 P, an apostle of Jesus Christ by the will
3. 1 P., the prisoner of Jesus Christ for you
Phil. 1. 1 P. and Timotheus, the servants of Jesus
Col. 1. 1 P., an apostle of Jesus Christ by the will
1. 23 whereof I P. am made a minister
4. 18 The salutation by the hand of me P. Re.
1 Th. 1. 1 P., and Silvanus, and Timotheus, unto
2. 18 we would have come unto you, even I P.
2 Th. 1. 1 P., and Silvanus, and Timotheus, unto
3. 17 The salutation of P. with mine own hand
1 Ti. 1. 1 P., an apostle of Jesus Christ by the
2 Ti. 1. 1 P., an apostle of Jesus Christ by the will
Titus 1. 1 P., a servant of God, and an apostle of
Phm. 1 P., a prisoner of Jesus Christ, and Timo.
9 being such an one as P. the aged, and now
19 I P. have written (it) with mine own hand
2 Pe. 3. 15 as our beloved brother P. also, according

PAVED, (being) —
1. *White work*, לִבְנָה *libnah*.
Exod 24. 10 as it were..paved work of a sapphire stone
2. *To pave, cover, overlay*, רָצַף *ratsaph*.
Song 3. 10 the midst thereof being paved (with) love

PAVEMENT —
1. *Pavement*, מַרְצֶפֶת *martsepheth*.
2 Ki. 16. 17 king Ahaz..put it upon a pavement of s.
2. *Pavement, floor*, רִצְפָּה *ritspah*.
2 Ch. 7. 3 with their faces to the ground upon the p.
Esth. 1. 6 a pavement of red, and blue, and white
Eze. 40. 17 pavement made for the court round about
40. 17 thirty chambers (were) upon the pavement
40. 18 And the pavement..(was) the lower pave.
42. 3 the pavement which (was) for the outer co.
3. *Paved with stone*, λιθόστρωτος *lithostrōtos*.
John 19. 13 in a place that is called the Pavement, but

PAVILION —
1. *A covering*, סֹךְ *sok*.
Psa. 27. 5 he shall hide me in his pavilion: in the
2. *A booth*, סֻכָּה *sukkah*.
2 Sa. 22. 12 made darkness pavilions round about him
1 Ki. 20. 12 he and the kings in the pavilions, that he
20. 16 drinking himself drunk in the pavilions
Psa. 18. 11 his pavilion round about him (were) dark
31. 20 thou shalt keep them secretly in a pavilion

PAW —
1. *Hand*, יָד *yad*.
1 Sa. 17. 37 the paw of the lion, and out of the paw of
2. *Palm (of the hand)*, כַּף *kaph*.
Lev. 11. 27 whatsoever goeth upon his paws, among

PAW, to —
To dig, paw, חָפַר *chaphar*.
Job 39. 21 He paweth in the valley, and rejoiceth in

PAY —
To give a price, נָתַן מֶכֶר *nathan meker*.
Num 20. 19 I will pay for it: I will only, without..a.

PAY (again), to —
1. *To give*, נָתַן *nathan*.
Exod 21. 19 only he shall pay (for) the loss of his time
21. 22 and he shall pay as the judges (determine)
Jon. 1. 3 he paid the fare thereof, and went down
2. *To give*, נְתַן *nethan*.
Ezra 4. 13 will they not pay toll, tribute, and custom
3. *To make complete*, שָׁלַם *shalam*, 3.
Exod 21. 36 he shall surely pay ox for ox; and the d.
22. 7 if the thief be found, let him pay double
22. 9 For..he shall pay double unto his neighb.
Deut 23. 21 thou shalt not slack to pay it: for the L.
2 Sa. 15. 7 let me go and pay my vow, which I have
2 Ki. 4. 7 and pay thy debt, and live thou and thy
Job 22. 27 hear thee, and thou shalt pay thy vows
Psa. 22. 25 I will pay my vows before them that fear
37. 21 The wicked borroweth, and payeth not
50. 14 and pay thy vows unto the most High
66. 13 I will go into thy house..I will pay thee
76. 11 pay unto the LORD your God: let all that
116. 14, 18 I will pay my vows unto the LORD now
Prov. 7. 14 offerings with me; this day have I paid my
19. 17 that..he hath given will he pay him again
22. 27 If thou hast nothing to pay, why should
Eccl. 5. 4 defer not to pay it..pay that which thou
5. 5 than that thou shouldest vow and not p.
Jon. 2. 9 sacrifice..I will pay (that) that I have v.

4. *To weigh out,* שָׁקַל *shaqal.*

Exod 22. 17 he shall pay money according to the dow.
1 Ki. 20. 39 or else thou shalt pay a talent of silver
Esth. 3. 9 I will pay ten thousand talents of silver
4. 7 Haman had promised to pay to the king's

5. *To cause to turn back,* שׁוּב *shub,* 5.

2 Ch. 27. 5 So much did the children of Ammon pay

6. *To give away or back,* ἀποδίδωμι *apodidōmi.*

Matt. 5. 26 till thou hast paid..uttermost farthing
18. 25 as he had not to pay, his lord commanded
18. 26, 29 patience with me, and I will pay thee
18. 28 took (him)..saying, Pay me that thou ow.
18. 30 cast him into prison, till he should pay
18. 34 till he should pay all that was due unto
Luke 7. 42 when they had nothing to pay, he frankly
12. 59 not..till thou hast paid the very last mi.

7. *To pay,* τελέω *teleō.*

Matt 17. 24 said, Doth not your master pay tribute?
Rom 13. 6 For, for this cause pay ye tribute also: for

PAY, to make to —

To cause to go up, impose, עָלָה *alah,* 5.

2 Ch. 8. 8 Solomon make to pay tribute until this

PAYMENT to be made —

To give away or back, ἀποδίδωμι *apodidōmi.*

Matt 18. 25 all that he had, and payment to be made

PEACE —

1. *Rest, ease, security,* שַׁלְוָה *shalvah.*

Dan. 8. 25 by peace shall destroy many: he shall also

2. *Completeness, peace,* שָׁלוֹם *shalom.*

Gen. 15. 15 shalt go to thy fathers in peace; thou
26. 29 have sent thee away in peace: thou (art)
26. 31 and they departed from him in peace
28. 21 come again to my father's house in peace
41. 16 God shall give Pharaoh an answer of peace
43. 23 Peace (be) to you, fear not: your God, and
44. 17 as for you, get you up in peace unto your
Exod. 4. 18 And Jethro said to Moses, Go in peace
18. 23 people shall also go to their place in peace
Lev. 26. 6 I will give peace in the land, and ye shall
Num. 6. 26 lift up his countenance..and give thee p.
25. 12 I give unto him my covenant of peace
Deut. 2. 26 sent messengers. with words of peace, s.
20. 10 When thou comest nigh..proclaim peace
20. 11 shall be, if it make thee answer of peace
23. 6 Thou shalt not seek their peace nor their
29. 19 I shall have peace, though I walk in the
Josh. 9. 15 Joshua made peace with them, and made
10. 21 all the people returned..in peace: none
Judg. 4. 17 peace between Jabin the king of Hazor and
6. 23 Peace (be) unto thee; fear not: thou shalt
8. 9 When I come again in peace, I will break
11. 31 when I return in peace from the children
18. 6 Go in peace: before the LORD (is) your way
19. 20 Peace (be) with thee: howsoever (let) all
1 Sa. 1. 17 Go in peace: and the God of Israel grant
7. 14 there was peace between Israel and the A.
20. 7 thy servant shall have peace: but if he be
20. 13 that thou mayest go in peace: and the L.
20. 21 for (there is) peace to thee, and no hurt
20. 42 Go in peace, forasmuch as we have sworn
25. 6 Peace (be) both to thee, and peace (be) to
25. 6 and peace (be) unto all that thou hast
25. 35 Go up in peace to thine house; see, I have
29. 7 return, and go in peace, that thou displ.
2 Sa. 3. 21 sent Abner away; and he went in peace
3. 22 sent him away, and he was gone in peace
3. 23 sent him away, and he is gone in peace
15. 9 king said unto him, Go in peace. So he a.
15. 27 return into the city in peace, and your
17. 3 returned: (so) all the people shall be in p.
19. 24 departed..the day he came (again) in pe.
19. 30 my lord the king is come again in peace
1 Ki. 2. 5 shed the blood of war in peace, and put
2. 6 hoar head go down to the grave in peace
2. 33 shall there be peace for ever from the L.
4. 24 had peace on all sides round about him
5. 12 was peace between Hiram and Solomon
20. 18 Whether they be come out for peace, take
22. 17 return every man to his house in peace
22. 27 water of affliction, until I come in peace
22. 28 If thou return at all in peace, the LORD
2 Ki. 5. 19 said unto him, Go in peace. So he departed
9. 17 to meet them, and let him say, (Is it) pe.?
9. 18, 19 Thus saith the king, (Is it) peace? And
9. 18, 19 What hast thou to do with peace? turn
9. 22 (Is it) peace..he answered, What peace, so
9. 31 (Had) Zimri peace, who slew his master?
20. 19 not (good), if peace and truth be in my d.?
22. 20 shalt be gathered into thy grave in peace
1 Ch. 12. 18 peace, peace (be) unto thee, and peace (be)
22. 9 give peace and quietness unto Israel in his
2 Ch. 15. 5 in those times (there was) no peace to him
18. 16 return..every man to his house in peace
18. 26 water of affliction, until I return in peace
18. 27 If thou certainly return in peace, (then)
19. 1 returned to his house in peace to Jerusalem
34. 28 shalt be gathered to thy grave in peace
Ezra 9. 12 seek their peace or their wealth for ever
Esth. 9. 30 sent the letters..(with) words of peace
10. 3 and speaking peace to all his seed
Job 5. 24 know that thy tabernacle (shall be) in pe.
25. 2 with him; he maketh peace in his high p.
Psa. 4. 8 will both lay me down in peace, and sleep
28. 3 which speak peace to their neighbours, but
29. 11 the LORD will bless his people with peace
Psa. 34. 14 Depart from evil, and do good; seek peace
35. 20 For they speak not peace; but they devise
37. 11 shall delight..in the abundance of peace
37. 37 upright: for the end of (that) man (is) pe.
55. 18 He hath delivered my soul in peace from
72. 3 mountains shall bring peace to the people
72. 7 abundance of peace so long as the moon e.
85. 8 for he will speak peace unto his people, and
85. 10 righteousness and peace have kissed (each
119. 165 Great peace have they which love thy law
120. 6 hath long dwelt with him that hateth pe.
120. 7 peace: but when I speak, they (are) for
122. 6 Pray for the peace of Jerusalem: they shall
122. 7 Peace be within thy walls..prosperity wi.
122. 8 sakes, I will now say, Peace (be) within
125. 5 the workers of iniquity..peace..upon Isr.
128. 6 children's children, (and) peace upon Isr.
147. 14 He maketh peace (in) thy borders, (and)
Prov. 3. 2 long life, and peace, shall they add to thee
3. 17 pleasantness, and all her paths (are) peace
12. 20 but to the counsellors of peace (is) joy
Eccl. 3. 8 A time..a time of war, and a time of pe.
Isa. 9. 6 The everlasting Father, The Prince of P.
9. 7 Of the increase of..government and peace
26. 12 thou wilt ordain peace for us: for thou
27. 5 make peace with me..he shall make peace
32. 17 the work of righteousness shall be peace
33. 7 ambassadors of peace shall weep bitterly
38. 17 for peace I had great bitterness; but thou
39. 8 there shall be peace and truth in my days
45. 7 I make peace, and create evil: I the LORD
48. 18 then had thy peace been as a river, and
48. 22 (There is) no peace, saith the LORD, unto
52. 7 that publisheth peace; that bringeth good
53. 5 the chastisement of our peace (was) upon
54. 10 neither shall the covenant of my peace be
54. 13 and great (shall be) the peace of thy chi.
55. 12 ye shall go..be led forth with peace: the
57. 2 He shall enter into peace: they shall rest
57. 19 Peace, peace to (him that is) far off, and
57. 21 (There is) no peace, saith my God, to the
59. 8 The way of peace they know not; and (th.)
59. 8 whosoever goeth therein..not know peace
60. 17 I will also make thy officers peace, and
66. 12 I will extend peace to her like a river, and
Jer. 4. 10 saying, Ye shall have peace; whereas the
6. 14 Peace, peace; when (there is) no peace
8. 11 Peace, peace; when (there is) no peace
8. 15 We looked for peace, but no good (came)
12. 5 in the land of peace, (wherein) thou trus.
12. 12 sword..devour..no flesh shall have peace
14. 13 I will give you assured peace in this place
14. 19 we looked for peace, and (there is) no good
16. 5 I have taken away my peace from this p.
23. 17 The LORD hath said, Ye shall have peace
28. 9 The prophet which prophesieth of peace
29. 7 seek the peace of the city whither I have
29. 7 for in the peace thereof shall ye have pe.
29. 11 thoughts of peace, and not of evil, to give
30. 5 voice of trembling, of fear, and not of pe.
33. 6 reveal unto them the abundance of peace
34. 5 thou shalt die in peace: and with the b.
43. 12 and he shall go forth from thence in peace
Lam. 3. 17 hast removed my soul far off from peace
Eze. 7. 25 they shall seek peace, and (there shall be)
13. 10 saying, Peace; and (there was) no peace
13. 16 of peace for her, and (there is) no peace
34. 25 I will make with them a covenant of peace
37. 26 I will make a covenant of peace with them
Dan. 10. 19 peace (be) unto thee; be strong, yea, be
Mic. 3. 5 that bite with their teeth, and cry, Peace
5. 5 And this..shall be the peace, when the A.
Nah. 1. 15 feet of him..that publisheth peace! O J.
Hag. 2. 9 in this place will I give peace, saith the L.
Zech. 6. 13 the counsel of peace shall be between them
8. 10 neither (was there any) peace to him that
8. 16 execute the judgment of truth and peace
8. 19 feasts; therefore love the truth and peace
9. 10 and he shall speak peace unto the heathen
Mal. 2. 5 My covenant was with him of life and p.
2. 6 he walked with me in peace and equity

3. *Completeness, peace,* שְׁלָם *shelam.*

Ezra 4. 17 (unto) the rest..Peace, and at such a time
5. 7 written thus; Unto Darius the king, all p.
Dan. 4. 1 unto all people..Peace be multiplied unto
6. 25 Darius wrote..Peace be multiplied unto

4. *Peace, unity, concord,* εἰρήνη *eirēnē.*

Matt 10. 13 let your peace come..let your peace return
10. 34 peace on earth: I came not to send peace
Mark 5. 34 go in peace, and be whole of thy plague
Luke 1. 79 to guide our feet into the way of peace
2. 14 and on earth peace, good will toward men
2. 29 now lettest thou thy servant depart in p.
7. 50 Thy faith hath saved thee; go in peace
8. 48 thy faith hath made thee whole; go in p.
10. 5 whatsoever house ye enter, first say, Peace
10. 6 if the son of peace be there, your peace
11. 21 keepeth his palace, his goods are in peace
12. 51 Suppose ye that I am come to give peace
14. 32 sendeth..and desireth conditions of peace
19. 38 peace in heaven, and glory in the highest
19. 42 the things (which belong) unto thy peace
24. 36 [saith unto them, Peace (be) unto you]
John 14. 27 Peace I leave with you, my peace I give
16. 33 I have spoken..that in me ye might have p.
20. 19 and saith unto them, Peace (be) unto you
20. 21 Peace (be) unto you: as (my) Father hath
20. 26 stood in the midst, and said, Peace (be)
Acts 10. 36 preaching peace by Jesus Christ: he is L.
12. 20 desired peace; because their country was
15. 33 they were let go in peace from the breth.
Acts 16. 36 told..now therefore depart, and go in p.
Rom. 1. 7 Grace to you and peace from God our Fa.
2. 10 peace, to every man that worketh good
3. 17 And the way of peace have they not kno.
5. 1 we have peace with God through our Lo.
8. 6 to be spiritually minded (is) life and peace
10. 15 of them that preach the gospel [of peace]
14. 17 and peace, and joy in the Holy Ghost
14. 19 follow after the things which make for p.
15. 13 with all joy and peace in believing, that
15. 33 Now the God of peace (be) with you all
16. 20 the God of peace shall bruise Satan under
1 Co. 1. 3 peace, from God our Father, and (from)
7. 15 depart..but God hath called us to peace
14. 33 not (the author) of confusion but of pea.
16. 11 conduct him forth in peace, that he may
2 Co. 1. 2 peace from God our Father, and (from)
13. 11 the God of love and peace shall be with
Gal. 1. 3 peace from God the Father, and (from)
5. 22 peace, long suffering, gentleness, goodne.
6. 16 peace (be) on them, and mercy, and upon
Eph. 1. 2 peace, from God our Father, and (from)
2. 14 he is our peace, who hath made both one
2. 15 of twain one new man, (so) making peace
2. 17 preached peace to you which were afar off
4. 3 the unity of the spirit in the bond of pe.
6. 15 with the preparation of the gospel of pe.
6. 23 Peace (be) to the brethren, and love with
Phil. 1. 2 peace, from God our Father, and (from)
4. 7 the peace of God, which passeth all unde.
4. 9 and the God of peace shall be with you
Col. 1. 2 peace, from God our Father and the Lord
3. 15 let the peace of God rule in your hearts
1 Th. 1. 1 peace, from God our Father, and the Lord
5. 3 when they shall say, Peace and safety, t.
5. 23 the very God of peace sanctify you wholly
2 Th. 1. 2 peace, from God our Father and the Lord
3. 16 the Lord of peace himself give you peace
1 Ti. 1. 2 peace, from God our Father and Jesus C.
2 Ti. 1. 2 peace, from God the Father and Christ J.
2. 22 follow righteousness, faith, charity, peace
Titus 1. 4 peace, from God the Father and the Lord
Phm. 3 peace, from God our Father and the Lord
Heb. 7. 2 also king of Salem, which is, king of pe.
11. 31 when she had received the spies with pe.
12. 14 Follow peace with all (men), and holiness
13. 20 the God of peace, that brought again from
Jas. 2. 16 Depart in peace, be (ye) warmed and filled
3. 18 is sown in peace of them that make peace
1 Pe. 1. 2 Grace unto you, and peace, be multiplied
3. 11 do good; let him seek peace, and ensue it
5. 14 Peace (be) with you all that are in Christ
2 Pe. 1. 2 peace be multiplied unto you through the
3. 14 that ye may be found of him in peace
2 John 3 peace, from God the Father, and from the
3 John 14 Peace (be) to thee. (Our) friends salute
Jude 2 Mercy unto you, and peace; Rev. 1. 4, 6. 4.

PEACE, to be at, have, or live in —

1. *To be complete, at peace,* שָׁלַם *shalam.*

Job 22. 21 be at peace: thereby good shall come unto
Psa. 7. 4 evil unto him that was at peace with me

2. *To be caused to be at peace,* שָׁלַם *shalam,* 6.

Job 5. 23 the beasts of the field shall be at peace

3. *To make peace,* שָׁלַם *shalam,* 5.

Prov 16. 7 maketh even his enemies to be at peace

4. *To be peaceable, desire peace,* εἰρηνεύω *eirēneuō.*

Mark 9. 50 Have salt in yourselves, and have peace
2 Co. 13. 11 live in peace; and the God of love and
1 Th. 5. 13 (And) be at peace among yourselves

PEACE, to hold one's —

1. *To be dumb, silent,* דָּמַם *damam.*

Lev. 10. 3 Then Moses said..And Aaron held his p.

2. *To become or keep silent,* הָסָה *hasah,* 3 or 1.

Neh. 8. 11 saying, Hold your peace, for; Zeph. 1. 7.

3. *The (nobles') voice was hidden,* קוֹל נֶחְבָּא [*qol*].

Job 29. 10 The nobles held their peace, and their

4. *To be silent, deaf,* חָרַשׁ *charash.*

Psa. 39. 12 hold not thy peace at my tears: for I (am)
83. 1 hold not thy peace, and be not still, O God
109. 1 Hold not thy peace, O God of my praise

5. *To keep silent,* חָרַשׁ *charash,* 5.

Gen. 24. 21 the man wondering at her held his peace
34. 5 Jacob held his peace until they were come
Exod 14. 14 fight for you, and ye shall hold your peace
Num 30. 4 and her father shall hold his peace at her
30. 7, 14 held his peace at her in the day that
30. 14 hold his peace at her from day to day
30. 14 because he held his peace at her in the d.
Judg 18. 19 Hold thy peace, lay thine hand upon thy
1 Sa. 10. 27 brought..no presents. But he held his p.
2 Sa. 13. 20 hold now thy peace, my sister: he (is) thy
2 Ki. 18. 36 the people held their peace, and answered
Neh. 5. 8 Then held they their peace, and found not.
Esth. 4. 14 if thou altogether holdest thy peace at
Job 11. 3 Should thy lies make men hold their pea.
13. 5 that ye would altogether hold your peace
13. 13 Hold your peace, let me alone, that I may
33. 31 hearken..hold thy peace, and I will speak
33. 33 hold thy peace, and I shall teach thee w.
Prov 11. 12 a man of understanding holdeth his peace
17. 28 Even a fool, when he holdeth his peace
Isa. 36. 21 they held their peace, and answered him
Jer. 4. 19 I cannot hold my peace, because thou hast

6. *To be silent,* חָשָׁה *chashah.*

Isa. 62. 1 For Zion's sake will I not hold my peace

Isa. 62. 6 shall never hold their peace day nor night
64. 12 wilt thou hold thy peace, and afflict us

7. *To keep silent*, חָשָׁה *chashah*, 5.
2 Ki. 2. 3, 5 Yea, I know (it;) hold ye your peace
7. 9 a day of good tidings, and we hold our p.
Psa. 39. 2 I held my peace, (even) from good; and
Isa. 42. 14 I have long time holden my peace; I have
57. 11 have not I held my peace even of old, and

8. *To be silent, not to speak*, σιγάω *sigaō*.
Luke 20. 26 marvelled at his answer, and held..peace
Acts 12. 17 beckoning..with the hand..to hold..pea.
15. 13 after they had held their peace, James
1 Co. 14. 30 If..be revealed..let the first hold his pe.

9. *To be silent, cease speaking*, σιωπάω *siōpaō*.
Matt 20. 31 because they should hold their peace: but
26. 63 But Jesus held his peace. And the high
Mark 3. 4 lawful..to kill? But they held their pea.
9. 34 they held their peace: for by the w. 4. 39.
10. 48 charged him that he should hold his pe.
14. 61 But he held his peace, and answered no.
Luke 18. 39 rebuked him, that [he should hold his p.]
19. 40 if these should hold their peace, the sto.
Acts 18. 9 Be not afraid..and hold not thy peace

10. *To be quiet*, ἡσυχάζω *hēsuchazō*.
Luke 14. 4 they held their peace. And he took (him)
Acts 11. 18 they held their peace, and glorified God

11. *To muzzle, gag*, φιμόω *phimoō*.
Mark 1. 25 saying, Hold thy peace..come Lu. 4. 35.

PEACE, to make (to be at) —
1. *To cause or make peace*, שָׁלַם *shalam*, 5.
Deut 20. 12 if it will make no peace with thee, but
Josh. 10. 1 the inhabitants of Gibeon had made peace
10. 4 it hath made peace with Joshua, and with
11. 19 There was not a city that made peace with
2 Sa. 10. 19 they made peace with Israel, and served
1 Ki. 22. 44 Jehoshaphat made peace with the king of
1 Ch. 19. 19 they made peace with David, and became
2. *To make peace*, εἰρηνοποιέω *eirēnopoieō*.
Col. 1. 20 having made peace through the blood of

PEACE, men that were at —
Men of peace, אַנְשֵׁי שְׁלוֹם [*anashim*]; Obad. 7.

PEACE offering —
1. *Peace offering*, שֶׁלֶם *shelem*.
Exod 20. 24 thy peace offerings, thy sheep, and thine
24. 5 sacrificed peace offerings of oxen unto the
29. 28 of the sacrifice of their peace offerings
32. 6 And they rose..and brought peace offer.
Lev. 3. 1 if his oblation (be) a sacrifice of peace off.
3. 3 offer of the sacrifice of the peace offering
3. 6 sacrifice of peace offering unto the LORD
4. 10, 26, 31, 35 the sacrifice of peace offerings
6. 12 he shall burn..the fat of the peace offer.
7. 11, 20, 21, 37 the sacrifice of peace offerings
7. 13 sacrifice of thanksgiving of his peace off.
7. 14 sprinkleth the blood of the peace offerings
7. 15, 18, 29, 29 sacrifice of his peace offerings
7. 32 the sacrifices of your peace offerings
7. 33 offereth the blood of the peace offerings
7. 34 from off the sacrifices of their peace offe.
9. 4 Also a bullock and a ram for peace offer.
9. 18 a sacrifice of peace offerings which (was)
9. 22 and the burnt offering, and peace offering
10. 14 out of the sacrifices of peace offerings of
17. 5 offer them (for) peace offerings unto the
19. 5 if ye offer a sacrifice of peace offerings unto
22. 21 offereth a sacrifice of peace offerings unto
23. 19 two lambs..for a sacrifice of peace offer.
Num. 6. 14 ram without blemish for peace offerings
6. 17 the ram (for) a sacrifice of peace offerin.
6. 18 (is) under the sacrifice of the peace offer
7. 17 for a sacrifice of peace offerings, two
So in verse 23, 29, 35, 41, 47, 53, 59, 65, 71, 77, 83.
7. 88 oxen, for the sacrifice of the peace offerin.
10. 10 over the sacrifices of your peace offerings
15. 8 a vow, or peace offerings unto the LORD
29. 39 ye shall do..for your peace offerings
Deut 27. 7 thou shalt offer peace offerings, and shalt
Josh. 8. 31 offered..and sacrificed peace offerings
22. 27 sacrifices, and with our peace offerings
Judg 20. 26 burnt offerings and peace offerings before
21. 4 offered burnt offerings and peace offerings
1 Sa. 10. 8 down..to sacrifice sacrifices of peace off.
11. 15 the sacrificed sacrifices of peace offerings
13. 9 burnt offering to me, and peace offerings
2 Sa. 6. 17 offered burnt offerings and peace offerings
6. 18 of offering burnt offerings and peace offer.
24. 25 offered burnt offerings and peace offerings
1 Ki. 3. 15 offered peace offerings, and made a feast
8. 63 Solomon offered a sacrifice of peace offer.
8. 64, 64 and the fat of peace offerings
9. 25 peace offerings upon the altar which he
2 Ki. 16. 13 sprinkled the blood of his peace offerings
1 Ch. 16. 1 offered burnt sacrifices and peace offerings
16. 2 the burnt offerings and the peace offerings
21. 26 offered burnt offerings and peace offerings
2 Ch. 7. 7 offered..the fat of the peace offerings
29. 35 with the fat of the peace offerings, and the
30. 22 offering peace offerings, and making con.
31. 2 for burnt offerings and for peace offerings
33. 16 sacrificed thereon peace offerings..thank.
Eze. 43. 27 priests shall make..your peace offerings
45. 15, 17 peace offerings, to make reconciliation
46. 2, 12, burnt offering, and his peace offerings
46. 12 or peace offerings voluntarily; Amos 5. 22.
2. *Sacrifices of peace offerings*, זִבְחֵי שְׁלָמִים [*zebach*].
Josh. 22. 23 or if to offer peace offerings; Prov. 7. 14.

PEACE with him, such as be at —
His peaceful ones (?), שְׁלֹמָיו [*shalom*].
Psa. 55. 20 against such as be at peace with him

PEACE, perfect —
Peace, peace, שָׁלוֹם שָׁלוֹם [*shalom*]. Isa. 26. 3.

PEACEABLE —
1. *Completeness, peace*, שָׁלוֹם *shalom*.
Isa. 32. 18 my people shall dwell in a peaceable hab.
Jer. 25. 37 peaceable habitations are cut down bec.
2. *At rest, at ease*, שָׁלֵיו, שָׁלֵו *shalev*.
1 Ch. 4. 40 land (was) wide, and quiet, and peaceable
3. *To be complete, at peace*, שָׁלַם *shalam*.
2 Sa. 20. 19 peaceable (and) faithful in Israel: thou s.
4. *Complete, peaceable*, שָׁלֵם *shalem*.
Gen. 34. 21 These men (are) peaceable with us; ther.
5. *Peaceable*, εἰρηνικός *eirēnikos*.
Heb. 12. 11 afterward it yieldeth the peaceable fruit
Jas. 3. 17 first pure, then peaceable, gentle, (and)
6. *Quiet*, ἡσύχιος *hēsuchios*.
1 Ti. 2. 2 that we may lead a quiet and peaceable

PEACEABLY —
1. *In security* or *peace*, בְּשַׁלְוָה *be-shalvah*.
Dan. 11. 21 he shall come in peaceably, and obtain
11. 24 He shall enter peaceably even upon the
2. *In peace*, (בְּשָׁלוֹם, לְשָׁלוֹם), שָׁלוֹם *shalom*.
Gen. 37. 4 and could not speak peaceably unto him
Judg 11. 13 therefore restore those (lands) again pea.
21. 13 Rimmon, and to call peaceably unto them
1 Sa. 16. 4 trembled..and said, Comest thou peace.?
16. 5 said, Peaceably: I am come to sacrifice
1 Ki. 2. 13 Comest thou peaceably? And he said, P.
1 Ch. 12. 17 If ye be come peaceably unto me to help
Jer. 9. 8 speaketh peaceably to his neighbour with

PEACEABLY, to live —
To be peaceable, desire peace, εἰρηνεύω *eirēneuō*.
Rom. 12. 18 If it be possible..live peaceably with all

PEACEMAKER —
A peacemaker, εἰρηνοποιός *eirēnopoios*.
Matt. 5. 9 Blessed (are) the peacemakers: for they

PEACOCKS —
1. *Peacocks*, תֻּכִּיִּים *tukkiyyim*.
1 Ki. 10. 22 and silver, ivory, and apes, and peacocks
2 Ch. 9. 21 and silver, ivory, and apes, and peacocks
2. *Ostrich hens*, רְנָנִים *renanim*.
Job 39. 13 the goodly wings unto the peacocks? or

PEARL —
1. *Chrystal*, גָּבִישׁ *gabish*.
Job 28. 18 mention shall be made of coral, or of pe.
2. *A pearl*, μαργαρίτης *margaritēs*.
Matt 7. 6 neither cast ye your pearls before swine
13. 45 a merchant man seeking goodly pearls
13. 46 when he had found one pearl of great pr.
1 Ti. 2. 9 with broidered hair, or gold, or pearls, or
Rev. 17. 4 precious stones, and pearls, having a gol.
18. 12 silver, and precious stones, and of pearls
18. 16 decked with..precious stones, and pearls
21. 21 twelve pearls; every several gate..one p.

PECULIAR (treasure) —
1. *Peculiar treasure, enclosure*, סְגֻלָּה *segullah*.
Exod 19. 5 ye shall be a peculiar treasure unto me a.
Deut 14. 2 LORD hath chosen thee to be a peculiar p.
26. 18 avouched thee this day to be his peculiar
Psa. 135. 4 hath chosen..Israel for his peculiar trea.
Eccl. 2. 8 peculiar treasure of kings and of the pri.
2. *Peculiar, beyond ordinary*, περιούσιος *periousios*.
Titus 2. 14 and purify unto himself a peculiar people
3. *For acquisition*, εἰς περιποίησιν [*peripoiēsis*].
1 Pe. 2. 9 But ye (are)..a peculiar people; that ye

PE-DA'-HEL, פְּדַהְאֵל *God delivers.*
The chief of Naphtali chosen to divide the land W. of the Jordan. B.C. 1452.
Num. 34. 28 prince of the tribe...P. the son of Ammih.

PE-DAH-ZUR, פְּדָהצוּר *the rock delivers.*
The father of Gamaliel the chief of Manasseh, chosen to number the people. B.C. 1452.
Num. 1. 10 of Manasseh; Gamaliel the son of P.
2. 20 captain..(shall be) Gamaliel the son of P.
7. 54 eighth day (offered) Gamaliel the son of P.
7. 59 the offering of Gamaliel the son of P.
10. 23 over the host..(was) Gamaliel the son of P.

PE-DA'-IAH, פְּדָיָה, פְּדָיָהוּ *Jah delivers*
1. Grandfather of king Josiah. B.C. 640.
2 Ki. 23. 36 (was) Zebudah, the daughter of P. of Ru
2. Son or grandson of Jeconiah son of king Jehoiakim, and father of Zerubbabel. B.C. 570.
1 Ch. 3. 18 and P., and Shenazar, Jecamiah, Hosha.
3. 19 the son of P. (were) Zerubbabel, and Shi.
3. Father of Joel, ruler of Manasseh W. of Jordan in the days of David. B.C. 1040.
1 Ch. 27. 20 half tribe of Manasseh; J. the son of P.
4. One of the sons of Parosh who helped to repair the wall after Nehemiah came. B.C. 446.
Neh. 3. 25 After him P. the son of Parosh
5. A prince, priest, or Levite who stood on Ezra's left hand when he read the law to the people. B.C. 445.
Neh. 8. 4 P., and Mishael, and Malchiah, and Has.
13. 13 and of the Levites, P.: and next to them
6. A Benjamite whose great grandson Sallu dwelt in Jerusalem. B.C. 530.
Neh. 11. 7 the son of P., the son of Kolaiah, the son

PEDIGREE, to declare —
To show one's birth or pedigree, יָלַד *yalad*, 7.
Num. 1. 18 declared their pedigrees after their famil.

PEELED —
1. *To pluck off, peel, polish*, מָרַט *marat*.
Eze. 29. 18 every shoulder (was) peeled; yet had he
2. *To be plucked off, peeled, polished*, מָרַט *marat*, 4.
Isa. 18. 2 to a nation scattered and peeled, to a pe.
18. 7 people scattered and peeled, and from a

PEEP, to —
To chatter, whisper, צָפַף *tsaphaph*, 3a.
Isa. 8. 19 unto wizards that peep and that mutter
10. 14 none that moved the wing..or peeped

PE'-KAH, פֶּקַח *watchfulness.*
Son of Remaliah, and an officer of Pekahiah, against whom he conspired and reigned in his stead, and who was himself slain by Hoshea son of Elah. B.C. 759-739.
2 Ki. 15. 25 But P. the son of Remaliah, a captain of
15. 27 P. the son of Remaliah began to reign over
15. 29 In the days of P. king of Israel came Ti.
15. 30 made a conspiracy against P. the son of
15. 31 And the rest of the acts of P., and all th.
15. 32 In the second year of P. the son of Rem.
15. 37 Rezin the king of Syria, and P. the son of
16. 1 In the seventeenth year of P. the son of
16. 5 Then Rezin king of Syria and P. son of R.
2 Ch. 28. 6 For P. the son of Remaliah slew in Judah
Isa. 7. 1 Rezin the king of Syria, and P. the son of

PE-KAH'-IAH, פְּקַחְיָה *Jah watches.*
Son of Menahem king of Israel, and slain by Pekah son of Remaliah, after reigning two years. B.C. 761.
2 Ki. 15. 22 and P. his son reigned in his stead
15. 23 P. the son of Menahem began to reign o.
15. 26 And the rest of the acts of P., and all that

PE'-KOD, פְּקוֹד *visitation.*
A symbolic name for Chaldea; perhaps the *Pactyians*, whom Herodotus names with the Armenians and Caspians.
Jer. 50. 21 Go up against..the inhabitants of P.: w.
Eze. 23. 23 P., and Shoa, and Koa, (and) all the Ass.

PE-LA'-IAH, פְּלָיָה *Jah is distinguished.*
1. A son of Elivenai, of the family of David. B.C. 445.
1 Ch. 3. 24 sons of Elioenai (were)..Eliashib, and P.
2. A priest who explained the law when Ezra read it. B.C. 445.
Neh. 8. 7 P. and the Levites, caused the people to
3. A Levite that, with Nehemiah, sealed the covenant. B.C. 445.
Neh. 10. 10 And their brethren..Kelita, P., Hanan

PE-LAL-I'AH, פְּלַלְיָה *Jah judges.*
A priest whose grandson Adaiah dwelt in Jerusalem after the exile. B.C. 500
Neh. 11. 12 P., the son of Amzi, the son of Zechariah

PE-LAT-I'AH, פְּלַטְיָה, פְּלַטְיָהוּ *Jah delivers.*
1. Son of Hananiah, descendant of Salathiel, of the family of David. B.C. 470.
1 Ch. 3. 21 And the sons of Hananiah; P., and Jesa.
2. A Simeonite captain. B.C. 715.
1 Ch. 4. 42 having for their captains P., and Neariah
3. A family that sealed the covenant. B.C. 445.
Neh. 10. 22 P., Hanan, Anaiah
4. Son of Benaiah, seen in vision by Ezekiel the prophet. B.C. 594.
Eze. 11. 1 P. the son of Benaiah, princes of the peo.
11. 13 came to pass..that P. the son of Benaiah

PE'-LEG, פֶּלֶג, פָּלֶג *division.*
A son of Eber, of the family of Shem, in whose days the earth was divided. B.C. 2222.
Gen. 10. 25 the name of one (was) P.; for in his days
11. 16 Eber lived four and thirty...and begat P.
11. 17 And Eber lived after he begat P. four hu.
11. 18 And P. lived thirty years, and begat Reu
11. 19 and P. lived after he begat Reu two hun.
1 Ch. 1. 19 the name of the one (was) P., because in
1. 25 Eber, P., Reu

PE'-LET, פֶּלֶט *escape.*
1. A son of Jahdai of the family of Caleb, son of Hezron. B.C. 1450.
1 Ch 2. 47 And the sons of Jahdai..P., and Ephah
2. A son of Azmaveth, who was also one of David's captains, 1 Ch. 11. 33. B.C. 1058.
1 Ch. 12. 3 Jeziel, and P., the sons of Azmaveth; and

PE'-LETH, פֶּלֶת *flight, haste.*
1. A Reubenite and father of On who joined Korah, Dathan, and Abiram against Moses and Aaron. B.C. 1510.
Num 16. 1 On the son of P., sons of Reuben, took
2. A son of Jonathan, and descendant of Pharez son of Judah. B.C. 1370.
1 Ch. 2. 33 And the sons of Jonathan; P., and Zaza

PE-LETH-ITES, פְּלֵתִי.
A company of David's body guard, like the Cherethites (*i.e.* Cretans); perhaps a contraction of *Philistines.*
2 Sa. 8. 18 And Benaiah..(was over)..the P.s; and
15. 18 all the P.s..passed on before the king
20. 7 the P.s, and all the mighty men: and the
20. 23 (was) over the Cherethites and over the P.
1 Ki. 1. 38 and the P.'s, went down, and caused Sol.
1. 44 And the king hath sent with him..P.s
1 Ch.18. 17 And Benaiah..(was) over..the P.s; and

PELICAN —
The pelican, קָאַת *qaath.*
Lev. 11. 18 swan, and the pelican, and the gier eagle
Deut14. 17 pelican, and the gier eagle, and the corm.
Psa.102. 6 I am like a pelican of the wilderness; I

PE-LON-ITE, פְּלוֹנִי.
1. An appellation of Helez an Ephraimite, one of David's valiant men; perhaps the same as *Paltite,* 2 Sam. 23. 26.
1 Ch.11. 27 Shammoth the Harorite, Helez the P.
27. 10 The seventh (captain)..(was) Helez the P.
2. An appellation of Ahijah the prophet.
1 Ch.11. 36 Hepher the Mecherathite, Ahijah the P.

PEN —
1. *A graving tool or pen,* חֶרֶט *cheret.*
Isa. 8. 1 write in it with a man's pen concerning
2. *A pen,* עֵט *et.*
Job 19. 24 they were graven with an iron pen and
Psa. 45. 1 my tongue (is) the pen of a ready writer
Jer. 8. 8 in vain made he (it); the pen of the scribes
17. 1 written with a pen of iron, (and) with the
3. *A rod, reed,* שֵׁבֶט *shebet.*
Judg. 5. 14 they that handle the pen of the writer
4. *A reed, pen,* κάλαμος *kalamos.*
3 John 13 I will not with ink and pen write unto t.

PE-NI'-EL, פְּנִיאֵל *face of God.*
A city where Jacob wrestled, S. of Jabbok, some distance from the Jordan and from Succoth, also called *Penuel.*
Gen. 32. 30 And Jacob called the name of the place P.

PE-NIN'-NAH, פְּנִנָּה *coral.*
A wife of Elkanah father of Samuel the prophet. B.C. 1170.
1 Sa. 1. 2 Hannah, and the name of the other P.
1. 2 and P. had children, but Hannah had no
1. 4 he gave to P. his wife, and to all her sons

PEN KNIFE —
A scribe's knife, תַּעַר סֹפֵר *taar sopher.*
Jer. 36. 23 cut it with the penknife, and cast (it) into

PENNY, PENCE, PENNYWORTH —
A denary (10 *asses, or* 7½*d.*), δηνάριον *dēnarion.*
Matt 18. 28 owed him an hundred pence; and he laid
20. 2 when he had agreed..for a penny day, he
20. 9 hour, they received every man a penny
20. 10 they likewise received every man a penny
20. 13 didst not thou agree with me for a penny?
22. 19 And they brought unto him a penny
Mark 6. 37 Shall we go and buy two hundred penny.
12. 15 bring me a penny, that I may see (it)
14. 5 sold for more than three hundred pence
Luke 7. 41 one owed five hundred pence, and the oth.
10. 35 took out two pence, and gave (them) to
20. 24 Show me a penny. Whose image and su.
John 6. 7 Two hundred penny worth of bread is not
12. 5 ointment sold for three hundred pence
Rev. 6. 6 A measure of wheat for a penny, and
6. 6 three measures of barley for a penny, and

PENTECOST —
Feast on fiftieth day after Passover, πεντηκοστή.
Acts 2. 1 when the day of Pentecost was fully come
20. 16 to be at Jerusalem the day of Pentecost
1 Co. 16. 8 But I will tarry at Ephesus until Pentecost

PE-NU'-EL, פְּנוּאֵל *face of God.*
1. The same as *Peniel* above.
Gen. 32. 31 And as he passed over P. the sun rose upon
Jud. 8. 8 And he went up thence to P., and spake
8. 8 and the men of P. answered him as the
8. 9 And he spake also unto the men of P.
8. 17 And he beat down the tower of P., and
1 Ki. 12. 25 and went out from thence, and built P.
2. Father or chief of Gedar. B.C. 1450.
1 Ch. 4. 4 And P. the father of Gedor, and Ezer the
3. A Benjamite. B.C. 1300.
1 Ch. 8. 25 And Iphedeiah, and P., the sons of Shashak

PENURY —
1. *Lack, want,* מַחְסוֹר *machsor.*
Prov.14. 23 talk of the lips (tendeth) only to penury
2. *Penury, deficiency,* ὑστέρημα *husterēma.*
Luke21. 4 but she of her penury hath cast in all the

PEOPLE —
1. *A man, individual,* אִישׁ *ish.*
2 Sa. 20. 13 all the people went on after Joab, to pu.
2. *Nations, people,* אֻמִּים, אֻמּוֹת *ummim, ummoth.*
Num25. 15 head over a people, (and) of a chief house
Psa.117. 1 all ye nations: praise him, all ye people
3. *A (mortal) man,* אֱנוֹשׁ *enosh.*
Jon. 3. 5 So the people of Nineveh believed God, and
4. *Sons of,* בְּנֵי *bene.*
Gen. 29. 1 came into the land of the people of the
5. *The sons (members) of the people,* בְּנֵי הָעָם [*ben*].
Lev. 20. 17 shall be cut off in the sight of their people
2 Ch.35. 5 of the fathers of your brethren the people
35. 7 Josiah gave to the people, of the flock, l.
35. 12 to the divisions of the families of the pe.
35. 13 divided (them) speedily among all the pe.
6. *Nation, corporate body,* גּוֹי *goi.*
Josh. 3. 17 until all the people were passed clean over
4. 1 when all the people were clean passed o.
5. 6 till all the people (that were) men of war
5. 8 had done circumcising all the people, that
10. 13 until the people had avenged themselves
Judg. 2. 20 Because that this people hath transgressed
2 Ki. 6. 18 Smite this people, I pray thee, with blind.
Dan. 11. 23 shall become strong with a small people
Joel 3. 8 shall sell them..to a people far off: for
Zeph. 2. 9 remnant of my people shall possess them
Zech.12. 3 though all the people of the earth be gath.
7. *Nation, people,* לְאֹם *leom.*
Gen. 25. 23 two manner of people shall be separated
25. 23 people shall be stronger than (the other) p.
Psa. 2. 1 Why do..the people imagine a vain thing?
7. 7 So shall the congregation of the people c.
9. 8 he shall minister judgment to the people
44. 2 didst afflict the people, and cast them out
44. 14 a shaking of the head among the people
65. 7 Which stilleth..the tumult of the people
105. 44 and they inherited the labour of the peo.
148. 11 Kings of the earth, and all people; prin.
149. 7 To execute..punishments upon the peop.
Prov 11. 26 He that withholdeth corn, the people shall
14. 28 in the want of people (is) the destruction
14. 34 nation: but sin (is) a reproach to any pe.
Isa. 34. 1 hearken, ye people: let the earth hear, and
41. 1 let the people renew (their) strength: let
43. 4 therefore will I give men for thee, and p.
43. 9 let the people be assembled: who among
49. 1 hearken, ye people, from far; The LORD
55. 4 given him (for) a witness to the people
55. 4 a leader and commander to the people
60. 2 gross darkness the people: but the LORD
8. *A company,* עֵדָה *edah.*
Lev. 10. 6 and lest wrath come upon all the people
9. *A people,* עַם, עָם *am.*
Gen. 11. 6 people (is) one, and they have all one lan.
14. 16 goods, and the woman also, and the peo.
17. 14 that soul shall be cut off from his people
17. 16 of nations: kings of people shall be of her
19. 4 both old and young, all the people from
23. 7 bowed himself to the people of the land
23. 11 in the presence of the sons of my people
23. 12 bowed down himself before the people of
23. 13 in the audience of the people of the land
25. 8, 17 and was gathered to his people
26. 10 one of the people might lightly have lien
26. 11 Abimelech charged all (his) people, saying
27. 29 Let people serve thee, and nations bow d.
28. 3 that thou mayest be a multitude of peop.
32. 7 he divided the people that (was) with him
34. 16 will dwell with you, and..become one p.
34. 22 consent unto us..to be one people, if ev.
35. 6 he, and all the people that (were) with him
35. 29 and died, and was gathered unto his peo.
41. 40 according unto thy word shall all my pe.
41. 55 people cried to Pharaoh for bread: and P.
42. 6 that sold to all the people of the land: and
47. 21 as for the people, he removed them to ci.
47. 23 Then Joseph said unto the people, Behold
48. 4 I will make of thee a multitude of people
48. 19 he also shall become a people, and he also
49. 10 unto him (shall) the gathering of the peo.
49. 16 Dan shall judge his people, as one of the
49. 29 I am to be gathered unto my people: bury
49. 33 Jacob..was gathered unto his people
50. 20 as (it is) this day, to save much people a.
Exod. 1. 9 said unto his people, Behold, the people
1. 20 people multiplied, and waxed very mighty
1. 22 Pharaoh charged all his people, saying
3. 7 have surely seen the affliction of my peo.
3. 10 that thou mayest bring forth my people
3. 12 When thou hast brought forth the people
3. 21 will give this people favour in the sight
4. 16 he shall be thy spokesman unto the peo.
4. 21 harden..that he shall not let the people
4. 30 did the signs in the sight of the people
4. 31 people believed: and when they heard th.
5. 1 Let my people go, that they may hold a.
5. 4 Wherefore do ye..let the people from th.
5. 5 people of the land now (are) many, and
5. 6 commanded..the taskmasters of the pe.
5. 7 Ye shall no more give the people straw
5. 10 taskmasters of the people went out, and
5. 10 spake to the people, saying, Thus saith P.
5. 12 So the people were scattered abroad thr.
5. 16 beaten; but the fault (is) in thine own p.
5. 22 wherefore..thou (so) evil entreated..p.?
5. 23 people; neither hast thou delivered thy p.
6. 7 I will take you to me for a people, and I
7. 4 bring forth..my people the children of I.
7. 14 hardened, he refuseth to let the people go
7. 16 Let my people go, that they may serve me
8. 1, 20 Let my people go, that they may serve
8. 3 upon thy people, and into thine ovens, and
8. 4 upon thy people, and upon all thy serva.
8. 8 from my people; and I will let the people
Exod 8. 9 when shall I entreat..for thy people, to
8. 11 frogs shall depart..from thy people; they
8. 21 Else, if thou wilt not let my people go, b.
8. 21 send swarms (of flies)..upon thy people
8. 22 land of Goshen, in which my people dwell
8. 23 division between my people and thy peo.
8. 29 swarms (of flies) may depart..from his pe.
8. 29 in not letting the people go to sacrifice to
8. 31 removed..from his people: there remained
8. 32 also, neither would he let the people go
9. 1, 13 Let my people go, that they may serve
9. 7 hardened, and he did not let the people
9. 14 send..my plagues..upon my people; that
9. 15 that I may smite thee and thy people with
9. 17 exaltest thou thyself against my people
9. 27 righteous, and I and my people (are) wic.
10. 3 let my people go, that they may serve me
10. 4 if thou refuse to let my people go, behold
11. 2 Speak now in the ears of the people, and
11. 3 gave the people favour in the sight of the
11. 3 very great..in the sight of the people
11. 8 Get thee out, and all the people that foll.
12. 27 people bowed the head and worshipped
12. 31 get you forth from among my people, both
12. 33 Egyptians were urgent upon the people
12. 34 people took their dough before it was le.
12. 36 gave the people favour in..sight of the E.
13. 3 said unto the people, Remember this day
13. 17 when Pharaoh had let the people go, that
13. 17 Lest peradventure the people repent when
13. 18 But God led the people about, (through)
13. 22 took not away the pillar..before the peo.
14. 5 told the king of Egypt that the people fled
14. 5 turned against the people, and they said
14. 6 made ready his chariot, and took his peo.
14. 13 Moses said unto the people, Fear ye not
14. 31 people feared the LORD, and believed the L.
15. 13 Thou in thy mercy hast led forth the pe.
15. 14 people shall hear, (and) be afraid: sorrow
15. 16 till thy people pass over, O LORD, till the
15. 16 people pass over, (which) thou hast purc.
15. 24 people murmured against Moses, saying
16. 4 people shall go out and gather a certain
16. 27 there went out (some) of the people on the
16. 30 So the people rested on the seventh day
17. 1 (there was) no water for the people to d
17. 2 Wherefore the people did chide with M.
17. 3 people thirsted..and the people murmur.
17. 4 What shall I do unto this people? they
17. 5 Go on before the people, and take with
17. 6 water out of it, that the people may drink
17. 13 discomfited Amalek and his people with
18. 1 done for Israel, and for Israel his people
18. 10 delivered the people from under the hand
18. 13 sat to judge the people: and the people
18. 14 saw all that he did to the people, he said
18. 14 this thing that thou doest to the people?
18. 14 people stand by thee from morning unto
18. 15 Because the people come unto me to enq.
18. 18 both thou and this people that (is) with
18. 19 Be thou for the people to God ward, that
18. 21 provide out of..the people able men, such
18. 22 let them judge the people at all seasons
18. 23 all this people shall also go to their place
18. 25 made them heads over the people, rulers
18. 26 judged the people at all seasons: the hard
19. 5 peculiar treasure unto me above all people
19. 7 came and called for the elders of the pe.
19. 8 people answered together, and said, All
19. 8 Moses returned the words of the people
19. 9 that the people may hear when I speak
19. 9 told the words of the people unto the L.
19. 10 Go unto the people, and sanctify them to
19. 11 come down in the sight of all the people
19. 12 thou shalt set bounds unto the people ro.
19. 14 unto the people, and sanctified the people
19. 15 he said unto the people, Be ready against
19. 16 all the people that (was) in the camp tre.
19. 17 Moses brought forth the people out of the
19. 21 Go down, charge the people, lest they br.
19. 23 people cannot come up to mount Sinai: for
19. 24 let not the priests and the people break
19. 25 So Moses went down unto the people, and
20. 18 all the people saw the thunderings, and
20. 18 when the people saw (it), they removed
20. 20 Moses said unto the people, Fear not: for
20. 21 people stood afar off: and Moses drew near
22. 25 If thou lend money to (any of) my people
22. 28 Thou shalt not..curse the ruler of thy p.
23. 11 that the poor of thy people may eat: and
23. 27 will destroy all the people to whom thou
24. 2 neither shall the people go up with him
24. 3 told the people..all the people answered
24. 7 read in the audience of the people: and
24. 8 sprinkled (it) on the people, and said, Be.
30. 33, 38 shall even be cut off from his people
31. 14 soul shall be cut off from among his peo.
32. 1 when the people saw that Moses delayed
32. 1 people gathered themselves together unto
32. 3 the people brake off the golden ear rings
32. 6 the people sat down to eat and to drink
32. 7 for thy people, which thou broughtest out
32. 9 seen this people..it (is) a stiff necked pe.
32. 11 thy wrath wax hot against thy people, wh.
32. 12 and repent of this evil against thy people
32. 14 evil which he thought to do unto his pe.
32. 17 when Joshua heard the noise of the people
32. 21 What did this people unto thee, that thou
32. 22 thou knowest the people, that they (are
32. 25 when Moses saw that the people (were)
32. 28 there fell of the people that day about
32. 30 Moses said unto the people, Ye have sin.

Exod32. 31 Oh, this people have sinned a great sin
32. 34 lead the people unto (the place) of which
32. 35 plagued the people, because they made
33. 1 thou and the people which thou hast bro.
33. 3 for thou (art) a stiff necked people ; lest I
33. 4 when the people heard these evil tidings
33. 5 Ye (are) a stiff necked people : I will come
33. 8 all the people rose up, and stood every
33. 10 people saw the cloudy pillar..people rose
33. 12 thou sayest unto me, Bring up this people
33. 13 and consider that this nation (is) thy pe.
33. 16 known here that I and thy people have
33. 16 so shall we be separated, I and thy peop.
33. 16 people that (are) upon the face of the ea.
34. 9 go among us; for it (is) a stiff necked pe.
34. 10 before all thy people..and all the people
36. 5 people bring much more than enough for
36. 6 So the people were restrained from bring.
Lev. 4. 3 do sin according to the sin of the people
4. 27 if any one of the common people sin thr.
7. 20, 21, 25, 27 shall be cut off from his people
9. 7 atonement for thyself, and for the people
9. 7 offer the offering of the people, and make
9. 15 brought the people's offering, and took
9. 15 which (was) the sin offering for the people
9. 18 peace offerings which (was) for the people
9. 22 lifted up his hand toward the people, and
9. 23 came out, and blessed the people : and the
9. 23 the glory..appeared unto all the people
9. 24 when all the people saw, they shouted, and
10. 3 before all the people I will be glorified
16. 15 goat of the sin offering that (is) for the p.
16. 24 burnt offering of the people..and for the p.
16. 33 and for all the people of the congregation
17. 4, 9 shall be cut off from among his people
17. 10 will cut him off from among his people
18. 29 shall be cut off from among their people
19. 8 soul shall be cut off from among his peo.
19. 16 a tale bearer among thy people; neither
19. 18 grudge against the children of thy people
20. 2 people of the land shall stone him with st
20. 3, 6 will cut him off from among his people
20. 4 if the people of the land do any ways hide
20. 5 will cut him off..from among their people
20. 18 shall be cut off from among their people
20. 24 which have separated you from (other) p.
20. 26 severed you from (other) people, that ye
21. 1 be defiled for the dead among his people
21. 4 chief man among his people, to profane
21. 14 he shall take a virgin of his own people
21. 15 Neither..profane his seed among his pe.
23. 29 he shall be cut off from among his people
23. 30 soul will I destroy from among his people
26. 12 be your God, and ye shall be my people
Num. 5. 21 a curse and an oath among thy people
5. 27 woman shall be a curse among her people
9. 13 shall be cut off from among his people : be.
11. 1 people complained, it displeased the LORD
11. 2 people cried unto Moses; and when Moses
11. 8 people went about, and gathered (it), and
11. 10 Moses heard the people weep throughout
11. 11 layest the burden of all this people upon
11. 12 Have I conceived all this people ? have I
11. 13 should I have flesh to give unto all this p.
11. 14 I am not able to bear all this people alone
11. 16 knowest to be the elders of the people, and
11. 17 they shall bear the burden of the people
11. 18 say thou unto the people, Sanctify yours.
11. 21 people, among whom I (am, are) six hun.
11. 24 told the people the words of the LORD, and
11. 24 the seventy men of the elders of the peo.
11. 29 Would God that all the LORD'S people were
11. 32 people stood up all that day, and all (that)
11. 33 wrath..was kindled against the people
11. 33 smote the people with a very great plague
11. 34 there they buried the people that lusted
11. 35 the people journeyed from Kibroth-hatt.
12. 15 people journeyed not till Miriam was br.
12. 16 afterward the people removed from Haz.
13. 18 and the people that dwelleth therein, w.
13. 28 Nevertheless the people (be) strong that
13. 30 Caleb stilled the people before Moses, and
13. 31 We be not able to go up against the people
13. 32 all the people that we saw in it (are) men
14. 1 cried; and the people wept that night
14. 9 neither fear ye the people of the land ; for
14. 11 How long will this people provoke me?
14. 13 for thou broughtest up this people in thy
14. 14 heard..thou, LORD, (art) among this pe.
14. 15 Now, (if) thou shalt kill (all) this people
14. 16 not able to bring this people into the land
14. 19 Pardon..the iniquity of this people acco.
14. 19 as thou hast forgiven this people, from E.
14. 39 told these sayings..and the people mour.
15. 26 be forgiven..seeing all the people (were)
15. 30 soul shall be cut off from among his peo
16. 41 saying, Ye have killed the people of the L.
16. 47 the plague was begun among the people
16. 47 and made an atonement for the people
20. 1 people abode in Kadesh; and Miriam d.
20. 3 people chode with Moses, and spake, say.
20. 20 came out against him with much people
20. 24 Aaron shall be gathered unto his people
21. 2 If thou wilt indeed deliver this people into
21. 4 soul of the people was much discouraged
21. 5 people spake against God, and against Mo.
21. 6 LORD sent fiery serpents among the people
21. 6 bit the people ; and much people of Israel
21. 7 people came..And Moses prayed for the p.
21. 16 Gather the people together, and I will give
21. 18 nobles of the people digged it, by (the di.
21. 23 but Sihon gathered all his people together
Num 21. 29 thou art undone, O people of Chemosh! he
21. 33 he, and all his people, to the battle at E.
21. 34 for I have delivered..all his people, and
21. 35 So they smote him..and all his people, un.
22. 3 Moab was sore afraid of the people, because
22. 5 of the land of the children of his people
22. 5 there is a people come out from Egypt: be.
22. 6, 17 therefore, I pray thee, curse me this p.
22. 11 people come out of Egypt, which covereth
22. 12 thou shalt not curse the people : for they
22. 41 he might see the utmost (part) of the pe.
23. 9 the people shall dwell alone, and shall not
23. 24 people shall rise up as a great lion, and
24. 14 now, behold, I go unto my people : come
24. 14 what this people shall do to thy people in
25. 1 people began to commit whoredom with
25. 2 called the people..and the people did eat
25. 4 Take all the heads of the people, and hang
27. 13 thou also shalt be gathered unto thy peo.
31. 2 shalt thou be gathered unto thy people
31. 3 Moses spake unto the people, saying, Arm
32. 15 leave..and ye shall destroy all this people
33. 14 where was no water for the people to drink
Deut. 1. 28 The people (is) greater and taller than we
2. 4 command thou the people, saying, Ye (are)
2. 10, 21 a people great, and many, and tall, as
2. 16 consumed and dead from among the peo.
2. 32 he and all his people, to fight at Jahaz
2. 33 smote him, and his sons, and all his peo.
3. 1 he and all his people, to battle at Edrei
3. 2 for I will deliver him, and all his people
3. 3 the king of Bashan, and all his people: and
3. 28 for he shall go over before this people, and
4. 6 nation (is) a wise and understanding peo.
4. 10 Gather me the people together, and I will
4. 20 to be unto him a people of inheritance, as
4. 33 Did (ever) people hear the voice of God
5. 28 heard the voice of the words of this people
6. 14 of the gods of the people which (are) round
7. 6 thou (art) an holy people unto the LORD
7. 6 people unto himself, above all people that
7. 7 people ; for ye (were) the fewest of all pe.
7. 14 Thou shalt be blessed above all people
7. 16 the people which the LORD thy God shall
7. 19 all the people of whom thou art afraid
9. 2 A people great and tall, the children of
9. 6 Understand..thou (art) a stiff necked peo.
9. 12 thy people which thou hast brought forth
9. 13 this people..it (is) a stiff necked people
9. 26 destroy not thy people and thine inherit.
9. 27 look not unto the stubbornness of this peo.
9. 29 they (are) thy people and thine inherit.
10. 11 take (thy) journey before the people, that
10. 15 he chose..(even) you above all people, as
13. 7 the people which (are) round about you, n.
13. 9 and afterwards the hand of all the people
14. 2, 21 thou (art) an holy people unto the LORD
14. 2 to be a peculiar people unto himself, ab.
16. 18 shall judge the people with just judgment
17. 7 and afterward the hands of all the people
17. 13 the people shall hear, and fear, and do no
17. 16 nor cause the people to return to Egypt
18. 3 shall be the priest's due from the people
20. 1 a people more than thou, be not afraid of
20. 2 shall approach and speak unto the people
20. 5 the officers shall speak unto the people
20. 8 officers shall speak further unto the peo.
20. 9 made an end of speaking unto the people
20. 9 captains of the armies to lead the people
20. 11 the people (that is) found therein shall
20. 16 of the cities of these people, which the L.
21. 8 thy people Israel, whom thou hast redee.
21. 8 lay not innocent blood unto thy people of
26. 15 bless thy people Israel, and the land wh.
26. 18 avouched thee..to be his peculiar people
26. 19 be an holy people unto the LORD thy God
27. 1 the elders of Israel commanded the peo.
27. 9 this day thou art become the people of the
27. 11 And Moses charged the people the same
27. 12 These shall stand..to bless the people, w.
27. 15 all the people shall answer and say, Amen
27. 16 And all the people shall say, Amen
So in verse 17, 18, 19, 20, 21, 22, 23, 24, 25, 26.
28. 9 establish thee an holy people unto hims.
28. 10 all people of the earth shall see that thou
28. 32 (shall be) given unto another people, and
28. 64 LORD shall scatter thee among all people
29. 13 establish thee..for a people unto himself
31. 7 thou must go with this people unto the la.
31. 12 Gather the people together, men, and w.
31. 16 this people will rise up, and go a whoring
32. 6 O foolish people and unwise? (is) not he thy
32. 8 he set the bounds of the people according
32. 9 For the LORD'S portion (is) his people ; Ja.
32. 21 jealousy with (those which are) not a pe.
32. 36 LORD shall judge his people, and repent
32. 43 Rejoice..his people..merciful..to his p.
32. 44 came and spake..in the ears of the people
32. 50 be gathered unto thy people ; as Aaron
32. 50 A..died..and was gathered unto his peo.
33. 3 Yea, he loved the people ; all his saints
33. 5 when the heads of the people (and) the
33. 7 of Judah, and bring him unto his people
33. 17 he shall push the people together to the
33. 19 shall call the people unto the mountain
33. 21 he came with the heads of the people, he
33. 29 O people saved by the LORD, the shield of
Josh. 1. 2 over this Jordan, thou, and all this people
1. 6 unto this people shalt thou divide for
1. 10 commanded the officers of the people, say.
1. 11 command the people, saying, Prepare you
3. 3 they commanded the people, saying, When
Josh. 3. 5 And Joshua said unto the people, Sanctify
3. 6 before the people..and went before the p.
3. 14 when the people removed from their tents
3. 14 the ark of the covenant before the people
3. 16 the people passed over right against Jer.
4. 2 Take you twelve men out of the people
4. 10 to speak unto the people..and the people
4. 11 all the people..in the presence of the pe.
4. 19 the people came up out of Jordan on the
4. 24 That all the people of the earth might kn.
5. 4 All the people that came out of Egypt
5. 5 all the people that came out were circu.
5. 5 all the people..born in the wilderness by
6. 5 the people shall shout with a great shout
6. 5 the people shall ascend up every man str.
6. 7 he said unto the people, Pass on, and co.
6. 8 when Joshua had spoken unto the people
6. 10 Joshua had commanded the people, saying
6. 16 Joshua said unto the people, Shout ; for
6. 20 the people shouted when (the priests) blew
6. 20 when the people heard the sound of the
6. 20 the people shouted with a great shout, that
6. 20 the people went up into the city, every m.
7. 3 Let not all the people go up; but let about
7. 3 make not all the people to labour thither
7. 4 there went up thither of the people about
7. 5 hearts of the people melted, and became
7. 7 hast thou at all brought this people over
7. 13 Up, sanctify the people, and say, Sanctify
8. 1 take all the people of war with thee, and
8. 1 and his people, and his city, and his land
8. 3 Joshua arose, and all the people of war, to
8. 5 the people that (are) with me, will appro.
8. 9 Joshua lodged that night among the peo.
8. 10 in the morning, and numbered the people
8. 10 Joshua..went up..before the people to
8. 11 the people..that (were) with him, went
8. 13 when they had set the people, (even) all
8. 14 he and all his people, at a time appointed
8. 16 all the people that (were) in Ai were call.
8. 20 the people that fled to the wilderness tu.
8. 33 that they should bless the people of Isra.
10. 7 the people of war with him, and all the
10. 21 the people returned to the camp to Josh.
10. 33 Joshua smote him and his people, until
11. 4 much people, even as the sand that (is)
11. 7 came, and all the people of war with him
14. 8 brethren..made the heart of the people
17. 14 seeing I (am) a great people, forasmuch
17. 15 If thou (be) a great people, (then) get thee
17. 17 Thou (art) a great people, and hast great
24. 2, 27 And Joshua said unto all the people
24. 16 the people answered and said, God forbid
24. 17 among all the people through whom we
24. 18 drave out from before us all the people
24. 19 And Joshua said unto the people, Ye can.
24. 21 the people said unto Joshua, Nay ; but we
24. 22 And Joshua said unto the people, Ye (are)
24. 24 the people said unto Joshua, The LORD
24. 25 made a covenant with the people that d.
24. 28 So Joshua let the people depart, every m.
Judg. 1. 16 and they went and dwelt among the peo.
2. 4 the people lifted up their voice, and wept
2. 6 And when Joshua had let the people go
2. 7 the people served the LORD all the days
2. 12 of the people that (were) round about them
3. 18 sent away the people that bare the prese
4. 13 people that (were) with him, from Haros.
5. 2 when the people willingly offered thems.
5. 9 that offered..willingly among the people
5. 11 people of the LORD go down to the gates
5. 13 dominion over the nobles among the pe.
5. 14 after thee, Benjamin, among thy people
5. 18 Zebulun and Naphtali (were) a people (t.)
7. 1 people that (were) with him, rose up ear.
7. 2 The people that (are) with thee (are) too
7. 3 proclaim in the ears of the people, saying
7. 3 there returned of the people twenty and
7. 4 The people (are) yet (too) many ; bring th.
7. 5 he brought down the people unto the wa.
7. 6 the people bowed down upon their knees
7. 7 let all the (other) people go every man u.
7. 8 the people took victuals in their hand, and
8. 5 Give..bread unto the people that follow
9. 29 would to God this people were under my
9. 32 thou and the people that (is) with thee
9. 33 (when) he and the people that (is) with
9. 34 and all the people that (were) with him
9. 35 rose up, and the people that (were) with
9. 36 when Gaal saw the people..come people
9. 37 there come people down by the middle of
9. 38 this the people that thou hast despised?
9. 42 the people went out into the field ; and
9. 43 he took the people, and divided them into
9. 43 the people (were) come forth (out) of the
9. 45 slew the people that (was) therein, and
9. 48 he and all the people that (were) with him
9. 48 said unto the people that (were) with him
9. 49 the people likewise cut down every man
10. 18 the people (and) princes of Gilead said one
11. 11 people made him head and captain over
11. 20 Sihon gathered all his people together, and
11. 21 and all his people into the hand of Israel
11. 23 the Amorites from before his people Israel
12. 2 my people were at great strife with the
14. 3 of thy brethren, or among all my people
14. 16 a riddle unto the children of my people
14. 17 the riddle to the children of her people
16. 24 when the people saw him, they praised
16. 30 and upon all the people that (were) there
18. 7 saw the people that (were) therein, how
18. 10 ye shall come unto a people secure, and

Judg 18. 20 and he..went in the midst of the people
18. 27 unto a people (that were) at quiet and s.
20. 2 the chief of all the people..of all the tri.
20. 2 in the assembly of the people of God, four
20. 8 the people arose as one man, saying, We
20. 10 to fetch victual for the people, that they
20. 16 Among all this people (there were) seven
20. 22 the people, the men of Israel, encouraged
20. 26 people, went up, and came unto the house
20. 31 Benjamin went out against the people,
20. 31 and they began to smite of the people, (and)
21. 2 the people came to the house of God, (and)
21. 4 the people rose early, and built there an
21. 9 the people were numbered, and, behold
21. 15 And the people repented them for Benja.
Ruth 1. 6 had visited his people in giving them br.
1. 10 we will return with thee unto thy people
1. 15 sister in law is gone back unto her people
1. 16 thy people..my people, and thy God my
2. 11 people which thou knewest not heretofore
3. 11 the city of my people doth know that thou
4. 4 Buy (it)..before the elders of my people
4. 9 said unto the elders, and (unto) all the p.
4. 11 the people that (were) in the gate, and the
1 Sa. 2. 13 the priest's custom with the people (was)
2. 23 I hear of your evil dealings by all this pe.
2. 24 ye make the LORD'S people to transgress
2. 29 of all the offerings of Israel my people
4. 3 the people were come into the camp, the
4. 4 the people sent to Shiloh, that they might
4. 17 also a great slaughter among the people
5. 10 brought..to us, to slay us and our people
5. 11 that it slay us not, and our people: for
6. 19 he smote of the people fifty thousand and
6. 19 the people lamented, because the LORD
6. 19 had smitten..of the people with a great s.
8. 7 Hearken unto the voice of the people in
8. 10 unto the people that asked of him a king
8. 19 the people refused to obey the voice of S
8. 21 Samuel heard all the words of the people
9. 2 (he was) higher than any of the people
9. 12 (there is) a sacrifice of the people to day
9. 13 the people will not eat until he come
9. 16 him (to be) captain over my people Israel
9. 16 he may save my people out of the hand of
9. 16 have looked upon my people, because th.
9. 17 Behold..this same shall reign over my p.
9. 24 since I said, I have invited the people
10. 11 the people said one to another, What (is)
10. 17 Samuel called the people together unto
10. 23 and when he stood among the people, he
10. 23 he was higher than any of the people from
10. 24 Samuel said to all the people, See ye him
10. 24 (there is) none like him among all the p.
10. 24 the people shouted, and said, God save the
10. 25 Samuel told the people..sent all the peo.
11. 4 told the tidings in the ears of the people
11. 4 the people lifted up their voices, and wept
11. 5 What (aileth) the people that they weep?
11. 7 the fear of the LORD fell on the people, and
11. 11 Saul put the people in three companies
11. 12 the people said unto Samuel, Who (is) he
11. 14 Then said Samuel to the people, Come, and
11. 15 the people went to Gilgal; and there they
12. 6 And Samuel said unto the people, (It is)
12. 18 people greatly feared the LORD and Sam.
12. 19 all the people said unto Samuel, Pray for
12. 20 Samuel said unto the people, Fear not: ye
12. 22 the LORD will not forsake his people for
12. 22 hath pleased the LORD to make you his p.
13. 2 the rest of the people he sent every man
13. 4 the people were called together after S.
13. 5 people as the sand which (is) on the sea
13. 6 the people were distressed, then the peo.
13. 7 and all the people followed him trembling
13. 8 and the people were scattered from him
13. 11 that the people were scattered from me
13. 14 commanded him (to be) captain over his
13. 15 Saul numbered the people (that were) p.
13. 16 and the people (that were) present with
13. 22 people that (were) with Saul and Jonathan
14. 2 the people that (were) with him (were) a.
14. 3 people knew not that Jonathan was gone
14. 15 in the field, and among all the people
14. 17 Then said Saul unto the people that (were)
14. 20 the people that (were) with him assembled
14. 24 Saul had adjured the people, saying, Cu.
14. 24 So none of the people tasted (any) food
14. 26 when the people were come into the wood
14. 26 no man put his hand..for the people fea.
14. 27 father charged the people with the oath
14. 28 Then answered one of the people, and said
14. 28 straitly charged the people with an oath
14. 28 eateth..food this day And the people w.
14. 30 if haply the people had eaten freely to day
14. 31 smote the Philistines..and the people w.
14. 32 the people flew upon the spoil, and took
14. 32 the people did eat (them) with the blood
14. 33 the people sin against the LORD, in that
14. 34 Disperse yourselves among the people
14. 34 the people brought every man his ox with
14. 38 ye near hither all the chief of the people
14. 39 (there was) not a man among all the peo.
14. 40 the people said unto Saul, Do what seem.
14. 41 Saul and Jonathan..but the people esca.
14. 45 the people said unto Saul, Shall Jonathan
14. 45 people rescued Jonathan, that he died not
15. 1 to anoint thee (to be) king over his people
15. 4 Saul gathered the people together, and
15. 8 destroyed all the people with the edge of
15. 9 the people spared Agag, and the best of
15. 15 people spared the best of the sheep and

1 Sa 15. 21 the people took of the spoil, sheep and o.
15. 24 feared the people, and obeyed their voice
15. 30 before the elders of my people, and before
17. 27 the people answered him after this man.
17. 30 the people answered him again after the
18. 5 was accepted in the sight of all the people
18. 13 he went out and came in before the people
23. 8 Saul called all the people together to war
26. 5 and the people pitched round about him
26. 7 Abishai came to the people by night: and
26. 7 Abner and the people lay round about him
26. 14 David cried to the people, and to Abner
26. 15 there came one of the people in to destroy
27. 12 He hath made his people Israel utterly to
30. 4 the people that (were) with him lifted up
30. 6 the people spake of stoning him, because
30. 6 the soul of all the people was grieved, ev.
30. 21 and to meet the people that (were) with
30. 21 when David came near to the people, he
31. 9 house of their idols, and among the people
2 Sa. 1. 4 the people are fled from the battle, and
1 4 many of the people also are fallen and d.
1 12 for the people of the LORD, and for the h.
2. 26 bid the people return from following their
2. 27 the people had gone up every one from
2. 28 the people stood still, and pursued after
2. 30 when he had gathered all the people tog.
3. 18 I will save my people Israel out of the h.
3. 31 and to all the people that (were) with him
3. 32 at the grave of Abner; and all the people
3. 34 And all the people wept again over him
3. 35 the people came to cause David to eat m.
3. 36 all the people took notice (of it), and it
3. 36 whatsoever the king did pleased..the pe.
3. 37 the people, and all Israel, understood that
5. 2 Thou shalt feed my people Israel, and th.
5. 12 his kingdom for his people Israel's sake
6. 2 with all the people that (were) with him
6. 18 he blessed the people in the name of the
6. 19 he dealt among all the people, (even) am.
6. 19 the people departed every one to his ho.
6. 21 ruler over the people of the LORD, over I.
7. 7 I commanded to feed my people Israel
7. 8 I took thee..to be ruler over my people
7. 10 I will appoint a place for my people Israel
7. 11 judges (to be) over my people Israel, and
7. 23 what one nation..(is) like thy people, (e.)
7. 23 went to redeem for a people to himself
7. 23 thy people, which thou redeemedst to thee
7. 24 thy people Israel (to be) a people unto
8. 15 judgment and justice unto all his people
10. 10 the rest of the people he delivered into the
10. 12 let us play the men for our people, and for
10. 13 drew nigh, and the people that (were) w.
11. 7 how the people did, and how the war pr.
11. 17 fell..of the people of the servants of Dav.
12. 28 gather the rest of the people together, and
12. 29 David gathered all the people together
12. 31 brought forth the people..all the people
13. 34 there came much people by the way of the
14. 13 thought such a thing against the people
14. 15 the people have made me afraid: and thy
15. 12 people increased continually with Absa.
15. 17 went forth, and all the people after him
15. 23 all the people passed over: the king also
15. 23 all the people passed over, toward the
15. 24 until all the people had done passing out
15. 30 the people that (was) with him covered
16. 6 and all the people and all the mighty men
16. 14 the people that (were) with him, came w.
16. 15 people the men of Israel, came to Jerusa.
16. 18 and this people, and all the men of Israel
17. 2 the people that (are) with him shall flee
17. 3 I will bring back all the people unto thee
17. 3 as if all..(so) all the people shall be in p.
17. 8 thy father..will not lodge with the people
17. 9 There is a slaughter among the people that
17. 16 king..and all the people that (are) with
17. 22 and all the people that (were) with him
17. 29 for the people. The people (is) hungry, and
18. 1 numbered the people that (were) with him
18. 2 part of the people under the hand of Joab
18. 2 the king said unto the people, I will sur.
18. 3 the people answered, Thou shalt not go
18. 4 all the people came out by hundreds, and
18. 5 the people heard when the king gave all
18. 6 the people went out into the field against
18. 7 Where the people of Israel were slain bef.
18. 8 the wood devoured more people that day
18. 16 people returned..Joab held back the pe.
19. 2 unto all the people: for the people heard
19. 3 the people gat them by stealth that day
19. 3 as people being ashamed steal away when
19. 8 And they told unto all the people, saying
19. 8 the people came before the king; for Isr.
19. 9 all the people were at strife throughout
19. 39 And all the people went over Jordan. And
19. 40 all the people of Judah..also half the pe.
20. 12 the man saw that all the people stood s.
20. 15 the people that (were) with Joab battered
20. 22 went unto all the people in her wisdom
22. 28 And the afflicted people thou wilt save
22. 44 delivered me from the strivings of my p.
22. 44 a people (which) I knew not shall serve
22. 48 that bringeth down the people under me
23. 10 the people returned after him only to sp.
23. 11 and the people fled from before the Phil.
24. 2 to Beer-sheba, and number ye the people
24. 2 that I may know the number of the peo.
24. 3 the LORD thy God add unto the people, how
24. 4 went out..to number the people of Israel
24. 9 the sum of the number of the people unto

2 Sa. 24. 10 after that he had numbered the people
24. 15 there died of the people from Dan even
24. 16 said to the angel that destroyed the peo.
24. 17 when he saw the angel that smote the pe.
24. 21 the plague may be stayed from the people
1 Ki. 1. 39 all the people said, God save king Solomon
1. 40 all the people..and the people piped with
3. 2 Only the people sacrificed in high places
3. 8 thy people..a great people, that cannot
3. 9 understanding heart to judge thy people
3. 9 who is able to judge..so great a people?
4. 34 there came of all people to hear the wisd.
5. 7 given..a wise son over this great people
5. 16 ruled over the people that wrought in the
6. 13 will dwell..and will not forsake my peo.
8. 16 day that I brought forth my people Israel
8. 16 I chose David to be over my people Israel
8. 30 hearken thou to..thy people Israel, when
8. 33 When thy people Israel be smitten down
8. 34 forgive the sin of thy people Israel, and
8. 36 forgive the sin..of thy people Israel, that
8. 36 land, which thou hast given to thy people
8. 38 by any man, (or) by all thy people Israel
8. 41 stranger, that (is) not of thy people Israel
8. 43 people of the earth may know thy name
8. 43 to fear thee, as (do) thy people Israel; and
8. 44 If thy people go out to battle against th.
8. 50 forgive thy people that have sinned agai.
8. 51 they (be) thy people, and thine inheritance
8. 52 unto the supplication of thy people Israel
8. 53 separate them from among all the people
8. 56 that hath given rest unto his people Israel
8. 59 cause of his people Israel at all times, as
8. 60 all the people of the earth may know that
8. 66 On the eighth day he sent the people away
8. 66 that the LORD had done for..his people
9. 7 a proverb and a byword among all people
9. 20 all the people (that were) left of the Am.
9. 23 bare rule over the people that wrought in
12. 5 Depart yet (for) three days..And the peo.
12. 6 ye advise that I may answer this people?
12. 7 If thou wilt be a servant unto this people
12. 9 that we may answer this people, who have
12. 10 Thus shalt thou speak unto this people that
12. 12 all the people came to Rehoboam the third
12. 13 answered the people roughly, and forsook
12. 15 the king hearkened not unto the people
12. 16 people answered the king, saying, What
12. 23 Speak unto..the remnant of the people
12. 27 If this people go up to do sacrifice in the
12. 27 then shall the heart of this people turn
12. 30 for the people went (to worship) before
12. 31 made priests of the lowest of the people
13. 33 but made again of the lowest of the people
14. 2 told me that (I should be) king over this p
14. 7 as I exalted thee from among the people
14. 7 made thee prince over my people Israel
16. 2 made thee prince over my people Israel
16. 2 hast made my people Israel to sin, to pro.
16. 15 people (were) encamped against Gibbethon
16. 16 people (that were) encamped heard say, Z.
16. 21 Then were the people of Israel divided into
16. 21 half of the people followed Tibni the son
16. 22 the people that followed Omri prevailed
16. 22 against the people that followed Tibni the
18. 21 Elijah came unto all the people, and said
18. 21 And the people answered him not a word
18 22 Then said Elijah unto the people, I, (even)
18. 24 all the people answered and said, It is well
18. 30 Elijah said unto all the people, Come near
18. 30 all the people came near unto him: and
18. 37 this people may know that thou (art) the
18. 39 when all the people saw (it), they fell on
19. 21 gave unto the people, and they did eat
20. 8 all the people, said unto him, Hearken not
20. 10 suffice for handfuls for all the people that
20. 15 after them he numbered all the people
20. 42 for his life, and thy people for his people
21. 9, 12 and set Naboth on high among the p.
21. 13 in the presence of the people, saying, N.
22. 4 my people as thy people, my horses as thy
22. 28 said, Hearken, O people, every one of you
22. 43 people offered and burnt incense yet
2 Ki. 3. 7 my people as thy people, (and) my horses as
4. 13 answered, I dwell among mine own people
4. 41 Pour out for the people, that they may eat
4. 42 Give unto the people, that they may eat
4. 43 Give the people, that they may eat: for
6. 30 people looked, and, behold, (he had) sack.
7. 16 people went out, and spoiled the tents of
7. 17, 20 people trode upon him in the gate, and
8. 21 So Joram..smote..and the people fled into
9. 6 anointed thee king over the people of the
10. 9 said to all the people, Ye (be) righteous
10. 18 Jehu gathered all the people together, and
11. 13 the people, she came to the people into
11. 14 all the people of the land rejoiced, and
11. 17 a covenant between the LORD..and the p.
11. 17 that they should be the LORD'S people
11. 17 between the king also and the people
11. 18 all the people of the land went into the
11. 19 he took..all the people of the land; and
11. 20 all the people of the land rejoiced, and
12. 3 people still sacrificed and burnt incense
12. 8 to receive no (more) money of the people
13. 7 Neither did he leave of the people to J.
14. 4 as yet the people did sacrifice and burnt
14. 21 all the people of Judah took Azariah, wh.
15. 4 people sacrificed and burnt incense still in
15. 5 over the house, judging the people of the
15. 10 smote him before the people, and slew him
15. 35 the people sacrificed and burnt incense

2 Ki. 16. 15 with the burnt offering of all the people
18. 26 in the ears of the people that (are) on the
18. 36 people held their peace, and answered him
20. 5 tell Hezekiah the captain of my people, T.
21. 24 people of the land..people of the land m.
22. 4 which the keepers..have gathered of the p.
22. 13 enquire of the LORD..for the people, and
23. 2 and all the people, both small and great
23. 3 and all the people stood to the covenant
23. 6 upon the graves of the children of the pe.
23. 21 commanded all the people, saying, Keep
23. 30 people of the land took Jehoahaz the son
23. 35 exacted the silver..of the people of the l.
24. 14 save the poorest sort of the people of the
25. 3 there was no bread for the people of the
25. 11 Now the rest of the people (that were) left
25. 19 which mustered the people of the land, and
25. 19 threescore men of the people of the land
25. 22 people that remained in the land of Judah
25. 26 all the people, both small and great, and
1 Ch. 5. 25 a whoring after the gods of the people of
10. 9 tidings unto their idols, and to the people
11. 2 said..Thou shalt feed my people Israel
11. 2 thou shalt be ruler over my people Israel
11. 13 the people fled from before the Philistines
13. 4 thing was right in the eyes of all the peo.
14. 2 lifted up on high, because of his people I.
16. 2 he blessed the people in the name of the
16. 8 make known his deeds among the people
16. 20 and from (one) kingdom to another peop.
16. 26 For all the gods of the people (are) idols
16. 28 ye kindreds of the people, give unto the
16. 36 the people said, Amen, and praised the L.
16. 43 all the people departed every man to his
17. 6 whom I commanded to feed my people, sa.
17. 7 thou shouldest be ruler over my people I.
17. 9 I will ordain a place for my people Israel
17. 10 commanded judges (to be) over my people
17. 21 what one nation..(is) like thy people Isr.
17. 21 God went to redeem (to be) his own peo.
17. 21 driving out nations from before thy peo.
17. 22 people Israel didst thou make thine own
18. 14 executed judgment..among all his people
19. 7 hired..the king of Maachah and his peo.
19. 11 rest of the people he delivered unto the
19. 13 behave ourselves valiantly for our people
19. 14 Joab and the people that (were) with him
20. 3 brought out the people..all the people re.
21. 2 said to Joab, and to the rulers of the pe.
21. 3 make his people an hundred times so many
21. 5 gave the sum of the number of the people
21. 17 (Is it) not I (that) commanded the people
21. 17 not on thy people, that they should be pl.
21. 22 the plague may be stayed from the people
22. 18 the land is subdued..before his people
23. 25 hath given rest unto his people, that they
28. 2 Hear me, my brethren, and my people
28. 21 all the people (will be) wholly at thy com.
29. 9 people rejoiced, for that they offered wil.
29. 14 what (is) my people, that we should be
29. 17 now have I seen with joy thy people, whi.
29. 18 of the thoughts of the heart of thy people
2 Ch. 1. 9 thou hast made me king over a people like
1. 10 may go out and come in before this people
1. 10 for who can judge this thy people, (that is
1. 11 that thou mayest judge my people, over
2. 11 Because the LORD hath loved his people
2. 18 six hundred overseers to set the people
6. 5 Since the day that I brought forth my p.
6. 5 any man to be a ruler over my people Is.
6. 6 chosen David to be over my people Israel
6. 21 supplications..of thy people Israel, which
6. 24 if thy people Israel be put to the worse be.
6. 25 forgive the sin of thy people Israel, and
6. 27 forgive the sin..of thy people Israel, when
6. 27 which thou hast given unto thy people for
6. 29 made of any man, or of all thy people Is.
6. 32 stranger, which is not of thy people Israel
6. 33 people..fear thee, as (doth) thy people I.
6. 34 If thy people go out to war against their
6. 39 forgive thy people which have sinned ag.
7. 4 all the people offered sacrifices before the
7. 5 all the people dedicated the house of God
7. 10 he sent the people away into their tents
7. 10 and to Solomon, and to Israel his people
7. 13 or if I send pestilence among my people
7. 14 If my people, which are called by my name
8. 7 all the people (that were) left of the Hit.
8. 10 officers..that bare rule over the people
10. 5 said..Come again..And the people depar.
10. 6 give ye (me) to return answer to this pe.?
10. 7 If thou be kind to this people, and please
10. 9 that we may return answer to this people
10. 10 Thus shalt thou answer the people that
10. 12 Jeroboam and all the people came to R.
10. 15 So the king hearkened not unto the peo.
10. 16 people answered the king, saying, What
12. 3 people (were) without number that came
13. 17 Abijah and his people slew them with a
14. 13 Asa and the people that (were) with him
16. 10 oppressed (some) of the people the same
17. 9 they..went about..and taught the people
18. 2 killed sheep..for the people that (he had)
18. 3 as thou (art), and my people as thy people
18. 27 And Micaiah said..Hearken, all ye people
19. 4 he went out again through the people
20. 7 drive out..before thy people Israel, and
20. 21 when he had consulted with the people
20. 25 when Jehoshaphat and his people came
20. 33 for as yet the people had not prepared
21. 14 smite thy people, and thy children, and
21. 19 his people made no burning for him, like

2 Ch. 23. 5 all the people (shall be) in the courts of
23. 6 all the people shall keep the watch of the
23. 10 he set all the people, every man having
23. 12 when Athaliah heard the noise of the pe.
23. 12 she came to the people into the house of
23. 13 all the people of the land rejoiced, and
23. 16 made a covenant between..all the people
23. 16 and..that they should be the LORD'S pe.
23. 17 all the people went to the house of Baal
23. 20 governors of the people, and all the peo.
23. 21 all the people of the land rejoiced: and
24. 10 princes and all the people rejoiced, and
24. 20 which stood above the people, and said
24. 23 the princes of the people from among the p.
25. 11 led forth his people, and went to the val.
25. 15 hast thou sought after the gods of the p.
25. 15 which could not deliver their own people
26. 1 Then all the people of Judah took Uzziah
26. 21 over the king's house, judging the people
27. 2 And the people did yet corruptly
29. 36 people, that God had prepared the people
30. 3 neither had the people gathered themsel.
30. 13 assembled at Jerusalem much people to
30. 18 For a multitude of the people, (even) many
30. 20 the LORD hearkened..and healed the pe.
30. 27 the priests..arose and blessed the people
31. 4 commanded the people that dwelt in Je.
31. 8 they blessed the LORD, and his people I.
31. 10 for the LORD hath blessed his people; and
32. 4 there was gathered much people together
32. 6 he set captains of war over the people, and
32. 8 people rested themselves upon the words
32. 13 my fathers have done unto all the people
32. 14 could deliver his people out of mine hand
32. 15 was able to deliver his people out of mine
32. 17 have not delivered their people out of mine
32. 17 the God of Hezekiah deliver his people out
32. 18 unto the people of Jerusalem that (were)
32. 19 as against the gods of the people of the
33. 10 LORD spake..to his people; but they wo.
33. 17 Nevertheless the people did sacrifice still
33. 25 the people..and the people of the land
34. 30 Levites, and all the people, great and small
35. 3 serve now the LORD your God, and his p.
35. 8 his princes gave willingly unto the people
36. 1 Then the people of the land took Jehoahaz
36. 14 people transgressed very much after all
36. 15 because he had compassion on his people
36. 16 wrath of the LORD arose against his peo.
36. 23 who (is there) among you of all his people?
Ezra 1. 3 Who (is there) among you of all his people?
2. 2 number of the men of the people of Israel
2. 70 (some) of the people..dwelt in their cities
3. 1 people gathered themselves together as
3. 3 fear (was) upon them because of the peo.
3. 11 all the people shouted with a great shout
3. 13 So that the people could not discern the
3. 13 weeping of the people: for the people sh.
4. 4 people..weakened the hands of the people
8. 15 viewed the people and the priests, and f.
8. 36 furthered the people, and the house of God
9. 1 people..have not separated..from the p.
9. 2 have mingled themselves with the people
9. 11 with the filthiness of the people of the l.
9. 14 join in affinity with the people of these a.
10. 1 assembled..for the people wept very sore
10. 2 have taken strange wives of the people of
10. 9 all the people sat in the street of the house
10. 11 separate yourselves from the people of the
10. 13 people (are) many..(it is) a time of much
Neh. 1. 10 these (are) thy servants and thy people
4. 6 joined..for the people had a mind to work
4. 13 I even set the people after their families
4. 14, 19 said..to the rest of the people
4. 22 at the same time said I unto the people
5. 1 there was a great cry of the people, and
5. 13 the people did according to this promise
5. 15 before me were chargeable unto the peo.
5. 15 their servants bare rule over the people
5. 18 the bondage was heavy upon this people
5. 19 to all that I have done for this people
7. 4 people (were) few therein, and the houses
7. 5 put into mine heart to gather..the people
7. 7 The number..of the men of the people of
7. 72 (that) which the rest of the people gave
7. 73 So the priests..and (some) of the people
8. 1 all the people gathered themselves toge.
8. 3 ears of all the people (were attentive) unto
8. 5 the people; for he was above all the peo.
8. 5 when he opened it, all the people stood up
8. 6 all the people answered, Amen, Amen, with
8. 7 caused the people to understand..the p.
8. 9 taught the people, said unto all the people
8. 9 all the people wept, when they heard the
8. 11 So the Levites stilled all the people, say.
8. 12 all the people went their way to eat, and
8. 13 chief of the fathers of all the people, the
8. 16 So the people went forth, and brought (t.)
9. 10 showedst signs..on all the people of his l.
9. 24 with their kings, and the people of the l.
9. 30 gavest thou them into the hand of the p.
9. 32 on all thy people, since the time of the k.
10. 14 chief of the people; Parosh, Pahath-moab
10. 28 rest of the people, the priests, the Levites
10. 30 not give our daughters unto the people of
10. 31 (if) the people of the land bring ware or
10. 34 we cast the lots among..the people, for the
11. 1 rulers of the people..rest of the people
11. 2 people blessed all the men that willingly
11. 24 hand in all matters concerning the people
12. 30 purified the people, and the gates, and the
12. 38 half of the people upon the wall, from be.

Neh. 13. 1 they read..in the audience of the people
13. 24 according to the language of each people
Esth. 1. 5 king made a feast unto all the people that
1. 11 show the people and the princes her bea.
1. 16 to all the people that (are) in all the pro.
1. 22 to every people..the language of every p.
2. 10 Esther had not showed her people nor her
2. 20 not (yet) showed her kindred nor her pe.
3. 6 for they had showed him the people of M.
3. 6 Haman sought to destroy..the people of
3. 8 There is a certain people scattered abroad
3. 8 dispersed among the people in all the pr.
3. 8 their laws (are) diverse from all people
3. 11 silver (is) given to thee, the people also
3. 12 every people..and (to) every people
3. 14 was published unto all people, that they
4. 8 to make request before him for her people
4. 11 people of the king's provinces, do know
7. 3 let my life be given..and my people at my
7. 4 For we are sold, I and my people, to be
8. 6 see the evil that shall come unto my peo.
8. 9 unto every people after their language
8. 11 all the power of the people and province
8. 13 (was) published unto all people, and that
8. 17 many of the people of the land became J.
9. 2 for the fear of them fell upon all people
10. 3 seeking the wealth of his people, and sp.
Job 12. 2 No doubt but ye (are) the people, and wi
12. 24 the heart of the chief of the people of the
17. 6 hath made me also a byword of the people
18. 19 son nor nephew among his people, nor any
34. 20 people shall be troubled at midnight, and
34. 30 That the hypocrite reign not, lest the pe.
36. 20 Desire not the night, when people are cut
36. 31 by them judgeth he the people; he giveth
Psa. 3. 6 I will not be afraid of ten thousands of p.
3. 8 thy blessing (is) upon thy people. Selah
7. 8 The LORD shall judge the people: judge
9. 11 declare among the people his doings
14. 4 who eat up my people (as) they eat bread
14. 7 bringeth back the captivity of his people
18. 27 For thou wilt save the afflicted people; but
18. 43 delivered me from the strivings of the p.
18. 43 people (whom) I have not known shall se.
18. 47 (It is) God that..subdueth the people un.
22. 6 reproach of men, and despised of the pe.
22. 31 unto a people that shall be born, that he
28. 9 Save thy people, and bless thine inherit.
29. 11 The LORD will give strength unto his peo.
29. 11 the LORD will bless his people with peace
33. 10 maketh the devices of the people of none
33. 12 people (whom) he hath chosen for his own
35. 18 I will praise thee among much people
44. 12 Thou sellest thy people for nought, and
45. 5 Thine arrows (are) sharp..the people fall
45. 10 forget also thine own people, and thy fa.
45. 12 rich among the people shall entreat thy
45. 17 therefore shall the people praise thee for
47. 1 clap your hands, all ye people; shout unto
47. 3 He shall subdue the people under us, and
47. 9 princes of the people..the people of the G.
49. 1 Hear this, all (ye) people; give ear, all (ye)
50. 4 He shall call..that he may judge his peo.
50. 7 Hear, O my people, and I will speak; O
53. 4 who eat up my people (as) they eat bread
53. 6 bringeth back the captivity of his people
56. 7 in (thine) anger cast down the people, O
57. 9 will praise thee, O LORD, among the peo.
59. 11 Slay them not, lest my people forget, scatter
60. 3 Thou hast showed thy people hard things
62. 8 ye people, pour out your heart before him
66. 8 bless our God, ye people, and make the
67. 3, 5 Let the people praise..let all the peo.
67. 4 thou shalt judge the people righteously
68. 7 when thou wentest forth before thy peo.
68. 30 of the bulls, with the calves of the people
68. 30 scatter thou the people (that) delight in
68. 35 giveth strength and power unto (his) pe.
72. 2 He shall judge thy people with righteous.
72. 3 mountains shall bring peace to the people
72. 4 He shall judge the poor of the people, he
73. 10 Therefore his people return hither; and
74. 14 gavest him (to be) meat to the people in.
74. 18 foolish people have blasphemed thy name
77. 14 hast declared thy strength among the pe.
77. 15 hast with (thine) arm redeemed thy peo.
77. 20 Thou leddest thy people like a flock by
78. 1 Give ear, O my people, (to) my law: inc.
78. 20 Behold..can he provide flesh for his peo.
78. 52 made his own people to go forth like sheep
78. 62 He gave his people over also unto the sw.
78. 71 he brought him to feed Jacob his people
79. 13 we thy people, and sheep of thy pasture
80. 4 be angry against the prayer of thy people
81. 8 Hear, O my people, and I will testify un.
81. 11 my people would not hearken to my voice
81. 13 O that my people had hearkened unto me
83. 3 have taken crafty counsel against thy pe.
85. 2 Thou hast forgiven the iniquity of thy p.
85. 6 revive us..that thy people may rejoice
85. 8 he will speak peace unto his people, and
87. 6 shall count, when he writeth up the peo.
89. 15 Blessed (is) the people that know the joy.
89. 19 I have exalted (one) chosen out of the p.
89. 50 bear..(the reproach of) all the mighty p.
94. 5 They break in pieces thy people, O LORD
94. 8 Understand, ye brutish among the people
94. 14 For the LORD will not cast off his people
95. 7 we (are) the people of his pasture, and
95. 10 It (is) a people that do err in their heart
96. 3 Declare..his wonders among all people
96. 7 O ye kindreds of the people, give unto the

Psa. 96. 10 LORD..shall judge the people righteously
96. 13 he shall judge..the people with his truth
97. 6 declare his righteousness, and all the pe.
98. 9 judge the world, and the people with eq.
99. 1 The LORD reigneth; let the people trem.
99. 2 LORD (is) great..he (is) high above all pe.
100. 3 (are) his people, and the sheep of his pa.
102. 18 the people which shall be created shall
102. 22 When the people are gathered together
105. 1 make known his deeds among the people
105. 13 went..from (one) kingdom to another pe.
105. 20 the ruler of the people, and let him go f.
105. 24 he increased his people greatly, and made
105. 25 He turned their heart to hate his people
105. 43 And he brought forth his people with joy
106. 4 the favour (that thou bearest unto) thy p.
106. 40 was the wrath..kindled against his people
106. 48 let all the people say, Amen. Praise ye
107. 32 exalt him..in the congregation of the pe.
110. 3 Thy people (shall be) willing in the day of
111. 6 He hath showed his people the power of
111. 9 He sent redemption unto his people: he
113. 8 may set (him)..with the princes of his p.
114. 1 house of Jacob from a people of strange
116. 14, 18 pay..now in the presence of all his peo.
125. 2 round about his people from henceforth
135. 12 And gave..an heritage unto Israel his p.
135. 14 the LORD will judge his people, and he
136. 16 which led his people through the wilder.
144. 2 and (he)..who subdueth my people under
144. 15 Happy (is that) people that is in such a
144. 15 happy (is that) people whose God (is) the
148. 14 He also exalteth the horn of his people
148. 14 children of Israel, a people near unto him
149. 4 the LORD taketh pleasure in his people: he
Prov 11. 14 Where no counsel (is), the people fall: but
14. 28 In the multitude of people (is) the king's
24. 24 him shall the people curse, nations shall
28. 15 (so is) a wicked ruler over the poor people
29. 2 the righteous are in authority, the people
29. 2 the wicked beareth rule, the people mourn
29. 18 Where (there is) no vision, the people pe.
30. 25 The ants (are) a people not strong, yet they
Eccl. 4. 16 (There is) no end of all the people..of all
12. 9 he still taught the people knowledge; yea
Isa. 1. 3 doth not know, my people doth not cons.
1. 4 people laden with iniquity, a seed of evil
1. 10 give ear unto the law..people of Gomor.
2. 3 people shall go and say, Come ye, and let
2. 4 shall rebuke many people; and they shall
2. 6 thou hast forsaken thy people the house
3. 5 the people shall be oppressed, every one
3. 7 saying..make me not a ruler of the people
3. 12 my people, children (are) their oppressors
3. 12 O my people, they which lead thee cause
3. 13 The LORD standeth up..to judge the pe.
3. 14 judgment with the ancients of his people
3. 15 What mean ye (that) ye beat my people to
5. 13 Therefore my people are gone into capti.
5. 25 is the anger..kindled against his people
6. 5 in the midst of a people of unclean lips
6. 9 and tell this people, Hear ye indeed, but
6. 10 Make the heart of this people fat, and ma.
7. 2 was moved, and the heart of his people
7. 8 Ephraim be broken, that it be not a peo.
7. 17 upon thy people, and upon thy father's
8. 6 this people refuseth the waters of Shiloah
8. 9 Associate yourselves, O ye people, and ye
8. 11 I should not walk in the way of this peo.
8. 12 (to) whom this people shall say, A confed.
8. 19 should not a people seek unto their God?
9. 2 The people that walked in darkness have
9. 9 all the people shall know, (even) Ephraim
9. 13 the people turneth not unto him that sm.
9. 16 the leaders of this people cause (them) to
9. 19 the people shall be as the fuel of the fire
10. 2 take..the right from the poor of my peop.
10. 6 against the people of my wrath will I give
10. 13 I have removed the bounds of the people
10. 14 found as a nest the riches of the people
10. 22 people Israel be as the sand of the sea
10. 24 O my people that dwellest in Zion, be not
11. 10 shall stand for an ensign of the people
11. 11 set..to recover the remnant of his people
11. 16 an highway for the remnant of his people
12. 4 declare his doings among the people, make
13. 4 noise..like as of a great people; a tumult.
13. 14 shall every man turn to his own people
14. 2 the people shall take them, and bring them
14. 6 He who smote the people in wrath with
14. 20 destroyed thy land, (and) slain thy people
14. 32 and the poor of his people shall trust in
17. 12 Woe to the multitude of many people, (w.)
18. 2, 7 a people terrible from their beginning
18. 7 present..of a people scattered and peeled
19. 25 Blessed (be) Egypt my people, and Assyria
22. 4 the spoiling of the daughter of my people
23. 13 this people was not, (till) the Assyrian
24. 2 as with the people, so with the priest; as
24. 4 haughty people of the earth do languish
24. 13 the midst of the land among the people
25. 3 Therefore shall the strong people glorify
25. 6 shall the LORD of hosts make unto all pe.
25. 7 the face of the covering cast over all the p.
25. 8 the rebuke of his people shall he take away
26. 11 be ashamed for (their) envy at the people
26. 20 Come, my people, enter thou into thy ch.
27. 11 for it (is) a people of no understanding
28. 5 a diadem..unto the residue of his people
28. 11 another tongue will he speak to this peo.
28. 14 rule this people which (is) in Jerusalem
29. 13 this people draw near (me) with their m.

Isa. 29. 14 to do a marvellous work among this peo.
30. 5 of a people (that) could not profit them
30. 6 carry..to a people (that) shall not profit
30. 9 this (is) a rebellious people, lying children
30. 19 people shall dwell in Zion at Jerusalem
30. 26 LORD bindeth up the breach of his people
30. 28 a bridle in the jaws of the people, causing
32. 13 Upon the land of my people shall come up
32. 18 And my people shall dwell in a peaceable
33. 3 At the noise of the tumult the people fled
33. 12 the people shall be (as) the burnings of l.
33. 19 shalt not see a fierce people, a people of
33. 24 the people that dwell therein (shall be)
34. 5 upon the people of my curse, to judgment
36. 11 in the ears of the people that (are) on the
40. 1 Comfort ye, comfort ye my people, saith
40. 7 grass withereth..surely the people (is) g.
42. 5 giveth bread unto the people upon it
42. 6 give thee for a covenant of the people, for
42. 22 this (is) a people robbed and spoiled; (th.)
43. 8 Bring forth the blind people that have
43. 20 to give drink to my people, my chosen
43. 21 This people have I formed for myself; th.
44. 7 since I appointed the ancient people? and
47. 6 was wroth with my people, I have pollu.
49. 8 give thee for a covenant of the people, to
49. 13 the LORD hath comforted his people, and
49. 22 and set up my standard to the people
51. 4 Hearken unto me, my people; and give
51. 4 judgment to rest for a light of the people
51. 5 mine arms shall judge the people: the is.
51. 7 Hearken..the people in whose heart (is)
51. 16 and say unto Zion, Thou (art) my people
51. 22 God (that) pleadeth the cause of his people
52. 4 My people went down aforetime into Eg.
52. 5 that my people is taken away for nought
52. 6 my people shall know my name: therefore
52. 9 the LORD hath comforted his people, he
53. 8 for the trangression of my people was he
56. 3 hath utterly separated me from his people
56. 7 be called an house of prayer for all people
57. 14 stumbling block out of the way of my pe.
58. 1 show my people their transgression, and
60. 21 Thy people also (shall be) all righteous
61. 9 and their offspring among the people
62. 10 prepare ye the way of the people; cast up
62. 10 cast up..lift up a standard for the people
62. 12 The holy people, The redeemed of the L.
63. 3 and of the people (there was) none with
63. 6 will tread down the people in mine anger
63. 8 they (are) my people, children (that) will n.
63. 11 he remembered..Moses, (and) his people
63. 14 so didst thou lead thy people, to make t.
63. 18 The people of thy holiness have possessed
64. 9 see, we beseech thee, we (are) all thy pe.
65. 2 have spread out..unto a rebellious people
65. 3 A people that provoketh me to anger
65. 10 place..for my people that have sought me
65. 18 Jerusalem a rejoicing, and her people a
65. 19 rejoice in Jerusalem, and joy in my people
65. 22 the days of a tree (are) the days of my p.
Jer. 1. 18 brasen walls..against the people of the l.
2. 11 my people have changed their glory for
2. 13 my people have committed two evils; they
2. 31 Wherefore say my people, We are lords
2. 32 my people have forgotten me days with.
4. 10 greatly deceived this people and Jerusa.
4. 11 that time shall it be said to this people
4. 11 wind..toward the daughter of my people
4. 22 people (is) foolish, they have not known me
5. 14 I will make..this people wood, and it sh.
5. 21 foolish people, and without understand.
5. 23 people hath a revolting and a rebellious
5. 26 For among my people are found wicked
5. 31 my people love (to have it) so: and what
6. 14 the hurt (of the daughter) of my people
6. 19 I will bring evil upon this people, (even)
6. 21 I will lay stumbling blocks before this p.
6. 22 a people cometh from the north country
6. 26 O daughter of my people, gird (thee) with
6. 27 a tower (and) a fortress among my people
7. 12 did..for the wickedness of my people Is.
7. 16 pray not thou for this people, neither lift
7. 23 will be your God, and ye shall be my pe.
7. 33 the carcases of this people shall be meat
8. 5 Why..is this people of Jerusalem slidden
8. 7 my people know not the judgment of the
8. 11, 21 the hurt of the daughter of my people
8. 19 of the cry of the daughter of my people
8. 22 not the health of the daughter of my pe.
9. 1 the slain of the daughter of my people
9. 2 I might leave my people, and go from th.
9. 7 how shall I do for..daughter of my peo.
9. 15 I will feed them, (even) this people, with
10. 3 the customs of the people (are) vain; for
11. 4 so shall ye be my people, and I will be
11. 14 pray not thou for this people, neither lift
12. 14 have caused my people Israel to inherit
12. 16 will diligently learn the ways of my peo.
12. 16 they taught my people to swear by Baal
12. 16 they be built in the midst of my people
13. 10 This evil people, which refuse to hear my
13. 11 they might be unto me for a people, and
14. 10 Thus saith the LORD unto this people, Th.
14. 11 Pray not for this people for (their) good
14. 16 the people to whom they prophesy shall
14. 17 the virgin daughter of my people is bro.
15. 1 my mind (could) not (be) toward this pe.
15. 7 I will destroy my people, (since) they re.
15. 20 I will make thee unto this people a fen.
16. 5 have taken away my peace from this pe.
16. 10 shalt show this people all these words

Jer. 17. 19 in the gate of the children of the people
18. 15 my people hath forgotten me, they have
19. 1 (take) of the ancients of the people, and
19. 11 so will I break this people, and this city
19. 14 and he stood..and said to all the people
21. 7 the people, and (such as are) left in this
21. 8 unto this people thou shalt say, Thus sa.
22. 2 and thy people that enter in by these ga.
22. 4 enter..he, and his servants, and his peo.
23. 2 against the pastors that feed my people
23. 13 they prophesied..and caused my people
23. 22 had caused my people to hear my words
23. 27 Which think to cause my people to forget
23. 32 cause my people to err by their lies, and
23. 32 they shall not profit this people at all
23. 33 when this people, or the prophet, or a p.
23. 34 the people, that shall say, The burden of
24. 7 shall be my people, and I will be their God
25. 1 concerning all the people of Judah in the
25. 2 prophet spake unto all the people of Jud.
25. 19 Pharaoh..and his princes, and all his pe.
26. 7 the people heard Jeremiah speaking these
26. 8 commanded (him) to speak unto all the p.
26. 8 all the people took him, saying, Thou sh.
26. 9 the people were gathered against Jeremiah
26. 11, 12 unto..the princes, and to all the peo.
26. 16 Then said the princes and all the people
26. 17 spake to all the assembly of the people
26. 18 spake to all the people of Judah, saying
26. 23 body into the graves of the common peo.
26. 24 not give him into the hand of the people
27. 12 and serve him and his people, and live
27. 13 Why will ye die, thou and thy people
27. 16 spake to the priests, and to all this people
28. 1 spake..in the presence..of all the people
28. 5 in the presence of all the people that stood
28. 7 that I speak..in the ears of all the people
28. 11 spake in the presence of all the people
28. 15 but thou makest this people to trust in a
29. 1 to all the people whom Nebuchadnezzar
29. 16 of all the people that dwelleth in this city
29. 25 sent letters in thy name unto all the peo.
29. 32 have a man to dwell among this people
29. 32 behold the good that I will do for my pe.
30. 3 bring again the captivity of my people I.
30. 22 ye shall be my people, and I will be your
31. 1 families of Israel, and they shall be my p.
31. 2 The people (which were) left of the sword
31. 7 LORD, save thy people, the remnant of I.
31. 14 people shall be satisfied with my goodness
31. 33 be their God, and they shall be my people
32. 21 hast brought forth thy people Israel out
32. 38 they shall be my people, and I will be their
32. 42 brought all this great evil upon this peo.
33. 24 Considerest thou not what this people h.
33. 24 have despised my people, that they should
34. 1 all the people, fought against Jerusalem
34. 8 covenant with all the people which (were)
34. 10 all the people, which had entered into the
34. 19 all the people of the land, which passed
35. 16 this people hath not hearkened unto me
36. 6 in the ears of the people, in the LORD'S
36. 7 LORD hath pronounced against this people
36. 9 people in Jerusalem, and to all the people
36. 10 Then read Baruch..in the ears of all the p.
36. 13 Baruch read the book in the ears of the p.
36. 14 thou hast read in the ears of the people
37. 2 neither he, nor his servants, nor the peo.
37. 4 came in and went out among the people
37. 12 separate..thence in the midst of the peo.
37. 18 against thy servants, or against this people
38. 1 Jeremiah had spoken unto all the people
38. 4 he weakeneth..the hands of all the people
38. 4 man seeketh not the welfare of this people
39. 8 burned..the houses of the people, with fire
39. 9 remnant of the people..rest of the people
39. 10 left of the poor of the people, which had
39. 14 carry him home: so he dwelt among the p.
40. 5 dwell with him among the people; or go
40. 6 dwelt with him among the people that w.
41. 10 residue of the people..and all the people
41. 13 when all the people which (were) with I.
41. 14 So all the people that Ishmael had carried
41. 16 all the remnant of the people whom he had
42. 1, 8 all the people from the least even unto
43. 1 made an end of speaking unto all the pe.
43. 4 all the people, obeyed not the voice of the
44. 15 all the people that dwelt in the land of E.
44. 20, 24 Jeremiah said unto all the people
44. 20 the people which had given him (that) a
44. 21 people of the land, did not the LORD re.
46. 16 Arise, and let us go again to our own peo.
46. 24 shall be delivered into the hand of the p.
48. 42 Moab shall be destroyed from (being) a p.
48. 46 people of Chemosh perisheth: for thy so.
49. 1 doth their king inherit Gad, and his people
50. 6 My people hath been lost sheep; their s.
50. 16 they shall turn every one to his people, and
50. 41 people shall come from the north, and a
51. 45 My people, go ye out of the midst of her
51. 58 people shall labour in vain, and the folk
52. 6 so that there was no bread for the people
52. 15 people, and the residue of the people that
52. 25 who mustered the people of the land; (and
52. 25 threescore men of the people of the land
52. 28 This (is) the people whom Nebuchadrezz.
Lam. 1. 1 city sit solitary (that was) full of people
1. 7 when her people fell into the hand of the
1. 11 All her people sigh, they seek bread; they
1. 18 hear, I pray you, all people, and behold
2. 11 the destruction of the daughter of my p
3. 14 I was a derision to all my people..their

Lam. 3. 45 made us (as)..refuse in the midst of the p.
3. 48 the destruction of the daughter of my p.
4. 3 the daughter of my people (is become) c.
4. 6 iniquity of the daughter of my people is
4. 10 the destruction of the daughter of my p.
Eze. 3. 5 thou (art) not sent to a people of a strange
3. 6 Not to many people of a strange speech
3. 11 go..unto the children of thy people, and
7. 27 the hands of the people of the land shall
11. 1 five and twenty men..princes of the peo.
11. 17 I will even gather you from the people, and
11. 20 they shall be my people, and I will be their
12. 19 say unto the people of the land, Thus saith
13. 9 shall not be in the assembly of my people
13. 10 even because they have seduced my peo.
13. 17 against the daughters of thy people, which
13. 18 Will ye hunt the souls of my people, and
13. 19 will ye pollute me among my people for
13. 19 by your lying to my people that hear (your)
13. 21 deliver my people out of your hand, and
13. 23 will deliver my people out of your hand
14. 8 cut him off from the midst of my people
14. 9 destroy him from the midst of my people
14. 11 but that they may be my people, and I
17. 9 without great power or many people to p.
17. 15 might give him horses and much people
18. 18 (that) which (is) not good among his peo.
20. 34 I will bring you out from the people, and
20. 35 bring you into the wilderness of the peo.
20. 41 when I bring you out from the people, and
21. 12 for it shall be upon my people, it (shall
21. 12 terrors..shall be upon my people: smite
22. 29 The people of the land have used oppres.
23. 24 with an assembly of people, (which) shall
24. 18 So I spake unto the people in the morn.
24. 19 people said unto me, Wilt thou not tell us
25. 7 I will cut thee off from the people, and I
25. 14 by the hand of my people Israel: and they
26. 2 she is broken (that was) the gates of the
26. 7 horsemen, and companies, and much peo.
26. 11 he shall slay thy people by the sword, and
26. 20 bring thee down..with the people of old
27. 3 a merchant of the people for many isles
27. 33 thou filledst many people; thou didst en.
27. 36 The merchants among the people shall
28. 19 All they that know thee among the people
28. 25 from the people among whom they are s.
29. 13 from the people whither they were scatt.
30. 11 He and his people with him, the terrible
31. 12 all the people of the earth are gone down
32. 3 over thee with a company of many peop.
32. 9 I will also vex the hearts of many people
32. 10 I will make many people amazed at thee
33. 2 Speak to the children of thy people, and
33. 2 if the people of the land take a man of
33. 3 he blow the trumpet and warn the peop.
33. 6 blow not the trumpet, and the people be
33. 12 say unto the children of thy people, The
33. 17 Yet the children of thy people say, The
33. 30 children of thy people still are talking a.
33. 31 they come unto thee as the people cometh
33. 31 and they sit before thee (as) my people
34. 13 I will bring them out from the people, and
34. 30 (that) they..(are) my people, saith the L.
36. 3 of talkers, and (are) an infamy of the pe.
36. 8 yield your fruit to my people of Israel; for
36. 12 I will cause men..(even) my people Israel
36. 15 shalt thou bear the reproach of the people
36. 20 These (are) the people of the LORD, and
36. 28 ye shall be my people, and I will be your
37. 12 O my people, I will open your graves, and
37. 13 when I have opened your graves, O my p.
37. 18 when the children of thy people shall sp.
37. 23 so shall they be my people, and I will be
37. 27 be their God, and they shall be my people
38. 6 all his bands; (and) many people with th
38. 8 gathered out of many people, against the
38. 9 all thy bands, and many people with thee
38. 12 upon the people (that are) gathered out
38. 14 In that day when my people of Israel dw.
38. 15 many people with thee, all of them riding
38. 16 thou shalt come up against my people of
38. 22 upon the many people that (are) with him
39. 4 all thy bands, and the people that (is) w.
39. 7 name known in the midst of my people I.
39. 13 all the people of the land shall bury (them)
39. 27 I have brought them again from the peo.
42. 14 to (those things) which (are) for the peop.
44. 11 offering and the sacrifice for the people
44. 19 go forth..into the outer court to the peo.
44. 19 they shall not sanctify the people with t.
44. 23 they shall teach my people (the difference)
45. 8 my princes shall no more oppress my pe.
45. 9 take away your exactions from my people
45. 16 All the people of the land shall give this
45. 22 and for all the people of the land a bull.
46. 3 Likewise the people of the land shall wo.
46. 9 when the people of the land shall come
46. 18 shall not take of the people's inheritance
46. 18 that my people be not scattered every m.
46. 20 into the outer court, to sanctify the peo.
46. 24 ministers..shall boil the sacrifice of the p.
Dan. 8. 24 shall destroy the mighty and the holy pe.
9. 6 which spake..to all the people of the land
9. 15 hast brought thy people forth out of the
9. 16 thy people (are become) a reproach to all
9. 19 for thy city and thy people are called by
9. 20 confessing my sin and the sin of my peo.
9. 24 Seventy weeks are determined upon thy p.
9. 26 people of the prince that shall come shall
10. 14 what shall befall thy people in the latter
11. 14 robbers of thy people shall exalt themsel.
Dan. 11. 15 not withstand, neither his chosen people
11. 32 people that do know their God shall be st.
11. 33 they that understand among the people
12. 1 standeth for the children of thy people
12. 1 at that time thy people shall be delivered
12. 7 to scatter the power of the holy people
Hos. 1. 9 for ye (are) not my people, and I will not
1. 10 Ye (are) not my people, (there) it shall be
2. 23 will say to (them which were) not my pe.
2. 23 Thou (art my) people; and they shall say
4. 4 for thy people (are) as they that strive w.
4. 6 My people are destroyed for lack of kno.
4. 8 They eat up the sin of my people, and th.
4. 9 there shall be, like people, like priest: and
4. 12 My people ask counsel at their stocks, and
4. 14 the people (that) doth not understand sh.
6. 11 when I returned the captivity of my peo.
7. 8 he hath mixed himself among the people
9. 1 Rejoice not..as (other) people: for thou
10. 5 for the people thereof shall mourn over it
10. 10 the people shall be gathered against them
10. 14 shall a tumult arise among thy people, and
11. 7 my people are bent to backsliding from me
Joel 2. 2 a great people and a strong; there hath
2. 5 as a strong people set in battle array
2. 6 Before their face the people shall be much
2. 16 Gather the people, sanctify the congrega.
2. 17 Spare thy people, O LORD, and give not
2. 17 wherefore should they say among the pe.
2. 18 be jealous for his land, and pity his peop.
2. 19 the LORD will answer and say unto his p.
2. 26, 27 and my people shall never be ashamed
3. 2 will plead with them there for my people
3. 3 they have cast lots for my people; and h.
3. 16 but the LORD (will be) the hope of his pe.
Amos 1. 5 people of Syria shall go into captivity un
3. 6 Shall a trumpet be blown..and the peop.
7. 8 set a plumb line in the midst of my people
7. 15 LORD said..Go, prophesy unto my people
8. 2 The end is come upon my people of Israel
9. 10 All the sinners of my people shall die by
9. 14 bring again the captivity of my people of
Obad. 13 have entered into the gate of my people
Jon. 1. 8 what (is) thy country? and of what people
Mic. 1. 2 Hear, all ye people; hearken, O earth, and
1. 9 is come unto the gate of my people, (even)
2. 4 he hath changed the portion of my people
2. 8 Even of late my people is risen up as an
2. 9 The women of my people have ye cast out
2. 11 he shall even be the prophet of this peo.
3. 3 Who also eat the flesh of my people, and
3. 5 the prophets that make my people err
4. 1 shall be exalted..and people shall flow un.
4. 3 shall judge among many people, and reb.
4. 5 For all people will walk every one in the
4. 13 and thou shalt beat in pieces many peop.
5. 7, 8 remnant..shall be in the midst of..pe.
6. 2 LORD hath a controversy with his people
6. 3 O my people, what have I done unto thee?
6. 5 O my people, remember now what Balak
6. 16 ye shall bear the reproach of my people
7. 14 Feed thy people with thy rod, the flock of
Nah. 3. 13 thy people in the midst of thee (are) wo.
3. 18 thy people is scattered upon the mountains
Hab. 2. 5 also, because he..heapeth unto him all p.
2. 8 all the remnant of the people shall spoil
2. 10 shame..by cutting off many people, and
2. 13 the people shall labour in the very fire, and
3. 13 wentest forth for the salvation of thy pe.
3. 16 when he cometh up unto the people, he
Zeph. 1. 11 all the merchant people are cut down; all
2. 8 whereby they have reproached my people
2. 9 residue of my people shall spoil them, and
2. 10 magnified (themselves) against the people
3. 9 For then will I turn to the people a pure
3. 12 also leave..an afflicted and poor people
3. 20 a praise among all people of the earth, w.
Hag. 1. 2 This people say, The time is not come, the
1. 12 Joshua..with all the remnant of the peo.
1. 12 and the people did fear before the LORD
1. 13 in the LORD'S message unto the people
1. 14 spirit of all the remnant of the people; and
2. 2 Speak now..to the residue of the people
2. 4 be strong, all ye people of the land, saith
2. 14 So (is) this people, and so (is) this nation
Zech. 2. 11 nations shall be joined..shall be my peo.
7. 5 Speak unto all the people of the land, and
8. 6 in the eyes of the remnant of this people
8. 7 I will save my people from the east cou.
8. 8 they shall be my people, and I will be th.
8. 11 I (will) not (be) unto the residue of this p.
8. 12 cause the remnant of this people to poss.
8. 20 there shall come people, and the inhabi.
8. 22 many people and strong nations shall co.
9. 16 shall save them..as the flock of his people
10. 9 I will sow them among the people: and
11. 10 covenant..I had made with all the people
12. 2 cup of trembling unto all the people rou.
12. 3 make..a burdensome stone for all people
12. 4 will smite every horse of the people with
12. 6 they shall devour all the people round a.
13. 9 I will say, It (is) my people; and they s.
14. 2 residue of the people shall not be cut off
14. 12 wherewith the LORD will smite all the p.
Mal. 1. 4 people against whom the LORD hath indi.
2. 9 contemptible and base before all the pe.

10. *People*, עַם *am.*

Ezra 5. 12 and carried the people away into Babylon
6. 12 destroy all kings and people that shall put
7. 13 make a decree, that all they of the people
7. 16 with the freewill offering of the people, and
Ezra 7. 25 judges, which may judge all the people th.
Dan. 2. 44 kingdom shall not be left to other people
3. 4 To you it is commanded, O people, nations
3. 7 when all the people heard..all the people
3. 29 I make a decree, That every people, nation
4. 1 unto all people, nations, and languages
5. 19 for the majesty that he gave him, all pe.
6. 25 king Darius wrote unto all people, nations
7. 14 all people, nations, and languages, should
7. 27 the people of the saints of the most high

11. *People, populace*, δῆμος *dēmos.*

Acts 12. 22 the people gave a shout, (saying, It is) the
17. 5 and sought to bring them out to the peo.
19. 30 Paul would have entered in unto the peo.
19. 33 would have made his defence unto the p.

12. *Nation*, ἔθνος *ethnos.*

Acts 8. 9 bewitched the people of Samaria, giving
Rom. 10. 19 provoke you..by (them that are) no peo

13. *People*, λαός *laos.*

Matt. 1. 21 he shall save his people from their sins
2. 4 the chief priests and scribes of the peop.
2. 6 Governor, that shall rule my people Israel
4. 16 The people which sat in darkness saw gr.
4. 23 and all manner of disease among the peo.
9. 35 sickness and every disease, [among the p.]
13. 15 this people's heart is waxed gross, and
15. 8 This people draweth nigh unto me with
21. 23 the elders of the people came unto him
26. 3 the scribes, and the elders of the people
26. 5 lest there be an uproar among the people
26. 47 the chief priests and elders of the people
27. 1 the chief priests and elders of the people
27. 25 Then answered all the people, and said
27. 64 steal him away, and say unto the people
Mark 7. 6 This people honoureth me with (their) lips
11. 32 they feared the people: for all (men) cou.
14. 2 Not..lest there be an uproar of the people
Luke 1. 10 the people were praying without at the
1. 17 make ready a people prepared for the L.
1. 21 people waited for Zacharias, and marvel.
1. 68 he hath visited and redeemed his people
1. 77 To give knowledge of salvation unto his p.
2. 10 of great joy, which shall be to all people
2. 31 hast prepared before the face of all peop.
2. 32 A light..and the glory of thy people Isr.
3. 15 as the people were in expectation, and all
3. 18 other things..preached he unto the peo
3. 21 when all the people were baptised, it ca.
6. 17 a great multitude of people out of all Ju.
7. 1 his sayings in the audience of the people
7. 16 saying..That God hath visited his people
7. 29 people that heard (him), and the publicans
8. 47 declared unto him before all the people
9. 13 should go and buy meat for all this peop.
18. 43 the people, when they saw (it), gave praise
19. 47 chief of the people sought to destroy him
19. 48 the people were very attentive to hear him
20. 1 he taught the people in the temple, and
20. 6 the people will stone us: for they be pe.
20. 9 Then began he to speak to the people this
20. 19 they feared the people: for they perceived
20. 26 take hold of his words before the people
20. 45 in the audience of all the people, he said
21. 23 there shall be..wrath upon this people
21. 38 the people came early in the morning to
22. 2 might kill him; for they feared the peo.
22. 66 the elders of the people, and the chief pr.
23. 5 He stirreth up the people, teaching thro.
23. 13 chief priests and the rulers and the peo.
23. 14 unto me, as one that perverteth the peo.
23. 27 there followed him a great company of p.
23. 35 the people stood beholding. And the ru.
24. 19 a prophet..before God and all the people
John 8. 2 [the people came unto him; and he sat]
11. 50 one man should die for the people, and
18. 14 that one man should die for the people
Acts 2. 47 and having favour with all the people
3. 9 people saw him walking and praising God
3. 11 the people ran together unto them in the
3. 12 he answered unto the people, Ye men of
3. 23 shall be destroyed from among the people
4. 1 as they spake unto the people, the priests
4. 2 that they taught the people, and preached
4. 8 ye rulers of the people, and elders of Isr.
4. 10 Be it known..to all the people of Israel
4. 17 it spread no further among the people
4. 21 might punish them, because of the people
4. 25 Why did..the people imagine vain things
4. 27 the people of Israel, were gathered toge.
5. 12 and wonders wrought among the people
5. 13 no man..but the people magnified them
5. 20 speak in the temple to the people all the
5. 25 are..in the temple, and teaching the pe.
5. 26 they feared the people, lest they should
5. 34 had in reputation among all the people
5. 37 drew away much people after him: he also
6. 8 did..wonders and miracles among the p.
6. 12 they stirred up the people, and the elders
7. 17 the people grew and multiplied in Egypt
7. 34 affliction of my people which is in Egypt
10. 2 which gave much alms to the people, and
10. 41 Not to all the people, but unto witnesses
10. 42 he commanded us to preach unto the pe.
12. 4 intending..to bring him forth to the peo.
12. 11 the expectation of the people of the Jews.
13. 15 any word of exhortation for the people
13. 17 The God of this people of Israel chose our
13. 17 exalted the people when they dwelt as
13. 24 of repentance to all the people of Israel
13. 31 them..who are his witnesses unto the p.

Acts 15. 14 to take out of them a people for his name
18. 10 to hurt..for I have much people in this
19. 4 saying unto the people, that they should
21. 28 teacheth..every where against the people
21. 30 the people ran together: and they took
21. 36 the people followed after, crying, Away
21. 39 said..suffer me to speak unto the people
21. 40 beckoned with the hand unto the people
23. 5 shalt not speak evil of the ruler of thy p.
26. 17 Delivering thee from the people, and (f.)
26. 23 should show light unto the people, and
28. 17 have committed nothing against the peo.
28. 26 Go unto this people, and say, Hearing ye
28. 27 the heart of this people is waxed gross
Rom. 9. 25 call..my people, which were not my peo.
9. 26 Ye (are) not my people; there shall they
10. 21 unto a disobedient and gainsaying people
11. 1 Hath God cast away his people? God for
11. 2 God hath not cast away his people which
15. 10 saith, Rejoice, ye Gentiles, with his peop.
15. 11 all ye Gentiles; and laud him, all ye peo.
1 Co. 10. 7 The people sat down to eat and drink, and
14. 21 With..other lips will I speak unto..peo.
2 Co. 6. 16 be their God, and they shall be my peop.
Titus 2. 14 and purify unto himself a peculiar people
Heb. 2. 17 make reconciliation for the sins of the p.
4. 9 remaineth therefore a rest to the people
5. 3 as for the people, so also for himself, to
7. 5 commandment to take tithes of the peop.
7. 11 for under it the people received the law
7. 27 for his own sins, and then for the people's
8. 10 a God, and they shall be to me a people
9. 7 for himself, and..the errors of the people
9. 19 had spoken every precept to all the peop.
9. 19 sprinkled both the book, and all the peop.
10. 30 And again, The Lord shall judge his peo.
11. 25 suffer affliction with the people of God
13. 12 might sanctify the people with his own b.
1 Pe. 2. 9 priesthood..holy nation, a peculiar peo.
2. 10 (were) not a people but (are) now the pe.
2 Pe. 2. 1 there were false prophets among the pe.
Jude 5 saved the people out of the land of Egypt
Rev. 5. 9 kindred, and tongue, and people, and n.
7. 9 of all nations, and kindreds and people
10. 11 must prophesy again before many peoples
11. 9 the people, and kindreds, and tongues, and
14. 6 nation, and kindred, and tongue, and pe.
17. 15 peoples, and multitudes, and nations, and
18. 4 Come out of her, my people, that ye be not
21. 3 they shall be his people, and God himself

14. *Crowd,* ὄχλος *ochlos.*
Matt. 7. 28 the people were astonished at his doctri.
9. 23 saw the minstrels and the people making
9. 25 when the people were put forth, he went
12. 23 the people were amazed, and said, Is not
12. 46 While he yet talked to the people, behold
14. 13 when the people had heard (thereof), they
21. 26 we fear the people; for all hold John as a
27. 15 wont to release unto the people a prisoner
Mark 5. 21 much people gathered unto him: and he
5. 24 much people followed him, and thronged
6. 33 [the people] saw them departing, and m
6. 34 Jesus..saw much people, and was moved
6. 45 and to go..while he sent away the people
7. 14 when he had called all the people (unto
7. 17 was entered into the house from the peo.
8. 6 he commanded the people to sit down on
8. 6 the loaves..and they did set..before the p.
8. 34 when he had called the people..with his
9. 15 people, when they beheld him, were gre.
9. 25 saw that the people came running toget.
10. 1 the people resort unto him again: and, as
11. 18 all the people was astonished at his doc.
12. 12 to lay hold on him, but feared the people
12. 37 And the common people heard him gladly
12. 41 how the people cast money into the trea
15. 11 the chief priests moved the people, that
15. 15 Pilate, willing to content the people, re.
Luke 3. 10 the people asked him, saying, What shall
4. 42 the people sought him, and came unto h.
5. 1 the people pressed upon him to hear the
5. 3 sat..and taught the people out of the ship
7. 9 said unto the people that followed him
7. 11 his disciples went with him, and much p.
7. 12 and much people of the city was with her
7. 24 to speak unto the people concerning John
8. 4 when much people were gathered togeth.
8. 40 the people (gladly) received him: for they
8. 42 But as he went the people thronged him
9. 11 the people, when they knew (it), followed
9. 18 saying, Whom say the people that I am?
9. 37 when they were come..much people met
11. 14 the dumb spake; and the people wondered
11. 29 when the people were gathered thick to
12. 1 gathered..innumerable multitude of peo.
12. 54 he said also to the people, When ye see
13. 14 said unto the people, There are six days
13. 17 all the people rejoiced for all the glorious
23. 4 to the chief priests and (to) the people, I
23. 48 the people that came together to that si.
John 6. 22 the people which stood on the other side
6. 24 the people therefore saw that Jesus was
7. 12 murmuring among the people concerning
7. 12 others said, Nay; but he deceiveth the p.
7. 20 The people answered and said, Thou hast
7. 31 the people believed on him, and said, W.
7. 32 people murmured such things concerning
7. 40 the people therefore, when they heard t.
7. 43 a division among the people because of him
7. 49 people who knoweth not the law are cur.
11. 42 because of the people which stand by I s.
John 12. 9 Much people of the Jews therefore knew
12. 12 much people that were come to the feast
12. 17 The people therefore that was with him
12. 18 the people also met him, for that they h.
12. 29 The people therefore that stood by, and
12. 34 The people answered him, We have heard
Acts 8. 6 the people with one accord gave heed unto
11. 24 and much people was added unto the Lo.
11. 26 they assembled..and taught much people
14. 11 when the people saw what Paul had done
14. 13 would have done sacrifice with the people
14. 14 they..ran in among the people, crying out
14. 18 scarce restrained they the people, that they
14. 19 persuaded the people, and, having stoned
17. 8 they troubled the people and the rulers of
17. 13 came thither..and stirred up the people
19. 26 persuaded and turned away much people
19. 35 when the town clerk had appeased the p.
21. 27 stirred up all the people, and laid hands
21. 35 was borne..for the violence of the people
24. 12 [neither raising up the people, neither in]
Rev. 19. 1 a great voice of much people in heaven

PEOPLE, number of or mingled —

1. *Mixture, rabble,* עֶרֶב *ereb.*
Jer. 25. 20 the mingled people, and all the kings of
25. 24 mingled people that dwell in the desert
50. 37 mingled people that (are) in the midst of
Eze. 30. 5 the mingled people, and Chub, and the

2. *Crowd,* ὄχλος *ochlos.*
Mark 10. 46 disciples and a great number of people

PEOPLE or Children of the East –

1. The inhabitants of Haran.
Gen. 29. 1 Jacob..came into the land of..P. of the E.

2. A tribe dwelling near the Amalekites and Midianites.
Judg 6. 3 C. of the E., even they came up against
6. 33 the C. of the E. were gathered together
7. 12 all the C. of the E. lay along in the valley
8. 10 left of all the hosts of the C. of the E.
1 Ki. 4. 30 excelled the wisdom of all the C. of the E.

PE'-OR, פְּעוֹר *opening.*

1. A mountain in Moab, part of the Abarim range, near Pisgah.
Num 23. 28 Balak brought Balaam unto the top of P.

2. The Moabite god of uncleanness.
Num 25. 18 they have beguiled you in..matter of P.
25. 18 slain in the day of the plague for P.'s sake
31. 16 against the LORD in the matter of P.
Josh. 22. 17 (Is) the iniquity of P. too little for us, from

PERADVENTURE (lest) —

1. *If so be, it may be,* אוּלַי, אֻלַי *ulai.*
Exod 32. 30 peradventure I shall make an atonement
Josh. 9. 7 Peradventure ye dwell among us; and h.
1 Ki. 18. 5 peradventure we may find grass to save
18. 27 peradventure he sleepeth, and must be a.

2. *It may be, if, peradventure,* לוּ *lu.*
Gen. 50. 15 Joseph will peradventure hate us, and w.

3. *Fronting, facing, lest,* פֶּן *pen.*
Gen. 31. 31 Peradventure thou wouldest take by force
42. 4 Lest peradventure mischief befall him

4. *Peradventure, perhaps,* τάχα *tacha.*
Rom. 5. 7 peradventure for a good man some would

PERCEIVE, to —

1. *To understand,* בִּין *bin.*
1 Sa. 3. 8 Eli perceived that the LORD had called the
2 Sa. 12. 19 David perceived that the child was dead
Job 9. 11 he passeth on also, but I perceive him not
14. 21 are brought low, but he perceiveth (it) not
23. 8 and backward, but I cannot perceive him

2. *To understand,* בִּין *bin, 7a.*
Job 38. 18 Hast thou perceived the breadth of the e.

3. *To taste, perceive,* טָעַם *taam.*
Prov 31. 18 perceiveth that her merchandise (is) good

4. *To know, be acquainted with,* יָדַע *yada.*
Gen. 19. 33, 35 he perceived not when she lay down
Deut 29. 4 hath not given you an heart to perceive
Josh 22. 31 we perceive that the LORD (is) among us
1 Sa. 12. 17 may perceive and see that your wicked.
28. 14 Saul perceived that it (was) Samuel, and
2 Sa. 5. 12 And David perceived that the LORD had
14. 1 son of Zeruiah perceived that the king's
19. 6 I perceive, that if Absalom had lived, and
2 Ki. 4. 9 perceive that this (is) an holy man of God
1 Ch. 14. 2 David perceived that the LORD had confi
Neh. 6. 16 they perceived that this work was wrou.
13. 10 I perceived that the portions of the Lev.
Esth. 4. 1 When Mordecai perceived all that was d.
Prov 14. 7 when thou perceivest not..the lips of k.
Eccl. 1. 17 I perceived that this also is vexation of
2. 14 perceived also that one event happeneth
Isa. 6. 9 and see ye indeed, but perceive not

5. *To discern,* נָכַר *nakar,* 5.
Neh. 6. 12 I perceived that God had not sent him

6. *To see,* רָאָה *raah.*
Judg. 6. 22 when Gideon perceived that he (was) an
1 Ki. 22. 33 when the captains of the chariots perce.
2 Ch. 18. 32 when the captains of the chariots perce.
Eccl. 3. 22 I perceive that (there is) nothing better
Jer. 23. 18 For who..hath perceived and heard his

7. *To behold,* שׁוּר *shur.*
Job 33. 14 God speaketh once..(yet man) perceiveth

8. *To hear, hearken,* שָׁמַע *shamea.*
Isa. 33. 19 of deeper speech than thou canst perceive

9. *To perceive,* αἰσθάνομαι *aisthanomai.*
Luke 9. 45 was hid from them, that they perceived

10. *To see, perceive, understand,* βλέπω *blepō.*
2 Co. 7. 8 perceive that the same epistle hath made

11. *To begin to know,* γινώσκω *ginōskō.*
Matt 16. 8 when Jesus perceived, he said unto them
21. 45 when the..Pharisees had heard..they pe.
22. 18 Jesus perceived their wickedness and said
Luke 8. 46 for I perceive that virtue is gone out of
20. 19 they perceived that he had spoken this p.
John 6. 15 When Jesus therefore perceived that they
Acts 23. 6 when Paul perceived that the one part w.
Gal. 2. 9 perceived the grace that was given unto
1 Jo. 3. 16 Hereby perceive we the love (of God), be.

12. *To see, know, be acquainted with,* οἶδα *oida.*
Matt 13. 14 seeing ye shall see, and shall not perceive
Mark 4. 12 That seeing they may see, and not perce.
12. 28 [perceiving] that he had answered them
Luke 9. 47 Jesus, perceiving the thought of their h.
Acts 14. 9 perceiving that he had faith to be healed
28. 26 and seeing ye shall see, and not perceive

13. *To know about, fully,* ἐπιγινώσκω *epiginōskō.*
Mark 2. 8 Jesus perceived in his spirit that they so
Luke 1. 22 they perceived that he had seen a vision
5. 22 when Jesus perceived their thoughts, he

14. *To find, discover,* εὑρίσκω *heuriskō.*
Acts 23. 29 Whom I perceived to be accused of ques.

15. *To see, perceive,* θεωρέω *theōreō.*
John 4. 19 Sir, I perceive that thou art a prophet
12. 19 Perceive ye how ye prevail nothing? beh.
Acts 17. 22 perceive that in all things ye are too sup.
27. 10 perceive that this voyage will be with hurt

16. *To take thoroughly, apprehend,* καταλαμβάνω.
Acts 4. 13 perceived that they were unlearned and
10. 34 Of a truth I perceive that God is no resp.

17. *To observe thoroughly with the mind,* κατανοέω.
Luke 6. 41 perceivest not the beam that is in thine
20. 23 he perceived their craftiness, and said u.

18. *To observe with the mind,* νοέω *noeō.*
Mark 7. 18 Do ye not perceive, that whatsoever thing
8. 17 perceive ye not yet, neither understand?

19. *To see,* ὁράω *horaō.*
Acts 8. 23 For I perceive that thou art in the gall of

PERCEIVE by the ear, to —

To give ear, אָזַן *azan,* 5.
Isa. 64. 4 have not heard, nor perceived by the ear

PERCEIVED, to be —

To be heard, שָׁמַע *shamea,* 2.
Jer. 38. 27 left off..for the matter was not perceived

PERDITION —

Loss, destruction, ἀπώλεια *apōleia.*
John 17. 12 none of them is lost, but the son of perd.
Phil. 1. 28 is to them an evident token of perdition
2 Th. 2. 3 man of sin be revealed, the son of perdi.
1 Ti. 6. 9 which drown men in destruction and per.
Heb. 10. 39 are not of them who draw back unto per.
2 Pe. 3. 7; Rev. 17. 8; 17. 11

PERES—*To divide, part,* פְּרַס *peras,* Dan. 5. 28.

PE'-RESH, פֶּרֶשׁ *separate.*

A son of Machir, son of Manasseh. B.C. 1400.
1 Ch. 7. 16 and she called his name P.; and the name

PE'-REZ, פֶּרֶץ *bursting through.*

An ancestor of Jashobeam, captain of the first division in David's army; perhaps the same as Pharez son of Judah, Gen. 38. 29. B.C. 1700.
1 Ch. 27. 3 Of the children of P. (was) the chief of all

PE-REZ UZ'-ZAH, פֶּרֶץ עֻזָּא, פֶּרֶץ עֻזָּה *breach of Uzza.*

A place where the Lord smote Uzzah for touching the ark.
2 Sa. 6. 8 and he called the name of the place P.-U.
1 Ch. 13. 11 wherefore that place is called P.-U. to this

PERFECT, PERFECTLY, (more)

1. *With understanding,* בִּינָה *binah.*
Jer. 23. 20 latter days ye shall consider it perfectly

2. *To perfect, complete,* גְּמַר *gemar.*
Ezra 7. 12 unto Ezra the priest..perfect (peace), and

3. *To be prepared,* כּוּן *kun,* 2.
Prov. 4. 18 shineth more and more unto the perfect

4. *Complete,* כָּלִיל *kalil.*
Eze. 16. 14 for it (was) perfect through my comeliness
27. 3 O Tyrus, thou hast said, I (am) of perfect
28. 12 Thou sealest up the sum..perfect in bea.

5. *Completion, perfection,* מִכְלוֹת *mikloth.*
2 Ch. 4. 21 tongs, (made he of) gold, (and) that perfect

6. *Finished, perfect, whole,* שָׁלֵם *shalem.*
Deut 25. 15 shalt have a perfect and just weight, a p.
1 Ki. 8. 61 Let your heart therefore be perfect with
11. 4 his heart was not perfect with the LORD
15. 3 his heart was not perfect with the LORD
15. 14 Asa's heart was perfect with the LORD all
2 Ki. 20. 3 how I have walked..with a perfect heart
1 Ch. 12. 38 came with a perfect heart to Hebron, to
28. 9 serve him with a perfect heart, and with
29. 9 because with perfect heart they offered

1 Ch.29. 19 give unto Solomon my son a perfect hea.
2 Ch.15. 17 nevertheless the heart of Asa was perfect
16. 9 behalf of (them) whose heart (is) perfect
19. 9 saying, Thus shall ye do..with a perfect
25. 2 he did..right..but not with a perfect h.
Isa. 38. 3 how I have walked..with a perfect heart

7. *Perfection, completion,* תַּכְלִית *taklith.*
Psa.139. 22 I hate them with perfect hatred; I count

8. *Perfect, plain,* תָּם *tam.*
Job 1. 1 that man was perfect and upright, and one
1. 8 a perfect and an upright man, one that
2. 3 a perfect and an upright man, one that
8. 20 God will not cast away a perfect (man)
9. 20 (if I say), I (am) perfect, it shall also pr.
9. 21 (Though) I (were) perfect, (yet) would I
9. 22 He destroyeth the perfect and the wicked
Psa. 37. 37 Mark the perfect (man), and behold the
64. 4 That they may shoot in secret at the pe.

9. *Perfection, integrity,* תֹּם *tom.*
Psa.101. 2 walk within my house with a perfect he

10. *Perfect, plain, whole, complete,* תָּמִים *tamim.*
Gen. 6. 9 Noah was a just man (and) perfect in his
17. 1 said..walk before me, and be thou perfect
Lev. 22. 21 it shall be perfect to be accepted; there
Deut18. 13 Thou shalt be perfect with the LORD thy
32. 4 (He is) the rock, his work (is) perfect, for
1 Sa. 14. 41 Therefore Saul said..Give a perfect (lot)
2 Sa. 22. 31 (As for) God, his way (is) perfect; the word
22. 33 (and) power: and he maketh my way pe.
Job 36. 4 he that is perfect in knowledge (is) with
37. 16 wondrous works of him which is perfect
Psa. 18. 30 (As for) God, his way (is) perfect: the w.
18. 32 (It is) God that..maketh my way perfect
19. 7 law of the LORD (is) perfect, converting
101. 2 I will behave myself wisely in a perfect
101. 6 he that walketh in a perfect way, he sha.
Prov. 2. 21 upright shall dwell..the perfect shall re.
11. 5 The righteousness of the perfect shall di.
Eze. 28. 15 Thou (wast) perfect in thy ways from the

11. *Accurately, diligently,* ἀκριβῶς *akribōs.*
Luke 1. 3 having had perfect understanding of all
Acts 18. 26 expounded..the way of God more perfe.
23. 15 would enquire something more perfectly
23. 20 enquire somewhat of him more perfectly
24. 22 having more perfect knowledge of (that)
1 Th. 5. 2 For yourselves know perfectly, that the

12. *Fitted, perfected,* ἄρτιος *artios.*
2 Ti. 3. 17 That the man of God may be perfect, th

13. *To fill, make full,* πληρόω *plēroō.*
Rev. 3. 2 for I have not found thy works perfect be

14. *Ended, complete,* τέλειος *teleios.*
Matt. 5. 48 perfect, even as your Father..is perfect
19. 21 If thou wilt be perfect, go (and) sell that
Rom 12. 2 good, and acceptable, and perfect will of
Eph. 4. 13 Till we all come..unto a perfect man, unto
Phil. 3. 15 Let us therefore, as many as be perfect, be
Col. 1. 28 that we may present every man perfect in
4. 12 that ye may stand perfect and complete
Heb. 9. 11 by a greater and more perfect tabernacle
Jas. 1. 4 (her) perfect work, that ye may be perfect
1. 17 Every good gift and every perfect gift is
1. 25 whoso looketh into the perfect law of lib.
3. 2 same (is) a perfect man, (and) able also
1 Jo. 4. 18 perfect love casteth out fear: because fear

PERFECT, to (be or make) —

1. *To perfect, complete,* גָּמַר *gamar.*
Psa.138. 8 LORD will perfect (that which) concerneth

2. *To perfect,* כָּלַל *kalal.*
Eze. 27. 4 thy builders have perfected thy beauty
27. 11 the Gammadims..made thy beauty perf.

3. *To perfect, finish,* תָּמַם *tamam.*
Isa. 18. 5 afore the harvest, when the bud is perfect

4. *To make perfect, finish,* תָּמַם *tamam,* 5.
Job 22. 3 gain..that thou makest thy ways perfect?

5. *To make an end of, complete,* ἐπιτελέω *epiteleō.*
2 Co. 7. 1 spirit, perfecting holiness in the fear of G
Gal. 3. 3 spirit, are ye now made perfect by the fle

6. *To fit thoroughly, adjust,* καταρτίζω *katartizō.*
Matt21. 16 Out of the mouth of babes..thou hast pe.
Luke 6. 40 every one that is perfect shall be as his
1 Co. 1. 10 but (that) ye be perfectly joined together
2 Co.13. 11 Be perfect, be of good comfort, be of one
1 Th. 3. 10 might perfect that which is lacking in your
Heb.13. 21 Make you perfect in every good work to
1 Pe. 5. 10 make you perfect, stablish, strengthen

7. *To end, complete,* τελειόω *teleioō.*
Luke13. 32 cures..and the third (day) I shall be per.
John17. 23 that they may be made perfect in one
2 Co.12. 9 for my strength [is made perfect] in wea.
Phil. 3. 12 either were already perfect; but I follow
Heb. 2. 10 to make the captain of their salvation pe.
5. 9 being made perfect, he became the author
7. 19 For the law made nothing perfect; but
9. 9 make him that did the service perfect, as
10. 1 can never..make the comers thereunto p.
10. 14 For by one offering he hath perfected for
11. 40 they without us should not be made per.
12. 23 and to the spirits of just men made perf.
Jas. 2. 22 and by works was faith made perfect
1 Jo. 4. 17 Herein is our love made perfect, that we
4. 18 He that feareth is not made perfect in lo.

PERFECT, that is or are —

1. *To be completed, finished, complete,* שָׁלַם *shalam,* 4.
Isa. 42. 19 who (is) blind as (he that is) perfect, and

2. *Ended, complete, perfect,* τέλειος *teleios.*
1 Co. 2. 6 speak wisdom among them that are perf.
13. 10 when that which is perfect is come, then

PERFECT manner —

Exactness, accuracy, ἀκρίβεια *akribeia.*
Acts 22. 3 taught according to the perfect manner

PERFECTED, (to be) —

1. *Lengthening went up,* עָלְתָה אֲרוּכָה [*arukah*].
2 Ch.24. 13 work was perfected by them, and they set

2. *Finished, perfect, whole,* שָׁלֵם *shalem.*
2 Ch. 8. 16 (So) the house of the LORD was perfected

3. *To end, complete,* τελειόω *teleioō.*
1 Jo. 2. 5 in him verily is the love of God perfected
4. 12 God dwelleth in us, and his love is perfe.

PERFECTING —

Perfecting, complete adjustment, καταρτισμός.
Eph. 4. 12 For the perfecting of the saints, for the

PERFECTION, PERFECTNESS —

1. *Complete,* כָּלִיל *kalil.*
Lam. 2. 15 this the city that (men) call The perfection

2. *Perfection,* מִכְלָל *miklal.*
Psa. 50. 2 Out of Zion, the perfection of beauty, God

3. *Continuance, possession,* מִנְלֶה *minleh.*
Job 15. 29 neither shall he prolong the perfection th.

4. *Perfection,* תִּכְלָה *tiklah.*
Psa.119. 96 I have seen an end of all perfection, (but)

5. *Perfection, end,* תַּכְלִית *taklith.*
Job 11. 7 canst thou find out the Almighty unto p.
28. 3 searcheth out all perfection: the stones

6. *Perfect, integrity,* תֹּם *tom.*
Isa. 47. 9 they shall come upon thee in their perfe.

7. *Thorough adjustment, fitness,* κατάρτισις *katart.*
2 Co.13. 9 and this also we wish, (even) your perfe.

8. *Completeness,* τελειότης *teleiotēs.*
Col. 3. 14 charity, which is the bond of perfectness
Heb 6. 1 let us go on unto perfection; not laying

9. *A completion,* τελείωσις *teleiōsis.*
Heb. 7. 11 If therefore perfection were by the Levi.

PERFECTION, to bring fruit to —

To bear on to completion or perfection, τελεσφορέω.
Luke 8. 14 are choked..and bring no fruit to perfec.

PERFORM, to —

1. *To cut off,* בָּצַע *batsa,* 3.
Isa. 10. 12 when the LORD hath performed his whole

2. *To complete, perfect,* גָּמַר *gamar.*
Psa. 57. 2 unto God..that performeth (all things) for

3. *To give,* נָתַן *nathan.*
Mic. 7. 20 Thou wilt perform the truth to Jacob, (a.)

4. *To do,* עָשָׂה *asah.*
Exod18. 18 thou art not able to perform it thyself a.
Deut. 4. 13 which he commanded you to perform, (e.)
23. 23 That which..thou shalt keep and perform
2 Sa. 14. 15 will perform the request of his handmaid
21. 14 they performed all that the king comma.
2 Ch.34. 31 perform the words of the covenant which
Esth. 1. 15 she hath not performed the commandm.
5. 8 to grant my petition, and to perform my
Psa.119. 112 I have inclined mine heart to perform
Isa. 9. 7 zeal of the LORD of hosts will perform this
Jer. 1. 12 for I will hasten my word to perform it
44. 25 surely perform our vows that we have v.
44. 25 accomplish..and surely perform your vows
Eze. 12. 25 will I say the word, and will perform it
37. 14 I the LORD have spoken (it), and perform.

5. *To separate,* פָּלָא *pala,* 3.
Num 15. 3 a sacrifice in performing a vow, or in a
15. 8 in performing a vow, or peace offerings

6. *To war, serve, perform,* צָבָא *tsaba.*
Num. 4. 23 all that enter in to perform the service

7. *To raise up, confirm,* קוּם *qum,* 3.
Psa.119. 106 I have sworn, and I will perform (it), that

8. *To cause to rise up, confirm,* קוּם *qum,* 5.
Gen. 26. 3 I will perform the oath which I sware u.
Deut. 9. 5 he may perform the word which the LORD
1 Sa. 3. 12 I will perform against Eli all..which I
15. 11 and hath not performed my commandm.
15. 13 have performed the commandment of the
1 Ki. 6. 12 then will I perform my word with thee
8. 20 hath performed his word that he spake
12. 15 he might perform his saying, which the
2 Ki.23. 3 to perform the words of this covenant that
23. 24 that he might perform the words of the
2 Ch. 6. 10 performed his word that he hath spoken
10. 15 the LORD might perform his word, which
Neh. 5. 13 that performeth not this promise, even
9. 8 and hast performed thy words; for thou
Jer. 11. 5 I may perform the oath which I have sw.
23. 20 till he have performed the thoughts of his
28. 6 the LORD perform thy words which thou
29. 10 perform my good word toward you, in c.
30. 24 until he have performed the intents of his
33. 14 I will perform that good thing which I h.
34. 18 which have not performed the words of
35. 16 the sons of Jonadab..have performed the

9. *To finish, complete,* שָׁלַם *shalam,* 3.
Psa. 61. 8 I sing..that I may daily perform my vows
Isa. 19. 21 vow a vow unto the LORD, and perform (it)
Nah. 1. 15 perform thy vows: for the wicked shall

10. *To finish, complete,* שָׁלַם *shalam,* 5.
Job 23. 14 he performeth (the thing that is) appoin
Isa. 44. 26 performeth the counsel of his messengers
44. 28 shall perform all my pleasure: even say.

11. *To give away,* ἀποδίδωμι *apodidōmi.*
Matt5. 33 shalt perform unto the Lord thine oaths

12. *To make an end of, complete,* ἐπιτελέω *epiteleō.*
Rom 15. 28 I have performed this, and have sealed
2 Co. 8. 11 Now therefore perform the doing (of it)
Phil. 1. 6 will perform (it) until the day of Jesus

13. *To work out thoroughly,* κατεργάζομαι *katergaz.*
Rom. 7. 18 to perform that which is good I find not

14. *To do, make,* ποιέω *poieō.*
Luke 1. 72 perform the mercy (promised) to our fat.
Rom. 4. 21 what he had promised..also to perform

15. *To end, complete,* τελέω *teleō.*
Luke 2. 39 they had performed all things according

PERFORMANCE —

1. *To make an end of, complete,* ἐπιτελέω *epiteleō.*
2 Co. 8. 11 (there may be) a performance also out of

2. *An ending, completion,* τελείωσις *teleiōsis.*
Luke 1. 45 for there shall be a performance of those

PERFORMED, to be —

1. *To be done,* עָשָׂה *asah,* 2.
Esth. 5. 6 half of the kingdom shall it be performed
7. 2 it shall be performed..to the half of the

2. *To rise up,* קוּם *qum.*
Jer. 51. 29 every purpose of the LORD shall be perf.

3. *To be raised up, confirmed,* קוּם *qum,* 6.
Jer. 35. 14 The words..he commanded..are perfor.

4. *To be completed,* שָׁלַם *shalam,* 4.
Psa. 65. 1 and unto thee shall the vow be performed

5. *To become, happen, come to pass,* γίνομαι *ginomai.*
Luke 1. 20 day that these things shall be performed

PERFUME —

1. *Perfume, incense,* קְטֹרֶת *qetoreth.*
Exod30. 35 thou shalt make it a perfume, a confect.
30. 37 the perfume which thou shalt make, ye
Prov.27. 9 Ointment and perfume rejoice the heart

2. *Confectionaries, compounds,* רִקֻּחִים *riqquchim.*
Isa. 57. 9 didst increase thy perfumes, and didst s.

PERFUME, be perfumed, to —

1. *To wave, sprinkle,* נוּף *nuph.*
Prov. 7. 17 I have perfumed my bed with myrrh, aloes

2. *To be perfumed,* קָטַר *qatar,* 4.
Song 3. 6 perfumed with myrrh and frankincense

PER'-GA, Πέργη.
The capital of Pamphylia, situated on the river Cestrus; it had a famous temple of Diana or Artemis.
Acts 13. 13 they came to P. in Pamphylia: and John
13. 14 But when they departed from P., they ca.
14. 25 when they had preached the word in P.

PER-GA'-MOS, Πέργαμος.
A celebrated city of Mysia, near the river Caicus. Here parchment was first perfected, and a library of 200,000 volumes formed, which was eventually sent to Alexandria. It had also a famous temple of Esculapius, who was represented under the figure of a serpent.
Rev. 1. 11 send (it)..unto P., and unto Thyatira, and
2. 12 And to the angel of the church in P. write

PERHAPS, (lest) —

1. *Indeed, in truth,* ἄρα *ara.*
Acts 8. 22 if perhaps the thought of thine heart may

2. *Lest by any means,* μήπως *mēpōs.*
2 Co. 2. 7 lest perhaps such a one should be swall.

3. *Perhaps,* τάχα *tacha.*
Phm. 15 perhaps he therefore departed for a seas.

PE-RI'-DA, פְּרִידָא *separation.*
One of the servants of Solomon whose descendants returned with Zerubbabel; called *Peruda* in Ezra 2. 55. B.C. 536.
Neh. 7. 57 children of Sophereth, the children of P.

PERIL —

Danger, peril, κίνδυνος *kindunos.*
Rom. 8. 35 famine, or nakedness, or peril, or sword
2 Co.11. 26 perils of waters..perils of robbers..perils
11. 26 perils by the heathen..perils in the city
11. 26 perils in the wilderness..perils in the sea
11. 26 the sea, (in) perils among false brethren

PERILOUS —

Hard, difficult, perilous, fierce, χαλεπός *chalepos.*
2 Ti. 3. 1 in the last days perilous times shall come

PERISH, to —

1. *To be lost,* אָבַד *abad.*
Lev. 26. 38 ye shall perish among the heathen, and
Num 16. 33 they perished from among the congrega.
17. 12 Behold, we die, we perish, we all perish
21. 30 Heshbon is perished even unto Dibon, and
Deut. 4. 26 ye shall soon utterly perish from off the
8. 19 I testify..this day ye shall surely per.

Deut. 8. 20 so shall ye perish; because ye would not
11. 17 (lest) ye perish quickly from off the good
28. 20 until thou perish quickly; because of the
28. 22 they shall pursue thee, until thou perish
30. 18 ye shall surely perish, (and that) ye shall
Josh. 23. 13 until ye perish from off this good land
23. 16 ye shall perish quickly from off the good
Judg 5. 31 let all thine enemies perish, O LORD: but
2 Sa. 1. 27 How are..the weapons of war perished
2 Ki. 9. 8 the whole house of Ahab shall perish: and
Esth. 4. 16 so will I go in..and if I perish, I perish
Job 3. 3 Let the day perish wherein I was born
4. 7 who (ever) perished, being innocent? or
4. 9 By the blast of God they perish, and by
4. 11 The old lion perisheth for lack of prey, and
4. 20 they perish for ever without any regard.
6. 18 The paths..they go to nothing, and per.
8. 13 and the hypocrite's hope shall perish
18. 17 remembrance shall perish from the earth
20. 7 he shall perish for ever like his own dung
30. 2 (profit) me, in whom old age was perished?
31. 19 If I have seen any perish for want of clo.
Psa. 1. 6 but the way of the ungodly shall perish
2. 12 lest he be angry, and ye perish (from) the
9. 3 they shall fall and perish at thy presence
9. 6 cities: their memorial is perished with th.
9. 18 the expectation of the poor shall (not) pe.
10. 16 the heathen are perished out of his land
37. 20 the wicked shall perish, and the enemies
41. 5 When shall he die, and his name perish?
49. 10 the fool and the brutish person perish, and
68. 2 the wicked perish at the presence of God
73. 27 they that are far from thee shall perish
80. 16 they perish at the rebuke of thy counten.
83. 17 yea, let them be put to shame, and perish
92. 9 thine enemies shall perish, all the workers
102. 26 They shall perish, but thou shalt endure
112. 10 the desire of the wicked shall perish
119. 92 I should then have perished in mine affl.
146. 4 goeth..in that very day his thoughts pe.
Prov 10. 28 the expectation of the wicked shall perish
11. 7 shall perish: and the hope of unjust..pe.
11. 10 when the wicked perish, (there is) shout.
19. 9 and (he that) speaketh lies shall perish
21. 28 A false witness shall perish: but the man
28. 28 but when they perish, the righteous incr.
Eccl. 5. 14 those riches perish by evil travail; and
7. 15 there is a just (man) that perisheth in his
9. 6 their hatred, and their envy, is now peri.
Isa. 29. 14 the wisdom of their wise (men) shall per.
41. 11 and they that strive with thee shall perish
57. 1 The righteous perisheth, and no man lay.
60. 12 For the nation and kingdom..shall perish
Jer. 4. 9 the heart of the king shall perish, and the
6. 21 the neighbour and his friend shall perish
7. 28 truth is perished, and is cut off from their
9. 12 the land perisheth (and) is burnt up like
10. 15 the time of their visitation they shall pe.
18. 18 the law shall not perish from the priest
27. 10 should drive you out, and ye should per.
27. 15 ye might perish, ye, and the prophets that
40. 15 scattered, and the remnant in Judah per.
48. 8 the valley also shall perish, and the plain
48. 36 the riches (that) he hath gotten are peri.
48. 46 the people of Chemosh perisheth: for thy
49. 7 is counsel perished from the prudent? is
51. 18 the time of their visitation they shall pe.
Lam. 3. 18 and my hope is perished from the LORD
Eze. 7. 26 the law shall perish from the priest, and
Joel 1. 11 because the harvest of the field is perished
Amos 1. 8 the remnant of the Philistines shall perish
2. 14 the flight shall perish from the swift, and
3. 15 the houses of ivory shall perish, and the
Jon. 1. 6 God will think upon us, that we perish n.
1. 14 let us not perish for this man's life, and
3. 9 will turn and repent..that we perish not
4. 10 came..in a night, and perished in a night
Mic. 4. 9 is thy counsellor perished? for pangs ha.
7. 2 The good (man) is perished out of the ea.
Zech. 9. 5 king shall perish from Gaza, and Ashkel.

2. *To be lost,* אָבַד *abad.*
Jer. 10. 11 they shall perish from the earth, and from

3. *Unto perishing,* עֲדֵי אֹבֵד *ade obed.*
Num 24. 20 his latter end..that he perish for ever
24. 24 afflict Eber, he also shall perish for ever

4. *To be lost,* אֲבַד *abad,* 5.
Dan. 2. 18 his fellows should not perish with the re.

5. *To expire,* גָּוַע *gava.*
Josh. 22. 20 that man perished not alone in his iniq.
Job 34. 15 All flesh shall perish together, and man

6. *To cease, be cut off,* דָּמָה *damah,* 2.
Psa. 49. 12 abideth not: he is like the beasts (that) p.
49. 20 Man (that is)..is like the beasts (that) per.

7. *To be cut off,* כָּרַת *karath,* 2.
Gen. 41. 36 that the land perish not through the fam.

8. *To fall,* נָפַל *naphal.*
Exod 19. 21 lest they..gaze, and many of them perish

9. *To be ended, consumed,* סוּף *suph.*
Esth. 9. 28 memorial of them perish from their seed

10. *To be ended, consumed,* סָפָה *saphah,* 2.
1 Sa. 26. 10 he shall descend into battle, and perish
27. 1 I shall now perish one day by the hand of

11. *To pass over,* עָבַר *abar.*
Job 33. 18 and his life from perishing by the sword
36. 12 they shall perish by the sword, and they

12. *To become naked,* פָּרַע *para,* 2.
Prov 29. 18 Where (there is) no vision, the people per.

13. *To corrupt, mar, destroy,* שָׁחַת *shachath,* 3.
Exod 21. 26 if a man smite the eye..that it perish

14. *To be destroyed, cut off, laid waste,* שָׁמַד *shamad,* 2.
Psa. 83. 10 (Which) perished at En-dor: they became

15. *To die off or away,* ἀποθνήσκω *apothnēskō.*
Matt. 8. 32 into the sea, and perished in the waters

16. *To loose, loose away, destroy,* ἀπόλλυμι *apollumi.*
Matt. 5. 29, 30 that one of thy members should perish
8. 25 awoke him, saying, Lord, save us: we p.
9. 17 the wine runneth out, and the bottles pe.
18. 14 that one of these little ones should perish
26. 52 they that take the sword [shall perish] w.
Mark 4. 38 Master, carest thou not that we perish?
Luke 5. 37 be spilled, and the bottle shall perish
8. 24 awoke him, saying, Master, master, we p.
11. 51 perished between the altar and the temp.
13. 3, 5 except ye repent, ye shall..likewise p.
13. 33 it cannot be that a prophet perish out of
13. 35 except ye repent, ye shall all..perish
15. 17 bread enough..and I perish with hunger
21. 18 there shall not an hair of your head perish
John 3. 15 whosoever believeth..should not perish
3. 16 [whosoever believeth..should not perish]
6. 27 Labour not for the meat which perisheth
10. 28 they shall never perish, neither shall any
11. 50 one..and that the whole nation perish not
Acts 5. 37 he also perished; and all, (even) as many
Rom. 2. 12 have sinned without law shall also perish
1 Co. 1. 18 For the preaching..is to them that perish
8. 11 shall the weak brother perish, for whom
15. 18 they also..asleep in Christ are perished
2 Co. 2. 15 sweet savour of Christ..in them that pe.
2 Th. 2. 10 with all deceivableness..in them that pe.
Heb. 1. 11 They shall perish; but thou remainest
Jas. 1. 11 and the grace of the fashion of it perisheth
1 Pe. 1. 7 more precious than of gold that perisheth
2 Pe. 3. 6 being overflowed with water, perished
3. 9 not willing that any should perish, but
Jude 11 and perished in the gainsaying of Core

17. *To be for loss or destruction,* εἰμὶ εἰς ἀπώλειαν.
Acts 8. 20 Thy money perish with thee, because thou

18. *To make disappear,* ἀφανίζω *aphanizō.*
Acts 13. 41 Behold, ye despisers, and wonder, and p.

19. *To corrupt thoroughly,* διαφθείρω *diaphtheirō.*
2 Co. 4. 16 though our outward man perish, yet the

20. *Corruption,* φθορά *phthora.*
Col. 2. 22 Which all are to perish with the using

PERISH, to cause, make, be ready to —

1. *To be lost,* אָבַד *abad.*
Deut 26. 5 A Syrian ready to perish (was) my father
Job 29. 13 The blessing of him that was ready to pe.
Prov 31. 6 Give..drink unto him that is ready to pe.
Isa. 27. 13 which were ready to perish in the land of

2. *To cause to be lost,* אָבַד *abad,* 3, 5.
Esth. 3. 13 to cause to perish, all Jews, both young
7. 4 to be destroyed, to be slain, and to perish
8. 11 to cause to perish, all the power of the p.
Isa. 26. 14 hast thou..made all their memory to pe.
Eze. 25. 7 I will cause thee to perish out of the cou.

PERISH utterly, to —

To corrupt utterly, καταφθείρω *kataphtheirō.*
2 Pe. 2. 12 [shall utterly perish] in their own corrup.

PERISH with, to —

To destroy together, συναπόλλυμι *sunapollumi.*
Heb. 11. 31 perished not with them that believed not

PE-RIZ-ZITE, פְּרִזִּי.

A tribe in the hill country of Judah driven out by the Ephraimites.

Gen. 13. 7 Canaanite and the P. dwelt then in the land
15. 20 Hittites, and the P., and the Rephaims
34. 30 among the Canaanites and the P.: and I
Exod. 3. 8, 17 Hittites, and the Amorites, and the P.
23. 23 bring thee in unto..the P., and the Cana.
33. 2 I will drive out..the P., the Hivite, and
34. 11 drive out before thee..the P., and the H.
Deut. 7. 1 Canaanites, and the P., and the Hivites
20. 17 utterly destroy..the P., the Hivites, and
Josh. 3. 10 drive out from before you..the P., and the
9. 1 the P., the Hivite, and the Jebusite, heard
11. 3 P., and the Jebusite in the mountains, and
12. 8 the P., the Hivites, and the Jebusites
17. 15 in the land of the P., and of the giants, if
24. 11 P., and the Canaanites, and the Hittites
Judg. 1. 4 delivered the Canaanites and the P. into
1. 5 and they slew the Canaanites and the P.
3. 5 Amorites, and P., and Hivites, and Jebu.
1 Ki. 9. 20 all the people (that were) left of the..P.
2 Ch. 8. 7 all the people (that were) left of the..P.
Ezra 9. 1 of the Canaanites, the Hittites, the P., the
Neh. 9. 8 to give the land of the..P., and the Jebu.

PERJURED person —

One who has broken an oath, ἐπίορκος *epiorkos.*
1 Ti. 1. 10 for perjured persons, and if there be any

PERMISSION —

A joint opinion, concession, συγγνώμη *suggnōmē.*
1 Co. 7. 6 But I speak this by permission, (and) not

PERMIT, to —

To turn over on, suffer, ἐπιτρέπω *epitrepō.*
Acts 26. 1 Thou art permitted to speak for thyself
1 Co. 14. 34 it is not permitted unto them to speak
1 Co. 16. 7 tarry a while with you, if the Lord permit
Heb. 6. 3 And this will we do, if God permit

PERNICIOUS ways —

Destruction, ἀπώλεια *apōleia.*
2 Pe. 2. 2 many shall follow their [pernicious ways]

PERPETUAL —

1. *To be pre-eminent, perpetual,* נָצַח *natsach,* 2.
Jer. 8. 5 slidden back by a perpetual backsliding

2. *Pre-eminence, perpetuity,* נֵצַח, נֶצַח *netsach.*
Psa. 9. 6 destructions are come to a perpetual end
74. 3 Lift up thy feet unto the perpetual deso.
Jer. 15. 18 Why is my pain perpetual, and my wou.

3. *An age, indefinite time,* עוֹלָם *olam.*
Gen. 9. 12 token of the covenant..for perpetual ge.
Exod 29. 9 priest's office shall be theirs for a perpet.
31. 16 shall keep the sabbath..(for) a perpetual
Lev. 3. 17 perpetual statute for your generations th.
24. 9 offerings..made by fire by a perpetual st.
25. 34 may not be sold; for it (is) their perpetual
Num 19. 21 it shall be a perpetual statute unto them
Psa. 78. 66 smote..he put them to a perpetual repro.
Jer. 5. 22 the bound of the sea by a perpetual decree
18. 16 make their land desolate, (and) a perpet.
23. 40 perpetual shame, which shall not be for.
25. 9 make them an astonishment..and perpe.
25. 12 punish..and will make it perpetual deso.
49. 13 all the cities thereof shall be perpetual
50. 5 let us join ourselves..in a perpetual cov.
51. 39, 57 sleep a perpetual sleep, and not wake
Eze. 35. 5 Because thou hast had a perpetual hatred
35. 9 I will make thee perpetual desolations
46. 14 a meat offering continually by a perpetual
Hab. 3. 6 perpetual hills did bow: his ways (are) e.
Zeph. 2. 9 Moab shall be..a perpetual desolation

4. *Continuity, continual,* תָּמִיד *tamid.*
Exod 30. 8 perpetual incense before the LORD thro.
Lev. 6. 20 fine flour for a meat offering perpetual

PERPETUALLY —

1. *Perpetuity, continuity,* עַד *ad.*
Amos 1. 11 his anger did tear perpetually, and he kept

2. *All the days,* כָּל־הַיָּמִים *kol-hay-yamim.*
1 Ki. 9. 3 and mine heart shall be there perpetually
2 Ch. 7. 16 and mine heart shall be there perpetually

PERPLEXED, to be (much) —

1. *To be perplexed, entangled,* בּוּךְ *buk,* 2.
Esth. 3. 15 drink; but the city Shushan was perple.
Joel 1. 18 herds of cattle are perplexed, because th.

2. *To be perplexed, without a passage,* ἀπορέομαι.
2 Co. 4. 8 (We are) troubled..perplexed, but not in

3. *To be thoroughly perplexed,* διαπορέω *diaporeō.*
Luke 9. 7 he was perplexed, because that it was said
24. 4 as [they were much perplexed] thereabout

PERPLEXITY —

1. *Perplexity, entanglement,* מְבוּכָה *mebukah.*
Isa. 22. 5 For (it is) a day..of perplexity by the L.
Mic. 7. 4 best of them..now shall be their perple.

2. *Perplexity, without a passage out,* ἀπορία *aporia.*
Luke 21. 25 distress of nations, with perplexity; the

PERSECUTE, to —

1. *To burn, pursue hotly after,* דָּלַק *dalaq.*
Psa. 10. 2 The wicked in (his) pride doth persecute t.

2. *To pursue after,* רָדַף אַחַר *radaph achar.*
Jer. 29. 18 will persecute them with the sword, with

3. *To pursue,* רָדַף *radaph.*
Deut 30. 7 on them that hate thee, which persecuted
Job 19. 22 Why do ye persecute me as God, and are
19. 28 Why persecute we him, seeing the root of
Psa. 7. 1 save me from all them that persecute me
31. 15 deliver me..from them that persecute me
35. 3 stop (the way) against them that persecute
35. 6 and let the angel of the LORD persecute
69. 26 they persecute (him) whom thou hast sm.
71. 11 God hath forsaken him: persecute and ta.
83. 15 So persecute them with thy tempest, and
109. 16 but persecuted the poor and needy man
119. 84 execute judgment on them that persecute
119. 86 they persecute me wrongfully; help thou
119. 161 Princes have persecuted me without a c.
143. 3 For the enemy hath persecuted my soul
Jer. 17. 18 Let them be confounded that persecute
Lam. 3. 43 Thou hast covered with anger, and pers.
3. 66 Persecute and destroy them in anger from

4. *To pursue,* רְדַף *radaph,* 3.
Psa. 7. 5 Let the enemy persecute my soul, and take

5. *To pursue,* διώκω *diōkō.*
Matt. 5. 10 Blessed (are) they which are persecuted
5. 11 Blessed are ye when (men) shall..persec.
5. 12 for so persecuted they the prophets which
5. 44 and pray for them which..persecute you
10. 23 when they persecute you in this city, flee
23. 34 scourge in your synagogues, and persecute
Luke 21. 12 shall lay their hands on you, and persec.
John 5. 16 therefore did the Jews persecute Jesus
15. 20 have persecuted me, they will also perse.
Acts 7. 52 Which..have not your fathers persecuted?
9. 4 saying unto him, Saul, Saul, why persec.
9. 5 Lord said, I am Jesus whom thou perse.
22. 4 persecuted this way unto the death, bind.
22. 7 saying unto me, Saul, Saul, why persecu.
22. 8 I am Jesus of Nazareth, whom thou pers.
26. 11 I persecuted (them) even unto strange c.

Acts 26. 14 why persecutest thou me? (It is) hard for
26. 15 he said, I am Jesus, whom thou persecu.
Rom. 12. 14 Bless them which persecute you: bless, an.
1 Co. 4. 12 being reviled, we bless; being persecuted
15. 9 because I persecuted the church of God
2 Co. 4. 9 Persecuted, but not forsaken; cast down
Gal. 1. 13 how that beyond measure I persecuted
1. 23 that he which persecuted us in times past
4. 29 he that was born after the flesh persecuted
Phil. 3. 6 Concerning zeal, persecuting the church]
Rev. 12. 13 persecuted the woman which brought fo.

6. *To chase out, pursue diligently*, ἐκδιώκω *ekdiōkō.*
Luke 11. 49 (some) of them that they shall slay and p.
1 Th. 2. 15 have persecuted us; and they please not G.

PERSECUTED —

Pursued, מֻרְדָּף *murdaph.*
Isa. 14. 6 he that ruled the nations in anger, is pe.

PERSECUTION —

1. *Pursuit*, διωγμός *diōgmos.*
Matt 13. 21 when tribulation or persecution ariseth
Mark 4. 17 when affliction or persecution ariseth for
10. 30 receive..children, and lands, with perse.
Acts 8. 1 at that time there was a great persecution
13. 50 raised persecution against Paul and Bar.
Rom. 8. 35 tribulation, or distress, or persecution, or
2 Co. 12. 10 take pleasure..in persecutions, in distre.
2 Th. 1. 4 faith in all your persecutions and tribula.
2 Ti. 3. 11 Persecutions, afflictions, which came unto
3. 11 what persecutions I endured: but out of

2. *Oppression, affliction*, θλῖψις *thlipsis.*
Acts 11. 19 which were scattered abroad upon the p.

PERSECUTION, to be under or suffer —

1. *To be pursued*, רָדַף *radaph*, 2.
Lam. 5. 5 Our necks (are) under persecution: we la.

2. *To pursue*, διώκω *diōkō.*
Gal. 5. 11 why do I yet suffer persecution? then is
6. 12 only lest they should suffer persecution
2 Ti. 3. 12 all that will live godly..shall suffer pers.

PERSECUTOR —

1. *To burn, pursue hotly*, דָּלַק *dalaq.*
Psa. 7. 13 ordaineth his arrows against the persecu.

2. *To pursue*, רָדַף *radaph.*
Neh. 9. 11 persecutors thou threwest into the deeps
Psa. 119. 157 Many (are) my persecutors and mine ene
142. 6 deliver me from my persecutors; for they
Jer. 15. 15 revenge me of my persecutors; take me
20. 11 therefore my persecutors shall stumble
Lam. 1. 3 all her persecutors overtook her between
4. 19 Our persecutors are swifter than the eag.

3. *A pursuer*, διώκτης *diōktēs.*
1 Ti. 1. 13 Who was before a blasphemer, and a pe.

PERSEVERANCE —

Perseverance, enduring constancy, προσκαρτέρησις.
Eph. 6. 18 with all perseverance and supplication for

PERSIA, פָּרַס.

A country in Asia (anciently called *Elam*), receiving its name from its chief province called *Fars* or Farsistan; now bounded on the W. by Asiatic Turkey, N. by Transcaucasia and the Caspian Sea, E. by Afghanistan and Beluchoostan, and S. by the Persian Gulf and the Arabian Sea: its area is about 500,000 square miles; it has thirteen provinces, viz., Azarbyan, Irak Ajemi, Ardelan, Laristan, Khuzistan, Fars, Laristan, Kerman, Ghilan, Mazanderan, Astrabad, Khorasan, and Yezd. Its first ruler was Kaiomars, B.C. 2160; in 2010 it became subject to Syria; in 1740 its king Nodar is attacked and defeated by Pashang king of Turan; in 1730 Zur (*or* Zoab) defeats Afrasiab; in 1661 the Pischdadian dynasty is subverted; in 642 Cyaxares expels the Turano; and set up the Kaianite dynasty; in 640 it is subject to the Scythians; in 612 they are expelled; in 606 he takes Nineveh; in 596 Egypt, Syria, and Asia Minor are subdued by the Persians; in 559 Cyrus became king; in 551 he annexes Media; in 538 he conquers Babylon; in 536 Zoroaster flourishes; in 522 Cambyses is slain and Smerdis usurps authority; in 517 Darius takes Babylon; in 497 a war between Persia and Greece; in 480 Xerxes I. invades Greece; in 465 he is killed; in 458 Ahasuerus marries Esther; in 401 occurs the retreat of the 10,000 Greeks; in 350 Ochus subdues Egypt; in 334 Alexander the Great invades Persia; in 250 it passes under the Parthian dynasty of the Arsacidae.

In A.D. 226 Artaxerxes, or Ardshir, founds the dynasty of the Sassanides; in 326 Christianity is prohibited; in 430 the Huns invade Persia; in 636 the Arabs invade it; in 651 it passes under the Saracen yoke; in 813 the Taherite dynasty commences; in 872 the Sopharide dynasty; in 874 the Saminide dynasty; in 1026 Ferdusi flourishes; in 1038 the Seljakian Turkish dynasty; in 1223 the Mongols succeed; in 1393 Timour reduces all Persia; in 1502 Ismail Shah Soop expels the Turks of the White Sheep, and sets up the Soofite dynasty; in 1724 Russia and Turkey agree to partition Persia; in 1800 Persia allies itself to Britain; in 1826 Russia declares war; in 1854 a treaty is concluded; in 1858 Mahammed Khasim Khan dies, aged 12 years.

2 Ch. 36. 20 until the reign of the kingdom of P.
36. 22 king of P...the spirit of Cyrus king of P.
36. 23 Thus saith Cyrus king of P., All the kin.
Ezra 1. 1 king of P...the spirit of Cyrus king of P.
1. 2 Thus saith Cyrus king of P., The LORD G.
1. 8 Even those did Cyrus king of P. bring fo.
3. 7 grant that they had of Cyrus king of P.
Ezra 4. 3 as king Cyrus the king of P. hath comma.
4. 5 Cyrus king of P...until..Darius king of P.
4. 7 companions, unto Artaxerxes king of P.
4. 24 the second year of..Darius king of P.
6. 14 and Darius, and Artaxerxes king of P.
7. 1 in the reign of Artaxerxes king of P., Ezra
9. 9 unto us in the sight of the kings of P., to
Esth. 1. 3 power of P. and Media, the nobles and p.
1. 14 seven princes of P. and Media, which saw
1. 18 shall the ladies of P. and Media say this
10. 2 chronicles of the kings of Media and P.?
Eze. 27. 10 They of P. and of Lud and of Phut were
38. 5 P., Ethiopia, and Libya with them; all of
Dan. 8. 20 The ram..(are) the kings of Media and P.
10. 1 In the third year of Cyrus king of P. a th.
10. 13 of the kingdom of P...the kings of P.
10. 20 will I return to fight with the prince of P.
11. 2 shall stand up yet three kings in P.; and

PERSIAN, פַּרְסָיָא, פָּרַס, הַפַּרְסִי, פָּרְסִי.

An inhabitant of Persia.
Neh. 12. 22 the priests, to the reign of Darius the P.
Esth. 1. 19 written among the laws of the P. and the
Dan. 5. 28 is divided and given to the Medes and P.
6. 8, 12 according to the law of the Medes..P.
6. 15 that the law of the Medes and P. (is), That
6. 28 Darius, and in the reign of Cyrus the P.

PER'-SIS, Περσίς.

A female disciple in Rome to whom Paul sends a salutation.
Rom. 16. 12 [Salute the beloved P., which laboured]

PERSON —

1. *A man, a human being*, אָדָם *adam.*
Num 31. 28 of the persons, and of the beeves, and of
31. 30 of the persons, of the beeves, of the asses
Prov. 6. 12 A naughty person, a wicked man, walketh
Eze. 44. 25 they shall come at no dead person to def.
Jon. 4. 11 are more than six score thousand persons

2. *A man, an individual*, אִישׁ *ish.*
Judg. 9. 2 threescore and ten persons, reign over you
9. 5, 18 threescore and ten persons, upon one
20. 39 began to smite..about thirty persons; for
1 Sa. 9. 2 (there was) not..a goodlier person than
9. 22 among them..which (were) about thirty p.
16. 18 a comely person, and the LORD (is) with
22. 18 slew on that day fourscore and five pers.
2 Sa. 4. 11 wicked men have slain a righteous person
2 Ki. 10. 6 Now the king's sons, (being) seventy per.
10. 7 slew seventy persons, and put their heads

3. *A man, a mortal man*, אֱנוֹשׁ *enosh.*
Judg. 9. 4 Abimelech hired vain and light persons
Zeph. 3. 4 prophets (are) light (and) treacherous per.

4. *Owner, master, lord*, בַּעַל *baal.*
Prov. 24. 8 He..shall be called a mischievous person

5. *Men*, מְתִים *methim.*
Psa. 26. 4 I have not sat with vain persons, neither

6. *Soul, breath*, נֶפֶשׁ *nephesh.*
Gen. 14. 21 Give me the persons, and take the goods
36. 6 Esau took his wives..and all the persons
Exod 16. 16 (according to) the number of your persons
Lev. 27. 2 person (shall be) for the LORD by thy est
Num. 5. 6 commit any sin..and that person be gui.
31. 19 whosoever hath killed any person, and w.
35. 11 slayer..which killeth any person at una.
35. 15 every one that killeth any person unawa.
35. 30 Whoso killeth any person, the murderer
35. 30 witness shall not testify against any per.
Deut 10. 22 went down..with threescore and ten per.
27. 25 taketh reward to slay an innocent person
Josh. 20. 3 slayer that killeth (any) person unawares
20. 9 whosoever killeth (any) person at unawa.
1 Sa. 22. 22 occasioned (the death) of all the persons
2 Sa. 14. 14 neither doth God respect (any) person: yet
Prov 28. 17 doeth violence to the blood of (any) person
Jer. 43. 6 every person that Nebuzar-adan the cap.
52. 29 eight hundred thirty and two persons
52. 30 persons: all the persons (were) four tho.
Eze. 16. 5 to the loathing of thy person, in the day
17. 17 and building forts, to cut off many persons
27. 13 they traded the persons of men and vessels
33. 6 come..take (any) person from among them

7. *Soul of man*, נֶפֶשׁ אָדָם *nephesh adam.*
Num 31. 35 thirty and two thousand persons in all, of
31. 40 persons (were) sixteen thousand; of which
31. 46 And sixteen thousand persons

8. *Num 19. 18 clean person shall take hyssop, and dip
† 19. 18 and upon the persons that were there
* Heb. as No. 2. † Heb. as No. 6.

9. *Face*, פָּנִים *panim.*
Lev. 19. 15 person of the poor, nor honour the person
Deut. 1. 17 Ye shall not respect persons in judgment
10. 17 regardeth not persons, nor taketh reward
16. 19 thou shalt not respect persons, neither take
28. 50 which shall not regard the person of the
1 Sa. 25. 35 hearkened..and have accepted thy person
2 Sa. 17. 11 that thou go to battle in thine own person
2 Ch. 19. 7 nor respect of persons, nor taking of gifts
Job 13. 8 Will ye accept his person? will ye contend
13. 10 reprove you, if ye do secretly accept per.
34. 19 that accepteth not the persons of princes
Psa. 82. 2 How long will ye..accept the persons of
Prov 18. 5 not good to accept the person of the wic.
24. 23 not good to have respect of persons in j.
28. 21 To have respect of persons (is) not good
Jer. 52. 25 that (were) near the king's person, which
Lam. 4. 16 they respected not the persons of the pr.
Mal. 1. 8 will he..accept thy person? saith the LO.
1. 9 will he regard your persons? saith the L.

10. *Face, countenance*, πρόσωπον *prosōpon.*
Matt 22. 16 for thou regardest not the person of men
Mark 12. 14 for thou regardest not the person of men
Luke 20. 21 neither acceptest thou the person (of any)
2 Co. 1. 11 by the means of many persons thanks may
2. 10 for your sakes (forgave I it) in the person
Gal. 2. 6 God accepteth no man's person: for they

11. *Substratum, what lies under*, ὑπόστασις *hupos.*
Heb. 1. 3 express image of his person, and uphold.

[*See also* Brutish, men's, perjured, profane, respect without respect of, uncircumcised, vile.]

PERSONS, to have respect to —

To accept faces or persons, προσωποληπτέω *prosō.*
Jas. 2. 9 if ye have respect to persons, ye commit

PERSONS, respecter of —

Acceptor of faces or persons, προσωπολήπτης *pros.*
Acts 10. 34 I perceive that God is no respecter of pe.

PERSONS, respect of —

Acceptance of faces or persons, προσωποληψία.
Rom. 2. 11 For there is no respect of persons with G.
Eph. 6. 9 neither is there respect of persons with
Col. 3. 25 shall receive..there is no respect of per.
Jas. 2. 1 have not the faith..with respect of pers.

PERSUADE, to —

1. *To move, persuade, remove*, סוּת *suth*, 5.
2 Ki. 18. 32 when he persuadeth you, saying, The Lo.
2 Ch. 18. 2 persuaded him to go up (with him) to R.
32. 11 Doth not Hezekiah persuade you to give
32. 15 let not Hezekiah..persuade you on this
Isa. 36. 18 lest Hezekiah persuade you, saying, The

2. *To entice, persuade*, פָּתָה *pathah*, 3.
1 Ki. 22. 20 Who shall persuade Ahab, that he may
22. 21 came forth a spirit..and said, I will per.
22. 22 Thou shalt persuade (him), and prevail

3. *To persuade again*, ἀναπείθω *anapeithō.*
Acts 18. 13 This (fellow) persuadeth men to worship

4. *To persuade*, πείθω *peithō.*
Matt 27. 20 persuaded the multitude that they should
28. 14 if this come..we will persuade him, and
Acts 13. 43 persuaded them to continue in the grace
14. 19 who persuaded the people, and, having
18. 4 and persuaded the Jews and the Greeks
19. 8 persuading the things concerning the ki.
19. 26 Paul hath persuaded and turned away
26. 28 Almost thou persuadest me to be a Chris.
28. 23 persuading them concerning Jesus, both
2 Co. 5. 11 we persuade men: but we are made man.
Gal. 1. 10 For do I now persuade men, or God? or do

PERSUADED, to be (fully) —

1. *To be enticed, persuaded*, פָּתָה *pathah*, 4.
Prov. 25. 15 By long forbearing is a prince persuaded

2. *To persuade*, πείθω *peithō.*
Luke 16. 31 neither will they be persuaded though one
20. 6 they be persuaded that John was a prop.
Acts 21. 14 when he would not be persuaded, we ce.
26. 26 for I am persuaded that none of these th.
Rom. 8. 38 For I am persuaded, that neither death
14. 14 I know, and am persuaded by the Lord
15. 14 I myself also am persuaded of you, my
2 Ti. 1. 5 and I am persuaded that in thee also
1. 12 for I know..and am persuaded that he is
Heb. 6. 9 we are persuaded better things of you, and
11. 13 [were persuaded of (them)] and embraced

3. *To bear through fully*, πληροφορέω *plērophoreō.*
Rom. 4. 21 being fully persuaded that what he had
14. 5 Let every man be fully persuaded in his

PERSUASION —

Persuasion, πεισμονή *peismonē.*
Gal. 5. 8 This persuasion (cometh) not of him that

PERTAIN (to), to —

1. *To be*, הָיָה *hayah.*
1 Sa. 27. 6 Ziklag pertaineth unto the kings of Judah
2 Sa. 9. 9 given unto thy master's son all that per.

2. *Instrument, vessel*, כְּלִי *keli.*
Deut 22. 5 woman shall not wear that which pertai.

3. *To hold with, partake with*, μετέχω *metechō.*
Heb. 7. 13 he of whom these things are spoken per

4. *Toward*, πρός (acc.) *pros.*
Rom 15. 17 glory..in those things which pertain to

PERTAINING —

About, concerning, περί (*gen.*) *peri.*
Acts 1. 3 speaking of the things pertaining to the

PE-RU'-DA, פְּרוּדָא *separation, isolation.*

One of the servants of Solomon whose descendants returned from exile with Zerubbabel. B.C. 536. See *Perida.*
Ezra 2. 55 children of Sophereth, the children of P.

PERVERSE, (to be, have, or prove) —

1. *Turns about with*, הָפַךְ בְּ *haphak (2) be.*
Prov 17. 20 he that hath a perverse tongue falleth into

2. *To turn over, be perverse*, יָרַט *yarat.*
Num 22. 32 went out..because (thy) way is perverse

3. *To be perverse, perverted*, לוּז *luz*, 2.
Prov 14. 2 (he that is) perverse in his ways despiseth

4. *Perverseness*, לְזוּת *lezuth.*
Prov. 4. 24 a froward mouth, and perverse lips put

5. *To become perverse*, עָוָה *avah*, 2.
1 Sa. 20. 30 Thou son of the perverse rebellious (wo.)
Prov 12. 8 he that is of a perverse heart shall be de.

6. *Perversities*, עִוְעִים *ivim.*
Isa. 19. 14 LORD hath mingled a perverse spirit in

7. *To declare perverse*, עָקַשׁ *aqash.*
Job 9. 20 I (am) perfect, it shall also prove me per.

8. *To be perverse*, עָקַשׁ *aqash*, 2.
Prov28. 18 (he that is) perverse (in his) ways shall f.

9. *Perverse, perverted*, עִקֵּשׁ *iqqesh.*
Deut 32. 5 (they are) a perverse and crooked gener.
Prov. 8. 8 (there is) nothing froward or perverse in
19. 1 Better..than (he that is) perverse in his
28. 6 Better..than (he that is) perverse (in his)

10. *To turn diversely, perversely*, διαστρέφω *diastre.*
Matt17. 17 O faithless and perverse generation, how
Luke 9. 41 O faithless and perverse generation! how
Phil. 2. 15 in the midst of a crooked and perverse

PERVERSE things —

1. *Mischief, calamity, desire*, הַוָּה *havvah.*
Job 6. 30 cannot my taste discern perverse things?

2. *Perverseness, frowardness*, תַּהְפֻּכוֹת *tahpukoth.*
Prov23. 33 and thine heart shall utter perverse thin.

3. *To turn diversely, perversely*, διαστρέφω *diastre.*
Acts 20. 30 shall men arise, speaking perverse things

PERVERSELY, to deal or do —

1. *To do perversely*, עָוָה *avah*, 5.
2 Sa. 19. 19 thy servant did perversely the day that
1 Ki. 8. 47 We have sinned, and have done pervers.

2. *To do perversely*, עָוַת *avath*, 3.
Psa 119. 78 dealt perversely with me without a cause

PERVERSENESS —

1. *To be perverse, perverted*, לוּז *luz*, 2.
Isa. 30. 12 trust in oppression and perverseness, and

2. *Perverseness*, מֻטֶּה *mutteh.*
Eze. 9. 9 and the city full of perverseness: for they

3. *Perverseness*, סֶלֶף *seleph.*
Prov 11. 3 the perverseness of transgressors shall d.
15. 4 perverseness therein (is) a breach in the

4. *Perverseness, perversity*, עַוְלָה *avlah.*
Isa. 59. 3 your tongue hath muttered perverseness

5. *Labour, perverseness, misery*, עָמָל *amal.*
Num23. 21 neither hath he seen perverseness in Isr.

PERVERT, to —

1. *To turn, overturn*, הָפַךְ *haphak.*
Jer. 23. 36 have perverted the words of the living God

2. *To cause to incline*, נָטָה *natah*, 5.
Deut 24. 17 Thou shalt not pervert the judgment of
27. 19 he that perverteth the judgment of the
1 Sa. 8. 3 and took bribes, and perverted judgment
Prov.17. 23 taketh a gift out of the bosom to pervert

3. *To overthrow, pervert*, סָלַף *salaph*, 3.
Exod 23. 8 and perverteth the words of the righteous
Deut 16. 19 and pervert the words of the righteous
Prov.19. 3 The foolishness of man perverteth his way

4. *To do perversely, pervert*, עָוָה *avah*, 5.
Job 33. 27 and perverted (that which was) right, and
Jer. 3. 21 they have perverted their way..they have

5. *To use perversely*, עָוַת *avath*, 3.
Job 8. 3 Doth God pervert judgment? or..pervert
34. 12 neither will the Almighty pervert judgm.

6. *To pervert*, עָקַשׁ *aqash*, 3.
Prov 10. 9 he that perverteth his ways shall be known
Mic. 3. 9 that abhor judgment, and pervert all equi.

7. *To turn or bring back*, שׁוּב *shub*, 3a.
Isa. 47. 10 it hath perverted thee; and thou hast s.

8. *To change, transfer*, שָׁנָה *shanah*, 3.
Prov 31. 5 and pervert the judgment of any of the

9. *To turn away or off*, ἀποστρέφω *apostrephō.*
Luke23. 14 this man..one that perverteth the people

10. *To turn diversely, perversely*, διαστρέφω *diastr.*
Luke23. 2 We found this (fellow) perverting the n.
Acts 13. 10 not..to pervert the right ways of the L.

11. *To turn away*, μεταστρέφω *metastrephō.*
Gal. 1. 7 some that..would pervert the gospel of

PESTILENCE —

1. *Pestilence, plague*, דֶּבֶר *deber.*
Exod 5. 3 lest he fall upon us with pestilence, or wi.
9. 15 smite thee and thy people with pestilence
Lev. 26. 25 I will send the pestilence among you; and
Num14. 12 I will smite them with the pestilence, and
Deut28. 21 shall make the pestilence cleave unto thee
2 Sa. 24. 13 or that there be three days' pestilence in
24. 15 So the LORD sent a pestilence upon Israel
1 Ki. 8. 37 if there be pestilence, blasting, mildew
1 Ch.21. 12 even the pestilence, in the land, and the
21. 14 So the LORD sent pestilence upon Israel
2 Ch. 6. 28 if there be pestilence, if there be blasting
7. 13 or if I send pestilence among my people
20. 9 sword, judgment, or pestilence, or famine
Psa. 78. 50 but gave their life over to the pestilence
91. 3 deliver thee..from the noisome pestilence
91. 6 for the pestilence, (that) walketh in dark.
Jer. 14. 12 and by the famine, and by the pestilence
21. 6 inhabitants..shall die of a great pestilence
21. 7 left in this city from the pestilence, from
21. 9 and by the famine, and by the pestilence
24. 10 the sword, the famine, and the pestilence
27. 8 with the pestilence, until I have consumed
27. 13 by the pestilence, as the LORD hath spoken
28. 8 prophesied both..of evil, and of pestilence
29. 17 the sword, the famine, and the pestilence
29. 18 with the famine, and with the pestilence
32. 24 and of the famine, and of the pestilence
32. 36 and by the famine, and by the pestilence
34. 17 sword, to the pestilence, and to the famine
38. 2 sword, by the famine, and by the pestile.
42. 17, 22 by the famine, and by the pestilence
44. 13 sword, by the famine, and by the pestile.
Eze. 5. 12 third part..shall die with the pestilence
5. 17 pestilence and blood shall pass through
6. 11 sword, by the famine, and by the pestile.
6. 12 He that is far off shall die of the pestilence
7. 15 and the pestilence and the famine within
7. 15 famine and pestilence shall devour him
12. 16 from the famine, and from the pestilence
14. 19 Or (if) I send a pestilence into that land
14. 21 the pestilence, to cut off from it man and
28. 23 For I will send into her pestilence, and
33. 27 and in the caves shall die of the pestilence
38. 22 I will plead against him with pestilence
Amos 4. 10 I have sent among you the pestilence after
Hab. 3. 5 Before him went the pestilence, and bur.

2. *A plague, pestilence*, λοιμός *loimos.*
Matt24. 7 there shall be famines, [and pestilences]
Luke21. 11 famines, and pestilences; and fearful si.

PESTILENT —

A plague, pestilence, λοιμός *loimos.*
Acts 24. 5 we have found this man (a) pestilent (fe.)

PESTLE —

A pestle, עֱלִי *eli.*
Prov 27. 22 in a mortar among wheat with a pestle

PET'-ER, Πέτρος *a stone.*

The surname of Simon brother of Andrew, and son of Jona (or Johanan); a native of Bethsaida, and a fisherman; called to be one of the twelve apostles of Christ; follows him, leaving all; acknowledges, and rebukes Christ, and is rebuked; denies him; sees him after the resurrection; addresses the disciples regarding the choice of an apostle, also the Jews on the day of Pentecost; cures a lame man at the gate of the temple; is imprisoned with John; performs many cures; is again imprisoned and released, speaks boldly before the magistrates, communicates the gifts of the Spirit to the Samaritans, confounds Simon Magus, cures Æneas of palsy, raises Dorcas to life, preaches to Cornelius, defends himself to the church; is imprisoned by Herod, and freed by a messenger of God; addresses the assembly at Jerusalem concerning circumcision; is opposed by Paul for his inconsistency; commends Paul's Epistles, writes two Epistles to the Jews scattered abroad. Tradition asserts that he died at Rome a martyr.

Matt. 4. 18 saw two brethren, Simon called P., and
8. 14 when Jesus was come into P.'s house, he
10. 2 The first, Simon, who is called P., and A.
14. 28 P. answered him and said, Lord, if it be
14. 29 when P. was come down out of the ship
15. 15 Then answered P. and said unto him, De.
16. 16 And Simon P. answered and said, Thou
16. 18 That thou art P., and upon this rock I will
16. 22 Then P. took him, and began to rebuke
16. 23 But he turned, and said unto P., Get thee
17. 1 Jesus taketh P...and bringeth them up
17. 4 Then answered P., and said unto Jesus, L.
17. 24 came to P., and said, Doth not your mas.
17. 26 [P. saith unto him, Of strangers. Jesus]
18. 21 Then came P. to him, and said, Lord, how
19. 27 Then answered P. and said unto him, Be.
26. 33 P. answered and said unto him, Though
26. 35 P. said unto him, Though I should die wi.
26. 37 And he took with him P. and the two sons
26. 40 saith unto P., What! could ye not watch
26. 58 But P. followed him afar off unto the high
26. 69 Now P. sat without in the palace: and a
26. 73 said to P., Surely thou also art (one) of th.
26. 75 P. remembered the word of Jesus, which
Mark 3. 16 And Simon he surnamed P.
5. 37 he suffered no man to follow him, save P.
8. 29 P. answereth and saith unto him, Thou art
8. 32 And P. took him, and began to rebuke him
8. 33 he rebuked P., saying, Get thee behind
9. 2 after six days Jesus taketh (with him) P.
9. 5 P. answered and said to Jesus, Master, it
10. 28 Then P. began to say unto him, Lo, we ha.
11. 21 P. calling to remembrance saith unto him
13. 3 P. and James and John..asked him priv.
14. 29 But P. said unto him, Although all shall
14. 33 he taketh with him P. and James and J.
14. 37 and saith unto P., Simon, sleepest thou?
14. 54 P. followed him afar off, even into the p.
14. 66 as P. was beneath in the palace, there
14. 67 when she saw P. warming himself, she lo.
14. 70 they that stood by said again to P., Surely
14. 72 And P. called to mind the word that Jesus
16. 7 tell his disciples and P. that he goeth be.
Luke 5. 8 When Simon P. saw (it), he fell down at
6. 14 Simon, whom he also named P., and A.
8. 45 When all denied, P. and they that were
8. 51 suffered no man to go in, save P. and Ja.
9. 20 whom say ye that I am? P. answering said
9. 28 he took P. and John and James, and went
9. 32 But P. and they that were with him were
9. 33 P. said unto Jesus, Master, it is good for
12. 41 Then P. said unto him, Lord, speakest thou
18. 28 Then P. said, Lo, we have left all, and fol.
22. 8 he sent P. and John, saying, Go and pre.
22. 34 And he said, I tell thee, P., the cock shall
22. 54 Then took they him..And P. followed afar
22. 55 when they..were set down together, P.
22. 58 Thou art also of them. And P. said, Man
22. 60 P. said, Man, I know not what thou say.
22. 61 looked upon P. And P. remembered the
22. 62 And [P.] went out, and wept bitterly
24. 12 [Then arose P., and ran unto the sepulc.]
John 1. 40 One of the two..was Andrew, Simon P.'s
1. 44 Philip was of Bethsaida, the city of..P.
6. 8 Andrew, Simon P.'s brother, saith unto
6. 68 Then Simon P. answered him, Lord, to wh.
13. 6 Then cometh he to Simon P.: and [P.] sa.
13. 8 P. saith unto him, Thou shalt never wash
13. 9 Simon P. saith unto him, Lord, not my f.
13. 24 Simon P. therefore beckoned to him, that
13. 36 Simon P. said unto him, Lord, whither go.
13. 37 P. said unto him, Lord, why cannot I follow
18. 10 Then Simon P. having a sword drew it, and
18. 11 Then said Jesus unto P., Put up thy swo.
18. 15 And Simon P. followed Jesus, and (so did)
18. 16 But P. stood at the door without. Then
18. 16 disciple..spake unto..and brought in P.
18. 17 Then saith the damsel..unto P., Art not
18. 18 and P. stood with them, and warmed him.
18. 25 Simon P. stood and warmed himself. They
18. 26 being (his) kinsman whose ear P. cut off
18. 27 P. then denied again: and immediately
20. 2 Then she runneth, and cometh to Simon P.
20. 3 P. therefore went forth, and that other d.
20. 4 the other disciple did outrun P., and came
20. 6 Then cometh Simon P. following him, and
21. 2 There were together Simon P., and Tho.
21. 3 Simon P. saith unto them, I go a fishing
21. 7 disciple whom Jesus loved saith unto P.
21. 7 Now when Simon P. heard that it was the
21. 11 Simon P. went up, and drew the net to
21. 15 Jesus saith to Simon P., Simon, (son) of J.
21. 17 P. was grieved because he said unto him
21. 20 Then P., turning about, seeth the discip.
21. 21 P. seeing him saith to Jesus, Lord, and
Acts 1. 13 into an upper room, where abode both P.
1. 15 in those days P. stood up in the midst of
2. 14 But P., standing up with the eleven, lifted
2. 37 said unto P. and to the rest of the apost.
2. 38 Then P. said unto them, Repent, and be
3. 1 Now P. and John went up together into
3. 3 Who seeing P. and John about to go into
3. 4 P., fastening his eyes upon him with J.
3. 6 Then P. said, Silver and gold have I none
3. 11 which was healed held P. and John, all
3. 12 And when P. saw (it), he answered unto the
4. 8 Then P., filled with the Holy Ghost, said
4. 13 they saw the boldness of P. and John
4. 19 But P. and John answered and said unto
5. 3 But P. said, Ananias, why hath Satan fil.
5. 8 And P. answered unto her, Tell me whe.
5. 9 Then P. said unto her, How is it that ye
5. 15 that at the least the shadow of P. passing
5. 29 Then P. and the (other) apostles answered
8. 14 they sent unto them P. and John
8. 20 But P. said unto him, Thy money perish
9. 32 as P. passed throughout all (quarters), he
9. 34 And P. said unto him, Æneas, Jesus Chr.
9. 38 had heard that P. was there, they sent
9. 39 Then P. arose and went with them. When
9. 40 But P. put them all forth, and kneeled
9. 40 and when she saw P., she sat up
10. 5 call for (one) Simon, whose surname is P.
10. 9 P. went up upon the house top to pray a.
10. 13 came a voice to him, Rise, P.; kill, and
10. 14 P. said, Not so, Lord; for I have never e.
10. 17 P. doubted in himself what this vision
10. 18 whether Simon, which was surnamed P.
10. 19 While P. thought on the vision, the spirit
10. 21 P. went down to the men which were sent
10. 23 [P.] went away with them, and certain bre.
10. 25 as P. was coming in, Cornelius met him
10. 26 P. took him up, saying, Stand up; I my.
10. 32 call hither Simon, whose surname is P.
10. 34 P. opened (his) mouth, and said, Of a truth
10. 44 While P. yet spake these words, the Holy
10. 45 were astonished, as many as came with P.
10. 46 Then answered P., Can any man forbid w.
11. 2 when P. was come up to Jerusalem, they
11. 4 P. rehearsed (the matter) from the begin.
11. 7 voice saying unto me, Arise, P.; slay, and
11. 13 and call for Simon, whose surname is P.
12. 3 he proceeded further to take P. also
12. 5 P. therefore was kept in prison: but pr.
12. 6 P. was sleeping between two soldiers, b.
12. 7 he smote P. on the side, and raised him
12. 11 when P. was come to himself, he said, Now
12. 13 as [P.] knocked at the door of the gate, a
12. 14 when she knew P.'s voice, she opened not
12. 14 ran..and told how P. stood before the g.
12. 16 P. continued knocking: and when they
12. 18 was no small stir..what was become of P.
15. 7 P. rose up, and said unto them, Men (and)
Gal. 1. 18 I went up to Jerusalem to see [P.], and a.
2. 7 (the gospel) of..circumcision (was) unto P.
2. 8 For he that wrought effectually in P. to the
2. 11 when [P.] was come to Antioch, I withstood
2. 14 I said unto [P.] before (them) all, If thou
1 Pe. 1. 1 P., an apostle of Jesus Christ, to the stran.
2 Pe. 1. 1 P., a servant and an apostle of Jesus Ch.

PE-THAH-I'AH, פְּתַחְיָה *Jah opens.*
1. A priest in the days of David appointed over the nineteenth charge of the sanctuary. B.C. 1015.
1 Ch.24. 16 The nineteenth to P., the twentieth to Je.
2. A Levite that had taken a strange wife. B.C. 445.
Ezra 10. 23 the same (is) Kelita, P., Judah, and Elie
3. A Levite who regulated the devotions of the people after Ezra had finished reading the Book of the Law to them. B.C. 445.
Neh. 9. 5 P.,said, Stand up (and) bless the LORD your
4. A son of Meshezabeel, and of the family of Zerah son of Judah, whom the king of Persia employed in matters concerning the returned exiles. B.C. 445.
Neh. 11. 24 P. the son of Meshezabeel, of the children

PE'-THOR, פְּתוֹר *extension.*
A city in Mesopotamia near the Euphrates, where Balaam the prophet the son of Beor dwelt, when Balak king of Moab sent for him to curse Israel.
Num22. 5 sent..unto Balaam the son of Beor, to P.
Deut23. 4 Balaam the son of Beor of P. of Mesopo.

PE-THU'-EL, פְּתוּאֵל *God delivers.*
Father of Joel the prophet. B.C. 800.
Joel 1. 1 word of the LORD that came to..son of P.

PETITION —
1. *Petition, prayer,* בָּעוּ *bau.*
Dan. 6. 7 whosoever shall ask a petition of any god
6. 13 but maketh his petition three times a day
2. *Asking,* מִשְׁאָלָה *mishalah.*
Psa. 20. 5 banners: the LORD fulfil all thy petitions
3. *Asking,* שְׁאֵלָה, שֵׁלָה *shelah, sheelah.*
1 Sa. 1. 17 grant (thee) thy petition that thou hast
1. 27 LORD hath given me my petition which
1 Ki. 2. 16 now I ask one petition of thee, deny me
2. 20 I desire one small petition of thee; (I pr.
Esth. 5. 6 What (is) thy petition? and it shall be g.
5. 7 answered Esther, and said, My petition
5. 8 if it please the king to grant my petition
7. 2 What (is) thy petition, queen Esther? and
7. 3 let my life be given me at my petition, and
9. 12 what (is) thy petition? and it shall be gr.
4. *An asking, petition,* αἴτημα *aitēma.*
1 Jo. 5. 15 we know that we have the petitions that

PE-UL'-THAI, פְּעֻלְּתַי *Jah works.*
A Kohathite, son of Obed-edom, and a gate keeper of the tabernacle in the days of David. B.C. 1015.
1 Ch.26. 5 Issachar the seventh; P. the eighth: for

PHA'-LEC, Φαλέκ *division,*
Father of Ragau, an ancestor of Jesus. See *Peleg.*
Luke 3. 35 which was (the son) of P., which was (the

PHAL'-TI, פַּלְטִי *Jah causes to escape.* (**PHALTIEL.**)
A Benjamite to whom Saul gave Michal his daughter, David's wife. B.C. 1060. See *Paltiel.*
1 Sa. 25. 44 had given Michal..to P. the son of Laish

PHA-NU'-EL, Φανουήλ.
An Asherite, mother of Anna the prophetess who came into the temple when Jesus was presented there by his parents, and spoke of him to those who looked for redemption in Israel.
Luke 2. 36 there was one Anna..the daughter of P.

PHAR'-AOH, פַּרְעֹה *sun.*
1. A king of Egypt in the days of Abram. B.C. 1896.
Gen. 12. 15 The princes also of P. saw her, and com.
12. 15 before P...the woman was taken into P.'s
12. 17 LORD plagued P. and his house with great
12. 18 P. called Abram, and said, What (is) this
12. 20 P. commanded (his) men concerning him
2. Another king of Egypt, in the days of Joseph. B.C. 1725.
Gen. 37. 36 an officer of P.'s,(and) captain of the guard
39. 1 an officer of P., captain of the guard
40. 2 P. was wroth against two (of) his officers
40. 7 he asked P.'s officers that (were) with him
40. 11 P.'s cup (was) in my hand: and I took the
40. 11 into P.'s cup, and I gave the cup into P.'s
40. 13, 19 within three days shall P. lift up thine
40. 13 thou shalt deliver P.'s cup into his hand
40. 14 make mention of me unto P.,and bring me
40. 17 (was) of all manner of bake meats for P.
40. 20 the third day, (which was) P.'s birthday
40. 21 and he gave the cup into P.'s hand
41. 1 P. dreamed: and, behold, he stood by the
41. 4 kine did eat up the..fat kine. So P. awoke
41. 7 And P. awoke, and, behold, (it was) a dr.
41. 8 P. told them his dreams; but (there was)
41. 8 none that could interpret them unto P.
41. 9 Then spake the chief butler unto P., say.
41. 10 P. was wroth with his servants, and put
41. 14 P. sent and called Joseph, and they bro.
41. 14 changed his raiment, and came in unto P.
41. 15 P. said unto Joseph, I have dreamed a d.
41. 16 Joseph answered P., saying, (It is) not in
41. 16 God shall give P. an answer of peace
41. 17 P. said unto Joseph, In my dream, behold
41. 25 P., The dream of P. (is) one: God hath sh.
41. 28 (is) the thing which I have spoken unto P.
41. 28 What God (is)..to do he showeth unto P.
41. 32 for that the dream was doubled unto P.
41. 33 let P. look out a man discreet and wise
41. 34 P. do (this), and let him appoint officers
41. 35 lay up corn under the hand of P., and
41. 37 the thing was good in the eyes of P., and
41. 38 P. said unto his servants, Can we find (such
41. 39 P. said unto Joseph..(there is) none so d.
Gen. 41. 41 P. said unto Joseph, See, I have set thee
41. 42 P. took off his ring from his hand, and
41. 44 P. said unto Joseph, I (am) P., and with.
41. 45 P. called Joseph's name Zaphnath-paane.
41. 46 And Joseph..stood before P. king of E.
41. 46 Joseph went out from the presence of P.
41. 55 people cried to P. for bread: and P. said
42. 15 By the life of P. ye shall not go forth he.
42. 16 or else, by the life of P. surely ye (are) s.
44. 18 not thine anger burn..thou (art)..as P.
45. 2 the Egyptians and the house of P. heard
45. 8 he hath made me a father to P., and lord
45. 16 fame..was heard in P.'s house..pleased P.
45. 17 P. said unto Joseph, Say unto thy brethren
45. 21 according to the commandment of P.
46. 5 the waggons which P. had sent to carry
46. 31 I will go up, and show P., and say unto
46. 33 it shall come to pass, when P. shall call
47. 1 Then Joseph came and told P., and said
47. 2 he took some..and presented them unto P.
47. 3 P. said unto his brethren, What (is) your
47. 3 they said unto P., Thy servants (are) she.
47. 4 They said, moreover, unto P., For to soj.
47. 5 P. spake unto Joseph, saying, Thy father
47. 7 set him before P.: and Jacob blessed P.
47. 8 And P. said unto Jacob, How old (art) t.?
47. 9 Jacob said unto P., The days of the years
47. 10 blessed P., and went out from before P.
47. 11 in the land of Rameses, as P. had comm.
47. 14 Joseph brought the money into P.'s house
47. 19 we and our land..will be servants unto P.
47. 20 Joseph bought all the land of Egypt for P.
47. 20 famine prevailed..so the land became P.'s
47. 22 priests had a portion (assigned them) of P.
47. 22 did eat their portion which P. gave them
47. 23 I have bought you this day..for P.: lo
47. 24 that ye shall give the fifth (part) unto P.
47. 25 And they said..we will be P.'s servants
47. 26 P. should have the fifth (part); except the
47. 26 land of the priests only..became not P.'s
50. 4 Joseph spake unto the house of P., saying
50. 4 speak, I pray you, in the ears of P., saying
50. 6 P. said, Go up and bury thy father, acc.
50. 7 with him went up all the servants of P.
3. A third king of Egypt, in the infancy of Moses. B.C. 1571.
Exod 1. 11 they built for P. treasure cities, Pithom
1. 19 the midwives said unto P., Because the
1. 22 P. charged all his people, saying, Every
2. 5 And the daughter of P. came down to w.
2. 7 Then said his sister to P.'s daughter, Shall
2. 8 P.'s daughter said to her, Go And the m.
2. 9 P.'s daughter said unto her, Take this ch.
2. 10 child grew, and she brought him unto P.'s
Heb. 11. 24 Moses..refused to be called the son of P.'s
4. A fourth king of Egypt, when Moses was grown up. B.C. 1531.
Exod. 2. 15 Now when P. heard this thing, he sought
2. 15 But Moses fled from the face of P., and
5. A fifth king of Egypt, who was reigning when Moses returned. B.C. 1491.
Exod 3. 10 Come now..and I will send thee unto P., th.
3. 11 Who (am) I., that I should go unto P., and
4. 21 see..thou do all those wonders before P.
4. 22 thou shalt say unto P., Thus saith the L.
5. 1 Moses and Aaron went in, and told P.
5. 2 P. said, Who (is) the LORD, that I should
5. 5 P. said, Behold, the people of the land n.
5. 6 P. commanded the same day the taskma.
5. 10 Thus saith P., I will not give you straw
5. 14 the officers..which P.'s taskmasters had
5. 15 Then the officers..came and cried unto P.
5. 20 Moses and Aaron..as they came forth..P.
5. 21 savour to be abhorred in the eyes of P.
5. 23 For since I came to P. to speak in thy na.
6. 1 Now shalt thou see what I will do to P.
6. 11 Go in, speak unto P. king of Egypt, that
6. 12 how then shall P. hear me, who (am) of
6. 13 gave them a charge..unto P. king of Eg.
6. 27 These (are) they which spake to P. king
6. 29 speak thou unto P. king of Egypt all that
6. 30 Behold..how shall P. hearken unto me?
7. 1 See, I have made thee a god to P.; and
7. 2 Aaron thy brother shall speak unto P., th.
7. 3 I will harden P.'s heart, and multiply
7. 4 But P. shall not hearken unto you, that I
7. 7 fourscore..when they spake unto P.
7. 9 When P. shall speak unto you, saying, S.
7. 9 Take thy rod, and cast (it) before P., (and)
7. 10 And Moses and Aaron went in unto P., and
7. 10 Aaron cast down his rod before P., and
7. 11 P. also called the wise men and the v. 13.
7. 14 P.'s heart (is) hardened, he refuseth to
7. 15 Get thee unto P. in the morning; lo, he
7. 20 he lifted up the rod..in the sight of P., and
7. 22 P.'s heart was hardened, neither did he
7. 23 P. turned and went into his house, neith.
8. 1 the LORD spake unto Moses, Go unto P.
8. 8 Then P. called for Moses and Aaron, and
8. 9 Moses said unto P., Glory over me: when
8. 12 Moses..Aaron went out from P.: and M.
8. 12 the frogs which he had brought against P.
8. 15 But when P. saw that there was respite
8. 19 Then the magicians said unto P., This (is)
8. 19 P.'s heart was hardened, and he hearke.
8. 20 Rise up early..and stand before P.; lo, he
8. 24 came..swarm (of flies) into..house of P.
8. 25 P. called for Moses and for Aaron, and
8. 28 P. said, I will let you go, that ye may sa.
8. 29 the swarms (of flies) may depart from P.
8. 29 but let not P. deal deceitfully any more
Exod.8. 30 Moses went out from P. and entreated
8. 31 he removed the swarms (of flies) from P.
8. 32 P. hardened his heart at this time also
9. 1 the LORD said unto Moses, Go in unto P.
9. 7 P. sent..And the heart of P. was hard v. 35.
9. 8 and let Moses sprinkle..in the sight of P.
9. 10 they took ashes..and stood before P.; and
9. 12 And the LORD hardened the heart of P.
9. 13 Rise up early..and stand before P., and
9. 20 He that feared..among the servants of P.
9. 27 P. sent, and called for Moses and Aaron
9. 33 Moses went out of the city from P., and
9. 34 P. saw that the rain and the hail..were
10. 1 the LORD said unto Moses, Go in unto P.
10. 3 Moses and Aaron came in unto P., and s.
10. 6 he turned himself, and went out from P.
10. 7 P.'s servants said unto him, How long sh.
10. 8 Moses and Aaron were brought..unto P.
10. 11 And they were driven out from P.'s pres.
10. 16 Then P. called for Moses and Aaron in h.
10. 18 he went out from P., and entreated the L.
10. 20, 27 But the LORD hardened P.'s heart, so th.
10. 24 P. called unto Moses, and said, Go ye, se.
10. 28 And P. said unto him, Get thee from me
11. 1 Yet..I bring one plague (more) upon P.
11. 3 Moses (was) very great..in..sight of P.'s
11. 5 the first born of P. that sitteth upon his t.
11. 8 And he went out from P. in a great anger
11. 9 the LORD said..P. shall not hearken unto
11. 10 before P.: and the LORD hardened P.'s he.
12. 29 first born of P. that sat on his throne
12. 30 And P. rose up in the night, he, and all
13. 15 when P. would hardly let us go, that the
13. 17 when P. had let the people go, that God
14. 3 P. will say of the children of Israel, They
14. 4 I will harden P.'s heart, that he shall fo.
14. 4 I will be honoured upon P., and upon all
14. 5 the heart of P. and of his servants was
14. 8 the LORD hardened the heart of P. king
14. 9 horses (and) chariots of P., and his horse.
14. 10 when P. drew nigh, the children of Israel
14. 17 I will get me honour upon P., and upon
14. 18 I have gotten me honour upon P., and up.
14. 23 P.'s horses, his chariots, and his horsemen
14. 28 host of P. that came into the sea after
15. 4 P.'s chariots and his host hath he cast
15. 19 the horse of P. went in with his chariots
18. 4 God..delivered me from the sword of P.
18. 8 all that the LORD had done unto P. and to
18. 10 hath delivered you..out of the hand of P.
Deut. 6. 21 We were P.'s bondmen in Egypt; and the
6. 22 upon P., and upon all his household, before
7. 8 redeemed..from the hand of P. king of E.
7. 18 remember what the LORD thy God did unto
11. 3 did in the midst of Egypt unto P. the ki.
29. 2 the LORD did..in the land of Egypt unto
34. 11 sent him to do in the land of Egypt to P.
1 Sa. 2. 27 when they were in Egypt, in P.'s house?
6. 6 the Egyptians and P. hardened their hea.?
2 Ki. 17. 7 from under the hand of P., king of Egypt
Neh. 9. 10 shewedst signs and wonders upon P., and
Psa.135. 9 tokens..upon P., and upon all his servants
136. 15 overthrew P. and his host in the Red sea
Acts 7. 10 gave him favour..in the sight of P. king
7. 13 Joseph's kindred was made known unto P.
7. 21 P.'s daughter took him up, and nourished
Rom. 9. 17 For the scripture saith unto P., Even for
6. A king of Egypt in the days of Solomon. B.C. 1015.
1 Ki. 3. 1 affinity with P. king of Egypt, and took P.
7. 8 Solomon made also an house for P.'s dau.
9. 16 (For) P. king of Egypt had gone up and
9. 24 P.'s daughter came up out of the city of
11. 1 together with the daughter of P., women
11. 18 they came to Egypt, unto P. king of Egy.
11. 19 found great favour in the sight of P.
11. 20 his son, whom Taphenes weaned in P.'s h.
11. 20 was in P.'s household among the sons of P
11. 21 Hadad said to P., Let me depart, that I
11. 22 P. said unto him, But what hast thou la.
2 Ch. 8. 11 Solomon brought up the daughter of P.
Song 1. 9 to a company of horses in P.'s chariots
7. A king of Egypt in the days of Isaiah. B.C. 720.
Isa. 19. 11 wise counsellors of P...how say ye to P.
30. 2 strengthen themselves in the strength of P.
30. 3 Therefore shall the strength of P. be your
36. 6 so (is) P. king of Egypt to all that trust in
8. Father of Bithiah wife of Mered, who was of the tribe of Judah. B.C. 1400.
1 Ch. 4. 18 the sons of Bithiah the daughter of P.

PHAR-AOH HOPH'-RA, פַּרְעֹה חָפְרַע *priest of the sun.*
A king of Egypt whose overthrow by Nebuchadnezzar was foretold by Jeremiah the prophet. B.C. 570. Herodotus reports his death by a rival king, Amasis.
Jer. 44. 30 I will give P. king of Egypt into the hand

PHAR-AOH (NECH-OH *or* **NECHO)**, פַּרְעֹה נְכֹה *or* נְכוֹ.
A king of Egypt, a successor of Psammetichus, who fought against Nabopolassar king of Assyria, slew king Josiah at Megiddo, bound Jehoahaz at Riblah, and made Eliakim his brother king in his stead. B.C. 610.
2 Ki. 18. 21 so (is) P. king of Egypt unto all that trust
23. 29 P. king of Egypt went up against the ki.
23. 33 P. put him in bands at Riblah in the land
23. 34 P. made Eliakim the son of Josiah king in
23. 35 Jehoiakim gave the silver and..gold to P.
23. 35 money according to..commandment of P.
23. 35 according to his taxation..to give..unto P.
Jer. 25. 19 P. king of Egypt, and his servants, and his
37. 5 P.'s army was come forth out of Egypt: and
37. 7 P.'s army which is come forth to help you

Jer. 37. 11 army..was broken up..for fear of P.'s army
43. 9 at the entry of P.'s house in Tahpanhes
46. 2 against the army of P. king of Egypt which
46. 17 P. king of Egypt (is but) a noise; he hath
46. 25 and P., and Egypt, with their gods, and
46. 25 even P., and (all) them that trust in him
47. 1 word..that came..before that P. smote G.
Eze. 17. 17 Neither shall P. with (his) mighty army
29. 2 set thy face against P. king of Egypt, and
29. 3 P. king of Egypt, the great dragon that
30. 21 I have broken the arm of P. king of Egy.
30. 22 I (am) against P. king of Egypt, and will
30. 24 I will break P.'s arms, and he shall groan
30. 25 the arms of P. shall fall down and they
31. 2 Son..speak unto P. king of Egypt, and to
31. 18 This (is) P. and all his multitude, saith
32. 2 take up a lamentation for P. king of Egypt
32. 31 P. shall see them, and shall be comforted
32. 31 P. and all his army slain by the sword
32. 32 (even) P. and all his multitude, saith the

PHA'-RES, Φαρές *breach* (*from Heb.* פֶּרֶץ).
Elder son of Judah by Thamar, and father of Esrom. B.C. 1700. See also the following.

Matt. 1. 3 Judas begat P...P. begat Esrom; and
Luke 3. 33 Esrom, which was (the son) of P., which

PHA'-REZ, PE'-REZ, פֶּרֶץ, פָּרֶץ *breaking forth.*
Elder son of Judah by Tamar his daughter in law, and father of Hezron and Hamul. B.C. 1700. See *Perez.*

Gen. 38. 29 therefore his name was called P.
46. 12 And the sons of P. were Hezron and Ham.
46. 12 Onan, and Shelah, and P., and Zarah
Num 26. 20 of P., the family of the Pharzites: of Ze.
26. 21 the sons of P. were; of Hezron, the fam.
Ruth 4. 12 let thy house be like the house of P., wh.
4. 18 these (are) the generations of P.; P. begat
1 Ch. 2. 4 Tamar his daughter in law bare him P. and
2. 5 The sons of P.; Hezron, and Hamul
4. 1 P., Hezron, and Carmi, and Hur, and Sh.
9. 4 Bani, of the children of P. the son of Judah
Neh. 11. 4 Mahalaleel, of the children of P.; 11. 6.

PHAROSH. *See* **PAROSH.**

PHA-RI-SEES, Φαρισαῖοι, (*from Heb.* פָּרַשׁ) *separate.*
The largest of the three or four Jewish sects; noted for their self conceit and long prayers; paid unnecessary tithes, fasted often, made broad their phylacteries, held to traditions, &c.

Matt. 3. 7 he saw many of the P. and Sadducees co.
5. 20 (the righteousness) of the scribes and P.
9. 11 And when the P. saw (it), they said unto
9. 14 the P. fast oft, but thy disciples fast not
9. 34 the P. said, He casteth out devils through
12. 2 But when the P. saw (it), they said unto
12. 14 the P. went out, and held a council again.
12. 24 when the P. heard (it), they said, This (f.)
12. 38 [the P.] answered, saying, Master, we wo.
15. 1 Then came to Jesus scribes and P., which
15. 12 Knowest thou that the P. were offended
16. 1 The P. also with the Sadducees came, and
16. 6, 11 leaven of the P. and of the Sadducees
16. 12 the doctrine of the P. and of the Sadduc.
19. 3 The P. also came unto him, tempting him
21. 45 when the chief priests and P. had heard
22. 15 Then went the P., and took counsel how
22. 34 P. had heard that he had put the Saddu.
22. 41 While the P. were gathered together, Je.
23. 2 The scribes and the P. sit in Moses' seat
23. 13, 15, 23, 25, 27 woe unto you, scribes and P.
23. 14 [Woe unto you, scribes and P., hypocrites]
23. 26 (Thou) blind P., cleanse first that (which
23. 29 Woe unto you, scribes and P., hypocrites!
27. 62 priests and P. came together unto Pilate
Mark 2. 16 [P.] saw him eat with publicans and sinne.
2. 18 disciples of John and [of..P.] used to fast
2. 18 Why do the disciples of John and of..P.
2. 24 the P. said unto him, Behold, why do they
3. 6 the P. went forth, and straightway took
7. 1 Then came together unto him the P., and
7. 3 the P., and all the Jews, except they wash
7. 5 the P. and scribes asked him, Why
8. 11 the P. came forth, and began to question
8. 15 beware of the leaven of the P., and (of) the
10. 2 the P. came to him, and asked him, Is it
12. 13 certain of the P. and of the Herodians
Luke 5. 17 there were P. and doctors of the law
5. 21 the P. began to reason, saying, Who is
5. 30 P. murmured against his disciples, saying
5. 33 and likewise (the disciples) of the P.
6. 2 the P. said unto them, Why do ye that w.
6. 7 the scribes and P. watched him, whether
7. 30 the P. and lawyers rejected the counsel
7. 36 one of the P. desired him that he would
7. 36 he went into the P.'s house, and sat down
7. 37 that (Jesus) sat at meat in the P.'s house
7. 39 when the P. which had bidden him saw
11. 37 a certain P. besought him to dine with
11. 38 when the P. saw (it), he marvelled that he
11. 39 ye P. make clean the outside of the cup
11. 42 But woe unto you, P.! for ye tithe mint
11. 43 Woe unto you, P.! for ye love the upper.
11. 44 [Woe unto you, scribes and P., hypocrites]
11. 53 the scribes and the P. began to urge (him)
12. 1 Beware ye of the leaven of the P., which
13. 31 The same day there came certain of the P.
14. 1 went into the house of one of the chief P.
14. 3 Jesus answering spake unto the..P., say.
15. 2 the P. and scribes murmured, saying, This
16. 14 the P. also..heard all these things: and
17. 20 when he was demanded of the P., when
18. 10 the one a P., and the other a publican
Luke 18. 11 The P. stood and prayed thus with hims.
19. 39 some of the P...said unto him, Master
John 1. 24 And they which were sent were of the P.
3. 1 There was a man of the P., named Nico.
4. 1 the Lord knew how the P. had heard that
7. 32 The P. heard that the people murmured
7. 32 the P. and the chief priests sent officers
7. 45 Then came the officers to the..P.; and
7. 47 Then answered them the P., Are ye also
7. 48 Have any of the rulers or of the P. belie.
8. 3 [the scribes and P. brought unto him a w.]
8. 13 The P. therefore said unto him, Thou b.
9. 13 They brought to the P. him that..was bl.
9. 15 Then again the P. also asked him how he
9. 16 Therefore said some of the P., This man
9. 40 (some) of the P...heard these words, and
11. 46 some of them went their ways to the P.
11. 47 Then gathered the..P. a council, and said
11. 57 Now..the P. had given a commandment
12. 19 The P. therefore said among themselves
12. 42 because of the P. they did not confess
18. 3 officers from the chief priests and P., co.
Acts 5. 34 stood there up one in the council, a P.
15. 5 there rose up certain of the sect of the P.
23. 6 perceived that the one part were..[P.]
23. 6 I am a P., [the son of a P.]: of the hope and
23. 7 there arose a dissension between the P.
23. 8 neither angel, nor spirit; but the P. con.
23. 9 the scribes (that were) of the P.s' part
26. 5 after the..straitest sect..I lived a P.
Phil. 3. 5 Circumcised..as touching the law, a P.

PHAR'-PAR, פַּרְפַּר *swift.*
The river *el-Sibarani*, flowing from Hermon past Damascus, or the little one at *el-Faigah* which falls into the Barada; or the *Awaj* from eastern Hermon, and now called *Barber.*

2 Ki. 5. 12 (Are) not Abana and P...better than all

PHAR-ZITES, הַפַּרְצִי *the Partsi.*
The family of Pharez son of Judah. Num. 26. 20.

PHASEAH. *See* **PASEAH.**

PHE'-BE, Φοίβη.
A female minister in Corinth or Cenchrea, who had helped Paul, and going to Rome, was recommended by Paul.

Rom 16. 1 I commend unto you P. our sister, which

PHE-NICE, Φοίνιξ.
A harbour on the S. of Crete.

Acts 27. 12 if by any means they might attain to P.

PHE-NICE, PHE-NI'-CIA, Φοινίκη.
The E. coast of the Mediterranean, commencing at the promontory of Carmel, and stretching 120 miles northward, with an average breadth of 20 miles; Tyre and Sidon were its chief cities. It was originally peopled by the sons of Anak, B.C. 2800; Agenor was its first king, 1184; in 878 it sent forth a colony, led by Elissa or Dido, to Africa, which founded Carthage; in 721 it was invaded by Shalmanezer; in 587 by Nebuchadnezzar; in 536 by Cyrus; in 466 the Phœnicians were totally defeated by Cimon at the naval battle of Eurymedon; in 352 they revolted from Persia; in 331 they were subdued by Alexander; in 323 the country was annexed to Egypt; in 315 it was seized by Antigonus of Phrygia; in 83 it passed to Tigranes king of Armenia; in 62 it became part of the Roman province of Syria; in 20 it was deprived by Augustus of all its liberties. It was annexed to Turkey in A.D. 1516.

Acts 11. 19 Now they..travelled as far as P., and C.
15. 3 they passed through P. and Samaria, de.
21. 2 finding a ship sailing over unto P., we we.

PHI'-BE-SETH, פִּי־בֶסֶת *the cat goddess Basht.*
A capital city in Lower Egypt, called also Bubastis, on the E. of Pelusiac branch of the Nile.

Eze. 30. 17 The young men of Aven and of P. shall

PHIC'-HOL, פִּיכֹל *great, strong, tamarisk.*
Chief captain of Abimelech king of the Philistines in the days of Abraham. B.C. 1880.

Gen. 21. 22 Abimelech and P. the chief captain..spa.
21. 32 then Abimelech rose up, and P. the chief
26. 26 Abimelech went..and P. the chief captain

PHIL-A-DELPH'-IA, Φιλαδέλφεια.
The second city of Lydia in the W. of Asia Minor, 26 miles S.E. of Sardis, and 70 N.E. of Smyrna; it was founded by Attalus Philadelphus king of Pergamos; in A.D. 17 it was almost destroyed by an earthquake; it was taken by Bazazet I. in A.D. 1390; it is now called *Allah shair*, "city of God," and still contains about 15,000 inhabitants, and the ruins of many ancient churches.

Rev. 1. 11 unto Sardis, and unto P., and unto Laod.
3. 7 And to the angel of the church in P. write

PHIL-E'-MON, Φιλήμων.
A person in Colosse to whom Paul addressed a letter in behalf of his spiritual son Onesimus.

Phm. 1 Paul..unto P. our dearly beloved, and f.

PHIL-E'-TUS, Φίλητος.
A person condemned (along with one Hymeneus) by Paul for error regarding the resurrection.

2 Ti. 2. 17 of whom is Hymeneus and P.

PHIL'-IP, Φίλιππος *a lover of horses.*
1. One of the twelve apostles, from Bethsaida.

Matt 10. 3 P., and Bartholomew; Thomas, and Ma.
Mark 3. 18 P., and Bartholomew, and Matthew, and
Luke 6. 14 Andrew..James and John, P. and Barth.
John 1. 43 findeth P., and saith unto him, Follow me
1. 44 P. was of Bethsaida, the city of Andrew
1. 45 P. findeth Nathanael, and saith unto him
1. 46 P. saith unto him, Come and see
1. 48 Before that P. called thee, when thou wast
6. 5 he saith unto P., Whence shall we buy b.
6. 7 P. answered him, Two hundred penny w.
12. 21 The same came therefore to P., which was
12. 22 P. cometh and telleth Andrew
12. 22 and again Andrew and P. tell Jesus
14. 8 P. saith unto him, Lord, show us the Fa.
14. 9 you, and yet hast thou not known me, P.?
Acts 1. 13 P., and Thomas, Bartholomew, and Mat.

2. A son of Herod the Great, and husband of Herodias.

Matt. 14. 3 for Herodias's sake, his brother [P.'s] wife
Mark 6. 17 for Herodias' sake, his brother P.'s wife
Luke 3. 19 for Herodias his brother [P.'s] wife, and

3. Another son who was tetrarch of Iturea.

Luke 3. 1 his brother P. tetrarch of Ituræa and of

4. One of the seven chosen to serve tables; he also preached and baptized.

Acts 6. 5 P., and Prochorus, and Nicanor, and Ti.
8. 5 P. went down to the city of Samaria, and
8. 6 gave heed unto those things which P. spa.
8. 12 when they believed P. preaching the th.
8. 13 he continued with P., and wondered
8. 26 the angel of the Lord spake unto P., say.
8. 29 the Spirit said unto P., Go near, and join
8. 30 P. ran thither to (him), and heard him read
8. 31 he desired P. that he would come up and
8. 34 the eunuch answered P., and said, I pray
8. 35 P. opened his mouth, and began at the s.
8. 37 [P. said, If thou believest with all thine]
8. 38 both into the water, both P. and the eu.
8. 39 the spirit of the Lord caught away P.
8. 40 P. was found at Azotus: and passing th.
21. 8 entered into..house of P. the evangelist

PHIL-IP'-PI, Φίλιπποι.
A chief city in proconsular Macedonia, E. of Amphipolis in ancient Thrace, and about seventy miles N.E. of Thessalonica; once called *Krenides;* fortified by Philip father of Alexander the Great, it received his name; near it were mines of gold, silver &c.; Brutus and Cassius were here defeated; it is now in ruins; in Matt. 16. 13 and Mark 8. 27 it is used as an adjunct to *Cæsarea*, N. of Palestine, near the sources of the Jordan.

Acts 16. 12 from thence to P., which is the chief city
20. 6 we sailed away from P. after the days of
Phil. 1. 1 the saints in Christ Jesus which are at P.
1 Th. 2. 2 were shamefully entreated as ye know at P

PHI-LIP-PIANS, Φιλιππήσιοι.
The (believing) inhabitants of Philippi in Macedonia, whom Paul addresses in his Epistle.

Phil. 4. 15 ye P., know also, that in the beginning of

PHI-LIST'-IA, פְּלֶשֶׁת *migration.*
The sea coast on the west of Dan and Simeon; from a little N. of Joppa to a little S. of Gaza, or about forty miles long by ten or twenty broad; its chief cities were Ekron, Ashdod, Askelon, Gaza, and Gath, to which may be added Gerar.

Psa. 60. 8 P., triumph thou because of me
87. 4 behold P., and Tyre, with Ethiopia; this
108. 9 Moab (is) my washpot..over P. will I tr.

PHI-LIST-IM, פְּלִשְׁתִּים.
The descendants of Casluhim the sixth son of Mizraim, who migrated from Egypt northward to Canaan keeping by the sea coast.

Gen. 10. 14 Casluhim, out of whom came P., and Ca.

PHI-LIS-TINES, פְּלִשְׁתִּים.
The same as the above. Pompey incorporated their country into the Roman province of Syria, B.C. 62.

Gen. 21. 32 and they returned into the land of the P.
21. 34 Abraham sojourned in the P.'s land many
26. 1 Isaac went unto Abimelech king of the P.
26. 8 king of the P. looked out at a window, and
26. 14 store of servants: and the P. envied him
26. 15 the P. had stopped them, and filled them
26. 18 the P. had stopped them after the death
Exod 13. 17 not (through) the way of the land of the P.
23. 31 the Red sea even unto the sea of the P.
Josh 13. 2 all the borders of the P., and all Geshuri
13. 3 five lords of the P.; the Gazathites, and
Judg. 3. 3 five lords of the P., and all the Canaanites
3. 31 which slew of the P. six hundred men w.
10. 6 served..and the gods of the P., and fors.
10. 7 he sold them into the hands of the P., and
10. 11 from the children of Ammon..from the P.?
13. 1 delivered them into the hand of the P.
13. 5 deliver Israel out of the hand of the P.
14. 1, 2 woman in Tim. of..daughters of the P.
14. 3 to take a wife of the uncircumcised P.?
14. 4 he sought an occasion against the P.
14. 4 that time the P. had dominion over Israel
15. 3 Now shall I be more blameless than the P.
15. 5 let (them) go into..standing corn of the P.
15. 6 the P. said, Who hath done this? And th.
15. 6 P. came up, and burnt her and her father
15. 9 the P. went up, and pitched in Judah, and
15. 11 Knowest thou not..P. (are) rulers over us?
15. 12 may deliver thee into the hand of the P.
15. 14 the P. shouted against him: and the spi.
15. 20 he judged Israel in the days of the P.
16. 5, 18 the lords of the P. came up unto her

Judg16. 8 the lords of the P. brought up to her
16. 9, 12, 14, 20 said unto him, The P. (be) upon th.
16. 18 called for the lords of the P., saying, Come
16. 21 the P. took him, and put out his eyes, and
16. 23 the lords of the P. gathered them together
16. 27 the lords of the P. (were) there; and (t.)
16. 28 I may be at once avenged of the P. for my
16. 30 Samson said, Let me die with the P. And
1 Sa. 4. 1 Israel went out against the P. to battle
4. 1 Ebenezer: and the P. pitched in Aphek
4. 2 P. put themselves in array against Israel
4. 2 Israel was smitten before the P.: and th.
4. 3 hath the LORD smitten us..before the P.?
4. 6 when the P. heard the noise of the shout
4. 7 the P. were afraid: for they said, God is
4. 9 quit yourselves like men, O ye P.! that ye
4. 10 the P. fought, and Israel was smitten, and
4. 17 Israel is fled before the P., and there
5. 1, 2 the P. took the ark of God, and brought
5. 8 gathered all the lords of the P. unto them
5. 11 gathered together all the lords of the P.
6. 1 was in the country of the P. seven months
6. 2 P. called for the priests and the diviners
6. 4 (according to)..number of the lords of..P.
6. 12 the lords of the P. went after them unto
6. 16 when the five lords of the P. had seen (it)
6. 17 the golden emerods which the P. returned
6. 18 cities of the P. (belonging) to the five lords
6. 21 The P. have brought again the ark of the
7. 3 will deliver you out of the hand of the P.
7. 7 the P. heard that the children of Israel
7. 7 the lords of the P. went up against Israel
7. 7 when the children of Israel heard (it,) they
7. 8 he will save us out of the hand of the P.
7. 10 the P. drew near to battle against Israel
7. 10 a great thunder on that day upon the P.
7. 11 pursued the P., and smote them, until
7. 13 the P. were subdued, and they came no
7. 13 the hand of the LORD was against the P.
7. 14 the cities which the P. had taken from
7. 14 Israel deliver out of the hands of the P.
9. 16 save my people out of the hand of the P.
10. 5 the hill..where (is) the garrison of the P.
12. 9 into the hand of the P., and into the hand
13. 3 garrison of the P...in Geba; and the P. h.
13. 4 Saul had smitten a garrison of the P., and
13. 4 I...was had in abomination with the P.
13. 5 the P. gathered themselves together to
13. 11 the P. gathered themselves together at
13. 12 P. will come down now upon me to Gilgal
13. 16 but the P. encamped in Michmash
13. 17 spoilers came out of the camp of the P.
13. 19 the P. said, Lest the Hebrews make (them)
13. 20 all the Israelites went down to the P., to
13. 23 And the garrison of the P. went out to the
14. 1 Come, and let us go over to the Ps.' garr.
14. 4 Jonathan sought to go over unto the Ps.'
14. 11 both..discovered themselves unto..the P.
14. 11 the P. said, Behold, the Hebrews come f.
14. 19 noise that (was) in the host of the P. went
14. 21 Moreover the Hebrews..were with the P.
14. 22 (when) they heard that the P. fled, even
14. 30 a much greater slaughter among the P.?
14. 31 they smote the P. that day from Michm
14. 36 Let us go down after the P. by night, and
14. 37 Shall I go down after the P.? wilt thou de
14. 46 Then Saul went up from following the P.
14. 46 and the P. went to their own place
14. 47 So Saul..fought..against the P. and
14. 52 there was sore war against the P. all the
17. 1 Now the P. gathered together their arm.
17. 2 and set the battle in array against the P.
17. 3 the P. stood on a mountain on the one s.
17. 4 there went out a champion..of the P., n.
17. 8 (am) not I a P., and ye servants to Saul?
17. 10 the P. said, I defy the armies of Israel
17. 11 all Israel heard those words of the P.
17. 16 the P. drew near morning and evening, a.
17. 19 Saul, and they..(were)..fighting with the P.
17. 21 Israel and the P. had put the battle in ar.
17. 23 there came up the champion the P. of G.
17. 23 Goliath..out of the armies of the P., and
17. 26 be done to the man that killeth this P.
17. 26 for who (is) this uncircumcised P., that
17. 32 thy servant will go and fight with this P.
17. 33 Thou art not able to go against this P. to
17. 36 this uncircumcised P. shall be as one of
17. 37 will deliver me out of the hand of this P.
17. 40 in his hand: and he drew near to the P.
17. 41 the P. came on and drew near unto David
17. 42 when the P. looked about, and saw David
17. 43 the P. said unto David..And the P. cursed
17. 44 the P. said to David, Come to me, and I
17. 45 Then said David to the P., Thou comest
17. 46 I will give the carcases of..the P...unto
17. 48 it came to pass, when the P. arose, and
17. 48 D...ran toward the army to meet the P.
17. 49 David..smote the P. in his forehead, that
17. 50 So David prevailed over the P. with a sl.
17. 50 smote the P., and slew him; but (there
17. 51 David ran, and stood upon the P., and to.
17. 51 when the P. saw their champion was de.
17. 52 men of Israel pursued the P., until tho.
17. 52 the wounded of the P. fell down by the
17. 53 Israel returned from chasing after the P.
17. 54 David took the head of the P., and brou.
17. 55 Saul saw David go forth against the P.
17. 57 returned from the slaughter of the P., A.
17. 57 before Saul, with the head of the P. in his
18. 6 returned from the slaughter of the P., th.
18. 17 Saul said..let the hand of the P. be upon
18. 21 that the hand of the P. may be against h.

1 Sa. 18. 25 desireth..an hundred foreskins of the P.
18. 25 to make David fall by the hand of the P.
18. 27 David..slew of the P. two hundred men
18. 30 Then the princes of the P. went forth: and
19. 5 For he..slew the P., and the LORD wroug.
19. 8 David went out and fought with the P.
21. 9 The sword of Goliath the P...(is here) w.
22. 10 he..gave him the sword of Goliath the P.
23. 1 the P. fight against Keilah, and they rob
23. 2 saying, Shall I go and smite these P.? And
23. 2 Go and smite the P., and save Keilah
23. 3 if we come..against the armies of the P.?
23. 4 for I will deliver the P. into thine hand
23. 5 So David and his men..fought with the P.
23. 27 come; for the P. have invaded the land
23. 28 Saul returned..and went against the P.
24. 1 Saul was returned from following the P.
27. 1 speedily escape into the land of the P.; and
27. 7 when David dwelt in the country of the P.
27. 11 while he dwelleth in the country of the P.
28. 1 the P. gathered their armies together for
28. 4 the P. gathered themselves together, and
28. 5 when Saul saw the host of the P., he was
28. 15 the P. make war against me, and God is
28. 19, 19 deliver Israel..into the hand of the P.
29. 1 the P. gathered together all their armies
29. 2 lords of the P. passed on by hundreds and
29. 3 Then said the princes of the P., What (do)
29. 3 Achish said unto the princes of the P.
29. 4 the princes of the P. were wroth with him
29. 4 princes of the P. said unto him, Make th.
29. 7 that thou displease not the lords of the P.
29. 9 notwithstanding the princes of the P. h.
29. 11 return into the land of the P.: and the P.
30. 16 they had taken out of the land of the P.
31. 1 Now the P. fought against Israel: and the
31. 1 fled from before the P., and fell down sl.
31. 2 the P. followed hard..and the P. slew J.
31. 7 fled; and the P. came and dwelt in them
31. 8 when the P. came to strip the slain, that
31. 9 sent into the land of the P. round about
31. 11 heard of that which the P. had done to
2 Sa. 1. 20 lest the daughters of the P. rejoice, lest
3. 14 to me for an hundred foreskins of the P.
3. 18 people Israel out of the hand of the P.
5. 17 the P. heard that they had anointed Dav.
5. 17 the P. came up to seek David; and David
5. 18 The P. also came and spread themselves
5. 19 Shall I go up to the P.? wilt thou deliver
5. 19 doubtless deliver the P. into thine hand
5. 22 P. came up yet again, and spread thems.
5. 24 LORD go out..to smite the host of the P.
5. 25 smote the P. from Geba until thou come
8. 1 David smote the P., and subdued them
8. 1 Metheg-ammah out of the hand of the P.
8. 12 of the P., and of Amalek, and of the spoil
19. 9 he delivered us out of the hand of the P.
21. 12 the P. had hanged them, when the P. had
21. 15 the P. had yet war again with Israel; and
21. 15 David..fought against the P.: and David
21. 17 smote the P., and killed him. Then the
21. 18, 19 was again a battle with the P. at Gob
23. 9 defied the P. (that) were there gathered
23. 10 smote the P., until his hand was weary, and
23. 11 the P. were gathered together into a troop
23. 11 and the people fled from the P.
23. 12 he stood..and defended it, and slew the P.
23. 13 troop of the P. pitched in the valley of
23. 14 garrison of the P. (was) then (in) Beth-le.
23. 16 mighty men brake..the host of the P.
1 Ki. 4. 21 from the river unto the land of the P.
15. 27 at Gibbethon, which (belonged) to the P.
15. 15 Gibbethon, which (belonged) to the P.
2 Ki. 8. 2 sojourned in the land of the P. seven ye.
8. 3 woman returned out of the land of the P.
18. 8 He smote the P., (even) unto Gaza, and
1 Ch. 1. 12 Casluhim, of whom came the P., and Cap.
10. 1 the P. fought against Israel; and the m
10. 1 Israel fled from before the P., and fell
10. 2 the P. followed hard after Saul, and after
10. 2 P. slew Jonathan, and Abinadab, and M.
10. 7 and the P. came and dwelt in them
10. 8 when the P. came to strip the slain, that
10. 9 sent into the land of the P. round about
10. 11 heard all that the P. had done to Saul
11. 13 the P. were gathered together to battle
11. 13 and the people fled from before the P.
11. 14 slew the P.; and the LORD saved (them) by
11. 15 the P. encamped in the valley of Rephaim
11. 16 the P.s' garrison (was) then at Beth-lehem
11. 18 three brake through the host of the P.
12. 19 he came with the P. against Saul to battle
12. 19 the lords of the P. upon advisement sent
14. 8 the P. heard that David was anointed k.
14. 8 the P. went up to seek David: and David
14. 9 the P. came and spread themselves in the
14. 10 Shall I go up against the P.? and wilt thou
14. 13 the P. yet again spread themselves abroad
14. 15 God is gone..to smite the host of the P.
14. 16 they smote the host of the P. from Gibeon
18. 1 David smote the P., and subdued them
18. 1 and her towns out of the hand of the P.
18. 11 the children of Ammon, and from the P.
20. 4 there arose war at Gezer with the P.; at
20. 5 there was war again with the P.; and E.
2 Ch. 9. 26 from the river even unto the land of the P.
17. 11 the P. brought Jehoshaphat presents, and
21. 16 LORD stirred up..the spirit of the P.
26. 6 warred against the P., and brake down the
26. 6 built cities about Ashdod, and among..P.
26. 7 God helped him against the P., and against
28. 18 The P. also had invaded the cities of the

Psa. 56. *title* Michtam..when the P. took him in G.
83. 7 Amalek; the P. with the inhabitants of
Isa. 2. 6 (are) soothsayers like the P., and they
9. 12 The Syrians before, and the P. behind; and
11. 14 they shall fly upon the shoulders of the P.
Jer. 25. 20 kings of the land of the P., and Ashkelon
47. 1 word of the LORD..came..against the P.
47. 4 the day that cometh to spoil all the P.
47. 4 the LORD will spoil the P., the remnant of
Eze. 16. 27 the daughters of the P., which are ashamed
16. 57 the daughters of the P., which despise
25. 15 P. have dealt by revenge, and have taken
25. 16 I will stretch out mine hand upon the P.
Amos 1. 8 the remnant of the P. shall perish, saith
6. 2 go down to Gath of the P.: (be they) bet.
9. 7 P. from Caphtor, and the Syrians from K.?
Obad. 19 (they of) the plain the P.: and they shall
Zeph. 2. 5 the land of the P., I will even destroy thee
Zech. 9. 6 and I will cut off the pride of the P.

PHI-LO-LO'-GUS, Φιλόλογος *a lover of words.*
A believer in Rome to whom Paul sends a salutation.
Rom. 16. 15 Salute P., and Julia, Nereus, and his sis.

PHILOSOPHER —
A lover of wisdom, φιλόσοφος *philosophos.*
Acts 17. 18 Then certain philosophers of the Epicur.

PHILOSOPHY —
Love of wisdom, φιλοσοφία *philosophia.*
Col. 2. 8 spoil you through philosophy and vain d.

PHI-NE'-HAS, פִּינְחָס *oracle.*
1. A son of Eleazar, one of Aaron's sons, who slew Zimri and Cozbi. B.C. 1452.
Exod 6. 25 and she bare him P.: these (are) the heads
Num25. 7 when P...saw (it), he rose up from among
25. 11 P...hath turned my wrath away from the
31. 6 Moses sent them to the war..them and P.
Josh. 22. 13, 31, 32 P. the son of Eleazar the priest
22. 30 when P. the priest..heard the words that
24. 33 buried him in a hill (that pertained to) P.
Judg20. 28 P...stood before it in those days, saying
1 Ch. 6. 4 Eleazar begat P., P. begat Abishua
6. 50 Eleazar his son, P. his son, Abishua his
9. 20 P...was the ruler over them in time past
Ezra 7. 5 The son of Abishua, the son of P., the son
8. 2 Of the sons of P.; Gershom: of the sons of
Psa. 106. 30 Then stood up P., and executed judgment
2. Younger son of Eli the priest and judge of Israel. B.C. 1140.
1 Sa. 1. 3 the two sons of Eli, Hophni and P...(were)
2. 34 that shall come upon..Hophni and P.; in
4. 4, 11 and the two sons of Eli, Hophni and P.
4. 17 thy two sons also, Hophni and P., are d.
4. 19 Ps.' wife, was with child, (near) to be de.
14. 3 P., the son of Eli, the LORD'S priest in S.
3. Father of Eleazar, a priest who returned with Ezra. B.C. 445.
Ezra 8. 33 and with him (was) Eleazar the son of P.

PHLE'-GON, Φλέγων *burning.*
A believer in Rome to whom Paul sends a salutation.
Rom. 16. 14 Salute Asyncritus, P., Hermas, Patrobas

PHRY'-GIA, Φρυγία.
An inland province of Asia Minor, having Bithynia and Galatia on the N., Cappadocia and Lycaonia on the E., Lycia, Pisidia, and Isauria on the S., and Caria, Lydia, and Mysia on the W. In early times it seems to have included most of Asia Minor; latterly it was divided into Phrygia Major in the S., and Phrygia Minor on the N.W. The Romans divided it into three parts, Phrygia Salutarias on the E., Phrygia Pocatiana on the W., and Phrygia Katckekaumene in the middle. Its cities mentioned in the New Testament are Laodicea, Hierapolis, and Colossae, also Antioch of Pisidia.
Acts 2. 10 P., and Pamphylia, in Egypt, and in the
16. 6 Now when they had gone throughout P.
18. 23 went over (all) the country of..P. in or.

PHU'-RAH, פֻּרָה *beauty.*
A servant of Gideon who went down with him to visit the host of Midian. B.C. 1249.
Judg. 7. 10 go thou with P. thy servant down to the
7. 11 Then went he down with P. his servant

PHUT, PUT, פּוּט *bow.*
1. The third son of Ham. B.C. 2300.
Gen. 10. 6 Cush, and Mizraim, and P., and Canaan
1 Ch. 1. 8 sons of Ham; Cush, and Mizraim, P., and
2. His dwelling Lybia, W. of Egypt.
Eze. 27. 10 They of Persia and of Lud and of P. were
3. His descendants who hired themselves out as mercenary auxiliaries to the Tyrians, &c.
Nah. 3. 9 (it was) infinite; P. and Lubim were thy

PHU'-VAH, PU'-A, PU'-AH, פֻּוָּה, פּוּאָה *utterance.*
1. The second son of Issachar. B.C. 1700.
Gen. 46. 13 Tola, and P., and Job, and Shimron
Num26. 23 the Tolaites: of P., the family of the P.
1 Ch. 7. 1 Now..sons of Issachar (were) Tola, and P.
2. Father of Tola of the tribe of Issachar, who judged Israel after the death of Abimelech. B.C. 1240.
Judg10. 1 Tola the son of P., the son of Dodo, a m.

PHY-GELLUS, Φύγελλος.
One who along with Hermogenes turned away from Paul in Asia.
2 Ti. 1. 15 of whom are P. and Hermogenes

PHYLACTERY --
Phylactery, a guard, charm, φυλακτήριον *phulak.*
Matt23. 5 they make broad their phylacteries, and

PHYSICIAN —
1. *To heal, repair,* רָפָא *rapha.*
Gen. 50. 2 commanded..the physicians..and the p.
2 Ch.16. 12 sought not to the LORD, but to the phys.
Job 13. 4 forgers of lies, ye (are) all physicians of
Jer. 8. 22 (is there) no physician there? why then

2. *A healer, physician,* ἰατρός *iatros.*
Matt 9. 12 They that be whole need not a physician
Mark 2. 17 whole have no need of the physician, but
5. 26 suffered many things of many physicians
Luke 4. 23 say unto me this proverb, Physician, heal
5. 31 They that are whole need not a physician
8. 43 spent all her living upon phy.; Col. 4. 14.

PIBESETH. *See* **PHIBESETH.**

PICK out, to —
To pick out, נָקַר *naqar.*
Prov.30. 17 the ravens of the valley shall pick it out

PICTURE —
1. *Imagery, imagination,* מַשְׂכִּית *maskith.*
Num 33. 52 destroy all their pictures, and destroy all
Prov.25. 11 (is like) apples of gold in pictures of silver

2. *Picture, object,* שְׂכִיָּה *sekiyyah.*
Isa. 2. 16 of Tarshish, and upon all pleasant pictu.

PIECE, (in pieces) —
1. *A separate piece,* בָּדָל *badal.*
Amos 3. 12 two legs, or a piece of an ear; so shall the

2. *A separate piece,* בֶּתֶר *bether.*
Gen. 15. 10 and laid each piece one against another

3. *A part cut off,* גֶּזֶר *gezer.*
Gen. 15. 17 lamp that passed between those pieces

4. *A piece cut off,* הַדָּם *haddam.*
Dan. 2. 5 ye shall be cut in pieces, and your houses
3. 29 shall be cut in pieces, and their houses

5. *A circular cake,* כִּכָּר *kikkar.*
Prov. 6. 26 (a man is brought) to a piece of bread, and
Jer. 37. 21 they should give him daily a piece of br.

6. *A measured thing,* מִדָּה *middah.*
Neh. 3. 11 repaired the other piece, and the tower
3. 19 another piece over against the going up
3. 20 Baruch..earnestly repaired the other pi.
3. 21 another piece, from the door of the house
3. 24 another piece, from the house of Azariah
3. 27 Tekoites repaired another piece, over ag.
3. 30 repaired Hananiah..another piece. After

7. *A part cut off,* נֵתַח *nethach.*
Exod29. 17 thou shalt cut the ram in pieces, and w.
29. 17 put (them) unto his pieces, and unto his
Lev. 1. 6 he shall flay..and cut it into his pieces
1. 12 he shall cut it into his pieces, with his h.
8. 20 cut the ram into pieces..and the pieces
9. 13 they presented..the pieces thereof, and
Judg19. 29 divided her..into twelve pieces, and sent
Eze. 24. 4 Gather the pieces..every good piece, the
24. 6 bring it out piece by piece; let no lot fall

8. *A slice,* פֶּלַח *pelach.*
Judg. 9. 53 a certain woman cast a piece of a mill stone
1 Sa. 30. 12 they gave him a piece of a cake of figs, and
2 Sa. 11. 21 did not a woman cast a piece of a mill st.
Job 41. 24 yea, as hard as a piece of the nether (mi.)
Song 4. 3 like a piece of a pomegranate within thy
6. 7 As a piece of a pomegranate (are) thy te.

9. *A morsel,* פַּת *path.*
Lev. 2. 6 Thou shalt part it in pieces, and pour oil
6. 21 the baken pieces of the meat offering shalt
1 Sa. 2. 36 Put me..that I may eat a piece of bread
Prov 28. 21 for a piece of bread (that) man will tran.

10. *A morsel,* פְּתוֹת *pethoth.*
Eze. 13. 19 for handfuls of barley and for pieces of b.

11. *Rent pieces, rags,* קְרָעִים *qeraim.*
1 Ki.11. 30 Ahijah caught..and rent it (in) twelve p.
11. 31 Take thee ten pieces; for thus saith the
2 Ki. 2. 12 he took hold..and rent them in two pieces

12. *A piece of silver,* רַץ *rats.*
Psa. 68. 30 (till every one) submit himself with pieces

13. *To be cut,* עֲרַט *sarat.*
Zech 12. 3 all that burden .shall be cut in pieces, th.

14. *A patch, piece put upon another,* ἐπίβλημα.
Matt. 9. 16 No man putteth a piece of new cloth unto
Mark 2. 21 No man also seweth a piece of new cloth
Luke 5. 36 No man [putteth a piece of a new garment]
5. 36 [piece] that was (taken) out of the new ag.

15. *Part,* μέρος *meros.*
Luke24. 42 they gave him a piece of a broiled fish, and
[*See also* Beaten out, money, silver, whole.]

PIECE (of flesh), good —
A good gift or present, אֶשְׁפָּר *eshpar.*
2 Sa. 6. 19 to every one..a good piece (of flesh), and
1 Ch.16. 3 a good piece of flesh, and a flagon (of w.)

PIECE (of ground or land) —
A portion, חֶלְקָה *chelqah.*
2 Sa. 23. 11 where was a piece of ground full of lent.
2 Ki. 3. 19 mar every good piece of land with stones
3. 25 on every good piece of land cast, Amos 4. 7
A field, ἀγρός *agros,* Luke 14. 18.

PIECE (of silver) —
1. *A wage of silver,* אֲגוֹרַת כֶּסֶף [*agorah*].
1 Sa. 2. 36 for a piece of silver and a morsel of bread

2. *A drachma, denarius, penny,* δραχμή *drachmē.*
Luke 15. 8 having ten pieces of silver..lose one p.
15. 9 for I have found the piece which I had l.

PIECE that filled up —
Fulness, filling up, πλήρωμα *plērōma.*
Mark 2. 21 new piece that filled it up taketh away f.

PIECES —
[*See* Baken, beat, beaten, break, broken, chop, cut, cut in, dash, dashed, dasheth, hew, hew in, pull, pull in, rend in, rent in, shake, silver, strong, tear in, torn in.]

PIECES, to break in —
To beat or dash in pieces, נָפַץ *naphats,* 3.
Jer. 51. 20, 21, 21, 22, 22, 22, 23, 23 will I break in p.
51. 23 I will also break in pieces with thee the

PIECES, cut in —
To cut self off, מוּל *mul,* 7a.
Psa. 58. 7 he bendeth..let them be as cut in pieces

PIERCE (through), to —
1. *As a lion,* כָּאֲרִי *ka-ari* [A.V. as if from כָּרָה *karah*].
Psa. 22. 16 they pierced my hands and my feet

2. *To pierce through,* דָּקַר *daqar.*
Zech 12. 10 shall look upon me whom they have pier.

3. *To smite, dash,* מָחַץ *machats.*
Num24. 8 and pierce (them) through with his arrows
Judg. 5. 26 when she had pierced and stricken thro.

4. *To pierce,* נָקַב *naqab.*
2 Ki.18. 21 it will go into his hand, and pierce it: so
Job 40. 24 his eyes; (his) nose pierceth through snares
Isa. 36. 6 it will go into his hand, and pierce it: so

5. *To come or go through,* διέρχομαι *dierchomai.*
Luke 2. 35 a sword shall pierce through thy own soul

6. *To arrive or come through,* διϊκνέομαι *diikneomai.*
Heb. 4. 12 piercing even to the dividing asunder of

7. *To pierce or stab through,* ἐκκεντέω *ekkenteō.*
John 19. 37 They shall look on him whom they pierced
Rev. 1. 7 he cometh..and they (also) which pierced

8. *To stab, pierce,* νύττω *nuttō.* νύσσω *nussō.*
John19. 34 one of the soldiers with a spear pierced

9. *To pierce all around,* περιπείρω *peripeirō.*
1 Ti. 6. 10 pierced themselves through with many s.

PIERCED, to be —
To pick out, pierce, נָקַר *naqar,* 3.
Job 30. 17 My bones are pierced in me in the night

PIERCING —
1. *Fleeing,* בָּרִיחַ *bariach.*
Isa. 27. 1 shall punish leviathan the piercing serp.

2. *Piercings,* מַדְקְרוֹת *madqaroth.*
Prov 12. 18 There is that speaketh like the piercings

PIETY—[See *Show.*]

PIGEON, (young) —
1. *A young bird,* גּוֹזָל *gozal.*
Gen. 15. 9 Take me an heifer..and a young pigeon

2. *A dove,* יוֹנָה *yonah.*
Lev. 1. 14 offering of turtle doves, or of young pig.
5. 7 he shall bring..two young pigeons, unto
5. 11 not able to bring..two young pigeons
12. 6 she shall bring..a young pigeon, or a tu.
12. 8 shall bring two turtles, or two young pi.
14. 22 two young pigeons, such as he is able to
14. 30 or of the young pigeons, such as he can
15. 14 shall take to him..two young pigeons, and
15. 29 she shall take unto her..two young pige.
Num. 6. 10 he shall bring..two young pigeons, to the

3. *A dove, pigeon,* περιστερά *peristera.*
Luke 2. 24 A pair of turtle doves, or two young pig.

PI HA-HI'-ROTH, פִּי הַחִירֹת *the place of meadows.*
A place on the west side of Heroopolis (the west gulf of Red Sea), at its N. end.
Exod14. 2 Speak..that..turn and encamp before P.
14. 9 overtook them encamping..beside P., b.
Num33. 7 And they..turned again unto P., which
33. 8 departed from before P., and passed thr.

PILATE, Πιλάτος.
The surname of the fifth Roman procurator of Judea, A.D. 26-36, who after vainly attempting to set Jesus free, gave him up to be crucified; being accused, he was recalled by Tiberius, banished by Caligula to Vienna in Gaul, where he died A.D. 41.
Matt27. 2 and delivered him to Pontius P. the gov.
27. 13 Then said P. unto him, Hearest thou not
27. 17 P. said unto them, Whom will ye that I
27. 22 P. saith unto them, What shall I do then
27. 24 When P. saw that he could prevail noth.
27. 58 He went to P., and begged the body of Je.
27. 58 Then P. commanded the body to be deli.
27. 62 chief priests and Pharisees came..unto P.
27. 65 P. said unto them, Ye have a watch: go
Mark15. 1 carried (him)..and delivered (him) to P.
15. 2 P. asked him, Art thou the king of the J.?
15. 4 P. asked him again, saying, Answerest
15. 5 Jesus yet answered nothing; so that P.
15. 9 But P. answered them, saying, Will ye th.
15. 12 P. answered and said again unto them
15. 14 Then P. said unto them, Why, what evil
15. 15 P...released Barabbas unto them, and de.
Mark15. 43 Joseph..came, and went in boldly unto P
15. 44 P. marvelled if he were already dead: and
Luke 3. 1 Pontius P. being governor of Judea, and
13. 1 whose blood P. had mingled with their
23. 1 the whole multitude..led him unto P.
23. 3 P. asked him, saying, Art thou the king
23. 4 Then said P. to the chief priests and (to)
23. 6 When P. heard of Galilee, he asked whe.
23. 11 set him at nought..and sent him...to P.
23. 12 P. and Herod were made friends together
23. 13 P...called together the chief priests and
23. 20 P. therefore, willing to release Jesus, sp.
23. 24 P. gave sentence that it should be as they
23. 52 This (man) went unto P., and begged the
John18. 29 P. then went out unto them, and said W.
18. 31 Then said P. unto them, Take ye him, and
18. 33 Then P. entered into the judgment hall
18. 35 P. answered, Am I a Jew?..what hast thou
18. 37 P. therefore said unto him, Art thou a ki.
18. 38 P. saith unto him, What is truth? And
19. 1 Then P. therefore took Jesus, and scourged
19. 4 P. therefore went forth again, and saith
19. 6 P. saith unto them, Take ye him, and cr.
19. 8, 13 When P. therefore heard that saying
19. 10 Then saith P. unto him, Speakest thou n.
19. 12 And from thenceforth P. sought to release
19. 15 P. saith unto them, Shall I crucify your
19. 19 P. wrote a title, and put (it) on the cross
19. 21 Then said the chief priests..to P., Write
19. 22 P. answered, What I have written I have
19. 31 The Jews..besought P. that their legs mi.
19. 38 Joseph..besought P...and P. gave (him)
Acts 3. 13 ye..denied him in the presence of P., when
4. 27 Pontius P., with the Gentiles..were gath.
13. 28 yet desired they P. that he should be sl.
1 Ti. 6. 13 who before Pontius P. witnessed a good

PIL'-DASH, פִּלְדָּשׁ *flame of fire.*
Sixth son of Nahor, Abraham's brother. B.C. 1860.
Gen. 22. 22 Chesed, and Hazo, and P., and Jidlaph

PILE (for fire) —
A pile, dwelling, מְדוּרָה *medurah.*
Isa. 30. 33 the pile thereof (is) fire and much wood
Eze. 24. 9 I will even make the pile for fire great

PIL-E'-HA, פִּלְחָא *worship.*
A person or family who, with Nehemiah, sealed the covenant. B.C. 445.
Neh. 10. 24 Hallohesh, P., Shobek

PILGRIMAGE —
Sojourn, sojourning, מָגוּר *magur.*
Gen. 47. 9 days of the years of my pilgrimage (are)
47. 9 my fathers in the days of their pilgrimage
Exod. 6. 4 land of their pilgrimage, wherein they
Psa.119. 54 been my songs in the house of my pilgri.

PILGRIM —
A sojourner, παρεπίδημος *parepidēmos.*
Heb. 11. 13 they were strangers and pilgrims on the
1 Pe. 2. 11 I beseech (you) as strangers and pilgrims

PILL, to —
To peel, פָּצַל *patsal,* 3.
Gen. 30. 37 pilled white strakes in them, and made
30. 38 set the rods which he had pilled before

PILLAR —
1. *Pillars,* אֹמְנוֹת *omenoth.*
2 Ki.18. 16 pillars which Hezekiah king of Judah had

2. *Support,* מִסְעָד *misad.*
1 Ki.10. 12 pillars for the house of the LORD, and for

3. *A thing set up, a standing pillar,* מַצֵּבָה *matstsebah.*
Gen. 28. 18 set it up (for) a pillar, and poured oil upon
28. 22 this stone, which I have set (for) a pillar
31. 13 where thou anointedst the pillar, (and)
31. 45 Jacob took a stone, and set it up (for) a p.
31. 51 Behold this heap, and behold (this) pillar
31. 52 (this) pillar be witness, that I will not p.
31. 52 shalt not pass over this heap and this pil.
35. 14 set up a pillar..(even) a pillar of stone
35. 20 Jacob set a pillar..that (is) the pillar of
Exod24. 4 builded..twelve pillars, according to the
Deut12. 3 break their pillars, and burn their groves
2 Sa. 18. 18 Now Absalom..reared up for himself a p.
18. 18 called the pillar after his own name: and
Isa. 19. 19 a pillar at the border thereof to the LORD

4. *Any thing fixed, a fixture,* מָצוּק *matsuq.*
1 Sa. 2. 8 for the pillars of the earth (are) the LORD'S

5. *To be set up,* נָצַב *natsab,* 6.
Judg. 9. 6 by the plain of the pillar that (was) in S.

6. *Any thing set up, a monument,* נְצִיב *netsib.*
Gen. 19. 26 looked back..and she became a pillar of

7. *A pillar, column,* עַמּוּד *ammud.*
Exod13. 21 before them by day in a pillar of a cloud
13. 21 by night in a pillar of fire, to give them
13. 22 the pillar of the cloud by day, nor the pi.
14. 19 the pillar of the cloud went from before
14. 24 through the pillar of fire and of the cloud
26. 32 four pillars of shittim (wood) overlaid
26. 37 shalt make..five pillars (of) shittim (wo.)
27. 10 twenty pillars thereof, and their twenty
27. 10, 11 hooks of the pillars and their fillets
27. 11 twenty pillars and their twenty sockets
27. 12 And..their pillars ten, and their sockets
27. 14, 15 pillars three, and their sockets three
27. 16 their pillars (shall be) four, and their so.
27. 17 All the pillars round about the court (sh.)
33. 9 the cloudy pillar descended, and stood

Exod33. 10 all the people saw the cloudy pillar stand
35. 11 his boards, his bars, his pillars, and his s.
35. 17 his pillars, and their sockets, and the ha.
36. 36 he made thereunto four pillars (of) shittim
36. 38 And the five pillars of it with their hooks
38. 10 Their pillars (were) twenty, and their br.
38. 10, 11, 12, 17 the hooks of the pillars and
38. 11 their pillars (were) twenty, and their soc.
38. 12 their pillars ten, and their sockets ten
38. 14, 15 pillars three, and their sockets three
38. 17 sockets for the pillars..hooks of the pill.
38. 17 pillars of the court (were) filleted with s.
38. 19 their pillars (were) four, and their sockets
38. 28 he made hooks for the pillars, and overl.
39. 33 his bars, and his pillars, and his sockets
39. 40 his pillars, and his sockets, and the han.
40. 18 put in the bars..and reared up his pillars
Num. 3. 36 the pillars thereof, and the sockets ther.
3. 37 the pillars of the court round about, and
4. 31 and the pillars thereof, and the sockets
4. 32 the pillars of the court round about, and
12. 5 LORD came down in the pillar of the cloud
14. 14 in a pillar of a cloud, and in a pillar of fire
Deut31. 15 in a pillar of a cloud: and the pillar of the
Judg16. 25 they called and..set him between the p.
16. 26 that I may feel the pillars whereupon the
16. 29 middle pillars upon which the house stood
20. 40 to arise up out of the city with a pillar of
1 Ki. 7. 2 pillars, with cedar beams upon the pillars
7. 3 that (lay) on forty five pillars, fifteen (in) a
7. 6 And he made a porch of pillars, the length
7. 6 the (other) pillars and the thick beam (w.)
7. 15 For he cast two pillars of brass, of eighteen
7. 16 chapiters..to set upon the tops of the pi.
7. 17, 19, 41, 41, chapiters..upon the top of..p.
7. 18 he made the pillars, and two rows round
7. 20 the chapiters upon the two pillars (had
7. 21 the pillars..the right pillar..the left pil.
7. 22 top of the pillars..the work of the pillars
7. 41 The two pillars, and the (two) bowls of the
7. 41 top of the two pillars..top of the pillars
7. 42 the chapiters that (were) upon the pillars
2 Ki. 11. 14 the king stood by a pillar, as the manner
23. 3 the king stood by a pillar, and made a
25. 13 the pillars of brass..in the house of the L.
25. 16 The two pillars, one sea, and the bases w.
25. 17 The height of the..pillar (was) eighteen
25. 17 like unto these had the second pillar with
1 Ch. 18. 8 and the pillars, and the vessels of brass
2 Ch. 3. 15 two pillars of thirty and five cubits high
3. 16 put (them) on the heads of the pillars; and
3. 17 he reared up the pillar before the temple
4. 12 the two pillars, and the pommels, and the
4. 12 top of the two pillars..the top of the pil.
4. 13 the chapters which (were) upon the pillars
23. 13 king stood at his pillar at the entering in
Neh. 9. 12 a cloudy pillar; and in the night by a pi.
9. 19 the pillar of the cloud..the pillar of fire
Esth. 1. 6 fastened to silver rings and pillars of
Job 9. 6 shaketh the earth..and the pillars thereof
26. 11 The pillars of heaven tremble and are af.
Psa 75. 3 earth..I bear up the pillars of it. Selah
99. 7 He spake unto them in the cloudy pillar
Prov. 9. 1 Wisdom..hath hewn out her seven pillars
Song 3. 10 He made the pillars thereof (of) silver, the
5. 15 His legs (are as) pillars of marble set upon
Jer 1. 18 an iron pillar, and brasen walls against
27. 19 concerning the pillars, and concerning the
52. 17 the pillars of brass that (were) in the ho.
52. 20 The two pillars, one sea, and twelve bra.
52. 21 the pillars, the height of one pillar (was)
52. 22 the second pillar also and the pomegran
Eze. 40. 49 pillars by the posts, one on this side, and
42. 6 had not pillars as the pillars of the courts

8. *Palm trees, pillars,* תִּימָרוֹת *timeroth.*
Song 3. 6 this that cometh out..like pillars of sm.
Joel 2. 30 wonders..blood, and fire, and pillars of

9. *A pillar, column,* στύλος *stulos.*
Gal. 2. 9 Cephas, and John, who seemed to be pil.
1 Ti. 3. 15 God..the pillar and ground of the truth
Rev. 3. 12 I make a pillar in the temple of my God
10. 1 as it were the sun, and his feet as pillars

PILLOW —

1. *A mattress,* כְּבִיר *kebir.*
1 Sa. 19. 13, 16 a pillow of goats' (hair) for his bolster

2. *Pillows,* כְּסָתוֹת *kesathoth.*
Eze. 13. 18 that sew pillows to all arm holes, and m.
13. 20 I (am) against your pillows, wherewith ye

3. *Bolster, pillow,* מְרַאֲשֹׁת *meraashoth.*
Gen. 28. 11 put (them for) his pillows, and lay down
28. 18 the stone that he had put (for) his pillows

4. *A pillow, stern,* προσκεφάλαιον *proskephalaion*
Mark 4. 38 was in the hinder part..asleep on a pillow

PILOT —

A pilot, חֹבֵל *chobel.*
Eze. 27. 8 thy wise (men)..in thee, were thy pilots
27. 27 thy pilots, thy calkers, and the occupiers
27. 28 shake at the sound of the cry of thy pilots
27. 29 all the pilots of the sea, shall come down

PIL'-TAI, פִּלְטַי *Jah causes to escape.*
A priest in Jerusalem in the days of Joiakim, grandson of Jozadak. B.C. 600.
Neh. 12. 17 Zichri; of Miniamin, of Moadiah, P.

PIN —

A pin, nail, יָתֵד *yathed.*
Exod27. 19 all the pins thereof, and all the pins of the
35. 18 The pins of the tabernacle, and the pins
38. 20 all the pins of the tabernacle, and of the
38. 31 pins of the tabernacle, and all the pins of
39. 40 his pins, and all the vessels of the service
Num. 3. 37 their sockets, and their pins, and their c.
4. 32 their pins, and their cords, with all their
Judg16. 14 she fastened (it) with the pin, and said unto
16. 14 went away with the pin of the beam and
Eze. 15. 3 will (men) take a pin of it to hang any

PINE (tree) —

1. *Pine, elm, plane or fir,* תִּדְהָר *tidhar.*
Isa. 41. 19 (and) the pine, and the box tree together
60. 13 the pine tree, and the box together, to be.

2. *A tree of oil, very fruitful,* עֵץ שֶׁמֶן *ets shemen.*
Neh. 8. 15 pine branches, and myrtle branches, and

PINE away, to —

1. *To flow away,* זוּב *zub.*
Lam. 4. 9 these pine away, stricken through for (wa.

2. *To become wasted or consumed away,* מָקַק *maqaq,* 2.
Lev. 26. 39 they that are left of you shall pine away
26. 39 and also..shall they pine away with them
Eze. 24. 23 ye shall pine away for your iniquities, and
33. 10 sins (be) upon us, and we pine away in th.

3. *To dry up, wither,* ξηραίνω *xērainō.*
Mark 9. 18 gnashed with his teeth, and pineth away

PINING sickness —

Weakness, heaviness, דַּלָּה *dallah.*
Isa. 38. 12 he will cut me off with pining sickness

PINNACLE —

A little wing, πτερύγιον *pterugion.*
Matt. 4. 5 and setteth him on a pinnacle of the temple
Luke 4. 9 set him on a pinnacle of the temple, and

PI'-NON, פִּינֹן *ore pit.*
A duke of Edom of the family of Esau. B.C. 1470.
Gen. 36. 41 Duke Aholibamah, duke Elah, duke P.
1 Ch. 1. 52 Duke Aholibamah, duke Elah, duke P.

PIPE —

1. *A pipe or flute,* חָלִיל *chalil.*
1 Sa. 10. 5 tabret, and a pipe, and a harp, before them
1 Ki. 1. 40 the people piped with pipes, and rejoiced
Isa. 5. 12 the tabret and pipe, and wine, are in their
30. 29 when one goeth with a pipe to come into
Jer. 48. 36 mine heart shall sound for Moab like pi.
48. 36 mine heart shall sound like pipes for the

2. *A pipe, a casting,* מוּצֶקֶת *mutseqeth.*
Zech. 4. 2 seven pipes to the seven lamps, which (are)

3. *A bezal for precious stones,* נֶקֶב *neqeb.*
Eze. 28. 13 workmanship of thy tabrets and of thy p.

4. *Pipes, tubes,* צַנְתָּרוֹת *tsantaroth.*
Zech. 4. 12 which through the two golden pipes em.

5. *A pipe or flute,* αὐλός *aulos.*
1 Co. 14. 7 whether pipe or harp, except they give a

PIPE, to —

1. *To pipe,* חָלַל *chalal,* 3.
1 Ki. 1. 40 the people piped with pipes, and rejoiced

2. *To play on a pipe or flute,* αὐλέω *auleō.*
Matt11. 17 We have piped unto you, and ye have not
Luke 7. 32 We have piped unto you, and ye have not
1 Co. 14. 7 shall it be known what is piped or harped?

PIPER —

One that plays on a pipe or flute, αὐλητής *aulētēs.*
Rev. 18. 22 musicians, and of pipers, and trumpeters

PIR'-AM, פִּרְאָם *wild, roving.*
A king of the Amorites or Canaanites who dwelt at Jarmuth and was slain by Joshua. B.C. 1451.
Josh. 10. 3 Adoni-zedek..sent..unto P. king of Jar.

PIR-A'-THON, פִּרְעָתוֹן *peak, top.*
An elevation in the hill of the Amalekites in Ephraim, where Abdon the son of Hillel was buried, after judging Israel eight years; now *Ferata.*
Judg12. 15 And Abdon..was buried in P. in the land

PIRATHONITE, פִּרְעָתֹנִי.
An inhabitant of the preceding place.
Judg12. 13, 15 Abdon the son of Hillel the P.
2 Sa. 23. 30 Benaiah the P., Hiddai of the brooks of
1 Ch. 11. 31 Ithai the son of Ribai..Benaiah the P.
27. 14 The eleventh (captain..was) Benaiah the P.

PIS'-GAH, פִּסְגָּה *peak, point.*
That ridge of the mountains of Abarim, of which Nebo is the highest point, in the kingdom of Sihon which he had taken from Moab.
Num21. 20 from Bamoth (in) the valley..to..top of P.
23. 14 he brought him..to the top of P., and b.
Deut. 3. 27 Get thee up into the top of P., and lift up
4. 49 sea of the plain, under the springs of P.
34. 1 Moses went up..to the top of P., that (is)

PI-SI-DI'A, Πισιδία.
A province forming part of the great table land in Asia Minor, having Pamphylia on the S., Phrygia on the N.; its chief city was Antioch, a Roman colony.
Acts 13. 14 they came to Antioch in P., and went into
14. 24 after they had passed throughout P., they

PI'-SON, פִּישׁוֹן *freely flowing.*
One of the four rivers of Eden, supposed to have been the Phasis, *i.e.* Araxes; the *Besynga,* the *Indus,* the *Ganges,* the *Hyphasis,* the *Nile* or the *Goshap.*
Gen. 2. 11 The name of the first (is) P.: that (is) it

PIS'-PAH, פִּסְפָּה *expansion.*
An Asherite, a son of Jether. B.C. 1500.
1 Ch. 7. 38 And the sons of Jether; Jephunneh, and P.

PISS —

1. *Urine,* שֵׁינַיִם *shenim.* (older reading of No. 2).
2 Ki. 18. 27 they may..drink their own piss with you
Isa. 36. 12 they may..drink their own piss with you

2. *Water of the feet, urine,* מֵי רַגְלַיִם *me raglayim.*
2 Ki. 18. 27 they may..drink their own piss with you?
Isa. 36. 12 they may..drink their own piss with you?

PISS, to —

To make water, שָׁתַן *shathan,* 5.
1 Sa. 25. 22, 34 any that pisseth against the wall
1 Ki. 14. 10 cut off..him that pisseth against the wall
16. 11 he left him not one that pisseth against a
21. 21 cut off..him that pisseth against the wall
2 Ki. 9. 8 cut off..him that pisseth against the wall

PIT —

1. *A pit or well,* בְּאֵר *beer.*
Gen. 14. 10 the vale of Siddim (was full of) slime pits
Psa. 55. 23 bring them down into the pit of destruc.
69. 15 and let not the pit shut her mouth upon
Prov 23. 27 and a strange woman (is) a narrow pit

2. *A pit or well,* בּוֹר *bor.*
Gen. 37. 20 let us slay him, and cast..into some pit
37. 22 cast him into this pit that (is) in the will.
37. 24 cast him into a pit: and the pit (was) em.
37. 28 lifted up Joseph out of the pit, and sold
37. 29 Reuben returned into the pit; and, beh.
37. 29 Joseph (was) not in the pit; and he rent
Exod21. 33 open a pit, or if a man shall dig a pit
21. 34 The owner of the pit shall make (it) good
Lev. 11. 36 a fountain or pit, (wherein there is) plen.
1 Sa. 13. 6 in rocks, and in high places, and in pits
2 Sa. 23. 20 slew a lion in the midst of a pit in time
2 Ki. 10. 14 slew them at the pit of the shearing hou.
1 Ch. 11. 22 and slew a lion in a pit in a snowy day
Psa. 7. 15 He made a pit, and digged it, and is fall.
28. 1 I become like them that go..into the pit
30. 3 that I should not go down to the pit
40. 2 brought me up also out of an horrible pit
88. 4 counted with them that go..into the pit
88. 6 Thou hast laid me in the lowest pit, in d.
143. 7 like unto them that go down into the pit
Prov. 1. 12 whole, as those that go down into the pit
28. 17 man that doeth violence..flee to the pit
Isa. 14. 15 be brought..to hell, to the sides of the pit
14. 19 that go down to the stones of the pit; as
24. 22 (as) prisoners are gathered in the pit, and
38. 18 they that go down into the pit cannot hope
51. 1 the hole of the pit (whence) ye are digged
Jer. 41. 7 into the midst of the pit, he, and the men
41. 9 the pit wherein Ishmael had cast all the
Eze. 26. 20 down with them that descend into the pit
26. 20 with them that go down to the pit, that
31. 14 delivered..with them that go..to the pit
31. 16 with them that descend into the pit: and
32. 18, 24, 25, 29, 30 them that go down to the pit
32. 23 Whose graves are set in the sides of the p.
Zech. 9. 11 sent..out of the pit wherein (is) no water

3. *A ditch, marshy place,* גֵּב *geb.*
Jer. 14. 3 they came to the pits, (and) found no w.

4. *A ditch, marshy place,* גֶּבֶא *gebe.*
Isa. 30. 14 or to take water (withal) out of the pit

5. *A pit,* גּוּמָּץ *gummats.*
Eccl. 10. 8 He that diggeth a pit shall fall into it

6. *Opening, hole,* פַּחַת *pachath.*
2 Sa. 17. 9 he is hid now in some pit, or in some (o.)
18. 17 cast him into a great pit in the wood, and
Isa. 24. 17 the pit, and the snare, (are) upon thee, O
24. 18 he who fleeth..shall fall into the pit; and
24. 18 that cometh up out of the midst of the pit
Jer. 48. 43 the pit, and the snare, (shall be) upon thee
48. 44 He that fleeth..shall fall into the pit; and
48. 44 he that getteth up out of the pit shall be

7. *Under world, hades,* שְׁאוֹל *sheol.*
Num16. 30 and they go down quick into the pit; then
16. 33 went down alive into the pit, and the ea.
Job 17. 16 They shall go down to the bars of the pit

8. *A pit, corruption,* שׁוּחָה *shuchah.*
Prov22. 14 The mouth of strange women (is) a deep p.
Jer. 2. 6 led..through a land of deserts and of pits
18. 20 for they have digged a pit for my soul
18. 22 they have digged a pit to take me, and hid

9. *A pit, corruption,* שְׁחוּת *shechuth.*
Prov 28. 10 he shall fall himself into his own pit: but

10. *A pit, corruption,* שְׁחִית *shechith.*
Lam. 4. 20 the anointed..was taken in their pits, of

11. *A pit, corruption,* שַׁחַת *shachath.*
Job 33. 18 He keepeth back his soul from the pit, and
33. 24 Deliver him from going down to the pit; I
33. 28 deliver his soul from going into the pit, and
33. 30 bring back his soul from the pit, to be en.
Psa. 9. 15 heathen are sunk down in the pit (that)
30. 9 What profit..when I go down to the pit?
35. 7 they hid for me their net (in) a pit, (which)
94. 13 rest..until the pit be digged for the wic.
Prov 26. 27 Whoso diggeth a pit shall fall therein; and
Isa. 38. 17 thou hast..(delivered it) from the pit of c.
51. 14 that he should not die in the pit, nor that
Eze. 19. 4, 8 he was taken in their pit
28. 8 They shall bring thee down to the pit, and

12. *A pit, corruption,* שְׁחִיתָה *shichah.*
Psa. 57. 6 they have digged a pit before me, into the
119. 85 The proud have digged pits for me, which
Jer. 18. 22 for they have digged a pit to take me, and

13. *A deep place,* βόθυνος *bothunos.*
Matt 12. 11 if it fall into a pit on the sabbath day, will

14. *A pit, dungeon,* φρέαρ *phrear.*
Luke 14. 5 shall have an ass or an ox fallen into a pit
Rev. 9. 1 was given the key of the bottomless pit
9. 2 [opened the bottomless pit]..out of the p.
9. 2 darkened by reason of the smoke of the pit

PITCH —

1. *Pitch,* זֶפֶת *zepheth.*
Exod. 2. 3 daubed it with slime and with pitch, and
Isa. 34. 9 streams thereof shall be turned into pitch
34. 9 land thereof shall become burning pitch

2. *Cypress,* כֹּפֶר *kopher.*
Gen. 6. 14 shalt pitch it within and without with p.

PITCH, be pitched, to —

1. *To sink down, encamp,* חָנָה *chanah.*
Exod 17. 1 pitched in Rephidim: and (there was) no
19. 2 had pitched in the wilderness: and there
Num. 1. 51 when the tabernacle is to be pitched, the
1. 52 the children of Israel shall pitch their te.
1. 53 Levites shall pitch round about the tabe.
2. 2 shall pitch..far off..shall they pitch
2. 3 shall they.. of the camp of Judah pitch
2. 5 those that do pitch next unto him (shall
2. 12 those which pitch by him (shall be) the t.
2. 34 so they pitched by their standards, and
3. 23 shall pitch behind the tabernacle westw.
3. 29, 35 shall pitch on the side of the tabern.
9. 18 at the commandment of the LORD they p.
12. 16 and pitched in the wilderness of Paran
21. 10 children of Israel set forward, and pitched
21. 11 pitched at Ije-abarim, in the wilderness
21. 12 removed, and pitched in the valley of Z.
21. 13 removed, and pitched on the other side
22. 1 pitched in the plains of Moab on this side
33. 5 removed from Rameses, and pitched in S.
33. 6 pitched in Etham, which (is) in the edge
33. 7 turned..and they pitched before Migdol
33. 8 went three day's journey..pitched in M.
33. 9 and came unto Elim..and they pitched
33. 15 they departed from Rephidim, and pitc.
33. 16 removed..and pitched at Kibroth-hatta.
33. 18 they departed from Hazeroth, and pitched
33. 19 departed from Rithmah, and pitched at R.
33. 20 departed from Rimmon-parez, and pitched
33. 21 removed from Libnah, and pitched at R.
33. 22 journeyed from Rissah, and pitched in K.
33. 23 went from Kehelathah, and pitched in m.
33. 25 they removed from Haradah, and pitched
33. 27 departed from Tahath, and pitched at T.
33. 28 removed from Tarah, and pitched in M.
33. 29 went from Mithcah, and pitched in Hash.
33. 31 departed from Moseroth..pitched in Be.
33. 33 went from Hor-hagidgad..pitched in Jo.
33. 36 pitched in the wilderness of Zin, which
33. 37 pitched in mount Hor, in the edge of the
33. 41 departed from mount Hor, and pitched
33. 42 departed from Zalmonah..pitched in P.
33. 43 departed from Punon, and pitched in O.
33. 44 departed from Oboth, and pitched in Ij.
33. 45 departed from Iim, and pitched in Dibon.
33. 47 pitched in the mountains of Abarim, be.
33. 48 pitched in the plains of Moab, by Jordan
33. 49 pitched by Jordan, from Beth-jesimoth
Josh. 8. 11 pitched on the north side of Ai: now (th.
11. 5 pitched together at the waters of Merom
Judg 6. 33 went over, and pitched in the valley of J.
7. 1 pitched beside the well of Harod: so that
11. 18 pitched on the other side of Arnon, but
11. 20 pitched in Jahaz, and fought against Isr.
15. 9 pitched in Judah, and spread themselves
18. 12 and pitched in Kirjath-jearim, in Judah
1 Sa. 4. 1 Now Israel..pitched beside Eben-ezer
4. 1 and the Philistines pitched in Aphek
13. 5 pitched in Michmash, eastward from Bet.
17. 1 pitched between Shochoh and Azekah, in
17. 2 pitched by the valley of Elah, and set the
26. 3 Saul pitched in the hill of Hachilah, wh.
26. 5 came to the place where Saul had pitched
26. 5 and the people pitched round about him
28. 4 came and pitched in Shunem..and they
29. 1 pitched by a fountain which (is) in Jezreel
2 Sa. 17. 26 and Absalom pitched in the land of Gil.
23. 13 troop of the Philistines pitched in the v.
24. 5 passed over Jordan, and pitched in Aroer
1 Ki. 20. 27 pitched before them like two little flocks
20. 29 they pitched one over against the other s.
2 Ki. 25. 1 pitched against it; and they built forts
1 Ch. 19. 7 king..who came and pitched before Mede.
Jer. 52. 4 pitched against it, and built forts against

2. *To cover,* כָּפַר *kaphar.*
Gen. 6. 14 and shalt pitch it within and without with

3. *To incline,* נָטָה *natah.*
Gen. 12. 8 pitched his tent, (having) Bethel on the w.
26. 25 pitched his tent there: and there Isaac's s.
Exod 33. 7 pitched it without the camp, afar off from
Judg 4. 11 pitched his tent unto the plain of Zaanaim
2 Sa. 6. 17 tabernacle that David had pitched for it
1 Ch. 15. 1 prepared a place..and pitched for it a te.
16. 1 midst of the tent that David had pitched
2 Ch. 1. 4 for he had pitched a tent for it at Jerus.

4. *To cause to stand, raise up,* קוּם *qum,* 5.
Josh. 4. 20 twelve stones..did Joshua pitch in Gilgal

5. *To strike, fix,* תָּקַע *taqa.*
Gen. 31. 25 Jacob had pitched..his brethren pitched
Jer. 6. 3 they shall pitch (their) tents against her

6. *To join together, unite, fix, pitch a tent,* πήγνυμι.
Heb. 8. 2 tabernacle, which the Lord pitched, and

PITCH a tent, to —

1. *To move one's tent,* אָהַל *ahal.*
Gen. 13. 12 and Lot..pitched (his) tent toward Sodom

2. *To move one's tent,* אָהַל *ahal,* 3.
Isa. 13. 20 neither shall the Arabians pitch tent th.

3. *To encamp, sink down,* חָנָה *chanah.*
Gen. 26. 17 and pitched his tent in the valley of Gerar
33. 18 Jacob..pitched his tent before the city
Num 9. 17 the children of Israel pitched their tents
Deut. 1. 33 search you out a place to pitch your tents

PITCHER —

1. *A pitcher,* כַּד *kad.*
Gen. 24. 14 Let down thy pitcher, I pray thee, that I
24. 15 Rebekah came out..with her pitcher upon
24. 16 went down to the well, and filled her pi.
24. 17 Let me..drink a little water of thy pitch.
24. 18 let down her pitcher upon her hand, and
24. 20 and emptied her pitcher into the trough
24. 43 Give me..a little water of thy pitcher to
24. 45 Rebekah came forth with her pitcher on
24. 46 made haste, and let down her pitcher fr.
Judg. 7. 16 empty pitchers, and lamps within the pi.
7. 19, 20 blew the the trumpets, and brake the p.
Eccl. 12. 6 or the pitcher be broken at the fountain

2. *A bottle, flagon,* נֵבֶל, נֶבֶל *nebel.*
Lam. 4. 2 how are they esteemed as earthen pitch.

3. *A clay or earthen pitcher,* κεράμιον *keramion.*
Mark 14. 13 meet you a man bearing a pitcher of wa.
Luke 22. 10 man meet you, bearing a pitcher of water

PI'-THOM, פִּתֹם *narrow pass.*
A city in Lower Egypt, in Goshen, E. of the Nile, twenty four miles from Heroopolis; a city in Upper Egypt, three days' journey from Cairo, (called also *Fayyum*), has the same name.
Exod. 1. 11 they built for Pharaoh treasure cities, P.

PI'-THON, פִּיתוֹן *harmless.*
A son of Micah, grandson of Jonathan son of Saul. B.C. 1000.
1 Ch. 8. 35 the sons of Michah (were) P., and Melech
9. 41 the sons of Micah (were) P., and Melech

PITIED, to be —

Mercies, bowels, רַחֲמִים *rachamim.*
Psa. 106. 46 He made them also to be pitied of all th.

PITIFUL, (very)—

1. *Merciful,* רַחְמָנִי *rachmani.*
Lam. 4. 10 The hands of the pitiful women have so.

2. *Tender hearted, compassionate,* εὔσπλαγχνος.
1 Pe. 3. 8 love as brethren, (be) pitiful, (be) court.

3. *Very tender hearted, or compa.* πολύσπλαγχνος.
Jas. 5. 11 the Lord is [very pitiful], and of tender

PITY —

1. *Pity,* חֶמְלָה *chemlah.*
Isa. 63. 9 in his love and in his pity he redeemed

2. *Loving kindness,* חֶסֶד *chesed.*
Job 6. 14 To him that is afflicted pity (should be s.)

3. *Mercies, bowels,* רַחֲמִים *rachamim.*
Amos 1. 11 did cast off all pity, and his anger did t.

PITY (on or upon), to have or take —

1. *To spare, pity,* חוּס *chus.*
Deut. 7. 16 thine eye shall have no pity upon them
13. 8 neither shall thine eye pity him, neither
19. 13 Thine eye shall not pity him: but thou
19. 21 thine eye shall not pity..life..for life, e.
25. 12 cut off her hand, thine eye shall not pity
Eze. 16. 5 None eye pitied thee, to do any of these
Jon. 4. 10 Thou hast had pity on the gourd, for the

2. *To have pity, spare,* חָמַל *chamal.*
2 Sa. 12. 6 restore the lamb..because he had no pity
Jer. 13. 14 I will not pity, nor spare, nor have mercy
15. 5 who shall have pity upon thee, O Jerus.?
21. 7 shall not spare them, neither have pity
Lam. 2. 2 Lord..hath not pitied: he hath thrown
2. 17 hath thrown down, and hath not pitied
2. 21 thou hast slain (them..and) not pitied
3. 43 thou hast slain, thou hast not pitied
Eze. 5. 11 eye spare, neither will I have any pity
7. 4 neither will I have pity: but I will
7. 9 shall not spare, neither will I have pity
8. 18 shall not spare, neither will I have pity
9. 5 let not your eye spare, neither have ye p.
9. 10 shall not spare, neither will I have pity
36. 21 But I had pity for mine holy name, which
Joel 2. 18 Then will the LORD be jealous..and pity
Zech. 11. 5 and their own shepherds pity them not
11. 6 For I will no more pity the inhabitants

3. *To be gracious,* חָנַן *chanan.*
Job 19. 21 Have pity upon me, have pity upon me
Prov 19. 17 He that hath pity upon the poor lendeth
28. 8 he shall gather it for him that will pity

4. *Pity, object of pity,* מַחְמָל *machmal.*
Eze. 24. 21 that which your soul pitieth; and your

5. *To move, bemoan,* נוּד *nud.*
Psa. 69. 20 and I looked (for some) to take pity, but

6. *To love, pity,* רָחַם *racham,* 3.
Psa. 103. 13 father pitieth (his) children, (so) the LORD
Isa. 13. 18 shall have no pity on the fruit of the womb

7. *To be kind, tender,* ἐλεέω *eleeō.*
Matt 18. 33 compassion..even as I had pity on thee?

PLACE —

1. *A place,* אֲתַר *athar.*
Ezra 5. 15 let the house of God be builded in his pl.
6. 3 place where they offered sacrifices, and
6. 5 vessels..be restored..(every one) to his p.
6. 7 Jews, build this house of God in his place
Dan. 2. 35 no place was found for them; and the st.

2. *A house,* בַּיִת *bayith.*
Exod 25. 27 shall the rings be for places of the staves
26. 29 make their rings (of) gold (for) places for
30. 4 they shall be for places for the staves to
36. 34 made their rings (of) gold (to be) places
37. 14 the places for the staves to bear the tabl
37. 27 to be places for the staves to bear it with
38. 5 the grate of brass, (to be) places for the
2 Sa. 15. 17 and tarried in a place that was far off
1 Ch. 28. 11 thereof, and of the place of the mercy seat
Neh. 2. 3 place of my fathers' sepulchres, (lieth) wa.
Esth. 7. 8 returned..into the place of the banquet
Job 8. 17 wrapped about..(and) seeth the place of
Prov. 8. 2 She standeth..in the places of the paths
Eze. 41. 9 place of the side chambers that (were) w.
46. 24 These (are) the places of them that boil

3. *Border,* גְּבוּלָה *gebulah.*
Isa. 28. 25 appointed barley, and the rye, in their p.?

4. *Hand,* יָד *yad.*
Num. 2. 17 every man in his place by their standards
Deut. 2. 37 unto any place of the river Jabbok, nor
23. 12 Thou shalt have a place also without the
1 Sa. 15. 12 he set him up a place, and is gone about
2 Sa. 18. 18 it is called unto this day, Absalom's place
Psa. 141. 6 their judges are overthrown in stony pla.
Isa. 56. 5 within my walls a place and a name better
Jer. 6. 3 they shall feed every one in his place
Eze. 21. 19 choose thou a place, choose (it) at the he.

5. *To sit down or still,* יָשַׁב *yashab.*
2 Sa. 23. 7 utterly burned with fire in the..place

6. *Station, base,* כֵּן *ken.*
Gen. 40. 13 restore thee unto thy place: and thou sh.

7. *A base, fixed place,* מָכוֹן *makon.*
Exod 15. 17 the place..thou hast made for thee to dw.
1 Ki. 8. 13 a settled place for thee to abide in for ever
8. 39, 43 hear thou in heaven thy dwelling pl.
8. 49 hear..in heaven thy dwelling place, and
2 Ch. 6. 2 an house..and a place for thy dwelling
6. 30 hear thou from heaven thy dwelling pla.
6. 33 hear thou..from thy dwelling place, and
6. 39 hear thou..from thy dwelling place, their
Ezra 2. 68 for the house of God to set it up in his p.
Psa. 33. 14 From the place of his habitation he look.
Dan. 8. 11 the place of his sanctuary was cast down

8. *Habitation,* מְעוֹנָה *meonah.*
Job 37. 8 go into dens, and remain in their places

9. *Station, standing,* מַעֲמָד *maamad.*
2 Ch. 35. 15 singers..(were) in their place, according to

10. *A place of standing,* מָקוֹם *maqom.*
Gen. 1. 9 waters..be gathered together unto one p.
12. 6 passed through the land unto the place of
13. 3 unto the place where his tent had been at
13. 4 Unto the place of the altar, which he had
13. 14 look from the place where thou art north.
18. 24 not spare the place for the fifty righteous
18. 26 then I will spare all the place for their s.
18. 33 and Abraham returned unto his place
19. 12 whatsoever..bring (them) out of this place
19. 13 For we will destroy this place, because the
19. 14 said, Up, get you out of this place; for the
19. 27 to the place where he stood before the L.
20. 11 Surely the fear of God (is) not in this pl.
20. 13 at every place whither we shall come, say
21. 31 Wherefore he called that place Beer-sheba
22. 3 went unto the place of which God had t.
22. 4 lifted up his eyes, and saw the place afar
22. 9 came to the place which God had told him
22. 14 Abraham called the name of that place J.
26. 7 the men of the place asked (him) of his
26. 7 men of the place should kill me for Reb.
28. 11 lighted upon a certain place, and tarried
28. 11 and he took of the stones of that place, and
28. 11 pillows, and lay down in that place to sl.
28. 16 Surely the LORD is in this place; and I k.
28. 17 afraid, and said, How dreadful (is) this p.!
28. 19 he called the name of that place Beth-el
29. 3 again upon the well's mouth in his place
29. 22 gathered together all the men of the place
30. 25 I may go unto mine own place, and to my
31. 55 Laban departed, and returned unto his p.
32. 2 he called the name of that place Mahan.
32. 30 Jacob called the name of the place Peniel
33. 17 therefore the name of the place is called
35. 7 built there an altar, and called the place
35. 13 God went up from him in the place where
35. 14 set up a pillar in the place where he tal.
35. 15 Jacob called the name of the place where
36. 40 after their places, by their names; duke
38. 21 Then he asked the men of that place, say.
38. 22 also the men of the place said, (that) there
39. 20 a place where the king's prisoners (were)

Gen. 40. 3 prison, the place where Joseph (was) bo.
Exod. 3. 5 place whereon thou standest (is) holy gr.
3. 8 place of the Canaanites, and the Hittites
16. 29 let no man go out of his place on the sev.
17. 7 he called the name of the place Massah
18. 23 all..shall also go to their place in peace
20. 24 In all places where I record my name I
21. 13 appoint thee a place whither he shall flee
23. 20 thee into the place which I have prepared
29. 31 shalt..seethe his flesh in the holy place
33. 21 (there is) a place by me, and thou shalt s.
Lev. 1. 16 on the east part, by the place of the ashes
4. 12 without the camp unto a clean place, wh.
4. 24, 33 in the place where they kill the burnt
4. 29 and slay..in the place of the burnt offer.
6. 11 carry..without the camp unto a clean p.
6. 16 shall it be eaten in the holy place; in the
6. 25 In the place where the burnt offering is
6. 26 in the holy place shall it be eaten, in the
6. 27 whereon it was sprinkled in the holy pla.
7. 2 In the place where they kill the burnt of.
7. 6 it shall be eaten in the holy place: it (is)
10. 13 ye shall eat it in the holy place, because
10. 14 wave breast..shall ye eat in a clean place
10. 17 not eaten the sin offering in the holy pla.
13. 19 in the place of the boil there be a white r.
14. 13 in the place where he shall kill the sin
14. 13 and the burnt offering, in the holy place
14. 28 place of the blood of the trespass offering
14. 40 cast them into an unclean place without
14. 41 off without the city into an unclean place
14. 45 forth out of the city into an unclean place
16. 24 wash his flesh with water in..holy place
24. 9 they shall eat it in the holy place: for it
Num. 9. 17 in the place where the cloud abode, there
10. 29 We are journeying unto the place of whi.
11. 3, 34 And he called the name of the place
13. 24 The place was called the brook Eshcol, b.
14. 40 the place which the LORD hath promised
18. 31 ye shall eat it in every place, ye and your
19. 9 lay..up without the camp in a clean pla.
20. 5 in unto this evil place? it (is) no place of
21. 3 he called the name of the place Hormah
22. 26 stood in a narrow place, where (was) no
23. 13 Come, I pray..with me unto another pla.
23. 27 Come, I..will bring thee unto another pla.
24. 11 flee thou to thy place: I thought to prom.
24. 25 returned to his place: and Balak also w.
32. 1 behold, the place (was) a place for cattle
32. 17 until we have brought them unto their p.
Deut. 1. 31 that ye went, until ye came into this place
1. 33 to search you out a place to pitch your ten.
9. 7 until ye came unto this place, ye have been
11. 5 what he did..until ye came into this pla.
11. 24 Every place whereon the soles of your fe.
12. 2 the places wherein the nations which ye
12. 3 and destroy the names..out of that place
12. 5 the place which the LORD your God shall
12. 11 there shall be a place which the LORD your
12. 13 offer not thy burnt offerings in every pl.
12. 14 in the place which the LORD shall choose
12. 18 in the place which the LORD thy God shall
12. 21 place which the LORD thy God hath chosen
12. 26 unto the place which the LORD shall cho.
14. 23 the place which he shall choose to place
14. 24 if the place be too far from thee, which
14. 25 place which the LORD thy God shall choose
15. 20 in the place which the LORD shall choose
16. 2 the place which the LORD shall choose to
16. 6, 7, 11, 15, in the place which the LORD thy
16. 16 in the place which he shall choose; in the
17. 8 place which the LORD thy God shall choose
17. 10 of that place which the LORD shall choose
18. 6 unto the place which the LORD shall cho.
21. 19 his city, and unto the gate of his place
23. 16 that place which he shall choose in one
26. 2 the place which the LORD thy God shall
26. 9 he hath brought us into this place, and
29. 7 when ye came unto this place, Sihon the
31. 11 in the place which he shall choose, thou
Josh. 1. 3 Every place that the sole of your foot sh.
3. 3 ye shall remove from your place, and go
4. 18 waters of Jordan returned unto their pl.
5. 9 the place is called Gilgal unto this day
5. 15 the place whereon thou standest (is) holy
7. 26 that place was called, The valley of Achor
8. 19 ambush arose quickly out of their place
9. 27 even..in the place which he should choose
20. 4 give him a place, that he may dwell am.
Judg. 2. 5 they called the name of that place Bochim
7. 7 let all..people go every man unto his pla.
9. 55 they departed every man unto his place
11. 19 Let us..through thy land into my place
15. 17 that he..called that place Ramath-lehi
18. 10 a place where (there is) no want of any
18. 12 they called that place Mahaneh-dan unto
19. 13 let us draw near to one of these places to
19. 16 but the men of the place (were) Benjami.
19. 28 man rose up, and gat him unto his place
20. 22 in the place where they put themselves
20. 33 men of Israel rose up out of their place
20. 33 liers in wait..came..out of their places
20. 36 men of Israel gave place to the Benjamites
Ruth 1. 7 went forth out of the place where she w.
3. 4 shalt mark the place where he shall lie
4. 10 brethren, and from the gate of his place
1 Sa. 3. 2 Eli (was) laid down in his place, and his
3. 9 So Samuel went and lay down in his place
5. 3 took Dagon, and set him in his place ag.
5. 11 let it go again to his own place, that it
6. 2 us wherewith we shall send it to his place
7. 16 and judged Israel in all those places

1 Sa. 9. 22 the chiefest place among them that were
12. 8 the LORD..made them dwell in this place
14. 46 the Philistines went to their own place
20. 19 the place where thou didst hide thyself
20. 25 by Saul's side, and David's place was em.
20. 27 David's place was empty: and Saul said
20. 37 the place of the arrow which Jonathan
21. 2 appointed..servants to such and such a p.
23. 22 see his place where his haunt is, (and) w.
23. 28 they called that place Sela-hammahlekoth
26. 5 came to the place where Saul had pitched
26. 5 David beheld the place where Saul lay, and
26. 25 David went..and Saul returned to his p.
27. 5 give..a place in some town in the count.
29. 4 he may go again to his place which thou
30. 31 the places where David himself and his
2 Sa. 2. 16 that place was called Helkath-hazzurim
2. 23 as many as came to the place where Asa.
5. 20 called the name of that place Baal-pera.
6. 8 called the name of the place Perez-uz.
6. 17 set it in his place, in the midst of the ta.
7. 10 will appoint a place for my people Israel
11. 16 a place where he knew that valiant men
15. 19 return to thy place, and abide with the
15. 21 in what place my lord the king shall be
17. 9 he is hid now in some pit, or in some..p.
17. 12 in some place where he shall be found
19. 39 Barzillai..returned unto his own place
1 Ki. 4. 28 unto the place where (the officers) were
5. 9 unto the place that thou shalt appoint
8. 6 the ark of the covenant..unto his place
8. 7 (their) two wings over the place of the
8. 21 And I have set there a place for the ark
8. 29 the place of which thou hast said, My na.
8. 29 thy servant shall make toward this place
8. 30 when they shall pray toward this place
8. 30 hear thou in heaven thy dwelling place
8. 35 if they pray toward this place, and confe.
10. 19 on either side on the place of the seat
13. 8 eat bread nor drink water in this place
13. 16 nor drink water with thee in this place
13. 22 the place of the which (the LORD) did say
20. 24 Take the kings..every man out of his pl.
21. 19 the place where dogs licked the blood of
2 Ki. 5. 11 strike his hand over the place, and recover
6. 1 the place where we dwell with thee is too
6. 2 let us make us a place there, where we m.
6. 6 he showed him the place. And he cut
6. 8 In such and such a place (shall be) my ca.
6. 9 Beware that thou pass not such a place
6. 10 the place which the man of God told him
18. 25 Am I now come up..against this place to
22. 16 will bring evil upon this place, and upon
22. 17 wrath shall be kindled against this place
22. 19 I spake against this place, and against
22. 20 the evil which I will bring upon this pla.
23. 14 filled their places with the bones of men
1 Ch. 13. 11 that place is called Perez-uzza to this day
14. 11 called the name of that place Baal-peraz.
15. 1 prepared a place for the ark of God, and
15. 3 unto his place which he had prepared for
16. 27 strength and gladness (are) in his place
17. 9 will ordain a place for my people Israel
21. 22 Grant me the place of (this) threshing fl.
21. 25 So David gave to Ornan for the place six
2 Ch. 3. 1 in the place that David had prepared in
5. 7 in the ark of the covenant..unto his place
5. 8 spread forth (their) wings over the place
6. 20 the place whereof thou hast said that thou
6. 20 which thy servant prayeth toward this p.
6. 21 place: hear thou from thy dwelling place
6. 26 if they pray toward this place, and confess
6. 40 unto the prayer (that is made) in this pl.
7. 12 have chosen this place to myself for an
7. 15 unto the prayer (that is made) in this pl.
9. 18 stays on each side of the sitting place
20. 26 the same place was called, The valley of
24. 11 took it, and carried it to his place again
33. 19 and the places wherein he built..and set
34. 24 will bring evil upon this place, and upon
34. 25 wrath shall be poured out upon this place
34. 27 thou heardest his words against this place
34. 28 the evil that I will bring upon this place
Ezra 1. 4 remaineth in any place where he sojourn.
1. 4 the men of his place help him with silver
8. 17 unto Iddo the chief at the place Casiphia
8. 17 the Nethinims, at the place Casiphia, that
9. 8 to give us a nail in his holy place, that our
Neh. 1. 9 the place that I have chosen to set my
2. 14 (there was) no place for the beast (that
4. 12 From all places whence ye shall return u.
4. 13 in the lower places behind the wall, (and)
4. 20 In what place (therefore) ye hear the sound
12. 27 sought the Levites out of all their places
Esth. 4. 14 arise to the Jews from another place; but
Job 2. 11 they came every one from his own place
6. 17 hot, they are consumed out of their place
7. 10 neither shall his place know him any more
8. 18 If he destroy him from his place, then (it)
9. 6 Which shaketh the earth out of her place
14. 18 and the rock is removed out of his place
16. 18 O earth, cover not..let my cry have no p.
18. 4 shall the rock be removed out of his place?
18. 21 this (is)..place (of him that) knoweth not
20. 9 neither shall his place any more behold
27. 21 and as a storm hurleth him out of his p.
27. 23 clap..and shall hiss him out of his place
28. 1 and a place for gold (where) they fine (it)
28. 6 The stones of it (are) the place of sapph.
28. 12, 20 where (is) the place of understanding?
28. 23 God understandeth..he knoweth the place
37. 1 trembleth, and is moved out of his place

Job 38. 12 caused the day spring to know his place
38. 19 (for) darkness, where (is) the place thereof
Psa. 24. 3 and who shall stand in his holy place?
26. 8 and the place where thine honour dwell.
37. 10 thou shalt diligently consider his place
44. 19 thou hast sore broken us in the place of
103. 16 the place thereof shall know it no more
103. 22 his works in all places of his dominion
104. 8 place which thou hast founded for them
132. 5 Until I find out a place for the LORD, an
Prov 15. 3 The eyes of the LORD (are) in every place
25. 6 and stand not in the place of great (men)
27. 8 so (is) a man that wandereth from his pl.
Eccl. 1. 5 and hasteth to his place where he arose
1. 7 unto the place from whence the rivers c.
3. 16 I saw under the sun the place of judgment
3. 16 and the place of righteousness, (that) ini.
3. 20 All go unto one place; all are of the dust
6. 6 seen no good: do not all go to one place?
8. 10 gone from the place of the holy, and they
10. 4 leave not thy place; for yielding pacifieth
11. 3 in the place where the tree falleth, there
Isa. 5. 8 till (there be) no place, that they may be
7. 23 every place shall be, where there were a
13. 13 the earth shall remove out of her place
14. 2 bring them to their place: and the house
18. 7 to the place of the name of the LORD of
22. 23 will fasten him (as) a nail in a sure place
22. 25 the nail that is fastened in the sure place
26. 21 LORD cometh out of his place to punish
28. 8 full of vomit..(so that there is) no place
33. 21 us a place of broad rivers (and) streams
45. 19 not spoken in secret, in a dark place of
46. 7 and set him in his place, and he standeth
49. 20 shall say..The place (is) too strait for me
54. 2 Enlarge the place of thy tent, and let them
60. 13 to beautify the place of my sanctuary; and
60. 13 I will make the place of my feet glorious
66. 1 house..and where (is) the place of my r.?
Jer. 4. 7 he is gone forth from his place to make
7. 3 and I will cause you to dwell in this place
7. 6 and shed not innocent blood in this place
7. 7 Then will I cause you to dwell in this pl.
7. 12 go ye..unto my place which (was) in Shi.
7. 14 the place which I gave to you and to your
7. 20 fury shall be poured out upon this place
7. 32 shall bury in Tophet, till there be no place
8. 3 the places whither I have driven them
13. 7 took the girdle from the place where I
14. 13 will give you assured peace in this place
16. 2 neither..sons or daughters in this place
16. 3 the daughters that are born in this place
16. 9 I will cause to cease out of this place in
17. 12 high throne..(is) the place of our sanctuary
19. 3 I will bring evil upon this place, the which
19. 4 have estranged this place, and have burnt
19. 4 have filled this place with the blood of
19. 6 this place shall no more be called Tophet
19. 7 will make void the counsel..in this place
19. 11 in Tophet, till (there be) no place to bury
19. 12 Thus will I do unto this place, saith the
19. 13 shall be defiled as the place of Tophet
22. 3 neither shed innocent blood in this place
22. 11 Shallum..which went forth out of this p.
22. 12 place whither they have led him captive
24. 5 whom I have sent out of this place into
24. 9 in all places whither I shall drive them
27. 22 bring them..and restore them to this p.
28. 3 will I bring again into this place all the
28. 3 king of Babylon took away from this place
28. 4 I will bring again to this place Jeconiah
28. 6 away captive, from Babylon into this place
29. 10 in causing you to return to this place
29. 14 from all the places whither I have driven
29. 14 I will bring you again into the place wh.
32. 37 I will bring them again unto this place
33. 10 there shall be heard in this place, which
33. 12 this place, which is desolate without man
40. 2 hath pronounced this evil upon this place
40. 12 all the Jews returned out of all places w.
42. 18 saith the LORD..ye shall see this place no
42. 22 the place whither ye desire to go (and) to
44. 29 I will punish you in this place, that ye
45. 5 a prey in all places whither thou goest
51. 62 thou hast spoken against this place, to
Eze. 3. 12 Blessed (be)..glory of the LORD from his p.
6. 13 place where they did offer sweet savour
10. 11 the place whither the head looked they
12. 3 remove from thy place to another place
17. 16 the place (where) the king (dwelleth) that
21. 30 in the place where thou wast created, in
34. 12 will deliver them out of all places where
38. 15 come from thy place out of the north pa.
39. 11 a place there of graves in Israel, the val.
41. 11 and the breadth of the place that was left
42. 13 the trespass offering; for the place (is) h.
43. 7 the place of my throne, and the place of
45. 4 it shall be a place for their houses, and
46. 19 there (was) a place on the two sides wes.
46. 20 This (is) the place where the priests shall
Hos. 1. 10 in the place where it was said unto them
5. 15 I will go (and) return to my place, till th.
Joel 3. 7 of the place whither ye have sold them
Amos 4. 6 and want of bread in all your places: yet
8. 3 (shall be) many dead bodies in every pl.
Mic. 1. 3 the LORD cometh forth out of his place
Nah. 1. 8 will make an utter end of the place ther.
3. 17 their place is not known where they (are)
Zeph. 1. 4 cut..the remnant of Baal from this place
2. 11 every one from his place, (even) all the
Hag. 2. 9 in this place will I give peace, saith the
Zech 14. 10 gate unto the place of the first gate, unto

Mal. 1. 11 in every place incense (shall be) offered

11. *Standing, station, place,* עֹמֶד *omed.*
2 Ch.30. 16 they stood in their place after their man.
34. 31 the king stood in his place, and made a
35. 10 the priests stood in their place, and the
Neh. 8. 7 law: and the people (stood) in their place
9. 3 they stood up in their place, and read in
13. 11 I gathered..and set them in their place

12. *See* Open.
Gen. 38. 14 sat in an open place, which (is) by the w.

13. *Under, beneath,* תַּחַת *tachath.*
Lev. 14. 42 and put (them) in the place of those sto.

14. *Hole, opening,* ὀπή *opē.*
Jas. 3. 11 a fountain send forth at the same place

15. *Passage, paragraph,* περιοχή *periochē.*
Acts 8. 32 The place of the Scripture which he read

16. *Place,* τόπος *topos.*
Matt 12. 43 he walketh through dry places, seeking
14. 13 departed thence by ship into a desert pl.
14. 15 This is a desert place, and the time is now
14. 35 the men of that place had knowledge of
24. 7 pestilences, and earthquakes, in divers p.
24. 15 the abomination..stand in the holy place
26. 52 Put up again thy sword into his place: for
27. 33 when they were come unto a place called
27. 33 Golgotha, that is to say, A place of a sk.
28. 6 Come, see the place where the Lord lay
Mark 1. 35 departed into a solitary place, and there
1. 45 the city, but was without in desert places
6. 31 Come..yourselves apart into a desert pl.
6. 32 they departed into a desert place by ship
6. 35 This is a desert place, and now the time
13. 8 there shall be earthquakes in divers pla.
15. 22 they bring him unto the place Golgotha
15. 22 which is, being interpreted, The place of
16. 6 Jesus..behold the place where they laid
Luke 4. 17 he found the place where it was written
4. 37 into every place of the country round ab.
4. 42 he departed and went into a desert place
9. 10 [desert place belonging to the city called]
9. 12 victuals: for we are here in a desert place
10. 1 into every city and place, whither he him.
10. 32 when he was at the place, came and look.
11. 1 as he was praying in a certain place, when
11. 24 walketh through dry places, seeking rest
14. 9 say to thee, Give this man place; and thou
16. 28 lest they also come into this place of tor.
19. 5 when Jesus came to the place, he looked
21. 11 great earthquakes shall be in divers plac.
22. 40 when he was at the place, he said unto
23. 33 come to the place which is called Calvary
John 4. 20 Jerusalem is the place where men ought
5. 13 away, a multitude being in (that) place
6. 10 there was much grass in the place. So
6. 23 nigh unto the place where they did eat
10. 40 into the place where John at first baptiz.
11. 6 abode..still in the same place where he
11. 30 was in that place where Martha met him
11. 48 and take away both our place and nation
14. 2 mansions..I go to prepare a place for you
14. 3 if I go and prepare a place for you, I will
18. 2 Judas..which betrayed him, knew the p.
19. 13 in a place that is called the Pavement, but
19. 17 And he..went forth into a place called
19. 20 the place where Jesus was crucified was
19. 41 in the place where he was crucified there
20. 7 but wrapped together in a place by itself
Acts 1. 25 fell, that he might go to his own place
4. 31 place was shaken where they were assem.
6. 13 blasphemous words against this holy place
6. 14 Jesus of Nazareth shall destroy this place
7. 7 come forth, and serve me in this place
7. 33 place where thou standest is holy ground
7. 49 what house..what (is) the place of my re.?
12. 17 he departed, and went into another place
21. 28 the people, and the law, and this place
21. 28 and further..hath polluted this holy place
27. 8 a place which is called the Fair Havens
27. 41 falling into a place where two seas met
Rom. 9. 26 in the place where it was said unto them
12. 19 give place unto wrath: for it is written
15. 23 having no more place in these parts, and
1 Co. 1. 2 with all that in every place call upon the
2 Co. 2. 14 savour of his knowledge by us in every pl.
Eph. 4. 27 Neither give place to the devil
1 Th. 1. 8 in every place your faith to God ward is
Heb. 8. 7 then should no place have been sought
11. 8 place which he should after receive for
12. 17 he found no place of repentance, though
2 Pe. 1. 19 unto a light that shineth in a dark place
Rev. 2. 5 will remove thy candlestick out of his pl.
6. 14 mountain and island..moved out of..pl.
12. 6 where she hath a place prepared of God
12. 8 neither was their place found any more
12. 14 into her place, where she is nourished for
16. 16 into a place called in the Hebrew tongue
20. 11 and there was found no place for them

17. *A little place, spot,* χωρίον *chōrion.*
Matt 26. 36 with them unto a place called Gethsemane
Mark 14. 32 came to a place which was named Geths.

[*See also* Another, appointed, besieged, broad, burying, certain, chiefest, close, couching, crooked, dark, decayed, deep, desolate, dry, dwelling, eminent, empty, even, every, feeding, from, fruitful, give, good, hearing, hiding, high, higher, hollow, holy, in, inhabited, large, lie down, lodge, lodging, low, lurking, market, miry, ordered, pass, pleasant, profane, refuge, rest, resting, secret, separate, settled, slippery, solitary, steep, stood, strong, this, threshing, void, waste, what, yonder.]

PLACE, (give or have), to —

1. *To cause to rest, set down,* נוּחַ *nuach,* 5.
2 Ch. 1. 14 which he placed in the chariot cities, and
4. 8 and placed (them) in the temple, five on
Eze. 37. 14 I shall place you in your own land: then

2. *To cause to sit down,* יָשַׁב *yashab,* 5.
Gen. 47. 11 Joseph placed his father and his brethren
2 Ki. 17. 6 placed them in Halah and in Habor (by)
17. 24 and placed (them) in the cities of Samaria
17. 26 removed, and placed in the cities of Sam.
Hos. 11. 11 I will place them in their houses, saith the

3. *To take,* לָקַח *laqach.*
Eze. 17. 5 he placed (it) by great waters, (and) set

4. *To put down, place,* נָחַת *nechath,* 5.
Ezra 6. 5 be restored..and place (them) in the ho.

5. *To give,* נָתַן *nathan.*
2 Ch. 17. 2 he placed forces in all the fenced cities
Isa. 46. 13 will place salvation in Zion, for Israel
Eze. 37. 26 I will place them, and multiply them, and
Dan. 11. 31 they shall place the abomination that

6. *To cause to stand,* עָמַד *amad,* 5.
1 Ki. 12. 32 he placed in Beth-el the priests of the

7. *To put, place,* שׂוּם, שִׂים *sum, sim.*
Exod 18. 21 place (such) over them, (to be) rulers of
Jer. 5. 22 which have placed the sand (for) the bo.

8. *To tabernacle, cause to settle down,* שָׁכַן *shaken,* 3.
Deut 14. 23 he shall choose to place his name there
16. 2 LORD shall choose to place his name there
16. 6 thy God shall choose to place his name
16. 11 God hath chosen to place his name there
26. 2 God shall choose to place his name there
Psa. 78. 60 Shiloh, the tent (which) he placed among

9. *To tabernacle, cause to settle down,* שָׁכַן *shaken,* 5.
Gen. 3. 24 he placed at the east of the garden of E.

10. *To give place, withdraw,* ἀναχωρέω *anachōreō.*
Matt. 9. 24 Give place; for the maid is not dead, but

11. *To have place for,* χωρέω *chōreō.*
John 8. 37 to kill me, because my word hath no pl.

PLACE, to bring again to one's —

To cause to sit down, יָשַׁב *yashab,* 5.
Zech 10. 6 and I will bring them again to place them

PLACE, (dwelling) —

A tent, אֹהֶל *ohel.*
Job 21. 28 where (are)..dwelling places of the wic.?

PLACE, in or to this or of that, where two ways meet—

1. *One residing in a place,* ἐντόπιος *entopios.*
Acts 21. 12 they of that place, besought him not to

2. *Here, in this place,* ὧδε *hōde.*
Matt 12. 6 in this place is (one) greater than the te.
Luke 23. 5 beginning from Galilee to this place

PLACE, where one is, same —

Under, beneath, תַּחַת *tachath.*
2 Sa. 2. 23 he fell down..and died in the same place
Jer. 38. 9 to die for hunger in the place where he is

PLACES, in all —

Every where, in every place, πανταχοῦ *pantachou.*
Acts 24. 3 We accept (it) always, and in all places

PLACED, to be —

1. *To be caused to sit down,* יָשַׁב *yashab,* 6.
Isa. 5. 8 they may be placed alone in the midst of

2. *To put, place,* שׂוּם, שִׂים *sum, sim.*
Job 20. 4 of old, since man was placed upon earth

PLACES —

[*See also* Boiling, desolate, drawing water, highest, latest, parched, rough, round, steep, walk.]

PLACES about —

Round about, סָבִיב *sabib.*
Jer. 17. 26 they shall come..from the places about J.

PLAGUE —

1. *Pestilence,* דֶּבֶר *deber.*
Hos. 13. 14 O death, I will be thy plagues; O grave, I

2. *Plague, smiting,* מַגֵּפָה *maggephah.*
Exod 9. 14 I will at this time send all my plagues upon
Num 14. 37 Even those men..died by the plague bef.
16. 48 stood between the dead..the plague was
16. 49 they that died in the plague were fourteen
16. 50 Aaron returned..and the plague was sta.
25. 8 plague was stayed from the children of I.
25. 9 those that died in the plague were twenty
25. 18 which was slain in the day of the plague
26. 1 came to pass after the plague, that the L.
31. 16 there was a plague among the congrega.
1 Sa. 6. 4 for one plague (was) on you all, and on yo.
2 Sa. 24. 21 the plague may be stayed from the people
24. 25 and the plague was stayed from Israel
1 Ch. 21. 22 the plague may be stayed from the people
2 Ch. 21. 14 with a great plague will the LORD smite
Psa. 106. 29 they provoked..and the plague brake in
106. 30 executed judgment: and (so) the plague
Zech. 14. 12 this shall be the plague wherewith the L.
14. 15 And so shall be the plague..as this plague
14. 18 there shall be the plague wherewith the

3. *A smiting,* מַכָּה *makkah.*
Lev. 26. 21 I will bring seven times more plagues upon
Num 11. 33 smote the people with a very great plague
Deut 28. 59 make thy plagues wonderful, and the pl.
28. 59 great plagues, and of long continuance
28. 61 every plague, which (is) not written in the
29. 22 when they see the plagues of that land
1 Sa. 4. 8 smote the Egyptians with all the plagues
Jer. 19. 8 and hiss because of all the plagues thereof
49. 17 and shall hiss at all the plagues thereof
50. 13 every one..shall..hiss at all her plagues

4. *A touch, smiting,* נֶגַע *nega.*
Gen. 12. 17 with great plagues because of Sarai, Abr.
Exod 11. 1 Yet will I bring one plague (more) upon
Lev. 13. 2 (like) the plague of leprosy; then he shall
13. 3 priest shall look on the plague in the skin
13. 3 hair in the plague is turned white, and the
13. 3 plague in sight (be) deeper than the skin
13. 3 it (is) a plague of leprosy: and the priest
13. 4 priest shall shut up (him that hath) the p
13. 5 (if) the plague in his sight be at a stay, (and)
13. 6 plague spread not in the skin, the priest
13. 6 plague (be) somewhat dark, (and) the pl.
13. 9 When the plague of leprosy is in a man
13. 12 the plague from his head even to his foot
13. 13, 17 pronounce..clean (that hath) the pla.
13. 17 the plague be turned into white; then t.
13. 20 plague of leprosy broken out of the boil
13. 22 shall pronounce him unclean: it (is) a p.
13. 25, 27 pronounce him unclean: it (is) the p.
13. 29 If a man or woman have a plague upon
13. 30 Then the priest shall see the plague: and
13. 31 if the priest look on the plague of the sc.
13. 31 shut up (him that hath) the plague of the
13. 32 seventh day the priest shall look on the p.
13. 44 he (is) unclean..his plague (is) in his head
13. 45 leper in whom the plague (is), his clothes
13. 46 All the days wherein the plague (shall be)
13. 47 garment also that the plague of leprosy is
13. 49 if the plague be greenish..it (is) a plague
13. 50 And the priest shall look upon the plague
13. 50 shut up (it that hath) the plague seven d.
13. 51 look on the plague..if the plague be spr.
13. 51 plague (is) a fretting leprosy; it (is) unc.
13. 52 any thing of skin, wherein the plague is
13. 53 the plague be not spread in the garment
13. 54 that they wash (the thing) wherein the pl.
13. 55 look on the plague..(if) the plague have
13. 55 and the plague be not spread; it (is) unc.
13. 56 plague (be) somewhat dark after the wa.
13. 57 thou shalt burn that wherein the plague
13. 58 if the plague be departed from them, then
13. 59 This (is) the law of the plague of leprosy
14. 3 the plague of leprosy be healed in the le.
14. 32 law (of him) in whom (is) the plague of l.
14. 34 I put the plague of leprosy in a house of
14. 35 seemeth to me (there is) as it were a pla.
14. 36 priest go (into it) to see the plague, that
14. 37 look on the plague..(if) the plague (be) in
14. 39 the plague be spread in the walls of the
14. 40 take away the stones in which the plague
14. 43 if the plague come again, and break out
14. 44 the plague be spread in the house, it (is)
14. 48 plague hath not spread in the house, after
14. 48 the house clean, because the plague is h.
14. 54 This (is) the law for all manner of plague
Deut. 24. 8 Take heed in the plague of leprosy, that
1 Ki. 8. 37 whatsoever plague, whatsoever sickness
8. 38 which shall know every man the plague
Psa. 91. 10 neither shall any plague come nigh thy

5. *A stumbling, plague,* נֶגֶף *negeph.*
Exod 12. 13 plague shall not be upon you to destroy
30. 12 that there be no plague among them, wh.
Num. 8. 19 that there be no plague among the child.
16. 46 there is wrath..the plague is begun
16. 47 the plague was begun among the people
Josh. 22. 17 there was a plague in the congregation of

6. *A scourge, whip, plague,* μάστιξ *mastix.*
Mark 3. 10 for to touch him, as many as had plagues
5. 29 felt..that she was healed of that plague
5. 34 go in peace, and be whole of thy plague
Luke 7. 21 cured many of (their) infirmities and pla.

7. *A stroke, plague,* πληγή *plēgē.*
Rev. 9. 20 which were not killed by these plagues
11. 6 to smite the earth with all plagues, as of.
15. 1 seven angels having the seven last plagues
15. 6 having the seven plagues, clothed in pure
15. 8 till the seven plagues of the seven angels
16. 9 which hath power over these plagues: and
16. 21 because of the plague..for the plague th.
18. 4 and that ye receive not of her plagues
18. 8 Therefore shall her plagues come in one
21. 9 seven vials full of the seven last plagues
22. 18 God shall add unto him the plagues that

PLAGUE, to —

1. *To touch, smite, plague,* נָגַע *naga,* 3.
Gen. 12. 17 LORD plagued Pharaoh and his house with

2. *To smite, plague,* נָגַף *nagaph.*
Exod 32. 35 LORD plagued the people, because they
Josh. 24. 5 I plagued Egypt, according to that which
Psa. 89. 23 I will beat down..and plague them that

PLAGUED, to be —

1. *Plague, stroke, slaughter,* מַגֵּפָה *maggephah.*
1 Ch. 21. 17 not on thy people, that they should be p.

2. *To be touched, smitten,* נָגַע *naga,* 4.
Psa. 73. 5 neither are they plagued like (other) men

3. *To touch, smite,* נָגַע *naga.*
Psa. 73. 14 For all the day long have I been plagued

PLAIN, (low) —
1. *A grassy meadow,* אָבֵל *abel.*
Judg 11. 33 unto the plain of the vineyards, with a

2. *A plain,* אֵלוֹן *elon.*
Gen. 12. 6 place of Sichem, unto the plain of Moreh
13. 18 and came and dwelt in the plain of Mamre
14. 13 he dwelt in the plain of Mamre the Amo.
18. 1 appeared unto him in the plains of Mamre
Deut 11. 30 over against Gilgal, beside the plains of
Judg. 4. 11 pitched his tent unto the plain of Zaanim
9. 6 by the plain of the pillar that (was) in S.
9. 37 another company come along by the plain
1 Sa. 10. 3 thou shalt come to the plain of Tabor and

3. *A valley, vale,* בִּקְעָה *biqah.*
Dan. 3. 1 he set it up in the plain of Dura, in the

4. *A valley, vale,* בִּקְעָה *biqah.*
Gen. 11. 2 they found a plain in the land of Shinar
Neh. 6. 2 (some one of) the villages in the plain of
Isa. 40. 4 made straight, and the rough places plain
Eze. 3. 22 Arise, go forth into the plain, and I will
3. 23 I arose, and went forth into the plain: and
8. 4 according to the vision..I saw in the plain
Amos 1. 5 cut off the inhabitant from the plain of A.

5. *A circle, circuit,* כִּכָּר *kikkar.*
Gen. 13. 10 beheld all the plain of Jordan, that it (was)
13. 11 Then Lot chose him all the plain of Jordan
13. 12 Lot dwelt in the cities of the plain, and p.
19. 17 neither stay thou in all the plain; escape
19. 25 overthrew those cities, and all the plain
19. 28 looked..toward all the land of the plain
19. 29 when God destroyed the cities of the plain
Deut 34. 3 plain of the valley of Jericho, the city of
2 Sa. 18. 23 Ahimaaz ran by the way of the plain, and
1 Ki. 7. 46 In the plain of Jordan did the king cast
2 Ch. 4. 17 In the plain of Jordan did the king cast
Neh. 3. 22 repaired the priests, the men of the plain
12. 28 out of the plain country round about Jer.

6. *A plain, level place,* מִישׁוֹר *mishor*
Deut. 3. 10 All the cities of the plain and all Gilead
4. 43 Bezer in the wilderness, in the plain cou.
Josh 13. 9 and all the plain of Medeba unto Dibon
13. 16 midst of the river, and all the plain by
13. 17 her cities that (are) in the plain: Dibon
13. 21 all the cities of the plain, and all the ki.
20. 8 upon the plain out of the tribe of Reuben
1 Ki. 20. 23 let us fight against them in the plain, and
20. 25 we will fight against them in the plain
2 Ch. 26. 10 both in the low country, and in the plains
Psa 27. 11 lead me in a plain path, because of mine
Jer. 21 13 against thee, O..rock of the plain, saith
48. 8 plain shall be destroyed, as the LORD hath
48. 21 judgment is come upon the plain country
Zech. 4. 7 before Zerubbabel (thou shalt become) a p.

7. *A wilderness, obscure place,* עֲרָבָה *arabah.*
Num 22. 1 pitched in the plains of Moab on this..J
26. 3 spake with them in the plains of Moab by
26. 63 numbered the children..in the plains of
31. 12 unto the camp at the plains of Moab, w.
33. 48 pitched in the plains of Moab, by Jordan
33. 49 (even) unto Abel-shittim in the plains of
33. 50 spake unto Moses in the plains of Moab
35. 1 the plains of Moab by Jordan (near) Jeri
36. 13 the plains of Moab by Jordan (near) Jeri.
Deut. 1. 1 the plain over against the Red (sea), bet.
1. 7 in the plain, in the hills, and in the vale
2. 8 the way of the plain from Elath, and from
3. 17 The plain also, and Jordan, and the coast
3. 17 Chinnereth even unto the sea of the plain
4. 49 the plain on this side Jordan eastward
4. 49 the sea of the plain under the springs
34. 1 Moses went up from the plains of Moab
34. 8 And..wept for Moses in the plains of M.
Josh. 3. 16 came down toward the sea of the plain
4. 13 over..unto battle, to the plains of Jericho
5. 10 passover..at even in the plains of Jericho
8. 14 out..at a time appointed before the plain
11. 2 the plains south of Chinneroth, and in the
11. 16 the plain, and the mountain of Israel, and
12. 1 unto..Hermon, and all the plain on the
12. 3 from the plain to the sea of Chinneroth, on
12. 3 unto the sea of the plain..the salt sea on
12. 8 in the plains, and in the springs, and in
13. 32 the plains of Moab, on the other side Jo.
1 Sa. 23. 24 in the plain on the south of Jeshimon
2 Sa. 2. 29 walked all that night through the plain
4. 7 gat them away through the plain all night
* 15. 28 will tarry in the plain of the wilderness
* 17. 16 Lodge not..in the plains of the wildern.
2 Ki. 14. 25 from..Hamath unto the sea of the plain
25. 4 (the king) went the way toward the plain
25. 5 and overtook him in the plains of Jericho
Jer. 39 4 and he went out the way of the plain
39. 5 overtook Zedekiah in the plains of Jeric.
52. 7 all the men..went by the way of the pla.
52. 8 overtook Zedekiah in the pl.; Zech. 14. 10
* V. L. עברות [*abarah*].

8. *A low place or plain,* שְׁפֵלָה *shephelah.*
1 Ch. 27. 28 sycamore trees that (were) in the low pl.
2 Ch. 9. 27 sycamore trees that (are) in the low plains
Jer. 17. 26 from the plain, and from the mountains
Obad. 19 and (they of) the plain the Philistines: and
Zech. 7. 7 (men) inhabited the south and the plain

9. *A level place,* τόπου πεδινοῦ *topou pedinou.*
Luke 6. 17 stood in the plain, and the company of his

PLAIN —
1. *Straight forward,* נָכֹחַ *nakoach.*
Prov. 8. 9 (are) all plain to him that understandeth

2. *Plain, perfect, simple,* תָּם *tam.*
Gen. 25. 27 Jacob (was) a plain man, dwelling in tents

3. *Rightly,* ὀρθῶς *orthōs.*
Mark 7. 35 his tongue was loosed, and he spake plain

PLAIN, to make or be made —
1. *To explain, engrave,* בָּאַר *baar,* 3.
Hab. 2. 2 make (it) plain upon tables that he may

2. *To make level, equal,* שָׁוָה *shavah,* 3
Isa. 28. 25 When he hath made plain the face thereof

3. *To exalt, raise up,* סָלַל *salal.*
Prov 15. 19 but the way of the righteous (is) made p.

PLAINLY —
1. *To say,* אָמַר *amar.*
Exod 21. 5 if the servant shall plainly say, I love my

2. *To explain,* בָּאַר *baar,* 3.
Deut 27. 8 write..all the words of this law very pla.

3. *To be uncovered, revealed,* גָּלָה *galah,* 2.
1 Sa. 2. 27 Did I plainly appear unto the house of thy

4. *To put before one,* נָגַד *nagad,* 5.
1 Sa. 10. 16 He told us plainly that the asses were

5. *To spread out,* פָּרַשׁ *perash,* 3.
Ezra 4. 18 letter..hath been plainly read before me

6. *Clear,* צַח *tsach.*
Isa. 32. 4 stammerers shall be ready to speak pla.

7. *Boldness,* παῤῥησία *parrhēsia.*
John 10. 24 said..If thou be the Christ, tell us plainly
11. 14 Then said Jesus unto them plainly, Laza.
16. 25 I shall show you plainly of the Father
16. 29 now speakest thou [plainly], and speakest

PLAINNESS of speech —
Boldness, παῤῥησία *parrhēsia.*
2 Co. 3. 12 Seeing..we use great plainness of speech

PLAISTER, PLASTER —
1. *Chalk,* גִּיר *gir.*
Dan. 5. 5 the plaster of the wall of the king's pala.

2. *Plaster, lime,* שִׂיד *sid.*
Deut 27. 2 great stones, and plaster them with plas.
27. 4 and thou shalt plaster them with plaster

PLAISTER or PLASTER, to (lay for a) —
1. *To daub, plaster,* טוּחַ *tuach.*
Lev. 14. 42 other mortar, and shall plaster the house

2. *To spread out, plaster,* מָרַח *marach.*
Isa. 38. 21 lay (it) for a plaister upon the boil, and

3. *To plaster,* שִׂיד *sid.*
Deut 27. 2 great stones, and plaster them with pla.
27. 4 and thou shalt plaster them with plaster

PLAISTERED or PLASTERED, to be —
To be daubed, plastered, טוּחַ *tuach,* 2.
Lev. 14. 43 if the plague come..after it is plastered
14. 48 not spread..after the house was plastered

PLAIT or PLAT, to —
To plait, braid, fold, twist, πλέκω *plekō.*
Matt 27. 29 when they had platted a crown of thorns
Mark 15. 17 platted a crown of thorns, and put it ab
John 19. 2 soldiers platted a crown of thorns, and put

PLAITING (the hair) —
Plaiting or folding in, ἐμπλοκή *emplokē.*
1 Pe. 3. 3 that outward (adorning) of plaiting the h.

PLANES —
Carving tools, corners, מַקְצֻעוֹת *maqtsuoth.*
Isa. 44. 13 he fitteth it with planes, and he marketh

PLANETS —
Constellations, מַזָּלוֹת *mazzaloth.*
2 Ki. 23. 5 to the planets, and to all the host of hea.

PLANK (thick) —
1. *Any thing thick* (?), עָבִים [*ob*].
Eze. 41. 26 side chambers of the house, and thick pl.

2. *Wooden threshold* (?), עָב עֵץ *ab ets.*
Eze. 41. 25 thick planks upon the face of the porch

3. *A rib, side,* צֵלָע *tsela.*
1 Ki. 6. 15 covered the floor of the house with planks

PLANT, planting, plantation —
1. *A plant, planting,* מַטָּע *matta.*
Isa. 60. 21 the branch of my planting, the work of
61. 3 planting of the LORD, that he might be g.
Eze. 17. 7 water it by the furrows of her plantation
31. 4 her rivers running round about his plants
34. 29 I will raise up for them a plant of renown
Mic. 1. 6 will make Samaria..as plantings of a vine

2. *Branches, tendrils, twigs,* נְטִישׁוֹת *netishoth.*
Jer. 48. 32 thy plants are gone over the sea, they re.

3. *A plant,* נֶטַע *neta.*
1 Ch. 4. 23 those that dwelt among plants and hedges
Job 14. 9 bud, and bring forth boughs like a plant
Isa. 5. 7 and the men of Judah his pleasant plant
17. 10 therefore shalt thou plant pleasant plants
17. 11 In the day shalt thou make thy plant to

4. *Plants,* נְטָעִים *netiim.*
Psa. 144. 12 That our sons (may be) as plants grown

5. *Shrub,* שִׂיחַ *siach.*
Gen. 2. 5 every plant of the field before it was in the

6. *A shoot,* שֶׁלַח *shelach.*
Song 4. 13 Thy plants (are) an orchard of pomegran.

7. *A plant,* שָׁתִל *shethil.*
Psa. 128. 3 children like olive plants round about

8. *Plant, plantation,* φυτεία *phuteia.*
Matt 15. 13 Every plant, which my heavenly Father

PLANT, to —
1. *To plant,* נָטַע *nata.*
Gen. 2. 8 God planted a garden eastward of Eden
9. 20 husbandman, and he planted a vineyard
21. 33 planted a grove in Beer-sheba, and called
Exod 15. 17 plant them in the mountain of thine inh.
Lev. 19. 23 shall have planted all manner of trees for
Num 24. 6 which the LORD hath planted, (and) as ce.
Deut. 6. 11 olive trees, which thou plantedst not; wh.
16. 21 Thou shalt not plant thee a grove of any
20. 6 what man (is he) that hath planted a vin.
28. 30 thou shalt plant a vineyard, and shalt not
28. 39 Thou shalt plant vineyards, and dress (th.)
Josh 24. 13 of the vineyards..which ye planted not do
2 Sa. 7. 10 plant them, that they may dwell in a pl.
2 Ki. 19. 29 plant vineyards, and eat the fruits thereof
1 Ch. 17. 9 will plant them, and they shall dwell in
Psa. 44. 2 drive..the heathen..and plantedst them
80. 8 thou hast cast out the heathen, and plan.
80. 15 vineyard which thy right hand hath plan.
94. 9 He that planted the ear, shall he not hear?
104. 16 cedars of Lebanon, which he hath planted
107. 37 sow the fields, and plant vineyards, which
Prov 31. 16 with the fruit of her hands she planteth
Eccl. 2. 4 I builded me houses; I planted me vine.
2. 5 I planted trees in them of all (kind of) fr.
3. 2 a time to plant, and a time to pluck up
Isa. 5. 2 planted it with the choicest vine, and bu.
17. 10 therefore shalt thou plant..and shalt set
37. 30 plant vineyards, and eat the fruit thereof
44. 14 he planteth an ash, and the rain doth n.
51. 16 that I may plant the heavens, and lay the
65. 21 they shall plant vineyards, and eat the f.
65. 22 they shall not plant, and another eat: for
Jer. 1. 10 and to throw down, to build, and to plant
2. 21 Yet I had planted thee a noble vine, wh.
11. 17 LORD of hosts, that planted thee, hath p.
12. 2 Thou hast planted them, yea, they have
18. 9 concerning a kingdom, to build and to p.
24. 6 I will plant them, and not pluck (them)
29. 5, 28 plant gardens, and eat the fruit of th.
31. 5 Thou shalt yet plant vines upon the mo.
31. 5 shall plant, and shall eat (them) as com.
31 28 watch over them, to build, and to plant
32. 41 plant them in this land assuredly with
35. 7 Neither shall ye..plant vineyard, nor h.
42. 10 will plant you, and not pluck (you) up
45. 4 that which I have planted I will pluck up
Eze. 28. 26 shall build houses, and plant vineyards
36. 36 know that I..plant that that was desolate
Dan. 11. 45 he shall plant the tabernacles of his pal.
Amos 5. 11 ye have planted pleasant vineyards, but
9. 14 they shall plant vineyards, and drink the
9. 15 I will plant them upon their land, and
Zeph. 1. 13 plant vineyards, but not drink the wine

2. *To plant,* שָׁתַל *shathal.*
Eze. 17. 22 will plant (it) upon an high mountain
17. 23 In the mountain..will I plant it; and it

3. *To plant,* φυτεύω *phuteuō.*
Matt 15. 13 which my heavenly Father hath not pla.
21. 33 which planted a vineyard, and hedged it
Mark 12. 1 A (certain) man planted a vineyard, and
Luke 13. 6 had a fig tree planted in his vineyard; and
17. 6 plucked up..and be thou planted in the
17. 28 bought, they sold, they planted, they bu.
20. 9 A certain man planted a vineyard, and
1 Co. 3. 6 I have planted, Apollos watered; but G.
3. 7 So then neither is he that planteth any
3. 8 he that planteth and he that watereth are
9. 7 who planteth a vineyard, and eateth not

PLANTED, to be —
1. *To plant, fasten,* נָטַע *nata.*
Eccl. 3. 2 a time to pluck up (that which is) planted

2. *To be planted,* נָטַע *nata,* 2.
Isa. 40. 24 they shall not be planted; yea, they shall

3. *To plant,* שָׁתַל *shathal.*
Psa. 1. 3 like a tree planted by the rivers of water
92. 13 Those that be planted in the house of the
Jer. 17. 8 he shall be as a tree planted by the waters
Eze. 17. 8 It was planted in a good soil by great w.
17 10 (being) planted, shall it prosper? shall it
19. 10 a vine in thy blood, planted by the waters
19. 13 she (is) planted in the wilderness, in a d.
Hos. 9. 13 Ephraim, as I saw Tyrus, (is) planted in

PLANTED together —
Planted together, σύμφυτος *sumphutos.*
Rom. 6. 5 if we have been planted together in the

PLANTER —
To plant, נָטַע *nata.*
Jer. 31. 5 the planters shall plant, and shall eat

PLANTS, principal —
Branches, שְׂרוּקִּים *seruqqim.*
Isa. 16. 8 have broken down the principal plants

PLAT —

Portion, חֶלְקָה *chelqah.*

2 Ki. 9. 26 I will requite thee in this plat, saith the
9. 26 cast him into the plat (of ground), accor.

PLATE (thin) —

1. *Tablet, board,* לוּחַ *luach.*

1 Ki. 7. 36 on the plates of the ledges thereof, and

2. *Axle, prince,* סֶרֶן *seren.*

1 Ki. 7. 30 had four brasen wheels, and plates of br.

3. *Plate,* פַּח *pach.*

Exod39. 3 they did beat the gold into thin plates
Num16 38 broad plates (for) a covering of the altar

4. *Blossom, flower, wing,* צִיץ *tsits.*

Exod28. 36 thou shalt make a plate (of) pure gold, and
39. 30 And they made the plate of the holy cro.
Lev. 8. 9 did he put the golden plate, the holy cro.

PLATTER —

1. *A dish or platter for food,* παροψίς *paropsis.*

Matt 23 25 the outside of the cup and of the platter
23 26 that (which is) within the cup [and plat.

2. *A board, flat dish,* πίναξ *pinax.*

Luke 11. 39 clean the outside of the cup and the pla.

PLAY, to —

1. *To play on a stringed instrument,* נָגַן *nagan,* 3.

1 Sa. 16 16 he shall play with his hand, and thou sh.
16. 17 Provide me now a man that can play well
16 23 David took an harp, and played with his
18. 10 David played with his hand, as at other
19. 9 sat in his house . . and David played with
2 Ki. 3. 15 when the minstrel played, that the hand
Psa. 33. 3 Sing unto him a new song; play skilfully
Eze. 33. 32 song of one that . . can play well on an in.

2. *To play with, mock,* צָחַק *tsachaq,* 3.

Exod32. 6 the people sat down . . and rose up to play

3. *To laugh, play, deride, mock,* שָׂחַק *sachaq,* 3.

1 Sa. 18. 7 women answered (one another) as they p.
2 Sa. 2 14 Let the young men now arise and play be.
6. 5 David and all the house of Israel played
6. 21 Israel: therefore will I play before the L.
1 Ch. 13 8 David and all Israel played before God w
15 29 saw king David dancing and playing; and
Job 40. 20 food, where all the beasts of the field play
41. 5 Wilt thou play with him as (with) a bird?
Psa. 104. 26 leviathan, (whom) thou hast made to play
Zech. 8. 5 shall be full of boys and girls playing in

4. *To play, delight self,* שָׁעַע *shaa,* 3a.

Isa. 11. 8 sucking child shall play on the hole of the

5. *To play, behave as a boy,* παίζω *paizō.*

1 Co 10. 7 people sat down to eat . . and rose up to p.

PLAYER (on instruments), playing —

1. *To play on a stringed instrument,* נָגַן *nagan.*

Psa. 68. 25 the players on instruments (followed) af.

2. *To play on a stringed instrument,* נָגַן *nagan,* 3.

1 Sa. 16. 16 man, (who is) a cunning player on an harp
16. 18 cunning in playing, and a mighty valiant

PLEA —

Judgment, plea, cause, דִּין *din.*

Deut 17. 8 between plea and plea, and between str.

PLEAD (the cause), to —

1. *To plead, judge, strive,* דִּין *din.*

Prov 31 9 plead the cause of the poor and needy
Jer. 30. 13 none to plead thy cause, that thou may

2. *To reason, reprove, decide,* יָכַח *yakach,* 5.

Job 16. 21 Oh that one might plead for a man with
19. 5 magnify . . against me, and plead against

3. *To reason,* יָכַח *yakach,* 7.

Mic. 6. 2 a controversy . . and he will plead with I

4. *To strive, plead,* רִיב *rib.*

Judg. 6. 31 Will ye plead . . he that will plead for him
6. 31 let him plead for himself, because (one)
6 32 Let Baal plead against him, because he
1 Sa. 24. 15 plead my cause, and deliver me out of t.
25. 39 hath pleaded the cause of my reproach
Job 13. 19 Who (is) he (that) will plead with me? for
23. 6 Will he plead against me with (his) great p.?
Psa. 35. 1 Plead . . O LORD, with them that strive w
43. 1 plead my cause against an ungodly nation
74. 22 plead thine own cause: remember how the
119. 154 Plead my cause, and deliver me: quicken
Prov 22. 23 For the LORD will plead their cause, and
23. 11 Redeemer . . shall plead their cause with
Isa. 1. 17 judge the fatherless, plead for the widow
3. 13 LORD standeth up to plead, and standeth
51. 22 thy God (that) pleadeth the cause of his p
Jer. 2. 9 I will yet plead with you, saith the LORD
2. 9 with your children's children will I plead
2. 29 Wherefore will ye plead with me? ye all
12. 1 Righteous (art) thou . . when I plead with
50. 34 he shall throughly plead their cause, that
51. 36 I will plead thy cause, and take vengeance
Lam. 3. 58 thou hast pleaded the causes of my soul
Hos. 2. 2 Plead with your mother plead; for she
Mic. 7 9 until he plead my cause, and execute ju.

5. *To be judged, to plead,* שָׁפַט *shaphat,* 2.

Isa. 43. 26 Put me in remembrance: let us plead to.
59 4 None calleth for justice, nor (any) plead.
66 16 will the LORD plead with all flesh: and the
Jer. 2 35 I will plead with thee, because thou say
25. 31 he will plead with all flesh; he will give

Eze. 17. 20 will plead with him there for his trespass
20. 35 and there will I plead with you face to face
20. 36 Like as I pleaded . . so will I plead with you
38. 22 I will plead against him with pestilence
Joel 3. 2 will plead with them there for my people

PLEADING —

Strife, pleading, cause, רִיב *rib.*

Job 13. 6 and hearken to the pleadings of my lips

PLEASANT (place or thing) —

1. *Desire,* חֶמֶד *chemed.*

Isa. 32. 12 for the pleasant fields, for the fruitful v.
Amos 5. 11 ye have planted pleasant vineyards, but

2. *Desire,* חֶמְדָּה *chemdah.*

2 Ch. 32. 27 and for all manner of pleasant jewels
Psa. 106. 24 Yea, they despised the pleasant land, they
Isa. 2. 16 all the ships . . and upon all pleasant pic
Jer. 3. 19 give thee a pleasant land, a goodly heri
12. 10 they have made my pleasant portion a d.
25. 34 and ye shall fall like a pleasant vessel
Eze. 26. 12 destroy thy pleasant houses: and they
Hos. 13 15 spoil the treasure of all pleasant vessels
Nah. 2. 9 glory out of all the pleasant furniture
Zech. 7 14 for they laid the pleasant land desolate

3. *Desirable objects,* חֲמוּדוֹת *chamudoth.*

Dan. 10 3 I ate no pleasant bread, neither came fle
11. 38 with precious stones, and pleasant things

4. *Grace,* חֵן *chen.*

Prov. 5 19 the loving hind and pleasant roe; let her

5. *Delighting, willing, desiring,* חָפֵץ *chephets.*

Isa 54. 12 and all thy borders of pleasant stones

6. *Good,* טוֹב *tob.*

2 Ki. 2. 19 situation of this city (is) pleasant, as my
Eccl 11. 7 pleasant (thing it is) for the eyes to beho.

7. *Fair,* יָפֶה *yapheh.*

Eze. 33 32 song of one that hath a pleasant voice, and

8. *Precious thing,* מֶגֶד *meged*

Song 4 13 with pleasant fruits; camphire, with sp.
4. 16 come into his garden, and eat his pleasant
7. 13 at our gates (are) all manner of pleasant

9. *Desirable thing,* מַחְמָד *machmad.*

1 Ki. 20. 6 whatsoever is pleasant in thine eyes, they
Isa. 64. 11 and all our pleasant things are laid waste
Lam. 1 10 his hand upon all her pleasant things: for
1. 11 they have given their pleasant things for
2. 4 slew all (that were) pleasant to the eye in
Hos. 9. 6 the pleasant (places) for their silver, net
Joel 3. 5 have carried . . my goodly pleasant things

10. *Desirable things,* מַחֲמַדִּים *machamuddim.*

Lam. 1. 7 all her pleasant things that she had in the
1 11 they have given their pleasant things for

11. *Comely place,* נָאָה *naah.*

Jer. 23 10 pleasant places of the wilderness are dr

12. *Comeliness,* נָוֶה *naveh.*

Hos. 9. 13 Ephraim . . (is) planted in a pleasant place

13. *Pleasant, sweet,* נָעִים *naim.*

2 Sa. 1. 23 Saul and Jonathan (were) lovely and ple
Psa. 16. 6 The lines are fallen unto me in pleasant
81. 2 bring hither the timbrel, the pleasant harp
133. 1 how good and how pleasant . . for brethren
135. 3 sing praises unto his name; for (it is) pl.
147 1 for (it is) pleasant; (and) praise is comely
Prov 22. 18 For (it is) a pleasant thing if thou keep t.
24 4 filled with all precious and pleasant riches
Song 1 16 thou (art) fair, my beloved, yea, pleasant

14. *Pleasantness,* נֹעַם *noam.*

Prov 15. 26 but (the words) of the pure (are) pleasant
16. 24 Pleasant words (are as) an honey comb

15. *Pleasant things,* נַעֲמָנִים *naamanim.*

Isa. 17 10 therefore shalt thou plant pleasant plants

16. *Delight,* עֹנֶג *oneg.*

Isa. 13. 22 dragons in (their) pleasant palaces: and

17. *Beauty, desire,* צְבִי *tsebi.*

Dan. 8 9 toward the east, and toward the pleasant

18. *Delights,* שַׁעֲשֻׁעִים *shaashuim.*

Isa. 5. 7 and the men of Judah his pleasant plant
Jer. 31. 20 Ephraim my dear son? (is he) a pleasant

19. *Desire,* תַּאֲוָה *taavah.*

Gen. 3. 6 when the woman saw . . that it (was) plea.

20. *Delight, luxury,* תַּעֲנוּג *taanug.*

Mic. 2. 9 have ye cast out from their pleasant ho.

PLEASANT, to be —

1. *To be desired,* חָמַד *chamad,* 2.

Gen. 2. 9 to grow every tree that is pleasant to the

2. *To be pleasant,* נָעֵם *naam.*

Gen. 49. 15 the land that (it was) pleasant; and bowed
2 Sa. 1 26 very pleasant hast thou been unto me: thy
Prov 2. 10 and knowledge is pleasant unto thy soul
9. 17 sweet, and bread (eaten) in secret is plea.
Song 7. 6 How fair and how pleasant art thou, O l.

3. *To be sweet,* עָרֵב *arab.*

Mal. 3. 4 Then shall the offering . . be pleasant unto

PLEASANTNESS —

Pleasantness, נֹעַם *noam.*

Prov 3. 17 Her ways (are) ways of pleasantness, and

PLEASE not —

Be evil in eyes of, רָעָה בְּעֵינֵי [*ra*].

Gen. 28 8; Exod. 21. 8.

PLEASE, to —

1. *To have delight, to please,* חָפֵץ *chaphets.*

Psa. 115. 3 he hath done whatsoever he hath pleased
135. 6 Whatsoever the LORD pleased, (that) did he
Eccl. 8. 3 for he doeth whatsoever pleaseth him
Song 2. 7 charge . . that ye stir not up . . till he please
3. 5 charge . . that ye stir not up . . till he please
8. 4; Isa. 53. 10; 55 11; 56. 4; Jon. 1. 14.

2. *To be good as regards,* טוֹב עַל *tob al.*

Neh. 2. 5, 7 said unto the king, If it please the king
Esth. 1. 19 If it please the king, let there go a royal
3. 9 If it please the king, let it be written that
5. 8 if it please the king to grant my petition
7. 3 if it please the king, let my life be given

3. *Good as regards,* טוֹב עַל *tob al.*

Esth. 9. 13 If it please the king, let it be gran.; 18.5.

4. *Delighting, willing,* חָפֵץ *chaphets.*

1 Ki. 21. 6 if it please thee, I will give thee (another)

5. *To be pleased, desirous,* יָאַל *yaal,* 5.

1 Sa. 12 22 hath pleased the LORD to make you his p.
2 Sa. 7 29 let it please thee to bless the house of thy
1 Ch. 17. 27 let it please thee to bless the house of thy
Job 6. 9 Even that it would please God to destroy

6. *To be good,* יָטַב *yatab.*

Neh 2. 6 So it pleased the king to send me: and I
Esth. 5. 14 the thing pleased Haman; and he caused

7. *To be good in the eyes of,* יָטַב בְּעֵינֵי *yatab be-ene.*

Gen. 34. 18 their words pleased Hamor, and Shechem
Josh. 22. 30 And when Phinehas . . heard . . it pleased
22. 33 the thing pleased the children of Israel
2 Sa. 3. 36 people took notice . . and it pleased them
1 Ki. 3. 10 speech pleased the LORD, that Solomon
Esth. 1. 21 the saying pleased the king and the prin.
2. 4 let the maiden which pleaseth the king be
2. 4 the thing pleased the king; and he did so
2. 9 maiden pleased him, and she obtained

8. *To become or seem good,* יָטַב *yatab,* 5.

1 Sa. 20 13 but if it please my father (to do) thee evil

9. *To be pleasing,* רָצָה *ratsah.*

2 Ch 10 7 If thou be kind to this people, and please
Prov 16. 7 When a man's ways please the LORD, he

10. *To be fair before,* שְׁפַר קֳדָם *shephar qodam.*

Dan. 6. 1 It pleased Darius to set over the kingdom

11. *To be right in the eyes of,* יָשַׁר בְּעֵינֵי *yashar be-ene.*

Num 23 27 peradventure it will please God that thou
1 Sa 18. 20 they told Saul, and the thing pleas. 18 26.
1 Ki 9 12 had given him; and they pleased him not
2 Ch. 30 4 pleased the king and all the congregation

12. *Good before,* טוֹב לִפְנֵי *tob li-phene.*

Eccl 7. 26 whoso pleaseth God shall escape from her

13. *Good in the eyes of,* טוֹב בְּעֵינֵי *tob be-ene.*

Gen. 16 6 Abram said . . do to her as it pleaseth thee
20. 15 before thee: dwell where it pleaseth thee
2 Sa. 3 36 whatsoever the king did pleas.; Num. 24. 1.

14. *To please,* ἀρέσκω *areskō.*

Matt 14. 6 danced before them, and pleased Herod
Mark 6 22 pleased Herod and them that sat with him
Acts 6. 5 the saying pleased the whole multitude
Rom. 8 8 they that are in the flesh cannot please G.
15 1 ought to bear . . and not to please ourselves
15 2 Let every one of us please (his) neighbour
15. 3 For even Christ pleased not himself; but
1 Co. 7. 32 He . . careth . . how he may please the Lord
7 33 he . . careth . . how he may please (his) wife
7 34 careth . . how she may please (her) husband
10 33 Even as I please all (men) in all (things)
Gal. 1 10 seek to please men? for if I yet pleased m.
1 Th. 2. 4 not as pleasing men, but God, which trieth
2. 15 they please not God, and are contrary to
4. 1 how ye ought to walk and to please God
2 Ti. 2. 4 that he may please him who hath chosen

15. *To please well,* εὐαρεστέω *euaresteō.*

Heb. 11. 5 had this testimony, that he pleased God
11 6 But without faith (it is) impossible to pl.

16. *To be pleasing,* (εἰμί) ἀρεστός *eimi arestos.*

Acts 12. 3 because he saw it pleased the Jo. 8. 29.

17. *To think, deem,* δοκέω *dokeō.*

Acts 15. 22 Then pleased it the apostles and elders
15. 34 [Notwithstanding it pleased Silas to abide]

18. *To think well,* εὐδοκέω *eudokeō.*

Rom. 15. 26 For it hath pleased them of Macedonia and
15. 27 It hath pleased them verily; and their d.
1 Co. 1 21 pleased God by the foolishness of preach.
Gal. 1. 15 when it pleased God, who separated me
Col. 1. 19 For it pleased (the Father) that in him sh.

19. *To wish, will,* θέλω *thelō.*

1 Co. 12. 18 God set the members . . as it hath pleased
15. 38 God giveth it a body as it hath pleased him

PLEASE better, to —

To be good to, יָטַב לְ *yatab le.*

Psa. 69. 31 (This) also shall please the LORD better

PLEASE selves, to —

To strike hands, שָׂפַק *saphaq,* 5.

Isa. 2. 6 please themselves in the children of stra.

PLEASE well, to —

1. *To be good in the eyes of,* יָטַב בְּעֵינֵי *yatab be-ene.*

Deut. 1. 23 saying pleased me well: and I; Gen 45 16.

2. *To be right in the eyes of*, יָשַׁר בְּעֵינֵי *yashar be-ene.*
Judg14. 3 Get her for me; for she pleaseth me well
14 7 with the woman; and she pleased S. well
1 Sa. 18. 26 pleased David well to be the king's son in
2 Sa. 17. 4 the saying pleased Absalom well, and all
19. 6 died this day, then it had pleased thee w.
3. *To please well*, εὐαρεστέω *euaresteō.*
Heb. 13. 16 for with such sacrifices God is well pleased
4. *To be well pleasing*, εἰμὶ εὐάρεστος *eimi euarestos.*
Titus 2. 9 to please (them) well in all (things); not
PLEASE, to seek to —
To please, amuse, רָצָה *ratsah*, 3.
Job 20. 10 His children shall seek to please the poor
PLEASED, to be (well) —
1. *To have delight, desire*, חָפֵץ *chaphets.*
Judg13. 23 If the LORD were pleased to kill us, he w
1 Ki 9 1 Solomon's desire which he was pleased to
Psa 51. 19 Then shalt thou be pleased with the sac.
Isa. 42. 21 LORD is well pleased for his righteousness'
2. *To be pleased*, רָצָה *ratsah.*
Psa. 40 13 Be pleased, O LORD, to deliver me: O L.
Mic. 6. 7 Will the LORD be pleased with thousands
Mal 1. 8 will he be pleased with thee, or accept thy
3. *To think well together*, συνευδοκέω *suneudokeō.*
1 Co. 7. 12 she be pleased to dwell with him, let him
7 13 if he be pleased to dwell with her, let her
4. *To be well pleased*, εὐδοκέω *eudokeō*, Matt 3. 17;
12 18; 17. 5; Mr. 1. 11; Lu. 3 22; 1 Co. 10. 5; 2 Pe. 1. 17.
PLEASED with, to be —
To be pleased, רָצָה *ratsah.*
Gen. 33 10 face of God, and thou wast pleased with
PLEASING, (to be) —
1. *Good*, טוֹב *tob.*
Esth. 8. 5 right before the king, and I (be) pleasing in
2. *To be sweet*, עָרֵב *arab.*
Hos. 9. 4 neither shall they be pleasing unto him
3. *Pleasing, pleasure*, ἀρέσκεια *areskeia.*
Col 1 10 walk worthy of the Lord unto all pleasing
4. *Pleasing*, ἀρεστός *arestos.*
1 Jo. 3 22 do those things that are pleasing in his
PLEASE, things that —
Pleasing, ἀρεστός *arestos.*
John 8. 29 I do always those things that please him
PLEASURE, (good) —
1. *Desire, inclination*, אַוָּה *avvah.*
Jer. 2. 24 snuffeth up the wind at her pleasure; in
2. *Delight, pleasure*, חֵפֶץ *chephets.*
Job 21 21 For what pleasure (hath) he in his house
22. 3 (Is it) any pleasure to the Almighty, that
Psa. 111. 2 sought out of all them that have pleasure
Eccl. 5 4 for (he hath) no pleasure in fools: pay that
12. 1 thou shalt say, I have no pleasure in them
Isa. 44. 28 shall perform all my pleasure: even saying
46 10 shall stand, and I will do all my pleasure
48. 14 he will do his pleasure on Babylon, and
53 10 pleasure of the LORD shall prosper in his
58. 3 in the day of your fast ye find pleasure and
58 13 doing thy pleasure on my holy day; and
58. 13 nor finding thine own pleasure, nor spea.
Jer. 22. 28; 48 38: Hos 8 8; Mal. 1. 10.
3. *Desire, delight*, חֵשֶׁק *chesheq.*
Isa. 21. 4 night of my pleasure hath he turned into
4. *Good, benefit*, טוֹב *tob.*
Job. 21. 25 And another..never eateth with pleasure
Eccl. 2. 1 enjoy pleasure: and, behold, this also (is)
5. *Soul, breath, desire*, נֶפֶשׁ *nephesh.*
Deut 23. 24 eat grapes thy fill at thine own pleasure
Psa. 105 22 To bind his princes at his pleasure and
Jer. 34 16 whom he had set at liberty at their plea.
6. *Delight*, עֵדֶן *eden.*
Psa. 36. 8 make them drink of the river of thy ple.
7. *Delight*, עֶדְנָה *ednah.*
Gen 18. 12 After I am waxed old shall I have pleas.
8. *Thought, will, desire*, רְעוּת *reuth.*
Ezra 5. 17 let the king send his pleasure to us con.
9. *Good will or pleasure*, רָצוֹן *ratson.*
Ezra 10. 11 make confession..and do his pleasure; and
Neh. 9. 37 they have dominion..at their pleasure
Esth. 1. 8 should do according to every man's plea.
Psa. 51 18 Do good in thy good pleasure unto Zion
103. 21 (ye) ministers of his, that do his pleasure
10. *Pleasant, sweet*, נָעִים *naim.*
Job 36. 11 they shall spend..their years in pleasures
Psa. 16 11 at thy right hand (there are) pleasures for
11. *Rejoicing, joy*, שִׂמְחָה *simchah.*
Prov 21. 17 He that loveth pleasure (shall be) a poor
12. *Good thought*, εὐδοκία *eudokia.*
Eph. 1 5 according to the good pleasure of his will
1 9 according to his good pleasure which he
Phil. 2. 13 both to will and to do of (his) good pleas.
2 Th. 1. 11 fulfil all the good pleasure of (his) good.
13. *Sweetness, pleasure*, ἡδονή *hēdonē.*
Luke 8 14 choked with cares and riches and pleasures
Titus 3. 3 serving divers lusts and pleasures, living
2 Pe. 2. 13 they that count it pleasure to riot in the
14. *Wish, will*, θέλημα *thelēma.*
Rev. 4. 11 for thy pleasure they are and were created
15. *Grace, favour*, χάρις *charis.*
Acts 24. 27 Felix, willing to show the Jews a pleasure
25. 9 Festus, willing to do the Jews a pleasure
PLEASURE, after their own —
According to their judgment, κατὰ τὸ δοκοῦν αὐτοῖς
Heb 12. 10 chastened (us) after their own pleasure
PLEASURE, to be the good —
To think well, εὐδοκέω *eudokeō.*
Luke 12. 32 for it is your Father's good pleasure to g.
PLEASURE, to have, live in, take —
1. *To have delight*, חָפֵץ *chaphets.*
Eze. 18 23 Have I any pleasure at all that the wicked
18. 32 I have no pleasure in the death of him t.
33. 11 I have no pleasure in the death of the wi.
2. *Delighting*, חָפֵץ *chaphets.*
Psa. 5 4 For thou (art) not a God that hath pleas.
35 27 which hath pleasure in the prosperity of
3. *To be sweet*, עָרֵב *arab.*
Eze. 16. 37 lovers, with whom thou hast taken pleas.
4. *To be pleased*, רָצָה *ratsah.*
1 Ch. 29. 17 I know also, my God, that thou..hast pl
Psa 102 14 For thy servants take pleasure in her st.
147 10 taketh not pleasure in the legs of a man
147. 11 taketh pleasure in them that fear him, in
149 4 For the LORD taketh pleasure in his peo
Hag. 1. 8 will take pleasure in it, and I will be gl.
5. *To think well*, εὐδοκέω *eudokeō.*
2 Co 12. 10 Therefore I take pleasure in infirmities, in
2 Th. 2. 12 believed not the truth, but had pleasure
Heb 10 6 In burnt offerings..thou hast had no pl.
10. 8 thou wouldest not, neither hadst pleasure
10. 38 my soul shall have no pleasure in him
6. *To live voluptuously*, σπαταλάω *spatalaō.*
1 Ti. 5 6 she that liveth in pleasure is dead while
7 *To think well together*, συνευδοκέω *suneudokeō.*
Rom. 1. 32 but have pleasure in them that do them
8. *To live luxuriously*, τρυφάω *truphaō.*
Jas. 5 5 Ye have lived in pleasure on the earth, and
PLEASURES, given to —
Given to delights, עֲדִין *adin.*
Isa. 47 8 hear now this, thou (that art) given to p.
PLEDGE —
1. *Pledge*, חֲבֹל *chabol.*
Eze 18 12 hath not restored the pledge, and hath l
18. 16 hath not withholden the pledge, neither
33. 15 (If) the wicked restore the pledge, give
2. *Pledge*, חֲבֹלָה *chabolah.*
Eze 18 7 hath restored to the debtor his pledge, hath
3. *Pledge*, עֲבוֹט *abot.*
Deut 24 10 not go into his house to fetch his pledge
24. 11 shall bring out the pledge abroad unto thee
24. 12 poor, thou shalt not sleep with his pledge
24. 13 thou shalt deliver him the pledge again
4. *Surety*, עֲרֻבָּה *arubbah.*
1 Sa 17 18 how thy brethren fare, and take their pl.
5. *Surety*, עֵרָבוֹן *erabon.*
Gen. 38 17 Wilt thou give (me) a pledge till thou send
38 18 What pledge shall I give thee? And she
38. 20 to receive (his) pledge from the woman's
PLEDGE, to lay to, or take a —
To take a pledge, חָבַל *chabal.*
Exod 22 26 take thy neighbour's raiment to pledge
Deut 24. 6 shall take the nether..millstone to pledge
24 6 for he taketh (a man's) life to pledge
24. 17 shalt not..take a widow's raiment to ple
Job 22. 6 For thou hast taken a pledge from thy b.
24. 3 they take the widow's ox for a pledge
24. 9 pluck the fatherless..and take a pledge of
Prov 20 16 take a pledge of him for a strange woman
27 13 take a pledge of him for a strange woman
Amos 2. 8 upon clothes laid to pledge by every altar
PLEDGES, to give —
To give surety for one's self, עָרַב *arab*, 7.
2 Ki. 18. 23 give pledges to my lord the king of Assy
Isa. 36. 8 give pledges, I pray thee, to my master the
PLE-IA-DES, כִּימָה *the cluster of seven stars.*
Job 9. 9 Which maketh Arcturus, Orion, and P.
38. 31 Canst thou bind the sweet influences of P.
PLENTEOUS —
1. *Fat, firm*, בָּרִיא *bari.*
Hab 1 16 portion (is) fat, and their meat plenteous
2. *Abundant*, רַב *rab.*
Psa. 86 5 plenteous in mercy unto all them that call
86. 15 longsuffering, and plenteous in mercy and
103. 8 slow to anger, and plenteous in mercy
3. *To make abundant*, רָבָה *rabah*, 5.
Psa. 130. 7 for with the LORD..(is) plenteous redem.
4. *Satiety, fulness*, שָׂבָע *saba.*
Gen. 41 34 land of Egypt in the seven plenteous years
41 47 in the seven plenteous years the earth br.
5. *Oily, fat, plenteous*, שָׁמֵן *shamen.*
Isa. 30. 23 it shall be fat and plenteous: in that day
6. *Much, many, abundant*, πολύς *polus.*
Matt. 9. 37 The harvest truly (is) plenteous, but the
PLENTEOUS, to make —
To cause to remain over, יָתַר *yathar*, 5.
Deut 28. 11 shall make thee plenteous in goods, in the
30 9 will make thee plenteous in every work
PLENTEOUSNESS —
1. *What remains over, superfluity*, מוֹתָר *mothar.*
Prov 21. 5 thoughts of the diligent (tend) only to pl.
2. *Satiety, fulness*, שָׂבָע *saba.*
Gen. 41 53 seven years of plenteousness that was in
PLENTIFUL (field) —
1. *Fruitful place or field*, כַּרְמֶל *karmel.*
Isa. 16 10 joy out of the plentiful field; and in the
Jer. 2 7 I brought you into a plentiful country, to
48 33 gladness is taken from the plentiful field
2. *Willing gift or offering*, נְדָבָה *nedabah.*
Psa. 68. 9 Thou, O God, didst send a plentiful rain
PLENTIFULLY —
1. *Superfluity*, יֶתֶר *yether.*
Psa. 31 23 and plentifully rewardeth the proud doer
2. *Abundance*, רֹב *rob.*
Job 26 3 hast thou plentifully declared the thing
PLENTY —
1. *Abundance*, רֹב *rob.*
Gen 27 28 fatness of the earth, and plenty of corn
2 Ch. 31 10 had enough to eat, and have left plenty
2. *To make abundant*, רָבָה *rabah*, 5.
1 Ki. 10. 11 great plenty of almug trees, and precious
3. *Satiety, fulness*, שָׂבָע *saba.*
Gen. 41 29 come seven years of great plenty throug.
41 30 all the plenty shall be forgotten in the
41. 31 plenty shall not be known in the land by
Prov 3. 10 So shall thy barns be filled with plenty
4. *Heights, glitterings*, תּוֹעָפוֹת *toaphoth.*
Job 22. 25 defence, and thou shalt have plenty of
5. *To eat*, אָכַל *akal* (adv inf.).
Joel 2. 26 ye shall eat in plenty, and be satisfied, and
PLENTY of, to have —
To be satiated, satisfied, שָׂבַע *sabea.*
Prov 28 19 tilleth his land shall have plenty of bread
Jer 44 17 for (then) had we plenty of victuals, and
PLENTY —
Collection, מִקְוֶה *miqveh.*
Lev 11 36 (wherein there is) plenty of water, shall
PLOT, to —
To devise, design, זָמַם *zamam.*
Psa. 37 12 wicked plotteth against the just, and g.
PLOUGH —
A plough, ἄροτρον *arotron.*
Luke 9. 62 No man, having put his hand to the plo.
PLOUGH, PLOW, to —
1. *To plough, grave*, חָרַשׁ *charash.*
Deut 22. 10 Thou shalt not plow with an ox and an ass
Judg 14. 18 If ye had not ploughed with my heifer, ye
1 Ki. 19 19 who (was) ploughing (with) twelve yoke
Job 1 14 The oxen were plowing, and the asses fe.
4. 8 they that plow iniquity, and sow wicked.
Psa. 129. 3 The plowers plowed upon my back; they
Prov 20. 4 sluggard will not plow by reason of the
Isa. 28 24 Doth the plowman plow all day to sow?
Hos 10. 11 Judah shall plow, (and) Jacob shall break
10 13 Ye have ploughed wickedness, ye have r.
Amos 6. 12 will (one) plow (there) with oxen? for ye
2. *To plough*, ἀροτριάω *arotriaō.*
Luke 17 7 which of you, having a servant plowing
1 Co. 9. 10 that he that plougheth should plow in h.
PLOWED, to be —
To be ploughed, חָרַשׁ *charash*, 2.
Jer 26 18 Zion shall be plowed (like) a field, and J.
Mic 3 12 Therefore shall Zion for your sake be pl.
PLOWER, PLOWMAN —
1. *Ploughman, husbandman*, אִכָּר *ikkar.*
Isa 61. 5 sons of the alien (shall be) your plowmen
Jer. 14 4 plowmen were ashamed, they covered th.
2. *To plough, plow*, חָרַשׁ *charash.*
Psa. 129 3 The plowers..made long their furrows
Isa. 28 24 Doth the plowman plow all day to sow?
Amos 9 13 the plowman shall overtake the reaper
PLOWING, PLOUGHSHARE —
1. *Coulter, ploughshare*, אֵת *eth.*
Isa. 2. 4 shall beat their swords into ploughshares
Joel 3. 10 Beat your ploughshares into swords, and
Mic. 4. 3 shall beat their swords into ploughshares
2. *Tilling, tillage*, נִיר *nir.*
Prov 21. 4 An high look..(and) the plowing of the
PLUCK (off, out, up), to —
1. *To pluck*, אָרָה *arah.*
Psa. 80. 12 all they which pass by the way do pluck
2. *To snatch violently away*, גָּזַל *gazal.*
2 Sa. 23. 21 plucked the spear out of the Egyptian's
1 Ch. 11. 23 plucked the spear out of the Egyptian's
Job 24. 9 They pluck the fatherless from the breast
Mic. 3. 2 who pluck off their skin from off them, and

3. *To cause to go or come out,* יָצָא *yatsa,* 5.
Exod. 4. 7 plucked it out of his bosom, and, behold
Psa. 25. 15 for he shall pluck my feet out of the net

4. *To make an end of, remove,* כָּלָה *kalah,* 3.
Psa. 74. 11 even thy right hand? pluck (it) out of thy

5. *To peel off, pluck out,* מָרַט *marat.*
Ezra 9. 3 plucked off the hair of my head and of my
Neh. 13. 25 plucked off their hair, and made them s.
Isa. 50. 6 my cheeks to them that plucked off the

6. *To pull away or down,* נָסַח *nasach.*
Psa. 52. 5 pluck thee out of (thy) dwelling place, and

7. *To draw away or out,* נָתַק *nathaq.*
Jer. 22. 24 (As) I live..yet would I pluck thee thence

8. *To draw away or out,* נָתַק *nathaq,* 3.
Eze. 23. 34 pluck off thine own breasts: for I have s.

9. *To pluck up,* נָתַשׁ *nathash.*
Jer. 12. 14 will pluck them out of their land, and p.
12. 15 after that I have plucked them out, I will
12. 17 I will utterly pluck up and destroy that
18. 7 to pluck up, and to pull down, and to d.
24. 6 I will plant them, and not pluck (them)
31. 28 to pluck up, and to break down, and to
42. 10 I will plant you, and not pluck (you) up
45. 4 that which I have planted, I will pluck up
Mic. 5. 14 I will pluck up thy groves out of the midst

10. *To root out,* עָקַר *aqar.*
Eccl. 3. 2 a time to pluck up (that which is) planted

11. *To crop, pluck,* קָטַף *qataph.*
Deut 23. 25 thou mayest pluck the ears with thine h

12. *To cause to cast away,* שָׁלַךְ *shalak,* 5.
Job 29. 17 and I..plucked the spoil out of his teeth

13. *To draw off or out,* שָׁלַף *shalaph.*
Ruth 4. 7 a man plucked off his shoe, and gave (it)

14. *To snatch at or away,* ἁρπάζω *harpazō.*
John 10. 28 neither shall any pluck them out of my
10. 29 and none is able to pluck..out of my Fa.

15. *To cast out,* ἐκβάλλω *ekballō.*
Mark 9. 47 if thine eye offend thee, pluck it out: it

16. *To take out or away,* ἐξαιρέω *exaireō.*
Matt. 5. 29 pluck it out, and cast (it) from thee: for
18. 9 pluck it out, and cast (it) from thee: it is

17. *To dig out,* ἐξορύττω *exoruttō.*
Gal. 4. 15 ye would have plucked out your own eyes

18. *To pluck or pull,* τίλλω *tillō.*
Matt 12. 1 began to pluck the ears of corn, and to eat
Mark 2. 23 began, as they went, to pluck the ears of
Luke 6. 1 his disciples plucked the ears of corn, and

PLUCK asunder or away, to —
1. *To (cause to) turn aside,* סוּר *sur,* 5.
Lev. 1. 16 he shall pluck away his crop with his fe.

2. *To draw asunder,* διασπάω *diaspaō.*
Mark 5. 4 chains had been plucked asunder by him

PLUCK down, to —
1. *To break or throw down,* הָרַס *haras.*
Prov. 14. 1 the foolish plucketh it down with her h.

2. *To destroy, cut off, lay waste,* שָׁמַד *shamad,* 5.
Num 33. 52 and quite pluck down all their high places

PLUCK off hair, to —
To peel, polish, מָרַט *marat.*
Neh. 13. 25 plucked off their hair, and made them s.

PLUCK up by the root, to —
1. *To pluck up,* נָתַשׁ *nathash.*
2 Ch. 7. 20 Then will I pluck them up by the roots

2. *To root out,* ἐκριζόω *ekrizoō.*
Luke 17. 6 Be thou plucked up by the root, and be
Jude 12 trees..twice dead, plucked up by the roots

PLUCKED (away, off or up), to be —
1. *To be peeled, polished,* מָרַט *merat.*
Dan. 7. 4 I beheld till the wings thereof were plu.

2. *To be pulled away,* נָסַח *nasach,* 2.
Deut 28. 63 ye shall be plucked from off the land

3. *To be snatched away,* נָצַל *natsal,* 6.
Amos 4. 11 as a fire brand plucked out of the burning
Zech. 3. 2 (is) not this a brand plucked out of..fire?

4. *To be drawn away or out,* נָתַק *nathaq,* 2.
Jer. 6. 29 in vain; for the wicked are not plucked a.

5. *To be plucked up,* נָתַשׁ *nathash,* 2.
Jer. 31. 40 it shall not be plucked up, nor thrown d.
Dan. 11. 4 his kingdom shall be plucked up, even for

6. *To be plucked up,* נָתַשׁ *nathash,* 6.
Eze. 19. 12 she was plucked up in fury, she was cast

7. *Torn off,* טָרָף *taraph.*
Gen. 8. 11 in her mouth (was) an olive leaf pluckt off

PLUMB LINE, PLUMMET —
1. *Plumb line,* אֲנָךְ *anak.*
Amos 7. 7 (made) by a plumb line, with a plumb line
7. 8 what seest thou? And I said, A plumb l.
7. 8 I will set a plumb line in the midst of my

2. *Plummet,* מִשְׁקֹלֶת, מִשְׁקֶלֶת *mishqoleth, mishqeleth.*
2 Ki. 21. 13 the line of Samaria, and the plummet of
Isa. 28. 17 will I lay..righteousness to the plummet

3. *A stone of tin,* אֶבֶן בְּדִיל *eben bedil.*
Zech. 4. 10 and shall see the plummet in the hand of

PLUNGE, to —
To sprinkle, dip, defile, טָבַל *tabal.*
Job 9. 31 Yet shalt thou plunge me in the ditch, and

PO-CHE'-RETH, פֹּכֶרֶת *binding.*
A servant of Solomon whose descendants returned with Zerubbabel. B.C. 636.
Ezra 2. 57 the children of P. of Zebaim, the children
Neh. 7. 59 the children of P. of Zebaim, the children

POET —
A maker, doer, poet, ποιητής *poiētēs.*
Acts 17. 28 as certain also of your own [poets] have

POINT —
1. *Turning, slaughter,* אִבְחָה *ibchah.*
Eze. 21. 15 I have set the point of the sword against

2. *Point, nail,* צִפֹּרֶן *tsipporen.*
Jer. 17. 1 (is) written..with the point of a diamond

POINT, to be at the —
1. *To go, go on,* הָלַךְ *halak.*
Gen. 25. 32 I (am) at the point to die; and what profit

2. *To be about to,* μέλλω *mellō.*
John 4. 47 heal his son: for he was at the point of d.

POINT of death —
Last, extreme point, ἐσχάτως *eschatōs.*
Mark 5. 23 My..daughter lieth at the point of death

POINT out, to —
1. *To point out, show, indicate,* אָוָה *avah,* 7.
Num 34. 10 ye shall point out your east border from

2. *To mark out,* תָּאָה *taah,* 3.
Num 34. 7 from the great sea ye shall point out for
34. 8 From mount Hor ye shall point out (your

POINTED (sharp) things —
Sharp pointed, חָרוּץ *charuts.*
Job 41. 30 he spreadeth sharp pointed things upon

POINTS, in —
Over against, just as, עֻמָּה *ummah.*
Eccl. 5. 16 in all points as he came, so shall he go

POISON —
1. *Heat, fury, poison,* חֵמָה *chemah.*
Deut 32. 24 with the poison of serpents of the dust
32. 33 Their wine (is) the poison of dragons, and
Job 6. 4 the poison whereof drinketh up my spirit
Psa. 58. 4 Their poison (is) like the poison of a serp.
140. 3 adders' poison (is) under their lips. Selah

2. *Venom,* רֹאשׁ *rosh.*
Job 20. 16 He shall suck the poison of asps: the vip.

3. *Poison, venom,* ἰός *ios.*
Rom. 3. 13 the poison of asps (is) under their lips
Jas. 3. 8 (it is) an unruly evil, full of deadly poison

POLE —
Sign, banner, נֵס *nes.*
Num 21. 8 Make..a fiery serpent, and set it upon a p.
21. 9 a serpent of brass, and put it upon a pole

POLICY —
Understanding, skill, שֶׂכֶל, שֵׂכֶל *sekel.*
Dan. 8. 25 through his policy also he shall cause c.

POLISHED, polishing, (to be) —
1. *To clear, purify,* בָּרַר *barar.*
Isa. 49. 2 he hid me, and made me a polished shaft

2. *To be hewn, carved,* חָטַב *chatab,* 4.
Psa. 144. 12 polished (after) the similitude of a palace

3. *Bright,* קָלָל *qalal.*
Dan. 10. 6 and his feet like in colour to polished br.

4. *Cutting, form, polishing,* גִּזְרָה *gizrah.*
Lam. 4. 7 in body..their polishing (was) of sapphire

POLL —
Scull, poll, גֻּלְגֹּלֶת *gulgoleth.*
Num. 1. 2 of (their) names, every male by their polls
1. 18 twenty years old and upward, by their p.
1. 20, 22 the number of the names, by their p.
3. 47 even take five shekels a piece by the poll
1 Ch. 23. 3 their number by their polls, man by man
23. 24 counted by number of names by their p.

POLL, to —
1. *To cut off or down, shave, shear,* גָּזַז *gazaz.*
Mic. 1. 16 and poll thee for thy delicate children

2. *To shave, poll one's head,* גָּלַח *galach,* 3.
2 Sa. 14. 26 And when he polled his head, for it
14. 26 was at every year's end that he polled (it

3. *To poll or shear the head,* כָּסַם *kasam.*
Eze. 44. 20 to grow..they shall only poll their heads

POLLUTE, to —
1. *To pollute,* גָּאַל *gaal,* 3.
Mal. 1. 7 and ye say, Wherein have we polluted thee

2. *To pierce, pollute,* חָלַל *chalal,* 3.
Exod 20. 25 lift up thy tool..thou hast polluted it
Num 18. 32 neither shall ye pollute the holy things
Isa. 47. 6 I have polluted mine inheritance, and
56. 6 keepeth the sabbath from polluting it
Jer. 34. 16 polluted my name, and caused every man
Lam 2. 2 hath polluted the kingdom and the princes
Eze. 7. 21 give it..for a spoil; and they shall pollute
7. 22 they shall pollute my secret (place): for
13. 19 And will ye pollute me among my people
20. 13 my sabbaths they greatly polluted: then
20. 16 Because they..polluted my sabbaths: for
20. 21 they polluted my sabbaths: then I said, I
20. 24 had polluted my sabbaths, and their eyes
20. 39 pollute ye my holy name no more with
44. 7 to be in my sanctuary, to pollute it, (even)
Dan. 11. 31 shall pollute the sanctuary of strength
Zeph. 3. 4 her priests have polluted the sanctuary

3. *To profane, defile,* חָנֵף *chaneph,* 5.
Num 35. 33 shall not pollute the land wherein ye (are)
Jer. 3. 2 and thou hast polluted the land with thy

4. *To defile, make unclean,* טָמֵא *tame,* 3.
2 Ki. 23. 16 polluted it, according to the word of the
2 Ch. 36. 14 polluted the house of the LORD which he
Jer. 7. 30 set..abominations in the house..to pollu.
Eze. 20. 26 I polluted them in their own gifts, in that
36. 18 their idols (wherewith) they had polluted

5. *To make common, pollute,* κοινόω *koinoō.*
Acts 21. 28 and further..hath polluted this holy pla.

POLLUTE selves, to —
1. *To be polluted,* גָּאַל *gaal,* 2.
Lam. 4. 14 they have polluted themselves with blood

2. *To be defiled,* טָמֵא *tame,* 2.
Eze. 20. 31 ye pollute yourselves with all your idols

POLLUTED, to be —
1. *To be trodden down,* בּוּס *bus,* 7a.
Eze. 16. 6 and saw thee polluted in thine own blood
16. 22 and bare, (and) wast polluted in thy blood

2. *To be polluted,* גָּאַל *gaal,* 2.
Zeph. 3. 1 Woe to her that is filthy and polluted, to

3. *To be polluted,* גָּאַל *gaal,* 4.
Ezra 2. 62 therefore were they, as polluted, put from
Neh. 7. 64 therefore were they, as polluted, put from
Mal. 1. 7 Ye offer polluted bread upon mine altar
1. 12 The table of the LORD (is) polluted; and

4. *To be pierced, polluted,* חָלַל *chalal,* 2.
Isa. 48. 11 do (it): for how should (my name) be po.
Eze. 20. 9, 14, 22 that it should not be polluted

5. *To be profaned,* חָנֵף *chaneph.*
Psa. 106. 38 and the land was polluted with blood
Jer. 3. 1 shall not that land be greatly polluted?

6. *To be unclean,* טָמֵא *tame.*
Eze. 23. 17 she was polluted with them, and her m.
Mic. 2. 10 because it is polluted, it shall destroy (you)

7. *To be or become unclean,* טָמֵא *tame,* 2.
Jer 2. 23 I am not polluted, I have not gone after
Eze. 20. 30 Are ye polluted after the manner of your
23. 30 because thou art polluted with their idols

8. *To be or become unclean,* טָמֵא *tame,* 4.
Eze. 4. 14 behold, my soul hath not been polluted

9. *To make self unclean,* טָמֵא *tame,* 7.
Eze. 14. 11 neither be polluted any more with all t.
Hos. 9. 4 all that eat thereof shall be polluted: for

10. *Unclean,* טָמֵא *tame.*
Amos 7. 17 thou shalt die in a polluted land: and I.

11. *Crooked, slippery,* עָקֹב *aqob.*
Hos. 6. 8 Gilead (is) a city..polluted with blood

POLLUTION —
1. *Unclean,* טָמֵא *tame.*
Eze. 22. 10 humbled her that was set apart for poll.

2. *Pollution,* ἀλίσγημα *alisgēma.*
Acts 15. 20 they abstain from pollutions of idols, and

3. *Defilement, pollution,* μίασμα *miasma.*
2 Pe. 2. 20 after they have escaped the pollutions of

POLLUX, *the twin brother of Castor.*
Acts 28 11 in the isle, whose sign was Castor and P.

POMEGRANATE (tree) —
Pomegranate, רִמּוֹן *rimmon.*
Exod 28. 33 thou shalt make pomegranates (of) blue
28. 34 pomegranate, a golden bell and a pome.
39. 24 made upon the hems..pomegranates (of)
39. 25 the pomegranates upon the hem of the r.
39. 25 round about between the pomegranates
39. 26 a pomegranate, a bell and a pomegranate
Num 13. 23 (they brought) of the pomegranates, and
20. 5 or of figs, or of vines, or of pomegranates
Deut. 8. 8 and vines, and fig trees, and pomegrana.
1 Sa. 14. 2 under a pomegranate tree which (is) in
1 Ki. 7. 18 that (were) upon the top with pomegran.
7. 20 the pomegranates (were) two hundred, in
7. 42 hundred pomegranates for the two net w.
7. 42 two rows of pomegranates for one net w.
2 Ki. 25. 17 and pomegranates upon the chapiter rou.
2 Ch. 3. 16 made an hundred pomegranates, and put
4. 13 hundred pomegranates on the two wreaths
4. 13 two rows of pomegranates on each wreath
Song 4. 3 temples (are) like a piece of a pomegranate
4. 13 Thy plants (are) an orchard of pomegra.
6. 7 As a piece of a pomegranate (are) thy te.
6. 11 to see whether..the pomegranates budded
7. 12 see..(whether)..the pomegranates bud f.
8. 2 spiced wine of the juice of my pomegran.
Jer. 52. 22 pomegranates upon the chapiters round
52. 22 and the pomegranates (were) like unto t.
52. 23 were ninety and six pomegranates on a

Jer. 52. 23 the pomegranates upon the net work (w.)
Joel 1. 12 the pomegranate tree, the palm tree also
Hag. 2. 19 pomegranate, and the olive tree, hath not

POMMEL —

Bowl, oil vessel, גֻּלָּה *gullah.*
2 Ch. 4. 12 two pillars, and the pommels, and the c.
4. 12, 13 to cover the two pommels of the cha.

POMP —

1. *Pride, rising, excellency,* גָּאוֹן *gaon.*
Isa. 14. 11 Thy pomp is brought down to the grave
Eze. 7. 24 I will also make the pomp of the strong to
30. 18 the pomp of her strength shall cease in her
32. 12 they shall spoil the pomp of Egypt, and
33. 28 and the pomp of her strength shall cease

2. *Wasting, desolation, noise,* שָׁאוֹן *shaon.*
Isa. 5. 14 and their pomp..shall descend into it

3. *Appearance, pomp,* φαντασία *phantasia.*
Acts 25. 23 when Agrippa was come..with great po.

POND, POOL —

1. *Pond,* אֲגַם *agam.*
Exod. 7. 19 stretch out thine hand..upon their ponds
8. 5 Stretch forth thine hand..over the ponds
Isa. 14. 23 I will also make it..pools of water: and
19. 10 all that make sluices (and) ponds for fish
35. 7 the parched ground shall become a pool
41. 18 I will make the wilderness a pool of wat.
42. 15 rivers islands, and I will dry up the pools

2. *Pool,* בְּרָכָה *berakah.*
Psa. 84. 6 passing through..rain also filleth the po.

3. *Pool,* בְּרֵכָה *berekah.*
2 Sa. 2. 13 met together by the pool of Gibeon: and
2. 13 one side of the pool..other side of the p.
4. 12 hanged (them) up over the pool in Hebron
1 Ki. 22. 38 washed the chariot in the pool of Samaria
2 Ki. 18. 17 and stood by the conduit of the upper p.
20. 20 how he made a pool, and a conduit, and
Neh. 2. 14 Then I went on..to the king's pool: but
3. 15 wall of the pool of Siloah by the king's g.
3. 16 to the pool that was made, and unto the
Eccl. 2. 6 I made me pools of water, to water ther.
Song 7. 4 thine eyes (like) the fish pools in Heshbon
Isa. 7. 3 the end of the conduit of the upper pool.
22. 9 ye gathered together the waters of the..p.
22. 11 the two walls for the water of the old pool
36. 2 stood by the conduit of the upper pool in
Nah. 2. 8 But Nineveh (is) of old like a pool of water

4. *Collection,* מִקְוֶה *miqveh.*
Exod. 7. 19 upon all their pools of water, that they

5. *Pool, bath,* κολυμβήθρα *kolumbēthra.*
John 5. 2 Now there is at Jerusalem..a pool, which
5. 4 [down at a certain season into the pool]
5. 7 have no man..put me into the pool: but
9. 7 wash in the pool of Siloam, which is, by
9. 11 Go to [the pool of] Siloam, and wash: and

PONDER, to —

1. *To ponder,* פָּלַס *palas,* 3.
Prov. 4. 26 Ponder the path of thy feet, and let all
5. 6 Lest thou shouldest ponder the path of
5. 21 the LORD, and he pondereth all his goings

2. *To weigh, ponder,* תָּכַן *takan.*
Prov 21. 2 right..but the LORD pondereth the hearts
24. 12 doth not he that pondereth the heart co.

3. *To cast together,* συμβάλλω *sumballō.*
Luke 2. 19 But Mary..pondered (them) in her heart

PONTIUS, Πόντιος.
The name of the Roman governor of Judea. A.D. 26–36. See *Pilate.*
Matt 27. 2 they..delivered him to P. Pilate the gov.
Luke 3. 1 P. Pilate being governor of Judæa, and H.
Acts 4. 27 P. Pilate, with the Gentiles..were gathe.
1 Ti. 6. 13 who before P. Pilate witnessed a good co.

PON'-TUS, Πόντος.
The N.E. province of Asia Minor, having the Euxine Sea on the N., Cappadocia on the S., Colchis on the E., and Paphlagonia and Galatia on the W. It was originally a part of Cappadocia, and a satrapy of the Persian empire; in 480 B.C. it was given to Artabazes; in 112–110 Mithridates the Great greatly enlarged it, and assisted the Greeks against the Scythians, and in 108–105 he formed connections as far W. as the Danube; in 89–85 he lost Bithynia, Cappadocia and Paphlagonia; in 84–81 he was still losing, and in 75–64 Pontus became a Roman province. Its kings were Ariobarzanes II. B.C. 363; Mithridates II. 337; Mithridates III. 302; Ariobarzanes III. 266; Mithridates IV. 240; Pharnaces I. 190, Mithridates V. 156; Mithridates VI. 120; Pharnaces II. 63.
Acts 2. 9 the dwellers in Mesopotamia..in P., and
18. 2 a certain Jew named Aquila, born in P.
1 Pe. 1. 1 to the strangers scattered throughout P.

POOR (man) —

1. *Desirous, needy, poor,* אֶבְיוֹן *ebyon.*
Exod 23. 6 shalt not wrest the judgment of thy poor
23. 11 that the poor of thy people may eat: and
Deut 15. 4 Save when there shall be no poor among
15. 7 If there be among you a poor man of one
15. 7 nor shut thine hand from thy poor brother
15. 9 thine eye be evil against thy poor brother
15. 11 For the poor shall never cease out of the
Esth. 9. 22 of sending portions..and gifts to the poor
Job 5. 15 But he saveth the poor from the sword
29. 16 I (was) a father to the poor: and the cause
30. 25 was (not) my soul grieved for the poor?
31. 19 If I have seen..any poor without covering
Psa. 49. 2 Both low and high, rich and poor, toget.
69. 33 For the LORD heareth the poor, and desp.
107. 41 Yet setteth he the poor on high from affl.
109. 31 shall stand at the right hand of the poor
112. 9 He hath dispersed, he hath given to the p.
132. 15 I will abundantly..satisfy her poor with
140. 12 LORD will maintain..the right of the poor
Prov. 14. 31 honoureth him hath mercy on the poor
Isa. 29. 19 poor among men shall rejoice in the holy
Jer. 2. 34 the blood of the souls of the poor innoce.
20. 13 for he hath delivered the soul of the poor
Amos. 2. 6 because they sold..the poor for a pair of
5. 12 they turn aside the poor in the gate (from

2. *Lean, poor, weak,* דַּל *dal.*
Gen. 41. 19 poor and very ill favoured and lean flesh.
Exod 23. 3 Neither shalt thou countenance a poor m.
30. 15 poor shall not give less, than half a shek.
Lev. 14. 21 if he (be) poor, and cannot get so much
19. 15 shalt not respect the person of the poor
Judg. 6. 15 my family (is) poor in Manasseh, and I
Ruth 3. 10 followedst not young men, whether poor
1 Sa. 2. 8 He raiseth up the poor out of the dust
Job 5. 16 So the poor hath hope, and iniquity stop.
20. 10 His children shall seek to please the poor
20. 19 he..oppressed (and) hath forsaken the p.
31. 16 If I have withheld the poor from (their) d.
34. 19 regardeth the rich more than the poor?
34. 28 So that they cause the cry of the poor to
Psa. 41. 1 Blessed (is) he that considereth the poor
72. 13 He shall spare the poor and needy, and
82. 3 Defend the poor and fatherless; do just.
82. 4 Deliver the poor and needy: rid (them)
113. 7 He raiseth up the poor out of the dust
Prov. 10. 15 the destruction of the poor (is) their pov.
14. 31 He that oppresseth the poor reproacheth
19. 4 the poor is separated from his neighbour
19. 17 He that hath pity upon the poor lendeth
21. 13 stoppeth his ears at the cry of the poor
22. 9 for he giveth of his bread to the poor
22. 16 He that oppresseth the poor to increase
22. 22 Rob not the poor, because he (is) poor, neit.
28. 3 man that oppresseth the poor (is like) a
28. 8 gather it for him that will pity the poor
28. 11 poor that hath understanding searcheth
28. 15 (so is) a wicked ruler over the poor peop.
29. 7 righteous considereth the cause of the p.
29. 14 The king that faithfully judgeth the poor
Isa. 11. 4 with righteousness shall he judge the po.
14. 30 first born of the poor shall feed, and the
25. 4 For thou hast been a strength to the poor
Jer. 5. 4 Surely these (are) poor; they are foolish
39. 10 left of the poor of the people, which had
Amos 2. 7 dust of the earth on the head of the poor
4. 1 which oppress the poor, which crush the
5. 11 as your treading (is) upon the poor, and
8. 6 That we may buy the poor for silver, and
Zeph. 3. 12 leave..an afflicted and poor people, and

3. *Poverty, weakness,* דַּלָּה *dallah.*
2 Ki. 25. 12 left of the poor of the land (to be) vine
Jer. 40. 7 poor of the land, of them that were not c.
52. 15 carried away captive (certain) of the poor
52. 16 left (certain) of the poor of the land for

4. *Thy army* (?), חֵלְכָה *chelekah.*
Psa. 10. 8 his eyes are privily set against the poor
10. 14 the poor committeth himself unto thee

5. *One that lacks,* מַחְסוֹר *machsor.*
Prov 21. 17 He that loveth pleasure (shall be) a poor m.

6. *Poor, useful,* מִסְכֵּן *misken.*
Eccl. 4. 13 Better (is) a poor and a wise child than an
9. 15 Now there was found in it a poor wise m.
9. 15 yet no man remembered that same poor m.
9. 16 nevertheless the poor man's wisdom (is)

7. *Humble, poor,* עָנֶה *aneh.*
Dan. 4. 27 by showing mercy to the poor; if it may

8 *Poor, oppressed,* עָנִי *ani* [V.L. עָנָו].
Job 24. 4 poor of the earth hide themselves togeth.
Psa. 9. 18 expectation of the poor shall (not) perish
Prov 14. 21 but he that hath mercy on the poor, happy
Isa. 32. 7 deviseth wicked devices to destroy the p.
Amos 8. 4 even to make the poor of the land to fail

9. *Poor, oppressed,* עָנִי *ani.*
Exod 22. 25 money to (any of) my people (that is) poor
Lev. 19. 10 thou shalt leave them for the poor and s.
23. 22 thou shalt leave them unto the poor, and
Deut 15. 11 to thy poor, and to thy needy, in thy land
24. 12 if the man (be) poor, thou shalt not sleep
24. 14 not oppress an hired servant (that is) poor
24. 15 for he (is) poor, and setteth his heart upon
Job 24. 9 They pluck..and take a pledge of the poor
24. 14 rising with the light killeth the poor and
29. 12 Because I delivered the poor that cried
36. 6 preserveth..but giveth right to the poor
36. 15 He delivereth the poor in his affliction, and
Psa. 9. 18 expectation of the poor shall (not) perish
10. 2 The wicked..doth persecute the poor: let
10. 9 he lieth in wait to catch the poor: he do.
10. 9 catch the poor, when he draweth him into
12. 5 For the oppression of the poor, for the s.
14. 6 Ye have shamed the counsel of the poor
34. 6 This poor man cried, and the LORD heard
35. 10 which deliverest the poor from him that
35. 10 poor and the needy from him that spoileth
Psa. 37. 14 cast down the poor and needy, (and) to s.
40. 17 But I (am) poor and needy; (yet) the L.
68. 10 hast prepared of thy goodness for the po.
69. 29 But I (am) poor and sorrowful: let thy s.
70. 5 But I (am) poor and needy; make haste
72. 2 He shall judge..thy poor with judgment
72. 4 He shall judge the poor of the people, he
72. 12 he shall deliver..the poor also, and (him)
74. 19 forget not the congregation of thy poor
74. 21 let the poor and needy praise thy name
86. 1 Bow down thine ear..for I (am) poor and
109. 16 but persecuted the poor and needy man
109. 22 poor and needy, and my heart is wounded
Prov 14. 21 he that hath mercy on the poor, happy
30. 14 to devour the poor from off the earth, and
31. 9 and plead the cause of the poor and needy
Eccl. 6. 8 what hath the poor, that knoweth to walk
Isa. 3. 14 the spoil of the poor (is) in your houses
3. 15 grind the faces of the poor? saith the L.
10. 2 take away the right from the poor of my
10. 30 cause it to be heard unto Laish, O poor A.
14. 32 and the poor of his people shall trust in it
26. 6 feet of the poor, (and) the steps of the n.
32. 7 devices to destroy the poor with lying w.
41. 17 (When) the poor and needy seek water, and
58. 7 that thou bring the poor that are cast out
66. 2 to (him that is) poor, and of a contrite s.
Jer. 22. 16 judged the cause of the poor and needy
Eze. 16. 49 strengthen the hand of the poor and needy
18. 12 Hath oppressed the poor and needy, hath
18. 17 hath taken off his hand from the poor, (th.)
22. 29 have vexed the poor and needy; yea they
Amos 8. 4 even to make the poor of the land to fail
Hab. 3. 14 their rejoicing (was) as to devour the poor
Zech. 7. 10 oppress not the widow..nor the poor; and
11. 7 feed the flock..(even) you, O poor of the
11. 11 so the poor of the flock that waited upon

10. *To be poor, impoverished,* רוּשׁ *rush.*
1 Sa. 18. 23 seeing that I (am) a poor man, and lightly
2 Sa. 12. 1 two men..the one rich, and the other po.
12. 3 But the poor (man) had nothing, save one
12. 4 took the poor man's lamb, and dressed it
Prov 10. 4 He becometh poor that dealeth (with) a
13. 8 his riches: but the poor heareth not reb.
13. 23 Much food (is in) the tillage of the poor
14. 20 The poor is hated even of his own neigh.
17. 5 Whoso mocketh the poor reproacheth his
18. 23 The poor useth entreaties; but the rich a.
19. 1 Better (is) the poor that walketh in his i.
19. 7 All the brethren of the poor do hate him
19. 22 kindness: and a poor man (is) better than
22. 2 The rich and poor meet together: the L.
22. 7 The rich ruleth over the poor, and the b.
28. 3 A poor man that oppresseth..(is like) a s.
28. 6 Better (is) the poor that walketh in his u.
28. 27 He that giveth unto the poor shall not l.
29. 13 The poor and the deceitful man meet to.
Eccl. 4. 14 that is) born in his kingdom becometh p.
5. 8 If thou seest the oppression of the poor

11. *Afflicted,* חֵלְכָּאִים *chelkaim* [V.L. חֵל כָּאִים *chel kaim*].
Psa. 10. 10 that the poor may fall by his strong ones

12. *Labourer, poor man,* πένης *penēs.*
2 Co. 9. 9 he hath given to the poor: his righteous.

13. *Very poor,* πενιχρός *penichros.*
Luke 21. 2 saw also a certain poor widow casting in

14. *Trembling, poor,* πτωχός *ptōchos.*
Matt 5. 3 Blessed (are) the poor in spirit: for theirs
11. 5 the poor have the gospel preached to th
19. 21 sell that thou hast, and give to the poor
26. 9 been sold for much, and given to the po.
26. 11 For ye have the poor always with you; but
Mark 10. 21 give to the poor, and thou shalt have tre.
12. 42 there came a certain [poor] widow, and
12. 43 this poor widow hath cast more in than
14. 5 have been sold..and..given to the poor
14. 7 For ye have the poor with you always, and
Luke 4. 18 anointed me to preach..to the poor; he
6. 20 Blessed (be ye) poor: for yours is the kin.
7. 22 how that ..to the poor the gospel is pre.
14. 13 when thou makest a feast, call the poor
14. 21 bring in hither the poor, and the maimed
18. 22 distribute unto the poor, and thou shalt
19. 8 the half of my goods I give to the poor
21. 3 this poor widow hath cast in more than
John 12. 5 was not this ointment..given to the p.?
12. 6 he said, not that he cared for the poor, but
12. 8 For the poor always ye have with you; b.
13. 29 that he should give something to the po.
Rom. 15. 26 certain contribution for the poor saints
2 Co. 6. 10 as poor, yet making many rich; as having
Gal. 2. 10 that we should remember the poor; the
Jas. 2. 2 there come in also a poor man in vile ra.
2. 3 say to the poor, Stand thou there, or sit
2. 5 Hath not God chosen the poor of this wo
2. 6 But ye have despised the poor. Do not
Rev. 3. 17 art wretched, and miserable, and poor
13. 16 rich and poor, free and bond, to receive

POOR or poorer, to be, become, or wax —

1. *To become impoverished,* יָרַשׁ *yarash,* 2.
Prov 30. 9 Who (is) the LORD? or lest I be poor, and

2. *To be or become low or poor,* מוּךְ *muk.*
Lev. 25. 25 If thy brother be waxen poor, and hath
25. 35 if thy brother be waxen poor, and fallen
25. 39 if thy brother..be waxen poor, and be sold
25. 47 thy brother (that dwelleth) by him wax p.
27. 8 But if he be poorer than thy estimation

3. *To be or become poor*, πτωχεύω *ptōcheuō*.
2 Co. 8. 9 he became poor, that ye through his pov.

POOR, to make (self) —

1. *To dispossess*, יָרַשׁ *yarash*, 5.
1 Sa. 2. 7 The LORD maketh poor, and maketh rich

2. *To impoverish self*, רוּשׁ *rush*, 7a.
Prov 13. 7 (there is) that maketh himself poor, yet

POOREST sort —

Poverty, weakness, דַּלָּה *dallah*.
2 Ki. 24. 14 the poorest sort of the people of the land

POPLAR —

Poplar, לִבְנֶה *libneh*.
Gen. 30. 37 Jacob took him rods of green poplar, and
Hos. 4. 13 burn incense..under oaks and poplars and

POPULOUS —

1. *A multitude, one nourished*, אָמוֹן *amon*.
Nah. 3. 8 Art thou better than populous No, that

2. *Numerous, abundant*, רַב *rab*.
Deut 26. 5 became..nation, great, mighty, and pop.

PO-RA'-THA, פּוֹרָתָא.
One of the sons of Haman the Agagite B.C. 510.
Esth. 9. 8 And P., and Adalia, and Aridatha

PORCH —

1. *Porch, arch*, אֻלָם, אוּלָם *ulam*.
1 Ki. 6. 3 the porch before the temple of the house
7. 6 he made a porch of pillars; the length
7. 6 the porch (was) before them; and the (o.)
7. 7 he made a porch for the throne where he
7. 7 the porch of judgment: and (it was) cov.
7. 8 house..(had) another court within the po
7. 8 made also an house..like unto this porch
7. 12 cedar beams..for the porch of the house
7. 19 chapiters..(were) of lily work in the por.
7. 21 the pillars in the porch of the temple
1 Ch. 28. 11 gave to Solomon..the pattern of the po.
2 Ch. 3. 4 porch that (was) in the front (of the ho.)
8. 12 altar..which he had built before the po.
15. 8 altar..that (was) before the porch of the
29. 7 they have shut up the doors of the porch
29. 17 on the eighth day..came they to the por.
Eze. 8. 16 between the porch and the altar, (were)
40. 7 by the porch of the gate within..one reed
40. 8 measured also the porch of the gate with
40. 9 the porch of the gate..the porch of the
40. 15 unto the face of the porch of the inner
40. 39 in the porch of the gate (were) two tables
40. 40 side, which (was) at the porch of the gate
40. 48 he brought me to the porch of the house
40. 48 measured (each) post of the porch, five c.
40. 49 The length of the porch (was) twenty cu.
41. 15 inner temple, and the porches of the co.
41. 25 planks upon the face of the porch without
41. 26 on the sides of the porch, and (upon) the
44. 3 enter by the way of the porch of (that) g.
46. 2 enter by the way of the porch of (that) gate
46. 8 go in by the way of the porch of (that) g.
Joel 2. 17 weep between the porch and the altar, and

2. *Porch*, מִסְדְּרוֹן *misderon*.
Judg. 3. 23 Ehud went forth through the porch, and

3. *Vestibule*, προαύλιον *proaulion*.
Mark 14. 68 went out into the porch; and the cock

4. *A gateway*, πυλών *pulōn*.
Matt 26. 71 when he was gone out into the porch, an.

5. *A standing place, portico*, στοά *stoa*.
John 5. 2 Now there is..a pool..having five porches
10. 23 walked in the temple, in Solomon's porch
Acts 3. 11 in the porch that is called Solomon's
5. 12 all with one accord in Solomon's porch

POR-CI'-US, Πόρκιος.
The procurator of the Jews who succeeded Felix A.D. 60, and who sent Paul to Rome.
Acts 24. 27 after two years P. Festus came into Felix'

PORT —

Gate, שַׁעַר *shaar*.
Neh. 2. 13 the dragon well, and to the dung port

PORTER —

1. *To (at) the gate*, שַׁעַר *shaar*.
1 Ch. 16. 42 And the sons of Jeduthun (were) porters

2. *Gate keeper*, שׁוֹעֵר *shoer*.
2 Sa. 18. 26 the watchman called unto the porter, and
2 Ki. 7. 10 came and called unto the porter of the
7. 11 he called the porters; and they told (it)
1 Ch. 9. 17 the porters (were) Shallum, and Akkub
9. 18 they (were) porters in the companies of
9. 21 the son of Meshelemiah (was) porter of the
9. 22 All these..chosen to be porters in the g.
9. 24 In four quarters were the porters, toward
9. 26 the four chief porters, were in (their) set
15. 18 with them..Obed-edom, and Jeiel, the p.
16. 38 son of Jeduthun, and Hosah, (to be) port.
23. 5 four thousand (were) porters; and four
26. 1 Concerning the divisions of the porters: Of
26. 12 Among these..the divisions of the porters
26. 19 the divisions of the porters among the sons
2 Ch. 8. 14 the porters also by their courses at every
23. 4 third part..(shall be) porters of the doors
23. 19 he set the porters at the gates of the house
31. 14 the porter toward the east, (was) over the
34. 13 (there were) scribes, and officers, and po.
35. 15 the porters (waited) at every gate; they m
Ezra 2. 42 The children of the porters: the children
2. 70 the porters, and the Nethinims, dwelt in
7. 7 singers, and the porters, and the Nethin.
10. 24 of the porters; Shallum, and Telem, and
Neh. 7. 1 the porters and the singers and the Levi.
7. 45 The porters: the children of Shallum, the
7. 73 Levites, and the porters, and the singers
10. 28 the porters, the singers, the Nethinims
10. 39 the priests that minister, and the porters
11. 19 porters: Akkub, Talmon, and their breth.
12. 25 Talmon, Akkub, (were) porters, keeping
12. 45 the porters kept the ward of their God, and
12. 47 the portions of the singers and the porters
13. 5 Levites, and the singers, and the porters

3. *Gate or door keeper*, תָּרָע *tara*.
Ezra 7. 24 porters, Nethinims, or ministers of this

4. *Door keeper, gate keeper*, θυρωρός *thurōros*.
Mark 13. 34 and commanded the porter to watch
John 10. 3 To him the porter openeth; and the sheep

PORTION —

1. *To lay or keep hold on*, אָחַז *achaz*.
Num 31. 30 thou shalt take one portion of fifty, of
31. 47 Moses took one portion of fifty, (both) of

2. *A word, thing, matter*, דָּבָר *dabar*.
2 Ch. 31 16 his daily portion for their service in their
Neh. 12. 47 and the porters, every day his portion: and
Job 26. 14 but how little a portion is heard of him?
Jer. 52. 34 every day a portion until the day of his

3. *A cord, line, portion*, חֶבֶל, חֶבֶל *chebel*.
Josh 17. 5 there fell ten portions to Manasseh, besi.
17. 14 one portion to inherit, seeing I (am) a
19. 9 the portion of the children of Judah (was)
Eze. 47. 13 the land..Joseph (shall have two) portions

4. *A portion, share*, חֵלֶק *cheleq*.
Gen. 14. 24 the portion of the men which went with
14. 24 Eshcol, and Mamre; let them take their p.
31. 14 (Is there) yet any portion or inheritance
Lev. 6. 17 their portion of my offerings made by fire
Num 31. 36 the portion of them that went out to war
Deut 18. 8 They shall have like portions to eat, be.
32. 9 For the LORD'S portion (is) his people; J.
1 Ki. 12. 16 saying, What portion have we in David?
2 Ki. 9. 10 dogs shall eat Jezebel in the portion of J.
9. 36 In the portion of Jezreel shall dogs eat
9. 37 upon the face of the field in the portion
2 Ch. 10. 16 saying, What portion have we in David?
Neh. 2. 20 but ye have no portion, nor right, nor m
Job 20. 29 This (is) the portion of a wicked man from
27. 13 This (is) the portion of a wicked man w.
31. 2 For what portion of God (is there) from
Psa. 17. 14 men of the world, (which have) their por.
73. 26 strength of my heart, and my portion for
119. 57 (Thou art) my portion, O LORD: I have
142. 5 Thou (art) my refuge (and) my portion in
Eccl. 2. 10 and this was my portion of all my labour
2. 21 therein shall he leave it (for) his portion
3. 22 for that (is) his portion: for who shall
5. 18 which God giveth him; for it (is) his por.
5. 19 take his portion, and to rejoice in his la.
9. 6 neither have they any more a portion for
9. 9 for that (is) thy portion in (this) life, and
11. 2 Give a portion to seven, and also to eight
Isa. 17. 14 This (is) the portion of them that spoil us
57. 6 of the stream (is) thy portion; they, they
61 7 confusion they shall rejoice in their port.
Jer. 10. 16 The portion of Jacob (is) not like them: for
51. 19 The portion of Jacob (is) not like them
Lam. 3. 24 LORD (is) my portion, saith my soul; the.
Eze. 45. 7 over against one of the portions, from the
48. 21 over against the portions for the prince
Hos. 5. 7 month devour them with their portions
Mic. 2. 4 he hath changed the portion of my people
Hab. 1. 16 because by them their portion (is) fat, and
Zech. 2. 12 LORD shall inherit Judah his portion in

5. *Portion, share*, חָלַק *chalaq*.
Ezra 4. 16 by this means thou shalt have no portion
Dan. 4. 15, 23 and (let) his portion (be) with the be.

6. *Portion, share*, חֶלְקָה *chelqah*.
Deut 33. 21 (in) a portion of the law giver, (was he)
2 Ki. 9. 21 met him in the portion of Naboth the Je.
9. 25 cast him in the portion of the field of N.
Job 24. 18 their portion is cursed in the earth: he
Jer. 12. 10 they have trodden my portion under foot
12. 10 have made my pleasant portion a desolate

7. *A statute, portion*, חֹק *choq*.
Gen. 47. 22 had a portion..and did eat their portion
Prov 31. 15 She..giveth..a portion to her maidens

8. *Course, division*, מַחֲלֹקֶת *machaloqeth*.
Eze. 48. 29 these (are) their portions, saith the Lord

9. *Portion, part*, מָנָה *manah*.
1 Sa. 1. 4 to all her sons and her daughters, portions
1. 5 unto Hannah he gave a worthy portion
9. 23 Bring the portion which I gave thee, of
2 Ch. 31. 19 to give portions to all the males among
Neh. 8. 10 send portions unto them for whom nothing
8. 12 to send portions, and to make great mirth
Esth. 9. 19, 22 and of sending portions one to another
Psa. 16. 5 LORD (is) the portion of mine inheritance
Jer. 13. 25 thy lot, the portion of thy measures from

10. *Portion, part*, מְנָת *menath*.
2 Ch. 31. 3 (He appointed) also the king's portion of
31. 4 to give the portion of the priests and the
Neh. 12. 44 the portions of the law for the priests
12. 47 portions of the singers and the porters
13. 10 I perceived that the portions of the Lev.
Psa. 11. 6 Upon the wicked..the portion of their c.
63. 10 They..they shall be a portion for foxes

11. *The mouth*, פֶּה *peh*.
Deut 21. 17 by giving him a double portion of all
2 Ki. 2. 9 let a double portion of thy spirit be upon

12. *The shoulder*, שְׁכֶם *shekem*.
Gen. 48. 22 I have given to thee one portion above thy

13. *Part, portion, share, division*, μέρος *meros*.
Matt 24. 51 appoint (him) his portion with the hypo.
Luke 12. 46 appoint him his portion with the unbeli.
15. 12 give me the portion of goods that falleth

PORTION of meat —

1. *A portion of food*, פַּתְבַּג *pathbag*.
Dan. 1. 8 with the portion of the king's meat, nor
1. 13 that eat of the portion of the king's meat
1. 15 which did eat the portion of the king's m.
1. 16 Melzar took away the portion of their m.
11. 26 they that feed of the portion of his meat

2. *A measure of corn*, σιτομέτριον *sitometrion*.
Luke 12. 42 to give (them their) portion of meat in due

PORTION, to take away a —

To apportion, share, חָלַק *chalaq*.
2 Ch. 28. 21 took away a portion (out) of the house of

POSSESS, to —

1. *To strengthen, possess*, חָסַן *chasan*, 5.
Dan. 7. 18 possess the kingdom for ever, even for e.
7. 22 came that the saints possessed the kingd.

2. *To possess, take possession of*, יָרַשׁ *yarash*.
Gen. 22. 17 seed shall possess the gate of his enemies
24. 60 possess the gate of those which hate them
Lev. 20. 24 I will give it unto you to possess it, a land
Num 13. 30 Let us go up at once, and possess it; for
21. 24 possessed his land from Arnon unto Jab.
21. 35 they smote him..and they possessed his
27. 11 unto his kinsman..and he shall possess
33. 53 for I have given you the land to possess
36. 8 that possesseth an inheritance in any tri.
Deut. 1. 8 possess the land which the LORD sware
1. 21 possess (it), as the LORD God of thy fath.
1. 39 will I give it, and they shall possess it
2. 24 begin to possess (it), and contend with h.
2. 31 begin to possess, that thou mayest inher.
3. 12 this land, (which) we possessed at that t.
3. 18 God hath given you this land to possess
3. 20 they also possess the land which the LORD
4. 1 possess the land which the LORD God of
4. 5 in the land whither ye go to possess it
4. 14 the land whither ye go over to possess it
4. 22 shall go over, and possess that good land
4. 26 land whereunto ye go over Jordan to po.
4. 47 they possessed his land, and the land of
5. 31 the land which I give them to possess it
5. 33 live..in the land which ye shall possess
6. 1 in the land whither ye go to possess it
6. 18 and possess the good land which the LORD
7. 1 the land whither thou goest to possess it
8. 1 possess the land which the LORD sware
9. 1 to possess nations greater and mightier
9. 4 hath brought me in to possess this land
9. 5 Not for thy righteousness..dost thou..p.
9. 6 not this good land to possess it for thy ri.
9. 23 possess the land which I have given you
10. 11 possess the land which I sware unto their
11. 8 possess the land, whither ye go to possess
11. 10 the land, whither thou goest in to possess
11. 11 the land, whither ye go to possess it, (is)
11. 23 shall possess greater nations and mightier
11. 29 the land whither thou goest to possess it
11. 31 to possess the land which the LORD your
11. 31 and ye shall possess it, and dwell therein
12. 1 the LORD God..giveth thee to possess it
12. 2 the nations which ye shall possess served
12. 29 whither thou goest to possess them, and
15. 4 giveth..(for) an inheritance to possess it
17. 14 shalt possess it, and shalt dwell therein
18. 14 these nations, which thou shalt possess
19. 2, 14 LORD thy God giveth thee to possess
21. 1 the LORD thy God giveth thee to possess
23. 20 the land whither thou goest to possess it
25. 19 giveth thee (for) an inheritance to possess
26. 1 come in unto the land..and possessest it
28. 21, 63 off the land whither thou goest to pos.
30. 5 fathers possessed, and thou shalt possess
30. 16 in the land whither thou goest to possess
30. 18 thou passest over Jordan to go to possess
31. 3 will destroy..and thou shalt possess them
31. 13 whither ye go over Jordan to possess it
32. 47 whither ye go over Jordan to possess it
33. 23 O Naphtali..possess thou the west and the
Josh. 1. 11 to go in to possess the land, which the
1. 11 LORD your God giveth you to possess it
1. 15 they also have possessed the land which
12. 1 possessed their land on the other side J.
18. 3 to go to possess the land, which the LORD
19. 47 smote..and possessed it, and dwelt ther.
21. 43 and they possessed it, and dwelt therein
23. 5 ye shall possess their land, as the LORD
24. 4 I gave unto Esau mount Seir, to possess
24. 8 that ye might possess their land; and I
Judg. 2. 6 unto his inheritance to possess the land
3. 13 went..and possessed the city of palm trees
11. 21 so Israel possessed all the land of the A.
11. 22 they possessed all the coasts of the Amo.
11. 23 dispossessed..and shouldest thou possess
11. 24 Wilt not thou possess..them will we pos.
18. 9 slothful to go..to enter to possess the la.
1 Ki. 21. 18 whither he is gone down to possess it

2 Ki.17. 24 they possessed Samaria, and dwelt in the
1 Ch.28. 8 that ye may possess this good land, and
Ezra 9. 11 The land, unto which ye go to possess it
Neh. 9. 15 possess the land which thou hadst sworn
9. 22 they possessed the land of Sihon, and the
9. 23 broughtest..that they should go in to po.
9. 24 So the children went in and possessed the
9. 25 possessed houses full of all goods, wells
Isa. 14. 21 nor possess the land, nor fill the face of
34. 11 the bittern shall possess it; the owl also
34. 17 they shall possess it for ever, from gene.
61. 7 in their land they shall possess the double
63. 18 The people of thy holiness have possessed
Jer. 30. 3 to the land..and they shall possess it
32. 23 they came in, and possessed it; but they
Eze. 7. 24 and they shall possess their houses: I will
33. 25 shed blood: and shall ye possess the land
33. 26 ye defile..and shall ye possess the land?
35. 10 shall be mine, and we will possess it
36. 12 they shall possess thee, and thou shalt be
Hos. 9. 6 nettles shall possess them: thorns (shall)
Amos 2. 10 led you..to possess the land of the Amo.
9. 12 they may possess the remnant of Edom
Obad. 17 the house of Jacob shall possess their po.
19 shall possess the mount..they shall poss.
20 captivity..shall possess the cities of the s.
Hab. 1. 6 to possess the dwelling places..not theirs

3. *To (cause to) possess, take possession,* יָרַשׁ *yarash,* 5.
Num14. 24 the land..and his seed shall possess it

4. *To inherit,* נָחַל *nachal.*
Isa. 57. 13 he that putteth..trust in me shall possess
Zeph 2. 9 remnant of my people shall possess them

5. *To inherit for one's self,* נָחַל *nachal,* 7.
Isa. 14. 2 the house of Israel shall possess them in

6. *To acquire, set up,* קָנָה *qanah.*
Psa.139. 13 thou hast possessed my reins: thou hast
Prov. 8. 22 The LORD possessed me in the beginning

7. *To hold down or firm,* κατέχω *katechō.*
1 Co. 7. 30 they that buy, as though they possessed
2 Co. 6. 10 having nothing, and (yet) possessing all

8. *To acquire, possess,* κτάομαι *ktaomai.*
Luke 18. 12 I fast..I give tithes of all that I possess
21. 19 In your patience possess ye your souls
1 Th. 4. 4 should know how to possess his vessel in

POSSESS, to cause, give, make —
1. *To cause to take possession,* יָרַשׁ *yarash,* 5.
Judg 11. 24 Chemosh thy god giveth thee to possess?
Job 13. 26 makest me to possess the iniquities of my

2. *To cause to inherit,* נָחַל *nachal,* 5.
Zech. 8. 12 will cause the remnant..to possess all th.

POSSESS, to be made to —
To be caused to inherit, נָחַל *nachal,* 6.
Job 7. 3 So am I made to possess months of vanity

POSSESSED (with), to be —
1. *To be laid hold of or on,* אָחַז *achaz,* 2.
Josh.22. 9 whereof they were possessed, according

2. *To take possession,* יָרַשׁ *yarash.*
Josh.13. 1 remaineth yet very much land to be poss.

3. *To be acquired, possessed,* קָנָה *qanah,* 2.
Jer. 32. 15 vineyards shall be possessed again in this

4. *To have, hold,* ἔχω *echō.*
Acts 8. 7 came out of many that were possessed (w.
16. 16 damsel possessed with a spirit of divinat.

POSSESSED with or of devils, to be —
To be demonized, be as a demon, δαιμονίζομαι.
Matt. 4. 24 those which were possessed with devils
8. 16 many that were possessed with devils: and
8. 28 there met him two possessed with devils
8. 33 what was befallen to the possessed of the d.
9. 32 brought to him a. man possessed with a d.
12. 22 one possessed with a devil, blind and du.
Mark 1. 32 and them that were possessed with devils
5. 15 see him that was possessed with the devil
5. 16 befell to him that was possessed with the d.
5. 18 he that had been possessed with the devil
Luke 8. 36 he that was possessed of the devils was

POSSESSETH, things which one —
Possessions, substance, τὰ ὑπάρχοντα *ta huparchon.*
Luke 12. 15 abundance of the things which he posse.
Acts 4. 32 things which he possessed was his own

POSSESSION —
1. *Possession, what is held fast,* אֲחֻזָּה *achuzzah.*
Gen. 17. 8 Canaan, for an everlasting possession; and
23. 4 give me a possession of a burying place
23. 9, 20 for a possession of a burying place
36. 43 habitations in the land of their possession
47. 11 gave them a possession in the land of E.
48. 4 give this land..(for) an everlasting pos.
49. 30 bought..for a possession of a burying pl.
50. 13 bought..for a possession of a burying p.
Lev. 14. 34 Canaan, which I give to you for a posses.
14. 34 in a house of the land of your possession
25. 10, 13 shall return every man unto his poss.
25. 24 in all the land of your possession ye shall
25. 25 hath sold away (some) of his possession
25. 27 that he may return unto his possession
25. 28 and he shall return unto his possession
25. 32 the houses of the cities of their possession
25. 33 city of his possession, shall go out in (the
25. 33 their possession among the children of I.
25. 34 may not be sold; for it (is) their..posses.
Lev. 25. 41 unto the possession of his fathers shall he
25. 45 land: and they shall be your possession
25. 46 to inherit (them for) a possession; they
27. 16 sanctify..(some part) of a field of his po.
27. 21 the possession thereof shall be the priest's
27. 22 which (is) not of the fields of his possession
27. 24 to him to whom the possession of the la.
27. 28 beast, and of the field of his possession
Num27. 4 a possession among the brethren of our
27. 7 thou shalt surely give them a possession
32. 5 given unto thy servants for a possession
32. 22 this land shall be your possession before
32. 29 give them the land of Gilead for a posse.
32. 32 that the possession of our inheritance on
35. 2 give..of the inheritance of their possess.
35. 8 of the possession of the children of Israel
35. 28 shall return into the land of his possess.
Deut32. 49 unto the children of Israel for a possess.
Josh21. 12 gave they to Caleb..for his possession
21. 41 All the cities of the Levites within the p.
22. 4 unto the land of your possession, which
22. 9 to the land of their possession, whereof
22. 19 if the land of your possession (be) unclean
22. 19 unto the land of the possession of the L.
1 Ch. 7. 28 their possessions and habitations (were)
9. 2 inhabitants that (dwelt) in their possess.
2 Ch.11. 14 left their suburbs, and their possession
31. 1 returned, every man to his possession, into
Neh. 11. 3 dwelt every one in his possession in their
Psa. 2. 8 uttermost parts of the earth (for) thy po.
Eze. 44. 28 no possession in Israel; I (am) their pos.
45. 5 for a possession for twenty chambers
45. 6 ye shall appoint the possession of the city
45. 7 of the possession..before the possession
45. 8 In the land shall be his possession in Is.
46. 16 it (shall be) their possession by inherita.
46. 18 thrust them out of their possession; (but)
46. 18 sons inheritance out of his own possession
46. 18 scattered every man from his possession
48. 20 ye shall offer..with the possession of the
48. 21 of the possession of the city, over against
48. 22 from the possession..and from the poss.

2. *Possession, occupancy,* יְרֵשָׁה *yereshah.*
Num24. 18 Edom shall be a possession, Seir also shall
24. 18 be a possession for his enemies; and Isr.

3. *Possession, occupancy,* יְרֻשָּׁה *yerushshah.*
Deut. 2. 5 given mount Seir unto Esau (for) a poss.
2. 9 I will not give thee of their land (for) a p.
2. 9 Ar unto the children of Lot (for) a posse.
2. 12 Israel did unto the land of his possession
2. 19 for I will not give thee..(any) possession
2. 19 unto the children of Lot (for) a possession
3. 20 ye return every man unto his possession
Josh. 1. 15 ye shall return unto the land of your po.
12. 6 gave it (for) a possession unto the Reub.
12. 7 gave unto the tribes of Israel (for) a poss.
2 Ch.20. 11 to come to cast us out of thy possession

4. *Possession,* מוֹרָשׁ *morash.*
Isa. 14. 23 I will also make it a possession for the b.
Obad. 17 house of Jacob shall possess their posses.

5. *Possession, occupancy,* מוֹרָשָׁה *morashah.*
Eze. 11. 15 unto us is this land given in possession
25. 4 deliver thee to the men of the east for a p.
25. 10 will give them in possession, that the A.
36. 2 the ancient high places are ours in poss.
36. 3 ye might be a possession unto the residue
36. 5 appointed my land into their possession

6. *Work, deed,* מַעֲשֶׂה *maaseh.*
1 Sa. 25. 2 man in Maon, whose possessions (were)

7. *Acquisition, possession,* מִקְנֶה *miqneh.*
Gen. 26. 14 he had possession of flocks, and possession
1 Ch.28. 1 over all the substance and possession of
2 Ch.32. 29 possessions of flocks and herds in abund.
Eccl. 2. 7 also I had great possessions of great and

8. *Acquisition, possession,* מִקְנָה *miqnah.*
Gen. 23. 18 Unto Abraham for a possession in the p.

9. *Inheritance,* נַחֲלָה *nachalah.*
Num26. 56 According to the lot shall the possession

10. *Foot,* רֶגֶל *regel.*
Deut 11. 6 the substance that (was) in their possess.

11. *Possession, occupation, holding firm,* κατάσχεσις.
Acts 7. 5 that he would give it to him for a posses.
7. 45 brought in with Jesus into the possession

12. *Possession, acquisition,* κτῆμα *ktēma.*
Matt19. 22 went away sorrowful: for he had great p.
Mark10. 22 went away grieved: for he had great po.
Acts 2. 45 sold their possessions and goods, and pa.
5. 1 certain man named Ananias..sold a pos.

13. *A little place, spot,* χωρίον *chōrion.*
Acts 28. 7 In the same quarters were possessions of

POSSESSION, purchased —
Acquirement, περιποίησις *peripoiēsis.*
Eph. 1. 14 the redemption of the purchased posses.

POSSESSION, to get, take, have in —
1. *To be laid or kept hold of or on,* אָחַז *achaz,* 2.
Gen. 34. 10 trade ye therein, and get you possessions
47. 27 they had possessions therein, and grew
Num32. 30 they shall have possessions among you in
Josh 22. 19 take possession among us; but rebel not

2. *To take or have in possession,* יָרַשׁ *yarash.*
1 Ki.21. 15 take possession of the vineyard of Naboth
21. 16 rose up to go down..to take possession
21. 19 Hast thou killed, and also taken possess.
Psa. 44. 3 For they got not the land in possession
69. 35 may dwell there, and have it in possession
83. 12 take to ourselves the houses of God in p.

3. *To inherit,* נָחַל *nachal.*
Prov 28. 10 upright shall have good (things) in poss.

POSSESSOR —
1. *To acquire, get, set up,* קָנָה *qanah.*
Gen. 14. 19, 22 most high God, possessor of heaven
Zech 11. 5 Whose possessors slay them, and hold

2. *A possessor, acquirer,* κτήτωρ *ktētōr.*
Acts 4. 34 for as many as were possessors of lands

POSSIBLE —
1. *Powerful, able, capable,* δυνατός *dunatos.*
Matt19. 26 but with God all things are possible
24. 24 if (it were) possible, they shall deceive
26. 39 if it be possible, let this cup pass from me
Mark 9. 23 all things (are) possible to him that beli.
10. 27 with God: for with God all things are p.
13. 22 to seduce, if (it were) possible, even the
14. 35 if it were possible, the hour might pass
14. 36 Father, all things (are) possible unto thee
Luke18. 27 impossible with men are possible with G.
Acts 2. 24 it was not possible that he should be ho.
20. 16 hasted, if it were possible for him, to be at
Rom 12. 18 If it be possible, as much as lieth in you
Gal. 4. 15 if (it had been) possible, ye would have p.

2. *To be able, capable,* δύναμαι *dunamai.*
Acts 27. 39 if it were possible, to thrust in the ship

POSSIBLE, not —
Not able, not capable, ἀδύνατος *adunatos.*
Heb. 10. 4 not possible that the blood of bulls and

POST, (door or side) —
1. *A ram, post,* אַיִל *ayil.*
Eze. 40. 9 the posts thereof, two cubits; and the p.
40. 10 posts had one measure on this side and
40. 14 He made also posts of threescore cubits
40. 14 the post of the court round about the gate
40. 16 to their posts..and upon (each) post (w.)
40. 21, 29, 33, 36 the posts thereof, and the arc.
40. 24 measured the posts thereof, and the arc.
40. 26 another on that side, upon the posts th.
40. 31, 34, 37 and palm trees (were) upon the p.
40. 37 the posts thereof (were) toward the outer
40. 38 entries thereof (were) by the posts of the
40. 48 measured (each) post of the porch, five c.
40. 49 pillars by the posts, one on this side, and
41. 1 measured the posts, six cubits broad on
41. 3 measured the post of the door two cubits

2. *Pedestal,* אַמָּה *ammah.*
Isa. 6. 4 posts of the door moved at the voice of

3. *Side post,* מְזוּזָה *mezuzah.*
Exod12. 7 strike (it) on the two side posts and on
12. 22 strike the lintel and the two side posts
12. 23 he seeth the blood..on the two side posts
21. 6 bring him to the door, or unto the door p.
Deut. 6. 9 thou shalt write them upon the posts of
11. 20 shalt write them upon the door posts of
Judg16. 3 took the doors of the gate..and the two p.
1 Sa. 1. 9 Eli the priest sat upon a seat by a post of
1 Ki. 6. 31 lintel (and) side posts (were) a fifth part
6. 33 made he for the door of the temple posts
7. 5 all the doors and posts (were) square, w.
Prov. 8. 34 my gates, waiting at the posts of my doors
Isa. 57. 8 Behind the doors also and the posts hast
Eze. 41. 21 The posts of the temple (were) squared
43. 8 their post by my posts, and the wall be.
45. 19 put (it) upon the posts of the house, and
45. 19 upon the posts of the gate of the inner c.
46. 2 shall stand by the post of the gate, and

4. *Threshold, lintel,* סַף *saph.*
2 Ch. 3. 7 He overlaid also the house..the posts, and
Eze. 41. 16 The door posts, and the narrow windows
Amos 9. 1 Smite the lintel..that the posts may shake

POSTERITY —
1. *After,* אַחַר *achar.*
1 Ki. 16. 3 will take away the posterity..and the po.
21. 21 will take away thy posterity, and will cut
Psa. 49. 13 yet their posterity approve their sayings

2. *Latter end,* אַחֲרִית *acharith.*
Psa.109. 13 Let his posterity be cut off; (and) in the
Dan. 11. 4 not to his posterity, nor according to his
Amos 4. 2 take you away with hooks, and your post.

3. *Generation,* דּוֹר *dor.*
Num. 9. 10 If any man of you or of your posterity shall

4. *Remnant, rest, residue,* שְׁאֵרִית *sheerith.*
Gen. 45. 7 to preserve you a posterity in the earth

POSTS —
Runners, רוּץ *ruts.*
2 Ch.30. 6 So the posts went with the letters from
30. 10 So the posts passed from city to city thr.
Esth. 3. 13 letters were sent by posts into all the ki.
3. 15 posts went out, being hastened by the k.
8. 10 sent letters by posts on horseback, (and)
8. 14 posts that rode upon mules (and) camels
Job 9. 25 Now my days are swifter than a post: they
Jer. 51. 31 One post shall run to meet another, and

POT —
1. *Pot,* אָסוּךְ *asuk.*
2 Ki. 4. 2 not any thing in the house, save a pot of

2. *Goblet, cup, calyx,* גְּבִיעַ *gabia.*
Jer. 35. 5 I set..pots full of wine, and cups, and I

3. *Kettle, basket,* דּוּד *dud.*
Job 41. 20 smoke, as (out) of a seething pot or cald.
Psa. 81. 6 his hands were delivered from the pots

4. *Vessel,* כְּלִי *keli.*
Lev. 6. 28 and if it be sodden in a brasen pot, it shall

5. *Pot,* סִיר *sir.*
Exod16. 3 when we sat by the flesh pots, (and) when
38. 3 made all the vessels of the altar, the pots
1 Ki. 7. 45 pots, and the shovels, and the basins: and
2 Ki. 4. 38 Set on the great pot, and seethe pottage
4. 39 came and shred (them) into the pot of po.
4. 40 man of God, (there is) death in the pot. And
4. 41 bring meal: and he cast (it) into the pot
4. 41 eat. And there was no harm in the pot
25. 14 pots, and the shovels, and the snuffers, and
2 Ch. 4. 11 Huram made the pots, and the shovels
4. 16 pots also, and the shovels, and the flesh
35. 13 sod they in pots, and in caldrons, and in
Job 41. 31 He maketh the deep to boil like a pot; he
Psa. 58. 9 Before your pots can feel the thorns, he
60. 8 Moab (is) my wash pot; over Edom will
108. 9 Moab (is) my wash pot; over Edom will
Eccl. 7. 6 For as the crackling of thorns under a pot
Jer. 1. 13 I see a seething pot; and the face thereof
Eze. 24. 3 Set on a pot, set (it) on, and also pour w.
24. 6 to the pot whose scum (is) therein, and wh
Mic. 3. 3 as for the pot, and as flesh within the ca.
Zech.14. 20 the pots in the LORD's house shall be like
14. 21 every pot in Jerusalem and in Judah shall

6. *Pan, pot,* פָּרוּר *parur.*
Judg. 6. 19 he put the broth in a pot, and brought
1 Sa. 2. 14 into the pan, or kettle, or caldron, or pot

7. *Basket, pot,* צִנְצֶנֶת *tsintseneth.*
Exod16. 33 Take a pot, and put an omer full of man

8. *Hooks,* שְׁפַתַּיִם *shephattayim.*
Psa. 68. 13 Though ye have lien among the pots, (yet)

9. *A measure,* ($1\frac{1}{2}$ *pints English*), ξέστης *xestēs.*
Mark 7. 4 the washing of cups, and pots, brasen ve.
7. 8 [the washing of pots and cups: and many]

10. *A pot, jar,* στάμνος *stamnos.*
Heb. 9. 4 the golden pot that had manna, and Aar.
[*See also* Fining, ointment, ranges, washpot.]

POTENTATE —
One that is powerful, δυνάστης *dunastēs.*
1 Ti. 6. 15 the blessed and only potentate, the king

PO-TI'-PHAR, פּוֹטִיפַר.
An officer of Pharaoh and captain of the guard, to whom Joseph was sold by the Midianites. B.C. 1730.
Gen. 37. 36 the Midianites sold him..unto P., an offi.
39. 1 P...bought him of the hands of the Ishm.

PO-TI PHE'-RAH, פּוֹטִי פֶרַע.
A priest of On (or Heliopolis), father of Asenath, Joseph's wife. B.C. 1730.
Gen. 41. 45 he gave him to wife..the daughter of P.
41. 50 which Asenath the daughter of P...bare
46. 20 which Asenath the daughter of P...bare

POTSHERD —
Potsherd, earthenware, חֶרֶשׂ *cheres.*
Job 2. 8 he took him a potsherd to scrape himself
Psa. 22. 15 My strength is dried up like a potsherd
Prov.26. 23 (like) a potsherd covered with silver dross
Isa. 45. 9 the potsherd (strive) with the potsherds

POTTAGE —
Pottage, נָזִיד *nazid.*
Gen. 25. 29 Jacob sod pottage: and Esau came from
25. 34 Jacob gave Esau bread and pottage of le.
2 Ki. 4. 38 seethe pottage for the sons of the prophets
4. 39 came and shred (them) into the pot of po.
4. 40 as they were eating of the pottage, that
Hag. 2. 12 bread, or pottage, or wine, or oil, or any

POTTER —
1. *To form, fashion, frame, make,* יָצַר *yatsar.*
1 Ch. 4. 23 These (were) the potters, and those that
Psa. 2. 9 dash them in pieces like a potter's vessel
Isa. 29. 16 shall be esteemed as the potter's clay
30. 14 the potter's vessel that is broken in pieces
41. 25 upon princes..as the potter treadeth clay
64. 8 we (are) the clay, and thou our potter; and
Jer. 18. 2 go down to the potter's house, and there
18. 3 I went down to the potter's house; and
18. 4 vessel..was marred in the hand of the p.
18. 4 as seemed good to the potter to make (it)
18. 6 cannot I do with you as this potter? saith
18. 6 as the clay (is) in the potter's hand, so (are)
19. 1 Go and get a potter's earthen bottle, and
19. 11 as (one) breaketh a potter's vessel, that
Lam. 4. 2 pitchers, the work of the hands of the p.
Zech 11. 13 Cast it unto the potter: a goodly price
11. 13 cast them to the potter in the house of

2. *Potter,* פֶּחָר *pechar.*
Dan. 2. 41 part of potter's clay, and part of iron, the

3. *A potter,* κεραμεύς *kerameus.*
Matt27. 7 and bought with them the potter's field
27. 10 gave them for the potter's field, as the L.
Rom. 9. 21 Hath not the potter power over the clay

4. *Belonging to a potter, earthen,* κεραμικός *keram.*
Rev. 2. 27 as the vessels of a potter shall they be b.

POUND —
1. *Manah, a pound weight,* מָנֶה *maneh.*
1 Ki.10. 17 three pound of gold went to one shield
Ezra 2. 69 five thousand pound of silver, and one
Neh. 7. 71 thousand and two hundred pound of silv.
7. 72 thousand pound of silver, and threescore

2. *A Mina, sum of money,* μνᾶ *mna.*
Luke19. 13 delivered them ten pounds, and said unto
19. 16 Lord, thy pound hath gained ten pounds
19. 18 Lord, thy pound hath gained five pounds
19. 20 (here is) thy pound, which I have kept l.
19. 24 said unto them..Take from him the pound
19. 24 and give (it) to him that hath ten pounds
19. 25 said unto him, Lord, he hath ten pounds

3. *Litra, a pound,* λίτρα *litra* (*Lat. libra*).
John12. 3 a pound of ointment of spikenard, very
19. 39 and aloes, about an hundred pound (wei.)

POUR (down or out), to —
1. *To drop, drop down,* דָּלַף *dalaph.*
Job 16. 20 (but) mine eye poureth out (tears) unto G.

2. *To refine, pour down,* זָקַק *zaqaq.*
Job 36. 27 they pour down rain according to the

3. *To pour or be poured out,* זָרַם *zaram, 3a.*
Psa. 77. 17 the clouds poured out water; the skies

4. *To cast, pour out,* יָצַק *yatsaq.*
Gen. 28. 18 stone..and poured oil upon the top of it
35. 14 drink offering thereon, and he poured oil
Exod29. 7 and pour (it) upon his head, and anoint h.
Lev. 2. 1 he shall pour oil upon it, and put franki.
2. 6 Thou shalt part it in pieces, and pour oil
8. 12 he poured of the anointing oil upon Aar.
8. 15 poured the blood at the bottom of the
9. 9 poured out the blood at the bottom of the
14. 15 pour (it) into the palm of his own left h.
14. 26 the priest shall pour of the oil into the pa.
Num. 5. 15 he shall pour no oil upon it, nor put fran.
1 Sa. 10. 1 poured (it) upon his head, and kissed him
2 Sa. 13. 9 poured (them) out before him: but he re.
1 Ki.18. 33 pour (it) on the burnt sacrifice, and on the
2 Ki. 3. 11 which poured water on the hands of Eli.
4. 4 shalt pour out into all those vessels, and
4. 40 So they poured out for the men to eat: and
4. 41 Pour out for the people, that they may eat
9. 3 pour (it) on his head, and say, Thus saith
9. 6 he poured the oil on his head, and said
Isa. 44. 3 will pour water upon him that is thirsty
44. 3 I will pour my Spirit upon thy seed, and
Eze. 24. 3 Set on a pot, set (it) on, and also pour w.

5. *To pour out,* יָצַק *yatsaq,* 3, 5.
2 Ki. 4. 5 So she went from him..and she poured

6. *To cause to flow out,* נָבַע *naba,* 5.
Prov. 1. 23 I will pour out my spirit unto you, I will
15. 2 the mouth of fools poureth out foolish.
15. 28 the mouth of the wicked poureth out evil

7. *To cause to run, pour out,* נָגַר *nagar,* 5.
Psa. 75. 8 he poureth out of the same: but the dregs
Jer. 18. 21 pour out their (blood) by the force of the
Mic. 1. 6 I will pour down the stones thereof into

8. *To give* נָתַן *nathan.*
Lev. 14. 18 he shall pour upon the head of him that

9. *To flow,* נָזַל *nazal.*
Num24. 7 He shall pour the water out of his buckets
Isa. 45. 8 and let the skies pour down righteousness

10. *To pour out,* נָסַךְ *nasak.*
Exod30. 9 neither shall ye pour drink offering there.
Isa. 29. 10 the LORD hath poured out upon you the

11. *To pour out,* נָסַךְ *nasak,* 3.
1 Ch.11. 18 David would not drink (of) it, but poured

12. *To pour out,* נָסַךְ *nasak,* 5.
Gen. 35. 14 he poured a drink offering thereon, and
2 Sa. 23. 16 would not drink..but poured it out unto
2 Ki. 16. 13 poured his drink offering, and sprinkled
Jer. 7. 18 to pour out drink offerings unto other gods
19. 13 poured out drink offerings unto other gods
32. 29 poured out drink offerings unto other gods
44. 17, 18, 19, 25 pour out drink offerings unto
44. 19 when we..poured out drink offerings unto
Eze. 20. 28 and poured out there their drink offerings

13. *To pour out, melt,* נָתַךְ *nathak,* 5.
Job 10. 10 Hast thou not poured me out as milk, and

14. *To make naked, bare, empty,* עָרָה *arah,* 5.
Isa. 53. 12 because he hath poured out his soul unto

15. *To pour out,* צוּק *tsuq.*
Job 29. 6 and the rock poured me out rivers of oil
Isa. 26. 16 poured out a prayer (when) thy chastening

16. *To draw out, empty,* רוּק *ruq,* 5.
Mal. 3. 10 pour you out a blessing, that (there shall)

17. *To pour or shed out,* שָׁפַךְ *shaphak.*
Exod. 4. 9 pour (it) upon the dry (land): and the w.
29. 12 pour all the blood beside the bottom of
Lev. 4. 7 shall pour all the blood of the bullock at
4. 18, 30, 34 shall pour out all the blood
4. 25 shall pour out his blood at the bottom of
14. 41 and they shall pour out the dust that they
17. 13 he shall even pour out the blood thereof
Deut12. 16, 24 shall pour it upon the earth as water
15. 23 shalt pour it upon the ground as water
Judg. 6. 20 and pour out the broth. And he did so
1 Sa. 1. 15 have poured out my soul before the LORD
7. 6 poured (it) out before the LORD, and fasted
Job 12. 21 He poureth contempt upon princes, and
16. 13 he poureth out my gall upon the ground
Psa. 42. 4 I pour out my soul in me: for I had gone
62. 8 pour out your heart before him: God (is)
69. 24 Pour out thine indignation upon them, and
Psa. 79. 6 Pour out thy wrath upon the heathen that
102. *title* poureth out his complaint before the L.
107. 40 He poureth contempt upon princes, and
142. 2 I poured out my complaint before him; I
Isa. 42. 25 poured upon him the fury of his anger
57. 6 to them hast thou poured a drink offering
Jer. 6. 11 will pour it out upon the children abroad
10. 25 Pour out thy fury upon the heathen that
14. 16 for I will pour their wickedness upon th.
Lam. 2. 4 he stood..he poured out his fury like fire
2. 19 pour out thine heart like water before
4. 11 he hath poured out his fierce anger, and
Eze. 7. 8 Now will I shortly pour out my fury upon
9. 8 thy pouring out of thy fury upon Jerusa.
14. 19 and pour out my fury upon it in blood
16. 15 pouredst out thy fornications on every one
20. 8 I will pour out my fury upon them, to a.
20. 13, 21 I would pour out my fury upon them
21. 31 I will pour out mine indignation upon th.
22. 22 I the LORD have poured out my fury upon
22. 31 I poured out mine indignation upon them
23. 8 and they..poured their whoredom upon
24. 7 she poured it not upon the ground, to c.
30. 15 will pour my fury upon Sin, the strength
36. 18 I poured my fury upon them for the blood
39. 29 I have poured out my spirit upon the ho.
Hos. 5. 10 I will pour out my wrath upon them like
Joel 2. 28 I will pour out my spirit upon all flesh
2. 29 And..in those days will I pour out my sp.
Amos 5. 8 poureth them out upon the face of the
9. 6 poureth them out upon the face of the
Zeph. 3. 8 to pour upon them mine indignation, (e.)
Zech 12. 10 I will pour upon the house of David, and

18. *To pour out,* ἐκχέω *ekcheō.*
John 2. 15 poured out the changers' money, and over
Acts 2. 17 I will pour out of my spirit upon all flesh
2. 18 will pour out in those days of my spirit
Rev. 16. 1 pour out the vials of the wrath of God upon
16. 2, 3, 4, 8, 10, 12, 17 angel poured out his vial

19. *To pour out,* ἐκχύνω *ekchunō.*
Acts 10. 45 was poured out the gift of the Holy Ghost

20. *To mix, infuse,* κεράννυμι *kerannumi* -ύω.
Rev. 14. 10 which is poured out without mixture into

21. *To cast, throw,* βάλλω *ballō.*
Matt26. 12 she hath poured this ointment on my body
John13. 5 he poureth water into a bason, and began

22. *To pour down,* καταχέω *katacheō.*
Matt26. 7 poured (it) on his head, as he sat (at m.)
Mark14. 3 brake the box, and poured (it) on his h.

POUR in, to —
To pour upon, ἐπιχέω *epicheō.*
Luke10. 34 pouring in oil and wine, and set him on

POURED, (down, forth, out), to be —
1. *To be poured forth,* יָסַךְ *yasak.*
Exod30. 32 Upon man's flesh shall it not be poured

2. *To be poured out,* יָצַק *yatsaq,* 6.
Lev. 21. 10 upon whose head the anointing oil was p.
Psa. 45. 2 grace is poured into thy lips: therefore

3. *To be poured out,* נָתַךְ *nathak.*
2 Ch.12. 7 my wrath shall not be poured out upon
34. 25 my wrath shall be poured out upon this
Job 3. 24 roarings are poured out like the waters
Jer. 42. 18 so shall my fury be poured forth upon you
44. 6 and mine anger was poured forth, and was
Dan. 9. 11 the curse is poured upon us, and the oath
9. 27 that determined shall be poured upon the

4. *To be drawn away or out,* נָתַךְ *nathak,* 2.
Exod 9. 33 the rain was not poured upon the earth
2 Ch.34. 21 the wrath of the LORD that is poured out
Jer. 7. 20 fury shall be poured out upon this place
42. 18 my fury hath been poured forth upon the
Nah. 1. 6 his fury is poured out like fire, and the

5. *To be poured out,* נָגַר *nagar,* 6.
Mic. 1. 4 waters (that are) poured down a steep p.

6. *To be emptied,* עָרָה *arah,* 2.
Isa. 32. 15 Until the spirit be poured upon us from

7. *To be emptied out,* רוּק *ruq,* 6.
Song 1. 3 thy name (is as) ointment poured forth

8. *To pour or shed out,* שָׁפַךְ *shaphak.*
Eze. 20. 33 with fury poured out, will I rule over you
20. 34 stretched out arm..with fury poured out

9. *To be poured or shed out,* שָׁפַךְ *shaphak,* 2.
Deut12. 27 the blood..shall be poured out upon the
1 Ki.13. 3 the ashes..upon it shall be poured out
13. 5 and the ashes poured out from the altar
Psa. 22. 14 I am poured out like water, and all my
Lam. 2. 11 my liver is poured upon the earth, for the
Eze. 16. 36 Because thy filthiness was poured out

10. *To be poured or shed out,* שָׁפַךְ *shaphak,* 4.
Zeph. 1. 17 their blood shall be poured out as dust

11. *To pour self out,* שָׁפַךְ *shaphak,* 7.
Job 30. 16 And now my soul is poured out upon me
Lam. 2. 12 when their soul was poured out into their
4. 1 the stones of the sanctuary are poured out

12. *Pouring out,* שֶׁפֶךְ *shephek.*
Lev. 4. 12 place, where the ashes are poured out, and
4. 12 where the ashes are poured out shall he

POURED, to cause to be —
To (cause to) pour out, נָסַךְ *nasak,* 5.
Num28. 7 cause the strong wine to be poured unto

POURTRAY —
1. *To grave,* חָקַק *chaqaq.*
Eze. 4. 1 pourtray upon it the city, (even) Jerusalem
23. 14 images of the Chaldeans pourtrayed with
2. *To be graved,* חָקָה *chaqah,* 4.
Eze. 8. 10 pourtrayed upon the wall round about
23. 14 when she saw men pourtrayed upon the
POVERTY —
1. *Lack,* חֶסֶר *cheser.*
Prov 28. 22 considereth not that poverty shall come
2. *Lack,* מַחְסוֹר *machsor.*
Prov 11. 24 withholdeth..but (it tendeth) to poverty
3. *Poverty,* רֵאשׁ *resh.*
Prov. 6. 11 So shall thy poverty come as one that tr.
30. 8 give me neither poverty nor riches; feed
4. *Poverty,* רֵישׁ *resh.*
Prov 10. 15 the destruction of the poor (is) their pov.
13. 18 Poverty and shame (shall be to) him that
24. 34 So shall thy poverty come (as) one that
5. *Poverty,* רִישׁ *rish.*
Prov 28. 19 he that followeth..shall have poverty en.
31. 7 Let him drink, and forget his poverty, and
6. *Poverty, beggary,* πτωχεία *ptōcheia.*
2 Co. 8. 2 poverty abounded unto the riches of their
8. 9 that ye through his poverty might be rich
Rev. 2. 9 know thy works, and tribulation, and po.
POVERTY, to come to —
To become dispossessed, poor, יָרַשׁ *yarash,* 2.
Gen. 45. 11 lest thou, and thy house...come to poverty
Prov 20. 13 Love not sleep, lest thou come to poverty
23. 21 and the glutton shall come to poverty; and
POWDER —
1. *Small crushed powder,* אָבָק *abaq.*
Deut 28. 24 shall make the rain of thy land powder
2. *Small crushed powder,* אֲבָקָה *abaqah.*
Song 3. 6 perfumed..with all powders of the merc.
3. *Dust,* עָפָר *aphar.*
2 Ki. 23. 6 to powder, and cast the powder thereof
23. 15 stamped (it) small to powder, and burned
POWDER, to grind or beat to —
1. *To be small, beaten small,* דָּקַק *daqaq.*
Exod 32. 20 burnt (it) in the fire, and ground (it) to p.
2. *To beat small,* דָּקַק *daqaq,* 5.
2 Ch. 34. 7 had beaten the graven images into powder
3. *To winnow, shatter,* λικμάω *likmaō.*
Matt 21. 44 whomsoever..it will grind him to powder
Luke 20. 18 whomsoever..it will grind him to powder
POWER —
1. *Might, strength,* אֵל *el.*
Gen. 31. 29 It is in the power of my hand to do you
Prov. 3. 27 when it is in the power of thine hand to
Mic. 2. 1 because it is in the power of their hand
2. *Might,* גְּבוּרָה *geburah.*
1 Ch. 29. 11 Thine, O Lord, (is)..the power, and the g.
Job 26. 14 but the thunder of his power who can u.
Psa. 21. 13 strength: (so) will we sing and praise thy p.
65. 6 Which..setteth..(being) girded with pow.
66. 7 He ruleth by his power for ever; his eyes
71. 18 (and) thy power to every one (that is) to
106. 8 that he might make his mighty power to
145. 11 They shall speak..and talk of thy power
3. *Word of might,* דְּבַר גְּבוּרָה [*dabar*].
Job 41. 12 I will not conceal his parts, nor his power
4. *Arm,* זְרוֹעַ *zeroa.*
Psa. 79. 11 according to the greatness of thy power
Eze. 17. 9 even without great power or many people
22. 6 every one were in thee to their power to
5. *Force, valour,* חַיִל *chayil.*
1 Sa. 9. 1 a Benjamite, a mighty man of power
2 Sa. 22. 33 God (is) my strength (and) power: and he
1 Ch. 20. 1 Joab led forth the power of the army, and
Ezra 4. 23 and made them to cease by force and po.
Esth. 1. 3 power of Persia and Media, the nobles and
8. 11 all the power of the people and province
Job 21. 7 live, become old, yea, are mighty in power
Psa. 59. 11 scatter them by thy power; and bring them
110. 3 (shall be) willing in the day of thy power
Zech. 9. 4 and he will smite her power in the sea
6. *Strength,* חֹסֶן *chesen.*
Dan. 2. 37 hath given thee a kingdom, power, and
4. 30 by the might of my power, and for the
7. *Hand,* יָד *yad.*
Deut 32. 36 when he seeth that (their) power is gone
Josh. 8. 20 they had no power to flee this way or that
2 Ki. 19. 26 their inhabitants were of small power, they
Job 1. 12 Behold, all that he hath (is) in thy power
5. 20 and in war from the power of the sword
Prov 18. 21 Death and life (are) in the power of the
Isa. 37. 27 inhabitants (were) of small power, they w.
47. 14 shall not deliver themselves from the po.
Dan. 6. 27 who hath delivered Daniel from the power
12. 7 to scatter the power of the holy people
Hos. 13. 14 I will ransom them from the power of the
8. *Power,* כֹּחַ *koach.*
Gen. 31. 6 know that with all my power I have served
Exod 9. 16 for to show (in) thee my power; and that
15. 6 Thy right hand..is become glorious in p.
32. 11 hast brought forth..with great power, and
Num 14. 17 let the power of my lord be great, accor.
Deut. 4. 37 brought thee out..with his mighty power
8. 17 My power and the might of (mine) hand
8. 18 for (it is) he that giveth thee power to get
9. 29 broughtest out by thy mighty power and
Josh 17. 17 a great people, and hast great power: thou
1 Sa. 30. 4 wept, until they had no more power to w.
2 Ki. 17. 36 who brought you up..with great power
1 Ch. 29. 12 in thine hand (is) power and might; and
2 Ch. 14. 11 many, or with them that have no power
20. 6 in thine hand (is there not) power and m.
22. 9 the house of Ahaziah had no power to k.
25. 8 God hath power to help, and to cast down
26. 13 that made war with mighty power, to help
Neh. 1. 10 thou hast redeemed by thy great power
Job 23. 6 Will he plead against me with..great po.
24. 22 draweth also the mighty with his power
26. 2 How hast thou helped (him..) without p.
26. 12 He divideth the sea with his power, and
36. 22 God exalteth by his power: who teacheth
37. 23 (he is) excellent in power, and in judgm
Psa. 111. 6 showed his people the power of his works
147. 5 Great (is) our LORD, and of great power
Eccl. 4. 1 on the side of..oppressors (there was) p.
Isa. 40. 26 for that (he is) strong in power; not one
40. 29 giveth power to the faint; and to (them
50. 2 have I no power to deliver? behold, at my
Jer. 10. 12 He hath made the earth by his power, he
27. 5 by my great power and by my outstretch.
32. 17 by thy great power and stretched out arm
51. 15 He hath made the earth by his power, he
Dan 8. 6 and ran unto him in the fury of his power
8. 7 no power in the ram to stand before him
8. 22 kingdoms shall stand..not in his power
8. 24 power shall be mighty..by his..power
11. 6 she shall not retain the power of the arm
11. 25 shall stir up his power and his courage
Mic. 3. 8 I am full of power by the spirit of the L.
Nah. 1. 3 LORD (is) slow to anger, and great in pow.
2. 1 make (thy) loins strong, fortify (thy) po.
Hab. 1. 11 (imputing) this his power unto his god
Zech. 4. 6 Not by might, nor by power, but by my
9. *Palm, hand,* כַּף *kaph.*
Hab. 2. 9 may be delivered from the power of evil
10. *Rule,* מֶמְשָׁלָה *memshalah.*
2 Ch. 32. 9 against Lachish, and all his power with
11. *Strength,* עַז *az.*
Gen. 49. 3 of dignity, and the excellency of power
12. *Strength, hardness,* עֹז *oz.*
Lev. 26. 19 I will break the pride of your power; and
Ezra. 8. 22 his power and his wrath (is) against all th.
Psa. 59. 16 I will sing of thy power; yea, I will sing
62. 11 heard this, that power (belongeth) unto
63. 2 To see thy power and thy glory, so (as) I
66. 3 through the greatness of thy power shall
78. 26 by his power he brought in the south w.
90. 11 Who knoweth the power of thine anger?
150. 1 praise him in the firmament of his power
Eze. 30. 6 the pride of her power shall come down
Hab. 3. 4 and there (was) the hiding of his power
13. *Strong, hard,* עִזּוּז *izzuz.*
Isa. 43. 17 chariot and horse, the army and the power
14. *Rule, dominion,* שִׁלְטוֹן *shilton.*
Eccl. 8. 4 where the word of a king (is, there is) p.
8. 8 neither (hath he) power in the day of de.
15. *Might, substance,* תַּעֲצֻמוֹת *taatsumoth.*
Psa. 68. 35 giveth strength and power unto (his) pe.
16. *Strength, might,* תְּקֹף *toqeph.*
Esth 10. 2 the acts of his power, and of his might
17. *Power of the hand,* אֵל יָד *el yad.*
Neh. 5. 5 neither (is it) in our power (to redeem t.)
18. *Beginning, principality,* ἀρχή *archē.*
Luke 20. 20 the power and authority of the governor
19. *Ability, power,* δύναμις *dunamis.*
Matt. 6. 13 [the kingdom, and the power, and the g.]
22. 29 not knoweth the Scriptures, nor the pow.
24. 29 the powers of the heavens shall be shaken
24. 30 coming in..with power and great glory
26. 64 sitting on the right hand of power, and
Mark 9. 1 seen the kingdom of God come with power
12. 24 know not the Scriptures, neither the po.
13. 25 powers that are in heaven shall be shaken
13. 26 in the clouds with great power and glory
14. 62 sitting on the right hand of power, and
Luke 1. 17 in the spirit and power of Elias, to turn
1. 35 power of the Highest shall overshadow t.
4. 14 Jesus returned in the power of the spirit
4. 36 with authority and power he commandeth
5. 17 power of the Lord was (present) to heal t.
9. 1 power and authority over all devils, and
10. 19 and over all the power of the enemy: and
21. 26 for the powers of heaven shall be shaken
21. 27 in a cloud, with power and great glory
22. 69 on the right hand of the power of God
24. 49 until ye be endued with power from on
Acts 1. 8 ye shall receive power, after that the
3. 12 by our own power or holiness we had ma.
4. 7 By what power, or by what name, have ye
4. 33 with great power gave the apostles witness
6. 8 Stephen, full of faith and power, did gr.
8. 10 saying, This man is the great power of G.
10. 38 Jesus..with the Holy Ghost and with p.
Rom. 1. 4 declared (to be) the Son of God with po.
1. 16 the power of God unto salvation to every
1. 20 his eternal power and Godhead; so that
8. 38 nor powers, nor things present, nor things
Rom. 9. 17 I might show my power in thee, and that
15. 13 abound..through the power of the Holy
15. 19 wonders, by the power of the spirit of God
1 Co. 1. 18 unto us which are saved it is the power
1. 24 the power of God, and the wisdom of God
2. 4 demonstration of the spirit and of power
2. 5 the wisdom of men, but in the power of G.
4. 19 not the speech of them..but the power
4. 20 kingdom of God (is) not in word, but in p.
5. 4 with the power of our Lord Jesus Christ
6. 14 and will also raise up us by his own power
15. 24 put down all rule and..authority and po.
15. 43 is sown in weakness; it is raised in power
2 Co. 4. 7 the excellency of the power may be of G.
6. 7 by the power of God, by the armour of r.
8. 3 For to (their) power, I bear record, yea
8. 3 beyond (their) power, (they were) willing
12. 9 that the power of Christ may rest upon me
13. 4 crucified..yet he liveth by the power of
13. 4 shall live..by the power of God toward
Eph. 1. 19 the exceeding greatness of his power to
3. 7 given..by the effectual working of his p.
3. 20 according to the power that worketh in
Phil. 3. 10 the power of his resurrection, and the
1 Th. 1. 5 in power, and in the Holy Ghost, and in
2 Th. 1. 11 and fulfil..the work of faith with power
2. 9 all power and signs and lying wonders
2 Ti. 1. 7 of power, and of love, and of a sound m.
1. 8 partaker..according to the power of God
3. 5 godliness, but denying the power thereof
Heb. 1. 3 upholding all..by the word of his power
6. 5 tasted..the powers of the world to come
7. 16 Who is made..after the power of an end.
1 Pe. 1. 5 Who are kept by the power of God through
3. 22 and powers being made subject unto him
2 Pe. 1. 3 his divine power hath given unto us all
1. 16 power and coming of our Lord Jesus Chr.
Rev. 4. 11 to receive glory and honour and power
5. 12 the Lamb that was slain to receive power
7. 12 power, and might, (be) unto our God for
11. 17 thou hast taken to thee thy great power
13. 2 the dragon gave him his power, and his
15. 8 from the glory of God, and from his pow.
17. 13 shall give their power and strength unto
19. 1 honour, and power, unto the Lord our G.
20. *The power,* τὸ δυνατόν *to dunaton.*
Rom. 9. 22 to make his power known, endured with
21. *Privilege, authority,* ἐξουσία *exousia.*
Matt. 9. 6 Son..hath power on earth to forgive sins
9. 8 God, which had given such power unto m.
10. 1 gave them power (against) unclean spirits
28. 18 All power is given unto me in heaven and
Mark 2. 10 the Son..hath power on earth to forgive
3. 15 to have power to heal sicknesses, and to
6. 7 and gave them power over unclean spirits
Luke 4. 6 this power will I give thee, and the glory
4. 32 astonished..for his word was with power
5. 24 hath power upon earth to forgive sins
10. 19 give unto you power to tread on serpents
12. 5 after he hath killed hath power to cast
12. 11 bring you..(unto) magistrates, and powers
22. 53 this is your hour, and..power of darkness
John 1. 12 gave he power to become the sons of God
10. 18 power to lay it down, and I have power
17. 2 As thou hast given him power over all fl.
19. 10 have power to crucify thee, and have po.
19. 11 couldest have no power (at all) against me
Acts 1. 7 which the Father hath put in his own p.
5. 4 was it not in thine own power? why hast
8. 19 Give me also this power, that on whom.
26. 18 (from) the power of Satan unto God, that
Rom. 9. 21 Hath not the potter power over the clay
13. 1 Let every soul be subject unto the..pow.
13. 1 there is no power but of God: the powers
13. 2 Whosoever therefore resisteth the power
13. 3 Wilt thou then not be afraid of the power?
1 Co. 7. 37 hath power over his own will, and hath
9. 4 Have we not power to eat and to drink?
9. 5 Have we not power to lead about a sister
9. 6 or..have not we power to forbear working
9. 12 If others be partakers of (this) power over
9. 12 we have not used this power; but suffer
9. 18 that I abuse not my power in the gospel
11. 10 ought the woman to have power on (her)
2 Co. 13. 10 the power which the Lord hath given me
Eph. 1. 21 power, and might, and dominion, and ev.
2. 2 to the prince of the power of the air, the
3. 10 principalities and powers in heavenly
6. 12 against powers, against the rulers of the
Col. 1. 13 delivered us from the power of darkness
1. 16 or dominions, or principalities, or powers
2. 10 the head of all principality and power
2. 15 having spoiled principalities and powers
2 Th. 3. 9 Not because we have not power, but to
Titus 3. 1 be subject to principalities and powers
Jude 25 dominion and power, both now and ever
Rev. 2. 26 to him will I give power over the nations
6. 8 power was given unto them over the four.
9. 3 and unto them was given power, as
9. 3 the scorpions of the earth have power
9. 10 their power (was) to hurt men five mont.
9. 19 their power is in their mouth, and in
11. 6 These have power to shut heaven, that it
11. 6 have power over waters to turn them to
12. 10 the kingdom of our God, and the power
13. 4 dragon which gave power unto the beast
13. 5 power was given unto him to continue f.
13. 7 power was given him over all kindreds, and
13. 12 all the power of the first beast before him
14. 18 another angel..which had power over fire
16. 9 God, which hath power over these plagues

Rev. 17. 12 receive power as kings one hour with the
18. 1 come down from heaven, having great p.
20. 6 on such the second death hath no power

22. *Strength, force, ἰσχύς ischus.*
2 Th. 1. 9 be punished..from the glory of his power
2 Pe. 2. 11 which are greater in power and might

23. *Strength, power, κράτος kratos.*
Eph. 1. 19 according to the working of his mighty p.
6. 10 be strong in the Lord, and in the power of
Col. 1. 11 according to his glorious power, unto all
1 Ti. 6. 16 to whom (be) honour and power everlast.
Heb. 2. 14 destroy him that had the power of death
Rev. 5. 13 glory, and power, (be) unto him that sit.

POWER, in great —
Terrible, עָרִיץ arits.
Psa. 37. 35 I have seen the wicked in great power, and

POWER to stand —
Upstanding, תְּקוּמָה tequmah.
Lev. 26. 37 ye shall have no power to stand before y

POWER, that hath —
Ruler, שַׁלִּיט shallit.
Eccl. 8. 8 no man that hath power over the spirit

POWER, mighty —
Greatness, μεγαλειότης megaleiotēs
Luke 9. 43 were all amazed at the mighty power of

POWER as a prince, to have —
To be prince, have princely power, שָׂרָה sarah.
Gen. 32. 28 as a prince hast thou power with God and

POWER, to give, have, or be of —
1. *To be able, יָכֹל yakol.*
Num 22. 38 have I now any power at all to say any

2. *To rule, מָשַׁל mashal.*
Exod 21. 8 he shall have no power seeing he hath
Dan. 11. 43 But he shall have power over the treasur

3. *To be prince, שׂוּר sur.*
Hos. 12. 4 had power over the angel, and prevailed

4. *To be prince, have princely power, שָׂרָה sarah.*
Hos. 12. 3 and by his strength he had power with G.

5. *To rule, שָׁלַט shalat.*
Esth. 9. 1 Jews hoped to have power over them, th.

6. *To cause to rule, שָׁלַט shalat, 5.*
Eccl. 5. 19 hath given him power to eat thereof, and
6. 2 God giveth him not power to eat thereof

7. *To rule, שֶׁלֶט shelet.*
Dan. 3. 27 upon whose bodies the fire had no power

8. *To give, δίδωμι didōmi.*
Rev. 13. 14 had power to do in the sight of the beast
13. 15 had power to give life unto the image of

9. *To be able, have power, δύναμαι dunamai.*
Rom 16. 25 Now to him that is of power to stablish

10. *To exercise privilege or authority, ἐξουσιάζω.*
1 Co. 7. 4 The wife hath not power of her own body
7. 4 likewise also the husband hath not power

POWER of, to bring under the —
To exercise privilege or authority, ἐξουσιάζω exou.
1 Co. 6. 12 will not be brought under the power of

POWERFUL —
1. *Power, כֹּחַ koach.*
Psa. 29. 4 The voice of the LORD (is) powerful, the

2. *Energetic, efficacious, ἐνεργής energēs.*
Heb. 4. 12 For the word of God (is) quick, and pow.

3. *Strong, robust, ἰσχυρός ischuros.*
2 Co. 10. 10 For (his) letters..(are) weighty and pow.

PRACTISE, to —
1. *To do over and over, עָלַל alal, 7a.*
Psa. 141. 4 to practise wicked works with men that

2. *To do, make, עָשָׂה asah.*
Isa. 32. 6 to practise hypocrisy, and to utter error
Dan. 8. 12 cast down..and it practised, and prospe.
8. 24 shall prosper, and practise, and shall de.
Mic. 2. 1 when the morning is light, they practise.

PRACTISE secretly, to —
To keep silent, חָרַשׁ charash, 5.
1 Sa. 23. 9 David knew that Saul secretly practised

PRÆTORIUM —
Prœtor's hall, πραιτώριον praitōrion (L. prœtorium).
Mark 15. 16 led him away into the hall called P., and

PRAISE —
1. *Praises, thanksgivings, הִלּוּלִים hillulim.*
Lev. 19. 24 shall be holy, to praise the LORD (withal)

2. *Praise, מַהֲלָל mahalal.*
Prov 27. 21 furnace for gold; so (is) a man to his p.

3. *Praise, psalm, תְּהִלָּה tehillah.*
Exod 15. 11 glorious in holiness, fearful (in) praises
Deut 10. 21 He (is) thy praise, and he (is) thy God
26. 19 which he hath made, in praise, and in
1 Ch. 16. 35 we may give thanks..(and) glory in thy p.
2 Ch. 20. 22 when they began to sing and to praise
Neh. 9. 5 which is exalted above all blessing and
12. 46 songs of praise and thanksgiving unto

Psa. 9. 14 That I may show forth all thy praise in
22. 3 (O thou) that inhabitest the praises of I.
22. 25 My praise (shall be) of thee in the great
33. 1 Rejoice..(for) praise is comely for the up.
34. 1 his praise (shall) continually (be) in my
35. 28 tongue shall speak ..of thy praise all the
40. 3 praise unto our God: many shall see (it)
48. 10 so (is) thy praise unto the ends of the ea
51. 15 and my mouth shall show forth thy praise
65. 1 Praise waiteth for thee, O God, in Zion
66. 2 Sing forth the honour.. make his praise
66. 8 and make the voice of his praise to be h.
71. 6 my praise (shall be) continually of thee
71. 8 Let my mouth be filled (with) thy praise
71. 14 and will yet praise thee more and more
78. 4 showing..the praises of the LORD, and his
79. 13 will show forth thy praise to all generat.
100. 4 Enter..into his courts with praise: be th.
102. 21 declare the name..and his praise in Jer.
106. 2 can utter..(who) can show forth all his p.?
106. 12 believed they his words; they sang his p.
106. 47 thy holy name, (and) to triumph in thy p.
109. 1 Hold not thy peace, O God of my praise
111. 10 fear of the LORD..his praise endureth for
119. 171 My lips shall utter praise, when thou h.
145. *title.* David's (Psalm) of praise
145. 21 My mouth shall speak the praise of the L.
147. 1 for (it is) pleasant; (and) praise is comely
148. 14 exalteth..the praise of all his saints; (e.)
149. 1 (and) his praise in the congregation of sa.
Isa. 42. 8 neither my praise to graven images
42. 10 Sing..his praise from the end of the earth
42. 12 give glory..and declare his praise in the
43. 21 This people..shall show forth my praise
48. 9 for my praise will I refrain for thee
60. 6 shall show forth the praises of the LORD
60. 18 thy walls salvation, and thy gates praise
61. 3 the garment of praise for the spirit of
61. 11 God will cause righteousness and praise
62. 7 till he make Jerusalem a praise in the
63. 7 I will mention..the praises of the LORD
Jer. 13. 11 a name, and for a praise, and for a glory
17. 14 I shall be saved: for thou (art) my praise
33. 9 a praise and an honour before all the
48. 2 (There shall be) no more praise of Moab
49. 25 How is the city of praise not left, the
51. 41 and how is the praise of the whole earth
Hab. 3. 3 and the earth was full of his praise
Zeph. 3. 19 get them praise and fame in every land
3. 20 a praise among all people of the earth

4. *Confession, thanksgiving, תּוֹדָה todah.*
Psa. 42. 4 with the voice of joy and praise, with
50. 23 Whoso offereth praise glorifieth me: and
56. 12 O God: I will render praises unto thee
100. *title.* A Psalm of praise

5. *Praise, αἴνεσις ainesis.*
Heb. 13. 15 let us offer the sacrifice of praise to God

6. *Praise, αἶνος ainos.*
Matt 21. 16 out of the mouth of babes..perfected pr.
Luke 18. 43 when they saw (it), gave praise unto God

7. *Courage, excellency, ἀρετή aretē.*
1 Pe. 2. 9 that ye should show forth the praises of

8. *Glory, δόξα doxa.*
John 9. 24 said unto him, Give God the praise: we
12. 43 loved the praise of men more than the p.
1 Pe. 4. 11 to whom be praise and dominion for ever

9. *Praise, commendation, ἔπαινος epainos.*
Rom. 2. 29 whose praise (is) not of men, but of God
13. 3 and thou shalt have praise of the same
1 Co 4. 5 then shall every man have praise of God
2 Co. 8. 18 whose praise (is) in the gospel throughout
Eph. 1. 6 To the praise of the glory of his grace, w.
1. 12 That we should be to the praise of his g.
1. 14 possession, unto the praise of his glory
Phil. 1. 11 Christ, unto the glory and praise of God
4. 8 if (there be) any praise, think on these t.
1 Pe. 1. 7 might be found unto praise and honour
2. 14 and for the praise of them that do well

PRAISE, to —
1. *To bless, declare blessed, בָּרַךְ barak, 3.*
Judg. 5. 2 Praise ye the LORD for the avenging of I.
Psa. 72. 15 continually; (and) daily shall he be prai.

2. *To praise, הָלַל halal, 3.*
Judg 16. 24 when the people saw him, they praised
2 Sa. 14. 25 there was none to be so much praised as
1 Ch. 16. 4 to thank and praise the LORD God of Isr
16. 36 all the people said, Amen, and praised
23. 5 four thousand praised the LORD with the
23. 5 which I made, (said David), to praise the.
23. 30 stand every morning to thank and praise
25. 3 to give thanks, and to praise the LORD
29. 13 we thank thee, and praise thy glorious n.
2 Ch. 5. 13 to make one sound to be heard in praising
5. 13 praised the LORD, (saying), For (he is) g.
7. 6 when David praised by their ministry; and
8. 14 to praise and minister before
20. 19 stood up to praise the LORD God of Israel
20. 21 and that should praise the beauty of holin.
23. 12 the people running and praising the king
30. 21 Levites and the priests praised the LORD
31. 2 to praise in the gates of the tents of the L.
Ezra 3. 10 to praise the LORD, after the ordinance of
3. 11 they sang together by course in praising
3. 11 praise the LORD, because the foundation
Neh. 5. 13 congregation said, Amen, and praised the
12. 24 to praise (and) to give thanks, according

Psa. 22. 22 midst of the congregation will I praise t.
22. 23 Ye that fear the LORD, praise him; all y
22. 26 they shall praise the LORD that seek him
35. 18 I will praise thee among much people
56. 4 In God I will praise his word: in God I
56. 10 I praise (his) word; in the LORD will I p.
63. 5 my mouth shall praise (thee) with joyful
69. 30 I will praise the name of God with a song
69. 34 Let the heaven and earth praise him, the
74. 21 let the poor and needy praise thy name
84. 4 they will be still praising thee. Selah
102. 18 people which shall be created shall praise
104. 35 Praise ye the LORD
So in 105. 45; 106. 1, 48; 111. 1; 112. 1; 113. 1, 9; 116. 19; 117. 2; 135. 1, 21; 146. 1, 10; 147. 1; 148. 1, 1, 14; 149. 1, 9; 150. 1, 6.
107. 32 praise him in the assembly of the elders
109. 30 yea, I will praise him among the multi.
113. 1 Praise, O ye servants of the LORD, praise
115. 17 The dead praise not the LORD, neither any
115. 18 But we will bless the LORD..Praise the L.
117. 1 O praise the LORD, all ye nations..all ye p.
119. 164 Seven times a day do I praise thee beca.
119. 175 Let my soul live, and it shall praise thee
135. 1 Praise ye the name of the LORD; praise
135. 3 Praise the Lord; for the LORD (is) good
145. 2 and I will praise thy name for ever and
146. 1 ye the LORD. Praise the LORD, O my soul
146. 2 While I live will I praise the LORD; I will
147. 12 the LORD, O Jerusalem; praise thy God
148. 1 from the heavens: praise him in the heig.
148. 2 Praise ye him, all his angels: praise ye him
148. 3 Praise ye him, sun and moon: praise him
148. 4 Praise him, ye heavens of heavens, and ye
148. 5, 13 Let them praise the name of the LORD
148. 7 Praise the LORD from the earth, ye drag.
149. 3 Let them praise his name in the dance: let
150. 1 Praise God in his sanctuary: praise him
150. 2 Praise him for his mighty acts: praise him
150. 3 Praise him with the sound..praise him
150. 4 Praise him..praise him with stringed in.
150. 5 Praise him..praise him upon the high so.
150. 6 Let every thing that hath breath praise
Prov. 27. 2 Let another man praise thee, and not th.
28. 4 They that forsake the law praise the wic.
31. 28 her husband (also), and he praiseth her
31. 31 let her own works praise her in the gates
Song 6. 9 daughters saw her..and they praised her
Isa. 62. 9 shall eat it, and praise the LORD; and they
64. 11 house where our fathers praised thee, is
Jer. 20. 13 Sing unto the LORD, praise ye the LORD
31. 7 publish ye, praise ye, and say, O LORD, save
Joel 2. 26 praise the name of the LORD your God

3. *To give praise, זָמַר zamar, 3.*
Psa. 21. 13 (so) will we sing and praise thy power

4. *To stretch out the hand, confess, יָדָה yadah, 5.*
Gen. 29. 35 Now will I praise the LORD: therefore she
49. 8 thou (art he) whom thy brethren shall p.
2 Ch. 7. 3 praised the LORD, (saying), For (he is) go.
7. 6 which David the king had made to praise
20. 21 Praise the LORD; for his mercy..for ever
Psa. 7. 17 I will praise the LORD according to his r.
9. 1 I will praise (thee), O LORD, with my wh.
28. 7 rejoiceth; and with my song will I praise
30. 9 Shall the dust praise thee? shall it declare
33. 2 Praise the LORD with harp: sing unto him
42. 5 for I shall yet praise him (for) the help of
42. 11 for I shall yet praise him, (who is) the he.
43. 4 upon the harp will I praise thee, O God
43. 5 for I shall yet praise him, (who is) the h.
44. 8 boast all the day long, and praise thy n.
45. 17 therefore shall the people praise thee for
49. 18 praise thee, when thou doest well to thy.
52. 9 I will praise thee for ever, because thou
54. 6 I will praise thy name, O LORD, for (it is)
57. 9 I will praise thee, O LORD, among the p.
67. 3, 5 praise thee, O God; let all the people p.
71. 22 I will also praise thee with the psaltery
76. 10 Surely the wrath of man shall praise thee
86. 12 I will praise thee, O Lord my God, with
88. 10 shall the dead arise (and) praise thee? S.
89. 5 And the heavens shall praise thy wonders
99. 3 Let them praise thy great and terrible n.
107. 8, 15, 21, 31 Oh that (men) would praise the
108. 3 I will praise thee, (O LORD), among the p.
109. 30 I will greatly praise the LORD with my
111. 1 I will praise the LORD with (my) whole h.
118. 19 I will go in to them, (and) I will praise
118. 21 I will praise thee: for thou hast heard
118. 28 Thou (art) my God, and I will praise thee
119. 7 I will praise thee with uprightness of he.
138. 1 I will praise thee with my whole heart
138. 2 praise thy name for thy loving kindness
138. 4 All the kings of the earth shall praise thee
139. 14 I will praise thee; for I am fearfully (and)
142. 7 that I may praise thy name: the right.
145. 10 All thy works shall praise thee, O LORD
Isa. 12. 1 shalt say, O LORD, I will praise thee: th.
12. 4 Praise the LORD, call upon his name, de.
25. 1 I will exalt thee, I will praise thy name
38. 18 For the grave cannot praise thee, death
38. 19 The living, the living, he shall praise thee
Jer. 33. 11 Praise the LORD of hosts: for the LORD (is)

5. *To praise, glorify, שָׁבַח shabach, 3.*
Psa. 63. 3 better than life, my lips shall praise thee
117. 1 all ye nations: praise him, all ye people
145. 4 One generation shall praise thy works to
147. 12 Praise the LORD, O Jerusalem;
Eccl. 4. 2 I praised the dead which are already dead

6. *To give praise,* שְׁבַח *shebach,* 3.
Dan. 2. 23 I thank thee, and praise thee, O thou God
4. 34 I praised and honoured him that liveth
4. 37 Now I Nebuchadnezzar praise and extol
5. 4 They drank wine, and praised the gods of
5. 23 thou hast praised the gods of silver, and

7. *To speak well of,* εὐλογέω *eulogeō.*
Luke 1. 64 tongue (loosed), and he spake, and prais.

8. *To praise,* αἰνέω *aineō.*
Luke 2. 13 multitude of the heavenly host praising
2. 20 shepherds returned, glorifying and prais.
19. 37 began to rejoice and praise God with a
24. 53 were continually in the temple, praising
Acts 2. 47 Praising God, and having favour with all
3. 8 walking, and leaping, and praising God
3. 9 people saw him walking and praising God
Rom 15. 11 Praise the Lord, all ye Gentiles; and laud
Rev. 19. 5 saying, Praise our God, all ye his servants

9. *To give praise to,* ἐπαινέω *epaineō.*
1 Co. 11. 2 Now I praise you, brethren, that ye rem.
11. 17 I praise (you) not, that ye come together
11. 22 shall I praise you in this? I praise (you)

PRAISES, to give or sing —

1. *To give praise,* זָמַר *zamar,* 3.
2 Sa. 22. 50 and I will sing praises unto thy name
Psa. 7. 17 will sing praise to the name of the LORD
9. 2 I will sing praise to thy name, O thou
9. 11 Sing praises to the LORD, which dwelleth
18. 49 Therefore will I..sing praises unto thy
27. 6 yea, I will sing praises unto the LORD
30. 12 (my) glory may sing praise to thee, and not
47. 6 Sing praises to God, sing praises
47. 6 sing praises unto our King, sing praises
47. 7 sing ye praises with understanding
57. 7 heart is fixed; I will sing and give praise
61. 8 will I sing praise unto thy name for ever
68. 4 sing praises to his name: extol him that
68. 32 ye kingdoms..sing praises unto the Lord
75. 9 I will sing praises to the God of Jacob
92. 1 to sing praises unto thy name, O Most H.
98. 4 make a..noise, and rejoice, and sing pra.
104. 33 I will sing praise to my God while I have
108. 1 sing and give praise, even with my glory
108. 3 I will sing praises unto thee among the
135. 3 sing praises unto his name; for (it is)
138. 1 before the gods will I sing praise unto
144. 9 upon a psaltery..will I sing praises
146. 2 I will sing praises unto my God while I
147. 1 (it is) good to sing praises unto our God
147. 7 sing praise upon the harp unto our God
149. 3 sing praises unto him with the timbrel

2. *To boast, praise,* הָלַל *halal,* 3.
2 Ch. 23. 13 singers..and such as taught to sing praise
29. 30 sing praise unto the LORD with the words
29. 30 they sang praises with gladness, and they

3. *To hymn,* ὑμνέω *humneō.*
Acts 16. 25 Silas prayed, and sang praises unto God
Heb. 2. 12 midst of the church will I sing praise

PRAISED, (worthy) to be —

1. *To bless, declare blessed,* בָּרַךְ *barak,* 3.
Psa. 72. 15 prayer also..(and) daily shall he be prais.

2. *To be praised,* הָלַל *halal,* 4.
2 Sa. 22. 4 on the LORD, (who is) worthy to be praised
1 Ch. 16. 25 great (is) the LORD, and..to be praised: he
Psa. 18. 3 upon the LORD, (who is worthy) to be pr.
48. 1 to be praised in the city of our God
96. 4 LORD (is) great, and greatly to be praised
113. 3 the LORD'S name (is) to be praised
145. 3 Great (is) the LORD, and..to be praised

3. *To praise self,* הָלַל *halal,* 7.
Prov. 31. 30 a woman (that) feareth..shall be praised

PRANCE, to —
To prance, דָּהַר *dahar.*
Nah. 3. 2 of the prancing horses, and of the jump.

PRANCING —
Prancing, דַּהֲרָה *daharah.*
Judg. 5. 22 the means of the prancings, the prancings

PRATE against, to —
To prattle, prate, φλυαρέω *phluareō.*
3 John 10 prating against us with malicious words

PRATING —
Of lips, שָׂפָה *saphah.*
Prov 10. 8 The wise..receive..but a prating fool sh.
10. 10 causeth sorrow: but a prating fool shall

PRAY, to —

1. *To petition, pray,* בְּעָה, בָּעָא *bea, beah.*
Dan. 6. 11 praying and making supplication before

2. *To entreat grace,* חָנַן *chanan,* 7.
2 Ch. 6. 37 and pray unto thee in the land of their

3. *To entreat, make supplication,* עָתַר *athar.*
Job 33. 26 He shall pray unto God, and he will be

4. *To come up, strike against, intercede,* פָּגַע *paga.*
Job 21. 15 and what profit..if we pray unto him?

5. *To judge self, pray habitually,* פָּלַל *palal,* 7.
Gen. 20. 7 shall pray for thee, and thou shalt live
20. 17 Abraham prayed unto God: and God hea.
Num 11. 2 when Moses prayed unto the LORD, the
21. 7 pray unto the LORD..And Moses prayed
Deut. 9. 20 and I prayed for Aaron also the same time
9. 26 I prayed therefore unto the LORD, and s.
1 Sa. 1. 10 and prayed unto the LORD, and wept sore
1. 12 as she continued praying before the LORD
1. 26 stood by thee here, praying unto the L.
1. 27 I prayed; and the LORD hath given me
2. 1 Hannah prayed, and said, My heart rejo.
7. 5 and I will pray for you unto the LORD
8. 6 a king to judge us. And Samuel prayed
12. 19 Pray for thy servants unto the LORD thy
12. 23 I should sin..in ceasing to pray for you
2 Sa. 7. 27 thy servant found in his heart to pray
1 Ki. 8. 28 thy servant prayeth before thee to day
8. 30 when they shall pray toward this place
8. 33 pray, and make supplication unto thee in
8. 35 they pray toward this place, and confess
8. 42 he shall come and pray toward this house
8. 44 shall pray unto the LORD toward the city
8. 48 pray unto thee toward their land which
8. 54 Solomon had made an end of praying all
13. 6 pray for me that my hand may be resto.
2 Ki. 4. 33 shut the door..and prayed unto the LORD
6. 17 And Elisha prayed, and said..open his eyes
6. 18 Elisha prayed unto the LORD, and said, S.
19. 15 Hezekiah prayed before the LORD, and s.
19. 20 thou hast prayed to me against Sennach.
20. 2 turned..and prayed unto the LORD, say.
1 Ch. 17. 25 hath found (in his heart) to pray before t.
2 Ch. 6. 19, 20 the prayer which thy servant prayeth
6. 24 pray and make supplication before thee
6. 26 they pray toward this place, and confess
6. 32 Moreover..if they come and pray in this
6. 34 they pray unto thee toward this city which
6. 38 pray toward their land, which thou gavest
7. 1 when Solomon had made an end of pray.
7. 14 pray, and seek my face, and turn from their
30. 18 Hezekiah prayed for them, saying, The
32. 20 the son of Amoz, prayed and cried to he.
32. 24 prayed unto the LORD: and he spake unto
33. 13 prayed unto him: and he was entreated
Ezra 10. 1 when Ezra had prayed, and when he had
Neh. 1. 4 fasted, and prayed before the God of he.
1. 6 which I pray before thee now, day and n.
2. 4 So I prayed to the God of heaven
Job 42. 8 my servant Job shall pray for you; for
42. 10 turned the captivity of Job, when he pr.
Psa. 5. 2 and my God: for unto thee will I pray
32. 6 shall every one that is godly pray unto thee
Isa. 16. 12 that he shall come to his sanctuary to p.
37. 15 And Hezekiah prayed unto the LORD, say.
37. 21 thou hast prayed to me against Sennach.
38. 2 turned his face..and prayed unto the L.
44. 17 prayeth unto it, and saith, Deliver me
45. 20 and pray unto a god (that) cannot save
Jer. 7. 16 pray not thou for this people, neither lift
11. 14 pray not thou for this people, neither lift
14. 11 Pray not for this people for (their) good
29. 7 pray unto the LORD for it: for in the peace
29. 12 pray unto me, and I will hearken unto you
32. 16 I had delivered the evidence..I prayed
37. 3 Pray now unto the LORD our God for us
42. 2 and pray for us unto the LORD thy God
42. 4 behold, I will pray unto the LORD your God
42. 20 Pray for us unto the LORD our God; and
Dan. 9. 4 I prayed unto the LORD my God, and made
9. 20 praying, and confessing my sin and the
Jon. 2. 1 Jonah prayed unto the LORD his God out
4. 2 And he prayed unto the LORD, and said, I

6. *To bend, bow, pray,* צְלָא *tsela,* 3.
Ezra 6. 10 pray for the life of the king, and of his
Dan. 6. 10 prayed, and gave thanks before his God

7. *To bow down, meditate, pray,* שִׂיחַ *siach.*
Psa. 55. 17 at noon, will I pray, and cry aloud; and

8. *To ask,* שָׁאַל *shaal.*
Psa. 122. 6 Pray for the peace of Jerusalem: they s.

9. *To smooth down, deprecate,* חָלָה *chalah,* 3.
Zech. 7. 2 When they had sent..to pray before the
8. 21 Let us go speedily to pray before the L.
8. 22 come to seek..and to pray before the L.

10. *To want, pray, beseech,* δέομαι *deomai.*
Matt. 9. 38 Pray ye therefore the Lord of the harvest
Luke 10. 2 pray ye therefore the Lord of the harvest
21. 36 Watch ye therefore, and pray always, that
22. 32 But I have prayed for thee, that thy faith
Acts 4. 31 when they had prayed, the place was sh.
8. 22 pray God, if perhaps the thought of thine
8. 24 Pray ye to the Lord for me, that none of
8. 34 I pray thee, of whom speaketh the prop.
10. 2 gave much alms to the people, and prayed
2 Co. 5. 20 we pray (you) in Christ's stead, be ye rec.
8. 4 Praying us with much entreaty that we
1 Th. 3. 10 praying exceedingly that we might see y.

11. *To ask, interrogate,* ἐρωτάω *erōtaō.*
Luke 5. 3 prayed him that he would thrust out a
14. 18, 19 I pray thee have me excused
16. 27 I pray thee therefore, father, that thou
John 4. 31 In the meanwhile his disciples prayed him
14. 16 I will pray the Father, and he shall give
16. 26 I say not unto you, that I will pray the F.
17. 9 I pray for them: I pray not for the world
17. 15 I pray not that thou shouldest take them
17. 20 Neither pray I for these alone, but for th.
Acts 10. 48 Then prayed they him to tarry certain d.
23. 18 prayed me to bring this young man unto
1 Jo. 5. 16 I do not say that he shall pray for it

12. *To pray, wish,* εὔχομαι *euchomai.*
2 Co. 13. 7 Now I pray to God that ye do no evil: not
Jas. 5. 16 pray one for another, that ye may be he.

13. *To call for, or alongside of,* παρακαλέω *parak.*
Matt 26. 53 Thinkest thou that I cannot now pray to
Mark 5. 17 began to pray him to depart out of their
5. 18 prayed him that he might be with him
Acts 16. 9 prayed him, saying, Come over into Mac.
24. 4 I pray thee that thou wouldest hear us of
27. 34 Wherefore I pray you to take (some) meat

14. *To pray or wish for,* προσεύχομαι *proseuchomai.*
Matt. 5. 44 pray for them which despitefully use you
6. 5 when thou prayest..for they love to pray
6. 6 when thou prayest..pray to thy Father wh.
6. 7 when ye pray, use not vain repetitions, as
6. 9 After this manner therefore pray ye: Our
14. 23 went up into a mountain apart to pray
19. 13 he should put (his) hands on them, and
24. 20 pray ye that your flight be not in the wint.
26. 36 Sit ye here, while I go and pray yonder
26. 39 fell on his face, and prayed, saying, O my
26. 41 Watch and pray, that ye enter not into
26. 42 prayed, saying, O my Father, if this cup
26. 44 prayed the third time, saying the same
Mark 1. 35 went..into a solitary place, and there p.
6. 46 he departed into a mountain to pray
11. 24 when ye pray, believe that ye receive (t.)
11. 25 when ye stand praying, forgive, if ye have
13. 18 pray ye that your flight be not in the
13. 33 watch and pray: for ye know not when
14. 32 he saith..Sit ye here, while I shall pray
14. 35 prayed that, if it were possible, the hour
14. 38 Watch ye and pray, lest ye enter into te.
14. 39 he went away, and prayed, and spake the
Luke 1. 10 the people were praying without at the
3. 21 Jesus also being baptized, and praying
5. 16 withdrew..into the wilderness, and pra.
6. 12 he went out into a mountain to pray, and
6. 28 pray for them which despitefully use you
9. 18 as he was alone praying, his disciples we.
9. 28 and went up into a mountain to pray
9. 29 as he prayed, the fashion of his counten.
11. 1 as he was praying in a certain place, wh.
11. 1 teach us to pray, as John also taught his
11. 2 When ye pray, say, Our Father which art
18. 1 men ought always to pray, and not to f.
18. 10 Two men went up into the temple to pr.
18. 11 prayed thus with himself, God, I thank
22. 40 said..Pray that ye enter not into tempt.
22. 41 withdrawn..kneeled down, and prayed
22. 44 [he prayed more earnestly: and his sweat]
22. 46 and pray, lest ye enter into temptation
Acts 1. 24 they prayed, and said, Thou, Lord, which
6. 6 when they had prayed, they laid (their) h.
8. 15 prayed for them, that they might receive
9. 11 Saul, of Tarsus: for, behold, he prayeth
9. 40 kneeled down, and prayed; and turning
10. 9 Peter went up upon the house top to pray
10. 30 I prayed in my house, and, behold, a man
11. 5 I was in the city of Joppa praying: and
12. 12 where many were gathered together pra.
13. 3 when they had fasted and prayed, and la.
14. 23 when they..had prayed with fasting, they
16. 25 Silas prayed, and sang praises unto God
20. 36 kneeled down, and prayed with them all
21. 5 we kneeled down on the shore, and prayed
22. 17 while I prayed in the temple, I was in a
28. 8 and prayed, and laid his hands on him, and
1 Co. 11. 4 Every man praying or prophesying, having
11. 5 every woman that prayeth or prophesieth
11. 13 is it comely that a woman pray unto God
14. 13 let him that speaketh..pray that he may
14. 14 pray in..(unknown) tongue, my spirit pr.
14. 15 will pray with the spirit, and I will pray
Eph. 6. 18 Praying always with all prayer and supli.
Phil. 1. 9 I pray, that your love may abound yet m.
Col. 1. 3 We give thanks..praying always for you
1. 9 do not cease to pray for you, and to des.
4. 3 praying also for us, that God would open
1 Th. 5. 17 Pray without ceasing
5. 25 Brethren, pray for us
2 Th. 1. 11 pray always for you, that our God would
3. 1 pray for us, that the word of the Lord may
1 Ti. 2. 8 I will therefore that men pray every wh.
Heb. 13. 18 Pray for us: for we trust we have a good
Jas. 5. 13 Is any among you afflicted? let him pray
5. 14 let them pray over him, anointing him
5. 18 he prayed again, and the heaven gave rain
Jude 20 But ye, beloved..praying in the Holy G.

PRAY (I, we) thee, you —

1. *Ah pray!* אָנָּה, אָנָּא *ana, anah.*
Gen. 50. 17 we pray thee, forgive the trespass of the
Jon. 4. 2 I pray thee, O LORD, (was) not this my s.

2. *O that!* לוּ *lu.*
Gen. 23. 13 I pray thee, hear me: I will give thee

3. *Pray!* נָא *na.*
Gen. 12. 13 Say, I pray thee, thou (art) my sister: th.
18. 4 Let a little water, I pray you, be fetched
Judg. 9. 38 Go out, I pray now, and fight with them

PRAY earnestly (or for), to —
To pray to or toward, προσεύχομαι *proseuchomai.*
Rom. 8. 26 we know not what we should pray for as
Jas. 5. 17 prayed earnestly that it might not rain

PRAYER —

1. *A whisper,* לַחַשׁ *lachash.*
Isa. 26. 16 poured out a prayer (when) thy chasten.

2. *Meditation,* שִׂיחַ, שִׂיחָה *sichah, siach.*
Job 15. 4 Yea, thou..restrainest prayer before God
Psa. 64. 1 Hear my voice, O God, in my prayer, pres.

3. *Prayer, song of praise,* תְּפִלָּה *tephillah.*
2 Sa. 7. 27 hath..found in his heart to pray this pra.
1 Ki. 8. 28 Yet have thou respect unto the prayer of
8. 28 to the prayer which thy servant prayeth
8. 29 the prayer which thy servant shall make
8. 38 What prayer and supplication soever be
8. 45, 49 their prayer and their supplication
8. 54 praying all this prayer and supplication
9. 3 heard thy prayer and thy supplication
2 Ki. 19. 4 lift up (thy) prayer for the remnant that
20. 5 I have heard thy prayer, I have seen thy
2 Ch. 6. 19 Have respect therefore to the prayer of
6. 19, 20 the prayer which thy servant prayeth
6. 29 what prayer (or) what supplication soever
6. 35, 39 their prayer and their supplication
6. 40 the prayer (that is made) in this place
7. 12 I have heard thy prayer, and have chosen
7. 15 the prayer (that is made) in this place
30. 27 their prayer came (up) to his holy dwell.
33. 18 his prayer unto his God, and the words of
33. 19 His prayer also, and (how God) was entr.
Neh. 1. 6 thou mayest hear the prayer of thy serv.
1. 11 the prayer of thy servant, and to the pra.
11. 17 principal to begin the thanksgiving in p.
Job 16. 17 Not..injustice..also my prayer (is) pure
Psa. 4. 1 have mercy upon me, and hear my prayer
6. 9 heard..the LORD will receive my prayer
17. *title.* A prayer of David. Hear the right
17. 1 give ear unto my prayer, (that goeth) not
35. 13 my prayer returned into mine own bosom
39. 12 Hear my prayer, O LORD, and give ear u.
42. 8 (and) my prayer unto the God of my life
54. 2 Hear my prayer, O God ; give ear to the
55. 1 Give ear to my prayer, O God ; and hide
61. 1 Hear my cry, O God ; attend unto my pr.
65. 2 thou that hearest prayer, unto thee shall
66. 19 he hath attended to the voice of my pra.
66. 20 which hath not turned away my prayer
69. 13 as for me, my prayer (is) unto thee, O L.
72. 20 The prayers of David the son of Jesse
80. 4 be angry against the prayer of thy people
84. 8 hear my prayer : give ear, O God of Jacob
86. *title* A prayer of David Bow down thine
86. 6 Give ear, O LORD, unto my prayer ; and
88. 2 Let my prayer come before thee : incline
88. 13 in..morning shall my prayer prevent thee
90. *title* A prayer of Moses the man of God. L.
102. *title* A prayer of the afflicted, when he is ov
102. 1 Hear my prayer, O LORD, and let my cry
102. 17 He will regard the prayer..their prayer
109. 4 adversaries : but I (give myself unto) pra.
109. 7 condemned ; and let his prayer become
141. 2 Let my prayer be set forth before thee (as)
141. 5 yet my prayer also..in their calamities
142. *title.* David ; A prayer when he was in the c.
143 1 Hear my prayer, O LORD, give ear to my
Prov 15 8 the prayer of the upright (is) his delight
15. 29 he heareth the prayer of the righteous
28. 9 He that turneth away..even his prayer
Isa. 1. 15 when ye make many prayers, I will not
37. 4 lift up (thy) prayer for the remnant that
38. 5 I have heard thy prayer, I have seen thy
56 7 make them joyful in my house of prayer
56. 7 shall be called an house of prayer for all
Jer. 7 16 neither lift up cry nor prayer for them
11 14 neither lift up a cry or prayer for them
Lam. 3. 8 when I cry..he shutteth out my prayer
3. 44 that (our) prayer should not pass through
Dan. 9. 3 to seek by prayer and supplication, with
9. 17 hear the prayer of thy servant, and his s.
9. 21 whiles I (was) speaking in prayer, even
Jon. 2. 7 my prayer came in unto thee, into thine
Hab. 3. 1 A prayer of Habakkuk the prophet upon

4. *Beseeching, prayer, supplication,* δέησις *deēsis.*
Luke 1. 13 thy prayer is heard ; and thy wife Elisa
2. 37 with fastings and prayers night and day
5 33 make prayers, and likewise (the disciples)
Rom 10. 1 my heart's desire and prayer to God for I
2 Co. 1. 11 Ye also helping together by prayer for us
9. 14 by their prayer for you, which long after
Phil. 1. 4 Always in every prayer of mine for you all
1. 19 turn to my salvation through your prayer
2 Ti. 1. 3 have remembrance of thee in my prayers
Heb. 5. 7 when he had offered up prayers and supl.
Jas. 5. 16 The effectual fervent prayer of a righteous
1 Pe. 3. 12 his ears (are open) unto their prayers : but

5. *Intercession, prayer,* ἔντευξις *enteuxis.*
1 Ti. 4. 5 sanctified by the word of God and prayer

6. *A wish, supplication,* εὐχή *euchē.*
Jas. 5. 15 the prayer of faith shall save the sick

7. *A prayer, pouring out,* προσευχή *proseuchē.*
Matt 17. 21 [goeth not out but by prayer and fasting]
21. 13 house shall be called the house of prayer
21. 22 whatsoever ye shall ask in prayer, believ
Mark 9. 29 by nothing but by prayer and fasting
11. 17 called of all nations the house of prayer
Luke 6. 12 and continued all night in prayer to God
19. 46 My house is the house of prayer : but ye
22. 45 when he rose up from prayer, and was c.
Acts 1. 14 with one accord in prayer and supplication
2. 42 and in breaking of bread, and in prayers
3. 1 into the temple at the hour of prayer
6. 4 will give ourselves continually to prayer
10. 4 Thy prayers and thine alms are come up
10. 31 thy prayer is heard, and thine alms are
12. 5 prayer was made without ceasing of the
16. 13 river side, where prayer was wont to be
16. 16 as we went to prayer, a certain damsel
Rom. 1. 9 make mention of you always in my pray.
Rom 12. 12 patient..continuing instant in prayer
15. 30 strive together with me in (your) prayers
1 Co. 7. 5 may give yourselves to fasting and prayer
Eph. 1. 16 making mention of you in my prayers
6. 18 all prayer and supplication in the spirit
Phil. 4. 6 prayer and supplication with thanksgiving
Col. 4. 2 Continue in prayer, and watch in the same
4. 12 labouring fervently for you in prayers
1 Th. 1. 2 making mention of you in our prayers
1 Ti. 2. 1 prayers, intercessions, (and) giving of tha.
5. 5 supplications and prayers night and day
Phm. 4 making mention of thee..in my prayers
22 trust that through your prayers I shall
1 Pe. 3. 7 dwell..that your prayers be not hindered
4. 7 be ye therefore sober..watch unto prayer
Rev. 5. 8 odours, which are the prayers of saints
8. 3 should offer (it) with the prayers of all s.
8. 4 (which came) with the prayers of the sai.

PRAYER, to make —

1. *To smooth down, deprecate,* חָלָה *chalah,* 3.
Dan. 9. 13 made we not our prayer before the LORD

2. *To entreat, make supplication,* עָתַר *athar,* 5.
Job 22. 27 Thou shalt make thy prayer unto him, and

3. *To judge self, pray habitually,* פָּלַל *palal,* 7.
1 Ki. 8. 29 the prayer which thy servant shall make
Neh. 4. 9 we made our prayer unto our God, and
Psa. 72. 15 prayer..shall be made for him continually

4. *To pray toward, pour out to,* προσεύχομαι *pros.*
Matt 23. 14 [for a pretence make long prayer : there.]
Mark 12. 40 for a pretence make long prayers : these
Luke 20. 47 Which..for a show make long prayers : the

PREACH (good tidings) to, unto, to—

1. *To bring or tell good tidings,* בָּשַׂר *basar,* 3.
Psa. 40. 9 I have preached righteousness in the gr.
Isa. 61. 1 to preach good tidings unto the meek ; he

2. *To call, proclaim, preach,* קָרָא *qara.*
Neh. 6. 7 thou hast also appointed prophets to pre.
Jon. 3. 2 preach unto it the preaching that I bid

3. *To tell or announce thoroughly,* διαγγέλλω *diag*
Luke 9. 60 but go thou and preach the kingdom of

4. *To speak throughout,* διαλέγομαι *dialegomai.*
Acts 20. 7 Paul preached unto them, ready to depart
20. 9 as Paul was long preaching, he sunk down

5. *To tell good news or tidings,* εὐαγγελίζω *euagg.*
Luke 3 18 many other things..preached he unto the
4. 43 I must preach the kingdom of God to ot.
16. 16 the kingdom of God is preached and ev.
Acts 5. 42 they ceased not to teach and preach Jesus
8. 4 they..went every where preaching the w.
8. 12 preaching the things concerning the kin
8. 35 and began..and preached unto him Jesus
8 40 he preached in all the cities, till he came
10 36 preaching peace by Jesus Christ : he is
11. 20 And some..spake..preaching the Lord J.
14. 15 preach unto you that ye should turn from
15. 35 preaching the word of the Lord, with many
17. 18 he preached unto them Jesus and the re
1 Co. 15. 1 the gospel which I preached unto you
15. 2 keep in memory what I preached unto you
2 Co. 11. 7 preached to you the gospel of God freely
Gal. 1. 8 than that which we have preached unto
1. 11 the gospel which was preached of me is
1. 16 that I might preach him among the hea.
1. 23 preacheth the faith which once he destr.
Eph. 2 17 preached peace to you which were afar
3 8 I should preach among the Gentiles the
Heb. 4. 2 unto us was the gospel preached, as well
4. 6 they to whom it was first preached
Rev. 14. 6 to preach unto them that dwell on the

6. *To tell thoroughly,* καταγγέλλω *kataggellō.*
Acts 4. 2 preached through Jesus the resurrection
13. 5 they preached the word of God in the sy.
13. 38 through this man is preached unto you the
15. 36 we have preached the word of the Lord
17. 3 Jesus, whom I preach unto you, is Christ
17. 13 word of God was preached of Paul at B.
1 Co. 9. 14 they which preach the gospel should live
Phil. 1. 16 The one preach Christ of contention, not
1. 18 in pretence, or in truth, Christ is preached
Col. 1. 28 we preach, warning every man, and teac.

7. *To cry or proclaim as a herald,* κηρύσσω *kērussō.*
Matt. 3. 1 came..preaching in the wilderness of Ju.
4. 17 Jesus began to preach, and to say, Repent
4. 23 preaching the gospel of the kingdom, and
9. 35 preaching the gospel of the kingdom, and
10. 7 preach, saying, The kingdom of heaven is
10. 27 what ye hear in the ear .preach ye upon
11. 1 departed..to teach and to preach in their
24. 14 gospel of the kingdom shall be preached
26. 13 Wheresoever this gospel shall be preached
Mark 1. 4 preach the baptism of repentance for the
1. 7 preached, saying, There cometh one mig.
1. 14 preaching the gospel of the kingdom of
1. 38 I may preach there also : for therefore c.
1. 39 preached in their synagogues throughout
3. 14 that he might send them forth to preach
6. 12 went..and preached that men should re.
14. 9 Wheresoever this gospel shall be preached
16. 15 Go ye..and preach the gospel to every c.
16. 20 they went forth, and preached every where
Luke 3. 3 preaching the baptism of repentance for
4. 18 to preach deliverance to the captives, and
4. 19 To preach the acceptable year of the Lord
4. 44 And he preached in the synagogues of G.
Luke 8. 1 preaching and showing the glad tidings
9. 2 sent them to preach the kingdom of God
24. 47 should be preached in his name among all
Acts 8. 5 Philip went down..and preached Christ
9. 20 straightway he preached Christ in the sy.
10. 37 after the baptism which John preached
10. 42 commanded us to preach unto the people
15. 21 hath in every city them that preach him
19. 13 adjure you by Jesus whom Paul preacheth
20. 25 among whom I have gone preaching the
28. 31 Preaching the kingdom of God, and teac.
Rom. 2. 21 thou that preachest a man should not st.
10. 8 that is, the word of faith, which we preach
10. 15 how shall they preach except they be se.?
1 Co. 1. 23 But we preach Christ crucified, unto the
9. 27 when I have preached to others, I myself
15. 11 I or they, so we preach, and so ye believ.
15. 12 Now if Christ be preached that he rose
2 Co. 1. 19 Christ, who was preached among you by
4. 5 For we preach not ourselves, but Christ
11. 4 preacheth another..whom we have not p.
Gal. 2. 2 which I preach among the Gentiles, but
5. 11 if I yet preach circumcision, why do I yet
Phil. 1. 15 Some indeed preach Christ even of envy
Col. 1. 23 which was preached to every creature w.
1 Th. 2. 9 we preached unto you the gospel of God
1 Ti. 3. 16 preached unto the Gentiles, believed on
2 Ti. 4. 2 Preach the word ; be instant in season, out
1 Pe. 3. 19 he went and preached unto the spirits in

8. *To talk, discourse,* λαλέω *laleō.*
Mark 2. 2 and he preached the word unto them
Acts 8. 25 when they had testified and preached the
11. 19 preaching the word to none but unto the
13. 42 might be preached to them the next sab.
14. 25 when they had preached the word in Pe.
16. 6 were forbidden of the Holy Ghost to pre.

PREACH the gospel (of, to, in, into), to—

To tell or announce good news, εὐαγγελίζω *euagg.*
Matt 11. 5 the poor have the gospel preached to th.
Luke 4. 18 anointed me to preach the gospel to the
7. 22 raised, to the poor the gospel is preached
9. 6 preaching the gospel, and healing every.
20. 1 as he taught..and preached the gospel, the
Acts 8. 25 preached the gospel in many villages of
14. 21 when they had preached the gospel, 14. 7.
16. 10 called us for to preach the gospel unto th.
Rom 1. 15 I am ready to preach the gospel to you
10 15 feet of them that preach the gospel of pe.
15. 20 so have I strived to preach the gospel, not
1 Co. 1. 17 For Christ sent me..to preach the gospel
9. 16 For though I preach the gospel, I have no.
9. 16 woe is unto me, if I preach not the gospel !
9. 18 when I preach the gospel, I may make the
2 Co. 10. 16 To preach the gospel in the (regions) bey.
Gal. 1. 8 preach any other gospel unto you than
1. 9 If any (man) preach any other gospel unto
4. 13 I preached the gospel unto you at the first
Heb. 4. 2 For unto us was the gospel preached, as
1 Pe. 1. 12 them that have preached the gospel unto
1. 25 word which by the gospel is preached unto
4. 6 for this cause was the gospel preached also

PREACH before or first, to—

To cry or proclaim beforehand, προκηρύσσω *prok.*
Acts 3 20 Christ, which before was preached unto you
13. 24 John had first preached before his coming

PREACH before the gospel, to —

To tell good news beforehand, προευαγγελίζομαι.
Gal. 3. 8 preached before the gospel unto Abraham

PREACH boldly, to —

To use boldness, be free in speech, παρρησιάζομαι *parr.*
Acts 9. 27 how he had preached boldly at Damascus

PREACHED (fully) —

1. *To fill, make full,* πληρόω *plēroō.*
Rom. 15. 19 I have fully preached the gospel of Christ

2. *Hearing, what is heard by the ear,* ἀκοή *akoē.*
Heb. 4. 2 but the word preached did not profit them

PREACHER —

1. *Caller, congregator, preacher,* קֹהֶלֶת *qoheleth.*
Eccl. 1. 1 words of the preacher, the son of David
1 2 Vanity of vanities, saith the preacher, v.
1. 12 I the preacher was king over Israel in J.
7. 27 Behold, this have I found, saith the prea.
12. 8 Vanity of vanities, saith the preacher ; all
12. 9 because the preacher was wise, he still t.
12. 10 preacher sought to find out acceptable w.

2. *Crier, proclaimer, herald,* κῆρυξ *kērux.*
1 Ti. 2. 7 Whereunto I am ordained a preacher, and
2 Ti. 1. 11 Whereunto I am appointed a preacher, and
2 Pe. 2. 5 but saved Noah..a preacher of righteous.

3. *To cry or proclaim as a herald,* κηρύσσω *kērus.*
Rom. 10. 14 and how shall they hear without a pre. ?

PREACHING —

1. *Cry, proclamation, preaching,* קְרִיאָה *qeriah.*
Jon. 3. 2 preach unto it the preaching that I bid t.

2. *A cry, proclamation,* κήρυγμα *kērugma.*
Matt 12. 41 because they repented at the preaching
Luke 11. 32 for they repented at the preaching of Jo.
Rom 16. 25 the preaching of Jesus Christ, according
1 Co. 1. 21 pleased God by the foolishness of preach.
2. 4 my speech and my preaching (was) not
15 14 then (is) our preaching vain, and your fa.
2 Ti. 4. 17 by me the preaching might be fully kno.
Titus 1 3 manifested his word through preaching

3. *A word*, λόγος *logos*.
1 Co. 1. 18 For the preaching of the cross is to them

PRECEPT —

1. *Command, thing set up*, מִצְוָה *mitsvah*.
Neh. 9. 14 commandedst them precepts,statutes,and
Isa. 29. 13 fear toward me is taught by the precept
Jer. 35. 18 kept all his precepts, and done according
Dan. 9. 5 even by departing from thy precepts and

2. *Charges*, פִּקּוּדִים *piqqudim*.
Psa. 119. 4 commanded (us) to keep thy precepts dilig.
119. 15 I will meditate in thy precepts, and have
119. 27 to understand the way of thy precepts : so
119. 40 I have longed after thy precepts : quicken
119. 45 will walk at liberty : for I seek thy prec.
119. 56 This I had, because I kept thy precepts
119. 63 companion..of them that keep thy prece.
119. 69 will keep thy precepts with (my) whole
119. 78 (but) I will meditate in thy precepts
119. 87 consumed..but I forsook not thy precepts
119. 93 I will never forget thy precepts : for with
119. 94 save me ; for I have sought thy precepts
119. 100 I understand..because I keep thy prec.
119. 104 Through thy precepts I get understand.
119. 110 laid a snare..yet I erred not from thy p.
119. 128 Therefore I esteem all (thy) precepts (c.)
119. 134 Deliver me..so will I keep thy precepts
119. 141 despised ; (yet) do not I forget thy prec.
119. 159 Consider how I love thy precepts : quic.
119. 168 I have kept thy precepts and thy testim.
119. 173 help me : for I have chosen thy precepts

3. *Command, thing set up*, צַו, צָו *tsav*.
Isa. 28. 10 precept..upon precept, precept upon pr.
28. 13 precept upon precept, precept upon pre.

4. *A charge*, ἐντολή *entolē*.
Mark 10. 5 For the hard..he wrote you this precept
Heb. 9. 19 For when Moses had spoken every prece.

PRECIOUS (things or fruits) —

1. *Desire*, חֶמְדָּה *chemdah*.
Dan. 11. 8 with their precious vessels of silver and

2. *Desired or desirable objects*, חֲמוּדוֹת *chamudoth*.
2 Ch. 20. 25 both riches with the dead bodies, and pr
Ezra 8. 27 two vessels of fine copper, precious as go
Dan. 11. 43 and over all the precious things of Egypt

3. *Grace*, חֵן *chen*.
Prov 17. 8 A gift (is as) a precious stone in the eyes

4. *Outspreading* (?), חֹפֶשׁ *chophesh*.
Eze. 27. 20 Dedan (was) thy merchant in precious cl.

5. *Good*, טוֹב *tob*.
2 Ki. 20. 13 showed them..the precious ointment, and
Psa. 133. 2 (It is) like the precious ointment upon the
Isa. 39. 2 showed them..the precious ointment, and

6. *Rare, precious*, יָקָר *yaqar*.
1 Sa. 3. 1 word of the LORD was precious in those
2 Sa. 12. 30 a talent of gold with the precious stones
1 Ki. 10. 2 she came to Jerusalem with..precious sto.
10. 10 she gave the king..precious stones : there
10. 11 great plenty of almug trees, and precious
1 Ch. 20. 2 precious stones in it ; and it was set upon
29. 2 all manner of precious stones, and marble
2 Ch. 3. 6 garnished the house with precious stones
9. 1 gold in abundance, and precious stones
9. 9 she gave the king..precious stones : neit.
9. 10 servants..brought algum trees and prec.
32. 27 made himself treasuries..for precious st.
Job 28. 16 It cannot be valued..with the precious on.
Psa. 116. 15 Precious in the sight of the LORD (is) the
Prov. 1. 13 We shall find all precious substance, we
3. 15 She (is) more precious than rubies : and all
6. 26 the adulteress will hunt for the precious
12. 27 the substance of a diligent man (is) prec.
24. 4 filled with all precious and pleasant riches
Isa. 28. 16 a precious corner (stone), a sure founda.
Jer. 15. 19 if thou take forth the precious from the
Lam. 4. 2 precious sons of Zion, comparable to fine
Eze. 27. 22 occupied in thy fairs..with all precious
28. 13 every precious stone (was) thy covering
Dan. 11. 38 shall he honour..with precious stones

7. *Rare, precious*, יְקָר *yeqar*.
Job 28. 10 cutteth..and his eye seeth every precious
Prov 20. 15 but the lips of knowledge (are) a precious
Jer. 20. 5 I will deliver..all the precious things th.
Eze. 22. 25 have taken the treasure and precious th.

8. *Precious thing*, מֶגֶד *meged*.
Deut 33. 13 for the precious things of heaven, for the
33. 14 precious fruits..and for the precious th.
33. 15 for the precious things of the lasting hills
33. 16 for the precious things of the earth and

9. *Precious things*, מִגְדָּנוֹת *migdanoth*.
Gen. 24. 53 gave also..to her mother precious things
2 Ch. 21. 3 their father gave them..precious things
Ezra 1. 6 precious things, besides all (that) was w.

10. *Acquisition, scattering*, מֶשֶׁךְ *meshek*.
Psa. 126. 6 He that goeth forth..bearing precious s.

11. *Spices*, נְכֹת *nekoth*.
2 Ki. 20. 13 the house of his precious things, the sil.
Isa. 39. 2 house of his precious things, the silver

12. *Held in honour or preciousness*, ἔντιμος *entimos*.
1 Pe. 2. 4 of men, but chosen of God, (and) precious
2. 6 lay in Sion a chief corner stone, elect, p.

13. *Honour, reverence, preciousness*, τιμή *timē*.
1 Pe. 2. 7 Unto you..which believe (he is) precious

14. *Honourable, honoured, precious*, τίμιος *timios*.
1 Co. 3. 12 gold, silver, precious stones, wood, hay
Jas. 5. 7 husbandman waiteth for the precious fr.
1 Pe. 1. 7 being much more precious than of gold
1. 19 with the precious blood of Christ, as of a
2 Pe. 1. 4 exceeding great and precious promises
Rev. 17. 4 decked with gold, and precious stones
18. 12 merchandise of gold..and precious ston.
18. 12 all manner vessels of most precious wood
18. 16 decked with gold, and precious stones, and
21. 11 light (was) like unto a stone most precious
21. 19 garnished with all manner of precious st.

PRECIOUS, like —

Equally honourable or precious, ἰσότιμος *isotimos*.
2 Pe. 1. 1 to them that have obtained like precious

PRECIOUS, very —

1. *Very precious*, βαρύτιμος *barutimos*.
Matt 26. 7 an alabaster box of very precious ointme.

2. *Very expensive*, πολυτελής *polutelēs*.
Mark 14. 3 box of ointment of spikenard very preci.

PRECIOUS, to be or make —

1. *To be precious, rare*, יָקַר *yaqar*.
1 Sa. 26. 21 because my soul was precious in thine e.
2 Ki. 1. 13 pray thee, let my life..be precious in thy
1. 14 therefore let my life now be precious in
Psa. 49. 8 For the redemption of their soul (is) prec.
72. 14 and precious shall their blood be in his
139. 17 How precious also are thy thoughts unto
Isa. 43. 4 Since thou wast precious in my sight, th.

2. *To make precious or rare*, יָקַר *yaqar*, 5.
Isa. 13. 12 I will make a man more precious than fi.

PREDESTINATE, to —

To mark off first or beforehand, προορίζω *proorizō*.
Rom. 8. 29 he also did predestinate (to be) conformed
8. 30 whom he did predestinate, them he also
Eph. 1. 5 Having predestinated us unto the adop.
1. 11 being predestinated according to the pur.

PRE-EMINENCE —

What is over and above, מוֹתָר *mothar*.
Eccl. 3. 19 so that a man hath no pre-eminence above

PRE-EMINENCE, (to love) to have the —

1. *To be first*, πρωτεύω *prōteuō*.
Col. 1. 18 in all (things) he might have the pre-emi.

2. *To love to be first*, φιλοπρωτεύω *philoprōteuō*.
3 John 9 who loveth to have the pre-eminence am.

PREFER, BE PREFERRED, to —

1. *To cause to go up*, עָלָה *alah*, 5.
Psa. 137. 6 if I prefer not Jerusalem above my chief

2. *To be pre-eminent*, נְצַח *netsach*, 4.
Dan. 6. 3 Then this Daniel was preferred above the

3. *To change, transfer*, שָׁנָה *shanah*, 3.
Esth. 2. 9 preferred her and her maids unto the best

4. *To become*, γίνομαι *ginomai*.
John 1. 15 He that cometh after me is preferred be.
1. 27 He it is, who coming after me, is prefer.
1. 30 After me cometh a man which is preferred

5. *To lead before*, προηγέομαι *proēgeomai*.
Rom 12. 10 kindly affectioned..in honour preferring

PREFERRING one before another —

Preference, prejudice, πρόκριμα *prokrima*.
1 Ti. 5. 21 without preferring one before another, d.

PREMEDITATE, to —

To take concern, μελετάω *meletaō*.
Mark 13. 11 neither do ye premeditate ; but whatsoe.

PREPARATION —

1. *To prepare, establish*, כּוּן *kun*, 5.
Nah. 2. 3 flaming torches in the day of his prepar.

2. *Arrangement, disposing*, מַעֲרָךְ *maarak*.
Prov 16. 1 The preparations of the heart in man, and

3. *Preparation, readiness*, ἑτοιμασία *hetoimasia*.
Eph. 6. 15 your feet shod with the preparation of the

4. *A making ready*, παρασκευή *paraskeuē*.
Matt 27. 62 that followed the day of the preparation
Mark 15. 42 because it was the preparation, that is, the
Luke 23. 54 that day was the preparation, and the s.
John 19. 14 it was the preparation of the passover, and
19. 31 because it was the preparation, that the
19. 42 because of the Jews' preparation (day) ; for

PREPARATION, to make —

To prepare, establish, כּוּן *kun*, 5.
1 Ch. 22. 5 I will (therefore) now make preparation

PREPARE (self), to —

1. *To bind, gird*, אָסַר *asar*.
1 Ki. 18. 44 Prepare (thy chariot), and get thee down

2. *To appoint, prepare*, זְמַן *zeman*, 2.
Dan. 2. 9 for ye have prepared lying and corrupt w.

3. *To be prepared, established*, כּוּן *kun*, 2.
2 Ch. 35. 4 prepare (yourselves) by the houses of your
Amos 4. 12 I will do this unto thee, prepare to meet

4. *To prepare, establish*, כּוּן *kun*, 3a.
Job 8. 8 prepare thyself to the search of their fat.
Psa. 9. 7 he hath prepared his throne for judgment
107. 36 that they may prepare a city for habitati.

5. *To prepare, establish*, כּוּן *kun*, 5.
Exod 16. 5 they shall prepare (that) which they bring
Exod 23. 20 bring thee into the place which I have p
Num 23. 1 prepare me here seven oxen and seven r.
23. 29 prepare me here seven bullocks and sev.
Deut 19. 3 Thou shalt prepare thee a way, and divide
Josh. 1. 11 Prepare you victuals ; for within three d.
4. 4 twelve men, whom he had prepared of the
1 Sa. 7. 3 prepare your hearts unto the LORD, and
23. 22 Go, I pray you, prepare yet, and know and
1 Ki. 5. 18 so they prepared timber and stones to bu.
6. 19 the oracle he prepared in the house with
1 Ch. 9. 32 over the showbread, to prepare (it) every
12. 39 for their brethren had prepared for them
15. 1 prepared a place for the ark of God, and
15. 3 unto his place which he had prepared for
15. 12 unto (the place that) I have prepared for
22. 3 David prepared iron in abundance for the
22. 5 So David prepared abundantly before his
22. 14 in my trouble I have prepared for the h.
22. 14 timber also and stone have I prepared ; and
29. 2 Now I have prepared with all my might
29. 3 above all that I have prepared for the h.
29. 16 all this store that we have prepared to b.
29. 18 keep this..and prepare their heart unto
2 Ch. 1. 4 (the place which) David had prepared for
2. 9 Even to prepare me timber in abundance
3. 1 place that David had prepared in the th.
12. 14 he prepared not his heart to seek the L.
19. 3 and hast prepared thine heart to seek God
20. 33 for as yet the people had not prepared th.
26. 14 Uzziah prepared for them, throughout all
27. 6 became mighty, because he prepared his
29. 19 vessels..have we prepared and sanctified
29. 36 Hezekiah rejoiced..that God had prepar.
30. 19 prepareth his heart to seek God, the LORD
31. 11 commanded to prepare..and they prepar.
35. 4 And prepare (yourselves) by the houses
35. 6 prepare your brethren, that (they) may
35. 14 therefore the Levites prepared for them.
35. 15 for their brethren the Levites prepared
35. 20 when Josiah had prepared the temple, N.
Ezra 7. 10 For Ezra had prepared his heart to seek
Esth. 6. 4 on the gallows that he had prepared for
7. 10 on the gallows that he had prepared for
Job 11. 13 If thou prepare thine heart, and stretch
15. 35 conceive mischief..their belly prepareth
27. 16 Though he heap up silver..and prepare
27. 17 He may prepare (it), but the just shall put
28. 27 he prepared it, yea, and searched it out
29. 7 (when) I prepared my seat in the street !
Psa. 7. 13 He hath also prepared for him the instru.
10. 17 thou wilt prepare their heart, thou wilt
57. 6 They have prepared a net for my steps
65. 9 thou preparest them corn, when thou ha.
68. 10 hast prepared of thy goodness for the po.
74. 16 thou hast prepared the light and the sun
103. 19 LORD hath prepared his throne in the he.
147. 8 who prepareth rain for the earth, who m.
Prov. 8. 27 When he prepared the heavens, I (was) t.
24. 27 Prepare thy work without, and make it
30. 25 yet they prepare their meat in the summ.
Isa. 14. 21 Prepare slaughter for his children for the
40. 20 cunning workman to prepare a graven i.
Jer. 46. 14 Stand fast, and prepare thee ; for the sw.
51. 12 set up the watchmen, prepare the ambu.
Eze. 38. 7 prepare for thyself, thou, and all thy co.
Zeph. 1. 7 for the LORD hath prepared a sacrifice, he

6. *To prepare or establish self*, כּוּן *kun*, 7a.
Psa. 59. 4 They run and prepare themselves without

7. *To dig, prepare*, כָּרָה *karah*.
2 Ki. 6. 23 he prepared great provision for them : and

8. *To number, count, appoint*, מָנָה *manah*, 3.
Psa. 61. 7 O prepare mercy and truth, (which) may
Jon. 1. 17 Now the LORD had prepared a great fish
4. 6 God prepared a gourd, and made (it) to
4. 7 God prepared a worm when the morning
4. 8 that God prepared a vehement east wind

9. *To arrange, set in array*, עָרַךְ *arak*.
Num 23. 4 I have prepared seven altars, and I have
Psa. 23. 5 Thou preparest a table before me in the p.
Isa. 21. 5 Prepare the table, watch in the watch t.
65. 11 that prepare a table for that troop, and

10. *To do, make*, עָשָׂה *asah*.
Gen. 27. 17 bread, which she had prepared, into the
Exod 12. 39 neither had they prepared for themselves
Num 15. 5 shalt thou prepare with the burnt offer.
15. 6 thou shalt prepare (for) a meat offering
15. 8 when thou preparest a bullock (for) a bu.
15. 12 According to the number that ye shall p.
Josh 22. 26 Let us now prepare to build us an altar
2 Sa. 15. 1 prepared him chariots and horses, and fi.
1 Ki. 1. 5 he prepared him chariots and horsemen
Neh. 13. 5 had prepared for him a great chamber, w.
13. 7 in preparing him a chamber in the courts
Esth. 5. 4 unto the banquet that I have prepared for
5. 5 to the banquet that Esther had prepared
5. 8 come to the banquet that I shall prepare
5. 12 unto the banquet that she had prepared
6. 14 unto the banquet that Esther had prepa.
Isa. 64. 4 he hath prepared for him that waiteth for
Eze. 4. 15 and thou shalt prepare thy bread therew.
12. 3 prepare thee stuff for removing, and rem.
35. 6 I will prepare thee unto blood, and blood
43. 25 shalt thou prepare..they shall also prep.
45. 17 he shall prepare the sin offering, and the
45. 22 upon that day shall the prince prepare for
45. 23 seven days of the feast he shall prepare
45. 24 he shall prepare a meat offering of an ep.
46. 2 the priests shall prepare his burnt offer.
46. 7 he shall prepare a meat offering, an eph.

Eze. 46. 12 prince shall prepare..he shall prepare his
46. 13 Thou shalt daily prepare..thou shalt pr.
46. 14 thou shalt prepare a meat offering for it
46. 15 Thus shall they prepare the lamb, and the
Hos. 2. 8 multiplied her silver..(which) they prep.

11. *To make ready the face or front,* פָּנָה *panah,* 3.
Gen. 24. 31 for I have prepared the house, and room
Psa. 80. 9 Thou preparedst (room) before it, and d.
Isa. 40. 3 Prepare ye the way of the LORD, make s.
57. 14 prepare the way, take up the stumbling
62. 10 prepare ye the way of the people; cast up
Mal. 3. 1 he shall prepare the way before me: and

12. *To set apart, consecrate,* קָדַשׁ *qadesh,* 3.
Jer. 6. 4 Prepare ye war against her; arise, and let
22. 7 I will prepare destroyers against thee, ev.
51. 27 prepare the nations against her, call toge.
51. 28 Prepare against her the nations with the
Joel 3. 9 Prepare war, wake up the mighty men
Mic. 3. 5 they even prepare war against him

13. *To set apart, consecrate,* קָדַשׁ *qadesh,* 5.
Jer. 12. 3 and prepare them for the day of slaughter

14. *To make ready,* ἑτοιμάζω *hetoimazō.*
Matt. 3. 3 Prepare ye the way of the Lord, make his
20. 23 to them) for whom it is prepared of my F.
22. 4 I have prepared my dinner: my oxen and
25. 34 inherit the kingdom prepared for you from
25. 41 fire, prepared for the devil and his angels
26. 17 Where wilt thou that we prepare for thee
Mark 1. 3 Prepare ye the way of the Lord, make his
10. 40 (it shall be given to them) for whom it is p.
14. 12 Where wilt thou that we go and prepare
Luke 1. 76 go before the face of the Lord to prepare
2. 31 Which thou hast prepared before the face
3. 4 Prepare ye the way of the Lord, make his
12. 47 prepared not (himself), neither did acco.
22. 8 Go and prepare us the passover, that we
22. 9 said..Where wilt thou that we prepare?
23. 56 prepared spices and ointments; and rested
24. 1 bringing the spices which they had prep.
John 14. 2 would have told you. I go to prepare a
14. 3 if I go and prepare a place for you, I will
1 Co. 2. 9 things which God hath prepared for them
2 Ti. 2. 21 meet for the master's use, (and) prepared
Phm. 22 But withal prepare me also a lodging: for
Heb. 11. 16 not ashamed..for he hath prepared for th.
Rev. 8. 6 the seven angels..prepared themselves to
9. 7 (were) like unto horses prepared unto ba.
9. 15 which were prepared for an hour, and a
12. 6 where she hath a place prepared of God
16. 12 way of the kings of the east might be pr.
21. 2 prepared as a bride adorned for her hus.

15. *To fit or adjust thoroughly,* καταρτίζω *katartizō.*
Heb. 10. 5 wouldest not, but a body hast thou pre.

16. *To make thoroughly ready,* κατασκευάζω *katas.*
Matt 11. 10 messenger..which shall prepare thy way
Mark 1. 2 messenger..which shall prepare thy way
Luke 1. 17 make ready a people prepared for the L.
7. 27 messenger..which shall prepare thy way
Heb. 11. 7 prepared an ark to the saving of his ho.
1 Pe. 3. 20 while the ark was a preparing, wherein f.

17. *To make ready for,* παρασκευάζω *paraskeuazō.*
1 Co. 14. 8 who shall prepare himself to the battle?

PREPARE afore, to —
To make ready beforehand, προετοιμάζω *proetoim.*
Rom. 9. 23 which he had afore prepared unto glory

PREPARED, (to be) —

1. *To arm,* חָלַץ *chalats* (pass. partic.).
Josh. 4. 13 About forty thousand prepared for war

2. *To be prepared, established,* כּוּן *kun,* 2.
2 Ch. 8. 16 Now all the work of Solomon was prepa.
35. 10 So the service was prepared, and the pri.
35. 16 So all the service of the LORD was prepa.
Neh. 8. 10 unto them for whom nothing is prepared
Prov 19. 29 Judgments are prepared for scorners, and
Eze. 38. 7 Be thou prepared..and all thy company
Hos. 6. 3 his going forth is prepared as the morning

3. *To be prepared, established,* כּוּן *kun,* 4a.
Eze. 28. 13 was prepared in thee in the day that thou

4. *To be prepared, established,* כּוּן *kun,* 6.
Prov. 21. 31 horse (is) prepared against the day of ba.
Isa. 30. 33 yea, for the king it is prepared: he hath
Nah. 2. 5 thereof, and the defence shall be prepared

5. *To prepare or establish self,* כּוּן *kun,* 7a.
Num 21. 27 let the city of Sihon be built and prepared

6. *To arrange, set in order,* עָרַךְ *arak.*
Eze. 23. 41 a stately bed, and a table prepared before

7. *To compound,* רָקַח *raqach,* 4.
2 Ch. 16. 14 odours..prepared by the apothecaries' art

8. *Ready, prepared,* ἕτοιμος *hetoimos.*
Mark 14. 15 large upper room furnished (and) prepa.

PREPARED, ready —
To arm, חָלַץ *chalats* (pass. partic.).
2 Ch. 17. 18 fourscore thousand ready prepared for

PRESBYTERY —
An assembly of elders, πρεσβυτέριον *presbuterion.*
1 Ti. 4. 14 the laying on of the hands of the presby.

PRESCRIBE, to—

1. *To write,* כָּתַב *kathab,* 3.
Isa. 10. 1 write grievousness (which) they have pr.

2. *To write,* כְּתַב *kethab.*
Ezra 7. 22 baths of oil, and salt without prescribing

PRESENCE —

1. *Before, over against, front,* נֶגֶד *neged.*
1 Ki. 8. 22 in the presence of all the congregation of
Prov 14. 7 Go from the presence of a foolish; Ps. 23. 5.

2. *Eyes,* עַיִן *[ayin].*
Gen. 23. 11 in the presence of the sons of my people
23. 18 for a possession in the presence of the c.
Deut 25. 9 come unto him in the presence of the el.
Jer. 28. 1 in the presence of the priests, and of all
28. 5 presence of the priests, and in the prese.
28. 11 spake in the presence of all the people, s.
32. 12 presence of the witnesses that subscribed

3. *Face, countenance,* פָּנִים *panim.*
Gen. 3. 8 hid themselves from the presence of the
4. 16 Cain went out from the presence of the L.
16. 12 shall dwell in the presence of all his bret.
25. 18 he died in the presence of all his brethren
27. 30 scarce gone out from the presence of Isa.
41. 46 Joseph went out from the presence of P.
45. 3 for they were troubled at his presence
Exod 10. 11 were driven out from Pharaoh's presence
33. 14 My presence shall go (with thee), and I
33. 15 If thy presence go not (with me), carry us
35. 20 congregation..departed from the presence
Lev. 22. 3 that soul shall be cut off from my prese.
Num 20. 6 went from the presence of the assembly
Josh. 4. 11 and the priests, in the presence of the peo.
8. 32 which he wrote in the presence of the c.
1 Sa. 18. 11 And David avoided out of his presence t.
19. 7 and he was in his presence, as in times p.
19. 10 but he slipped away out of Saul's prese.
2 Sa. 16. 19 (should I) not (serve) in the presence of
16. 19 father's presence, so will I be in thy pre.
24. 4 went out from the presence of the king
1 Ki. 1. 28 came into the king's presence, and stood
12. 2 for he was fled from the presence of king
2 Ki. 5. 27 went out from his presence a leper (as w.)
13. 23 neither cast he them from his presence
24. 20 until he had cast them out from his pres.
25. 19 of them that were in the king's presence
1 Ch. 16. 27 Glory and honour (are) in his presence
16. 33 sing out at the presence of the LORD, be.
24. 31 cast lots..in the presence of David the k.
2 Ch. 9. 23 sought the presence of Solomon, to hear
10. 2 whither he had fled from the presence of
20. 9 stand before this house, and in thy pres.
Neh. 2. 1 I had not been (before time) sad in his p.
Esth. 1. 10 served in the presence of Ahasuerus the
8. 15 Mordecai went out from the presence of
Job 1. 12 Satan went forth from the presence of the
2. 7 So went Satan forth from the presence of
23. 15 Therefore am I troubled at his presence
Psa. 16. 11 show me the path of life: in thy presence
17. 2 Let my sentence come forth from thy pr.
31. 20 shalt hide them in the secret of thy pres.
51. 11 Cast me not away from thy presence; and
68. 2 the wicked perish at the presence of God
68. 8 heavens also dropped at the presence of
95. 2 Let us come before his presence with th.
97. 5 at the presence of the LORD, at the presence
114. 7 at the presence of the LORD, at the pres.
139. 7 or whither shall I flee from thy presence?
140. 13 the upright shall dwell in thy presence
Prov 17. 18 becometh surety in the presence of his fr.
25. 6 Put not forth thyself in the presence of the
25. 7 thou shouldest be put lower in the pres.
Isa. 19. 1 idols of Egypt shall be moved at his pres.
63. 9 and the angel of his presence saved them
64. 1 mountains might flow down at thy prese.
64. 2 the nations may tremble at thy presence!
64. 3 mountains flowed down at thy presence
Jer. 4. 26 broken down at the presence of the LORD
5. 22 will ye not tremble at my presence, which
52. 3 he had cast them out from his presence
Eze. 38. 20 all the men..shall shake at my presence
Jon. 1. 3, 3 unto Tarshish from the presence of the
1. 10 that he fled from the presence of the LORD
Nah. 1. 5 earth is burned at his presence, yea, the
Zeph. 1. 7 Hold thy peace at the presence of the L.

4. *Before,* קֳדָם *qodam.*
Dan. 2. 27 Daniel answered in the presence of the k.

5. *Presence, a being alongside,* παρουσία *parousia.*
2 Co. 10. 10 but (his) bodily presence (is) weak, and
Phil. 2. 12 not as in my presence only but now much

6. *Face, countenance,* πρόσωπον *prosōpon.*
Acts 3. 13 denied him in the presence of Pilate, when
3. 19 shall come from the presence of the Lord
5. 41 departed from the presence of the council
2 Co. 10. 1 I Paul..who in presence (am) base among
1 Th. 2. 17 taken from you for a short time in prese.
2 Th. 1. 9 destruction from the presence of the Lord
Heb. 9. 24 now to appear in the presence of God for

PRESENCE (of), in or before the —

1. *Over against,* ἀπέναντι *apenanti.*
Acts 3. 16 perfect soundness in the presence of you

2. *Before, in front of, in presence of,* ἔμπροσθεν.
1 Th. 2. 19 (Are) not even ye in the presence of our

3. *In the face or sight of,* ἐνώπιον *enōpion.*
Luke 1. 19 I am Gabriel, that stand in the presence of
13. 26 We have eaten and drunk in thy presence
14. 10 worship in the presence of them that sit
15. 10 There is joy in the presence of the angels of
John 20. 30 did Jesus in the presence of his disciples
Acts 27. 35 gave thanks to God in presence of them
1 Co. 1. 29 That no flesh should glory in his presence
Rev. 14. 10 presence of the holy angels, and in the p.

4. *Fully in the presence of,* κατενώπιον *katenōpion.*
Jude 24 faultless before the presence of his glory

PRESENT —

1. *A reward,* אֶשְׁכָּר *eshkar.*
Eze. 27. 15 they brought thee (for) a present horns of

2. *A blessing,* בְּרָכָה *berakah.*
1 Sa. 30. 26 Behold a present for you of the spoil of
2 Ki. 18. 31 Make (an agreement) with me by a present
Isa. 36. 16 Make (an agreement) with me (by) a pre.

3. *Precious things,* מִגְדָּנוֹת *migdanoth.*
2 Ch. 32. 23 many brought..presents to Hezekiah king

4. *Present, offering,* מִנְחָה *minchah.*
Gen. 32. 13 and took..a present for Esau his brother
32. 18 it (is) a present sent unto my lord Esau
32. 20 appease him with the present that goeth
32. 21 So went the present over before him: and
33. 10 then receive my present at my hand: for
43. 11 carry down the man a present, a little ba.
43. 15 men took that present, and they took do.
43. 25 they made ready the present against Jo.
43. 26 brought him the present which (was) in
Judg. 3. 15 sent a present unto Eglon the king of M.
3. 17 brought the present unto Eglon king of
3. 18 he had made an end to offer the present
3. 18 sent away the people that bare the pres.
6. 18 bring forth my present, and set (it) bef.
1 Sa. 10. 27 despised him, and brought him no pres.
1 Ki. 4. 21 they brought presents, and served Solo.
10. 25 they brought every man his present, ve.
2 Ki. 8. 8 Take a present in thine hand, and go, m.
8. 9 took a present with him, even of every
17. 3 became his servant, and gave him prese.
17. 4 brought no present to the king of Assyria
20. 12 sent letters and a present unto Hezekiah
2 Ch. 9. 24 they brought every man his present, ves.
17. 5 Judah brought to Jehoshaphat presents
17. 11 Philistines brought Jehoshaphat presents
Psa. 72. 10 kings of Tarshish..shall bring presents
Isa. 39. 1 sent letters and a present to Hezekiah
Hos. 10. 6 carried unto Assyria (for) a present to k.

5. *Bribe, reward,* שֹׁחַד *shochad.*
1 Ki. 15. 19 I have sent unto thee a present of silver
2 Ki. 16. 8 sent (it for) a present to the king of Ass.

6. *Sent away,* שִׁלּוּחִים *shilluchim.*
1 Ki. 9. 16 given it (for) a present unto his daughter
Mic. 1. 14 Therefore shalt thou give presents to Mo.

7. *A present,* שַׁי *shai.*
Psa. 68. 29 Because of thy temple..kings bring pre.
76. 11 all that be round about him bring presents
Isa. 18. 7 In that time shall the present be brought

8. *A present,* תְּשׁוּרָה *teshurah.*
1 Sa. 9. 7 not a present to bring to the man of God

9. *To be found,* מָצָא *matsa,* 2.
Ezra 8. 25 and all Israel (there) present, had offered
Psa. 46. 1 our refuge and strength, a very present

10. *Now, at present, already,* ἄρτι *arti.*
1 Co. 4. 11 Even unto this present hour we both hu.
15. 6 the greater part remain unto this present

11. *To put or place in,* ἐνίστημι *enistēmi.*
Rom. 8. 38 powers, nor things present, nor things to
1 Co. 3. 22 death, or things present, or things to come
7. 26 that this is good for the present distress
Gal. 1. 4 he might deliver us from this present evil
Heb. 9. 9 Which (was) a figure for the time then p.

12. *To place upon, place by,* ἐφίστημι *ephistēmi.*
Acts 28. 2 because of the present rain, and because

13. *Now,* νῦν *nun.*
Rom. 8. 18 reckon that the sufferings of this present
11. 5 Even so then at this present time also there
2 Ti. 4. 10 having loved this present world, and is d.
Titus 2. 12 should live soberly..in this present world

14. *To be alongside,* πάρειμι *pareimi.*
Heb. 12. 11 no chastening for the present seemeth to
2 Pe. 1. 12 and be established in the present truth

PRESENT (self), to —

1. *To set up one's self,* יָצַב *yatsab,* 7.
Deut 31. 14 present yourselves in the tabernacle of the
31. 14 presented themselves in the tabernacle of
Josh. 24. 1 and they presented themselves before God
Judg 20. 2 presented themselves in the assembly of
1 Sa. 10. 19 present yourselves before the LORD by
17. 16 drew near..and presented himself forty
Job 1. 6 the sons of God came to present themse.
2. 1 the sons of God came to present themse.
2. 1 Satan came also..to present himself bef.

2. *To set up,* יָצַג *yatsag,* 5.
Gen. 47. 2 took..five men, and presented them unto

3. *To cause to find, present,* מָצָא *matsa,* 5.
Lev. 9. 12, 18 Aaron's sons presented unto him the
9. 13 they presented the burnt offering unto him

4. *To cause to come or draw nigh,* נָגַשׁ *nagash,* 5.
Judg. 6. 19 brought (it) out unto him..and presented

5. *[Their supplication will] fall,* נָפַל *naphal.*
Jer. 36. 7 It may be they will present their suppli.

6. *To cause to fall, present,* נָפַל *naphal,* 5.
Jer. 38. 26 I presented my supplication before the
42. 9 ye sent me to present your supplication

Dan. 9. 18 for we do not present our supplications
9. 20 presenting my supplication before the L.

7. *To be set up,* נָצַב *natsab,* 2.
Exod34. 2 present thyself there to me in the top of

8. *To cause to stand,* עָמַד *amad,* 5.
Lev. 14. 11 shall present the man that is to be made
16. 7 present them before the LORD (at) the door
27. 8 then he shall present himself before the
27. 11 then he shall present the beast before the
Num. 3. 6 and present them before Aaron the priest

9. *To give,* נָתַן *nathan.*
Eze. 20. 28 there they presented the provocation of

10. *To cause to come or draw near,* קָרַב *qarab,* 5.
Lev. 2. 8 and when it is presented unto the priest
7. 35 in the day (when) he presented them to

11. *To be seen,* רָאָה *raah,* 2.
Gen. 46. 29 presented himself unto him; and he fell

12. *To set, place, station,* ἵστημι *histēmi.*
Jude 24 able..to present (you) faultless before the

13. *To set alongside,* παρίστημι *paristēmi.*
Luke 2. 22 brought him to Jerusalem, to present (him)
Acts 9. 41 when he had called..presented her alive
23. 33 when they came to Cesarea..presented P.
Rom12. 1 that ye present your bodies a living sacr.
2 Co. 4. 14 Knowing that he..shall present (us) with
11. 2 that I may present (you as) a chaste vir.
Eph. 5. 27 That he might present it to himself a gl.
Col. 1. 22 to present you holy and unblameable and
1. 28 may present every man perfect in Christ

PRESENT unto, to —
To bear toward or to, προσφέρω *prospherō.*
Matt. 2. 11 they presented unto him gifts; gold, and

PRESENT (with), to be (here) —
1. *To be nourished, sustained,* כּוּל *kul,* 3b.
1 Ki. 20. 27 children of Israel..were all present, and

2. *To be found,* מָצָא *matsa,* 2.
1 Sa. 13. 15 Saul numbered the people (that were) p.
13. 16 and the people (that were) present with
21. 3 bread in mine hand, or what there is pr.
1 Ch.29. 17 people, which are present here, to offer
2 Ch. 5. 11 for all the priests (that were) present were
29. 29 king and all that were present with him
30. 21 children of Israel that were present at J.
31. 1 all Israel that were present went out to
34. 32 caused all that were present in Jerusalem
34. 33 made all that were present in Israel to se.
35. 7 for all that were present, to the number
35. 17 children of Israel that were present kept
35. 18 all Judah and Israel that were present, and
Esth. 1. 5 feast unto all the people that were present
4. 16 gather together all the Jews (that are) p.

3. *To stand,* עָמַד *amad.*
2 Sa. 20. 4 Then said the king..be thou here present

4. *To be among one's people,* ἐνδημέω *endēmeō.*
2 Co. 5. 8 absent from the body, and to be present
5. 9 whether present or absent, we may be ac.

5. *To remain,* μένω *menō.*
John14. 25 spoken unto you, being (yet) present with

6. *To come alongside,* παραγίνομαι *paraginomai.*
Acts 21. 18 Paul went in..and all the elders were p.

7. *To lie alongside,* παράκειμαι *parakeimai.*
Rom. 7. 18 for to will is present with me; but (how)
7. 21 when I would do good, evil is present with

8. *To be alongside,* πάρειμι *pareimi.*
Luke13. 1 There were present at that season some
Acts 10. 33 therefore are we all here present before
1 Co. 5. 3 as absent in body, but present in spirit
5. 3 judged already, as though I were present
2 Co. 10. 2 that I may not be bold when I am present
10. 11 (we be) also in deed when we are present
11. 9 when I was present with you, and wanted
13. 2 and foretell you as if I were present, the
13. 10 lest being present I should use sharpness
Gal. 4. 18 and not only when I am present with you
4. 20 I desire to be present with you now, and

PRESENT with, to be here —
To be alongside with, συμπάρειμι *sumpareimi.*
Acts 25. 24 all men which are here present with us, ye

PRESENTED, to be —
1. *To be caused to stand,* עָמַד *amad,* 6.
Lev. 16. 10 shall be presented alive before the LORD

2. *To cause to come or draw near,* קָרַב *qarab,* 5.
Lev. 2. 8 when it is presented unto the priest, he

PRESENTLY —
1. *In the day,* בַּיּוֹם *bay-yom.*
Prov.12. 16 A fool's wrath is presently known: but a

2. *At the same moment,* ἐξαυτῆς *exautēs.*
Phil. 2. 23 Him therefore I hope to send presently

3. *Along with the matter,* παραχρῆμα *parachrēma.*
Matt.21. 19 And presently the fig tree withered away
[*See* Give.]

PRESERVE, to —
1. *To give or preserve life,* חָיָה *chayah,* 3.
Gen. 19. 32, 34 that we may preserve seed of our fat.
Neh. 9. 6 preservest them all; and the host of he.

2. *To give ease, safety,* יָשַׁע *yasha,* 5.
2 Sa. 8. 6, 14 preserved David whithersoever he went
1 Ch.18. 6, 13 LORD preserved David whithersoever
Psa. 36. 6 O LORD, thou preservest man and beast

3. *To cause to be over and above,* יָתַר *yathar,* 5.
Psa. 79. 11 preserve thou those that are appointed to

4. *To cause to slip away,* מָלַט *malat,* 5.
Isa. 31. 5 deliver (it); and passing over he will pre.

5. *To keep, watch, reserve,* נָצַר *natsar.*
Psa. 12. 7 thou shalt preserve them from this gene.
25. 21 Let integrity and uprightness preserve me
31. 23 (for) the LORD preserveth the faithful, and
32. 7 thou shalt preserve me from trouble; thou
40. 11 let thy loving kindness..continually pre.
61. 7 prepare mercy and truth, (which) may pr.
64. 1 preserve my life from fear of the enemy
140. 1, 4 O LORD..preserve me from the violent
Prov20. 28 Mercy and truth preserve the king; and
22. 12 The eyes of the LORD preserve knowledge
Isa. 49. 8 preserve thee, and give thee for a coven.

6. *To put, place,* שׂוּם, שִׂים *sum, sim.*
Gen. 45. 7 God sent me before you to preserve you

7. *To keep, observe,* שָׁמַר *shamar.*
Josh 24. 17 preserved us in all the way wherein we w.
1 Sa. 30. 23 preserved us, and delivered the company
Job 10. 12 thy visitation hath preserved my spirit
29. 2 as (in) the days (when) God preserved me
Psa. 16. 1 Preserve me, O God: for in thee do I put
41. 2 LORD will preserve him, and keep him al.
86. 2 Preserve my soul, for I (am) holy: O thou
97. 10 he preserveth the souls of his saints; he
116. 6 LORD preserveth the simple: I was brou.
121. 7 shall preserve thee from all evil: he shall
121. 8 shall preserve thy going out, and thy co.
145. 20 LORD preserveth all them that love him
146. 9 LORD preserveth the strangers; he reliev.
Prov. 2. 8 keepeth the paths of judgment, and pres.
2. 11 Discretion shall preserve thee, understa.
4. 6 Forsake her not, and she shall preserve
14. 3 but the lips of the wise shall preserve th.
16. 17 he that keepeth his way preserveth his

8. *To preserve alive,* ζωογονέω *zōogoneō.*
Luke17. 33 whosoever shall lose his life shall preserve

9. *To make sound or whole,* σώζω *sōzō.*
2 Ti. 4. 18 will preserve (me) unto his heavenly kin.

PRESERVE (alive or life), to —
1. *To give or preserve life,* חָיָה *chayah,* 3.
Deut. 6. 24 might preserve us alive, as (it is) at this
Job 36. 6 He preserveth not the life of the wicked
Jer. 49. 11 I will preserve (them) alive; and let thy

2. *A life preserver,* מִחְיָה *michyah.*
Gen. 45. 5 did send me before you to preserve life

PRESERVED, to be —
1. *One kept, watched, reserved,* נָצִיר *natsir.*
Isa. 49. 6 and to restore the preserved of Israel; I

2. *To be snatched away,* נָצַל *natsal,* 2.
Gen. 32. 30 I have seen God..and my life is preserv.

3. *To be kept,* שָׁמַר *shamar,* 2.
Psa. 37. 28 forsaketh not his saints; they are preser.
Hos. 12. 13 Egypt, and by a prophet was he preserved

4. *To keep together,* συντηρέω *suntēreō.*
Matt. 9. 17 into new bottles, and both are preserved
Luke 5. 38 into new bottles; [and both are preserved]

5. *To keep,* τηρέω *tēreō.*
1 Th. 5. 23 be preserved blameless unto the coming
Jude 1 to them that are..preserved in Jesus Ch.

PRESERVER —
To keep watch, reserve, נָצַר *natsar.*
Job 7. 20 O thou preserver of men? why hast thou

PRESIDENTS —
Presidents, סָרְכִין *sarekin*
Dan. 6. 2 over these three presidents, of whom D.
6. 3 Daniel was preferred above the presidents
6. 4 Then the presidents and princes sought
6. 6 Then these presidents and princes assem.
6. 7 All the presidents of the kingdom, the g.

PRESS (fat) —
1 *Wine press or vat,* גַּת *gath.*
Joel 3. 13 for the press is full, the fats overflow: for

2. *Wine or oil press or vat,* יֶקֶב *yeqeb.*
Prov. 3. 10 thy presses shall burst out with new wine
Isa. 16. 10 shall tread out no wine in (their) presses
Hag. 2. 16 when (one) come to the press fat for to

3. *Wine press or vat,* פּוּרָה *purah.*
Hag. 2. 16 for to draw out fifty (vessels) out of the p.

PRESS —
A crowd, ὄχλος *ochlos.*
Mark 2. 4 could not come nigh unto him for the p.
5. 27 came in the press behind, and touched
5. 30 turned him about in the press, and said
Luke 8. 19 and could not come at him for the press
19. 3 could not for the press, because he was

PRESS, (down, sore, toward, upon), to —
1. *To come or go down,* נָחַת *nachath.*
Psa. 38. 2 stick fast..and thy hand presseth me so.

2. *To press,* פָּצַר *patsar.*
Gen. 19. 3 pressed upon them greatly; and they tu.
19. 9 pressed sore upon the man, (even) Lot, and

3. *To break, spread, or burst forth,* פָּרַץ *parats.*
2 Sa. 13. 25 pressed him: howbeit he would not go
13. 27 Absalom pressed him, that he let Amnon

4. *To distress, oppress, straiten,* צוּק *tsuq,* 5.
Judg16. 16 she pressed him daily with her words, and

5. *To press,* שָׂחַט *sachat.*
Gen. 40. 11 pressed them into Pharaoh's cup, and I

6. *To press away or off,* ἀποθλίβω *apothlibō.*
Luke 8. 45 the multitude throng thee and press (th.

7. *To force, use force,* βιάζομαι *biazomai.*
Luke16. 16 preached, and every man presseth into it

8. *To pursue,* διώκω *diōkō.*
Phil. 3. 14 I press toward the mark for the prize of

9. *To lie or be laid upon,* ἐπίκειμαι *epikeimai.*
Luke 5. 1 pressed upon him to hear the word of G.

10. *To fall upon,* ἐπιπίπτω *epipiptō.*
Mark 3. 10 insomuch that they pressed upon him for

11. *To press (with the foot),* πιέζω *piezō.*
Luke 6. 38 good measure, pressed down, and shaken

12. *To hold together,* συνέχω *sunechō.*
Acts 18. 5 Paul was pressed in the spirit, and testi.

PRESSED (on), to be —
1. *To hasten, press,* דָּחַף *dachaph.*
Esth. 8. 14 being hastened and pressed on by the k.

2. *To be bruised,* מָעַךְ *maak,* 4.
Eze. 23. 3 there were their breasts pressed, and th.

3. *To press,* עוּק *uq,* 5.
Amos 2. 13 I am pressed..as a cart is pressed (that

4. *To be weighed down,* βαρέομαι *bareomai.*
2 Co. 1. 8 that we were pressed out of measure, a.

PRESUME, to —
1. *To act proudly, presume,* זִיד, זוּד *zud, zid,* 5.
Deut18. 20 prophet which shall presume to speak a

2. *To fill in, be full,* מָלֵא *male.*
Esth. 7. 5 where is he, that durst presume in his h.

3. *To presume, lift self up,* עָפַל *aphal,* 5.
Num14. 44 they presumed to go up unto the hill top

PRESUMPTUOUS, PRESUMPTUOUSLY (to come)
1. *To act proudly, presume,* זִיד, זוּד *zud, zid,* 5.
Exod21. 14 But if a man come presumptuously upon
Deut. 1. 43 and went presumptuously up into the h.
17. 13 and fear, and do no more presumptuously

2. *Proud, presumptuous,* זֵד *zed.*
Psa. 19. 13 Keep back thy servant also from presum.

3. *Pride, presumption,* זָדוֹן *zadon.*
Deut17. 12 man that will do presumptuously, and w.
18. 22 the prophet hath spoken it presumptuos.

4. *With a high hand,* בְּיָד רָמָה *be-yad ramah.*
Num15. 30 the soul that doeth (ought) presumptuos.

5. *Bold, daring,* τολμητής *tolmētēs.*
2 Pe. 2. 10 Presumptuous (are they), self willed, they

PRETENCE —
A pretence, pretext, πρόφασις *prophasis.*
Matt23. 14 [and for a pretence make long prayer]
Mark12. 40 for a pretence make long prayers: these
Phil. 1. 18 in pretence, or in truth, Christ is preach.

PREVAIL (against), to —
1. *To be or become strong or courageous,* אָמַץ *amats.*
2 Ch.13. 18 the children of Judah prevailed, because

2. *To be or become mighty,* גָּבַר *gabar.*
Gen. 7. 18 the waters prevailed, and were increased
7. 19 the waters prevailed exceedingly upon the
7. 20 Fifteen cubits upward did the waters pre.
7. 24 the waters prevailed upon the earth an
49. 26 The blessings of thy father have prevailed
Exod17. 11 Moses held up his hand..Israel prevailed
17. 11 when he let down his hand, Amalek pre.
1 Sa. 2. 9 silent..for by strength shall no man pre
2 Sa. 11. 23 the men prevailed against us, and came
1 Ch. 5. 2 Judah prevailed above his brethren, and
Psa. 65. 3 Iniquities prevail against me: (as for) our
Lam. 1. 16 are desolate, because the enemy prevailed

3. *To make mighty,* גָּבַר *gabar,* 5.
Psa. 12. 4 With our tongue will we prevail; our lips

4. *To make or show self mighty,* גָּבַר *gabar,* 7.
Isa. 42. 13 The LORD..shall prevail against his ene.

5. *To lay or keep hold on,* חָזַק *chdzaq.*
Gen. 47. 20 because the famine prevailed over them
1 Sa. 17. 50 David prevailed over the Philistine with
2 Sa. 24. 4 the king's word prevailed against Joab, and
1 Ki. 16. 22 people that followed..prevailed against
2 Ki. 25. 3 the famine prevailed in the city, and there
1 Ch. 21. 4 the king's word prevailed against Joab
2 Ch. 8. 3 And Solomon went..and prevailed against
27. 5 He fought..and prevailed against them

6. *To make strong, take hold on,* חָזַק *chazaq,* 5.
Job 18. 9 (and) the robber shall prevail against him
Dan. 11. 7 shall deal against them, and shall prevail

7. *To be able,* יָכֹל *yakol,* 1, 6.
Gen. 30. 8 I wrestled with my sister, and I have pr.
32. 25 when he saw that he prevailed not against
32. 28 hast thou power with God..and hast pre.
Num22. 6 peradventure I shall prevail, (that) we may
Judg16. 5 by what (means) we may prevail against

1 Sa. 17. 9 if I prevail against him, and kill him, then
26. 25 thou shalt both do great (things), and..p.
1 Ki. 22. 22 Thou shalt persuade (him), and prevail
2 Ch. 18. 21 thou shalt also prevail: go out, and do
Esth. 6. 13 thou shalt not prevail against him, but
Psa. 13. 4 I have prevailed against him; (and) those
129. 2 yet they have not prevailed against me
Isa. 16. 12 come..to pray; but he shall not prevail
Jer. 1. 19 they shall not prevail against thee; for
5. 22 toss themselves, yet can they not prevail
15. 20 they shall not prevail against thee: for
20. 7 thou art stronger..and hast prevailed
20. 10 we shall prevail against him, and we sh.
20. 11 and they shall not prevail: they shall be
38. 22 Thy friends..have prevailed against thee
Hos. 12. 4 had power over the angel, and prevailed
Obad. 7 deceived thee, (and) prevailed against thee

8. *To be able*, יְכִל *yekil.*
Dan. 7. 21 horn made war..and prevailed against t.

9. *To be heavy, weighty*, כָּבֵד *kabed.*
Judg. 1. 35 the hand of the house of Joseph prevailed

10. *To eat, consume*, לָחַם *lacham*, 2.
Isa. 7. 1 went..but could not prevail against it

11. *To be or become or make strong*, עָזַז *azaz.*
Judg. 3. 10 hand prevailed against Chushan-rishath.
6. 2 hand of Midian prevailed against Israel

12. *To keep in, restrain, detain, retain*, עָצַר *atsar.*
2 Ch. 14. 11 O LORD..let not man prevail against thee

13. *To fear, be afraid, terrified*, עָרַץ *arats.*
Isa. 47. 12 able to profit, if so be thou mayest prevail

14. *To rule, cause to rule*, רָדָה *radah.*
Lam. 1. 13 sent fire..and it prevaileth against them

15. *To strengthen, prevail*, תָּקַף *taqaph.*
Job 14. 20 Thou prevailest for ever against him, and
15. 24 they shall prevail against him, as a king
Eccl. 4. 12 And if one prevail against him, two shall

16. *Sharp, hard*, קָשֶׁה *qasheh.*
Judg. 4. 24 and prevailed against Jabin the king of

17. *To be strong, prevail*, ἰσχύω *ischuō.*
Acts 19. 16 prevailed against them, so that they fled
19. 20 So mightily grew the word..and prevailed
Rev. 12. 8 And prevailed not; neither was their pl.

18. *To be very strong, prevail greatly*, κατισχύω.
Matt 16. 18 gates of hell shall not prevail against it
Luke 23. 23 the voices..of the chief priests prevailed

19. *To conquer, obtain victory*, νικάω *nikaō.*
Rev. 5. 5 hath prevailed to open the book, and to

20. *To profit, benefit*, ὠφελέω *ōpheleō.*
Matt 27. 24 he could prevail nothing, but (that) rath.
John 12. 19 Perceive ye how ye prevail nothing? be.

PREVENT, to —

1. *To be, go, come, or put before*, קָדַם *qadam*, 3.
2 Sa. 22. 6 sorrows..the snares of death prevented
22. 19 prevented me in the day of my calamity
Job 3. 12 Why did the knees prevent me? or why the
30. 27 boiled..the days of affliction prevented me
Psa. 18. 5 sorrows..the snares of death prevented
18. 18 prevented me in the day of my calamity
21. 3 thou preventest him with the blessings of
59. 10 The God of my mercy shall prevent me
79. 8 let thy tender mercies speedily prevent us
88. 13 in the morning shall my prayer prevent
119. 147 I prevented the dawning of the morning
119. 148 Mine eyes prevent the (night) watches, th.
Isa. 21. 14 prevented with their bread him that fled

2. *To put before*, קָדַם *qadam*, 5.
Job 41. 11 Who hath prevented me, that I should r.
Amos 9. 10 The evil shall not overtake nor prevent us

3. *To come before, anticipate*, προφθάνω *prophthanō.*
Matt 17. 25 Jesus prevented him, saying, What think.

4. *To precede*, φθάνω *phthanō.*
1 Th. 4. 15 shall not prevent them which are asleep

PREY —

1. *Eating, food*, אֹכֶל *okel.*
Job 9. 26 are..as the eagle (that) hasteth to the prey
39. 29 From thence she seeketh the prey..her e.

2. *Prey*, בַּז *baz.*
Num 14. 3 our wives and..children should be a prey?
14. 31 your little ones..ye said should be a prey
31. 32 the prey which the men of war had caught
Deut. 1. 39 little ones, which ye said should be a prey
2 Ki. 21. 14 a prey and a spoil to all their enemies
Isa. 10. 6 to take the prey, and to tread them down
33. 23 great spoil divided; the lame take the p.
42. 22 they are for a prey, and none delivereth
Jer. 30. 16 all that prey upon thee will I give for a p.
Eze. 7. 21 I will give it into the hands..for a prey
29. 19 take her prey; and it shall be the wages
34. 8 my flock became a prey, and my flock be.
34. 22 they shall no more be a prey; and I will
34. 28 they shall no more be a prey to the heat.
36. 4 a prey and derision to the residue of the
36. 5 have appointed..to cast it out for a prey
38. 12 to take a prey; to turn thine hand upon
38. 13 thou gathered thy company to take a p.

3. *Prey*, בִּזָּה *bizzah.*
Neh. 4. 4 for a prey in the land of captivity
Esth. 9. 15 but on the prey they laid not their hand
9. 16 but they laid not their hands on the prey
Dan. 11. 24 he shall scatter among them the prey, and

4. *What is snatched at*, חֶתֶף *chetheph.*
Prov 23. 28 She also lieth in wait as (for) a prey, and

5. *To tear, tear off*, טָרַף *taraph.*
Psa. 17. 12 as a lion (that) is greedy of his prey, and

6. *Torn thing, prey*, טֶרֶף *tereph.*
Gen. 49. 9 from the prey, my son, thou art gone up
Num 23. 24 not lie down until he eat (of) the prey
Job 4. 11 The old lion perisheth for lack of prey, a.
24. 5 rising betimes for a prey: the wilderness
38. 39 Wilt thou hunt the prey for the lion, or
Psa. 76. 4 more glorious..than the mountains of p.
104. 21 The young lions roar after their prey, and
124. 6 hath not given us (as) a prey to their teeth
Isa. 5. 29 lay hold of the prey, and shall carry (it)
31. 4 and the young lion roaring on his prey
Eze. 19. 3 it learned to catch the prey; it devoured
19. 6 learned to catch the prey, (and) devoured
22. 25 like a roaring lion ravening the prey: th.
22. 27 like wolves ravening the prey, to shed bl.
Amos 3. 4 Will a lion roar..when he hath no prey?
Nah. 2. 12 filled his holes with prey, and his dens
2. 13 I will cut off thy prey from the earth
3. 1 all full of lies (and) robbery; the prey de.

7. *What is taken or caught*, מַלְקוֹחַ *malqoach.*
Num 31. 11 and all the prey, (both) of men and of bea.
31. 12 they brought the captives, and the prey
31. 26 Take the sum of the prey that was taken
31. 27 divide the prey into two parts, between
Isa. 49. 24 Shall the prey be taken from the mighty
49. 25 the prey of the terrible shall be delivered

8. *Prey, booty*, עַד *ad.*
Gen. 49. 27 in the morning he shall devour the prey
Isa. 33. 23 then is the prey of a great spoil divided
Zeph. 3. 8 until the day that I rise up to the prey

9. *Spoil*, שָׁלָל *shalal.*
Judg. 5. 30 have they (not) divided the prey; to every
5. 30 a prey of divers colours, a prey of divers
8. 24 give me every man the ear rings of his prey
8. 25 did cast therein..the ear rings of his prey
Isa. 10. 2 that widows may be their prey, and (that)
Jer. 21. 9 and his life shall be unto him for a prey
38. 2 he shall have his life for a prey, and shall
39. 18 but thy life shall be for a prey unto thee
45. 5 thy life will I give unto thee for a prey in

PREY, to take for or make (self) a —

1. *To take prey*, בָּזַז *bazaz.*
Deut. 2. 35 Only the cattle we took for a prey unto
3. 7 the spoil..we took for a prey to ourselves
Josh. 8. 2 shall ye take for a prey unto yourselves
8. 27 Israel took for a prey unto themselves
11. 14 Israel took for a prey unto themselves
Esth. 3. 13 and (to take) the spoil of them for a prey
8. 11 and (to take) the spoil of them for a prey
Jer. 30. 16 and all that prey upon thee will I give for
Eze. 26. 12 and make a prey of thy merchandise; and

2. *To make self a spoil*, שָׁלַל *shalal*, 7a.
Isa. 59. 15 he (that) departeth..maketh himself a p.

PRICE —

1. *Price, preciousness*, יְקָר *yeqar.*
Zech. 11. 13 a goodly price that I was prised at of

2. *Silver*, כֶּסֶף *keseph.*
Lev. 25. 50 the price of his sale shall be according to
1 Ch. 21. 22 thou shalt grant it me for the full price
21. 24 but I will verily buy it for the full price

3. *Hire, price*, מְחִיר *mechir.*
Deut 23. 18 the hire of a whore, or the price of a dog
2 Sa. 24. 24 but I will surely buy (it) of thee at a pr.
1 Ki. 10. 28 merchants received the linen yarn at a p.
2 Ch. 1. 16 merchants received the linen yarn at a p.
Job 28. 15 neither shall silver be weighed..the price
Psa. 44. 12 and dost not increase..by their price
Prov 17. 16 Wherefore..a price in the hand of a fool
27. 26 and the goats (are) the price of the field
Isa. 45. 13 not for price nor reward, saith the LORD
55. 1 buy wine..without money, and without p.
Jer. 15. 13 will I give to the spoil without price, and

4. *What is to be sold, wares, price*, מֶכֶר *meker.*
Prov 31. 10 Who can find a virtuous woman?..her p.

5. *Acquisition, possession*, מִקְנָה *miqnah.*
Lev. 25. 16 increase the price..diminish the price of

6. *Acquisition, scattering*, מֶשֶׁךְ *meshek.*
Job 28. 18 for the price of wisdom (is) above rubies

7. *Arrangement, valuation*, עֵרֶךְ *erek.*
Job 28. 13 Man knoweth not the price thereof; nei.

8. *Hire, reward, price*, שָׂכָר *sakar.*
Zech 11. 12 give (me) my price..weighed for my pri.

9. *Honour, preciousness, price*, τιμή *timē.*
Matt 27. 6 It is not lawful..it is the price of blood
27. 9 the price of him that was valued, whom
Acts 4. 34 brought the prices of the things that we.
5. 2 kept back (part) of the price, his wife also
5. 3 keep back (part) of the price of the land
19. 19 they counted the price of them, and found
1 Co. 6. 20 For ye are bought with a price: therefore
7. 23 Ye are bought with a price; be not ye the

PRICE, of great —

1. *Very expensive*, πολυτελής *polutelēs.*
1 Pe. 3. 4 which is in the sight of God of great price

2. *Very precious*, πολύτιμος *polutimos.*
Matt 13. 46 when he had found one pearl of great pr.

PRICK —

1. *A prick*, שֵׂךְ *sek.*
Num. 33. 55 (shall be) pricks in your eyes, and thorns

2. *A prick, goad*, κέντρον *kentron.*
Acts 9. 5 [hard for thee to kick against the pricks]
26. 14 hard for thee to kick against the pricks

PRICK, to —

1. *To act bitterly, make bitter*, מָאַר *maar*, 5.
Eze. 28. 24 a pricking brier unto the house of Israel

2. *To sharpen or prick self*, שָׁנַן *shanan*, 7a.
Psa. 73. 21 was grieved, and I was pricked in my re.

3. *To stab, pierce thoroughly*, κατανύσσω *katanussō.*
Acts 2. 37 they were pricked in their heart, and sa.

PRIDE —

1. *Pride*, גֵּאָה *geah.*
Prov. 8. 13 pride, and arrogancy, and the evil way

2. *Pride, rising, excellency*, גַּאֲוָה *gaavah.*
Job 41. 15 scales (are his) pride, shut up together (as
Psa. 10. 2 The wicked in (his) pride doth persecute
36. 11 Let not the foot of pride come against me
73. 6 pride compasseth them about as a chain
Prov 14. 3 the mouth of the foolish (is) a rod of pride
29. 23 A man's pride shall bring him low: but
Isa. 9. 9 that say in the pride and stoutness of he.
25. 11 he shall bring down their pride together
Jer. 48. 29 his pride, and the haughtiness of his heart
Zeph. 3. 11 take away..them that rejoice in thy pride

3. *Pride, rising, excellency*, גָּאוֹן *gaon.*
Lev. 26. 19 I will break the pride of your power; and
Job 35. 12 they cry..because of the pride of evil m.
Psa. 59. 12 let them even be taken in their pride; and
Prov 16. 18 Pride (goeth) before destruction, and an
Isa. 16. 6 We have heard of the pride of Moab; he
16. 6 of his haughtiness, and his pride, and his
23. 9 to stain the pride of all glory..to bring in.
Jer. 13. 9 the pride of Judah, and the great pride of
48. 29 We have heard the pride of Moab, he is
Eze. 16. 49 pride, fulness of bread; and abundance of
16. 56 was not mentioned..in the day of thy pr.
30. 6 the pride of her power shall come down
Hos. 5. 5 the pride of Israel doth testify to his face
7. 10 the pride of Israel testifieth to his face
Zeph. 2. 10 This shall they have for their pride, bec
Zech. 9. 6 will cut off the pride of the Philistines
10. 11 the pride of Assyria shall be brought down
11. 3 a voice..for the pride of Jordan is spoiled

4. *Pride, rising, excellency*, גֵּאוּת *geuth.*
Isa. 28. 1 Woe to the crown of pride, to the drunk.
28. 3 The crown of pride, the drunkards of Ep.

5. *Height, loftiness, haughtiness*, גֹּבַהּ *gobah.*
2 Ch. 32. 26 humbled himself for the pride of his hea.
Psa. 10. 4 through the pride of his countenance

6. *Pride, lifting up*, גֵּוָה *gevah.*
Job 33. 17 may withdraw..and hide pride from m.
Jer. 13. 17 shall weep in secret places for (your) pr.
Dan. 4. 37 those that walk in pride he is..to abase

7. *Pride, presumption*, זָדוֹן *zadon.*
1 Sa. 17. 28 I know thy pride, and the naughtiness of
Prov. 11. 2 pride cometh, then cometh shame: but
13. 10 by pride cometh contention: but with the
Jer. 49. 16 (and) the pride of thine heart, O thou that
Eze. 7. 10 the rod hath blossomed, pride hath bud.
Obad. 3 The pride of thine heart hath deceived

8. *To act proudly, presume*, זוּד *zud*, 5.
Dan. 5. 20 lifted up, and his mind hardened in pride

9. *Entanglement, artifice*, רֹכֶס *rokes.*
Psa 31. 20 Thou shalt hide them..from the pride of

10. *Pride*, שַׁחַץ *shachats.*
Job 41. 34 he (is) a king over all the children of pride

11. *Vain boasting or glory, ostentation*, ἀλαζονεία.
1 Jo. 2. 16 the pride of life, is not of the Father, but

12. *Arrogance*, ὑπερηφανία *huperēphania.*
Mark 7. 22 an evil eye, blasphemy, pride, foolishness

[*See* Lift up with.]

PRIEST—

1. *Priest, prince, minister*, כֹּהֵן *kohen.*
Gen. 14. 18 he (was) the priest of the most high God
41. 45, 50 daughter of Poti-pherah priest of On
46. 20 the daughter of Poti-pherah priest of On
47. 22 On the land of the priests bought he not
47. 22 the priests had a portion (assigned them)
47. 26 except the land of the priests only, (which)
Exod. 2. 16 the priest of Midian had seven daughters
3. 1 Jethro, his father in law, the priest of M.
18. 1 Jethro the priest of Midian, Moses' father
19. 6 ye shall be unto me a kingdom of priests
19. 22 let the priests also, which come near to
19. 24 let not the priests and the people break
29. 30 that son that is priest in his stead shall
31. 10 the holy garments for Aaron the priest
35. 19 the holy garments for Aaron the priest
38. 21 hand of Ithamar, son to Aaron the priest
39. 41 the holy garments for Aaron the priest
Lev. 1. 5, 8, 11 and the priests, Aaron's sons, shall
1. 7 the sons of Aaron the priest shall put fire
1. 9 and the priest shall burn all on the altar
1. 12 the priest shall lay them in order on the
1. 13 the priest shall bring (it) all, and burn
1. 15 the priest shall bring it unto the altar, and
1. 17 and the priest shall burn it upon the alt.
2. 2 he shall bring it to Aaron's sons the prie.
2. 2 the priest shall burn the memorial of it

Lev. 2. 8 when it is presented unto the priest, he
2. 9 priest shall take from the meat offering
2. 16 the priest shall burn the memorial of it
3. 2 the priests shall sprinkle the blood upon
3. 11 And the priest shall burn it upon the al.
3. 16 the priest shall burn them upon the altar
4. 3 If the priest that is anointed do sin acc.
4. 5, 16 And the priest that is anointed shall
4. 6, 17 And the priest shall dip his finger
4. 7 the priest shall put (some) of the blood
4. 10, 35 priest shall burn them upon the altar
4. 20 the priest shall make an atonement for
4. 25, 30, 34 the priest shall take of the blood
4. 26, 31, 35 the priest shall make an atoneme.
4. 31 the priest shall burn (it) upon the altar
5. 6, 10, 13, 16, 18 priest shall make an atone.
5. 8 he shall bring them unto the priest, who
5. 12 shall he bring it to the priest, and the p.
5. 13 shall be the priest's, as a meat offering
5. 16 the fifth part..and give it unto the priest
5. 18 for a trespass offering, unto the priest
6. 6 for a trespass offering, unto the priest
6. 7 the priest shall make an atonement for
6. 10 the priest shall put on his linen garment
6. 12 the priest shall burn wood on it every m.
6. 22 the priest of his sons that is anointed in
6. 23 every meat offering for the priest shall be
6. 26 the priest that offereth it for sin shall eat
6. 29 All the males among the priests shall eat
7. 5 the priest shall burn them upon the altar
7. 6 Every male among the priests shall eat
7. 7 priest that maketh atonement therewith
7. 8 the priest that offereth any man's burnt
7. 8 the priest shall have to himself the skin
7. 9 all..shall be the priest's that offereth it
7. 14 it shall be the priest's that sprinkleth the
7. 31 the priest shall burn the fat upon the al.
7. 32 right shoulder shall ye give unto the pr.
7. 34 have given them unto Aaron the priest
12. 6 she shall bring a lamb..unto the priest
12. 8 the priest shall make an atonement for
13. 2 the priest, or unto one of his sons the pr.
13. 3, 3, 5, 6, 25, 27, 32, 34 the priest shall look
So in v. 34, 36, 39, 43, 50, 53, 55.
13. 4, 31, 33 the priest shall shut up (him that
13. 5, 21, 26 the priest shall shut him up seven
13. 6 the priest shall pronounce
So in v. 8, 11, 17, 20, 22, 23, 25, 27, 28, 30, 37, 44.
13. 7 been seen of the priest..of the priest ag.
13. 8 And (if) the priest see that, behold, the
13. 9 then he shall be brought unto the priest
13. 10, 17 the priest shall see (him:) and, behold
13. 12 all the skin..wheresoever the priest look.
13. 13 Then the priest shall consider: and, beh.
13. 15 And the priest shall see the raw flesh, and
13. 16 be changed..he shall come unto the prie.
13. 19 and..reddish, and it be showed to the p.
13. 20 And if, when the priest seeth it, behold
13. 21, 26 if the priest look on it, and, behold
13. 30 Then the priest shall see the plague: and
13. 31 And if the priest look on the plague of the
13. 36 the priest shall not seek for yellow hair
13. 49 and shall be showed unto the priest
13. 54 the priest shall command that they wash
13. 56 if the priest look, and, behold, the plague
14. 2 the leper..shall be brought unto the pri.
14. 3 the priest shall go forth out of the camp
14. 3 the priest shall look, and, behold, (if) the
14. 4 Then shall the priest command to take for
14. 5 the priest shall command that one of the
14. 11 the priest that maketh (him) clean shall
14. 12 the priest shall take one he lamb, and off.
14. 13 as the sin offering (is) the priest's, (so is) the
14. 14 the priest shall take (some) of the blood
14. 14 the priest shall put (it) upon the tip of the
14. 15 the priest shall take (some) of the log of
14. 16 the priest shall dip his right finger in the
14. 17 of the oil that (is) in his hand shall the p.
14. 18 the remnant of the oil that (is) in the pr.
14. 18, 20, 31 the priest shall make an atonement
14. 19 the priest shall offer the sin offering, and
14. 20 the priest shall offer the burnt offering
14. 23 bring them on the eighth..unto the priest
14. 24 the priest shall take..the priest shall wave
14. 25 the priest shall take (some) of the blood
14. 26 the priest shall pour of the oil into the p.
14. 27 the priest shall sprinkle with his right fi.
14. 28 the priest shall put of the oil that (is) in
14. 29 the rest of the oil that (is) in the priest's
14. 35 shall come and tell the priest, saying, It
14. 36 the priest shall command that they empty
14. 36 before the priest go (into it) to see the p.
14. 36 afterward the priest shall go in to see the
14. 38 the priest shall go out of the house to the
14. 39 the priest shall come again the seventh
14. 40 the priest shall command that they take
14. 44 the priest shall come and look, and, beh.
14. 48 And if the priest shall come in, and look
14. 48 the priest shall pronounce the house cl.
15. 14 young pigeons..and give them unto the
15. 15 the priest shall offer them, the one (for)
15. 15, 30 the priest shall make an atonement
15. 29 bring them unto the priest, to the door
15. 30 the priest shall offer the one (for) a sin
16. 32 the priest whom he shall anoint, and w
16. 33 he shall make an atonement for the pri.
17. 5 unto the priest, and offer them (for) pe.
17. 6 the priest shall sprinkle the blood upon
19. 22 the priest shall make an atonement for
21. 1 Speak unto the priests the sons of Aaron
21. 9 the daughter of any priest, if she profane
21. 10 the high priest among his brethren, upon

Lev. 21. 21 No man..of the seed of Aaron the priest
22. 10 a sojourner of the priest, or an hired ser.
22. 11 if the priest buy (any) soul with his money
22. 12 If the priest's daughter also be (married)
22. 13 But if the priest's daughter be a widow, or
22. 14 shall give (it) unto the priest with the holy
23. 10 first fruits of your harvest unto the priest
23. 11 on the morrow after the sabbath the prie.
23. 20 the priest shall wave them with the bread
23. 20 they shall be holy to the LORD for the p.
27. 8 before the priest, and the priest shall va.
27. 8 according to his ability..shall the priest
27. 11 he shall present the beast before the pri.
27. 12 the priest shall value it, whether it be
27. 12 as thou valuest it, (who art) the priest, so
27. 14 the priest shall estimate it, whether it be
27. 14 as the priest shall estimate it, so shall it
27. 18, 23 the priest shall reckon unto him the
27. 21 the possession thereof shall be the priest's
Num. 3. 3 the priests which were anointed, whom he
3. 6 present them before Aaron the priest, that
3. 32 And Eleazar the son of Aaron the priest
4. 16 office of Eleazar the son of Aaron the pri.
4. 28, 33 Ithamar the son of Aaron the priest
5. 8 unto the LORD..to the priest, beside the
5. 9 offering..which they bring unto the priest
5. 10 whatsoever any man giveth the priest
5. 15 shall the man bring his wife unto the pr.
5. 16 the priest shall bring her near, and set her
5. 17 the priest shall take..the priest shall ta.
5. 18 the priest shall set..the priest shall have
5. 19 the priest shall charge her by an oath, and
5. 21 the priest shall charge..the priest shall
5. 23 the priest sh. ll write these curses in a b.
5. 25 Then the priest shall take the jealousy
5. 26 the priest shall take an handful of the
5. 30 the priest shall execute upon her all this
6. 10 two young pigeons, to the priest, to the
6. 11 the priest shall offer the one for a sin off.
6. 16 the priest shall bring..before the LORD
6. 17 the priest shall offer also his meat offer.
6. 19 the priest shall take the sodden shoulder
6. 20 the priest shall wave them (for) a wave of.
6. 20 this (is) holy for the priest, with the wave
7. 8 of Ithamar the son of Aaron the priest
10. 8 the priests, shall blow with the trumpets
15. 25, 28 the priest shall make an atonement for
16. 37 Eleazar the son of Aaron the priest, that
16. 39 Eleazar the priest took the brasen censers
18. 28 LORD'S heave offering to Aaron the priest
19. 3 ye shall give her unto Eleazar the priest
19. 4 Eleazar the priest shall take of her blood
19. 6 the priest shall take cedar wood, and hy.
19. 7 the priest shall wash his clothes, and he
19. 7 the priest shall be unclean until the even
25. 7, 11 Eleazar, the son of Aaron the priest
26. 1 unto Eleazar the son of Aaron the priest
26. 3 Moses and Eleazar the priest spake with
26. 63 by Moses and Eleazar the priest, who nu.
26. 64 whom Moses and Aaron the priest numb.
27. 2, 22 before Eleazar the priest, and before
27. 19 set him before Eleazar the priest, and b.
27. 21 he shall stand before Eleazar the priest
31. 6 and Phinehas the son of Eleazar the priest
31. 12 unto Moses, and Eleazar the priest, and
31. 13, 31, 51, 54 And Moses, and Eleazar the p.
31. 21 the priest said unto the men of war whi.
31. 26 the priest, and the chief fathers of the c.
31. 29 give (it) unto Eleazar the priest, (for) an
31. 41 heave offering, unto Eleazar the priest
32. 2 to Eleazar the priest, and unto the prin.
32. 28 Eleazar the priest, and Joshua the son of
33. 38 Aaron the priest went up into mount Hor
34. 17 Eleazar the priest, and Joshua the son of
35. 25, 28, 28 the death of the high priest
35. 32 again to dwell..until the death of the pr.
Deut. 17. 9 thou shalt come unto the priests the Lev.
17. 12 the priest that standeth to minister there
17. 18 out of (that which is) before the priests
18. 1 The priests the Levites, (and) all the tri.
18. 3 this shall be the priests' due from the p.
18. 3 they shall give unto the priest the shoul.
19. 17 before the priests and the judges which
20. 2 the priest shall approach and speak unto
21. 5 the priests the sons of Levi shall come n.
24. 8 all that the priests the Levites shall teac.
26. 3 thou shalt go unto the priest that shall be
26. 4 the priest shall take the basket out of thine
27. 9 Moses and the priests the Levites spake
31. 9 delivered it unto the priests the sons of
Josh. 3. 3 and the priests the Levites bearing it
3. 6 Joshua spake unto the priests, saying, Take
3. 8, 13, 15, 17 the priests that bear the ark
3. 14 the priests bearing the ark of the coven.
4. 3 out of the place where the priests' feet s.
4. 9, 10, 16, 18 the priests which bear the ark
4. 11 the ark..passed over, and the priests, in
4. 17 Joshua therefore commanded the priests
4. 18 the soles of the priests' feet were lifted up
6. 4 seven priests shall bear before the ark se.
6. 4 the priests shall blow with the trumpets
6. 6 Joshua the son of Nun called the priests
6. 6 let seven priests bear seven trumpets of
6. 8, 13 seven priests bearing the seven trum.
6. 9 the priests that blew with the trumpets
6. 12 the priests took up the ark of the LORD
6. 16 when the priests blew with the trumpets
8. 33 before the priests the Levites, which bare
14. 1 Eleazar the priest, and Joshua the son of
17. 4 they came near before Eleazar the priest
19. 51 Eleazar the priest, and Joshua the son of
20. 6 until the death of the high priest that sh.

Josh 21. 1 unto Eleazar the priest, and unto Joshua
21. 4, 13 the children of Aaron the priest
21. 19 the cities of the children of Aaron, the p.
22. 13, 31, 32 Phinehas the son of Eleazar the p.
22. 30 when Phinehas the priest, and the princes
Judg 17. 5 made..one of his sons, who became his p.
17. 10 be unto me a father and a priest, and I
17. 12 the young man became his priest, and was
17. 13 good, seeing I have a Levite to (my) priest
18. 4 Micah..hath hired me, and I am his priest
18. 6 And the priest said unto them, Go in pe.
18. 17 the priest stood in the entering of the g.
18. 18 Then said the priest unto them, What do
18. 19 go with us..be to us a father and a priest
18. 19 be a priest unto the house of one man
18. 19 or that thou be a priest unto a tribe and
18. 20 the priest's heart was glad; and he took
18. 24 Ye have taken away..the priest, and ye
18. 27 they took..the priest which he had, and
18. 30 he and his sons were priests to the tribe
1 Sa. 1. 3 the two sons of Eli..the priests of the L.
1. 9 Eli the priest sat upon a seat by a post of
2. 11 child did minister..before Eli the priest
2. 13 And the priest's custom with the people
2. 13 the priest's servant came, while the flesh
2. 14 all..brought up the priest took for hims.
2. 15 the priest's servant came, and said to the
2. 15 Give flesh to roast for the priest; for he
2. 28 (to be) my priest, to offer upon mine altar
2. 35 I will raise me up a faithful priest, (that)
5. 5 neither the priests of Dagon, nor any that
6. 2 the Philistines called for the priests and
14. 3 the son of Eli, the LORD'S priest in Shiloh
14. 19 while Saul talked unto the priest, that the
14. 19 Saul said unto the priest, Withdraw thine
14. 36 Then said the priest, Let us draw near h.
21. 1 came David to Nob to Ahimelech the pr.
21. 2 And David said unto Ahimelech the priest
21. 4 And the priest answered David, and said
21. 5 David answered the priest, and said unto
21. 6 So the priest gave him hallowed (bread)
21. 9 the priest said, The sword of Goliath the
22. 11 the king sent to call Ahimelech the priest
22. 11 and all his father's house, the priests that
22. 17 slay the priests of the LORD; because th.
22. 17 would not..fall upon the priests of the L.
22. 18 Doeg, Turn thou, and fall upon the priests
22. 18 he fell upon the priests, and slew on that
22. 19 Nob, the city of the priests, smote he with
22. 21 showed..that Saul had slain the LORD'S p.
23. 9 he said to Abiathar the priest, Bring hit.
30. 7 And David said to Abiathar the priest
2 Sa. 8. 17 And Zadok..and Ahimelech..(were) the p.
15. 27 The king said also unto Zadok the priest
15. 35 (hast thou) not there with thee..the pr.?
15. 35 tell (it) to Zadok and Abiathar the priests
17. 15 said..unto Zadok and to Abiathar the p.
19. 11 sent to Zadok and to Abiathar the priests
20. 25 and Zadok and Abiathar (were) the priests
1 Ki. 1. 7 And he conferred..with Abiathar the pr.
1. 8, 26 the priest, and Benaiah the son of
1. 19 Abiathar the priest, and Joab the captain
1. 25 captains of the host, and Abiathar the p.
1. 32, 38, 44, 45 the priest, and Nathan the pr.
1. 34 let Zadok the priest, and Nathan the pr.
1. 39 Zadok the priest took an horn of oil out
1. 42 Jonathan the son of Abiathar the priest
2. 22 for Abiathar the priest, and for Joab the
2. 26 And unto Abiathar the priest said the k.
2. 27 thrust out Abiathar from being priest un.
2. 35 Zadok the priest did the king put in the
4. 2 Azariah the son of Zadok the priest
4. 4 and Zadok and Abiathar (were) the priests
8. 3 the elders of Israel came, and the priests
8. 4 those did the priests and the Levites bring
8. 6 the priests brought in the ark of the cov.
8. 10 when the priests were come out of the h.
8. 11 So that the priests could not stand to m.
12. 31 made priests of the lowest of the people
12. 32 the priests of the high places which he had
13. 2 upon thee shall he offer the priests of the
13. 33 made..of the lowest of the people priests
13. 33 he became (one) of the priests of the high
2 Ki. 10. 11 great men, and his kinsfolks, and his pri.
10. 19 of Baal, all his servants, and all his prie.
11. 9 to all..that Jehoiada the priest command.
11. 9 every man..and came to Jehoiada the p.
11. 10 to the captains over hundreds did the p.
11. 15 the priest commanded the captains of the
11. 15 the priest had said, Let her not be slain
11. 18 slew Mattan the priest of Baal before the
11. 18 the priest appointed officers over the ho.
12. 2 wherein Jehoiada the priest instructed
12. 4 Jehoash said to the priests, All the mon.
12. 5 Let the priests take (it) to them, every m.
12. 6 the priests had not repaired the breaches
12. 7 Jehoiada the priest, and the (other) pries.
12. 8 the priests consented to receive no (more)
12. 9 the priest took a chest, and bored a hole
12. 9 the priest that kept the door put therein
12. 10 king's scribe and the high priest came up
12. 16 the trespass money..it was the priests'
16. 10 Ahaz sent to Urijah the priest the fashion
16. 11 Urijah the priest, built an altar according
16. 11 Urijah the priest made (it) against king A.
16. 15 king Ahaz commanded Urijah the priest
16. 16 Thus did Urijah the priest, according to
17. 27 one of the priests whom ye brought from
17. 28 one of the priests, whom they had carried
17. 32 made..of the lowest of them priests of the
19. 2 the elders of the priests, covered with sa.
22. 4 Go up to Hilkiah the high priest, that he

2 Ki.22. 8 Hilkiah the high priest said unto Shaphan
22. 10 Hilkiah the priest hath delivered me a b.
22. 12 the king commanded Hilkiah the priest
22. 14 So Hilkiah the priest, and Ahikam. and
23. 2 the priests, and the prophets, and all the
23. 4 Hilkiah the high priest, and the priests of
23. 8 he brought all the priests out of the cities
23. 8 places where the priests had burnt incense
23. 9 the priests of the high places came not up
23. 20 he slew all the priests of the high places
23. 24 the book that Hilkiah the priest found in
25. 18 chief priest, and Zephaniah the second p.
1 Ch. 9. 2 the priests, Levites, and the Nethinims
9. 10 of the priests; Jedaiah, and Jehoiarib, and
9. 30 of the sons of the priests made the oint.
13. 2 to the priests and Levites (which are) in
15. 11 called for Zadok and Abiathar the priests
15. 14 So the priests and the Levites sanctified
15. 24 the priests, did blow with the trumpets
16. 6 the priests with trumpets continually be.
16. 39 the priest, and his brethren the priests
18. 16 Zadok. and Abimelech (were) the priests
23. 2 princes..with the priests and the Levites
24. 6 Zadok the priest, and Ahimelech the son
24. 6, 31 the fathers of the priests and Levites
27. 5 Benaiah the son of Jehoiada, a chief pri.
28. 13, 21 courses of the priests and the Levites
29. 22 the chief governor, and Zadok (to be) pr
2 Ch. 4. 6 but the sea (was) for the priests to wash
4. 9 he made the court of the priests, and the
5. 5 these did the priests (and) the Levites bring
5. 7 the priests brought in the ark of the cov.
5. 11 when the priests were come out of the h
5. 11 the priests (that were) present were san
5. 12 and twenty priests sounding with trump.
5. 14 So that the priests could not stand to m
6. 41 let thy priests, O LORD God, be clothed
7. 2 the priests could not enter into the house
7. 6 And the priests waited on their offices; the
7. 6 the priests sounded trumpets before them
8. 14 the courses of the priests to their service
8. 14 to praise and minister before the priests
8. 15 commandment of the king unto the priests
11. 13 the priests and the Levites that (were) in
11. 15 ordained him priests for the high places
13. 9 Have ye not cast out the priests of the L.
13. 9 and have made you priests after the man.
13. 9 may be a priest of (them that are) no gods
13. 10 the priests, which minister unto the LORD
13. 12 his priests with sounding trumpets to cry
13. 14 and the priests sounded with the trumpets
15. 3 without a teaching priest, and without
17. 8 with them Elishama and Jehoram, priests
19. 8 (of) the priests, and of the chief of the f
19. 11 Amariah the chief priest (is) over you in
22. 11 So Jehoshabeath..the wife of..the priest
23. 4 third..of the priests and of the Levites
23. 6 save the priests, and they that minister
23. 8 that Jehoiada the priest had commanded
23. 8 Jehoiada the priest dismissed not the co
23. 9 the priest delivered to the captains of h.
23. 14 the priest brought out the captains of h.
23. 14 the priest said, Slay her not in the house
23. 17 slew Mattan the priest of Baal before the
23. 18 by the hand of the priests the Levites
24. 2 right..all the days of Jehoiada the priest
24. 5 he gathered together the priests and the
24. 11 the high priest's officer came and emptied
24. 20 Zechariah the son of Jehoiada the priest
24. 25 the blood of the sons of Jehoiada the pri
26. 17 Azariah the priest went in after him, and
26. 17 and with him fourscore priests of the L.
26. 18 but to the priests the sons of Aaron, that
26. 19 and while he was wroth with the priests
26. 19 before the priests in the house of the Lo
26. 20 the chief priest, and all the priests, look.
29. 4 he brought in the priests and the Levites
29. 16 the priests went into the inner part of
29. 21 he commanded the priests the sons of Aar
29. 22 and the priests received the blood, and
29. 24 the priests killed them, and they made
29. 26 Levites..and the priests with the trump.
29. 34 the priests were too few, so that they co
29. 34 the (other) priests had sanctified themse.
29. 34 more upright in heart..than the priests
30. 3 the priests had not sanctified themselves
30. 15 the priests and the Levites were ashamed
30. 16 the priests sprinkled the blood..of the h.
30. 21 the priests praised the LORD day by day
30. 24 a great number of priests sanctified the.
30. 25 with the priests and the Levites, and all
30. 27 the priests the Levites arose and blessed
31. 2 of the priests and the Levites after their
31. 2 the priests and Levites for burnt offerings
31. 4 the portion of the priests and the Levites
31. 9 Hezekiah questioned with the priests and
31. 10 Azariah the chief priest of the house of
31. 15 in the cities of the priests, in..set office
31. 17 to the genealogy of the priests by the h.
31. 19 the priests, (which were) in the fields of
31. 19 to all the males among the priests, and to
34. 5 he burnt the bones of the priest upon th.
34. 9 when they came to Hilkiah the high pri.
34. 14 Hilkiah the priest found a book of the l.
34. 18 Hilkiah the priest hath given me a book
34. 30 the priests, and the Levites, and all the
35. 2 he set the priests in their charges, and e.
35. 8 unto the people, to the priests, and to the
35. 8 gave unto the priests for the passover off.
35. 10 the priests stood in their place, and the
35. 11 priests sprinkled (the blood) from their
35. 14 for the priests: because the priests the sons
2 Ch. 35. 14 prepared..for the priests the sons of Aa.
35. 18 the priests, and the Levites, and all Jud.
36. 14 the priests and the people transgressed
Ezra 1. 5 and the priests, and the Levites, with all
2. 36 The priests: the children of Jedaiah, of
2. 61 of the children of the priests: the children
2. 63 till there stood up a priest with Urim and
2. 69 They gave..one hundred priests garme.
2. 70 So the priests, and the Levites, and (some)
3. 2 the priests, and Zerubbabel the son of S.
3. 8 the priests and the Levites, and all they
3. 10 they set the priests in their apparel with
3. 12 of the priests and Levites, and chief of the
6. 20 the priests and the Levites were purified
6. 20 for their brethren the priests, and for th.
7. 5 Eleazar, the son of Aaron the chief priest
7. 7 of the priests, and the Levites, and the s.
7. 11 king Artaxerxes gave unto Ezra the priest
8. 15 I viewed the people and the priests, and
8. 24 of the priests, Sherebiah, Hashabiah, and
8. 29 of the priests and the Levites, and chief
8. 30 So took the priests and the Levites the w.
8. 33 of Meremoth the son of Uriah the priest
9. 1 and the priests, and the Levites, have not
9. 7 have we, our kings, (and) our priests, been
10. 5 the chief priests, the Levites, and all Isr.
10. 10 the priest stood up, and said unto them
10. 16 the priest, (with) certain chief of the fat.
10. 18 among the sons of the priests there were
Neh. 2. 16 nor to the priests, nor to the nobles, nor
3. 1 the high priest rose up, with his brethren
3. 1 the priests..they builded the sheep gate
3. 20 door of the house of Eliashib the high pr.
3. 22 after him repaired the priests, the men of
3. 28 above the horse gate repaired the priests
5. 12 I called the priests, and took an oath of
7. 39 The priests: the children of Jedaiah, of
7. 63 of the priests: the children of Habaiah
7. 65 their stood (up) a priest with Urim and
7. 70 five hundred and thirty priests' garments
7. 72 and threescore and seven priests' garme.
7. 73 So the priests, and the Levites, and the p.
8. 2 Ezra the priest brought the law before t.
8. 9 Ezra the priest the scribe, and the Levites
8. 13 all the people, the priests, and the Levites
9. 32 on our priests, and on our prophets, and
9. 34 Neither have..our priests, nor our fathe
9. 38 and our princes, Levites, (and) priests, se
10. 8 Bilgai, Shemaiah: these (were) the priests
10. 28 the priests, the Levites, the porters, the
10. 34 the priests, the Levites, and the people
10. 36 the priests that minister in the house
10. 37 unto the priests, to the chambers of the
10. 38 the priest the son of Aaron shall be with
10. 39 the priests that minister and the porters
11. 3 priests and the Levites, and the Nethin.
11. 10 Of the priests: Jedaiah the son of Joiarib
11. 20 the priests (and) the Levites, (were) in all
12. 1 the priests and the Levites that went up
12. 7 These..the chief of the priests and of th.
12. 12 in the days of Joiakim were priests, the
12. 22 also the priests, to the reign of Darius the
12. 26 in the days..of Ezra the priest, the scribe
12. 30 the priests and the Levites purified them
12. 35 And..of the priests' sons with trumpets
12. 41 the priests; Eliakim, Maaseiah, Miniamin
12. 44 portions of the law for the priests and L.
12. 44 for the priests and for the Levites that
13. 4 the priest, having the oversight of the c.
13. 5 the oil, and the offerings of the priests
13. 13 Shelemiah the priest, and Zadok the scr.
13. 28 Joiada, the son of Eliashib the high priest
13. 30 of the priests and the Levites, every one
Psa. 78. 64 Their priests fell by the sword; and their
99. 6 Aaron among his priests, and Samuel am.
110. 4 Thou (art) a priest for ever after the order
132. 9 Let thy priests be clothed with righteou.
132. 16 I will also clothe her priests with salvat.
Isa. 8. 2 Uriah the priest, and Zechariah the son
24. 2 And..as with the people, so with the p.
28. 7 the priest and the prophet have erred th.
37. 2 the elders of the priests, covered with sa.
61. 6 ye shall be named the priests of the LORD
66. 21 And I will also take of them for priests
Jer. 1. 1 of the priests that (were) in Anathoth in
1. 18 against the priests thereof, and against
2. 8 The priests said not, Where (is) the LORD?
2. 26 their kings and their priests, and their
4. 9 the priests shall be astonished, and the
5. 31 and the priests bear rule by their means
6. 13 from the prophet even unto the priest ev.
8. 1 the bones of the priests, and the bones of
8. 10 from the prophet even unto the priest ev.
13. 13 the priests, and the prophets, and all the
14. 18 the prophet and the priest go about into
18. 18 the law shall not perish from the priest
19. 1 Go and get..of the ancients of the priests
20. 1 Pashur the son of Immer the priest, who
21. 1 Zephaniah the son of Maaseiah the priest
23. 11 both prophet and priest are profane: yea
23. 33 when..a priest, shall ask thee, saying, Wh.
23. 34 the priest, and the people, that shall say
26. 7, 8 the priests and the prophets and all
26. 11 Then spake the priests and the prophets
26. 16 said..unto the priests and to the prophets
27. 16 I spake to the priests, and to all this
28. 1, 5 in the presence of the priests, and
29. 1 to the priests, and to the prophets, and to
29. 25 Maaseiah the priest, and to all the priests
29. 26 priest in the stead of Jehoiada the priest
29. 29 the priest read this letter in the ears of J.
31. 14 I will satiate the soul of the priests with
Jer. 32. 32 their priests, and their prophets, and the
33. 18 Neither shall the priests the Levites want
33. 21 with the Levites the priests, my ministers
34. 19 the priests, and all the people of the land
37. 3 Zephaniah the son of Maaseiah the priest
48. 7 (with) his priests and his princes together
49. 3 (and) his priests and his princes together
52. 24 priest, and Zephaniah the second priest
Lam. 1. 4 her priests sigh, her virgins are afflicted
1. 19 my priests and mine elders gave up the
2. 6 hath despised..the king and the priest
2. 20 shall the priest and the prophet be slain
4. 13 her priests, that have shed the blood of
4. 16 respected not the persons of the priests
Eze. 1. 3 unto Ezekiel the priest, the son of Buzi
7. 26 the law shall perish from the priest, and
22. 26 Her priests have violated my law, and
40. 45, 46 the priests, the keepers of the charge
42. 13 the priests that approach unto the LORD
42. 14 When the priests enter therein, then shall
43. 19 thou shalt give to the priests the Levites
43. 24 the priests shall cast salt upon them, and
43. 27 priests shall make your burnt offerings
44. 15 the priests the Levites, the sons of Zadok
44. 21 Neither shall any priest drink wine when
44. 22 take..a widow that had a priest before
44. 30 first..of your oblations, shall be the prie.
44. 30 ye shall also give unto the priest the first
44. 31 priests shall not eat of any thing that is
45. 4 shall be for the priests the ministers of the
45. 19 priest shall take of the blood of the sin of.
46. 2 the priests shall prepare his burnt offering
46. 19 into the holy chambers of the priests, w.
46. 20 This (is) the place where the priests shall
48. 10 (even) for the priests, shall be (this) holy
48. 11 for the priests that are sanctified of the
48. 13 over against the borders of the priests the
Hos. 4. 4 people (are) as they that strive with the p.
4. 9 there shall be, like people, like priest: and
5. 1 Hear ye this, O priests; and hearken, ye
6. 9 company of priests murder in the way by
Joel 1. 9 the priests, the LORD'S ministers, mourn
1. 13 Gird yourselves, and lament, ye priests
2. 17 Let the priests..weep between the porch
Amos 7. 10 Then Amaziah the priest of Beth-el sent
Mic. 3. 11 priests thereof teach for hire, and the p.
Zeph. 1. 4 the name of the Chemarims with the pr.
3. 4 her priests have polluted the sanctuary
Hag. 1. 1, 12, 14 Joshua the son of Josedech the h. p.
2. 2, 4 to Joshua the son of Josedech the..pr.
2. 11 Ask now the priests (concerning) the law
2. 12 And the priests answered and said, No
2. 13 priests answered and said, It shall be un.
Zech. 3. 1 showed me Joshua the high priest, stand.
3. 8 Hear now, O Joshua the high priest, thou
6. 11 Joshua the son of Josedech, the high pr
6. 13 he shall be a priest upon his throne: and
7. 3 speak unto the priests which (were) in the
7. 5 Speak unto..the priests saying, When ye
Mal. 1. 6 O priests, that despise my name. And ye
2. 1 O ye priests, this commandment (is) for
2. 7 For the priest's lips should keep knowle.

2. *Priest, prince, minister,* כֹּהֵן *kahen.*
Ezra 6. 9 according to the appointment of the pri.
6. 16 the priests..kept the dedication of this
6. 18 set the priests in their divisions, and..L.
7. 12 unto Ezra the priest, a scribe of the law
7. 13 his priests and Levites, in my realm, wh.
7. 16 with the freewill offering..of the priests
7. 21 that whatsoever Ezra the priest, the scribe
7. 24 touching any of the priests and Levites

3. *Idolatrous priests,* כְּמָרִים *kemarim.*
Hos. 10. 5 priests thereof (that) rejoiced; Zeph. 1.4.

4. *A priest,* ἱερεύς *hiereus.*
Matt. 8. 4 show thyself to the priest, and offer the
12. 4 which were with him, but only for the p.?
12. 5 how that on the sabbath days the priests
Mark 1. 44 show thyself to the priest, and offer for
2. 26 which is not lawful to eat but for the pr.
Luke 1. 5 a certain priest named Zacharias, of the
5. 14 show thyself to the priest, and offer for
6. 4 not lawful to eat but for the priests alone?
10. 31 by chance there came down a certain pr.
17. 14 Go show yourselves unto the priests. And
John 1. 19 when..Jews sent priests and Levites from
Acts 4. 1 spake unto the people, the priests, and the
6. 7 company of the priests were obedient to
14. 13 Then the priest of Jupiter, which was be.
Heb. 5. 6 Thou (art) a priest for ever after the order
7. 1 For this Melchisedec..priest of the most
7. 3 Without father..abideth a priest contin.
7. 11 that another priest should rise after the
7. 15 after the similitude..ariseth another pr.
7. 17, 21 Thou (art) a priest for ever, after the
7. 21 For those priests were made without an
7. 23 they truly were many priests, because t.
8. 4 be a priest, seeing that there are [priests]
9. 6 priests went always into the first tabern.
10. 11 every [priest] standeth daily ministering
10. 21 (having) an high priest over the house of
Rev. 1. 6 hath made us kings and priests unto God
5. 10 made us unto our God kings and priests
20. 6 they shall be priests of God and of Christ

PRIEST, chief or high —

1. *A chief priest,* ἀρχιερεύς *archiereus.*
Matt. 2. 4 when he had gathered all the chief priests
16. 21 many things of the elders and chief priests
20. 18 shall be betrayed unto the chief priests and
21. 15 when the chief priests and scribes saw the

Matt21. 23 chief priests..came unto him as he was t.
21. 45 when the chief priests..had heard his p.
26. 3 Then assembled together the chief priests
26. 3 unto the palace of the high priest, who was
26. 14 one of the twelve..went unto the chief p.
26. 47 from the chief priests and elders of the p.
26. 51 struck a servant of the high priest, and s.
26. 57 led (him) away to Caiaphas the high priest
26. 58 afar off unto the high priest's palace, and
26. 59 Now the chief priests, and elders, and all
26. 62 the high priest arose, and said unto him
26. 63 high priest answered and said unto him
26. 65 Then the high priest rent his clothes, say
27. 1 chief priests and elders of the people took
27. 3 thirty pieces of silver to the chief priests
27. 6 chief priests took the silver pieces, and s.
27. 12 when he was accused of the chief priests
27. 20 But the chief priests and elders persuaded
27. 41 Likewise also the chief priests, mocking
27. 62 chief priests and Pharisees came together
28. 11 showed unto the chief priests all the thi.
Mark 2. 26 in the days of Abiathar the high priest, and
8. 31 be rejected of..chief priests, and scribes
10. 33 shall be delivered unto the chief priests
11. 18 scribes and chief priests heard (it), and s.
11. 27 there come to him the chief priests, and
14. 1 chief priests and the scribes sought how
14. 10 went unto the chief priests, to betray him
14. 43 from the chief priests and the scribes and
14. 47 smote a servant of the high priest, and cut
14. 53 they led Jesus away to the high priest: and
14. 53 assembled all the chief priests and the e.
14. 54 even into the palace of the high priest: and
14. 55 chief priests..sought for witness against
14. 60 high priest stood up in the midst, and as.
14. 61 high priest asked him, and said unto him
14. 63 Then the high priest rent his clothes, and
14. 66 cometh one of the maids of the high priest
15. 1 chief priests held a consultation with the
15. 3 the chief priests accused him of many th.
15. 10 knew that the chief priests had delivered
15. 11 chief priests moved the people, that he
15. 31 chief priests mocking said among them.
Luke 3. 2 Annas and Caiaphas being the high priests
9. 22 rejected of the elders and chief priests and
19. 47 chief priests and the scribes and the chief
20. 1 the [chief] priests and the scribes came
20. 19 chief priests and the scribes the same ho.
22. 2 chief priests and scribes sought how they
22. 4 communed with the chief priests and ca.
22. 50 smote the servant of the high priest, and cut
22. 52 Then Jesus said unto the chief priests, and
22. 54 brought him into the high priest's house
22. 66 chief priests..came together, and led him
23. 4 Then said Pilate to the chief priests and
23. 10 chief priests and scribes stood and vehe.
23. 13 when he had called together the chief p.
23. 23 voices of them [and of the chief priests] p.
24. 20 how the chief priests and our rulers del.
John 7. 32 and the chief priests sent officers to take
7. 45 Then came the officers to the chief priests
11. 47 Then gathered the chief priests and the P.
11. 49 being the high priest that same year, said
11. 51 being high priest that year, he prophesied
11. 57 Now both the chief priests and the Phar.
12. 10 chief priests consulted that they might
18. 3 having received..from the chief priests
18. 10 smote the high priest's servant, and cut
18. 13 Caiaphas, which was the high priest that
18. 15 disciple was known unto the high priest
18. 15 went in..into the palace of the high priest
18. 16 disciple which was known unto the h. pr.
18. 19 The high priest then asked Jesus of his d.
18. 22 saying, Answerest thou the high priest so?
18. 24 sent him bound unto Caiaphas the high pr.
18. 26 One of the servants of the high priest, b
18. 35 the chief priests have delivered thee unto
19. 6 When the chief priests..saw him, they
19. 15 chief priests answered, We have no king
19. 21 Then said the chief priests of the Jews to
Acts 4. 6 Annas the high priest, and Caiaphas, and
4. 23 reported all that the chief priests and el.
5. 17 high priest rose up, and all they that w.
5. 21 But the high priest came, and they that
5. 24 when..the [chief] priests heard these th.
5. 27 before the council: and the high priest
7. 1 Then said the high priest, Are these thi.
9. 1 Saul, yet breathing..went unto the high p
9. 14 authority from the chief priests to bind
9. 21 might bring them bound unto the chief p.
19. 14 a Jew, (and) chief of the priests, which
22. 5 As also the high priest doth bear me wi.
22. 30 commanded the chief priests and all their
23. 2 high priest Ananias commanded them t.
23. 4 they..said, Revilest thou God's high pri.?
23. 5 I wist not..that he was the high priest
23. 14 they came to the chief priests and elders
24. 1 after five days Ananias the high priest d.
25. 2 high priest and the chief of the Jews in.
25. 15 chief priests and the elders of the Jews
26. 10 received authority from the chief priests
26. 12 and commission from the chief priests
Heb. 2. 17 a merciful and faithful high priest in th.
3. 1 consider the apostle and high priest of our
4. 14 Seeing then that we have a great high p.
4. 15 For we have not an high priest which ca.
5. 1 For every high priest taken from among
5. 5 glorified not himself to be made an high p.
5. 10 Called of God an high priest after the or.
6. 20 made an high priest for ever, after the o.
7. 26 For such an high priest became us, (who
7. 27 Who needeth not daily, as those high pr.
Heb. 7. 28 For the law maketh men high priests w.
8. 1 We have such an high priest, who is set
8. 3 For every high priest is ordained to offer
9. 7 But into the second (went) the high priest
9. 11 But Christ being come an high priest of
9. 25 as the high priest entereth into the holy
13. 11 brought into the sanctuary by the high p.

2. *Priest*, ἱερεύς *hiereus*.
Acts 5. 24 Now when the high priest and the capt.

PRIEST, of the high —

Belonging to the chief priest, ἀρχιερατικός *archie.*
Acts 4. 6 as were of the kindred of the high priest

PRIEST, to be —

To be or act as a priest, כָּהַן *kahan*, 3.
Hos. 4. 6 that thou shalt be no priest to me: seeing

PRIESTHOOD —

1. *Priesthood*, כְּהֻנָּה *kehunnah*.
Exod40. 15 shall surely be an everlasting priesthood
Num16. 10 with thee: and seek ye the priesthood
18. 1 shall bear the iniquity of your priesthood
25. 13 the covenant of an everlasting priesthood
Josh.18. 7 for the priesthood of the LORD (is) their
Ezra 2. 62 therefore were they..put from the priest.
Neh. 7. 64 therefore were they..put from the priest.
13. 29 because they have defiled the priesthood
13. 29 the covenant of the priesthood, and of the

2. *Priesthood, assembly of priests*, ἱεράτευμα *hiera.*
1 Pe. 2. 5 a spiritual house, an holy priesthood, to
2. 9 a chosen generation, a royal priesthood

3. *Priesthood, priestly office*, ἱερωσύνη *hierōsunē*.
Heb. 7. 11 perfection were by the Levitical priesth.
7. 12 For the priesthood being changed, there
7. 14 Moses spake nothing concerning [priest.]
7. 24 continueth ever, hath an unchangeable p.

PRIEST'S OFFICE —

1. *Priesthood*, כְּהֻנָּה *kehunnah*.
Exod29. 9 priest's office shall be theirs for a perpet.
Num. 3. 10 and they shall wait on their priest's office
18. 7 shall keep your priest's office for every th.
18. 7 I have given your priest's office (unto you)
1 Sa. 2. 36 Put me..into one of the priest's offices

2. *Priesthood, priestly office*, ἱερατεία *hierateia*.
Luke 1. 9 According to the custom of the priest's o.

PRIEST'S OFFICE, to do, execute or minister in the —

1. *To act as a priest*, כָּהַן *kahan*, 3.
Exod28. 1, 3, 4, 41 minister unto me in the priest's o.
29. 1 to minister unto me in the priest's office
29. 44 his sons, to minister to me in the priest's o.
30. 30 may minister unto me in the priest's office
31. 10 his sons, to minister in the priest's office
35. 19 his sons, to minister in the priest's office
39. 41 garments, to minister in the priest's office
40. 13, 15 may minister unto me in the priest's of.
Lev. 7. 35 minister unto the LORD in the priest's of.
16. 32 to minister in the priest's office in his fa.
Num. 3. 3 consecrated to minister in the priest's of.
3. 4 Ithamar ministered in the priest's office
Deut10. 6 son ministered in the priest's office in his
1 Ch. 6. 10 he (it is) that executed the priest's office
24. 2 and Ithamar executed the priest's office
2 Ch.11. 14 from executing the priest's office unto the
Eze. 44. 13 to do the office of a priest unto me, nor

2. *To act as a priest*, ἱερατεύω *hierateuō*.
Luke 1. 8 while he executed the priest's office before

PRINCE —

1. *Satraps*, אֲחַשְׁדַּרְפְּנַיָּא *achashdarpenayya*.
Dan. 3. 2 king sent to gather together the princes
3. 3 Then the princes..were gathered togeth.
3. 27 princes..being gathered together, saw th.
6. 1 an hundred and twenty princes, which sh.
6. 2 the princes might give accounts unto th.
6. 3 preferred above the presidents and prin.
6. 4 princes sought to find occasion against D.
6. 6 princes assembled together to the king
6. 7 princes..have consulted together to esta.

2. *Fat ones*, חַשְׁמַנִּים *chashmannim*.
Psa. 68. 31 Princes shall come out of Egypt; Ethiopia

3. *Priest, prince, minister*, כֹּהֵן *kohen*.
Job 12. 19 He leadeth princes away spoiled, and ov.

4. *Leader*, נָגִיד *nagid*.
1 Ki 14. 7 and made thee prince over my people Isr.
16. 2 and made thee prince over my people Is.
Job 31. 37 as a prince would I go near unto him
Psa. 76. 12 He shall cut off the spirit of princes: he
Prov 28. 16 prince that wanteth understanding (is)
Eze. 28. 2 Son of man, say unto the prince of Tyrus
Dan. 9. 25 build Jerusalem unto the Messiah the p.
9. 26 people of the prince that shall come shall
11. 22 broken; yea, also the prince of the cove

5. *Willing, noble*, נָדִיב *nadib*.
1 Sa. 2. 8 set (them) among princes, and to make
Job 12. 21 He poureth contempt upon princes, and
21. 28 For ye say, Where (is) the house of the p.?
34. 18 (Is it fit) to say..to princes, (Ye are) un.?
Psa. 47. 9 princes of the people are gathered toget.
107. 40 poureth contempt upon princes, and ca.
113. 8 with princes, (even) with the princes of
118. 9 (It is) better..than to put confidence in p.
146. 3 Put not your trust in princes, (nor) in the
Prov.17. 7 becometh not..much less do lying lips a p.
17. 26 not good, (nor) to strike princes for equity
19. 6 Many will entreat the favour of the prince
Prov25. 7 put lower in the presence of the prince
Song 7. 1 How beautiful..O prince's daughter! the

6. *Anointed*, נָסִיךְ *nasik*.
Psa. 83. 11 all their princes as Zebah and as Zalmu.
Eze. 32. 30 There (be) the princes of the north, all of
Dan. 11. 8 their gods, with their princes, (and) with

7. *Lifted up, exalted*, נָשִׂיא *nasi*.
Gen. 17. 20 twelve princes shall he beget, and I will
23. 6 Thou (art) a mighty prince among us: in
25. 16 twelve princes according to their nations
34. 2 prince of the country, saw her, he took her
Num. 1. 16 princes of the tribes of their fathers, heads
1. 44 princes of Israel, (being) twelve men, each
7. 2 That the princes of Israel..the princes of
7. 3 a wagon for two of the princes, and for e.
7. 10 princes offered..even the princes offered
7. 11 offer their offering, each prince on his day
7. 18 On the second day..prince of Issachar, did
7. 24, 30, 36, 42, 48 prince of the children of
7. 54, 60, 66, 72, 78 prince of the children of
7. 84 when it was anointed, by the princes of I.
10. 4 princes..shall gather themselves unto thee
16. 2 two hundred and fifty princes of the asse.
17. 2 of all their princes, according to the house
17. 6 every one of their princes..for each prince
25. 14 prince of a chief house among the Simeon.
25. 18 daughter of a prince of Midian, their sister
27. 2 before the princes and all the congregation
31. 13 all the princes of the congregation, went
32. 2 unto the princes of the congregation, say.
34. 18 ye shall take one prince of every tribe, to
34. 22, 24, 25, 26, 27, 28 the prince of the tribe of
34. 23 The prince of the children of Joseph, for
36. 1 spake before Moses, and before the princes
Josh. 9. 15 princes of the congregation sware unto t.
9. 18 princes of the congregation had sworn un.
9. 18 congregation murmured against the pri.
9. 19 all the princes said unto all the congrega.
9. 21 princes said unto them..as the princes had
13. 21 whom Moses smote with the princes of M.
17. 4 they came near before..the princes, saying
22. 14 ten princes; of each chief house a prince
22. 30 princes of the congregation, and heads of
22. 32 princes, returned from the children of R.
1 Ki.11. 34 but I will make him prince all the days of
1 Ch. 2. 10 begat Nahshon, prince of the children of
4. 38 mentioned by (their) names (were) princes
5. 6 Beerah his son..he (was) prince of the R.
7. 40 mighty men of valour, chief of the princes
Ezra 1. 8 numbered them unto Sheshbazzar, the p.
Eze. 7. 27 the prince shall be clothed with desolation
12. 10 This burden (concerneth) the prince in J.
12. 12 prince that (is) among them shall bear upon
19. 1 take thou up a lamentation for the princes
21. 12 it (shall be) upon all the princes of Israel
21. 25 profane wicked prince of Israel, whose day
22. 6 princes of Israel, every one were in thee
26. 16 Then all the princes of the sea shall come
27. 21 the princes of Kedar, they occupied with
30. 13 there shall be no more a prince of the land
32. 29 all her princes, which with their might are
34. 24 my servant David a prince among them; I
37. 25 my servant David (shall be) their prince
38. 2, 3 the chief prince of Meshech and Tubal
39. 1 the chief prince of Meshech and Tubal
39. 18 drink the blood of the princes of the earth
44. 3 (It is) for the prince; the prince, he shall
45. 7 for the prince on the one side and on the
45. 8 my princes shall no more oppress my pe.
45. 9 Let it suffice you, O princes of Israel, rem.
45. 16 shall give this oblation for the prince in
45. 17 it shall be the prince's part (to give) burnt
45. 22 upon that day shall the prince prepare for
46. 2 prince shall enter by the way of the porch
46. 4 burnt offering that the prince shall offer
46. 8 when the prince shall enter, he shall go
46. 10 prince in the midst of them, when they go
46. 12 Now when the prince shall prepare a vo.
46. 16 If the prince give a gift unto any of his s.
46. 17 after it shall return to the prince: but his
46. 18 Moreover the prince shall not take of the
48. 21 residue (shall be) for the prince, on the
48. 21 over against the portions for the prince
48. 22 in the midst (of that) which is the prince's
48. 22 border of Benjamin, shall be for the prince

8. *Prefects*, סְגָנִים *seganim*.
Isa. 41. 25 he shall come upon princes as (upon) mo.

9. *Foremost*, פַּרְתְּמִים *partemim*.
Dan. 1. 3 and of the king's seed, and of the princes

10. *Decider, consul*, קָצִין *qatsin*.
Prov.25. 15 By long forbearing is a prince persuaded
Dan. 11. 18 but a prince for his own behalf shall cau.
Mic. 3. 1 ye princes of the house of Israel; (Is it)
3. 9 princes of the house of Israel, that abhor

11. *Great, elder*, רַב *rab*.
Jer. 39. 13 and all the king of Babylon's princes
41. 1 princes of the king, even ten men with him

12. *Very great*, רַבְרְבָן *rabreban*.
Dan. 5. 2, 3 king, and his princes, his wives, and his

13. *A secret or heavy one, noble*, רָזוֹן *razon*.
Prov 14. 28 want of people (is) the destruction of the p.

14. *Princes, rulers*, רֹזְנִים [*razan*].
Judg. 5. 3 Hear, O ye kings; give ear, O ye princes
Prov. 8. 15 By me kings reign, and princes decree j.
31. 4 kings to drink wine, nor for princes stro.

Isa. 40. 23 That bringeth the princes to nothing; he
Hab. 1. 10 and the princes shall be a scorn unto them

15. *Head, official, captain,* שַׂר *sar.*

Gen. 12. 15 princes also of Pharaoh saw her, and co.
Exod. 2. 14 Who made thee a prince and a judge over
Num 21. 18 princes digged the well, the nobles of the
22. 8 and the princes of Moab abode with Bal.
22. 13 said unto the princes of Balak, Get you
22. 14 princes of Moab rose up, and they went
22. 15 Balak sent yet again princes, more, and
22. 21 saddled his ass, and went with the prin.
22. 35 So Balaam went with the princes of Bal.
22. 40 sent to Balaam, and to the princes that
23. 6 he stood..he, and all the princes of Moab
23. 17 stood by his burnt offering, and the prin.
Judg. 5. 15 the princes of Issachar (were) with Debo.
7. 25 they took two princes of the Midianites
8. 3 hath delivered into your hands the prin.
8. 6 princes of Succoth said, (Are) the hands
8. 14 described unto him the princes of Succoth
10. 18 princes of Gilead said one to another, W.
1 Sa. 18. 30 Then the princes of the Philistines went
29. 3, 3, 4, 4, 9 the princes of the Philistines
2 Sa. 3. 38 Know ye not that there is a prince and a
10. 3 princes of the children of Ammon said un.
19. 6 that thou regardest neither princes nor s.
1 Ki. 4. 2 these (were) the princes which he had; A.
9. 22 his princes, and his captains, and rulers
20. 14, 15, 17, 19 young men of the princes of the
2 Ki. 11. 14 the princes and the trumpeters by the ki.
24. 12 his princes, and his officers: and the king
24. 14 carried away all Jerusalem, and all the p.
1 Ch. 19. 3 But the princes of the children of Ammon
22. 17 David also commanded all the princes of
23. 2 gathered together all the princes of Israel
24. 6 wrote them before the king and the prin.
27. 22 These (were) the princes of the tribes of
28. 1 all the princes of Israel, the princes of
28. 21 also the princes and all the people (will
29. 6 Then the chief of the fathers and princes
29. 24 all the princes, and the mighty men, and
2 Ch. 12. 5 Then came Shemaiah..(to) the princes of
12. 6 Whereupon the princes of Israel and the
17. 7 third year of his reign he sent to his pri.
21. 4 and (divers) also of the princes of Israel
21. 9 Then Jehoram went forth with his prin.
22. 8 found the princes of Judah, and the sons
23. 13 and the princes and the trumpets by the
24. 10 all the princes and all the people rejoiced
24. 17 after the death of Jehoiada came the pri.
24. 23 destroyed all the princes of the people f.
28. 14 before the princes and all the congregat.
28. 21 took away a portion..of the princes, and
29. 30 Hezekiah the king and the princes com.
30. 2 king had taken counsel, and his princes
30. 6 letters from the king and his princes th.
30. 12 commandment of the king and of the pr.
30. 24 princes gave to the congregation a thous.
31. 8 when Hezekiah and the princes came and
32. 3 He took counsel with his princes and his
32. 31 ambassadors of the princes of Babylon
35. 8 his princes gave willingly unto the people
36. 18 the treasures of the king, and of his pri.
Ezra 7. 28 and before all the king's mighty princes
8. 20 princes had appointed for the service of
9. 1 princes came to me, saying, The people
9. 2 hand of the princes and rulers hath been
10. 8 according to the counsel of the princes
Neh. 9. 32 come upon us, on our kings, on our prin.
9. 34 Neither have our kings, our princes, our
9. 38 our princes, Levites, (and) priests, seal (un.
12. 31 Then I brought up the princes of Judah
12. 32 went Hoshaiah, and half of the princes of
Esth. 1. 3 made a feast unto all his princes and his
1. 3 nobles and princes of the provinces, (being)
1. 11 to show the people and the princes her b.
1. 14 seven princes of Persia and Media, which
1. 16 answered before the king and the princes
1. 16 also to all the princes, and to all the peo.
1. 18 say this day unto all the king's princes
1. 21 the saying pleased the king and the prin.
2. 18 made a great feast unto all his princes and
3. 1 set his seat above all the princes that (w.)
5. 11 how he had advanced him above the pri.
6. 9 of one of the king's most noble princes
Job 3. 15 Or with princes that had gold, who filled
29. 9 princes refrained talking, and laid (their)
34. 19 that accepteth not the persons of princes
Psa. 45. 16 whom thou mayest make princes in all
68. 27 princes of Judah (and) their council, the
68. 27 princes of Zebulun, (and) the princes of N.
82. 7 die like men, and fall like one of the pri.
105. 22 To bind his princes at his pleasure, and
119. 23 Princes also did sit (and) speak against me
119. 161 Princes have persecuted me without a
148. 11 Kings of the earth, and all people; prin.
Prov. 8. 16 By me princes rule and nobles, (even) all
19. 10 seemly..for a servant to have rule over p.
28. 2 many (are) the princes thereof: but by a
Eccl. 10. 7 princes walking as servants upon the ea.
10. 16 when thy king (is) a child, and thy princes
10. 17 thy princes eat in due season, for streng.
Isa. 1. 23 The princes (are) rebellious, and compa.
3. 4 I will give children (to be) their princes
3. 14 ancients of his people, and the princes th.
9. 6 The everlasting Father, The Prince of Pe
10. 8 saith, (Are) not my princes altogether ki.
19. 11 Surely the princes of Zoan (are) fools, the
19. 13 princes of Zoan are become fools, the pr.
21. 5 eat, drink: arise, ye princes, (and) anoint
23. 8 whose merchants (are) princes, whose tr.
Isa. 30. 4 For his princes were at Zoan, and his am.
31. 9 princes shall be afraid of the ensign, saith
32. 1 reign in righteousness, and princes shall
34. 12 none (shall be) there, and all her princes
43. 28 Therefore I have profaned the princes of
49. 7 princes also shall worship, because of the
Jer. 1. 18 against the princes thereof, against the
2. 26 their princes, and their priests, and their
4. 9 shall perish, and the heart of the princes
8. 1 bones of his princes, and the bones of the
17. 25 kings and princes..they, and their princes
24. 1 princes of Judah, with the carpenters and
24. 8 So will I give Zedekiah..and his princes
25. 18 kings thereof, and the princes thereof, to
25. 19 Pharaoh king of Egypt..and his princes
26. 10 When the princes of Judah heard these
26. 11 Then spake the priests..unto the princes
26. 12 Then spake Jeremiah unto all the princes
26. 16 Then said the princes and all the people
26. 21 with all his mighty men, and all the prin.
29. 2 princes of Judah and Jerusalem, and the
32. 32 their princes, their priests, and their pro.
34. 10 Now when all the princes, and all the pe.
34. 19 princes of Judah, and the princes of Jer.
34. 21 Zedekiah king of Judah, and his princes
35. 4 which (was) by the chamber of the princ.
36. 12 all the princes sat there..and all the pri.
36. 14 Therefore all the princes sent Jehudi the
36. 19 Then said the princes unto Baruch, Go
36. 21 in the ears of all the princes which stood
37. 14 took Jeremiah, and brought him to the p.
37. 15 the princes were wroth with Jeremiah, and
38. 4 princes said unto the king, We beseech
38. 17, 18, 22 forth unto the king of Babylon's p.
38. 25 But if the princes hear that I have talked
38. 27 Then came all the princes unto Jeremiah
39. 3, 3 princes..with all the residue of the p.
44. 17 our fathers, our kings, and our princes, in
44. 21 your fathers, your kings, and your princes
48. 7 into captivity (with) his priests and his p.
49. 3 (and) his priests and his princes together
49. 38 destroy from thence the king and the pr.
50. 35 and upon her princes, and upon her wise
51. 57 I will make drunk her princes, and her
51. 59 reign. And (this) Seraiah (was) a quiet p.
52. 10 slew also all the princes of Judah in Rib.
Lam. 1. 6 her princes are become like harts (that)
2. 2 polluted the kingdom and the princes th.
2. 9 king and her princes (are) among the Ge.
5. 12 Princes are hanged up by their hand: the
Eze. 11. 1 five and twenty men..princes of the peo.
17. 12 hath taken..the princes thereof, and led
22. 27 Her princes in the midst thereof (are) like
Dan. 1. 7 Unto whom the prince of the eunuchs gave
1. 8 requested of the prince of the eunuchs that
1. 9 into favour and tender love with the pri.
1. 10 prince of the eunuchs said unto Daniel, I
1. 11 Melzar, whom the prince of the eunuchs
1. 18 then the prince of the eunuchs brought
8. 11 magnified (himself) even to the prince of
8. 25 stand up against the prince of princes; but
9. 6 which spake in thy name to..our princes
9. 8 confusion of face, to our kings, to our p.
10. 13 But the prince of the kingdom of Persia
10. 13 one of the chief princes, came to help me
10. 20 now will I return to fight with the prince
10. 20 when I am gone forth, lo, the prince of G.
10. 21 none that holdeth..but Michael your pr.
11. 5 shall be strong, and (one) of his princes
12. 1 great prince which standeth for the chil.
Hos. 3. 4 shall abide..without a prince, and without
5. 10 princes of Judah were like them that re.
7. 3 make the king glad..and the princes with
7. 5 In the day of our king the princes have
7. 16 their princes shall fall by the sword for
8. 10 sorrow..for the burden of the king of p.
9. 15 I will love them no more: all their princes
13. 10 thou saidst, Give me a king and princes?
Amos 1. 15 he and his princes together, saith the
2. 3 will slay all the princes thereof with him
Mic. 7. 3 the prince asketh, and the judge (asketh)
Zeph. 1. 8 that I will punish the princes, and the k.
3. 3 Her princes within her (are) roaring lions

16. *A warrior, knight,* שָׁלִישׁ *shalish.*

Eze. 23. 15 all of them princes to look to, after the

17. *A chief leader,* ἀρχηγός *archēgos.*

Acts 3. 15 killed the prince of life, whom God hath
5. 31 exalted..(to be) a prince and a Saviour, for

18. *Chief, prince,* ἄρχων *archōn.*

Matt. 9. 34 He casteth out devils through the prince
12. 24 but by Beelzebub the prince of the devils
20. 25 Ye know that the princes of the Gentiles
Mark 3. 22 by the prince of the devils casteth he out
John 12. 31 now shall the prince of this world be cast
14. 30 for the prince of this world cometh, and
16. 11 because the prince of this world is judged
1 Co. 2. 6 nor of the princes of this world, that come
2. 8 Which none of the princes of this world
Eph. 2. 2 according to the prince of the power of
Rev. 1. 5 and the prince of the kings of the earth

19. *A leader,* ἡγεμών *hēgemōn.*

Matt. 2. 6 art not the least among the princes of J

PRINCE, to make (self) a—

1. *To make prince,* שׂוּר *sur,* 5.

Hos. 8. 4 they have made princes, and I knew (it)

2. *To make self prince,* שָׂרַר *sarar,* 7.

Num 16. 13 except thou make thyself altogether a p.

PRINCESS —

Princess, שָׂרָה *sarah.*

1 Ki. 11. 3 he had seven hundred wives, princesses
Lam. 1. 1 princess among the provinces, (how) is

PRINCIPAL (thing, officer, plant) —

1. *Father,* אָב *ab.*

1 Ch. 24. 6 one principal household being taken for

2. *Honourable, mighty,* אַדִּיר *addir.*

Jer. 25. 34 wallow yourselves..ye principal of the fl.
25. 35 nor the principal of the flock to escape
25. 36 and an howling of the principal of the fl.

3. *Anointed,* נָסִיךְ *nasik.*

Mic. 5. 5 seven shepherds, and eight principal men

4. *Priest, prince, minister,* כֹּהֵן *kohen.*

1 Ki. 4. 5 Zabud the son of Nathan (was) principal o.

5. *Head, chief,* רֹאשׁ *rosh.*

Exod 30. 23 Take thou also unto thee principal spices
Lev. 6. 5 he shall even restore it in the principal
Num. 5. 7 recompense his trespass with the princi.
1 Ch. 24. 31 principal fathers over against their you.
Neh. 11. 17 the principal to begin the thanksgiving

6. *Beginning,* רֵאשִׁית *reshith.*

Prov. 4. 7 Wisdom (is)..principal thing; (therefore)

7. *A row, range,* שׂוֹרָה *sorah.*

Isa. 28. 25 cast in the principal wheat, and the app.

8. *Head, prince, chief,* שַׂר *sar.*

Jer. 52. 25 principal scribe of the host, who mustered
2 Ki. 25. 19 principal scribe of the host, which mustered

9. *Intertwining branches,* שְׂרוּקִּים *seruqqim.*

Isa. 16. 8 broken down the principal plants thereof

10. *According to pre-eminence,* κατ' ἐξοχὴν ὤν.

Acts 25. 23 with the chief captains and principal men

PRINCIPALITY —

1. *Principalities,* מַרְאָשׁוֹת *marashoth.*

Jer. 13. 18 for your principalities shall come down

2. *Beginning, principality,* ἀρχή *archē.*

Rom. 8. 38 principalities, nor powers, nor things pr.
Eph. 1. 21 Far above all principality, and power, and
3. 10 intent that now unto the principalities and
6. 12 but against principalities, against powers
Col. 1. 16 principalities, or powers: all things were
2. 10 which is the head of all principality and
2. 15 having spoiled principalities and powers
Titus 3. 1 to be subject to principalities and powers

PRINCIPLE —

1. *Step, element, principle,* στοιχεῖον *stoicheion.*

Heb. 5. 12 which (be) the first principles of the ora.

2. *Beginning,* ἀρχή *archē.*

Heb. 6. 1 leaving the principles of the doctrine of

PRINT —

A stroke, mark, type, τύπος *tupos.*

John 20. 25 Except I shall see in his hands the print
20. 25 put my finger into the [print] of the nails

PRINT, to (set a) —

1. *To set a circle or limit,* חָקָה *chaqah,* 7.

Job 13. 27 thou settest a print upon the heels of my

2. *To give,* נָתַן *nathan.*

Lev. 19. 28 Ye shall not..print any marks upon you

PRINTED, to be —

To be graven, חָקַק *chaqaq,* 6.

Job 19. 23 now written! oh that they were printed

PRIS'-CA, Πρίσκα.

A female believer in Ephesus to whom Paul sends a salutation; without doubt the same as *Priscilla.*

2 Ti. 4. 19 Salute P. and Aquila, and the household

PRIS-CIL'-LA, Πρίσκιλλα.

The wife of Aquila of Pontus, who had been driven from Rome by Claudius, accompanied Paul a little, and afterwards instructed Apollos of Alexandria.

Acts 18. 2 And found a certain Jew..with his wife P.
18. 18 sailed thence..and with him P. and Aqu.
18. 26 whom when Aquila and P. had heard, they
Rom. 16. 3 Greet [P.] and Aquila my helpers in Christ
1 Co. 16. 19 Aquila and P. salute you much in the Lo.

PRISON —

1. *[House] of the bound,* אֲסוּרִים [V.L. אסירים] *[asar].*

Judg 16. 21 he did grind in the prison house; 16. 25.

1a. *House of the bound,* בֵּית הָסוּרִים *beth hā-surim.*

Eccl. 4. 14 for out of prison he cometh to reign

2. *House of bondage,* בֵּית אֵסוּר *beth esur.*

Jer. 37. 15 put him in prison in the house of Jonat.

3. *House of restraint,* בֵּית כֶּלֶא *beth kele.*

1 Ki. 22. 27 Put this (fellow) in the prison, and feed
2 Ki. 17. 4 the king of Assyria..bound him in prison
25. 27 lift up the head of Jehoiachin..out of pr.
2 Ch. 18. 26 Put this (fellow) in the prison, and feed
Jer. 37. 18 that ye have put me in prison; 37. 15.

3a. *House of restraint,* בית כליא [V.L. בֵּית כְּלוּא] *beth kelu.*

Jer. 37. 4 they had not put him into prison; 52. 31.

4. *Round house, or tower,* בֵּית סֹהַר *beth sohar.*

Gen. 39. 20 into the prison..he was there in the pri.
39. 21 favour in the sight of the keeper of the p.
39. 22 keeper of the prison committed to Joseph's
39. 22 all the prisoners that (were) in the prison
39. 23 The keeper of the prison looked not to
40. 3 into the prison, the place where Joseph
40. 5 butler and the baker..bound in the prison

5 *Restraint*, כֶּלֶא *kele.*
2 Ki.25. 29 And changed his prison garments : and he
Isa. 42. 7 to bring out the prisoners from the prison
42. 22 they are hid in prison houses: they are for
Jer. 52. 33 And changed his prison garments : and he

6. *House of inspection*, בֵּית פְּקֻדָּה *beth pequddah.*
Jer. 52. 11 put him in prison till the day of his death

7. *Torture, stocks, pillory*, מַהְפֶּכֶת *mahpeketh.*
2 Ch.16. 10 put him in a prison house ; for (he was) in
Jer. 29. 26 thou shouldest put him in prison, and in

8. *Prison, watch*, מַטָּרָה *mattarah.*
Neh. 3. 25 house, that (was) by the court of the pri.
12. 39 gate: and they stood still in the prison gate
Jer. 32. 2 prophet was shut up in the court of the p.
32. 8 came to me in the court of the prison, a.
32. 12 the Jews that sat in the court of the pri.
33. 1 was yet shut up in the court of the prison
37. 21 commit Jeremiah into the court of the p.
37. 21 Jeremiah remained in the court of the p.
38. 6 that (was) in the court of the prison : and
38. 13 Jeremiah remained in the court of the pr.
38. 28 Jeremiah abode in the court of the prison
39. 14 took Jeremiah out of the court of the pr.
39. 15 while he was shut up in the court of the p.

9. *Prison, enclosed or secure place*, מַסְגֵּר *masger.*
Psa.142. 7 Bring my soul out of prison, that I may
Isa. 24. 22 shall be shut up in the prison, and after
42. 7 bring out the prisoners from the prison

10. *Restraint*, עֹצֶר *otser.*
Isa. 53 8 He was taken from prison and from jud.

11. *Ward*, מִשְׁמָר *mishmar.*
Gen. 42 19 brethren be bound in the house of your p.

12. *Band, prison*, קוֹחַ *qoach.*
Isa. 61. 1 opening of the prison to (them that are)

13. *Place of bonds, prison*, δεσμωτήριον *desmōtērion.*
Matt 11. 2 when John had heard in the prison the
Acts 5. 21 sent to the prison to have them brought
5. 23 prison truly found we shut with all safety
16. 26 foundations of the prison were shaken

14. *House*, οἴκημα *oikēma.*
Acts 12 7 light shined in the prison : and he smote

15. *A keeping, place of keeping*, τήρησις *tērēsis.*
Acts 5. 18 and put them in the common prison

16. *A guarding, place of guarding*, φυλακή *phulakē.*
Matt. 5 25 lest at any time..thou be cast into prison
14 3 put (him) in prison for Herodias sake his
14. 10 he sent, and beheaded John in the prison
18. 30 but went and cast him into prison, till he
25 36 I was in prison, and ye came unto me
25 39 Or when saw we thee sick or in prison
25. 43 sick, and in prison, and ye visited me not
25. 44 sick, or in prison, and did not minister
Mark 6. 17 bound him in prison for Herodias' sake
6. 27 he went and beheaded him in the prison
Luke 3 20 this above all, that he shut up John in p.
12 58 officer, and the officer cast thee into pris.
21 12 into prisons, being brought before kings
22. 33 ready to go with thee, both into prison
23 19 for a certain sedition..was cast into pris.
23 25 for sedition and murder was cast into p.
John 3. 24 For John was not yet cast into prison
Acts 5. 19 angel..opened the prison doors, and bro.
5. 22 found them not in the prison, they retur.
5 25 men whom ye put in prison are standing
8. 3 men and women, committed (them) to p.
12. 4 apprehended him, he put (him) in prison
12. 5 Peter therefore was kept in prison : but
12. 6 the keepers before the door kept the pr.
12 17 the Lord had brought him out of the pr
16. 23 cast (them) into prison, charging the jai.
16 24 thrust them into the inner prison, and
16. 27 seeing the prison doors open, he drew out
16. 37 have cast (us) into prison ; and now do they
16. 40 they went out of the prison, and entered
22. 4 binding and delivering into prison both
26 10 many of the saints did I shut up in prison
2 Co. 11. 23 in prisons more frequent, in deaths oft
1 Pe. 3. 19 went and preached unto the spirits in pr.
Rev. 2. 10 the devil shall cast (some) of you into pr.
20. 7 Satan shall be loosed out of his prison

PRISON, to be put or cast into —
To give along, up, over, παραδίδωμι *paradidōmi.*
Matt 4. 12 had heard that John was cast into prison
Mark 1 14 after that John was put in prison, Jesus

PRISONER (fellow)—
1. *One bound*, אָסִיר *asir.*
Gen. 39. 20 place where the king's prisoners (were) b.
39. 22 committed..all the prisoners that (were)
Job 3. 18 prisoners rest together ; they hear not the
Psa. 69. 33 For the LORD..despiseth not his prisoners
79. 11 Let the sighing of the prisoner come before
102 20 To hear the groaning of the prisoner ; to
Isa. 14. 17 (that) opened not the house of his priso ?
Lam. 3 34 To crush under his feet all the prisoners
Zech. 9. 11 I have sent forth thy prisoners out of the
9 12 Turn you to the stronghold, ye prisoners

2. *One bound*, אַסִּיר *assir.*
Isa. 10. 4 they shall bow down under the prisoners
24. 22 prisoners are gathered in the pit, and shall
42. 7 to bring out the prisoners from the prison

3. *To bind*, אָסַר *asar* (pass. partic.).
Psa 146. 7 The LORD looseth the prisoners
Isa. 49. 9 That thou mayest say to the prisoners, Go

4. *Captive*, שְׁבִי *shebi.*
Num 21. 1 against Israel, and took (some) of them p.
Isa. 20. 4 lead away the Egyptians prisoners, and the

5. *One bound*, δέσμιος *desmios.*
Matt 27. 15 wont to release unto the people a priso.
27 16 they had then a notable prisoner, called
Mark15. 6 released unto them one prisoner, whom.
Acts 16. 25 sang praises .and the prisoners heard th.
16. 27 supposing that the prisoners had been fled
23. 18 Paul the prisoner called me unto (him), and
25 27 unreasonable to send a prisoner, and not
28. 16 [centurion delivered the prisoners to..c.]
28. 17 yet was I delivered prisoner from Jerusa.
Eph. 3. 1 the prisoner of Jesus Christ for you Gen.
4. 1 I therefore, the prisoner of the Lord, be.
2 Ti. 1. 8 ; Phm. 1. 9.

6. *Fellow captive*, συναιχμάλωτος *sunaichmalōtos.*
Rom. 16 7 ; Col. 4. 10 ; Phil. 23.

7. *One bound*, δεσμώτης *desmōtēs.*
Acts 27. 1 delivered Paul and certain other prisoners
27 42 soldiers' counsel was to kill the prisoners

PRIVATE, PRIVATELY —
1. *One's own*, ἴδιος *idios.*
2 Pe. 1. 20 no prophecy of the Scripture is of any pr.

2. *By one's self*, κατ' ἰδίαν *kat' idian.*
Matt24. 3 disciples came unto him privately, saying
Mark 6. 32 departed into a desert place by ship priv.
9 28 disciples asked him privately, Why could
13. 3 and John and Andrew asked him privately
Luke 9. 10 went aside privately into a desert place
10. 23 said privately, Blessed (are) the eyes wh
Acts 23. 19 went (with him) aside privately, and asked
Gal. 2. 2 privately to them which were of reputation

PRIVILY —
1. *In darkness*, בְּמוֹ אֹפֶל *bemo ophel.*
Psa 11 2 may privily shoot at the upright in heart

2. *In secret, secretly*, בַּלָּט [*lat*].
1 Sa. 24. 4 and cut off the skirt of Saul's robe privily

3. *In secret*, בַּסֵּתֶר [*sether*]
Psa.101. 5 Whoso privily slandereth his neighbour

4. *In deceit*, בְּתָרְמָה [*tormah*].
Judg 9. 31 sent messengers unto Abimelech privily

5. *Hidingly, secretly*, λάθρα *lathra.*
Matt. 1. 19 Joseph..was minded to put her away pr
2. 7 when he had privily called the wise men
Acts 16. 37 now do they thrust us out privily? nay

PRIVILY bring in, to —
To lead in sideways, παρεισάγω *pareisagō.*
2 Pe 2. 1 who privily shall bring in damnable her.

PRIVY chamber, to enter a —
To go into an inner chamber, חָדַר *chadar.*
Eze 21 14 which entereth into their privy chambers

PRIVY MEMBER —
Urethra, שָׁפְכָה *shophkah.*
Deut23. 1 He that..hath his privy member cut off

PRIVY (to), to be —
1. *To know, be acquainted with*, יָדַע *yada.*
1 Ki. 2. 44 wickedness which thine heart is privy to

2. *To know with*, σύνοιδα *sunoida.*
Acts 5. 2 his wife also being privy (to it), and brou.

PRIZE —
A prize crown or garland, βραβεῖον *brabeion.*
1 Co 9. 24 run all, but one receiveth the prize? So
Phil 3 14 I press toward the mark for the prize of

PRIZED, to be —
To be precious, prized, priced, יָקַר *yaqar.*
Zech.11 13 a goodly price that I was prized at of them

PROCEED (forth, further, out of), to —
1. *To add*, יָסַף *yasaph.*
Isa. 29. 14 I will proceed to do a marvellous work

2. *To (cause to) add*, יָסַף *yasaph*, 5.
Job 36. 1 Elihu also proceeded, and said
40. 5 yea, twice ; but I will proceed no further

3. *To go out or forth*, יָצָא *yatsa.*
Gen. 24. 50 The thing proceedeth from the LORD : we
Exod25. 35 branches that proceed out of the candle.
Num30. 2 do according to all that proceedeth out of
32. 24 do that which hath proceeded out of your
Josh. 6. 10 neither shall (any) word proceed out of
Judg11 36 that which hath proceeded out of thy m.
1 Sa. 24. 13 Wickedness proceedeth from the wicked
2 Sa. 7 12 which shall proceed out of thy bowels, and
Eccl.10. 5 an error (which) proceedeth from the ru.
Isa. 51. 4 a law shall proceed from me, and I will
Jer. 9. 3 for they proceed from evil to evil, and t.
30 19 out of them shall proceed thanksgiving
30. 21 shall proceed from the midst of them ; and
Lam. 3. 38 Out of the mouth..proceedeth not evil and
Hab. 1 4 righteous ; therefore wrong judgment p.
1. 7 and their dignity shall proceed of thems.

4. *Outgoing*, מוֹצָא *motsa.*
Num30. 12 whatsoever proceeded out of her lips co
Deut. 8. 3 proceedeth out of the mouth of the LORD

5. *To go on out of*, ἐκπορεύομαι *ekporeuomai.*
Matt. 4. 4 by every word that proceedeth out of the
15 18 things which proceed out of the mouth co.
Mark 7. 21 out of the heart of men, proceed evil tho.
Luke 4. 22 gracious words which proceeded out of his
John15. 26 which proceedeth from the Father, he sh.
Eph. 4. 29 Let no corrupt communication proceed
Rev. 4. 5 out of the throne proceeded
11. 5 fire proceedeth out of their mouth, and
19. 21 which (sword) [proceeded] out of his mou.
22. 1 proceeding out of the throne of God and

6. *To come or go out of*, ἐξέρχομαι *exerchomai.*
Matt15. 19 For out of the heart proceed evil thoughts
John 8. 42 for I proceeded forth and came from God
Jas. 3. 10 Out of the same mouth proceedeth bless.

7. *To strike forward*, προκόπτω *prokoptō.*
2 Ti. 3. 9 But they shall proceed no further, for t.

8. *To put to or toward, add*, προστίθημι *prostithēmi.*
Acts 12. 3 he proceeded further to take Peter also

PROCESS of time, in —
1. *At the end of days*, מִקֵּץ יָמִים [*qets*].
Gen. 4. 3 in process of time it came to pass, that

2. *In those many days*, בַּיָּמִים הָרַבִּים הָהֵם [*yom*].
Exod. 2. 23 it came to pass in process of time, that the

3. *When the days increased*, וַיִּרְבּוּ הַיָּמִים [*yom*].
Gen 38. 12 in process of time the daughter of Shuah

4. *After days*, מִיָּמִים *miy-yamim.*
Judg11. 4 it came to pass in process of time, that
2 Ch 21. 19 in process of time, after the end of two

PRO-CHO'-RUS, Πρόχορος.
One of the seven chosen to serve tables for the poor.
Acts 6. 5 they chose Stephen..and P., and Nicanor

PROCLAIM, to —
1. *To cause a voice to pass over*, עָבַר קוֹל *abar* (5) *qol.*
Neh. 8. 15 should publish and proclaim in all their

2. *To call*, קָרָא *qara.*
Exod33 19 will proclaim the name of the LORD bef.
34. 5 stood with him there, and proclaimed the
34. 6 proclaimed, The LORD, The LORD God, m.
Lev. 23. 2, 37 ye shall proclaim (to be) holy convoc.
23. 4 which ye shall proclaim in their seasons
23 21 ye shall proclaim on the self same day
25. 10 proclaim liberty throughout (all) the land
Deut20 10 When thou comest nigh..proclaim peace
Judg 7. 3 proclaim in the ears of the people, saying
1 Ki. 21. 9 Proclaim a fast, and set Naboth on high
21. 12 proclaimed a fast, and set Naboth on high
2 Ki. 10. 20 assembly for Baal. And they proclaimed
23. 16 man of God proclaimed, who proclaimed
23. 17 proclaimed these things that thou hast d.
2 Ch.20. 3 proclaimed a fast throughout all Judah
Ezra 8. 21 Then I proclaimed a fast there, at the ri.
Esth. 6. 9 proclaim before him, Thus shall it be do.
6. 11 and proclaimed before him, Thus shall it
Prov.12. 23 the heart of fools proclaimeth foolishness
20. 6 Most men will proclaim every one his own
Isa. 61. 1 to proclaim liberty to the captives, and
61. 2 To proclaim the acceptable year of the L.
Jer. 3. 12 Go and proclaim these words toward the
7. 2 proclaim there this word, and say, Hear
11. 6 Proclaim all these words in the cities of
19. 2 proclaim there the words that I shall tell
34. 8 made a covenant..to proclaim liberty un.
34. 15 proclaiming liberty every man to his ne.
34. 17 proclaiming liberty..I proclaim a liberty
36. 9 proclaimed a fast before the LORD to all
Joel 3. 9 Proclaim ye this among the Gentiles ; Pr.
Amos 4. 5 proclaim (and) publish the free offerings
Jon. 3. 5 proclaimed a fast, and put on sackcloth

3. *To set apart, sanctify*, קָדַשׁ *qadesh*, 3.
2 Ki. 10. 20 said, Proclaim a solemn assembly for B.

4. *To cause to hear*, שָׁמַע *shamea*, 5.
Isa. 62. 11 hath proclaimed unto the end of the wo.

5. *To cry or proclaim as a herald*, κηρύσσω *kērussō.*
Luke12. 3 shall be proclaimed upon the house tops
Rev. 5. 2 saw a strong angel proclaiming with a

PROCLAIMED, to cause to be —
1. *To cause to cry*, זָעַק *zaaq*, 5.
Jon. 3. 7 caused (it) to be proclaimed and published

2. *To cause voice to pass*, עָבַר קוֹל *abar* (5) *qol.*
Exod36. 6 caused it to be proclaimed throughout the

PROCLAMATION –
1. *Voice*, קוֹל *qol.*
2 Ch.24. 9 made a proclamation through Judah and

2. *Loud cry, proclamation, singing*, רִנָּה *rinnah.*
1 Ki.22. 36 there went a proclamation throughout the

PROCLAMATION, to make a —
1. *To cause to cry as a herald*, כְּרַז *keraz*, 5.
Dan. 5. 29 and made a proclamation concerning him

2. *To cause a voice to pass over*, עָבַר קוֹל *abar*, 5.
2 Ch.30. 5 to make proclamation throughout all Is.
36. 22 that he made a proclamation throughout
Ezra 1. 1 that he made a proclamation throughout
10. 7 they made proclamation throughout Jud.

3. *To call*, קָרָא *qara.*
Exod32. 5 Aaron made proclamation, and said, To.

4. *To cause to hear*, שָׁמַע *shamea*, 5.
1 Ki 15. 22 made a proclamation throughout all Jud.

PROCURE, to —
1. *To seek, enquire, require*, בָּקַשׁ *baqash*, 3.
Prov11. 27 He that diligently seeketh good procureth

2. *To do, make,* עָשָׂה *asah.*
Jer. 2. 17 Hast thou not procured this unto thyself
4. 18 Thy way and thy doings have procured
26. 19 Thus might we procure great evil against
33. 9 for all the prosperity, that I procure unto

PRODUCE, to —
To bring near, קָרַב *qarab,* 3.
Isa. 41. 21 Produce your cause..bring forth your str.

PROFANE (person or place) —
1. *Common, polluted,* חֹל *chol.*
Eze. 22. 26 no difference between the holy and prof.
42. 20 between the sanctuary and the profane p.
44. 23 between the holy and profane, and cause
48. 15 shall be a profane (place) for the city, for

2. *Pierced, polluted, common,* חָלָל *chalal.*
Lev. 21. 7 shall not take a wife (that is)..profane; n.
21. 14 widow, or a divorced woman, or profane
Eze. 21. 25 profane wicked prince of Israel, whose day

3. *Profane, impious,* βέβηλος *bebēlos.*
1 Ti. 1. 9 but for the..unholy and profane, for mur.
4. 7 refuse profane and old wives' fables, and
6. 20 avoiding profane (and) vain babblings, and
2 Ti. 2. 16 But shun profane (and) vain babblings; for
Heb. 12. 16 profane person, as Esau, who for one m.

PROFANE (self), cast as, to —
1. *To be polluted, common,* חָלַל *chalal,* 2.
Lev. 21. 4 shall not defile himself..to profane him.
21. 9 if she profane herself by playing the whore

2. *To pollute, make common,* חָלַל *chalal,* 3.
Lev. 18. 21 neither shalt thou profane the name of
19. 8 because he hath profaned the hallowed
19. 12 neither shalt thou profane the name of
20. 3 defile my sanctuary, and to profane my h.
21. 6 They shall be holy..and not profane the
21. 9 by playing the whore, she profaneth her
21. 12 nor profane the sanctuary of his God; for
21. 15 Neither shall he profane his seed among
21. 23 that he profane not my sanctuaries: for
22. 2 and that they profane not my holy name
22. 9 die therefore, if they profane it: I the L.
22. 15 they shall not profane the holy things of
22. 32 Neither shall ye profane my holy name
Neh. 13. 17 What evil thing (is) this that ye do, and p.
13. 18 bring more wrath upon Israel by profan.
Psa. 89. 39 thou hast profaned his crown (by casting
Isa. 43. 28 I have profaned the princes of the sanct.
Eze. 22. 8 Thou hast despised..and hast profaned
22. 26 Her priests..have profaned mine holy t.
23. 38 they have defiled..and have profaned my
23. 39 they came..into my sanctuary to profane
24. 21 will profane my sanctuary, the excellency
28. 16 will cast thee as profane out of the mou.
36. 20 whither they went, they profaned my holy
36. 21 which the house of Israel had profaned
36. 22 which ye have profaned among the heat.
36. 23 which ye have profaned in the midst of
Amos 2. 7 father will go in..to profane my holy n.
Mal. 1. 12 But ye have profaned it, in that ye say
2. 10 by profaning the covenant of our fathers?
2. 11 Judah hath profaned the holiness of the

3. *To profane,* βεβηλόω *bebēloō.*
Matt 12. 5 priests in the temple profane the sabbath
Acts 24. 6 also hath gone about to profane the tem.

PROFANE, to be —
To be profane, חָנֵף *chaneph.*
Jer. 23. 11 For both prophet and priest are profane

PROFANED, to be —
1. *To be polluted,* חָלַל *chalal,* 2.
Eze. 22. 26 hid their eyes..and I am profaned amo.
25. 3 against my sanctuary, when it was profa.

2. *To be polluted,* חָלַל *chalal,* 4.
Eze. 36. 23 which was profaned among the heathen

PROFANENESS —
Profaneness, profanity, חֲנֻפָּה *chanuppah.*
Jer. 23. 15 is profaneness gone forth into all the land

PROFESS, to —
1. *To put before,* נָגַד *nagad,* 5.
Deut 26. 3 I profess this day unto the LORD thy God
2. *To announce, promise,* ἐπαγγέλλομαι *epaggellomai.*
1 Ti. 2. 10 which becometh women professing godl.
6. 21 Which some professing have erred conc.

3. *To say publicly, confess,* ὁμολογέω *homologeō.*
Matt. 7. 23 then will I profess unto them, I never k.
1 Ti. 6. 12 hast professed a good profession before
Titus 1. 16 They profess that they know God; but in

4. *To say, assert, affirm,* φάσκω *phaskō.*
Rom. 1. 22 Professing themselves to be wise, they be.

PROFESSED, PROFESSION —
A saying the same thing, ὁμολογία *homologia.*
1 Ti. 6. 12 hast professed a good profession before
2 Co. 9. 13 they glorify God for your professed subj.
Heb. 3. 1 consider the apostle..of our profession
4. 14 Son of God, let us hold fast (our) profess.
10. 23 Let us hold fast the profession of (our)

PROFIT —
1. *Dishonest gain,* בֶּצַע *betsa.*
Gen. 37. 26 What profit (is it) if we slay our brother
Psa. 30. 9 What profit (is there) in my blood, when
Mal. 3. 14 what profit (is it) that we have kept his

2. *What is over and above,* יוֹתֵר *yother.*
Eccl. 7. 11 (by it there is) profit to them that see the

3. *To profit,* יָעַל *yaal,* 5.
Isa. 30. 5 nor be an help nor profit, but a shame, and
Jer. 16. 19 vanity..(things) wherein (there is) no p.

4. *What is over and above,* יִתְרוֹן *yithron.*
Eccl. 1. 3 What profit hath a man of all his labour
2. 11 vexation of spirit, and (there was) no pro.
3. 9 What profit hath he that worketh in that
5. 9 Moreover the profit of the earth is for all
5. 16 what profit hath he that hath laboured

5. *What is over and above,* מוֹתָר *mothar.*
Prov 14. 23 In all labour there is profit: but the talk

6. *To be equal, profitable, compared,* שָׁוָה *shavah.*
Esth. 3. 8 it (is) not for the king's profit to suffer th.

7. *To bear together, advantage,* συμφέρω *sumpherō.*
1 Co. 7. 35 this I speak for your own profit; not that
10. 33 please all..not seeking mine own [profit]
Heb. 12. 10 but he for (our) profit, that (we) might be

8. *Useful, profitable,* χρήσιμος *chrēsimos.*
2 Ti. 2. 14 they strive not about words to no profit

9. *Profit,* ὠφέλεια *ōpheleia.*
Rom. 3. 1 or what profit (is there) of circumcision

PROFIT, to (have), be profited —
1. *To make or give profit,* יָעַל *yaal,* 5.
1 Sa. 12. 21 which cannot profit nor deliver; for they
Job 21. 15 what profit should we have, if we pray un.
35. 3 What profit shall I have, (if I be cleansed)
Prov 10. 2 Treasures of wickedness profit nothing
11. 4 Riches profit not in the day of wrath: but
Isa. 30. 5 ashamed of a people that could not profit
30. 6 to a people (that) shall not profit (them)
44. 9 and their delectable things shall not pro.
47. 12 if so be thou shalt be able to profit, if so
48. 17 thy God which teacheth thee to profit, wh.
57. 12 and thy works; for they shall not profit
Jer. 2. 8 and walked after (things that) do not pr.
2. 11 their glory for (that which) doth not profit
7. 8 ye trust in lying words, that cannot profit
12. 13 put themselves to pain, (but) shall not pr.
23. 32 therefore they shall not profit this people
Hab. 2. 18 What profiteth the graven image that the

2. *To profit,* סָכַן *sakan.*
Job 34. 9 It profiteth a man nothing that he should

3. *To be equal, profitable, compared,* שָׁוָה *shavah.*
Job 33. 27 perverted (that which was) right, and it p.

4. *Profit,* ὄφελος *ophelos.*
Jas. 2. 14 What (doth it) profit, my brethren, tho.
2. 16 needful to the body; what (doth it) profit?

5. *To bear together, advantage,* συμφέρω *sumpherō.*
1 Co. 12. 7 is given to every man to profit withal

6. *To strike forward,* προκόπτω *prokoptō.*
Gal. 1. 14 profited in the Jews' religion above many

7. *To profit,* ὠφελέω *ōpheleō.*
Matt 15. 5 by whatsoever thou mightest be profited
16. 26 what is a man profited, if he shall gain the
Mark 7. 11 by whatsoever thou mightest be profited
8. 36 what shall it profit a man, if he shall gain
John 6. 63 flesh profiteth nothing: the words that
Rom. 2. 25 For circumcision verily profiteth, if thou
1 Co. 13. 3 have not charity, it profiteth me nothing
14. 6 what shall I profit you, except I shall sp.
Gal. 5. 2 if ye be circumcised, Christ shall profit
Heb. 4. 2 but the word preached did not profit them
13. 9 not with meats, which have not profited

8. *To be profitable,* εἰμὶ ὠφέλιμος *eimi ōphelimos.*
1 Ti. 4. 8 For bodily exercise profiteth little; but

PROFITABLE —
1. *What is over and above,* יִתְרוֹן *yithron.*
Eccl. 10. 10 more strength: but wisdom (is) profitable

2. *Very useful,* εὔχρηστος *euchrēstos.*
2 Ti. 4. 11 for he is profitable to me for the ministry
Phm. 11 unprofitable, but now profitable to thee

3. *Profitable,* ὠφέλιμος *ōphelimos.*
1 Ti. 4. 8 but godliness is profitable unto all things
2 Ti. 3. 16 and (is) profitable for doctrine, for reproof
Titus 3. 8 These things are good and profitable unto

PROFITABLE (for), to be —
1. *To make or give profit,* יָעַל *yaal,* 5.
Isa. 44. 10 graven image (that) is profitable for not.?

2. *To profit,* סָכַן *sakan.*
Job 22. 2 Can a man be profitable unto God, as he
22. 2 is wise may be profitable unto himself

3. *To prosper,* צָלֵחַ *tsaleach.*
Jer. 13. 7 girdle was marred, it was profitable for

4. *To bear together, advantage,* συμφέρω *sumpherō.*
Matt. 5. 29, 30 for it is profitable for thee that one of
Acts 20. 20 I kept back nothing that was profitable

PROFITING —
A striking forward, προκοπή *prokopē.*
1 Ti. 4. 15 that thy profiting may appear to all

PROFOUND, to be —
To make deep, עָמַק *amaq,* 5.
Hos. 5. 2 the revolters are profound to make slau.

PROGENITOR —
To conceive, הָרָה *harah.*
Gen. 49. 26 blessings of my progenitors unto the u.

PROGNOSTICATOR —
To know, be acquainted with, יָדַע *yada,* 5.
Isa. 47. 13 prognosticators, stand up and save thee

PROLONG, to —
1. *To make long, prolong,* אָרַךְ *arak,* 5.
Deut. 4. 26 ye shall not prolong (your) days upon it
4. 40 that thou mayest prolong (thy) days upon
5. 33 may prolong (your) days in the land which
11. 9 may prolong (your) days in the land which
17. 20 he may prolong (his) days in his kingdom
22. 7 and (that) thou mayest prolong (thy) days
30. 18 ye shall not prolong (your) days upon the
32. 47 through this thing ye shall prolong (your)
Job 6. 11 what (is) mine end, that I should prolong
Prov 28. 16 he that hateth covetousness shall prolong
Eccl. 7. 15 that prolongeth (his life) in his wickedn.
8. 13 neither shall he prolong (his) days, (which
Isa. 53. 10 he shall prolong (his) days, and the plea.

2. *To (cause to) add,* יָסַף *yasaph,* 5.
Psa. 61. 6 Thou wilt prolong the king's life; (and)
Prov 10. 27 The fear of the LORD prolongeth days: but

3. *To stretch out, incline to,* נָטָה *natah.*
Job 15. 29 neither shall he prolong the perfection

PROLONGED, to be —
1. *To be long,* אָרַךְ *arak.*
Eze. 12. 22 days are prolonged, and every vision fail?

2. *To make long,* אָרַךְ *arak,* 5.
Deut. 5. 16 days may be prolonged, and that it may
6. 2 life; and that thy days may be prolonged
Prov 28. 2 knowledge the state (thereof) shall be p.
Eccl. 8. 12 his (days) be prolonged, yet surely I know

3. *Length [in lives] was given,* אַרְכָה יְהִיבַת בְּ *[arekah].*
Dan. 7. 12 lives were prolonged for a season and t.

4. *To draw out,* מָשַׁךְ *mashak,* 2.
Isa. 13. 22 to come, and her days shall not be prolo.
Eze. 12. 25 it shall be no more prolonged; for in your
12. 28 There shall none of my words be prolon.

PROMISE —
1. *Saying,* אֹמֶר *omer.*
Psa. 77. 8 gone for ever? doth (his) promise fail for

2. *Word,* דָּבָר *dabar.*
1 Ki. 8. 56 not failed one word of all his good pr.
Neh. 5. 12 that they should do according to this pr.
5. 13 performeth not this promise, even thus
Psa. 105. 42 For he remembered his holy promise, (and)

3. *A promise,* ἐπαγγελία *epaggelia.*
Luke 24. 49 I send the promise of my Father upon y.
Acts 1. 4 wait for the promise of the Father, which
2. 33 having received of the Father the prom.
2. 39 For the promise is unto you, and to your
7. 17 But when the time of the promise drew
13. 23 God, according to (his) promise, raised un.
13. 32 the promise which was made unto the fa.
23. 21 ready, looking for a promise from thee
26. 6 am judged for the hope of the promise
Rom. 4. 13 For the promise, that he should be the
4. 14 void, and the promise made of none effect
4. 16 to the end the promise might be sure to
4. 20 staggered not at the promise of God thr.
9. 4 and the service (of God), and the promis.
9. 8 children of the promise are counted for
9. 9 For this (is) the word of promise, At this
15. 8 confirm the promises (made) unto the fa.
2 Co. 1. 20 For all the promises of God in him (are)
7. 1 Having therefore these promises, dearly
Gal. 3. 14 that we might receive the promise of the
3. 16 to Abraham and his seed were the prom.
3. 17 it should make the promise of none effect
3. 18 no more of promise..to Abraham by pro.
3. 21 (Is) the law then against the promises of
3. 22 promise by faith of Jesus Christ might be
3. 29 seed, and heirs according to the promise
4. 23 but he of the free woman (was) by prom.
4. 28 as Isaac was, are the children of promise
Eph. 1. 13 were sealed with that holy spirit of pro.
2. 12 strangers from the covenants of promise
3. 6 partakers of his promise in Christ by the
6. 2 which is the first commandment with p.
1 Ti. 4. 8 having promise of the life that now is, and
2 Ti. 1. 1 according to the promise of life which is
Heb. 4. 1 promise being left (us) of entering into
6. 12 through faith and patience inherit the p.
6. 15 patiently endured, he obtained the prom.
6. 17 unto the heirs of promise the immutabil.
7. 6 and blessed him that had the promises
8. 6 which was established upon better prom.
9. 15 might receive the promise of eternal inh.
10. 36 that, after..ye might receive the promise
11. 9 By faith he sojourned in the land of pro.
11. 9 the heirs with him of the same promise
11. 13 died in faith, not having received the pr.
11. 17 he that had received the promises offered
11. 33 obtained promises, stopped the mouths of
11. 39 through faith, received not the promise
2 Pe. 3. 4 Where is the promise of his coming? for
3. 9 The Lord is not slack concerning his pro.
1 Jo. 2. 25 this is the promise that he hath promised

4. *A promise,* ἐπάγγελμα *epaggelma.*
2 Pe. 1. 4 exceeding great and precious promises
3. 13 Nevertheless we, according to his promise

PROMISE, to (make) —

1. *To say,* אָמַר *amar.*

Num 14. 40 unto the place which the LORD hath pro.
2 Ki. 8. 19 promised him to give him alway a light
2 Ch. 21. 7 as he promised to give a light to him and
Neh. 9. 15 promisedst them that they should go in
9. 23 which thou hadst promised to their fathers
Esth. 4. 7 promised to pay to the king's treasuries

2. *To speak,* דָּבַר *dabar.*

Jer. 32. 42 all the good that I have promised them

3. *To speak,* דָּבַר *dabar,* 3.

Exod 12. 25 according as he hath promised, that ye
Deut 1. 11 and bless you, as he hath promised you!
6. 3 LORD God of thy fathers hath promised
9. 28 bring them into the land which he prom.
10. 9 according as the LORD thy God promised
12. 20 enlarge thy border, as he hath promised
15. 6 thy God blesseth thee, as he promised th.
19. 8 give thee all the land which he promised
23. 23 which thou hast promised with thy mouth
26. 18 peculiar people, as he hath promised thee
27. 3 LORD God of thy fathers hath promised
Josh. 9. 21 Let them live..as the princes had prom.
22. 4 hath given rest..as he promised them
23. 5 as the LORD your God hath promised unto
23. 10 fighteth for you, as he hath promised you
23. 15 which the LORD your God promised you
2 Sa. 7. 28 hast promised this goodness unto thy se.
1 Ki. 2. 24 hath made me an house, as he promised
5. 12 gave Solomon wisdom, as he promised h.
8. 20 sit on the throne..as the LORD promised
8. 24 that thou promisedst him: thou spakest
8. 25 that thou promisedst him, saying, There
8. 56 according to all that he promised: there
8. 56 which he promised by the hand of Moses
9. 5 as I promised to David thy father, saying
1 Ch. 17. 26 hast promised this goodness unto thy se.
2 Ch. 6. 10 set on the throne..as the LORD promised
6. 15 hast kept..that which thou hast promis.
6. 16 keep..that which thou hast promised h.
Jer. 33. 14 that good thing which I have promised

4. *To say publicly, profess,* ὁμολογέω *homologeō.*

Matt 14. 7 he promised with an oath to give her what

5. *Say out publicly,* ἐξομολογέομαι *exomologeomai.*

Luke 22. 6 [And he promised], and sought opportu.

6. *To profess, promise,* ἐπαγγέλλομαι *epaggellomai.*

Mark 14. 11 were glad, and promised to give him mo
Acts 7. 5 yet he promised that he would give it to
Rom. 4. 21 persuaded that what he had promised he
Gal. 3. 19 should come to whom the promise was
Titus 1. 2 which God..promised before the world
Heb. 6. 13 For when God made promise to Abraham
10. 23 wavering; for he (is) faithful that promised
11. 11 she judged him faithful who had promised
12. 26 now he hath promised, saying, Yet once
Jas. 1. 12 which the Lord hath promised to them t.
2. 5 kingdom which he hath promised to them
2 Pe. 2. 19 While they promise them liberty, they t.
1 Jo. 2. 25 this is the promise that he hath promised

PROMISE afore, to —

To profess or promise before, προεπαγγέλλομαι.

Rom. 1. 2 Which he had promised afore by his pr.

PROMISE life, to —

To give or promise life, חָיָה *chayah,* 5.

Eze. 13. 22 from his wicked way, by promising him l.

PROMOTE, to —

1. *To make great,* גָּדַל *gadal,* 3.

Esth. 3. 1 did king Ahasuerus promote Haman the
5. 11 wherein the king had promoted him, and

2. *To make heavy, weighty, honoured,* כָּבֵד *kabed,* 3.

Num 24. 11 I thought to promote thee unto great h.

3. *To cause to prosper,* צָלַח *tselach,* 5.

Dan. 3. 30 Then the king promoted Shadrach, Mesh.

4. *To make high,* רוּם *rum,* 3a.

Prov. 4. 8 Exalt her, and she shall promote thee; she

PROMOTE to honour, to —

To make heavy, weighty, honoured, כָּבֵד *kabed,* 3.

Num 22. 17 I will promote thee unto very great hon.
22. 37 not able indeed to promote thee to honour?

PROMOTED, to be —

To move, shake, נוּעַ *nua.*

Judg. 9. 9, 11, 13 and go to be promoted over the trees?

PROMOTION —

To make high, רוּם *rum,* 5.

Psa. 75. 6 For promotion (cometh) neither from the
Prov 3. 35 but shame shall be the promotion of fools

PRONOUNCE, to —

1. *To speak idly,* בָּטָה *batah,* 3.

Lev. 5. 4 swear, pronouncing with (his) lips to do
5. 4 that a man shall pronounce with an oath

2. *To speak,* דָּבַר *dabar,* 3.

Judg 12. 6 he could not frame to pronounce (it) right
Neh. 6. 12 he pronounced this prophecy against me
Jer. 11. 17 hath pronounced evil against thee, for the
16. 10 Wherefore hath the LORD pronounced all
18. 8 If that nation, against whom I have pro.
19. 15 all the evil that I have pronounced agai.
25. 13 all my words which I have pronounced
26. 13 repent him of the evil that he hath pron.
26. 19 evil which he had pronounced against th.?
34. 5 for I have pronounced the word, saith the
35. 17 all the evil that I have pronounced agai.
36. 7 fury that the LORD hath pronounced aga.
36. 31 evil that I have pronounced against them
40. 2 God hath pronounced this evil upon this

3. *To call,* קָרָא *qara.*

Jer. 36. 18 pronounced all these words unto me with

PROOF —

Proof, trial, δοκιμή *dokimē.*

2 Co. 2. 9 that I might know the proof of you, wh.
13. 3 Since ye seek a proof of Christ speaking
Phil 2. 22 But ye know the proof of him, that, as a

PROOF, infallible.

1. *A sure token,* τεκμήριον *tekmērion.*

Acts 1. 3 showed himself..by many infallible proo.

2. *A showing in, pointing out,* ἔνδειξις *endeixis.*

2 Co. 8. 24 show ye to them..the proof of your love, and

PROPER —

1. *Belonging to the city, well born,* ἀστεῖος *asteios.*

Heb. 11. 23 because they saw (he was) a proper child

2. *One's own,* ἴδιος *idios.*

Acts 1. 19 that field is called in their proper tongue
1 Co. 7. 7 every man hath his proper gift of God, one

PROPER good —

A peculiar treasure, סְגֻלָּה *segullah.*

1 Ch. 29. 3 I have of mine own proper good, of gold

PROPHECY —

1. *What is lifted up, a burden, message,* מַשָּׂא *massa.*

Prov 30. 1 words of Agur..(even) the prophecy: the
31. 1 the prophecy that his mother taught him

2. *Prophecy,* נְבוּאָה *nebuah.*

2 Ch. 9. 29 in the prophecy of Ahijah the Shilonite
15. 8 when Asa heard..the prophecy of Oded
Neh. 6. 12 that he pronounced this prophecy against

3. *A prophet,* נָבִיא *nabi.*

Dan. 9. 24 to seal up the vision and prophecy, and to

4. *Prophecy, public exposition,* προφητεία *prophēteia.*

Matt 13. 14 in them is fulfilled the prophecy of Esaias
Rom 12. 6 whether prophecy, (let us prophesy) acc.
1 Co. 12. 10 to another prophecy; to another discern.
13. 8 but whether (there be) prophecies, they
1 Ti. 1. 18 according to the prophecies which went
4. 14 which was given thee by prophecy, with
2 Pe. 1. 20 no prophecy of the scripture is of any
1. 21 For the prophecy came not in old time
Rev. 1. 3 they that hear the words of this prophecy
11. 6 it rain not in the days of their prophecy
19. 10 the testimony of Jesus is the spirit of pr.
22. 7 he that keepeth the sayings of the proph.
22. 10 Seal not the sayings of the prophecy of t.
22. 18 that heareth the words of the prophecy of
22. 19 from the words of the book of this proph.

5. *Prophetic,* προφητικός *prophētikos.*

2 Pe. 1. 19 We have also a more sure word of proph.

PROPHECY, (the gift of) —

Prophecy, προφητεία *prophēteia.*

1 Co. 13. 2 though I have (the gift of) prophecy, and

PROPHESY, to —

1. *To see (in vision),* חָזָה *chazah.*

Isa. 30. 10 Prophesy not unto us right things..prop.

2. *To prophesy, flow forth,* נָבָא *naba,* 2.

1 Sa. 10. 11 he prophesied among the prophets, then
1 Ki. 22. 12 all the prophets prophesied so, saying, Go
1 Ch. 25. 1 who should prophesy with harps, with
25. 2 which prophesied according to the order
25. 3 who prophesied with a harp, to give tha.
2 Ch. 18. 11 all the prophets prophesied so, saying, Go
Jer. 2. 8 prophesied by Baal, and walked after (t.
5. 31 prophesy falsely, and the priests bear rule
11. 21 Prophesy not in the name of the LORD, th.
14. 14 The prophets prophesy lies in my name: I
14. 15 concerning the prophets that prophesy in
14. 16 people to whom they prophesy shall be c.
19. 14 whither the LORD had sent him to proph.
20. 1 heard that Jeremiah prophesied these thi.
20. 6 friends, to whom thou hast prophesied l.
23. 16 words of the prophets that prophesy unto
23. 21 I have not spoken to them, yet they p.
23. 25 that prophesy lies in my name, saying, I
23. 26 in the heart of the prophets that prophe.
23. 32 against them that prophesy false dreams
25. 13 which Jeremiah hath prophesied against
25. 30 Therefore prophesy thou against them all
26. 9 Why hast thou prophesied in the name of
26. 11 for he hath prophesied against this city
26. 12 LORD sent me to prophesy against this h.
26. 18 Micah the Morasthite prophesied in the
26. 20 who prophesied against this city, and ag.
27. 10 For they prophesy a lie unto you, to rem.
27. 14 Ye shall not serve..for they prophesy a
27. 15 yet they prophesy a lie in my name; that
27. 15 and the prophets that prophesy unto you
27. 16 that prophesy..for they prophesy a lie un.
28. 6 perform thy words which thou hast pro.
28. 8 prophesied both against many countries
28. 9 The prophet which prophesieth of peace
29. 9 For they prophesy falsely unto you in my
29. 21 which prophesy a lie unto you in my na.
29. 31 Because that Shemaiah hath prophesied
32. 3 Wherefore dost thou prophesy, and say
Jer. 37. 19 Where (are) now your prophets which pr.
Eze. 4. 7 uncovered, and thou shalt prophesy aga.
6. 2 set thy face toward the mountains..and p.
11. 4 Therefore prophesy against them, proph.
11. 13 when I prophesied, that Pelatiah the son
12. 27 he prophesieth of the times (that are) far
13. 2 prophesy against the prophets..that pro.
13. 16 prophets of Israel, which prophesy conc.
13. 17 set thy face..and prophesy thou against
20. 46 prophesy against the forest of the south
21. 2 set thy face toward Jerusalem..and pro.
21. 9 Son of man, prophesy, and say, Thus sa.
21. 14 prophesy, and smite (thine) hands toget.
21. 28 thou, son of man, prophesy, and say, Th.
25. 2 Son of man, set thy face..and prophesy
28. 21 set thy face against Zidon, and prophesy
29. 2 prophesy against him, and against all E.
30. 2 prophesy and say, Thus saith the Lord G.
34. 2 prophesy against the shepherds..prophe.
35. 2 set thy face against mount Seir, and pro.
36. 1 prophesy unto the mountains of Israel
36. 3 Therefore prophesy and say, Thus saith
36. 6 Prophesy therefore concerning the land
37. 4 Prophesy upon these bones, and say unto
37. 7 So I prophesied..and as I prophesied, th.
37. 9 Prophesy unto the wind, prophesy, son of
37. 12 prophesy and say unto them, Thus saith
38. 2 set thy face against Gog..and prophesy
38. 14 prophesy and say unto Gog, Thus saith the
38. 17 which prophesied in those days (many) y.
39. 1 prophesy against Gog, and say, Thus saith
Joel 2. 28 sons and your daughters shall prophesy
Amos 2. 12 commanded the prophets, saying, Proph.
3. 8 Lord GOD hath spoken, who can but pro.?
7. 12 and there eat bread, and prophesy there
7. 13 But prophesy not again any more at Bet.
7. 15 LORD said unto me, Go, prophesy unto my
7. 16 Prophesy not against Israel, and drop not
Zech. 13. 3 when any shall yet prophesy, then his f.
13. 3 shall thrust him through when he proph.
13. 4 shall be ashamed..when he hath proph.

3. *To show self a prophet,* נָבָא *naba,* 7.

Num 11. 25 when the spirit rested..they prophesied
11. 26 spirit rested..and they prophesied in the c.
11. 27 Eldad and Medad do prophesy in the ca.
1 Sa. 10. 5 prophets coming down..and they shall p.
10. 6 thou shalt prophesy with them, and shalt
10. 10 prophets met him..and he prophesied am.
18. 10 and he prophesied in the midst of the h.
19. 21 they prophesied likewise..they prophes.
19. 23 went on and prophesied, until he came to
19. 20 messengers of Saul, and they also proph.
19. 24 stripped off his clothes also, and prophe.
1 Ki. 18. 29 they prophesied until the (time) of the o.
22. 8 for he doth not prophesy good concerning
22. 10 and all the prophets prophesied before th.
22. 18 Did I not tell thee that he would proph.
2 Ch. 18. 7 for he never prophesied good unto me, but
18. 9 and all the prophets prophesied before
18. 17 Did I not tell thee (that) he would not pr.
20. 37 prophesied against Jehoshaphat, saying
Jer. 14. 14 they prophesy unto you a false vision and
23. 13 they prophesied in Baal, and caused my
26. 20 there was also a man that prophesied in
Eze. 13. 17 daughters..which prophesy out of their
37. 10 So I prophesied, as he commanded me, and

4. *To prophesy,* נְבָא *neba,* 2.

Ezra 5. 1 prophesied unto the Jews that (were) in

5. *To cause to drop, let drop,* נָטַף *nataph,* 5.

Mic. 2. 6 Prophesy ye not, (say they to them that)
2. 6 shall not prophesy to them, (that) they
2. 11 I will prophesy unto thee of wine and of

6. *A prophet,* נָבִיא *nabi.*

Eze. 13. 2 say thou unto them that prophesy out of

7. *To prophesy, publicly expound,* προφητεύω *proph.*

Matt. 7. 22 have we not prophesied in thy name? and
11. 13 For all the prophets and the law prophe.
15. 7 hypocrites, well did Esaias prophesy of
26. 68 Prophesy unto us, thou Christ, Who is he
Mark 7. 6 Well hath Esaias prophesied of you hyp.
14. 65 say unto him, Prophesy: and the servants
Luke 1. 67 filled with the Holy Ghost, and prophesied
22. 64 saying, Prophesy, who is it that smote
John 11. 51 he prophesied that Jesus should die for
Acts 2. 17 sons and your daughters shall prophesy
2. 18 pour out in those days..and they shall p.
19. 6 and they spake with tongues, and proph.
21. 9 four daughters, virgins, which did proph.
1 Co. 11. 4 Every man praying or prophesying, having
11. 5 every woman that prayeth or prophesieth
13. 9 For we know in part, and we prophesy in
14. 1 but rather that ye may prophesy
14. 3 But he that prophesieth speaketh unto
14. 4 but he that prophesieth edifieth the chu.
14. 5 prophesied: for greater (is) he that prop.
14. 24 if all prophesy, and there come in one that
14. 31 For ye may all prophesy one by one, that
14. 39 covet to prophesy, and forbid not to speak
1 Pe. 1. 10 who prophesied of the grace (that should
Jude 14 prophesied of these, saying, Behold, the
Rev. 10. 11 Thou must prophesy again before many
11. 3 they shall prophesy a thousand two hund.

PROPHESYING —

1. *To prophesy,* נָבָא *naba,* 2.

1 Sa. 19. 20 saw the company of the prophets prophes.

2. *To show self a prophet,* נָבָא *naba,* 7.

1 Sa. 10. 13 when he had made an end of prophesying

3. *Prophecy*, נְבוּאָה *nebuah.*
Ezra 6. 14 prospered through the prophesying of H.

4. *Prophecy*, προφητεία *prophēteia.*
1 Co. 14. 6 or by knowledge, or by prophesying, or
14. 22 prophesying (serveth) not for them that
1 Th. 5. 20 Despise not prophesyings

PROPHET —

1. *A seer*, חֹזֶה *chozeh.*
Isa. 30. 10 Which say . to the prophets, Prophesy not

2. *A prophet*, נָבִיא *nabi.*
Gen. 20. 7 for he (is) a prophet, and he shall pray for
Exod 7. 1 and Aaron thy brother shall be thy proph.
Num 11. 29 that all the LORD'S people were prophets
12. 6 If there be a prophet among you, (I) the
Deut 13. 1 If there arise among you a prophet, or a
13. 3 not hearken unto the words of that prop.
13. 5 that prophet, or that dreamer of dreams
18. 15 God will raise up unto thee a prophet fr.
18. 18 I will raise them up a prophet from amo.
18. 20 the prophet which shall presume..that p
18. 22 When a prophet speaketh in the name of
18. 22 the prophet hath spoken it presumptuou.
34. 10 there arose not a prophet since in Israel
Judg. 6. 8 the LORD sent a prophet unto the children
1 Sa. 3. 20 established (to be) a prophet of the LORD
9. 9 a prophet was beforetime called a seer
10. 5 a company of prophets coming down from
10. 10 a company of prophets met him; and the
10. 11 behold, he prophesied among the proph.
10. 11, 12 (Is) Saul also among the prophets?
19. 20 prophets prophesying, and Samuel stand.
19. 24 they say, (Is) Saul also among the proph.
22. 5 the prophet Gad said unto David, Abide
28. 6 neither by dreams, nor by Urim, nor by p.
28. 15 answereth..neither by prophets, nor by
2 Sa. 7. 2 the king said unto Nathan the prophet, S.
12. 25 sent by the hand of Nathan the prophet
24. 11 word of the LORD came unto the prophet
1 Ki. 1. 8 the prophet, and Shimei, and Rei, and the
1. 10 the prophet, and Benaiah, and the mighty
1. 22 And, lo..Nathan the prophet also came in
1. 23 told the king..Behold Nathan the prophet
1. 32 the prophet, and Benaiah the son of Jeh.
1. 34, 38, 44, 45 the priest and Nathan the pro.
11. 29 the prophet Ahijah the Shilonite found
13. 11 there dwelt an old prophet in Beth-el, and
13. 18 I (am) a prophet also as thou (art); and an
13. 20, 26 the prophet that brought him back
13. 23 for the prophet whom he had brought ba.
13. 25 told..in the city where the old prophet d.
13. 29 the prophet took up the carcase of the man
13. 29 the old prophet came to the city, to mou.
14. 2 Ahijah the prophet, which told me that
14. 18 by the hand of his servant Ahijah the pr.
16. 7 also by the hand of the prophet Jehu the
16. 12 spake against Baasha by Jehu the prophet
18. 4 Jezebel cut off the prophets of the LORD
18. 4 Obadiah took an hundred prophets, and
18. 13 when Jezebel slew the prophets of the L.
18. 13 hid an hundred men of the LORD'S proph.
18. 19 the prophets of Baal four hundred and fi.
18. 19 the prophets of the groves four hundred
18. 20 gathered the prophets together unto m.
18. 22 I..a prophet of the LORD; but Baal's p.
18. 25 Elijah said unto the prophets of Baal
18. 36 the prophet came near, and said, LORD G.
18. 40 Take the prophets of Baal; let not one of
19. 1 had slain all the prophets with the sword
19. 10, 14 and slain thy prophets with the sword
19. 16 shalt thou anoint (to be) prophet in thy
20. 13 there came a prophet unto Ahab king of
20. 22 the prophet came to the king of Israel
20. 35 a certain man of the sons of the prophets
20. 38 the prophet departed, and waited for the
20. 41 discerned him that he (was) of the proph
22. 6 the king of Israel gathered the prophets
22. 7 not here a prophet of the LORD besides
22. 10 all the prophets prophesied before them
22. 12 the prophets prophesied so, saying, Go up
22. 13 the words of the prophets (declare) good
22. 22, 23 lying spirit in the mouth of..prophets
2 Ki 2. 3, 5 the sons of the prophets that (were) at
2. 7 of the sons of the prophets went, and st.
2. 15 when the sons of the prophets which (w.)
3. 11 not here a prophet of the LORD, that we
3. 13 the prophets of thy father, and to the p.
4. 1 of the wives of the sons of the prophets
4. 38 the sons of the prophets (were) sitting be.
4. 38 seethe pottage for the sons of the proph.
5. 3 (were) with the prophet that (is) in Sam.
5. 8 he shall know that there is a prophet in
5. 13 (if) the prophet had bid thee (do some) g.
5. 22 two young men of the sons of the prophets
6. 1 the sons of the prophets said unto Elisha
6. 12 Elisha, the prophet that (is) in Israel, tell.
9. 1 prophet called one of the children of the
9. 4 So..the prophet, went to Ramoth-gilead
9. 7 the blood of my servants the prophets, and
10. 19 call unto me all the prophets of Baal, all
14. 25 the prophet, which (was) of Gath-hepher
17. 13 by all the prophets, (and by) all the seers
17. 13 sent to you by my servants the prophets
17. 23 as he had said by all his servants the pr.
19. 2 to Isaiah the prophet, the son of Amoz
20. 1 the prophet Isaiah the son of Amoz came
20. 11 And Isaiah the prophet cried unto the L.
20. 14 Then came Isaiah the prophet unto king
21. 10 the LORD spake by his servants the prop.
23. 2 the prophets, and all the people, both sm.
23. 18 of the prophet that came out of Samaria
2 Ki. 24. 2 which he spake by his servants the proph.
1 Ch. 16. 22 Touch not..and do my prophets no harm
17. 1 David said to Nathan the prophet, Lo, I
29. 29 in the book of Nathan the prophet, and
2 Ch. 9. 29 in the book of Nathan the prophet, and
12. 5 Then came Shemaiah the prophet to Re.
12. 15 in the book of Shemaiah the prophet, and
13. 22 written in the story of the prophet Iddo
15. 8 heard..the prophecy of Oded the prophet
18. 5 the king..gathered together of prophets
18. 6 not here a prophet of the LORD besides
18. 9 all the prophets prophesied before them
18. 11 all the prophets prophesied so, saying
18. 12 the words of the prophets (declare) good
18. 21, 22 lying spirit in the mouth of..prophets
20. 20 believe his prophets, so shall ye prosper
21. 12 a writing to him from Elijah the prophet
24. 19 he sent prophets to them, to bring them
25. 15 he sent unto him a prophet, which said
25. 16 the prophet forbare, and said, I know th.
26. 22 did..the prophet, the son of Amoz, write
28. 9 But a prophet of the LORD was there, wh.
29. 25 Gad the king's seer, and Nathan the pro.
29. 25 the commandment of the LORD by his pr.
32. 20 the prophet Isaiah the son of Amoz, pra.
32. 32 in the vision of Isaiah the prophet, the son
35. 18 And..from the days of Samuel the proph.
36. 12 humbled not himself before..the prophet
36. 16 misused his prophets, until the wrath of
Ezra 9. 11 hast commanded by thy servants the pro.
Neh. 6. 7 prophets to preach of thee at Jerusalem
6. 14 prophets, that would have put me in fear
9. 26 thy prophets which testified against them
9. 30 testifiedst..by thy spirit in thy prophets
9. 32 on our prophets, and on our fathers, and
Psa. 51. *title.* the prophet came unto him, after he had
74. 9 (there is) no more any prophet: neither
105. 15 Touch not mine anointed, and do my pro.
Isa. 3. 2 the prophet, and the prudent, and the an.
9. 15 the prophet that teacheth lies, he (is) the
28. 7 the priest and the prophet have erred th.
29. 10 the prophets and your rulers, the seers
37. 2 unto Isaiah the prophet, the son of Amoz
38. 1 the prophet, the son of Amoz, came unto
39. 3 Then came Isaiah the prophet unto king
Jer. 1. 5 ordained thee a prophet unto the nations
2. 8 the prophets prophesied by Baal, and w.
2. 26 they..and their priests, and their proph.
2. 30 your own sword hath devoured your pr.
4. 9 And..at that day..the prophets shall w.
5. 13 the prophets shall become wind, and the
5. 31 The prophets prophesy falsely, and the p.
6. 13 from the prophet even unto the priest e.
7. 25 sent unto you all my servants the proph.
8. 1 the bones of the prophets, and the bones
8. 10 from the prophet even unto the priest e.
13. 13 the prophets, and all the inhabitants of
14. 13 the prophets say unto them, Ye shall not
14. 14 The prophets prophesy lies in my name
14. 15 the prophets that prophesy in my name
14. 15 By sword and famine shall those prophets
14. 18 the prophet and the priest go about into
18. 18 nor counsel..nor the word from the pro.
20. 2 Pashur smote Jeremiah the prophet, and
23. 9 Mine heart..is broken because of the pr.
23. 11 both prophet and priest are profane: yea
23. 13 I have seen folly in the prophets of Sam.
23. 14 I have seen also in the prophets of Jeru
23. 15 saith the LORD..concerning the prophets
23. 15 from the prophets of Jerusalem is profan.
23. 16 of the prophets that prophesy unto you
23. 21 I have not sent these prophets, yet they
23. 25 I have heard what the prophets said, that
23. 26 in the heart of the prophets that prophesy
23. 26 prophets of the deceit of their own heart
23. 28 The prophet that hath a dream, let him
23. 30, 31 I (am) against the prophets, saith the L.
23. 33 or the prophet, or a priest, shall ask thee
23. 34 the prophet, and the priest, and the peo.
23. 37 Thus shalt thou say to the prophet, What
25. 2 the prophet spake unto all the people of
25. 4 hath sent unto you all his servants the p.
26. 5 the prophets, whom I sent unto you, both
26. 7 So..the prophets and all the people heard
26. 8 the prophets and all the people took him
26. 11 Then spake the priests and the prophets
26. 16 said..unto the priests and to the prophets
27. 9 hearken not ye to your prophets, nor to
27. 14 the prophets that speak unto you, saying
27. 15 and the prophets that prophesy unto you
27. 16 of your prophets that prophesy unto you
27. 18 if they (be) prophets, and if the word of
28. 1 of Azur the prophet, which (was) of Gib.
28. 5 prophet Jeremiah said unto the prophet
28. 6 Even the prophet Jeremiah said, Amen
28. 8 The prophets that have been before me and
28. 9 The prophet which prophesieth of peace
28. 9 when the word of the prophet shall come
28. 9 (then) shall the prophet be known, that
28. 10 prophet took the yoke from off the proph.
28. 11 And the prophet Jeremiah went his way
28. 12 Hananiah the prophet had broken the y.
28. 12 from off the neck of the prophet Jeremiah
28. 15 Then said the prophet..unto..the proph.
28. 17 So Hananiah the prophet died the same
29. 1 the prophet sent from Jerusalem unto the
29. 1 and to the prophets, and to all the people
29. 8 Let not your prophets and your diviners
29. 15 hath raised us up prophets in Babylon
29. 19 which I sent..by my servants the proph.
29. 29 read..in the ears of Jeremiah the prophet
32. 2 the prophet was shut up in the court of the
Jer. 32. 32 their prophets, and the men of Judah, and
34. 6 the prophet spake all these words unto Z.
35. 15 I have sent..you all my servants the pro.
36. 8 all that Jeremiah the prophet commanded
36. 26 Baruch the scribe, and Jeremiah the pro.
37. 2 which he spake by the prophet Jeremiah
37. 3 And..the king sent..to the prophet Jere.
37. 6 came the word of the LORD unto the pro.
37. 13 he took Jeremiah the prophet, saying, Th.
37. 19 your prophets which prophesied unto you
38. 9 the prophet, whom they have cast into
38. 10 take up Jeremiah the prophet out of the
38. 14 took Jeremiah the prophet unto him into
42. 2 said unto Jeremiah the prophet, Let, we
42. 4 the prophet said unto them, I have heard
43. 6 the prophet, and Baruch the son of Ner.
44. 4 I sent unto you all my servants the proph.
45. 1 the prophet spake unto Baruch the son of
46. 1 which came to Jeremiah the prophet ag.
46. 13 that the LORD spake to Jeremiah the pr.
47. 1 that came to Jeremiah the prophet agai.
49. 34 that came to Jeremiah the prophet agai.
50. 1 the LORD spake..by Jeremiah the prophet
51. 59 the prophet commanded Seraiah the son
Lam. 2. 9 prophets also find no vision from the LORD
2. 14 Thy prophets have seen vain and foolish
2. 20 shall the priest and the prophet be slain
4. 13 For the sins of her prophets, (and) the ini.
Eze. 2. 5 that there hath been a prophet among th.
7. 26 then shall they seek a vision of the proph.
13. 2 the prophets of Israel that prophesy, and
13. 3 Woe unto the foolish prophets, that follow
13. 4 thy prophets are like the foxes in the de.
13. 9 upon the prophets that see vanity, and
13. 16 the prophets of Israel, which prophesy c.
14. 4 Every man..that..cometh to the prophet
14. 7 and cometh to a prophet to enquire of him
14. 9 if the prophet be deceived when he hath
14. 9 I the LORD have deceived that prophet
14. 10 the punishment of the prophet shall be
22. 25 a conspiracy of her prophets in the midst
22. 28 her prophets have daubed them with un.
33. 33 know that a prophet hath been among th.
38. 17 the prophets of Israel, which prophesied
Dan. 9. 2 the word..came to Jeremiah the prophet
9. 6 the prophets, which spake in thy name to
9. 10 laws, which he set before us by..the pro.
Hos. 4. 5 the prophet also shall fall with thee in
6. 5 Therefore have I hewed (them) by the p.
9. 7 the prophet (is) a fool, the spiritual man
9. 8 the prophet (is) a snare of a fowler in all
12. 10 I have also spoken by the prophets, and
12. 10 used similitudes, by the ministry of the p.
12. 13 by a prophet the LORD brought..by a pr.
Amos 2. 11 I raised up of your sons for prophets, and
2. 12 and commanded the prophets, saying
3. 7 he revealeth his secret unto..the proph.
7. 14 I (was) no prophet, neither (was) I a pro.
Mic. 3. 5 the prophets that make my people err
3. 6 the sun shall go down over the prophets
3. 11 the prophets thereof divine for money: yet
Hab. 1. 1 The burden which Habakkuk the proph.
3. 1 A prayer of Habakkuk the prophet upon
Zeph. 3. 4 Her prophets (are) light (and) treacherous
Hag. 1. 1, 3 word of the LORD by Haggai the proph.
1. 12 the words of Haggai the prophet, as the
2. 1, 10 word of the LORD by the prophet Ha.
Zech. 1. 1, 7 the word of the LORD unto..the proph.
1. 4 unto whom the former prophets have cr.
1. 5 and the prophets, do they live for ever?
1. 6 which I commanded my servants the pr.
7. 3 to speak..to the prophets, saying, Should
7. 7 LORD hath cried by the former prophets
7. 12 sent in his spirit by the former prophets
8. 9 these words by the mouth of the prophets
13. 2 the prophets and the unclean spirit to
13. 4 the prophets shall be ashamed every one
13. 5 I (am) no prophet, I (am) an husbandman
Mal. 4. 5 I will send you Elijah the prophet before

3. *A prophet*, נְבִיא *nebi.*
Ezra 5. 1 prophets, Haggai the prophet, and Zech.
5. 2 with them..the prophets of God helping
6. 14 the prophet and Zechariah the son of Id.

4. *To (cause to) drop*, נָטַף *nataph*, 5.
Mic. 2. 11 he shall even be the prophet of this peo.

5. *A prophet, public expounder*, προφήτης *prophētēs.*
Matt. 1. 22 fulfilled which was spoken..by the proph.
2. 5 of Judea: for thus it is written by the p.
2. 15 be fulfilled which was spoken..by the p.
2. 17 that which was spoken by Jeremy the p.
2. 23 be fulfilled which was spoken by the pr.
3. 3 this is he that was spoken of by the pro
4. 14 which was spoken by Esaias the prophet
5. 12 for so persecuted they the prophets wh.
5. 17 am come to destroy the law, or the proph.
7. 12 do..for this is the law and the prophets
8. 17 which was spoken by Esaias the prophet
10. 41 receiveth a prophet in..name of a proph.
10. 41 He..shall receive a prophet's reward; and
11. 9 A prophet? yea..and more than a proph
11. 13 the prophets and the law prophesied un.
12. 17 which was spoken by Esaias the prophet
12. 39 no sign..but the sign of the prophet [illegible]
13. 17 That many prophets and righteous (men)
13. 35 fulfilled which was spoken by the prophet
13. 57 A prophet is not without honour, save in
14. 5 because they counted him as a prophet
16. 4 unto it, but the sign of [the prophet] Jonas
16. 14 and others, Jeremias, or one of the proph.
21. 4 fulfilled which was spoken by the prophet

Matt21. 11 Jesus the prophet of Nazareth of Galilee
21. 26 we fear..for all hold John as a prophet
21. 46 But..because they took him for a prophet
22. 40 On these..hang all the law and the prop.
23. 29 ye build the tombs of the prophets, and
23. 30 been partakers..in the blood of the pro.
23. 31 children of them which killed the proph.
23. 34 I send unto you prophets, and wise men
23. 37 (thou)that killest the prophets and stonest
24. 15 desolation, spoken of by Daniel the pro.
26. 56 that the scriptures of the prophets might
27. 9 that which was spoken by Jeremy the p.
27. 35 [fulfilled which was spoken by the prop.]
Mark 1. 2 As it is written in [the prophets], Behold
6. 4 A prophet is not without honour, but in
6. 15 That it is a prophet, or as one of the pro.
8. 28 (say), Elias, and others, One of the proph.
11. 32 counted John, that he was a prophet in.
13. 14 [desolation, spoken of by Daniel the pro.]
Luke 1. 70 As he spake by the mouth of his holy pr.
1. 76 shalt be called the prophet of the Highest
3. 4 in the book of the words of Esaias the p.
4. 17 delivered unto him the book of the prop.
4. 24 No prophet is accepted in his own coun.
4. 27 lepers..in the time of Eliseus the prophet
6. 23 in the like..did their fathers unto the p.
7. 16 a great prophet is risen up among us; and
7. 26 A prophet? Yea..much more than a pro.
7. 28 not a greater [prophet] than John the B.
7. 39 This man, if he were a prophet, would h.
9. 8 that one of the old prophets was risen a.
9. 19 that one of the old prophets is risen again
10. 24 many prophets and kings have desired to
11. 29 no sign..but the sign of Jonas [the prop.]
11. 47 for ye build the sepulchres of the prophets
11. 49 I will send them prophets and apostles
11. 50 the blood of all the prophets, which was
13. 28 the prophets, in the kingdom of God, and
13. 33 be that a prophet perish out of Jerusalem
13. 34 which killest the prophets, and stonest t.
16. 16 The law and the prophets (were) until J.
16. 29 They have Moses and the prophets; let t.
16. 31 If they hear not Moses and the prophets
18. 31 all things that are written by the proph.
20. 6 they be persuaded that John was a proph.
24. 19 a prophet mighty in deed and word before
24 25 believe all that the prophets have spoken
24. 27 beginning at Moses and all the prophets
24. 44 and (in) the prophets, and (in) the Psalms
John 1. 21 Art thou that prophet? And he answered
1. 23 Make straight the way..said the prophet
1. 25 not..Christ, nor Elias, neither that prop.
1. 45 of whom Moses in the law, and the prop.
4. 19 saith..Sir, I perceive that thou art a pr.
4. 44 prophet hath no honour in his own coun.
6. 14 prophet that should come into the world
6. 45 It is written in the prophets, And they s.
7. 40 Many..said, Of a truth this is the prophet
7. 52 Search..for out of Galilee ariseth no pr.
8. 52 Abraham is dead, and the prophets, and
8. 53 Abraham, which is dead? and the proph.
9. 17 What sayest thou..He said, He is a pro.
12. 38 the saying of Esaias the prophet might
Acts 2. 16 that which was spoken by the prophet J.
2. 30 being a prophet, and knowing that God
3. 18 had showed by the mouth of all his pro.
3. 21 spoken by the mouth of all his holy pro.
3. 22 A prophet shall the Lord your God raise
3. 23 every soul, which will not hear that prop.
3. 24 the prophets from Samuel and those that
3. 25 Ye are the children of the prophets, and
7. 37 A prophet shall the Lord your God raise
7. 42 as it is written in the book of the proph.
7. 48 Howbeit the most High..as saith the pro.
7. 52 Which of the prophets have not your fa.
8. 28 sitting in his chariot read Esaias the pr.
8. 30 heard him read the prophet Esaias, and
8. 34 of whom speaketh the prophet this? of h.
10. 43 To him give all the prophets witness, that
11. 27 these days came prophets from Jerusalem
13. 1 was at Antioch certain prophets and tea.
13. 15 after the reading of the law and the prop.
13. 20 he gave..judges..until Samuel the prop.
13. 27 the prophets which are read every sabb.
13. 40 that..which is spoken of in the prophets
15. 15 And to this agree the words of the proph.
15. 32 being prophets also themselves, exhorted
21. 10 from Judea a certain prophet, named A.
24. 14 written in the law and in the prophets
26. 22 than those which the prophets and Moses
26. 27 believest thou the prophets? I know that
28. 23 out of the law of Moses, and (out of) the p.
28. 25 Well spake the Holy Ghost by..the prop.
Rom. 1. 2 by his prophets in the holy Scriptures
3. 21 being witnessed by the law and the prop.
11. 3 they have killed thy prophets, and digged
1 Co. 12. 28 secondarily prophets, thirdly teachers
12. 29 all apostles?..all prophets?..all teachers?
14. 29 Let the prophets speak two or three, and
14. 32 spirits of the prophets..subject to the pr.
14. 37 If any man think himself to be a prophet
Eph. 2. 20 the foundation of the apostles and proph.
3. 5 revealed unto his holy apostles and prop.
4. 11 some, prophets; and some, evangelists
1 Th. 2. 15 killed the Lord Jesus and their own pro.
Titus 1. 12 a prophet of their own, said, The Cretians
Heb. 1. 1 God..spake..unto the fathers by the pro.
11. 32 David also, and Samuel, and (of) the pro.
Jas. 5. 10 the prophets, who have spoken in the name
1 Pe. 1. 10 the prophets have enquired and searched
2 Pe. 2. 16 dumb ass..forbade the madness of the p.
3. 2 which were spoken before by the holy p.

Rev. 10. 7 hath declared to his servants the proph.
11. 10 two prophets tormented them that dwelt
11. 18 give reward unto thy servants the proph.
16. 6 have shed the blood of saints and proph.
18. 20 heaven, and (ye) holy apostles and proph.
18. 24 in her was found the blood of prophets
22. 6 the Lord God of the holy prophets sent
22. 9 of thy brethren the prophets, and of them

6. *Prophetic*, προφητικός *prophētikos*.
Rom. 16. 26 But now..by the scriptures of the proph.

PROPHET, to make self a —

To show self a prophet, נָבָא *naba*, 7.
Jer. 29. 26 (that is) mad, and maketh himself a pro.
29. 27 which maketh himself a prophet to you?

PROPHET, false —

A false prophet, ψευδοπροφήτης *pseudoprophētēs*.
Matt. 7. 15 Beware of false prophets, which come to
24. 11 many false prophets shall rise, and shall
24. 24 there shall arise false Christs, and false p.
Mark13. 22 false prophets shall rise, and shall show
Luke 6. 26 for so did their fathers to the false proph.
Acts 13. 6 a false prophet, a Jew, whose name (was)
2 Pe. 2. 1 were false prophets also among the peo.
1 Jo. 4. 1 false prophets are gone out into the world
Rev. 16. 13 and out of the mouth of the false prophet
19. 20 the false prophet that wrought miracles
20. 10 where the beast and the false prophet

PROPHETESS —

1. *A prophetess, female preacher*, נְבִיאָה *nebiah*.
Exod15. 20 Miriam the prophetess, the sister of Aar.
Judg. 4. 4 Deborah, a prophetess, the wife of Lapid.
2 Ki.22. 14 the prophetess, the wife of Shallum the
2 Ch.34. 22 Huldah the prophetess, the wife of Shal.
Neh. 6. 14 on the prophetess Noadiah, and the rest
Isa. 8. 3 I went unto the prophetess; and she co.

2. *A prophetess, female preacher*, προφῆτις *proph.*
Luke 2. 36 Anna, a prophetess, the daughter of Ph.
Rev. 2. 20 Jezebel, which calleth herself a prophet.

PROPITIATION —

1. *What appeases, propitiates*, ἱλασμός *hilasmos*.
1 Jo. 2. 2 he is the propitiation for our sins; and not
4. 10 his Son (to be) the propitiation for our s.

2. *Place of propitiation*, ἱλαστήριον *hilastērion*.
Rom. 3. 25 a propitiation through faith in his blood

PROPORTION —

1. *Void or open space*, מַעַר *maar*.
1 Ki. 7. 36 according to the proportion of every one

2. *Array*, עֵרֶךְ *erek*.
Job 41. 12 nor his power, nor his comely proportion

3. *Proportion, equality*, ἀναλογία *analogia*.
Rom12. 6 (let..) according to the proportion of faith

PROSELYTE —

Proselyte, one who comes toward, προσήλυτος *pro.*
Matt23. 15 compass sea and land to make one prose.
Acts 2. 10 and strangers of Rome, Jews and prosel.
6. 5 Parmenas, and Nicolas a proselyte of A.
13. 43 religious proselytes followed Paul and B.

PROSPECT —

Face, פָּנִים *panim*.
Eze. 40. 44 and their prospect (was) toward the south
40. 44 one..(having) the prospect toward the n.
40. 45, 46 chamber, whose prospect (is) toward
42. 15 gate whose prospect (is) toward the east
43. 4 gate whose prospect (is) toward the east

PROSPER, to —

1. *To go on*, הָלַךְ *halak*.
Judg. 4. 24 Israel prospered, and prevailed against

2. *To be or go right*, כָּשֵׁר *kasher*.
Eccl. 11. 6 for thou knowest not whether shall pro.

3. *To cause to prosper*, צְלַח *tselach*, 5.
Ezra 5. 8 this work goeth fast on, and prospereth
6. 14 prospered through the prophesying of H.
Dan. 6. 28 So this Daniel prospered in the reign of

4. *To go on prosperously*, צָלֵחַ *tsaleach*.
Num14. 41 ye transgress..but it shall not prosper
Isa. 53. 10 pleasure of the LORD shall prosper in his
54. 17 No weapon..formed against thee shall p.
Jer. 12. 1 Wherefore doth the way of the wicked p.?
22. 30 a man (that) shall not prosper in his days
22. 30 no man of his seed shall prosper, sitting
Eze. 16. 13 and thou didst prosper into a kingdom
17. 9 Thus saith the Lord GOD; Shall it prosper?
17. 10 Yea, behold, (being) planted, shall it pr.?
17. 15 Shall he prosper? shall he escape that do.
Dan. 11. 27 but it shall not prosper: for yet the end

5. *To (cause to) go on prosperously*, צָלֵחַ *tsaleach*, 5.
Gen. 24. 40 will send his angel with thee, and prosper
24. 42 if now thou do prosper my way which I
24. 56 seeing the LORD hath prospered my way
Deut 28. 29 thou shalt not prosper in thy ways: and
1 Ki.22. 12 Go up to Ramoth-gilead, and prosper: for
22. 15 Go, and prosper: for the LORD shall de.
1 Ch.22. 11 prosper thou, and build the house of the
22. 13 Then shalt thou prosper, if thou takest
29. 23 Solomon sat on the throne..and prospered
2 Ch.13. 12 fight ye not..for ye shall not prosper
14. 7 rest on every side. So they built and pr.
18. 11 Go up to Ramoth-gilead, and prosper; for
18. 14 Go ye up, and prosper, and they shall be
20. 20 believe his prophets, so shall ye prosper

2 Ch. 24. 20 Why transgress ye..that ye cannot pro.?
31. 21 he did (it) with all his heart, and prospered
32. 30 And Hezekiah prospered in all his works
Neh. 1. 11 prosper, I pray thee, thy servant this day
2. 20 will prosper us; therefore we his servants
Psa. 1. 3 and whatsoever he doeth shall prosper
37. 7 fret not thyself because of him who pros.
Prov 28. 13 He that covereth his sins shall not prosper
Isa. 55. 11 shall prosper (in the thing) whereto I sent
Jer. 2. 37 LORD hath rejected..thou shalt not pros.
5. 28 judge not the cause..yet they prosper; and
32. 5 though ye fight..ye shall not prosper
Dan. 8. 12 cast down..and it practised, and prospered
8. 24 shall prosper, and practise, and shall de.
11. 36 shall prosper till the indignation be acc.

6. *To cause to act wisely*, שָׂכַל *sakal*, 5.
Deut29. 9 do them, that ye may prosper in all that
Josh. 1. 7 mayest prosper whithersoever thou goest
1 Ki. 2. 3 mayest prosper in all that thou doest, and
2 Ki. 18. 7 he prospered withersoever he went forth
Prov 17. 8 whithersoever it turneth, it prospereth
Jer. 10. 21 therefore they shall not prosper, and all
20. 11 for they shall not prosper: (their) everla.
23. 5 a king shall reign and prosper, and shall

7. *To be at rest*, שָׁלָו *shalav*.
Job 12. 6 tabernacles of robbers prosper, and they
Psa. 122. 6 peace of Jerusalem: they shall prosper
Lam. 1. 5 her enemies prosper; for the LORD hath

8. *Peace, completeness*, שָׁלוֹם *shalom*.
2 Sa. 11. 7 how the people did, and how the war p.

9. *Safe, at ease, at rest*, שָׁלֵו, שָׁלֵיו *shalev*.
Psa. 73. 12 ungodly, who prosper in the world; they

10. *To be complete, finished, at peace*, שָׁלַם *shalam*.
Job 9. 4 hardened (himself) against him, and..p.?

11. *To have a good journey, go on well*, εὐοδόομαι.
1 Co. 16. 2 lay by him in store, as (God) hath prosp.
3 John 2 thou mayest prosper..even as thy soul p.

PROSPER, to cause or make to —

To cause to prosper or go on, צָלֵחַ *tsaleach*, 5.
Gen. 39. 3 made all that he did to prosper in his h.
39. 23 which he did, the LORD made (it) to pros.
2 Ch.26. 5 sought the LORD, God made him to pros.
Dan. 8. 25 he shall cause craft to prosper in his hand

PROSPERITY —

1. *Good*, טוֹב *tob*.
Deut 23. 6 Thou shalt not seek..their prosperity all
1 Ki. 10. 7 prosperity exceedeth the fame which I h.
Job 36. 11 they shall spend their days in prosperity
Eccl. 7. 14 In the day of prosperity be joyful, but in
Lam. 3. 17 hast removed my soul..I forgat prosperity
Zech. 1. 17 My cities through prosperity shall yet be

2. *Rest, ease, security*, שָׁלֵו *shelev*.
Psa. 30. 6 in my prosperity I said, I shall never be

3. *Safe, at ease, at rest*, שָׁלֵו *shalev*.
Zech. 7. 7 when Jerusalem was..in prosperity, and

4. *Rest, ease, security*, שַׁלְוָה *shalvah*.
Psa. 122. 7 Peace be within thy walls, (and) prosper.
Prov. 1. 32 and the prosperity of fools shall destroy
Jer. 22. 21 I spake unto thee in thy prosperity; (but)

5. *Peace, completeness*, שָׁלוֹם *shalom*.
Job 15. 21 in prosperity the destroyer shall come u.
Psa. 35. 27 which hath pleasure in the prosperity of
73. 3 (when) I saw the prosperity of the wicked
Jer. 33. 9 for all the prosperity, that I procure unto

PROSPERITY, to send —

To cause to prosper, צָלֵחַ *tsaleach*, 5.
Psa. 118. 25 O LORD, I beseech thee, send now prosp.

PROSPEROUS, PROSPEROUSLY, to make —

1. *To prosper*, צָלֵחַ *tsaleach*.
Psa. 45. 4 in thy majesty ride prosperously, because

2. *To cause to prosper*, צָלֵחַ *tsaleach*, 5.
Gen. 24. 21 had made his journey prosperous or not
39. 2 he was a prosperous man; and he was in
Josh. 1. 8 then thou shalt make thy way prosperous
Judg18. 5 may know whether our way..shall be pr.
2 Ch. 7. 11 and in his own house, he prosperously eff.
Isa. 48. 15 brought him, and he shall make his way p.

3. *To finish, complete*, שָׁלַם *shalam*, 3.
Job 8. 6 surely..make the habitation..prosperous

4. *Peace, completeness*, שָׁלוֹם *shalom*.
Zech. 8. 12 For the seed (shall be) prosperous; the

PROSTITUTE, to —

To pierce, pollute, make common, חָלַל *chalal*, 3.
Lev. 19. 29 Do not prostitute thy daughter, to cause

PROTECTION —

Hiding, secrecy, סִתְרָה *sithrah*.
Deut 32. 38 rise up and help you, (and) be your prot.

PROTEST by, I —

Yea, (*adv. of affirmation or adjuring*), νή *nē*.
1 Co. 15. 31 I protest by your rejoicing which I have

PROTEST (earnestly), to —

To protest, (*cause to testify*), עוּד *ud*, 5.
Gen. 43. 3 The man did solemnly protest unto us, s.
1 Sa. 8. 9 howbeit yet protest solemnly unto..and
1 Ki. 2. 42 protested unto thee, saying, Know for a
Jer. 11. 7 For I earnestly protested unto your fath.
11. 7 rising early and protesting, saying, Obey
Zech. 3. 6 angel of the LORD protested unto Joshua

PROUD (thing, most, proudly) —

1. *Gay, proud,* גֵּא *ge.*
Isa. 16. 6 he (is) very proud: (even) of his haughti.

2. *Proud, gay,* גֵּאֶה *geeh.*
Job 40. 11 behold every one (that is) proud, and ab.
40. 12 Look on every one (that is) proud, (and)
Psa. 94. 2 Lift up thyself..render a reward to the p.
140. 5 proud have hid a snare for me, and cords
Prov 15. 25 The LORD will destroy the house of the p.
16. 19 better..than to divide the spoil with the p.
Isa. 2. 12 upon every (one that is) proud and lofty
Jer. 48. 29 he is exceeding proud, his loftiness, and

2a. *Proud,* גאיונים *gwayonim* [V.L. גְּאֵי יוֹנִים], Ps. 123. 4.

3. *Pride, rising, excellency,* גָּאוֹן *gaon.*
Job 38. 11 and here shall thy proud waves be stayed?

4. *Pride, rising, excellency,* גֵּאוּת *geuth.*
Psa. 17. 10 with their mouth they speak proudly

5. *To be or become proud, haughty, high,* גָּבַהּ *gabah.*
Prov 16. 5 Every one (that is) proud in heart (is) an
Eccl. 7. 8 patient in spirit (is) better than the proud

6. *High, haughty,* גָּבֹהַּ, גָּבֹהַּ *gaboah.*
1 Sa. 2. 3 Talk no more so exceeding proudly; let
Psa. 138. 6 but the proud he knoweth afar off

7. *Proud,* זֵד *zed.*
Psa. 86. 14 O God, the proud are risen against me, and
119. 21 Thou hast rebuked the proud (that are)
119. 51 The proud have had me greatly in derision
119. 69 The proud have forged a lie against me
119. 78 Let the proud be ashamed; for they dealt
119. 85 The proud have digged pits for me, which
119. 122 Be surety..let not the proud oppress me
Prov 21. 24 Proud (and) haughty scorner (is) his name
Isa. 13. 11 will cause the arrogancy of the proud to
Jer. 43. 2 all the proud men, saying unto Jeremiah
Mal. 3. 15 now we call the proud happy; yea, they
4. 1 all the proud, yea, and all that do wick.

8. *Pride, presumption, proud one,* זָדוֹן *zadon.*
Prov 21. 24 (is) his name who dealeth in proud wrath
Jer. 50. 31 I (am) against thee, (O thou) most proud
50. 32 most proud shall stumble and fall, and n.

9. *Great,* גָּדוֹל *gadol.*
Psa. 12. 3 (and) the tongue that speaketh proud th.

10. *Pride, rising, excellency,* גַּאֲוָה *gaavah.*
Psa. 31. 18 which speak grievous things proudly and
31. 23 and plentifully rewardeth the proud doer

11. *Proud,* זֵידוֹן *zedon.*
Psa. 124. 5 Then the proud waters had gone over our

12. *Haughty,* יָהִיר *yahir.*
Hab. 2. 5 a proud man, neither keepeth at home

13. *To oppress, break,* יָנָה *yanah.*
Psa. 123. 4 filled..with the contempt of the proud

14. *Breadth, width, pride,* רַהַב *rahab.*
Job 9. 13 the proud helpers do stoop under him
26. 12 by his understanding he smiteth..the p.

15. *Broad, wide, proud,* רָהָב *rahab.*
Psa. 40. 4 respecteth not the proud, nor such as turn

16. *To be high,* רוּם *rum.*
Prov 6. 17 A proud look, a lying tongue and hands

17. *Broad, wide, proud,* רָחָב *rachab.*
Psa. 101. 5 him that hath an high look and a proud
Prov 21. 4 An high look, and a proud heart, (and) the
28. 25 He that is of a proud heart stirreth up s.

18. *Exceeding proud,* ὑπερήφανος *huperēphanos.*
Luke 1. 51 he hath scattered the proud in the imag.
Rom. 1. 30 haters of God, despiteful, proud, boasters
2 Ti. 3. 2 For men shall be..proud, blasphemers
Jas. 4. 6 God resisteth the proud, but giveth grace
1 Pe. 5. 5 for God resisteth the proud, and giveth

PROUD, to be —

1. *To be high or haughty,* גָּבַהּ *gabah.*
Jer. 13. 15 Hear ye, and give ear; be not proud: for

2. *To be proud,* זוּד, זִיד *zud, zid.*
Jer. 50. 29 for she hath been proud against the LORD

3. *To be puffed up,* τυφόομαι *tuphoomai.*
1 Ti. 6. 4 He is proud, knowing nothing, but doting

PROUDLY, to deal, behave self, have spoken —

1. *To be proud,* זוּד *zud.*
Exod 18. 11 for in the thing wherein they dealt proud.

2. *To act proudly,* זוּד *zud,* 5.
Neh. 9. 10 for thou knewest that they dealt proudly
9. 16 But they and our fathers dealt proudly
9. 29 yet they dealt proudly, and hearkened

3. *To make great the mouth,* גָּדַל פֶּה [*gadal,* 5].
Obad. 12 neither shouldest thou have spoken pro.

4. *To stir against,* רָהַב *rahab.*
Isa. 3. 5 child shall behave himself proudly agai.

PROVE, to —

1. *To try, prove, test,* בָּחַן *bachan.*
Psa. 17. 3 Thou hast proved mine heart; thou hast
66. 10 For thou, O God, hast proved us: thou
81. 7 I proved thee at the waters of Meribah
95. 9 When your fathers tempted me, proved
Mal. 3. 10 prove me now herewith, saith the LORD

2. *To try, prove,* נָסָה *nasah,* 3.
Exod 15. 25 an ordinance, and there he proved them
16. 4 may prove them, whether they will walk
Exod 20. 20 God is come to prove you, and that his f.
Deut. 8. 2 to prove thee, to know what (was) in thi.
8. 16 that he might prove thee, to do thee good
13. 3 for the LORD your God proveth you, to k.
33. 8 whom thou didst prove at Massah, (and
Judg. 2. 22 That through them I may prove Israel
3. 1 which the LORD left, to prove Israel by t.
3. 4 they were to prove Israel by them, to kn.
6. 39 let me prove, I pray thee, but this once
1 Sa. 17. 39 he assayed to go; for he had not proved
17. 39 for I have not proved (them). And David
1 Ki. 10. 1 she came to prove him with hard quest.
2 Ch. 9. 1 she came to prove Solomon with hard qu.
Psa. 26. 2 Examine me, O LORD, and prove me; try
Eccl. 2. 1 Go to now, I will prove thee with mirth
7. 23 All this have I proved by wisdom: I said
Dan. 1. 12 Prove thy servants, I beseech thee, ten d.
1. 14 So he consented..and proved them ten

3. *To show off,* ἀποδείκνυμι *apodeiknumi.*
Acts 25. 7 complaints..which they could not prove

4. *To try, prove,* δοκιμάζω *dokimazō.*
Luke 14. 19 I go to prove them: I pray thee have me
Rom. 12. 2 that ye may prove what (is) that good, and
2 Co. 8. 8 and to prove the sincerity of your love
8. 22 whom we have oftentimes proved diligent
13. 5 prove your own selves. Know ye not your
Gal. 6. 4 let every man prove his own work, and
Eph. 5. 10 Proving what is acceptable unto the Lord
1 Th. 5. 21 Prove all things: hold fast that which is
1 Ti. 3. 10 these also first be proved; then let them
Heb. 3. 9 [When your fathers tempted me, proved]

5. *To set alongside, prove, demonstrate,* παρίστημι.
Acts 24. 13 Neither can they prove the things where.

6. *To attempt, try, put to the proof,* πειράζω *peirazō.*
John 6. 6 this he said to prove him: for he himself

7. *To cause to go up together, construct,* συμβιβάζω.
Acts 9. 22 confounded the Jews..proving that this

PROVE before, to —

To accuse before or first, προαιτιάομαι *proaitiaomai.*
Rom. 3. 9 for we have before proved both Jews and

PROVED, to be —

To be tried, proved, tested, בָּחַן *bachan,* 2.
Gen. 42. 15 Hereby ye shall be proved: By the life of
42. 16 that your words may be proved, whether

PROVENDER —

1. *Provender, mixed food,* בְּלִיל *belil.*
Isa. 30. 24 the young asses..shall eat clean proven.

2. *Fodder, provender,* מִסְפּוֹא *mispo.*
Gen. 24. 25 We have both straw and provender enou.
24. 32 gave straw and provender for the camels
42. 27 to give his ass provender in the inn, he e.
43. 24 their feet; and he gave their asses prov.
Judg 19. 19 Yet there is both straw and provender

PROVENDER, to give —

To mix, mingle, בָּלַל *balal.*
Judg 19. 21 gave provender unto the asses: and they

PROVERB —

1. *Acute saying, hidden thing,* חִידָה *chidah.*
Hab. 2. 6 take up..a taunting proverb against him

2. *A ruling saying, proverb, similitude,* מָשָׁל *mashal.*
Deut 28. 37 thou shalt become..a proverb, and a by
1 Sa. 10. 12 Therefore it became a proverb, (Is) Saul
24. 13 As saith the proverb of the ancients, Wic.
1 Ki. 4. 32 And he spake three thousand proverbs
9. 7 Israel shall be a proverb and a by word
2 Ch. 7. 20 make it (to be) a proverb and a by word
Psa. 69. 11 made sackcloth..and I became a proverb
Prov. 1. 1 proverbs of Solomon the son of David, k.
1. 6 To understand a proverb, and the interp.
10. 1 The proverbs of Solomon. A wise son ma.
25. 1 These (are) also proverbs of Solomon, w.
Eccl. 12. 9 sought out, (and) set in order many prov.
Isa. 14. 4 That thou shalt take up this proverb agai.
Jer. 24. 9 a proverb, a taunt and a curse, in all pla.
Eze. 12. 22 what (is) that proverb (that) ye have in the
12. 23 I will make this proverb to cease, and t.
14. 8 and will make him a sign and a proverb
18. 2 What mean ye, that ye use this proverb
18. 3 have (occasion) any more to use this pro.

3. *Parable, comparison, similitude,* παραβολή *par.*
Luke 4. 23 Ye will surely say unto me this proverb

4. *Proverb, obscure saying,* παροιμία *paroimia.*
John 16. 25 things have I spoken unto you in proverbs
16. 25 shall no more speak unto you in proverbs
16. 29 speakest thou plainly, and speakest no p.
2 Pe. 2. 22 according to the true proverb, The dog

PROVERB, to speak or use as a —

To use a similitude or ruling saying, מָשַׁל *mashal.*
Num 21. 27 Wherefore they that speak in proverbs say
Eze. 12. 23 they shall no more use it as a proverb in
16. 44 one that useth proverbs shall use (this) p.

PROVIDE (for) to —

1. *To see, look after,* חָזָה *chazah.*
Exod 18. 21 Moreover thou shalt provide out of all the

2. *To prepare,* כּוּן *kun,* 5.
2 Ch. 2. 7 cunning men..whom D. my father did p.
Job 38. 41 Who provideth for the raven his food? w.
Psa. 65. 9 preparest them corn..thou hast so prov.
78. 20 can he give bread also? can he provide fl.
Prov. 6. 8 Provideth her meat in the summer, (and)

3. *To do, make,* עָשָׂה *asah.*
Gen. 30. 30 now when shall I provide for mine own h.
2 Ch. 32. 29 Moreover he provided him cities, and po.

4. *To see, look after,* רָאָה *raah.*
Gen. 22. 8 God will provide himself a lamb for a bu.
Deut 33. 21 provided the first part for himself, because
1 Sa. 16. 1 I have provided me a king among his sons
16. 17 Provide me now a man that can play well

5. *To make ready,* ἑτοιμάζω *hetoimazō.*
Luke 12. 20 those things be which thou hast provided?

6. *To acquire, prepare, possess,* κτάομαι *ktaomai.*
Matt 10. 9 Provide neither gold, nor silver, nor brass

7. *To set alongside,* παρίστημι *paristēmi.*
Acts 23. 24 provide (them) beasts, that they may set

8. *To do, make,* ποιέω *poieō.*
Luke 12. 33 provide yourselves bags which wax not old

9. *To look before or forward,* προβλέπω *problepō.*
Heb. 11. 40 God having provided some better thing

10. *To know or think beforehand,* προνοέω *pronoeō.*
Rom. 12. 17 Provide things honest in the sight of all
2 Co. 8. 21 Providing for honest things, not only in
1 Ti. 5. 8 But if any provide not for his own, and

PROVIDENCE —

Forethought, πρόνοια *pronoia.*
Acts 24. 2 done unto this nation by thy providence

PROVINCE —

1. *Jurisdiction,* מְדִינָה *medinah.*
1 Ki. 20. 14, 15, 17, 19 men of the princes of the prov.
Ezra 2. 1 these (are) the children of the province
4. 15 hurtful unto kings and provinces, and that
5. 8 went into the province of Judea, to the h.
6. 2 in the palace that (is) in the province of
7. 16 canst find in all the province of Babylon
Neh. 1. 3 left of the captivity there in the province
7. 6 These (are) the children of the province, th.
11. 3 Now these (are) the chief of the province
Esth. 1. 1 an hundred and seven and twenty provin.
1. 3 nobles and princes of the provinces, (be.)
1. 16 people that (are) in all the provinces of
1. 22 into all the king's provinces, into every pr.
2. 3 appoint officers in all the provinces of his
2. 18 made a release to the provinces, and gave
3. 8 dispersed among the people in all the pr.
3. 12 governors that (were) over every province
3. 12 to the rulers of every people of every pro.
3. 13 sent by posts into all the king's provinces
3. 14 commandment to be given in every provin.
4. 3 in every province, whithersoever the ki.
4. 11 people of the king's provinces, do know
8. 5 Jews which (are) in all the king's provin.
8. 9 deputies and rulers of the provinces whi.
8. 9 provinces, unto every province according
8. 11 all the power of the people and province
8. 12 Upon one day, in all the provinces of king
8. 13 commandment to be given in every prov.
8. 17 in every province, and in every city, whi.
9. 2 throughout all the provinces of the king
9. 3 rulers of the provinces, and the lieutene.
9. 4 fame went out throughout all the provin.
9. 12 have they done in the rest of the king's p.
9. 16 other Jews that (were) in the king's pro.
9. 20 Jews that (were) in all the provinces of
9. 28 kept throughout every..province, and
9. 30 to the hundred twenty and seven prov.
Eccl. 2. 8 peculiar treasure of kings and of the pr.
5. 8 perverting of..justice in a province, ma.
Lam. 1. 1 princess among the provinces, (how) is
Eze. 19. 8 on every side from the provinces, and sp.
Dan. 2. 48 made him ruler over the whole province
2. 49 over the affairs of the province of Babyl.
3. 1 in the plain of Dura, in the province of B.
3. 2 gather together..all the rulers of the p.
3. 3 all the rulers of the provinces, were gat.
3. 12 hast set over the affairs of the province
3. 30 king promoted Shadrach..in the province
8. 2 palace, which (is) in the province of Elam
11. 24 even upon the fattest places of the prov.

2. *What is ruled over, a province, district,* ἐπαρχία.
Acts 23. 34 he asked of what province he was. And
25. 1 when Festus was come into the province

PROVISION (for) —

1. *A word, matter, thing,* דָּבָר *dabar.*
Dan. 1. 5 appointed them a daily provision of the

2. *Provision, what is prepared,* כֵּרָה *kerah.*
2 Ki. 6. 23 he prepared great provision for them: and

3. *Bread, food,* לֶחֶם *lechem.*
1 Ki. 4. 22 Solomon's provision for one day was th.

4. *Hunting, what is gained by hunting,* צַיִד *tsayid.*
Josh. 9. 5 all the bread of their provision was dry
Psa. 132. 15 I will abundantly bless her provision: I

5. *Hunting, what is gained by hunting,* צֵידָה *tsedah.*
Gen. 42. 25 to give them provision for the way: and
45. 21 Joseph..gave them provision for the way

6. *Forethought,* πρόνοια *pronoia.*
Rom 13. 14 make not provision for the flesh, to (ful.)

PROVISION, to make or take —

1. *To contain, comprehend, provide,* כּוּל *kul,* 3a.
1 Ki. 4. 7 each man his month in a year made pro.

2. *To prepare, establish,* כּוּן *kun,* 5.
1 Ch. 29. 19 palace, (for) the which I have made pro.

3. *To hunt for one's self,* צוּד *tsud,* 7.
Josh. 9. 12 This our bread we took hot (for) our pr.

PROVOCATION —

1. *Provocation, cause of anger, sadness,* כַּעַס *kaas.*
1 Ki. 15. 30 by his provocation wherewith he provo.
21. 22 provocation wherewith thou hast provo
2 Ki. 23. 26 because of all the provocations that Ma.
Eze. 20. 28 presented the provocation of their offer.

2. *To make bitter,* מָרָה *marah,* 5.
Job 17. 2 doth not mine eye continue in their pro.

3. *Strife, contention,* מְרִיבָה *meribah.*
Psa. 95. 8 Harden not your heart, as in the provoc.

4. *Despisings, blasphemies,* נֶאָצוֹת *neatsoth.*
Neh. 9. 18 thy god that..wrought great provocatio.
9. 26 rebelled..and they wrought great provo

5. *A very bitter provocation,* παραπικρασμός *para.*
Heb. 3. 8, 15 Harden not your hearts, as in the pr

PROVOKE (to anger, wrath, emulation, jealousy), to —

1. *To anger, provoke,* כַּעַס *kaas,* 3.
1 Sa. 1. 6 her adversary also provoked her sore for

2. *To make angry, provoke,* כַּעַס *kaas,* 5.
Deut. 4. 25 shall do evil..to provoke him to anger
9. 18 in doing wickedly..to provoke him to a
31. 29 provoke him to anger through the work
32. 16 They provoked him to jealousy with str
32. 21 they have provoked me to anger with th.
32. 21 I will provoke them to anger with a fool.
Judg. 2. 12 bowed themselves..and provoked the L
1 Sa. 1. 7 so she provoked her; therefore she wept
1 Ki. 14. 9 molten images, to provoke me to anger
14. 15 their groves, provoking the LORD to anger
15. 30 provoked the LORD God of Israel to anger
16. 2 to provoke me to anger with their sins
16. 7 in provoking him to anger with the work
16. 13 provoking the LORD God of Israel to an.
16. 26, 33 provoke the LORD God of Israel to an.
21. 22 wherewith thou hast provoked (me) to a
22. 53 provoked to anger the LORD God of Israel
2 Ki. 17. 11 wicked things to provoke the LORD to an.
17. 17 sold to do evil. to provoke him to anger
21. 6 much wickedness..to provoke (him) to an.
21. 15 have provoked me to anger, since the day
22. 17 that they might provoke me to anger with
23. 19 Israel..made to provoke (the LORD) to an
23. 26 that Manasseh had provoked him withal
2 Ch. 28. 25 provoked to anger the LORD God of his
33. 6 wrought much evil..to provoke him to a
34. 25 that they might provoke me to anger with
Neh. 4. 5 for they have provoked (thee) to anger b.
Psa. 78. 58 provoked him to anger with their high p
106. 29 provoked (him) to anger with their inve
Isa. 65. 3 people that provoketh me to anger cont
Jer. 7. 18 gods, that they may provoke me to anger
7. 19 Do they provoke me to anger? saith the L.
8. 19 Why have they provoked me to anger w
11. 17 provoke me to anger in offering incense
25. 6 provoke me not to anger with the works
25. 7 that ye might provoke me to anger with
32. 29 unto other gods. to provoke me to anger
32. 30 have only provoked me to anger with the
32. 32 they have done to provoke me to anger
44. 3 have committed to provoke me to anger
44. 8 In that ye provoke me unto wrath with
Eze. 8. 17 have returned to provoke me to anger: and
16. 26 thy whoredoms, to provoke me to anger
Hos. 12. 14 Ephraim provoked (him) to anger most b.

3. *To make bitter,* מָרָה *marah,* 5.
Psa. 78. 40 How oft did they provoke him in the wil
78. 56 Yet they tempted and provoked the most
106. 7 provoked (him) at the sea, (even) at the R.
106. 33 Because they provoked his spirit, so that
106. 43 but they provoked (him) with their coun.
Isa. 3. 8 against the LORD, to provoke the eyes of

4. *To make bitter,* מָרַר *marar,* 5.
Exod. 23. 21 Beware of him, and obey his voice, prov.

5. *To despise, blaspheme,* נָאַץ *naats,* 3.
Num. 14. 11 How long will this people provoke me?
14. 23 neither shall any of them that provoked
16. 30 understand that these men have provoked
Deut. 31. 20 serve them, and provoke me, and break
Isa. 1. 4 provoked the holy one of Israel unto an.

6. *To move, persuade,* סוּת *suth,* 5.
1 Ch. 21. 1 stood up..and provoked David to number

7. *To show self wroth, cause wrath,* עָבַר *abar,* 7.
Prov. 20. 2 provoketh him to anger sinneth (against)

8. *To make angry,* רָגַז *ragaz,* 5.
Job 12. 6 they that provoke God are secure; into

9. *To make angry,* רְגַז *regaz,* 5.
Ezra 5. 12 after that our fathers had provoked the G

10. *To rouse to strife,* ἐρεθίζω *erethizō.*
2 Co. 9. 2 and your zeal hath provoked very many
Col. 3. 21 Fathers, provoke not your children (to a.)

11. *To be very zealous,* παραζηλόω *parazēloō.*
Rom. 10. 19 I will provoke you to jealousy by (them
11. 11 the Gentiles, for to provoke them to jea.
11. 14 If by any means I may provoke to emula.
1 Co. 10. 22 Do we provoke the Lord to jealousy? are

12. *To irritate beyond measure,* παροργίζω *parorgizō.*
Eph. 6. 4 fathers, provoke not your children to w.

13. *To provoke bitterly,* παραπικραίνω *parapikrainō*
Heb. 3. 16 some, when they had heard, did provoke

14. *To call forth or forward,* προκαλέομαι *prokale.*
Gal. 5. 26 provoking one another, envying one ano

PROVOKE (to speak) unto, to —

1. *To make to speak offhand,* ἀποστοματίζω *apost.*
Luke 11. 53 and to provoke him to speak of many th.

2. *Paroxysm, excitement,* παροξυσμός *paroxusmos.*
Heb. 10. 24 let us consider one another to provoke un.

PROVOKED, to be easily —

To be greatly excited, παροξύνομαι *paroxunomai.*
1 Co. 13. 5 is not easily provoked, thinketh no evil

PROVOKING —

1. *Provocation, cause of anger, sadness,* כַּעַס *kaas.*
Deut. 32. 19 because of the provoking of his sons and

2. *To make bitter,* מָרָה *marah,* 5.
Psa. 78. 17 sinned yet more against him by provoking

PRUDENCE —

1. *Prudence, craftiness, subtility,* עָרְמָה *ormah.*
Prov. 8. 12 I wisdom dwell with prudence, and find

2. *Understanding, wisdom, meaning,* שֶׂכֶל, שֵׂכֶל *sekel.*
2 Ch. 2. 12 endued with prudence and understanding

3. *Prudence, wisdom, mental feeling,* φρόνησις
Eph. 1. 8 hath abounded toward us in all..prudence

PRUDENT —

1. *To understand, consider,* בִּין *bin.*
Jer. 49. 7 is counsel perished from the prudent? is

2. *To be intelligent, have understanding,* בִּין *bin,* 2.
Prov. 18. 15 The heart of the prudent getteth knowle.
Isa. 29. 14 understanding of their prudent (men) sh.

3. *Prudent, crafty,* עָרוּם *arum.*
Prov. 12. 16 fool's wrath is presently known: but a p.
12. 23 A prudent man concealeth knowledge: but
13. 16 Every prudent (man) dealeth with know.
14. 8 wisdom of the prudent (is) to understand
14. 15 the prudent (man) looketh well to his go.
14. 18 but the prudent are crowned with know
22. 3 prudent (man) forseeth the evil, and hid.
27. 12 prudent (man) forseeth the evil, (and) hi.

4. *To divine, use divination,* קָסַם *qasam.*
Isa. 3. 2 prophet, and the prudent, and the ancient

5. *To cause to act wisely, understand,* שָׂכַל *sakal,* 5.
Prov. 19. 14 inheritance of fathers and a prudent wife
Amos 5. 13 prudent shall keep silence in that time; for

6. *Intelligent,* συνετός *sunetos.*
Matt. 11. 25 hid these things from the wise and prud.
Luke 10. 21 hid these things from the wise and prud
Acts 13. 7 prudent man; who called for Barnabas
1 Co. 1. 19 to nothing the understanding of the prud

PRUDENT, to be —

1. *To be intelligent, have understanding,* בִּין *bin,* 2.
1 Sa. 16. 18 prudent in matters, and a comely person
Prov. 16. 21 The wise in heart shall be called prudent
Isa. 5. 21 Woe unto (them that are)..prudent in th
10. 13 for I am prudent: and I have removed the
Hos. 14. 9 Who (is)..prudent, and he shall know th.?

2. *To act prudently, craftily,* עָרַם *aram,* 5.
Prov. 15. 5 but he that regardeth reproof is prudent

PRUDENTLY, to deal —

To cause to act wisely, שָׂכַל *sakal,* 5.
Isa. 52. 13 my servant shall deal prudently, he shall

PRUNE, be pruned, to —

1. *To prune,* זָמַר *zamar.*
Lev. 25. 3 six years thou shalt prune thy vineyard
25. 4 thou shalt neither sow thy field, nor prune

2. *To be pruned,* זָמַר *zamar,* 2.
Isa. 5. 6 it shall not be pruned nor digged; but th.

PRUNING HOOKS —

Pruning hooks, מְזַמְּרוֹת *mazmeroth.*
Isa. 2. 4 shall beat..their spears into pruning ho
18. 5 both cut off the sprigs with pruning hoo.
Joel 3. 10 Beat your..pruning hooks into spears: let
Mic. 4. 3 shall beat..their spears into pruning ho

PSALM, PSALMIST —

1. *A pruned song or psalm of praise,* זָמִיר *zemir.*
2 Sa. 23. 1 and the sweet psalmist of Israel, said
Psa. 95. 2 make a joyful noise unto him with psalms

2. *A song of praise,* זִמְרָה *zimrah.*
Psa. 81. 2 Take a psalm, and bring hither the timb.
98. 5 Sing unto the LORD with..voice of a psa.

3. *A song of praise,* מִזְמוֹר *mizmor.*
Psa. 3. *title.* A Psalm of David
[So in Ps. 4, 5, 6, 8, 9, 12, 13, 15, 19, 20, 21, 22, 23, 24, 29, 31, 38, 39, 40, 41, 51, 62, 63, 64, 101, 109, 110, 139, 140, 141, 143.]
Psa. 30. *title* A Psalm (and) Song..of David
[So in Ps. 65, 68, 108.]
47. *title.* A Psalm..for the sons of Korah
[So in Ps. 48, 49, 84, 85, 87, 88.]
50. A Psalm of Asaph
[So in Ps. 73, 75, 76, 77, 79, 80, 82, 83.]
66. *title* To the chief Musician, a Song (or) Ps.
67. ,, Musician on Neginoth, A Psalm (or) So.
92. ,, A Psalm (or) Song for the sabbath day
98. ,, A Psalm
100. ,, A Psalm of praise. Make a joyful noise

4. *A song of praise (on an instrument),* ψαλμός.
Luke 20. 42 David himself saith in the book of Psalms
24. 44 which were written in..the Psalms, con.
Acts 1. 20 For it is written in the book of Psalms
13. 33 as it is also written in the second psalm
1 Co. 14. 26 every one of you hath a psalm, hath a d.
Eph. 5. 19 Speaking to yourselves in psalms and h.
Col. 3. 16 admonishing one another in psalms and

PSALMS, to sing —

1. *To sing songs of praise,* זָמַר *zamar,* 3.
1 Ch. 16. 9 sing psalms unto him, talk ye of all his
Psa. 105. 2 sing psalms unto him: talk ye of all his

2. *To sing songs of praise,* ψάλλω *psallō.*
Jas. 5. 13 let him pray. Is any merry? let him sing p.

PSALTERY —

1. *A wind instrument,* כְּלִי נֶבֶל *keli nebel.*
1 Ch. 16. 5 Jeiel with psalteries and with harps; but
Psa. 71. 22 I will also praise thee with the psaltery

2. *A wind instrument, lyre,* נֶבֶל, נֵבֶל *nebel.*
1 Sa. 10. 5 prophets coming down..with a psaltery
2 Sa. 6. 5 played before the LORD..on psalteries
1 Ki. 10. 12 harps also and psalteries for singers: there
1 Ch. 13. 8 with harps, and with psalteries, and with
15. 16 psalteries and harps and cymbals, sound.
15. 20 and Benaiah, with psalteries on Alamoth
15. 28 making a noise with psalteries and harps
25. 1 should prophesy with harps, with psalter.
25. 6 with cymbals, psalteries, and harps, for
2 Ch. 5. 12 having cymbals, and psalteries, and harps
9. 11 psalteries for singers: and there were n.
20. 28 came to Jerusalem with psalteries and
29. 25 psalteries, and with harps, according to
Neh. 12. 27 with singing, (with) cymbals, psalteries
Psa. 33. 2 sing unto him with the psaltery (and) an
57. 8 Awake up, my glory; awake, psaltery and
81. 2 the pleasant harp with the psaltery
92. 3 Upon an instrument..and upon the psal.
108. 2 Awake, psaltery and harp; I (myself) will
144. 9 upon a psaltery (and) an instrument of ten
150. 3 praise him with the psaltery and harp

3. *Psaltery, lyre, harp,* פְּסַנְטֵרִין, פְּסַנְתֵּרִין *pesanterin.*
Dan. 3. 5, 7, 10, 15 sackbut, psaltery..all kinds of

PTO-LE-MA'-IS, Πτολεμαΐς.
A seaport in Asher between Carmel and Tyre, Hebrew Accho, now Akka or St Jean d Acre.
Acts 21. 7 we came to P., and saluted the brethren

PUAH. *See* **PHUAH.**

PUBLICAN —

A tax gatherer, public official, τελώνης *telōnēs.*
Matt. 5. 46 what reward have ye? do not even the p.
5. 47 salute your brethren..do not even the [p.]
9. 10 many publicans and sinners came and sat
9. 11 Why eateth your Master with publicans
10. 3 Thomas and Matthew the publican; Ja.
11. 19 wine bibber a friend of publicans and s.
18. 17 unto thee as an heathen man and a pub.
21. 31 That the publicans and the harlots go into
21. 32 the publicans and the harlots believed him
Mark 2. 15 many publicans and sinners sat also tog.
2. 16 saw him eat with publicans and sinners
Luke 3. 12 Then came also publicans to be baptized
5. 27 saw a publican, named Levi, sitting at
5. 29 there was a great company of publicans
5. 30 Why do ye eat and drink with publicans
7. 29 publicans, justified God, being baptized
7. 34 wine bibber, a friend of publicans and si.
15. 1 Then drew near unto him all the publicans
18. 10 the one a Pharisee, and the other a publ.
18. 11 unjust, adulterers, or even as this publi.
18. 13 publican, standing afar off, would not lift

PUBLICANS, chief among the —

A chief tax gatherer, ἀρχιτελώνης *architelōnēs.*
Luke 19. 2 which was the chief among the publicans

PUBLICLY —

Publicly, in a public place, δημοσίᾳ *dēmosia.*
Acts 18. 28 convinced the Jews, (and that) publicly
20. 20 have taught you publicly, and from house

PUBLISH, to —

1. *To say,* אָמַר *amar.*
Jon. 3. 7 published through Nineveh by the decree

2. *To tell good news,* בָּשַׂר *basar,* 3.
1 Sa. 31. 9 to publish (it in) the house of their idols
2 Sa. 1. 20 publish (it) not in the streets of Askelon
Psa. 68. 11 great (was) the company..that published

3. *To call,* קָרָא *qara.*
Deut. 32. 3 Because I will publish the name of the L.

4. *To cause to hear,* שָׁמַע *shamea,* 5.
Neh. 8. 15 they should publish and proclaim in all
Psa. 26. 7 That I may publish with the voice of th.
Isa. 52. 7 publisheth peace..that publisheth salva.
Jer. 4. 5 Declare ye in Judah, and publish in Jer.
4. 15 and publisheth affliction from mount Ep.
4. 16 publish against Jerusalem, (that) watch.
5. 20 Declare this..and publish it in Judah, s.
31. 7 publish ye, praise ye, and say. O LORD, s
46. 14 publish in Migdol, and publish in No.
50. 2 publish, and set up a standard; publish
Amos 3. 9 Publish in the palaces at Ashdod, and in
4. 5 proclaim (and) publish the free offerings
Nah. 1. 15 the feet of him..that publisheth peace! O

5. *To cry as a herald,* κηρύσσω *kērussō.*
Mark 1. 45 went out, and began to publish (it) much

Mark. 5. 20 began to publish in Decapolis how great
7. 36 so much the more a great deal they pub.
Luke 8. 39 published throughout the whole city how

PUBLISHED, to be —

1. *To uncover, reveal,* גָּלָה *galah.*
Esth. 3. 14 was published unto all people, that they
8. 13 copy..(was) published unto all people, and

2. *To speak,* דָּבַר *dabar,* 3.
Esth. 1. 22 should be published according to the la.

3. *To be heard,* שָׁמַע *shamea,* 2.
Esth. 1. 20 shall be published throughout all his em.

4. *To become, begin to be,* γίνομαι *ginomai.*
Acts 10. 37 which was published throughout all Jud.

5. *To bear or carry through,* διαφέρω *diapherō.*
Acts 13. 49 word of the Lord was published through

6. *To cry as a herald,* κηρύσσω *kērussō.*
Mark 13. 10 gospel must first be published among all

PUB'-LIUS, Πόπλιος *common.*
The chief man in Melita when Paul was shipwrecked.
Acts 28. 7 the same quarters were possessions of..P.
28. 8 the father of P. lay sick of a fever and of

PU'-DENS, Πούδης *shamefaced.*
A believer in Rome who unites with Paul in sending salutation to Timothy.
2 Ti. 4. 21 Eubulus greeteth thee, and P., and Linus

PUFF (up), to —

1. *To breathe, blow, puff up,* פּוּחַ *puach,* 5.
Psa. 10. 5 (as for) all his enemies, he puffeth at them
12. 5 will set (him) in safety (from him that) p.

2. *To breathe, puff up,* φυσιόω *phusioō.*
1 Co. 4. 6 that no one of you be puffed up for one
4. 18 Now some are puffed up, as though I w.
4. 19 not the speech of them which are puffed up
5. 2 ye are puffed up, and have not rather m.
8. 1 Knowledge puffeth up, but charity edifi.
13. 4 charity vaunteth not itself, is not puffed up
Col. 2. 18 vainly puffed up by his fleshly mind

PUHITES, הַפּוּתִי *Puthite.*
A family in Kirjath-jearim, descended from Caleb son of Hur.
1 Ch. 2. 53 the Ithrites, and the P., and the Shuma.

PUL, פּוּל *strong.*
1 A king of Assyria who invaded Israel in the days of Menahem, B.C. 771, and was bribed to depart.
2 Ki. 15. 19 P. the king of Assyria came against the l.
15. 19 Menahem gave P. a thousand talents of s.
1 Ch. 5. 26 God..stirred up the spirit of P. king of A.
2 A place or tribe in Africa near Libya.
Isa. 66. 19 Tarshish, P., and Lud, that draw the bow

PULL, (be pulled away, down, in, off, out, up), to —

1. *To cause to go or come in,* בּוֹא *bo,* 5.
Gen. 8. 9 took her, and pulled her in unto him in.
19. 10 pulled Lot into the house to them, and s.

2. *To break or throw down,* הָרַס *haras.*
Isa. 22. 19 from thy state shall he pull thee down
Jer. 24. 6 I will build them, and not pull (them) d.
42. 10 then will I build you, and not pull (you) d.

3. *To cause to go out or forth,* יָצָא *yatsa,* 5.
Psa. 31. 4 Pull me out of the net that they have laid

4. *To pull away or down,* נְסַח *nesach,* 2.
Ezra 6. 11 let timber be pulled down from his house

5. *To give (make) rebellious,* נָתַן סָרֶרֶת *[nathan].*
Zech. 7. 11 pulled away the shoulder, and stopped th.

6. *To break down,* נָתַץ *nathats.*
Jer. 1. 10 to pull down, and to destroy, and to throw
18. 7 to pluck up, and to pull down, and to de.

7. *To draw away, out, up, off,* נָתַק *nathaq,* 3.
Eze. 17. 9 shall he not pull up the roots thereof, and

8. *To draw away or out,* נָתַק *nathaq,* 5.
Jer. 12. 3 pull them out like sheep for the slaugh.

9. *To be plucked up,* נָתַשׁ *nathash,* 2.
Amos 9. 15 shall no more be pulled up out of their

10. *To put or strip off,* פָּשַׁט *pashat,* 5.
Mic. 2. 8 ye pull off the robe with the garment from

11. *To cause to turn back,* שׁוּב *shub,* 5.
1 Ki. 13. 4 so that he could not pull it in again to him

12. *To draw up or back,* ἀνασπάω *anaspaō.*
Luke 14. 5 will not straightway pull him out on the

13. *To snatch at or away,* ἁρπάζω *harpazō.*
Jude 23 pulling (them) out of the fire; hating even

14. *To cast out or forth,* ἐκβάλλω *ekballō.*
Matt. 7. 4 Let me pull out the mote out of thine eye
Luke 6. 42 let me pull out the mote that is in thine
6. 42 then shalt thou see clearly to pull out the

15. *To take down,* καθαιρέω *kathaireō.*
Luke 12. 18 This will I do: I will pull down my barns

PULL (be pulled) in pieces, to —

1. *To pull in pieces, or violently,* פָּשַׁח *pashach,* 3.
Lam. 3. 11 pulled me in pieces: he hath made me de.

2. *To draw asunder,* διασπάω *diaspaō.*
Acts 23. 10 Paul should have been pulled in pieces of

PULLING down —
A taking down, καθαίρεσις *kathairesis.*
2 Co. 10. 4 mighty through God to the pulling down

PULPIT —
High place, מִגְדָּל *migdal.*
Neh. 8. 4 Ezra the scribe stood upon a pulpit of w.

PULSE —

1. *Seeds, pulse,* זֵרֹעִים *zeroim.*
Dan. 1. 12 let them give us pulse to eat, and water

2. *Seeds, pulse,* זֵרְעֹנִים *zereonim.*
Dan. 1. 16 took away the portion..and gave them p.

PUNISH, to —

1. *To darken, keep back, restrain,* חָשַׂךְ *chasak.*
Ezra 9. 13 seeing that thou our God hast punished us

2. *To chasten, instruct, teach,* יָסַר *yasar,* 3.
Lev. 26. 18 I will punish you seven times more for your

3. *To (cause to) smite,* נָכָה *nakah,* 5.
Lev. 26. 24 will punish you yet seven times for your

4. *To fine, punish,* עָנַשׁ *anash.*
Prov. 17. 26 Also to punish the just (is) not good, (nor)

5. *To inspect, look after,* (עַל) פָּקַד *paqad (al).*
Isa. 10. 12 I will punish the fruit of the stout heart
13. 11 I will punish the world for (their) evil, and
24. 21 shall punish the host of the high ones (that
26. 21 cometh out of his place to punish the in.
27. 1 shall punish leviathan the piercing serp.
Jer. 9. 25 I will punish all (them which are) circu.
11. 22 I will punish them: the young men shall
13. 21 What wilt thou say when he shall punish
21. 14 punish you according to the fruit of your
23. 34 I will even punish that man and his house
25. 12 I will punish the king of Babylon, and that
27. 8 that nation will I punish, saith the LORD
29. 32 I will punish Shemaiah the Nehelamite
30. 20 and I will punish all that oppress them
36. 31 punish him and his seed and his servants
44. 13 I will punish..as I have punished Jerus.
44. 29 punish you in this place, that ye may know
46. 25 will punish the multitude of No, and Ph.
50. 18 I will punish..as I have punished the k.
51. 44 will punish Bel in Babylon, and I will br.
Hos. 4. 9 punish them for their ways, and reward
4. 14 punish your daughters when they commit
12. 2 punish Jacob according to his ways; acc.
Amos 3. 2 therefore I will punish you for all your
Zeph. 1. 8 punish the princes, and the king's child.
1. 9 punish all those that leap on the thresh.
1. 12 punish the men that are settled on their
3. 7 howsoever I punished them: but they
Zech 10. 3 punished the goats: for the LORD of hosts

6. *To treat ill,* רָעַע *raa,* 5.
Zech. 8. 14 As I thought to punish you, when your

7. *To restrain, punish,* κολάζω *kolazō.*
Acts 4. 21 finding nothing how they might punish t.

8. *To punish, avenge,* τιμωρέω *timōreō.*
Acts 22. 5 bound unto Jerusalem, for to be punished
26. 11 I punished them oft in every synagogue

PUNISHED, to be —

1. *To be avenged,* נָקַם *naqam,* 2.
Exod 21. 20 smite his servant..he shall be surely pu.

2. *To be avenged,* נָקַם *naqam,* 6.
Exod 21. 21 he shall not be punished: for he (is) his

3. *To punish, fine,* עָנַשׁ *anash.*
Prov 21. 11 When the scorner is punished, the simp.

4. *To be punished, fined,* עָנַשׁ *anash,* 2.
Exod 21. 22 he shall be surely punished, according as
Prov 22. 3 but the simple pass on, and are punished
27. 12 (but) the simple pass on, (and) are punis.

5. *To pay justice,* δίκην τίω *dikēn tiō.*
2 Th. 1. 9 Who shall be punished with everlasting

6. *To restrain, punish,* κολάζω *kolazō.*
2 Pe. 2. 9 to reserve the unjust..to be punished

PUNISHMENT (of iniquity, sin) —

1. *Error, erring, sin,* חֵטְא *chet.*
Lam. 3. 39 a man for the punishment of his sins.

2. *Erring, error, (punishment for) sin,* חַטָּאת *chattath.*
Lam. 4. 6 than the punishment of the sin of Sodom
Zech 14. 19 This shall be the punishment..and the p.

3. *Perversity, (punishment for) iniquity,* עָוֹן *avon.*
Gen. 4. 13 My punishment (is) greater than I can
Lev. 26. 41, 43 accept of the punishment of their in.
1 Sa. 28. 10 there shall no punishment happen to thee
Job 19. 29 for wrath (bringeth) the punishments of
Lam. 4. 6 For the punishment of the iniquity of the
4. 22 punishment of thine iniquity is accompli.
Eze. 14. 10 bear the punishment of their iniquity
14. 10 punishment..shall be even as the punish.

4. *Punishment, fine,* עֹנֶשׁ *onesh.*
Prov 19. 19 man of great wrath shall suffer punishm.

5. *Reproof,* תּוֹכֵחָה *tokechah.*
Psa. 149. 7 To execute..punishments upon the peo.

6. *Full justice,* ἐκδίκησις *ekdikēsis.*
1 Pe. 2. 14 for the punishment of evil doers, and for

7. *Penalty, burden,* ἐπιτιμία *epitimia.*
2 Co. 2. 6 Sufficient to such a man (is) this punish.

8. *Restraint,* κόλασις *kolasis.*
Matt 25. 46 shall go away into everlasting punishm.

9. *Punishment, vengeance,* τιμωρία *timōria.*
Heb. 10. 29 Of how much sorer punishment, suppose

PUNITES, הַפּוּנִי *the Puni.*
The family of Pua, son of Issachar.
Num 26. 23 the Tolaites: of Pua, the family of the P.

PU'-NON, פּוּנֹן *ore-pit.*
A city in the E. of Edom between Selah and Zoar; the 35th station from Egypt, 24th from Sinai and 4th from Ezion-geber; N. of M. Hor, and E. of S. and of Salt Sea; now *Phanon.*
Num 33. 42 departed from Zalmonah, and pitched in P.
33. 43 they departed from P., and pitched in O.

PUR, PU'-RIM, *lots,* פּוּרִים, פּוּר *lots.*
A festival of the Jews commemorating their deliverance from Haman.
Esth. 3. 7 they cast P., that (is), the lot, before H.
9. 24 had cast P., that (is), the lot, to consume
9. 26 called these days P., after the name of P.
9. 28 (that) these days of P. should not fail from
9. 29 to confirm this second letter of P.
9. 31 To confirm these days of P. in their times
9. 32 decree of Esther confirmed these..of P.

PURCHASE —

1. *Acquisition, purchase,* מִקְנָה *miqnah.*
Jer. 32. 11 So I took the evidence of the purchase, (bo.)
32. 12 gave the evidence of the purchase unto
32. 12 subscribed the book of the purchase, be.
32. 14 evidence of the purchase, both which is
32. 16 delivered the evidence of the purchase un.

2. *Acquisition, purchase,* מִקְנֶה *miqneh.*
Gen. 49. 32 The purchase of the field and of the cave

PURCHASE, (be purchased), to —

1. *To free, avenge,* גָּאַל *gaal.*
Lev. 25. 33 if a man purchase of the Levites, then the

2. *To acquire, purchase,* קָנָה *qanah.*
Gen. 25. 10 field which Abraham purchased of the s.
Exod 15. 16 people pass over, (which) thou hast pur.
Ruth 4. 10 Ruth the Moabitess..have I purchased
Psa. 74. 2 congregation, (which) thou hast purchas.
78. 54 mountain, (which) his right hand had pu.

3. *To acquire, prepare, possess,* κτάομαι *ktaomai.*
Acts 1. 18 this man purchased a field with the rew.
8. 20 gift of God may be purchased with money

4. *To acquire,* περιποιέομαι *peripoieomai.*
Acts 20. 28 which he hath purchased with his own bl.
1 Ti. 3. 13 purchase to themselves a good degree, and

PURE, PURER —

1. *Clear, choice, chosen,* בַּר *bar.*
Psa. 19. 8 commandment of the LORD (is) pure, en.
24. 4 He that hath clean hands, and a pure he.

2. *To clear, choose,* בָּרַר *barar.*
Zeph. 3. 9 For then will I turn to the people a pure

3. *To be clear,* בָּרַר *barar,* 2.
2 Sa. 22. 27 With the pure..and with the froward th.
Psa. 18. 26 With the pure..and with the froward thou

4. *Liberty, wildness,* דְּרוֹר *deror.*
Exod 30. 23 Take thou also..of pure myrrh five hun.

5. *Pure,* זַךְ, זָךְ *zak.*
Exod 27. 20 bring thee pure oil olive beaten for the
30. 34 sweet spices with pure frankincense: of
Lev. 24. 2 bring unto thee pure oil olive beaten for
24. 7 thou shalt put pure frankincense upon
Job 8. 6 If thou (wert) pure and upright; surely
11. 4 My doctrine (is) pure, and I am clean in
16. 17 Not for (any) injustice..my prayer (is) p.
Prov 20. 11 whether his work (be) pure, and whether
21. 8 strange: but (as for) the pure, his work

6. *Clean, pure,* טָהוֹר *tahor.*
Exod 25. 11 thou shalt overlay it with pure gold, wit.
25. 17 thou shalt make a mercy seat (of) pure g.
25. 24 thou shalt overlay it with pure gold, and
25. 29 cover withal: (of) pure gold shalt thou m.
25. 31 thou shalt make a candlestick (of) pure
25. 36 all it (shall be) one beaten work (of) p.
25. 38 snuff dishes thereof, (shall be of) pure g.
25. 39 a talent of pure gold shall he make it, w.
28. 14 two chains (of) pure gold at the ends; (of)
28. 22 at the ends (of) wreathen work (of) pure
28. 36 thou shalt make a plate (of) pure gold, and
30. 3 thou shalt overlay it with pure gold, the
30. 35 shalt make it a perfume..pure (and) holy
31. 8 the pure candlestick with all his furnit.
37. 2 overlaid it with pure gold within and w.
37. 6 he made the mercy seat (of) pure gold: two
37. 11 overlaid it with pure gold, and made th.
37. 16 and his covers to cover withal, (of) pure
37. 17 made the candlestick (of) pure gold: (of)
37. 22 all of it (was) one beaten work (of) pure
37. 23 snuffers, and his snuff dishes, (of) pure
37. 24 a talent of pure gold made he it, and all
37. 26 overlaid it with pure gold, (both) the top
37. 29 pure incense of sweet spices, according to
39. 15 at the ends, of wreathen work (of) pure
39. 25 made bells (of) pure gold, and put the bells
39. 30 made the plate of the holy crown (of) pure
39. 37 The pure candlestick, (with) the lamps
Lev. 24. 4 He shall order the lamps upon the pure
24. 6 six on a row, upon the pure table before
1 Ch. 28. 17 Also pure gold for the flesh hooks, and the
2 Ch. 3. 4 And he overlaid it within with pure gold
9. 17 Moreover the king..overlaid it with pure

2 Ch. 13. 11 also (set they in order) upon the pure ta.
Ezra 6. 20 all of them (were) pure, and killed the p.
Job 28. 19 neither shall it be valued with pure gold
Psa. 12. 6 words of the LORD (are) pure words: (as)
Prov 15. 26 but (the words) of the pure (are) pleasant
30. 12 generation (that are) pure in their own e.
Hab. 1. 13 (Thou art) of purer eyes than to behold
Mal. 1. 11 offered unto my name, and a pure offering

7. *Beaten*, כָּתִית *kathith*.
1 Ki. 5. 11 twenty measures of pure oil: thus gave S.

8. *Fermented*, חֶמֶר *chemer*.
Deut 32. 14 thou didst drink the pure blood of the g.

9. *Free, innocent, acquitted*, נְקֵא *neqe*.
Dan. 7. 9 and the hair of his head like the pure w.

10. *To shut up, close, refine*, סָגַר *sagar*.
1 Ki. 6. 20 overlaid it with pure gold; and (so) cov.
6. 21 overlaid the house within with pure gold
7. 49 candlesticks of pure gold, five on the right
7. 50 and the spoons, and the censers, (of) pure
10. 21 pure gold; none (were of) silver: it was
2 Ch. 4. 20 after the manner before the oracle, of p.
4. 22 and the spoons, and the censers, (of) pure
9. 20 pure gold: none (were of) silver; it was

11. *To refine, try, purify*, צָרַף *tsaraph*.
Psa. 119. 140 Thy word (is) very pure: therefore thy
Prov 30. 5 Every word of God (is) pure: he (is) a s.

12. *Chaste, pure*, ἁγνός *hagnos*.
Phil. 4. 8 whatsoever things (are) pure, whatsoever
1 Ti. 5. 22 neither be partaker..keep thyself pure
Jas. 3. 17 the wisdom that is from above is first pure
1 Jo. 3. 3 every man..purifieth himself..as he is p.

13. *Sincere, pure*, εἰλικρινής *eilikrinēs*.
2 Pe. 3. 1 in (both) which I stir up your pure minds

14. *Clean, pure, clear*, καθαρός *katharos*.
Matt. 5. 8 Blessed (are) the pure in heart: for they
Acts 20. 26 that I (am) pure from the blood of all (m.)
Rom 14. 20 All things indeed (are) pure; but (it is)
1 Ti. 1. 5 charity out of a pure heart, and (of) a good
3. 9 Holding the mystery of the faith in a pure
2 Ti. 1. 3 whom I serve from (my) forefathers..pure
2. 22 them that call on the Lord out of a pure
Titus 1. 15 Unto the pure all things (are) pure: but
1. 15 are defiled and unbelieving (is) nothing p.
Heb. 10. 22 and our bodies washed with pure water
Jas. 1. 27 Pure religion and undefiled before God
1 Pe. 1. 22 love one another with [a pure] heart fer.
Rev. 15. 6 clothed in pure and white linen, and ha
21. 18 the city (was) pure gold, like unto clear
21. 21 street of the city (was) pure gold, as it w.
22. 1 showed me a [pure] river of water of life

PURE, PURER, (to be, count, show self) —

1. *To purify self, show self pure*, בָּרַר *barar*, 7.
2 Sa. 22. 27 thou wilt show thyself pure; and with the
Psa. 18. 26 thou wilt show thyself pure; and with the

2. *To be (reckoned) pure*, זָכָה *zakah*.
Mic. 6. 11 Shall I count (them) pure with the wicked

3. *To be pure*, זָכַךְ *zakak*.
Job 25. 5 yea, the stars are not pure in his sight
Lam. 4. 7 Her Nazarites were purer than snow, th.

4. *To be clean, cleansed*, טָהֵר *taher*.
Job 4. 17 shall a man be more pure than his maker?
Prov. 20. 9 I have made my heart clean, I am pure

PURELY, PURENESS —

1. *Cleanness, purity*, בֹּר *bor*.
Job 22. 30 is delivered by the pureness of thine ha.
Isa. 1. 25 I will turn my hand upon thee, and pur.

2. *Clean, pure, cleanness, purity*, טָהוֹר *tahor*.
Prov. 22. 11 He that loveth pureness of heart, (for) the

3. *Chastity, purity*, ἁγνότης *hagnotēs*.
2 Co. 6. 6 By pureness, by knowledge, by long suff.

PURGE (away, throughly, out), to —

1. *To clear, purify, chose*, בָּרַר *barar*.
Eze. 20. 38 I will purge out from among you the re.

2. *To clear, cleanse*, בָּרַר *barar*, 3.
Dan. 11. 35 to try them, and to purge, and to make

3. *To cast out, force away*, דּוּחַ *duach*, 5.
Isa. 4. 4 shall have purged the blood of Jerusalem

4. *To refine, pour down*, זָקַק *zaqaq*, 3.
Mal. 3. 3 purge them as gold and silver, that they

5. *To cleanse from error*, חָטָא *chata*, 3.
Psa. 51. 7 Purge me with hyssop and I shall be clean

6. *To cleanse, pronounce clean*, טָהֵר *taher*, 3.
2 Ch. 34. 3 began to purge Judah and Jerusalem from
34. 8 when he had purged the land, and the h.
Eze. 24. 13 because I have purged thee, and thou w.

7. *To cover, pacify*, כָּפַר *kaphar*, 3.
Psa. 65. 3 transgressions, thou shalt purge them a.
79. 9 and purge away our sins, for thy name's
Eze. 43. 20 thus shalt thou cleanse and purge it
43. 26 Seven days shall they purge the altar and

8. *To refine, try, purify*, צָרַף *tsaraph*.
Isa. 1. 25 purge away thy dross, and take away all

9. *To cleanse thoroughly*, διακαθαρίζω *diakatharizō*.
Matt. 3. 12 he will throughly purge his floor, and
Luke 3. 17 he will throughly purge his floor, and

10. *To cleanse out*, ἐκκαθαίρω *ekkathairō*.
1 Co. 5. 7 Purge out therefore the old leaven, that ye
2 Ti. 2. 21 If a man therefore purge himself from th.

11. *To cleanse, make a cleansing*, καθαρίζω *kathar.*
Mark 7. 19 goeth out into the draught, purging all
Heb. 9. 14 purge your conscience from dead works
9. 22 almost all things are by the law purged

12. *To cleanse*, καθαίρω *kathairō*.
John 15. 2 every (branch) that beareth fruit he pur.
Heb 10. 2 because that the worshippers once [purged]

13. *To make a cleansing*, ποιέω καθαρισμόν [*poieō*].
Heb. 1. 3 when he had by himself purged our sins

PURGED, to be —

1. *To be clean, cleansed*, טָהֵר *taher*.
Eze. 24. 13 wast not purged, thou shalt not be purg.

2. *To be covered, pardoned*, כָּפַר *kaphar*, 4.
Prov 16. 6 By mercy and truth iniquity is purged
Isa. 6. 7 iniquity is taken away, and thy sin purg.
22. 14 Surely this iniquity shall not be purged
27. 9 therefore shall the iniquity of Jacob be p.

3. *To be covered, pardoned*, כָּפַר *kaphar*, 7.
1 Sa. 3. 14 iniquity of Eli's house shall not be purg.

4. *A purification, cleansing*, καθαρισμός *katharism.*
2 Pe. 1. 9 hath forgotten that he was purged from

PURIFICATION (for sin, things for) —

1. *Offering for error or sin*, חַטָּאת *chattath*.
Num 19. 9 of separation: it (is) a purification for sin
19. 17 of the burnt heifer of purification for sin

2. *Cleansing, purity*, טָהֳרָה *tohorah*.
2 Ch. 30. 19 according to the purification of the sanc.
Neh. 12. 45 ward of the purification, according to the

3. *Things emptied out, ointments*, מְרוּקִים *meruqim*.
Esth. 2. 12 for so were the days of their purifications

4. *Thing rubbed in, ointment*, תַּמְרוּק *tamruq*.
Esth. 2. 3 let their things for purification be given
2. 9 speedily gave her her things for purifica.

5. *Purification*, ἁγνισμός *hagnismos*.
Acts 21. 26 accomplishment of the days of purificati.

6. *A cleansing*, καθαρισμός *katharismos*.
Luke 2. 22 when the days of her purification accord.

PURIFIED, to be —

1. *To clear or purify self*, בָּרַר *barar*, 7.
Dan. 12. 10 Many shall be purified, and made white

2. *To be refined*, זָקַק *zaqaq*, 4.
Psa. 12. 6 silver tried in a furnace of earth, purified

3. *To show self clean, become cleansed*, חָטָא *chata*, 7.
Num. 8. 21 Levites were purified, and they washed
31. 23 it shall be purified with the water of sep.

4. *To cleanse self, show self cleansed*, טָהֵר *taher*, 7.
Ezra 6. 20 the priests and Levites were purified tog.

5. *To separate self, show self separate*, קָדַשׁ *qadesh*, 7.
2 Sa. 11. 4 for she was purified from her uncleanne.

PURIFIER —

To cleanse, pronounce clean, טָהֵר *taher*, 3.
Mal. 3. 3 he shall sit (as) a refiner and purifier of s.

PURIFY (self), to —

1. *To show self clean, cleanse self*, חָטָא *chata*, 7.
Num 19. 12 He shall purify himself with it on the th.
19. 12 but if he purify not himself the third day
19. 13 Whosoever..purifieth not himself, defile.
19. 20 But the man that..shall not purify him.
31. 19 purify (both) yourselves and your captiv.
31. 20 purify all (your) raiment, and all that is
Job 41. 25 by reason of breakings they purify them.

2. *To cleanse from error or sin*, חָטָא *chata*, 3.
Lev. 8. 15 purified the altar, and poured the blood
Num 19. 19 on the seventh day he shall purify hims.

3. *To cleanse, pronounce clean*, טָהֵר *taher*, 3.
Neh. 12. 30 priests and the Levites..purified the peo.
Eze. 43. 26 Seven days shall they..purify it; and th.
Mal. 3. 3 he shall purify the sons of Levi, and pur.

4. *To cleanse self, show self clean*, טָהֵר *taher*, 7.
Neh. 12. 30 purified themselves..and the gates, and
Isa. 66. 17 purify themselves in the gardens behind

5. *To cleanse, make clean*, ἁγνίζω *hagnizō*.
John 11. 55 went out of the country..to purify them.
Acts 21. 24 purify thyself with them, and be at cha.
21. 26 the next day purifying himself with them
24. 18 found me purified in the temple, neither
Jas. 4. 8 and purify (your) hearts, (ye) double mi.
1 Pet. 1. 22 Seeing ye have purified your souls in ob.
1 Jo. 3. 3 that hath this hope in him purifieth him.

6. *To make clean*, καθαρίζω *katharizō*.
Acts 15. 9 put no difference..purifying their hearts
Titus 2. 14 purify unto himself a peculiar people, zea.
Heb. 9. 23 patterns..should be purified with these

PURIFYING, PURITY —

1. *Offering for error or sin*, חַטָּאת *chattath*.
Num. 8. 7 Sprinkle water of purifying upon them

2. *Cleanness, cleansing*, טֹהַר *tohar*.
Lev. 12. 4 until the days of her purifying be fulfilled
12. 6 when the days of her purifying are fulfil.

3. *Cleansing, purity*, טָהֳרָה *tohorah*.
Lev. 12. 4, 5 continue in the blood of her purifying
1 Ch. 23. 28 in the purifying of all holy things, and

4. *Thing rubbed in, ointment*, תַּמְרוּק *tamruq*.
Esth. 2. 12 with (other) things for the purifying of

5. *Chastity, purity*, ἁγνεία *hagneia*.
1 Ti. 4. 12 be thou an example..in faith, in purity
5. 2 the younger as sisters, with all purity

6. *A cleansing*, καθαρισμός *katharismos*.
John 2. 6 after the manner of the purifying of the
3. 25 Then there arose a question..about pur

7. *Cleanness, purity*, καθαρότης *katharotēs*.
Heb. 9. 13 sanctifieth to the purifying of the flesh

PURLOIN, to —

To purloin, secrete, νοσφίζομαι *nosphizomai*.
Titus 2. 10 Not purloining, but showing all good fi.

PURPLE —

1. *Purple*, אַרְגְּוָן *argevan*.
2 Ch. 2. 7 work in gold..and in purple, and crimson

2. *Purple, red*, אַרְגָּמָן *argaman*.
Exod 25. 4 blue, and purple, and scarlet, and fine li.
26. 1, 31 curtains (of) fine twined linen..and pu.
26. 36 purple, and scarlet, and fine twined linen
27. 16 hanging of twenty cubits, (of) blue, and p.
28. 5 they shall take gold, and blue, and purple
28. 6 make the ephod (of) gold..purple, (of) sc.
28. 8 purple, and scarlet, and fine twined linen
28. 15 purple, and (of) scarlet, and (of) fine tw.
28. 33 make pomegranates (of) blue, and (of) p.
35. 6 blue, and purple, and scarlet, and fine li.
35. 25 of purple, (and) of scarlet, and of fine li.
35. 35 in blue, and in purple, in scarlet, and in
36. 8 fine twined linen, and blue, and purple
36. 35 made a veil (of) blue, and purple, and sc.
36. 37 made an hanging..(of) blue, and purple
38. 18 needlework, (of) blue, and purple, and s.
38. 23 embroiderer in blue, and in purple, and
39. 1 of the blue, and purple, and scarlet, they
39. 2, 5, 8 gold, blue, and purple, and scarlet
39. 3 to work (it) in the blue, and in the purple
39. 24 blue, and purple, and scarlet, (and) twi.
39. 29 blue, and purple, and scarlet, (of) needl.
Num. 4. 13 altar, and spread a purple cloth thereon
Judg. 8. 26 purple raiment that (was) on the kings of
2 Ch. 2. 14 skilful to work in gold..in purple, in blue
3. 14 made the veil (of) blue, and purple, and
Esth. 1. 6 fastened with cords of fine linen and pu.
8. 15 with a garment of fine linen and purple
Prov 31. 22 tapestry; her clothing (is) silk and purp.
Song 3. 10 He made..the covering of it (of) purple
7. 5 hair of thine head like purple: the king
Jer. 10. 9 blue and purple (is) their clothing: they
Eze. 27. 7 blue and purple from the isles of Elishah
27. 16 occupied in thy fairs with emeralds, pur.

3. *Purple garment*, πορφύρα *porphura*.
Mark 15. 17 clothed him with purple, and platted a
15. 20 took off the purple from him, and put his
Luke 16. 19 rich man, which was clothed in purple, and
Rev. 17. 4 woman was arrayed in purple and scarlet
18. 12 The merchandise of gold..and purple, and

4. *Purple, of a purple colour*, πορφύρεος, πορφυροῦς.
John 19. 2 on his head, and they put on him a purp.
19. 5 came Jesus forth, wearing..the purple
Rev. 18. 16 that was clothed in fine line linen, and p.

PURPLE, seller of —

A seller of purple, πορφυρόπωλις *porphuropōlis*.
Acts 16. 14 woman named Lydia, a seller of purple

PURPOSE —

1. *A word, thing*, דָּבָר *dabar*.
Neh 8. 4 which they had made for the purpose; and

2. *Device, thought*, זִמָּה *zimmah*.
Job 17. 11 My days are past, my purposes are broken

3. *Delight, pleasure, desire*, חֵפֶץ *chephets*.
Eccl. 3. 1 a time to every purpose under the heaven
3. 17 a time there for every purpose and for e.
8. 6 Because to every purpose there is time and

4. *Thought, device*, מַחֲשָׁבָה, מַחֲשֶׁבֶת *machashabah*.
Prov 15. 22 Without counsel purposes are disappoin.
20. 18 (Every) purpose is established by counsel
Jer. 49. 20 purposes that he hath purposed against
49. 30 and hath conceived a purpose against you
50. 45 purposes, that he hath purposed against
51. 29 every purpose of the LORD shall be perf

5. *Deed, act, work*, מַעֲשֶׂה *maaseh*.
Job 33. 17 he may withdraw man (from his) purpose

6. *Counsel*, עֵצָה *etsah*.
Ezra 4. 5 frustrate their purpose, all the days of C
Isa. 14. 26 This (is) the purpose that is purposed

7. *Wish, will, desire*, צְבוּ *tsebu*.
Dan. 6. 17 purpose might not be changed concern.

8. *Foundation, prince*, שָׁת *shath*.
Isa. 19. 10 they shall be broken in the purposes the.

9. *Purpose, intention*, βούλημα *boulēma*.
Acts 27. 43 kept them from (their) purpose; and co.

10. *A setting before, purpose*, πρόθεσις *prothesis*.
Acts 11. 23 that with purpose of heart they would c.
27. 13 they had obtained (their) purpose, loosing
Rom. 8. 28 who are the called according to (his) pur.
9. 11 that the purpose of God according to ele.
Eph. 1. 11 being predestinated according to the pur.
3. 11 According to the eternal purpose which
2 Ti. 1. 9 but according to his own purpose and gr.
3. 10 hast fully known my purpose, faith, long

PURPOSE, to —

1. *To say,* אָמַר *amar.*
1 Ki. 5. 5 I purpose to build an house unto the na.
2 Ch.28. 10 now ye purpose to keep under the child.

2. *To devise, think,* זָמַם *zamam.*
Psa. 17 3 I am purposed (that) my mouth shall not
Jer. 4. 28 I have purposed (it), and will not repent

3. *To think, reckon,* חָשַׁב *chashab.*
Psa.140. 4 who have purposed to overthrow my go.
Jer. 26. 3 repent me of the evil which I purpose to
36. 3 will hear all the evil which I purpose to
49. 20 that he hath purposed against the inhab.
50. 45 that he hath purposed against the land of
Lam. 2. 8 LORD hath purposed to destroy the wall

4. *To counsel,* יָעַץ *yaats.*
Isa. 14. 24 and as I have purposed, (so) shall it stand
14. 26 This (is) the purpose that is purposed
14. 27 For the LORD of hosts hath purposed, and
19. 12 know what the LORD of hosts hath purp.
23. 9 LORD of hosts hath purposed it, to stain

5. *To form, frame,* יָצַר *yatsar.*
Isa. 46. 11 will also bring it to pass; I have purposed

6. *To set, place,* שׂוּם, שִׂים *sum, sim.*
Dan. 1. 8 purposed in his heart that he would not

7. *His face was,* פָּנָיו [*panim*].
2 Ch. 32 2 he was purposed to fight against Jerusa.

8. *To counsel, deliberate,* βουλεύομαι *bouleuomai.*
2 Co. 1 17 the things that I purpose, do I purpose

9. *A resolution was made,* ἐγένετο γνώμη [*ginomai*].
Acts 20. 3 he purposed to return through Macedo.

10. *To do, make,* ποιέω *poieō.*
Eph. 3. 11 which he purposed in Christ Jesus our L.

11. *To take beforehand, determine,* προαιρέομαι.
2 Co. 9. 7 Every man according as he purposeth in

12. *To put or place before, propose,* προτίθημι *prot.*
Rom. 1. 13 that oftentimes I purposed to come unto
Eph. 1. 9 good pleasure which he hath purposed in

13. *To put, place,* τίθημι *tithēmi.*
Acts 19. 21 Paul purposed in the spirit, when he had p.

PURPOSE, of; to no —

1. *Empty, vain, to no purpose,* רִיק *riq.*
Isa. 30. 7 the Egyptians shall help..to no purpose

2. *To give spoil,* שָׁלַל *shalal.*
Ruth 2. 16 let fall also (some) of the handfuls of pur.

PURSE —

1. *Cup, bag, purse,* כִּיס *kis.*
Prov. 1. 14 Cast in thy lot..let us all have one purse

2. *A bag, purse,* βαλάντιον *balantion.*
Luke10. 4 Carry neither purse, nor scrip, nor shoes
22. 35 When I sent you without purse, and scrip
22. 36 he that hath a purse, let him take (it), and

3. *A girdle, purse,* ζώνη *zōnē.*
Matt10. 9 Provide neither gold..nor brass in your p.
Mark 6. 8 no scrip, no bread, no money in (their) p.

PURSUE (hard or hotly), to —

1. *After,* אַחַר *achar.*
1 Ki.22. 33 that they turned back from pursuing him
2 Ch.18. 32 they turned back again from pursuing him

2. *To (cause to) cleave to,* דָּבַק *dabaq,* 5.
Judg20. 45 pursued hard after them unto Gidom, and

3. *To burn, pursue hotly,* דָּלַק *dalaq.*
Gen. 31. 36 what (is) my sin, that thou hast so hotly p.
Lam. 4. 19 they pursued us upon the mountains, they

4. *To go after,* יָלַךְ אַחֲרֵי *yalak achare.*
Jer. 48. 2 O Madmen: the sword shall pursue thee

5. *Going aside (?) is to [him],* שִׂיג לְ *sig le.*
1 Ki.18. 27 either he is talking, or he is pursuing, or

6. *To pursue,* רָדַף *radaph.*
Gen. 14. 14 armed his trained (servants)..and pursued
14. 15 pursued them unto Hobah, which (is) on
31. 23 pursued after him seven days' journey; and
35. 5 they did not pursue after the sons of Jac.
Exod14. 8 and he pursued after the children of Isr.
14. 9 Egyptians pursued after them, all the h.
14. 23 Egyptians pursued, and went in after th.
15. 9 enemy said, I will pursue, I will overtake
Lev. 26. 17 and ye shall flee when none pursueth you
26. 36 and they shall fall when none pursueth
26. 37 And they shall fall..when none pursueth
Deut11. 4 to overflow them, as they pursued after
19. 6 Lest the avenger of the blood pursue the
28. 22 and they shall pursue thee until thou p.
28. 45 shall come upon thee, and shall pursue
Josh. 2. 5 pursue after them quickly; for ye shall
2. 7 men pursued after them the way to Jor.
2. 7 as soon as they which pursued after them
8. 16 to pursue after them: and they pursued
8. 17 left the city open, and pursued after Israel
10. 19 pursue after your enemies, and smite the
20. 5 if the avenger of blood pursue after him
24. 6 pursued after your fathers with chariots
Judg. 1. 6 they pursued after him, and caught him
4. 16 Barak pursued after the chariots, and af.
4. 22 as Barak pursued Sisera, Jael came out to
7. 23 men of Israel..pursued after the Midian.
7. 25 pursued Midian, and brought the heads
8. 4 passed over..faint, yet pursuing (them)
8. 5 I am pursuing after Zebah and Zalmunna
Judg. 8. 12 pursued after them, and took the two k.
1 Sa. 7. 11 pursued the Philistines, and smote them
17. 52 pursued the Philistines, until thou come
23. 25 pursued after David in the wilderness of
23. 28 Wherefore Saul returned from pursuing
24. 14 after whom dost thou pursue? after a dead
25. 29 Yet a man is risen to pursue thee, and to
26. 18 Wherefore doth my lord thus pursue after
30. 8 Shall I pursue..he answered him, Pursue
30. 10 David pursued, he and four hundred men
2 Sa. 2. 19 Asahel pursued after Abner; and in going
2. 24 Joab also and Abishai pursued after Abner
2. 28 pursued after Israel no more, neither fo.
17. 1 I will arise and pursue after David this n.
18. 16 people returned from pursuing after Isr.
20. 6 pursue after him, lest he get him fenced c.
20. 7 went out of Jerusalem, to pursue after S.
20. 10 Joab and Abishai his brother pursued af.
20. 13 all the people went on after Joab, to pur.
22. 38 I have pursued mine enemies, and destr.
24. 13 wilt thou flee..while they pursue thee? or
1 Ki.20. 20 the Syrians fled, and Israel pursued them
2 Ki.25. 5 army of the Chaldees pursued after the k.
2 Ch.13. 19 Abijah pursued after Jeroboam, and took
14. 13 people that (were) with him pursued them
Job 13. 25 and wilt thou pursue the dry stubble?
30. 15 Terrors are turned upon me: they pursue
Psa. 18. 37 I have pursued mine enemies, and over.
34. 14 Depart from evil..seek peace, and pursue
Prov28. 1 The wicked flee when no man pursueth
Isa. 30. 16 therefore shall they that pursue you be
41. 3 pursued them, (and) passed safely; (even)
Jer. 39. 5 Chaldeans' army pursued after them, and
52. 8 army of the Chaldeans pursued after the
Eze. 35. 6 blood shall pursue..even blood shall pur.
Hos. 8. 3 Israel hath cast off..enemy shall pursue
Amos 1. 11 because he did pursue his brother with the

7. *To pursue,* רָדַף *radaph,* 3.
Prov11. 19 so he that pursueth evil (pursueth it) to
13. 21 Evil pursueth sinners but to the righte.
19. 7 pursueth (them with) words, (yet) they
Nah. 1. 8 and darkness shall pursue his enemies

PURSUER —

To pursue, רָדַף *radaph.*
Josh. 2. 16 Get you to the mountain, lest the pursu.
2. 16 hide yourselves..until the pursuers be re.
2. 22 pursuers were returned: and the pursuer
8. 20 people..turned back upon the pursuers
Lam. 1. 6 gone without strength before the pursuer

PURTENANCE —

Inwards, heart, קֶרֶב *qereb.*
Exod12. 9 with his legs, and with the purtenance th.

PUSH (away, down, used or wont to), to —

1. *To gore, push,* נָגַח *nagach.*
Exod21. 32 If the ox shall push a man servant or

2. *To gore, push,* נָגַח *nagach,* 3.
Deut33. 17 with them he shall push the people toge.
1 Ki.22. 11 With these thou shalt push the Syrians
2 Ch.18. 10 With these thou shalt push Syria until
Psa. 44. 5 Through thee will we push down our en.
Eze. 34. 21 pushed all the diseased with your horns
Dan. 8. 4 I saw the ram pushing westward, and no.

3. *To push self on or forward,* נָגַח *nagach,* 7.
Dan. 11. 40 shall the king of the south push at him

4. *One accustomed to push,* נַגָּח *naggach.*
Exod21. 29 if the ox were wont to push with; 21.36.

5. *To send forth or out,* שָׁלַח *shalach,* 3.
Job 30. 12 they push away my feet, and they raise

PUT. *See* **PHUT.**

PUT, to —

1. *To cause to go or come in,* בּוֹא *bo,* 5.
Exod25. 14 thou shalt put the staves into the rings by
26. 11 put the taches into the loops, and couple th.
37. 5 put the staves into the rings by the sides
38. 7 put the staves into the rings on the sides
Neh. 3. 5 nobles put not their necks to the work of

2. *To put, guide,* הָדָה *hadah.*
Isa. 11. 8 shall put his hand on the cockatrice den

3. *To put, set, place,* שׂוּם, שִׂים *sum, sim.*
Mic. 2. 12 will put them together as the sheep of B.

4. *To bind up,* חָבַשׁ *chabash.*
Exod29. 9 put the bonnets on them: and the priest's
Lev. 8. 13 girded them..and put bonnets upon them

5. *To rest, set down,* נוּחַ *nuach,* 5.
Gen. 2. 15 put him into the garden of Eden to dress
Lev. 24. 12 put him in ward, that the mind of the L.
Num15. 34 put him in ward, because it was not dec.
1 Ki. 8. 9 tables of stone, which Moses put there at
2 Ki. 17. 29 put (them) in the houses of the high pla.

6. *To add,* יָסַף *yasaph.*
Lev. 22. 14 then he shall put the fifth (part) thereof

7. *To cause to go out,* יָצַג *yatsag,* 5.
Judg. 6. 37 will put a fleece of wool in the floor; (and)
8. 27 made an ephod thereof, and put it in his

8. *To (cause to) clothe or put on,* לָבַשׁ *labesh,* 5.
Gen. 27. 15 and put them upon Jacob her younger son
27. 16 put the skins of the kids of the goats upon
Exod28. 41 thou shalt put them upon Aaron thy bro.
29. 5 put upon Aaron the coat, and the robe of
40. 13 thou shalt put upon Aaron the holy gar.
Num20. 26, 28 and put them upon Eleazar his son

9. *A sending forth,* מִשְׁלַח *mishlach.*
Deut12. 7 rejoice in all that ye put your hand unto
12. 18 in all that thou puttest thine hands unto
15. 10 in all that thou puttest thine hand unto

10. *To lead, put in,* נָחָה *nachah,* 5.
2 Ki.18. 11 put them in Halah and in Habor (by) the

11. *To cause to reach, attain,* נָשַׂג *nasag,* 5.
1 Sa. 14. 26 but no man put his hand to his mouth: for

12. *To give,* נָתַן *nathan.*
Gen. 38. 28 that (the one) put out (his) hand: and the
39. 4 and all (that) he had he put into his hand
39. 20 took him, and put him into the prison a
40. 3 put them in ward in the house of the ca.
41. 10 put me in ward in the captain of the gu.
41. 42 put it upon Joseph's hand, and arrayed
Exod. 5. 21 to put a sword in their hand to slay us
16. 33 Take a pot, and put an omer full of man.
25. 12 put (them) in..four corners thereof; and
25. 16 thou shalt put into the ark the testimony
25. 26 put the rings in the four corners that (are)
25. 21 thou shalt put the mercy seat above upon
25. 21 in the ark thou shalt put the testimony
26. 34 thou shalt put the mercy seat upon the a.
26. 35 thou shalt put the table on the north side
27. 5 thou shalt put it under the compass of the
28. 23 shalt put the two rings on the two ends of
28. 24 shalt put the two wreathen (chains) of g.
28. 25 put (them) on the shoulder pieces of the
28. 27 shalt put them on the two sides of the e.
28. 30 thou shalt put in the breastplate of jud.
29. 3 shalt put them into one basket, and bring
29. 6 and put the holy crown upon the mitre
29. 12 put (it) upon the horns of the altar with
29. 17 put (them) unto his pieces, and unto his
29. 20 put (it) upon the tip of the right ear of A.
30. 6 thou shalt put it before the veil that (is)
30. 18 thou shalt put it..and thou shalt put wa.
30. 33 whosoever putteth (any) of it upon a str.
30. 36 put of it before the testimony in the tab.
31. 6 in the hearts..I have put wisdom, that
34. 33 (till) Moses had done speaking..he put a
35. 34 he hath put in his heart that he may te.
36. 1 in whom the LORD put wisdom and und.
36. 2 in whose heart the LORD had put wisdom
37. 13 put the rings upon the four corners that
39. 16 put the two rings in the two ends of the
39. 17 they put the two wreathen chains of gold
39. 18 put them on the shoulder pieces of the e.
39. 20 put them on the two sides of the ephod
39. 25 put the bells between the pomegranates
40. 7 set the laver..and shalt put water therein
40. 18 put in the bars thereof, and reared up his
40. 20 put the testimony..and put the mercy s.
40. 22 put the table in the tent of the congrega.
40. 30 set the laver..and put water there, to w.
Lev. 1. 7 put fire upon the altar, and lay the wood
2. 1 shall pour oil upon it, and put frankince.
2. 15 thou shalt put oil upon it, and lay frank.
4. 7 priest shall put (some) of the blood upon
4. 18 he shall put (some) of the blood upon the
4. 25, 30, 34 put (it) upon the horns of the altar
5. 11 neither shall he put (any) frankincense th.
8. 7 put upon him the coat..and put the ephod
8. 8 also he put in the breastplate the Urim
8. 15 put (it) upon the horns of the altar round
8. 23 put (it) upon the tip of Aaron's right ear
8. 24 put of the blood upon the tip of their rig.
8. 27 put all upon Aaron's hands, and upon his
9. 9 and put (it) upon the horns of the altar
10. 1 put fire therein, and..offered strange fire
14. 17, 25 put..upon the tip of the right ear of
14. 14 priest shall put (it) upon the tip of the
14. 28 put of the oil that (is) in his hand upon
14. 29 he shall put upon the head of him that is
14. 34 put the plague of leprosy in a house of the
16. 13 he shall put the incense upon the fire be.
16. 18 put (it) upon the horns of the altar round
16. 21 putting them upon the head of the goat
19. 14 not curse the deaf, nor put a stumbling
24. 7 shalt put pure frankincense upon (each)
Num. 4. 6 shall put thereon the covering of badgers
4. 7 put thereon the dishes and the spoons, and
4. 10 they shall put it..and shall put (it) upon
4. 12 put (them) in a cloth..and shall put (the.)
5. 15 shall pour no oil upon it, nor put franki.
5. 17 priest shall take, and put (it) into the w.
5. 18 put the offering of memorial in her hands
6. 18 put (it) in the fire which (is) under the s.
6. 19 put (them) upon the hands of the Nazar.
11. 29 the LORD would put his spirit upon them!
15. 38 put upon the fringe of the borders a rib.
16. 7 put fire therein..it shall be (that) the m.
16. 17 put incense in them, and bring ye before
16. 18 put fire in them, and laid incense thereon
16. 46 Take a censer, and put fire therein from
16. 47 put on incense, and made an atonement
19. 17 running water shall be put thereto in a
27. 20 thou shalt put (some) of thine honour up.
Deut. 2. 25 This day will I begin to put the dread of
11. 29 shalt put the blessing upon mount Gerizim
18. 18 will put my words in his mouth; and he
23. 24 but thou shalt not put (any) in thy vessel
28. 48 shall put a yoke of iron upon thy neck
30. 7 will put all these curses upon thine enem.
Josh. 6. 24 put into the treasury of the house of the
17. 13 that they put the Canaanites to tribute
Judg. 7. 16 put a trumpet in every man's hand, with
1 Sa. 17. 38 put an helmet of brass upon his head; a.
2 Sa. 20. 3 put them in ward, and fed them, but w.
1 Ki. 2. 5 put the blood of war upon his girdle that

1 Ki. 2. 35 king put Benaiah the son of Jehoiada in
2. 35 did the king put in the room of Abiathar
5. 3 LORD put them under the soles of his feet
7. 39 put five bases on the right side of the ho.
7. 51 did he put among the treasures of the h.
10. 17 king put them in the house of the forest
10. 24 hear his wisdom, which God had put in
12. 4 heavy yoke which he put upon us, lighter
12. 9 Make the yoke which thy father did put
12. 29 set the one in Beth-el, and the other put
22. 23 LORD hath put a lying spirit in the mouth
2 Ki. 16. 14 and put it on the north side of the altar
16. 17 and put it upon a pavement of stones
18. 14 that which thou puttest on me will I bear
23. 33 Pharaoh-nechoh put him in bands at Ribl.
2 Ch. 3. 16 put (them) on the heads..and put (them)
4. 6 put five on the right hand, and five on the
5. 1 all the instruments, put he among the t.
5. 10 two tables which Moses put (therein) at
9. 16 king put them in the house of the forest
9. 23 hear his wisdom, that God had put in his
10. 4 ease..his heavy yoke that he put upon us
10. 9 Ease..the yoke that thy father did put
11. 11 put captains in them, and store of victual
16. 10 put him in a prison house; for (he was)
17. 19 besides (those) whom the king put in the
18. 22 hath put a lying spirit in the mouth of
22. 11 put him and his nurse in a bed chamber
23. 11 put upon him the crown, and (gave him)
34. 10 put (it) in the hand of the workmen that
35. 3 Put the holy ark in the house which Sol.
36. 7 and put them in his temple at Babylon
Ezra 1. 7 and had put them in the house of his gods
7. 27 which hath put (such a thing) as this in
Neh. 2. 12 what my God had put in my heart to do
7. 5 God put into mine heart to gather toget.
Psa. 4. 7 Thou hast put gladness in my heart, more
15. 5 putteth not out his money to usury, nor
40. 3 he hath put a new song in my mouth, (e.)
78. 66 smote his enemies..he put them to a pe.
Prov. 8. 1 Doth not..understanding put forth her
Isa. 42. 1 I have put my spirit upon him; he shall
Jer. 1. 9 Then the LORD put forth his hand, and t.
1. 9 Behold, I have put my words in thy mo.
20. 2 put him in the stocks that (were) in the
27. 2 Make thee bonds and yokes, and put them
27. 8 that will not put their neck under the yo.
28. 14 I have put a yoke of iron upon the neck
29. 26 shouldest put him in prison, and in the s.
31. 33 I will put my law in their inward parts
32. 14 put them in an earthen vessel, that they
32. 40 but I will put my fear in their hearts, that
37. 4 among the people; for they had not put
37. 15 put him in prison in the house of Jonath.
37. 18 What have I offended..that ye have put
38. 7 heard that they had put Jeremiah in the
52. 11 Then he put out the eyes of Zedekiah; and
Lam. 3. 29 putteth his mouth in the dust, if so be th.
Eze. 3. 25 they shall put bands upon thee, and shall
4. 9 put them in one vessel, and make thee br.
10. 7 put (it) into the hands of (him that was)
11. 19 will put a new spirit within you; and I
14. 3 put the stumbling block of their iniquity
16. 11 I put bracelets upon thy hands, and a ch.
16. 12 I put a jewel on thy forehead, and ear r.
19. 9 they put him in ward in chains, and brou.
23. 42 which put bracelets upon their hands, and
29. 4 will put hooks in thy jaws, and I will ca.
30. 13 and I will put a fear in the land of Egypt
30. 24 put my sword in his hand: but I will br.
30. 25 put my sword into the hand of the king
36. 26 new spirit will I put within you; and I
36. 27 will put my spirit within you, and cause
37. 6 put breath in you, and ye shall live; and
37. 14 shall put my spirit in you, and ye shall
37. 19 will put them with him, (even) with the
38. 4 put hooks into thy jaws, and I will bring
43. 20 put (it) on the four horns of it, and on the
45. 19 put (it) upon the posts of the house, and
Mic. 3. 5 and he that putteth not into their mouths

13. *To turn aside,* סוּר *sur,* 5.
Gen. 38. 14 she put her widow's garments off from her
Deut. 21. 13 she shall put the raiment of her captivity
1 Sa. 17. 39 proved (them). And David put them off

14. *To sustain, support,* סָמַךְ *samak.*
Exod. 29. 10, 15, 19 shall put their hands upon the h.
Lev. 1. 4 he shall put his hand upon the head of the
Num. 8. 10 children of Israel shall put their hands up.

15. *To add,* סָפָה *saphah.*
Jer. 7. 21 Put your burnt offerings unto your sacri.

16. *To add,* סָפַח *saphach.*
1 Sa. 2. 36 Put me, I pray thee, into one of the pri.

17. *To add,* סָפַח *saphach,* 3.
Hab. 2. 15 Woe unto him..that puttest thy bottle to

18. *To cause to go up,* עָלָה *alah,* 5.
Josh. 7. 6 fell to the earth..and put dust upon their

19. *To lay on, load,* עָמַס *amas,* 5.
2 Ch. 10. 11 For whereas my father put a heavy yoke

20. *To do, make,* עָשָׂה *asah.*
1 Sa. 8. 16 he will take..your asses, and put (them)

21. *To cause to ride,* רָכַב *rakab,* 5.
2 Ki. 13. 16 Put thine hand upon the bow. And he put

22. *To set, put, place,* שִׂים, שׂוּם *sum, sim.*
Gen. 2. 8 there he put the man whom he had formed
21. 14 putting (it) on her shoulder, and the child
24. 2 Put, I pray thee, thy hand under my thigh
24. 9 servant put his hand under the thigh of A.
24. 47 put the ear ring upon her face, and the b.
28. 11 put (them for) his pillows, and lay down
28. 18 took the stone that he had put (for) his p.
30. 42 when the cattle were feeble, he put (them)
31. 34 put them in the camel's furniture, and sat
32. 16 and put a space betwixt drove and drove
33. 2 put the handmaids and their children fo.
37. 34 put sackcloth upon his loins, and mourned
40. 15 that they should put me into the dungeon
41. 42 fine linen, and put a gold chain about his
43. 22 we cannot tell who put our money in our
44. 1 put every man's money in his sack's mo.
44. 2 put my cup, the silver cup, in the sack's
47. 29 put, I pray thee, thy hand under my thi.
48. 18 Not so..put thy right hand upon his head
Exod. 2. 3 put the child therein; and she laid (it) in
3. 22 ye shall put (them) upon your sons, and
4. 15 thou shalt speak unto him, and put words
4. 21 those wonders..which I have put in thine
8. 23 I will put a division between my people
15. 26 I will put none of these diseases upon thee
17. 12 took a stone, and put (it) under him, and
24. 6 put (it) in basins; and half of the blood he
28. 12 thou shalt put the two stones upon the s.
28. 26 thou shalt put them upon the two ends of
28. 37 thou shalt put it on a blue lace, that it may
29. 6 and put the holy crown upon the mitre
29. 24 thou shalt put all in the hands of Aaron
32. 27 Put every man his sword by his side, (and)
33. 22 that I will put thee in a clift of the rock
39. 7 he put them on the shoulders of the ephod
39. 19 put (them) on the two ends of the breast.
40. 3 thou shalt put therein the ark of the tes.
40. 5 put the hanging of the door to the taber.
40. 19 put the covering of the tent above upon
40. 24 put the candlestick in the tent of the co.
40. 26 put the golden altar in the tent of the co.
40. 29 put the altar of burnt offering (by) the
Lev. 5. 11 he shall put no oil upon it, neither shall
6. 10 his linen breeches shall he put upon his
8. 8 And he put the breastplate upon him: also
8. 9 put the mitre upon his head; also upon
8. 9 did he put the golden plate, the holy
8. 26 and put (them) on the fat, and upon
9. 20 put the fat upon the breasts, and he burnt
10. 1 put incense thereon, and offered strange
Num. 4. 6, 8 and shall put in the staves thereof
6. 27 shall put my name upon the children of
11. 17 will put (it) upon them; and they shall
16. 7 put incense in them before the LORD to
21. 9 made a serpent of brass, and put it upon
22. 38 the word that God putteth in my mouth
23. 5 the LORD put a word in Balaam's mouth
23. 12 speak that which the LORD hath put in
23. 16 put a word in his mouth, and said, Go ag.
24. 21 Strong is thy dwelling place, and thou pu.
Deut. 7. 15 will put none of the evil diseases of Egypt
10. 2 I will write..and thou shalt put them in
10. 5 put the tables in the ark which I had m.
12. 5 shall choose out of all your tribes to put
12. 21 place which the LORD..hath chosen to put
26. 2 shalt put (it) in a basket, and shalt go unto
27. 15 man that maketh..and putteth (it) in (a)
31. 19 put it in their mouths, that this song may
31. 26 Take this book of the law, and put it in
33. 10 they shall put incense before thee, and
Josh. 7. 11 they have put (it) even among their own
10. 24 put your feet..And they..put their feet
24. 7 he put darkness between you and the E.
Judg. 1. 28 that they put the Canaanites to tribute
6. 19 flesh he put in a basket, and he put the
9. 49 put (them) to the hold, and set the hold
12. 3 I put my life in my hands, and passed o.
15. 4 put a fire brand in the midst between
16. 3 put (them) upon his shoulders, and carr.
18. 21 put the little ones and the cattle and the
Ruth 3. 3 put thy raiment upon thee, and get thee
1 Sa. 6. 8 put the jewels of gold, which ye return
6. 15 wherein the jewels of gold (were), and put
11. 11 Saul put the people in three companies
17. 40 put them in a shepherd's bag which he
17. 54 brought it to Jerusalem: but he put his
19. 5 For he did put his life in his hand, and s.
19. 13 put a pillow of goat's (hair) for his bolster
21. 6 to put hot bread in the day when it was
28. 21 have put my life in my hand, and have h.
31. 10 they put his armour in the house of Ash.
2 Sa. 8. 6 Then David put garrisons in Syria of Da.
8. 14 he put garrisons in Edom..all they of Edom
8. 14 throughout all Edom put he garrisons: and
12. 31 put (them) under saws, and under harr.
14. 3 So Joab put the words in her mouth
14. 19 put all these words in the mouth of thine
1 Ki. 9. 3 to put my name there for ever; and mine
11. 36 city which I have chosen me to put my
14. 21 city which the LORD did choose..to put
18. 23, 23 and lay (it) on wood, and put no fire
18. 25 call on the name of your gods, but put no
18. 42 and put his face between his knees
20. 6 shall put (it) in their hand, and take (it)
20. 24 Take the kings away..and put captains
20. 31 let us, I pray thee, put sackcloth on our
21. 27 put sackcloth upon his flesh, and fasted
22. 27 Put this (fellow) in the prison, and feed him
2 Ki. 2. 20 Bring me a new cruse, and put salt ther.
4. 34 put his mouth upon his mouth, and his
9. 13 put (it) under him on the top of the stairs
10. 7 put their heads in baskets, and sent him
13. 16 and he put his hand (upon it): and Elisha
19. 28 therefore I will put my hook in thy nose
2 Ki. 21. 4 the LORD said, In Jerusalem will I put my
21. 7 In this house..will I put my name for e.
1 Ch. 10. 10 they put his armour in the house of their
18. 6 Then David put (garrisons) in Syria-dam.
18. 13 put garrisons in Edom; and all the Edo.
2 Ch. 1. 5 he put before the tabernacle of the LORD
6. 11 in it have I put the ark, wherein (is) the
6. 20 said that thou wouldest put thy name th.
12. 13 LORD had chosen..to put his name there
18. 26 Put this (fellow) in the prison, and feed
33. 7 and in Jerusalem..will I put my name for
33. 14 and put captains of war in all the fenced
Job 13. 14 take my flesh in my teeth, and put my l.
13. 27 Thou puttest my feet also in the stocks
23. 6 No; but he would put (strength) in me
33. 11 He putteth my feet in the stocks, he ma.
41. 2 Canst thou put an hook into his nose? or
Psa. 56. 8 put thou my tears into thy bottle: (are t.)
Prov. 23. 2 put a knife to thy throat, if thou (be) a
Isa. 5. 20 that put darkness for light..that put bit.
37. 29 therefore will I put my hook in thy nose
51. 16 have put my words in thy mouth, and h.
51. 23 I will put it into the hand of them that
59. 21 my words which I have put in thy mouth
63. 11 where (is) he that put his holy spirit wit.
Jer. 13. 1 put it upon thy loins, and put it not in
13. 2 So I got a girdle..and put (it) on my loins
38. 12 Put now (these) old cast clouts and rotten
40. 10 put (them) in your vessels, and dwell in
Eze. 14. 4, 7 putteth the stumbling block of his in.
16. 14 comeliness, which I had put upon thee
24. 17 put on thy shoes upon thy feet, and cover
30. 21 to put a roller to bind it, to make it strong
Mic. 2. 12 I will put them together as the sheep of

23. *To cause to turn back,* שׁוּב *shub,* 5.
1 Sa. 14. 27 put his hand to his mouth; and his eyes

24. *To set, put, place,* שִׁית *shith.*
Gen. 3. 15 will put enmity between thee and the w.
30. 40 he put his own flocks by themselves
30. 40 and put them not unto Laban's cattle
46. 4 Joseph shall put his hand upon thine eyes
Exod. 23. 1 put not thine hand with the wicked to be
Job 38. 36 Who hath put wisdom in the inward pa.?
Psa. 8. 6 thou hast put all (things) under his feet
9. 20 Put them in fear, O LORD: (that) the na.
73. 28 I have put my trust in the Lord GOD, that
Jer. 3. 19 How shall I put thee among the children

25. *To send forth,* שָׁלַח *shalach.*
Exod. 22. 8 whether he have put his hand unto his n.
22. 11 hath not put his hand unto his neighbo.
Judg. 5. 26 She put her hand to the nail, and her ri.
1 Sa. 17. 49 David put his hand in his bag, and took
1 Ch. 13. 10 because he put his hand to the ark: and
Eze. 8. 17 and, lo, they put the branch to their nose

26. *To send forth,* שְׁלַח *shelach.*
Ezra 6. 12 people that shall put to their hand to al

27. *To cast, throw, put,* βάλλω *ballō.*
Matt. 9. 17 Neither do men put new wine into old b.
9. 17 but they put new wine into new bottles
25. 27 Thou oughtest therefore to have put my
27. 6 It is not lawful for to put them into the
Mark 2. 22 no man putteth new wine into old bottles
7. 33 put his fingers into his ears, and he spit
Luke 5. 37 no man putteth new wine into old bottles
John 5. 7 I have no man..to put me into the pool
12. 6 had the bag, and bare what was put ther.
13. 2 devil having now put into the heart of J.
20. 25 put my finger into the print of the nails
Jas. 3. 3 we put bits in the horses' mouths, that t.
Rev. 2. 24 I will put upon you none other burden

28. *To give,* δίδωμι *didōmi.*
Luke 15. 22 put a ring on his hand, and shoes on (his)
2 Co. 8. 16 which put the same earnest care into the
Heb. 8. 10 I will put my laws into their mind, and
10. 16 I will put my laws into their hearts, and
Rev. 17. 17 For God hath put in their hearts to fulfil

29. *To do, make,* ποιέω *poieō.*
Acts 5. 34 commanded to put the apostles forth a l.

30. *To put, place,* τίθημι *tithēmi.*
Matt. 5. 15 Neither do men light a candle, and put
12. 18 I will put my spirit upon him, and he sh.
14. 3 put (him) in prison for Herodias' sake, his
Mark 4. 21 Is a candle brought to be put under a bu.
10. 16 put (his) hands upon them, and blessed t.
Luke 8. 16 covereth it with a vessel, or putteth (it)
11. 33 when he hath lighted a candle, putteth
John 19. 19 Pilate wrote a title, and put (it) on the
Acts 1. 7 which the Father hath put in his own p.
4. 3 laid hands on them, and put (them) in h.
5. 18 laid their hands on the apostles, and put
5. 25 men whom ye put in prison are standing
12. 4 put (him) in prison, and delivered (him)
Rom. 14. 13 that no man put a stumbling block, or an
1 Co. 15. 25 till he hath put all enemies under his feet
2 Co. 3. 13 not as Moses, (which) put a veil over his.
1 Ti. 1. 12 counted me faithful, putting me into the
Rev. 11. 9 not suffer their dead bodies to be put in

PUT again, to —
To cause to turn back, שׁוּב *shub,* 5.
Gen. 29. 3 put the stone again upon the well's mouth
Exod. 4. 7 said, Put thine hand into thy bosom again
4. 7 And he put his hand into his bosom again
34. 35 Moses put the veil upon his face again, un.

PUT altogether, to —

To gather, אָסַף *asaph.*

Gen. 42. 17 he put them altogether into ward three d.

PUT apart, to —

A putting or driving away, נִדָּה *niddah.*

Lev. 15. 19 she shall be put apart seven days; and
18. 19 as long as she is put apart for her uncle.

PUT about, or asunder, to —

1. *To put around,* περιτίθημι *peritithēmi.*

Mark15. 17 platted a crown of thorns, and put it ab.

2. *To put apart,* χωρίζω *chōrizō.*

Matt 19. 6 joined together, let not man put asunder
Mark10. 9 joined together, let not man put asunder

PUT (far, far away), to (be) —

1. *To cause to burn, consume,* בָּעַר *baar,* 3.

Deut 13. 5 so shalt thou put the evil away from the
17. 7 So thou shalt put the evil away from am.
17. 12 and thou shalt put away the evil from I.
19. 13 thou shalt put away (the guilt of) innocent
19. 19 so shalt thou put the evil away from am.
21. 9 put away the (guilt of) innocent blood fr.
21. 21 so shalt thou put evil away from among
22. 21 so shalt thou put evil away from among
22. 22 so shalt thou put away evil from Israel
22. 24 so thou shalt put away evil from among
24. 7 thou shalt put evil away from among you
Judg 20. 13 that we may..put away evil from Israel
2 Ki.23 24 Josiah put away, that he might perform

2. *To cast out,* גָּרַשׁ *garash.*

Lev. 21 7 neither shall they take a woman put aw.
Eze. 44. 22 nor her that is put away; but they shall

3. *To cause to go out,* יָצָא *yatsa,* 5.

Ezra 10. 3 covenant with our God to put away all
10. 19 gave their hands that they would put aw.

4. *To drive away,* נָדָה *nadah,* 3.

Amos 6 3 Ye that put far away the evil day, and c.

5. *To cause to stretch out, turn aside,* נָטָה *natah,* 5,

Psa. 27. 9 put not thy servant away in anger: thou

6. *To cause to turn aside,* סוּר *sur,* 5.

Gen. 35. 2 Put away the strange gods that (are) am.
Josh.24 14 put away the gods which your fathers s.
24. 23 put away..the strange gods which (are)
Judg 10. 16 put away the strange gods from among
1 Sa. 1. 14 How long wilt thou be drunken? put aw.
7. 3 put away the strange gods and Ashtaroth
7. 4 children of Israel did put away Baalim
28. 3 Saul had put away those that had famil
2 Sa 7. 15 took (it) from Saul, whom I put away be.
2 Ki 3. 2 put away the image of Baal that his fath.
Psa. 18. 22 and I did not put away his statutes from
Prov. 4. 24 Put away from thee a froward mouth, and
Isa. 1. 16 put away the evil of your doings from b.
Jer. 4. 1 if thou wilt put away thine abominations
Hos. 2. 2 let her therefore put away her whoredoms

7. *To cause to pass over,* עָבַר *abar,* 5.

2 Sa. 12. 13 LORD also hath put away thy sin: thou
2 Ch.15. 8 put away the abominable idols out of all
Esth. 8. 3 besought him with tears to put away the
Eccl.11. 10 put away evil from thy flesh: for childh.

8. *To put far off,* רָחַק *rachaq,* 3.

Eze. 43. 9 Now let them put away their whoredom

9. *To put far off,* רָחַק *rachaq,* 5.

Job 11. 14 put it far away, and let not wickedness
19. 13 He hath put my brethren far from me
22. 23 thou shalt put away iniquity far from thy
Psa. 88. 8 Thou hast put away mine acquaintance f.
88. 18 Lover and friend hast thou put far from
Prov. 4. 24 a froward mouth, and perverse lips put far

10. *To cause to rest or keep sabbath,* שָׁבַת *shabath,* 5.

Exod12. 15 even the first day ye shall put away leav.
Psa.119. 119 Thou puttest away all the wicked of the

11. *To send forth,* שָׁלַח *shalach,* 3.

Deut 22 19, 29 he may not put her away all his days
Isa. 50. 1 whom I have put away? or which of my
Jer. 3. 1 If a man put away his wife, and she go
3. 8 I had put her away, and given her a bill

12. *To be sent forth,* שָׁלַח *shalach,* 4.

Isa. 50. 1 for your transgressions is your mother p. a.

13. *A putting away, rejecting,* ἀθέτησις *athetēsis.*

Heb. 9. 26 hath he appeared to put away sin by the

14. *To lift up,* αἴρω *airō.*

Eph. 4. 31 Let all bitterness..be put away from you

15. *To loose away,* ἀπολύω *apoluō.*

Matt. 1. 19 Joseph..was minded to put her away pr.
5. 31 Whosoever shall put away his wife, let
5 32 That whosoever shall put away his wife
19. 3 Is it lawful for a man to put away his w.
19. 7 Why did Moses then command..to put her a.
19. 8 suffered you to put away your wives: but
19. 9 Whosoever shall put away his wife, exc.
19. 9 whoso marrieth her which is put away d.
Mark10. 2 Is it lawful for a man to put away (his)
10. 4 they said, Moses suffered..to put (her) a.
10. 11 Whosoever shall put away his wife, and
10. 12 if a woman shall put away her husband
Luke16. 18 Whosoever putteth away his wife, and m.
16. 18 whosoever marrieth her that is put away

16. *To put away,* ἀποτίθημι *apotithēmi.*

Eph. 4. 25 putting away lying, speak every man tr.

17. *To push away,* ἀπωθέω *apōtheō.*

1 Ti. 1. 19 which some having put away, concerning

18. *To send away,* ἀφίημι *aphiēmi.*

1 Co. 7. 11 and let not the husband put away (his)
7. 12 let him not put her away

19. *To take out,* ἐξαίρω *exairō.*

1 Co. 5. 13 Therefore put away from among yourse.

20. *To do away entirely,* καταργέω *katargeō.*

1 Co.13. 11 when I became a man, I put away child.

PUT down, to —

1. *To cause to go down,* יָרַד *yarad,* 5.

Isa. 10. 13 I have put down the inhabitants like a v.

2. *To cause to turn aside,* סוּר *sur,* 5.

2 Ch.36. 3 king of Egypt put him down at Jerusale.

3. *To cause to rest or keep sabbath,* שָׁבַת *shabath,* 5.

2 Ki.23. 5 put down the idolatrous priests, whom the

4. *To make low or humble,* שָׁפֵל *shaphel,* 5.

Psa. 75. 7 he putteth down one, and setteth up ano.

5. *To make low or humble,* שְׁפַל *shephal,* 5.

Dan. 5. 19 set up, and whom he would he put down

6. *To take down,* καθαιρέω *kathaireō.*

Luke 1. 52 He hath put down the mighty from (their)

7. *To do away entirely,* καταργέω *katargeō.*

1 Co 15. 24 when he shall have put down all rule and

PUT forth (self), to (be) —

1. *What is cast out, produced,* גֶּרֶשׁ *geresh.*

Deut33. 14 for the precious things put forth by the

2. *To honour self,* הָדַר *hadar,* 7.

Prov25. 6 Put not forth thyself in the presence of

3. *To put forth a riddle,* חוּד *chud.*

Judg14. 12 will now put forth a riddle unto you: if
14. 13 Put forth thy riddle, that we may hear it
14. 16 thou hast put forth a riddle unto the chi.
Eze. 17. 2 put forth a riddle, and speak a parable un.

4. *To embalm, ripen,* חָנַט *chanat.*

Song 2. 13 fig tree putteth forth her green figs, and

5. *To give,* נָתַן *nathan.*

Prov. 8. 1 Doth not..understanding put forth her

6. *To send forth,* שָׁלַח *shalach.*

Gen. 3. 22 lest he put forth his hand, and take also
8. 9 then he put forth his hand, and took her
19. 10 men put forth their hand, and pulled Lot
Exod. 4. 4 Put forth thine hand..And he put forth
Deut25 11 putteth forth her hand, and taketh him
Judg. 3. 21 Ehud put forth his left hand, and took the
6. 21 put forth the end of the staff that (was)
15. 15 put forth his hand and took it, and slew
1 Sa. 14. 27 wherefore he put forth the end of the rod
22. 17 servants of the king would not put forth
24. 10 will not put forth mine hand against my
2 Sa. 6. 6 Uzzah put forth (his hand) to the ark of
15. 5 he put forth his hand, and took him, and
18. 12 would I not put forth mine hand against
1 Ki.13. 4 that he put forth his hand from the altar
13. 4 his hand, which he put forth against him
1 Ch 13. 9 Uzza put forth his hand to hold the ark
Job 1. 11 But put forth thine hand now, and touch
1. 12 only upon himself put not forth thine h.
2. 5 But put forth thine hand now, and touch
28. 9 He putteth forth his hand upon the rock
Psa. 55. 20 He hath put forth his hands against such
125. 3 lest the righteous put forth their hands
Jer. 1. 9 put forth his hand, and touched my mouth
Eze. 8. 3 put forth the form of an hand, and took

7. *To cast out,* ἐκβάλλω *ekballō.*

Matt. 9. 25 when the people were put forth, he went
John10. 4 when he putteth forth his own sheep, he
Acts 9. 40 Peter put them all forth, and kneeled down

8. *To stretch out,* ἐκτείνω *ekteinō.*

Matt. 8. 3 Jesus put forth (his) hand, and touched
Mark 1 41 put forth (his) hand, and touch him, and
Luke 5. 13 put forth (his) hand, and touched him, sa.

9. *To put forth, produce,* ἐκφύω *ekphuō.*

Matt 24. 32 When his branch..putteth forth leaves, ye
Mark13. 28 branch is yet tender, and putteth forth le.

10. *To say,* λέγω *legō.*

Luke14. 7 put forth a parable to those which were

11. *To put alongside,* παρατίθημι *paratithēmi.*

Matt 13. 24, 31 Another parable put he forth unto th.

PUT forward, from, to —

1. *To push away,* ἀπωθέομαι *apōtheomai.*

Acts 13. 46 but seeing ye put it from you, and judge

2. *To cast forth,* προβάλλω *proballō.*

Acts 19. 33 the Jews putting him forward. And Al.

PUT in, to —

1. *To send forth,* שָׁלַח *shalach.*

Song 5. 4 My beloved put in his hand by the hole
Joel 3. 13 Put ye in the sickle; for the harvest is r.

2. *To send forth,* שָׁלַח *shalach,* 3.

Exod22. 5 If a man..shall put in his beast, and shall

3. *To send forth or away,* ἀποστέλλω *apostellō.*

Mark 4. 29 he putteth in the sickle, because the har

4. *To cause to go up on, or into,* ἐμβιβάζω *embibazō.*

Acts 27. 6 found a ship of Alex...and he put us..in

[*See also* Away far, confidence, covering, death, difference, far away, lower, more, order, prison, silence, surety, trust.]

[*See also* Array, execution, fear, mind, order, remembrance, subjection.]

PUT in bands or in mind, to —

1. *To bind,* אָסַר *asar.*

2 Ki.23. 33 Pharaoh-nechoh put him in bands at Riblah

2. *To cause to remember again,* ἐπαναμιμνήσκω.

Rom.15. 15 putting you in mind, because of the grace

PUT off, to —

1. *To draw off,* חָלַץ *chalats.*

Isa. 20. 2 put off thy shoe from thy foot. And he

2. *To cause to go or come down,* יָרַד *yarad,* 5.

Exod33 5 therefore now put off thy ornaments from

3. *To cover, pardon,* כָּפַר *kaphar,* 3.

Isa. 47. 11 thou shalt not be able to put it off: and

4. *To cast off or out,* נָשַׁל *nashal.*

Exod. 3. 5 Draw not nigh hither: put off thy shoes

5. *To strip, put off,* פָּשַׁט *pashat.*

Lev. 6. 11 he shall put off his garments..and carry
16. 23 shall put off the linen garments which he
Neh. 4. 23 none of us put off our clothes, (saving that)
Song 5. 3 I have put off my coat; how shall I
Eze. 26. 16 put off their broidered garments: they
44. 19 they shall put off their garments wherein

6. *To open up or out,* פָּתַח *pathach,* 3.

1 Ki 20. 11 boast himself as he that putteth it off
Psa. 30. 11 thou hast put off my sackcloth, and gir.

7. *What is sent or put forth,* שֶׁלַח *shelach.*

Neh. 4. 23 (saving that) every one put them off for

8. *To unclothe oneself,* ἀπεκδύομαι *apekduomai.*

Col. 3. 9 seeing that ye have put off the old man

9. *A putting off,* ἀπόθεσις *apothesis.*

2 Pe. 1. 14 Knowing that shortly I must put off (this)

10. *To put away,* ἀποτίθεμαι *apotithemai.*

Eph. 4. 22 That ye put off, concerning the former c.
Col. 3. 8 But now ye also put off all these; anger

11. *To loose,* λύω *luō.*

Acts 7. 33 Put off thy shoes from thy feet: for the

PUT, must be —

To be thrown or cast, βλητέον *blēteon.*

Mark 2. 22 [but new wine must be put into new bot.]
Luke 5. 38 But new wine must be put into new bot.

PUT on or upon, to —

1. *To clothe,* לָבַשׁ *labesh.*

Gen. 28. 20 give me bread to eat, and raiment to put o.
38. 19 and put on the garments of her widowhood
Exod29. 30 shall put them on seven days, when he c.
Lev. 6. 10 priest shall put on his linen garment, and
6. 10 his linen breeches shall he put upon his
6. 11 put on other garments, and carry forth
16. 4 He shall put on the holy linen coat, and
16. 4 wash his flesh in water, and (so) put them o.
16. 23 linen garments which he put on when he
16. 24 put on his garments, and come forth, and
16. 32 put on the linen clothes, (even) the holy
21. 10 that is consecrated to put on the garme.
Deut22. 5 neither shall a man put on a woman's g.
1 Sa. 28. 8 put on other raiment, and he went, and
2 Sa. 14. 2 put on now mourning apparel, and ano.
1 Ki.22. 30 enter into the battle; but put thou on thy
2 Ch.18. 29 will go to the battle; but put thou on thy
Esth. 4. 1 put on sackcloth with ashes, and went out
5. 1 Esther put on (her) royal (apparel), and
Job 27. 17 prepare (it), but the just shall put (it) on
29. 14 I put on righteousness, and it clothed me
Song 5. 3 how shall I put it on? I have washed my
Isa. 51. 9 put on strength, O arm of the LORD; a.!
52. 1 put on thy strength, O Zion; put on thy
59. 17 For he put on righteousness as a breast
59. 17 and he put on the garments of vengeance
Jer. 46. 4 furbish the spears, (and) put on the brig.
Eze. 42. 14 shall put on other garments, and shall ap.
44. 19 shall put on other garments; and they s.
Jon. 3. 5 put on sackcloth, from the greatest of th.

2. *To be clothed,* לָבַשׁ *labesh,* 4.

1 Ki.22. 10 having put on their robes, in a void place

3. *To clothe one,* לָבַשׁ *labesh,* 5.

Exod29. 8 shalt bring his sons, and put coats upon
Lev. 8. 13 put coats upon them, and girded them

4. *To cover, wrap up, veil,* עָטָה *atah.*

Jer. 43. 12 as a shepherd putteth on his garment; and

5. *To cause to go up,* עָלָה *alah,* 5.

2 Sa. 1. 24 who put on ornaments of gold upon your

6. *To set, put, place,* שׂוּם, שִׂים *sum, sim.*

Num16. 46 put on incense, and go quickly unto the

7. *To set, put, place,* שִׁית *shith.*

Exod33. 4 and no man did put on him his ornaments

8. *To clothe, go into clothing,* ἐνδύω *enduō.*

Matt. 6. 25 Take no thought..what ye shall put on
27. 31 put his own raiment on him, and led him
Mark 6. 9 shod with sandals: and not put on two c.
15. 20 put his own clothes on him, and led him
Luke12. 22 neither for the body, what ye shall put on
15. 22 Bring forth the best robe, and put (it) on
Rom13. 12 and let us put on the armour of light
13. 14 put ye on the Lord Jesus Christ, and m.
1 Co.15. 53 this corruptible must put on incorruption
15. 53 and this mortal (must) put on immortality

1 Co. 15. 54 So when this corruptible shall have put
15. 54 this mortal shall have put on immortality
Gal. 3. 27 For as many of you..have put on Christ
Eph. 4. 24 that ye put on the new man, which after
6. 11 Put on the whole armour of God, that ye
Col. 3. 10 have put on the new (man), which is ren.
3. 12 Put on therefore, as the elect of God, holy
1 Th. 5. 8 putting on the breastplate of faith and love

9. *To put upon,* ἐπιτίθημι *epitithēmi.*
Matt 19. 13 that he should put (his) hands on them
21. 7 put on them their clothes, and they set
27. 29 they put (it) upon his head, and a reed in
Mark 7. 32 they beseech him to put his hand upon
8. 23 when he had..put his hands upon him, he
8. 25 After that he put (his) hands again [upon]
John 9. 15 He put clay upon mine eyes, and I washed
19. 2 soldiers platted a crown..and put (it) on
Acts 9. 12 putting (his) hand on him, that he might
9. 17 putting his hands on him, said, Brother S.
15. 10 to put a yoke upon the neck of the disci.

10. *To cast around,* περιβάλλω *periballō.*
John 19. 2 on his head, and they put on him a purple

11. *To put around,* περιτίθημι *peritithēmi.*
Matt 27. 28 they stripped him, and put on him a sca
27. 48 put (it) on a reed, and gave him to drink
Mark 15. 36 put (it) on a reed, and gave him to drink
John 19. 29 put (it) upon hyssop, and put (it) to his

PUT on, to be able to —
To gird, be restrained, חָגַר *chagar.*
2 Ki. 3. 21 gathered all that were able to put on ar.

PUT on account, to —
To reckon in, bring into the account, ἐλλογέω.
Phm. 18 If he..oweth..ought, put that on mine a.

PUT out, to —
1. *To quench,* כָּבָה *kabah,* 3.
2 Ch. 29. 7 put out the lamps, and have not burnt in.
Eze. 32. 7 when I shall shall put thee out, I will cover

2. *To wipe away, blot out,* מָחָה *machah.*
Exod 17. 14 utterly put out the remembrance of Am.
Psa. 9. 5 thou hast put out their name for ever and

3. *To pick out, pierce,* נָקַר *naqar,* 3.
Num 16. 14 wilt thou put out the eyes of these men?
Judg 16. 21 Philistines took him, and put out his eyes

4. *To cast out or off,* נָשַׁל *nashal.*
Deut. 7. 22 will put out those nations before thee by

5. *To blind,* עָוַר *avar,* 3.
2 Ki. 25. 7 put out the eyes of Zedekiah, and bound
Jer. 39. 7 Moreover he put out Zedekiah's eyes, and
52. 11 then he put out the eyes of Zedekiah; and

6. *To send forth,* שָׁלַח *shalach.*
2 Sa. 13. 17 Put now this (woman) out from me, and
2 Ki. 6. 7 And he put out his hand, and took it

7. *To send forth,* שָׁלַח *shalach,* 3.
Num. 5. 2 that they put out of the camp every leper
5. 3 Both male and female shall ye put out
5. 4 did so, and put them out without the ca.

8. *To cast out,* ἐκβάλλω *ekballō.*
Mark 5. 40 when he had put them all out, he taketh
Luke 8. 54 [he put them all out, and took her by the]

9. *To remove, transfer,* μεθιστάνω *methistanō.*
Luke 16. 4 when I am put out of the stewardship, th.

PUT out, to be —
1. *To be extinguished,* דָּעַךְ *daak.*
Job 18. 5 light of the wicked shall be put out, and
18. 6 and his candle shall be put out with him
21. 17 How oft is the candle of the wicked put o.
Prov 13. 9 the lamp of the wicked shall be put out
20. 20 lamp shall be put out in obscure darkness
24. 20 the candle of the wicked shall be put out

2. *To be quenched,* כָּבָה *kabah.*
Lev. 6. 12 fire upon the altar..shall not be put out

3. *To be wiped away, blotted out,* מָחָה *machah,* 2.
Deut 25. 6 that his name be not put out of Israel
[*See also* Confusion, death, flight, grief, shame, worse.]

PUT to or unto, to —
1. *To set, put, place,* שׂוּם, שִׂים *sum, sim.*
Num. 4. 11, 14 they shall spread..and shall put to t.

2. *To cast or throw upon,* ἐπιβάλλω *epiballō.*
Matt. 9. 16 putteth a piece of new cloth unto an old
Luke 5. 36 No man putteth a piece of a new gar.upon
9. 62 No man, having put his hand to the plo.

3. *To bear toward,* προσφέρω *prospherō.*
John 19. 29 filled a spunge..and put (it) to his mouth

PUT to death, to be —
1. *Slain of death,* הֲרוּגֵי מָוֶת *[harag].*
Jer. 18. 21 let their men be put to death; (let) their

2. *To lead away, destroy,* ἀπάγω *apagō* (pass.).
Acts 12. 19 commanded that (they) should be put to d.

PUT to more strength, to —
To use might, גָּבַר *gabar,* 3.
Eccl. 10. 10 then must he put to more strength: but

PUT to silence, to —
To cause to be dumb, דָּמַם *damam,* 5.
Jer. 8. 14 for the LORD our God hath put us to sile.

PUT under, to —
To set in array under, ὑποτάσσω *hupotassō.*
1 Co. 15. 27 For he hath put all things under his feet
1 Co. 15. 27 saith, All things are put under (him, it is)
15. 27 is excepted which did put all things under
15. 28 unto him that put all things under him
Eph. 1. 22 hath put all (things) under his feet, and
Heb. 2. 8 we see not yet all things put under him

PUT under, not —
Not arranged under, ἀνυπότακτος *anupotaktos.*
Heb. 2. 8 he left nothing (that is) not put under him

PUT up self, to —
To be gathered, אָסַף *asaph,* 2.
Jer. 47. 6 Put up thyself into thy scabbard, rest, and

PUT (up) again, to —
1. *To cause to turn back,* שׁוּב *shub,* 5.
1 Ch. 21. 27 put up his sword again into the sheath t.

2. *To turn from,* ἀποστρέφω *apostrephō.*
Matt 26. 52 Put up again thy sword into his place: for

3. *To cast, throw,* βάλλω *ballō.*
John 18. 11 Put up thy sword into the sheath: the c.

PUT up in bags, to —
To compass, bind up, צוּר *tsur.*
2 Ki. 12. 10 they put up in bags, and told the money

PUT, to be —
1. *To be caused to go in,* בּוֹא *bo,* 6.
Exod 27. 7 staves shall be put into the rings, and the
Lev. 11. 32 it must be put into water, and it shall be

2. *To be added,* יָסַף *yasaph,* 2.
Num 36. 3 shall be put to the inheritance of the tribe
36. 4 then shall their inheritance be put unto

3. *To (cause to) add,* יָסַף *yasaph,* 5.
Eccl. 3. 14 nothing can be put to it, nor any thing t.

4. *To put, place,* שׂוּם *yasam.*
Gen. 50. 26 and he was put in a coffin in Egypt

5. *To be brought nigh,* נָגַשׁ *nagash,* 6.
2 Sa. 3. 34 hands (were) not bound, nor thy feet put

6. *To be given,* נָתַן *nathan,* 2.
2 Ch. 2. 14 find out every device which shall be put
Eze. 32. 25 he is put in the midst of (them that be) s.

7. *To be caused to give,* נָתַן *nathan,* 6.
Lev. 11. 38 if (any) water be put upon the seed, and

8. *To give,* נָתַן *nathan.*
Num 19. 17 running water shall be put thereto in a v.

9. *To go up,* עָלָה *alah.*
1 Ch. 27. 24 neither was the number put in the account

PU-TE-O'-LI, Ποτίολοι.
A seaport of Campania in Italy, six miles W. of Naples; once called Dicæ-archia, now Pozzuoli; it was founded by a colony of Samians, B.C. 521; in 215 fortified against Hannibal; in 212 became the chief port of the Roman army. In A.D. 60 it was passed by Paul on his way to Rome; in 410 was captured by Alaric; in 455 by Genseric; in 545 by Totila; in 1119 it was destroyed by an eruption of the Solfatara, and in 1538 by a volcanic disturbance of the Monte Nuova.
Acts 28. 13 and we came the next day to P.

PU-TI'-EL, פּוּטִיאֵל *God enlightens.*
Father in law of Eleazar, son of Aaron. B.C. 1500.
Exod 6. 25 Aaron's son, took him..daughters of P.

PUTRIFYING —
Fresh, raw, torn, טָרִי *tari.*
Isa. 1. 6 wounds, and bruises, and putrifying sores

PUTTING (away, forth, off, on, upon) —
1. *To give,* נָתַן *nathan.*
Lev. 16. 21 putting them upon the head of the goat

2. *To send forth,* שָׁלַח *shalach.*
Isa. 58. 9 putting forth of the finger, and speaking

3. *To send forth,* שָׁלַח *shalach,* 3.
Mal. 2. 16 saith that he hateth putting away: for

4. *A stripping off or away,* ἀπέκδυσις *apekdusis.*
Col. 2. 11 in putting off the body of the sins of the

5. *A putting off or away,* ἀπόθεσις *apothesis.*
1 Pe. 3. 21 not the putting away of the filth of the fl.

6. *A putting on, going into,* ἔνδυσις *endusis.*
1 Pe. 3. 3 wearing of gold, or of putting on of app.

7. *A putting on or upon,* ἐπίθεσις *epithesis.*
2 Ti. 1. 6 which is in thee by the putting on of my

PYGARG —
Species of antelope, דִּישֹׁן *dishon.*
Deut 14. 5 the pygarg, and the wild ox, and the cha.

Q

QUAILS —
A quail, שְׂלָיו, שְׂלוּ *selav.*
Exod 16. 13 at even the quails came up, and covered
Num 11. 31 brought quails from the sea, and let (them)
11. 32 gathered the quails: he that gathered le.
Psa. 105. 40 brought quails, and satisfied them with

QUAKE, to —
1. *To tremble, trouble self,* חָרַד *charad.*
Exod 19. 18 and the whole mount quaked greatly

2. *To be angry, troubled, to tremble,* רָגַז *ragaz.*
1 Sa. 14. 15 and the earth quaked: so it was a very gr.
Joel 2. 10 earth shall quake before them; the hea.

3. *To shake, tremble,* רָעַשׁ *raash.*
Nah. 1. 5 mountains quake at him, and the hills m.

4. *To shake, trouble, disturb,* σείω *seiō.*
Matt 27. 51 the earth did quake, and the rocks rent

5. *To be frightened, terrified,* εἰμὶ ἔντρομος *[eimi].*
Heb 12. 21 Moses said, I exceedingly fear and quake

QUAKING —
1. *Trembling, fear, trouble,* חֲרָדָה *charadah.*
Dan. 10. 7 a great quaking fell upon them, so that

2. *A shaking, trembling,* רַעַשׁ *raash.*
Eze. 12. 18 eat thy bread with quaking, and drink

QUARREL —
1. *Vengeance,* נָקָם *naqam.*
Lev. 26. 25 shall avenge the quarrel of (my) covenant

2. *Blame, complaint,* μομφή *momphē.*
Col. 3. 13 if any man have a quarrel against any

QUARREL against, to have or seek a —
1. *To present self, seek a quarrel,* אָנָה *anah,* 7.
2 Ki. 5. 7 see how he seeketh a quarrel against me

2. *To hold in,* ἐνέχω *enechō.*
Mark 6. 19 Herodias had a quarrel against him, and

QUARRIES —
Graven images, פְּסִילִים *pesilim.*
Judg. 3. 19 from the quarries that (were) by Gilgal
3. 26 passed beyond the quarries, and escaped

QUARTER —
1. *Border,* גְּבוּל *gebul.*
Exod 13. 7 neither..leaven seen..in all thy quarters

2. *Extremities,* יַרְכְּתַיִם *[yarekah].*
Eze. 38. 6 house of Togarmah of the north quarters

3. *Wing,* כָּנָף *kanaph.*
Deut 22. 12 make thee..upon the four quarters of thy

4. *Side, border,* עֵבֶר *eber.*
Isa. 47. 15 they shall wander every one to his quar.

5. *Corner,* פֵּאָה *peah.*
Num. 34. 3 south quarter shall be from the wildern.
Josh. 15. 5 border in the north quarter (was) from
18. 14 Kirjath-jearim..this (was) the west quar
18. 15 And the south quarter (was) from the end

6. *End, extremity,* קָצָה *qatsah.*
Jer. 49. 36 the four winds from the four quarters of

7. *End, extremity,* קָצֶה *qatseh.*
Gen. 19. 4 old and young..people from every quart.
Isa. 56. 11 every one for his gain, from his quarter

8. *Wind,* רוּחַ *ruach.*
1 Ch. 9. 24 In four quarters were the porters, toward

9. *Corner, angle,* γωνία *gōnia.*
Rev. 20. 8 which are in the four quarters of the ea.

10. *Place,* τόπος *topos.*
Acts 16. 3 of the Jews which were in those quarters
28. 7 In the same quarters were possessions of

QUARTER, from every —
From every place, πανταχόθεν *pantachothen.*
Mark 1. 45 and they came to him from every quarter

QUARTUS, Κούαρτος *fourth.*
A believer in Rome to whom Paul sends a salutation.
Rom. 16. 23 Erastus..saluteth you, and Q. a brother

QUATERNION —
A company of four, τετράδιον *tetradion.*
Acts 12. 4 four quaternions of soldiers to keep him

QUEEN —
1. *Mighty one, mistress,* גְּבִירָה *gebirah.*
1 Ki. 11. 19 to wife..the sister of Tahpenes the queen
15. 13 her he removed from (being) queen, bec.
2 Ki. 10. 13 go down to salute..the children of the q.
2 Ch. 15. 16 he removed her from (being) queen, bec.
Jer. 13. 18 Say unto the king and to the queen, Hu.
29. 2 the queen, and the eunuchs, and the pri.

2. *A queen,* מַלְכָּה *malkah.*
1 Ki. 10. 1 when the queen of Sheba heard of the fa.
10. 4 when the queen of Sheba had seen all So.
10. 10 which the queen of Sheba gave to king S
10. 13 Solomon gave unto the queen of Sheba all
2 Ch. 9. 1 when the queen of Sheba heard of the fa.
9. 3 when the queen of Sheba had seen the wi.
9. 9 as the queen of Sheba gave king Solomon
9. 12 Solomon gave to the queen of Sheba all
Esth. 1. 9 Vashti the queen made a feast for the w.
1. 11 To bring Vashti the queen before the king
1. 12 queen Vashti refused to come at the kin.
1. 15 What shall we do unto the queen Vashti
1. 16 the queen hath not done wrong to the
1. 17 (this) deed of the queen shall come abroad
1. 17 Ahasuerus commanded Vashti the queen
1. 18 which have heard of the deed of the que.
2. 22 who told (it) unto Esther the queen; and
4. 4 Then was the queen exceedingly grieved
5. 2 Esther the queen standing in the court
5. 3 What wilt thou, queen Esther? and what
5. 12 the queen did let no man come in with t.
7. 1 Haman..to banquet with Esther the qu.
7. 2 What (is) thy petition, queen Esther? and
7. 3 Esther the queen answered and said, If I

Esth. 7. 5 answered and said unto Esther the queen
7. 6 was afraid before the king and the queen
7. 7 request for his life to Esther the queen
7. 8 Will he force the queen also before me
8. 1 the house of Haman..unto Esther the q.
8. 7 king Ahasuerus said unto Esther the qu.
9. 12 And the king said unto Esther the queen
9. 29 Then Esther the queen, the daughter of
9. 31 and Esther the queen had enjoined them
Song 6. 8 There are threescore queens, and fourscore
6. 9 the queens, and the concubines, and th.
Dan. 5. 10 the queen, by reason of the words of the
5. 10 the queen spake, and said, O king, live for

3. *Queen*, מַלְכֶת *meleketh.*
Jer. 7. 18 to make cakes to the queen of heaven, and
44. 17, 18, 19, 25 incense unto the queen of hea.

4. *A princess*, שָׂרָה *sarah.*
Isa. 49. 23 and their queens thy nursing mothers

5. *A wife, queen*, שֵׁגָל *shegal.*
Neh. 2. 6 the king said..the queen also sitting by
Psa. 45. 9 right..did stand the queen in gold of Op.

6. *A queen*, βασίλισσα *basilissa.*
Matt12. 42 The queen of the south shall rise up in
Luke11. 31 The queen of the south shall rise up in
Acts 8. 27 under Candace queen of the Ethiopians
Rev. 18. 7 I sit a queen, and am no widow, and shall

QUEEN, to be or make —

1. *To be queen, to reign*, מָלַךְ *malak.*
Esth. 2. 4 let the maiden which pleaseth..be queen

2. *To make queen, to cause to reign*, מָלַךְ *malak*, 5.
Esth. 2. 17 the king..made her queen instead of Va.

QUENCH, to —

1. *To quench*, כָּבָה *kabah*, 3.
2 Sa. 14. 7 so they shall quench my coal which is l.
21. 17 go..that thou quench not the light of I.
Song 8. 7 Many waters cannot quench love, neither
Isa. 1. 31 burn together, and none shall quench (t.)
42. 3 and the smoking flax shall he not quench
Jer. 4. 4 burn that none can quench (it), because of
21. 12 burn that none can quench (it), because
Amos 5. 6 and (there be) none to quench (it) in Be.

2. *To break in pieces, destroy*, שָׁבַר *shabar.*
Psa.104. 11 They give drink..the wild asses quench

3. *To quench*, σβέννυμι *sbennumi.*
Matt12. 20 smoking flax shall he not quench, till he
Mark 9. 44, 46, 48 [Where..the fire is not quenched]
Eph. 6. 16 to quench all the fiery darts of the wicked
1 Th. 5. 19 Quench not the spirit
Heb.11. 34 Quenched the violence of fire, escaped the

QUENCHED, (not) to be —

1. *To be extinguished*, דָּעַךְ *daak*, 4.
Psa.118. 12 they are quenched as the fire of thorns

2. *To be quenched*, כָּבָה *kabah.*
2 Ki.22. 17 therefore my wrath..shall not be quen.
2 Ch.34. 25 therefore my wrath..shall not be quen.
Isa. 34. 10 It shall not be quenched night nor day
43. 17 they are extinct, they are quenched as tow
66. 24 neither shall their fire be quenched; and
Jer. 7. 20 it shall burn, and shall not be quenched
17. 27 shall devour..and it shall not be quenched
Eze. 20. 47 the flaming flame shall not be quenched
20. 48 have kindled it: it shall not be quenched

3. *To sink*, שָׁקַע *shaqa.*
Num11. 2 when Moses prayed..the fire was quen.

4. *Unquenched, unquenchable*, ἄσβεστος *asbestos.*
Mark 9. 43, 45 [the fire that never shall be quenched]

QUESTION, (hard) —

1. *A word, matter, thing*, דָּבָר *dabar.*
1 Ki. 10. 3 And Solomon told her all her questions
2 Ch. 9. 2 And Solomon told her all her questions

2. *Acute saying, hidden thing*, חִידָה *chidah.*
1 Ki. 10. 1 she came to prove him with hard quest.
2 Ch. 9. 1 came to prove Solomon with hard ques.

3. *Question, enquiry*, ζήτημα *zētēma.*
Acts 15. 2 go up to Jerusalem..about this question
18. 15 if it be a question of words and names
23. 29 Whom I perceived to be accused of ques.
25. 19 had certain questions against him of their
26. 3 and questions which are among the Jews

4. *A question, questioning, enquiry*, ζήτησις *zētēsis.*
John 3. 25 Then there arose a question between (some)
Acts 25. 20 because I doubted of such manner of qu.
1 Ti. 1. 4 endless genealogies, which minister que.
6. 4 doting about questions and strifes of words
2 Ti. 2. 23 unlearned questions avoid, knowing that
Titus 3. 9 foolish questions, and genealogies, and

5. *A word, matter, thing*, λόγος *logos.*
Mark11. 29 I will also ask of you one question, and

QUESTION (with), call in, ask, one with another, to —

1. *To seek, enquire, require*, דָּרַשׁ *darash.*
2 Ch.31. 9 Hezekiah questioned with the priests and

2. *To call into (court)*, ἐγκαλέω *egkaleō.*
Acts 19. 40 to be called in question for this day's

3. *To ask upon or about*, ἐπερωτάω *eperōtaō.*
Luke 2. 46 both hearing them, and asking them qu.
23. 9 he questioned with him in many words

4. *To judge*, κρίνω *krinō.*
Acts 23. 6 hope..of the dead I am called in question
24. 21 Touching..the dead I am called in ques.

5. *To seek together*, συζητέω *suzēteō.*
Mark 1. 27 they questioned among themselves, say.
8. 11 began to question with him, seeking of him
9. 10 questioning one with another what the
9. 14 he saw..the scribes questioning with them
9. 16 he asked..What question ye with them?

QUICK —

1. *Alive, living*, חַי *chai.*
Num16. 30 and they go down quick into the pit; then
Psa. 55. 15 (and) let them go down quick into hell: for
124. 3 they had swallowed us up quick, when th.

2. *Quickening, life giving, preserving*, מִחְיָה *michyah.*
Lev. 13. 10 and (there be) quick raw flesh in the rising
13. 24 the quick (flesh) that burneth have a white

3. *To live, have life*, ζάω *zaō.*
Acts 10. 42 he..(to be) the Judge of quick and dead
2 Ti. 4. 1 who shall judge the quick and the dead
Heb. 4. 12 the word of God (is) quick, and powerful
1 Pe. 4. 5 is ready to judge the quick and the dead

QUICKEN (together with), be quickened, to —

1. *To keep, preserve or give life*, חָיָה *chayah*, 3.
Psa. 71. 20 shalt quicken me again, and shalt bring
80. 18 quicken us, and we will call upon thy n.
119. 25 quicken thou me according to thy word
119. 37 Turn away mine eyes..quicken thou me
119. 40 Behold..quicken me in thy righteousness
119. 50 my comfort..for thy word hath quickened
119. 88 Quicken me after thy loving kindness; so
119. 93 for with them thou hast quickened me
119. 107 quicken me, O LORD, according unto thy
119. 149 LORD, quicken me according to thy judg.
119. 154 deliver..quicken me according to thy w.
119. 156 quicken me according to thy judgments
119. 159 quicken me, O LORD, according to thy
143. 11 Quicken me, O LORD, for thy name's sake

2. *To give or preserve life*, ζωοποιέω *zōopoieō.*
John 5. 21 raiseth up the dead, and quickeneth (th.)
5. 21 even so the Son quickeneth whom he will
6. 63 It is the spirit that quickeneth; the flesh
Rom. 4. 17 who quickeneth the dead, and calleth t.
8. 11 shall also quicken your mortal bodies by
1 Co.15. 36 that which thou sowest is not quickened
15. 45 last Adam (was made) a quickening spirit
1 Ti. 6. 13 in the sight of God, who [quickeneth] all
1 Pe. 3. 18 put to death..but quickened by the spirit

3. *To give or preserve life together*, συζωοποιέω.
Eph. 2. 5 hath quickened us together with Christ
Col. 2. 13 hath he quickened together with him, ha.

QUICKLY —

1. *Might, with might*, מְאֹד *meod.*
1 Sa.20. 19 thou shalt go down quickly, and come to

2. *Hasting, hastily*, מַהֵר *maher.*
Exod32. 8 They have turned aside quickly out of the
Deut. 9. 3 destroy them quickly, as the LORD hath
9. 12 Arise, get thee down quickly from hence
9. 12 they are quickly turned aside out of the
9. 16 ye had turned aside quickly out of the
28. 20 until thou perish quickly; because of the
Josh. 2. 5 pursue after them quickly; for ye shall
Judg. 2. 17 they turned quickly out of the way which

3. *Haste*, מְהֵרָה *meherah.*
Num.16. 46 go quickly unto the congregation, and m.
Deut 11. 17 ye perish quickly from off the good land
Josh. 8. 19 ambush arose quickly out of their place
10. 6 come up to us quickly, and save us, and
23. 16 ye shall perish quickly from off the good
2 Sa. 17. 16 send quickly, and tell David, saying, Lo.
17. 18 they went both of them away quickly, and
17. 21 pass quickly over the water: for thus ha.
2 Ki. 1. 11 thus hath the king said, Come down qui.
Eccl. 4. 12 a three fold cord is not quickly broken

4. *To hasten, make haste*, מָהַר *mahar*, 3.
Gen. 27. 20 How (is it)..thou hast found (it) so quic.

5. *Quickly, speedily*, ταχέως *tacheōs.*
Luke14. 21 Go out quickly into the streets and lanes
16. 6 Take thy bill, and sit down quickly, and

6. *More quickly or speedily*, τάχιον *tachion.*
John13. 27 Then said Jesus..That thou doest, do q.

7. *In or with speed*, ἐν τάχει *en tachei.*
Acts 12. 7 and raised him up, saying, Arise up quic.
22. 18 get thee quickly out of Jerusalem: for t.

8. *Quickly, speedily*, ταχύ *tachu.*
Matt. 5. 25 Agree with thine adversary quickly whi.
28. 7 go quickly, and tell his disciples that he
28. 8 they departed quickly from the sepulchre
Mark16. 8 they went out [quickly] and fled from t.
John11. 29 As soon as she heard..she arose quickly
Rev. 2. 5 I will come unto thee [quickly], and will
2. 16 I will come unto thee quickly, and will
3. 11 I come quickly: hold that fast which th.
11. 14 (and), behold, the third woe cometh qui.
22. 7 I come quickly: blessed (is) he that kee.
22. 12 I come quickly; and my reward (is) with
22. 20 I come quickly. Amen. Even so, come

QUICKLY, to fetch or make ready —

To make haste, cause to make haste, מָהַר *mahar*, 3.
Gen. 18. 6 Make ready quickly three measures of fi.
2 Ch.18. 8 Fetch quickly Micaiah the son of Imla

QUICKSANDS —

A sand bank, quicksand, σύρτις *surtis.*
Acts 27. 17 lest they should fall into the quicksands

QUIET (that are), at —

1. *Rest, place of rest*, מְנוּחָה *menuchah.*
Jer. 51. 59 And (this) Seraiah (was) a quiet prince

2. *Descent, rest, quietness*, נַחַת *nachath.*
Eccl. 9. 17 The words of wise (men are) heard in qu.

3. *Quiet*, רָגֵעַ *ragea.*
Psa. 35. 20 against (them that are) quiet in the land

4. *Quiet, ease*, שַׁאֲנָן *shaanan.*
Isa. 32. 18 sure dwellings, and in quiet resting plac.
33. 20 shall see Jerusalem a quiet habitation

5. *Safe, at ease, at rest*, שָׁלֵיו, שָׁלֵו *shalev.*
Job 21. 23 One dieth..being wholly at ease and quiet

6. *Finished, perfect, peaceable*, שָׁלֵם *shalem.*
Nah. 1. 12 Though (they be) quiet, and likewise ma.

7. *To be quiet, at rest*, שָׁקַט *shaqat.*
Judg18. 7 how they dwelt careless..quiet and secu.
18. 27 a people (that were) at quiet and secure
1 Ch. 4. 40 the land (was) wide, and quiet, and peac.

8. *Quiet*, ἤρεμος *ēremos.*
1 Ti. 2. 2 quiet and peaceable life in all godliness

9. *Mild, tranquil, gentle*, ἡσύχιος *hēsuchios.*
1 Pe. 3. 4 a meek and quiet spirit, which is in the

QUIET (self), to —

1. *To cause or let rest*, נוּחַ *nuach*, 5.
Zech. 6. 8 have quieted my spirit in the north cou.

2. *To be quiet, at rest*, שָׁקַט *shaqat*, 5.
Job 37. 17 he quieteth the earth by the south (wind)

3. *To be silent, to cease, stand still*, דָּמַם *damam*, 3a.
Psa.131. 2 I have behaved and quieted myself, as a

4. *To send down, appease, pacify*, καταστέλλω.
Acts 19. 36 ought to be quiet, and to do nothing ras.

QUIET, to be (in) —

1. *To keep self silent*, חָרַשׁ *charash*, 7.
Judg16. 2 were quiet all the night, saying, In the

2. *To (be at) rest*, נוּחַ *nuach.*
Job 3. 26 rest, neither was I quiet; yet trouble ca.

3. *To be quiet, at ease, secure*, שָׁאַן *shaan*, 3a.
Prov. 1. 33 whoso hearkeneth..shall be quiet from f.
Jer. 30. 10 shall be in rest, and be quiet, and none

4. *To be quiet, at rest*, שָׁקַט *shaqat.*
2 Ki.11. 20 city was in quiet: and they slew Athaliah
2 Ch.14. 1 In his days the land was quiet ten years
14. 5 and the kingdom was quiet before him
20. 30 the realm of Jehoshaphat was quiet; for
23. 21 the city was quiet, after that they had
Job 3. 13 should I have lain still and been quiet
Isa. 14. 7 The whole earth is at rest, (and) is quiet
Jer. 47. 6 how long (will it be) ere thou be quiet?
47. 7 How can it be quiet, seeing the LORD ha.
Eze 16. 42 will be quiet, and will be no more angry

5. *To cause to be quiet, or be at rest*, שָׁקַט *shaqat*, 5.
Isa. 7. 4 be quiet; fear not, neither be faint hea.
Jer. 49. 23 is) sorrow on the sea; it cannot be quiet

6. *To cease, be quiet, calm*, שָׁתַק *shathaq.*
Psa.107. 30 Then are they glad because they be quiet

7. *To rest, keep quiet*, ἡσυχάζω *hēsuchazō.*
1 Th. 4. 11 that ye study to be quiet, and to do your

QUIETLY —

In quietness, בַּשֶּׁלִי *bash-sheli.*
2 Sa. 3. 27 in the gate, to speak with him quietly

QUIETNESS —

1. *Descent, rest, quietness*, נַחַת *nachath.*
Eccl. 4. 6 Better (is) an handful (with) quietness, th.

2. *Safe, at ease, at rest*, שָׁלֵיו, שָׁלֵו *shalev.*
Job 20. 20 he shall not feel quietness in his belly

3. *Rest, ease, security*, שַׁלְוָה *shalvah.*
Prov.17. 1 Better (is) a dry morsel, and quietness th.

4. *To cause to be quiet or at rest*, שָׁקַט *shaqat*, 5.
Isa. 30. 15 in quietness and in confidence shall be your
32. 17 effect..quietness and assurance for ever

5. *Rest, quietness*, שֶׁקֶט *sheqet.*
1 Ch.22. 9 will give..quietness unto Israel in his d.

6. *Peace, concord, harmony*, εἰρήνη *eirēnē.*
Acts 24. 2 that by thee we enjoy great quietness, and

7. *Quietness, silence*, ἡσυχία *hēsuchia.*
2 Th. 3. 12 with quietness they work, and eat their

QUIETNESS, to give or be in —

1. *To be quiet, at rest*, שָׁקַט *shaqat.*
Judg. 8. 28 the country was in quietness forty years

2. *To cause to be quiet or at rest*, שָׁקַט *shaqat*, 5.
Job 34. 29 When he giveth quietness, who then can

QUIT, (to be) —

1. *Innocent, free, acquitted, exempt, clean*, נָקִי *naqi.*
Exod21. 28 but the owner of the ox (shall be) quit
Josh. 2. 20 we will be quit of thine oath which thou

2. *To be innocent, free, empty, acquitted*, נָקָה *naqah*, 2.
Exod21. 19 then shall he that smote (him) be quit: on.

QUIT selves, to —

1. *To be*, הָיָה *hayah.*
1 Sa. 4. 9 quit yourselves like men, O ye Philistines

2. *To act like a man*, ἀνδρίζομαι *andrizomai.*
1 Co.16. 13 Watch ye..quit you like men, be strong

QUITE —
Naked, bare, עֶרְיָה *eryah.*
Hab. 3. 9 Thy bow was made quite naked, (accord.)
[*See also* Driven, take away.]

QUIVER —
1. *A quiver,* אַשְׁפָּה *ashpah.*
Job 39. 23 The quiver rattleth against him, the glit.
Psa. 127. 5 Happy (is) the man that hath his quiver
Isa. 22. 6 Elam bare the quiver with chariots of m.
49. 2 made me a polished shaft; in his quiver
Jer. 5. 16 Their quiver (is) as an open sepulchre they
Lam. 3. 13 He hath caused the arrows of his quiver
2. *A quiver or sword,* תְּלִי *teli.*
Gen. 27. 3 thy weapons, thy quiver and thy bow, and

QUIVER, to —
To quiver, tingle, צָלַל *tsalal.*
Hab. 3. 16 my lips quivered at the voice: rottenness

R

RAA'-MAH, רַעְמָה *trembling.* (1 Ch. 1. 9*a*, רַעְמָא).
1. The fourth son of Cush eldest son of Ham. B.C. 2250.
Gen. 10. 7 Havilah, and Sabtah, and R., and Sabte.
10. 7 and the sons of R.; Sheba, and Dedan
1 Ch. 1. 9 Havilah, and Sabta, and R., and Sabte.
1. 9 And the sons of R.; Sheba, and Dedan
2. A place in the S.E. of Arabia, or on the Persian Gulf.
Eze. 27. 22 The merchants of Sheba and R., they (w).

RA-AM'-IAH, רַעַמְיָה *Jah causes trembling.*
A chief that returned with Zerubbabel. B.C. 536.
Neh. 7. 7 Nehemiah, Azariah, R., Nahamani, Mor.

RA-AM'-SES, רַעַמְסֵס *son of the sun.*
A treasure city built by the Israelites, *i.e.* Belbeis or Pelusium, a day's journey N.E of Cairo, on the Syro—Egyptian road, and capital of the province *Schaikyyah.*
Exod 1. 11 they built for Pharaoh..Pithom and R.

RAB'-BATH, RAB'-BAH, רַבָּה, רַבַּת *great.*
1. Chief city of Ammon, on the N. of Arnon, now *Amman,* twenty-two miles E. of Jordan, and fourteen N.E. of Heshbon.
Deut 3. 11 (is) it not in R. of the children of Ammon?
Josh. 13. 25 coast was..unto Aroer that (is) before R.
2 Sa. 11. 1 and they..besieged R. But David tarried
12. 26 Joab fought against R. of the children of
12. 27 I have fought against R., and have taken
12. 29 David gathered..people..and went to R.
17. 27 Nahash of R. of the children of Ammon
1 Ch. 20. 1 Joab led forth the..army..besieged R.
20. 1 And Joab smote R., and destroyed it
Jer. 49. 2 cause an alarm of war to be heard in R.
49. 3 cry, ye daughters of R., gird you with sa.
Eze. 21. 20 that the sword may come to R of the A.
25. 5 And I will make R. a stable for camels
Amos 1. 14 But I will kindle a fire in the wall of R.
2. A city in Judah, near Kirjath-jearim.
Josh. 15. 60 Kirjath-baal..Kirjath-jearim, and R.; two

RABBI —
A great man, teacher, (*from Ch.* רַבִּי), ῥαββί *rabbi.*
Matt 23. 7 greetings..be called of men, Rabbi, [Rab.]
23. 8 be not ye called Rabbi: for one is your M
John 1. 38 Rabbi, which is to say, being interpreted
1. 49 Rabbi, thou art the Son of God; thou art
3. 2 Rabbi, we know that thou art a teacher
3. 26 Rabbi, he that was with thee beyond Jo.
6. 25 they said..Rabbi, when camest thou hi.?

RAB'-BITH, הָרַבִּית *the great place.*
A city in Issachar, near Kishion and Abez; now called *Arrabeh.*
Josh. 19. 20 And R., and Kishion, and Abez

RABBONI —
My rabbi, (*Aramaic* רַבֹּן), ῥαββουνί *rhabbouni.*
John 20. 16 and saith..Rabboni! which is to say, M.

RAB'-MAG, רַב־מָג *head of the Magi.*
An officer of Nebuchadnezzar king of Babylon. B.C. 588.
Jer. 39. 3 R., with all the residue of the princes of
39. 13 R., and all the king of Babylon's princes

RAB-SA'-RIS, רַב־סָרִיס *head of the eunuchs.*
1. An officer of Nebuchadnezzar king of Babylon B.C. 588.
Jer. 39. 3 R..with all the residue of the princes of
39. 13 R..and all the king of Babylon's princes
2. An officer of Sennacherib king of Assyria. B.C. 710.
2 Ki. 18. 17 the king of Assyria sent Tartan, and R.

RAB-SHA'-KEH, רַבְשָׁקֵה *head of the cup bearers.*
An officer of Sennacherib king of Assyria in the days of Hezekiah. B.C. 710.
2 Ki. 18. 17 the king of Assyria sent..R., from Lachish
18. 19 R. said unto them, Speak ye now to Hez.
18. 26 Then said Eliakim..unto R., Speak, I pray
18. 27 But R. said unto them, Hath my master
18. 28 Then R. stood, and cried with a loud voice
18. 37 Eliakim..and told him the words of R.
19. 4 LORD thy God will hear..the words of R.
19. 8 So R. returned, and found the king..wa.
Isa. 36. 2 And the king of Assyria sent R. from La.
36. 4 And R. said unto them, Say ye now to H.
36. 11 Then said Eliakim..unto R., Speak, I pray
36. 12 But R. said, Hath my master sent me to
36. 13 Then R. stood, and cried with a loud vo.
36. 22 Eliakim .. told him the words of R.
37. 4 LORD thy God will hear the words of R.
37. 8 So R. returned, and found the king of A.

RACA —
Vain, empty, (*Aramaic* רֵיקָא) ῥακά *rhaka.*
Matt. 5. 22 whosoever shall say to his brother, Raca

RACE —
1. *Path, way, custom,* אֹרַח *orach.*
Psa. 19. 5 rejoiceth as a strong man to run a race
2. *A race,* מֵרוֹץ *merots.*
Eccl. 9. 11 the race (is) not to the swift, nor the ba.
3. *A race course, contest,* ἀγών *agōn.*
Heb. 12. 1 let us run with patience the race that is
4. *A race course, stadium, furlong,* στάδιον *stadion.*
1 Co. 9. 24 they which run in a race run all, but one

RACHAB. *See* **RAHAB.**

RA'-CHAL, רָכָל *place of traffic.*
A city in Judah, near Eshtemoa.
1 Sa. 30. 29 And to (them) which (were) in R., and to

RA'-CHEL, רָחֵל, Ῥαχήλ *a lamb.*
Younger daughter of Laban, and the best beloved wife of Jacob, to whom she bare Joseph and Benjamin. She died at Ephratah, B.C. 1729. Her tomb is said to be about a mile N. of Bethlehem; but from 1 Sa. 10. 2 it would seem to have been at *Zelzah.* In Jer. 31. 15 English *Rahel.*
Gen. 29. 6 behold, R. his daughter cometh with the
29. 9 R. came with her father's sheep; for she
29. 10 when Jacob saw R. the daughter of Laban
29. 11 And Jacob kissed R., and lifted up his v.
29. 12 Jacob told R. that he (was) her father's b.
29. 16 and the name of the younger (was) R.
29. 17 but R. was beautiful and well favoured
29. 18 And Jacob loved R.; and said, I will serve
29. 18 I will serve thee seven years for R. thy
29. 20 And Jacob served seven years for R.
29. 25 did not I serve with thee for R.? wherefore
29. 28 and he gave him R. his daughter to wife
29. 29 And Laban gave to R. his daughter Bil.
29. 30 And he went in also unto R.
29. 30 and he loved also R. more than Leah
29. 31 he opened her womb: but R. (was) barren
30. 1 when R. saw that she bare J. no children
30. 1 R..said unto Jacob, Give me children, or
30. 2 And Jacob's anger was kindled against R.
30. 6 R. said, God hath judged me..and hath
30. 7 And Bilhah, R.'s maid, conceived again
30. 8 R. said, With great wrestlings have I w.
30. 14 Then R. said to Leah, Give me, I pray thee
30. 15 And R. said, Therefore he shall lie with
30. 22 God remembered R., and God hearkened
30. 25 it came to pass, when R. had born J.
31. 4 And Jacob sent and called R. and Leah
31. 14 And R. and Leah answered and said unto
31. 19 R. had stolen the images that (were) her
31. 32 For Jacob knew not that R. had stolen
31. 33 Then went he out..and entered into R.'s
31. 34 Now R. had..put them in the camel's fu.
33. 1 he divided the children unto Leah, and..R.
33. 2 And he put..R. and Joseph hindermost
33. 7 and after came Joseph near and R., and
35. 16 and R. travailed, and she had hard labour
35. 19 And R. died, and was buried in the way
35. 20 that (is) the pillar of R.'s grave unto this
35. 24 The sons of R.; Joseph and Benjamin
35. 25 the sons of Bilhah, R.'s handmaid; D.
46. 19 The sons of R., Jacob's wife; Joseph, and
46. 22 These (are) the sons of R., which were b.
46. 25 Bilhah, which Laban gave unto R. his d.
48. 7 R. died by me in the land of Canaan in the
Ruth 4. 11 The Lord make the woman..like R. and
1 Sa. 10. 2 thou shalt find two men by R.'s sepulchre
Jer. 31. 15 R. weeping for her children, refused to be
Matt 2. 18 R. weeping (for) her children, and would

RAD'-DAI, רַדַּי *Jah subdues.*
Fifth son of Jesse the father of David. B.C. 1060.
1 Ch. 2. 14 Nethaneel the fourth, R. the fifth

RAFTER —
A rafter, gallery, רָהִיט *rahit.*
Song 1. 17 The beams..(are) cedar, (and) our rafters

RAG (rotten) —
1. *Cloak, garment, covering,* בֶּגֶד *beged.*
Isa. 64. 6 all our righteousnesses (are) as filthy rags
2. *Rotten rags,* מְלָחִים *melachim.*
Jer. 38. 11, 12 old cast clouts and old rotten rags
3. *Rents, pieces, rags,* קְרָעִים *qeraim.*
Prov 23. 21 drowsiness shall clothe (a man) with rags

RA'-GAU, Ῥαγαῦ. See *Reu.*
Father of Saruch, an ancestor of Jesus.
Luke 3. 35 Saruch, which was (the son) of R., which

RAGE, RAGING —
1. *Pride, rising, excellency,* גֵּאוּת *geuth.*
Psa. 89. 9 Thou rulest the raging of the sea: when
2. *Indignation, insolence,* זַעַם *zaam.*
Hos. 7. 16 shall fall..for the rage of their tongue
3. *Wrath, rage, raging,* זַעַף *zaaph.*
2 Ch. 16. 10 (he was) in a rage with him because of this
28. 9 in a rage (that) reacheth up unto heaven
Jon. 1. 15 and the sea ceased from her raging
4. *Heat, fury, poison,* חֵמָה *chemah.*
2 Ki. 5. 12 So he turned, and went away in a rage
Prov. 6. 34 jealousy (is) the rage of a man; therefore
5. *Wrath, transgression,* עֶבְרָה *ebrah.*
Job 40. 11 Cast abroad the rage of thy wrath: and
Psa. 7. 6 Arise..because of the rage of mine enem.
6. *Anger,* רֹגֶז *regaz.*
Dan. 3. 13 Then Nebuchadnezzar in..rage and fury
7. *To show self angry,* רָגַז *ragaz,* 7.
2 Ki. 19. 27 and thy coming in, and thy rage against
19. 28 thy rage against me and thy tumult is c.
Isa. 37. 28 and thy coming in, and thy rage against
37. 29 thy rage against me, and thy tumult, is
8. *Trembling, trouble, anger, rage,* רֹגֶז *rogez.*
Job 39. 24 He swalloweth the ground with..rage
9. *Rural, rustic, wild,* ἄγριος *agrios.*
Jude 13 Raging waves of the sea, foaming out their
10. *Rushing, raging,* κλύδων *kludōn.*
Luke 8. 24 rebuked the wind and the raging of the

RAGE, to —
1. *To show self foolish,* הָלַל *halal,* 7*a.*
Jer. 46. 9 rage, ye chariots; and let the mighty men
Nah. 2. 4 The chariots shall rage in the streets, they
2. *To roar, sound, make a noise,* הָמָה *hamah.*
Psa. 46. 6 The heathen raged, the kingdoms were
Prov 20. 1 strong drink (is) raging; and whosoever
3. *To show self wroth,* עָבַר *abar,* 7.
Prov 14. 16 A wise (man) feareth..but the fool rageth
4. *To be angry, troubled,* רָגַז *ragaz.*
Prov 29. 9 whether he rage or laugh, (there is) no r.
5. *To assemble,* רָגַשׁ *ragash.*
Psa. 2. 1 Why do the heathen rage, and the people
6. *To snort, rage,* φρυάσσω *phruassō.*
Acts 4. 25 Why did the heathen rage, and the people

RA-GU'-EL, רְעוּאֵל *Jah is friend.*
Father in law of Moses, called also *Jethro* and *Reuel.* B.C. 1530.
Num 10. 29 Moses said unto Hobab, the son of R.

RA'-HAB, רַהַב *tumult.*
A poetic and symbolic name for Egypt.
Psa. 87. 4 I will make mention of R. and Babylon
89. 10 Thou hast broken R. in pieces, as one that
Isa. 51. 9 (Art) thou not it that hath cut R., (and)

RA'-HAB, RA'-CHAB, רָחָב Ῥαάβ, Ῥαχάβ *breadth.*
1. A woman in Jericho who received and concealed the two spies. B.C. 1452.
Josh. 2. 1 came into an harlot's house, named R.
2. 3 And the king of Jericho sent unto R., sa.
6. 17 R. the harlot shall live..because she hid
6. 23 young men..went in, and brought out R.
6. 25 And Joshua saved R. the harlot alive, and
Heb. 11. 31 the harlot R. perished not with them that
Jas. 2. 25 Likewise also, was not R. the harlot justi.
2. The wife of Salmon, and mother of Booz. *See* Salmon.
Matt. 1. 5 And Salmon begat Booz of Rachab;

RA'-HAM, רַחַם *pity, love.*
Son of Shema the son of Hebron, descended from Caleb.
1 Ch. 2 44 And Shema begat R. the father of Jork.

RAHEL. *See* **RACHEL.**

RAIL (on), to —
1. *To reproach,* חָרַף *charaph,* 3.
2 Ch. 32. 17 letters to rail on the LORD God of Israel
2. *To flee ravenously,* עִיט *it.*
1 Sa. 25. 14 salute our master; and he railed on them
3. *To speak injuriously,* βλασφημέω *blasphēmeō.*
Mark 15. 29 they that passed by railed on him, wag.
Luke 23. 39 And one of the malefactors..railed on him

RAILER, RAILING —
1. *Injurious speaking,* βλασφημία *blasphēmia.*
1 Ti. 6. 4 cometh envy, strife, railings, evil surm.
Jude 9 not bring against him a railing accusation
2. *Injurious speaker,* βλάσφημος *blasphēmos.*
2 Pe. 2. 11 bring not railing accusation against them
3. *Reviling,* λοιδορία *loidoria.*
1 Pe. 3. 9 or railing for railing: but contrariwise
4. *Reviler,* λοίδορος *loidoros.*
1 Co. 5. 11 or a railer, or a drunkard, or an extort.

RAIMENT —
1. *Cloak, garment, covering,* בֶּגֶד *beged.*
Gen. 24. 53 jewels of gold, and raiment, and gave (th.)
27. 15 took goodly raiment of her eldest son Esau
27. 27 and he smelled the smell of his raiment
28. 20 give..bread to eat, and raiment to put on
Lev. 11. 32 or raiment, or skin, or sack, whatsoever
Num 31. 20 purify all (your) raiment, and all that is
Deut 24. 17 nor take a widow's raiment to pledge
Judg. 8. 26 raiment that (was) on the kings of Midian
1 Sa. 28. 8 put on other raiment, and he went, and
2 Ki. 5. 5 (pieces) of gold, and ten changes of rai.
7. 8 and gold, and raiment, and went and hid
Esth. 4. 4 she sent raiment to clothe Mordecai, and
2. *Covering,* כְּסוּת *kesuth.*
Exod 21. 10 her raiment, and her duty of marriage
3. *Clothing,* לְבוּשׁ *lebush.*
Isa. 14. 19 the raiment of those that are slain, thrust
4. *Long robe,* מַד *mad.*
Judg. 3. 16 he did gird it under his raiment upon his
5. *Clothing,* מַלְבּוּשׁ *malbush.*
Job 27. 16 Though he..prepare raiment as the clay

Isa. 63. 3 sprinkled..and I will stain all my raim.
Eze. 16. 13 thy raiment (was of) fine linen, and silk
6. *Outer garment,* שַׂלְמָה *salmah.*
Exod22. 9 raiment, (or) for any manner of lost thing
22. 26 take thy neighbour's raiment to pledge
Deut24. 13 that he may sleep in his own raiment, and
Josh 22. 8 and with iron, and with very much raiment
2 Ch. 9. 24 raiment, harness, and spices, horses, and
7. *Raiment, garment, a cloth,* שִׂמְלָה *simlah.*
Gen. 41. 14 changed his raiment, and came in unto P.
45. 22 he gave each man changes of raiment; but
45. 22 gave..of silver, and five changes of raim.
Exod 3. 22 of silver, and jewels of gold, and raiment
12. 35 of silver, and jewels of gold and raiment
22. 27 it (is) his raiment for his skin: wherein
Deut. 8. 4 Thy raiment waxed not old upon thee, n.
10. 18 and loveth..in giving him food and rai.
21. 13 she shall put the raiment of her captivity
22. 3 so shalt thou do with his raiment; and
Ruth 3. 3 put thy raiment upon thee, and get thee
8. *Clothing, garment,* ἔνδυμα *enduma.*
Matt. 3. 4 John had his raiment of camel's hair, and
6. 25 more than meat, and the body than rai.
6. 28 And why take ye thought for raiment?
28. 3 was like lightning, and his raiment white
Luke12. 23 is more than meat, and the body..than r.
9. *A robe, raiment,* ἐσθής *esthēs.*
Jas. 2. 2 there come in also a poor man in vile ra.
10. *Garment,* ἱμάτιον *himation.*
Matt11. 8 A man clothed in soft [raiment]? Behold
17. 2 transfigured..and his raiment was white
27. 31 put his own raiment on him, and led him
Mark 9. 3 his raiment became shining, exceeding w.
Luke 7. 25 A man clothed in soft raiment? Behold
23. 34 And they parted his raiment, and cast lots
John 19. 24 They parted my raiment among them, and
Acts 18. 6 he shook (his) raiment, and said unto them
22. 20 and kept the raiment of them that slew
Rev. 3. 5 the same shall be clothed in white raim.
3. 18 white raiment, that thou mayest be clot
4. 4 clothed in white raiment; and they had
11. *Garment, raiment,* ἱματισμός *himatismos.*
Luke 9. 29 and his raiment (was) white (and) glister.
12. *A covering,* σκέπασμα *skepasma.*
1 Ti. 6. 8 having food and raiment let us be there.

RAIMENT (of needlework), change of —
1. *Costly apparel,* מַחֲלָצוֹת *machalatsoth.*
Zech. 3. 4 I will clothe thee with change of raiment
2. *Embroidery,* רִקְמָה *riqmah.*
Psa. 45. 14 shall be brought..in raiment of needlew.

RAIN —
1. *Heavy rain, shower,* גֶּשֶׁם *geshem.*
Gen. 7. 12 the rain was upon the earth forty days and
8. 2 and the rain from heaven was restrained
Lev. 26. 4 I will give you rain in due season, and the
1 Ki. 17. 7 because there had been no rain in the l.
17. 14 (that) the LORD sendeth rain upon the e.
18. 41 for (there is) a sound of abundance of rain
18. 44 get thee down, that the rain stop thee not
18. 45 there was a great rain. And Ahab rode
2 Ki. 3. 17 neither shall ye see rain; yet that valley
Ezra 10. 9 sat..trembling because of..the great rain
10. 13 a time of much rain, and we are not able
Job 37. 6 the earth; likewise to the small rain
Psa. 68. 9 didst send a plentiful rain, whereby thou
105. 32 He gave them hail for rain, (and) flaming
Prov 25. 14 (is like) clouds and wind without rain
25. 23 The north wind driveth away rain; so (d.)
Eccl. 11. 3 If the clouds be full of rain, they empty
12. 2 nor the clouds return after the rain
Song 2. 11 For, lo, the winter is past, the rain is o.
Isa. 44. 14 he planteth an ash, and the rain doth n.
55. 10 as the rain cometh down, and the snow f.
Jer. 5. 24 that giveth rain, both the former and the
14. 4 there was no rain in the earth, the plow.
Eze. 1. 28 that is in the cloud in the day of rain
38. 22 an overflowing rain, and great hail stones
Hos. 6. 3 he shall come unto us as the rain, as the
Joel 2. 23 will cause to come down for you the rain
Amos 4. 7 I have withholden the rain from you, when
Zech 10. 1 give them showers of rain, to every one g.
14. 17 not come up..upon them shall be no rain
2. *Sprinkling rain,* מוֹרֶה *moreh.*
Psa. 84. 6 make it a well; the rain also filleth the p.
Joel 2. 23 the former rain..the former rain, and the
3. *Rain,* מָטָר *matar.*
Exod. 9. 33 the rain was not poured upon the earth
9. 34 the rain and the hail and the thunders
Deut11. 11 (and) drinketh water of the rain of heaven
11. 14 I will give (you) the rain of your land in his
11. 17 that there be no rain, and that the land
28. 12 give the rain unto thy land in his season
28. 24 The LORD shall make the rain of thy land
32. 2 My doctrine shall drop as the rain, my s.
1 Sa. 12. 17 he shall send thunder and rain; that ye
12. 18 the LORD sent thunder and rain that day
2 Sa. 1. 21 neither (let there be) rain upon you, nor
23. 4 out of the earth by clear shining after r.
1 Ki. 8. 35 there is no rain because they have sinned
8. 36 give rain upon thy land, which thou hast
17. 1 there shall not be dew nor rain these yea.
18. 1 Go..and I will send rain upon the earth
2 Ch. 6. 26 there is no rain, because they have sinn.
6. 27 send rain upon thy land, which thou hast
7. 13 If I shut up heaven that there be no rain
Job 5. 10 Who giveth rain upon the earth, and se.
28. 26 he made a decree for the rain, and a way
29. 23 they waited for me as for the rain; and
36. 27 they pour down rain according to the va.
37. 6 and to the great rain of his strength
38. 28 Hath the rain a father? or who hath be.
Psa. 72. 6 He shall come down like rain upon the
135. 7 he maketh lightnings for the rain: he br.
147. 8 who prepareth rain for the earth, who m.
Prov.26. 1 as rain in harvest; so honour is not see.
28. 3 a sweeping rain which leaveth no food
Isa. 4. 6 and for a covert from storm and from rain
5. 6 the clouds that they rain no rain upon it
30. 23 Then shall he give the rain of thy seed
Jer. 10. 13 maketh lightnings with rain, and bringe.
51. 16 maketh lightnings with rain, and brin.
Zech 10. 1 Ask ye of the LORD rain in the time of the
4. *Violent rain,* βροχή *brochē.*
Matt. 7. 25, 27 the rain descended, and the floods ca.
5. *A shower of rain,* ὑετός *huetos.*
Acts 14. 17 gave us rain from heaven, and fruitful se.
28. 2 because of the present rain, and because
Heb. 6. 7 the rain that cometh oft upon it, and br.
Jas. 5. 7 until he receive the early and latter [rain]
5. 18 the heaven gave rain, and the earth bro.

RAIN, first, former, latter, small —
1. *Sprinkling rain,* יוֹרֶה *yoreh.*
Deut.11. 14 That I will give (you)..the first rain, and
2. *To cast forth sprinkling showers,* יָרָה *yarah.*
Hos. 6. 3 come..as the..former rain unto the earth
3. *Gathered rain,* מַלְקוֹשׁ *malqosh.*
Deut 11. 14 the latter rain, that thou mayest gather
Job 29. 23 opened their mouth..for the latter rain
Prov.16. 15 his favour (is) as the cloud of the latter r.
Jer. 3. 3 there hath been no latter rain; and thou
Hos. 6. 3 come..as the latter..rain unto the earth
Joel 2. 23 and the latter rain in the first (month)
Zech 10. 1 Ask ye..in the time of the latter rain
4. *Showers,* שְׂעִירִים *seirim.*
Deut 32. 2 as the small rain upon the tender herb, and

RAIN, to cause or send —
1. *To cause or send or give rain,* גָּשַׁם *gasham,* 5.
Jer. 14. 22 Are there (any)..that can cause rain? or
2. *To cast forth sprinkling showers,* יָרָה *yarah,* 5.
Hos. 10. 12 till he come and rain righteousness upon
3. *To cause or send or give rain,* מָטַר *matar,* 5.
Gen. 2. 5 had not caused it to rain upon the earth
7. 4 I will cause it to rain upon the earth forty
19. 24 Then the LORD rained upon Sodom and u.
Exod 9. 18 I will cause it to rain a very grievous hail
9. 23 LORD rained hail upon the land of Egypt
16. 4 I will rain bread from heaven for you; and
Job 20. 23 shall rain (it) upon him while he is eating
38. 26 To cause it to rain on the earth, (where)
Psa. 11. 6 Upon the wicked he shall rain snares, fire
78. 24 had rained down manna upon them to eat
78. 27 He rained flesh also upon them as dust
Isa. 5. 6 the clouds that they rain no rain upon it
Eze. 38. 22 will rain upon him, and upon his bands
Amos 4. 7 I caused it to rain upon one city, and
4. 7 caused it not to rain upon another city
4. 7 piece whereupon it rained not withered
4. *To rain,* βρέχω *brechō.*
Matt. 5. 45 sendeth rain on the just and on the
Luke17. 29 rained fire and brimstone from heaven
Jas. 5. 17 that it might not rain; and it rained not
5. *To rain rain,* βρέχω ὑετόν *brechō hueton.*
Rev. 11. 6 it rain not in the days of their prophecy

RAINBOW —
A rainbow, ἶρις *iris.*
Rev. 4. 3 (there was) a rainbow round about the t.
10. 1 a rainbow (was) upon his head, and his

RAINED upon, (to be) —
1. *Its rain* (?), גֻּשְׁמָהּ [A.V. as if *gasham,* 4].
Eze. 22. 24 nor rained upon in the day of indignation
2. *To be rained on,* מָטַר *matar,* 2.
Amos 4. 7 one piece was rained upon, and the piece

RAINY, very —
Heavy shower, סַגְרִיר *sagrir.*
Prov 27. 15 A continual dropping in a very rainy day

RAISE (again, together, up), to —
1. *To make erect,* זָקַף *zaqaph.*
Psa. 145. 14 raiseth up all (those that) be bowed down
146. 8 LORD raiseth (them that are) bowed do.
2. *To lift up,* נָשָׂא *nasa.*
Exod23. 1 Thou shalt not raise a false report: put
Hab. 1. 3 there are (that) raise up strife and conte.
3. *To exalt, raise up,* סָלַל *salal.*
Job 19. 12 raise up their way against me, and encamp
30. 12 they raise up against me the ways of their
4. *To awake up, lift up,* עוּר *ur,* 3a.
Job 3. 8 who are ready to raise up their mourning
Song 8. 5 I raised thee up under the apple tree: th.
Isa. 15. 5 for..they shall raise up a cry of destruc.
Zech. 9. 13 raised up thy sons, O Zion, against thy sons
5. *To awake up,* עוּר *ur,* 5.
Ezra 1. 5 with all (them) whose spirit God had rai.
Isa. 41. 2 Who raised up the righteous (man) from
41. 25 I have raised up (one) from the
Isa. 45. 13 I have raised him up in righteousness, and
Jer. 50. 9 I will raise, and cause to come up against
51. 1 I will raise up against Babylon, and aga.
51. 11 LORD hath raised up the spirit of the kings
Eze. 23. 22 I will raise up thy lovers against thee
Joel 3. 7 I will raise them out of the place whither
6. *To stir up,* עִיר *ir.*
Hos. 7. 4 (who) ceaseth from raising after he hath
7. *To cause to go or come up,* עָלָה *alah,* 5.
1 Ki. 5. 13 king Solomon raised a levy out of all Is.
9. 15 reason of the levy which..Solomon raised
2 Ch.32. 5 raised (it) up to the towers, and another
8. *To cause to stand still,* עָמַד *amad,* 5.
Exod. 9. 16 I raised thee up, for to show (in) thee my
Psa.107. 25 raiseth the stormy wind, which lifteth up
9. *To make bare,* עָרַר *arar,* 3a.
Isa. 23. 13 they raised up the palaces thereof..he br.
10. *To raise up,* קוּם *qum,* 3a.
Isa. 44. 26 I will raise up the decayed places thereof
58. 12 thou shalt raise up the foundations of ma.
61. 4 they shall raise up the former desolations
11. *To cause to rise up,* קוּם *qum,* 5.
Gen. 38. 8 marry her, and raise up seed to thy bro.
Deut 18. 15 God will raise up unto thee a prophet from
18. 18 I will raise them up a prophet from amo.
25. 7 to raise up unto his brother a name in I.
Josh. 5. 7 children, (whom) he raised up in their st.
7. 26 they raised over him a great heap of stones
8. 29 and raise thereon a great heap of stones
Judg. 2. 16 LORD raised up judges, which delivered
2. 18 when the LORD raised them up judges, t.
3. 9 LORD raised up a deliverer to the childr.
3. 15 the LORD raised them up a deliverer, Eh.
Ruth 4. 5, 10 to raise up the name of the dead upon
1 Sa. 2. 8 He raiseth up the poor out of the dust
2. 35 I will raise me up a faithful priest, (that)
2 Sa. 12. 11 I will raise up evil against thee out of
12. 17 to raise him up from the earth: but he
1 Ki.14. 14 LORD shall raise him up a king over Isra.
1 Ch.17. 11 I will raise up thy seed after thee, which
Psa. 41. 10 and raise me up, that I may requite them
113. 7 He raiseth up the poor out of the dust
Isa. 14. 9 it hath raised up from their thrones all
29. 3 I will camp..I will raise forts against th.
49. 6 my servant to raise up the tribes of Jacob
Jer. 23. 5 will raise unto David a righteous branch
29. 15 hath raised us up prophets in Babylon
30. 9 their king, whom I will raise up unto th.
50. 32 and fall, and none shall raise him up
Eze. 34. 29 will raise up for them a plant of renown
Hos. 6. 2 he will raise us up, and we shall live in
Amos 2. 11 I raised up of your sons for prophets, and
5. 2 forsaken..(there is) none to raise her up
6. 14 I will raise up against you a nation, O
9. 11 In that day will I raise up the tabernacle
9. 11 I will raise up his ruins, and I will build
Mic. 5. 5 we raise against him seven shepherds, and
Hab. 1. 6 I raise up the Chaldeans, (that) bitter and
Zech.11. 16 I will raise up a shepherd in the land
12. *To set or place up again,* ἀνίστημι *anistēmi.*
Matt 22. 24 marry..and raise up seed unto his brot.
John 6. 39 should raise it up again at the last day
6. 40, 44, 54 will raise him up at the last day
Acts 2. 24 Whom God hath raised up, having loosed
2. 30 [would raise up Christ to sit on his throne]
2. 32 Jesus hath God raised up, whereof we all
3. 22 prophet shall the Lord your God raise up
3. 26 having raised up his Son Jesus, sent him
7. 37 prophet shall the Lord your God raise up
13. 33 in that he hath raised up Jesus again; as
13. 34 he raised him up from the dead, (now) no
17. 31 in that he hath raised him from the dead
13. *To raise or rouse up,* ἐγείρω *egeirō.*
Matt. 3. 9 God is able of these stones to raise up c.
10. 8 [raise the dead], cast out devils: freely ye
Luke 1. 69 hath raised up an horn of salvation for
3. 8 God is able of these stones to raise up ch.
John 2. 19 Destroy..in three days I will raise it up
5. 21 Father raiseth up the dead, and quickeneth
12. 1 Lazarus was..whom he raised from the
12. 9 Lazarus..whom he had raised from the
12. 17 when he called..and raised him from the
Acts 3. 15 prince..whom God hath raised from the
4. 10 whom God raised from the dead..by him
5. 30 God of our fathers raised up Jesus, whom
10. 40 Him God raised up the third day, and sh.
12. 7 and raised him up, saying, Arise up qui.
13. 22 [he raised up] unto them David to be th.
13. 23 God..raised unto Israel a Saviour, Jesus
13. 30 But God raised him from the dead
13. 37 But he, whom God raised again, saw no
26. 8 incredible with you, that God should raise
Rom. 4. 24 raised up Jesus our Lord from the dead
8. 11 of him that raised up Jesus from the dead
8. 11 he that raised up Christ from the dead s.
10. 9 that God hath raised him from the dead
1 Co. 6. 14 God hath both raised up the Lord, and
15. 15 raised up Christ: whom he raised not up
2 Co. 1. 9 trust..in God which raiseth the dead
4. 14 raised up the Lord Jesus shall raise up
Gal. 1. 1 the Father, who raised him from the dead
Eph. 1. 20 he raised him from the dead, and set (him)
Col. 2. 12 God, who hath raised him from the dead
1 Th. 1. 10 he raised from the dead, (even) Jesus, w
Heb. 11. 19 God (was) able to raise (him) up, even from
Jas. 5. 15 the Lord shall raise him up; and if he have
1 Pe. 1. 21 that raised him up from the dead, and

14. *To raise up upon,* ἐπεγείρω *epegeirō.*
Acts 13. 50 raised persecution against Paul and Bar.

15. *To set or put up out,* ἐξανίστημι *exanistēmi.*
Mark12. 19 take..and raise up seed unto his brother
Luke20. 28 take..and raise up seed unto his brother

16. *To raise up out,* ἐξεγείρω *exegeirō.*
Rom. 9. 17 have I raised thee up, that I might show
1 Co. 6. 14 and will also raise up us by his own power

17. *To raise up together,* συνεγείρω *sunegeirō.*
Eph. 2. 6 hath raised (us) up together, and made (us)

RAISE up self, great height, to —

1. *To make high, go up high,* גָּבַהּ *gabah,* 5.
2 Ch.33. 14 raised it up a very great height, and put

2. *To cause to rise up,* קוּם *qum,* 5.
Dan. 7. 5 it raised up itself on one side, and (it had)

3. *Rising, swelling,* שְׂאֵת *seth.*
Job 41. 25 When he raiseth up himself, the mighty

RAISE to life again, to —

A setting or raising up, ἀνάστασις *anastasis (gen.)*
Heb. 11. 35 received their dead raised to life again

RAISED (again, up,) to be —

1. *To be awaked up,* עוּר *ur,* 2.
Job 14. 12 not awake, nor be raised out of their sleep
Jer. 6. 22 a great nation shall be raised from the
25. 32 a great whirlwind shall be raised up from
50. 41 kings shall be raised up from the coasts
Zech. 2. 13 he is raised up out of his holy habitation

2. *To be caused to rise,* קוּם *qum,* 6.
2 Sa. 23. 1 the man (who was) raised up on high, the

3. *To raise up thoroughly,* διεγείρω *diegeirō.*
Matt. 1. 24 Joseph, [being raised] from sleep, did as

4. *To raise up,* ἐγείρω *egeirō.*
Matt 11. 5 the dead are raised up, and the poor have
16. 21 killed, and be raised again the third day
17. 23 and the third day [he shall be raised again]
Luke 7. 22 dead are raised, to the poor the Gospel
9. 22 and be slain, and [be raised] the third day
20. 37 that the dead are raised, even Moses sh.
Rom. 4. 25 and was raised again for our justification
6. 4 Christ was raised up from the dead by the
6. 9 being raised from the dead dieth no more
7. 4 to him who is raised from the dead, that
1 Co.15. 16 dead rise not, then is not Christ raised
15. 17 if Christ be not raised, your faith (is) vain
15. 35 How are the dead raised up? and with
15. 42 It is sown in corruption; it is raised in in.
15. 43 sown in dishonour; it is raised in glory
15. 43 sown in weakness; it is raised in power
15. 44 it is raised a spiritual body. There is a.
15. 52 the dead [shall be raised] incorruptible
2 Ti. 2. 8 Christ of the seed of David was raised

RAISER of taxes —

(One) sending a collector, מַעֲבִיר נוֹגֵשׂ *[abar].*
Dan. 11. 20 stand up in his estate a raiser of taxes

RAISING up —

To make a concourse, ποιέω ἐπισύστασιν *[poieō].*
Acts 24. 12 neither [raising up] the people, neither

RAISINS, bunches or clusters of —

Dried fruits, צִמּוּקִים *tsimmuqim.*
1 Sa. 25. 18 an hundred clusters of raisins, and two
30. 12 cake of figs, and two clusters of raisins
2 Sa. 16. 1 an hundred bunches of raisins, and an
1 Ch. 12. 40 bunches of raisins, and wine, and oil, and

RA'-KEM, *friendship,* רֶקֶם.
Son of Sheresh grandson of Manasseh. B.C. 1400.
1 Ch. 7. 16 and his sons (were) Ulam and R.

RAK'-KATH, רַקַּת *bank, flowing.*
A fenced city in Naphtali for Manasseh, near Hammath and Chinneroth; supposed by the Rabbins to have been afterwards the site of Tiberias. Now called *Kerak.*
Josh 19. 35 And the fenced cities (are) Ziddim..R., a.

RAK'-KON, הָרַקּוֹן *well watered.*
A city in Dan, near Joppa; now called *Oyun Kara.*
Josh.19. 46 And Me-jarkon, and R., with the border

RAM, רָם *high.*
1. Father of Aminadab, and son of Hezron son of Pharez. B.C. 1620.
Ruth. 4. 19 And Hezron begat R., and R. begat Amm.
1 Ch. 2. 9 The sons also of Hezron..Jerahmeel..R.
2. 10 And R. begat Amminadab; and Ammina.
2. Son of Jerahmeel brother of Ram. B.C. 1600.
1 Ch. 2. 25 And the sons of Jerahmeel..were R. the
2. 27 the sons of R. the first born of Jerahmeel
3. Head of the family of Elihu, who reasoned with Job. B.C. 1880.
Job 32. 2 Barachel the Buzite, of the kindred of R.

RAM —

1. *A ram,* אַיִל *ayil.*
Gen. 15. 9 a ram of three years old, and a turtledove
22. 13 a ram caught in a thicket by his horns
22. 13 took the ram, and offered him up for a
31. 38 and the rams of thy flock have I not eaten
32. 14 goats, two hundred ewes, and twenty ra.
Exod25. 5 rams' skins dyed red, and badgers' skins
26. 14 for the tent (of) rams' skins dyed red, and
29. 1 young bullock, and two rams without bl.
29. 3 bring..with the bullock and the two rams
29. 15 Thou shalt also take one ram; and Aaron
Exod29. 15, 19 their hands upon the head of the ram
29. 16 thou shalt slay the ram, and thou shalt
29. 17 thou shalt cut the ram in pieces, and w.
29. 18 thou shalt burn the whole ram upon the
29. 19 thou shalt take the other ram; and Aaron
29. 20 Then shalt thou kill the ram, and take of
29. 22 thou shalt take of the ram the fat, and
29. 22 shalt take..for it (is) a ram of consecrat.
29. 26 breast of the ram of Aaron's consecration
29. 27 the ram of the consecration, (even) of (t.)
29. 31 shalt take the ram of the consecration
29. 32 his sons shall eat the flesh of the ram
35. 7 rams' skins dyed red, and badgers' skins
35. 23 and red skins of rams, and badgers' skins
36. 19 for the tent (of) rams' skins dyed red, and
39. 34 the covering of rams' skins dyed red, and
Lev. 5. 15, 18 ram without blemish out of the flock
5. 16 with the ram of the trespass offering, and
6. 6 a ram without blemish out of the flock
8. 2 two rams, and a basket of unleavened b.
8. 18 he brought the ram for the burnt offering
8. 18 laid their hands upon the head of the ram
8. 20 he cut the ram into pieces; and Moses b.
8. 21 Moses burnt the whole ram upon the al.
8. 22 he brought the other ram, the ram of co.
8. 22 laid their hands upon the head of the ram
8. 29 of the ram of consecration it was Moses'
9. 2 ram for a burnt offering, without blem.
9. 4 a bullock and a ram for peace offerings
9. 18 the ram (for) a sacrifice of peace offerings
9. 19 the fat of the bullock and of the ram, the
16. 3 bullock..and a ram for a burnt offering
16. 5 kids..and one ram for a burnt offering
19. 21 shall bring..a ram for a trespass offering
19. 22 with the ram of the trespass offering be.
23. 18 one young bullock, and two rams: they
Num. 5. 8 beside the ram of the atonement, where.
6. 14 ram without blemish for peace offerings
6. 17 the ram (for) a sacrifice of peace offerings
6. 19 shall take the sodden shoulder of the ram
7. 15 One young bullock, one ram
[So in verse 21, 27, 33, 39, 45, 51, 57, 63, 69, 75, 81.]
7. 17 peace offerings, two oxen, five rams
[So in verse 23, 29, 35, 41, 47, 53, 59, 65, 71, 77, 83.]
7. 87 the rams twelve, the lambs of the first
7. 88 the rams sixty, the he goats sixty, the la.
15. 6 for a ram, thou shalt prepare (for) a meat
15. 11 done..for one ram, or for a lamb, or a kid
23. 1 prepare me here seven oxen and seven r.
23. 2, 4, 14, 30 on (every) altar a bullock and a r.
23. 29 prepare me..seven bullocks and seven r.
28. 11, 19, 27 one ram, seven lambs of the first
28. 12 offering, mingled with oil, for one ram
28. 14 the third (part) of an hin unto a ram, and
28. 20 shall ye offer..two tenth deals for a ram
28. 28 with oil..two tenth deals unto one ram
29. 2, 8, 36 one ram, (and) seven lambs of the first
29. 3, 9, with oil..(and) two tenth deals for a ram
29. 13, 17, 20, 23, 26, 29, 32 two rams, (and) fou.
29. 14 tenth deals to each ram of the two rams
29. 18, 21, 24, 27, 30, 33, 37 for the ram, and for
Deut32. 14 rams of the breed of Bashan, and goats
1 Sa. 15. 22 (and) to hearken than the fat of rams
2 Ki. 3. 4 an hundred thousand rams, with the w.
1 Ch.15. 26 they offered seven bullocks and seven rams
29. 21 a thousand rams, (and) a thousand lambs
2 Ch.13. 9 with a young bullock and seven rams, (the)
17. 11 seven hundred rams, and seven thousand
29. 21 seven rams, and seven lambs, and seven
29. 22 when they had killed the rams, they spr.
29. 32 an hundred rams, (and) two hundred lambs
Ezra 8. 35 ninety and six rams, seventy and seven
10. 19 (they offered) a ram of the flock for their
Job 42. 8 take unto you now..seven rams, and go
Psa. 66. 15 burnt sacrifices..with the incense of rams
114. 4 mountains skipped like rams, (and) the
114. 6 Ye mountains, (that) ye skipped like rams
Isa. 1. 11 I am full of the burnt offerings of rams
34. 6 with the fat of the kidneys of rams: for
60. 7 rams of Nebaioth shall minister unto thee
Jer. 51. 40 I will bring them down..like rams with
Eze. 27. 21 occupied with thee in lambs, and rams
34. 17 I judge..between the rams and the he g.
39. 18 drink the blood..of rams, of lambs, and
43. 23 and a ram out of the flock without blem.
43. 25 a ram out of the flock, without blemish
45. 23 seven rams without blemish daily the se.
45. 24 an ephah for a ram, and an hin of oil for
46. 4 burnt offering..(shall be)..a ram without
46. 5 meat offering (shall be) an ephah for a ram
46. 6 six lambs, and a ram; they shall be with.
46. 7 he shall prepare..an ephah for a ram, and
46. 11 an ephah to a ram, and to the lambs as he
Dan. 8. 3 there stood before the river a ram which
8. 4 I saw the ram pushing westward, and no.
8. 6 came to the ram that had (two) horns, wh.
8. 7 close unto the ram..and smote the ram
8. 7 there was no power in the ram to stand
8. 7 none that could deliver the ram out of his
8. 20 ram which thou sawest having (two) ho.
Mic. 6. 7 LORD be pleased with thousands of rams

2. *A ram,* דְּכַר *dekar.*
Ezra 6. 9 both young bullocks, and rams, and lambs
6. 17 two hundred rams, four hundred; 7. 17.

2a. *Ram, (ram's horn),* יוֹבֵל *yobel.*
Josh. 6. 5 they make a long (blast) with the ram's h.

3. *A stout ram,* כַּר *kar.*
Eze. 4. 2 set (battering) rams against it; 21. 22.

4. *He goat, ram, chief,* עַתּוּד *attud.*
Gen. 31. 10 rams which leaped upon the cattle (were) r.
Gen. 31. 12 rams which leap upon the cattle (are) ri.

RA'-MA, Ῥαμᾶ, *from Heb.* רָמָה *height.*
A city in Benjamin; same as succeeding.
Matt. 2. 18 In R. was there a voice heard, lamentat.

RA'-MAH, הָרָמָה *the height.*
1. A city in Benjamin, half an hour W. of Gibeon, and forty stadia or two hours or five miles N. of Jerusalem; now called *el-Ram.* It formed the frontier hold between Israel and Judah, 1 Ki. 15. 17.
Josh.18. 25 Gibeon, and R., and Beeroth
Judg. 4. 5 the palm tree of Deborah between R. and
19. 13 let us draw near to one of these places..R.
1 Ki. 15. 17 Baasha king of Israel went..and built R.
15. 21 he left off building of R., and dwelt in T.
15. 22 and they took away the stones of R., and
2 Ch.16. 1 Baasha king of Israel came..and built R.
16. 5 he left off building of R., and let his work
16. 6 and they carried away the stones of R.
Ezra 2. 26 The children of R. and Gaba, six hundred
Neh. 7. 30 The men of R. and Gaba, six hundred tw.
11. 33 Hazor, R., Gittaim
Isa. 10. 29 R. is afraid; Gibeah of Saul is fled
Jer. 40. 1 captain of the guard had let him go..R.
Hos. 5. 8 Blow ye..the trumpet in R.: cry aloud (at)
2. A city in Napthali, near Adamah and Hazor; now called *Rameh.*
Josh.19. 29 And (then) the coast turneth to R., and to
19. 36 And Adamah, and R., and Hazor
3. A city in Ephraim (also called Ramathaim Zophim), where Samuel the prophet dwelt, and near Bethel.
1 Sa. 1. 19 they rose up..and came to their house to R.
2. 11 And Elkanah went to R. to his house
7. 17 And his return (was) to R.; for there (was)
8. 4 Then all the elders of Israel..came..R.
15. 34 Then Samuel went to R.; and Saul went
16. 13 So Samuel rose up, and went to R.
19. 18 So David fled..and came to Samuel to R.
19. 19 Behold, David (is) at Naioth in R.
19. 22 Then went he also to R., and came to a
19. 22 (one) said, Behold, (they be) at Naioth in R.
19. 23 And he went thither to Naioth in R.
19. 23 he went on..until he came to Naioth in R.
20. 1 And David fled from Naioth in R., and
22. 6 Saul abode in Gibeah under a tree in R.
25. 1 the Israelites..buried him in his house at R.
28. 3 Israel had lamented him, and buried..in R.
Jer. 31. 15 A voice was heard in R., lamentation, (an.)
4. A contraction of Ramoth-*Gilead.*
2 Ki. 8. 29 wounds which the Syrians had given..R.
2 Ch.22. 6 of the wounds which were given him at R.

RA'-MATH, רָמַת *height.*
A city in Simeon called Ramoth "of the south;" now called *Kurnab.*
Josh.19. 8 R. of the south. This (is) the inheritance

RA-MA-THA-IM ZO'-PHIM, הָרָמָתַיִם צוֹפִים.
A city in Mount Ephraim, where Samuel the prophet dwelt, and more commonly called simply *Ramah.*
1 Sa. 1. 1 Now there was a certain man of R., of mo.

RAM-A-THITE, רָמָתִי.
An inhabitant of Ramah in Benjamin
1 Ch. 27. 27 And over..vineyards (was) Shimei the R.

RAM-ATH LE'-HI רָמַת לְחִי *high place of the jaw bone.*
A place in Judah, near Dan.
Judg15. 17 he cast away the jawbone..and called..R.

RA-MATH MIZ'-PEH, רָמַת הַמִּצְפֶּה *place of watch tower.*
A city of Gad in Gilead, fifteen miles N.W. of Rabbath Ammon, at the Jabbok.
Josh.13. 26 And from Heshbon unto R., and Betonim

RA-ME'-SES, רַעְמְסֵס *son of the sun.* See *Raamses.*
A city or district in Goshen, on the E. of the Nile. Perhaps *Pelusium* or *Belbeis.*
Gen. 47. 11 Joseph..possession..in the land of R.
Exod12. 37 the children of Israel journeyed from R.
Num33. 3 And they departed from R. in the first m.
33. 5 And..children of Israel removed from R.

RAM'-IAH, רַמְיָה *Jah is high.*
A son of Parosh who had taken a strange wife. B.C. 456.
Ezra 10. 25 of the sons of Parosh; R., and Jeziah, and

RA'-MOTH, רָאמוֹת, רָמֹת *heights.*
1. A Levitical city of Gilead in Gad, the same as Ramoth-*Gilead* and Ramoth-*mizpeh.*
Deut. 4. 43 and R. in Gilead, of the Gadites; and G.
Josh.20. 8 and R. in Gilead out of the tribe of Gad
21. 38 And out of the tribe of Gad, R.; 1 Ki.22.3.
1 Ch. 6. 80 And out of the tribe of Gad; R. in Gilead
2. A Levitical city in Issachar, perhaps the same as *Jarmuth* in Josh. 21. 29, and *Remath* in Josh 19. 21.
1 Ch. 6. 73 And R. with her suburbs, and Anem with
3. One of the sons of Bani that had taken a strange wife. B.C. 456.
Ezra 10. 29 of the sons of Bani Meshullam..and R.

RA-MOTH GIL'-EAD, רָמֹת גִּלְעָד.
A city of Gad in Gilead; sometimes simply called *Ramoth.* In 1 Ki. 22. 3 the Heb. is Ramoth Gilead.
1 Ki. 4. 13 The son of Geber, in R.; to him (pertained)
22. 4 Wilt thou go with me to battle to R.?
22. 6 Shall I go against R. to battle, or shall I
22. 12 saying, Go up to R., and prosper
22. 15 Micaiah, shall we go against R. to battle

1 Ki. 22. 20 that he may go up and fall at R.?
22. 29 Jehoshaphat..king of Judah went..to R.
2 Ki. 8. 28 went..to the war against Hazael..in R.
9. 1 Gird up thy loins..and go to R.
9. 4 the young man the prophet, went to R.
9. 14 Now Joram had kept R., he and all Israel
2 Ch. 18. 2 persuaded him to go up (with him) to R.
18. 3 Wilt thou go with me to R.?
18. 5 Shall we go to R. to battle, or shall I for.?
18. 11 saying, Go up to R., and prosper; for the
18. 14 shall we go to R. to battle, or shall I fo.?
18. 19 that he may go up and fall at R.?
18. 28 Jehosh. the king of Judah went up to R.
22. 5 to war against Hazael king of Syria at R.

RA'-MOTH, (South), רָמוֹת נֶגֶב.
A city of Simeon in the Negeb or south country. See *Ramath*
1 Sa. 30. 27 and to (them) which (were) in south R.

RAMPART —
Army, force, bulwark, חֵיל, חֵל *chel.*
Lam. 2. 8 made the rampart and the wall to lament
Nah. 3. 8 whose rampart (was) the sea, (and) her w.

RAMS' horn —
Ram's horn, יוֹבֵל *yobel.*
Josh. 6. 4 shall bear..seven trumpets of rams' horns
6. 6 bear seven trumpets of rams' horns before
6. 8 bearing the seven trumpets of rams' horns
6. 13 bearing seven trumpets of rams' horns be.

RANGE, to —
To run to and fro, שָׁקַק *shaqaq.*
Prov. 28. 15 (As) a roaring lion, and a ranging bear; (so

RANGE (for pots) —
1. *Abundance, range*, יְתוּר *yethur.*
Job 39. 8 The range of the mountains (is) his past.
2. *Range or row*, שְׂדֵרָה *sederah.*
2 Ki. 11. 8 he that cometh within the ranges, let him
11. 15 Have her forth without the ranges: and
2 Ch. 23. 14 Have her forth of the ranges: and whoso
3. *Double range for pots*, כִּירַיִם *kirayim.*
Lev. 11. 35 (whether it be) oven, or ranges for pots

RANK —
1. *Path, way, custom, traveller*, אֹרַח *orach.*
Joel 2. 7 and they shall not break their ranks
2. *Fat, firm*, בָּרִיא *bari.*
Gen. 41. 5 came up upon one stalk, rank and good
41. 7 seven thin ears devoured the seven rank
3. *Rank, arrangement*, מַעֲרָכָה *maarakah.*
1 Ch. 12. 38 All these men of war, that could keep rank
4. *Step, foot, time*, פַּעַם *paam.*
1 Ki 7. 4, 5 and light (was) against light (in) three r.
5. *A row, company*, πρασιά *prasia.*
Mark 6. 40 sat down in ranks, by hundreds, and by

RANK, to keep —
To keep rank, be in order, עָדַר *adar.*
1 Ch. 12. 33 fifty thousand, which could keep rank: (th.)

RANSOM —
1. *A covering*, כֹּפֶר *kopher.*
Exod 30. 12 then shall they give every man a ransom
Job 33. 24 saith, Deliver him..I have found a ransom
36. 18 then a great ransom cannot deliver thee
Psa. 49. 7 None (of them) can..give to God a rans.
Prov. 6. 35 He will not regard any ransom; neither
13. 8 The ransom of a man's life (are) his riches
21. 18 wicked (shall be) a ransom for the righ.
Isa. 43. 3 I gave Egypt (for) thy ransom, Ethiopia
2. *Freedom*, פִּדְיוֹן *pidyon.*
Exod 21. 30 then he shall give for the ransom of his l.
3. *A corresponding price*, ἀντίλυτρον *antilutron.*
1 Ti. 2. 6 gave himself a ransom for all, to be test.
4. *A price, ransom*, λύτρον *lutron.*
Matt 20. 28 and to give his life a ransom for many
Mark 10. 45 to minister, and to give his life a ransom

RANSOM, to —
1. *To free*, גָּאַל *gaal.*
Isa. 51. 10 depths of the sea a way for the ransomed
Jer. 31. 11 ransomed him from the hand of (him that
2. *To free*, פָּדָה *padah.*
Isa. 35. 10 And the ransomed of the LORD shall ret.
Hos. 13. 14 I will ransom them from the power of the

RA'-PHA, רָפָא, רָפָה *fearful.*
1. The fifth son of Benjamin. B.C. 1700.
1 Ch 8. 2 Nohah the fourth, and R. the fifth
2. A Benjamite of Saul's family. B.C. 730.
1 Ch. 8. 37 R. (was) his son, Eleasah his son, Azel his
3. An ancestor of certain Philistine warriors slain in the days of David, and here translated "the giant."
2 Sa. 21. 16, 18 which (was) of the sons of the giant
21. 20 and he also was born to the giant
21. 22 These four were born to the giant in Gath
1 Ch. 20. 4 Sippai, (that was) of the children of the g.
20. 6 and he also was the son of the giant
20. 8 These were born unto the giant in Gath

RA'-PHU, רָפוּא *feared.*
A Benjamite, father of Palti, one of those sent out to spy the land of Canaan by Moses. B.C. 1500.
Num 13. 9 the tribe of Benjamin, Palti the son of R.

RARE —
Rare, precious, יַקִּיר *yaqqir.*
Dan. 2. 11 rare thing that the king requireth; and

RASE, to —
To make naked or bare, עָרָה *arah*, 3.
Psa. 137. 7 Rase (it), rase (it, even) to the foundation

RASH, (to be), rashly —
1. *To trouble, hasten*, בָּהַל *bahel*, 3.
Eccl. 5. 2 Be not rash with thy mouth, and let not
2. *To be hasty, hastened*, מָהַר *mahar*, 2.
Isa. 32. 4 heart also of the rash shall understand k.
3. *Precipitate*, προπετής *propetēs.*
Acts 19. 36 ought to be quiet, and to do nothing ras.

RASOR, RAZOR —
1. *A knife, razor*, תַּעַר *taar.*
Num. 6. 5 there shall no razor come upon his head
Psa. 52. 2 mischiefs; like a sharp razor, working de.
Isa. 7. 20 LORD shave with a razor that is hired..by
Eze. 5. 1 take thee a barber's razor, and cause (it)
2. *A razor*, מוֹרָה *morah.*
Judg 13. 5 no razor shall come on his head: for the
16. 17 There hath not come a razor upon mine
1 Sa. 1. 11 and there shall no razor come upon his

RATE —
A word, matter, thing, דָּבָר *dabar.*
Exod 16. 4 gather a certain rate every day, that I
1 Ki. 10. 25 horses, and mules, a rate year by year
2 Ki. 25. 30 a daily rate for every day, all the days of
2 Ch. 8. 13 after a certain rate every day, offering ac.
9. 24 spices, horses, and mules, a rate year by

RATHER (than), (be, have, the) —
1. *And not*, וְאַל *ve-al.*
Prov 17. 12 meet a man, rather than a fool in his folly
2. *To choose*, בָּחַר *bachar.*
Psa. 84. 10 I had rather be a doorkeeper in the house
3. *Than*, ἤ *ē.*
Matt 18. 8 rather than having two hands or two feet
18. 9 rather than having two Lu. 12. 51; 18. 14.
4. *To will, wish*, θέλω *thelō.*
1 Co. 14. 19 I had rather speak five ..than ten thous.
5. *More, rather*, μᾶλλον *mallon.*
Matt 10. 6 go rather to the lost sheep of the house
10. 28 rather fear him which is able to destroy
25. 9 go ye rather to them that sell, and buy
27. 24 prevail nothing, but (that) rather a tum.
Mark 5. 26 was nothing bettered, but rather grew w.
15. 11 should rather release Barabbas unto them
Luke 10. 20 [rather] rejoice, because your names are
John 3. 19 men loved darkness rather than light, b.
Acts 5. 29 said, We ought to obey God rather than
Rom. 8. 34 yea rather, that is risen again, who is ev.
14. 13 but judge this rather that no man put a
1 Co. 5. 2 are puffed up, and have not rather mou.
6. 7 Why do ye not rather take wrong? why
6. 7 not rather (suffer yourselves to) be defr.
7. 21 if thou mayest be made free, use (it) rat.
9. 12 (are) not we rather? Nevertheless we h.
14. 1 desire spiritual (gifts), but rather that ye
14. 5 but rather that ye prophesied: for grea.
2 Co. 2. 7 So that contrariwise ye (ought) rather to
3. 8 ministration of the spirit be rather glori.
5. 8 willing rather to be absent from the body
12. 9 gladly therefore will I rather glory in my
Gal. 4. 9 after that ye have known God, or rather
Eph. 4. 28 but rather let him labour, working with
5. 4 nor jesting..but rather giving of thanks
5. 11 have no fellowship with..but rather rep.
Phil. 1. 12 have fallen out rather unto the furthera.
1 Ti. 1. 4 rather than godly edifying which is in fa.
6. 2 rather do (them) service, because they are
Phm. 9 Yet for love's sake I rather beseech (thee)
Heb. 11. 25 Choosing rather to suffer affliction with
12. 9 shall we not much rather be in subjection
12. 13 turned out of the way; but let it rather
2 Pe. 1. 10 Wherefore the rather, brethren, give di.
6. *More abundantly*, περισσοτέρως *perissoterōs.*
Heb. 13. 19 But I beseech (you) the rather to do this

RATTLE, to —
1. *To sing, rattle*, רָנָה *ranah.*
Job 39. 23 quiver rattleth against him, the glittering
2. *A shaking, trembling, rushing, rattling*, רַעַשׁ *raash.*
Nah. 3. 2 noise of the rattling of the wheels, and of

RAVEN —
1. *A raven*, עֹרֵב *oreb.*
Gen. 8. 7 sent forth a raven, which went forth to
Lev. 11. 15 Every raven after his kind
Deut 14. 14 And every raven after his kind
1 Ki. 17. 4 have commanded the ravens to feed thee
17. 6 ravens brought him bread and flesh in the
Job 38. 41 Who provideth for the raven his food? wh.
Psa. 147. 9 He giveth..to the young ravens which cry
Prov. 30. 17 the ravens of the valley shall pick it out
Song 5. 11 his locks (are) bushy, (and) black as a ra.
Isa. 34. 11 the owl also and the raven shall dwell in
2. *A raven or crow*, κόραξ *korax.*
Luke 12. 24 Consider the ravens: for they neither sow

RAVEN, RAVIN, to —
1. *To tear*, טָרַף *taraph.*
Gen. 49. 27 Benjamin shall ravin (as) a wolf: in the
Psa. 22. 13 They gaped..(as) a ravening and a roaring
Eze. 22. 25 like a roaring lion ravening the prey: th.
22. 27 Her princes..(are) like wolves ravening
2. *A torn thing, prey, rapine*, טְרֵפָה *terephah.*
Nah. 2. 12 holes with prey, and his dens with ravin

RAVENING, RAVENOUS (bird) —
1. *A ravenous bird or fowl*, עַיִט *ayit.*
Isa. 46. 11 Calling a ravenous bird from the east, the
Eze. 39. 4 I will give thee unto the ravenous birds
2. *A burglar, destroyer*, פָּרִיץ *parits.*
Isa. 35. 9 nor (any) ravenous beast shall go up the.
3. *A snatching at or away, prey*, ἁρπαγή *harpagē.*
Luke 11. 39 inward part is full of ravening and wick.
4. *Snatching, ravenous*, ἅρπαξ *harpax.*
Matt. 7. 15 but inwardly they are ravening wolves

RAVISH (the heart), to —
1. *To embolden, give heart*, לָבַב *labab*, 3.
Song 4. 9, 9 Thou hast ravished my heart
2. *To afflict, humble*, עָנָה *anah*, 3.
Lam. 5. 11 They ravished the women in Zion, (and) the

RAVISHED, to be —
1. *To err, go astray, magnify self*, שָׁגָה *shagah.*
Prov. 5. 19 and be thou ravished always with her love
5. 20 why wilt thou..be ravished with a strange
2. *To be ravished*, שָׁכַב *shakab*, 2 [V.L. שָׁגַל *shagal*, 2].
Isa. 13. 16 shall be spoiled, and their wives ravished
Zech 14. 2 the houses rifled, and the women ravished

RAW —
1. *Living, alive*, חַי *chai.*
Lev. 13. 10 (there be) quick raw flesh in the rising
13. 14 when raw flesh appeareth in him, he shall
13. 15 see the raw flesh..the raw flesh (is) uncle.
13. 16 Or if the raw flesh turn again, and be ch.
1 Sa. 2. 15 not have sodden flesh of thee, but raw
2. *Raw*, נָא *na.*
Exod 12. 9 Eat not of it raw, nor sodden at all with

REACH (forth, to, unto, up), to —
1. *To cause to flee or reach*, בָּרַח *barach*, 5.
Exod 26. 28 the middle bar..shall reach from end to
2. *To smite*, מָחָה *machah.*
Num 34. 11 shall reach unto the side of the sea of C.
3. *To reach, come, arrive*, מְטָה, מְטָא *meta, metah.*
Dan. 4. 11 height thereof reached unto heaven, and
4. 20 whose height reached unto the heaven, a.
4. 22 reacheth unto heaven, and thy dominion
4. *To touch, come upon, strike*, נָגַע *naga.*
Jer. 4. 10 whereas the sword reacheth unto the soul
4. 18 because it reacheth unto thine heart
48. 32 they reach (even) to the sea of Jazer: the
51. 9 for her judgment reacheth unto heaven
5. *To cause to reach, attain, overtake*, נָשַׂג *nasag*, 5.
Lev 26. 5 reach unto the vintage..reach unto the
6. *To touch, come upon, meet with*, פָּגַע *paga.*
Josh 19. 11 reached to Dabbasheth, and reached to the
19. 22 reacheth to Tabor, and Shahazimah, and
19. 26 reacheth to Carmel westward, and to Sh.
19. 27 reacheth to Zebulun, and to the valley of
19. 34 reacheth to Zebulun..and reacheth to A.
7. *To reach out, give*, צָבַט *tsabat.*
Ruth 2. 14 he reached her parched (corn), and she did
8. *To cause to touch or come upon*, נָגַע *naga*, 5.
Gen. 28. 12 top of it reached to heaven: and behold
2 Ch. 3. 11 reaching to the wall..reaching to the wi.
3. 12 reaching to the wall of the house; and
28. 9 slain them in a rage (that) reacheth up
Job 20. 6 Though..his head reach unto the clouds
Isa. 8. 8 he shall reach (even) to the neck: and the
Zech 14. 5 valley of the mountains shall reach unto
9. *To send forth*, שָׁלַח *shalach*, 3.
Prov 31. 20 she reacheth forth her hands to the n.
10. *To follow*, ἀκολουθέω *akoloutheō.*
Rev. 18. 5 For her sins [have reached] unto heaven
11. *To reach out, stretch out toward*, ἐπεκτείνομαι.
Phil. 3. 13 reaching forth unto those things which
12. *To come upon, arrive at*, ἐφικνέομαι *ephikneomai.*
2 Co. 10. 13 to us, a measure to reach even unto you
10. 14 as though we reached not unto you: for
13. *To bear, carry*, φέρω *pherō.*
John 20. 27 Reach hither thy finger..reach hither thy

READ, to (be) —
1. *To call, read*, קָרָא *qara.*
Exod 24. 7 read in the audience of the people: and
Deut 17. 19 shall read therein all the days of his life
31. 11 thou shalt read this law before all Israel
Josh. 8. 34 afterward he read all the words of the law
8. 35 which Joshua read not before all the con.
2 Ki. 5. 7 when the king of Israel had read the let.
19. 14 Hezekiah received the letter..and read it
22. 8 gave the book to Shaphan, and he read it
22. 10 And Shaphan read it before the king
22. 16 book which the king of Judah hath read
23. 2 read in their ears all the words of the book
2 Ch. 34. 18 And Shaphan read it before the king

2 Ch.34. 24 which they have read before the king of
34. 30 read in their ears all the words of the book
Neh. 8. 3 read therein before the street that (was)
8. 8 So they read in the book, in the law of
8. 18 he read in the book of the law of God
9. 3 read in the book of the law of the LORD
Isa. 29. 11, 12 Read this, I pray thee: and he saith
34. 16 Seek ye out of the book..and read; no one
37. 14 received the letter ... and read it: and H.
Jer. 29. 29 Zephaniah the priest read this letter in
36. 6 read in the roll..shalt read them in the
36. 8 reading in the book the words of the LORD
36. 10 Then read Baruch in the book the words
36. 13 Baruch read the book in the ears of the
36. 14 the roll wherein thou hast read in the e.
36. 15 read it in our ears. So Baruch read (it)
36. 21 Jehudi read it in the ears of the king, and
36. 23 when Jehudi had read three or four leaves
51. 61 shalt see, and shalt read all these words
Hab. 2. 2 plain..that he may run that readeth it

2. *To be called, read,* קָרָא *qara,* 2.
Neh 13. 1 On that day they read in the book of Mo.
Esth. 6. 1 Chronicles; and they were read before the

3. *To call, read,* קְרָא *qera.*
Ezra 4. 18 The letter..hath been plainly read before
4. 23 letter (was) read before Rehum, and Shi.
Dan. 5. 7 Whosoever shall read this writing, and s.
5. 8 but they could not read the writing, nor
5. 15 that they should read this writing, and
5. 16 now if thou canst read the writing, and
5. 17 yet I will read the writing unto the king

4. *To know well, read,* ἀναγινώσκω *anaginōskō.*
Matt 12. 3 Have ye not read what David did, when
12. 5 Or have ye not read in the law, how that
19. 4 Have ye not read, that he which made (t.)
21. 16 Yea; have ye never read, Out of the mo.
21. 42 Did ye never read in the Scriptures, The
22. 31 have ye not read that which was spoken
24. 15 whoso readeth, let him understand
Mark 2. 25 Have ye never read what David did, when
12 10 have ye not read this scripture; The stone
12 26 have ye not read in the book of Moses, how
13. 14 let him that readeth understand, then let
Luke 4. 16 the sabbath day, and stood up for to read
6 3 Have ye not read so much as this, what
10 26 What is written in the law? how readest
John 19 20 This title then read many of the Jews; for
Acts 8. 28 sitting in his chariot read Esaias the pro.
8. 30 heard him read the prophet Esaias, and
8. 30 Understandest thou what thou readest?
8. 32 place of the Scripture which he read was
13. 27 prophets which are read every sabbath day
15 21 being read in the synagogues every sabbath
15. 31 when they had read, they rejoiced for the
23. 34 when the governor had read (the letter), he
2 Co. 1. 13 none other things..than what ye read or
3. 2 written in our hearts, known and read of
3. 15 even unto this day, when Moses is read
Eph. 3. 4 Whereby, when ye read, ye may underst.
Col. 4. 16 And when this epistle is read among you
4. 16 cause that it be read also in the church
4. 16 that ye likewise read the (epistle) from
1 Th. 5. 27 that this epistle be read unto all the
Rev. 1. 3 Blessed (is) he that readeth, and they that
5. 4 [to read] the book, neither to look thereon

READING —

1. *A calling, reading,* מִקְרָא *miqra.*
Neh 8. 8 and caused (them) to understand the re.

2. *To call, read,* קְרָא *qara.*
Jer 51. 63 when thou hast made an end of reading

3. *A reading, knowing again,* ἀνάγνωσις *anagnōsis.*
Acts 13. 15 the reading of the law and the prophets
2 Co 3. 14 the same veil untaken away in the read.
1 Ti. 4. 13 give attendance to reading, to exhortation

READINESS (of mind) —

1. *Ready,* ἕτοιμος *hetoimos.*
2 Co.10. 6 a readiness to revenge all disobedience

2. *Readiness, forwardness,* προθυμία *prothumia.*
Acts 17. 11 received the word with..readiness of m.
2 Co. 8. 11 as (there was) a readiness to will, so (there

READY (mind) —

1. *To make haste, enjoy,* חוּשׁ *chush.*
Num 32. 17 we ourselves will go ready armed before

2. *Good,* טוֹב *tob.*
Isa. 41. 7 saying, It (is) ready for the soldering: and

3. *To be formed, prepared, ready,* כּוּן *kun,* 2.
Exod 19. 11 be ready against the third day: for the
19. 15 Be ready against the third day: come not
34. 2 be ready in the morning, and come up in
Josh. 8. 4 not very far from the city..be ye all ready
Job 12. 5 He that is ready to slip with (his) feet (is
15. 23 the day of darkness is ready at his hand
18. 12 destruction (shall be) ready at his side
Psa. 38. 17 For I (am) ready to halt, and my sorrow

4. *Ready, hasting,* מָהִיר *mahir.*
Ezra 7. 6 (was) a ready scribe in the law of Moses
Psa. 45. 1 my tongue (is) the pen of a ready writer

5. *To find,* מְצָא *matsa.*
2 Sa. 18. 22 seeing that thou hast no tidings ready

6. *Ready, prepared,* עָתִיד *athid* [V.L. עתוד Est. 8.13].
Esth. 3. 14 that they should be ready against that day
8. 13 the Jews should be ready against that day
Job 3. 8 who are ready to raise up their mourning
15. 24 prevail..as a king ready to the battle

7. *Ready, prepared,* עֲתִיד *athid.*
Dan. 3. 15 if ye be ready that at what time ye hear

8. *Nigh,* ἐγγύς *eggus.*
Heb. 8. 13 that which decayeth..(is) ready to vanish

9. *Ready,* ἕτοιμος *hetoimos.*
Matt 22. 4 all things (are) ready: come unto the m.
22. 8 The wedding is ready, but they which were
24. 44 be ye also ready: for in such an hour as
25. 10 they that were ready went in with him to
Luke 12. 40 Be ye therefore ready also: for the Son
14. 17 to say..Come; for all things are now re.
22. 33 I am ready to go with thee, both into pri.
John 7. 6 not yet come: but your time is alway ready
Acts 23. 15 we, or ever he come near, are ready to kill
23. 21 now are they ready, looking for a promise
2 Co. 9. 5 the same might be ready, as (a matter of)
Titus 3. 1 Put them in mind..to be ready to every
1 Pe. 1. 5 salvation ready to be revealed in the last
3. 15 (be) ready always to (give) an answer to

10. *Readiness, forwardness,* προθυμία *prothumia.*
2 Co. 8. 19 same Lord, and (declaration of) your r. m.

11. *Readily,* ἑτοίμως *hetoimōs.*
Acts 21. 13 I am ready not to be bound only, but also
2 Co.12. 14 I am ready to come to you; and I will
1 Pe. 4. 5 him that is ready to judge the quick and

12. *To be about to,* μέλλω *mellō.*
Luke 7. 2 centurion's servant.. was sick, and ready
Acts 20. 7 preached..ready to depart on the morrow

13. *Ready, prompt,* πρόθυμος *prothumos.*
Mark 14. 38 The spirit truly (is) ready, but the flesh
Rom. 1. 15 I am ready to preach the gospel to you

[*See also* Armed, burst, dressed, fall, forgive, made, make, offered, prepared, quickly.]

READY, to be or become —

1. *To be ready, make,* הוּן *hun,* 5.
Deut. 1. 41 And..ye were ready to go up into the hill

2. *To form, prepare, make ready,* כּוּן *kun,* 3a.
Isa. 51. 13 oppressor, as if he were ready to destroy

3. *To move, slip, fail,* מוֹט *mot.*
Prov 24. 11 drawn unto death, and..ready to be slain

4. *To show self ready,* עָתַד *athad,* 7.
Job 15. 28 houses..which are ready to become hea.

5. *Hasten,* מהר *maher,* 2.
Isa. 32. 4 the tongue..shall be ready to speak plain.

6. *To be about to,* μέλλω *mellō.*
Rev. 3. 2 things which remain, that are ready, 12.4

7. *To make ready beside,* παρασκευάζω *paraskeuazō.*
2 Co. 9. 2 Achaia was ready a year ago; and; 9. 3.

READY, to make or be made —

1. *To gird,* אָסַר *asar.*
Gen. 46. 29 Joseph made ready his chariot, and went
Exod 14. 6 he made ready his chariot, and took his
2 Ki. 9. 21 Make ready. And his chariot was made r.

2. *To form, prepare, establish,* כּוּן *kun,* 3a.
Psa. 7. 12 he hath bent his bow, and made it ready
11. 2 they make ready their arrow upon the st.
21. 12 thou shalt make ready (thine arrows) upon

3. *To prepare, establish,* כּוּן *kun,* 5.
Gen. 43. 16 made ready; for (these) men shall dine
43. 25 they made ready the present against Jos.
1 Ch. 28. 2 God, and had made ready for the building
2 Ch. 35. 14 they made ready for themselves, and for
Eze. 7. 14 blown the trumpet, even to make all re.

4. *To bring near,* קָרַב *qarab,* 3.
Hos. 7. 6 have made ready their heart like an oven

5. *To make ready,* ἑτοιμάζω *hetoimazō.*
Matt 26. 19 the disciples..made ready the passover
Mark 14. 15 a large upper room..there make ready for
14. 16 his disciples..made ready the passover
Luke 1. 17 to make ready a people prepared for the
9. 52 entered into a village..to make ready for
17. 8 Make ready wherewith I may sup, and g.
22. 12 a large upper room..there make ready
22. 13 And they went, and..made ready the pa.
Acts 23. 23 Make ready two hundred soldiers to go to
Rev. 19. 7 and his wife hath made herself ready

6. *To make ready beside,* παρασκευάζω *paraskeuazō.*
Acts 10. 10 while they made ready, he fell into a tr.

READY to our hand, made —
Ready, ἕτοιμος *hetoimos.*
2 Co.10. 16 another man's line..made ready to our h.

READY, more —
Near, קָרוֹב *qarob.*
Eccl. 5. 1 be more ready to hear than to give the s.

READY to distribute —
Ready to give over or share with, εὐμετάδοτος.
1 Ti. 6. 18 ready to distribute, willing to communi.

RE-A'-IAH, RE-A'-IA, רְאָיָה *Jah sees.*

1. Son of Shobal son of Judah. B.C. 1670.
1 Ch. 4. 2 And R. the son of Shobal begat Jahath

2. Grandfather of Beerah prince of Reuben when Israel was carried away to Assyria. B.C. 1500.
1 Ch. 5. 5 Micah his son, Reaia his son, Baal his

3. One of the Nethinim whose descendants returned with Zerubbabel. B.C. 536
Ezra 2. 47 the children of Gahar, the children of R.
Neh. 7. 50 The children of R., the children of Rezin

REALM —

1. *Kingdom,* מַלְכוּ *maleku.*
Ezra. 7. 13 and (of) his priests and Levites, in my rea.
7. 23 there be wrath against the realm of the
Dan. 6. 3 thought to set him over the whole realm

2. *Kingdom,* מַלְכוּת *malekuth.*
2 Ch. 20. 30 the realm of Jehoshaphat was quiet; for
Dan. 1. 20 (and) astrologers that (were) in all his re.
9. 1 made king over the realm of the Chaldea.
11. 2 shall stir up all against the realm of Gre.

REAP (wholly, down), **to** —

1. *To finish,* כָּלָה *kalah,* 3.
Lev. 19. 9 thou shalt not wholly reap the corners of

2. *To shorten, reap,* קָצַר *qatsar.*
Lev. 19. 9 when ye reap the harvest of your land, th.
23. 10 When ye..shall reap the harvest thereof
23. 22 when ye reap the harvest of your land
23. 22 not make clean riddance..when thou re.
25. 5 thou shalt not reap, neither gather the g.
25. 11 neither reap that which groweth of itself
Ruth 2. 9 thine eyes (be) on the field that they dor.
1 Sa. 8. 12 and to reap his harvest, and to make his
2 Ki. 19. 29 reap, and plant vineyards, and eat the fr.
Job 4. 8 they that..sow wickedness, reap the same
24. 6 They reap (every one) his corn in the field
Psa. 126. 5 They that sow in tears shall reap in joy
Prov. 22. 8 He that soweth iniquity shall reap vanity
Eccl. 11. 4 he that regardeth the clouds shall not re.
Isa. 17. 5 reapeth the ears with his arm; and it sh.
37. 30 reap, and plant vineyards, and eat the fr.
Jer. 12. 13 They have sown wheat, but shall reap th.
Hos. 8. 7 they shall reap the whirlwind: it hath no
10. 12 reap in mercy; break up your fallow gro.
10. 13 ye have reaped iniquity; ye have eaten the
Mic. 6. 15 thou shalt not reap; thou shalt tread the

3. *To reap, mow, gather together,* ἀμάω *amaō.*
Jas. 5. 4 labourers who have reaped down your

4. *To reap, gather in the harvest,* θερίζω *therizō.*
Matt. 6. 26 neither do they reap, nor gather into ba.
25. 24 reaping where thou hast not sown, and
25. 26 I reap where I sowed not, and gather wh.
Luke 12. 24 they neither sow nor reap; which neither
19. 21 thou..reapest that thou didst not sow
19. 22 taking up..and reaping that
John 4. 36 he that reapeth receiveth wages, and ga.
4. 36 he that soweth and he that reapeth may
4. 37 saying true, One soweth, and another re.
4. 38 I sent you to reap that whereon ye best.
1 Co. 9. 11 a great thing if we shall reap your carnal
2 Co. 9. 6 He which soweth sparingly shall reap also
9. 6 he which soweth bountifully shall reap
Gal. 6. 7 whatsoever a man soweth..shall he alsor
6. 8 For he..shall of the flesh reap corruption
6. 8 he..shall of the spirit reap life everlasting
6. 9 in due season we shall reap, if we faint
Jas. 5. 4 cries of them which have reaped are en.
Rev. 14. 15 Thrust in thy sickle and reap: for the time
14. 15 is come for thee to reap; for the harvest
14. 16 thrust in his sickle..and the earth was r.

REAPER, REAPING —

1. *To shorten, reap,* קָצַר *qatsar.*
Ruth 2. 3 gleaned in the field after the reapers: and
2. 4 said unto the reapers, The LORD (be) with
2. 5, 6 servant that was set over the reapers
2. 7 let me glean and gather after the reapers
2. 14 she sat beside the reapers: and he reached
1 Sa. 6. 13 reaping their wheat harvest in the valley
2 Ki. 4. 18 he went out to his father to the reapers
Amos 9. 13 that the plowman shall overtake the re.

2. *A reaper,* θεριστής *theristēs.*
Matt 13. 30 I will say to the reapers, Gather ye toge.
13. 39 is the end of the world; and the reapers

REAR (up), **to** —

1. *To set up,* נָצַב *natsab,* 5.
2 Sa. 18. 18 taken and reared up for himself a pillar

2. *To cause to rise,* קוּם *qum,* 5.
Exod 26. 30 thou shalt rear up the tabernacle accor.
40. 18 Moses reared up the tabernacle, and fas.
40. 18 put in the bars thereof, and reared up his
40. 33 he reared up the court round about the
Lev. 26. 1 neither rear you up a standing image
2 Sa. 24. 18 Go up, rear an altar unto the LORD in the
1 Ki. 16. 32 he reared up an altar for Baal in the house
2 Ki. 21. 3 he reared up altars for Baal, and made a
2 Ch. 3. 17 he reared up the pillars before the temple
33. 3 he reared up altars for Baalim and made

3. *To lift, raise or rouse up,* ἐγείρω *egeirō.*
John 2. 20 this temple..wilt thou rear it up in three

REARED up, to be —

1. *To cause to rise,* קוּם *qum,* 5.
Num. 9. 15 the day that the tabernacle was reared up

2. *To be caused to rise,* קוּם *qum,* 6.
Exod 40. 17 came to pass..tabernacle was reared up

REASON —

1. *A word,* דָּבָר *dabar.*
1 Ki. 9. 15 this (is) the reason of the levy which..S.

2. *Reason, device, reckoning,* חֶשְׁבּוֹן *cheshbon.*
Eccl. 7 25 and to seek out wisdom, and the reason

3. *Taste, discretion,* טַעַם *taam.*
Prov 26. 16 than seven men that can render a reason

4. *Knowledge, understanding,* מַנְדַּע *manda.*
Dan. 4. 36 my reason returned unto me; and for the

5. *Understanding, skilfulness,* תְּבוּנָה *tebunah.*
Job 32. 11 I gave ear to your reasons, whilst ye sea.
6. *Agreeable, pleasing, grateful,* ἀρεστός *arestos.*
Acts 6. 2 It is not reason that we should leave the
7. *A word,* λόγος *logos.*
1 Pe. 3. 15 a reason of the hope that is in you with

REASON (together, with), to —
1. *To be reasoned with,* יָכַח *yakach,* 2.
Isa. 1. 18 Come now, and let us reason together, saith
2. *To reason, reprove, decide,* יָכַח *yakach,* 5.
Job 13. 3 I would speak..I desire to reason with God
15. 3 Should he reason with unprofitable talk?
3. *To be judged,* שָׁפַט *shaphat,* 2.
1 Sa. 12. 7 I may reason with you before the LORD of
4. *To discourse, reason,* διαλέγομαι *dialegomai.*
Acts 17. 2 reasoned with them out of the Scriptures
18. 4 reasoned in the synagogue every sabbath
18. 19 entered into the synagogue, and reasoned
24. 25 as he reasoned of righteousness, temper.
5. *To reckon, reason thoroughly,* διαλογίζομαι.
Matt 16. 7 they reasoned among themselves, saying
16. 8 why reason ye among yourselves, because
21. 25 they reasoned with themselves, saying
Mark 2. 6 sitting there, and reasoning in their he.
2. 8 that they so reasoned within themselves
2. 8 Why reason ye these things in your hearts?
8. 16 they reasoned among themselves, saying
8. 17 Why reason ye because ye have no bread?
Luke 5. 21 scribes and the Pharisees began to reason
5. 22 he..said..Why reason ye in your hearts?
20. 14 they reasoned among themselves, saying
6. *To reckon,* λογίζομαι *logizomai.*
Mark 11. 31 [they reasoned] with themselves, saying
7. *To seek together, discuss,* συζητέω *suzēteō.*
Mark 12. 28 having heard them reasoning together
Luke 24. 15 while they communed (together) and re.
8. *To reckon together,* συλλογίζομαι *sullogizomai.*
Luke 20. 5 they reasoned with themselves, saying, If

REASON of, by —
1. *From, out of, by reason of,* מִן *min.*
Exod. 2. 23 their cry came up unto God by reas. of
2. *With,* עִם *im.*
2 Ch. 21. 19 his bowels fell out by reason of his sick.
3. *Before, at the front of,* לִפְנֵי *li-phene.*
Gen. 41. 31 shall not be known in the land by reas. of
Exod 3. 7 heard their cry by reason of their taskm.
8. 24 land was corrupted by reason of the swarm
Deut. 5. 5 ye were afraid by reason of the fire, and
Psa. 44. 16 For..by reason of the enemy and avenger
4. *Before, in the presence of,* קֳבֵל, קֳבֵל *qobel, qebel.*
Dan. 5. 10 by reason of the words of the king and his
5. *Because of,* διά (acc.) *dia.*
John 12. 11 by reason of him many of the Jews went
Rom. 8. 20 by reason of him who hath subjected (the
Heb. 5. 3 [by reason hereof] he ought, as for the p.
5. 14 who by reason of use have their senses ex.
2 Pe. 2. 2 by reason of whom the way of truth shall
6. *Out of,* ἐκ *ek.*
Rev. 8. 13 by reason of the other voices of the tru.
9. 2 darkened by reason of the smoke of the
18. 19 were made rich..by reason of her costli.
7. *For the sake of,* ἕνεκα *heneka.*
2 Co. 3. 10 had..by reason of the glory that excelleth

REASON would—
According to reason, κατὰ λόγον, Acts 18. 14.

REASONABLE —
Rational, reasonable, λογικός *logikos.*
Rom 12. 1 sacrifice..(which is) your reasonable ser.

REASONING —
1. *Reproof, correction,* תּוֹכַחַת *tokachath.*
Job 13. 6 Hear now my reasoning, and hearken to
2. *A reckoning throughout,* διαλογισμός *dialogismos.*
Luke 9. 46 there arose a reasoning among them, w.
3. *A seeking together,* συζήτησις *suzētēsis.*
Acts 28. 29 [had great reasoning among themselves]

RE'-BA, רֶבַע *sprout, offspring.*
A king of Midian, slain by Israel while they were in the plains of Moab. B.C. 1456.
Num 31. 8 Evi, and Rekem, and Zur, and Hur..R.
Josh. 13. 21 Hur, and R., (which were), dukes of Sihon

RE-BEC'-CA, Ῥεβέκκα. *Same as the succeeding.*
Rom. 9. 10 R. also had conceived by one, (even) by our

RE-BEK'-AH, רִבְקָה *flattering.*
Daughter of Bethuel the nephew of Abraham. She became wife of Isaac, and mother of Esau and Jacob. B.C. 1838.
Gen. 22. 23 And Bethuel begat R.: these eight Milcah
24. 15 R. came out, who was born to Bethuel, son
24. 29 R. had a brother, and his name (was) Laban
24. 30 and when he heard the words of R. his s.
24. 45 R. came forth with her pitcher on her sh.
24. 51 Behold, R. (is) before thee, take (her), and
24. 53 servant brought forth jewels..to R.: he
24. 58 And they called R., and said unto her
24. 59 And they sent away R. their sister, and
24. 60 And they blessed R., and said unto her
24 61 And R. arose, and her damsels, v. 61, 64.
Gen. 24. 67 Isaac..took R., and she became his wife
25. 20 Isaac..took R. to wife, the daughter of B.
25. 21 the Lord was entreated..and R. his wife c.
25. 28 And Isaac loved Esau..but R. loved Jacob
26. 7 the men of the place should kill me for R.
26. 8 behold, Isaac (was) sporting with R. his w.
26. 35 were a grief of mind unto Isaac and to R.
27. 5 R. heard when Isaac spake to Esau his s.
27. 6 And R. spake unto Jacob her son, saying
27. 11 And Jacob said to R. his mother, Behold
27. 15 R. took goodly raiment of her eldest son
27. 42 And these words of Esau..were told to R.
27. 46 And R. said to Isaac, I am weary of my l.
28. 5 he went..unto Laban..the brother of R.
29. 12 Jacob told Rachel..that he (was) R.'s son
35. 8 But Deborah, R.'s nurse, died, and she was
49. 31 there they buried Isaac and R. his wife

REBEL —
1. *To rebel,* מָרַד *marad.*
Eze. 20. 38 I will purge out from among you the re.
2. *To be or make bitter, provoke, rebel,* מָרָה *marah.*
Num 20. 10 Hear now, ye rebels; must we fetch you
3. *A son of rebellion,* בֶּן־מְרִי *ben meri.*
Num 17. 10 to be kept for a token against the rebels

REBEL (against), to —
1. *To rebel,* מָרַד *marad.*
Gen. 14. 4 and in the thirteenth year they rebelled
Num 14. 9 Only rebel not ye against the LORD, neith.
Josh 22. 16 ye might rebel this day against the LORD
22. 18 (seeing) ye rebel to day against the LORD
22. 19 rebel not against the LORD, nor rebel ag.
22. 29 God forbid that we should rebel against
2 Ki. 18. 7 he rebelled against the king of Assyria, and
18. 20 whom dost thou trust, that thou rebellest a.
24. 1 then he turned and rebelled against him
24. 20 Zedekiah rebelled against the king of Ba.
2 Ch. 13. 6 Jeroboam..hath rebelled against his lord
36. 13 he also rebelled against king Nebuchad.
Neh. 2. 19 What (is) this..will ye rebel against the
6. 6 the Jews think to rebel: for which cause
9. 26 rebelled against thee, and cast thy law
Job 24. 13 They are of those that rebel against the
Isa. 36. 5 whom dost thou trust, that thou rebell. a.
Jer. 52. 3 Zedekiah rebelled against the king of B.
Eze. 2. 3 a rebellious nation that hath rebelled ag.
17. 15 he rebelled against him in sending his am.
Dan. 9. 5 have rebelled, even by departing from thy
9. 9 God..though we have rebelled against him
2. *To be or make bitter, provoke, rebel,* מָרָה *marah.*
Num 20. 24 ye rebelled against my word at the water
27. 14 ye rebelled against my commandment in
1 Sa. 12. 15 rebel against the commandment of the L.
Psa. 5. 10 Destroy..for they have rebelled against
105. 28 He sent darkness..they rebelled not aga.
Isa. 1. 20 ye refuse and rebel, ye shall be devoured
63. 10 they rebelled, and vexed his Holy Spirit
Lam. 1. 18 have rebelled against his commandment
1. 20 I have grievously rebelled: abroad the s.
3. 42 We have transgressed and have rebelled
Hos. 13. 16 she hath rebelled against her God: they
3. *To make bitter, provoke, rebel,* מָרָה *marah,* 5.
Deut. 1. 26, 43 rebelled against the commandment of
9. 23 ye rebelled against the commandment of
Josh. 1. 18 that doth rebel against thy commandment
1 Sa. 12. 14 rebel against the commandment of the
Psa. 107. 11 they rebelled against the words of God
Eze. 20. 8 they rebelled against me, and would not
20. 13 But..rebelled against me in the wildern.
20. 21 the children rebelled against me: they w.
4. *To turn aside,* סוּר *sur.*
Hos. 7. 14 they assemble themselves..they rebel ag.
5. *To transgress, rebel,* פָּשַׁע *pasha.*
1 Ki. 12. 19 Israel rebelled against the house of David
2 Ki. 1. 1 Moab rebelled against Israel after the de.
3. 5 king of Moab rebelled against the king
3. 7 The king of Moab hath rebelled against
2 Ch. 10. 19 Israel rebelled against the house of David
Isa. 1. 2 brought up children..they have rebelled a.

REBELLION —
1. *To rebel,* מְרַד *merad.*
Ezra 4. 19 rebellion and sedition have been made th.
2. *Rebellion,* מֶרֶד *mered.*
Josh. 22. 22 in rebellion, or if in transgression against
3. *Rebellion, bitterness,* מְרִי *meri.*
Deut 31. 27 For I know thy rebellion, and thy stiff n.
1 Sa. 15. 23 For rebellion (is as) the sin of witchcraft
Neh. 9. 17 in their rebellion appointed a captain to
Prov. 17. 11 An evil (man) seeketh only rebellion; th.
4. *A turning aside,* סָרָה *sarah.*
Jer. 28. 16 thou hast taught rebellion against the L.
29. 32 he hath taught rebellion against the LORD
5. *Transgression,* פֶּשַׁע *pesha.*
Job 34. 37 For he addeth rebellion unto his sin; he

REBELLIOUS, (to be most) —
1. *To rebel,* מָרַד *marad.*
Eze. 2. 3 to a rebellious nation that hath rebelled
2. *Rebellious,* מָרָד *marad.*
Ezra 4. 12 building the rebellious and the bad city
4. 15 this city (is) a rebellious city, and hurtful
3. *Rebellion,* מַרְדּוּת *marduth.*
1 Sa. 20. 30 Thou son of the perverse rebellious (wo.)
4. *To be or make bitter, provoke, rebel,* מָרָה *marah.*
Deut 21. 18 a man have a stubborn and rebellious son
21. 20 This our son (is) stubborn and rebellious
Psa. 78. 8 be..a stubborn and rebellious generation
Isa. 50. 5 I was not rebellious, neither turned away
Jer. 4. 17 she hath been rebellious against me, saith
5. 23 this people hath..a rebellious heart; they
5. *To make bitter, provoke, rebel,* מָרָה *marah,* 5.
Deut. 9. 7, 24 Ye have been rebellious against the L.
31. 27 ye have been rebellious against the LORD
6. *Rebellion,* מְרִי *meri.*
Isa. 30. 9 this (is) a rebellious people, lying child.
Eze. 2. 5 forbear, for they (are) a rebellious house
2. 6 be not afraid..though they (be) a rebell.
2. 7 will forbear; for they (are) most rebelli.
2. 8 rebellious like that rebellious house: open
3. 9 fear them not..though they (be) a rebel.
3. 26, 27 for they (are) a rebellious house
12. 2 thou dwellest in the midst of a rebellious
12. 2 hear not: for they (are) a rebellious house
12. 3 consider, though they (be) a rebellious ho.
12. 9 hath not the house of Israel, the rebelli.
12. 25 in your days, O rebellious house, will I say
17. 12 Say now to the rebellious house, Know ye
24. 3 utter a parable unto the rebellious house
44. 6 And thou shalt say to the rebellious
7. *To turn aside,* סָרַר *sarar.*
Psa. 66. 7 let not the rebellious exalt themselves
68. 6 but the rebellious dwell in a dry (land)
68. 18 (for) the rebellious also, that the LORD G.
Isa. 1. 23 Thy princes (are) rebellious, and compa.
30. 1 Woe to the rebellious children, saith the
65. 2 I have spread out my hands..unto a reb.

REBUKE, REBUKING —
1. *Rebuke,* גְּעָרָה *gearah.*
2 Sa. 22. 16 at the rebuking of the LORD, at the blast
Psa. 18. 15 foundations..were discovered at thy reb.
76. 6 At thy rebuke, O God of Jacob, both the
80. 16 perish at the rebuke of thy countenance
104. 7 At thy rebuke they fled; at the voice of
Prov 13. 1 but a scorner heareth not rebuke
13. 8 riches: but the poor heareth not rebuke
Eccl. 7. 5 better to hear the rebuke of the wise, than
Isa. 30. 17 at the rebuke of one; at the rebuke of five
50. 2 at my rebuke I dry up the sea, I make the
51. 20 fury of the LORD, the rebuke of thy God
66. 15 to render..his rebuke with flames of fire
2. *Reproach,* חֶרְפָּה *cherpah.*
Isa. 25. 8 the rebuke of his people shall he take a.
Jer. 15. 15 that for thy sake I have suffered rebuke
3. *Rebuking,* מִגְעֶרֶת *migereth.*
Deut 28. 20 cursing, vexation, and rebuke, in all that
4. *Reproof, correction,* תּוֹכֵחָה *tokechah.*
2 Ki. 19. 3 day of trouble, and of rebuke, and blasp.
Isa. 37. 3 day of trouble, and of rebuke, and of bla.
Hos. 5. 9 Ephraim shall be desolate in the day of r.
5. *Reproof, correction,* תּוֹכַחַת *tokachath.*
Psa. 39. 11 When thou with rebukes dost correct man
Prov 27. 5 Open rebuke (is) better than secret love
Eze. 5. 15 anger and in fury and in furious rebukes
25. 17 vengeance upon them with furious rebuk.

REBUKE, without —
Without blemish, spotless, blameless, ἀμώμητος.
Phil. 2. 15 without rebuke, in the midst of a crooked

REBUKE, to —
1. *To rebuke,* גָּעַר *gaar.*
Gen. 37. 10 his father rebuked him, and said unto him
Ruth 2. 16 she may glean (them), and rebuke her not
Psa. 9. 5 Thou hast rebuked the heathen, thou ha.
68. 30 Rebuke the company of spearmen, the
106. 9 He rebuked the Red sea also, and it was
119. 21 Thou hast rebuked the proud (that are)
Isa. 17. 13 (God) shall rebuke them, and they shall
54. 9 would not be wroth with thee, nor rebu.
Nah. 1. 4 He rebuketh the sea, and maketh it dry
Zech. 3. 2 The LORD rebuke thee, O Satan; even the
3. 2 LORD that hath chosen Jerusalem rebuke
Mal. 3. 11 will rebuke the devourer for your sakes
2. *To reason, reproof, decide,* יָכַח *yakach,* 5.
Gen. 31. 42 God hath seen..and rebuked (thee) yester.
Lev. 19. 17 thou shalt in any wise rebuke thy neigh.
1 Ch. 12. 17 God of our fathers look..and rebuke (it)
Psa. 6. 1 rebuke me not in thine anger, neither ch.
38. 1 rebuke me not in thy wrath: neither ch.
Prov. 9. 7 he that rebuketh a wicked (man getteth)
9. 8 rebuke a wise man, and he will love thee
24. 25 to them that rebuke (him) shall be delig.
28. 23 He that rebuketh a man, afterwards shall
Isa. 2. 4 and shall rebuke many people; and they
Amos 5. 10 They hate him that rebuketh in the gate
Mic. 4. 3 rebuke strong nations afar off; and they
3. *To strive, plead,* רִיב *rib.*
Neh. 5. 7 I rebuked the nobles, and the rulers, and
4. *To strike upon, blame, chide, reprove,* ἐπιπλήττω.
1 Ti. 5. 1 Rebuke not an elder, but entreat (him) as
5. *To convince, convict,* ἐλέγχω *elegchō.*
1 Ti. 5. 20 Them that sin rebuke before all, that ot.
Titus 1. 13 rebuke them sharply, that they may be
2. 15 and exhort, and rebuke with all authority
Heb. 12. 5 nor faint when thou art rebuked of him
Rev. 3. 19 As many as I love, I rebuke and chasten
6. *To have a reproof,* ἔχω ἔλεγξιν *echō elegxin.*
2 Pe. 2. 16 But was rebuked for his iniquity: the du.

7. *To set a weight upon, chide,* ἐπιτιμάω *epitimaō.*
Matt. 8. 26 rebuked the winds and the sea; and there
16. 22 began to rebuke him, saying, Be it far fr.
17. 18 Jesus rebuked the devil, and he departed
19. 13 children..and the disciples rebuked them
20. 31 the multitude rebuked them, because they
Mark 1. 25 Jesus rebuked him, saying, Hold thy peace
4. 39 rebuked the wind, and said unto the sea
8. 32 Peter took him, and began to rebuke him
8. 33 he rebuked Peter saying, Get thee behind
9. 25 he rebuked the foul spirit, saying unto him
10. 13 disciples rebuked those that brought(them)
Luke 4. 35 Jesus rebuked him, saying, Hold thy pea.
4. 39 and rebuked the fever; and it left her
4. 41 he, rebuking (them), suffered them not to
8. 24 rebuked the wind and the raging of the
9. 42 And Jesus rebuked the unclean spirit, and
9. 55 rebuked them, and said, Ye know not wh.
17. 3 brother trespass against thee, rebuke him
18. 15 when (his) disciples saw (it), they rebuked
18. 39 they which went before rebuked him, that
19. 39 said unto him, Master, rebuke thy discip.
23. 40 the other answering rebuked him, saying
2 Ti. 4. 2 rebuke, exhort, with all long suffering and
Jude 9 durst not..but said, The Lord rebuke thee

REBUKER —
Instruction, chastisement, מוּסָר *musar.*
Hos. 5. 2 though I (have been) a rebuker of them

RECALL, to —
To turn back, שׁוּב *shub,* 5.
Lam. 3. 21 This I recall to my mind, therefore have

RECEIVE, to —
1. *To gather,* אָסַף *asaph,* 3.
Judg 19. 18 there (is) no man that receiveth me to
2. *To lay hold, seize,* חָזַק *chazaq,* 5.
2 Ch. 4. 5 received and held three thousand baths
3. *To receive a portion,* חָלַק *chalaq.*
Josh 18. 2 which had not yet received their inherit.
4. *To contain, bear,* כּוּל *kul,* 5.
1 Ki. 8. 64 too little to receive the burnt offerings
2 Ch. 7. 7 was not able to receive the burnt offer.
5. *To take, receive,* לָקַח *laqach.*
Gen. 4. 11 receive thy brother's blood from thy hand
33. 10 then receive my present at my hand; for
38. 20 to receive (his) pledge from the woman's
Exod 29. 25 thou shalt receive them of their hands
32. 4 he received (them) at their hand, and fa.
36. 3 they received of Moses all the offering
Num 18. 28 which ye receive of the children of Israel
23. 20 I have received (commandment) to bless
34. 14 have received (their inheritance); and h.
34. 15 The two tribes and the half tribe have r.
Deut. 9. 9 When I was gone up into the mount to r.
Josh. 13. 8 Gadites have received their inheritance
18 7 have received their inheritance beyond
Judg 13. 23 would not have received a burnt offering
1 Sa. 10. 4 which thou shalt receive of their hands
12. 3 of whose hand have I received (any) bribe
25. 35 So David received of her hand (that) wh.
1 Ki. 10. 28 merchants received the linen yarn at a
2 Ki. 5. 16 before whom I stand, I will receive none
5. 26 time to receive money, and to receive ga.
12. 7 now therefore receive no (more) money
12. 8 priests consented to receive no (more) m.
19. 14 Hezekiah received the letter of the hand
2 Ch. 1. 16 merchants received the linen yarn at a p.
Job 4. 12 a thing was..brought..and mine ear rec.
22. 22 Receive, I pray thee, the law from his m.
27. 13 (which) they shall receive of the Almighty
35. 7 If thou be righteous..what receiveth he
Psa. 6. 9 LORD hath heard..will receive my prayer
49. 15 redeem my soul..for he shall receive me
68. 18 thou hast received gifts for men; yea, (for)
73. 24 guide me..and afterward receive me (to)
75. 2 When I shall receive the congregation I
Prov. 1. 3 receive the instruction of wisdom, justice
2. 1 My son, if thou wilt receive my words, and
4. 10 Hear, O my son, and receive my sayings
8. 10 Receive my instruction, and not silver
10. 8 wise in heart will receive commandments
21. 11 when the wise is instructed, he receiveth
24. 32 I looked upon (it, and) received instruct.
Isa. 37. 14 Hezekiah received the letter from the h.
40. 2 for she hath received of the LORD'S hand
Jer. 2. 30 they received no correction: your own s.
5. 3 they have refused to receive correction
7. 28 obeyeth not..nor receiveth correction: t.
9. 20 let your ear receive the word of his mouth
17. 23 they might not hear, nor receive instruc.
32. 33 yet they have not hearkened to receive
35. 13 Will ye not receive instruction to hearken
Eze. 3. 10 words that I shall speak unto thee receive
16. 61 when thou shalt receive thy sisters, thine
18. 17 hath not received usury nor increase, hath
36. 30 ye shall receive no more reproach of fa.
Hos. 10. 6 Ephraim shall receive shame, and Israel
14. 2 receive (us) graciously: so will we render
Mic. 1. 11 Pass ye..he shall receive of you his stan.
Zeph. 3. 2 received not correction; she trusted not
3. 7 thou wilt receive instruction; so their d.
Mal. 2. 13 receiveth (it) with good will at your hand
6. *To find,* מָצָא *matsa.*
Gen. 26. 12 received in the same year an hundredfold
7. *To lift up,* נָשָׂא *nasa.*
Deut 33. 3 sat down at thy feet; (every one) shall r.
1 Ki. 5. 9 be discharged there, and thou shalt rece.
Psa. 24. 5 He shall receive the blessing from the L.
8. *To take, receive,* קָבַל *qabal,* 3.
1 Ch. 12. 18 Then David received them, and made them
2 Ch. 29. 22 priests received the blood, and sprinkled
Esth. 4. 4 sackcloth from him: but he received (it) not
Job 2. 10 shall we receive good..and..not receive
Prov 19. 20 Hear counsel, and receive instruction, th.
9. *To take, receive,* קְבַל *qebal,* 3.
Dan. 2. 6 ye shall receive of me gifts and rewards
10. *To weigh out, pay, spend,* שָׁקַל *shaqal.*
2 Sa. 18. 12 Though I should receive a thousand (sh.)
11. *To receive again or back,* ἀναδέχομαι *anadech.*
Acts 28. 7 received us, and lodged us three days co.
Heb. 11. 17 he that had received the promises offered
12. *To hold off or away, or fully,* ἀπέχω *apechō.*
Luke 6. 24 woe unto you..for ye have received your
Phm. 15 that thou shouldest receive him for ever
13. *Receive in, welcome,* ἀποδέχομαι *apodechomai.*
Acts 18. 27 exhorting the disciples to receive him: w.
28. 30 and received all that came in unto him
14. *To receive or take back,* ἀπολαμβάνω *apolambanō.*
Luke 6. 34 lend (to them) of whom ye hope [to receive]
15. 27 because he hath received him safe and s.
16. 25 thou in thy life time receivedst thy good
18. 30 Who shall not [receive] manifold more in
23. 41 for we receive the due reward of our de.
Rom. 1. 27 receiving in themselves that recompence
Gal. 4. 5 that we might receive the adoption of s.
Col. 3. 24 Knowing that of the Lord ye shall receive
2 John 8 lose not..but that we receive a full rew.
3 John 8 We therefore ought [to receive] such, that
15. *To receive,* δέχομαι *dechomai.*
Matt 10. 14 whosoever shall not receive you, nor hear
10. 40 He that receiveth you, receiveth me; and
10. 40 he that receiveth me, receiveth him that
10. 41 He that receiveth..and he that receiveth
11. 14 if ye will receive (it), this is Elias, which
18. 5 whoso shall receive one such..receiveth
Mark 6. 11 whosoever shall not receive you, nor hear
9. 37 Whosoever shall receive one..receiveth
9. 37 whosoever shall receive me, receiveth not
10. 15 Whosoever shall not receive the kingdom
Luke 8. 13 receive the word with joy; and these have
9. 5 whosoever will not receive you, when ye
9. 11 [received] them, and spake unto them of
9. 48 receive this child in my name receiveth
9. 48 whosoever shall receive me receiveth him
9. 53 they did not receive him, because his face
10. 8, 10 whatsoever city ye enter, and they re.
16. 4 they may receive me into their houses
16. 9 they may receive you into everlast. 18. 17.
John 4. 45 Galileans received him, having seen all
Acts 3. 21 Whom the heaven must receive until the
7. 38 who received the lively oracles to give u.
7. 59 and saying, Lord Jesus, receive my spirit
8. 14 Samaria had received the word of God, t.
11. 1 heard that the Gentiles had also received
17. 11 in that they received the word with all
21. 17 when we were come to Jerusalem..[rece.]
22. 5 from whom also I received letters unto the
28. 21 We neither received letters out of Judea
1 Co. 2. 14 receiveth not the things of the spirit of
2 Co. 6. 1 beseech (you) also that ye receive not the
7. 15 with fear and trembling ye received him
8. 4 with much entreaty that [we would rec.]
11. 16 if otherwise, yet as a fool receive me, that
Gal. 4. 14 but received me as an angel of God, (ev.)
Phil. 4. 18 having received of Epaphroditus the thi.
Col. 4. 10 Marcus..if he come unto you, receive him
1 Th. 1. 6 having received the word in much afflic.
2. 13 ye received (it) not (as) the word of men
2 Th. 2. 10 because they received not the love of the
Heb. 11. 31 when she had received the spies with pe.
Jas. 1. 21 receive with meekness the ingrafted word
16. *To give,* δίδωμι *didōmi.*
Rev. 13. 16 caused all..to receive a mark in their ri.
17. *To receive into,* εἰσδέχομαι *eisdechomai.*
2 Co. 6. 17 touch not the unclean..and I will receive
18. *To receive on or upon,* ἐπιδέχομαι *epidechomai.*
3 John 9 pre-eminence among them, receiveth us
10 neither doth he himself receive the bret.
19. *To bring,* κομίζω *komizō.*
Matt 25. 27 at my coming I should have received mi.
2 Co. 5. 10 that every one may receive the things (d.)
Eph. 6. 8 same shall he receive of the Lord, whether
Heb. 10. 36 done the will of God, ye might receive the
11. 19 from whence also he received him in a fi.
11. 39 having obtained a good report..received
1 Pe. 1. 9 Receiving the end of your faith, (even) the
5. 4 ye shall receive a crown of glory that fa.
2 Pe. 2. 13 shall receive the reward of unrighteous.
20. *To take, receive,* λαμβάνω *lambanō.*
Matt. 7. 8 For every one that asketh receiveth; and
10. 8 cast out devils: freely ye have received
10. 41 shall receive a prophet's reward; and he
10. 41 man shall receive a righteous man's rew.
13. 20 heareth..and anon with joy receiveth it
17. 24 they that received tribute (money) came
19. 29 receive an hundredfold, and shall inherit
20. 7 [whatsoever is right, (that) shall ye rece.]
20. 9 when they came..they received every man
20. 10 received more; and they likewise received
20. 11 when they had received (it), they murm.
21. 22 ask in prayer, believing, ye shall receive
21. 34 that they might receive the fruits of it
23. 14 ye shall receive the greater damnation]
Matt 25. 16 Then he that had received the five talents
25. 18 he that had received one went and digged
25. 20 so he that had received five talents came
25. 22 [He also that had received] two talents c.
25. 24 Then he which had received the one tal.
Mark 4. 16 immediately receive it with gladness
10. 30 But he shall receive an hundredfold now
11. 24 believe that ye receive (them), and ye sh.
12. 2 that he might receive from the husband.
12. 40 these shall receive greater damnation
15. 23 gave him to drink..but he received (it) not
Luke 11. 10 For every one that asketh receiveth; and
19. 12 went into a far country to receive for hi.
19. 15 returned, having received the kingdom, t.
20. 47 the same shall receive greater damnation
John 1. 12 But as many as received him, to them g.
1. 16 of his fulness have all we received, and g.
3. 11 testify that we have seen: and ye receive
3. 27 man can receive nothing, except it be gi.
3. 32 and no man receiveth his testimony
3. 33 He that hath received his testimony hath
4. 36 he that reapeth receiveth wages, and ga.
5. 34 But I receive not testimony from man
5. 41 I receive not honour from men
5. 43 ye receive me not..him ye will receive
5. 44 How can ye believe, which receive hono.
6. 21 Then they willingly received him into the
7. 23 If a man on the sabbath day receive cir.
7. 39 they that believe on him should receive
10. 18 This commandment have I received of
12. 48 He that rejecteth me, and receiveth not
13. 20 receiveth whomsoever I send receiveth
13. 20 receiveth me receiveth him that sent me
13. 30 He then having received the sop went im.
14. 17 cannot receive, because it seeth him not
16. 14 for he shall receive of mine, and shall s.
16. 24 ask, and ye shall receive, that your joy
17. 8 they have received (them), and have kno.
18. 3 having received a band (of men) and offi.
19. 30 When Jesus therefore had received the
20. 22 saith unto them, Receive ye the Holy G.
Acts 1. 8 receive power, after that the Holy Ghost
2. 33 having received of the Father the prom.
2. 38 ye shall receive the gift of the Holy Gho.
3. 5 expecting to receive something of them
7. 53 Who have received the law by the dispo.
8. 15 prayed for them, that they might receive
8. 17 them, and they received the Holy Ghost
8. 19 lay hands, he may receive the Holy Ghost
9. 19 when he had received meat, he was stre.
10. 43 whosoever believeth in him shall receive
10. 47 have received the Holy Ghost as well as
16. 24 Who, having received such a charge, th.
17. 15 receiving a commandment unto Silas and
19. 2 Have ye received the Holy Ghost since
20. 24 ministry which I have received of the L.
20. 35 It is more blessed to give than to receive
26. 10 having received authority from the chief
26. 18 that they may receive forgiveness of sins
Rom. 1. 5 By whom we have received grace and ap.
4. 11 received the sign of circumcision, a seal
5. 11 by whom we have now received the ato.
5. 17 much more they which receive abundance
8. 15 For ye have not received the spirit of bo.
8. 15 but ye have received the spirit of adopt.
13. 2 they that resist shall receive to themsel.
1 Co. 2. 12 Now we have received, not the spirit of
3. 8 every man shall receive his own reward
3. 14 If any man's work abide..he shall receive
4. 7 what hast thou that thou didst not rece.?
4. 7 now if thou didst receive (it), why dost
4. 7 thou glory, as if thou hadst not received
9. 24 run all, but one receiveth the prize? So
14. 5 that the church may receive edifying
2 Co. 11. 4 receive another..which ye have not rec.
11. 24 Of the Jews five times received I forty (st.)
Gal. 3. 2 Received ye the spirit by the works of the
3. 14 that we might receive the promise of the
Col. 4. 10 touching whom ye received commandm.
Heb. 2. 2 received a just recompence of reward
7. 5 who receive the office of the priesthood
7. 8 here men that die receive tithes; but there
7. 9 who receiveth tithes, payed tithes in Ab.
9. 15 they which are called might receive the
10. 26 if we sin wilfully after that we have re.
11. 8 which he should after [receive] for an in.
11. 11 Through faith also Sara herself received
11. 13 not [having received] the promises, but h.
11. 35 Women received their dead raised to life
Jas. 1. 7 let not that man think that he shall rec.
1. 12 receive the crown of life, which the Lord
3. 1 knowing that we shall receive the greater
4. 3 Ye ask, and receive not, because ye ask
5. 7 until he receive the early and latter rain
1 Pe. 4. 10 every man hath received the gift, (even so)
2 Pe. 1. 17 For he received from God the Father ho.
1 Jo. 2. 27 But the anointing which ye have received
3. 22 whatsoever we ask, we receive of him, b.
5. 9 If we receive the witness of men, the wi.
2 Jo. 4 as we have received a commandment from
10 receive him not into (your) house, neither
Rev. 2. 17 no man knoweth saving he that receiveth
2. 27 broken to shivers: even as I received of
3. 3 Remember therefore how thou hast rece.
4. 11 Thou art worthy, O Lord, to receive glory
5. 12 Worthy is the Lamb..to receive power, and
14. 9 receive (his) mark in his forehead, or in
14. 11 whosoever receiveth the mark of his name
17. 12 received no kingdom as yet; but receive
18. 4 and that ye receive not of her plagues
19. 20 deceived them that had received the mark
20. 4 neither had received (his) mark upon their

21. *To take along with, share,* μεταλαμβάνω *metal.*
Heb. 6. 7 For the earth..receiveth blessing from God

22. *To receive beside,* παραδέχομαι *paradechomai.*
Mark 4. 20 such as hear the word, and receive (it), and
Acts 16. 21 which are not lawful for us to receive. n.
22. 18 they will not receive thy testimony con.
1 Ti. 5. 19 Against an elder receive not an accusation
Heb. 12. 6 scourgeth every son whom he receiveth

23. *To take or receive beside,* παραλαμβάνω *parala.*
Mark 7. 4 things there be which they have received
John 1. 11 came unto his own, and his own received
14. 3 come again, and receive you unto myself
1 Co. 11. 23 For I have received of the Lord that wh.
15. 1 which also ye have received, and wherein
15. 3 first of all that which I also received, how
Gal. 1. 9 any other gospel..than that ye have rec.
1. 12 For I neither received it of man, neither
Phil. 4. 9 which ye have both learned, and received
Col. 2. 6 As ye have therefore received Christ Jesus
4. 17 ministry which thou hast received in the
1 Th. 2. 13 when ye received the word of God which
4. 1 that as ye have received of us how ye ou.
2 Th. 3. 6 after the tradition which he received of
Heb. 12. 28 we receiving a kingdom which cannot be

24. *To receive to (one's self),* προσδέχομαι *prosdech.*
Luke 15. 2 This man receiveth sinners, and eateth
Rom 16. 2 That ye receive her in the Lord, as beco.
Phil. 2. 29 Receive him therefore in the Lord with

25. *To take or receive to (one's self),* προσλαμβάνω.
Acts 28. 2 received us every one, because of the pr.
Rom. 14. 1 Him that is weak in the faith receive ye
14. 3 not judge him..for God hath received
15. 7 receive ye one another, as Christ also re.
Phm. 12 therefore [receive] him that is mine own
17 If thou count me therefore a partner, re.

26. *To receive under (one's roof),* ὑποδέχομαι *hupo.*
Luke 10. 38 certain woman named Martha received
19. 6 and came down, and received him joyfu.
Acts 17. 7 Whom Jason hath received: and these
Jas. 2. 25 when she had received the messengers

27. *To take or receive under,* ὑπολαμβάνω *hupolam.*
Acts 1. 9 a cloud received him out of their sight

28. *To have place for, contain, receive,* χωρέω *chōreō.*
Matt 19. 12 He that is able to receive (it), let him re.
2 Co. 7. 2 Receive us; we have wronged no man

[*See also* Comfort, damage, law, mercy, seed, sight, strength, tithes.]

RECEIVE (again, for), to —

1. *To take or receive from,* ἀπολαμβάνω *apolambanō.*
Luke 6. 34 lend to sinners, to receive as much again

2. *To bring,* κομίζω *komizō.*
Col. 3. 25 But he that doeth wrong shall receive for

RECEIVE ashes, to —

To remove ashes, דָּשֵׁן *dashen,* 3.
Exod 27. 3 shalt make his pans to receive his ashes

RECEIVE (gladly), to —

To receive in, welcome, ἀποδέχομαι *apodechomai.*
Luke 8. 40 people (gladly) received him: for they
Acts 2. 41 Then they that gladly received his word
15. 4 [they were received] of the church, and

RECEIVE, can, to be room to —

To have place, contain, receive, χωρέω *chōreō.*
Matt 19. 11 All (men) cannot receive this saying, save
Mark 2. 2 insomuch that there was no room to rec.

RECEIVED (up), to be —

1. *To be gathered,* אָסַף *asaph,* 2.
Num 12. 14 and after that let her be received in (ag.)

2. *To take up,* ἀναλαμβάνω *analambanō.*
Mark 16. 19 [he was received up into heaven, and sat]
Acts 10. 16 vessel was received up again into heaven
1 Ti. 3. 16 believed on in the world, received up into

3. *A taking or receiving back,* ἀνάληψις *analēpsis.*
Luke 9. 51 was come that he should be received up

4. *To take, receive,* λαμβάνω *lambanō.*
1 Ti. 4. 4 nothing to be refused, if it be received

5. *A receiving or sharing with,* μετάληψις,-λημψις.
1 Ti. 4. 3 which God hath created to be received

RECEIVER, RECEIVING —

1. *To take, receive,* לָקַח *laqach.*
2 Ki. 5. 20 spared Naaman..in not receiving at his

2. *To weigh out, pay, spend,* שָׁקַל *shaqal.*
Isa. 33. 18 where (is) the receiver? where (is) he that

3. *A receiving, reception,* λῆψις *lēpsis.*
Phil. 4. 15 as concerning giving and receiving, but

4. *A receiving to (one's self),* πρόσληψις *proslēpsis.*
Rom 11. 15 what (shall) [the receiving] (of them be)

RE'-CHAB, רֵכָב *companionship.*

1. A son of Rimmon the Beerothite; with the help of his brother Baanah he assassinated Ish-bosheth son of Saul in his bed, and were put to death for it by David. B.C. 1048.
2 Sa. 4. 2 and the name of the other R., the sons of
4. 5 And the sons of Rimmon..R. and Baanah
4. 6 and R. and Baanah his brother escaped
4. 9 David answered R. and Baanah his brother

2. Father of Jehonadab, B.C. 930, and founder of a tribe whom he charged to abstain from wine, live in tents, &c.: and who are still found N.E. of Medina.
2 Ki. 10. 15 he lighted on Jehonadab the son of R. (c.)
10. 23 Jehu went, and Jehonadab the son of R.
Jer. 35. 6 Jonadab the son of R. our father comma.
35. 8 obeyed the voice of Jonadab..son of R.
35. 14 The words of Jonadab the son of R., that
35. 16 the sons of Jonadab the son of R. have p.
35. 19 Jonadab the son of R. shall not want a m.

3. A descendant of Hemath a Kenite. B.C. 930.
1 Ch. 2. 55 Hemath, the father of the house of R.

4. Father of Malchiah, a chief man who returned from exile and helped to repair the wall after Nehemiah came. B.C. 455.
Neh. 3. 14 dung gate repaired Malchiah the son of R.

RE-CHAB-ITES, רֵכָבִים.

The tribe or family of the preceding Rechab, and of Jonadab or Jehonadab his son.
Jer. 35. 2 Go unto the house of the R., and speak
35. 3 Then I took..the whole house of the R.
35. 5 And I set before..the R. pots full of wine
35. 18 Jeremiah said unto the house of the R.

RE'-CHAH, רֵכָה *declivity.*

A city in Judah, not yet identified.
1 Ch. 4. 12 These (are) the men of R.

RECKON, to —

1. *To reckon,* חָשַׁב *chashab,* 3.
Lev. 25. 50 he shall reckon with him that bought him
27. 18 priest shall reckon unto him the money
27. 23 Then the priest shall reckon unto him the
2 Ki. 12. 15 Moreover they reckoned not with the men

2. *To number, write, cypher,* סָפַר *saphar.*
Eze. 44. 26 they shall reckon unto him seven days

3. *To visit, inspect, lay a charge on,* פָּקַד *paqad.*
Num. 4. 32 by name ye shall reckon the instruments

4. *To make equal, compare, place,* שָׁוָה *shavah,* 3.
Isa. 38. 13 I reckoned till morning, (that,) as a lion

5. *To reckon,* λογίζομαι *logizomai.*
Luke 22. 37 he was reckoned among the transgressors
Rom. 4. 4 is the reward not reckoned of grace, but
4. 9 we say that faith was reckoned to Abrah.
4. 10 How is it then reckoned? when he was in
6. 11 Likewise reckon ye also yourselves to be
8. 18 For I reckon that the sufferings of this p.

6. *To take account together,* συναίρω λόγον [*sunairō*].
Matt 25. 19 lord of those servants cometh, and reck.

7. *To take up together,* συναίρω *sunairō.*
Matt 18. 24 when he had begun to reckon, one was b.

RECKONED (by genealogies), to be —

1. *To be reckoned,* חָשַׁב *chashab,* 2.
Num 18. 27 your heave offering shall be reckoned un.
2 Sa. 4. 2 for Beeroth also was reckoned to Benjamin

2. *To reckon self,* חָשַׁב *chashab,* 7.
Num 23. 9 shall not be reckoned among the nations

3. *Be reckoned genealogically,* יָחַשׂ *yachash,* 7.
1 Ch. 5. 1 the genealogy is not to be reckoned after
5. 7 genealogy of their generations was reck.
5. 17 All these were reckoned by genealogies
7. 5 reckoned in all by their genealogies four.
7. 7 were reckoned by their genealogies twen.
9. 1 all Israel were reckoned by genealogies
9. 22 These were reckoned by their genealogy
2 Ch. 31. 19 were reckoned by genealogies among the
Ezra 2. 62 those that were reckoned by genealogy
8. 3 were reckoned by genealogy of the males
Neh. 7. 5 might be reckoned by genealogy; 7. 64.

RECKONING, (to be made) —

1. *To be reckoned,* חָשַׁב *chashab,* 2.
2 Ki. 22. 7 there was no reckoning made with them

2. *Inspection, visitation, charge,* פְּקֻדָּה *pequddah.*
1 Ch. 23. 11 therefore they were in one reckoning, ac.

RECOMMENDED, to be —

To give beside, παραδίδωμι *paradidōmi.*
Acts 14. 26 whence they had been recommended to
15. 40 being recommended by the brethren unto

RECOMPENCE (of reward) —

1. *Recompence, deserving, deed,* גְּמוּל *gemul.*
Prov 12. 14 recompence of a man's hands shall be re.
Isa. 35. 4 vengeance, (even) God (with) a recompe.
59. 18 fury to his adversaries, recompence to his
59. 18 to the islands he will repay recompence
66. 6 that rendereth recompence to his enemies
Jer. 51. 6 he will render unto her a recompence
Lam 3. 64 Render unto them a recompence, O LORD
Joel. 3. 4 will ye render me a recompence? and if
3. 4, 7 return your recompence upon your own

3. *Recompence, deserving, deed,* גְּמוּלָה *gemulah.*
Jer. 51. 56 God of recompences shall surely requite

4. *Recompence,* שִׁלּוּם *shillum.*
Isa. 34. 8 of recompences for the controversy of Zion
Hos. 9. 7 the days of recompence are come; Israel

5. *Recompence,* שִׁלֵּם *shillem.*
Deut 32. 35 To me (belongeth) vengeance and recom.

6. *Change, exchange, recompence,* תְּמוּרָה *temurah.*
Job 15. 31 Let not..for vanity shall be his recomp.

7. *Retaliation, recompence,* ἀνταπόδομα *antapodoma.*
Luke 14. 12 bid thee..and a recompence be made thee
Rom 11. 9 stumbling block, and a recompence unto

8. *A corresponding reward,* ἀντιμισθία *antimisthia.*
Rom. 1. 27 recompence of their error which was meet
2 Co. 6. 13 Now for a recompence in the same, I speak

9. *A giving away or back a reward,* μισθαποδοσία.
Heb. 2. 2 if..received a just recompence of reward
10. 35 which hath great recompence of reward
11. 26 respect unto the recompence of the reward

RECOMPENSE (again), to —

1. *To recompense, do,* גָּמַל *gamal.*
2 Sa. 19. 36 why should the king recompense it me
Joel 3. 4 if ye recompense me, swiftly (and) speedily

2. *To give,* נָתַן *nathan.*
2 Ch. 6. 23 recompensing his way upon his own head
Eze. 7. 3 and will recompense upon thee all thine
7. 4 I will recompense thy ways upon thee, and
7. 8 recompense thee for all thine abominat.
7. 9 I will recompense thee according to thy
9. 10 will recompense their way upon their head
11. 21 I will recompense their way upon their
16. 43 will recompense thy way upon (thine) h.
17. 19 it will I recompense upon his own head
22. 31 their own way have I recompensed upon
23. 49 they shall recompense your lewdness upon

3. *To turn back,* שׁוּב *shub,* 5.
Num. 5. 7 he shall recompense his trespass with the
5. 8 if the man have no kinsman to recompense
2 Sa. 22. 21 to the cleanness of my hands..he recom.
22. 25 LORD hath recompensed me according to
Psa. 18. 20 to the cleanness of my hands..he recom.
18. 24 LORD recompensed me according to my
Hos. 12. 2 according to his doings will he recomp.

4. *To finish, complete, recompense,* שָׁלַם *shalam,* 3.
Ruth 2. 12 The LORD recompense thy work, and a
Job 34. 33 he will recompense it, whether thou re.
Prov 20. 22 Say not thou, I will recompense evil; (but)
Isa. 65. 6 will recompense, even recompense into
Jer. 16. 18 I will recompense their iniquity and their
25. 14 I will recompense them according to their
32. 18 recompensest the iniquity of the fathers
50. 29 recompense her according to her work

5. *To give away, back, fully,* ἀποδίδωμι *apodidōmi.*
Rom. 12. 17 Recompense to no man evil for evil

6. *Give in return,* ἀνταποδίδωμι *antapodidōmi.*
Luke 14. 14 they cannot recompense thee; for thou
14. 14 be recompensed at the resurrection of the
Rom. 11. 35 it shall be recompensed unto him again
2 Th. 1. 6 to recompense tribulation to them that
Heb. 10. 30 I will recompense, saith the Lord. And

RECOMPENSED, to be —

1. *To be caused to turn back,* שׁוּב *shub,* 6.
Num. 5. 8 let the trespass be recompensed unto the

2. *To be completed, repaid, recompensed,* שָׁלַם *shalam,* 4.
Prov 11. 31 the righteous shall be recompensed in the
Jer. 18. 20 Shall evil be recompensed for good? for.

RECONCILE (self), to —

1. *To cover, make atonement,* כָּפַר *kaphar,* 3.
Lev. 6. 30 is brought..to reconcile..in the holy (place)
16. 20 when he hath made an end of reconciling
Eze. 45. 20 so thou shalt do..so shall ye reconcile the

2. *To make self pleasing,* רָצָה *ratsah,* 7.
1 Sa. 29. 4 wherewith should he reconcile himself

3. *To change thoroughly from,* ἀποκαταλλάττω.
Eph. 2. 16 he might reconcile both unto God in one
Col. 1. 20 by him to reconcile all things unto him.
1. 21 And you, that were..enemies..hath he r.

4. *To change thoroughly,* καταλλάσσω *katallassō.*
2 Co. 5. 18 who hath reconciled us to himself by Jesus
5. 19 reconciling the world unto himself, not

RECONCILED, to be —

1. *To be changed throughout,* διαλλάττομαι *diallatt.*
Matt. 5. 24 be reconciled to thy brother, and then

2. *To change thoroughly,* καταλλάσσω *katallassō.*
Rom. 5. 10 we were reconciled to God by the death
5. 10 being reconciled, we shall be saved by his
1 Co. 7. 11 let her..be reconciled to (her) husband
2 Co. 5. 20 we pray..in Christ's stead, be ye reconc.

RECONCILING, RECONCILIATION —

A thorough change, καταλλαγή *katallagē.*
Rom 11. 15 if the casting away of them (be) the rec
2 Co. 5. 18 hath given to us the ministry of reconcil.
5. 19 hath committed unto us the word of rec.

RECONCILIATION (for), to make —

1. *To offer or receive a sin offering,* חָטָא *chata,* 3.
2 Ch. 29. 24 they made reconciliation with their blood

2. *To cover, make atonement,* כָּפַר *kaphar,* 3.
Lev. 8. 15 sanctified it, to make reconciliation upon
Eze. 45. 15 to make reconciliation for them, saith the
45. 17 to make reconciliation for the house of I.
Dan. 9. 24 to make reconciliation for iniquity, and

3. *To appease, propitiate,* ἱλάσκομαι *hilaskomai.*
Heb. 2. 17 make reconciliation for the sins of the

RECORD —

1. *A record,* דִּכְרוֹן, דָּכְרָן *dokran, dikron.*
Ezra 4. 15 made in the book of the records of thy f.
4. 15 so shalt thou find in the book of the rec.
6. 2 and therein (was) a record thus written

2. *A memorial,* זִכָּרוֹן *zikkaron.*
Esth. 6. 1 to bring the book of records of the C.
3. *A testimony, witness,* שָׂהֵד *sahed.*
Job 16. 19 my witness (is) in heaven, and my record
4. *A martyr, witness,* μάρτυς *martus.*
2 Co. 1. 23 I call God for a record upon my soul, that
Phil. 1. 8 God is my record, how greatly I long after
5. *Testimony, witness,* μαρτυρία *marturia.*
John 1. 19 this is the record of John, when the Jews
8. 13 said unto him..thy record is not true
8. 14 my record is true: for I know whence I
19. 35 his record is true: and he knoweth that
1 Jo. 5. 10 he believeth not the record that God gave
5. 11 this is the record, that God hath given to
3 John 12 good report..and ye know that our record

RECORD, to (bear, call, take to) —
1. *To cause to remember,* זָכַר *zakar,* 5.
Exod 20. 24 In all places where I record my name I
1 Ch. 16. 4 to record, and to thank and praise the
2. *To cause to testify,* עוּד *ud,* 5.
Deut 30. 19 I call heaven and earth to record this day
31. 28 call heaven and earth to record against t.
Isa. 8. 2 I took unto me faithful witnesses to rec.
3. *To write,* כָּתַב *kathab.*
Neh. 12. 22 (were) recorded chief of the fathers: also
4. *To bear testimony or witness,* μαρτυρέω *martureō.*
John 1. 32 John bare record, saying, I saw the spirit
1. 34 I saw, and bare record that this is the Son
8. 13 said..Thou bearest record of thyself; thy
8. 14 said..Though I bear record of myself, (yet)
12. 17 The people..that was with him..bare rec.
19. 35 And he that saw (it) bare record, and his
Rom 10. 2 I bear them record that they have a zeal
2 Co. 8. 3 For to (their) power, I bear record, yea, and
Gal. 4. 15 for I bear you record, that, if..possible, ye
Col. 4. 13 I bear him record, that he hath a great
1 Jo. 5. 7 [there are three that bear record in hea.]
3 John 12 we (also) bear record; and ye know that
Rev. 1. 2 Who bare record of the word of God, and of
5. *To testify or bear witness,* μαρτύρομαι *marturomai.*
Acts 20. 26 I take you to record this day, that I (am)

RECORDER —
To cause to remember, זָכַר *zakar,* 5.
2 Sa. 8. 16 Jehoshaphat the son of Alihud (was) rec.
20. 24 Jehoshaphat the son of Alihud (was) rec.
1 Ki. 4. 3 Jehoshaphat the son of Alihud, the reco
2 Ki. 18. 18, 37 and Joah the son of Asaph the recorder
1 Ch. 18. 15 Jehoshaphat the son of Alihud, recorder
2 Ch. 34. 8 and Joah the son of Joahaz the recorder
Isa. 36. 3 the scribe, and Joah, Asaph's son, the r
36. 22 scribe and Joah the son of Asaph, the rec.

RECOUNT, to —
To remember, זָכַר *zakar.*
Nah. 2. 5 He shall recount his worthies: they shall

RECOVER (self, strength), to —
1. *To gather,* אָסַף *asaph.*
2 Ki. 5. 3 prophet..would recover him of his lepr
5. 6 thou mayest recover him of his leprosy
5. 7 that this man doth send unto me to rec
5. 11 strike his hand over the place, and reco.
2. *To brighten up, encourage,* בָּלַג *balag,* 5.
Psa. 39. 13 that I may recover strength, before I go
3. *To live, revive,* חָיָה *chayah.*
2 Ki. 1. 2 enquire..whether I shall recover of this
8. 8, 9 saying, Shall I recover of this disease
8. 10 Thou mayest certainly recover: howbeit
8. 14 He told me..thou shouldest surely reco.
20. 7 took and laid (it) on the boil, and he rec.
Isa. 38. 9 when he had been sick, and was recovered
38. 21 lay [it] for a plaister..and he shall recover
4. *To keep safe, recover,* חָלַם *chalam,* 5.
Isa. 38. 16 so wilt thou recover me, and make me to
5. *Life preserver, quickening,* מִחְיָה *michyah*
2 Ch. 14. 13 that they could not recover themselves
6. *To snatch away, deliver, spoil,* נָצַל *natsal,* 5.
Judg 11. 26 did ye not recover (them) within that time
1 Sa. 30. 8 overtake (them), and without fail recover
30. 18 David recovered all that the Amalekites
30. 22 not give..of the spoil that we have reco.
Hos. 2. 9 and will recover my wool and my flax (g.)
7. *To keep in, restrain, detain,* עָצַר *atsar.*
2 Ch. 13. 20 Neither did Jeroboam recover strength
8. *To get, acquire, possess,* קָנָה *qanah.*
Isa. 11. 11 to recover the remnant of his people, wh.
9. *To cause to turn back,* שׁוּב *shub,* 5.
1 Sa. 30. 19 was nothing lacking..David recovered all
2 Sa. 8. 3 recover his border at the river Euphrates
2 Ki. 13. 25 beat him, and recovered the cities of Is.
14. 28 he recovered Damascus, and Hamath, (w.
16. 6 Rezin king of Syria recovered Elath to S.
Jer. 41. 16 of the people whom he had recovered from
10. *To become sober again,* ἀνανήφω *ananēphō.*
2 Ti. 2. 26 they may recover themselves out of the
11. *To hold well,* ἔχω καλῶς *echō kalōs.*
Mark 16. 18 [hands on the sick, and they shall recover]

RECOVERED, to be —
1. *To be or become strong,* חָזַק *chazaq.*
Isa. 39. 1 that he had been sick, and was recovered
2. *To go up,* עָלָה *alah.*
Jer. 8. 22 why..is not the health of..my people re.

RED (marble, wine), redness —
1. *Red, ruddy,* אָדֹם *adom.*
Gen. 25. 30 Feed me, I pray thee, with that same red
Num 19. 2 that they bring thee a red heifer without
2 Ki. 3. 22 saw the water on the other side..red as
Isa. 63. 2 Wherefore (art thou) red in thine apparel
Zech. 1. 8 behold a man riding upon a red horse, and
1. 8 and behind him..red horses, speckled and
6. 2 In the first chariot..red horses, and in the
2. *Red, ruddy,* אַדְמוֹנִי, אַדְמֹנִי *admoni.*
Gen. 25. 25 the first came out red, all over like an
3. *Refreshed, fiery,* חַכְלִילִי *chaklili.*
Gen. 49. 12 His eyes..red with wine, and his teeth
4. *Refreshment, fierceness,* חַכְלִלוּת *chakliluth.*
Prov 23. 29 who hath wounds..who hath redness of
5. *Fermented,* חָמַר *chemer.*
Isa. 27. 2 sing ye unto her, A vineyard of red wine
6. *Fiery, red,* πυῤῥός *purrhos.*
Rev. 6. 4 there went out another horse (that was) r.
12. 3 a great red dragon, having seven heads and
7. *White or shining marble,* בַּהַט *bahat.*
Esth. 1. 6 a pavement of red, and blue, and white

RED SEA, יַם סוּף *yam suph.*
The sea between Egypt and Arabia: the Hebrew name is *Yam Suph,* the "sea of weeds." The upper part of it has two arms: the western one being called the Gulf of *Suez,* which is 190 miles long; while the eastern one is called the Gulf of *Akaba,* and is about 112 miles in length. The head of the former (over which Israel passed), is said to have retired 50 miles since the birth of Christ. The name *Red* is perhaps a translation of *Edom.*
Exod 10. 19 And the LORD..cast them into the R. sea
[See under *Sea,* for other passages.]

RED, to be (made) —
1. *To be made red,* אָדַם *adam,* 4.
Exod 25. 5 rams' skins dyed red, and badgers' skins
26. 14 make a covering..(of) rams' skins dyed r.
35. 7 rams' skins dyed red, and badgers' skins
35. 23 and red skins of rams, and badgers' skin
36. 19 made a covering..(of) rams' skins dyed red
39. 34 the covering of rams' skins dyed red, and
Nah. 2. 3 The shield of his mighty men is made red
2. *To make red,* אָדַם *adam,* 5.
Isa. 1. 18 though they be red like crimson, they shall
3. *To show self red,* אָדַם *adam,* 7.
Prov. 23. 31 Look not thou upon the wine when it is r.
4. *To be red* (or *foam, ferment*), חָמַר *chamar.*
Psa. 75. 8 and the wine is red; it is full of mixture
5. *To be fire-coloured,* πυῤῥάζω *purrhazō.*
Matt 16. 2 (It will be) fair weather; for the sky is red
16. 3 foul weather to day; for the sky is red and

REDDISH (somewhat) —
Reddish, very red, אֲדַמְדָּם *adamdam.*
Lev. 13. 19 a bright spot, white, and somewhat red.
13. 24 bright spot, somewhat reddish, or white
13. 42 if there be..a white reddish sore: it (is) a
13. 43 (if) the rising of the sore (be) white reddish
13. 49 if the plague be greenish or reddish in the
14. 37 with hollow strakes, greenish or reddish

REDEEM (self), to —
1. *To free (by avenging or repaying),* גָּאַל *gaal.*
Gen. 48. 16 The Angel which redeemed me from all
Exod. 6. 6 will redeem you with a stretched out arm
15. 13 led..the people (which) thou hast redee.
Lev. 25. 25 come to redeem it, then shall he redeem
25. 26 if the man have none to redeem it, and hi.
25. 48 After..one of his brethren may redeem
25. 49 his uncle or his uncle's son, may redeem
27. 13 if he will at all redeem it, then he shall
27. 15 if he that sanctified it will redeem his ho.
27. 19 if he..will in any wise redeem it, then he
27. 20 if he will not redeem the field, or if he ha.
27. 31 if a man will at all redeem..of his tithes
Ruth 4. 4 If thou wilt redeem (it), redeem (it); but
4. 4 if thou wilt not redeem (it, then) tell me
4. 4 none to redeem (it)..he said, I will rede.
4. 6 I cannot redeem (it) for myself, lest I mar
4. 6 redeem thou my right..I cannot redeem
Psa. 69. 18 Draw nigh unto my soul, (and) redeem
72. 14 He shall redeem their soul from deceit
74. 2 thine inheritance, (which) thou hast red.
77. 15 Thou hast with (thine) arm redeemed thy
103. 4 Who redeemeth thy life from destruction
106. 10 redeemed them from the hand of the en.
107. 2 whom he hath redeemed from the hand
Isa. 43. 1 for I have redeemed thee, I have called
44. 22 return unto me; for I have redeemed thee
44. 23 LORD hath redeemed Jacob, and glorified
48. 20 LORD hath redeemed his servant Jacob
52. 9 for the LORD..he hath redeemed Jerusa.
63. 9 in his pity he redeemed them; and he b.
Lam. 3. 58 hast pleaded..thou hast redeemed my l.
Hos. 13. 14 I will redeem them from death: O death
Mic. 4. 10 LORD shall redeem thee from the hand of
2. *To be freed,* גָּאַל *gaal,* 2.
Lev. 25. 49 or, if he be able, he may redeem himself
3. *Freedom, redemption,* גְּאֻלָּה *geullah.*
Lev. 25. 26 if the man..himself be able to redeem it
25. 29 he may redeem it within a whole year a.
25. 29 (within) a full year may he redeem it
25. 32 cities..may the Levites redeem at any ti.
4. *To free, redeem,* פָּדָה *padah.*
Exod 13. 13 every firstling of an ass thou shalt redeem
13. 13 if thou wilt not redeem it, then thou shalt
13. 13 the first born of man..shalt thou redeem
13. 15 all the first born of my children I redeem
34. 20 the firstling of an ass thou shalt redeem
34. 20 if thou redeem (him) not, then shalt thou
34. 20 the first born of thy sons thou shalt red.
Lev. 27. 27 he shall redeem (it) according to thine es.
Num 18. 15 first born of man shalt thou surely rede.
18. 15 firstling of unclean beasts shalt thou re.
18. 16 And..from a month old shalt thou redeem
18. 17 firstling of a goat, thou shalt not redeem
Deut. 7. 8 redeemed you out of the house of bond
9. 26 which thou hast redeemed through thy
13. 5 redeemed you out of the house of bond.
15. 15 God redeemed thee: therefore I comman.
21. 8 thy people Israel, whom thou hast rede.
24. 18 God redeemed thee thence: therefore I
2 Sa. 4. 9 who hath redeemed my soul out of all a.
7. 23 God went to redeem for a people to him.
7. 23 which thou redeemedst to thee from Eg.
1 Ki. 1. 29 hath redeemed my soul out of all distress
1 Ch. 17. 21 God went to redeem (to be) his own peo.
17. 21 whom thou hast redeemed out of Egypt
Neh. 1. 10 thou hast redeemed by thy great power
Job 5. 20 he shall redeem thee from death; and in
6. 23 or, Redeem me from the hand of the mi.
Psa. 25. 22 Redeem Israel, O God, out of all his tro.
26. 11 But..redeem me, and be merciful unto
31. 5 thou hast redeemed me, O LORD God of
34. 22 LORD redeemeth the soul of his servants
44. 26 Arise..and redeem us for thy mercies' s.
49. 7 None..can by any means redeem his bro.
49. 15 God will redeem my soul from the power
71. 23 and my soul, which thou hast redeemed
130. 8 he shall redeem Israel from all his iniq.
Isa. 29. 22 thus saith the LORD, who redeemed Abr.
Jer. 15. 21 I will redeem thee out of the hand of the
31. 11 LORD hath redeemed Jacob, and ransom.
Hos. 7. 13 though I have redeemed them, yet they
Mic. 6. 4 redeemed thee out of the house of serva.
Zech. 10. 8 for I have redeemed them: and they sh.
5. *Separation, redemption,* פְּדוּת *peduth.*
Isa. 50. 2 Is my hand shortened..that it cannot re.
6. *To break off, rend, deliver,* פָּרַק *paraq.*
Psa. 136. 24 hath redeemed us from our enemies: for
7. *To acquire, get,* קָנָה *qanah.*
Neh. 5. 8 have redeemed our brethren the
8. *To acquire at the forum,* ἀγοράζω *agorazō.*
Rev. 5. 9 hast redeemed us to God by thy blood out
14. 3 And..which were redeemed from the ea.
14. 4 These were redeemed from among men
9. *To acquire out of the forum,* ἐξαγοράζω *exagorazō.*
Gal. 3. 13 Christ hath redeemed us from the curse
4. 5 To redeem them that were under the law
Eph. 5. 16 Redeeming the time, because the days are
Col. 4. 5 Walk in wisdom..redeeming the time
10. *To loose by a price,* λυτρόω *lutroō.*
Luke 24. 21 he which should have redeemed Israel
Titus 2. 14 that he might redeem us from all iniquity
1 Pe. 1. 18 ye know that ye were not redeemed with
11. *To make a loosing,* ποιέω λύτρωσιν *poieō lutrōsin.*
Luke 1. 68 he hath visited and redeemed his people

REDEEMED, to (let) be —
1. *To be or become freed,* גָּאַל *gaal,* 2.
Lev. 25. 30 if it be not redeemed within the space of
25. 54 if he be not redeemed in these (years), th.
27. 20 the field..shall not be redeemed any mo.
27. 27 or if it be not redeemed, then it shall be
27. 28 no devoted thing..shall be sold or rede.
27. 33 if he change it..it shall not be redeemed
Isa. 52. 3 and ye shall be redeemed without money
2. *To be freed, redeemed,* פָּדָה *padah,* 2.
Lev. 19. 20 not at all redeemed, nor freedom given
27. 29 None..devoted of men, shall be redeemed
Isa. 1. 27 Zion shall be redeemed with judgment
3. *To free, redeem,* פָּדָה *padah,* 5.
Exod 21. 8 If she please not..let her be redeemed: to
4. *Freed or redeemed ones,* פְּדוּיִם *peduyim.*
Num. 3. 48 the odd number of them is to be redeemed

REDEEMED (that are or were to be) —
1. *To free by avenging or repaying,* גָּאַל *gaal.*
Psa. 107. 2 Let the redeemed of the LORD say (so)
Isa. 35. 9 No lion..but the redeemed shall walk (th.)
62. 12 The holy people, The redeemed of the L.
63. 4 and the year of my redeemed is come
2. *To free, redeem,* פָּדָה *padah.*
Num 18. 16 those that are to be redeemed from a m.
Isa. 51. 11 Therefore the redeemed of the LORD shall
3. *Freed ones,* פְּדוּיִם *peduyim* [V.L. פדים Num. 3. 51].
Num. 3. 46 for those that are to be redeemed of the
3. 49 them that were redeemed by the Levite
3. 51 gave the money of them that were redeem.

REDEEMER —
To free (by avenging or repaying), גָּאַל *gaal.*
Job 19. 25 For I know (that) my redeemer liveth, and
Psa. 19. 14 Let..acceptable..my strength, and my re.
78. 35 they remembered..the high God their re.

Prov 23. 11 their redeemer (is) mighty; he shall plead
Isa. 41. 14 and thy redeemer, the holy one of Israel
43. 14 Thus saith the LORD, your redeemer, the
44. 6 Thus saith the LORD..and his redeemer
44. 24 Thus saith the LORD, thy redeemer, and
47. 4 our redeemer, the LORD of hosts (is) his n.
48. 17 Thus saith the LORD, thy redeemer, the h.
49. 7 Thus saith the LORD, the redeemer of Is.
49. 26 thy redeemer, the mighty one of Jacob
54. 5 thy redeemer the holy one of Israel
54. 8 will I have mercy on thee, saith..thy re.
59. 20 the redeemer shall come to Zion, and unto
60. 16 and thy redeemer, the mighty one of Ja.
63. 16 thou, O LORD, (art) our Father, our red.
Jer. 50. 34 Their redeemer (is) strong; The LORD of

REDEMPTION (price of), redeeming —

1. *Right or price of redemption*, גְּאֻלָּה *geullah*.
Lev. 25. 24 ye shall grant a redemption for the land
25. 51 he shall give again the price of his rede.
25. 52 give him again the price of his redempt.
Ruth 4. 7 concerning redeeming, and concerning c.
Jer. 32. 7 for the right of redemption (is) thine to
32. 8 right of inheritance (is) thine, and the re.

2. *Separation, redemption*, פְּדוּת *peduth*.
Psa. 111. 9 He sent redemption unto his people: he
130. 7 and with him (is) plenteous redemption

3. *Separation, redemption*, פִּדְיוֹם *pidyom*.
Num. 3. 49 Moses took the redemption money of them

4. *Separation, redemption*, פִּדְיוֹן *pidyon*.
Psa. 49. 8 the redemption of their soul (is) precious

5. *A loosing away*, ἀπολύτρωσις *apolutrōsis*.
Luke 21. 28 look up..for your redemption draweth ni.
Rom. 3. 24 through the redemption that is in Christ
8. 23 adoption, (to wit), the redemption of our
1 Co. 1. 30 made unto us..sanctification, and rede.
Eph. 1. 7 In whom we have redemption through h.
1. 14 until the redemption of the purchased p.
4. 30 whereby ye are sealed unto the day of re.
Col. 1. 14 In whom we have redemption through h.
Heb. 9. 15 for the redemption of the transgressions

6. *A loosing*, λύτρωσις *lutrōsis*.
Luke 2. 38 to all them that looked for redemption in
Heb. 9. 12 entered..having obtained eternal redem.

REDOUND, to —

To be over and above, περισσεύω *perisseuō*.
2 Co. 4. 15 grace might..redound to the glory of God

REED —

1. *A reed*, אֲגַם *agam*.
Jer. 51. 32 the reeds they have burned with fire, and

2. *A stalk, cane, reed, beam*, קָנֶה *qaneh*.
1 Ki. 14. 15 LORD shall smite Israel, as a reed is sha.
2 Ki. 18. 21 trustest upon the staff of this bruised reed
Job 40. 21 He lieth..in the covert of the reed, and
Isa. 19. 6 dried up: the reeds and flags shall wither
35. 7 where each lay, (shall be) grass, with re.
36. 6 trustest in the staff of this broken reed
42. 3 bruised reed shall he not break, and the
Eze. 29. 6 because they have been a staff of reed to
40. 3 flax in his hand, and a measuring reed
40. 5 breadth..one reed; and the height, one r.
40. 6 (which was) one reed broad, and the other
40. 6 threshold (of the gate, which was) one r.
40. 7 chamber (was) one reed long, and one re.
40. 7 threshold of the gate..(was) one reed
40. 8 also the porch of the gate within, one re.
41. 8 foundations..a full reed of six great cub.
42. 16 He measured..with the measuring reed
42. 16 with the measuring reed round about
42. 17, 18, 19 hundred reeds, with the measuring

3. *A stalk, reed, cane*, κάλαμος *kalamos*.
Matt 11. 7 What went ye out..to see? A reed shaken
12. 20 bruised reed shall he not break, and sm.
27. 29 they put (it) upon his head, and a reed in
27. 30 took the reed, and smote him on the head
27. 48 put (it) on a reed, and gave him to drink
Mark 15. 19 they smote him on the head with a reed
15. 36 put (it) on a reed, and gave him to drink
Luke 7. 24 What went ye out..to see? A reed shaken
Rev. 11. 1 there was given me a reed like unto a rod
21. 15 he that talked with me had a golden reed
21. 16 he measured the city with the reed, twe.

REEL (to and fro), to —

1. *To reel to and fro*, חָגַג *chagag*.
Psa. 107. 27 They reel to and fro, and stagger like a

2. *To move, stagger*, נוּעַ *nua*.
Isa. 24. 20 shall reel to and fro like a drunkard, and

RE-E-LA'-IAH, רְעֵלָיָה *Jah causes trembling*.
One of the principal men that returned with Zerubbabel. B.C. 536.
Ezra 2. 2 Nehemiah, Seraiah, R., Mordecai

REFINE, (well) refined, refiner, to —

1. *To be refined*, זָקַק *zaqaq*, 4.
1 Ch. 28. 18 for the altar of incense refined gold by w.
29. 4 seven thousand talents of refined silver
Isa. 25. 6 marrow, of wines on the lees well refined

2. *To refine, try, purify*, צָרַף *tsaraph*.
Isa. 48. 10 I have refined thee, but not with silver; I
Zech. 13. 9 through the fire, and will refine them as

3. *To refine, try, purify*, צָרַף *tsaraph*, 3.
Mal. 3. 2 for he (is) like a refiner's fire, and like fu.
3. 3 shall sit (as) a refiner and purifier of silver

REFINED, to be —

To refine, try, purify, צָרַף *tsaraph*.
Zech. 13. 9 as silver is refined, and will try them as

REFORMATION —

A making thoroughly right, διόρθωσις *diorthōsis*.
Heb. 9. 10 imposed (on them) until the time of refo.

REFORMED, to be —

To be instructed, chastised, יָסַר *yasar*, 2.
Lev. 26. 23 if ye will not be reformed by me by these

REFRAIN, (self, from), to —

1. *To refrain or force self*, אָפַק *aphaq*, 7.
Gen. 43. 31 refrained himself, and said, Set on bread
45. 1 Joseph could not refrain himself before
Esth. 5. 10 Nevertheless Haman refrained himself
Isa. 42. 14 I have been still, (and) refrained myself
64. 12 Wilt thou refrain thyself for these (thi.)

2. *To refrain*, חָטַם *chatam*.
Isa. 48. 9 for my praise will I refrain for thee, that

3. *To darken, keep back*, חָשַׂךְ *chasak*.
Job 7. 11 Therefore I will not refrain my mouth; I
Prov. 10. 19 sin: but he that refraineth his lips (is) w.
Jer. 14. 10 they have not refrained their feet; there.

4. *To shut, restrain*, כָּלָא *kala*.
Psa. 40. 9 I have not refrained my lips, O LORD, t.
119. 101 I have refrained my feet from every evil

5. *To withhold, keep back*, מָנַע *mana*.
Prov. 1. 15 My son..refrain thy foot from their path
Jer. 31. 16 Refrain thy voice from weeping, and thi.

6. *To keep in, restrain, detain*, עָצַר *atsar*.
Job 29. 9 princes refrained talking, and laid (their)

7. *To be or keep far off*, רָחַק *rachaq*.
Eccl. 3. 5 time to embrace, and a time to refrain fr.

8. *To set off from*, ἀφίστημι *aphistēmi*.
Acts 5. 38 Refrain from these men, and let them al.

9. *To cease, refrain*, παύομαι *pauomai*.
1 Pe. 3. 10 let him refrain his tongue from evil, and

REFRESH (self), to —

1. *To be refreshed*, נָפַשׁ *naphash*, 2.
2 Sa. 16. 14 came weary, and refreshed themselves

2. *To support, refresh*, סָעַד *saad*.
1 Ki. 13. 7 Come home with me, and refresh thyself

3. *To cause to turn back*, שׁוּב *shub*, 5.
Prov 25. 13 for he refresheth the soul of his masters

4. *To give rest again*, ἀναπαύω *anapauō*.
1 Co. 16. 18 For they have refreshed my spirit and yo.
2 Co. 7. 13 because his spirit was refreshed by you
Phm. 20 Yea, brother..refresh my bowels in the

5. *To cool or refresh again*, ἀναψύχω *anapsuchō*.
2 Ti. 1. 16 for he oft refreshed me, and was not ash.

6. *To obtain much attention*, τυγχάνω ἐπιμελείας.
Acts 27. 3 liberty to go unto his friends to refresh him

REFRESHED (with), to be —

1. *To be refreshed*, נָפַשׁ *naphash*, 2.
Exod 23. 12 and the stranger may be refreshed
31. 17 seventh day he rested, and was refreshed

2. *To have breath, be refreshed*, רָוַח *ravach*.
1 Sa. 16. 23 so Saul was refreshed, and was well, and
Job 32. 20 I will speak, that I may be refreshed

3. *To give rest again*, ἀναπαύω *anapauō*.
Phm. 7 bowels of the saints are refreshed by thee

4. *To rest again with*, συναναπαύομαι *sunanapauomai*
Rom. 15. 32 [come unto you..and may with you be r.]

REFRESHING —

1. *Refreshing*, מַרְגֵּעָה *margeah*.
Isa. 28. 12 this (is) the refreshing: yet they would

2. *A cooling or refreshing again*, ἀνάψυξις *anapsu*.
Acts 3. 19 when the times of refreshing shall come

REFUGE, (place of) —

1. *A refuge, place of refuge*, מַחְסֶה *machseh*.
Psa. 14. 6 of the poor, because the LORD (is) his re.
46. 1 God (is) our refuge and strength, a very
62. 7 rock of my strength, (and) my refuge, (is)
62. 8 pour out your heart..God (is) a refuge for
71. 7 unto many: but thou (art) my strong ref.
91. 2 my refuge and my fortress: my God; in
91. 9 thou hast made the LORD (which is) my r.
94. 22 and my God (is) the rock of my refuge
104. 18 high hills (are) a refuge for the wild goats
142. 5 Thou (art) my refuge (and) my portion in
Prov 14. 26 and his children shall have a place of re.
Isa. 4. 6 for a place of refuge, and for a covert from
25. 4 refuge from the storm, a shadow from the
28. 15 for we have made lies our refuge, and un.
28. 17 the hail shall sweep away the refuge of

2. *Flight, place of flight*, מָנוֹס *manos*.
2 Sa. 22. 3 my refuge, my saviour; thou savest me fr.
Psa. 59. 16 for thou hast been my defence and refuge
142. 4 refuge failed me; no man cared for my so.
Jer. 16. 19 refuge in the day of affliction, the Gentiles

3. *Habitation, den*, מְעוֹנָה *meonah*.
Deut 33. 27 eternal God (is thy) refuge, and underne.

4. *Asylum, refuge, restricted place*, מִקְלָט *miqlat*.
Num 35. 6 six cities for refuge, which ye shall appo.
35. 11 appoint you cities to be cities of refuge
Num 35. 12 they shall be unto you cities for refuge
35. 13 shall give, six cities shall ye have for ref.
35. 14 of Canaan, (which) shall be cities of refuge
35. 15 These six cities shall be a refuge, (both)
35. 25 shall restore him to the city of his refuge
35. 26, 27 the border of the city of his refuge
35. 28 have remained in the city of his refuge
35. 32 him that is fled to the city of his refuge
Josh 20. 2 Appoint out for you cities of refuge, wh.
20. 3 shall be your refuge from the avenger of
21. 13, 21, 27, 32, 38 a city of refuge for the sla.
1 Ch. 6. 57 Hebron, (the city) of refuge, and Libnah
6. 67 they gave unto them, (of) the cities of re.

5. *High place, tower*, מִשְׂגָּב *misgab*.
Psa. 9. 9 will be a refuge for the oppressed, a ref.
46. 7, 11 the God of Jacob (is) our refuge. Se.
48. 3 God is known in her palaces for a refuge

REFUGE, to make —

To take refuge, חָסָה *chasah*.
Psa. 57. 1 shadow of thy wings will I make my ref.

REFUSE, (to) —

1. *To refuse*, מָאֵן *maan*, 3.
Gen. 37. 35 he refused to be comforted: and he said
39. 8 he refused, and said unto his master's w.
48. 19 his father refused and said, I know (it)
Exod. 4. 23 if thou refuse to let him go, behold, I w.
7. 14 Pharaoh's heart (is) hardened, he refuseth
10. 3 How long wilt thou refuse to humble th.
16. 28 How long refuse ye to keep my comman.
22. 17 If her father utterly refuse to give her u.
Num 20. 21 Thus Edom refused to give Israel passage
22. 13 LORD refuseth to give me leave to go with
22. 14 said, Balaam refuseth to come with us
Deut 25. 7 My husband's brother refuseth to raise up
1 Sa. 8. 19 the people refused to obey the voice of S.
28. 23 But, he refused, and said, I will not eat
2 Sa. 2. 23 he refused to turn aside: wherefore Ab.
13. 9 he refused to eat. And Amnon said, Have
1 Ki. 20. 35 And the man refused to smite him
21. 15 which he refused to give thee for money
2 Ki. 5. 16 he urged him to take (it); but he refused
Neh. 9. 17 refused to obey, neither were mindful of
Esth. 1. 12 Vashti refused to come at the king's com.
Job 6. 7 The things (that) my soul refused to tou.
Psa. 77. 2 sore ran..my soul refused to be comforted
78. 10 kept not..and refused to walk in his law
Prov. 1. 24 I have called, and ye refused; I have
21. 7 destroy..because they refuse to do judg.
21. 25 killeth him; for his hands refuse to lab.
Isa. 1. 20 if ye refuse and rebel, ye shall be devou.
Jer. 3. 3 thou hadst a whore's forehead, thou ref.
5. 3 they have refused..have refused to retu.
8. 5 they hold fast deceit, they refuse to ret.
9. 6 they refuse to know me, saith the LORD
11. 10 forefathers, which refused to hear my w.
15. 18 incurable, (which) refuseth to be healed
25. 28 if they refuse to take the cup at thine h.
31. 15 refused to be comforted for her children
50. 33 held them fast; they refused to let them
Hos. 11. 5 shall be his king, because they refused to
Zech. 7. 11 they refused to hearken, and pulled away

2. *Refusing*, מָאֵן *maen*.
Exod. 8. 2 if thou refuse to let (them) go, behold, I
9. 2 if thou refuse to let (them) go, and wilt
10. 4 Else, if thou refuse to let my people go
Jer. 38. 21 if thou refuse to go forth, this (is) the w.

3. *Refusing*, מֵאֲנִים *meanim*.
Jer. 13. 10 This evil people which refuse to hear my

4. *To loathe, despise, reject*, מָאַס *maas*.
1 Sa. 16. 7 Look not..because..I have refused him
Job 34. 33 whether thou refuse, or whether thou ch.
Psa. 78. 67 he refused the tabernacle of Joseph, and
118. 22 The stone..the builders refused is become
Isa. 7. 15, 16 know to refuse the evil, and choose
8. 6 as this people refuseth the waters of Shi.
Eze. 5. 6 they have refused my judgments and my

5. *To forsake*, עָזַב *azab*.
Prov. 10. 17 but he that refuseth reproof erreth

6. *To make free, void, refuse*, פָּרַע *para*.
Prov. 8. 33 Hear instruction..be wise..refuse it not
13. 18 shame (shall be) to him that refuseth ins.
15. 32 He that refuseth instruction despiseth his

7. *To deny, disown*, ἀρνέομαι *arneomai*.
Acts 7. 35 This Moses whom they refused, saying, W,
Heb. 11. 24 refused to be called the son of Pharaoh's

8. *To ask off, deprecate*, παραιτέομαι *paraiteomai*.
Acts 25. 11 I refuse not to die: but if there be none
1 Ti. 4. 7 refuse profane and old wives' fables, and
5. 11 the younger widows refuse: for when they
Heb. 12. 25 See that ye refuse not him that speaketh
12. 25 who refused him that spake on earth, much

REFUSE —

1. *To loathe, despise, reject*, מָאַס *maas*.
Lam. 3. 45 Thou hast made us..refuse in the midst

2. *To be melted, wasted*, מָסַס *masas*, 2.
1 Sa. 15. 9 vile and refuse, that they destroyed utte.

3. *Refuse, flakes*, מַפָּל *mappal*.
Amos 8. 6 may buy..and sell the refuse of the wh.

REFUSED, to be —

1. *To be loathed, despised, rejected*, מָאַס *maas*, 2.
Isa. 54. 6 a wife of youth, when thou wast refused

2. *What is to be cast away*, ἀπόβλητος *apoblētos*.
1 Ti. 4. 4 nothing to be refused, if it be received

REGARD of, in —

On account of the matter of, עַל־דִּבְרַת *al dibrath.*

Eccl. 8. 2 and (that) in regard of the oath of God

REGARD, to (have) —

1. *To understand, consider, attend,* בִּין *bin.*

Psa. 28. 5 Because they regard not the works of the
94. 7 neither shall the God of Jacob regard (it)
Prov 29. 7 (but) the wicked regardeth not to know
Dan. 11. 37 Neither shall he regard the God..nor re.

2. *To understand, consider, attend,* בִּין *bin, 7a.*

Job 30. 20 I stand up, and thou regardest me (not)

3. *To seek, inquire, require,* דָּרַשׁ *darash.*

Job 3. 4 let not God regard it from above, neither

4. *To let the eye spare,* חוּס עַיִן *[ayin].*

Gen. 45. 20 Also regard not your stuff; for the good

5. *To think, reckon, esteem,* חָשַׁב *chashab.*

Isa. 13. 17 which shall not regard silver; and (as for)
33. 8 he hath despised the cities, he regardeth

6. *To know,* יָדַע *yada.*

Prov 12. 10 righteous (man) regardeth the life of his

7. *To set the taste or desire,* שׂוּם טְעֵם *sum teem.*

Dan. 3. 12 these men, O king, have not regarded thee
6. 13 regardeth not thee, O king, nor the dec.

8. *To (cause to) behold,* נָבַט *nabat, 5.*

Isa. 5. 12 but they regard not the work of the LORD
Lam. 4. 16 he will no more regard them: they respe.
Amos 5. 22 neither will I regard the peace offerings
Hab. 1. 5 regard, and wonder marvellously: for (I)

9. *To discern,* נָכַר *nakar, 3.*

Job 34. 19 nor regardeth the rich more than the poor?

10. *To lift up,* נָשָׂא *nasa.*

Deut 10. 17 which regardeth not persons, nor taketh
28. 50 which shall not regard the person of the
2 Ki. 3. 14 were it not that I regard the presence of
Mal. 1. 9 will he regard your persons? saith the L.

11. *To face, front, look,* פָּנָה *panah.*

Lev. 19. 31 Regard not them that have familiar spir.
Job 36. 21 Take heed, regard not iniquity: for this
Psa. 102. 17 He will regard the prayer of the destitute
Mal. 2. 13 insomuch that he regardeth not the offe.

12. *To lift up the face,* נָשָׂא פָּנִים *nasa phanim.*

Prov. 6. 35 He will not regard any ransom; neither

13. *To give attention,* קָשַׁב *qashab, 5.*

Prov. 1. 24 stretched out my hand, and no man reg.

14. *Attention,* קֶשֶׁב *qesheb.*

1 Ki. 18. 29 nor any to answer, nor any that regarded

15. *To see,* רָאָה *raah.*

1 Ch. 17. 17 hast regarded me according to the estate
Psa 66. 18 If I regard iniquity in my heart, the LORD
106. 44 Nevertheless he regarded their affliction
Eccl. 11. 4 he that regardeth the clouds shall not r.

16. *To set, put, place,* שׂוּם *sum, 5.*

Job 4. 20 they perish for ever without any regarding

17. *To set the heart,* לֵב (שִׁית or) שׂוּם *sum (or shith) leb.*

Exod. 9. 21 he that regarded not the word of the Lo.
1 Sa. 4. 20 she answered not, neither did she regard
25. 25 I pray thee, regard this man of Belial, (e.)
2 Sa. 13. 20 he (is) thy brother; regard not this thing

18. *To behold, look,* שׁוּר *shur.*

Job 35. 13 vanity, neither will the Almighty regard

19. *To hear, hearken,* שָׁמַע *shamea.*

Job 39. 7 neither regardeth he the crying of the d.

20. *To observe, watch, take heed, keep,* שָׁמַר *shamar.*

Psa. 31. 6 I have hated them that regard lying van.
Prov. 5. 2 That thou mayest regard discretion, and
13. 18 that regardeth reproof shall be honoured
15. 5 but he that regardeth reproof is prudent
Eccl. 5. 8 higher than the highest regardeth; and

21. *To look, glance at,* שָׁעָה *shaah.*

Exod. 5. 9 labour therein; and let them not regard

22. *To see, perceive, understand,* βλέπω *blepō.*

Matt22. 16 for thou regardest not the person of men
Mark12. 14 for thou regardest not the person of men

23. *To turn self in or away,* ἐντρέπομαι *entrepomai.*

Luke18. 2 which feared not God, neither regarded
18. 4 Though I fear not God, nor regard man

24. *To look upon,* ἐπιβλέπω *epiblepō.*

Luke 1. 48 For he hath regarded the low estate of

25. *To hold toward,* προσέχω *prosechō.*

Acts 8. 11 to him they had regard, because that of

26. *To think, set the mind,* φρονέω *phroneō.*

Rom 14. 6 He that regardeth the day, regardeth (it)
14. 6 [he that regardeth not..doth not regard]

REGARD, not to —

1. *To be careless,* ἀμελέω *ameleō.*

Heb. 8. 9 and I regarded them not, saith the Lord

2. *To consult amiss,* παραβουλεύομαι *parabouleuomai.*

Phil. 2. 30 [not regarding] his life, to supply your l.

RE'-GEM, רֶגֶם *friendship, association.*

A son of Jahdai, of the family of Caleb son of Jephunneth. B.C. 1470.

1 Ch. 2. 47 And the sons of Jahdai: R.. and Jotham

RE-GEM ME'-LECH, רֶגֶם מֶלֶךְ.

One whom the people sent into the temple to pray and to consult the priests and prophets regarding a day of humiliation in memory of the destruction of the temple. B.C. 518.

Zech. 7. 2 they had sent..Sherezer and R., and

REGENERATION —

A re-creation, regeneration, παλιγγενεσία *paliggenesia.*

Matt19. 28 in the regeneration, when the Son of man
Titus 3. 5 by the washing of regeneration, and ren.

REGION that lieth (round about) —

1. *A cord, line, coast,* חֶבֶל, חֶבֶל *chebel.*

Deut. 3. 4 all the region of Argob, the kingdom of
3. 13 all the region of Argob, with all Bashan
1 Ki. 4. 13 the region of Argob, which (is) in Bashan

2. *An elevated place,* נָפָה *naphah.*

1 Ki. 4. 11 in all the region of Dor; which had Tap.

3. *A climate, region, district,* κλίμα *klima.*

2 Co. 11. 10 of this boasting in the regions of Achaia
Gal. 1. 21 I came into the regions of Syria and Cil.

4. *The place all around,* περίχωρος *perichōros.*

Matt. 3. 5 Then went out..all the region round ab.
Mark 1. 28 throughout all the region round about G.
6. 55 ran through that whole region [round a.]
Luke 4. 14 fame..through all the region round about
7. 17 and throughout all the region round about
Acts 14. 6 and unto the region that lieth round about

5. *A place, region, field,* χώρα *chōra.*

Matt. 4. 16 to them which sat in the region and sha.
Luke 3. 1 of the region of Trachonitis, and Lysanias
Acts 8. 1 throughout the regions of Judea and Sa.
13. 49 was published throughout all the region
16. 6 throughout Phrygia and the region of Ga.

REGISTER —

1. *A writing,* כְּתָב *kethab.*

Ezra 2. 62 These sought their register (among) those
Neh. 7. 64 These sought their register (among) those

2. *A book, letter, account,* סֵפֶר *sepher.*

Neh. 7. 5 I found a register of the genealogy of them

RE-HAB'-IAH, רְחַבְיָה, רְחַבְיָהוּ *Jah is a widener.*

Eldest son of Eliezer son of Moses. B.C. 1390.

1 Ch. 23. 17 And the sons of Eliezer (were) R. the ch.
23. 17 but the sons of R. were very many
24. 21 concerning R.: of the sons of R.
26. 25 And his brethren by Eliezer; R. his son

REHEARSE, to —

1. *To speak,* דָּבַר *dabar, 3.*

1 Sa. 8. 21 he rehearsed them in the ears of the LORD

2. *To bring forward, tell, declare,* נָגַד *nagad, 5.*

1 Sa. 17. 31 they rehearsed (them) before Saul; and

3. *To sit, place, put,* שׂוּם *sum.*

Exod 17. 14 Write..and rehearse..in the ears of Jos.

4. *To give, give forth,* תָּנָה *tanah, 3.*

Judg. 5. 11 rehearse the righteous acts of the LORD

5. *To tell back or again,* ἀναγγέλλω *anaggellō.*

Acts 14. 27 rehearsed all that God had done with them

REHEARSE from the beginning, to —

To begin, commence, ἄρχομαι *archomai.*

Acts 11. 4 Peter rehearsed..from the beginning, and

RE'-HOB, רְחֹב *width.*

1. A Levitical city in Asher, near the source of the Jordan, the farthest place northward to which the spies went; now called *Hunin.*

Num 13. 21 went up, and searched the land..unto R.
Josh. 19. 28 And Hebron, and R., and Hammon, and
19. 30 Ummah also, and Aphek, and R.: twenty
21. 31 Helkath with her suburbs, and R. with
Judg. 1. 31 Neither did Asher drive out the inh...of R.
2 Sa. 10. 8 and the Syrians..of R...(were) by thems.
1 Ch. 6. 75 Hukok with her suburbs, and R. with her

2. Father of Hadadezer, king of Zobah in the days of David. B.C. 1040.

2 Sa. 8. 3 David smote also Hadadezer..son of R.
8. 12 and of the spoil of Hadadezer, son of R.

3. A Levite that with Nehemiah sealed the covenant. B.C. 445.

Neh. 10. 11 Micha, R., Hashabiah

RE-HO-BO'-AM, רְחַבְעָם *freer of the people.*

Son and successor of Solomon, from whom the ten tribes revolted. B.C. 975.

1 Ki. 11. 43 and R. his son reigned in his stead
12. 1 And R. went to Shechem: for all Israel
12. 3 And Jeroboam..came, and spake unto R.
12. 6 And king R. consulted with the old men
12. 12 Jeroboam..came to R. the third day, as
12. 17 the cities of Judah, R. reigned over them
12. 18 Then king R. sent Adoram, who (was) over
12. 18 R. made speed to get him up to his cha.
12. 21 And when R. was come to Jerusalem, he
12. 21 to bring the kingdom again to R. the son
12. 23 Speak unto R., the son of Solomon, king
12. 27 the heart of this people turn..unto R.
12. 27 they shall kill me, and go again to R. king
14. 21 R. the son of Solomon reigned in Judah
14. 21 R.(was) forty and one years old when he
14. 25 it came to pass, in..fifth year of king R.
14. 27 king R. made in their stead brasen shie.
14. 29 Now the rest of the acts of R...(are)..w.
1 Ki. 14. 30 And there was war between R. and Jero.
14. 31 And R. slept with his fathers, and was
15. 6 And there was war between R. and Jero.
1 Ch. 3. 10 And Solomon's son (was) R., Abia his son
2 Ch. 9. 31 and R. his son reigned in his stead
10. 1 And R. went to Shechem: for to Shechem
10. 3 Jeroboam and all Israel..spake to R., say.
10. 6 king R. took counsel with the old men
10. 12 all the people came to R. on the third day
10. 13 and king R. forsook the counsel of the old
10. 17 the cities of J., R. reigned over them
10. 18 R. sent Hadoram that (was) over the trib.
10. 18 R. made speed to get him up to (his) cha.
11. 1 And when R. was come to Jerusalem, he
11. 1 he might bring the kingdom again to R.
11. 3 Speak unto R. the son of Solomon, king
11. 5 And R. dwelt in Jerusalem, and built cities
11. 17 So they..made R. the son of Solomon st.
11. 18 And R. took him Mahalath the daughter
11. 21 And R. loved Maachah the daughter of A.
11. 22 R. made Abijah the son of Maachah the
12. 1 when R. had established the kingdom..he
12. 2 came to pass..in the fifth year of king R.
12. 5 Then came Shemaiah the prophet to R.
12. 10 Instead of which king R. made shields of
12. 13 So king R. strengthened himself in Jeru.
12. 13 R. (was) one and forty years old when he
12. 15 Now the acts of R...(are)..written in the
12. 15 (there were) wars between R. and Jerob.
12. 16 And R. slept with his fathers, and was b.
13. 7 against R. the son of Solomon, when R. was
Matt. 1. 7 And Solomon begat R.; and R. begat A.

RE-HO'-BOTH, רְחֹבֹת, רְחֹבוֹת *enlargement.*

1. A city in Assyria, built in Nimrod, near Nineveh and Calab, on the Euphrates.

Gen. 10. 11 Asshur..builded Nineveh..the city R.
36. 37 and Saul of R...reigned in his stead
1 Ch. 1. 48 Shaul of R. by the river reigned in his st.

2. A well which Isaac digged, perhaps *Ruchaibah* three miles S. of *Elusa.*

Gen. 26. 22 and he called the name of it R.; and he

RE'-HUM, רְחוּם *pity.*

1. A chief man that returned with Zerubbabel. B.C. 536.

Ezra 2. 2 Bilshan, Mispar, Bigvai, R., Baanah
Neh. 12. 3 Shechaniah, R., Meremoth

2. A chancellor of Artaxerxes. B.C. 522.

Ezra 4. 8 R. the chancellor..wrote a letter against
4. 9 Then (wrote) R. the chancellor, and Shi.
4. 17 (Then) sent the king an answer unto R.
4. 23 Artaxerxes' letter (was) read before R., and

3. A Levite that helped to repair the wall. B.C. 445.

Neh. 3. 17 after him repaired the Levites, R. the son

4. A person that with Nehemiah sealed the covenant. B.C. 445.

Neh. 10. 25 R., Hashabnah, Maaseiah

RE'-I, רֵעִי *Jah is a friend.*

A friend of David when Adonijah attempted to become king. B.C. 1015.

1 Ki. 1. 8 But Zadok..and R...were not with Adon.

REIGN —

1. *To reign, be a king,* מָלַךְ *malak.*

1 Ki. 6. 1 in the fourth year of Solomon's reign over
2 Ki. 24. 12 took him in the eighth year of his reign
25. 1 in the ninth year of his reign, in the tenth
1 Ch. 4. 31 These (were) their cities unto the reign
2 Ch. 16. 13 in the one and fortieth year of his reign
17. 7 in the third year of his reign he sent to
29. 3 He, in the first year of his reign, in the fi.
34. 3 in the eighth year of his reign, while he
34. 8 in the eighteenth year of his reign, when
36. 20 servants..until the reign of the kingdom
Esth. 1. 3 In the third year of his reign, he made a
Jer. 1. 2 came..in the thirteenth year of his reign
51. 59 he went..in the fourth year of his reign
52. 4 in the ninth year of his reign, in the tenth
Dan. 9. 2 In the first year of his reign, I Daniel un.

2. *Kingdom,* מַלְכוּ *maleku.*

Ezra 4. 24 ceased unto the second year of the reign
6. 15 sixth year of the reign of Darius the king
Dan. 6. 28 in the reign of Darius, and in the reign of

3. *Kingdom,* מַלְכוּת *malekuth.*

1 Ch. 26. 31 In the fortieth year of the reign of David
29. 30 With all his reign and his might, and the
2 Ch. 3. 2 second month, in the fourth year of his r.
15. 10 in the fifteenth year of the reign of Asa
15. 19 five and thirtieth year of the reign of Asa
16. 1 In the six and thirtieth year of the reign
16. 12 in the thirty and ninth year of his reign
29. 19 Ahaz in his reign did cast away in his tran.
35. 19 In the eighteenth year of the reign of J.
Ezra 4. 5 until the reign of Darius king of Persia
4. 6 And in the reign of Ahasuerus, in the be.
4. 6 beginning of his reign, wrote they (unto
7. 1 in the reign of Artaxerxes king of Persia
8. 1 chief..in the reign of Artaxerxes the king
Neh. 12. 22 priests, to the reign of Darius the Persian
Esth. 2. 16 was taken..in the seventh year of his re.
Jer. 49. 34 in the beginning of the reign of Zedekiah
52. 31 in the (first) year of his reign lifted up the
Dan. 1. 1 In the third year of the reign of Jehoiakim
2. 1 in the second year of the reign of Nebuc.
8. 1 In the third year of the reign of king Be.

4. *Kingdom, reign,* מַמְלָכָה *mamlakah.*

Jer. 27. 1 In the beginning of the reign of Jehoiakim
28. 1 in the beginning of the reign of Zedekiah

5. *Kingdom,* מַמְלְכוּת *mamlakuth.*
Jer. 26. 1 In the beginning of the reign of Jehoiakim

6. *Leadership,* ἡγεμονία *hēgemonia.*
Luke 3. 1 in the fifteenth year of the reign of Tibe.

REIGN (over, with), to —

1. *To reign, be a king,* מָלַךְ *malak.*
Gen. 36. 31 the kings that reigned in the land of Ed.
36. 31 before there reigned any king over the c.
36. 32 And Bela the son of Beor reigned in Edom
36. 33 Jobab the son of Zerah of Bozrah reigned
36. 34 Husham of the land of Temani reigned in
36. 35 Husham died, and Hadad..reigned in his
36. 36 Samlah of Masrekah reigned in his stead
36. 37 Saul of Rehoboth (by) the river reigned
36. 38 Baal-hanan the son of Achbor reigned in
36. 39 Hadar reigned in his stead: and the name
37. 8 Shalt thou indeed reign over us? or shalt
Exod15. 18 The LORD shall reign for ever and ever
Josh.13. 10, 21 king of the Amorites, which reigned
13. 12 which reigned in Ashtaroth and in Edrei
Judg. 4. 2 Jabin king of Canaan, that reigned in Ha.
9. 8 said unto the olive tree, Reign thou over
9. 10, 12, 14 said..Come thou, (and) reign over
1 Sa. 8. 7 rejected me, that I should not reign over
8. 9 manner of the king that shall reign over
8. 11 the manner of the king that shall reign
11. 12 Who (is) he that said, Shall Saul reign ov.
12. 12 said..Nay; but a king shall reign over us
12. 14 and also the king that reigneth over you
13. 1 Saul reigned one year..when he had rei.
16. 1 have rejected him from reigning over Is.
2 Sa 2. 10 Ish-bosheth, Saul's son..reigned two ye.
3. 21 that thou mayest reign over all that thine
5. 4 thirty years old..(and) he reigned forty y.
5. 5 In Hebron he reigned over Judah seven
5. 5 he reigned thirty and three years over all
8. 15 David reigned over all Israel; and David
10. 1 and..his son reigned in his stead
[So in 1 Ki. 11. 43; 14. 20, 31; 15. 8, 24; 16. 6, 28; 22. 40, 50; 2 Ki. 8. 15, 24; 10. 35; 12. 21; 13. 9, 24; 14. 16, 29; 15. 7, 22, 38; 16. 20; 19. 37; 20. 21; 21. 18, 26; 24. 6; 1 Ch. 19. 1; 29. 28; 2 Ch. 9. 31; 12. 16; 14. 1; 17. 1; 21. 1; 24. 27; 26. 23; 27. 9; 28. 27; 32. 33; 33. 20; 36. 8.]
2 Sa. 15. 10 ye shall say, Absalom reigneth in Hebron
16. 8 Saul, in whose stead thou hast reigned
1 Ki. 1. 11 the son of Haggith doth reign, and David
1. 13, 17, 30 thy son shall reign after me, and
1. 13 saying..why then doth Adonijah reign?
1. 18 Adonijah reigneth; and now, my lord the
1. 24 Adonijah shall reign after me, and he sh.
2. 11 And the days that David reigned over Is.
2. 11 seven years reigned he in Hebron, and th.
2. 11 and three years reigned he in Jerusalem
2. 15 set their faces on me, that I should reign
6. 1 in the fourth year of Solomon's reign over
11. 24 dwelt therein, and reigned in Damascus
11. 25 he abhorred Israel, and reigned over Sy.
11. 37 thou shalt reign according to all that
11. 42 reigned in Jerusalem over all Israel
12. 17 the cities of Judah, Rehoboam reigned over
14. 19 how he warred, and how he reigned, beh.
14. 20 the days which Jeroboam reigned (were)
14. 21 Rehoboam the son of Solomon reigned in
14. 21 he reigned seventeen years in Jerusalem
15. 1 the eighteenth year..reigned Abijam over
15. 2 Three years reigned he in Jerusalem, and
15. 9 twentieth year of Jeroboam..re. Asa over
15. 10 forty and one years reigned he in Jerusa.
15. 25 And Nadab..reigned over Israel two ye.
15. 28 did Baasha slay him, and reigned in his
15. 29 when he reigned, (that) he smote all the
16. 10 and killed him..and reigned in his stead
16. 15 did Zimri reign seven days in Tirzah. And
16. 22 prevailed..so Tibni died, and Omri reig.
16. 23 began Omri..six years reigned he in Tir.
16. 29 Ahab the son of Omri reigned over Israel
22. 42 he reigned twenty and five years in Jeru.
22. 51 Ahaziah..reigned two years over Israel
2 Ki 1. 17 Jehoram reigned in his stead, in the sec.
3. 1 Jehoram the son of Ahab..reigned twelve
3. 27 son, that should have reigned in his stead
8. 17 and he reigned eight years in Jerusalem
10. 36 the time that Jehu reigned over Israel in
11. 3 And Athaliah did reign over the land
12. 1 forty years reigned he in Jerusalem. And
14. 1 reigned Amaziah the son of Joash king of
14. 2 reigned twenty and nine years in Jerusa.
15. 2 he reigned two and fifty years in Jerusa.
15. 8 did..reign over Israel in Samaria six mo.
15. 10, 14, 30 slew him, and reigned in his stead
15. 13 and he reigned a full month in Samaria
15. 25 and he killed him, and reigned in his room
15. 33 and he reigned sixteen years in Jerusalem
16. 2 and reigned sixteen years in Jerusalem
18. 2 he reigned twenty and nine years in Jer.
21. 1 reigned fifty and five years in Jerusalem
21. 19 and he reigned two years in Jerusalem
22. 1 reigned thirty and one years in Jerusalem
23. 31 and he reigned three months in Jerusalem
23. 33 put him..that he might not reign in Jer.
23. 36 and he reigned eleven years in Jerusalem
24. 8 he reigned in Jerusalem three months
24. 18 and he reigned eleven years in Jerusalem
1 Ch. 1. 43 these (are) the kings that reigned in the
1. 43 before (any) king reigned over the children
1. 44 Jobab the son of Zerah of Bozrah reigned
1. 45 Husham of the land of the Temanites re.
1. 46 Hadad the son of Bedad..reigned in his
1. 47 Samlah of Masrekah reigned in his stead
1. 48 Shaul of Rehoboth by the river reigned in
1 Ch. 1. 49 And..the son of Achbor reigned in his st.
1. 50 Hadad reigned in his stead: and the name
3. 4 there he reigned seven years and six mo.
3. 4 in Jerusalem he reigned thirty and three
16. 31 say among the nations, The LORD reigneth
18. 14 So David reigned over all Israel, and ex.
29. 26 Thus David the son of Jesse reigned over
29. 27 And the time that he reigned over Israel
29. 27 seven years reigned he in Hebron, and
29. 27 thirty and three (years) reigned he in Je.
2 Ch. 1. 13 Solomon came..and reigned over Israel
9. 30 And Solomon reigned in Jerusalem over
10. 17 cities of Judah, Rehoboam reigned over
12. 13 Rehoboam strengthened himself..and r.
12. 13 he reigned seventeen years in Jerusalem
13. 2 He reigned three years in Jerusalem. His
20. 31 And Jehoshaphat reigned over Judah, (He
20. 31 he reigned twenty and five years in Jer.
21. 5 and he reigned eight years in Jerusalem
21. 20 he reigned in Jerusalem eight years, and
22. 1 the son of Jehoram king of Judah reigned
22. 2 and he reigned one year in Jerusalem
22. 12 and Athaliah reigned over the land
23. 3 the king's son shall reign, as the LORD h.
24. 1 and he reigned forty years in Jerusalem
25. 1 he reigned twenty and nine years in Jer.
26. 3 he reigned fifty and two years in Jerusa.
27. 1 and he reigned sixteen years in Jerusalem
27. 8 and reigned sixteen years in Jerusalem
28. 1 and he reigned sixteen years in Jerusalem
29. 1 he reigned nine and twenty years in Jer.
33. 1 reigned fifty and five years in Jerusalem
33. 21 Amon..reigned two years in Jerusalem
34. 1 reigned in Jerusalem one and thirty years
36. 2 and he reigned three months in Jerusalem
36. 5 and he reigned eleven years in Jerusalem
36. 9 reigned three months and ten days in Je.
36. 11 and reigned eleven years in Jerusalem
Esth. 1. 1 Ahasuerus which reigned from India even
Job 34. 30 That the hypocrite reign not, lest the pe.
Psa. 47. 8 God reigneth over the heathen: God sit.
93. 1 The LORD reigneth; he is clothed with
96. 10 Say among the heathen..the LORD reign.
97. 1 The LORD reigneth; let the earth rejoice
99. 1 The LORD reigneth; let the people trem.
146. 10 The LORD shall reign for ever..thy God
Prov. 8. 15 By me kings reign, and princes decree j.
30. 22 For a servant when he reigneth; and a
Eccl. 4. 14 For out of prison he cometh to reign, whe.
Isa. 24. 23 when the LORD of hosts shall reign in m.
32. 1 a king shall reign in righteousness, and
37. 38 and Esar-haddon his son reigned in his
52. 7 that saith unto Zion, Thy God reigneth
Jer. 22. 11 which reigned instead of Josiah his fath.
22. 15 Shalt thou reign, because thou closest (t.)
23. 5 a King shall reign and prosper, and shall
33. 21 that he should not have a son to reign u.
37. 1 Zedekiah the son of Josiah reigned inste.
52. 1 and he reigned eleven years in Jerusalem
Mic. 4. 7 LORD shall reign over them in mount Zion

2. *To rule,* מָשַׁל *mashal.*
Deut15. 6 thou shalt reign over..they shall not rei.
Josh.12. 5 reigned in mount Hermon, and in Salcah
Judg. 9. 2 that all..reign over you, or that one rei.
1 Ki. 4. 21 Solomon reigned over all kingdoms from
1 Ch.29. 12 thou reignest over all; and in thine hand
2 Ch. 9. 26 he reigned over all the kings from the ri.

3. *To rule,* רָדָה *radah.*
Lev. 26. 17 they that hate you shall reign over you

4. *To restrain,* עָצַר *atsar.*
1 Sa. 9. 17 Behold..this same shall reign over my p.

5. *To be a prince,* שׂוּר *sur.*
Judg. 9. 22 When Abimelech had reigned three years

6. *To be first or chief,* ἄρχω *archō.*
Rom.15. 12 he that shall rise to reign over the Gent.

7. *To reign, be a king,* βασιλεύω *basileuō.*
Matt. 2. 22 when he heard that Archelaus did reign
Luke 1. 33 he shall reign over the house of Jacob for
19. 14 We will not have this..to reign over us
19. 27 which would not that I should reign over
Rom. 5. 14 death reigned from Adam to Moses, even
5. 17 if by one man's offence death reigned by
5. 17 they..shall reign in life by one, Jesus C.
5. 21 That as sin hath reigned unto death, even
5. 21 so might grace reign through righteous.
6. 12 Let not sin therefore reign in your mortal
1 Co. 4. 8 ye have reigned as kings without us: and
4. 8 I would to God ye did reign, that we also
15. 25 he must reign, till he hath put all enemies
Rev. 5. 10 kings and priests: and we shall reign on
11. 15 saying..and he shall reign for ever and e.
11. 17 taken..thy great power, and hast reigned
19. 6 for the Lord God omnipotent reigneth
20. 4 and reigned with Christ a thousand years
20. 6 and shall reign with him a thousand years
22. 5 and they shall reign for ever and ever

8. *To have a kingdom,* ἔχω βασιλείαν *echō basileian.*
Rev. 17. 18 which reigneth over the kings of the earth

9. *To reign or be a king with,* συμβασιλεύω *sumba.*
1 Co. 4. 8 I would..that we also might reign with
2 Ti. 2. 12 If we suffer, we shall also reign with (him)

REIGN, to begin to, make to —

1. *To be a king, reign,* מָלַךְ *malak.*
2 Sa. 2. 10 when he began to reign.
[So in 5. 4; 1 Ki. 14. 21; 16. 11; 22. 42; 2 Ki. 8. 17, 26; 11. 21; 14. 2; 15. 2, 33; 16. 2; 18. 2; 21. 1, 19; 22. 1; 23. 31, 36; 24. 8, 18; 25. 27; 2 Ch. 12. 13; 20. 31; 21. 5, 20; 22. 2; 24. 1; 26. 3; 27. 1, 8; 28. 1; 33. 1, 21; 34. 1; 36. 2, 5, 9, 11; Jer. 52. 1.]
1 Ki.15. 25 Nadab the son of Jeroboam began to reign
22. 41 Jehoshaphat the son of Asa began to reign
22. 51 the son of Ahab began to reign over Israel
2 Ki. 3. 1 the son of Ahab began to reign over Israel
8. 16 J. the son of Jehoshaphat..began to reign
8. 25 did..the son of Jehoram..begin to reign
9. 29 the eleventh year..began Ahaziah to reign
12. 1 Jehoash began to reign: and forty years
13. 1 Jehoahaz the son of Jehu began to reign
13. 10 began Jehoash the son of Jehoahaz to re.
14. 23 Jeroboam..began to reign in Samaria, (a.)
15. 1 began Azariah son of Amaziah..to reign
15. 13 Shallum the son of Jabesh began to reign
15. 17 began Menahem the son of Gadi to reign
15. 23 Pekahiah the son of Menahem began to r.
15. 27 Pekah the son of Remaliah began to reign
15. 32 began Jotham the son of Uzziah..to reign
16. 1 son of Jotham king of Judah began to re.
17. 1 began Hoshea the son of Elah to reign in
18. 1 son of Ahaz king of Judah began to reign
2 Ch.25. 1 twenty and five..(when) he began to reign
29. 1 Hezekiah began to reign (when he was)

2. *To cause to reign, make a king,* מָלַךְ *malak,* 5.
2 Ch. 1. 8 and hast made me to reign in his stead

REINS —

1. *Loins,* חֲלָצַיִם *chalatsayim.*
Isa. 11. 5 and faithfulness the girdle of his reins

2. *Kidneys, reins,* כְּלָיוֹת *kelayoth.*
Job 16. 13 he cleaveth my reins asunder, and doth
19. 27 (though) my reins be consumed within me
Psa. 7. 9 righteous God trieth the hearts and reins
16. 7 my reins also instruct me in the night se.
26. 2 Examine me..try my reins and my heart
73. 21 was grieved, and I was pricked in my re.
139. 13 For thou hast possessed my reins: thou
Prov23. 16 my reins shall rejoice when thy lips speak
Jer. 11. 20 that triest the reins and the heart, let me
12. 2 in their mouth, and far from their reins
17. 10 (I) try the reins, even to give every man
20. 12 seest the reins and the heart, let me see
Lam. 3. 13 caused the arrows..to enter into my reins

3. *Reins, kidneys,* νεφρός *nephros.*
Rev. 2. 23 he which searcheth the reins and hearts

REJECT, to —

1. *To loathe, despise, reject,* מָאַס *maas.*
1 Sa. 8. 7 not rejected thee, but they have rejected
10. 19 ye have this day rejected your God, who
15. 23, 26 thou hast rejected the word of the L.
15. 23 he hath also rejected thee from (being) k.
15. 26 LORD hath rejected thee from being king
16. 1 seeing I have rejected him from reigning
2 Ki. 17. 15 they rejected his statutes, and his cove.
17. 20 LORD rejected all the seed of Israel, and
Jer. 2. 37 LORD hath rejected thy confidences, and
6. 19 not hearkened..to my law, but rejected
6. 30 because the LORD hath rejected them
7. 29 LORD hath rejected and forsaken the gen.
8. 9 they have rejected the word of the LORD
14. 19 Hast thou utterly rejected Judah? hath
Lam. 5. 22 thou hast utterly rejected us; thou art
Hos. 4. 6 hast rejected knowledge, I will also reject

2. *To put away or aside,* ἀθετέω *atheteō.*
Mark 6. 26 for their sakes..he would not reject her
7. 9 Full well ye reject the commandment of
Luke 7. 30 lawyers rejected the counsel of God agai.
John12. 48 He that rejecteth me, and receiveth not

3. *To disapprove of,* ἀποδοκιμάζω *apodokimazō.*
Matt21. 42 stone which the builders rejected, the
Mark 8. 31 must suffer many things, and be rejected
12. 10 stone which the builders rejected is bec.
Luke 9. 22 must suffer many things, and be rejected
17. 25 suffer many things, and be rejected of this
20. 17 stone which the builders rejected, the sa.
Heb. 12. 17 he was rejected: for he found no place of

4. *To spit out,* ἐκπτύω *ekptuō.*
Gal. 4. 14 despised not, nor rejected; but received

5. *To ask off, deprecate,* παραιτέομαι *paraiteomai.*
Titus 3. 10 heretic after the..second admonition re.

REJECTED —

1. *To cease, leave off, forbear,* חָדַל *chadel.*
Isa. 53. 3 He is despised and rejected of men, a man

2. *Not approved of,* ἀδόκιμος *adokimos.*
Heb. 6. 8 But that which beareth thorns..(is) reje.

REJOICE (greatly), to —

1. *To spring about, rejoice, be joyful,* גִּיל ,גּוּל *gul, gil.*
1 Ch.16. 31 heavens be glad, and let the earth rejoice
Psa. 2. 11 Serve the LORD with fear, and rejoice with
9. 14 daughter of Zion: I will rejoice in thy s.
13. 4 those that trouble me rejoice when I am
13. 5 my heart shall rejoice in thy salvation
14. 7 Jacob shall rejoice, (and) Israel shall be
16. 9 my heart is glad, and my glory rejoiceth
21. 1 in thy salvation how greatly shall he rej.
31. 7 I will be glad and rejoice in thy mercy
32. 11 Be glad in the LORD, and rejoice, ye rig.
51. 8 bones (which) thou hast broken may rej.
53. 6 Jacob shall rejoice, (and) Israel shall be
89. 16 In thy name shall they rejoice all the day
97. 1 let the earth rejoice; let the multitude of
97. 8 daughters of Judah rejoiced because of

Psa 118. 24 LORD hath made; we will rejoice and be
Prov. 2. 14 Who rejoice to do evil..delight in the fr.
23. 24 The father of the righteous shall greatly r.
23. 25 glad, and she that bare thee shall rejoice
Isa. 9. 3 as (men) rejoice when they divide the sp.
29. 19 poor among men shall rejoice in the Holy
35. 1 desert shall rejoice, and blossom as the
35. 2 It shall blossom abundantly, and rejoice
41. 16 thou shalt rejoice in the LORD, (and) shalt
65. 18 But be ye glad and rejoice for ever (in that)
65. 19 will rejoice in Jerusalem, and joy in my
Hos. 10. 5 priests thereof (that) rejoiced on it, for
Zech. 9. 9 Rejoice greatly, O daughter of Zion; sh.
10. 7 their heart shall rejoice in the LORD

2. *To gird on joy,* חָגַר גִּיל *chagar gil.*
Psa. 65. 12 and the little hills rejoice on every side

3. *To rejoice,* חָדָה *chadah.*
Exod 18. 9 Jethro rejoiced for all the goodness which

4. *Joy, rejoicing,* מָשׂוֹשׂ *masos.*
Isa. 8. 6 and rejoice in Rezin and Remaliah's son
62. 5 (as) the bridegroom rejoiceth over the b.

5. *To rejoice, exult,* עָלַז *alaz.*
Psa. 28. 7 therefore my heart greatly rejoiceth, and
60. 6 I will rejoice, I will divide Shechem, and
68. 4 Sing unto God..and rejoice before him
108. 7 I will rejoice, I will divide Shechem, and
Prov 23. 16 my reins shall rejoice when thy lips speak
Isa. 23. 12 Thou shalt no more rejoice, O thou oppr.
Jer. 11. 15 when thou doest evil, then thou rejoicest
15. 17 I sat not in the assembly..nor rejoiced
50. 11 Because ye were glad, because ye rejoiced
51. 39 make them drunken, that they may rejo.
Hab. 3. 18 Yet I will rejoice in the LORD, I will joy
Zeph. 3. 14 be glad and rejoice with all the heart, O

6. *To rejoice, exult,* עָלַס *alas.*
Job 20. 18 restitution (be), and he shall not rejoice

7. *To rejoice, exult,* עָלַץ *alats.*
1 Sa. 2. 1 my heart rejoiceth in the LORD; mine h.
1 Ch. 16. 32 let the fields rejoice, and all that (is) th.
Psa. 9. 2 I will be glad and rejoice in thee: I will
68. 3 let them rejoice before God; yea, let them
Prov 11. 10 When it goeth well..the city rejoiceth
28. 12 When righteous (men) do rejoice, (there

8. *To cry aloud, rejoice,* צָהַל *tsahal.*
Esth. 8. 15 the city of Shushan rejoiced and was glad

9. *To sing, cry aloud,* רָנַן *ranan.*
Isa. 61. 7 confusion they shall rejoice in their por.

10. *To sing, cry aloud,* רָנַן *ranan,* 3.
Psa. 20. 5 We will rejoice in thy salvation, and in
33. 1 Rejoice in the LORD, O ye righteous; (for)
63. 7 in the shadow of thy wings will I rejoice
71. 23 My lips shall greatly rojoice when I sing
89. 12 Tabor and Hermon shall rejoice in thy n.
90. 14 that we may rejoice and be glad all our
96. 12 then shall all the trees of the wood rejoice
98. 4 make a loud noise, and rejoice, and sing

11. *To (cause to) sing or cry aloud,* רָנַן *ranan,* 5.
Deut 32. 43 Rejoice, O ye nations, (with) his people

12. *To enjoy, rejoice,* שׂוּשׂ, שִׂישׂ *sus, sis.*
Deut 28. 63 as the LORD rejoiced..so the LORD will
30. 9 rejoice over thee for good, as he rejoiced
Job 39. 21 He paweth in the valley, and rejoiceth in
Psa. 19. 5 rejoiceth as a strong man to run a race
35. 9 soul shall be joyful..it shall rejoice in
40. 16 Let all those that seek thee rejoice and
68. 3 before God; yea, let them exceedingly rej.
70. 4 Let all those that seek thee rejoice and
119. 14 I have rejoiced in the way of thy testim.
119. 162 I rejoice at thy word, as one that find.
Isa. 61. 10 I will greatly rejoice in the LORD, my so.
62. 5 the bride, (so) shall thy God rejoice over
64. 5 Thou meetest him that rejoiceth and wo.
66. 10 rejoice for joy with her, all ye that mourn
66 14 when ye see (this), your heart shall rejoice
Jer. 32. 41 I will rejoice over them to do them good
Lam. 4. 21 Rejoice and be glad, O daughter of Edom
Zeph. 3. 17 he will rejoice over thee with joy; he will

13. *To laugh, deride, play, rejoice,* שָׂחַק *sachaq.*
Prov 31. 25 and she shall rejoice in time to come

14. *To laugh, deride, play, rejoice,* שָׂחַק *sachaq,* 3.
Prov. 8. 30 daily (his) delight, rejoicing always before
8. 31 Rejoicing in the habitable part of his ea.

15. *To shine, rejoice, joy, be glad,* שָׂמַח *sameach.*
Lev. 23. 40 ye shall rejoice before the LORD your God
Deut 12. 7 ye shall rejoice in all that ye put your h.
12. 12 ye shall rejoice before the LORD your God
12. 18 thou shalt rejoice before the LORD thy G.
14. 26 shalt rejoice, thou, and thine household
16. 11 thou shalt rejoice before the LORD thy G.
16. 14 thou shalt rejoice in thy feast, thou, and
26. 11 thou shalt rejoice in every good (thing)
27. 7 eat there, and rejoice before the LORD thy
33. 18 Rejoice, Zebulun, in thy going out; and
Judg. 9. 19 rejoice ye..and let him also rejoice in you
19. 3 when the father..saw him, he rejoiced to
1 Sa. 2. 1 enlarged..because I rejoice in thy salva.
6. 13 and saw the ark, and rejoiced to see (it)
11. 15 and all the men of Israel rejoiced greatly
19. 5 thou sawest (it), and didst rejoice: wher.
2 Sa. 1. 20 lest the daughters of the Philistines rej.
1 Ki. 5. 7 rejoiced greatly, and said, Blessed (be) the
2 Ki. 11. 20 all the people of the land rejoiced, and the
1 Ch. 16. 10 let the heart of them rejoice that seek t.
29. 9 people rejoiced..the king also rejoiced w.
2 Ch. 6. 41 and let thy saints rejoice in goodness
15. 15 all Judah rejoiced at the oath: for they
23. 21 all the people of the land rejoiced: and
24. 10 princes and all the people rejoiced, and
29. 36 Hezekiah rejoiced, and all the people, that
30. 25 the strangers..that dwelt in Judah, rejo.
Neh. 12. 43 rejoiced..and the children rejoiced: so
Job 21. 12 take the timbrel and harp, and rejoice at
31. 25 If I rejoiced because my wealth (was) gr.
31. 29 If I rejoiced at the destruction of him th.
Psa. 5. 11 all those that put their trust in thee rej.
31. 7 I will be glad and rejoice in thy mercy: for
33. 21 For our heart shall rejoice in him; because
35. 15 But in mine adversity they rejoiced, and
35. 19 Let not them..wrongfully rejoice over me
35. 24 Judge me..and let them not rejoice over
38. 16 lest (otherwise) they should rejoice over
40. 16 Let all those that seek thee rejoice and be
48. 11 Let mount Zion rejoice, let the daughters
58. 10 righteous shall rejoice when he seeth the
63. 11 king shall rejoice in God; every one that
66. 6 flood on foot: there did we rejoice in him
85 6 revive us..that thy people may rejoice in
96. 11 Let the heavens rejoice, and let the earth
97. 12 Rejoice in the LORD, ye righteous; and
104. 31 ever: the LORD shall rejoice in his works
105. 3 the heart of them rejoice that seek the L
106. 5 that I may rejoice in the gladness of thy
107. 42 The righteous shall see (it), and rejoice
109. 28 be ashamed; but let thy servant rejoice
149. 2 Let Israel rejoice in him that made him
Prov. 5. 18 and rejoice with the wife of thy youth
13. 9 light of the righteous rejoiceth: but the
23. 15 thine heart be wise, my heart shall rejoice
24. 17 Rejoice not when thine enemy falleth, and
29. 2 righteous are in authority, the people re.
Eccl. 3. 12 no good in them, but for (a man) to rejo.
3. 22 than that a man should rejoice in his own
4. 16 they also that come after shall not rejoice
5. 19 take his portion, and to rejoice in his la.
11. 8 live many years, (and) rejoice in them all
11. 9 Rejoice, O young man, in thy youth, and
Song 1. 4 we will be glad and rejoice in thee; we
Isa. 14. 8 Yea, the fir trees rejoice at thee, (and) the
14. 29 Rejoice not thou, whole Palestina, because
25. 9 we will be glad and rejoice in his salvation
65. 13 my servants shall rejoice, but ye shall be
66. 10 Rejoice ye with Jerusalem, and be glad
Jer. 31. 13 Then shall the virgin rejoice in the dance
Eze. 7. 12 let not the buyer rejoice, nor the seller
25. 6 rejoiced in heart with all thy despite ag.
35. 14 When the whole earth rejoiceth, I will
Hos. 9. 1 Rejoice not, O Israel, for joy, as (other)
Joel 2. 21 Fear not, O land; be glad and rejoice: for
2. 23 Be glad then..and rejoice in the LORD your
Obad. 12 neither shouldest thou have rejoiced over
Mic. 7. 8 Rejoice not against me, O mine enemy
Hab. 1. 15 therefore they rejoice and are glad
Zech. 2. 10 Sing and rejoice, O daughter of Zion: for
4. 10 for they shall rejoice, and shall see the
10. 7 their heart shall rejoice as through wine

16. *To make joyful, or glad,* שָׂמַח *sameach,* 3.
Psa. 19. 8 statutes of the LORD (are) right, rejoicing
86. 4 Rejoice the soul of thy servant; for unto
Prov 15. 30 The light of the eyes rejoiceth the heart
27. 9 Ointment and perfume rejoice the heart
29. 3 Whoso loveth wisdom rejoiceth his father
Jer. 31. 13 Then shall the virgin rejoice in the dance

17. *Rejoicing, joy,* שִׂמְחָה *simchah.*
Judg 16. 23 to offer a great sacrifice..and to rejoice
Neh. 12. 44 for Judah rejoiced for the priests and for
Eze. 35. 15 As thou didst rejoice at the inheritance

18. *To leap much for joy, exult,* ἀγαλλιάω *agalliaō.*
Luke 1. 47 my spirit hath rejoiced in God my Saviour
10. 21 In that hour Jesus rejoiced in spirit, and
John 5. 35 ye were willing for a season to rejoice in
8. 56 Your father Abraham rejoiced to see my
Acts 16. 34 he set meat before them, and rejoiced, be.
1 Pe. 1. 6 Wherein ye greatly rejoice, though now
1. 8 rejoice with joy unspeakable and full of
Rev. 19. 7 Let us be glad and rejoice, and give hon.

19. *To make glad, well pleased,* εὐφραίνω *euphrainō.*
Acts 2. 26 Therefore did my heart rejoice, and my t.
7. 41 rejoiced in the works of their own hands
Rom 15. 10 saith, Rejoice, ye Gentiles, with his people
Gal. 4. 27 Rejoice, (thou) barren that bearest not.
Rev. 12. 12 rejoice, (ye) heavens, and ye that dwell in
18. 20 Rejoice over her, (thou) heaven, and (ye)

20. *To boast,* καυχάομαι *kauchaomai.*
Rom. 5. 2 wherein we stand, and rejoice in hope of
Phil. 3. 3 rejoice in Christ Jesus, and have no con.
Jas. 1. 9 Let the brother of low degree rejoice in
4. 16 But now ye rejoice in your boastings: all

21. *A matter, cause of boasting,* καύχημα *kauchēma.*
Phil. 2. 16 that I may rejoice in the day of Christ, t.

22. *To rejoice, be glad,* χαίρω *chairō.*
Matt. 2. 10 they rejoiced with exceeding great joy
5. 12 Rejoice, and be exceeding glad; for great
18. 13 he rejoiceth more of that (sheep), than of
Luke 1. 14 and many shall rejoice at his birth
6. 23 Rejoice ye in that day, and leap for joy
10. 20 in this rejoice not..but rather rejoice, be.
13. 17 people rejoiced for all the glorious things
15. 5 he layeth (it) on his shoulders, rejoicing
19. 37 disciples began to rejoice and praise God
John 3. 29 rejoiceth greatly because of the bridegr.
4. 36 soweth and he that reapeth may rejoice
14. 28 If ye loved me, ye would rejoice, because
16. 20 world shall rejoice: and ye shall be sorr.
16. 22 see you again, and your heart shall rejo.
Acts 5. 41 rejoicing that they were counted worthy
8. 39 and he went on his way rejoicing
15. 31 when they had read, they rejoiced for the
Rom 12. 12 Rejoicing in hope; patient in tribulation
12. 15 Rejoice with them that do rejoice, and w.
1 Co. 7. 30 they that rejoice, as though they rejoiced
13. 6 Rejoiceth not in iniquity, but..in the truth
2 Co. 2. 3 sorrow from them of whom I ought to r.
6. 10 As sorrowful, yet alway rejoicing; as po.
7. 7 toward me; so that I rejoiced the more
7. 9 Now I rejoice, not that ye were made so.
7. 16 I rejoice therefore that I have confidence
Phil. 1. 18 I therein do rejoice, yea, and will rejoice
2. 28 when ye see him again, ye may rejoice
3. 1 Finally, my brethren, rejoice in the Lord
4. 4 Rejoice in the Lord..again I say, Rejoice
4. 10 But I rejoiced in the Lord greatly, that
Col. 1. 24 Who now rejoice in my sufferings for you
1 Th. 5. 16 Rejoice evermore
1 Pe. 4. 13 But rejoice, inasmuch as ye are partakers
2 John 4 rejoiced greatly that I found of thy child.
3 John 3 For I rejoiced greatly when the brethren
Rev. 11. 10 shall rejoice over them, and make

REJOICE, to cause or make to —

1. *To (cause to) sing, cry aloud,* רָנַן *ranan,* 5.
Psa. 65. 8 thou makest the outgoings..to rejoice

2. *To make to rejoice, make joyful,* שָׂמַח *sameach,* 3.
2 Ch. 20. 27 had made them to rejoice over their ene.
Neh. 12. 43 God had made them rejoice with great
Psa. 30. 1 hast not made my foes to rejoice over me
Jer. 31. 13 and make them rejoice from their sorrow
Lam. 2. 17 hath caused (thine) enemy to rejoice over

3. *To cause to rejoice,* שָׂמַח *sameach,* 5.
Psa. 89. 42 thou hast made all his enemies to rejoice

REJOICE, rejoiced (that or which) —

1. *Rejoicing, exulting,* עָלֵז *alez.*
Isa. 5. 14 and he that rejoiceth, shall descend into

2. *Rejoicing, exulting,* עַלִּיז *alliz.*
Isa. 13. 3 (even) them that rejoice in my highness
24. 8 noise of them that rejoice endeth, the joy
Zeph. 3. 11 them that rejoice in thy pride, and thou

3. *Rejoicing,* שָׂמֵחַ *sameach.*
Deut 16. 15 hands, therefore thou shalt surely rejoice
1 Ki. 1. 40 rejoiced with great joy, so that the earth
2 Ki. 11. 14 all the people of the land rejoiced, and
2 Ch. 23. 13 all the people of the land rejoiced, and s.
Job 3. 22 Which rejoice exceedingly, (and) are glad
Psa. 35. 26 brought to confusion together that rejoice
Prov. 2. 14 Who rejoice to do evil, (and) delight in
29. 6 but the righteous doth sing and rejoice
Eccl. 2. 10 for my heart rejoiced in all my labour, and
Amos 6. 13 Ye which rejoice in a thing of nought, whi.

REJOICE against, in, with, to —

1. *To boast against,* κατακαυχάομαι *katakauchaomai.*
Jas. 2. 13 and mercy rejoiceth against judgment

2. *To rejoice together with,* συγχαίρω *sugchairō.*
Luke 1. 58 Showed great mercy..and they rejoiced w.
15. 6, 9 saying..Rejoice with me; for I have fo.
1 Co. 12. 26 honoured, all the members rejoice with
13. 6 not in iniquity, but rejoiceth in the truth
Phil. 2. 17 if I be offered..I joy and rejoice with yo.
2. 18 same cause also do ye joy and rejoice with

REJOICING —

1. *Joy, rejoicing,* גִּיל *gil.*
Psa. 45. 15 With gladness and rejoicing shall they

2. *Joy, rejoicing,* גִּילָה *gilah.*
Isa. 65. 18 I create Jerusalem a rejoicing, and her

3. *Rejoicing, exulting,* עַלִּיז *alliz.*
Zeph. 2. 15 This (is) the rejoicing city that dwelt ca.

4. *Rejoicing, exultation,* עֲלִיצוּת *alitsuth.*
Hab. 3. 14 rejoicing (was) as to devour the poor sec.

5. *Loud cry, proclamation, singing,* רִנָּה *rinnah.*
Psa. 107. 22 let them..declare his works with rejoic.
118. 15 voice of rejoicing and salvation (is) in the
126. 6 shall doubtless come again with rejoicing

6. *Rejoicing,* שָׂמֵחַ *sameach.*
1 Ki. 1. 45 and they are come up from thence rejoic

7. *Rejoicing, joy,* שִׂמְחָה *simchah.*
2 Ch. 23. 18 with rejoicing and with singing, (as it was
Jer. 15. 16 the joy and rejoicing of mine heart: for I

8. *Joy, rejoicing, gladness,* שָׂשׂוֹן *sason.*
Psa. 119. 111 Thy testimonies..(are) the rejoicing of

9. *Shout, shouting, blowing,* תְּרוּעָה *teruah.*
Job 8. 21 Till he fill..thy lips with rejoicing

10. *A matter or subject of boasting,* καύχημα *kauch.*
2 Co. 1. 14 that we are your rejoicing, even as ye also
Gal. 6. 4 then shall he have rejoicing in himself al.
Phil. 1. 26 That your rejoicing may be more abund.
Heb. 3. 6 if we hold fast the..rejoicing of the hope

11. *Boasting,* καύχησις *kauchēsis.*
1 Co. 15. 31 I protest by your rejoicing which I have
2 Co. 1. 12 For our rejoicing is this, the testimony of
1 Th. 2. 19 For what (is) our..crown of rejoicing?
Jas. 4. 16 But now ye rejoice..all such rejoicing is

RE'-KEM, רֶקֶם *friendship.*
1. A prince of Midian, slain by Phinehas when in the plains of Moab. B.C. 1452.
Num 31. 8 Evi, and R., and Zur, and Hur, and Reba

Josh 13. 21 Evi, and R., and Zur, and Hur, and Reba

2. A son of Hebron, and father of Shammai. B.C. 1490.
1 Ch. 2. 43 Korah, and Tappuah, and R., and Shema
2. 44 father of Jorkoam, and R. begat Shammai

3. A city in Benjamin, near Irpeel; now called *Ain-Karim.*
Josh 18. 27 And R., and Irpeel, and Taralah

RELEASE —

1. *Release, rest,* הֲנָחָה *hanachah.*
Esth. 2. 18 and he made a release to the provinces

2. *Release,* שְׁמִטָּה *shemittah.*
Deut 15. 1 end of..seven years thou shalt make a r.
15. 2 the manner of the release..the LORD'S re.
15. 9 The seventh year, the year of release, is
31. 10 in the solemnity of the year of release, in

RELEASE, to —

1. *To release, let go, throw down,* שָׁמַט *shamat.*
Deut 15. 2 Every creditor..shall release (it); he sh.

2. *To (cause to) release,* שָׁמַט *shamat,* 5.
Deut 15. 3 with thy brother thine hand shall release

3. *To loose away, or off,* ἀπολύω *apoluō.*
Matt 27. 15 governor was wont to release unto the p.
27. 17 Whom will ye that I release unto you? B.
27. 21 Whether of the twain will ye that I rele.
27. 26 Then released he Barabbas unto them
Mark 15. 6 Now at (that) feast he released unto them
15. 9 Will ye that I release unto you the king
15. 11 that he should rather release Barabbas
15. 15 released Barabbas unto them, and deliv.
Luke 23. 16 I will therefore chastise him, and release
23. 17 [For of necessity he must release one un.]
23. 18 Away with this (man), and release unto
23. 20 Pilate therefore, willing to release Jesus
23. 25 released unto them him that for sedition
John 18. 39 custom, that I should release unto you
18. 39 will ye therefore that I release unto you
19. 10 knowest thou not that I have power..to r.
19. 12 Pilate sought to release him: but the J.

RELIEF —

Thorough service, ministration, διακονία *diakonia.*
Acts 11. 29 determined to send relief unto the bret.

RELIEVE, to —

1. *To declare happy, or upright,* אָשַׁר *ashar,* 3.
Isa. 1. 17 relieve the oppressed, judge the fatherless

2. *To take or keep firm hold,* חָזַק *chazaq,* 5.
Lev. 25. 35 thou shalt relieve him; (yea, though he

3. *To cause to stand,* עוּד *ud,* 3a.
Psa. 146. 9 The LORD..relieveth the fatherless and

4. *To cause to turn back,* שׁוּב *shub,* 5.
Lam. 1. 11 pleasant things for meat to relieve the s.
1. 16 comforter that should relieve my soul is
1. 19 they sought their meat to relieve their s.

5. *To suffice for,* ἐπαρκέω *eparkeō.*
1 Ti. 5. 10 if she have relieved the afflicted, if she
5. 16 let them relieve them, and let not the c.
5. 16 it may relieve them that are widows in.

RELIGION — [*See* Jews'.]

Outward religious service, θρησκεία *thrēskeia.*
Acts 26. 5 most straitest sect of our religion I lived
Jas. 1. 26 deceiveth his own heart, this man's reli.
1. 27 Pure religion and undefiled before God

RELIGIOUS —

1. *Religious, superstitious,* θρῆσκος *thrēskos.*
Jas. 1. 26 If any man among you seem to be religious

2. *To venerate, worship, adore,* σέβομαι *sebomai.*
Acts 13. 43 many of the Jews and religious proselytes

RELY, to —

To be supported, lean on, שָׁעַן *shaan,* 2.
2 Ch. 13. 18 they relied upon the LORD God of their
16. 7 Because thou hast relied on the king of
16. 7 not relied on the LORD thy God, therefore
16. 8 because thou didst rely on the LORD, he

REMAIN, (things which), to —

1. *To draw self up, sojourn,* גּוּר *gur.*
Judg. 5. 17 why did Dan remain in ships? Asher co.

2. *To sit down or still,* יָשַׁב *yashab.*
Gen. 38. 11 Remain a widow at thy father's house
Num 35. 28 Because he should have remained in the
Deut 21. 13 shall remain in thine house, and bewail
Josh. 1. 14 shall remain in the land which Moses g.
1 Sa. 20. 19 go down quickly..and shalt remain by the
23. 14 remained in a mountain in the wilderness
24. 3 his men remained in the sides of the cave
2 Sa. 13. 20 Tamar remained desolate in her brother
1 Ki. 11. 16 For six months did Joab remain there w.
1 Ch. 13. 14 ark of God remained with the family of
Isa. 32. 16 righteousness remain in the fruitful field
44. 13 beauty of a man; that it may remain in
65. 4 Which remain among the graves, and lo.
Jer. 17. 25 Jerusalem; and this city shall remain for
30. 18 palace shall remain after the manner th.
37. 16 and Jeremiah had remained there many
37. 21 Jeremiah remained in the court of the p.
38. 2 He that remaineth in this city shall die
38. 13 Jeremiah remained in the court of the p.
51. 30 they have remained in (their) holds: their
51. 62 to cut it off, that none shall remain in it
Lam. 5. 19 Thou, O LORD, remainest for ever; thy t.
Eze. 3. 15 remained there astonished among them

3. *To be left,* יָתַר *yathar,* 2.
Exod 10. 15 there remained not any green thing in
12. 10 that which remaineth of it until the mo.
29. 34 if ought of the flesh..remain unto the m.
Lev. 8. 32 that which remaineth of the flesh and of
10. 12 Take the meat offering that remaineth of
19. 6 if ought remain until the third day, it sh.
27. 18 money according to the years that rema.
Josh. 18. 2 there remained among the children of I.
21. 20 which remained of the children of Koha.
21. 26 of the children of Kohath that remained
Judg 21. 7, 16 shall we do for wives for them that r.
1 Ki. 18. 22 I only, remain a prophet of the LORD; but
Prov. 2. 21 in the land, and the perfect shall remain
Isa. 4. 3 (he that) remaineth in Jerusalem, shall
Jer. 27. 19 residue of the vessels that remain in this
27. 21 concerning the vessels that remain (in)
Eze. 39. 14 bury with the passengers those that rem.
Dan. 10. 13 I remained there with the kings of Persia
Amos 6. 9 if there remain ten men in one house, that

4. *All the days of,* כָּל יְמֵי *kol yeme.*
Gen. 8. 22 While the earth remaineth, seed time and

5. *To pass the night,* לוּן, לִין *lun, lin.*
Exod 23. 18 neither shall the fat of my sacrifice rem.
Deut 16. 4 even, remain all night until the morning
21. 23 His body shall not remain all night upon
Job 19. 4 have erred, mine error remaineth with
41. 22 In his neck remaineth strength, and sor.
Psa. 55. 7 would I wander far off, (and) remain in
Zech. 5. 4 it shall remain in the midst of his house

6. *To rest, be at rest,* נוּחַ *nuach.*
Prov 21. 16 shall remain in the congregation of the d.

7. *To be over and above, superfluous,* עָדַף *adaph.*
Exod 16. 23 that which remaineth over lay up for you
26. 12 remnant that remaineth of the curtains of
26. 12 curtain that remaineth shall hang over
26. 13 that which remaineth in the length of the

8. *To stand still,* עָמַד *amad.*
2 Ki. 13. 6 there remained the grove also in Samaria
Eccl. 2. 9 also my wisdom remained with me
Isa. 10. 32 As yet shall he remain at Nob that day
66. 22 earth, which I will make, shall remain b.
66. 22 so shall your seed and your name remain
Jer. 48. 11 therefore his taste remained in him, and
Dan. 10. 17 straightway there remained no strength in
Hag. 2. 5 so my spirit remaineth among you: fear

9. *To rise up,* קוּם *qum.*
Josh. 2. 11 neither did there remain any more courage

10. *To remain over,* שָׂרַד *sarad.*
Josh 10. 20 rest (which) remained of them entered

11. *Remnant, remaining one,* שָׂרִיד *sarid.*
Num 24. 19 shall destroy him that remaineth of the
Deut. 2. 34 destroyed the men..we left none to rem.
Josh. 8. 22 so that they let none of them remain or
10. 28 he let none remain: and he did to the king of
10. 30 he let none remain in it; but did unto the
Judg. 5. 13 he made him that remaineth have domin.
Job 27. 15 Those that remain of him shall be buried
Jer. 42. 17 none of them shall remain or escape from
44. 14 So that none..shall escape or remain, that
47. 4 to cut off..every helper that remaineth
Lam. 2. 22 so that..none escaped nor remained: tho.
Obad. 14 delivered up those of his that did remain

12. *To remain, be left,* שָׁאַר *shaar.*
1 Sa. 16. 11 There remaineth yet the youngest, and

13. *To remain, be left,* שָׁאַר *shaar,* 2.
Gen. 7. 23 Noah only remained (alive), and they that
14. 10 they that remained fled to the mountain
Exod 8. 9 (that) they may remain in the river only?
8. 11 depart..they shall remain in the river
8. 31 from his people: there remained not one
10. 5 which remaineth unto you from the hail
10. 19 there remained not one locust in all the
14. 28 there remained not so much as one of them
Lev. 25. 52 if there remain but few years unto the ye.
Num 11. 26 there remained two (of the) men in the c.
Deut. 3. 11 For only Og king of Bashan remained of
19. 20 those which remain shall hear, and fear
Josh 11. 22 in Gath, and in Ashdod, there remained
13. 1 there remaineth yet very much land to be
13. 2 This (is) the land that yet remaineth: all
13. 12 who remained of the remnant of the giants
23. 4 remain, to be an inheritance for your tribes
23. 7 these that remain among you; neither
23. 12 these that remain among you, and shall
Judg. 7. 3 two thousand; and there remained ten th.
1 Sa. 11. 11 that they which remained were scattered
16. 11 There remaineth yet the youngest, and
1 Ki. 22. 46 remnant of the Sodomites, which remain.
2 Ki. 7. 13 five of the horses that remain, which are
10. 11 So Jehu slew all that remained of the ho.
10. 17 slew all that remained unto Ahab in Sam.
24. 14 none remained, save the poorest sort of
25. 22 people that remained in the land of Judah
Ezra 1. 4 whosoever remaineth in any place where
9. 15 for we remain yet escaped, as (it is) this
Job 21. 34 in your answers there remaineth falseh.?
Jer. 8. 3 remain of this evil family, which remain
24. 8 that remain in this land, and them that
34. 7 for these defenced cities remained of the
37. 10 there remained (but) wounded men among
38. 4 hands of the men of war that remain in
39. 9 remnant of the people that remained in
39. 9 with the rest of the people that remained
41. 10 all the people that remained in Mizpah
52. 15 residue of the people that remained in the

Eze. 6. 12 he that remaineth and is besieged shall
17. 21 they that remain shall be scattered toward
Dan. 10. 8 there remained no strength in me: for my
Zech 9. 7 but he that remaineth, even he, (shall be)
12. 14 All the families that remain, every family

14. *Remnant, rest, posterity,* שְׁאֵרִית *sheerith.*
Jer. 44. 7 to cut off..to leave you none to remain

15. *To tabernacle,* שָׁכַן *shaken.*
Lev. 16. 16 remaineth among them in the midst of
Eze. 31. 13 shall all the fowls of the heaven remain

16. *To watch,* שָׁקַד *shaqad.*
Job 21. 32 brought to the grave, and shall remain in

17. *To leave off,* ἀπολείπω *apoleipō.*
Heb. 4. 6 Seeing therefore it remaineth that some
4. 9 There remaineth therefore a rest to the
10. 26 there remaineth no more sacrifice for sins

18. *To remain throughout,* διαμένω *diamenō.*
Luke 1. 22 beckoned unto them, and remained spe.
Heb. 1. 11 They shall perish; but thou remainest

19. *The things left,* τὰ λοιπά *ta loipa.*
Rev. 3. 2 strengthen the things which remain, that

20. *The thing left is,* τὸ λοιπόν ἐστιν *to loipon estin.*
1 Co. 7. 29 it remaineth, that both they that have w.

21. *To remain,* μένω *menō.*
Matt 11. 23 it would have remained until this day
Luke 10. 7 in the same house remain, eating and dr.
John 1. 33 see the spirit descending, and remaining
9. 41 say, We see; therefore your sin remaineth
15. 11 that my joy [might remain] in you, and
15. 16 your fruit should remain; that whatsoe.
19. 31 bodies should not remain upon the cross
Acts 5. 4 Whiles it remained, was it not thine own?
27. 41 stuck fast, and remained unmoveable, but
1 Co. 7. 11 if she depart, let her remain unmarried
15. 6 of whom the greater part remain unto th.
2 Co. 3. 11 much more that which remaineth (is) gl.
3. 14 for until this day remaineth the same veil
9. 9 his righteousness remaineth for ever
Heb. 12. 27 things which cannot be shaken may rem.
1 Jo. 2. 24 remain in you, ye also shall continue in
3. 9 for his seed remaineth in him: and he ca.

22. *To be left all around,* περιλείπομαι *perileipomai.*
1 Th. 4. 15, 17 we which are alive (and) remain unto

23. *To be over and above,* περισσεύω *perisseuō.*
Matt 14. 20 took up of the fragments that remained
Luke 9. 17 was taken up of fragments that remained
John 6. 12 Gather up the fragments that remain, th.

REMAIN, to let or cause to —

1. *To cause to be abundant,* יָתַר *yathar,* 5.
Exod 12. 10 ye shall let nothing of it remain until the
Num 33. 55 that those which ye let remain of them

2. *To cause to tabernacle,* שָׁכַן *shaken,* 5.
Eze. 32. 4 will cause all the fowls..to remain upon

REMAIN long, over and above, to —

1. *To be old, aged,* יָשַׁן *yashan,* 2.
Deut. 4. 25 ye shall have remained long in the land

2. *To be over and above,* περισσεύω *perisseuō.*
John 6. 13 which remained over and above unto them

REMAINDER —

1. *To be left, to remain,* יָתַר *yathar,* 2.
Exod 29. 34 thou shalt burn the remainder with fire
Lev. 6. 16 the remainder thereof shall Aaron and his
7. 16 on the morrow also the remainder of it s.
7. 17 the remainder of the flesh of the sacrifice

2. *Remnant,* שְׁאֵרִית *sheerith.*
2 Sa. 14. 7 (neither) name nor remainder upon the e.
Psa. 76. 10 remainder of wrath shalt thou restrain

REMAINING, (to be) —

1. *To set up or station self,* יָצַב *yatsab,* 7.
2 Sa. 21. 5 we should be destroyed from remaining

2. *To be left over,* יָתַר *yathar,* 2.
Josh. 21. 40 which were remaining of the families of

3. *Remaining one, remnant,* שָׂרִיד *sarid.*
Deut. 3. 3 until none was left to him remaining
Josh 10. 33 until he had left him none remaining
10. 37 he left none remaining, according to all
10. 39 he left none remaining: as he had done
10. 40 he left none remaining, but utterly dest.
11. 8 smote..until they left them none remain.
2 Ki. 10. 11 slew..until he left him none remaining
Job 18. 19 neither..any remaining in his dwellings
Obad. 18 there shall not be (any) remaining of the

4. *To tabernacle,* שָׁכַן *shaken.*
Num. 9. 22 tarried upon the tabernacle, remaining

RE-MAL'-IAH, רְמַלְיָהוּ *Jah increases.*

Father of Pekah who slew Pekahiah and reigned in his stead. B.C. 769.
2 Ki. 15. 25 But Pekah the son of R...conspired against
15. 27 Pekah the son of R. began to reign over
15. 30 a conspiracy against Pekah the son of R.
15. 32 In the second year of Pekah the son of R.
15. 37 the LORD began to send against..son of R.
16. 1 In the seventeenth year of..the son of R.
16. 5 Pekah son of R...came up to Jerusalem
2 Ch. 28. 6 Pekah the son of R. slew in Judah an h.
Isa. 7. 1 Pekah the son of R...went up toward J.
7. 4 for the fierce anger..of the son of R.
7. 5 Because Syria..and the son of R., have
7. 9 and the head of Samaria (is) R.'s son
8. 6 this people..rejoice in Rezin and R.'s son

REMEDY —
Healing, מַרְפֵּא *marpe.*
2 Ch.36. 16 wrath..arose..till(there was) no remedy
Prov. 6. 15 suddenly shall he be broken without re.
29. 1 shall..be destroyed, and that without re.

REMEMBER (earnestly), to —
1. *To remember, imprint,* זָכַר *zakar.*
Gen. 8. 1 God remembered Noah, and every living
9. 15 I will remember my covenant, which (is)
9. 16 I may remember the everlasting covenant
19. 29 God remembered Abraham, and sent Lot
30. 22 God remembered Rachel, and God heark.
40. 23 Yet did not the chief butler remember J.
42. 9 And Joseph remembered the dreams wh.
Exod. 2. 24 God remembered his covenant with Abr.
6. 5 heard..and I have remembered my cove.
13. 3 Remember this day, in which ye came out
20. 8 Remember the sabbath day, to keep it h.
32. 13 Remember Abraham, Isaac, and Israel
Lev. 26. 42 Then will I remember my covenant with
26. 42 I remember; and I will remember the l.
26. 45 But I will for their sakes remember the
Num 11. 5 We remember the fish which we did eat
15. 39 remember..the commandments of the L.
15. 40 may remember, and do all my command.
Deut. 5. 15 remember that thou wast a servant in
7. 18 shalt well remember what the LORD thy
8. 2 thou shalt remember all the way which
8. 18 thou shalt remember the LORD thy God
9. 7 Remember, (and) forget not, how thou p.
9. 27 Remember thy servants, Abraham, Isaac
15. 15 thou shalt remember that thou wast a
16. 3 thou mayest remember the day when thou
16. 12 thou shalt remember that thou wast a bo.
24. 9 Remember what the LORD thy God did un.
24. 18, 22 thou shalt remember that thou wast a
25. 17 Remember what Amalek did unto thee by
32. 7 Remember the days of old, consider the
Josh. 1. 13 Remember the word which Moses the s.
Judg. 8. 34 Israel remembered not the LORD their God
9. 2 remember also that I (am) your bone and
16. 28 remember me, I pray thee, and strengthen
1 Sa. 1. 11 remember me, and not forget thine hand.
1. 19 his wife; and the LORD remembered her
25. 31 my lord, then remember thine handmaid
2 Sa. 14. 11 let the king remember the LORD thy God
19. 19 neither do thou remember that which thy
2 Ki. 9. 25 remember how that, when I and thou rode
20. 3 remember now how I have walked before
1 Ch.16. 12 Remember his marvellous works that he
2 Ch. 6. 42 remember the mercies of David thy serv.
24. 22 the king remembered not the kindness
Neh. 1. 8 Remember, I beseech thee, the word that
4. 14 remember the LORD, (which is) great and
13. 14, 22 Remember me, O my God, concerning
13. 29 Remember them, O my God, because they
13. 31 Remember me, O my God, for good
Esth. 2. 1 he remembered Vashti, and what she had
Job 4. 7 Remember, I pray thee who (ever) perish.
7. 7 remember that my life (is) wind: mine eye
10. 9 Remember, I beseech thee, that thou h.
11. 16 (and) remember (it) as waters (that) pass
14. 13 appoint me a set time, and remember me
21. 6 when I remember I am afraid, and trem.
36. 24 Remember that thou magnify his work
41. 8 Lay thine hand upon him, remember the
Psa. 9. 12 he remembereth them: he forgetteth not
20. 3 Remember all thy offerings, and accept
22. 27 the ends of the world shall remember
25. 6 Remember, O LORD, thy tender mercies
25. 7 Remember not the sins of my youth, nor
25. 7 remember thou me for thy goodness' sake
42. 4 I remember these (things), I pour out my
42. 6 I remember thee from the land of Jordan
63. 6 I remember thee upon my bed, (and) m.
74. 2 Remember thy congregation (which) thou
74. 18 Remember this..the enemy hath reproa.
74. 22 remember how the foolish man reproach.
77. 3 I remembered God, and was troubled: I
*77. 11 I will remember the works of the LORD
77. 11 surely I will remember thy wonders of old
78. 35 they remembered that God (was) their
78. 39 For he remembered that they (were but)
78. 42 They remembered not his hand, (nor) the
79. 8 remember not against us former iniquities
88. 5 the dead..whom thou rememberest no
89. 47 Remember how short my time is: where.
89. 50 Remember, LORD, the reproach of thy s.
98. 3 He hath remembered his mercy and his
103. 14 he knoweth..remembereth that we (are)
103. 18 to those that remember his commandm.
105. 5 Remember his marvellous works that he
105. 8 He hath remembered his covenant for e.
105. 42 For he remembered his holy promise, (and)
106. 4 Remember me, O LORD, with the favour
106. 7 they remembered not the multitude of thy
106. 45 he remembered for them his covenant, and
109. 16 Because that he remembered not to show
119. 49 Remember the word unto thy servant, up.
119. 52 I remembered thy judgments of old, O
119. 55 I have remembered thy name O LORD, in
132. 1 LORD, remember David..all his afflictions
136. 23 Who remembered us in our low estate: for
137. 1 yea, we wept, when we remembered Zion
137. 6 If I do not remember thee, let my tongue
137. 7 Remember, O LORD, the children of Edom
143. 5 I remember the days of old; I meditate
Prov 31. 7 Let him drink..and remember his misery
Eccl. 5. 20 he shall not much remember the days of
9. 15 no man remembered that same poor man
11. 8 let him remember the days of darkness
Eccl.12. 1 Remember now thy Creator in the days
Isa. 38. 3 Remember now, O LORD, I beseech thee
43. 18 Remember ye not the former things, nei.
43. 25 I, (am) he that..will not remember thy
44. 21 Remember these, O Jacob and Israel; for
46. 8 Remember this, and show yourselves men
46. 9 Remember the former things of old: for
47. 7 neither didst remember the latter end of
54. 4 shalt not remember the reproach of thy
57. 11 hast not remembered me, nor laid (it) to
63. 11 Then he remembered the days of old, M.
64. 5 (those that) remember thee in thy ways
64. 9 neither remember iniquity for ever: be.
Jer. 2. 2 I remember thee, the kindness of thy yo.
3. 16 neither shall they remember it, neither
14. 10 he will now remember their iniquity, and
14. 21 remember, break not thy covenant with
15. 15 remember me, and visit me, and revenge
17. 2 their children remember their altars and
18. 20 Remember that I stood before thee to sp.
31. 20 I do earnestly remember him still: there.
31. 34 and I will remember their sin no more
44. 21 did not the LORD remember them, and
51. 50 remember the LORD afar off, and let Jer.
Lam. 1. 7 Jerusalem remembered in the days of her
1. 9 she remembereth not her last end; ther.
2. 1 remembered not his footstool in the day
3. 19 Remembering mine affliction and my m.
5. 1 Remember, O LORD, what is come upon
Eze. 6. 9 they that escape of you shall remember
16. 22, 43 thou hast not remembered the days
16. 60 I will remember my covenant with thee
16. 61 Then thou shalt remember thy ways, and
16. 63 thou mayest remember, and be confoun.
20. 43 there shall ye remember your ways, and
23. 27 thou shalt not..remember Egypt any mo.
36. 31 Then shall ye remember your own evil
Hos. 7. 2 they consider not..(that) I remember all
8. 13 now will he remember their iniquity, and
9. 9 he will remember their iniquity, he will
Amos 1. 9 and remembered not the brotherly cove.
Jon. 2. 7 I remembered the LORD: and my prayer
Mic. 6. 5 remember now what Balak king of Moab
Hab. 3. 2 revive thy work..in wrath remember me.
Zech.10. 9 they shall remember me in far countries
Mal. 4. 4 Remember ye the law of Moses my servant
[* V.L. as No. 2.]

2. *To cause to remember, imprint,* זָכַר *zakar,* 5.
Gen. 41. 9 saying, I do remember my faults this day
Psa. 20. 7 we will remember the name of the LORD
Song 1. 4 we will remember thy love more than w.

3. *To look after, inspect,* פָּקַד *paqad.*
1 Sa. 15. 2 I remember (that) which Amalek did to

4. *To remind again,* ἀναμιμνήσκω *anamimnēskō.*
2 Co. 7. 15 he remembereth the obedience of you all

5. *To be mindful,* μιμνήσκομαι *mimnēskomai.*
Heb. 13. 3 Remember them that are in bonds, as bo.

6. *To remember,* μνάομαι *mnaomai.*
Matt. 5. 23 there rememberest that thy brother hath
26. 75 Peter remembered the word of Jesus, wh
27. 63 we remember that that deceiver said, wh.
Luke 1. 72 To perform..and to remember his holy c.
16. 25 Son, remember that thou in thy lifetime
23. 42 remember me when thou comest into thy
24. 6 remember how he spake unto you when
24. 8 And they remembered his words
John 2. 17 And his disciples remembered that it was
2. 22; 12. 16; Acts 11. 16; 1 Co. 11. 2; Heb. 8.
12; 10. 17; Jude 17.

7. *To remember,* μνημονεύω *mnēmoneuō.*
Matt.16. 9; Mark 8. 18; Luke 17. 32; John 15. 20
16. 4, 21; Acts 20. 31, 35; Gal. 2. 10; Eph. 2. 11; Col. 4
18; 1 Th. 1. 3; 2. 9; 2 Th. 2. 5; 2 Ti. 2. 8; Heb. 13. 7;
Rev. 2. 5; 3. 3; 18. 5.

8. *To remind gradually,* ὑπομιμνήσκω *hupomimnēskō.*
Luke22. 61 Peter remembered the word of the Lord
3 John 10 I will remember his deeds which he doeth

REMEMBERED, (to make) to be —
1. *To be remembered, imprinted,* זָכַר *zakar,* 2.
Num10. 9 ye shall be remembered before the LORD
Esth. 9. 28 these days (should be) remembered and
Job 24. 20 he shall be no more remembered; and
Psa.109. 14 Let the iniquity of his fathers be remem.
Isa. 23. 16 sing..that thou mayest be remembered
65. 17 the former shall not be remembered, nor
Jer. 11. 19 that his name may be no more remembe.
Eze. 3. 20 his righteousness..shall not be remembe.
21. 32 thou shalt be no (more) remembered: for
25. 10 the Ammonites may not be remembered
33. 13 all his righteousnesses shall not be reme.
Hos. 2. 17 they shall no more be remembered by th.
Zech.13. 2 they shall no more be remembered; and

2. *To cause to remember, imprint,* זָכַר *zakar,* 5.
Psa. 45. 17 I will make thy name to be remembered
Eze. 21. 24 have made your iniquity to be remembe.

3. *Remembrance,* זֵכֶר, זֶכֶר *zeker.*
Psa.111. 4 hath made his wonderful works to be re.

REMEMBRANCE (again) of —
1. *Remembrance,* זֵכֶר, זֶכֶר *zeker.*
Exod17. 14 I will utterly put out the remembrance
Deut25. 19 thou shalt blot out the remembrance of
32. 26 I would make the remembrance of them
Job 18. 17 His remembrance shall perish from the e.
Psa. 6. 5 For in death (there is) no remembrance
30. 4 give thanks at the remembrance of his h.
34. 16 to cut off the remembrance of them from
Psa. 97. 12 give thanks at the remembrance of his
102. 12 and thy remembrance unto all generations
112. 6 the righteous shall be in everlasting rem.
Isa. 26. 8 desire of (our) soul (is)..to the remembr.

2. *Remembrance, memorial,* זִכָּרוֹן *zikkaron.*
Job 13. 12 Your remembrances (are) like unto ashes
Eccl. 1. 11 no remembrance of former..neither..re.
2. 16 no remembrance of the wise more than
Isa. 57. 8 Behind..hast thou set up thy remembra.
Mal. 3. 16 a book of remembrance was written befo.

3. *A remembering again,* ἀνάμνησις *anamnēsis.*
Luke22. 19 saying..this do in remembrance of me
1 Co.11. 24 Take, eat..this do in remembrance of me
11. 25 as oft as ye drink (it), in remembrance of
Heb. 10. 3 (there is) a remembrance again (made) of

4. *To remember,* μνάομαι *mnaomai.*
Luke 1. 54 holpen his servant Israel, in remembr. of

5. *Remembrance, mention, memory,* μνεία *mneia.*
Phil. 1. 3 I thank my God upon every remembrance
1 Th. 3. 6 ye have good remembrance of us always
2 Ti. 1. 3 have remembrance of thee in my prayers

6. *Remembrance, memory,* μνήμη *mnēmē.*
2 Pe. 1. 15 have these things always in remembrance

7. *Remembrance, recollection,* ὑπόμνησις *hupomnēsis.*
2 Ti. 1. 5 call to remembrance the unfeigned faith
2 Pe. 1. 13 stir you up by putting (you) in remembra.
3. 1 I stir up your pure minds by way of rem.

REMEMBRANCE, to bring or call to —
1. *To remember,* זָכַר *zakar.*
Psa 77. 6 call to remembrance my song in the night
Eze. 23. 19 in calling to remembrance the days of

2. *To cause to remember,* זָכַר *zakar,* 5.
Num. 5. 15 an offering..bringing iniquity to remem.
1 Ki. 17. 18 come unto me to call my sin to rememb.
Psa. 38. *title.* A psalm of David, to bring to remem.
70. *title.* (A psalm) of David, to bring to remem.
Eze. 21. 23 but he will call to remembrance the ini.
29. 16 which bringeth (their) iniquity to remem.

3. *To inspect, visit,* פָּקַד *paqad.*
Eze. 23. 21 Thus thou calledst to remembrance the l.

4. *To remind again,* ἀναμιμνήσκω *anamimnēskō.*
Mark11. 21 Peter calling to remembrance saith unto
1 Co. 4. 17 who shall bring you into remembrance of
Heb. 10. 32 But call to remembrance the former days

5. *To remind gradually,* ὑπομιμνήσκω *hupomim.*
John 14. 26 and bring all things to your remembrance

REMEMBRANCE, to be, come, have, keep, put, in —
1. *To be remembered,* זָכַר *zakar,* 2.
Psa. 83. 4 name of Israel may be no more in remem.
Eze. 21. 24 that ye are come to remembrance, ye shall

2. *To cause to remember,* זָכַר *zakar,* 5.
2 Sa. 18. 18 no son to keep my name in remembrance
Lam. 3. 20 My soul hath (them) still in remembrance
Isa. 43. 26 Put me in remembrance: let us plead to.

3. *To be mindful again,* ἀναμιμνήσκω *anamimnēskō.*
2 Ti. 1. 6 Wherefore I put thee in remembrance t.

4. *To remember,* μνάομαι *mnaomai.*
Acts 10. 31 alms are had in remembrance in the sight
Rev. 16. 19 great Babylon came in remembrance be.

5. *To be privately mindful,* ὑπομιμνήσκω *hupomim.*
2 Ti. 2. 14 Of these things put (them) in remembrance
2 Pe. 1. 12 negligent to put you always in remembr.
Jude 5 I will therefore put you in remembrance

6. *To place under, suggest,* ὑποτίθημι *hupotithēmi.*
1 Ti. 4. 6 If thou put the brethren in remembrance

RE'-METH, רֶמֶת *height.*
A Levitical city in Issachar, near Engannim; now called *Yarmuth.*
Josh 19. 21 And R., and En-gannim, and En-haddah

REMISSION —
1. *A sending away,* ἄφεσις *aphesis.*
Matt26. 28 is shed for many for the remission of sins
Mark 1. 4 baptism of repentance for the remission
Luke 1. 77 knowledge of salvation..by the remission
3. 3 baptism of repentance for the remission of
24. 47 that repentance and remission of sins sh.
Acts 2. 38 be baptized..for the remission of sins, and
10. 43 believeth in him shall receive remission of
Heb. 9. 22 without shedding of blood is no remission
10. 18 Now where remission of these (is, there

2. *A sending over, passing by,* πάρεσις *paresis.*
Rom. 3. 25 declare his righteousness for the remission

REMIT, be remitted, to —
To send away, ἀφίημι *aphiēmi.*
John20. 23 Whose soever sins ye remit, [they are re.]

REM'-MON, רִמּוֹן. See *Rimmon.*
A city in Judah or Simeon, near Ain and Ether; now called *Romaneh.*
Josh 19. 7 Ain, R., and Ether, and Ashan; four cities

REM-MON ME-THO'-AR, רִמּוֹן הַמְּתֹאָר.
A city in Zebulun, N. of Nazareth, now called *Rummanah.*
Josh 19. 13 And from thence..goeth out to R., to Neah

REMNANT —
1. *After, after parts,* אַחֲרֵי *achare.*
1 Ki. 14. 10 will take away the remnant of the house

2. *Latter end*, אַחֲרִית *acharith*.
Eze. 23. 25 and thy remnant shall fall by the sword
3. *To be left over*, יָתַר *yathar*, 2.
Lev. 2. 3 remnant of the meat offering (shall be) A.
14. 18 remnant of the oil that (is) in the priest's
1 Ch. 6. 70 for the family of the remnant of the sons
4. *What is left over*, יֶתֶר *yether*.
Deut. 3. 11 remained of the remnant of giants; beh.
28. 54 toward the remnant of his children which
Josh 12. 4 of the remnant of the giants, that dwelt
13. 12 who remained of the remnant of the gia.
23. 12 cleave unto the remnant of these nations
2 Sa. 21. 2 but of the remnant of the Amorites; and
1 Ki. 12. 23 Speak..to the remnant of the people, sa.
22. 46 remnant of the sodomites, which remain.
2 Ki. 25. 11 with the remnant of the multitude, did N.
Job 22. 20 but the remnant of them the fire consu.
Jer. 39. 9 remnant of the people that remained in
Mic. 5. 3 then the remnant of his brethren shall r.
Hab. 2. 8 all the remnant of the people shall spoil
Zeph. 2. 9 the remnant of my people shall possess
5. *Loose or spread out part*, סֶרַח *serach*.
Exod 26. 12 remnant that remaineth of the curtains
6. *Escape, escaping*, פְּלֵיטָה *peletah*.
Eze. 14. 22 therein shall be left a remnant that shall
7. *Remaining one, remnant*, שָׂרִיד *sarid*.
Isa. 1. 9 had left unto us a very small remnant, we
Joel 2. 32 in the remnant whom the LORD shall call
8. *To be left, to remain*, שָׁאַר *shaar*, 2.
2 Ki. 19. 30 remnant that is escaped of the house of
2 Ch. 30. 6 he will return to the remnant of you that
Neh. 1. 3 remnant that are left of the captivity th.
Isa. 37. 31 remnant that is escaped of the house of
9. *Remnant, rest*, שְׁאָר *shear*.
Ezra 3. 8 remnant of their brethren the priests and
Isa. 10. 20 remnant of Israel, and such as are escaped
10. 21 remnant shall return, (even) the remnant
10. 22 remnant of them shall return: the consu.
11. 11 second time to recover the remnant of his
11. 16 there shall be an highway for the remnant
14. 22 cut off from Babylon the name, and rem.
16. 14 the remnant (shall be) very small (and)
17. 3 kingdom from Damascus, and the remn.
Zeph. 1. 4 will cut off the remnant of Baal from this
10. *Remnant, residue*, שְׁאֵרִית *sheerith*.
2 Ki. 19. 4 wherefore lift up (thy) prayer for the re.
19. 31 out of Jerusalem shall go forth a remnant
21. 14 forsake the remnant of mine inheritance
2 Ch. 34. 9 of all the remnant of Israel, and of all J.
Ezra 9. 14 (there should be) no remnant nor escaping?
Isa. 14. 30 with famine, and he shall slay thy remnant
15. 9 lions..upon the remnant of the land
37. 4 wherefore lift up (thy) prayer for the re.
37. 32 out of Jerusalem shall go forth a remnant
46. 3 all the remnant of the house of Israel, w.
Jer. 6. 9 They shall throughly glean the remnant
11. 23 there shall be no remnant of them: for I
23. 3 I will gather the remnant of my flock out
25. 20 and Ekron, and the remnant of Ashdod
31. 7 save thy people, the remnant of Israel
40. 11 king of Babylon had left a remnant of J.
40. 15 be scattered, and the remnant in Judah
41. 16 all the remnant of the people whom he
42. 2 pray for us..(even) for all this remnant
42. 15 hear the word of the LORD, ye remnant
42. 19 O ye remnant of Judah; Go ye not into
43. 5 took all the remnant of Judah, that were
44. 12 will take the remnant of Judah, that have
44. 14 So that none of the remnant of Judah, w.
44. 28 all the remnant of Judah, that are gone
47. 4 the remnant of the country of Caphtor
47. 5 Ashkelon is cut off (with) the remnant of
Eze. 5. 10 whole remnant of thee will I scatter into
11. 13 wilt thou make a full end of the remnant
25. 16 and destroy the remnant of the sea coast
Amos 1. 8 remnant of the Philistines shall perish
5. 15 will be gracious unto the remnant of Jo.
9. 12 That they may possess the remnant of E.
Mic. 2. 12 I will surely gather the remnant of Israel
4. 7 I will make her that halted a remnant, and
5. 7 remnant of Jacob shall be in the midst of
5. 8 remnant of Jacob shall be among the G.
7. 18 passeth by the transgression of the remn.
Zeph. 2. 7 coast shall be for the remnant of the ho.
3. 13 The remnant of Israel shall not do iniquity
Hag. 1. 12 with all the remnant of the people, obeyed
1. 14 spirit of all the remnant of the people; and
Zech. 8. 6 marvellous in the eyes of the remnant of
8. 12 I will cause the remnant of this people to
11. *Remnant* (?), שֵׁרוּת *sheruth* [V.L. שָׂרָה *sharah*, 3].
Jer. 15. 11 Verily it shall be well with thy remnant
12. *What is left fully*, κατάλειμμα *kataleimma*.
Rom. 9. 27 sand of the sea, [a remnant] shall be sav.
13. *What is left*, λεῖμμα *leimma*.
Rom 11. 5 there is a remnant according to the elec.
14. *Remaining, left*, λοιπός *loipos*.
Matt 22. 6 remnant took his servants, and entreated
Rev. 11. 13 remnant were affrighted, and gave glory
12. 17 went to make war with the remnant of her
19. 21 remnant were slain with the sword of him

REMNANT, to leave a —
To let or cause to be over, יָתַר *yathar*, 5.
Eze. 6. 8 Yet will I leave a remnant, that ye may

REMOVE (away), to —
1. *To remove*, גָּלָה *galah*.
Eze. 12. 3 remove by day..thou shalt remove from
2. *To cause to remove*, גָּלָה *galah*, 5.
2 Ki. 17. 26 nations which thou hast removed, and
1 Ch. 8. 6 and they removed them to Manahath
8. 7 he removed them, and begat Uzza and A.
3. *To roll*, גָּלַל *galal*.
Psa. 119. 22 Remove from me reproach and contempt
4. *To remove*, מוּשׁ *mush*.
Zech. 3. 9 remove the iniquity of that land in one d.
14. 4 half of the mountain shall remove toward
5. *To (cause to) remove*, מוּשׁ *mush*, 5.
Isa. 46. 7 from his place shall he not remove: yea
Mic. 2. 3 from which ye shall not remove your ne.
2. 4 how hath he removed (it) from me! turn.
6. *To move*, נוּד *nud*.
Jer. 4. 1 wilt put away..then shalt thou not rem.
50. 3 they shall remove, they shall depart, both
50. 8 Remove out of the midst of Babylon, and
7. *To cause to move*, נוּד *nud*, 5.
Psa. 36. 11 let not the hand of the wicked remove me
8. *To move, shake*, נוּעַ *nua*.
Exod 20. 18 when the people saw (it), they removed
9. *To remove*, נָסַג *nasag*, 5.
Deut 19. 14 Thou shalt not remove thy neighbour's
27. 17 Cursed (be) he that removeth his neighb.
Prov 22. 28 Remove not the ancient landmark, which
23. 10 Remove not the old landmark; and enter
Hos. 5. 10 princes..were like them that remove the
10. *To remove, journey*, נָסַע *nasa*.
Exod 14. 19 removed and went behind them; and the
Num 12. 16 afterward the people removed from Haz.
21. 12, 13 From thence they removed, and pitc.
33. 5 children of Israel removed from Rameses
33. 7, 9, 10, 11, 14, 16, 21 And they removed from
[So in v. 24, 25, 26, 28, 32, 34, 36, 37, 46, 47.]
Josh. 3. 1 Joshua rose early..and they removed from
3. 3 then ye shall remove from your place, and
3. 14 when the people removed from their tents
11. *To cause to remove or journey*, נָסַע *nasa*, 5.
Job 19. 10 mine hope hath he removed like a tree
Eccl. 10. 9 Whoso removeth stones shall be hurt th.
12. *To cause to reach, attain, overtake*, נָשַׂג *nasag*, 5.
Job 24. 2 (Some) remove the landmarks: they vi.
13. *To be, go, turn or bring round about*, סָבַב *sabab*, 2.
Num 36. 7 remove from tribe to tribe; for every one
36. 9 Neither shall the inheritance remove from
14. *To turn or bring round about*, סָבַב *sabab*, 5.
2 Sa. 20. 12 removed Amasa out of the highway into
15. *To cause to turn aside*, סוּר *sur*, 5.
Gen. 8. 13 removed the covering of the ark, and lo.
30. 35 removed that day the he goats that were
48. 17 to remove it from Ephraim's head unto M.
Exod. 8. 31 removed the swarm (of flies) from Pharaoh
Judg. 9. 29 then would I remove Abimelech. And he
1 Sa. 18. 13 Therefore Saul removed him from him, and
2 Sa. 6. 10 So David would not remove the ark of the
1 Ki. 15. 12 removed all the idols that his fathers had
15. 13 even her he removed from (being) queen
2 Ki. 16. 17 removed the laver from off them; and t.
17. 18 removed them out of his sight: there was
17. 23 Until the LORD removed Israel out of his
18. 4 removed the high places, and brake the
23. 27 I will remove..as I have removed Israel
24. 3 to remove (them) out of his sight, for the
2 Ch. 15. 16 removed her from (being) queen, because
33. 8 Neither will I any more remove the foot
35. 12 removed the burnt offerings, that they
Job 12. 20 He removeth away the speech of the tru.
27. 5 till I die I will not remove mine integrity
Psa. 39. 10 Remove thy stroke away from me: I am
81. 6 I removed his shoulder from the burden
119. 29 Remove from me the way of lying; and
Prov. 4. 27 Turn not..remove thy foot from evil
Eccl. 11. 10 Therefore remove sorrow from thy heart
Isa. 10. 13 I have removed the bounds of the people
Jer. 32. 31 that I should remove it from before my
Eze. 21. 26 Remove the diadem, and take off the cr.
45. 9 remove violence and spoil, and execute
16. *To cause to move, remove, persuade*, סוּת *suth*, 5.
Job 36. 16 Even so would he have removed thee out
17. *To cause to pass over*, עָבַר *abar*, 5.
Gen. 47. 21 removed them to cities from (one) end of
18. *To cause to pass on or by*, עָדָה *adah*, 5.
Dan. 2. 21 he removeth kings, and setteth up kings
19. *To remove, transcribe, leave off*, עָתַק *athaq*, 5.
Gen. 12. 8 he removed from thence unto a mountain
26. 22 removed from thence, and digged another
Job 9. 5 Which removeth the mountains, and they
20. *To shake, tremble*, רָעַשׁ *raash*.
Isa. 13. 13 earth shall remove out of her place, in the
21. *To move, shake*, κινέω *kineō*.
Rev. 2. 5 will remove thy candlestick out of his pl.
22. *To set over or beyond*, μεθίστημι *methistēmi*.
Acts 13. 22 when he had removed him, he raised up
1 Co 13. 2 that I could remove mountains, and have
23. *To go up over or beyond*, μεταβαίνω *metabainō*.
Matt 17. 20 Remove hence..and it shall remove: and
24. *To put over or beyond*, μετατίθημι *metatithēmi*.
Gal. 1. 6 I marvel that ye are so soon removed fr.
25. *To bear away*, παραφέρω *parapherō*.
Luke 22. 42 if thou be willing, remove this cup from

REMOVE a tent, to —
To move a tent, אָהַל *ahal*.
Gen. 13. 18 removed (his) tent, and came and dwelt

REMOVE far (away or off), to —
1. *To cast off*, זָנַח *zanach*.
Lam. 3. 17 thou hast removed my soul far off from
2. *To put far off*, רָחַק *rachaq*, 3.
Isa. 6. 12 LORD have removed men far away, and
26. 15 thou hast removed (it) far (unto) all the
29. 13 but have removed their heart far from
3. *To put far off*, רָחַק *rachaq*, 5.
Psa. 103. 12 (so) far hath he removed our transgressi.
Prov. 5. 8 Remove thy way far from her, and come
30. 8 Remove far from me vanity and lies; give
Jer. 27. 10 remove you far from your land; and that
Joel 2. 20 But I will remove far off from you the n.
3. 6 that ye might remove them far from their

REMOVE into, to —
To make a change of dwelling, μετοικίζω *metoikizō*.
Acts 7. 4 removed him into this land, wherein ye

REMOVED, to be —
1. *To be removed*, גָּלָה *galah*, 2.
Isa. 38. 12 is removed from me as a shepherd's tent
2. *Removal* (? *ill-treatment*), זַעֲוָה *zaavah* [In Jer. V.L. זְוָעָה]. Deut. 28. 25.
Jer. 15. 4 cause them to be removed into all kingd.
24. 9 will deliver them to be removed into all
29. 18 will deliver them to be removed to all the
34. 17 I will make you to be removed into all the
Eze. 23. 46 and will give them to be removed and sp.
3. *To remove*, יָגָה *yagah*, 5.
2 Sa. 20. 13 When he was removed out of the highway
4. *To be covered or removed*, כָּנַף *kanaph*, 2.
Isa. 30. 20 yet shall not thy teachers be removed into
5. *To move, slip, fail*, מוֹט *mot*, 1, 5.
Psa. 104. 5 the earth, (that) it should not be removed
125. 1 cannot be removed, (but) abideth for ever
Prov. 10. 30 The righteous shall never be removed: but
Isa. 54. 10 shall depart, and the hills be removed; but
54. 10 shall the covenant of my peace be remo.
6. *To exchange, change*, מוּר *mur*, 5.
Psa. 46. 2 though the earth be removed, and though
7. *To remove, depart*, מוּשׁ *mush*.
Isa. 22. 25 shall the nail that is fastened..be removed
8. *To move, wander or flee away*, נָדַד *nadad*.
Isa. 10. 31 Madmenah is removed; the inhabitants
9. *To move or bemoan self*, נוּד *nud*, 7a.
Isa. 24. 20 shall be removed like a cottage; and the
10. *Separation, impurity*, נִדָּה *niddah*.
Eze. 7. 19 gold shall be removed: their silver and
11. *A removal*, נִידָה *nidah*.
Lam. 1. 8 therefore she is removed: all that honou.
12. *To pluck up*, נָסַע *nasa*.
Isa. 33. 20 not one of the stakes..shall ever be rem.
13. *To turn aside*, סוּר *sur*.
1 Sa. 6. 3 known to you why his hand is not remo.
Amos 6. 7 and the banquet..shall be removed
14. *To be removed, old*, עָתַק *athaq*.
Job 14. 18 and the rock is removed out of his place
18. 4 shall the rock be removed out of his place
15. *To lift up, carry away*, αἴρω *airō*.
Matt 21. 21 say unto this mountain, Be thou removed
Mark 11. 23 say unto this mountain, Be thou removed

REMOVED woman —
Separation, impurity, נִדָּה *niddah*.
Eze. 36. 17 as the uncleanness of a removed woman

REMOVING (to and fro) —
1. *Removal, exile*, גּוֹלָה *golah*.
Eze. 12. 3 prepare thee stuff for removing, and
12. 4 bring forth..as stuff for removing: and
2. *To turn aside*, סוּר *sur*.
Isa. 49. 21 a captive, and removing to and fro? and
3. *To cause to turn aside*, סוּר *sur*, 5.
Gen. 30. 32 removing from thence all the speckled
4. *A putting over*, μετάθεσις *metathesis*.
Heb. 12. 27 signifieth the removing of those things

REM'-PHAN, Ῥεμφάν.
An idol worshipped by Israel in the wilderness; perhaps the same as *Chiun* (Amos 5. 26) or *Saturn*.
Acts 7. 43 Yea, ye took up..the star of your god R.

REND (off or in pieces), be rent, to —
1. *To cleave, rend*, בָּקַע *baqa*.
Eze. 29. 7 didst break, and rend all their shoulder
2. *To cleave, rend*, בָּקַע *baqa*, 3.
Eze. 13. 11 shall fall; and a stormy wind shall rend
13. 13 I will even rend (it) with a stormy wind
3. *To rend*, פָּרַם *param*.
Lev. 10. 6 Uncover not your heads, neither rend your
21. 10 shall not uncover his head, nor rend his

4. *To break off,* פָּרַק *paraq.*
Psa. 7. 2 Lest he tear my soul like a lion, rending

5. *To break off,* פָּרַק *paraq,* 3.
1 Ki.19. 11 great and strong wind rent the mountains

6. *To rend away, cut out,* קָרַע *qara.*
Gen. 37. 29 Joseph (was) not in the pit; and he rent
37. 34 Jacob rent his clothes, and put sackcloth
44. 13 Then they rent their clothes, and laded
Lev. 13. 56 then he shall rend it out of the garment
Num14. 6 Joshua the son of Nun, and Caleb..rent
Josh. 7. 6 Joshua rent his clothes, and fell to the e.
Judg11. 35 rent his clothes, and said, Alas, my daugh.
1 Sa. 15. 28 The LORD hath rent the kingdom of Israel
28. 17 for the LORD hath rent the kingdom out
2 Sa. 1. 11 David took hold on his clothes, and rent
3. 31 Rend your clothes, and gird you with sa.
13. 19 rent her garment of divers colours that
1 Ki.11. 11 I will surely rend the kingdom from thee
11. 12 I will rend it out of the hand of thy son
11. 13 I will not rend away all the kingdom; (but)
11. 30 caught the new garment..and rent it (in)
11. 31 will rend the kingdom out of the hand of
14. 8 rent the kingdom away from the house of
21. 27 rent his clothes, and put sackcloth upon
2 Ki. 2. 12 he took hold..and rent them in two pie
5. 7 rent his clothes, and said, (Am) I God, to
5. 8 heard that the king of Israel had rent his
5. 8 Wherefore hast thou rent thy clothes? let
6. 30 rent his clothes; and he passed by upon
11. 14 Athaliah rent her clothes, and cried, Tr.
17. 21 For he rent Israel from the house of Dav.
19. 1 rent his clothes, and covered himself with
22. 11 when the king had heard..he rent his cl.
22. 19 hast rent thy clothes, and wept before me
2 Ch.23. 13 Athaliah rent her clothes, and said, Tre.
34. 19 heard the words of the law, that he rent
34. 27 didst rend thy clothes, and weep before
Ezra 9. 3 rent my garment and my mantle, and pl.
9. 5 having rent my garment and my mantle
Esth. 4. 1 Mordecai rent his clothes, and put on sa.
Job 1. 20 Then Job arose, and rent his mantle, and
2. 12 rent every one his mantle, and sprinkled
Eccl. 3. 7 A time to rend, and a time to sew; a time
Isa. 37. 1 rent his clothes, and covered himself with
64. 1 Oh that thou wouldest rend the heavens
Jer. 4. 30 though thou rentest thy face with paint.
36. 24 Yet they were not afraid, nor rent their g.
Hos. 13. 8 will rend the caul of their heart, and there
Joel 2. 13 rend your heart, and not your garments

7. *To cleave, rend,* שָׁסַע *shasa,* 3.
Judg14. 6 he rent him as he would have rent a kid

8. *To burst through, rend thoroughly,* διαῤῥήσσω.
Matt26. 65 Then the high priest rent his clothes, say.
Mark14. 63 Then the high priest rent his clothes, and
Acts 14. 14 rent their clothes, and ran in among the

9. *To rend all around,* περιῤῥήγνυμι *perirrhēgnumi.*
Acts 16. 22 and the magistrates rent off their clothes

10. *To rend, burst,* ῥήγνυμι *rhēgnumi.*
Matt. 7. 6 trample..and turn again and rend you

11 *To tear, lacerate,* σπαράσσω *sparassō.*
Mark 9. 26 cried, and rent him sore, and came out of

12. *To rend, tear,* σχίζω *schizō.*
Matt27. 51 veil of the temple was rent in twain from
27. 51 the earth did quake, and the rocks rent
Mark15. 38 veil of the temple was rent in twain from
Luke23. 45 the veil of the temple was rent in the m.
John19. 24 Let us not rend it, but cast lots for it, w.

RENDER (again), to —

1. *To give,* נָתַן *nathan.*
2 Ch. 6. 30 render unto every man according unto all

2. *To cause to turn back,* שׁוּב *shub,* 5.
Num 18. 9 which they shall render unto me, (shall be)
Deut32. 41 I will render vengeance to mine enemies
32. 43 will render vengeance to his adversaries
Judg.9. 56 Thus God rendered the wickedness of A.
9. 57 all the evil..did God render upon their
1 Sa.26. 23 render to every man his righteousness
2 Ki. 3. 4 rendered unto the king of Israel an hund.
2 Ch.32. 25 Hezekiah rendered not again according to
Job 33. 26 he will render unto man his righteousness
Psa. 28. 4 of their hands; render to them their des.
79. 12 render unto our neighbours sevenfold into
94. 2 Lift up thyself..render a reward to the
116. 12 What shall I render unto the LORD (for)
Prov24. 12 shall (not) he render to (every) man acco.
24. 29 will render to the man according to his
26. 16 than seven men that can render a reason
Isa. 66. 15 render his anger with fury, and his rebu.
Lam. 3. 64 Render unto them a recompence, O LORD
Zech. 9. 12 even to day do I declare (that) I will ren.

3. *To finish, complete,* שָׁלַם *shalam,* 3.
Job 34. 11 For the work of a man shall he render un.
Psa. 38. 20 They also that render evil for good are
56. 12 vows (are) upon me, O God: I will rend.
62. 12 for thou renderest to every man according
Isa. 66. 6 voice of the LORD that rendereth recom.
Jer. 51. 6 he will render unto her a recompence
51. 24 I will render unto Babylon and to all the
Hos. 14. 2 so will we render the calves of our lips
Joel 3. 4 will ye render me a recompence? and if

4. *To give back in return,* ἀνταποδίδωμι *antapodid.*
1 Th. 3. 9 what thanks can we render to God again

5. *To give back,* ἀποδίδωμι *apodidōmi.*
Matt21. 41 shall render him the fruits in their seasons
Matt22. 21 Render therefore unto Cesar the things
Mark12. 17 Render to Cesar the things that are Ces.
Luke20. 25 Render therefore unto Cesar the things
Rom. 2. 6 Who will render to every man according
13. 7 Render therefore to all their dues: tribu.
1 Co. 7. 3 render unto the wife due benevolence: and
1 Th. 5. 15 See that none render evil for evil unto an.
1 Pe. 3. 9 Not rendering evil for evil, or railing for

RENDERED, to be —

To (cause to) turn back, שׁוּב *shub,* 5 [V.L. 1].
Prov12. 14 recompence..shall be rendered unto him

RENEW, to —

1. *To renew, repair,* חָדַשׁ *chadash,* 3.
1 Sa.11. 14 let us go to Gilgal, and renew the kingdom
2 Ch.15. 8 renewed the altar of the LORD that (was)
Job 10. 17 Thou renewest thy witnesses against me
Psa. 51. 10 Create in me a clean heart..and renew a
104. 30 and thou renewest the face of the earth
Lam. 5. 21 we shall be turned; renew our days as of

2. *To change, pass on,* חָלַף *chalaph,* 5.
Isa. 40. 31 they that wait upon the LORD shall renew
41. 1 let the people renew (their) strength: let

3. *To make new again,* ἀνακαινίζω *anakainizō.*
Heb. 6. 6 If they shall fall away, to renew them a.

RENEWED, to be

1. *To renew self, be renewed,* חָדַשׁ *chadash,* 7.
Psa.103. 5 so that) thy youth is renewed like the ea.

2. *To change, pass on, renew,* חָלַף *chalaph,* 5.
Job 29. 20 and my bow was renewed in my hand

3. *To make new again,* ἀνακαινόω *anakainoō.*
2 Co. 4. 16 yet the inward (man) is renewed day by
Col. 3. 10 which is renewed in knowledge after the

4. *To be renewed again,* ἀνανεόομαι *ananeoomai.*
Eph. 4. 23 And be renewed in the spirit of your mind

RENEWING —

A making new again, ἀνακαίνωσις *anakainōsis.*
Rom12. 2 but be ye transformed by the renewing of
Titus 3. 5 regeneration, and renewing of the Holy

RENOUNCE, to —

To speak off or away, ἀπεῖπον *apeipon.*
2 Co. 4. 2 have renounced the hidden things of dis.

RENOWN, renowned —

1. *To be shining, praised,* הָלַל *halal,* 4.
Eze. 26. 17 renowned city, which wast strong in the

2. *To call,* קָרָא *qara.*
Eze. 23. 23 great lords and renowned, all of them ri.

3. *To be called,* קָרָא *qara,* 2.
Isa. 14. 20 seed of evil doers shall never be renowned

4. *To call,* קָרָא *qara* (pass. partic.) [V.L. קריא].
Num. 1. 16 These (were) the renowned of the congr.

5. *A name,* שֵׁם *shem.*
Gen. 6. 4 men which (were) of old, men of renown
Num16. 2 famous in the congregation, men of ren.
Eze. 16. 14 thy renown went forth among the heathen
16. 15 playedst the harlot because of thy renown
34. 29 I will raise up for them a plant of renown
39. 13 it shall be to them a renown, the day that
Dan. 9. 15 and hast gotten thee renown, as at this

RENT —

1. *A rope or rent thing,* נִקְפָּה *niqpah.*
Isa. 3. 24 instead of a girdle a rent; and instead of

2. *To rend,* פָּרַם *param.*
Lev. 13. 45 his clothes shall be rent, and his head b.

3. *To rend away, cut out,* קָרַע *qara.*
1 Sa. 4. 12 his clothes rent, and with earth upon his
2 Sa. 1. 2 his clothes rent, and earth upon his head
13. 31 servants stood by with their clothes rent
15. 32 came to meet him with his coat rent, and
2 Ki. 18. 37 came..to Hezekiah, with (their) clothes r.
Isa. 36. 22 came..to Hezekiah with (their) clothes r.
Jer. 41. 5 their beards shaven, and their clothes r.

4. *A rent, dissension,* σχίσμα *schisma.*
Matt. 9. 16 taketh from the garment, and the rent is
Mark 2. 21 taketh away from the old, and the rent is

RENT (asunder, in pieces), to be —

1. *To be cleft,* בָּקַע *baqa,* 2.
1 Ki. 1. 40 that the earth rent with the sound of them
Job 26. 8 the waters..the cloud is not rent under
Eze. 30. 16 and No shall be rent asunder, and Noph

2. *To be cleft,* בָּקַע *baqa,* 4.
Josh. 9. 4 wine bottles, old, and rent, and bound up

3. *To cleave self, be cleft,* בָּקַע *baqa,* 7.
Josh. 9. 13 behold, they be rent: and these our garm.

4. *To be torn,* טָרַף *taraph,* 4.
Gen. 37. 33 Joseph is without doubt rent in pieces

5. *To be rent away,* קָרַע *qara,* 2.
Exod 28. 32 shall have a binding..that it be not rent
39. 23 a band round..that it should not rend
1 Sa. 15. 27 he laid hold upon the skirt..and it rent
1 Ki.13. 3 the altar shall be rent, and the ashes that
13. 5 The altar also was rent, and the ashes p.

RENT, to make a —

To rend, σχίζω *schizō.*
Luke 5. 36 the new maketh a rent, and the piece that

REPAIR, to —

1. *To repair a breach,* בָּדַק *badaq.*
2 Ch.34. 10 wrought..to repair and amend the house

2. *To build,* בָּנָה *banah.*
Judg21. 23 and repaired the cities, and dwelt in them
2 Ch. 33. 16 he repaired the altar of the LORD, and s.

3. *To renew,* חָדַשׁ *chadash,* 3.
2 Ch.24. 4 was minded to repair the house of the L.
24. 12 hired masons and carpenters to repair the
Isa. 61. 4 they shall repair the waste cities, the de

4. *To strengthen, harden, fix,* חָזַק *chazaq,* 3.
2 Ki. 12. 5 let them repair the breaches of the house
12. 6 the priests had not repaired the breaches
12. 7 Why repair ye not the breaches of the h.
12. 8 neither to repair the breaches of the ho.
12. 12 to repair the breaches of the house of the
12. 14 repaired therewith the house of the LORD
22. 5 give..to repair the breaches of the house
22. 6 timber and hewn stone to repair the ho.
2 Ch.24. 5 to repair the house of your God from year
29. 3 opened the doors..and repaired them
32. 5 repaired Millo (in) the city of David, and
34. 8 to repair the house of the LORD his God
Neh. 3. 19 next to him repaired Ezer the son of Jes.

5. *To strengthen,* חָזַק *chazaq,* 5.
Neh. 3. 4 next unto them repaired Meremoth the s.
3. 4 next unto them repaired Meshullam the
3. 4 next unto them repaired Zadok the son of
3. 5 next unto them the Tekoites repaired, but
3. 6 the old gate repaired Jehoiada the son of
3. 7 And next unto them repaired Melatiah
3. 8 Next unto him repaired Uzziel the son of
3. 8 Next unto him also repaired Hananiah the
3. 9 next unto them repaired Rephaiah the s.
3. 10 next unto them repaired Jedaiah the son
3. 10 next unto him repaired Hattush the son
3. 11 repaired the other piece, and the tower
3. 12 next unto him repaired Shallum the son
3. 13 The valley gate repaired Hanun, and the
3. 14 the dung gate repaired Malchiah the son
3. 15 the gate of the fountain repaired Shallum
3. 16 After him repaired Nehemiah the son of
3. 17 after him repaired the Levites, Rehum
3. 17 Next unto him repaired Hasbabiah, the
3. 18 After him repaired their brethren, Bavai
3. 20 Baruch the son of Zabbai earnestly repai.
3. 21 After him repaired Meremoth the son of
3. 22 after him repaired the priests, the men of
3. 23 After him repaired Benjamin and Hashub
3. 23 After him repaired Azariah the son of M.
3. 24 After him repaired Binnui the son of H.
3. 27 After them the Tekoites repaired another
3. 28 From above the horse gate repaired the
3. 29 After them repaired Zadok the son of Im.
3. 29 After him repaired also Shemaiah the son
3. 30 After him repaired Hananiah the son of
3. 30 After him repaired Meshullam the son of
3. 31 After him repaired Malchiah the goldsm.
3. 32 repaired the goldsmiths and the mercha.

6. *Strength, firm hold,* חֶזְקָה *chozqah.*
2 Ki. 12. 12 all that was laid out for the house to re.

7. *To keep living or alive,* חָיָה *chayah,* 3.
1 Ch.11. 8 built..and Joab repaired the rest of the

8. *To shut up or in,* סָגַר *sagar.*
1 Ki. 11. 27 repaired the breaches of the city of David

9. *To cause to stand still,* עָמַד *amad,* 5.
Ezra 9. 9 to repair the desolations thereof, and to

10. *To heal,* רָפָא *rapha,* 3.
1 Ki. 18. 30 and he repaired the altar of the LORD

REPAIRER, repairing —

1. *To wall or hedge,* גָּדַר *gadar.*
Isa. 58. 12 The repairer of the breach, The restorer

2. *Foundation,* יְסוֹד *yesod.*
2 Ch.24. 27 the repairing of the house of God, behold

REPAY, be repayed, to —

1. *To finish, complete, repay,* שָׁלַם *shalam,* 3.
Deut. 7. 10 repayeth them that hate him to their face
7. 10 he will not be slack..he will repay him to
Job 21. 31 who shall repay him (what) he hath done
41. 11 Who hath prevented me, that I should r.
Prov 13. 21 but to the righteous good shall be repaid
Isa. 59. 18 he will repay..he will repay recompence

2. *To give back in return,* ἀνταποδίδωμι *antapodid.*
Rom 12. 19 Vengeance (is) mine; I will repay, saith

3. *To give back or away,* ἀποδίδωμι *apodidōmi.*
Luke 10. 35 more, when I come again, I will repay

4. *To pay away or back,* ἀποτίνω *apotinō.*
Phm. 19 I will repay (it): albeit I do not say to

REPEAT, to —

To do a thing twice, repeat, שָׁנָה *shanah.*
Prov 17. 9 but he that repeateth a matter separateth

REPENT (self), to —

1. *To be penitent, comforted, eased,* נָחַם *nacham,* 2.
Gen. 6. 6 it repented the LORD that he had made
6. 7 for it repenteth me that I have made th.
Exod13. 17 the people repent when they see war, and
32. 12 and repent of this evil against thy people
32. 14 the LORD repented of the evil which he
Judg. 2. 18 it repented the LORD because of their gr
21. 6 Israel repented them for Benjamin their
21. 15 And the people repented them for Benj

1 Sa. 15. 11 It repenteth me that I have set up Saul
15. 29 strength of Israel will not lie nor repent
15. 29 for he (is) not a man, that he should repe.
15. 35 the LORD repented that he had made Saul
2 Sa. 24. 16 the LORD repented him of the evil, and
1 Ch.21. 15 he repented him of the evil, and said to
Job 42. 6 Wherefore I abhor..and repent in dust
Psa. 90. 13 let it repent thee concerning thy servants
106. 45 repented according to the multitude of
110. 4 The LORD hath sworn, and will not repent
Jer. 4. 28 I have purposed (it), and will not repent
8. 6 no man repented him of his wickedness
18. 8 I will repent of the evil that I thought to
18. 10 I will repent of the good wherewith I said
20. 16 which the LORD overthrew, and repented
26. 3 that I may repent me of the evil which I
26. 13 the LORD will repent him of the evil that
26. 19 LORD repented him of the evil which he
31. 19 I repented; and after that I was instru.
42. 10 I repent me of the evil that I have done
Eze. 24. 14 neither will I repent: according to thy
Joel 2. 13 of great kindness, and repenteth him of
2. 14 (if) he will return and repent, and leave
Amos 7. 3 LORD repented for this: It shall not be
7. 6 LORD repented for this: This also shall not
Jon. 3. 9 God will turn and repent, and turn away
3. 10 God repented of the evil that he had said
4. 2 Knew that thou..repentest thee of the e.
Zech. 8. 14 provoked me to wrath..and I repented

2. *To comfort self, be penitent,* נָחַם *nacham,* 7.
Num 23. 19 neither the son of man, that he should r.
Deut 32. 36 repent himself for his servants, when he
Psa. 135. 14 he will repent himself concerning his se.

3. *To turn back,* שׁוּב *shub.*
1 Ki. 8. 47 repent, and make supplication unto thee
Eze. 14. 6 Repent, and turn..from your idols; and
18. 30 Repent, and turn..from all your transg.

4. *To be careful or concerned with,* μεταμέλομαι.
Matt 21. 29 said, I will not: but afterward he repen.
21. 32 repented not afterward, that ye might b.
27. 3 repented himself, and brought again the
2 Co. 7. 8 I do not repent, though I did repent
Heb. 7. 21 The Lord sware and will not repent, Thou

5. *To have another mind,* μετανοέω *metanoeō.*
Matt. 3. 2 Repent ye: for the kingdom of heaven is
4. 17 Repent: for the kingdom of heaven is at
11. 20 to upbraid..because they repented not
11. 21 they would have repented long ago in sa.
12. 41 they repented at the preaching of Jonas
Mark 1. 15 saying..repent ye, and believe the gospel
6. 12 And they..preached that men should re.
Luke 10. 13 they had a great while ago repented, sit.
11. 32 they repented at the preaching of Jonas
13. 3, 5 except ye repent, ye shall all likewise
15. 7, 10 joy..over one sinner that repenteth
16. 30 if one went unto them..they will repent
17. 3 rebuke him; and if he repent, forgive him
17. 4 turn again to thee, saying, I repent; thou
Acts 2. 38 Repent, and be baptized every one of you
3. 19 Repent ye therefore, and be converted, th.
8. 22 Repent therefore of this thy wickedness
17. 30 commandeth all men every where to repent
26. 20 they should repent and turn to God, and
2 Co. 12. 21 have not repented of the uncleanness, and
Rev. 2. 5 repent, and do the first works; or else I
2. 5 remove thy candlestick..except thou re
2. 16 Repent; or else I will come unto thee q
2. 21 repent of her fornication; and she repen.
2. 22 I will cast..except they repent of their d.
3. 3 Remember..and hold fast, and repent
3. 19 chasten: be zealous therefore, and repent
9. 20 repented not of the works of their hands
9. 21 Neither repented they of their murders
16. 9 and they repented not to give him glory
16. 11 blasphemed..and repented not of their

REPENTANCE —

1. *Penitence, comfort,* נֹחַם *nocham.*
Hos. 13. 14 repentance shall be hid from mine eyes

2. *A change of mind,* μετάνοια *metanoia.*
Matt. 3. 8 Bring forth..fruits meet for repentance
3. 11 I..baptize you with water unto repentance
9. 13 come to call the..sinners [to repentance]
Mark 1. 4 baptism of repentance for the remission
2. 17 I came..to call..sinners [to repentance]
Luke 3. 3 baptism of repentance for the remission
3. 8 Bring forth..fruits worthy of repentance
5. 32 I came..to call..sinners to repentance
15. 7 just persons, which need no repentance
24. 47 repentance and remission of sins should
Acts 5. 31 give repentance to Israel, and forgiveness
11. 18 Then hath God..granted repentance unto
13. 24 the baptism of repentance to all the people
19. 4 baptized with the baptism of repentance
20. 21 repentance toward God, and faith toward
26. 20 turn..and do works meet for repentance
Rom. 2. 4 goodness of God leadeth thee to repenta.
2 Co. 7. 9 ye sorrowed to repentance: for ye were
7. 10 godly sorrow worketh repentance to sal.
2 Ti. 2. 25 peradventure will give them repentance
Heb. 6. 1 foundation of repentance from dead works
6. 6 to renew them again unto repentance
12. 17 he found no place of repentance, though
2 Pe. 3. 9 but that all should come to repentance

REPENTANCE (without), not to be repented of —
Not to be careful or concerned with, ἀμεταμέλητος.
Rom 11. 29 gifts and calling..(are) without repenta.
2 Co 7. 10 to salvation not to be repented of: but

REPENTING —

1. *To be penitent, comforted,* נָחַם *nacham,* 2.
Jer. 15. 6 destroy thee; I am weary with repenting

2. *Comforts, repentings,* נִחוּמִים *nichumim.*
Hos. 11. 8 How..my repentings are kindled together

REPETITIONS, to use vain —
To speak emptily, βαττολογέω *battologeō.*
Matt. 6. 7 when ye pray, use not vain repetitions, as

RE-PHA'-EL, רְפָאֵל *God is a healer.*
A Kohathite, son of Shemaiah the first born of Obed-edom, and a gatekeeper of the tabernacle. B.C. 1020.
1 Ch. 26. 7 The sons of Shemaiah; Othni, and R., and

RE'-PHAH, רֶפַח *healing, support.*
A grandson of Ephraim, through Beriah. B.C. 1680.
1 Ch. 7. 25 And R. (was) his son, also Resheph, and

RE-PHA-I'AH, רְפָיָה *Jah heals.*
1. A head of a family of the house of David. B.C. 500.
1 Ch. 3. 21 the sons of R., the sons of Arnan, the sons
2. A captain of Simeon when they smote the Amalekites. B.C. 715.
1 Ch. 4. 42 Neariah, and R., and Uzziel, the sons of I.
3. A son of Tola, son of Issachar. B.C. 1400.
1 Ch. 7. 2 And the sons of Tola; Uzzi, and R., and
4. A Benjamite called in 1 Ch. 8. 37 *Rapha* B.C. 900.
1 Ch. 9. 43 R. his son, Eleasah his son, Azel his son
5. One who helped to repair the wall of Jerusalem after Nehemiah came from Shushan. B.C. 445.
Neh. 3. 9 And next unto them repaired R. the son

RE-PHA'-IM(S), רְפָאִים *strong.*
1. A race dwelling around the S. of Jerusalem, and eastward beyond Jordan, in Bashan, Ammon and Moab, in Ashteroth Karnaim and Shaveh Kiriathaim; variously called Zamzummim, Zuzim, and Emim; also Anakim.
Gen. 14. 5 the kings..smote the R. in Ashteroth K.
15. 20 the Hittites, and the Perizzites, and the R.
2. A valley S.W. of Jerusalem, and N. of Bethlehem, now called *el-Bukaa.* This was the boundary between Judah and Benjamin, Josh. 15. 8.
2 Sa. 5. 18 Philistines..spread themselves in the..R.
5. 22 Philistines..spread themselves in the..R.
23. 13 the Philistines pitched in the valley of R.
1 Ch. 11. 15 Philistines encamped in the valley of R.
14. 9 Philistines..spread themselves in the..R.
Isa. 17. 5 he that gathereth ears in the valley of R.

RE-PHI'-DIM, רְפִידִים *plains.*
A station of Israel where, after leaving Alush, they fought with Amalek; near Horeb, between the wilderness of Sin and of Sinai, here they murmured for water, and Moses struck a rock in Horeb, and supplied their need.
Exod 17. 1 all..Israel journeyed..and pitched in R.
17. 8 came Amalek, and fought with Isr. in R.
19. 2 For they were departed from R., and were
Num 33. 14 they removed from Alush..encamped at R.
33. 15 And they departed from R., and pitched

REPLENISH, to —

1. *To fill, be full,* מָלֵא *male.*
Gen. 1. 28 Be fruitful..and replenish the earth, and
9. 1 Be fruitful, and multiply, and replenish

2. *To fill, make full,* מָלֵא *male,* 3.
Isa. 23. 2 thou whom the merchants..have replen.
Jer. 31. 25 I have replenished every sorrowful soul

REPLENISHED, to be —

1. *To fill, be full,* מָלֵא *male.*
Isa. 2. 6 because they be replenished from the east

2. *To be filled,* מָלֵא *male,* 2.
Eze. 26. 2 I shall be replenished..she is laid waste
27. 25 and thou wast replenished, and made v.

REPLY against, to —
To judge back in return, ἀνταποκρίνομαι *antapok.*
Rom. 9. 20 but..who art thou that repliest against

REPORT —

1. *Word,* דָּבָר *dabar.*
1 Ki. 10. 6 It was a true report that I heard in mine
2 Ch. 9. 5 (It was) a true report which I heard in

2. *Name,* שֵׁם *shem.*
Neh. 6. 13 they might have (matter) for an evil rep.

3. *What is heard,* שְׁמוּעָה *shemuah.*
1 Sa. 2. 24 (it is) no good report that I hear: ye make
Prov 15. 30 (and) a good report maketh the bones fat
Isa. 28. 19 a vexation only (to) understand the rep.
53. 1 Who hath believed our report? and to w.

4. *Hearing, report,* שֵׁמַע *shema.*
Exod 23. 1 Thou shalt not raise a false report: put
Deut. 2. 25 who shall hear report of thee, and shall
Isa. 23. 5 As at the report concerning Egypt, (so)
23. 5 shall they be sorely pained at the report
Jer. 50. 43 The king of Babylon hath heard the rep.

5. *Hearing, a rumour,* ἀκοή *akoē.*
John 12. 38 who hath believed our report? and to w.
Rom. 10. 16 saith, Lord, who hath believed our report?

6. *Testimony, witness,* μαρτυρία *marturia.*
1 Ti. 3. 7 he must have a good report of them which

REPORT, (evil) —
A bad report, δυσφημία *dusphēmia.*
2 Co. 6. 8 By honour and dishonour by evil report

REPORT (to have or obtain), good or honest —

1. *A good report,* εὐφημία *euphēmia.*
2 Co. 6. 8 By honour and dishonour, by..good rep.

2. *Well reported, sounding well,* εὔφημος *euphēmos*
Phil. 4. 8 whatsoever things (are) of good report; if

3. *To testify, bear witness,* μαρτυρέω *martureō.*
Acts 6. 3 seven men of honest report, full of the H.
10. 22 of good report among all the nation of the
22. 12 having a good report of all the Jews which
Heb. 11. 2 For by it the elders obtained a good repo.
11. 39 having obtained a good report through f.
3 John 12 Demetrius hath good report of all..and of

REPORT, to —

1. *To say,* אָמַר *amar.*
Neh. 6. 19 they reported his good deeds before me

2. *To bring forward, tell, declare,* נָגַד *nagad,* 5.
Jer. 20. 10 Report, (say they), and we will report it

3. *To tell or announce again,* ἀναγγέλλω *anaggellō.*
1 Pe. 1. 12 the things which are now reported unto

4. *To tell off or away,* ἀπαγγέλλω *apaggellō.*
Acts 4. 23 reported all that the chief priests and el.
1 Co. 14. 25 and report that God is in you of a truth

REPORTED, to be slanderously —
To speak injuriously, βλασφημέω *blasphēmeō.*
Rom. 3. 8 as we be slanderously reported, and as

REPORTED, to be —

1. *To say,* אָמַר *amar.*
Esth. 1. 17 they shall despise..when it shall be rep.

2. *To be heard,* שָׁמַע *shamea,* 2.
Neh. 6. 6 It is reported among the heathen, and G.
6. 7 and now shall it be reported to the king

3. *To hear, hearken,* ἀκούω *akouō.*
1 Co. 5. 1 It is reported commonly (that there is) fo.

REPORTED of, to be well —
To testify, bear witness, μαρτυρέω *martureō.*
Acts 16. 2 Which was well reported of by the bret.
1 Ti. 5. 10 Well reported of for good works; if she

REPROACH —

1. *Reviling,* גִּדּוּף *gidduph.*
Isa. 43. 28 given Jacob to the curse, and Israel to re.

2. *Disgrace, shame,* חֶסֶד *chesed.*
Prov. 14. 34 exalteth a nation: but sin (is) a reproach

3. *To reproach,* חָרַף *charaph,* 3.
Psa. 57. 3 save me (from) the reproach of him that

4. *Reproach,* חֶרְפָּה *cherpah.*
Gen. 30. 23 and said, God hath taken away my repro.
34. 14 We cannot..for that (were) a reproach un.
Josh. 5. 9 This day have I rolled away the reproach
1 Sa. 11. 2 and lay it (for) a reproach upon all Israel
17. 26 and taketh away the reproach from Israel
25. 39 that hath pleaded the cause of my repro.
Neh. 1. 3 remnant..(are) in great affliction and re
2. 17 let us build..that we be no more a rep.
4. 4 turn their reproach upon their own head
5. 9 the reproach of the heathen our enemies
Job 19. 5 and plead against me my reproach
Psa. 15. 3 taketh up a reproach against his neighb.
22. 6 a reproach of men..despised of the peop.
31. 11 I was a reproach among all mine enemies
39. 8 make me not the reproach of the foolish
44. 13 Thou makest us a reproach to our neigh.
69. 7 for thy sake I have borne reproach; sha.
69. 9 the reproaches of them that reproached
69. 10 soul with fasting, that was to my reproach
69. 19 Thou hast known my reproach, and my
69. 20 Reproach hath broken my heart, and I
71. 13 let them be covered (with) reproach and
78. 66 And..he put them to a perpetual reproach
79. 4 We are become a reproach to our neighb.
79. 12 render..sevenfold into..bosom their re
89. 41 All..spoil him: he is a reproach to his
89. 50 Remember, Lord, the reproach of thy se.
109. 25 I became also a reproach unto them: (wh.)
119. 22 Remove from me reproach and contempt
119. 39 Turn away my reproach which I fear; for
Prov. 6. 33 and his reproach shall not be wiped away
18. 3 (then) cometh also..with ignominy repr.
Isa. 4. 1 called by thy name, to take away our re.
30. 5 nor profit, but a shame, and also a repr.
51. 7 fear ye not the reproach of men, neither
54. 4 and shalt not remember the reproach of
Jer. 6. 10 word of the LORD is unto them a reproach
20. 8 the word of the LORD was made a reproach
23. 40 I will bring an everlasting reproach upon
24. 9 a reproach and a proverb, a taunt and a
29. 18 a reproach, among all the nations whither
31. 19 because I did bear the reproach of my y.
42. 18 astonishment, and a curse, and a reproach
44. 8 a reproach among all the nations of the
44. 12 astonishment, and a curse, and a reproach
49. 13 a desolation, a reproach, a waste, and a c.
51. 51 because we have heard reproach: shame
Lam. 3. 30 smiteth him: he is filled full with reproach
3. 61 Thou hast heard their reproach, O LORD
5. 1 O LORD..consider, and behold our repr.
Eze. 5. 14 I will make thee waste, and a reproach
5. 15 So it shall be a reproach and a taunt, an
16. 57 as at the time of (thy) reproach of the da.
21. 28 Thus saith the Lord..concerning their re.
22. 4 I made thee a reproach unto the heathen
36. 15 neither shalt thou bear the reproach of
36. 30 ye shall receive no more reproach of fam.

Dan. 9. 16 thy people (are become) a reproach to all
11. 18 shall cause the reproach offered by him
11 18 without his own reproach he shall cause
Hos. 12. 14 his reproach shall his Lord return unto
Joel 2. 17 give not thine heritage to reproach, that
2. 19 make you a reproach among the heathen
Mic. 6 16 ye shall bear the reproach of my people
Zeph. 2. 8 I have heard the reproach of Moab, and
3. 18 (to whom) the reproach of it (was) a bur.

5. *Blushing, shame,* כְּלִמָּה *kelimmah.*
Job 20. 3 I have heard the check of my reproach, and

6. *Lightness, confusion,* קָלוֹן *qalon.*
Prov 22. 10 Cast out the scorner, and..reproach shall

7. *Dishonour,* ἀτιμία *atimia.*
2 Co. 11. 21 I speak as concerning reproach, as though

8. *Reproach, insult,* ὀνειδισμός *oneidismos.*
Rom 15. 3 The reproaches of them that reproached
1 Ti 3 7 lest he fall into reproach and the snare
Heb 10. 33 made a gazing stock both by reproaches
11. 26 Esteeming the reproach of Christ greater
13. 13 Let us go forth..without..bearing his re.

9. *Reproach, disgrace,* ὄνειδος *oneidos.*
Luke 1. 25 to take away my reproach among men

10. *Contumely, insult,* ὕβρις *hubris.*
2 Co. 12. 10 in infirmities, in reproaches, in necessities

REPROACH, to (bring or suffer) —

1. *To revile,* גָּדַף *gadaph,* 3.
Num 15. 30 the same reproacheth the LORD; and that

2. *To make ashamed, confound,* חָפֵר *chapher,* 5.
Prov 19. 26 that causeth shame, and bringeth reproa

3. *To reproach,* חָרַף *charaph.*
Job 27 6 my heart shall not reproach (me) so long
Psa 69. 9 the reproaches of them that reproached
119 42 to answer him that reproacheth me: for
Prov 27. 11 that I may answer him that reproacheth

4. *To reproach,* חָרַף *charaph,* 3.
2 Ki. 19. 4 king..hath sent to reproach the living G.
19 22 Whom hast thou reproached and blasph.
19. 23 By thy messengers thou hast reproached
Neh. 6. 13 an evil report, that they might reproach
Psa. 42. 10 mine enemies reproach me; while they
44. 16 of him that reproacheth and blasphemeth
55. 12 (it was) not an enemy (that) reproached me
74. 10 how long shall the adversary reproach?
74. 18 Remember this..the enemy hath reproac.
79. 12 wherewith they have reproached thee, O
89. 51 Wherewith thine enemies have reproached
89. 51 they have reproached the footsteps of th
102 8 enemies reproach me all the day; and th.
Prov 14. 31 He that oppresseth the poor reproacheth
17. 5 Whoso mocketh the poor reproacheth his
Isa. 37. 4. 17 hath sent to reproach the living God
37. 23 Whom hast thou reproached and blasph.
37. 24 thou reproached the LORD, and hast said
Zeph. 2. 8 whereby they have reproached my people
2. 10 they have reproached and magnified (them)

5. *Thy reproach from (the foolish),* חֶרְפָּה מִן [*cherpah*].
Psa. 74. 22 how the foolish man reproacheth thee d.

6. *To cause to blush,* כָּלַם *kalam,* 5.
Ruth 2. 15 Let her glean even ..and reproach her not
Job 19. 3 These ten times have ye reproached me

7. *To reproach,* ὀνειδίζω *oneidizō.*
Luke 6. 22 shall reproach (you), and cast out your
Rom 15 3 The reproaches of them that reproached
1 Ti. 4. 10 we both labour and [suffer reproach], be.
1 Pe. 4. 14 If ye be reproached for the name of Chr.

8. *To insult, treat with contumely,* ὑβρίζω *hubrizō.*
Luke 11. 45 Master, thus saying thou reproachest us

REPROACHFULLY, (to speak)—

1. *Reproach,* חֶרְפָּה *cherpah.*
Job 16. 10 smitten me upon the cheek reproachfully

2. *Because of reviling,* χάριν λοιδορίας [*charin*].
1 Ti. 5 14 give none occasion..to speak reproachfu.

REPROBATE —

1. *To loathe, despise, reject,* מָאַס *maas,* 2.
Jer. 6. 30 Reprobate silver shall (men) call them

2. *Disapproved,* ἀδόκιμος *adokimos.*
Rom. 1. 28 gave them over to a reprobate mind, to
2 Co. 13. 5 Christ is in you, except ye be reprobates?
13. 6 ye shall know that we are not reprobates
13. 7 which is honest, though we be as reprob.
2 Ti. 3. 8 men of corrupt minds reprobate concer.
Titus 1. 16 disobedient, and unto every good work re

REPROOF —

1. *Rebuke,* גְּעָרָה *gearah.*
Job 26. 11 tremble and are astonished at his reproof
Prov. 17. 10 reproof entereth more into a wise man

2. *Reproof, correction,* תּוֹכַחַת *tokachath.*
Psa. 38. 14 and in whose mouth (are) no reproofs
Prov 1. 23 Turn you at my reproof: behold, I will p.
1. 25 But ye..would none of my reproof
1. 30 my counsel; they despised all my reproof
5. 12 instruction, and my heart despised repro.
6. 23 reproofs of instruction (are) the way of life
10. 17 but he that refuseth reproof erreth
12. 1 but he that hateth reproof (is) brutish
13. 18 he that regardeth reproof shall be honou.
15. 5 but he that regardeth reproof is prudent
15. 10 (and) he that hateth reproof shall die
15. 31 ear that heareth the reproof of life abideth
Prov 15. 32 that heareth reproof getteth understand.
29. 15 rod and reproof give wisdom: but a child

3. *Conviction,* ἔλεγχος *elegchos.*
2 Ti. 3. 16 profitable for doctrine, for [reproof], for

REPROVE, REPROVER, to —

1. *To rebuke,* גָּעַר *gaar.*
Jer. 29. 27 why hast thou not reproved Jeremiah of

2. *To reason, reprove, decide,* יָכַח *yakach,* 5.
Gen. 21 25 reproved Abimelech because of a well of
2 Ki. 19. 4 will reprove the words which the LORD
1 Ch. 16 21 yea, he reproved kings for their sakes
Job 6. 25 words! but what doth your arguing repr.
6. 26 Do ye imagine to reprove words, and the
13. 10 He will surely reprove you, if ye do secr.
22 4 Will he reprove thee for fear of thee? will
40. 2 he that reproveth God, let him answer it
Psa. 50. 8 will not reprove thee for thy sacrifices or
50. 21 I will reprove thee, and set (them) in or.
105. 14 yea, he reproved kings for their sakes
141 5 let him reprove me; (it shall be) an exc.
Prov. 9. 8 Reprove not a scorner, lest he hate thee
15. 12 scorner loveth not one that reproveth him
19. 25 reprove one that hath understanding, (and)
25. 12 (so is) a wise reprover upon an obedient
30. 6 lest he reprove thee, and thou be found
Isa. 11 3 neither reprove after the hearing of his
11. 4 reprove with equity for the meek of the
29 21 lay a snare for him that reproveth in the
37. 4 will reprove the words which the LORD
Jer. 2. 19 and thy backslidings shall reprove thee
Eze 3. 26 shalt not be to them a reprover: for the
Hos 4. 4 Yet let no man strive, nor reprove anot.

3. *To instruct, correct,* יָסַר *yasar.*
Prov. 9. 7 He that reproveth a scorner getteth to

4. *To convict,* ἐλέγχω *elegchō.*
Luke 3. 19 being reproved by him for Herodias his
John 3 20 light, lest his deeds should be reproved
16. 8 he will reprove the world of sin and of
Eph. 5. 11 have no fellowship..but rather reprove
5. 13 But all things that are reproved are made
2 Ti. 4 2 reprove, rebuke, exhort, with all longsu.

REPROVED, to be (often) —

1. *To be reasoned with,* יָכַח *yakach,* 2.
Gen. 20. 16 and with all (other): thus she was repro.

2. *Reproof, correction,* תּוֹכַחַת *tokachath.*
Prov 29. 1 He that, being often reproved, hardeneth
Hab 2. 1 what I shall answer when I am reproved

REPUTATION, (to be of, have in, make of no) —

1. *One rare, precious,* יָקָר *yaqar.*
Eccl. 10. 1 him that is in reputation for wisdom (and)

2. *To think, seem,* δοκέω *dokeō.*
Gal. 2. 2 privately to them which were of reputa.

3. *To have or hold in honour,* ἔχω ἔντιμον [*echō*].
Phil. 2. 29 all gladness; and hold such in reputation

4. *To empty,* κενόω *kenoō.*
Phil. 2. 7 But made himself of no reputation, and

5. *Honourable, prized,* τίμιος *timios.*
Acts 5 34 had in reputation among all the people

REPUTED, to be —

To think, reckon, devise, חָשַׁב *chashab.*
Dan. 4. 35 the inhabitants of the earth (are) reputed

REQUEST —

1. *Request, desire,* אֲרֶשֶׁת *aresheth.*
Psa. 21. 2 hast not withholden the request of his lips

2. *Request, inquiry,* בַּקָּשָׁה *baqqashah.*
Ezra. 7. 6 king granted him all his request, accord.
Esth. 5. 3 what (is) thy request? it shall be even giv.
5 6 what (is) thy request? even to the half of
5. 7 Then answered Esther, and said..my re.
5. 8 if it please the king..to perform my req.
7. 2 what (is) thy request? and it shall be perfo.
7. 3 petition, and my people at my request
9. 12 what (is) thy request further? and it shall

3. *A word,* דָּבָר *dabar.*
2 Sa. 14. 15 king will perform the request of his hand.
14. 22 king hath fulfilled the request of his serv.

4. *Asking, request, demand,* שְׁאֵלָה *sheelah.*
Judg. 8. 24 would desire a request of you, that ye w
Job 6 8 Oh that I might have my request; and that
Psa 106. 15 he gave them their request; but sent lean.

5. *Request, petition,* αἴτημα *aitēma.*
Phil. 4. 6 let your requests be made known unto God

6. *Supplication,* δέησις *deēsis.*
Phil. 1. 4 in every prayer of mine..making request

REQUEST, to (make) —

1. *To seek, pray,* בְּעָא *bea.*
Dan. 2. 49 Then Daniel requested of the king, and he

2. *To seek, inquire,* בָּקַשׁ *baqash,* 3.
Neh. 2. 4 For what dost thou make request? So I
Esth. 4. 8 to make request before him for her people
7. 7 Haman stood up to make request for his
Dan. 1. 8 requested of the prince of the eunuchs th.

3. *To ask, demand,* שָׁאַל *shaal.*
Judg 8. 26 of the golden ear rings that he requested
1 Ki. 19. 4 he requested for himself that he might die
1 Ch. 4. 10 God granted him that which he requested

4. *To be in want of, to supplicate,* δέομαι *deomai.*
Rom. 1. 10 Making request if by any means now at

REQUIRE, to —

1. *To say,* אֲמַר *amar.*
Ruth 3. 11 I will do to thee all that thou requirest

2. *To choose, try, fix on,* בָּחַר *bachar.*
2 Sa. 19. 38 and whatsoever thou shalt require of me

3. *To seek, inquire,* בָּקַשׁ *baqash,* 3.
Gen. 31. 39 of my hand didst thou require it, (whether)
43. 9 of my hand shalt thou require him: if I
Josh 22. 23 thereon, let the LORD himself require (it)
1 Sa. 20. 16 Let the LORD even require (it) at the hand
2 Sa. 4. 11 shall I not therefore now require his bl.
1 Ch. 21. 3 why then doth my lord require this thing?
Neh. 5. 12 will require nothing of them; so will we
5. 18 yet for all this required not I the bread
Esth. 2. 15 she required nothing but what Hegai the
Eccl. 3. 15 and God requireth that which is past
Isa. 1. 12 who hath required this at your hand, to
Eze. 3. 18 but his blood will I require at thine hand
3. 20 but his blood will I require at thine hand
33. 8 but his blood will I require at thine hand

4. *To seek, inquire, require,* דָּרַשׁ *darash.*
Gen. 9. 5 surely your blood of your lives will I re.
9. 5 at the hand of every beast will I require
9. 5 hand of every man's brother will I require
Deut 18. 19 speak in my name, I will require (it) of him
23. 21 for the LORD thy God will surely require
2 Ch. 24. 6 Why hast thou not required of the Levites
24. 22 said, The LORD look upon (it), and require
Psa 10. 13 said in his heart, Thou wilt not require (it)
Eze. 20. 40 there will I require your offerings, and the
33. 6 his blood will I require at the watchman's
34. 10 and I will require my flock at their hand
Mic. 6. 8 what doth the LORD require of thee, but to

5. [*See* haste].
1 Sa. 21. 8 because the king's business required haste

6. *To ask, demand,* שָׁאַל *shaal.*
Deut. 10. 12 what doth the LORD thy God require of t.
2 Sa. 3. 13 but one thing I require of thee, that is, T.
12. 20 when he required, they set bread before
Ezra 8. 22 For I was ashamed to require of the king
Psa 40. 6 and sin offering hast thou not required
137. 3 they that carried us away captive required
Prov 30. 7 Two (things) have I required of thee; deny

7. *To ask, demand,* שְׁאֵל *sheel.*
Ezra 7. 21 whatsoever Ezra ..shall require of you, it
Dan. 2. 11 rare thing that the king requireth; and

8. *To ask,* αἰτέω *aiteō.*
Luke 23. 23 requiring that he might be crucified: and
1 Co. 1. 22 For the Jews require a sign, and the Gr.

9. *Request, petition,* αἴτημα *aitēma.*
Luke 23. 24 gave sentence that it should be as they re.

10. *To become,* γίνομαι *ginomai.*
1 Co. 7. 36 need so require, let him do what he will

11. *To do,* πράσσω *prassō.*
Luke 19. 23 might have required mine own with usury?

REQUIRED, to be —

1. *To be sought,* דָּרַשׁ *darash,* 2.
Gen. 42 22 therefore, behold, also his blood is requi.

2. *To ask off or away,* ἀπαιτέω *apaiteō.*
Luke 12. 20 this night thy soul shall be required of

3. *To seek out,* ἐκζητέω *ekzēteō.*
Luke 11 50 That the blood..may be required of this
11. 51 It shall be required of this generation

4. *To seek,* ζητέω *zēteō.*
Luke 12. 48 of him shall be much required; and to w.
1 Co. 4. 2 Moreover it is required in stewards, that

REQUIRED (shall require), as [it] —

In its day, בְּיוֹמוֹ [*be*].
1 Ki. 8. 59 at all times, as the matter shall require
1 Ch. 16. 37 continually, as every day's work required
2 Ch 8. 14 the duty of every day required; Ezra 3. 4.

REQUITE, to —

1. *To recompense, do,* גָּמַל *gamal.*
Deut 32. 6 Do ye thus requite the LORD, O foolish p

2. *To give,* נָתַן *nathan.*
Psa. 10. 14 to requite (it) with thy hand: the poor

3. *To do, make,* עָשָׂה *asah.*
2 Sa. 2. 6 and I also will requite you this kindness

4. *To cause to turn back,* שׁוּב *shub,* 5.
Gen. 50. 15 will certainly requite us all the evil which
1 Sa 25. 21 and he hath requited me evil for good
2 Sa. 16. 12 will requite me good for his cursing this
2 Ch. 6. 23 judge thy servants, by requiting the wic.

5. *To finish, complete, repay,* שָׁלַם *shalam,* 3.
Judg. 1. 7 as I have done, so God hath requited me
2 Ki. 9. 26 and I will requite thee in this plat, saith
Psa. 41. 10 and raise me up, that I may requite them
Jer 51. 56 LORD God of recompenses shall surely r.

6. *To give back a recompence,* ἀποδίδωμι ἀμοιβάς.
1 Ti. 5. 4 requite their parents: for that is good

REREWARD, (to be) —

1. *Behind, last, furthest,* אַחֲרוֹן *acharon.*
1 Sa. 29. 2 men passed on in the rereward with Achish

2. *To gather,* אָסַף *asaph.*
Isa. 58. 8 the glory of the LORD shall be thy rereward

3. *To gather,* אָסַף *asaph,* 3.
Num 10. 25 the rereward of all the camps throughout
Josh. 6. 9 rereward came after the ark, (the priests)

Josh. 6. 13 the rereward came after the ark of the L.
Isa. 52. 12 and the God of Israel (will be) your rere.

RESCUE, to —

1. *To give ease,* יָשַׁע *yasha*, 5.
Deut28. 31 and thou shalt have none to rescue (them)

2. *To snatch away,* נָצַל *natsal*, 5.
1 Sa. 30. 18 carried away; and David rescued his two
Hos. 5. 14 I will take away, and none shall rescue

3. *To snatch away,* נְצַל *netsal*, 5.
Dan. 6. 27 He delivereth and rescueth, and he work.

4. *To free,* פָּדָה *padah.*
1 Sa. 14. 45 So the people rescued Jonathan, that he

5. *To cause to turn back,* שׁוּב *shub*, 5.
Psa. 35. 17 rescue my soul from their destructions

6. *To take away, lift up out of,* ἐξαιρέω *exaireō.*
Acts 23. 27 then came I with an army, and rescued

RESEMBLANCE —

Eye, appearance, עַיִן *ayin.*
Zech. 5. 6 This (is) their resemblance through all the

RESEMBLE, (to) —

1. [*Be*] *like the form of,* כְּתֹאַר [*toar*].
Judg. 8. 18 each one resembled the children of a king

2. *To liken,* ὁμοιόω *homoioō.*
Luke13. 18 like? and whereunto shall I resemble it?

RES'-EN, רֶסֶן *fortress.*

A city between Nineveh and Caleh, now called *Kuyyundshite*, once *Mespila.*
Gen 10. 12 And R. between Nineveh and Calah: the

RESERVE, be reserved, to —

1. *To keep back, lay up,* אָצַל *atsal.*
Gen. 27 36 Hast thou not reserved a blessing for me?

2. *To darken, keep back, restrain,* חָשַׂךְ *chasak.*
Job 38. 23 Which I have reserved against the time?

3. *To be kept back,* חָשַׂךְ *chasak*, 2.
Job 21. 30 That the wicked is reserved to the day of

4. *To cause to be abundant,* יָתַר *yathar*, 5.
Ruth 2. 18 gave to her that she had reserved after
2 Sa. 8. 4 but reserved of them (for) an hundred ch.
1 Ch.18. 4 but reserved of them an hundred chariots

5. *To take,* לָקַח *laqach.*
Judg21. 22 because we reserved not to each man his

6. *To keep,* נָטַר *natar.*
Jer. 3. 5 Will he reserve (his anger) for ever? will
Nah. 1. 2 and he reserveth (wrath) for his enemies

7. *To leave,* שָׁאַר *shaar*, 5.
Jer 50. 20 for I will pardon them whom I reserve

8. *To keep,* שָׁמַר *shamar.*
Jer. 5. 24 he reserveth unto us the appointed weeks

9. *To leave thoroughly,* καταλείπω *kataleipō.*
Rom 11. 4 I have reserved to myself seven thousand

10. *To keep,* τηρέω *tēreō.*
Acts 25. 21 when Paul had appealed to be reserved
1 Pe. 1. 4 that fadeth not away, reserved in heaven
2 Pe. 2. 4 darkness, [to be reserved] unto judgment
2. 9 reserve the unjust unto the day of judgm.
2. 17 to whom the mist of darkness is reserved
3. 7 reserved unto fire against the day of jud.
Jude 6 he hath reserved in everlasting chains,un.
13 to whom is reserved the blackness of dar.

RE'-SHEPH, רֶשֶׁף *haste.*

A son of Rephah, grandson of Sarah the daughter of Ephraim. B.C. 1680.
1 Ch. 7. 25 And Rephah (was) his son, also R., and

RESIDUE—

1. *Latter end, posterity,* אַחֲרִית *acharith.*
Eze. 23. 25 and thy residue shall be devoured by the

2. *To be over and above,* יָתַר *yathar*. 2.
Eze. 34. 18 ye must foul the residue with your feet
48 18 residue in length over against the oblat.
48. 21 residue (shall be) for the prince, on the

3. *What is over and above,* יֶתֶר *yether.*
Exod10. 5 they shall eat the residue of that which
Isa. 38. 10 I am deprived of the residue of my years
44. 19 shall I make the residue thereof an abo
Jer. 27. 19 concerning the residue of the vessels that
29. 1 sent from Jerusalem unto the residue of
52 15 residue of the people that remained in the
Eze. 34. 18 must tread down with your feet the resi
Zech 14. 2 residue of the people shall not be cut off

4. *Remnant, rest,* שְׁאָר *shear.*
Neh. 11 20 residue of Israel, of the priests (and) the
Isa. 21. 17 residue of the number of archers the mi
28. 5 diadem of beauty, unto the residue of his
Dan. 7 7 stamped the residue with the feet of it
7. 19 and stamped the residue with his feet
Mal. 2. 15 Yet had he the residue of the spirit. And

5. *Remnant, residue,* שְׁאֵרִית *sheerith.*
Isa 44. 17 residue thereof he maketh a god, (even)
Jer. 8. 3 chosen rather than life by all the residue
15. 9 residue of them will I deliver to the sword
24. 8 residue of Jerusalem, that remain in this
39. 3 residue of the princes of the king of Bab.
41. 10 Ishmael carried away captive all the res.
Eze. 9. 8 wilt thou destroy all the residue of Israel
36. 3 might be a possession unto the residue of
36. 4 derision to the residue of the heathen that
Eze. 36. 5 spoken against the residue of the heathen
Zeph. 2. 9 residue of my people shall spoil them, and
Hag. 2. 2 Speak..to the residue of the people, say.
Zech. 8. 11 But now I (will) not (be) unto the residue

6. *Thoroughly left,* κατάλοιπος *kataloipos.*
Acts 15. 17 That the residue of men might seek after

7. *Left,* λοιπός *loipos.*
Mark16. 13 [they went and told (it) unto the residue]

RESIST, to —

1. *To oppose, accuse, hate,* שָׂטַן *satan.*
Zech. 3. 1 Satan standing at his right hand to resist

2. *To set over against,* ἀνθίστημι *anthistēmi.*
Matt 5. 39 That ye resist not evil; but whosoever s.
Luke21. 15 shall not be able to gainsay nor resist
Acts 6. 10 they were not able to resist the wisdom
Rom. 9. 19 find fault? for who hath resisted his will
13. 2 resisteth the ordinance..and they that r.
2 Ti. 3. 8 so do these also resist the truth: men of
Jas 4. 7 Resist the devil, and he will flee from you
1 Pe. 5. 9 Whom resist stedfast in the faith, know.

3. *To set down over against,* ἀντικαθίστημι *antika*
Heb.12. 4 Ye have not yet resisted unto blood striv

4. *To fall over against,* ἀντιπίπτω *antipiptō.*
Acts 7. 51 ye do always resist the Holy Ghost: as yo.

5. *To set self in array over against,* ἀντιτάσσομαι
Rom 13. 2 Whosoever therefore resisteth the power
Jas. 4. 6 God resisteth the proud, but giveth grace
5. 6 killed the just; (and) he doth not resist
1 Pe. 5. 5 God resisteth the proud, and giveth grace

RESOLVED, to be —

To begin to know, γινώσκω *ginōskō.*
Luke 16. 4 I am resolved what to do, that, when I

RESORT, to —

1. *To go or come in,* בּוֹא *bo.*
Psa 71. 3 whereunto I may continually resort: thou

2. *To set self up,* יָצַב *yatsab*, 7.
2 Ch.11 13 Israel resorted to him out of all their co.

3. *To be squeezed, gathered together,* קָבַץ *qabats*, 2.
Neh. 4. 20 resort ye thither unto us: our God shall

4. *To come,* ἔρχομαι *erchomai.*
Mark 2. 13 all the multitude resorted unto him, and
John10. 41 many resorted unto him, and said, John

5. *To pass through together,* συμπορεύομαι *sumpor*
Mark10. 1 people resort unto him again: and, as he

6. *To lead together,* συνάγω *sunagō.*
John 18. 2 Jesus ofttimes resorted thither with his

7. *To come together,* συνέρχομαι *sunerchomai.*
John18. 20 temple, whither the Jews always resort
Acts 16. 13 spake unto the women which resorted

RESPECT (of persons) without—

1. *Acceptance (of persons),* מַשּׂא *masso*
2 Ch.19. 7 nor respect of persons, nor taking of gifts

2. *A part, particular,* μέρος *meros.*
2 Co. 3. 10 had no glory in this respect, by reason of
Col. 2. 16 or in respect of an holy day, or of the new

3. *Acceptance of faces,* προσωποληψία *prosōpolēpsia.*
Rom. 2. 11 For there is no respect of persons with God
Eph. 6. 9; Col. 3. 25; Jas. 2. 1.

4. *Without acceptance of faces,* ἀπροσωπολήπτως.
1 Pe. 1. 17 the Father, who without respect of per.

RESPECT to (persons), to have —

To accept faces, προσωποληπτέω *prosōpolēpteō.*
Jas. 2. 9 But if ye have respect to persons, ye com.

RESPECT to, to (have)—

1. *To know, be acquainted with,* יָדַע *yada.*
Exod. 2. 25 God looked..and God had respect unto

2. *To (cause to) look attentively,* נָבַט *nabat*, 5.
Psa. 74. 20 Have respect unto the covenant: for the
119. 6 when I have respect unto all thy comma.
119 15 meditate in thy precepts, and have resp.

3. *To discern,* נָכַר *nakar*, 5.
Deut. 1. 17 Ye shall not respect persons in judgment
16. 19 thou shalt not respect persons, neither t.
Prov24. 23 not good to have respect of persons in ju.
28. 21 To have respect of persons (is) not good

4. *To lift up,* נָשָׂא *nasa.*
Lev. 19. 15 thou shalt not respect the person of the
2 Sa.14. 14 neither doth God respect (any) person: yet
Lam. 4. 16 respected not the persons of the priests

5. *To face, front, look,* פָּנָה *panah.*
Lev 26. 9 For I will have respect unto you, and m.
Num16 15 Respect not thou their offering: I have
1 Ki. 8 28 Yet have thou respect unto the prayer of
2 Ki 13. 23 had respect unto them because of his co.
2 Ch. 6 19 Have respect therefore to the prayer of
Psa 40. 4 respecteth not the proud, nor such as tu.

6. *To see,* רָאָה *raah.*
Job 37. 24 he respecteth not any (that are) wise of h.
Psa.138. 6 yet hath he respect unto the lowly: but
Isa. 17. 7 shall have respect to the Holy One of Is.
17. 8 neither shall respect (that) which his fin.
22. 11 neither had respect unto him that fashion.

7. *To glance, look,* שָׁעָה *shaah.*
Gen. 4. 4 had respect unto Abel and to his offering
4. 5 to his offering he had not respect. And
Psa.119. 117 have respect unto thy statutes continu.

8. *To look away,* ἀποβλέπω *apoblepō.*
Heb. 11. 26 for he had respect unto the recompence

9. *To look upon,* ἐπιβλέπω *epiblepō.*
Jas. 2. 3 ye have respect to him that weareth the

RESPECTER of persons —

Acceptor of faces, προσωπολήπτης *prosōpolēptēs.*
Acts 10. 34 perceive that God is no respecter of per.

RESPITE, (to give) —

1. *Breathing, respite,* רְוָחָה *revachah.*
Exod. 8. 15 when Pharaoh saw that there was respite

2. *To let fall or go, desist,* רָפָה *raphah*, 5.
1 Sa. 11. 3 Give us seven days respite, that we may

REST (of)—

1. *Silence,* דֳּמִי *domi.*
Isa. 62. 7 give him no rest, till he establish, and till

2. *To be over and above,* יָתַר *yathar*, 2 (partic.).
Gen. 30. 36 and Jacob fed the rest of Laban's flocks
Exod28. 10 six names of the rest on the other stone
Lev. 14. 29 rest of the oil that (is) in the priest's hand
Josh.17. 2 There was also (a lot) for the rest of the
17. 6 rest of Manasseh's sons had the land of
21. 5 rest of the children of Kohath (had) by
21. 34 rest of the Levites, out of the tribe of Ze.
1 Ki.20. 30 rest fled to Aphek, into the city; and (th)
2 Ki 4. 7 and live thou and thy children of the rest
1 Ch. 6. 77 Unto the rest of the children of Merari
24. 20 rest of the sons of Levi (were these): Of

3. *What is over and above,* יֶתֶר *yether.*
Lev. 14. 17 of the rest of the oil that (is) in his hand
Num31. 32 rest of the prey which the men of war had
Deut. 3. 13 rest of Gilead, and all Bashan, (being) the
Josh.13. 27 rest of the kingdom of Sihon king of He.
Judg. 7. 6 rest of the people bowed down upon their
1 Sa.13. 2 rest of the people he sent every man to his
2 Sa. 10. 10 rest of the people he delivered into the
12. 28 Now therefore gather the rest of the peo.
1 Ki.11 41 And the rest of the acts of
[So in 14. 19; 2 Ki. 8. 23; 12 19; 13. 12; 14. 18; 15. 6, 11, 15, 21, 26, 31; 20 20; 2 Ch. 13. 22.]
1 Ki. 14 29 Now the rest of the acts of
[So in 15. 7, 31; 16. 5, 14, 20, 27; 22. 39, 45; 2 Ki. 1. 18; 10. 34; 13. 8; 14. 15, 28; 15. 36; 16. 19; 21. 17, 25; 23. 28; 24. 5; 2 Ch. 20. 34; 25. 26; 26. 22; 27. 7; 32. 32; 33. 18; 35. 26; 36. 8.]
1 Ki.15. 23 rest of all the acts of Asa, and all his mig.
2 Ki 25. 11 Now the rest of the people (that were) left
1 Ch.19 11 And the rest of the people he delivered
Neh. 2. 16 neither had I as yet told (it) to..the rest
4. 14, 19 said unto the nobles..and to the rest
6. 1 rest of our enemies, heard that I had bu.
6 14 rest of the prophets, that would have put
Psa. 17 14 leave the rest of their (substance) to their
Jer. 39. 9 with the rest of the people that remained
52. 15 carried away captive..the rest of the mu.
Eze. 48. 23 As for the rest of the tribes, from the east

4. *Place of rest, rest,* מָנוֹחַ *manoach.*
Gen. 8. 9 But the dove found no rest for the sole of
Deut28. 65 neither shall the soul of thy foot have re.
Ruth 3. 1 shall I not seek rest for thee that it may
Psa.116. 7 Return unto thy rest, O my soul; for the
Lam. 1. 3 she findeth no rest: all her persecutors

5. *Place of rest, rest,* מְנוּחָה *menuchah.*
Gen 49. 15 saw that rest (was) good, and the land
Deut12. 9 For ye are not as yet come to the rest and
Ruth 1. 9 LORD grant you that ye may find rest, each
1 Ki. 8. 56 that hath given rest unto his people Isr.
1 Ch.22. 9 who shall be a man of rest; and I will
28. 2 build an house of rest for the ark of the
Psa. 95. 11 that they should not enter into my rest
132. 8 Arise, O LORD, into thy rest; thou, and
132. 14 This (is) my rest for ever: here will I dw.
Isa. 11. 10 to it shall the Gentiles seek: and his rest
28. 12 This (is) the rest (wherewith) ye may ca.
66. 1 unto me? and where (is) the place of my r.?
Jer. 45. 3 I fainted in my sighing, and I find no re.
Mic. 2. 10 for this (is) not (your) rest; because it is
Zech. 9. 1 Damascus (shall be) the rest thereof: when

6. *Remaining,* יוֹתֵר *yother.*
1 Sa. 15. 15 and the rest we have utterly destroyed

7. *Rest,* מַרְגּוֹעַ *margoa.*
Jer. 6. 16 walk therein, and ye shall find rest for

8. [*See* have rest.]
Esth. 9. 16 had rest from their enemies, and slew of

9. *A coming down, settling,* נַחַת *nachath.*
Job 17 16 when (our) rest together (is) in the dust
Prov29 9 whether he rage or laugh, (there is) no r.
Eccl. 6. 5 this hath more rest than the other
Isa. 30. 15 In returning and rest shall ye be saved

10. *Rest, intermission,* פּוּגָה *pugah.*
Lam. 2. 18 give thyself no rest; let not the apple of

11. *Remaining one,* שָׂרִיד *sarid.*
Josh.10. 20 rest (which) remained of them entered in.

12. *Cessation, sabbath,* שַׁבָּתוֹן *shabbathon.*
Exod16. 23 Tomorrow (is) the rest of the holy sabbath
31. 15 but in the seventh (is) the sabbath of rest
35. 2 sabbath of rest to the LORD: whosoever
Lev. 16. 31 sabbath of rest unto you, and ye shall af.
23. 3 but the seventh day (is) the sabbath of r.
23. 32 unto you a sabbath of rest, and ye shall
25. 4 the seventh year shall be a sabbath of rest
25. 5 (for) it is a year of rest unto the land

13. *Completeness, peace,* שָׁלוֹם *shalom.*
Psa. 38. 3 neither (is there any) rest in my bones b.

14. *To be left, remain,* שָׁאַר *shaar,* 2.
Lev. 5. 9 rest of the blood shall be wrung out at
Zech. 11. 9 let the rest eat every one the flesh of an.

15. *Remnant, rest,* שְׁאָר *shear.*
1 Ch. 11. 8 and Joab repaired the rest of the city
16. 41 rest that were chosen, who were expressed
2 Ch. 9. 29 Now the rest of the acts of Solomon, first
24. 14 they brought the rest of the money before
Ezra 4. 3 rest of the chief of the fathers of Israel
4. 7 rest of their companions, unto Artaxerxes
4. 9 and the rest of their companions ; the D
4. 10 rest of the nations..and the rest (that are)
4. 17 rest of their companions..and..the rest
6. 16 the rest of the children of the captivity
7. 18 to do with the rest of the silver and the
Neh. 10. 28 rest of the people, the priests, the Levites
11. 1 the rest of the people also cast lots, to br
Esth. 9. 12 what have they done in the rest of the ki.
Isa. 10. 19 the rest of the trees of his forest shall be
Dan. 2. 18 should not perish with the rest of the wise
7. 12 As concerning the rest of the beasts, they

16. *Remnant, residue,* שְׁאֵרִית *sheerith.*
1 Ch. 4. 43 they smote the rest of the Amalekites that
12. 38 all the rest also of Israel (were) of one h.
Neh. 7. 72 (that) which the rest of the people gave

17. *A ceasing again, resting up,* ἀνάπαυσις *anapa.*
Matt 11. 29 and ye shall find rest unto your souls
12. 43 walketh through dry places, seeking rest
Luke 11. 24 walketh through dry places, seeking rest
Rev 14. 11 they have no rest day nor night, who w.

18. *A sending up or back,* ἄνεσις *anesis.*
2 Co. 2. 13 I had no rest in my spirit, because I found
7. 5 our flesh had no rest, but we were troub.
2 Th. 1. 7 And to you who are troubled rest with us

19. *Peace, concord,* εἰρήνη *eirēnē.*
Acts 9. 31 Then had the churches rest throughout

20. *Remaining or left upon or over,* ἐπίλοιπος *epil.*
1 Pe. 4. 2 That he no longer should live the rest of

21. *A place of resting down,* κατάπαυσις *katapausis.*
Acts 7. 49 what house..what (is) the place of my r.
Heb 3. 11 I sware..They shall not enter into my r.
3. 18 that they should not enter into his rest
4. 1 being left (us) of entering into his rest, any
4. 3 into rest..If they shall enter into my rest
4. 5 (place) again, If they shall enter into my r.
4. 10 For he that is entered into his rest, he also
4. 11 labour therefore to enter into that rest

22. *Remaining, left,* λοιπός *loipos.*
Matt 27. 49 The rest said, Let be, let us see whether
Luke 12. 26 least, why take ye thought for the rest?
24. 9 told all these things unto..all the rest
Acts 2. 37 said unto Peter and to the rest of the ap.
5. 13 of the rest durst no man join himself to
27. 44 And the rest, some on boards, and some
Rom 11. 7 election hath obtained it, and the rest w.
1 Co 7. 12 But to the rest speak I, not the Lord : If
11. 34 And the rest will I set in order when I c.
Rev. 2. 24 But unto you I say, and unto the rest in
9. 20 rest of the men, which were not killed by
20. 5 But the rest of the dead lived not again

23. *A sabbath rest,* σαββατισμός *sabbatismos.*
Heb. 4. 9 There remaineth therefore a rest to the

REST, to —

1. *To lay hold,* אָחַז *achaz.*
1 Ki. 6. 10 they rested on the house with timber of

2. *To be still, keep silence,* דָּמַם *damam.*
Job 30. 27 My bowels boiled, and rested not ; the d.
Psa. 37. 7 Rest in the LORD, and wait patiently for

3. *To cease, forbear, leave off,* חָדַל *chadal.*
Job 14. 6 Turn from him, that he may rest, till he

4. *To rush (on), fall (on),* חוּל *chul.*
2 Sa. 3. 29 Let it rest on the head of Joab, and on all

5. *To hold one's peace, keep silent,* חָרַשׁ *charash,* 5.
Zeph 3. 17 he will rest in his love ; he will joy over

6. As No. 7.
Esth. 9. 17 fourteenth day of the same rested they
9. 18 the fifteenth (day) of the same they rested

7. *To be at rest,* נוּחַ *nuach.*
Gen 8. 4 And the ark rested in the seventh month
Exod 10. 14 locusts..rested in all the coasts of Egypt
20. 11 rested the seventh day : wherefore the
23. 12 that thine ox and thine ass may rest, and
Num 10. 36 when it rested, he said, Return, O LORD
11. 25 when the spirit rested upon them, they
11. 26 spirit rested upon them ; and they (were)
Deut. 5. 14 maid servant may rest as well as thou
Josh. 3. 13 soles of the feet..shall rest in the waters
2 Sa. 21. 10 suffered neither the birds of the air to r.
2 Ki. 2. 15 The spirit of Elijah doth rest on Elisha
Esth. 9. 22 As the days wherein the Jews rested from
Psa. 125. 3 For the rod of the wicked shall not rest
Prov 14. 33 Wisdom resteth in the heart of him that
Eccl. 7. 9 for anger resteth in the bosom of fools
Isa. 7. 19 shall rest all of them in the desolate val
11. 2 spirit of the LORD shall rest upon him, the
25. 10 shall the hand of the LORD rest..and Moab
57. 2 they shall rest in their beds, (each one)
Dan. 12. 13 for thou shalt rest, and stand in thy lot
Hab. 3. 16 that I might rest in the day of trouble

8. *To rest, be quiet,* רָגַע *raga,* 2.
Jer. 47. 6 Put up thyself into thy scabbard, rest, and

9. *To (cause to) rest, give quietness,* רָגַע *raga,* 5.
Isa. 34. 14 screech owl also shall rest there, and find

10. *To be at ease, quiet, rest,* שָׁאַן *shaan,* 3a.
Job 3. 18 prisoners rest together ; they hear not the

11. *To cease, rest, keep sabbath,* שָׁבַת *shabath.*
Gen. 2. 2 rested on the seventh day from all his w.
2. 3 because that in it he had rested from all
Exod 16. 30 So the people rested on the seventh day
23. 12 on the seventh day thou shalt rest ; that
31. 17 seventh day he rested, and was refreshed
34. 21 but on the seventh day thou shalt rest : in
34. 21 earing time and in harvest thou shalt rest
Lev 26. 34 then shall the land rest, and enjoy her sa.
26. 35 it shall rest ; because it did not rest in yo.

12. *To tabernacle,* שָׁכַן *shaken.*
Num 10. 12 cloud rested in the wilderness of Paran
Psa. 16. 9 rejoiceth : my flesh also shall rest in hope
55. 6 (for then) I would fly away, and be at rest

13. *To lean or rely on,* שָׁעַן *shaan,* 2.
2 Ch. 14. 11 help us, O LORD our God ; for we rest on
Job 24. 23 whereon he resteth, yet his eyes (are) up.

14. *To be quiet, have rest,* שָׁקַט *shaqat.*
Josh. 11. 23 their tribes. And the land rested from
Isa. 62. 1 and for Jerusalem's sake I will not rest

15. *To cause quiet or rest,* שָׁקַט *shaqat,* 5.
Isa. 57. 20 troubled sea, when it cannot rest, whose

16. *To have a resting again, or back,* ἔχω ἀνάπαυσιν.
Rev. 4. 8 and they rest not day and night, saying

17. *To rest again or back,* ἀναπαύομαι *anapauomai.*
Mark 6. 31 rest a while : for there were many coming
1 Pe. 4. 14 for the spirit of glory and of God resteth
Rev. 6. 11 that they should rest yet for a little season
14. 13 that [they may rest] from their labours

18. *To keep quiet, rest,* ἡσυχάζω *hēsuchazō.*
Luke 23. 56 rested the sabbath day, according to the

19. *To rest down or thoroughly, cease,* καταπαύομαι.
Heb. 4. 4 God did rest the seventh day from all his

20. *To tabernacle down or thoroughly,* κατασκηνόω.
Acts 2. 26 moreover also my flesh shall rest in hope

REST, to cause, give, have, let, make, take —

1. *Resting, place of rest,* מָנוֹחַ *manoach.*
1 Ch. 6. 31 David set over..after that the ark had rest

2. *To be at rest,* נוּחַ *nuach.*
Neh. 9. 28 after they had rest, they did evil ; Est. 9. 16
Isa. 23. 12 Chittim ; there also shalt thou have no r.

3. *To cause to rest,* נוּחַ *nuach,* 5.
Exod 33. 14 shall go (with thee), and I will give thee r
Deut. 3. 20 Until the LORD have given rest unto your
12. 10 giveth you rest from all your enemies ro.
25. 19 LORD thy God hath given thee rest from
Josh. 1. 13 LORD your God hath given you rest, and
1. 15 the LORD have given your brethren rest
21. 44 LORD gave them rest round about, accor.
22. 4 now the LORD your God hath given rest
23. 1 after that the LORD had given rest unto
2 Sa. 7. 1 LORD had given him rest round about from
7. 11 caused thee to rest from all thine enemies
1 Ki. 5. 4 my God hath given me rest on every side
1 Ch. 22. 9 give him rest from all his enemies round
22. 18 hath he (not) given you rest on every side?
23. 25 LORD God of Israel hath given rest unto
2 Ch. 14. 6 And..because the LORD had given him r.
14. 7 and he hath given us rest on every side
15. 15 and the LORD gave them rest round about
20. 30 quiet ; for his God gave him rest round
Prov 29. 17 Correct thy son, and he shall give thee rest
Isa. 14. 3 LORD shall give thee rest from thy sorrow
28. 12 ye may cause the weary to rest ; and this
63. 14 the spirit of the LORD caused him to rest
Eze. 5. 13 and I will cause my fury to rest upon them
16. 42 will I make my fury toward thee to rest
21. 17 cause my fury to rest : I the LORD have
24. 13 till I have caused my fury to rest upon
44. 30 may cause the blessing to rest in thine

4. *To be caused to rest, have rest,* נוּחַ *nuach,* 6.
Lam. 5. 5 persecution : we labour, (and) have no rest

5. *To cause to lie down,* רָבַץ *rabats,* 5.
Song 1. 7 where thou makest (thy flock) to rest at

6. *To (cause to) rest, give quietness,* רָגַע *raga,* 5.
Isa. 51. 4 make my judgment to rest for a light of
Jer. 31. 2 Israel, when I went to cause him to rest
50. 34 that he may give rest to the land, and di.

7. *To cause to cease or rest,* שָׁבַת *shabath,* 5.
Exod. 5. 5 and ye make them rest from their burdens

8. *To release, let go,* שָׁמַט *shamat.*
Exod 23. 11 But the seventh (year) thou shalt let it r.

9. *To be quiet, have rest,* שָׁקַט *shaqat.*
Josh. 14. 15 And the land had rest from war
Judg. 3. 11 land had rest forty years. And Othniel
3. 30 And the land had rest fourscore years
5. 31 And the land had rest forty years
2 Ch. 14. 6 for the land had rest, and he had no war
Job 3. 26 I was not in safety, neither had I rest, n.
Isa. 18. 4 will take my rest, and I will consider in

10. *To cause quiet or rest,* שָׁקַט *shaqat,* 5.
Psa. 94. 13 That thou mayest give him rest from the

11. *To rest again or back,* ἀναπαύω, *-ομαι.*
Matt 11. 28 Come unto me..and I will give you rest
26. 45 Sleep on now, and take (your) rest : beh.
Mark 14. 41 Sleep on now, and take (your) rest : it is

12. *To rest down or thoroughly,* καταπαύομαι *katapau.*
Heb. 4. 8 For if Jesus had given them rest, then

REST, to be at or in —

1. *To be at rest,* נוּחַ *nuach.*
Job 3. 13 should have slept : then had I been at r.
3. 17 troubling ; and there the weary be at rest
Isa. 14. 7 whole earth is at rest, (and) is quiet : they

2. *To be at rest,* שְׁלֵה *shelah.*
Dan 4. 4 Nebuchadnezzar was at rest in mine house

3. *To be quiet, have rest,* שָׁקַט *shaqat.*
Ruth 3. 18 for the man will not be in rest until he
Jer. 30. 10 shall be in rest, and be quiet, and none
46. 27 Jacob shall return, and be in rest and at
Zech. 1. 11 all the earth sitteth still, and is at rest
Eze. 38. 11 I will go to them that are at rest, that

REST in, on, or upon, to —

1. *To lean or rely on,* שָׁעַן *shaan,* 2.
Job 24. 23 whereon he resteth, yet his eyes (are) upon

2. *To rest back upon,* ἐπαναπαύομαι *epanapauomai.*
Luke 10. 6 your peace shall rest upon it : if not, it
Rom. 2. 17 restest in the law, and makest thy boast

3. *To tabernacle on,* ἐπισκηνόω *episkēnoō.*
2 Co. 12. 9 that the power of Christ may rest upon

REST, taking of —

A lying down to sleep, κοίμησις *koimēsis.*
John 11. 13 that he had spoken of taking of rest in sl.

REST content, to —

To be willing, inclined, אָבָה *abah.*
Prov. 6. 35 neither will he rest content, though thou

REST in a tent, to —

To encamp, pitch, חָנָה *chanah.*
Num 9. 18 as long..they rested in their tents
9. 23 rested in the tents, and at the comman.

REST selves, to —

1 *To lay or support self, be supported,* סָמַךְ *samak,* 2.
2 Ch. 32. 8 people rested themselves upon the words

2. *To bear or rely on,* שָׁעַן *shaan,* 2.
Gen. 18. 4 wash your feet and rest yourselves under

REST, resting place, place of —

1. *Rest, place of rest,* מָנוֹחַ *manoach.*
Isa. 34. 14 there, and find for herself a place of rest

2. *Rest, place of rest,* מְנוּחָה *menuchah.*
Num 10. 33 to search out a resting place for them
Isa. 32. 18 sure dwellings, and in quiet resting places

3. *Rest,* נוּחַ *nuach* (infin).
2 Ch. 6. 41 arise..into thy resting place, thou, and

4. *Lying or crouching down,* רֵבֶץ *rebets.*
Prov. 24. 15 Lay not wait..spoil not his resting place
Jer. 50. 6 they have forgotten their resting place

RESTITUTION —

1. *Exchange, restitution,* תְּמוּרָה *temurah.*
Job 20. 18 according to (his) substance (shall) the r.

2. *A putting down again, restoration,* ἀποκατάστασις.
Acts 3. 21 until the times of restitution of all things

RESTITUTION, to make —

To make whole, complete, שָׁלֵם *shalam,* 3.
Exod 22. 3 (for) he should make full restitution : if
22. 5 and of the best..shall he make restitution
22. 6 kindled the fire shall surely make restit.
22. 12 shall make restitution unto the owner th.

RESTORE (again, to life), to —

1. *To make alive,* חָיָה *chayah,* 5.
2 Ki. 8. 1, 5 woman, whose son he had restored to l.
8. 5 how he had restored a dead body to life
8. 5 her son, whom Elisha restored to life

2. *To give,* נָתַן *nathan.*
2 Ch. 8. 2 That the cities which Huram had restored

3. *To cause to go up,* עָלָה *alah,* 5.
Jer. 30. 17 For I will restore health unto thee, and I

4. *To turn back,* שׁוּב *shub,* 3a.
Psa. 23. 3 He restoreth my soul : he leadeth me in

5. *To cause to turn back,* שׁוּב *shub,* 5.
Gen. 20. 7 restore the man (his) wife..if thou restore
20. 14 gave (them) unto Abraham, and restored
40. 13 restore thee unto thy place : and thou s.
40. 21 restored the chief butler unto his butler.
41. 13 me he restored unto mine office, and him
42. 25 to restore every man's money into his sack
Lev. 6. 4 restore that which he took violently away
25. 27 restore the overplus unto the man to wh.
25. 28 But if he be not able to restore (it) to him
Num. 35. 25 shall restore him to the city of his refuge
Deut. 22. 2 and thou shalt restore it to him again
Judg 11. 13 therefore restore those (lands) again pea.
17. 3 when he had restored the eleven hundred
17. 3 now therefore I will restore it unto thee
17. 4 Yet he restored the money unto his mot.
1 Sa. 12. 3 whose ox have I taken..I will restore it
2 Sa. 9. 7 will restore thee all the land of Saul thy
16. 3 house of Israel restore me the kingdom
1 Ki. 20. 34 cities which my father took..I will rest.
2 Ki. 8. 6 Restore all that (was) her's, and all the

2 Ki. 14. 22 He built Elath, and restored it to Judah
14. 25 He restored the coast of Israel from the
2 Ch. 26. 2 He built Eloth, and restored it to Judah
Neh. 5. 11 Restore, I pray you, to them, even this
5. 12 We will restore (them), and will require
Job 20. 10 and his hands shall restore their goods
20. 18 That which he laboured for shall he res.
Psa. 51. 12 Restore unto me the joy of thy salvation
69. 4 then I restored (that) which I took not a.
Isa. 1. 26 I will restore thy judges as at the first, and
42. 22 they are..for a spoil, and none saith, Re.
49. 6 to restore the preserved of Israel; I will
Jer. 27. 22 will I bring them up, and restore them to
Eze. 18 7 hath restored to the debtor his pledge
18 12 hath not restored the pledge, and hath li.
33. 15 (If) the wicked restore the pledge give ag.
Dan. 9. 25 commandment to restore and to build Je.

6. *To make whole, complete*, שָׁלַם *shalam*, 3.
Exod 22. 1 he shall restore five oxen for an ox, and
22. 4 ox, or ass, or sheep, he shall restore dou.
Lev. 6. 5 he shall even restore it in the principal
24. 21 that killeth a beast, he shall restore it: and
2 Sa. 12 6 shall restore the lamb fourfold, because he
Prov 6. 31 (if) he be found, he shall restore sevenfold
Isa. 57. 18 restore comforts unto him, and to his m
Joel 2. 25 I will restore to you the years that the lo.

7. *To give away or back*, ἀποδίδωμι *apodidōmi*.
Luke 19 8 if I have taken any thing..I restore (him)

8. *To place down again, restore*, ἀποκαθίστημι.
Matt 17. 11 Elias truly shall first come, and restore all
Mark 9 12 Elias verily cometh first, and restoreth all
Acts 1. 6 wilt thou at this time restore again the

9. *To make thoroughly right*, καταρτίζω *katartizō*.
Gal 6. 1 ye which are spiritual restore such an one

RESTORED (again), to be —

1. *To turn back, return*, שׁוּב *shub*.
Deut 28 31 shall not be restored to thee: thy sheep
1 Sa. 7. 14 cities..were restored to Israel, from Ek.
1 Ki 13. 6 that my hand may be restored me again
13. 6 king's hand was restored him again, and

2. *To be caused to turn back*, שׁוּב *shub*, 6.
Gen. 42 28 My money is restored; and, lo, (it is) even

3. *To cause to turn back*, תּוּב *tub*, 5.
Ezra 6 5 be restored, and brought again unto the

4. *To place down again, restore*, ἀποκαθίστημι.
Matt 12. 13 it was restored whole, like as the other
Mark 3. 5 his hand was restored whole as the other
8. 25 was restored, and saw every man clearly
Luke 6. 10 his hand was restored whole as the other
Heb 13 19 that I may be restored to you the sooner

RESTORER —

1. *To turn back*, שׁוּב *shub*, 3*a*.
Isa. 58 12 called..The restorer of paths to dwell in

2. *To cause to turn back*, שׁוּב *shub*, 5.
Ruth 4 15 he shall be unto thee a restorer of (thy)

RESTRAIN, to —

1. *To diminish*, גָּרַע *gara*.
Job 15 4 castest off fear, and restrainest prayer be.
15. 8 and dost thou restrain wisdom to thyself?

2. *To gird*, חָגַר *chagar*.
Psa. 76 10 the remainder of wrath shalt thou restrain

3. *To make dim or faint*, כָּהָה *kahah*, 3.
1 Sa. 3 13 made themselves vile, and he restrained

4. *To withhold*, מָנַע *mana*.
Eze. 31. 15 restrained the floods thereof, and the gr.

5. *To shut up, restrain*, עָצַר *atsar*.
Gen 16. 2 LORD hath restrained me from bearing: I

6. *To cause to rest thoroughly*, καταπαύω *katapauō*.
Acts 14 18 restrained they the people, that they had

RESTRAINED, to be —

1. *To force self, be restrained*, אָפַק *aphaq*, 7.
Isa. 63. 15 mercies toward me? are they restrained?

2. *To be fenced off*, בָּצַר *batsar*, 2.
Gen. 11. 6 now nothing will be restrained from them

3. *To be restrained*, כָּלָא *kala*, 2.
Exod 36. 6 So the people were restrained from bring.
Gen. 8. 2 and the rain from heaven was restrained

RESTRAINT —

Restraint, hindrance, מַעְצוֹר *matsor*.
1 Sa. 14. 6 no restraint to the LORD to save by many

RESURRECTION —

1. *A standing or rising up*, ἀνάστασις *anastasis*.
Matt 22 23 which say that there is no resurrection
22 28 in the resurrection whose wife shall she
22 30 For in the resurrection they neither marry
22 31 as touching the resurrection of the dead
Mark 12. 18 which say there is no resurrection; and
12 23 In the resurrection therefore, when they
Luke 14. 14 recompensed at the resurrection of the just
20. 27 which deny that there is any resurrection
20. 33 in the resurrection whose wife of them is
20 35 resurrection from the dead neither marry
20. 36 being the children of the resurrection
John 5 29 resurrection of life..resurrection of dam.
11. 24 rise again in the resurrection at the last
11. 25 Jesus said unto her, I am the resurrection
Acts 1. 22 to be a witness with us of his resurrection
2. 31 spake of the resurrection of Christ, that
4. 2 preached through Jesus the resurrection
Acts 4. 33 gave the apostles witness of the resurrec.
17. 18 because he preached unto them..the res.
17. 32 when they heard of the resurrection of the
23. 6 of the hope and resurrection of the dead
23. 8 the Sadducees say that there is no resur.
24. 15 there shall be a resurrection of the dead
24. 21 Touching the resurrection of the dead I am
Rom. 1. 4 declared..by the resurrection from the d.
6. 5 be also (in the likeness) of (his) resurrec.
1 Co. 15. 12 that there is no resurrection of the dead?
15. 13 if there be no resurrection of the dead
15. 21 by man..also the resurrection of the dead
15. 42 So also (is) the resurrection of the dead
Phil. 3. 10 the power of his resurrection, and 3 11
2 Ti. 2 18 saying that the resurrection is past alre.
Heb. 6. 2 of resurrection of the dead, and of eter.
11 35 that they might obtain a better resurrec.
1 Pe. 1 3 by the resurrection of Jesus Christ from
3. 21 save us..by the resurrection of Jesus Ch.
Rev. 20. 5 were finished. This (is) the first resurrec.
20. 6 he that hath part in the first resurrection

2. *A raising*, ἔγερσις *egersis*.
Matt 27. 53 came out of the graves after his resurrec.

3. *A standing up out of*, ἐξανάστασις *exanastasis*.
Phil. 3. 11 I might attain unto the resurrection of

RETAIN, to —

1. *To take fast hold*, חָזַק *chazaq*, 5.
Judg 7 8 and retained those three hundred men
19. 4 the damsel's father, retained him; and
Job 2. 9 Dost thou still retain thine integrity?
Mic 7. 18 he retaineth not his anger for ever, beca.

2. *To restrain*, כָּלָא *kala*.
Eccl 8. 8 no man that hath power..to retain the

3. *To shut up, restrain*, עָצַר *atsar*.
Dan. 10. 8 was left alone..and I retained no strength
10. 16 O my lord..I have retained no strength
11 6 she shall not retain the power of the arm

4. *To hold up*, תָּמַךְ *tamak*.
Prov. 3 18 and happy (is every one) that retaineth
4 4 Let thine heart retain my words: keep
11. 16 retaineth honour; and strong (men) retain

5. *To have or hold*, ἔχω *echō*.
Rom 1 28 even as they did not like to retain God in

6. *To hold down or fast*, κατέχω *katechō*.
Phm. 13 Whom I would have retained with me, that

7. *To lay fast hold of*, κρατέω *krateō*.
John 20 23 whose soever..ye retain, they are retained

RETIRE, to —

1. *To turn, overturn*, הָפַךְ *haphak*.
Judg 20. 39 when the men of Israel retired in the ba.

2. *To cause to haste*, עוּז *uz*, 5.
Jer. 4. 6 retire, stay not; for I will bring evil from

3. *To scatter*, פּוּץ *puts*.
2 Sa. 20. 22 they retired from the city every man to

4. *To turn back*, שׁוּב *shub*.
2 Sa. 11. 15 retire ye from him, that he may be smit.

RETURN —

1. *To turn back, return*, שׁוּב *shub*.
Gen. 14. 17 after his return from the slaughter of C.

2. *A return*, תְּשׁוּבָה *teshubah*.
1 Sa. 7 17 And his return (was) to Ramah; for there
1 Ki. 20. 22 at the return of the year the king of Syria
20. 26 it came to pass at the return of the year

RETURN (back or again), to —

1. *To return*, שׁוּב *shub* [V. L. יָשַׁב ?].
Eze 35 9 thy cities shall not return; and ye shall

2. *To be turned round about, compassed*, סָבַב *sabab*, 2.
2 Sa. 14. 24 Absalom returned to his own house, and
1 Ch. 16. 43 and David returned to bless his house

3. *To face, front, look*, פָּנָה *panah*.
Josh. 22. 4 return ye, and get you unto your tents

4. *To turn back, return*, שׁוּב *shub*.
Gen. 3. 19 till thou return unto the ground; for out
3 19 thou (art), and unto dust shalt thou ret.
8. 3 the waters returned from off the earth co.
8. 9 she returned unto him into the ark, for
8. 12 which returned not again unto him any
14. 7 And they returned, and came to En-mis.
16. 9 Return to thy mistress, and submit thy.
18. 10 I will certainly return unto thee accord
18. 14 I will return unto thee, according to the
18. 33 and Abraham returned unto his place
21. 32 returned into the land of the Philistines
22. 19 Abraham returned unto his young men
31. 3 Return unto the land of thy fathers, and
31. 13 and return unto the land of thy kindred
31. 55 departed, and returned unto his place
32. 6 the messengers returned to Jacob, saying
32 9 Return unto thy country, and to thy kin.
33. 16 Esau returned that day on his way unto
37. 29 Reuben returned unto the pit; and, beho.
37 30 he returned unto his brethren, and said
38. 22 he returned to Judah, and said, I cannot
42. 24 returned to them again, and communed
43. 10 now we had returned this second time
44. 13 laded every man his ass, and returned to
50. 14 Joseph returned into Egypt, he, and his
Exod. 4. 18 returned to Jethro his father in law, and
4. 18 return unto my brethren which (are) in E
4. 20 Moses..he returned to the land of Egypt
Exod. 4. 19 return into Egypt: for all the men are
4. 21 When thou goest to return into Egypt, see
5. 22 Moses returned unto the LORD, and said
13. 17 peradventure the people..return to Egypt
14. 27 the sea returned to his strength when
14. 28 the waters returned, and covered the ch.
32. 31 Moses returned unto the LORD, and said
34. 31 all the rulers of the congregation returned
Lev. 25 10, 13 ye shall return every man unto his p.
25. 10 ye shall return every man unto his family
25. 27 the man..that he may return unto his p.
25. 28 and he shall return unto his possession
25. 41 shall return unto his own family, and
25. 41 and unto the possession..shall he return
27. 24 shall return unto him of whom it was
Num 10. 36 Return, O LORD, unto the many thousands
13. 25 they returned from searching of the land
14. 3 Were it not better for us to return into E.
14 4 Let us make a captain, and let us return
14. 36 who returned, and made all the congreg.
16. 50 Aaron returned unto Moses unto the door
23. 5 Return unto Balak, and thus thou shalt
23 6 he returned unto him, and, lo, he stood
24. 25 returned to his place: and Balak also
32. 18 We will not return unto our houses, until
32. 22 ye shall return, and be guiltless before the
35. 28 the slayer shall return into the land of his
Deut. 1. 45 ye returned and wept before the LORD; but
3. 20 shall ye return every man unto his posse.
17 16 Ye shall henceforth return no more that
20. 5, 6, 7, 8 let him go and return to his house
30. 2 And shalt return unto the LORD thy God
30. 3 will return and gather thee from all the
30. 8 thou shalt return, and obey the voice of
Josh. 1. 15 ye shall return unto the land of your
2 23 So the two men returned, and descended
4. 18 the waters of Jordan returned unto their
6. 14 they compassed the city once, and return.
7. 3 they returned to Joshua, and said unto
8. 24 the Israelites returned unto Ai, and smote
10. 15, 38, 43 Joshua returned, and all Israel wi.
10. 21 the people returned to the camp to Joshua
20. 6 then shall the slayer return, and come un.
22. 8 Return with much riches unto your tents
22. 9 the half tribe of Manasseh, returned, and
22 32 returned from the children of Reuben, and
Judg. 2. 19 they returned, and corrupted (themselves)
7. 3 let him return and depart early from mo.
7. 3 there returned of the people twenty and
7 15 returned into the host of Israel, and said
8. 13 Gideon the son of Joash returned from ba.
11 31 I return in peace from the children of
11 39 she returned unto her father, who did w.
14 8 after a time he returned to take her, and
21 23 and returned unto their inheritance, and
Ruth 1. 6 that she might return from the country of
1. 7 they went on the way to return unto the
1. 8 Go, return each to her mother's house: the
1 10 we will return with thee unto thy people
1 15 Behold..return thou after thy sister in l.
1 16 (or) to return from following after thee
1. 22 Naomi returned, and Ruth the Moabitess
1. 22 which returned out of the country of M.
1 Sa. 1. 19 returned, and came to their house to R.
6. 16 the five lords..returned to Ekron the same
7. 3 If ye do return unto the LORD with all
9. 5 Come, and let us return; lest my father
15 26 I will not return with thee: for thou hast
17. 15 David went and returned from Saul to fe.
17 53 Israel returned from chasing after the Ph.
17 57 as David returned from the slaughter of
23. 28 Saul returned from pursuing after David
26 21 return, my son David; for I will no more
26 25 David went on his way, and Saul returned
27. 9 And David..returned, and came to Achish
29 7 return, and go in peace, that thou displea.
29 11 return into the land of the Philistines
2 Sa. 1 22 the sword of Saul returned not empty
2. 26 ere thou bid the people return from foll
2. 30 And Joab returned from following Abner
3. 16 said Abner. Go, return. And he returned
6. 20 Then David returned to bless his househ.
8. 13 he returned from smiting of the Syrians
10. 5 said, Tarry at Jericho..and (then) return
10. 14 Joab returned from the children of Am.
11. 4 with her..and she returned unto her ho.
12 23 shall go to him, but he shall not return
12. 31 all the people returned unto Jerusalem
15. 19 return to thy place, and abide with the
15. 20 return thou, and take back thy brethren
15 27 return into the city in peace, and your
15. 34 if thou return to the city, and say unto
16. 8 The LORD hath returned upon thee all the
17. 3 the man whom thou seekest (is)..returned
17. 20 when they had sought..they returned to
18 16 the people returned from pursuing after
19. 14 they sent..Return thou, and all thy ser.
19. 15 So the king returned, and came to Jordan
19. 39 Barzillai..he returned unto his own place
20 22 Joab returned to Jerusalem unto the ki.
23. 10 the people returned after him only to sp.
1 Ki. 2 33 Their blood shall therefore return upon
8 48 And (so) return unto thee with all their
12 24 return every man to his house; for this
12 24 and returned to depart, according to the
12 26 Now shall the kingdom return to the ho.
13 10 returned not by the way that he came to
13 16 I may not return with thee, nor go in w.
13 33 Jeroboam returned not from his evil way
19. 15 return on thy way to the wilderness of
19. 21 he returned back from him, and took a
22. 17 let them return every man to his house

1 Ki. 22. 28 If thou return at all in peace, the LORD
2 Ki. 2. 25 and from thence he returned to Samaria
3. 27 they departed from him, and returned to
4. 35 he returned, and walked in the house to
5. 15 he returned to the man of God, he and
7. 15 the messengers returned, and told the k.
8. 3 the woman returned out of the land of
14. 14 took all the gold..and returned to Sama.
18. 14 return from me: that which thou puttest
19. 7 shall return to his own land; and I will
19. 8 Rab-shakeh returned, and found the king
19. 33 by the same shall he return, and shall not
19. 36 went and returned, and dwelt at Nineveh
20. 10 let the shadow return backward ten deg.
23. 20 he slew all the priests..and returned to
1 Ch. 19. 5 said, Tarry at Jericho..and (then) return
20. 3 and all the people returned to Jerusalem
2 Ch. 6. 24 shall return and confess thy name, and
6. 38 If they return to thee with all their heart
10. 2 when Jeroboam..heard..Jeroboam retu.
11. 4 return every man to his house; for this
11. 4 and returned from going against Jeroboam
14. 15 smote also the tents..and returned to Je.
18. 16 let them return..every man to his house
18. 26 put..in the prison..until I return in peace
18. 27 If thou certainly return in peace, (then)
19. 1 the king of Judah returned to his house
19. 8 did..set..when they returned to Jerus.
20. 27 Then they returned, every man of Judah
22. 6 And he returned to be healed in Jezreel
25. 10 and they returned home in great anger
25. 24 took) all the gold..and returned to Sam.
28. 15 brought them to Jericho..then they ret.
30. 6 he will return to the remnant of you that
30. 9 God (is) gracious..if ye return unto him
31. 1 Israel returned every man to his posses.
32. 21 he returned with shame of face to his own
34. 7 And when he had broken down..he retu.
34. 9 delivered the money..and they returned
Neh. 2. 6 For how long..and when wilt thou return
2. 15 and entered by the gate..and (so) return.
4. 12 From all places whence ye shall return
4. 15 we returned all of us to the wall, every
9. 17 appointed a captain to return to their b.
9. 28 when they returned, and cried unto thee
Esth. 2. 14 she returned into the second house of the
7. 8 the king returned out of the palace garden
9. 25 should return upon his own head, and that
Job 1. 21 Naked came I out..naked shall I return
6. 29 Return, I pray you, let it not be iniquity
6. 29 return again, my righteousness (is) in it
7. 10 He shall return no more to his house, ne.
10. 21 Before I go (whence) I shall not return
15. 22 not that he shall return out of darkness
16. 22 then I shall go the way..I shall not return
17. 10 do ye return, and come now: for I cannot
22. 23 If thou return to the Almighty, thou shalt
33. 25 he shall return to the days of his youth
36. 10 commandeth that they return from iniq.
39. 4 they go forth, and return not unto them
Psa. 6. 4 Return, O LORD, deliver my soul: oh save
6. 10 let them return (and) be ashamed suddenly
7. 7 for their sakes therefore return thou on
7. 16 His mischief shall return upon his own
35. 13 my prayer returned into mine own bosom
59. 6 They return at evening: they make a noise
59. 14 let them return; and let them make a n.
60. *title* Joab returned, and smote of Edom in the
73. 10 his people return hither; and waters of a
74. 21 let not the oppressed return ashamed: let
78. 34 they returned and enquired early after G.
80. 14 Return, we beseech thee, O God of hosts
90. 3 and sayest, Return, ye children of men
90. 13 Return, O LORD, how long? and let it re.
94. 15 judgment shall return unto righteousness
104. 29 thou takest away..they die, and return
116. 7 Return unto thy rest, O my soul; for the
146. 4 he returned to his earth; in that very day
Prov. 2. 19 None that go unto her return again, nei.
26. 11 As a dog returneth to his vomit, (so) a fool
26. 27 he that rolleth a stone, it will return upon
Eccl. 1. 6 the wind returneth again according to his
1. 7 they return again [with inf. of *halak*]
4. 1 So I returned, and considered all the op.
4. 7 I returned, and I saw vanity under the s.
5. 15 naked shall he return to go as he came
9. 11 I returned, and saw under the sun, that
12. 2 be not darkened, nor the clouds return
12. 7 Then shall the dust return to the earth
12. 7 spirit shall return unto God who gave it
Song 6. 13 Return, return, O Shulamite; return, ret.
Isa. 6. 13 (it) shall return, and shall be eaten: as a
10. 21 The remnant shall return, (even) the rem.
10. 22 a remnant of them shall return: the con.
19. 22 they shall return..to the LORD, and he
21. 12 if ye will enquire, enquire ye: return, come
35. 10 the ransomed of the LORD shall return, and
37. 7 he shall..return to his own land; and I
37. 8 Rabshakeh returned, and found the king
37. 34 by the same shall he return, and shall not
37. 37 went and returned, and dwelt at Nineveh
38. 8 So the sun returned ten degrees, by which
44. 22 return unto me; for I have redeemed thee
45. 23 the word is gone out..and shall not return
51. 11 the redeemed of the LORD shall return
55. 7 let him return unto the LORD, and he will
55. 10 returneth not thither, but watereth the
55. 11 it shall not return unto me void, but it
63. 17 Return for thy servant's sake, the tribes
Jer. 3. 1 shall he return unto her again? shall not
3. 1 yet return again to me, saith the LORD
3. 7 **but she returned not. And her treacher.**
Jer. 3. 12 Return, thou backsliding Israel, saith the
3. 22 Return, ye backsliding children, (and) I
4. 1 return, O Israel, saith the LORD, return
5. 3 O LORD..they have refused to return
8. 4 saith..shall he turn away, and not return?
8. 5 they hold fast deceit, they refuse to return
12. 15 will return, and have compassion on them
14. 3 they returned with their vessels empty
15. 7 I will destroy..they return not from th.
15. 19 If thou return, then will I bring thee again
15. 19 let them return unto thee; but return not
18. 11 return ye now every one from his evil way
22. 10 shall return no more, nor see his native
22. 11 Shallum..shall not return thither any
22. 27 to return, thither shall they not return
23. 14 that none doth return from his wickedness
23. 20 The anger of the LORD shall not return
24. 7 they shall return unto me with their wh.
30. 10 Jacob shall return, and shall be in rest
30. 24 fierce anger of the LORD shall not return
31. 8 Behold..a great company shall return th.
35. 15 Return ye now every man from his evil
36. 3 may return every man from his evil way
36. 7 will return every one from his evil way
37. 7 shall return to Egypt into their own land
40. 12 Even all the Jews returned out of all pl.
41. 14 returned, and went unto Johanan the son
44. 14 that they should return into the land of
44. 14 a desire to return..none shall return but
44. 28 number that escape the sword shall retu.
46. 27 Jacob shall return, and be in rest and at
50. 9 their arrows..none shall return in vain
Eze. 1. 14 the living creatures ran and returned as
7. 13 the seller shall not return to that which
7. 13 multitude thereof, (which) shall not ret.
8. 17 and have returned to provoke me to anger
13. 22 he should not return from his wicked w.
16. 55, 55 shall return to their former estate
16. 55 then thou and thy daughters shall return
18. 23 not that he should return from his ways
21. 5 out of his sheath: it shall not return any
35. 7 that passeth out and him that returneth
35. 9 thy cities shall not return; and ye shall
46. 9 he shall not return by the way of the gate
46. 17 after it shall return to the prince: but his
47. 7 Now when I had returned, behold, at the
Dan. 10. 20 return to fight with the prince of Persia
11. 9 the king of the south shall return into his
11. 10 then shall he return, and be stirred up
11. 13 the king of the north shall return, and sh.
11. 28 Then shall he return into his land with
11. 28 and he shall do..and return to his own l.
11. 29 he shall return, and come toward the so.
11. 30 return, and have indignation against the
11. 30 he shall even return, and have intellige.
Hos. 2. 7 I will go and return to my first husband
2. 9 Therefore will I return, and take away
3. 5 Afterward shall the children of Israel re.
5. 15 I will go (and) return to my place, till th.
6. 1 let us return unto the LORD: for he hath
6. 11 when I returned the captivity of my peo.
7. 10 they do not return to the LORD their God
7. 16 They return, (but) not to the most High
8. 13 and visit their sins: they shall return to
9. 3 Ephraim shall return to Egypt, and they
11. 5 He shall not return into the land of Egy.
11. 5 his king, because they refuse to return
11. 9 I will not return to destroy Ephraim: for
14. 1 return unto the LORD thy God; for thou
14. 7 They that dwell under his shadow..retu.
Joel 2. 14 (if) he will return and repent, and leave
Amos 4. 6, 8, 9, 10, 11 yet have ye not returned unto
Obad. 15 thy reward shall return upon thine own
Mic. 1. 7 they shall return to the hire of an harlot
5. 3 the remnant of his brethren shall return
Zech. 1. 6 they returned and said, Like as the LORD
7. 14 no man passed through nor returned: for
9. 8 because of him that returneth: and no op
Mal. 1. 4 will return and build the desolate places
3. 7 Return unto me, and I will return unto
3. 7 But ye said, Wherein shall we return?
3. 18 Then shall ye return, and discern between

5. *To cause to turn back,* שׁוּב *shub,* 5.
Exod 10. 8 Moses returned the words of the people
Judg 5. 29 yea, she returned answer to herself
1 Sa. 6. 3 in any wise return him a trespass offering
6. 4 offering which we shall return to him
6. 8 which ye return him..a trespass offering
6. 17 the Philistines returned (for) a trespass
25. 39 LORD hath returned the wickedness of N.
2 Sa. 16. 8 LORD hath returned upon thee all the bl
24. 13 see what answer I shall return to him th.
1 Ki. 2. 32 LORD shall return his blood upon his own
2. 44 LORD shall return thy wickedness upon
2 Ch. 10. 6 What counsel give ye (me) to return ans.
10. 9 that we may return answer to this people
Esth. 4. 15 Esther bade (them) return Mordecai this
Joel 3. 4 speedily will I return your recompence
3. 7 return your recompence upon your own

6. *To do a second time, double, repeat,* שָׁנָה *shanah.*
Prov 26. 11 As a dog..(so) a fool returneth to his folly

7. *To turn back, return,* תּוּב *tub.*
Dan. 4. 34 mine understanding returned unto me
4. 36 my reason returned unto me; and for the
4. 36 mine honour and brightness returned un.

8. *To cause to turn back,* תּוּב *tub,* 5.
Ezra 5. 11 they returned us answer, saying, We are

9. *To bend up or back,* ἀνακάμπτω *anakamptō.*
Matt. 2. 12 **that they should not return to Herod, th.**
Acts 18. 21 I will return again unto you, if God will
Heb. 11. 15 have had opportunity to have returned

10. *To loose again,* ἀναλύω *analuō.*
Luke 12. 36 when he will return from the wedding

11. *To turn round again,* ἀναστρέφω *anastrephō.*
Acts 5. 22 not in the prison, they returned, and told
15. 16 After this I will return, and will build a.

12. *To lead up or back upon,* ἐπανάγω *epanagō.*
Matt 21. 18 as he returned into the city, he hungered

13. *To come back upon,* ἐπανέρχομαι *epanerchomai.*
Luke 19. 15 when he was returned, having received

14. *To turn upon,* ἐπιστρέφω *epistrephō.*
Matt 12. 44 I will return into my house from 10. 13.
24. 18 Neither let him..which is in the field re.
Luke 2. 20 And the shepherds [returned], glorifying
17. 31 let him likewise..return back, 1 Pe. 2. 25.

15. *To be about to return,* μέλλω ὑποστρέφειν.
Acts 13. 34 no more to return to corruption, he said

16. *To turn back,* ὑποστρέφω *hupostrephō.*
Mark 14. 40 [when he returned, he found them asleep]
Luke 1. 56 Mary abode..three months, and returned
2. 39 they returned into Galilee, to their own
2. 43 as they returned, the child Jesus tarried
4. 1 returned from Jordan, and was led by the
4. 14 Jesus returned in the power of the spirit
7. 10 they that were sent, returning to the ho.
8. 37 into the ship, and returned back again
8. 39 Return to thine own house, and show how
8. 40 that, when Jesus was returned, the peo.
9. 10 the apostles, when they were returned
10. 17 the seventy returned again with joy, say.
11. 24 I will return unto my house whence I came
17. 18 There are not found that returned to give
19. 12 receive for himself a kingdom, and to re.
23. 48 people..smote their breasts, and returned
23. 56 returned, and prepared spices and ointm.
24. 9 returned from the sepulchre, and told all
24. 33 returned to Jerusalem, and found the el.
24. 52 and returned to Jerusalem with great joy
Acts 1. 12 Then returned they unto Jerusalem from
8. 25 returned to Jerusalem, and preached the
8. 28 Was returning, and sitting in his chariot
12. 25 Barnabas and Saul returned from Jerusa.
13. 13 departing from them returned to Jerusa.
13. 34 no more to return to corruption, he said
14. 21 returned again to Lystra, and (to) Iconi.
20. 3 purposed to return through Macedonia
21. 6 took ship; and they returned home again
23. 32 left the horsemen..and returned to the
Gal. 1. 17 went into Arabia, and returned again unto
Heb. 7. 1 returning from the slaughter of the kings

RETURN an answer, to —
To cause to turn back, return, תּוּב *tub,* 5.
Ezra 5. 5 they returned answer by letter concerning

RETURN, to cause or make to —
1. *To cause to return,* שׁוּב *shub,* 5 [V.L. 1].
Jer 33. 26 cause their captivity to return, and have

2. *To cause to turn back, return,* שׁוּב *shub,* 5.
Deut 17. 16 nor cause the people to return to Egypt
1 Sa. 29. 4 Make this fellow return, that he may go
Jer. 29. 10 in causing you to return to this place
30. 3 will cause them to return to the land that
32. 44 for I will cause their captivity to return
33. 7 will cause..captivity of Israel, to return
33. 11 For I will cause to return the captivity of
34. 11 caused the servants..to return, and bro.
34. 16 caused every man his servant..to return
34. 22 cause them to return to this city; and
37. 20 cause me not to return to the house of J.
38. 26 that he would not cause me to return to
42. 12 and cause you to return to your own land
Eze. 21. 30 Shall I cause (it) to return into his sheath?
29. 14 cause them to return (into) the land of P.
47. 6 caused me to return to the brink of the r

RETURNED, to be —
To turn back, return, שׁוּב *shub.*
Gen 43. 18 the money that was returned in our sacks
Lev. 22. 13 and is returned unto her father's house
Josh. 2. 16 until the pursuers be returned: and after.
2. 22 until the pursuers were returned: and the
1 Sa. 18. 6 David was returned from the slaughter of
24. 1 when Saul was returned from following
2 Sa. 1. 1 David was returned from the slaughter of
3. 27 when Abner was returned to Hebron, Joab
2 Ki. 9. 15 Joram was returned to be healed in Jez.
Jer. 43. 5 that were returned from all nations
Zech. 1. 16 I am returned to Jerusalem with mercies
8. 3 I am returned unto Zion, and will dwell

RETURNING —
Returning, turning back, שׁוּבָה *shubah.*
Isa. 30. 15 In returning and rest shall ye be saved; in

RE'-U, רְעוּ *friendship.*
A son of Peleg, the fourth from Shem, and father of Serug. B.C. 2200.
Gen. 11. 18 And Peleg lived thirty years, and begat R.
11. 19 Peleg lived after he begat R. two hundred
11. 20 And R. lived two and thirty years, and
11. 21 R. lived after he begat Serug two hundred
1 Ch. 1. 25 Eber, Peleg, R.

RE-U'-BEN, רְאוּבֵן *behold a son.* Ῥουβήν.
1. The eldest son of Jacob and Leah. B.C. 1752.
Gen. 29. 32 Leah..bare a son, and..called his name R.
30. 14 **And R. went in the days of wheat harvest**

Gen. 35. 22 R. went and lay with Bilhah his father's
35. 23 The sons of Leah; R., Jacob's first born
37. 21 R. heard (it), and he delivered him out of
37. 22 And R. said unto them, Shed no blood
37. 29 And R. returned unto the pit; and beho.
42. 22 And R. answered them, saying, Spake I
42. 37 And R. spake unto his father, saying, Slay
46. 8 Jacob and his sons; R., Jacob's first born
46. 9 And the sons of R.; Hanoch, and Phallu
48. 5 as R. and Simeon, they shall be mine
49. 3 R., thou (art) my first born, my might, and
Exod. 1. 2 R., Simeon, Levi, and Judah
6. 14 The sons of R. the first born of Israel
6. 14 these (be) the families of R.
Num. 1. 20 And the children of R., Israel's eldest son
16. 1 Now Korah..and On..sons of R., took
26. 5 R. the eldest son of Israel
26. 5 the children of R.; Hanoch, (of whom c.)
Deut 11. 6 he did unto..sons of Eliab, the son of R.
Josh 15 6 went up to the stone of Bohan the son of R.
18. 17 to the stone of Bohan the son of R.
1 Ch. 2. 1 These (are) the sons of Israel; R., Simeon
5. 1 Now the sons of R. the first born of Israel
5. 3 The sons. (I say), of R. the first born of I.

2. His descendants and their territory E. of Jordan and of the Salt Sea

Num. 1. 5 of (the tribe of) R.; Elizur the son of She.
1. 21 that were numbered..of the tribe of R.
2. 10 south side (shall be) the standard..of R.
2. 10 the captain of the children of R. (shall)
2. 16 All that were numbered in the camp of R.
7. 30 Elizur..prince of the children of R., (did
10. 18 the standard of the camp of R. set forw.
13. 4 of the tribe of R., Shammua the son of Z
32. 1 the children of R...had a very great mult
32. 2 the children of R. came and spake unto
32. 6 And Moses said..to the children of R.
32. 25 and the children of R. spake unto Moses
32. 29 the children of R. will pass with you over
32. 31 and the children of R. answered, saying
32. 33 And Moses gave..to the children of R.
32. 37 And the children of R. built Heshbon
34. 14 the children of R...have received (their
Deut27. 13 R., Gad, and Asher, and Zebulun, Dan, and
33. 6 Let R. live, and not die; and let (not) his
Josh. 4. 12 the children of R...passed over armed b
13. 15 Moses gave unto the..children of R. (in)
13. 23 And the border of the children of R. was
13. 23 (was) the inheritance of the children of R.
18. 7 Gad, and R...have received their inheri.
20. 8 they assigned Bezer..out of the tribe of R.
21. 7 children of Merari..(had) out..tribe of R.
21. 36 And out of the tribe of R., Bezer with her
22. 9, 10, 11 the children of R., and the children
22. 13 children of Israel sent unto the chil. of R.
22. 15 And they came unto the children of R.
22. 21 Then the children of R...answered and
22. 25 ye children of R. and children of Gad
22. 30 P...heard the words that the children of R.
22. 31 Phinehas..said unto the children of R.
22. 32 Phinehas..returned from..children of R.
22. 33 wherein the children of R. and Gad
22. 34 And the children of R..called the altar
Judg. 5. 15, 16 For the divisions of R. (there were)
1 Ch. 5. 18 The sons of R., and the Gadites, and half
6. 63 Unto the sons of Merari (were given)..R.
6. 78 (were given them) out of the tribe of R.
Eze. 48. 6 the border of Ephraim..a (portion for) R.
48. 7 by the border of R...a (portion for) Judah
48. 31 one gate of R., one gate of Judah, one g.
Rev. 7. 5 Of the tribe of R. (were) sealed twelve th.

The following are the chief localities in the territory of Reuben: Abarim, Aroer, Ashdoth-Pisgah, Bamoth (Baal), Beon, (Beth) Baal-Meon, Beth-Jeshimoth, Beth-Peor, Bezer, Dibon, Elealeh, Heshbon Jahaza, Kedemoth, Kirjathaim, Medeba, Mephaath, Nebo, Sebam, (Shibmah or Sibmah), Zareth-Shahar, &c.

REUBENITES, הָראוּבֵנִי *the Reubenite.*

The descendants of Reuben. With the tribe of Gad and Manasseh they applied to Moses for an inheritance on the E. of the Jordan, and obtained it; they were consequently the first of the ten tribes that were carried to Assyria by Tiglath-pileser. B.C. 740.

Num26. 7 These (are) the families of the R.
Deut. 3. 12 the cities thereof, gave I unto the R.
3. 16 And unto the R...I gave from Gilead even
4. 43 (Namely) Bezer in the wilderness..of the R.
29. 8 we..gave it for an inheritance unto the R.
Josh. 1. 12 to the R., and to the Gadites..spake Jos
12. 6 Moses..gave it (for) a possession unto the R.
13. 8 With whom the R...have received their
22. 1 Then Joshua called the R., and the Gadites
2 Ki. 10. 33 all the land of Gilead, the Gadites, and R.
1 Ch. 5. 6 he (was) prince of the R.
5. 26 and he carried them away, even the R.
11. 42 Adina the son of Shiza the R.
11. 42 a captain of the R., and thirty with him
12. 37 And on the other side of Jordan, of the R.
26. 32 whom king David made rulers over the R.
27. 16 the ruler of the R. (was) Eliezer the son

RE-U'-EL, רְעוּאֵל *God is friend.*

1. A son of Esau by Bashemath daughter of Ishmael. B.C. 1750.

Gen. 36. 4 and Bashemath bare R.
36. 10 R. the son of Bashemath the wife of Esau
36. 13 And these (are) the sons of R.; Nahath
36. 17 And these (are) the sons of R. Esau's son
36. 17 these (are) the dukes (that came) of R.
1 Ch. 1. 35 The sons of Esau; Eliphaz, R., and Jeush
1. 37 The sons of R.; Nahath, Zerah, Shammah

2. Father-in-law of Moses, called also *Jethro* and *Raguel.* B.C. 1530

Exod. 2. 18 And when they came to R. their father, he

3. Father of Eliasaph, a captain of Gad, called in Num. 1. 14 *Deuel.* B.C. 1530

Num. 2. 14 and the captain..(shall be) Eliasaph..R.

4. A Benjamite in Jerusalem. B.C. 536.

1 Ch. 9. 8 Meshullam the son of Shephathiah..R.

RE-U'-MAH, רְאוּמָה *pearl, coral.*

A concubine of Nahor, Abraham's brother. B.C. 1860.

Gen. 22. 24 R...bare also Tebah, and Gaham, and Ta.

REVEAL (self), to —

1. *To uncover the ear,* גָּלָה אֹזֶן *galah ozen.*

2 Sa. 7. 27 hast revealed to thy servant, saying, I will

2. *To uncover, remove,* גָּלָה *galah.*

Prov. 20. 19 He that goeth about (as) a tale bearer re.
Amos 3. 7 revealeth his secret unto his servants the

3. *To be uncovered, removed,* גָּלָה *galah,* 2.

1 Sa. 3. 21 for the LORD revealed himself to Samuel

4. *To uncover, remove,* גָּלָה *galah,* 3.

Job 20. 27 The heavens shall reveal his iniquity; and
Prov 11. 13 A tale bearer revealeth secrets: but he
Jer. 11. 20 for unto thee have I revealed my cause
33. 6 will reveal unto them the abundance of

5. *To uncover, remove,* גְּלָה *gelah.*

Dan. 2. 19 Then was the secret revealed unto Daniel
2. 22 He revealeth the deep and secret things
2. 28 there is a God in heaven that revealeth
2. 29 he that revealeth secrets maketh known
2. 30 this secret is not revealed to me for (any)
2. 47 and a revealer..seeing thou couldest reveal

6. *To uncover, unveil,* ἀποκαλύπτω *apokaluptō.*

Matt11. 25 because thou..hast revealed them unto
11. 27 (he) to whomsoever the Son [will reveal]
16. 17 for flesh and blood hath not revealed (it)
Luke10 21 thank thee..that thou..hast revealed th
10. 22 (he) to whom the Son will reveal (him)
1 Co. 2. 10 But God hath revealed (them) unto us by
Gal. 1 16 To reveal his Son in me, that I might pr.
Phil. 3. 15 otherwise minded, God shall reveal even

REVEALED, to be —

1. *To be uncovered,* גָּלָה *galah,* 2.

Deut29. 29 but those (things which are) revealed (b.)
1 Sa. 3. 7 neither was the word..yet revealed unto
Isa. 22 14 it was revealed in mine ears by the LORD
23. 1 from the land of Chittim it is revealed to
40. 5 glory of the LORD shall be revealed, and
53 1 to whom is the arm of the LORD revealed?
56. 1 and my righteousness to be revealed
Dan. 10. 1 a thing was revealed unto Daniel, whose

2. *To uncover, unveil,* ἀποκαλύπτω *apokaluptō.*

Matt10 26 nothing covered, that shall not be revealed
Luke 2 35 thoughts of many hearts may be revealed
12. 2 nothing covered, that shall not be revealed
17. 30 the day when the Son of man is revealed
John12 38 hath the arm of the Lord been revealed?
Rom. 1 17 therein is the righteousness of God reve.
1. 18 For the wrath of God is revealed from h.
8. 18 with the glory which shall be revealed in
1 Co. 3 13 because it shall be revealed by fire; and
14. 30 If (any thing) be revealed to another that
Gal. 3 23 faith which should afterwards be revealed
Eph. 3. 5 as it is now revealed unto his holy apostles
2 Th. 2. 3 that man of sin be revealed, the son of pe.
2. 6 that he might be revealed in his time
2. 8 then shall that wicked be revealed, whom
1 Pe. 1. 5 kept..ready to be revealed in the last time
1. 12 Unto whom it was revealed, that not unto
5 1 partaker of the glory that shall be revea.

3. *An uncovering,* ἀποκάλυψις *apokalupsis.*

2 Th. 1. 7 when the Lord Jesus shall be revealed fr.
1 Pe. 4. 13 when his glory shall be revealed, ye may

4. *To utter an oracle,* χρηματίζω *chrēmatizō.*

Luke 2. 26 it was revealed unto him by the Holy Gh.

REVEALER —

To remove, uncover, unveil, גְּלָה *gelah* (partic.).

Dan. 2 47 and a revealer of secrets, seeing thou co.

REVELATION —

An uncovering, ἀποκάλυψις *apokalupsis.*

Rom. 2. 5 revelation of the righteous judgment of
16. 25 according to the revelation of the mystery
1 Co. 14. 6 I shall speak to you either by revelation
14. 26 every one of you..hath a revelation, hath
2 Co. 12. 1 will come to visions and revelations of the
12. 7 through the abundance of the revelations
Gal. 1. 12 but by the revelation of Jesus Christ
2. 2 I went up by revelation, and communica.
Eph. 1. 17 may give unto you the spirit of..revelat.
3. 3 How that by revelation he made known
1 Pe. 1. 13 brought unto you at the revelation of J.
Rev. 1. 1 The revelation of Jesus Christ, which G.

REVELLING —

Revelry, wantonness, (from Lat. comus), κῶμος.

Gal. 5. 21 Envyings, murders, drunkenness, revellings
1 Pe 4. 3 when we walked in..revellings, banquet.

REVENGE, REVENGING —

1. *Vengeance,* נְקָמָה *neqamah.*

Psa. 79. 10 the revenging of the blood of thy servants
Jer 20 10 and we shall take our revenge on him
Eze. 25. 15 Because the Philistines have dealt by re.

2. *Locks of hair, princes of the people,* פְּרָעוֹת *peraoth.*

Deut32. 42 from the beginning of revenges upon the

3. *Vengeance, full justice,* ἐκδίκησις *ekdikēsis.*

2 Co. 7. 11 yea, (what) revenge! In all (things) ye ha.

REVENGE (self), to —

1. *To avenge,* נָקַם *naqam.*

Nah. 1. 2 the LORD revengeth; the LORD revengeth

2. *To be avenged,* נָקַם *naqam,* 2.

Jer. 15. 15 revenge me of my persecutors; take me

3. *To avenge, exact full justice,* ἐκδικέω *ekdikeō.*

2 Co 10. 6 having in a readiness to revenge all disob.

REVENGER —

1. *To free (by avenging or repaying),* גָּאַל *gaal.*

Num35. 19 revenger of blood himself shall slay the
35 21 revenger of blood shall slay the murderer
35. 24 between the slayer and the revenger of b.
35. 25 out of the hand of the revenger of blood
35. 27 revenger of blood find him without the b.
35. 27 revenger of blood kill the slayer; he shall
2 Sa. 14. 11 wouldest not suffer the revengers of blood

2. *Avenger, exactor of full justice,* ἔκδικος *ekdikos.*

Rom 13 4 revenger to (execute) wrath upon him that

REVENUE —

1. *Revenue or income,* אַפְּתֹם *appethom.*

Ezra 4. 13 shalt endamage the revenue of the king

2. *Increase, revenue,* תְּבוּאָה *tebuah.*

Prov. 8. 19 and my revenue than choice silver
15. 6 but in the revenues of the wicked is trou.
16. 8 Better (is) a little..than great revenues
Isa. 23. 3 harvest of the river, (is) her revenue; and
Jer. 12. 13 they shall be ashamed of your revenues

REVERENCE —

Modesty, decency, αἰδώς *aidōs.*

Heb 12. 28 serve God acceptably with [reverence] and

REVERENCE, to (do, give, be had in) —

1. *To fear, be afraid, reverence,* יָרֵא *yare.*

Lev. 19 30 shall keep my sabbaths, and reverence my
26. 2 shall keep my sabbaths, and reverence my

2. *To be feared, reverenced,* יָרֵא *yare,* 2.

Psa. 89. 7 to be had in reverence of all (them that

3. *To bow down self,* שָׁחָה *shachah,* 7*a.*

2 Sa. 9. 6 fell on his face, and did reverence. And
1 Ki. 1. 31 did reverence to the king, and said, Let
Esth. 3. 2 bowed, and reverenced Haman: for the k.
3. 2, 5 Mordecai bowed not, nor did (him) reve.

4. *To turn in to, reverence,* ἐντρέπομαι *entrepomai.*

Matt21 37 sent..saying, They will reverence my son
Mark12. 6 sent..saying, They will reverence my son
Luke20 13 it may be they will reverence (him) when
Heb 12 9 corrected (us), and we gave (them) rever.

5. *To be terrified, affrighted, afraid,* φοβέομαι *phobe.*

Eph. 5. 33 the wife (see) that she reverence (her) hu.

REVEREND —

To be feared, reverenced, יָרֵא *yare,* 2.

Psa. 111. 9 for ever: holy and reverend (is) his name

REVERSE, to —

To cause to turn back, שׁוּב *shub,* 5.

Num. 23 20 he hath blessed; and I cannot reverse it
Esth. 8. 5 let it be written to reverse the letters de.
8. 8 writing which is written..may no man re.

REVILE (again), to —

1. *To declare light, despised or vile,* קָלַל *qalal,* 3.

Exod 22. 28 Thou shalt not revile the gods, nor curse

2. *To revile in return,* ἀντιλοιδορέω *antiloidoreō.*

1 Pe. 2. 23 Who..reviled not again; when he suffer.

3. *To speak injuriously,* βλασφημέω *blasphēmeō.*

Matt 27. 39 they that passed by reviled him, wagging

4. *To revile, rail,* λοιδορέω *loidoreō.*

John 9. 28 Then they reviled him, and said, Thou art
Acts 23 4 they that stood by said, Revilest thou G.
1 Co. 4. 12 being reviled, we bless; being persecuted
1 Pe. 2. 23 Who, when he was reviled..when he suff.

5. *To upbraid, revile,* ὀνειδίζω *oneidizō.*

Matt. 5. 11 Blessed are ye when (men) shall revile you
Mark15. 32 they that were crucified with him reviled

REVILER, REVILING —

1. *Reviling,* גִּדּוּף *gidduph.*

Isa. 51. 7 neither be ye afraid of their revilings
Zeph. 2. 8 the revilings of the children of Ammon

2. *Reviling, railing,* λοίδορος *loidoros.*

1 Co. 6. 10 nor revilers, nor extortioners, shall inhe.

REVIVE, to —

1. *To live, revive,* חָיָה *chayah.*

Gen. 45. 27 the spirit of Jacob their father revived
Judg15. 19 and..his spirit came again, and he revived
1 Ki. 17. 22 soul..came into him again, and he revived
2 Ki. 13. 21 when the man was let down..he revived

2. *To keep or make alive, revive,* חָיָה *chayah,* 3.

Neh. 4. 2 will they revive the stones out of the he.
Psa. 85 6 Wilt thou not revive us again, that thy p.
138. 7 thou wilt revive me; thou shalt stretch
Hos. 6. 2 After two days will he revive us: in the
14. 7 they shall revive (as) the corn, and grow
Hab. 3. 2 revive thy work in the midst of the years

3. *To cause to live,* חָיָה *chayah,* 5.

Isa. 57. 15 to revive the spirit..and to revive the h.

4. *To live again, revive,* ἀναζάω *anazaō.*
Rom. 7. 9 when the commandment came, sin reviv.
14. 9 Christ both died, and [rose, and revived]

REVIVING —
Preservation or means of life, מִחְיָה *michyah.*
Ezra 9. 8 give us a little reviving in our bondage
9. 9 give us a reviving, to set up the house of

REVOLT, revolted —
A turning aside, סָרָה *sarah.*
Isa. 1. 5 ye will revolt more and more. The whole
31. 6 from) whom the children..have deeply re.
59. 13 speaking oppression and revolt, conceiving

REVOLT, to —
To transgress, trespass, פָּשַׁע *pasha.*
2 Ki. 8 20 In his days Edom revolted from under the
8 22 Yet Edom revolted. Then Libnah revolted
2 Ch. 21. 8, 10 the Edomites revolted from under the
21. 10 same time (also) did Libnah revolt from

REVOLTED, to be —
To turn aside, סוּר *sur.*
Jer. 5. 23 But this people..are revolted and gone

REVOLTER, revolting —
1. *To turn aside,* סָרַר *sarar.*
Jer. 5. 23 But this people hath a revolting..heart
6 28 They (are) all grievous revolters, walking
Hos. 9 15 no more: all their princes (are) revolters
2. *Turning aside,* שֵׂטִים *setim.*
Hos. 5 2 revolters are profound to make slaughter

REWARD —
1. *Latter end,* אַחֲרִית *acharith.*
Prov 24. 14 there shall be a reward, and thy expect.
24. 20 For there shall be no reward to the evil
2. *A gift,* אֶתְנָה *ethnah.*
Hos 2. 12 These (are) my rewards that my lovers have
3. *A gift,* אֶתְנַן *ethnan.*
Eze 16. 34 that thou givest a reward, and no reward
Hos 9 1 hast loved a reward upon every corn floor
4. *Recompence, deed,* גְּמוּל *gemul*
Psa. 94 2 Lift up thyself..render a reward to the
Isa 3 11 reward of his hands shall be given him
Obad. 15 thy reward shall return upon thine own
5. *Recompence, deed,* גְּמוּלָה *gemulah.*
2 Sa 19. 36 why..recompense it me with such a rew.
6. *What is lifted up,* מַשְׂאֵת *maseth*
Jer 40. 5 the guard gave him victuals and a reward
7. *Wage, reward,* מַשְׂכֹּרֶת *maskoreth.*
Ruth 2. 12 a full reward be given thee of the LORD
8. *A gift,* מַתָּת *mattath.*
1 Ki. 13. 7 Come home..and I will give thee a reward
9. *A largess, gift,* נְבִזְבָּה *nebizbah.*
Dan. 2 6 ye shall receive of me gifts and rewards
5 17 give thy rewards to another; yet I will
10. *Heel, consequence,* עֵקֶב *eqeb.*
Psa. 19 11 in keeping of them (there is) great reward
40 15 Let them be desolate for a reward of their
70 3 let them be turned back for a reward of
11. *Work,* פְּעֻלָּה *peullah*
Psa 109 20 this (be) the reward of mine adversaries
12. *Fruit,* פְּרִי *peri.*
Psa. 58. 11 (there is) a reward for the righteous: ver.
13. *Reward,* שָׂכָר *sakar.*
Gen 15. 1 thy shield (and) thy exceeding great rew.
Num 18. 31 it (is) your reward for your service in the
Psa 127. 3 (and) the fruit of the womb (is his) reward
Eccl. 4. 9 they have a good reward for their labour
9. 5 neither have they any more a reward; for
Isa. 40. 10 his reward (is) with him, and his work be.
62. 11 his reward (is) with him, and his work be.
14. *Reward,* שֶׂכֶר *seker.*
Prov. 11. 18 to him that soweth..(shall be) a sure re.
15. *Bribe,* שֹׁחַד *shochad.*
Deut 10. 17 regardeth not persons, nor taketh reward
27. 25 he that taketh reward to slay an innocent
Psa 15 5 nor taketh reward against the innocent
Prov. 21. 14 and a reward in the bosom strong wrath
Isa. 5. 23 Which justify the wicked for reward, and
45. 13 not for price nor reward, saith the LORD
Mic. 3. 11 The heads thereof judge for reward, and
16. *A completing, recompence,* שִׁלּוּם *shillum.*
Mic. 7. 3 the judge (asketh) for a reward; and the
17. *A completion, recompence,* שִׁלֻּמָה *shillumah.*
Psa. 91. 8 behold and see the reward of the wicked
18. *Recompences,* שַׁלְמֹנִים *shalmonim.*
Isa. 1. 23 followeth after rewards: they judge not
19. *A giving back again,* ἀνταπόδοσις *antapodosis.*
Col. 3. 24 receive the reward of the inheritance
20. *Hire, wage, reward,* μισθός *misthos.*
Matt. 5. 12 great (is) your reward in heaven: for so
5. 46 what reward have ye? do not even the
6. 1 ye have no reward of your Father which is
6. 2, 5, 16 I say unto you, They have their rew
10. 41 He..shall receive a prophet's reward: and
10. 41 he shall receive a righteous man's reward
10. 42 verily..he shall in no wise lose his reward
Mark 9. 41 I say unto you, he shall not lose his rew.
Luke 6. 23 your reward (is) great in heaven: for in
6. 35 your reward shall be great, and ye shall
Acts 1. 18 this man purchased a field with the rew.
Rom 4. 4 reward not reckoned of grace, but of debt
1 Co. 3 8 every man shall receive his own reward
3. 14 work abide..he shall receive a reward
9. 17 I do this thing willingly, I have a reward
9. 18 What is my reward then? (Verily) that
1 Ti. 5. 18 and, The labourer (is) worthy of his reward
2 Pe. 2. 13 shall receive the reward of unrighteous.
2 John 8 lose not..but that we receive a full reward
Jude 11 ran greedily after the error..for reward
Rev 11. 18 that thou shouldest give reward unto thy
22. 12 my reward (is) with me, to give every ma..

REWARD, be rewarded, to (give) —
1 *To do, recompense, benefit,* גָּמַל *gamal.*
1 Sa 24. 17 rewarded me good, whereas I have rew.
2 Sa. 22. 21 The LORD rewarded me according to my
2 Ch. 20. 11 they reward us, to come to cast us out of
Psa 7 4 If I have rewarded evil unto him that was
18 20 The LORD rewarded me according to my
103. 10 nor rewarded us according to our iniqu.
Isa. 3. 9 they have rewarded evil unto themselves
2. *To set, put, lay,* שִׂים, שׂוּם *sum, sim.*
Psa 109. 5 they have rewarded me evil for good, and
3 *To hire, reward,* שָׂכַר *sakar.*
Prov 26 10 both rewardeth the fool and rewardeth
4. *There shall be reward to,* יֵשׁ שָׂכָר לְ *yesh sakar le.*
2 Ch. 15. 7 Be ye strong..your work shall be rewarded
Jer. 31. 16 thy work shall be rewarded, saith the L.
5. *To (cause to) turn back,* שׁוּב *shub,* 5 [V.L. 1]
Psa. 54 5 He shall reward evil unto mine enemies
6. *To cause to turn back,* שׁוּב *shub,* 5.
Prov 17. 13 Whoso rewardeth evil for good, evil shall
Hos. 4. 9 and I will..reward them their doings
7. *To bribe, hire,* שָׁחַד *shachad.*
Job 6 22 Give a reward for me of your substance
8 *To make whole, complete, repay,* שָׁלַם *shalam,* 3.
Gen. 44 4 Wherefore have ye rewarded evil for good?
Deut 32 41 If I whet..I..will reward them that hate
1 Sa. 24. 19 the LORD reward thee good for that thou
2 Sa. 3 39 LORD shall reward the doer of evil accor
Job 21. 19 he rewardeth him, and he shall know (it)
Psa. 31. 23 and plentifully rewardeth the proud doer
35 12 They rewarded me evil for good, (to) the
137 8 happy (shall he be) that rewardeth thee
Prov 25 22 heap coals of fire..LORD shall reward thee
9. *To be made whole, complete, perfect,* שָׁלַם *shalam,* 4.
Prov 13 13 but he that feareth shall be rewarded
10. *To give away or back,* ἀποδίδωμι *apodidōmi.*
Matt 6. 4, 6, 18 thy Father shall reward thee ope.
16 27 he shall reward every man according to
2 Ti. 4 14 Lord reward him according to his works
Rev 18. 6 Reward her even as she rewarded you, and

REWARDER —
A giver of wages, μισθαποδότης *misthapodotēs.*
Heb. 11 6 he is a rewarder of them that diligently

RE'ZEPH, רֶצֶף *stronghold.*
A city in East Syrian Palmyrene, between Racca and Emesa, near Haran and Gozan, and taken by Sennacherib.
2 Ki. 19 12 (as) Gozan, and Haran, and R. and the
Isa. 37. 12 (as) Gozan, and Haran, and R., and the ch.

REZ'IA, רִצְיָא *Jah is pleasing.*
An Asherite, a son of Ulla. B.C. 1452.
1 Ch. 7. 39 sons of Ulla; Arah, and Hanniel, and R.

RE'ZIN, רְצִין *dominion.*
1. The last king of Syria, in the days of Jothan king of Judah, and slain by Tiglath pileser. B.C. 742.
2 Ki. 15. 37 the LORD began to send..R the king of S.
16. 5 R. king of Syria ..came up to Jerusalem to
16. 6 R king of Syria recovered Elath to Syria
16. 9 the king of Assyria went up..and slew R.
Isa. 7 1 R the king of Syria..went up toward J
7. 4 fear not..for the fierce anger of R. with
7 8 For the..head of Damascus (is) R.; and w.
8. 6 and rejoice in R and Remaliah's son
9. 11 the LORD shall set up the adversaries of R
2 One of the Nethinim whose descendants returned with Zerubbabel. B C 536
Ezr. 2. 48 The children of R., the children of Nek.
Neh. 7 50 The children of Reaiah, the children of R.

RE'ZON, רְזוֹן *prince, noble.*
Son of Eliadah, and a subject of Hadadezer king of Zobah, from whom he fled to Damascus, where he founded a kingdom and opposed Solomon. B.C. 1000.
1 Ki. 11. 23 God stirred him up..R. the son of Eliadah

RHE-GI-UM, Ῥήγιον *breach.*
A port in the S.W. of Italy, opposite Messina in Sicily; here Paul landed on his way to Rome. It is now called *Reggio,* and is the capital of Calabria.
Acts 28. 13 we fetched a compass, and came to R.

RHE'-SA, Ῥησά *an ancestor of Jesus.*
Luke 3. 27 of Joanna, which was (the son) of R. wh.

RHO'-DA, Ῥόδη *a rose.*
A damsel in the house of Mary the mother of John Mark, and who opened the door for Peter.
Acts 12. 13 And..a damsel came to hearken, named R.

RHO'-DES, Ῥόδος.
An island in the Mediterranean Sea, W. of Lydia, and 75 miles E. of Crete. It is 120 miles in circumference, and was held by a branch of the Doric race about the time of the Trojan war, B.C. 1184; in 408 its capital city was built; in 431 it was compelled to pay tribute to Athens; in 412 it changed sides; in 396 it changed sides again; in 390 the aristocrats recovered power; in 357-355 it opposed Athens; in 323 it submitted to Alexander; in 304 it was besieged by Demetrius Poliorcetes; in 108 it fought against Mithridites; in 50 it helped Cæsar against Pompey, but in 42 it was subdued. In A.D. 330 it was made the capital of the Provincia Isularium; in 616 it was taken by the Persians; in 651 by the Saracens; in 1309 by the Knights of St John; in 1480 it repelled Mohammed II; in 1522 it was taken by Soliman II. It was noted for its colossal statute of Apollos, 70 cubits or 105 feet high (built by Chares, a pupil of Lysippus, and by Laches), which was completed B.C. 280; it was erected over the entrance of the harbour, and was overthrown by an earthquake. B.C. 224.
Acts 21. 1 we came..unto R., and from thence unto

RIB —
1. *A rib,* עֲלַע *ala.*
Dan. 7 5 three ribs in the mouth of it between the
2. *A rib,* צֵלָע *tsela.*
Gen. 2. 21 he took one of his ribs, and closed up the
2. 22 the rib, which the LORD God had taken

RI'BAI, רִיבַי *Jah contends.*
Father of Ittai one of David's valiant men, from Gibeah of Benjamin. B.C. 1070.
2 Sa 23. 29 Ittai the son of R. out of Gibeah of..Be.
1 Ch 11. 31 Ithai the son of R. of Gibeah..of Benja.

RIBBAND —
A thread, ribband, פְּתִיל *pathil.*
Num 15. 38 they put upon the fringe..a ribband of bl.

RIB'LAH, רִבְלָה *bare place.* See *Diblath.*
A city on the Orontes N. of the *Bikea,* now called *Ribleh.*
Num 34. 11 And the coast shall go down..to R, on the
2 Ki. 23. 33 Pharaoh-nechoh put him in bands at R.
25 6, 20 brought..to the king of Babylon to R.
25. 21 And the king of Babylon..slew them at R.
Jer 39. 5 they brought him..to R. in the land of H.
39. 6 the king..slew the sons of Zedekiah in R.
52. 9 they took the king..to R in the land of
52. 10 he slew also all the princes of Judah in R.
52 26 brought them to the king of Babylon to R.
52. 27 And the king..put them to death in R.

RICH (man) —
1. *Rich,* עָשִׁיר *ashir.*
Exod 30 15 The rich shall not give more, and the poor
Ruth 3. 10 followedst not..men, whether poor or r.
2 Sa. 12. 1 There were two..in one city; the one rich
12. 2 The rich..had exceeding many flocks and
12. 4 there came a traveller unto the rich man
Job 27 19 The rich man shall lie down, but he shall
Psa. 45. 12 the rich among the people shall entreat
49 2 Both low and high, rich and poor, together
Prov 10 15 The rich man's wealth (is) his strong city
14. 20 is hated..but the rich (hath) many friends
18. 11 The rich man's wealth (is) his strong city
18. 23 The poor useth entreaties; but the rich
22. 2 The rich and poor meet together: the L.
22. 7 The rich ruleth over the poor, and the b.
22 16 he that giveth to the rich, (shall) surely
28. 6 perverse (in his) ways, though he (be) rich
28. 11 The rich man (is) wise in his own conceit
Eccl. 5. 12 the abundance of the rich will not suffer
10. 6 Folly is set in great dignity, and the rich
10. 20 curse not the rich in thy bed chamber: for
Isa. 53. 9 made his grave..with the rich in his de.
Jer. 9 23 let not the rich (man) glory in his riches
Mic. 6. 12 the rich men thereof are full of violence
2. *Rich, wide, bountiful,* שׁוֹעַ *shoa.*
Job 34. 19 nor regardeth the rich more than the poor
3. *Rich,* πλούσιος *plousios.*
Matt 19. 23 That a rich man shall hardly enter into
19. 24 than for a rich man to enter into the kin.
27 57 there came a rich man of Arimathea, na.
Mark 10. 25 than for a rich man to enter into the kin.
12. 41 and many that were rich cast in much
Luke 6. 24 woe unto you that are rich! for ye have
12. 16 The ground of a certain rich man brought
14. 12 not..thy kinsmen, nor (thy) rich neighb.
16. 1 a certain rich man which had a steward
16. 19 a certain rich man, which was clothed in
16. 21 crumbs which fell from the rich man's t.
16. 22 the rich man also died, and was buried
18. 23 he was very sorrowful: for he was very r.
18. 25 than for a rich man to enter into the kin.
19. 2 a man named Zaccheus..and he was rich
21. 1 saw the rich men casting their gifts into
2 Co. 8. 9 though he was rich, yet for your sakes he
Eph. 2. 4 God, who is rich in mercy, for his great
1 Ti. 6. 17 Charge them that are rich in this world
Jas. 1. 10 But the rich, in that he is made low: be.
1. 11 so also shall the rich man fade away in his
2. 5 the poor of this world rich in faith, and
2. 6 Do not rich men oppress you, and draw
5. 1 Go to now..rich men, weep and howl for
Rev. 2. 9 I know thy..poverty, but thou art rich
3. 17 I am rich, and increased with goods, and
6. 15 the rich men, and the chief captains, and
13. 16 both small and great, rich and poor, free

4. *To be or become rich*, πλουτέω *plouteō*.
Luke 1. 53 and the rich he hath sent empty away

RICH (richer), to be, be made, become, wax —

1. *Wealth, substance, sufficiency*, הוֹן *hon*.
Prov 28. 22 He that hasteth to be rich hath an evil eye
2. *To be heavy, weighty, honourable*, כָּבֵד *kabed*.
Gen. 13. 2 Abram (was) very rich in cattle, in silver
3. *To reach to, overtake*, נָשַׂג *nasag*, 5.
Lev. 25. 47 if a sojourner or stranger wax rich by thee
4. *To be rich*, עָשַׁר *ashar*.
Job 15. 29 He shall not be rich, neither shall his su.
Hos. 12. 8 Yet I am become rich, I have found me
5. *To make rich*, עָשַׁר *ashar*, 5.
Psa. 49. 16 Be not thou afraid when one is made rich
Prov 21. 17 that loveth wine and oil shall not be rich
23. 4 Labour not to be rich; cease from thine
28. 20 he that maketh haste to be rich shall not
Jer. 5. 27 they are become great, and waxen rich
Dan. 11. 2 the fourth shall be far richer than (they)
Zech. 11. 5 Blessed (be) the LORD; for I am rich: and
6. *To be or become rich*, πλουτέω *plouteō*.
Luke 12. 21 So (is) he that..is not rich toward God
Rom. 10. 12 same Lord over all is rich unto all that
1 Co. 4. 8 Now ye are full, now ye are rich, ye have
2 Co. 8. 9 that ye through his poverty might be rich
1 Ti. 6. 9 they that will be rich fall into temptation
6. 18 that they be rich in good works, ready to
Rev. 3. 18 that thou mayest be rich; and white rai.
18. 3 merchants of the earth are waxed rich th.
18. 15 merchants..which were made rich by her
18. 19 wherein were made rich all that had ships

RICH, to make (self) —

1. *To make rich*, עָשַׁר *ashar*, 5.
Gen. 14. 23 shouldest say, I have made Abram rich
1 Sa. 2. 7 maketh poor, and maketh rich: he bring
Prov 10. 4 but the hand of the diligent maketh rich
10. 22 The blessing of the LORD, it maketh rich
2. *To make self rich*, עָשַׁר *ashar*, 7.
Prov 13. 7 There is that maketh himself rich, yet (ha.)
3. *To make rich*, πλουτίζω *ploutizō*.
2 Co. 6. 10 yet making many rich; as having nothing

RICHES —

1. *Substance, riches*, הוֹן *hon*.
Psa. 119. 14 I have rejoiced..as (much as) in all riches
Prov. 8. 18 (are) with me; (yea), durable riches and ri.
11. 4 Riches profit not in the day of wrath: but
13. 7 maketh himself poor, yet (hath) great ri.
19. 14 House and riches (are) the inheritance of
24. 4 filled with all precious and pleasant riches
Eze. 27. 12 thy merchant..of all (kind of) riches; with
27. 18 for the multitude of all riches; in the wi.
27. 27 Thy riches, and thy fairs, thy merchandise
27. 33 enrich..with the multitude of thy riches
2. *Multitude*, הָמוֹן *hamon*.
Psa. 37. 16 better than the riches of many wicked
3. *Force, might*, חַיִל *chayil*.
Job 20. 15 He hath swallowed down riches, and he
Psa. 62. 10 if riches increase, set not your heart (upon
73. 12 prosper in the world; they increase (in) r.
Isa. 8. 4 riches of Damascus and the spoil of Sam.
10. 14 my hand hath found as a nest the riches
30. 6 they will carry their riches upon the sho.
61. 6 ye shall eat the riches of the Gentiles, and
Eze. 26. 12 they shall make a spoil of thy riches, and
28. 4 thou hast gotten thee riches, and hast go
28. 5 traffic hast thou increased thy riches, and
28. 5 thine heart is lifted up because of thy ri.
4. *Thing laid or treasured up*, חֹסֶן *chosen*.
Prov. 27. 24 For riches (are) not for ever: and doth the
5. *What is over and above*, יִתְרָה *yithrah*.
Jer. 48. 36 the riches (that) he hath gotten are peris.
6. *Goods, what is covered or concealed*, נְכָסִים *nekasim*.
Josh. 22. 8 Return with much riches unto your tents
7. *Riches*, עֹשֶׁר *osher*.
Gen. 31. 16 For all the riches which God hath taken
1 Sa. 17. 25 king will enrich him with great riches, and
1 Ki. 3. 11 neither hast asked riches for thyself, nor
3. 13 have also given thee..both riches and ho.
10. 23 exceeded all the kings..for riches and for
1 Ch. 29. 12 Both riches and honour (come) of thee, and
29. 28 died..full of days, riches, and honour: and
2 Ch. 1. 11 hast not asked riches, wealth, or honour
1. 12 give thee riches, and wealth, and honour
9. 22 passed all the kings..in riches and wisdom
17. 5 he had riches and honour in abundance
18. 1 Jehoshaphat had riches and honour in a.
32. 27 had exceeding much riches and honour
Esth. 1. 4 When he showed the riches of his glorious
5. 11 told them of the glory of his riches, and
Psa. 49. 6 boast..in the multitude of their riches
52. 7 trusted in the abundance of his riches
112. 3 Wealth and riches (shall be) in his house
Prov. 3. 16 (and) in her left hand riches and honour
8. 18 Riches and honour (are) with me; (yea)
11. 16 honour; and strong (men) retain riches
11. 28 He that trusteth in his riches shall fall
13. 8 The ransom of a man's life (are) his riches
14. 24 The crown of the wise (is) their riches; (but
22. 1 rather to be chosen than great riches, (and)
22. 4 fear of the LORD. (are) riches, honour, and
30. 8 give me neither poverty nor riches; feed
Eccl. 4. 8 neither is his eye satisfied with riches
Eccl. 5. 13 riches kept for the owners thereof to th.
5. 14 But those riches perish by evil travail
5. 19 to whom God hath given riches and we.
6. 2 to whom God hath given riches, wealth
9. 11 nor yet riches to men of understanding
Jer. 9. 23 let not the rich (man) glory in his riches
17. 11 he that getteth riches, and not by right
Dan. 11. 2 by his strength through his riches he sh.
8. *Acquisition*, קִנְיָן *qinyan*.
Psa. 104. 24 made them all: the earth is full of thy ri.
9. *What is collected, goods, substance*, רְכוּשׁ *rekush*.
Gen 36. 7 For their riches were more than they that
2 Ch. 20. 25 found among them..both riches with the
Dan. 11. 13 with a great army and with much riches
11. 24 scatter among them the prey..and riches
11. 28 he return into his land with great riches
10. *Riches, bountifulness*, שׁוּעַ *shua*.
Job 36. 19 Will he esteem thy riches? (no), not gold
11. *Riches*, πλοῦτος *ploutos*.
Matt 13. 22 deceitfulness of riches, choke the word
Mark 4. 19 deceitfulness of riches, and the lusts of
Luke 8. 14 choked with cares and riches and pleas.
Rom 2. 4 Or despisest thou the riches of his good.
9. 23 that he might make known the riches of
11. 12 Now if the fall of them (be) the riches of
11. 12 diminishing of them the riches of the G.
11. 33 the depth of the riches both of the wisd.
2 Co. 8. 2 abounded unto the riches of their liber.
Eph. 1. 7 sins, according to the riches of his grace
1. 18 riches of the glory of his inheritance in
2. 7 might show the exceeding riches of his gr.
3. 8 I should preach..the unsearchable riches
3. 16 according to the riches of his glory, to be
Phil. 4. 19 supply all your need according to his ri.
Col. 1. 27 would make known what (is) the riches
2. 2 unto all riches of the full assurance of un.
1 Ti. 6. 17 nor trust in uncertain riches, but in the
Heb. 11. 26 reproach of Christ greater riches than the
Jas. 5. 2 Your riches are corrupted, and your gar.
Rev. 5. 12 that was slain to receive power, and riches
18. 17 For in one hour so great riches is come to
12. *Goods*, χρῆμα *chrēma*.
Mark 10. 23 How hardly shall they that have riches
10. 24 how hard is it for them that trust in ri.
Luke 18. 24 How hardly shall they that have riches

RICHES, hidden —

Hidden treasures or riches, מַטְמוֹן *matmon*.
Isa. 45. 3 I will give thee..hidden riches of secret

RICHLY —

Richly, πλουσίως *plousiōs*.
Col. 3. 16 Let the word of Christ dwell in you richly
1 Ti. 6. 17 who giveth us richly all things to enjoy

RID, to —

1. *To snatch at or away, deliver*, נָצַל *natsal*, 5.
Gen. 37. 22 that he might rid him out of their hands
Exod 6. 6 will rid you out of their bondage, and I
Psa. 82. 4 Deliver the poor and needy: rid (them)
2. *To open*, פָּצָה *patsah*.
Psa. 144. 7 rid me, and deliver me out of great waters
144. 11 Rid me, and deliver me from the hand of
3. *To cause to cease or rest*, שָׁבַת *shabath*, 5.
Lev. 26. 6 and I will rid evil beasts out of the land

RIDDANCE, (to make clean) —

1. *To end, consume*, כָּלָה *kalah*.
Zeph. 1. 18 for he shall make even a speedy riddance
2. *To make an end, consume*, כָּלָה *kalah*, 3.
Lev. 23. 22 shalt not make clean riddance of the co.

RIDDLE —

A hidden saying, חִידָה *chidah*.
Judg 14. 12 I will now put forth a riddle unto you: if
14. 13 Put forth thy riddle, that we may hear it
14. 14 could not in three days expound the rid.
14. 15 that he may declare unto us the riddle
14. 16 thou hast put forth a riddle unto the ch.
14. 17 told the riddle to the children of her pe.
14. 18 If..not..ye had not found out my riddle
14. 19 gave..unto them which expounded the ri.
Eze. 17. 2 Son of man, put forth a riddle, and speak

RIDE, to cause or make —

To cause or make to ride, רָכַב *rakab*, 5.
Gen. 41. 43 he made him to ride in the second chariot
Deut 32. 13 He made him ride on the high places of
1 Ki. 1. 33 cause Solomon my son to ride upon mine
1. 38 caused Solomon to ride upon king David's
1. 44 caused him to ride upon the king's mule
2 Ki. 10. 16 So they made him ride in his chariot
Job 30. 22 thou causest me to ride (upon it), and d.
Psa. 66. 12 Thou hast caused men to ride over our
Isa. 58. 14 cause thee to ride upon the high places of
Hos. 10. 11 I will make Ephraim to ride; Judah shall

RIDE (on, upon, in a chariot), to —

To ride, רָכַב *rakab*.
Gen. 24. 61 they rode upon the camels, and followed
Lev. 15. 9 what saddle soever he rideth upon that
Num 22. 30 upon which thou hast ridden ever since
Deut 33. 26 rideth upon the heaven in thy help, and
Judg. 5. 10 Speak, ye that ride on white asses, ye th.
10. 4 thirty sons that rode on thirty ass colts
12. 14 that rode on threescore and ten ass colts
1 Sa. 25. 20 it was (so, as) she rode on the ass, that
25. 42 hasted, and arose, and rode upon an ass
30. 17 young men, which rode upon camels, and
2 Sa. 16. 2 for the king's household to ride on: and
18. 9 Absalom rode upon a mule, and the mule
19. 26 saddle me an ass, that I may ride thereon
22. 11 rode upon a cherub, and did fly; and he
1 Ki. 13. 13 saddled him the ass: and he rode thereon
18. 45 And Ahab rode, and went to Jezreel
2 Ki. 9. 16 So Jehu rode in a chariot, and went to J.
9. 25 when I and thou rode together after Ah.
Neh. 2. 12 with me, save the beast that I rode upon
Esth. 6. 8 and the horse that the king rideth upon
8. 14 posts that rode upon mules (and) camels
Psa. 18. 10 rode upon a cherub, and did fly; yea, he
45. 4 in thy majesty ride prosperously, because
68. 4 extol him that rideth upon the heavens
68. 33 To him that rideth upon the heavens of
Isa. 19. 1 the LORD rideth upon a swift cloud, and
30. 16 We will ride upon the swift; therefore shall
Jer. 6. 23 they ride upon horses, set in array as men
50. 42 shall ride upon horses, (every one) put in
Hos. 14. 3 we will not ride upon horses; neither will
Amos 2. 15 neither shall he that rideth the horse de.
Hab. 3. 8 that thou didst ride upon thine horses
Hag. 2. 22 overthrow the chariots, and those that r.

RIDER, RIDING —

To ride, רָכַב *rakab*.
Gen. 49. 17 biteth the horse heels, so that his rider
Exod 15. 1, 21 horse and his rider hath he thrown in.
Num 22. 22 Now he was riding upon his ass, and his
2 Ki. 4. 24 slack not (thy) riding for me, except I bid
18. 23 if thou be able on thy part to set riders
Esth. 8. 10 riders on mules, camels, (and) young dr.
Job 39. 18 she scorneth the horse and his rider
Isa. 36. 8 if thou be able on thy part to set riders
Jer. 17. 25 riding in chariots and on horses, they, and
22. 4 riding in chariots and on horses, he, and
51. 21 break in pieces the horse and his rider; and
51. 21 I break in pieces the chariot and his rid.
Eze. 23. 6 young men, horsemen riding upon horses
23. 12 horsemen riding upon horses, all of them
23. 23 renowned, all of them riding upon horses
38. 15 all of them riding upon horses, a great c.
Hag. 2. 22 horses and their riders shall come down
Zech. 1. 8 and behold a man riding upon a red horse
9. 9 riding upon an ass, and upon a colt the
10. 5 the riders on horses shall be confounded
12. 4 smite every horse..and his rider with m.

RIDGE —

A furrow, ridge, תֶּלֶם *telem*.
Psa. 65. 10 Thou waterest the ridges thereof abunda.

RIE, RYE —

Prickly spelt or vetch, כֻּסֶּמֶת *kussemeth*.
Exod. 9. 32 But the wheat and the rye were not sm.
Isa. 28. 25 appointed barley, and the rye, in their p.?

RIFLED, to be —

To be rifled, spoiled, robbed, שָׁסַס *shasas*, 2.
Zech 14. 2 city shall be taken, and the houses rifled

RIGHT —

1. *Truth*, אֱמֶת *emeth*.
Gen. 24. 48 which had led me in the right way to take
Neh. 9. 33 for thou hast done right, but we have d.
Jer. 2. 21 planted thee a noble vine, wholly a right
2. *Right of freeing or redeeming*, גְּאֻלָּה *geullah*.
Ruth 4. 6 redeem thou my right to thyself; for I
3. *Right hand or side*, יָמִין *yamin*.
Gen. 48. 17 saw that his father laid his right hand up.
Exod 29. 22 the right shoulder; for it (is) a ram of
Lev. 7. 32 the right shoulder shall ye give unto the
7. 33 shall have the right shoulder for (his) part
8. 25 two kidneys, and their fat, and the right
8. 26 on the fat, and upon the right shoulder
9. 21 breasts and the right shoulder Aaron w.
Num 18. 18 as the wave breast and as the right shoul.
Judg. 3. 16 gird it under his raiment upon his right
3. 21 took the dagger from his right thigh, and
7. 20 the trumpets in their right hands to blow
1 Sa. 11. 2 that I may thrust out all your right eyes
2 Sa. 20. 9 took Amasa by the beard with the right
1 Ki. 7. 39 five bases on the right side of the house
7. 49 five on the right (side), and five on the left
Job 30. 12 Upon (my) right (hand) rise the youth; th.
Psa. 73. 23 thou hast holden (me) by my right hand
121. 5 the LORD (is) thy shade upon thy right h.
Jer. 22. 24 were the signet upon my right hand, yet
Eze. 39. 3 cause thine arrows to fall out of thy right
Zech. 4. 3 one upon the right (side) of the bowl, and
4. 11 these two olive trees upon the right (side)
11. 17 upon his right eye..his right eye shall be
4. *Right hand or side*, יְמִינִי *yemini*.
Eze. 4. 6 lie again on thy right side, and thou shalt
5. *Right hand or side*, יְמָנִי *yemani*.
Exod 29. 20 upon the tip of the right ear of
29. 20 thumb of their right hand..right foot
Lev. 8. 23 put (it) upon the tip of Aaron's right ear
8. 23 and upon the thumb of his right hand
8. 23 and upon the great toe of his right foot
8. 24 the blood upon the tip of their right ear
8. 24 and upon the thumbs of their right hands
8. 24 and upon the great toes of their right feet
14. 14, 17, 25, 28 right ear..right..right foot
14. 16 priest shall dip his right finger in the oil
14. 27 priest shall sprinkle with his right finger
1 Ki. 6. 8 The door..(was) in the right side of the
7. 21 he set up the right pillar, and called the
7. 39 put five bases on the right side of the ho.
2 Ki. 11. 11 from the right corner of the temple to the
2 Ch. 4. 10 set the sea on the right side of the east

2 Ch.23. 10 from the right side of the temple to the
Eze. 4. 6 lie again on thy right side, and thou shalt
47. 1 from the right side of the house, at the
47. 2 behold, there ran out waters on the right s.

6. *One right, upright,* יָשָׁר *yashar.*
Exod15. 26 and wilt do that which is right in his sig.
Deut. 6. 18 thou shalt do (that which is) right and g.
12. 8 every man whatsoever(is)right in his own
12. 25 (that which is) right in the sight of the L.
So in 21. 9; 1 Ki. 15. 5; 2 Ki. 12. 2; 14. 3; 15. 3, 34; 16.
2; 18 3; 22. 2; 2 Ch. 20. 32; 24. 2, 25. 2; 26. 4; 27. 2; 28.
1; 29. 2; 34. 2.
Deut 12. 28 thou doest (that which is) good and right
13. 18 to do (that which is) right in the eyes of
32. 4 and without iniquity, just and right (is)
Josh. 9. 25 as it seemeth good and right unto thee to
Judg17. 6 every man did (that which was) right in
21. 25 every man did (that which was) right in
1 Sa. 12. 23 will teach you the good and the right way
1 Ki.11. 33 to do (that which is) right in mine eyes
11. 38 do (that is) right in my sight, to keep my
14. 8 to do (that) only (which was) right in mi.
15. 11 Asa did (that which was) right in the eyes
22. 43 doing (that which was) right in the eyes
2 Ki. 10. 15 Is thine heart right, as my heart (is) with
10. 30 done well in executing (that which is) ri.
2 Ch. 14. 2 Asa did (that which was) good and right
31. 20 wrought (that which was) good and right
Ezra 8. 21 to seek of him a right way for us, and for
Neh. 9. 13 gavest them right judgments, and true
Job 33. 27 perverted (that which was) right, and it
Psa. 19 8 statutes of the LORD (are) right, rejoicing
33. 4 For the word of the LORD (is) right; and all
107. 7 he led them forth by the right way, that
Prov. 8 9 and right to them that find knowledge
12 15 The way of a fool (is) right in his own eyes
14. 12 There is a way which seemeth right unto
16. 13 and they love him that speaketh right
16. 25 There is a way that seemeth right unto
20. 11 his work (be) pure, and whether (it be) r
21. 2 Every way of a man (is) right in his own
21. 8 but (as for) the pure, his work (is) right
Jer. 34. 15 had done right in my sight, in proclaim.
Hos. 14. 9 for the ways of the LORD (are) right, and

7. *Right, uprightness,* יֹשֶׁר *yosher.*
Job 6. 25 How forcible are right words! but what
Prov. 4. 11 taught thee..I have led thee in right pa.

8. *To be prepared, ready, established,* כּוּן *kun,* 2.
Job 42. 7 not spoken of me (the thing that is) right
42. 8 not spoken of me (the thing which is) ri.
Psa. 51. 10 and renew a right spirit within me
78. 37 For their heart was not right with him

9. *So, prepared, right,* כֵּן *ken.*
Num27. 7 The daughters of Zelophehad speak right

10. *Rightness, uprightness,* כִּשְׁרוֹן *kishron.*
Eccl. 4. 4 every right work, that for this a man is

11. *Upright place or thing,* מִישׁוֹר *mishor.*
Psa. 45. 6 sceptre of thy kingdom (is) a right sceptre

12. *Judgment, right, cause, manner,* מִשְׁפָּט *mishpat.*
Gen 18. 25 Shall not the judge of all the earth do ri.?
Deut21. 17 beginning of his strength: the right of the
Job 34. 6 Should I lie against my right? my wound
34. 17 Shall even he that hateth right govern?
35. 2 Thinkest thou this to be right, (that) thou
36. 6 the wicked: but giveth right to the poor
Psa. 9. 4 thou hast maintained my right and my
140. 12 cause of the afflicted, (and) the right of
Prov.12. 5 The thoughts of the righteous (are) right
16. 8 Better..than great revenues without rig.
Isa. 10. 2 to take away the right from the poor of
32 7 words, even when the needy speaketh ri.
Jer. 5. 28 and the right of the needy do they not
17. 11 he that getteth riches, and not by right
32. 7 for the right of redemption (is) thine to
32. 8 for the right of inheritance (is) thine, and
Lam. 3 35 To turn aside the right of a man before
Eze. 21 27 until he come whose right it is; and I w.

13. *Straight forward,* נָכֹחַ *nakoach.*
2 Sa. 15. 3 See, thy matters (are) good and right; but
Prov24 26 shall kiss (his) lips that giveth a right an
Amos 3. 10 For they know not to do right, saith the

14. *Rightness, justice,* צֶדֶק *tsedeq.*
Psa. 9. 4 thou satest in the throne judging right
17. 1 Hear the right, O LORD, attend unto my
119. 75 that thy judgments (are) right, and (that)

15. *Rightness, justice,* צְדָקָה *tsedaqah.*
2 Sa. 19. 28 what right therefore have I yet to cry any
Neh. 2 20 ye have no portion, nor right, nor memo.
Eze. 18 5, 19, 21, 27 that which is lawful and right
33. 14, 16, 19 that which is lawful and right

16. *Right (hand, foot, or side),* δεξιός *dexios.*
Matt. 5. 29 if thy right eye offend thee, pluck it out
5. 30 if thy right hand offend thee, cut if off, and
5. 39 whosoever shall smite thee on thy right
Luke 6. 6 was a man whose right hand was withered
22. 50 smote a servant..and cut off his right ear
John18. 10 Then Simon Peter..cut off his right ear
21. 6 Cast the net on the right side of the ship
Acts 3. 7 he took him by the right hand, and lifted
Rev. 1. 16 he had in his right hand seven stars; and
1. 17 laid his right hand upon me, saying unto
10. 2 set his right foot upon the sea, and (his)
13. 16 to receive a mark in their right hand, or

17. *Right, just,* δίκαιος *dikaios.*
Matt20. 4 and whatsoever is right I will give you
Matt20. 7 [whatsoever is right, (that) shall ye receive]
Luke12. 57 of yourselves judge ye not what is right?
Acts 4. 19 Whether it be right in the sight of God to
Eph. 6. 1 Children, obey your parents..this is right

18. *Privilege,* ἐξουσία *exousia.*
Heb. 13. 10 whereof they have no right to eat which
Rev. 22. 14 may have right to the tree of life, and may

19. *Straight, upright, correct,* εὐθύς *euthus.*
Acts 8. 21 thy heart is not right in the sight of God
13. 10 to pervert the right ways of the Lord
2 Pe. 2. 15 Which have forsaken the right way, and

20. *Right, upright, erect,* ὀρθῶς *orthōs.*
Luke10. 28 Thou hast answered right: this do, and

RIGHT, to be, esteem, go on —

1. *To be right or upright,* יָשַׁר *yashar.*
1 Ch.13. 4 for the thing was right in the eyes of all

2. *To esteem or go right,* יָשַׁר *yashar,* 3.
Psa.119. 128 I esteem all (thy) precepts..(to be) right
Prov. 9. 15 To call passengers who go right on their

3. *To be right or upright,* כָּשֵׁר *kasher.*
Esth. 8. 5 and the thing (seem) right before the king

RIGHT (early, forth, on) —

1. *Straightforward, over against, right on,* נֹכַח *nokach.*
Prov. 4. 25 Let thine eyes look right on, and let thine

2. *To face, front, look,* פָּנָה *panah.*
Psa. 46. 5 God shall help her, (and that) right early

3. *Face,* פָּנִים *panim.*
Jer. 49. 5 shall be driven out every man right forth

RIGHT hand or side —

1. *Right hand or side,* יָמִין *yamin.*
Gen. 13. 9 or if (thou depart) to the right hand then
24. 49 I may turn to the right hand, or to the
48. 13 Ephraim in his right hand toward Israel's
48. 13 Manasseh .toward Israel's right hand, and
48. 14 Israel stretched out his right hand, and
48. 18 Not so..put thy right hand upon his head
Exod14. 22, 29 wall unto them on their right hand
15. 6 Thy right hand..thy right hand, O LORD
15. 12 Thou stretchedst out thy right hand, the
Num20 17 we will not turn to the right hand nor to
22. 26 no way to turn either to the right hand
Deut. 2. 27 will neither turn unto the right hand nor
5. 32 ye shall not turn aside to the right hand
17. 11 thou shalt not decline..(to) the right ha.
17. 20 turn not aside..(to) the right hand, or (to)
28. 14 not go aside..(to) the right hand or (to)
33. 2 from his right hand (went) a fiery law for
Josh. 1. 7 turn not from it (to) the right hand or (to)
17. 7 border went along on the right hand unto
23. 6 turn not aside therefrom (to) the right h.
Judg. 5. 26 right hand to the workmen's hammer
16. 29 of the one with his right hand, and of the
1 Sa. 6. 12 turned not aside (to) the right hand or (to)
2 Sa. 2. 19 turned not to the right hand nor to the
2. 21 Turn thee aside to thy right hand or to
16. 6 mighty men (were) on his right hand and
24. 5 on the right side of the city that (lieth) in
1 Ki. 2. 19 sat down..and she sat on his right hand
22 19 standing by him on his right hand and on
2 Ki.12. 9 on the right side as one cometh into the
22. 2 turned not aside to the right hand or to
23. 13 which (were) on the right hand of the m.
1 Ch. 6. 39 brother Asaph, who stood on his right h.
2 Ch. 3. 17 one on the right hand, and the other on
4. 6, 7, 8 five on the right hand, and five on
18. 18 standing on his right hand and (on) his
34. 2 declined (neither) to the right hand nor
Neh. 8 4 Maaseiah, on his right hand; and on his
12. 31 went on the right hand upon the wall to.
Job 23. 9 he hideth himself on the right hand, th.
40. 14 that thine own right hand can save thee
Psa. 16. 8 (is) at my right hand, I shall not be moved
16. 11 at thy right hand. pleasures for evermore
17. 7 thou that savest by thy right hand them
18. 35 thy right hand hath holden me up, and
20. 6 with the saving strength of his right hand
21. 8 thy right hand shall find out those that
26. 10 In whose hands (is) mischief..their right h.
44. 3 thy right hand, and thine arm, and the
45. 4 thy right hand shall teach thee terrible
45. 9 upon thy right hand did stand the queen
48. 10 thy right hand is full of righteousness
60. 5 save (with) thy right hand, and hear me
63. 8 followeth hard after thee: thy right hand
74. 11 Why withdrawest thou..thy right hand?
77. 10 the years of the right hand of the most
78. 54 mountain .his right hand had purchased
80. 15 vineyard which thy right hand hath pla.
80. 17 hand be upon the man of thy right hand
89. 13 strong is thy hand..high is thy right ha.
89. 25 I will set..his right hand in the rivers
89. 42 Thou hast set up the right hand of his ad.
91. 7 and ten thousand at thy right hand; (but)
98. 1 his right hand, and his holy arm, hath g.
108. 6 save (with) thy right hand, and answer me
109. 6 and let Satan stand at his right hand
109. 31 he shall stand at the right hand of the
110. 1 Sit thou at my right hand, until I make
110. 5 The Lord at thy right hand shall strike
118. 15, 16 right hand of the LORD doeth valiantly
118. 16 The right hand of the LORD is exalted
137. 5 If I forget thee..let my right hand forget
138. 7 stretch forth..thy right hand shall save
139. 10 Even there..thy right hand shall hold me
142. 4 I looked on (my) right hand, and beheld
Psa.144. 8, 11 right hand (is) a right hand of falseh.
Prov. 3. 16 Length of days (is) in..right hand; (and)
4. 27 Turn not to the right hand nor to the left
27. 16 and the ointment of his right hand, (which)
Eccl.10. 2 A wise man's heart (is) at his right hand
Song 2. 6 and his right hand doth embrace me
8. 3 and his right hand should embrace me
Isa. 9. 20 he shall snatch on the right hand, and be
41. 10 with the right hand of my righteousness
41. 13 thy God will hold thy right hand, saying
44. 20 say, (Is there) not a lie in my right hand
45. 1 whose right hand I have holden, to subd.
48. 13 my right hand hath spanned the heavens
54. 3 thou shalt break forth on the right hand
62. 8 The LORD hath sworn by his right hand
63. 12 That led (them) by the right hand of Mo.
Lam. 2. 3 he hath drawn back his right hand from
2. 4 stood with his right hand as an adversary
Eze. 1. 10 and the face of a lion on the right side
10. 3 the cherubim stood on the right side of
16. 46 sister, that dwelleth at thy right hand
21. 22 At his right hand was the divination for
Dan. 12. 7 when he held up his right hand and his
Jon. 4. 11 their right hand and their left hand; and
Hab. 2. 16 the cup of the LORD'S right hand shall be
Zech. 3. 1 standing at his right hand to resist him
12. 6 on the right hand and on the left: and

2. *Right hand, side,* יְמָנִי, יְמִינִי *yemani, yemini.*
2 Ch. 3. 17 called the name of that on the right hand

3. *Right hand, side,* δεξιός *dexios.*
Matt. 6. 3 thy left hand know what thy right hand
20. 21 the one on thy right hand, and the other
20. 23 to sit on my right hand, and on my left
22. 44 Sit thou on my right hand, till I make
25. 33 he shall set the sheep on his right hand
25. 34 the king say unto them on his right hand
26. 64 see..sitting on the right hand of power
27. 29 they put..a reed in his right hand: and
27. 38 one on the right hand, and another on the
Mark10. 37 one on thy right hand, and the other on
10. 40 to sit on my right hand and on my left
12. 36 Sit thou on my right hand, till I make
14. 62 sitting on the right hand of power, and
15. 27 the one on his right hand, and the other
16. 5 saw a young man sitting on the right side
16. 19 [up into heaven, and sat on the right hand]
Luke 1. 11 standing on the right side of the altar of
20. 42 The LORD said..Sit thou on my right hand
22. 69 shall the Son of man sit on the right hand
23. 33 one on the right hand, and the other on
Acts 2. 25 he is on my right hand, that I should not
2. 33 being by the right hand of God exalted
2. 34 The LORD said..Sit thou on my right hand
5. 31 Him hath God exalted with his right ha.
7. 55 Jesus standing on the right hand of God
7. 56 Son of man standing on the right hand of
Rom. 8. 34 who is even at the right hand of God, w.
2 Co. 6. 7 armour..on the right hand and on the le.
Gal. 2. 9 they gave..the right hands of fellowship
Eph. 1. 20 and set (him) at his own right hand in the
Col. 3. 1 where Christ sitteth on the right hand of
Heb. 1. 3 on the right hand of the majesty on high
1. 13 Sit on my right hand, until I make thine
8. 1 who is set on the right hand of the throne
10. 12 this man .sat down on the right hand of
12. 2 at the right hand of the throne of God
1 Pe. 3. 22 Who is..on the right hand of God; angels
Rev. 1. 20 stars which thou sawest in my right hand
2. 1 holdeth the seven stars in his right hand
5. 1 I saw in the right hand of him that sat on
5. 7 took the book out of the right hand of him

RIGHT hand, to go, turn, or use the —

1. *To turn to the right hand,* אָמַן *aman,* 5.
Isa. 30. 21 when ye turn to the right hand, and when

2. *To go, turn, or use the right hand,* יָמַן *yaman,* 5.
Gen. 13. 9 then I will go to the right; or if (thou d.)
2 Sa. 14. 19 none can turn to the right hand or to the
1 Ch. 12. 2 could use both the right hand and the
Eze. 21. 16 (either) on the right hand, (or) on the left

RIGHT thing —

1. *Upright things, uprightness,* מֵישָׁרִים *mesharim.*
Prov. 8. 6 opening of my lips (shall be) right things
23. 16 rejoice when thy lips speak right things
Isa. 45 19 I the LORD..declare things that are right

2. *Straightforwardness,* נְכֹחָה *nekochah.*
Isa. 30. 10 Prophesy not unto us right things, speak

RIGHTEOUS (man or cause) —

1. *Upright, right,* יָשָׁר *yashar.*
Num23. 10 Let me die the death of the righteous, and
Job 4. 7 Remember..where were the righteous cut
23. 7 the righteous might dispute with him; so
Psa.107. 42 The righteous shall see (it), and rejoice
Prov. 2. 7 layeth up sound wisdom for the righteous
3. 32 the LORD..his secret (is) with the righte.
14. 9 but among the righteous (there is) favour
15. 19 but the way of the righteous (is) made p.
28. 10 Whoso causeth the righteous to go astray

2. *Righteous, just,* צַדִּיק *tsaddiq.*
Gen. 7. 1 thee have I seen righteous before me in
18. 23 Wilt thou also destroy the righteous with
18. 24 there be fifty righteous within the city?
18. 24 for the fifty righteous that (are) therein
18. 25 That be far from thee..to slay the righteous
18. 25 that the righteous should be as the wicked
18. 26 If I find in Sodom fifty righteous within
18. 28 there shall lack five of the fifty righteous
20. 4 Lord, wilt thou slay also a righteous na.?
Exod. 9. 27 LORD (is) righteous, and I and my people

Exod 23. 7 the innocent and righteous slay thou not
23. 8 and perverteth the words of the righteous
Deut. 4. 8 judgments (so) righteous as all this law
16. 19 and pervert the words of the righteous
25. 1 then they shall justify the righteous, and
1 Sa. 24. 17 Thou (art) more righteous than I; for thou
2 Sa. 4. 11 wicked men have slain a righteous person
1 Ki. 2. 32 two men more righteous and better than
8. 32 justifying the righteous, to give him acc.
2 Ki. 10 9 Ye (be) righteous: behold, I conspired ag.
2 Ch. 6. 23 by justifying the righteous, by giving him
12. 6 the princes..said, The LORD (is) right.
Ezra 9. 15 O LORD God of Israel, thou (art) righteous
Neh. 9. 8 performed thy words; for thou (art) righ.
Job 17. 9 The righteous also shall hold on his way
22. 19 The righteous see (it), and are glad; and
32. 1 because he (was) righteous in his own eyes
36 7 He withdraweth not his eyes from the rig.
Psa. 1. 5 sinners in the congregation of the right
1. 6 the LORD knoweth the way of the right
5. 12 thou, LORD wilt bless the righteous; with
7. 9 righteous God trieth the hearts and reins
7. 11 God judgeth the righteous, and God is an.
11. 3 be destroyed, what can the righteous do?
11. 5 The LORD trieth the righteous; but the
11. 7 the righteous LORD loveth righteousness
14 5 God (is) in the generation of the righteous
31. 18 and contemptuously against the righteous
32. 11 rejoice, ye righteous: and shout for joy
33. 1 Rejoice in the LORD, O ye righteous
34 15 The eyes of the LORD (are) upon the righ.
34. 19 Many (are) the afflictions of the righteous
34. 21 they that hate the righteous shall be des
37. 16 A little that a righteous man hath is) bet
37. 17 but the LORD upholdeth the righteous
37. 21 the righteous showeth mercy, and giveth
37. 25 yet have I not seen the righteous forsaken
37. 29 The righteous shall inherit the land, and
37. 30 The mouth of the righteous speaketh wi.
37. 32 The wicked watcheth the righteous, and
37. 39 the salvation of the righteous (is) of the
52. 6 The righteous also shall see, and fear, and
55. 22 he shall never suffer the righteous to be
58 10 The righteous shall rejoice when he seeth
58. 11 (there is) a reward for the righteous: ver.
64. 10 The righteous shall be glad in the LORD
68. 3 let the righteous be glad: let them rejoice
69. 28 and not be written with the righteous
72. 7 In his days shall the righteous flourish
75. 10 the horns of the righteous shall be exalted
92. 12 The righteous shall flourish like the palm
94. 21 They gather..against the soul of the rig
97. 11 Light is sown for the righteous, and gl.
97 12 Rejoice in the LORD, ye righteous; and
112. 4 gracious, and full of compassion, and ri.
112. 6 the righteous shall be in everlasting rem.
116. 5 Gracious (is) the LORD, and righteous; yea
118. 15 voice..(is) in the tabernacles of the right.
118 20 This gate..into which the righteous shall
119. 137 Righteous (art) thou, O LORD, and upri.
125. 3 shall not rest upon the lot of the righteous
125. 3 the righteous put forth their hands unto
129. 4 The LORD (is) righteous: he hath cut asu.
140. 13 the righteous shall give thanks unto thy
141. 5 Let the righteous smite me; (it shall be)
142. 7 the righteous shall compass me about; for
145. 17 The LORD (is) righteous in all his ways
146. 8 bowed down; the LORD loveth the righte.
Prov. 2 20 thou mayest..keep the paths of the righ.
10. 3 suffer the soul of the righteous to famish
10. 11 mouth of a righteous (man is) a well of
10. 16 labour of the righteous (tendeth) to life
10. 21 The lips of the righteous feed many: but
10. 24 desire of the righteous shall be granted
10. 25 the righteous (is) an everlasting foundation
10. 28 The hope of the righteous (shall be) glad.
10. 30 The righteous shall never be removed; but
10. 32 The lips of the righteous know what is ac.
11. 8 The righteous is delivered out of trouble
11. 10 When it goeth well with the righteous
11. 21 seed of the righteous shall be delivered
11 23 The desire of the righteous (is) only good
11. 28 but the righteous shall flourish as a branch
11. 30 The fruit of the righteous (is) a tree of life
11. 31 the righteous shall be recompensed in the
12. 3 the root of the righteous shall not be mo.
12. 5 The thoughts of the righteous (are) right
12. 7 the house of the righteous shall stand
12. 10 A righteous (man) regardeth the life of his
12. 12 the root of the righteous yieldeth (fruit)
12. 26 The righteous (is) more excellent than his
13. 5 A righteous (man) hateth lying: but a wi.
13. 9 The light of the righteous rejoiceth: but
13. 21 but to the righteous good shall be repaid
13. 25 The righteous eateth to the satisfying of
14. 19 the wicked at the gates of the righteous
14. 32 but the righteous hath hope in his death
15. 6 In the house of the righteous (is) much
15. 28 The heart of the righteous studieth to an.
15. 29 but he heareth the prayer of the righteous
18 5 not good..to overthrow the righteous in
18. 10 the righteous runneth into it, and is safe
21. 12 The righteous (man) wisely considereth
21. 18 wicked (shall be) a ransom for the righteous
21. 26 but the righteous giveth and spareth not
23. 24 The father of the righteous shall greatly
24. 15 Lay not wait..against the dwelling of the ri.
24. 24 saith unto the wicked. Thou (art) righteo.
25. 26 A righteous man falling down before the
28. 1 flee..but the righteous are bold as a lion
28. 12 When righteous..do rejoice, (there is) gr.
28. 28 when they perish, the righteous increase
Prov 29. 2 When the righteous are in authority, the
29. 6 but the righteous doth sing and rejoice
29. 7 The righteous considereth the cause of
29. 16 but the righteous shall see their fall
Eccl. 3. 17 God shall judge the righteous and the
7. 16 Be not righteous overmuch; neither make
8. 14 according to the work of the righteous
9. 1 the righteous, and the wise, and their w.
9. 2 one event to the righteous, and to the w.
Isa. 3. 10 Say ye to the righteous, that (it shall be)
5. 23 take away the righteousness of the right.
24. 16 have we heard songs..glory to the right.
26. 2 that the righteous nation which keepeth
41. 26 that we may say, (He is) righteous? yea
53. 11 by his knowledge shall my righteous ser.
57. 1 The righteous perisheth, and no man lay
57. 1 the righteous is taken away from the evil
60. 21 Thy people also (shall be) all righteous
Jer. 12. 1 Righteous (art) thou, O LORD, when I p.
20. 12 O LORD of hosts, that triest the righteous
23. 5 will raise unto David a righteous
Lam. 1. 18 The LORD is righteous; for I have rebel.
Eze. 3. 20 When a righteous (man) doth turn from
3. 21 warn the righteous (man), that the right.
13. 22 have made the heart of the righteous sad
18. 20 the righteousness of the righteous shall
18. 24 when the righteous turneth away from
18. 26 When a righteous (man) turneth away
21. 3, 4 will cut off from thee the righteous
23. 45 the righteous men, they shall judge them
33. 12 The righteousness of the righteous shall
33. 12 neither shall the righteous be able to live
33. 13 shall say to the righteous, (that) he shall
33. 18 righteous turneth from his righteousness
Dan. 9. 14 the LORD our God (is) righteous in all his
Amos 2. 6 they sold the righteous for silver, and
Hab. 1 4 wicked doth compass about the righteous
1. 13 (the man that is) more righteous than he
Mal. 3. 18 discern between the righteous and the w.

3. *Rightness, justice,* צֶדֶק *tsedeq.*
Psa. 35. 27 be glad, that favour my righteous cause
119. 7 shall have learned thy righteous judgm.
119. 62 thanks..because of thy righteous judgm.
119. 106 that I will keep thy righteous judgments
119 138 Thy testimonies..(are) righteous and
119. 160 thy righteous judgments (endureth) for
119. 164 I praise thee because of thy righteous
Prov 16. 13 Righteous lips (are) the delight of kings
Isa. 41. 2 Who raised up the righteous (man) from

4. *Right, righteous, just,* δίκαιος *dikaios.*
Matt. 9. 13 I am not come to call the righteous, but
10. 41 a righteous man in the name of a righte.
10. 41 he..shall receive a righteous man's rew.
13. 17 many prophets and righteous (men) have
13. 43 Then shall the righteous shine forth as
23. 28 Even so ye also outwardly appear righte.
23. 29 and garnish the sepulchres of the righte.
23. 35 righteous blood..from the blood of righ.
25. 37 Then shall the righteous answer him, say.
25. 46 these shall go away..but the righteous in
Mark 2. 17 came not to call the righteous, but sinners
Luke 1. 6 they were both righteous before God, wa.
5. 32 came not to call the righteous, but sinne
18. 9 trusted in themselves that they were rig.
23. 47 saying, Certainly this was a righteous m.
John 7. 24 appearance, but judge righteous judgm.
17 25 O righteous Father, the world hath not
Rom. 3. 10 As it is written, There is none righteous
5. 7 For scarcely for a righteous man will one
5. 19 obedience of one shall many be made rig.
2 Th. 1. 5 manifest token of the righteous judgme.
1. 6 Seeing (it is) a righteous thing with God
1 Ti. 1. 9 the law is not made for a righteous man
2 Ti. 4. 8 which the Lord, the righteous judge, sh.
Heb. 11. 4 he obtained witness that he was righteo
Jas. 5. 16 prayer of a righteous man availeth much
1 Pe. 3. 12 the eyes of the Lord (are) over the right.
4. 18 if the righteous scarcely be saved, where
2 Pe. 2. 8 that righteous man..vexed (his) righteous
1 Jo. 2. 1 have an advocate..Jesus Christ the righ.
2. 29 If ye know that he is righteous, ye know
3. 7 he..is righteous, even as he is righteous
3. 12 works were evil, and his brother's righte.
Rev. 16. 5 Thou art righteous, O LORD, which art
16. 7 Lord God Almighty, true and righteous
19. 2 For true and righteous (are) his judgments
22. 11 let him be filthy still: and he that is rig.

RIGHTEOUS act or judgment —

1. *Rightness, justice,* צְדָקָה *tsedaqah.*
Judg. 5. 11 there shall they rehearse the righteous acts
5. 11 righteous acts (toward the inhabitants) of
1 Sa. 12. 7 all the righteous acts of the LORD, which

2. *Right or just judgment,* δικαιοκρισία *dikaiokrisia.*
Rom 2. 5 revelation of the righteous judgment of G

RIGHTEOUS, to be —

1. *To be right, just,* צָדַק *tsadaq.*
Gen. 38. 26 She hath been more righteous than I; be.
Job 9. 15 though I were righteous, (yet) would I not
10. 15 (if) I be righteous, (yet) will I not lift up my
15. 14 born of a woman, that he should be right.?
22. 3 (Is it) any pleasure..that thou art right.?
34. 5 For Job hath said, I am righteous: and G.
35. 7 If thou be righteous, what givest thou him?
40. 8 condemn me, that thou mayest be right.?
Psa. 19. 9 judgments of the LORD (are) true (and) r.
Eze. 16. 52 they are more righteous than thou: yea

2. *To make right, just,* δικαιόω *dikaioō.*
Rev. 22. 11 [let him be righteous] still: and he that is

RIGHTEOUSLY —

1. *Upright place or thing,* מִישׁוֹר *mishor.*
Psa. 67. 4 for thou shalt judge the people righteous.

2. *Upright things, uprightness,* מֵישָׁרִים *mesharim.*
Psa. 96. 10 he shall judge the people righteously

3. *Rightness, justice,* צֶדֶק *tsedeq.*
Deut. 1. 16 judge righteously between (every) man
Prov. 31. 9 Open thy mouth, judge righteously, and
Jer. 11. 20 LORD of hosts, that judgest righteously

4. *Rightness, justice,* צְדָקָה *tsedaqah.*
Isa. 33. 15 He that walketh righteously, and speak.

5. *Rightly, justly,* δικαίως *dikaiōs.*
Titus 2 12 righteously, and godly, in this present wo.
1 Pe. 2. 23 committed (himself)..that judgeth right.

RIGHTEOUSNESS —

1. *Rightness, justice,* צֶדֶק *tsedeq.*
Lev. 19 15 in righteousness shalt thou judge thy ne.
Deut 33. 19 they shall offer sacrifices of righteousness
Job 6. 29 return again, my righteousness (is) in it
8. 6 make the habitation of thy righteousness
29. 14 I put on righteousness, and it clothed me
35. 2 saidst, My righteousness (is) more than G.
36. 3 and will ascribe righteousness to my
Psa. 4. 1 Hear me..O God of my righteousness: th.
4. 5 Offer the sacrifices of righteousness, and
7. 8 according to my righteousness, and acco.
7. 17 praise the LORD according to his righteo.
9. 8 he shall judge the world in righteousness
15. 2 walketh uprightly, and worketh righteo.
17. 15 I will behold thy face in righteousness: I
18. 20 rewarded me according to my righteous.
18. 24 recompensed me according to my righte.
23. 3 leadeth me in the paths of righteousness
35 24 Judge me..according to thy righteousness
35. 28 my tongue shall speak of thy righteousness
37. 6 he shall bring forth thy righteousness as
40. 9 I have preached righteousness in the gr.
45. 4 because of truth and meekness (and) rig.
45. 7 Thou lovest righteousness, and hatest w.
48. 10 thy right hand is full of righteousness
50. 6 the heavens shall declare his righteousn.
51 19 pleased with the sacrifices of righteousn.
52. 3 lying rather than to speak righteousness
58. 1 Do ye indeed speak righteousness, O con.
65. 5 terrible things in righteousness wilt thou
72. 2 shall judge thy people with righteousness
85. 10 righteousness and peace have kissed (each
85. 11 righteousness shall look down from hea.
85 13 Righteousness shall go before him, and sh.
94 15 But judgment shall return unto righteou.
96. 13 shall judge the world with righteousness
97. 2 righteousness and judgment (are) the ha.
97. 6 The heavens declare his righteousness, and
98. 9 with righteousness shall he judge the w.
118. 19 Open to me the gates of righteousness: I
119. 123 and for the word of thy righteousness me
119. 142 an everlasting righteousness: and thy law
119. 144 The righteousness of thy testimonies (is)
119. 172 all thy commandments (are) righteousn.
132. 9 Let thy priests be clothed with righteou.
Prov. 2. 9 Then shalt thou understand righteousness
8. 8 All the words of my mouth (are) in right.
12. 17 speaketh truth showeth forth righteous.
25. 5 throne shall be established in righteousn.
Eccl. 3. 16 place of righteousness, (that) iniquity (was)
7. 15 just (man) that perisheth in his righteou.
Isa. 1. 21 righteousness lodged in it; but now mu.
1. 26 shalt be called, The city of righteousness
11. 4 with righteousness shall he judge the poor
11. 5 righteousness shall be the girdle of his lo.
16 5 seeking judgment, and hasting righteou.
26. 9 inhabitants of the world will learn right.
26. 10 will he not learn righteousness: in the la.
32. 1 king shall reign in righteousness, and pr.
41. 10 uphold thee with the right hand of my ri.
42. 6 I the LORD have called thee in righteous.
42. 21 is well pleased for his righteousness' sake
45. 8 and let the skies pour down righteousness
45. 13 I have raised him up in righteousness, and
45. 19 I the LORD speak righteousness, I declare
51. 1 ye that follow after righteousness, ye that
51. 5 My righteousness (is) near; my salvation
51. 7 Hearken unto me, ye that know righteo.
58. 8 thy righteousness shall go before thee; the
61. 3 they might be called Trees of righteousn.
62. 1 until the righteousness thereof go forth as
62. 2 the Gentiles shall see thy righteousness
64. 5 that rejoiceth and worketh righteousness
Jer. 23. 6 shall be called; The LORD our righteous.
33. 16 shall be called, The LORD our righteous.
Eze. 3. 20 doth turn from his righteousness, and co.
Dan. 9. 24 and to bring in everlasting righteousness
Hos. 2. 19 I will betroth thee unto me in righteous.
10. 12 Sow to yourselves, in righteousness, reap
Zeph. 2. 3 seek righteousness seek meekness: it may

2. *Rightness, justice,* צְדָקָה *tsedaqah.*
Gen. 15. 6 and he counted it to him for righteousn.
30. 33 So shall my righteousness answer for me
Deut. 6. 25 it shall be our righteousness, if we observe
9. 4 For my righteousness the LORD hath bro.
9. 5 Not for thy righteousness, or for the up.
9. 6 land to possess it for thy righteousness
24 13 it shall be righteousness unto thee before
1 Sa. 26. 23 LORD render to every man his righteous.
2 Sa. 22. 21 rewarded me according to my righteous.
22. 25 recompensed me according to my righteo.
1 Ki. 3. 6 walked before thee..in righteousness, and
8. 32 to give him according to his righteousness

2 Ch. 6. 23 by giving him according to his righteous.
Job 27. 6 My righteousness I hold fast, and will not
33. 26 he will render unto man his righteousness
35. 8 thy righteousness (may profit) the son of
Psa. 5. 8 Lead me..in thy righteousness because of
11. 7 For the righteous LORD loveth righteous.
22. 31 shall declare his righteousness unto a pe.
24. 5 receive..righteousness from the God of
31. 1 ashamed..deliver me in thy righteousness
33. 5 He loveth righteousness and judgment
36. 6 Thy righteousness (is) like the great mo.
36. 10 thy righteousness to the upright in heart
40. 10 I have not hid thy righteousness within
51. 14 tongue shall sing aloud of thy righteous.
69. 27 let them not come into thy righteousness
71. 2 Deliver me in thy righteousness, and cause
71. 15 My mouth shall show forth thy righteou.
71. 16 will make mention of thy righteousness
71. 19 Thy righteousness also, O God, (is) very
71. 24 My tongue also shall talk of thy righteo.
72. 1 Give..thy righteousness unto the king's
72. 2 shall judge thy people with righteousness
88. 12 thy righteousness in the land of forgetfu.
89. 16 in thy righteousness shall they be exalted
98. 2 his righteousness hath he openly showed
99. 4 executest judgment and righteousness in
103 6 executeth righteousness and judgment for
103. 17 his righteousness unto children's children
106. 3 he that doeth righteousness at all times
106. 31 counted unto him for righteousness unto
111. 3 and his righteousness endureth for ever
112. 3, 9 his righteousness endureth for ever
119. 40 precepts: quicken me in thy righteousn.
119. 142 Thy righteousness..and thy law (is) the
143. 1 in thy faithfulness..in thy righteousness
143. 11 for thy righteousness' sake bring my soul
145. 7 utter..and shall sing of thy righteousness
Prov. 8. 18 with me; (yea), durable riches and righte.
8. 20 lead in the way of righteousness, in the
10. 2 but righteousness delivereth from death
11. 4 but righteousness delivereth from death
11. 5 righteousness of the perfect shall direct
11. 6 righteousness of the upright shall deliver
11. 18 but to him that soweth righteousness (shall
11. 19 As righteousness (tendeth) to life; so he
12. 28 In the way of righteousness (is) life; and
13. 6 Righteousness keepeth (him that is) uprig.
14. 34 Righteousness exalteth a nation: but sin
15. 9 loveth him that followeth after righteou.
16. 8 Better (is) a little with righteousness, than
16. 12 the throne is established by righteousness
16. 31 it be found in the way of righteousness
21. 21 He that followeth after righteousness and
21. 21 findeth life, righteousness, and honour
Isa. 1. 27 and her converts with righteousness
5. 7 looked for..righteousness, but behold a
5. 16 God..shall be sanctified in righteousness
5. 23 take away the righteousness of the right.
10. 22 consumption..shall overflow with right.
28. 17 righteousness to the plummet; and the
32. 16 and righteousness remain in the fruitful
32. 17 work of righteousness shall be peace; and
32. 17 effect of righteousness, quietness and as.
33. 5 filled Zion with judgment and righteous.
45. 8 and let righteousness spring up together
45. 23 is gone out of my mouth (in) righteousness
45. 24 In the LORD have I righteousness and str.
46. 12 stout hearted, that (are) far from righteo.
46. 13 I bring near my righteousness; it shall not
48. 1 mention..not in truth, nor in righteous.
48. 18 thy righteousness as the waves of the sea
51. 6 my righteousness shall not be abolished
51. 8 but my righteousness shall be for ever, and
54. 14 In righteousness shalt thou be established
54. 17 their righteousness (is) of me, saith the
56. 1 near to come, and my righteousness to be
57. 12 will declare thy righteousness, and thy
58. 2 a nation that did righteousness, and fors.
59. 16 and his righteousness, it sustained him
59. 17 For he put on righteousness as a breastpl.
60. 17 peace, and thine exactors righteousness
61. 10 covered me with the robe of righteousness
61. 11 cause righteousness and praise to spring
63. 1 I that speak in righteousness, mighty to
64. 6 and all our righteousness (are) as filthy rags
Jer. 4. 2 in truth, in judgment, and in righteousn.
9. 24 judgment and righteousness in the earth
22. 3 Execute ye judgment and righteousness
33. 15 will I cause the branch of righteousness
33. 15 execute judgment and righteousness in
51. 10 LORD hath brought forth our righteous.
Eze. 3. 20 When a righteous (man) doth turn from
14. 14 their own souls by their righteousness
14. 20 deliver their own souls by their righteo.
18. 20 righteousness of the righteous shall be
18. 22 in his righteousness that he hath done he
18. 24, 26 turneth away from his righteousness
18. 24 All his righteousness that he hath done
33. 12 righteousness of the righteous shall not
33. 13 if he trust to his own righteousness, and
33. 13 all his righteousness shall not be remem.
33. 18 the righteous turneth from his righteous.
Dan. 9. 7 righteousness (belongeth) unto thee, but
9. 16 according to all thy righteousness, I be.
9. 18 supplications before thee for our righte.
Hos. 10. 12 Sow to yourselves in righteousness, reap
Amos 5. 7 and leave off righteousness in the earth
5. 24 judgment run down as waters, and righ.
6. 12 the fruit of righteousness into hemlock
Mic. 6. 5 ye may know the righteousness of the L.
7. 9 light, (and) I shall behold his righteous.
Zech. 8. 8 their God, in truth and in righteousness
Mal. 3. 3 they may offer..an offering in righteous.
4. 2 shall the Sun of righteousness arise with

3. *Rightness, justice,* צְדָקָה *tsidqah.*
Dan. 4. 27 break off thy sins by righteousness, and

4. *Rightness, justice,* δικαιοσύνη *dikaiosunē.*
Matt. 3. 15 it becometh us to fulfil all righteousness
5. 6 do hunger and thirst after righteousness
5. 10 they which are persecuted for righteous.
5. 20 except your righteousness shall exceed
6. 33 kingdom of God, and his righteousness
21. 32 came unto you in the way of righteousness
Luke 1. 75 In holiness and righteousness before him
John 16. 8 and of righteousness, and of judgment
16. 10 Of righteousness, because I go to my Fat.
Acts 10. 35 worketh righteousness, is accepted with
13. 10 enemy of all righteousness, wilt thou not
17. 31 he will judge the world in righteousness
24. 25 he reasoned of righteousness, temperance
Rom. 1. 17 For therein is the righteousness of God re.
3. 5 commend the righteousness of God, what
3. 21 But now the righteousness of God without
3. 22 Even the righteousness of God (which is)
3. 25 declare his righteousness for the remission
3. 26 declare..at this time his righteousness
4. 3 was counted unto him for righteousness
4. 5 his faith is counted for righteousness
4. 6 unto whom God imputeth righteousness
4. 9 reckoned to Abraham for righteousness
4. 11 seal of the righteousness of the faith which
4. 11 righteousness might be imputed unto th.
4. 13 but through the righteousness of faith
4. 22 it was imputed to him for righteousness
5. 17 receive..of the gift of righteousness shall
5. 21 so might grace reign through righteous.
6. 13 (as) instruments of righteousness unto God
6. 16 whether..of obedience unto righteousness
6. 18 ye became the servants of righteousness
6. 19 members servants to righteousness unto
6. 20 servants of sin, ye were free from righte.
8. 10 the spirit (is) life because of righteous.
9. 28 [cut (it) short in righteousness: because]
9. 30 righteousness, have attained to righteou.
9. 30 even the righteousness which is of faith
9. 31 which followed after the law of righteou.
9. 31 hath not attained to the law [of righteo.]
10. 3 they being ignorant of God's righteous.
10. 3 going about to establish their own [rig.]
10. 3 submitted themselves unto the righteous.
10. 4 Christ (is) the end of the law for righteo.
10. 5 Moses describeth the righteousness which
10. 6 righteousness which is of faith speaketh
10. 10 with the heart man believeth unto right.
14. 17 righteousness, and peace, and joy in the
1 Co. 1. 30 made unto us wisdom, and righteousness
2 Co. 3. 9 much more doth the ministration of rig.
5. 21 be made the righteousness of God in him
6. 7 by the armour of righteousness on the ri.
6. 14 for what fellowship hath righteousness
9. 9 poor: his righteousness remaineth for ever
9. 10 increase the fruits of your righteousness
11. 15 transformed as the ministers of righteous.
Gal. 2. 21 for if righteousness (come) by the law, th.
3. 6 it was accounted to him for righteousness
3. 21 righteousness should have been by the law
5. 5 for the hope of righteousness by faith
Eph. 4. 24 which after God is created in righteous.
5. 9 in all goodness and righteousness, and tr.
6. 14 having on the breast plate of righteousness
Phil. 1. 11 Being filled with the fruits of righteous.
3. 6 touching the righteousness which is in the
3. 9 not having mine own righteousness which
3. 9 the righteousness which is of God by faith
1 Ti. 6. 11 follow after righteousness, godliness, fa.
2 Ti. 2. 22 follow righteousness, faith, charity, peace
3. 16 for correction, for instruction in righteous.
4. 8 laid up for me a crown of righteousness
Titus 3. 5 Not by works of righteousness which we
Heb. 1. 9 Thou hast loved righteousness, and hated
5. 13 unskilful in the word of righteousness; for
7. 2 by interpretation King of righteousness
11. 7 became heir of the righteousness which
11. 33 wrought righteousness, obtained promises
12. 11 yieldeth the peaceable fruit of righteous.
Jas. 1. 20 wrath of man worketh not the righteous.
2. 23 was imputed unto him for righteousness
3. 18 fruit of righteousness is sown in peace of
1 Pe. 2. 24 dead to sins, should live unto righteous.
3. 14 and if ye suffer for righteousness' sake
2 Pe. 1. 1 through the righteousness of God and our
2. 5 preacher of righteousness, bringing in the
2. 21 to have known the way of righteousness
3. 13 new earth, wherein dwelleth righteousness
1 Jo. 2. 29 every one that doeth righteousness is born
3. 7 he that doeth righteousness is righteous
3. 10 [whosoever doeth not righteousness is not]
Rev. 19. 11 in righteousness he doth judge and make

5. *A judicial sentence,* δικαίωμα *dikaiōma.*
Rom. 2. 26 if the uncircumcision keep the righteous.
5. 18 even so by the righteousness of one (the
8. 4 That the righteousness of the law might
Rev. 19. 8 for the fine linen is the righteousness of

6. *Uprightly, justly, rightly,* δικαίως *dikaiōs.*
1 Co. 15. 34 Awake to righteousness, and sin not; for

7. *Straightforwardness, rectitude,* εὐθύτης *euthutēs.*
Heb. 1. 8 sceptre of righteousness (is) the sceptre

RIGHTEOUSNESS, to turn to —
To make righteous or just, צָדַק *tsadaq,* 5.
Dan. 12. 3 they that turn many to righteousness as

RIGHTLY —
1. *That,* כִּי *ki.*
Gen. 27. 36 Is not he rightly named Jacob? for he h.
2. *Rightly,* ὀρθῶς *orthōs.*
Luke 7. 43 said unto him, Thou hast rightly judged
20. 21 know that thou sayest and teachest righ.

RIGOUR —
Rigour, פֶּרֶךְ *perek.*
Exod. 1. 13 the children of Israel to serve with rigour
1. 14 bitter..all their service..(was) with rigour
Lev. 25. 43 Thou shalt not rule over him with rigour
25. 46 not rule one over another with rigour
25. 53 not rule with rigour over him in thy sight

RIM'-MON, רִמֹּן, רִמּוֹן *pomegranate.*
1. A city in Simeon, now called *Um-er-Rumamim.*
Josh 15. 32 Lebaoth, and Shilhim, and Ain, and R.
Zech 14. 10 the land shall be turned as a plain..to R.
2. A rock in Benjamin near Gibeah, now called *Rummon* or *Rammun.*
Judg 20. 45 they turned and fled..unto the rock of R.
20. 47 six hundred men..fled..unto the rock R.
20. 47 and abode in the rock R. four months
21. 13 children..that (were) in the rock R., and
3. Father of two captains of Ish-bosheth, from Beeroth in Benjamin.
2 Sa. 4. 2 Baanah, and..Rechab, the sons of R.
4. 5 the sons of R. the Beerothite, Rechab and
4. 9 David answered..the sons of R. the Beer.
4. A Syrian god, representing a certain aspect of Adonis.
2 Ki. 5. 18 my master goeth into the house of R. to
5. 18 and I bow myself in the house of R.: when
5. 18 I bow down myself in the house of R., the
5. A city in Simeon, near Tochen.
1 Ch. 4. 32 their villages (were), Etam, and Ain, R.
6. A Levitical city in Zebulon. Heb. Rimmono.
1 Ch. 6. 77 R. with her suburbs, Tabor with her sub.

RIM'-MON PA'-REZ, רִמֹּן פֶּרֶץ.
The fifteenth station of Israel from Egypt, and fourth from Sinai, between Rithmah and Libnah.
Num 33. 19 departed from Rithmah, and pitched at R.
33. 20 they departed from R., and pitched in L.

RING —
1. *Rim, felloe,* גַּב *gab.*
Eze. 1. 18 As for their rings..their rings (were) full
2. *Folding (of a door), cylinder,* גָּלִיל *galil.*
Esth. 1. 6 fastened..to silver rings and pillars of m.
Song 5. 14 His hands (are as) gold rings set with the
3. *Ring,* טַבַּעַת *tabbaath.*
Gen. 41. 42 Pharaoh took off his ring from his hand
Exod 25. 12 thou shalt cast four rings of gold for
25. 12 two rings (shall be) in the one side of
25. 12 and two rings in the other side of it
25. 14 into the rings by the sides of the ark
25. 15 staves shall be in the rings of the ark
25. 26 four rings of gold, and put the rings in
25. 27 against the border shall the rings be
26. 24 shall be coupled together..unto one ring
26. 29 rings (of) gold (for) places for the bars
27. 4 brasen rings in the four corners thereof
27. 7 the staves shall be put into the rings
28. 23 upon the breast plate two rings of gold
28. 23 shalt put the two rings on the two ends
28. 24 the two rings (which are) on the ends of
28. 26 thou shalt make two rings of gold, and
28. 27 two (other) rings of gold thou shalt make
28. 28 by the rings thereof unto the rings of
30. 4 two golden rings shalt thou make to it
35. 22 and rings, and tablets, all jewels of gold
36. 29 coupled together at the head..to one ring
36. 34 rings (of) gold (to be) places for the bars
37. 3, 13 And he cast for it four rings of gold
37. 3 even two rings upon the one side of it
37. 3 and two rings upon the other side of it
37. 5 into the rings by the sides of the ark
37. 13 put the rings upon the four corners that
37. 14 against the border were the rings, the
37. 27 he made two rings of gold for it under
38. 5 he cast four rings for the four ends of
38. 7 he put the staves into the rings on the
39. 16 two gold rings, and put the two rings in
39. 17 two rings on the ends of the breastplate
39. 19 they made two rings of gold, and put (th.)
39. 20 they made two (other) golden rings, and
39. 21 by his rings unto the rings of the ephod
Num 31. 50 and bracelets, rings, ear rings, and tablets
Esth. 3. 10 the king took his ring from his hand, and
3. 12 written, and sealed with the king's ring
8. 2 the king took off his ring, which he had
8. 8 Write ye also..seal (it) with the king's ring
8. 8 the writing..sealed with the king's ring
8. 10 sealed (it) with the king's ring: and sent
Isa. 3. 21 The rings, and nose jewels
4. *A finger ring,* δακτύλιος *daktulios.*
Luke 15. 22 put a ring on his hand, and shoes on (his)

RING again, to —
To be moved, noisy, הוּם *hum,* 2.
1 Sa. 4. 5 great shout, so that the earth rang again
1 Ki. 1. 45 the city rang again. This (is) the noise th.

RINGLEADER —
One who stands first, πρωτοστάτης *prōtostatēs.*
Acts 24. 5 a ringleader of the sect of the Nazarenes

RINGSTRAKED —
Straked, notched, עָקֹד *aqod.*
Gen 30. 35 the he goats that were ringstraked and
30 39 brought forth cattle ringstraked, speckled
30 40 toward the ringstraked and all the brown
31. 8 The ringstraked shall be thy hire
31. 8 then bare all the cattle ringstraked
31 10 the cattle (were) ringstraked, speckled
31. 12 all the rams which leap..(are) ringstraked

RIN'-NAH, רִנָּה *a shout, strength.*
A son of Shimon, a descendant of Caleb son of Jephunneh B C 1400.
1 Ch. 4 20 the sons of Shimon (were) Amnon, and R.

RINSE, to —
To overflow, rinse, שָׁטַף *shataph.*
Lev. 15 11 and hath not rinsed his hands in water

RINSED, to be —
1. *To be overflowed, rinsed,* שָׁטַף *shataph,* 2.
Lev. 15 12 every vessel of wood shall be rinsed in
2. *To be overflowed, rinsed,* שָׁטַף *shataph,* 4.
Lev. 6. 28 be both scoured, and rinsed in water

RIOT, rioting, riotous (livers) —
1. *To flow, squander, be vile,* זָלַל *zalal.*
Prov 23. 20 Be not..among riotous eaters of flesh
28. 7 a companion of riotous (men) shameth his
2. *Spendthriftness, extravagance,* ἀσωτία *asōtia.*
Titus 1 6 children not accused of riot or unruly
1 Pe. 4 4 not with (them) to the same excess of riot
3. *In a spendthrift manner,* ἀσώτως *asōtōs.*
Luke 15. 13 wasted his substance with riotous living
4. *Revelry, (Lat. comus),* κῶμος *kōmos.*
Rom 13. 13 not in rioting and drunkenness, not in
5. *Luxurious living, expenditure,* τρυφή *truphē.*
2 Pe 2 13 count it pleasure to riot in the day time

RIP up, be ripped up, to —
1. *To cleave through,* בָּקַע *baqa.*
Amos 1 13 they have ripped up the women with child
2. *To cleave through,* בָּקַע *baqa,* 3.
2 Ki. 8 12 and wilt..rip up their women with child
15 16 women..that were with child he ripped up
3. *To be cleft through,* בָּקַע *baqa,* 4
Hos. 13. 16 their women with child shall be ripped up

RIPE, to be (fully) —
1. *To boil, ripen, seethe,* בָּשַׁל *bashal.*
Joel 3. 13 the harvest is ripe: come get you down
2. *To make or give ripe fruit,* בָּשַׁל *bashal,* 5.
Gen 40 10 clusters thereof brought forth ripe grapes
3. *To bloom, arrive at maturity,* ἀκμάζω *akmazō.*
Rev. 14. 18 and gather..for her grapes are fully ripe

RIPEN, to —
1. *To do, make ready or ripe,* גָּמַל *gamal.*
Isa. 18 5 the sour grape is ripening in the flower
2. *To dry up, wither, be ripe,* ξηραίνω *xērainō.*
Rev. 14 15 reap; for the harvest of the earth is ripe

RI'-PHATH, רִיפַת.
A son of Gomer, son of Japheth, and his descendants the Celts who marched across the Riphaen mountains, *i.e.* the Carpathian, into the farthest regions of Europe B.C. 2250. In 1 Ch. another reading is Diphath.
Gen. 10. 3 And the sons of Gomer; Ashkenaz, and R
1 Ch. 1 6 And the sons of Gomer; Ashchenaz, and R.

RISE (up, up again), that should—
1. *To arise,* זָרַח *zarach.*
Gen 32. 31 the sun rose upon him and he halted upon
Deut 33. 2 The LORD..rose up from Seir unto them
2 Sa. 23 4 light of the morning (when) the sun riseth
2 Ch. 26 19 the leprosy even rose up in his forehead
Job. 9 7 commandeth the sun, and it riseth not
Isa. 58 10 then shall thy light rise in obscurity
2. *To go up,* עָלָה *alah.*
Judg. 6. 21 there rose up fire out of the rock, and
Neh. 4. 21 from the rising of the morning till the
Eccl 10. 4 If the spirit of the ruler rise up against
Jer 46 8 Egypt riseth up like a flood, and (his)
47 2 waters rise up out of the north, and shall
Amos 8. 8 it shall rise up wholly as a flood; and
9. 5 it shall rise up wholly like a flood, and
Jon 4. 7 when the morning rose the next day, and
Zech. 14 13 rise up against the hand of his neighbour
3. *To rise up,* קוּם *qum.*
Gen. 4. 8 Cain rose up against Abel his brother, and
18. 16 the men rose up from thence, and looked
19 1 and Lot seeing (them) rose up to meet them
21. 32 Abimelech rose up and Phichol the chief
22 3 Abraham rose up early in the morning
22 19 they rose up and went together to Beer.
24. 54 they rose up in the morning; and he said
25. 34 he did eat and drink and rose up, and
31. 17 Jacob rose up and set his sons and his
31. 21 he rose up and passed over the river, and
31. 35 that I cannot rise up before thee; for the
32. 22 he rose up that night, and took his two
37. 35 all his daughters rose up to comfort him
43. 15 rose up, and went down to Egypt, and st.
46. 5 Jacob rose up from Beer-sheba: and the
Exod 10. 23 neither rose any from his place for three
12 30 Pharaoh rose up in the night, he, and all
Exod 12. 31 Rise up, (and) get you forth from among
15. 7 overthrown them that rose up against thee
21. 19 If he rise again, and walk abroad upon his
24. 13 Moses rose up, and his minister Joshua
32. 6 And they rose up early on the morrow, and
32. 6 sat down to eat and to drink, and rose up
33. 8 the people rose up, and stood every man
33. 10 the people rose up and worshipped, every
Lev. 19. 32 Thou shalt rise up before the hoary head
Num 10. 35 Rise up, LORD, and let thine enemies be
16. 2 they rose up before Moses, with certain
16. 25 Moses rose up, and went unto Dathan and
22. 13, 21 And Balaam rose up in the morning, and
22. 14 the princes of Moab rose up, and they we
22. 20 rise up (and) go with them: but yet the
23. 18 Rise up Balak, and hear: hearken unto
23. 24 the people shall rise up as a great lion
24. 17 a sceptre shall rise out of Israel, and shall
24. 25 Balaam rose up, and went and returned
25. 7 he rose up from among the congregation
Deut. 2. 13 rise up, (said I), and get you over the brook
2. 24 Rise ye up, take your journey, and pass
6. 7 thou liest down, and when thou risest up
11. 19 thou liest down, and when thou risest up
19. 11 and rise up against him, and smite him
19. 15 One witness shall not rise up against a
19. 16 If a false witness rise up against any
22. 26 a man riseth against his neighbour, and
28. 7 thine enemies that rise up against thee
29. 22 your children that shall rise up after you
31. 16 this people will rise up, and go a whoring
32. 38 let them rise up and help you, (and) be
33. 11 smite through..that they rise not again
Josh. 3. 16 rose up upon an heap very far from the
6. 26 riseth up and buildeth this city Jericho
8. 7 ye shall rise up from the ambush and
18. 4 they shall rise and go through the land
Judg. 8. 21 Rise thou, and fall upon us; for as the
9. 34, 35 Abimelech rose up, and the people that
9. 43 he rose up against them, and smote them
19 5 he rose up to depart: and the damsel's
19. 7, 9 And when the man rose up to depart
19 10 but he rose up and departed, and came
19. 27 her lord rose up in the morning, and op.
19. 28 the man rose up, and gat him unto his p.
20. 5 the men of Gibeah rose against me, and
20. 19 children of Israel rose up in the morning
20 33 all the men of Israel rose up out of their p.
Ruth 3. 14 she rose up before one could know another
1 Sa. 1. 9 Hannah rose up after they had eaten in
16. 13 So Samuel rose up, and went to Ramah
22. 13 he should rise against me, to lie in wait
24. 7 not to rise against Saul. But Saul rose
28. 25 Then they rose up, and went away that
2 Sa. 12. 21 when the child was dead, thou didst rise
18. 31 of all them that rose up against thee
18. 32 that rise against thee to do (thee) hurt
22. 40 them that rose up against me hast thou
22. 49 high above them that rose up against me
1 Ki 1. 49 and rose up, and went every man his way
2. 19 the king rose up to meet her, and bowed
3. 21 when I rose in the morning to give my ch
21. 16 Ahab rose up to go down to the vineyard
2 Ki. 3. 24 Israelites rose up and smote the Moabites
7. 5 they rose up in the twilight, to go unto
8. 21 he rose by night, and smote the Edomites
16. 7 king of Israel, which rise up against me
2 Ch. 21. 9 rose up by night, and smote the Edomites
28. 15 men which were expressed by name rose up
Ezra 1. 5 Then rose up the chief of the fathers of
10. 6 Ezra rose up from before the house of
Neh. 2. 18 And they said, Let us rise up and build
3. 1 the high priest rose up, with his brethren
4. 14 I looked, and rose up, and said unto the
Job 14. 12 man lieth down, and riseth not: till the
16. 8 and my leanness rising up in me beareth
24. 14 murderer rising with the light killeth the
24. 22 he riseth up, and no (man) is sure of life
30 12 Upon (my) right (hand) rise the youth; th
31. 14 What then shall I do when God riseth up?
Psa. 3. 1 many (are) they that rise up against me
18. 38 they were not able to rise: they are fallen
27. 3 though war should rise against me in this
35. 11 False witnesses did rise up: they laid to
36. 12 cast down, and shall not be able to rise
41. 8 (now) that he lieth he shall rise up no
92 11 of the wicked that rise up against me
94. 16 Who will rise up for me against the evil
119. 62 I will rise to give thanks unto thee because
124. 2 on our side when men rose up against us
127. 2 (It is) vain for you to rise up early, to
140. 10 into deep pits, that they rise not up again
Prov. 24. 22 For their calamity shall rise suddenly
28. 12 but when the wicked rise, a man is hidden
28. 28 When the wicked rise, men hide themse.
31. 15 She riseth also while it is yet night, and
Eccl. 12. 4 he shall rise up at the voice of the bird
Song 2. 10 Rise up, my love, my fair one, and come
3. 2 I will rise now, and go about the city in
5. 5 I rose up to open to my beloved; and my
Isa. 14. 21 they do not rise, nor possess the land, nor
14. 22 I will rise up against them, saith the LORD
24. 20 and it shall fall, and not rise again
26. 14 they shall not rise: therefore hast thou
28. 21 LORD shall rise up as (in) mount Perazim
32. 9 Rise up, ye women that are at ease; hear
33. 10 Now will I rise, saith the LORD; now will
43. 17 they shall not rise: they are extinct, they
54. 17 every tongue (that) shall rise against thee
Jer. 25. 27 rise no more, because of the sword which
26. 17 Then rose up certain of the elders of the
37. 10 they rise up every man in his tent, and
Jer. 49. 14 come against her, and rise up to the battle
51. 64 shall not rise from the evil that I will
Lam. 1. 14 (from whom) I am not able to rise up
Dan. 8 27 I rose up, and did the king's business
Amos 5. 2 she shall no more rise: she is forsaken
7 9 I will rise against the house of Jeroboam
8. 14 they shall fall, and never rise up again
Obad 1 and let us rise up against her in battle
Jon 1. 3 Jonah rose up to flee unto Tarshish from
Mic. 7 6 the daughter riseth up against her mother
Nah. 1. 9 affliction shall not rise up the second time
Hab. 2. 7 Shall they not rise up suddenly that
Zeph 3. 8 until the day that I rise up to the prey
4. *To raise self up,* קוּם *qum, 7a.*
Job 20 27 and the earth shall rise up against him
Psa. 17. 7 from those that rise up (against them)
5. *To rise up,* קוּם *qum.*
Ezra 5 2 Then rose up Zerubbabel the son of Sheal.
Dan 3 24 rose up in haste, (and) spake, and said unto
6. *To go up,* ἀναβαίνω *anabainō.*
Rev. 13. 1 and saw a beast rise up out of the sea
19 3 And her smoke rose up for ever and ever
7. *A standing up,* ἀνάστασις *anastasis.*
Acts 26. 23 that he should be the first that should rise
8. *To rise or spring up,* ἀνατέλλω *anatellō.*
Luke 12 54 When ye see a cloud rise out of the west
9 *To set up,* ἀνίστημι *anistēmi.*
Matt 12. 41 The men of Nineve shall rise in judgment
20. 19 and the third day [he shall rise again]
Mark 1. 35 rising up a great while before day, he
3. 26 if Satan rise up against himself, and be
8. 31 be killed, and after three days rise again
9. 31 after that he is killed, he shall rise the
10. 34 and the third day he shall rise again
10. 50 he, casting away his garment, [rose], and
12. 23 [when they shall rise], whose wife shall
12. 25 For when they shall rise from the dead
Luke 4. 29 rose up, and thrust him out of the city, and
5. 25 immediately he rose up before them, and
5. 28 And he left all, rose up, and followed him
11. 7 Trouble me not..I cannot rise and give
11. 8 Though he will not rise and give him, be.
11. 32 men of Nineve shall rise up in the judgm.
16. 31 persuaded though one rose from the dead
18. 33 and the third day he shall rise again
22. 45 when he rose up from prayer, and was co.
22. 46 rise and pray, lest ye enter into temptat.
24. 7 and be crucified, and the third day rise ag.
24. 33 they rose up the same hour, and returned
24. 46 and to rise from the dead the third day
John 11. 23 saith unto her, Thy brother shall rise ag.
11. 24 know that he shall rise again in the res.
11. 31 that she rose up hastily and went out, fo.
20. 9 that he must rise again from the dead
Acts 5. 17 Then the high priest rose up, and all they
5. 36 For before these days rose up Theudas
5. 37 After this man rose up Judas of Galilee in
10. 13 there came a voice to him, Rise, Peter
10. 41 drink with him after he rose from the de.
14. 20 rose up, and came into the city: and the
15. 7 Peter rose up, and said unto them, Men
17. 3 suffered, and risen again from the dead
26. 16 But rise, and stand upon thy feet: for I
26. 30 king rose up, and the governor, and Ber.
Rom 14. 9 For to this end Christ both died, and [ro.]
15. 12 he that shall rise to reign over the Gent.
1 Co. 10. 7 sat down to eat and drink, and rose up to
1 Th. 4. 14 if we believe that Jesus died and rose ag.
4. 16 and the dead in Christ shall rise first
Heb. 7. 11 should rise after the order of Melchisedec
10. *To lift or raise up,* ἐγείρω *egeirō.*
Matt 11. 11 there hath not risen a greater than John
12. 42 queen of the south shall rise up in the
24. 7 For nation shall rise against nation, and
24. 11 many false prophets shall rise, and shall
26. 46 Rise, let us be going: behold, he is at ha.
27. 63 said..After three days I will rise again
Mark 4. 27 should sleep, and rise night and day, and
10. 49 Be of good comfort, [rise]; he calleth thee
12. 26 as touching the dead, that they rise; have
13. 8 For nation shall rise against nation and
13. 22 false prophets shall rise, and shall show
14. 42 Rise up, let us go; lo, he that betrayeth
Luke 5. 23 forgiven thee; or to say, [Rise up] and wa.
6. 8 [Rise up], and stand forth in the midst
11. 8 Though he will not rise and give him be.
11. 31 queen of the south shall rise up in the ju.
21. 10 Nation shall rise against nation, and kin.
John 5. 8 saith unto him, [Rise], take up thy bed
13. 4 He riseth from supper, and laid aside his
Acts 3. 6 In the name of Jesus..[rise up] and walk
1 Co. 15. 4 that he was buried, and that he rose ag.
15. 12 Now if Christ be preached that he rose
15. 14 if Christ be not risen, then (is) our preac.
15. 15 raised not up, if so be that the dead rise
15. 16 For if the dead rise not, then is not Christ
15 29 if the dead rise not at all? why are they
15. 32 advantageth it me, if the dead rise not?
2 Co. 5. 15 him which died for them, and rose again
Rev. 11. 1 saying, [Rise], and measure the temple of
11. *To set up out of,* ἐξανίστημι *exanistēmi.*
Acts 15. 5 But there rose up certain of the sect of

RISE (up, against, together, with), to —
1. *To rise up,* קוּם *qum.*
Exod 15. 7 hast overthrown them that rose up agai.
Deut 33. 11 through the loins of them that rise against

2 Sa. 22. 40 them that rose up against me hast thou
22. 49 high above them that rose up against me
Psa. 18. 39 subdued under me those that rose up ag.
18. 48 liftest me up above those that rise up ag.
44. 5 we tread them under that rise up against
74. 23 tumult of those that rise up against thee
Prov 24. 16 falleth seven times, and riseth up again
Jer 51. 1 midst of them that rise up against me, a
Lam. 3. 62 The lips of those that rose up against me

2. *To raise self up*, קוּם *qum*, 7a.
Job 27. 7 that riseth up against me as the unright.
Psa. 59. 1 defend me from them that rise up against

3. *An upriser*, תְּקוֹמֵם *teqomem*.
Psa. 139 21 grieved with those that rise up against th.

4. *To rise up against*, ἐπανίσταμαι *epanistamai*.
Matt 10. 21 children shall rise up against (their) par.
Mark 13. 12 children shall rise up against (their) par.

5. *Stand together against*, συνεφίστημι *sunephistēmi*.
Acts 16. 22 the multitude rose up together against th.

RISE (up) betimes or early, to —

1. *To seek early or earnestly*, שָׁחַר *shachar*, 3.
Job 24. 5 rising betimes for a prey: the wilderness

2. *To rise up early*, שָׁכַם *shakam*, 5.
Gen. 19. 2 shall rise up early, and go on your ways
20. 8 Abimelech rose early in the morning, and
21. 14 Abraham rose up early in the morning, and
22. 3 Abraham rose up early in the morning, and
26. 31 they rose up betimes in the morning, and
28. 18 Jacob rose up early in the morning, and
31. 55 early in the morning Laban rose up, and
Exod. 8. 20 Rise up early in the morning, and stand
9. 13 Rise up early in the morning, and stand
24. 4 rose up early in the morning, and builded
32. 6 they rose up early on the morrow, and off.
34. 4 Moses rose up early in the morning, and
Num 14. 40 they rose up early in the morning, and gat
Josh. 3. 1 Joshua rose early in the morning; and th.
6. 12 Joshua rose early in the morning, and the
6. 15 rose early, about the dawning of the day
7. 16 So Joshua rose up early in the morning
8. 10 Joshua rose up early in the morning, and
8. 14 hasted, and rose up early, and the men of
Judg. 6. 38 for he rose up early on the morrow, and
7. 1 rose up early, and pitched beside the well
9. 33 thou shalt rise early, and set upon the city
21 4 people rose early, and built there an altar
1 Sa. 1. 19 rose up in the morning early, and worsh.
15. 12 rose early to meet Saul in the morning, it
17. 20 David rose up early in the morning, and
29. 10 Wherefore rise up early in the morn.
29. 11 men rose up early to depart in the morn.
2 Sa. 15. 2 Absalom rose up early, and stood beside
2 Ki. 3. 22 they rose up early in the morning, and the
6. 15 servant of the man of God was risen early
2 Ch. 20. 20 they rose early in the morning, and went
29 20 Hezekiah the king rose early, and gathered
Job 1. 5 rose up early in the morning, and offered
Isa. 5. 11 Woe unto them that rise up early in the
Zeph. 3. 7 but they rose early, (and) corrupted all th.

RISE (up), to make to —

1. *To cause to go up*, עָלָה *alah*, 5.
Judg 20. 38 make a great flame..to rise up out of the

2. *To (cause to) rise, spring, grow up*, ἀνατέλλω.
Matt. 5. 45 he maketh his sun to rise on the evil and

RISEN (up, again, with), to be —

1. *To rise or grow up*, גָּאָה *gaah*.
Eze. 47. 5 for the waters were risen, waters to swim

2. *To rise up*, זָרַח *zarach*.
Exod 22. 3 If the sun be risen upon him, (there shall
Isa. 60. 1 and the glory of the LORD is risen upon

3. *To go out or forth*, יָצָא *yatsa*.
Gen. 19. 23 sun was risen upon the earth when Lot en.

4. *To rise up*, קוּם *qum*.
Num 32 14 ye are risen up in your father's stead, an
Judg 9. 18 ye are risen up against my father's house
Ruth 2. 15 when she was risen up to glean, Boaz co
1 Sa. 25. 29 Yet a man is risen to pursue thee, and to
2 Sa. 14. 7 family is risen against thine handmaid
1 Ki. 8. 20 am risen up in the room of David my fat.
2 Ki. 6. 15 servant of the man of God was risen early
2 Ch. 6. 10 for I am risen up in the room of David my
13. 6 Yet Jeroboam ..is risen up, and hath reb.
21. 4 Now when Jehoram was risen up to the
Psa. 20. 8 fallen; but we are risen, and stand upri.
27. 12 for false witnesses are risen up against me
54. 3 For strangers are risen up against me, and
86. 14 the proud are risen against me, and the
Prov. 24. 16 falleth seven times, and riseth up again
Jer. 51. 1 midst of them that rise up against me
Lam. 3 62 The lips of those that rose up against me
Eze. 7. 11 Violence is risen up into a rod of wickedn.

5. *To raise up*, קוּם *qum*, 3a.
Mic. 2. 8 my people is risen up as an enemy: ye

6. *To rise or spring up*, ἀνατέλλω *anatellō*.
Jas. 1. 11 For the sun is no sooner risen with a bu.

7. *To set up*, ἀνίστημι *anistēmi*.
Matt 17 9 Son of man [be risen again] from the dead
Mark 9. 9 till the Son of man were risen from the d.
16. 9 [when (Jesus) was risen early the first]
Luke 9. 8, 19 that one of the old prophets was risen a.

8. *To lift or raise up*, ἐγείρω *egeirō*.
Matt 14. 2 he is risen from the dead; and therefore
26. 32 But after I am risen again, I will go bef.
27. 64 He is risen from the dead: so the last err.
28. 6 for he is risen, as he said. Come, see the
28. 7 tell his disciples that he is risen from the
Mark 6. 14 John the Baptist was risen from the dead
6. 16 It is John, whom I beheaded: he is risen
14. 28 after that I am risen, I will go before you
16. 6 he is risen; he is not here: behold the pl.
16. 14 [which had seen him after he was risen]
Luke 7. 16 That a great prophet is risen up among
9. 7 said of some, that John was risen from
13. 25 When..the master of the house is risen up
24. 6 He is not here, but is risen: remember
24. 34 Lord is risen indeed, and hath appeared
John 2. 22 When therefore he was risen from the
21. 14 showed himself..after that he was risen
Rom. 8. 34 that died, yea rather, that is risen again
1 Co. 15. 13 no resurrection..then is Christ not risen
15. 14 if Christ be not risen, then (is) our preac.
15. 20 But now is Christ risen from..dead, (and)

9. *To raise together with*, συνεγείρω *sunegeirō*.
Col. 2. 12 wherein also ye are risen with (him) th.
3. 1 If ye then be risen with Christ, seek those

RISETH, from whence it —

Its rising, שַׁחְרָה [*shachar*].
Isa. 47. 11 thou shalt not know from whence it riseth

RISING (again, early, up, betimes) —

1. *A rising up*, זֶרַח *zerach*.
Isa. 60. 3 and kings to the brightness of thy rising

2. *Region of the rising of the sun*, מִזְרָח *mizrach*.
Num 21 11 (is) before Moab, toward the sun rising
Deut. 4. 41, 47 this side Jordan, toward the sun rising
Josh. 1. 15 this side Jordan toward the sun rising
12. 1 toward the rising of the sun, from the
13. 5 toward the sun rising, from Baal-gad un.
19. 12 toward the sun rising unto the border of
19. 27 turneth toward the sun rising to Beth-D.
19. 34 Judah upon Jordan toward the sun rising
Judg 20 43 over against Gibeah toward the sun rising
Psa. 50. 1 from the rising of the sun unto the going
113. 3 From the rising of the sun unto the going
Isa. 41. 25 from the rising of the sun shall he call
45 6 they may know from the rising of the sun
59. 19 and his glory from the rising of the sun
Mal. 1. 11 from the rising of the sun, even unto the

3. *To go up*, עָלָה *alah*.
Neh. 4. 21 from the rising of the morning till the s.

4. *Uprising*, קִימָה *qimah*.
Lam. 3. 63 their sitting down, and their rising up

5. *Lifting or rising up*, שְׂאֵת *seeth*.
Lev. 13. 2 have in the skin of his flesh a rising, a
13. 10 (if) the rising (be) white in the skin, and
13. 10 (there be) quick raw flesh in the rising
13. 19 a white rising, or a bright spot, white
13. 28 it (is) a rising of the burning, and the
13. 43 the rising of the sore (be) white reddish
14. 56 for a rising, and for a scab, and for a

6. *To rise up early*, שָׁכַם *shakam*, 5.
2 Ch 36. 15 rising up betimes, and sending; because
Prov 27. 14 He that blesseth his friend..rising early
Jer. 7. 13 rising up early and speaking, but ye
7. 25 daily rising up early and sending (them)
11. 7 rising early and protesting, saying, Obey
25. 3 I have spoken unto you, rising early and
25. 4 prophets, rising early and sending (them)
26. 5 both rising up early, and sending (them)
29. 19 prophets, rising up early and sending (th)
32. 33 rising up early and teaching (them), yet th.
35. 14 I have spoken unto you, rising early and
35. 15 rising up early and sending (them), saying
44. 4 prophets, rising early, and sending (them)

7. *To go up, ascend*, ἀναβαίνω *anabainō*.
Mark 9. 10 what the rising from the dead should mean

8. *To rise or spring up*, ἀνατέλλω *anatellō*.
Mark 16. 2 they came unto the sepulchre at the rising

9. *A standing or rising up*, ἀνάστασις *anastasis*.
Luke 2. 34 fall and rising again of many in Israel

RISING of the sun, sunrising —

Place of the rising of the sun, the east, מִזְרָח *mizrach*.
Num. 2. 3 east side toward the rising of the sun
34. 15 Jericho eastward, toward the sun rising

RISING up, no —

No standing up(?), אַלְקוּם *alqum*.
Prov. 30. 31 king, against whom (there is) no rising up

RIS'-SAH, רִסָּה *heap of ruins*.
The 17th Station of Israel from Egypt, and 6th from Sinai, between Libnah and Kehelathah.
Num 33. 21 removed from Libnah, and pitched at R.
33. 22 And they journeyed from R., and pitched

RITE —

Statute, חֻקָּה *chuqqah*.
Num. 9. 3 according to all the rites of it, and accord.

RITH'-MAH, רִתְמָה *broom*.
The 14th station of Israel from Egypt, and 3d from Sinai, between Hazeroth and Rimmon-parez; perhaps the same as Kadesh. Num. 13 26. (*Erthariah?*).
Num 33. 18 departed from Hazeroth..pitched in R.
33. 19 And they departed from R., and pitched

RIVER —

1. *What flows forth, a stream, canal*, אוּבָל, אֻבָל *ubal*.
Dan. 8. 2 saw in a vision, and I was by the river
8. 3 there stood before the river a ram which
8. 6 which I had seen standing before the riv.

2. *A channel, stream*, אָפִיק *aphiq*.
Song 5. 12 (the eyes) of doves by the rivers of waters
Eze. 6. 3 and to the hills, to the rivers, and to the
31. 12 are broken by all the rivers of the land
32. 6 and the rivers shall be full of thee
34. 13 upon the mountains of Israel by the rivers
35. 8 in all thy rivers, shall they fall that are
36. 4, 6 to the rivers, and to the valleys, to the
Joel 1. 20 the rivers of waters are dried up, and the
3. 18 the rivers of Judah shall flow with waters

3. *The Nile, a stream*, יְאֹר (יְאוֹר) *yeor*.
Gen. 41. 1 dreamed: and, behold, he stood by the ri.
41. 2 there came up out of the river seven well
41. 3 kine came up after them out of the river
41. 3 (other) kine upon the brink of the river
41. 17 behold, I stood upon the bank of the river
41. 18 there came up out of the river seven kine
Exod. 1. 22 Every son..ye shall cast into the river
2. 3 laid (it) in the flags by the river's brink
2. 5 came down to wash (herself) at the river
2. 5 maidens walked along by the river's side
4. 9 thou shalt take of the water of the river
4. 9 water which thou takest out of the river
7. 15 stand by the river's brink against he come
7. 17 upon the waters which (are) in the river
7. 18 the fish that (is) in the river shall die, and
7. 18 the river shall stink; and the Egyptians
7. 18 loathe to drink of the water of the river
7. 19 upon their rivers, and upon their ponds
7. 20 smote the waters that (were) in the river
7. 20 the waters that (were) in the river were
7. 21 the fish that (was) in the river died; and
7. 21 and the river stank, and the Egyptians
7. 21, 24 could not drink of the water of the ri.
7. 24 Egyptians digged round about the river
7. 25 after that the LORD had smitten the river
8. 3 river shall bring forth frogs abundantly
8. 5 over the rivers, and over the ponds, and
8. 9 (that) they may remain in the river only
8. 11 they shall remain in the river only
17. 5 thy rod, wherewith thou smotest the river
2 Ki. 19. 24 dried up all the rivers of besieged places
Job 28. 10 He cutteth out rivers among the rocks
Psa. 78. 44 And had turned their rivers into blood
Isa. 7. 18 the uttermost part of the rivers of Egypt
23. 3 the harvest of the river, (is) her revenue
23. 10 Pass through thy land as a river, O dau.
37. 25 dried up all the rivers of the besieged pl.
Eze. 29. 3 that lieth in the midst of his rivers
29. 3 My river (is) mine own, and I have made
29. 4 I will cause the fish of thy rivers to stick
29. 4 bring..up out of the midst of thy rivers
29. 4 the fish of thy rivers shall stick unto thy
29. 5 thee and all the fish of thy rivers: thou
29. 9 said, The river (is) mine, and I have made
29. 10 (am) against thee, and against thy rivers
30. 12 I will make the rivers dry, and sell the
Dan. 12. 5 on this side of the bank of the river, and
12. 5 other on that side of the bank of the river
12. 6, 7 which (was) upon the waters of the river
Nah. 3. 8 No, that was situate among the rivers
Zech. 10. 11 all the deeps of the rivers shall dry up

4. *A stream, canal*, יוּבַל *yubal*.
Jer. 17. 8 (that) spreadeth out her roots by the river

5. *A river*, נָהָר *nahar*.
Gen. 2. 10 a river went out of Eden to water the ga.
2. 13 And the name of the second river (is) G.
2. 14 the name of the third river (is) Hiddekel
2. 14 the east of Assyria. And the fourth river
15. 18 have I given this land, from the river of
15. 18 unto the great river, the river Euphrates
31. 21 passed over the river, and set his face
36. 37 Saul of Rehoboth (by) the river reigned in
Exod 23. 31 bounds..from the desert unto the river
Num 22. 5 the river of the land of the children of
24. 6 gardens by the river's side, as the trees
Deut. 1. 7 unto the great river, the river Euphrates
11. 24 from the river, the river Euphrates, even
Josh. 1. 4 even unto the great river, the river Eup.
2 Sa. 8. 3 recover his border at the river Euphrates
10. 16 the Syrians that (were) beyond the river
1 Ki. 4. 21 reigned over all kingdoms from the river
4. 24 all (the region) on this side the river
4. 24 over all the kings on this side the river
14. 15 and shall scatter them beyond the river
2 Ki. 5. 12 not Abana and Pharpar, rivers of Dama.
17. 6 in Habor (by) the river of Gozan, and in
18. 11 in Habor (by) the river of Gozan, and in the
23. 29 king of Egypt went..to the river Euphr.
24. 7 had taken from..the river Euphrates all
1 Ch. 1. 48 Shaul of Rehoboth by the river reigned
5. 9 the wilderness from the river Euphrates
5. 26 and Habor, and Hara, and to the river G.
18. 3 went to stablish his dominion by the river
19. 16 the Syrians that (were) beyond the river
2 Ch. 9. 26 reigned over all the kings from the river
Ezra 8. 15 gathered them together to the river that
8. 21 I proclaimed a fast there, at the river
8. 31 we departed from the river of Ahava on
8. 36 to the governors on this side the river
Neh. 2. 7 given me to the governors beyond the ri.
2. 9 I came to the governors beyond the river
3. 7 of the governor on this side the river
Job 40. 23 he drinketh up a river, (and) hasteth not

Psa. 46. 4 (There is) a river, the streams wherof sh.
72. 8 from the river unto the ends of the earth
74. 15 the flood: thou driedst up mighty rivers
78. 16 and caused waters to run down like rivers
80. 11 She sent out..her branches unto the rivers
89. 25 I will set..his right hand in the rivers
105. 41 they ran in the dry places (like) a river
107. 33 He turneth rivers into a wilderness, and
137. 1 By the rivers of Babylon, there we sat do.
Isa. 7. 20 by them beyond the river, by the king of
8. 7 up upon them the waters of the river
11. 15 shall he shake his hand over the river
18. 1 which (is) beyond the rivers of Ethiopia
18. 2, 7 whose land the rivers have spoiled
19. 5 the river shall be wasted and dried up
19. 6 And they shall turn the rivers far away
27. 12 beat off from the channel of the river
33. 21 (will be) unto us a place of broad rivers
41. 18 I will open rivers in high places, and
42. 15 I will make the rivers islands, and I will
43. 2 the rivers, they shall not overflow thee
43. 19, 20 wilderness, (and) rivers in the desert
44. 27 saith..Be dry, and I will dry up thy rivers
47. 2 uncover the thigh, pass over the rivers
48. 18 then had thy peace been as a river, and
50. 2 I make the rivers a wilderness: their fish
66. 12 I will extend peace to her like a river
Jer. 2. 18 to do..to drink the waters of the river
46. 2 was by the river Euphrates in
46. 6 toward the north by the river Euphrates
46. 7 whose waters are moved as the rivers?
46. 8 and (his) waters are moved like the rivers
46. 10 the north country by the river Euphrates
Eze. 1. 1 among the captives by the river of Chebar
1. 3 land of the Chaldeans, by the river Cheb.
3. 15 I came to them..that dwelt by the river
3. 23 glory which I saw by the river of Chebar
10. 15 creature that I saw by the river of Cheb.
10. 20 living creature that I saw..by the river
10. 22 faces which I saw by the river of Chebar
31. 4 her rivers running round about his plants
32. 2 and thou camest forth with thy rivers
32. 2 and troubledst..and fouledst their rivers
32. 14 and cause their rivers to run like oil
43. 3 the vision that I saw by the river Chebar
Dan. 10. 4 as I was by the side of the great rivers
Mic. 7. 12 from the fortress even to the river, and
Nah. 1. 4 maketh it dry, and drieth up all the riv.
2. 6 The gates of the rivers shall be opened
Hab. 3. 8 Was the LORD displeased against..rivers
3. 8 (was) thine anger against the rivers? (w.)
3. 9 Thou didst cleave the earth with rivers
Zeph. 3. 10 From beyond the rivers of Ethiopia my
Zech. 9. 10 from the river (even) to the ends of the

6. *A river*, נָהָר *nehar*.
Ezra 4. 10 the rest (that are) on this side the river
4. 11 servants the men on this side the river
4. 16 have no portion on this side the river
4. 17 answer..(unto) the rest beyond the river
4. 20 ruled over all (countries) beyond the riv.
5. 3, 6 Tatnai, governor on this side the river
5. 6 Apharsachites..on this side the river
6. 6 Tatnai, governor beyond the river, Shet.
6. 6 Apharsachites, which (are) beyond the ri.
6. 8 goods, (even) of the tribute beyond the ri.
6. 13 Tatnai, governor on this side the river
7. 21 the treasurers which (are) beyond the ri.
7. 25 all the people that (are) beyond the river

7. *A dividing brook in a valley*, נַחַל *nachal*.
Lev. 11. 9 the waters, in the seas, and in the rivers
11. 10 and in the rivers, of all that move in the
Num34. 5 from Azmon unto the river of Egypt, and
Deut. 2. 24 pass over the river Arnon: behold, I have
2. 36 (is) by the brink of the river of Arnon, and
2. 36 (from) the city that (is) by the river, even
2. 37 (nor) unto any place of the river Jabbok
3. 8 from the river of Arnon unto mount He.
3. 12 Aroer, which (is) by the river Arnon, and
3. 16 even unto the river Arnon half the valley
3. 16 and the border even unto the river Jabbok
4. 48 which (is) by the bank of the river Arnon
10. 7 to Jotbath, a land of rivers of waters
Josh. 12. 1 from the river Arnon unto mount Herm.
12. 2 which (is) upon the bank of the river Ar.
12. 2 from the middle of the river, and from
12. 2 the river Jabbok, (which is) the border of
13. 9, 16 that (is) upon the bank of the river A.
13. 9, 16 city that (is) in the midst of the river
15. 4 went out unto the river of Egypt; and the
15. 7 which (is) on the south side of the river
15. 47 unto the river of Egypt, and the great sea
16. 8 Tappuah westward unto the river Kanah
17. 9 the river Kanah, southward of the river
17. 9 coast..(was) on the north side of the river
19. 11 and reached to the river that (is) before
Judg. 4. 7 will draw unto thee, to the river Kishon
4. 13 from Harosheth..unto the river of Kish.
5. 21 The river..that ancient river, the river K.
2 Sa. 17. 13 we will draw it into the river, until there
24. 5 (lieth) in the midst of the river of Gad
1 Ki. 8. 65 entering in of Hamath unto the river of
2 Ki. 10. 33 from Aroer, which (is) by the river Arnon
24. 7 taken from the river of Egypt unto the ri.
2 Ch. 7. 8 entering in of Hamath unto the river of
Psa. 36. 8 make them drink of the river of thy ple.
Eccl. 1. 7 All the rivers run into the sea; yet the
1. 7 unto the place from whence the rivers
Jer. 31. 9 will cause them to walk by the rivers of
Lam. 2. 18 let tears run down like a river day and
Eze. 47. 5 river that I could not pass over..river that
47. 6 caused me to return to the brink of the ri.
Eze. 47. 7 at the bank of the river (were) very many
47. 9 whithersoever the rivers shall come, shall
47. 9 every thing shall live whither the river co.
47. 12 by the river upon the bank thereof, on
Amos 6. 14 entering in of Hemath unto the river of
Mic. 6. 7 be pleased..with ten thousands of rivers

8. *A brook in a valley*, נַחְלָה *nachalah*.
Eze. 47. 19 waters of strife (in) Kadesh, the river to
48. 28 (and) to the river toward the great sea

9. *A division, artificial water course*, פֶּלֶג *peleg*.
Job 29. 6 and the rock poured me out rivers of oil
Psa. 1. 3 shall be like a tree planted by the rivers
65. 9 the river of God, (which) is full of water
119. 136 Rivers of waters run down mine eyes, b.
Prov. 5. 16 dispersed abroad, (and) rivers of waters in
21. 1 The king's heart..(as) the rivers of water
Isa. 30. 25 rivers (and) streams of waters in the day
32. 2 as rivers of water in a dry place; as the sh
Lam. 3. 48 Mine eye runneth down with rivers of wa.

10. *A division, artificial water course*, פְּלַגָּה *pelaggah*.
Job 20. 17 He shall not see the rivers, the floods, the

11. *A flowing, a river, flood*, ποταμός *potamos*.
Mark 1. 5 were all baptized of him in the river of J.
John 7. 38 out of his belly shall flow rivers of living
Acts 16. 13 we went out of the city by a river side
Rev. 8. 10 and it fell upon the third part of the riv.
9. 14 which are bound in the great river Eup.
16. 4 poured out his vial upon the rivers and
16. 12 poured out his vial upon the great river
22. 1 showed me a pure river of water of life
22. 2 on either side of the river, (was there) the

RIVER, little —
A trench or conduit, תְּעָלָה *tealah*.
Eze. 31. 4 sent out her little rivers unto all the trees

RIZ'-PAH, רִצְפָּה *variegated*.
A daughter of Aiah and concubine of Saul, whom Abner took after Saul's death, and whose two sons were given up by David to the Gibeonites and hanged. B.C. 1070.
2 Sa. 3. 7 Saul had a concubine, whose name..R.
21. 8 But the king took the two sons of R. the
21. 10 And R. the daughter of Aiah took sackc.
21. 11 And it was told David what R...had done

ROAD, to make a —
To strip off, פָּשַׁט *pashat*.
1 Sa. 27. 10 Whither have ye made a road to day? And

ROAR, to —
1. *To meditate, mutter*, הָגָה *hagah*.
Isa. 31. 4 Like as the lion and the young lion roar.

2. *To make a noise*, הָמָה *hamah*.
Psa. 46. 3 the waters thereof roar (and) be troubled
Isa. 51. 15 that divided the sea, whose waves roared
59. 11 We roar all like bears, and mourn sore
Jer. 5. 22 though they roar, yet can they not pass
6. 23 their voice roareth like the sea; and they
31. 35 when the waves thereof roar; The LORD
50. 42 their voice shall roar like the sea, and they
51. 55 when her waves do roar like great waters

3. *To be disquieted, troubled*, נָהַם *naham*.
Isa. 5. 29 like young lions; yea, they shall roar, and
5. 30 in that day they shall roar against them

4. *To shriek, cry aloud or out*, צָרַח *tsarach*, 5.
Isa. 42. 13 shall cry, yea, roar; he shall prevail ag.

5. *To roar, be troubled*, רָעַם *raam*.
1 Ch. 16. 32 Let the sea roar, and the fulness thereof
Psa. 96. 11 let the sea roar, and the fulness thereof
98. 7 Let the sea roar, and the fulness thereof

6. *To roar*, שָׁאַג *shaag*.
Judg 14. 5 behold, a young lion roared against him
Job 37. 4 After it a voice roareth: he thundereth
Psa. 22. 13 gaped..(as) a ravening and a roaring lion
38. 8 I have roared by reason of the disquiet.
74. 4 Thine enemies roar in the midst of thy
104. 21 The young lions roar after their prey, and
Isa. 5. 29 they shall roar like young lions; yea, they
Jer. 2. 15 The young lions roared upon him, (and)
25. 30 The LORD shall roar from on high, and
25. 30 he shall mightily roar upon his habitation
51. 38 They shall roar together like lions they
Eze. 22. 25 like a roaring lion ravening the prey: they
Hos. 11. 10 roar like a lion: when he shall roar, then
Joel 3. 16 The LORD also shall roar out of Zion, and
Amos 1. 2 LORD will roar from Zion, and utter his
3. 4 Will a lion roar in the forest when he hath
3. 8 lion hath roared, who will not fear? the
Zeph. 3. 3 Her princes within her (are) roaring lions

7. *To sound*, ἠχέω *ēcheō*.
Luke 21. 25 perplexity; the sea and the waves [roaring]

8. *To low, bellow, roar*, μυκάομαι *mukaomai*.
Rev. 10. 3 cried with a loud voice, .. lion roareth

9. *To roar, bellow, howl, bark*, ὠρύομαι *ōruomai*.
1 Pe. 5. 8 your adversary the devil, as a roaring

ROARING —
1. *To be disquieted, troubled*, נָהַם *naham*.
Prov 28. 15 roaring lion, and a ranging bear; (so is)

2. *Disquietude, trouble*, נַהַם *naham*.
Prov 19. 12 king's wrath (is) as the roaring of a lion
20. 2 fear of a king (is) as the roaring of a lion

3. *Disquietude, trouble*, נְהָמָה *nehamah*.
Isa. 5. 30 against them like the roaring of the sea

4. *Roar, roaring*, שְׁאָגָה *sheagah*.
Job 3. 24 my roarings are poured out like the waters
4. 10 The roaring of the lion, and the voice of
Psa. 22. 1 me, (and from) the words of my roaring
32. 3 my bones waxed old through my roaring
Isa. 5. 29 Their roaring (shall be) like a lion, they
Eze. 19. 7 was desolate..by the noise of his roaring
Zech 11. 3 voice of the roaring of young lions; for

ROAST, to roast, —
1. *To boil, ripen, cook*, בָּשַׁל *bashal*, 3.
Deut 16. 7 thou shalt roast and eat (it) in the place
2 Ch. 35. 13 roasted the passover with fire according

2. *To roast or singe*, חָרַךְ *charak*.
Prov 12. 27 slothful (man) roasteth not that which he

3. *To roast*, צָלָה *tsalah*.
1 Sa. 2. 15 Give flesh to roast for the priest; for he
Isa. 44. 16 he roasteth roast, and is satisfied: yea, he
44. 19 I have roasted flesh, and eaten (it): and

4. *Roasting*, צְלִי *tsali*.
Exod 12. 8 roast with fire, and unleavened bread, and
12. 9 but roast (with) fire; his head with his legs
Isa. 44. 16 roast, and is satisfied: yea, he warmeth

5. *To parch, roast, burn*, קָלָה *qalah*.
Jer. 29. 22 whom the king of Babylon roasted in the

ROB, to —
1. *To take prey or spoil*, בָּזַז *bazaz*.
Isa. 10. 2 and (that) they may rob the fatherless!
17. 14 that spoil us, and the lot of them that rob
Eze. 39. 10 rob those that robbed them, saith the L.

2. *To snatch away*, גָּזַל *gazal*.
Lev. 19. 13 not defraud thy neighbour, neither rob
Judg. 9. 25 robbed all that came along that way by
Prov. 22. 22 Rob not the poor, because he (is) poor, ne.
28. 24 Whoso robbeth his father or his mother

3. *To surround, compass, ensnare*, עוּד *ud*, 3.
Psa. 119. 61 The bands of the wicked have robbed me

4. *To circumvent*, קָבַע *qaba*.
Mal. 3. 8 Will a man rob God? Yet ye have robbed
3. 8 ye say, Wherein have we robbed thee? In
3. 9 for ye have robbed me, (even) this whole na.

5. *To rifle, spoil*, שָׁסָה *shasah*, 1, 3a.
1 Sa. 23. 1 the Philistines..rob the threshing floors
Isa. 10. 13 robbed their treasures, and I have put do.

6. *To spoil, rob, plunder*, συλάω *sulaō*.
2 Co. 11. 8 robbed other churches, taking wages (of

ROB of children or whelps, to —
1. *To bereave*, שָׁכֹל *shakol*, 3.
Lev. 26. 22 which shall rob you of your children, and

2. *Bereaved*, שַׁכּוּל *shakkul*.
2 Sa. 17. 8 as a bear robbed of her whelps in the field
Prov 17. 12 Let a bear robbed of her whelps meet a

ROBBED, to be, that he had —
1. *To take as prey or spoil*, בָּזַז *bazaz*.
Isa. 42. 22 But this (is) a people robbed and spoiled

2. *To be taken as prey or spoil*, בָּזַז *bazaz*, 4.
Jer. 50. 37 upon her treasures; and they shall be ro.

3. *A snatching away*, גְּזֵלָה *gezelah*.
Eze. 33. 15 give again that he had robbed, walk in the

ROBBER — [*See* Churches.]
1. *To take prey or spoil*, בָּזַז *bazaz*.
Isa. 42. 24 Jacob for a spoil, and Israel to the robbers

2. *A breaker up, burglar*, פָּרִיץ *parits*.
Jer. 7. 11 become a den of robbers in your eyes? Be.
Eze. 7. 22 for the robbers shall enter into it, and
18. 10 If he beget a son (that is) a robber, a she.

3. *Son of a burglar*, בֶּן־פָּרִיץ *ben parits*.
Dan. 11. 14 robbers of thy people shall exalt themse.

4. *A designing one, noose*, צַמִּים *tsammim*.
Job 5. 5 the robber swalloweth up their substance
18. 9 (and) the robber shall prevail against him

5. *To spoil or waste*, שָׁדַד *shadad*.
Job 12. 6 tabernacles of robbers prosper, and they
Obad. 5 If thieves came to thee, if robbers by night

6. *Robber, plunderer*, λῃστής *lēstēs*.
John 10. 1 He that entereth not..is a thief and a ro.
10. 8 All..are thieves and robbers: but the sh.
18. 40 but Barabbas. Now Barabbas was a rob.
2 Co. 11. 26 perils of robbers, (in) perils by (mine own)

ROBBERY —
1. *A snatching away*, גָּזֵל *gazel*.
Psa. 62. 10 become not vain in robbery: if riches in.
Isa. 61. 8 hate robbery for burnt offering; and I w.
Eze. 22. 29 have used oppression, and exercised rob.

2. *A breaking up or forth*, פֶּרֶק *pereq*.
Nah. 3. 1 it (is) all full of lies (and) robbery; the p.

3. *Spoiling, waste*, שֹׁד *shod*.
Prov 21. 7 robbery of the wicked shall destroy them
Amos 3. 10 store up violence and robbery in their pa.

4. *A snatching away*, ἁρπαγμός *harpagmos*.
Phil. 2. 6 thought it not robbery to be equal with G.

ROBE, (long) —
1. *An ornamental mantle*, אֶדֶר *eder*.
Mic. 2. 8 ye pull off the robe with the garment from

2. *An ornamental mantle*, אַדֶּרֶת *addereth*.
Jon. 3. 6 laid his robe from him, and covered (him)

3. *Garment, cloth,* בֶּגֶד *beged.*
1 Ki.22. 10 having put on their robes, in a void place
22. 30 but put thou on thy robes. And the king
2 Ch.18. 9 clothed in (their) robes, and they sat in a
18. 29 go to the battle ; but put thou on thy ro.

4. *A coat, tunic,* כְּתֹנֶת, (כֻּתֹּנֶת *kethoneth), kuttoneth.*
Isa. 22. 21 will clothe him with thy robe, and stren.

5. *Robe, mantle,* מְעִיל *meil.*
Exod28. 4 robe, and a broidered coat, a mitre, and
28. 31 shalt make the robe of the ephod all (of)
28. 34 upon the hem of the robe round about
29. 5 put upon Aaron the coat, and the robe of
39. 22 made the robe of the ephod (of) woven
39. 23 an hole in the midst of the robe, as the ho.
39. 24 made upon the hems of the robe pomegr.
39. 25 upon the hem of the robe, round about b.
39. 26 round about the hem of the robe to min.
Lev. 8 7 clothed him with the robe, and put the ep.
1 Sa. 18. 4 Jonathan stripped himself of the robe th.
24 4 and cut off the skirt of Saul's robe privily
24. 11 see the skirt of thy robe in my hand : for
24. 11 for in that I cut off the skirt of thy robe
2 Sa. 13. 18 with such robes were the king's daughters
1 Ch. 15 27 David (was) clothed with a robe of fine li.
Job 29 14 my judgment (was) as a robe and a diad.
Isa 61 10 covered me with the robe of righteousness
Eze. 26. 16 lay away their robes, and put off their br.

6. *Garment, robe, raiment,* ἐσθής *esthēs*
Luke23. 11 arrayed him in a gorgeous robe, and sent

7. *Garment, mantle,* ἱμάτιον *himation.*
John19. 2 head, and they put on him a purple robe
19 5 the crown of thorns, and the purple robe

8. *A long garment, robe,* στολή *stolē.*
Luke15 22 Bring forth the best robe, and put (it) on
20. 46 which desire to walk in long robes, and
Rev. 6. 11 white robes were given unto every one of
7. 9 clothed with white robes, and palms in th.
7. 13 are these which are arrayed in white ro.?
7. 14 have washed their robes, and made them

9. *A cloak, robe, loose garment,* χλαμύς *chlamus.*
Matt 27. 28 stripped him, and put on him a scarlet ro.
27. 31 they took the robe off from him, and put

RO-BO'-AM, Ῥοβοάμ. See *Rehoboam.*
Son of Solomon and father of Abijah, kings of Judah.
B.C. 975
Matt. 1. 7 And Solomon begat R. ; and R. begat A.

ROCK, (ragged) —

1. *Flint, flinty rock,* חַלָּמִישׁ *challamish.*
Job 28. 9 He putteth forth his hand upon the rock

2. *Rocks,* כֵּפִים *kephim.*
Job 30. 6 To dwell in the cliffs..and (in) the rocks
Jer. 4. 29 thickets, and climb up upon the rocks

3. *Strong place, strength,* מָעוֹז *maoz.*
Judg. 6. 26 build an altar..upon the top of this rock

4. *A cliff, rock, (from its elevation),* סֶלַע *sela.*
Num20. 8 speak ye unto the rock before their eyes
20. 8 bring forth to them water out of the rock
20. 10 gathered..together before the rock, and
20. 10 must we fetch you water out of this rock
20. 11 with his rod he smote the rock twice ; and
24. 21 and said..thou puttest thy nest in a rock
Deut32. 13 suck honey out of the rock, and oil out of
Judg. 1. 36 going up to Akrabbim, from the rock, and
6. 20 lay (them) upon this rock, and pour out
15. 8 went down and dwelt in the top of the ro.
15 11 went to the top of the rock Etam, and said
15. 13 bound..and brought him up from the ro.
20. 45 fled toward the wilderness unto the rock
20. 47 unto the rock..and abode in the rock R.
21. 13 children..that(were)in the rock Rimmon
1 Sa. 13. 6 hide themselves..in rocks, and in high pl.
14. 4 rock on the one side, and a sharp rock on
23. 25 wherefore he came down into a rock, and
2 Sa 22. 2 LORD (is) my rock, and my fortress, and
1 Ki 19. 11 brake in pieces the rocks, before the LORD
2 Ch.25. 12 brought them unto the top of the rock, and
25. 12 cast them down from the top of the rock
Neh. 9. 15 water for them out of the rock for their
Job 39. 1 time when the wild goats of the rock br.
39 28 on the rock, upon the crag of the rock
Psa. 18. 2 LORD (is) my rock, and my fortress, and
31. 3 For thou (art) my rock and my fortress
40. 2 set my feet upon a rock, (and) established
42. 9 I will say unto God my rock, Why hast
71. 3 for thou (art) my rock and my fortress
78. 16 He brought streams also out of the rock
104 18 refuge for the wild goats, (and) the rocks
Prov.30. 26 yet make they their houses in the rocks
Song 2. 14 my dove, (that art) in the clefts of the ro.
Isa. 2. 21 and into the tops of the ragged rocks
7 19 in the holes of the rocks, and upon all th.
22. 16 graveth an habitation for himself in a ro.?
32. 2 the shadow of a great rock in a weary la.
33. 16 defence (shall be) the munitions of rocks
42. 11 let the inhabitants of the rock sing, let
57 5 in the valleys under the clifts of the roc.?
Jer. 5. 3 made their faces harder than a rock ; th.
13. 4 and hide it there in a hole of the rock
16 16 hunt them..out of the holes of the rocks
23 29 like a hammer (that) breaketh the rock in
48. 28 dwell in the rock, and be like the dove
49. 16 thou that dwellest in the clefts of the ro.
51 25 roll thee down from the rocks, and will
Eze. 24. 7 she set it upon the top of a rock ; she po.
24. 8 have set her blood upon the top of a rock
26. 4 will also..make her like the top of a rock
26. 14 I will make thee like the top of a rock : th.
Amos 6. 12 Shall horses run upon the rock? will (one)
Obad. 3 thou that dwellest in the clefts of the ro.

5. *A rock, (from its sharpness),* צוּר *tsur.*
Exod17. 6 will stand before thee there upon the ro.
17. 6 smite the rock, and there shall come wa.
33. 21 by me, and thou shalt stand upon a rock
33. 22 that I will put thee in a clift of the rock
Num23. 9 For from the top of the rocks I see him
Deut. 8. 15 brought thee forth water out of the rock
32. 4 (He is) the rock, his work (is) perfect ; for
32. 13 made him to suck..oil of the flinty rock
32. 15 lightly esteemed the rock of his salvation
32. 18 Of the rock (that) begat thee thou art un.
32. 30 except their rock had sold them, and the
32. 31 For their rock (is) not as our rock, even
32. 37 Where (are) their gods, (their) rock in wh.
Judg. 6. 21 there rose up fire out of the rock, and co.
7. 25 slew Oreb upon the rock Oreb, and Zeeb
13. 19 took a kid..and offered (it) upon a rock
1 Sa. 2. 2 none..neither (is their) any rock like our
24. 2 his men upon the rocks of the wild goats
2 Sa. 21. 10 spread it for her upon the rock, from the
22. 3 God of my rock ; in him will I trust : (he
22. 32 save the LORD? and who (is) a rock, save
22. 47 The LORD liveth ; and blessed (be) my ro
22. 47 exalted be the God of the rock of my sal.
23. 3 The God of Israel said, the rock of Israel
1 Ch. 11. 15 went down to the rock to David, into the
Job 14. 18 and the rock, is removed out of his place
18. 4 shall the rock be removed out of his place
19. 24 they were graven..in the rock for ever!
24. 8 and embrace the rock for want of a she.
28. 10 He cutteth out rivers among the rocks
29. 6 and the rock poured me out rivers of oil
Psa. 18. 31 save the LORD? or who (is) a rock save our
18. 46 The LORD liveth ; and blessed (be) my ro.
27 5 hide me ; he shall set me up upon a rock
28. 1 Unto thee will I cry, O LORD my rock ; be
31 2 be thou my strong rock, for an house of
61. 2 lead me to the rock (that) is higher than
62. 2 He only (is) my rock and my salvation ; he
62. 7 rock of my strength, (and) my refuge, (is)
78. 15 He clave the rocks in the wilderness, and
78. 20 smote the rock, that the waters gushed
78. 35 they remembered that God (was) their ro.
81. 16 with honey out of the rock should I have
89. 26 my God, and the rock of my salvation
92. 15 my rock, and (there is) no unrighteousn.
94. 22 my defence ; and my God (is) the rock of
95 1 let us make a joyful noise to the rock of
105 41 opened the rock, and the waters gushed
114 8 Which turned the rock (into) a standing
Prov.30. 19 way of a serpent upon a rock, the way of
Isa. 2. 10 Enter into the rock, and hide thee in the
2. 19 they shall go into the holes of the rocks
2. 21 To go into the clefts of the rocks, and in.
8. 14 for a rock of offence to both the houses
10. 26 slaughter of Midian at the rock of Oreb
17. 10 hast not been mindful of the rock of thy
48. 21 caused the waters to flow out of the rock
48. 21 clave the rock also, and the waters gush.
51. 1 look unto the rock (whence) ye are hewn
Jer. 18. 14 (which cometh) from the rock of the field
21. 13 I (am) against thee, O..rock of the plain
Nah. 1. 6 fury is poured out like fire, and the rocks

6. *A rock, stone,* πέτρα *petra.*
Matt. 7. 24 man, which built his house upon a rock
7. 25 fell not : for it was founded upon a rock
16. 18 and upon this rock I will build my church
27. 51 the earth did quake, and the rocks rent
27. 60 tomb, which he had hewn out in the rock
Mark15. 46 a sepulchre which was hewn out of a rock
Luke 6. 48 laid the foundation on a rock : and when
6. 48 [could not shake it ; for it was..upon a ro.]
8. 6 some fell upon a rock ; and as soon as it
8. 13 They on the rock (are they), which, when
Rom. 9. 33 lay..a stumbling stone and rock of offence
1 Co 10. 4 rock that followed them ; and that rock
1 Pe. 2. 8 a rock of offence, (even to them) which
Rev. 6. 15 dens and in the rocks of the mountains
6. 16 said to the mountains and rocks, Fall on

7. *Rough or rugged places,* τραχεῖς τόπους [*trachus*].
Acts 27. 29 fearing..we should have fallen upon rocks

ROD —

1. *A rod, shoot, twig, sprout,* חֹטֶר *choter.*
Prov 14. 3 In the mouth of the foolish (is) a rod of
Isa. 11. 1 there shall come forth a rod out of the

2. *A staff,* מַקֵּל *maqqel.*
Gen. 30. 37 Jacob took him rods of green poplar, and
30. 37 made the white appear...in the rods
30. 38 set the rods which he had pilled before
30. 39 the flocks conceived before the rods, and
30. 41 Jacob laid the rods before the eyes of the
30. 41 that they might conceive among the rods
Jer. 1. 11 And I said, I see a rod of an almond tree
48. 17 strong staff broken, (and) the beautiful rod

3. *A rod,* מַטֶּה *matteh.*
Exod. 4. 2 What (is)..in thine hand? And he said, Ar.
4. 4 caught it, and became a rod in his hand
4. 17 thou shalt take this rod in thine hand
4. 20 and Moses took the rod of God in his ha.
7. 9 Take thy rod, and cast (it) before Pharaoh
7. 10 Aaron cast down his rod before Pharaoh
7. 12 they cast down every man his rod, and
7. 12 but Aaron's rod swallowed up their rods
7. 15 the rod which was turned to a serpent
7. 17 I will smite with the rod that (is) in mine
7. 19 Take thy rod, and stretch out thine hand
7. 20 lifted up the rod, and smote the waters
8. 5 Stretch forth thine hand with thy rod
8. 16 Stretch out thy rod, and smite the dust
8. 17 Aaron stretched out his hand with his rod
9. 23 stretched forth his rod toward heaven
10. 13 Moses stretched forth his rod over the
14. 16 lift thou up thy rod, and stretch out thine
17. 5 thy rod, wherewith thou smotest the river
17. 9 stand on the top of the hill with the rod
Num17. 2 take of every one of them a rod according
17. 2 the house of their fathers twelve rods
17. 2 write thou every man's name upon his rod
17. 3 upon the rod of Levi: for one rod (shall be)
17. 5 the man's rod, whom I shall choose, shall
17. 6 every one of their princes gave him a rod
17. 6 to their fathers' houses, (even) twelve rods
17. 6 and the rod of Aaron (was) among their ro.
17. 7 Moses laid up the rods before the LORD
17. 8 the rod of Aaron for the house of Levi was
17. 9 Moses brought out all the rods from before
17. 9 they looked, and took every man his rod
17. 10 Bring Aarons rod again before the testim.
20. 8 Take the rod, and gather thou the assem.
20. 9 Moses took the rod from before the LORD
20. 11 and with his rod he smote the rock twice
1 Sa. 14. 27 the end of the rod that (was) in his hand
14. 43 the end of the rod that (was) in mine hand
Psa.110. 2 send the rod of thy strength out of Zion
Isa. 10. 26 (as) his rod (was) upon the sea, so shall he
Eze. 7. 10 the rod hath blossomed, pride hath bud.
7. 11 Violence is risen up into a rod of wickedness
19. 11 she had strong rods for the sceptres of
19. 12 her strong rods were broken and withered
19. 14 fire is gone out of a rod of her branches
19. 14 hath no strong rod (to be) a sceptre to rule
Mic. 6. 9 hear ye the rod, and who hath appointed

4. *A sceptre, rod,* שֵׁבֶט *shebet.*
Exod21. 20 smite his servant, or his maid, with a rod
Lev. 27. 32 whatsoever passeth under the rod, the te.
2 Sa. 7. 14 I will chasten him with the rod of men
Job 9. 34 Let him take his rod away from me, and
21. 9 (are) safe from fear, neither (is) the rod of
Psa. 2. 9 Thou shalt break them with a rod of iron
23. 4 thou (art) with me ; thy rod and thy staff
74. 2 the rod of thine inheritance, (which) thou
89. 32 I visit their transgression with the rod
125. 3 the rod of the wicked shall not rest upon
Prov.10. 13 a rod (is) for the back of him that is void
13. 24 He that spareth his rod hateth his son
22. 8 and the rod of his anger shall
22. 15 the rod of correction shall drive it far
23. 13 (if) thou beatest him with the rod, he shall
23. 14 Thou shalt beat him with the rod, and sh.
26. 3 a bridle for the ass, and a rod for the fool's
29. 15 The rod and reproof give wisdom : but a
Isa. 9. 4 thou hast broken..the rod of his oppres.
10. 5 the rod of mine anger, and the staff in
10. 15 the rod should shake (itself) against them
10. 24 he shall smite thee with a rod, and shall
11. 4 smite the earth with the rod of his mouth
14. 29 the rod of him that smote thee is broken
28. 27 with a staff, and, the cummin with a rod
30. 31 be beaten down, (which) smote with a rod
Jer. 10. 16 and Israel (is) the rod of his inheritance
51. 19 and (Israel is) the rod of his inheritance
Lam. 3. 1 seen affliction by the rod of his wrath
Eze. 20 37 I will cause you to pass under the rod
21 10 it contemneth the rod of my son, (as) ev.
21. 13 what if (the sword) contemn even the rod?
Mic. 5. 1 shall smite the judge of Israel with a rod
7. 14 Feed thy people with thy rod, the flock

5. *A rod, staff, sceptre,* ῥάβδος *rhabdos.*
1 Co. 4. 21 shall I come unto you with a rod, or in love
Heb 9. 4 Aaron's rod that budded, and the tables
Rev. 2. 27 And he shall rule them with a rod of iron
11. 1 there was given me a reed like unto a rod
12. 5 was to rule all nations with a rod of iron
19. 15 and he shall rule them with a rod of iron

ROE, roebuck, (young) —

1. *A wild goat, roe,* יַעֲלָה *yaalah.*
Prov. 5. 19 (be as) the loving hind and pleasant roe

2. *Young roe or hart,* עֹפֶר צְבִיָּה *opher tsebiyyah.*
Song 4. 5 (are) like two young roes that are twins
7. 3 (are) like two young roes (that are) twins

3. *A roe, roebuck,* צְבִי *tsebi.*
Deut 12. 15 as of the roebuck, and as of the hart
12. 22 Even as the roebuck and the hart is eaten
14. 5 the roebuck, and the fallow deer, and the
15. 22 shall eat it) alike, as the roebuck, and as
2 Sa. 2. 18 Asahel (was as) light of foot as a wild roe
1 Ki. 4. 23 roebucks, and fallow deer, and fatted fo.
1 Ch.12. 8 as swift as the roes upon the mountains
Prov. 6. 5 Deliver thyself as a roe from the hand
Song 2. 7 by the roes, and by the hinds of the field
2. 9 My beloved is like a roe or a young hart
2. 17 be thou like a roe or a young hart upon
3. 5 by the roes, and by the hinds of the field
8. 14 be thou like to a roe or to a young hart
Isa. 13. 14 And it shall be as the chased roe, and as a

RO-GE'-LIM, רֹגְלִים *fullers' place.*
A city in Gilead, in Gad or Manasseh.
2 Sa. 17. 27 that Shobi..and Barzillai the Gileadite of R.
19. 31 Barzillai the Gileadite came down from R.

ROH'-GAH, רָהְגָּה *outcry, alarm.*
A son of Shamer, grandson of Beriah son of Asher. B.C. 1600.
1 Ch. 7. 34 Ahi, and R., Jehubbah, and Aram

ROLL —

1. *Polished writing table,* גִּלָּיוֹן *gillayon.*
Isa. 8. 1 Take thee a great roll, and write in it with

2. *A roll, volume,* מְגִלָּה *megillah.*
Ezra 6. 2 there was found at Achmetha..a roll, and
Jer. 36. 2 Take thee a roll of a book, and write
36. 4 and Baruch wrote..upon a roll of a book
36. 6 read in the roll, which thou hast written
36. 14 Take in thine hand the roll wherein thou
36. 14 son of Neriah took the roll in his hand
36. 20 they laid up the roll in the chamber of
36. 21 the king sent Jehudi to fetch the roll
36. 23 the roll was consumed in the fire that (was)
36. 25 that he would not burn the roll; but he
36. 27 the king had burnt the roll, and the words
36. 28 Take thee again another roll, and write
36. 28 former words that were in the first roll
36. 29 Thou hast burnt this roll, saying, Why hast
36. 32 Then took Jeremiah another roll, and gave
Eze. 2. 9 and, lo, a roll of a book (was) therein
3. 1 eat this roll, and go speak unto the house
3. 2 mouth, and he caused me to eat that roll
3. 3 fill thy bowels with this roll that I give
Zech. 5. 1 Then I turned..and, behold, a flying roll
5. 2 I see a flying roll; the length thereof, the

3. *A book, scroll,* סֵפֶר *sephar.*
Ezra 6. 1 search was made in the house of the rolls

ROLL (selves, away, back, down, to, together, unto), to—

1. *To roll,* גָּלַל *galal.*
Gen. 29. 3 rolled the stone from the well's mouth
29. 8 they roll the stone from the well's mouth
Josh. 5. 9 I rolled away the reproach of Egypt from
10. 18 Roll great stones upon the mouth of the
1 Sa. 14. 33 Ye have transgressed: roll a great stone
Prov 26. 27 he that rolleth a stone, it will return upon

2. *To roll,* גָּלַל *galal, 3a.*
Jer. 51. 25 roll thee down from the rocks, and will

3. *To (cause to) roll,* גָּלַל *galal, 5.*
Gen. 29. 10 rolled the stone from the well's mouth, and

4. *To roll self,* גָּלַל *galal, 7a.*
Job 30. 14 in the desolation they rolled themselves

5. *To press or roll self through,* פָּלַשׁ *palash, 7.*
Mic. 1. 10 in the house of Aphrah roll thyself in the

6. *To roll off or away,* ἀποκυλίζω *apokulizō.*
Matt28. 2 rolled back the stone from the door, and
Mark16. 3 Who shall roll us away the stone from the
16. 4 they saw that the stone was rolled away
Luke24. 2 they found the stone rolled away from the

7. *To roll round or up,* εἱλίσσω *heilissō,* ἑλίσσω.
Rev. 6. 14 as a scroll when it is rolled together; and

8. *To roll toward,* προσκυλίω *proskuliō.*
Matt 27. 60 he rolled a great stone to the door of
Mark15. 46 and rolled a stone unto the door of the

ROLLED together, to be —

1. *To be rolled,* גָּלַל *galal, 2.*
Isa. 34. 4 shall be rolled together as a scroll, and

2. *To be rolled,* גָּלַל *galal, 4a.*
Isa. 9. 5 noise, and garments rolled in blood

ROLLER, rolling thing —

1. *A rolling thing, wheel,* גַּלְגַּל *galgal.*
Isa. 17. 13 like a rolling thing before the whirlwind

2. *A bandage,* חִתּוּל *chittul.*
Eze. 30. 21 put a roller to bind it, to make it strong

RO-MAM-TI E'-ZER, רוֹמַמְתִּי עֶזֶר *highest help.*
A son of Heman, appointed by lot over the service of song in the tabernacle in the days of David. B.C. 1015.
1 Ch.25. 4 R., Joshbekashah, Mallothi, Hothir, (and)
25. 31 The four and twentieth to R., (he), his sons

RO'-MAN, Ῥωμαῖος, *belonging to Rome.*
John 11. 48 R. shall come and take away..our..nat.
Acts 16. 21 which are not lawful for us..being R.
16. 37 beaten us openly uncondemned, being R.
16. 38 feared, when they heard that they were R.
22. 25 Is it lawful..to scourge a man that is a R.
22. 26 saying, Take heed..for this man is a R.
22. 27 Tell me, art thou a R.? He said, Yea
22. 29 afraid, after he knew that he was a R.
23. 27 rescued..having understood..he was a R.
25. 16 It is not the manner of the R. to deliver
28. 17 was I delivered..into the hands of the R.

ROME, Ῥώμη.
The capital of Italy, on the Tiber, about fifteen miles from its mouth; founded about 750 B.C., and covered seven hills; in 716 Romulus its founder was killed; in 615 the Capital was founded; in 578 the first Roman money was coined; in 566 the first census was taken and its citizens were reckoned at 84,700; in 550 Servius Tullius divided them into six classes, instituted the Comitia Centuriata; in 520 the Sibylline books removed from Cuma to Rome; in 510 the Tarquins expelled and consular government established; in 499 the Dictatorship is instituted; 493 the Comitia Tributa instituted; in 486 the first law proposed; in 451 the Decemviri appointed; in 433 temple of Apollo dedicated; in 406 the army first receives regular pay; in 403 all bachelors taxed; in 400 the first public banquet of the gods celebrated; in 390 Rome burnt by the Gauls; in 387 the Capitoline games established; in 362 M. Curtius leaps into the gulf; in 269 the first silver coinage struck at Rome; in 235 the temple of Janus closed; in 181 discovery of the Sacred Books of Numa Pompilius; in 167 the first public library opened; in 102 the eagle becomes the standard; in 100 Julius Cæsar born; in 64 Pompey annexes Syria; in 55 Cæsar invades Britain; in 29 temple of Janus again closed; in 12 Augustus made Supreme Pontiff. In A.D. 17 Cappadocia annexed to Rome; in 44 Judea annexed; in 50 Caractacus carried to Rome; in 64 Rome nearly burnt by Nero; in 65 Paul, Peter, Seneca, and Lucan put to death; in 71 Titus and Vespasian receive a triumph, and the temple of Janus closed; in 75 the temple of peace completed; in 131-135 war with the Jews; in 274 Aurelian founds the temple of the Sun; in 306 Constantine dies at York; in 312 Constantine establishes Christianity as the religion of the state; in 330 it is again formally recognised at Constantinople; in 360 Julian abjures Christianity; in 364 division into the Eastern and the Western Empires; in 410 Rome taken by Alaric; in 600, according to Gibbon, Rome had reached its lowest point; in 728 it comes under the sovereignty of the Pope; in 846 threatened by the Arabs; in 1155 Arnold of Brescia burnt for heresy and sedition; in 1278 Charles of Anjou compelled to abdicate by the Pope; in 1309 the Pope removes to Avignon; in 1434 the Romans revolt against the Pope; in 1626 dedication of St Peter's at Rome; in 1773 the Jesuits expelled; in 1798 the Pope deprived of his temporal power; in 1814 he returns to Rome; in 1846 Pius IX. elected Pope, and in 1878 Leo XIII.
Acts 2. 10 and strangers of R., Jews and proselytes
18. 2 commanded all Jews to depart from R.
19. 21 After I have been there, I must also see R.
23. 11 so must thou bear witness also at R.
28. 14 found brethren..so we went toward R.
28. 16 And when we came to R., the centurion
Rom. 1. 7 To all that be in R., beloved of God, cal.
1. 15 ready to preach the gospel to you..at R.
2 Ti. 1. 17 But, when he was in R., he sought me out

ROOF (of the house, or mouth) —

1. *Roof or top, upper part,* גַּג *gag.*
Deut22. 8 shalt make a battlement for thy roof, that
Josh. 2. 6 brought them up to the roof of the house
2. 6 which she had laid in order upon the roof
2. 8 she came up unto them upon the roof
Judg16. 27 upon the roof about three thousand men
2 Sa. 11. 2 walked upon the roof of the king's house
11. 2 from the roof he saw a woman washing
18. 24 watchman went up to the roof over the
Neh. 8. 16 every one upon the roof of his house, and
Jer. 19. 13 upon whose roofs they have burned inc.
32. 29 houses upon whose roofs they have offered
Eze. 40. 13 roof of (one) little chamber to the roof of

2. *A beam,* קוֹרָה *qorah.*
Gen. 19. 8 came they under the shadow of my roof

3. *The palate, mouth,* חֵךְ *chek.*
Job 29. 10 tongue cleaved to the roof of their mouth
Psa.137. 6 my tongue cleave to the roof of my mouth
Song 7. 9 roof of thy mouth like the best wine for
Lam. 4. 4 cleaveth to the roof of his mouth for thirst
Eze. 3. 26 tongue cleave to the roof of thy mouth

4. *A covering, flat roof,* στέγη *stegē.*
Matt. 8. 8 that thou shouldest come under my roof
Mark 2. 4 they uncovered the roof where he was
Luke 7. 6 that thou shouldest enter under my roof

ROOM (chief, highest, large, upper, uppermost, in the)—

1. *A place, standing ground,* מָקוֹם *maqom.*
Gen. 24. 23 is there room (in) thy father's house for
24. 25 We have both straw..and room to lodge
24. 31 prepared the house, and room for the ca.

2. *A nest,* קֵן *qen.*
Gen. 6. 14 rooms shalt thou make in the ark, and

3. *Broad place,* מֶרְחָב *merchab.*
Psa. 31. 8 thou hast set my feet in a large room

4. *Under, instead of,* תַּחַת *tachath.* (1 Ch. 4. 41.)
2 Sa. 19. 13 before me continually in the room of Jo.

5. *Over against, in the place of,* ἀντί *anti.*
Matt. 2. 22 did reign in Judea in the room of his fa.

6. *Successor,* διάδοχος *diadochos.*
Acts 24. 27 Porcius Festus came into Felix' room: and

7. *Foremost seat for reclining,* πρωτοκλισία *prōtok.*
Matt23. 6 love the uppermost rooms at feasts, and
Mark12. 39 chief seats..and the uppermost rooms at
Luke 14. 7 marked how they chose out the chief ro.
14. 8 sit not down in the highest room; lest a
20. 46 love greetings..and the chief rooms at f.

8. *A place,* τόπος *topos.*
Luke 2. 7 there was no room for them in the inn
14. 9 begin with shame to take the lowest room
14. 10 go and sit down in the lowest room
14. 22 Lord, it is done..and yet there is room
1 Co. 14. 16 how shall he that occupieth the room of

9. *An upper chamber,* ὑπερῷον *huperōon.*
Acts 1. 13 they went up into an upper room, where

ROOM, to make —

To make broad or wide, רָחַב *rachab, 5.*
Gen. 26. 22 For now the LORD hath made room for
Prov.18. 16 man's gift maketh room for him, and

ROOT —

1. *Root,* שֹׁרֶשׁ *shoresh.*
Deut29. 18 a root that beareth gall and wormwood
Judg. 5. 14 Out of Ephraim (was there) a root of th.
2 Ki.19. 30 house of Judah shall yet again take root
Job 8. 17 His roots are wrapped about the heap
14. 8 Though the root thereof wax old in the
18. 16 His roots shall be dried up beneath, and
19. 28 seeing the root of the matter is found in
28. 9 overturneth the mountains by the roots
29. 19 My root (was) spread out by the waters
30. 4 cut up mallows..and juniper roots (for)
Prov.12. 3 root of the righteous shall not be moved
12. 12 but the root of the righteous yieldeth fr.
Isa. 5. 24 their root shall be as rottenness, and th.
11. 1 and a branch shall grow out of his roots
11. 10 in that day there shall be a root of Jesse
14. 29 for out of the serpent's root shall come
14. 30 kill thy root with famine, and he shall
37. 31 house of Judah shall again take root do.
53. 2 shall grow up..as a root out of a dry gro.
Jer. 17. 8 spreadeth out her roots by the river, and
Eze. 17. 6 roots thereof were under him: so it bec.
17. 7 this vine did bend her roots towards him
17. 9 shall he not pull up the roots thereof, and
17. 9 people to pluck it up by the roots thereof
31. 7 branches: for his root was by great waters
Dan. 11. 7 But out of a branch of her roots shall (one)
Hos. 9. 16 Ephraim is smitten, their root is dried up
14. 5 grow as the lily, and cast forth his roots
Amos 2. 9 yet I destroyed..his roots from beneath
Mal. 4. 1 that it shall leave them neither root nor

2. *A root,* שֹׁרֶשׁ *shoresh.*
Dan. 4. 15 leave the stump of his roots in the earth
4. 23 yet leave the stump of the roots thereof
4. 26 leave the stump of the tree roots; thy ki.

3. *A root,* ῥίζα *rhiza.*
Matt. 3. 10 now also the axe is laid unto the root of
13. 6 because they had no root, they withered
13. 21 Yet hath he not root in himself, but dur.
Mark 4. 6 because it had no root, it withered away
4. 17 have no root in themselves, and so endu.
11. 20 saw the fig tree dried up from the roots
Luke 3. 9 now also the ax is laid unto the root of the
8. 13 these have no root, which for a while be.
Rom.11. 16 and if the root (be) holy, so (are) the bra.
11. 17 partakest of the root and fatness of the
11. 18 thou bearest not the root, but the root th.
15. 12 There shall be a root of Jesse, and he that
1 Ti. 6. 10 For the love of money is the root of all evil
Heb. 12. 15 lest any root of bitterness springing up
Rev. 5. 5 Root of David, hath prevailed to open the
22. 16 I am the root and the offspring of David

ROOT, (to cause) to take —

1. *To take root,* שָׁרַשׁ *sharash, 3.*
Isa. 40. 24 their stock shall not take root in the earth

2. *To be rooted out, take root,* שָׁרַשׁ *sharash, 3b.*
Jer. 12. 2 planted them, yea, they have taken root

3. *To cause to take root,* שָׁרַשׁ *sharash, 5.*
Job 5. 3 have seen the foolish taking root: but
Psa. 80. 9 didst cause it to take deep root, and it fil.
Isa. 27. 6 He shall cause them..to take root: Israel

ROOT out or up, to —

1. *To pluck up,* נָתַשׁ *nathash.*
Deut29. 28 LORD rooted them out of their land in an.
1 Ki.14. 15 shall root up Israel out of this good land
Jer. 1. 10 to root out, and to pull down, and to de.

2. *To root up or out,* שָׁרַשׁ *sharash, 3.*
Job 31. 12 and would root out all mine increase
Psa. 52. 5 and root thee out of the land of the living

3. *To root out,* ἐκριζόω *ekrizoō.*
Matt13. 29 while ye gather up the tares, ye root up

ROOTED (out or up), to be —

1. *To be plucked out or up,* נָסַח *nasach.*
Prov. 2. 22 the transgressors shall be rooted out of it

2. *To be broken off or away,* נָתַק *nathaq, 2.*
Job 18. 14 His confidence shall be rooted out of his

3. *To be uprooted,* עָקַר *aqar, 2.*
Zeph. 2. 4 shall drive out..Ekron shall be rooted up

4. *To be rooted up or out,* שָׁרַשׁ *sharash, 4.*
Job 31. 8 let me sow..let my offspring be rooted out

5. *To root out,* ἐκριζόω *ekrizoō.*
Matt15. 13 said, Every plant..shall be rooted up

6. *To be rooted,* ῥιζόομαι *rhizoomai.*
Eph. 3. 17 that ye, being rooted and grounded in love
Col. 2. 7 Rooted and built up in him, and stablis.

ROOTS, to pluck (or be plucked) up by the —

1. *To pluck up,* נָתַשׁ *nathash.*
2 Ch. 7. 20 Then will I pluck them up by the roots out

2. *To be uprooted,* עָקַר *aqar, 2.*
Dan. 7. 8 three..horns plucked up by the roots: and

3. *To root out,* ἐκριζόω *ekrizoō.*
Luke17. 6 Be thou plucked up by the root, and be
Jude 12 fruit, twice dead, plucked up by the roots

ROPE —

1. *Cord, line, rope,* חֶבֶל *chebel.*
2 Sa.17. 13 then shall all Israel bring ropes to that
1 Ki.20. 31 put sackcloth on our loins, and ropes upon
20. 32 ropes on their heads, and came to the king

2. *Thick band,* עֲבֹת *aboth.*
Judg16. 11 If they bind me fast with new ropes that
16. 12 Delilah therefore took new ropes, and bo.
Isa. 5. 18 draw..sin as it were with a cart rope

3. *A rope made of bulrushes,* σχοινίον *schoinion.*
Acts 27. 32 Then the soldiers cut off the ropes of the

ROSE —
Meadow saffron or narcissus, חֲבַצֶּלֶת *chabatstseleth*
Song 2. 1 the rose of Sharon, (and) the lily of the va.
Isa. 35. 1 desert shall rejoice, and blossom as the r.

ROSH, ראשׁ *head.*
A son of Benjamin. B.C. 1700.
Gen. 46. 21 And the sons of Benjamin (were)..R., M.

ROT, (to make) to —
1. *To fall,* נָפַל *naphal.*
Num. 5. 21 LORD doth make thy thigh to rot, and thy
5. 27 belly shall swell, and her thigh shall rot

2. *To cause to fall,* נָפַל *naphal,* 5.
Num. 5. 22 (thy) belly to swell, and (thy) thigh to rot

3. *To rot,* רָקַב *raqab.*
Prov. 10. 7 but the name of the wicked shall rot
Isa. 40. 20 chooseth a tree (that) will not rot; he se.

ROTTEN, to be —
To be putrid, עָבַשׁ *abash.*
Joel 1 17 seed is rotten under their clods, the gar.

ROTTEN, (rags, thing,) rottenness —
1. *Rags, tatters,* מְלָחִים *melachim.*
Jer. 38. 11 old cast clouts and old rotten rags, and
38. 12 now (these) old cast clouts and rotten rags

2. *Rottenness, putridity, fœtor,* מַק *maq.*
Isa. 5. 24 their root shall be as rottenness, and their

3. *Rotten,* רָקָב *raqab.*
Job 13 28 as a rotten thing, consumeth, as a garment
Prov 12. 4 she that maketh ashamed (is) as rottenn.
14. 30 but envy the rottenness of the bones
Hos . 5. 12 and to the house of Judah as rottenness
Hab. 3. 16 rottenness entered into my bones, and I

4. *Rottenness,* רִקָּבוֹן *riqqabon.*
Job 41 27 iron as straw, (and) brass as rotten wood

ROUGH (places) —
1. *Mighty,* אֵיתָן, אֵתָן *ethan*
Deut 21. 4 bring down the heifer unto a rough valley

2. *Rough, bristling,* סָמָר *samar.*
Jer 51. 27 cause the horses to come up as the rough

3. *Gathered together, heaped up,* רְכָסִים *rekasim.*
Isa. 40. 4 made straight, and the rough places plain

4. *Sharp, hard,* קָשֶׁה *qasheh.*
Isa. 27. 8 he stayeth his rough wind in the day of

5. *Hairy,* שָׂעִיר *sair.*
Dan. 8. 21 And the rough goat (is) the king of Grecia

6. *Hair,* שֵׂעָר *sear.*
Zech. 13. 4 neither shall they wear a rough garment

7. *Rough, rugged, hard, uneven,* τραχύς *trachus.*
Luke 3. 5 and the rough ways (shall be) made smooth

ROUGHLY —
1. *Strong, fierce,* עַז *az.*
Prov 18. 23 useth entreaties..rich answereth roughly

2. *Sharp, hard,* קָשֶׁה *qasheh.*
Gen. 42. 7 Joseph..spake roughly unto them; and he
42. 30 spake roughly to us, and took us for spies
1 Sa 20. 10 what (if) thy father answer thee roughly
1 Ki. 12. 13 the king answered the people roughly, and
2 Ch. 10. 13 the king answered them roughly: and ki.

ROUND (thing) —
1. *To be scaly,* חַסְפַּס *chaspas.*
Exod16. 14 a small round thing, (as) small as the hoar

2. *Roundness,* סַהַר *sahar.*
Song 7. 2 Thy navel (is like) a round goblet, (which)

3. *Round,* עָגֹל *agol.*
1 Ki. 7. 23 (it was) round all about, and his height
7 31 the mouth thereof (was) round, (after) the
7. 31 with their borders, foursquare, not round
7. 35 a round compass of half a cubit high: and
10. 19 the top of the throne (was) round behind
2 Ch. 4. 2 he made a molten sea..round in compass
[*See also* Beset, compass, go, inclose, tires like the moon, shine].

ROUND, to —
To go or compass round about, נָקַף *naqaph,* 5.
Lev. 19 27 Ye shall not round the corners of your

ROUND about —
1. *Like a circle,* כַּדּוּר *kad-dur.*
Isa. 29. 3 I will camp against thee round about, and

2. *Environs, round about, a circle,* מֵסַב *mesab.*
1 Ki. 6. 29 all the walls of the house round about
Job 37. 12 it is turned round about by his counsels

3. *Round about,* סָבִיב *sabib.*
Gen. 23. 17 that (were) in all the borders round about
35 5 the cities that (were) round about them
41 48 food of the field, which (was) round about
Exod. 7 24 Egyptians digged round about the river
16. 13 in the morning the dew lay round about
19. 12 set bounds unto the people round about
Exod25. 11 make upon it a crown of gold round about
25. 24 make thereto a crown of gold round about
25 25 a border of an hand breadth round about
25. 25 crown to the border thereof round about
27. 17 the pillars round about the court (shall be)
28. 32 of woven work round about the hole of it
28 33 pomegranates..round about the hem the.
28. 33 bells of gold between them round about
28. 34 upon the hem of the robe round about
29. 16 sprinkle (it) round about upon the altar
29. 20 the blood upon the altar round about
30. 3 and the sides thereof round about, and
30. 3 make unto it a crown of gold round abo.
37. 2 made a crown of gold to it round about
37. 11 made thereunto a crown of gold round a.
37. 12 a border of an hand breadth round about
37. 12 a crown..for the border thereof round a.
37. 26 and the sides thereof round about, and
37. 26 made unto it a crown of gold round about
38. 16 hangings of the court round about (were)
38. 20 tabernacle, and of the court round about
38. 31 the sockets of the court round about, and
38. 31 and all the pins of the court round about
39. 23 a band round about the hole, that it sho.
39. 25 round about between the pomegranates
39. 26 round about the hem of the robe to min
40. 8 thou shalt set up the court round about
40. 33 round about the tabernacle and the altar
Lev. 1. 5, 11 sprinkle the blood round about upon
3 2 sprinkle the blood upon the altar round a.
3. 8 blood thereof round about upon the altar
3. 13 blood thereof upon the altar round about
7. 2 blood thereof shall he sprinkle round ab.
8. 15 upon the horns of the altar round about
8. 19, 24 the blood upon the altar round about
9. 12 he sprinkled round about upon the altar
9. 18 he sprinkled upon the altar round about
14. 41 house to be scraped within round about
16. 18 upon the horns of the altar round about
25. 31 villages which have no wall round about
25 44 of the heathen that are round about you
Num. 1. 50 shall encamp round about the tabernacle
1. 53 the Levites shall pitch round about the
3. 26 by the altar round about and the cords
3. 37 the pillars of the court round about, and
4. 26 which (is)..by the altar round about, and
4. 32 the pillars of the court round about. and
11. 24 and set them round about the tabernacle
11. 31 on the other side, round about the camp
11 32 they spread (them)..round about the camp
16. 34 Israel that (were) round about them fled
22. 4 company lick up all (that are) round about
32. 33 (even) the cities of the country round ab.
34. 12 land with the coasts thereof round about
35. 2 suburbs for the cities round about them
35 4 and outward a thousand cubits round ab.
Deut. 6 14 of the people which (are) round about you
12. 10 rest from all your enemies round about
13. 7 gods of the people which (are) round ab
21 2 the cities which (are) round about him th.
25 19 rest from all thine enemies round about
Josh. 15. 12 coast of the children of Judah round ab.
18. 20 the coasts thereof round about, according
19. 8 the villages that were round about these
21 11 with the suburbs thereof round about it
21. 42 every one with their suburbs round about
21. 44 And the LORD gave them rest round about
23 1 rest .from all their enemies round about
Judg. 2. 12 of the people that (were) round about th.
2 14 the hands of their enemies round about
7. 21 stood every man in his place round about
20. 29 Israel set liers in wait round about Gibeah
1 Sa. 14. 21 into the camp (from the country) round a.
26. 5 and the people pitched round about him
26. 7 Abner and the people lay round about him
31. 9 into the land of the Philistines round ab.
2 Sa 5. 9 And David built round about from Millo
7. 1 the LORD had given him rest round about
22. 12 he made darkness pavilions round about
1 Ki. 3. 1 house..and the wall of Jerusalem round a.
4. 24 he had peace on all sides round about him
4. 31 and his fame was in all nations round ab.
6. 5 he built chambers round about, (against)
6. 5 the walls of the house round about, (both)
6. 5 oracle: and he made chambers round ab.
6. 6 he made narrowed rests round about, that
7. 12 the great court round about (was) with
7. 18 two rows round about upon the one net
7. 20 in rows round about upon the other ch.
7. 23 (it was) round all about, and his height
7. 23 thirty cubits did compass it round about
7 24 under the brim of it round about (there
7. 24 ten in a cubit, compassing the sea round a.
7. 36 according to the..additions round about
18. 35 the water ran round about the altar; and
2 Ki. 6. 17 horses and chariots of fire round about
11. 8 ye shall compass the king round about
11. 11 round about the king, from the right co.
17. 15 went after the heathen that (were) round a.
25. 1 and they built forts against it round about
25 4 Chaldees (were) against the city round ab.
25. 10 brake down the wall of Jerusalem round a.
25. 17 pomegranates upon the chapiter round a.
1 Ch. 4. 33 their villages that (were) round about the
6. 55 and the suburbs thereof round about it
9. 27 they lodged round about the house of God
10. 9 into the land of the Philistines round ab.
11. 8 round about, even from Millo round about
22. 9 give him rest from all his enemies round a.
28. 12 and of all the chambers round about of
2 Ch. 4. 2 thirty cubits did compass it round about
4. 3 oxen, which did compass it round about
2 Ch. 4. 3 ten in a cubit compassing the sea round a
14. 14 they smote all the cities round about G.
15. 15 and the LORD gave them rest round about
17. 10 of the lands that (were) round about Ju.
20. 30 quiet; for his God gave him rest round a.
23. 7 Levites shall compass the king round ab.
23. 10 set all the people..by the king round ab.
34. 6 unto Naphtali, with their mattocks ro. ab.
Neh. 12. 28 the plain country round about Jerusalem
12. 29 had builded them villages round about J.
Job 10. 8 and fashioned me together round about
19. 12 and encamp round about my tabernacle
22. 10 snares (are) round about thee, and sudd.
41. 14 his face? his teeth (are) terrible round
Psa. 3. 6 have set (themselves) against me ro. abo.
18. 11 his pavilion round about him (were) dark
27. 6 up above mine enemies round about me
34. 7 The angel of the LORD encampeth round a.
44. 13 a derision to them that are round about
50. 3 it shall be very tempestuous round about
76. 11 let all that be round about him bring pr.
78. 28 he let (it) fall..round about their habita.
79. 3 shed like water round about Jerusalem
79. 4 derision to them that are round about us
89. 8 or to thy faithfulness round about thee?
97. 2 Clouds and darkness (are) round about
97. 3 and burneth up his enemies round about
125. 2 (As) the mountains (are) round about Je.
125 2 so the LORD (is) round about his people
128. 3 thy children like olive plants round abo.
Isa. 42. 25 it hath set him on fire round about, yet
49. 18 Lift up thine eyes round about, and beh.
60. 4 Lift up thine eyes round about, and see
Jer. 1. 15 against all the walls thereof round about
4. 17 As keepers..are they against her round ab.
6. 3 pitch (their) tents against her round abo.
12. 9 the birds round about (are) against her
21. 14 it shall devour all things round about it
25. 9 and against all the nations round about
46. 5 (for) fear (was) round about, saith the L.
46 14 the sword shall devour round about thee
50. 14 in array against Babylon round about
50. 15 Shout against her round about: she hath
50. 29 camp against it round about, let none th.
50. 32 and it shall devour all round about him
51. 2 for..they shall be against her round ab.
52. 4 and built forts against it round about
52. 7 Chaldeans (were) by the city round about
52. 14 brake down all the walls of Jerusalem ro.a.
52 22 pomegranates upon the chapiters round a.
52 23 pomegranates..(were) an hundred round a.
Lam. 1. 17 his adversaries (should be) round about
2 3 flaming fire, (which) devoureth round ab.
2. 22 Thou hast called..my terrors round abo.
Eze. 1. 18 their rings (were) full of eyes round abo.
1. 27 the appearance of fire round about within
1. 27 I saw..and it had brightness round about
1. 28 appearance of the brightness round about
4. 2 set (battering) rams against it round ab.
5. 5 and countries that are round about her
5. 6 than the countries that (are) round about
5. 7 than the nations that (are) round about
5. 7 of the nations that (are) round about you
5. 12 shall fall by the sword round about thee
5. 14 among the nations that (are) round about
5. 15 unto the nations that (are) round about
6. 5 I will scatter your bones round about your
6. 13 among their idols round about their altars
8. 10 pourtrayed upon the wall round about
10. 12 the wheels, (were) full of eyes round about
11. 12 of the heathen that (are) round about you
16. 37 I will even gather them round about aga.
16 57 Syria, and all (that are) round about her
16 57 daughters..which despise thee round ab.
23. 24 and shield and helmet round about
27. 11 The men..(were) upon thy walls round ab.
27. 11 their shields upon thy walls round about
28. 24 thorn of all (that are) round about them
28. 26 those that despise them round about them
31. 4 her rivers running round about his plants
32. 23 and her company is round about her grave
32. 24 all her multitude round about her grave
32. 25, 26 her graves (are) round about him; all
36. 4 residue of the heathen that (are) round ab.
36. 36 the heathen that are left round about you
37. 2 caused me to pass by them round about
40. 5 on the outside of the house round about
40. 14 the post of the court round about the gate
40. 16 to their posts within the gate round about
40. 16 and windows (were) round about inward
40. 17 a pavement made for the court round ab.
40. 25, 29, 33 and in the arches thereof round ab.
40. 30 the arches round about (were) five and tw.
40 36 the windows to it round about: the length
40. 43 within (were) hooks..fastened round ab.
41. 5 four cubits, round about the house on ev.
41. 6 the house for the side chambers round ab.
41. 7 went still upward round about the house
41. 8 also the height of the house round about
41. 10 the wideness of twenty cubits round about
41 11 and the breadth..(was) five cubits round a.
41 12 the wall..(was) five cubits thick round ab.
41. 16 the galleries round about on their three
41 16 the door, cieled with wood round about
41. 17 and by all the wall round about, within
41 19 made through all the house round about
42. 15 toward the gate..and measured it round a.
42. 16, 17 reeds, with the measuring reed round a.
42. 28 it had a wall round about, five hundred
43. 12 the whole limit thereof round about (shall
43. 13 the border..by the edge thereof round ab.
43. 20 and put (it)..upon the border round about

Eze. 45. 1 holy in all the borders thereof round ab.
45. 2 round about; and fifty cubits round ab.
46. 23 a row..round about in them, round about
46. 23 boiling places under the rows round about
48. 35 round about eighteen thousand (measures)
Joel 3. 11 and gather yourselves together round ab.
3. 12 sit to judge all the heathen round about
Amos 3. 11 adversary..even round about the land
Nah. 3. 8 the waters round about it, whose rampart
Zech. 2. 5 be unto her a wall of fire round about
7. 7 cities thereof round about her, when (m.)
12. 2 trembling unto all the people round abo.
12. 6 shall devour all the people round about
14. 14 wealth of all the heathen round about

4. *Round about*, κυκλόθεν *kuklothen*.
Rev. 4. 3 rainbow round about the throne, in sight
4. 4 round about the throne (were) four and
5. 11 heard the voice of many angels [round ab.]

5. *A circle*, κύκλος *kuklos*, (*dat*).
Mark 3. 34 looked round about on them which sat
6. 6 went round about the villages, teaching
6. 36 they may go into the country round about
Luke 9. 12 into the towns and country round about
Rom 15. 19 from Jerusalem, and round about unto
Rev. 4. 6 round about the throne, (were) four bea.
7. 11 the angels stood round about the throne

6. *From every quarter, on all sides*, πάντοθεν.
Heb. 9. 4 overlaid round about with gold, wherein

7. *Surrounding, round about*, περίξ *perix*.
Acts 5. 16 the cities round about unto Jerusalem
[*See also* Come, country, dwell, go, hedge, look, region, stand].

ROUND about, to come, compass, or stand —
To be, go, turn round about, סָבַב *sabab*.
Gen. 37. 7 your sheaves stood round about, and ma.
Job 16. 13 His archers compass me round about; he
40. 22 the willows of the brook compass him ab.
Psa. 88. 17 They came round about me daily like w.

ROUND about, to beset, close or go —
1. *To go, turn, or be turned round about*, סָבַב *sabab*, 2.
Gen 19. 4 compassed the house round, both old and
Judg 19. 22 beset the house round about, (and) beat
2. *To be, go, turn round about*, סָבַב *sabab*, 3*a*.
Psa. 59. 6 noise like a dog, and go round about the
Jon. 2. 5 depth closed me round about, the weeds

ROUND about, places —
1. *Environs, circle*, מֵסַב *mesab*.
2 Ki. 23. 5 places round about Jerusalem; them also
2. *Round about*, סָבִיב *sabib*.
Eze. 34. 26 them and the places round about my hill

ROUSE up, to —
To cause to rise up, קוּם *qum*, 5.
Gen. 49. 9 as an old lion; who shall rouse him up?

ROW —
1. *A row*, טוּר *tur*.
Exod 28. 17 four rows of stones: (the first) row (shall
28. 17 a carbuncle: (this shall be) the first row
28. 18 second row shall be an emerald, a sapph.
28. 19 third row a ligure, an agate, and an ame.
28. 20 fourth row a beryl, and an onyx, and a
39. 10 set in it four rows of stones: (the first) r.
39. 10 and a carbuncle: this (was) the first row
39. 11 second row, an emerald, a sapphire, and
39. 12 third row, a ligure, an agate, and an am.
39. 13 fourth row, a beryl, an onyx, and a jasper
1 Ki. 6. 36 three rows of hewed stone, and a row of
7. 2 upon four rows of cedar pillars, with ce.
7. 3 that (lay) on forty five pillars..(in) a row
7. 4 windows (in) three rows, and light (was)
7. 12 three rows of hewed stones, and a row of
7. 18 made the pillars, and two rows round ab.
7. 20 in rows round about upon the other cha.
7. 24 knops (were) cast in two rows when it
7. 42 two rows of pomegranates for one net w.
2 Ch. 4. 3 Two rows of oxen (were) cast, when it was
4. 13 two rows of pomegranates on each wreath
Eze. 46. 23 a row (of building) round about in them
2. *A row*, טִירָה *tirah*.
Eze. 46. 23 boiling places under the rows round ab.
3. *Array, arrangement*, מַעֲרָכָה *maarakah*.
Lev. 24. 6 And thou shalt set them in two rows, six
4. *Array, arrangement*, מַעֲרֶכֶת *maareketh*.
Lev. 24. 6 six on a row, upon the pure table before
24. 7 put pure frankincense upon (each) row
5. *A layer or row*, נִדְבָּךְ *nidbak*.
Ezra 6. 4 three rows of great stones, and a row of
6. *A row*, תּוֹר *tor*.
Song 1. 10 Thy cheeks are comely with rows (of je.)

ROW, rowers, to —
1. *To dig, dig through*, חָתַר *chathar*.
Jon. 1. 13 Nevertheless the men rowed hard to br.
2. *To move to and fro*, שׁוּט *shut*.
Eze. 27. 26 Thy rowers have brought thee into great
3. *To drive or push forward, row*, ἐλαύνω *elaunō*.
Mark 6. 48 he saw them toiling in rowing; for the
John 6. 19 So when they had rowed about five and

ROYAL —
1. *Kingdom*, מְלוּכָה *melukah*.
2 Ki. 25. 25 Ishmael..of the seed royal, came, and ten
Isa. 62. 3 and a royal diadem in the hand of thy G.
Jer. 41. 1 Ishmael..of the seed royal, and the pri.
2. *A king*, מֶלֶךְ *melek*.
Gen. 49. 20 (shall be) fat, and he shall yield royal da.
1 Ki. 10. 13 which Solomon gave her of his royal bo.
Dan. 6. 7 consulted together to establish a royal
3. *Kingdom*, מַלְכוּת *malkuth*.
Esth. 1. 7 royal wine in abundance, according to the
1. 9 (in) the royal house which (belonged) to
1. 11 To bring Vashti..with the crown royal
1. 19 let there go a royal commandment from
1. 19 let the king give her royal estate unto
2. 16 Esther was taken..into his house royal
2. 17 he set the royal crown upon her head, and
5. 1 Esther put on (her) royal (apparel), and st.
5. 1 upon his royal throne in the royal house
6. 8 Let the royal apparel be brought which
6. 8 the crown royal which is set upon his he.
8. 15 in royal apparel of blue and white, and
4. *Kingdom, reign*, מַמְלָכָה *mamlakah*.
Josh 10. 2 Gibeon (was) a great city, as one of the ro.
1 Sa. 27. 5 why should thy servant dwell in the royal
2 Ki. 11. 1 she arose and destroyed all the seed royal
2 Ch. 22. 10 destroyed all the seed royal of the house
5. *Belonging to the king*, βασίλειος *basileios*.
1 Pe. 2. 9 a chosen generation, a royal priesthood
6. *Kingly*, βασιλικός *basilikos*.
Acts 12. 21 Herod, arrayed in royal apparel, sat upon
Jas. 2. 8 If ye fulfil the royal law according to the

ROYAL CITY, עִיר הַמְּלוּכָה *city of the kingdom*.
A part of the chief city of the Ammonites, called also Rabbah and the city of Waters.
2 Sa. 12. 26 And Joab fought..and took the royal city

ROYAL PAVILION —
A canopy, arched roof, שַׁפְרִיר, *shaphrir* [V.L. שפרור].
Jer. 43. 10 he shall spread his royal pavilion over

RUB, to —
To rub, break in pieces, ψώχω *psōchō*.
Luke 6. 1 and did eat, rubbing (them) in (their) hands

RUBBISH —
Dust, עָפָר *aphar*.
Neh. 4. 2 the heaps of the rubbish which are burnt
4. 10 (there is) much rubbish; so that we are

RUBIES —
Coral, red pearl, gem. פְּנִיִּים, פְּנִינִים *peniyyim, peninim*
Job 28. 18 for the price of wisdom (is) above rubies
Prov. 3. 15 She (is) more precious than rubies: and
8. 11 For wisdom (is) better than rubies; and
20. 15 There is gold, and a multitude of rubies
31. 10 a virtuous woman..her price (is)..above r.
Lam. 4. 7 they were more ruddy in body than rubies

RUDDER —
A rudder, broad flat oar, πηδάλιον *pēdalion*.
Acts 27. 40 loosed the rudder bands, and hoised up

RUDDY —
1. *Red, ruddy*, אָדֹם *adom*.
Song 5. 10 My beloved (is) white and ruddy, the ch.
2. *Red*, אַדְמֹנִי ,אַדְמוֹנִי *admoni*.
1 Sa. 16. 12 Now he (was) ruddy, (and) withal of a be.
17. 42 he was (but) a youth, and ruddy, and of

RUDDY, to be —
To be red, ruddy, or firm, אָדַם *adam*.
Lam. 4. 7 they were more ruddy in body than rubies

RUDE —
Private, uninstructed, ἰδιώτης *idiōtēs*.
2 Co. 11. 6 But though (I be) rude in speech, yet not

RUDIMENT —
An element, first step or principle, στοιχεῖον *stoich*.
Col. 2. 8 after the rudiments of the world, and not
2. 20 if ye be dead..from the rudiments of the

RUE —
Rue, πήγανον *pēganon*.
Luke 11. 42 ye tithe mint and rue, and all manner of

RU'-FUS, Ῥοῦφος (*Lat. Rufus*) *red*.
1. A son of Simon the Cyrenian who was compelled to bear the cross after Jesus.
Mark 15. 21 Simon a Cyrenian..the father of..R.
2. A believer in Rome to whom Paul sends a salutation.
Rom. 16. 13 Salute R. chosen in the Lord, and his mo.

RU-HA'-MAH, רֻחָמָה *pitied*.
A symbolic name of Israel.
Hos. 2. 1 Say ye unto..your sisters, R.

RUIN —
1. *A ruin*, הֲרִיסָה *harisah*.
Amos 9. 11 I will raise up his ruins, and I will build
2. *Overthrow*, מִדְחֶה *midcheh*.
Prov 26. 28 and a flattering mouth worketh ruin
3. *Downfall*, מְחִתָּה *mechittah*.
Psa. 89. 40 thou hast brought his strong holds to ruin
4. *Ruin, stumbling stone*, מִכְשׁוֹל *mikshol*.
Eze. 18. 30 so iniquity shall not be your ruin
21. 15 that (their) heart may faint, and (their) r.
5. *What has stumbled, a ruin*, מַכְשֵׁלָה *makshelah*.
Isa. 3. 6 be thou our ruler, and (let) this ruin (be)
6. *What has fallen, fall*, מַפָּלָה *mappelah*.
Isa. 23. 13 palaces thereof; (and) he brought it to ru.
25. 2 hast made..(of) a defenced city a ruin
7. *What has fallen*, מַפֶּלֶת *mappeleth*.
Eze. 27. 27 the midst of the seas in the day of thy r.
31. 13 Upon his ruin shall all the fowls of the
8. *Ruin, calamity*, פִּיד *pid*.
Prov 24. 22 and who knoweth the ruin of them both?
9. *To dig down*, κατασκάπτω *kataskaptō*.
Acts 15. 16 I will build again the ruins thereof, and
10. *Breakage, a breaking down*, ῥῆγμα *rhēgma*.
Luke 6. 49 fell; and the ruin of that house was great

RUIN of, to be the —
To cause to stumble, כָּשַׁל *kashal*, 5.
2 Ch. 28. 23 they were the ruin of him, and of all Is.

RUINED, (to be) —
1. *To be broken or thrown down*, הָרַס *haras*, 2.
Eze. 36. 35 the waste and desolate and ruined cities
36. 36 I the LORD build the ruined (places, and)
2. *To stumble*, כָּשַׁל *kashal*.
Isa. 3. 8 For Jerusalem is ruined, and Judah is

RUINOUS —
1. *What has fallen*, מַפָּלָה *mappalah*.
Isa. 17. 1 Behold, Damascus..shall be a ruinous
2. *To become ruinous, bare, burnt up*, נָצָה *natsah*, 2.
2 Ki. 19. 25 lay waste fenced cities into ruinous heaps
Isa. 37. 26 lay waste fenced cities (into) ruinous he.

RULE —
1. *Restraint*, מַעְצָר *matsar*.
Prov 25. 28 He that (hath) no rule over his own spirit
2. *Beginning, pre-eminence*, ἀρχή *archē*.
1 Co. 15. 24 he shall have put down all rule and all
3. *A rule (of measure or of conduct)*, κανών *kanōn*.
2 Co. 10. 13 the measure of the rule which God hath
10. 15 be enlarged by you according to our rule
Gal. 6. 16 as many as walk according to this rule
Phil. 3. 16 [let us walk by the same rule, let us mind

RULE (over), to (bear or have) —
1. *To be a king, reign*, מָלַךְ *malak*.
Eze. 20. 33 with fury poured out, will I rule over you
2. *Rule, dominion*, מֶמְשֶׁלֶת *memsheleth*.
Gen 1. 16 rule the day, and the lesser light to rule
Psa. 136. 8 The sun to rule by day: for his mercy
136. 9 The moon and stars to rule by night: for
3. *To rule*, מָשַׁל *mashal*.
Gen. 1. 18 to rule over the day and over the night
3. 16 thy husband..he shall rule over thee
4. 7 (shall be) his desire, and thou shalt rule o.
24. 2 servant of his house, that ruled over all
Josh 12. 2 ruled from Aroer, which (is) upon the b.
Judg. 8. 22 Rule thou over us, both thou and thy son
8. 23 I will not rule over you, neither shall my
8. 23 rule over you: the LORD shall rule over
2 Sa. 23. 3 He that ruleth over men (must be) just
2 Ch. 20. 6 rulest (not) thou over all the kingdoms
Psa. 59. 13 let them know that God ruleth in Jacob
66. 7 He ruleth by his power for ever; his eyes
89. 9 Thou rulest the raging of the sea: when
103. 19 prepared his throne..his kingdom ruleth o.
106. 41 and they that hated them ruled over them
Prov 12. 24 The hand of the diligent shall bear rule
16. 32 he that ruleth his spirit than he that ta.
17. 2 A wise servant shall have rule over a son
19. 10 much less for a servant to have rule over
22. 7 The rich ruleth over the poor, and the bo.
29. 2 when the wicked beareth rule, the people
Eccl. 9. 17 than the cry of him that ruleth among fo.
Isa. 3. 4 their princes, and babes shall rule over
3. 12 (As for) my people..women rule over them
19. 4 a fierce king shall rule over them, saith
28. 14 that rule this people which (is) in Jerus.
40. 10 his arm shall rule for him; behold, his
52. 5 They that rule over them make them to
63. 19 thou never barest rule over them; they
Jer. 22. 30 sitting upon the throne..and ruling any
Lam. 5. 8 Servants have ruled over us: (there is) no.
Eze. 19. 11 rods for the sceptres of them that bare ru.
19. 14 hath no strong rod (to be) a sceptre to r.
Dan. 11. 3 that shall rule with great dominion, and
11. 4 according to his dominion which he ruled
Joel 2. 17 that the heathen should rule over them
Zech. 6. 13 shall sit and rule upon his throne: and
4. *To rule*, רָדָה *radah*.
Lev. 25. 43 Thou shalt not rule over him with rigour
25. 46 ye shall not rule one over another with
25. 53 the other) shall not rule with rigour over
1 Ki. 5. 16 which ruled over the people that wrought
9. 23 which bare rule over the people that wro.
2 Ch. 8. 10 two hundred and fifty, that bare rule over
Psa. 110. 2 rule thou in the midst of thine enemies
Isa. 14. 2 and they shall rule over their oppressors
14. 6 he that ruled the nation in anger, is pers.
Jer. 5. 31 and the priests bear rule by their means
Eze. 29. 15 they shall no more rule over the nations
34. 4 with force and with cruelty have ye ruled
5. *To rule*, רוּד *rud*.
Hos. 11. 12 Judah yet ruleth with God, and is faithful
6. *To be a prince*, שָׂרַר *sarar*.
Esth. 1. 22 every man should bear rule in his own
Prov. 8. 16 By me princes rule, and nobles, (even) all
Isa. 32. 1 Behold..princes shall rule in judgment

7. *To rule, have power or authority,* שְׁלַט *shalat.*
Neh. 5. 15 their servants bare rule over the people
Esth. 9. 1 the Jews had rule over them that hated
Eccl. 2. 19 yet shall he have rule over all my labour
8. 9 one man ruleth over another to his own

8. *To rule,* שְׁלֵט *shelet.*
Dan. 2. 39 which shall bear rule over all the earth

9. *Ruling, ruler,* שַׁלִּיט *shallit.*
Ezra 4. 20 kings also over Jerusalem, which have ru.
Dan. 4. 17, 25, 32 that the Most High ruleth in the
4. 26 shalt have known that the heavens do rule
5. 21 till he knew that the Most High God ruled

10. *To judge, be a magistrate,* שָׁפַט *shaphat.*
Ruth 1. 1 in the days when the judges ruled, that

11. *To be first, pre-eminent,* ἄρχω *archō.*
Mark 10. 42 they which are accounted to rule over the

12. *To act as judge or president,* βραβεύω *brabeuō.*
Col. 3. 15 let the peace of God rule in your hearts

13. *To lead, guide, govern,* ἡγέομαι *hēgeomai.*
Heb. 13. 7 Remember them which have rule over you
13. 17 Obey them that have the rule over you
13. 24 Salute all them that have the rule over you

14. *To shepherd, guide, govern,* ποιμαίνω *poimainō.*
Matt. 2. 6 a governor, that shall rule my people Is.
Rev. 2. 27 And he shall rule them with a rod of iron
12. 5 who was to rule all nations with a rod of
19. 15 and he shall rule them with a rod of iron

15. *To set or place over or before,* προΐστημι *proistēmi*
Rom 12. 8 he that ruleth, with diligence; he that
1 Ti. 3. 4 One that ruleth well his own house, hav.
3. 5 if a man know not how to rule his own ho
3. 12 ruling their children and their own houses
5. 17 Let the elders that rule well be counted

RULE, to cause or make to —

1. *To cause to rule,* רָדָה *radah,* 5.
Isa. 41. 2 Who raised up..and made (him) rule over

2. *To cause to rule,* מָשַׁל *mashal,* 5.
Dan. 11. 39 he shall cause them to rule over many, and

RULED, to be, or that —

1. *Ruler, rule, dominion,* מִמְשָׁל *mimshal.*
1 Ch. 26. 6 that ruled throughout the house of their

2. *To kiss or salute,* נָשַׁק *nashaq.*
Gen. 41. 40 acording unto thy word shall all..be ru.

RULER, (chief) —

1. *A shield,* מָגֵן *magen.*
Hos. 4. 18 her rulers (with) shame do love, Give ye

2. *To rule,* מָשַׁל *mashal.*
Gen. 45. 8 and a ruler throughout all the land of Eg.
Judg 15. 11 that the Philistines (are) rulers over us
2 Ch. 7. 18 There shall not fail thee a man (to be) ru.
Psa. 105. 20 The king sent and loosed him; (even) r
105. 21 He made him lord of his house, and ruler
Prov. 6. 7 Which having no guide, overseer, or ruler
23. 1 When thou sittest to eat with a ruler, con.
28. 15 (so is) a wicked ruler over the poor people
29. 12 If a ruler hearken to lies, all his servants
29. 26 Many seek the ruler's favour; but (every)
Eccl. 10. 4 If the spirit of the ruler rise up against th.
Isa. 14. 5 hath broken..the sceptre of the rulers
16. 1 Send ye the lamb to the ruler of the land
49. 7 to a servant of rulers, kings shall see and
Jer. 33. 26 I will not take (any) of his seed (to be) ru.
51. 46 and violence in the land, ruler against ru.
Mic. 5. 2 come forth unto me (that is) to be ruler in
Hab. 1. 14 as the creeping things, (that have) no ruler

3. *A leader,* נָגִיד *nagid.*
1 Sa. 25. 30 shall have appointed thee ruler over Isr
2 Sa. 6. 21 to appoint me ruler over the people of the
7. 8 to be ruler over my people, over Israel
1 Ki. 1. 35 I have appointed him to be ruler over Is.
1 Ch. 5. 2 and of him (came) the chief ruler; but the
9. 11 the son of Ahitub, the ruler of the house
9. 20 the son of Eleazar was the ruler over them
11. 2 thou shalt be a ruler over my people Isr.
17. 7 thou shouldest be ruler over my people
26. 24 And Shebuel..(was) ruler of the treasures
27. 4 of his course (was) Mikloth also the ruler
27. 16 the ruler of the Reubenites (was) Eliezer
28. 4 for he hath chosen Judah (to be) the rul.
2 Ch. 6. 5 neither chose I any man to be a ruler ov.
11. 22 Rehoboam made Abijah..(to be) ruler
19. 11 the son of Ishmael, the ruler of the house
31. 12 over which Cononiah the Levite (was) ru.
31. 13 and Azariah the ruler of the house of God
35. 8 Zechariah and Jehiel, rulers of the house
Neh. 11. 11 son of Ahitub, (was) the ruler of the ho.

4. *One lifted up,* נָשִׂיא *nasi.*
Exod 16. 22 rulers of the congregation came and told
22. 28 not revile the gods, nor curse the ruler of
34. 31 all the rulers of the congregation return.
35. 27 rulers brought onyx stones, and for the
Lev. 4. 22 When a ruler hath sinned, and done (so.)
Num 13. 2 send a man, every one a ruler among th.

5. *Captain, ruler, judge,* קָצִין *qatsin.*
Isa. 1. 10 Hear the word of the LORD, ye rulers of
3. 6 Thou hast clothing, be thou our ruler
3. 7 nor clothing: make me not a ruler of the
22. 3 All thy rulers are fled together, they are

6. *A head,* רֹאשׁ *rosh.*
Deut. 1. 13 and I will make them rulers over you
Isa. 29. 10 prophets and your rulers, the seers hath

7. *To rule,* רָדָה *radah.*
Psa. 68. 27 There (is) little Benjamin (with) their ru.

8. *Princes,* רוֹזְנִים [*razan*].
Psa. 2. 2 rulers take counsel together, against the

9. *Officer, controller,* שַׂר *sar.*
Gen. 47. 6 then make them rulers over my cattle
Exod 18. 21, 25 rulers of thousands, (and) rulers of hu.
18. 21, 25 rulers of fifties, and rulers of tens
Judg. 9. 30 when Zebul the ruler of the city heard
2 Ki. 10. 1 sent to Samaria, unto the rulers of Jezre.
11. 4 fetched the rulers over hundreds, with the
11. 19 took the rulers over hundreds, and the ca.
1 Ch. 21. 2 David said to Joab, and to the rulers of
27. 31 All these (were) the rulers of the substa.
29. 6 with the rulers of the king's work, offered
2 Ch. 29. 20 gathered the rulers of the city, and went
Ezra 10. 14 Let now our rulers of all the congregation
Neh. 3. 9, 12, 16, 17, 18 the ruler of the half part of
3. 14 the ruler of part of Beth-haccerem; he bu.
3. 15 Shallum the son of Col-hozeh, the ruler
3. 19 Ezer the son of Jeshua, the ruler of Miz.
4. 16 the rulers (were) behind all the house of
7. 2 gave..Hananiah the ruler of the palace
11. 1 rulers of the people dwelt at Jerusalem
Esth. 3. 12 to the rulers of every people of every pr.
8. 9 deputies and rulers of the provinces wh.
9. 3 all the rulers of the provinces, and the li.

10. *To be an overseer, one in authority,* שֹׁטֵר *shatar.*
2 Ch. 26. 11 Maaseiah the ruler, under the hand of H.

11. *Rule, authority,* שִׁלְטוֹן *shilton.*
Dan. 3. 2 all the rulers of the provinces, to come to
3. 3 rulers of the provinces, were gathered

12. *Rule, ruling,* שַׁלִּיט *shallit.*
Eccl. 10. 5 an error (which) proceeded from the ruler
Dan. 2. 10 therefore (there is) no king, lord, nor ruler
5. 29 should be the third ruler in the kingdom

13. *Prefects,* סְגָנִים *seganim.*
Ezra 9. 2 hand of the princes and rulers hath been
Neh. 2. 16 rulers knew not whether I went, or what
2. 16 nor to the rulers, nor to the rest that did
4. 14 to the rulers, and to the rest of the people
4. 19 I said unto the nobles, and to the rulers
5. 7 rebuked the nobles, and the rulers, and
5. 17 hundred and fifty of the Jews and rulers
7. 5 gather together the nobles, and the rulers
12. 40 and I, and the half of the rulers with me
13. 11 Then contended I with the rulers, and said
Jer. 51. 23 will I break in pieces captains and rulers
51. 28 all the rulers thereof, and all the land of
51. 57 her wise (men), her captains, and her ru.
Eze. 23. 6 clothed with blue, captains and rulers, all
23. 12 captains and rulers clothed most gorgeo.
23. 23 captains and rulers, great lords and ren.

14. *Ruler, chief magistrate,* ἄρχων *archōn.*
Matt. 9. 18 there came a certain ruler, and worship.
9. 23 when Jesus came into the ruler's house
Luke 8. 41 ruler of the synagogue: and he fell down
18. 18 certain ruler asked him, saying, Good M.
23. 13 when he had called together..the rulers
23. 35 the rulers also with them derided (him)
24. 20 how the chief priests and our rulers del.
John 3. 1 There was a man..a ruler of the Jews
7. 26 Do the rulers know indeed that this is the
7. 48 Have any of the rulers or of the Pharisees
12. 42 among the chief rulers also many believed
Acts 3. 17 that through ignorance..(did) also your r.
4. 5 that their rulers, and elders, and scribes
4. 8 Ye rulers of the people, and elders of Is.
4. 26 rulers were gathered together against the
7. 27, 35 Who made thee a ruler and a judge
7. 35 the same did God send to be a ruler and
13. 27 their rulers, because they knew him not
14. 5 also of the Jews with their rulers, to use
16. 19 drew..into the market place unto the ru.
23. 5 Thou shalt not speak evil of the ruler of
Rom 13. 3 For rulers are not a terror to good works

15. *A leader, guide,* ἡγεμών *hēgemōn.*
Mark 13. 9 ye shall be brought before rulers and ki.
Luke 21. 12 brought before kings and rulers for my

16. *World-ruler,* κοσμοκράτωρ *kosmokratōr.*
Eph. 6. 12 against the rulers of the darkness of this

RULER, chief of the city, feast, synagogue —

1. *Chief of a city,* πολιτάρχης *politarchēs.*
Acts 17. 6 drew Jason..unto the rulers of the city
17. 8 troubled the..rulers of the city, when

2. *Chief of a festive party,* ἀρχιτρίκλινος *architrik.*
John 2. 9 When the ruler of the feast had tasted the

3. *Chief of a synagogue,* ἀρχισυνάγωγος *archisun.*
Mark 5. 22 there cometh one of the rulers of the sy.
5. 35 came from the ruler of the synagogue's
5. 36 he saith unto the ruler of the synagogue
5. 38 to the house of the ruler of the synagog.
Luke 8. 49 cometh one from the ruler of the synago.
13. 14 ruler of the synagogue answered with in.
Acts 13. 15 rulers of the synagogue sent unto them
18. 8 Crispus, the chief ruler of the synagogue
18. 17 Sosthenes, the chief ruler of the synago.

RULER, to be or make a —

1. *To appoint,* פָּקַד *paqad,* 5.
2 Ki. 25. 22 made Gedaliah..ruler; 1 Kings 11. 28.
1 Ch. 26. 32 whom king David made rulers over the R.

2. *To rule, have power,* שְׁלֵט *shelet.*
Dan. 5. 7, 16 shall be the third ruler in the kingdom

3. *To cause to rule,* שְׁלֵט *shelet,* 5. Dan. 2. 38, 48.

4. *To set down* καθίστημι *kathistēmi.*
Matt. 24. 45, 47; 25. 21, 23; Luke 12. 42, 44.

RULING —

To rule, מָשַׁל *mashal.*
2 Sa. 23. 3 (must be) just, ruling in the fear of God
Jer. 22. 30 sitting upon the throne..and ruling any

RU'-MAH, רוּמָה *height.*
The native place of Pedaiah father of Zebudah the mother of Jehoiakim king of Judah. B.C. 610.
2 Ki. 23. 36 Zebudah, the daughter of Pedaiah of R.

RUMBLING —

Multitude, noise, הָמוֹן *hamon.*
Jer. 47. 3 the rumbling of his wheels, the fathers

RUMOUR —

1. *What is heard, report, tidings,* שְׁמוּעָה *shemuah.*
2 Ki. 19. 7 shall hear a rumour, and shall return to
Isa. 37. 7 shall hear a rumour, and return to his
Jer. 49. 14 I have heard a rumour from the LORD
51. 46 fear for the rumour..a rumour shall both
51. 46 after that in (another) year (shall come) a r.
Eze. 7. 26 rumour shall be upon rumour; then sh.
Obad 1. We have heard a rumour from the LORD

2. *What is heard, report, rumour,* ἀκοή *akoē.*
Matt 24. 6 ye shall hear of wars and rumours of wa.
Mark 13. 7 ye shall hear of wars and rumours of wa.

3. *A word,* λόγος *logos.*
Luke 7. 17 this rumour of him went forth througho.

RUMP —

Rump, tail, אַלְיָה *alyah.*
Exod 29. 22 shalt take of the ram the fat, and the ru.
Lev. 3. 9 the whole rump, it shall he take off hard
7. 3 rump, and the fat that covereth the inw.
8. 25 took the fat, and the rump, and all the
9. 19 ram, the rump, and that which covereth

RUN, to —

1. *To go in,* בּוֹא *bo.*
Ezra 8. 15 the river that runneth to Ahava; and th.

2. *To go on,* הָלַךְ *halak.*
Psa. 105. 41 waters gushed out; they ran in the dry
Eccl. 1. 7 All the rivers run into the sea; yet the
Eze. 31. 4 with her rivers running round about his

3. *To go on,* הָלַךְ *halak,* 3.
Psa. 104. 10 into the valleys, (which) run among the

4. *To go on continually or habitually,* הָלַךְ *halak,* 7.
Psa. 58. 7 Let them melt away as waters (which) run

5. *To flow,* זוּב *zub.*
Lev. 15. 25 or if it run beyond the time of her separ.

6. *To be poured or spread out,* נָגַר *nagar,* 2.
Psa. 77. 2 my sore ran in the night, and ceased not

7. *To come or fall up, come against,* פָּגַע *paga.*
Judg 18. 25 lest angry fellows run upon thee, and th.

8. *To run,* רוּץ *ruts.*
Gen. 18. 2 he ran to meet them from the tent door
18. 7 Abraham ran unto the herd, and fetched
24. 17 servant ran to meet her, and said, Let me
24. 20 ran again unto the well to draw (water)
24. 28 damsel ran, and told (them of) her moth.
24. 29 Laban ran out unto the man, unto the we.
29. 12 Rebekah's son: and she ran and told her
29. 13 ran to meet him, and embraced him, and
33. 4 Esau ran to meet him, and embraced him
Num 11. 27 there ran a young man, and told Moses
16. 47 ran into the midst of the congregation
Josh. 7. 22 Joshua sent messengers, and they ran un.
8. 19 they ran as soon as he had stretched out
Judg. 7. 21 and all the host ran, and cried, and fled
13. 10 woman made haste, and ran, and showed
1 Sa. 3. 5 ran unto Eli, and said, Here (am) I; for
4. 12 there ran a man of Benjamin out of the
8. 11 and (some) shall run before his chariots
10. 23 they ran and fetched him thence: and wh.
17. 22 ran into the army, and came and saluted
17. 48 ran toward the army to meet the Philist.
17. 51 Therefore David ran, and stood upon the
20. 6 that he might run to Beth-lehem his city
20. 36 said..Run..(And) as the lad ran, he shot
2 Sa. 15. 1 prepared him..fifty men to run before
18. 19 Let me now run and bear the king tidings
18. 21 Cushi bowed himself unto Joab, and ran
18. 22 let me, I pray thee, also run after Cushi
18. 22 Joab said, Wherefore wilt thou run, my
18. 23 let me run. And he said unto him, Run
18. 23 Ahimaaz ran by the way of the plain, and
1 Ki. 1. 5 prepared him..fifty men to run before him
18. 46 ran before Ahab to the entrance of Jezr.
19. 20 left the oxen, and ran after Elijah, and
2 Ki. 4. 22 that I may run to the man of God, and
4. 26 Run now, I pray thee, to meet her; and
5. 20 will run after him, and take somewhat of
Job 15. 26 He runneth upon him, (even) on (his) ne.
16. 14 breach; he runneth upon me like a giant
Psa. 19. 5 (and) rejoiceth as a strong man to run a
59. 4 They run and prepare themselves without
119. 32 I will run the way of thy commandments
147. 15 sendeth forth..his word runneth very sw.
Prov. 1. 16 For their feet run to evil, and make haste
4. 12 when thou runnest, thou shalt not stum.
18. 10 the righteous runneth into it, and is safe
Song 1. 4 Draw me, we will run after thee. The ki.
Isa. 40. 31 they shall run, and not be weary; (and)
55. 5 nations (that) knew thee not shall run
59. 7 Their feet run to evil, and they make ha.

Jer. 12. 5 If thou hast run with the footmen, and
23. 21 have not sent these prophets, yet they r.
51. 31 One post shall run to meet another, and
Dan. 8. 6 and ran unto him in the fury of his pow,
Joel 2. 4 and as horsemen, so shall they run
2. 7 They shall run like mighty men; they
2. 9 they shall run upon the wall; they shall
Amos 6. 12 Shall horses run upon the rock? will (one)
Hab. 2. 2 make (it) plain..that he may run that re.
Hag. 1. 9 and ye run every man unto his own hou.
Zech. 2. 4 Run, speak to this young man, saying, J.

9. *To run*, רוּץ *ruts*, 3a.
Nah. 2. 4 seem like torches, they shall run like the

10. *To (cause to) run*, רוּץ *ruts*, 5.
1 Sa. 17. 17 and run to the camp to thy brethren

11. *To run, flow*, רוּר *rur*.
Lev. 15. 3 whether his flesh run with his issue, or

12. *To run*, רָצָא *ratsa*.
Eze. 1. 14 living creatures ran and returned as the

13. *To overflow, rush*, שָׁטַף *shataph*.
2 Ch. 32. 4 brook that ran through the midst of the

14. *To run to and fro*, שָׁקַק *shaqaq*.
Isa. 33. 4 to and fro of locusts shall he run upon

15. *To rush impetuously*, ὁρμάω *hormaō*.
Acts 7. 57 stopped their ears, and ran upon him wi.

16. *To run toward or to*, προστρέχω *prostrechō*.
Mark 10. 17 there came one running, and kneeled to

17. *To run together with*, συντρέχω *suntrechō*.
Mark 6. 33 ran a foot thither out of all cities, and

18. *To run*, τρέχω *trechō*.
Matt 27. 48 straightway one of them ran, and took a
28. 8 departed..and did run to bring his disci.
Mark 5. 6 when he saw Jesus afar off, he ran and
15. 36 one ran and filled a sponge full of vinegar
Luke 15. 20 ran, and fell on his neck, and kissed him
24. 12 [Then arose Peter, and ran unto the sep.]
John 20. 2 Then she runneth, and cometh to Simon
20. 4 So they ran both together: and the other
Rom. 9. 16 nor of him that runneth, but of God that
1 Co. 9. 24 Know..that they which run in a race run
9. 24 but one receiveth the prize? So run, that
9. 26 I therefore so run, not as uncertainly; so
Gal. 2. 2 by any means I should run, or had run
5. 7 Ye did run well; who did hinder you that
Phil. 2. 16 that I have not run in vain, neither lab.
Heb 12. 1 let us run with patience the race that is
Rev 9. 9 of chariots of many horses running to ba.

RUN (aground, along, away), to —

1. *To go on*, הָלַךְ *halak*.
Exod. 9. 23 and the fire ran along upon the ground

2. *To flee*, בָּרַח *barach*.
1 Ki 2. 39 ran away unto Achish son of Maachah ki.

3. *To dash against or upon, run aground*, ἐποκέλλω.
Acts 27. 41 ran the ship aground: and the fore part

RUN (down, out, over, through), to —

1. *To go in*, בּוֹא *bo*.
Eze. 24. 16 nor weep, neither shall thy tears run do.

2. *To be rolled*, גָּלַל *galal*, 2.
Amos 5. 24 But let judgment run down as waters, and

3. *To run out*, יָצַק *yatsaq*.
1 Ki 22. 35 blood ran out of the wound into the midst

4. *To go or come down*, יָרַד *yarad*.
Psa. 119. 136 Rivers of waters run down mine eyes, be.
133. 2 ran down upon the beard, (even) Aaron's
Jer. 9. 18 that our eyes may run down with tears
13. 17 run down with tears, because the LORD'S
14. 17 Let mine eyes run down with tears night
Lam. 1. 16 mine eye runneth down with water, bec.
2. 18 let tears run down like a river day and ni.
3. 48 Mine eye runneth down with rivers of wa.

5. *To flow, run out*, פָּכָה *pakah*, 3.
Eze. 47. 2 behold, there ran out waters on the right

6. *To step, tread*, צָעַד *tsaad*.
Gen. 49. 22 bough..(whose) branches run over the wa.

7. *To run*, רוּץ *ruts*.
2 Sa. 22. 30 For by thee I have run through a troop
Psa. 18. 29 For by thee I have run through a troop

8. *Fulness*, רְוָיָה *revayah*.
Psa. 23. 5 anointest my head..my cup runneth over

9. *To pour out*, ἐκχέω *ekcheō*.
Matt. 9. 17 the bottles break, and the wine runneth

10. *To run down*, κατατρέχω *katatrechō*.
Acts 21. 32 ran down unto them: and when they saw

11. *To run around about*, περιτρέχω *peritrechō*.
Mark 6. 55 ran through that whole region round about

12. *To run over, overflow*, ὑπερεκχύνομαι *huperek*.
Luke 6. 38 and shaken together, and running over

RUN (away or down), to cause or make to —

1. *To cause to go on*, יָלַךְ *yalak*, 5.
Eze. 32. 14 Then will I..cause their rivers to run like

2. *To cause to run down*, יָרַד *yarad*, 5.
Psa. 78. 16 and caused waters to run down like rivers

3. *To cause to run*, רוּץ *ruts*, 5.
Jer. 49. 19 but I will suddenly make him run away
50. 44 but I will make them suddenly run away

RUN before, greedily, in, to, thither to, to —

1. *To pour out*, ἐκχύνω *ekchunō*.
Jude 11 ran greedily after the error of Balaam

2. *To leap or rush in*, εἰσπηδάω *eispēdaō*.
Acts 14. 14 and [ran in] among the people, crying

3. *To run to or into*, εἰστρέχω *eistrechō*.
Acts 12. 14 but ran in, and told how Peter stood be.

4. *To run toward or to*, προστρέχω *prostrechō*.
Mark 9. 15 were greatly amazed, and running to (him)
Acts 8. 30 Philip ran thither to (him), and heard him

5. *To run forward or before*, προτρέχω *protrechō*.
Luke 19. 4 ran before, and climbed up into a sycam.

RUN to and fro, upon, to —

1. *To push against, strip off*, פָּשַׁט *pashat*.
Judg 9. 44 two (other) companies ran upon all (the

2. *To go to and fro*, שׁוּט *shut*, 3a.
2 Ch. 16. 9 For the eyes of the LORD run to and fro
Jer. 5. 1 Run ye to and fro through the streets of
Dan. 12. 4 many shall run to and fro, and knowledge
Amos 8. 12 they shall run to and fro to seek the word
Zech. 4. 10 which run to and fro through the whole

3. *To go to and fro*, שׁוּט *shut*, 7a.
Jer. 49. 3 lament, and run to and fro by the hedges

4. *To go or run to and fro, or along*, שָׁקַק *shaqaq*.
Joel 2. 9 They shall run to and fro in the city; they

RUN together, under, violently, with, to —

1. *To rush impetuously*, ὁρμάομαι *hormaomai*.
Matt. 8. 32 whole herd of swine ran violently down
Mark 5. 13 herd ran violently down a steep place into
Luke 8. 33 herd ran violently down a steep place into

2. *There was a concourse*, ἐγένετο συνδρομή.
Acts 21. 30 people ran together: and they took Paul

3. *To run together with*, συντρέχω *suntrechō*.
Acts 3. 11 all the people ran together unto them in
1 Pe. 4. 4 they think it strange that ye run not with

4. *To run under or below*, ὑποτρέχω *hupotrechō*.
Acts 27 16 running under a certain island which is

RUNNING (together, to and fro, to come) —

1. *Living*, חַי *chai*.
Lev. 14. 5, 50 in an earthen vessel over running wa.
14. 6 the bird (that was) killed over the runn.
14. 51 dip them..in the running water, and sp
14. 52 cleanse the house..with the running wa.
15. 13 bathe his flesh in running water, and shall
Num 19. 17 running water shall be put thereto in a

2. *Running*, מְרוּצָה,מְרֻצָה *merutsah*.
2 Sa. 18. 27 running of the foremost is like the runn.

3. *A running to and fro*, מַשָּׁק *mashshaq*.
Isa. 33. 4 as the running to and fro of locusts shall

4. *To run*, רוּץ *ruts*.
2 Sa. 18. 24 looked, and behold a man running alone
18. 26 the watchman saw another man running
18. 26 said, Behold (another) man running alone
2 Ki. 5. 21; 2 Ch. 23. 12; Prov. 6. 18.

5. *To run together*, ἐπισυντρέχω, Mark. 9. 25.

RUNNING issue, to have a —

To flow, issue, זוּב *zub*.
Lev. 15. 2 When any man hath a running issue out
22. 4 What man..hath a running issue, he shall

RUNNING water —

To flow on, נָזַל *nazal*.
Prov. 5. 15 and running waters out of thine own well

RUSH —

1. *A reed*, אַגְמוֹן *agmon*.
Isa. 9. 14 the LORD will cut off..branch and rush
19. 15 which the head or tail, branch or rush, may

2. *A rush, reed*, גֹּמֶא *gome*.
Job 8. 11 Can the rush grow up without mire? can
Isa. 35. 7 where each lay, (shall be)..reeds and ru.

RUSH, to —

1. *To push against, strip off*, פָּשַׁט *pashat*.
Judg. 9. 44 rushed forward, and stood in the entering
20. 37 the liers in wait hasted, and rushed upon

2. *To be wasted, desolate*, שָׁאָה *shaah*, 2.
Isa. 17. 13 The nations shall rush like..many waters

3. *To overflow, rush*, שָׁטַף *shataph*.
Jer. 8. 6 turned to his course, as the horse rusheth

4. *To rush impetuously*, ὁρμάομαι *hormaomai*.
Acts 19. 29 they rushed with one accord into the th.

RUSHING (to make a) —

1. *A shaking, trembling, rushing*, רַעַשׁ *raash*.
Jer. 47. 3 at the rushing of his chariots, (and at) the
Eze. 3. 12 heard behind me a voice of a great rush.
3. 13 (I heard) also..a noise of a great rushing

2. *Wasting, desolation, noise*, שָׁאוֹן *shaon*.
Isa. 17. 12 the rushing of nations..like the rushing
17. 13 The nations..like the rushing of many wa.

3. *To be wasted, desolate*, שָׁאָה *shaah*, 2.
Isa. 17. 12 of nations, (that) make a rushing like the

4. *To bear on, carry*, φέρω *pherō*
Acts 2. 2 a rushing mighty wind, and it filled all

RUST —

1. *Eating, a devouring*, βρῶσις *brōsis*.
Matt. 6. 19 where moth and rust doth corrupt, and
6. 20 where neither moth nor rust doth corrupt

2. *Metallic rust*, ἰός *ios*.
Jas. 5. 3 the rust of them shall be a witness against

RUTH, רוּת, Ῥούθ *friendship*.
A Moabitess who became the wife of Mahlon, elder son of Elimelech and Naomi, and afterwards of Boaz, to whom she bare Obed father of Jesse father of David.
B.C. 1312.
Ruth 1. 4 one (was) Orpah..the name of the other R.
1. 14 Orpah kissed her..but R. clave unto her
1. 16 And R. said, Entreat me not to leave thee
1. 22 So Naomi returned, and R. the Moabitess
2. 2 R. the Moabitess..Let me now go to the
2. 8 Then said Boaz unto R., Hearest thou not
2. 21 And R. the Moabitess said, He said unto
2. 22 And Naomi said unto R. her daughter in
3. 9 And she answered, I (am) R. thine hand.
4. 5 thou must buy (it) also of R. the Moabitess
4. 10 R. the Moabitess..have I purchased to
4. 13 So Boaz took R., and she was his wife
Matt. 1. 5 Booz begat Obed of R; and Obed begat J.

S

SABACHTHANI —

Hast thou forsaken me (Aramaic שְׁבַקְתַּנִי) σαβαχθανί.
Matt 27. 46 Eli! Eli! lama sabachthani? that is to say
Mark 15. 34 Eloi! Eloi! lama sabachthani? which is

SA-BA'-OTH, σαβαώθ, (*from Heb.* צְבָאוֹת) *hosts*.
An appellation of the Lord as Ruler over all.
Rom. 9. 29 Except the Lord of S. had left us a seed
Jas. 5. 4 cries..entered into..ears of the Lord of S.

SABBATH (day) —

1. *Cessation, sabbath*, שַׁבָּת *shabbath*.
Exod 16. 23 Tomorrow (is) the rest of the holy sabbath
16. 25 today (is) a sabbath unto the LORD: to day
16 26 the seventh day, (which is) the sabbath
16. 29 that the LORD hath given you the sabbath
20. 8 Remember the sabbath day, to keep it holy
20. 10 the seventh day (is) the sabbath of the L.
20. 11 wherefore the LORD blessed the sabbath
31. 13 my sabbaths ye shall keep: for it (is) a si.
31. 14 ye shall keep the sabbath therefore; for
31. 15 the seventh (is) the sabbath of rest, holy to
31. 15 whosoever doeth (any) work in the sabbath
31. 16 keep the sabbath, to observe the sabbath
35. 2 shall be to you an holy day, a sabbath of
35. 3 ye shall kindle no fire..upon the sabbath d.
Lev. 16. 31 It (shall be) a sabbath of rest unto you, and
19. 3 and keep my sabbaths: I (am) the LORD
19. 30 Ye shall keep my sabbaths, and reverence
23. 3 the seventh day (is) the sabbath of rest, an
23. 3 it (is) the sabbath of the LORD in all your
23. 11 the morrow after the sabbath the priest
23. 15 count..from the morrow after the sabbath
23. 15 from the day..seven sabbaths shall be co.
23. 16 unto the morrow after the seventh sabb.
23. 32 (It shall be) unto you a sabbath of rest, and
23. 32 unto even, shall ye celebrate your sabbath
23. 38 Beside the sabbaths of the LORD, and be.
24. 8 Every sabbath he shall set it in order be.
25. 2 then shall the land keep a sabbath unto
25. 4 a sabbath of rest unto the land, a sabbath
25. 6 the sabbath of the land shall be meat for
25. 8 thou shalt number seven sabbaths of years
25. 8 the space of the seven sabbaths of years
26. 2 Ye shall keep my sabbaths, and reverence
26. 34 Then shall the land enjoy her sabbaths
26. 34 then shall the land..enjoy her sabbaths
26. 35 it did not rest in your sabbaths, when ye
26. 43 shall enjoy her sabbaths, while she lieth
Num 15. 32 that gathered sticks upon the sabbath day
28. 9 on the sabbath day two lambs of the first
28. 10 (This is) the burnt offering of every sabb.
Deut 5. 12 Keep the sabbath day to sanctify it, as the
5. 14 the seventh day (is) the sabbath of the L.
5. 15 commanded thee to keep the sabbath day
2 Ki. 4. 23 to day? (it is) neither new moon nor sab.
11. 5 part of you that enter in on the sabbath
11. 7 of all you that go forth on the sabbath
11. 9 men that were to come in on the sabbath
11. 9 them that should go out on the sabbath
16. 18 And the covert for the sabbath that they
1 Ch. 9. 32 the show bread, to prepare (it) every sab.
23. 31 sacrifices unto the LORD in the sabbaths
2 Ch. 2. 4 on the sabbaths, and on the new moons
8. 13 on the sabbaths, and on the new moons
23. 4 third part of you entering on the sabbath
23. 8 men that were to come in on the sabbath
23. 8 them that were to go (out) on the sabbath
31. 3 the burnt offerings for the sabbaths, and
36. 21 until the land had enjoyed her sabbaths
Neh. 9. 14 madest known unto them thy holy sabb.
10. 31 or any victuals on the sabbath day to sell
10. 31 would not buy it of them on the sabbath
10. 33 of the sabbaths, of the new moons, for the
13. 15 treading wine presses on the sabbath, and
13. 15 brought into Jerusalem on the sabbath day
13. 16 sold on the sabbath unto the children of
13. 17 that ye do, and profane the sabbath day?

Neh. 13. 18 bring more wrath..by profaning the sab.
13. 19 gates..began to be dark before the sabb.
13. 19 should not be opened till after the sabbath
13. 19 no burden be brought in on the sabbath d.
13. 21 From that..came they no (more) on the sa.
13. 22 keep the gates, to sanctify the sabbath day
Psa. 92 *title.* A Psalm (or) Song for the sabbath d.
Isa. 1. 13 the new moons and sabbaths, the calling
56. 2, 6 that keepeth the sabbath from pollut.
56. 4 unto the eunuchs that keep my sabbaths
58. 13 If thou turn away thy foot from the sab.
58. 13 call the sabbath a delight, the holy of the
66. 23 from one sabbath to another, shall all fle.
Jer. 17. 21 bear no burden on the sabbath day, nor
17. 22 a burden out of your houses on the sabb. d.
17. 22 hallow ye the sabbath day, as I comman.
17. 24 the sabbath day, but hallow the sabbath d.
17. 27 hearken unto me to hallow the sabbath d.
17. 27 entering in at the gates..on the sabbath d.
Lam. 2. 6 caused the solemn feasts and sabbaths to
Eze. 20. 12 also I gave them my sabbaths, to be a sign
20. 13 and my sabbaths they greatly polluted
20. 16 polluted my sabbaths: for their heart
20. 20 hallow my sabbaths; and they shall be a
20. 21 they polluted my sabbaths: then I said, I
20. 24 polluted my sabbaths, and their eyes were
22. 8 despised..and hast profaned my sabbaths
22. 26 have hid their eyes from my sabbaths, and
23. 38 defiled my sanctuary..profaned my sabb.
44. 24 and they shall hallow my sabbaths
45. 17 the new moons, and in the sabbaths, and
46. 1 on the sabbath it shall be opened, and in
46. 3 in the sabbaths and in the new moons
46. 4 offer unto the LORD in the sabbath day
46. 12 shall prepare..as he did on the sabbath d.
Hos. 2. 11 and her sabbaths, and all her solemn fe.
Amos 8. 5 the sabbath, that we may est set forth wh.

2. *A cessation, sabbath,* שַׁבָּתוֹן *shabbathon.*
Lev. 23. 24 shall ye have a sabbath, a memorial of
23. 39 on the first day (shall be) a sabbath
23. 39 and on the eighth day (shall be) a sabbath

3. *Cessations, desolations,* מִשְׁבַּתִּים *mishbattim.*
Lam. 1. 7 saw her, (and) did mock at her sabbaths

4. *Sabbath,* σάββατα *sabbata.*
Matt 12. 1 Jesus went on the sabbath day through
12. 5 on the sabbath days the priests in the
12. 10 Is it lawful to heal on the sabbath days?
12. 11 if it fall into a pit on the sabbath day, will
12. 12 it is lawful to do well on the sabbath day
28. 1 In the end of the sabbath, as it began to
Mark 1. 21 on the sabbath day he entered into the
2. 23 went through the fields on the sabbath
2. 24 why do they on the sabbath day that wh.
3. 2 whether he would heal him on the sab. d.
3. 4 Is it lawful to do good on the sabbath day
Luke 4. 16 went into the synagogue on the sabbath d.
4. 31 and taught them on the sabbath days
6. 2 which is not lawful to do on the sabbath d.
6. 9 Is it lawful on the sabbath days to do go.
13. 10 in one of the synagogues on the sabbath
Acts 13. 14 went into the synagogue on the sabbath d.
16. 13 on the sabbath we went out of the city
17. 2 three sabbath days reasoned with them
Col. 2. 16 or of the new moon, or of the sabbath

5. *Sabbath,* σάββατον *sabbaton.*
Matt 12. 2 which is not lawful to do upon the sab. d.
12. 5 priests in the temple profane the sabbath
12. 8 Son of man is Lord even of the sabb. day
24. 20 that your flight be not..on the sabbath day
Mark 2. 27 he said unto them, The sabbath was
2. 27 made for man, and not man for the sabb.
2. 28 The Son of man is Lord also of the sabb.
6. 2 when the sabbath day was come, he beg.
16. 1 when the sabbath was past, Mary Magd.
Luke 6. 1 on the second sabbath after the first, that
6. 5 the Son of man is Lord also of the sabba.
6. 6 it came to pass also on another sabbath
6. 7 whether he would heal on the sabbath day
13. 14 Jesus had healed on the sabbath day, and
13. 14 in them..be healed, and not on the sab. d.
13. 15 doth not each one of you on the sabbath
13. 16 be loosed from this bond on the sabbath d.
14. 1 into the house..to eat bread on the sab. d.
14. 3 Is it lawful to heal on the sabbath day
14. 5 straightway pull him out on the sabbath d.
23. 54 that day was the preparation, and the sa.
23. 56 rested the sabbath day, according to the
John 5. 9 walked: and on the same day was the sa.
5. 10 It is the sabbath day: it is not lawful for
5. 16 he had done these things on the sabbath
5. 18 he not only had broken the sabbath, but
7. 22 ye on the sabbath day circumcise a man
7. 23 If a man on the sabbath day receive
7. 23 every whit whole on the sabbath day
9. 14 it was the sabbath day when Jesus made
9. 16 because he keepeth not the sabbath day
19. 31 on the sabbath day, for that sabbath day
Acts 1. 12 from Jerusalem a sabbath day's journey
13. 27 Prophets which are read every sabbath d.
13. 42 might be preached to them the next sab.
13. 44 the next sabbath day came almost the
15. 21 read in the synagogues every sabbath day
18. 4 he reasoned in the synagogue every sab.

SABBATH, day before the —
Day before the sabbath, προσάββατον *prosabbaton.*
Mark 15. 42 preparation, that is, [the day before the sa.]

SABBATH, to keep —
To cease, keep sabbath, שָׁבַת *shabath.*
2 Ch. 36. 21 as long as she lay desolate she kept sabb.

SA-BE-ANS, סְבָאִים, סְבָאִים [V. L. סובאים Eze.]
The descendants of Seba (the eldest son of Cush or of Sheba his grandson) in N. Ethiopia, including Meroe.
Isa. 45. 14 and merchandise of Ethiopia and of the S.
Eze. 23. 42 with the men..(were) brought S. from the

SA-BE-ANS, שְׁבָאִים, שְׁבָא.
The descendants of Sheba, son of Yokshan son of Abraham, in Edom and Syria and Arabia.
Job 1. 15 the S. fell (upon them), and took them aw.
Joel 3. 8 they shall sell them to the S., to a people

SAB'-TAH, SAB'-TA, סַבְתָּה, סַבְתָּא.
Third son of Cush, whose descendants dwelt in the middle of S. Arabia, N. of Kane (*Periplus*). B.C. 2300.
Gen. 10. 7 the sons of Cush; Seba..Havilah, and S.
1 Ch. 1. 9 the sons of Cush; Seba..Havilah, and S.

SAB-TE'-CHA, SAB-TE'-CHAH, סַבְתְּכָא.
Fifth son of Cush son of Ham, and his descendants on the E. side of Persian Gulf, in Carmania, or on the E. of Ethiopia. B.C. 2250.
Gen. 10. 7 sons of Cush..Sabtah, and Raamah, and S.
1 Ch. 1. 9 the sons of Cush..Sabta, and Raamah..S.

SA'-CAR, שָׂכָר *hired.*
1. Father of Ahiham, one of David's valiant men (in 2 Sa. 23. 33 Sharar). B.C. 1048.
1 Ch. 11. 35 Ahiham the son of S. the Hararite, Eliphal
2. A Kohathite, son of Obed-edom, a gatekeeper of the tabernacle in the days of David. B.C. 1040.
1 Ch. 26. 4 Joah the third, and S. the fourth, and N.

SACK —
1. *Bag, sack,* אַמְתַּחַת *amtachath.*
Gen. 42. 27 for, behold, it (was) in his sack's mouth
42. 28 My money is restored..(it is) even in my s.
43. 12 brought again in the mouth of your sacks
43. 18 the money that was returned in our sacks
43. 21 that we opened our sacks, and, behold
43. 21 (every) man's money..in the mouth of his s.
43. 22 cannot tell who put our money in our sa.
43. 23 God..hath given you treasure in your sa.
44. 1 Fill the men's sacks (with) food, as much
44. 1 put every man's money in his sack's mo.
44. 2 put my cup, the silver cup, in the sack's
44. 8 the money which we found in our sack's
44. 11 took down every man his sack to the gr.
44. 11 Then they..opened every man his sack
44. 12 and the cup was found in Benjamin's sa.

2. *Vessel,* כְּלִי *keli.*
Gen. 42. 25 Joseph commanded to fill their sacks with

3. *Sack,* שַׂק *saq.*
Gen. 42. 25 to restore every man's money into his sack
42. 27 as one of them opened his sack, to give
42. 35 as they emptied their sacks, that, behold
42. 35 every man's bundle of money (was) in his s.
Lev. 11. 32 whether (it be)..raiment, or skin, or sack
Josh. 9. 4 took old sacks upon their asses, and wine

SACKBUT —
Sackbut, harp-like instrument, שַׂבְּכָא, סַבְּכָא *sabbeka.*
Dan. 3. 5, 7, 10, 15 cornet, flute, harp, sackbut, psal.

SACKCLOTH, sackclothes —
1. *A sack, dress of sackcloth,* שַׂק *saq.*
Gen. 37. 34 and put sackcloth upon his loins, and
2 Sa. 3. 31 gird you with sackcloth, and mourn bef.
21. 10 the daughter of Aiah took sackcloth, and
1 Ki. 20. 31 put sackcloth on our loins, and ropes up.
20. 32 they girded sackcloth on their loins, and
21. 27 and put sackcloth upon his flesh, and fa.
21. 27 and lay in sackcloth, and went softly
2 Ki. 6. 30 behold, (he had) sackcloth within upon
19. 1 covered himself with sackcloth, and went
19. 2 And he sent Eliakim..covered with sack.
1 Ch. 21. 16 elders (of Israel, who were) clothed in sa.
Neh. 9. 1 and with sackclothes, and earth upon th.
Esth. 4. 1 put on sackcloth with ashes, and went out
4. 2 into the king's gate clothed with sackclo.
4. 3 and many lay in sackcloth and ashes
4. 4 and to take away his sackcloth from him
Job 16. 15 I have sewed sackcloth upon my skin, and
Psa. 30. 11 thou hast put off my sackcloth, and gird.
35. 13 when they were sick, my clothing (was) s.
69. 11 I made sackcloth also my garment; and
Isa 3. 24 instead of a stomacher a girding of sack.
15. 3 they shall gird themselves with sackcloth
20. 2 loose the sackcloth from off thy loins, and
22. 12 to baldness, and to girding with sackcloth
37. 1 covered himself with sackcloth, and went
37. 2 And he sent Eliakim..covered with sack.
50. 3 I clothe..and I make sackcloth their cov.
58. 5 and to spread sackcloth and ashes (under
Jer. 4. 8 gird you with sackcloth, lament and howl
6. 26 gird (thee) with sackcloth, and wallow th.
48. 37 cuttings, and upon the loins sackcloth
49. 3 gird you with sackcloth; lament, and run
Lam. 2. 10 they have girded themselves with sackcl.
Eze. 7. 18 They shall also gird (themselves) with sa.
27. 31 gird them with sackcloth, and they shall
Dan. 9. 3 with fasting, and sackcloth, and ashes
Joel 1. 8 Lament like a virgin girded with sackcl.
1. 13 lie all night in sackcloth, ye ministers of
Amos 8. 10 I will bring up sackcloth upon all loins
Jon. 3. 5 put on sackcloth, from the greatest of
3. 6 covered (him) with sackcloth, and sat in
3. 8 let man and beast be covered with sackc.

2. *A sack, dress of sackcloth,* σάκκος *sakkos.*
Matt 11. 21 repented long ago in sackcloth and ashes
Luke 10. 13 repented, sitting, in sackcloth and ashes
Rev. 6. 12 the sun became black as sackcloth of ha.
11. 3 they shall prophesy..clothed in sackcloth

SACRIFICE —
1. *A slaughter, slaughtered animal,* דְּבַח *debach.*
Ezra 6. 3 the place where they offered sacrifices

2. *A slaughter, slaughtered animal,* זֶבַח *zebach.*
Gen. 31. 54 Jacob offered sacrifice upon the mount
46. 1 offered sacrifices unto the God of his fat.
Exod 10. 25 Thou must give us also sacrifices and bu.
12. 27 It (is) the sacrifice of the LORD'S passover
18. 12 took a burnt offering and sacrifices for G.
23. 18 shalt not offer the blood of my sacrifice
29. 28 of the sacrifice of their peace offerings
34. 15 (one) call thee, and thou eat of his sacri.
34. 25 shalt not offer the blood of my sacrifice
34. 25 neither shall the sacrifice of the feast of
Lev. 3. 1 if his oblation (be) a sacrifice of peace off.
3. 3, 9 he shall offer of the sacrifice of the pe.
3. 6 if his offering for a sacrifice of peace offe.
4. 10 taken off from the bullock of the sacrifice
4. 26 as the fat of the sacrifice of peace offering
4. 31 the fat is taken away from off the sacrifice
4. 35 taken away from the sacrifice of the pea.
7. 11 the law of the sacrifice of peace offerings
7. 12 then he shall offer with the sacrifice of
7. 13 the sacrifice of thanksgiving of his peace
7. 15 And the flesh of the sacrifice of his peace
7. 16 if the sacrifice of his offering (be) a vow
7. 16 the same day that he offereth his sacrifice
7. 17 the remainder of the flesh of the sacrifice
7. 18 (any) of the flesh of the sacrifice of his
7. 20, 21 flesh of the sacrifice of peace offerings
7. 29 He that offereth the sacrifice of his peace
7. 29 shall bring his oblation..of the sacrifice
7. 32 an heave offering of the sacrifices of your
7. 34 from off the sacrifices of their peace offe.
7. 37 and of the sacrifice of the peace offerings
9. 18 (for) a sacrifice of peace offerings which
10. 14 (which) are given out of the sacrifices of
17. 5 Israel may bring their sacrifices, which
17. 7 they shall no more offer their sacrifices
17. 8 that offereth a burnt offering or sacrifice
19. 5 if ye offer a sacrifice of peace offerings un.
22. 21 And whosoever offereth a sacrifice of pe.
22. 29 when ye will offer a sacrifice of thanksgi.
23. 19 two lambs of the first year for a sacrifice
23. 37 a meat offering, a sacrifice, and drink off.
Num. 6. 17 he shall offer the ram (for) a sacrifice of pe.
6. 18 the fire which (is) under the sacrifice of
7. 17 And for a sacrifice of peace offerings, two
[So in verse 23, 29, 35, 41, 47, 53, 59, 65, 71, 77, 83.]
7. 88 the oxen, for the sacrifice of the peace off.
10. 10 and over the sacrifices of your peace off.
15. 3 or a sacrifice in performing a vow, or in
15. 5 prepare with the burnt offering or sacrifi.
15. 8 or (for) a sacrifice in performing a vow
25. 2 they called the people unto the sacrifices
Deut 12. 6, 11 your burnt offerings, and your sacrifi.
12. 27 the blood of thy sacrifices shall be poured
18. 3 from them that offer a sacrifice, whether
32. 38 Which did eat the fat of their sacrifices
33. 19 they shall offer sacrifices of righteousness
Josh 22. 26, 28 not for burnt offerings, nor for sacrifice
22. 27 with our sacrifices, and with our peace off.
22. 29 for meat offerings, or for sacrifices. besides
Judg. 6. 26 offer a burnt sacrifice with the wood of
1 Sa. 1. 21 offer unto the LORD the yearly sacrifice
2. 13 when any man offered sacrifice, the pri.
2. 19 she came..to offer the yearly sacrifice
2. 29 Wherefore kick ye at my sacrifice and at
3. 14 shall not be purged with sacrifice nor off.
6. 15 sacrificed sacrifices the same day unto the
9. 12 (there is) a sacrifice of the people today
9. 13 because he doth bless the sacrifice; (and)
10. 8 (and) to sacrifice sacrifices of peace offering
11. 15 they sacrificed sacrifices of peace offerings
15. 22 delight in burnt offerings and sacrifices
15. 22 to obey (is) better than sacrifice, (and) to
16. 3 call Jesse to the sacrifice, and I will show
16. 5 sanctify..and come with me to the sacri.
16. 5 sanctified..and called them to the sacrifi.
20. 6 a yearly sacrifice there for all the family
20. 29 for our family hath a sacrifice in the city
2 Sa. 15. 12 sent..while he offered sacrifices: and the
1 Ki. 8. 62 all Israel with him, offered sacrifice before
8. 63 And Solomon offered a sacrifice of peace
12. 27 If this people go up to do sacrifice in the
2 Ki. 5. 17 offer neither burnt offering nor sacrifice
10. 19 for I have a great sacrifice (to do) to Baal
10. 24 when they went in to offer sacrifices and
16. 15 sprinkle upon it..blood of the sacrifice
1 Ch. 29. 21 they sacrificed sacrifices unto the LORD
29. 21 and sacrifices in abundance for all Israel
2 Ch. 7. 1 consumed the burnt offering and the sac.
7. 4 the people offered sacrifices before the L.
7. 5 Solomon offered a sacrifice of twenty and
7. 12 have chosen this..for an house of sacrifice
29. 31 bring sacrifices and thank offerings into
29. 31 the congregation brought in sacrifices and
Neh. 12. 43 they offered great sacrifices, and rejoiced
Psa. 4. 5 Offer the sacrifices of righteousness, and
27. 6 therefore will I offer..sacrifices of joy
40. 6 Sacrifice and offering thou didst not des.
50. 5 have made a covenant with me by sacrifi.
50. 8 I will not reprove thee for thy sacrifices
51. 16 thou desirest not sacrifice, else would I
51. 17 The sacrifices of God (are) a broken spirit

Psa. 51. 19 shalt thou be pleased with the sacrifices
106. 28 joined themselves..and ate the sacrifices
107. 22 let them sacrifice the sacrifices of thank.
116. 17 offer to thee the sacrifice of thanksgiving
Prov 15. 8 sacrifice of the wicked (is) an abomination
17. 1 than an house full of sacrifices (with) str.
21. 3 more acceptable to the LORD than sacrifi.
21. 27 The sacrifice of the wicked (is) abomina.
Eccl. 5. 1 more ready to hear than to give the sacr.
Isa. 1. 11 what..(is) the multitude of your sacrifices
19. 21 and shall do sacrifice and oblation; yea
34. 6 the LORD hath a sacrifice in Bozrah, and
43. 23 neither..honoured me with thy sacrifices
43. 24 neither..filled me with the fat of thy sacr.
56. 7 their sacrifices (shall be) accepted upon
57. 7 even thither wentest thou up to offer sa.
Jer. 6. 20 (are) not acceptable, nor your sacrifices
7. 21 Put your burnt offerings unto your sacri.
7. 22 concerning burnt offerings or sacrifices
17. 26 sacrifices, and meat offerings, and incense
33. 18 kindle meat offerings, and to do sacrifice
46. 10 the Lord GOD of hosts hath a sacrifice in
Eze. 20. 28 they offered there their sacrifices, and
39. 17 gather yourselves..to my sacrifice that I
39. 17 a great sacrifice upon the mountains of Is.
39. 19 till ye be drunken, of my sacrifice which
40. 42 slew the burnt offering and the sacrifice
44. 11 slay the burnt offering and the sacrifice
46. 24 the ministers..shall boil the sacrifice
Dan. 9. 27 he shall cause the sacrifice and the obla.
Hos. 3. 4 without a sacrifice, and without an image
4. 19 shall be ashamed because of their sacrifi.
6. 6 For I desired mercy, and not sacrifice; and
8. 13 flesh (for) the sacrifices of mine offerings
9. 4 their sacrifices (shall be) unto them as the
Amos 4. 4 bring your sacrifices every morning, (and)
5. 25 Have ye offered unto me sacrifices and
Jon. 1. 16 offered a sacrifice unto the LORD, and
Zeph. 1. 7 the LORD hath prepared a sacrifice, he
1. 8 in the day of the LORD'S sacrifice, that

3. *To sacrifice*, זֶבַח *zabach.*
Mal. 1. 8 if ye offer the blind for sacrifice, (is it) not

4. *A festival*, חַג *chag.*
Exod 23. 18 neither shall the fat of my sacrifice remain
Psa. 118. 27 bind the sacrifice with cords, (even) unto
Isa. 29. 1 add ye year to year; let them kill sacrifi.

5. *Offering, present*, מִנְחָה *minchah.*
1 Ki. 18. 29, 36 the offering of the (evening) sacrifice
Ezra 9. 4 I sat astonied until the evening sacrifice
9. 5 at the evening sacrifice I arose up from
Psa. 141. 2 lifting up of my hands (as) the evening s.

6. *A slaughter, slaughtered animal*, θυσία *thusia.*
Matt. 9. 13 I will have mercy, and not sacrifice: for
12. 7 I will have mercy, and not sacrifice, ye
Mark 9. 49 [and every sacrifice shall be salted with]
12. 33 than all whole burnt offerings and sacri.
Luke 2. 24 offer a sacrifice according to that which
13. 1 blood Pilate had mingled with their sac.
Acts 7. 41 offered sacrifice unto the idol, and rejoi.
7. 42 offered to me slain beasts and sacrifices
Rom 12. 1 ye present your bodies a living sacrifice
1 Co. 10. 18 are not they which eat of the sacrifices p.
Eph. 5. 2 an offering and a sacrifice to God for a sa.
Phil. 2. 17 Yea, and if I be offered upon the sacrifice
4. 18 a sacrifice acceptable, well pleasing to G.
Heb. 5. 1 that he may offer both gifts and sacrifices
7. 27 to offer up sacrifice, first for his own sins
8. 3 priest is ordained to offer gifts and sacri.
9. 9 in which were offered..sacrifices, that co.
9. 23 heavenly things..with better sacrifices
9. 26 appeared to put away sin by the sacrifice
10. 1 can never with those sacrifices which th.
10. 5 Sacrifice and offering thou wouldest not
10. 8 Sacrifice and offering and burnt offerings
10. 11 and offering oftentimes the same sacrifices
10. 12 after he had offered one sacrifice for sins
10. 26 there remaineth no more sacrifice for sins
11. 4 more excellent sacrifice than Cain, by wh.
13. 15 By him therefore let us offer the sacrifice
13. 16 for with such sacrifices God is well pleas.
1 Pe. 2. 5 to offer up spiritual sacrifices, acceptable
[*See also* Burn, burnt, do, offer, whole.]

SACRIFICE made by fire, of praise —

1. *A fire offering*, אִשֶּׁה *ishsheh.*
Lev. 10. 13 of the sacrifices of the LORD made by fire
Num 15. 25 sacrifice made by fire unto the LORD, and
28. 2 my bread for my sacrifices made by fire
28. 6, 13 a sacrifice made by fire unto the LORD
28. 8 sacrifice made by fire, of a sweet savour
28. 19 But ye shall offer a sacrifice made by fire
28. 24 the meat of the sacrifice made by fire, of
29. 6 a sacrifice made by fire unto the LORD
29. 13, 36 sacrifice made by fire, of a sweet sav.
Josh. 13. 14 sacrifices of the LORD..made by fire, (are)

2. *A thank offering*, תּוֹדָה *todah.*
Jer. 17. 26 bringing sacrifices of praise, unto the ho.
33. 11 them that shall bring the sacrifice of pr.

SACRIFICE to idols, (offered in) —

What is sacrificed to an idol, εἰδωλόθυτον *eidōlot.*
1 Co. 8. 4 that are offered in sacrifice unto idols, we
10. 19 that which is offered in sacrifices to idols
10. 28 This is offered in sacrifice unto idols, eat
Rev. 2. 14 to eat things sacrificed unto idols, and to
2. 20 and to eat things sacrificed unto idols

SACRIFICE, be sacrificed, to (do) —

1. *To slaughter, sacrifice*, זָבַח *zabach.*
Exod. 3. 18 that we may sacrifice to the LORD our G.
5. 3 sacrifice unto the LORD our God; lest he
5. 8 saying, Let us go (and) sacrifice to our G.
5. 17 say, Let us go (and) do sacrifice to the L.
8. 8 that they may do sacrifice unto the LORD
8. 25 Go ye, sacrifice to your God in the land
8. 26 for we shall sacrifice the abomination of
8. 26 shall we sacrifice the abomination of the
8. 27 sacrifice to the LORD our God, as he shall
8. 28 that ye may sacrifice to the LORD your G.
8. 29 in not letting the people go to sacrifice
13. 15 sacrifice to the LORD all that openeth the
20. 24 shalt sacrifice thereon thy burnt offerings
22. 20 He that sacrificeth unto (any) god, save
24. 5 sacrificed peace offerings of oxen unto the
32. 8 worshipped it, and have sacrificed there.
34. 15 do sacrifice unto their gods, and (one) ca.
Lev. 9. 4 to sacrifice before the LORD; and a meat
Deut 15. 21 shalt not sacrifice it unto the LORD thy
16. 2 Thou shalt therefore sacrifice the passover
16. 4 which thou sacrificedst the first day at
16. 5 Thou mayest not sacrifice the passover
16. 6 there thou shalt sacrifice the passover at
17. 1 Thou shalt not sacrifice unto the LORD
32. 17 They sacrificed unto devils, not to God
Josh. 8. 31 offered thereon..and sacrificed peace off.
Judg. 2. 5 and they sacrificed there unto the LORD
1 Sa. 1. 3 to worship and to sacrifice unto the LORD
2. 15 said to the man that sacrificed, Give flesh
6. 15 offered burnt offerings and sacrificed sac.
10. 8 to offer burnt offerings, (and) to sacrifice
11. 15 there they sacrificed sacrifices of peace off.
15. 15 to sacrifice unto the LORD thy God; and
15. 21 to sacrifice unto the LORD thy God in G.
16. 2 say, I am come to sacrifice to the LORD
16. 5 I am come to sacrifice unto the LORD, sac.
2 Sa. 6. 13 had gone six paces, he sacrificed oxen and
1 Ki. 3. 4 king went to Gibeon to sacrifice there, for
2 Ki. 17. 35 Ye shall not fear..nor sacrifice to them
17. 36 ye worship, and to him shall he do sacri.
1 Ch. 21. 28 when David saw..then he sacrificed the.
29. 21 they sacrificed sacrifices unto the LORD
2 Ch. 11. 16 to sacrifice unto the LORD God of their fa.
28. 23 For he sacrificed unto the gods of Dama.
33. 16 sacrificed thereon peace offerings and th.
33. 17 Nevertheless the people did sacrifice still
34. 4 upon the graves of them that had sacrifi.
Ezra 4. 2 we do sacrifice unto him since the days of
Neh. 4. 2 will they sacrifice? will they make an end
Psa. 54. 6 I will freely sacrifice unto thee: I will pr.
106. 37 sacrificed their sons and their daughters
107. 22 let them sacrifice the sacrifices of thank.
Eccl. 9. 2 him that sacrificeth, and to him that sac.
Isa. 65. 3 that sacrificeth in gardens, and burneth
66. 3 he that sacrificeth a lamb, (as if) he cut
Eze. 16. 20 thou sacrificed unto them to be devoured
39. 17 to my sacrifice that I do sacrifice upon the
39. 19 my sacrifice which I have sacrificed for
Hos. 8. 13 They sacrifice flesh (for) the sacrifice of
13. 2 Let the men that sacrifice kiss the calves
Jon. 2. 9 But I will sacrifice unto thee with the vo.
Zech. 14. 21 all they that sacrifice shall come and take
Mal. 1. 14 and sacrificeth unto the Lord a corrupt

2. *To slaughter, sacrifice*, זָבַח *zabach*, 3.
1 Ki. 3. 2 Only the people sacrificed in high places
3. 3 only he sacrificed and burnt incense in hi.
8. 5 sacrificing sheep and oxen, that could not
11. 8 which burnt incense, and sacrificed unto
12. 32 sacrificing unto the calves that he had ma.
2 Ki. 12. 3 people still sacrificed and burnt incense
14. 4 people did sacrifice and burnt incense on
15. 4, 35 people sacrificed and burnt incense still
16. 4 sacrificed and burnt incense in the high
2 Ch. 5. 6 sacrificed sheep and oxen, which could
28. 4 He sacrificed also and burnt incense in the
28. 23 will I sacrifice to them, that they may help
33. 22 for Amon sacrificed unto all the carved
Psa. 106. 38 whom they sacrificed unto the idols of C.
Hos. 4. 13 They sacrifice upon the tops of the moun.
4. 14 they sacrifice with harlots: therefore the
11. 2 they sacrificed unto Baalim, and burnt in.
12. 11 they sacrifice bullocks in Gilgal; yea, th.
Hab. 1. 16 Therefore they sacrifice unto their net, and

3. *To do, make*, עָשָׂה *asah.*
Lev. 23. 19 two lambs of the first year for a sacrifice
2 Ki. 17. 32 which sacrificed for them in the houses of

4. *To slaughter, sacrifice*, θύω *thuō.*
Acts 14. 13 would have done sacrifice with the people
14. 18 that they had not done sacrifice unto them
1 Co. 5. 7 even Christ our passover is sacrificed for
10. 20 which the Gentiles sacrifice, they sacrifice

SACRILEGE, to commit —

To rob a temple, commit sacrilege, ἱεροσυλέω *hier.*
Rom. 2. 22 abhorrest idols, dost thou commit sacril.

SAD, sadly, sadness —

1. *To be wroth, sad, morose*, זָעַף *zaaph.*
Gen. 40. 6 looked upon them..behold, they (were) s.

2. *Sour, sulky*, סַר *sar.*
1 Ki. 21. 5 Why is thy spirit so sad, that thou eatest

3. *Evil, sad*, רַע *ra.*
Neh. 2. 1 Now I had not been (beforetime) sad in
2. 2 Why (is) thy countenance sad, seeing thou

4. *Evil, sadness*, רֹעַ *roa.*
Eccl. 7. 3 for by the sadness of the countenance the

5. *Of a sad, rueful, morose countenance*, σκυθρωπός.
Luke 24. 17 one to another, as ye walk, and are sad?
[*See also* Countenance.]

SAD, to be or make —

1. *To be evil*, רָעַע *raa.*
Neh. 2. 3 why should not my countenance be sad

2. *To pain, mar*, כָּאַב *kaab*, 5.
Eze. 13. 22 whom I have not made sad; and streng.

3. *To give pain*, כָּאָה *kaah*, 5.
Eze. 13. 22 have made the heart of the righteous sad

4. *To be dark, gloomy*, στυγνάζω *stugnazō.*
Mark 10. 22 he was sad at that saying, and went away

SADDLE, (to) —

1. *Riding seat, saddle*, מֶרְכָּב *merkab.*
Lev. 15. 9 what saddle soever he rideth upon that

2. *To bind up, gird*, חָבַשׁ *chabash.*
Gen. 22. 3 saddled his ass, and took two of his young
Num 22. 21 saddled his ass, and went with the princes
Judg 19. 10 two asses saddled; his concubine also (was)
2 Sa. 16. 1 with a couple of asses saddled, and upon
17. 23 he saddled (his) ass, and arose, and gat
19. 26 I will saddle me an ass, that I may ride
1 Ki. 2. 40 saddled his ass, and went to Gath to Ac.
13. 13 Saddle me the ass. So they saddled him
13. 23 he saddled for him the ass, (to wit), for
13. 27 Saddle me the ass. And they saddled (him)
2 Ki. 4. 24 she saddled an ass, and said to her servant

SAD-DU-CEES, Σαδδουκαῖοι.

A sect of the Jews, denying the resurrection and the existence of angels and spirits, who derived their origin from Sadok, a follower of Antigonus of Socho, B.C. 250, a president of the Sanhedrim.
Matt. 3. 7 he saw many of the..S. come to his bapt.
16. 1 The Pharisees also with the S. came, and
16. 6, 11 beware of the leaven..of the S.?
16. 12 the doctrine of the Pharisees and of the S.
22. 23 The same day came to him the S., which
22. 34 Pharisees had heard that he had put the S.
Mark 12. 18 Then come unto him the S., which say th.
Luke 20. 27 Then came to (him) certain of the S., wh.
Acts 4. 1 the priests..and the S., came upon them
5. 17 which is the sect of the S., and were filled
23. 6 perceived that the one part were S., and
23. 7 dissension between the Pharisees and the S.
23. 8 For the S. say that there is no resurrect.

SADOC, Σαδώκ (*from Heb.* צָדוֹק) *righteous, just.*

Son of Azor, and father of Achim; an ancestor of Jesus.
Matt. 1. 14 And Azor begat S.; and S. begat Achim

SAFE, safely, safety —

1. *Confidence, trust*, בֶּטַח *betach.*
Lev. 25. 18 and ye shall dwell in the land in safety
25. 19 eat your fill, and dwell therein in safety
26. 5 shall eat..and dwell in your land safely
Deut 12. 10 giveth you rest..that ye dwell in safety
33. 12 beloved of the LORD shall dwell in safety
33. 28 Israel then shall dwell in safety alone: the
1 Sa. 12. 11 LORD..delivered you..and ye dwelled safe
1 Ki. 4. 25 Israel dwelt safely, every man under his
Job 11. 18 (and) thou shalt take thy rest in safety
24. 23 (Though) it be given him (to be) in safety
Psa. 4. 8 thou, LORD, only makest me dwell in sa.
78. 53 he led them on safely, so that they feared
Prov. 1. 33 whoso hearkeneth..shall dwell safely, and
3. 23 Then shalt thou walk in thy way safely
Isa. 14. 30 and the needy shall lie down in safety
Jer. 23. 6 Israel shall dwell safely; and this (is) his
32. 37 and I will cause them to dwell safely
33. 16 Jerusalem shall dwell safely: and this (is
Eze. 28. 26 they shall dwell safely therein, and shall
34. 25 they shall dwell safely in the wilderness
34. 27 they shall be safe in their land, and shall
34. 28 they shall dwell safely, and none shall m.
38. 8 and they shall dwell safely all of them
38. 11 them that are at rest, that dwell safely
38. 14 when my people of Israel dwelleth safely
39. 26 they dwelt safely in their land, and none
Hos. 2. 18 and will make them to lie down safely
Zech 14. 11 but Jerusalem shall be safely inhabited

2. *Safety, deliverance*, יֵשַׁע, יֶשַׁע *yesha.*
Job 5. 4 His children are far from safety, and they
5. 11 those which mourn may be exalted to sa.
Psa. 12. 5 I will set (him) in safety (from him that)

3. *Peace, completeness*, שָׁלוֹם *shalom.*
2 Sa. 18. 29, 32 Is the young man Absalom safe? And
Job 21. 9 Their houses (are) safe from fear, neither
Isa. 41. 3 pursued them, (and) passed safely; even

4. *Safety, deliverance*, תְּשׁוּעָה *teshuah.*
Psa. 33. 17 An horse (is) a vain thing for safety: ne.
Prov 11. 14 in the multitude of counsellors (there is) s.
21. 31 The horse (is) prepared..but safety (is) of
24. 6 in multitude of counsellors (there is) saf.

5. *Security, firmness, certainty*, ἀσφάλεια *asphaleia.*
Acts 5. 23 The prison truly found we shut with all s.
1 Th. 5. 3 when they shall say, Peace and safety

6. *Secure, firm, certain*, ἀσφαλής *asphalēs.*
Phil. 3. 1 to me..not grievous, but for you (it is) sa.

7. *Securely, firmly*, ἀσφαλῶς *asphalōs.*
Mark 14. 44 that same is he..lead (him) away safely
Acts 16. 23 charging the jailor to keep them safely
[*See also* Bring, carry away, escape.]

SAFE and sound —

To be in health, sound, whole, ὑγιαίνω *hugiainō.*
Luke 15. 27 because he hath received him safe and so.

SAFE, to be or being —
1. *To be in safety*, יָשַׁע *yasha*, 2.
Psa.119. 117 Hold thou me up, and I shall be safe
2. *To be or become high or strong*, שָׂגַב *sagab*, 2.
Prov 18. 10 the righteous runneth into it, and is safe
3. *To become high, be set on high*, שָׂגַב *sagab*, 4.
Prov 29. 25 but whoso putteth his trust..shall be safe

SAFEGUARD —
Guard, charge, ward, מִשְׁמֶרֶת *mishmereth*.
1 Sa. 22. 23 but with me thou (shalt be) in safe guard

SAFETY, to be in —
To be safe, at rest, שָׁלֵו, שָׁלָה *shalah, shalav*.
Job 3. 26 I was not in safety, neither had I rest, ne.

SAFFRON —
Indian saffron, crocus, כַּרְכֹּם *karkom*.
Song 4. 14 Spikenard and saffron; calamus and cin.

SAID, (to be) —
1. *To be said*, אָמַר *amar*, 2.
Gen. 10. 9 it is said, Even as Nimrod the mighty hu.
22. 14 as it is said (to) this day, In the mount of
Num 21. 14 it is said in the book of the wars of the
23. 23 it shall be said of Jacob and of Israel, W.
Job 34. 31 it is meet to be said unto God, I have bo.
Psa. 87. 5 of Zion it shall be said, This and that man
Isa. 32. 5 liberal, nor the churl said (to be) bounti.
Jer. 4. 11 At that time shall it be said to this peo.
16. 14 it shall no more be said, The LORD liveth
Eze. 13. 12 shall it not be said unto you, Where (is)
Hos. 1. 10 in the place where it was said unto them
1. 10 it shall be said unto them, (Ye are) the
Zeph 3. 16 it shall be said to Jerusalem, Fear thou
2. *A word*, דָּבָר *dabar*.
Gen. 47. 30 And he said, I will do as thou hast said
1 Sa. 9. 10 Well said; come, let us go So they went
1 Ki. 13. 17 it was said to me by the word of the LORD
Ezra 10. 12 with a loud voice As thou hast said, so
Esth 5. 8 I will do tomorrow as the king hath said

SAID, of the —
Of the same, αὐτῆς *autēs*.
Mark 6. 22 the daughter of the said Herodias came

SAIL —
1. *Sign, ensign, banner, sail*, נֵס *nes*.
Isa. 33. 23 they could not spread the sail: then is
Eze. 27. 7 which thou spreadest forth to be thy sail
2. *A vessel, instrument*, σκεῦος *skeuos*.
Acts 27. 17 fearing lest they should fall..strake sail

SAIL, away, by, thence, to —
1. *To lead up, put to sea*, ἀνάγω *anagō*.
Acts 18. 21 bade them farewell..And he sailed from
20. 3 as he was about to sail into Syria, he pu
20. 13 we went before to ship, and sailed unto
2. *To sail off or away*, ἀποπλέω *apopleō*.
Acts 13. 4 and from thence they sailed to Cyprus
14. 26 thence sailed to Antioch, from whence
20. 15 we sailed thence, and came the next (day)
27. 1 it was determined that we should sail
3. *To sail out*, ἐκπλέω *ekpleō*.
Acts 15. 39 Barnabas took Mark, and sailed unto C.
18. 18 sailed thence into Syria, and with him
20. 6 we sailed away from Philippi after the
4. *To sail*, πλέω *pleō*.
Luke 8. 23 as they sailed he fell asleep: and there
Acts 21. 3 and sailed into Syria, and landed at Tyre
27. 2 we launched, meaning to sail by the coast
27. 6 found a ship of Alexandria sailing into
27. 24 God hath given thee all them that sail
5. *To lie near to or alongside*, παραλέγομαι *parale.*
Acts 27. 13 loosing (thence), they sailed close by C.
6. *To sail near or alongside*, παραπλέω *parapleō*.
Acts 20. 16 Paul had determined to sail by Ephesus

SAIL over, slowly, under —
1. *To pass over, through*, διαπεράω *diaperaō*.
Acts 21. 2 finding a ship sailing over unto Phenicia
2. *To sail through*, διαπλέω *diapleō*.
Acts 27. 5 when we had sailed over the sea of Cilic.
3. *To sail heavily or slowly*, βραδυπλοέω *braduplo.*
Acts 27. 7 when we had sailed slowly many days
4. *To sail under or beneath*, ὑποπλέω *hupopleō*.
Acts 27. 4 we sailed under Cyprus, because the wind
27. 7 we sailed under Crete, over against Salm.

SAILING, sailor —
1. *A sailor*, ναύτης *nautēs*.
Rev. 18. 17 all the company in ships, and sailors, and
2. *Sailing, navigation*, πλόος *ploos*.
Acts 27. 9 when sailing was now dangerous, because

SAINT —
1. *Kind, pious*, חָסִיד *chasid*.
1 Sa. 2. 9 He will keep the feet of his saints, and the
2 Ch. 6. 41 and let thy saints rejoice in goodness
Psa. 30. 4 Sing unto the LORD, O ye saints of his
31. 23 O love the LORD, all ye his saints: (for)
37. 28 For the LORD..forsaketh not his saints
50. 5 Gather my saints together unto me: th.
52. 9 thy name, for (it is) good before the sa.
79. 2 the flesh of thy saints unto the beasts of
Psa. 85. 8 peace unto his people, and to his saints
97. 10 he preserveth the souls of his saints; he
116. 15 Precious..(is) the death of his saints
132. 9 Let thy priests..let thy saints shout for
132. 16 and her saints shall shout aloud for joy
145. 10 thy works shall praise thee..thy saints
148. 14 exalteth..the praise of all his saints
149. 1 (and) his praise in the congregation of sa.
149. 5 Let the saints be joyful in glory: let them
149. 9 this honour have all his saints. Praise ye
Prov. 2. 8 keepeth..and preserveth the way of his sa.
2. *Set apart, separate, holy*, קָדוֹשׁ *qadosh*.
Deut 33. 3 his saints (are) in thy hand: and they sat
Job 5. 1 and to which of the saints wilt thou turn?
15. 15 he putteth no trust in his saints: yea, the
Psa. 16. 3 to the saints that (are) in the earth, and
34. 9 fear the LORD, ye his saints: for (there
89. 5 also in the congregation of the saints
89. 7 to be feared in the assembly of the saints
106. 16 They envied..Aaron the saint of the LORD
Dan. 8. 13 heard one saint speaking, and another sa.
Hos. 11. 12 ruleth..and is faithful with the saints
Zech 14. 5 God shall come, (and) all the saints with
3. *Set apart, separate, holy*, קַדִּישׁ *qaddish*.
Dan. 7. 18 the saints of the most High shall take
7. 21 the same horn made war with the saints
7. 22 judgment was given to the saints of the
7. 22 the time came that the saints possessed the
7. 25 shall wear out the saints of the most High
7. 27 shall be given to the people of the saints
4. *Separation, holiness*, קֹדֶשׁ *qodesh*.
Deut 33. 2 and he came with ten thousands of saints
5. *Set apart, separate, holy*, ἅγιος *hagios*.
Matt 27. 52 many bodies of the saints which slept arose
Acts 9. 13 how much evil he hath done to thy saints
9. 32 he came down also to the saints which
9. 41 when he had called the saints and widows
26. 10 many of the saints did I shut up in prison
Rom. 1. 7 To all that be in Rome..called (to be) sa
8. 27 because he maketh intercession for the sa.
12. 13 Distributing to the necessity of saints; gi.
15. 25 But now I go..to minister unto the saints
15. 26 for the poor saints which are at Jerusalem
15. 31 my service..may be accepted of the saints
16. 2 That ye receive her..as becometh saints
16. 15 and all the saints which are with them
1 Co. 1. 2 to them that are..called (to be) saints wi.
6. 1 before the unjust, and not before the sa.
6. 2 Do ye not know that the saints shall jud
14. 33 of peace, as in all churches of the saints
16. 1 concerning the collection for the saints
16. 15 addicted..to the ministry of the saints
2 Co. 1. 1 all the saints which are in all Achaia
8. 4 fellowship of the ministering to the saints
9. 1 touching the ministering to the saints
9. 12 not only supplieth the want of the saints
13. 13 All the saints salute you
Eph. 1. 1 to the saints which are at Ephesus, and
1. 15 I heard of your..love unto all the saints
1. 18 the glory of his inheritance in the saints
2. 19 fellow citizens with the saints, and of the
3. 8 who am less than the least of all [saints]
3. 18 May be able to comprehend with all sa.
4. 12 For the perfecting of the saints, for the
5. 3 let it not be..named..as becometh sain.
6. 18 watching..with..supplication for all sa.
Phil. 1. 1 to all the saints in Christ Jesus which are
4. 21 Salute every saint in Christ Jesus. The
4. 22 the saints salute you, chiefly they that
Col. 1. 2 To the saints and faithful brethren in
1. 4 of the love (which ye have) to all the sa
1. 12 partakers of the inheritance of the saints
1. 26 but now is made manifest to his saints
1 Th. 3. 13 coming of our Lord..with all his saints
2 Th. 1. 10 he shall come to be glorified in his saints
1 Ti. 5. 10 if she have washed the saints' feet, if she
Phm. 5 toward the Lord Jesus, and toward all sa.
7 the bowels of the saints are refreshed by
Heb. 6. 10 that ye have ministered to the saints, and
13. 24 Salute all..over you, and all the saints
Jude 3 which was once delivered unto the saints
14 cometh with ten thousand of his saints
Rev. 5. 8 odours, which are the prayers of saints
8. 3 offer (it) with the prayers of all saints
8. 4 (which came) with the prayers of the sa.
11. 18 the saints, and them that fear thy name
13. 7 [to make war with the saints, and to ov.]
13. 10 the patience and the faith of the saints
14. 12 Here is the patience of the saints: here
15. 3 and true (are) thy ways, thou King [of s.]
16. 6 they have shed the blood of saints and
17. 6 drunken with the blood of the saints and
18. 24 of saints, and of all that were slain upon
19. 8 fine linen is the righteousness of saints
20. 9 compassed the camp of the saints about

SAKE —
1. *Causes, reasons, circumstances*, אוֹדֹת *odoth*.
Exod 18. 8 that the LORD had done..for Israel's sake
2. *Word, matter*, דָּבָר *dabar*.
Gen. 20. 11 and they will slay me for my wife's sake
Num 25. 18 slain in the day of the plague for Peor's sa.
Deut. 4. 21 the LORD was angry with me for your sa.
3. *Word, matter*, דִּבְרָה *dibrah*.
Dan. 2. 30 for (their) sakes that shall make known
4. *In order to, to the intent that*, לְמַעַן *le-maan*.
1 Ki. 8. 41 out of a far country for thy name's sake
5. *Because of, for the purpose of*, עֲבוּר *abur*.
Gen. 8. 21 curse the ground any more for man's sake
6. *Zeal, jealousy, envy*, קִנְאָה *qinah*.
Num 25. 11 while he was zealous for my sake among
7. *Which, whom*, שֶׁל *shel*.
Jon. 1. 12 know that for my sake this great tempest
8. *Under, instead of, because*, תַּחַת *tachath*.
Exod 21. 26 he shall let him go free for his eye's sake
9. *On account of, because of*, χάριν *charin*.
Titus 1. 11 which they ought not, for filthy lucre's sa.
10. *Above, in behalf of*, ὑπέρ (*gen.*) *huper*.
John 13. 37 now? I will lay down my life for thy sake
13. 38 Wilt thou lay down thy life for my sake?
17. 19 for their sakes I sanctify myself, that they
Acts 9. 16 how..he must suffer for my name's sake
2 Co. 12. 10 take pleasure..in distresses, for Christ's
Phil. 1. 29 not only..but also to suffer for his sake
Col. 1. 24 for his body's sake, which is the church
3 John 7 Because that for his name's sake they we.
[*See also* For the sake of.]

SA'-LA, SA'-LAH, שָׁלַח, שֶׁלַח, Σαλά.
Son of Arphaxad third son of Shem, and father of Eber. B.C. 2255. *See* Shelah.
Gen. 10. 24 And Arphaxad begat S.; and S. begat E.
11. 12 And Arphaxad lived..and begat S.
11. 13 And Arphaxad lived after he begat S. four
11. 14 And S. lived thirty years, and begat Eber
11. 15 S. lived after he begat Eber four hundred
Luke 3. 35 (the son) of Heber..was (the son) of Sala.

SA-LA'-MIS, Σαλαμίς.
A chief city in the S. E. of Cyprus; afterwards called *Constantia*, and *Famagusta*, and now *Kebres*.
Acts 13. 5 And when they were at S., they preached

SA-LA-THI'-EL, SHE-AL-TI'-EL, שְׁאַלְתִּיאֵל, שְׁלְתִּיאֵל, Σαλαθιήλ.
Son or grandson of Jeconiah son of Jehoiakim king of Judah. B.C. 580.
1 Ch. 3. 17 the sons of Jeconiah, Assir, Salathiel
Ezra 3. 2 Zerubbabel the son of S. and his brethren
3. 8 month, began Zerubbabel the son of S.
5. 2 Then rose up Zerubbabel the son of S.
Neh. 12. 1 that went up with Zerubbabel..son of S.
Hag. 1. 1 the word of the LORD..unto..the son of S.
1. 12 Then Zerubbabel the son of S...obeyed the
1. 14 LORD stirred up the spirit of..the son of S.
2. 2 Speak now to Zerubbabel the son of S.
2. 23 Zerubbabel my servant the son of Sheal.
Matt. 1. 12 Jechonias begat S.; and Salathiel begat
Luke 3. 27 Zorobabel, which was (the son) of Salath.

SAL'-CHAH, SAL'-CAH, סַלְכָה *wandering*.
A city of Gad in the N.E. of Bashan; now called *Zalchat*, or *Sulkhad*, seven miles E. of Bostra.
Deut. 3. 10 and all Bashan, unto S. and Edrei, cities
Josh 12. 5 And reigned in mount Hermon, and in S.
13. 11 all mount Hermon, and all Bashan unto S.
1 Ch. 5. 11 dwelt..in the land of Bashan, unto S.

SALE, (that which cometh of the) —
Sale, thing sold, wares, מִמְכָּר *mimkar*.
Lev. 25. 27 Then let him count the years of sale the.
25. 50 price of his sale shall be according unto
Deut 18. 8 that which cometh of the sale of his pat.

SA'-LEM, שָׁלֵם, Σαλήμ *summit*.
The city of Melchizedek who met Abraham; supposed to be Jerusalem; rather the same as the following (*Salim*)
Gen. 14. 18 Melchizedek king of S. brought forth br.
Psa. 76. 2 In S. also in his tabernacle, and his dwel.
Heb. 7. 1 Melchisedec, king of S...met Abraham re.
7. 2 and after that also King of S., which is

SA'-LIM, Σαλείμ, (*from Heb.* שָׁלֵם) *completeness*.
A city near Ænon, on the W. of Jordan; now called *Shalem*.
John 3. 23 John also was baptizing in Ænon, near..S.

SAL'-LAI, סַלַּי *rejecter*.
1. A leading Benjamite, son of Meshullam, dwelling in Jerusalem. B.C. 445.
Neh. 11. 8 after him Gabbai, S. nine hundred twenty
2. A priest that returned with Zerubbabel; also called *Sallu* in 12. 7. B.C. 536.
Neh. 12. 20 Of S., Kallai; of Amok, Eber

SAL'-LU, סַלּוּ *contempt, rejection*. See *Sallai*.
A priest that returned with Zerubbabel. B.C. 536.
Neh. 12. 7 S., Amok, Hilkiah, Jedaiah These were

SAL'-LU, סַלּוּא, סַלֻּא *weighed, dear*.
A Benjamite, grandson of Joed, dwelling in Jerusalem after the exile. B.C. 445.
1 Ch. 9. 7 S. the son of Meshullam, the son of Hod.
Neh. 11. 7 S. the son of Meshullam, the son of Joed

SAL'-MA, שַׂלְמָא *strength, firmness*.
A son of Caleb son of Hur, and father of Bethlehem. B.C. 1450.
1 Ch. 2. 51 S. the father of Beth-lehem, Hareph
2. 54 The sons of S.; Beth-lehem, and the Net.

SAL'-MON, SAL'-MA, שַׂלְמוֹן, שַׂלְמָה, שַׂלְמָא, Σαλμών.
The father of Boaz husband of Ruth, and grandfather of Jesse father of David. B.C. 1380.
Ruth 4. 20 A. begat Nahshon, and Nahshon begat S.
4. 21 And S. begat Boaz, and Boaz begat Obed

1 Ch. 2. 11 And Nahshon begat S., and S. begat Boaz
Matt. 1. 4 begat Naasson; and Naasson begat S.
1. 5 And S. begat Booz of Rachab
Luke 3. 32 Booz, which was (the son) of S., which was

SAL'-MON, צַלְמוֹן *terrace, ascent.* See *Zalmon.*
A mount in Samaria, near Shechem.
Psa. 68. 14 scattered..it was (white) as snow in S

SAL-MO'-NE, Σαλμώνη.
A promontory at the E. of Crete.
Acts 27. 7 we sailed under Crete, over against S

SA-LO'-ME, Σαλώμη.
One of the women who followed Jesus from Galilee and who stood afar off witnessing his crucifixion.
Mark 15. 40 the mother of James the less and of J & S.
16. 1 and Mary the (mother) of James, and S.

SALT, (land, pit) —
1. *Salt,* מֶלַח *melach.*
Gen. 14. 3 vale of Siddim, which is the salt sea
19. 26 looked back..and she became a pillar of s
Lev. 2. 13 every oblation..shalt thou season with s.
2. 13 neither shalt thou suffer the salt of the
2. 13 with all thine offerings thou shalt offer s.
Num. 18. 19 it (is) a covenant of salt for ever before
34. 3 shall be the outmost coast of the salt sea
34. 12 the goings out of it shall be at the salt sea
Deut. 3. 17 the salt sea, under Ashdoth-pisgah eastw.
29. 23 salt, (and) burning, (that) it is not sown
Josh. 3. 16 toward the sea of the plain, (even) the s.
12. 3 sea of the plain, (even) the salt sea on the
15. 2 border was from the shore of the salt sea
15. 5 east border (was) the salt sea, (even) 15. 62.
18. 19 north bay of the salt sea at the south end
Judg. 9. 45 beat down the city, and sowed it with salt
2 Sa. 8. 13 smiting of the Syrians in the valley of S.
2 Ki. 2. 20 Bring me a new cruse, and put salt the
2. 21 cast the salt in there, and said, Thus saith
14. 7 He slew of Edom in the valley of Salt
1 Ch. 18. 12 slew of the Edomites in the valley of Salt
2 Ch. 13. 5 to him and to his sons by a covenant of s?
25. 11 went to the valley of Salt, and smote of
Job 6. 6 which is unsavoury be eaten without sa?
Psa. 60 title. smote of Edom in the valley of Salt
Eze. 43. 24 priests shall cast salt upon them, and they
47. 11 not be healed; they shall be given to salt
Zeph. 2. 9 salt pits, and a perpetual desolation: the

2. *Salt,* מְלַח *melach.*
Ezra 6. 9 they have need of..wheat, salt, wine, and
7. 22 and salt without prescribing (how much)

3. *Salt place, barren land,* מְלֵחָה *melechah.*
Jer. 17. 6 wilderness, (in) a salt land and not inha.

4. *Salt,* ἅλας *halas.*
Matt. 5. 13 Ye are the salt of the earth: but if the s.
Mark 9. 50 Salt (is) good; but if the salt have lost his
9. 50 Have salt in yourselves, and have peace
Luke 14. 34 Salt (is) good: but if the salt have lost his
Col. 4. 6 seasoned with salt, that ye may know how

5. *Salt,* ἅλς *hals.*
Mark 9. 49 [and every sacrifice shall be salted with s.]

6. *Salt, brackish,* ἁλυκός *halukos.*
Jas. 3. 12 no fountain both yield salt water and fresh

SALTED, to be —
1. *To be salted, rubbed with salt,* מָלַח *malach,* 6.
Eze. 16. 4 thou wast not salted at all, nor swaddled

2. *To be salted,* ἁλίζομαι *halizomai.*
Matt. 5. 13 lost his savour, wherewith shall it be sa
Mark 9. 49 For every one shall be salted with fire, and
9. 49 every sacrifice [shall be salted with salt]

SALTNESS, to lose—
To become saltless, γίνομαι ἄναλος *ginomai analos.*
Mark 9. 50 lost his saltness, wherewith will ye seas

SA'-LU, סָלוּא *miserable, unfortunate.*
A Simeonite, father of Zimri who was slain by Phinehas son of Aaron. B.C. 1492.
Num. 25. 14 name of the Israelite..Zimri, the son of S.

SALUTATION —
A salutation, embrace, ἀσπασμός *aspasmos.*
Mark 12. 38 and (love) salutations in the market pla.
Luke 1. 29 cast in her mind what manner of saluta
1. 41 when Elizabeth heard the salutation of M.
1. 44 as soon as the voice of thy salutation so.
1 Co. 16. 21 salutation of (me) Paul with mine own ha.
Col. 4. 18 The salutation by the hand of me Paul
2 Th. 3. 17 The salutation of Paul with mine own ha.

SALUTE, to —
1. *To bless,* בָּרַךְ *barak,* 3.
1 Sa. 13. 10 to meet him, that he might salute him

2. *To bless, declare blessed,* בָּרַךְ *barak,* 3.
1 Sa. 25. 14 David sent messengers..to salute our ma.
2 Ki. 4. 29 salute him not; and if any salute thee
10. 15 he saluted him, and said to him, Is thine

3. *To ask of the peace,* שָׁאַל לְשָׁלוֹם *shaal le-shalom.*
Judg. 18. 15 came to..the house of Micah, and saluted
1 Sa. 10. 4 they will salute thee, and give thee two
17. 22 ran into the army, and came and saluted
30. 21 David came near to the people, he saluted
2 Sa. 8. 10 to salute him, and to bless him, because

4. *Peace, completeness,* שָׁלוֹם *shalom.*
2 Ki. 10. 13 we go down to salute the children of the

5. *To salute, embrace, draw together,* ἀσπάζομαι.
Matt. 5. 47 if ye salute your brethren only, what do
Matt. 10. 12 And when ye come into an house, salute
Mark 9. 15 were..amazed, and running to (him) sal.
15. 18 began to salute him, Hail, King of the J.
Luke 1. 40 And entered into the house..and saluted
10. 4 Carry neither purse, nor scrip..and salute
Acts 18. 22 when he had..saluted the church, he went
21. 7 we came to Ptolemais, and saluted the
21. 19 when he had saluted them, he declared
25. 13 Bernice came unto Cesarea to salute Fes.
Rom. 16. 5 Salute my well beloved Epenetus, who
16. 7 Salute Andronicus and Junia, my kinsmen
16. 9 Salute Urbane our helper in Christ, and
16. 10 Salute Apelles approved in Christ. Salute
16. 11 Salute Herodion my kinsman. Greet them
16. 12 Salute Tryphena and Tryphosa, who labo.
16. 12 [Salute the beloved Persis, which laboured]
16. 13 Salute Rufus chosen in the Lord, and his
16. 14 Salute Asyncritus, Phlegon, Hermas, Pa.
16. 15 Salute Philologus, and Julia, Nereus, and
16. 16 Salute one another with an holy kiss
16. 16 The churches of Christ salute you
16. 21 Jason, and Sosipater, my kinsmen, salute
16. 22 I Tertius, who wrote (this) epistle salute
16. 23 mine host, and of the whole church sal.
16. 23 the chamberlain of the city saluteth you
1 Co. 16. 19 salute you. Aquila and Priscilla salute
2 Co. 13. 13 All the saints salute you
Phil. 4. 21 Salute every saint in Christ Jesus. The
4. 22 the saints salute you, chiefly they that are
Col. 4. 10 my fellow prisoner saluteth you, and M.
4. 12 a servant of Christ, saluteth you, always
4. 15 Salute the brethren which are in Laodicea
2 Ti. 4. 19 Salute Prisca and Aquila, and the house.
Titus 3. 15 All that are with me salute thee. Greet
Phm. 23 There salute thee Epaphras, my fellow p.
Heb. 13. 24 Salute all them that have the rule over
13. 24 and all the saints. They of Italy salute
1 Pe. 5. 13 The (church that is) at Babylon..saluteth
3 John 14 (Our) friends salute thee. Greet the friends

SALVATION —
1. *Safety, ease,* יְשׁוּעָה *yeshuah.*
Gen. 49. 18 I have waited for thy salvation, O LORD
Exod. 14. 13 see the salvation of the LORD, which he
15. 2 he is become my salvation: he (is) my G.
Deut. 32. 15 lightly esteemed the rock of his salvation
1 Sa. 2. 1 because I rejoice in thy salvation
14. 45 who hath wrought this great salvation in
2 Sa. 22. 51 (He is) the tower of salvation for his king
1 Ch. 16. 23 show forth from day to day his salvation
2 Ch. 20. 17 and see the salvation of the LORD with you
Job 13. 16 He also (shall be) my salvation: for an hy
Psa. 3. 8 Salvation (belongeth) unto the LORD: thy
9. 14 in the gates..I will rejoice in thy salvation
13. 5 my heart shall rejoice in thy salvation
14. 7 Oh that the salvation of Israel (were come)
20. 5 We will rejoice in thy salvation, and in
21. 1 in thy salvation how greatly shall he rej.
21. 5 His glory is great in thy salvation, honour
35. 3 say unto my soul, I (am) thy salvation
35. 9 my soul..it shall rejoice in his salvation
53. 6 Oh that the salvation of Israel (were come)
62. 1 upon God: from him (cometh) my salvati.
62. 2 He only (is) my rock and my salvation; he.
68. 19 Blessed (be) the Lord..God of our salva.
69. 29 let thy salvation, O God, set me up on high
70. 4 let such as love thy salvation say contin.
74. 12 working salvation in the midst of the earth
78. 22 Because they..trusted not in his salvation
88. 1 O LORD God of my salvation, I have cried
89. 26 my God, and the rock of my salvation
91. 16 With long life will I..show him my salv.
96. 2 show forth his salvation from day to day
98. 2 The LORD hath made known his salvation
98. 3 the ends of the earth have seen the salv.
106. 4 Remember me..O visit me with thy salv.
116. 13 I will take the cup of salvation, and call
118. 14 The LORD (is) my strength and..my salv.
118. 15 The voice of rejoicing and salvation (is)
118. 21 thou hast heard me, and art..my salvat.
119. 123 Mine eyes fail for thy salvation, and for
119. 155 Salvation (is) far from the wicked: for
119. 166 I have hoped for thy salvation, and done
119. 174 I have longed for thy salvation, O LORD
140. 7 O GOD the Lord, the strength of my salv
149. 4 he will beautify the meek with salvation
Isa. 12. 2 God (is) my salvation; I will trust, and not
12. 2 the LORD JEHOVAH..is become my salva.
12. 3 ye draw water out of the wells of salvat.
25. 9 we will be glad and rejoice in his salvat.
26. 1 salvation will (God) appoint (for) walls
33. 2 our salvation also in the time of trouble
33. 6 of thy times, (and) strength of salvation
49. 6 thou mayest be my salvation unto the end
49. 8 in a day of salvation have I helped thee
51. 6 my salvation shall be for ever, and my
51. 8 my salvation from generation to generat.
52. 7 that publisheth salvation; that saith unto
52. 10 the ends of the earth shall see the salvat.
56. 1 for my salvation (is) near to come, and my
59. 11 we look..for salvation, (but) it is far off
59. 17 and an helmet of salvation upon his head
60. 18 thou shalt call thy walls salvation, and
62. 1 the salvation thereof as a lamp (that) bur
Jon. 2. 9 I will sacrifice..Salvation (is) of the LORD
Hab. 3. 8 thine horses, (and) thy chariots of salva.

2. *Safety, ease,* יֶשַׁע, יֵשַׁע *yesha.*
2 Sa. 22. 3 the horn of my salvation, my high tower
22. 36 also given me the shield of thy salvation
22. 47 and exalted be..the rock of my salvation
23. 5 (this is) all my salvation, and all my des.
1 Ch. 16. 35 Save us, O God of our salvation, and gat.
Psa. 18. 2 the horn of my salvation, (and) my high
18. 35 also given me the shield of thy salvation
18. 46 and let the God of my salvation be exal.
24. 5 righteousness from the God of his salva.
25. 5 thou (art) the God of my salvation; on
27. 1 The LORD (is) my light and my salvation
27. 9 neither forsake me, O God of my salvation
50. 23 to him..will I show the salvation of God
51. 12 Restore unto me the joy of thy salvatio.
62. 7 In God (is) my salvation and my glory: th.
65. 5 O God of our salvation; (who art) the co.
69. 13 hear me, in the truth of thy salvation
79. 9 Help us, O God of our salvation, for the
85. 4 Turn us, O God of our salvation, and ca.
85. 7 Show us thy mercy..grant us thy salvat.
85. 9 his salvation (is) nigh them that fear him
95. 1 a joyful noise to the rock of our salvation
132. 16 I will also clothe her priests with salvation
Isa. 17. 10 thou hast forgotten the God of thy salva.
45. 8 and let them bring forth salvation, and
51. 5 my salvation is gone forth, and mine ar.
61. 10 clothed me with the garments of salvation
62. 11 Behold, thy salvation cometh; behold, his
Mic. 7. 7 I will wait for the God of my salvation
Hab. 3. 13 salvation of thy people, (even) for salvat.
3. 18 Yet..I will joy in the God of my salvati.

3. *Safety, deliverances,* מוֹשָׁעוֹת *moshaoth.*
Psa. 68. 20 our God (is) the God of salvation; and un.

4. *Safety, ease,* תְּשׁוּעָה *teshuah.*
1 Sa. 11. 13 the LORD hath wrought salvation in Isr.
19. 5 the LORD wrought a great salvation for
2 Ch. 6. 41 let thy priests..be clothed with salvation
Psa. 37. 39 the salvation of the righteous (is) of the L.
38. 22 Make haste to help me, O Lord my salv.
40. 10 declared thy faithfulness and thy salvat.
40. 16 let such as love thy salvation say contin.
51. 14 Deliver me..O God, thou God of my sal.
71. 15 thy righteousness (and) thy salvation all
119. 41 Let thy mercies come..(even) thy salvat.
119. 81 My soul fainteth for thy salvation; (but)
144. 10 (It is he) that giveth salvation unto kings
Isa. 45. 17 be saved..with an everlasting salvation
46. 13 it shall not be far off, and my salvation
46. 13 I will place salvation in Zion for Israel
Jer. 3. 23 in the LORD our God (is) the salvation of
Lam. 3. 26 and quietly wait for the salvation of the

5. *Safety, soundness,* σωτηρία *sōtēria.*
Luke 1. 69 hath raised up an horn of salvation for us
1. 77 To give knowledge of salvation unto his
19. 9 This day is salvation come to this house
John 4. 22 we know what we worship: for salvation
Acts 4. 12 [Neither is there salvation in any other]
13. 26 to you is the word of this salvation sent
13. 47 thou shouldest be for salvation unto the
16. 17 which show unto us the way of salvation
Rom. 1. 16 it is the power of God unto salvation to
10. 10 with the mouth confession is..unto salv.
11. 11 through their fall salvation (is come) unto
13. 11 now is our salvation nearer than when we
2 Co. 1. 6 (it is) for your consolation and salvation
6. 2 in the day of salvation have I succoured
6. 2 now (is) the accepted time..the day of sa.
7. 10 sorrow worketh repentance to salvation
Eph. 1. 13 heard..the gospel of your salvation: in
Phil. 1. 19 I know that this shall turn to my salvat.
1. 28 but to you of salvation, and that of God
2. 12 work out your own salvation with fear and
1 Th. 5. 8 and for an helmet the hope of salvation
5. 9 to obtain salvation by our Lord Jesus C.
2 Th. 2. 13 chosen you to salvation through sanctific.
2 Ti. 2. 10 that they may also obtain the salvation
3. 15 make thee wise unto salvation through
Heb. 1. 14 for them who shall be heirs of salvation
2. 3 escape, if we neglect so great salvation
2. 10 make the captain of their salvation perf.
5. 9 he became the author of eternal salvation
6. 9 things that accompany salvation, though
9. 28 the second time without sin unto salvat.
1 Pe. 1. 5 through faith unto salvation ready to be
1. 9 end of your faith, (even) the salvation of
1. 10 Of which salvation the prophets have en.
2 Pe. 3. 15 the long suffering of our Lord (is) salvat.
Jude 3 write unto you of the common salvation
Rev. 7. 10 Salvation to our God which sitteth upon
12. 10 Now is come salvation, and strength, and
19. 1 Salvation, and glory, and honour, and po.

6. *Safety, soundness,* σωτήριον *sōtērion.*
Luke 2. 30 For mine eyes have seen thy salvation
3. 6 And all flesh shall see the salvation of God
Acts 28. 28 that the salvation of God is sent unto the
Eph. 6. 17 take the helmet of salvation, and the sw.

SALVATION, to bring or have —
1. *To be saved, have safety,* יָשַׁע *yasha,* 2.
Zech. 9. 9 he (is) just, and having salvation; lowly

2. *To give or cause safety,* יָשַׁע *yasha,* 5.
Isa. 59. 16 therefore his arm brought salvation unto
63. 5 therefore mine own arm brought salvation

3. *Saving, sound,* σωτήριος *sōtērios.*
Titus 2. 11 grace of God that bringeth salvation hath

SA-MA'-RIA, שֹׁמְרוֹן Σαμάρεια *watch.*
1. A hill and city in Ephraim, the capital of the ten tribes of Israel, forty two miles N. of Jerusalem; built about B.C. 925 by Omri, the sixth king of Israel; its inhabitants were carried away to Assyria by Shalmanezer, B.C. 720, and their place supplied by persons from Babylon, Cuthah, Ava, Hamath, and Sepharvaim, who

brought their gods with them. It is six miles N.W. of Shechem, and nineteen miles E. of the Mediterranean; the small village of *Sebustieh*, (a corruption of the Greek *Sebaste*, which Herod called it in honour of Cæsar Augustus,) now occupies part of the ancient site.

1 Ki. 16. 24 And they bought the hill S. of Shemer
16. 24 called the name of the city which he..S.
16. 28 So Omri slept..and was buried in S., and
16. 29 Ahab the son of Omri reigned over..in S.
16. 32 house of Baal, which he had built in S.
18. 2 And (there was) a sore famine in S.
20. 1 and he went up and besieged S., and wa.
20. 10 if the dust of S. shall suffice for handfuls
20. 17 told him..There are men come out of S.
20. 34 shalt make streets..my father made in S.
20. 43 And the king of Israel..came to S.
21. 18 Arise, go..to meet Ahab..which (is) in S.
22. 10 place in the entrance of the gate of S.
22. 37 brought to S.; and..buried the king in S.
22. 38 (one) washed the chariot in the pool of S.
22. 51 Ahaziah..began to reign over Israel in S.
2 Ki. 1. 2 a lattice in his..chamber that (was) in S.
2. 25 Carmel; and..thence he returned to S.
3. 1 began to reign over Israel in S. the eight.
3. 6 king Jehoram went out of Samaria the s.
5. 3 my lord (were) with the prophet..in S.!
6. 19 man whom ye seek. But he led them to S.
6. 20 came to pass, when they were come into S.
6. 20 and, behold, (they were) in the midst of S.
6. 24 that Ben-hadad..went up, and besieged S.
6. 25 And there was a great famine in S.: and
7. 1, 18 measures of barley..in the gate of S.
10. 1 Ahab had seventy sons in S. And Jehu
10. 1 sent to S., unto the rulers of Jezreel
10. 12 he arose and departed, and came to S.
10. 17 when he came to S., he slew all that rem.
10. 17 unto Ahab in S., till he had destroyed him
10. 35 Jehu slept..and they buried him in S. A.
10. 36 time that Jehu reigned over Israel in S.
13. 1 Jehoahaz..began to reign over Israel in S.
13. 6 and there remained the grove also in S.
13. 9 Jehoahaz slept..and they buried him in S.
13. 10 began Jehoash..to reign over Israel in S.
13. 13 Joash was buried in S. with the kings of
14. 14 he took all the gold..and returned to S.
14. 16 Jehoash..was buried in S. with the kings
14. 23 Joash king of Israel began to reign in S.
15. 8 did Zachariah..reign over Israel in S. six
15. 13 Shallum..he reigned a full month in S.
15. 14 For Menahem the son of Gadi..came to S.
15. 14 and smote Shallum the son of Jabesh in S.
15. 17 Menahem..(reigned) ten years in S
15. 23, 27 Pekahiah..began to reign over Is. in S.
15. 25 conspired against..and smote him in S.
17. 1 began Hoshea..to reign in S. over Israel
17. 5 Then the king of Assyria..went up to S.
17. 6 the king of Assyria took S., and carried
17. 28 one of the priests..from S., came and dw.
18. 9 Shalmaneser..of Assyria came..against S.
18. 10 in the sixth year of Hezekiah..S. was ta.
18. 34 have they delivered S. out of mine hand?
21. 13 I..stretch over Jerusalem the line of S.
2 Ch. 18. 2 after..years he went down to Ahab to S.
18. 9 place at the entering in of the gate of S.
22. 9 and they caught him, for he was hid in S.
25. 13 the cities of J., from S. even unto Beth.
25. 24 (he took) all the gold..and returned to S.
28. 8 children of Israel..brought the spoil to S.
28. 9 went out before the host that came to S.
28. 15 brought them..then they returned to S.
Isa. 7. 9 head of Ephraim (is) S...the head of S.
8. 4 the riches..of S. shall be taken away be.
9. 9 the people shall know..inhabitant of S.
10. 9 (is) not Hamath as Arpad? (is) not S. as
10. 10 whose graven images did excel them of..S.
10. 11 Shall I not, as I have done unto S and her
Jer. 41. 5 from Shiloh, and from S...fourscore men
Eze. 16. 46 thine elder sister (is) S., she and her daugh
16. 51 Neither hath S. committed half of thy s.
16. 53 and the captivity of S. and her daughters
16. 55 S. and her daughters shall return to their
23. 4 S. (is) Aholah, and Jerusalem Aholibah
23. 33 Thou shalt be filled..with the cup of..S.
Hos. 13. 16 S. shall become desolate; for she hath re.
Amos 3. 12 the children of Israel..that dwell in S. in
Mic. 1. 1 which he saw concerning S. and Jerusalem
1. 5 the transgression of Jacob? (is it) not S.?
1. 6 Therefore I will make S. as an heap of the
Acts 8. 5 Then Philip went down to the city of S
8. 9 a certain man..bewitched the people of S.
8. 14 the apostles..heard that S. had received

2. Their whole territory, but in New Testament times only the land of Ephraim and Manasseh W. of the Jordan, having Galilee on the N., the Jordan on the E., Judea on the S., and the Mediterranean on the W.

1 Ki. 13. 32 high places which (are) in the cities of S.
21. 1 hard by the palace of Ahab king of S.
2 Ki. 1. 3 to meet the messengers of the king of S
17. 24 king of Assyria..placed..in the cities of S.
17. 24 they possessed S., and dwelt in the cities
17. 26 thou hast removed, and placed in..S.
23. 18 bones of the prophet that came out of S.
23. 19 high places that (were) in the cities of S.
Ezra 4. 10 whom..Asnapper..set in the cities of S.
4. 17 rest of their companions that dwell in S.
Neh. 4. 2 he spake before..the army of S., and said
Isa. 36. 19 have they delivered S. out of my hand
Jer. 23. 13 I have seen folly in the prophets of S.
31. 5 yet plant vines upon the mountains of S.
Hos. 7. 1 would have healed..the wickedness of S.
8. 5 Thy calf, O S., hath cast..off; mine ang.
Hos. 8. 6 the calf of S. shall be broken in pieces
10. 5 S. shall fear because of the calves of Bet.
10. 7 S., her king is cut off as the foam upon
Amos 3. 9 Assem..selves upon the mountains of S.
4. 1 ye kine..that (are) in the mountain of S.
6. 1 them (that)..trust in the mountain of S.
8. 14 They that swear by the sin of S., and say
Obad. 19 and they shall possess..the fields of S.
Luke 17. 11 passed through the midst of S. and Gali.
John 4. 4 And he must needs go through S.
4. 5 Then cometh he to a city of S., which is
4. 7 There cometh a woman of S. to draw wa.
4. 9 Then saith the woman of S. unto him
4. 9 thou..askest drink of me..a woman of S.?
Acts 1. 8 and ye shall be witnesses unto me..in S.
8. 1 were, all scattered abroad throughout..S.
9. 31 had the churches rest throughout..S.
15. 3 they passed through Phenice and S., decl.

SA-MA-RI-TANS, שֹׁמְרֹנִים Σαμαρεῖτης.

The Samaritans were a mixed race descended partly from the Ten Tribes, partly from heathen immigrants (Assyrians). They inhabited central Palestine, between Judæa and Galilee. Their faith and practice was founded on the Pentateuch alone, and they rejected the whole of the other Jewish books. Our Lord, before His ascension, expressly included the Samaritans, with the Gentiles, in His commission to preach the Gospel (Acts 1. 8).

2 Ki. 17. 29 of the high places which the S. had made
Matt 10. 5 into (any) city of the S. enter ye not
Luke 9. 52 went, and entered into a village of the S.
10. 33 But a certain S...compassion (on him)
17. 16 giving him thanks: and he was a S.
John 4. 9 for the Jews have no dealings with the S.
4. 39 many of the S. of..city believed on him
4. 40 So when the S. were come unto him
8. 48 Say we not well that thou art a S., and
Acts 8. 25 preached the gospel in..villages of the S.

SAME, (the or that, this or these)—

1. *Midst*, גַּו *gav.*

Ezra 4. 15 moved sedition within the same of old

2. *This*, דֵּךְ *dek.*

Ezra 5. 16 Then came the same Sheshbazzar, (and)

3. *This*, דִּכֵּן *dikken.*

Dan. 7. 21 the same horn made war with the saints

4. *He, he himself*, הוּא *hu.*

Gen. 19. 37 the same (is) the father of the Moabites

5. *She, it*, הַהִיא, הִיא *ha-hi, hi.*

Gen. 14. 8 the king of Bela, the same (is) Zoar; and
Lev. 23. 30 the same soul will I destroy from among
2 Ki. 8. 22 Then Libnah revolted at the same time

6. *They*, הֵם, הֵמָּה *hemah, hem.*

Gen. 6. 4 the same (became) mighty men which (w.)
Eze. 10. 16 the same wheels also turned not from be.
10. 22 likeness of their faces (was) the same fa.

7. *This*, הַזֶּה, זֶה *zeh, haz-zeh.*

Gen. 7. 11 the same day were all the fountains of the
Psa. 75. 8 poureth out of the same: but the dregs

8. *This (fem.)*, זֹאת *zoth.*

Eze. 21. 26 this (shall) not (be) the same: exalt (him

9. *Bone, substance*, עֶצֶם *etsem.*

Lev. 23. 28 ye shall do no work in that same day; for
23. 29 shall not be afflicted in that same day, he
23. 30 that doeth any work in that same day, the
Eze. 24. 2 the name of the day, (even) of this same
24. 2 set himself against Jerusalem this same

10. *He, he himself, it, it itself*, αὐτός *autos.*

Matt 25. 16 went and traded with the same, and made
Luke 7. 21 in that same hour he cured many of (their)
10. 7 in the same house remain, eating and
Luke 10. 10 go..out into the streets of the same, and
Rom. 9. 17 Even for this same purpose have I raised
12. 16 of the same mind one toward another
1 Co. 1. 10 the same thing..the same mind..the same
2 Co. 2. 3 I wrote this same unto you, lest, when I
Phil. 4. 2 that they be of the same mind in the L.
Heb. 1. 12 but thou art the same, and thy years
13. 8 Jesus Christ the same yesterday..ever
1 Pe. 4. 1 arm yourselves likewise with the same

11. *He, she, it, that very*, ἐκεῖνος *ekeinos.*

Matt 10. 19 for it shall be given you in [that same]
13. 1 The same day went Jesus out of the house
15. 22 woman of Canaan came out of the same
18. 1 the same time came the disciples unto J.
18. 28 the [same] servant went out, and found
22. 23 The same day came to him the Sadducees
26. 55 In that same hour said Jesus to the mul.
Mark 4. 35 the same day, when the even was come
John 1. 33 same said unto me, Upon whom thou shalt
4. 53 father knew that (it was) at the same ho.
5. 9 and on the same day was the sabbath
5. 11 the same said unto me, Take up thy bed
10. 1 climbeth up some other way, the same is
11. 49 being the high priest that same year, said
12. 48 the same shall judge him the last day
18. 13 which was the high priest that same year
20. 19 Then the same day at evening, being the
Acts 2. 41 same day there were added (unto them)
12. 6 the same night Peter was sleeping betw.
16. 33 took them the same hour of the night, and
19. 23 the same time there arose no small stir
28. 7 In the same quarters were possessions of
2 Co. 7. 8 I perceive that the same epistle, Re. 11. 13.

12. *And, even*, καί *kai*, Gal. 2. 8.

13. *This, that*, οὗτος *houtos.*

Matt. 5. 19 the same shall be called great in the king.
13. 20 the same is he that heareth the word, and
Matt 18. 4 the same is greatest in the kingdom of
21. 42 the same is become the head of the corner
24. 13 he that shall endure..the same shall be
26. 23 He that dippeth..the same shall betray
Mark 3. 35 the same is my brother, and my sister, and
8. 35 whosoever shall lose his life..[the same]
13. 13 he that shall endure..the same shall be
Luke 2. 25 the same man (was) just and devout, wa.
9. 24 whosoever will lose his life..the same sh.
9. 48 least among you all, the same shall be gr.
16. 1 the same was accused unto him that he
20. 17 the same is become the head of the cor.?
23. 51 The same had not consented to the cou.
John 1. 2 The same was in the beginning with God
1. 7 The same came for a witness, to bear wit.
1. 33 [the same] is he which baptizeth with the
3. 2 The same came to Jesus by night, and sa.
3. 26 the same baptizeth, and all (men) come
7. 18 the same is true, and no unrighteousness
15. 5 the same bringeth forth much fruit; for
Acts 1. 11 this same Jesus, which is taken up from
7. 19 The same dealt subtilely with our kindred
14. 9 The same heard Paul speak: who stedfa.
1 Co. 8. 3 But if any man love God, the same is kn.
2 Co. 8. 19 administered by us to the glory of the [s.]
Eph. 6. 8 the same shall he receive of the Lord, wh.
Jas. 3. 2 the same (is) a perfect man, (and) able also
1 Pe. 2. 7 the same is made the head of the corner
Rev. 3. 5 He that overcometh, [the same] shall be

14. *These, those*, οὗτοι *houtoi.*

Luke 20. 47 the same shall receive greater damnation
John 12. 21 The same came therefore to Phil Ac. 24. 20.
Gal. 3. 7 Know ye..the same are the children of

15. *This*, αὕτη *hautē.*

Acts 16. 17 The same followed Paul and us, and cried

16. *These, those*, ταῦτα *tauta.*

1 Co. 9. 8 man? or saith not the law the same also?
2 Ti. 2. 2 the same commit thou to faithful men, who

17. *In this*, ταύτῃ *tautē.*

1 Co. 7. 20 Let every man abide in the same calling
2 Co. 9. 4 should be ashamed in this same confident

18. *This*, ταύτην *tautēn.*

Acts 13. 33 God hath fulfilled the same unto us their
2 Co. 8. 6 would also finish in you the same grace
9. 5 that the same might be ready, as (a mat.

19. *This*, ταύτης *tautēs.*

Acts 8. 35 began at the same scripture, and preached

20. *This itself*, αὐτὸ τοῦτο *auto touto.*

Gal. 2. 10 the same which I also was for. Eph. 6. 8.
Col. 4. 8 Whom I have sent unto you for the same

21. *This*, τοῦτον *touton.*

Acts 7. 35 the same did God send (to be) a ruler and

22. *To this*, τούτῳ *toutō.*

Acts 21. 9 the same man had four daughters, virgins
2 Pe. 2. 19 of the same is he brought in bondage

[*See also* Body, care, cause, craft, day, hour, manner, mind, place, purpose, quarter, rank, springeth, springeth up, that.]

SAM-GAR NE'-BO, סַמְגַּר־נְבוֹ.

A prince of the king of Babylon, who sat in the middle gate of Jerusalem. B.C. 588.

Jer. 39. 3 Nergal-sharezer, S., Sarsechim, Rabsaris

SAM'-LAH, שַׂמְלָה *garment.*

The fifth of the ancient kings of Edom, of the city of *Masrekah*. B.C. 1500.

Gen. 36. 36 and S. of Masrekah reigned in his stead
36. 37 And S. died, and Saul..reigned in his st.
1 Ch. 1. 47 S. of Masrekah reigned in his stead
1. 48 when S. was dead, Shaul..reigned in his

SA'-MOS, Σάμος.

An island in the Ægean Sea, nine miles off the coast of Lydia in Asia Minor, a few miles S.W. of Ephesus, and about seventy-two miles in circumference; noted for its worship of Juno, its valuable pottery, and as the birth-place of Pythagoras.

Acts 20. 15 the next (day) we arrived at S., and tarried

SA-MO-THRA-CI-A, Σαμοθρᾴκη.

A small island in the N.E. of the Ægean Sea, above the Hellespont, and ten miles S. of Thrace, seventeen miles in circumference; once called Dardana, Leucania, and also Samos; now called *Samandrachi* or *Samothraki*.

Acts 16. 11 we came with a straight course to S., and

SAM'-SON, שִׁמְשׁוֹן *distinguished, strong*, Σαμψών.

A Danite, son of Manoah a native of Zorah; he judged the S.W. of Israel twenty years; his birth was foretold, also his manner of life; his great strength enabled him to kill a lion, thirty Philistines, to break the strongest bands, to smite 1000 men, to carry off the gates of Gaza, and at last to pull down the house of Dagon. B.C. 1120.

Judg 13. 24 woman bare a son, and called his name S
14. 1 S. went down to Timnath, and saw a wo.
14. 3 S. said unto his father, Get her for me
14. 5 Then went S. down, and his father and
14. 7 And he went down..and she pleased S.
14. 10 S. made there a feast; for so used the yo.
14. 12 S. said unto them, I will now put forth a
14. 15 they said unto S.'s wife, Entice thy husb.
14. 16 S.'s wife wept before him, and said, Thou
14. 20 S.'s wife was (given) to his companion, wh.
15. 1 S. visited his wife with a kid; and he said
15. 3 S. said concerning them, Now shall I be
15. 4 S. went and caught three hundred foxes
15. 6 they answered, S., the son in law of the
15. 7 S. said unto them, Though ye have done
15. 10 they answered, To bind S. are we come up

Judg15. 11 three thousand men of Judah..said to S.
15. 12 S. said unto them, Swear unto me, that
15. 16 S. said, With the jawbone of an ass, heaps
16. 1 Then went S. to Gaza, and saw there an
16. 2 (it was told) the Gazites, saying, S. is come
16. 3 S. lay till midnight, and arose at midnight
16. 6 Delilah said to S., Tell me, I pray thee, wh.
16. 7 S. said unto her, If they bind me with
16. 9, 12, 14, 20 The Philistines (be) upon thee S.
16. 10 Delilah said unto S., Behold, thou hast
16. 13 Delilah said unto S., Hitherto thou hast
16. 23 Our god hath delivered S. our enemy into
16. 25 Call for S., that he may make us sport
16. 25 they called for S. out of the prison house
16. 26 S. said unto the lad that held him by the
16. 27 and women, that beheld while S. made sp.
16. 28 S. called unto the LORD, and said, O Lord
16. 29 S. took hold of the two middle pillars upon
16. 30 S. said, Let me die with the Philistines
Heb. 11. 32 to tell of Gideon..(of) S., and (of) Jephth.

SA-MU'-EL, שְׁמוּאֵל Σαμουήλ *heard of God.*

A Levite, son of Elkanah and Hannah, of Ramathaim-Zophim in Mount Ephraim; the last of the Judges, and the first of the Prophets (after Moses), a class of men who continued till Malachi and John; he was asked of God, and for him, was devoted to him from childhood, spoken to by him, persuaded Israel to abandon idolatry at Mizpeh, had two wicked sons, explained the usages of kings, received Saul, anointed him, asserted his integrity, reproved Saul, leaves him, anoints David, and dies. B.C. 1171-1060.

1 Sa. 1. 20 she bare a son, and called his name S.
2. 18 S. ministered before the LORD, (being) a
2. 21 And the child S. grew before the LORD
2. 26 the child S. grew on, and was in favour
3. 1 the child S. ministered unto the LORD be.
3. 3 went out..and S. was laid down (to sleep)
3. 4 the LORD called S.: and he answered, Here
3. 6 the LORD called yet again, S. And S. arose
3. 7 Now S. did not yet know the LORD, neith.
3. 8 the LORD called S. again the third time
3. 9 Eli said unto S., Go, lie down. so S. went
3. 10 the LORD..called as at other times, S., S.
3. 10 S. answered, Speak; for thy servant hear.
3. 11 the LORD said to S., Behold, I will do a
3. 15 S. lay until the morning..And S. feared
3. 16 Then Eli called S., and said, S., my son
3. 18 S. told him every whit, and hid nothing
3. 19 S. grew, and the LORD was with him, and
3. 20 all Israel..knew that S. (was) established
3. 21 the LORD revealed himself to S. in Shiloh
4. 1 And the word of S. came to all Israel
7. 3 S. spake unto all the house of Israel, say.
7. 5 S. said, Gather all Israel to Mizpeh, and
7. 6 S. judged the children of Israel in Mizpeh
7. 8 the children of Israel said to S., Cease not
7. 9 And S. took a sucking lamb, and offered
7. 9 and S. cried unto the LORD for Israel; and
7. 10 as S. was offering up the burnt offering
7. 12 S. took a stone, and set (it) between Miz.
7. 13 against the Philistines all the days of S.
7. 15 S. judged Israel all the days of his life
8. 1 And it came to pass, when S. was old, that
8. 4 Then all the elders..came to S. unto Ra.
8. 6 the thing displeased S...And S. prayed
8. 7 the LORD said unto S., Hearken unto the
8. 10 S. told all the words of the LORD unto
8. 19 the people refused to obey the voice of S.
8. 21 S. heard all the words of the people, and
8. 22 the LORD said to S., Hearken unto their
8. 22 S. said unto the men of Israel, Go ye ev.
9. 14 S. came out against them, for to go up to
9. 15 the LORD had told S. in his ear a day be.
9. 17 when S. saw Saul, the LORD said unto him
9. 18 Saul drew near to S. in the gate, and said
9. 19 S. answered Saul, and said, I (am) the se.
9. 22 S. took Saul and his servant, and brought
9. 23 S. said unto the cook, Bring the portion
9. 24 So Saul did eat with S. that day; v. 25.
9. 26 S. called Saul to the top of the house, say.
9. 26 they went out both of them, he and S., ab.
9. 27 S. said to Saul, Bid the servant pass on
10. 1 S. took a vial of oil, and poured (it) upon
10. 9 when he had turned his back to go from S.
10. 14 we saw that..no where, we came to S.
10. 15 Tell me, I pray thee, what S. said unto you
10. 16 of the matter of the kingdom, whereof S.
10. 17 S. called the people together unto the L.
10. 20 S. had caused all the tribes of Israel to co.
10. 24 S. said to all the people, See ye him whom
10. 25 S. told the people the manner of the kin.
10. 25 S. sent all the people away, every man to
11. 7 Who. cometh not..after Saul and after S.
11. 12 the people said unto S., Who (is) he that
11. 14 Then said S. to the people, Come, and let
12. 1 S. said unto all Israel, Behold, I have hear.
12. 6 S. said unto the people, (It is) the LORD th.
12. 11 the LORD sent Jerubbaal..and S., and de
12. 18 So S. called unto the LORD; and the LORD
12. 18 the people greatly feared the LORD and S.
12. 19 all the people said unto S., Pray for thy se.
12. 20 S. said unto the people, Fear not: ye have
13. 8 according to the set time that S. (had ap.)
13. 8 but S. came not to Gilgal; and the people
13. 10 it came to pass..behold, S. came; and S.
13. 11 S. said, What hast thou done? And Saul
13. 13 S. said to Saul, Thou hast done foolishly
13. 15 S. arose, and gat him up from Gilgal unto
15. 1 S. also unto Saul, The LORD sent me to an.
15. 10 Then came the word of the LORD unto S.
15. 11 grieved S.; and he cried unto the LORD

1 Sa. 15. 12 when S. rose early to meet Saul in the mo.
15. 12 it was told S., saying, Saul came to Carmel
15. 13 S. came to Saul: and Saul said unto him
15. 14 S. said, What..then this bleating of the sh.
15. 16 S. said unto Saul, Stay, and I will tell thee
15. 17 S. said, When thou (wast) little in thine
15. 20 Saul said unto S., Yea, I have obeyed the
15. 22 S. said, Hath the LORD (as great) delight
15. 24 Saul said unto S., I have sinned: for I h.
15. 26 S. said unto Saul, I will not return with
15. 27 as S. turned about to go away, he laid
15. 28 S. said unto him, The LORD hath rent the
15. 31 So S. turned again after Saul; and Saul
15. 32 Then said S., Bring ye hither to me Agag
15. 33 S. said, As thy sword hath made women
15. 33 S. hewed Agag in pieces before the LORD
15. 34 S. went to Ramah; and Saul went up to
15. 35 S. came no more to see Saul until..his de.
15. 35 nevertheless S. mourned for Saul: and
16. 1 the LORD said unto S., How long wilt thou
16. 2 S. said, How can I go? if Saul hear (it), he
16. 4 S. did that which the LORD spake, and ca.
16. 7 the LORD said unto S., Look not on his co.
16. 8 Abinadab, and made him pass before S.
16. 10 made seven of his sons to pass before S.
16. 10 S. said unto Jesse, The LORD hath not ch.
16. 11 S. said unto Jesse, Are here all (thy) chi.?
16. 11 S. said unto Jesse, Send and fetch him: for
16. 13 Then S. took the horn of oil, and anointed
16. 13 So S. rose up, and went to Ramah
19. 18 So David fled, and escaped, and came to S.
19. 18 And he and S. went and dwelt in Naioth
19. 20 and S. standing (as) appointed over them
19. 22 he asked and said, Where (are) S. and D.?
19. 24 he..prophesied before S. in like manner
25. 1 S. died; and all the Israelites were gath.
28. 3 Now S. was dead, and all Israel had lam.
28. 11 Whom..And he said, Bring me up S.
28. 12 when the woman saw S., she cried with a
28. 14 Saul perceived that it (was) S., and he st.
28. 15 S. said to Saul, Why hast thou disquieted
28. 16 Then said S., Wherefore then dost thou ask
28. 20 sore afraid, because of the words of S.
1 Ch. 6. 28 the sons of S.; the first born Vashni, and
9. 22 whom David and S. the seer did ordain in
11. 3 according to the word of the LORD by S.
26. 28 And all that S. the seer..had dedicated
29. 29 they (are) written in the book of S. the se.
2 Ch. 35. 18 passover like to that..from the days of S.
Psa. 99. 6 and S. among them that call upon his na.
Jer. 15. 1 Though Moses..S. stood before me, (yet)
Acts 3. 24 the prophets from S. and those that follow
13. 20 after that he gave..judges..until S. the p
Heb. 11. 32 David also, and S., and (of) the prophets

SAN-BAL'-LAT, סַנְבַלַּט.

A Horonite (from Bethhoron in Ephraim, or Horonaim in Moab), an enemy of the Jews who opposed Nehemiah in the days of Artaxerxes Longimanus. B.C. 445.

Neh. 2. 10, 19 When S. the Horonite, and Tobiah the
4. 1 when S. heard that we builded the wall,
4. 7 S...heard that the walls of Jerusalem were
6. 1 when S..heard that I had builded the wall
6. 2 S. and Geshem sent unto me, saying, Come
6. 5 Then sent S. his servant unto me in like
6. 12 for Tobiah and S. had hired him
6. 14 My God, think thou upon Tobiah and S.
13. 28 And (one..was) son in law to S. the Hor.

SANCTIFICATION —

Separation, a setting apart, ἁγιασμός *hagiasmos.*

1 Co. 1. 30 righteousness, and sanctification, and red.
1 Th. 4. 3 this is the will of God, (even) your sancti.
4. 4 how to possess his vessel in sanctification
2 Th. 2. 13 chosen you to salvation through sanctific.
1 Pe. 1. 2 through sanctification of the spirit, unto

SANCTIFIED, (to be) —

1. *To be separate, set apart,* קָדַשׁ *qadesh.*

1 Sa. 21. 5 though it were sanctified this day in the

2. *To be separated, set apart,* קָדַשׁ *qadesh,* 2.

Exod29. 43 (the tabernacle) shall be sanctified by my
Lev. 10. 3 will be sanctified in them that come nigh
Num20. 13 strove with the LORD, and he was sancti.
Isa. 5. 16 holy, shall be sanctified in righteousness
Eze. 20. 41 will be sanctified in you before the heat.
28. 22 when I..shall be sanctified in her
28. 25 shall be sanctified in them in the sight of
36. 23 I shall be sanctified in you before their
38. 16 when I shall be sanctified in thee, O Gog
39. 27 am sanctified in them in the sight of ma.

3. *To be separated, set apart,* קָדַשׁ *qadesh,* 4.

Eze. 48. 11 for the priests that are sanctified of the

4. *To separate, set self apart,* קָדַשׁ *qadesh,* 7.

2 Ch. 5. 11 the priests (that were) present were sanc.
30. 17 many..that were not sanctified: therefore

5. *To separate, set apart,* ἁγιάζω *hagiazō.*

Acts 20. 32 inheritance among all them which are sa.
26. 18 inheritance among them which are sanc.
Rom 15. 16 being sanctified by the Holy Ghost
1 Co. 1. 2 to them that are sanctified in Christ Jesus
6. 11 but ye are washed, but ye are sanctified
7. 14 For the unbelieving husband is sanctified
7. 14 unbelieving wife is sanctified by the hus.
1 Ti. 4. 5 For it is sanctified by the word of God
2 Ti. 2. 21 he shall be a vessel unto honour, sanctified
Heb. 2. 11 they who are sanctified (are) all of one, for
10. 10 By the which will we are sanctified thro.
10. 14 perfected for ever them that are sanctified
10. 29 wherewith he was sanctified, an unholy
Jude 1 to them [that are sanctified] by God the

SANCTIFIED (one) —

1. *To be separated, set apart,* קָדַשׁ *qadesh,* 4.

Isa. 13. 3 I have commanded my sanctified ones, I

2. *To separate, set apart,* ἁγιάζω *hagiazō.*

John17. 19 also might be sanctified through the truth

SANCTIFY (self), to —

1. *To separate, set apart,* קָדַשׁ *qadesh,* 3.

Gen. 2. 3 God blessed the seventh day, and sancti.
Exod13. 2 Sanctify unto me all the first born, what.
19. 10 sanctify them today and to morrow, and
19. 14 sanctified the people; and they washed th.
19. 23 saying, Set bounds..and sanctify it
28. 41 sanctify them, that they may minister unto
29. 27 thou shalt sanctify the breast of the wave
29. 33 made to consecrate (and) to sanctify them
29. 36 and thou shalt anoint it, to sanctify it
29. 37 atonement for the altar, and sanctify it
29. 44 sanctify the tabernacle..will sanctify also
30. 29 sanctify them, that they may be most holy
31. 13 know that I (am) the LORD that doth san.
40. 10 sanctify the altar: and it shall be an altar
40. 11 anoint the laver and his foot, and sanctify
40. 13 sanctify him; that he may minister unto
Lev. 8. 10 anointed the tabernacle..and sanctified
8. 11 both the laver and his foot, to sanctify th.
8. 12 poured of the anointing oil..to sanctify th.
8. 15 sanctified it, to make reconciliation upon
8. 30 sanctified Aaron, (and) his garments, and
10. 3 will be sanctified in them that come nigh
20. 8 do them: I (am) the LORD which sanctify
21. 8 Thou shalt sanctify..for I..which sanctify
21. 15, 23 for I the LORD do sanctify them
22. 9, 16 I the LORD do sanctify them
Num. 7. 1 had anointed it, and sanctified it, and all
7. 1 and had anointed them, and sanctified th.
Deut. 5. 12 Keep the sabbath day to sanctify it, as th.
32. 51 sanctified me not in the midst of the chi.
Josh. 7. 13 sanctify the people, and say..thus saith
1 Sa. 7. 1 sanctified Eleazar his son to keep the ark
16. 5 sanctified Jesse and his sons, and called
2 Ch.29. 5 sanctify the house of the LORD God of your
29. 17 began..to sanctify..so they sanctified the
Neh. 3. 1 they sanctified it, and set up the doors of
3. 1 unto the tower of Meah they sanctified it
13. 22 keep the gates, to sanctify the sabbath day
Job 1. 5 Job sent and sanctified them, and rose up
Eze. 20. 12 know that I (am) the LORD that sanctify th.
36. 23 I will sanctify my great name, which was
37. 28 shall know that I the LORD do sanctify
44. 19 they shall not sanctify the people with th.
46. 20 into the outer court, to sanctify the peo.
Joel 1. 14 Sanctify ye a fast, call a solemn assembly
2. 15 sanctify a fast, call a solemn assembly
2. 16 Gather the people, sanctify the congreg.

2. *To separate, set apart,* קָדַשׁ *qadesh,* 5.

Lev. 27. 14 when a man shall sanctify his house (to be)
27. 15 if he that sanctified it will redeem his ho.
27. 16 if a man shall sanctify unto the LORD (so.
27. 17 If he sanctify his field from the year of J.
27. 18 But if he sanctify his field after the jubi.
27. 19 if he that sanctified the field will in any
27. 22 sanctify unto the LORD a field which he
27. 26 no man shall sanctify it: whether (it be)
Num. 8. 17 all the first born..I sanctified them for
20. 12 Because ye believed me not, to sanctify
27. 14 sanctify me at the water before their eyes
Deut15. 19 thou shalt sanctify unto the LORD thy G.
1 Ch.23. 13 should sanctify the most holy things, he
2 Ch. 7. 16 For now have I chosen and sanctified this
7. 20 house, which I have sanctified for my na.
20. 19 have we prepared and sanctified, and, be.
30. 8 which he hath sanctified for ever; and se.
30. 17 had the charge..to sanctify (them) unto
Neh. 12. 47 sanctified..and the Levites sanctified (th.)
Isa. 8. 13 Sanctify the LORD of hosts himself; and
29. 23 they shall sanctify my name, and sanctify
Jer. 1. 5 before thou camest forth..I sanctified th.

3. *To separate or set self apart,* קָדַשׁ *qadesh,* 7.

Exod19. 22 sanctify themselves, lest the LORD break
Lev. 11. 44 therefore sanctify yourselves, and ye shall
20. 7 Sanctify yourselves therefore, and be ye
Num11. 18 Sanctify yourselves against to morrow, and
Josh. 3. 5 Sanctify yourselves: for to morrow the L.
7. 13 Sanctify yourselves against to morrow, for
1 Sa. 16. 5 sanctify yourselves, and come with me to
1 Ch.15. 12 sanctify yourselves, (both) ye and your
15. 14 sanctified themselves to bring up the ark
2 Ch. 5. 11 the priests (that were) present were sanc.
29. 5 sanctify now yourselves..and carry forth
29. 15 sanctified themselves, and came, according
29. 34 until the (other) priests had sanctified th.
29. 34 more upright in heart to sanctify themsel.
30. 3 had not sanctified themselves sufficiently
30. 15 sanctified themselves, and brought in the
30. 24 great number of priests sanctified thems.
31. 18 in their set office they sanctified themse.
35. 6 So kill the passover, and sanctify yourse.
Isa. 66. 17 They that sanctify themselves, and purify
Eze. 38. 23 will I magnify myself, and sanctify mys.

4. *To set apart,* ἁγιάζω *hagiazō.*

Matt23. 17 gold, or the temple that sanctifieth the g.?
23. 19 gift, or the altar that sanctifieth the gift
John10. 36 of him, whom the Father hath sanctified
17. 17 Sanctify them through thy truth, thy word
17. 19 for their sakes I sanctify myself, that they
Eph. 5. 26 That he might sanctify and cleanse it with
1 Th. 5. 23 the very God of peace sanctify you wholly
Heb. 2. 11 For both he that sanctifieth and they who

Heb. 9. 13 sanctifieth to the purifying of the flesh
13. 12 might sanctify the people with his own bl.
1 Pe. 3. 15 But sanctify the Lord God in your hearts

SANCTUARY —

1. *Place set apart*, מִקְדָּשׁ *miqdash.*
Exod 15. 17 sanctuary..(which) thy hands have esta.
25. 8 let them make me a sanctuary; that I may
Lev. 12. 4 nor come into the sanctuary, until the da.
16. 33 make an atonement for the holy sanctuary
19. 30 keep my sabbaths, and reverence my san.
20. 3 defile my sanctuary, and to profane my ho.
21. 12 sanctuary, nor profane the sanctuary of
21. 23 that he profane not my sanctuaries: for I
26. 2 keep my sabbaths, and reverence my san.
26. 31 bring your sanctuaries unto desolation
Num. 3. 38 keeping the charge of the sanctuary for the
10. 21 Kohathites set forward, bearing the san.
18. 1 shall bear the iniquity of the sanctuary
19. 20 because he hath defiled the sanctuary of
Josh 24. 26 oak that (was) by the sanctuary of the L.
1 Ch. 22. 19 build ye the sanctuary of the LORD God, to
28. 10 chosen thee to build an house for the sa.
2 Ch. 20. 8 dwelt therein, and have built thee a san.
26. 18 go out of the sanctuary; for thou hast tr.
29. 21 for the sanctuary, and for Judah. And he
30. 8 enter into his sanctuary, which he hath s.
36. 17 the sword in the house of their sanctuary
Neh. 10. 39 where (are) the vessels of the sanctuary
Psa. 73. 17 Until I went into the sanctuary of God
74. 7 They have cast fire into thy sanctuary, they
78. 69 he built his sanctuary like high (palaces)
96. 6 strength and beauty (are) in his sanctuary
Isa. 8. 14 he shall be for a sanctuary; but for a sto.
16. 12 he shall come to his sanctuary to pray, but
60. 13 to beautify the place of my sanctuary, and
63. 18 adversaries have trodden down thy sanc.
Jer. 17. 12 high throne..(is) the place of our sanctu.
51. 51 strangers are come into the sanctuaries of
Lam. 1. 10 heathen entered into her sanctuary, whom
2. 7 he hath abhorred his sanctuary, he hath
2. 20 prophet be slain in the sanctuary of the
Eze. 5. 11 because thou hast defiled my sanctuary
8. 6 I should go far off from my sanctuary? B.
9. 6 begin at my sanctuary. Then they began
11. 16 yet will I be unto them as a little sanctu.
23. 38 have defiled my sanctuary in the same day
23. 39 came the same day into my sanctuary to
24. 21 I will profane my sanctuary, the excelle.
25. 3 against my sanctuary, when it was profa.
28. 18 Thou hast defiled thy sanctuaries by the
37. 26 will set my sanctuary in the midst of them
37. 28 when my sanctuary shall be in the midst
43. 21 place of the house, without the sanctuary
44. 1 way of the gate of the outward sanctuary
44. 5 with every going forth of the sanctuary
44. 7 to be in my sanctuary, to pollute it, (even)
44. 8 set keepers of my charge in my sanctuary
44. 9 shall enter into my sanctuary, of any str.
44. 11 Yet they shall be ministers in my sanctu.
44. 15 that kept the charge of my sanctuary when
44. 16 They shall enter into my sanctuary, and
45. 3 in it shall be the sanctuary (and) the most
45. 4 for the priests the ministers of the sanct.
45. 4 houses, and an holy place for the sanctu.
45. 18 without blemish, and cleanse the sanctu.
47. 12 waters they issued out of the sanctuary
48. 8 and the sanctuary shall be in the midst of
48. 10, 21 the sanctuary..in the midst thereof
Dan. 8. 11 the place of his sanctuary was cast down
9. 17 cause thy face to shine upon thy sanctu.
11. 31 they shall pollute the sanctuary of stren.
Amos 7. 9 the sanctuaries of Israel shall be laid wa.

2. *Separation*, קֹדֶשׁ *qodesh.*
Exod 30. 13, 24 shekel after the shekel of the sanctuary
36. 1 of work for the service of the sanctuary
36. 3 the work of the service of the sanctuary
36. 4 that wrought all the work of the sanctu.
36. 6 more work for the offering of the sanctu.
38. 24, 25, 26 after the shekel of the sanctuary
38. 27 were cast the sockets of the sanctuary
Lev. 4. 6 sprinkle..before the veil of the sanctuary
5. 15 of silver, after the shekel of the sanctuary
10. 4 carry your brethren from..the sanctuary
27. 3 of silver, after the shekel of the sanctuary
27. 25 according to the shekel of the sanctuary
Num. 3. 28 keeping the charge of the sanctuary
3. 31 the vessels of the sanctuary wherewith
3. 32 them that keep the charge of the sanctuary
3. 47, 50 after the shekel of the sanctuary
4. 12 wherewith they minister in the sanctuary
4. 15 have made an end of covering the sanct.
4. 15 and all the vessels of the sanctuary, as
4. 16 of all that therein (is), in the sanctuary
7. 9 the service of the sanctuary belonging un.
7. 13 shekels, after the shekel of the sanctuary
[So in verse 19, 25, 31, 37, 43, 49, 55, 61, 67, 73, 79, 85, 86.]
8. 19 children of Israel come..unto the sanctua.
18. 3 come nigh the vessels of the sanctuary
18. 5 ye shall keep the charge of the sanctuary
18. 16 after the shekel of the sanctuary, which
1 Ch. 9. 29 the instruments of the sanctuary, and the
24. 5 the governors of the sanctuary, and gove.
2 Ch. 30. 19 according to the purification of the sanc.
Psa. 20. 2 Send thee help from the sanctuary, and
63. 2 so (as) I have seen thee in the sanctuary
68. 24 the goings of my God..in the sanctuary
74. 3 enemy hath done wickedly in the sanctu.
77. 13 Thy way, O God, (is) in the sanctuary: who
78. 54 to the border of his sanctuary, (even to)
102. 19 down from the height of his sanctuary
Psa. 114. 2 Judah was his sanctuary, (and) Israel his
134. 2 Lift up your hands (in) the sanctuary, and
150. 1 Praise God in his sanctuary: praise him
Isa. 43. 28 profaned the princes of the sanctuary, and
Lam. 4. 1 the stones of the sanctuary are poured out
Eze. 41. 21 (were) squared, (and) the face of the sanc.
41. 23 the temple and the sanctuary had two do.
42. 20 a separation between the sanctuary and
44. 27 in the day that he goeth into the sanctu.
44. 27 to minister in the sanctuary, he shall offer
45. 2 there shall be for the sanctuary five hun.
Dan. 8. 13 to give both the sanctuary and the host
8. 14 then shall the sanctuary be cleansed
9. 26 shall destroy the city and the sanctuary
Zeph. 3. 4 her priests have polluted the sanctuary

3. *Place set apart*, ἅγιον *hagion.*
Heb. 8. 2 A minister of the sanctuary, and of the
9. 1 also ordinances..and a worldly sanctuary
9. 2 the first..which is called [the sanctuary]
13. 11 whose blood is brought into the sanctuary

SAND —

1. *Sand*, חוֹל *chol.*
Gen. 22. 17 as the sand which (is) upon the sea shore
32. 12 make thy seed as the sand of the sea, which
41. 49 Joseph gathered corn as the sand of the
Exod. 2. 12 slew the Egyptian, and hid him in the sand
Deut 33. 19 shall suck..(of) treasures..hid in the sand
Josh 11. 4 as the sand that (is) upon the sea shore in
Judg. 7. 12 as the sand by the sea side for multitude
1 Sa. 13. 5 people as the sand which (is) on the sea
2 Sa. 17. 11 as the sand that is by the sea shore for
1 Ki. 4. 20 as the sand which (is) by the sea in multi.
4. 29 even as the sand that (is) on the sea shore
Job 6. 3 it would be heavier than the sand of the
29. 18 and I shall multiply (my) days as the sand
Psa. 78. 27 feathered fowls like as the sand of the sea
139. 18 they are more in number than the sand
Prov. 27. 3 A stone (is) heavy, and the sand weighty
Isa. 10. 22 though thy people Israel be as the sand
48. 19 Thy seed also had been as the sand, and
Jer. 5. 22 which have placed the sand (for) the bo.
15. 8 are increased to me above the sand of the
33. 22 neither the sand of the sea measured
Hos. 1. 10 children of Israel shall be as the sand of
Hab. 1. 9 they shall gather captivity as the sand

2. *Sand*, ἄμμος *ammos.*
Matt. 7. 26 man, which built his house upon the sand
Rom. 9. 27 children of Israel be as the sand of the sea
Heb. 11. 12 and as the sand which is by the sea shore
Rev. 13. 1 I stood upon the sand of the sea, and saw
20. 8 the number of whom (is) as the sand of the

SANDAL —

Sandal, σανδάλιον *sandalion.*
Mark 6. 9 (be) shod with sandals; and not put on two
Acts 12. 8 bind on thy sandals. And so he did And

SAN-SAN'-NAH, סַנְסַנָּה *instruction.*
A city in S. of Judah, near Madmannah. See *Kirjath-senneh.*
Josh. 15. 31 And Ziklag, and Madmannah, and S.

SAPH, סַף *preserver.*
A descendant of Rapha the progenitor of the giants or Rephaim; called *Sippai* in 1 Ch. 20. 4. B.C. 1048.
2 Sa. 21. 18 then Sibbechai the Hushathite slew S., w.

SA'-PHIR, שָׁפִיר *beautiful, thorny.* See *Shamir.*
A city in Ephraim or Judah, now *el-Savafir.*
Mic. 1. 11 Pass ye away, thou inhabitant of S., hav.

SAP-PHI'-RA, Σαπφείρη *sapphire.*
Wife of Ananias, who joined with him in trying to impose on the church, and was subjected to the same punishment.
Acts 5. 1 a certain man..with S. his wife, sold a po.

SAPPHIRE —

1. *Sapphire*, סַפִּיר *sappir.*
Exod 24. 10 as it were a paved work of a sapphire stone
28. 18 an emerald, a sapphire, and a diamond
39. 11 an emerald, a sapphire, and a diamond
Job 28. 6 The stones of it (are) the place of sapphi.
28. 16 with the precious onyx, or the sapphire
Song 5. 14 (is as) bright ivory overlaid (with) sapphires
Isa. 54. 11 and lay thy foundations with sapphires
Lam. 4. 7 Nazarites..their polishing (was) of sap.
Eze. 1. 26 as the appearance of a sapphire stone
10. 1 over them as it were a sapphire stone
28. 13 the sapphire, the emerald, and the car.

2. *Sapphire*, σάπφειρος *sappheiros.*
Rev. 21. 19 the second, sapphire, the third, a chal.

SA'-RAH, שָׂרָה Σάῤῥα *princess.*
1. The later name of Sarai wife of Abram, who bare Isaac when above ninety years of age, and died at Kirjath-arba or Hebron, aged 127 years, and was buried at Machpelah. B.C. 1950. In Heb. 11. 11 Sara.
Gen. 17. 15 thou shalt not call her name Sarai, but S.
17. 17 shall S., that is ninety years old, bear?
17. 19 S. thy wife shall bear thee a son indeed
17. 21 Isaac, which S. shall bear unto thee at
18. 6 Abraham hastened into the tent unto S.
18. 9 they said unto him, Where (is) S. thy wi.?
18. 10 S. thy wife shall have a son. And S. heard
18. 11 Abraham and S. (were) old..well stricken
18. 11 it ceased to be with S. after the manner
18. 12 Therefore S. laughed within herself, say.
18. 13 And the LORD said..Wherefore did S. la.
18. 14 I will return unto thee..and S. shall have
18. 15 Then S. denied, saying, I laughed not
Gen. 20. 2 Abraham said of S. his wife, She (is) my
20. 2 Abimelech king of Gerar sent, and took S
20. 14 And Abimelech..restored him S. his wife
20. 16 unto S. he said, Behold, I have given thy
20. 18 closed up all the wombs..because of S.
21. 1 the LORD visited S...the LORD did unto S.
21. 2 For S. conceived, and bare Abraham a son
21. 3 Abraham called..his son..whom S. bare
21. 6 And S. said, God hath made me to laugh
21. 7 that S. should have given children suck?
21. 9 S. saw the son of Hagar the Egyptian, wh.
21. 12 in all that S. hath said unto thee, hearken
23. 1 S. was an hundred and seven and twenty
23. 1 (these were) the years of the life of S.
23. 2 S. died in Kirjath-arba; the same (is) H.
23. 2 Abraham came to mourn for S., and to we.
23. 19 Abraham buried S. his wife in the cave of
24. 36 S. my master's wife bare a son to my ma.
24. 67 Isaac brought her into his mother S.'s tent
25. 10 there was Abraham buried, and S. his w.
25. 12 whom Hagar the Egyptian, S.'s handmaid
49. 31 There they buried Abraham and S. his wi.
Isa. 51. 2 Look unto Abraha. your father, and unto S.
Rom. 4. 19 considered not..the deadness of S.'s womb
9. 9 At this time will I come, and S. shall have
Heb. 11. 11 S. herself received strength to conceive
1 Pe. 3. 6 Even as S. obeyed Abraham, calling him
2. A daughter of Asher. B.C. 1690. *See* Serah.
Num 26. 46 the name of the daughter of Asher (was) S.

SA'-RAI, שָׂרַי *Jah is prince.*
The original name of Sarah, wife of Abraham, and also his half-sister on his father Terah's side. (Gen. 20. 12).
Gen. 11. 29 the name of Abram's wife (was) S.; and
11. 30 But S. was barren; she (had) no child
11. 31 Terah took Abram his son..and S. his da.
12. 5 Abram took S. his wife, and Lot his brot.
12. 11 it came to pass..that he said unto S. his
12. 17 the LORD plagued Pharaoh..because of S.
16. 1 Now S., Abram's wife, bare him no children
16. 2 S. said unto Abram, Behold now, the Lo.
16. 2 And Abram hearkened to the voice of S.
16. 3 S., Abram's wife, took Hagar her maid, the
16. 5 S. said unto Abram, My wrong (be) upon
16. 6 Abram said unto S., Behold, thy maid (is)
16. 6 when S. dealt hardly with her, she fled
16. 8 he said, Hagar, S.'s maid, whence camest
16. 8 I flee from the face of my mistress S.
17. 15 S. thy wife, thou shalt not call her name S.

SA'-RAPH, שָׂרָף *burning.*
A descendant of Shelah son of Judah, who had dominion in Moab. B.C. 1300.
1 Ch. 4. 22 Joash, and S., who had the dominion in

SARDINE, SARDIUS —

1. *Ruby*, אֹדֶם *odem.*
Exod 28. 17 (the first) row (shall be) a sardius, a topaz
39. 10 (the first) row (was) a sardius, a topaz, and
Eze. 28. 13 the sardius, topaz, and the diamond, the

2. *Sardine*, σάρδινος *sardinos.*
Rev. 4. 3 like a jasper and a sardine stone: and

3. *Sardine*, σάρδιον, σάρδιος *sardion, sardios.*
Rev. 21. 20 the sixth, sardius; the seventh, chrysop.

SAR-DIS, Σάρδεις.
The capital of *Lydia* in Asia Minor, which had Smyrna on the W., Thyatira on the N., and Philadelphia on the E., at the foot of Mount Tmolus on the river Pactolus; and now called *Sest-Kalessi*; it was taken by the Cimmerians about 635 B.C; in 617 they were expelled; in 584 it was taken by the Persians; in 504 by the Ionians, assisted by the Athenians; in 395 the Greeks defeated the Persians in its vicinity; in 334 it surrendered to Alexander; in 283 it was taken by Seleucus; in 214 Antiochus the Great seized it; in 189 it was given up to the Romans; in A.D. 14-37 it was destroyed by an earthquake and rebuilt by Tiberius; it was taken by the Turks in the 11th century, and again in the 14th; it was also taken by Tamerlane.
Rev. 1. 11 send (it)..unto S., and unto Philadelphia
3. 1 unto the angel of the church in S. write
3. 4 Thou hast a few names even in S. which

SAR-DITES, הַסַּרְדִּי *the Sardite.*
The family of Sered, a son of Zebulun. B.C. 1700.
Num 26. 26 of Sered, the family of the S.: of Elon, the

SARDONYX —

Sardonyx, σαρδόνυξ *sardonux.*
Rev. 21. 20 The fifth sardonyx, the sixth, sardius, the

SA-REP'-TA, Σάρεπτα. See *Zarephath.*
A city midway between Tyre and Sidon, now called *Sarfend* or *Surafend.*
Luke 4. 26 unto none of them was Elias sent, save..S.

SAR-GON, סַרְגוֹן.
A king of Assyria, B.C. 718-715, successor of Shalmanezar, and predecessor of Sennacherib, and whose general was *Tartan.*
Isa. 20. 1 when S. the king of Assyria sent him, and

SA'-RID, שָׂרִיד *refuge.*
A city in Zebulun or Issachar.
Josh 19. 10 the border of their inheritance was unto S.
19. 12 And turned from S. eastward toward the

SA'-RON, Σάρων.
The sea coast between Joppa and Cæsarea.
Acts 9. 35 all that dwelt in Lydda and S. saw him

SAR-SE'-CHIM, שַׂרְסְכִים *chief of the eunuchs.*
A prince of Babylon when Nebuchadnezzar took Jerusalem, and who sat at the gate. B.C. 588.
Jer. 39. 3 Samgar-nebo, S., Rabsaris, Nergal-shar.

SA'-RUCH, Σαρούχ, Σερούχ. See *Serug.*
Father of Nachor and son of Ragau, an ancestor of Jesus. B.C. 2180.
Luke 3. 35 Which was (the son) of S., which was (the

SA'-TAN, שָׂטָן הַשָּׂטָן, Σατανᾶς, Σατᾶν *the hater, accuser.*
1. An adversary of David. B.C. 1017.
1 Ch.21. 1 S. stood up against Israel, and provoked
2. An adversary, opposing spirit.
Job 1. 6 sons of God came..and S. came also among
1. 7 the LORD said unto S., Whence comest th.?
1. 7, 9 S. answered the LORD, and said
1. 8 the LORD said unto S., Hast thou consid.
1. 12 the LORD said unto S., Behold, all that
1. 12 S. went forth from the presence of the L.
2. 1 S. came also among them to present him
2. 2 LORD said unto S., From whence comest
2. 2 S. answered the LORD, and said, From
2. 3 the LORD said unto S., Hast thou con.v.4.
2. 6 LORD said unto S., Behold, he (is) in thine
2. 7 So went S. forth from the presence of the
Psa 109. 6 and let S. stand at his right hand
Zech. 3. 1 S. standing at his right hand to resist him
3. 2 LORD said unto S., The LORD rebuke thee
Matt 4. 10 Then saith Jesus unto him, Get. hence, S.
12. 26 if S. cast out S., he is divided against him
16. 23 Get thee behind me, S.: thou art an off
Mark 1. 13 was there in the wilderness..tempted of S.
3. 23 And he..said..How can S. cast out S.?
3. 26 if S. rise up against himself..he cannot
4. 15 when they have heard, S. cometh immed.
8. 33 he rebuked Peter..Get thee behind me, S.
Luke 4. 8 [And Jesus..said Get thee behind me, S.]
10. 18 I beheld S. as lightning fall from heaven
11. 18 If S. also be divided against himself, how
13. 16 whom S. hath bound, lo, these eighteen
22. 3 Then entered S. into Judas surnamed I.
22. 31 Simon, behold, S. hath desired (to have)
John 13. 27 And after the sop S. entered into him
Acts 5. 3 Ananias, why hath S. filled thine heart
26. 18 to turn..(from) the power of S. unto God
Rom 16. 20 the God of peace shall bruise S. under your
1 Co. 5. 5 To deliver such an one unto S. for the de.
7. 5 that S. tempt you not for your incontin.
2 Co. 2. 11 Lest S. should get an advantage of us
11. 14 S. himself is transformed into an angel
12. 7 the messenger of S. to buffet me, lest I
1 Th. 2. 18 we would have come..but S. hindered us
2 Th. 2. 9 whose coming is after the working of S.
1 Ti. 1. 20 whom I have delivered unto S., that they
5. 15 For some are already turned aside after S.
Rev. 2. 9 and are not, but (are) the synagogue of S.
2. 13 where thou dwellest, (even) where Satan's
2. 13 who was slain among you, where S. dwe.
2. 24 which have not known the depths of S.
3. 9 I will make them of the synagogue of S.
12. 9 and S., which deceiveth the whole world
20. 2 he laid hold on the dragon..S., and bound
20. 7 And..S. shall be loosed out of his prison

SATIATE, to —
1. *To fill, water, satisfy,* רָוָה *ravah,* 3.
Jer. 31. 14 I will satiate the soul of the priests with
2. *To fill, water, satisfy,* רָוָה *ravah,* 5.
Jer. 31. 25 I have satiated the weary soul, and I have

SATIATE, to be—
To be satisfied, satiated, full, שָׂבֵעַ *sabea.*
Jer. 46. 10 it shall be satiate and made drunk with

SATISFACTION —
Atonement, covering, כֹּפֶר *kopher.*
Num 35. 31 ye shall take no satisfaction for the life
35. 32 ye shall take no satisfaction for him that

SATISFIED (abundantly, with), to be —
1. *To be full,* מָלֵא *male.*
Exod 15. 9 my lust shall be satisfied upon them; I
2. *To be satisfied, watered,* רָוָה *ravah.*
Psa. 36. 8 They shall be abundantly satisfied with
3. *To be satisfied, satiated,* שָׂבֵעַ *sabea.*
Lev. 26. 26 and ye shall eat, and not be satisfied
Deut 14. 29 shall come, and shall eat and be satisfied
Job 19. 22 Why do ye persecute..and are not satis. w.
27. 14 his offspring shall not be satisfied with
31. 31 Oh that we had of his flesh! we cannot be s.
Psa. 17. 15 I shall be satisfied, when I awake, with
22. 26 The meek shall eat and be satisfied: they
37. 19 in the days of famine they shall be satis
59. 15 Let them..grudge if they be not satisfied
63. 5 My soul shall be satisfied as (with) marrow
65. 4 we shall be satisfied with the goodness of
104. 13 the earth is satisfied with the fruit of thy
Prov 12. 11 He that tilleth his land shall be satisfied
12. 14 A man shall be satisfied with good by the
18. 20 A man's belly shall be satisfied with the
20. 13 open thine eyes, (and) thou shalt be sat. w.
27. 20 so the eyes of man are never satisfied
30. 15 There are three (things that) are never sa.
Eccl. 1. 8 the eye is not satisfied with seeing, nor
4. 8 neither is his eye satisfied with riches
5. 10 He that loveth silver shall not be satis w.
Isa. 9. 20 shall eat..and they shall not be satisfied
44. 16 he roasteth roast, and is satisfied: yea
53. 11 He shall see..(and) shall be satisfied: by
Isa. 66. 11 That ye may suck, and be satisfied with
Jer. 31. 14 people shall be satisfied with my goodness
50. 10 all that spoil her shall be satisfied, saith
50. 19 his soul shall be satisfied upon mount E.
Lam. 5. 6 We have given the hand..to be satisfied w.
Eze. 16. 28 played the harlot..yet couldest not be sa.
16. 29 and yet thou wast not satisfied herewith
Joel 2. 19 send you corn..and ye shall be satisfied
2. 26 ye shall eat in plenty, and be satisfied
Amos 4. 8 to drink water; but they were not satisfi.
Mic 6. 14 Thou shalt eat, but not be satisfied; and
Hab. 2. 5 (is) as death, and cannot be satisfied, but
4. *Satisfied, satiated,* שָׂבֵעַ *sabea.*
Deut 33. 23 O Naphtali, satisfied with favour, and
Prov 19. 23 and (he that hath it) shall abide satisfied

SATISFY (with), to —
1. *To fill,* מָלֵא *male,* 3.
Prov. 6. 30 if he steal to satisfy his soul when he is
2. *To water, satiate,* רָוָה *ravah,* 3.
Prov. 5. 19 let her breasts satisfy thee at all times
3. *To satisfy, satiate,* שָׂבֵעַ *sabea,* 3.
Psa. 90 14 O satisfy us early with thy mercy; that
Eze. 7. 19 they shall not satisfy their souls, neither
4. *To (cause to) satisfy,* שָׂבֵעַ *sabea,* 5.
Job 38. 27 To satisfy the desolate and waste (ground)
Psa. 81. 16 with honey..should I have satisfied thee
91. 16 With long life will I satisfy him, and sh.
103. 5 Who satisfieth thy mouth with good (th.)
105. 40 satisfied them with the bread of heaven
107. 9 he satisfieth the longing soul, and filleth
132. 15 I will abundantly bless..I will satisfy
145. 16 and satisfiest the desire of every living th.
Isa. 58. 10 (if) thou..satisfy the afflicted soul; then
58. 11 satisfy thy soul in drought, and make fat
5. *Satiety, satisfaction,* שָׂבְעָה *sobah.*
Isa. 55. 2 your labour for (that which) satisfieth not
6. *To feed, fill, satisfy,* χορτάζω *chortazō.*
Mark 8. 4 whence can a man satisfy these (men) w.

SATISFYING —
1. *Satiety, satisfaction,* שֹׂבַע *soba.*
Prov 13. 25 The righteous eateth to the satisfying of
2. *Fulness,* πλησμονή *plēsmonē.*
Col. 2. 23 not in any honour to the satisfying of the

SATYR —
Hairy one, kid, goat, שָׂעִיר *sair.*
Isa. 13. 21 owls shall dwell there, and satyrs shall
34. 14 the satyr shall cry to his fellow; the sc.

SAUL, SHAUL, שָׁאוּל Σαούλ, Σαῦλος *asked.*
1. The sixth of the ancient kings of Edom, from Rehoboth on the Euphrates. B.C. 1490.
Gen. 36. 37 S. of Rehoboth..reigned in his stead
36. 38 S. died, and Baal-hanan..reigned in his st.
1 Ch. 1. 48 S. of Rehoboth by the river reigned in..s.
1. 49 when S. was dead, Baal-hanan..reigned
2. A Benjamite, the first king of Israel. B.C. 1096-56.
He was sent to seek his father's asses applied to Samuel, was anointed by him, filled with the spirit, chosen king, restricted in his powers, delivers Jabesh-gilead arms the people against the Philistines, defeats them, vows and sacrifices rashly, his success, left by Samuel, sends for David, tries to kill him, prophesies, pursues David, slays the priests of Nob, is spared by David in the cave, again at Hachilah, consults a witch at Endor, is slain at Gilboa with his three sons, was succeeded by David, seven of his sons given up to the Gibeonites, and hanged.
1 Sa 9. 2 And he had a son, whose name (was) S., a
9. 3 the asses of Kish, S.'s father were lost
9. 3 Kish said to S. his son..go seek the asses
9. 5 S. said to the servant that (was) with him
9. 7 Then said S. to his servant, But, behold
9. 8 the servant answered S. again, and said
9. 10 Then said S. to his servant, Well said; co.
9. 15 Now the LORD had told Samuel..before S.
9. 17 when Samuel saw S., the LORD said unto
9. 18 Then S. drew near to Samuel in the gate
9. 19 Samuel answered S., and said, I (am) the
9. 21 S. answered and said, (Am) not I a Benj.
9. 22 And Samuel took S. and his servant
9. 24 took up the shoulder..and set (it) before S.
9. 24 So S. did eat with Samuel that day
9. 25 (Samuel) communed with S. upon the top
9. 26 Samuel called S. to the top of the house
9. 26 S. arose, and they went out both of them
9. 27 Samuel said to S., Bid the servant pass on
10. 11, 12 (Is) S. also among the prophets?
10. 14 S.'s uncle said unto him and to his serva.
10. 15 S.'s uncle said, Tell me, I pray thee, what
10. 16 S. said unto his uncle, He told us plainly
10. 21 S. the son of Kish was taken: and when
10. 26 S. also went home to Gibeah; and there
11. 4 Then came the messengers to Gibeah of S.
11. 5 S. came after the herd out of the field
11. 5 S. said, What (aileth) the people that they
11. 6 the Spirit of God came upon S. when he
11. 7 Whosoever cometh not forth after S. and
11. 11 that S. put the people in three companies
11. 12 Who (is) he that said Shall S. reign over
11. 13 S. said, There shall not a man be put to
11. 15 there they made S. king before the LORD
11. 15 there S. and all the men of Israel rejoiced
13. 1 S. reigned one year; and when he had re.
13. 2 S. chose him three thousand (men) of Is.
13. 2 (whereof) two thousand were with S. in
13. 3 S. blew the trumpet throughout all the
1 Sa. 13. 4 S. had smitten a garrison of the Philistines
13. 4 the people were gathered together after S.
13. 7 As for S...all the people followed him tr.
13. 9 S. said, Bring hither a burnt offering to
13. 10 S. went out to meet him, that he might
13. 11 S. said, Because I saw that the people w.
13. 13 Samuel said to S., Thou hast done foolishly
13. 15 Saul numbered the people (that were) pr.
13. 16 S., and Jonathan..abode in Gibeah of B.
13. 22 the people that (were) with S. and Jona.
13. 22 with S. and with Jonathan his son was
14. 1 S. said unto the young man that bare his
14. 2 S. tarried in the uttermost part of Gibeah
14. 16 the watchmen of S. in Gibeah of Benjamin
14. 17 S. said unto the people that (were) with
14. 18 S. said unto Ahiah, Bring hither the ark
14. 19 it came to pass, when S. talked unto the
14. 19 S. said unto the priest, Withdraw thine
14. 20 S. and all the people..assembled thems.
14. 21 the Israelites that (were) with S. and Jo.
14. 24 for S. had adjured the people, saying, C.
14. 33 Then they told S., saying, Behold. the p.
14. 34 S. said, Disperse yourselves among the p.
14. 35 And S. built an altar unto the LORD
14. 36 S. said, Let us go down after the Philist.
14. 37 S. asked counsel of God, Shall I go down
14. 38 S. said, Draw ye near hither all the chief
14. 40 the people said unto S., Do what seemeth g.
14. 41 Therefore S. said unto the LORD God of
14. 41 S. and Jonathan were taken: but the pe.
14. 42 S. said, Cast (lots) between me and Jon.
14. 43 S. said to Jonathan, Tell me what thou
14. 44 S. answered, God do so and more also: for
14. 45 the people said unto S., Shall Jonathan
14. 46 S. went up from following the Philistines
14. 47 S. took the kingdom over Israel. and fou.
14. 49 Now the sons of S. were Jonathan, and
14. 50 the name of S.'s wife (was) Ahinoam, the
14. 50 captain..(was) Abner, the son of Ner, S.'s
14. 51 Kish (was) the father of S.; and Ner the
14. 52 And there was sore war..all the days of S.
14. 52 when S. saw any strong man..he took him
15. 1 Samuel also said unto S., The LORD sent
15. 4 S. gathered the people together, and num.
15. 5 S. came to a city of Amalek, and laid wai.
15. 6 S. said unto the Kenites, Go, depart, get
15. 7 S. smote the Amalekites from Havilah
15. 9 S. and the people spared Agag, and the
15. 11 It repenteth me that I have set up S. (to be)
15. 12 Samuel rose early to meet S. in the v. 12
15. 13 And Samuel came to S: and S. said unto him
15. 15 S. said, They have brought them from the
15. 16 Samuel said unto S., Stay, and I will tell
15. 20 S. said unto Samuel, Yea, I have obeyed
15. 24 S. said unto Samuel, I have sinned: for I
15. 26 Samuel said unto S., I will not return with
15. 31 So Samuel turned again after S.; and S.
15. 34 S. went up to his house in Gibeah of S.
15. 35 Samuel came no more to see S. until the day
15. 35 nevertheless Samuel mourned for S.: and
15. 35 the LORD repented that he had made S.
16. 1 How long wilt thou mourn for S., seeing
16. 2 How can I go? if S. hear (it), he will kill
16. 14 the Spirit of the LORD departed from S.
16. 15 S.'s servants said unto him, Behold now
16. 17 S. said unto his servants, Provide me now
16. 19 Wherefore S. sent messengers unto Jesse
16. 20 and sent (them) by David his son unto S.
16. 21 David came to S., and stood before him
16. 22 S. sent to Jesse, saying, Let David..stand
16. 23 when the (evil) spirit from God was upon S.
16. 23 S. was refreshed, and was well, and the
17. 2 S. and the men of Israel were gathered
17. 8 not I a Philistine, and ye servants to S.?
17. 11 When S. and all Israel heard those words
17. 12 man went..an old man in the days of S.
17. 13 the three eldest sons..followed S. to the
17. 14 youngest: and the three eldest followed S.
17. 15 David went and returned from S. to feed
17. 19 Now S., and they..(were) in the valley of
17. 31 words were heard..rehearsed..before S.
17. 32 David said to S., Let no man's heart fail
17. 33 S. said to David, Thou art not able to go
17. 34 David said unto S., Thy servant kept his
17. 37 S. said unto David, Go, and the LORD be
17. 38 S. armed David with his armour, and he
17. 39 David said unto S., I cannot go with th.
17. 55 when S. saw David go forth against the P.
17. 57 Abner took him..brought him before S.
17. 58 S. said to him, Whose son (art) thou. (th.)
18. 1 when he..made an end of speaking unto S.
18. 2 S. took him that day, and would let him
18. 5 David went out whithersoever S. sent him
18. 5 and S. set him over the men of war; and
18. 5 was accepted..in the sight of S.'s servants
18. 6 the women came out..to meet king S., wi.
18. 7 S. hath slain his thousands, and David his
18. 8 S. was very wroth, and the saying disple.
18. 9 S. eyed David from that day and forward
18. 10 that the evil spirit from God came upon S.
18. 10 and (there was) a javelin in S.'s hand
18. 11 S. cast the javelin; for he said, I will sm.
18. 12 S. was afraid of David, because the LORD
18. 12 was with him, and was departed from S.
18. 13 Therefore S. removed him from him, and
18. 15 when S. saw that he behaved himself very
18. 17 S. said to David, Behold my elder daugh.
18. 17 S. said, Let not mine hand be upon him
18. 18 David said unto S., Who (am) I? and wh.
18. 19 S.'s daughter, should have been given to D.
18. 20 And Michal S.'s daughter loved David
18. 20 and they told S., and the thing pleased him

1 Sa. 18. 21 S. said, I will give him her, that she may
18. 21 Wherefore S. said to David, Thou shalt
18. 22 S. commanded his servants..Commune
18. 23 S.'s servants spake those words in the ears
18. 24 the servants of S. told him, saying, On
18. 25 S. said, Thus shall ye say to David, The
18. 25 S. thought to make David fall by the hand
18. 27 S. gave him Michal his daughter to wife
18. 28 S. saw and knew that the LORD (was) with
18. 28 and (that) Michal, S.'s daughter, loved him
18. 29 And S. was yet the more afraid of David
18. 29 and S. became David's enemy continually
18. 30 more wisely than all the servants of S., so
19. 1 S. spake to Jonathan his son, and to all
19. 2 Jonathan, S.'s son, delighted much in David
19. 2 S. my father seeketh to kill thee: now
19. 4 Jonathan spake good of David unto S., and
19. 6 S. hearkened unto the voice of Jonathan
19. 6 S. sware, (As) the LORD liveth, he shall
19. 7 Jonathan brought David to S., and he was
19. 9 the evil spirit from the LORD was upon S.
19. 10 S. sought to smite David even to the wall
19. 10 but he slipped away out of S.'s presence
19. 11 S. also sent messengers unto David's ho.
19. 14 when S. sent messengers to take David
19. 15 S. sent the messengers (again) to see Da.
19. 17 S. said unto Michal, Why hast thou dec.
19. 17 Michal answered S., He said unto me, Let
19. 18 David..told him all that S. had done to
19. 19 it was told S., saying, Behold, David (is)
19. 20 S. sent messengers to take David: and
19. 20 spirit of God..upon the messengers of S.
19. 21 when it was told S., he sent other messe.
19. 21 S. sent messengers again the third time
19. 24 Wherefore they say, (Is) S. also among
20. 25 Abner sat by S.'s side, and David's place
20. 26 Nevertheless S. spake not anything that
20. 27 S. said unto Jonathan his son, Wherefore
20. 28 Jonathan answered S., David earnestly as.
20. 30 S.'s anger was kindled against Jonathan
20. 32 Jonathan answered S. his father, and said
20. 33 And S. cast a javelin at him to smite him
21. 7 Now a certain man of the servants of S.
21. 7 the chiefest of the herdmen that..to S.
21. 10 arose, and fled that day for fear of S.
21. 11 S. hath slain his thousands, and David his
22. 6 When S. heard that David was discovered
22. 6 now S. abode in Gibeah under a tree in R.
22. 7 S. said unto his servants that stood about
22. 9 Doeg..which..set over the servants of S.
22. 12 And S. said, Hear now, thou son of Ahitub
22. 13 S. said unto him, Why have ye conspired
22. 21 Abiathar showed David that S. had slain
22. 22 I knew..that day. he would surely tell S.
23. 7 it was told S. that David was come to
23. 7 S. said, God hath delivered him into mine
23. 8 S. called all the people together to war
23. 9 David knew that S. secretly practised m.
23. 10 thy servant hath certainly heard that S.
23. 11 will S. come down, as thy servant hath
23. 12 Will the men..deliver..into..hand of S.?
23. 13 it was told S. that David was escaped from
23. 14 S. sought him every day; but God delive
23. 15 D. saw that S. was come out to seek his
23. 16 Jonathan, S.'s son, arose, and went to Da.
23. 17 for the hand of S. my father shall not find
23. 17 and that also S. my father knoweth
23. 19 Then came up the Ziphites to S. to Gib.
23. 21 S. said, Blessed (be) ye of the LORD, for
23. 24 they arose, and went to Ziph before S.
23. 25 S. also and his men went to seek (him)
23. 25 And when S. heard..he pursued after D.
23. 26 S. went on this side of the mountain, and
23. 26 David made haste..get away for fear of S.
23. 26 for S. and his men compassed David and
23. 27 there came a messenger unto S., saying
23. 28 S. returned from pursuing after David
24. 1 when S. was returned from following the
24. 2 S. took three thousand chosen men out of
24. 3 a cave: and S. went in to cover his feet
24. 4 David arose, and cut off the skirt of S.'s
24. 5 heart smote him, because he..cut off S.'s
24. 7 David..suffered them..to rise against S.
24. 7 S. rose up out of the cave, and went on
24. 8 David also arose afterward..cried after S.
24. 8 when S. looked behind him, David stoop.
24. 9 David said to S., Wherefore hearest thou
24. 16 David..made an end of speaking..unto S.
24. 16 S. said, (Is) this thy voice..David? And S.
24. 22 And David sware unto S. And S. went ho.
25. 44 S. had given Michal his daughter..to P.
26. 1 the Ziphites came unto S. to Gibeah, say.
26. 2 S. arose, and went down to the wildern.
26. 3 S. pitched in the hill of Hachilah, which
26. 3 he saw that S. came after him into the w.
26. 4 David..understood that S. was come in
26. 5 David..came to the place where S. had
26. 5 and David beheld the place where S. lay
26. 5 S. lay in the trench, and the people pitc.
26. 6 Who will go down with me to S. to the
26. 7 behold, S. lay sleeping within the trench
26. 12 David took..the cruse of water from S.'s
26. 17 S. knew David's voice, and said, (Is) this
26. 21 Then said S., I have sinned: return, my
26. 25 S. said to David, Blessed (be) thou, my
26. 25 David went on his way, and S. returned
27. 1 I shall..perish one day by the hand of S.
27. 1 S. shall despair of me, to seek me any mo.
27. 4 it was told S. that David was fled to Gath
28. 3 S. had put away those that had familiar
28. 4 S. gathered all Israel together, and they
28. 5 when S. saw the host of the Philistines
1 Sa. 28. 6 when S. enquired of the LORD, the LORD
28. 7 Then said S. unto his servants, Seek me
28. 8 S. disguised himself, and put on other ra.
28. 9 Behold, thou knowest what S. hath done
28. 10 And S. sware to her by the LORD, saying
28. 12 and the woman spake to S...thou (art) S.
28. 13 the woman said unto S., I saw gods asce.
28. 14 S. preceived that it (was) Samuel, and he
28. 15 Samuel said to S., Why hast thou disquie.
28. 15 S. answered, I am sore distressed; for the
28. 20 S. fell straightway all along on the earth
28. 21 the woman came unto S., and saw that
28. 25 she brought (it) before S., and before his
29. 3 (Is) not this David, the servant of S. the
29. 5 S. slew his thousands, and David his ten
31. 2 And the Philistines followed hard upon S.
31. 2 Philistines slew Jonathan..Abinadab..S.'s
31. 3 the battle went sore against S., and the
31. 4 Then said S. unto his armour bearer, Draw
31. 4 Therefore S. took a sword, and fell upon
31. 5 when his armour bearer saw that S. was
31. 6 S. died, and his three sons, and his armour
31. 7 the men..saw..that S. and his sons were
31. 8 they found S. and his three sons fallen in
31. 11 that which the Philistines had done to S.
31. 12 the valiant men..took the body of S. and
2 Sa. 1. 1 Now it came to pass after the death of S.
1. 2 a man came out of the camp from S., with
1. 4 and S. and Jonathan his son are dead also
1. 5 How knowest thou that S. and Jonathan
1. 6 S. leaned upon his spear; and, lo, the ch.
1. 12 mourned..and fasted until even, for S.
1. 17 David lamented..over S. and over Jon.
1. 21 shield..vilely cast away, the shield of S.
1. 22 and the sword of S. returned not empty
1. 23 S. and Jonathan..lovely and pleasant in
1. 24 Ye daughters of Israel, weep over S., who
2. 4 the men of Jabesh-gilead..that buried S.
2. 5 ye have showed this kindness..unto S., and
2. 7 for your master S. is dead, and also the
2. 8 Abner the son of Ner, captain of S.'s host
2. 8 took Ish-bosheth the son of S., and brought
2. 10 S.'s son (was) forty years old when he be.
2. 12 the servants of Ish-bosheth the son of S.
2. 15 (pertained) to Ish-bosheth the son of S.
3. 1 there was a..war between the house of S.
3. 1 and the house of S. waxed weaker and
3. 6 there was war between the house of S.
3. 6 A. made himself strong for the house of S.
3. 7 S. had a concubine, whose name (was) R.
3. 8 I..show kindness..unto the house of S.
3. 10 translate the kingdom from..house of S.
3. 13 except thou first bring Michal, S.'s daug.
3. 14 David sent messengers to Ish-bosheth, S.'s
4. 1 when S.'s son heard that Abner was dead
4. 2 S.'s son had two men (that were) captains
4. 4 S.'s son, had a son (that was) lame of (his)
4. 4 five years old when the tidings came of S.
4. 8 Behold the head of Ish-bosheth..son of S.
4. 8 LORD hath avenged my lord..this day of S.
4. 10 When one told me, saying, Behold, S. is
5. 2 Also in time past, when S. was king over
6. 16 Michal, S.'s daughter, looked through a wi.
6. 20 Michal the daughter of S. came out to me.
6. 23 Therefore Michal the daughter of S. had
7. 15 as I took (it) from S., whom I put away
9. 1 Is there..any that is left of the house of S.
9. 2 And (there was) of the house of S. a serv.
9. 3 (Is) there not yet any of the house of S.
9. 6 Mephibosheth..son of Jonathan..son of S.
9. 7 will restore thee all the land of S. thy fa.
9. 9 Then the king called to Ziba, S.'s servant
9. 9 I have given..all that pertained to S. and
12. 7 and I delivered thee out of the hand of S.
16. 5 thence came out a man..of the house of S.
16. 8 hath returned upon thee..the blood..of S.
19. 17 and Ziba, the servant of the house of S.
19. 24 Mephibosheth the son of S. came down
21. 1 (It is) for S., and for (his) bloody house
21. 2 S. sought to slay them in his zeal to the
21. 4 We will have no silver nor gold of S., nor
21. 6 hang them up unto..LORD in Gibeah of S.
21. 7 spared..the son of Jonathan, the son of S.
21. 7 (was)..between David and..the son of S.
21. 8 two sons of Rizpah..whom she bare unto S.
21. 8 the five sons of Michal the daughter of S.
21. 11 what Rizpah..the concubine of S., had
21. 12 And David went and took the bones of S.
21. 12 when the Philistines had slain S. in Gil.
21. 13 he brought up from thence the bones of S.
21. 14 the bones of S...buried they in..Benjam.
22. 1 LORD..delivered him..out of the hand of S.
1 Ch. 5. 10 in the days of S. they made war with the
8. 33 Ner begat Kish, and Kish begat S., and S.
9. 39 Kish begat S.; and S. begat Jonathan, and S.
10. 2 And the Philistines followed hard after S.
10. 2 and the Philistines slew..the sons of S.
10. 3 the battle went sore against S., and the
10. 4 Then said S. to his armour bearer, Draw
10. 4 So S. took a sword, and fell upon it
10. 5 when his armour bearer saw that S. was
10. 6 So S. died..and all his house died togeth.
10. 7 the men..saw..that S. and his sons were
10. 8 they found S. and his sons fallen in mount
10. 11 all that the Philistines had done to S.
10. 12 They arose..and took away the body of S.
10. 13 S. died for his transgression which he co.
11. 2 in time past, even when S. was king, thou
12. 1 while he..kept himself close because of S.
12. 2 (even) of S.'s brethren of Benjamin
12. 19 he came with the Philistines against S to
12. 19 He will fall to his master S. to (the jeop.
1 Ch. 12. 23 ready armed..to turn the kingdom of S. to
12. 29 children of Benjamin, the kindred of S.
12. 29 them had kept the ward of the house of S.
13. 3 for we enquired not at it in the days of S.
15. 29 Michal the daughter of S...saw king Da.
26. 28 all that..S. the son of Kish..had dedica.
Psa. 18. *title.* LORD delivered..from the hand of S.
52. ,, Doeg the Edomite came and told S., and
54. ,, when the Ziphims came and said to S.
57. ,, when he fled from S. in the cave
59. ,, when S. sent, and they watched the ho.
Isa. 10. 29 Ramah is afraid; Gibeah of S. is fled
Acts 13. 21 and God gave unto them S. the son of Cis

3. The original name of PAUL, a native of Tarsus in Cilicia, first a persecutor, and afterwards an apostle of Jesus the Christ. See *Paul.* A.D. 3–70.

Acts 7. 58 at a young man's feet, whose name was S.
8. 1 And S. was consenting unto his death
8. 3 As for S., he made havock of the church
9. 1 And S., yet breathing out threatenings and
9. 4 saying unto him, S., S., why persecutest
9. 8 S. arose from the earth; and when his ey.
9. 11 in the house of Judas for (one) called S.
9. 17 Brother S., the Lord, (even) Jesus..hath
9. 19 Then was [S.] certain days with the disc.
9. 22 S. increased the more in strength, and
9. 24 But their laying await was known of S.
9. 26 when [S.] was come to Jerusalem, he ass.
11. 25 departed Barnabas to Tarsus..to seek S.
11. 30 sent it to the elders by the hands of..S.
12. 25 Barnabas and S. returned from Jerusalem
13. 1 brought up with Herod the tetrach..S.
13. 2 Separate me Barnabas and S. for the work
13. 7 who called for Barnabas and S., and des.
13. 9 Then S., who also (is called) Paul, filled
22. 7 saying unto me, S., S., why persecutest
22. 13 and said unto me, Brother S., receive thy
26. 14 saying..S., S., why persecutest thou me?

SAVE, SAVING, (for) **save that, only —**

1. *Only,* אַךְ *ak.*
Exod 12. 16 save (that) which every man must eat, th,

2. *But; rather, except,* כִּי אִם *ki im.*
Gen. 39. 6 he knew not ought he had, save the bread
2 Ch. 2. 6 that I should build him an house, save
Eccl. 5. 11 saving the beholding (of them) with their

3. *End, cessation,* אֶפֶס *ephes.*
Deut 15. 4 Save when there shall be no poor among
Amos 9. 8 saving that I will not utterly destroy the

4. *Without, save, besides,* בִּלְעֲדֵי *bilade.*
Gen. 14. 24 Save only that which the young have eaten
Psa. 18. 31 who (is) God save the LORD? or who (is)

5. *Without, save, not,* בִּלְתִּי *bilti.*
Exod 22. 20 He that sacrificeth unto (any) god, save

6. *Save, except, besides,* זוּלָה *zulah.*
Deut. 1. 36 Save Caleb the son of Jephunneh; he shall
Josh 11. 13 burned none of them, save Hazor only
1 Sa. 21. 9 take (it); for (there is) no other save that
1 Ki. 3. 18 no stranger..in the house, save we two in
2 Ki. 24. 14 save the poorest sort of the people of the
Psa. 18. 31 who (is) God..who (is) a rock save our God;

7. *Therefore, except, but,* לָהֵן *lahen.*
Dan. 6. 7 whosoever shall ask a petition..save of

8. *Only, surely, nevertheless,* רַק *raq.*
1 Ki. 8. 9 (There was) nothing in the ark save the

9. *But,* ἀλλά *alla.*
Matt 19. 11 All (men) cannot receive this saying, save
Mark 9. 8 they saw no man any more, [save] Jesus

10. *If not, except,* εἰ μή *ei mē.*
Matt 11. 27 neither knoweth any man the Father, save
13. 57 A prophet is not without honour, save in
17. 8 And..they saw no man, save Jesus only
Mark 5. 37 he suffered no man to follow him, save P.
6. 5 save that he laid his hands upon a few si
6. 8 nothing for their journey, save a staff only
Luke 4. 26 unto none of them was Elias sent, save
4. 27 none of them was cleansed, saving Naa.
8. 51 he suffered no man to go in, save Peter and
17. 18 There are not found that returned..sav
18. 19 none (is) good, save one, (that is), God
John 6. 22 save that one whereinto his disciples were
6. 46 save he which is of God, he hath seen the
Acts 21. 25 [save only that they keep themselves from
1 Co. 2. 2 not to know any thing among you, save
2. 11 save the spirit of man which is in him
Gal. 1. 19 other of the apostles saw I none, save Ja
6. 14 save in the cross of our Lord Jesus Chris
Rev. 2. 17 which no man knoweth saving he that
13. 17 that no man might buy or sell, save he

11. *Than,* ἤ *ē.*
John 13. 10 He that is washed needeth not [save] to

12 *To the side of,* παρά *(acc.) para.*
2 Co. 11. 24 five times received I forty (stripes) save

13. *Outside, without, except,* παρεκτός *parektos.*
Matt. 5. 32 whosoever shall put away his wife, sav.

14. *But, yet, besides,* πλήν *plēn.*
Acts 20. 23 Save that the Holy Ghost witnesseth in

SAVE (alive, life), **to —**

1. *To live,* חָיָה *chayah.*
1 Sa. 10. 24 the people shouted, and said, God save

2 Sa. 16. 16 God save the king, God save the king
1 Ki. 1. 25 they eat and drink..and say, God save
1. 34 blow ye..and say, God save king Solomon
1. 39 the people said, God save king Solomon
2 Ki.11. 12 clapped their hands, and said, God save
2 Ch.23. 11 anointed him, and said, God save the king

2. *To keep living, quicken,* חָיָה *chayah,* 3.
Gen. 12. 12 will kill me but they will save thee alive
Exod. 1. 17 the midwives..saved the men children
1. 18 and have saved the men children alive
1. 22 saying..every daughter ye shall save alive
Num 31. 15 said..Have ye saved all the women alive?
Deut 20. 16 thou shalt save alive nothing that breat.
Judg 21. 14 gave them wives which they had saved a.
1 Sa. 27. 11 David saved neither man nor woman alive
1 Ki. 18. 5 grass to save the horses and mules alive
20. 31 the king..peradventure he will save thy l.
2 Ki. 7. 4 if they save us alive, we shall live; and
Eze. 3. 18 speakest to warn the wicked..to save his l.
13. 18 and will ye save the souls alive (that come)
13. 19 to save the souls alive that should not live
18. 27 turneth away..he shall save his soul alive

3. *To give or preserve life,* חָיָה *chayah,* 5.
Gen. 19. 19 thou hast showed unto me in saving my l.
45. 7 to save your lives by a great deliverance
47. 25 Thou hast saved our lives: let us find gr.
50. 20 God meant it..to save much people alive
Num 22. 33 also I had slain thee, and saved her alive
Josh. 2. 13 ye will save alive my father, and my mo.
6. 25 Joshua saved Rahab the harlot alive, and
Judg 8. 19 if ye had saved them alive, I would not

4. *To preserve life,* חַיַי *chayai.*
Neh. 6. 11 would go into the temple to save his life

5. *Safety or ease,* יְשׁוּעָה *yeshuah.*
Psa. 80. 2 stir up thy strength, (and) come and save

6. *To save, give safety or ease,* יָשַׁע *yasha,* 5.
Exod 14. 30 the LORD saved Israel that day out of the
Deut 20. 4 to fight for you against your enemies, to
22. 27 damsel cried, and (there was) none to sa.
28. 29 only oppressed..and no man shall save
Josh. 10. 6 come up to us quickly, and save us, and
22. 22 if (it be) in rebellion..save us not this
Judg. 6. 14 thou shalt save Israel from the hand of
6. 15 wherewith shall I save Israel? behold, my
6. 31 Will ye plead for Baal? will ye save him?
6. 36, 37 thou wilt save Israel by mine hand, as
7. 2 saying, Mine own hand hath saved me
7. 7 By the three hundred men..will I save
1 Sa. 4. 3 it may save us out of the hand of our en.
7. 8 he will save us out of the hand of the P.
9. 16 he may save my people out of the hand
10. 19 who himself saved you out of all your ad.
10. 27 How shall this man save us? And they de.
11. 3 if (there be) no man to save us, we will
14. 6 (there is) no restraint to the LORD to save
14. 23 the LORD saved Israel that day: and the
14. 39 (as) the LORD liveth, which saveth Israel
17. 47 the LORD saveth not with sword and spear
23. 2 smite the Philistines, and save Keilah
23. 5 David saved the inhabitants of Keilah
2 Sa. 3. 18 I will save my people Israel out of the ha.
22. 3 my saviour; thou savest me from violence
22. 28 the afflicted people thou wilt save: but
22. 42 They looked, but (there was) none to save
2 Ki.14. 27 he saved them by the hand of Jeroboam
16. 7 save me out of the hand of the king of
19. 19 save thou us out of his hand, that all the
19. 34 I will defend this city to save it, for mine
1 Ch.11. 14 the LORD saved (them) by a great deliver.
16. 35 Save us, O God of our salvation, and ga.
2 Ch.32. 22 the LORD saved Hezekiah and the inhab.
Neh. 9. 27 saved them out of the hand of their ene.
Job 5. 15 he saveth the poor from the sword, from
22. 29 and he shall save the humble person
26. 2 savest thou the arm (that hath) no stren.
40. 14 that thine own right hand can save thee
Psa. 3. 7 save me, O my God: for thou hast smitten
6. 4 deliver my soul: oh save me for thy merci.
7. 1 save me from all them that persecute me
7. 10 My defence (is) of God, which saveth the
17. 7 thou that savest by thy right hand them
18. 27 thou wilt save the afflicted people; but
18. 41 They cried, but (there was) none to save
20. 6 Now know I that the LORD saveth his an.
20. 9 Save, LORD: let the king hear us when we c.
22. 21 Save me from the lion's mouth: for thou
28. 9 Save thy people, and bless thine inheri.
31. 2 rock, for an house of defence to save me
31. 16 Make thy face to shine..save me for thy
34. 6 the LORD heard (him), and saved him out
34. 18 and saveth such as be of a contrite spirit
37. 40 and save them, because they trust in him
44. 3 neither did their own arm save them; but
44. 6 my bow, neither shall my sword save me
44. 7 thou hast saved us from our enemies, and
54. 1 Save me, O God, by thy name, and judge
55. 16 I will call..and the LORD shall save me
57. 3 save me (from) the reproach of him that
59. 2 Deliver me..and save me from bloody men
60. 5 save (with) thy right hand, and hear me
69. 1 Save me, O God; for the waters are come
69. 35 God will save Zion, and will build the ci.
71. 2 incline thine ear unto me, and save me
71. 3 thou hast given commandment to save
72. 4 he shall save the children of the needy
72. 13 He shall..save the souls of the needy
76. 9 God arose to judgment, to save all the
86 2 save thy servant that trusteth in thee

Psa. 86. 16 give thy strength..and save the son of
106. 8 he saved them for his name's sake, that
106. 10 he saved them from the hand of him that
106. 47 Save us, O LORD our God, and gather us
107. 13 19 (and) he saved them out of their dist.
108. 6 save (with) thy right hand, and answer
109. 26 Help me, O LORD my God: O save me
109. 31 to save (him) from those that condemn
118. 25 Save now, I beseech thee, O LORD: O LORD
119. 94 I (am) thine, save me; for I have sought
119. 146 save me, and I shall keep thy testimonies
138. 7 thou..and thy right hand shall save me
145. 19 he also will hear their cry, and will save
Prov.20. 22 wait on the LORD, and he shall save thee
Isa. 25. 9 we have waited for him, and he will save
33. 22 the LORD (is) our king; he will save us
35. 4 behold, your God..he will come and save
37. 20 save us from his hand, that all the kingd.
37. 35 I will defend this city to save it, for mine
38. 20 The LORD (was ready) to save me: theref.
43. 12 I have declared, and have saved, and I ha.
45. 20 and pray unto a god (that) cannot save
46. 7 yet can he not answer, nor save him out
47. 13 save thee from (these things) that shall co.
47. 15 they shall wander..none shall save thee
49. 25 I will contend..I will save thy children
59. 1 hand is not shortened, that it cannot save
63. 1 speak in righteousness, mighty to save
63. 9 and the angel of his presence saved them
Jer. 2. 27 but..they will say, Arise, and save us
2. 28 if they can save thee in the time of thy tr.
11. 12 they shall not save them at all in the time
14. 9 astonied, as a mighty man (that) cannot
15. 20 I (am) with thee to save thee, and to del.
17. 14 Heal me..save me..for thou (art) my pr.
30. 10 I will save thee from afar, and thy seed
30. 11 I (am) with thee, saith the LORD, to save
31. 7 LORD, save thy people, the remnant of Is.
42. 11 for I (am) with you to save you, and to
46. 27 I will save thee from afar off, and thy seed
Lam. 4. 17 watched for a nation (that) could not save
Eze. 34. 22 Therefore will I save my flock, and they
36. 29 also save you from all your uncleannesses
37. 23 I will save them out of all their dwelling
Hos. 1. 7 will save them by the LORD their God, and
1. 7 will not save them by bow, nor by sword
13. 10 where (is any other) that may save thee
14. 3 Asshur shall not save us; we will not ride
Hab. 1. 2 cry out unto thee..and thou wilt not save
Zeph. 3. 17 he will save, he will rejoice over thee with
3. 19 I will save her that halteth, and gather
Zech. 8. 7 I will save my people from the east coun.
8. 13 so will I save you, and ye shall be a bles.
9. 16 God shall save them in that day as the fl
10. 6 I will save the house of Joseph, and I will
12. 7 The LORD also shall save the tents of Ju.

7. *To let or cause to escape, slip away,* מָלַט *malat,* 3.
1 Sa. 19. 11 If thou save not thy life to-night, to-morrow
2 Sa. 19. 5 servants, which this day have saved thy life
1 Ki. 1. 12 thou mayest save thine own life, and the
Job 20. 20 he shall not save of that which he desired
Jer. 48. 6 save your lives, and be like the heath in

8. *To snatch away,* נָצַל *natsal,* 5.
2 Sa. 19. 9 The king saved us out of the hand of our

9. *To keep, preserve,* שָׁמַר *shamar.*
Job 2. 6 Behold, he (is) in thine hand; but save his l.

10. *To bring safely through,* διασώζω *diasōzō.*
Acts 27. 43 the centurion, willing to save Paul, kept
1 Pe. 3. 20 wherein few, that is, eight souls were sa.

11. *To save, keep sound,* σώζω *sōzō.*
Matt. 1. 21 for he shall save his people from their sins
8. 25 awoke him, saying, Lord, save us: we pe.
14. 30 beginning to sink, he cried..Lord, save
16. 25 whosoever will save his life shall lose it
18. 11 [the son of man is come to save that which]
27. 40 Thou that destroyest the temple..save
27. 42 He saved others; himself he cannot save
27. 49 let us see whether Elias will come to save
Mark 3. 4 Is it lawful..on the sabbath..to save life
8. 35 whosoever will save his life shall lose it
8. 35 whosoever shall lose his life..shall save
15. 30 Save thyself, and come down from the cr.
15. 31 He saved others; himself he cannot save
Luke 6. 9 Is it lawful on the sabbath..to save life
7. 50 Thy faith hath saved thee; go in peace
9. 24 whosoever will save his life shall lose it
9. 24 whosoever will lose his life..shall save it
9. 56 [not come to destroy men's lives, but to s.]?
17. 33 Whosoever shall seek [to save] his life sh.
18. 42 Receive thy sight: thy faith hath saved
19. 10 come to seek and to save that which was
23. 35 He saved others; let him save himself, if
23. 37 If thou be the king of the Jews, save thy.
23. 39 If thou be Christ, save thyself and us
John 12. 27 Father, save me from this hour: but for
12. 47 came not to judge the world, but to save
Rom.11. 14 If by any means I..might save some of
1 Co. 1. 21 it pleased God..to save them that believe
7. 16, 16 knowest thou..whether thou shalt sa.
9. 22 that I might by all means save some
1 Ti. 1. 15 Jesus came into the world to save sinners
4. 16 thou shalt both save thyself, and them th.
2 Ti. 1. 9 Who hath saved us, and called (us) with
Titus 3. 5 he saved us, by the washing of regenera.
Heb. 5. 7 unto him that was able to save him from
7. 25 he is able also to save them to the utter.
Jas. 1. 21 the ingrafted word, which is able to save
2. 14 and have not works? can faith save him

Jas. 4. 12 There is one law giver, who is able to save
5. 15 the prayer of faith shall save the sick, and
5. 20 shall save a soul from death, and shall
1 Pe. 3. 21 whereunto (even) baptism doth also save
Jude 5 having saved the people out of the land
23 others save with fear, pulling them out

12. *To guard,* φυλάσσω *phulassō.*
2 Pe. 2. 5 saved Noah, the eighth (person), a preacher

SAVE self, to —

1. *To be kept, preserved,* שָׁמַר *shamar,* 2.
2 Ki. 6. 10 saved himself there, not once nor twice

2. *To save, keep sound,* σώζω *sōzō.*
Acts 2. 40 Save yourselves from this untoward gen.

SAVED, to be —

1. *To be saved or eased,* יָשַׁע *yasha,* 2.
Num 10. 9 and ye shall be saved from your enemies
Deut 33. 29 who (is) like unto thee, O people saved by
2 Sa. 22. 4 so shall I be saved from mine enemies
Psa. 18. 3 so shall I be saved from mine enemies
33. 16 There is no king saved by the multitude
80. 3, 7, 19 Turn us again..we shall be saved
Prov 28. 18 Whoso walketh uprightly shall be saved?
Isa. 30. 15 In returning and rest shall ye be saved
45. 17 Israel shall be saved in the LORD with an
45. 22 be ye saved, all the ends of the earth; for
64. 5 in those is continuance..we shall be sav.
Jer. 4. 14 wash thine heart..that thou mayest be s.
8. 20 the summer is ended, and we are not sav.
17. 14 and I shall be saved: for thou (art) my
23. 6 Judah shall be saved, and Israel shall
30. 7 trouble..But he shall be saved out of it
33. 16 In those days shall Judah be saved, and

2. *To make or keep sound or safe,* σώζω *sōzō.*
Matt 10. 22 he that endureth to the end shall be sav.
19. 25 amazed, saying, Who then can be saved?
24. 13 But he that shall endure..shall be saved
24. 22 there should no flesh be saved: but for the
Mark 10. 26 saying among themselves, Who..can be s.
13. 13 but he that shall endure..shall be saved
13. 20 no flesh should be saved: but for the elect's
16. 16 [He that believeth..shall be saved; but he]
Luke 8. 12 lest they should believe and be saved
13. 23 Lord, are there few that be saved? And
18. 26 they that heard (it) said, Who..can be sa.
John 3. 17 the world through him might be saved
5. 34 these things I say, that ye might be saved
10. 9 if any man enter in, he shall be saved, and
Acts 2. 21 (that) whosoever shall call..shall be saved
2. 47 to the church daily such as should be sa.
4. 12 none other name..whereby we must be sa.
11. 14 thou and all thy house shall be saved
15. 1 Except ye be circumcised..ye cannot be s.
15. 11 we believe..we shall be saved, even as they
16. 30 and said, Sirs, what must I do to be saved?
16. 31 and thou shalt be saved, and thy house
27. 20 all hope that we should be saved was then
27. 31 Except these abide..ye cannot be saved
Rom. 5. 9 we shall be saved from wrath through h.
5. 10 being reconciled, we shall be saved by his
8. 24 we are saved by hope: but hope that is
9. 27 be as the sand..a remnant shall be saved
10. 9 if thou..shalt believe..thou shalt be sav.
10. 13 upon the name of the Lord shall be saved
11. 26 Israel shall be saved: as it is written, Th.
1 Co. 1. 18 unto us which are saved it is the power
3. 15 he himself shall be saved; yet so as by fire
5. 5 the spirit may be saved in the day of the
10. 33 the (profit) of many, that they may be sa.
15. 2 By which also ye are saved, if ye keep in
2 Co. 2. 15 in them that are saved, and in them that
Eph. 2. 5 hath quickened us..by grace ye are saved
2. 8 by grace are ye saved through faith; and
1 Th. 2. 16 to the Gentiles that they might be saved
2 Th. 2. 10 received not the love..they might be sav.
1 Ti. 2. 4 Who wi.. have all men to be saved, and
2. 15 she shall be saved in child bearing, if they
1 Pe. 4. 18 if the righteous scarcely be saved, where
Rev. 21. 24 the nations [of them which are saved] sh.

3. *Safety,* σωτηρία *sōteria.*
Luke 1. 71 That we should be saved from our enem.
Rom 10. 1 my..prayer..is, that they might be saved

SAVING (health) —

1. *Safety, ease,* יְשׁוּעָה *yeshuah.*
Psa. 28. 8 he (is) the saving strength of his anointed
67. 2 thy saving health among all nations

2. *Safety, ease,* יֶשַׁע *yesha.*
Psa. 20. 6 with the saving strength of his right hand

3. *A laying up, acquiring,* περιποίησις *peripoiēsis.*
Heb. 10. 39 of them that believe to the saving of the

4. *Safety, ease,* σωτηρία *sōtēria.*
Heb. 11. 7 prepared an ark to the saving of his ho.

SAVIOUR —

1. *To save, give ease,* יָשַׁע *yasha,* 5.
2 Sa. 22. 3 my high tower, and my refuge, my savi.
2 Ki. 13. 5 the LORD gave Israel a saviour, so that th.
Neh. 9. 27 thou gavest them saviours, who saved th.
Psa 106. 21 They forgat God their saviour, which had
Isa. 19. 20 he shall send them a saviour, and a great
43. 3 God, the holy One of Israel, thy saviour
43. 11 I..(am) the LORD; and..(there is) no sav.
45. 15 hidest thyself, O God of Israel, the savio.
45. 21 and a saviour; (there is) none besides me
49. 26 that I the LORD (am) thy saviour and thy
60. 16 that I the LORD (am) thy saviour and thy

Isa. 63. 8 (are) my people..so he was their saviour
Jer. 14. 8 O the hope of Israel, the saviour thereof
Hos. 13. 4 no god but me; for (there is) no saviour
Obad. 21 saviours shall come up on mount Zion to

2. *A saviour, preserver*, σωτήρ *sōtēr*.
Luke 1. 47 my spirit hath rejoiced in God my saviour
2. 11 in the city of David, a saviour, which is
John 4. 42 this is indeed the Christ, the saviour of
Acts 5. 31 (to be) a prince and a saviour, for to give
13. 23 hath God..raised unto Israel a saviour, J.
Eph. 5. 23 as Christ..he is the saviour of the body
Phil. 3. 20 from whence also we look for the saviour
1 Ti. 1. 1 the commandment of God our saviour, and
2. 3 acceptable in the sight of God our savi.
4. 10 who is the saviour of all men, specially of
2 Ti. 1. 10 manifest by the appearing of our saviour
Titus 1. 3 the commandment of God our saviour
1. 4 and the Lord Jesus Christ our saviour
2. 10 adorn the doctrine of God our saviour in
2. 13 appearing of the great God and our savi.
3. 4 the kindness and love of God our saviour
3. 6 Which he shed on us..through..our sav.
2 Pe. 1. 1 the righteousness of God and our saviour
1. 11 kingdom of our Lord and saviour Jesus
2. 20 the knowledge of the Lord and saviour
3. 2 of us the apostles of the Lord and saviour
3. 18 the knowledge of our Lord and saviour
1 Jo. 4. 14 the Father sent the Son (to be) the savio.
Jude 25 To the only wise God our saviour, (be) g.

SAVOUR, (ill) —
1. *Stench*, צַחֲנָה *tsachanah*.
Joel 2. 20 his ill savour shall come up, because he

2. *Smell, savour, fragrance*, רֵיחַ *reach*.
Gen. 8. 21 the LORD smelled a sweet savour; and
Exod. 5. 21 ye have made our savour to be abhorred
29. 18, 41 a sweet savour, an offering made by
29. 25 for a burnt offering, for a sweet savour
Lev. 1. 9, 13, 17 of a sweet savour unto the LORD
2. 2, 9 an offering made by fire, of a sweet sa.
2. 12 be burnt on the altar for a sweet savour
3. 5 an offering made by fire, of a sweet sav.
3. 16 offering made by fire for a sweet savour
4. 31 burn (it) upon the altar for a sweet sav.
6. 15 burn it upon the altar (for) a sweet sav.
6. 21 shalt thou offer (for) a sweet savour unto
8. 21 it (was) a burnt sacrifice for a sweet sav.
8. 28 they (were) consecrations for a sweet sav.
17. 6 burn the fat for a sweet savour unto the
23. 13 offering made by fire..(for) a sweet sav.
23. 18 an offering made by fire, of sweet savour
26. 31 I will not smell the savour of your sweet
Num. 15. 3 to make a sweet savour unto the LORD
15. 7 an hin of wine, for a sweet savour unto
15. 10, 13, 14 of a sweet savour unto the LORD
15. 24 a burnt offering, for a sweet savour unto
18. 17 an offering made by fire, for a sweet sav.
28. 2 sacrifices made by fire, (for) a sweet sav.
28. 6 for a sweet savour, a sacrifice made by fire
28. 8 a sacrifice made by fire, of a sweet savour
28. 13 a burnt offering of a sweet savour, a sav
28. 24 sacrifice made by fire, of a sweet savour
28. 27 offer the burnt offering for a sweet savour
29. 2 offer a burnt offering for a sweet savour
29. 6 for a sweet savour, a sacrifice made by
29. 8 offer a burnt offering..(for) a sweet sav.
29. 13, 36 sacrifice made by fire, of a sweet sav.
Song 1. 3 Because of the savour of thy good oint.
Eze. 6. 13 the place where they did offer sweet sav.
16. 19 even set it before them for a sweet sav.
20. 28 there also they made their sweet savour
20. 41 I will accept you with your sweet savour

3. *A smell, odour*, ὀσμή *osmē*.
2 Co. 2. 14 maketh manifest the savour of his know.
2. 16 To the one (we are) the savour of death
2. 16 and to the other the savour of life unto li.
Eph. 5. 2 sacrifice to God for a sweet smelling sav.

SAVOUR, sweet —
1. *Rest, sweetness*, נִיחוֹחַ *nichoach*.
Ezra 6. 10 they may offer sacrifices of sweet savours

2. *Sweet smell, fragrance*, εὐωδία *euōdia*.
2 Co. 2. 15 we are unto God a sweet savour of Christ

SAVOUR, to lose —
To make insipid, foolish, μωραίνω *mōrainō*.
Matt. 5. 13 if the salt have lost his savour, wherewith
Luke 14. 34 if the salt have lost his savour, wherewith

SAVOUR, to —
To set the mind on, φρονέω *phroneō*.
Matt 16. 23 thou savourest not the things that be of
Mark 8. 33 thou savourest not the things that be of

SAVOURY meat —
Tasteful things, מַטְעַמִּים *matammim*.
Gen. 27. 4 make me savoury meat, such as I love, and
27. 7 make me savoury meat, that I may eat
27. 9 I will make them savoury meat for thy
27. 14 his mother made savoury meat, such as his
27. 17 she gave the savoury meat and the bread
27. 31 And he also had made savoury meat, and

SAW —
1. *A saw*, מְגֵרָה *megerah*.
2 Sa. 12. 31 put them under saws, and under harrows
1 Ki. 7. 9 sawed with saws, within and without, ev.
1 Ch. 20. 3 cut (them) with saws and with harrows of

2. *A saw*, מַשּׂוֹר *massor*.
Isa. 10. 15 shall the saw magnify itself against him

SAWN or **sawed** (asunder), to be —
1. *To saw*, גָּרַר *garar*, 4a.
1 Ki. 7. 9 sawed with saws, within and without, ev.

2. *To saw*, πρίζω *prizō*.
Heb. 11. 37 they were sawn asunder, were tempted, w.

SAY, to —
1. *To say, lift up the voice*, אָמַר *amar*.
Gen. 1. 3 And God said, Let there be light: and
See v. 6, 9, 11, 14, 20, 24, 26, 28, 29; 2. 18, 23; 3. 1, 1, 2, 3, 4, 9, 10, 11, 12, 13, 13, 14, 16, 17, 22; 4. 1, 6, 8, 9, 9, 10, 13, 15, 23; 6. 3, 7, 13; 7. 1; 8. 21; 9. 1, 8, 12, 17, 25, 26; 11. 3, 4, 6; 12. 1, 7, 11, 12, 13, 18, 19; 13. 8, 14; 14. 19, 21, 22, 23; 15. 2, 3, 5, 5, 7, 8, 9, 13; 16. 2, 5, 6, 6, 9, 10, 11, 13; 17. 1, 9, 15, 17, 18, 19; 18. 3, 5, 6, 9, 9, 10, 13, 15, 17, 20, 23, 26, 27, 28, 29, 29, 30, 30, 31, 31. 32, 32; 19. 2, 2, 5, 7, 9, 9, 12, 14, 17, 18, 21, 31, 34; 20. 2, 3, 4, 5, 5, 6, 9, 10, 11, 13, 13, 15, 16; 21. 1, 6, 7, 10, 12, 12, 16, 17, 24, 26, 29, 30; 22. 1, 1, 2, 5, 7, 7, 8, 11, 11, 12, 16; 24. 2, 5, 6, 12, 14, 14, 17, 18, 19, 23, 24, 25, 27, 31, 33, 33, 34, 39, 40, 42, 43, 44, 45, 46, 47, 47, 50, 54, 55, 56, 57, 57, 60, 65, 65; 25. 22, 23, 30, 31, 32, 33; 26. 2, 7, 7, 9, 9, 9, 9, 10, 16, 22, 24, 27, 28, 28, 32; 27. 1, 1, 2, 11, 13, 18, 18, 19, 20, 20, 21, 22, 24, 24, 25, 26, 27, 31, 32, 32, 33, 34, 35, 36, 36, 37, 38, 39, 41, 42, 46; 28. 1, 13, 16, 17; 29. 4, 4, 5, 5, 6, 6, 7, 8, 14, 15, 18, 19, 21, 25, 26, 32, 33, 34, 35; 30. 1, 2, 3, 6, 8, 11, 13, 14, 15, 15, 16, 18, 20, 23, 24, 25, 27, 28, 29, 29, 29, 34; 31. 3, 5, 8, 8, 11, 12, 14, 16, 24, 26, 31, 31, 35, 36, 43, 46, 48, 49, 51; 32. 2, 4, 8, 9, 9, 12, 16, 18, 20, 20, 26, 26, 27, 27, 28, 29, 29; 33. 5, 5, 8, 8, 9, 10, 12, 13, 15, 15; 34. 11, 11, 12, 14, 30, 31; 35. 1, 2, 10, 11, 17; 37. 6, 8, 9, 10, 13, 13, 14, 16, 17, 17, 19, 20, 21, 22, 26, 30, 32, 33, 35; 38. 8, 11, 11, 16, 16, 17, 17, 21, 22, 22, 23, 24 25, 26, 29; 39. 7, 8; 40. 8, 8, 9, 12, 16, 18; 41. 15, 15, 24, 25, 38, 39, 41, 44, 54, 55, 55; 42. 1, 2, 4, 7, 7, 9, 10, 12, 13, 14, 18, 21, 28, 31, 33, 36, 38; 43. 2, 5, 6, 7, 7, 8, 11, 16, 18, 20, 23, 27, 29, 29, 31; 44. 4, 4, 7, 10, 15, 16, 17, 18, 20, 21, 22, 23, 25, 26, 27, 28; 45. 3, 4, 4, 9, 17, 17, 24, 28; 46. 2, 2, 3, 30, 31, 31, 33, 34; 47. 1, 3, 3, 4, 8, 9, 16, 18, 23, 25, 29, 30, 31; 48. 2, 3, 4, 8, 9, 9, 11, 15, 18, 19, 21; 49. 1, 29; 50. 6, 11, 15, 17, 18, 19, 24.

Exod. 1. 9, 15, 16, 18, 19, 19; 2. 6, 7, 8, 9 10, 13, 14, 14, 18, 19, 20, 22; 3. 3, 4, 4, 5, 6, 7, 11, 12, 13, 13. 13, 13, 14, 14, 15, 15, 16, 17, 18; 4. 1, 1, 2, 2, 3, 4, 6, 7, 10, 11, 13, 14, 18, 18, 19, 21, 22, 22, 23, 25, 26, 27; 5. 1, 2, 3, 4, 5, 10, 16, 17, 17, 21, 22; 6. 1, 2, 6, 26, 30; 7. 1, 9, 14, 16, 17, 19; 8. 1, 5, 8, 9, 10, 10, 16, 16, 19, 20, 20, 25, 26, 28, 29; 9. 1, 1, 8, 13, 13, 13, 22, 27, 29; 10. 1, 3, 3, 7, 8, 10, 12, 16, 21, 24, 25, 28, 29; 11. 1, 4, 4, 9; 12. 21, 26, 27, 31, 33, 43; 13. 3. 14; 14. 3, 5, 11, 13, 15, 25, 26; 15. 1, 9, 26; 16. 3, 4, 6, 8, 9, 15, 15, 19, 23, 25, 28, 32, 33; 17. 2, 2, 3, 5, 8, 10, 14, 16; 18. 3, 6, 10, 14, 15, 17, 24; 19. 3, 8, 9, 10, 15, 21, 23, 24; 20. 19, 20, 22, 22; 21. 5; 23. 13; 24. 1, 3, 7, 8, 12, 14; 30. 34; 32. 1, 2, 4, 5, 8, 9, 11, 12, 17, 18, 21, 22, 23, 24, 26, 27, 27, 29, 30, 31, 33; 33. 5, 5, 12, 12, 14, 15, 17. 18, 19, 20, 21; 34. 1, 9, 10, 27; 35. 1, 30.

Lev. 1. 2; 8. 5, 31; 9. 2, 6, 7; 10. 3, 4, 6; 15. 2; 16. 2; 17. 2, 8, 12, 14; 18. 2; 19. 2; 20. 2, 24; 21. 1, 1; 22. 3, 18; 23. 2, 10; 25. 2, 20; 27. 2; 33. 12.

Num. 3. 40; 5. 12, 19, 21, 22; 6. 2; 7. 11; 8. 2; 9. 7, 8; 10. 29, 29, 30. 31, 35, 36; 11. 4, 11, 12, 16, 21, 21, 23, 27, 28, 29; 12. 2, 6, 11, 14; 13. 17, 27, 30, 31; 14. 2, 4, 11, 13, 20, 28, 31, 41; 15. 2, 18, 35; 16. 3, 8, 12, 15, 16, 22, 28, 34, 46; 17. 10; 18. 1, 24, 26, 30; 20. 10, 14, 18, 19, 20; 21. 2, 7, 8, 27, 34; 22. 4, 8, 9, 10, 12, 13, 14, 16, 16, 17, 18, 19, 20, 28, 29, 30, 30, 30, 32, 34, 35, 37, 38; 23. 1, 3, 4, 5, 7, 11, 12, 13, 15, 16, 17, 18, 19, 25, 26, 27, 29, 30; 24. 3, 10, 12, 15, 20, 21, 23; 25. 4. 5, 12; 26. 65; 27. 12, 18; 28. 2, 3; 31. 15, 21, 49; 32. 5, 6, 16, 20, 29; 33. 51; 34. 2; 35. 10; 36. 2.

Deut. 1. 14, 20, 22, 25, 27, 29, 39, 41, 42, 42; 2. 9, 31; 3. 2, 26; 4. 6, 10; 5. 1, 24, 27, 28, 30; 6. 21; 7. 17; 8. 17; 9. 12, 13, 25, 26, 28; 10. 1, 11; 12. 20; 15. 16; 17. 14, 16; 18. 17, 21; 20. 3, 8; 21. 7, 20; 22. 14, 16; 25. 7, 8, 9; 26. 3, 5, 13; 27. 14, 15, 16, 17, 18, 19, 20, 21, 22, 23, 24, 25, 26; 28. 67, 67, 68; 29. 2, 22, 24, 25; 31. 2, 2, 7, 14, 16, 17, 23; 32. 20, 26, 27, 37, 40, 46; 33. 2, 7, 8, 9, 12, 13, 18, 20, 22, 23, 24, 27; 34. 4.

Josh. 2. 4, 9, 16, 17, 21, 24; 3. 5, 7, 9, 10; 4. 5; 5. 2, 9, 13, 14, 14, 15; 6. 2, 6, 16, 22; 7. 3, 7, 8, 10, 13, 13, 19, 20, 25; 8. 1, 6, 18; 9. 6, 7, 8, 8, 9, 11, 19, 21, 24; 10. 8, 12, 18, 22, 24, 25; 11. 6; 13. 1; 14. 6; 15. 16, 18; 17. 16; 18. 3; 22. 2, 11, 16, 26, 27, 28, 28, 28, 31; 23. 2; 24. 2, 2, 16, 19, 21, 22, 22, 24, 27.

Judg. 1. 2, 3, 7, 12, 14, 15, 24; 2. 1, 1, 3, 20; 3. 19, 19, 20, 24, 28; 4. 6, 8, 9, 14, 18, 19, 20, 20, 20, 22; 5. 23; 6. 8, 8, 10, 12, 13, 14, 15, 16, 17, 18, 20, 22, 23, 25, 29, 29, 30, 31, 36, 39; 7. 2, 4, 4, 4, 5, 7, 9, 13, 14, 15, 17, 18; 8. 1, 2, 5, 6, 7, 15, 18, 19, 20, 21, 22, 23, 24; 9. 3, 7, 8, 9, 10, 11, 12, 13, 14, 15, 28, 29, 36, 36, 37, 38, 38, 48, 54, 54; 10. 11, 15, 18; 11. 2, 6, 7, 8, 9, 10, 15, 15, 19, 30, 35, 36, 37, 38; 12. 1, 2, 4, 5, 5, 5, 6, 6, 6; 13. 3, 7, 8, 10, 11, 11, 12, 13, 13, 15, 16, 17, 18, 22, 23; 14. 2, 3, 3, 12, 13, 14, 15, 16, 16, 18, 18; 15. 1, 2, 3, 6, 6, 7, 10, 11, 11, 12, 12, 13, 16, 18; 16. 5, 6, 7, 9, 10, 11, 12, 13, 13, 14, 15, 15, 17, 20, 20, 23, 24, 25, 26, 28, 30; 17. 2, 2, 3, 9, 9, 10, 13; 18. 2, 3, 4, 5, 6, 8, 9, 14, 18, 19, 23, 24, 24, 25; 19. 5, 6, 8, 9, 11, 12, 13, 17, 18, 20, 23, 28, 30; 20. 3, 4, 18, 18, 23, 28, 32, 32, 39; 21. 3, 5, 6, 8, 16, 17, 19, 22.

Ruth 1. 8, 10, 11, 12, 15, 16, 19, 20; 2. 2, 2, 4, 5, 6, 7, 8, 10, 11, 13, 14, 19, 19, 20, 20, 21, 21, 22; 3. 1, 5, 9, 10, 14, 15, 16, 17, 17, 18; 4. 1, 2, 3, 4, 5, 6, 8, 9, 11, 14.

1 Sa. 1. 8, 11, 14, 15, 17, 18, 22, 23, 26; 2. 1, 15, 16, 20, 23, 27, 27, 30, 36; 3. 5, 5, 6, 8, 9, 9, 11, 16, 17, 18; 4. 3, 6, 7, 7, 14, 16, 16, 17, 22; 5. 7, 8, 11; 6. 3, 4, 20; 7. 5, 6, 8; 8. 5, 6, 7, 7, 11, 19, 22, 22; 9. 3, 5, 6, 7, 8, 10, 11, 12, 18, 19, 21, 23, 23, 24, 24, 27; 10. 1, 2, 11, 12, 14, 14, 15, 15, 16, 18, 18, 19, 24, 24, 27; 11. 1, 3, 5, 9, 9, 10, 12, 12, 13, 14; 12. 1, 1, 4, 5, 6, 10, 12, 19, 20; 13. 4, 9, 11, 11, 12, 13, 19; 14. 1, 6. 7, 8, 9, 10, 11, 12, 12, 17, 18, 19, 28, 29, 33, 34, 34; 14. 36, 36, 36, 38, 40, 40, 41, 42, 43, 43, 45; 15. 1, 2, 6, 13, 14, 15, 16, 16, 17, 18, 20, 22, 24, 26, 28, 30, 32, 32, 33; 16. 1, 2, 2, 2, 4, 5, 6, 7, 8, 9, 10, 11, 11, 11, 12, 15, 17, 18, 19; 17. 8, 10, 17, 25, 28, 29, 32, 33, 34, 37, 37, 39, 43, 44, 45, 55, 55, 56, 58; 18. 7, 8, 11, 17, 17, 18, 21, 21, 22, 23, 25, 25; 19. 4, 14, 17, 17, 22, 22, 24; 20. 1, 2, 3, 3, 4, 5, 6, 7, 9, 10, 11, 12, 18, 21, 22, 27, 29, 30, 32, 36, 37, 40, 42; 21. 1, 2, 2, 4, 5, 8, 9, 9, 11, 14; 22. 3, 5, 7, 9, 12, 13, 14, 16, 17, 18, 22; 23. 2, 3, 4, 7, 9, 10, 11, 12, 12, 17, 21; 24. 4, 4, 6, 9, 10, 13, 16, 17; 25. 5, 6, 10, 13, 19, 21, 24, 32, 35, 39, 41; 26. 6, 6, 8, 9, 10, 14, 15, 17, 17, 18, 21, 22, 25; 27. 1, 5, 10, 10; 28. 1, 2, 2, 7, 7, 8, 9, 11, 11, 13, 13, 14, 14, 15, 16, 21, 23; 29. 3, 3, 4, 6, 8, 9, 9; 30. 7, 13, 13, 15, 15, 20, 22, 23; 31. 4.

2 Sa. 1. 3, 3, 4, 5, 6, 8, 9, 13, 14, 15, 16; 2. 1, 1, 1, 5, 14, 14, 20, 21, 26, 27; 3. 7, 8, 13, 16, 21, 24, 28, 31, 33, 38; 4. 8, 9; 5. 2, 8, 8, 19, 20, 23; 6. 9, 20, 21; 7. 2, 3, 5, 8, 8, 18; 9. 1, 2, 2, 3, 3, 4, 4, 6, 7, 8, 9, 11; 10. 2, 3, 5, 11; 11. 3, 5, 8, 10, 11, 12, 20, 21, 23, 25, 25; 12. 1, 5, 7, 7, 11, 13, 13, 18, 19, 19, 21, 22, 22, 27; 13. 4, 4, 5, 5, 6, 9, 10, 11, 15, 16, 17, 20, 24, 25, 26, 26, 28, 32, 35; 14. 2, 4, 5, 7, 8, 9, 10, 11, 11, 12, 12, 13, 15, 17, 18, 18, 19, 19, 21, 22, 24, 24, 30, 31, 32; 15. 2, 2, 3, 4, 7, 9, 10, 14, 15, 19, 21, 22, 25, 26, 27, 31, 33, 34; 16. 2, 2, 3, 3, 3, 4, 4, 7, 9, 10, 10, 10, 11, 16, 17, 18, 20, 21; 17. 1, 5, 6, 7, 8, 9, 14, 15, 20, 20, 21, 29; 18. 2, 4, 10, 11, 12, 14, 18, 19, 20, 21, 22, 22, 23, 25, 26, 26, 27, 27, 28 28, 29, 30, 31, 32, 33; 19. 2, 5, 13, 19, 21, 22, 23, 25, 26, 29, 29, 30, 33, 34, 41, 43; 20. 1, 4, 6, 9, 11, 16, 17, 17, 20, 21; 21. 2, 3, 4, 4, 4, 6; 22. 2; 23. 3, 15, 17; 24. 1, 2, 3, 10, 12, 13, 14, 16, 17, 18, 21, 21, 22, 23, 24.

1 Ki. 1. 2, 13, 16, 17, 24, 24, 25, 28, 29, 31, 33, 32, 34, 36, 36, 39, 41, 42, 43, 48, 52, 53; 2. 4, 13, 13, 14, 14, 15, 16, 17, 18, 20, 20, 21, 22, 26, 30, 30, 31, 51, 36, 38, 42, 42, 44; 3. 5, 6, 11, 17, 22, 22, 23, 23, 24, 25, 26, 26, 27; 5. 7; 8. 12, 15, 18, 23, 29; 9. 3, 8, 13; 10. 6; 11. 2, 11, 21, 22, 31, 31; 12. 5, 6, 9, 24, 26, 28; 13. 2, 2, 6, 8, 13, 14, 14, 15, 16, 18, 21, 26; 14. 2, 5, 6, 7, 16, 16; 17. 1, 10, 11, 12, 13, 14, 18, 19, 20, 21, 23, 24; 18. 5, 7, 9, 10, 11, 14, 15, 17, 21, 22, 24, 25, 27, 30, 33, 34, 34, 36, 39, 40, 41, 43, 43, 43, 44, 44, 44; 19. 4, 5, 7, 9, 10, 11, 13, 14, 15, 20, 20; 20. 2, 2, 4, 5, 7, 8, 9, 10, 11, 12, 13, 14, 14, 14, 14, 18, 22, 23, 28, 28, 28, 31, 32, 32, 32, 33, 33, 34, 35, 36, 37, 39, 39, 40, 42, 42; 21. 3, 4, 6, 7, 15, 19, 19, 20; 22. 3, 4, 4, 5, 6, 6, 7, 8, 8, 8, 9, 11, 11, 14, 14, 15, 16, 17, 17, 18, 19, 20, 20, 20, 21, 22, 22, 22, 24, 25, 26, 27, 27, 28, 28, 30, 32, 34, 49.

2 Ki. 1. 2, 4, 5, 6, 6, 6, 8, 11, 16; 2. 2, 2, 3, 3, 4, 4, 5, 6, 6, 9, 9, 10, 14, 15, 16, 16, 17, 18, 18, 19, 20, 21, 21, 23; 3. 7, 8, 10, 11, 11, 12, 13, 13, 14, 16, 16, 17, 23; 4. 2, 2, 3, 6, 6, 7, 9, 12, 13, 13, 14, 15, 16, 16, 19, 19, 22, 23, 23, 24, 25, 26, 27, 28, 28, 29, 30, 36, 36, 38, 40, 41, 41, 42, 43, 43, 43; 5. 3, 5, 7, 11, 13, 13, 15, 16, 17, 19, 20, 21, 22, 23, 25, 25, 26; 6. 1, 3, 5, 6, 7, 11, 12, 13, 15, 17, 18, 19, 20, 21, 27, 28, 28, 29, 31, 32, 33; 7. 1, 1, 2, 2, 3, 4, 6, 9, 12, 13, 19, 19; 8. 5, 8, 9, 10, 10, 12, 13, 14, 14; 9. 1, 3, 3, 5, 5, 5, 6, 6, 11, 11, 12, 12, 12, 15, 17, 17, 17, 18, 18, 18, 19, 19, 21, 22, 23, 25, 27, 31, 32, 33, 34, 36, 37; 10. 4, 8, 9, 13, 14, 15, 16, 18, 20, 22, 23, 24, 25, 30; 11. 12, 15, 15; 12. 4, 7; 13. 14, 15, 16, 17, 17, 17, 18, 18, 19; 17. 12; 18. 11, 19, 20, 22, 22, 25, 26, 27, 29, 31; 19. 3, 3, 6, 6, 6, 9, 15, 20, 23, 32; 20. 1, 1, 5, 7, 8, 9, 14, 14, 14, 15, 16, 17, 19, 19; 21. 4, 7, 12; 22. 8, 9, 15, 15, 16, 18, 18; 23. 17, 18, 27, 27; 25. 24.

1 Ch. 10. 41; 11. 2, 5, 6, 17, 19; 12. 17; 13. 2, 4; 14. 10, 11, 14; 15. 2, 12; 16 31, 35, 36; 17. 1, 2, 4, 7, 7, 16; 19. 2, 3, 5. 12; 21. 2, 8, 10, 11, 11, 13, 15, 17, 22, 23, 24; 22. 1, 5, 7, 18; 23. 25; 27. 23; 28. 2, 3, 6, 20; 29. 1, 10, 20.

2 Ch. 1. 7, 8, 11; 2. 12; 6. 1, 1, 4, 8, 14, 20; 7. 12, 21; 8. 11; 9. 5; 10. 5, 9, 10; 11. 4; 12. 5, 5, 6; 13. 4, 7, 11; 15. 2; 16. 7; 18. 3, 4, 5, 5, 6, 7, 7, 7, 8, 10, 10, 13, 13, 14, 14, 15, 16, 16, 17, 18, 19, 20, 20, 21, 21, 23, 24, 25, 26, 27, 27, 31, 33; 19. 2, 6; 20. 6, 15, 15, 20, 21; 21. 12; 22. 9; 23. 3, 11, 13, 14, 14; 24. 5, 6, 20, 20, 22; 25. 9, 15, 16, 16, 19; 26. 18, 23; 28. 9, 13, 23; 29. 5, 18, 31; 31. 10; 32. 10; 33. 4, 7; 34. 15, 23, 24, 26, 26; 35. 3, 23; 36. 23.

Ezra 1. 2; 2. 63; 4. 2, 3; 8. 28; 9. 6, 10; 10. 2, 10, 12;
Neh. 1. 3, 5; 2. 2, 3, 4, 5, 6, 7, 17, 18, 19; 2. 20; 4. 2, 3, 10, 11, 12, 14, 10, 22; 5. 2, 3, 4, 7, 8, 9, 12, 12, 13, 13; 6. 6, 8, 10, 11; 7. 3, 65; 8. 9, 10; 9. 5, 18; 13. 11, 17, 21;
Esth. 1. 13, 18; 2. 2; 3. 3, 8, 11; 5. 3, 5, 6, 7, 12, 14; 6. 3, 3, 4, 5, 5, 6, 10, 13; 7. 2, 3, 6, 8, 9, 9; 8. 5, 7; 9. 12, 13.

Job 1. 5, 7, 7, 8, 9, 12 14, 16, 17, 18, 21; 2. 2, 2, 3, 4, 6, 9, 10; 3. 2; 4. 1; 6. 1, 22; 7. 4, 13; 8. 1; 9. 1, 12, 22, 27; 10. 2; 11. 1, 4; 12. 1; 15. 1; 16. 1; 18. 1; 19. 1, 28; 20. 1, 7; 21. 1, 14. 28; 22. 1, 13, 17, 29; 23. 1, 5; 25. 1; 26. 1; 27. 1; 28. 14, 22, 28; 29. 1, 18; 31. 24, 31; 32. 6, 7, 10, 13; 33. 24, 27; 34. 1, 5, 9, 18; 35. 1, 2; 3. 10, 14; 36. 1, 23; 37. 6, 19; 38. 1, 11, 35; 39. 25; 40. 1, 3, 6; 42. 1, 7.

Psa. 2. 7; 3. 2; 4. 6; 10. 6, 11, 13; 11. 1; 12. 4, 5; 13. 14; 14. 1; 16. 2; 18. *title*; 27. 8; 30. 6; 31. 22; 32. 5; 35. 3, 10, 21, 25, 25, 27; 38. 16; 39. 1; 40. 7, 15, 16; 41. 4; 42. 39, 10; 50. 16; 52. *title*; 53. 1; 54. *title*; 55. 6; 58. 11; 64. 5; 66. 3; 68. 22; 70. 3, 4; 73. 11, 15; 74. 8; 75. 4; 77. 10; 78. 19; 79. 10; 82. 6; 83. 4, 12; 89. 2, 19; 90. 3; 91. 2; 94. 7, 18; 95. 10; 96. 10; 102. 24; 106. 23, 48; 107. 2; 115. 2; 116. 11; 118. 2, 3, 4; 119. 57; 122. 1; 124. 1; 126. 2; 129. 1, 8; 137. 7; 139. 11; 140. 6; 142 5;
Prov. 1. 11; 3. 28; 4. 4; 5. 12; 7. 4, 13; 9. 4, 16; 20. 9, 14, 22; 22. 13; 23. 7; 24. 12, 24, 29; 25. 7; 26. 13, 19; 30. 9, 15, 16, 26; 28. 24.

Eccl. 1. 2, 10; 2. 1, 2, 15; 3. 17, 18; 5. 6; 6. 3; 7. 10, 23, 27; 8. 4, 14; 9. 16; 10. 3; 12. 1, 8; Song 2. 10; 7. 8.

Isa. 1. 11, 18; 2. 3; 3. 10, 16; 5. 19; 6. 3, 5, 7, 8, 9, 11; 7. 3, 4, 7, 12, 13; 8. 1, 3, 12, 12, 19; 9. 9; 10. 8, 13, 24; 12. 1, 4; 14. 4, 10, 13; 18. 4; 19. 11; 20. 3, 6; 21. 6, 9, 12, 16; 22. 4, 14, 15; 23. 4, 12; 24. 16; 25. 9; 28. 12, 15, 16; 29. 11, 12, 13, 15, 16, 16, 22; 30. 10, 10, 15, 16, 22; 33, 10, 24; 35. 4; 36. 4, 4, 4, 5, 7, 7, 10, 11, 12, 13, 14, 16; 37. 3, 3, 6, 6, 6, 9, 21, 24, 33; 38. 1, 1, 3, 5, 5, 10, 11, 21, 23; 39. 3, 3, 3, 4, 5, 6, 8, 8; 40. 1, 6, 6, 9, 25, 27; 41. 6, 9, 21, 21, 26; 42. 5, 17, 22; 43. 1, 6, 9, 14, 16; 44. 2, 5, 6, 16, 17, 20, 24, 26, 27, 28; 45. 1, 9, 10, 11, 14, 18, 19, 24; 47. 7, 8

10, 10; 48. 5, 7, 17, 20, 22; 49. 3, 4, 5, 6, 7, 8, 9, 14, 20, 21, 22, 25; 50. 1; 51. 16, 22, 23; 52. 3, 4, 7; 54. 1, 6, 8, 10; 56. 1, 3, 4; 57. 10, 14, 15, 19, 21; 58. 9; 59. 21, 21; 62. 11; 63. 8, 5; 65. 1, 7, 8, 8, 13, 25; 66. 1, 5, 9, 9, 12, 20, 21, 23.

Jer. 1. 6, 7, 7, 9, 11, 12, 13, 14; 2. 2, 2, 5, 6, 8, 20, 23, 25, 27, 31, 35; 3. 1, 6, 7, 11, 12, 16, 19, 19; 4. 3, 5, 5, 10, 27; 5. 2, 4, 12, 14, 19, 24; 6. 6, 9, 15, 16, 16, 17, 21, 22; 7. 2, 3, 10, 20; 8. 4. 8, 12; 9. 7, 13, 15, 17, 23; 10. 2, 18, 19; 11. 3, 3, 5, 5, 6, 9, 11, 21, 22; 12. 4. 14; 13. 1, 6, 9, 12, 12, 13, 18, 21, 22; 14. 10, 11, 13, 13, 14, 15, 15, 17; 15. 1, 2, 2, 11, 19; 16. 3, 5, 9, 10, 11, 19; 17. 5, 15, 19, 20, 21; 18. 10, 11, 12, 13, 18; 19. 1, 3, 3, 11, 11, 14, 15; 20. 3, 4, 9; 21. 3, 3, 3, 4, 8, 8, 12, 13; 22. 1, 2, 3, 6, 8, 11, 14, 18, 21, 30; 23. 7, 7, 15, 16, 17, 17, 25, 33, 34, 35, 37, 38, 38, 38, 38; 24. 3, 3, 5, 8; 25. 5, 8, 15, 27, 27, 28, 28, 30, 32; 26. 2, 4, 16, 18; 27. 2, 4, 4, 4, 16, 19, 21; 28. 1, 2, 5, 6, 11, 13, 14, 15, 16; 29. 4, 8, 10, 15, 16, 17, 21, 25, 31, 32; 31. 2, 7, 7, 10, 15, 16, 23; 30. 2, 3, 5, 12, 18; 31. 29, 35, 37; 32. 3, 3, 6, 8, 14, 15, 25, 28, 36, 36, 42, 43; 33. 2, 4, 10, 10, 11, 11, 12, 13, 17, 20, 25; 34. 2, 2, 4, 13, 17; 35. 5, 6, 11, 13, 13, 17, 18, 18, 19; 36. 15, 16, 19, 29, 29, 30; 37. 7, 7. 9, 14, 17, 17, 17, 18; 38. 2, 3, 4, 5, 12, 14, 15, 17, 17, 19, 20, 22, 24, 25, 26; 39. 16; 40. 2, 14, 16; 41. 6, 8; 42. 2, 4, 5, 9, 9, 13, 15, 18, 20; 43. 10, 10; 44. 2, 7, 11, 20, 24, 25, 26, 30; 45. 2, 3, 4, 4; 46. 8, 14, 16, 25; 47. 2; 48. 1, 14, 17, 19, 40; 49. 1, 2, 7, 12, 18, 28, 35; 50. 2, 7, 18, 33; 51. 1, 33, 35, 35, 36, 58, 61, 62, 64.

Lam. 2. 12, 16; 3. 18, 24, 27, 54, 57; 4. 15, 20.

Eze. 2. 1, 3, 4; 3. 1, 3, 4, 10, 11, 18, 22, 24, 27; 4. 13, 14, 15, 16; 5. 5, 7, 8; 6. 3, 12, 14; 7. 2, 5; 8. 5, 6, 8, 9, 12, 12, 13, 15, 17; 9. 4, 5, 7, 8, 9, 9; 10. 2; 11. 2, 3, 5, 5, 7, 13, 15, 16, 16, 17, 17; 12. 9. 10, 10, 11, 19, 19, 23, 27, 28, 28; 13. 2, 3, 7, 7, 8, 11, 13, 15, 18, 20; 14. 4, 6, 6, 17, 21; 15. 6; 16. 3, 6, 6, 36, 59; 17. 3, 9, 9, 12, 19, 22; 18. 19, 25, 29; 19. 2, 20, 3, 5, 7, 8, 13, 18, 21, 27, 29, 30, 30, 32, 47, 47, 49, 49; 21. 3, 3, 7, 9, 9, 24, 26, 28, 28, 28; 22. 3, 3, 19, 24, 28; 23. 22, 28, 32, 35, 36, 43, 46; 24. 3, 3, 6, 9, 19, 21; 25. 3, 3, 3, 6, 8, 8, 12, 13, 15, 16; 26. 2, 3, 7, 15, 17, 19; 27. 3, 3, 3; 28. 2, 2, 2, 6, 9, 12, 12, 22, 22, 25; 29. 3, 3, 3, 8, 9, 13, 19; 30. 2, 2, 6, 10, 13, 22; 31. 10, 15; 32. 2, 3, 11; 33. 2, 8, 10, 11, 12, 13, 14, 17, 20, 25, 25, 27, 27; 34. 2, 10, 11, 17, 20; 35. 3, 10, 14; 36. 1, 2, 2, 3, 4, 5, 6, 6, 7, 13, 13, 20, 22, 22, 33, 35, 37; 37. 3, 4, 4, 5, 9, 9, 11, 11, 12, 19, 21; 38. 3, 10, 11, 13. 14, 17; 39. 1, 17, 25; 41. 4; 42. 13; 43. 7, 18, 18; 44. 2, 5, 6, 9; 45. 9, 18; 46. 1, 16, 20, 24; 47. 6, 8, 13.

Dan. 1. 10, 11, 18; 2. 3; 8. 13, 14, 16, 17, 19; 9. 4, 22; 10. 11, 12. 16, 19, 19. 20; 12. 6, 8, 9.

Hos. 1. 2, 4, 6, 9; 2. 1, 5, 7, 12, 23, 23; 3. 1, 3; 10. 3, 8; 12. 8; 12. 8; 13, 2, 10; 14. 2, 3.

Joel 2. 17, 17, 19, 32; 3 10; Amos 1. 2, 3, 5, 6, 8, 9, 11, 13, 15; 2. 1, 3, 4, 6; 3. 9, 11, 12; 4. 1; 5. 3, 4, 14, 16, 16, 17, 27; 6. 10, 10, 10, 13; 7. 2, 3, 5, 6, 8, 8, 8, 11, 12, 14, 15, 16, 17; 8. 2, 2, 2, 14; 9. 1, 10, 15.

Obad. 1. 3; Jon. 1. 6, 7, 8, 9, 10, 11, 12, 14; 2. 2, 4; 3. 4; 4. 2, 4, 8, 9, 9, 10; Mic. 2. 3, 4; 3. 1, 5, 11; 4; 2. 11; 6. 1, 7, 10; Nah. 1. 12; 3. 7; Hab. 2. 2, 6, 19; Zeph. 1. 12; 2. 15; 3. 7, 20; Hag. 1. 2, 5, 7, 8; 2. 6, 7, 9, 11, 12, 13, 13, 14; Zech. 1. 3, 3, 4, 6, 9, 9, 10, 11, 12, 14, 14, 16, 17, 19, 21; 2. 2, 2, 4, 8; 3. 2, 4, 5, 7; 4. 2, 2, 5, 5. 6, 11, 12, 13, 13, 14; 5. 2, 3, 5, 6, 6, 6, 8, 10, 11; 6. 4, 5, 7; 7. 13; 8. 2, 3, 4, 6, 7, 9, 14, 14, 19, 20, 23; 11. 4, 5, 9, 12, 13, 15; 12. 5; 13. 3, 5, 6, 9, 9.

Mal. 1. 2, 2, 4, 4, 5, 6, 6, 7, 7, 8, 9, 10, 11, 12, 13, 13, 13, 14; 2. 2, 4, 8, 14, 16, 16, 17, 17; 3. 1, 5, 7, 7, 8, 10. 11, 12, 13, 14, 17; 4. 1, 3.

2. *To say, lift up the voice,* אֲמַר *amar.*

Ezra 5. 3 said thus unto them, Who hath comman.
5. 4 Then said we unto them after this man.
5. 9 Then asked we those elders, (and) said
5. 15 said unto him, Take these vessels, go ca.
Jer. 10. 11 Thus shall ye say unto them, The gods
Dan. 2. 5 king answered and said unto the Caldeans
2. 7 They answered again and said, Let the ki.
2. 8 king answered and said, I know of certa.
2. 10 Chaldeans answered..and said, There is
2. 15 He answered and said to Arioch the king's
2. 20 Daniel answered and said, Blessed be the
2. 24 he went and said thus unto him; Destroy
2. 25 said thus unto him, I have found a man
2. 26 king answered and said to Daniel, whose
2. 27 Daniel answered..and said, The secret wh.
2. 47 The king answered unto Daniel, and said
3. 9 They spake and said to the king Nebuch.
3. 14 Nebuchadnezzar spake and said unto th.
3. 16 Abednego, answered and said to the king
3. 24 said unto his counsellors, Did not we cast
3. 24 They answered and said unto the king, T.
3. 25 He answered and said, Lo, I see four men
3. 26 spake, and said, Shadrach, Meshach, and A.
3. 28 Nebuchadnezzar spake, and said, Blessed
4. 14 He cried aloud, and said thus, Hew down
4. 19 king spake, and said, Belteshazzar, let not
4. 19 answered and said, My lord, the dream
4. 23 saying, Hew the tree down, and destroy
5. 7 king spake, and said to the wise (men) of
5. 10 queen spake, and said, O king, live for ev.
5. 13 king spake and said unto Daniel, (Art)
5. 17 Daniel answered and said before the king
6. 5 Then said these men, We shall not find
6. 6 said thus unto him, King Darius, live for
6. 12 king answered and said, The thing (is) true
6. 13 said before the king, That Daniel, which
6. 15 said unto the king, Know, O king, that
6. 16 king spake and said unto Daniel, Thy God
6. 20 king spake and said to Daniel, O Daniel
7. 2 Daniel spake, and said, I saw in my vis.
7. 5 said thus unto it, Arise, devour much fl.
7. 23 Thus he said, The fourth beast shall be

3. *To speak,* דָּבַר *dabar.*

Exod. 6. 29 Speak thou..all that I say unto thee
Num 32. 27 before the LORD to battle, as my lord sa.
36. 5 tribe of the sons of Joseph hath said well

4. *To speak,* דָּבַר *dabar,* 3.

Gen. 17. 23 in the selfsame day, as God said unto him
18. 5 shall pass on..So do, as thou hast said
34. 13 said, because he had defiled Dinah their
41. 17 Pharaoh said unto Joseph, In my dream
44. 7 unto him, Wherefore saith my lord these
45. 27 which he had said unto them: and when
Exod. 4. 12 and I will..teach thee what thou shalt s.
7. 13 he hearkened not..as the LORD had said
7. 22 neither did he hearken..as the LORD had s.
8. 15, 19 hearkened not..as the LORD had said
12. 31 and go, serve the LORD, as ye have said
12. 32 take your flocks..as ye have said, and be
16. 23 This (is that) which the LORD hath said
24. 3 All the words which the LORD hath said
24. 7 All that the LORD hath said will we do, and
32. 7 LORD said unto Moses, Go, get thee down
32. 13 saidst unto them, I will multiply your se.
33. 1 LORD said unto Moses, Depart, (and) go
Lev. 10. 5 So they..carried them..as Moses had said
10. 19 Aaron said unto Moses, Behold, this day
Num 14. 35 I the LORD have said, I will surely do it
16. 40 the LORD said to him by the hand of M.
22. 19 that I may know what the LORD will say
22. 20 yet the word which I shall say unto thee
22. 38 have I now any power at all to say any.
23. 16 said, Go again unto Balak, and say thus
24. 13 what the LORD saith, that will I speak
32. 31 As the LORD hath said unto thy servants
Deut. 1. 21 as the LORD God of thy fathers hath said
9. 3 quickly, as the LORD hath said unto thee
11. 25 lay the fear..as he hath said unto you
18. 2 LORD (is) their inheritance, as he hath sa.
29. 13 as he hath said unto thee, and as he hath
31. 3 go over before thee, as the LORD hath said
Josh. 1. 3 that have I given unto you, as I said unto
5. 14 What saith my lord unto his servant
11. 23 according to all that the LORD said unto
13. 14, 33 their inheritance, as he said unto them
14. 6 thing that the LORD said unto Moses the
14. 10 kept me alive, as he said, these forty and
14. 12 be able to drive them out, as the LORD sa.
22. 21 answered and said unto the heads of the
Judg. 1. 20 they gave Hebron unto Caleb, as Moses s.
2. 15 as the LORD had said, and as the LORD
6. 27 did as the LORD had said unto him: and
6. 36, 37 wilt save Israel..as thou hast said
7. 11 thou shalt hear what they say; and after.
8. 3 abated toward him, when he had said that
1 Sa. 3. 17 thing that (the LORD) hath said unto thee?
3. 17 of all the things that he said unto thee
4. 20 women that stood by her said unto her
9. 6 all that he saith cometh surely to pass
15. 16 what the LORD hath said to me this night
2 Sa. 7. 20 what can David say more unto thee? for
7. 25 establish (it)..and do as thou hast said
14. 10 Whosoever saith (ought) unto thee, bring
24. 12 say unto David, Thus saith the LORD, I
1 Ki. 2. 30 Thus said Joab, and thus he answered me
2. 31 Do as he hath said, and fall upon him, and
12. 10 thus shalt thou say unto them, My little
13. 7 the king said unto the man of God, If th.
13. 12 their father said unto them, What way
13. 22 the place of the which (the LORD) did say
14. 5 thus and thus shalt thou say unto her; for
21. 6 he said unto her, Because I spake unto
2 Ki. 1. 3 the angel of the LORD said to Elijah the
1. 6 turn again unto the king..and say unto
1. 7 he said unto them, What manner of man
1. 9 Thou man of God, the king hath said, C.
1. 10 Elijah answered and said to the captain
1. 11 he answered and said unto him, O man
1. 12 Elijah answered and said unto them, If
1. 13 besought him, and said unto him, O man
1. 15 the angel of the LORD said unto Elijah, G.
1. 16 he said unto him. Forasmuch as thou ha.
4. 17 at that season that Elisha had said unto
5. 4 thus said the maid that (is) of the land of
7. 17 he died, as the man of God had said, who
14. 27 the LORD said not that he would blot out
17. 23 as he had said by all his servants the pr.
24. 13 carried out thence..as the LORD had said
1 Ch. 17. 23 Therefore now, LORD..do as thou hast sa.
22. 11 build the house..as he hath said of thee
2 Ch. 18. 15 that thou say nothing but the truth to
23. 3 as the LORD hath said of the sons of David
Ezra 8. 17 I told them what they should say unto I.
Esth. 6. 10 take the apparel..as thou hast said, and
Psa. 122. 8 For my companions' sakes, I will now say
Eccl. 2. 15 I said in my heart, that this also (is) van.
Isa. 38. 15 What shall I say? he hath both spoken
Jer. 5. 15 neither understandest what they say
23. 17 The LORD hath said, Ye shall have peace
38. 25 what thou hast said..what the king said
39. 12 do unto him even as he shall say unto th.
40. 3 and done according as he hath said: be.
42. 19 The LORD hath said concerning you, O ye
Eze. 2. 8 But thou, son of man, hear what I say un.
6. 10 I have not said in vain that I would do
12. 23 say unto them, The days are at hand, and
12. 25 will I say the word, and will perform it
21. 17 I will also smite..I the LORD have said
37. 19 Say unto them..Behold, I will take the
37. 21 And say unto them..Behold, I will take
40. 4 the man said unto me, Son of man, beh.
40. 45 he said unto me, This chamber, whose pr.
41. 22 he said unto me, This (is) the table that
Eze. 44. 5 all that I say unto thee concerning all the
Jon. 3. 10 the evil that he had said that he would do
Hab. 2. 1 will watch to see what he will say unto

5. *To speak, say,* מְלַל *malal,* 3.

Gen. 21. 7 Who would have said unto Abraham, th.

6. *To speak, say,* מְלַל *melal,* 3.

Dan. 6. 21 Then said Daniel unto the king, O king

7. *To affirm, utter an affirmation,* נְאֻם *naam.*

Gen. 22. 16 By myself have I sworn, saith the LORD
Num 14. 28 I live, saith the LORD, as ye have spoken
24. 3, 15 Baalam the son of Beor hath said, and
24. 3, 15 the man whose eyes are open hath said
24. 4, 16 He hath said, which heard the words
1 Sa. 2. 30 Wherefore the LORD God of Israel saith
2. 30 but now the LORD saith, Be it far from
2 Sa. 23. 1 David the son of Jesse said, and the man
23. 1 and the sweet psalmist of Israel, said
2 Ki. 9. 26 saith the LORD..I will requite..saith the
19. 33 shall not come into this city, saith the L.
22. 19 I also have heard (thee), saith the LORD
2 Ch. 34. 27 I have even heard..also, saith the LORD
Psa. 36. 1 saith within my heart, (that there is) no
110. 1 LORD said unto my Lord, Sit thou at my
Isa. 1. 24 saith the LORD

So in 3. 15; 14. 22, 22, 23; 17. 3, 6; 19. 4; 22. 25; 30 1; 31. 9; 37. 34; 41. 14; 43. 10, 12; 49. 18; 52. 5, 5; 54. 17; 55. 8; 59. 20; 66. 2, 17, 22.

Isa. 56. 8 saith, Yet will I gather (others) to him
Jer. 1. 8, 15, 19; 2. 3, 9, 12 saith the LORD

So in 2. 19, 22, 29; 3. 1, 10, 12, 12, 13, 14, 16, 20; 4. 1, 9, 17; 5. 9, 11, 15, 18, 22, 29; 6. 12; 7. 11, 13, 19, 30, 32; 8. 1, 3, 13, 17; 9. 3, 6, 9, 22, 24, 25; 12. 17; 13. 11, 14, 25; 15. 3, 6, 9, 20; 16. 5, 11, 14, 16; 17. 24; 18. 6; 19. 6, 12; 21. 7, 10, 13, 14; 22. 5, 16, 24; 23. 1, 2, 4, 5, 7, 11, 12, 23, 24, 24, 28, 29, 30, 31.

Jer. 23. 31 prophets..that use their tongues..He sa.
23. 32, 32, 33 saith the LORD

So in 25. 7, 9, 12, 29, 31; 27. 8, 11, 15, 22; 28. 4; 29. 9, 11, 14, 14, 19, 19, 23, 32; 30. 3, 8, 10, 11, 12, 21; 31. 1, 14, 16, 17, 20, 27, 28, 31, 32, 33, 34, 36, 37, 38; 32. 5, 30, 44; 33. 14; 34. 5, 17, 22; 35. 13; 39. 17, 18; 42. 11; 44. 29; 45. 5; 46. 5.

Jer. 46. 18; 48. 15; 51, 57 saith the King, whose name
46. 23, 26, 28; 48. 12 saith the LORD

So in 48. 25, 30, 35, 38, 43, 44, 47; 49 2, 5, 6, 13, 16, 26, 30, 31, 32, 37, 38, 39; 50. 4, 10, 20, 21, 30, 31, 35, 40; 51. 24, 25, 26, 39, 48, 52, 53; Eze. 5. 11; 11. 8, 21; 12. 25, 28.

Eze. 13. 6 The LORD saith: and the LORD hath not
13. 7 The LORD saith (it); albeit I have not sp.
13. 8, 16; 14. 11, 14, 16, 18, 20, 23 saith the LORD

So in 15. 8; 16. 8, 14, 19, 23, 30, 43, 48; 16. 58, 63.

17. 16 saith the Lord GOD

So in 18. 3, 9, 23, 30, 32; 20. 3, 31, 33, 36, 40, 44; 21. 7, 13; 22. 12, 31; 23. 34; 24. 14; 25. 14; 26. 5, 14, 21; 28. 10; 29. 20, 30. 6; 31. 18; 32. 8, 14, 16, 31, 32; 33. 11; 34. 8, 15, 30, 31; 35. 6, 11; 36. 14, 15, 23, 32.

Eze. 37. 14 saith the LORD
38. 18, 21; 39. 5, 8, 10, 13, 20, 29; saith the L. G.

So in 43. 19, 27; 44. 12, 15, 27; 45 9, 15; 47. 23; 48. 29; Hos. 2. 13, 16, 21; 11. 11; Joel 2. 12; Amos 2. 11, 16; 3. 10, 15; 4. 3; 3. 13; 4. 5; 8. 3, 9, 11; 4. 6, 8, 9, 10, 11; 6. 8, 14; 9. 7, 8, 12, 13; Obad. 4. 8; Mic. 4. 6; 5. 10; Nah. 2. 13; Zeph. 1. 2, 3, 10; 2, 9; 3. 8; Hag. 1. 9, 13; 2. 4. 4, 8, 9, 14, 17, 23, 23, 23; Zech. 1. 3, 4, 16; 2. 5, 6, 6, 10; 3. 9, 10; 5. 4; 8. 6, 11, 17; 10. 12; 11. 6; 12. 1, 4; 13. 2, 7, 8; Mal. 1. 2.

8. *To answer, respond,* עָנָה *anah.*

1 Sa. 9. 17 LORD said unto him, Behold the man, wh.

9. *To call, cry,* קָרָא *qara.*

Job 17. 14 I have said to corruption, Thou (art) my

10. *To utter, speak sententiously,* ἀποφθέγγομαι.

Acts 2. 14 Peter..said unto them, Ye men of Judea

[*eipein.*

11. *To speak, use an expression,* ἔπος εἰπεῖν *epos*

Heb. 7. 9 as I may so say, Levi also, who receiveth

12. *To speak,* εἶπον *eipon.*

Matt. 2. 5 they said unto him, In Bethlehem of J.
2. 8 he sent them to Bethlehem, and said, Go

See also 3. 7, 15; 4. 3, 4; 5. 11, [22], 22; 8. 10, 13, 19, 21, 22, 32; 9. 2, [3,] 4, 5, 5, [11] 12, 15, 22; 11. 3, 4, 25; 12. 2, 3, 11, 24, 25, 39, 47, 48, 49; 13. 10, 11, 27, [28,] 37, [52,] 57; 14. 2, 16, 18, 28, 29; 15. 3, 5, 10, [11,] 13, 15. 16, 24, 26, 27, 28, 32, 34; 16. 2, 6, 8, 14, 16, 17, 23, 24; 17. 4, 7, 11, 17, 19, [20], 22, 24; 18. 3, 21; 19. 4, 5, 11, 14, 16, 17, 18, 23, 26, 27, 28; 20. 4, 13, 17, 21, 22, 25, 32; 21. 3, 5, 16, 21, 21, 24, 25, 26, 27, 28, 29, 30, 30, 38; 22. 13, 18, 24, 29, [37,] 44; 23. 39; 24. 2, 4, 23, 26, 48; 25 8, 12, 22, 24, 26; 26. 1, 10, 15, 18, 18, 21, 23, 25, 25, 26, 33, 35, 49, 50, 55, 61, 62, 63, 64, 66, 73; 27. 4, 6, 17, 21, 21, 25, 43, 63, 64; 28. 5, 6, 13.

Mark 1. 17, 44; 2. [8,] 9, 9, 19; 3. [32]; 4. 39, 40; 5. [7,] 34; 6. [16,] 22, 24, 24, [31,] 37; 7. 6, 10, 11, [27,] 29; 8. 5, [20,] 34; 9. [17,] 21, 23, 29, 36, 39; 10. 3, 4, 5, 14, 18, [20,] 21, [29,] 36, 37, 38, 39, 39, 51, 52; 11. 3, 3, 6, 14, 23, [23], 29, 31, 32; 12. 7, 15, [16,] 17, [24,] 32, 32, 34, 36, [36]; 13. 2, 21; 14. 6, 14, 16, 18, 20, 22, 24, 48, 62, 72; 15. [2, 12,] 39; 16. 7, 8, [15].

Luke 1. 13, 18, 19, 28, 30, 34, 35, 38, 42, 46, 60, 61; 2. 10, [15,] 28, 34, 48, 49; 3. 12, 13, 14; 4. 3, 6, 8, 9, 12, 23, 24, 43; 5. 4, 5, 10, [13,] 20, 22, 23, 23, 24, 27, 31, 33, 34; 6. 2, 3, 8, 9, 10; 7. 7, 9, 13, 14, 20, 22, [31,] 40, 40, 43, 43, 48, 50; 8. 10, 21, 22, 25, 28, 30, 45, 45, 46, 48, 52; 9. 3, 9, 12, 13, 13, 14, 19, 20, 20, 33, 41, 43, 48, 49, 50, 54, [55,] 57, 58, 59, 59, 60, 61, 62; 10. 10, 18, 21, 23, 26, 27, 28, 29, 30, 35, 37, 37, 40, 41; 11. 1, 2, 5, [5,] 7, 15, 17, 27, 28, 39, 46,

19; 12. 11, 12, 13, 14, 15, 18, 20, 22, 41, 42, 45; 13. 2, 7, 12, 15, 20, 23, 23, 32, 35; 14. [10,] 15, 16, 17, 18, 19, 20, 21, 22, 23, 25; 15. 11, 12, [17,] 21, 22, 27, 29, 31; 16. 2, 3, 6, 6, 7, 7, 15, 24, 25, 27, 30, 31; 17. 1, 5, 6, 14, 17, 19, 20, 22, 37; 18. 4, 6, 16, 19, 21, 22, 24, 26, 27, 28, 29, 31, 41, 42; 19. 5, 8, 9, 12, 13, 17, 19, 24, 25, [30], 32, 33, 34, 39, 40; 20. 3, 5, 6, 8, 13, 16, 17, 23, 24, 25, 34, 39, 39, 41, 42, 45; 21. 3, 5, 8; 22. 9, 10, 15, 17, 25, [31,] 33, 34, 35, 35, 36, 38, 38, 40, 46, 48, 49, 51, 52, 56, 58, 60, 61, 67, 70, 71; 23. 4, 14, 22, 28, 43, 46, 46; 24. 5, 17, 18, 19, 19, 24, 25, 32, 38, 40, 41, 44, 46.

John 1. 22, 23, 25, 30, 33, 38, 42, 46, 48, 50, 50; 2. 16, 18, 19, 20, 22; 3. 2, 3, 7, 9, 10, 26, 27, 28; 4. 10, 13, 17, 17, 27, 32, 48, 52, 53; 5. 11, 12, 14, 19; 6. 10, 25, 26, 28, 29, 30, 32, 34, 35, 36, 41, 43, 53, 59, 60, 61, 67; 7. 3, 9, 16, [20], 21, 33, 35, 36, 38, 42, 45, 52; 8. [7, 10, 11, 11,] 13, 14, 21, [23,] 24, 25, 28, 39, 41, 42, 48, 52, 55, 57, 58; 9. 7, [11,] 11, 12, 15, 17, 20, 23, 24, [25], 26, 28, 30, 34, 35, 36, 37, 39, 40, 41; 10. 7, [26, 34,] 36; 11. 4, 11, 12, 14, 16, 21, 25, 28, 34, 37, 40, 41, 42, 49; 12. 6, 7, 19, 27, 30, 35, 39, 41, 44, 49; 13. 7, 11, 12, 21, 21, 33; 14. 23, 26, 28, [28]; 15. 20; 16. 4, 15, 17, 19, 19; 17. 1; 18. [4,] 6, 7, 11, 21, 25, 25, [29,] 30, 31, 31, 33, 37, 38; 19. 21, 24, 30; 20. 14, [17,] 20, 21, 22, 25, 26, 28; 21. 6, 17, 17, 20, 23.

Acts 1. 7, 11, 15, 24; 2. 34, 37; 34. 6, 22; 4. 8, 19, 23, 24, 25; 5. 3, 8, [9,] 19, 29, 35; 6. 2; 7. 1, 3, 7, 33, 37, 56, 60; 8. 20, 24, 29, 30, 31, 34, [37, 37]; 9. 5, [5, 6,] 10, 10, 15, 17, 34, 40; 10. 4, 4, 14, 19, 21, 22, 34; 11. 8, 13; 12. 8, 11, 15, 17; 13. 2, 10, 16, 22, 46; 14. 10; 15. 7, 36; 16. 18, 31; 17. 32; 18. 6, 14; 19. 2, [2,] 3, 3, 4, 15, 25; 20. 10, 18, 35; 21. 11, 20, 37, 39; 22. 8, 10, 10, 13, 14, 19, 21, 25, 27, 27, 23, 1, 3, 4, 11, 14, 20; 24. 20, 22; 25. 9, 10; 26. [15,] 15, [29]; 27. 21; 31; 28. 21, 26, [29].

Rom. 10. 6; 1 Co. 1. 15; 10. 28; 11. 22, 24; 12. 3, 15, 16, 21; 15. 27; 2 Co. 4. 6; 6. 16; Gal. 2. 14; Col. 4. 7; Ti. 1. 12; Heb. 1. 12; 3. 10; 7. 9; 10. 7, 30; 12. 21; Jas. 2. 3, 3, 11, 11, 16; 1 Jo. 1. 6. 8, 10; 4. 20; Jude 9; Rev 7 14; 17. 7; 21. 5, 6; 22. [6.] 17.

13. *To say, speak, tell, declare,* ἐρῶ *erō,* ἐρέω *ereō.*

Matt. 7. 4 Or how wilt thou say to thy brother, Let
7. 22 Many will say to me in that day, Lord, L.
13. 30 I will say to the reapers, Gather ye toge.
17. 20 shall say unto this mountain, Remove he.
21. 3 ye shall say, The Lord hath need of them
21. 25 will say unto us, Why did ye not then be.
25. 34 Then shall the king say unto them on his
25. 40 king shall answer and say unto them, Ve.
25. 41 Then shall he say also unto them on the.
26. 75 remembered the word of Jesus, which sa.
Mark 11. 31 he will say, Why then did ye not believe
Luke 2. 24 according to that which is said in the law
4. 12 It is said, Thou shalt not tempt the Lord
4. 23 Ye will surely say unto me this proverb
12. 19 I will say to my soul, Soul, thou hast mu.
13. 25 and he shall answer and say unto you, I
13. 27 shall say, I tell you, I know you not wh.
14. 9 he that bade thee and him come and say
15. 18 will say unto him, Father, I have sinned
17. 7 will say unto him by and by, when he is
17. 8 will not rather say unto him, Make ready
17. 21 Neither shall they say, Lo here! or, lo th.!
17. 23 they shall say to you. See here! or, see
19. 31 thus shall ye say unto him, Because the
20. 5 he will say, Why then believed ye him not?
22. 11 say unto the good man of the house, The
22. 13 found as he had said unto them: and they
23. 29 in the which they shall say, Blessed (are)
John 4. 18 not thy husband: in that saidst thou tr.
6. 65 Therefore said I unto you, that no man
12. 50 even as the Father said unto me, so I sp.
Acts 13. 34 he said on this wise, I will give you the
17. 28 poets have said, For we are also his offs.
Rom. 3. 5 what shall we say? (Is) God unrighteous
4. 1 What shall we then say that Abraham our
6. 1 What shall we say then? Shall we conti.
7. 7 What shall we say then? (Is) the law sin?
8. 31 What shall we then say to these things?
9. 14, 30 What shall we say then?
9. 19 Thou wilt say then unto me, Why doth
9. 20 Shall the thing formed say to him that
11. 19 Thou wilt say then, The branches were
1 Co. 14. 16 how shall he..say Amen at thy giving of
14. 23 unbelievers, will they not say that ye are
15. 35 will say, How are the dead raised up? and
2 Co. 12. 6 for I will say the truth: but (now) I forb.
12. 9 said unto me, My grace is sufficient for
Phil. 4. 4 Rejoice in the Lord alway: (and) again I
Heb. 1. 13 But to which of the angels said he at any
4. 3 as he said, As I have sworn in my wrath
4. 7 as [it is said,] To day if ye will hear his.
10. 9 Then said he, Lo, I come to do thy will
13. 5 for he hath said, I will never leave thee
Jas. 2. 18 man may say, Thou hast faith, and I have
Rev. 7. 14 said unto him, Sir, thou knowest. And he
19. 3 again they said, Alleluia! And her smoke

14. *To talk, speak, tell,* λαλέω *laleō.*

Mark 9. 6 For he wist not what [to say]; for they
John 8. 25 Even (the same) that I said unto you from
8. 26 I have many things to say and to judge
16. 6 But because I have said these things unto
16. 18 A little while? we cannot tell what he sa.
18. 20 resort; and in secret have I said nothing
18. 21 ask them..what I have said unto them
Acts 3. 22 hear..whatsoever he shall say unto you
23. 7 [when he had so said,] there arose a disp.
23. 18 young man..who hath something to say
26. 22 which the prophets and Moses did say
Rom. 3. 19 it saith to them who are under the law
1 Co. 9. 8 Say I these things as a man? or..not the
Heb. 5. 5 but he that saith unto him, Thou art my
11. 18 Of whom it was said, That in Isaac shall

15. *To say, speak, declare, lay out,* λέγω *legō.*

Matt. 3. 9 think not to say within yourselves, We
3. 9 for I say unto you, that God is able of th.

See also 4. [6, 9,] 10, 17, 19; 5. 18, 20, 22, 26, 28, 32, 34, 36, 44; 6. 2, 5, 6, 25, 29; 7. 21; 8. 4, 7, 9, 10, 11, 20, 26; 9. 6, 9, 21, 24, 28, 28, 34, 37; 10. 15, 23, 42; 11. 7, 9, 11, 18, 19, 22, 24; 12. 6, 13, 23, 31, 36, 44; 13. 14, 17, [51,] 51, 54; 14. 4, 17, 31; 15. 5, 33, 34; 16. 2, 13, 15, 15, 18, 28; 17. 5, 10, 12, 20, 25, [26]; 18. 1, 10, 13, 18, 19, 22, 32; 19. 7, 8, 9, 10, [18,] 20, 23, 24, 28; 20. 6, 7, 7, 8, 21, 22, 23, 33; 21. 11, 13, 16, 16, 19, 21, 23, 31, 31, 31, 41, 42, 43; 22. 1, 8, 12, 20, 21, 21, 23, 42, 43; 23. 3, 16, 30, 36, 39; 24. 2, 34, 47; 25. 12, 40, 45; 26. 5, 13, 18, 21, 22, 25, 29, 31, 34, 35, 36, 38, 40, 45, 52, 64, 64, 70, 71; 27. 11, 13, 22, 22, [33,] 41, 47, [49]; 28. 10.

Mark 1. 37, 38, 41, 44; 2. 5, 10, 11, 14, 16, 17, 18, 24, 25, 27; 3. 3, 4, 5, 21, 22, 23, 28, 30, 34; 4. 2, 9, 11, 13, 21, 24, 26, 30, 35, 38, 41; 5. 8, 19, 28, 30, 31, 35, 36, 39, 41, 41; 6. 4, 10, [11,] 14, 15, 15, 18, 35, 37, 38, 38, 50; 7. 9, 11, 14, 18, 20, 28, 34; 8. 1, 12, 12, 17, 19, 21, [24,] 27, [29,] 29, 29; 9. 1, 5, 11, 13, 19, 24, 26, 31, 35, 41; 10. 11, 15, 23, 24, 27, 28, 29, 42, 47, [51]; 11. 2, 5, 21, 22, 23, [23,] 24, 28, 33, 33; 12. 14, 16, 18, 35, 35, 38, [43,] 43; 13. 1, 5, 30, 37, 37; 14. 2, [4,] 9, 12, 13, 14, 18, 19, 25, 27, 30, 30, 31, 32, 34, 36, 37, 41, 45, 58, 61, 63, 65, 67, 68, 69, 70; 15. 2, 14, [28], 31, 35; 16. 3, 6.

Luke 3. 7, 8, 8, 11, [22]; 4. 21, 22, 24; 5. 24, 39; 6. 5, 20, 27, 42, 46; 7. 8, 9, 14, 26, 28, 33, 34, 47, 49; 8. 8, [20;] 9, 7, 18, 20, 23, 33; 10. 2, 5, 9, 12; 11. 2, 8, 9, 18, 24, 29; 45, 51, [53]; 12. 1, 4, 5, 8, 22, 27, 37, 44, 54, 54, 55; 13. 8, 14, 17, 18, 24, 26, 35; 14. 12, 24; 15. 7, 10; 16. 1, 5, 7, 9, 29; 17. 6, 10, 13, 37; 18. 6, 17, 29; 19. 22, 26; 20. 21, 41, 42; 21. 3, 10, 32; 22. 11, 16, 18, 37, 60, 70; 23. 3, 30, [34,] 42, 43; 24. 23, [30.]

John 1. 21, 22, 29, 36, 38, 38, 39, 41, 43, 45, 46, 47, 48, [49,] 51, 51; 2. 3, 4, 5, 5, 7, 8, 10, 22; 3. 3, 4, 5, 11; 4. 7, 9, 10, 11, 15, 16, 17, 19, 20, 21, 25, 26, 28, 33, 34, 35, 35, 42, 49, 50; 5. 6, 8, 10, 18, 19, 24, 25, 34; 6. 5, 6, 8, 12, 14, 20, 26, 32, 42, 42, 47, 53, 65; 7. 6, 11, 12, 12, 25, 26, 31, 40, 41, 41, 50; 8. [4, 5, 6,] 19, 22, 22, 25, 31, 33, 34, 39, 46, 48, 51, 52, 54, 58; 9. 8, 9, 9, 10, 12, 16, 16, 17, 17, 19, 41; 10. 1, 7, 20, 21, 24, 36, 41; 11. 7, 8, 11, 23, 24, 27, 34, 36, 39, 39, 40, 44, 47; 12. 4, 24, 29, 29, 33, 34; 13. 6, 8, 9, 10, 13, 16, 20, 21, 25, 27, 29, 31, 33, 36, 37, 38; 14. 5, 6, 8, 9, 9, 12, 22; 16. 12, 17, 18, 20, 23, 26, 29; 18. 5, 17, 26, 34, 37, 38; 19. 3, 4, 5, 6, 9, 10, 14, 15, 17, 21, [24], 26, 27, 28, 35, 37; 20. 2, 13, 13, 15, 15, 16, 16, 17, 22, 25, 27, 29; 21. 3, 3, 5, 7, 10, 12, 15, 15, 15, 16, 16, 16, 17, 17, 18, 19, 21, 22.

Acts 2. 13, 17, 34; 4. 32; 5. 38; 6. 11, 13, 14; 7. 48, 49; 9. 21; 11. 16; 12. 8, [15;] 13. 25, 35; 15. 17; 17. 18, 18; 21. 4, 11, 23, 37; 22. 22; 23. 8, 30; 27. 10; 28. 4, 6, 17.

Rom. 2. 22; 3. 8, 19; 4. 3, 9; 7. 7; 9. 1, 15, 17, 25; 10. 8, 11, 16, 18, 19, 19, 20, 21; 11. 1, 2, 4, 9, 11; 12. 3, 19; 14. 11; 15. 8, 10, 12.

1 Co. 1. 12, 12; 3. 4; 7. 8; 9. 8, 10; 10. 29; 14. 16, 21, 34; 15. 12.

2 Co. 6. 2, 17, 18; 9. 3, 4; 11. 16; Gal. 1. 9; 3. 16, 17; 4. 1, 30; 5. 2, 16; Eph. 4. 8, 17; 5. 14; Col. 2. 4; 1 Th. 4. 15; 5. 3; 1 Ti. 1. 7; 5. 18; 2 Ti. 2. 7; Titus 2. 8; Phil. 19. 21; Heb. 1. 6, 7; 3. 7, 15; 5. 6; 7. 21; 8. 8, 9, 10, 13; 10. 5, 8, 16, [30]; 11. 14, 32; 13. 6; Jas. 1. 13; 2. 14. 23; 4. 5. 6. 13. 15; 1 Jo. 2. 4, 6, 9; 5. 16.

Rev. 1. 8; 2. 1, 7, 8, 9. 11. 12. 17. 18, 24, 29; 3. 1, 6, 7, 9, 13, 14, 17, 22; 4. 1; 5. 5, 14; 6. 3. 5, 6, 7, 16; 10. 8 9. 9, 11; 14. 13; 16. 5, 7; 17. [15]; 18 7; 19. 9. 9, 10; 21. 5; 22. 9, 10, 17, 20.

16. *To speak, say,* ἐρῶ *erō,* ῥέω *rheō.*

Matt. 5. 21, 27 ye have heard that it was said by them
5. 31 It hath been said, Whosoever shall put
5. 33, 38, 43 ye have heard that it hath been s.
Rom. 9. 12 It was said unto her, The elder shall serve
9. 26 in the place where it was said unto them
Rev. 6. 11 it was said unto them, that they should rest

17. *To say, assert, affirm,* φάσκω *phaskō.*

Rev. 2. 2 [thou hast tried them which say they are]

18. *To say, affirm,* φημί *phēmi.*

Matt. 4. 7 Jesus said unto him, It is written again
8. 8 The centurion answered and said, Lord
13. 28 The servants said unto him, Wilt thou th.
13. 29 he said, Nay; lest, while ye gather up the
14. 8 she, being before instructed..said, Give
17. 26 Jesus saith unto him, Then are the children
19. 21 Jesus [said] unto him, If thou wilt be pe.
21. 27 he said unto them, Neither tell I you by
25. 21 His lord said unto him, Well done, (thou)
25. 23 His lord said unto him, Well done, good
26. 34 Jesus said unto him, Verily I say unto
26. 61 This (fellow) said, I am able to destroy
27. 11 Art thou the king of the Jews? Jesus said
27. 23 the governor said, Why, what evil hath he
27. 65 Pilate said unto them, Ye have a watch
Mark 14. 29 Peter said unto him, Although all shall
Luke 7. 40 Simon, I have somewhat..And he saith
7. 44 he turned to the woman, and said unto S.
22. 58 another saw him, and said, Thou art also
22. 70 Art thou then the Son of God? And he sa.
23. 3 And he answered him and said, Thou sa.
John 1. 23 He said, I (am) the voice of one crying in
9. 38 he said, Lord, I believe. And he worship.
Acts 2. 38 Peter [said] unto them, Repent, and be
7. 2 he said, Men, brethren, and fathers, hea.
8. 36 the eunuch said, See, (here is) water; what
10. 28 he said unto them, Ye know how that it
10. 30 Cornelius said, Four days ago I was fast.
10. 31 said, Cornelius, thy prayer is heard, and
16. 30 brought them out, and said, Sirs, what mu.
16. 37 Paul said unto them, They have beaten
17. 22 said, (Ye) men of Athens, I perceive that
19. 35 he said, (Ye) men of Ephesus, what man
21. 37 captain..Who said, Canst thou speak G.?
Acts 22. 2 they kept the more silence: and he saith
22. 27 Tell me, art thou a Roman? He said, yea
22. 28 And Paul said, But I was (free) born
23. 5 Then said Paul, I wist not, brethren, that
23. 17 said, Bring this young man unto the chief
23. 18 brought (him) to the chief captain, and
23. 35 I will hear thee, said he, when thine acc.
25. 5 Let them therefore, said he, which among
25. 22 Agrippa [said] unto Festus, I would also
25. 22 To morrow, said he, thou shalt hear him
25. 24 Festus said, King Agrippa, and all men
26. 1 Agrippa said unto Paul, Thou art permi.
26. 24 Festus said with a loud voice, Paul, thou
26. 25 he said, I am not mad, most noble Festus
26. 28 Agrippa [said] unto Paul, Almost thou
26. 32 Then said Agrippa unto Festus, This man
1 Co. 6. 16 is one body? for two, [saith he,] shall be one
7. 29 But this I say, brethren, the time (is) sh.
10. 15 I speak as to wise men; judge ye what I say
10. 19 What say I then? that the idol is any th.
15. 50 this I say, brethren, that flesh and blood
2 Co. 10. 10 (his) letters, say they, (are) weighty and
Heb. 8. 5 See, saith he, (that) thou make all things

19. *The word,* ὁ λόγος *ho logos.*

Heb. 5. 11 we have many things to say, and hard to

SAY against, to —

To speak against, ἀντεῖπον *anteipon.*

Acts 4. 14 And beholding..they could say nothing a

SAY before, to —

To say beforehand, publicly, προερέω *proereō.*

Rom. 9. 29 as Esaias said before, Except the Lord of
2 Co. 7. 3 for I have said before, that ye are in our
Gal. 1. 9 As we said before, so say I now again, If
Heb. 10. 15 a witness..for after that [he had said be.]

SAY on, to —

1. *To speak,* דָּבַר *dabar,* 3.

1 Sa. 15. 16 Stay, and I will tell thee..Say on
2 Sa. 14. 12 speak (one) word..And he said, Say on
1 Ki. 2. 14 I have somewhat..unto thee..Say on
2. 16 now I ask one petition of thee..Say on

2. *To speak, tell, declare,* εἶπον, *eipon.*

Luke 7. 40 Simon, I have somewhat..Master, say on

3. *To lay out, say, speak,* λέγω *legō.*

Acts 13. 15 if ye have any word of exhortation..say on

SAY anything, or what, to —

Word, מִלָּה *millah.*

Job 32. 11 waited..whilst ye searched out what to say
33. 32 If thou hast any thing to say, answer me

SAY nay, to —

To send back the face of, שׁוּב פָּנִים *shub* (5) *panim.*

1 Ki. 2. 17 Speak..for he will not say thee nay, that
2. 20 I desire one small petition..say me not n.
2. 20 Ask on, my mother..I will not say thee n.

SAY —

In [*his*] *mouth,* בְּפִיו [*peh*].

2 Sa. 17. 5 and let us hear likewise what he saith

SAY, somewhat to —

A word, דָּבָר *dabar.*

1 Ki. 2. 14 I have somewhat to say unto thee. And

SAYING —

1. *A saying,* אֵמֶר *emer.*

Prov. 4. 10 Hear, O my son, and receive my sayings
4. 20 My son..incline thine ear unto my saying

2. *To say, lift up the voice,* אָמַר *amar.*

Gen. 1. 22 And God blessed them, saying

See also 2. 16; 3. 17; 5. 2; 8. 15; 9. 8; 15. 1, 4, 18; 17. 3; 18. 12, 13, 15; 19. 15; 21. 22; 22. 20; 23. 3, 5, 8, 10, 13, 14; 24. 7, 30, 37; 26. 11, 20; 27. 6, 6; 28. 6, 20; 31. 1, 29; 32. 4, 6, 17, 17, 19; 34. 4, 8, 20; 37. 15; 38. 13, 21, 24, 25, 28; 39. 12, 14, 17, 19; 40. 7; 41. 9, 16; 42. 14, 22, 22, 28, 29, 37; 43. 3, 3, 7; 44. 1, 19, 32; 45. 16, 26; 47. 5; 48. 20, 20; 50. 4, 4, 5, 16, 16, 25.

Exod 1. 22; 3. 16; 5. 6, 8, 10, 13, 15; 6. 10, 12, 29; 7. 8, 9, 16; 9. 5; 11. 8; 12. 1, 3; 13. 1, 8, 14, 19; 14. 1, 12; 15. 1, 24; 16. 11, 12; 17. 4, 7; 19. 3, 12, 23; 20. 1; 25. 1; 30. 11, 17, 22, 31; 31. 1, 12, 13; 33. 1; 35. 4, 4; 36. 5, 6; 40. 1.

Lev. 1. 1; 4. 1, 2; 5. 14; 6. 1, 8, 9, 19, 24, 25; 7. 22, 23, 28, 29; 8. 1, 31; 9. 3; 10. 3, 8, 16; 11. 1, 2; 12. 1, 2; 13. 1; 14. 1, 33, 35; 15. 1; 17. 1, 2; 18. 1; 19. 1, 2; 20. 1; 21. 16, 17; 22. 1, 17, 26; 23. 1, 9, 23, 24, 26, 33, 34; 24. 1, 13, 15; 25. 1; 27. 1.

Num. 1. 1, 48; 2. 1; 3. 5, 11, 14, 44; 4. 1, 17, 21; 5. 1, 5, 11; 6. 1, 22, 23, 23; 7. 4; 8. 1, 5, 23; 9. 1, 9, 10; 10. 1; 11. 13, 18, 20; 12. 13; 13. 1, 32; 14. 7, 15, 17, 26, 40; 15. 1, 17, 37; 16. 5, 20, 23, 24, 26, 36, 41, 44; 17. 1, 12; 18. 25; 19. 1, 2; 20. 3, 7, 23; 21. 21; 22. 5; 23. 26; 24. 12; 25. 10; 26. 1, 3, 52; 27. 2, 6, 8, 15; 28. 1; 30. 1, 3, 25; 32. 2, 10, 25, 31; 33. 50; 34. 1, 13, 16; 35. 1, 9; 36. 5, 6.

Deut. 1. 5, 6, 9, 16, 28, 34, 37; 2. 2, 4, 17, 26; 3. 18, 21, 23; 5. 5; 6. 20; 9. 4, 13, 23; 12. 30; 13. 2, 6, 12, 13; 15. 9, 11; 18. 16; 19. 7; 20. 5; 22. 17; 27. 1, 9, 11; 29. 19; 31. 10, 25; 32. 48; 34. 4.

Josh. 1. 1, 10, 11, 12, 13, 16; 2. 1, 2, 3; 3. 3, 6, 8, 9; 4. 1, 3, 6, 15, 17, 21, 21, 22; 6. 10, 26; 7. 2; 8. 4; 9. 11, 22, 22; 10. 3, 6, 17; 14. 9; 17. 4, 14, 17; 18. 8; 20. 1, 2; 21. 2; 22. 8, 15, 24.

Judg. 1. 1; 5. 1; 6. 13, 32; 7. 2, 3, 24; 8. 9, 15; 9. 1, 31; 10. 10; 11. 12, 17; 13. 6; 15. 13; 16. 2, 2, 18; 19. 22; 20. 8, 12, 23, 28; 21. 1, 5, 10, 18, 20.

Ruth 2. 15; 4. 4, 17; 1 Sa. 4. 21; 5. 10; 6. 2, 21; 7. 3; 9. 15, 26; 10. 2; 11. 7; 13. 3; 14. 24, 28, 33; 15. 10, 12; 16. 22; 17. 26, 27; 18. 24; 19. 2, 11, 15, 19; 20. 42; 21. 11; 23. 1, 2.

19, 27; 24. 1, 8, 9; 25. 14, 40; 26. 1, 6, 14, 19; 27. 11, 11, 12; 28. 10, 12; 29. 5; 30. 8, 26.
2 Sa. 1. 16, 2, 1, 4; 3. 12, 12, 14, 17, 18, 23, 35; 4. 10; 5. 1, 6, 19; 6. 12; 7. 4, 26; 11. 10, 15, 19; 13. 7, 28, 30; 14. 32; 15. 8, 10, 13, 31; 17. 6, 16; 18. 5, 12; 19. 8, 9, 11, 11; 20. 18, 18; 21. 17; 24. 11.
1 Ki. 1. 5, 6, 11, 13, 23, 30, 47, 51, 51; 2. 1, 4, 8, 23, 29, 30, 39, 42; 5. 2, 5, 8; 6. 11; 8. 15, 25, 47, 55; 9. 5; 12. 3, 7, 9, 10, 10, 12, 14, 16, 22, 23; 13. 3, 4, 9, 18, 21, 27, 31; 15. 18; 16. 1; 17. 2, 8; 18. 1, 26, 31; 19. 2; 20. 5, 5, 17; 21. 2, 9, 10, 13, 14, 17, 19, 19, 23, 28; 22. 12, 13, 31, 36.
2 Ki. 3. 7; 4. 1, 31; 5. 4, 6, 8, 10, 22; 6. 8, 9, 13, 26; 7. 10, 12, 14, 18; 8. 1, 4, 6, 7, 8, 9; 9. 12, 18, 20, 36; 10. 1, 5, 6, 8; 11. 5; 14. 6, 8, 9, 9; 15. 12; 16. 7, 15; 17. 13, 26, 27, 35; 18. 14, 30, 32, 36; 19. 9, 10, 10, 20; 20. 6, 4; 21. 10; 22. 3, 10, 12; 23. 21.
1 Ch. 4. 9, 10; 11. 1; 12. 19; 13. 12; 14. 10; 16. 18; 17. 3, 6, 24; 21. 9, 10; 22. 8; 2 Ch. 2. 3; 6. 4, 16, 37; 7. 18; 10. 3, 6, 7, 9, 10, 10, 12, 14, 16; 11. 2, 3; 12. 7; 16. 2; 18. 11, 12, 19, 19, 30; 19. 9; 20. 2, 8, 37; 21. 12; 25. 4, 7, 17, 18, 18; 30. 6, 18; 32. 4, 6, 9, 11, 12, 17; 34. 16, 18, 20; 35. 21; 36. 22.
Ezra 1. 1; 8. 22; 9. 1, 11; Neh. 1. 8; 6. 2, 3, 7, 8, 9; 8. 11, 15; Job 24. 15; Psa. 71. 11; 105. 11; 119. 82; Eccl. 1. 16.
Isa. 3. 7; 4. 1; 6. 8; 7. 2, 5, 10; 8. 5, 11; 14. 24; 16. 14; 19. 25; 20. 2; 23. 4; 29. 11, 12; 30. 21; 36. 15, 18, 21; 7.39, 10, 10, 15, 21; 38. 4; 41. 7, 13; 44. 28; 46. 10; 56. 3,
Jer. 1. 4, 11, 13; 2. 1, 2, 27; 4. 10; 5. 20; 6. 14; 7. 1, 4. 23; 8. 6, 11; 11. 1, 4, 6, 7, 21; 13. 3, 8; 18. 1, 5, 11; 20. 15; 21 1; 23. 25; 33. 38; 24. 4; 25. 2; 36. 1, 8, 9, 11, 12, 17, 18; 27. 1, 9, 12, 14, 16, 16; 28. 1, 2, 11, 12, 13; 29. 3, 22, 24, 25, 25, 28, 30, 31; 30. 1, 2; 31. 34; 32. 3, 6, 7, 13, 16, 26; 33. 1, 19, 23, 24; 34. 1, 12, 13; 35 1, 6, 12, 15; 36. 1, 5, 14, 17, 27, 29, 29; 37. 3, 6, 9, 13, 19; 38. 1, 8, 10, 16; 39. 11, 15, 16; 40. 9, 15; 42. 14, 20; 43. 8; 43. 2; 44. 1, 4, 15, 20, 25, 25, 26; 45. 1; 49. 34.
Eze. 3. 16; 6. 1; 7. 1; 9. 1, 11; 10. 6; 11. 14; 12. 1, 8, 17, 21, 22, 26; 13. 1, 6, 10; 14. 2, 12; 15. 1; 16. 1, 44; 17. 1, 11; 18. 1, 2; 20. 2, 5, 45; 21. 1, 8, 18; 22. 1, 17, 23, 28; 23. 1; 24. 1, 15, 20; 25. 1; 26. 1; 27. 1; 28. 1, 11, 20; 29. 1, 17; 30. 1, 20; 31. 1; 32. 1, 17; 33. 1, 10, 21, 23, 24, 30; 34. 1; 35. 1, 12; 36. 16; 37. 15, 18; 38. 1.
Amos 2. 12; 3. 1; 7. 10; 8. 5; Jon. 1. 1; 3. 1, 7; Hag. 1. 1, 2, 13; 2. 1, 2, 10, 11, 20, 21; Zech. 1. 1, 4, 7, 14, 17, 21; 2. 4; 3. 4, 6; 4. 4, 6, 6, 8; 6. 8, 9, 12, 12; 7. 3, 4, 5, 8, 9; 8. 1, 18, 21, 23.

3. *To say, lift up the voice,* אָמַר *amar.*
Ezra 5. 11 they returned us answer saying We are

4. *A word,* דָּבָר *dabar.*
Gen. 37. 11 envied..but his father observed the say.
Num 14. 39 Moses told these sayings unto all the ch.
1 Sa. 18. 8 Saul was very wroth, and the saying dis.
1 Ki. 12. 15 that he might perform his saying, which
13. 32 the saying which he cried by the word of
15. 29 according unto the saying of the LORD, wh.
17. 15 and did according to the saying of Elijah
20. 4 according to thy saying, I (am) thine, and
2 Ki. 2. 22 according to the saying of Elisha which
5. 14 according to the saying of the man of God
8. 2 and did after the saying of the man of God
10. 17 according to the saying of the LORD, which
1 Ch. 21. 19 David went up at the saying of God, wh.
2 Ch. 13. 22 his sayings, (are) written in the story of
33. 19 they (are) written among the sayings of
Esth. 1. 21 the saying pleased the king and the prin.
Jon. 4. 2 (was) not this my saying when I was yet

5. *Mouth,* פֶּה *peh.*
Psa. 49. 13 yet their posterity approve their sayings

6. *Talk,* λαλιά *lalia.*
John 4. 42 Now we believe, not because of thy saying

7. *Word,* λόγος *logos.*
Matt. 7. 24 whosoever heareth these sayings of mine
7. 26 every one that heareth these sayings of
7. 28 when Jesus had ended these sayings, the
15. 12 offended, after they heard this saying
19. 1 when Jesus had finished these sayings, he
19. 11 All (men) cannot receive this saying, save
19. 22 when the young man heard that saying
26. 1 when Jesus had finished all these sayings
28. 15 this saying is commonly reported among
Mark 7. 29 For this saying go thy way; the devil is
8. 32 he spake that saying openly. And Peter
9. 10 And they kept that saying with themsel.
10. 22 he was sad at that saying, and went away
Luke 1. 29 she was troubled [at his saying], and cast
6. 47 and heareth my sayings, and doeth them
9. 28 eight days after these sayings, he took P.
9. 44 Let these sayings sink down into your ears
John 4. 37 herein is that saying true, One soweth, and
4. 39 believed on him for the saying of the wo.
6. 60 This is an hard saying; who can hear it?
7. 36 What (manner of) saying is this that he
7. 40 therefore when they heard this saying, sa.
8. 51, 52 If a man keep my saying, he shall ne.
8. 55 but I know him, and keep his saying
10. 19 division..among the Jews for these say.
12. 38 That the saying of Esaias the prophet
14. 24 He that loveth me not keepeth not my sa.
15. 20 if they have kept my saying, they will keep
18. 9 That the saying might be fulfilled which
18. 32 That the saying of Jesus might be fulfilled
19. 8, 13 When Pilate therefore heard that sa.
21. 23 Then went this saying abroad among the
Acts 6. 5 And the saying pleased the whole multi.
7. 29 Then fled Moses at this saying, and was
16. 36 the keeper of the prison told this saying
Rom. 3. 4 thou mightest be justified in thy sayings
13. 9 it is briefly comprehended in this saying
1 Co. 15. 54 then shall be brought to pass this saying
1 Ti. 1. 15 This (is) a faithful saying, and worthy of
3. 1 This (is) a true saying, If a man desire the
4. 9 This (is) a faithful saying, and worthy of
2 Ti. 2. 11 (It is) a faithful saying: For if we be dead
Titus 3. 8 (This is) a faithful saying, and these things
Rev. 19. 9 saith unto me, These are the true sayings
22. 6 These sayings (are) faithful and true: and
22. 7 blessed (is) he that keepeth the sayings of
22. 9 of them which keep the sayings of this
22. 10 Seal not the sayings of the prophecy of th.

8. *Saying, speech,* ῥῆμα *rhēma.*
Mark 9. 32 they understood not that saying, and were
Luke 1. 65 these sayings were noised abroad throug.
2. 17 they made known abroad the saying wh.
2. 50 they understood not the saying which he
2. 51 his mother kept all these sayings in her
7. 1 when he had ended all these sayings in the
9. 45 they understood not this saying, and it
9. 45 and they feared to ask him of that saying
18. 34 this saying was hid from them, neither

9. *To speak, tell, utter,* εἶπον *eipon.*
Matt 26. 44 prayed the third time, saying the same
Luke 5. 13 touched him, saying, I will: be thou clean
9. 22 Saying, The Son of man must suffer many
14. 5 answered them, saying, Which of you sh.
19. 30 Saying, Go ye into the village over against
John 11. 28 called Mary her sister, secretly, saying, T.
18. 22 saying, Answerest thou the high priest so?
Acts 7. 26 saying, Sirs, ye are brethren; why do ye
7. 27 thrust him away, saying, Who made thee
7. 40 Saying unto Aaron, Make us gods to go
10. 3 coming in to him, and saying unto him
16. 20 brought them to the magistrates, saying
19 21 to go to Jerusalem, saying, After I have
21. 14 we ceased, saying, The will of the Lord
23. 23 he called unto (him) two centurions, sa.

10. *To lay out, say, speak,* λέγω *legō.*
Matt. 1. 20 appeared unto him in a dream, saying, J.
Also in v. 22; 2. 2, 13, 15, 17, 20; 3. 2, 3, 14, 17; 4. 14; 5. 2; 6. 31; 8. 2, 3, 6, 17, 25, 27, 29, 31; 9. 14, 18, 27, 29, 30, 33; 10. 5, 7; 11. 17; 12. 10, 17; 13. 3, 24, 31, 35, 36; 14. 15, 26, 27, 30, 33; 15 1, [4,] 7, 22, 23, 25; 16. 7, 13, 22; 17. 9, 10, 14, 25; 18. 1, 26, 28, 29; 19. 3, 25; 20. 12, 30, 31; 21. 2, 4, 9, 10, 15, 20, 25, 37; 22. 4, 16, 24, 31, [35,] 42, 43; 23. 2; 24. 3, 5; 25. 9, 11, 20, 37, 44, 45; 26. 8, 17, 27, 39, 42, 48, 65, 68, 69, 70; 27. 4, 9, 11, 19, 23, 24, 29, 40, 46, 54, 63; 28. 9, 13, 18.
Mark 1. 7, 15, 24, 25, 27, 40; 2. [12]; 3. 11, 33; 5. 9, 12, 23. 31; 6. 2, 25; 7. 37; 8. 15, [16,] 26, 27, 33; 9. [7,] 11, 25, 38; 10. 26. 35, 49; 11. [9,] 17, 31; 12. 6, 18, 26; 13. 6; 14. 44, 57, 60, 68; 15. 4, 9, 29, [34,] 36.
Luke 1. 24, 63, 66, 67; 2. 13; 3. [4], 10, 14, 16; 4. [4,] [34,] 35, 36, 41; 5. 8, 12, 21, 26, [30]; 7. 4, 6, 16, 19, 20, 32, 39; 8. 9, 24, 25, 30, 38, 49, 50, 54; 9. 18, 35, 38; 10. 17, 25; 11. 45; 12. 16, 17; 13. 25, 31; 14. [3,] 7, 30; 15. 2, 3, 6, 9; 17. 4; 18. 2, 3, 13, 18, 38, [41]; 19. 7, 14, 16, 18, 20, 38, 42, 46; 20. [2,] 5, 14, 21, 28; 21. 7, 8; 22. 19, 20, 42, 57, 59, 64, 66; 23. 2, 2, 3, 5, 18, 21, 35, 37, [39,] [40,] 47; 24. 7, 23, 29, 34.
John 1. 15, 26, 32; 4. 31, 51; 6. 52; 7. 15, 28, 37; 8. 12; 9. 2, 19; 10. [33,] 11. 3, [31,] 32; 12. 21, 23; 18. 40; 19. 6, 12.
Acts 1. 6; 2. 7, 12, 40; 3. 25; 4. 16; 5. 23, [25,] 28; 7; 56; 8. 10, 19, 26; 9. 4; 10. 26; 11. 3, 4, 7, 18; 12. 7; 13. 15; 14. 11, 15, 18; 15. 5, 13, [24]; 16. 9, 15, 17, 28, 35; 17. 7, 19; 18. 13; 19. 4, 13, 26, 28; 20. 23, 21, 21, 40; 22. 7, 18, 26; 23. 9, 12; 24. 2; 25. 14; 26. [14,] 22, 31; 27. 24, 33; 28. 26.
Rom. 11. [2]; 1 Co. 11. 25; 2 Ti. 2. 18; Heb. 2. 6, 12; 4. 7; 6. 15; 8. 11; 9. 20; 12. 26; 2 Pe. 3. 4; Jude 14; Rev. 1. 11, 17; 4. 8, 10; 5. 9, 12, 13; 6. 1, 10; 7. 3, 10, 12, 13; 8. 13; 9. 14; 10. 4; 11. 1, 12, 15, 17; 12. 10; 13. 4, 14; 14. 7, 8, 9, 13, 18; 15. 3; 16. 1, 17; 17. 1; 18. 2, 4, 10, 16, 18, 19, 21; 19. 1, 4, 5, 6, 17; 21. 3, 9.

11. *To assert, affirm,* φάσκω *phaskō.*
Acts 24. 9 the Jews also assented, saying that these

SAYING, dark —
Acute or hidden thing, חִידָה *chidah.*
Psa. 49. 4 I will open my dark saying upon the harp
78. 2 I will open..I will utter dark sayings of
Prov. 1. 6 words of the wise, and their dark sayings

SCAB, scabbed —
1. *Scurvy,* גָּרָב *garab.*
Deut 28. 27 with the emerods, and with the scab, and
2. *A scab,* מִסְפַּחַת *mispachath.*
Lev. 13. 6 pronounce him clean: it (is but) a scab
13. 7 if the scab spread much abroad in the skin
13. 8 that, behold, the scab spreadeth in the skin
3. *A scab,* סַפַּחַת *sappachath.*
Lev. 13. 2 When a man shall have in the skin..a sc.
14. 56 for a rising, and for a scab, and for a br.
4. *Itch, scab, scurvy,* יַלֶּפֶת *yallepheth.*
Lev. 21. 20 or be scurvy, or scabbed, or hath his st.
22. 22 or having a wen, or scurvy, or scabbed

SCAB, to smite with a —
To scab, שָׂפַח *saphach,* 3.
Isa. 3. 17 the LORD will smite with a scab the crown

SCABBARD —
Scabbard, sheath, תַּעַר *taar.*
Jer. 47. 6 Put up thyself into thy scabbard, rest, and

SCAFFOLD —
A pulpit, כִּיּוֹר *kiyyor.*
2 Ch. 6. 13 Solomon had made a brasen scaffold, of

SCALE, to —
To go up, עָלָה *alah.*
Prov. 21. 22 A wise (man) scaleth the city of the mig.

SCALES —
1. *Scales, armour,* קַשְׂקֶשֶׂת *qasqeseth.*
Lev. 11. 9 whatsoever hath fins and scales in the wa.
11. 10 all that have not fins and scales in the
11. 12 Whatsoever hath no fins nor scales in the
Deut 14. 9 all that have fins and scales shall ye eat
14. 10 whatsoever hath not fins and scales ye
Eze. 29. 4 cause the fish..to stick unto thy scales
29. 4 fish of thy rivers shall stick unto thy scales
2. *Strong or firm of shield,* אָפִיק מָגֵן *aphiq magen.*
Job 41. 15 (His) scales (are his) pride, shut up toget.
3. *Balance, beam of scales,* פֶּלֶס *peles.*
Isa. 40. 12 weighed the mountains in scales, and the
4. *A scale,* λεπίς *lepis.*
Acts 9. 18 there fell from his eyes as it had been sc.

SCALL —
A scall, נֶתֶק *netheq.*
Lev. 13. 30 it (is) a dry scall, (even) a leprosy upon
13. 31 the priest look on the plague of the scall
13. 31 (him that hath) the plague of the scall se.
13. 32 (if) the scall spread not, and there be in it
13. 32 the scall (be) not in sight deeper than the
13. 33 He shall be shaven, but the scall shall be
13. 33 shall shut up (him that hath) the scall se.
13. 34 look on the scall: and, behold, (if) the sc.
13. 35 But if the scall spread much in the skin
13. 36 if the scall be spread in the skin, the pri.
13. 37 if the scall be in his sight at a stay, and
13. 37 scall is healed, he (is) clean: and the pr.
14. 54 all manner of plague of leprosy, and scall

SCALP —
Crown of head, pate, קָדְקֹד *qodqod.*
Psa. 68. 21 hairy scalp of such an one as goeth on st.

SCANT —
Leanness, scantiness, רָזוֹן *razon.*
Mic. 6. 10 and the scant measure (that is) abomin.?

SCAPE GOAT —
A goat for going away, עֲזָאזֵל *azazel.*
Lev. 16. 8 LORD, and the other lot for the scape goat
16. 10 on which the lot fell to be the scape goat
16. 10 let him go for a scape goat into the wild.
16. 26 he that let go the goat for the scape goat

SCARCE, scarcely —
1. *To go out or forth,* יָצָא *yatsa.*
Gen. 27. 30 Jacob was yet scarce gone out from the pr.
2. *Hardly,* μόλις *molis.*
Acts 14. 18 with these sayings scarce restrained they
27. 7 scarce were come over against Cnidus, the
Rom. 5. 7 scarcely for a righteous man will one die
1 Pe. 4. 18 if the righteous scarcely be saved, where

SCARCENESS —
Scarcity, מִסְכֵּנֻת *miskenuth.*
Deut. 8. 9 wherein thou shalt eat bread without sc.

SCARE, to —
To break down, affright, חָתַת *chathath,* 3.
Job 7. 14 Then thou scarest me with dreams, and

SCARLET (colour or thread) —
1. *Purple,* אַרְגְּוָן *argevan.*
Dan. 5. 7, 16 be clothed with scarlet, and (have) a
5. 29 clothed Daniel with scarlet, and (put) a
2. *(Cochineal) crimson,* (שְׁנִי תוֹלַעַת), (תּוֹלַעַת) *[shani].*
Gen. 38. 28 bound upon his hand a scarlet thread, sa.
38. 30 that had the scarlet thread upon his hand
Exod 25. 4 blue, and purple, and scarlet, and fine li.
26. 1, 31, 36 blue, and purple, and scarlet
27. 16 blue, and purple, and scarlet, and fine tw.
28. 5, 8 blue, and purple, and scarlet, and fine
28. 6 (of) blue, and (of) purple, (of) scarlet, and
28. 15, 33 (of) blue, and (of) purple, and (of) sca.
35. 6, 23 blue, and purple, and scarlet, and fine
35. 25 blue, and of purple, (and) of scarlet, and of
35. 35 in blue, and in purple, in scarlet, and in
36. 8 curtains (of)..blue, and purple, and scar.
36. 35, 37 blue, and purple, and scarlet, and fine
38. 18 blue, and purple, and scarlet, and fine tw.
38. 23 embroiderer in blue..and in scarlet, and
39. 1 of the blue, and purple, and scarlet, they
39. 2, 5, 8, 24, 29 blue, and purple, and scarlet
39. 3 in the purple, and in the scarlet, and in
Lev. 14. 4, 49 and cedar wood, and scarlet, and hys.
14. 6 take it, and the cedar wood, and the sca.
14. 51 take the cedar wood..and the scarlet, and
14. 52 and with the hyssop, and with the scarlet
Num. 4. 8 shall spread upon them a cloth of scarlet
19. 6 take cedar wood, and hyssop, and scarlet
Josh. 2. 18 thou shalt bind this line of scarlet thread
2. 21 she bound the scarlet line in the window
2 Sa. 1. 24 clothed you in scarlet, with (other) delic.
Prov 31. 21 all her household (are) clothed with sca.
Song 4. 3 Thy lips (are) like a thread of scarlet, and
Isa. 1. 18 Though your sins be as scarlet, they shall
3. *Cochineal, crimson, scarlet,* תּוֹלָע *tola.*
Lam. 4. 5 brought up in scarlet embrace dunghills
4. *To be in scarlet, dyed,* תָּלַע *tala,* 4.
Nah. 2. 3 valiant men (are) in scarlet: the chariots
5. *Scarlet,* κόκκινος *kokkinos.*
Matt 27. 28 stripped him, and put on him a scarlet

Heb. 9. 19 with water, and scarlet wool, and hyssop
Rev. 17. 3 saw a woman sit upon a scarlet coloured
17. 4 was arrayed in purple and scarlet colour
18. 12 fine linen, and purple, and silk, and scar
18. 16 clothed in fine linen, and purple, and sc

SCATTER (abroad, away, into corners), to —

1. *To scatter,* בְּדַר *bedar,* 3.
Dan. 4. 14 shake off his leaves, and scatter his fruit

2. *To scatter,* בְּזַר *bazar.*
Dan. 11. 24 he shall scatter among them the prey, and

3. *To scatter,* בָּזַר *bazar,* 3.
Psa. 68. 30 scatter thou the people (that) delight in

4. *To scattter, winnow, spread,* זָרָה *zarah.*
Num 16. 37 scatter thou the fire yonder; for they are
Eze. 5. 2 third part thou shalt scatter in the wind

5. *To scatter, winnow, spread,* זָרָה *zarah,* 3.
Lev. 26. 33 will scatter you among the heathen, and
1 Ki. 14. 15 and shall scatter them beyond the river
Psa. 44. 11 and hast scattered us among the heathen
106. 27 To overthrow..and to scatter them in the
Prov 20. 8 A king..scattereth away all evil with his
20. 26 A wise king scattereth the wicked, and
Jer. 31. 10 He that scattered Israel will gather him
49. 32 scatter into all winds them (that are) in
49. 36 will scatter them toward all those winds
Eze. 5. 10 remnant of thee will I scatter into all the
5. 12 I will scatter a third part into all the wi
6. 5 I will scatter your bones round about your
12. 14 I will scatter toward every wind all that
Zech. 1. 19, 21 the horns which have scattered Judah
1. 21 horn over the land of Judah to scatter it

6. *To sprinkle,* זָרַק *zaraq.*
Isa. 28. 25 scatter the cummin, and cast in the prin.
Eze. 10. 2 scatter (them) over the city. And he went

7. *To cause to move, shake,* נוּעַ *nua,* 5.
Psa. 59. 11 scatter them by thy power; and bring th.

8. *To dash or beat in pieces, spread out,* נָפַץ *naphats,* 3.
Dan. 12. 7 when he shall have accomplished to sca.

9. *To blow away,* פָּאָה *paah,* 5.
Deut 32. 26 I said, I would scatter them into corners

10. *To scatter,* פּוּץ *puts,* 5.
Gen. 11. 8 So the LORD scattered them abroad from
11. 9 scatter them abroad upon the face of the
49. 7 divide them in Jacob, and scatter them in
Deut. 4. 27 LORD shall scatter you among the nations
28. 64 LORD shall scatter thee among all people
30. 3 whither the LORD thy God hath scattered
2 Sa. 22. 15 sent out arrows, and scattered them; li
Neh. 1. 8 I will scatter you abroad among the nat.
Job 37. 11 he wearieth the thick cloud; he scattereth
38. 24 (which) scattereth the east wind upon the
Psa. 18. 14 he sent out his arrows and scattered them
144. 6 Cast forth lightning, and scatter them
Isa. 24. 1 scattereth abroad the inhabitants thereof
41. 16 the whirlwind shall scatter them: and th.
Jer. 9. 16 I will scatter them also among the heat.
13. 24 Therefore will I scatter them as the stu
18. 17 I will scatter them as with an east wind
23. 1 that destroy and scatter the sheep of my
23. 2 Ye have scattered my flock, and driven
30. 11 end of all nations whither I have scatte.
Eze. 11. 16 I have scattered them among the count.
12. 15 I shall scatter them among the nations, and
20. 23 I would scatter them among the heathen
22. 15 I will scatter thee among the heathen, and
29. 12 I will scatter the Egyptians among the na.
30. 23, 26 I will scatter the Egyptians among the
34. 21 pushed..till ye have scattered them abr.
36. 19 I scattered them among the heathen and
Hab. 3. 14 they came out as a whirlwind to scatter

11. *To scatter,* פָּזַר *pazar,* 3.
Psa. 53. 5 God hath scattered the bones of him that
89. 10 thou hast scattered thine enemies with
147. 16 he scattereth the hoar frost like ashes
Prov 11. 24 There is that scattereth, and yet increa.
Jer. 3. 13 hast scattered thy ways to the strangers
Joel 3. 2 whom they have scattered among the na.

12. *To break off,* פָּרַץ *parats.*
Psa. 60. 1 thou hast scattered us, thou hast been di.

13. *To spread out or forth,* פָּרַשׂ *paras,* 3.
Psa. 68. 14 When the Almighty scattered kings in it

14. *To scatter thoroughly,* διασκορπίζω *diaskorpizō.*
Luke 1. 51 he hath scattered the proud in the imag.

15. *To scatter,* σκορπίζω *skorpizō.*
Matt 12. 30 he that gathereth not with me scattereth a.
Luke 11. 23 he that gathereth not with me scattereth
John 10. 12 the wolf catcheth them, and scattereth

SCATTERED (abroad), to be —

1. *To be scattered, winnowed, spread,* זָרָה *zarah,* 2.
Eze. 6. 8 ye shall be scattered through the countr.

2. *To be scattered, winnowed, spread,* זָרָה *zarah,* 4.
Job 18. 15 brimstone shall be scattered upon his ha

3. *To be prolonged, drawn out,* מָשַׁךְ *mashak,* 4.
Isa. 18. 2 to a nation scattered and peeled, to a pe.
18. 7 of a people scattered and peeled, and fr.

4. *To dash or beat in pieces,* נָפַץ *naphats.*
1 Sa. 13. 11 I saw that the people were scattered from
Isa. 33. 3 at the lifting up..nations were scattered

5. *To scatter, be scattered,* פּוּץ *puts.*
Gen. 11. 4 lest we be scattered abroad upon the face
Num 10. 35 Rise up..let thine enemies be scattered
1 Sa. 11. 11 they which remained were scattered, so
Psa. 68. 1 Let God arise, let his enemies be scattered
Eze. 34. 5 they were scattered, because (there is) no
34. 15 they became meat..when they were scat.
46. 18 that my people be not scattered every m.
Zech 13 7 smite..and the sheep shall be scattered

6. *To be scattered,* פּוּץ *puts,* 2.
2 Sa. 18. 8 For the battle was there scattered over
1 Ki. 22. 17 I saw all Israel scattered upon the hills
2 Ki. 25. 5 and all his army were scattered from him
2 Ch 18. 16 I did see all Israel scattered upon the mo
Jer. 10. 21 therefore their flocks shall be scattered
40. 15 that all the Jews should be scattered and
52. 8 and all his army were scattered from him
Eze. 11 17 countries where ye have been scattered
20. 34 out of the countries wherein ye are scatt.
20. 41 countries wherein ye have been scattered
28. 25 the people among whom they were scatt.
29. 13 from the people whither they were scatt.
34. 6 My flock was scattered upon all the face
34. 12 all places where they have been scattered

7. *To scatter, break in pieces,* פּוּץ *puts,* 5.
Exod. 5. 12 the people were scattered abroad throug.
1 Sa 13 8 and the people were scattered from him

8. *To scatter selves, be scattered,* פּוּץ *puts,* 7a.
Hab 3 6 the everlasting mountains were scattered

9. *To be increased, scattered,* פּוּשׁ *push,* 2.
Nah. 3. 18 thy people is scattered upon the mounta.

10. *To scatter,* פָּזַר *pazar.*
Jer 50. 17 Israel (is) a scattered sheep; the lions have

11. *To be scattered,* פָּזַר *pazar,* 2.
Psa. 141. 7 Our bones are scattered at the grave's mo.

12. *To be scattered,* פָּזַר *pazar,* 4.
Esth. 3. 8 There is a certain people scattered abroad

13. *To separate selves,* פָּרַד *parad,* 7.
Job 4. 11 the stout lion's whelps are scattered abr
Psa 92 9 all the workers of iniquity shall be scatt.

14. *To be spread out or forth,* פָּרַשׂ *paras,* 2.
Eze 17 21 they that remain shall be scattered tow.

15. *To be spread abroad,* פָּרַשׁ *parash,* 2.
Eze. 34 12 he is among his sheep (that are) scattered

16. *To be dissolved,* διαλύομαι *dialuomai.*
Acts 5. 36 as many as obeyed him, were scattered

17. *To scatter thoroughly,* διασκορπίζω *diaskorpizō.*
Matt 26. 31 the sheep of the flock shall be scattered a.
Mark 14. 27 smite and the sheep shall be scattered
John 11. 52 children of God that were scattered abr.

18. *To scatter diversely, disperse,* διασπείρω *diasp.*
Acts 8. 1 they were all scattered abroad throughout
8. 4 they that were scattered abroad went ev.
11. 19 they which were scattered abroad upon

19. *A dispersion, dispersed portion,* διασπορά *dias.*
Jas 1. 1 twelve tribes which are scattered abroad
1 Pe 1. 1 the strangers scattered throughout Pontus

20. *To throw down,* ῥίπτω *rhiptō.*
Matt 9 36 they fainted, and were scattered abroad

21. *To scatter,* σκορπίζω *skorpizō.*
John 16. 32 ye shall be scattered, every man to his own

SCATTERING —

Scattering, נֶפֶץ *nephets.*
Isa. 30. 30 (with) scattering, and tempest, and hails.

SCENT —

1. *Memorial, remembrance,* זֵכֶר, זֶכֶר *zeker.*
Hos. 14. 7 the scent thereof (shall be) as the wine of L.

2. *Smell, savour, fragrance,* רֵיחַ *reach.*
Job 14 9 through the scent of water it will bud, and
Jer. 48. 11 his taste remained in him, and his scent

SCEPTRE —

1. *Reed, rod, sceptre,* שֵׁבֶט *shebet.*
Gen. 49. 10 The sceptre shall not depart from Judah
Num 24. 17 a sceptre shall rise out of Israel, and shall
Psa. 45. 6 the sceptre of thy kingdom (is) a right sc.
Isa. 14. 5 The LORD hath broken..the sceptre of the
Eze. 19. 11 she had strong rods for the sceptres of
19. 14 she hath no strong rod (to be) a sceptre to
Amos 1. 5, 8 and him that holdeth the sceptre from
Zech 10. 11 and the sceptre of Egypt shall depart aw.

2. *Sceptre,* שַׁרְבִיט *sharebit.*
Esth. 4 11 the king shall hold out the golden sceptre
5 2 held out to Esther the golden sceptre that
5 2 So Esther..touched the top of the sceptre
8. 4 the king held out the golden sceptre tow.

3. *Rod, sceptre, staff,* ῥάβδος *rhabdos.*
Heb 1. 8 a sceptre of righteousness (is) the sceptre

SCE'-VA, Σκευᾶς.
A Jewish priest at Ephesus, father of seven sons who attempted to cast out a demon in the name of Jesus, but who were wounded by it and had to flee. A.D. 58.
Acts 19. 14 And there were seven sons of..S., a Jew

SCHOLAR —

1. *To answer, respond,* עָנָה *anah.*
Mal. 2. 12 The LORD will cut off..the scholar, out

2. *One who is being taught,* תַּלְמִיד *talmid.*
1 Ch. 25. 8 cast lots..as well..teacher as the scholar

SCHISM —

Rent, schism, σχίσμα *schisma.*
1 Co. 12. 25 That there should be no schism in the bo.

SCHOOL —

A school, σχολή *scholē.*
Acts 19. 9 disputing daily in the school of one Tyr.

SCHOOLMASTER —

Child conductor, παιδαγωγός *paidagōgos.*
Gal. 3. 24 the law was our schoolmaster (to bring us)
3. 25 we are no longer under a schoolmaster

SCIENCE —

1. *Knowledge,* מַדָּע, מַדַּע *madda.*
Dan. 1. 4 understanding science, and such as (had)

2. *Knowledge,* γνῶσις *gnōsis.*
1 Ti. 6. 20 and oppositions of science falsely so call.

SCOFF, to —

To show self a derider, scoffer, קָלַס *qalas,* 7.
Hab. 1. 10 they shall scoff at the kings, and the pr.

SCOFFER —

Childish trifler, ἐμπαίκτης *empaiktēs.*
2 Pe. 3. 3 that there shall come in the last days sc.

SCORCH, be scorched, to —

To parch, wither with heat, καυματίζω *kaumatizō.*
Matt 13. 6 when the sun was up, they were scorched
Mark 4. 6 But when the sun was up, it was scorched
Rev. 16. 8 power was given unto him to scorch men
16. 9 men were scorched with great heat, and

SCORN, scorning, scornful, scorner —

1. *Scorn, scorning,* לַעַג *laag.*
Job 34. 7 Job, (who) drinketh up scorning like w.
Psa. 44. 13 a scorn and a derision to them that are
79. 4 a scorn and derision to them that are ro.
123. 4 with the scorning of those that are at ea.

2. *Laughter,* מִשְׂחָק *mischaq.*
Hab. 1. 10 the princes shall be a scorn unto them: they

3. *To scorn,* לִיץ *luts.*
Psa. 1. 1 nor sitteth in the seat of the scornful
Prov. 1. 22 the scorners delight in their scorning, and
3. 34 he scorneth the scorners: but he giveth
9. 7 He that reproveth a scorner getteth to
9. 8 Reprove not a scorner, lest he hate thee
13. 1 A wise son (heareth)..a scorner heareth
14. 6 A scorner seeketh wisdom, and (findeth
15. 12 A scorner loveth not one that reproveth
19. 25 Smite a scorner, and the simple will bew.
19. 29 Judgments are prepared for scorners, and
21. 11 When the scorner is punished, the simple
21 24 haughty scorner (is) his name who dealeth
22. 10 Cast out the scorner, and contention shall
24. 9 and the scorner (is) an abomination to men
Isa. 29. 20 the scorner is consumed, and all that wat.

4. *Scorning,* לָצוֹן *latson.*
Prov. 1. 22 delight in their scorning, and fools hate
29. 8 Scornful men bring a city into a snare: but
Isa. 28. 14 hear the word of the LORD, ye scornful

5. *To be a scorner,* לָצַץ *latsats.*
Hos. 7. 5 he stretched out his hand with scorners

SCORN, (laugh to, think) to —

1. *To despise, contemn,* בָּזָה *bazah.*
Esth. 3. 6 he thought scorn to lay hands on Morde.

2. *To scorn,* לִיץ *luts.*
Prov. 9. 12 but (if) thou scornest, thou alone shalt

3. *To scorn,* לִיץ *luts,* 5.
Job 16. 20 My friends scorn me: (but) mine eye po.
Prov. 3. 34 Surely he scorneth..but he giveth grace
19. 28 An ungodly witness scorneth judgment

4. *To scorn,* לָעַג *laag.*
2 Ki. 19. 21 despised thee, (and) laughed thee to scorn
Job 22. 19 and the innocent laugh them to scorn
Isa. 37. 22 despised thee, (and) laughed thee to scorn

5. *To scorn,* לָעַג *laag,* 5.
Neh. 2. 19 they laughed us to scorn, and despised
Psa. 22. 7 All they that see me laugh me to scorn

6. *Laughter,* צְחֹק *tsechoq.*
Eze. 23. 32 thou shalt be laughed to scorn, and had

7. *To deride, scoff,* קָלַס *qalas,* 3.
Eze. 16. 31 been as an harlot, in that thou scornest

8. *To laugh, deride, play,* שָׂחַק *sachaq.*
Job 39. 7 He scorneth the multitude of the city, n.
39. 18 lifteth up herself on high, she scorneth

9. *To laugh, deride, play,* שָׂחַק *sachaq,* 5.
2 Ch. 30. 10 laughed them to scorn, and mocked them

SCORPION —

1. *A scorpion,* עַקְרָב *aqrab.*
Deut 8. 15 scorpions, and drought, where (there was)
1 Ki. 12. 11, 14 but I will chastise you with scorpions
2 Ch. 10. 11, 14 but I (will chastise you) with scorpio.
Eze. 2. 6 and thou dost dwell among scorpions: be

2. *A scorpion,* σκορπίος *skorpios.*
Luke 10. 19 power to tread on serpents and scorpions
11. 12 ask an egg, will he offer him a scorpion?
Rev. 9. 3 as the scorpions of the earth have power
9. 5 torment (was) as the torment of a scorpion
9. 10 they had tails like unto scorpions, and

SCOURED, to be —

To be scoured, polished, מָרַק *maraq,* 4.
Lev. 6. 28 it shall be both scoured, and rinsed in wa.

SCOURGE, scourged, scourging —

1. *Investigation,* בִּקֹּרֶת *biqqoreth.*
Lev. 19. 20 she shall be scourged; they shall not be

2. *A scourge, whip, rod,* שׁוֹט *shot.*
Job 5. 21 Thou shalt be hid from the scourge of the
9. 23 If the scourge slay suddenly, he will laugh
Isa. 10. 26 LORD of hosts shall stir up a scourge for
28. 18 when the overflowing scourge shall pass

3. *A scourge,* שֹׁטֵט *shotet.*
Josh. 23. 13 scourges in your sides, and thorns in your

4. *A scourge,* שׁוֹט *shot* [V. L. שׁיט].
Isa. 28. 15 when the overflowing scourge shall pass

5. *A scourge, whip,* μάστιξ *mastix.*
Acts 22. 24 he should be examined by scourging,
Heb. 11. 36 others had trial of.. mockings and scour

6. *A scourge, whip, (Lat. flagellum),* φραγέλλιον.
John 2. 15 when he had made a scourge of small co

SCOURGE, to —

1. *To whip, scourge, flog,* μαστιγόω *mastigoō.*
Matt 10. 17 they will scourge you in their synagogues
20. 19 deliver him to the Gentiles.. to scourge
23. 34 (some) of them shall ye scourge in your
Mark 10. 34 shall mock him, and shall scourge him
Luke 18. 33 shall scourge (him), and put him to death
John 19. 1 Pilate therefore took Jesus, and scourged
Heb. 12. 6 and scourgeth every son whom he receiv.

2. *To scourge, whip,* μαστίζω *mastizō.*
Acts 22. 25 Is it lawful for you to scourge a man that

3. *To flagellate,* φραγελλόω *phragelloō.*
Matt 27. 26 when he had scourged Jesus, he delivered
Mark 15. 15 delivered Jesus, when he had scourged

SCRABBLE, to —

To make a mark, scribble, תָּוָה *tavah,* 3
1 Sa. 21. 13 scrabbled on the doors of the gate, and

SCRAPE (off, self), to —

1. *To scrape self,* גָּרַד *garad,* 7.
Job 2. 8 took him a potsherd to scrape himself wi

2. *To scrape,* סָחָה *sachah,* 3.
Eze. 26. 4 I will also scrape her dust from her, and

3. *To scrape off,* קָצָה *qatsah,* 5.
Lev. 14. 41 scrape off without the city into an uncle
14. 43 hath scraped the house, and after it is pl.

SCRAPED, to cause to be —

To cause to be scraped, קָצַע *qatsa,* 5.
Lev. 14. 41 he shall cause the house to be scraped wi.

SCREECH OWL —

Night owl, לִילִית *lilith.*
Isa. 34. 14 screech owl also shall rest there, and find

SCRIBE —

1. *To cypher, number, write,* סָפַר *saphar.*
2 Sa. 8. 17 (were) the priests, and Seraiah (was).. sc.
20. 25 Sheva (was) scribe; and Zadok and Abia.
1 Ki. 4. 3 Elihoreph and Ahiah.. scribes; Jehoshap
2 Ki. 12. 10 king's scribe and the high priest came up
18. 18, 37 Shebna the scribe, and Joah the son
19. 2 sent Eliakim and Shebna the scribe, and
22. 3 son of Meshullam, the scribe to the ho
22. 8 high priest said unto Shaphan the scribe
22. 9 Shaphan the scribe came to the king and
22. 10 Shaphan the scribe showed the king, say
22. 12 Shaphan the scribe, and Asahiah a servant
25. 19 principal scribe of the host, which must
1 Ch. 2. 55 the families of the scribes which dwelt at
18. 16 (were) the priests; and Shavsha (was) scr
24. 6 the son of Nethaneel the scribe, (one) of
27. 32 was a counsellor, a wise man, and a scribe
2 Ch. 24. 11 the king's scribe and the high priest's off.
26. 11 their account by the hand of Jeiel the sc.
34. 13 of the Levites (there were) scribes, and
34. 15 answered and said to Shaphan the scribe
34. 18 the scribe told the king, saying, Hilkiah
34. 20 Shaphan the scribe, and Asaiah a servant
Ezra 7. 6 he (was) a ready scribe in the law of Moses
7. 11 the scribe, (even) a scribe of the words of
Neh. 8. 1 they spake unto Ezra the scribe to bring
8. 4 the scribe stood upon a pulpit of wood, wh.
8. 9 Ezra the priest the scribe, and the Levites
8. 13 and the Levites, unto Ezra the scribe, ev.
12. 26 in the days.. of Ezra the priest, the scribe
12. 36 David the man of God, and Ezra the scri.
13. 13 Shelemiah the priest, and Zadok the scr.
Esth. 3. 12 Then were the king's scribes called on the
8. 9 Then were the king's scribes called at that
Isa. 33. 18 Where (is) the scribe? where (is) the rec.?
36. 3 Shebna the scribe, and Joah, Asaph's son
36. 22 Shebna the scribe, and Joah the son of A.
37. 2 Shebna the scribe, and the elders of the
Jer. 8. 8 in vain made he (it); the pen of the scri.
36. 10 Gemariah the son of Shaphan the scribe
36. 12 he went down.. into the scribe's chamber
36. 12 Elishama the scribe, and Delaiah the son
36. 20 in the chamber of Elishama the scribe
36. 21 took it out of Elishama the scribe's cham.
36. 26 to take Baruch the scribe, and Jeremiah
36. 32 gave it to Baruch the scribe, the son of N
37. 15 in the house of Jonathan the scribe; for
37. 20 return to the house of Jonathan the scri
52. 25 the principal scribe of the host, who mu

2. *Scribe, writer,* סֹפֵר *sapher.*
Ezra 4. 8 Shimshai the scribe wrote a letter against
4. 9 the chancellor, and Shimshai the scribe
4. 17 (to) Shimshai the scribe, and (to) the rest
4. 23 Rehum, and Shimshai the scribe, and th.
7. 12. 21 scribe of the law of the God of heaven

3. *Scribe, writer, clerk,* γραμματεύς *grammateus.*
Matt. 2. 4 gathered all the chief priests and scribes
5. 20 (the righteousness) of the scribes and Ph.
7. 29 having authority, and not as the scribes
8. 19 a certain scribe came, and said unto him
9. 3 certain of the scribes said within themse.
12. 38 certain of the scribes and of the Pharisees
13. 52 every scribe (which is) instructed unto the
15. 1 Then came to Jesus scribes and Pharisees
16. 21 the elders and chief priests and scribes, and
17. 10 Why then say the scribes that Elias must
20. 18 the chief priests and unto the scribes
21. 15 when the chief priests and scribes saw the
23. 2 The scribes and the Pharisees sit in Moses'
23. 13, 15, 23, 25, 27, 29 woe unto you, scribes and
23. 14 [Woe unto you, scribes and Pharisees, h].
23. 34 prophets, and wise men and scribes: and
26. 3 the chief priests, [and the scribes,] and the
26. 57 where the scribes and the elders were as.
27. 41 mocking (him), with the scribes and elders
Mark 1. 22 for he taught them.. not as the scribes
2. 6 there were certain of the scribes sitting
2. 16 when the scribes and Pharisees saw him
3. 22 the scribes which came down from Jeru.
7. 1 certain of the scribes, which came from J.
7. 5 the Pharisees and scribes asked him, Why
8. 31 and (of) the chief priests, and scribes, and
9. 11 Why say the scribes that Elias must first
9. 14 and the scribes questioning with them
9. 16 he asked [the scribes,] What question ye
10. 33 unto the chief priests, and unto the scribes
11. 18 the scribes and chief priests heard (it), and
11. 27 the chief priests, and the scribes, and the
12. 28 one of the scribes came, and having heard
12. 32 the scribe said unto him, Well Master, th.
12. 35 How say the scribes that Christ is the son
12. 38 Beware of the scribes, which love to go in
14. 1 the scribes sought how they might take
14. 43 from the chief priests and the scribes and
14. 53 priests and the elders and the scribes
15. 1 the elders and scribes and the whole con.
15. 31 said among themselves with the scribes
Luke 5. 21 the scribes and the Pharisees began to re
5. 30 their scribes and Pharisees murmured ag.
6. 7 the scribes and Pharisees watched him
9. 22 of the elders and chief priests and scribes
11. 44 [Woe unto you, scribes and Pharisees, hy.]
11. 53 the scribes and the Pharisees began to ur.
15. 2 the Pharisees and scribes murmured, sa.
19. 47 the scribes and the chief of the people so.
20. 1 the scribes came upon (him) with the el.
20. 19 the scribes the same hour sought to lay
20. 39 certain of the scribes answering said, M.
20. 46 Beware of the scribes, which desire to wa.
22. 2 the chief priests and scribes sought how
22. 66 the scribes, came together, and led him
23. 10 the chief priests and scribes stood and
John 8. 3 [the scribes and Pharisees brought unto]
Acts 4. 5 that their rulers, and elders, and scribes
6. 12 the people and the elders, and the scribes
23. 9 [the scribes that were of the Pharisees' p.]
1 Co. 1. 20 where (is) the scribe? where (is) the disp.

SCRIP —

1. *Scrip, bag, purse,* יַלְקוּט *yalqut.*
1 Sa. 17. 40 put them in a shepherd's bag.. in a scrip

2. *Bag, satchel,* πήρα *pēra.*
Matt 10. 10 Nor scrip for (your) journey, neither two
Mark 6. 8 no scrip, no bread, no money in (their) pu
Luke 9. 3 neither staves, nor scrip, neither bread
10. 4 Carry neither purse, nor scrip, nor shoes
22. 35 When I sent you without purse, and scrip
22. 36 let him take (it), and likewise (his) scrip

SCRIPTURE —

1. *Writing,* כְּתָב *kethab.*
Dan. 10. 21 that which is noted in the scripture of tr.

2. *What is written, literature,* γράμμα *gramma.*
2 Ti. 3. 15 thou hast known the Holy Scriptures, wh.

3. *Writing, anything written,* γραφή *graphē.*
Matt 21. 42 Did ye never read in the scriptures, The
22. 29 Ye do err, not knowing the scriptures, nor
26. 54 how then shall the scriptures be fulfilled
26. 56 that the scriptures of the prophets might
Mark 12. 10 have ye not read this scripture; The stone
12. 24 ye know not the scriptures, neither the
14. 49 ye took me not: but the scriptures must
15. 28 [the scripture was fulfilled, which saith]
Luke 4. 21 This day is this scripture fulfilled in your
24. 27 expounded unto them in all the scriptures
24. 32 and while he opened to us the scriptures
24. 45 that they might understand the scriptures
John 2. 22 they believed the scripture, and the word
5. 39 Search the scriptures; for in them ye th.
7. 38 He that believeth on me, as the scripture
7. 42 Hath not the scripture said, That Christ
10. 35 and the scripture cannot be broken
13. 18 that the scripture may be fulfilled, He
17. 12 that the scripture might be fulfilled
19. 24, 28 that the scripture might be fulfilled
19. 36 these things were done, that the scripture
19. 37 another scripture saith, They shall look on
20. 9 they knew not the scripture, that he must
Acts 1. 16 this scripture must needs have been fulfi.
8. 32 The place of the scripture which he read
8. 35 began at the same scripture, and preached
17. 2 reasoned with them out of the scriptures
17. 11 searched the scriptures daily, whether th
18. 24 eloquent man, (and) mighty in the script.
18. 28 showing by the scriptures that Jesus was
Rom. 1. 2 afore by his prophets in the holy scriptu.
4. 3 what saith the scripture? Abraham belie
9. 17 the scripture saith unto Pharaoh, Even
10. 11 the scripture saith, Whosoever believeth
11. 2 Wot ye not what the scripture saith of E.?
15. 4 that we through.. comfort of the scriptu.
16. 26 made manifest, and by the scriptures of
1 Co. 15. 3 Christ died.. according to the scriptures
15. 4 rose again.. according to the scriptures
Gal. 3. 8 the scripture, foreseeing that God would
3. 22 the scripture hath concluded all under sin
4. 30 what saith the scripture? Cast out the bo.
1 Ti. 5. 18 the scripture saith, Thou shalt not muzzle
2 Ti. 3. 16 All scripture (is) given by inspiration of G.
Jas. 2. 8 the royal law according to the scripture
2. 23 the scripture was fulfilled which saith
4. 5 Do ye think that the scripture saith in va.
1 Pe. 2. 6 it is contained in the scripture, Behold, I
2 Pe. 1. 20 no prophecy of the scripture is of any pr.
3. 16 wrest, as (they do) also the other scriptu.

SCROLL —

1. *Scroll, roll, book,* סֵפֶר *sepher.*
Isa. 34. 4 heavens shall be gathered together as a sc.

2. *Small scroll, roll, book,* βιβλίον *biblion.*
Rev. 6. 14 the heaven departed as a scroll when it is

SCULL, SKULL —

Scull, skull, poll, גֻּלְגֹּלֶת *gulgoleth.*
Judg. 9. 53 piece of a millstone.. all to brake his skull
2 Ki. 9. 35 they found no more of her than the scull

SCUM —

Scum, rust, חֶלְאָה *chelah.*
Eze. 24. 6 whose scum (is) therein, and whose scum
24. 11 may be molten in it, (that) the scum of it
24. 12 scum went not forth out of her: her scum

SCURVY —

Scurvy, גָּרָב *garab.*
Lev. 21. 20 or be scurvy, or scabbed, or hath his stones
22. 22 or having a wen, or scurvy, or scabbed

SCY-TH-I-AN, Σκύθης *belonging to Scythia.*
Col. 3. 11 Where there is neither.. Barbarian, S., bo.

SEA —

1. הַיָּם הַגָּדוֹל *hay-yam hag-gadol, The Great Sea,* i.e., *the Mediterranean.* Θάλασσα *thalassa.*
Num 34. 6 ye shall even have the great sea for a bor.
34. 7 from the great sea ye shall point out for
Josh. 1. 4 unto the great sea toward the going down
9. 1 the coasts of the great sea over against L.
15. 12 And the west border (was) to the great sea
15. 47 unto the river of Egypt, and the great sea
Eze. 47. 10 fish shall be.. as the fish of the great sea
47. 15 (shall be) the border.. from the great sea
47. 19 (in) Kadesh, the river to the great sea
47. 20 The west side also (shall be) the great sea
48. 28 (and) to the river toward the great sea
Acts 10. 6 Simon a tanner, whose house is by the sea
10. 32 the house of.. Simon a tanner by the sea
27. 30 they had let down the boat into the sea
27. 38 And.. they.. cast out the wheat into the s.
27. 40 they committed (themselves) unto the sea
28. 4 whom, though he hath escaped the sea
2 Co. 11. 26 (in) perils in the sea, (in) perils among fa.

2. הַיָּם הָאַחֲרוֹן *hay-yam ha-acharon, the hinder or uttermost or uttermost Sea,* i.e., *the Mediterranean.*
Deut 11. 24 even unto the uttermost sea, shall your co.
34. 2 all the land of Judah, unto the utmost sea
Joel 2. 20 and his hinder part toward the utmost sea
Zech 14. 8 and half of them toward the hinder sea

3. יָם יָפוֹא *yam yapho, the sea of Japho,* i.e., *the Mediterranean.*
Ezra 3. 7 to bring cedar trees.. to the sea of Joppa

4. יָם פְּלִשְׁתִּים *, the sea of the Philistines,* i.e., *the Med.*
Exod 23. 31 from the Red sea.. unto the sea of the Ph.

5. יָם הַמֶּלַח *the Salt Sea, that into which Jordan falls.*
Num 34. 3 shall be the outmost coast of the salt sea
34. 12 the goings out of it shall be at the salt sea
Deut. 3. 17 (even) the salt sea, under Ashdoth-pisgah
Josh. 3. 16 those that came down toward.. the salt s.
15. 2 was from the shore of the salt sea, from
15. 5 the east border (was) the salt sea.. unto the
18. 19 of the salt sea at the south end of Jordan

6. הַיָּם הַקַּדְמֹנִי *hay-yam haq-qadmoni, the East or former Sea, that into which the Jordan falls.*
Eze. 47. 18 measure.. from the border unto the east s.
Joel 2. 20 desolate, with his face toward the east sea
Zech. 14. 8 half of them toward the former sea: in

7. יָם הָעֲרָבָה *yam ha-arabah, the Sea of the Plain or of Arabah, that into which the Jordan falls.*
Deut. 3. 17 from Chinnereth.. unto the sea of the pl.
Josh 3. 16 that came down toward the sea of the pl.
12. 3 unto the sea of the plain.. the salt sea on
2 Ki. 14. 25 entering of Hamath unto the sea of the pl.

8. יָם סוּף *yam suph, the Red Sea,* i.e., *the sea between Egypt and Arabia, the Gulf of Suez.* Θάλασσα.
Exod 10. 19 wind, which.. cast them into the Red sea

Exod13. 18 the way of the wilderness of the Red sea
15. 4 his..captains also..drowned in the Red s.
15. 22 So Moses brought Israel from the Red sea
23. 31 I will set thy bounds from the Red sea
Num14. 25 the wilderness by the way of the Red sea
21. 4 from Mount Hor by the way of the Red s.
21. 14 What he did in the Red sea, and in the br.
33. 10 removed..and encamped by the Red sea
33. 11 they removed from the Red sea, and enc.
Deut. 1. 1 in the plain over against the Red (sea)
1. 40 the wilderness by the way of the Red sea
2. 1 the wilderness by the way of the Red sea
11. 4 he made the water of the Red sea to over.
Josh. 2. 10 dried up the water of the Red sea for you
4. 23 as the LORD your God did to the Red sea
24. 6 with chariots and horsemen unto the Red s.
Judg11. 16 walked through the wilderness..the Red s.
1 Ki. 9. 26 on the shore of the Red sea, in the land
Neh. 9. 9 and heardest their cry by the Red sea
Psa.106. 7 provoked (him) at the sea..at the Red sea
106. 9 He rebuked the Red sea also, and it was
106. 22 (and) terrible things by the Red sea
136. 13 To him which divided the Red sea into pa.
136. 15 overthrew Pharaoh and..host in the Red s.
Jer. 49. 21 the noise thereof was heard in the Red sea
Acts 7. 36 in the land of Egypt, and in the Red sea
1 Co. 10. 1 the cloud, and all passed through the sea
10. 2 unto Moses in the cloud and in the sea
Heb. 11. 29 By faith they passed through the Red sea

9. יָם מִצְרַיִם *yam mitsrayim, the Egyptian Sea,* i.e., *the sea between Egypt and Arabia.*
Isa. 11. 15 shall utterly destroy the tongue of the E.s.

10. יָם כִּנֶּרֶת *or* כִּנְּרוֹת *yam kinneroth or kinnereth, sea of Chinnereth,* i.e., *that through which Jordan passes.*
Num34. 11 unto the side of the sea of C. eastward
Josh.12. 3 from the plain to the sea of C. on the east
13. 27 unto the edge of the sea of C. on the other

11. Θάλασσα τῆς Γαλιλαίας, *the sea of Galilee.*
The same as the preceding, and sometimes called the Lake of Gennesereth, or of Tiberias. It is about thirteen miles long, six miles wide, and 150 feet deep. Its surface is 328 feet below the level of the Mediterranean.
Matt. 4. 15 the way of the sea, beyond Jordan, Galilee
4. 18 Jesus, walking by the sea of G., saw two
8. 24 there arose a great tempest in the sea, in.
8. 26 arose, and rebuked the winds and the sea
8. 27 that even the winds and the sea obey him
8. 32 violently down a steep place into the sea
13. 1 out of the house, and sat by the sea side
14. 24 [the ship was now in the midst of the sea]
14. 25 Jesus went unto them, walking on the sea
14. 26 the disciples saw him walking on the sea
15. 29 and came nigh unto the sea of G.; and went
17. 27 lest we should offend them, go..to the sea
Mark 1. 16 Now as he walked by the sea of G., he
1. 16 he saw Simon..casting a net into the sea
2. 13 And he went forth again by the sea side
3. 7 withdrew..with his disciples to the sea
4. 1 he began again to teach by the sea side
4. 1 he entered into a ship, and sat in the sea
4. 1 the whole multitude was by the sea on the
4. 39 And he..said unto the sea, Peace, be still
4. 41 that even the wind and the sea obey him?
5. 1 came over unto the other side of the sea
5. 13 into the sea..and were choked in the sea
5. 21 And when Jesus..was nigh unto the sea
6. 47 the ship was in the midst of the sea, and
6. 48 cometh unto them, walking upon the sea
7. 31 he came unto the sea of G., through the
John 6. 1 went over the sea of G. which is..of Tib.
6. 16 And his disciples went down unto the sea
6. 17 entered unto a ship, and went over the s.
6. 18 the sea arose, by reason of a great wind
6. 19 they see Jesus walking on the sea, and
6. 22 which stood on the other side of the sea
21. 1 Jesus showed himself..at the sea of Tib.
21. 7 Simon Peter..did cast himself into the s.

12. יָם יַעְזֵר *yam yazer, the sea of Jazer, a small lake in Gad, six hours from Heshbon and four from Rabbah, where a spring,* Wady-Seir, *is still found.*
Jer. 48. 32 they reach..to the sea of Jazer: the spo.

SEA —

1. *Sea, lake, pool,* יָם *yam.*
Gen. 1. 10 gathering..of the waters called he seas
1. 22 fill the waters in the seas, and let fowl
1. 26, 28 have dominion over the fish of the sea
9. 2 and upon all the fishes of the sea; unto your
14. 3 the vale of Siddim, which is the salt sea
22. 17 as the sand which (is) upon the sea shore
32. 12 make thy seed as the sand of the sea, wh.
41. 49 gathered corn as the sand of the sea, very
49. 13 Zebulun shall dwell at..haven of the sea
Exod10. 19 And the LORD..cast them into the Red sea
13. 18 the way of the wilderness of the Red sea
14. 2 between Migdol and the sea, over against
14. 2 before it shall ye encamp by the sea
14. 9 overtook them encamping by the sea, bes.
14. 16, 26 stretch out thine hand over the sea
14. 16 shall go..through the midst of the sea
14. 21 Moses stretched out his hand over the sea
14. 21 the LORD caused the sea to go (back) by
14. 21 made the sea dry (land), and the waters
14. 22 Israel went into the midst of the sea upon
14. 23 in after them to the midst of the sea
14. 27 his hand over the sea, and the sea retur.
14. 27 the Egyptians in the midst of the sea

Exod14. 28 the host of Pharaoh that came into the sea
14. 29 walked upon..(land) in the midst of the sea
14. 30 saw the Egyptians dead upon the sea sh.
15. 1, 21 his rider hath he thrown into the sea
15. 4 and his host hath he cast into the sea
15. 4 captains also are drowned in the Red sea
15. 8 were congealed in the heart of the sea
15. 10 Thou didst blow with thy wind, the sea
15. 19 and with his horsemen into the sea, and
15. 19 LORD brought again the waters of the sea
15. 19 went on dry (land) in the midst of the sea
15. 22 So Moses brought Israel from the Red sea
20. 11 the LORD made heaven and earth, the sea
23. 31 from the Red sea even unto the sea of the
Lev. 11. 9 in the waters, in the seas, and in the rivers
11. 10 that have not fins and scales in the seas
Num 11. 22 shall all the fish of the sea be gathered to.
11. 31 brought quails from the sea, and let (them)
13. 29 the Caananites dwell by the sea, and by
14. 25 the wilderness by the way of the Red sea
21. 4 from mount Hor by the way of the Red sea
33. 8 passed through the midst of the sea into
33. 10 removed..and encamped by the Red sea
33. 11 they removed from the Red sea, and en.
34. 3 the outmost coast of the salt sea eastward
34. 5 the goings out of it shall be at the sea
34. 6 ye shall even have the great sea for a bo.
34. 7 from the great sea ye shall point out for
34. 11 shall reach unto the side of the sea of C.
34. 12 the goings out of it shall be at the salt sea
Deut. 1. 7 by the sea side, to the land of the Canaa.
1. 40 the wilderness by the way of the Red sea
2. 1 the wilderness by the way of the Red sea
3. 17 the sea of the plain, (even) the salt sea
4. 49 even unto the sea of the plain, under the
11. 4 how he made the water of the Red sea to
11. 24 even unto the uttermost sea, shall your
30. 13 Neither (is) it beyond the sea, that thou
30. 13 Who shall go over the sea for us, and br.
33. 19 shall suck (of) the abundance of the seas
34. 2 all the land of Judah, unto the utmost sea
Josh. 1. 4 unto the great sea toward the going down
2. 10 LORD dried up the water of the Red sea
3. 16 the sea of the plain, (even) the salt sea
4. 23 as the LORD your God did to the Red sea
5. 1 the kings of the Canaanites..by the sea
9. 1 in all the coasts of the great sea over ag.
11. 4 as the sand that (is) upon the sea shore
12. 3 from the plain to the sea of Chinneroth
12. 3 the sea of the plain, (even) the salt sea on
13. 27 unto the edge of the sea of Chinnereth on
15. 2 border was from the shore of the salt sea
15. 4 goings out of that coast were at the sea
15. 5 the east border (was) the salt sea, (even)
15. 5 from the bay of the sea at the uttermost
15. 11 goings out of the border were at the sea
15. 12 the west border (was) to the great sea, and
15. 46 From Ekron even unto the sea, all that
15. 47 unto the river of Egypt, and the great sea
16. 3 and the goings out thereof are at the sea
16. 6 And the border went out toward the sea
16. 8 and the goings out thereof were at the s.
17. 9 and the outgoings of it were at the sea
17. 10 northward (it was) Manasseh's, and the s.
18. 14 compassed the corner of the sea southw.
18. 19 at the north bay of the salt sea at the so.
19. 11 their border went up toward the sea, and
19. 29 the outgoings thereof are at the sea from
23. 4 cut off, even unto the great sea westward
24. 6 ye came unto the sea; and the Egyptians
24. 6 the Egyptians pursued..unto the Red sea
24. 7 brought the sea upon them, and covered
Judg. 5. 17 Asher continued on the sea shore, and ab.
7. 12 as the sand by the sea side for multitude
11. 16 through the wilderness unto the Red sea
1 Sa. 13. 5 people as the sand which (is) on the sea
2 Sa. 17. 11 as the sand that (is) by the sea for multi.
22. 16 And the channels of the sea appeared, the
1 Ki. 4. 20 as the sand which (is) by the sea in mul.
4. 29 even as the sand that (is) on the sea
5. 9 unto the sea..convey them by sea in flo.
7. 23 made a molten sea, ten cubits from the
7. 24 ten in a cubit, compassing the sea round
7. 25 sea (was set) above upon them, and all th.
7. 39 set the sea on the right side of the house
7. 44 one sea, and twelve oxen under the sea
9. 26 on the shore of the Red sea, in the land
9. 27 that had knowledge of the sea, with
10. 22 For the king had at sea a navy of Thara.
18. 43 looked toward the sea. And he went up
18. 44 there ariseth a little cloud out of the sea
2 Ki. 14. 25 entering of Hamath unto the sea of the
16. 17 took down the sea from off the brasen o.
25. 13 brasen sea, (that was) in the house of the
25. 16 two pillars, one sea, and the bases which
1 Ch. 16. 32 Let the sea roar, and the fulness thereof
18. 8 wherewith Solomon made the brasen sea
2 Ch. 2. 16 we will bring it to thee in floats by sea to
4. 2 made a molten sea of ten cubits from br.
4. 3 ten in a cubit, compassing the sea round
4. 4 sea (was set) above upon them, and all th.
4. 6 but the sea (was) for the priests to wash
4. 10 set the sea on the right side of the east
4. 15 One sea, and twelve oxen under it
8. 17 to Eloth, at the sea side in the land of E.
8. 18 servants that had knowledge of the sea
20. 2 against thee from beyond the sea on this
Ezra 3. 7 from Lebanon to the sea of Joppa, accor.
Neh. 9. 6 the seas, and all that (is) therein, and th.
9. 9 and heardest their cry by the Red sea
9. 11 thou didst divide the sea before them, so
9. 11 they went through the midst of the sea on

Esth 10. 1 the land, and (upon) the isles of the sea
Job 6. 3 would be heavier than the sand of the sea
7. 12 (Am) I a sea, or a whale, that thou settest
9. 8 and treadeth upon the waves of the sea
11. 9 than the earth, and broader than the sea
12. 8 the fishes of the sea shall declare unto
14. 11 waters fail from the sea, and the flood de.
26. 12 divideth the sea with his power, and by
28. 14 depth saith, It (is) not in me; and the sea
36. 30 Behold, he..covereth the bottom of the s.
38. 8 (who) shut up the sea with doors, when it
38. 16 Hast thou entered into..springs of the s.?
41. 31 he maketh the sea like a pot of ointment
Psa. 8. 8 The fowl of the air, and the fish of the s.
8. 8 passeth through the paths of the seas
24. 2 For he hath founded it upon the seas, and
33. 7 He gathereth the waters of the sea toget.
46. 2 the mountains be carried into..the sea
65. 5 and of them that are afar off (upon) the s.
65. 7 Which stilleth the noise of the seas, the
66. 6 He turned the sea into dry (land): they
68. 22 I will bring..from the depths of the sea
69. 34 the seas, and every thing that moveth th.
72. 8 shall have dominion also from sea to sea
74. 13 Thou didst divide the sea by thy strength
77. 19 Thy way (is) in the sea, and thy path in
78. 13 He divided the sea, and caused them to
78. 27 feathered fowls..as the sand of the sea
78. 53 but the sea overwhelmed their enemies
80. 11 She sent out her boughs unto the sea, and
89. 9 Thou rulest the raging of the sea: when
89. 25 I will set his hand also in the sea, and his
93. 4 (yea, than) the mighty waves of the sea
95. 5 The sea (is) his, and he made it: and his
96. 11 let the earth be glad; let the sea roar, and
98. 7 Let the sea roar, and the fulness thereof
104. 25 (So is) this great and wide sea, wherein
106. 7 provoked (him) at the sea..at the Red s.
106. 9 He rebuked the Red sea also, and it was
106. 22 Wondrous..terrible things by the Red s.
107. 23 They that go down to the sea in ships, th.
114. 3 The sea saw (it,) and fled: Jordan was dr.
114. 5 What (ailed) thee, O thou sea, that thou
135. 6 in earth, in the seas, and all deep places
136. 13 To him which divided the Red sea into p.
136. 15 Pharaoh and his host in the Red sea
139. 9 (and) dwell in the uttermost parts of the s.
146. 6 Which made heaven and earth, the sea
Prov. 8. 29 When he gave to the sea his decree, that
23. 34 he that lieth down in the midst of the sea
30. 19 the way of a ship in the midst of the sea
Eccl. 1. 7 the rivers run into the sea; yet the sea
Isa. 5. 30 shall roar..like the roaring of the sea
9. 1 grievously afflict (her by) the way of the s.
10. 22 thy people Israel be as the sand of the s.
10. 26 (as) his rod (was) upon the sea, so shall he
11. 9 shall be full..as the waters cover the sea
11. 11 Hamath, and from the islands of the sea
11. 15 destroy the tongue of the Egyptian sea
16. 8 her branches..they are gone over the sea
17. 12 make a noise like the noise of the sea
18. 2 That sendeth ambassadors by the sea, ev.
19. 5 the waters shall fail from the sea, and the
21. 1 The burden of the desert of the sea. As
23. 2 merchants of Zidon, that pass over the s.
23. 4 sea hath spoken..the strength of the sea
23. 11 He stretched out his hand over the sea; he
24. 14 sing..they shall cry aloud from the sea
24. 15 glorify ye the LORD..in..isles of the sea
27. 1 he shall slay the dragon that (is) in the sea
42. 10 ye that go down to the sea, and all that
43. 16 which maketh a way in the sea, and a pa.
48. 18 thy righteousness as the waves of the sea
50. 2 at my rebuke I dry up the sea, I make the
51. 10 (Art) thou not it which hath dried the sea
51. 10 that hath made the depths of the sea away
51. 15 the LORD thy God, that divided the sea
57. 20 the wicked (are) like the troubled sea, wh.
60. 5 the abundance of the sea shall be conver.
63. 11 he that brought them up out of the sea wi.
Jer. 5. 22 the bound of the sea by a perpetual decree
6. 23 their voice roareth like the sea; and they
15. 8 increased..above the sand of the seas: I
25. 22 kings of the isles which (are) beyond the
27. 19 concerning the sea, and concerning the
31. 35 which divided the sea when the waves th.
33. 22 neither the sand of the sea measured; so
46. 18 and as Carmel by the sea, (so) shall he co.
47. 7 given it a charge..against the sea shore?
48. 32 over the sea, they reach (even) to the sea
49. 21 noise thereof was heard in the Red sea
49. 23 sorrow on the sea; it cannot be quiet
50. 42 their voice shall roar like the sea, and th.
51. 36 will dry up her sea, and make her springs
51. 42 sea is come up upon Babylon: she is cov.
52. 17 brasen sea that (was) in the house of the
52. 20 two pillars, one sea, and twelve brasen
Lam. 2. 13 for thy breach (is) great like the sea; who
Eze. 25. 16 and destroy the remnant of the sea coast
26. 3 as the sea causeth his waves to come up
26. 5 spreading of nets in the midst of the sea
26. 16 Then all the princes of the sea shall come
26. 17 city, which wast strong in the sea, she and
26. 18 isles that (are) in the sea shall be troubled
27. 3 thou that art situate at the entry of the sea
27. 4 Thy borders (are) in the midst of the seas
27. 9 ships of the sea with their mariners were
27. 25 made very glorious in the midst of the seas
27. 26 hath broken thee in the midst of the seas
27. 27 shall fall into the midst of the seas in the
27. 29 all the pilots of the sea, shall come down
27. 32 like the destroyed in the midst of the sea?

Eze. 27. 33 When thy wares went forth out of the seas
27. 34 thou shalt be broken by the seas in the de.
28. 2 the seat of God, in the midst of the seas
28. 8 (them that are) slain in the midst of the s.
32. 2 thou (art) as a whale in the seas; and thou
38. 20 So that the fishes of the sea, and the fowls
39. 11 valley..on the east of the sea; and it sha.
47. 8 down into the desert, and go into the sea
47. 8 brought forth into the sea, and the waters
47. 10 as the fish of the great sea, exceeding ma.
47. 15 from the great sea, the way of Hethlon, as
47. 17 border from the sea shall be Hazer-enan
47. 18 from the border unto the east sea. And
47. 19 Kadesh, the river to the great sea. And
47. 20 west side also (shall be) the great sea from
48. 28 (and) to the river toward the great sea
Dan. 7. 2 winds of the heaven strove upon the..sea
7. 3 four great beasts came up from the sea
11. 45 palace between the seas in the glorious
Hos. 1. 10 as the sand of the sea, which cannot be
4. 3 fishes of the sea also shall be taken away
Joel 2. 20 with his face toward the east sea, and his
2. 20 hinder part toward the utmost sea, and his
Amos 5. 8 that calleth for the waters of the sea, and
8. 12 they shall wander from sea to sea, and
9. 3 hid..in the bottom of the sea, thence will
9. 6 he that calleth for the waters of the sea
Jon. 1. 4 LORD sent out a great wind into the sea
1. 4 there was a mighty tempest in the sea, so
1. 5 cast forth the wares..into the sea, to lig.
1. 9 which hath made the sea and the (land)
1. 11 sea may be calm unto us? for the sea wr.
1. 12 cast me forth into the sea; so shall the s.
1. 13 for the sea wrought, and was tempestuous
1. 15 cast him forth into the sea; and the sea
1. 15 and the sea ceased from her raging
2. 3 into the deep, in the midst of the seas
Mic. 7. 12 from sea to sea, and (from) mountain to
7. 19 all their sins into the depths of the sea
Nah. 1. 4 He rebuketh the sea, and maketh it dry
3. 8 the sea, (and) her wall (was) from the sea?
Hab. 1. 14 makest men as the fishes of the sea, as the
2. 14 be filled..as the waters cover the sea
3. 8 thy wrath against the sea, that thou didst
3. 15 Thou didst walk through the sea with th.
Zeph. 1. 3 I will consume the..fishes of the sea, and
2. 5 Woe unto the inhabitants of the sea coast
2. 6 sea coast shall be dwellings (and) cottages
Hag. 2. 6 I will shake the heavens..and the sea, and
Zech. 9. 4 and he will smite her power in the sea
9. 10 his dominion (shall be) from sea (even) to s.
10. 11 shall pass through the sea with affliction
10. 11 shall smite the waves in the sea, and all
14. 8 half of them toward the former sea, and
14. 8 half of them toward the hinder sea: in su.

2. *A sea, lake, pool,* θάλασσα *thalassa.*
Matt. 4. 15 the way of the sea, beyond Jordan, Galilee
4. 18 Jesus, walking by the sea of Galilee, saw
4. 18 casting a net into the sea: for they were
8. 24 there arose a great tempest in the sea, in.
8. 26 rebuked the winds and the sea; and there
8. 27 that even the winds and the sea obey him
8. 32 ran..down a steep place into the sea, and
13. 1 out of the house, and sat by the sea side
13. 47 net, that was cast into the sea, and gath.
14. 24 [the ship was now in the midst of the sea]
14. 25 Jesus went unto them, walking on the sea
14. 26 the disciples saw him walking on the sea
15. 29 came nigh unto the sea of Galilee; and
17. 27 go thou to the sea, and cast an hook, and
18. 6 he were drowned in the depth of the sea
21. 21 be thou cast into the sea; it shall be done
23. 15 compass sea and land to make one prose.
Mark 1. 16 Now as he walked by the sea of Galilee, he
1. 16 casting a net into the sea: for they were
2. 13 he went forth again by the sea side; and
3. 7 Jesus withdrew himself..to the sea: and
4. 1 began again to teach by the sea side: and
4. 1 he entered into a ship, and sat in the sea
4. 1 whole multitude was by the sea on the l.
4. 39 said unto the sea, Peace, be still And
4. 41 that even the wind and the sea obey him?
5. 1 over unto the other side of the sea, into
5. 13 into the sea..and were choked in the sea
5. 21 unto him: and he was nigh unto the sea
6. 47 ship was in the midst of the sea, and he
6. 48 walking upon the sea, and would have pa.
6. 49 when they saw him walking upon the sea
7. 31 he came unto the sea of Galilee, through
9. 42 his neck, and he were cast into the sea
11. 23 shall say..be thou cast into the sea; and
Luke 17. 2 he cast into the sea, than that he should
17. 6 be thou planted in the sea; and it should
21. 25 with perplexity; the sea and the waves
John 6. 1 Jesus went over the sea of Galilee, which
6. 16 his disciples went down unto the sea
6. 17 and went over the sea toward Capernaum
6. 18 sea arose, by reason of a great wind that
6. 19 see Jesus walking on the sea, and drawing
6. 22 which stood on the other side of the sea
6. 25 found him on the other side of the sea, th.
21. 1 showed himself..at the sea of Tiberias
21. 7 Simon Peter..did cast himself into the s.
Acts 4. 24 hast made..the sea, and all that in them
7. 36 showed wonders..in the Red sea, and in
10. 6 a tanner, whose house is by the sea side
10. 32 house of (one) Simon a tanner by the sea
14. 15 made..the sea, and all things that are th.
17. 14 sent away Paul, to go as it were to the s.
27. 30 they had let down the boat into the sea
27. 38 and cast out the wheat into the sea
Acts 27. 40 they commited (themselves) unto the sea
28. 4 whom, though he hath escaped the sea, yet
Rom. 9. 27 number..be as the sand of the sea, a re.
1 Co. 10. 1 that all our fathers..passed through the s.
10. 2 were all baptized unto Moses..in the sea
2 Co. 11. 26 perils in the sea, (in) perils among false
Heb. 11. 12 sand which is by the sea shore innumer.
11. 29 By faith they passed through the Red sea
Jas. 1. 6 like a wave of the sea, driven with the w.
Jude 13 Raging waves of the sea, foaming out their
Rev. 4. 6 before the throne (there was) a sea of gl.
5. 13 such as are in the sea, and all that are in
7. 1 not blow on the earth, nor on the sea, nor
7. 2 it was given to hurt the earth and the sea
7. 3 Hurt not the earth, neither the sea, nor
8. 8 burning with fire was cast into the sea
8. 8 and the third part of the sea became blo.
8. 9 of the creatures which were in the sea, and
10. 2 he set his right foot upon the sea, and (his)
10. 5 angel which I saw stand upon the sea and
10. 6 [sea, and the things which are therein]
10. 8 angel which standeth upon the sea and
12. 12 the inhabiters of the earth and of the sea!
13. 1 sea, and saw a beast rise up out of the s.
14. 7 made heaven, and earth, and the sea, and
15. 2 saw as it were a sea of glass mingled with
15. 2 stand on the sea of glass, having the har.
16. 3 angel poured out his vial upon the sea
16. 3 and every living soul died in the sea
18. 17 as many as trade by sea, stood afar off
18. 19 made rich all that had ships in the sea by
18. 21 cast (it) into the sea, saying, Thus with
20. 8 number of whom (is) as the sand of the s.
20. 13 sea gave up the dead which were in it, and
21. 1 passed away; and there was no more sea

3. *The deep open sea,* πέλαγος *pelagos.*
Acts 27. 5 when we had sailed over the sea of Cilicia

SEA coast (upon the) —

1. *Along the lake,* παραθαλάσσιος *parathalassios.*
Matt 4. 13 Capernaum, which is upon the sea coast

2. *Along the (salt) sea,* παράλιος *paralios.*
Luke 6. 17 from the sea coast of Tyre and Sidon, wh.

SEA, (things) in the —

Belonging to or in the (salt) water, ἐνάλιος *enalios.*
Jas. 3 7 every kind..of things in the sea, is tamed

SEA monster —

Howlers, jackals, dragons, תַּנִּין *tannin.*
Lam 4. 3 the sea monsters draw out the breast, th.

SEAFARING men —

Seas, יַמִּים *yammim.*
Eze. 26. 17 (that wast) inhabited of seafaring men, the

SEAL —

1. *Seal, signet,* חוֹתָם *chotham.*
1 Ki. 21. 8 sealed (them) with his seal, and sent the
Job 38. 14 It is turned as clay (to) the seal; and they
41. 15 pride shut up together (as with) a close se.
Song 8. 6 Set me as a seal upon thine heart..a seal

2. *A seal, impression, inscription,* σφραγίς *sphragis.*
Rom. 4. 11 a seal of the righteousness of the faith wh.
1 Co. 9. 2 the seal of mine apostleship are ye in the
2 Ti. 2. 19 having this seal, The Lord knoweth them
Rev. 5. 1 and on the back side, sealed with seven s.
5. 2 to open the book, and to loose the seals t.
5. 5 open the book, and to loose the seven se.
5. 9 Thou art worthy..to open the seals ther
6. 1 when the Lamb opened one of the seals
6. 3, 5, 7, 9, 12 when he had opened the..seal
7. 2 angel..having the seal of the living God
8. 1 when he had opened the seventh seal, th.
9. 4 those men which have not the seal of God

SEAL (up, set a seal), to —

1. *To seal, seal up, finish,* חָתַם *chatham.*
Deut 32. 34 (Is) not this..sealed up among my treas.
1 Ki. 21. 8 wrote letters in Ahab's name, and sealed
Neh. 9. 38 princes, Levites, (and) priests, seal (unto it)
10. 1 Now those that sealed (were) Nehemiah
Esth. 8. 8 seal it with the king's ring: for the writ.
8. 10 sealed (it) with the king's ring; and sent
Job 9. 7 Which commandeth the sun..and sealeth u.
14. 17 My transgression (is) sealed up in a bag
33. 16 he openeth the ears of men, and sealeth
37. 7 He sealeth up the hand of every man; th.
Song 4. 12 A garden..(is) my sister..a fountain sea.
Isa. 8. 16 Bind up the testimony, seal the law amo.
29. 11 as the words of a book that is sealed, wh.
29. 11 and he saith, I cannot; for it (is) sealed
Jer. 32. 10 I subscribed the evidence, and sealed (it)
32. 11 that which was sealed (according) to the
32. 14 both which is sealed, and this evidence
32. 44 subscribe evidences, and seal (them), and
Eze. 28. 12 Thou sealest up the sum, full of wisdom
Dan. 9. 24 to seal up the vision and prophecy, and
12. 4 seal the book, (even) to the time of the end
12. 9 the words (are) closed up and sealed till

2. *To seal, seal up,* חֲתַם *chatham.*
Dan. 6. 17 the king sealed it with his own signet

3. *To seal, impress,* σφραγίζω *sphragizō.*
Matt 27. 66 made the sepulchre sure, sealing the stone
John 3. 33 He..hath set to his seal that God is true
6. 27 the Son..him hath God the Father sealed
Rom 15. 28 When therefore I..have sealed to them th.
2 Co. 1. 22 Who hath also sealed us, and given the ea.
Eph. 1. 13 ye were sealed with the Holy Spirit of
4. 30 whereby ye are sealed unto the day of
Rev. 7. 3 till we have sealed the servants of our G.
7. 4 which were sealed: (and there were) sealed
Rev. 7. 5, 6, 7, 8 Of the tribe..(were) sealed twelve
10. 4 Seal up those things which the seven th.
20. 3 set a seal upon him, that he should dece.
22. 10 Seal not the sayings of the prophecy of th.

SEALED, to be —

1. *To be sealed, sealed up,* חָתַם *chatham,* 2.
Esth. 3. 12 was it written, and sealed with the king's
8. 8 is written in the king's name, and sealed

2. *To seal down,* κατασφραγίζω *katasphragizō.*
Rev. 5. 1 written within and on the back side, sea.

SEAM, without —

Without a seam, ἄῤῥαφος *arrhaphos.*
John 19. 23 the coat was without seam, woven from

SEARCH, searching, secret —

1. *A search,* חֵפֶשׂ *chephes.*
Psa. 64. 6 they accomplish a diligent search: both

2. *A search, searching,* חֵקֶר *cheqer.*
Judg. 5. 16 For the divisions(..were) great searchings
Job 8. 8 prepare thyself to the search of their fath.
11. 7 Canst thou by searching find out God? ca.
38. 16 hast thou walked in the search of the de.
Isa. 40. 28 (there is) no searching of his understand.

3. *Digging, or breaking through,* מַחְתֶּרֶת *machtereth.*
Jer. 2. 34 I have not found it by secret search, but

SEARCH (diligently, for, out), to —

1. *To seek, inquire,* בָּקַר *baqar,* 3.
Lev. 27. 33 He shall not search whether it be good or

2. *To seek, require,* דָּרַשׁ *darash.*
1 Ch. 28. 9 the LORD searcheth all hearts, and under.
Job 10. 6 enquirest after mine iniquity, and searc.
39. 8 and he searcheth after every green thing
Jer. 29. 13 when ye shall search for me with all your
Eze. 34. 6 and none did search or seek (after them)
34. 8 neither did my shepherds search for my
34. 11 I, (even) I, will both search my sheep, and

3. *To seek, dig, search,* חָפַר *chaphar.*
Deut. 1. 22 they shall search us out the land, and
Josh. 2. 2 there came men..to search out the coun.
2 3 they be come to search out all the country

4. *To search out for,* חָפַשׂ *chaphas.*
Psa. 64. 6 They search out iniquities; they accompl.
Prov 2. 4 and searchest for her as (for) hid treasures
20. 27 searching all the inward parts of the belly
Lam 3. 40 Let us search and try our ways, and turn

5. *To search, search out for,* חָפַשׂ *chaphas,* 3.
Gen. 31 35 And he searched, but found not the im.
44. 12 he searched, (and) began at the eldest, and
1 Sa. 23. 23 I will search him out throughout all the
1 Ki. 20. 6 they shall search thine house, and the h.
2 Ki. 10. 23 Search, and look that there be here with
Amos 9. 3 I will search and take them out thence
Zeph. 1. 12 I will search Jerusalem with candles, and

6. *To search, search out, investigate,* חָקַר *chaqar.*
Judg 18 2 to spy out the land, and to search it
18. 2 they said unto them, Go, search the land
2 Sa. 10. 3 to search the city, and to spy it out, and
1 Ch. 19. 3 his servants come unto thee for to search
Job 5. 27 Lo this, we have searched it, so it (is)
13. 9 Is it good that he should search you out?
28. 3 setteth an end to darkness, and searcheth
28. 27 he prepared it, yea, and searched it out
29. 16 the cause (which) I knew not I searched o.
32. 11 I gave ear..whilst ye searched out what
Psa. 44. 21 Shall not God search this out? for he kn.
139. 1 thou hast searched me, and known (me)
139. 23 Search me, O God, and know my heart
Prov 18. 17 his neighbour cometh and searcheth him
25. 2 the honour of kings (is) to search out a
28. 11 that hath understanding searcheth him out
Jer. 17. 10 I the LORD search the heart, (I) try the
Eze. 39. 14 after the..seven months shall they search

7. *Search, searching,* חֵקֶר *cheqer.*
Prov 25. 27 so (for men) to search their own glory (is

8. *To feel, search, grope,* מָשַׁשׁ *mashash,* 3.
Gen. 31. 34 Laban searched all the tent, but found
31. 37 Whereas thou hast searched all my stuff

9. *To traverse, spy out,* רָגַל *ragal,* 3.
Deut. 1 24 came unto the valley of Eshcol, and they

10. *To go about, spy out, search,* תּוּר *tur.*
Num 10. 33 to search out a resting place for them
13. 2 Send thou men, that they may search the
13. 21 they went up, and searched the land from
13. 25 they returned from searching of the land
13. 32 of the land which they had searched
13. 32 through which we have gone to search
14. 6 (which were) of them that searched the
14. 7 The land, which we passed through to se.
14. 34 the number of the days in which ye sear.
14. 36 the men which Moses sent to search the
14. 38 of the men that went to search the land
Deut. 1. 33 to search you out a place to pitch your
Eccl. 1. 13 I gave my heart to seek and search out
7. 25 to search and to seek out wisdom, and

11. *To judge or sift again,* ἀνακρίνω *anakrinō.*
Acts 17. 11 searched the scriptures daily, whether

12. *To trace out,* ἐξερευνάω *exereunaō.*
1 Pe. 1. 10 the prophets have enquired and searched

13. *To search out,* ἐξετάζω *exetazō.*
Matt. 2. 8 Go and search diligently for the young

14. *To trace, track,* ἐρευνάω *ereunaō.*
John 5. 39 Search the scriptures; for in them ye th.

John 7. 52 Art thou also of Galilee? Search, and look
Rom. 8. 27 he that searcheth the hearts knoweth wh.
1 Co. 2. 10 the spirit searcheth all things, yea, the
1 Pe. 1. 11 Searching what, or what manner of time
Rev. 2. 23 I am he which searcheth the reins and the

SEARCH, to make (diligent) —

1. *To seek, inquire,* בָּקַר *beqar,* 3.
Ezra 4. 15 That search may be made in the book of
4. 19 I commanded, and search hath been ma.
6. 1 search was made in the house of the rolls

2. *To seek, inquire,* בְּקַר *beqar,* 4.
Ezra 5. 17 let there be search made in the king's

3. *To search out for,* חָפַשׂ *chaphas,* 3.
Psa. 77. 6 and my spirit made diligent search

4. *To search out, investigate,* חָקַר *chaqar.*
Deut 13. 14 enquire, and make search, and ask dilig.

SEARCHED (out), to be —

1. *To be searched out,* חָפַשׂ *chaphas,* 2.
Obad. 6 How are (the things) of Esau searched out!

2. *To be searched out,* חָקַר *chaqar,* 2.
Jer. 31. 37 the foundations of the earth searched out
46. 23 cut down her forest..it cannot be searched

3. *A search, searching,* חֵקֶר *cheqer.*
Job 36. 26 neither can the number..be searched out

SEARED with a hot iron, to be —

To sear, brand, burn with hot iron, καυτηριάζομαι.
1 Ti. 4. 2 having their conscience seared with a hot i.

SEAS meet, where two —

Between two seas, διθάλασσος *dithalassos.*
Acts 27. 41 falling into a place where two seas met

SEASON (appointed, convenient, due) —

1. *An appointed time or season,* זְמָן,זְמַן *zeman.*
Eccl. 3. 1 To every (thing there is) a season, and a
Dan. 2. 21 And he changeth the times and the seas.
7. 12 their lives were prolonged for a season and

2. *Days,* יָמִים *yamim.*
Gen. 40. 4 and they continued a season in ward
Josh. 24. 7 ye dwelt in the wilderness a long season
2 Ch. 15. 3 for a long season Israel (hath been) witho.

3. *An appointed time or season,* מוֹעֵד *moed.*
Gen. 1. 14 let them be for signs, and for seasons, and
Exod 13. 10 therefore keep this ordinance in his season
Lev. 23. 4 which ye shall proclaim in their seasons
Num. 9. 2 also keep the passover at his appointed se.
9. 3 ye shall keep it in his appointed season
9. 7 offer an offering..in his appointed season
9. 13 offering of the LORD in his appointed sea.
28. 2 observe to offer unto me in their due seas.
Deut 16. 6 at the season that thou camest forth out
2 Ki. 4. 16 About this season, according to the time
4. 17 bare a son at that season that Elisha had
Psa. 104. 19 He appointed the moon for seasons: the
Hos. 2. 9 and my wine in the season thereof, and

4. *Time,* עֵת *eth.*
Exod 18. 22 And let them judge the people at all sea.
18. 26 And they judged the people at all seasons
Lev. 26. 4 Then I will give you rain in due season
Deut 11. 14 the rain of your land in his due season
28. 12 to give the rain unto thy land in his due s.
1 Ch. 21. 29 (were) at that season in the high place at
Job 5. 26 as a shock of corn cometh in his season
38. 32 Canst thou bring..Mazzaroth in his seas.?
Psa. 1. 3 that bringeth forth his fruit in his season
104. 27 mayest give (them) their meat in due se.
145. 15 thou givest them their meat in due season
Prov 15. 23 a word (spoken) in due season, how good
Eccl. 10. 17 thy princes eat in due season, for strength
Jer. 5. 24 both the former and the latter, in his sea.
33. 20 should not be day and night in their sea.
Eze. 34. 26 cause the shower to come down in his se.

5. *A time or season,* καιρός *kairos.*
Matt 21. 41 shall render him the fruits in their seasons
24. 45 made ruler..to give them meat in due se.
Mark 12. 2 at the season he sent to the husbandmen
Luke 1. 20 which shall be fulfilled in their season
4. 13 the devil..departed from him for a season
12. 42 give..(their) portion of meat in due season
13. 1 There were present at that season some
20. 10 And at the season he sent a servant to the
John 5. 4 [an angel went down at a certain season]
Acts 1. 7 for you to know the times or the seasons
13. 11 be blind, not seeing the sun for a season
14. 17 rain from heaven, and fruitful seasons
24. 25 when I have a convenient season I will
Gal. 6. 9 in due season we shall reap, if we faint
1 Th. 5. 1 of the times and the seasons, brethren, ye

6. *Time, delay,* χρόνος *chronos.*
Acts 19. 22 but he himself stayed in Asia for a season
20. 18 I have been with you at all seasons
Rev. 6. 11 that they should rest yet for a little season
20. 3 after that he must be loosed a little season

7. *An hour, time,* ὥρα *hōra.*
John 5. 35 ye were willing for a season to rejoice in
2 Co. 7. 8 made you sorry, though .. but for a season
Phm. 15 perhaps he therefore departed for a season

SEASON, for a, in, out of —

1. *Out of season, in good season,* ἀκαίρως, εὐκαίρως.
2 Ti. 4. 2 be instant in season, out of season; reprove

2. *Little,* ὀλίγον *oligon.*
1 Pe. 1. 6 ye greatly rejoice, though now for a seas.

3. *For a time,* πρόσκαιρος *proskairos.*
Heb. 11. 25 than to enjoy the pleasures of sin for a se.

SEASON, to —

1. *To salt,* מָלַח *malach.*
Lev. 2. 13 every oblation..shalt thou season with se.

2. *To fit, prepare,* ἀρτύω *artuō.*
Mark 9. 50 lost his saltness, wherewith will ye season
Luke 14. 34 his savour, wherewith shall it be season.
Col. 4. 6 Let your speech (be) alway with grace se.

SEAT, (seated) —

1. *To sit down or still,* יָשַׁב *yashab.*
1 Ki. 10. 19 on either side on the place of the seat, and
Amos 6. 3 cause the seat of violence to come near

2. *A seat, throne,* כִּסֵּא *kisse.*
Judg. 3. 20 he was sitting..And he arose out of (his) s.
1 Sa. 1. 9 Eli the priest sat upon a seat by a post of
4. 13 Eli sat upon a seat by the way side watc.
4. 18 he fell from off the seat backward by the
1 Ki. 2. 19 caused a seat to be set for the king's mo.
Esth. 3. 1 set his seat above all the princes that (w.)
Prov. 9. 14 on a seat in the high places of the city

3. *A seat, place of sitting down,* מוֹשָׁב *moshab.*
1 Sa. 20. 18 thou shalt be missed, because thy seat
20. 25 the king sat upon his seat..a seat by the
Job 29. 7 (when) I prepared my seat in the street
Psa. 1. 1 nor sitteth in the seat of the scornful
Eze. 8. 3 where (was) the seat of the image of jeal.
28. 2 I sit (in) the seat of God, in the midst of

4. *A seat, sitting,* שֶׁבֶת *shebeth.*
2 Sa. 23. 8 The Tachmonite that sat in the seat, ch.

5. *Prepared place or seat,* תְּכוּנָה *tekunah.*
Job 23. 3 Oh..(that) I might come (even) to his seat!

6. *To cover, be concealed,* סָפַן *saphan.*
Deut 33. 21 (in) a portion of the lawgiver, (was he) se.

7. *A seat, throne,* θρόνος *thronos.*
Luke 1. 52 He hath put down the mighty from..se.
Rev. 2. 13 thou dwellest, (even) where Satan's seat
4. 4 four and twenty seats: and upon the seats
11. 16 elders which sat before God on their seats
13. 2 dragon gave him his power, and his seat
16. 10 angel poured out his vial upon the seat of

8. *A seat, chair, stool,* καθέδρα *kathedra.*
Matt 21. 12 and the seats of them that sold doves
23. 2 and the Pharisees sit in Moses' seat
Mark 11. 15 and the seats of them that sold doves

SEAT, chief, highest, uppermost —

First seat or chair, πρωτοκαθεδρία *prōtokathedria.*
Matt 23. 6 and the chief seats in the synagogues
Mark 12. 39 And the chief seats in the synagogues, and
Luke 11. 43 ye love the uppermost seats in the synag.
20. 46 the highest seats in the synagogues, and

SE'-BA, סְבָא.

1. Eldest son of Cush, son of Ham. B.C. 2250.
Gen. 10. 7 And the sons of Cush; S., and Havilah
1 Ch. 1. 9 And the sons of Cush; S., and Havilah, and

2. His land, the N. part of Ethiopia, including Meroe.
Psa. 72. 10 the kings of Sheba and S. shall offer gifts
Isa. 43. 3 I gave Egypt..ransom, Ethiopia and S.

SE'-BAT, שְׁבָט.

The eleventh month of the Jewish year, beginning with the new moon of February.
Zech. 1. 7 eleventh month, which (is) the month S.

SE-CA'-CAH, סְכָכָה *enclosure.*

A city in the plain of Judah, near Middin.
Josh 15. 61 In the wilderness, Beth-arabah..and S.

SE'-CHU, שֶׂכוּ *watchplace.*

A city in Benjamin, near Ramah.
1 Sa. 19. 22 he..came to a great well that (is) in S.

SECOND (order, time, rank) —

1. *Second, a copy, double,* מִשְׁנֶה *mishneh.*
Gen. 41. 43 he made him to ride in the second chariot
1 Sa. 8. 2 Joel, and the name of his second, Abiah
2 Sa. 3. 3 his second, Chileab, of Abigail the wife of
2 Ki. 23. 4 and the priests of the second order, and
25. 18 Zephaniah the second priest, and the th.
1 Ch. 15. 18 with them their brethren of the second
2 Ch. 35. 24 and put him in the second chariot that
Ezra 1. 10 silver basins of a second (sort) four hun.
Neh. 11. 9 Judah the son of Senuah (was) second ov.
11. 17 Bakbukiah the second among his breth.
Jer. 52. 24 Zephaniah the second priest, and the th.
Zeph. 1. 10 an howling from the second, and a great

2. *Second, other, again,* שֵׁנִי *sheni.*
Gen. 1. 8 evening and the morning were the second
2. 13 And the name of the second river (is) Gi.
6. 16 (with) lower, second, and third (stories)
7. 11 in the second month, the seventeenth day
8. 14 in the second month, on the seven and tw.
22. 15 LORD called..Abraham..the second time
30. 7 conceived again, and bare Jacob a second
30. 12 Zilpah, Leah's maid, bare Jacob a second
32. 19 so commanded he the second, and the th.
41. 5 he slept and dreamed the second time
41. 52 the name of the second called he Ephraim
47. 18 they came unto him the second year, and
Exod. 2. 13 when he went out the second time, beho.
16. 1 on the fifteenth day of the second month
26. 4 and likewise..in the coupling of the sec.
26. 5 that (is) in the coupling of the second, that
Exod 26. 10 of the curtain which coupleth the second
26. 20 for the second side of the tabernacle, on
28. 18 And the second row (shall be) an emerald
36. 11, 12 in the coupling of the second
36. 17 of the curtain which coupleth the second
39. 11 the second row, an emerald, a sapphire
40. 17 in the first month in the second year, on
Lev. 5. 10 he shall offer the second (for) a burnt off.
13. 58 it shall be washed the second time, and
Num. 1. 1, 18 on the first (day) of the second month
1. 1 in the second year after they were come
2. 16 And they shall set forth in the second ra.
7. 18 On the second day Nethaneel the son of
9. 1 in the first month of the second year after
9. 11 The fourteenth day of the second month
10. 6 When ye blow an alarm the second time
10. 11 of the second month, in the second year
29. 17 on the second day (ye shall offer) twelve
Josh. 5. 2 circumcise..children of Israel a second ti.
6. 14 the second day they compassed the city
10. 32 which took it on the second day, and sm.
19. 1 the second lot came forth to Simeon, (even)
Judg. 6. 25 even the second bullock of seven years old
6. 26 take the second bullock, and offer a burnt
6. 28 the second bullock was offered upon the
20. 24 the children of Israel came..the second
20. 25 Benjamin went forth..the second day, and
1 Sa. 20. 27 (which was) the second (day) of the month
20. 34 did eat no meat the second day of the mo.
2 Sa. 14. 29 when he sent again the second time, he wo.
1 Ki. 6. 1 in the month Zif, which (is) the second m.
9. 2 LORD appeared to Solomon the second ti.
19. 7 angel of the LORD came again the second t.
2 Ki. 9. 19 he sent out a second on horseback, which
10. 6 he wrote a letter the second time to them
19. 29 in the second year that which springeth
25. 17 like unto these had the second pillar with
1 Ch. 2. 13 Abinadab the second, and Shimma the th.
3. 1 the second, Daniel, of Abigail the Carme.
3. 15 the second Jehoiakim, the third Zedekiah
7. 15 and the name of the second (was) Zeloph.
8. 1 Ashbel the second, and Aharah the third
8. 39 Ulam his first born, Jehush the second
12. 9 Ezer the first, Obadiah the second, Eliab
23. 11 Jahath was the chief, and Zizah the second
23. 19 Amariah the second, Jahaziel the third
23. 20 Micah the first, and Jesiah the second
24. 7 first lot came..to Jehoiarib, the second
24. 23 Amariah the second, Jahaziel the third
25. 9 the second to Gedaliah, who with his br.
26. 2 Jediael the second, Zebadiah the third
26. 4 Jehozabad the second, Joah the third, and
26. 11 Hilkiah the second, Tebaliah the third
27. 4 over the course of the second month (was)
29. 22 the son of David king the second time
2 Ch. 3. 2 to build in the second (day) of the second
27. 5 pay unto him, both the second year and
30. 2 to keep the passover in the second month
30. 13 to keep the feast..in the second month
30. 15 on the fourteenth (day) of the second mo.
Ezra 3. 8 in the second year of their coming unto
3. 8 in the second month, began Zerrubabel
Neh. 8. 13 on the second day were gathered together
Esth. 2. 14 she returned into the second house of the
2. 19 virgins were gathered together the second
7. 2 king said again unto Esther on the second
9. 29 wrote..to confirm this second letter of P.
Job 42. 14 the name of the second, Kezia; and the
Eccl. 4. 8 There is one (alone), and (there is) not a
4. 15 with the second child that shall stand up
Isa. 11. 11 LORD shall set his hand again the sec. time
37. 30 the second year that which springeth of
Jer. 1. 13 word of the LORD came unto me the sec. ti.
13. 3 word of the LORD came unto me the sec. ti.
33. 1 word..came unto Jeremiah the second ti.
41. 4 the second day after he had slain Gedaliah
52. 22 the second pillar also and the pomegran.
Eze. 10. 14 the second face (was) the face of a man
43. 22 on the second day thou shalt offer a kid
Jon. 3. 1 word..came unto Jonah the second time
Zech. 6. 2 and in the second chariot black horses

3. *Two, both,* שְׁנַיִם *shenayim.*
1 Ki. 15. 25 began to reign over Israel in the second
2 Ki. 1. 17 Jehoram reigned in his stead in the second
14. 1 In the second year of Joash son of Jehoa.
15. 32 In the second year of Pekah the son of R.
Dan. 2. 1 And in the second year of the reign of
Hag. 1. 1, 15 In the second year of Darius the king
2. 10 in the second year of Darius, came the
Zech. 1. 1, 7 in the second year of Darius, came the

4. *Second,* תִּנְיָן *tinyan.*
Dan. 7. 5 another beast, a second, like to a bear, and

5. *Second,* תְּרֵין *teren.*
Ezra 4. 24 it ceased unto the second year of the reign

6. *Second,* δεύτερος *deuteros.*
Matt 21. 30 And he came to [the second], and said li.
22. 26 Likewise the second also, and the third
22. 39 the second (is) like unto it, Thou shalt lo.
26. 42 He went away again the second time, and
Mark 12. 21 the second took her, and died, neither le.
12. 31 the second (is) like, (namely) this, Thou
14. 72 the second time the cock crew. And Peter
Luke 12. 38 if he shall come in the second watch, or
19. 18 the second came, saying, Lord, thy pound
20. 30 second took her to wife, and he died chil.
John 3. 4 can he enter the second time into his mo.
4. 54 This (is) again the second miracle (that)
21. 16 He saith to him again the second time
Acts 7. 13 at the second (time) Joseph was made kn.

Acts10. 15 voice (spake) unto him again the second
12. 10 When they were past the first and the se.
13. 33 as it is also written in [the second] psalm
1 Co. 15. 47 the second man (is) the Lord from heaven
2 Co. 1. 15 before, that ye might have a second ben.
13. 2 as if I were present, the second time; and
Titus 3. 10 after the first and second admonition rej.
Heb. 8. 7 no place have been sought for the second
9. 3 after the second veil, the tabernacle wh.
9. 7 into the second (went) the high priest al.
9. 28 appear the second time without sin unto
10. 9 the first, that he may establish the second
2 Pe. 3. 1 second epistle, beloved, I now write unto
Rev. 2. 11 He..shall not be hurt of the second death
4. 7 second beast like a calf, and the third be.
6. 3 when he had opened the second seal, I
6. 3 heard the second beast say, Come and see
8. 8 second angel sounded, and as it were a gre.
11. 14 The second woe is past; (and), behold, the
16. 3 second angel poured out his vial upon the
20. 6 on such the second death hath no power
20. 14 lake of fire. This is the second death
21. 8 and brimstone: which is the second death
21. 19 second, sapphire; the third, a chalcedony

SECOND after the first, the —
Second-first, δευτερόπρωτος deuteroprōtos.
Luke 6. 1 on the [second] sabbath [after the first], th.

SECOND time, (to do) the —
To repeat, do it a second time, שָׁנָה shanah.
1 Sa. 26. 8 and I will not (smite) him the second time
1 Ki. 18. 34 And he said, Do (it) the second time: and
18. 34 did (it) the second time. And he said, Do

SECONDARILY —
Second, δεύτερον deuteron.
1 Co. 12. 28 secondarily prophets, thirdly teachers, af.

SECRET (chamber, counsel, part, place, thing, in)—
1. *In quietness, לָאַט la-at.*
Job 15. 11 is there any secret thing with thee?
2. *Secret hiding place, מִסְתָּר mistar.*
Psa. 10. 8 in the secret places doth he murder the in.
17. 12 were a young lion lurking in secret places
64. 4 That they may shoot in secret at the per.
Isa. 45. 3 hidden riches of secret places, that thou
Jer. 13. 17 my soul shall weep in secret places for (yo.)
23. 24 Can any hide himself in secret places that
49. 10 have uncovered his secret places, and he
Lam. 3. 10 lying in wait, (and as) a lion in secret pl.
3. *Parts of shame, מְבֻשִׁים mebushim.*
Deut25. 11 her hand, and taketh him by the secrets
4. *Secret, counsel, סוֹד sod.*
Gen. 49. 6 O my soul, come not thou into their secret
Job 15. 8 Hast thou heard the secret of God? and
29. 4 when the secret of God (was) upon my ta.
Psa. 25. 14 secret of the LORD (is) with them that fear
64. 2 Hide me from the secret counsel of the wi.
Prov. 3. 32 but his secret (is) with the righteous
11. 13 tale bearer revealeth secrets: but he that
20. 19 tale bearer revealeth secrets; therefore m.
25. 9 and discover not a secret to another
Amos 3. 7 revealeth his secret unto his servants the
5. *To stop, hide, סָתַם satham.*
Eze. 28. 3 there is no secret that they can hide from
6. *To be hidden, absent, סָתַר sathar, 2.*
Deut29. 29 secret (things belong) unto the LORD our
Psa. 19. 12 (his) errors? cleanse thou me from secret
7. *To be hidden, to hide, סָתַר sathar, 4.*
Prov 27. 5 Open rebuke (is) better than secret love
8. *To hide, סְתַר sethar, 3.*
Dan. 2. 22 He revealeth the deep and secret things
9. *Hiding or secret place, סֵתֶר sether.*
Deut 27. 15 putteth (it) in (a) secret (place). And all
Judg. 3. 19 I have a secret errand unto thee, O king
1 Sa. 19. 2 abide in a secret (place), and hide thyself
Psa. 18. 11 He made darkness his secret place; his pa.
27. 5 in the secret of his tabernacle shall he hi.
31. 20 Thou shalt hide them in the secret of thy
81. 7 answered thee in the secret place of thun.
91. 1 He that dwelleth in the secret place of the
139. 15 when I was made in secret, (and) curiou.
Prov. 9. 17 sweet, and bread (eaten) in secret is plea.
21. 14 gift in secret pacifieth anger, and a reward
Song 2. 14 in the secret (places) of the stairs, let me
Isa. 45. 19 I have not spoken in secret, in a dark pl.
48. 16 I have not spoken in secret from the beg.
10. *To be hidden, concealed, עָלַם alam.*
Psa. 90. 8 secret (sins) in the light of thy countena.
11. *To be hidden, עָלַם alam, 2.*
Eccl. 12. 14 with every secret thing, whether (it be)
12. *Wonderful, פִּלְאִי ,פֶּלִאי peli, pili.*
Judg 13. 18 Why askest thou..seeing it (is) secret?
13. *To hide, lay up, conceal, צָפַן tsaphan.*
Job 20. 26 darkness (shall be) hid in his secret pla.
Eze. 7. 22 and they shall pollute my secret (place)
14. *A secret, רָז raz.*
Dan. 2. 18 desire mercies..concerning this secret
2. 19 Then was the secret revealed unto Daniel
2. 27 The secret which the king hath demanded
2. 28 a God in heaven that revealeth secrets
2. 29 he that revealeth secrets maketh known
2. 30 this secret is not revealed to me for (any)
2. 47 a Lord of kings, and a revealer of secrets
Dan. 2. 47 seeing thou couldest reveal this secret
4. 9 I know that..no secret troubleth thee
15. *Hinge, opening, simplicity, פֹּת poth.*
Isa. 3. 17 the LORD will discover their secret parts
16. *Hidden thing, secret, תַּעֲלֻמָה taalumah.*
Job 11. 6 he would show thee the secrets of wisdom
Psa. 44. 21 for he knoweth the secrets of the heart
17. *To hide, secrete, טָמַן taman.*
Job 40. 13 Hide them..(and) bind their faces in se.
18. *Concealed, hidden, secret, κρυπτός kruptos.*
Matt. 6. 4 That thine alms may be in secret: and
6. 4 thy Father which seeth in secret himself
6. 6 which is in secret..which seeth in secret
6. 18 but unto thy Father which is [in secret]
6. 18 and thy Father, which seeth [in secret]
Luke 8. 17 nothing is secret that shall not be made
11. 33 No man..putteth (it) in a secret place, ne.
John 7. 4 no man (that) doeth any thing in secret
7. 10 went..not openly, but as it were in secret
18. 20 I spake openly..in secret have I said no.
Rom. 2. 16 when God shall judge the secrets of men
1 Co. 14. 25 thus are the secrets of his heart made ma.
19. *In secret, secretly, κρυφῇ kruphē.*
Eph. 5. 12 things which are done of them in secret
20. *A secret chamber, storehouse, ταμεῖον tameion.*
Matt 24. 26 (he is) in the secret chambers; believe (it)

SECRET, to keep or be kept —
1. *To (cause to) hide, סָתַר sathar, 5.*
Job 14. 13 that thou wouldest keep me in secret, un.
2. *Hidden away, ἀπόκρυφος apokruphos.*
Mark 4. 22 neither was any thing kept secret, but
3. *To hide, conceal, κρύπτω kruptō.*
Matt 13. 35 things which have been kept secret from
4. *To be silent, quiet, σιγάω sigaō.*
Rom. 16. 25 which was kept secret since the world be.

SECRET parts, to have in —
To be hidden, broken forth, שָׁתַר sathar, 2.
1 Sa. 5. 9 and they had emerods in their secret pa.

SECRETLY —
1. *Silence, חֶרֶשׁ cheresh.*
Josh. 2. 1 son of Nun sent..two men to spy secretly
2. *In secret, בַּלָּט bal-lat.*
1 Sa. 18 22 Commune with David secretly, and say
3. *In a secret place, בַּמִּסְתָּר be-mistar.*
Psa. 10. 9 He lieth in wait secretly as a lion in his
Hab. 3. 14 rejoicing (was) as to devour the poor se.
4. *In secret, בַּסֵּתֶר [sether].*
Deut 13. 6 entice thee secretly, saying, Let us go and
27. 24 he that smiteth his neighbour secretly. A.
28. 57 eat them..secretly in the siege and strait.
2 Sa. 12. 12 For thou didst (it) secretly; but I will do
Job 13. 10 reprove you, if ye do secretly accept per.
31. 27 my heart hath been secretly enticed, or
Jer. 37. 17 king asked him secretly in his house, and
38. 16 So Zedekiah the king sware secretly unto
40. 15 spake to Gedaliah in Mizpah secretly, say.
5. *To hide, conceal, κρύπτω kruptō.*
John19. 38 being a disciple of Jesus, but secretly for
6. *Privately, secretly, λάθρα lathra.*
John11. 28 called Mary her sister secretly saying, T.

SECRETLY, to do, practise, be brought —
1. *To be furtively brought, גָּנַב ganab, 4.*
Job 4. 12 Now a thing was secretly brought to me
2. *To be hidden, hid self, חָבָא chaba, 2.*
Gen. 31. 27 Wherefore didst thou flee away secretly
3. *To do covertly, חָפָא chapha, 3.*
2 Ki. 17. 9 did secretly (those) things that (were) not
4. *To keep or remain silent, conceal, חָרַשׁ charash, 5.*
1 Sa. 23. 9 knew that Saul secretly practised misch.

SECT —
Act of choosing, party, αἵρεσις hairesis.
Acts 5. 17 which is the sect of the Sadducees, and
15. 5 rose up certain of the sect of the Pharis.
24. 5 ringleader of the sect of the Nazarenes
26. 5 after the most straitest sect of our relig.
28. 22 for as concerning this sect, we know that

SE-CUN'-DUS, Σεκοῦνδος.
A believer of Thessalonica, and companion of Paul on his return from Greece on his way to Syria.
Acts 20. 4 of the Thessalonians, Aristarchus and S.

SECURE, securely, (to be) —
1. *Confidence, trust, בֶּטַח betach.*
Judg. 8. 11 and smote the host: for the host was sec.
Prov. 3. 29 seeing he dwelleth securely by thee
Mic. 2. 8 pass by securely as men averse from war
2. *Confidences, confident ones, בַּטֻּחוֹת battuchoth.*
Job 12. 6 they that provoke God are secure; into
3. *To lean on, trust, be confident, בָּטַח batach.*
Judg 18. 7 they dwelt careless..quiet and secure; and
18. 10 ye shall come unto a people secure, and
18. 27 unto a people (that were) at quiet and se.
Job 11. 18 thou shalt be secure, because there is ho.

SECURE, to —
To make without anxiety, ποιέω ἀμέριμνον [poieō].
Matt 28. 14 we will persuade him, and secure you

SECURITY —
Sufficient, ἱκανός hikanos.
Acts 17. 9 when they had taken security of Jason

SEDITION —
1. *Sedition, אֶשְׁתַּדּוּר eshtaddur.*
Ezra 4. 15 that they have moved sedition within the
4. 19 rebellion and sedition have been made th.
2. *A standing apart, διχοστασία dichostasia.*
Gal. 5. 20 emulations, wrath, strife, seditions, her.
3. *A standing up, στάσις stasis.*
Luke23. 19 Who for a certain sedition made in the ci.
23. 25 released unto them him that for sedition
Acts 24. 5 mover of sedition among all the Jews th.

SEDUCE, to —
1. *To cause to err or wander, טָעָה taah, 5.*
Eze. 13. 10 even because they have seduced my peo.
2. *To cause to err or wander, תָּעָה taah, 5.*
2 Ki. 21. 9 Manasseh seduced them to do more evil
Prov 12. 26 but the way of the wicked seduceth them
Isa. 19. 13 they have also seduced Egypt, (even they
3. *To lead away astray, ἀποπλανάω apoplanaō.*
Mark13. 22 to seduce, if (it were) possible. even the
4. *To seduce, lead astray, πλανάω planaō.*
1 Jo. 2. 26 written..concerning them that seduce
Rev. 2. 20 seduce my servants to commit fornicati.

SEDUCER, seducing —
1. *Groaner, conjuror, juggler, γόης goēs.*
2 Ti. 3. 13 evil men and seducers shall wax worse
2. *Wandering, seducing, πλάνος planos.*
1 Ti. 4. 1 giving heed to seducing spirits, and doc.

SEE —
1. *Lo! הִנֵּה hinneh.*
Gen. 19. 21 See, I have accepted thee concerning this
[This particle occurs very frequently.]
2. *See! רְאֵה [raah].*
Job 10. 15 confusion; therefore see thou mine affli.
3. *See, behold, ἴδε ide.*
Mark13. 1 see what manner of stones and what bu.
4. *See, behold, lo! ἰδού idou.*
Luke17. 23 say to you, See here! or, see there! go
Acts 8. 36 said, See, (here is) water; what doth hi.

SEE (to), to —
1. *To see (in vision), חָזָה chazah.* [*See also* No. 10.]
Exod. 24. 11 also they saw God, and did eat and drink
Num 24. 4, 16 saw the vision of the Almighty, falling
Job 8. 17 wrapped about the heap, (and) seeth the
15. 17 and that (which) I have seen I will decl.
19. 26 destroy..yet in my flesh shall I see God
19. 27 Whom I shall see for myself, and mine
24. 1 do they that know him not see his days?
27. 12 all ye yourselves have seen (it); why then
34. 32 I see not, teach thou me; if I have done
36. 25 Every man may see it, man may behold
Psa. 58. 8 pass away..(that) they may not see the
58. 10 righteous shall rejoice when he seeth the
63. 2 thy power and thy glory, so (as) I have se.
Prov 22. 29 Seest thou a man diligent in his business
24. 32 Then I saw, (and) considered (it) well; I
29. 20 Seest thou a man (that is) hasty in his w.?
Song 6. 13 What will ye see in the Shulamite? As it
Isa. 1. 1 which he saw concerning Judah and Jer.
2. 1 son of Amoz saw concerning Judah and
13. 1 which Isaiah the son of Amoz did see
26. 11 they will not see: (but) they shall see, and
33. 17 Thine eyes shall see the king in his beau.
48. 6 Thou hast heard, see all this; and will
57. 8 thou lovedst their bed where thou sawest
Lam. 2. 14 Thy prophets have seen vain and foolish
2. 14 have seen for thee false burdens, and ca.
Eze. 12. 27 The vision that he seeth (is) for many da.
13. 6 They have seen vanity and lying divinat.
13. 7 Have ye not seen a vain vision, and have
13. 8 ye have spoken vanity, and seen lies, th.
13. 23 Therefore ye shall see no more vanity, nor
21. 29 Whiles they see vanity unto thee, whiles
Amos 1. 1 which he saw concerning Israel in the
Mic. 1. 1 which he saw concerning Samaria and J.
Hab. 1. 1 which Habakkuk the prophet did see
Zech. 10. 2 diviners have seen a lie, and have told fa.
2. *To see (in vision), חֲזָה, חֲזָא chaza, chazah*
Ezra 4. 14 not meet for us to see the king's dishon.
Dan. 2. 8 because ye see the thing is gone from me
2. 26 make known..the dream which I have se.
2. 31 Thou, O king, sawest, and, behold, a gr.
2. 34 Thou sawest till that a stone was cut out
2. 41 whereas thou sawest the feet and toes
2. 41, 43 thou sawest the iron mixed with miry
2. 45 Forasmuch as thou sawest that the stone
3. 25 see four men loose, walking in the midst
3. 27 saw these men, upon whose bodies the fire
4. 5 saw a dream which made me afraid, and
4. 9 visions of my dream that I have seen, and
4. 10 I saw, and behold a tree in the midst of
4. 13 I saw in the visions of my head upon my
4. 18 dream I king Nebuchadnezzar have seen
4. 20 tree that thou sawest, which grew, and
4. 23 whereas the king saw a watcher and an
5. 5 king saw the part of the hand that wrote
5. 23 praised the gods..which see not, nor he.
7. 2 saw in my vision by night, and, behold
7. 7 After this I saw in the night visions, and
7. 13 saw in the night visions, and, behold, (one)

3. *Vision, sight, appearance, aspect,* מַרְאָה *mareh.*
Josh.22. 10 an altar by Jordan, a great altar to see

4. *To (cause to) behold attentively,* נָבַט *nabat,* 5.
1 Sa. 2. 32 thou shalt see an enemy (in my) habitat.
Psa. 92. 11 Mine eye also shall see (my desire) on mi.
94. 9 he that formed the eye, shall he not see?
Isa. 64. 9 see, we beseech thee, we (are) all thy pe.

5. *To see, behold, look, consider, enjoy,* רָאָה *raah.*
Gen. 1. 4 God saw the light, that (it was) good: and
1. 10, 12, 18, 21, 25 and God saw that (it was)
1. 31 God saw every thing that he had made
2. 19 brought (them) unto Adam to see what
3. 6 when the woman saw that the tree (was)
6. 2 sons of God saw the daughters of men th.
6. 5 God saw that the wickedness of man (w.)
7. 1 for thee have I seen righteous before me
8. 8 to see if the waters were abated from off
9. 22 saw the nakedness of his father, and told
9. 23 and they saw not their father's nakedness
11. 5 came down to see the city and the tower
12. 12 when the Egyptians shall see thee, that
12. 15 princes also of Pharaoh saw her, and co.
13. 15 For all the land which thou seest, to thee
16. 4, 5 when she saw that she had conceived
18. 2 when he saw (them), he ran to meet them
18. 21 will go down now, and see whether they
19. 1 and Lot seeing (them) rose up to meet
20. 10 What sawest thou, that thou hast done
21. 9 Sarah saw the son of Hagar the Egyptian
21. 16 Let me not see the death of the child. And
21. 19 she saw a well of water; and she went
22. 4 lifted up his eyes, and saw the place afar
24. 30 when he saw the earring, and bracelets
24. 63 lifted up his eyes, and saw, and, behold
24. 64 when she saw Isaac, she lighted off the ca.
26. 8 looked out at a window, and saw, and, be
26. 28 We saw certainly that the LORD was with
27. 1 eyes were dim, so that he could not see
27. 27 See, the smell of my son (is) as the smell
28. 6 When Esau saw that Isaac had blessed Ja.
28. 8 Esau seeing that the daughters of Canaan
29. 10 when Jacob saw Rachel the daughter of
29. 31 when the LORD saw that Leah (was) hated
30. 1 when Rachel saw that she bare Jacob no
30. 9 When Leah saw that she had left bearing
31. 5 I see your father's countenance, that it (is)
31. 10 lifted up mine eyes, and saw in a dream
31. 12 Lift up now thine eyes and see, all the ra
31. 12 have seen all that Laban doeth unto thee
31. 42 God hath seen mine affliction and the la
31. 43 all that thou seest (is) mine: and what can
31. 50 see, God (is) witness betwixt me and thee
32. 2 when Jacob saw them, he said, This (is)
32. 20 afterward I will see his face; peradvent
32. 25 saw that he prevailed not against him
32. 30 seen God face to face, and my life is pre
33. 5 saw the women and the children, and said
33. 10 seen thy face, as though I had seen the fa
34. 1 went out to see the daughters of the land
34. 2 saw her, he took her, and lay with her, and
37. 4 when his brethren saw that their father
37. 14 see whether it be well with thy brethren
37. 18 when they saw him afar off, even before
37. 20 shall see what will become of his dreams
38. 2 saw there a daughter of a certain Canaan.
38. 14 for she saw that Shelah was grown, and
38. 15 When Judah saw her, he thought her (to
39. 3 his master saw that the LORD (was) with
39. 13 when she saw that he had left his garment
39. 14 See, he hath brought in an Hebrew unto
40. 16 baker saw that the interpretation was go.
41. 19 such as I never saw in all the land of Eg.
41. 22 saw, in my dream, and, behold, seven ears
41. 41 See, I have set thee over all the land of E.
42. 1 when Jacob saw that there was corn in E.
42. 7 Joseph saw his brethren, and he knew th.
42. 9, 12 to see the nakedness of the land ye are
42. 21 in that we saw the anguish of his soul, w.
42. 35 saw the bundles of money, they were afr.
43. 3, 5 Ye shall not see my face, except your br.
43. 16 when Joseph saw Benjamin with them, he
43. 29 saw his brother Benjamin, his mother's
44. 23 come down with you, ye shall see my face
44. 26 for we may not see the man's face, except
44. 28 Surely he is torn in pieces; and I saw him
44. 31 when he seeth that the lad (is) not (with
44. 34 lest peradventure I see the evil that shall
45. 12 your eyes see, and the eyes of my brother
45. 13 tell my father..of all that ye have seen
45. 27 when he saw the wagons which Joseph had
45. 28 Israel said..I will go and see him before
46. 30 let me die, since I have seen thy face, be.
48. 10 were dim for age, (so that) he could not
48. 11 I had not thought to see thy face; and, lo
48. 17 when Joseph saw that his father laid his
49. 15 saw that rest (was) good, and the land that
50. 11 saw the mourning in the floor of Atad, they
50. 15 when Joseph's brethren saw that their fa.
50. 23 Joseph saw Ephraim's children of the th.
Exod. 1. 16 see (them) upon the stools, if it (be) a son
2. 2 when she saw him that he (was a) goodly
2. 5 when she saw the ark among the flags, she
2. 6 when she had opened (it), she saw the ch.
2. 12 when he saw that (there was) no man, he
3. 3 will now turn aside, and see this great
3. 4 LORD saw that he turned aside to see, God
3. 7 have surely seen the affliction of my peo.
3. 9 have also seen the oppression wherewith
4. 14 when he seeth thee, he will be glad in his
4. 18 Let me go..and see whether they be yet

Exod. 4. 21 see that thou do all those wonders before
5. 19 officers of the children of Israel did see
6. 1 Now shalt thou see what I will do to Ph.
7. 1 See, I have made thee a god to Pharaoh
8. 15 when Pharaoh saw that there was respite
9. 34 when Pharaoh saw that the rain and the
10. 5 that one cannot be able to see the earth
10. 6 have seen, since the day that they were
10. 23 They saw not one another, neither rose any
10. 28 see my face no more..seest my face thou
10. 29 Thou hast spoken well, I will see thy face
12. 13 when I see the blood, I will pass over you
12. 23 when he seeth the blood upon the lintel
13. 17 the people repent when they see war, and
14. 13 see the salvation of the LORD, which he
14. 13 seen today, ye shall see them again no more
14. 30 saw the Egyptians dead upon the sea sh.
14. 31 saw that great work which the LORD did
16. 7 then ye shall see the glory of the LORD
16. 15 when the children of Israel saw (it), they
16. 29 See, for that the LORD hath given you the
16. 32 that they may see the bread wherewith
18. 14 when Moses' father in law saw all that
19. 4 Ye have seen what I did unto the Egypt.
20. 18 people saw..when the people saw (it), they
20. 22 Ye have seen that I have talked with you
23. 5 If thou see the ass of him that hateth thee
24. 10 they saw the God of Israel: and (there was)
31. 2 See, I have called by name Bezaleel the son
32. 1 when the people saw that Moses delayed
32. 5 when Aaron saw (it), he built an
32. 9 have seen this people, and, behold, it (is)
32. 19 saw the calf, and the dancing: and Moses'
32. 25 when Moses saw that the people (were)
33. 10 all the people saw the cloudy pillar stand
33. 12 See, thou sayest unto me, Bring up this
33. 20 not see..for there shall no man see me
33. 23 thou shalt see my back parts; but my face
34. 10 people..shall see the work of the LORD
34. 30 all the children of Israel saw Moses, be.
34. 35 children of Israel saw the face of Moses, th.
35. 30 See, the LORD hath called by name Beza.
Lev. 5. 1 whether he hath seen or known (of it); if
9. 24 when all the people saw, they shouted, and
13. 8 priest see that, behold, the scab spreadeth
13. 10 priest shall see (him): and, behold, (if)
13. 15 priest shall see the raw flesh, and pronou.
13. 17 priest shall see him: and, behold, (if) the
13. 20 when the priest seeth it, behold, it (be) in
13. 30 Then the priest shall see the plague: and
14. 36 before the priest go (into it) to see the pla.
14. 36 afterward the priest shall go in to see the
20. 17 see her nakedness, and she see his naked.
Num. 4. 20 they shall not go in to see when the holy th.
11. 15 and let me not see my wretchedness
11. 23 thou shalt see now whether my word shall
13. 18 see the land, what it (is); and the people
13. 28 moreover we saw the children of Anak th.
13. 32 all the people that we saw in it (are) men
13. 33 there we saw the giants, the sons of Anak
14. 22 Because all those men which have seen my
14. 23 Surely they shall not see the land which I
14. 23 shall any of them that provoked me see it
20. 29 when all the congregation saw that Aaron
22. 2 Balak the son of Zippor saw all that Israel
22. 23, 25, 27 the ass saw the angel of the LORD
22. 31 he saw the angel of the LORD standing in
22. 33 ass saw me, and turned from me these
22. 41 he might see the utmost (part) of the peo.
23. 9 For from the top of the rocks I see him
23. 13 see them: thou shalt see but the utmost
23. 13 shalt not see them all; and curse me them
23. 21 neither hath he seen perverseness in Israel
24. 1 when Balaam saw that it pleased the LORD
24. 2 saw Israel abiding (in his tents) according
24. 17 shall see him, but not now; I shall behold
25. 7 when Phinehas..saw (it), he rose up from
27. 12 see the land which I have given unto the
27. 13 when thou hast seen it, thou also shalt be
32. 1 when they saw the land of Jazer, and the
32. 8 sent them from Kadesh-barnea, to see the
32. 9 when they..saw the land, they discourag.
32. 11 shall see the land which I sware unto A.
35. 23 with any stone..seeing (him) not, and cast
Deut. 1. 19 which ye saw by the way of the mountain
1. 28 we have seen the sons of the Anakims the.
1. 31 seen how that the LORD thy God bare thee
1. 35 there shall not one of these men..see that
1. 36 he shall see it, and to him will I give the
3. 21 Thine eyes have seen all that the LORD your
3. 25 let me go over and see the good land that
3. 28 to inherit the land which thou shalt see
4. 3 Your eyes have seen what the LORD did
4. 9 forget the things which thine eyes have
4. 12 saw no similitude; only (ye heard) a voice
4. 15 for ye saw no manner of similitude on the
4. 19 when thou seest the sun, and the moon
4. 28 which neither see, nor hear, nor eat, nor
5. 24 we have seen this day that God doth talk
7. 19 The great temptations which thine eyes sa.
9. 13 seen this people, and, behold, it (is) a stiff
10. 21 terrible things which thine eyes have seen
11. 2 which have not seen the chastisement of
11. 7 your eyes have seen all the great acts of th.
12. 13 offerings in every place that thou seest
18. 16 neither let me see this great fire any more
20. 1 seest horses and chariots, (and) a people
21. 7 not shed..neither have our eyes seen (it)
21. 11 seest among the captives a beautiful wo.
22. 1, 4 Thou shalt not see..hide thyself from
23. 14 that he see no unclean thing in thee, and
28. 10 all people of the earth shall see that thou

Deut. 28. 34, 67 sight of thine eyes which thou shalt see
28. 68 Thou shalt see it no more again: and th.
29. 2 Ye have seen all that the LORD did before
29. 3 temptations which thine eyes have seen, the
29. 4 not given you..eyes to see, and ears to he.
29. 17 ye have seen their abominations, and th.
29. 22 when they see the plagues of that land
30. 15 See, I have set before thee this day life
32. 19 when the LORD saw (it), he abhorred (them)
32. 20 I will see what their end (shall be): for
32. 36 when he seeth that (their) power is gone
32. 39 See now that I, (even) I, (am) he, and (th.
32. 52 Yet thou shalt see the land before (thee)
33. 9 said..I have not seen him; neither did
Josh. 3. 3 When ye see the ark of the covenant of
6. 2 See, I have given into thine hand Jericho
7. 21 When I saw among the spoils a goodly B.
8. 1 see, I have given into thy hand the king
8. 8 shall ye do. See, I have commanded you
8. 14 when the king of Ai saw (it), that they h.
8. 20 they saw, and, behold, the smoke of the
8. 21 when Joshua and all Israel saw that the
23. 3 ye have seen all that the LORD your God
24. 7 your eyes have seen what I have done in
Judg. 1. 24 spies saw a man come forth out of the ci.
2. 7 who had seen all the great works of the
3. 24 when they saw that, behold, the doors of
6. 22 have seen an angel of the LORD face to fa.
9. 36 when Gaal saw the people, he said to Ze.
9. 36 Thou seest the shadow of the mountains
9. 48 What ye have seen me do, make haste
9. 55 when the men of Israel saw that Abime.
11. 35 came to pass, when he saw her, that he
12. 3 when I saw that ye delivered (me) not, I
13. 22 shall surely die, because we have seen G.
14. 1 saw a woman in Timnath of the daught.
14. 2 I have seen a woman in Timnath of the
14. 8 turned aside to see the carcase of the lion
14. 11 came to pass, when they saw him, that
16. 1 saw there an harlot, and went in unto h.
16. 5 see wherein his great strength (lieth), and
16. 18 when Delilah saw that he had told her all
16. 24 when the people saw him, they praised
18. 7 saw the people that (were) therein, how
18. 9 for we have seen the land, and, behold
18. 26 Micah saw that they (were) too strong for
19. 3 when the father of the damsel saw him
19. 17 saw a wayfaring man in the street of the
19. 30 And it was so, that all that saw it said
20. 36 children of Benjamin saw that they were
20. 41 they saw that evil was come upon them
21. 21 see, and, behold, if the daughters of Shi.
Ruth 1. 18 When she saw that she was stedfastly mi.
2. 18 mother in law saw what she had gleaned
1 Sa. 3. 2 began to wax dim, (that) he could not see
4. 15 his eyes were dim, that he could not see
5. 7 when the men of Ashdod saw that (it w.)
6. 9 see, if it goeth up by the way of his own
6. 13 and saw the ark, and rejoiced to see (it)
6. 16 when the five lords..had seen (it), they
9. 17 when Samuel saw Saul, the LORD said unto
10. 11 when all that knew him before time saw
10. 14 To seek the asses: and when we saw th.
10. 24 See ye him whom the LORD hath chosen
12. 12 when ye saw that Nahash the king of the
12. 16 Now therefore stand and see this great th.
12. 17 may perceive and see that your wickedn.
13. 6 When the men of Israel saw that they w.
13. 11 Because I saw that the people were scat.
14. 17 Number now, and see who is gone from
14. 29 see, I pray you, how mine eyes have been
14. 38 know and see wherein this sin hath been
14. 52 when Saul saw any strong man, or any va.
15. 35 Samuel came no more to see Saul until the
16. 7 not as man seeth; for man looketh on the
16. 18 I have seen a son of Jesse the Beth-lehe.
17. 24 when they saw the man, fled from him
17. 25 Have ye seen this man that is come up?
17. 28 art come down that thou mightest see the
17. 42 when the Philistine..saw David, he dis.
17. 51 when the Philistines saw their champion
17. 55 when Saul saw David go forth against the
18. 15 when Saul saw that he behaved himself
18. 28 Saul saw and knew that the LORD (was)
19. 3 and what I see, that I will tell thee
19. 5 thou sawest (it), and didst rejoice: where
19. 15 sent the messengers (again) to see David
19. 20 they saw the company of the prophets pr.
20. 29 let me get away..and see my brethren
21. 14 Lo, ye see the man is mad: wherefore
22. 9 I saw the son of Jesse coming to Nob, to
23. 15 David saw that Saul was come out to seek
23. 22 know and see his place where his haunt
23. 22 who hath seen him there: for it is told
23. 23 See therefore, and take knowledge of all
24. 10 this day thine eyes have seen how that the
24. 11 see, yea, see the skirt of thy robe in my
24. 11 know thou and see that (there is) neither
24. 15 see, and plead my cause, and deliver me
25. 23 when Abigail saw David, she hasted, and
25. 25 thine handmaid saw not the young men
25. 35 see, I have hearkened to thy voice, and
26. 3 saw that Saul came after him into the wil.
26. 12 no man saw (it), nor knew (it), neither aw.
26. 16 now see where the king's spear (is), and
28. 5 saw the host of the Philistines, he was af.
28. 12 when the woman saw Samuel, she cried
28. 13 what sawest thou..I saw gods ascending
28. 21 saw that he was sore troubled, and said
31. 5 when his armour bearer saw that Saul was
31. 7 saw that the men of Israel fled, and that S.
2 Sa. 1. 7 when he had looked behind him, he saw

2 Sa. 3. 13 Thou shalt not see my face, except thou
3. 13 daughter, when thou comest to see my fa.
6. 16 saw king David leaping and dancing be.
7. 2 See now, I dwell in an house of cedar, but
10. 6 when the children of Ammon saw that th.
10. 9 When Joab saw that the front of the ba.
10. 14 when the children of Ammon saw that
10. 15 when the Syrians saw that they were sm.
10. 19 saw that they were smitten before Israel
11. 2 from the roof he saw a woman washing
12. 19 when David saw that his servants whisp.
13. 5 when thy father cometh to see thee, say
13. 5 that I may see (it), and eat (it) at her hand
13. 6 when the king was come to see him, Am.
14. 24 let him not see my face. So Absalom re.
14. 24 to his own house, and saw not the king's
14. 28 dwelt..in Jerusalem, and saw not the ki.
14. 30 See, Joab's field is near mine, and he hath
14. 32 now therefore let me see the king's face
15. 3 See, thy matters (are) good and right; but
15. 28 See, I will tarry in the plain of the wild.
17. 18 Nevertheless a lad saw them, and told A.
17. 23 when Ahithophel saw that his counsel was
18. 10 certain man saw (it), and..said..I saw A.
18. 11 thou sawest (him), and why didst thou not
18. 21 Go tell the king what thou hast seen. A.
18. 26 watchman saw another man running: and
18. 29 saw a great tumult, but I knew not what
20. 12 when the man saw that all the people st.
20. 12 when he saw that every one that came by
24. 3 that the eyes of my lord the king may see
24. 13 see what answer I shall return to him th.
24. 17 when he saw the angel that smote the pe.
24. 20 saw the king and his servants coming on
1 Ki. 3. 28 for they saw that the wisdom of God (w)
9. 12 came out from Tyre to see the cities which
10. 4 when the queen of Sheba had seen all So.
10. 7 mine eyes had seen (it); and, behold, the
11. 28 Solomon seeing the young man that he was
12. 16 So when all Israel saw that the king hea.
12. 16 now see to thine own house, David. So
13. 12 For his sons had seen what way the man
13. 25 saw the carcase cast in the way, and the
14. 4 Ahijah could not see; for his eyes were set
16. 18 when Zimri saw that the city was taken
17. 23 and Elijah said, See, thy son liveth
18. 17 when Ahab saw Elijah, that Ahab said un.
18. 39 when all the people saw (it), they fell on
19. 3 when he saw (that), he arose, and went
20. 7 see how this (man) seeketh mischief: for
20. 13 Hast thou seen all this great multitude
20. 22 see what thou doest: for at the return of
21. 29 Seest thou how Ahab humbleth himself
22. 17 I saw all Israel scattered upon the hills
22. 19 I saw the LORD sitting on his throne, and
22. 25 thou shalt see in that day, when thou sh.
22. 32 when the captains of the chariots saw J.
2 Ki. 2. 10 if thou see me (when I am) taken from
2. 12 Elisha saw (it)..And he saw him no more
2. 15 when the sons of the prophets..saw him
2. 19 pleasant, as my lord seeth; but the water
3. 14 would not look toward thee, nor see thee
3. 17 not see wind, neither shall ye see rain
3. 22 saw the water on the other side (as) red
3. 26 when the king of Moab saw that the bat.
4. 25 when the man of God saw her afar off, th.
5. 7 see how he seeketh a quarrel against me
5. 21 when Naaman saw (him) running after
6. 17 open his eyes, that he may see..and he saw
6. 20 LORD, open the eyes..that they may see
6. 20 opened their eyes, and they saw; and, be.
6. 21 when he saw them, My father, shall I s.
6. 32 See ye how this son of a murderer hath
7. 2 shalt see (it) with thine eyes, but shalt
7. 13 answered and said..let us send and see
7. 14 and the king sent..saying, Go and see
7. 19 thou shalt see it with thine eyes, but sh.
8. 29 went down to see Joram the son of Ahab
9. 16 king of Judah was come down to see Jo.
9. 17 said, I see a company. And Joram said
9. 22 when Joram saw Jehu, that he said, (Is
9. 26 Surely I have seen yesterday the blood of
9. 27 when Ahaziah the king of Judah saw (th.)
10. 16 Come with me, and see my zeal for the L.
11. 1 when Athaliah..saw that her son was de.
12. 10 when they saw that (there was) much m.
13. 4 for he saw the oppression of Israel, bec.
14. 26 saw the affliction of Israel, (that it was)
16. 10 saw an altar that (was) at Damascus: and
16. 12 saw the altar: and the king approached to
19. 16 open, LORD, thine eyes, and see; and he.
20. 5 I have heard thy prayer, I have seen thy
20. 15 said, What have they seen in thine house?
20. 15 All..that (are) in mine house have they se.
22. 20 thine eyes shall not see all the evil which
23. 17 Then he said, What title (is) that that I see
23. 29 slew him at Megiddo, when he had seen
1 Ch. 10. 5 when his armour bearer saw that Saul was
10. 7 men of Israel that (were) in the valley saw
15. 29 looking out at a window, saw king David
19. 6 the children of Ammon saw that they had
19. 10 Joab saw that the battle was set against
19. 15 the children of Ammon saw that the Syr.
19. 16 the Syrians saw that they were put to the
19. 19 the servants of Hadar-ezer saw that they
21. 16 saw the angel of the LORD stand between
21. 20 Ornan turned back, and saw the angel; and
21. 21 Ornan looked, and saw David, and went
21. 28 David saw that the LORD had answered
29. 17 now have I seen with joy thy people, wh.
2 Ch. 7. 3 the children of Israel saw how the fire ca.
9. 3 the queen of Sheba had seen the wisdom

2 Ch. 9. 6 until I came, and mine eyes had seen (it)
10. 16 (and) now, David, see to thine own house
12. 7 the LORD saw that they humbled themse
15. 9 they saw that the LORD his God (was) with
18. 16 I did see all Israel scattered upon the mo.
18. 18 I saw the LORD sitting upon his throne
18. 24 thou shalt see on that day when thou sh.
18. 31 the captains of the chariots saw Jehosh.
20. 17 see the salvation of the LORD with you
22. 6 went down to see Jehoram the son of A.
22. 10 the mother of Ahaziah saw that her son
24. 11 when they saw that (there was) much mo.
29. 8 and to hissing, as ye see with your eyes
30. 7 gave them up to desolation, as ye see
31. 8 and the princes came and saw the heaps
32. 2 Hezekiah saw that Sennacherib was come
34. 28 neither shall thine eyes see all the evil th.
Ezra 3. 12 ancient men, that had seen the first house
Neh. 2. 17 Ye see the distress that we (are) in, how
4. 11 They shall not know, neither see, till we
6. 16 the heathen that were about us saw (these)
9. 9 didst see the affliction of our fathers in E.
13. 15 In those days saw I in Judah (some) tr.
13. 23 In those days also saw I Jews (that) had
Esth. 1. 14 which saw the king's face, (and) which sat
3. 4 to see whether Mordecai's matters would
3. 5 Haman saw that Mordecai bowed not, nor
5. 2 the king saw Esther the queen standing
5. 9 Haman saw Mordecai in the king's gate
5. 13 I see Mordecai the Jew sitting at the king's
7. 7 he saw that there was evil determined ag
8. 6 how can I endure to see the evil that
8. 6 how can I endure to see the destruction
9. 26 (of that) which they had seen concerning
Job 2. 13 for they saw that (his) grief was very great
3. 9 neither let it see the dawning of the day
3. 16 I had not been; as infants (which) never
4. 8 as I have seen, they that plough iniquity
5. 3 I have seen the foolish taking root: but
6. 21 ye see (my) casting down, and are afraid
7. 7 remember..mine eye shall no more see go.
7. 8 The eye of him..shall see me no (more), th.
8. 18 (it) shall deny him, (saying), I have not seen
9. 11 he goeth by me, and I see (him) not: he
9. 25 they flee away, they see no good
10. 4 Hast thou eyes..seest thou as man seeth?
10. 15 (I am) full of confusion; therefore see th.
10. 18 given up the ghost, and no eye had seen
11. 11 he seeth wickedness also; will he not th.
13. 1 mine eye hath seen all (this), mine ear hath
20. 7 they which have seen him shall say, Wh.
20. 17 He shall not see the rivers, the floods, the
21. 20 His eyes shall see his destruction, and he
22. 11 Or darkness, (that) thou canst not see; and
22. 14 clouds (are) a covering to him that he se.
22. 19 The righteous see (it), and are glad; and
23. 9 he hideth himself..that I cannot see (him)
28. 10 and his eye seeth every precious thing
28. 24 (and) seeth under the whole heaven
28. 27 Then did he see it, and declare it; he
29. 8 The young men saw me, and hid themsel.
29. 11 when the eye saw (me), it gave witness to
31. 4 Doth not he see my ways, and count all
31. 19 If I have seen any perish for want of clot.
31. 21 If I have lifted up mine hand..when I saw
32. 5 Elihu saw that (there was) no answer in the
33. 26 he shall see his face with joy: for he will
33. 28 deliver his soul..and his life shall see the
34. 21 eyes (are) upon the ways of man, and he
35. 5 Look unto the heavens, and see; and be
37. 21 (men) see not the bright light which (is)
38. 17 hast thou seen the doors of the shadow of
38. 22 or hast thou seen the treasures of the hail
42. 5 I have heard of thee..mine eye seeth thee
42. 16 saw his sons, and his sons' sons, (even) fo.
Psa. 10. 11 he hideth his face; he will never see (it)
10. 14 Thou hast seen (it); for thou beholdest mi.
14. 2 to see if there were any that did under.
16. 10 neither..suffer thine Holy One to see co.
22. 7 they that see me laugh me to scorn: they
27. 13 unless I had believed to see the goodness
31. 11 they that did see me without fled from me
34. 8 O taste and see that the LORD (is) good
34. 12 (and) loveth (many) days, that he may see
35. 21 (and) said, Aha, aha! our eye hath seen (it)
35. 22 (This) thou hast seen, O LORD: keep not
36. 9 For with thee..in thy light shall we see
37. 13 The Lord shall laugh at him; for he seeth
37. 25 yet have I not seen the righteous forsa.
37. 34 the wicked are cut off, thou shalt see (it)
37. 35 I have seen the wicked in great power
40. 3 many shall see (it), and fear, and shall tr.
41. 6 if he come to see (me,) he speaketh van.
48. 5 They saw (it, and) so they marvelled; they
48. 8 so have we seen in the city of the LORD
49. 9 should still live for ever, (and) not see
49. 10 he seeth (that) wise men die, likewise the
49. 19 He shall go..they shall never see light
50. 18 When thou sawest a thief, then thou co.
52. 6 The righteous also shall see, and fear, and
53. 2 to see if there were (any) that did under.
54. 7 mine eye hath seen (his desire) upon mine
55. 9 I have seen violence and strife in the city
63. 2 To see thy power and thy glory, so (as) I
64. 5 they commune..they say, Who shall see
64. 8 So they..all that see them shall flee away
66. 5 Come and see the works of God: (he is)
68. 24 They have seen thy goings, O God; (even)
69. 23 Let their eyes be darkened, that they see
69. 32 The humble shall see (this, and) be glad
73. 3 (when) I saw the prosperity of the wicked
74. 9 We see not our signs: (there is) no more

Psa. 77. 16 The waters saw thee, O God, the waters s.
86. 17 that they which hate me may see (it), and
89. 48 What man (..that) liveth, and shall not
90. 15 (and) the years (wherein) we have seen ev.
91. 8 with thine eyes shalt thou behold and see
94. 7 The LORD shall not see, neither shall the
95. 9 tempted me, proved me, and saw my wo.
97. 4 enlightened the world: the earth saw, and
97. 6 The heavens declare..the people see his
98. 3 the ends of the earth have seen the salv.
106. 5 That I may see the good of thy chosen, th.
107. 24 These see the works of the LORD, and his
107. 42 The righteous shall see (it,) and rejoice
112. 8 until he see (his desire) upon his enemies
112. 10 The wicked shall see (it,) and be grieved
114. 3 The sea saw (it), and fled: Jordan was dr.
115. 5 speak not; eyes have they, but they see
118. 7 therefore shall I see (my desire) upon them
119. 74 They..will be glad when they see me; be.
119. 96 I have seen an end of all perfection: (but)
128. 5 thou shalt see the good of Jerusalem all
128. 6 thou shalt see thy children's children, (and)
135. 16 speak not; eyes have they, but they see
139. 16 Thine eyes did see my substance, yet be.
139. 24 see if (there be any) wicked way in me, and
Prov 24. 18 Lest the LORD see (it), and it displease him
25. 7 of the prince whom thine eyes have seen
26. 12 Seest thou a man wise in his own conceit?
29. 16 but the righteous shall see their fall
Eccl. 1. 8 the eye is not satisfied with seeing, nor
1. 10 whereof it may be said, See, this (is) new
1. 14 I have seen all the works that are done
2. 3 till I might see what (was) that good for
2. 13 I saw that wisdom excelleth folly, as far
2. 24 This also I saw, that it (was) from the ha.
3. 10 I have seen the travail which God hath
3. 16 I saw under the sun the place of judgm.
3. 18 that they might see that they themselves
3. 22 who shall bring him to see what shall be
4. 3 who hath not seen the evil work that is
4. 7 I returned, and I saw vanity under the
5. 8 If thou seest the oppression of the poor
5. 13 There is a sore evil (which) I have seen
5. 18 Behold (that) which I have seen: (it is)
6. 1 There is an evil which I have seen under
6. 5 he hath not seen the sun, nor known (any
6. 6 yet hath he seen no good: do not all go
7. 11 there is) profit to them that see the sun
7. 15 All (things) have I seen in the days of my
8. 9 All this have I seen, and applied my he.
8. 10 I saw the wicked buried, who had come
8. 16 to see the business that is done under the
8. 16 (there is that) neither day nor night seeth
9. 11 I returned, and saw under the sun, that
9. 13 This wisdom have I seen also under the
10. 5 There is an evil (which) I have seen under
10. 7 I have seen servants upon horses, and pr.
Song 3. 3 (I said), Saw ye him whom my soul love.?
6. 9 The daughters saw her, and blessed her
6. 11 to see the fruits of the valley, (and) to see
7. 12 let us see if the vine flourish, (whether)
Isa. 5. 19 (and) hasten his work, that we may see
6. 1 I saw also the LORD sitting upon a throne
6. 5 mine eyes have seen the King, the LORD
6. 9 and see ye indeed, but perceive not
6. 10 lest they see with their eyes, and hear wi.
9. 2 people that walked in darkness have seen
14. 16 They that see thee shall narrowly look up.
18. 3 see ye, when he lifteth up an ensign on the
21. 3 Therefore..I was dismayed at the seeing
21. 6 a watchman, let him declare what he se.
21. 7 he saw a chariot (with) a couple of horse.
22. 9 Ye have seen also the breaches of the city
28. 4 he that looketh upon it seeth, while it is
29. 15 they say, Who seeth us? and who know.
29. 18 the eyes of the blind shall see out of obsc.
29. 23 when he seeth his children, the work of
30. 10 Which say to the seers, See not; and to
30. 20 but thine eyes shall see thy teachers
32. 3 the eyes of them that see shall not be dim
33. 19 Thou shalt not see a fierce people, a peo.
33. 20 thine eyes shall see Jerusalem a quiet ha.
35. 2 they shall see the glory of the LORD, (and)
37. 17 open thine eyes, O LORD, and see; and he.
38. 5 I have heard thy prayer, I have seen thy
38. 11 I shall not see the LORD, (even) the LORD
39. 4 Then said he, What have they seen in th.
39. 4 All that (is) in mine house have they seen
40. 5 all flesh shall see (it) together: for the m.
41. 5 The isles saw (it), and feared; the ends of
41. 20 That they may see, and know, and consi.
42. 18 Hear..and look, ye blind, that ye may see
44. 9 they see not, nor know; that they may be
44. 16 Aha, I am warm, I have seen the fire
44. 18 hath shut their eyes, that they cannot see
47. 10 thou hast said, None seeth me. Thy wis.
49. 7 kings shall see and arise, princes also sh.
52. 8 they shall see eye to eye, when the LORD
52. 10 the ends of the earth shall see the salvat.
52. 15 (that) which had not been told..they see
53. 2 when we shall see him, (there is) no bea.
53. 10 he shall see (his) seed, he shall prolong
53. 11 He shall see of the travail of his soul, (and)
57. 18 I have seen his ways, and will heal him; I
58. 3 Wherefore have we fasted..and thou seest
58. 7 when thou seest the naked, that thou co.
59. 15 the LORD saw (it), and it displeased him
59. 16 he saw that (there was) no man, and wo.
60. 4 Lift up thine eyes round about, and see
60. 5 Then thou shalt see, and flow together, and
61. 9 all that see them shall acknowledge them
62. 2 the Gentiles shall see thy righteousness

Isa. 64. 4 neither hath the eye seen, O God, besides
66. 8 Who hath heard such a thing? who hath
66. 14 when ye see (this), your heart shall rejoice
66. 18 and they shall come, and see my glory
66. 19 not heard my fame, neither have seen my
Jer. 1. 10 See, I have this day set thee over the na.
1. 11 Jeremiah, what seest thou? And I said, I
1. 12 Thou hast well seen: for I will hasten my
1. 13 saying, What seest thou? And I said, I see
2. 10 pass over the isles of Chittim, and see; and
2. 10 consider diligently, and see if there be su.
2. 19 see that (it is) an evil (thing) and bitter
2. 23 See thy way in the valley, know what th.
2. 31 O generation, see ye the word of the LORD
3. 2 and see where thou hast not been lien with
3. 6 Hast thou seen (that) which backsliding Is.
3. 7 And her treacherous sister Judah saw (it)
3. 8 I saw, when for all the causes whereby ba
4. 21 How long shall I see the standard, (and)
5. 1 see now, and know, and seek in the broad
5. 12 neither shall we see sword nor famine
5. 21 which have eyes, and see not; which have
6. 16 Stand ye in the ways and see, and ask for
7. 11 Behold, even I have seen it saith (it), saith
7. 12 see what I did to it for the wickedness of
7. 17 Seest thou not what they do in the cities
11. 20 let me see thy vengeance on them; for un.
12. 3 thou hast seen me, and tried mine heart
12. 4 they said, He shall not see our last end
13. 27 I have seen thine adulteries, and thy nei.
14. 13 Ye shall not see the sword, neither shall
17. 6 shall not see when good cometh; but sh.
17. 8 shall not see when heat cometh, but her
20. 12 seest the reins and the heart let me see
20. 18 Wherefore came I forth..to see labour and
22. 10 he shall return no more, nor see his native
22. 12 he shall die..and shall see this land no mo
23. 13 I have seen folly in the prophets of Sam.
23. 14 I have seen also in the prophets of Jerus.
23. 24 in secret places that I shall not see him
24. 3 Then said the LORD unto me What seest
30. 6 see whether a man doth travail with ch.?
30. 6 wherefore do I see every man with his ha.
32. 24 is come to pass; and, behold thou seest
39. 4 the king of Judah saw them, and all the
41. 13 the people which (were) with Ishmael saw
42. 14 where we shall see no war, nor hear the
42 18 a reproach; and ye shall see this place no
44. 2 Ye have seen all the evil that I have bro.
44. 17 for (then) had we plenty..and saw no evil
46. 5 Wherefore have I seen them dismayed
51. 61 and shalt see, and shalt read all these w.
Lam. 1. 7 the adversaries saw her, (and) did mock
1. 8 they have seen her nakedness: yea, she
1. 10 she hath seen (that) the heathen entered
1. 11 see, O LORD, and consider; for I have bec.
1. 12 see if there be any sorrow like unto my
2. 16 day that we looked for..we have seen (it)
3. 1 I (am) the man (that) hath seen affliction
3. 59 thou hast seen my wrong; judge thou my
3 60 Thou hast seen all their vengeance (and) all
Eze. 1. 1 the heavens were opened, and I saw visi
1. 27 I saw as the colour of amber as the app
1. 27 I saw as it were the appearance of fire
1. 28 when I saw (it) I fell upon my face and
3. 23 as the glory which I saw by the river of
8. 4 according to the vision that I saw in the
8. 6 Son of man, seest thou what they do? (e)
8. 6 (and) thou shalt see greater abominations
8. 10 I went in and saw; and, behold every fo.
8. 12 hast thou seen what the ancients of the
8. 12 The LORD seeth us not; the LORD hath fo.
8. 13 thou shalt see greater abominations that
8. 15 Then said he unto me Hast thou seen (th)
8. 15 thou shalt see greater abominations than
8. 17 Hast thou seen (this). O son of man? Is it
9. 9 LORD hath forsaken..the LORD seeth not
10. 15, 20 This (is) the living creature that I saw
10. 22 the same faces which I saw by the river
11. 1 among whom I saw Jaazaniah the son of
11. 24 the vision that I had seen went up from
12. 2 which have eyes to see, and see not; they
12. 6 thou shalt cover thy face, that thou see
12. 12 he shall cover his face, that he see not the
12. 13 yet shall he not see it, though he shall die
13. 3 follow their own spirit, and have seen no
14. 22 and ye shall see their way and their doings
16. 6 and saw thee polluted in thine own blood
16. 37 that they may see all thy nakedness
16. 50 therefore I took them away as I saw (go.)
18. 14 that seeth all his father's sins which he
19. 5 when she saw that she had waited. (and)
20. 28 they saw every high hill, and all the thick
20. 48 all flesh shall see that I the LORD have
23. 11 when her sister Aholibah saw (this). she
23. 13 I saw that she was defiled, (that) they (t.)
23. 14 she saw men pourtrayed upon the wall
32. 31 Pharaoh shall see them, and shall be co.
33. 3 when he seeth the sword come upon the
33. 6 if the watchman see the sword come, and
39. 15 when (any) seeth a man's bone, then shall
39. 21 the heathen shall see my judgment that
40. 4 declare all that thou seest to the house of
41. 8 I saw also the height of the house round
43. 3 the appearance of the vision which I saw
43. 3 the vision that I saw when I came to de
43. 3 the vision that I saw by the river Chebar
47. 6 he said unto me, Son of man, hast thou seen
Dan. 1. 10 why should he see your faces worse liking
1. 13 and as thou seest, deal with thy servants
8. 2 I saw in a vision; and it came to pass, wh
8. 2 I saw, that I (was) at Shushan (in) the pa.

Dan. 8. 2 I saw in a vision, and I was by the river
8. 3 I lifted up mine eyes, and saw, and, beh.
8. 4 I saw the ram pushing westward, and no.
8. 6 which I had seen standing before the ri.
8. 7 I saw him come close unto the ram, and
8. 15 I Daniel, had seen the vision, and sought
8. 20 The ram which thou sawest having (two)
9. 21 whom I had seen in the vision at the be.
10. 7 And I Daniel alone saw the vision: for
10. 7 the men that were with me saw not the
10. 8 I was left alone, and saw this great vision
Hos. 5. 13 When Ephraim saw his sickness, and Ju.
6. 10 I have seen an horrible thing in the house
9. 10 I saw your fathers as the first ripe in the
9. 13 Ephraim, as I saw Tyrus, (is) planted in
Joel 2. 28 dream dreams, your young men shall see
Amos 6. 2 Pass ye unto Calneh, and see; and from
7. 8 Amos, what seest thou? And I said, A pl.
8. 2 Amos, what seest thou? And I said, A
9. 1 I saw the LORD standing upon the altar
Jon. 3. 10 God saw their works, that they turned fr.
4. 5 till he might see what would become of
Mic. 6. 9 and (the man of) wisdom shall see thy na.
7. 10 (she that is) mine enemy shall see it, and
7. 16 The nations shall see, and be confounded
Hab. 2. 1 will watch to see what he will say unto
3. 7 saw the tents of Cushan in affliction: (and)
3 10 The mountains saw thee (and) they trem
Zeph. 3. 15 in the midst of thee: thou shalt not see
Hag. 2. 3 Who (is) left among you that saw this ho.
2. 3 how do ye see it now? (is it) not in your
Zech. 1. 8 I saw by night, and behold a man riding
1. 18 Then lifted I up mine eyes, and saw, and
2. 2 To measure Jerusalem, to see what (is) the
4. 2 said unto me What seest thou? And I said
4. 10 and shall see the plummet in the hand of
5. 2 What seest thou? And I answered, I see a
5. 5 Lift up now thine eyes, and see what (is)
9. 5 Ashkelon shall see (it) and fear; Gaza also
9. 8 for now have I seen with mine eyes
10. 7 yea, their children shall see (it), and be
Mal. 1. 5 your eyes shall see, and ye shall say, The

6. [*God*] *of seeing*, רֳאִי *roi.*
Gen. 16. 13 she called the name..Thou God seest me

6*a*. *Him that seeth* (*hath seen*), רָאָה *raah* (partic.).
Gen. 16 13 looked after him that seeth me; Job 7. 8.

7. *To behold, look*, שׁוּר *shur.*
Job 7. 8 The eye of him..shall see me no (more)
17. 15 where (is) now my hope?..who shall see
24 15 No eye shall see me and disguiseth (his)
35 14 Although thou sayest thou shalt not see

8. *To see, behold, scorch*, שָׁזַף *shazaph.*
Job 20 9 The eye also (which) saw him shall..no more
28 7 and which the vulture's eye hath not seen

9. *To fear, reverence, be afraid*, יָרֵא *yare.*
Isa. 60. 5 thou shalt see, and flow together, and th.

10 *A seer*, חֹזֶה *chozeh.*
Eze. 13. 9 shall be upon the prophets that see vanity
13. 16 and which see visions of peace for her, and

11. *To look up, behold again*, ἀναβλέπω *anablepō.*
Luke 7. 22 how that the blind see, the lame walk, the

12. *To look away, look at*, ἀπεῖδον *apeidon.*
Phil. 2 23 so soon as I shall see how it will go with

13. *To see, perceive, understand*, βλέπω *blepō.*
Matt. 6. 4 6. 18 and thy Father which seeth in secret
11. 4 those things which ye do hear and see
12. 22 the blind and dumb both spake and saw
13 13 they seeing, see not; and hearing, they hear
13 14 seeing ye shall see, and shall not perceive
13. 16 blessed (are) your eyes, for they see: and
13. 17 (those things) which ye see, and have not
14. 30 when he saw the wind boisterous, he was
15. 31 when they saw the dumb to speak, the m.
15. 31 the lame to walk, and the blind to see
24. 2 Jesus said unto them, See ye not all these
Mark 4. 12 That seeing they may see, and not perce.
5. 31 Thou seest the multitude thronging thee
8. 18 Having eyes, see ye not? and having ears
8 23 hands upon him, he asked him if he saw o.
8. 24 he looked up, and said, I see men as trees
13. 2 Seest thou these great buildings? there sh.
Luke 7. 44 said unto Simon, Seest thou this woman
8. 10 that seeing they might not see, and hear.
8. 16 that they which enter in may see the light
10. 23 the eyes which see the things that ye see
10. 24 those things which ye see, and have not
11. 33 that they which come in may see the light
21. 30 ye see and know of your own selves that
John 1. 29 John seeth Jesus coming unto him, and
5. 19 Son can do nothing..but what he seeth
9. 7 He went his way..washed, and came see.
9. 15 He put clay upon mine eyes, and I..do see
9. 19 was born blind? how then doth he now see
9. 21 by what means he now seeth, we know not
9. 25 that, whereas I was blind, now I see
9. 39 that they which see not might see, and
9. 39 that they which see might be made blind
9. 41 but now ye say, We see; therefore your sin
11. 9 he stumbleth not, because he seeth the
20. 1 seeth the stone taken away from the sep.
20. 5 looking in), saw the linen clothes lying
21. 9 [they saw] a fire of coals there, and fish
21. 20 seeth the disciple whom Jesus loved foll.
Acts 2. 33 he hath shed forth this, which ye now see
8. 6 hearing and seeing the miracles which he
9. 8 when his eyes were opened, he saw no ma.

Acts 12. 9 and wist not..but thought he saw a vision
13. 11 thou shalt be blind, not seeing the sun for
28. 26 and seeing ye shall see, and not perceive
Rom. 7. 23 I see another law in my members, warring
8. 24 is seen is not hope: for what a man seeth
8. 25 if we hope for that we see not, (then) do
11. 8 eyes that they should not see, and ears th.
11. 10 eyes be darkened, that they may not see
1 Co. 1. 26 ye see your calling, brethren, how that
13. 12 now we see through a glass darkly; but th.
16. 10 see that he may be with you without fear
2 Co. 4. 18 we look not at the things which are seen
4. 18 but at the things which are not seen; for
4. 18 the things which are seen (are) temporal
4. 18 the things which are not seen (are) eter.
12. 6 think of me above that which he seeth me
Eph. 5. 15 See then that ye walk circumspectly, not
Heb. 2. 9 we see Jesus, Who was made a little low.
3. 19 we see that they could not enter in becau.
10. 25 so much the more as ye see the day appr.
11. 1 faith is..the evidence of things not seen
11. 3 things which are seen were not made of
11. 7 being warned of God of things not seen as
12. 25 See that ye refuse not him that speaketh
Jas. 2. 22 Seest thou how faith wrought with his wo.
Rev. 1. 11 What thou seest, write in a book, and send
1. 12 I turned to see the voice that spake with
3. 18 anoint thine eyes..that thou mayest see
6. 1 one of the four beasts saying, Come and [s.]
6. 3 heard the second beast say, Come [and see]
6. 5 I heard the third beast say, Come and [s.]
6. 7 heard..the fourth beast say, Come and [s.]
9. 20 which neither can see, nor hear, nor walk
11. 9 shall see their dead bodies three days and
16. 15 lest he walk naked, and they see his shame
18. 9 when they shall see the smoke of her bur.
22. 8 I John saw these things, and heard (them)
22. 8 when I had heard and [seen], I fell down

14. *To know, be acquainted, see*, εἶδον *eidon.*
Matt. 2. 2 we have seen his star in the east, and are
2. 9 the star, which they saw in the east, went
2. 10 when they saw the star, they rejoiced with
2. 16 when he saw that he was mocked of the
3. 7 And when he saw many of the Pharisees
3. 16 he saw the spirit of God descending like a
4. 16 The people which sat in darkness saw great
4. 18 Jesus, walking by the sea of Galilee, saw
4 21 he saw other two brethren, James (the son)
5. 1 seeing the multitudes, he went up into a
5. 16 that they may see your good works, and
8. 14 he saw his wife's mother laid, and sick of a
8. 18 when Jesus saw great multitudes about
8. 34 when they saw him, they besought (him)
9. 2 Jesus, seeing their faith, said unto the sick
9. 8 when the multitudes saw (it), they marv.
9 9 he saw a man, named Matthew, sitting at
9. 11 when the Pharisees saw (it), they said un.
9 22 when he saw her, he said, Daughter, be of
9 23 saw the minstrels and the people making
9. 36 when he saw the multitudes, he was mov.
11. 8 what went ye out for to see? A man cloth.
11 9 what went ye out for to see? A prophet
12. 2 when the Pharisees saw (it), they said un.
12. 38 saying, Master, we would see a sign from
13. 15 lest at any time they should see with (their)
13 17 desired to see..and have not seen
14. 14 Jesus went forth, and saw a great multi.
14. 26 when the disciples saw him walking on the
16 28 till they see the son of man coming in his
17 8 they had lifted up their eyes, they saw no
18. 31 when his fellow servants saw what was
20. 3 saw others standing idle in the market pl.
21. 15 when the chief priests and scribes saw the
21. 19 when he saw a fig tree in the way, he came
21. 20 when the disciples saw (it,) they marvelled
21. 32 ye, when ye had seen (it), repented not after
21. 38 when the husbandmen saw the son, they
22. 11 he saw there a man which had not on a
23 39 Ye shall not see me henceforth, till ye sha.
24. 15 When ye therefore shall see the abomin.
24. 33 likewise ye, when ye shall see all these
25 37, 44 Lord, when saw we thee an hungered
25 38 When saw we thee a stranger, and took
25. 39 when saw we thee sick, or in prison, and
26 8 when his disciples saw (it), they had indi.
26. 58 and sat with the servants, to see the end
26. 71 another (maid) saw him, and said unto th.
27. 3 when he saw that he was condemned, re.
27. 24 When Pilate saw that he could prevail no.
27. 49 let us see whether Elias will come to save
27. 54 saw the earthquake, and those things th.
28. 6 Come, see the place where the Lord lay
28. 17 when they saw him, they worshipped him
Mark 1. 10 he saw the heavens opened, and the spirit
1. 16 he saw Simon, and Andrew his brother ca.
1. 19 he saw James the (son) of Zebedee, and J.
2. 5 When Jesus saw their faith, he said unto
2. 12 saying, We never saw it on this fashion
2. 14 he saw Levi the (son) of Alpheus sitting at
2. 16 when the scribes and Pharisees saw him
5. 6 when he saw Jesus afar off, he ran and
5 14 they went out to see what it was that was
5. 16 they that saw (it) told them how it befell
5. 22 and when he saw him, he fell at his feet
5. 32 he looked round about to see her that had
6. 33 the people saw them departing, and many
6. 34 Jesus, when he came out, saw much peo.
6. 38 saith..How many loaves have ye? go and s.
6. 48 he saw them toiling in rowing; for the wind
6. 49 when they saw him walking upon the sea
6. 50 For they all saw him, and were troubled

Mark 7. 2 when they saw some of his disciples eat
9. 1 till they have seen the kingdom of God co.
9. 8 they saw no man any more, save Jesus only
9. 9 tell no man what things they had seen, till
9. 14 he saw a great multitude about them, and
9. 20 when he saw him, straightway the spirit
9. 25 When Jesus saw that the people came ru.
9. 38 we saw one casting out devils in thy name
10. 14 when Jesus saw (it), he was much displea.
11. 13 seeing a fig tree afar off having leaves, he
11. 20 they saw the fig tree dried up from the
12. 15 bring me a penny, that I may see (it)
12. 34 when Jesus saw that he answered discre.
13. 14 But when ye shall see the abomination of
13. 29 when ye shall see these things come to p.
14. 67 when she saw Peter warming himself, she
14. 69 a maid saw him again, and began to say
15. 32 Let Christ..descend..that we may see and
15. 36 let us see whether Elias will come to take
15. 39 saw that he so cried out, and gave up the
16. 5 they saw a young man sitting on the right
Luke 1. 12 when Zacharias saw (him), he was troub.
1. 29 [when she saw (him),)] she was troubled
2. 15 see this thing which is come to pass, wh.
2. 17 when they had seen (it), they made known
2. 20 the things that they had heard and seen
2. 26 should not see death, before he had seen
2. 30 For mine eyes have seen thy salvation
2. 48 when they saw him, they were amazed
5. 2 saw two ships standing by the lake: but
5. 8 When Simon Peter saw (it), he fell down
5. 12 who, seeing Jesus, fell on (his) face, and
5. 20 when he saw their faith, he said unto him
5. 26 saying, We have seen strange things to.
7. 13 when the Lord saw her, he had compass.
7. 22 tell John what things ye have seen and
7. 25 what went ye out for to see? A man clo.
7. 26 what went ye out for to see? A prophet?
7. 39 the Pharisee which had bidden him saw
8. 20 thy brethren stand without, desiring to s.
8. 28 When he saw Jesus, he cried out, and fell
8. 34 When they that fed (them) saw what was
8. 35 Then they went out to see what was done
8. 36 They also which saw (it) told them by wh.
8. 47 when the woman saw that she was not hid
9. 9 but who is this..And he desired to see
9. 27 which shall not taste of death, till they see
9. 32 when they were awake, they saw his gl.
9. 49 we saw one casting out devils in thy name
9. 54 when his disciples James and John saw
10. 24 desired to see..and have not seen them
10. 31 when he saw him, he passed by on the
10. 33 when he saw him, he had compassion (on
11. 38 when the Pharisee saw (it), he marvelled
12. 54 When ye see a cloud rise out of the west
13. 12 when Jesus saw her, he called (her to him)
13. 35 Ye shall not see me, until (the time) come
14. 18 I must needs go and see it: I pray thee
15. 20 his father saw him, and had compassion
17. 14 when he saw (them), he said unto them
17. 15 one of them, when he saw that he was
17. 22 when ye shall desire to see one of the
18. 15 when (his) disciples saw (it), they rebuked
18. 24 when Jesus saw that he was very sorrow.
18. 43 the people, when they saw (it), gave pra.
19. 3 he sought to see Jesus who he was; and
19. 4 climbed up into a sycamore tree to see
19. 5 he looked up, and saw him, and said unto
19. 7 when they saw (it), they all murmured, s.
19. 37 all the mighty works that they had seen
20. 13 they will reverence (him) [when they see]
20. 14 when the husbandmen saw him, they re.
21. 1 he looked up, and saw the rich men cast.
21. 2 he saw also a certain poor widow casting
21. 20 when ye shall see Jerusalem compassed
21. 31 likewise ye, when ye see these things co.
22. 49 When they which were about him saw w.
22. 58 another saw him, and said, Thou art also
23. 8 when Herod saw Jesus, he was exceeding
23. 8 he was desirous to see him of a long (se.)
23. 8 he hoped to have seen some miracle done
23. 47 when the centurion saw what was done
24. 24 found (it) even so..but him they saw not
24. 39 handle me and see; for a spirit hath not
John 1. 33 Upon whom thou shalt see the Spirit de.
1. 39 Come and [see]. They came and saw where
1. 46 Philip saith unto him, Come and see
1. 47 Jesus saw Nathanael coming to him, and
1. 48 when thou wast under the fig tree, I saw
1. 50 Because I said unto thee, I saw thee under
3. 3 Except a man be born again, he cannot s.
4. 29 see a man which told me all things that
4. 48 Except ye see signs and wonders, ye will
5. 6 When Jesus saw him lie, and knew that
6. 14 when they had seen the miracle that Je.
6. 22 saw that there was none other boat there
6. 24 When the people therefore saw that Je.
6. 26 Ye seek me, not because ye saw the mir.
6. 30 What sign showest thou..that we may s.
8. 56 rejoiced to see my day; and he saw (it)
9. 1 he saw a man which was blind from (his)
11. 31 when they saw Mary, that she rose up h.
11. 32 saw him, she fell down at his feet, say.
11. 33 When Jesus therefore saw her weeping
11. 34 They said unto him, Lord, come and see
12. 9 but that they might see Lazarus also, wh.
12. 21 desired him, saying, Sir, we would see J.
12. 40 that they should not see with (their) eyes
12. 41 These things said Esaias, when he saw his
18. 26 Did not I see thee in the garden with him
19. 6 the chief priests therefore and officers saw
19. 26 When Jesus therefore saw his mother, and
John 19. 33 when they came to Jesus, and saw that
20. 8 came first to the sepulchre, and he saw
20. 20 Then were the disciples..when they saw
20. 25 Except I shall see in his hands the print
20. 29 blessed (are) they that have not seen, and
21. 21 Peter seeing him saith to Jesus, Lord, and
Acts 2. 27 neither..suffer thine Holy One to see cor.
2. 31 neither his flesh did see corruption
3. 3 Who seeing Peter and John about to go
3. 9 the people saw him walking and praising
3. 12 when Peter saw (it), he answered unto the
4. 20 the things which we have seen and heard
6. 15 saw his face as it had been the face of an
7. 24 seeing one (of them) suffer wrong, he de.
7. 31 When Moses saw (it), he wondered at the
7. 34 I have seen, I have seen the affliction of
7. 55 saw the glory of God, and Jesus standing
8. 39 the eunuch saw him no more: and he we.
9. 12 hath seen in a vision a man named Ana.
9. 27 declared unto them how he had seen the
9. 35 all that dwelt in Lydda and Saron saw him
9. 40 she opened her eyes: and when she saw
10. 3 He saw in a vision evidently, about the
10. 17 what this vision which he had seen should
11. 5 in a trance I saw a vision, A certain ves.
11. 6 I considered, and saw four footed beasts
11. 13 he showed us how he had seen an angel
11. 23 when he came, and had seen the grace of
12. 3 And because he saw it pleased the Jews
12. 16 when they had opened (the door), and saw
13. 12 the deputy, when he saw what was done
13. 35 Thou shalt not suffer thine Holy One to see
13. 36 was laid unto his fathers, and saw corru.
13. 37 he, whom God raised again, saw no cor.
13. 45 when the Jews saw the multitudes, they
14. 11 when the people saw what Paul had done
16. 10 after he had seen the vision, immediately
16. 19 when her masters saw that the hope of
16. 27 awaking out of his sleep, and seeing the
16. 40 when they had seen the brethren, they
19. 21 After I have been there, I must also see
21. 32 when they saw the chief captain and the
22. 14 shouldest know his will, and see that just
22. 18 saw him saying unto me, Make haste, and
26. 13 I saw in the way a light from heaven
26. 16 of these things which thou hast seen, and
28. 4 when the barbarians saw the (venomous)
28. 15 whom when Paul saw, he thanked God
28. 20 have I called for you, to see (you), and to
28. 27 lest they should see with (their) eyes, and
Rom. 1. 11 I long to see you, that I may impart unto
1 Co. 2. 9 Eye hath not seen, nor ear heard, neither
8. 10 if any man see thee which hast knowledge
16. 7 For I will not see you now by the way
Gal. 1. 19 other of the apostles saw I none, save Ja.
2. 7 contrariwise, when they saw that the go.
2. 14 when I saw that they walked not upright.
6. 11 Ye see how large a letter I have written
Phil. 1. 27 that whether I come and see you, or else
1. 30 Having the same conflict which ye saw in
2. 28 that, when ye see him again, ye may rej.
4. 9 Those things, which ye have..seen in me
1 Th. 2. 17 endeavoured the more abundantly to see
3. 6 desiring greatly to see us, as we also (to)
3. 10 praying exceedingly that we might see
1 Ti. 6. 16 whom no man hath seen, nor can see: to
2 Ti. 1. 4 Greatly desiring to see thee, being mind.
Heb. 3. 9 proved me, and saw my works forty years
11. 5 was translated that he should not see de.
11. 13 but having seen them afar off, and were
11. 23 they saw (he was) a proper child; and they
Jas. 5. 11 have seen the end of the Lord; that the
1 Pe. 1. 8 Whom having not seen, ye love; in wh.
3. 10 he that will love life, and see good days
1 Jo. 5. 16 If any man see his brother sin a sin (wh.
3 John 14 I trust I shall shortly see thee, and we sh.
Rev. 1. 2 bare record..of all things that he saw
1. 12 being turned I saw seven golden candles.
1. 17 when I saw him, I fell at his feet as dead
1. 19 Write the things which thou hast seen, and
1. 20 mystery of the seven stars which thou saw.
1. 20 the seven candlesticks [which thou sawe.]
4. 4 [I saw] four and twenty elders sitting, cl.
5. 1 I saw in the right hand of him that sat on
5. 2 I saw a strong angel proclaiming with a
6. 1 I saw, when the Lamb opened one of the
6. 2 [I saw,] and behold a white horse; and
6. 9 I saw under the altar the souls of them
7. 1 I saw four angels standing on the four co.
7. 2 I saw another angel ascending from the
8. 2 I saw the seven angels which stood before
9. 1 I saw a star fall from heaven unto the ea.
9. 17 I saw the horses in the vision, and them
10. 1 I saw another mighty angel come down
10. 5 the angel which I saw stand upon the sea
12. 13 when the dragon saw that he was cast un.
13. 1 saw a beast rise up out of the sea, having
13. 2 the beast which I saw was like unto a le.
13. 3 [I saw] one of his heads as it were woun.
14. 6 I saw another angel fly in the midst of
15. 1 I saw another sign in heaven, great and
15. 2 I saw as it were a sea of glass mingled
16. 13 I saw three unclean spirits like frogs (c.)
17. 3 I saw a woman sit upon a scarlet colour.
17. 6 I saw the woman drunken with the blood
17. 6 when I saw her, I wondered with great
17. 8 The beast that thou sawest was, and is
17. 12 the ten horns which thou sawest, are ten
17. 15 The waters which thou sawest, where the
17. 16 the ten horns which thou sawest upon the
17. 18 the woman which thou sawest is that gr.
18. 1 I saw another angel come down from he.
Rev. 18. 7 and am no widow, and shall see no sorrow
19. 11 I saw heaven opened, and behold a white
19. 17 I saw an angel standing in the sun; and
19. 19 I saw the beast, and the kings of the ea.
20. 1 I saw an angel come down from heaven
20. 4 I saw thrones, and they sat upon them
20. 11 I saw a great white throne, and him that
20. 12 I saw the dead, small and great, stand b.
21. 1 I saw a new heaven and a new earth: for
21. 2 I John saw the holy city, new Jerusalem
21. 22 I saw no temple therein: for the Lord G.

15. *To look on*, ἐμβλέπω *emblepō*.
Mark 8. 25 he was restored, and saw every man cle
Acts 22. 11 when I could not see for the glory of that

16. *To find (by search)*, εὑρίσκω *heuriskō*.
Matt. 2. 11 [they saw] the young child with Mary his

17. *To view, behold attentively*, θεάομαι *theaomai*.
Matt 11. 7 What went ye..into the wilderness to see?
22. 11 when the king came in to see the guests
Mark 16. 14 [they believed not them which had seen]
Luke 5. 27 he went forth, and [saw] a publican, na.
7. 24 What went ye..into the wilderness..to s.
John 1. 32 I saw the Spirit descending from heaven
1. 38 Jesus turned, and saw them following, and
6. 5 Jesus then lifted up (his) eyes, and saw a
8. 10 [When Jesus had lifted up himself, and s.]
11. 45 and had seen the things which Jesus did
Acts 1. 11 come in like manner as ye have seen him
8. 18 when Simon [saw] that through laying on
21. 27 the Jews..when they saw him in the tem.
22. 9 they that were with me saw indeed the
Rom 15. 24 I trust to see you in my journey, and to
1 Jo. 4. 12 No man hath seen God at any time. If we
4. 14 we have seen and do testify that the Fat.

18. *To view, see*, θεωρέω *theōreō*.
Matt 28. 1 and the other Mary to see the sepulchre
Mark 3. 11 unclean spirits, when they saw him, fell
5. 15 see him that was possessed with the devil
5. 38 seeth the tumult, and them that wept and
16. 4 they saw that the stone was rolled away
Luke 24. 37 and supposed that they had seen a spirit
24. 39 a spirit hath not flesh..as ye see me have
John 2. 23 when they saw the miracles which he did
6. 19 they see Jesus walking on the sea, and
6. 40 that every one which seeth the Son, and
6. 62 if ye shall see the Son of man ascend up
7. 3 that thy disciples also may see the works
8. 51 keep my saying, he shall never see death
9. 8 they which before had seen him that he
10. 12 seeth the wolf coming, and leaveth the sh.
12. 45 he that seeth me seeth him that sent me
14. 17 because it seeth him not, neither know.
14. 19 the world seeth me no more; but ye see
16. 10 because I go to my Father, and ye see me
16. 16, 17, 19 A little while, and ye shall not see
20. 6 went into the sepulchre, and seeth the li.
20. 12 seeth two angels in white sitting, the one
20. 14 she turned herself back, and saw Jesus
Acts 3. 16 hath made this man strong, whom ye see
4. 13 when they saw the boldness of Peter and
7. 56 I see the heavens opened, and the Son of
9. 7 speechless, hearing a voice, but seeing no
10. 11 saw heaven opened, and a certain vessel
17. 16 when he saw the city wholly given to ido.
19. 26 ye see and hear, that not alone at Ephes.
20. 38 that they should see his face no more
21. 20 Thou seest brother, how many thousands
25. 24 ye see this man, about whom all the
28. 6 they had looked a great while, and saw
1 Jo. 3. 17 whoso hath this world's good, and seeth
Rev. 11. 11 great fear fell upon them which saw them

19. *To know*, ἱστορέω *historeō*.
Gal. 1. 18 I went up to Jerusalem to see Peter, and

20. *To see, discern, take heed*, ὁράω *horaō*.
Matt. 5. 8 Blessed (are) the pure..for they shall see
8. 4 See thou tell no man; but go thy way, sh.
9. 30 charged them, saying, See (that) no man
24. 6 see that ye be not troubled: for all (these
24. 30 they shall see the Son of man coming in
26. 64 Hereafter shall ye see the Son of man sit.
27. 4 they said, What (is that) to us? see thou
27. 24 saying, I am innocent..see ye (to it)
28. 7 there shall ye see him: lo, I have told you
28. 10 go into Galilee, and there shall they see
Mark 1. 44 See thou say nothing to any man: but go
13. 26 then shall they see the Son of man coming
14. 62 ye shall see the Son of man sitting on the
16. 7 there shall ye see him, as he said unto y.
Luke 1. 22 they perceived that he had seen a vision
3. 6 And all flesh shall see the salvation of G.
9. 36 any of those things which they had seen
13. 28 when ye shall see Abraham, and Isaac
16. 23 seeth Abraham afar off, and Lazarus in
17. 22 of the Son of man, and ye shall not see
21. 27 then shall they see the Son of man com.
24. 23 they had also seen a vision of angels, wh.
John 1. 18 No man hath seen God at any time; the
1. 34 I saw, and bare record that this is the
1. 50 thou shalt see greater things than these
1. 51 ye shall see heaven open, and the angels
3. 11 We..testify that we have seen: and ye r.
3. 32 what he hath seen and heard, that he tes.
3. 36 he that believeth not the Son shall not see
4. 45 having seen all the things that he did at
5. 37 neither heard his voice..nor seen his sh.
6. 2 [they saw] his miracles which he did on
6. 36 That ye also have seen me, and believe
6. 46 Not that any man hath seen the Father
6. 46 he which is of God, he hath seen the Fa

John 8. 38 I speak that which I have seen with my
8. 38 ye do that which [ye have seen] with yo.
8. 57 Thou art not yet fifty..and hast thou se.
9. 37 Thou hast both seen him, and it is he th.
11. 40 thou shouldest see the glory of God
14. 7 henceforth ye know him, and have seen
14. 9 he that hath seen me hath seen the Fat.
15. 24 now have they both seen and hated both
16. 16, 17 again, a little while, and ye shall see
16. 19 and again, a little while, and ye shall see
16. 22 I will see you again, and your heart shall
19. 35 he that saw (it) bare record, and his rec.
20. 18 told the disciples that she had seen the
20. 25 said unto him, We have seen the Lord
20. 29 because thou hast seen me, thou hast be.
Acts 2. 17 your young men shall see visions, and yo.
7. 44 according to the fashion that he had se.
13. 31 he was seen many days of them which ca.
20. 25 I know that ye..shall see my face no mo.
22. 15 unto all men of what thou hast seen and
Rom 15. 21 whom he was not spoken of, they shall s.
1 Co 9. 1 have I not seen Jesus Christ our Lord?
15. 5 he was seen of Cephas, then of the twelve
15. 6 he was seen of above five hundred breth.
15. 7 he was seen of James; then of all the ap.
15. 8 he was seen of me also, as of one born out
Col. 2. 1 as many as have not seen my face in the
2. 18 into those things which he hath not seen
1 Th. 5. 15 See that none render evil for evil unto
1 Ti. 3. 16 justified in the spirit, seen of angels, pre.
Heb. 2. 8 But now we see not yet all things put un
8. 5 See, saith he, (that) thou make all things
11. 27 he endured, as seeing him who is invisi.
12. 14 without which no man shall see the Lord
13. 23 with whom, if he come shortly, I will see
Jas. 2. 24 Ye see then how that by works a man is
1 Pe. 1. 8 though now ye see (him) not, yet believing
1 Jo. 1. 1 which we have seen with our eyes, which
1. 2 the life was manifested, and we have se.
1. 3 That which we have seen and heard dec.
3. 2 we shall be like him; for we shall see h.
3. 6 whosoever sinneth hath not seen him, n.
4. 20 loveth not his brother whom he hath seen
4. 20 can he love God whom he hath not seen?
3 John 11 but he that doeth evil hath not seen God
Rev. 1. 7 every eye shall see him, and they (also) w.
11. 19 there was seen in his temple the ark of
18. 18 cried [when they saw] the smoke of her
19. 10 See (thou do it) not: I am thy fellow se.
22. 4 they shall see his face; and his name (sh.
22. 9 See (thou do it) not: for I am thy fellow,

SEE afar off, cannot —

To shut or wink the eyes, μυωπάζω *muōpazō.*
2 Pe. 1. 9 is blind, and cannot see afar off, and hath

SEE before, to —

1. *To see before,* προεῖδον *proeidon.*
Acts 2. 31 He, seeing this before, spake of the resu.

2. *To see before,* προοράω *prooraō.*
Acts 21. 29 they had seen before with him in the ci.

SEE clearly, to —

1. *To see or look through,* διαβλέπω *diablepō.*
Matt. 7. 5 then shalt thou see clearly to cast out the
Luke 6. 42 then shalt thou see clearly to pull out the

2. *To see thoroughly,* καθοράω *kathoraō.*
Rom. 1. 20 invisible things of him..are clearly seen

SEE, to make, cause or let —

1. *To cause to see,* רָאָה *raah,* 5.
Deut 34. 4 I have caused thee to see (it) with thine
Psa. 59. 10 God shall let me see (my desire) upon mine
Song 2. 14 let me see thy countenance, let me hear

2. *To enlighten,* φωτίζω *phōtizō.*
Eph. 3. 9 to make all (men) see what (is) the fellow

SEE one another, to —

To look at one another, רָאָה *raah,* 7.
2 Ch. 25. 17 Come, let us see one another in the face
25. 21 they saw one another in the face, (both)

SEED (sown, time) —

1. *Seed, seed time, progeny,* זֶרַע *zera*
Gen. 1. 11 the herb yielding seed, (and) the fruit tree
1. 11 whose seed (is) in itself upon the earth
1. 12 brought forth grass, (and) herb yielding s.
1. 12 the tree yielding fruit, whose seed (was)
1. 29 I have given you every herb bearing seed
1. 29 which (is) the fruit of a tree yielding seed
3. 15 put enmity..between thy seed and her se.
4. 25 hath appointed me another seed instead
7. 3 keep seed alive upon the face of all the ea.
8. 22 seed time and harvest, and cold and heat
9. 9 with you, and with your seed after you
12. 7 Unto thy seed will I give this land: and
13. 15 to thee will I give it, and to thy seed for
13. 16 I will make thy seed as the dust of the e.
13. 16 (then) shall thy seed also be numbered
15. 3 to me thou hast given no seed: and, lo, one
15. 5 and he said unto him, So shall thy seed be
15. 13 thy seed shall be a stranger in a land (that
15. 18 Unto thy seed have I given this land, from
16. 10 I will multiply thy seed exceedingly, that
17. 7 between me and thee and thy seed after
17. 7 to be a God unto thee, and to thy seed af.
17. 8 I will give unto thee, and to thy seed after
17. 9 and thy seed after thee in their generat.
17. 10 between me and you and thy seed after
17. 12 of any stranger, which (is) not of thy seed
Gen. 17. 19 will establish my covenant..with his seed
19. 32, 34 that we may preserve seed of our fath.
21. 12 for in Isaac shall thy seed be called
21. 13 also of the son..because he (is) thy seed
22. 17 I will multiply thy seed as the stars of the
22. 17 thy seed shall possess the gate of his ene.
22. 18 in thy seed shall all the nations of the ea.
24. 7 saying, Unto thy seed will I give this land
24. 60 let thy seed possess the gate of those wh.
26. 3 unto thy seed, I will give all these count
26. 4 I will make thy seed to multiply as the st.
26. 4 will give unto thy seed all these countries
26. 4 in thy seed shall all the nations of the earth
26. 24 will bless thee, and multiply thy seed, for
28. 4 to thee, and to thy seed with thee; that thou
28. 13 to thee will I give it, and to thy seed
28. 14 thy seed shall be as the dust of the earth
28. 14 in thy seed shall all the families of the ea.
32. 12 make thy seed as the sand of the sea, wh.
35. 12 to thy seed after thee will I give the land
38. 8 marry her, and raise up seed to thy bro.
38. 9 Onan knew that the seed should not be his
38. 9 lest that he should give seed to his brother
46. 6 came into Egypt, Jacob, and all his seed
46. 7 all his seed, brought he with him into Eg.
47. 19 give (us) seed, that we may live, and not
47. 23 (here is) seed for you, and ye shall sow the
47. 24 four parts shall be your own, for seed of
48. 4 will give this land to thy seed after thee
48. 11 and lo, God hath showed me also thy seed
48. 19 his seed shall become a multitude of nat.
Exod 16. 31 it (was) like coriander seed, white; and the
28. 43 a statute for ever unto him and his seed
30. 21 to his seed throughout their generations
32. 13 I will multiply your seed as the stars of
32. 13 all this land..will I give unto your seed
33. 1 to Jacob, saying, Unto thy seed will I gi.
Lev. 11. 37 fall upon any sowing seed which is to be.
11. 38 if (any) water be put upon the seed, and
15. 16 if any man's seed of copulation go out fr.
15. 17 every skin, whereon is the seed of copul.
15. 18 with whom man shall lie (with) seed of
15. 32 (of him) whose seed goeth from him, and
18. 21 thou shalt not let any of thy seed pass
20. 2 that giveth any of his seed to Molech, he
20. 3 he hath given of his seed unto Molech, to
20. 4 when he giveth of his seed unto Molech
21. 15 Neither shall he profane his seed among
21. 17 Whosoever (he be) of thy seed in their ge.
21. 21 No man that hath a blemish of the seed
22. 3 Whosoever (he be) of all your seed among
22. 4 What man soever of the seed of Aaron (is)
22. 4 or a man whose seed goeth from him
26. 16 ye shall sow your seed in vain, for your
27. 16 shall be according to the seed thereof
27. 16 an homer of barley seed (shall be valued)
27. 30 (whether) of the seed of the land, (or) of
Num. 5. 28 she shall be free, and shall conceive seed
11. 7 the manna (was) as coriander seed, and
14. 24 him will I bring..and his seed shall pos.
16. 40 no stranger, which (is) not of the seed of
18. 19 unto thee and to thy seed with thee
20. 5 it (is) no place of seed, or of figs, or of vi.
24. 7 his seed (shall be) in many waters, and his
25. 13 he shall have it, and his seed after him
Deut. 1. 8 to give unto them and to their seed after
4. 37 he chose their seed after them, and brou.
10. 15 he chose their seed after them, (even) you
11. 9 to give unto them, and to their seed, a land
11. 10 where thou sowedst thy seed, and water
14. 22 tithe all the increase of thy seed, that the
22. 9 lest the fruit of thy seed which thou hast
28. 38 Thou shalt carry much seed out into the
28. 46 And they shall be..upon thy seed for ever
28. 59 the plagues of thy seed, (even) great pla.
30. 6 thine heart, and the heart of thy seed, to
30. 19 choose life, that both thou and thy seed
31. 21 forgotten out of the mouths of their seed
34. 4 I will give it unto thy seed. I have cau.
Josh 24. 3 multiplied his seed, and gave him Isaac
Ruth 4. 12 of the seed which the LORD shall give th.
1 Sa. 2. 20 The LORD give thee seed of this woman
8. 15 he will take the tenth of your seed, and
20. 42 between my seed and thy seed for ever
24. 21 thou wilt not cut off my seed after me, and
2 Sa. 4. 8 avenged my lord..of Saul, and of his seed
7. 12 I will set up thy seed after thee, which
22. 51 unto David, and to his seed for evermore
1 Ki. 2. 33 and upon the head of his seed for ever
2. 33 upon David, and upon his seed, and upon
11. 14 the Edomite: he (was) of the king's seed
11. 39 I will for this afflict the seed of David, but
18. 32 as would contain two measures of seed
2 Ki. 5. 27 shall cleave unto thee, and unto thy seed
11. 1 she arose and destroyed all the seed royal
17. 20 the LORD rejected all the seed of Israel
25. 25 the son of Elishama, of the seed royal, ca.
1 Ch. 16. 13 O ye seed of Israel his servant, ye child.
17. 11 I will raise up thy seed after thee, which
2 Ch. 20. 7 gavest it to the seed of Abraham thy fri.
22. 10 she arose and destroyed all the seed royal
Ezra 2. 59 they could not show..their seed, whether
9. 2 the holy seed have mingled themselves wi.
Neh. 7. 61 they could not show..their seed, whether
9. 2 the seed of Israel separated themselves
9. 8 to give (it, I say,) to his seed, and hast
Esth. 6. 13 (If) Mordecai (be) of the seed of the Jews
9. 27 took upon them, and upon their seed, and
9. 28 nor the memorial..perish from their seed
9. 31 decreed for themselves, and for their seed
10. 3 seeking..and speaking peace to all his se.
Job 5. 25 Thou shalt know also that thy seed (shall
Job 21. 8 Their seed is established in their sight wi.
39. 12 that he will bring home thy seed, and ga.
Psa. 18. 50 to David, and to his seed for evermore
21. 10 their seed from among the children of men
22. 23 all ye the seed of Jacob, glorify him
22. 23 and fear him, all ye the seed of Israel
22. 30 A seed shall serve him; it shall be acco.
25. 13 His soul shall dwell at ease; and his seed
37. 25 yet have I not seen..his seed begging br.
37. 26 (He is) ever merciful..and his seed (is) bl.
37. 28 but the seed of the wicked shall be cut off
69. 36 The seed also of his servants shall inherit
89. 4 Thy seed will I establish for ever, and bu.
89. 29 His seed also will I make (to endure) for
89. 36 His seed shall endure for ever, and his th.
102. 28 their seed shall be established before th.
105. 6 O ye seed of Abraham his servant, ye ch.
106. 27 To overthrow their seed also among the
112. 2 His seed shall be mighty upon earth, the
126. 6 He that goeth forth..bearing precious se.
Prov 11. 21 the seed of the righteous shall be delive.
Eccl. 11. 6 In the morning sow thy seed, and in the
Isa. 1. 4 a people laden with iniquity, a seed of evil
5. 10 the seed of an homer shall yield an ephah
6. 13 the holy seed (shall be) the substance th.
14. 20 the seed of evil doers shall never be ren.
17. 11 in the morning shalt thou make thy seed
23. 3 by great waters the seed of Sihor, the ha.
30. 23 Then shall he give the rain of thy seed, th.
41. 8 Jacob whom I have chosen, the seed of
43. 5 I will bring thy seed from the east, and
44. 3 I will pour my spirit upon thy seed, and
45. 19 I said not unto the seed of Jacob, Seek ye
45. 25 In the LORD shall all the seed of Israel be
48. 19 Thy seed also had been as the sand, and
53. 10 he shall see (his) seed, he shall prolong
54. 3 thy seed shall inherit the Gentiles, and
55. 10 that it may give seed to the sower, and
57. 3 ye sons of the sorceress, the seed of the
57. 4 (are) ye not children of transgression, a s.
59. 21 not depart..out of the mouth of thy seed
59. 21 nor out of the mouth of thy seed's seed
61. 9 their seed shall be known among the Ge.
61. 9 they (are) the seed (which) the LORD ha.
65. 9 I will bring forth a seed out of Jacob, and
65. 23 they (are) the seed of the blessed of the L.
66. 22 so shall your seed and your name remain
Jer. 2. 21 I had planted thee..a right seed: how th.
7. 15 all your brethren, (even) the whole seed
22. 28 wherefore are they cast out, he and his se.
22. 30 no man of his seed shall prosper, sitting
23. 8 which led the seed of the house of Israel out
29. 32 I will punish Shemaiah..and his seed: he
30. 10 I will save thee from afar, and thy seed from
31. 27 with the seed of man, and with the seed
31. 36 the seed of Israel also shall cease from be.
31. 37 I will also cast off all the seed of Israel for
33. 22 so will I multiply the seed of David my
33. 26 Then will I cast away the seed of Jacob, and
33. 26 (any) of his seed (to be) rulers over the seed
35. 7 Neither shall ye build house, nor sow seed
35. 9 neither have we vineyard..field, nor seed
36. 31 I will punish him and his seed and his
41. 1 the son of Elishama, of the seed royal, and
46. 27 I will save thee from afar off, and thy seed
49. 10 his seed is spoiled, and his brethren, and
Eze. 17. 5 He took also of the seed of the land, and
17. 13 hath taken of the king's seed, and made a
20. 5 lifted up mine hand unto the seed of the
43. 19 the priests the Levites that be of the seed
44. 22 they shall take maidens of the seed of the
Dan. 1. 3 and of the king's seed, and of the princes
9. 1 the son of Ahasuerus, of the seed of the
Amos 9. 13 the treader of grapes him that soweth se.
Hag. 2. 19 Is the seed yet in the barn? yea, as yet
Zech. 8. 12 the seed (shall be) prosperous; the vine
Mal 2. 3 I will corrupt your seed, and spread dung
2. 15 That he might seek a godly seed. There.

2. *Seed, progeny,* זְרַע *zera.*
Dan. 2. 43 they shall mingle themselves with the se.

3. *What are separated,* פְּרֻדוֹת *perudoth.*
Joel 1. 17 The seed is rotten under their clods, the

4. *A laying down of seed,* שִׁכְבַת זֶרַע *shikbath zera.*
Lev. 15. 32 (of him) whose seed goeth from him, and is
22. 4 or a man whose seed goeth from him

5. *Seed, progeny,* σπέρμα *sperma.*
Matt 13. 24 a man which sowed good seed in his field
13. 27 didst not thou sow good seed in thy field
13. 32 Which indeed is the least of all seeds; but
13. 37 He that soweth the good seed is the Son of
13. 38 the good seed are the children of the king.
22. 24 shall marry his wife, and raise up seed un.
Mark 4. 31 (It is) like a grain of mustard seed, which
12. 19 should take his wife, and raise up seed un.
12. 20 the first took a wife, and dying left no se.
12. 21 took her, and died, neither left he any se.
12. 22 the seven had her, and left no seed: last
Luke 1. 55 to Abraham, and to his seed for ever
20. 28 should take his wife, and raise up seed
John 7. 42 Christ cometh of the seed of David, and
8. 33 We be Abraham's seed, and were never in
8. 37 I know that ye are Abraham's seed; but
Acts 3. 25 in thy seed shall all the kindreds of the
7. 5 to him for a possession, and to his seed
7. 6 his seed should sojourn in a strange land
13. 23 Of this man's seed hath God, according to
Rom. 1. 3 which was made of the seed of David acc.
4. 13 (was) not to Abraham, or to his seed, th.
4. 16 the promise might be sure to all the seed

Rom. 4. 18 that which was spoken, So shall thy seed
9. 7 Neither, because they are the seed of Ab.
9. 7 but, In Isaac shall thy seed be called
9. 8 the children..are counted for the seed
9. 29 Except the Lord..had left us a seed, we
11. 1 I also am an Israelite, of the seed of Abr.
1 Co. 15. 38 God giveth..to every seed his own body
2 Co. 9. 10 that ministereth [seed] to the sower, both
11. 22 Are they the seed of Abraham? so (am) I
Gal. 3. 16 to Abraham and his seed were the prom.
3. 16 saith not, And to seeds..but..to thy seed
3. 19 till the seed should come to whom the pr.
3. 29 then are ye Abraham's seed, and He. 2. 16.
2 Ti. 2. 8 Remember that Jesus Christ of the seed
Heb. 11. 11 Sara..received strength to conceive seed
11. 18 That in Isaac shall thy seed be called
1 Jo. 3. 9 his seed remaineth in him: and he cannot
Rev. 12. 17 make war with the remnant of her seed

6. *Seed for sowing*, σπορά *spora.*
1 Pe. 1. 23 Being born again, not of corruptible seed

7. *Seed for sowing*, σπόρος *sporos.*
Mark 4. 26 as if a man should cast seed into the ground
4. 27 and the seed should spring and grow up
Luke 8. 5 A sower went out to sow his seed: and
8. 11 the parable is this: The seed is the word
2 Co. 9. 10 multiply your seed sown, and increase the
[*See also* Conceive, mingled, divers].

SEED, to receive —

To be sown, receive seed, σπείρομαι *speiromai.*
Matt 13. 19 This is he which received seed by the way
13. 20 he that received the seed into stony pla.
13. 22 He also that received seed among the th.
13. 23 he that received seed into the good gro.

SEEING (that, then) —

1. *After that*, אַחֲרֵי אֲשֶׁר *achare asher.*
Judg. 19. 23 seeing that this man is come into mine

2. *If, since*, אִם *im.*
Job 14. 5 Seeing his days (are) determined, the nu.

3. *That*, דִּי *di.*
Dan. 2. 47 seeing thou couldest reveal this secret

4. *Because, since*, יַעַן *yaan.*
Eze. 21. 4 Seeing then that I will cut off from thee

5. *That, because*, כִּי *ki.*
Exod 23. 9 seeing ye were strangers in the land of E.

6. *Open eyed*, פִּקֵּחַ *piqqeach.*
Exod. 4. 11 the dumb, or deaf, or the seeing, or the

7. *To see*, רָאָה *raah.*
Exod 22. 10 be hurt, or driven away, no man seeing
1 Ki. 1. 48 sit on my throne..mine eyes even seeing
Prov 20. 12 The hearing ear, and the seeing eye, the
Isa. 21. 3 it); I was dismayed at the seeing (of it)
33. 15 and shutteth his eyes from seeing evil
42. 20 Seeing many things, but thou observest

8. *Look, cast of countenance*, βλέμμα *blemma.*
2 Pe. 2. 8 in seeing and hearing, vexed (his) right.

9. *For*, γάρ *gar.*
Acts 2. 15 seeing it is (but) the third hour of the day

10. *If, truly*, εἴ περ *ei per.*
2 Th. 1. 6 Seeing (it is) a righteous thing with God

11. *After that, since, for then*, ἐπεί *epei.*
Luke 1. 34 How shall this be, seeing I know not a m.
2 Co. 11. 18 Seeing that many glory after the flesh, I
Heb. 4. 6 Seeing therefore it remaineth that some
5. 11 hard to be uttered, seeing ye are dull of

12. *When truly, since truly*, ἐπειδή *epeidē.*
Acts 13. 46 seeing ye put it from you, and judge you.
1 Co. 14. 16 seeing he understandeth not what thou

13. *Since, truly*, ἐπείπερ *epeiper.*
Rom. 3. 30 Seeing (it is) one God which shall justify

SEEK (after, carefully, for), to —

1. *To seek, pray*, בָּעָא, בְּעָה *bea.*
Dan. 2. 13 they sought Daniel and his fellows to be
4. 36 my counsellors and my lords sought unto
6. 4 sought to find occasion against Daniel co.

2. *To seek, inquire*, בָּקַר *baqar*, 3.
Lev. 13. 36 the priest shall not seek for yellow hair

3. *To seek, inquire, require*, בָּקַשׁ *baqash*, 3.
Gen. 37. 15 the man asked him, saying, What seekest
37. 16 I seek my brethren: tell me, I pray thee
43. 30 he sought (where) to weep; and he ente.
Exod. 2. 15 when Pharaoh heard this thing, he soug
4. 19 the men are dead which sought thy life
4. 24 the LORD met him, and sought to kill him
33. 7 every one which sought the LORD went
Lev. 19. 31 neither seek after wizards, to be defiled by
Num 16. 10 brought thee..seek ye the priesthood also
35. 23 (was) not his enemy, neither sought his
Deut. 4. 29 if from thence thou shalt seek the LORD
13. 10 he hath sought to thrust thee away from
Josh. 2. 22 the pursuers sought (them) throughout
Judg. 4. 22 I will show thee the man whom thou se.
14. 4 he sought an occasion against the Philis.
18. 1 the tribe of the Danites sought them an
Ruth 3. 1 shall I not seek rest for thee, that it may
1 Sa. 9. 3 Kish said to Saul..go seek the asses
10. 2 The asses which thou wentest to seek are
10. 14 To seek the asses: and when we saw that
10. 21 when they sought him, he could not be fo.
13. 14 the LORD hath sought him a man after
14. 4 by which Jonathan sought to go over un.
1 Sa. 16. 16 to seek out a man, (who is) a cunning pla.
19. 2 my father seeketh to kill thee: now ther.
19. 10 Saul sought to smite David even to the
20. 1 what (is) my sin..that he seeketh my life?
22. 23 he that seeketh my life seeketh thy life
23. 10 Saul seeketh to come to Keilah, to destroy
23. 14 Saul sought him every day; but God de.
23. 15 that Saul was come out to seek his life
23. 25 Saul also and his men went to seek (him)
24. 2 went to seek David and his men upon the
24. 9 saying, Behold, David seeketh thy hurt
25. 26 they that seek evil to my lord, be as Na.
25. 29 is risen to pursue thee, and to seek thy
26. 2 to seek David in the wilderness of Ziph
26. 20 the king of Israel is come out to seek a
27. 1 to seek me any more in the coast of Isr.
27. 4 and he sought no more again for him
28. 7 Seek me a woman that hath a familar sp.
2 Sa. 3. 17 Ye sought for David in times past (to be)
4. 8 Saul thine enemy, which sought thy life
5. 17 all the Philistines came up to seek David
16. 11 Behold, my son..seeketh my life: how
17. 3 the man whom thou seekest (is) as if all
17. 20 when they had sought and could not find
20. 19 thou seekest to destroy a city and a mot.
21. 2 Saul sought to slay them in his zeal to the
1 Ki. 1. 2 Let there be sought for my lord the king
1. 3 they sought for a fair damsel throughout
2. 40 went to Gath to Achish to seek his serva.
10. 24 all the earth sought to Solomon, to hear
11. 22 thou seekest to go to thine own country
11. 40 Solomon sought therefore to kill Jeroboam
18. 10 whither my lord hath not sent to seek thee
19. 10, 14 and they seek my life, to take it away
20. 7 and see how this (man) seeketh mischief
2 Ki. 2. 16 let them go, we pray thee, and seek thy
2. 17 they sought three days, but found him not
6. 19 I will bring you to the man whom ye seek
1 Ch. 4. 39 went..to seek pasture for their flocks
14. 8 all the Philistines went up to seek David
16. 10 let the heart of them rejoice that seek the
16. 11 and his strength, seek his face continually
2 Ch. 7. 14 pray, and seek my face, and turn from th.
9. 23 the kings of the earth sought the presence
11. 16 such as set their hearts to seek the LORD
15. 4 and sought him, he was found of th.
15. 15 and sought him with their whole desire
20. 4 out of all the cities..they came to seek
22. 9 he sought Ahaziah: and they caught him
Ezra 2. 62 These sought their register (among) those
8. 21 to seek of him a right way for us, and for
8. 22 (is) upon all them for good that seek him
Neh. 2. 10 there was come a man to seek the welfare
7. 64 These sought their register (among) those
12. 27 they sought the Levites out of all their pl.
Esth. 2. 2 Let there be fair young virgins sought for
2. 21 were wroth, and sought to lay hand on the
3. 6 Haman sought to destroy all the Jews th.
6. 2 who sought to lay hand on the king Ah.
9. 2 to lay hand on such as sought their hurt
Psa. 4. 2 (how long) will ye love vanity, (and) seek a.
24. 6 This (is) the generation..that seek thy fa.
27. 4 One (thing) have I desired..that will I s.
27. 8 (When thou saidst), Seek ye my face; my
27. 8 said unto thee, Thy face, LORD, will I se.
34. 14 Depart from evil, and do good; seek pe.
35. 4 Let them be confounded..that seek after
37. 32 The wicked watcheth the righteous, and s.
37. 36 I sought him, but he could not be found
38. 12 They also that seek after my life lay sn.
40. 14 Let them be ashamed..that seek after my
40. 16 Let all those that seek thee rejoice and be
54. 3 oppressors seek after my soul: they have
63. 9 those (that) seek my soul, to destroy (it)
69. 6 let not those that seek thee be confounded
70. 2 Let them be ashamed..that seek after my
70. 4 Let all those that seek thee rejoice and be
71. 13 covered (with) reproach..that seek my hu.
71. 24 they are brought unto shame, that seek
83. 16 that they may seek thy name, O LORD
86. 14 the assemblies of violent (men) have so.
104. 21 young lions roar after their prey, and se.
105. 3 let the heart of them rejoice that seek the
105. 4 and his strength; seek his face evermore
119. 176 seek thy servant; for I do not forget thy
122. 9 Because of the house of..God I will seek
Prov. 2. 4 If thou seekest her as silver, and search.
14. 6 A scorner seeketh wisdom, and (findeth
15. 14 him that hath understanding seeketh kn.
17. 9 He that covereth a transgression seeketh
17. 11 An evil (man) seeketh only rebellion; th.
17. 19 he that exalteth his gate seeketh destru.
18. 1 seeketh (and) intermeddleth with all wis.
18. 15 and the ear of the wise seeketh knowledge
21. 6 tossed to and fro of them that seek death
23. 35 when shall I awake? I will seek it yet ag.
28. 5 they that seek the LORD understand all
29. 10 The blood thirsty hate..but the just seek
29. 26 Many seek the ruler's favour: but (every)
Eccl. 7. 25 to seek out wisdom, and the reason (of th.)
7. 28 Which yet my soul seeketh, but I find not
7. 29 they have sought out many inventions
8. 17 though a man labour to seek (it) out, yet
12. 10 The preacher sought to find out accepta.
Song 3. 1 I sought him whom my soul loveth: I so.
3. 2 I will seek him whom my soul loveth: I
5. 6 I sought him, but I could not find him; I
6. 1 whither is thy beloved..that we may seek
Isa. 40. 20 he seeketh unto him a cunning workman
41. 12 Thou shalt seek them, and shalt not find
41. 17 the poor and needy seek water, and (the.
45. 19 I said not unto the seed of Jacob, Seek
Isa. 51. 1 Hearken to me..ye that seek the LORD
65. 1 I am found of (them that) sought me no
Jer. 2. 24 they that seek her will not weary them.
2. 33 Why trimmest thou thy way to seek love,
4. 30 lovers will despise thee, they will seek thy
5. 1 seek in the broad places thereof, if ye can
5. 1 (any) that executeth judgment, that seek.
11. 21 the men of Anathoth, that seek
19. 7 by the hands of them that seek their lives
19. 9 they that seek their lives, shall straiten
21. 7 into the hand of those that seek their life
22. 25 into the hand of them that seek thy life
26. 21 the king sought to put him to death, but
29. 13 ye shall seek me, and find (me), when ye
34. 20, 21 into the hand of them that seek their
38. 16 into the hand of these men that seek thy
44. 30 into the hand of them that seek his life
44. 30 of Nebuchadrezzar..that sought his life
45. 5 seekest thou great things for thyself? se.
46. 26 into the hand of those that seek their li.
49. 37 to be dismayed..before them that seek th.
50. 4 they shall go, and seek the LORD their God
Lam. 1. 11 her people sigh, they seek bread; they ha.
1. 19 they sought their meat to relieve their so.
Eze. 7. 25 they shall seek peace, and (there shall be)
7. 26 then shall they seek a vision of the prop.
22. 30 I sought for a man among them, that sh.
34. 4 neither have ye sought that which was lo.
34. 6 and none did search or seek (after them)
34. 16 I will seek that which was lost, and bring
Dan. 8. 15 I Daniel, had seen the vision, and sought
9. 3 to seek by prayer and supplications, with
Hos. 2. 7 she shall seek them, but shall not find (th.)
3. 5 seek the LORD their God, and David their
5. 6 They shall go with..their herds to seek the
5. 15 acknowledge their offence, and seek my
7. 10 they do not return..nor seek him for all
Amos 8. 12 they shall run to and fro to seek the word
Nah. 3. 7 whence shall I seek comforters for thee?
3. 11 thou also shalt seek strength because of
Zeph. 1. 6 (those) that have not sought the LORD, nor
2. 3 Seek ye the LORD, all ye meek of the ea.
2. 3 seek righteousness, seek meekness: it may
Zech. 6. 7 the bay went forth, and sought to go th.
8. 21 to pray before the LORD, and to seek the
8. 22 strong nations shall come to seek the Lo.
11. 16 neither shall seek the young one, nor he.
12. 9 I will seek to destroy all the nations that
Mal. 2. 7 they should seek the law at his mouth
2. 15 wherefore one? That he might seek a go.
3. 1 the Lord, whom ye seek, shall suddenly

4. *To seek, dig, search*, חָפַר *chaphar.*
Job 39. 29 From thence she seeketh the prey, (and)

5. *To search, investigate*, חָקַר *chaqar.*
Prov 23. 30 that tarry long..that go to seek mixed

6. *To search*, חָקַר *chaqar*, 3.
Eccl. 12. 9 he gave good heed, and sought out, (and)

7. *To seek, inquire, require*, דָּרַשׁ *darash.*
Lev. 10. 16 Moses diligently sought the goat of the
Deut. 4. 29 if from thence thou shalt seek the LORD
4. 29 if thou seek him with all thy heart and
12. 5 (even) unto his habitation shall ye seek
22. 2 shall be with thee until thy brother seek a.
23. 6 Thou shalt not seek their peace nor their
1 Ch. 15. 13 we sought him not after the due order
16. 11 Seek the LORD and his strength..contin.
22. 19 set your heart and your soul to seek the L.
28. 8 seek for all the commandments of the L.
28. 9 if thou seek him, he will be found of thee
2 Ch. 1. 5 Solomon and the congregation sought unto
12. 14 he prepared not his heart to seek the L.
14. 4 commanded Judah to seek the LORD God
14. 7 sought the LORD our God, we have soug.
15. 2 if ye seek him, he will be found of you
15. 12 they entered into a covenant to seek the L.
15. 13 whosoever would not seek the LORD God
16. 12 in his disease he sought not to the LORD
17. 3 he walked in the first ways..and sought
17. 4 sought to the (LORD) God of his father, and
19. 3 and hast prepared thine heart to seek God
20. 3 Jehoshaphat feared, and set himself to se.
22. 9 who sought the LORD with all his heart
25. 15 Why hast thou sought after the gods of the
25. 20 because they sought after the gods of E.
26. 5 he sought God in the days of Zechariah
26. 5 as long as he sought the LORD, God made
30. 19 (That) prepareth his heart to seek God
31. 21 in every work that he began..to seek his
34. 3 he began to seek after the God of David
Ezra 4. 2 we seek your God, as ye (do); and we do
6. 21 separated themselves..to seek the LORD
7. 10 Ezra had prepared his heart to seek the
9. 12 nor seek their peace or their wealth for
Esth 10. 3 seeking the wealth of his people, and sp.
Job 5. 8 I would seek unto God, and unto God wo.
Psa. 9. 10 hast not forsaken them that seek thee
10. 4 The wicked..will not seek (after God): G
14. 2 any that did understand, (and) seek God
22. 26 they shall praise the LORD that seek him,
24. 6 This (is) the generation of them that seek
34. 4 I sought the LORD, and he heard me, and
34. 10 they that seek the LORD shall not want
38. 12 they that seek my hurt speak mischievous
53. 2 (any) that did understand, that did seek
69. 32 and your heart shall live that seek God
77. 2 In the day of my trouble I sought the L.
78. 34 When he slew them, then they sought him
105. 4 Seek the LORD, and his strength..evermore
109. 10 let them seek (their bread) also out of th.

Psa.119. 2 Blessed (are) they (..that) seek him with
119. 10 With my whole heart have I sought thee
119. 45 will walk at liberty: for I seek thy prec.
119. 94 save me; for I have sought thy precepts
119. 155 far from the wicked: for they seek not
Prov 11. 27 he that seeketh mischief, it shall come un.
31. 13 She seeketh wool and flax, and worketh
Eccl. 1. 13 gave my heart to seek and search out by
Isa. 1. 17 seek judgment, relieve the oppressed, ju.
8. 19 Seek unto them that have familiar spirits
8. 19 should not a people seek unto their God?
9. 13 neither do they seek the LORD of hosts
11. 10 to it shall the Gentiles seek: and his rest
16. 5 seeking judgment, and hasting righteous.
19. 3 shall seek to the idols, and to the charm.
31. 1 but they look not..neither seek the LORD!
34. 16 Seek ye out of the book of the LORD, and
55. 6 Seek ye the LORD while he may be found
58. 2 Yet they seek me daily, and delight to kn.
65. 10 a place..for my people that have sought
Jer. 8. 2 whom they have sought, and whom they
10. 21 For the pastors..have not sought the Lo.
29. 7 seek the peace of the city whither I have
30. 14 they seek thee not: for I have wounded
30. 17 This (is) Zion, whom no man seeketh after
38. 4 for this man seeketh not the welfare of th.
Lam. 3. 25 LORD (is) good..to the soul (that) seeketh
Eze. 14. 10 as the punishment of him that seeketh
Hos. 10. 12 for (it is) time to seek the LORD, till he co
Amos 5. 4 thus saith the LORD..Seek ye me, and ye
5. 5 seek not Bethel, nor enter into Gilgal, and
5. 6 Seek the LORD, and ye shall live; lest he
5. 14 Seek good, and not evil, that ye may live

8. *To call, call for, meet,* קָרָא *qara.*
Num24. 1 went not..to seek for enchantments, but

9. *To search, spy out,* תּוּר *tur.*
Num15. 39 seek not after your own heart and your
Eccl. 2. 3 sought in mine heart to give myself unto

10. *To seek up, out, again,* ἀναζητέω *anazēteō.*
Luke 2. 44 sought him among (their) kinsfolk and ac.
Acts 11. 25 departed Barnabas to Tarsus, for to seek

11. *To seek out,* ἐκζητέω *ekzēteō.*
Acts 15. 17 That the residue of men might seek after
Rom. 3. 11 there is none that seeketh after

12. *To seek about, or after,* ἐπιζητέω *epizēteō.*
Matt. 6. 32 after all these things do the Gentiles seek
12. 39 evil and adulterous generation seeketh af.
16. 4 adulterous generation seeketh after a sign
Mark 8. 12 Why doth this generation [seek after] a si
Luke11. 29 is an evil generation: they seek a sign
12. 30 do the nations of the world seek after: and
Acts 12. 19 when Herod had sought for him, and found
Rom 11. 7 not obtained that which he seeketh for
Heb. 11. 14 declare plainly that they seek a country
13. 14 no continuing city, but we seek one to co.

13. *To seek, desire, require, question,* ζητέω *zēteō.*
Matt. 2. 13 will seek the young child to destroy him
2. 20 for they are dead which sought the young
6. 33 But seek ye first the kingdom of God, and
7. 7 seek, and ye shall find; knock, and it sh.
7. 8 he that seeketh findeth; and to him that
12. 43 he walketh through dry places, seeking re.
13. 45 is like unto a merchantman seeking goodly
18. 12 goeth into the mountains, and seeketh th
21. 46 when they sought to lay hands on him, th.
26. 16 from that time he sought opportunity to
26. 59 the council, sought false witness against
28. 5 for I know that ye seek Jesus, which was
Mark 1. 37 they said unto him, All (men) seek for th.
3. 32 and thy brethren without seek for thee
8. 11 seeking of him a sign from heaven, temp.
11. 18 and sought how they might destroy him
12. 12 they sought to lay hold on him, but feared
14. 1 the scribes sought how they might take
14. 11 he sought how he might conveniently be.
14. 55 the council sought for witness against Je.
16. 6 Ye seek Jesus of Nazareth, which was cr.
Luke 2. 45 turned back again to Jerusalem, [seeking]
2. 48 thy father and I have sought thee sorrow.
2. 49 How is it that ye sought me? wist ye not
4. 42 the people [sought] him, and came unto
5. 18 they sought (means) to bring him in, and to
6. 19 the whole multitude sought to touch him
11. 9 seek, and ye shall find; knock, and it sh.
11. 10 he that seeketh findeth; and to him that
11. 16 others, tempting (him), sought of him a sign
11. 24 he walketh through dry places, seeking re.
11. 54 [seeking] to catch something out of his mo.
12. 29 seek not ye what ye shall eat, or what ye
12. 31 seek ye the kingdom of God; and all these
13. 6 he came and sought fruit thereon, and fo.
13. 7 these three years I come seeking fruit on
13. 24 many, I say unto you, will seek to enter
15. 8 sweep the house, and seek diligently till
17. 33 Whosoever shall seek to save his life, sh.
19. 3 he sought to see Jesus who he was; and
19. 10 the son of man is come to seek and to save
19. 47 the chief of the people sought to destroy
20. 19 sought to lay hands on him; and they fe.
22. 2 scribes sought how they might kill him
22. 6 sought opportunity to betray him unto
24. 5 Why seek ye the living among the dead?
John 1. 38 saith unto them, What seek ye? They said
4. 23 for the Father seeketh such to worship him
4. 27 yet no man said, What seekest thou? or
5. 16 [sought to slay him, because he had done]
5. 18 Therefore the Jews sought the more to kill
5. 30 because I seek not mine own will, but the
John 5. 44 seek not the honour that (cometh) from G.
6. 24 and came to Capernaum, seeking for Jesus
6. 26 Ye seek me, not because ye saw the mir.
7. 1 because the Jews sought to kill him
7. 4 he himself seeketh to be known openly
7. 11 Then the Jews sought him at the feast
7. 18 seeketh his own glory: but he that seek.
7. 25 Is not this he whom they seek to kill?
7. 30 Then they sought to take him: but no man
7. 34, 36 Ye shall seek me, and shall not find
8. 21 shall seek me, and shall die in your sins
8. 37 seek to kill me, because my word hath no
8. 40 But now ye seek to kill me, a man that ha.
8. 50 seek not mine own glory..one that seeketh
10. 39 Therefore they sought again to take him
11. 8 Jews of late sought to stone thee; and go.
11. 56 Then sought they for Jesus, and spake
13. 33 Ye shall seek me: and as I said unto the
18. 4 went forth, and said unto them, Whom s.
18. 7 Then asked he them again, Whom seek
18. 8 therefore ye seek me, let these go their
19. 12 sought to release him: but the Jews cried
20. 15 why weepest thou? whom seekest thou?
Acts 10. 19 said unto him, Behold, three men seek th.
10. 21 said, Behold, I am he whom ye seek: what
13. 8 seeking to turn away the deputy from the
13. 11 seeking some to lead him by the hand
17. 5 sought to bring them out to the people
17. 27 should seek the Lord, if haply they might
Rom. 2. 7 seek for glory and honour and immortality
10. 20 I was found of them that sought me not
11. 3 and I am left alone, and they seek my life
1 Co. 1. 22 Jews require a sign, and the Greeks seek a.
7. 27 bound unto a wife? seek not to be loosed
7. 27 Art thou loosed from a wife? seek not a
10. 24 Let no man seek his own, but every man
10. 33 not seeking mine own profit, but the pr.
13. 5 seeketh not her own, is not easily provoked
14. 12 seek that ye may excel to the edifying of
2 Co. 12. 14 for I seek not yours, but you: for the ch.
13. 3 Since ye seek a proof of Christ speaking
Gal. 1. 10 do I seek to please men? for if I yet plea.
2. 17 But if, while we seek to be justified by C.
Phil. 2. 21 For all seek their own, not the things wh.
Col. 3. 1 seek those things which are above, where
1 Th. 2. 6 Nor of men sought we glory, neither of
2 Ti. 1. 17 he sought me out very diligently, and fo.
Heb 8. 7 then should no place have been sought for
1 Pe. 3. 11 do good; let him seek peace, and ensue
5. 8 walketh about, seeking whom he may de.
Rev. 9. 6 in those days shall men seek death, and

SEEK a quarrel or occasion, to —

1. *To present self, seek a quarrel,* אָנָה *anah,* 7.
2 Ki. 5. 7 see how he seeketh a quarrel against me

2. *To roll self,* גָּלַל *galal,* 7a.
Gen. 43. 18 that he may seek occasion against us, and

SEEK betimes, diligently, early (in the morning), to —

1. *To seek early or earnestly,* שָׁחַר *shachar.*
Prov.11. 27 He that diligently seeketh good procureth

2. *To seek early or earnestly,* שָׁחַר *shachar,* 3.
Job 7. 21 and thou shalt seek me in the morning
8. 5 If thou wouldest seek unto God betimes
Psa. 63. 1 early will I seek thee: my soul thirsteth
Prov. 1. 28 they shall seek me early, but they shall
7. 15 diligently to seek thy face, and I have fo.
8. 17 and those that seek me early shall find me
Isa. 26. 9 seek thee early: for when thy judgments
Hos. 5. 15 in their affliction they will seek me early

3. *To seek out,* ἐκζητέω *ekzēteō.*
Heb. 11. 6 rewarder of them that diligently seek

SEEK out, to —

1. *To seek, inquire,* בָּקַר *baqar,* 3.
Eze. 34. 11 both search my sheep, and seek them out
34. 12 so will I seek out my sheep, and will del.

2. *A seeking, inquiry, investigation,* בַּקָּרָה *baqqarah.*
Eze. 34. 12 As a shepherd seeketh out his flock in the

3. *To seek, inquire, require,* דָּרַשׁ *darash.*
Psa. 10. 15 seek out his wickedness (till) thou

SEEM (good, ill to, unto), to —

1. *Appearance,* מַרְאֶה *mareh.*
Nah. 2. 4 they shall seem like torches, they shall

2. *To be seen, appear,* רָאָה *raah,* 2.
Lev. 14. 35 seemeth to me (there is) as it were a plague

3. *To be in the eyes of,* הָיָה בְּעֵינֵי *hayah be-ene.*
Gen. 19. 14 But he seemed as one that mocked unto
27. 12 and I shall seem to him as a deceiver; and
29. 20 seemed unto him (but) a few days, for the
Josh. 9. 25 as it seemeth good and right unto thee
24. 15 if it seem evil unto you to serve the LORD
Judg 10. 15 whatsoever seemeth good unto thee; del.
19. 24 do with them what seemeth good unto
1 Sa. 1. 23 Do what seemeth thee good; tarry until
3. 18 the LORD: let him do what seemeth him
11. 10 ye shall do with us all that seemeth good
14 36 Do whatsoever seemeth good unto thee
14. 40 said unto Saul, Do what seemeth good un.
18. 23 Seemeth it to you (a) light (thing) to be a
24. 4 do to him as it shall seem good unto thee
2 Sa. 3. 19 to speak..all that seemed good to Israel
3. 19 that seemed good to the whole house of B.
10. 12 the LORD do that which seemeth him good
15. 26 let him do to me as seemeth good unto him
19. 37 do to him what shall seem good unto thee
2 Sa. 19. 38 do to him that which shall seem good unto
1 Ki.21. 2 if it seem good to thee, I will give thee the
Esth. 3. 11 to do with them as it seemeth good to th.
Jer. 18. 4 as seemed good to the potter to make (it)
26. 14 do with me as seemeth good and meet un.
27. 5 given it unto whom it seemed meet unto
40. 4 If it seem good....if it seem ill unto thee
40. 4 whither it seemeth good and convenient

4. *There was approval,* ἐγένετο εὐδοκία [*eudokia*].
Matt 11. 26 Even so,...for so it seemed good [Lu. 10 2]

5. *To seem good,* δοκέω *dokeō.*
Luke 1. 3 It seemed good to me also, having had pe.
8. 18 taken even that which he seemeth to ha.
Acts 15. 25 It seemed good unto us, being assembled
15. 28 For it seemed good to the Holy Ghost, and
17. 18 seemeth to be a setter forth of strange go.
25. 27 For it seemeth to me unreasonable to send
1 Co. 3. 18 If any man among you seemeth to be wise
11. 16 But if any man seem to be contentious
12. 22 those members..which seem to be more
2 Co.10. 9 That I may not seem as if I would terrify
Gal. 2. 6 But of these who seemed to be somewhat
2. 6 for they who seemed (to be somewhat) in
2. 9 when James..and John, who seemed to
Heb. 4. 1 any of you should seem to come short of
12. 11 no chastening for the present seemeth to
Jas. 1. 26 If any man among you seem to be religious

6. *To make to appear, to manifest,* φαίνω *phainō.*
Luke24. 11 their words seemed to them as idle tales

[*See also* Best, good, hard, light thing, little, meat, vile.]

SEEMLY —

Comely, נָאוֶה *naveh.*
Prov.19. 10 Delight is not seemly for a fool; much less
26. 1 so honour is not seemly for a fool

SEEN, to (can) be —

1. *To be seen,* רָאָה *raah,* 2.
Gen. 8. 5 on the first (day)..were the tops..seen
9. 14 that the bow shall be seen in the cloud
22. 14 In the mount of the LORD it shall be seen
Exod13. 7 there shall no leavened bread be seen with
13. 7 neither shall there be leaven seen with
33. 23 back parts; but my face shall not be seen
34. 3 neither let any man be seen throughout
Lev. 13. 7 after that he hath been seen of the priest
13. 7 cleansing, he shall be seen of the priest
Num 14. 14 that thou, LORD, art seen face to face; and
Deut.16. 4 there shall be no leavened bread seen with
Judg. 5. 8 spear seen among forty thousand in Israel
19. 30 There was no such deed done nor seen fr.
2 Sa. 17. 17 for they might not be seen to come into
22. 11 he was seen upon the wings of the wind
1 Ki. 6. 18 all (was) cedar; there was no stone seen
8. 8 ends of the staves were seen out in the
8. 8 they were not seen without: and there
10. 12 no such almug trees, nor were seen unto
2 Ch. 5. 9 that the ends of the staves were seen from
5. 9 but they were not seen without. And
9. 11 there were none such seen before in the
Psa. 18. 15 Then the channels of waters were seen, and
Isa. 16. 12 when it is seen that Moab is weary on the
47. 3 thy shame shall be seen: I will take veng.
60. 2 and his glory shall be seen upon thee
Zech. 9. 14 LORD shall be seen over them, and his ar.

2. *To be seen,* רָאָה *raah,* 4.
Job 33. 21 his bones (that) were not seen stick out

3. *Vision, sight,* רֳאִי *roi.*
Job 33. 21 His flesh..that it cannot be seen; and his

4. *To view, behold attentively,* θεάομαι *theaomai.*
Matt. 6. 1 do not your alms before men, to be seen
23. 5 their works they do for to be seen of men
Mark16. 11 [and had been seen of her, believed not]

5. *To cause to appear, be manifest,* φαίνω *phainō.*
Matt. 6. 5 that they may be seen of men. Verily I
9. 33 saying, It was never so seen in Israel

6. *To see, behold,* ὄπτομαι, ὀπτάνομαι *optanomai.*
Acts 1. 3 being seen of them forty days, and speak.

SEETHE, seething —

1. *To boil, cook, ripen,* בָּשַׁל *bashal.*
Eze. 24. 5 and let them seethe the bones of it

2. *To boil, cook, ripen,* בָּשַׁל *bashal,* 3.
Exod16. 23 seethe that ye will seethe; and that whi.
23. 19 thou shalt not seethe a kid in his mother's
29. 31 and seethe his flesh in the holy place
34. 26 Thou shalt not seethe a kid in his mother's
Deut14. 21 Thou shalt not seethe a kid in his mother's
1 Sa. 2. 13 came, while the flesh was in seething,
2 Ki. 4. 38 seethe pottage for the sons of the prophets
Zech 14. 21 come and take of them, and seethe therein

3. *To blow, breathe out, boil,* נָפַח *naphach.*
Job 41. 20 smoke, as (out) of a seething pot or caldron
Jer. 1. 13 I see a seething pot; and the face thereof

SEER —

1. *A seer,* חֹזֶה *chozeh.*
2 Sa. 24. 11 came unto the prophet Gad, David's seer
2 Ki. 17. 13 by all the prophets, (and by) all the seers
1 Ch.21. 9 LORD spake unto Gad, David's seer, saying
25. 5 sons of Heman the king's seer in the wor.
29. 29 prophet, and in the book of Gad the seer
2 Ch. 9. 29 in the visions of Iddo the seer against Jer.
12. 15 of Iddo the seer concerning genealogies?

2 Ch.19. 2 Jehu the son of Hanani the seer went out
29. 25 of Gad the king's seer, and Nathan the pr.
29. 30 words of David, and of Asaph the seer : and
33. 18 words of the seers that spake to him in the
33. 19 (are) written among the sayings of the see.
35. 15 and Heman, and Jeduthun the king's seer
Isa. 29. 10 prophets and your rulers, the seers hath
Amos 7. 12 said unto Amos, O thou seer, go, flee thee
Mic. 3. 7 Then shall the seers be ashamed, and the

2. *A seer*, רֹאֶה *roeh*.
1 Sa. 9. 9 Come, and let us go to the seer : for (he th.
9. 9 a prophet was beforetime called a seer
9. 11 draw water, and said unto them, Is the s.
9. 18 Tell me, I pray thee, where the seer's ho.
9. 19 answered Saul, and said, I (am) the seer
2 Sa. 15. 27 (Art not) thou a seer? return into the city
1 Ch. 9. 22 Samuel the seer did ordain in their set of.
26. 28 all that Samuel the seer, and Saul the son
29. 29 written in the book of Samuel the seer, and
2 Ch. 16. 7 at that time Hanani the seer came to Asa
16. 10 Then Asa was wroth with the seer, and
Isa. 30. 10 Which say to the seers, See not; and to the

SE'-GUB, שְׂגוּב *might, protection*.
1. The younger son of Hiel the Bethelite, who rebuilt Jericho in the time of Ahab king of Israel, B.C. 918.
1 Ki. 16. 34 set up the gates..in his youngest (son) S
2. A son of Hezron grandson of Judah. B.C. 1490.
1 Ch. 2. 21 whom he married..and she bare him S.
2. 22 And S. begat Jair, who had three and twen.

SE'-IR, שֵׂעִיר *rough, wooded*.
1. A hilly region S. of the Salt Sea and reaching to the Elanitic Gulf; it was occupied in succession by the Horites, Deut. 2. 12, the Esauites, Gen. 32. 4, and the Edomites, Deut. 2. 4.
Gen. 14. 6 And the Horites in their mount S., unto
32. 3 Jacob sent..to Esau..unto the land of S.
33. 14 on..until I come unto my lord unto S.
33. 16 Esau returned that day on his way unto S.
36. 8 Thus dwelt Esau in mount S: Esau (is) E.
36. 9 Esau..father of the Edomites in mount S.
36. 30 these (are)..their dukes in the land of S.
Num 24. 18 S. also shall be a possession for his ene.
Deut. 1. 2 by the way of mount S. unto Kadesh-barnea
1. 44 the Amorites..destroyed you in S...unto
2. 1 and we compassed mount S. many days
2. 4, 29 children of Esau, which dwell in S.
2. 5 I have given mount S. unto Esau..a pos.
2. 8, 22 children of Esau, which dwelt in S.
2. 12 The Horims also dwelt in S. beforetime
33. 2 The LORD..rose up from S. unto them
Josh 11. 17 the mount Halak, that goeth up to S.
12. 7 unto the mount Halak, that goeth up to S.
15. 10 the border compassed..unto mount S.
24. 4 I gave unto Esau mount S., to possess it
Judg. 5. 4 when thou wentest out of S...the earth
1 Ch. 4. 42 five hundred men, went to mount S., ha.
2 Ch. 20. 10 the children of Ammon..and mount S
20. 22 children of Ammon, Moab, and mount S.
20. 23 up against the inhabitants of mount S.
20. 23 had made an end of the inhabitants of S.
25. 11 and smote of the children of S. ten thou.
25. 14 he brought the gods of the children of S.
Isa. 21. 11 He calleth to me out of S., Watchman
Eze. 25. 8 Because that Moab and S. do say, Behold
35. 2 Son of man, set thy face against mount S.
35. 3 Behold, O mount S., I (am) against thee
35. 7 Thus will I make mount S. most desolate
35. 15 thou shalt be desolate, O mount S.. and
2. The grandfather of Hori, ancestor of the Horites. B.C. 1840.
Gen. 36. 20 These (are) the sons of S the Horite, who
36. 21 the children of S. in the land of Edom
1 Ch. 1. 38 the sons of S ; Lotan, and Shobal, and Z.

SE-I'-RATH, הַשְּׂעִירָה *the wooded*.
A city in Ephraim, near Gilgal.
Judg. 3. 26 And Ehud..passed..and escaped unto S.

SEIZE (on or upon), to —
1. *To take or keep fast hold*, חָזַק *chazaq*, 5.
Jer. 49. 24 fear hath seized on (her); anguish and so.
2. *To take possession*, יָרַשׁ *yarash*, 5.
Josh. 8. 7 rise up from the ambush, and seize upon
3. *To take, receive*, לָקַח *laqach*.
Job 3. 6 let darkness seize upon it; let it not be jo.
4. *To take away*, נָשָׁא *nasha*, 5.
Psa. 55. 15 Let death seize upon them, (and) let them
5. *To hold down or firm*, κατέχω *katechō*.
Matt 21. 38 kill him, and [let us seize on] his inheritance

SE-LA HAM-MAH-LE'-KOTH, סֶלַע הַמַּחְלְקוֹת *rock of the separations*.
A hill in the wilderness of Maon, in the south of Judah.
1 Sa. 23. 28 therefore they called that place S.-ham.

SE'-LA, SE'-LAH, הַסֶּלַע *the rock or cliff*.
The capital of Edom, called also *Petra*, in the valley *Wady Musi*, between the Salt Sea and the Elanitic Gulf; called *Joktheel* by Amaziah king of Judah after his taking it, B.C. 839–822.
2 Ki. 14. 7 He slew..ten thousand, and took S. by
Isa. 16. 1 to the ruler of the land from S. to the w.

SELAH —
A pause, or musical note, סֶלָה.
Psa. 3. 2, 4, 8; 4. 2, 4; 7. 5; 9. 16, 20; 20. 3; 21. 2; 24. 6, 10; 32. 4, 5, 7; 39. 5, 11; 44. 8; 46. 3, 7, 11; 47. 4; 48. 8; 49. 13, 15; 50. 6; 52. 3, 5; 54. 3; 55. 7, 19; 57. 3, 6; 59. 5, 13; 60. 4; 61. 4; 62. 4, 8; 66. 4, 7, 15; 67. 1, 4; 68. 7, 19, 32; 75. 3; 76. 3, 9; 77. 3, 9, 15; 81. 7; 82. 2; 83. 8; 84. 4, 8; 85. 2; 87. 3, 6; 88. 7, 10; 89. 4, 37, 45, 48; 140. 3, 5, 8; 143. 6; Hab. 3. 3, 9, 13.

SE'-LED, סֶלֶד *exultation*.
A descendant of Jehahmeel, grandson of Pharez son of Judah. B.C. 1400.
1 Ch. 2. 30 sons of Nadab; S., and Appaim: but S.

SE-LEU-CI-A, Σελεύκεια.
A city of Syria, fourteen miles W. of Antioch, and five miles N. of the mouth of the Orontes; called also *S. Pieria* (from Mount Pierius) and *S. ad mare* (from the proximity to the sea, and to distinguish it from others of the same name). Strabo says it was founded by Seleucus Nicator, B.C. 280; in 245 it was taken by Ptolemy Euergetes; in 220 by Antiochus the Great.
Acts 13. 4 sent..by the Holy Ghost, departed unto S.

SELF, SELVES —
1. *My flesh*, בָּשָׂר *basar*.
Eccl. 2. 3 I sought in mine heart to give myself un.
2. *My life, soul*, נֶפֶשׁ *nephesh*.
Lev. 11. 43 Ye shall not make yourselves abominable
11. 44 neither shall ye defile yourselves with any
Deut. 4. 15 Take ye therefore good heed unto yourse.
Josh. 23. 11 Take good heed therefore unto yourselves
1 Ki. 19. 4 he requested for himself that he might die
Esth. 4. 13 Think not with thyself that thou
9. 31 as they had decreed for themselves, and
Job 18. 4 He teareth himself in his anger : shall the
32. 2 because he justified himself rather than
Psa. 131. 2 Surely I have behaved and quieted myself
Isa 5. 14 Therefore hell hath enlarged herself, and
46. 2 but themselves are gone into captivity
47. 14 they shall not deliver themselves from the
Jer. 3. 11 Israel hath justified herself more than tr.
17. 21 Take heed to yourselves, and bear no bu.
37. 9 Deceive not yourselves, saying, The Chal.
51. 14 The LORD of hosts hath sworn by himself
Amos 2. 14 neither shall the mighty deliver himself
2. 15 he that rideth the horse deliver himself
6. 8 The Lord GOD hath sworn by himself, sai.
Jon. 4. 8 wished in himself to die, and said, (It is)
3. *He, he himself*, αὐτός *autos*.
1 Pe. 2. 24 Who his own self bare our sins in his own
See also Herself, himself, itself, mine own self, myself, ourselves, themselves, thyself, your own self, yourselves. —(*Also*) Abase, acquaint, advise, adventure, afflict, anoint, answer, array, assemble, associate, avenge, make bald, bathe, behave, bemoan, be beside, bestir, bethink, bewail, bind, boast, bow, burden, call, cast, catch, circumcise, clad, clean, cleanse, clear, clearing, clothe, comfort, commit, condemned, corrupt, cover, cut, deck, defile, delight, deliver, destroy, discover, disguise, disperse, divide, ease, encourage, make fair, make fat, feign, fill, force, forswear, fret, show (self) friendly, show (self) froward, gather, gird, glorify, hang, harden, heed, hide, hire out, hold, honour, humble, behave (self) ill, join, justify, keep, known, lift, lift up, lifting up, loose, lothe, lover of, show (self) mad, magnify, make (self) many, show (self) marvellous, show (selves) men, show (self) merciful, mingle, mix, make naked, make (self) odious, oppose, put selves to pain, present, make (self) a prey, make (self) a prince, profane, make (self) a prophet, behave (self) proudly, show (self) pure, purify, put forth, put up, quiet, quit, raise up, reconcile, recover, redeem, refrain, refresh, repent, rest, reveal, revenge, make rich, roll, sanctify, save, scrap, sell, separate, separating, serve, set, sever, shake, show, showing, shut, make sick, solace, sport, spread, stay, stir up, make (self) strange, behave (self) strangely, strengthen, stretch, stretch out, strip, show (self) strong, submit, thrust, toss, turn, make (self) unclean, uncover, show (self) unsavoury, show (self) upright, behave (self) valiantly, vaunt, wallow, warm, wash, weary, make wise behave wisely, withdraw, withhold, within, wrap.

SELF, of —
Of its own accord, αὐτόματος *automatos*.
Mark 4. 28 the earth bringeth forth fruit of herself

SELF same (thing) —
1. *Substance*, עֶצֶם *etsem*.
Gen. 7. 13 In the self same day entered Noah, and S.
17. 23 flesh of their foreskin in the self same day
17. 26 In the self same day was Abraham circu.
Exod 12. 17 for in this self same day have I brought
12. 41 even the self same day it came to pass, th.
12. 51 it came to pass the self same day, (that)
Lev. 23. 14 until the self same day that ye have brou.
23. 21 ye shall proclaim on the self same day, (th.)
Deut 32. 48 LORD spake unto Moses that self same day
Josh. 5. 11 did eat..parched (corn) in the self same
Eze. 40. 1 in the self same day the hand of the LORD
2. *This very thing*, αὐτὸ τοῦτο *auto touto*.
2 Co. 5. 5 hath wrought us for the self same thing
3. *That very*, ἐκεῖνος *ekeinos*.
Matt. 8. 13 servant was healed in the self same hour

SELF will, self willed —
1. *Good will, good pleasure*, רָצוֹן *ratson*.
Gen. 49. 6 in their self will they digged down a wall
2. *Pleasing one's self*, αὐθάδης *authadēs*.
Titus 1. 7 not self willed, not soon angry, not given
2 Pe. 2. 10 Presumptuous (are they), self willed, they

SELL (away, self) to —
1. *To sell*, מָכַר *makar*.
Gen. 25. 31 Jacob said, Sell me this day thy birthright
25. 33 sware unto him: and he sold his birthrig.
31. 15 for he hath sold us, and hath quite devo.
37. 27 Come, and let us sell him to the Ishmeel.
37. 28 sold Joseph to the Ishmeelites for twenty
37. 36 sold him into Egypt unto Potiphar, an offi.
45. 4 Joseph your brother, whom ye sold into
45. 5 angry with yourselves that ye sold me hi.
47. 20 for the Egyptians sold every man his field
47. 22 them; wherefore they sold not their lands
Exod 21. 7 if a man sell his daughter to be a maid ser.
21. 8 to sell her unto a strange nation he shall
21. 16 he that stealeth a man, and selleth him
21. 35 then they shall sell the live ox, and divide
22. 1 steal an ox, or a sheep, and kill it, or sell
Lev. 25. 14 if thou sell ought unto thy neighbour, or
25. 15 according unto the number..he shall sell
25. 16 number..of the fruits doth he sell unto
25. 25 hath sold away (some) of his possession
25. 27 unto the man to whom he sold it, that he
25. 29 if a man sell a dwelling house in a walled
27. 20 if he have sold the field to another man
Deut 14. 21 or thou mayest sell it unto an alien : for
21. 14 thou shalt not sell her at all for money, th.
24. 7 maketh merchandise of him, or selleth
32. 30 except their Rock had sold them, and the
Judg. 2. 14 sold them into the hands of their enemies
3. 8 sold them into the hand of Chushan-risha.
4. 2 LORD sold them into the hand of Jabin
4. 9 for the LORD shall sell Sisera into the hand
10. 7 sold them into the hands of the Philistines
Ruth 4. 3 selleth a parcel of land, which (was) our
1 Sa. 12. 9 sold them unto the hand of Sisera, capta.
2 Ki. 4. 7 Go, sell the oil, and pay thy debt, and li.
Neh. 5. 8 will ye even sell your brethren? or shall
10. 31 any victuals on the sabbath day to sell, th.
13. 15 in the day wherein they sold victuals
13. 16 sold on the sabbath unto the children of
Psa. 44. 12 Thou sellest thy people for nought, and
Prov 23. 23 Buy the truth, and sell (it) not; (also) wi.
31. 24 She maketh fine linen, and selleth (it); and
Isa. 50. 1 to whom I have sold you? Behold; 52. 3.
Eze. 30. 12 sell the land into the hand of the wicked
48. 14 they shall not sell of it, neither exchange
Joel 3. 3 sold a girl for wine, that they might drink
3. 6 sold unto the Grecians, that ye might re.
3. 7 whither ye have sold them, and will ret.
3. 8 I will sell your sons and your daughters
3. 8 they shall sell them to the Sabeans, to a
Amos 2. 6 because they sold the righteous for silver
Nah. 3. 4 selleth nations through her whoredoms
Zech. 11. 5 they that sell them say, Blessed (be) the
2. *To be sold*, מָכַר *makar*, 2.
Lev. 25. 47 sell himself unto the stranger (or) sojou.
3. *To sell self*, מָכַר *makar*, 7.
1 Ki. 21. 20 because thou hast sold thyself to work e.
21. 25 which did sell himself to work wickedness
2 Ki. 17. 17 sold themselves to do evil in the sight of
4. *To break, sell corn*, שָׁבַר *shabar*.
Gen. 41. 56 sold unto the Egyptian; and the famine
5. *To break, sell corn*, שָׁבַר *shabar*, 5.
Gen. 42. 6 he (it was) that sold to all the people of
Deut. 2. 28 Thou shalt sell me meat for money, that
Prov 11. 26 upon the head of him that selleth (it)
Amos 8. 5 new moon be gone, that we may sell corn?
8. 6 (yea), and sell the refuse of the wheat?
6. *To give away*, ἀποδίδωμι *apodidōmi*.
Acts 5. 8 Tell me whether ye sold the land for so
7. 9 patriarchs, moved with envy, sold Joseph
Heb. 12. 16 who for one morsel of meat sold his birt.
7. *To sell, dispose of*, πιπράσκω *pipraskō*.
Matt 13. 46 went and sold all that he had, and bought
Acts 2. 45 sold their possessions and goods, and pa.
8. *To sell*, πωλέω *pōleō*.
Matt 13. 44 selleth all that he hath, and buyeth that
19. 21 go (and) sell that thou hast, and give to
21. 12 cast out all them that sold and bought in
21. 12 overthrew..the seats of them that sold d.
25. 9 but go ye rather to them that sell, and
Mark 10. 21 go thy way, sell whatsoever thou hast, and
11. 15 cast out them that sold and bought in the
11. 15 overthrew..the seats of them that sold d.
Luke 12. 33 Sell that ye have, and give alms; provide
17. 28 they bought, they sold, they planted, they
18. 22 sell all that thou hast, and distribute un.
19. 45 began to cast out them that sold therein
22. 36 let him sell his garment, and buy one
John 2. 14 found in the temple those that sold oxen
2. 16 said unto them that sold doves, Take th.
Acts 4. 34 sold them, and brought the prices of the
4. 37 Having land, sold (it), and brought the
5. 1 certain man named Ananias..sold a pos.
Rev. 13. 17 that no man might buy or sell, save he

SELLER (of purple) —
1. *To sell*, מָכַר *makar*.
Neh. 13. 20 sellers of all kind of ware, lodged without
Isa. 24. 2 as with the buyer, so with the seller; as
Eze 7. 12 let not the buyer rejoice, nor the seller
7. 13 For the seller shall not return to that wh.
2. *A seller of purple*, πορφυρόπωλις *porphuropōlis*.
Acts 16. 14 woman named Lydia, a seller of purple

SELVEDGE, selvage —
End, extremity, קָצָה *qatsah.*
Exod26. 4 from the selvage in the coupling ; and li.
36. 11 edge of one curtain from the selvage in

SELVES, themselves, yourselves —
Of one another, ἀλλήλων *allēlōn.*
Mark 8. 16 reasoned among themselves, saying, (It is)
9. 34 they had disputed among themselves, who
15. 31 said among themselves with the scribes
Luke 4. 36 spake among themselves, saying, What a
John 6. 43 said..Murmur not among yourselves
6. 52 Jews therefore strove among themselves
11. 56 spake among themselves, as they stood in
16. 17 said..among themselves, What is this that
16. 19 Do ye enquire among yourselves of that I
19. 24 They said therefore among themselves, Let
Acts 4. 15 council, they conferred among themselves
26. 31 they talked between themselves, saying
28. 4 said among themselves, No doubt this man
28. 25 when they agreed not among themselves
1 Th. 5. 11 Wherefore comfort yourselves together
5. 15 that which is good, both among yoursel.

SEM, Σήμ. *See Shem.*
Son of Noah, and father of Arphaxad. B.C. 2448.
Luke 3. 36 which was (the son) of S., which was (the

SE-MACH'-IAH, סְמַכְיָהוּ *Jah supports.*
Son of Shemaiah, a Kohathite, a gatekeeper of the tabernacle in the days of David. B.C. 1015.
1 Ch.26. 7 whose brethren..strong men, Elihu, and S.

SE-ME'-I, Σεμεΐ. *An ancestor of Jesus.* See *Shimei.*
Luke 3. 26 which was (the son) of [S]., which was

SE-NA'-AH, הַסְּנָאָה *thorn-hedge.* See *Hassenaah.*
A city in Judah, some of whose inhabitants returned with Zerubbabel from exile. B.C. 536.
Ezra 2. 35 children of S., three thousand..six hun.
Neh. 7. 38 children of S., three thousand nine hun.

SENATE, SENATOR —
1. *Elder, aged, senior,* זָקֵן *zaqen.*
Psa. 105. 22 To bind his princes..and teach his sena.
2. *Senate, assembly of elders,* γερουσία *gerousia.*
Acts 5. 21 and all the senate of the children of Israel

SEND (again, away, earnestly, forth, many, out), to —
1. *To cause to go or come in,* בּוֹא *bo,* 5.
Lev. 26. 36 I will send a faintness into their hearts
2. *Multiply,* רָבָה *rabah,* 5.
Neh. 6. 17 the nobles of Judah sent many letters un.
3. *To cast up and down,* טוּל *tul,* 5.
Jon. 1. 4 the LORD sent out a great wind into the
4. *To set over, or give a charge to,* צָוָה *tsavah,* 3.
Ezra 8. 17 I sent them with commandment unto I.
5. *To belch out, send forth,* נָבַע *naba,* 5.
Eccl. 10. 1 flies cause the ointment..to send forth
6. *To wave, shake out,* נוּף *nuph,* 5.
Psa. 68. 9 Thou, O God didst send a plentiful rain
7. *To give,* נָתַן *nathan.*
Exod. 9. 23 the LORD sent thunder and hail, and the
Deut 11. 15 I will send grass in thy fields for thy ca.
1 Sa. 12. 17 I will call unto the LORD, and he shall se.
12. 18 the LORD sent thunder and rain that day
2 Sa. 24. 15 the LORD sent a pestilence upon Israel
1 Ki. 17. 14 the day (that) the LORD sendeth rain up.
18. 1 show thyself unto Ahab ; and I will send
2 Ki. 19. 7 I will send a blast upon him, and he shall
1 Ch.21. 14 the LORD sent pestilence upon Israel : and
2 Ch. 6. 27 send rain upon thy land, which thou hast
Psa. 68. 33 he doth send out his voice, (and that) a
77. 17 the skies sent out a sound : thine arrows
Song 1. 12 my spikenard sendeth forth the smell th.
Isa. 37. 7 I will send a blast upon him, and he shall
8. *To send,* שָׁלַח *shalach.*
Gen. 20. 2 Abimelech king of Gerar sent and took S.
24. 7 he shall send his angel before thee, and
24. 40 will send his angel with thee, and prosp.
27. 42 she sent and called Jacob her younger son
27. 45 then I will send and fetch thee from th.
28. 5 Isaac sent away Jacob : and he went to
31. 4 Jacob sent and called Rachel and Leah
32. 3 Jacob sent messengers before him to Es.
32. 5 I have sent to tell my lord, that I may find
37. 13 come, and I will send thee unto them
37. 14 he sent him out of the vale of Hebron, and
38. 17 Wilt thou give..a pledge, till thou send
38. 20 Judah sent the kid by the hand of his fr.
38. 23 I sent this kid, and thou hast not found
38. 25 she sent to her father in law, saying, By
41. 8 he sent and called for all the magicians
41. 14 Pharaoh sent and called Joseph, and they
42. 4 Benjamin, Joseph's brother, Jacob sent
42. 16 Send one of you, and let him fetch your
43. 8 Send the lad with me, and we will arise
45. 5 God did send me before you to preserve
45. 7 God sent me before you to preserve you
45. 8 (it was) not you (that) sent me hither, but
45. 23 And to his father he sent after this (m.)
45. 27 saw the wagons which Joseph had sent
46. 5 in the wagons which Pharaoh had sent to
46. 28 he sent Judah before him unto Joseph, to
Exod. 2. 5 when she saw the ark..she sent her maid
3. 10 I will send thee unto Pharaoh, that thou
3. 12 a token unto thee that I have sent thee
3. 13 The God of your fathers hath sent
Exod. 3. 14 Thus shalt thou say..I AM hath sent me
3. 15 the God of Jacob, hath sent me unto you
4. 13 And he said, O my Lord, send, I pray thee
4. 13 by the hand (of him whom) thou wilt se.
4. 28 the words of the LORD who had sent him
5. 22 Lord..why (is) it (that) thou hast sent me?
7. 16 The LORD God of the Hebrews hath sent
9. 7 Pharaoh sent, and, behold, there was not
9. 14 I will at this time send all my plagues up.
9. 19 Send therefore now, (and) gather thy ca.
9. 27 Pharaoh sent, and called for Moses, and
23. 20 I send an angel before thee, to keep thee
23. 28 I will send hornets before thee, which sh.
24. 5 he sent young men of the children of Isr.
33. 2 I will send an angel before thee : and I
33. 12 hast not let me know whom thou wilt se.
Num13. 2 Send thou men, that they may search the
13. 2 of every tribe of their fathers shall ye se.
13. 3 sent them from the wilderness of Paran
13. 16 the men which Moses sent to spy out the
13. 17 Moses sent them to spy out the land of C.
13. 27 we came unto the land whither thou sent.
14. 36 the men which Moses sent to search the
16. 12 Moses sent to call Dathan and Abiram, the
16. 28 ye shall know that the LORD hath sent me
16. 29 If these men die..the LORD hath not sent
20. 14 Moses sent messengers from Kadesh unto
20. 16 he heard our voice, and sent an angel, and
21. 21 Israel sent messengers unto Sihon king of
21. 32 Moses sent to spy out Jaazer, and they to.
22. 5 He sent messengers therefore unto Bala.
22. 10 Balak..king of Moab, hath sent unto me
22. 15 Balak sent yet again princes, more and
22. 37 Did I not earnestly send unto thee to call
24. 12 thy messengers which thou sentest unto
31. 4 Of every tribe a thousand..shall ye send
31. 6 Moses sent them to the war, a thousand
32. 8 when I sent them from Kadesh-barnea to
Deut. 1. 22 We will send men before us, and they sh.
2. 26 I sent messengers out of the wilderness of
9. 23 when the LORD sent you from Kadesh-b.
19. 12 the elders of his city shall send and fetch
34. 11 the wonders which the LORD sent him to
Josh. 1. 16 whithersoever thou sendest us we will go
2. 1 the son of Nun sent out of Shittim two men
2. 3 the king of Jericho sent unto Rahab, say.
6. 17 she hid the messengers that we sent
6. 25 the messengers which Joshua sent to spy
7. 2 Joshua sent men from Jericho to Ai, wh.
7. 22 Joshua sent messengers, and they ran unto
8. 3 men of valour, and sent them away by ni.
8. 9 Joshua therefore sent them forth : and
10. 3 Adoni-zedec king of Jerusalem sent unto
10. 6 the men of Gibeon sent unto Joshua to the
11. 1 he sent to Jobab king of Madon, and to
14. 7 Moses the servant of the LORD sent me fr.
14. 11 this day as (I was) in the day that Moses
18. 4 I will send them, and they shall rise and
22. 13 the children of Israel sent unto the chil.
24. 5 I sent Moses also and Aaron, and I plag.
24. 9 sent and called Baalam the son of Beor to
24. 12 I sent the hornet before you, which drave
Judg. 3. 15 by him the children of Israel sent a pre.
4. 6 And she sent and called Barak the son of
6. 8 the LORD sent a prophet unto the childr.
6. 14 Go in this thy might..have not I sent th.?
6. 35 he sent messengers throughout all Mana.
6. 35 and he sent messengers unto Asher, and
7. 24 Gideon sent messengers throughout all
9. 23 God sent an evil spirit between Abimelech
9. 31 he sent messengers unto Abimelech priv.
11. 12 Jephthah sent messengers unto the king
11. 14 Jephthah sent messengers again, unto the
11. 17 Israel sent messengers unto the king of E.
11. 17 in like manner they sent unto the king of
11. 19 Israel sent messengers unto Sihon king of
11. 28 the words of Jephthah which he sent him
11. 38 he sent her away (for) two months: and she
13. 8 let the man of God which thou didst send
16. 18 she sent and called for the lords of the P.
18. 2 the children of Dan sent of their family
20. 12 the tribes of Israel sent men through all
21. 10 the congregation sent thither twelve th.
21. 13 the whole congregation sent (some) to sp.
1 Sa. 4. 4 the people sent to Shiloh, that they mig.
5. 8 They sent therefore, and gathered all the
5. 11 they sent and gathered together all the
6. 21 they sent messengers to the inhabitants
9. 16 I will send..a man out of the land of Be.
11. 3 that we may send messengers unto all the
12. 8 the LORD sent Moses and Aaron, which
12. 11 And the LORD sent Jerubbaal, and Bedan
15. 1 The LORD sent me to anoint thee (to be) ki.
15. 18 the LORD sent thee on a journey, and said
15. 20 have gone the way which the LORD sent
16. 1 I will send thee to Jesse the Beth-lehem.
16. 11 Send and fetch him : for we will not sit
16. 12 he sent and brought him in. Now he (was)
16. 19 Saul sent messengers unto Jesse, and said
16. 20 and sent (them) by David his son unto Sa.
16. 22 Saul sent to Jesse, saying, Let David, I
18. 5 David went out whithersoever Saul sent
19. 11 Saul also sent messengers unto David's
19. 14 when Saul sent messengers to take David
19. 15 Saul sent the messengers (again) to see D.
19. 20 Saul sent messengers to take David : and
19. 21 he sent other messengers, and they prop.
19. 21 Saul sent messengers again the third time
20. 12 and I then send not unto thee, and show
20. 21 I will send a lad, (saying,) Go, find out the
20. 31 send and fetch him unto me, for he shall
21. 2 of the business whereabout I send thee
1 Sa. 22. 11 the king sent to call Ahimelech the priest
25. 5 David sent out ten young men ; and Dav.
25. 14 David sent messengers out of the wilder.
25. 25 saw not the young men..thou didst send
25. 32 which sent thee this day to meet me
25. 39 David sent and communed with Abigail
25. 40 David sent us unto thee, to take thee to
26. 4 David therefore sent out spies, and und.
2 Sa. 2. 5 David sent messengers unto the men of
3. 12 Abner sent messengers unto David on his
3. 14 David sent messengers to Ish-bosheth, S.
3. 15 Ish-bosheth sent, and took her from (her)
3. 26 he sent messengers after Abner, which
5. 11 Hiram king of Tyre sent messengers to
8. 10 Toi sent Joram his son unto king David
9. 5 David sent, and fetched him out of the h.
10. 2 David sent to comfort him by the hand of
10. 3 that he hath sent comforters unto thee?
10. 3 hath not David (rather) sent his servants
10. 5 he sent to meet them, because the men we.
10. 6 the children of Ammon sent and hired
10. 7 he sent Joab, and all the host of the mi.
10. 16 Hadarezer sent, and brought out the Syr.
11. 1 David sent Joab, and his servants with
11. 3 And David sent and enquired after the w.
11. 4 And David sent messengers and took her
11. 5 the woman conceived, and sent and told
11. 6 David sent to Joab, (saying), Send me U.
11. 6 And Joab sent Uriah to David
11. 14 David wrote a letter to Joab, and sent (it)
11. 18 Then Joab sent and told David all the th.
11. 22 showed David all that Joab had sent him
11. 27 David sent and fetched her to his house
12. 1 And the LORD sent Nathan unto David
12. 25 he sent by the hand of Nathan the prop.
12. 27 Joab sent messengers to David, and said
13. 7 David sent home to Tamar, saying, Go now
14. 2 Joab sent to Tekoah, and fetched thence
14. 29 Absalom sent for Joab, to have sent him
14. 29 when he sent again a second time, he wo.
14. 32 Behold, I sent unto thee, saying, Come hi.
14. 32 that I may send thee to the king, to say
15. 10 Absalom sent spies throughout all the tr.
15. 12 Absalom sent for Ahithophel the Gilonite
15. 36 by them ye shall send unto me every th.
17. 16 send quickly, and tell David, saying, Lo.
18. 29 When Joab sent the king's servant, and
19. 11 David sent to Zadok and to Abiathar the
19. 14 they sent (this word) unto the king, Re.
22. 15 he sent out arrows, and scattered them
22. 17 He sent from above, he took me ; he drew
24. 13 what answer I shall return to him that se.
1 Ki. 1. 44 the king hath sent with him Zadok the pr.
1. 53 Solomon sent, and they brought him down
2. 25 Solomon sent by the hand of Benaiah the
2. 29 Solomon sent Benaiah the son of Jehoiada
2. 36 the king sent and called for Shimei, and
2. 42 the king sent and called for Shimei and
5. 1 Hiram king of Tyre sent his servants unto
5. 2 And Solomon sent to Hiram, saying
5. 8 Hiram sent to Solomon, saying, I have
5. 8 considered the things which thou sentest
5. 14 he sent them to Lebanon, ten thousand a
7. 13 Solomon sent and fetched Hiram out of T.
8. 44 whithersoever thou shalt send them, and
9. 14 Hiram sent to the king six score talents
9. 27 Hiram sent in the navy his servants, shi.
12. 3 they sent and called him. And Jeroboam
12. 18 Rehoboam sent Adoram, who (was) over
12. 20 they sent and called him unto the congr.
15. 18 Asa sent them to Ben-hadad, the son of
15. 19 I have sent unto thee a present of silver
15. 20 sent the captains of the host which he had
18. 10 whither my lord hath not sent to seek th.
18. 19 send, (and) gather to me all Israel unto
18. 20 Ahab sent unto all the children of Israel
19. 2 Jezebel sent a messenger unto Elijah, say.
20. 2 he sent messengers to Ahab king of Israel
20. 5 Although I have sent unto thee, saying
20. 6 I will send my servants unto thee tomor.
20. 7 he sent unto me for my wives, and for my
20. 9 All that thou didst send for to thy serv.
20. 10 Ben-hadad sent unto him, and said, Th
20. 17 Ben-hadad sent out, and they told him
21. 8 sent the letters unto the elders and to the
21. 11 did as Jezebel had sent unto them, (and)
21. 11 written in the letters which she had sent
21. 14 they sent to Jezebel, saying, Naboth is st.
2 Ki. 1. 2 he sent messengers, and said unto them
1. 6 turn again unto the king that sent you
1. 6 thou sendest to enquire of Baal-zebub the
1. 9 the king sent unto him a captain of fifty
1. 11 he sent unto him another captain of fifty
1. 13 he sent again a captain of the third fifty
1. 16 thou hast sent messengers to enquire of
2. 2, 4, 6 tarry here..for the LORD hath sent
2. 16 And he said, Ye shall not send
2. 17 he said, Send. They sent therefore fifty
3. 7 he went and sent to Jehoshaphat the king
4. 22 Send me, I pray thee one of the young
5. 5 I will send a letter unto the king of Israel
5. 6 I have (therewith) sent Naaman my serv.
5. 7 that this man doth send unto me to reco.
5. 8 he sent to the king, saying, Wherefore ha.
5. 10 Elisha sent a messenger unto him, saying
5. 22 My master hath sent me, saying, Behold
6. 9 the man of God sent unto the king of Is.
6. 10 the king of Israel sent to the place which
6. 13 spy where he (is), that I may send and fet.
6. 14 Therefore sent he thither horses, and ch
6. 32 and (the king) sent a man from before him
6. 32 this son of a murderer hath sent to take

2 Ki. 7. 13 take..five of the horses..and let us send
7. 14 the king sent after the host of the Syrians
8. 9 Ben-hadad king of Syria hath sent me to
9 17 Take an horseman, and send to meet them
9. 19 he sent out a second on horseback, which
10. 1 Jehu wrote letters, and sent to Samaria
10. 5 the bringers up (of the children), sent to J.
10. 7 put their heads in baskets, and sent him
10. 21 And Jehu sent through all Israel; and all
11. 4 Jehoiada sent and fetched the rulers over
12. 18 sent (it) to Hazael king of Syria: and he
14. 8 Amaziah sent messengers to Jehoash, the
14. 9 the king of Israel sent to Amaziah king
14. 9 thistle that (was) in Lebanon sent to the
14. 19 they sent after him to Lachish, and slew
16. 7 Ahaz sent messengers to Tiglath-pileser
16. 8 sent (it for) a present to the king of Assy.
16. 10 Ahaz sent to Urijah the priest the fashion
16. 11 according to all that king Ahaz had sent
17. 4 he had sent messengers to So king of Eg.
17. 13 which I sent to you by my servants the pr.
18. 14 Hezekiah king of Judah sent to the king
18. 17 the king of Assyria sent Tartan, and Rab.
18. 27 Hath my master sent me to thy master
19. 2 he sent Eliakim, which (was) over the ho.
19. 4 the king of Assyria his master hath sent
19. 9 he sent messengers again unto Hezekiah
19. 16 which hath sent him to reproach the liv.
19. 20 the son of Amoz sent to Hezekiah, saying
20. 12 sent letters and a present unto Hezekiah
22. 3 the king sent Shaphan the son of Azaliah
22. 15 Thus saith the LORD..Tell the man that s.
22. 18 the king of Judah, which sent you to enq.
23. 1 the king sent, and they gathered unto him
23. 16 sent, and took the bones out of the sepu.
1 Ch. 13. 2 let us send abroad unto our brethren every
14. 1 Hiram king of Tyre sent messengers to D.
18. 10 He sent Hadoram his son to king David
19. 2 David sent messengers to comfort him co.
19. 3 that he hath sent comforters unto thee
19. 5 he sent to meet them: for the men were
19. 6 the children of Ammon sent a thousand
19 8 he sent Joab, and all the host of the mig.
19. 16 they sent messengers, and drew forth the
21. 12 what word I shall bring..to him that sent
21. 15 God sent an angel unto Jerusalem to des
2 Ch. 2. 3 Solomon sent to Huram the king of Tyre
2. 3 didst send him cedars to build him an ho
2. 7 Send me now therefore a man cunning to
2. 8 Send me also cedar trees, fir trees, and
2. 11 answered in writing, which he sent to S.
2. 13 I have sent a cunning man, endued with
2. 15 the oil, and the wine..let him send unto
6. 34 by the way that thou shalt send them, and
8. 18 Huram sent him, by the hands of his ser.
10. 3 they sent and called him. So Jeroboam
10 18 Rehoboam sent Hadoram that (was) over
16. 2 sent to Ben-hadad king of Syria, that dw.
16. 3 I have sent thee silver and gold; go, break
16. 4 sent the captains of his armies against the
17. 7 he sent to his princes, (even) to Ben-hail
24. 19 he sent prophets to them, to bring them
25. 15 he sent unto him a prophet, which said
25. 17 sent to Joash, the son of Jehoahaz, the son
25. 18 Joash king of Israel sent to Amaziah king
25. 18 The thistle that (was) in Lebanon sent to
25. 27 they sent to Lachish after him, and slew
28. 16 At that time did king Ahaz send unto the
30. 1 Hezekiah sent to all Israel and Judah, and
32. 9 this did Sennacherib king of Assyria send
32. 21 the LORD sent an angel, which cut off all
34. 8 he sent Shaphan the son of Azaliah, and
34. 23 saith the LORD..Tell ye the man that sent
34. 26 the king of Judah, who sent you to enquire
34. 29 the king sent and gathered together all the
35. 21 he sent ambassadors to him, saying
36. 10 Nebuchadnezzar sent and brought him to
36. 15 the LORD God of their fathers sent to them
36. 15 rising up betimes, and sending; because
Ezra 8. 16 Then sent I for Eliezer, for Ariel, for Sh
Neh. 2. 5 that thou wouldest send me unto Judah
2. 6 it pleased the king to send me; and I set
2. 9 the king had sent captains of the army and
6. 2 Geshem sent unto me, saying, Come, let
6. 3 I sent messengers unto them, saying, I
6. 4 they sent unto me four times after this so
6. 5 Then sent Sanballat his servant unto me
6. 8 I sent unto him, saying, There are no such
6. 12 lo, I perceived that God had not sent him
6. 19 (And) Tobiah sent letters to put me in fear
8. 10 send portions unto them for whom nothing
Esth. 1. 22 he sent letters into all the king's provin.
4. 4 she sent raiment to clothe Mordecai, and
5. 10 he sent and called for his friends, and Ze
8. 10 sent letters by posts on horseback, (and)
9. 20 sent letters unto all the Jews that (were)
9. 30 he sent the letters unto all the Jews, to the
Job 1. 4 sent and called for their three sisters, to
1. 5 Job sent and sanctified them, and rose up
5. 10 Who giveth rain..and sendeth waters up.
Psa. 18. 14 he sent out his arrows, and scattered them
18. 16 He sent from above, he took me, he drew
20. 2 Send thee help from the sanctuary, and
43. 3 O send out thy light and thy truth: let
57. 3 He shall send from heaven, and save me
57. 3 God shall send forth his mercy and his tr.
59. *title.* when Saul sent, and they watched
78. 25 Man did eat angels' food: he sent them
105. 17 He sent a man before them, (even) Joseph
105. 20 The king sent and loosed him; (even) the
105. 26 He sent Moses his servant, (and) Aaron
105. 28 He sent darkness, and made it dark; and

Psa. 107. 20 He sent his word, and healed them, and
110. 2 The LORD shall send the rod of thy stre.
111. 9 He sent redemption unto his people: he
135. 9 (Who) sent tokens and wonders into the
144. 7 Send thine hand from above; rid me, and
147. 15 He sendeth forth his commandment (up.)
147. 18 He sendeth out his word, and melteth th.
Prov. 9. 3 She hath sent forth her maidens: she cr.
10. 26 so (is) the sluggard to them that send him
22. 21 answer the words of truth to them that s.
25 13 (so is) a faithful messenger to them that s.
26. 6 He that sendeth a message by the hand
Isa. 6. 8 heard the voice..saying, Whom shall I se.
6. 8 who will go for us? Then said I..send me
9. 8 The Lord sent a word into Jacob, and it
16. 1 Send ye the lamb to the ruler of the land
18. 2 That sendeth ambassadors by the sea, ev.
19. 20 shall send them a saviour, and a great one
20. 1 Sargon the king of Assyria sent him, and
36. 2 king of Assyria sent Rabshakeh from Lac.
36. 12 Hath my master sent me to thy master
37. 2 sent Eliakim, who (was) over the househ.
37. 4, 17 hath sent to reproach the living God
37. 9 he sent messengers to Hezekiah, saying
37. 21 Isaiah the son of Amoz sent unto Hezek.
39. 1 sent letters and a present to Hezekiah
42. 19 deaf, as my messenger (that) I sent? who
48. 16 the Lord GOD, and his spirit, hath sent
55. 11 shall prosper (in the thing) whereto I sent
61. 1 hath sent me to bind up the broken hea.
Jer. 1. 7 for thou shalt go to all that I shall send
2. 10 send unto Kedar, and consider diligen.
7. 25 I have even sent unto you all my servants
7. 25 daily rising up early and sending (them)
9. 17 send for cunning (women), that they may
14. 3 have sent their little ones to the waters
14. 14 sent them not, neither have I commanded
14. 15 sent them not, yet they say, Sword and
16. 16 I will send..and after will I send for ma.
19. 14 whither the LORD had sent him to proph.
21. 1 when king Zedekiah sent unto him Pashur
23. 21 I have not sent these prophets, yet they
23. 32 yet I sent them not, nor commanded them
23. 38 I have sent unto you, saying, Ye shall not
25. 4 LORD hath sent unto you all his servants
25. 4 rising early and sending (them); but ye
25. 9 I will send and take all the families of the
25. 15 cause all the nations, to whom I send th.
25. 16, 27 because of the sword that I will send
25. 17 nations..unto whom the LORD had sent
26. 5 sent..rising up early, and sending (them)
26. 12 LORD sent me to prophesy against this ho.
26. 15 hath sent me unto you to speak all these
26. 22 Jehoiakim the king sent men into Egypt
27. 15 For I have not sent them, saith the LORD
28. 9 known, that the LORD hath truly sent him
28. 15 LORD hath not sent thee; but thou mak.
29. 1 sent from Jerusalem unto the residue of
29. 3 sent unto Babylon to Nebuchadnezzar ki.
29. 9 I have not sent them, saith the LORD
29. 19 sent..rising up early and sending (them)
29. 25 sent letters in thy name unto all the pe.
29. 28 For therefore he sent unto us (in) Babylon
29. 31 Send to all them of the captivity, saying
29. 31 sent him not, and he caused you to trust
35. 15 I have sent also unto you all my servants
35. 15 rising up early and sending (them), saying
36. 14 the princes sent Jehudi the son of Neth.
36. 21 the king sent Jehudi to fetch the roll: and
37. 3 the king sent Jehucal the son of Shelemiah
37. 7 the king of Judah, that sent you unto me
37. 17 the king sent, and took him out; and the
38. 14 the king sent, and took Jeremiah the pr.
39. 13 Nebuzar-adan the captain of the guard se.
39. 14 they sent, and took Jeremiah out of the
40. 14 the king of the Ammonites hath sent Is.
42. 5 for the which the LORD thy God shall send
42. 6 the LORD our God, to whom we send thee
42. 9 unto whom ye sent me to present your su.
42. 20 when ye sent me unto the LORD your God
42. 21 nor any (thing) for the which he hath sent
43. 1 for which the LORD their God had sent
43. 2 the LORD our God hath not sent thee to
43. 10 I will send and take Nebuchadrezzar the
44. 4 I sent unto you all my servants the prop.
44. 4 rising early and sending (them), saying
Lam. 1. 13 he sent fire into my bones, and it prevail.
Eze. 2. 3 I send thee to the children of Israel, to a
2. 4 I do send thee unto them; and thou sh.
3. 6 had I sent thee to them, they would have
13. 6 LORD hath not sent them: and they have
17. 15 But he rebelled against him in sending his
23. 16 sent messengers unto them into Chaldea
23. 40 that ye have sent for men to come from
Hos. 5. 13 sent to king Jareb: yet could he not heal
Joel 2. 19 I will send you corn, and wine, and oil, and
Amos 7. 10 sent to Jeroboam king of Israel, saying
Mic. 6. 4 sent before thee Moses, Aaron, and Mir.
Hag. 1. 12 as the LORD their God had sent him, and
Zech. 1. 10 whom the LORD hath sent to walk to and
2. 8 After the glory hath he sent me unto the
2. 9, 11 that the LORD of hosts hath sent me
4. 9 know that the LORD of hosts hath sent me
6. 15 know that the LORD of hosts hath sent me
7. 2 When they had sent unto the house of God
7. 12 words which the LORD of hosts hath sent
Mal. 3. 1 I will send my messenger and he shall pr.
4. 5 I will send you Elijah the prophet before

9. *To send*, שָׁלַח *shalach*, 3.

Gen. 3. 23 Therefore the LORD God sent him forth
8. 7 sent forth a raven which went forth to and

Gen. 8. 8 Also he sent forth a dove from him, to see
8. 10 again he sent forth the dove out of the ark
8. 12 sent forth the dove; which returned not
12. 20 sent him away, and his wife, and all that
19. 13 and the LORD hath sent us to destroy it
19. 29 sent Lot out of the midst of the overthrow
21. 14 shoulder, and the child, and sent her away
24. 54 he said, Send me away unto my master
24. 56 send me away that I may go to my master
24. 59 they sent away Rebekah their sister, and
25. 6 sent them away from Isaac his son, while
26. 27 hate me, and have sent me away from you?
26. 29 have sent thee away in peace: thou (art)
26. 31 Isaac sent them away, and they departed
28. 6 sent him away to Padan-aram, to take him
30. 25 Send me away, that I may go unto mine
31. 27 might have sent thee away with mirth, and
31. 42 surely thou hadst sent me away now em.
37. 32 they sent the coat of (many) colours, and
38. 17 he said, I will send..a kid from the flock
43. 4 If thou wilt send our brother with us, we
43. 5 But if thou wilt not send (him), we will not
43. 14 that he may send away your other brother
45. 24 So he sent his brethren away, and they de.
Exod. 7. 2 that he send the children of Israel out of
12. 33 that they might send them out of the land
15. 7 thou sentest forth thy wrath, (which) co
23. 27 I will send my fear before thee, and will
Lev. 16. 21 send (him) away by the hand of a fit man
26. 25 I will send the pestilence among you; and
Num. 21. 6 LORD sent fiery serpents among the peo.
22. 40 sent to Balaam, and to the princes that
Deut. 7. 20 will send the hornet among them, until
15. 13 when thou sendest him out free from thee
15. 18 when thou sendest him away free from th.
24. 1 give (it) in her hand, and send her out of
24. 3 sendeth her out of his house; or if the la.
24. 4 former husband, which sent her away, may
28. 20 LORD shall send upon thee cursing, vexat.
28. 48 which the LORD shall send against thee, in
32. 24 I will also send the teeth of beasts upon
Josh. 2. 21 she sent them away, and they departed
22. 6 Joshua blessed them, and sent them away
22. 7 when Joshua sent them away also unto th.
Judg. 3. 18 sent away the people that bare the present
7. 8 he sent all (the rest of) Israel every man
12. 9 sent abroad, and took in thirty daughters
19. 29 and sent her into all the coasts of Israel
20. 6 sent her throughout all the country of the
1 Sa. 5. 10 Therefore they sent the ark of God to Ek.
5. 11 Send away the ark of the God of Israel, and
6. 2 wherewith we shall send it to his place
6. 3 If ye send away..send it not empty; but
6. 8 thereof; and send it away, that it may go
9. 26 saying, Up, that I may send thee away
10. 25 Samuel sent all the people away, every
11. 7 sent (them) throughout all the coasts of
13. 2 the rest of the people he sent every man
19. 17 sent away mine enemy, that he is escaped?
20. 13 I will show it thee, and send thee away
20. 22 thy way: for the LORD hath sent thee away
30. 26 he sent of the spoil unto the elders of Ju.
31. 9 sent into the land of the Philistines round
2 Sa. 3. 21 sent Abner away; and he went in peace
3. 22 for he had sent him away, and he was gone
3. 23 hath sent him away, and he is gone in pe.
3. 24 why (is) it (that) thou hast sent him away
10. 4 to their buttocks, and sent them away
13. 16 this evil in sending me away (is) greater
18. 2 David sent forth a third part of the people
1 Ki. 8. 66 On the eighth day he sent the people away
20. 34 I will send thee away with this covenant
20. 34 he made a covenant..and sent him away
2 Ki. 6. 23 sent them away, and they went to their
17. 25 LORD sent lions among them, which slew
17. 26 therefore he hath sent lions among them
24. 2 sent against him bands of the Chaldees, and
24. 2 sent them against Judah to destroy it, ac.
1 Ch. 8. 8 after he had sent them away; Hushim and
10. 9 sent into the land of the Philistines round
12. 19 for the lords..sent him away, saying, He
19. 4 cut off their garments..and sent them a.
2 Ch. 7. 10 he sent the people away into their tents
7. 13 or if I send pestilence among my people
24. 23 sent all the spoil of them unto the king
32. 31 who sent unto him to enquire of the won.
Neh. 8. 12 to send portions, and to make great mirth
Job 12. 15 also he sendeth them out, and they over.
14. 20 his countenance, and sendeth him away
21. 11 They send forth their little ones like a flo.
22. 9 Thou hast sent widows away empty, and
38. 35 Canst thou send lightnings, that they may
39. 5 Who hath sent out the wild ass free? or
Psa. 78. 45 He sent divers sorts of flies among them
80. 11 She sent out her boughs unto the sea, and
104. 10 He sendeth the springs into the valleys
104. 30 Thou sendeth forth thy spirit, they are cr.
106. 15 gave them their request; but sent leanness
Isa. 10. 6 I will send him against an hypocritical
10. 16 send among his fat ones leanness; and un
32. 20 send forth (thither) the feet of the ox an
43. 14 For your sake I have sent to Babylon, and
57. 9 didst send thy messengers far off, and di.
66. 19 will send those that escape of them unto
Jer. 8. 17 I will send serpents, cockatrices, among
9. 16 send a sword after them, till I have cons.
24. 5 Judah, whom I have sent out of this place
24. 10 I will send the sword, the famine, and the
27. 3 send them to the king of Edom, and to the
29. 17 will send upon them the sword, the famine
29. 20 whom I have sent from Jerusalem to Bab.
48. 12 that I will send unto him wanderers, that

Jer. 49. 37 send the sword after them, till I have co.
51. 2 will send unto Babylon fanners, that sh.
Eze. 5. 16 When I shall send upon them the evil ar.
5. 16 Which I will send to destroy you: and I
5. 17 So will I send upon you famine and evil
7. 3 I will send mine anger upon thee, and wi.
14. 19 Or (if) I send a pestilence into that land
14. 21 How much more when I send my four so.
28. 23 For I will send into her pestilence, and
31. 4 sent out her little rivers unto all the trees
39. 6 will send a fire on Magog, and among th.
Hos. 8. 14 but I will send a fire upon his cities, and
Joel 2. 25 my great army which I sent among you
Amos 1. 4, 7, 10, 12 But I will send a fire
2. 2, 5 But I will send a fire..and it shall
4. 10 I have sent among you the pestilence after
Zech. 9. 11 have sent forth thy prisoners out of the
Mal. 2. 2 will even send a curse upon you, and I
2. 4 ye shall know that I have sent this com.

10. *To send forth*, שָׁלַח *shalach*, 5.
Exod. 8. 21 I will send swarms (of flies) upon thee, and
Lev. 26. 22 I will also send wild beasts among you
2 Ki. 15. 37 the LORD began to send against Judah R.
Eze. 14. 13 will send famine upon it, and will cut off
Amos 8. 11 I will send a famine in the land, not a fa.

11. *To send, send forth*, שְׁלַח *shelach*.
Ezra 4. 11 This (is) the copy of the letter that they sent
4. 14 therefore have we sent and certified the
4. 17 (Then) sent the king an answer unto Re.
4. 18 The letter which ye sent unto us hath be.
5. 6 The copy of the letter that Tatnai..sent
5. 7 They sent a letter unto him, wherein was
5. 17 let the king send his pleasure to us conc.
6. 13 to that which Darius the king had sent
Dan. 3. 2 the king sent to gather together the prin.
3. 28 who hath sent his angel, and delivered his
6. 22 God hath sent his angel, and hath shut

12. *To send up, again*, ἀναπέμπω *anapempō*.
Luke 23. 7 he sent him to Herod, who himself also was
23. 11 arrayed him in a gorgeous robe, and sent
23. 15 I sent you to him; and, lo, nothing worthy
Phm. 12 Whom I have sent [again]: thou therefore

13. *To loose off or away*, ἀπολύω *apoluō*.
Matt 14. 15 send the multitude away, that they may
14. 22 go before..while he sent the multitude a.
14. 23 when he had sent the multitudes away
15. 23 send her away; for she crieth after us
15. 32 I will not send them away fasting, lest
15. 39 he sent away the multitude, and took sh.
Mark 6. 36 Send them away, that they may go into
6. 45 to go to the other side..while he sent aw.
8. 3 if I send them away fasting to their own
8. 9 about four thousand; and he sent them aw.
Luke 8. 38 be with him: but Jesus sent him away
9. 12 Send the multitudes away, that they may
Acts 13. 3 laid (their) hands on them, they sent (th.)

14. *To send away, forth*, ἀποστέλλω *apostellō*.
Matt 2. 16 sent forth, and slew all the children that
10. 5 Jesus sent forth, and commanded them
10. 16 I send you forth as sheep in the midst of
10. 40 receiveth me, receiveth him that sent me
11. 10 I send my messenger before thy face, wh.
13. 41 The Son of man shall send forth his angels
14. 35 they sent out into all that country round
15. 24 I am not sent but unto the lost sheep of
20. 2 when he had agreed..he sent them into
21. 1 when they drew nigh..then sent Jesus
21. 3 Lord hath need..straightway he will send
21. 34 he sent his servants to the husbandmen
21. 36 Again, he sent other servants more than
21. 37 he sent unto them his son, saying, They
22. 3 sent forth his servants to call them that
22. 4 he sent forth other servants, saying, Tell
22. 16 they sent out unto him their disciples wi.
23. 34 I send unto you prophets, and wise men
23. 37 and stonest them which are sent unto th.
24. 31 he shall send his angels with a great sou.
27. 19 his wife sent unto him, saying, Have thou
Mark 1. 2 I send my messenger before thy face, wh.
3. 14 that he might send them forth to preach
3. 31 his brethren..sent unto him, calling him
5. 10 that he would not send them away out of
6. 7 began to send them forth by two and two
6. 17 Herod himself had sent forth and laid hold
6. 27 the king sent an executioner, and comm.
8. 26 he sent him away to his house, saying
9. 37 receiveth not me, but him that sent me
11. 1 at the mount of Olives, he sendeth forth
11. 3 and straightway he will send him hither
12. 2 he sent to the husbandmen a servant, th.
12. 3 they caught..and beat him, and sent..away
12. 4 again he sent unto them another servant
12. 4 and [sent (him) away] shamefully handled
12. 5 he sent another; and him they killed, and
12. 6 he sent him also last unto them, saying
12. 13 they send unto him certain of the Phari.
13. 27 then shall he send his angels, and shall
14. 13 he sendeth forth two of his disciples, and
Luke 1. 19 and am sent to speak unto thee, and to
1. 26 the angel Gabriel was sent from God unto
4. 18 he hath sent me to heal the broken hear.
4. 43 I must preach..for therefore am I sent
7. 3 he sent unto him the elders of the Jews
7. 20 John Baptist hath sent us unto thee, sa.
7. 27 I send my messenger before thy face, wh.
9. 2 he sent them to preach the kingdom of G.
9. 48 shall receive me receiveth him that sent
9. 52 sent messengers before his face: and they
10. 1 sent them two and two before his face into
Luke 10. 3 I send you forth as lambs among wolves
10. 16 despiseth me despiseth him that sent me
11. 49 I will send them prophets and apostles
13. 34 and stonest them that are sent unto thee
14. 17 sent his servant at supper time to say to
14. 32 he sendeth an ambassage, and desireth
19. 14 his citizens hated him, and sent a message
19. 29 when he was come nigh..he sent two of
19. 32 they that were sent went their way, and
20. 10 he sent a servant to the husbandmen, th.
20. 20 they watched (him), and sent forth spies
22. 8 he sent Peter and John, saying, Go and pr.
22. 35 I sent you without purse, and scrip, and
24. 49 [I send] the promise of my Father upon
John 1. 6 There was a man sent from God, whose
1. 19 the Jews sent priests and Levites from J.
1. 24 they which were sent were of the Pharis.
3. 17 God sent not his son into the world to co.
3. 28 I am not the Christ, but that I am sent
3. 34 he whom God hath sent speaketh the wo.
4. 38 I sent ye to reap that whereon ye besto.
5. 33 Ye sent unto John, and he bare witness
5. 36 bear witness..that the Father hath sent
5. 38 for whom he hath sent, him ye believe not
6. 29 that ye believe on him whom he hath sent
6. 57 As the living Father hath sent me, and I
7. 29 for I am from him, and he hath sent me
7. 32 the chief priests sent officers to take
8. 42 neither came I of myself, but he sent me
10. 36 whom the Father hath sanctified, and sent
11. 3 his sisters sent unto him, saying, Lord, be.
11. 42 they may believe that thou hast sent me
17. 3 and Jesus Christ, whom thou hast sent
17. 8 they have believed that thou didst send
17. 18 As thou hast sent me into the world, even
17. 18 so have I also sent them into the world
17. 21 world may believe that thou hast sent me
17. 23 world may know that thou hast sent me
17. 25 these have known that thou hast sent me
18. 24 Annas had sent him bound unto Caiaphas
20. 21 as (my) Father hath sent me. even so
Acts 3. 20 he shall send Jesus Christ, which before
3. 26 having raised up his Son Jesus, sent him
5. 21 sent to the prison to have them brought
7. 14 Then sent Joseph, and called his father J.
7. 34 now come, I will send thee into Egypt
7. 35 the same did God send (to be) a ruler and
8. 14 they sent unto them Peter and John
9. 17 hath sent me, that thou mightest receive
9. 38 they sent unto him..men, desiring (him)
10. 8 when he had declared all..he sent them
10. 17 the men which were sent from Cornelius
10. 20 go..doubting nothing: for I have sent th.
10. 21 [went down to the men which were sent]
10. 36 The word which (God) sent unto the chil.
11. 11 there were three men..sent from Cesarea
11. 13 Send men to Joppa, and call for Simon
11. 30 sent it to the elders by the hands of Bar.
13. 15 rulers of the synagogue sent unto them, sa.
13. 26 to you is the word of this salvation [sent]
15. 27 We have sent therefore Judas and Silas
16. 35 the magistrates sent the serjeants, saying
16. 36 The magistrates have sent to let you go
19. 22 he sent into Macedonia two of them that
26. 17 the Gentiles, unto whom now I send thee
28. 28 the salvation of God is sent unto the Gen.
Rom 10. 15 how shall they preach except they be sent
1 Co. 1. 17 Christ sent me not to baptize, but to pre.
2 Co. 12. 17 a gain of you by any of them whom I sent
2 Ti. 4. 12 And Tychicus have I sent to Ep; He. 1. 14.
1 Pe. 1. 12 with the Holy Ghost sent down from hea.
1 Jo. 4. 9 God sent his only begotten Son into the
4. 10 sent his Son (to be) the propitiation for
4. 14 the Father sent the Son (to be) the Saviour
Rev. 1. 1 he sent and signified (it) by his angel unto
5. 6 which are the seven spirits of God sent fo.
22. 6 the Lord God of the holy prophets sent his

15. *To arrange off*, ἀποτάσσομαι *apotassomai*.
Mark 6. 46 when he had sent them away, he departed

16. *To send off or away, let go*, ἀφίημι *aphiēmi*.
Matt 13. 36 Jesus sent the multitude away, and went
Mark 4. 36 when they had sent away the multitude

17. *To cast*, βάλλω *ballō*.
Matt 10. 34 send peace on earth: I came not to send
Luke 12. 49 I am come to send fire on the earth; and

18. *To gush forth abundantly*, βρύω *bruō*.
Jas. 3. 11 Doth a fountain send forth at the same pl.

19. *To cast out*, ἐκβάλλω *ekballō*.
Matt. 9. 38 that he will send forth labourers into his
12. 20 till he send forth judgment unto victory
Mark 1. 43 charged him, and forthwith sent him away
Luke 10. 2 that he would send forth labourers into his
Jas. 2. 25 had received the messengers, and had sent

20. *To send out*, ἐκπέμπω *ekpempō*.
Acts 13. 4 So they, being sent forth by the Holy Ghost
17. 10 the brethren immediately sent away Paul

21. *To send away out*, ἐξαποστέλλω *exapostellō*.
Luke 1. 53 and the rich he hath sent empty away
20. 10 husbandmen beat him, and sent..away
20. 11 entreated..shamefully, and sent..away em.
Acts 7. 12 when Jacob heard..he sent out our fathers
9. 30 brought him down..and sent him forth to
11. 22 they sent forth Barnabas, that he should
12. 11 the Lord hath sent his angel, and hath
17. 14 the brethren sent away Paul, to go as it
22. 21 I will send thee far hence unto the Gent.
Gal. 4. 4 God sent forth his Son, made of a woman
4. 6 God hath sent forth the spirit of his Son

22. *To send*, πέμπω *pempō*.
Matt. 2. 8 he sent them to Bethlehem, and said, Go
11. 2 when John had heard..he sent two of his
14. 10 he sent, and beheaded John in the prison
22. 7 he sent forth his armies, and destroyed th.
Mark 5. 12 Send us into the swine, that we may enter
Luke 4. 26 unto none of them was Elias sent, save
7. 6 the centurion sent friends to him, saying
7. 10 they that were sent, returning to the hou.
7. 19 John..sent (them) to Jesus, saying, Art
15. 15 and he sent him into his fields to feed sw.
16. 24 send Lazarus, that he may dip the tip of
16. 27 that thou wouldest send him to my father's
20. 11 he sent another servant: and they beat h.
20. 12 he sent a third: and they wounded him
20. 13 I will send my beloved son: it may be th.
John 1. 22 we may give an answer to them that sent
1. 33 he that sent me to baptize with water, the
4. 34 My meat is to do the will of him that sent
5. 23 honoureth not the Father which hath sent
5. 24 He that..believeth on him that sent me
5. 30 the will of the Father which hath sent me
5. 37 the Father himself, which hath sent me
6. 38 I came..to do..the will of him that sent
6. 39 this is the Father's will which hath sent
6. 40 this is the will [of him that sent] me, that
6. 44 except the Father which hath sent me dr.
7. 16 My doctrine is not mine, but his that sent
7. 18 he that seeketh his glory that sent him, the
7. 28 he that sent me is true, whom ye know
7. 33 a little while..I go unto him that sent me
8. 16 not alone; but I and the Father that sent
8. 18 the Father that sent me beareth witness
8. 26 he that sent me is true; and I speak to
8. 29 he that sent me is with me: the Father ha.
9. 4 I must work the works of him that sent
12. 44 believeth not on me, but on him that sent
12. 45 he that seeth me seeth him that sent me
12. 49 but the Father which sent me, he gave me
13. 16 neither he..greater than he that sent him
13. 20 He that receiveth whomsoever I send re.
13. 20 that receiveth me receiveth him that sent
14. 24 not mine, but the Father's which sent me
14. 26 the Holy Ghost, whom the Father will se.
15. 21 because they know not him that sent me
15. 26 whom I will send unto you from the Fat.
16. 5 I go my way to him that sent me; and n.
16. 7 but if I depart, I will send him unto you
20. 21 Then said Jesus..even so send I you
Acts 10. 5 send men to Joppa, and call for (one) Sim.
10. 32 Send therefore to Joppa, and call hither S.
10. 33 Immediately therefore I sent to thee; and
11. 29 determined to send relief unto the brethr.
15. 22 to send chosen men of their own company
15. 25 to send chosen men unto you with our
19. 31 sent unto him, desiring (him) that he wo.
20. 17 he sent to Ephesus, and called the elders
23. 30 I sent straightway to thee, and gave com.
25. 21 commanded..to be kept till [I might s.]
25. 25 I found..I have determined to send him
25. 27 it seemeth to me unreasonable to send a
Rom. 8. 3 sending his own son in the likeness of s.
1 Co. 4. 17 I sent unto you Timotheus, who is my be.
16. 3 them will I send to bring your liberality
2 Co. 9. 3 Yet have I sent the brethren, lest our b.
Eph. 6. 22 Whom I have sent unto you for the same
Phil. 2. 19 I trust in the Lord Jesus to send
2. 23 Him therefore I hope to send presently
2. 25 Yet I supposed it necessary to send to you
2. 28 I sent him therefore the more carefully
4. 16 in Thessalonica ye sent once and again
Col. 4. 8 Whom I have sent unto you for the same
1 Th. 3. 2 sent Timotheus, our brother, and minister
3. 5 I sent to know your faith, lest by some
2 Th. 2. 11 God shall send them strong delusion, that
Titus 3. 12 I shall send Artemas unto thee, or Tych.
1 Pe. 2. 14 as unto them that are sent by him for the
Rev. 1. 11 send (it) unto the seven churches which are
11. 10 make merry, and [shall send] gifts one to
22. 16 I Jesus have sent mine angel to testify un.

SEND back, for, over, with, to —

1. *To take, receive*, לָקַח *laqach*.
1 Sa. 17. 31 rehearsed (them) before Saul..he sent for

2. *To cause to pass over*, עָבַר *abar*, 5.
Gen. 32. 23 sent them over the brook, and sent over

3. *To cause to turn back*, שׁוּב *shub*, 5.
2 Ch. 25. 13 soldiers of the army which Amaziah sent b.

4. *To send after*, μεταπέμπω *metapempō*.
Acts 10. 22 warned from God by an holy angel to send f.
10. 29 Therefore came I..as soon as I was s. for
10. 29 I ask..for what intent ye have sent for me
24. 24 he sent for Paul, and heard him concern.
24. 26 he sent for him the oftener, and commun.
25. 3 that he would send for him to Jerusalem

5. *To send with*, συμπέμπω *sumpempō*.
2 Co. 8. 18 And we have sent with him the brother
8. 22 And we have sent with them our brother

6. *To send away with*, συναποστέλλω *sunapostellō*.
2 Co. 12. 18 I desired Titus, and with (him) I sent a

SEND good speed, to —

To cause to meet, קָרָה *qarah*, 5.
Gen. 24. 12 send me good speed this day, and show

SEND rain, to —

To rain, cause rain, βρέχω *brechō*.
Matt. 5. 45 sendeth rain on the just and on the un

SEND to descry, to —
To cause to spy out, תּוּר *tur,* 5.
Judg. 1. 23 the house of Joseph sent to descry Beth-el

SENDING (away, forth) —
1. *A sending,* מִשְׁלָח *mishlach.*
Isa. 7. 25 it shall be for the sending forth of oxen
2. *A sending,* מִשְׁלוֹחַ *mishloach.*
Esth. 9. 19, 22 and of sending portions one to anoth.
3. *A sending,* מִשְׁלַחַת *mishlachath.*
Psa. 78. 49 He cast upon them..trouble, by sending
4. *To send,* שָׁלַח *shalach,* 3.
2 Sa. 13. 16 this evil in sending me away (is) greater

SE'-NEH, סֶנֶּה *pointed rock.*
A rock in Benjamin, near Gibeah, at the pass of Michmash, where the Philistines had a garrison in the days of Saul.
1 Sa. 14. 4 one..Bozez, and the name of the other S.

SE'-NIR, שְׂנִיר *peak or snowy mountain.*
A mountain N.E. of Jordan, between Amanah and Hermon. See *Shenir.*
1 Ch. 5. 23 they increased from Bashan unto..S., and
Eze. 27. 5 have made..thy..boards of fir trees of S.

SEN-NA-CHE'-RIB, סַנְחֵרִיב.
An Assyrian king, B.C. 714–696, who invaded Judah in the days of Hezekiah, and whose army was destroyed in one night; he was slain by two of his sons in Nineveh in the temple of Nisroch.
2 Ki. 18. 13 did S. king of Assyria come up against
19. 16 hear the words of S., which hath sent him
19. 20 against S. king of Assyria I have heard
19. 36 S. king of Assyria departed, and went and
2 Ch. 32. 1 S. king of Assyria came, and entered into
32. 2 when Hezekiah saw that S. was come, and
32. 9 After this did S...send his servants to J.
32. 10 Thus saith S. king of Assyria, Whereon
32. 22 from the hand of S. the king of Assyria
Isa. 36. 1 S...came up against all the defenced cit.
37. 17 hear all the words of S., which hath sent
37. 21 Whereas thou hast prayed..against S. ki.
37. 37 So S...departed, and went and returned

SENSE, SENSES —
1. *Understanding, wisdom, meaning,* שֶׂכֶל, שֵׂכֶל *sekel.*
Neh. 8. 8 they read in the book..and gave the sen.
2. *Organ of sense, mental faculty,* αἰσθητήριον.
Heb. 5. 14 have their senses exercised to discern both

SENSUAL —
Animal, sensual, sensuous, ψυχικός *psuchikos.*
Jas. 3. 15 This wisdom..(is) earthly, sensual, devil.
Jude 19 These be they..sensual, having not the

SENT (back) —
1. *To send,* שָׁלַח *shalach.*
Gen. 32. 18 it (is) a present sent unto my lord Esau
1 Ki. 14. 6 for I (am) sent to thee (with) heavy (tid.)
Jer. 49. 14 an ambassador is sent unto the heathen
Eze. 2. 9 behold, an hand (was) sent unto me, and
3. 5 thou (art) not sent to a people of a stran
23. 40 men..unto whom a messenger (was) sent
2. *Sending,* שִׁלּוּחִים *shilluchim.*
Exod 18. 2 took Zipporah..after he had sent her ba.
3. *To send off or away,* ἀποστέλλω *apostellō.*
John 9. 7 Siloam, which is, by interpretation, Sent
4. *One sent off or away,* ἀπόστολος *apostolos.*
John 13. 16 neither he that is sent greater than he th.

SENT (away, forth), to be —
1. *To be sent,* שָׁלַח *shalach,* 2.
Esth. 3. 13 the letters were sent by posts into all the
2. *To be sent,* שָׁלַח *shalach,* 4.
Gen. 44. 3 the men were sent away, they and their
Judg. 5. 15 Barak: he was sent on foot into the val.
Prov 17. 11 a cruel messenger shall be sent against
Dan. 10. 11 stand upright: for unto thee am I now se.
Obad. 1 an ambassador is sent among the heath.
3. *To send,* שְׁלַח *shelach.*
Ezra 7. 14 Forasmuch as thou art sent of the king
Dan. 5. 24 Then was the part of the hand sent from
4. *To be sent off or away,* ἀποστέλλομαι *apostellomai.*
Heb. 1. 14 Are they not all ministering spirits, s. fo.

SENTENCE, dark, divine, hard —
1. *An acute or sharp saying,* אֲחִידָה *achidah.*
Dan. 5. 12 showing of hard sentences, and dissolv.
2. *A word, utterance,* דָּבָר *dabar.*
Deut 17. 9 they shall show thee the sentence of jud.
17. 11 shalt not decline from the sentence
3. *Acute saying, hidden thing, riddle,* חִידָה *chidah.*
Dan. 8. 23 a king..understanding dark sentences
4. *The mouth,* פֶּה *peh.*
Deut 17. 11 According to the sentence of the law wh.
5. *Word, utterance,* דָּבָר *dabar.*
Deut 17. 10 thou shalt do according to the sentence
6. *Judgment,* מִשְׁפָּט *mishpat.*
Psa. 17. 2 Let my sentence come forth from thy pr.
Jer. 4. 12 now also will I give sentence against th.
7. *Word, matter, sentence,* פִּתְגָם *pithgam.*
Eccl. 8 11 Because sentence against an evil work is
8. *Divination, oath,* קֶסֶם *qesem.*
Prov 16. 10 A divine sentence (is) in the lips of the k.
9. *A judicial sentence,* ἀπόκριμα *apokrima.*
2 Co. 1. 9 we had the sentence of death in ourselves

SENTENCE, to be or give —
1. *To judge upon or about,* ἐπικρίνω *epikrinō.*
Luke 23. 24 Pilate gave sentence that it should be as
2. *To judge,* κρίνω *krinō.*
Acts 15. 19 my sentence is, that we trouble not them

SE-NU'-AH, הַסְּנוּאָה *the violated.* See *Hasenuah.*
A Benjamite, father of Judah who was second over Jerusalem in the days of Nehemiah. B.C. 445.
Neh. 11. 9 Judah the son of S. (was) second over the

SE-O'-RIM, שְׂעֹרִים *fear, distress.*
A priest in the days of David, to whom the fourth charge of the sanctuary was given by lot. B.C. 1015.
1 Ch. 24. 8 The third to Harim, the fourth to S.

SEPARATE, separated —
Separate, נָזִיר *nazir.*
Gen. 49. 26 of him that was separate from his breth.
Deut 33. 16 of him (that was) separated from his br.

SEPARATE (selves), to —
1. *To be separated,* בָּדַל *badal,* 2.
Num 16. 21 Separate yourselves from among this co.
Ezra 6. 21 all such as had separated themselves un.
9. 1 have not separated themselves from the
10. 8 himself separated from the congregation
10. 11 separate yourselves from the people of
1 Ch. 12. 8 there separated themselves unto David
Neh. 9. 2 the seed of Israel separated themselves
10. 28 they that had separated themselves from
2. *To separate,* בָּדַל *badal,* 5.
Lev. 20. 24 which have separated you from (other) pe.
20. 25 which I have separated from you as unc.
Num. 8. 14 Thus shalt thou separate the Levites from
16. 9 that the God of Israel hath separated you
Deut 10. 8 the LORD separated the tribe of Levi, to
19. 2, 7 Thou shalt separate three cities for th.
29. 21 the LORD shall separate him unto evil out
1 Ki. 8. 53 thou didst separate them from among all
1 Ch. 25. 1 Moreover David..separated to the service
2 Ch. 25. 10 Amaziah separated them, (to wit), the ar.
Ezra 8. 24 I separated twelve of the chief of the pr.
Neh. 13. 3 that they separated from Israel all the mi.
Isa. 56. 3 The LORD hath utterly separated me from
59. 2 your iniquities have separated between
3. *To give or take a portion,* חָלַק *chalaq,* 5.
Jer. 37. 12 to separate himself thence in the midst
4. *To be separated,* נָזַר *nazar,* 2.
Lev. 22. 2 that they separate themselves from the
Eze. 14. 7 which separateth himself from me, and
Hos. 9. 10 and separated themselves unto (that) sh.
Zech. 7. 3 separating myself, as I have done these
5. *To separate,* נָזַר *nazar,* 5.
Lev. 15. 31 Thus shall ye separate the children of Is.
Num. 6. 2 to vow a vow..to separate (themselves)
6. 3 He shall separate (himself) from wine and
6. 5 in the which he separateth (himself) unto
6. 6 All the days that he separateth (himself)
6. *To do any thing wonderful,* פָּלָא *pala.*
Num. 6. 2 either man or woman shall separate (th.)
7. *To be parted, separated,* פָּרַד *parad,* 2.
Gen. 13. 9 separate thyself, I pray thee, from me
13. 11 they separated themselves the one from
Prov 18. 1 a man, having separated himself, seeketh
8. *To part, separate,* פָּרַד *parad,* 5.
Gen. 30. 40 Jacob did separate the lambs, and set the
Deut 32. 8 when he separated the sons of Adam, he
Prov 16. 28 and a whisperer separateth chief friends
17. 9 he that repeateth a matter separateth..f.
9. *To border off thoroughly,* ἀποδιορίζω *apodiorizō.*
Jude 19 These be they who separate themselves
10. *To border off,* ἀφορίζω *aphorizō.*
Matt 25. 32 he shall separate them one from another
Luke 6. 22 when they shall separate you (from their
Acts 13. 2 Separate me Barnabas and Saul for the
19. 9 separated the disciples, disputing daily
Rom. 1. 1 an apostle, separated unto the gospel of
Gal. 1. 15 who separated me from my mother's wo.
2. 12 he withdrew and separated himself, fear.
11. *To put apart,* χωρίζω *chōrizō.*
Rom. 8. 35 Who shall separate us from the love of C.
8. 39 shall be able to separate us from the love

SEPARATE cities or place —
1. *A cut off place,* גִּזְרָה *gizrah.*
Eze. 41. 12 building that (was) before the separate p.
41. 13 the separate place, and the building, wi.
41. 14 and of the separate place toward the east
41. 15 the building over against the separate pl.
42. 1 that (was) over against the separate place
42. 10 over against the separate place, and over
42. 13 which (are) before the separate place, the
2. *Separate cities,* מִבְדָּלוֹת *mibdaloth.*
Josh. 16. 9 the separate cities for the children of E.

SEPARATE, separated, to be —
1. *To be separated,* בָּדַל *badal,* 2.
1 Ch. 23. 13 Aaron was separated, that he should sa.
Ezra 10. 16 all of them by (their) names, were separ.
2. *To be made wonderful or separate,* פָּלָה *palah,* 2.
Exod 33. 16 so shall we be separated, I and thy people
3. *To be parted,* פָּרַד *parad,* 2.
Gen. 13. 14 after that Lot was separated from him
25. 23 two manner of people shall be separated
Neh. 4. 19 we are separated upon the wall, one far
Prov 19. 4 the poor is separated from his neighbour
4. *To part,* פָּרַד *parad,* 3.
Hos. 4. 14 themselves are separated with whores, and
5. *To border off,* ἀφορίζω *aphorizō.*
2 Co. 6. 17 be ye separate, saith the Lord, and touch
6. *To put apart,* χωρίζω *chōrizō.*
Heb. 7. 26 holy, harmless, undefiled, separate from

SEPARATION, (to make a) —
1. *To cause a separation,* בָּדַל *badal,* 5.
Eze. 42. 20 to make a separation between the sanct.
2. *Separation, impurity,* נִדָּה *niddah.*
Lev. 12. 2 according to the days of the separation
12. 5 be unclean two weeks, as in her separat.
15. 20 that she lieth upon in her separation
15. 25 many days out of the time of her separa.
15. 25 if it run beyond the time of her separat.
15. 25 shall be as the days of her separation
15. 26 be unto her as the bed of her separation
15. 26 as the uncleanness of her separation
Num 19. 9 shall be kept..for a water of separation
19. 13 the water of separation was not sprinkled
19. 20 the water of separation hath not been sp.
19. 21 the water of separation shall wash his cl.
19. 21 he that toucheth the water of separation
31. 23 be purified with the water of separation
3. *Separation,* נֵזֶר *nezer.*
Num. 6. 4 All the days of his separation shall he e.
6. 5 All the days of the vow of his separation
6. 8 All the days of his separation he (is) holy
6. 12 consecrate..the days of his separation
6. 12 lost, because his separation was defiled
6. 13 when the days of his separation are fulfi.
6. 18 shall shave the head of his separation (at)
6. 18 take the hair of the head of his separati.
6. 19 after (the hair of) his separation is shaven
6. 21 offering unto the LORD for his separation
6. 21 he must do after the law of his separation

SE'-PHAR, סְפָר.
A mount of the East in the S.W. of Arabia, on the S. of Yemen; or *Thafor* in Hadramaut, at the sea, in Arabia Felix.
Gen. 10. 30 as thou goest unto S., a mount of the east

SE-PHA'-RAD, סְפָרַד.
The ancient Iberia or Georgia, between Colchis and Albania; or Spain, so Targums, Peshito, Ben Gannach, Kimchi, etc.
Obad. 20 captivity of Jerusalem, which (is) in S.

SE-PHAR-VA'-IM, סְפַרְוַיִם.
A city in S. Mesopotamia (called also *Sipphara* and *Sifris*), joined with Babylon, Cutha, Ava, Hamath, Arpad, Hena, Ivah, Gozan, Carchemish, Haran, Rezeph, Telassar, as being conquered by Shalmanezer. B.C. 710.
2 Ki. 17. 24 from Ava, and from Hamath, and from S.
17. 31 Adrammelech..Anammelech..gods of S.
18. 34 where (are) the gods of S., Hena, and Ivah?
19. 13 Where (is) the king..of the city of S., of
Isa. 36. 19 where (are) the gods of S.? and have
37. 13 Where (is) the king..of the city of S., He.

SE-PHAR-VITES, סְפַרְוִים.
The inhabitants of Sepharvaim; they were accustomed to burn their children in the fire to Adrammelech and Anammelech their gods, even after their removal to Samaria.
2 Ki. 17. 31 the S. burnt their children in fire to Adr.

SEPULCHRE —
1. *Grave,* קְבוּרָה *qeburah.*
Deut 34. 6 no man knoweth of his sepulchre unto
1 Sa. 10. 2 thou shalt find two men by Rachel's sep.
2 Ki. 9. 28 buried him in his sepulchre with his fat.
21. 26 he was buried in his sepulchre in the ga.
23. 30 and buried him in his own sepulchre
2. *Grave,* קֶבֶר *qeber.*
Gen. 23. 6 in the choice of our sepulchres bury thy
23. 6 none of us shall withhold..his sepulchre
Judg. 8. 32 was buried in the sepulchre of Joash his
2 Sa. 2. 32 buried him in the sepulchre of his father
4. 12 buried (it) in the sepulchre of Abner in
17. 23 was buried in the sepulchre of his father
21. 14 in Zelah, in the sepulchre of Kish his fat.
1 Ki. 13. 22 carcase shall not come unto the sepulchre
13. 31 bury me in the sepulchre wherein the man
2 Ki 13. 21 they cast the man into the sepulchre of
23. 16 he spied the sepulchres that (were) there
23. 16 took the bones out of the sepulchres, and
23. 17 (It is) the sepulchre of the man of God, wh.
2 Ch. 16. 14 they buried him in his own sepulchres, wh.
21. 20 but not in the sepulchres of the kings
24. 25 they buried him not in the sepulchres of
28. 27 they brought him not into the sepulchres
32. 33 buried him in the chiefest of the sepulch,
35. 24 was buried in (one of) the sepulchres of
Neh. 2. 3 the place of my fathers' sepulchres (lieth)
2. 5 unto the city of my fathers' sepulchres
3. 16 (the place) over against the sepulchres of
Psa. 5. 9 their throat (is) an open sepulchre; they
Isa. 22. 16 thou hast hewed thee out a sepulchre here
22. 16 he that heweth him out a sepulchre on
Jer. 5. 16 Their quiver (is) as an open sepulchre, th.

3. *Monument, tomb,* μνῆμα *mnēma.*
Luke 23. 53 laid it in a sepulchre that was hewn in
24. 1 they came unto the sepulchre, bringing
Acts 2. 29 and his sepulchre is with us unto this day
7. 16 laid in the sepulchre that Abraham boug.

4. *Monument, tomb,* μνημεῖον *mnēmeion.*
Matt 23. 29 and garnish the sepulchres of the righteo.
27. 60 a great stone to the door of the sepulchre
28. 8 they departed quickly from the sepulchre
Mark 15. 46 laid him in a sepulchre which was hewn
15. 46 rolled a stone unto the door of the sepul.
16. 2 they came unto the sepulchre at the rising
16. 3 the stone from the door of the sepulchre
16. 5 entering into the sepulchre, they saw a
16. 8 fled from the sepulchre; for they trembled
Luke 11. 47 ye build the sepulchres of the prophets
11. 48 killed them, and ye build their [sepulch.]
23. 55 beheld the sepulchre, and how his body
24. 2 the stone rolled away from the sepulchre
24. 9 returned from the sepulchre, and told all
24. 12 Then arose Peter, and ran unto the sepul.
24. 22 women..which were early at the sepulchre
24. 24 [certain of them..went to the sepulchre]
John 19. 41 in the garden a new sepulchre, wherein
19. 42 for the sepulchre was nigh at hand
20. 1 cometh Mary Magdalene..unto the sepu.
20. 1 seeth the stone taken..from the sepulchre
20. 2 taken away the Lord out of the sepulchre
20. 3 went forth..and came to the sepulchre
20. 4 other disciple..came first to the sepulchre
20. 6 went into the sepulchre, and seeth the li.
20. 8 disciple which came first to the sepulchre
20. 11 Mary stood without at the sepulchre we.
20. 11 stooped down, (and looked) into the sep.
Acts 13. 29 took (him) down..and laid (him) in a sep.

5. *Burying place,* τάφος *taphos.*
Matt 23. 27 ye are like unto whited sepulchres, which
27. 61 Mary, sitting over against the sepulchre
27. 64 Command..that the sepulchre be made
27. 66 they went, and made the sepulchre sure
28. 1 came Mary Magdalene..to see the sepul.
Rom. 3. 13 Their throat (is) an open sepulchre: with

SE'-RAH, SA'-RAH, שֶׂרַח, שָׂרַח *extension.*
A daughter of Asher, and sister of Jimnah, Ishuah, and Beriah, who went down to Egypt with Jacob. B.C. 1706.
Gen. 46. 17 Ishuah, and Isui, and Beriah, and S. their
Num 26. 46 name of the daughter of Asher (was) S.
1 Ch. 7. 30 Isuah, and Ishuai, and Beriah, and S. the

SE-RA'-IAH, שְׂרָיָהוּ, שְׂרָיָה *Jah is prince*
1. David's scribe. B.C. 1020.
2 Sa. 8. 17 (were) the priests; and S. (was) the scribe
2. The Son of Azariah, and chief priest at Jerusalem when Nebuchadnezzar took it. B.C. 588.
2 Ki. 25. 18 the captain of the guard took S. the chief
1 Ch. 6. 14 Azariah begat S., and S. begat Jehozadak
Ezra 7. 1 Ezra the son of S., the son of Azariah, the
Jer. 52. 24 the captain of the guard took S. the chief
3. Son of Tanhumeth, from Netophah, whom Gedaliah advised to submit to the Chaldeans. B.C. 588.
2 Ki. 25. 23 Johanan..and S. the son of Tanhumeth
Jer. 40. 8 Johanan..and S. the son of Tanhumeth
4. A son of Kenaz, and brother of Othniel, and father of Joab. B.C. 1450.
1 Ch. 4. 13 the sons of Kenaz; Othniel, and S.: and
4. 14 S. begat Joab, the father of the valley of
5. A Simeonite, son of Asiel. B.C. 700.
1 Ch. 4. 35 Josibiah, the son of S., the son of Asiel
6. A priest that returned with Zerubbabel. B.C. 536.
Ezra 2. 2 Nehemiah, S., Reelaiah, Mordecai, Bils.
Neh. 10. 2 S., Azariah, Jeremiah
12. 1 these..went up..Jeshua: S., Jeremiah, E.
12. 12 of S., Meraiah; of Jeremiah, Hananiah
7. A priest, son of Hilkiah, dwelling in Jerusalem after the exile and called "ruler of the house of God." B.C. 445.
Neh. 11. 11 S. the son of Hilkiah, the son of Meshullam
8. A chief man, son of Aziel, and sent by Jehoiakim to take Jeremiah and Baruch. B.C. 606.
Jer. 36. 26 But the king commanded..S. the son of
9. A prince of Judah, and son of Neriah; he went to Babylon with Zedekiah. B.C. 595.
Jer. 51. 59 Jeremiah the prophet commanded S. the
51. 59 And (this) S. (was) a quiet prince
51. 61 Jeremiah said to S., When thou comest to

SE-RA'-PHIM, שְׂרָפִים *burning, noble.*
Symbolic beings seen in vision, with six wings each, in attendance on the Lord.
Isa. 6. 2 Above it stood the seraphim: each one
6. 6 Then flew one of the seraphim unto me

SE'-RED, סֶרֶד *escape, deliverance.*
The eldest son of Zebulun. B.C. 1700.
Gen. 46. 14 the sons of Zebulun; S., and Elon, and
Num 26. 26 of S., the family of the Sardites: of Elon

SER-GI'-US, Σέργιος.
The Roman deputy of Cyprus when Paul and Barnabas visited it in A.D. 45, and who was converted by Elymas or Bar-Jesus being struck with blindness.
Acts 13. 7 was with the deputy of the country, S. P.

SERJEANT —
One holding a rod, lictor, serjeant, ῥαβδοῦχος.
Acts 16. 35 the magistrates sent the serjeants, saying
16. 38 And the serjeants told these words unto

SERPENT, (fiery) —
1. *To be fearful* or *creep,* זָחַל *zachal* (partic.).
Deut 32. 24 with the poison of serpents of the dust

2. *A serpent,* נָחָשׁ *nachash.*
Gen. 3. 1 the serpent was more subtil than any be.
3. 2 the woman said unto the serpent, We may
3. 4 the serpent said unto the woman, Ye sh.
3. 13 The serpent beguiled me, and I did eat
3. 14 God said unto the serpent, Because thou
49. 17 Dan shall be a serpent by the way, an ad.
Exod. 4. 3 it became a serpent; and Moses fled from
7. 15 rod which was turned to a serpent shalt
Num 21. 6 LORD sent fiery serpents among the peo.
21. 7 that he take away the serpents from us
21. 9 Moses made a serpent of brass, and put
21. 9 that if a serpent had bitten any man, wh.
21. 9 he beheld the serpent of brass, he lived
Deut. 8. 15 (wherein were) fiery serpents, and scorp.
2 Ki. 18. 4 brake in pieces the brasen serpent that M.
Job 26. 13 his hand hath formed the crooked serpent
Psa. 58. 4 Their poison (is) like the poison of a ser.
140. 3 have sharpened their tongues like a ser.
Prov 23. 32 At the last it biteth like a serpent, and
30. 19 the way of a serpent upon a rock, the way
Eccl. 10. 8 whoso breaketh an hedge, a serpent shall
10. 11 Surely the serpent will bite without ench.
Isa. 14. 29 for out of the serpent's root shall come
27. 1 shall punish leviathan the piercing serp.
27. 1 even leviathan that crooked serpent; and
65. 25 dust (shall be) the serpent's meat. They
Jer. 8. 17 I will send serpents, cockatrices, among
46. 22 The voice thereof shall go like a serpent
Amos 5. 19 leaned his hand on the wall, and a serp.
9. 3 thence will I command the serpent, and
Mic. 7. 17 They shall lick the dust like a serpent, th.

3. *A burning, fiery, stinging serpent,* שָׂרָף *saraph.*
Num 21. 8 Make thee a fiery serpent, and set it up.
Isa. 14. 29 and his fruit (shall be) a fiery flying serp.
30. 6 the viper and fiery flying serpent, they

4. *Howler, dragon,* תַּנִּין *tannin.*
Exod. 7. 9 before Pharaoh, (and) it shall become a se.
7. 10 cast down his rod..and it became a serpent
7. 12 they became serpents: but Aaron's rod

5. *A creeping thing, reptile,* ἑρπετόν *herpeton.*
Jas. 3. 7 For every kind of beasts..and of serpents

6. *A serpent,* ὄφις *ophis.*
Matt. 7. 10 Or if he ask a fish, will he give him a ser.
10. 16 be ye therefore wise as serpents, and ha.
23. 33 serpents, (ye) generation of vipers, how
Mark 16. 18 [They shall take up serpents; and if they]
Luke 10. 19 give unto you power to tread on serpents
11. 11 a fish, will he for a fish give him a serpent
John 3. 14 Moses lifted up the serpent in the wilder.
1 Co. 10. 9 tempted, and were destroyed of serpents
2 Co. 11. 3 as the serpent beguiled Eve through his
Rev. 9. 19 for their tails (were) like unto serpents
12. 9 that old serpent, called the Devil, and Sa.
12. 14 half a time, from the face of the serpent
12. 15 serpent cast out of his mouth water as a
20. 2 that old serpent, which is the Devil, and

SE'-RUG, שְׂרוּג *strength, firmness.*
Grandson of Peleg, and father of Nahor father of Terah. B.C. 2180.
Gen. 11. 20 lived two and thirty years, and begat S.
11. 21 after he begat S. two hundred and seven
11. 22 And S. lived thirty years, and begat Nahor
11. 23 S. lived after he begat Nahor two hundr.
1 Ch. 1. 26 S., Nahor, Terah

SERVANT —
1. *Men,* אֲנָשִׁים *anashim.*
1 Sa. 24. 7 So David stayed his servants with these

2. *A young person, youth, servant,* נַעַר *naar.*
Num 22. 22 riding upon his ass, and his two servants
Judg. 7. 10 go thou with Phurah thy servant down to
7. 11 Then went he down with Phurah his ser.
19. 3 having his servant with him, and a couple
19. 9 he, and his concubine, and his servant, his
19. 11 servant said unto his master, Come, I pr.
19. 13 said unto his servant, Come, and let us
Ruth 2. 5, 6 servant that was set over the reapers
1 Sa. 2. 13 priest's servant came, while the flesh was
2. 15 priest's servant came, and said to the man
9. 3 Take now one of the servants with thee
9. 5 Saul said to his servant that (was) with
9. 7 Then said Saul to his servant, But behold
9. 8 servant answered Saul again, and said, B.
9. 10 Then said Saul to his servant, Well said
9. 22 Samuel took Saul and his servant, and br.
9. 27 Bid the servant pass on before us, and
10. 14 uncle said unto him and to his servant
16. 18 Then answered one of the servants, and
21. 2 have appointed (my) servants to such and
25. 19 said unto her servants, Go on before me
2 Sa. 9. 9 called to Ziba, Saul's servant, and said
13. 17 Then he called his servant that minister.
13. 28 Now Absalom had commanded his serva.
13. 29 servants of Absalom did unto Amnon as
16. 1 Ziba the servant of Mephibosheth met him
19. 17 servant of the house of Saul, and his fift.
1 Ki. 18. 43 said to his servant, Go up now, look tow.
19. 3 came to Beersheba..and left his servant
2 Ki. 4. 12 said to Gahazi his servant, Call this Shu.
4. 24 she saddled an ass, and said to her serv.
2 Ki. 4. 25 that he said to Gehazi his servant, Behold
4. 38 said unto his servant, Set on the great pot
5. 20 Gehazi, the servant of Elisha the man of
5. 23 laid (them) upon two of his servants, and
6. 15 his servant said unto him. Alas, my mas.
8. 4 king talked with Gehazi, the servant of
19. 6 with which the servants of the king of A.
Neh. 4. 16 half of my servants wrought in the work
4. 22 Let every one with his servant lodge with
4. 23 neither I, nor my brethren, nor my serv.
5. 10 I likewise, (and) my brethren, and my se.
5. 15 even their servants bare rule over the p.
5. 16 all my servants (were) gathered thither
6. 5 Then sent Sanballat his servant unto me
13. 19 servants set I at the gates, (that) there sh.
Esth. 2. 2 Then said the king's servants that minis.
6. 3 Then said the king's servants that minis.
6. 5 servants said unto him, Behold, Haman
Job 1. 15, 17 the servants with the edge of the swo.
1. 16 burnt up the sheep, and the servants, and
Isa. 37. 6 wherewith the servants of the king of A.

3. *To serve, do, till,* עָבַד *abad.* (partic.).
Gen. 49. 15 bowed his shoulder..and became a servant
2 Ki. 10. 19 call unto me..all his servants, and all his
Zech. 2. 9 and they shall be a spoil to their servants

4. *A servant, doer, tiller, slave,* עֶבֶד *ebed.*
Gen. 9. 25 servant of servants shall he be unto his
9. 26, 27 and Canaan shall be his servant
14. 15 divided himself..he and his servants, by
18. 3 pass not away, I pray thee, from thy ser.
18. 5 for therefore are ye come to your servant
19. 2 turn in, I pray you, into your servant's ho.
19. 19 thy servant hath found grace in thy sight
20. 8 called all his servants, and told all these
21. 25 which Abimelech's servants had violently
24. 2 Abraham said unto his eldest servant of
24. 5 servant said unto him, Peradventure the
24. 9 servant put his hand under the thigh of A.
24. 10 servant took ten camels of the camels of
24. 14 thou hast appointed for thy servant Isaac
24. 17 servant ran to meet her, and said, Let me
24. 34 And he said, I (am) Abraham's servant
24. 52 when Abraham's servant heard their wo.
24. 53 servant brought forth jewels of silver, and
24. 59 sent away..her nurse, and Abraham's se.
24. 61 servant took Rebekah, and went his way
24. 65 For she (had) said unto the servant, What
24. 65 servant (had) said, It (is) my master: the.
24. 66 servant told Isaac all things that he had
26. 15 For all the wells which his father's serv.
26. 19 And Isaac's servants digged in the valley
26. 24 multiply thy seed, for my servant Abrah.
26. 25 and there Isaac's servants digged a well
26. 32 the same day, that Isaac's servants came
27. 37 brethren have I given to him for servants
32. 4 Thy servant Jacob saith thus, I have soj.
32. 10 which thou hast showed unto thy servant
32. 16 delivered (them) into the hand of his ser.
32. 16 said unto his servants, Pass over before
32. 18 (They be) thy servant Jacob's; it (is) a pr.
32. 20 Behold, thy servant Jacob (is) behind us
33. 5 which God hath graciously given thy ser.
33. 14 Let my lord..pass over before his servant
39. 17 servant, which thou hast brought unto us
39. 19 After this manner did thy servant to me
40. 20 he made a feast unto all his servants, and
40. 20 and of the chief baker among his servants
41. 10 Pharaoh was wroth with his servants, and
41. 12 man, an Hebrew, servant to the captain
41. 37 was good..in the eyes of all his servants
41. 38 Pharaoh said unto his servants, Can we
42. 10 but to buy food are thy servants come
42. 11 we (are) true (men), thy servants are no
42. 13 Thy servants (are) twelve brethren, the
43. 28 Thy servant our father (is) in good health
44. 7 God forbid that thy servants should do ac.
44. 9 With whomsoever of thy servants it be
44. 10 he with whom it is found shall be my se.
44. 16 hath found out the iniquity of thy serva.
44. 16 behold, we (are) my lord's servants, both
44. 17 he shall be my servant; and as for you
44. 18 let thy servant..speak a word in my lord's
44. 18 thine anger burn against thy servant, for
44. 19 My lord asked his servants, saying, Have
44. 21 thou saidst unto thy servants, Bring him
44. 23 thou saidst unto thy servants, Except yo.
44. 24 when we came up unto thy servant my fa.
44. 27 And thy servant my father said unto us
44. 30 when I am come to thy servant my father
44. 31 he will die: and thy servants shall bring
44. 31 the grey hairs of thy servant our father
44. 32 For thy servant became surety for the lad
44. 33 let thy servant abide instead of the lad a
45. 16 it pleased Pharaoh well, and his servants
46. 34 Thy servants' trade hath been about cat.
47. 3 Thy servants (are) shepherds, both..and
47. 4 for thy servants have no pasture for their
47. 4 let thy servants dwell in the land of Go.
47. 19 we and our land will be servants unto P.
47. 25 lord, and we will be Pharaoh's servants
50. 2 Joseph commanded his servants the ph.
50. 7 with him went up all the servants of Ph.
50. 17 forgive the trespass of the servants of the
50. 18 and they said, Behold, we (be) thy serva.
Exod. 4. 10 thou hast spoken unto thy servant; but
5. 15 Wherefore dealest thou thus with thy se.
5. 16 There is no straw given unto thy servants
5. 16 behold, thy servants (are) beaten; but the
5. 21 in the eyes of his servants, to put a sword
7. 10 down his rod..before his servants, and it

Exod. 7. 20 in the sight of his servants; and all the
8. 3 into the house of thy servants, and upon
8. 4 upon thy people, and upon all thy serva.
8. 9 when shall I entreat..for thy servants, and
8. 11 from thy servants, and from thy people
8. 21 upon thy servants. and upon thy people
8. 24 servant's houses, and into all the land of
8. 29, 31 from his servants, and from his peop.
9. 14 upon thy servants, and upon thy people
9. 20 He that feared..among the servants of P.
9. 20 made his servants and his cattle flee into
9. 21 left his servants and his cattle in the field
9. 30 But as for thee and thy servants, I know
9. 34 hardened his heart, he and his servants
10. 1 hardened..the heart of his servants, that
10. 6 fill..the houses of all thy servants, and
10. 7 Pharaoh's servants said unto him, How
11. 3 favour..in the sight of Pharaoh's serva.
11. 8 all these thy servants shall come down
12. 30 Pharaoh rose up..and all his servants
12. 44 But every man's servant that is bought
14. 5 heart of Pharaoh and of his servants was
14. 31 believed the LORD, and his servant Moses
21. 2 If thou buy an Hebrew servant, six years
21. 5 if the servant shall plainly say, I love my
21. 20 if a man smite his servant, or his maid
21. 26 if a man smite the eye of his servant, or
32. 13 Remember Abraham, Isaac..thy servants
Lev. 25. 6 meat for you; for thee, and for thy serv.
25. 42, 55 they (are) my servants, which I brou.
25. 55 unto me the children of Israel (are) serv.
Num 11. 11 Wherefore hast thou afflicted thy serva.
12. 7 My servant Moses (is) not so, who (is) fa.
12. 8 not afraid to speak against my servant
14. 24 But my servant Caleb, because he had an.
22. 18 said unto the servants of Balak, If Balak
31. 49 Thy servants have taken the sum of the
32. 4 land for cattle, and thy servants have ca.
32. 5 let this land be given unto thy servants
32. 25 servants will do as my lord commandeth
32. 27 But thy servants will pass over, every m.
32. 31 As the LORD hath said unto thy servants
Deut. 3. 24 thou hast begun to show thy servant thy
5. 15 remember that thou wast a servant in
9. 27 Remember thy servants, Abraham, Isaac
15. 17 and he shall be thy servant for ever. And
23. 15 servant which is escaped from his master
29. 2 unto all his servants, and unto all his land
32. 36 repent himself for his servants, when he
32. 43 for he will avenge the blood of his serva.
34. 5 So Moses the servant of the LORD died th.
34. 11 and to all his servants, and to all his land
Josh. 1. 1 after the death of Moses the servant of
1. 2 Moses my servant is dead; now therefore
1. 7 law which Moses my servant commanded
1. 13 Remember the word of which Moses the s.
1. 15 which Moses the LORD'S servant gave you
5. 14 What saith my LORD unto his servant?
8. 31 As Moses the servant of the LORD comm.
8. 33 as Moses the servant of the LORD had co.
9. 8 said unto Joshua, We (are) thy servants
9. 9 From a very far country thy servants are
9. 11 We (are) your servants: therefore now ma.
9. 24 Because it was certainly told thy servants
9. 24 commanded his servant Moses to give you
10. 6 Slack not thy hand from thy servants, come
11. 12 Moses the servant of the LORD comman.
11. 15 As the LORD commanded Moses his serv.
12. 6 Them did Moses the servant of the LORD
12. 6 servant of the LORD gave it (for) a posses.
13. 8 as Moses the servant of the LORD gave th.
14. 7 Forty years old (was) I when Moses the s.
18. 7 which Moses the servant of the LORD gave
22. 2 Ye have kept all that Moses the servant
22. 4, 5 which Moses the servant of the LORD
24. 29 servant of the LORD died, (being) an hun.
Judg. 2. 8 servant of the LORD died, (being) an hun.
3. 24 When he was gone out, his servants came
6. 27 Then Gideon took ten men of his servants
15. 18 deliverance into the hand of thy servant
19. 19 young man (which is) with thy servants
1 Sa. 3. 9 say, Speak, LORD; for thy servant heareth
3. 10 answered, Speak; for thy servant heareth
8. 14 take your fields..and give (them) to his se.
8. 15 and give to his officers, and to his servants
8. 17 of your sheep: and ye shall be his servants
12. 19 Pray for thy servants unto the LORD thy
16. 15 Saul's servants said unto him, Behold now
16. 16 Let our LORD now command thy servants
16. 17 Saul said unto his servants, Provide me
17. 8 (am) not I a Philistine, and ye servants to
17. 9 kill me, then will we be your servants, but
17. 9 then shall ye be our servants, and serve us
17. 32 servant will go and fight with this Philist.
17. 34 thy servant kept his father's sheep, and
17. 36 Thy servant slew both the lion and the bear
17. 58 son of thy servant Jesse the Beth-lehem.
18. 5 and also in the sight of Saul's servants
18. 22 Saul commanded his servants, (saying)
18. 22 delight in thee, and all his servants love
18. 23 Saul's servants spake those words in the
18. 24 servants of Saul told him, saying, On this
18. 26 when his servants told David these words
18. 30 more wisely than all the servants of Saul
19. 1 Saul spake..to all his servants, that they
19. 4 Let not the king sin against his servant
20. 7 (It is) well; thy servant shall have peace
20. 8 thou shalt deal kindly with thy servant
20. 8 thou hast brought thy servant into a cove.
21. 7 a certain man of the servants of Saul (was)
21. 11 the servants of Achish said unto him, (Is)
21. 14 Then said Achish unto his servants, Lo

1 Sa. 22. 6 all his servants (were) standing about him
22. 7 Saul said unto his servants that stood ab.
22. 8 my son hath stirred up my servant against
22. 9 which was set over the servants of Saul
22. 14 who (is so) faithful among all thy servants
22. 15 Let not the king impute..unto his servant
22. 15 thy servant knew nothing of all this, less
22. 17 the servants of the king would not put fo.
23. 10 thy servant hath certainly heard that Saul
23. 11 will Saul come down, as thy servant hath
23. 11 O LORD..I beseech thee, tell thy servant
25. 8 give..whatsoever cometh..unto thy serv.
25. 10 Nabal answered David's servants, and said
25. 10 There be many servants now a days that
25. 39 and hath kept his servant from evil
25. 40 when the servants of David were come to
25. 41 to wash the feet of the servants of my lo.
26. 18 doth my lord thus pursue after his servant
26. 19 let my lord..hear the words of his servant
27. 5 why should thy servant dwell in the royal
27. 12 therefore he shall be my servant for ever
28. 2 thou shalt know what thy servant can do
28. 7 Then said Saul unto his servants, Seek me
28. 7 his servants said to him, Behold, (there
28. 23 But his servants, together with the woman
28. 25 And she brought (it)..before his servants
29. 3 (Is) not this David, the servant of Saul the
29. 8 what hast thou found in thy servant, so
29. 10 with thy master's servants that are come
30. 13 I (am) a young man of Egypt, servant to
2 Sa. 2. 12 the servants of Ish-bosheth the son of Saul
2. 13 the servants of David, went out, and met
2. 15 and twelve of the servants of David
2. 17 Abner was beaten..before the servants of
2. 30 there lacked of David's servants nineteen
2. 31 the servants of David had smitten of Ben.
3. 18 By the hand of my servant David I will sa.
3. 22 the servants of David and Joab came from
3. 38 the king said unto his servants, Know ye
6. 20 in the eyes of the handmaids of his serv.
7. 5 tell my servant David, Thus saith the Lo.
7. 8 so shalt thou say unto my servant David
7. 19 thou hast spoken also of thy servant's ho.
7. 20 for thou, Lord GOD, knowest thy servant
7. 21 hast thou done all..to make thy servant
7. 25 thou hast spoken concerning thy servant
7. 26 and let the house of thy servant David be
7. 27 hast revealed to thy servant, saying, I w.
7. 27 therefore hath thy servant found in his
7. 28 hast promised this goodness unto thy se.
7. 29 to bless the house of thy servant, that it
7. 29 let the house of thy servant be blessed for
8. 2 (so) the Moabites became David's servants
8. 6 Syrians became servants to David, (and)
8. 7 the shields of gold that were on the serv.
8. 14 all they of Edom became David's servants
9. 2 (there was) of the house of Saul a servant
9. 2 (Art) thou Ziba? And he said, Thy serva.
9. 6 And he answered, Behold thy servant!
9. 8 What (is) thy servant, that thou shouldest
9. 10 thy servants, shall till the land for him
9. 10 Ziba had fifteen sons and twenty servants
9. 11 the king hath commanded his servant
9. 12 And all..(were) servants unto Mephibos.
10. 2 to comfort him by the hand of his serva.
10. 2 David's servants came into the land of the
10. 3 hath not David (rather) sent his servants
10. 4 Hanun took David's servants, and shaved
10. 19 the kings (that were) servants to Hadare.
11. 1 David sent Joab, and his servants with
11. 9 Uriah slept..with all the servants of his
11. 11 the servants of my lord, are encamped in
11. 13 to lie on his bed with the servants of his
11. 17 there fell (some) of the people of the ser.
11. 21 Thy servant Uriah the Hittite is dead al.
11. 24 shot from off the wall upon thy servants
11. 24 the king's servants be dead, and thy ser.
12. 18 the servants of David feared to tell him
12. 19 David saw that his servants whispered
12. 19 David said unto his servants, Is the child
12. 21 Then said his servants unto him, What
13. 24 Behold now, thy servant hath sheep she.
13. 24 let..his servants go with thy servant
13. 31 his servants stood by with their clothes
13. 35 the king's sons come: as thy servant said
13. 36 the king also and all his servants wept
14. 19 thy servant Joab, he bade me, and he put
14. 20 hath thy servant Joab done this thing
14. 22 thy servant knoweth that I have found
14. 22 king hath fulfilled the request of his ser.
14. 30 he said unto his servants, See, Joab's field
14. 30 And Absalom's servants set the field on
14. 31 Wherefore have thy servants set my field
15. 2 Thy servant (is) of one of the tribes of Is.
15. 8 thy servant vowed a vow while I abode
15. 14 David said unto all his servants that
15. 15 And the king's servants said unto the ki.
15. 15 thy servants (are ready to do) whatsoever
15. 18 his servants passed on beside him; and
15. 21 even there also will thy servant be
15. 34 say unto Absalom, I will be thy servant
15. 34 (as) I (have been) thy father's servant hit.
15. 34 so (will) I now also (be) thy servant: then
16. 6 he cast stones..at all the servants of king
16. 11 said to Abishai, and to all his servants
17. 20 when Absalom's servants came to the wo.
18. 7 the people..were slain before the servants
18. 9 And Absalom met the servants of David
18. 29 sent the king's servant, and (me) thy ser.
19. 5 shamed this day the faces of all thy serv.
19. 6 thou regardest neither princes nor serv.
19. 7 and speak comfortably unto thy servants

2 Sa. 19. 14 (this word)..Return thou, and all thy se.
19. 17 his fifteen sons and his twenty servants
19. 19 neither..remember that which thy serv.
19. 20 thy servant doth know that I have sinned
19. 26 my servant deceived me: for thy servant
19. 26 go to the king; because thy servant (is) la.
19. 27 he hath slandered thy servant unto my
19. 28 yet didst thou set thy servant among th.
19. 35 can thy servant taste what I eat or what
19. 35 wherefore then should thy servant be yet
19. 36 Thy servant will go a little way over Jor.
19. 37 Let thy servant, I pray thee, turn back ag.
19. 37 behold thy servant Chimham; let him go
20. 6 take thou thy lord's servants, and pursue
21. 15 David went down, and his servants with
21. 22 and fell..by the hand of his servants
24. 10 LORD take away the iniquity of thy serv.
24. 20 saw the king and his servants coming on
24. 21 Wherefore is..the king come to his serv.
1 Ki. 1. 2 his servants said unto him, Let there be
1. 9 all the men of Judah the king's servants
1. 19 Solomon thy servant hath he not called
1. 26 But me, (even) me thy servant, and Zadok
1. 26 and thy servant Solomon, hath he not called
1. 27 thou hast not showed (it) unto thy serv.
1. 33 Take with you the servants of your lord
1. 47 the king's servants came to bless our lord
1. 51 that he will not slay his servant with the
2. 38 as..the king hath said, so will thy servant
2. 39 two of the servants of Shimei ran away
2. 39 saying, Behold, thy servants (be) in Gath
2. 40 went to Gath to Achish to seek his serv.
2. 40 Shimei went, and brought his servants fr.
3. 6 Thou hast showed unto thy servant David
3. 7 thou hast made thy servant king instead
3. 8 thy servant (is) in the midst of thy people
3. 9 Give therefore thy servant an understan.
3. 15 and made a feast to all his servents
5. 1 Hiram king of Tyre sent his servants unto
5. 6 and my servants shall be with thy servants
5. 6 unto thee will I give hire for thy servants
5. 9 My servants shall bring (them) down from
8. 23 who keepest covenant..with thy servants
8. 24 Who hast kept with thy servant David my
8. 25 keep with thy servant David my father
8. 26 which thou spakest unto thy servant Da.
8. 28 have..respect unto the prayer of thy ser.
8. 28, 29 the prayer which thy servant
8. 30 hearken..to the supplication of thy serv.
8. 32 judge thy servants, condemning the wic.
8. 36 forgive the sin of thy servants, and of thy
8. 52 open unto the supplication of thy servant
8. 53 spakest by the hand of Moses thy servant
8. 56 promised by the hand of Moses his servant
8. 59 that he maintain the cause of his servant
8. 66 that the LORD had done for David his se.
9. 22 his servants, and his princes, and his cap.
9. 27 Hiram sent..his servants..with the serv.
10. 5 the sitting of his servants, and the atten.
10. 8 happy (are) these thy servants, which st.
10. 13 went to her own country..and her serva.
11. 11 I will surely..give it to thy servant
11. 13 give one tribe..for David my servant's sa.
11. 17 certain Edomites of his father's servants
11. 26 Solomon's servant, whose mother's name
11. 32 he shall have one tribe for my servant Da.
11. 34 make him prince..for David my servants
11. 36 David my servant may have a light alway
11. 38 keep my statutes..as David my servant
12. 7 If thou wilt be a servant unto this people
12. 7 then they will be thy servants for ever
14. 8 thou hast not been as my servant David
14. 18 which he spake by the hand of his servant
15. 18 delivered them into the hand of his serv.
15. 29 which he spake by his servant Ahijah the
16. 9 his servant Zimri, captain of half (his) ch.
18. 9 that thou wouldest deliver thy servant into
18. 12 I thy servant fear the LORD from my yo.
18. 36 (that) I (am) thy servant, and (that) I have
20. 6 I will send my servants unto thee tomor.
20. 6 thine house, and the houses of thy serva.
20. 9 All that thou didst send for to thy serva.
20. 12 he said unto his servants, Set (yourselves
20. 23 the servants of the king of Syria said unto
20. 31 his servants said unto him, Behold now
20. 32 Thy servant Ben-hadad saith, I pray thee
20. 39 Thy servant went out into the midst of the
20. 40 as thy servant was busy here and there
22. 3 the king of Israel said unto his servants
22. 49 Let my servants go with thy servants in
2 Ki. 1. 13 let..the life of these fifty thy servants, be
2. 16 there be with thy servants fifty strong men
3. 11 one of the king of Israel's servants answ.
4. 1 Thy servant my husband is dead; and thou
4. 1 knowest that thy servant did fear the L.
5. 6 sent Naaman my servant to thee, that th.
5. 13 servants came near, and spake unto him
5. 15 I pray thee, take a blessing of thy servant
5. 17 be given to thy servant two mules' burden
5. 17 for thy servant will henceforth offer nei.
5. 18 LORD pardon thy servant..pardon thy se.
5. 25 And he said, Thy servant went no whither
6. 3 go with thy servants. And he answered, I.
6. 8 took counsel with his servants, saying, In
6. 11 called his servants, and said unto them
6. 12 one of his servants said, None my lord, O
7. 12 said unto his servants, I will now show you
7. 13 one of his servants answered and said, Let
8. 13 (is) thy servant a dog, that he should do
8. 19 destroy Judah for David his servants' sake
9. 7 I may avenge the blood of my servants
9. 7 blood of all the servants of the LORD, at

2 Ki. 9. 11 Then Jehu came forth to the servants of
9. 28 servants carried him in a chariot to Jeru.
9. 36 which he spake by his servant Elijah the
10. 5 We (are) thy servants, and will do all that
10. 10 (that) which he spake by his servant Elij.
10. 23 here with you none of the servants of the
12. 20 his servants arose, and made a conspiracy
12. 21 his servants, smote him, and he died; and
14. 5 slew his servants which had slain the king
14. 25 which he spake by the hand of his servant
16. 7 I (am) thy servant, and thy son; come up
17. 3 became his servant, and gave him presents
17. 13 which I sent to you by my servants the
17. 23 as he had said by all his servants the pro.
18. 12 all that Moses the servant of the LORD co.
18. 24 captain of the least of my master's serv.
18. 26 Speak..to thy servants in the Syrian lan.
19. 5 So the servants of king Hezekiah came to
19. 34 for mine own sake, and for my servant D.
20. 6 for mine own sake, and for my servant D.
21. 8 according to all the law that my servant
21. 10 LORD spake by his servants the prophets
21. 23 servants of Amon conspired against him
22. 9 Thy servants have gathered the money
22. 12 scribe, and Asahiah a servant of the king's
23. 30 servants carried him in a chariot dead fr.
24. 1 Jehoiakim became his servant three years
24. 2 which he spake by his servants the proph.
24. 10 At that time the servants of Nebuchadn.
24. 11 came against the city, and his servants did
24. 12 he, and his mother, and his servants, and
25. 8 servant of the king of Babylon, unto Jer.
25. 24 Fear not to be the servants of the Chaldees
Ch. 2. 34 Sheshan had a servant, an Egyptian, wh.
2. 35 gave his daughter to Jarha his servant to
6. 49 Moses the servant of God had commanded
16. 13 O ye seed of Israel his servant, ye children
17. 4 Go and tell David my servant, Thus saith
17. 7 thus shalt thou say unto my servant Dav.
17. 17 for thou hast (also) spoken of thy servant's
17. 18 thy servant? for thou knowest thy serva.
17. 19 O LORD, for thy servant's sake, and acco
17. 23 thou hast spoken concerning thy servant
17. 24 house of David thy servant (be) established
17. 25 hast told thy servant..thy servant hath fo.
17. 26 promised this goodness unto thy servant
17. 27 please thee to bless the house of thy serv.
18. 2 Moabites became David's servants, (and)
18. 6 Syrians became David's servants, (and) br.
18. 7 shields of gold that were on the servants
18. 13 all the Edomites became David's servants
19. 2 servants of David came into the land of the
19. 3 are not his servants come unto thee for to
19. 4 Wherefore Hanun took David's servants
19. 19 when the servants of Hadarezer saw that
20. 8 they fell..by the hand of his servants
21. 3 (are) they not all my lord's servants? why
21. 8 do away the iniquity of thy servant; for
Ch. 1. 3 which Moses the servant of the LORD had
2. 8 for I know that thy servants can skill to
2. 8 my servants (shall be) with thy servants
2. 10 will give to thy servants, the hewers that
2. 15 the wheat..let him send unto his servants
6. 14 mercy unto thy servants that walk before
6. 15 Thou which hast kept with thy servant
6. 16 keep with thy servant David my father th.
6. 17 which thou hast spoken unto thy servant
6. 19 respect therefore to the prayer of thy ser.
6. 19, 20 the prayer which thy servant prayeth
6. 21 unto the supplications of thy servant, and
6. 23 judge thy servants, by requiting the wic.
6. 27 forgive the sin of thy servants, and of thy
6. 42 remember the mercies of David thy serv.
8. 9 did Solomon make no servants for his wo.
8. 18 sent him, by the hands of his servants, sh.
8. 18 servants that had knowledge of the sea
8. 18 they went with the servants of Solomon
9. 4 sitting of his servants, and the attendance
9. 7 happy (are) these thy servants, which st.
9. 10 servants also of Huram, and the servants
9. 12 and went away..she and her servants
9. 21 went to Tarshish with the servants of H.
10. 7 be kind..they will be thy servants for ever
12. 8 Nevertheless they shall be his servants
13. 6 the servant of Solomon the son of David
24. 6 of Moses the servant of the LORD, and of
24. 9 Moses the servant of God (laid) upon Isr.
24. 25 his own servants conspired against him
25. 3 slew his servants that had killed the king
32. 9 did Sennacherib..send his servants to
32. 16 his servants spake..against his servant
33. 24 servants conspired against him, and slew
34. 16 All that was committed to thy servants
34. 20 commanded..Asaiah a servant of the ki.
35. 23 king said to his servants, Have me away
35. 24 servants therefore took him out of that c.
36. 20 where they were servants to him and his
Ezra 2. 55, 58 the children of Solomon's servants
2. 65 Besides their servants and their maids, of
9. 11 Which thou hast commanded by thy ser.
Neh. 1. 6 thou mayest hear the prayer of thy serv.
1. 6 for the children of Israel thy servants, and
1. 7, 8 thou commandedst thy servant Moses
1. 10 Now these (are) thy servants and thy pe.
1. 11 be attentive to the prayer of thy servant
1. 11 to the prayer of thy servants, who desire to
1. 11 prosper, I pray thee, thy servant this day
2. 5 if thy servant have found favour in thy si.
2. 10, 19 and Tobiah the servant, the Ammonite
2. 20 therefore we his servants will arise and
5. 5 bring into bondage our sons..to be serv.
7. 57, 60 the children of Solomon's servants
Neh. 9. 10 on all his servants, and on all the people
9. 14 and laws, by the hand of Moses thy serv.
9. 36 Behold, we (are) servants this day; and
9. 36 thereof, behold, we (are) servants in it
10. 29 which was given by Moses the servant of
11. 3 and the children of Solomon's servants
Esth. 1. 3 feast unto all his princes and his servants
2. 18 feast unto all his princes and his servants
3. 2 all the king's servants, that (were) in the
3. 3 Then the king's servants, which (were) in
4. 11 All the king's servants, and the people of
5. 11 advanced him above the..servants of the
Job 1. 8 Hast thou considered my servant Job, that
2. 3 Hast thou considered my servant Job, that
3. 19 small and great are there; and the serv.
4. 18 Behold, he put no trust in his servants
7. 2 As a servant earnestly desireth the shad.
19. 16 called my servant, and he gave (me) no
41. 4 wilt thou take him for a servant for ever
42. 7 not spoken of me..as my servant Job (ha.)
42. 8 go to my servant..and my servant Job
42. 8 (the thing which is) right, like my serva.
Psa. 18. *title.* (A Psalm) of David the servant of the
19. 11 Moreover by them is thy servant warned
19. 13 Keep back thy servant also from presum.
27. 9 put not thy servant away in anger: thou
31. 16 Make thy face to shine upon thy servant
34. 22 LORD redeemeth the soul of his servants
35. 27 pleasure in the prosperity of his servant
36. *title.* (A Psalm) of David the servant of the L.
69. 17 hide not thy face from thy servant; for
69. 36 The seed also of his servants shall inher.
78. 70 He chose David also his servant, and took
79. 2 The dead bodies of thy servants have they
79. 10 revenging of the blood of thy servants (wh.
86. 2 save thy servant that trusteth in thee
86. 4 Rejoice the soul of thy servant: for unto
86. 16 give thy strength unto thy servant, and
89. 3 I have sworn unto David my servant
89. 20 I have found David my servant; with my
89. 39 hast made void the covenant of thy serv.
89. 50 Remember, Lord, the reproach of thy se.
90. 13 let it repent thee concerning thy servants
90. 16 Let thy work appear unto thy servants
102. 14 For thy servants take pleasure in her st.
102. 28 children of thy servants shall continue
105. 6 O ye seed of Abraham his servant, ye ch.
105. 17 (even) Joseph, (who) was sold for a serv.
105. 25 turned..to deal subtilely with his servants
105. 26 He sent Moses his servant, (and) Aaron
105. 42 he remembered..Abraham his servant
109. 28 let them be ashamed; but let thy servant
113. 1 Praise, O ye servants of the LORD, praise
116. 16 truly I (am) thy servant; I (am) thy serv.
119. 17 Deal bountifully with thy servant, (that)
119. 23 thy servant did meditate in thy statutes
119. 38 Stablish thy word unto thy servant, who
119. 49 Remember the word unto thy servant, up.
119. 65 Thou hast dealt well with thy servant, O
119. 76 according to thy word unto thy servant
119. 84 How many (are) the days of thy servant?
119. 91 They continue..for all (are) thy servants
119. 122 Be surety for thy servant for good: let
119. 124 Deal with thy servant according unto thy
119. 125 I (am) thy servant; give me understand
119. 135 Make thy face to shine upon thy servant
119. 140 Thy word (is) very pure..thy servant lo.
119. 176 seek thy servant; for I do not forget thy
123. 2 as the eyes of servants (look) unto the hand
132. 10 For thy servant David's sake turn not away
134. 1 bless ye the LORD, all (ye) servants of the
135. 1 praise (him), O ye servants of the LORD
135. 9 upon Pharaoh, and upon all his servants
135. 14 will repent himself concerning his serva
136. 22 (Even) an heritage unto Israel his servant
143. 2 enter not into judgment with thy servant
143. 12 destroy all them..for I (am) thy servant
144. 10 who delivereth David his servant from the
Prov 11. 29 the fool (shall be) servant to the wise of
12. 9 (He that is) despised, and hath a servant
14. 35 The king's favour (is) toward a wise serv.
17. 2 A wise servant shall have rule over a son
19. 10 much less for a servant to have rule over
22. 7 and the borrower (is) servant to the lender
29. 19 A servant will not be corrected by words
29. 21 He that delicately bringeth up his servant
30. 10 Accuse not a servant unto his master, lest
30. 22 For a servant when he reigneth; and a fo.
Eccl. 2. 7 I got (me) servants and maidens, and had
7. 21 lest thou hear thy servant curse thee
10. 7 I have seen servants upon horses, and
10. 7 princes walking as servants upon the ea.
Isa. 14. 2 shall possess them..for servants and ha.
20. 3 Like as my servant Isaiah hath walked na.
22. 20 I will call my servant Eliakim the son of
24. 2 as with the servant, so with his master
36. 9 captain of the least of my master's serv.
36. 11 Speak, I pray thee, unto thy servants in
37. 5 the servants of king Hezekiah came to I.
37. 24 By thy servants hast thou reproached the
37. 35 I will defend this city..for my servant D.
41. 8 thou, Israel, (art) my servant, Jacob wh.
41. 9 Thou (art) my servant; I have chosen th.
42. 1 Behold my servant, whom I uphold; mi.
42. 19 Who (is) blind, but my servant? or deaf
42. 19 who (is)..blind as the LORD'S servant?
43. 10 and my servant whom I have chosen
44. 1 hear, O Jacob my servant; and Israel, wh.
44. 2 Fear not, O Jacob, my servant; and thou
44. 21 thou (are) my servant: I have formed th.
44. 21 thou (art) my servant: O Israel, thou sh.
44. 26 That confirmeth the word of his servant
Isa. 45. 4 For Jacob my servant's sake, and Israel
48. 20 The LORD hath redeemed his servant Ja.
49. 3 Thou (art) my servant, O Israel, in whom
49. 5 formed me from the womb (to be) his ser.
49. 6 that thou shouldest be my servant to ra.
49. 7 to a servant of rulers, Kings shall see and
50. 10 that obeyeth the voice of his servant, that
52. 13 my servant shall deal prudently, he shall
53. 11 by his knowledge shall my righteous ser.
54. 17 This (is) the heritage of the servants of
56. 6 to be his servants, every one that keepeth
63. 17 Return for thy servants' sake, the tribes
65. 8 so will I do for my servants' sakes, that
65. 9 mine elect shall inherit it, and my serv.
65. 13 my servants shall eat, but ye shall be hu.
65. 13 my servants shall drink, but ye shall be
65. 13 my servants shall rejoice, but ye shall be
65. 14 my servants shall sing for joy of heart, but
65. 15 GOD shall..call his servants by another n.
66. 14 shall be known toward his servants, and
Jer. 2. 14 (Is) Israel a servant? (is) he a home born
7. 25 I have even sent unto you all my servants
21. 7 Zedekiah king of Judah, and his servants
22. 2 thou, and thy servants, and thy people th.
22. 4 riding in chariots..he, and his servants
25. 4 the LORD hath sent unto you all his serv.
25. 9 and Nebuchadrezzar the king..my serv.
25. 19 his servants, and his princes, and all his
26. 5 To hearken to the words of my servants
27. 6 into the hand of Nebuchadnezzar..my se.
29. 19 which I sent unto them by my servants
30. 10 fear thou not, O my servant Jacob, saith
33. 21 covenant be broken with David my serv.
33. 22 will I multiply the seed of..my servant
33. 26 will I cast away the seed of..my servant
34. 11 they turned, and caused the servants and
34. 11 brought them into subjection for servants
34. 16 caused every man his servant, and every
34. 16 to be unto you for servants and for hand.
35. 15 I have sent also unto you all my servants
36. 24 nor any of his servants that heard all th.
36. 31 punish him and his seed and his servants
37. 2 neither he, nor his servants, nor the peo.
37. 18 What have I..against thy servants, or ag.
43. 10 I will send and take..my servant, and will
44. 4 sent unto you all my servants the proph.
46. 26 deliver them..into the hand of his serv.
46. 27 fear not thou, O my servant Jacob, and
46. 28 Fear thou not, O Jacob my servant, saith
Lam. 5. 8 Servants have ruled over us: (there is) no.
Eze. 28. 25 land that I have given to my servant Ja.
34. 23 he shall feed them, (even) my servant D.
34. 24 and my servant David a prince among
37. 24 David my servant (shall be) king over th.
37. 25 that I have given unto Jacob my servant
37. 23 my servant David (shall be) their prince
38. 17 I have spoken in old time by my servants
46. 17 if he give a gift..to one of his servants
Dan. 1. 12 Prove thy servants, I beseech thee, ten
1. 13 and as thou seest, deal with thy servants
9. 6 we hearkened unto thy servants the pro.
9. 10 which he set before us by his servant the
9. 11 written in the law of Moses the servant
9. 17 O our God, hear the prayer of thy servant
10. 17 how can the servant of this my lord talk
Joel 2. 29 upon the servants and upon the handm.
Amos 3. 7 he revealeth his secret unto his servants
Mic. 6. 4 redeemed thee out of the house of serva.
Hag. 2. 23 will I take thee, O Zerubbabel, my serv.
Zech. 1. 6 which I commanded my servants the pr.
3. 8 I will bring forth my servant The
Mal. 1. 6 A son honoureth (his) father, and a serv.
4. 4 Remember ye the law of Moses my serv.

5. *A servant, doer, tiller, slave,* עֲבַד *abad.* (partic.).

Ezra 4. 11 Thy servants the men on this side the ri.
5. 11 We are the servants of the God of heaven
Dan. 2. 4 tell thy servants the dream, and we will
2. 7 Let the king tell his servants the dream
3. 26 ye servants of the most high God, come
3. 28 delivered his servants that trusted in him
6. 20 O Daniel, servant of the living God, is thy

6. *To minister,* שָׁרַת *sharath,* 3. (partic.).

Exod 33. 11 his servant Joshua, the son of Nun, a yo.
Num 11. 28 the servant of Moses, (one) of his young
2 Sa. 13. 17 he called his servant that ministered un.
13. 18 his servant brought her out, and bolted
2 Ki. 6. 15 when the servant of the man of God, was
Prov 29. 12 If a ruler hearken to lies, all his servants

7. *A minister,* διάκονος *diakonos.*

Matt 22. 13 Then said the king to the servant, Bind
23. 11 he that is greatest..shall be your servant
Mark 9. 35 (the same) shall be last of all, and servant
John 2. 5 His mother saith unto the servants, Wh.
2. 9 but the servants which drew the water k.
12. 26 where I am, there shall also my servant
Rom 16. 1 Phebe our sister, which is a servant of the

8. *A servant, enslaved,* δοῦλος *doulos.*

Rom. 6. 19 yielded your members servants to uncle.
6. 19 yield your members servants to righteo.

9. *A servant, slave,* δοῦλος *doulos.*

Matt. 8. 9 to my servant, Do this, and he doeth (it)
10. 24 is not above (his) master, nor the servant
10. 25 as his master, and the servant as his lord
13. 27 the servants of the householder came and
13. 28 The [servants] said unto him, Wilt thou
18. 23 which would take account of his servants
18. 26 The servant therefore fell down, and wo.
18. 27 the lord of that servant was moved with
18. 28 the same servant went out and found one
18. 32 O thou wicked servant, I forgave thee all

Matt 20. 27 whosoever will be chief..be your servant
21. 34 he sent his servants to the husbandmen
21. 35 the husbandmen took his servants, and
21. 36 he sent other servants more than the first
22. 3 sent forth his servants to call them that
22. 4 he sent forth other servants, saying, Tell
22. 6 the remnant took his servants, and entre.
22. 8 Then saith he to his servants, The wedd.
22. 10 those servants went out into the highways
24. 45 Who then is a faithful and wise servant
24. 46 Blessed (is) that servant whom his lord wh.
24. 48 if that evil servant shall say in his heart
24. 50 The lord of that servant shall come in a
25. 14 (who) called his own servants, and deliv.
25. 19 the lord of those servants cometh, and re.
25. 21 Well done, (thou) good and faithful serv.
25. 23 Well done, good and faithful servant: th.
25. 26 (Thou) wicked and slothful servant, thou
25. 30 cast ye the unprofitable servant into outer
26. 51 struck a servant of the high priest, and
Mark 10. 44 will be the chiefest, shall be servant of all
12. 2 he sent to the husbandmen a servant, that
12. 4 he sent unto them another servant, and
13. 34 gave authority to his servants, and to ev.
14. 47 smote a servant of the high priest, and cut
Luke 2. 29 now lettest thou thy servant depart in pe.
7. 2 a certain centurion's servant, who was de.
7. 3 that he would come and heal his servant
7. 8 to my servant, Do this, and he doeth (it)
7. 10 found the servant whole that had been si.
12. 37 Blessed (are) those servants, whom the
12. 38 find (them) so, blessed are [those servants]
12. 43 Blessed (is) that servant, whom his lord
12. 45 if that servant say in his heart, My lord
12. 46 The lord of that servant will come in a day
12. 47 that servant, which knew his lord's will
14. 17 sent his servant at supper time to say to
14. 21 that servant came, and showed his lord
14. 21 being angry, said to his servant, Go out
14. 22 the servant said, Lord, it is done as thou
14. 23 the lord said unto the servant, Go out in.
15. 22 the father said to his servants, Bring fo.
17. 7 which of you, having a servant plowing
17. 9 Doth he thank that servant because he
17. 10 We are unprofitable servants: we have do.
19. 13 he called his ten servants, and delivered
19. 15 he commanded these servants to be called
19. 17 Well, thou good servant: because thou
19. 22 will I judge thee, (thou) wicked servant
20. 10 he sent a servant to the husbandmen, th.
20. 11 he sent another servant: and they beat
22. 50 one of them smote the servant of the hi.
John 4. 51 his servants met him, and told (him), say.
8. 34 Whosoever committeth sin is the servant
8. 35 the servant abideth not in the house for
13. 16 The servant is not greater than his lord
15. 15 I call you not servants; for the servant
15. 20 The servant is not greater than his lord
18. 10 smote the high priest's servant, and cut
18. 10 The servant's name was Malchus
18. 18 the servants and officers stood there who
18. 26 One of the servants of the high priest, be.
Acts 2. 18 on my servants and on my handmaidens
4. 29 grant unto thy servants, that with all bo.
16. 17 These men are the servants of the most
Rom. 1. 1 Paul, a servant of Jesus Christ, called (to
6. 16 servants to obey, his servants ye are to
6. 17 God be thanked, that ye were the servants
6. 20 when ye were the servants of sin, ye were
1 Co. 7. 21 Art thou called (being) a servant? care not
7. 22 he that is called in the Lord, (being) a s.
7. 22 he that is called, (being) free, is Christ's s.
7. 23 Ye are bought..be not ye the servants of
2 Co. 4. 5 and ourselves your servants for Jesus' sa.
Gal. 1. 10 pleased men, I should not be the servant
4. 1 the heir..differeth nothing from a serva.
4. 7 thou art no more a servant, but a son
Eph. 6. 5 Servants, be obedient to them that are (y.)
6. 6 as the servants of Christ, doing the will of
Phil. 1. 1 Paul and Timotheus, the servants of Jesus
2. 7 and took upon him the form of a servant
Col. 3. 22 Servants, obey in all things (your) master
4. 1 give unto (your) servants that which is
4. 12 Epaphras, who is (one) of you, a servant
1 Ti. 6. 1 Let as many servants as are under the
2 Ti. 2. 24 the servant of the Lord must not strive
Titus 1. 1 Paul, a servant of God, and an apostle of
2. 9 (Exhort) servants to be obedient unto th.
Phm. 16 Not now as a servant, but above a serva.
Jas. 1. 1 James, a servant of God and of the Lord
1 Pe. 2. 16 not using (your) liberty..but as the serv.
2 Pe. 1. 1 Simon Peter, a servant and an apostle of
2. 19 they themselves are the servants of corr.
Jude 1 Jude, the servant of Jesus Christ, and br.
Rev. 1. 1 to show unto his servants things which
1. 1 signified (it) by his angel unto his servant
2. 20 to seduce my servants to commit fornic.
7. 3 till we have sealed the servants of our G.
10. 7 as he hath declared to his servants the
11. 18 shouldest give reward unto thy servants
15. 3 they sing the song of Moses the servant
19. 2 hath avenged the blood of his servants at
19. 5 Praise our God, all ye his servants, and
22. 3 no more curse..and his servants shall se.
22. 6 sent his angel to show unto his servants

10. *An attendant, servant,* θεράπων *therapōn.*
Heb. 3. 5 Moses verily (was) faithful..as a servant

11. *A domestic, house servant,* οἰκέτης *oiketēs.*
Luke 16. 13 No servant can serve two masters: for
Rom. 14. 4 thou that judgest another man's servant?
1 Pe. 2. 18 Servants, (be) subject to your masters wi.

12. *A child, boy, servant,* παῖς *pais.*
Matt. 8. 6 my servant lieth at home sick of the palsy
8. 8 speak the word only, and my servant sh.
8. 13 his servant was healed in the self same
12. 18 Behold my servant, whom I have chosen
14. 2 said unto his servants, This is John the
Luke 1. 54 He hath holpen his servant Israel, in re.
1. 69 for us in the house of his servant David
7. 7 say in a word, and my servant shall be
15. 26 he called one of the servants, and asked
Acts 4. 25 Who by the mouth of thy servant David

13. *An under rower, underling,* ὑπηρέτης *hupēretēs.*
Matt 26. 58 went in, and sat with the servants, to see
Mark 14. 54 he sat with the servants, and warmed hi.
14. 65 the servants did strike him with the pal.
John 18. 36 then would my servants fight, that I sho.

SERVANT, (hired, born, fellow)—

1. *Hired servant, hireling,* שָׂכִיר *sakir.*
Exod 12. 45 and an hired servant shall not eat thereof
Lev. 22. 10 an hired servant, shall not eat (of) the holy
25. 6 and for thy maid, and..thy hired servant
25. 40 as an hired servant, (and) as a sojourner
25. 50 according to the time of an hired servant
25. 53; Deut. 15. 18; 24. 14.

2. *Fellow slave,* σύνδουλος, Matt. 18. 28, 29, 31, 33, 24, 49; Col. 1. 7; 4. 7; Rev. 6. 11; 19. 10; 22. 9.

3. *A son of the house,* בֶּן־בַּיִת *ben bayith.*
Eccl. 2. 7 and had servants born in my house; also

4. *A hired servant, hireling,* μίσθιος *misthios.*
Luke 15. 17 How many hired servants of my father's
15. 19 make me as one of thy hired servants

5. *A hireling, hired servant,* μισθωτός *misthōtos*
Mark 1. 20 in the ship with the hired servants, and

SERVANTS, to be, become, make —

1. *To be or become a servant,* עָבַד *abad.*
1 Sa. 4. 9 that ye be not servants unto the Hebrews
1 Ch. 19. 19 they made peace..and became his serva.

2. *To make one a servant or slave,* δουλόω *douloō.*
Rom. 6. 18 ye became the servants of righteousness
6. 22 made free from sin, and become servants
1 Co. 9. 19 yet have I made myself servant unto all

SERVANTS, store of —
Service, עֲבֻדָּה *abuddah.*
Gen. 26. 14 possession of herds, and great store of se.

SERVE (self), to —

1. *To serve,* עָבַד *abad.*
Gen. 14. 4 Twelve years they served Chedorlaomer
15. 13 Know..that thy seed..shall serve them
15. 14 that nation, whom they shall serve, will
25. 23 and the elder shall serve the younger
27. 29 Let people serve thee, and nations bow
27. 40 shalt thou live, and shalt serve thy bro.
29. 15 shouldest thou therefore serve me for no.
29. 18 I will serve thee seven years for Rachel
29. 20 And Jacob served seven years for Rachel
29. 25 did not I serve with thee for Rachel? wh.
29. 27 for the service which thou shalt serve with
29. 30 and served with him yet seven other ye.
30. 26 Give (me) my wives..for whom I have se.
30. 29 Thou knowest how I have served thee, and
31. 6 with all my power I have served your fa.
31. 41 I served thee fourteen years for thy two
Exod. 3. 12 ye shall serve God upon this mountain
4. 23 Let my son go, that he may serve me, and
7. 16 that they may serve me in the wilderness
8. 1, 20 Let my people go, that they may serve
9. 1, 13 Let my people go, that they may serve
10. 3 let my people go, that they may serve me
10. 7 that they may serve the LORD their God
10. 8 he said unto them, Go, serve the LORD yo.
10. 11 go now ye (that are) men, and serve the
10. 24 Go ye, serve the LORD; only let your flo.
10. 26 thereof must we take to serve the LORD
10. 26 we know not with what we must serve the
12. 31 and go, serve the LORD, as ye have said
14. 12 Let us alone, that we may serve the Egy.
14. 12 (it had been) better for us to serve the E.
21. 2 Hebrew servant, six years he shall serve
21. 6 bore his ear..he shall serve him for ever
23. 25 ye shall serve the LORD your God, and he
23. 33 if thou serve their gods, it will surely be
Lev. 25. 40 (and) shall serve thee unto the year of ju.
Num. 4. 24 This (is) the service..to serve, and for
4. 26 that is made for them: so shall they serve
8. 25 shall cease waiting..and shall serve no m.
18. 7 ye shall serve: I have given your priest's
18. 21 for their service which they serve, (even)
Deut. 4. 19 be driven to worship them, and serve th.
4. 28 ye shall serve gods, the work of men's ha.
6. 13 Thou shalt fear the LORD thy God, and se.
7. 4 turn away..that they may serve other go.
7. 16 neither shalt thou serve their gods; for th.
8. 19 walk after other gods, and serve them
10. 12 to serve the LORD thy God with all thy
10. 20 him shalt thou serve, and to him shalt th.
11. 13 to serve him with all your heart and with
11. 16 and serve other gods, and worship them
12. 2 the places wherein the nations..served
12. 30 How did these nations serve their gods?
13. 4 ye shall serve him, and cleave unto him
13. 6, 13 Let us go and serve other gods, which
15. 12 be sold unto thee, and serve thee six years
17. 3 hath gone and served other gods, and wo.
20. 11 all the people..they shall serve thee

Deut 28. 14 not go aside..after other gods to serve th.
28. 36 there shalt thou serve other gods, wood
28. 47 thou servedst not the LORD thy God with
28. 48 Therefore shalt thou serve thine enemies
28. 64 thou shalt serve other gods, which neither
29. 18 to go (and) serve the gods of these nations
29. 26 they went and served other gods, and wo.
30. 17 and worship other gods, and serve them
31. 20 serve them, and provoke me, and break
Josh 16. 10 unto this day, and serve under tribute
22. 5 serve him with all your heart, and with
23. 7 neither serve them, nor bow yourselves
23. 16 have gone and served other gods, and bo.
24. 2 Your fathers dwelt..and they served other
24. 14 and serve him in sincerity and in truth
24. 14 which your fathers served on the other si.
24. 14 put away the gods..and serve ye the LORD
24. 15 if it seem evil unto you to serve the LORD
24. 15 choose you this day whom ye will serve
24. 15 the gods which your fathers served, that
24. 15 as for me and my house, we will serve the
24. 16 should forsake the LORD, to serve other
24. 18 will we also serve the LORD; for he (is) our
24. 19 said unto the people, Ye cannot serve the
24. 20 forsake the LORD, and serve strange gods.
24. 21 said unto Joshua, Nay; but we will serve
24. 22 have chosen you the LORD, to serve him
24. 24 LORD our God will we serve, and his voice
24. 31 Israel served the LORD all the days of Jo.
Judg. 2. 7 people served the LORD all the days of Jo.
2. 11 children of Israel did evil..and served Ba.
2. 13 forsook the LORD, and served Baal and As.
2. 19 in following other gods to serve them, and
3. 6 gave their daughters..and served their go.
3. 7 forgat the LORD their God, and served Ba.
3. 8 the children of Israel served Cushan-risha.
3. 14 served Eglon the king of Moab eighteen
9. 28 who (is) Shechem, that we should serve him
9. 28 serve the men..for why should we serve
9. 38 Who (is) Abimelech, that we should serve
10. 6 served Baalim, and Ashtaroth, and the gods
10. 6 forsook the LORD, and served not him
10. 10 forsaken our God, and also served Baalim
10. 13 have forsaken me, and served other gods
10. 16 put away the strange gods..and served
1 Sa. 7. 3 serve him only; and he will deliver you out
7. 4 put away Baalim..and served the LORD
8. 8 have forsaken me, and served other gods
11. 1 Make a covenant..and we will serve thee
12. 10 and have served Baalim and Ashtaroth
12. 10 now deliver us..and we will serve thee
12. 14 If ye will fear the LORD, and serve him, and
12. 20 turn not aside..but serve the LORD with
12. 24 Only fear the LORD, and serve him in tr.
17. 9 then shall ye be our servants, and serve us.
26. 19 driven me out..saying, Go, serve other g.
2 Sa. 10. 19 they made peace with Israel, and served
15. 8 to Jerusalem, then I will serve the LORD
16. 19 whom should I serve..served in thy fat.
22. 44 a people (which) I knew not shall serve
1 Ki. 4. 21 and served Solomon all the days of his l.
9. 6 but go and serve other gods, and worship
9. 9 have worshipped them, and served them
12. 4 make thou..lighter, and we will serve th.
12. 7 wilt serve them, and answer them, and
16. 31 went and served Baal, and worshipped
22. 53 For he served Baal, and worshipped him
2 Ki. 10. 18 served Baal a little, (but) Jehu shall serve
17. 12 For they served idols, whereof the LORD
17. 16 worshipped all the host of heaven, and s
17. 33 They feared the LORD, and served their
17. 35 nor bow yourselves to them, nor serve t.
17. 41 served their graven images, both their c.
18. 7 rebelled against the king..and served him
21. 3 worshipped all the host of heaven, and s.
21. 21 served the idols that his fathers served
25. 24 dwell in the land, and serve the king of
1 Ch. 28. 9 serve him with a perfect heart, and with
2 Ch. 7. 19 go and serve other gods, and worship th.
7. 22 laid hold on other gods..and served them
10. 4 therefore ease..and we will serve thee
24. 18 served groves and idols: and wrath came
30. 8 serve the LORD..that the fierceness of his
33. 3 worshipped all the host..and served them
33. 16 commanded Judah to serve the LORD God
33. 22 for Amon sacrificed..and served them
34. 33 all that were present..to serve the LORD
35. 3 serve now the LORD your God, and his p.
Neh. 9. 35 For they have not served thee in their k.
Job 21. 15 What (is) the Almighty, that we should s.
36. 11 If they obey and serve (him), they shall
39. 9 Will the unicorn be willing to serve thee
Psa. 2. 11 Serve the LORD with fear, and rejoice w.
18. 43 people (whom) I have not known shall s.
22. 30 A seed shall serve him; it shall be acco.
72. 11 before him; all nations shall serve him
97. 7 Confounded be all they that serve graven
100. 2 Serve the LORD with gladness; come be.
102. 22 are gathered together..to serve the LORD
106. 36 served their idols which were a snare un.
Isa. 19. 23 Egyptians shall serve with the Assyrians
60. 12 kingdom that will not serve thee shall p.
Jer. 5. 19 Like as ye have..served strange gods in
5. 19 so shall ye serve strangers in a land (th.
8. 2 loved, and whom they have served, and
11. 10 they went after other gods to serve them
13. 10 walk after other gods, to serve them, and
16. 11 walked after other gods, and have served
16. 13 there shall ye serve other gods day and
22. 9 and worshipped other gods, and served
25. 6 go not after other gods to serve them, and
25. 11 these nations shall serve the king of Ba.

Jer. 25. 14 great kings shall serve themselves of th.
27. 6 the beasts..have I given..to serve
27. 7 all nations shall serve him, and his son, and
27. 7 great kings shall serve themselves of him
27. 8 nation and kingdom which will not serve
27. 9 Ye shall not serve the king of Babylon
27. 11 the nations that..serve him, those will I
27. 12 and serve him and his people, and live
27. 13 the nation that will not serve the king of
27. 14 Ye shall not serve the king of Babylon
27. 17 serve the king of Babylon, and live: where.
28. 14 that they may serve Nebuchadnezzar ki.
28. 14 they shall serve him: and I have given
30. 8 strangers shall no more serve themselves
30. 9 they shall serve the LORD their God, and
34. 9 none should serve himself of them, (to
34. 10 none should serve themselves of them any
34. 14 when he hath served thee six years, thou
35. 15 go not after other gods to serve them, and
40. 9 Fear not to serve the Chaldeans: dwell
40. 9 serve the king of Babylon, and it shall be
44. 3 to serve other gods, whom they knew not
Eze. 20. 39 serve ye every one his idols, and hereaf.
20. 40 there shall all the house..serve me: th
29. 18 for the service that he had served against
29. 20 (for) his labour wherewith he served ag
34. 27 out of the hand of those that served the
48. 18 for food unto them that serve the city
48. 19 they that serve the city shall serve it out
Hos. 12. 12 Israel served for a wife, and for a wife he
Zeph. 3. 9 call upon the name of the LORD, to serve
Mal. 3. 14 It (is) vain to serve God; and what profit
3. 17 as a man spareth his own son that serv.
3. 18 him that serveth God and him that serv

2. *To be caused to serve*, עָבַד *abad*, 6.
Exod 20. 5 Thou shalt not bow down..nor serve th.
23. 24 Thou shalt not bow down..nor serve th.
Deut. 5. 9 Thou shalt not bow down ..nor serve th.
13. 2 go after other gods..and let us serve th.

3. *Service*, עֲבֹדָה *abodah*.
Num. 3. 36 all the vessels thereof, and all that serv

4. *To stand before*, עָמַד לִפְנֵי *amad li-phene*.
Jer. 40. 10 I will dwell at Mizpah, to serve the Cha.
52. 12 came Nebuzar-adan..(which) served the

5. *To do thing to*, עָשָׂה דָבָר לְ *asah dabar le*.
Judg. 8. 1 Why hast thou served us thus, that thou

6. *To cleave, break up, till, serve*, פְּלַח *pelach*.
Dan. 3. 12 they serve not thy gods, nor worship the
3. 14 do not ye serve my gods, nor worship the
3. 17 our God whom we serve is able to deliver
3. 18 we will not serve thy gods, nor worship
3. 28 that they might not serve nor worship any
6. 16 Thy God, whom thou servest continually
6. 20 is thy God, whom thou servest continually
7. 14 that all..nations, and languages, should s.
7. 27 and all dominions shall serve and obey

7. *To minister*, שָׁרַת *sharath*, 3.
Gen. 39. 4 Joseph found grace..and he served him
40. 4 charged Joseph with them, and he served
1 Ch. 27. 1 their officers that served the king in any
2 Ch. 29. 11 chosen you to stand before him, to serve
Esth. 1. 10 the seven chamberlains that served in the
Psa. 101. 6 walketh in a perfect way, he shall serve
Isa. 56. 6 to serve him, and to love the name of the
Eze. 20. 32 We will be as the heathen..to serve wood

8. *To do a deed*, גָּמַל גְּמוּל *gamal gemul*.
Psa. 137. 8 that rewardeth thee as thou hast served

9. *To wait on, minister to*, διακονέω *diakoneō*.
Luke 10. 40 that my sister hath left me to serve alone
12. 37 that he shall gird himself..and serve them
17. 8 serve me, till I have eaten and drunken
22. 26 and he that is chief, as he that doth serve
22. 27 he that sitteth at meat, or he that serveth
22. 27 but I am among you as he that serveth
John 12. 2 made him a supper; and Martha served
12. 26 If any man serve me,..if any man serve me
Acts 6. 2 It is not reason that we should..serve ta.

10. *To serve, be a slave*, δουλεύω *douleuō*.
Matt. 6. 24 No man can serve two masters: for either
6. 24 Ye cannot serve God and mammon
Luke 15. 29 Lo, these many years do I serve thee, ne.
16. 13 No servant can serve two masters: for eit.
16. 13 Ye cannot serve God and mammon
Acts 20. 19 Serving the Lord with all humility of mi.
Rom. 6. 6 that henceforth we should not serve sin
7. 6 we should serve in newness of spirit, and
7. 25 with the mind I myself serve the law of
9. 12 It was said..The elder shall serve the yo.
12. 11 Not slothful..fervent in spirit; serving
14. 18 he that in these things serveth Christ (is)
16. 18 they that are such serve not our Lord J.
Gal. 5. 13 (use) not liberty..but by love serve one
Phil. 2. 22 as a son with the father, he hath served
Col. 3. 24 ye shall receive the reward..for ye serve
1 Th. 1. 9 turned to God from idols to serve the li.
Titus 3. 3 serving divers lusts and pleasures, living

11. *To serve (God)*, λατρεύω *latreuō*.
Matt. 4. 10 thy God, and him only shalt thou serve
Luke 1. 74 that we..might serve him without fear
2. 37 served (God) with fastings and prayers ni.
4. 8 thy God, and him only shalt thou serve
Acts 7. 7 after that shall they come forth, and serve
26. 7 our twelve tribes, instantly serving (God)
27. 23 of God, whose I am, and whom I serve
Rom. 1. 9 God is my witness, whom I serve with my
1. 25 served the creature more than the Crea.
2 Ti. 1. 3 I thank God, whom I serve from (my) for.
Heb. 8. 5 Who serve unto the example and shadow
9. 14 purge your conscience..to serve the liv.
12. 28 let us have grace, whereby we may serve
13. 10 they have no right to eat which serve the
Rev. 7. 15 and serve him day and night in his tem.
22. 3 no more curse..and his servants shall se.

12. *To row as an underling*, ὑπηρετέω *hupēreteō*.
Acts 13. 36 David, after he had served his own gen.

SERVE, to cause or make to —

1. *To work by*, עָבַד בְּ *abad be*.
Exod. 1. 14 wherein they made them serve, Lev. 25. 39.

2. *To cause to serve*, עָבַד *abad*, 5.
Exod. 1. 13 made the children of Israel to serve with
2 Ch. 34. 33 and made all that were present..to serve
Isa. 43. 23 I have not caused thee to serve with an
43. 24 thou hast made me to serve with thy sins
Jer. 17. 4 I will cause thee to serve thine enemies
Eze. 29. 18 caused his army to serve a great service

SERVE, to be made to —

To be made to serve, עָבַד *abad*, 4.
Isa. 14. 3 bondage wherein thou wast made to serve

SERVED, to be —

To be served, עָבַד *abad*, 2.
Eccl. 5. 9 the king (himself) is served by the field

SERVICE, servile, serving, servitor, servitude, divine—

1. *Hands, side, help*, יָד [*yad*].
1 Ch. 6. 31 (they) whom David set over the service of
29. 5 who (then) is willing to consecrate his se.

2. *To serve*, עָבַד *abad*.
Exod 14. 5 that we have let Israel go from serving
Deut 15. 18 a double hired servant (to thee), in serving

3. *Service*, עֲבֹדָה *abodah*.
Gen. 29. 27 we will give thee this also for the service
30. 26 thou knowest my service which I have do.
Exod. 1. 14 and in all manner of service in the field
1. 14 all their service wherein they made them
12. 25 when ye be come..ye shall keep this serv.
12. 26 say unto you, What mean ye by this ser.
13. 5 thou shalt keep this service in this mo.
27. 19 vessels of the tabernacle in all the service
30. 16 shalt appoint it for the service of the ta.
35. 21 for all his service, and for the holy garm.
35. 24 shittim wood, for any work of the service
36. 1 work all manner of work for the service
36. 3 for the work of the service of the sanctu.
36. 5 much more than enough for the service
38. 21 as it was counted..(for) the service of the
39. 40 all the vessels of the service of the taber.
Lev. 23. 7, 8, 21, 25, 35, 36 ye shall do no servile work
Num. 3. 7, 8, to do the service of the tabernacle
3. 26 the cords of it, for all the service thereof
3. 31 the hanging, and all the service thereof
4. 4 This (shall be) the service of the sons of
4. 19 and appoint them every one to his service
4. 23 all that enter in to perform the service
4. 24, 28, 33 This (is) the service of the families
4. 26 all the instruments of their service, and
4. 27 his sons shall be all the service of the sons
4. 27 all their burdens, and in all their service
4. 31, 33 according to all their service in the ta.
4. 32 their instruments, and with all their ser.
4. 47 the service of the ministry, and the serv.
4. 49 every one according to his service, and
7. 5 that they may be to do the service of the
7. 5 give..to every man according to his ser.
7. 7 the sons of Gershon, according to their se.
7. 8 he gave..according unto their service, un.
7. 9 the service of the sanctuary belonging un.
8. 11 they may execute the service of the LORD
8. 19 to do the service of the children of Israel
8. 22 to do their service in the tabernacle of
8. 24 shall go in to wait upon the service of the
8. 25 they shall cease waiting upon the service
8. 26 to keep the charge, and shall do no serv.
16. 9 to do the service of the tabernacle of the
18. 4 keep the charge..for all the service of the
18. 6 to do the service of the tabernacle of the
18. 7 given your priest's office..as a service of
18. 21 service which they serve, (even) the ser.
18. 23 the Levites shall do the service of the ta.
18. 31 it (is) your reward for your service in the
28. 18 ye shall do no manner of servile work
28. 25, 26 ye shall do no servile work
29. 1, 12 ye shall do no servile work: it is a d.
29. 35 ye shall do no servile work (therein)
Josh. 22. 27 that we might do the service of the LORD
1 Ki. 12. 4 make thou the grievous service of thy fa.
1 Ch. 6. 48 (were) appointed unto all manner of ser.
9. 13 able men for the work of the service of
9. 19 Korahites, (were) over the work of the se.
23. 24 that did the work for the service of the
23. 26 nor any vessels of it for the service ther.
23. 28 for the service of the house of the LORD
23. 28 the work of the service of the house of
23. 32 in the service of the house of the LORD
24. 3 according to their offices in their service
24. 19 the orderings of them in their service to
25. 1 separated to the service of the sons of A.
25. 1 of the workmen according to their serv.
25. 6 harps, for the service of the house of God
26. 8 able men for strength for the service, (we.)
26. 30 the business of the LORD, and in the ser.
28. 13 the work of the service of the house of
28. 13 the vessels of service in the house of the
28. 14 for all instruments of all manner of ser.
1 Ch. 28. 14 for all instruments of every kind of serv.
28. 20 the work for the service of the house of
28. 21 they shall be with thee) for all the serv.
28. 21 willing skilful man, for any manner of s.
29. 7 gave for the service of the house of God
2 Ch. 8. 14 the courses of the priests to their service
10. 4 ease thou somewhat the grievous servit.
12. 8 they may know my service, and the serv.
24. 12 gave it to such as did the work of the se.
29. 35 the service of the house of the LORD was
31. 2 every man according to his service, the
31. 16 his daily portion for their service in their
31. 21 every work that he began in the service
34. 13 wrought the work in any manner of serv.
35. 2 encouraged them to the service of the ho.
35. 10 the service was prepared, and the priests
35. 15 they might not depart from their service
35. 16 the service of the LORD was prepared the
Ezra 8. 20 the princes had appointed for the service
Neh. 10. 32 for the service of the house of our God
Psa. 104. 14 grass to grow..and herb for the service of
Lam. 1. 3 captivity..because of great servitude
Eze. 29. 18 caused his army to serve a great service
29. 18 yet had he no wages..for the service that
44. 14 for all the service thereof, and for all that

4. *Service*, עֲבִידָא *abida*.
Ezra 6. 18 for the service of God, which (is) at Jeru.

5. *Service*, פָּלְחָן *polchan*.
Ezra 7. 19 for the service of the house of thy God

6. *A host, service of the host*, צָבָא *tsaba*.
Num. 4. 23 all that enter in to perform the service, to
4. 30, 35, 39, 43 every one that entereth..serv.
8. 24 they shall go in to wait upon the service

7. *Coloured or twined cloth*, שְׂרָד *serad*.
Exod 31. 10 the cloths of service, and the holy garm.
35. 19 The cloths of service..the holy garments
39. 1 of the blue..they made cloths of service
39. 41 The cloths of service..and the holy gar.

8. *To minister*, שָׁרַת *sharath*, 3.
2 Ki. 4. 43 his servitor said, What! should I set this

9. *Ministration, service*, διακονία *diakonia*.
Luke 10. 40 Martha was cumbered about much serving
Rom 15. 31 that my [service] which (I have) for Jeru.
Rev. 2. 19 I know thy works, and charity, and serv.

10. *Public or reverential service*, λατρεία *latreia*.
John 16. 2 yea..will think that he doeth God service
Rom. 9. 4 the giving of the law, and the service (of
12. 1 sacrifice..(which is) your reasonable ser.
Heb. 9. 1 had also ordinances of divine service
9. 6 priests went..accomplishing the service

11. *Public work*, λειτουργία *leitourgia*.
2 Co. 9. 12 the administration of this service not only
Phil. 2. 17 if I be offered upon the sacrifice and serv.
2. 30 to supply your lack of service toward me

SERVICE, to do or use the —

1. *To serve*, עָבַד *abad*.
Num. 4. 37, 41 all that might do service in the taber.
8. 15 go in to do the service of the tabernacle
18. 23 But the Levites shall do the service of the
Jer. 22. 13 useth his neighbour's service without wa.

2. *To minister*, שָׁרַת *sharath*, 3.
Exod 39. 1 to do service in the holy (place), and made

3. *Ministration*, διακονία *diakonia*.
2 Co. 11. 8 robbed other churches..to do you service

4. *To serve, be a slave*, δουλεύω *douleuō*.
Gal. 4. 8 ye did service unto them which by nature
Eph. 6. 7 With good will doing service, as
1 Ti. 6. 2 but rather do (them) service, because they

5. *To serve (God)*, λατρεύω *latreuō*.
Heb. 9. 9 not make him that did the service perfect

SET —

1. *To be founded*, יָסַד *yasad*, 4.
Song 5. 15 His legs (are as) pillars of marble set upon

2. *To be appointed*, יָעַד *yaad*, 6.
Eze. 21. 16 Go thee..whithersoever thy face (is) set

3. *To be filled, full*, מָלֵא *male*, 4.
Song 5. 14 hands (are as) gold rings set with the be.

4. *Arranged, fixed*, τακτός *taktos*.
Acts 12. 21 upon a set day Herod, arrayed in royal

5. *To arrange, set in array*, τάσσω *tassō*.
Luke 7. 8 For I also am a man set under authority

SET (self), to —

1. *To set a border*, גָּבַל *gabal*.
Deut 19. 14 which they of old time have set in thine

2. *To grave, decree*, חָקַק *chaqaq*.
Prov. 8. 27 when he set a compass upon the face of

3. *To give*, יָהַב *yahab*.
2 Sa. 11. 15 Set ye Uriah in the fore front of the hot

4. *To cause to rest, place*, נוּחַ *nuach*, 5.
Gen. 19. 16 and set him without the city
Deut 26. 10 thou shalt set it before the LORD thy God
Judg. 6. 18 bring forth my present, and set (it) before
Isa. 14. 1 set them in their own land: and the str.
46. 7 set him in his place, and he standeth; from

5. *To station self*, יָצַב *yatsab*, 7.
2 Sa. 18. 13 thou thyself wouldest have set thyself ag.
1 Ch. 11. 14 set themselves in the midst of (that) parcel
2 Ch. 20. 17 set yourselves, stand ye (still), and see the

Psa. 2. 2 kings of the earth set themselves, and the
36. 4 he setteth himself in a way (that is) not go.
Hab. 2. 1 set me upon the tower, and will watch to

6. *To set up, place,* יָצַג *yatsag,* 5.
Gen. 30. 38 set the rods which he had pilled before the
43. 9 if I bring him not unto thee, and set him
Deut 28. 56 which would not adventure to set the sole
Judg. 7. 5 him shalt thou set by himself; likewise ev.
1 Sa. 5. 2 brought it into the house of Dagon, and s.
2 Sa. 6. 17 set it in his place, in the midst of the ta.
1 Ch. 16. 1 set it in the midst of the tent that David
Hos. 2. 3 set her as in the day that she was born

7. *To set down,* יָשַׁב *yashab,* 3.
Eze. 25. 4 they shall set their palaces in thee, and m.

8. *To cause to sit down,* יָשַׁב *yashab,* 5.
1 Sa. 2. 8 to set (them) among princes, and to make
1 Ki. 2. 24 set me on the throne of David my father
21. 9, 12 and set Naboth on high among the pe.
21. 10 set two men, sons of Belial, before him, to
2 Ch. 23. 20 set the king upon the throne of the king.
Psa. 68. 6 God setteth the solitary in families: he
113. 8 That he may set (him) with princes, (even)
Lam. 3. 6 He hath set me in dark places, as (they
Eze. 26. 20 shall set thee in the low parts of the ear.

9. *To cause to sit down,* יְתִב *yethib,* 5.
Ezra 4. 10 set in the cities of Samaria, and the rest

10. *To set up, prepare,* כּוּן *kun,* 5.
Ezra 3. 3 they set the altar upon his bases; for fear
Eze. 4. 3 and set thy face against it, and it shall be
4. 7 Therefore thou shalt set thy face toward

11. *To fill up or in,* מָלֵא *male,* 3.
Exod 28. 17 thou shalt set in it settings of stones, (ev.)
31. 5 in cutting of stones, to set (them), and in
35. 33 in the cutting of stones, to set (them), and
39. 10 they set in it four rows of stones: (the first)

12. *To appoint,* מָנָה *manah,* 3.
Dan. 1. 11 prince of the eunuchs had set over Dani.

13. *To appoint,* מְנָא *mena,* 3.
Ezra 7. 25 set magistrates and judges, which may ju.
Dan. 2. 49 set Shadrach, Meshach, and Abed-nego
3. 12 certain Jews whom thou hast set over the

14. *Any thing lifted up,* מַשָּׂא *massa.*
Eze. 24. 25 and that whereupon they set their minds

15. *A sending forth,* מִשְׁלַח *mishlach.*
Deut 23. 20 bless thee in all that thou settest thine
28. 8, 20 in all that thou settest thine hand unto

16. *To cause to rest,* נוּחַ *nuach,* 5.
Eze. 40. 2 set me upon a very high mountain, by wh.

17. *To cause to move,* נוּעַ *nua,* 5.
Dan. 10. 10 an hand touched me, which set me upon

18. *To pour out, anoint,* נָסַךְ *nasak.*
Psa. 2. 6 Yet have I set my king upon my holy hill

19. *To cause to stand, set up,* נָצַב *natsab,* 5.
Gen. 21. 28 Abraham set seven ewe lambs of the flock
21. 29 these seven ewe lambs which thou hast s.
35. 20 Jacob set a pillar upon her grave: that
Deut 32. 8 he set the bounds of the people according
Psa. 41. 12 upholdest me in mine integrity, and set.
74. 17 Thou hast set all the borders of the earth
Jer. 5. 26 they lay wait..they set a trap, they catch
Lam. 3. 12 He hath bent his bow, and set me as a m.

20. *To lift up,* נָשָׂא *nasa.*
Gen. 31. 17 and set his sons and his wives upon cam.
Deut 24. 15 he (is) poor, and setteth his heart upon it
Hos. 4. 8 and they set their heart on their iniquity

21. *To give,* נָתַן *nathan.*
Gen. 1. 17 God set them in the firmament of the he.
9. 13 I do set my bow in the cloud, and it shall
18. 8 took butter and milk..and set (it) before
30. 40 and set the faces of the flocks toward the
41. 41 I have set thee over all the land of Egypt
Exod 25. 30 thou shalt set upon the table showbread
40. 5 thou shalt set the altar of gold for the in.
40. 6 thou shalt set the altar of the burnt offering
40. 7 thou shalt set the laver between the tent
40. 33 and set up the hanging of the court gate
Lev. 17. 10 I will even set my face against that soul
20. 3 I will set my face against that man, and
20. 6 I will even set my face against that soul
26. 1 neither shall ye set up (any) image of st.
26. 11 I will set my tabernacle among you, and
26. 17 I will set my face against you, and ye sh.
Deut. 1. 8 I have set the land before you: go in and
1. 21 God hath set the land before thee: go up
4. 8 this law, which I set before you this day?
11. 26 I set before you this day a blessing and a
11. 32 judgments which I set before you this day
17. 15 thou mayest not set a stranger over thee
28. 1 God will set thee on high above all nations
30. 1 blessing and the curse, which I have set b.
30. 15 I have set before thee this day life and go.
30. 19 I have set before you life and death, bles.
1 Sa. 12. 13 behold, the LORD hath set a king over you
1 Ki. 5. 5 Thy son, whom I will set upon my throne
6. 19 to set there the ark of the covenant of the
6. 27 he set the cherubim within the inner ho.
7. 16 two chapiters of molten brass, to set up.
7. 39 he set the sea on the right side of the ho.
9. 6 my statutes which I have set before you
10. 9 which delighted in thee, to set thee on
2 Ki. 4. 43 should I set this before an hundred men?
4. 44 he set (it) before them, and they did eat
12. 9 set it beside the altar, on the right side
2 Ki. 18. 23 if thou be able on thy part to set riders
25. 28 set his throne above the throne of the ki.
1 Ch 22. 19 set your heart and your soul to seek the
2 Ch 4. 7 set (them) in the temple, five on the right
4. 10 he set the sea on the right side of the ea.
6. 13 and had set it in the midst of the court
7. 19 my commandments, which I have set be.
9. 8 to set thee on his throne, (to be) king for
11. 16 such as set their hearts to seek the LORD
17. 2 set garrisons in the land of Judah, and in
20. 3 set himself to seek the LORD, and procla.
20. 22 the LORD set ambushments against the ch.
24. 8 set it without at the gate of the house of
32. 6 he set captains of war over the people and
Neh. 2. 6 it pleased the king to send me; and I set
5. 7 And I set a great assembly against them
9. 37 unto the kings whom thou hast set over
Psa. 8. 1 who hast set thy glory above the heavens
Eccl. 3. 11 also he hath set the world in their heart
Isa. 27. 4 who would set the briers (and) thorns ag.
36. 8 if thou be able on thy part to set riders
Jer. 1. 15 they shall set every one his throne at the
6. 27 I have set thee (for) a tower and a fortr.
9. 13 forsaken my law which I set before them
21. 8 I set before you the way of life, and the
26. 4 to walk in my law, which I have set bef.
35. 5 And I set before the sons of the house of
44. 10 my statutes, that I set before you and
52. 32 set his throne above the throne of the ki.
Eze. 4. 2 set the camp also against it, and..(batt.)
4. 3 set it (for) a wall of iron between thee and
7. 20 therefore have I set it far from them
12. 6 I have set thee (for) a sign unto the house
14. 8 I will set my face against that man, and
15. 7 I will set my face against them; they sh
16. 18 thou hast set mine oil and mine incense
16. 19 thou hast even set it before them for a sw
17. 22 branch of the high cedar, and will set (it)
19. 8 the nations set against him on every side
21. 15 I have set the point of the sword against
23. 24 I will set judgment before them, and they
23. 25 I will set my jealousy against thee, and
24. 8 I have set her blood upon the top of a ro.
26. 9 he shall set engines of war against thy wa.
26. 20 I shall set glory in the land of the living
27. 10 they hanged the shield..in thee; they set
28. 2 though thou set thine heart as the heart
28. 6 thou hast set thine heart as the heart of
28. 14 I have set thee (so): thou wast upon the
30. 8 when I have set a fire in Egypt, and (wh.)
30. 14 and will set fire in Zoan, and will execute
30. 16 I will set fire in Egypt: Sin shall have gr.
32. 8 will I make dark over thee, and set dark.
32. 25 They have set her a bed in the midst of the
33. 2 take a man of their coasts, and set him for
33. 7 I have set thee a watchman unto the ho.
37. 26 will set my sanctuary in the midst of them
39. 21 I will set my glory among the heathen, and
Dan. 9. 3 I set my face unto the LORD God, to seek by
9. 10 to walk in his laws, which he set before us
10. 12 thou didst set thine heart to understand
10. 15 I set my face toward the ground, and I be.

22. *To stir up, join together,* סָכַךְ *sakak,* 3a.
Isa. 19. 2 I will set the Egyptians against the Egy.

23. *To sustain, support, lean,* סָמַךְ *samak.*
Eze. 24. 2 the king of Babylon set himself against

24. *To cause to fly,* עוּף *uph,* 5 [V.L. 1].
Prov. 23. 5 Wilt thou set thine eyes upon that which

25. *To cause to go up,* עָלָה *alah,* 5.
2 Ch. 3. 5 and set thereon palm trees and chains

26. *To cause to stand,* עָמַד *amad,* 5.
Gen. 47. 7 brought in Jacob..and set him before Ph.
Num. 5. 16 the priest shall bring her near, and set her
5. 18, 30 shall set the woman before the LORD
8. 13 thou shalt set the Levites before Aaron
11. 24 and set them round about the tabernacle
27. 19 set him before Eleazar the priest, and be.
27. 22 he took Joshua, and set him before Eleazar
Judg 16. 25 he made them sport: and they set him be.
2 Sa. 22. 34 and setteth me upon my high places
1 Ch. 22. 2 he set masons to hew wrought stones to
2 Ch. 19. 5 he set judges in the land, throughout all
19. 8 in Jerusalem did Jehoshaphat set of the
23. 10 he set all the people, every man having his
23. 19 he set the porters at the gates of the house
24. 13 they set the house of God in his state, and
29. 25 he set the Levites in the house of the Lo.
35. 2 he set the priests in their charges, and
Ezra 3. 10 they set the priests in their apparel with
Neh. 4. 9 and set a watch against them day and nig.
4. 13 Therefore set I in the lower places behind
4. 13 I even set the people after their families
13. 11 I gathered them together, and set them in
13. 19 (some) of my servants set I at the gates
Job 34. 24 break in pieces mighty men..and set oth.
Psa. 18. 33 maketh my feet like hind's (feet), and se.
31. 8 thou hast set my feet in a large room
Isa. 21. 6 set a watchman, let him declare what he
Eze. 2. 2 the spirit entered into me..and set me up.
3. 24 the spirit entered unto me, and set me up.
24. 11 set it empty upon the coals thereof, that
Dan. 8. 18 but he touched me, and set me upright

27. *To do, make, use,* עָשָׂה *asah.*
2 Ch. 2. 18 he set threescore and ten thousand of th.
Prov 22. 28 ancient land mark..thy fathers have set
Eccl. 7. 14 God also hath set the one over against the

28. *To inspect, appoint,* פָּקַד *paqad.*
Num 27. 16 Let the LORD..set a man over the congre.

29. *To (cause to) appoint,* פָּקַד *paqad,* 5.
Josh. 10. 18 Roll great stones..and set men by it for to
Psa. 109. 6 Set thou a wicked man over him, and let
Isa. 62. 6 I have set watchmen upon thy walls, O J.
Jer. 1. 10 I have this day set thee over the nations
40. 11 that he had set over them Gedaliah the son

30. *To push out, rush,* פָּשַׁט *pashat.*
Judg. 9. 33 thou shalt rise early, and set upon the city

31. *To cause to rise,* קוּם *qum,* 5.
Deut 28. 36 thy king which thou shalt set over thee
Judg. 7. 19 and they had but newly set the watch
Ezra 6. 18 they set the priests in their divisions, and
Psa. 40. 2 set my feet upon a rock, (and) established
Jer. 6. 17 I set watchmen over you, (saying), Hear.
Dan. 6. 1 It pleased Darius to set over the kingdom
6. 3 the king thought to set him over the whole

32. *To cause to ride,* רָכַב *rakab,* 5.
Exod. 4. 20 took his wife and his sons, and set them
2 Sa. 6. 3 they set the ark of God upon a new cart

33. *To put, set, place,* שׂוּם, שִׂים *sum, sim.*
Gen. 4. 15 the LORD set a mark upon Cain, lest any
6. 16 the door of the ark shalt thou set in the
28. 22 this stone, which I have set (for) a pillar
30. 36 he set three days' journey betwixt himself
31. 21 and set his face (toward) the mount Gilead
31. 37 set (it) here before my brethren and thy
44. 21 Bring him..that I may set mine eyes upon
48. 20 and he set Ephraim before Manasseh
Exod. 1. 11 they did set over them taskmasters to affl.
21. 1 the judgments which thou shalt set before
26. 35 thou shalt set the table without the veil
40. 20 and set the staves on the ark, and put the
40. 30 he set the laver between the tent of the
Lev. 20. 5 I will set my face against that man, and
24. 6 thou shalt set them in two rows, six on a
Num 21. 8 Make thee a fiery serpent, and set it upon
Deut. 4. 44 this (is) the law which Moses set before
14. 24 thy God shall choose to set his name the.
17. 14 I will set a king over me, like as all the n.
17. 15 Thou shalt in any wise set (him) king over
17. 15 from among thy brethren shalt thou set
32. 46 Set your hearts unto all the words which
Josh. 8. 12 set them to lie in ambush between Beth-el
8. 13 when they had set the people, (even) all
24. 25 set them a statute and an ordinance in S.
Judg. 7. 22 set every man's sword against his fellow
9. 25 men of Shechem set liers in wait for him
20. 29 Israel set liers in wait round about Gibe.
20. 36 liers in wait which they had set beside
1 Sa. 7. 12 took a stone, and set (it) between Mizpeh
9. 20 set not thy mind on them; for they are fo.
9. 23 of which I said unto thee, set it by thee
9. 24 set (it) before Saul..set (it) before thee
10. 19 said unto him, (Nay), but set a king over
18. 5 Saul set him over the men of war; and he
28. 22 let me set a morsel of bread before thee
2 Sa. 12. 20 they set bread before him, and he did eat
18. 1 set captains of thousands and captains of
23. 23 and David set him over his guard
1 Ki. 2. 15 and (that) all Israel set their faces on me
8. 21 I have set there a place for the ark, whe.
12. 29 set the one in Beth-el, and the other put
20. 12 Set (yourselves in array): and they set (th.
2 Ki. 4. 10 let us set for him there a bed, and a table
6. 22 Set bread and water before them, that th.
10. 3 set (him) on his father's throne, and fight
12. 17 Hazael set his face to go up to Jerusalem
21. 7 set a graven image of the grove that he had
1 Ch. 11. 25 and David set him over his guard
2 Ch. 33. 7 set a carved image, the idol which he had
Esth. 2. 17 so that he set the royal crown upon her
3. 1 set his seat above all the princes that (were)
8. 2 Esther set Mordecai over the house of H.
Job 7. 12 a whale, that thou settest a watch over
7. 20 why hast thou set me as a mark against
19. 8 cannot pass, and he hath set darkness in
28. 3 He setteth an end to darkness, and sear.
34. 14 If he set his heart upon man, (if) he gather
38. 10 brake up for it my decreed (place), and set
38. 33 canst thou set the dominions thereof in
Psa. 19. 4 In them hath he set a tabernacle for the
54. 3 they have not set God before them. Selah
78. 7 That they might set their hope in God, and
85. 13 and shall set (us) in the way of his steps
86. 14 sought after my soul, and have not set th.
89. 25 I will set his hand also in the sea, and his
104. 9 Thou hast set a bound that they may not
Song 8. 6 Set me as a seal upon thine heart, as a seal
Isa. 41. 19 I will set in the desert the fir tree, (and)
42. 4 till he have set judgment in the earth: and
50. 7 therefore have I set my face like a flint
57. 7 Upon a..high mountain hast thou set thy
66. 19 I will set a sign among them, and I will
Jer. 7. 30 they have set their abominations in the
21. 10 For I have set my face against this city for
24. 6 For I will set mine eyes upon them for go.
32. 20 Which hast set signs and wonders in the
32. 34 they set their abominations in the house
42. 15 If ye wholly set your faces to enter into
42. 17 men that set their faces to go into Egypt
43. 10 will set his throne upon these stones that
44. 11 I will set my face against you for evil, and
44. 12 that have set their faces to go into the la.
49. 38 set my throne in Elam, and will destroy
Eze. 4. 2 set (battering) rams against it round abo.
5. 5 I have set it in the midst of the nations
6. 2 set thy face toward the mountains of Isr.
7. 20 As for the beauty of his ornament, he set

Eze. 13. 17 set thy face against the daughters of thy
15. 7 when I set my face against them
17. 4 carried it into a land of traffic; he set it
17. 5 placed (it) by great waters, (and) set it (as)
20. 46 Son of man, set thy face toward the south
21. 2 set thy face toward Jerusalem, and drop
23. 24 shall set against thee buckler and shield
23. 41 whereupon thou hast set mine incense and
24. 7 she set it upon the top of a rock; she po.
25. 2 set thy face against the Ammonites, and
28. 21 set thy face against Zidon, and prophesy
29. 2 set thy face against Pharaoh king of Eg.
35. 2 set thy face against mount Seir, and pro.
38. 2 set thy face against Gog, the land of Ma.
40. 4 set thine heart upon all that I shall show
44. 8 ye have set keepers of my charge in my
Dan. 6. 14 set (his) heart on Daniel to deliver him
11. 17 He shall also set his face to enter with the
Hos. 11. 8 shall I set thee as Zeboim? Mine heart is
Amos 7. 8 I will set a plumb line in the midst of my
9. 4 will set mine eyes upon them for evil, and
Obad 4 though thou set thy nest among the stars
Nah. 3. 6 make thee vile, and will set thee as a ga.
Hab. 2. 9 that he may set his nest on high, that he
Zech. 3. 5, 5 set a fair mitre upon his head
6. 11 set (them) upon the head of Joshua the

34. *To set, place, put,* שָׁוָה *shavah,* 3.
Psa. 16. 8 I have set the LORD always before me: be.

35. *To set, put, place,* שִׁית *shith.*
Gen. 41. 33 let Pharaoh..set him over the land of E.
Exod. 7. 23 neither did he set his heart to this also
23. 31 will set thy bounds from the Red sea ev.
Num 24. 1 but he set his face toward the wilderness
1 Sa. 2. 8 and he hath set the world upon them
2 Sa. 19. 28 yet didst thou set thy servant among th.
Job 7. 17 that thou shouldest set thine heart upon
30. 1 I would have disdained to have set with
Psa. 3. 6 people that have set (themselves) against
12. 5 I will set (him) in safety (from him that)
17. 11 they have set their eyes bowing down to
21. 3 thou settest a crown of pure gold on his
62. 10 if riches increase, set not your heart (up.
73. 18 thou didst set them in slippery places
90. 8 Thou hast set our iniquities before thee
101. 3 I will set no wicked thing before mine
132. 11 Of the fruit of thy body will I set upon
140. 5 The proud..they have set gins for me
141. 3 Set a watch, O LORD, before my mouth
Isa. 22. 7 the horsemen shall set themselves in ar.
Jer. 31. 21 set thine heart toward the highway, (ev.)
Hos. 2. 3 set her like a dry land, and slay her with
6. 11 he hath set an harvest for thee, when I re.

36. *To cover,* שָׂכַךְ *shakak.*
Jer. 5. 26 they lay wait, as he that setteth snares

37. *To make to settle down, tabernacle,* שָׁכַן *shaken,* 3.
Neh. 1. 9 that I have chosen to set my name there
Jer. 7. 12 Shiloh, where I set my name at the first

38. *To send out or forth,* שָׁלַח *shalach,* 3.
Judg. 1. 8 and smitten..and set the city on fire
20. 48 they set on fire all the cities that they ca.
2 Ki. 8. 12 their strong holds wilt thou set on fire
Jer. 34. 16 whom he had set at liberty at their plea.

39. *To set, put,* שָׁתַת *shathath.*
Psa. 73. 9 They set their mouth against the heavens

40. *To give,* δίδωμι *didōmi.*
Rev. 3. 8 I have set before thee an open door, and

41. *To go in (as the sun),* δύνω *dunō.*
Mark 1. 32 at even, when the sun did set, they bro.
Luke 4. 40 when the sun was setting, all they that h.

42. *To set, place, put,* ἵστημι *histēmi.*
Matt. 4. 5 setteth him on a pinnacle of the temple
18. 2 called a little child, and set him in the
25. 33 he shall set the sheep on his right hand
Mark 9. 36 he took a child, and set him in the midst
Luke 4. 9 and set him on a pinnacle of the temple
9. 47 Jesus..took a child, and set him by him
John 8. 3 [and when they had set her in the midst]
Acts 4. 7 when they had set them in the midst, th.
5. 27 when they had brought them, they set
6. 6 Whom they set before the apostles: and
22. 30 brought Paul down, and set him before

43. *To cause to sit down,* καθίζω *kathizō.*
1 Co. 6. 4 set them to judge who are least esteemed
Eph. 1. 20 set (him) at his own right hand in the he.

44. *To set down,* καθίστημι *kathistēmi.*
Heb. 2. 7 [didst set him over the works of thy hands]

45. *To put, set, place,* τίθημι *tithēmi.*
Acts 13. 47 I have set thee to be a light of the Gent.
1 Co. 12. 18 now hath God set the members every one
12. 28 God hath set some in the church, first a.
Rev. 10. 2 he set his right foot upon the sea, and (his)

[*See also* Affection, aright, in array, bounds, evidently, a feast, fire, forward, fully, a king, love, open in order, a print, seal, steadfastly, in uproar, at variance, work.]

SET (down), to be—

1. *To go in,* בּוֹא *bo.*
Gen. 28. 11 tarried there..because the sun was set

2. *To be built up,* בָּנָה *banah,* 2.
Mal. 3. 15 they that work wickedness are set up; yea

3. *To be caused to rest, placed,* נוּחַ *nuach,* 6.
Zech. 5. 11 shall be established, and set there upon

4. *To be set, placed, put,* שׂוּם, שִׂים *sum, sim,* 6 [V.L. יִשַׁם].
Gen. 24. 33 there was set (meat) before him to eat: but

5. *To sit down, abide,* יָשַׁב *yashab.*
2 Ch. 6. 10 am set on the throne of Israel, as the Lo.
Psa 122. 5 For there are set thrones of judgment, the
Song 5. 12 of waters, washed with milk, (and) fitly set

6. *To cause to sit down, set down,* יְתִב *yethib.*
Dan. 7. 10 judgment was set, and the books were op.

7. *Fillings in,* מִלֻּאִים *milluim.*
Exod 25. 7 Onyx stones, and stones to be set in the
35. 9, 27 stones to be set for the ephod, and for
1 Ch. 29. 2 to be set, glistering stones, and of divers

8. *To be set up, appointed,* נָצַב *natsab,* 2.
Isa. 21. 8 and I am set in my ward whole nights

9. *To be given,* נָתַן *nathan,* 2.
Esth 6. 8 crown royal which is set upon his head
Eccl. 10. 6 Folly is set in great dignity, and the rich
Eze. 32. 23 Whose graves are set in the sides of the

10. *To be caused to go round,* סָבַב *sabab,* 6.
Exod 28. 11 thou shalt make them to be set in ouches

11. *An inspector,* פָּקִיד *paqid.*
2 Ki. 25. 19 he took an officer that was set over the men

12. *To rise or stand up,* קוּם *qum.*
1 Ki. 14. 4 for his eyes were set by reason of his age

13. *To be embroidered, set, fastened,* שָׁבַץ *shabats,* 4.
Exod 28. 20 they shall be set in gold in their inclosings

14. *To come,* ἔρχομαι *erchomai.*
Acts 19. 27 our craft is in danger to be set at nought

15. *To set down,* καθίζω *kathizō.*
Matt. 5. 1 when he was set, his disciples came unto
Heb. 8. 1 who is set on the right hand of the

16. *To lie, be laid,* κεῖμαι *keimai.*
Matt. 5. 14 city that is set on an hill cannot be hid
Luke 2. 34 this (child) is set for the fall and rising ag.
John 2. 6; 19. 29; Phil. 1. 17; Rev. 4. 2.

17. *To fall back,* ἀναπίπτω *anapiptō.*
John 13. 12 So after he..was set down again

SET (a mark), to —

To scribble, make a mark, תָּוָה *tavah,* 5.
Eze. 9. 4 set a mark upon the foreheads of the men

SET a time, to —

To cause to meet, convene, יָעַד *yaad,* 5
Job 9. 19 if of judgment, who shall set me a time

SET about, to —

1. *To fence,* סוּג *sug.*
Song 7. 2 belly (is like) an heap of wheat set about

2. *To put around,* περιτίθημι *peritithēmi.*
Mark 12. 1 set an hedge about (it), and digged (a pl.

SET again (at one), to —

1. *To cause to turn back,* שׁוּב *shub,* 5.
1 Sa. 5. 3 took Dagon, and set him in his place again

2. *To lead together into peace,* συνελαύνω εἰς εἰρήνην.
Acts 7. 26 [would have set them at one again], saying

SET apart, or aside, to (be) —

1. *Separation, impurity,* נִדָּה *niddah.*
Eze. 22. 10 humbled her that was set apart for pollu.

2. *To cause to remove, journey,* נָסַע *nasa,* 5.
2 Ki. 4. 4 and thou shalt set aside that which is full

3. *To cause to pass over,* עָבַר *abar,* 5.
Exod 13. 12 That thou shalt set apart unto the LORD

4. *To separate,* פָּלָה *palah,* 5.
Psa. 4. 3 know that the LORD hath set apart him th.

SET at (liberty, nought), to —

1. *Array, arrangement,* עֵרֶךְ *erek.*
2 Ki. 12. 4 money that every man is set at, (and) all

2. *To free, make naked or void, refuse,* פָּרַע *para.*
Prov. 1. 25 But ye have set at nought all my counsel

3. *To send away,* ἀποστέλλω *apostellō.*
Luke 4. 18 to set at liberty them that are bruised

4. *To make of no importance,* ἐξουδενόω *exoudenoō.*
Mark 9. 12 suffer many things, and be set at nought

5. *To make of no importance,* ἐξουθενέω *exoutheneō.*
Luke 23. 11 Herod..set him at nought, and mocked
Acts 4. 11 This is the stone which was set at nought
Rom 14. 10 why dost thou set at nought thy brother

SET by, to be (much) —

1. *To be or become great,* גָּדַל *gadal.*
1 Sa. 26. 24 as thy life was much set by this day in mi.
26. 24 so let my life be much set by in the eyes

2. *To be or become precious,* יָקַר *yaqar.*
1 Sa. 18. 30 Saul; so that his name was much set by

SET, to cause to be —

To set, place, put, שׂוּם, שִׂים *sum, sim.*
1 Ki. 2. 19 caused a seat to be set for the king's mot.

SET before, down, together, fast, to —

1. *To cause to rest, put down,* נוּחַ *nuach,* 5.
Deut 26. 4 set it down before the altar of the LORD
1 Sa. 6. 18 whereon they set down the ark of the Lo.

2. *To make firm,* יָצַג *yatsag,* 5.
2 Sa. 15. 24 set down the ark of God; and Abiathar we

3. *To prepare, establish,* כּוּן *kun,* 5.
Psa. 65. 6 by his strength setteth fast the mountains

4. *To cause to rest, put down,* נוּחַ *nuach,* 5.
Eze. 37. 1 set me down in the midst of the valley wh.

5. *To set down,* καθίζω *kathizō.*
Heb. 12. 2 is set down at the right hand of the throne
Rev. 3. 21 am set down with my Father on his throne

6. *To put alongside of,* παρατίθημι *paratithēmi.*
Mark 6. 41 gave (them) to his disciples to set before
8. 6 set before (them); and they did set before
8. 7 commanded to set them also before (them)
Luke 9. 16 gave to the disciples to set before the mu.
10. 8 And..eat such things as are set before you
11. 6 to me, and I have nothing to set before him
Acts 16. 34 he set meat before them, and rejoiced, be.
1 Co. 10. 27 whatsoever is set before you eat, asking no

7. *To lie before or forward,* πρόκειμαι *prokeimai.*
Heb. 6. 18 refuge to lay hold upon the hope set be.
12. 1 run with patience the race that is set
12. 2 who for the joy that was set before him

8. *To set down together,* συγκαθίζω *sugkathizō.*
Luke 22. 55 kindled a fire..and [were set down tog.]

SET eyes or foot on, to —

1. *To gaze intently,* ἀτενίζω *atenizō.*
Acts 13. 9 Saul who also (is..) Paul..set his eyes on

2. *A foot breadth,* βῆμα ποδός *bēma podos.*
Acts 7. 5 not (so much as) to set his foot on: yet he

SET (on) fire, to — [*See* fire.]

1. *To cause light, set on fire,* אוֹר *or,* 5.
Isa. 27. 11 the women come, (and) set them on fire

2. *To consume, cause to burn,* בָּעַר *baar,* 3.
Eze. 39. 9 shall set on fire and burn the weapons

3. *To kindle fire in,* בָּעַר אֵשׁ בְּ *baar (5) esh be.*
Judg 15. 5 when he had set the brands on fire, he let

4. *To kindle, burn,* יָצַת *yatsath,* 5.
Josh. 8. 8 ye shall set the city on fire: according to
8. 19 took it, and hasted and set the city on fi.
Judg. 9. 49 set the hold on fire upon them: so that
2 Sa. 14. 30 he hath barley there; go and set it on fi.
14. 30 And Absalom's servants set the field on
14. 31 have thy servants set my field on fire
Jer. 32. 29 shall come and set fire on this city, and

SET forth (evidently), forward, to —

1. *To be prepared, established,* כּוּן *kun,* 2.
Psa. 141. 2 Let my prayer be set forth before thee

2. *To overlook, be pre-eminent,* נָצַח *natsach,* 3.
1 Ch. 23. 4 set forward the work of the house of the
2 Ch. 34. 12 to set (it) forward; and (other of) the L.
Ezra 3. 8 set forward the work of the house of the
3. 9 to set forward the workmen in the house

3. *To give,* נָתַן *nathan.*
Eze. 27. 10 They of Persia..set forth thy comeliness

4. *To cause to stand,* עָמַד *'amad,* 5.
Dan. 11. 11 he shall set forth a great multitude; but
11. 13 shall set forth a multitude greater than

5. *To open, open up,* פָּתַח *pathach.*
Amos 8. 5 may set forth wheat, making the ephah

6. *To lead up or forth,* ἀνάγω *anagō.*
Acts 21. 2 finding a ship..we went aboard, and set f.

7. *To show off,* ἀποδείκνυμι *apodeiknumi.*
1 Co. 4. 9 God hath set forth us the apostles last, as

8. *To write or describe before,* προγράφω *prographō*
Gal. 3. 1 Christ hath been evidently set forth

9. *To lie or be laid before,* πρόκειμαι *prokeimai.*
Jude 7 are set forth for an example, suffering the

10. *To put before,* προτίθημι *protithēmi.*
Rom. 3. 25 Whom God hath set forth (to be) a propit.

11. *To put, place,* τίθημι *tithēmi.*
John 2. 10 Every man at the beginning doth set forth

SET (forth) in order or array, to —

1. *To bind, direct, join,* אָסַר *asar.*
2 Ch. 13. 3 Abijah set the battle in array with an ar.

2. *To array, arrange,* עָרַךְ *arak.*
Exod 40. 4 bring in the table, and set in order the
40. 23 he set the bread in order upon it before
Lev. 24. 8 he shall set it in order before the LORD
Judg 20. 22 set their battle again in array, in the place
1 Sa. 17. 2 set the battle in array against the Philist.
17. 8 Why..come out to set (your) battle in ar.?
2 Sa. 10. 17 the Syrians set themselves in array against
1 Ch. 19. 11 they set (themselves) in array against the
19. 17 and set (the battle) in array against them
2 Ch. 13. 3 Jeroboam also set the battle in array agai.
14. 10 they set the battle in array in the valley
Job 6. 4 the terrors of God do set themselves in ar.
33. 5 set (thy words) in order before me, stand
Psa. 50. 21 I will reprove thee, and set (them) in or.
Isa. 44. 7 shall declare it, and set it in order for me
Jer. 6. 23 they ride upon horses, set in array as men
50. 9 they shall set themselves in array against
Joel. 2. 5 as a strong people set in battle array

3. *Array, arrangement,* עֵרֶךְ *erek.*
Exod 40. 4 the things that are to be set in order up.
40. 23 he set the bread in order upon it before

4. *To be set up, prepared,* כּוּן *kun,* 2.
2 Ch. 29. 35 the service of the house..was set in order

5. *To set up, command,* צָוָה *tsavah,* 3.
2 Ki. 20. 1 Set thine house in order; for thou shalt
Isa. 38. 1 Set thine house in order: for thou shalt
6. *To make straight or right,* תָּקַן *taqan,* 3.
Eccl. 12. 9 sought out, (and) set in order many pro.
7. *To be joined,* שָׁלַב *shalab,* 4.
Exod 26. 17 Two tenons..set in order one against an.
8. *To set up (or again) in array,* ἀνατάσσομαι.
Luke 1. 1 to set forth in order a declaration of tho.
9. *To arrange throughout or thoroughly,* διατάσσομαι.
1 Co. 11. 34 And the rest will I set in order when I co.
10. *To make right also,* ἐπιδιορθόω *epidiorthoō.*
Titus 1. 5 that thou shouldest set in order the things

SET light (by one), to —
1. *To esteem lightly,* קָלָה *qalah,* 5.
Deut 27. 16 Cursed (be) he that setteth light by his fa.
2. *To make light of,* קָלַל *qalal,* 5.
Eze. 22. 7 In thee have they set light by father and

SET office —
Steadfastness, stability, אֱמוּנָה *emunah.*
1 Ch. 9. 22 whom..the seer did ordain in their set offi.
9. 26 four chief porters, were in (their) set office
9. 31 Mattithiah..had the set office over the th.
2 Ch. 31. 15 in the cities of the priests, in (their) set off.
31. 18 in their set office they sanctified themse.

SET on, to (be) —
1. *A setting down, what is set down,* נַחַת *nachath.*
Job 36. 16 that which should be set on thy table (sh.
2. *To move, persuade,* סוּת *suth,* 5.
Jer. 38. 22 Thy friends have set thee on, and have pr.
43. 3 the son of Neriah setteth thee on against
3. *To set, place, put,* שׂוּם, שִׂים *sum, sim.*
Gen. 43. 31 refrained himself, and said, Set on bread
43. 32 they set on for him by himself, and for th.
4. *To set on, appoint,* שָׁפַת *shaphath.*
2 Ki. 4. 38 Set on the great pot, and seethe pottage
Eze. 24. 3 set on a pot, set (it) on, and also pour wa.
5. *To cause to go up on,* ἐπιβιβάζω *epibibazō.*
Luke 10. 34 set him on his own beast, and brought him
19. 35 upon the colt, and they set Jesus thereon
Acts 23. 24 that they may set Paul on, and bring (him)
6. *To cause to sit upon,* ἐπικαθίζω *epikathizō.*
Matt 21. 7 brought the ass..and [set (him) thereon]
7. *To put upon,* ἐπιτίθημι *epitithēmi.*
Mark 4. 21 Is a candle..not to be set on a candlestick
Luke 8. 16 setteth (it) on a candlestick, that they wh.
Acts 18. 10 and no man shall set on thee to hurt thee

SET stedfastly, to —
To fix firmly, στηρίζω *stērizō.*
Luke 9. 51 he stedfastly set his face to go to Jerus.

SET over, (to be) —
1. *To be set, set up,* נָצַב *natsab,* 2.
Ruth 2. 5, 6 servant that was set over the reapers
1 Sa. 22. 9 which was set over the servants of Saul
2. *To cause to stand,* עָמַד *amad,* 5.
1 Ch. 6. 31 these (are they) whom David set over the
3. *To inspect, appoint,* פָּקַד *paqad.*
2 Ch. 23. 14 captains of hundreds that were set over

SET, to be privily —
To watch secretly, צָפַן *tsaphan.*
Psa. 10. 8 his eyes are privily set against the poor

SET time —
A limit, set or appointed time, חֹק *choq.*
Job 14. 13 that thou wouldest appoint me a set time

SET up, to —
1. *To build, build up,* בָּנָה *banah.*
Eze. 39. 15 then shall he set up a sign by it till the
2. *To perfect, finish,* כְּלַל *kelal,* 8.
Ezra 5. 11 a great king of Israel builded and set up
3. *To perfect, finish,* כְּלַל *kelal,* 8a.
Ezra 4. 12 have set up the walls (thereof), and joined
4. 13 this city be builded, and the walls set up
4. 16 be builded..and the walls thereof set up
4. *To set up,* נָצַב *natsab,* 5.
Gen. 35. 14 Jacob set up a pillar in the place where
Josh. 6. 26 in his youngest (son) shall he set up the
1 Sa. 15. 12 he set him up a place, and is gone about
1 Ki. 16. 34 set up the gates thereof in his youngest
2 Ki. 17. 10 they set them up images and groves in
Jer. 31. 21 Set thee up way marks, make thee high
6. *To lift up,* נָשָׂא *nasa.*
Isa. 11. 12 he shall set up an ensign for the nations
45. 20 that set up the wood of their graven
Jer. 4. 6 Set up the standard toward Zion: retire
6. 1 and set up a sign of fire in Beth-haccerem
50. 2 set up a standard; publish, (and) conceal
51. 12 Set up the standard upon the walls of B.
51. 27 Set ye up a standard in the land, blow the
6. *To give (up, forth),* נָתַן *nathan.*
Dan. 12. 11 abomination that maketh desolate set up
7. *To cause to go up,* עָלָה *alah,* 5.
Eze. 14. 7 setteth up his idols in his heart, and pu.
8. *To cause to go up,* עָלָה *alah,* 5.
Eze. 14. 3 these men have set up their idols in their
14. 4 Every man..that setteth up his idols in
9. *To cause to stand,* עָמַד *amad,* 5.
2 Ch. 25. 14 set them up (to be) his gods, and bowed
33. 19 set up groves and graven images, before
Ezra 2. 68 offered..for the house of God to set it up
Neh. 3. 1 they sanctified it, and set up the doors of
3. 3, 6, 13, 14, 15 set up the doors thereof, the
6. 1 I had not set up the doors upon the gates
7. 1 wall was built, and I had set up the doors
10. *To cause to rise up,* קוּם *qum,* 5.
Exod 40. 2 shalt thou set up the tabernacle of the te.
Num. 1. 51 the Levites shall set it up: and the stra.
7. 1 the day that Moses had fully set up the
10. 21 (the other) did set up the tabernacle ag.
Deut 16. 22 Neither shalt thou set thee up (any) im.
27. 2 thou shalt set thee up great stones, and
27. 4 ye shall set up these stones, which I co.
Josh. 4. 9 Joshua set up twelve stones in the midst
24. 26 set it up there under an oak that (was) by
Judg 18. 30 the children of Dan set up the graven im.
2 Sa. 3. 10 and to set up the throne of David over Is.
7. 12 I will set up thy seed after thee, which
1 Ki. 7. 21 he set up the pillars in the porch of the
7. 21 he set up the right pillar, and called the
7. 21 he set up the left pillar, and called the
15. 4 to set up his son after him, and to estab.
1 Ch. 21. 18 David should go up, and set up an altar
Job 16. 12 shaken me to pieces, and set me up for
Isa. 23. 13 they set up the towers thereof, they rai.
Jer. 10. 20 (there is) none..to set up my curtains
23. 4 I will set up shepherds over them which
51. 12 Set up the watchmen, prepare the ambu.
Eze. 34. 23 I will set up one shepherd over them, and
Dan. 2. 21 he removeth kings, and setteth up kings
2. 44 shall the God of heaven set up a kingdom
3. 1 he set it up in the plain of Dura, in the
3. 2, 3, 3, 7 that Nebuchadnezzar..had set up
3. 5 that Nebuchadnezzar the king hath set up
3. 12, 18 the golden image which thou hast set up
3. 14 the golden image which I have set up
4. 17 and setteth up over it the basest of men
11. *To raise up,* רוּם *rum,* 3a.
Ezra 9. 9 to set up the house of our God, and to re.
Psa. 27. 5 hide me; he shall set me up upon a rock
Eze. 31. 4 the deep set him up on high with her r.
12. *To cause to rise, raise up,* רוּם *rum,* 5.
Gen. 31. 45 Jacob took a stone, and set it up (for) a
Psa. 75. 7 he putteth down one, and setteth up an.
89. 42 Thou hast set up the right hand of his a
Isa. 49. 22 I will..set up my standard to the people
Lam. 2. 17 hath set up the horn of thine adversaries
Dan. 5. 19 whom he would he set up, and whom he
13. *To make or set on high,* שָׂגַב *sagab,* 3.
Isa. 9. 11 the LORD shall set up the adversaries of
14. *To set, place, put,* שׂוּם, שִׂים *sum, sim.*
Gen. 28. 18 set it up (for) a pillar, and poured oil up.
Exod 40. 8 thou shalt set up the court round about
40. 18 set up the boards thereof, and put in the
40. 21 set up the veil of the covering, and cove.
40. 28 he set up the hanging (at) the door of the
Job 5. 11 To set up on high those that be low; that
Psa. 74. 4 Thine enemies..they set up their ensigns
Isa. 57. 8 Behind the doors..hast thou set up thy
Jer. 11. 13 have ye set up altars to (that) shameful
15. *To cause to settle down,* שָׁכַן *shaken,* 5.
Josh. 18. 1 set up the tabernacle of the congregation
16. *To make right again,* ἀνορθόω *anorthoō.*
Acts 15. 16 I will build again..and I will set it up
17. *To put over or upon,* ἐπιτίθημι *epitithēmi.*
Matt. 27. 37 set up over his head his accusation writ.
18. *To set, place, put,* ἵστημι *histēmi.*
Acts 6. 13 set up false witnesses, which said, This

SET up, to be —
1. *To make erect,* זְקַף *zeqaph.*
Ezra 6. 11 being set up, let him be hanged thereon
2. *To be anointed,* נָסַךְ *nasak,* 2.
Prov. 8. 23 I was set up from everlasting, from the
3. *To be set up,* נָצַב *natsab,* 6.
Gen. 28. 12 behold a ladder set up on the earth, and

SET with, to —
To sow, זָרַע *zara.*
Isa. 17. 10 plant pleasant plants, and shalt set it wi.

SETH, SHETH, שֵׁת *compensation, sprout,* Σήθ.
1. The son of Adam and Eve, born after the death of Abel. B.C. 3874–2962.
Gen. 4. 25 and she bare a son, and called his name S.
4. 26 to S., to him also there was born a son
5. 3 after his image; and called his name S.
5. 4 the days of Adam after he had begotten S.
5. 6 And S. lived an hundred and five years
5. 7 S. lived after he begat Enos eight hundred
5. 8 the days of S. were nine hundred and tw.
1 Ch. 1. 1 Adam, S., Enosh
Luke 3. 38 of Enos, which was (the son) of S., which
2. An unknown king or race.
Num 24. 17 and shall..destroy all the children of S.

SE'-THUR, סְתוּר *secreted, hidden.*
An Asherite, son of Michael, whom Moses sent to spy out the land. B.C. 1490.
Num. 13. 13 Of the tribe of Asher S. the son of Michael

SETTER forth —
A teller forth, announcer, καταγγελεύς *kataggeleus.*
Acts 17. 18 He seemeth to be a setter forth of strange

SETTING —
1. *A filling in,* מִלֻּאָה *milluah.*
Exod 28. 17 thou shalt set in it settings of stones, (e.)
2. *To give,* נָתַן *nathan.*
Eze. 43. 8 In their setting of their threshold by my
3. *With,* μετά *(gen.) meta.*
Matt 27. 66 sealing the stone, and setting a watch

SETTLE —
A border, עֲזָרָה *azarah.*
Eze. 43. 14 (even) to the lower settle (shall be) two
43. 14 from the lesser settle (even) to the..set.
43. 17 the settle (shall be) fourteen cubits long
43. 20 on the four corners of the settle, and up.
45. 19 the four corners of the settle of the altar

SETTLE, to —
1. *To cause to sit down,* יָשַׁב *yashab,* 5.
Eze. 36. 11 I will settle you after your old estates, a.
2. *To deepen, make go down,* נָחַת *nachath,* 3.
Psa. 65. 10 thou settlest the furrows thereof; thou
3. *To cause to stand still,* עָמַד *amad,* 5.
2 Ki. 8. 11 he settled his countenance stedfastly, un.
1 Ch. 17. 14 I will settle him in mine house and in my
4. *To be quiet, at rest,* שָׁקַט *shaqat.*
Jer. 48. 11 he hath settled on his lees, and hath not
5. *To lay a foundation, establish firmly,* θεμελιόω.
1 Pe. 5. 10 make you perfect..strengthen, [settle]
6. *To put, place, set,* τίθημι *tithēmi.*
Luke 21. 14 [Settle] (it) therefore in your hearts, not

SETTLED, to be —
1. *To be sunk, settled, fastened,* טָבַע *taba,* 6.
Prov. 8. 25 Before the mountains were settled, before
2. *To be set up,* נָצַב *natsab,* 2.
Psa. 119. 89 For ever, O LORD, thy word is settled in

SETTLED (place, that are) —
1. *A prepared place,* מָכוֹן *makon.*
1 Ki. 8. 13 a settled place for thee to abide in for ev.
2. *To be congealed, hardened,* קָפָא *qapha.*
Zeph. 1. 12 punish the men that are settled on their
3. *Seated, settled,* ἑδραῖος *hedraios.*
Col. 1. 23 continue in the faith grounded and settled

SEVEN (fold, times), seventh —
1. *Weeks,* שְׁבֻעַ *[shabua].*
Eze. 45. 21 have the passover, a feast of seven days
2. *Seven,* שֶׁבַע, שִׁבְעָה *sheba, shibah.*
Gen. 4. 24 truly Lamech seventy and sevenfold
5. 7 Seth lived..eight hundred and seven ye.
5. 25 lived an hundred eighty and seven years
5. 26 lived after he begat Lamech seven hun.
5. 31 seven hundred seventy and seven years
7. 2 thou shalt take to thee by sevens, the m.
7. 3 Of fowls also of the air by sevens, the ma.
7. 4 yet seven days, and I will cause it to rain
7. 10 it came to pass after seven days, that the
8. 10, 12 And he stayed yet other seven days
8. 14 on the seven and twentieth day of the
11. 21 Reu lived..two hundred and seven years
21. 28 Abraham set seven ewe lambs of the flock
21. 29 What (mean) these seven ewe lambs wh.
21. 30 For (these) seven ewe lambs shalt thou ta.
23. 1 Sarah was an hundred and seven and tw.
25. 17 an hundred and thirty and seven years
29. 18 I will serve thee seven years for Rachel
29. 20 Jacob served seven years for Rachel; and
29. 27 thou shalt serve with me yet seven other
29. 30 and served with him yet seven other ye.
31. 23 pursued after him seven days' journey; and
33. 3 bowed himself to the ground seven times
41. 2, 18 there came up out of the river seven
41. 3 seven other kine came up after them out
41. 4 did eat up the seven well favoured and
41. 5 seven ears of corn came up upon one st.
41. 6 seven thin ears and blasted with the east
41. 7 the seven thin ears devoured the seven r.
41. 19 seven other kine came up after them, poor
41. 20 ill favoured kine did eat up the first sev.
41. 22 seven ears came up in one stalk, full and
41. 23 seven ears, withered, thin, (and) blasted
41. 24 the thin ears devoured the seven good e.
41. 26 The seven good kine (are) seven years, a.
41. 26 the seven good ears (are) seven years: the
41. 27 And the seven thin and ill favoured kine
41. 27 that came up after them (are) seven yea.
41. 27 the seven empty ears..shall be seven ye.
41. 29 there come seven years of great plenty
41. 30 there shall arise after them seven years
41. 34 take up the fifth part. in the seven plen.
41. 36 for store to the land against the seven y.
41. 47 in the seven plenteous years the earth br.
41. 48 he gathered up all the food of the seven
41. 53 the seven years of plenteousness that was
41. 54 the seven years of dearth began to come
46. 25 she bare these..all the souls (were) seven
47. 28 age of Jacob was an hundred forty and s.
50. 10 he made a mourning for his father seven

Exod. 2. 16 Now the priest of Midian had seven dau.
6. 16 (were) an hundred thirty and seven years
6. 20 (were) an hundred and thirty and seven
7. 25 seven days were fulfilled, after that the
12. 15 Seven days shall ye eat unleavened bread
12. 19 Seven days shall there be no leaven found
13. 6 Seven days thou shalt eat unleavened br.
13. 7 Unleavened bread shall be eaten seven da.
22. 30 seven days it shall be with his dam; on
23. 15 thou shalt eat unleavened bread seven d.
25. 37 thou shalt make the seven lamps thereof
29. 30 shall put them on seven days, when he
29. 35 seven days shalt thou consecrate them
29. 37 Seven days thou shalt make an atonem.
34. 18 Seven days thou shalt eat unleavened br.
37. 23 he made his seven lamps, and his snuffers
38. 24 seven hundred and thirty shekels, after
38. 25 a thousand seven hundred and threescore
38. 28 of the thousand seven hundred seventy
Lev. 4. 6 sprinkle of the blood seven times before
4. 17 sprinkle (it) seven times before the LORD
8. 11 sprinkled thereof upon the altar seven ti
8. 33 ye shall not go out..(in) seven days, until
8. 33 for seven days shall he consecrate you
8. 35 Therefore shall ye abide..seven days, and
12. 2 she shall be unclean seven days; accord.
13. 4 shut up (him that hath) the plague seven
13. 5, 21, 26 priest shall shut him up seven da.
13. 31 shut up (him that hath) the plague..sev.
13. 33 shut up (him that hath) the scall seven d.
13. 50 shut up (it that hath) the plague seven da.
13. 54 and he shall shut it up seven days more
14. 7 he shall sprinkle upon him..seven times
14. 8 shall tarry abroad out of his tent seven da.
14. 16 sprinkle of the oil with his finger seven
14. 27 sprinkle..(some) of the oil..seven times
14. 38 the priest shall..shut up the house seven
14. 51 And he shall..sprinkle the house seven ti.
15. 13 he shall number to himself seven days for
15. 19 she shall be put apart seven days; and
15. 24 he shall be unclean seven days; and all
15. 28 she shall number to herself seven days, and
16. 14 shall he sprinkle of the blood..seven times
16. 19 shall sprinkle of the blood..seven times
22. 27 then it shall be seven days under the dam
23. 6 seven days ye must eat unleavened bread
23. 8 ye shall offer an offering..seven days
23. 15 seven sabbaths shall be complete
23. 18 ye shall offer with the bread seven lambs
23. 34 the feast of tabernacles (for) seven days un.
23. 36 Seven days ye shall offer an offering made
23. 39 keep a feast unto the LORD seven days
23. 40 rejoice before the LORD your God seven
23. 41 keep it a feast unto the LORD seven days
23. 42 ye shall dwell in booths seven days; all
25. 8 thou shalt number seven sabbaths of ye.
25. 8 seven times seven years; and the space of
25. 8 the seven sabbaths of years shall be unto
26. 18 I will punish you seven times more for your
26. 21 I will bring seven times more plagues upon
26. 24 will punish you yet seven times for your
26. 28 I, will chasten you seven times for your
Num. 1. 31 fifty and seven thousand and four hundred
1. 39 threescore and two thousand and seven
2. 8 fifty and seven thousand and four hundr.
2. 26 threescore and two thousand and seven
2. 31 an hundred thousand and fifty and seven
3. 22 (were) seven thousand and five hundred
4. 36 two thousand seven hundred and fifty
8. 2 the seven lamps shall give light over ag.
12. 14 should she not be ashamed seven days?
12. 14 let her be shut out from the camp seven
12. 15 Miriam was shut out from the camp seven
13. 22 Hebron was built seven years before Zoan
16. 49 fourteen thousand and seven hundred
19. 4 and sprinkle of her blood..seven times
19. 11 He that toucheth..shall be unclean seven
19. 14 and all..shall be unclean seven days
19. 16 whosoever toucheth..be unclean seven da
23. 1, 29 said unto Balak, Build me here seven
23. 1 prepare me here seven oxen and seven
23. 4 I have prepared seven altars, and I have
23. 14 built seven altars, and offered a bullock
23. 29 prepare me here seven bullocks and sev.
26. 7 forty and three thousand and seven hun.
26. 34 fifty and two thousand and seven hundr
26. 51 and a thousand seven hundred and thirty
28. 11 seven lambs of the first year without sp.
28. 17 seven days shall unleavened bread be ea.
28. 19, 27 one ram, and seven lambs of the first
28. 21, 29 tenth deal..throughout the seven la.
28. 24 ye shall offer daily, throughout the seven
29. 2, 8, 36 one ram, (and) seven lambs of the fi.
29. 4, 10 for one lamb, throughout the seven
29. 12 shall keep a feast unto the LORD seven
29. 32 seven bullocks, two rams, (and) fourteen
31. 19 do ye abide without the camp seven days
31. 36 three hundred thousand and seven and
31. 43 seven thousand and five hundred sheep
31. 52 sixteen thousand seven hundred and fifty
Deut. 7. 1 seven nations greater and mightier than
15. 1 At the end of (every) seven years thou sh.
15. 9 The seventh year, the year of release, is
16. 3 seven days shalt thou eat unleavened br.
16. 4 there shall be no leavened bread..seven
16. 9 Seven weeks shalt thou number unto th.
16. 9 begin to number the seven weeks from
16. 13 observe the feast of the tabernacles seven
16. 15 Seven days shalt thou keep a solemn fea.
28. 7 they shall..flee before thee seven ways
28. 25 thou shalt..flee seven ways before them
31. 10 At the end of (every) seven years, in the
Josh. 6. 4 seven priests shall bear before the ark se.
6. 4 ye shall compass the city seven times, and
6. 6 let seven priests bear seven trumpets of
6. 8, 13 seven priests bearing the seven trum.
6. 15 and compassed the city..seven times: on.
6. 15 that day they compassed the city seven ti.
18. 2 among the children of Israel seven tribes
18. 5 they shall divide it into seven parts: Ju.
18. 6 describe the land (into) seven parts, and
18. 9 described it by cities into seven parts in
Judg. 6. 1 delivered..into the hand of Midian seven
6. 25 even the second bullock of seven years old
8. 26 a thousand and seven hundred (shekels)
12. 9 and he judged Israel seven years
14. 12 declare it me within the seven days of the
14. 17 she wept before him the seven days
16. 7 If they bind me with seven green withs
16. 8 the lords..brought up to her seven green
16. 13 If thou weavest the seven locks of my head
16. 19 caused him to shave off the seven locks of
20. 15 which were numbered seven hundred ch.
20. 16 seven hundred chosen men left handed
Ruth 4. 15 which is better to thee than seven sons
1 Sa. 2. 5 the barren hath born seven; and she that
6. 1 in the country of the Philistines seven mo.
10. 8 seven days shalt thou tarry, till I come to
11. 3 Give us seven days' respite, that we may se.
13. 8 he tarried seven days, according to the set
16. 10 Jesse made seven of his sons to pass before
31. 13 buried (them) under a tree..and fasted se.
2 Sa. 2. 11 the time that David was king..was seven
5. 5 he reigned over Judah seven years and six
8. 4 seven hundred horsemen, and twenty th.
10. 18 David slew (the men of) seven hundred ch.
21. 6 Let seven men of his sons be delivered unto
21. 9 they fell (all) seven together, and were put
23. 39 Uriah the Hittite: thirty and seven in all
24. 13 Shall seven years of famine come unto thee
1 Ki. 2. 11 seven years reigned he in Hebron, and th.
6. 6 the third (was) seven cubits broad: for wi.
6. 38 So was he seven years in building it
7. 17 seven for the one chapiter, and seven for
8. 65 seven days and seven days, (even) fourteen
11. 3 he had seven hundred wives, princesses, a.
16. 10, 15 in the twenty and seventh year of Asa
16. 15 did Zimri reign seven days in Tirzah. And
18. 43 nothing. And he said, Go again seven tim.
19. 18 I have left (me) seven thousand in Israel
20. 15 the children of Israel, (being) seven thou.
20. 29 pitched one over against the other seven
20. 30 a wall fell upon twenty and seven thous.
2 Ki. 3. 9 they fetched a compass of seven day's jo.
3. 26 he took with him seven hundred men that
4. 35 the child sneezed seven times, and the chil.
5. 10 Go and wash in Jordan seven times, and thy
5. 14 and dipped himself seven times in Jordon
8. 1 it shall also come upon the land seven years
8. 2 sojourned in the land of the Philistines se.
8. 3 it came to pass at the seven years' end, that
11. 21 Seven years old (was) Jehoash when he b.
12. 1 In the seventh year of Jehu, Jehoash be.
13. 10 In the thirty and seventh year of Joash ki.
15. 1 In the twenty and seventh year of Jerob.
24. 16 all the men of might, (even) seven thous
25. 8 in the fifth month, on the seventh (day)
25. 27 the seven and thirtieth year of the cap.
25. 27 on the seven and twentieth (day) of the
1 Ch. 3. 4 there he reigned seven years and six mo.
3. 24 And the sons of Elioenai (were)..seven
5. 13 and Jachan, and Zia, and Heber, seven
5. 18 four and forty thousand seven hundred
7. 5 reckoned..fourscore and seven thousand
9. 13 a thousand and seven hundred and thre.
9. 25 (were) to come after seven days from time
10. 12 buried their bones..and fasted seven da.
12. 25 men of valour for the war, seven thousa.
12. 27 with him (were) three thousand and seven
12. 34 with them..thirty and seven thousand
15. 26 they offered seven bullocks and seven ra.
18. 4 seven thousand horsemen, and twenty th.
19. 18 David slew of the Syrians seven thousand
26. 30 men of valour, a thousand and seven hu.
26. 32 two thousand and seven hundred chief
29. 4 seven thousand talents of refined silver
29. 27 seven years reigned he in Hebron, and
2 Ch. 7. 8 Solomon kept the feast seven days, and
7. 9 dedication..seven days, and the feast se.
13. 9 with a young bullock and seven rams, (the
15. 11 seven hundred oxen and seven thousand
17. 11 seven thousand and seven hundred rams
17. 11 seven thousand and seven hundred he go.
24. 1 Joash (was) seven years old when he be.
26. 13 seven thousand and five hundred, that ma.
29. 21 they brought seven bullocks, and seven
29. 21 seven lambs, and seven he goats, for a sin
30. 21 kept the feast of unleavened bread seven
30. 22 they did eat throughout the feast seven da.
30. 23 other seven days: and they kept (other) s.
30. 24 a thousand bullocks and seven thousand
35. 17 and the feast of unleavened bread seven
Ezra 2. 5 The children of Arah, seven hundred se.
2. 9 the children of Zaccai, seven hundred and
2. 25 The children of..Beeroth, seven hundred
2. 33 The children of Lod..seven hundred tw.
2. 38 a thousand two hundred forty and seven
2. 65 seven thousand three hundred thirty and s.
2. 66 Their horses (were) seven hundred thirty
2. 67 six thousand seven hundred and twenty
6. 22 kept the feast of unleavened bread seven
7. 7 in the seventh year of Artaxerxes the ki.
8. 35 seventy and seven lambs, twelve he goats
Neh. 7. 14 The children of Zaccai, seven hundred and
Neh. 7. 18 Adonikam, six hundred threescore and se.
7. 19 Bigvai, two thousand threescore and sev
7. 29 The men of..Beeroth, seven hundred fo
7. 37 The children of Lod..seven hundred twe.
7. 41 a thousand two hundred forty and seven
7. 67 seven thousand three hundred thirty..se-
7. 68 Their horses, seven hundred thirty and
7. 69 six thousand seven hundred and twenty
7. 72 and threescore and seven priest's garme.
8. 18 they kept the feast seven days; and on
Esth. 1. 1 an hundred and seven and twenty provi.
1. 5 the king made a feast..seven days, in the
1. 10 the seven chamberlains that served in the
1. 14 the seven princes of Persia and Media, wh.
2. 9 seven maidens, (which were) meet to be
2. 16 taken..into his house..in the seventh ye.
8. 9 an hundred twenty and seven provinces
9. 30 to the hundred twenty and seven provin.
Job 1. 2 there were born unto him seven sons and
1. 3 His substance also was seven thousand
2. 13 sat down with him..seven days and seven
5. 19 yea, in seven there shall no evil touch th.
42. 8 take unto you now seven bullocks and se.
Psa. 119. 164 Seven times a day do I praise thee beca.
Prov. 6. 16 yea, seven (are) an abomination unto him
9. 1 she hath hewn out her seven pillars
24. 16 a just (man) falleth seven times, and ris.
26. 16 than seven men that can render a reason
26. 25 (there are) seven abominations in his he.
Eccl. 11. 2 Give a portion to seven, and also to eight
Isa. 4. 1 seven women shall take hold of one man
11. 15 shall smite it in the seven streams, and ma.
30. 26 light of the sun..as the light of seven da.
Jer. 15. 9 She that hath born seven languisheth
34. 14 At the end of seven years let ye go every
52. 25 seven men of them that were near the ki.
52. 28 In the seventh year three thousand Jews
52. 30 carried away captive..seven hundred fo.
52. 31 in the seven and thirtieth year of the ca.
Eze. 3. 15 I sat..astonished among them seven days
3. 16 it came to pass at the end of seven days
29. 17 it came to pass in the seven and twentieth
30. 20 in the first (month), in the seventh (day)
39. 9 they shall burn them with fire seven yea.
39. 12 seven months shall the house of Israel be
39. 14 after the end of seven months shall they
40. 22 and they went up unto it by seven steps
40. 26 (there were) seven steps to go up to it, and
41. 3 and the breadth of the door seven cubits
43. 25 Seven days shalt thou prepare every day
43. 26 Seven days shall they purge the altar and
44. 26 they shall reckon unto him seven days
45. 20 so thou shalt do the seventh (day) of the
45. 23 seven days of the feast he shall prepare a
45. 23 seven bullocks and seven rams..the seven
45. 25 In the seventh (month), in the fifteenth day
Dan. 9. 25 (shall be) seven weeks, and threescore and
Mic. 5. 5 then shall we raise against him seven sh.
Zech. 3. 9 upon one stone (shall be) seven eyes: be.
4. 2 seven lamps..and seven pipes to the seven
4. 10 shall see the plummet..(with) those seven

3. *Seventh*, שְׁבִיעִי *shebii*.

Gen. 2. 2 on the seventh day God ended his work
2. 2 he rested on the seventh day from all his
2. 3 God blessed the seventh day and sanctified
8. 4 the ark rested in the seventh month, on the
Exod. 12. 15 from the first day until the seventh day
12. 16 in the seventh day there shall be an holy
13. 6 in the seventh day (shall be) a feast to the
16. 26 on the seventh day, (which is) the sabbath
16. 27 there went out (some)..on the seventh day
16. 29 let no man go out of his place on the sev.
16. 30 So the people rested on the seventh day
20. 10 the seventh day (is) the sabbath of the L.
20. 11 the LORD..rested the seventh day: where.
21. 2 in the seventh he shall go out free for no.
23. 11 the seventh (year) thou shalt let it rest and
23. 12 on the seventh day thou shalt rest; that
24. 16 the seventh day he called unto Moses out
31. 15 but in the seventh (is) the sabbath of rest
31. 17 on the seventh day he rested, and was re.
34. 21 on the seventh day thou shalt rest: in ea.
35. 2 on the seventh day there shall be to you
Lev. 13. 5 the priest shall look on him the seventh
13. 6 shall look on him again the seventh day
13. 27 the priest shall look upon him the seventh
13. 32, 34 in the seventh day the priest shall lo.
13. 51 he shall look on the plague on the seventh
14. 9 it shall be on the seventh day, that he sh.
14. 39 the priest shall come again the seventh day
16. 29 in the seventh month, on the tenth (day)
23. 3 the seventh day (is) the sabbath of rest, an
23. 8 in the seventh day (is) an holy convocation
23. 16 unto the morrow after the seventh sabbath
23. 24 In the seventh month, in the first (day) of
23. 27 on the tenth (day) of this seventh month
23. 34 The fifteenth day of this seventh month
23. 39 in the fifteenth day of the seventh month
23. 41 ye shall celebrate it in the seventh month
25. 4 in the seventh year shall be a sabbath
25. 9 to sound on the tenth (day) of the seventh
25. 20 What shall we eat the seventh year? be.
Num. 6. 9 on the seventh day shall he shave it
7. 48 On the seventh day Elishama the son of
19. 12 and on the seventh day he shall be clean
19. 12 then the seventh day he shall not be clean
19. 19 on the seventh day; and on the seventh day
28. 25 on the seventh day ye shall have an holy
29. 1 in the seventh month, on the first (day) of
29. 7 have on the tenth (day) of this seventh mo.
29. 12 on the fifteenth day of the seventh month

Num 29. 32 on the seventh day seven bullocks, two ra.
31. 19 on the third day, and on the seventh day
31. 24 ye shall wash your clothes on the seventh
Deut. 5. 14 the seventh day (is) the sabbath of the L.
15. 12 in the seventh year thou shalt let him go
16. 8 on the seventh day (shall be) a solemn
Josh. 6. 4 and the seventh day ye shall compass the
6. 15 it came to pass on the seventh day, that
6. 16 it came to pass at the seventh time, when
19. 40 the seventh lot came out for the tribe of
Judg 14. 15, 17 it came to pass on the seventh day th.
14. 18 said unto him on the seventh day before
2 Sa. 12. 18 it came to pass on the seventh day, that
1 Ki. 8. 2 Ethanim, which (is) the seventh month
18. 44 it came to pass at the seventh time, that
20. 29 in the seventh day the battle was joined
2 Ki. 11. 4 the seventh year Jehoiada sent and fetched
18. 9 which (was) the seventh year of Hoshea
25. 25 it came to pass in the seventh month, that
1 Ch. 2. 15 Ozem the sixth, David the seventh
12. 11 Attai the sixth, Eliel the seventh
24. 10 The seventh to Hakkoz, the eighth to Ab.
25. 14 The seventh to Jesharelah, (he), his sons
26. 3 Jehohanan the sixth, Elioenai the seventh
26. 5 Issachar the seventh, Peulthai the eighth
27. 10 The seventh (captain) for the seventh mo.
2 Ch. 5. 3 the feast which (was) in the seventh mo.
7. 10 three and twentieth day of the seventh mo.
23. 1 in the seventh year Jehoiada strengthened
31. 7 and finished (them) in the seventh month
Ezra 3. 1 when the seventh month was come, and
3. 6 From the first day of the seventh month
7. 8 which (was) in the seventh year of the ki.
Neh. 7. 73 when the seventh month came, the child.
8. 2 upon the first day of the seventh month
8. 14 in booths in the feast of the seventh mo.
10. 31 and (that) we would leave the seventh year
Esth. 1. 10 On the seventh day, when the heart of the
Jer. 28. 17 died the same year, in the seventh month
41. 1 it came to pass in the seventh month, (th.)
Eze. 20. 1 it came to pass in the seventh year, in the
45. 25 In the seventh (month), in the fifteenth
Hag. 2. 1 In the seventh (month), in the one and tw.
Zech. 7. 5 and mourned in the fifth and seventh (mo.)
8. 19 the fast of the seventh, and the fast of the

4. *Seven*, שִׁבְעָה *shibah.*
Ezra 7. 14 sent of the king, and of his seven couns.
Dan. 3. 19 seven times more than it was wont to be
4. 16 and let seven times pass over him
4. 23 with the beasts..till seven times pass over
4. 25 seven times shall pass over thee, till thou

5. *Seven*, שִׁבְעָנָה *shibanah.*
Job 42. 13 He had also seven sons and three daugh.

6. *Sevenfold*, שִׁבְעָתַיִם *shibathayim.*
Gen. 4. 15 vengeance shall be taken on him sevenf.
4. 24 If Cain shall be avenged sevenfold, truly
2 Sa. 21. 9 they fell (all) seven together, and were put
Psa. 12. 6 (as) silver tried..purified seven times
79. 12 render unto our neighbours sevenfold into
Prov. 6. 31 But (if) he be found, he shall restore sev.
Isa. 30. 26 and the light of the sun shall be sevenfold

7. *The seventh*, ἕβδομος *hebdomos.*
John 4. 52 Yesterday at the seventh hour the fever
Heb. 4. 4 he spake in a certain place of the seventh
4. 4 God did rest the seventh day from all his
Jude 14 Enoch, also, the seventh from Adam, pr.
Rev. 8. 1 when he had opened the seventh seal, th.
10. 7 in the days of the voice of the seventh an.
11. 15 the seventh angel sounded; and there we.
16. 17 the seventh angel poured out his vial into
21. 20 the seventh, chrysolyte; the eighth, beryl

8. *Seven*, ἑπτά *hepta.*
Matt 12. 45 taketh with himself seven other spirits
15. 34 And they said, Seven, and a few little fi.
15. 36 he took the seven loaves and the fishes
15. 37 the broken (meat) that was left seven ba.
16. 10 Neither the seven loaves of the four tho.
18. 22 Jesus saith..Until seventy times seven
22. 25 there were with us seven brethren: and
22. 26 second also, and the third, unto the sev.
22. 28 whose wife shall she be of the seven? for
Mark 8. 5 How many loaves have ye?..they said, S.
8. 6 he took the seven loaves, and gave thanks
8. 8 took up of the broken (meat)..seven bas.
8. 20 And when the seven among four thousand
8. 20 how many baskets full..And they said, S.
12. 20 there were seven brethren: and the first
12. 22 And the seven had her, and left no seed
12. 23 whose wife shall she be..for the seven had
16. 9 [Mary..out of whom he had cast seven]
Luke 2. 36 had lived with an husband seven years fr.
8. 2 Magdalene, out of whom went seven de.
11. 26 taketh (to him) seven other spirits more
20. 29 There were therefore seven brethren: and
20. 31 in like manner the seven also: and they
20. 33 whose wife of them is she? for seven had
Acts 6. 3 look ye out among you seven men of ho.
13. 19 when he had destroyed seven nations in
19. 14 there were seven sons of (one) Sceva, a Jew
20. 6 came..to Troas..where we abode seven d.
21. 4 finding disciples, we tarried there seven d.
21. 8 the evangelist, which was (one) of the se.
21. 27 when the seven days were almost ended
28. 14 were desired to tarry with them seven d.
Heb. 11. 30 after they were compassed about seven d.
Rev. 1. 4 John to the seven churches which are in
1. 4 from the seven spirits which are before his
1. 11 send (it) unto the [seven] churches which
1. 12 being turned I saw seven golden candlest.
Rev. 1. 13 in the midst of the [seven] candlesticks
1. 16 And he had in his right hand seven stars
1. 20 The mystery of the seven stars which th.
1. 20 and the seven golden candlesticks
1. 20 seven stars are the angels of the seven ch.
1. 20 the seven candlesticks..are the seven ch.
2. 1 he that holdeth the seven stars in his right
2. 1 who walketh in the midst of the seven go.
3. 1 the [seven] spirits of God, and the seven
4. 5 seven lamps..which are the seven spirits
5. 1 a book written..sealed with seven seals
5. 5 to open the book, and to loose the seven
5. 6 having seven horns and seven eyes, which
5. 6 the [seven] spirits of God sent forth into
8. 2 I saw the seven angels which stood before
8. 2 and to them were given seven trumpets
8. 6 the seven angels which had the seven tr.
10. 3 when he had cried, seven thunders uttered
10. 4 when the seven thunders had uttered their
10. 4 Seal up those things which the [seven] th.
11. 13 in the earthquake were slain..seven tho.
12. 3 having seven heads and ten horns, and se.
13. 1 having seven heads and ten horns, and up.
15. 1 seven angels having the seven last plagues
15. 6 the seven angels..having the seven plag.
15. 7 gave unto the seven angels seven golden
15. 8 till the seven plagues of the seven angels
16. 1 I heard a great voice..saying to the seven
17. 1 one of the seven angels which had the se.
17. 3 a scarlet coloured beast..having seven h.
17. 7 which hath the seven heads and ten hor.
17. 9 The seven heads are seven mountains, on
17. 10 there are seven kings: five are fallen, and
17. 11 he, is the eighth, and is of the seven, and
21. 9 there came unto me one of the seven an.
21. 9 the seven vials full of the seven last pla.

9. *Seven times*, ἑπτάκις *heptakis.*
Matt 18. 21 how oft shall..I forgive him? till seven ti.
18. 22 Until seven times; but, Until seventy ti.
Luke 17. 4 seven times in a day, and seven times in

SE-VEN STARS, כִּימָה *Kimah.*
The Pleiades: their names are Alcyone, Merope, Maia, Electra, Tayegeta, Sterope, and Celaeno; they are also called Atlantides and Hesperides.
Amos 5. 8 him) that maketh the seven stars and O.

SEVEN thousand —
Seven thousand, ἑπτακισχίλιοι *heptakischilioi.*
Rom 11. 4 I have reserved to myself seven thousand

SEVENTEEN, seventeenth —
1. *Seven and ten*, שִׁבְעָה וַעֲשָׂרָה *shibah va-asarah.*
Jer. 32. 9 the money, (even) seventeen shekels of si.

2. *Seventy and seven*, שִׁבְעִים וְשִׁבְעָה *shibim ve-shibah.*
Judg. 8. 14 he described..threescore and seventeen

3. *Seven (and) ten*, שִׁבְעָה עָשָׂר or שְׁבַע עֶשְׂרֵה [*sheba*].
Gen. 7. 11 in the second month, the seventeenth day
8. 4 on the seventeenth day of the month, up.
37. 2 Joseph, (being) seventeen years old, was
47. 28 Jacob lived in the land of Egypt sevent.
1 Ki. 14. 21 Rehoboam..reigned seventeen years in J.
22. 51 the seventeenth year of Jehoshaphat king
2 Ki. 13. 1 Jehoahaz..began to reign..seventeen ye.
16. 1 In the seventeenth year of Pekah the son
1 Ch. 7. 11 seventeen thousand and two hundred ..fit
24. 15 The seventeenth to Hezir, the eighteenth
25. 24 The seventeenth to Joshbekashah, (he)
2 Ch. 12. 13 he reigned seventeen years in Jerusalem
Ezra 2. 39 children of Harim, a thousand and seve.
Neh. 7. 42 children of Harim, a thousand and seven.

SEVENTY (times) —
1. *Seventy*, שִׁבְעִים *shibim.*
Gen. 4. 24 truly Lamech seventy and sevenfold
5. 12 And Cainan lived seventy years, and be.
5. 31 seven hundred seventy and seven years
11. 26 Terah lived seventy years, and begat Ab.
12. 4 Abram (was) seventy and five years old
Exod. 1. 5 all the souls that came..were seventy so.
24. 1, 9 Abihu, and seventy of the elders of Is.
38. 28 of the thousand seven hundred seventy
38. 29 the brass of the offering (was) seventy ta.
Num. 7. 13 one silver bowl of seventy shekels, after
[So in verse 19, 25, 31, 37, 43, 49, 55, 61, 67, 73, 79.]
7. 85 hundred and thirty (shekels), each bowl s.
11. 16 Gather unto me seventy men of the elders
11. 24 gathered the seventy men of the elders of
11. 25 and gave (it) unto the seventy elders: and
31. 32 six hundred thousand and seventy thou.
Judg. 9. 56 which he did..in slaying his seventy br.
2 Sa. 24. 15 there died of the people..seventy thou.
2 Ki. 10. 1 And Ahab had seventy sons in Samaria
10. 6 the king's sons, (being) seventy persons
10. 7 slew seventy persons, and put their heads
1 Ch. 21. 14 there fell of Israel seventy thousand men
Ezra 2. 3 thousand an hundred seventy and two
2. 4 children..three hundred seventy and two
2. 5 children of Arah, seven hundred seventy
2. 36 The priests..nine hundred seventy and
2. 40 of the children of Hodaviah, seventy and
8. 7 the son of Athaliah, and with him seventy
8. 14 Uthai, and Zabbud, and with them seve.
8. 35 seventy and seven lambs, twelve he goats
Neh. 7. 8 two thousand an hundred seventy and two
7. 9 of Shephatiah, three hundred seventy and
7. 39 The priests..nine hundred seventy and th.
7. 43 of the children of Hodevah, seventy and
11. 19 their brethren..(were) an hundred seventy
Esth. 9. 16 slew of their foes seventy and five thous.
Isa. 23. 15 that Tyre shall be forgotten seventy years
23. 15 after the end of seventy years shall Tyre
23. 17 after the end of seventy years, that the
Jer. 25. 11 these nations shall serve..seventy years
25. 12 when seventy years are accomplished
29. 10 after seventy years be accomplished at
Eze. 8. 11 there stood before them seventy men of
41. 12 the building..(was) seventy cubits broad
Dan. 9. 2 that he would accomplish seventy years
9. 24 Seventy weeks are determined upon thy
Zech. 7. 5 When ye fasted..those seventy years, did

2. *Seventy*, ἑβδομήκοντα *hebdomēkonta.*
Luke 10. 1 the Lord appointed other seventy also
10. 17 the seventy returned again with joy, say.

3. *Seventy times*, ἑβδομηκοντάκις *hebdomēkontakis.*
Matt 18. 22 Until seven times; but, Until seventy ti.

SEVER (out, self), to —
1. *To separate*, בָּדַל *badal*, 5.
Lev. 20. 26 have severed you from (other) people, that
Deut. 4. 41 Moses severed three cities on this side J.
Eze. 39. 14 they shall sever out men of continual em.

2. *To separate, make wonderful*, פָּלָה *palah*, 5.
Exod. 8. 22 I will sever in that day the land of Goshen
9. 4 the LORD shall sever between the cattle

3. *To be parted*, פָּרַד *parad*, 2.
Judg. 4. 11 Heber..had severed himself from the K.

4. *To boundary off*, ἀφορίζω *aphorizō.*
Matt 13. 49 and sever the wicked from among the just

SEVERAL, severally —
1. *Freedom, separation*, חָפְשִׁית *chophshith* [V. L. חפשות]
2 Ch. 26. 21 and dwelt in a several house, (being) a

2. *Free, separate*, חָפְשִׁית *chophshith.*
2 Ki. 15. 5 he was a leper..and dwelt in a several

3. *One's own*, ἴδιος *idios.*
Matt 25. 15 to every man according to his several ab.
1 Co. 12. 11 dividing to every man severally as he will

SEVERITY —
A cutting off, severity, ἀποτομία *apotomia.*
Rom 11. 22 severity of God: on them which fell, sev.

SEW (on, together, up), to —
1. *To sew up*, טָפַל *taphal.*
Job 14. 17 My transgression (is) sealed..thou sewest up

2. *To sew*, תָּפַר *taphar.*
Gen. 3. 7 they sewed fig leaves together, and made
Job 16. 15 I have sewed sackcloth upon my skin, and
Eccl. 3. 7 A time to rend, and a time to sew; a time

3. *To sew upon*, ἐπιρράπτω *epirrhaptō.*
Mark 2. 21 No man also seweth a piece of new cloth

SEW, (women) that —
To sew, תָּפַר *taphar*, 3.
Eze. 13. 18 Woe to the (women) that sew pillows to

SHA-A-LAB'-BIN, שַׁעַלְבִין *jackals.*
A city in Dan, near Ajalon, on the slope of Mount Ephraim; called Selebi by Jerome, but now *Silbit*; or *Salaba*, on the borders of Sebaste, according to Eusebius.
Josh. 19. 42 And S., and Ajalon, and Jethlah

SHA-AL'-BIM, שַׁעַלְבִים. *Same as preceding.*
Judg. 1. 35 the Amorites would dwell..in S.: yet the
1 Ki. 4. 9 The son of Dekar, in Makaz, and in S., and

SHA-AL-BO-NITE, שַׁעַלְבֹנִי.
Patronymic of Eliahba, a native of Shaalabbin.
2 Sa. 23. 32 Eliahba the S., of the sons of Jashen, Jo.
1 Ch. 11. 33 Azmaveth the Baharumite, Eliahba the S.

SHA'-APH, שַׁעַף *union, friendship.*
1. A son of Jahdai son of Caleb by his concubine Ephah. B.C. 1470.
1 Ch. 2. 47 and Gesham, and Pelet, and Ephah, and S.
2. Son of Caleb son of Hezron by his concubine Maachah. B.C. 1470.
1 Ch. 2. 49 She bare also S. the father of Madmannah

SHA-A-RA'-IM, SHA-RA'-IM, שַׁעֲרַיִם *double cleft.*
A city in Judah or Simeon, near Adithaim and Beth-birei; now called *Shilhim.*
Josh. 15. 36 S., and Adithaim, and Gederah, and G.
1 Sa. 17. 52 the wounded..fell down by the way to S.
1 Ch. 4. 31 And at Beth-marcaboth..and at S.

SHA-ASH'-GAZ, שַׁעַשְׁגַז.
A chamberlain of Ahasuerus king of Persia, who had the charge of the king's concubines. B.C. 515.
Esth. 2. 14 to the custody of S., the king's chamberl.

SHAB-BE'-THAI, שַׁבְּתַי *sabbath-born.*
1. A Levite who helped in the matter of those that had taken strange wives. B.C. 445.
Ezra 10. 15 Meshullam and S. the Levite helped them
2. One who explained the law to the people after Ezra had read it to them. B.C. 445.
Neh. 8. 7 Akkub, S., Hodijah, Maaseiah, Kelita A.
3. A chief Levite in Jerusalem after the exile. B.C. 445.
Neh. 11. 16 S..(had) the oversight of the outward bus.

SHACH'-IA, שָׂכְיָה *fame of Jah.*
A son of Shaharaim a Benjamite; some Hebrew copies read *Shobia.* B.C. 1350.
1 Ch. 8. 10 Jeuz, and S., and Mirma. These (were) his

SHADE, shadow, shadowing —

1. *Shadow, shade, defence,* צֵל *tsel.*

Gen. 19. 8 therefore came they under the shadow of
Judg. 9. 15 (then) come (and) put your trust in my sh.
9. 36 Thou seest the shadow of the mountains
2 Ki. 20. 9 shall the shadow go forward ten degrees
20. 10 It is a light thing for the shadow to go
20. 10 let the shadow return backward ten deg.
20. 11 he brought the shadow ten degrees back.
1 Ch. 29. 15 our days on the earth (are) as a shadow
Job 7. 2 As a servant earnestly desireth the shad.
8. 9 because our days upon earth (are) a sha.
14. 2 he fleeth also as a shadow, and continu.
17. 7 and all my members (are) as a shadow
Psa. 17. 8 hide me under the shadow of thy wings
36. 7 put their trust under the shadow of thy
57. 1 in the shadow of thy wings will I make
63. 7 in the shadow of thy wings will I rejoice
80. 10 The hills were covered with the shadow
91. 1 shall abide under the shadow of the Alm.
102. 11 My days (are) like a shadow that decline.
109. 23 I am gone like the shadow when it decli.
121. 5 the LORD (is) thy shade upon thy right ha.
144. 4 his days (are) as a shadow that passeth a.
Eccl. 6. 12 the days..which he spendeth as a shadow
8. 13 prolong (his) days, (which are) as a shad.
Song 2. 3 I sat down under his shadow with great
Isa. 4. 6 there shall be a tabernacle for a shadow
16. 3 make thy shadow as the night in the mi.
25. 4 a shadow from the heat, when the blast
25. 5 (even) the heat with the shadow of a clo.
30. 2 and to trust in the shadow of Egypt
30. 3 the trust in the shadow of Egypt (your)
32. 2 as the shadow of a great rock in a weary
34. 15 lay, and hatch, and gather under her sh.
38. 8 I will bring again the shadow of the deg.
49. 2 in the shadow of his hand hath he hid me
51. 16 have covered thee in the shadow of mine
Jer. 48. 45 They that fled stood under the shadow of
Lam. 4. 20 Under his shadow we shall live among the
Eze. 17. 23 in the shadow of the branches thereof sh.
31. 6 under his shadow dwelt all great nations
31. 12 the people..are gone down from his sha.
31. 17 (that) dwelt under his shadow in the mi.
Hos. 4. 13 under oaks..because the shadow thereof
14. 7 They that dwell under his shadow shall
Jon. 4. 5 sat under it in the shadow, till he might
4. 6 that it might be a shadow over his head

2. *A shadow,* צְלָל *tselel.*

Job 40. 22 The shady trees cover him (with) their sh.
Song 2. 17 Until the day break, and the shadows flee
4. 6 Until the day break, and the shadows flee
Jer. 6. 4 the shadows of the evening are stretched

3. *To (cause a) shadow,* צָלַל *tsalal,* 5.

Eze. 31. 3 with fair branches, and with a shadowing

4. *A shadow, shadowed,* צִלְצַל *tselatsal.*

Isa. 18. 1 Woe to the land shadowing with wings

5. *A shadow,* ἀποσκίασμα *aposkiasma.*

Jas. 1. 17 no variableness, neither shadow of turn

6. *A shade, shadow,* σκιά *skia.*

Matt. 4. 16 which sat in the region and shadow of de.
Mark 4. 32 the fowls..may lodge under the shadow
Luke 1. 79 in darkness and (in) the shadow of death
Acts 5. 15 that at the least the shadow of Peter pa.
Col. 2. 17 Which are a shadow of things to come, but
Heb. 8. 5 Who serve unto the example and shadow
10. 1 the law having a shadow of good things

SHADOW, to (have) —

1. *To take shade,* טְלַל *telal,* 5.

Dan. 4. 12 the beasts of the field had shadow under

2. *To shadow, shade fully,* κατασκιάζω *kataskiazō.*

Heb. 9. 5 over it the cherubim of glory shadowing

SHADOW of death —

A great shade or shadow, צַלְמָוֶת *tsalmaveth.*

Job 3. 5 Let darkness and the shadow of death st.
10. 21 land of darkness, and the shadow of dea.
10. 22 of the shadow of death, without any ord.
12. 22 bringeth out to light the shadow of death
16. 16 and on my eyelids (is) the shadow of de.
24. 17 morning (is) to them even as the sha. of d.
24. 17 (they are in) the terrors of the shad. of d.
28. 3 the stones of darkness, and the shad. of d.
34. 22 (There is) no darkness, nor shadow of de.
38. 17 hast thou seen the doors of the shad. of d.
Psa. 23. 4 through the valley of the shadow of dea.
44. 19 and covered us with the shadow of death
107. 10 Such as sit in darkness, and in the sh. of d.
107. 14 out of darkness and the shadow of death
Isa. 9. 2 they that dwell in the land of the sh. of d.
Jer. 2. 6 a land of drought, and of the shadow of d.
13. 16 he turn it into the shadow of death, (and)
Amos 5. 8 turneth the shadow of death into the mo.

SHAD'-RACH, שַׁדְרַךְ.

The name which the chief of Nebuchadnezzar's eunuchs gave to Hananiah, one of the Jewish princes who were carried away to Babylon, and who was cast into the burning fiery furnace. B.C. 580.

Dan. 1. 7 to Hananiah, of S.; and to Mishael, of M.
2. 49 he set S..over the affairs of the province
3. 12 thou hast set..the affairs..of Babylon, S.
3. 13 Then Nebuchadnezzar..commanded..S.
3. 14 O S., Meshach, and Abednego, do not ye
3. 16 S...and Abednego, answered and said to
3. 19 form of his visage was changed against S.
3. 20 he commanded..mighty men..to bind S.
Dan. 3. 22 those men that took up S., Meshach, and
3. 23 S...fell down bound into the midst of the
3. 26 S., Meshach, and Abednego..come forth
3. 26 Then S...came forth of the midst of the
3. 28 Blessed (be) the God of S., Meshach, and
3. 29 which speak..amiss against the God of S.
3. 30 the king promoted S., Meshach, and Ab.

SHADY trees —

Shades, צֶאֱלִים *tseelim.*

Job 40. 21 He lieth under the shady trees, in the co.
40. 22 The shady trees cover him (with) their sh.

SHAFT —

1. *A handle, arrow,* חֵץ *chets.*

Isa. 49. 2 he hid me, and made me a polished shaft

2. *The thigh,* יָרֵךְ *yarek.*

Exod. 25. 31 his shaft, and his branches, his bowls, his
37. 17 his shaft, and his branch, his bowls, his kn.
Num. 8. 4 (was of) beaten gold, unto the shaft there.

SHA'-GE, שָׁגֵא *erring, wandering.*

Father of Jonathan the Hararite, one of David's valiant men. B.C. 1048.

1 Ch. 11. 34 Jonathan the son of S. the Hararite

SHA'-HAR. See *Aijeleth Shahar.*

SHA-HA-RA'-IM, שַׁחֲרַיִם *double dawn.*

A Benjamite who went to Moab and begat children there of his two wives Hushim and Baara. B.C. 1400.

1 Ch. 8. 8 S. begat..in the country of Moab, after

SHA-HA-ZI'-MAH, שַׁחֲצוּמָה *heights.*

A city in Issachar, between Tabor and Beth-shemesh.

Josh 19. 22 the coast reacheth to Tabor, and S., and

SHAKE (off, together), to —

1. *To shake, tremble,* גָּעַשׁ *gaash.*

Psa. 18. 7 the earth shook and trembled; the found.

2. *To shake self,* גָּעַשׁ *gaash,* 7.

2 Sa. 22. 8 Then the earth shook and trembled; the
22. 8 foundations of heaven moved and shook

3. *To pain, cause pain,* חִיל, חוּל *chul, chil,* 5.

Psa. 29. 8 shaketh the wilderness; the LORD shaketh

4. *To shake violently,* חָמַס *chamas.*

Job 15. 33 He shall shake off his unripe grape as the

5. *To move, slip, fail,* מוֹט *mot.*

Psa. 60. 2 heal the breaches thereof; for it shaketh

6. *To cause to move or shake,* נוּעַ *nua,* 5.

2 Ki. 19. 21 the daughter of Jerusalem hath shaken h.
Job 16. 4 heap up words against you, and shake
Psa. 22. 7 they shoot out the lip, they shake the head
109. 25 (when) they looked upon me they shaked
Isa. 37. 22 daughter of Jerusalem hath shaken her h.

7. *To wave,* נוּף *nuph,* 3a.

Isa. 10. 32 he shall shake his hand (against) the mount

8. *To cause to wave,* נוּף *nuph,* 5.

Isa. 10. 15 him that shaketh it? as if the rod should s.
11. 15 with his mighty wind shall he shake his
13. 2 exalt the voice unto them, shake the hand
19. 16 the hand of the LORD..which he shaketh
Zech. 2. 9 I will shake mine hand upon them, and th.

9. *To shake out or off,* נָעַר *naar.*

Neh. 5. 13 Also I shook my lap, and said, So God
Isa. 33. 9 and Bashan and Carmel shake off (their
33. 15 that shaketh his hands from holding of

10. *To shake out or off,* נָעַר *naar,* 3.

Neh. 5. 13 So God shake out every man from his ho.

11. *To shake off,* נָתַר *nethar,* 5.

Dan. 4. 14 shake off his leaves, and scatter his fruit

12. *To cause to shake,* רָגַז *ragaz,* 5.

Job 9. 6 Which shaketh the earth out of her place
Isa. 13. 13 I will shake the heavens, and the earth sh.
23. 11 he shook the kingdoms: the LORD hath

13. *To move, flutter,* רָחַף *rachaph.*

Jer. 23. 9 all my bones shake: I am like a drunken

14. *To shake, tremble,* רָעַשׁ *raash.*

Psa. 46. 3 the mountains shake with the swelling th.
68. 8 The earth shook, the heavens also dropp.
72. 16 the fruit thereof shall shake like Lebanon
77. 18 the lightnings lightened..earth..shook
Isa. 24. 18 and the foundations of the earth do sha.
Eze. 26. 10 thy walls shall shake at the noise of the
26. 15 Shall not the isles shake at the sound of
27. 28 The suburbs shall shake at the sound of
38. 20 all the men..shall shake at my presence
Joel 3. 16 and the heavens and the earth shall shake
Amos 9. 1 Smite the lintel..that the posts may sha.

15. *To cause to shake or tremble,* רָעַשׁ *raash,* 5.

Isa. 14. 16 (Is) this the man..that did shake kingdo.
Hag. 2. 6 I will shake the heavens, and the earth
2. 7 I will shake all nations, and the desire
2. 21 saying, I will shake the heavens and the

16. *To throw down,* שָׁמַט *shamat.*

2 Sa. 6. 6 and took hold of it; for the oxen shook

17. *To shake away,* ἀποτινάσσω *apotinassō.*

Luke 9. 5 shake off the very dust from your feet for
Acts 28. 5 he shook off the beast into the fire, and

18. *To shake out or off,* ἐκτινάσσω *ektinassō.*

Matt 10. 14 when ye depart..shake off the dust of yo.
Mark 6. 11 shake off the dust under your feet for a
Acts 13. 51 they shook off the dust of their feet aga.
18. 6 he shook (his) raiment, and said unto them

19. *To shake, agitate, toss,* σαλεύω *saleuō.*

Matt 11. 7 What went ye..see? A reed shaken with
24. 29 the powers of the heavens shall be shaken
Mark 13. 25 powers that are in heaven shall be shaken
Luke 6. 38 good measure, pressed down, and shaken t.
6. 48 could not shake it; for it was founded up.
7. 24 What went ye..to see? A reed shaken wi.
21. 26 for the powers of heaven shall be shaken
Acts 4. 31 the place was shaken where they were
16. 26 the foundations of the prison were shaken
2 Th. 2. 2 That ye be not soon shaken in mind, or
Heb. 12. 26 Whose voice then shook the earth, but
12. 27 the removing of those things that are sh.
12. 27 those things which cannot be shaken may

20. *To shake, tremble, disturb,* σείω *seiō.*

Matt 28. 4 for fear of him the keepers did shake, and
Heb. 12. 26 I shake not the earth only, but also hea.
Rev. 6. 13 a fig tree..when she is shaken of a mighty

SHAKE, to make to —

1. *To cause to slide, shake,* מָעַד *maad,* 5.

Psa. 69. 23 and make their loins continually to shake

2. *To cause to fear or tremble,* פָּחַד *pachad,* 5.

Job 4. 14 trembling, which made all my bones to sh.

3. *To cause to shake or tremble,* רָעַשׁ *raash,* 5.

Eze. 31. 16 I made the nations to shake at the sound

SHAKE self, (terribly, to pieces), to —

1. *To shake self, become shaken,* נָעַר *naar,* 2.

Judg 16. 20 and said, I will go out..and shake myself

2. *To shake self,* נָעַר *naar,* 7.

Isa. 52. 2 Shake thyself from the dust; arise, (and)

3. *To fear, make afraid, terrify,* עָרַץ *arats.*

Isa. 2. 19, 21 when he ariseth to shake terribly the

4. *To scatter, break in pieces,* פּוּץ *puts,* 3a.

Job 16. 12 shaken me to pieces, and set me up for his

SHAKEN (out, terribly), to be —

1. *To shake self, be shaken,* גָּעַשׁ *gaash,* 7.

Psa. 18. 7 the hills moved and were shaken, because

2. *To be driven away,* נָדַף *nadaph,* 2.

Lev. 26. 36 the sound of a shaken leaf shall chase th.

3. *To move,* נוּד *nud.*

1 Ki. 14. 15 shall smite Israel, as a reed is shaken in

4. *To be moved, shaken,* נוּעַ *nua.*

Nah. 3. 12 if they be shaken, they shall even fall into

5. *To shake out or off,* נָעַר *naar.*

Neh. 5. 13 even thus be he shaken out, and emptied

6. *To be shaken out or off,* נָעַר *naar,* 2.

Job 38. 13 that the wicked might be shaken out of

7. *To be caused to tremble,* רָעַל *raal,* 6.

Nah. 2. 3 and the fir trees shall be terribly shaken

SHAKING —

1. *A moving, shaking,* מָנוֹד *manod.*

Psa. 44. 14 a shaking of the head among the people

2. *A compassing,* נֹקֶף *noqeph.*

Isa. 17. 6 as the shaking of an olive tree, two (or)
24. 13 (there shall be) as the shaking of an olive

3. *A shaking, trembling,* רַעַשׁ *raash.*

Job 41. 29 he laugheth at the shaking of a spear
Eze. 37. 7 there was a noise, and behold a shaking
38. 19 there shall be a great shaking in the land

4. *Waving, shaking,* תְּנוּפָה *tenuphah.*

Isa. 19. 16 because of the shaking of the hand of the
30. 32 in battles of shaking will he fight with it

SHA'-LEM, שָׁלֵם *peace, summit.*

A city in Ephraim near Shechem; now *Salim,* E. of Nablus.

Gen. 33. 18 Jacob came to S. a city of Shechem, wh.

SHA'-LIM, שַׁעֲלִים *jackal.*

A district in Dan, in the way from Philistia to Ophrah.

1 Sa. 9. 4 then they passed through the land of S.

SHA-LI'-SHA, שָׁלִשָׁה *third ground.*

1. A district in Ephraim, containing Baal-shalishah, not far from Gilgal.

1 Sa. 9. 4 And he..passed through the land of S.

2. Probably the same as Beth-Shalisha, fifteen Roman miles N. of Diospolis in Lydda.

2 Ki. 4. 42 there came a man from Baal-S., and broug.

SHALL (be or have), that, because, who, which—

1. *There is, there are,* יֵשׁ *yesh.*

2 Ch. 15. 7 Be ye strong..for your work shall be rew.
16. 9 from henceforth thou shalt have wars
Prov 24. 14 there shall be a reward, and thy expect.
Jer. 23. 26 How long shall (this) be in the heart of the
31. 6 there shall be a day, (that) the watchmen
31. 16 thy work shall be rewarded, saith the L.

2. *To be about to,* μέλλω *mellō.*

Matt 16. 27 the Son of man shall come in the glory of
17. 12 Likewise shall also the Son of man suffer
17. 22 The Son of man shall be betrayed into the
20. 22 to drink of the cup that I shall drink of
24. 6 ye shall hear of wars and rumours of wars
Mark 13. 4 the sign when all these things shall be
Luke 9. 44 the Son of man shall be delivered into the
21. 7 sign..when these things shall come to pass
21. 36 all these things that shall come to pass
Acts 23. 3 God shall smite thee, (thou) whited wall
24. 15 there shall be a resurrection of the dead

Acts 26. 2 I shall answer for myself this day before
Rom. 4. 24 for us also, to whom it shall be imputed
8. 13 For if ye live after the flesh, ye shall die
8. 18 with the glory which shall be revealed in
2 Ti. 4. 1 who shall judge the quick and the dead
Heb. 1. 14 for them who shall be heirs of salvation
10. 27 fiery indignation, which shall devour the
Jas. 2. 12 as they that shall be judged by the law of
1 Pe. 5. 1 a partaker of the glory that shall be rev.
Rev 1. 19 and the things which shall be hereafter
2. 10 thou shalt suffer: behold, the devil shall
3. 10 the hour of temptation, which shall come
17. 8 shall ascend out of the bottomless pit, and

3. *Kind, gracious, hallowed,* ὅσιος *hosios.*
Rev. 16. 5 O Lord, which art, and wast, and [shalt be]

SHAL-LE'-CHETH, שַׁלֶּכֶת *casting out.*
A gate of the first temple.
1 Ch. 26. 16 westward, with the gate S., by the cause.

SHAL'-LUM (SHAL'-LUN), שַׁלֻּם, שַׁלּוּם *recompenser.*
1. A son of Jabesh who slew Zechariah son of Jeroboam II., and was himself slain by Menahem son of Gadi, after reigning one month. B.C. 772.
2 Ki. 15. 10 S. the son of Jabesh conspired against him
15. 13 S. the son of Jabesh began to reign in the
15. 14 Menahem..smote S. the son of Jabesh in
15. 15 And the rest of the acts of S...(are) written
2. The husband of Huldah the prophetess in the days of Josiah. B.C. 624.
2 Ki. 22. 14 Huldah the prophetess, the wife of S. the
2 Ch. 34. 22 Huldah the prophetess, the wife of S. the
3. Son of Sisamai and father of Jakamiah, a descendant of Jerahmeel grandson of Pharez. B.C. 1280.
1 Ch. 2. 40 Eleasah begat Sisamai..Sisamai begat S.
2. 41 S. begat Jekamiah, and Jekamiah begat
4. Fourth son of king Josiah. B.C. 610.
1 Ch. 3. 15 the sons of Josiah (were)..Zedekiah..S.
Jer. 22. 11 For thus saith the LORD touching S. the
5. Grandson of Simeon second son of Jacob. B.C. 1200.
1 Ch. 4. 25 S. his son, Mibsam his son, Mishma his son
6. Father of Hilkiah the priest who found the book of the law in the temple in the days of king Josiah. B.C. 700.
1 Ch. 6. 12 Ahitub begat Zadok, and Zadok begat S.
6. 13 S. begat Hilkiah, and Hilkiah begat Azar.
Ezra 7. 2 The son of S., the son of Zadok, the son
7. Fourth son of Naphtali the second son of Bilhah, Rachel's handmaid; called *Shillem* in Gen. 46. 24. B.C. 1690.
1 Ch. 7. 13 Guni, and Jezer, and S., the sons of Bil.
8. A Levite, a gate keeper of the tabernacle. B.C. 536.
1 Ch. 9. 17 the porters (were) S., and Akkub, and
9. 17 Ahiman, and their brethren: S. (was) the
9. 19 S. the son of Kore, the son of Ebiasaph
9. 31 Mattithiah..the first born of S. the Kor.
Ezra 2. 42 the children of S., the children of Ater
Neh. 7. 45 the children of S., the children of Ater
9. Father of Jehizkiah who opposed the reducing of the Jewish captives to slaves. B.C. 741.
2 Ch. 28. 12 Jehizkiah the son of S., and Amasa the
10. A gatekeeper of the sanctuary that had taken a strange wife. B.C. 445.
Ezra 10. 24 of the porters; S., and Telem, and Uri
11. One of the sons of Bani who had also taken a strange wife. B.C. 445.
Ezra 10. 42 S., Amariah, (and) Joseph
12. A son of Halohesh, ruler of the half of Jerusalem, who with his daughters helped to repair the wall. B.C. 445.
Neh. 3. 12 next unto him repaired S. the son of
13. Son of Col-Hozeh, ruler of part of Mizpah, who repaired the gate of the fountain. B.C. 445.
Neh. 3. 15 the gate of the fountain repaired Shallun
14. Father of Hanameel uncle to Jeremiah the prophet. B.C. 630.
Jer. 32. 7 Hanameel the son of S...shall come unto
15. Father of Maaseiah, an officer of the temple in the days of Jehoiakim son of Josiah. B.C. 607.
Jer. 35. 4 (was) above the chamber of..the son of S.

SHAL'-MAI, שַׁלְמַי, שַׂלְמַי *Jah is recompenser.*
One of the Nethinim whose descendants returned with Zerubbabel from exile. B.C. 536. (Ezr. 2. 46, V.L. שמלי).
Ezra 2. 46 the children of S., the children of Hanan
Neh. 7. 48 children of Hagaba, the children of S.

SHAL'-MAN, שַׁלְמַן.
An Assyrian king who laid waste Beth-Arbel, *i.e.*, Αρβηλα, near Gaugamela; apparently a predecessor of *Pul*, and not the same as the following.
Hos. 10. 14 as S. spoiled Beth-arbel in the day of ba.

SHAL-MAN-E'-SER, שַׁלְמַנְאֶסֶר.
Successor of Tiglath-pileser, and who invaded Israel, carrying off Hoshea and the ten tribes to Assyria. B.C. 730-716.
2 Ki 17. 3 Against him came up S. king of Assyria
18. 9 S. king of Assyria came up against Sam.

SHA'-MA, שָׁמָע *hearer.*
One of David's valiant men. B.C. 1048.
1 Ch. 11. 44 S. and Jehiel the sons of Hothan the Ar.

SHAMARIAH. *See* **SHEMARIAH.**

SHAMBLES —
Market place, (Lat. macellum), μάκελλον *makellon.*
1 Co. 10. 25 Whatsoever is sold in the shambles, (th.)

SHAME, shameful thing —
1. *To be ashamed,* בּוֹשׁ *bosh.*
Jer. 48. 39 how hath Moab turned the back with sh.
2. *Shame,* בּוּשָׁה *bushah.*
Psa. 89. 45 thou hast covered him with shame. Selah
Eze. 7. 18 shame (shall be) upon all faces, and bald.
Obad. 10 shame shall cover thee, and thou shalt be
Mic. 7. 10 shame shall cover her which said unto me
3. *Shame,* בָּשְׁנָה *boshnah.*
Hos. 10. 6 Ephraim shall receive shame, and Israel
4. *Shame, shameful thing,* בֹּשֶׁת *bosheth.*
2 Ch. 32. 21 he returned with shame of face to his own
Job 8. 22 They..shall be clothed with shame; and
Psa. 35. 26 let them be clothed with shame and dish.
40. 15 for a reward of their shame that say unto
44. 15 and the shame of my face hath covered
69. 19 Thou hast known..my shame, and my dis.
70. 3 turned back for a reward of their shame
132. 18 His enemies will I clothe with shame: but
Isa. 30. 3 the strength of Pharaoh be your shame
30. 5 nor be an help nor profit, but a shame, and
54. 4 thou shalt forget the shame of thy youth
61. 7 For your shame (ye shall have) double, and
Jer. 3. 24 shame hath devoured the labour of our f.
3. 25 We lie down in our shame, and our conf.
11. 13 have ye set up altars to (that) shameful th.
20. 18 my days should be consumed with shame
Hos. 9. 10 and separated themselves unto (that) sh.
Mic. 1. 11 Pass ye away..having thy shame naked
Hab. 2. 10 Thou hast consulted shame to thy house
Zeph. 3. 5 faileth not; but the unjust knoweth no sh.
5. *Reproach,* חֶרְפָּה *cherpah.*
2 Sa. 13. 13 And I, whither shall I cause my shame to
Isa. 47. 3 thy shame shall be seen; I will take ven.
Dan. 12. 2 some to shame (and) everlasting contempt
6. *Blushing, shame,* כְּלִמָּה *kelimmah.*
Psa. 4. 2 how long (will ye turn) my glory unto sh.?
69. 7 I have borne reproach: shame hath cov.
109. 29 Let mine adversaries be clothed with sh.
Prov 18. 13 He that answereth..it (is) folly and shame
Isa. 50. 6 I hid not my face from shame and spitting
Jer. 51. 51 shame hath covered our faces; for stran.
Eze. 16. 52 bear thine own shame for thy sins that th.
16. 52 be thou confounded also, and bear thy s.
16. 54 That thou mayest bear thine own shame
16. 63 never open thy mouth..because of thy s.
32. 24, 25 yet have they borne their shame with
32. 30 bear their shame with them that go down
34. 29 neither bear the shame of the heathen any
36. 6 ye have borne the shame of the heathen
36. 7 the heathen..they shall bear their shame
36. 15 to hear in thee the shame of the heathen
39. 26 After that they have borne their shame
44. 13 but they shall bear their shame, and th.
Mic. 2. 6 not prophesy..they shall not take shame
7. *Blushing, shame,* כְּלִמּוּת *kelimmuth.*
Jer. 23. 40 a perpetual shame, which shall not be fo.
8. *Nakedness,* עֶרְוָה *ervah.*
Isa. 20. 4 naked and barefoot..to the shame of Eg.
9. *Lightness, shame, confusion,* קָלוֹן *qalon.*
Psa. 83. 16 Fill their faces with shame; that they m.
Prov. 3. 35 but shame shall be the promotion of fools
9. 7 He that reproveth a scorner getteth..sh.
11. 2 (When) pride cometh, then cometh shame
12. 16 known: but a prudent (man) covereth sh.
13. 18 shame (shall be) to him that refuseth in.
Isa. 22. 18 the chariots of thy glory (shall be) the sh.
Jer. 13. 26 discover thy skirts..that thy shame may
46. 12 The nations have heard of thy shame, and
Hos. 4. 7 will I change their glory into shame
4. 18 her rulers (with) shame do love, Give ye
Nah. 3. 5 and I will show..the kingdoms thy shame
Hab. 2. 16 Thou art filled with shame for glory: dr.
10. *Contempt, detestation,* שִׁמְצָה *shimtsah.*
Exod 32. 25 had made them naked unto (their) shame
11. *Base thing,* αἰσχρόν *aischron.*
1 Co. 11. 6 if it be a shame for a woman to be shorn
14. 35 it is a shame for women to speak in the ch.
Eph. 5. 12 it is a shame even to speak of those thin.
12. *Baseness, dishonour,* αἰσχύνη *aischunē.*
Luke 14. 9 thou begin with shame to take the lowest
Phil. 3. 19 (whose) glory (is) in their shame, who mi.
Heb 12. 2 endured the cross, despising the shame, and
Jude 13 Raging waves..foaming out their own sh.
Rev. 3. 18 (that) the shame of thy nakedness do not
13. *Unseemliness,* ἀσχημοσύνη *aschēmosunē.*
Rev. 16. 15 lest he walk naked, and they see his shame
14. *Dishonour,* ἀτιμία *atimia.*
1 Co. 11. 14 if a man have long hair, it is a shame unto
15. *A turning in, shame,* ἐντροπή *entropē.*
1 Co. 6. 5 I speak to your shame. Is it so, that there
15. 34 some have not..I speak (this) to your sh.

SHAME, to bring, cause, do, come, put to —
1. *To put to shame, make shame,* בּוֹשׁ *bosh,* 5.
Psa. 14. 6 Ye have shamed the counsel of the poor
44. 7 and hast put them to shame that hated us
53. 5 thou hast put (them) to shame, because
119. 31 testimonies: O LORD, put me not to sha.
Prov. 10. 5 he that sleepeth in harvest..causeth sha.
14. 35 wrath is (against) him that causeth shame
17. 2 have rule over a son that causeth shame
19. 26 (is) a son that causeth shame, and bringe.
29. 15 a child left..bringeth his mother to sha.
2. *To put to shame,* חָסַד *chasad,* 3.
Prov. 25. 10 Lest he that heareth (it) put thee to sha.
3. *To make or become confounded,* חָפֵר *chapher,* 5.
Prov 13. 5 but a wicked (man)..cometh to shame
Isa. 54. 4 thou shalt not be put to shame: for thou
4. *To dry up, shame,* יָבֵשׁ *yabash,* 5.
2 Sa. 19. 5 Thou hast shamed this day the faces of
5. *To cause to blush, put to shame,* כָּלַם *kalam,* 5.
Judg 18. 7 that might put (them) to shame in (any)
1 Sa. 20. 34 because his father had done him shame
Psa. 44. 9 But thou hast cast off, and put us to sha.
Prov 25. 8 when thy neighbour hath put thee to sh.
28. 7 a companion of riotous (men) shameth his
6. *To turn inward, put to shame,* ἐντρέπω *entrepō.*
1 Co. 4. 14 I write not these things to shame you, but
7. *To make ashamed,* καταισχύνω *kataischunō.*
1 Co. 11. 22 despise ye the church of God, and shame

SHAME, to be brought unto or put to —
1. *Their shame,* בֹּשֶׁת *bosheth.*
Zeph. 3. 19 fame..where they have been put to sha.
2. *To be ashamed, confounded,* חָפֵר *chapher.*
Psa. 71. 24 they are brought unto shame, that seek
83. 17 yea, let them be put to shame, and perish
3. *To make or become confounded,* חָפֵר *chapher,* 5.
Isa. 54. 4 thou shalt not be put to shame: for thou sh.
4. *To blush, be ashamed,* כָּלַם *kalam,* 2.
Psa. 35. 4 Let them be confounded and put to shame
40. 14 let them be..put to shame that wish me

SHAME, to put to an open —
To make a show of openly, παραδειγματίζω *parad.*
Heb. 6. 6 they crucify..and put..to an open shame

SHAMED, shameful spewing —
1. *Contempt, despised thing,* בּוּז *buz.*
Gen. 38. 23 Let her take (it) to her, lest we be shamed
2. *Ignominy, shame,* קִיקָלוֹן *qiqalon.*
Hab. 2. 16 and shameful spewing (shall be) on thy gl.

SHA'-MED, (שֶׁמֶר *watcher,*) *destroyer.*
Third son of Elpaal. B.C. 1400.
1 Ch. 8. 12 S., who built Ono and Lod, with the to.

SHAMEFACEDNESS —
Shamefacedness, modesty, αἰδώς *aidōs.*
1 Ti. 2. 9 in modest apparel, with shamefacedness

SHAMEFULLY, to do, entreat, handle —
1. *To do or act shamefully,* יָבֵשׁ *yabash,* 5.
Hos. 2. 5 she that conceived..hath done shamefully
2. *To dishonour, disgrace,* ἀτιμάζω *atimazō.*
Luke 20. 11 entreated (him) shamefully, and sent (him)
3. *To dishonour, disgrace,* ἀτιμάω *atimaō.*
Mark 12. 4 and [sent (him) away shamefully handled]

SHAMELESSLY —
To be uncovered, revealed, גָּלָה *galah,* 2.
2 Sa. 6. 20 as one of the vain fellows shamelessly un.

SHA'-MER, שֶׁמֶר *preserver.*
1. Son of Mahli grandson of Merari. B.C. 1400.
1 Ch. 6. 46 son of Amzi, the son of Bani, the son of S.
2. Son of Heber, son of Beriah, son of Asher; in 1 Ch. 7. 32 it is spelt *Shomer.* B.C. 1600.
1 Ch. 7. 34 the sons of S.; Ahi, and Rohgah, Jehubb.

SHAM'-GAR, שַׁמְגַּר *cupbearer, fleer.*
The son of Anath, and third judge of Israel after the death of Joshua. He delivered Israel from the Philistines. B.C. 1326.
Judg. 3. 31 after him was S. the son of Anath, which
5. 6 In the days of S. the son of Anath, in the

SHAM'-HUTH, שַׁמְהוּת *fame, renown.*
An Izrahite, a captain of David's army, who served in the fifth month. B.C. 1048.
1 Ch. 27. 8 fifth captain for the fifth month (was) S.

SHA'-MIR, שָׁמִיר *thorn hedge, approved.*
1. A city in the hill country of Judah, near Jattir.
Josh 15. 48 in the mountains, S., and Jattir, and S.
2. A city in Mount Ephraim.
Judg 10. 1 and he dwelt in S. in mount Ephraim
10. 2 judged..and died, and was buried in S.
3. A son of Micah, a Levite and descendant of Uzziel. B.C. 1015.
1 Ch. 24. 24 Michah: of the sons of Michah; S.

SHAM'-MA, שַׁמָּא *fame, renown.*
A son of Zophah an Asherite. B.C. 1500.
1 Ch. 7. 37 Bezer, and Hod, and S., and Shilshah.

SHAM'-MAH, שַׁמָּה *fame, renown.*
1. A son of Reuel son of Esau. B.C. 1700.
Gen. 36. 13 Nahath, and Zerah, S., and Mizzah: th.
36. 17 duke Nahath, duke Zerah, duke S., duke
1 Ch. 1. 37 The sons of Reuel; Nahath, Zerah, S., and
2. Third son of Jesse father of David. B.C. 1060. *See* Shimma.
1 Sa. 16. 9 Then Jesse made S. to pass by. And he said
17. 13 the names..(were)..Abinadab; and..S.

3. Son of Agee the Hararite. and one of David's valiant men. B.C. 1048.
2 Sa. 23. 11 after him (was) S. the son of Agee the H.
4. Another of the same also a Hararite; in 1 Ch. 11. 27 it is *Shammoth*.
2 Sa. 23. 33 S. the Hararite, Ahiam the son of Sharar
5. Another of the same, a Harodite. B.C. 1048.
2 Sa. 23. 25 S. the Harodite, Elika the Harodite

SHAM'-MAI, שַׁמַּי *celebrated*.
1. A son of Onan son of Jerahmeel grandson of Judah. B.C. 1440.
1 Ch. 2. 28 And the sons of Onam were S., and Jada
2. 28 And the sons of S.; Nadab, and Abishur
2. 32 And the sons of Jada the brother of S.
2. Father of Maon, and son of Rekem a descendant of Caleb son of Hezron. B.C. 1440.
1 Ch. 2. 44 Shema begat Raham..and Rekem begat S.
2. 45 the son of S. (was) Maon: and Maon (was)
3. A son or grandson of Ezra, of the family of Caleb son of Jephunneh. B.C. 1400.
1 Ch. 4. 17 she bare Miriam, and S., and Ishbah the f.

SHAM'-MOTH, שַׁמּוֹת *fame, renown*.
A Harorite, one of David's valiant men. B.C. 1048.
1 Ch 11. 27 S. the Harorite, Helez the Pelonite

SHAM-MU'-A, SHAM-MU'-AH, שַׁמּוּעַ *famous*.
1. A Reubenite, son of Zaccur, and sent by Moses to spy out the land. B.C. 1491.
Num 13. 4 of the tribe of Reuben, S. the son of Zac.
2. A son of David, born to him after he became king; in 1 Ch. 3. 5 he is called *Shimei*. B.C. 1020.
2 Sa. 5. 14 S., and Shobab, and Nathan, and Solom.
1 Ch. 14. 4 these (are) the names..S., and Shobab
3. Grandson of Juduthun, and father of Abda or Obadiah, a Levite appointed to lead the worship in the temple after the exile. In 1 Ch. 9. 16 it is *Shemaiah* B.C. 470.
Neh. 11. 17 Abda the son of S., the son of Galal, the
4. A priest in the family of Bilgah in the days of Nehemiah. B.C. 445.
Neh. 12. 18 Of Bilgah, S.; of Shemaiah, Jehonathan

SHAM-SHE'-RAI, שַׁמְשְׁרַי *heroic*.
A son of Jeroham, a Benjamite. B.C. 1300.
1 Ch. 8. 26 And S., and Sheharìah, and Athaliah

SHAPE —
1. *Appearance, aspect*, εἶδος *eidos*.
Luke 3. 22 the Holy Ghost descended in a bodily sh
John 5. 37 neither heard his voice..nor seen his sh.
2. *Likeness, resemblance*, ὁμοίωμα *homoiōma*.
Rev 9. 7 the shapes of the locusts (were) like unto

SHAPEN, to be —
To be formed, brought forth, חוּל, חִיל *chul, chil*, 4.
Psa. 51. 5 I was shapen in iniquity; and in sin did

SHA'-PHAM, שָׁפָם *youthful, vigorous*.
A chief of Gad, second in rank. B.C. 1070.
1 Ch. 5. 12 Joel the chief, and S. the next, and Jaan

SHA'-PHAN, שָׁפָן *prudent, sly*.
1. A scribe, son of Azaliah, father of Gemariah, who lived in the days of king Josiah. B.C. 640
2 Ki. 22. 3 the king sent S. the son of Azaliah, the son
22. 8 Hilkiah the high priest said unto S. the s.
22. 8 Hilkiah gave the book to S., and he read it
22. 9 S. the scribe came to the king, and brou.
22. 10 S. the scribe showed the king, saying, Hi.
22. 10 And S. read it before the king
22. 12 the king commanded..S. the scribe, and
22. 14 S., and Asahiah, went unto Huldah the
2 Ch. 34. 8 he sent S. the son of Azaliah, and Maas.
34. 15 Hilkiah answered and said to S. the scribe
34. 15 And Hilkiah delivered the book to S.
34. 16 S. carried the book to the king, and bro.
34. 18 S. the scribe told the king, saying, Hilkiah
34. 18 And S. read it before the king
34. 20 the king commanded..S. the scribe and
Jer. 36. 10 in the chamber of Gemariah the son of S
36. 11 Michaiah..son of Gemariah, the son of S
36. 12 Gemariah the son of S...and all the pri.
2. Father of Ahikam a chief officer in the court of Josiah. B.C. 640.
2 Ki. 22. 12 king commanded..Ahikam the son of S
25. 22 Gedaliah the son of Ahikam, the son of S.
2 Ch. 34. 20 king commanded..Ahikam the son of S.
Jer. 26. 24 the hand of Ahikam the son of S. was with
39. 14 Gedaliah the son of Ahikam the son of S.
40. 5, 9, 11 Gedaliah..son of Ahikam the son of S.
41. 2 Gedaliah the son of Ahikam, the son of S.
43. 6 Gedaliah the son of Ahikam, the son of S.
3. Father of Elasah by whom Jeremiah the prophet sent a letter to the exiles in Babylon. B.C. 640.
Jer. 29. 3 By the hand of Elasah the son of S., and
4. Father of Jaazaniah whom Ezekiel saw in a vision enticing people to idolatry. B.C. 595.
Eze. 8. 11 in the midst of them stood..the son of S.

SHA'-PHAT, שָׁפָט *judge*.
1. A Simeonite, son of Hori, and sent by Moses to spy the land. B.C. 1492.
Num 13. 5 Of the tribe of Simeon, S. the son of Hori
2. Father of Elisha the prophet. B.C. 930.
1 Ki. 19. 16 Elisha the son of S., of Abel-meholah, sh.
19. 19 he..found Elisha the son of S., who (was)
2 Ki. 3. 11 Here (is) Elisha the son of S., which poured
6. 31 if the head of Elisha the son of S. shall st.
3. A grandson of Shechaniah, of the family of David. B.C. 450.
1 Ch. 3. 22 and Igeal, and Bariah, and Neariah, and S
4. A chief Gadite, in Bashan. B.C. 1070.
1 Ch. 5. 12 Joel the chief..Jaania, and S. in Bashan
5. Son of Adlai, and over David's herds in the valley. B.C. 1015.
1 Ch. 27. 29 over the herds..in the valleys..S. the son

SHA'-PHER, שָׁפֶר *fair*.
A mountain in the wilderness, the next station of Israel after Kehelathah and before Haradah.
Num 33. 23 And they went..and pitched in mount S.
33. 24 they removed from mount S., and encam.

SHA'-RAI, שָׁרַי *Jah is deliverer*.
One of the sons of Bani that had taken a strange wife. B.C. 445.
Ezra 10. 40 Machnadebai, Shashai, S.

SHARAIM. *See* **SHAARAIM**.

SHA'-RAR, שָׁרָר *strong*.
One of David's valiant men. *See* **Sacar**.
2 Sa. 23. 33 Shammah the Hararite, Ahiam the..of S.

SHARE —
Mattock, sickle, מַחֲרֶשֶׁת *macharesheth*.
1 Sa. 13. 20 to sharpen every man his share, and his

SHAR-E'-ZER, SHER-E'-ZER, שַׂרְאֶצֶר.
1. A son of Sennacherib king of Assyria, who with his brother Adrammelech slew their father in the temple of Nisroch at Nineveh, and escaped into the land of Ararat. B.C. 710.
2 Ki. 19. 37 Adrammelech and S. his sons smote him
Isa. 37. 38 Adrammelech and S. his sons smote him
2. One who was sent to consult the priests and prophets in the temple as to a day of humiliation. B.C. 519
Zech. 7. 2 they had sent unto the house of God S.

SHA'-RON, שָׁרוֹן *a plain*.
1. The W. of Ephraim and Manasseh, extending from Joppa to Cæsarea, noted for its rich pastures and vegetation. In the midst of the plain between the modern Lydda and Arsuf lay the city *Sharon* (now a hamlet), supposed to be that meant in Josh. 12. 18.
Josh. 12. 18 The king of Aphek, one; the king of L. S.
1 Ch. 27. 29 over the herds that fed in S. (was) Shitrai
Song 2. 1 I (am) the rose of S., (and) the lily of the
Isa. 33. 9 S. is like a wilderness; and Bashan and
35. 2 the excellency of Carmel and S.; they shall
65. 10 S. shall be a fold of flocks, and the valley
2. A plain or city in the E. of Jordan, in Gad.
1 Ch. 5. 16 they dwelt..in all the suburbs of S., upon

SHARONITE, שָׁרוֹנִי.
A patronymic of Shitrai who was over the king's herds in Sharon. B.C. 1015
1 Ch. 27. 29 And over the herds..(was) Shitrai the S.

SHARP (stone), sharper—
1. *Sharp*, חַד *chad*.
Psa 57. 4 and arrows, and their tongue a sharp sw.
Prov. 5. 4 her end is..sharp as a two edged sword
Isa. 49. 2 he hath made my mouth like a sharp sw.
Eze. 5. 1 take thee a sharp knife, take thee a barb.
2. *Sharp things*, חַדּוּדִים *chaddudim*.
Job 41. 30 Sharp stones (are) under him: he spread.
3. *A sharp pointed thing*, חָרוּץ *charuts*.
Job 41. 30 he spreadeth sharp pointed things upon
Isa 41. 15 I will make thee a new sharp threshing
4. *To be sharpened*, לָטַשׁ *latash*, 4.
Psa 52. 2 like a sharp razor, working deceitfully
5. *A rock, sharpness*, צוּר *tsur*.
Josh. 5. 2 Make thee sharp knives, and circumcise
5. 3 made him sharp knives, and circumcised
6. *Flint*, צֹר *tsor*.
Exod. 4. 25 Then Zipporah took a sharp stone, and
7. *A tooth*, שֵׁן *shen*.
1 Sa. 14. 4 sharp rock on the one side, and a sharp
8. *To sharpen, be sharp*, שָׁנַן *shanan*.
Psa. 45. 5 Thine arrows (are) sharp in the heart of
120. 4 Sharp arrows of the mighty, with coals of
Prov 25. 18 a maul, and a sword, and a sharp arrow
Isa. 5. 28 Whose arrows (are) sharp, and all their
9. *Sharp, swift, acute*, ὀξύς *oxus*.
Rev. 1. 16 out of his mouth went a sharp two edged
2. 12 saith he which hath the sharp sword with
14. 14 golden crown, and in his hand a sharp si.
14. 17 another angel came out..having a sharp
14. 18 loud cry to him that had the sharp sickle
14. 18 Thrust in thy sharp sickle, and gather the
19. 15 out of his mouth goeth a sharp sword, that
10. *More cutting, sharper*, τομώτερος *tomōteros*.
Heb. 4. 12 sharper than any two edged sword, pier.

SHARPEN, to —
1. *To make sharp, acute, light*, חָדַד *chadad*.
Prov 27. 17 Iron sharpeneth iron; so a man..the co.
2. *To make sharp*, חָדַד *chadad*, 5.
Prov 27. 17 so a man sharpeneth the countenance of
3. *To sharpen, instruct*, לָטַשׁ *latash*.
1 Sa. 13. 20 to sharpen every man his share, and his
Job 16. 9 mine enemy sharpeneth his eyes upon me
4. *To set up*, נָצַב *natsab*, 5.
1 Sa. 13. 21 and for the axes, and to sharpen the goads
5. *To sharpen*, שָׁנַן *shanan*.
Psa. 140. 3 They have sharpened their tongues like

SHARPENED, to be —
To be made sharp, חָדַד *chadad*, 6.
Eze. 21. 9 a sword is sharpened, and also furbished
21. 10 It is sharpened to make a sore slaughter
21. 11 sword is sharpened, and it is furbished

SHARPLY, sharpness —
1. *Strength, with strength*, חָזְקָה *chozqah*.
Judg. 8. 1 And they did chide with him sharply
2. *Cuttingly, severely*, ἀποτόμως *apotomōs*.
2 Co. 13. 10 lest being present I should use sharpness
Titus 1. 13 Wherefore rebuke them sharply, that th.

SHA-RU'-HEN, שָׁרוּחֶן *dwelling of grace*.
A city in Simeon near Beth-lebaoth: perhaps *Shaarim*.
Josh. 19. 6 Beth-lebaoth, and S.; thirteen cities and

SHA'-SHAI, שָׁשַׁי *noble, free*.
One of the sons of Bani that had taken a strange wife. B.C. 445.
Ezra 10. 40 Machnadebai, S. Sharai

SHA'-SHAK, שָׁשַׁק *assaulter, runner*.
A son of Elpal, a Benjamite. B.C. 1400.
1 Ch. 8. 14 And Ahio, S., and Jeremoth
8. 25 Iphedeiah, and Penuel, the sons of S.

SHA'-UL, שָׁאוּל *asked*.
1. A son of Simeon by a Canaanitish woman. B.C. 1690.
Gen. 46. 10 Zohar, and S. the son of a Canaanitish wo.
Exod. 6. 15 Zohar, and S. the son of a Canaanitish wo.
Num 26. 13 of S., the family of the Shaulites
1 Ch. 4. 24 The sons of Simeon (were)..Zerah, (and) S.
2. An ancient king of Edom called Saul in Gen. 36. 37. B.C. 1490.
1 Ch. 1. 48 S. of Rehoboth by the river reigned in
1. 49 when S. was dead, Baal-hanan..reigned
3. A son of Kohath son of Levi.
1 Ch. 6. 24 Uriel, his son, Uzziah his son. and S. his

SHAULITES, שָׁאוּלִי.
The family of the son of Simeon.
Num 26. 13 of Shaul, the family of the S.

SHAVE (off), to —
1. *To cut off, shave, shear*, גָּזַז *gazaz*.
Job 1. 20 shaved his head, and fell down upon the
2. *To shave, poll the head*, גָּלַח *galach*, 3.
Gen. 41. 14 shaved (himself), and changed his raiment
Lev. 13. 33 but the scall shall he not shave; and the
14. 8 shave off all his hair, and wash himself in
14. 9 shave all his hair off his head and his be.
14. 9 even all his hair he shall shave off: and
21. 5 neither shall they shave off the corner of
Num. 6. 9 then he shall shave his head in the day of
6. 9 on the seventh day shall he shave it
6. 18 Nazarite shall shave the head of his sep.
Deut 21. 12 she shall shave her head, and pare her
Judg 16. 19 caused him to shave off the seven locks
2 Sa. 10. 4 shaved off the one half of their beards, and
1 Ch. 19. 4 shaved them, and cut off their garments
Isa. 7. 20 the LORD shave with a razor that is hired
Eze. 44 20 Neither shall they shave their heads, nor
3. *To cause a razor to pass over*, עָבַר תַּעַר *abar* (5) *taar*
Num. 8. 7 let them shave all their flesh, and let th.
4. *To scrape, shave*, ξυράω *xuraō*.
Acts 21. 24 at charges with them, that they may sh.

SHA'-VEH, שָׁוֵה *level place*.
A valley at Salem or Salim, near Ænon.
Gen. 14. 17 at the valley of S., which (is) the king's d.

SHA-VEH KIR-IA-THA'-IM, שָׁוֵה קִרְיָתַיִם.
A place in Reuben, where the Emim dwelt, who were smitten by Chedorlaomer in the days of Abraham and Lot. B.C. 1917.
Gen. 14. 5 and smote..the Emims in S. Kiriathaim

SHAVEN, to be —
1. *To be shaven*, גָּלַח *galach*, 4.
Judg 16. 17 if I be shaven, then my strength will go
16. 22 began to grow again after he was shaven
Jer. 41. 5 fourscore men, having their beards shaven
2. *To shave self, be shaven*, גָּלַח *galach*, 7.
Lev. 13. 33 He shall be shaven, but the scall shall he
Num. 6. 19 after (the hair of) his separation is shaven
3. *To scrape, shave*, ξυράω *xuraō*.
1 Co. 11. 5 that is even all one as if she were shaven
11. 6 shame for a woman to be..shaven, let her

SHAV'-SHA, שַׁוְשָׁא *nobility, splendour, dominion*.
David's scribe; perhaps the same as Seraiah in 2 Sa. 8. 17; Sheva in 2 Sa. 20. 25; and Shisha in 1 Ki. 4. 3. B.C. 1048.
1 Ch. 18. 16 Zadok..and Abimelech..the priests..S.

SHE —
1. *He, it*, הוּא *hu*.
Job 39. 30 and where the slain (are), there (is) she
2. *She, it*, הִיא *hi*.
Gen. 3. 12 she gave me of the tree, and I did eat
20. 5 She (is) my sister? and she..He (is) my br.

3. *This,* זאת *zoth.*
Gen. 2. 23 Woman, because she was taken out of man

4. *To this,* לְזֹאת *le-zoth.*
Gen. 2. 23 This (is) now..flesh of my flesh: she shall

5. *She herself,* αὐτή [*autos*].
Luke 1. 57 full time came that she should be delive.
7. 12 only son of his mother, and [she] was a wi

6. *This one,* αὕτη [*houtos*].
Matt26. 12 in that she hath poured this ointment on
Mark12. 44 but she of her want did cast in all that
14. 8 hath done what [she] could
14. 9 also that she hath done shall be spoken
Luke 2. 36 she was of a great age, and had lived with
2. 37 [she] (was) a widow of about fourscore an
2. 38 [she] coming in that instant gave thanks
7. 44; 8. 42; 21. 4; Rom. 16. 2

7. *Of one's self,* ἑαυτῆς *heautēs.*
Mark 5. 26 and had spent all that she had

8. *That very one,* ἐκείνη [*ekeinos*].
Mark16. 10 she went and told them that had been wi.
John11. 29 As soon as she heard (that)..arose quickly
20. 15 She, supposing him to be the gardener, sa.
20. 16 She turned herself, and saith unto him, R.

9. *This, that one,* ἥδε (*f.*) *hēde.*
Luke10. 39 she had a sister called Mary, which also

SHE ass —
A she ass, strong one, אָתוֹן *athon.*
Gen.12. 16 he had sheep, and oxen..and she asses, and
32. 15 ten bulls, twenty she asses, and ten foals
45. 23 ten she asses laden with corn and bread
Job 1. 3 five hundred she asses, and a very great
42. 12 yoke of oxen, and a thousand she asses

SHEAF —
1. *A sheaf,* אֲלֻמָּה *alummah.*
Gen. 37. 7 binding sheaves..and, lo, my sheaf arose
37. 7 your sheaves..made obeisance to my sh.
Psa.126. 6 with rejoicing, bringing his sheaves (with

2. *A sheaf,* עָמִיר *amir.*
Amos 2. 13 as a cart is pressed (that is) full of sheaves
Mic. 4. 12 gather them as the sheaves into the floor
Zech.12. 6 like a torch of fire in a sheaf; and they s.

3. *A sheaf, omer,* עֹמֶר *omer.*
Lev. 23. 10 then ye shall bring a sheaf of the first fr.
23. 11 he shall wave the sheaf before the LORD
23. 12 shall offer that day when ye wave the sh.
23. 15 from the day that ye brought the sheaf
Deut24. 19 hast forgot a sheaf in the field, thou sha.
Ruth 2. 7 gather after the reapers among the shea.
2. 15 Let her glean even among the sheaves, and
Job 24. 10 they take away the sheaf (from) the hun.

4. *A heap,* עֲרֵמָה *aremah.*
Neh. 13. 15 bringing in sheaves, and lading asses, as

SHE'-AL, שְׁאָל *request.*
One of the sons of Bani that had taken a strange wife. B.C. 445.
Ezra 10. 29 Malluch, and Adaiah, Jashub, and S and

SHE-AL-TI'-EL, שְׁאַלְתִּיאֵל שַׁלְתִּיאֵל. *See* Salathiel.
Father of Zerubbabel who led the Jews back from their exile in Babylon. B.C. 536.
Ezra 3. 2 Then stood up..Zerubbabel the son of S.
3. 8 in the second month, began..the son of S.
5. 2 Then rose up Zerubbabel the son of S., and
Neh.12. 1 Levites that went up with..the son of S.
Hag. 1. 1 the word..unto Zerubbabel the son of S.
1. 12 Zerubbabel the son of S., and Joshua the
1. 14 stirred up the spirit of..the son of S.
2. 2 Speak now to Zerubbabel the son of S. 2. 23

SHEAR, to —
To cut off, shave, shear, גָּזַז *gazaz.*
Gen. 31. 19 Laban went to shear his sheep: and Ra.
38. 13 goeth up to Timnath to shear his sheep
Deut15. 19 shalt do no work..nor shear the firstling
1 Sa. 25. 2 and he was shearing his sheep in Carmel
25. 4 David heard..that Nabal did shear his sh.

SHEARER, shearing house —
1. *To cut off, shave, shear,* גָּזַז *gazaz.*
Gen. 38. 12 went up unto his sheep shearers to Tim.
1 Sa. 25. 7 now I have heard that thou hast shearers
25. 11 my flesh that I have killed for my shear.
Isa. 53. 7 as a sheep before her shearers is dumb

2. *Marking house (of shepherds),* (בֵּית עֵקֶד (הָרֹעִים [*beth*].
2 Ki.10. 12 as he (was) at the shearing house in the
10. 14 slew them at the pit of the shearing hou.

3. *To cut off, shear, shave,* κείρω *keirō.*
Acts 8. 32 like a lamb dumb before his shearer, so

SHE-AR'-IAH, שְׁעַרְיָה *Jah is decider.*
Son of Azel a Benjamite, of the family of Saul. B.C. 860.
1 Ch. 8. 38 Azrikam, Bocheru, and Ishmael, and S.
9. 44 Azrikam, Bocheru, and Ishmael, and S.

SHE-AR JA'-SHUB, שְׁאָר יָשׁוּב *a remnant returns.*
A symbolic name given to a son of Isaiah the prophet before the Syrians and the Ephraimites invaded Judah in the days of king Ahaz. B.C. 742.
Isa. 7. 3 Go forth now to meet Ahaz, thou, and S.

SHEATH —
1. *A sheath,* נָדָן *nadan.*
1 Ch.21. 27 put up his sword again into the sheath

2. *Scabbard,* תַּעַר *taar.*
1 Sa.17. 51 drew it out of the sheath thereof, and sle
2 Sa.20. 8 sword fastened upon his loins in the she.
Eze. 21. 3 will draw forth my sword out of his she.
21. 4 shall my sword go forth out of his sheath
21. 5 drawn forth my sword out of his sheath
21. 30 Shall I cause (it) to return into his shea.?

3. *A scabbard, sheath,* θήκη *thēkē.*
John18. 11 Put up thy sword into the sheath: the cup

SHE'-BA, שְׁבָא.
1. Son of Raamah son of Cush son of Ham in N. Ethiopia. B.C. 2240.
Gen. 10. 7 and the sons of Raamah; S., and Dedan
1 Ch. 1. 9 And the sons of Raamah; S., and Dedan

2. Son of Yoktan of the family of Shem. B.C. 2200.
Gen. 10. 28 And Obal, and Abimael, and S.
1 Ch. 1. 22 And Ebal, and Abimael, and S.

3. A son of Yokshan, son of Abraham by Keturah, in Edom. B.C. 1800.
Gen. 25. 3 and Jokshan begat S. and Dedan. And
1 Ch. 1. 32 And the sons of Jokshan; S., and Dedan

4. A land in S.W. of Arabia, or in Africa near the Straits of Babel-mandeb.
1 Ki.10. 1 the queen of S. heard of the fame of Sol.
10. 4 the queen of S. had seen all Solomon's wi.
10. 10 these which the queen of S. gave to king
10. 13 Solomon gave unto the queen of S. all her
2 Ch. 9. 1 the queen of S. heard of the fame of Sol.
9. 3 the queen of S. had seen the wisdom of So.
9. 12 Solomon gave to the queen of S. all her
Job 6. 19 looked, the companies of S. waited for th.
Psa. 72. 10 the kings of S. and Seba shall offer gifts
72. 15 to him shall be given of the gold of S.
Isa. 60. 6 all they from S. shall come: they shall br.
Jer. 6. 20 what purpose cometh..incense from S.
Eze. 27. 22 The merchants of S. and Raamah, they
27. 23 the merchants of S., Asshur, (and) Chilmad
38. 13 S., and Dedan, and the merchants of Tar.

SHE'-BA, שֶׁבַע *oath, covenant.*
1. A city in Simeon, near Beersheba and Moladah; perhaps *Beer-sheba.*
Josh 19. 2 And they had in their inheritance..Sheba

2. A son of Bichri, a Benjamite who rebelled against David after Absalom's death, and whose head was cut off by the people of Abel. B.C. 1022.
2 Sa. 20. 1 a man..whose name (was) S., the son of
20. 2 So every man..followed S. the son of Bi.
20. 6 Now shall S...do us more harm than (did)
20. 7, v. 13 to pursue after S. the son of Bichri
20. 10 So Joab..pursued after S. the son of Bic.
20. 21 S...hath lifted up his hand against the ki.
20 22 and they cut off the head of S. the son of

3. A chief Gadite.
1 Ch. 5. 13 S., and Jorai, and Jachan, and Zia, and

SHE'-BAH, שִׁבְעָה *oath.*
A well dug by Isaac's servants near Beer-sheba in Judah. B.C. 1818.
Gen. 26. 33 he called it S.: therefore the name of the

SHE'-BAM, שְׂבָם *balsam.*
A city in Reuben, once belonging to Moab, then to the Amorites; it is also called *Sibmah,* and *Shibmah,* and was 500 paces from Heshbon, and the centre of the Moabite vineyards.
Num 32. 3 Heshbon, and Elealeh, and S , and Nebo

SHE-BAN'-IAH, שְׁבַנְיָהוּ, שְׁבַנְיָה *Jah is powerful.*
1. A priest who aided in bringing up the ark from the house of Obed-edom to Jerusalem. B.C. 1042.
1 Ch.15. 24 S., and Jehoshaphat, and Nethaneel, and

2. A Levite who guided the devotions of the people after Ezra had read the book of the law to them. B.C. 536.
Neh. 9. 4 Kadmiel, S., Bunni, Sherebiah, Bani, (and)
9. 5 Sherebiah, Hodijah, S., (and) Pethahiah
10. 10 their brethren, S., Hodijah, Kelita, Pela.

3. A priest that with Nehemiah sealed the covenant. B.C. 445.
Neh. 10. 4 Hattush, S., Malluch
12. 14 Of Melicu, Jonathan; of S., Joseph

4. A Levite that did the same.
Neh.10. 12 Zaccur, Sherebiah, S.

SHE-BA'-RIM, שְׁבָרִים *breaches.*
A place near Ai, N. of Jericho, in Benjamin.
Josh. 7. 5 chased them (from) before the gate .to S.

SHE'-BER, שֶׁבֶר *breach.*
A son of Caleb, son of Jephunneh by his concubine Maachah. B.C. 1430.
1 Ch. 2. 48 Maachah, Caleb's concubine, bare S., and

SHEB'-NA, (שֶׁבְנָה 2 Ki. 18. 18, 26), שֶׁבְנָא *youthfulness.*
1. The scribe or secretary of king Hezekiah. B.C. 713.
2 Ki. 18. 18 S. the scribe, and Joah the son of Asaph
18. 26 said Eliakim the son of Hilkiah, and S.
18. 37 S. the scribe, and Joah the son of Asaph
19. 2 he sent Eliakim..and S. the scribe, and
Isa. 36. 3 S. the scribe, and Joah, Asaph's son, the
36. 11 Then said Eliakim and S. and Joah unto
36. 22 Then came Eliakim..and S. the scribe, and
37. 2 he sent Eliakim..and S. the scribe, and

2. The treasurer over the house who was to be supplanted by Eliakim son of Hilkiah. B.C. 700.
Isa. 22. 15 get thee unto this treasurer..unto S., wh.

SHE-BU'-EL, שְׁבוּאֵל *God is renown.*
1. A son of Gershom son of Levi. B.C. 1015.
1 Ch.23. 16 Of the sons of Gershom, S. (was) the ch.
26. 24 S. the son of Gershom, the son of Moses

2. A son of Haman chief singer in the sanctuary in the days of David; in verse 20 it is *Shubael.* B.C. 1015.
1 Ch.25. 4 Mattaniah, Uzziel, S., and Jerimoth, Ha.

SHECANIAH, שְׁכַנְיָהוּ.
1. A priest in the time of David; 1 Ch. 24. 11.
2. A priest in the time of Hezekiah; 2 Ch. 31. 15.

SHE-CHAN'-IAH, שְׁכַנְיָהוּ, שְׁכַנְיָה *Jah is a neighbour.*
1. Head of a family of the house of David. B.C. 470.
1 Ch. 3. 21 Arnan, the sons of Obadiah, the sons of S.
3. 22 the sons of S.; Shemaiah; and the sons of

2. A person some of whose descendants returned with Ezra in the days of Artaxerxes. B.C. 536.
Ezra 8. 3 Of the sons of S., of the sons of Pharosh

3. Another whose descendants did the same.
Ezra. 8. 5 Of the sons of S.; the son of Jahaziel, and

4. A son of Jehiel, and who first confessed the trespass of taking strange wives. B.C. 445.
Ezra10. 2 S...answered and said unto Ezra, We have

5. Father of Shemaiah who helped to repair the wall. B.C. 445.
Neh. 3. 29 After him repaired..Shemaiah..son of S.

6. Father in law of Tobiah the Ammonite who opposed Nehemiah. B.C. 445.
Neh. 6. 18 because he (was) the son in law of S. the

7. A priest who returned with Zerubbabel. B.C. 536.
Neh. 12. 3 S., Rehum, Meremoth

SHE'-CHEM, שְׁכֶם, שְׁכֶם *shoulder.*
1. A Levitical city and district in Mount Ephraim, on Gerizim and Ebal; it was also a city of refuge, and the first residence of the kings of Israel or of the ten tribes. In the time of the Romans it was called *Neapolis,* and at present Nablus, and is the seat of the Samaritan worship; it was the first city in Canaan visited by Abraham, B.C. 1921; here Joshua addressed for the last time the tribes of Israel, B.C. 1427; Abimelech was elected king by its inhabitants, B.C. 1235; and all Israel was assembled there to make Rehoboam king, B.C. 975; at Jacob's well, in its vicinity, Jesus met with the woman of Samaria, A.D. 27; and Justin Martyr was born here, about A.D. 100.
Gen. 33. 18 Jacob came to Shalem a city of S., which
35. 4 hid them under the oak which (was) by S.
37. 12 went to feed their father's flock in S.
37. 13 Do not thy brethren feed (the flock) in S?
37. 14 So he sent him out..and he came to S.
Josh.17. 7 Asher to Michmethah..(lieth) before S.
20. 7 they appointed..S. in mount Ephraim
21. 21 they gave them S. with her suburbs in mo.
24. 1 Joshua gathered..the tribes of Israel to S.
24. 25 set them a statute and an ordinance in S.
24. 32 the bones of Joseph..buried they in S., in
Judg. 8. 31 his concubine that (was) in S., she also bare
9. 1 Abimelech the son of Jerubbaal went to S.
9. 2 Speak..in the ears of all the men of S., W.
9. 3 spake..in the ears of all the men of S.
9. 6 the men of S. gathered together, and all
9. 6 by the plain of the pillar that (was) in S.
9. 7 Hearken unto me, ye men of S., that God
9. 18 made Abimelech..king over the men of S.
9. 20 let fire come..and devour the men of S.
9. 20 let fire come out from the men of S., and
9. 23 the men of S.; and the men of S. dealt
9. 24 upon the men of S., which aided him in
9. 25 the men of S. set liers in wait for him in
9. 26 went over to S.: and the men of S. put the
9. 31 Gaal..and his brethren, be come to S.
9. 34 they laid wait against S. in four compa.
9. 39 Gaal went out before the men of S., and
9. 41 that they should not dwell in S.
9. 46 when all the men of the tower of S. heard
9. 47 the men of the tower of S. were gathered
9. 49 all the men of the tower of S. died also
9. 57 the evil of the men of S. did God render
21. 19 highway that goeth up from Beth-el to S.
1 Ki.12. 1 went to S.: for all Israel were come to S.
12. 25 Jeroboam built S. in mount Ephraim, and
1 Ch. 6. 67 they gave unto them..S. in mount Eph.
7. 28 S. also and the towns thereof, unto Gaza.
2 Ch.10. 1 Rehoboam went to S.: for to S. were all
Psa. 60. 6 I will divide S., and mete out the valley
108. 7 I will divide S., and mete out the valley
Jer. 41. 5 That there came certain from S., from

2. A son of Hamor, a Hivite prince, who defiled Jacob's daughter Dinah, and was treacherously slain for it with all his followers by Simeon and Levi her maternal brothers. B.C. 1732.
Gen. 33. 19 at the hand of the children of Hamor, S.'s
34. 2 when S. the son of Hamor..saw her, he
34. 4 S. spake unto his father Hamor, saying
34. 6 Hamor the father of S. went out unto Ja.
34. 8 The soul of my son S. longeth for your
34. 11 S. said unto her father and unto her br.
34. 13 the sons of Jacob answered S. and Hamor
34. 18 their words pleased Hamor, and S., Ha.
34. 20 Hamor and S...came unto the gate of th.
34. 24 unto Hamor, and unto S. his son, heark.
34. 26 they slew Hamor and S. his son with the
34. 26 took Dinah out of S.'s house, and went out
Josh.24. 32 of the sons of Hamor the father of S.
Judg. 9. 28 Who (is) Abimelech, and who (is) S., that
9. 28 Serve the men of Hamor the father of S.

3. A son of Gilead, son of Manasseh. B.C. 1450.
Num 26. 31 and (of) S., the family of the Shechemites
Josh 17. 2 for the children of S., and for the childr.
4. A son of Shemidah, a Manassite. B.C. 1400.
1 Ch. 7. 19 the sons of Shemidah were Ahian, and S.

SHECHEMITE, הַשִּׁכְמִי.
The family of Shechem son of Gilead.
Num 26. 31 and (of) Shechem, the family of the S.

SHED (abroad, forth, out), be shed, to —
1. *To cause to pour out or run,* נָגַר *nagar,* 5.
Eze. 35. 5 hast shed (the blood of) the children of I.
2. *To place, set, put,* שׂוּם, שִׂים *sum, sim.*
1 Ki. 2. 5 shed the blood of war in peace, and put
3. *To pour or shed out,* שָׁפַךְ *shaphak.*
Gen. 9. 6 Whoso sheddeth man's blood, by man sh.
37. 22 Shed no blood, (but) cast him into this pit
Lev. 17. 4 he hath shed blood; and that man shall
Num 35. 33 but by the blood of him that shed it
Deut 21. 7 Our hands have not shed this blood, neit.
1 Sa. 25. 31 either that thou hast shed blood cause.
2 Sa. 20. 10 shed out his bowels to the ground, and
1 Ki. 2. 31 innocent blood, which Joab shed, from
2 Ki. 21. 16 Manasseh shed innocent blood very much
24. 4 also for the innocent blood that he shed
1 Ch. 22. 8 Thou hast shed blood abundantly, and ha.
22. 8 because thou hast shed much blood upon
28. 3 (hast been) a man of war, and hast shed
Psa. 79. 3 Their blood have they shed like water ro.
79. 10 of the blood of thy servants (which is) sh.
106. 38 shed innocent blood, (even) the blood of
Prov 1. 16 run to evil, and make haste to shed blood
6. 17 lying tongue, and hands that shed innoc.
Isa. 59. 7 they make haste to shed innocent blood
Jer. 7. 6 shed not innocent blood in this place, ne.
22. 3 neither shed innocent blood in this place
22. 17 for to shed innocent blood, and for oppre.
Lam. 4. 13 that have shed the blood of the just in
Eze. 16. 38 break wedlock and shed blood are judged
22. 3 The city sheddeth blood in the midst of
22. 4 guilty in thy blood that thou hast shed
22. 6 one were in thee to their power to shed
22. 9 In thee are men that carry tales to shed
22. 12 In thee have they taken gifts to shed bl.
22. 27 to shed blood, (and) to destroy souls, to
23. 45 after the manner of women that shed bl
33. 25 lift up your eyes..and shed blood: and sh.
36. 18 for the blood that they had shed upon the
Joel 3. 19 because they have shed innocent blood
4. *To be poured out, shed,* שָׁפַךְ *shaphak,* 2.
Gen. 9. 6 by man shall his blood be shed: for in the
Deut 19. 10 That innocent blood be not shed in thy
5. *To be poured out, shed,* שָׁפַךְ *shaphak,* 4.
Num 35. 33 cleansed of the blood that is shed therein
6. *To pour out, shed,* ἐκχέω *ekcheō.*
Acts 2. 33 he hath shed forth this, which ye now see
22. 20 blood of thy martyr Stephen [was shed]
Rom. 3. 15 Their feet (are) swift to shed blood
Titus 3. 6 Which he shed on us abundantly through
Rev. 16. 6 For they have shed the blood of saints and
7. *To pour out, shed,* ἐκχύνω *ekchunō.*
Matt 23. 35 may come all the righteous blood shed up.
26. 28 is shed for many for the remission of sins
Mark 14. 24 blood of the new testament, which is sh.
Luke 11. 50 which was shed from the foundation of the
22. 20 testament in my blood, which is shed for
Rom. 5. 5 because the love of God is shed abroad in

SHEDDER —
To pour out, שָׁפַךְ *shaphak.*
Eze. 18. 10 If he beget a son (that is)..a shedder of

SHEDDING of blood —
Pouring out of blood, αἱματεκχυσία *haimatekchusia.*
Heb. 9. 22 without shedding of blood is no remission

SHE-DE'-UR, שְׁדֵיאוּר *shedder of light.*
A Reubenite, father of Elizur, chosen to assist in numbering the people in the days of Moses. B.C. 1525.
Num. 1. 5 (the tribe of) Reuben; Elizur the son of S.
2. 10 captain..(shall be) Elizur the son of S
7. 30 On the fourth day Elizur the son of S.. pr.
7. 35 this (was) the offering of..the son of S.
10. 18 over his host (was) Elizur the son of S.

SHEEP —
1. *A lamb,* כֶּבֶשׂ *kebes.*
Exod 12. 5 ye shall take (it) out from the sheep, or
Job 31. 20 (not) warmed with the fleece of my sheep
2. *A lamb,* כֶּשֶׂב *keseb.*
Gen. 30. 32 all the brown cattle among the sheep, and
30. 33 one that (is) not..brown among the sheep
30. 35 all the brown among the sheep, and gave
Lev. 1. 10 if his offering (be)..of the sheep, or of the
7. 23 eat no manner of fat, of ox, or of sheep
22. 19 of the beeves, of the sheep, or of the goats
22. 27 When a bullock, or a sheep, or a goat, is
Num 18. 17 firstling of a sheep, or the firstling of a g.
Deut 14. 4 beasts which ye shall eat: The ox, the s.
3. *Sheep,* צֹאן *tson.*
Gen. 4. 2 Abel was a keeper of sheep, but Cain was
12. 16 he had sheep, and oxen, and he asses, and
20. 14 Abimelech took sheep, and oxen, and men
21. 27 Abraham took sheep and oxen, and gave
29. 2 there (were) three flocks of sheep lying by
29. 3 watered the sheep, and put the stone ag.
29. 6 Rachel his daughter cometh with the sh.
29. 7 water ye the sheep, and go (and) feed (th.)
29. 8 gathered together..then we water the sh.
29. 9 Rachel came with her father's sheep, for
29. 10 and the sheep of Laban his mother's bro.
31. 19 Laban went to shear his sheep: and Rac.
34. 28 They took their sheep, and their oxen, and
38. 13 goeth up to Timnath to shear his sheep
Exod 9. 3 camels, upon the oxen, and upon the sh.
20. 24 thy peace offerings, thy sheep, and thine
22. 1 five oxen for an ox, and four sheep for a
22. 30 Likewise shalt thou do..with thy sheep
Lev. 22. 21 a free will offering in beeves or sheep, it
Num 22. 40 offered oxen and sheep, and sent to Bala.
27. 17 congregation of the LORD be not as sheep
31. 28 beeves, and of the asses, and of the sheep
31. 32 seventy thousand and five thousand sheep
31. 36 and thirty thousand and five hundred sh.
31. 37 LORD'S tribute of the sheep was six hun.
31. 43 seven thousand and five hundred sheep
32. 36 Beth-haran, fenced cities; and folds for sh.
Deut. 7. 13 flocks of thy sheep, in the land which he
14. 26 for oxen, or for sheep, or for wine, or for
15. 19 bullock, nor shear the firstling of thy sh.
18. 4 first of the fleece of thy sheep, shalt thou
28. 4 Blessed (shall be)..the flocks of thy sheep
28. 18 Cursed (shall be)..the flocks of thy sheep
28. 31 thy sheep (shall be) given unto thine eni.
28. 51 not leave thee..flocks of thy sheep, until
32. 14 Butter of kine, and milk of sheep, with
Josh 7. 24 his sheep, and his tent, and all that he had
1 Sa. 8. 17 He will take the tenth of your sheep, and
14. 32 took sheep, and oxen, and calves, and sl.
15. 9 best of the sheep, and of the oxen, and of
15. 14 What (meaneth) then this bleating of the s.
15. 15 people spared the best of the sheep and of
15. 21 sheep and oxen, the chief of the things
16. 11 keepeth the sheep. And Samuel said unto
16. 19 Send me David..which (is) with the sheep
17. 15 returned from Saul to feed his father's sh.
17. 20 left the sheep with a keeper, and took, and
17. 28 with whom hast thou left those few sheep
17. 34 Thy servant kept his father's sheep, and
25. 2 had three thousand sheep..shearing his sh.
25. 4 David heard..that Nabal did shear his sh.
25. 16 while we were with them keeping the sh.
25. 18 five sheep ready dressed, and five measures
27. 9 took away the sheep, and the oxen, and the
2 Sa. 7. 8 I took thee..from following the sheep, to be
17. 29 honey, and butter, and sheep, and cheese
24. 17 but these sheep, what have they done? Let
1 Ki. 1. 9 Adonijah slew sheep and oxen and fat ca.
1. 19, 25 hath slain oxen and fat cattle and sheep
4. 23 an hundred sheep, beside harts, and roeb.
8. 5 sacrificing sheep and oxen, that could not
8. 63 an hundred and twenty thousand sheep
22. 17 scattered upon the hills, as sheep that ha.
2 Ki. 5. 26 (Is it) a time to receive..sheep, and oxen
1 Ch. 5. 21 of sheep two hundred and fifty thousand
12. 40 brought..oxen, and sheep abundantly: for
17. 7 I took thee..from following the sheep, th.
21. 17 but (as for) these sheep, what have they
2 Ch. 5. 6 sacrificed sheep and oxen, which could not
7. 5 an hundred and twenty thousand sheep
14. 15 carried away sheep and camels in abund.
15. 11 And they offered..seven thousand sheep
18. 2 killed sheep and oxen for him in abundance
18. 16 as sheep that have no shepherd: and the
29. 33 consecrated things (were)..three thous. s.
30. 24 seven thousand sheep..ten thousand she.
31. 6 also brought in the tithe of oxen and sheep
Neh. 3. 1 they builded the sheep gate; they sancti.
3. 32 unto the sheep gate repaired the goldsm.
5. 18 six choice sheep; also fowls were prepar.
12. 39 tower of Meah, even unto the sheep gate
Job 1. 3 substance also was seven thousand sheep
1. 16 hath burnt up the sheep, and the servants
42. 12 for he had fourteen thousand sheep, and s.
Psa. 44. 11 Thou hast given us like sheep (appointed)
44. 22 we are counted as sheep for the slaughter
49. 14 Like sheep they are laid in the grave; death
74. 1 doth thine anger smoke against the sheep
78. 52 made his own people to go forth like sheep
79. 13 So we thy people, and sheep of thy pasture
95. 7 people of his pasture, and the sheep of his
100. 3 his people, and the sheep of his pasture
144. 13 our sheep may bring forth thousands and
Isa. 7. 21 shall nourish a young cow and two sheep
13. 14 as a sheep that no man taketh up: they
22. 13 slaying oxen and killing sheep, eating flesh
53. 6 All we like sheep have gone astray; we
Jer. 12. 3 pull them out like sheep for the slaughter
23. 1 destroy and scatter the sheep of my past.
50. 6 My people hath been lost sheep; their sh.
Eze. 34. 6 My sheep wandered through all the mo.
34. 11 both search my sheep, and seek them out
34. 12 in the day that he is among his sheep (that)
34. 12 so will I seek out my sheep, and will de.
Joel 1. 18 yea, the flocks of sheep are made desolate
Mic. 2. 12 I will put them together as the sheep of
5. 8 young lion among the flocks of sheep; who
Zech 13. 7 sheep shall be scattered; and I will turn
4. *Sheep,* צֹאן *tson* [V.L. צאון].
Psa. 144. 13 our sheep may bring forth thousands and
5. *A sheep, sheep,* צֹנֶה, צֹנֶא *tsoneh, tsone.*
Num 32. 24 Build..folds for your sheep; and do that
Psa. 8. 7 All sheep and oxen, yea, and the beasts of
6. *A ewe, lamb,* רָחֵל *rachel.*
Song 6. 6 Thy teeth (are) as a flock of sheep which
Isa. 53. 7 as a sheep before her shearers is dumb
7. *A young lamb, kid, sheep,* שֶׂה *seh.*
Exod 22. 1 If a man shall steal an ox, or a sheep, and
22. 1 five oxen for an ox, and four..for a sheep
22. 4 whether it be ox, or ass, or sheep, he sh.
22. 9 for ox, for ass, for sheep, for raiment, (or)
22. 10 If a man deliver..a sheep, or any beast, to
34. 19 among thy cattle, (whether) ox or sheep
Lev. 27. 26 whether (it be) ox or sheep, it (is) the L.
Deut 17. 1 bullock or sheep wherein is blemish, (or)
18. 3 whether (it be) ox or sheep; and they sh.
22. 1 not see thy brother's ox or his sheep go
Josh. 6. 21 sheep, and ass, with the edge of the sword
Judg. 6. 4 no sustenance for Israel, neither sheep
1 Sa. 14. 34 Bring me hither..every man his sheep
15. 3 slay both..ox and sheep, camel and ass
22. 19 oxen, and asses, and sheep, with the edge
Psa. 119. 176 I have gone astray like a lost sheep, seek
Jer. 50. 17 Israel (is) a scattered sheep; the lions have
8. *A sheep, sheep,* πρόβατον *probaton.*
Matt. 7. 15 which come to you in sheep's clothing, but
9. 36 scattered abroad, as sheep having no sh.
10. 6 But go rather to the lost sheep of the ho.
10. 16 send you forth as sheep in the midst of
12. 11 What man..that shall have one sheep, and
12. 12 How much..is a man better than a sheep?
15. 24 I am not sent but unto the lost sheep of the
18. 12 If a man have an hundred sheep, and one
25. 32 as a shepherd divideth (his) sheep from
25. 33 he shall set the sheep on his right hand
26. 31 sheep of the flock shall be scattered ab.
Mark 6. 34 because they were as sheep not having a
14. 27 smite the shepherd, and the sheep shall
Luke 15. 4 What man..having an hundred sheep, if
15. 6 for I have found my sheep which was lost
John 2. 14 those that sold oxen and sheep and doves
2. 15 drove them all out..the sheep, and the
10. 2 But he..is the shepherd of the sheep
10. 3 sheep hear his voice..calleth his own sh.
10. 4 when he putteth forth his own [sheep], he
10. 4 sheep follow him: for they know his voice
10. 7 say unto you, I am the door of the sheep
10. 8 robbers: but the sheep did not hear them
10. 11 good shepherd giveth his life for the sheep
10. 12 hireling..whose own the sheep are not
10. 12 seeth the wolf..and leaveth the sheep
10. 12 [wolf catcheth them, and scattereth the s.]
10. 13 fleeth, because he..careth not for the sheep
10. 15 and I lay down my life for the sheep
10. 16 other sheep I have, which are not of this
10. 26 believe not, because ye are not of my sheep
10. 27 My sheep hear my voice, and I know them
21. 16, 17 saith unto him, Feed my [sheep]
Acts 8. 32 He was led as a sheep to the slaughter
Rom. 8. 36 we are accounted as sheep for the slaughter
Heb. 13. 20 Jesus, that great shepherd of the sheep
1 Pe. 2. 25 For ye were as sheep going astray; but are
Rev. 18. 13 sheep, and horses, and chariots, and slaves

SHEEP COTE, (fold, market) —
1. *A fence for the flock,* גִּדְרֹת צֹאן *gedereth tson.*
Num 32. 16 We will build sheep folds here for our ca.
1 Sa. 24. 3 came to the sheep cotes by the way, where
2. *Restraints for the flock,* מִכְלְאֹת צֹאן [*miklah*].
Psa. 78. 70 servant, and took him from the sheep fold
3. *Double places or folds,* מִשְׁפְּתַיִם *mishpethayim.*
Judg. 5. 16 Why abodest thou among the sheep folds
4. *Home, habitation, fold,* נָוֶה *naveh.*
2 Sa. 7. 8 I took thee from the sheep cote, from foll.
1 Ch. 17. 7 I took thee from the sheep cote, (even) fr.
5. *Court of the sheep,* αὐλὴ τῶν προβάτων [*aulē*].
John 10. 1 entereth not by the door into the sheep f.
6. *Of or belonging to sheep,* προβατικός *probatikos.*
John 5 2 at Jerusalem, by the sheep (market), a po.

SHEEP MASTER or shearer —
1. *To cut off, shave, shear,* גָּזַז *gazaz.*
2 Sa. 13. 23 Absalom had sheep shearers in Baal-hazor
13. 24 Behold now, thy servant hath sheep sh.
2. *To shear the flock,* גָּזַז צֹאן *gazaz tson.*
Gen. 38. 12 went up unto his sheep shearers to Tim.
3. *Herdsman, sheep master,* נֹקֵד *noqed.*
2 Ki. 3. 4 Mesha king of Moab was a sheep master

SHEEP (skin) —
Of or belonging to a sheep, μηλωτή *mēlōtē.*
Heb. 11. 37 they wandered about in sheep skins and

SHEET —
1. *Linen garments,* סָדִין *sadin.*
Judg 14. 12, 13 thirty sheets and thirty change of ga.
2. *A piece of linen, a linen sheet,* ὀθόνη *othonē.*
Acts 10. 11 a great sheet knit at the four corners, and
11. 5 as it had been a great sheet, let down from

SHE-HAR'-IAH, שְׁחַרְיָה *Jah is the dawn.*
A son of Jeroham, a Benjamite. B.C. 1360.
1 Ch. 8 26 And Shamsherai, and S., and Athaliah

SHEKEL —
A shekel, florin, שֶׁקֶל *sheqel.*
Gen. 23. 15 the land (is worth) four hundred shekels
23. 16 four hundred shekels of silver, current
Exod 21. 32 give unto their master thirty shekels of
30. 13 half a shekel after the shekel of the san.
30. 13 a shekel (is) twenty gerahs: an half shekel
30. 15 the poor shall not give less, than half a sh.
30. 24 five hundred..after the shekel of the sa.
38. 24, 25, 26 shekels, after the shekel of the sa.
38. 29 and two thousand and four hundred she.

Lev. 5. 15 shekels of silver, after the shekel of the
27. 3 shekels of silver, after the shekel of the
27. 4 then thy estimation shall be thirty shekels
27. 5 twenty shekels, and for the female ten s.
27. 6 five shekels of silver..three shekels of si.
27. 7 fifteen shekels, and for the female ten sh.
27. 16 seed (shall be valued) at fifty shekels of
27. 25 shekel..twenty gerahs shall be the shekel
Num. 3. 47 Thou shalt even take five shekels apiece
3. 47 after the shekel..the shekel (is) twenty
3. 50 took he..after the shekel of the sanctuary
7. 13 shekels, after the shekel of the sanctuary
[So in verse 19, 25, 31, 37, 43, 49, 55, 61, 67, 73, 79]
7. 85, 86 after the shekel of the sanctuary
18. 16 shekels, after the shekel of the sanctuary
31. 52 thousand seven hundred and fifty shekels
Josh. 7. 21 shekels of silver, and a wedge..fifty she.
1 Sa. 9. 8 here at hand the fourth part of a shekel
17. 5 weight of the coat (was) five thousand sh.
17. 7 spear's head (weighed) six hundred shek.
2 Sa. 14. 26 two hundred shekels after the king's we.
24. 24 bought the threshing floor..for fifty shek.
2 Ki. 7. 1 a measure of fine flour (be sold) for a sh.
7. 1, 16 two measures of barley for a shekel
7. 16 measure of fine flour was (sold) for a she.
7. 18 Two measures of barley for a shekel, and
7. 18 measure of fine flour for a shekel, shall
15. 20 of each man fifty shekels of silver, to give
1 Ch. 21. 25 six hundred shekels of gold by weight
2 Ch. 3. 9 weight of the nails (was) fifty shekels of
Neh. 5. 15 bread and wine, besides forty shekels of
10. 32 with the third part of a shekel for the se.
Jer. 32. 9 weighed him the money..seventeen she.
Eze. 4. 10 (shall be) by weight, twenty shekels a day
45. 12 shekel (shall be) twenty gerahs: twenty
45. 12 five and twenty shekels, fifteen shekels
Amos 8. 5 making the ephah small, and the shekel

SHEKEL, half a —

A drachma, a shilling, בֶּקַע *beqa.*

Gen. 24. 22 took a golden earring of half a shekel we.

SHE'-LAH, שֵׁלָה *peace.*

1. Youngest son of Judah, by the daughter of Shua the Canaanite. B.C. 1700.

Gen. 38. 5 she..bare a son; and called his name S.
38. 11 Remain a widow..till S. my son be grown
38. 14 she saw that S. was grown, and she was
38. 26 because that I gave her not to S. my son
46. 12 the sons of Judah; Er, and Onan, and S.
Num 26. 20 of S., the family of the Shelanites: of P.
1 Ch. 2. 3 The sons of Judah; Er, and Onan, and S.
4. 21 The sons of S. the son of Judah (were) Er

2. Son of Arphaxad (שֶׁלַח). In A.V. also called Salah.

1 Ch. 1. 18 And Arphaxad begat S., and S. begat E.
1. 24 Shem, Arphaxad, S.

SHELANITES, הַשֵּׁלָנִי.

The family of Shelah son of Judah.

Num 26. 20 of Shelah, the family of the S.: of Pharez

SHE-LEM'-IAH, שֶׁלֶמְיָה, שֶׁלֶמְיָהוּ *Jah is recompense.*

1. A Levite, a gatekeeper of the tabernacle in the days of David. B.C. 1015.

1 Ch. 26. 14 the lot eastward fell to S. Then for Zech.

2. One of the sons of Bani that had taken a strange wife. B.C. 445.

Ezra 10. 39 And S., and Nathan, and Adaiah

3. Another of the same family that had done the same.

Ezra 10. 41 Azareel, and S., Shemariah

4. Father of Hananiah that helped to repair the wall. B.C. 445.

Neh. 3. 30 After him repaired Hananiah the son of S.

5. A priest set over the treasuries by Nehemiah. B.C. 445.

Neh. 13. 13 I made treasurers over the treasuries, S. the

6. Son of Cushi and grandfather of Jehudi who was sent by the princes of Judah to bring Baruch before their council. B.C. 650

Jer. 36. 14 Nethaniah, the son of S., the son of Cushi

7. Son of Abdeel, and ordered by Jehoiakim to take Baruch the scribe and Jeremiah the prophet. B.C. 605.

Jer. 36. 26 the king commanded..S the son of Abd.

8. Father of Jehucal, who was sent by Zedekiah to ask the prayers of Jeremiah. B.C. 620.

Jer. 37. 3 the king sent Jehucal the son of S., and
38. 1 Jucal the son of S., and Pashur the son of

9. Father of Irijah captain of the guard at the gate of Benjamin, who apprehended Jeremiah when about to leave Jerusalem. B.C. 620.

Jer. 37. 13 whose name (was) Irijah, the son of S., the

SHE'-LEPH, שֶׁלֶף *drawn out.*

A son of Joktan of the family of Shem. B.C. 2210.

Gen. 10. 26 Joktan begat Almodad, and S., and Haz.
1 Ch. 1. 20 Joktan begat Almodad, and S., and Haza.

SHE'-LESH, שֵׁלֶשׁ *might.*

A son of Helem, grandson of Beriah, son of Asher. B.C. 1600.

1 Ch. 7. 35 Zophah, and Imna, and S., and Amal

SHE-LO'-MI, שְׁלֹמִי *Jah is peace.*

Father of Ahihud, a chief Asherite, one of those chosen to divide the land W. of the Jordan. B.C. 1510.

Num 34. 27 the prince..of Asher, Ahihud the son of S.

SHE-LO'-MITH, שְׁלֹמִית, שְׁלוֹמִית *peacefulness.*

1. The daughter of Dibri, of the tribe of Dan, and mother of the person stoned for blaspheming the name of the Lord in the wilderness, in the days of Moses. B.C. 1450.

Lev. 24. 11 his mother's name (was) S., the daughter

2. Daughter of Zerubbabel, grandson of Jeconiah son of Jehoiakim king of Judah. B.C. 500.

1 Ch. 3. 19 Meshullam, and Hananiah, and S. their

3. A son of Shimei, and descendant of Gershon son of Levi, in the days of David. B.C. 1015.

1 Ch. 23. 9 sons of Shimei; S., and Haziel, and Haran

4. A son of Izhar, a Kohathite. B.C. 1015.

1 Ch. 23. 18 Of the sons of Izhar; S. the chief.

5. A descendant of Eliezer son of Moses, set over the dedicated treasures in the days of David. B.C. 1015.

1 Ch. 26. 25 Joram his son, and Zichri his son, and S.
26. 26 S. and his brethren (were) over all the tr
26. 28 it was) under the hand of S., and of his

6. A son or daughter of king Rehoboam. B.C. 960.

2 Ch. 11. 20 bare him Abijah, and Attai, and Ziza, and S.

7. Ancestor of a family that returned with Ezra B.C. 536

Ezra 8. 10 of the sons of S.; the son of Josiphiah, and

SHE-LO'-MOTH, שְׁלֹמוֹת *peacefulness.*

A descendant of Izhar (*Cf.* Shelomith, 3 & 5). B.C. 1015.

1 Ch. 24. 22 Of the Izharites; S.: of the sons of S.; J.

SHELTER —

A refuge, מַחְסֶה *machseh.*

Job 24. 8 and embrace the rock for want of a shelter
Psa. 61. 3 For thou hast been a shelter for me, (and)

SHE-LU-MI'-EL, שְׁלֻמִיאֵל *God is peace*

The son of Zurishaddai and a chief of Simeon appointed to assist Moses in numbering the people. B.C. 1490.

Num. 1. 6 Of Simeon; S. the son of Zurishaddai.
2. 12 the captain..(shall be) S. the son of Zuri.
7. 36 S. the son of Zurishaddai, prince of the
7. 41 this (was) the offering of S. the son of Zu.
10. 19 over..Simeon (was) S. the son of Zurisha.

SHEM, שֵׁם *name, renown.*

A son of Noah, ancestor of Elam, Asshur, Arphaxad, Lud, and Aram. B.C. 2248.

Gen. 5. 32 and Noah begat S., Ham, and Japheth
6. 10 And Noah begat three sons, S., Ham, and
7. 13 In the selfsame day entered Noah, and S.
9. 18 the sons of Noah..were S., and Ham, and
9. 23 S. and Japheth took a garment, and laid
9. 26 he said, Blessed (be) the LORD God of S.
9. 27 he shall dwell in the tents of S., and Can.
10. 1 these (are)..the sons of Noah; S., Ham
10. 21 Unto S. also, the father of all the children
10. 22 The children of S.; Elam, and Asshur, and
10. 31 These (are) the sons of S., after their fam.
11. 10 These (are) the generations of S.: S. (was)
11. 11 S. lived after he begat Arphaxad five hu.
1 Ch. 1. 4 Noah, S., Ham, and Japheth
1. 17 The sons of S.; Elam, and Asshur, and
1. 24 S., Arphaxad, Shelah

SHE'-MA, שֶׁמַע, שְׁמַע, שֶׁמַע *fame, repute.*

1. A city in S. of Judah, near Anam.

Josh. 15. 26 Amam, and S., and Moladah

2. A son of Hebron, and father of Raham. B.C. 1530.

1 Ch. 2. 43 Korah, and Tappuah, and Rekem, and S.
2. 44 And S. begat Raham the father of Jork.

3. A Reubenite, father of Azaz. B.C. 1230.

1 Ch. 5. 8 Bela the son of Azaz, the son of S., the

4. A Benjamite head of the inhabitants of Aijalon. B.C. 1400.

1 Ch. 8. 13 Beriah also, and S., who (were) heads of

5. One who stood at Ezra's right hand. B.C. 445.

Neh. 8. 4 beside him stood Mattithiah, and S., and

SHE-MA'-AH, הַשְּׁמָעָה *the fame.*

A Gibeathite, father of two valiant men who joined David at Ziklag. B.C. 1088

1 Ch. 12. 3 chief (was) Ahiezer, then Joash..sons of S.

SHE-MA'-IAH, שְׁמַעְיָה, שְׁמַעְיָהוּ *Jah is fame.*

1. A prophet sent by God to prevent Rehoboam warring against Israel. B.C. 975.

1 Ki. 12. 22 the word of God came unto S. the man of
2 Ch. 11. 2 the word of the LORD came to S. the man
12. 5 Then came S. the prophet to Rehoboam
12. 7 the word of the LORD came to S., saying
12. 15 (are) they not written in the book of S.

2. Son of Shechaniah, and father of Hattush, a descendant of David through Jehoiakim. B.C. 480.

1 Ch. 3. 22 sons of Shechaniah; S.: and the sons of S.

3. Father of Shimri, and head of a family of Simeon. B.C. 800.

1 Ch. 4. 37 Jedaiah, the son of Shimri, the son of S.

4. Son of Joel, head of a family of Reuben. B.C. 1640.

1 Ch. 5. 4 The sons of Joel; S. his son, Gog his son

5. A Merarite. B.C. 445.

1 Ch. 9. 14 And of the Levites; S. the son of Hasshub
Neh. 11. 15 Also of the Levites: S. the son of Hash.

6. A Levite, father of Obadiah. B.C. 470.

1 Ch. 9. 16 Obadiah the son of S., the son of Galal, the

7. A Kohathite, whom David called to assist in bringing up the ark from the house of Obed-edom. B.C. 1015.

1 Ch. 15. 8 Of the sons of Elizaphan, S. the chief, and
15. 11 Asaiah and Joel, S., and Eliel, and Am.

8. A Levite, son of Nathaneel, who recorded the allotment of the priestly offices in the days of David. B.C. 1015.

1 Ch. 24. 6 S. the son of Nethaneel the scribe, (one)

9. A Kohathite, son of Obed-edom, a gate keeper for the tabernacle in the days of David. B.C. 1015.

1 Ch. 26. 4 The sons of Obed-edom (were) S. the first
26. 6 unto S. his son were sons born, that ruled
26. 7 The sons of S.; Othni, and Rephael, and

10. A Levite, whom Jehoshaphat sent to teach the people in the cities of Judah. B.C. 941.

2 Ch. 17. 8 with them (he sent) Levites, (even) S., and

11. A son of Jeduthun, who assisted in cleansing the temple in the days of Hezekiah. B.C. 726.

2 Ch. 29. 14 and of the sons of Jeduthun; S. and Uz.

12. A Levite in the days of Hezekiah who distributed the freewill offerings to the Levites in their cities. B.C. 726

2 Ch. 31. 15 next him (were) Eden..and S., Amariah

13. A chief Levite in the days of Josiah. B.C. 623.

2 Ch. 35. 9 Conaniah also, and S. and Nethaneel, his

14. A son of Adonikam who returned with Ezra in the days of Artaxerxes. B.C. 536.

Ezra 8. 13 whose names (are)..Eliphelet, Jeiel..S.

15. A person whom Ezra sent to Iddo to ask for ministers. B.C. 456.

Ezra 8. 16 Then sent I for Eliezer, for Ariel, for S.

16. A priest who had married a strange wife. B.C. 445.

Ezra 10. 21 of the sons of Harim; Maaseiah..and S.

17. A person that had done the same.

Ezra 10. 31 (of) the sons of Harim; Eliezer..S., Shi.

18. A person that helped to repair the wall. B.C. 445.

Neh. 3. 29 After him repaired also S. the son of Sh.

19. A person that tried to intimidate Nehemiah. B.C. 445

Neh. 6. 10 I came unto the house of S. the son of D.

20. A priest that with Nehemiah sealed the covenant. B.C. 445.

Neh. 10. 8 Maaziah, Bilgai, S.: these (were) the pri.
12. 6 S., and Joiarib, Jedaiah
12. 18 Of Bilgah, Shammua; of S., Jehonathan
12. 34 Judah, and Benjamin, and S., and Jere.
12. 35 Zechariah the son of Jonathan..son of S.

21. One who took part in the purification of the wall. B.C. 445.

Neh. 12. 36 his brethren, S., and Azarael, Milalai, G.

22. One that gave thanks at the dedication of the wall. B.C. 445.

Neh. 12. 42 Maaseiah, and S., and Eleazar, and Uzzi

23. Father of Uriah from Kirjath-jearim who was slain by Jehoiakim for prophesying against Jerusalem and Judah. B.C. 630

Jer. 26. 20 Urijah the son of S. of Kirjath-jearim, who

24. A Nehelamite that wrote from Babylon to the priests in Jerusalem to reprove Jeremiah. B.C. 606.

Jer. 29. 24 (Thus) shalt thou also speak to S. the N.
29. 31 Thus saith the LORD concerning S. the N.
29. 31 S. hath prophesied unto you, and I sent
29. 32 I will punish S. the Nehelamite, and his

25. Father of Delaiah a prince of the Jews to whom Baruch read the roll which he had written from the mouth of Jeremiah. B.C. 630.

Jer. 36. 12 Delaiah the son of S., and Elnathan the

SHE-MAR'-IAH, SHA-MAR'-IAH, שְׁמַרְיָה, שְׁמַרְיָהוּ.

1. A mighty man who joined David in Ziklag. B.C. 1048.

1 Ch. 12. 5 Bealiah, and S., and Shephatiah the Ha.

2. Son of Rehoboam son of Solomon. B.C. 975.

2 Ch. 11. 19 Which bare him children; Jeush, and S.

3. One of the family of Harim that had taken a strange wife. B.C. 445.

Ezra 10. 32 Benjamin, Malluch, (and) S.

4. One of the family of Bani that had done the same.

Ezra 10. 41 Azareel, and Shelemiah, S.

SHEM-E'-BER, שֶׁמְאֵבֶר *splendour of heroism.*

A king of Zeboim in the days of Abraham. B.C. 1917.

Gen. 14. 2 these) made war with..S. king of Zeboiim

SHE'-MER, שֶׁמֶר *watch.*

Owner of a hill which Omri purchased and on which he built Samaria. B.C. 925.

1 Ki. 16. 24 he bought the hill Samaria of S. for two
16. 24 called the name..after the name of S.,

SHE-MI'-DAH, SHE-MI'-DA שְׁמִידָע *fame of knowing*

Son of Gilead, grandson of Manasseh. B.C. 1450.

Num 26. 32 S., the family of the Shemidaites; and (of)
Josh 17. 2 There was..(a lot)..for the children of S.
1 Ch. 7. 19 the sons of S. were, Ahian, and Shechem

SHE-MI'-NITH —

The eighth, the octave, הַשְּׁמִינִית *hash-sheminith.*

1 Ch. 15. 21 Azaziah, with harps on the Sheminith to
Psa. 6. *title.* To the..Musician on Neginoth upon S
12. *title.* To the chief Musician upon Sheminith

SHEMIDAITES, הַשְּׁמִידָעִי.

Family of the preceding Shemidah.

Num 26. 32 And (of) Shemida the family of the S.

SHE-MI-RA'-MOTH, שְׁמִירָמוֹת *fame of the highest.*
1. A Levite appointed for the choral service of the tabernacle. B.C. 1015.
1 Ch.15. 18 S., and Jehiel, and Unni, Eliab, and Be.
15. 20 And Zechariah, and Aziel, and S., and J.
16. 5 Asaph the chief, and next to him..S., and
2. Another, whom Jehoshaphat sent to teach the people in the cities of Judah. B.C. 913.
2 Ch.17. 8 Asahel, and S., and Jehonathan, and Ad.

SHE-MU'-EL, שְׁמוּאֵל *heard of God.*
1. A chief Simeonite, appointed to divide the land W. of the Jordan. B.C. 1452.
Num 34. 20 of the tribe of the children of Simeon, S.
2. Samuel the prophet, father of Joel. (See 1 Sa. 1. 1 and 8. 2). B.C. 1171-1060.
1 Ch. 6 33 Heman a singer, the son of Joel..son of S.
3. Head of a family in Issachar.
1 Ch. 7. 2 Jibsam, and S., heads of their father's ho.

SHEN, שֵׁן *peak, tooth.*
A place in Benjamin, near Mizpeh, lying W. of Jerusalem, and E. of Kirjath-jearim.
1 Sa. 7. 12 Samuel.. set (it) between Mizpeh and S.

SHEN-A'-ZAR, שֶׁנְאַצַּר.
Son or grandson of Jeconiah son of Jehoiakim king of Judah. B.C. 580.
1 Ch. 3. 18 Malchiram also, and Pedaiah, and S., Je.

SHE'-NIR, SE'-NIR, שְׂנִיר, שְׁנִיר *peak, snow.*
The mountain between Amanah and Hermon, at the N.E. of Jordan.
Deut. 3. 9 (Which) Hermon..the Amorites call..S.
1 Ch. 5. 23 they increased from Bashan unto..S., and
Song 4. 8 from the top of S. and Hermon, from the
Eze. 27. 5 made all thy (ship) boards of fir trees of S.

SHE'-PHAM, שְׁפָם *fruitful.*
A place E. of the sea of Cinneroth, at the N., between Hazar-enan, Riblah, and Ain.
Num 34. 10 shall point out your east border..to S.
34. 11 the coast shall go down from S. to Riblah

SHE-PHAT'-IAH, שְׁפַטְיָה, שְׁפַטְיָהוּ *Jah is judge.*
1. Fifth son of David, by Abital. B.C. 1030.
2 Sa. 3. 4 and the fifth, S. the son of Abital
1 Ch. 3. 3 The fifth, S. of Abital; the sixth, Ithream
2. A Benjamite, father of Meshullam that dwelt in Jerusalem. B.C. 470. Shephathiah.
1 Ch. 9. 8 Meshullam the son of S., the son of Reuel
3. Another, a valiant man that joined David at Ziklag. B.C. 1048.
1 Ch.12. 5 Bealiah, and Shemariah, and S. the Har
4. A prince of Simeon in the days of David. B.C. 1015.
1 Ch.27. 16 of the Simeonites; S. the son of Maachah
5. A son of king Jehoshaphat. B.C. 890.
2 Ch.21. 2 Zechariah, and Azariah, and Michael..S.
6. A person whose descendants returned with Zerubbabel. B.C. 536
Ezra 2. 4 The children of S., three hundred seventy
Neh. 7. 9 The children of S., three hundred seventy
7. One of Solomon's servants whose descendants returned with Zerubbabel. B.C. 536.
Ezra 2. 57 The children of S., the children of Hattil
Neh. 7. 59 The children of S., the children of Hattil
8. One whose descendant Zebadiah and eighty males returned with Ezra. B.C. 536.
Ezra 8. 8 And of the sons of S.; Zebadiah the son of
9. A descendant of Pharez, some of whose descendants dwelt in Jerusalem. B.C. 550.
Neh.11. 4 Amariah, the son of S., the son of Maha.
10. Son of Mattan, a prince of Judah in the days of Zedekiah. B.C. 600.
Jer. 38. 1 S. the son of Mattan, and Gedaliah the

SHEPHERD —
1. *To feed sheep,* רָעָה *raah.*
Gen. 49. 24 from thence (is) the shepherd, the stone
Exod 2. 17 the shepherds came and drove them aw.
2. 19 delivered us out of the hand of the shep.
Num 27. 17 be not as sheep which have no shepherd
1 Sa. 17. 40 put them in a shepherd's bag which he
25. 7 now thy shepherds which were with us
1 Ki.22. 17 scattered..as sheep that have not a sheph.
2 Ch. 18. 16 scattered..as sheep that have no shep.
Psa. 23. 1 LORD (is) my shepherd, I shall not want
80. 1 Give ear, O shepherd of Israel, thou that
Eccl. 12. 11 assemblies, (which) are given from one sh.
Song 1. 8 feed thy kids beside the shepherds' tents
Isa. 13. 20 neither shall the shepherds make their
31. 4 when a multitude of shepherds is called
40. 11 He shall feed his flock like a shepherd; he
44. 28 (He is) my shepherd, and shall perform
56. 11 they (are) shepherds (that) cannot under.
63. 11 out of the sea with the shepherd of his fl.?
Jer 6. 3 The shepherds with their flocks shall come
23. 4 will set up shepherds over them which
25. 34 Howl ye shepherds, and cry; and wallow
25. 35 shepherds shall have no way to flee, nor
25. 36 A voice of the cry of the shepherds, and
31. 10 and keep him, as a shepherd (doth) his fl.
33. 12 shall be an habitation of shepherds caus.
43. 12 as a shepherd putteth on his garment; and
49. 19 who (is) that shepherd that will stand be.
50. 6 their shepherds have caused them to go
50. 44 who (is) that shepherd that will stand be.
Jer. 51. 23 break in pieces with thee the shepherd
Eze. 34. 2 prophesy against the shepherds of Israel
34. 2 unto the shepherds; Woe (be) to the shep.
34. 2 should not the shepherds feed the flocks?
34. 5 scattered, because (there is) no shepherd
34. 7 Therefore, ye shepherds, hear the word
34. 8 no shepherd, neither did my shepherds se.
34. 8 but the shepherds fed themselves, and fed
34. 9 Therefore, O ye shepherds, hear the word
34. 10 the shepherds..neither shall the shephe.
34. 12 As a shepherd seeketh out his flock in the
34. 23 one shepherd..and he shall be their shep.
37. 24 they all shall have one shepherd: they
Amos 1. 2 habitations of the shepherds shall mourn
3. 12 As the shepherd taketh out of the mouth
Mic. 5. 5 shall we raise against him seven shepherds
Nah. 3. 18 Thy shepherds slumber, O king of Assyria
Zeph. 2. 6 cottages for shepherds, and folds for flo.
Zech 10. 2 were troubled, because (there was) no sh.
10. 3 Mine anger was kindled against the shep.
11. 3 a voice of the howling of the shepherds
11. 5 and their own shepherds pity them not
11. 8 Three shepherds also I cut off in one mo.
11. 15 Take..the instruments of a foolish shep.
11. 16 For, lo, I will raise up a shepherd in the
13. 7 Awake, O sword, against my shepherd, and
13. 7 smite the shepherd, and the sheep shall
2. *Pasturer,* רֹעִי [*raah* (partic.)]
Isa. 38. 12 is removed from me as a shepherd's tent
Zech 11. 17 Woe to the idol shepherd that leaveth the
3. *To feed a flock,* רָעָה צֹאן *raah tson.*
Gen. 46. 32 the men (are) shepherds, for their trade
46. 34 every shepherd (is) an abomination unto
47. 3 Thy servants (are) shepherds, both we, (and
4. *A feeder, shepherd* (ἄνθρωπος) ποιμήν (*anthrōpos*).
Matt. 9. 36 were scattered abroad..having no sheph.
25. 32 as a shepherd divideth (his) sheep from the
26. 31 I will smite the shepherd, and the sheep
Mark 6. 34 they were as sheep not having a shepherd
14. 27 I will smite the shepherd, and the sheep
Luke 2. 8 there were in the same country shepherds
2. 15 the shepherds said one to another, Let us
2. 18 which were told them by the shepherds
2. 20 the shepherds returned, glorifying and pr.
John 10. 2 he that entereth in..is the shepherd of
10. 11 I am the good shepherd: the good sheph.
10. 12 he that is an hireling, and not the sheph.
10. 14 I am the good shepherd, and know my (s.)
10. 16 there shall be one fold, (and) one shepherd
Heb. 13. 20 our Lord Jesus, that great shepherd of
1 Pe. 2. 25 are now returned unto the shepherd and

SHEPHERD, chief —
Chief shepherd, ἀρχιποίμην *archipoimēn.*
1 Pe. 5. 4 when the chief shepherd shall appear, ye

SHE'-PHO, SHEPHI, שְׁפוֹ, שְׁפִי *unconcern.*
A son of Shobal, son of Seir the Horite. B.C. 1740.
Gen. 36. 23 Alvan, and Manahath, and Ebal, S., and
1 Ch. 1. 40 Alian, and Manahath, and Ebal, S., and

SHE-PHU'-PHAN, שְׁפוּפָן *serpent.*
A son of Bela, son of Benjamin. B.C. 1630.
1 Ch. 8. 5 And Gera, and S., and Huram

SHE'-RAH, שֶׁאֱרָה *blood-relationship.*
Daughter of Beriah, son of Ephraim, or daughter of Ephraim and sister of Beriah. B.C. 1450.
1 Ch. 7. 24 his daughter (was) S., who built Beth-ho.

SHERD —
Earthenware, potsherd, חֶרֶשׂ *cheres.*
Isa. 30. 14 there shall not be found..a sherd to take
Eze. 23. 34 thou shalt break the sherds thereof, and

SHE-REB'-IAH, שֵׁרֵבְיָה *Jah is originator.*
1. A priest with eighteen sons and brethren who were brought to Ezra to return to Jerusalem. B.C. 536.
Ezra 8. 18 S., with his sons and his brethren, eight.
8. 24 S., Hashabiah, and ten of their brethren
Neh. 8. 7 Jeshua, and Bani, and S., Jamin, Akkub
9. 4 Shebaniah, Bunni, S., Bani, (and) Chenani
9. 5 Hashabniah, S., Hodijah, Shebaniah, (and)
2. A Levite that with Nehemiah sealed the covenant. B.C. 445.
Neh. 10. 12 Zaccur, S., Shebaniah
12. 8 Jeshua, Binnui, Kadmiel, S., Judah, (and)
12. 24 Hashabiah, S., and Jeshua the son of Ka.

SHE'-RESH, שֶׁרֶשׁ *union.*
Son of Machir son of Manasseh. B.C. 1400.
1 Ch. 7. 16 the name of his brother (was) S.: and his

SHEREZER. *See* **SHAREZER.**

SHERIFFS —
Judges, supreme masters, prefects, תִּפְתָּיֵא *tiphtaye.*
Dan. 3. 2, 3 the sheriffs, and all the rulers of the p.

SHE'-SHACH, שֵׁשַׁךְ.
A mystical name of Babylon, alluding to its iron gates or idols.
Jer. 25. 26 and the king of S. shall drink after them
51. 41 How is S. taken; and how is the praise of

SHE'-SHAI, שֵׁשַׁי *free, noble.*
A son of Anak, in Hebron in the days of Joshua. B.C. 1450.
Num13. 22 where Ahiman, S., and Talmai, the chil.
Josh 15. 14 drove thence the three sons of Anak, S., and
Judg. 1. 10 and they slew S., and Ahiman, and Talmai

SHE'-SHAN, שֵׁשָׁן *free, noble.*
A descendant of Jerahmeel grandson of Pharez son of Judah. B.C. 1415.
1 Ch. 2. 31 the sons of Ishi; S. And the children of S.
2. 34 S. had no sons, but daughters. And S. had
2. 35 S. gave his daughter to Jarha his servant

SHESH-BAZ'-ZAR, שֵׁשְׁבַּצַּר.
The governor whom Cyrus set over Judah, elsewhere called *Zerubbabel.* B.C. 536.
Ezra 1. 8 numbered them unto S., the prince of J.
1. 11 (these) did S. bring up with (them of) the
5. 14 (one), whose name (was) S., whom he had
5. 16 Then came the same S., (and) laid the fo.

SHETH, שֵׁת.
Some Moabite chief or tribe.
Num 24. 17 smite..and destroy all the children of S.

SHE'-THAR, שֵׁתָר *star, commander.*
One of the seven princes of Persia and Media that saw the king's face at pleasure. B.C. 510.
Esth. 1. 14 the next unto him (was) Carshena, S., Ad.

SHE-THAR BOZ'-NAI, שְׁתַר בּוֹזְנַי *starry splendour.*
An official of the king of Persia in the district adjoining Judah. B.C. 445.
Ezra 5. 3 At the same time came to them..S., and
5. 6 S., and his companions the Apharsachites
6. 6 (therefore)..S., and your companions the
6. 13 Then Tatnai..S., and their companions

SHE'-VA, שְׁוָא *self-satisfying.*
1. A scribe or secretary of David. B.C. 1030. [V. L. שׁיא].
2 Sa. 20. 25 And S. (was) scribe; and Zadok and Abi.
2. Father of Machbenah and son of Maachah concubine of Caleb son of Jephunneh. B.C. 1450.
1 Ch. 2. 49 S. the father of Machbenah, and the father

SHEW, show—
1. *Discerning,* הַכָּרָה *hakkarah.*
Isa. 3. 9 The show of their countenance doth witness
2. *Word, matter,* λόγος *logos.*
Col. 2. 23 Which things have indeed a show of wis.
3. *Appearance, pretence,* πρόφασις *prophasis.*
Luke20. 47 devour widows' houses, and for a show

SHEW, to —
1. *To uncover the ear, reveal,* גָּלָה אֹזֶן *galah ozen.*
1 Sa. 20. 2 do nothing..but that he will shew it me
20. 12 I then send not unto thee, and shew it
20. 13 I will shew it thee, and send thee away
22. 8 (there is) none that sheweth me that my
22. 8 or sheweth unto me that my son hath st
22. 17 they knew..and did not shew it to me
2. *To shew, indicate,* חָוָה *chavah,* 3.
Job 15 17 I will shew thee, hear me; and that (wh.)
32. 6 I was afraid, and durst not shew you mine
32. 10 Hearken to me; I also will shew mine op.
32. 17 (I said)..I also will shew mine opinion
36. 2 I will shew thee that (I have) yet to speak
Psa. 19. 2 and night unto night sheweth knowledge
3. *To shew, indicate,* חֲוָא, חֲוָה *chava,* 3.
Dan. 2. 4 tell..and we will shew the interpretation
2. 11 there is none other that can shew it before
2. 24 will shew unto the king the interpretation
5. 7 Whosoever shall read this writing, and s
4. *To shew, indicate,* חֲוָה, חֲוָא *chava,* 5.
Dan. 2. 6 if ye shew the dream, and the interpreta.
2. 6 shew me the dream, and the interpretation
2. 7 and we will shew the interpretation of it
2. 9 I shall know that ye can shew me the
2. 10 There is not a man..that can shew the k.
2. 16 he would shew the king the interpretation
2. 27 cannot the wise (men)..shew unto the k.
4. 2 I thought it good to shew the signs and
5. 12 shewing of hard sentences, and dissolving
5. 15 they could not shew the interpretation of
5. *To cause to know,* יָדַע *yada,* 5.
Gen. 41. 39 God hath shewed thee all this, (there is)
Exod18. 20 shalt shew them the way wherein they
33. 13 shew me now thy way, that I may know
Num16. 5 the LORD will shew who (are) his, and (who)
1 Sa. 10. 8 till I come to thee, and shew thee what
14. 12 Come up to us, and we will shew you a
16. 3 and I will shew thee what thou shalt do
1 Ki. 1. 27 thou hast not shewed (it) unto thy servant
Job 10. 2 shew me wherefore thou contendest with
Psa. 16. 11 Thou wilt shew me the path of life: in thy
25. 4 Shew me thy ways, O LORD; teach me thy
25. 14 and he will shew them his covenant
Isa. 40. 14 shewed to him the way of understanding
Eze. 20. 11 I gave them my statutes, and shewed them
22. 2 thou shalt shew her all her abominations
22. 26 neither have they shewed (difference) be.
43. 11 shew them the form of the house and the
6. *To cast, shew, direct,* יָרָה *yarah,* 5.
Exod15. 25 the LORD shewed him a tree, (which) when
7. *To put or place before,* נָגַד *nagad,* 5.
Gen. 41. 25 God hath shewed Pharaoh what he (is) a
46. 31 I will go up, and shew Pharaoh, and say
Exod13. 8 thou shalt shew thy son in that day, say
Deut. 5. 5 I stood..to shew you the word of the LORD
17. 9 they shall shew thee the sentence of jud.
17. 10 which they of that place..shall shew thee
17. 11 from the sentence which they shall shew
32. 7 ask thy father, and he will shew thee

Judg. 4. 12 they shewed Sisera that Barak the son of
13. 10 shewed her husband, and said unto him
16. 18 Come up this once, for he hath shewed
Ruth 2. 19 she shewed her mother in law with whom
1 Sa. 3. 15 And Samuel feared to shew Eli the vision
8. 9 shew them the manner of the king that
9. 6 he can shew us our way that we should
11. 9 the messengers came and shewed (it) to
19. 7 and Jonathan shewed him all those things
22. 21 Abiathar shewed David that Saul had
24. 18 thou hast shewed this day how that thou
25. 8 Ask thy young men, and they will shew
2 Sa. 11. 22 came and shewed David all that Joab
2 Ki. 6. 11 Will ye not shew me which of us (is) for
7. 12 I will now shew you what the Syrians h.
22. 10 the scribe shewed the king, saying, Hilk.
Ezra 2. 59 they could not shew their father's house
Neh. 7. 61 they could not shew their father's house
Esth. 2. 10 Esther had not shewed her people nor her
2. 10 charged her that she should not shew (it)
2. 20 Esther had not (yet) shewed her kindred
3. 6 they had shewed him the people of Mor.
Job 11. 6 that he would shew thee the secrets of w.
33. 23 one..to shew unto man his uprightness
36. 9 he sheweth them their work, and their
36. 33 The noise thereof sheweth concerning it
Psa. 19. 1 and the firmament sheweth his handy w.
71. 18 until I have shewed thy strength unto
92. 15 To shew that the LORD (is) upright: (he
111. 6 He hath shewed his people the power of
142. 2 I poured out my complaint..I shewed be.
147. 19 He sheweth his word unto Jacob, his sta.
Isa. 41. 22 shew us what shall happen: let them shew
41. 23 Shew the things that are to come hereafter
41. 26 (there is) none that sheweth; yea, (there
44. 7 the things that are coming..let them sh.
58. 1 shew my people their transgression, and
Jer. 16. 10 thou shalt shew this people all these wo.
33. 3 shew thee great and mighty things, which
42. 3 God may shew us the way wherein we may
51. 31 to shew the king of Babylon that his city
Eze. 37. 18 Wilt thou not shew us what thou (mean.)
43. 10 shew the house to the house of Israel, that
Dan. 2. 2 to call the magicians..to shew the king
9. 23 I am come to shew (thee); for thou (art)
10. 21 I will shew thee that which is noted in
11. 2 now will I shew thee the truth. Behold
Mic. 6. 8 He hath shewed thee, O man, what (is)

8. *To incline, stretch out,* נָטָה *natah.*
Gen. 39. 21 the LORD was with Joseph, and shewed

9. *To give,* נָתַן *nathan.*
Exod. 7. 9 Pharaoh shall speak unto you, saying, S
Deut. 6. 22 the LORD shewed signs and wonders great
13. 17 shew thee mercy, and have compassion
Neh. 9. 10 shewedst signs and wonders upon Pharaoh
Jer. 16. 13 a land..where I will not shew you favour
42. 12 I will shew mercies unto you, that he
Joel 2. 30 I will shew wonders in the heavens and

10. *To do, make,* עָשָׂה *asah.*
Gen. 19. 19 thy mercy, which thou hast shewed unto
20. 13 thy kindness which thou shalt shew unto
24. 12 shew kindness unto my master Abraham
24. 14 thou hast shewed kindness unto my ma.
32. 10 which thou hast shewed unto thy servant
40. 14 shew kindness, I pray thee, unto me, and
Exod 14. 13 salvation of the LORD, which he will shew
20. 6 shewing mercy unto thousands of them
Num 14. 11 the signs which I have shewed among th.
Deut. 5. 10 shewing mercy unto thousands of them
34. 12 the great terror which Moses shewed in
Josh. 2. 12 Now..since I have shewed you kindness
2. 12 will also shew kindness unto my father's
Judg. 1. 24 into the city, and we will shew thee me
6. 17 shew me a sign that thou talkest with me
8. 35 Neither shewed they kindness to the ho.
8. 35 the goodness which he had shewed unto
1 Sa. 15. 6 ye shewed kindness to all the children of
20. 14 thou shalt not only while yet I live shew
2 Sa. 2. 5 ye have shewed this kindness unto your
2. 6 the LORD shew kindness and truth unto
3. 8 which against Judah do shew kindness th.
9. 1 that I may shew him kindness for Jon.
9. 3 that I may shew the kindness of God unto
9. 7 I will surely shew thee kindness for Jon.
10. 2 I will shew kindness unto Hanun the son
10 2 as his father shewed kindness unto me
22. 51 sheweth mercy to his anointed, unto D.
1 Ki. 2. 7 shew kindness unto the sons of Barzillai
3. 6 Thou hast shewed unto thy servant David
16. 27 acts of Omri..and his might that he shew.
22. 45 his might that he shewed, and how he
1 Ch. 19. 2 I will shew kindness unto Hanun the son
19. 2 because his father shewed kindness to me
2 Ch. 1. 8 Thou hast shewed great mercy unto David
7. 10 the goodness that the LORD had shewed
Psa. 18. 50 sheweth mercy to his anointed, to David
86. 17 Shew me a token for good; that they which
88. 10 Wilt thou shew wonders to the dead? shall
109. 16 that he remembered not to shew mercy
Jer. 32. 18 Thou shewest loving kindness unto thou.
Eze. 33. 31 with their mouth they shew much love
Zech. 7. 9 shew mercy and compassions every man

11. *To see,* רָאָה *raah* [A.V. as if 5].
Jer. 18. 17 I will shew them the back, and not the face

12. *To cause to see,* רָאָה *raah,* 5.
Gen. 12. 1 Get thee..unto a land that I will shew thee
41. 28 What God (is) about to do he sheweth un.
48. 11 lo, God hath shewed me also thy seed
Exod 9. 16 have I raised thee up, for to shew (in) thee
25. 9 According to all that I shew thee, (after)
27. 8 as it was shewed thee in the mount, so
33. 18 he said, I beseech thee, shew me thy glory
Num. 8. 4 the pattern which the LORD had shewed
13. 26 and shewed them the fruit of the land
23. 3 whatsoever he sheweth me I will tell thee
Deut. 1. 33 to shew you by what way ye should go
3. 24 thou hast begun to shew thy servant thy
4. 36 upon earth he shewed thee his great fire
5. 24 the LORD our God hath shewed us his gl.
34. 1 the LORD shewed him all the land of Gilead
Josh. 5. 6 he would not shew them the land which
Judg. 1. 24 Shew us, we pray thee, the entrance into
1. 25 he shewed them the entrance into the city
4. 22 I will shew thee the man whom thou seek.
13. 23 neither would he have shewed us all these
2 Sa. 15. 25 and shew me (both) it and his habitation
2 Ki. 6. 6 Where fell it? And he shewed him the pl.
8. 10 the LORD hath shewed me that he shall s.
8. 13 The LORD hath shewed me that thou (shalt
11. 4 took an oath..and shewed them the king's
20. 13 shewed them all the house of his precious
20. 13 nothing..that Hezekiah shewed them not
20. 15 there is nothing..I have not shewed them
Esth. 1. 4 he shewed the riches of his glorious king.
1. 11 to shew the people and the princes her b.
4. 8 to shew (it) unto Esther, and to declare (it)
Psa. 4. 6 (There be) many that say, Who will shew
50. 23 to him..will I shew the salvation of God
60. 3 Thou hast shewed thy people hard things
71. 20 (Thou), which hast shewed me great and
78. 11 and his wonders that he had shewed th.
85. 7 Shew us thy mercy, O LORD, and grant us
91. 16 With long life will I satisfy him, and shew
Isa. 30. 30 shall shew the lighting down of his arm
39. 2 shewed them the house of his precious th.
39. 2 nothing..that Hezekiah shewed them not
39. 4 there is nothing..I have not shewed th.
Jer. 11. 18 then thou shewedst me their doings
24 1 The LORD shewed me, and, behold, two
38. 21 this (is) the word that the LORD hath sh.
Eze. 11. 25 the things that the LORD had shewed me
40. 4 set thine heart upon all..I shall shew th.
40. 4 to the intent that I might shew (them)
Amos 7. 1, 4 Thus hath the Lord GOD shewed unto
7. 7 Thus he shewed me; and, behold, the L.
8. 1 Thus hath the Lord GOD shewed unto me
Mic. 7. 15 will I shew unto him marvellous (things)
Nah. 3. 5 will shew the nations thy nakedness, and
Hab. 1. 3 Why dost thou shew me iniquity, and ca.
Zech. 1. 9 said unto me, I will shew thee what these
1. 20 And the LORD shewed me four carpenters
3. 1 he shewed me Joshua the high priest st.

13. *To set, place, put,* שׂוּם, שִׂים *sum, sim.*
Psa. 105. 27 They shewed his signs among them and
Isa. 47. 6 thou didst shew them no mercy; upon the

14. *To set, place, put,* שִׁית *shith.*
Exod 10. 1 that I might shew these my signs before

15. *To cause to hear,* שָׁמַע *shamea,* 5.
1 Sa. 9. 27 that I may shew thee the word of God
Isa. 43. 9 who among them can declare this, and sh.
43. 12 I have shewed, when (there was) no str.
48. 3 went forth out of my mouth, and I shewed
48. 5 before it came to pass I shewed (it) thee
48. 6 I have shewed thee new things from this

16. *To tell back or again,* ἀναγγέλλω *anaggellō.*
John 16. 13 and he will shew you things to come
16. 14 he shall receive of mine, and shall shew
16. 15 he shall take of mine, and shall [shew]
16. 25 but [I shall shew] you plainly of the Fa.
Acts 19. 18 and confessed, and shewed their deeds
20. 20 have shewed you, and have taught you

17. *To shew clearly,* ἀναδείκνυμι *anadeiknumi.*
Acts 1. 24 shew whether of these two thou hast ch.

18. *To tell off or away,* ἀπαγγέλλω *apaggellō.*
Matt 12. 18 and he shall shew judgment to the Gen.
28. 11 shewed unto the chief priests all the thi.
Luke 7. 18 the disciples of John shewed him of all
14. 21 that servant came, and shewed his lord
Acts 11. 13 he shewed us how he had seen an angel
12. 17 shew these things unto James, and to the
26. 20 But shewed first unto them of Damascus
28. 21 neither any..shewed or spake any harm of
1 Th. 1. 9 they themselves shew of us what manner
1 Jo. 1. 2 shew unto you that eternal life which was

19. *To shew off or away,* ἀποδείκνυμι *apodeiknumi.*
2 Th. 2. 4 sitteth in the temple of God, shewing hi.

20. *To shew,* δεικνύω *deiknuō.*
Matt. 4. 8 sheweth him all the kingdoms of the wo.
8. 4 shew thyself to the priest, and offer the
16. 21 that time forth began Jesus to shew unto
Mark 1. 44 shew thyself to the priest, and offer for
14. 15 he will shew you a large upper room fur.
Luke 4. 5 shewed unto him all the kingdoms of the
5. 14 shew thyself to the priest, and offer for
22. 12 And he shall shew you a large upper room
John 2. 18 What sign shewest thou unto us, seeing
5. 20 sheweth him all things that himself doeth
5. 20 he will shew him greater works than these
10. 32 Many good works have I shewed you from
14. 8 Lord, shew us the Father, and it sufficeth
14. 9 how sayest thou (then), Shew us the Father
20. 20 he shewed unto them (his) hands and his
Acts 7. 3 come into the land which I shall shew th.
10. 28 God hath shewed me that I should not ca.
1 Co. 12. 31 yet shew I unto you a more excellent way
1 Ti. 6. 15 Which in his times he shall shew, (who is)
Heb. 8. 5 the pattern shewed to thee in the mount
Jas. 2. 18 shew me thy faith without thy works
2. 18 and I will shew thee my faith by my wo.
3. 13 let him shew out of a good conversation
Rev. 1. 1 to shew unto his servants things which
4. 1 I will shew thee things which must be
17. 1 I will shew unto thee the judgment of the
21. 9 I will shew thee the bride, the Lamb's wi.
21. 10 shewed me that great city, the holy Jeru.
22. 1 he shewed me a pure river of water of life
22. 6 sent his angel to shew unto his servants
22. 8 the angel which shewed me these things

21. *To manifest,* δηλόω *dēloō.*
2 Pe. 1. 14 as our Lord Jesus Christ hath shewed me

22. *To give,* δίδωμι *didōmi.*
Matt 24. 24 and shall shew great signs and wonders
Mark 13. 22 [shall shew] signs and wonders, to seduce

23. *To lead through, tell thoroughly,* διηγέομαι.
Luke 8. 39 shew how great things God hath done unto

24. *To manifest clearly,* ἐμφανίζω *emphanizō.*
Acts 23. 22 tell no man that thou hast shewed these

25. *To show clearly or inwardly,* ἐνδείκνυμι *endeik.*
Rom. 2. 15 Which shew the work of the law written
9. 17 that I might shew my power in thee, and
9. 22 (What) if God, willing to shew (his) wrath
2 Co. 8. 24 shew ye to them, and before the churches
Eph. 2. 7 he might shew the exceeding riches of his
Titus 2. 10 Not purloining, but shewing all good fid.
3. 2 (but) gentle, shewing all meekness unto
Heb. 6. 10 labour of love, which ye have shewed to.
6. 11 we desire that every one of you do shew

26. *To shew in addition,* ἐπιδείκνυμι *epideiknumi.*
Matt 16. 1 that he would shew them a sign from he.
22. 19 Shew me the tribute money. And they br.
24. 1 to shew him the buildings of the temple
Luke 17. 14 he said unto them, Go shew yourselves un.
20. 24 [Shew] me a penny. Whose image and su.
24. 40 [he shewed them (his) hands and (his) feet]
Acts 9. 39 shewing the coats and garments which D.
18. 28 shewing by the Scriptures that Jesus was
Heb. 6. 17 willing more abundantly to shew unto the

27. *To tell thoroughly,* καταγγέλλω *kataggellō.*
Acts 16. 17 which shew unto us the way of salvation
26. 23 should shew light unto the people, and to
1 Co. 11. 26 ye do shew the Lord's death till he come

28. *To put down, bestow,* κατατίθημι *katatithēmi.*
Acts 24. 27 willing to shew the Jews a pleasure, left

29. *To lay out, say, tell,* λέγω *legō.*
1 Co. 15. 51 I shew you a mystery; We shall not all

30. *To indicate, declare,* μηνύω *mēnuō.*
Luke 20. 37 even Moses shewed at the bush, when he
John 11. 57 he should shew (it), that they might take
1 Co. 10. 28 eat not for his sake that shewed it, and for

31. *To hold alongside,* παρέχω *parechō.*
Acts 28. 2 barbarous people shewed us no little kin.
Titus 2. 7 In all things shewing thyself a pattern of

32. *To set, or place near,* παρίστημι *paristēmi.*
Acts 1. 3 To whom also he shewed himself alive af.
2 Ti. 2. 15 Study to shew thyself approved unto God

33. *To do, make,* ποιέω *poieō.*
Luke 1. 51 He hath shewed strength with his arm
10. 37 And he said, He that shewed mercy on
John 6. 30 What sign shewest thou then, that we may
Acts 7. 36 after that he had shewed wonders and si
Jas. 2. 13 judgment without mercy that hath sh.

34. *To shew quietly,* ὑποδείκνυμι *hupodeiknumi.*
Luke 6. 47 I will shew you to whom he is like
Acts 9. 16 I will shew him how great things he must
20. 35 I have shewed you all things, how that so

35. *To manifest,* φανερόω *phaneroō.*
John 7. 4 If thou do these things, shew thyself to
21. 1 Jesus shewed himself again to the disci
21. 1 After these things..on this wise shewed
21. 14 the third time that Jesus shewed himself
Rom. 1 19 for God hath shewed (it) unto them

SHEW again, before, forth, openly, self, to —

1. *To tell good tidings,* בָּשַׂר *basar,* 3.
1 Ch. 16. 23 shew forth from day to day his salvation
Psa. 96. 2 shew forth his salvation from day to day
Isa. 60. 6 they shall shew forth the praises of the L.

2. *To be revealed, uncovered,* גָּלָה *galah,* 2.
Isa. 49. 9 to them that (are) in darkness, Shew your

3. *To uncover, reveal,* גָּלָה *galah,* 3.
Psa. 98. 2 his righteousness hath he openly shewed

4. *To (cause to) shine,* יָפַע *yapha,* 5.
Psa. 94. 1 God, to whom vengeance belongeth, shew

5. *To put before,* נָגַד *nagad,* 5.
Psa. 51. 15 and my mouth shall shew forth thy praise
92. 2 To shew forth thy loving kindness in the
Prov. 12. 17 speaketh truth sheweth forth righteous.

6. *To number, recount,* סָפַר *saphar,* 3.
Psa. 9. 1 I will shew forth all thy marvellous works
9. 14 That I may shew forth all thy praise in
71. 15 My mouth shall shew forth thy righteo.
79. 13 we will shew forth thy praise to all gen.
Isa. 43. 21 This people..shall shew forth my praise

7. *To be seen,* רָאָה *raah,* 2.
1 Ki.18. 1 shew thyself unto Ahab; and I will send
18. 2 And Elijah went to shew himself unto A.
Prov 27. 25 the tender grass sheweth itself, and herbs
8. *To cause to hear,* שָׁמַע *shamea,* 5.
Psa 106. 2 Who can utter..(who) can shew forth all his
9. *To tell off or away,* ἀπαγγέλλω *apaggellō.*
Matt 11. 4 shew John again those things which ye do
10. *To shew inwardly,* ἐνδείκνυμι *endeiknumi.*
1 Ti. 1. 16 Christ might shew forth all long suffering
11. *To work inwardly,* ἐνεργέω *energeō.*
Matt 14. 2 mighty works do shew forth themselves
Mark 6. 14 mighty works do shew forth themselves
12. *To tell out,* ἐξαγγέλλω *exaggellō.*
1 Pe. 2. 9 that ye should shew forth the praises of
13. *To see, appear,* ὄπτομαι *optomai.*
Acts 7. 26 he shewed himself unto them as they st.
14. *To tell thoroughly beforehand,* προκαταγγέλλω.
Acts 3. 18 those things, which God...shewed 7. 52
15. *To give to become,* δίδωμι γενέσθαι, Acts 10. 40.

SHEW (light, more), to —
1. *To give light,* אוֹר *or,* 5.
Neh. 9. 19 pillar of fire by night, to shew them light
Psa. 118. 27 the LORD, which hath shewed us light
2. *To do good,* יָטַב *yatab,* 5.
Ruth 3. 10 thou hast shewed more kindness in the lat.

SHEW (great, piety), to —
1. *To be pious, worship devoutly,* εὐσεβέω *eusebeō.*
1 Ti. 5. 4 let them learn first to shew piety at home
2. *To make great, magnify,* μεγαλύνω *megalunō.*
Luke 1. 58 the Lord had shewed great mercy upon

SHEW, to make a (fair) —
1. *To make a shew or example,* δειγματίζω *deigma.*
Col. 2. 15 he made a shew of them openly, triump.
2. *To have a good appearance,* εὐπροσωπέω *eupros.*
Gal. 6. 12 As many as desire to make a fair shew in

SHEW, (vain) —
An image, shadow, צֶלֶם *tselem.*
Psa. 39. 6 Surely every man walketh in a vain shew

SHEW bread —
1. *Arrangement,* מַעֲרֶכֶת *maareketh.*
1 Ch.28. 16 (he gave) gold for the tables of shew bre.
2 Ch. 2. 4 for the continual shew bread, and for the
29. 18 the shew bread table, with all the vessels
2. *Bread of arrangement,* לֶחֶם מַעֲרָכָה [*lechem*].
1 Ch. 9. 32 (were) over the shew bread, to prepare (it)
23. 29 for the shew bread, and for the fine flour
2 Ch.13. 11 the shew bread also (set they in order) up.
Neh. 10. 33 For the shew bread, and for the continual
3. *Bread of the presence,* לֶחֶם פָּנִים *lechem panim.*
Exod 25. 30 thou shalt set upon the table shew bread
35. 13 and all his vessels, and the shew bread
39. 36 (and) all the vessels thereof, and the s. b.
1 Sa. 21. 6 there was no bread there but the shew br.
1 Ki. 7. 48 table of gold, whereupon the shew bread
2 Ch. 4. 19 the tables whereon the shew bread (was
4. *Presence,* פָּנִים *panim.*
Num. 4. 7 upon the table of shew bread they shall
5. *Loaves to set before (God),* ἄρτοι τῆς προθέσεως.
Matt 12. 4 did eat the shew bread, which was not la.
Mark 2. 26 did eat the shew bread, which is not la.
Luke 6. 4 did take and eat the shew bread, and ga.
6. *A setting forth of the loaves,* πρόθεσις τῶν ἄρτων.
Heb. 9. 2 and the table, and the shew bread, which

SHEWED, to be —
1. *To be uncovered, revealed,* גָּלָה *galah,* 2.
Prov 26. 26 his wickedness shall be shewed before the
2. *To be put before,* נָגַד *nagad,* 6.
Ruth 2. 11 It hath fully been shewed me all that th.
3. *To explain, be explained,* פָּרַשׁ *parash.*
Lev. 24. 12 that the mind of the LORD might be she.
4. *To be seen, appear,* רָאָה *raah,* 2.
Lev. 13. 19 a bright spot..and it be shewed to the
5. *To be caused to see,* רָאָה *raah,* 6.
Exod 25. 40 pattern, which was shewed thee in the
26. 30 the fashion thereof which was shewed th.
Lev. 13. 49 it (is) a plague..and shall be shewed un.
Deut. 4. 35 Unto thee it was shewed, that thou mig.
6. *To become, happen,* γίνομαι *ginomai.*
Acts 4. 22 on whom this miracle of healing was sh.

SHEWING (self) —
1. *A shewing, indication,* אַחֲוָיָה *achavayah.*
Dan. 5. 12 shewing of hard sentences, and dissolv.
2. *To number, recount,* סָפַר *saphar,* 3.
Psa. 78. 4 shewing to the generation to come the pr.
3. *To bloom, flourish,* צוּץ *tsuts,* 5.
Song 2. 9 he looketh..shewing himself through the
4. *A shewing again,* ἀνάδειξις *anadeixis.*
Luke 1. 80 was in the deserts till the day of his she.

SHIB-BO'-LETH, שִׁבֹּלֶת *stream, ear of corn.*
A word used by the Gileadites on one occasion to distinguish the Ephraimites (from other Israelites) who called it *Sib-bo-leth.* B.C. 1150.
Judg 12. 6 Then said they unto him, Say now Shib.

SHIB'-MAH, שִׂבְמָה *balsam.*
A city in Reuben, once Moabite, near Kirjathaim and Jazer. *See* Sibmah.
Num 32. 38 And Nebo, and Baal-meon..and S.: and

SHIC'-RON, שִׁכְּרוֹן *fruitfulness.*
A city in N.W. of Judah.
Josh.15. 11 the border was drawn to S., and passed

SHIELD —
1. *Halbert, javelin,* כִּידוֹן *kidon.*
1 Sa. 17. 45 Thou comest to me with..a shield; but
Job 39. 23 the glittering spear and the shield
2. *Shield,* מָגֵן *magen.*
Gen. 15. 1 Fear not, Abram: I (am) thy shield, (and)
Deut 33. 29 O people saved by the LORD, the shield
Judg. 5. 8 was there a shield or spear seen among
2 Sa. 1. 21 for there the shield..the shield of Saul
22. 3 (he is) my shield, and the horn of my sa.
22. 36 Thou hast also given me the shield of thy
1 Ki.10. 17 three hundred shields (of) beaten gold
10. 17 pound of gold went to one shield; and the
14. 26 took away all the shields of gold which S.
14. 27 Rehoboam made in their stead brasen sh.
2 Ki.19. 32 nor come before it with shield, nor cast
2 Ch. 9. 16 three hundred shields (made he of) beaten
9. 16 three hundred..went to one shield
12. 9 he carried away also the shields of gold
12. 10 king Rehoboam made shields of brass, and
14. 8 out of Benjamin, that bare shields and dr.
17. 17 with him armed men with bow and shield
26. 14 Uzziah prepared for them..shields, and
32. 5 and made darts and shields in abundance
32. 27 for spices, and for shields, and for all ma.
Neh. 4. 16 held both the spears, the shields, and the
Psa. 3. 3 But thou, O LORD, (art) a shield for me
18. 35 hast also given me the shield of thy sal.
28. 7 The LORD (is) my strength and my shield
33. 20 for the LORD: he (is) our help and our sh.
35. 2 Take hold of shield and buckler, and stand
47. 9 for the shields of the earth (belong) unto
59. 11 and bring them down, O Lord our shield
76. 3 There brake he the..shield, and the sword
84. 9 God our shield, and look upon the face of
84. 11 For the LORD God (is) a sun and shield, the
115. 9, 10, 11 he (is) their help and their shield
119. 114 Thou (art) my hiding place and my shield
144. 2 my shield, and (he) in whom I trust; who
Prov 30. 5 he (is) a shield unto them that put their
Isa. 21. 5 arise, ye princes, (and) anoint the shield
22. 6 horsemen, and Kir uncovered the shield
37. 33 nor come before it with shields, nor cast
Jer. 46. 9 and the Libyans, that handle the shield
Eze. 23. 24 set against thee buckler and shield and
27. 10 they hanged the shield and helmet in thee
38. 4 great company (with) bucklers and shields
38. 5 Libya with them; all of them with shield
39. 9 both the shields and the bucklers, the bo.
Nah. 2. 3 shield of his mighty men is made red, the
3. *A buckler, target,* צִנָּה *tsinnah.*
1 Sa. 17. 7 and one bearing a shield went before him
17. 41 man that bare the shield (went) before him
1 Ch.12. 8 that could handle shield and buckler, wh.
12. 24 children of Judah that bare shield and sp.
12. 34 with them with shield and spear thirty and
2 Ch. 11. 12 in every several city (he put) shields and
25. 5 go forth to war, that could handle..shield
Psa. 5. 12 wilt thou compass him as (with) a shield
91. 4 his truth (shall be thy) shield and buckler
Jer. 46. 3 Order ye the buckler and shield, and dra.
4. *A shield, armour,* שֶׁלֶט *shelet.*
2 Sa. 8. 7 David took the shields of gold that were
2 Ki. 11. 10 priest give king David's spears and shie.
1 Ch. 18. 7 David took the shields of gold that were
2 Ch 23. 9 delivered to the captains..shields, that
Song 4. 4 thousand bucklers, all shields of mighty
Jer. 51. 11 Make bright the arrows; gather the shie.
Eze. 27. 11 they hanged their shields upon thy walls
5. *A large shield,* θυρεός *thureos.*
Eph. 6. 16 Above all, taking the shield of faith, wh.

SHIG-GA'-ION, SHIG-IO'-NOTH, שִׁגָּיוֹן *erring.*
Psa. 7. *title.* Shiggaion of David, which he sang unto
Hab. 3. 1 A prayer of Habakkuk..upon Shigionoth

SHI'-HON, שִׁיאוֹן *heaps of ruins.*
A city in Issachar, near Haphraim, and N. of Tabor, where are ruins still called *Khirbah Shaiin.*
Josh 19. 19 And Haphraim, and S., and Anaharath

SHI-HOR LIB'-NATH, שִׁיחוֹר לִבְנָת *glass river.*
A small river at the S. of Asher.
Josh 19. 26 reacheth to Carmel westward, and to S.

SHIHOR. *See* SIHOR.

SHIL'-HI, שִׁלְחִי *a warrior, one with darts.*
Father of Azubah mother of king Jehoshaphat. B.C. 925.
1 Ki. 22. 42 name (was) Azubah the daughter of S.
2 Ch. 20. 31 name (was) Azubah the daughter of S.

SHIL'HIM, שִׁלְחִים *fountains.*
A city in the S. of Judah near Lebaoth and Ain.
Josh.15. 32 Lebaoth, and S., and Ain, and Rimmon

SHIL'-LEM, שִׁלֵּם *recompense.*
The fourth son of Naphtali. B.C. 1690. *See* Shallum.
Gen. 46. 24 Jahzeel, and Guni, and Jezer, and S.
Num 26. 49 of S., the family of the Shillemites

SHILLEMITES, שִׁלֵּמִי.
The family of the preceding.
Num 26. 49 of Shillem, the family of the S.

SHI-LO'-AH, שִׁלֹחַ *sending forth.* See *Siloa.*
A fountain in the S. of the valley of the Tyropæon, between the upper and the lower parts of Jerusalem from which flowed a little brook past Sion and Moriah, and was lost in the gardens S. of Ophel.
Isa. 8. 6 this people refuseth the waters of S. that

SHI'-LOH, שִׁילֹה.
A description of Messiah, as the Prince of Peace; or as the "*Seed*" of Judah, so *Ben Gannach, Kimchi,* &c.
Gen. 49. 10 The sceptre shall not depart..until S. co.

SHI'-LOH, שִׁלֹה, שִׁלוֹ, שִׁילֹה, שִׁלֹה, שִׁילוֹ.
A city in Ephraim, N. of Bethel, and E. of the road from Bethel to Shechem, ten or twelve Roman miles distant from it, and S. of Lebonah. Under Joshua it was a central city, and till the time of Samuel it was the seat of the tabernacle. It was also the residence of Ahijah the prophet, and is now called *Seilun.*
Josh 18. 1 children of Israel assembled together at S.
18. 8 I..cast lots for you before the LORD in S.
18. 9 came (again) to Joshua to the host at S.
18. 10 cast lots for them in S. before the LORD
19. 51 divided for an inheritance by lot in S. be.
21. 2 spake unto them at S. in the land of Can.
22. 9 children of Reuben..departed..out of S.
22 12 gathered themselves together at S., to go
Judg 18. 31 the time that the house of God was in S.
21. 12 they brought them unto the camp to S.
21. 19 Behold, (there is) a feast of the LORD in S.
21. 21 daughters of S. come out to dance in da.
21. 21 every man his wife of the daughters of S.
1 Sa. 1. 3 to sacrifice unto the LORD of hosts in S.
1. 9 Hannah rose up after they had eaten in S.
1. 24 brought..unto the house of the LORD in S.
2. 14 So they did in S. unto all the Israelites
3. 21 the LORD appeared again in S.: for the
3. 21 revealed himself to Samuel in S. by the
4. 3 Let us fetch the ark..out of S. unto us
4. 4 So the people sent to S., that they might
4. 12 came to S. the same day, with his clothes
14. 3 Ahiah..the LORD's priest in S., wearing
1 Ki. 2. 27 spake concerning the house of Eli in S.
14. 2 Arise..disguise thyself..and get thee to S.
14. 4 Jeroboam's wife..arose, and went to S., and
Psa. 78. 60 So that he forsook the tabernacle of S., the
Jer. 7. 12 But go ye now unto my place..in S., wh.
7. 14 Therefore will I do..as I have done to S.
26. 6 Then will I make this house like S., and
26. 9 saying, This house shall be like S., and
41. 5 That there came certain from..S, and fr.

SHI-LO'-NI, הַשִּׁילֹנִי.
Father of Zechariah, of the sons of Parez (or Pharez) son of Judah. B.C. 630.
Neh. 11. 5 Joiarib, the son of Zechariah, the son of S.

SHILONITE, הַשִּׁילֹנִי, הַשִּׁלֹנִי, הַשִּׁילוֹנִי.
An inhabitant of Shiloh.
1 Ki. 11. 29 Ahijah the S. found him in the way; and
12. 15 which the LORD spake by Ahijah the S. un.
15. 29 he spake by his servant Ahijah the S.
1 Ch. 9. 5 And of the S.; Asaiah the first born, and
2 Ch. 9. 29 and in the prophecy of Ahijah the S., and
10. 15 he spake by the hand of Ahijah the S. to

SHIL'-SHAH, שִׁלְשָׁה *might, heroism.*
The ninth son of Zophah an Asherite. B.C. 1500.
1 Ch. 7. 37 Bezer, and Hod, and Shamma, and S., and

SHIM'-EAH, שִׁמְאָה *splendour.*
Son of Mikloth a Benjamite, of the family of Saul, the first king of Israel. B.C. 1100. *See* Shimeam.
1 Ch. 8. 32 Mikloth begat S. And these also dwelt

SHIM'-EAH, שִׁמְעָה (2 Sam. 21. 21 V.L. שמעי), *fame.*
One of David's brothers. *See* Shammah No. 2, and Shimea No. 1. B.C. 1060.
2 Sa.13. 3 Amnon had a friend..the son of S.; 13. 32.
21. 21 Jonathan the son of S., the brother of Da.

SHIMEA, שִׁמְעָא *fame, rumour.*
1. David's brother. 1 Ch. 20. 7. *See* Shimeah.
2. A son of David. *See* Shammuah No. 2. B.C. 1020.
1 Ch. 3. 5 S., and Shobab, and Nathan, and Solomon
3. A Merarite, father of Haggiah. B.C. 1015.
1 Ch. 6. 30 S. his son, Haggiah his son, Asaiah his son
4. Father of Berachiah, a Gershonite. B.C. 1060.
1 Ch. 6. 39 Asaph the son of Berachiah, the son of S.

SHIM'-EAM, שִׁמְאָם *fame, rumour.*
Son of Mikloth, a Benjamite whose family dwelt in Jerusalem, same as *Shimeah,* 1 Ch. 8. 32. B.C. 1100.
1 Ch. 9. 38 And Mikloth begat S. And they also dw.

SHIM'-EATH, שִׁמְעָת *fame.*
An Ammonitess, mother of Jozachar who was one of those that slew Jehoash king of Judah. B.C. 835.
2 Ki. 12. 21 For Jozachar the son of S., and Jehoza.
2 Ch.24. 26 Zabad the son of S. an Ammonitess, and

SHIMEATHITES, הַשִּׁמְעָתִים.
A family of scribes at Jabez, of Caleb son of Hur, first-born of Ephratah
1 Ch. 2. 55 the Tirathites, the S., (and) Suchathites.

SHIM'-EI, SHIM'-I, SHIM'-HI, שִׁמְעִי. *Jah is fame.*
1. A son of Gershon, son of Levi. B.C. 1600.
Exod. 6. 17 The sons of Gershon; Libni and Shimi

Num. 3. 18 names of..sons of Gershon..Libni, and S.
1 Ch. 6. 17 names of..sons of Gershom; Libni, and S.
6. 42 Ethan, the son of Zimmah, the son of S.
23. 7 Of the Gershonites (were) Laadan and S.
23. 10 the sons of S. (were) Jahath, Zina, and J.
23. 10 These four (were) the sons of S.

2. A Benjamite, son of Gera, who cursed David when fleeing from Absalom. B.C. 1012.

2 Sa. 16. 5 thence came..a man..whose name (was) S.
16. 7 thus said S. when he cursed, Come out, co.
16. 13 S. went along on the hill's side over against
19. 16 the son of Gera, a Benjamite, which (was)
19. 18 S. the son of Gera fell down before the ki.
19. 21 Shall not S. be put to death for this, bec.
19. 23 the king said unto S., Thou shalt not die
1 Ki. 2. 8 (thou hast) with thee S. the son of Gera
2. 36 the king sent and called for S., and said
2. 38 S. said unto the king, The saying (is) good
2. 38 And S. dwelt in Jerusalem many days
2. 39 two of the servants of S. ran away unto
2. 39 they told S., saying, Behold, thy servants
2. 40 S. arose, and saddled his ass, and went to
2. 40 S. went, and brought his servants from G.
2. 41 it was told Solomon that S. had gone from
2. 42 the king sent and called for S. and said un.
2. 44 The king said moreover to S., Thou kno.

3. An officer of David who remained stedfast when Adonijah usurped the throne. B.C. 1012.

1 Ki. 1. 8 S., and Rei, and the mighty men which (be.)

4. A son of Elah, one of the twelve purveyors of Solomon, in Benjamin. B.C. 1010.

1 Ki. 4. 18 S. the son of Elah in Benjamin

5. Grandson of Jeconiah, son of Jehoiakim king of Judah. B.C. 536.

1 Ch. 3. 19 sons of Pedaiah (were) Zerubbabel, and S.

6. Son of Zacchar, a Benjamite with sixteen sons and six daughters. B.C. 1040.

1 Ch. 4. 26 Hamuel his son Zacchur his son, S. his
4. 27 S. had sixteen sons and six daughters; but

7. A Reubenite, son of Gog. B C 1300.

1 Ch. 5. 4 Shemaiah his son, Gog his son, S. his son

8. A Merarite, son of Libni. B.C. 1012.

1 Ch. 6. 29 Libni his son, S. his son, Uzza his son

9. Father of a chief family in Judah. B.C. 1300.

1 Ch. 8. 21 and Beraiah, and Shimrath, the sons of S.

10. A Levite of the family of Laadan. B.C. 1012.

1 Ch. 23. 9 The sons of S.; Shelomith, and Haziel, and

11. A Levite to whom the tenth lot fell in the service of song in the sanctuary in the days of David. B.C. 1015.

1 Ch. 25. 17 The tenth to S., (he), his sons, and his br.

12. A Ramathite, who was over the vineyards in the days of David. B.C. 1015.

1 Ch. 27. 27 over the vineyards (was) S. the Ramath.

13. A descendant of Heman who assisted in cleansing the temple in the days of Hezekiah. B.C. 726.

2 Ch. 29. 14 of the sons of Heman; Jehiel and S.: and

14. A Levite with charge of the offerings in the days of Hezekiah. B.C. 726.

2 Ch. 31. 12 Cononiah the Levite (was) ruler, and S.
31. 13 under the hand of Cononiah and S. his br.

15. A Levite that had taken a strange wife. B.C. 445.

Ezra 10. 23 Also of the Levites; Jozabad, and S., and

16. One of the family of Heshum that had done the same.

Ezra 10. 33 Z., Eliphelet, Jeremai, Manasseh (and) S.

17. One of the family of Bani that had done the same.

Ezra 10. 38 And Bani, and Binnui, S.

18. A Benjamite, grandfather of Mordecai who brought up Esther. B.C. 550.

Esth. 2. 5 Jair, the son of S., the son of Kish a Be.

19. Perhaps the simple representative of the Gershonites.

Zech 12. 13 the family of S. apart, and their wives ap.

SHIM-E'-ON, שִׁמְעוֹן *hearing.*
One of the family of Harim. B.C. 445. Ezra 10. 31.

SHIMHI. *See* **SHIMEI,** No. 9.

SHIMI. *See* **SHIMEI,** No. 1.

SHIMITES, הַשִּׁמְעִי.
The family of Shimei, son of Gershon.

Num. 3. 21 Of Gershon, (was)..the family of the S.:

SHIM'-MA, שִׁמְעָא *fame, rumour.*
The third son of Jesse, also called *Shamma.* B.C. 1060.

1 Ch. 2. 13 Jesse begat his first born Eliab..and S.

SHI'-MON, שִׁימוֹן *trier, valuer.*
A descendant of Caleb son of Jephunneh. B.C. 1400.

1 Ch. 4. 20 And the sons of S. (were) Amnon, and

SHIM'-RATH, שִׁמְרָת *watch.*
A son of Shimri, a descendant of Benjamin. B.C. 1300.

1 Ch. 8. 21 and Beraiah, and S. the sons of Shimhi

SHIM'-RI, SIM'-RI, שִׁמְרִי *Jah is watching.*
1. Head of a family in Simeon. B.C. 930.

1 Ch. 4. 37 Allon, the son of Jedaiah, the son of S.

2. Father of Jediael, one of David's valiant men. B.C. 1070.

1 Ch. 11. 45 Jediael the son of S., and Joha his brother

3. A Merarite, son of Hosah, and gate keeper of the tabernacle in the days of David. B.C. 1015.

1 Ch. 26. 10 Hosah..had sons; S. the chief, for (though)

4. A Levite, son of Elizaphan, who assisted in cleansing the temple in the days of Hezekiah. B.C. 730.

2 Ch. 29. 13 of the sons of Elizaphan; S. and Jeiel: and

SHIM'-RITH, שִׁמְרִית *watch.*
A Moabitess, mother of Jehozabad who slew Joash king of Judah. B.C. 840.

2 Ch. 24. 26 and Jehozabad the son of S. a Moabitess

SHIM'-RON (SHIM'-ROM, 1 Ch. 7. 1), שִׁמְרוֹן *watch.*
1. Fourth son of Issachar B.C. 1700.

Gen. 46. 13 And the sons of Issachar..Job, and S.
Num 26. 24 of S., the family of the Shimronites
1 Ch. 7. 1 sons of Issachar (were) Tola and Puah..S.

2. A city in Zebulon, near Nahallal; also called *Shimron-meron.*

Josh. 11. 1 he sent..to the king of S., and to the king
19. 15 Kattath, and Nahallal, and S., and Idalah

SHIMRONITES, הַשִּׁמְרֹנִי.
The family of Shimron, son of Issachar.

Num 26. 24 of Shimron, the family of the S.

SHIM-RON MER'-ON, שִׁמְרוֹן מְראוֹן.
A city in Upper Galilee, near Giscala, and now called *Marun,* two hours W of Zaphet, where are the reputed graves of *Hillel* and *Shammai,* also a very old synagogue and an uncovered school. Here every year on the eighteenth Iyar is held a Jewish festival over the grave of *Simon ben Jochai,* to which thousands of pilgrims resort from Aleppo, Bagdad, Cairo, Constantinople, Damascus, &c.

Josh 12. 20 The king of S., one; the king of Achshaph

SHIM'-SHAI, שִׁמְשַׁי *Jah is splendour.*
A scribe who along with Rehum wrote to the king of Persia against the rebuilding of Jerusalem by Nehemiah. B.C. 522.

Ezra 4. 8 S. the scribe wrote a letter against Jerus.
4. 9 (wrote) Rehum the chancellor, and S. the
4. 17 (Then) sent the king an answer..(to) S. the
4. 23 Artaxerxes letter (was) read before S. the

SHI'-NAB, שִׁנְאָב.
King of Admah, in the days of Abraham B.C. 1913.

Gen. 14. 2 S. king of Admah, and Shemeber king of

SHI'-NAR, שִׁנְעָר.
Babylonia in its fullest extent. not including Assyria or Susiana. Its chief cities were Babylon, Erech, Accad and Calneh.

Gen. 10. 10 and Accad, and Calneh, in the land of S.
11. 2 that they found a plain in the land of S.
14. 1 in the days of Amraphel king of S., Arioch
14. 9 Amraphel king of S., and Arioch king of
Isa. 11. 11 recover the remnant of his people..from S.
Dan. 1. 2 which he carried into the land of S. to the
Zech. 5. 11 To build it an house in the land of S.: and

SHINE, to —

1. *To shine, become bright,* אָהַל *ahal,* 5.

Job 25. 5 Behold even to the moon, and it shineth

2. *To be or become bright,* אוֹר *or.*

Prov. 4. 18 shineth more and more unto the perfect
Isa. 60. 1 Arise, shine; for thy light is come, and

3. *To cause or give light,* אוֹר *or,* 5.

Psa. 139. 12 night shineth as the day: the darkness
Eze 43. 2 and the earth shined with his glory

4. *To shine,* הָלַל *halal.*

Job 29. 3 When his candle shined upon my head

5. *To (cause to) shine,* הָלַל *halal,* 5.

Job 31. 26 If I beheld the sun when it shined, or the
41. 18 By his neesings a light doth shine, and his

6. *To (cause to) shine,* זָהַר *zahar,* 5.

Dan. 12. 3 they that be wise shall shine as the brig.

7. *To rise,* זָרַח *zarach.*

2 Ki. 3. 22 sun shone upon the water, and the Moab.

8. *To (cause to) shine,* יָפַע *yapha,* 5.

Job 10. 3 and shine upon the counsel of the wicked
Psa. 50. 2 the perfection of beauty, God hath shined

9. *To shine,* נָגַהּ *nagah.*

Job 18. 5 and the spark of his fire shall not shine
22. 28 and the light shall shine upon thy ways
Isa. 9. 2 upon them hath the light shined

10. *To shine,* עָשַׁת *ashath.*

Jer. 5. 28 They are waxen fat, they shine: yea, they

11. *To have rays, shine,* קָרַן *qaran.*

Exod 34. 29 wist not that the skin of his face shone
34. 30 the skin of his face shone; and they were
34. 35 that the skin of Moses' face shone: and

12. *To flash as lightning,* ἀστράπτω *astraptō.*

Luke 24. 4 two men stood by them in shining garm.

13. *To beam forth,* αὐγάζω *augazō.*

2 Co. 4. 4 lest the light..[should shine] unto them

14. *To shine, give light,* λάμπω *lampō.*

Matt. 5. 16 Let your light so shine before men, that
17. 2 his face did shine as the sun, and his rai.
Luke 17. 24 shineth unto the other (part) under hea.
Acts 12. 7 light shined in the prison: and he smote
2 Co. 4. 6 God, who commanded the light to shine
4. 6 hath shined in our hearts, to (give) the li.

15. *To (cause to) appear, shine,* φαίνω *phainō.*

Matt 24. 27 shineth even unto the west; so shall also
John 1. 5 light shineth in darkness; and the dark.
5. 35 He was a burning and a shining light: and
Phil. 2. 15 among whom ye shine as lights in the wo.
2 Pe. 1. 19 as unto a light that shineth in a dark pl.
1 Jo. 2. 8 darkness is past, and the true light now
Rev. 1. 16 his countenance (was) as the sun shineth
8. 12 day shone not for a third part of it, and
18. 23 light of a candle shall shine no more at
21. 23 neither of the moon, to shine in it: for the

SHINE, to cause, let or make —

1. *To cause or give light, or cause to shine,* אוֹר *or,* 5.

Num 6. 25 LORD make his face shine upon thee, and
Job 41. 32 He maketh a path to shine after him; (one)
Psa. 31. 16 Make thy face to shine upon thy servant
67. 1 (and) cause his face to shine upon us. Se.
80. 3, 19 cause thy face to shine; and we shall
119. 135 Make thy face to shine upon thy servant
Eccl. 8. 1 man's wisdom maketh his face to shine
Dan. 9. 17 cause thy face to shine upon thy sanctu.

2. *To (cause to) shine,* יָפַע *yapha,* 5.

Job 3. 4 above, neither let the light shine upon it
37. 15 and caused the light of his cloud to shine?

3. *To cause to shine, enlighten,* נָגַהּ *nagah,* 5.

Isa. 13. 10 the moon shall not cause her light to sh.

4. *To cause to rejoice, make to shine,* צָהַל *tsahal,* 5.

Psa. 104. 15 oil to make (his) face to shine, and bread

SHINE forth, round about, to —

1. *To (cause to) shine,* יָפַע *yapha,* 5.

Deut 33. 2 shined forth from mount Paran, and he
Psa. 80. 1 Give ear, O shepherd of Israel..shine fo.

2. *To flee or move quickly,* עוּף *uph.*

Job 11. 17 thou shalt shine forth, thou shalt be as

3. *To shine out,* ἐκλάμπω *eklampō.*

Matt 13. 43 Then shall the righteous shine forth as

4. *To flash round about,* περιαστράπτω *periastraptō.*

Acts 9. 3 suddenly there shined round about him
22. 6 there shone..a great light round about

5. *To shine round about,* περιλάμπω *perilampō.*

Luke 2. 9 glory of the Lord shone round about th.
Acts 26. 13 shining round about me and them which

SHINING, (bright, clear) —

1. *Shining, brightness,* נֹגַהּ *nogah.*

2 Sa. 23. 4 out of the earth by clear shining after ra.
Prov. 4. 18 the path of the just (is) as the shining li.
Isa. 4. 5 and the shining of a flaming fire by night
Joel 2. 10 and the stars shall withdraw their shin.
3. 15 and the stars shall withdraw their shin.
Hab. 3. 11 (and) at the shining of thy glittering sp.

2. *A flash, bright shining,* ἀστραπή *astrapē.*

Luke 11. 36 as when the bright shining of a candle

3. *To shine, glisten,* στίλβω *stilbō.*

Mark 9. 3 his raiment became shining, exceeding

SHIP, (little, small) —

1. *A ship,* אֳנִיָּה *oniyyah.*

Gen. 49. 13 and he (shall be) for an haven of ships
Deut 28. 68 bring thee into Egypt again with ships, by
Judg. 5. 17 why did Dan remain in ships? Asher co.
1 Ki. 22. 48 Jehoshaphat made ships of Tarshish to
22. 48 for the ships were broken at Ezion-geber
22. 49 Let my servants go..in the ships: but
2 Ch. 9. 21 the king's ships went to Tarshish with the
9. 21 every three years once came the ships of
20. 36 he joined himself with him to make ships
20. 36 and they made the ships in Ezion gaber
20. 37 the ships were broken, that they were not
Job 9. 26 They are passed away as the swift ships
Psa. 48. 7 Thou breakest the ships of Tarshish with
104. 26 There go the ships; (there is) that leviat.
107. 23 They that go down to the sea in ships, that
Prov 30. 19 the way of a ship in the midst of the sea
31. 14 She is like the merchants' ships; she bri.
Isa. 2. 16 upon all the ships of Tarshish, and upon
23. 1 Howl, ye ships of Tarshish; for it is laid
23. 14 Howl, ye ships of Tarshish: for your str.
43. 14 and the Chaldeans, whose cry (is) in the sh.
60. 9 the isles shall wait for me, and the ships
Eze. 27. 9 the ships of the sea with their mariners
27. 25 The ships of Tarshish did sing of thee in
27. 29 the pilots..shall come down from their sh.
Dan. 11. 40 and with horsemen, and with many ships
Jon. 1. 3 and he found a ship going to Tarshish
1. 4 so that the ship was like to be broken
1. 5 cast forth the wares that (were) in the ship

2. *Ships,* אוֹנִיּוֹת *oniyyoth.*

2 Ch. 8. 18 Huram sent him..ships, and servants that

3. *A ship, vessel, what is roofed in,* סְפִינָה *sephinah.*

Jon. 1. 5 was gone down into the sides of the ship

4. *A ship,* צִי *tsi.*

Num 24. 24 the ships (shall come) from the coast of C.
Isa. 33. 21 neither shall gallant ship pass thereby
Eze. 30. 9 shall messengers go forth from me in ships
Dan. 11. 30 the ships of Chittim shall come against him

5. *A ship,* ναῦς *naus.*

Acts 27. 41 they ran the ship aground: and the fore

6. *A little ship or boat,* πλοιάριον *ploiarion.*

Mark 3. 9 that a small ship should wait on him be.
4. 36 were also with him other [little ships]
John 21. 8 the other disciples came in a little ship

7. *A ship, sailing vessel,* πλοῖον *ploion.*

Matt. 4. 21 John his brother, in a ship with Zebedee
4. 22 they immediately left the ship and their
8. 23 when he was entered into a ship, his dis.

Matt. 8. 24 that the ship was covered with the waves
9. 1 he entered into a ship, and passed over
13. 2 so that he went into a ship, and sat
14. 13 he departed thence by ship into a desert
14. 22 constrained his disciples to get into a ship
14. 24 the ship was now in the midst of the sea
14. 29 when Peter was come down out of the sh.
14. 32 when they were come into the ship, the
14. 33 they that were in the ship came and wo.
15. 39 he sent away the multitude, and took ship
Mark 1. 19 who also were in the ship mending their
1. 20 they left their father Zebedee in the ship
4. 1 he entered into a ship, and sat in the sea
4. 36 they took him even as he was in the ship
4. 37 the waves beat into the ship, so that it was
5. 2 when he was come out of the ship, im.
5. 18 when he was come into the ship, he that
5. 21 when Jesus was passed over again by ship
6. 32 they departed into a desert place by ship
6. 45 to get into the ship, and to go to the other
6. 47 the ship was in the midst of the sea, and
6. 51 And he went up unto them into the ship
6. 54 And when they were come out of the ship
8. 10 he entered into a ship with his disciples
8. 13 he left them, and, entering [into the ship]
8. 14 neither had they in the ship with them
Luke 5. 2 saw two [ships] standing by the lake: but
5. 3 he entered into one of the ships, which
5. 3 and taught the people out of the ship
5. 7 partners, which were in the other ship
5. 7 they came, and filled both the ships, so
5. 11 when they had brought their ships to land
8. 22 that he went into a ship with his disciples
8. 37 he went up into the ship, and returned ba.
John 6. 17 entered into a ship, and went over the sea
6. 19 walking..and drawing nigh unto the ship
6. 21 they willingly received him into the ship
6. 21 immediately the ship was at the land w.
21. 3 They went forth, and entered into a ship
21. 6 Cast the net on the right side of the ship
Acts 20. 13 we went before to ship, and sailed unto
20. 38 And they accompanied him unto the ship
21. 2 finding a ship sailing over unto Phenicia
21. 3 for there the ship was to unlade her bur.
21. 6 we took ship; and they returned home
27. 2 entering into a ship of Adramyttium
27. 6 the centurion found a ship of Alexandria
27. 10 not only of the lading and ship, but also
27. 15 when the ship was caught, and could not
27. 17 they used helps, undergirding the ship
27. 19 we cast out..the tackling of the ship
27. 22 for there shall be no loss..but of the ship
27. 30 shipmen were about to flee out of the ship
27. 31 Except these abide in the ship, ye cannot
27. 37 And we were in all in the ship two hun.
27. 38 they lightened the ship, and cast out the
27. 39 they were minded..to thrust in the ship
27. 44 and some on (broken pieces) of the ship
28. 11 we departed in a ship of Alexandria, wh.
Jas. 3. 4 Behold also the ships, which though (they
Rev. 8. 9 the third part of the ships were destroyed
18. 17 [all the company in ships, and sailors, and]
18. 19 wherein were made rich all that had shi.

SHIP master, owner of a ship —

1. *Master of the pilots,* רַב חֹבֵל *rab chobel.*
Jon. 1. 6 the ship master came to him, and said

2. *Pilot, steersman, governor,* κυβερνήτης *kubernēt.*
Rev. 18. 17 every ship master, and all the company

3. *Master or owner of a ship,* ναύκληρος *nauklēros.*
Acts 27. 11 the master and the owner of the ship

SHIP men, (to take) shipping —

1. *Ship men,* אַנְשֵׁי אֳנִיּוֹת *[anashim].*
1 Ki. 9. 27 ship men that had knowledge of the sea

2. *To go up into the ship,* ἐπιβαίνω εἰς τὸ πλοῖον.
Acts 21. 6 [we took] ship; and they returned home

3. *A sailor,* ναύτης *nautēs.*
Acts 27. 27 the ship men deemed that they drew near
27. 30 as the ship men were about to flee out of

4. *A ship, sailing vessel,* πλοῖον *ploion.*
John 6. 24 they also [took shipping], and came to C.

SHIPH'-I, שִׁפְעִי *Jah is fulness.*
Father of Ziza, a chief Simeonite. B.C. 830.
1 Ch. 4. 37 Ziza the son of S., the son of Allon, the son

SHIPH-MITE, שִׁפְמִי. See *Shepham.*
Patronymic of Zabdi who was over the increase of the vineyards for the wine cellars. B.C. 1015.
1 Ch. 27. 27 over the increase..(was) Zabdi the S.

SHIPH'-RAH, שִׁפְרָה *beauty.*
One of the Hebrew midwives at the time of the birth of Moses. B.C. 1571.
Exod. 1. 15 of which the name of the one (was) S., and

SHIPH'-TAN, שִׁפְטָן *judge.*
Father of Kemuel, a chief Ephraimite appointed to divide the land W. of the Jordan. B.C. 1510.
Num 34. 24 prince..of Ephraim, Kemuel the son of S.

SHIPWRECK, to make or suffer —
To be shipwrecked, ναυαγέω *nauageō.*
2 Co. 11. 25 thrice I suffered shipwreck, a night and
1 Ti. 1. 19 concerning faith have made shipwreck

SHI'-SHA, שִׁישָׁא *distinction, nobility.*
Father of Elihoreph and Ahiah, two of Solomon's scribes. B.C. 1048.
1 Ki. 4. 3 Elihoreph and Ahiah, the sons of S., scri.

SHI'-SHAK, שִׁישַׁק.
Sesconchis I. king of the twenty second Bubastic dynasty in Egypt; he protected Jeroboam against Solomon, invaded Judea under Rehoboam, took fenced cities, and plundered Jerusalem and the temple. B.C. 975.
1 Ki. 11. 40 and Jeroboam arose, and fled..unto S. ki.
14. 25 S. king of Egypt came up against Jerusa.
2 Ch. 12. 2 S. king of Egypt came up against Jerusa.
12. 5 that were gathered together..because of S.
12. 5 have I also left you in the hand of S.
12. 7 shall not be poured out..by the hand of S.
12. 9 S. king of Egypt came up against Jerusa.

SHIT'-RAI, שִׁטְרַי *Jah is deciding.*
A native of Sharon who was over the herds there in the days of David. B.C. 1015.
1 Ch. 27. 29 over the herds that fed in Sharon (was) S.

SHIT'-TIM, שִׁטִּים.
A place in Moab, E. of the Salt Sea, whence Joshua sent forth spies. See also *Abel* and *Beth.*
Num 25. 1 Israel abode in S., and the people began
Josh. 2. 1 Joshua..sent out of S. two men to spy se.
3. 1 and they removed from S., and came to
Joel 3. 18 a fountain..shall water the valley of S.
Mic. 6. 5 what Balaam..answered him from S. unto

SHITTIM, shittah tree —
Acacia, acacia wood, שִׁטָּה *shittah.*
Exod 25. 5 and badgers' skins, and shittim wood
25. 10 And they shall make an ark (of) shittim
25. 13 thou shalt make staves (of) shittim wood
25. 23 Thou shalt also make a table (of) shittim
25. 28 thou shalt make the staves (of) shittim w.
26. 15 thou shalt make boards..(of) shittim wo.
26. 26 thou shalt make bars (of) shittim wood
26. 32 four pillars of shittim (wood) overlaid w.
26. 37 thou shalt make..five pillars (of) shittim
27. 1 thou shalt make an altar (of) shittim wo.
27. 6 staves for the altar, staves (of) shittim w.
30. 1 (of) shittim wood shalt thou make it
30. 5 thou shalt make the staves (of) shittim w.
35. 7 and badgers' skins, and shittim wood
35. 24 every man with whom was found shittim
36. 20 he made boards..(of) shittim wood, stan.
36. 31 he made bars of shittim wood; five for
36. 36 he made thereunto four pillars (of) shit.
37. 1 Bezaleel made the ark (of) shittim wood
37. 4 15, 28 he made staves (of) shittim wood
37. 10 he made the table (of) shittim wood: two
37. 25 he made the incense altar (of) shittim wo.
38. 1 And he made the altar..(of) shittim wood
38. 6 And he made the staves (of) shittim wood
Deut 10. 3 I made an ark (of) shittim wood, and he.
Isa. 41. 19 I will plant..the shittah tree, and the

SHIVERS. *See* **BREAK.**

SHI'-ZA, שִׁיזָא *splendour.*
A Reubenite, one of David's valiant men. B.C. 1070.
1 Ch. 11. 42 Adina the son of S. the Reubenite, a cap.

SHO'-A, שׁוֹעַ *rich.*
A tribe named along with the Chaldeans and Pekod as an enemy of Israel.
Eze. 23. 23 Pekod, and S., and Koa, (and) all the As.

SHO'-BAB, שׁוֹבָב *returning.*
1. A son of David born after he became king of Israel. B.C. 1020.
2 Sa. 5. 14 Shammuah, and S., and Nathan, and Sol.
1 Ch. 3. 5 Shimea, and S., and Nathan, and Solomon
14. 4 Shammua, and S., Nathan, and Solomon
2. A son of Caleb, son of Hezron. B.C. 1540.
1 Ch. 2. 18 her sons (are) these; Jesher, and S., and

SHO'-BACH, שׁוֹבַךְ *expansion.*
Captain of the host of Hadarezer king of Zobah defeated and slain by Joab; called *Shophach,* 1 Chron. 19. 16. B.C. 1036.
2 Sa. 10. 16 S. the captain of the host..(went) before
10. 18 David..smote S. the captain of their host

SHO'-BAI, שֹׁבַי *Jah is glorious.*
A gate keeper of the tabernacle whose descendants returned with Zerubbabel. B.C. 536.
Ezra 2. 42 the children of S., (in) all an hundred th.
Neh. 7. 45 the children of S., an hundred thirty and

SHO'-BAL, שׁוֹבָל *wandering.*
1. A son of Seir. B.C. 1820.
Gen. 36. 20 sons of S..Lotan, and S., and Zibeon, and
36. 23 the children of S. (were) these; Alvan, and
36. 29 duke Lotan, duke S., duke Zibeon, duke
1 Ch. 1. 38 Lotan, and S., and Zibeon, and Anah, and
1. 40 The sons of S.; Alian, and Manahath, and
2. A son of Caleb, son of Hur. B.C. 1480.
1 Ch. 2. 50 These were the sons of Caleb..S. the fat.
2. 52 S. the father of Kirjath-jearim had sons
3. A son of Judah and father of Reaiah. B.C. 1670.
1 Ch. 4. 1 sons of Judah; Pharez..Carmi..Hur..S.
4. 2 And Reaiah the son of S. begat Jahath

SHO'-BEK, שׁוֹבֵק *free.*
A person or family that with Nehemiah sealed the covenant. B.C. 445.
Neh. 10. 24 Hallohesh, Pileha, S.

SHO'-BI, שֹׁבִי *Jah is glorious.*
A son of Nahash of Rabbah who received David when he fled from Absalom; perhaps the brother of Harun who succeeded his father Nahash, 1 Chron. 19. 1. B.C. 1023.
2 Sa. 17. 27 S. the son of Nahash of Rabbah of the ch.

SHOCK (of corn) —
A stalk, shock or heap of corn, גָּדִישׁ *gadish.*
Judg 15. 5 burnt up both the shocks, and also the
Job 5. 26 like as a shock of corn cometh in in his

SHO'-CO, SHO'-CHO. *See* **SOCHO.**

SHOCOH. *See* **SOCOH.**

SHOD, to be —
To be shod, ὑποδέομαι *hupodeomai.*
Mark 6. 9 (be) shod with sandals; and not put on two
Eph. 6. 15 your feet shod with the preparation of

SHOE, pair of shoes —

1. *A shoe,* נַעַל *naal.*
Exod. 3. 5 put off thy shoes from off thy feet, for the
12. 11 your shoes on your feet, and your staff in
Deut 25. 9 loose his shoe from off his foot, and spit
25. 10 The house of him that hath his shoe loos.
29. 5 thy shoe is not waxen old upon thy foot
Josh. 5. 15 Loose thy shoe from off thy foot; for the
9. 5 old shoes and clouted upon their feet, and
9. 13 our shoes are become old by reason of the
Ruth 4. 7 a man plucked off his shoe, and gave (it)
4. 8 Buy (it) for thee. So he drew off his shoe
1 Ki. 2. 5 put the blood..in his shoes that (were) on
Psa. 60. 8 over Edom will I cast out my shoe: Phi.
108. 9 over Edom will I cast out my shoe; over
Song 7. 1 How beautiful are thy feet with shoes, O
Isa. 5. 27 nor the latchet of their shoes be broken
20. 2 Go..and put off thy shoe from thy foot
Eze. 24. 17 put on thy shoes upon thy feet, and cover
24. 23 tires..upon your heads, and your shoes
Amos 2. 6 they sold..the poor for a pair of shoes
8. 6 we may buy..the needy for a pair of sh.

2. *Shoe,* מִנְעָל *minal.*
Deut 33. 25 Thy shoes (shall be) iron and brass; and

3. *A sandal,* ὑπόδημα *hupodēma.*
Matt. 3. 11 whose shoes I am not worthy to bear
10. 10 neither two coats, neither shoes, nor yet
Mark 1. 7 the latchet of whose shoes I am not wort.
Luke 3. 16 the latchet of whose shoes I am not wor
10. 4 Carry neither purse, nor scrip, nor shoes
15. 22 put a ring on his hand, and shoes on (his)
22. 35 without purse, and scrip, and shoes, lac.
John 1. 27 whose shoe's latchet I am not worthy to
Acts 7. 33 Put off thy shoes from thy feet: for the
13. 25 whose shoes of (his) feet I am not worthy

SHOE, to —

1. *To shoe,* נָעַל *naal.*
Eze. 16. 10 shod thee with badgers' skin, and I girded

2. *To shoe,* נָעַל *naal,* 5.
2 Ch. 28. 15 arrayed them, and shod them, and gave

SHOE latchet —
A shoe latchet, שְׂרוֹךְ נַעַל *serok naal.*
Gen. 14. 23 I will not (take)..even to a shoe latchet
Isa. 5. 27 nor the latchet of their shoes be broken

SHO'-HAM, שֹׁהַם *leek-green beryl.*
A Merarite. B.C. 1700.
1 Ch. 24. 27 The sons of Merari by Jaaziah; Beno..S..

SHO'-MER, שֹׁמֵר *watcher.*
1. A Moabitess, mother of Jehozabad, one of those who slew Jehoash king of Judah; called *Shimrith* in 2 Ch. 24. 26. B.C. 870.
2 Ki. 12. 21 Jehozabad the son of S..smote him, and
2. A great grandson of Asher; spelt *Shamer* in ver. 34. B.C. 1600.
1 Ch. 7. 32 Heber begat Japhlet, and S., and Hotham

SHOOT (forth, out, up), to —

1. *To flee, move on,* בָּרַח *barach.*
Exod 36. 33 he made the middle bar to shoot through

2. *To tread,* דָּרַךְ *darak.*
1 Ch. 5. 18 and to shoot with bow, and skilful in war

3. *To cast, throw,* יָדָה *yadah.*
Jer. 50. 14 all ye that bend the bow, shoot at her

4. *To go out or forth,* יָצָא *yatsa.*
Job 8. 16 and his branch shooteth forth in his gar

5. *To cast, throw,* יָרָא *yara.*
2 Ch. 26. 15 to shoot arrows and great stones withal

6. *To (cause to) cast, throw,* יָרָא *yara,* 5.
2 Sa. 11. 24 the shooters shot from off the wall upon

7. *To cast, throw, shoot,* יָרָה *yarah.*
Num 21. 30 We have shot at them: Heshbon is peris.
1 Sa. 20. 36 as the lad ran, he shot an arrow beyond
20. 37 of the arrow which Jonathan had shot
2 Ki. 13. 17 and he opened (it). Then Elisha said, S.
Psa. 11. 2 that they may privily shoot at the uprig.
64. 4 That they may shoot in secret at the per.

8. *To (cause to) throw, shoot,* יָרָה *yarah,* 5.
1 Sa. 20. 20 I will shoot three arrows on the side (th.)
20. 36 Run, find out now the arrows which I sh.
2 Sa. 11. 20 knew ye not that they would shoot from
2 Ki. 13. 17 and he shot. And he said, The arrow of
19. 32 He shall not come into this city, nor sho.
2 Ch. 35. 23 the archers shot at king Josiah: and the
Psa. 64. 4 suddenly do they shoot at him, and fear
64. 7 But God shall shoot at them (with) an ar

9. *To give,* נָתַן *nathan.*
Eze. 31. 10 he hath shot up his top among the thick
31. 14 neither shoot up their top among the th.
36. 8 ye shall shoot forth your branches, and

10. *To go up,* עָלָה *alah.*
Gen. 40. 10 it budded, (and) her blossoms shot forth
Amos 7. 1 in the beginning of the shooting up of the

11. *To (cause to) open,* פָּטַר *patar,* 5.
Psa. 22. 7 they shoot out the lip, they shake the

12. *To cast, shoot,* רָבַב *rabab.*
Gen. 49. 23 The archers have..shot (at him), and
Psa. 18. 14 he shot out lightnings, and discomfited

13. *To send,* שָׁלַח *shalach.*
Psa. 144. 6 shoot out thine arrows, and destroy th.

14. *To send,* שָׁלַח *shalach,* 3.
1 Sa. 20. 20 And I will..as though I shot at a mark
Isa. 27. 8 when it shooteth forth, thou wilt debate
Eze 17. 6 brought forth branches, and shot forth
17. 7 shot forth her branches toward him, th.
31. 5 branches became long..when he shot for.

15. *To do, make,* ποιέω *poieō.*
Mark 4. 32 becometh greater..and shooteth out gre.

16. *To cast or throw forth,* προβάλλω *proballō.*
Luke 21. 30 When they now shoot forth, ye see and

SHOOTER —
To (cause to) cast, throw, יָרָא *yara,* 5.
2 Sa. 11. 24 the shooters shot from off the wall upon

SHO'-PHACH, שׁוֹפַךְ *extension.*
Captain of the host of Hadarezer, king of Zobah in the days of David; called *Sho-bach* in 2 Sam. 10. 16. B.C. 1036.
1 Ch. 19. 16 S. the captain of the host of Hadarezer
19. 18 David..killed S. the captain of the host

SHO'-PHAN, שׁוֹפָן *nakedness.*
A city in Gad; or a denominative of the city *Atroth.*
Num 32. 35 Atroth, S., and Jaazer, and Jogbehah

SHORE —
1. *Haven, shore,* חוֹף *choph.*
Judg. 5. 17 Asher continued on the sea shore, and
Jer. 47. 7 against Ashkelon, and against the sea sh.

2. *End, extremity,* קָצֶה *qatseh.*
Josh 15. 2 their south border was from the shore of

3. *Lip, edge,* שָׂפָה *saphah.*
Gen. 22. 17 as the sand which (is) upon the sea shore
Exod 14. 30 saw the Egyptians dead upon the sea sh.
Josh 11. 4 as the sand that (is) upon the seashore in
1 Sa. 13. 5 people as the sand which (is) on the sea s.
1 Ki. 4. 29 even as the sand that (is) on the sea shore
9. 26 on the shore of the Red sea, in the land

4. *Sea shore,* αἰγιαλός *aigialos.*
Matt 13. 2 and the whole multitude stood on the sh.
13. 48 they drew to shore, and sat down, and ga.
John 21. 4 Jesus stood on the shore: but the disciples
Acts 21. 5 we kneeled down on the shore, and prayed
27. 39 discovered a certain creek with a shore
27. 40 and hoised up..and made toward shore

5. *Shore,* χεῖλος *cheilos.*
Heb. 11. 12 and as the sand which is by the sea shore

SHORE, to draw to the —
To draw a ship to the shore, προσορμίζω *prosormizō.*
Mark 6. 53 came into the land..and drew to the sh.

SHORN, (to be, having) —
1. *To cut, shear,* קָצַב *qatsab.*
Song 4. 2 like a flock (of sheep that are even) shorn

2. *To cut off, shear, shave,* κείρω *keirō.*
Acts 18. 18 having shorn (his) head in Cenchrea: for
1 Co. 11. 6 be not covered, let her also be shorn
11. 6 if it be a shame for a woman to be shorn

SHORT (space, time), shortly —
1. *Age, life time,* חֶלֶד *cheled.*
Psa. 89. 47 Remember how short my time is: where.

2. *To haste,* מָהַר *mahar,* 3.
Gen. 41. 32 and God will shortly bring it to pass

3. *Haste,* מְהֵרָה *meherah.*
Jer. 27. 16 the vessels..shall now shortly be brought

4. *Near,* קָרוֹב *qarob.*
Job 17. 12 the light (is) short because of darkness
20. 5 the triumphing of the wicked (is) short
Eze. 7. 8 Now will I shortly pour out my fury upon

5. *Season of an hour,* καιρὸς ὥρας *kairos hōras.*
1 Th. 2. 17 being taken from you for a short time in

6. *Straightly,* εὐθέως *eutheōs.*
3 John 14 I trust I shall shortly see thee, and we sh.

7. *Little, small, few, feeble,* ὀλίγος *oligos.*
Rev. 12. 12 he knoweth that he hath but a short time
17. 10 he cometh, he must continue a short sp.

8. *To cut off at once,* συντέμνω *suntemnō.*
Rom. 9. 28 For he will..cut (it) short in righteousness
9. 28 a short work will the Lord make upon

9. *To contract,* συστέλλω *sustellō.*
1 Co. 7 29 But this I say, brethren, the time (is) short

10. *Quickly, speedily,* ταχέως *tacheōs.*
1 Co. 4. 19 I will come to you shortly, if the Lord will
Phil. 2. 19 I trust..to send Timotheus shortly unto
Phil. 2. 24 I trust..I also myself shall come shortly
2 Ti. 4. 9 Do thy diligence to come shortly unto me

11. *Quick, speedy,* ταχινός *tachinos.*
2 Pe. 1. 14 knowing that shortly I must put off (this

12. *More quickly, more speedily,* τάχιον *tachion.*
1 Ti. 3. 14 write..hoping to come unto thee [shortly]
Heb. 13. 23 with whom, if he come shortly, I will see

13. *With or in speed,* ἐν τάχει *en tachei.*
Acts 25. 4 that he himself would depart shortly
Rom 16. 20 shall bruise Satan under your feet shortly
Rev. 1. 1 things which must shortly come to pass
22. 6 the things which must shortly be done

SHORTEN, be shorter, shortened, come short, to—
1. *To be or become shortened,* קָצַר *qatsar,* 3.
Psa. 102. 23 He weakened my strength..he shortened

2. *To shorten,* קָצַר *qatsar,* 5.
Psa. 89. 45 The days of his youth hast thou shortened

3. *To shorten,* קָצַר *qatsar.*
Num 11. 23 Is the LORD'S hand waxed short? thou sh.
Prov 10. 27 the years of the wicked shall be shortened
Isa. 28. 20 the bed is shorter than that (a man) can
50. 2 Is my hand shortened at all, that it can.
59. 1 the LORD'S hand is not shortened, that it
Eze. 42. 5 the upper chambers (were) shorter: for

4. *To cut off, shorten, amputate,* κολοβόω *koloboō.*
Matt 24. 22 except those days should be shortened
24. 22 for the elect's sake..shall be shortened
Mark 13. 20 except that the Lord had shortened v. 20.

5. *To be behind,* ὑστερέω *hustereō,* He. 4. 1; Ro. 3. 23.

SHO-SHAN'-NIM (Eduth), שֹׁשַׁנִּים עֵדוּת *or* שׁוֹשַׁנִּים.
Psa. 45. *title.* 69. *title.* To the chief musician upon S.
80. *title.* To the chief musician upon S.-E.

SHOT (out), to be —
1. *To be cast, thrown,* יָרָה *yarah,* 2.
Exod 19. 13 he shall surely be stoned, or shot through

2. *To slaughter,* שָׁחַט *shachat.*
Jer. 9. 8 Their tongue (is as) an arrow shot out; it

SHOULD (after, afterwards, hereafter, have) what th.—
1. *It behoveth, it is necessary,* δεῖ *dei.*
Matt 18. 33 Shouldest not thou also have had comp.
26. 35 Though I should die with thee, yet will I
Mark 14. 31 If I should die with thee, I Ac. 27. 21.

2. *To be about to,* μέλλω *mellō.*
Mark 10. 32 to tell them what things should happen
Luke 9. 31 which he should accomplish at Jerusalem
19. 11 the kingdom of God should immediately
22. 23 which of them it was that should do this
24. 21 that it had been he which should have r.
John 6. 71 he it was that should betray him, being
7. 39 which they that believe on him should r.
11. 51 prophesied that Jesus should die for that
12. 4 Simon's (son), which should betray him
12. 33 signifying what death he should die
18. 32 spake, signifying what death he should die
Acts 11. 28 that there should be great dearth thro.
19. 27 her magnificence should be destroyed, w.
20. 38 Sorrowing..that they should see his face
22. 29 they departed from him which should h.
23 27 This man..should have been killed of th.
26. 22 the prophets and Moses did say should
26. 23 should show light unto the people, and to
28. 6 they looked when he should have swollen
Gal. 3. 23 shut up unto the faith which should aft.
1 Th. 3. 4 we told you before that we should suffer
1 Ti. 1. 16 a pattern to them which should hereafter
Heb. 11. 8 a place which he should after receive for
2 Pe. 2. 6 unto those that after should live ungodly
Rev. 6. 11 brethren, that should be killed as they (w.)

3. *To owe, be obliged,* ὀφείλω *opheilō.*
1 Co. 9. 10 he that ploweth should plow in hope

SHOULDER, (blade, piece) —
1. *Arm,* זְרוֹעַ *zeroa.*
Num. 6. 19 the priest shall take the sodden shoulder
Deut 18 3 they shall give unto the priest the shoul.

2. *Shoulder,* כָּתֵף *katheph.*
Exod 28. 7 It shall have the two shoulder pieces th.
28. 12 put the two stones upon the shoulders o.
28. 12 bear their names..upon his two shoulders
28. 25 put (them) on the shoulder pieces of the
39. 4 They made shoulder pieces for it, to cou.
39. 7 he put them on the shoulders of the ephod
39. 18 put them on the shoulder pieces of the e.
Num. 7. 9 they should bear upon their shoulders
Deut 33. 12 and he shall dwell between his shoulders
Judg 16. 3 put (them) upon his shoulders, and carr.
1 Sa. 17. 6 and a target of brass between his should.
1 Ch. 15. 15 bare the ark of God upon their shoulders
2 Ch. 35. 3 (it shall) not (be) a burden upon (your) sh.
Neh. 9. 29 withdrew the shoulder, and hardened th.
Isa. 11. 14 they shall fly upon the shoulders of the
30. 6 will carry their riches upon the should.
46. 7 They bear him upon the shoulder, they c.
49. 22 shall be carried upon (their) shoulders
Eze. 12. 6 shalt thou bear (it) upon (thy) shoulders
12. 7 (and) I bare (it) upon (my) shoulder in their
12. 12 the prince..shall bear upon (his) shoulder
24. 4 every good piece, the thigh..the shoulder
29. 7 didst break, and rend all their shoulder
29. 18 every head (was) made bald, and every sh.
34. 21 ye have thrust with side and with shoul.
Zech. 7. 11 pulled away the shoulder, and stopped

3. *Leg,* שׁוֹק *shoq.*
Exod 29. 22 the two kidneys..and the right shoulder
29. 27 the shoulder of the heave offering, which
Lev. 7. 32 the right shoulder shall ye give unto the
7. 33 shall have the right shoulder for (his) pa.
7. 34 the heave shoulder have I taken of the c.
8. 25 and their fat, and the right shoulder
8. 26 on the fat, and upon the right shoulder
9. 21 the right shoulder Aaron waved (for) a
10. 14 the wave breast and heave shoulder shall
10. 15 The heave shoulder and the wave breast
Num. 6. 20 with the wave breast and heave shoulder
18. 18 as the wave breast and as the right shou.
1 Sa. 9. 24 the cook took up the shoulder, and (that)

4. *Shoulder,* שְׁכֶם *shekem.*
Gen. 9. 23 laid (it) upon both their shoulders, and
21. 14 gave (it)..putting (it) on her shoulder
24. 15 came..with her pitcher upon her should.
24. 45 came forth with her pitcher on her shoul.
49. 15 bowed his shoulder to bear, and became a
Exod 12. 34 bound up in their clothes upon their sho.
Josh. 4. 5 take..every man..a stone upon his shou.
Judg. 9. 48 laid (it) on his shoulder, and said unto the
1 Sa. 9. 2 from his shoulders and upward (he was)
10. 23 he was higher..from his shoulders and
Job 31. 36 I would take it upon my shoulder, (and)
Psa. 81. 6 I removed his shoulder from the burden
Isa. 9. 4 hast broken..the staff of his shoulder
9. 6 the government shall be upon his shoul.
10. 27 shall be taken away from off thy shoulder
Isa. 14. 25 his burden depart from off their should.
22. 22 And the key..will I lay upon his should.

5. *Shoulder,* שִׁכְמָה *shikmah.*
Job. 31. 22 let mine arm fall from my shoulder blade

6. *Shoulder,* ὦμος *ōmos.*
Matt 23. 4 they bind..and lay (them) on men's sho.
Luke 15. 5 he layeth (it) on his shoulders, rejoicing

SHOUT, shouting —
1. *A shout (of exultation),* הֵידָד *hedad.*
Isa. 16. 9 for the shouting for thy summer fruits, and
16. 10 I have made (their vintage) shouting to c.
Jer. 25. 30 he shall give a shout, as they that tread
48. 33 none shall tread with shouting
48. 33 (their) shouting (shall be) no shouting
51. 14 and they shall lift up a shout against th.

2. *Loud cry, singing,* רִנָּה *rinnah.*
Prov 11. 10 when the wicked perish, (there is) shout.

3. *Shout, shouting, blowing,* תְּרוּעָה *teruah.*
Num 23. 21 and the shout of a king (is) among them
Josh. 6. 5 the people shall shout with a great shout
6. 20 the people shouted with a great shout
1 Sa. 4. 5 Israel shouted with a great shout, so th.
4. 6 noise of the shout..the noise of this..sh.
2 Sa. 6. 15 Israel brought up the ark..with shouting
1 Ch. 15. 28 Israel brought up the ark..with shouting
2 Ch. 15. 14 with a loud voice, and with shouting, and
Ezra 3. 11 the people shouted with a great shout, wh.
3. 13 the noise of the shout of joy from the no.
3. 13 the people shouted with a loud shout
Job 39. 25 the thunder of the captains, and the sho.
Psa. 47. 5 God is gone up with a shout, the LORD
Jer. 20. 16 let him hear..the shouting at noontide
Eze. 21. 22 to lift up the voice with shouting, to ap.
Amos 1. 14 with shouting in the day of battle, with
2. 2 Moab shall die with tumult, with shout.

4. *Cry, crying, noise,* תְּשֻׁאוֹת *teshuoth.*
Zech. 4. 7 bring forth the head stone..(with) shou.

5. *A shout of encouragement,* κέλευσμα *keleusma.*
1 Th. 4. 16 shall descend from heaven with a shout

SHOUT (for joy, give a), to —
1. *To answer, respond,* עָנָה *anah.*
Exod 32. 18 (It is) not the voice of (them that) shout
Jer. 25. 30 he shall give a shout, as they that tread

2. *To cry aloud, rejoice, neigh,* צָהַל *tsahal,* 3.
Jer. 31. 7 and shout among the chief of the nations

3. *To cry out,* צָוַח *tsavach.*
Isa. 42. 11 let them shout from the top of the moun

4. *To shout,* רוּעַ *rua,* 5.
Josh. 6. 5 all the people shall shout with a great
6. 10 Ye shall not shout, nor make any noise
6. 10 day I bid you shout; then shall ye shout
6. 16 Shout; for the LORD hath given you the
6. 20 the people shouted when (the priests) blew
6. 20 and the people shouted with a great
Judg 15. 14 the Philistines shouted against him: and
1 Sa. 4. 5 when the ark..came..Israel shouted with
10. 24 the people shouted, and said, God save
17. 20 he came to the trench..and shouted for
17. 52 the men of Israel..shouted, and pursued
2 Ch. 13. 15 Then the men of Judah gave a shout: and
13. 15 as the men of Judah shouted, it came to
Ezra 3. 11 And all the people shouted with a great
3. 13 for the people shouted with a loud
Job 38. 7 and all the sons of God shouted for joy
Psa. 47. 1 shout unto God with the voice of triumph
Isa. 44. 23 shout, ye lower parts of the earth: break
Jer. 50. 15 Shout against her round about: she hath
Zeph. 3. 14 shout, O Israel; be glad and rejoice with
Zech. 9. 9 shout, O daughter of Jerusalem: behold

5. *To shout,* רוּעַ *rua,* 7a.
Psa. 65. 13 the valleys..shout for joy, they also sing

6. *To cry aloud, sing,* רָנַן *ranan.*
Lev. 9. 24 when all the people saw, they shouted, and
Psa. 35. 27 Let them shout for joy, and be glad, that
Isa. 12. 6 Cry out and shout, thou inhabitant of Zion

7. *To cry aloud, sing,* רָנַן *ranan,* 3.
Psa. 5. 11 let them ever shout for joy, because thou
132. 9 and let thy saints shout for joy
132. 16 and her saints shall shout aloud for joy

8. *To (cause to) cry aloud or sing,* רָנַן *ranan,* 5.
Psa. 32. 11 shout for joy, all (ye that are) upright in

9. *To cry aloud, sing,* רָנַן *ranan,* 7*a*.
Psa. 78. 65 a mighty man that shouteth by reason of

10. *A shout,* רֵעַ *rea.*
Exod32. 17 heard the noise of the people as they sh.

11. *To cry (aloud),* שָׁוַע *shava,* 3.
Lam. 3. 8 when I cry and shout, he shutteth out my

12. *With a shout,* בִּתְרוּעָה *bi-teruah.*
Ezra 3. 12 wept..and many shouted aloud for joy

13. *To sound over or besides,* ἐπιφωνέω *epiphōneō.*
Acts 12. 22 the people gave a shout, (saying, It is) the

SHOUTING, to be —
To shout, רוּעַ *rua,* 4*a*.
Isa. 16. 10 no singing, neither shall there be shout.

SHOVELS —
1. *Shovels,* יָעִים *yaim.*
Exod27. 3 his shovels, and his basins, and his flesh
38. 3 the pots, and the shovels, and the basins
Num. 4. 14 the flesh hooks, and the shovels, and the
1 Ki. 7. 40 Hiram made the lavers, and the shovels
7. 45 the pots, and the shovels, and the basins
2 Ki. 25. 14 the shovels, and the snuffers, and the sp
2 Ch. 4. 11 Huram made the pots, and the shovels, and
4. 16 the shovels, and the flesh hooks, and all
Jer. 52. 18 the shovels, and the snuffers and the bo.

2. *A winnowing shovel,* רַחַת *rachath.*
Isa. 30. 24 which hath been winnowed with the sh.

SHOW — See to Shew.

SHOWER —
1. *Heavy rain, shower,* גֶּשֶׁם *geshem.*
Eze. 13. 11, 13 there shall be an overflowing shower
34. 26 I will cause the shower to come down in
34. 26 there shall be showers of blessing
Zech.10. 1 give them showers of rain, to every one

2. *Inundation, flood, storm,* זֶרֶם *zerem.*
Job 24. 8 They are wet with the showers of the mo

3. *Showers,* רְבִיבִים *rebibim.*
Deut32. 2 as the small rain..and as the showers up
Psa. 65. 10 thou makest it soft with showers; thou
72. 6 He shall come down..as showers (that)
Jer. 3. 3 the showers have been withholden, and
14. 22 can the heavens give showers? (Art) not
Mic. 5. 7 as the showers upon the grass, that tarri.

4. *A flowing together, heavy shower,* ὄμβρος *ombros.*
Luke12. 54 ye say, There cometh a shower; and so

SHRANK, which —
A tendon, נָשֶׁה *nasheh.*
Gen. 32. 32 eat not (of) the sinew which shrank, wh.
32. 32 touched the hollow..in the sinew that sh.

SHRED, to —
To split, פָּלַח *palach,* 3.
2 Ki. 4. 39 came and shred (them) into the pot of po.

SHRINE —
Dwelling place, inner shrine, ναός *naos.*
Acts 19. 24 a silversmith, which made silver shrines

SHROUD —
A bough, חֹרֶשׁ *choresh.*
Eze. 31. 3 cedar..with a shadowing shroud, and of

SHRUBS —
A shrub, שִׂיחַ *siach.*
Gen. 21. 15 she cast the child under one of the shrubs

SHU'-A, שׁוּעָא *prosperity.*
Daughter of Heber, an Asherite. B.C. 1600.
1 Ch. 7. 32 and Shomer, and Hotham, and S. their s.

SHU'-AH, SHU'-A, שׁוּעַ *prosperity.*
A Canaanite of Adullam, whose daughter Judah took to wife. B.C. 1730.
Gen. 38. 2 Judah saw there..S.; and he took her
38. 12 the daughter of S., Judah's wife died, and
1 Ch. 2. 3 were born unto him of the daughter of S.

SHU'-AH, שׁוּחַ *depression.*
A son of Keturah by Abraham, and his posterity in Edom; comp. *Sakkaia*, E. of Bashan, *Shichan* in Moab, and *Siajcha*, E. of Aila. B.C. 1800.
Gen. 25. 2 and Medan, and Midian, and Ishbak..S.
1 Ch. 1. 32 and Medan, and Midian, and Ishbak..S.

SHU'-AH, שׁוּחָה *depression.*
Brother of Chelub, a descendant of Caleb son of Hur. B.C. 1430.
1 Ch. 4. 11 Chelub the brother of S. begat Mehir, wh.

SHU'-AL, שׁוּעָל *jackal.*
1. A district in Benjamin, on the way to Ophrah. See *Shalim* and *Hazar-shual.*
1 Sa. 13. 17 (that leadeth to)..to the land of S.

2. Third son of Zophah, an Asherite. B.C. 1500.
1 Ch. 7. 36 The sons of Zophah; Suah..and S., and

SHU-BA'-EL, שׁוּבָאֵל.
1. A son or descendant of Amram grandson of Levi. B.C. 1015.
1 Ch.24. 20 Of the sons of Amram; S.: of the sons of S
2. A singer in the sanctuary in the days of David; perhaps the same as *Shebuel* in 1 Ch. 25. 4. B.C. 1015.
1 Ch.25. 20 The thirteenth to S., (he), his sons, and

SHU'-HAM, שׁוּחָם *depression.*
A son of Dan; perhaps the same as *Husham*, Gen. 46. 23. B.C. 1700.
Num.26. 42 of S., the family of the Shuhamites

SHUHAMITES, הַשּׁוּחָמִי *the Shuchamite.*
The family of the preceding.
Num26. 42 of Shuham, the family of the S. These
26. 43 the families of the S., according to those

SHU-HITE, הַשּׁוּחִי *the Shuchi.*
A descendant of Shuah son of Keturah. B.C. 1580.
Job 2. 11 Bildad the S., and Zophar the Naamathite
8. 1 Then answered Bildad the S., and said
18. 1 Then answered Bildad the S., and said
25. 1 Then answered Bildad the S., and said
42. 9 Bildad the S (and) Zophar the Naamath.

SHULAMITE, הַשּׁוּלַמִּית *the Shulammith.*
A female inhabitant of *Shulem* (or *Shunem*), in Issachar.
Song 6. 13 return, O S; return, return, that we may
6. 13 What will ye see in the S.? As it were the

SHUMATHITES, הַשֻּׁמָתִי *the Shumathi.*
A family in Kirjath-jearim, descended from Shobal son of Caleb, son of Hur
1 Ch. 2. 53 the Puhites, and the S., and the Mishra.

SHUN, to —
1. *To set around, repress,* περιΐστημι *periistēmi.*
2 Ti. 2. 16 shun profane (and) vain babblings; for th.

2. *To send back, decline,* ὑποστέλλω *hupostellō.*
Acts 20. 27 I have not shunned to declare unto you

SHUNAMMITE, הַשּׁוּנַמִּית *the Shunammith.*
A female inhabitant of Shunem.
1 Ki. 1. 3 found Abishag a S., and brought her to
1. 15 and Abishag the S. ministered unto the
2. 17 that he gave me Abishag the S. to wife
2. 21 Let Abishag the S. be given to Adonijah
2. 22 why dost thou ask Abishag the S. for Ad.?
2 Ki. 4. 12 said to Gehazi..Call this S. And when he
4. 25 said to Gehazi..Behold, (yonder is) that S.
4. 36 he called Gehazi, and said, Call this S.

SHU'-NEM, שׁוּנֵם *uneven.*
A city in Issachar, near Chesulloth, on a steep slope of Gilboa; now called *Sulim* or *Salem.*
Josh.19. 18 their border was toward Jezreel..and S.
1 Sa. 28. 4 the Philistines..came and pitched in S.
2 Ki. 4. 8 Elisha passed to S., where (was) a great

SHU'-NI, שׁוּנִי *fortunate.*
Third son of Gad. B.C. 1700.
Gen. 46. 16 the sons of Gad; Ziphion, and Haggi, S.
Num26. 15 of S., the family of the Shunites

SHUNITES, הַשּׁוּנִי *the Shuni.*
The family of the preceding.
Num26. 15 of Shuni, the family of the S.

SHUPH'-AM, שְׁפוּפָם *serpent.*
A son of Benjamin; perhaps the same as *Shephaphen* son of Bela, 1 Ch. 8. 5. B.C. 1700.
Num 26. 39 Of S., the family of the Shuphamites: of H.

SHUPHAMITES, הַשּׁוּפָמִי *the Shuphami.*
The family of the preceding.
Num26. 39 Of Shupham, the family of the S.: of

SHUP'-PIM, שֻׁפִּם, שֻׁפִּים *serpent.*
1. A Benjamite. B.C. 1600.
1 Ch. 7. 12 S. also, and Huppim, the children of Ir
7. 15 Machir took to wife (the sister) of..S.
2. A Levite, a gate keeper of the tabernacle in the days of David. B.C. 1015
1 Ch.26. 16 To S. and Hosah (the lot came forth) we.

SHUR, שׁוּר.
A desert reaching from the E. border of Egypt as far as the habitations of Amalek and Ishmael.
Gen. 16. 7 found..by the fountain in the way to S.
20. 1 dwelled between Kadesh and S., and soj.
25. 18 they dwelt from Havilah unto S., that (is)
Exod15. 22 they went out into the wilderness of S.
1 Sa. 15. 7 (until) thou comest to S., that (is) over ag.
27. 8 as thou goest to S., even unto the land of

SHU'-SHAN, שׁוּשַׁן *lily.*
A city (also called *Susa*) in Elam, on the river Ulai (or *Eulius*), the seat of the Persian government; now called *Sus*, between the *Shapur* and the *Dizful* in the province *Hus* or *Chusistan.*
Neh. 1. 1 in the twentieth year, as I was in S. the
Esth. 1. 2 throne of his kingdom, which (was) in S.
1. 5 the people that were present in S. the p.
2. 3 gather..the fair young virgins unto S. the
2. 5 in S. the palace there was a certain Jew
2. 8 maidens were gathered together unto S.
3. 15 and the decree was given in S. the palace
3. 15 to drink; but the city S. was perplexed
4. 8 the decree that was given at S. to destroy
4. 16 gather..the Jews (that are) present in S.
8. 14 And the decree was given at S. the palace
8. 15 and the city of S. rejoiced and was glad
9. 6 in S the palace the Jews slew and destr.
9. 11 the number of those that were slain in S.
9. 12 slain and destroyed five hundred men in S.
9. 13 let it be granted..the Jews which (are) in S.
9. 14 the decree was given at S.; and they han.
9. 15 the Jews that (were) in S. gathered them.
9. 15 slew three hundred men at S.; but on the
9. 18 the Jews that (were) at S. assembled to.
Dan. 8. 2 I (was) at S. (in) the palace, which (is) in

SHU'-SHAN E'-DUTH, שׁוּשַׁן עֵדוּת *lily of testimony.*
A temple music choir.
Psa. 60. *title.* To the chief musician upon Sh. E.

SHUT (out, to, up, together, self), to —
1. *To be narrow, shut, stop,* אָטַם *atam.*
Prov17. 28 he that shutteth his lips (is esteemed) a

2. *To shut,* אָטַר *atar.*
Psa. 69. 15 and let not the pit shut her mouth upon

3. *To cause to shut,* גּוּף *guph,* 5.
Neh. 7. 3 while they stand by, let them shut the do

4. *To plaster, daub, overlay,* טוּחַ *tuach.*
Isa. 44. 18 he hath shut their eyes, that they cannot

5. *To shut in or up, restrain,* כָּלָא *kala.*
1 Sa. 6. 10 tied them to the cart, and shut up their
Psa. 88. 8 (I am) shut up, and I cannot come forth
Jer. 32. 2 the prophet was shut up in the court of the
32. 3 Zedekiah king of Judah had shut him up

6. *To bolt, fasten,* נָעַל *naal.*
Song 4. 12 a spring shut up, a fountain sealed

7. *To shut in or up,* סָגַר *sagar.*
Gen. 7. 16 commanded him..the LORD shut him in
19. 6 Lot went out..and shut the door after him
19. 10 pulled Lot into the house..and shut to the
Exod14. 3 entangled..the wilderness hath shut them
Josh. 2. 7 as soon as they..were gone out they shut
Judg. 3. 23 shut the doors of the parlour upon him, and
9. 51 shut (it) to them, and gat them up to the
1 Sa. 1. 5 but the LORD had shut up her womb
1. 6 because the LORD had shut up her womb
2 Ki. 4. 4 thou shalt shut the door upon thee and up.
4. 5 shut the door upon her and upon her sons
4. 21 and shut (the door) upon him, and went
4. 33 shut the door upon them twain, and prayed
6. 32 shut the door, and hold him fast at the do.
2 Ch.28. 24 shut up the doors of the house of the Lo.
29. 7 they have shut up the doors of the porch
Neh. 6. 10 let us shut the doors of the temple: for
Job 3. 10 it shut not up the doors of my (mother's)
12. 14 he shutteth up a man, and there can be no
41. 15 (His) scales (are his) pride, shut up toge.
Isa. 22. 22 none shall shut; and he shall shut, and
26. 20 shut thy doors about thee: hide thyself
Eze. 44. 1 gate of the outward sanctuary..(was) shut
44. 2 This gate shall be shut, it shall not be op.
44. 2 entered in by it, therefore it shall be shut
46. 1 the gate..shall be shut the six working d.
46. 12 after his going forth (one) shall shut the
Mal. 1. 10 Who (is there)..that would shut the doors

8. *To be shut in or up,* סָגַר *sagar,* 2.
Eze. 3. 24 said unto me, Go, shut thyself within th.

9. *To (cause to) shut in or up,* סָגַר *sagar,* 5.
Lev. 13. 4, 31, 33 the priest shall shut up (him that
13. 5, 21, 26 the priest shall shut him up seven
13. 11 shall not shut him up; for he (is) unclean
13. 50 shut up (it that hath) the plague seven d.
13. 54 and he shall shut it up seven days more
14. 38 the priest shall..shut up the house seven
14. 46 the house all the while that it is shut up
Deut 32. 30 except..the LORD had shut them up
Job 11. 10 If he cut off, and shut up, or gather toge.
Psa. 31. 8 hast not shut me up into the hand of the

10. *To shut in or up,* סְגַר *segar.*
Dan. 6. 22 God hath sent his angel, and hath shut

11. *To (cause to) cover, shut up,* סָכַךְ *sakak,* 5.
Job 38. 8 (who) shut up the sea with doors, when it

12. *To shut, close,* עָצָה *atsah.*
Prov 16. 30 He shutteth his eyes to devise froward th.

13. *To make firm, shut,* עָצַם *atsam.*
Isa. 33. 15 and shutteth his eyes from seeing evil

14. *To keep in, restrain,* עָצַר *atsar.*
Deut11. 17 he shut up the heaven, that there be no
32. 36 he seeth that..(there is) none shut up, or
1 Ki. 14. 10 (and) him that is shut up and left in Israel
21. 21 and him that is shut up and left in Israel
2 Ki. 9. 8 and him that is shut up and left in Israel
14. 26 (there was) not any shut up, nor any left
17. 4 the king of Assyria shut him up, and bo.
2 Ch. 7. 13 If I shut up heaven that there be no rain
Isa. 66. 9 shall I cause to bring forth, and shut (the
Jer. 20. 9 as a burning fire shut up in my bones, and
33. 1 while he was yet shut up in the court of
36. 5 I (am) shut up; I cannot go into the house
39. 15 while he was shut up in the court of the

15. *To bind up, distress,* צָרַר *tsarar.*
2 Sa. 20. 3 they were shut up unto the day of their

16. *To shut out, up or in,* סָתַם *satham.*
Dan. 8. 26 shut thou up the vision; for (it shall be)
12. 4 shut up the words, and seal the book, (ev.)

17. *To shut, contract,* קָפַץ *qaphats.*
Deut15. 7 nor shut thine hand from thy poor brother
Psa. 77. 9 hath he in anger shut up his tender mer.
Isa. 52. 15 the kings shall shut their mouths at him

18. *To delight, dazzle,* שָׁעַע *shaa,* 5.
Isa. 6. 10 make their ears heavy, and shut their eyes

19. *To shut up, out, in,* שָׂתַם *satham.*
Lam. 3. 8 when I cry and shout, he shutteth out

20. *To shut back,* ἀποκλείω *apokleiō.*
Luke13. 25 When once the Master..hath shut to the

21. *To shut down,* κατακλείω *katakleiō.*
Luke 3. 20 Added yet this above all, that he shut up
Acts 26. 10 many of the saints did I shut up in prison

22. *To shut,* κλείω *kleiō.*
Matt. 6. 6 when thou hast shut thy door, pray to thy
23. 13 ye shut up the kingdom of heaven against
25. 10 went in with him ..and the door was shut
Luke 4. 25 the heaven was shut up three years and
11. 7 the door is now shut, and my children are
John20. 19 the doors were shut where the disciples
20. 26 (Then) came Jesus, the doors being shut
Acts 5. 23 The prison truly found we shut with all
21. 30 drew him out..and..the doors were shut
1 Jo. 3. 17 shutteth up his bowels (of compassion) fr.
Rev. 3. 7 openeth, and no man shutteth; and shut.
3. 8 an open door, and no man can shut it
11. 6 These have power to shut heaven, that it
20. 3 shut him up, and set a seal upon him, that
21. 25 the gates of it shall not be shut at all by

23. *To shut together,* συγκλείω *sugkleiō.*
Gal. 3. 23 shut up unto the faith which should aft.

SHUT (in, out, up), to be —
1. *To be shut in or up,* סָגַר *sagar,* 2.
Num12. 14 let her be shut out from the camp seven
12. 15 Miriam was shut out from the camp seven
1 Sa. 23. 7 he is shut in, by entering into a town that
Neh. 13. 19 I commanded that the gates should be sh.
Isa. 45. 1 to open..and the gates shall not be shut
60. 11 they shall not be shut day nor night; that
Eze. 46. 2 the gate shall not be shut until the even.

2. *To be shut in or up,* סָגַר *sagar,* 4.
Josh. 6. 1 Jericho was straitly shut up because of the
Eccl.12. 4 the doors shall be shut in the streets, when
Isa. 24. 10 every house is shut up, that no man may
24. 22 shall be shut up in the prison, and after
Jer. 13. 19 The cities of the south shall be shut up

3. *To be kept in, restrained,* עָצַר *atsar,* 2.
1 Ki. 8. 35 When heaven is shut up, and there is no
2 Ch. 6. 26 When the heaven is shut up, and there is
Neh. 6. 10 the house of Shemaiah..who (was) shut up

SHUTHALHITES, הַשֻּׁתַלְחִי *the family of Shuthelah.*
Num26. 35 of Shuthelah, the family of the S.: of Bec.

SHU-THE'-LAH, שׁוּתֶלַח *setting of Telah.*
1. A son of Ephraim. B.C. 1680.
Num26. 35 of S., the family of the Shuthalhites: of
26. 36 these (are) the sons of S.: of Eran, the fa.
1 Ch. 7. 20 the sons of Ephraim; S., and Bered his son
2. Son of Zabad, a descendant of Ephraim in the fifth or sixth remove. B.C. 1530.
1 Ch. 7. 21 Zabad his son, and S. his son, and Ezer

SHUTTING —
To shut in or up, סָגַר *sagar.*
Josh. 2. 5 (about the time) of shutting of the gate,

SHUTTLE —
Weaving machine, אֶרֶג *ereg.*
Job 7. 6 My days are swifter than a weaver's shu.

SI-A'-HA, SI'-A, סִיעֲהָא, סִיעָא *congregation.*
One of the Nethinim whose descendants returned with Zerubbabel. B.C. 536.
Ezra 2. 44 The children of Keros, the children of S.
Neh. 7. 47 The children of Keros, the children of S.

SIB-BE'-CHAI, SIB-BE'-CAI, סִבְּכַי *Jah is intervening.*
One of the family of Hushah who slew Saph or Sappai, a Philistine giant, in the days of David. B.C. 1048.
2 Sa. 21. 18 S. the Hushathite slew Saph, which (was)
1 Ch.11. 29 S. the Hushathite, Ilai the Ahohite
20. 4 at which time S. the Hushathite slew
27. 11 eighth (captain) for the..month (was) S.

SIB-BO'-LETH, סִבֹּלֶת.
The Ephraimite pronunciation of *Shibboleth,* "an ear of corn."
Judg12. 6 Say now Shibboleth; and he said S., for

SIB'-MAH, שִׂבְמָה *balsam.*
A city in Reuben, called in Num. 32. 3 *Shebam,* and in ver. 38 *Shibmah;* near Jazer and Kirjathaim.
Josh.13. 19 Kirjathaim, and S., and Zareth-shahar
Isa. 16. 8 the fields..languish, (and) the vine of S.
16. 9 Therefore I will bewail..the vine of S.
Jer. 48. 32 O vine of S., I will weep for thee with the

SIB-RA'-IM, סִבְרַיִם *double hill.*
A city of Syria, between Damascus and Hamath.
Eze. 47. 16 Hamath, Berothah, S., which (is) between

SI'-CHEM, שְׁכֶם *ridge, shoulder.*
A place in the plain of Moreh in mount Ephraim, now called *Nablous.* See *Shechem.*
Gen. 12. 6 A. passed through..unto the place of S.

SICK (folk, people), very, sickly —
1. *To be or become sickly,* אָנַשׁ *anash,* 2.
2 Sa. 12. 15 struck the child..and it was very sick

2. *Menstruous,* דָּוֶה *daveh.*
Lev. 15. 33 of her that is sick of her flowers, and of

3. *Sicknesses, diseases,* תַּחֲלֻאִים *tachaluim.*
Jer. 14. 18 then behold them that are sick with fam.

4. *Not robust or strong,* ἄῤῥωστος *arrhōstos.*
Matt14. 14 Jesus went forth..and he healed their s.
Mark 6. 5 he laid his hands upon a few sick folk
16. 18 [they shall lay hands on the sick, and th.]
1 Co.11. 30 many (are) weak and sickly among you

5. *To be infirm, without strength,* ἀσθενέω *astheneō.*
Matt10. 8 Heal the sick, cleanse the lepers, raise
Mark 6. 56 they laid the sick in the streets, and bes.
Luke 4. 40 they that had any sick with divers disea.
9. 2 sent them to preach..and to heal [the si.]
John11. 1 a certain (man) was sick, (named) Lazarus
Acts 19. 12 from his body were brought unto the sick
2 Ti. 4. 20 but Trophimus have I left at Miletum si.

6. *Infirm, without strength,* ἀσθενής *asthenēs.*
Matt25. 39 when saw we thee [sick,] or in prison, and
25. 43 sick, and in prison, and ye visited me not
25. 44 a stranger, or naked, or sick, or in prison
Luke10. 9 heal the sick that are therein; and say
Acts 5. 15 they brought forth the sick into the, 5. 16

6a. *Held fast, seized,* κατεχόμενος [*katechō*], Acts28.8

7. *To be ill,* ἔχω κακῶς *echō kakōs.*
Matt. 4. 24 they brought unto him all sick people th.
Luke 7. 2 a certain centurion's servant..was sick

8. *To labour, suffer from fatigue,* κάμνω *kamnō.*
Jas. 5. 15 the prayer of faith shall save the sick, and

SICK, to be, fall, make self —
1. *To be sick, weak, diseased,* חָלָה *chalah.*
Gen 48 1 told Joseph, Behold, thy father (is) sick
1 Sa. 19. 14 And when Saul sent..she said, He (is) si.
30. 13 my master left me, because I fell sick
1 Ki. 14. 1 Abijah the son of Jeroboam fell sick
14. 5 ask a thing .for her son; for he (is) sick
17. 17 the son of the woman..fell sick; and his
2 Ki. 1. 2 fell down through a lattice..and was sick
8. 7 and Ben-hadad the king of Syria was sick
8. 29 went..to see Joram..because he was sick
13. 14 Elisha was fallen sick of his sickness wh.
20. 1 In those days was Hezekiah sick unto de.
20. 12 he had heard that Hezekiah had been si.
2 Ch.22. 6 went..to see Jehoram .because he was si.
32. 24 In those days Hezekiah was sick to the de.
Neh. 2. 2 seeing thou (art) not sick? this (is) nothing
Psa. 35. 13 when they were sick, my clothing (was) sa.
Prov.23. 35 They have stricken me..(and) I was not s.
Song 2. 5 comfort me with apples; for I (am) sick of
5. 8 that ye tell him, that I (am) sick of love
Isa. 33. 24 the inhabitant shall not say, I am sick
38. 1 In those days was Hezekiah sick unto de.
38. 9 when he had been sick, and was recovered
39. 1 he had heard that he had been sick, and
Eze 34. 4 neither have..healed that which was sick
34. 16 and will strengthen that which was sick
Mal. 1. 8 if ye offer the lame and sick, (is it) not
1. 13 brought (that which was) torn..and the s.

2. *To become sick, weak, diseased,* חָלָה *chalah,* 2.
Dan. 8. 27 I Daniel fainted, and was sick (certain) da.

3. *To cause sickness, weakness,* חָלָה *chalah,* 5.
Prov.13. 12 Hope deferred maketh the heart sick: but
Hos. 7. 5 the princes have made (him) sick with bo.
Mic. 6. 13 Therefore also will I make (thee) sick in

4. *To become or show self sick,* חָלָה *chalah,* 7.
2 Sa. 13. 2 Amnon was so vexed, that he fell sick for
13. 5 Lay thee down..and make thyself sick:
13. 6 Amnon lay down, and made himself sick

5. *Sickness, weakness,* חֳלִי *choli.*
Isa. 1. 5 The whole head is sick, and the whole he.

6. *Not robust or strong,* ἄῤῥωστος *arrhōstos.*
Mark 6. 13 anointed with oil many that were sick, and

7. *To be infirm, without strength,* ἀσθενέω *astheneō.*
Matt25. 36 I was sick, and ye visited me: I was in
Luke 7. 10 found..servant whole [that had been si.]
John 4. 46 a certain nobleman, whose son was sick
11. 2 Mary..whose brother Lazarus was sick
11. 3 Lord, behold, he whom thou lovest is sick
11. 6 he had heard therefore that he was sick
Acts 9. 37 it came to pass..that she was sick, and
Phil. 2. 26 that ye had heard that he had been sick
2. 27 he was sick nigh unto death: but God had
Jas. 5. 14 Is any sick among you? let him call for the

8. *To be ill,* ἔχω κακῶς *echō kakōs.*
Matt. 8. 16 and he..healed all that were sick
9. 12 not a physician, but they that are sick
Mark 1. 34 he healed many that were sick of divers
2. 17 no need..but they that are sick: I came
6. 55 carry about in beds those that were sick
Luke 5. 31 need not a physician; but they that are si.

SICKLE —
1. *A sickle, reaping hook,* חֶרְמֵשׁ *chermesh.*
Deut 16. 9 thou beginnest (to put) the sickle to the
23. 25 not move a sickle unto thy neighbour's st.

2. *A sickle, scythe, large knife,* מַגָּל *maggal.*
Jer. 50. 16 him that handleth the sickle in the time
Joel 3. 13 Put ye in the sickle; for the harvest is ripe

3. *A reaping hook, sickle,* δρέπανον *drepanon.*
Mark 4. 29 immediately he putteth in the sickle, bec
Rev. 14. 14 Son of man, having..in his hand a sharp s.
14. 15 Thrust in thy sickle, and reap: for the ti.
14. 16 he that sat on the cloud thrust in his sic.
14. 17 angel came..also having a sharp sickle
14. 18 cry to him that had the sharp sickle, say.
14. 18 Thrust in thy sharp sickle, and gather the
14. 19 angel thrust in his sickle into the earth

SICKNESS, (having) —
1. *Menstruous,* דָּוֶה *daveh.*
Lev. 20. 18 lie with a woman having her sickness, and

2. *Sickness, weakness,* חֳלִי *choli.*
Deut. 7. 15 LORD will take away from thee all sickn
28. 59 sore sicknesses, and of long continuance
28. 61 Also every sickness, and every plague, wh.
1 Ki.17. 17 sickness was so sore, that there was no br.
2 Ki.13. 14 Elisha was fallen sick of his sickness wh.
2 Ch.21. 15 thou (shalt have) great sickness by disease
21. 15 fall out by reason of the sickness day by
21. 19 bowels fell out by reason of his sickness
Psa. 41. 3 thou wilt make all his bed in his sickness
Eccl. 5. 17 much sorrow and wrath with his sickness
Isa. 38. 9 been sick, and was recovered of his sickn.
Hos. 5. 13 When Ephraim saw his sickness, and Jud.

3. *Sickness, disease,* מַחֲלָה *machalah.*
Exod23. 25 take sickness away from the midst of thee
1 Ki. 8. 37 whatsoever plague, whatsoever sickness
2 Ch. 6. 28 whatsoever sore, or whatsoever sickness

4. *Sicknesses, diseases,* תַּחֲלֻאִים *tachaluim.*
Deut29. 22 sicknesses which the LORD hath laid upon

5. *Infirmity,* ἀσθένεια *astheneia.*
John 11. 4 This sickness is not unto death, but for

6. *Unsoundness, sickness,* νόσος *nosos.*
Matt. 4. 23 healing all manner of sickness and all ma.
8. 17 took our infirmities, and bare (our) sickn.
9. 35 healing every sickness and every disease
10. 1 heal all manner of sickness, and all man.
Mark 3. 15 to have power [to heal sicknesses, and] to

SID'-DIM, שִׂדִּים *extension.*
The region on the shores of the Salt Sea wherein were Sodom, Gomorrah, Admah, and Zeboim.
Gen. 14. 3 were joined together in the vale of S., wh.
14. 8 joined battle with them in the vale of S.
14. 10 the vale of S. (was full of) slime pits, and

SIDE, (farther, other, this, yonder) —
1. *This, that,* הַלָּז *hallaz.*
1 Sa. 14. 1 garrison, that (is) on the other side. But

2. *Hand,* יָד *yad.*
Exod. 2. 5 maidens walked along by the river's side
1 Sa. 4. 13 Eli sat upon a seat by the way side watc.
4. 18 from off the seat backward by the side of
2 Sa. 18. 4 king stood by the gate side, and all the pe.
Psa 140. 5 they have spread a net by the way side, th.
Eccl. 4. 1 on the side of their oppressors (there was)
Dan.10. 4 as I was by the side of the great river wh.

3. *Thigh,* יָרֵךְ *yarek.*
Exod32. 27 Put every man his sword by his side, (and)
40. 22 upon the side of the tabernacle northward
40. 24 on the side of the tabernacle southward
Lev. 1. 11 kill it on the side of the altar northward
Num. 3. 29, 35 shall pitch on the side of the taberna.
2 Ki. 16. 14 and put it on the north side of the altar

4. *Thigh,* יַרְכָה *yarekah.*
Exod26. 22 for the sides of the tabernacle westward
26. 23 corners of the tabernacle in the two sides
26. 27 the tabernacle for the two sides westward
36. 27 for the sides of the tabernacle westward
36. 28 corners of the tabernacle in the two sides
36. 32 of the tabernacle for the sides westward
Judg19. 1 certain Levite sojourning on the side of
19. 18 from Beth-lehem-judah toward the side
1 Sa. 24. 3 his men remained in the sides of the cave
1 Ki. 6. 16 built twenty cubits on the side of the ho.
2 Ki.19. 23 am come up..to the sides of Lebanon, and
Psa. 48. 2 the sides of the north, the city of the gr.
128. 3 as a fruitful vine by the sides of thine ho.
Isa. 14. 13 will sit also..in the sides of the north
14. 15 shalt be brought down to hell, to the si.
37. 24 am I come up..to the sides of Lebanon
Jer. 6. 22 shall be raised from the sides of the earth
Eze. 32. 23 Whose graves are set in the sides of the
46. 19 there (was) a place on the two sides wes.
Amos 6. 10 shall say unto him that (is) by the sides
Jon. 1. 5 Jonah was gone down into the sides of the

5. *Shoulder,* כָּתֵף *katheph.*
Exod27. 14 hangings of one side (of the gate shall be)
27. 15 on the other side (shall be) hangings fift.
28. 27 shalt put them on the two sides of the ep.
38. 14 hangings of the one side (of the gate were)
38. 15 for the other side of the court gate, on
39. 20 put them on the two sides of the ephod
Num34. 11 shall reach unto the side of the sea of Ch.
Josh 15. 8 went up..unto the south side of the Jeb.
15. 10 passed along unto the side of mount Jea.
15. 11 border went out unto the side of Ekron no.
18. 12 border went up to the side of Jericho on
18. 13 to the side of Luz, which (is) Beth-el, so.
18. 16 descended..to the side of Jebusi on the
18. 18 passed along toward the side over against
18. 19 border passed along to the side of Beth-h.
1 Ki. 6. 8 The door..(was) in the right side of the ho.
7. 39 side of the house, and five on the left side
7. 39 he set the sea on the right side of the ho.

2 Ch. 4. 10 set the sea on the right side of the east end
23. 10 right side of the temple to the left side of
Eze. 25. 9 I will open the side of Moab from the ci.
40. 18 pavement by the side of the gates, over ag.
40. 40 at the side without..on the other side, wh.
40. 41 Four tables (were)..by the side of the gate
40. 44 which (was) at the side of the north gate
40. 44 one at the side of the east gate (having)
41. 2 the sides of the door (were) five cubits on
41. 26 the sides of the porch, and (upon) the..c.
46. 19 the entry, which (was) at the side of the
47. 1 from the right side of the house, at the
47. 2 there ran out waters on the right side

6. *Loins*, מָתְנַיִם *mothnayim.*
Neh. 4. 18 every one had his sword girded by his s.
Eze. 9. 2 with a writer's inkhorn by his side: and
9. 3 which (had) the writer's inkhorn by his s.
9. 11 man..which (had) the inkhorn by his side

7. *Margin, side*, עֵבֶר *eber.*
Exod 28. 26 which (is) in the side of the ephod inwa.
32. 15 tables (were) written on both their sides
39. 19 which (was) on the side of the ephod in
Num 21. 13 pitched on the other side of Arnon, whi
22. 1 pitched in the plains of Moab on this side
32. 19 on yonder side Jordan, or forward: bec.
32. 19 our inheritance is fallen to us on this side
32. 32 possession of our inheritance on this side
34. 15 received their inheritance on this side J.
35. 14 Ye shall give three cities on this side Jo.
Deut. 1. 1 Moses spake unto all Israel on this side J.
1. 5 On this side Jordan, in the land of Moab
3. 8 the land that (was) on this side Jordan, fr.
4. 41 Moses severed three cities on this side Jo.
4. 46 On this side Jordan, in the valley over ag.
4. 47 which (were) on this side Jordan, toward
4. 49 all the plain on this side Jordan eastwa.
11. 30 (Are) they not on the other side Jordan
Josh. 1. 14 land which Moses gave you on this side
1. 15 which Moses ..gave you on this side Jord.
2. 10 Amorites, that (were) on the other side J.
5. 1 Amorites, which (were) on the side of Jo.
7. 7 content and dwelt on the other side Jord.!
9. 1 kings which (were) on this side Jordan, in
12. 1 possessed their land on the other side J.
12. 7 Joshua..smote on this side Jordan on the
13. 27 Chinnereth on the other side Jordan east.
13. 32 on the other side Jordan, by Jericho, eas.
14. 3 an half tribe on the other side Jordan
17. 5 Bashan, which (were) on the other side J.
20. 8 on the other side Jordan by Jericho east.
22. 4 which Moses..gave you on the other side
22. 7 among their brethren on this side Jordan
24. 2 Your fathers dwelt on the other side of
24. 3 took your father..from the other side of
24. 8 which dwelt on the other side Jordan; and
24. 14 fathers served on the other side of the flo.
24. 15 that (were) on the other side of the flood
Judg. 7. 25 brought..to Gideon on the other side Jor.
10. 8 children..that (were) on the other side Jo.
11. 18 pitched on the other side of Arnon. but
1 Sa. 14. 1 garrison, that (is) on the other side
14. 4 (there was) a sharp rock on the one side
14. 4 sharp rock on the other side: and the na
14. 40 Be ye on one side, and I and Jonathan
14. 40 son will be on the other side. And the pe.
26. 13 Then David went over to the other side
31. 7 men of Israel that (were) on the other si.
31. 7 (they) that (were) on the other side Jord.
1 Ki. 4. 24 dominion over all (the region) on this si.
4. 24 over all the kings on this side the river
4. 24 had peace on all sides round about him
7. 30 under the laver..at the side of every ad.
1 Ch. 6. 78 on the other side Jordan, by Jericho on
12. 37 on the other side of Jordan, of the Reu.
26. 30 on this side Jordan westward, in all the
Ezra 8. 36 and to the governors on this side the riv.
Neh. 3. 7 throne of the governor on this side the ri.
Jer. 48. 28 maketh her nest in the sides of the hole's
49. 32 bring their calamity from all sides there.

8. *Margin, side*, עֲבַר *abar.*
Ezra 4. 10 rest (that are) on this side the river, and
4. 11 Thy servants the men on this side the ri.
4. 16 shalt have no portion on this side the riv.
5. 3, 6 Tatnai, governor on this side the river
5. 6 which (were) on this side the river, sent
6. 13 Then Tatnai, governor on this side the r.

9. *Corner*, פֵּאָה *peah.*
Exod 26. 18 twenty boards on the south side southw.
26. 20 on the north side, (there shall be) twenty
27. 9 for the south side southward (there shall
27. 9 of an hundred cubits long for one side
27. 11 likewise for the north side in length (there
27. 12 the breadth of the court on the west side
27. 13 the breadth of the court on the east side
36. 23 twenty boards for the south side southw.
38. 9 on the south side southward the hangings
38. 11 for the north side (the hangings were) an
38. 12 for the west side (were) hangings of fifty
38. 13 And for the east side eastward fifty cubits
Num 35. 5 east side..and on the south side two tho.
35. 5 west side..and on the north side two th.
Josh. 18. 12 their border on the north side was from
18. 20 Jordan was the border..on the east side
Eze. 45. 7 west side westward, and from the east side
47. 15 border of the land toward the north side
47. 17 border of Hamath. And (this is) the n. side
47. 18 the east side..And (this is) the east side
47. 19 south side southward..south side south.
47. 20 The west side..This (is) the west side

Eze. 48. 1 for these are his sides east (and) west; a
48. 2 from the east side unto the west side
[So in v. 4, 5, 8, 23, 24, 25, 26, 27.]
48. 3, 6, 7 from the east side even unto the west s.
48. 16 north side four thousand and five hundred
48. 16 south side four thousand and five hundred
48. 16 on the east side four thousand and five
48. 16 west side four thousand and five hundred
48. 28 border of Gad, at the south side southw.
48. 30 goings out of the city on the north side
48. 32 at the east side four thousand and five
48. 33 at the south side four thousand and five
48. 34 At the west side four thousand and five

10. *Side*, צַד *tsad.*
Gen. 6. 16 door of the ark shalt thou set in the side
Exod 25. 32 six branches shall come out of the sides
25. 32 three branches..out of the one side, and
25. 32 three branches..out of the other side
26. 13 it shall hang over the sides of the tabern.
30. 4 upon the two sides of it shalt thou make
37. 18 And six branches going out of the sides
37. 18 out of the one side..out of the other side
37. 27 upon the two sides thereof, to be places
Num 33. 55 thorns in your sides, and shall vex you in
Deut 31. 26 put it in the side of the ark of the covenant
Josh 23. 13 scourges in your sides, and thorns in your
Judg. 2. 3 but they shall be (as thorns) in your sides
1 Sa. 6. 8 put the jewels..in a coffer by the side th.
20. 20 I will shoot three arrows on the side (th.)
20. 25 Abner sat by Saul's side, and David's place
23. 26 Saul went on this side of the mountain
23. 26 David and his men on that side of the m.
2 Sa. 2. 16 and (thrust) his sword in his fellow's side
13. 34 much people by the way of the hill side
Psa. 91. 7 A thousand shall fall at thy side, and ten
Isa. 60. 4 thy daughters shall be nursed at (thy) side
66. 12 ye shall be borne upon (her) sides, and be
Eze. 4. 4 Lie thou also upon thy left side, and lay
4. 6 lie again on thy right side, and thou shalt
4. 8 shalt not turn thee from one side to ano.
4. 9 days that thou shalt lie upon thy side
34. 21 Because ye have thrust with side and with

11. *Rib*, צֵלָע *tsela.*
Exod 25. 12 and two rings (shall be) in the one side of
25. 12 and two rings in the other side of it
25. 14 put the staves into the rings by the sides
26. 20 And for the second side of the tabernacle
26. 26 five for the boards of the one side of the
26. 27 five bars for the boards of the other side
26. 27 five bars for the boards of the side of the
26. 35 on the side of the tabernacle toward the
26. 35 thou shalt put the table on the north side
27. 7 staves shall be upon the two sides of the
36. 25 for the other side of the tabernacle, (which
36. 31 five for the boards of the one side of the
36. 32 five bars for the boards of the other side
37. 3 even two rings upon the one side of it
37. 3 and two rings upon the other side of it
37. 5 staves into the rings by the sides of the
38. 7 put the staves into the rings on the sides
2 Sa. 16. 13 Shimei went along on the hill's side over
Job 18. 12 and destruction (shall be) ready at his side

12. *Wall*, קִיר *qir.*
Exod 30. 3 sides thereof round about, and the horns
37. 26 the top of it, and the sides thereof round
Lev. 1. 15 blood..shall be wrung out at the side of
5. 9 he shall sprinkle..upon the side of the al.

13. *End, extremity*, קָצֶה *qatseh.*
Deut 4. 32 from the one side of heaven unto the oth.

14. *Square, fourth part*, רֶבַע *reba.*
Eze. 1. 8 hands..under their wings on their four si.
1. 17 they went upon their four sides..they tu.
10. 11 went upon their four sides; they turned

15. *Wind*, רוּחַ *ruach.*
Jer. 52. 23 ninety..six pomegranates on a side; (and)
Eze. 42. 16 He measured the east side with the mea.
42. 17 He measured the north side, five hundred
42. 18 measured the south side, five hundred re.
42. 19 He turned about to the west side, (and)
42. 20 He measured it by the four sides: it had a

16. *Lip*, שָׂפָה *saphah.*
Exod 36. 11 likewise he made in the uttermost side of
Judg. 7. 12 as the sand by the sea side for multitude
2 Ch. 8. 17 to Eloth, at the sea side in the land of E.

17. *Side, authority*, שְׂטַר *shetar.*
Dan. 7. 5 it raised up itself on one side, and (it had)

18. *Part, division*, μέρος *meros.*
John 21. 6 Cast the net on the right side of the ship

19. *Beyond, over, on the other side*, πέραν *peran.*
Matt. 8. 18 commandment to depart unto the other si.
8. 28 when he was come to the other side, into
14. 22 to go before him unto the other side, whi.
16. 5 his disciples were come to the other side
Mark 4. 35 saith..Let us pass over unto the other side
5. 1 they came over to the other side of the sea
5. 21 passed over..unto the other side, much
6. 45 to go to the other side before unto Beth.
8. 13 and, entering..departed to the other side
10. 1 cometh..by the farther side of Jordan: and
Luke 8. 22 Let us go over unto the other side of the
John 6. 22 people which stood on the other side of the
6. 25 found him on the other side of the sea, th.

20. *The side, ribs*, πλευρά *pleura.*
John 19. 34 one of the soldiers..pierced his side, and
20. 20 showed unto them (his) hands and his side
John 20. 25 thrust my hand into his side, I will not
20. 27 thrust (it) into my side: and be not faith.
Acts 12. 7 smote Peter on the side, and raised him

SIDE, by the —
Alongside of, παρά (acc.) *para.*
Matt 13. 1 out of the house, and sat by the sea side
13. 4 some (seeds) fell by the way side, and the
13. 19 is he which received seed by the way side
20. 30 two blind men sitting by the way side, wh.
Mark 2. 13 he went forth again by the sea side; and
4. 1 began again to teach by the sea side: and
4. 4 as he sowed, some fell by the way side, and
4. 15 these are they by the way side, where the
10. 46 son of Timæus, sat by the highway side be.
Luke 8. 5 as he sowed, some fell by the way side
8. 12 Those by the way side are they 18. 35.
Acts 10. 6 a tanner, whose house is by the sea side
10. 32 he is lodged..by the sea side: who, when
16. 13 we went out of the city by a river side, wh.
[*See also* About on every, by, east, every, farther, floor, left, north, on, on this, other, the other, pass by, post, right, south, this, way side, west.]

SIDE chamber —
Rib, side room, צֵלָע *tsela.*
Eze. 41. 5 breadth of (every) side chamber four cubits
41. 6 side chambers (were) three, one over anot.
41. 6 which (was) of the house for the side ch.
41. 7 winding about still upward to the side ch.
41. 8 foundations of the side chambers (were) a
41. 9 wall, which (was) for the side chamber
41. 9 left (was) the place of the side chambers
41. 11 the doors of the side chambers (were) to.
41. 26 side chambers of the house, and thick pl.

SIDE, on every —
1. *To be girded, restrained*, חָגַר *chagar.*
Psa. 65. 12 drop..the little hills rejoice on every s.

2. *Round about*, סָבִיב *sabib.*
Num 16. 27 from the tabernacle of Korah..on every s.
Judg 7. 18 blow ye the trumpets also on every side
8. 34 hands of all their enemies on every side
1 Sa. 12. 11 the hand of your enemies on every side
14. 47 fought against..his enemies on every side
1 Ki. 5. 4 my God hath given me rest on every side
1 Ch. 22. 18 hath he (not) given you rest on every side?
2 Ch. 14. 7 and he hath given us rest on every side
32. 22 saved..and guided them on every side
Job 1. 10 and about all that he hath on every side?
18. 11 Terrors shall make him afraid on every si.
19. 10 He hath destroyed me on every side, and
Psa. 12. 8 The wicked walk on every side, when the
31. 13 fear (was) on every side: while they took
Jer. 6. 25 for the sword of the enemy..(is) on every s.
20. 10 fear on every side. Report, (say they), and
49. 29 shall cry unto them, Fear (is) on every si.
Eze. 16. 33 may come unto thee on every side for thy
19. 8 nations set against him on every side from
23. 22 will bring them against thee on every si.
28. 23 by the sword upon her on every side; and
36. 3 swallowed you up on every side, that ye
37. 21 will gather them on every side, and bring
39. 17 gather yourselves on every side to my sa.
41. 5, 10 round about the house on every side

3. *From every quarter*, πάντοθεν *pantothen.*
Luke 19. 43 enemies shall..keep thee in on every side

SIDE, right —
Right hand or side, δεξιός *dexios.*
Mark 16. 5 saw a young man sitting on the right side
Luke 1. 11 standing on the right side of the altar of

SIDE, (sea) —
Haven, shore, חוֹף *choph.*
Deut. 1. 7 by the sea side, to the land of the Canaan

SIDE, the one...the other, this.. that —
From here, מִפֹּה ,מִפּוֹ *mip-po, mip-poh.*
Eze. 40. 10 one measure on this side and on that side
41. 1 six cubits broad on the one side, and six
41. 1 cubits broad on the other side, (which was)

SI'-DON, צִידֹן ,צִידוֹן *fortified*, Σιδών.
1. The eldest son of Canaan son of Ham. B.C. 2200.
Gen. 10. 15 Canaan begat S. his first born, and Heth
2. The city founded by the Phœnicians, twenty miles N. of Tyre, and twenty S. of Beirut, now called *Saida*. It was founded by Sidon, first born of Canaan, B.C. 2750; in 1444 it fell to Asher, but was never occupied; in 1210 it was seized by the king of Ascalon, and its inhabitants fled to Tyre; in 1157 they oppressed Israel; in 728 it was taken by Shalmanezer; in 480 it furnished ships for the fleet of Xerxes; in 332 it revolted from Persia; in 351 it was betrayed to Ochus by Tennes, when the people burnt the city, and 40,000 perished by the flames; in 333 it submitted to Alexander the Great; in 323 it was annexed by Ptolemy; in 315 taken from him by Antigonus; in 65 it fell with the rest of Syria into the Roman power; in 20 it was deprived by Augustus of its ancient privileges; in A.D. 1108 it was invested by the Crusaders, and in 1111 it was taken by Baldwin; having been retaken by the Saracens it was recovered in 1197 by the Christians; in 1291, they abandoned it; in 1658 it established commercial relations with France, which had a monopoly of the trade till 1791 when they were driven out by Jezzar Pasha; in 1840 it was bombarded and taken by Admiral Napier; in 1839 Lady Hester Stanhope died at D'Joun, eight miles from Sidon. The manufacture of glass, for which

it was renowned, made from the fine sand on the coast near Mount Carmel, is referred to by Pliny, A.D. 77. See *Zidon*.

Gen. 10. 19 the border of the Canaanites was from S.
Matt11. 21 mighty works..had..done in Tyre and S.
11. 22 It shall be more tolerable for Tyre and S.
15. 21 departed into the coasts of Tyre and S.
Mark 3. 8 they about Tyre and S., a great multitude
7. 24 went into the borders of Tyre [and S.], and
7. 31 departing from the coasts of Tyre and S.
Luke 4. 26 save unto Sarepta, (a city) [of S.], unto a
6. 17 people..from the sea coast of Tyre and S.
10. 13 mighty works had..done in Tyre and S.
10. 14 it shall be more tolerable for Tyre and S.
Acts 12. 20 highly displeased..them of Tyre and S.
27. 3 the next (day) we touched at S. And Ju.

SIDONIANS, צִידֹנִי. See *Zidonians*.
The inhabitants of Sidon.

Deut. 3. 9 (Which) Hermon the S. call Sirion, and
Josh.13. 4 Mearah that (is) beside the S., unto Ap.
13. 6 the S., them will I drive out from before
Judg. 3. 3 the S., and the Hivites that dwelt in mo.
1 Ki. 5. 6 (there is) not among us any..like..the S.

SIEGE, (to lay) —

1. *Siege, bulwark,* מָצוֹר *matsor.*
Deut20. 19 not cut..to employ (them) in the siege
28. 53 in the siege, and in the straitness, where.
28. 55 he hath nothing left him in the siege, and
28. 57 shall eat them..secretly in the siege
2 Ch.32. 10 that ye abide in the siege in Jerusalem
Jer. 19. 9 in the siege and straitness wherewith their
Eze. 4. 2 lay siege against it, and build a fort ag.
4. 7 thou shalt set thy face toward the siege
4. 8 till thou hast ended the days of thy siege
5. 2 when the days of the siege are fulfilled
Mic. 5. 1 he hath laid siege against us; they shall
Nah. 3. 14 Draw thee waters for the siege, fortify thy
Zech12. 2 when they shall be in the siege both ag.

2. *To besiege,* צוּר *tsur.*
1 Ki.15. 27 Nadab and all Israel laid siege to Gibbe.
Isa. 29. 3 will lay siege against thee with a mount
Eze. 4. 3 and thou shalt lay siege against it

SIEVE —

1. *Sieve,* כְּבָרָה *kebarah.*
Amos 9. 9 like as (corn) is sifted in a sieve, yet shall

2. *A sieve, fan,* נָפָה *naphah.*
Isa. 30. 28 to sift the nations with the sieve of vanity

SIFT, be sifted, to —

1. *To be moved, shaken, sifted,* נוּעַ *nua,* 2.
Amos 9. 9 like as (corn) is sifted in a sieve, yet shall

2. *To cause to move, shake, sift,* נוּעַ *nua,* 5.
Amos 9. 9 I will sift the house of Israel among all

3. *To wave, shake, sift,* נוּף *nuph,* 5.
Isa. 30. 28 to sift the nations with the sieve of van.

4. *To sift, shake,* σινιάζω *siniazō.*
Luke22. 31 desired (to have) you, that he may sift (you)

SIGH, sighing —

1. *Sigh, sighing,* אֲנָחָה *anachah.*
Job 3. 24 For my sighing cometh before I eat, and
Psa. 31. 10 spent with grief, and my years with sig.
Isa. 21. 2 the sighing thereof have I made to cease
35. 10 and sorrow and sighing shall flee away
Jer. 45. 3 I fainted in my sighing, and I find no re.
Lam. 1. 22 my sighs (are) many, and my heart (is) fa.

2. *Groan, groaning,* אֲנָקָה *anaqah.*
Psa. 12. 5 for the sighing of the needy, now will I
79. 11 Let the sighing of the prisoner come bef.

SIGH (deeply), to —

1. *To sigh,* אָנַח *anach,* 2.
Exod. 2. 23 the children of Israel sighed by reason of
Isa. 24. 7 languisheth, all the merry hearted do sigh
Lam. 1. 4 her priests sigh, her virgins are afflicted
1. 11 her people sigh, they seek bread; they
1. 21 have heard that I sigh; (there is) none to
1. 8 yea, she sigheth, and turneth backward
Eze. 9. 4 the men that sigh and that cry for all the
21. 6 Sigh therefore, thou son of man, with the
21. 6 and with bitterness sigh before their eyes
21. 7 when they say unto thee, Wherefore sig.

2. *To groan again, be indignant,* ἀναστενάζω.
Mark 8. 12 he sighed deeply in his spirit, and saith

3. *To groan, be indignant,* στενάζω *stenazō.*
Mark 7. 34 he sighed, and saith unto him, Ephpha.

SIGHT, (fearful), in the sight of —

1. *Vision,* חָזוּת *chazoth.*
Dan. 4. 11 the sight thereof to the end of all the ea.
4. 20 and the sight thereof to all the earth

2. *Appearance,* מַרְאֶה *mareh.*
Gen. 2. 9 every tree that is pleasant to the sight and
Exod. 3. 3 and see this great sight, why the bush is
24. 17 the sight of the glory of the LORD (was)
Lev. 13. 3 the plague in sight (be) deeper than the sk.
13. 4 in sight (be) not deeper than the skin, and
13. 20 behold, it (be) in sight lower than the skin
13. 25 it (be in) sight deeper than the skin, it (is)
13. 30 if it (be) in sight deeper than the skin, and
13. 31 it (be) not in sight deeper than the skin
13. 32 scall (be) not in sight deeper than the skin
13. 34 nor (be) in sight deeper than the skin
Lev. 14. 37 which in sight (are) lower than the wall
Deut28. 34 thou shalt be mad for the sight of thine
28. 67 for the sight of thine eyes which thou sh.
Job 41. 9 shall not (one) be cast down..at the sight
Eccl. 6. 9 Better (is) the sight of the eyes than the
11. 9 walk in the ways..and in the sight of th.
Isa. 11. 3 he shall not judge after the sight of his

3. *Before,* נֶגֶד *neged.*
Psa. 78. 12 Marvellous things did he in the sight of

4. *Eye,* עַיִן *ayin.*
Gen. 18. 3 if now I have found favour in thy sight
19. 19 thy servant hath found grace in thy sight
21. 11 was very grievous in Abraham's sight
21. 12 Let it not be grievous in thy sight because
33. 8 (These are) to find grace in the sight of my
33. 10 if now I have found grace in thy sight, th.
33. 15 let me find grace in the sight of my lord
38. 7 Judah's first born, was wicked in the sight
39. 4 Joseph found grace in his sight, and he se.
39. 21 gave him favour in the sight of the keeper
47. 25 let us find grace in the sight of my lord
47. 29 If now I have found grace in thy sight, put
Exod. 3. 21 I will give this people favour in the sight
4. 30 and did the signs in the sight of the people
7. 20 in the sight of Pharaoh, and in the sight
9. 8 sprinkle it toward the heaven in the sight
11. 3 LORD gave the people favour in the sight
11. 3 the sight of Pharaoh's servants..the sight
12. 36 gave the people favour in the sight of the
15. 26 wilt do that which is right in his sight, and
17. 6 Moses did so in the sight of the elders of
19. 11 the LORD will come down in the sight of
33. 12 and thou hast also found grace in my si.
33. 13 if I have found grace in thy sight, show
33. 13 that I may find grace in thy sight
33. 16 and thy people have found grace in thy si.
33. 17 thou hast found grace in my sight, and I
34. 9 If now I have found grace in thy sight, O
40. 38 fire was on it by night, in the sight of all
Lev. 10. 19 should it have been accepted in the sight
13. 5 (if) the plague in his sight be at a stay, (and)
13. 37 if the scall be in his sight at a stay, and
20. 17 they shall be cut off in the sight of their
25. 53 rule with rigour over him in thy sight
26. 45 out of the land of Egypt in the sight of the
Num11. 11 have I not found favour in thy sight, that
11. 15 if I have found favour in thy sight; and
13. 33 we were in our own sight as grasshoppers
13. 33 and so we were in their sight
19. 5 (one) shall burn the heifer in his sight, her
20. 27 they went up into mount Hor in the sight
25. 6 in the sight of Moses, and in the sight of
27. 19 and give him a charge in their sight
32. 5 if we have found grace in thy sight, let this
32. 13 that had done evil in the sight of the LORD
33. 3 went out with an high hand in the sight
Deut. 4. 6 your understanding in the sight of the na.
4. 25 shall do evil in the sight of the LORD thy
6. 18 right and good in the sight of the LORD
9. 18 in doing wickedly in the sight of the LORD
12. 25 do (that which is) right in the sight of the
12. 28 (that which is) good and right in the sight
17. 2 that hath wrought wickedness in the sight
21. 9 do (that which is) right in the sight of the
31. 7 and said unto him in the sight of all Israel
31. 29 ye will do evil in the sight of the LORD, to
34. 12 terror which Moses showed in the sight
Josh. 3. 7 to magnify thee in the sight of all Israel
4. 14 the LORD magnified Joshua in the sight of
10. 12 he said in the sight of Israel, Sun, stand
24. 17 which did those great signs in our sight
Judg. 2. 11 the children of Israel did evil in the sight
3. 7 the children of Israel did evil in the sight
3. 12 Israel did evil again in the sight of the Lo.
3. 12 they had done evil in the sight of the LORD
4. 1 Israel again did evil in the sight of the L.
6. 1 Israel did evil in the sight of the LORD
6. 17 If now I have found grace in thy sight
6. 21 angel of the LORD departed out of his si.
10. 6 Israel did evil again in the sight of the L.
13. 1 Israel did evil again in the sight of the L.
Ruth 2. 13 Let me find favour in thy sight, my lord
1 Sa. 1. 18 Let thine handmaid find grace in thy sight
12. 17 which ye have done in the sight of the L.
15. 17 When thou (wast) little in thine own sight
15. 19 and didst evil in the sight of the LORD
16. 22 for he hath found favour in my sight
18. 5 he was accepted in the sight of all the pe.
18. 5 and also in the sight of Saul's servants
29. 6 and thy going out..(is) good in my sight
29. 9 I know that thou (art) good in my sight
2 Sa. 6. 22 And I will..be base in mine own sight
7. 19 this was yet a small thing in thy sight, O
12. 9 thou despised..to do evil in his sight
13. 5 dress the meat in my sight, that I may see
13. 6 make me a couple of cakes in my sight, th.
13. 8 made cakes in his sight, and did bake the
14. 22 I have found grace in thy sight, my lord
16. 4 (that) I may find grace in thy sight, my
16. 22 Absalom went in..in the sight of all Is.
1 Ki.11. 6 Solomon did evil in the sight of the LORD
11. 19 Hadad found great favour in the sight of
11. 38 do (that is) right in my sight, to keep my
14. 22 Judah did evil in the sight of the LORD
15. 26, 34 he did evil in the sight of the LORD
16. 7 the evil that he did in the sight of the L.
16. 19 he sinned in doing evil in the sight of the
16. 30 the son of Omri did evil in the sight of the
21. 20 sold thyself to work evil in the sight of
21. 25 to work wickedness in the sight of the L.
1 Ki.22. 52 he did evil in the sight of the LORD and
2 Ki. 1. 13 let my life..be precious in thy sight
1. 14 let my life now be precious in thy sight
3. 2 he wrought evil in the sight of the LORD
3. 18 this is (but) a light thing in the sight of
8. 18 and he did evil in the sight of the LORD
8. 27 did evil in the sight of the LORD, as (did)
12. 2 did (that which was) right in the sight of
13. 2, 11 he did (that which was) evil in the si.
14. 3 he did (that which was) right in the sight
14. 24 he did (that which was) evil in the sight
15. 3, 34 he did (that which was) right in the si.
15. 9, 18, 24, 28 (that which was) evil in the sight
16. 2 did not (that which was) right in the sight
17. 2 he did (that which was) evil in the sight
17. 17 sold themselves to do evil in the sight of
18. 3 he did (that which was) right in the sight
20. 3 have done (that which is) good in thy si.
21. 2, 16, 20 (that which was) evil in the sight
21. 6 he wrought much wickedness in the sight
21. 15 done (that which was) evil in my sight of
22. 2 he did (that which was) right in the sight
23. 32, 37 he did (that which was) evil in the si.
24. 9, 19 he did (that which was) evil in the si.
1 Ch. 2. 3 And Er..was evil in the sight of the LORD
19. 13 LORD do (that which is) good in his sight
28. 8 in the sight of all Israel the congregation
29. 25 magnified Solomon exceedingly in the si.
2 Ch.20. 32 doing (that which was) right in the sight
22. 4 he did evil in the sight of the LORD like
24. 2 Joash did (that which was) right in the si.
25. 2 he did (that which was) right in the sight
26. 4 he did (that which was) right in the sight
27. 2 he did (that which was) right in the sight
28. 1 did not (that which was) right in the sig.
29. 2 he did (that which was) right in the sight
32. 23 he was magnified in the sight of all nati.
33. 2 did (that which was) evil in the sight of
33. 6 he wrought much evil in the sight of the
33. 22 he did (that which was) evil in the sight
34. 2 he did (that which was) right in the sight
36. 5, 9, 12 did (that which was) evil in the si.
Neh. 8. 5 Ezra opened the book in the sight of all
Esth. 2. 15 Esther obtained favour in the sight of all
2. 17 she obtained favour in his sight: and the
5. 8 If I have found favour in the sight of the
7. 3 If I have found favour in thy sight, O ki.
8. 5 if I have found favour in his sight, and
Job 15. 15 yea, the heavens are not clean in his sight
18. 3 Wherefore are we..vile in your sight?
19. 15 a stranger: I am an alien in their sight
25. 5 yea, the stars are not pure in his sight
Psa. 5. 5 The foolish shall not stand in thy sight
51. 4 sinned, and done (this) evil in thy sight
72. 14 precious shall their blood be in his sight
79. 10 be known among the heathen in our sight
90. 4 a thousand years in thy sight (are but) as
98. 2 hath he openly showed in the sight of the
101. 7 telleth lies shall not tarry in my sight
116. 15 Precious in the sight of the LORD (is) the
Prov. 1. 17 in vain the net is spread in the sight of
3. 4 So shalt thou find favour..in the sight of
Isa. 38. 3 have done (that which is) good in thy si.
43. 4 Since thou wast precious in my sight, th.
Jer. 7. 30 the children..have done evil in my sight
19. 10 shalt thou break the bottle in the sight of
32. 12 in the sight of Hanameel mine uncle's (son)
34. 15 had done right in my sight, in proclaiming
43. 9 in Tahpanhes, in the sight of the men of
51. 24 that they have done in Zion in your sight
Eze. 5. 8 in the midst of thee in the sight of the na.
5. 14 a reproach..in the sight of all that pass
10. 2 said, Go in..And he went in in my sight
10. 19 and mounted up from the earth in my si.
12. 3 remove by day in their sight; and thou sh.
12. 3 remove..to another place in their sight
12. 4 bring forth thy stuff by day in their sight
12. 4 thou shalt go forth at even in their sight
12. 5 Dig thou through the wall in their sight
12. 6 In their sight shalt thou bear (it) upon
12. 7 I bare (it) upon (my) shoulder in their si.
16. 41 execute judgments upon thee in the sight
20. 9 in whose sight I made myself known unto
20. 14, 22 the heathen, in whose sight I brought
20. 22 it should not be polluted in the sight of
21. 23 as a false divination in their sight, to them
22. 16 take thine inheritance..in the sight of the
28. 18 in the sight of all them that behold thee
28. 25 sanctified in them in the sight of the hea.
36. 34 it lay desolate in the sight of all that pas.
39. 27 am sanctified in them in the sight of many
43. 11 write (it) in their sight, that they may k.
Hos. 2. 10 her lewdness in the sight of her lovers
Amos 9. 3 though they be hid from my sight in the
Jon. 2. 4 I said, I am cast out of thy sight; yet I
Mal. 2. 17 one that doeth evil (is) good in the sight

5. *Face,* פָּנִים *panim.*
Gen. 23. 4 that I may bury my dead out of my sight
23. 8 I should bury my dead out of my sight
47. 18 there is not ought left in the sight of my
Num. 3. 4 in the priest's office in the sight of Aaron
Deut. 4. 37 brought thee out in his sight with his mi.
Josh.23. 5 drive them from out of your sight; and
2 Sa. 7. 9 cut off all thine enemies out of thy sight
1 Ki. 8. 25 There shall not fail thee a man in my si.
9. 7 this house..I cast out of my sight; and
2 Ki. 17. 18 the LORD..removed them out of his sight
17. 20 until he had cast them out of his sight
17. 23 the LORD removed Israel out of his sight
23. 27 I will remove Judah also out of my sight
24. 3 to remove (them) out of his sight, for the

1 Ch.22. 8 thou hast shed much blood..in my sight
2 Ch. 6. 16 There shall not fail thee a man in my si.
7. 20 this house..will I cast out of my sight, and
Ezra 9. 9 extended mercy unto us in the sight of
Neh. 1. 11 and grant him mercy in the sight of this
2. 5 if thy servant have found favour in thy si.
Esth. 2. 17 she obtained grace and favour in his sig.
Job 21. 8 Their seed is established in their sight
Psa. 9. 19 let the heathen be judged in thy sight
19. 14 Let the words..be acceptable in thy sight
76. 7 who may stand in thy sight when once th.
143. 2 in thy sight shall no man living be justi.
Prov. 4. 3 tender and only (beloved) in the sight of
Eccl. 2. 26 giveth to a man that (is) good in his sight
8. 3 Be not hasty to go out of his sight: stand
Isa. 5. 21 (them that are)..prudent in their own si.
26. 17 so have we been in thy sight, O LORD
Jer. 4. 1 put..thine abominations out of my sight
7. 15 I will cast you out of my sight, as I have
15. 1 cast (them) out of my sight, and let them
18. 23 neither blot out their sin from thy sight
Eze. 20. 43 loathe yourselves in your own sight for
36. 31 shall loathe yourselves in your own sight
Hos. 2. 2 put away her whoredoms out of her sight
6. 2 raise us up, and we shall live in his sight

6. *To see*, רָאָה *raah.*
Job 34. 26 He striketh them..in the open sight of ot.

7. *To see*, βλέπω *blepō.*
Acts 9. 9 he was three days without sight Lu. 7. 21.

8. *Appearance*, εἶδος *eidos.*
2 Co. 5. 7 For we walk by faith, not by sight

9. *Before*, ἔμπροσθεν *emprosthen.*
Matt 11. 26 Even so..for so it seemed good in thy sight
Luke 10. 21 even so..for so it seemed good in thy si.
1 Th. 1. 3 in the sight of God and our Father

10. *Before, in over against*, ἐναντίον *enantion.*
Acts 7. 10 favour and wisdom in the sight of Pharaoh

11. *In the sight of*, ἐνώπιον *enōpion.*
Luke 1. 15 he shall be great in the sight of the Lord
15. 21 sinned against heaven, and in thy sight
16. 15 is abomination in the sight of God
Acts 4. 19 Whether it be right in the sight of God to
8. 21 thy heart is not right [in the sight of] God
10. 31 are had in remembrance in the sight of G.
Rom. 3. 20 there shall no flesh be justified in his sight
12. 17 Provide things honest in the sight of all
2 Co. 4. 2 commending ourselves..in the sight of G
7. 12 that our care for you in the sight of God
8. 21 sight of the Lord, but also in the sight of
1 Ti. 2. 3 this (is) good and acceptable in the sight
6. 13 I give thee charge in the sight of God, who
Heb. 4. 13 creature that is not manifest in his sight
13. 21 that which is well pleasing in his sight
Jas. 4. 10 Humble yourselves in the sight of the Lord
1 Pe. 3. 4 which is in the sight of God of great price
1 Jo. 3. 22 those things that are pleasing in his sight
Rev. 13. 13 maketh fire come down..in the sight of
13. 14 which he had power to do in the sight of

12. *A sight, spectacle*, θεωρία *theōria.*
Luke 23. 48 people that came together to that sight

13. *A sight, vision*, ὅραμα *horama.*
Acts 7. 31 Moses saw (it), he wondered at the sight

14. *Appearance, vision*, ὅρασις *horasis.*
Rev. 4. 3 a rainbow..in sight like unto an emerald

15. *Over against, in the face of*, κατενώπιον *katenō.*
2 Co. 2. 17 [in the sight of] God speak we in Christ
Col. 1. 22 unblameable and unreprovable in his sight

16. *Eye*, ὀφθαλμός *ophthalmos.*
Acts 1. 9 and a cloud received him out of their sight

17. *With or before*, παρά (dat.) *para.*
Gal. 3. 11 no man is justified by the law in the sight

18. *To be manifested, seen*, φαντάζομαι *phantazomai.*
Heb. 12. 21 so terrible was the sight, (that) Moses said

19. *Dreadful sight, terrific appearance*, φόβητρον.
Luke 21. 11 fearful sights and great signs shall there

SIGHT, to receive, recovering of —

1. *A seeing again, looking up*, ἀνάβλεψις *anablepsis.*
Luke 4. 18 and recovering of sight to the blind, to set

2. *To see again, look up*, ἀναβλέπω *anablepō.*
Matt 11. 5 The blind receive their sight, and the lame
20. 34 their eyes received sight, and they follo.
Mark 10. 51 Lord, that I might receive my sight
10. 52 he received his sight, and followed Jesus
Luke 18. 41 he said, Lord, that I may receive my sight
18. 42 Receive thy sight: thy faith hath saved
18. 43 immediately he received his sight, and fo.
John 9. 11 I went and washed, and I received sight
9. 15 asked him how he had received his sight
9. 18 he had been blind, and received his sight
9. 18 parents of him that had received his sight
Acts 9. 12 on him, that he might receive his sight
9. 17 that thou mightest receive thy sight, and
9. 18 he received sight forthwith, and arose, and
22. 13 said unto me, Brother Saul, receive thy si.

SIGN, appointed, of fire —

1. *A sign*, אוֹת *oth.*
Gen. 1. 14 let them be for signs, and for seasons, and
Exod. 4. 8 neither hearken to the voice of the first si.
4. 8 they will believe the voice of the latter si.
4. 9 they will not believe also these two signs
4. 17 this rod..wherewith thou shalt do signs
Exod. 4. 28 the signs which he had commanded him
4. 30 and did the signs in the sight of the peo.
7. 3 multiply my signs and my wonders in the
8. 23 a division..tomorrow shall this sign be
10. 1 I might show these my signs before him
10. 2 my signs which I have done among them
13. 9 it shall be for a sign unto thee upon thine
31. 13 it (is) a sign between me and you throug.
31. 17 It (is) a sign between me and the children
Num 14. 11 the signs which I have showed among th.
16. 38 they shall be a sign unto the children of
Deut. 4. 34 by signs, and by wonders, and by war, and
6. 8 thou shalt bind them for a sign upon thine
6. 22 the LORD showed signs and wonders, great
7. 19 the signs, and the wonders, and the mig.
11. 18 bind them for a sign upon your hand, that
13. 1 If..a prophet..giveth thee a sign or a wo.
13. 2 And the sign or the wonder come to pass
26. 8 with great terribleness, and with signs, and
28. 46 they shall be upon thee for a sign, and for
29. 3 The great temptations..the signs, and th.
34. 11 the signs and the wonders which the LORD
Josh. 4. 6 That this may be a sign among you, (th.)
24. 17 which did those great signs in our sight
Judg. 6. 17 show me a sign that thou talkest with me
1 Sa. 2. 34 this (shall be) a sign unto thee, that shall
10. 7 let it be, when these signs are come unto
10. 9 and all those signs came to pass that day
14. 10 Come up unto us..this (shall be) a sign
2 Ki. 19. 29 this (shall be) a sign unto thee, Ye shall
20. 8 What (shall be) the sign that the LORD
20. 9 This sign shalt thou have of the LORD
Neh. 9. 10 showedst signs and wonders upon Phara.
Psa. 74. 4 enemies..set up their ensigns (for) signs
74. 9 We see not our signs: (there is) no more
78. 43 How he had wrought his signs in Egypt
105. 27 They showed his signs among them, and
Isa. 7. 11 Ask thee a sign of the LORD thy God; ask
7. 14 the LORD himself shall give you a sign
8. 18 for signs and for wonders in Israel from
19. 20 it shall be for a sign and a witness unto
20. 3 (for) a sign and a wonder upon Egypt and
37. 30 this (shall be) a sign unto thee, Ye shall
38. 7 this (shall be) a sign unto thee from the L.
38. 22 What (is) the sign that I shall go up to the
55. 13 an everlasting sign (that) shall not be cut
66. 19 I will set a sign among them, and I will
Jer. 10. 2 be not dismayed at the signs of heaven
32. 20 Which hast set signs and wonders in the
32. 21 out of the land of Egypt with signs, and
44. 29 this (shall be) a sign unto you, saith the
Eze. 4. 3 This (shall be) a sign to the house of Isr.
14. 8 will make him a sign and a proverb, and
20. 12 to be a sign between me and them, that
20. 20 they shall be a sign between me and you

2. *Word or matter of a sign*, דְּבַר אוֹת *debar oth.*
Psa. 105. 27 They showed his signs among them, and

3. *Signs*, אָתִין *athin.*
Dan. 4. 2 I thought it good to show the signs and
4. 3 How great (are) his signs! and how mig.
6. 27 he worketh signs and wonders in heaven

4. *Wonder*, מוֹפֵת *mopheth.*
1 Ki. 13. 3 he gave a sign the same day, saying
13. 3 This (is) the sign which the LORD hath sp.
13. 5 according to the sign which the man of
2 Ch. 32. 24 spake unto him, and he gave him a sign
Eze. 12. 6 I have set thee (for) a sign unto the hou.
12. 11 Say, I (am) your sign: like as I have done
24. 24 Ezekiel is unto you a sign: according to
24. 27 thou shalt be a sign unto them; and they

5. *Sign, ensign, banner, sail*, נֵס *nes.*
Num 26. 10 that company died..and they became a s.

6. *A lifting up, signal*, מַשְׂאֵת *maseth.*
Jer. 6. 1 and set up a sign of fire in Beth-haccerem

7. *Sign, monument*, צִיּוּן *tsiyyun.*
Eze. 39. 15 then shall he set up a sign by it, till the

8. *A sign, mark, signal*, σημεῖον *sēmeion.*
Matt. 12. 38 Master, we would see a sign from thee
12. 39 An evil..generation seeketh after a sign
12. 39 shall no sign be given to it, but the sign
16. 1 that he would show them a sign from he.
16. 3 can ye not (discern) the signs of the times?
16. 4 A wicked..generation seeketh after a sign
16. 4 no sign be given unto it, but the sign of
24. 3 what (shall be) the sign of thy coming, and
24. 24 and shall show great signs and wonders
24. 30 then shall appear the sign of the Son of
26. 48 he that betrayed him gave them a sign
Mark 8. 11 seeking of him a sign from heaven, temp.
8. 12 Why doth this generation seek after a sign
8. 12 There shall no sign be given unto this ge.
13. 4 what (shall be) the sign when all these th.
13. 22 shall show signs and wonders, to seduce
16. 17 [these signs shall follow them that beli.]
16. 20 [confirming the word with signs following]
Luke 2. 12 this (shall be) a sign unto you; Ye shall
2. 34 for a sign which shall be spoken against
11. 16 others, tempting (him), sought of him a s.
11. 29 an evil generation: they seek a sign; and
11. 29 shall no sign be given it, but the sign of
11. 30 as Jonas was a sign unto the Ninevites, so
21. 7 what sign (will there be) when these things
21. 11 and great signs shall there be from heaven
21. 25 there shall be signs in the sun, and in the
John 2. 18 What sign showest thou unto us, seeing
4. 48 Except ye see signs and wonders, ye will
6. 30 What sign showest thou then, that we m.
20. 30 many other signs truly did Jesus in the
Acts 2. 19 wonders in heaven above, and signs in the
2. 22 by miracles and wonders and signs, which
2. 43 many wonders and signs were done by the
4. 30 that signs and wonders may be done by
5. 12 by the hands of the apostles were many s.
7. 36 he had showed wonders and signs in the
8. 13 beholding the miracles and signs which
14. 3 granted signs and wonders to be done by
Rom. 4. 11 he received the sign of circumcision, a
15. 19 Through mighty signs and wonders, by the
1 Co. 1. 22 the Jews require a sign, and the Greeks
14. 22 tongues are for a sign, not to them that be.
2 Co. 12. 12 the signs of an apostle were wrought am.
12. 12 in signs, and wonders, and mighty deeds
2 Th. 2. 9 with all power and signs and lying wond.
Heb. 2. 4 with signs and wonders, and with divers
Rev. 15. 1 I saw another sign in heaven, great and

SIGN was, whose —
Ensign, παράσημος *parasēmos.*
Acts 28. 11 a ship..whose sign was Castor and Pollux

SIGN, be signed, to (make) —

1. *To note down, write, sign*, רְשַׁם *resham.*
Dan. 6. 8 and sign the writing, that it be not chan.
6. 9 Darius signed the writing and the decree
6. 10 Daniel knew that the writing was signed
6. 12 Hast thou not signed a decree, that every
6. 13 nor the decree that thou hast signed, but

2. *To beckon to*, ἐννεύω *enneuō.*
Luke 1. 62 they made signs to his father, how he wo.

SIGNET —

1. *A seal, signet*, חוֹתָם *chotham.*
Gen. 38. 18 Thy signet, and thy bracelets, and thy st.
Exod 28. 11, 21, 36 (like) the engraving of a signet, sh.
39. 6 ouches of gold, graven, as signets are gr.
39. 14 (like) the engravings of a signet, every one
39. 30 a writing, (like to) the engravings of a si.
Jer. 22. 24 though Coniah..were the signet upon my
Hag. 2. 23 will make thee as a signet: for I have ch.

2. *Seal, signet*, חוֹתֶמֶת *chothemeth.*
Gen. 38. 25 whose (are) these, the signet, and brace.

3. *Signet*, עִזְקָא *izqa.*
Dan. 6. 17 with his own signet, and with the signet

SIGNIFICATION, without —
Without sound or sense, ἄφωνος *aphōnos.*
1 Co. 14. 10 and none of them (is) without signification

SIGNIFY, to —

1. *To manifest*, δηλόω *dēloō.*
Heb. 9. 8 The Holy Ghost this signifying, that the
12. 27 this (word), Yet once more, signifieth the
1 Pe. 1. 11 spirit..which was in them did signify

2. *To tell or declare thoroughly*, διαγγέλλω *diaggel.*
Acts 21. 26 to signify the accomplishment of the days

3. *To make manifest*, ἐμφανίζω *emphanizō.*
Acts 23. 15 Now therefore ye with the council sign

4. *To signify*, σημαίνω *sēmainō.*
John 12. 33 This he said, signifying what death he sh.
18. 32 which he spake, signifying what death he
21. 19 This spake he, signifying by what death
Acts 11. 28 signified by the spirit that there should
25. 27 not withal to signify the crimes (laid) ag.
Rev. 1. 1 signified (it) by his angel unto his servant

SI'-HON, סִיחֹן, סִיחוֹן *great, bold.*
An Amorite king in Heshbon, whose land lay N. of the land of Moab, from which he took all that lay to the N. of the Arnon. B.C. 1452.
Num 21. 21 Israel sent messengers unto S. king of the
21. 23 S. would not suffer Israel to pass through
21. 23 S. gathered all his people together, and we.
21. 26 Heshbon (was) the city of S. the king of
21. 27 let the city of S. be built and prepared
21. 28 For there is..a flame from the city of S.
21. 29 into captivity unto S. king of the Amorites
21. 34 thou shalt do to him as thou didst unto S.
32. 33 the kingdom of S. king of the Amorites
Deut. 1. 4 After he had slain S. the king of the Am.
2. 24 have given into thine hand S. the Amorite
2. 26 I sent messengers..unto S. king of Hesh.
2. 30 S. king of Heshbon would not let us pass
2. 31 I have begun to give S. and his land before
2. 32 S. came out against us, he and all his p.
3. 2 shalt do unto him as thou didst unto S.
3. 6 utterly destroyed them, as we did unto S.
4. 46 in the land of S. king of the Amorites
29. 7 S. the king of Heshbon, and Og the king
31. 4 LORD shall do unto them as he did to S.
Josh. 2. 10 S. and Og, whom ye utterly destroyed
9. 10 to S. king of Heshbon, and to Og king of
12. 2 S. king of the Amorites, who dwelt in H.
12. 5 half Gilead, the border of S. king of He.
13. 10 the cities of S. king of the Amorites, wh.
13. 21 S. king of the Amorites, which reigned in
13. 21 Hur, and Reba, (which were) dukes of S.
13. 27 the rest of the kingdom of S. king of H.
Judg 11. 19 Israel sent messengers unto S. king of the
11. 20 S. trusted not Israel to pass through his
11. 20 S. gathered all his people together, and
11. 21 the LORD God of Israel delivered S. and
1 Ki. 4. 19 (in) the country of S. king of the Amorites
Neh. 9. 22 they possessed the land of S., and the
Psa 135. 11 S. king of the Amorites, and Og king of
136. 19 S. king of the Amorites: for his mercy
Jer. 48. 45 shall come..a flame from the midst of S.

SI'-HOR, SHI'-HOR, שִׁיחוֹר *turbid, slimy.*
The *Wady-el-Arish* or *Rhinocolura,* the S. boundary of Canaan; also called the "river of Egypt," Gen. 15. 18. The word is also applied to the *Nile* itself.

Josh 13. 3 From S., which (is) before Egypt, even
1 Ch. 13. 5 David gathered..Israel together, from S.
Isa. 23. 3 by great waters the seed of S., the harvest
Jer. 2. 18 what hast thou..to drink the waters of S.?

SI'-LAS, Σίλας.
A believer who accompanied Paul through Asia Minor and Greece, and was imprisoned with him at Philippi; a contracted form of *Silvanus.*

Acts 15. 22 Judas surnamed Barsabas, and S., chief
15. 27 We have sent therefore Judas and S., who
15. 32 Judas and S., being prophets also them.
15. 34 [Notwithstanding it pleased S. to abide]
15. 40 Paul chose S., and departed, being rec.
16. 19 they caught Paul and S., and drew (them)
16. 25 at midnight Paul and S. prayed, and sang
16. 29 came..and fell down before Paul and S.
17. 4 believed, and consorted with Paul and S.
17. 10 brethren immediately sent..Paul and S.
17. 14 but S. and Timotheus abode there still
17. 15 receiving a commandment unto S. and
18. 5 when S. and Timotheus were come from

SILENCE, silent —
1. *Silence,* דּוּמָה *dumah.*
Psa. 94. 17 help, my soul had almost dwelt in silence
115. 17 neither any that go down into silence

2. *Silence,* דּוּמִיָּה *dumiyyah.*
Psa. 22. 2 cry in the day time..and am not silent
39. 2 I was dumb with silence; I held my pe.

3. *Silence,* דֳּמִי *domi.*
Psa. 83. 1 Keep not thou silence, O God: hold not
Isa. 62. 6 ye that make mention..keep not silence

4. *Silently,* דּוּמָם *dumam.*
Isa. 47. 5 Sit thou silent, and get thee into darkn

5. *Silence, calm,* דְּמָמָה *demamah.*
Job 4. 16 (there was) silence, and I heard a voice

6. *To be or keep silent,* הָסָה *hasah,* 3.
Amos 8. 3 they shall cast (them) forth with silence

7. *Quietness, stillness,* ἡσυχία *hēsuchia.*
Acts 22. 2 they kept the more silence: and he saith
1 Ti. 2. 11 Let the woman learn in silence with all
2. 12 suffer not..to teach..but to be in silence

8. *Silence,* σιγή *sigē.*
Acts 21. 40 when there was made a great silence, he
Rev. 8. 1 there was silence in heaven about the sp

SILENCE, to be brought to —
To be cut off, silenced, דָּמָה *damah,* 2.
Isa. 15. 1 Moab is laid waste, (and) brought to sil.

SILENCE, to keep or put to —
1. *To be silent, cease, stand still,* דָּמַם *damam.*
Job 29. 21 and waited, and kept silence at my cou.
31. 34 kept silence, (and) went not out of the
Lam. 2. 10 sit upon the ground, (and) keep silence
3. 28 He sitteth alone and keepeth silence, be.
Amos 5. 13 prudent shall keep silence in that time

2. *To cause silence, put to silence,* דָּמַם *damam,* 5.
Jer. 8. 14 for the LORD our God hath put us to sil.

3. *To be or keep silent,* הָסָה *hasah,* 3
Judg. 3. 19 who said, Keep silence And all that st.
Hab. 2. 20 let all the earth keep silence before him

4. *To be or become silent,* חָרַשׁ *charash.*
Psa. 35. 22 keep not silence: O LORD, be not far from
50. 3 God shall come, and shall not keep silen.

5. *To keep or remain silent,* חָרַשׁ *charash,* 5.
Psa. 32. 3 When I kept silence, my bones waxed old
50. 21 hast thou done, and I kept silence; thou
Isa. 41. 1 Keep silence before me, O islands; and

6. *To be silent,* חָשָׁה *chashah.*
Eccl. 3. 7 time to keep silence, and a time to speak
Isa. 65. 6 will not keep silence, but will recompense

7. *To be bound, silent,* אָלַם *alam,* 2.
Psa. 31. 18 Let the lying lips be put to silence; wh.

8. *To be silent, quiet,* σιγάω *sigaō.*
Acts 15. 12 Then all the multitude kept silence, and
1 Co. 14. 28 let him keep silence in the church; and
14. 34 Let your women keep silence in the chu.

9. *To muzzle, silence,* φιμόω *phimoō.*
Matt 22. 34 that he had put the Sadducees to silence
1 Pe. 2. 15 that with well doing ye may put to sile.

SILENT, to be —
1. *To be silent, cease, stand still,* דָּמַם *damam.*
Psa. 30. 12 may sing praises to thee, and not be sil.
31. 17 be ashamed, (and) let them be silent in

2. *To become silent, cease, stand still,* דָּמַם *damam,* 2.
1 Sa. 2. 9 and the wicked shall be silent in darkness
Jer. 8. 14 let us be silent there; for the LORD our

3. *To be or keep silent,* הָסָה *hasah,* 3.
Zech. 2. 13 Be silent, O all flesh, before the LORD: for

4. *To be silent,* חָרַשׁ *charash.*
Psa. 28. 1 be not silent to me: lest..I become like

5. *To be silent,* חָשָׁה *chashah.*
Psa. 28. 1 (if) thou be silent to me, I become like th.

SILK —
1. *Figured silk, silk, silk thread,* מֶשִׁי *meshi.*
Eze. 16. 10 fine linen, and I covered thee with silk
16. 13 thy raiment (was of) fine linen, and silk

2. *Fine white linen,* שֵׁשׁ *shesh.*
Prov 31. 22 coverings of tapestry; her clothing (is) si

3. *Silk, silken,* σηρικόν *sērikon.*
Rev. 18. 12 fine linen, and purple, and silk, and sca.

SIL'-LA, סִלָּא *highway.*
A locality near or in Jerusalem; the way going from the Jaffa gate, and ascending to a bank at the *Haram-*Area.

2 Ki. 12. 20 the house of Millo, which goeth down to S.

SILLY (one, women) —
1. *To be enticed, simple,* פָּתָה *pathah.*
Job 5. 2 foolish man, and envy slayeth the silly one
Hos. 7. 11 Ephraim also is like a silly dove without

2. *A silly woman,* γυναικάριον *gunaikarion.*
2 Ti. 3. 6 lead captive silly women laden with sins

SI-LO'-AH, שֶׁלַח, *sending forth.*
A pool at the king's gardens, S. of Jerusalem.

Neh. 3. 15 the wall of the pool of S. by the king's

SI-LO'-AM, Σιλωάμ. *Same as the preceding.*
Luke 13. 4 those eighteen, upon whom the tower in S.
John 9. 7 said unto him, Go, was in the pool of S.
9. 11 said unto me, Go to the pool of S., and

SIL-VA'-NUS, Σιλουανός.
1. Probably the same as *Silas.*

2 Co. 1. 19 who was preached..by me and S. and T.
1 Th. 1. 1 Paul, and S. and Timotheus, unto the ch.
2 Th. 1. 1 Paul and S. and Timotheus, unto the ch.

2 One by whom Peter sent his first Epistle to the Jews scattered abroad. A.D. 66.

1 Pe. 5. 12 By S., a faithful brother unto you, as I

SILVER, silverling, (piece of) —
1. *Silver, silverling,* כֶּסֶף *keseph.*
Gen. 13. 2 Abram (was) very rich in cattle, in silver
20. 16 given thy brother a thousand (pieces) of si.
23. 15, 16 four hundred shekels of silver
23. 16 Abraham weighed to Ephron the silver
24. 35 given him flocks, and herds, and silver
24. 53 servant brought forth jewels of silver, and
37. 28 sold Joseph..for twenty (pieces) of silver
44. 2 put my cup, the silver cup, in the sack's
44. 8 how then should we steal..silver or gold?
45. 22 he gave three hundred (pieces) of silver
Exod. 3. 22 jewels of silver, and jewels of gold, and
11. 2 let every man borrow..jewels of silver
12. 35 borrowed of the Egyptians jewels of silver
20. 23 Ye shall not make with me gods of silver
21. 32 shall give..thirty shekels of silver, and
25. 3 this (is) the offering..gold, and silver, and
26. 19 thou shalt make forty sockets of silver
26. 21 their forty sockets (of) silver; two sockets
26. 25 their sockets (of) silver, sixteen sockets
26 32 be of) gold, upon the four sockets of silv
27. 10 the pillars and their fillets (shall be of) s.
27. 11 hooks of the pillars and their fillets (of) s.
27. 17 All the pillars..filleted with silver; their
27. 17 hooks (shall be of) silver, and their sock
31. 4 to work in gold, and in silver, and in br
35. 5 an offering of the LORD; gold, and silver
35. 24 Every one that did offer an offering of si
35. 32 to work in gold, and in silver, and in br
36. 24 forty sockets of silver he made under the
36. 26 their forty sockets of silver; two sockets
36. 30 their sockets (were) sixteen sockets of sil.
36. 36 and he cast for them four sockets of silv.
38. 10 the hooks..and their fillets (were of) sil.
38. 11, 12, 17 the hooks..and their fillets (of) silv.
38. 17 the overlaying of their chapiters (of) silver
38. 17 pillars of the court (were) filleted with si.
38. 19 their hooks (of) silver, and the overlaying
38. 19 their chapiters and their fillets (of) silver
38. 25 silver of them that were numbered of the
38. 27 of the hundred talents of silver were cast
Lev. 5. 15 with thy estimation by shekels of silver
27. 3 estimation shall be fifty shekels of silver
27. 6 shekels of silver..three shekels of silver
27. 16 seed (shall be valued) at fifty shekels of si.
Num. 7. 13 his offering (was) one silver charger, the
7. 19, 25, 31, 37, 43, 49, 55, 61, 67, 73, 79 one silver
7. 84 twelve charges of silver, twelve silver bo.
7. 85 Each charger of silver (weighing) an hun.
7. 85 all the silver vessels (weighed) two thou.
10. 2 Make thee two trumpets of silver; of a wh.
22. 18 would give me his house full of silver and
24. 13 would give me his house full of silver and
31. 22 Only the gold, and the silver, the brass
Deut. 7. 25 thou shalt not desire the silver or gold
8. 13 and thy silver and thy gold is multiplied
17. 17 greatly multiply to himself silver and go.
22. 19 amerce him in an hundred (shekels) of sil.
22. 29 the damsel's father fifty (shekels) of silver
29. 17 their idols, wood and stone, silver and go.
Josh. 6. 19, 24 the silver, and gold, and vessels of brass
7. 21 two hundred shekels of silver, and a wedge
7. 21 behold, they (are) hid..and the silver under
7. 22 (it was) hid in his tent, and the silver un.
7. 24 the silver, and the garment, and the wedge
22. 8 with silver, and with gold, and with brass
Judg. 9. 4 three score and ten (pieces) of silver out of
16. 5 give thee..eleven hundred (pieces) of sil.
17. 2 The eleven hundred (shekels) of silver that
Judg 17. 2 behold, the silver (is) with me; I took it
17. 3 restored the eleven hundred (shekels) of s.
17. 3 I had wholly dedicated the silver unto the
17. 4 mother took two hundred (shekels) of si.
17. 10 I will give thee ten (shekels) of silver by
1 Sa. 2. 36 crouch to him for a piece of silver and a
9. 8 the fourth part of a shekel of silver
2 Sa. 8. 10 (Joram) brought with him vessels of silver
8. 11 with the silver and gold that he had dedi.
18. 11 I would have given thee ten (shekels) of s.
18. 12 a thousand (shekels) of silver in mine hand
21. 4 We will have no silver nor gold of Saul
24. 24 bought..the oxen for fifty shekels of sil.
1 Ki. 7. 51 the silver, and the gold, and the vessels
10. 21 none (were of) silver: it was nothing acco.
10. 22 bringing gold, and silver, ivory, and apes
10. 25 vessels of silver, and vessels of gold, and
10. 27 the king made silver (to be) in Jerusalem
10. 29 came..for six hundred (shekels) of silver
15. 15 he brought..silver, and gold, and vessels
15. 18 Asa took all the silver and the gold (that)
15. 19 I have sent unto thee a present of silver
16. 24 bought the hill..for two talents of silver
20. 3 Thy silver and thy gold (is) mine; thy wives
20. 5 Thou shalt deliver me thy silver, and thy
20. 7 he sent unto me for..my silver, and for my
20. 39 or else thou shalt pay a talent of silver
2 Ki. 5. 5 took with him ten talents of silver, and
5. 22 give them, I pray thee, a talent of silver
5. 23 bound two talents of silver in two bags
6. 25 an ass's head..fourscore (pieces) of silver
6. 25 cab of dove's dung for five (pieces) of sil.
7. 8 carried thence silver, and gold, and raim.
12. 13 bowls of silver, snuffers, basins, trumpets
12. 13 any vessels of gold, or vessels of silver, of
14. 14 he took all the gold and silver, and all the
15. 19 gave Pul a thousand talents of silver, that
15. 20 of each man fifty shekels of silver, to give
16. 8 Ahaz took the silver and gold (that was)
18. 14 three hundred talents of silver, and thirty
18. 15 Hezekiah gave (him) all the silver (that
20. 13 the silver, and the gold, and the spices
22. 4 that he may sum the silver which is bro.
23. 33 a tribute of an hundred talents of silver
23. 35 Jehoiakim gave the silver and the gold to
23. 35 he exacted the silver and the gold of the
25. 15 such things as (were)..of silver, (in) silver
1 Ch 18. 10 all manner of vessels of gold and silver and
18. 11 with the silver and the gold that he brou.
19. 6 sent a thousand talents of silver to hire
22. 14 and a thousand thousand talents of silver
22. 16 Of the gold, the silver, and the brass, and
28. 14 all instruments of silver by weight, for all
28. 15 for the candlesticks of silver by weight
28. 16 and (likewise) silver for the tables of sil.
28. 17 and..by weight for every basin of silver
29. 2 the silver for (things) of silver, and the br.
29. 3 of gold and silver, (which) I have given to
29. 4 seven thousand talents of refined silver, to
29. 5 the silver for (things) of silver, and for all
29. 7 of silver ten thousand talents, and of br.
2 Ch. 1. 15 the king made silver and gold at Jerusa.
1. 17 a chariot for six hundred (shekels) of sil.
2. 7, 14 to work in gold, and in silver, and in
5. 1 the silver, and the gold, and all the inst.
9. 14 governors..brought gold and silver to S.
9. 20 none (were of) silver; it was (not) any th.
9. 21 bringing gold, and silver, ivory, and apes
9. 24 vessels of silver, and vessels of gold, and
9. 27 the king made silver in Jerusalem as sto.
15. 18 that he himself had dedicated, silver, and
16. 2 Asa brought out silver and gold out of the
16. 3 I have sent thee silver and gold; go break
17. 11 the Philistines brought..tribute silver
21. 3 their father gave them great gifts of silver
24. 14 and spoons, and vessels of gold and silver
25. 6 hired..for an hundred talents of silver
25. 24 (he took) all the gold and the silver, and
27. 5 an hundred talents of silver, and ten tho
32. 27 he made himself treasuries for silver, and
36. 3 in an hundred talents of silver and a tal.
Ezra 1. 4 let the men of his place help him with sil.
1. 6 with vessels of silver, with gold, with go.
1. 9 a thousand chargers of silver, nine and tw.
1. 10 silver basins of a second (sort) four hun.
1. 11 All the vessels of gold and of silver (were)
2. 69 five thousand pound of silver, and one hu.
8. 25 weighed unto them the silver and the go.
8. 26 fifty talents of silver, and silver vessels an
8. 28 the silver and the gold (are) a free will off.
8. 30 the weight of the silver, and the gold, and
8. 33 on the fourth day was the silver and the
Neh. 5. 15 and wine, besides forty shekels of silver
7. 71 thousand and two hundred pound of sil.
7. 72 two thousand pound of silver, and three.
Esth. 1. 6 cords of fine linen and purple to silver ri.
1. 6 the beds (were of) gold and silver, upon a
3. 9 I will pay ten thousand talents of silver
3. 11 The silver (is) given to thee, the people
Job 3. 15 princes..who filled their houses with sil.
22. 25 and thou shalt have plenty of silver
27. 16 Though he heap up silver as the dust, and
27. 17 and the innocent shall divide the silver
28. 1 there is a vein for the silver, and a place
28. 15 neither shall silver be weighed (for) the
Psa. 12. 6 (as) silver tried in a furnace of earth, pu.
66. 10 thou..hast tried us, as silver is tried
68. 13 (as) the wings of a dove covered with sil.
68. 30 one) submit himself with pieces of silver
105. 37 He brought them forth also with silver
115. 4 Their idols (are) silver and gold, the work
119. 72 better..than thousands of gold and silver

Psa.135. 15 The idols of the heathen (are) silver and
Prov. 2. 4 If thou seekest her as silver, and search.
3. 14 (is) better than the merchandise of silver
8. 10 Receive my instruction, and not silver
8. 19 gold; and my revenue than choice silver
10. 20 The tongue of the just (is as) choice silver
16. 16 and to get understanding..than silver
17. 3 The fining pot (is) for silver, and the fur.
22. 1 loving favour rather than silver and gold
25. 4 Take away the dross from the silver, and
25. 11 (is like) apples of gold in pictures of silver
26. 23 (are like) a potsherd covered with silver
27. 21 (As) the fining pot for silver, and the fu.
Eccl. 2. 8 I gathered me also silver and gold, and
5. 10 silver shall not be satisfied with silver
12. 6 Or ever the silver cord be loosed, or the
Song 1. 11 make..borders of gold, with studs of silver
3. 10 He made the pillars thereof (of) silver, the
8. 9 we will build upon her a palace of silver
8. 11 was to bring a thousand (pieces) of silver
Isa. 1. 22 Thy silver is become dross, thy wine mi.
2. 7 Their land also is full of silver and gold
2. 20 a man shall cast his idols of silver, and his
7. 23 a thousand vines at a thousand silverlings
13. 17 the Medes..which shall not regard silver
30. 22 the covering of thy graven images of silver
31. 7 shall cast away his idols of silver, and his
39. 2 the silver, and the gold, and the spices, and
40. 19 and the goldsmith..casteth silver chains
46. 6 weigh silver in the balance, (and) hire a
48. 10 I have refined thee, but not with silver
60. 9 to bring thy sons from far, their silver and
60. 17 for iron I will bring silver, and for wood
Jer. 6. 30 Reprobate silver shall (men) call them, be.
10. 4 They deck it with silver and with gold; th.
10. 9 Silver spread into plates is brought from
32. 9 the money, (even) seventeen shekels of sil.
52. 19 (that) which (was) of silver (in) silver, took
Eze. 7. 19 They shall cast their silver in the streets
7. 19 their silver and their gold shall not be able
16. 13 Thus wast thou decked with gold and sil.
16. 17 fair jewels of my gold and of my silver, w.
22. 18 all they..are (even) the dross of silver
22. 20 they gather silver, and brass, and iron, and
22. 22 As silver is melted in the midst of the fu.
27. 12 with silver, iron, tin, and lead, they tra.
28. 4 hast gotten gold and silver into thy trea
38. 13 to carry away silver and gold, to take away
Dan. 11. 8 their precious vessels of silver and of gold
11. 38 shall he honour with gold, and silver, and
11. 43 over the treasures of gold and of silver
Hos. 2. 8 multiplied her silver and gold, (which)
3. 2 bought her to me for fifteen (pieces) of s.
8. 4 of their silver and their gold have they
9. 6 the pleasant (places) for their silver, net.
13. 2 made them molten images of their silver
Joel 3. 5 ye have taken my silver and my gold, and
Amos 2. 6 they sold the righteous for silver, and the
8. 6 That we may buy the poor for silver, and
Nah. 2. 9 Take ye the spoil of silver, take the spoil
Hab. 2. 19 it (is) laid over with gold and silver, and
Zeph 1. 11 all they that bear silver are cut off
1. 18 their silver nor their gold shall be able to
Hag. 2. 8 The silver (is) mine, and the gold (is) mine
Zech 6. 11 take silver and gold, and make crowns
9. 3 heaped up silver as the dust, and fine go.
11. 12 weighed for my price thirty (pieces) of si.
11. 13 I took the thirty (pieces) of silver, and ca.
13. 9 will refine them as silver is refined, and
14. 14 gold, and silver, and apparel, in great ab.
Mal. 3. 3 shall sit (as) a refiner and purifier of sil.
3. 3 purge them as gold and silver, that they

2. *Silver, silverling,* כֶּסֶף *kesaph.*
Ezra 5. 14 the vessels also of gold and silver of the
6. 5 let the golden and silver vessels of the ho.
7. 15 to carry the silver and gold, which the
7. 16 the silver and gold that thou canst find
7. 18 to do with the rest of the silver and the
7. 22 Unto an hundred talents of silver, and
Dan. 2. 32 his breast and his arms of silver, his belly
2. 35 the clay, the brass, the silver, and the go.
2. 45 the brass, the clay, the silver, and the go.
5. 2 to bring the golden and silver vessels wh.
5. 4 praised the gods of gold, and of silver, of
5. 23 thou hast praised the gods of silver, and

3. *A qesitah, a lamb,* קְשִׂיטָה *qesitah.*
Josh.24. 32 bought..for an hundred pieces of silver

4. *Made of silver,* ἀργύρεος *argureos.*
Acts 19. 24 a silversmith, which made silver shrines
2 Ti. 2. 20 not only vessels of gold and of silver, but
Rev. 9. 20 idols of gold, and silver, and brass, and

5. *Silver, money,* ἀργύριον *argurion.*
Matt 26. 15 covenanted..for thirty pieces of silver
27. 3 brought again the thirty pieces of silver
27. 5 he cast down the pieces of silver in the
27. 6 the chief priests took the silver pieces
27. 9 they took the thirty pieces of silver, the
Acts 3. 6 Silver and gold have I none; but such as
19. 19 and found (it) fifty thousand (pieces) of sil.
20. 33 I have coveted no man's silver, or gold, or
1 Pet 1. 18 with corruptible things, (as) silver, and go.

6. *Silver,* ἄργυρος *arguros.*
Matt 10. 9 Provide neither gold, nor silver, nor brass
Acts 17. 29 silver, or stone, graven by art and man's
1 Co. 3. 12 if any man build..gold, silver, precious
Jas. 5. 3 Your gold and silver is cankered; and
Rev. 18. 12 The merchandise of gold, and silver, and

SILVERSMITH —
A worker in silver, ἀργυροκόπος *argurokopos.*
Acts 19. 24 certain (man) named Demetrius, a silver.

SIM'-E-ON, שִׁמְעוֹן *hearing,* Συμεών.
1. The second son of Jacob by Leah. B.C. 1720.
Gen. 29. 33 bare a son..and she called his name S.
34. 25 S. and Levi, Dinah's brethren, took each
34. 30 Jacob said to S. and Levi, Ye have trou.
35. 23 The sons of Leah..S., and Levi, and Judah
42. 24 took from them S., and bound him before
42. 36 Joseph (is) not, and S. (is) not, and ye will
43. 23 And he brought S. out unto them
46. 10 And the sons of S.; Jemuel, and Jamin
48. 5 as Reuben and S., they shall be mine
49. 5 S. and Levi (are) brethren; instruments
Exod. 1. 2 Reuben, S., Levi, and Judah
6. 15 the sons of S.; Jemuel, and Jamin, and
6. 15 these (are) the families of S.

2. His posterity and their land.
Num 1. 6 Of S.; Shelumiel the son of Zurishaddai
1. 22 Of the children of S., by their generations
1. 23 of the tribe of S., (were) fifty and nine th.
2. 12 those which pitch by him (shall be)..S.
2. 12 the captain of the children of S. (shall
7. 36 Shelumiel..prince of the children of S.
10. 19 host of the tribe of the children of S.
13. 5 Of the tribe of S., Shaphat the son of Ho.
26. 12 The sons of S. after their families: of N.
34. 20 of the tribe of the children of S., Shemu.
Deut 27. 12 S., and Levi, and Judah, and Issachar, and
Josh.19. 1 the second lot came forth to S.
19. 1 (even) for the tribe of the children of S.
19. 8 This (is) the inheritance..of S. according
19. 9 (was) the inheritance of the children of S.
19. 9 the children of S. had their inheritance
21. 4 out of the tribe of S., and out of the tribe
21. 9 out of the tribe of the children of S., th.
Judg 1. 3 Judah said unto S. his brother, Come up
1. 3 and I likewise will go..So S. went with
1. 17 Judah went with S. his brother, and they
1 Ch. 2. 1 Reuben, S., Levi, and Judah, Issachar
4. 24 The sons of S. (were) Nemuel, and Jam.
4. 42 the sons of S., five hundred men, went to
6. 65 and out of the tribe of the children of S.
12. 25 Of the children of S., mighty men of va.
2 Ch. 15. 9 And he gathered..the strangers..out of S.
34. 6 cities of Manasseh, and Ephraim, and S.
Eze. 48. 24 by the border of Benjamin..S. (shall ha.)
48. 25 by the border of S., from the east side un.
48. 33 one gate of S., one gate of Issachar, one
Rev. 7. 7 Of the tribe of S. (were) sealed twelve th.

The following localities were in the territory of Simeon: Ain, Ashan, Azem, Baalah, Balah, Beth-birei, Beth-lebaoth, Beth-marcaboth, Bethuel, Bilhah, Chorashan, Eltolad, En-rimmon, Ether, Hazar-shual, Hazar-susah, Hormah, Moladah, Ramah, Sharuhen, Tochen, Tola, &c.

3. A just and devout man in Jerusalem, waiting for the consolation of Israel, who saw and blessed the child Jesus in the temple.
Luke 2. 25 a man in Jerusalem, whose name (was) S.
2. 34 S. blessed them, and said unto Mary his

4. An ancestor of Jesus.
Luke 3. 30 Which was (the son) of S., which was (the

5. A disciple and prophet at Antioch, and surnamed *Niger.*
Acts 13. 1 as Barnabas, and S. that was called Niger

6. The original name of a son of Jonas (or John), and brother of Andrew an apostle of Christ. See *Simon.*
Acts 15. 14 S. hath declared how God at the first did

SIMEONITES, שִׁמְעֹנִי.
The descendants of No. 1 above.
Num 25. 14 a prince of a chief house among the S.
26. 14 These (are) the families of the S., twenty
1 Ch.27. 16 of the S.; Shephatiah the son of Maachah

SIMILITUDE —
1. *Likeness,* דְּמוּת *demuth.*
2 Ch. 4. 3 under it (was) the similitude of oxen, wh.
Dan. 10. 16 (one) like the similitude of the sons of men

2. *Pattern, form, building,* תַּבְנִית *tabnith.*
Psa.106. 20 changed their glory into the similitude of
144. 12 polished (after) the similitude of a palace

3. *Form, similitude, likeness,* תְּמוּנָה *temunah.*
Num 12. 8 the similitude of the LORD shall he behold
Deut. 4. 12 heard the voice..but saw no similitude
4. 15 for ye saw no manner of similitude on the
4. 16 make you..the similitude of any figure

4. *Likeness,* ὁμοιότης *homoiotes.*
Heb. 7. 15 for that after the similitude of Melchise.

5. *Likeness,* ὁμοίωμα *homoiōma.*
Rom. 5. 14 that had not sinned after the similitude

6. *Likeness,* ὁμοίωσις *homoiōsis.*
Jas. 3. 9 men, which are made after the similitude

SIMILITUDES, to use —
To liken, compare, use similitudes, דָּמָה *damah,* 3.
Hos. 12. 10 used similitudes, by the ministry of the

SI'-MON, Σίμων *hearing.*
1. An early disciple and apostle of Jesus Christ; he was the son of Jonas (or John), and brother of Andrew, a fisherman at Bethsaida by the sea of Galilee. He was also surnamed *Peter, i.e.* a "stone," and *Cephas,* its equivalent in Syriac.
Matt.4. 18 S. called Peter, and Andrew his brother
10. 2 The first, S., who is called Peter, and An.
16. 16 S. Peter answered and said, Thou art the
16. 17 Blessed art thou, S. Bar-jona: for flesh and
17. 25 What thinkest thou, S.? of whom do the
Mark 1. 16 he saw S., and Andrew his brother casti.
1. 29 they entered into the house of S. and An.
1. 30 S.'s wife's mother lay sick of a fever, and
1. 36 S. and they that were with him followed
3. 16 And S. he surnamed Peter
14. 37 S., sleepest thou? couldest not thou wa.
Luke 4. 38 entered into S.'s house. And S.'s wife's
5. 3 entered..one of the ships, which was S.'s
5. 4 he said unto S., Launch out into the deep
5. 5 S. answering said unto him, Master, we
5. 8 When S. Peter saw (it), he fell down at
5. 10 partners with S. And Jesus said unto S.
6. 14 S., (whom he also named Peter), and An.
22. 31 the Lord said, S., S., behold, Satan hath
24. 34 The Lord is risen..and hath appeared to S.
John 1. 40 One of the two..was Andrew, S. Peter's
1. 41 He first findeth his own brother S., and
1. 42 Thou art S. the son of Jona: thou shalt
6. 8 Andrew, S. Peter's brother, saith unto him
6. 68 S. Peter answered him, Lord, to whom
13. 6 Then cometh he to S. Peter: and Peter
13. 9 S. Peter saith unto him, Lord, not my fe.
13. 24 S. Peter therefore beckoned to him, that
13. 36 S. Peter said unto him, Lord, whither go.
18. 10 S. Peter having a sword drew it, and sm.
18. 15 S. Peter followed Jesus, and (so did) an.
18. 25 S. Peter stood and warmed himself. 20. 2
20. 6 Then cometh S. Peter following him, and
21. 2 There were together S. Peter, and Thom.
21. 3 S. Peter saith unto them, I go a fishing
21. 7 when S. Peter heard that it was the Lord
21. 11 S. Peter went up, and drew the net to la.
21. 15 Jesus saith to S. Peter, S., (son) of Jonas
21. 16, 17 He saith..S., (son) of Jonas, lovest th.
Acts 10. 5 send men to Joppa, and call for (one) S.
10. 18 asked whether S., which was surnamed P.
10. 32 and call hither S., whose surname is Peter
11. 13 Send men to Joppa, and call for S., whose
2 Pe. 1. 1 [S.] Peter, a servant and an apostle of Jesus

2. Another of the twelve apostles, called the "Canaanite," from being a native of Cana in Galilee, or rather from the Hebrew *canna,* "zealous;" in Greek, *Zelotes.*
Matt 10. 4 S. the Canaanite, and Judas Iscariot, who
Mark 3. 18 James..and Thaddeus, and S. the Canaa.
Luke 6. 15 James the (son) of Alpheus, and S. called
Acts 1. 13 and S. Zelotes, and Judas (the brother) of

3. One of the brethren of our Lord.
Matt 13. 55 his brethren, James, and Joses, and S., and
Mark 6. 3 of James, and Joses, and of Juda, and S.?

4. A person in Bethany, a leper, in whose house the head of Jesus was anointed with oil.
Matt 26. 6 Jesus was in Bethany, in the house of S.
Mark 14. 3 being in Bethany, in the house of S. the

5. A Cyrenian who was compelled to bear the cross after Jesus.
Matt 27. 32 they found a man of Cyrene, S. by name
Mark 15. 21 they compel one S. a Cyrenian, who pas.
Luke 23. 26 they laid hold upon one S., a Cyrenian

6. A Pharisee, in whose house the feet of Jesus were washed with tears and anointed with ointment.
Luke 7. 40 S., I have somewhat to say unto thee. A.
7. 43 S. answered and said, I suppose that (he)
7. 44 he turned to the woman, and said unto S.

7. The father of Judas Iscariot.
John 6. 71 He spake of Judas Iscariot (the son) of S.
12. 4 Judas Iscariot, S.'s (son), which should
13. 2 put into the heart of Judas Iscariot, S.'s
13. 26 gave (it) to Judas Iscariot, (the son) of S.

8. A sorcerer in Samaria, who sought to purchase the gifts of the Spirit from the apostles with money.
Acts 8. 9 there was a certain man called S., which
8. 13 S. himself believed also: and when he was
8. 18 when S. saw that through laying on of the
8. 24 Then answered S., and said, Pray ye to the

9. A tanner at Joppa, with whom Simon Peter lodged when sent for by Cornelius the centurion at Cæsarea.
Acts 9. 43 tarried many days in Joppa with one S.
10. 6 He lodgeth with one S. a tanner, whose
10. 17 Cornelius had made enquiry for S.'s house
10. 32 he is lodged in the house of (one) S. a ta.

SIMPLE (one), simplicity —
1. *Simple,* פֶּתִי *pethi.*
Psa. 19. 7 testimony..(is) sure, making wise the si.
116. 6 LORD preserveth the simple: I was brou.
119. 130 it giveth understanding unto the simple
Prov. 1. 4 To give subtilty to the simple, to the yo.
1. 22 How long, ye simple ones, will ye love si.?
1. 32 For the turning away of the simple shall
7. 7 beheld among the simple ones, I discern.
8. 5 O ye simple, understand wisdom; and, ye
9. 4, 16 Whoso (is) simple, let him turn in hither
14. 15 The simple believeth every word: but the
14. 18 The simple inherit folly: but the prude.
19. 25 Smite a scorner, and the simple will be.
21. 11 When the scorner is punished, the simple
22. 3 but the simple pass on, and are punished
27. 12 (but) the simple pass on, (and) are punis.
Eze. 45. 20 so shalt thou do..for (him that is) simple

2. *Simplicity, simple one,* פְּתַיּוּת *pethayyuth.*
Prov. 9. 13 foolish woman (is) clamorous; (she is) si.

3. *Integrity, simplicity,* תֹּם *tom.*
2 Sa. 15. 11 they went in their simplicity, and they
4. *Harmless, without evil,* ἄκακος *akakos.*
Rom 16. 18 fair speeches deceive the hearts of the s.
5. *Harmless, without horns,* ἀκέραιος *akeraios.*
Rom 16. 19 that which is good, and simple concern.
6. *Simplicity,* ἁπλότης *haplotēs.*
Rom 12. 8 he that giveth, (let him do it) with simpl.
2 Co. 1. 12 that in [simplicity] and godly sincer., 11.3.
SIMRI. *See* **SHIMRI.**
SIN, סִין *cliff, place.*
1 A desert between Elim and Sinai on the E. of the g f of Suez.
Exod 16. 1 Israel came unto the wilderness of S., wh.
17. 1 Israel journeyed from the wilderness of S.
Num 33. 11 And they..encamped in the wilderness..S.
33. 12 their journey out of the wilderness of S.
2. The most easterly border of Egypt, usually called *Pelusium, i.e.,* marsh town.
Eze. 30. 15 I will pour my fury upon S, the strength of
30. 16 S. shall have great pain, and No shall be
SIN —
1. *Guilt, guilt offering,* אָשָׁם *asham.*
Prov 14. 9 Fools make a mock at sin: but among the
Isa. 53. 10 shalt make his soul an offering for sin, he
Jer. 51. 5 though their land was filled with sin aga.
2. *Guilt, guilt offering,* אַשְׁמָה *ashmah.*
Lev. 4. 3 according to the sin of the people; then
2 Ch. 28. 10 even with you, sins against the LORD yo.
Psa. 69. 5 and my sins are not hid from thee
Amos 8. 14 They that swear by the sin of Samaria, and
3. *Sin, error, failure,* חֵטְא *chet.*
Lev. 19 17 rebuke thy neighbour, and not suffer sin
20. 20 shall bear their sin; they shall die child
22. 9 lest they bear sin for it, and die therefo.
24. 15 Whosoever curseth..God shall bear his sin
Num. 9. 13 forbeareth..that man shall bear his sin
18. 22 Neither..come nigh..lest they bear sin
18 32 ye shall bear no sin by reason of it, when
27. 3 but died in his own sin, and had no sons
Deut 15. 9 cry unto the LORD..and it be sin unto th.
19. 15 not rise up against a man..in any sin th.
21. 22 if a man have committed a sin worthy of
22. 26 (there is) in the damsel no sin (worthy) of
23. 21 require it of thee; and it would be sin in
23. 22 if thou shalt forbear..it shall be no sin in
24. 15 lest he cry against..and it be sin unto th
24. 16 man shall be put to death for his own sin
2 Ki. 10. 29 Howbeit (from) the sins of Jeroboam the
14. 6 man shall be put to death for his own sin
2 Ch. 25. 4 but every man shall die for his own sin
Psa. 51. 5 and in sin did my mother conceive me
51. 9 Hide thy face from my sins, and blot out
103. 10 He hath not dealt with us after our sins
Isa. 1. 18 Though your sins be as scarlet they sha.
31. 7 own hands have made unto you (for) a sin
38. 17 thou hast cast all my sins behind thy ba.
53 12 bare the sin of many, and made interces.
Eze. 23. 49 ye shall bear the sins of your idols; and
Dan 9 16 because for our sins, and for the iniquit.
Hos. 12 8 find none iniquity in me that (were) sin
4. *Sin,* חֲטָאָה *chataah.*
Gen. 20. 9 brought..on my kingdom a great sin? th.
Exod 32. 21 that thou hast brought so great a sin up.
32. 30 Ye have sinned a great sin..and now I
32. 31 Oh, this people have sinned a great sin
2 Ki. 17. 21 Jeroboam..made them sin a great sin
Psa. 32 1 Blessed (is he whose)..sin (is) covered
109. 7 condemned; and let his prayer become s.
5. *Sin,* חַטָּאָה *chattaah.*
Exod 34. 7 forgiving iniquity..and sin, and that wi.
Isa. 5. 18 Woe unto them that draw..sin as it were
6. *Sin, sin offering,* חַטָּאת *chattath.*
Gen. 4 7 if thou doest not well, sin lieth at the d.
18 20 and because their sin is very grievous
31. 36 what (is) my sin, that thou hast so hotly
50. 17 trespass of thy brethren, and their sin
Exod 10. 17 forgive, I pray thee, my sin only this on.
32. 30 I shall make an atonement for your sin
32. 32 Yet now, if thou wilt forgive their sin
32. 34 when I visit I will visit their sin upon th.
34. 9 pardon our iniquity and our sin, and take
Lev. 4. 3 then let him bring for his sin, which he
4. 14 When the sin..is known, then the congr.
4. 14 shall offer a young bullock for the sin, and
4. 23, 28 Or if his sin..come to his knowledge
4. 26 make an atonement..as concerning his s.
4. 28 Or if his sin, which he hath sinned, come
4. 28 a female without blemish, for his sin wh.
4. 35 make an atonement for his sin that he h.
5. 6 offering unto the LORD for his sin which
5. 6 an atonement for him concerning his sin
5. 10 make an atonement for him for his sin
5. 13 atonement for him as touching his sin th.
16. 16, 21 transgressions in all their sins
16. 30 be clean from all your sins before the Lo.
16. 34 make an atonement..for all their sins, on.
19. 22 sin which he hath done: and the sin wh.
26. 18 punish you seven times more for your si.
26. 21 plagues upon you, according to your sins
26. 24 punish you yet seven times for your sins
26. 28 will chastise you seven times for your sins
Num. 5. 6 shall commit any sin that men commit
5. 7 they shall confess their sin which they ha.
12. 11 lay not the sin upon us, wherein we have
Num 16. 26 lest ye be consumed in all their sins
32. 23 and be sure your sin will find you out
Deut. 9. 18 because of all your sins, which ye sinned
9. 21 I took your sin, the calf which ye had ma.
9. 27 nor to their wickedness, nor to their sin
19. 15 not rise up against a man..for any sin..in
Josh 24. 19 forgive your transgressions nor your sins
1 Sa. 2. 17 the sin of the young men was very great
12. 19 we have added unto all our sins (this) evil
14. 38 see wherein this sin hath been this day
15. 23 rebellion (is as) the sin of witchcraft, and
15. 25 pardon my sin, and turn again with me
20. 1 what (is) my sin before thy father, that he
2 Sa. 12. 13 The LORD also hath put away thy sin; th.
1 Ki. 8. 34 forgive the sin of thy people Israel, and
8. 35 turn from their sin, when thou afflictest
8. 36 forgive the sin of thy servants, and of thy
12. 30 this thing became a sin: for the people
13. 34 this thing became sin unto the house of
14. 16 he shall give Israel up because of the sins
14. 22 provoked him to jealousy with their sins
15. 3 he walked in all the sins of his father, wh.
15 26, 34 and in his sin wherewith he made Is
15 30 Because of the sins of Jeroboam which he
16. 2 to provoke me to anger with their sins
16. 13 all the sins of Baasha, and the sins of E
16. 19 his sins which he sinned in doing evil in
16. 19 in his sin which he did, to make Israel to
16. 26 and in his sin wherewith he made Israel
16. 31 a light thing for him to walk in the sins
2 Ki. 3. 3 he cleaved unto the sins of Jeroboam the
10. 31 he departed not from the sins of Jeroboam
12. 16 The trespass money and sin money was not
13. 2 followed the sins of Jeroboam the son of
13. 6 they departed not from the sins of the ho.
13. 11 he departed not from all the sins of Jero.
14. 24 he departed not from all the sins of Jero.
15. 9, 24, 28 he departed not from the sins of J.
15. 18 he departed not all his days from the sins
17. 22 Israel walked in all the sins of Jeroboam
21. 16 besides his sin wherewith he made Judah
21. 17 all that he did, and his sins that he sinned
24. 3 for the sins of Manasseh, according to all
2 Ch. 6 25 forgive the sin of thy people Israel, and
6. 26 turn from their sin, when thou dost afflict
6. 27 forgive the sin of thy servants, and of thy
7. 14 will forgive their sin, and will heal their
28. 13 ye intend to add (more) to our sins and to
33. 19 his sins, and his trespass, and the places
Neh. 1. 6 confess the sins of the children of Israel
4. 5 let not their sin be blotted out from before
9. 2 confessed their sins, and the iniquities of
9. 37 thou hast set over us because of our sins
Job 10. 6 enquirest..and searchest after my sin
13. 23 How many (are) mine iniquities and sins?
13. 23 to know my transgression and my sin
14. 16 For now..dost thou not watch over my sin
34. 37 he addeth rebellion unto his sin; he cla
35. 3 What profit..(if I be cleansed) from my s ?
Psa. 25. 7 Remember not the sins of my youth, nor
25. 18 Look upon..my pains; and forgive all my s
32. 5 I acknowledged my sin unto thee, and mi.
32. 5 and thou forgavest the iniquity of my sin
38. 3 (any) rest in my bones because of my sin
38. 18 I will declare..I will be sorry for my sin
51. 2 Wash me..and cleanse me from my sin
51. 3 acknowledge my transgressions and my sin
59. 3 not (for) my transgression, nor (for) my s.
59 12 the sin of their mouth (and) the words of
79. 9 and purge away our sins, for thy name's
85. 2 hast forgiven..hast covered all their sin
109. 14 let not the sin of his mother be blotted out
Prov. 5. 22 shall be holden with the cords of his sins
10. 16 to life: the fruit of the wicked to sin
14. 34 Righteousness exalteth..but sin (is) a re.
20. 9 made my heart clean, I am pure from m.s.
21. 4 (and) the plowing of the wicked (is) sin
24. 9 The thought of foolishness (is) sin: and the
Isa. 3. 9 they declare their sin as Sodom, they hide
6. 7 iniquity is taken away, and thy sin purged
27. 9 this (is) all the fruit to take away his sin
30. 1 that cover..that they may add sin to sin
40. 2 hath received..double for all her sins
43. 24 thou hast made me to serve with thy sins
43. 25 I, (am) he that..will not remember thy si.
44. 22 I have blotted out..as a cloud, thy sins
58. 1 and show..the house of Jacob their sins
59. 2 your sins have hid (his) face from you, th.
59. 12 our sins testify against us: for our trans.
Jer. 5. 25 your sins have withholden good (things)
14. 10 will now remember..and visit their sins
15. 13 (that) for all thy sins, even in all thy bor.
16. 10 what (is) our sin that we have committed
16. 18 recompense their iniquity and their sin
17. 1 The sin of Judah (is) written with a pen of
17. 3 thy high places for sin, throughout all thy
18. 23 neither blot out their sin from thy sight
30 14 wounded thee..(because) thy sins were in.
30. 15 thy sins were increased, I have done these
31. 34 and I will remember their sin no more
36. 3 may forgive their iniquity and their sin
50. 20 the sins of Judah, and they shall not be
Lam. 4. 13 the sins of her prophets, (and) the iniqui.
4. 22 O daughter..he will discover thy sins
Eze. 3. 20 he shall die in his sin, and his righteous.
16. 51 Neither hath Samaria committed..thy sins
16. 52 bear thine own shame for thy sins that th.
18. 14 that seeth all his father's sins which he ha.
18. 21 if the wicked will turn from all his sins
18. 24 in his sin that he hath sinned, in them sh.
21. 24 so that in all your doings your sins do ap.
33. 10 If our transgressions and our sins (be) up.
Eze. 33. 14 if he turn from his sin, and do that which
33. 16 None of his sins that he hath committed
Dan. 9. 20 praying, and confessing my sin and the sin
9. 24 to make an end of sins, and to make rec.
Hos. 4. 8 They eat up the sin of my people, and th.
8. 13 now will he..visit their sins: they shall
9. 9 will remember..he will visit their sins
10. 8 The high places also of Aven, the sin of Is.
13. 12 The iniquity of Ephraim..his sin (is) hid
Amos 5. 12 For I know your..mighty sins: they aff
Mic. 1. 5 For the transgression..and for the sins of
1. 13 she (is) the beginning of the sin to the da
3. 8 his transgression, and to Israel his sin
6. 7 the fruit of my body (for) the sin of my so.
6. 13 making (thee) desolate because of thy sins
7. 19 thou wilt cast all their sins into the depths
Zech 13. 1 a fountain opened..for sin and for uncl.
7. *Sin,* חֲטָי *chatai.*
Dan. 4. 27 break off thy sins by righteousness, and
8. *Iniquity,* עָוֹן *avon.*
1 Ki 17. 18 art thou come unto me to call my sin to
9. *Trespass, transgression,* פֶּשַׁע *pesha.*
Prov 10. 12 stirreth up..but love covereth all sins
10. 19 multitude of words there wanteth not sin
28. 13 He that covereth his sins shall not prosper
10. *A sin, transgression,* ἁμάρτημα *hamartēma.*
Mark 3. 28 All sins shall be forgiven unto the sons of
4. 12 and [(their) sins] should be forgiven them
Rom. 3. 25 for the remission of sins that are past
1 Co. 6. 18 Every sin that a man doeth is without the
11. *Sin, error, sin offering,* ἁμαρτία *hamartia.*
Matt. 1. 21 for he shall save his people from their sins
3. 6 baptized of him..confessing their sins
9. 2 be of good cheer; thy sins be forgiven
9. 5 to say, (Thy) sins be forgiven thee; or to
9. 6 Son of man hath power..to forgive sins
12. 31 All manner of sin and blasphemy shall
26. 28 shed for many for the remission of sins
Mark 1. 4 of repentance for the remission of sins
1. 5 were all baptized..confessing their sins
2. 5 he said..Son, thy sins be forgiven thee
2. 7 who can forgive sins but God only?
2. 9 is it easier to say..(Thy) sins be forgiven
2. 10 Son of man hath power..to forgive sins
Luke 1. 77 knowledge..by the remission of their sins
3. 3 of repentance for the remission of sins
5. 20 he said unto him, Man, thy sins are for.
5. 21 Who can forgive sins but God alone?
5. 23 to say, Thy sins be forgiven thee; or to
5. 24 Son of man hath power..to forgive sins
7. 47 Her sins, which are many, are forgiven
7. 48 he said unto her, Thy sins are forgiven
7. 49 Who is this that forgiveth sins also?
11. 4 forgive us our sins; for we also forgive
24. 47 remission of sins should be preached in
John 1. 29 which taketh away the sin of the world
8. 21 shall seek me, and shall die in your sins
8. 24 that ye shall die in your sins: for if
8. 24 believe not..ye shall die in your sins
8. 34 committeth sin is the servant [of sin]
8. 46 Which of you convinceth me of sin? And
9. 34 Thou wast altogether born in sins, and do.
9. 41 If ye were blind, ye should have no sin
9. 41 We see; therefore your sin remaineth
15 22 If I had not come..they had not had sin
15. 22 but now they have no cloak for their sin
15. 24 they had not had sin: but now have they
16. 8 he will reprove the world of sin, and of
16 9 Of sin, because they believe not on me
19. 11 he that delivered..hath the greater sin
20. 23 Whose soever sins ye remit, they are re.
Acts 2. 38 be baptized..for the remission of sins
3. 19 that your sins may be blotted out, when
5 31 give repentance..and forgiveness of sins
7. 60 Lord, lay not this sin to their charge
10. 43 in him shall receive remission of sins
13. 38 preached unto you the forgiveness of sins
22. 16 wash away thy sins calling on the name
26. 18 that they may receive forgiveness of sins
Rom. 3. 9 proved both..that they are all under sin
3. 20 for by the law (is) the knowledge of sin
4. 7 Blessed (are) they..whose sins are covered
4. 8 to whom the Lord will not impute sin
5. 12 sin entered..the world, and death by sin
5. 13 sin was in the world: but sin is not imp.
5. 20 where sin abounded, grace did much more
5. 21 as sin hath reigned unto death, even so
6. 1 Shall we continue in sin, that grace may
6. 2 How shall we, that are dead to sin, live
6. 6 that the body of sin might be destroyed
6. 6 that henceforth we should not serve sin
6. 7 For he that is dead is freed from sin
6. 10 For in that he died, he died unto sin once
6. 11 to be dead indeed unto sin, but alive unto
6. 12 Let not sin therefore reign in your mortal
6. 13 instruments of unrighteousness unto sin
6. 14 sin shall not have dominion over you: for
6. 16 whether of sin unto death, or of obedience
6. 17 ye were the servants of sin, but ye have
6. 18 Being then made free from sin, ye became
6. 20 when ye were the servants of sin, ye were
6. 22 now being made free from sin, and become
6. 23 the wages of sin (is) death; but the gift of
7. 5 the motions of sins, which were by the law
7. 7 What shall we say then? (Is) the law sin?
7. 7 I had not known sin but by the law: for
7. 8, 11 sin, taking occasion by the command
7. 8 For without the law sin (was) dead

Rom. 7. 9 when the commandment came, sin revived
7. 13 sin that it might appear sin, working de.
7. 13 that sin by the commandment might be.
7. 14 spiritual: but I am carnal, sold under sin
7 17, 20 it is no more I that do it, but sin that
7. 23 to the law of sin which is in my members
7. 25 of God, but with the flesh the law of sin
8 2 hath made me free from the law of sin
8 3 and for sin, condemned sin in the flesh
8 10 the body (is) dead because of sin; but the
11. 27 covenant..when I shall take away their si.
14 23 for whatsoever (is) not of faith is sin
1 Co. 15. 3 Christ died for our sins according to the
15. 17 your faith (is) vain; ye are yet in your sins
15 56 (is) sin; and the strength of sin (is) the law
2 Co. 5. 21 made him (to be) sin for us, who knew no s
Gal. 1. 4 Who gave himself for our sins, that he mi.
2. 17 (is) therefore Christ the minister of sin?
3. 22 the Scripture hath concluded all under s.
Eph 2. 1 who were dead in trespasses and sins
Col. 1. 14 In whom we have..the forgiveness of sins
2. 11 in putting off the body [of the sins] of the
1 Th. 2. 16 might be saved, to fill up their sins alway
2 Th. 2. 3 that man of sin be revealed, the son of pe.
1 Ti. 5. 22 neither be partaker of other men's sins
5. 24 Some men's sins are open beforehand, go.
2 Ti. 3. 6 lead captive silly women laden with sins
Heb. 1. 3 when he had by himself purged our sins
2. 17 make reconciliation for the sins of the pe.
3. 13 hardened through the deceitfulness of sin
4. 15 tempted like as (we are, yet) without sin
5. 1 may offer both gifts and sacrifices for sins
5. 3 by reason hereof he ought..to offer for si.
7. 27 offer up sacrifice, first for his own sins
8. 12 sins and their iniquities will I remember
9. 26 hath he appeared to put away sin by the
9. 28 Christ was once offered to bear the sins
9. 28 appear the second time without sin unto
10. 2 should have had no more conscience of s.
10. 3 remembrance again (made) of sins every
10. 4 the blood..of goats should take away sins
10. 6 In burnt offerings and (sacrifices) for sin
10. 8 burnt offerings and (offering) for sin thou
10. 11 sacrifices, which can never take away si.
10. 12 after he had offered one sacrifice for sins
10. 17 their sins and iniquities will I remember
10. 18 where remission..no more offering for sin
10. 26 there remaineth no more sacrifice for sin
11. 25 than to enjoy the pleasures of sin for a se.
12. 1 let us lay aside..the sin which doth so ea.
12. 4 not yet resisted..striving against sin
13. 11 brought into the sanctuary..[for sin] are
Jas. 1. 15 bringeth forth sin; and sin, when it is fi.
2. 9 have respect to persons, ye commit sin
4. 17 knoweth..and doeth (it) not, to him it is s.
5. 15 if he have committed sins, they shall be
5. 20 death, and shall hide a multitude of sins
1 Pe. 2. 22 Who did no sin, neither was guile found
2. 24 bare our sins..that we, being dead to sins
3. 18 For Christ also hath once suffered for si.
4. 1 suffered in the flesh hath ceased from sin
4. 8 charity shall cover the multitude of sins
2 Pe. 1. 9 forgotten that he was purged from..[sins]
2. 14 cannot cease from sin; beguiling unstab.
1 Jo. 1. 7 blood of Jesus..cleanseth us from all sin
1. 8 If we say that we have no sin, we deceive
1. 9 If we confess our sins, he is faithful and
1. 9 forgive us (our) sins, and to cleanse us fr.
2. 2 he is the propitiation for our sins; and
2. 12 because your sins are forgiven you for his
3. 4 Whosoever committeth sin..for sin is the
3. 5 take away our sins; and in him is no sin
3. 8 He that committeth sin is of the devil
3. 9 born of God doth not commit sin; for his
4. 10 his Son (to be) the propitiation for..sins
5. 16 a sin (which is) not unto death, he shall
5. 16 There is a sin unto death: I do not say
5. 17 unrighteousness is sin: and there is a sin
Rev. 1. 5 and washed us from our sins in his own
18. 4 that ye be not partakers of her sins, and
18. 5 For her sins have reached unto heaven

12. *Fall, offence, trespass,* παράπτωμα *paraptōma.*
Eph. 1. 7 forgiveness of sins, according to the rich.
2. 5 Even when we were dead in sins, hath
Col. 2. 13 being dead in your sins, and the uncircu.
[*See also* Offer, offering, punishment, purification.]

SIN (already, heretofore, ignorantly), to —
1. *To sin, err, miss the mark,* חָטָא *chata.*
Gen. 20. 6 I also withheld thee from sinning against
39. 9 do this great wickedness, and sin against
42. 22 saying, Do not sin against the child; and
Exod. 9. 27 said unto them, I have sinned this time
9. 34 when Pharaoh saw..he sinned yet more
10. 16 I have sinned against the LORD your God
20. 20 may be before your faces, that ye sin not
32. 30 Ye have sinned..and now I will go up un.
32. 31 this people have sinned..and have made
32. 33 Whosoever hath sinned against me, him
Lev. 4. 2 If a soul shall sin through ignorance ag.
4. 3 If the priest that is anointed do sin acco.
4. 3 bring for his sin, which he hath sinned
4. 14 which they have sinned against it, is kn.
4. 22 When a ruler hath sinned, and done (so.)
4. 23 wherein he hath sinned, come to his kn.
4. 27 if any one of the common people sin thr.
4. 28 which he hath sinned, come to his know.
4. 28 offering..for his sin which he hath sinned
5. 1 if a soul sin, and hear the voice of swear.
5. 5 shall confess that he hath sinned in that
5. 6 offering..for his sin which he hath sinned

Lev. 5. 10 for his sin, which he hath sinned, and it
5. 11 then he that sinned shall bring for his of.
5. 13 as touching his sin that he hath sinned in
5. 15 If a soul commit a tresspass, and sin thr.
5. 17 if a soul sin, and commit any of these th.
6. 2 If a soul sin, and commit a trespass ag.
6. 3 all these that a man doeth, sinning ther.
6. 4 Then it shall be, because he hath sinned
Num. 6. 11 for that he sinned by the dead, and shall
12. 11 done foolishly, and wherein we have sin.
14. 40 Lo, we..will go up..for we have sinned
15. 27 if any soul sin through ignorance, then he
15. 28 when he sinneth by ignorance before the
16. 22 shall one man sin, and wilt thou be wroth
21. 7 We have sinned; for we have spoken ag.
22. 34 Balaam said..I have sinned; for I knew
32. 23 ye have sinned against the LORD: and be
Deut. 1. 41 We have sinned against the LORD, we will
9. 16 ye had sinned against the LORD your God
9. 18 ye sinned, in doing wickedly in the sight
19. 15 in any sin that he sinneth: at the mouth
20. 18 so should ye sin against the LORD your
Josh. 7. 11 Israel hath sinned, and they have also tr.
7. 20 Indeed I have sinned against the LORD
Judg 10. 10 We have sinned against thee both beca.
10. 15 We have sinned: do thou unto us what.
11. 27 Wherefore I have not sinned against thee
1 Sa. 2. 25 If one man sin..but if a man sin against
7. 6 said there, We have sinned against the L.
12. 10 We have sinned, because we have forsaken
12. 23 God forbid that I should sin against the L.
14. 33 people sin against the LORD, in that they
14. 34 sin not against the LORD in eating with
15. 24 said unto Samuel, I have sinned: for I ha.
15. 30 Then he said, I have sinned: (yet) honour
19. 4 Let not the king sin against his servant
19. 4 because he hath not sinned against thee
19. 5 wherefore then wilt thou sin against inn.
24. 11 have not sinned against thee; yet thou
26. 21 Then said Saul, I have sinned: return, my
2 Sa. 12 13 said unto Nathan, I have sinned against
19. 20 thy servant doth know that I have sinned
24. 10 have sinned greatly in that I have done
24. 17 have sinned, and I have done wickedly
1 Ki. 8. 33 because they have sinned against thee, and
8. 35 because they have sinned against thee: if
8. 46 sin against thee..no man that sinneth not
8. 47 We have sinned, and have done pervers.
8. 50 forgive thy people that have sinned aga.
14. 16 sins of Jeroboam, who did sin, and who
15. 30 sins of Jeroboam which he sinned, and
16. 13 sins of Elah his son, by which they sinned
16. 19 For his sins which he sinned in doing evil
18. 9 What have I sinned, that thou wouldest
2 Ki. 17. 7 children of Israel had sinned against the
21. 17 all that he did, and his sin that he sinned
1 Ch. 21. 8 I have sinned greatly because I have done
21. 17 even I it is that have sinned, and done ev.
2 Ch. 6. 22 If a man sin against his neighbour
6. 24, 26 because they have sinned against thee
6. 36 If they sin..for..no man which sinneth not
6. 37 We have sinned, we have done amiss, and
6. 39 forgive thy people which have sinned ag
Neh. 1. 6 sins..which we have sinned against thee
1. 6 both I and my father's house have sinned
6. 13 should be afraid, and do so, and sin, and
9. 29 sinned against thy judgments which if a
13. 26 Did not Solomon king of Israel sin by th
Job 1. 5 It may be that my sons have sinned, and
1. 22 In all this Job sinned not nor charged God
2. 10 In all this did not Job sin with his lips
5. 24 shalt visit thy habitation, and shalt not sin
7. 20 I have sinned: what shall I do unto thee
8. 4 If thy children have sinned against him
10. 14 If I sin, then thou markest me, and thou
24. 19 (so doth) the grave (those which) have si.
31. 30 Neither have I suffered my mouth to sin
33. 27 say, I have sinned, and perverted (that
35. 6 If thou sinnest, what doest thou against
Psa. 4. 4 Stand in awe, and sin not: commune with
39. 1 take heed..that I sin not with my tongue
41. 4 heal my soul; for I have sinned against th
51. 4 Against thee, thee only, have I sinned, and
78. 17 sinned yet more against him by provoking
78. 32 For all this they sinned still and believed
106. 6 We have sinned with our fathers, we have
119. 11 have I hid..that I might not sin against
Prov. 8. 36 But he that sinneth against me wrongeth
14. 21 He that despiseth his neighbour sinneth
19. 2 and he that hasteth with (his) feet sinneth
20. 2 provoketh him to anger sinneth (against)
Eccl. 7. 20 (there is) not a just man..that..sinneth
Isa. 42. 24 he against whom we have sinned? for they
43. 27 Thy first father hath sinned, and thy tea.
64. 5 thou art wroth; for we have sinned: in th.
Jer. 2. 35 because thou sayest, I have not sinned
3. 25 for we have sinned against the LORD our
8. 14 because we have sinned against the LORD
14. 7 backslidings are many; we have sinned
14. 20 We acknowledge..for we have sinned ag.
33. 8 whereby they have sinned against me; and
33. 8 their iniquities, whereby they have sinned
40. 3 ye have sinned against the LORD and have
44. 23 ye have sinned against the LORD and have
50. 7 they have sinned against the LORD, the
50. 14 for she hath sinned against the LORD
Lam. 1. 8 Jerusalem hath grievously sinned; there.
5. 7 Our fathers have sinned, (and) are not
5. 16 fallen..woe unto us, that we have sinned
Eze. 3. 21 the righteous sin not, and he doth not sin
14. 13 the land sinneth against me by trespassing
18. 4, 20 the soul that sinneth, it shall die

Eze. 18. 24 in his sin that he hath sinned, in them
28. 16 thou hast sinned: therefore I will cast
33. 12 (righteousness) in the day that he sinneth
37. 23 dwelling places, wherein they have sinned
Dan. 9. 5 We have sinned, and have committed in.
9. 8 because we have sinned against thee
9. 11 because we have sinned against him.
9. 15 we have sinned, we have done wickedly
Hos. 4 7 As they were increased, so they sinned a.
8. 11 altars to sin, altars shall be unto him to s.
10. 9 thou hast sinned from the days of Gibeah
13. 2 they sin more and more, and have made
Mic. 7. 9 because I have sinned against him, until
Hab. 2. 10 consulted shame..and hast sinned (agai.)
Zeph. 1. 17 because they have sinned against the Lo.

2. *To do, make,* עָשָׂה *asah.*
Num 15. 29 shall have one law for him that sinneth

3. *To err, go astray,* שָׁגַג *shagag.*
Num 15. 28 for the soul that sinneth ignorantly

4. *To err, go astray,* שָׁגָה *shagah.*
Lev. 4 13 if the whole congregation of Israel sin th.

5. *To sin, err, miss the mark,* ἁμαρτάνω *hamartanō.*
Matt 18. 21 how oft shall my brother sin against me
27. 4 I have sinned in that I have betrayed the
Luke 15. 18, 21 Father I have sinned against Heaven
John 5. 14 sin no more, lest a worse thing come unto
8. 11 [Neither do I condemn thee; go, and sin]
9. 2 who did sin, this man or his parents, that
9. 3 Neither hath this man sinned, nor his pa.
Rom. 2. 12 as many as have sinned without law shall
2. 12 as many as have sinned in the law shall be
3. 23 all have sinned, and come short of the
5. 12 upon all men, for that all have sinned
5. 14 over them that had not sinned after the
5. 16 not as (it was) by one [that sinned].
6. 15 shall we sin, because we are not under
1 Co. 6. 18 he that committeth fornication sinneth
7. 28 and if thou marry, thou hast not sinned
7. 28 and if a virgin marry, she hath not sinned
7. 36 let him do what he will he sinneth not
8. 12 when ye sin so..ye sin against Christ
15. 34 Awake to righteousness, and sin not; for
Eph 4. 26 Be ye angry, and sin not; let not the sun
1 Ti. 5. 20 Them that sin rebuke before all, that
Titus 3. 11 and sinneth, being condemned of himself
Heb. 3. 17 (was it) not with them that had sinned
10. 26 if we sin wilfully after that we have rec.
2 Pe. 2. 4 God spared not the angels that sinned
1 Jo. 1. 10 If we say that we have not sinned, we
2. 1 these things write I unto you, that ye sin
2. 1 if any man sin, we have an advocate with
3. 6 in him sinneth not: whosoever sinneth
3. 8 for the devil sinneth from the beginning
3. 9 he cannot sin, because he is born of God
5 16 If any man see his brother sin a sin (wh.
5. 16 he shall give him life for them that sin not
5. 18 whosoever is born of God sinneth not

6. *To sin beforehand or publicly,* προαμαρτάνω.
2 Co. 12. 21 I shall bewail many which have sinned
13 2 to them which heretofore have sinned

SIN, without —
Without sin, ἀναμάρτητος *anamartētos.*
John 8. 7 [He that is without sin among you, let him]

SIN, to cause, make to —
To cause to sin, חָטָא *chata,* 5.
Exod 23. 33 lest they make thee sin against me: for
Deut 24. 4 thou shalt not cause the land to sin, wh.
1 Ki. 14. 16 sins of Jeroboam..who made Israel to sin
15. 26, 34 his sin wherewith he made Israel to s.
15. 30 which he made Israel sin, by his provoc.
16. 2 hast made my people Israel to sin, to pr.
16. 13 by which they made Israel to sin, in pro.
16. 19 his sin which he did, to make Israel to s.
16. 26 his sin wherewith he made Israel to sin
21 22 wherewith thou hast..made Israel to sin
22 52 the son of Nebat, who made Israel to sin
2 Ki. 3 3 son of Nebat, which made Israel to sin
10 29 the son of Nebat, who made Israel to sin
10 31 sins of Jeroboam, which made Israel to sin
13. 2 son of Nebat, which made Israel to sin
13. 6 house of Jeroboam, who made Israel sin
13. 11 the son of Nebat, who made Israel sin
14. 24 the son of Nebat, who made Israel to sin
15. 9 18, 24 son of N., who made Israel to sin
15. 28 the son of Nebat, who made Israel to sin
17. 21 Jeroboam drave Israel..and made them s.
21. 11 hath made Judah also to sin with his id.
21. 16 his sin wherewith he made Judah to sin
23. 15 son of Nebat, who made Israel to sin, had
Neh. 13. 26 him did outlandish women cause to sin
Eccl. 5. 6 mouth to cause thy flesh to sin; neither s.
Jer. 32. 35 do this abomination, to cause Judah to sin

SIN offering —
1. *Sin offering,* חֲטָאָה *chataah.*
Psa. 40. 6 burnt offering and sin offering hast thou
2. *Sin offering,* חַטָּאָה *chattaah* [V.L. חטיא].
Ezra 6. 17 for a sin offering for all Israel, twelve
3. *Sin offering,* חַטָּאת *chattath.*
Exod. 29. 14 fire without the camp: it (is) a sin offer.
29. 36 offer every day a bullock (for) a sin offer.
30. 10 with the blood of the sin offering of ato.
Lev. 4. 3 bullock..unto the LORD for a sin offering
4. 8 the fat of the bullock for the sin offering
4. 20 did with the bullock for a sin offering, so

Lev. 4. 21 it (is) a sin offering for the congregation
4. 24 offering before the LORD: it (is) a sin off.
4. 25 shall take of the blood of the sin offering
4. 29, 33 hand upon the head of the sin offering
4. 29 sin offering in the place of the burnt off.
4. 32 if he bring a lamb for a sin offering, he sh.
4. 33 slay it for a sin offering in the place wh.
4. 34 shall take of the blood of the sin offering
5. 6 a kid of the goats, for a sin offering; and
5. 7 one for a sin offering, and the other for
5. 8 offer (that) which (is) for the sin offering
5. 9 sprinkle of the blood of the sin offering
5. 9, 11, 12 it (is) a sin offering
5. 11 an ephah of fine flour for a sin offering
6. 17 as (is) the sin offering, and as the trespass
6. 25 This (is) the law of the sin offering: In the
6. 25 shall the sin offering be killed before the
6. 30 no sin offering, whereof (any) of the blo.
7. 7 As the sin offering (is), so (is) the trespass
7. 37 This (is) the law..of the sin offering, and
8. 2 bullock for the sin offering, and two rams
8. 14 brought the bullock for the sin offering
8. 14 the head of the bullock for the sin offer.
9. 2 Take thee a young calf for a sin offering
9. 3 Take ye a kid of the goats for a sin offer.
9. 7 Go unto the altar, and offer thy sin offer.
9. 8 slew the calf of the sin offering which (was)
9. 10 the caul above the liver of the sin offer.
9. 15 took the goat, which (was) the sin offer.
9. 22 came down from offering of the sin offer.
10. 16 diligently sought the goat of the sin offe.
10. 17 Wherefore have ye not eaten the sin offe.
10. 19 this day have they offered their sin offeri.
10. 19 I had eaten the sin offering to day, should
12. 6 turtle dove, for a sin offering, unto the do.
12. 8 the other for a sin offering: and the priest
14. 13 where he shall kill the sin offering and the
14. 13 for as the sin offering (is) the priest's, (so
14. 19 priest shall offer the sin offering, and ma.
14. 22 one shall be a sin offering, and the other
14. 31 the one (for) a sin offering, and the other
15. 15 the one (for) a sin offering, and the other
15. 30 priest shall offer the one (for) a sin offer.
16. 3 with a young bullock for a sin offering, and
16. 5 two kids of the goats for a sin offering, and
16. 6 shall offer his bullock of the sin offering
16. 9 And Aaron shall..offer him (for) a sin off.
16. 11 shall bring the bullock of the sin offering
16. 11 kill the bullock of the sin offering which
16. 15 Then shall he kill the goat of the sin off.
16. 25 fat of the sin offering shall he burn upon
16. 27 sin offering, and the goat (for) the sin off.
23. 19 sacrifice one kid of the goats for a sin off
Num. 6. 11 priest shall offer the one for a sin offering
6. 14 one ewe lamb..for a sin offering, and one
6 16 offer his sin offering, and his burnt offeri.
7. 16 One kid of the goats for a sin offering
[So in verse 22, 28, 34, 40, 46, 52, 58, 64, 70, 76, 82]
7. 87 kids of the goats for sin offering twelve
8. 8 bullock shalt thou take for a sin offering
8. 12 thou shalt offer the one (for) a sin offering
15. 24 and one kid of the goats for a sin offering
15. 25 their sin offering before the LORD, for th.
15. 27 she goat of the first year for a sin offering
18. 9 every sin offering of theirs..which they
28 15 one kid of the goats for a sin offering un.
28. 22 one goat (for) a sin offering, to make an
29 5, 11 16, 19 25 kid of the goats (for) a sin o.
29 11 beside the sin offering of atonement, and
29 22, 28, 31, 34 38 one goat (for) a sin offering
2 Ch. 29. 21 they brought. seven he goats, for a sin off.
29. 23 (for) the sin offering before the king and
29. 24 burnt offering and the sin offering (should
Ezra 8. 35 twelve he goats (for) a sin offering: all (th.
Neh. 10. 33 for the sin offerings to make an atoneme.
Eze 40. 39 to slay thereon..the sin offering, and the
42. 13 the sin offering, and the trespass offering
43 19 shalt give..a young bullock for a sin off.
43. 21 take the bullock also of the sin offering
43. 22 shalt offer a kid..for a sin offering
43. 25 prepare every day a goat (for) a sin offer.
44. 27 he shall offer his sin offering, saith the L.
44. 29 and the sin offering, and the trespass off.
45. 17 he shall prepare the sin offering, and the
45. 19 shall take of the blood of the sin offering
45. 22 for all..a bullock (for) a sin offering
45. 23 a kid of the goats daily (for) a sin offering
45. 25 according to the sin offering, according to
46. 20 the trespass offering and the sin offering

SI'-NA, SI'-NAI, סִינַי *cliffs*, Σινᾶ.
A mountain between the gulfs of *Suez* and *Akaba*, with three large tops; the N.-Eastern one is called Horeb, and the S.-Western one St Catherine. The wilderness of Sinai is particularly the plain *Sebayeh* at the south of *Gebel Mousa*.
Exod 16. 1 wilderness .which (is) between Elim and S.
19. 1 came they (into) the wilderness of S.
19. 2 were come (to) the desert of S., and had
19. 11 the sight of..the people upon mount S.
19. 18 S. was altogether on a smoke, because the
19. 20 the LORD came down upon mount S., on
19. 23 The people cannot come up to mount S
24. 16 glory of the LORD abode upon mount S.
31. 18 of communing with him upon mount S.
34. 2 come up in the morning unto mount S.
34. 4 went up unto mount S., as the LORD had
34. 29 Moses came down from mount S with the
34 32 LORD had spoken with him in mount S.
Lev. 7. 38 the LORD commanded Moses in mount S.
7 38 their oblations unto the LORD, in..S
25. 1 the LORD spake unto Moses in mount S.
Lev. 26. 46 laws which the LORD made..in mount S.
27. 34 for the children of Israel in mount S.
Num. 1. 1 spake unto Moses in the wilderness of S.
1. 19 numbered them in the wilderness of S.
3. 1 the LORD spake with Moses in mount S.
3. 4 offered strange fire..in..wilderness of S.
3. 14 spake unto Moses in the wilderness of S.
9. 1 spake unto Moses in the wilderness of S.
9. 5 kept the passover..in the wilderness of S.
10. 12 their journeys out of the wilderness of S.
26. 64 numbered..Israel in the wilderness of S.
28. 6 which was ordained in mount S. for a sw.
33. 15 And they..pitched in the wilderness of S.
33. 16 And they removed from the desert of S.
Deut 33. 2 And he said, The LORD came from S., and
Judg. 5. 5 mountains melted..(even) that S. from bef.
Neh. 9. 13 Thou camest down also upon mount S.
Psa. 68. 8 S. itself (was moved) at the presence of
68. 17 the LORD (is) among them, (as) in S., in
Acts 7. 30 appeared..in the wilderness of mount S.
7. 38 which spake to him in the mount S., and
Gal. 4. 24 the one from the mount S., which gende.
4. 25 For this Agar is mount S. in Arabia, and

SINCE, even, that time —
1. *From then, from that time,* מֵאָז *me-az.*
Exod. 4. 10 neither heretofore, nor since thou hast sp.
Josh 14. 10 even since the LORD spake this word unto
Isa. 16. 13 spoken concerning Moab since that time
2. *After,* אַחַר *achar.*
Gen. 46. 30 let me die, since I have seen thy face, be.
3. *If,* אִם *im.*
Jer. 23. 38 since ye say, The burden of the LORD; the.
4. *That, since,* דַּי *dai.*
Jer. 20. 8 since I spake, I cried out, I cried violence
31. 20 for since I spake against him. I do earne.
48. 27 since thou spakest of him, thou skippedst
5. *From,* מִן *min.*
Exod 10. 6 since the day that they were upon the ea.
6. *Hitherto,* עַד הֵנָּה *ad henah.*
Gen. 44. 28 he is torn in pieces; and I saw him not si.
7. *That, because,* כִּי *ki.*
Josh. 2. 12 since I have showed you kindness, that ye
8. *From,* מִן *min.*
2 Ki. 21. 15 since the day their fathers came forth out
9. *Even from,* לְמִן *le-min.*
Exod. 9. 18 since the foundation thereof even until
10. *From,* מִן *min.*
Ezra 5. 16 since that time even until now hath it been
11. *Yet, still, again, while, any more,* עוֹד *od.*
Deut 34. 10 there arose not a prophet since in Israel
12. *From,* ἀπό (οὗ) *apo (hou)*
Matt 24. 21 since the beginning of the world to this
Luke 1. 70 which have been since the world began
7. 45 this woman since the time I came in hath
16. 16 since that time the kingdom of God is pr.
24. 21 to day is the third day since these things
Acts 3. 21 spoken by..his holy prophets since 24. 11.
Col. 1. 6 since the day ye heard (of it), and knew
1. 9 we also, since the day we heard (it), do
Heb. 9. 26 suffered since the foundation 2 Pe. 3. 4.
13. *Out of,* ἐκ *ek.*
John 9 32 Since the world began was it not heard
14. *If then, since then,* ἐπεί *epei.*
2 Co. 13. 3 Since ye seek a proof of Christ speaking
15. *Since then, truly,* ἐπειδή *epeidē.*
1 Co. 15. 21 since by man (came) death, by man (came)
16. *Into the midst of, after,* μετά (acc.) *meta.*
Heb. 7. 28 the word of the oath, which was since the
17. *So that,* ὡς *hōs.*
Mark 9. 21 How long is it ago since this came unto

SINCERE, sincerely, sincerity —
1. *Perfect, whole, complete, plain,* תָּמִים *tamim.*
Josh. 24. 14 and serve him in sincerity and in truth
Judg. 9. 16 if ye have done truly and sincerely, in that
9. 19 If ye then have dealt truly and sincerely
2. *Guileless,* ἄδολος *adolos.*
1 Pe. 2. 2 As new born babes desire the sincere mi.
3. *Purely,* ἁγνῶς *hagnōs.*
Phil. 1. 16 The one preach Christ..not sincerely, su.
4. *Incorruption,* ἀφθαρσία *aphtharsia.*
Eph. 6. 24 that love our Lord Jesus Christ in sinc.
Titus 2. 7 (showing) uncorruptness, gravity, [since.]
5. *Genuine, true,* γνήσιος *gnēsios.*
2 Co. 8. 8 and to prove the sincerity of your love
6. *Sincerity, unsullied brightness,* εἰλικρίνεια *eilik.*
1 Co. 5. 8 with the unleavened (bread) of sincerity
2 Co. 1. 12 in simplicity and godly sincerity, not wi.
2. 17 but as of sincerity, but as of God, in the
7. *Sincere, unsullied,* εἰλικρινής *eilikrinēs.*
Phil. 1. 10 that ye may be sincere and without offe.

SINEW —
1. *Sinew, nerve,* גִּיד *gid.*
Gen. 32. 32 the children of Israel eat not (of) the sinew
32. 32 the hollow of Jacob's thigh in the sinew
Job 10. 11 hast fenced me with bones and sinews
40. 17 the sinews of his stones are wrapped tog.
Isa. 48. 4 thy neck (is) an iron sinew, and thy brow
Eze. 37. 6 I will lay sinews upon you, and will bring
37. 8 the sinews and the flesh came up upon th.
2. *To flee, gnaw, wink,* עָרַק *araq.*
Job 30. 17 My bones are pierced..my sinews take no

SINFUL, sinner —
1. *To sin,* חָטָא *chata.*
Prov. 11. 31 much more the wicked and the sinner
13. 22 the wealth of the sinner (is) laid up for the
Eccl. 2. 26 to the sinner he giveth travail, to gather
7. 26 but the sinner shall be taken by her
8. 12 Though a sinner do evil an hundred times
9. 2 as (is) the good, so (is) the sinner; (and) he
9. 18 but one sinner destroyeth much good
Isa. 1. 4 Ah sinful nation, a people laden with in.
65. 20 the sinner, (being) an hundred years old
2. *Sinful, sinner, erring one,* חַטָּא *chatta.*
Gen 13. 13 men of Sodom (were) wicked and sinners
Num 16. 38 The censers of these sinners against their
32. 14 an increase of sinful men, to augment yet
1 Sa 15. 18 Go and utterly destroy the sinners the A.
Psa. 1. 1 nor standeth in the way of sinners, nor si.
1. 5 nor sinners in the congregation of the ri.
25. 8 therefore will he teach sinners in the way
26. 9 Gather not my soul with sinners, nor my
51. 13 and sinners shall be converted unto thee
104. 35 Let the sinners be consumed out of the
Prov. 1. 10 My son, if sinners entice thee, consent th.
13. 21 Evil pursueth sinners: but to the righte.
23. 17 Let not thine heart envy sinners: but (be
Isa. 1. 28 destruction..of the sinners (shall be) to.
13. 9 shall destroy the sinners thereof out of it
33. 14 sinners in Zion are afraid; fearfulness ha.
Amos 9. 10 All the sinners of my people shall die by
3. *Sin, error,* חַטָּאָה *chattaah.*
Amos 9. 8 eyes of the Lord GOD (are) upon the sin.
4. *Sin, error,* חַטָּאת *chattath.*
Prov 13. 6 but wickedness overthroweth the sinner
5. *Of sin, error,* ἁμαρτίας (gen.) *hamartias.*
Rom. 8. 3 his own Son in the likeness of sinful fle.
6. *Sinful, sinner, erring one,* ἁμαρτωλός *hamartōlos.*
Matt. 9. 10 many publicans and sinners came and sat
9. 11 Why eateth your Master with..sinners?
9. 13 not come to call the righteous, but sinners
11. 19 Behold..a friend of publicans and sinners
26. 45 is betrayed into the hands of sinners
Mark 2. 15 many publicans and sinners sat also toge.
2. 16 saw him eat with publicans and sinners
2. 16 and drinketh with publicans and sinners
2. 17 came not to call the righteous, but sinners
8. 38 in this adulterous and sinful generation
14. 41 is betrayed into the hands of sinners
Luke 5. 8 Depart from me; for I am a sinful man
5. 30 and drink with publicans and sinners
5. 32 came not to call the righteous, but sinners
6. 32 for sinners also love those that love them
6. 33 what thank have ye? for sinners also do
6. 34 sinners also lend to sinners, to receive as
7. 34 Behold..a friend of publicans and sinners
7. 37 a woman in the city, which was a sinner
7. 39 that toucheth him; for she is a sinner
13. 2 these Galileans were sinners above all the
15. 1 Then drew near..publicans and sinners for
15. 2 This man receiveth sinners, and eateth wi.
15. 7 joy shall be in heaven over one sinner th.
15. 10 There is joy..over one sinner that repen.
18. 13 saying, God be merciful to me a sinner
19. 7 to be guest with a man that is a sinner
24. 7 be delivered into the hands of sinful men
John 9. 16 How can a man that is a sinner do such
9. 24 we know that this man is a sinner
9. 25 Whether he be a sinner (or no), I know
9. 31 we know that God heareth not sinners: but
Rom 3. 7 why yet am I also judged as a sinner
5. 8 in that, while we were yet sinners, Christ
5. 19 For as by one..many were made sinners
7. 13 that sin..might become exceeding sinful
Gal. 2. 15 We (who are) Jews by nature, and not si.
2. 17 we ourselves also are found sinners, (is)
1 Ti. 1. 9 for sinners, for unholy and profane, for m.
1. 15 Jesus came into the world to save sinners
Heb. 7. 26 separate from sinners, and made higher
12. 3 that endured such contradiction of sinners
Jas. 4. 8 Cleanse (your) hands, (ye) sinners; and pu.
5. 20 he which converteth the sinner from the
1 Pe. 4. 18 where shall the ungodly and the sinner ap.
Jude 15 which ungodly sinners have spoken agai
7. *One owing, a debtor,* ὀφειλέτης *opheiletēs.*
Luke 13. 4 that they were sinners above all men that

SING (aloud, forth, out), to —
1. *To sing praise,* זָמַר *zamar,* 3.
Judg. 5. 3 I will sing (praise) to the LORD God of I.
Psa. 30. 4 Sing unto the LORD, O ye saints of his, and
33. 2 sing unto him with the psaltery (and) an
57. 9 I will sing unto thee among the nations
59. 17 Unto thee, O my strength, will I sing: for
66. 2 Sing forth the honour of his name; make
66. 4 shall sing unto thee; they shall sing (to)
71. 22 unto thee will I sing with the harp, O thou
71. 23 My lips shall greatly rejoice when I sing
98. 5 Sing unto the LORD with the harp; with
101. 1 of mercy..unto thee, O LORD, will I sing
Isa. 12. 5 Sing unto the LORD; for he hath done ex.
2. *To give forth the voice,* נָתַן קוֹל *nathan qol.*
Psa. 104. 12 the fowls..(which) sing among the bran.

3. *To answer, respond,* עָנָה *anah.*
Num21. 17 Spring up, O well; sing ye unto it
1 Sa. 21. 11 did they not sing one to another of him
29. 5 (Is) not this David, of whom they sang one
Psa.147. 7 Sing unto the LORD with thanksgiving
Hos. 2. 15 she shall sing there, as in the days of her

4. *To answer, respond,* עָנָה *anah,* 3.
Exod32. 18 (but) the noise of (them that) sing do I
Isa. 27. 2 In that day sing ye unto her, A vineyard

5. *Loud cry or singing,* רִנָּה *rinnah.*
2 Ch.20. 22 when they began to sing and to praise, the

6. *To sing or cry aloud,* רָנַן *ranan.*
Job 38. 7 When the morning stars sang together
Prov.29. 6 but the righteous doth sing and rejoice
Isa. 24. 14 they shall sing for the majesty of the Lo.
35. 6 Then shall..the tongue of the dumb sing
42. 11 let the inhabitants of the rock sing, let
44. 23 Sing, O ye heavens; for the LORD hath
49. 13 Sing, O heavens; and be joyful, O earth
54. 1 Sing, O barren, thou (that) didst not bear
65. 14 my servants shall sing for joy of heart, but
Jer. 31. 7 Sing with gladness for Jacob, and shout
Zeph. 3. 14 Sing, O daughter of Zion; shout, O Israel
Zech 2. 10 Sing and rejoice, O daughter of Zion: for

7. *To sing or cry aloud,* רָנַן *ranan,* 3.
1 Ch.16. 33 Then shall the trees of the wood sing out
Psa. 51. 14 my tongue shall sing aloud of thy
59. 16 I will sing aloud of thy mercy in the mo.
67. 4 O let the nations be glad, and sing for joy
95. 1 let us sing unto the LORD; let us make a
145. 7 They shall..sing of thy righteousness
149. 5 let them sing aloud upon their beds
Isa. 26. 19 Awake and sing, ye that dwell in dust
52. 8 with the voice together shall they sing
52. 9 sing together, ye waste places of Jerusa.
Jer. 31. 12 they shall come and sing in the height of
51. 48 all that (is) therein, shall sing for Babylon

8. *To cause to sing or cry aloud,* רָנַן *ranan,* 5.
Psa. 81. 1 Sing aloud unto God our strength: make

9. *To sing* (?), שׁוּר *shur* (probably error).
Eze. 27. 25 The ships of Tarshish did sing of thee in

10. *To sing,* שִׁיר *shir.*
Exod15. 1 Then sang Moses and the children of Isr.
15. 1 I will sing unto the LORD, for he hath tr.
15. 21 Sing ye to the LORD, for he hath triump.
Num21. 17 Then Israel sang this song, Spring up, O.
Judg 5. 1 Then sang Deborah and Barak the son of
5. 3 I, (even) I, will sing unto the LORD; I
1 Ki. 10. 12 harps also and psalteries for singers
1 Ch.16. 9 Sing unto him..talk ye of all his wondr.
16. 23 Sing unto the LORD, all the earth; show
Psa. 7. *title.* Shiggaion of David, which he sang unto
13. 6 will sing unto the LORD, because he hath
21. 13 Be thou exalted..(so) will we sing and pr.
27. 6 offer..sacrifices of joy; I will sing, yea, I
33. 3 Sing unto him a new song; play skilfully
57. 7 my heart is fixed; I will sing and give pr.
59. 16 But I will sing of thy power..for thou ha.
65. 13 covered..they shout for joy, they also sing
68. 4 Sing unto God..extol him that rideth upon
68. 32 Sing unto God, ye kingdoms of the earth
89. 1 will sing of the mercies of the LORD for
96. 1 O sing unto the LORD..sing unto the LORD
96. 2 Sing unto the LORD, bless his name; show
98. 1 O sing unto the LORD a new song; for he
101. 1 I will sing of mercy and judgment: unto
104. 33 I will sing unto the LORD as long as I live
105. 2 Sing unto him..talk ye of all his wondro.
106. 12 Then believed they his words; they sang
108. 1 I will sing and give praise, even with my
137. 3 (saying), Sing us (one) of the songs of Zion
137. 4 How shall we sing the LORD'S song in a st.
138. 5 Yea, they shall sing in the ways of the L.
144. 9 I will sing a new song unto thee, O God
149. 1 Sing unto the LORD a new song, (and) his
Prov 25. 20 he that singeth songs to an heavy heart
Isa. 5. 1 Now will I sing to my well beloved a song
42. 10 Sing unto the LORD a new song, (and) his
Jer. 20. 13 Sing unto the LORD, praise ye the LORD

11. *To sing,* שִׁיר *shir,* 3a.
Zeph.2. 14 (their) voice shall sing in the windows; de.

12. *A song,* שִׁירָה *shirah.*
Isa. 23. 15 after the end..shall Tyre sing as an harlot

13. *To sing an ode,* ᾄδω *adō.*
Eph. 5. 19 singing and making melody in your heart
Col. 3. 16 singing with grace in your hearts to the L.
Rev. 5. 9 they sung a new song, saying, Thou art
14. 3 they sung as it were a new song before the
15. 3 they sing the song of Moses the servant of

14. *To sing praise with a musical instrument,* ψάλλω.
Rom.15. 9 I will confess..and sing unto thy name
1 Co. 14. 15 will sing with the spirit, and I will sing

SING for joy, to cause to —
To cause to sing or cry aloud, רָנַן *ranan,* 5.
Job 29. 13 I caused the widow's heart to sing for j.

SING an hymn, praise, psalms, to —
1. *To boast, praise,* הָלַל *halal,* 3.
2 Ch.23. 13 singers..and such as taught to sing praise
29. 30 commanded the Levites to sing praise un.
29. 30 they sang praises with gladness, and they

2. *To sing praise with a musical instrument,* ψάλλω.
Jas. 5. 13 let him pray. Is any merry? let him sing ps.

3. *To hymn, sing a hymn,* ὑμνέω *humneō.*
Matt26. 30 when they had sung an hymn, they went
Mark14. 26 And when they had sung an hymn, they
Acts 16. 25 Silas prayed, and sang praises unto God
Heb. 2. 12 in the midst of the church will I sing pr.

SING together by course, to —
To answer, respond, עָנָה *anah.*
Ezra 3. 11 they sang together by course in praising and

SINGED, to be —
To be singed, חָרַךְ *charak,* 4.
Dan. 3. 27 nor was an hair of their head singed, nei.

SINGER, (chief, men, women) —
1. *Singer of praise, musician,* זַמָּר *zammar.*
Ezra 7. 24 any of the priests and Levites, singers, po.

2. *To overlook, be pre-eminent,* נָצַח *natsach,* 3.
Hab. 3. 19 To the chief singer on my stringed instr.

3. *A song,* שִׁיר *shir.*
2 Ch.29. 28 the singers sang, and the trumpeters sou.

4. *To sing,* שִׁיר *shir.*
1 Ki. 10. 12 harps also and psalteries for singers
2 Ch. 9. 11 and harps and psalteries for singers
Psa. 68. 25 The singers went before, the players on
87. 7 As well the singers as the players on ins.
Eccl. 2. 8 I gat me men singers and women singers
Eze. 40. 44 the chambers of the singers in the inner

5. *To sing,* שִׁיר *shir,* 3a.
1 Ch. 6. 33 Heman a singer, the son of Joel, the son
9. 33 these (are) the singers, chief of the fathers
15. 16 (to be) the singers with instruments of mu.
15. 19 the singers, Heman, Asaph, and Ethan
15. 27 Levites that bare the ark, and the singers
15. 27 the master of the song with the singers
2 Ch. 5. 12 the Levites (which were) the singers, all
5. 13 the trumpeters and singers (were) as one
20. 21 he appointed singers unto the LORD, and
23. 13 the singers with instruments of music, and
35. 15 the singers the sons of Asaph (were) in th.
Ezra 2. 41 The singers: the children of Asaph, an hu.
2. 70 the singers, and the porters, and the Net.
7. 7 the singers, and the porters, and the Net.
10. 24 Of the singers also; Eliashib: and of the
Neh. 7. 1 the singers and the Levites were appointed
7. 44 The singers: the children of Asaph, an hun.
7. 73 the singers, and (some) of the people, and
10. 28 the singers, the Nethinims, and all they
10. 39 priests..and the porters, and the singers
11. 22 the singers (were) over the business of the
11. 23 a certain portion should be for the singers
12. 28 the sons of the singers gathered themsel.
12. 29 the singers had builded them villages ro.
12. 42 the singers sang loud, with Jezrahiah (th.)
12. 45 the singers and the porters kept the ward
12. 46 (there were) chief of the singers, and songs
12. 47 gave the portions of the singers and the
13. 5 the singers, and the porters, and the off.
13. 10 the singers, that did the work, were fled

SINGING (man, woman)—
1. *Singing,* זָמִיר *zamir.*
Song 2. 12 the time of the singing (of birds) is come

2. *Loud cry or singing,* רִנָּה *rinnah.*
Psa.126. 2 with laughter, and our tongue with singing
Isa. 14. 7 is quiet: they break forth into singing
44. 23 break forth into singing, ye mountains, O
48. 20 with a voice of singing declare ye, tell th.
49. 13 and break forth into singing, O mountains
51. 11 shall return, and come with singing unto
54. 1 break forth into singing, and cry; 55. 12.
Zeph. 3. 17 he will joy over thee with singing

3. *To cry or sing aloud,* רָנַן *ranan,* 3.
Isa. 35. 2 and rejoice even with joy and singing

4. *Singing,* רְנָנָה *renanah.*
Psa.100. 2 come before his presence with singing

5. *To sing,* שִׁיר *shir.*
1 Sa. 18. 6 singing and dancing, to meet king Saul
2 Sa. 19. 35 the voice of singing men and singing wo.
2 Ch.35. 25 the singing men and the singing women

6. *To sing,* שִׁיר *shir,* 3a.
Ezra 2. 65 hundred singing men and singing women
Neh. 7. 67 they had..singing men and singing wo.

7. *A song, singing, singer,* שִׁיר *shir.*
1 Ch. 6. 32 they ministered..with singing, until Sol.
13. 8 with singing, and with harps, and with ps.
2 Ch.23. 18 with rejoicing and with singing, (as it was
Neh. 12. 27 with singing, (with) cymbals, psalteries

SINGING, to be —
To be crying or singing aloud, רָנַן *ranan,* 4.
Isa. 16. 10 in the vineyards there shall be no singing

SINGLE, singleness —
1. *Freedom from duplicity,* ἁπλότης *haplotēs.*
Eph. 6. 5 with fear and trembling, in singleness of
Col. 3. 22 but in singleness of heart, fearing God

2. *Free from defect, unspotted,* ἁπλοῦς *haplous.*
Matt. 6. 22 if therefore thine eye be single, thy who.
Luke11. 34 when thine eye is single, thy whole body

3. *Freedom from duplicity,* ἀφελότης *aphelotēs.*
Acts 2. 46 with gladness and singleness of heart

SINGULAR, to make —
To make wonderful, do wonderfully, פָּלָא *pala,* 5.
Lev. 27. 2 When a man shall make a singular vow

SI'-NIM, סִינִים.
A people in the far east; the *Chinese!*
Isa. 49. 12 Behold..and these from the land of S.

SINITE, סִינִי.
A tribe of Canaanites in the N. of Lebanon; or at Tripolis or Orthosia between Tripolis and Arca.
Gen. 10. 17 And the Hivite, and the Arkite, and the S.
1 Ch. 1. 15 And the Hivite, and the Arkite, and the S.

SINK (down, to begin to), to (let)—
1. *To sink,* טָבַע *taba.*
1 Sa. 17. 49 stone sunk into his forehead; and he fell
Psa. 69. 2 I sink in deep mire, where (there is) no
69. 14 Deliver me..and let me not sink: let me
Jer. 38. 6 no water, but mire: so Jeremiah sunk in

2. *To go down,* יָרַד *yarad.*
Exod15. 5 depths have covered them: they sank in.

3. *To bend or bow the knees,* כָּרַע *kara.*
2 Ki. 9. 24 smote Jehoram..and he sunk down in his

4. *To sink,* צָלַל *tsalal.*
Exod15. 10 sea covered them: they sank as lead in the

5. *To sink,* שָׁקַע *shaqa.*
Jer. 51. 64 Thus shall Babylon sink, and shall not rise

6. *To go down, sink down,* βυθίζω *buthizō.*
Luke 5. 7 both the ships, so that they began to sink

7. *To sink or go down into the sea,* καταποντίζομαι.
Matt 14. 30 beginning to sink, he cried, saying, Lord

8. *To bear or carry down,* καταφέρω *katapherō.*
Acts 20. 9 sunk down with sleep, and fell down from

9. *To put, set, place,* τίθημι *tithēmi.*
Luke 9. 44 Let these sayings sink down into your ears

SI'-ON, שִׂיאֹן *projecting,* Σιών.
1. The peak of Mount Hermon; called *Sirion* by the Sidonians, and *Shenir* by the Amorites.
Deut. 4. 48 even unto mount S., which (is) Hermon
2. The city of *Zion* or Jerusalem.
Matt21. 5 Tell ye the daughter of S., Behold, thy
John12. 15 Fear not, daughter of S.: behold, thy king
Rom. 9. 33 I lay in S. a stumbling stone and rock of
11. 26 There shall come out of S. the Deliverer
Heb.12. 22 But ye are come unto mount S., and unto
1 Pe. 2. 6 Behold, I lay in S. a chief corner stone
Rev. 14. 1 lo; a Lamb stood on the mount S., and wi.

SIPH'-MOTH, שִׂפְמוֹת *fruitful.*
A city in Judah.
1 Sa.30. 28 to (them) which (were) in S., and to (them)

SIP'-PAI, סִפַּי *Jah is preserver.*
A son or descendant of Rapha, the gigantic ancestor of the Rephaim; he is called *Saph* in 2 Sam. 21. 18, and was slain by Sibbechai the Hushathite in the days of David. B.C. 1048.
1 Ch.20. 4 at which time Sibbechai..slew S., (that was)

SIR —
1. *Lord, master, sir,* אָדוֹן *adon.*
Gen. 43. 20 said, O sir, we came indeed down at the

2. *A man, male, husband,* ἀνήρ *anēr.*
Acts 7. 26 Sirs, ye are brethren; why do ye wrong one
14. 15 saying, Sirs, why do ye these things? We
19. 25 Sirs, ye know that by this craft we have
27. 10 Sirs, I perceive that this voyage will be wi.
27. 21 Sirs, ye should have hearkened unto me
27. 25 Wherefore, sirs, be of good cheer: for I b.

3. *Lord, master, sir,* κύριος *kurios.*
Matt 13. 27 Sir, didst not thou sow good seed in thy
21. 30 he answered and said, I (go) sir; and we.
27. 63 Sir, we remember that that deceiver said
John 4. 11 Sir, thou hast nothing to draw with, and
4. 15 Sir, give me this water, that I thirst not
4. 19 Sir, I perceive that thou art a prophet
4. 49 saith unto him, Sir, come down ere my ch.
5. 7 Sir, I have no man..to put me into the
12. 21 desired him, saying, Sir, we would see Je.
20. 15 Sir, if thou have borne him hence, tell me
Acts 16. 30 and said, Sirs, what must I do to be saved
Rev. 7. 14 said unto him, Sir, thou knowest. And

SI'-RAH, סִרָה *turning aside.*
A pit, cistern, or well, near Hebron.
2 Sa. 3. 26 brought him again from the well of S.: but

SIR'-ION, שִׂרְיֹן, [V. L. שִׁרְיוֹן] *coat of mail.*
The name given by the Sidonians to Hermon, the S. part of Mount Anti-Libanus.
Deut. 3. 9 (Which) Hermon the Sidonians call S., and
Psa. 29. 6 maketh..Lebanon and S. like a young un.

SIS-A'-MAI, סִסְמַי *Jah is distinguished.*
Son of Eleasah, and father of Shallum, a descendant of Jerahmeel son of Pharez. B.C. 1280.
1 Ch. 2. 40 And Eleasah begat S., and S. begat Shal.

SI-SE'-RA, סִיסְרָא *mediation, array.*
1. Captain of the host of Jabin king of Canaan, and killed by Jael. B.C. 1300.
Judg. 4. 2 the captain of whose host (was) S., which
4. 7 I will draw unto thee..S., the captain of
4. 9 the LORD shall sell S. into the hand of a
4. 12 they showed S. that Barak..was gone up
4. 13 S. gathered together all his chariots, (even)
4. 14 the LORD hath delivered S. into thine ha.
4. 15 the LORD discomfited S., and all (his) ch.
4. 15 so that S. lighted down off (his) chariot

Judg. 4. 16 all the host of S. fell upon the edge of the
4. 17 S. fled away on his feet to the tent of Jael
4. 18 Jael went out to meet S., and said unto
4. 22 as Barak pursued S., Jael came out to me.
4. 22 S. lay dead, and the nail (was) in his tem.
5. 20 stars in their courses fought against S.
5. 26 with the hammer she smote S., she smote
5. 28 mother of S. looked out at a window, and
5. 30 to S. a prey of divers colours, a prey of di.
1 Sa. 12. 9 he sold them into the hand of S., captain
Psa. 83. 9 Do unto them..as (to) S., as (to) Jabin, at

2. One of the Nethinim whose descendants returned with Zerubbabel. B.C. 536.
Ezra 2. 53 The children of Barkos, the children of S.
Neh. 7. 55 The children of Barkos, the children of S.

SISTER —

1. *Sister*, אָחוֹת *achoth.*
Gen. 4. 22 and the sister of Tubal-cain (was) Naamah
12. 13 Say, I pray thee, thou (art) my sister: that
12. 19 Why saidst thou, She (is) my sister? so I
20. 2 said of Sarah his wife, She (is) my sister
20. 5 Said he not unto me, She (is) my sister?
20. 12 yet indeed (she is) my sister; she (is) the
24. 30 when he saw the..bracelets upon his sis.
24. 30 heard the words of Rebekah his sister, sa.
24. 59 they sent away Rebekah their sister, and
24. 60 Thou (art) our sister, be thou (the mother)
25. 20 took Rebekah to wife..the sister to Lab.
26. 7 said, She (is) my sister: for he feared to
26. 9 how saidst thou, She (is) my sister? And
28. 9 Mahalath..the sister of Nebajoth, to be
29. 13 heard the tidings of Jacob his sister's son
30. 1 Rachel envied her sister; and said unto
30. 8 wrestled with my sister, and I have pre.
34. 13 because he had defiled Dinah their sister
34. 14 to give our sister to one that is uncircum.
34. 27 because they had defiled their sister
34. 31 Should he deal with our sister as with an
36. 3 Ishmael's daughter, sister of Nebajoth
36. 22 and Hemam; and Lotan's sister (was) Ti.
46. 17 Isui, and Beriah, and Serah their sister
Exod. 2. 4 his sister stood afar off, to wit what wo.
2. 7 Then said his sister to Pharaoh's daughter
6 23 Elisheba, daughter of Amminadab, sister
15. 20 Miriam the prophetess, the sister of Aar.
Lev. 18. 9 The nakedness of thy sister, the daughter
18. 11 she (is) thy sister, thou shalt not uncover
18. 12 the nakedness of thy father's sister
18. 13 the nakedness of thy mother's sister
18. 18 Neither shalt thou take a wife to her sis.
20. 17 if a man shall take his sister, his father's
20. 17 he hath uncovered his sister's nakedness
20. 19 mother's sister, nor of thy father's sister
21. 3 for his sister a virgin, that is nigh unto
Num. 6. 7 his mother, for his brother, or for his sis.
25. 18 their sister, which was slain in the day of
26. 59 Aaron and Moses, and Miriam their sist.
Deut 27. 22 Cursed (be) he that lieth with his sister
Josh. 2. 13 my brethren, and my sisters, and all that
Judg 15. 2 (is) not her younger sister fairer than she?
2 Sa. 13. 1 the son of David had a fair sister, whose
13. 2 he fell sick for his sister Tamar; for she
13. 4 I love Tamar, my brother Absalom's sist.
13. 5, 6 I pray thee, let my sister Tamar come
13. 11 said unto her, Come lie with me, my sist.
13. 20 hold now thy peace, my sister: he (is) thy
13. 22 because he had forced his sister Tamar
13. 32 the day that he forced his sister Tamar
17. 25 the daughter of Nahash, sister to Zeruiah
1 Ki. 11. 19 the sister of his own wife, the sister of T.
11. 20 the sister of Tahpenes bare him Genubath
2 Ki. 11. 2 the daughter of king Joram, sister of A.
1 Ch. 1. 39 and Homam: and Timna (was) Lotan's si.
2. 16 Whose sisters (were) Zeruiah, and Abigail
3. 9 sons of David..and Tamar their sister.
3. 19 Hananiah, and Shelomith their sister
4. 3 and the name of their sister (was) Hazel.
4. 19 (his) wife Hodiah, the sister of Naham, the
7. 15 Shuppim, whose sister's name (was) Maa.
7. 18 his sister Hammoleketh bare Ishod, and
7. 30 Ishuai, and Beriah, and Serah their sister
7. 32 Shomer, and Hotham, and Shua their sis.
2 Ch. 22. 11 for she was the sister of Ahaziah
Job 1. 4 called for their three sisters, to eat and to
17. 14 said..(Thou art) my mother, and my sis.
42. 11 all his sisters, and all they that had been
Prov. 7. 4 Say unto wisdom, Thou (art) my sister, and
Song 4. 9 Thou hast ravished my heart, my sister
4. 10 How fair is thy love, my sister, (my) spo.
4. 12 A garden inclosed (is) my sister, (my) sp.
5. 1 I am come into my garden, my sister, (my)
5. 2 Open to me, my sister, my love, my dove
8. 8 We have a little sister, and she hath no
8. 8 what shall we do for our sister in the day
Jer. 3. 7 And her treacherous sister Judah saw (it)
3. 8 her treacherous sister Judah feared not
3. 10 her treacherous sister Judah hath not tu.
22. 18 (saying), Ah my brother! or, Ah sister!
Eze. 16. 45 and thou (art) the sister of thy sisters
16. 46 thine elder sister (is) Samaria, she and her
16. 46 thy younger sister, that dwelleth at thy
16. 48 thy sister hath not done, she nor her da.
16. 49 this was the iniquity of thy sister Sodom
16. 51 hast justified thy sisters in all thine abo.
16. 52 Thou also, which hast judged thy sisters
16. 52 in that thou hast justified thy sisters
16. 55 When thy sisters, Sodom and her daugh.
16. 56 thy sister Sodom, was not mentioned by
16. 61 when thou shalt receive thy sisters, thine
22. 11 another in thee hath humbled his sister
Eze. 23. 4 Aholah the elder, and Aholibah her sist.
23. 11 when her sister Aholibah saw (this,) she
23. 11 in her whoredoms more than her sister
23. 18 my mind was alienated from her sister
23. 31 Thou hast walked in the way of thy sister
23. 32 Thou shalt drink of thy sister's cup deep
23. 33 filled..with the cup of thy sister Samaria
44. 25 for brother, or for sister that hath had no
Hos. 2. 1 Say ye unto your brethren..your sisters

2. *Sister*, ἀδελφή *adelphē.*
Matt 12. 50 the same is my brother, and sister, and
13. 56 And his sisters, are they not all with us?
19. 29 hath forsaken houses, or brethren, or si.
Mark 3. 35 the same is my brother, and my sister, and
6. 3 are not his sisters here with us? And th.
10. 29 that hath left house, or brethren, or sist.
10. 30 sisters, and mothers, and children, and
Luke 10. 39 she had a sister called Mary, which also
10. 40 dost thou not care that my sister hath
14. 26 and children, and brethren, and sisters
John 11. 1 the town of Mary and her sister Martha
11. 3 his sisters sent unto him, saying, Lord, be.
11. 5 Jesus loved Martha, and her sister, and
11. 28 called Mary her sister secretly, saying, The
11. 39 the sister of him that was dead, saith unto
19. 25 his mother, and his mother's sister, Mary
Acts 23. 16 Paul's sister's son heard of their lying in
Rom 16. 1 I commend unto you Phebe our sister, wh.
16. 15 Julia, Nereus, and his sister, and Olym.
1 Co. 7. 15 a sister is not under bondage in such (ca.)
9. 5 Have we not power to lead about a sister
1 Ti. 5. 2 the younger as sisters, with all purity
Jas. 2. 15 If a brother or sister be naked, and desti.
2 John 13 The children of thy elect sister greet thee

SISTER'S son —

A cousin-german, sister's son, ἀνεψιός *anepsios.*
Col. 4. 10 Marcus, sister's son to Barnabas, touching

SISTER in law —

Brother's (brother in law's) wife, יְבֶמֶת *yebemeth.*
Ruth 1. 15 thy sister in law is gone back unto her pe.
1. 15 said..return thou after thy sister in law

SIT (by, down, with, still, up, together), to —

1. *To brood, hatch*, דָּגַר *dagar.*
Jer. 17. 11 (As) the partridge sitteth (on eggs), and

2. *To sit down or still*, יָשַׁב *yashab.*
Gen. 18. 1 he sat in the tent door in the heat of the
19. 1 Lot sat in the gate of Sodom: and Lot see.
21. 16 sat her down over against (him) a good way
21. 16 she sat over against (him), and lift up her
27. 19 sit and eat of my venison, that thy soul
31. 34 had taken the images..and sat upon them
37. 25 they sat down to eat bread: and they lif.
38. 14 sat in an open place, which (is) by the way
43. 33 they sat before him, the first born accor.
48. 2 Israel strengthened himself, and sat upon
Exod. 2. 15 But Moses fled..and he sat down by a w.
11. 5 the first born of Pharaoh that sitteth upon
12. 29 the first born of Pharaoh that sat on his
16. 3 when we sat by the flesh pots, (and) when
17. 12 put (it) under him, and he sat thereon
18. 13 on the morrow, that Moses sat to judge
18. 14 why sittest thou thyself alone, and all the
32. 6 the people sat down to eat and to drink
Lev. 15. 4 every thing whereon he sitteth shall be
15. 6 that sitteth on (any) thing whereon he sat
15. 20 every thing also that she sitteth upon sh.
15. 22 toucheth any thing that she sat upon sh.
15. 23 or on any thing whereon she sitteth, when
15. 26 whatsoever she sitteth upon shall be unc.
Num 32. 6 your brethren go to war, and shall ye sit
Deut. 6. 7 shalt talk of them when thou sittest in th.
11. 19 speaking of them when thou sittest in th.
17. 18 when he sitteth upon the throne of his ki.
Judg. 3. 20 he was sitting in a summer parlour, which
5. 10 ye that sit in judgment, and walk by the
6. 11 sat under an oak which (was) in Ophrah
13. 9 came again unto the woman as she sat
19. 6 they sat down, and did eat and drink both
19. 15 he sat him down in a street of the city
20. 26 sat there before the LORD, and fasted that
Ruth 2. 14 she sat beside the reapers: and he reached
3. 18 Sit still, my daughter, until thou know how
4. 1 went Boaz up to the gate, and sat him d.
4. 1 Ho, such a one turn aside, sit down here
4. 1 And he turned aside, and sat down
4. 2 said, Sit ye down here. And they sat do.
1 Sa. 1. 9 the priest sat upon a seat by a post of the
4. 13 Eli sat upon a seat by the way side watc.
19. 9 he sat in his house with his javelin in his
20. 5 I should not fail to sit with the king at me.
20. 24 the king sat him down to eat meat
20. 25 the king sat upon his seat, as at other ti.
20. 25 Abner sat by Saul's side, and David's pl.
28. 23 he arose from the earth, and sat upon the
2 Sa. 2. 13 they sat down, the one on the one side of
7. 1 it came to pass, when the king sat in his
7. 18 Then went king David in, and sat before
18. 24 David sat between the two gates: and the
19. 8 Then the king arose, and sat in the gate
23. 8 The Tachmonite that sat in the seat, chief
1 Ki. 1. 13. 17, 24 reign after me, and he shall sit
1. 20 who shall sit on the throne of my lord the
1. 27 who should sit on the throne of my lord
1. 30 he shall sit upon my throne in my stead
1. 35 that he may come and sit upon my throne
1. 46 Solomon sitteth on the throne of the kin.
1. 48 which hath given (one) to sit on my throne
2. 12 Then sat Solomon upon the throne of Da.
1 Ki. 2. 19 sat down on his throne, and caused a seat
2. 19 the king's mother; and she sat on his ri.
3. 6 thou hast given him a son to sit on his th.
8. 20 sit on the throne of Israel, as the LORD pr.
8. 25 not fail thee a man in my sight to sit on
13. 14 found him sitting under an oak: and he
13. 20 it came to pass, as they sat at the table
16. 11 as soon as he sat on his throne, (that) he
19. 4 came and sat down under a juniper tree
21. 13 there came in two men..and sat before
22. 10 the king of Judah sat each on his throne
22. 19 I saw the LORD sitting on his throne, and
2 Ki. 1. 9 and, behold, he sat on the top of an hill
4. 20 he sat on her knees till noon, and (then)
4. 38 the sons of the prophets (were) sitting be.
6. 32 Elisha sat in his house..the elders sat with
7. 3 they said one to another, Why sit we here
7. 4 if we sit still here, we die also. Now there.
9. 5 behold, the captains of the host (were) s.
10. 30 children of..fourth (generation) shall sit
11. 19 And he sat on the throne of the kings
13. 13 Jeroboam sat upon his throne: and Joash
15. 12 Thy sons shall sit on the throne of Israel
18. 27 (hath he)..(sent me) to the men which sit
1 Ch. 17. 1 it came to pass, as David sat in his house
17. 16 the king came and sat before the LORD
28. 5 he hath chosen Solomon my son to sit up.
29. 23 Solomon sat on the throne of the LORD as
2 Ch. 6. 16 not fail thee a man in my sight to sit upon
18. 9 and Jehoshaphat king of Judah sat either
18. 9 they sat in a void place at the entering in
18. 18 I saw the LORD sitting upon his throne
Ezra 9. 3 I rent my garment..and sat down aston.
9. 4 I sat astonied until the evening sacrifice
10. 9 the people sat in the street of the house
10. 16 sat down in the first day of the tenth mo.
Neh. 1. 4 I sat down and wept, and mourned (cer.)
2. 6 said unto me, the queen also sitting by
8. 17 made booths, and sat under the booths
Esth. 1. 2 the king Ahasuerus sat on the throne of
1. 14 (and) which sat the first in the kingdom
2. 19 then Mordecai sat in the king's gate
2. 21 while Mordecai sat in the king's gate, two
3. 15 the king and Haman sat down to drink
5. 1 the king sat upon his royal throne in the
5. 13 Mordecai the Jew sitting at the king's gate
6. 10 the Jew, that sitteth at the king's gate
Job 2. 8 he took him a potsherd..and he sat down
2. 13 they sat down with him upon the ground
29. 25 I chose out their way, and sat chief, and
Psa. 1. 1 nor sitteth in the seat of the scornful
2. 4 He that sitteth in the heavens shall laugh
9. 4 thou satest in the throne judging right
10. 8 He sitteth in the lurking places of the vi.
26. 4 I have not sat with vain persons, neither
26. 5 I have hated..and will not sit with the
29. 10 sitteth upon the flood; yea, the LORD sit.
47. 8 God sitteth upon the throne of his holin.
50. 20 Thou sittest (and) speakest against thy
69. 12 They that sit in the gate speak against
99. 1 he sitteth (between) the cherubim; let
107. 10 Such as sit in darkness, and in the shadow
110. 1 Sit thou at my right hand, until I make
119. 23 Princes also did sit (and) speak against me
127. 2 to sit up late, to eat the bread of sorrows
132. 12 their children shall also sit upon thy thr.
137. 1 we sat down: yea, we wept, when we re.
Prov. 9. 14 she sitteth at the door of her house, on a
20. 8 A king that sitteth in the throne of judg.
23. 1 When thou sittest to eat with a ruler, co.
31. 23 when he sitteth among the elders of the
Eccl. 10. 6 great dignity, and the rich sit in low pla.
Song 2. 3 I sat down under his shadow with great
Isa. 3. 26 she, (being) desolate, shall sit upon the
6. 1 I saw also the LORD sitting upon a throne
14. 13 I will sit also upon the mount of the con.
16. 5 he shall sit upon it in truth in the taber.
28. 6 a spirit of judgment to him that sitteth
36. 12 (hath he) not (sent me) to the men that s.
40. 22 (It is) he that sitteth upon the circle of
42. 7 them that sit in darkness out of the pris.
47. 1 sit in the dust, O virgin daughter of Bab.
47. 1 sit on the ground: (there is) no throne, O
47. 5 Sit thou silent, and get thee into darkness
47. 8 I shall not sit (as) a widow, neither shall
47. 14 (there shall) not (be) a..fire to sit before
52. 2 sit down, O Jerusalem: loose thyself from
Jer. 3. 2 in the ways hast thou sat for them, as the
8. 14 Why do we sit still? assemble yourselves
13. 13 even the kings that sit upon David's thr.
13. 18 Humble yourselves, sit down: for your
15. 17 I sat not in the assembly of the mockers
15. 17 I sat alone, because of thy hand: for thou
16. 8 to sit with them to eat and to drink
17. 25 princes sitting upon the throne of David
22. 2 O king of Judah, that sittest upon the th.
22. 4 kings sitting upon the throne of David
22. 30 sitting upon the throne of David, and ru.
26. 10 sat down in the entry of the new gate of
29. 16 the king that sitteth upon the throne of
32. 12 the Jews that sat in the court of the pri.
33. 17 David shall never want a man to sit upon
36. 12 all the princes sat there, (even) Elishama
36. 15 they said unto him, Sit down now, and re.
36. 22 the king sat in the winter house, in the
36. 30 He shall have none to sit upon the throne
38. 7 the king then sitting in the gate of Benj.
39. 3 sat in the middle gate, (even) Nergal-sha.
48. 18 come down from (thy) glory, and sit in th.
Lam. 1. 1 How doth the city sit solitary (that was)
2. 10 The elders of the daughter of Zion sit up.
3. 28 He sitteth alone and keepeth silence, be.

Eze. 3. 15 I sat where they sat, and remained there
8. 1 in the fifth (day) of the month, (as) I sat in
8. 1 and the elders of Judah sat before me
8. 14 behold, there sat women weeping for Ta.
14. 1 came certain of the elders..and sat before
20. 1 came to enquire of the LORD, and sat be.
23. 41 satest upon a stately bed, and a table pre.
26. 16 they shall sit upon the ground, and shall
28. 2 I sit (in) the seat of God, in the midst of
33. 31 they sit before thee (as) my people, and
44. 3 he shall sit in it to eat bread before the
Joel 3. 12 there will I sit to judge all the heathen
Jon. 3. 6 covered (him) with sackcloth, and sat in
4. 5 sat on the east side of the city, and there
4. 5 sat under it in the shadow, till he might
Mic. 4. 4 they shall sit every man under his vine
7. 8 when I sit in darkness, the LORD (shall be)
Zech. 1. 11 behold, all the earth sitteth still, and is
3. 8 thou, and thy fellows that sit before thee
5. 7 this (is) a woman that sitteth in the midst
6. 13 and shall sit and rule upon his throne; and
Mal. 3. 3 he shall sit (as) a refiner and purifier of

3. *To sit down or still,* יְתִב *yethib.*
Dan. 7. 9 the Ancient of days did sit, whose garm.
7. 26 the judgment shall sit, and they shall ta.

4. *A place,* מָקוֹם *maqom.* (*See* make sit.)
1 Sa. 9. 22 made them sit in the chiefest place among

5. *To be, come, go round about,* סָבַב *sabab*
1 Sa. 16. 11 we will not sit down till he come hither

6. *To lie down, crouch,* רָבַץ *rabats.*
Deut 22. 6 the dam sitting upon the young, or upon

7. *To be laid down,* תָּכָה *takah,* 4.
Deut 33. 3 they sat down at thy feet; (every one) sh.

8. *A sitting, session,* שֶׁבֶת *shebeth.*
Isa. 30. 7 have I cried..Their strength is (to) sit st.

9. *To sit up,* ἀνακαθίζω *anakathizō.*
Luke 7. 15 he that was dead [sat up], and began to sp.
Acts 9. 40 eyes: and when she saw Peter, she sat up

10. *To lie back, recline,* ἀνάκειμαι *anakeimai.*
Matt 26. 20 when the even was come, he sat down wi.
Mark 14. 18 as they sat and did eat, Jesus said, Verily

11. *To lay down or back, recline,* ἀνακλίνω *anaklinō.*
Matt. 8. 11 That many..shall sit down with Abraham
14. 19 commanded the multitude to sit down on
Luke 13. 29 and shall sit down in the kingdom of God

12. *To fall back, recline,* ἀναπίπτω *anapiptō.*
Matt 15. 35 he commanded the multitude to sit down
Mark 6. 40 they sat down in ranks, by hundreds, and
8. 6 he commanded the people to sit down on
Luke 14. 10 But..go and sit down in the lowest room
22. 14 when the hour was come, he sat down, and
John 6. 10, 10 Make the men sit down. So the men sat d.

13. *To sit down,* καθέζομαι *kathezomai.*
Matt 26. 55 I sat daily with you teaching in the tem.
Luke 2. 46 sitting in the midst of the doctors, both
John 4. 6 Je. therefore..sat thus on the well: (and)
11. 20 went and met him: but Mary sat (still) in
20. 12 seeth two angels in white sitting, the one
Acts 6. 15 all that sat in the council, looking stedf.

14. *To sit or put down,* κάθημαι *kathēmai.*
Matt. 4. 16 The people which sat in darkness saw gr.
4. 16 to them which sat in the region and sha.
9. 9 saw a man named Matthew, sitting at the
11. 16 like unto children sitting in the markets
13. 1 same day went Jesus..and sat by the sea
13. 2 so that he went into a ship, and sat; and
15. 29 went up into a mountain, and sat down
20. 30 two blind men sitting by the way side, wh.
22. 44 Sit thou on my right hand, till I make th.
23. 22 sweareth..by him that sitteth thereon
24. 3 as he sat upon the mount of Olives, the
26. 58 went in, and sat with the servants, to see
26. 64 see the Son of man sitting on the right ha.
26. 69 Now Peter sat without in the palace: and
27. 36 And sitting down they watched him v 19.
27. 61 other Mary, sitting over against the sep.
28. 2 and rolled back the stone..and sat upon
Mark 2. 6 there were certain of the scribes sitting
2. 14 saw Levi the (son) of Alpheus sitting at
3. 32 multitude sat about him; and they said
3. 34 looked round about on them which sat ab.
4. 1 he entered into a ship, and sat in the sea
5. 15 had the legion, sitting, and clothed, and
10. 46 son of Timeus, sat by the highway side be.
12. 36 [Sit thou] on my right hand, till I make
13. 3 as he sat upon the mount of Olives, over
14. 62 shall see the Son of man sitting on the ri.
16. 5 they saw a young man sitting on the right
Luke 1. 79 To give light to them that sit in darkness
5. 17 Pharisees and doctors of the law sitting by
5. 27 saw..Levi, sitting at the receipt of custom
7. 32 They are like unto children sitting in the
8. 35 found the man..sitting at the feet of Jesus
10. 13 great while ago repented, sitting in sack.
18. 35 certain blind man sat by the way side be.
20. 42 LORD said unto my Lord, Sit thou on my
22. 55 when they had kindled a fire..Peter sat do.
22. 56 certain maid beheld him as he sat by the
22. 69 Hereafter shall the Son of man sit on the
John 2. 14 And found..the changers of money sitting
6. 3 into a mountain, and there he sat with his
9. 8 said, Is not this he that sat and begged?
12. 15 thy king cometh, sitting on an ass's colt
Acts 2. 2 it filled all the house where [they were si.]
2. 34 said unto my Lord, Sit thou on my right

Acts 3. 10 knew that it was he which sat for alms at
8. 28 sitting in his chariot read Esaias the pro.
14. 8 there sat a certain man at Lystra, impot.
20. 9 [there sat] in a window a certain young
23. 3 for sittest thou to judge me after the law
1 Co. 14. 30 be revealed to another that sitteth by, let
Col. 3. 1 where Christ sitteth on the right hand of
Heb. 1. 13 Sit on my right hand, until I make thine
Jas. 2. 3 Sit thou here in a good place; and say to
2. 3 Stand thou there, or sit here under my fo.
Rev. 4. 2 throne was set in heaven, and (one) sat on
4. 3 [he that sat was to look upon like a jasper]
4. 4 saw four and twenty elders sitting, clothed
4. 9 honour and thanks to him that sat on the
4. 10 fall down before him that sat on the thr.
5. 1 saw in the right hand of him that sat on
5. 7 right hand of him that sat upon the thr.
5. 13 unto him that sitteth upon the throne, and
6. 2 behold a white horse: and he that sat on
6. 4 given to him that sat thereon to take pe.
6. 5 he that sat on him had a pair of balances
6. 8 his name that sat on him was Death, and
6. 16 hide us from the face of him that sitteth on
7. 10 Salvation to our God which sitteth upon
7. 15 he that sitteth on the throne shall dwell
9. 17 them that sat on them, having breastplates
11. 16 four and twenty elders which sat before
14. 14 upon the cloud (one) sat like unto the Son
14. 15 crying with a loud voice to him that sat on
14. 16 he that sat on the cloud thrust in his sic.
17. 1 great whore that sitteth upon many wat.
17. 3 saw a woman sit upon a scarlet coloured
17. 9 mountains, on which the woman sitteth
17. 15 where the whore sitteth, are peoples, and
18. 7 for she saith in her heart, I sit a queen, and
19. 4 fell down and worshipped God that sat on
19. 11 he that sat upon him (was) called Faithf.
19. 18 flesh of horses, and of them that sat on th.
19. 19 make war against him that sat on the ho.
19. 21 slain with the sword of him that sat upon
20. 11 great white throne, and him that sat on it
21. 5 he that sat upon the throne said, Behold

15. *To set or put down,* καθίζω *kathizō.*
Matt 13. 48 sat down, and gathered the good into ve.
19. 28 when the Son of man shall sit in the thro.
19. 28 ye also shall sit upon twelve thrones, ju.
20. 21 Grant that these my two sons may sit, the
20. 23 but to sit on my right hand, and on my left
23. 2 The scribes and the Pharisees sit in Moses'
25. 31 then shall he sit upon the throne of his gl.
26. 36 Sit ye here, while I go and pray yonder
Mark 9. 35 sat down, and called the twelve, and saith
10. 37 Grant unto us that we may sit, one on thy
10. 40 But to sit on my right hand and on my left
11. 2 find a colt tied, whereon never man sat
11. 7 brought the colt to Jesus..and he sat up.
12. 41 Jesus sat over against the treasury, and
14. 32 saith to his disciples, Sit ye here, while I
16. 19 [received up into heaven, and sat on the]
Luke 4. 20 gave (it) again to the minister, and sat do.
5. 3 sat down, and taught the people out of the
14. 28 which of you..sitteth not down first, and co.
14. 31 what king..sitteth not down first, and co.
16. 6 Take thy bill, and sit down quickly, and
19. 30 a colt tied, whereon yet never man sat: l.
22. 30 sit on thrones judging the twelve tribes of
John 8. 2 [people came unto him; and he sat down]
12. 14 when he had found a young ass, sat there.
19. 13 sat down in the judgment seat in a place
Acts 2. 3 like as of fire, and it sat upon each of them
2. 30 he would raise up Christ to sit on his thr.
8. 31 desired Philip that he would..sit with him
12. 21 sat upon his throne, and made an oration
13. 14 went into the synagogue..and sat down
16. 13 sat down, and spake unto the women wh.
25. 6 sitting on the judgment seat, commanded
25. 17 sat on the judgment seat, and commanded
1 Co. 10. 7 people sat down to eat and drink, and ro.
2 Th. 2. 4 so that he as God sitteth in the temple of
Heb. 1. 3 sat down on the right hand of the Majesty
10. 12 But this man..sat down on the right hand
Rev. 3. 21 will I grant to sit..in my throne, even as I
20. 4 I saw thrones, and they sat upon them, and

16. *To lay or lie down,* κατάκειμαι *katakeimai.*
Luke 5. 29 great company..that sat down with them

17. *To lay down,* κατακλίνω *kataklinō.*
Luke 14. 8 sit not down in the highest room; lest a

18. *To sit down alongside,* παρακαθίζω *parakathizō.*
Luke 10. 39 sister called Mary, which also sat at Jesus'

19. *To recline with,* συνανάκειμαι *sunanakeimai.*
Matt. 9. 10 came and sat down with him and his dis.
Mark 2. 15 sat also together with Jesus and his disc.
6. 22 pleased Herod and them that sat with him
6. 26 for their sakes which [sat with] him, he

SIT (down at meat with), to —

1. *To lie or lay down or back,* ἀνάκειμαι *anakeimai.*
Matt. 9. 10 as Jesus sat at meat in the house, behold
26. 7 poured (it) on his head, as he sat (at meat)
Mark 16. 14 [appeared..as they sat at meat, and upb.]
Luke 7. 37 when she knew that (Jesus) [sat at meat]
22. 27 whether (is) greater he that sitteth at meat
22. 27 (is) not he that sitteth at meat? but I am

2. *To recline,* ἀνακλίνω *anaklinō.*
Luke 7. 36 And he went..and [sat down to meat]

3. *To lay or lie down,* κατάκειμαι *katakeimai.*
Mark 2. 15 as Jesus sat at meat in his house, many

Mark 14. 3 as he sat at meat, there came a woman
1 Co. 8. 10 if any man see thee..sit at meat in the id.

4. *To lay down,* κατακλίνω *kataklinō.*
Luke 24. 30 as he sat at meat with them, he took bread

5. *To fall back or down,* ἀναπίπτω *anapiptō.*
Luke 11. 37 and he went in, and sat down to meat
17. 7 will say..Go and sit down to meat

6. *To lie down with,* συνανάκειμαι *sunanakeimai.*
Matt 14. 9 for..them which sat with him at meat, he
Luke 7. 49 they that sat at meat with him began to
14. 10 presence of them that sit at meat with thee
14. 15 when one of them that sat at meat with

SIT down to meat, to make to —

To lay down or back, recline, ἀνακλίνω *anaklinō.*
Luke 12. 37 make them to sit down to meat, and will

SIT (down, together), to make to —

1. *Give place to,* נָתַן מָקוֹם לְ [*nathan*]; 1 Sam. 9. 22.

2. *To lay down or back,* ἀνακλίνω *anaklinō.*
Mark 6. 39 commanded them [to make all sit down]
Luke 9. 15 And they did so, and [made them all sit d.]

3. *To lay down,* κατακλίνω *kataklinō.*
Luke 9. 14 Make them sit down by fifties in a comp.

4. *To sit down with,* συγκαθίζω *sugkathizō.*
Eph. 2. 6 made (us) sit together in heavenly (places)

SIT upon or with, to —

1. *To go up upon, mount,* ἐπιβαίνω *epibainō.*
Matt 21. 5 sitting upon an ass, and a colt the foal of

2. *To sit down with,* συγκάθημαι *sugkathēmai.*
Mark 14. 54 sat with the servants, and warmed him.
Acts 26. 30 and Bernice, and they that sat with them

SIT at the table with, to —

To recline with, συνανάκειμαι *sunanakeimai.*
John 12. 2 one of them that [sat at the table with]

SITH —

If, אִם *im.*
Eze. 35. 6 sith thou hast not hated blood, even blo.

SIT'-NAH, שִׂטְנָה *hatred.*

A name given to a well which Isaac's servants digged in Gerar, but which was seized by the servants of Abimelech; still called *Shutneh,* and is on the W. of Rehoboth or *Ruheibah.* B.C. 1897.
Gen. 26. 21 digged..and he called the name of it S.

SITTING (down) —

1. *To sit down or still,* יָשַׁב *yashab.*
2 Ch. 9. 18 stays on each side of the sitting place, and
Psa. 139. 2 Thou knowest my down sitting and mine
Lam. 3. 63 Behold their sitting down, and their ris.

2. *A seat,* מוֹשָׁב *moshab.*
1 Ki. 10. 5 sitting of his servants, and the attendance
2 Ch. 9. 4 sitting of his servants, and the attendance

SITUATE, situation, (to be) —

1. *To sit down or still,* יָשַׁב *yashab.*
Eze. 27. 3 O thou that art situate at the entry of the
Nah. 3. 8 that was situate among the rivers, (that

2. *A seat,* מוֹשָׁב *moshab.*
2 Ki. 2. 19 situation of this city (is) pleasant, as my

3. *What is fixed,* מָצוּק *matsuq.*
1 Sa. 14. 5 fore front of the one (was) situate north.

4. *Elevation,* נוֹף *noph.*
Psa. 48. 2 Beautiful for situation, the joy of the wh.

SI'-VAN, סִיוָן.

The third month of the Hebrew year, from the new moon of June to that of July.
Esth. 8. 9 the third month, that (is), the month S.

SIX, sixth —

1. *Six, sixth,* שִׁשָּׁה ,שֵׁשׁ *shesh, shishshah.*
Gen. 7. 6 Noah (was) six hundred years old when
7. 11 In the six hundredth year of Noah's life
8. 13 it came to pass in the six hundredth and
16. 16 Abram (was) fourscore and six years old
30. 20 because I have born him six sons: and she
31. 41 I served thee..six years for thy cattle: and
46. 26 all the souls (were) threescore and six
Exod 12. 37 about six hundred thousand on foot (that
14. 7 he took six hundred chosen chariots, and
16. 26 Six days ye shall gather it; but on the se.
20. 9 Six days shalt thou labour and do all thy
20. 11 (in) six days the LORD made heaven and
21. 2 six years he shall serve; and in the sev.
23. 10 six years thou shalt sow thy land, and sh.
23. 12 Six days thou shalt do thy work, and on
24. 16 the cloud covered it six days: and the se.
25. 32 six branches shall come out of the sides of
25. 33 the six branches that come out of the ca.
25. 35 the six branches that proceed out of the
26. 9 and six curtains by themselves, and shalt
26. 22 for the sides..thou shalt make six boards
28. 10 Six of their names on one stone, and (the
28. 10 six names of the rest on the other stone
31. 15 Six days may work be done; but in the
31. 17 (in) six days the LORD made heaven and
34. 21 Six days thou shalt work; but on the se.
35. 2 Six days shall work be done, but on the
36. 16 five curtains by themselves, and six curt.
36. 27 And for the sides..he made six boards
37. 18 six branches going out of the sides thereof

Exod37. 19 throughout the six branches going out of
37. 21 according to the six branches going out of
38. 26 six hundred thousand and three thousand
Lev. 12. 5 shall continue..threescore and six days
23. 3 Six days shall work be done: but the sev.
24. 6 thou shalt set them in two rows, six on a
25. 3 Six years thou shalt sow thy field, and six
Num. 1. 21 forty and six thousand and five hundred
1. 25 forty and five thousand six hundred and
1. 27 threescore and fourteen thousand and six
1. 46 six hundred thousand and three thousand
2. 4 and fourteen thousand and six hundred
2. 9 fourscore thousand and six thousand and
2. 11 forty and six thousand and five hundred
2. 15 forty and five thousand and six hundred
2. 31 fifty and seven thousand and six hundred
2. 32 six hundred thousand and three thousand
3. 28 eight thousand and six hundred, keeping
3. 34 those that were numbered..(were) six tho.
4. 40 two thousand and six hundred and thirty
7. 3 they brought..six covered wagons, and
11. 21 The people, among whom I (am are) six
26. 41 forty and five thousand and six hundred
26. 51 six hundred thousand and a thousand se.
31. 32 six hundred thousand and seventy thous.
31. 37 was six hundred and threescore and fift.
31. 38 And the beeves (were) thirty and six tho.
31. 44 And thirty and six thousand beeves
35. 6 there shall be six cities for refuge, which
35. 13 of these cities..six cities shall ye have for
35. 15 six cities shall be a refuge, (both) for the
Deut. 5. 13 Six days thou shalt labour, and do all thy
15. 12 be sold unto thee, and serve thee six ye.
15. 18 servant (to thee), in serving thee six yea.
16. 8 Six days thou shalt eat unleavened bread
Josh. 6. 3 And ye shall compass the city..six days
6. 14 returned into the camp: so they did six
7. 5 smote of them about thirty and six men
15. 59 and Eltekon, six cities with their villages
15. 62 and En-gedi; six cities with their villages
Judg. 3. 31 slew of the Philistines six hundred men
12. 7 Jephthah judged Israel six years. Then
18. 11 six hundred men appointed with weapons
18. 16 the six hundred men appointed with th.
18. 17 the six hundred men (that were) appoin.
20. 15 twenty and six thousand men that drew
20. 47 six hundred men turned and fled to the
Ruth 3. 15 he measured six (measures) of barley, and
3. 17 These six measures of barley gave he me
1 Sa. 13. 5 six thousand horsemen, and people as the
13. 15 present with him, about six hundred men
14. 2 people..with him (were) about six hundred
17. 4 Goliath..whose height (was) six cubits and
17. 7 his spear's head (weighed) six hundred sh.
23. 13 his men, (which were) about six hundred
27. 2 he passed over with the six hundred men
30. 9 and the six hundred men that (were) with
2 Sa. 2. 11 David was king..seven years and six mo.
5. 5 he reigned..seven years and six months
6. 13 when they..had gone six paces, he sacri.
15. 18 six hundred men which came after him
21. 20 six fingers, and on every foot six toes
1 Ki. 6. 6 the middle (was) six cubits broad, and the
10. 14 six hundred threescore and six talents of
10. 16 six hundred (shekels) of gold went to one
10. 19 The throne had six steps, and the top of
10. 20 twelve lions stood..upon the six steps: th.
10. 29 went out of Egypt for six hundred (she.)
11. 16 six months did Joab remain there with all
16. 8 In the twenty and sixth year of Asa king
16. 23 Omri..six years reigned he in Tirzah
2 Ki. 5. 5 six thousand (pieces) of gold, and ten ch.
11. 3 hid in the house of the LORD six years
13. 19 Thou shouldest have smitten five or six
15. 8 reign over Israel in Samaria six months
18. 10 in the sixth year of Hezekiah, that (is)
1 Ch. 3. 4 (These) six were born unto him in Hebr.
3. 4 there he reigned seven years and six mo.
3. 22 Bariah, and Neariah, and Shaphat, six
4. 27 Shimei had sixteen sons and six daughters
7. 2 two and twenty thousand and six hundred
7. 4 soldiers for war, six and thirty thousand
7. 40 the number..(was) twenty and six thous.
8. 38 Azel had six sons, whose names (are) th.
9. 6 and their brethren, six hundred and nin.
9. 9 brethren..nine hundred and fifty and six
9. 44 Azel had six sons, whose names (are) th.
12. 24 The children of Judah..(were) six thous.
12. 26 of Levi, four thousand and six hundred
12. 35 twenty and eight thousand and six hund.
20. 6 fingers and toes..six (on each hand), and s.
21. 25 David gave to Ornan for the place six hu.
23. 4 and six thousand (were) officers and jud.
25. 3 the sons of Juduthun..six, under the ha.
26. 17 Eastward (were) six Levites, northward
2 Ch. 1. 17 a chariot for six hundred (shekels) of silv.
2. 2 three thousand and six hundred to over.
2. 17 fifty thousand and three thousand and six
2. 18 three thousand and six hundred overseers
3. 8 fine gold, (amounting) to six hundred ta.
9. 13 six hundred and threescore and six talents
9. 15 six hundred (shekels) of beaten gold went
9. 18 (there were) six steps to the throne, with
9. 19 twelve lions stood..upon the six steps
16. 1 In the six and thirtieth year of the reign
22. 12 he was..hid in the house of God six years
26. 12 men of valour (were) two thousand and six
29. 33 the consecrated things (were) six hundred
35. 8 two thousand and six hundred (small ca.)
Ezra 2. 10 The children of Bani, six hundred forty
2. 11 The children of Bebai, six hundred twenty
2. 13 of Adonikam, six hundred sixty and six
Ezra 2. 14 of Bigvai, two thousand fifty and six
2. 22 The men of Netophah, fifty and six
2. 26 The children of Ramah and Gaba, six hu.
2. 30 of Magbish, an hundred fifty and six
2. 35 three thousand and six hundred and thi.
2. 60 the children of Nekoda, six hundred fifti.
2. 66 horses (were) seven hundred thirty and six
2. 67 (their) asses, six thousand seven hundred
8. 26 I even weighed unto their hand six hun.
8. 35 ninety and six rams, seventy and seven la.
Neh. 5. 18 one ox, (and) six choice sheep; also fowls
7. 10 The children of Arah, six hundred fifty and
7. 15 The children of Binnui, six hundred forty
7. 16 The children of Bebai, six hundred twenty
7. 18 The children of Adonikam, six hundred
7. 20 The children of Adin, six hundred fifty
7. 30 The men of Ramah and Gaba, six hundred
7. 62 the children of Nekoda, six hundred forty
7. 68 Their horses, seven hundred thirty and six
7. 69 six thousand seven hundred and twenty
Esth. 2. 12 six months with oil of myrrh, and six mo.
Job 5. 19 He shall deliver thee in six troubles; yea
42. 12 six thousand camels, and a thousand yoke
Prov. 6. 16 These six (things) doth the LORD hate, yea
Isa. 6. 2 each one had six wings; with twain he co.
Jer. 34. 14 when he hath served thee six years, thou
52. 23 there were ninety and six pomegranates
52. 30 persons (were) four thousand and six hu.
Eze. 9. 2 six men came from the way of the higher
40. 5 measuring reed of six cubits (long) by the
40. 12 six cubits on this side, and six cubits on
41. 1 six cubits broad on the one side, and six
41. 3 door six cubits, and the breadth of the do.
41. 5 measured the wall of the house six cubits
41. 8 the foundations..(were) a full reed of six
46. 1 The gate..shall be shut the six working
46. 4 six lambs without blemish, and a ram wi.
46. 6 a young bullock..and six lambs, and a ram

2. *Six, sixth*, שֵׁשׁ, שֵׁשׁ *sheth, shith.*
Ezra 6. 15 the sixth year of the reign of Darius the
Dan. 3. 1 (and) the breadth thereof six cubits: he

3. *Sixth*, שִׁשִּׁי *shishshi.*
Gen. 1. 31 evening and the morning were the sixth
30. 19 conceived again, and bare Jacob the sixth
Exod16. 5 the sixth day they shall prepare (that) wh.
16. 22 the sixth day they gathered twice as mu.
16. 29 he giveth you on the sixth day the bread
26. 9 shalt double the sixth curtain in the fore
Lev. 25. 21 command my blessing upon you in the si.
Num. 7. 42 On the sixth day Eliasaph the son of De.
29. 29 on the sixth day eight bullocks, two rams
Josh 19. 32 sixth lot came out to the children of Na.
2 Sa. 3. 5 the sixth, Ithream, by Eglah, David's wi.
1 Ch. 2. 15 Ozem the sixth, David the seventh
3. 3 the sixth, Ithream, by Eglah his wife
12. 11 Attai the sixth, Eliel the seventh
24. 9 The fifth to Malchijah, the sixth to Mija.
25. 13 The sixth to Bukkiah, (he), his sons, and
26. 3 Elam the fifth, Jehohanan the sixth, Eli.
26. 5 Ammiel the sixth, Issachar the seventh
27. 9 The sixth (captain) for the sixth month
Neh. 3. 30 Hanun the sixth son of Zalaph, another
Eze. 8. 1 in the sixth year, in the sixth (month), in
Hag. 1. 1 in the sixth month, in the first day of the
1. 15 In the four and twentieth day of the sixth

4. *Six*, ἕξ *hex.*
Matt 17. 1 after six days Jesus taketh Peter, James
Mark 9. 2 after six days Jesus taketh (with him) P.
Luke 4. 25 was shut up three years and six months
13. 14 There are six days in which men ought to
John 2. 6 there were set there six waterpots of sto.
2. 20 Forty and six years was this temple in bu.
12. 1 Jesus, six days before the passover, came
Acts 11. 12 these six brethren accompanied me, and
18. 11 he continued (there) a year and six months
Jas. 5. 17 by the space of three years and six mont
Rev. 4. 8 the four beasts had each of them six win.
13. 18 and his number (is)..threescore and six

5. *Sixth*, ἕκτος *hektos.*
Matt 20. 5 he went out about the sixth and ninth ho.
27. 45 from the sixth hour there was darkness
Mark 15. 33 when the sixth hour was come, there was
Luke 1. 26 in the sixth month the angel Gabriel was
1. 36 this is the sixth month with her, who was
23. 44 it was about the sixth hour, and there was
John 4. 6 sat thus..it was about the sixth hour
19. 14 it was..about [the sixth] hour: and he sa.
Acts 10. 9 Peter went..to pray about the sixth hour
Rev. 6. 12 beheld when he had opened the sixth seal
9. 12, 14; 16. 12; 21. 20

SIX HUNDRED, ἑξακόσιοι *hexakosioi*, Rev. 14. 20.

SIX HUNDRED threescore six, χξς', Rev. 13. 18.

SIX SCORE —

A hundred and twenty, מֵאָה וְעֶשְׂרִים *meah ve-esrim.*
1 Ki 9. 14 Hiram sent to the king six score talents of

SIX SCORE thousand —

Twelve myriads, שְׁתֵּים־עֶשְׂרֵה רִבּוֹ *shete esreh ribbo.*
Jon. 4. 11 wherein are more than sixscore thousand

SIXTEEN, sixteenth —

Sixteen, sixteenth, שֵׁשׁ עָשָׂר, שִׁשָּׁה עָשָׂר, שֵׁשׁ עֶשְׂרֵה *shesh esreh.*
Gen. 46. 18 these she bare unto Jacob, (even) sixteen
Exod26. 25 their sockets (of) silver, sixteen sockets
36. 30 their sockets (were) sixteen sockets of sil.
Num 26. 22 threescore and sixteen thousand and five
31. 40 the persons (were) sixteen thousand; of w.
31. 46 And sixteen thousand persons
Num31. 52 was sixteen thousand seven hundred
Josh. 15. 41 Makkedah; sixteen cities with their vill.
19. 22 Jordan; sixteen cities with their villages
2 Ki. 13. 10 began Jehoash..to reign..in Samaria..six.
14. 21 took Azariah, which (was) sixteen years
15. 2 Sixteen years old was he when he began
15. 33 and he reigned sixteen years in Jerusalem
16. 2 reigned sixteen years in Jerusalem, and
1 Ch 4. 27 Shimei had sixteen sons and six daughters
24. 4 sixteen chief men of the house of (their) fa.
24. 14 The fifteenth to Bilgah, the sixteenth to
25. 23 The sixteenth to Hananiah, (he), his sons
2 Ch. 13. 21 begat twenty and two sons, and sixteen d.
26. 1 took Uzziah, who (was) sixteen years old
26. 3 Sixteen years old (was) Uzziah when he
27. 1, 8 reigned sixteen years in Jerusalem
28. 1 and he reigned sixteen years in Jerusalem
29. 17 in the sixteenth day of the first month they

SIXTEEN, threescore and —

Seventy-six ἑβδομήκοντα ἕξ *hebdomēkonta hex.*
Acts 27. 37 two hundred threescore and sixteen souls

SIXTH part, (to give or leave but the) —

1. *To give or leave a sixth part*, שָׁשָׁא *shasha*, 3.
Eze. 39. 2 leave but the sixth part of thee, and will

2. *To give or leave a sixth part*, שָׁשָׁה *shashah*, 3.
Eze. 45. 13 give the sixth part of an ephah of an homer

3. *Sixth*, שִׁשִּׁי *shishshi.*
Eze 4. 11 sixth part of an hin: from time to time sh.
45. 13 the sixth part of an ephah of an homer of
46. 14 sixth part of an ephah, and the third part
[*See also* Hundred, thousand.]

SIXTY (fold) —

1. *Sixty*, שִׁשִּׁים *shishshim.*
Gen. 5. 15 Mahalaleel lived sixty and five years, and
5. 18 Jared lived an hundred sixty and two ye.
5. 20 days of Jared were nine hundred sixty and
5. 21 Enoch lived sixty and five years, and begat
5. 23 days of Enoch were three hundred sixty
5. 27 were nine hundred sixty and nine years
Lev. 27. 3 twenty years old even unto sixty years old
27. 7 if (it be) from sixty years old and above
Num. 7. 88 rams sixty..he goats sixty..lambs..sixty
Ezra 2. 13 children of Adonikam, six hundred sixty

2. *Sixty*, ἑξήκοντα *hexēkonta.*
Matt 13. 8 some an hundred fold, some sixty fold, so
13. 23 some an hundred fold, some sixty, some th.
Mark 4. 8 brought forth, some thirty, and some sixty
4. 20 some thirty fold, some sixty, and some an

SIZE —

1. *Measure*, מִדָּה *middah.*
Exod36. 9 cubits: the curtains (were) all of one size
36. 15 curtain: the eleven curtains (were)..one s.
1 Ch. 23. 29 and for all manner of measure and size

2. *Cut, cutting*, קֶצֶב *qetseb.*
1 Ki. 6. 25 cherubim..of one measure and one size
7. 37 all of them had one casting..one size

SKILFUL, man of skill —

1. *To understand, give understanding*, בִּין *bin*, 5.
1 Ch. 15. 22 about the song, because he (was) skilful

2. *Wisdom*, חָכְמָה *chokmah.*
1 Ch. 28. 21 every willing skilful man, for any manner

3. *Engraver, carver, artificer*, חָרָשׁ *charash.*
Eze. 21. 31 into the hand of brutish men, (and) skilful

4. *To know, be acquainted with*, יָדַע *yada.*
2 Ch. 2. 14 skilful to work in gold, and in silver, in
Eccl. 9. 11 nor yet favour to men of skill; but time
Amos 5. 16 such as we are skilful of lamentation to

5. *To learn, accustom self*, לָמַד *lamad.*
1 Ch. 5. 18 skilful in war, (were) four and forty thou

6 *To cause to act wisely*, שָׂכַל *sakal*, 5.
Dan. 1. 4 skilful in all wisdom, and cunning in kn.

SKILFULLY, skilfulness —

1. *To do good or well*, יָטַב *yatab*, 5.
Psa. 33. 3 Sing unto him a new song; play skilfully

2. *Understanding, skilfulness*, תְּבוּנָה *tebunah.*
Psa. 78. 72 guided them by the skilfulness of his hands

SKILL, can, to give —

1. *To cause to understand*, בִּין *bin*, 5.
2 Ch. 34. 12 all that could skill of instruments of mu.

2. *To know, be acquainted with*, יָדַע *yada.*
1 Ki. 5. 6 not among us any that can skill to hew t.
2 Ch. 2. 7 that can skill to grave with the cunning
2. 8 know that thy servants can skill to cut ti.

3. *To cause to act wisely*, שָׂכַל *sakal*, 5.
Dan. 1. 17 gave them knowledge and skill in all lea.
9. 22 come forth to give thee skill and underst.

SKIN —

1. *Flesh*, בָּשָׂר *basar.*
Psa. 102. 5 my groaning my bones cleave to my skin

2. *Skin, enclosure*, גֶּלֶד *geled.*
Job 16. 15 have sewed sackcloth upon my skin, and

3. *Skin*, עוֹר *or.*
Gen. 3. 21 did the LORD God make coats of skins, and
27. 16 put the skins of the kids of the goats upon
Exod22. 27 his raiment for his skin: wherein shall he
25. 5 rams' skins dyed red, and badgers' skins
26. 14 covering for the tent (of) rams' skins dyed

Exod26. 14 and a covering above (of) badgers' skins
29. 14 But the flesh of the bullock, and his skin
34. 29 Moses wist not that the skin of his face
34. 30 skin of his face shone; and they were af.
34. 35 saw..that the skin of Moses' face shone
35. 7 rams' skins dyed red, and badgers' skins
35. 23 red skins of rams, and badgers' skins, br.
36. 19 covering for the tent (of) rams' skins dyed
36. 19 and a covering (of) badgers' skin above (th.)
39. 34 covering of rams' skins..badgers' skins
Lev 4. 11 skin of the bullock, and all his flesh, with
7. 8 shall have to himself the skin of the burnt
11. 32 whether (it be) any..raiment, or skin, or
13. 2 When a man shall have in the skin of his
13. 2 it be in the skin of his flesh (like) the pla.
13. 3 priest shall look on the plague in the skin
13. 3 plague in sight (be) deeper than the skin
13. 4 If the bright spot (be) white in the skin
13. 4 in sight (be) not deeper than the skin, and
13. 5 plague spread not in the skin; then the
13. 6 plague spread not in the skin, the priest
13. 7 the scab spread much abroad in the skin
13. 8 scab spreadeth in the skin, then the priest
13. 10 behold, (if) the rising (be) white in the skin
13. 11 an old leprosy in the skin of his flesh, and
13. 12 if a leprosy break out abroad in the skin
13. 12 leprosy cover all the skin of (him that hath)
13. 18 in the skin thereof, was a boil, and is hea.
13. 20 behold, it (be) in sight lower than the skin
13. 21 lower than the skin, but (be) somewhat d.
13. 22 if it spread much abroad in the skin, then
13. 24 Or if there be (any) flesh, in the skin whe.
13. 25 it (be in) sight deeper than the skin, it (is)
13. 26 it (be) no lower than the (other) skin, but
13. 27 if it be spread much abroad in the skin
13. 28 spread not in the skin, but it (be) somewhat
13. 30 behold, if it (be)..deeper than the skin
13. 31 it (be) not in sight deeper than the skin, and
13. 32 scall (be) not in sight deeper than the skin
13. 34 (if) the scall be not spread in the skin, nor
13. 34 in sight deeper than the skin; then the
13. 35 But if the scall spread much in the skin
13. 36 if the scall be spread in the skin, the pr.
13. 38 If a man also or a woman have in the skin
13. 39 the bright spots in the skin of their flesh
13. 39 freckled spot (that) groweth in the skin
13. 43 as the leprosy appeareth in the skin of the
13. 48 whether in a skin, or..any thing made of s.
13. 49 in the skin..or in any thing of skin; it (is)
13. 51 skin, (or) in any work that is made of skin
13. 52 or any thing of skin, wherein the plague
13. 53, 57 or in the woof, or in any thing of skin
13. 56 out of the garment, or out of the skin, or
13. 58 warp or woof, or whatsoever thing of skin
13. 59 in the warp, or woof, or any thing of skin
15. 17 every garment, and every skin, whereon
16. 27 they shall burn in the fire their skins, and
Num. 4. 6 put thereon the covering of badgers' skins
4. 8, 11, 12 cover..a covering of badgers' skins
4. 10 put..within a covering of badgers' skins
4. 14 spread upon it a covering of badgers' sk.
19. 5 her skin, and her flesh, and her blood
31. 20 all that is made of skins, and all work of
Job 2. 4 Skin for skin, yea, all that a man hath will
7. 5 my skin is broken, and become loathsome
10. 11 Thou hast clothed me with skin and flesh
18. 13 It shall devour the strength of his skin
19. 20 My bone cleaveth to my skin and to my
19. 20 and I am escaped with the skin of my te
19. 26 (though) after my skin (worms) destroy
30. 30 My skin is black upon me, and my bones
41. 7 Canst thou fill his skin with barbed irons
Jer. 13. 23 Can the Ethiopian change his skin, or the
Lam. 3. 4 My flesh and my skin hath he made old
4. 8 their skin cleaveth to their bones; it is
5. 10 Our skin was black like an oven because
Eze. 37. 6 cover you with skin, and put breath in
37. 8 the skin covered them above: but (there
Mic. 3. 2 who pluck off their skin from off them
3. 3 Who also..flay their skin from off them

4. *A skin, hide, leather,* δέρμα *derma.*
Heb. 11. 37 wandered about in sheep..and goat skins

5. *Leathern, made of leather,* δερμάτινος *dermatinos.*
Mark 1. 6 and with a girdle of a skin about his loins

SKIP (for joy, to make to), to —

1. *To move or bemoan self,* נוּד *nud, 7a.*
Jer. 48. 27 thou spakest of him, thou skippedst for j.

2. *To skip, spring, dart,* קָפַץ *qaphats,* 3.
Song 2. 8 leaping upon the mountains, skipping up.

3. *To skip, dance,* רָקַד *raqad.*
Psa. 114. 4 mountains skipped like rams, (and) the
114. 6 mountains, (that) ye skipped like rams

4. *To cause to skip,* רָקַד *raqad,* 5.
Psa. 29. 6 He maketh them also to skip like a calf

SKIRT —

1. *Wing,* כָּנָף *kanaph.*
Deut 22. 30 man shall not..discover his father's skirt
27. 20 because he uncovereth his father's skirt
Ruth 3. 9 spread therefore thy skirt over thine ha.
1 Sa. 15. 27 he laid hold upon the skirt of his mantle
24. 4 and cut off the skirt of Saul's robe privily
24. 5 smote..because he had cut off Saul's skirt
24. 11 see the skirt of thy robe in my hand: for
24. 11 I cut off the skirt of thy robe, and killed
Jer. 2. 34 in thy skirts is found the blood of the souls
Eze. 5. 3 also take..and bind them in thy skirts
16. 8 I spread my skirt over thee, and covered
Hag. 2. 12 If one bear holy flesh in the skirt of his
Hag. 2. 12 with his skirt do touch bread, or pottage
Zech. 8. 23 shall take hold of the skirt of him that is

2. *Mouth,* פֶּה *peh.*
Psa. 133. 2 that went down to the skirts of his garm.

3. *Hem, skirt, train,* שׁוּל *shul.*
Jer. 13. 22 thy skirts discovered, (and) thy heels made
13. 26 Therefore will I discover thy skirts upon
Lam. 1. 9 Her filthiness (is) in her skirts; she reme.
Nah. 3. 5 I will discover thy skirts upon thy face

SKULL —

A scull, skull, κρανίον *kranion.*
Matt 27. 33 Golgotha, that is to say, A place of a sk.
Mark 15. 22 Golgotha, which is..The place of a skull
John 19. 17 into a place called (the place) of a skull

SKY —

1. *Small dust, thin cloud,* שַׁחַק *shachaq.*
Deut. 33. 26 (who) rideth..in his excellency on the sk.
2 Sa. 22. 12 dark waters, (and) thick clouds of the sk.
Job 37. 18 Hast thou with him spread out the sky
Psa. 18. 11 dark waters (and) thick clouds of the ski.
77. 17 the skies sent out a sound: thine arrows
Isa. 45. 8 and let the skies pour down righteousness
Jer. 51. 9 judgment..is lifted up (even) to the skies

2. *Heaven,* οὐρανός *ouranos.*
Matt 16. 2 (It will be) fair weather; for the sky is red
16. 3 (It will be) foul weather to day; for the sky
16. 3 ye can discern the face of the sky; but
Luke 12. 56 ye can discern the face of the sky and of
Heb. 11. 12 (so many) as the stars of the sky in mult.

SLACK, (to) be slack, slackness —

1. *To be behind, tarry, delay,* אָחַר *achar,* 3.
Deut. 7. 10 he will not be slack to him that hateth
23. 21 thou shalt not slack to pay it: for the L.

2. *To keep in, restrain,* עָצַר *atsar.*
2 Ki. 4. 24 slack not (thy) riding for me, except I bid

3. *To be feeble, faint, cease,* פּוּג *pug.*
Hab. 1. 4 the law is slacked, and judgment doth

4. *Sloth, remissness,* רְמִיָּה *remiyyah.*
Prov 10. 4 He becometh poor that dealeth (with) a sl.

5. *To be or become feeble, desist,* רָפָה *raphah.*
Zeph. 3. 16 (and to) Zion, Let not thine hands be slack

6. *To (cause to) become feeble, desist,* רָפָה *raphah,* 5.
Josh. 10. 6 Slack not thy hand from thy servants, co.

7. *To become or show self feeble,* רָפָה *raphah,* 7.
Josh. 18. 3 How long (are) ye slack to go to possess

8. *To be slow, delay,* βραδύνω *bradunō.*
2 Pe. 3. 9 The Lord is not slack concerning his pro.

9. *Slowness, tardiness, delay,* βραδυτής *bradutēs.*
2 Pe. 3. 9 Lord is not..as some men count slackness

SLAIN (man, beast) —

1. *To be pierced, wounded, slain,* חָלַל *chalal,* 4.
Eze. 32. 26 all of them uncircumcised, slain by the sw.

2. *Pierced, wounded, slain,* חָלָל *chalal.*
Gen. 34. 27 The sons of Jacob came upon the slain
Num 19. 16 whosoever toucheth one that is slain with
19. 18 him that touched a bone, or one slain or
23. 24 until he..drink the blood of the slain
31. 8 besides the rest of them that were slain
31. 19 whosoever hath touched any slain, purify
Deut. 21. 1 If (one) be found slain in the land which
21. 2 which (are) round about him that is slain
21. 3 the city (which is) next unto the slain man
21. 6 the elders (that are) next unto the slain
32. 42 with the blood of the slain and of the ca.
Josh. 11. 6 will I deliver them up all slain before Is
13. 22 among them that were slain by them
1 Sa. 31. 1 and fell down slain in mount Gilboa
31. 8 when the Philistines came to strip the sl
2 Sa. 1. 19 The beauty of Israel is slain upon thy high
1. 22 From the blood of the slain, from the fat
1. 25 O Jonathan, (thou wast) slain in thine high
1 Ki. 11. 15 Joab..was gone up to bury the slain, after
1 Ch. 5. 22 there fell down many slain, because the
10. 1 and fell down slain in mount Gilboa
10. 8 when the Philistines came to strip the sl.
11. 11 three hundred, slain (by him) at one time
2 Ch. 13. 17 there fell down slain of Israel five hundred
Job 39. 30 and where the slain (are), there (is) she
Psa. 88. 5 Free among the dead, like the slain that
89. 10 broken Rahab in pieces, as one that is sl.
Isa. 22. 2 thy slain (men are) not slain with the sw.
34. 3 Their slain also shall be cast out, and th.
66. 16 and the slain of the LORD shall be many
Jer. 9. 1 weep day and night for the slain of the
14. 18 then behold the slain with the sword, and
25. 33 slain of the LORD shall be at that day from
41. 9 Ishmael..filled it with (them that were) sl.
51. 4 Thus the slain shall fall in the land of the
51. 47 all her slain shall fall in the midst of her
51. 49 As Babylon (hath caused) the slain of Isr.
51. 49 so at Babylon shall fall the slain of all the
Lam. 4. 9 (They that be) slain with the sword are
4. 9 slain with hunger; for these pine away
Eze. 6. 4 cast down your slain (men) before your
6. 7 slain shall fall in the midst of you; and
6. 13 when their slain (men) shall be among th.
9. 7 fill the courts with the slain: go ye forth
11. 6 Ye have multiplied your slain in this city
11. 6 filled the streets thereof with the slain
11. 7 Your slain, whom ye have laid in the mi.
21. 14 let the sword..the sword of the slain: it (is)
21. 14 sword of the great (men that are) slain
Eze. 21. 29 upon the necks of (them that are) slain
28. 8 shalt die the deaths of (them that are) sl.
30. 4 when the slain shall fall in Egypt, and th
30. 11 and they shall..fill the land with the sl.
31. 17 unto (them that be) slain with the sword
31. 18 with (them that be) slain by the sword
32. 20 fall in the midst of (them that are) slain
32. 21 they lie uncircumcised, slain by the sword
32. 22, 23, 24 all of them slain, fallen by the sw.
32. 25 set her a bed in the midst of the slain
32. 25 all of them uncircumcised, slain by the sw.
32. 25 is put in the midst of (them that be) slain
32. 28 shalt lie with (them that are) slain with
32. 29 are laid by (them that were) slain by the sw.
32. 30 which are gone down with the slain
32. 30 uncircumcised with (them that be) slain
32. 31 Pharaoh and all his army slain by the sw.
32. 32 uncircumcised with (them that are) slain
35. 8 I will fill his moutains with his slain (men)
35. 8 shall they fall that are slain with the sw.
Dan. 11. 26 overflow; and many shall fall down slain
Nah. 3. 3 (there is) a multitude of slain, and a great
Zeph. 2. 12 Ye Ethiopians also, ye (shall be) slain by

3. *To slaughter,* שָׁחַט *shachat.*
Lev. 14. 51 dip them in the blood of the slain bird

4. *A slaughtered animal,* σφάγιον *sphagion.*
Acts 7. 42 have ye offered to me slain beasts and sa.

SLAIN, to be —

1. *To be slain,* הָרַג *harag,* 2.
Isa. 27. 7 is he slain according to the slaughter of
Lam. 2. 20 shall the priest and the prophet be slain
Eze. 26. 6 her daughters..shall be slain by the sw.

2. *Slaughter,* הֶרֶג *hereg.*
Prov 24. 11 and (those that are) ready to be slain

3. *To be wasted, destroyed,* חָרַב *chareb,* 2.
2 Ki. 3. 23 the kings are surely slain, and they have

4. *To die,* מוּת *muth.*
1 Sa. 4. 11 and the two sons of Eli..were slain

5. *To be caused to be put to death,* מוּת *muth,* 6.
1 Sa. 19. 6 (As) the LORD liveth, he shall not be slain
20. 32 Wherefore shall he be slain? what hath he
2 Ki. 11. 2 among the..slain..so that he was not s.
11. 8 cometh within the ranges, let him be sla.
11. 15 Let her not be slain in the house of the
11. 16 went by the way..and there was she slain
2 Ch. 22. 11 from among the king's sons that were slain
23. 14 whoso followeth her, let him be slain with

6. *To be plagued,* נָגַף *nagaph,* 2.
Lev. 26. 17 and ye shall be slain before your enemies
2 Sa. 18. 7 the people of Israel were slain before the

7. *To be smitten,* נָכָה *nakah,* 6.
Num 25. 14 Now the name of the Israelite that was sl.
25. 14 that was slain with the Midianitish wom.
25. 15 the Midianitish woman that was slain (w.)
25. 18 which was slain in the day of the plague
Jer. 18. 21 (let) their young men (be) slain by the sw.

8. *To slay,* קְטַל *qetal.*
Dan. 5. 30 that night was Belshazzar the king..slain
7. 11 I beheld (even) till the beast was slain, and

9. *To be slain,* קְטַל *qetal,* 2.
Dan. 2. 13 that the wise (men) should be slain; and

10. *To be slain,* קְטַל *qetal,* 4.
Dan. 2. 13 sought Daniel and his fellows to be slain

11. *To be murdered,* רָצַח *ratsach,* 2.
Judg 20. 4 the husband of the woman that was slain
Prov 22. 13 (There is) a lion without, I shall be slain

12. *To be murdered,* רָצַח *ratsach,* 4.
Psa. 62. 3 ye shall be slain all of you: as a bowing

13. *To be slaughtered,* שָׁחַט *shachat,* 2.
Num 11. 22 Shall the flocks and the herds be slain for

14. *To die off or away,* ἀποθνήσκω *apothnēskō.*
Heb. 11. 37 were tempted, were slain with the sword

SLANDER, slanderer —

1. *Evil account or report,* דִּבָּה *dibbah.*
Num 14. 36 by bringing up a slander upon the land
Psa. 31. 13 I have heard the slander of many: fear
Prov 10. 18 and he that uttereth a slander, (is) a fool

2. *Slander, traffic,* רָכִיל *rakil.*
Jer. 6. 28 grievous revolters, walking with slanders
9. 4 every neighbour will walk with slanders

3. *Devil, accuser, slanderer,* διάβολος *diabolos.*
1 Ti. 3. 11 so (must their) wives (be) grave, not sla

SLANDER, to —

1. *To give forth slander,* נָתַן דֹּפִי *nathan dophi.*
Psa. 50. 20 thou slanderest thine own mother's son

2. *To use the tongue, slander,* לָשַׁן *lashan,* 3a (or 3).
Psa. 101. 5 Whoso privily slandereth his neighbour

3. *To use the feet, slander,* רָגַל *ragal,* 3.
2 Sa. 19. 27 he hath slandered thy servant unto my

SLAUGHTER —

1. *Slaying, slaughter,* הֶרֶג *hereg.*
Esth. 9. 5 with the stroke of the sword, and slaug.
Isa. 27. 7 is he slain according to the slaughter of
30. 25 in the day of the great slaughter, when
Eze. 26. 15 when the slaughter is made in the midst
Jer. 7. 32 but, The valley of slaughter: for they sh.
12. 3 and prepare them for the day of slaugh.

Jer. 19. 6 be called Tophet..but The valley of sla.
Zech 11. 4 saith the LORD..Feed the flock of the sl.
11. 7 I will feed the flock of slaughter, (even)

3. *To slaughter*, טָבַח *tabach.*
Jer. 11. 19 (or)an ox(that) is brought to the slaughter
25. 34 the days of your slaughter and of your di.
51. 40 bring them down like lambs to the slau.

4. *Slaughter, slaughtered animal*, טֶבַח *tebach.*
Prov. 7. 22 as an ox goeth to the slaughter, or as a fo.
Isa. 34. 2 he hath delivered them to the slaughter
34. 6 a great slaughter in the land of Idumea
53. 7 he is brought as a lamb to the slaughter
65. 12 ye shall all bow down to the slaughter
Jer. 48. 15 young men are gone down to the slaugh.
50. 27 let them go down to the slaughter: woe
Eze. 21. 15 bright, (it is) wrapped up for the slaugh.
21. 28 the slaughter (it is) furbished, to consume

5. *Slaughter*, טִבְחָה *tibchah.*
Psa. 44. 22 we are counted as sheep for the slaughter
Jer. 12. 3 pull them out like sheep for the slaughter

6. *Plague, stroke*, מַגֵּפָה *maggephah.*
1 Sa. 4. 17 there hath been also a great slaughter am.
2 Sa. 17. 9 There is a slaughter among the people th.
18. 7 there was there a great slaughter that day

7. *Slaughter*, מַטְבֵּחַ *matbeach.*
Isa. 14. 21 Prepare slaughter for his children for the

8. *Smiting, stroke, blow*, מַכָּה *makkah.*
Josh. 10. 10 slew them with a great slaughter at Gib.
10. 20 slaying them with a very great slaughter
Judg 11. 33 smote them..with a very great slaughter
15. 8 he smote them..with a great slaughter
1 Sa. 4. 10 there was a very great slaughter, for there
6. 19 had smitten (many)..with a great slaugh.
14. 14 that first slaughter, which Jonathan and
14. 30 a much greater slaughter among the Phi.
19. 8 went..and slew them with a great slaug.
23. 5 and smote them with a great slaughter
1 Ki. 20. 21 slew the Syrians with a great slaughter
2 Ch. 13. 17 his people slew them with a great slaug.
28. 5 who smote him with a great slaughter
Isa. 10. 26 according to the slaughter of Midian at

9. *Slaughter axe*, מַפָּץ *mappats.*
Eze. 9. 2 every man a slaughter weapon in his hand

10. *To (cause to) smite*, נָכָה *nakah*, 5.
Gen. 14. 17 return from the slaughter of Chedorlaom.
1 Sa. 17. 57 David returned from the slaughter of the
18. 6 David was returned from the slaughter of
2 Sa. 1. 1 David was returned from the slaughter of
2 Ch. 25. 14 Amaziah was come from the slaughter of

11. *Slaughter, killing*, קֶטֶל *qetel.*
Obad. 9 every one..may be cut off by slaughter

12. *Murder*, רֶצַח *retsach.*
Eze. 21. 22 to open the mouth in the slaughter, to

13. *A smiting, slaughter*, κοπή *kopē.*
Heb. 7. 1 returning from the slaughter of the kings

14. *Slaughter*, σφαγή *sphagē.*
Acts 8. 32 He was led as a sheep to the slaughter
Rom. 8. 36 we are accounted as sheep for the slaugh.
Jas. 5. 5 nourished your hearts, as in a day of sla.

15. *Murder, slaughter, homicide*, φόνος *phonos.*
Acts 9. 1 breathing out threatenings and slaughter

SLAUGHTER, to make or be made a —

1. *To be slain*, הָרַג *harag*, 2.
Eze. 26. 15 when the slaughter is made in the midst

2. *To slaughter*, טָבַח *tabach.*
Eze. 21. 10 It is sharpened to make a sore slaughter

3. *To slaughter*, שָׁחַט *shachat.*
Hos. 5. 2 the revolters are profound to make slau.

SLAVE —

Body, person, σῶμα *sōma.*
Rev. 18. 13 horses, and chariots, and slaves and souls

SLAY (utterly), to —

1. *To slay*, הָרַג *harag.*
Gen. 4. 8 rose up against Abel his brother, and slew
4. 14 every one that findeth me shall slay me
4. 15 whosoever slayeth Cain, vengeance shall
4. 23 I have slain a man to my wounding, and
4. 25 another..instead of Abel, whom Cain slew
20. 4 Lord, wilt thou slay also a righteous nat.?
20. 11 and they will slay me for my wife's sake
27. 41 The days..are at hand; then will I slay
34. 25 came upon the city boldly, and slew all
34. 26 they slew Hamor and Shechem his son
37. 20 let us slay him, and cast him into some
37. 26 What profit (is it) if we slay our brother
49. 6 in their anger they slew a man, and in th.
Exod. 2. 15 when Pharaoh heard..he sought to slay
4. 23 behold, I will slay thy son, (even) thy first
5. 21 to put a sword in their hand to slay us
13. 15 the LORD slew all the first born in the la.
21. 14 But if a man come..to slay him with gu.
23. 7 the innocent and righteous slay thou not
32. 12 to slay them in the mountains, and to co.
32. 27 slay every man his brother, and every man
Lev. 20. 15 if a man lie with a beast..slay the beast
Num 22. 33 surely now also I had slain thee, and sav.
25. 5 Slay ye every one his men that were joined
31. 7 they warred..and they slew all the males
31. 8 they slew the kings of Midian, besides the
31. 8 Baalam also the son of Beor they slew with
Josh. 8. 24 when Israel had made an end of slaying
Josh. 9. 26 delivered them..that they slew them not
10. 11 (they) whom the children of Israel slew
13. 22 did the children of Israel slay with the s.
Judg. 7. 25 they slew Oreb upon the rock Oreb, and
7. 25 Zeeb they slew at the wine press of Zeeb
8. 17 he beat down the tower..and slew the
8. 18 What manner of men (were they) whom
8. 19 if ye had saved them..I would not slay
8. 20 said unto Jether his first born, Up, (and)s.
8. 21 Gideon arose, and slew Zebah and
9. 5 slew his brethren the sons of Jerubbaal
9. 18 have slain his sons, threescore and ten pe.
9. 24 Abimelech their brother, which slew them
9. 45 he took the city, and slew the people that
9. 54 that men say not of me, A woman slew him
9. 56 which he did unto his father, in slaying
20. 5 men of Gibeah..thought to have slain me
1 Sa. 22. 21 that Saul had slain the LORD'S priests
2 Sa. 3. 30 So Joab and Abishai his brother slew Ab.
4. 10 I took hold of him, and slew him in Ziklag
4. 11 when wicked men have slain a righteous
4. 12 they slew them, and cut off their hands
10. 18 David slew (the men of) seven hundred ch.
12. 9 hast slain him with the sword of the chil.
14. 7 for the life of his brother whom he slew
23. 21 plucked..and slew him with his own spear
1 Ki. 2. 5 Amasa the son of Jether, whom he slew
2. 32 who fell upon two men..and slew them
9. 16 slain the Canaanites that dwelt in the city
11. 24 captain over a band, when David slew them
18. 12 and he cannot find thee, he shall slay me
18. 13 when Jezebel slew the prophets of the L.
18. 14 Go, tell thy lord..and he shall slay me
19. 1 he had slain all the prophets with the sw.
19. 10, 14 and slain thy prophets with the sword
2 Ki. 8. 12 their young men wilt thou slay with the
9. 31 she said, (Had) Zimri peace, who slew his
10. 9 I conspired against my master, and slew
11. 18 slew Mattan the priest of Baal before the
17. 25 sent lions among them, which slew (some)
1 Ch. 7. 21 whom the men of Gath..slew, because th.
11. 23 went down..and slew him with his own
19. 18 David slew of the Syrians seven thousand
2 Ch. 21. 4 slew all his brethren with the sword, and
21. 13 hast slain thy brethren of thy father's ho.
22. 1 for the band of men..had slain all the el.
22. 8 when Jehu..found the princes..he slew
23. 17 slew Mattan the priest of Baal before the
24. 22 remembered not the kindness..but slew
24. 25 slew him on his bed, and he died: and th.
25. 3 slew his servants that had killed the king
28. 6 For Pekah the son of Remaliah slew in J.
28. 7 slew Maaseiah the king's son, and Azrik.
28. 9 ye have slain them in a rage (that) reacheth
36. 17 who slew their young men with the sword
Neh. 4. 11 slay them, and cause the work to cease
6. 10 shut the doors..for they will come to sl.
6. 10 yea, in the night will they come to slay
9. 26 slew thy prophets which testified against
Esth. 7. 4 to be destroyed, to be slain, and to perish
8. 11 to stand for their life, to destroy, to slay
9. 6 Jews slew and destroyed five hundred men
9. 10 The ten sons of Haman..slew they; but
9. 12 Jews have slain and destroyed five hun.
9. 15 slew three hundred men at Shushan: but
9. 16 slew of their foes seventy and five thou.
Job 20. 16 of asps: the viper's tongue shall slay him
Psa. 59. 11 Slay them not, lest my people forget: sc.
78. 31 slew the fattest of them, and smote down
78. 34 When he slew them, then they sought him
94. 6 They slay the widow and the stranger, and
135. 10 smote great nations, and slew mighty kings
136. 18 slew famous kings: for his mercy (endu.)
Prov. 1. 32 turning away of the simple shall slay th.
Isa. 14. 20 destroyed thy land, (and) slain thy people
14. 30 kill thy root..and he shall slay thy rem.
22. 13 slaying oxen and killing sheep, eating fl.
27. 1 he shall slay the dragon that (is) in the sea
Jer. 15. 3 the sword to slay, and the dogs to tear, and
Lam. 2. 4 slew all (that were) pleasant to the eye in
2. 21 thou hast slain (them) in the day of thine
3. 43 thou hast slain, thou hast not pitied
Eze. 9. 6 Slay utterly old (and) young, both maids
23. 10 slew her with the sword: and she became
23. 47 slay their sons and their daughters, and
26. 8 He shall slay with the sword thy daugh.
26. 11 he shall slay thy people by the sword, and
28. 9 Wilt thou yet say before him that slayeth
Hos. 6. 5 slain them by the words of my mouth: and
Amos 2. 3 will slay all the princes thereof with him
4. 10 your young men have I slain with the sw.
9. 1 I will slay the last of them with the sw.
9. 4 command the sword, and it shall slay th.
Hab. 1. 17 not spare continually to slay the nations
Zech 11. 5 Whose possessors slay them, and hold th.

2. *To slaughter, sacrifice*, זָבַח *zabach.*
1 Ki. 1. 9 Adonijah slew sheep and oxen and fat ca.
1. 19 hath slain oxen and fat cattle and sheep
1. 25 hath slain oxen and fat cattle and sheep
19. 21 slew them, and boiled their flesh with the
2 Ki. 23. 20 he slew all the priests of the high places

3. *To pierce*, חָלַל *chalal.*
Judg 16. 24 destroyer of our country, which slew ma.
2 Sa. 23. 8 eight hundred, whom he slew at one ti.
23. 18 slew (them), and had the name among th.
1 Ch. 11. 20 slew them, and had a name among the th.

4. *To pierce*, חָלַל *chalal*, 3.
Eze. 28. 9 no god, in the hand of him that slayeth

5. *To waste, be dried up*, חָרֵב *chareb.*
Jer. 50. 27 Slay all her bullocks; let them go down

6. *To devote to God* or *destruction*, חָרַם *charam*, **5.**
2 Ch. 20. 23 Ammon and Moab stood up..utterly to s

7. *To slaughter (a slaughter)*, (טֶבַח) טָבַח *tabach (tebach).*
Gen. 43. 16 (these) men home, and slay, Deut. 28. 31.
Psa. 37. 14 to slay such as be of upright conversation

8. *To put to death*, מוּת *muth*, 3a.
Judg. 9. 54 Draw thy sword, and slay me, that men
1 Sa. 14. 13 and his armour bearer slew after him
17. 51 slew him, and cut off his head therewith
2 Sa. 1. 9 Stand, I pray thee, upon me, and slay me
1. 10 I stood upon him, and slew him, because
1. 16 saying, I have slain the LORD'S anointed
Psa. 34. 21 Evil shall slay the wicked; and they that
109. 16 that he might even slay the broken in he.
Jer. 20. 17 Because he slew me not from the womb

9. *To (cause to) put to death*, מוּת *muth*, 5.
Gen. 18. 25 to slay the righteous with the wicked
37. 18 they conspired against him to slay him
38. 7 Er..was wicked..and the LORD slew him
38. 10 displeased the LORD: wherefore he slew
42. 37 Slay my two sons, if I bring him not to
Num 35. 19 The revenger of blood himself shall slay
35. 19 when he meeteth him, he shall slay him
35. 21 the revenger of blood shall slay the mur.
Deut. 9. 28 he hath brought them out to slay them
Josh. 10. 26 Joshua smote them, and slew them, and
11. 17 he took, and smote them, and slew them
Judg 16. 30 so the dead which he slew at his death we.
16. 30 more than (they) which he slew in his life
1 Sa. 2. 25 because the LORD would slay them
5. 10 brought about the ark..to us, to slay us
5. 11 let it go..that it slay us not, and our pe.
15. 3 slay both man and woman, infant and su.
17. 35 I caught (him) by his beard..and slew him
17. 50 and smote the Philistine, and slew him
19. 5 wilt thou sin..to slay David without a ca.
19. 11 to watch him, and to slay him in the mo.
19. 15 Bring him up to me..that I may slay him
20. 8 if there be in me iniquity, slay me thyself
20. 33 it was determined of his father to slay D.
22. 17 Turn, and slay the priests of the LORD
22. 18 slew on that day fourscore and five persons
30. 2 they slew not any, either great or small
2 Sa. 3. 30 he had slain their brother Asahel at
3. 37 it was not of the king to slay Abner the
4. 7 they smote him, and slew him, and beh.
13. 32 Let not my lord suppose (that) they h. s.
14. 6 but the one smote the other, and slew him
18. 15 compassed about and smote Absalom..sl.
21. 1 (It is) for Saul..because he slew the Gib.
1 Ki. 1. 51 he will not slay his servant with the sword
2. 34 went up, and fell upon him, and slew him
3. 26, 27 give her the..child, and in no wise slay
13. 24 a lion met him by the way, and slew him
13. 26 which hath torn him, and slain him, acc.
15. 28 in the third year..did Baasha slay him
17. 18 call..to remembrance, and to slay my son
17. 20 brought evil upon the widow..by slaying
18. 9 wouldest deliver thy servant..to slay me
19. 17 (that) him that escapeth..shall Jehu slay
19. 17 and him that escapeth..shall Elisha slay
2 Ki. 11. 20 they slew Athaliah with the sword (beside)
14. 6 the children of the murderers he slew not
14. 19 they sent after him to Lachish, and slew
15. 10 smote him before the people, and slew him
15. 14 and slew him, and reigned in his stead
15. 30 smote him, and slew him, and reigned in
16. 9 carried (the people of) it captive..and slew
17. 26 they slay them, because they know not
21. 23 conspired against him, and slew the king
23. 29 he slew him at Megiddo, when he had seen
25. 21 slew them at Riblah in the land of Ham.
1 Ch. 2. 3 evil in the sight of the LORD; and he slew
10. 14 he slew him, and turned the kingdom unto
2 Ch. 22. 9 when they had slain him, they buried him
22. 11 hid him from Athaliah, so that she slew
23. 14 said, Slay her not in the house of the L.
23. 15 by the king's house, they slew her there
23. 21 they had slain Athaliah with the sword
25. 4 he slew not their children, but (did) as (it
25. 27 sent to Lachish after him, and slew him
33. 24 conspired against him, and slew him in
Job 5. 2 killeth the foolish man, and envy slayeth
9. 23 If the scourge slay suddenly, he will laugh
Psa. 37. 32 The wicked watcheth..and seeketh to sl.
105. 29 turned their waters into blood, and slew
Isa. 11. 4 with the breath of his lips shall he slay the
65. 15 GOD shall slay thee, and call his servants
Jer. 41. 2 slew him, whom the king of Babylon had
41. 4 the second day after he had slain Gedaliah
41. 8 Slay us not; for we have treasures in the
41. 8 and slew them not among their brethren
Eze. 13. 19 to slay the souls that should not die, and
Hos. 2. 3 set her like a dry land, and slay her with
9. 16 yet will I slay (even) the beloved (fruit) of

9a. *For death*, לָמָוֶת [*maveth*]. Jer. 18. 23.

10. *To (cause to) smite*, נָכָה *nakah*, **5.**
Gen 34. 30 they shall gather themselves..and slay me
Exod 2. 12 he slew the Egyptian, and hid him in the
Deut. 1. 4 After he had slain Sihon the king of the
19. 6 Lest the avenger of the blood..slay him
Josh. 8. 21 they turned again, and slew the men of Ai
10. 10 slew them with a great slaughter at Gibe.
10. 20 Israel had made an end of slaying them
Judg. 1. 4 they slew of them in Bezek ten thousand
1. 5 they slew the Canaanites and the Perizz.
1. 10 they slew Sheshai, and Ahiman, and Ta.
1. 17 they slew the Canaanites that inhabited
3. 29 they slew of Moab at that time about ten
3. 31 which slew of the Philistines six hundred

Judg. 9. 44 two (other) companies ran..and slew them
14. 19 slew thirty men of them, and took their
15. 15 took it, and slew a thousand men there.
15. 16 with the jaw of an ass have I slain a tho.
20. 45 and slew two thousand men of them
1 Sa. 4. 2 they slew of the army in the field about
11. 11 slew the Ammonites until the heat of the
17. 36 Thy servant slew both the lion and the be.
18. 7 Saul hath slain his thousands, and David
18. 27 slew of the Philistines two hundred men
19. 5 slew the Philistine, and the LORD wrought
19. 8 and slew them with a great slaughter
21. 9 whom thou slewest in the valley of Elah
21. 11 Saul hath slain his thousands, and David
29. 5 Saul slew his thousands, and David his
31. 2 the Philistines slew Jonathan, and Abina.
2 Sa. 8. 5 David slew of the Syrians two and twenty
13. 30 Absalom hath slain all the king's sons, and
21. 2 Saul sought to slay them in his zeal to the
21. 12 when the Philistines had slain Saul in G.
21. 16 he, being girded..thought to have slain D.
21. 18 Sibbechai the Hushathite slew Saph, which
21. 19 slew (the brother of) Goliath the Gittite, the
21. 21 Jonathan the son of Shimeah..slew him
23. 12 and defended it, and slew the Philistines
23. 20 he slew two lion like men of Moab: he we.
23. 20 slew a lion in the midst of a pit in time
23. 21 And he slew an Egyptian, a goodly man
1 Ki. 16. 11 he slew all the house of Baasha: he left
16. 16 Zimri hath conspired, and hath also slain
20. 20 they slew every one his man: and the Sy.
20. 21 slew the Syrians with a great slaughter
20. 29 the children of Israel slew of the Syrians
20. 36 Then said he..a lion shall slay thee
20. 36 as soon as he was departed..a lion..slew
2 Ki. 10. 9 Ye (be) righteous..but who slew all these?
10. 11 Jehu slew all that remained of the house
10. 17 he slew all that remained unto Ahab
10. 25 Go in (and) slay them; let none come forth
12. 20 slew Joash in the house of Millo, which
14. 5 he slew his servants which had slain the
14. 7 He slew of Edom in the valley of salt ten
15. 30 smote him, and slew him, and reigned in
21. 24 the people of the land slew all them that
1 Ch 10. 2 the Philistines slew Jonathan, and Abin.
11. 14 and delivered it, and slew the Philistines
11. 22 he slew two lion like men of Moab
11. 22 and slew a lion in a pit in a snowy day
11. 23 he slew an Egyptian, a man of (great) sta.
18. 5 David slew of the Syrians two and twenty
18. 12 the son of Zeruiah slew of the Edomites
20. 4 Sibbechai the Hushathite slew Sippai, (th.)
20. 5 the son of Jair slew Lahmi the brother of
20. 7 the son of Shimea, David's brother, slew
2 Ch. 13. 17 Abijah and his people slew them with a gr.
33. 25 the people of the land slew all them that
Job 1. 15 they have slain the servants with the edge
1. 17 slain the servants with the edge of the sw.
Isa. 66. 3 He that killeth an ox (is as if) he slew a
Jer. 5. 6 a lion out of the forest shall slay them, (a.)
20. 4 shall carry them captive..and shall slay
26. 23 who slew him with the sword, and cast
29. 21 and he shall slay them before your eyes
33. 5 whom I have slain in mine anger, and in
40. 15 I will slay Ishmael the son of Nethaniah
40. 15 wherefore should he slay thee, that all the
41. 3 Ishmael also slew all the Jews that were
41. 16 he had slain Gedaliah the son of Ahikam
41. 18 the son of Nethaniah had slain Gedaliah
41. 9 the men, whom he had slain because of
Eze. 9. 7 And they went forth, and slew in the city
9. 8 it came to pass, while they were slaying th.

11. *Smite murderously (the blood of)*, (דָּם) נָכָה נֶפֶשׁ [*nakah*, 5].
Jer. 40. 14 Ishmael the son of N. to slay, Deut. 27. 25.

12. *To cause to fall*, נָפַל *naphal*, 5.
2 Ch. 32. 21 they that came..slew him there with the

13. *To kill*, קָטַל *qatal*.
Job 13. 15 Though he slay me, yet will I trust in him
Psa. 139. 19 thou wilt slay the wicked, O God: depart

14. *To kill*, קְטַל *qetal*.
Dan 5. 19 whom he would he slew, and whom he

15. *To kill*, קְטַל *qetal*, 3.
Dan. 2. 14 which was gone forth to slay the wise (m.)
3. 22 the flame of the fire slew those men that

16. *To murder a soul*, רָצַח נֶפֶשׁ *ratsach nephesh*.
Deut 22. 26 riseth against his neighbour, and slayeth

17. *To slaughter*, שָׁחַט *shachat*.
Gen. 22. 10 Abraham..took the knife to slay his son
Exod 29. 16 thou shalt slay the ram, and thou shalt
Lev. 4. 29 slay the sin offering in the place of the
4. 33 slay it for a sin offering in the place wh.
8. 15, 23 And he slew (it); and Moses took the
9. 8 slew the calf of the sin offering which (w.)
9. 12 he slew the burnt offering; and Aaron's so.
9. 15 slew it, and offered it for sin, as the first
9. 18 He slew also the bullock and the ram (for)
14. 13 he shall slay the lamb in the place where
Num 14. 16 therefore he hath slain them in the wil.
19. 3 bring her..and (one) shall slay her before
Judg 12. 6 and slew him at the passages of Jordan
1 Sa. 1. 25 they slew a bullock, and brought the ch.
14. 32 took sheep, and oxen, and calves, and sl.
14. 34 slay (them) here, and eat; and sin not ag.
14. 34 brought every man his ox..and slew (th.)
1 Ki. 18. 40 Elijah brought them..and slew them th.
2 Ki. 10. 7 slew seventy persons, and put their heads
10. 14 slew them at the pit of the shearing house
2 Ki. 25. 7 they slew the sons of Zedekiah before his
Isa. 57. 5 slaying the children in the valleys under
Jer. 39. 6 the king of Babylon slew the sons of Zec.
39. 6 the king of Babylon slew all the nobles of
41. 7 Ishmael the son of Nethaniah slew them
52. 10 the king of Babylon slew the sons of Ze.
52. 10 he slew also all the princes of Judah in R.
Eze. 16. 21 thou hast slain my children, and deliver.
23. 39 they had slain their children to their id.
40. 39 to slay thereon the burnt offering, and the
40. 41 eight tables, whereupon..slew (their sa.)
40. 42 they slew the burnt offering and the sac.
44. 11 shall slay the burnt offering and the sac.

18. *To take up or away*, ἀναιρέω *anaireō*.
Matt. 2. 16 slew all the children that were in Bethl.
Acts 2. 23 by wicked hands have crucified and slain
5. 33 they were cut..and took counsel to slay
5. 36 who was slain; and all, as many as obey.
9. 29 spake boldly..but they went about to slay
10. 39 whom they slew and hanged on a tree
13. 28 desired they Pilate that he should be sla.
22. 20 kept the raiment of them that slew him

19. *To kill off*, ἀποκτείνω *apokteinō*.
Matt 21. 39 cast (him) out of the vineyard, and slew
22. 6 entreated (them) spitefully, and slew (th.)
Luke 9. 22 and be slain, and be raised the third day
11. 49 (some) of them they shall slay and perse.
13. 4 the tower in Siloam fell, and slew them
John 5. 16 [sought to slay him, because he had done]
Acts 7. 52 they have slain them which showed before
23. 14 we will eat nothing until we have slain P.
Rom. 7. 11 For sin..deceived me, and by it slew (me)
Eph. 2. 16 reconcile both..having slain the enmity
Rev. 2. 13 my faithful martyr, who was slain among
9. 15 prepared..for to slay the third part of m.
11. 13 in the earthquake were slain of men sev.
19. 21 the remnant were slain with the sword of

20. *To handle severely*, διαχειρίζομαι *diacheirizomai*.
Acts 5. 30 Jesus, whom ye slew and hanged on a tr.

21. *To sacrifice, slaughter*, θύω *thuō*.
Acts 11. 7 a voice saying unto me, Arise, Peter; slay

22. *To slay utterly*, κατασφάττω *kataasphattō*, -άζω.
Luke 19. 27 bring hither, and slay (them) before me

23. *To slay, slaughter*, σφάττω *sphattō*, σφάζω.
1 Jo. 3. 12 slew his brother. And wherefore slew he
Rev. 5. 6 stood a Lamb as it had been slain, having
5. 9 thou wast slain, and hast redeemed us to
5. 12 Worthy is the Lamb that was slain to re.
6. 9 the souls of them that were slain for the
13. 8 the Lamb slain from the foundation of
18. 24 and of all that were slain upon the earth

24. *To murder*, φονεύω *phoneuō*.
Matt 23. 35 whom ye slew between the temple and

SLAYER —

1. *To slay*, הָרַג *harag*.
Eze. 21. 11 to give it into the hand of the slayer

2. *To (cause to) smite*, נָכָה *nakah*, 5.
Num 35. 24 shall judge between the slayer and the re.

3. *To murder*, רָצַח *ratsach*.
Num 35. 11 that the slayer may flee thither, which
35. 25 the congregation shall deliver the slayer
35. 26 if the slayer shall at any time come with.
35. 27 and the revenger of blood shall kill the sl.
35. 28 the slayer shall return into the land of his
Deut. 4. 42 That the slayer might flee thither, which
19. 3 three parts, that every slayer may flee th.
19. 4 this (is) the case of the slayer which shall
19. 6 the avenger of the blood pursue the slayer
Josh 20. 3 the slayer that killeth (any) person unawa.
20. 5 they shall not deliver up the slayer into
20. 6 then shall the slayer return, and come
21. 13, 21, 27, 32, 38 city of refuge for the slayer

SLEEP, one out of, sleeping, slept —

1. *Sleeping, one asleep*, יָשֵׁן *yashen*.
1 Sa. 26. 7 Saul lay sleeping within the trench, and
1 Ki. 3. 20 took my son..while thine handmaid slept
Psa. 78. 65 the Lord awaked as one out of sleep, (and)

2. *To be fast asleep, in a trance*, רָדַם *radam*, 2.
Jon. 1. 6 What meanest thou, O sleeper? arise, call

3. *Sleep*, שֵׁנָא *shena*.
Psa. 127. 2 (for) so he giveth his beloved sleep

4. *Sleep*, שֵׁנָה *shenah*.
Gen. 28. 16 Jacob awaked out of his sleep, and he sa.
31. 40 and my sleep departed from mine eyes
Judg 16. 14 he awaked out of his sleep, and went away
16. 20 he awoke out of his sleep, and said, I will
Job 14. 12 not awake, nor be raised out of their sleep
Esth. 6. 1 On that night could not the king sleep
Psa. 76. 5 The stout hearted..have slept their sleep
90. 5 they are (as) a sleep: in the morning (they)
Prov. 3. 24 thou shalt lie down, and thy sleep shall be
4. 16 their sleep is taken away, unless they ca.
6. 4 Give not sleep to thine eyes, nor slumber
6. 9 when wilt thou arise out of thy sleep?
6. 10 a little sleep, a little slumber, a little fol.
20. 13 Love not sleep, lest thou come to poverty
24. 33 a little sleep, a little slumber, a little fol.
Eccl. 5. 12 The sleep of a labouring man (is) sweet
8. 16 neither day nor night seeth sleep with his
Jer. 31. 26 I awaked, and beheld; and my sleep was
51. 39 may rejoice, and sleep a perpetual sleep
51. 57 they shall sleep a perpetual sleep, and not
Dan. 2. 1 his spirit was troubled, and his sleep br.
Zech. 4. 1 as a man that is wakened out of his sleep

5. *Sleep*, שֵׁנָה *shenah*.
Dan. 6. 18 passed the night fasting..his sleep went

6. *Sleep*, שְׁנַת *shenath*.
Psa. 132. 4 I will not give sleep to mine eyes, (or) sl.

7. *Sleep*, ὕπνος *hupnos*.
Matt. 1. 24 Joseph, being raised from sleep, did as the
Luke 9. 32 But Peter and they..were heavy with sl.
John 11. 13 he had spoken of taking of rest in sleep
Acts 20. 9 Eutychus, being fallen into a deep sleep
20. 9 he sunk down with sleep, and fell down
Rom 13. 11 now (it is) high time to awake out of sleep

SLEEP (on), to —

1. *To doze*, הָזָה *hazah*.
Isa. 56. 10 sleeping, lying down, loving to slumber

2. *Sleeping*, יָשֵׁן *yashen*.
1 Ki. 18. 27 peradventure he sleepeth, and must be a.
Song 5. 2 I sleep, but my heart waketh: (it is) the vo.
Dan. 12. 2 many of them that sleep in the dust of the
Hos. 7. 6 their baker sleepeth all the night; in the

3. *To sleep*, יָשֵׁן *yashen*.
Gen. 2. 21 sleep to fall upon Adam, and he slept
41. 5 he slept and dreamed the second time
1 Ki. 19. 5 as he lay and slept under a juniper tree
Job 3. 13 I should have slept: then had I been at
Psa. 3. 5 I laid me down and slept; I awaked; for
4. 8 I will both lay me down in peace, and sle.
13. 3 lighten mine eyes, lest I sleep the (sleep of)
44. 23 why sleepest thou, O LORD? arise, cast us
121. 4 Behold, he..shall neither slumber nor sl.
Prov. 4. 16 they sleep not, except they have done mi.
Isa. 5. 27 none shall slumber nor sleep; neither sh.
Jer. 51. 39 that they may rejoice, and sleep a perpe.
51. 57 and they shall sleep a perpetual sleep
Eze. 34. 25 they shall dwell safely..and sleep in the

4. *To slumber, sleep*, נוּם *num*.
Psa. 76. 5 stout hearted are spoiled, they have slept

5. *To be fast asleep, in a trance*, רָדַם *radam*, 2.
Prov 10. 5 he that sleepeth in harvest is a son that

6. *To lie down*, שָׁכַב *shakab*.
Gen. 28. 11 and he..lay down in that place to sleep
Exod 22. 27 it (is) his raiment..wherein shall he sleep?
Deut 24. 12 if the man (be) poor, thou shalt not sleep
24. 13 that he may sleep in his own raiment, and
31. 16 thou shalt sleep with thy fathers; and th.
2 Sa. 7. 12 and thou shalt sleep with thy fathers
11. 9 Uriah slept at the door of the king's house
1 Ki. 1. 21 when my lord the king shall sleep with his
2. 10 David slept with his fathers, and was bu.
11. 21 Hadad heard in Egypt that David slept wi.
11. 43 Solomon slept with his fathers, and was
14. 20 he slept with his fathers; and Nadab his
14. 31 Rehoboam slept with his fathers, and was
15. 8 Abijam slept with his fathers; and they
15. 24 Asa slept with his fathers, and was buried
16. 6 Baasha slept with his fathers, and was bu.
16. 28 Omri slept with his fathers, and was bur.
22. 40 Ahab slept with his fathers; and Ahaziah
22. 50 Jehoshaphat slept with his fathers, and
2 Ki. 8. 24 Joram slept with his fathers, and was bu.
10. 35 Jehu slept with his fathers: and they bu.
13. 9 Jehoahaz slept with his fathers; and they
13. 13 Joash slept with his fathers; and Jerobo.
14. 16 Jehoash slept with his fathers, and was
14. 22 after that the king slept with his fathers
14. 29 Jeroboam slept with his fathers, (even) wi
15. 7 Azariah slept with his fathers; and they
15. 22 Menahem slept with his fathers; and Pe.
15. 38 Jotham slept with his fathers, and was bu
16. 20 Ahaz slept with his fathers, and was bu.
20. 21 Hezekiah slept with his fathers: and Man
21. 18 Manasseh slept with his fathers, and wa
24. 6 Jehoiakim slept with his fathers: and Je.
2 Ch. 9. 31 Solomon slept with his fathers, and he
12. 16 Rehoboam slept with his fathers, and w.
14. 1 Abijah slept with his fathers, and they bu.
16. 13 Asa slept with his fathers, and died in the
21. 1 Jehoshaphat slept with his fathers, and
26. 2 after that the king slept with his fathers
26. 23 Uzziah slept with his fathers, and they bu.
27. 9 Jotham slept with his fathers, and they
28. 27 Ahaz slept with his fathers, and they bu.
32. 33 Hezekiah slept with his fathers, and they
33. 20 Manasseh slept with his fathers, and they
Job 7. 21 now shall I sleep in the dust; and thou
Prov. 6. 9 How long wilt thou sleep, O sluggard? wh
6. 10 a little folding of the hands to sleep
6. 22 when thou sleepest, it shall keep thee, and
24. 33 a little folding of the hands to sleep

7. *To sleep*, καθεύδω *katheudō*.
Matt. 9. 24 for the maid is not dead, but sleepeth
13. 25 while men slept, his enemy came and so.
25. 5 While the bridegroom tarried, they..slept
26. 45 Sleep on now, and (take) your rest: behold
Mark 4. 27 And should sleep, and rise night and day
5. 39 the damsel is not dead, but sleepeth
13. 36 Lest, coming suddenly, he find you sleep.
14. 37 he cometh, and findeth them sleeping, and
14. 37 Simon, sleepest thou? couldest not thou
14. 41 Sleep on now, and take (your) rest: it is en.
Luke 8. 52 Weep not; she is not dead, but sleepeth
22. 46 Why sleep ye? rise and pray, lest ye enter
Eph. 5. 14 Awake thou that sleepest, and arise from
1 Th. 5. 6 let us not sleep, as (do) others; but let us
5. 7 they that sleep sleep in the night; and th.
5. 10 whether we wake or sleep, we should live

8. *To lie down in sleep, κοιμάομαι koimaomai.*
Matt27. 52 many bodies of the saints which slept aro.
28. 13 disciples..stole him (away) while we slept
Luke22. 45 when he rose up..he found them sleeping
John11. 11 our friend Lazarus sleepeth; but I go, th.
11. 12 Then said his disciples, Lord, if he sleep
Acts 12. 6 Peter was sleeping between two soldiers
13. 36 fell on sleep, and was laid unto his fath.
1 Co.11. 30 many (are) weak and sickly..and many sl.
15. 20 become the first fruits of them that slept
15. 51 We shall not all sleep, but we shall all be
1 Th. 4. 14 even so them also which sleep in Jesus will

SLEEP, to be, make, or cast into a dead or deep —
1. *To make to sleep, יָשֵׁן yashen, 3.*
Judg16. 19 she made him sleep upon her knees: and
2. *To be in a fast sleep, in a trance, רָדַם radam, 2.*
Psa. 76. 6 chariot and horse are cast into a dead sl.
Dan. 8. 18 I was in a deep sleep on my face toward
10. 9 then was I in a deep sleep on my face, and

SLEIGHT —
Playing at dice, cheat, artifice, κυβεία kubeia.
Eph. 4. 14 by the sleight of men, (and) cunning cra.

SLIDE (back), to —
1. *To move, slip, fail, מוֹט mot.*
Deut32. 35 their foot shall slide in (due) time: for the
2. *To slide, מָעַד maad.*
Psa. 26. 1 I have trusted..(therefore) I shall not sl.
37. 31 in his heart; none of his steps shall slide
3. *To be refractory, stubborn, סָרַר sarar.*
Hos. 4. 16 Israel slideth back as a backsliding heifer
4. *To turn or bring back, שׁוּב shub, 3a.*
Jer. 8. 5 is this people of Jerusalem slidden back

SLIGHTLY —
In light (superficial) fashion, עַל־נְקַלָּה *[qalal, 2].*
Jer. 6. 14 healed also the hurt..of my people slightly
8. 11 healed the hurt..of my people slightly

SLIME —
Bitumen, חֵמָר chemar.
Gen. 11. 3 they had brick for stone, and slime had th.
14. 10 the vale of Siddim (was full of) slime pits
Exod. 2. 3 daubed it with slime and with pitch, and

SLING, slinger, sling stone —
1. *A sling stone, אֶבֶן קֶלַע eben qela.*
Job 41. 28 sling stones are turned with him into st.
Zech. 9. 15 devour, and subdue with sling stones
2. *A sling, heap of stones, מַרְגֵּמָה margemah.*
Prov26. 8 As he that bindeth a stone in a sling, so
3. *A sling, קֶלַע qela.*
1 Sa. 17. 40 his sling (was) in his hand: and he drew
17. 50 prevailed over the Philistine with a sling
25. 29 sling out, (as out) of the middle of a sling
2 Ch.26. 14 habergeons, and bows, and slings (to ca.)
4. *A slinger, קַלָּע qalla.*
2 Ki. 3. 25 howbeit the slingers went about (it), and

SLING (out), to —
1. *To sling out, קָלַע qala.*
Judg20. 16 every one could sling stones at an hair (br.)
Jer. 10. 18 I will sling out the inhabitants of the land
2. *To sling out, קָלַע qala, 3.*
1 Sa. 17. 49 took thence a stone, and slang (it), and
25. 29 them shall he sling out, (as out) of the mi.

SLIP —
A branch, slip, זְמוֹרָה zemorah.
Isa. 17. 10 and shalt set it with strange slips

SLIP away, to (let) —
1. *To move, slip, fail, מוֹט mot.*
Psa. 38. 16 when my foot slippeth, they magnify (th.)
94. 18 When I said, My foot slippeth; thy mercy
2. *To be moved, מוֹט mot, 2.*
Psa. 17. 5 Hold up my goings..(that) my footsteps s.
3. *To slide, מָעַד maad.*
2 Sa. 22. 37 enlarged my steps..my feet did not slip
Job 12. 5 He that is ready to slip with (his) feet (is)
Psa. 18. 36 enlarged my steps..my feet did not slip
4. *To cast out or off, slip or fall off, נָשַׁל nashal.*
Deut19. 5 the head slippeth from the helve, and li.
5. *To free, open, let away, פָּטַר patar.*
1 Sa. 19. 10 he slipped away out of Saul's presence, and
6. *To be poured out, to slip, שָׁפַךְ shaphak, 4.*
Psa. 73. 2 as for me..my steps had well nigh slipped
7. *To flow along or by, παραῤῥέω pararrheō.*
Heb. 2. 1 lest at any time we should let (them) slip

SLIPPERY (place) —
1. *A smooth thing or place, חֶלְקָה chelqah.*
Psa. 73. 18 thou didst set them in slippery places: th.
2. *Smooth thing or places, חֲלַקְלַקּוֹת chalaqlaqqoth.*
Psa. 35. 6 Let their way be dark and slippery: and
Jer. 23. 12 their way shall be unto them as slippery

SLOTHFUL, slothfulness, to be —
1. *To be slothful, עָצַל atsal, 2.*
Judg 18. 9 be not slothful to go, (and) to enter to p.
2. *Slothful, עָצֵל atsel.*
Prov15. 19 The way of the slothful (man is) as an he.
Prov19. 24 slothful (man) hideth his hand in (his) bo.
21. 25 desire of the slothful killeth him; for his
22. 13 slothful (man) saith, (There is) a lion with.
24. 30 went by the field of the slothful, and by
26. 13 slothful (man) saith, (There is) a lion in
26. 14 door turneth..so (doth) the slothful upon
26. 15 The slothful hideth his hand in (his) bos.
3. *Sloth, עַצְלָה atslah.*
Prov19. 15 Slothfulness casteth into a deep sleep; and
Eccl.10. 18 By much slothfulness the building decay.
4. *Remissness, deceit, רְמִיָּה remiyyah.*
Prov12. 24 bear rule: but the slothful shall be under
12. 27 slothful (man) roasteth not that which he
5. *To become or show self feeble, רָפָה raphah, 7.*
Prov18. 9 He also that is slothful in his work is br.
6. *Slothful, sluggish, νωθρός nōthros.*
Heb. 6. 12 That ye be not slothful, but followers of
7. *Motionless, slothful, idle, ὀκνηρός oknēros.*
Matt25. 26 wicked and slothful servant, thou knew.
Rom12. 11 Not slothful in business; fervent in spirit

SLOW (to anger) —
1. *Long, אֶרֶךְ erek.*
Neh. 9. 17 gracious and merciful, slow to anger, and
Psa.103. 8 gracious, slow to anger, and plenteous in
145. 8 full of compassion; slow to anger, and of
Prov14. 29 (He that is) slow to wrath (is) of great un.
15. 18 but (he that is) slow to anger appeaseth
16. 32 (He that is) slow to anger (is) better than
Joel 2. 13 merciful, slow to anger, and of great kin.
Jon. 4. 2 merciful, slow to anger, and of great kin.
Nah. 1. 3 LORD (is) slow to anger, and great in pow.
2. *Heavy, weighty, כָּבֵד kabed.*
Exod. 4. 10 but I (am) slow of speech, and of a slow
3. *Inactive, unprofitable, ἀργός argos.*
Titus 1. 12 Cretians (are) alway liars, evil beasts, slow
4. *Heavy, slow, sluggish, βραδύς bradus.*
Luke24. 25 slow of heart to believe all that the pro.
Jas. 1. 19 swift to hear, slow to speak, slow to wrath

SLUGGARD —
Slothful, עָצֵל atsel.
Prov. 6. 6 Go to the ant, thou sluggard; consider
6. 9 How long wilt thou sleep, O sluggard? wh.
10. 26 so (is) the sluggard to them that send him
13. 4 The soul of the sluggard desireth, and (ha.)
20. 4 sluggard will not plow by reason of the
26. 16 sluggard (is) wiser in his own conceit th.

SLUICE —
Hire, wage, reward, שֶׂכֶר seker.
Isa. 19. 10 all that make sluices (and) ponds for fish

SLUMBER, (slumbering, to) —
1. *To slumber, נוּם num.*
Psa.121. 3 he that keepeth thee will not slumber
121. 4 he that keepeth Israel shall neither slum.
Isa. 5. 27 none shall slumber nor sleep; neither
56. 10 sleeping, lying down, loving to slumber
Nah. 3. 18 Thy shepherds slumber, O king of Assyria
2. *Slumber, תְּנוּמָה tenumah.*
Job 33. 15 falleth upon men, in slumberings upon
Psa.132. 4 I will not give..slumber to mine eyelids
Prov. 6. 4 Give not sleep to thine eyes, nor slumber
6. 10 little slumber, a little folding of the han.
24. 33 little slumber, a little folding of the han.
3. *Deep sleep, κατάνυξις katanuxis.*
Rom11. 8 God hath given them the spirit of slumb.
4. *To nod, slumber, linger, νυστάζω nustazō.*
Matt25. 5 While the bridegroom tarried, they all sl.
2 Pe. 2. 3 and their damnation slumbereth not

SMALL (matter, one, quantity, thing, very) —
1. *Lean, thin, דַּק daq.*
Exod16. 14 small round thing, (as) small as the hoar
Lev. 16. 12 hands full of sweet incense beaten small
1 Ki. 19. 12 fire: and after the fire a still small voice
Isa. 29. 5 multitude..shall be like small dust, and
2. *Few, מִזְעָר mizar.*
Isa. 16. 14 the remnant (shall be) very small (and) fe.
3. *To do good or well, יָטַב yatab, 5.*
Deut. 9. 21 stamped it, (and) ground (it) very small
4. *A little, few, מְעַט meat.*
Gen. 30. 15 (Is it) a small matter that thou hast tak.
Num16. 9 small thing unto you, that the God of I.
16. 13 small thing that thou hast brought us up
Job 15. 11 (Are) the consolations of God small with
Isa. 1. 9 had left unto us a very small remnant, we
7. 13 small thing for you to weary men, but will
Eze. 16. 20 (Is this) of thy whoredoms a small matter
34. 18 small thing unto you to have eaten up the
Dan. 11. 23 shall become strong with a small people
5. *Men, a few, מְתִים methim.*
Jer. 44. 28 Yet a small number that escape the sw
6. *Little, small, מִצְעָר mitsar.*
2 Ch.24. 24 came with a small company of men, and
Job 8. 7 Though thy beginning was small, yet thy
7. *Little, small, young, צָעִיר tsair.*
Psa.119. 141 I (am) small and despised; (yet) do not
Isa. 60. 22 a small one a strong nation: Dan. 8. 9.
8. *Strait, close, צַר tsar.*
Prov24. 10 (If) thou faint thy strength (is) small
9. *Little, small, young, קָטָן qatan.*
Deut25. 13, 14 shalt not have..a great and a small
1 Sa. 9. 21 a Benjamite, of the smallest of the tribes
1 Ki. 2. 20 I desire one small petition of thee..say
2 Ch.31. 15 courses, as well to the great as to the sm.
34. 30 all the people, great and small; and he
36. 18 all the vessels..great and small, and the
Esth. 1. 5 all the people..both unto great and small
1. 20 husbands honour, both to great and sm.
Psa.104. 25 wherein (are) things..both small and gr.
115. 13 He will bless them..(both) small and gr.
Isa. 22. 24 all vessels of small quantity, from the ve.
Jer. 16. 6 Both the great and the small shall die in
Zech. 4. 10 who hath despised the day of small thi.?
10. *Little, small, young, קָטֹן qaton.*
Gen. 19. 11 smote the men..both small and great; so
Exod18. 22 but every small matter they shall judge
18. 26 every small matter they judged themsel.
Deut. 1. 17 ye shall hear the small as well as the gr.
1 Sa. 5. 9 smote the men of the city, both small and
20. 2 will do nothing, either great or small, but
30. 2 they slew not any, either great or small
30. 19 neither small nor great, neither sons nor
1 Ki. 22. 31 Fight neither with small nor great, save
2 Ki.23. 2 and all the people, both small and great
25. 26 all the people, both small and great, and
1 Ch.25. 8 as well the small as the great, the teacher
26. 13 cast lots, as well the small as the great
2 Ch.15. 13 whether small or great, whether man or
18. 30 Fight ye not with small or great, save only
Job 3. 19 small and great are there; and the servant
Isa. 54. 7 For a small moment have I forsaken thee
60. 22 a small one a strong nation: I the LORD will
Jer. 49. 15 will make thee small among the heathen
Amos 7. 2, 5 by whom shall Jacob arise? for he (is) s.
Obad. 2 have made thee small among the heathen
11. *Short, small, few, soon, קָצֵר qatser.*
2 Ki.19. 26 Therefore their inhabitants were of small
Isa. 37. 27 Therefore their inhabitants (were) of sm.
12. *Smallest, least, lowest, ἐλάχιστος elachistos.*
1 Co. 4. 3 But with me it is a very small thing that
6. 2 are ye unworthy to judge the smallest ma.?
Jas. 3. 4 they turned about with a very small helm
13. *Little, small, short, μικρός mikros.*
Acts 26. 22 witnessing both to small and great, saying
Rev. 11. 18 them that fear thy name, small and great
13. 16 caused all, both small and great, rich and
19. 5 and ye that fear him, both small and great
19. 18 the flesh of all (men)..both small and gre.
20. 12 saw the dead, small and great, stand be.
14. *Little, small, few, feeble, ὀλίγος oligos.*
Acts 12. 18 there was no small stir among the soldiers
15. 2 Paul and Barnabas had no small dissension
19. 23 same time there arose no small stir about
19. 24 brought no small gain unto the craftsmen
27. 20 no small tempest lay on (us), all hope that

SMALL towns —
Hamlets, חַוּוֹת chavvoth.
Num32. 41 took the small towns thereof, and called

SMALL, to be, beat, make, stamp —
1. *To diminish, גָּרַע gara, 3.*
Job 36. 27 For he maketh small the drops of water
2. *To be small, beaten small, דָּקַק daqaq.*
Deut. 9. 21 until it was as small as dust: and I cast the
Isa. 41. 15 beat (them) small, and shalt make the hills
3. *To beat small, דָּקַק daqaq, 5.*
Exod30. 36 thou shalt beat (some) of it very small, and
2 Ki. 23. 6 stamped (it) small to powder, and cast the
23. 15 stamped (it) small to powder, and burned
4. *To be small, little, young, צָעַר tsaar.*
Jer. 30. 19 glorify them, and they shall not be small
5. *To be small, little, unworthy, קָטֹן qaton.*
2 Sa. 7. 19 this was yet a small thing in thy sight, O
1 Ch.17. 17 this was a small thing in thine eyes, O
6. *To make little, קָטֹן qaton, 5.*
Amos 8. 5 making the ephah small, and the shekel

SMART, to —
Be (become) evil with evil, ירוֹעַ רַע *raa (2) ra.*
Prov.11 15 He that is surety for a stranger shall sm.

SMELL, (sweet), smelling —
1. *Spice, בֹּשֶׂם bosem.*
Isa. 3. 24 instead of sweet smell there shall be stink
2. *To go or pass over, עָבַר abar.*
Song 5. 5 my fingers (with) sweet smelling myrrh
5. 13 lips (like) lilies, dropping sweet smelling
3. *Smell, savour, fragrance, רֵיחַ reach.*
Gen. 27. 27 the smell of his raiment, and blessed him
27. 27 smell of my son (is) as the smell of a field
Song 1. 12 spikenard sendeth forth the smell thereof
2. 13 vines (with)..tender grape give a (good) s.
4. 10 how much better is..the smell of thine o.
4. 11 smell of thy garments (is) like the smell
7. 8 now also..the smell of thy nose like apples
7. 13 mandrakes give a smell, and at our gates
Dan. 3. 27 nor the smell of fire had passed on them
Hos. 14. 6 as the olive tree, and his smell as Leban.
4. *Sweet smell, fragrance, εὐωδία euōdia.*
Phil. 4. 18 an odour of a sweet smell, a sacrifice acc.
5. *Smelling, ὄσφρησις osphrēsis.*
1 Co.12. 17 whole (were) hearing, where (were) the s

SMELL, to —

To smell, refresh, רוּחַ *ruach*, 5.

Gen. 8. 21 LORD smelled a sweet savour; and the L.
27. 27 came near, and kissed him: and he sm.
Exod30. 38 shall make like unto that, to smell there.
Lev. 26. 31 will not smell the savour of your sweet sa.
Deut. 4. 28 neither see, nor hear, nor eat, nor smell
Job 39. 25 he smelleth the battle afar off, the thun.
Psa 115. 6 noses have they, but they smell not
Amos 5. 21 will not smell in your solemn assemblies

SMITE, to —

1. *To bruise,* דָּכָא *daka*, 3.

Psa. 143. 3 he hath smitten my life down to the gro.

2. *To beat, break,* הָלַם *halam.*

Psa. 141. 5 Let the righteous smite me; (it shall be)
Isa. 41. 7 smootheth (with) the hammer him that sm.

3. *To beat down or out,* כָּתַת *kathath*, 3.

Zech 11. 6 smite the land, and out of their hand I

4. *To smite,* מְחָא *mecha.*

Dan. 2. 34 which smote the image upon his feet (that
2. 35 stone that smote the image became a gr.

5. *To smite, dash,* מָחַץ *machats.*

Num 24. 17 shall smite the corners of Moab, and des.

6. *A smiting, stroke, blow,* מַכָּה *makkah.*

Isa. 27. 7 as he smote those..(or) is he slain according

7. *To plague, strike,* נָגַע *naga.*

1 Sa. 6. 9 know that (it is) not his hand (that) smote
Job 1. 19 smote the four corners of the house, and

8. *To plague,* נָגַע *naga*, 3.

2 Ki. 15. 5 LORD smote the king, so that he was a le
2 Ch. 26. 20 hasted..because the LORD had smitten him

9. *To smite, plague,* נָגַף *nagaph.*

Exod. 8. 2 behold, I will smite all thy borders with
12. 23 LORD will pass through to smite the Egy.
12. 23 to come in unto your houses to smite (you)
12. 27 when he smote the Egyptians, and deliv.
Judg 20. 35 LORD smote Benjamin before Israel: and
1 Sa. 4. 3 Wherefore hath the LORD smitten us to
25. 38 that the LORD smote Nabal, that he died
26. 10 LORD shall smite him; or his day shall co.
2 Ch. 13. 15 God smote Jeroboam and all Israel before
14. 12 So the LORD smote the Ethiopians before
21. 14 with a great plague will the LORD smite
21. 18 after all this the LORD smote him in his
Isa. 19. 22 LORD shall smite Egypt; he shall smite
Zech 14. 12, 18 plague wherewith the LORD will smite

10. *To (cause to) smite,* נָכָה *nakah*, 5.

Gen. 8. 21 neither will I again smite any more every
14. 5 smote the Rephaims in Ashteroth Karna.
14. 7 smote all the country of the Amalekites
14. 15 smote them, and pursued them unto Ho.
19. 11 smote the men that (were) at the door of
32. 8 If Esau come..and smite it, then the oth.
32. 11 I fear him, lest he will come and smite me
36. 35 who smote Midian in the field of Moab, re.
Exod. 2. 11 spied an Egyptian smiting an Hebrew, one
2. 13 he said..Wherefore smitest thou thy fel?
3. 20 smite Egypt with all my wonders which I
7. 17 will smite with the rod that (is) in mine
7. 20 smote the waters that (were) in the river
7. 25 after that the LORD had smitten the river
8. 16 Stretch out thy rod, and smite the dust of
8. 17 smote the dust of the earth, and it beca.
9. 15 smite thee and thy people with pestilence
9. 25 hail smote throughout all the land of Eg.
9. 25 hail smote every herb of the field, and br.
12. 12 will smite all the first born in the land of
12. 13 destroy (you), when I smite the land of E.
12. 29 at midnight the LORD smote all the first
17. 5 rod, wherewith thou smotest the river, ta.
17. 6 thou shalt smite the rock, and there shall
21. 12 He that smiteth a man, so that he die
21. 15 he that smiteth his father or mother shal
21. 18 one smite another with a stone, or with
21. 19 then shall he that smote (him) be quit
21. 20 if a man smite his servant, or his maid
21. 26 if a man smite the eye of his servant, or
Num. 3. 13 on the day that I smote all the first born
8. 17 on the day that I smote every first born in
11. 33 LORD smote the people with a very great
14. 12 I will smite them with the pestilence, and
14. 45 smote them, and discomfited them, (even)
20. 11 with his rod he smote the rock twice; and
21. 24 Israel smote him with the edge of the sw.
21. 35 So they smote him, and his sons, and all
22. 6 shall prevail, (that) we may smite them
22. 23 Balaam smote the ass, to turn her into the
22. 25 crushed Balaam's foot..and he smote her
22. 27 anger was kindled, and he smote the ass
22. 28 that thou hast smitten me these three ti.?
22. 32 Wherefore hast thou smitten thine ass th.
25. 17 Vex the Midianites, and smite them
32. 4 LORD smote before the congregation of Is.
33. 4 which the LORD had smitten among them
35. 16 if he smite him with an instrument of iron
35. 17 if he smite him with throwing a stone, wh.
35. 18 Or (if) he smite him with an hand weapon
35. 21 in enmity smite him..he that smote (him)
Deut. 2. 33 smote him, and his sons, and all his peop.
3. 3 smote him until none was left to him re.
4. 46 children of Israel smote, after they were
7. 2 thou shalt smite them, (and) utterly dest.
13. 15 Thou shalt surely smite the inhabitants
19. 11 smite him mortally that he die, and flee.
20. 13 thou shalt smite every male thereof with
Deut 25. 11 out of the hand of him that smiteth him
27. 24 Cursed (be) he that smiteth his neighbour
28. 22 LORD shall smite thee with a consumpti.
28. 27 LORD will smite thee with the botch of E.
28. 28 LORD shall smite thee with madness, and
28. 35 LORD shall smite thee in the knees, and
29. 7 against us unto battle, and we smote them
Josh. 7. 3 three thousand men go up and smite Ai
7. 5 men of Ai smote of them about thirty and
7. 5 smote them in the going down: wherefo.
8. 22 smote them, so that they let none of them
8. 24 and smote it with the edge of the sword
9. 18 children of Israel smote them not, beca.
10. 4 help me, that we may smite Gibeon: for
10. 10 smote them to Azekah, and unto Makked.
10. 26 afterward Joshua smote them, and slew
10. 28, 30, 32, 35, 37 smote it with the edge of
10. 33 smote him and his people, until he had
10. 39 they smote them with the edge of the sw.
10. 40 So Joshua smote all the country of the hi.
10. 41 Joshua smote them from Kadesh-barnea
11. 8 smote them, and chased them unto great
11. 8 smote them, until they left them none re.
11. 10 smote the king thereof with the sword
11. 11 smote all the souls that (were) therein wi.
11. 12 smote them with the edge of the sword
11. 14 every man they smote with the edge of the
11. 17 took, and smote them, and slew them
12. 1 which the children of Israel smote, and
12. 6 Them did Moses..smite: and Moses the
12. 7 children of Israel smote on this side Jor.
13. 12 for these did Moses smite, and cast them
13. 21 whom Moses smote with the princes of M.
15. 16 He that smiteth Kirjath-sepher, and tak.
19. 47 smote it with the edge of the sword, and
20. 5 smote his neighbour unwittingly, and ha.
Judg. 1. 8 smitten it with the edge of the sword, and
1. 12 He that smiteth Kirjath-sepher, and tak.
1. 25 smote the city with the edge of the sword
3. 13 smote Israel, and possessed the city of p.
6. 16 thou shalt smite the Midianites as one m.
7. 13 smote it that it fell, and overturned it
8. 11 and smote the host: for the host was se.
9. 43 he rose up against them, and smote them
11. 21 smote them: so Israel possessed all the
11. 33 smote them from Aroer, even till thou
12. 4 men of Gilead smote Ephraim, because
15. 8 smote them hip and thigh with a great sl.
18. 27 smote them with the edge of the sword
20. 31 they began to smite of the people, (and)
20. 37 smote all the city with the edge of the sw.
20. 39 Benjamin began to smite (and) kill of the
20. 48 smote them with the edge of the sword
21. 10 Go and smite the inhabitants of Jabesh-g.
1 Sa. 4. 8 these (are) the Gods that smote the Egy.
5. 6 smote them with emerods, (even) Ashdod
5. 9 smote the men of the city, both small and
6. 19 smote the men..even he smote of the pe.
6. 19 because the LORD had smitten (many) of
7. 11 smote them, until (they came) under Be.
13. 3 Jonathan smote the garrison of the Phil.
13. 4 Saul had smitten a garrison of the Phili.
14. 31 smote the Philistines that day from Mic.
14. 48 smote the Amalekites, and delivered Is.
15. 3 Now go and smite Amalek, and utterly
15. 7 Saul smote the Amalekites from Havilah
17. 35 smote him, and delivered (it) out of his
17. 35 caught (him) by his beard, and smote him
17. 46 will smite thee, and take thine head from
17. 49 smote the Philistine in his forehead, that
17. 50 David..smote the Philistine, and slew him
18. 11 I will smite David even to the wall (with
19. 10 Saul sought to smite David even..the wall
20. 33 Saul cast a javelin at him to smite him
22. 19 Nob..smote he with the edge of the sw.
23. 2 Shall I go and smite these Philistines? A.
23. 2 Go and smite the Philistines, and save K.
23. 5 smote them with a great slaughter. So D.
24. 5 David's heart smote him, because he had
26. 8 now therefore let me smite him, I pray
27. 9 David smote the land, and left neither man
30. 1 smitten Ziklag, and burnt it with fire
30. 17 David smote them from the twilight even
2 Sa. 1. 15 fall upon him. And he smote him that he
2. 22 wherefore should I smite thee to the gr.?
2. 23 with the hinder end of the spear smote him
2. 31 servants of David had smitten of Benja.
3. 27 smote him there under the fifth (rib), th.
4. 6 smote him under the fifth (rib): and Re.
4. 7 smote him, and slew him, and beheaded
5. 8 Whosoever..smiteth the Jebusites, and
5. 20 David smote them there, and said, The L.
5. 24 go out before thee, to smite the host of
5. 25 smote the Philistines from Geba until th.
6. 7 God smote him there for (his) error; and
8. 1 David smote the Philistines, and pursued
8. 2 smote Moab, and measured them with a
8. 3 David smote also Hadadezer, the son of
8. 9 heard that David had smitten all the host
8. 10 fought against Hadadezer, and smitten
8. 13 when he returned from smiting of the Sy.
10. 18 smote Shobach the captain of their host
11. 21 Who smote Abimelech the son of Jerub.
13. 28 Smite Amnon; then kill him, fear not; have
14. 6 but the one smote the other, and slew him
14. 7 Deliver him that smote his brother, that
15. 14 smite the city with the edge of the sword
17. 2 shall flee: and I will smite the king only
18. 11 why didst thou not smite him there to the
18. 15 compassed about and smote Absalom, and
20. 10 smote him therewith in the fifth (rib), and
21. 17 and smote the Philistines, and killed th.
2 Sa. 23. 10 He arose, and smote the Philistines, unt.
24. 10 David's heart smote him after that he had
24. 17 when he saw the angel that smote the pe.
1 Ki. 11. 15 after he had smitten every male in Edom
14. 15 For the LORD shall smite Israel, as a reed
15. 20 smote Ijon, and Dan, Abel-beth-maachah
15. 27 smote him at Gibbethon, which (belonged)
15. 29 when he reigned, (that) he smote all the
16. 10 Zimri went in and smote him, and killed
20. 21 smote the horses and chariots, and slew
20. 35 Smite me..And the man refused to smite
20. 37 found another man, and said, Smite me
20. 37 smote him, so that in smiting he wounded
22. 24 smote Micaiah on the cheek, and said, wh.
22. 34 drew a bow at a venture, and smote the
2 Ki. 2. 8 smote the waters, and they were divided
2. 14 smote the waters..when he also had smi.
3. 19 ye shall smite every fenced city, and every
3. 23 they have smitten one another: now th.
3. 24 smote the Moabites, so that they fled be.
3. 24 but they went forward smiting the Moab.
3. 25 the slingers went about (it), and smote it
6. 18 Smite this people.. And he smote them
6. 21 father, shall I smite (them)? shall I smite
6. 22 shalt not smite (them); wouldest thou sm.
8. 21 smote the Edomites which compassed him
9. 7 thou shalt smite the house of Ahab thy
9. 24 smote Jehoram between his arms, and the
9. 27 Smite him also in the chariot. (And they
10. 25 they smote them with the edge of the sw.
10. 32 Hazael smote them in all the coasts of Is.
12. 21 smote him, and he died; and they buried
13. 17 for thou shalt smite the Syrians in Aphek
13. 18 Smite upon the ground: and he smote th.
13. 19 Thou shouldest have smitten five or six
13. 19 hadst thou smitten Syria till thou hadst
13. 19 whereas now thou shalt smite Syria (but)
14. 10 Thou hast indeed smitten Edom, and thine
15. 10 smote him before the people, and slew him
15. 14 smote Shallum the son of Jabesh in Sam.
15. 16 Then Menahem smote Tiphsah, and all
15. 16 therefore he smote (it; and) all the women
15. 25 conspired against him, and smote him in
15. 30 smote him, and slew him, and reigned in
18. 8 He smote the Philistines, (even) unto Gaza
19. 35 smote in the camp of the Assyrians an h.
19. 37 Sharezer his sons smote him with the sw.
25. 21 king of Babylon smote them, and slew
25. 25 smote Gedaliah, that he died, and the J.
1 Ch. 1. 46 which smote Midian in the field of Moab
4. 41 smote their tents, and the habitations
4. 43 smote the rest of the Amalekites that were
11. 6 Whosoever smiteth the Jebusites first sh.
13. 10 smote him, because he put his hand to the
14. 11 came up to Baal-perazim; and David sm.
14. 15 God is gone forth before thee, to smite the
14. 16 smote the host of the Philistines from G.
18. 1 David smote the Philistines, and subdued
18. 2 smote Moab; and the Moabites became
18. 3 David smote Hadarezer king of Zobah unto
18. 9 heard how David had smitten all the host
18. 10 fought against Hadarezer, and smitten him
20. 1 And Joab smote Rabbah, and destroyed
21. 7 displeased with this thing; therefore he
2 Ch. 14. 14 they smote all the cities round about Ge.
14. 15 They smote also the tents of cattle, and
16. 4 they smote Ijon, and Dan, and Abel-maim
18. 23 smote Micaiah upon the cheek, and said
18. 33 smote the king of Israel between the joi.
21. 9 smote the Edomites which compassed him
22. 5 at Ramoth-gilead: and the Syrians smote
25. 11 and smote of the children of Seir ten tho.
25. 13 smote three thousand of them, and took
25. 16 forbear; why shouldest thou be smitten?
25. 19 Lo, thou hast smitten the Edomites; and
28. 5 smote him, and carried away a great mu.
28. 5 king of Israel, who smote him with a great
28. 17 again the Edomites had come and smitten
28. 23 smote him: and he said, Because the gods
Neh. 13. 25 smote certain of them, and plucked off
Esth. 9. 5 Thus the Jews smote all their enemies
Job 2. 7 smote Job with sore boils from the sole
16. 10 they have smitten me upon the cheek re.
Psa. 3. 7 for thou hast smitten all mine enemies
60. *title.* smote of Edom in the valley of Salt tw.
69. 26 persecute (him) whom thou hast smitten
78. 20 smote the rock, that the waters gushed
78. 51 smote all the first born in Egypt; the ch.
78. 66 he smote his enemies in the hinder part
105. 33 He smote their vines also and their fig tr.
105. 36 He smote also all the first born in their
121. 6 The sun shall not smite thee by day, nor
135. 8 Who smote the first born of Egypt, both
135. 10 Who smote great nations, and slew mig.
136. 10 To him that smote Egypt in their first b.
136. 17 To him which smote great kings: for his
Prov 19. 25 Smite a scorner, and the simple will bew.
Song 5. 7 they smote me, they wounded me; the
Isa. 5. 25 hath smitten them: and the hills did tr.
9. 13 people turneth not unto him that smiteth
10. 20 no more again stay upon him that smote
10. 24 he shall smite thee with a rod and shall
11. 4 he shall smite the earth with the rod of
11. 15 and shall smite it in the seven streams
14. 6 He who smote the people in wrath with a
14. 29 because the rod of him that smote thee is
27. 7 Hath he smitten him..that smote him?
30. 31 Assyrian be beaten down, (which) smote
37. 36 smote in the camp of the Assyrians a hu.
37. 38 his sons smote him with the sword; and
49. 10 neither shall the heat nor sun smite them
57. 17 was I wroth, and smote him: I hid me

Isa. 58. 4 and to smite with the fist of wickedness
60. 10 for in my wrath I smote thee, but in my
Jer. 2. 30 In vain have I smitten your children; they
14. 19 why hast thou smitten us, and (there is)
18. 18 come, and let us smite him with the ton.
20. 2 Then Pashur smote Jeremiah the prophet
21. 6 I will smite the inhabitants of this city
21. 7 shall smite them with the edge of the sw.
37. 10 For though ye had smitten the whole army
37. 15 smote him, and put him in prison in the
41. 2 smote Gedaliah the son of Ahikam, the
43. 11 when he cometh, he shall smite the land
46. 2 king of Babylon smote in the fourth year
46. 13 should come (and) smite the land of Eg.
47. 1 came to Jeremiah..before that Pharaoh s.
49. 28 which Nebuchadrezzar..shall smite, thus
52. 27 smote them, and put them to death in R.
Lam. 3. 30 giveth (his) cheek to him that smiteth him
Eze. 5. 2 smite about it with a knife; and a third
6. 11 Smite with thine hand, and stamp with
7. 9 shall know that I (am) the LORD that sm.
9. 5 Go ye after him..and smite; let not your
21. 14 smite (thine) hands together, and let the
21. 17 I will also smite mine hands together, and
22. 13 have smitten mine hand at thy dishonest
32. 15 when I shall smite all them that dwell th.
39. 3 I will smite thy bow out of thy left hand
Dan. 8. 7 smote the ram, and brake his two horns
Hos. 6. 1 he hath smitten, and he will bind us up
Amos 3. 15 smite the winter house with the summer
4. 9 I have smitten you with blasting and mil.
6. 11 he will smite the great house with breac.
9. 1 Smite the lintel of the door, that the posts
Jon. 4. 7 and it smote the gourd that it withered
Mic. 5. 1 they shall smite the judge of Israel with
6. 13 also will I make (thee) sick in smiting thee
Hag. 2. 17 I smote you with blasting and with mild.
Zech. 9. 4 and he will smite her power in the sea; and
10. 11 shall smite the waves in the sea, and all
12. 4 I will smite every horse with astonishment
12. 4 will smite every horse of the people with
13. 7 smite the Shepherd, and the sheep shall
Mal. 4. 6 lest I come and smite the earth with a cu.

11. *To smite*, נָקַשׁ *neqash*.
Dan. 5. 6 and his knees smote one against another

12. *To strike*, סָפַק *saphaq*.
Num 24. 10 smote his hands together: and Balak said
Jer. 31. 19 I smote upon (my) thigh: I was ashamed
Eze. 21. 12 my people: smite therefore upon (thy) th.

13. *To strike, clap, blow*, תָּקַע *taqa*.
Judg. 4. 21 smote the nail into his temples, and fast.

14. *To flay, beat, scourge, strike, smite*, δέρω *derō*.
Luke 22. 63 And the men that held Jesus..smote (him)
John 18. 23 Jesus answered him..why smitest thou
2 Co. 11. 20 For ye suffer..if a man smite you on the

15. *To strike, smite, beat, sting*, παίω *paiō*.
Matt 26. 68 Saying, Prophesy..Who is he that smote
Mark 14. 47 smote a servant of the high priest, and cut
Luke 22. 64 saying, Prophesy, who is it that smote thee?
John 18. 10 smote the high priest's servant, and cut

16. *To strike, smite*, πατάσσω *patassō*.
Matt 26. 31 will smite the shepherd, and the sheep of
Mark 14. 27 will smite the shepherd, and the sheep sh.
Luke 22. 49 Lord, shall we smite with the sword
22. 50 one of them smote a servant of the high
Acts 7. 24 avenged him that was oppressed, and sm.
12. 7 smote Peter on the side, and raised him
12. 23 immediately the angel of the Lord smote
Rev. 11. 6 power..to smite the earth with all plagues
19. 15 that with it he should smite the nations

17. *To slap*, ῥαπίζω *rhapizō*.
Matt 5. 39 but whosoever shall smite thee on thy ri.

18. *To strike*, τύπτω *tuptō*.
Matt 24. 49 shall begin to smite (his) fellow servants
27. 30 took the reed, and smote him on the head
Mark 15. 19 they smote him on the head with a reed
Luke 6. 29 unto him that smiteth thee on the (one)
18. 13 smote upon his breast, saying, God be me.
23. 48 all the people..smote their breasts, and
Acts 23. 2 commanded them..to smite him on the
23. 3 God shall smite thee, (thou) whited wall

SMITE down, off, out, through, together, to —

1. *To cause to bow or bend*, כָּרַע *kara*, 5.
Psa. 78. 31 and smote down the chosen (men) of Isr.

2. *To smite, dash*, מָחַץ *machats*.
Deut 33. 11 smite through the loins of them that rise
Job 26. 12 by his understanding he smiteth through

3. *To smite through*, מָחַק *machaq*.
Judg. 5. 26 smote off his head, when she had pierced

4. *To cause to fall*, נָפַל *naphal*, 5.
Exod 21. 27 if he smite out his man servant's tooth, or

5. *A melting together, tottering*, פִּיק *piq*.
Nah. 2. 10 heart melteth, and the knees smite toge.

6. *To take away or off*, ἀφαιρέω *aphaireō*.
Matt 26. 51 struck a servant of the high priest, and

SMITE with (the palm of) the hand, to —

1. *To give a slap*, δίδωμι ῥάπισμα *didōmi rhapisma*.
John 19. 3 and they smote him with their hands

2. *To slap*, ῥαπίζω *rhapizō*.
Matt 26. 67 smote (him) with the palms of their hands

SMITE with the hammer or scab, to —

1. *To beat, break*, הָלַם *halam*.
Judg. 5. 26 and with the hammer she smote Sisera

2. *To scab*, שָׂפַח *saphach*, 3.
Isa. 3. 17 Lord will smite with a scab the crown of

SMITER —

To (cause to) smite, נָכָה *nakah*, 5.
Isa. 50. 6 I gave my back to the smiters and my ch.

SMITH —

1. *Engraver, carver, artificer*, חָרָשׁ *charash*.
1 Sa. 13. 19 there was no smith found throughout all
Isa. 54. 16 I have created the smith that bloweth the

2. *To work in iron*, חָרַשׁ בַּרְזֶל *charash barzel*.
Isa. 44. 12 The smith with the tongs both worketh in

3. *Smith*, מַסְגֵּר *masger*.
2 Ki. 24. 14 carried away..all the craftsmen and smi.
24. 16 craftsmen and smiths a thousand, all (that
Jer. 24. 1 with the carpenters and smiths, from Je.
29. 2 the carpenters, and the smiths, were de.

SMITTEN (down), to be —

1. *To be beaten down or out*, כָּתַת *kathath*, 6.
Isa. 24. 12 and the gate is smitten with destruction

2. *To be plagued, smitten*, נָגַף *nagaph*, 2.
Num 14. 42 that ye be not smitten before your enemies
Deut. 1. 42 lest ye be smitten before your enemies
28. 7 shall cause thine enemies..to be smitten
28. 25 The LORD shall cause thee to be smitten
Judg 20. 32 They (are) smitten down before us, as at the
20. 36 Benjamin saw that they were smitten: for
20. 39 they are smitten down before us, as (in) the
1 Sa. 4. 2 Israel was smitten before the Philistines
4. 10 Israel was smitten, and they fled every man
7. 10 and they were smitten before Israel
2 Sa. 10. 15 the Syrians saw that they were smitten
10. 19 saw that they were smitten before Israel
1 Ki. 8. 33 When thy people Israel be smitten down
2 Ch. 20. 22 set ambushments..and they were smitten

3. *To be smitten*, נָכָה *nakah*, 2.
2 Sa. 11. 15 retire ye from him, that he may be smit.

4. *To be smitten*, נָכָה *nakah*, 4.
Exod. 9. 31 the flax and the barley was smitten; for
9. 32 the wheat and the rye were not smitten

5. *To be smitten*, נָכָה *nakah*, 6.
Exod 22. 2 If a thief..be smitten that he die, (there
1 Sa. 5. 12 the men that died not were smitten with
Psa. 102. 4 My heart is smitten, and withered like gr.
Isa. 53. 4 we did esteem him stricken, smitten of
Eze. 33. 21 came unto me, saying, The city is smitten
40. 1 after that the city was smitten, in the self
Hos. 9. 16 Ephraim is smitten, their root is dried up

6. *To smite, strike*, πλήσσω *plēssō*.
Rev. 8. 12 and the third part of the sun was smitten

7. *To strike*, τύπτω *tuptō*.
Acts 23. 3 commandest me to be smitten contrary to

SMOKE, smoking —

1. *Weak, dim*, כֵּהֶה *keheh*.
Isa. 42. 3 and the smoking flax shall he not quench

2. *Smoke*, עָשָׁן *ashan*.
Gen. 15. 17 behold a smoking furnace, and a burning
Exod 19. 18 the smoke thereof ascended as the smoke
Josh. 8. 20 the smoke of the city ascended up to he.
8. 21 Israel saw..that the smoke of the city as.
Judg 20. 38 should make a great flame with smoke to
20. 40 up out of the city with a pillar of smoke
2 Sa. 22. 9 There went up a smoke out of his nostrils
Job 41. 20 Out of his nostrils goeth smoke, as (out) of
Psa. 18. 8 There went up a smoke out of his nostrils
37. 20 they shall consume; into smoke shall they
68. 2 As smoke is driven away, (so) drive them
102. 3 my days are consumed like smoke, and my
Prov 10. 26 As vinegar to the teeth, and as smoke to
Song 3. 6 out of the wilderness like pillars of smoke
Isa. 4. 5 a cloud and smoke by day, and the shin.
6. 4 and the house was filled with smoke
9. 18 shall mount up (like) the lifting up of sm
14. 31 there shall come from the north a smoke
34. 10 the smoke thereof shall go up for ever: fr.
51. 6 the heavens shall vanish away like smoke
65. 5 These (are) a smoke in my nose, a fire th.
Hos. 13. 3 and as the smoke out of the chimney
Joel 2. 30 show wonders..fire, and pillars of smoke
Nah. 2. 13 I will burn her chariots in the smoke

3. *Smoking*, עָשֵׁן *ashen*.
Exod 20. 18 all the people saw..the mountain smok.
Isa. 7. 4 the two tails of these smoking firebrands

4. *Vapour, smoke*, קִיטוֹר *qitor*.
Gen. 19. 28 smoke of the country went up as the sm.
Psa. 119. 83 I am become like a bottle in the smoke

5. *Smoke*, καπνός *kapnos*.
Acts 2. 19 show wonders..fire, and vapour of smoke
Rev. 8. 4 the smoke of the incense, (which came)
9. 2 a smoke out of the pit, as the smoke of a
9. 2 darkened by reason of the smoke of the
9. 3 there came out of the smoke locusts upon
9. 17 out of their mouths issued fire and smoke
9. 18 by the fire, and by the smoke, and by the
14. 11 the smoke of their torment ascendeth up
15. 8 the temple was filled with smoke from the
18. 9 when they shall see the smoke of her bu.
18. 18 cried when they saw the smoke of her bu.
19. 3 And her smoke rose up for ever and ever

6. *To smoke*, τύφομαι *tuphomai*.
Matt 12. 20 smoking flax shall he not quench, till he

SMOKE, to (be on a) —

To smoke, עָשַׁן *ashan*.
Exod 19. 18 Sinai was altogether on a smoke, because
Deut 29. 20 his jealousy shall smoke against that man
Psa. 74. 1 (why) doth thine anger smoke against the
104. 32 he toucheth the hills, and they smoke
144. 5 touch the mountains, and they shall sm.

SMOOTH (thing) —

1. *A smooth thing*, חָלָק *chalaq*.
Gen. 27. 11 Esau..(is) a hairy man, and I (am) a sm.
Prov. 5. 3 a strange woman..her mouth (is) smooth

2. *A smooth thing*, חֵלֶק *cheleq*.
Isa. 57. 6 Among the smooth (stones) of the stream

3. *Smooth*, חַלּוּק *challuq*.
1 Sa. 17. 40 chose him five smooth stones out of the

4. *Smoothness, smooth thing*, חֶלְקָה *chelqah*.
Gen. 27. 16 put the skins..upon the smooth of his ne.
Isa. 30. 10 speak unto us smooth things, prophesy de.

5. *Smooth, plain*, λεῖος *leios*.
Luke 3. 5 and the rough ways (shall be) made smo.

SMOOTH, be smoother, to —

1. *To be smooth*, חָלַק *chalaq*.
Psa. 55. 21 (The words) of his mouth were smoother

2. *To make smooth*, חָלַק *chalaq*, 5.
Isa. 41. 7 he that smootheth (with) the hammer him

SMYR'-NA. Σμύρνα *myrrh*.
A city of Ionia, in the W. of Asia Minor, on the E. of Ægean Sea, fifty miles N. of Ephesus; now called *Ismir*.
Rev. 1. 11 unto S., and unto Pergamos, and unto T.
2. 8 unto the angel of the church in S. write

SNAIL —

1. *Lizard*, חֹמֶט *chomet*.
Lev. 11. 30 and the lizard, and the snail, and the mo.

2. *A snail, or festering sore*, שַׁבְּלוּל *shablul*.
Psa. 58. 8 As a snail (which) melteth, let (every one

SNARE —

1. *Destruction, snare, cord*, חֶבֶל, חֵבֶל *chebel*.
Job 18. 10 The snare (is) laid for him in the ground

2. *A snare, fowler*, יָקוּשׁ *yaqush*.
Jer. 5. 26 they lay wait, as he that setteth snares; th.

3. *A snare, fowler*, מוֹקֵשׁ *moqesh*.
Exod 10. 7 How long shall this man be a snare unto
23. 33 it will surely be a snare unto thee
34. 12 lest it be for a snare in the midst of thee
Deut. 7. 16 for that (will be) a snare unto thee
Judg. 2. 3 and their gods shall be a snare unto you
8. 27 which thing became a snare unto Gideon
1 Sa. 18. 21 that she may be a snare to him, and that
2 Sa. 22. 6 compassed me about; the snares of death
Job 40. 24 He taketh it..(his) nose pierceth through s.
Psa. 18. 5 compassed me about; the snares of death
64. 5 they commune of laying snares privily; th.
69. 22 Let their table become a snare before th.
106. 36 they served their idols which were a snare
Prov 13. 14 a fountain of life, to depart from the sn.
14. 27 a fountain of life, to depart from the sn.
18. 7 A fool's..lips (are) the snare of his soul
20. 25 (It is) a snare to the man (who) devoureth
22. 25 Lest thou learn his ways, and get a snare
29. 6 In the transgression..(there is) a snare: but
29. 25 The fear of man bringeth a snare: but wh.
Isa. 8. 14 for a snare to the inhabitants of Jerusal.

4. *Net*, מָצוֹד *matsod*.
Eccl. 7. 26 the woman whose heart (is) snares and nets

5. *Net*, מְצוּדָה *metsudah*.
Eze. 12. 13 he shall be taken in my snare: and I will
17. 20 and he shall be taken in my snare; and I

6. *A gin*, פַּח *pach*.
Josh 23. 13 they shall be snares and traps unto you
Job 22. 10 snares (are) round about thee, and sudden
Psa. 11. 6 Upon the wicked he shall rain snares
69. 22 Let their table become a snare before th.
91. 3 Surely he shall deliver thee from the sn.
119. 110 The wicked have laid a snare for me: yet
124. 7 out of the snare of the fowlers: the snare
140. 5 The proud have hid a snare for me, and
141. 9 Keep me from the snares..they have laid
142. 3 In the way..have they privily laid a sna.
Prov. 7. 23 as a bird hasteth to the snare, and know.
22. 5 Thorns..snares (are) in the way of the fr.
Eccl. 9. 12 as the birds that are caught in the snare
Isa. 24. 17 Fear, and the pit, and the snare (are) up.
24. 18 midst of the pit shall be taken in the sn.
Jer. 18. 22 they have digged a pit..and hid snares for
48. 43 Fear, and the pit, and the snare..upon th.
48. 44 out of the pit shall be taken in the snare
Hos. 5. 1 ye have been a snare on Mizpah, and a net
9. 8 the prophet (is) a snare of a fowler in all
Amos 3. 5 Can a bird fall in a snare upon the earth
3. 5 shall (one) take up a snare from the earth

7. *A pit, snare*, פַּחַת *pachath*.
Lam. 3. 47 a snare is come upon us, desolation and

8. *Net or wreathed work, snare*, שְׂבָכָה *sebakah*.
Job 18. 8 his own feet, and he walketh upon a snare

9. *A rope, snare*, βρόχος *brochos*.
1 Co. 7. 35 not that I may cast a snare upon you, but

10. *A fastening, net, snare,* παγίς *pagis.*
Luke21. 35 as a snare shall it come on all them that
Rom.11. 9 Let their table be made a snare, and a tr.
1 Ti. 3. 7 lest he fall into reproach and the snare
6. 9 they that will be rich fall into..a snare
2 Ti. 2. 26 may recover themselves out of the snare

SNARE, to bring into or lay a —

1. *To lay a snare,* יָקֹשׁ *yaqosh.*
Jer. 50. 24 I have laid a snare for thee, and thou art

2. *To lay a snare,* נָקַשׁ *naqash,* 3.
Psa. 38. 12 They..that seek after my life lay snares

3. *To lay a snare,* נָקַשׁ *naqash,* 7.
1 Sa. 28. 9 wherefore then layest thou a snare for my

4. *To breathe, inflame,* פּוּחַ *puach,* 5.
Prov 29. 8 Scornful men bring a city into a snare

5. *To lay a snare,* קוֹשׁ *qosh.*
Isa. 29. 21 lay a snare for him that reproveth in the

SNARED, to be —

1. *To be snared,* יָקֹשׁ *yaqosh,* 2.
Deut. 7. 25 lest thou be snared therein: for it (is) an
Prov. 6. 2 Thou art snared with the words of thy mo.
Isa. 8. 15 many among them shall..be snared, and
28. 13 and be broken, and snared, and taken

2. *To be snared,* יָקֹשׁ *yaqosh,* 6.
Eccl. 9. 12 so (are) the sons of men snared in an evil

3. *A snare, snarer,* מוֹקֵשׁ *moqesh.*
Prov 12. 13 The wicked is snared by the transgression

4. *To be snared,* נָקַשׁ *naqash.*
Psa. 9. 16 the wicked is snared in the work of his

5. *To be or become snared,* נָקַשׁ *naqash,* 2,
Deut 12. 30 Take heed to thyself that thou be not sn.

6. *To be or become snared,* פָּחַח *puchach,* 5.
Isa. 42. 22 (they are) all of them snared in holes, and

SNATCH, to —

To cut down or off, גָּזַר *gazar.*
Isa. 9. 20 he shall snatch on the right hand, and be

SNEEZE, to —

To sneeze, זָרַר *zarar,* 3a.
2 Ki. 4. 35 the child sneezed seven times and the ch.

SNORTING —

Snorting, נַחֲרָה *nacharah.*
Jer. 8. 16 The snorting of his horses was heard fr.

SNOUT —

Nose, אַף *aph.*
Prov 11. 22 (As) a jewel of gold in a swine's snout, (so)

SNOW, snowy, (to be as) —

1. *Snow,* שֶׁלֶג *sheleg.*
Exod 4. 6 behold, his hand (was) leprous as snow
Num12. 10 Miriam (became) leprous, (white) as snow
2 Sa. 23. 20 in the midst of a pit in time of snow
2 Ki. 5. 27 from his presence a leper (as white) as sn.
1 Ch.11. 22 and slew a lion in a pit in a snowy day
Job 6. 16 of the ice, (and) wherein the snow is hid
9. 30 If I wash myself with snow water, and
24. 19 Drought and heat consume the snow wa.
37. 6 he saith to the snow, Be thou (on) the ea.
38. 22 entered into the treasures of the snow?
Psa. 51. 7 wash me, and I shall be whiter than snow
147. 16 He giveth snow like wool: he scattereth
148. 8 Fire, and hail; snow, and vapour; stormy
Prov25. 13 As the cold of snow in the time of harvest
26. 1 As snow in summer, and as rain in harv.
31. 21 She is not afraid of the snow for her ho.
Isa. 1. 18 Though..scarlet, they shall be as..snow
55. 10 as the rain cometh down, and the snow
Jer. 18. 14 Will (a man) leave the snow of Lebanon
Lam. 4. 7 Her Nazarites were purer than snow, they

2. *To snow,* שָׁלַג *shalag,* 5.
Psa. 68. 14 scattered kings in it, it was (white) as sn.

3. *Snow,* תְּלַג *telag.*
Dan. 7. 9 whose garment (was) white as snow, and

4. *Snow,* χιών *chiōn.*
Matt28. 3 lightning, and his raiment white as snow
Mark 9. 3 his raiment..exceeding white [as snow]
Rev. 1. 14 hairs (were) white like wool, as white as s.

SNUFF (up), to —

1. *To cause to breathe out, snuff up,* נָפַח *naphach,* 5.
Mal. 1. 13 ye have snuffed at it, saith the LORD of ho.

2. *To swallow up, pant,* שָׁאַף *shaaph.*
Jer. 2. 24 snuffeth up the wind at her pleasure
14. 6 they snuffed up the wind like dragons

SNUFF DISH, snuffers —

1. *Snuffers, forceps,* מְזַמְּרוֹת *mezammeroth.*
1 Ki. 7. 50 the snuffers, and the basins, and the spo.
2 Ki.12. 13 bowls of silver, snuffers, basins, trumpets
25. 14 the snuffers, and the spoons, and all the
2 Ch. 4. 22 the snuffers, and the basins, and the spo.
Jer. 52. 18 the snuffers and the bowls, and the spo.

2. *Fire, coal, incense, or snuff dish,* מַחְתָּה *machtah.*
Exod25. 38 the snuff dishes thereof, (shall be of) pure
37. 23 he made..his snuff dishes, (of) pure gold
Num. 4. 9 his snuff dishes, and all the oil vessels th.

3. *Tongs, snuffers,* מַלְקָחַיִם *malqachayim.*
Exod37. 23 he made his seven lamps, and his snuff.

SO, סוֹא.

A king of Egypt, of Ethiopian descent; or *Sevechus,* the second king of the twenty-fifth dynasty in Manetho, who reigned fourteen years and was succeeded by Tirhakah; his alliance was sought for by Hoshea son of Elah, the last king of Israel, who had become tributary to Shalmanezer king of Assyria. B.C. 728.
2 Ki. 17. 4 he had sent messengers to So king of Eg.

SO —

1. *These,* אֵלֶּה *eleh.*
Deut22. 5 all that do so (are) abomination unto the

2. *This,* זֹאת *zoth.*
Gen. 44. 17 God forbid that I should do so: (but) the

3. *This,* הַזֹּאת *haz-zoth.*
Judg19. 24 but unto this man do not so vile a thing

4. *Thus,* כֹּה *koh.*
Gen. 15. 5 and he said unto him, So shall thy seed
Isa. 18. 4 For so the LORD said unto me, I will take

5. *Thus,* כָּכָה *kakah.*
Num15. 12 so shall ye do to every one according to

6. *So,* כֵּן *ken.*
Gen. 1. 7 and divided the waters..and it was so
Deut22. 3 so shalt thou do with his raiment; and

7. *Thus,* בְּכֵן *be-ken.*
Esth. 4. 16 so will I go in unto the king, which (is)
Eccl. 8. 10 so I saw the wicked buried, who had co.

8. *Thus, so,* כְּנֵמָא *kenema.*
Ezra 6. 13 that which Darius the king had sent, so

9. *Thus, according to these,* כָּהֵם *ka-hem.*
Eccl. 9. 12 so (are) the sons of men snared in an evil

10. *And, even,* καί *kai.*
Matt 27. 64 so the last..shall be worse than the first
[*See also* Luke 11. [2]; John 6. 57; 13. 33; 15. 9; Acts 7. 51; Rom. 11. 16; Gal. 1. 9; Phil. 1. 20; 1 Pe. 1. 15; 1 Jo. 4. 17; 2 Cor. 11. 22].

11. *Therefore, since,* ἄρα *ara.*
Rom 14. 12 So [then] every one of us shall give acco.

12. *Indeed,* μέν *men.*
Mark16. 19 [So then, after the Lord had spoken unto]

13. *Similarly, likewise,* ὁμοίως *homoiōs.*
Luke 5. 10 so (was) also James and John, the sons of

14. *Then, therefore,* οὖν *oun.*
Matt. 1. 17 So all the generations from Abraham to
Luke14. 33 So likewise, whosoever he be of you that
John 4. 40 So when the Samaritans were come unto
4. 46 So Jesus came again into Cana of Galilee
4. 53 So the father knew that (it was) at the s.
6. 10 [So] the men sat down, in number about fi.
6. 19 So when they had rowed about five and
7. 43 So there was a division among the people
13. 12 So after he had washed their feet, and had
21. 15 So when they had dined, Jesus saith to S.
Acts 13. 4 So they, being sent forth by the Holy Gh.
15. 30 So when they were dismissed, they came
23. 18 So he took him, and brought (him) to the
23. 22 So the chief captain (then) let the young
28. 9 [So] when this was done, others also, whi.

15. *Thus,* οὕτω, οὕτως *houtō, houtōs.*
Matt. 5. 12 for so persecuted they the prophets whi.
5. 16 Let your light so shine before men, that
5. 19 Whosoever..shall teach men so, he shall
5. 47 what do ye..not even the publicans [so]?
6. 30 if God so clothe the grass of the field, wh.
9. 33 saying, It was never so seen in Israel
11. 26 for so it seemed good in thy sight
12. 40 so shall the Son of man be three days and
13. 40 so shall it be in the end of this world
13. 49 So shall it be at the end of the world: the
18. 35 So likewise shall my heavenly Father do
19. 8 but from the beginning it was not so
19. 10 If the case of the man be so with (his) w.
19. 12 which were so born from (their) mother's
20. 16 So the last shall be first, and the first last
20. 26 it shall not be so among you: but whoso.
24. 27 so shall also the coming of the Son of man
24. 33 So likewise ye, when ye shall see all these
24. 37, 39 so shall also the coming of the Son of
24. 46 his lord when he cometh shall find so do.
Mark 2. [8]; 4. 26, [40]; 7. 18; 10. 43; 14. 59; 15. 39; Luke 6. [10]; 9. 15; 10. 21; 11. 30; 12. 21, 28, 38, 43, 54; 17. 10, 24, 26; 21. 31; 22. 26; 24. 24; John 3. 8, 16; 5. 21, 26; 8. [59]; 12. 50; 18. 22; Acts 1. 11; 3. 18; 7. 1, 8; 8. 32; 12. 8; 13. 8, 47; 14. 1; 17. 11, 33; 19. 20; 20. 11, 13, 35; 21. 11; 22. 24; 23. 11; 24. 9, 14; 27. 17, 44; 28. 14; Rom. 1. 15; 4. 18; 5. 12, 15, 18, 19, 21; 11. 5, 26; 12. 5; 15. 20; 1 Co. 2. 11; 3. 15; 4. 1; 5. 3, 0. 5; 7. 17, 17, 26, 36, 40; 8. 12; 9. 14, 15, 24, 26; 11. 28; 12. 12; 14. 9, 12, 25; 15. 11, 11, 22, 42, 45; 16. 1; 2 Co. 1. 5, 7; 7. 14; 8. 6, 11; 10. 7; 11. [3]; Gal. 1. 6; 3. 3; 4. 3, 29; 6. 2; Eph. 4. 20; 5. 24, 28, 33; Phil. 3. 17; 4. 1; Col. 3. 13; 1 Ti. 2. 8; 4. 17; 5. 2; 2 Th. 3. 17; 2 Ti. 3. 8; Heb. 5. 3, 5; 6. 15; 9. 28; 10. 33; 12. 21; Jas. 1. 11; 2. 12, 12, 17, 26; 3. 5, [6], 10, [12]; 1 Pe. 2. 15; 2 Pe. 1. 11; 1 Jo. 2. [6]; 4. 11; Rev. 2. 15; 3. 16; 16. 18.

16. *According to these,* κατὰ ταῦτα *kata tauta.*
Luke 6. 26 for so did their fathers to the false prop.

17. *These things,* ταῦτα *tauta.*
John11. 28 when she had so said, she went her way

18. *This,* τοῦτο *touto.*
John20. 20 when he had so said, he showed unto th.
Acts 19. 14 And there were seven sons..which did so
23. 7 when he had so said, there arose a disse.

Rom 12. 20 in so doing thou shalt heap coals of fire
1 Co. 7. 37 hath so decreed in his heart that he will

19. *As, so that,* ὡς *hōs.*
Heb. 3. 11 So I sware in my wrath, They shall not
[*See also* And, bad, called, evil, great, long as, mighty, much, not, soon, yet].

SO...and —

Also...also, גַּם...גַּם *gam...gam.*
Gen. 32. 19 so commanded he the second, and the th.

SO and much —

Thus...thus, כֹּה...כֹּה *koh...koh.*
1 Sa. 20. 13 The LORD do so and much more to Jona.

SO as —

1. *That, so that, so as,* ἵνα *hina.*
Rev. 8. 12 so as the third part of them was darkened

2. *Such, such as,* οἷα *hoia.*
Mark 9. 3 so as no fuller on earth can white them

SO be (it) —

1. *It is steadfast! be it steadfast!* אָמֵן *amen.*
Jer. 11. 5 Then answered I, and said, So be it, O L.

2. *Then, therefore, in truth,* ἄρα *ara.*
1 Co.15. 15 whom he raised not up, if so be that the

SO great —

1. *Heavy, weighty,* כָּבֵד *kabed.*
1 Ki. 3. 9 who is able to judge this thy so great a p.

2. *So great, so many,* τοσοῦτος *tosoutos.*
Matt. 8. 10 I have not found so great faith, no, not in
15. 33 Whence..bread..as to fill so great a mu.
Luke 7. 9 I have not found so great faith, no, not in
Heb.12. 1 compassed about with so great a cloud
Rev. 18. 17 in one hour so great riches is come to no.

SO long —

So great, so many, τοσοῦτος *tosoutos.*
John14. 9 Have I been so long time with you, and
Heb. 4. 7 saying in David, To day, after so long a

SO long as —

1. *From the day when,* מִיּוֹם אֲשֶׁר [*yom*].
1 Sa. 29. 8 so long as I have been with thee unto this

2. *All the days in which,* כָּל־הַיָּמִים אֲשֶׁר [*yom*].
2 Ch. 6. 31 so long as they live in the land which thou

3. *In* [*my*] *days,* מִיָּמָי [*yom*].
Job 27. 6 shall not reproach (me) so long as I live

4. *Until, as long as,* עַד *ad.*
2 Ki. 9. 22 so long as the whoredoms of thy mother

5. *During all the time that,* בְּכָל־עֵת אֲשֶׁר [*eth*].
Esth. 5. 13 all this availeth me nothing, so long as I

SO many (more) as —

1. *Like them,* כָּהֵם *ka-hem.*
1 Ch.21. 3 an hundred times so many more as they

2. *As many as,* ὅσος *hosos.*
Rom. 6. 3 so many of us as were baptized into Jesus

3. *So great, so many,* τοσοῦτος *tosoutos.*
John 6. 9 but what are they among so many?
12. 37 though he had done so many miracles be.
21. 11 for all there were so many, yet was not
1 Co.14. 10 There are, it may be, so many kinds of v.
Gal. 3. 4 Have ye suffered so many things in vain?

SO much (as) —

1. *Also, even,* גַּם *gam.*
2 Sa. 17. 12 there shall not be left so much as one

2. *This,* זֹאת *zoth.*
2 Ch.27. 5 So much did the children of Ammon pay

3. *Might, exceedingly,* מְאֹד *meod.*
2 Sa. 14. 25 there was none to be so much praised as
Jer. 2. 36 Why gaddest thou about so much to cha.

4. *Unto,* עַד *ad.*
Exod14. 28 there remained not so much as one of th.

5. *Neither, nor,* μήτε *mēte.*
Mark 3. 20 so that they could not so much as eat br.

6. *So great, so many,* τοσοῦτος *tosoutos.*
Matt 15. 33 Whence should we have so much bread
Acts 5. 8 whether ye sold the land for so much?
5. 8 And she said, Yea, for so much
Heb. 1. 4 Being made so much better than the ang.
7. 22 By so much was Jesus made a surety of
10. 25 so much the more as ye see the Re.18.7.

7. *Not even,* οὐδέ *oude,* Luke 18. 13.

SO much the more —

Much more, (πολλῷ) μᾶλλον (*pollō*) *mallon.*
Luke 5. 15 so much the more went there a fame ab.
18. 39 he cried so much the more, (thou) son of
Mark 7. 36 so much the more a great deal they pub.

SO sore —

Might, exceedingly, מְאֹד *meod.*
1 Ki.17. 17 his sickness was so sore, that there was

SO that —

1. *That,* אֲשֶׁר *asher.*
Gen. 13. 16 so that if a man can number the dust of

2. *That,* כִּי *ki.*
Deut 14. 24 so that thou art not able to carry it

3. *Till,* עַד *ad.*
Josh. 8. 22 they smote them, so that they let none of

4. *Only if*, רַק אִם *raq im.*
1 Ki. 8. 25 so that thy children take heed to their way
5. *With a view to*, εἰς *eis.*
Rom. 1. 20 so that they are without excuse
Heb. 11. 3 so that things which are seen were not
6. *That, so that, as that*, ἵνα *hina.*
Rev. 13. 13 so that he maketh fire come down from
7. *How, so that*, ὅπως *hopōs.*
Luke 16. 26 so that they which would pass from hence
8. *As, so that*, ὡς *hōs.*
Acts 20. 24 so that I might finish my course with joy
9. *As also, so that*, ὥστε *hōste.*
Matt. 8. 28 so that no man might pass by that way
13. 2 so that he went into a ship, and sat
13. 32 so that the birds of the air come and lodge
Mark 3. 20 multitude cometh together again, so that
4. 1 so that he entered into a ship, and sat in
4. 32 so that the fowls of the air may lodge un.
4. 37 the waves beat into the ship, so that it
15. 5 Jesus yet answered nothing; so that Pil.
Luke 5. 7 filled both the ships, so that they began
Acts 16. 26 so that the foundations of the prison were
19. 10 so that all they which dwelt in Asia heard
19. 12 So that from his body were brought unto
19. 16 so that they fled out of that house naked
Rom 15. 19 so that from Jerusalem, and round about
1 Co. 1. 7 So that ye come behind in no gift; wait.
13. 2 though I have all faith, so that I could
2 Co. 2. 7 So that contrariwise ye (ought) rather to
3. 7 so that the children of Israel could not
7. 7 your fervent mind toward me; so that I
Phil. 1. 13 So that my bonds in Christ are manifest
1 Th. 1. 7 So that ye were ensamples to all that be.
1. 8 so that we need not to speak any thing
2 Th. 1. 4 So that we ourselves glory in you in the
2. 4; Heb. 13. 6.

SO it was, συμβαίνω *to happen*, Acts 21. 35.

SO (that) no —
Without, so that no, מִבְּלִי *mib-beli.*
Eccl. 3. 11 so that no man can find out the work that

SO then —
1. *Then, now, therefore*, μὲν οὖν *men oun.*
Mark 16. 19 [So then, after the Lord had spoken unto]
2. *As also, so that*, ὥστε *hōste.*
Mark 10. 8 so then they are no more twain, but one
1 Co. 3. 7; 7. 38; 2 Co. 4. 12; Gal. 3. 9.
3. *Then*, ἄρα *ara*, Rom. 10. 17; Gal. 4. 31.
4. *Then indeed*, ἄρα οὖν, Ro. 7. 3, 25; 9. 16; 14. 12.
5. *But, and, also*, δέ *de*, Rom. 8. 8.
6. *So, so then*, οὕτως *houtōs*, Rev. 3. 16.

SOAP. See SOPE.

SOAKED —
To be filled, satisfied, watered, רָוָה *ravah*, 3.
Isa. 34. 7 their land shall be soaked with blood, and

SOBER, soberly, soberness, sobriety —
1. *Sober, vigilant*, νηφάλιος *nēphalios.*
1 Ti. 3. 11 not slanderers, sober, faithful in all things
Titus 2. 2 That the aged men be sober, grave, temp.
2. *To be sober, watchful*, νήφω *nēphō.*
1 Pe. 1. 13 be sober, and hope to the end for the gr.
3. *With a view to be sound minded*, εἰς τὸ σωφρονεῖν.
Rom 12. 3 to think soberly, according as God hath
4. *Temperately, prudently*, σωφρόνως *sōphronōs.*
Titus 2. 12 we should live soberly, righteously, and
5. *Prudence, moderation*, σωφροσύνη *sōphrosunē.*
Acts 26. 25 speak forth the words of truth and sober.
1 Ti. 2. 9 with shamefacedness and sobriety
2. 15 and charity and holiness with sobriety
6. *Sound minded, moderate*, σώφρων *sōphrōn.*
1 Ti. 3. 2 vigilant, sober, of good behaviour, given
Titus 1. 8 a lover of good men, sober, just, holy, te.

SOBER (minded, to teach) to be —
1. *To be sober, watchful*, νήφω *nēphō.*
1 Th. 5. 6 let us not sleep..but let us..be sober
5. 8 let us, who are of the day, be sober, put.
1 Pe. 5. 8 Be sober, be vigilant; because your adv.
2. *To be sound minded*, σωφρονέω *sōphroneō.*
2 Co. 5. 13 or whether we be sober, (it is) for your c.
Titus 2. 6 Young men..exhort to be sober minded
1 Pe. 4. 7 be ye therefore sober, and watch unto p.
3. *Make prudent*, σωφρονίζω *sōphronizō.*
Titus 2. 4 may teach the young women to be sober

SO'-CHO, SHO'-CO, SHO'-CHO, שׂוֹכוֹ.
1. A son of Heber. B.C. 1380.
1 Ch. 4. 18 Jehudijah bare..Heber the father of S.
2. A city in Judah, rebuilt by Rehoboam; perhaps *Socoh*, in the N.W. of the plain of Judah.
2 Ch. 11. 7 And Beth-zur, and S., and Adullam
28. 18 Gedoroth, and S. with the villages thereof

SOCKET —
A socket, אֶדֶן *eden.*
Exod 26. 19 thou shalt make forty sockets of silver u.
26. 19, 21, 25 two sockets under one board
26. 19, 21, 25 and two sockets under another bo.
26. 21 And their forty sockets (of) silver; two
26. 25 and their sockets (of) silver, sixteen soc.
26. 32 hooks (shall be of) gold, upon the four so.
Exod 26. 37 thou shalt cast five sockets of brass for
27. 10 and their twenty sockets, (shall be of) br.
27. 11 twenty pillars and their twenty sockets (of)
27. 12 their pillars ten, and their sockets ten
27. 14, 15 their pillars three, and their sockets
27. 16 pillars (shall be) four, and their sockets f.
27. 17 hooks (shall be of silver,) and their sock.
27. 18 fine twined linen, and their sockets (of) b.
35. 11 boards, his bars, his pillars, and his sock.
35. 17 his pillars, and their sockets, and the ha.
36. 24 forty sockets of silver he made under the
36. 24, 26 two sockets under one board for his
36. 26 And their forty sockets of silver; two
36. 24, 26 and two sockets under another board
36. 30 their sockets (were) sixteen sockets of
36. 30 eight boards..under every board two so.
36. 36 and he cast for them four sockets of silv.
36. 38 fillets with gold: but their five sockets (w.
38. 10 pillars (were) twenty, and their brazen so
38. 11 their pillars (were) twenty, and their so
38. 12 their pillars ten, and their sockets ten
38. 14, 15 their pillars three, and their sockets
38. 17 the sockets for the pillars (were of) brass
38. 19 their pillars (were) four, and their sockets
38. 27 sockets of the sanctuary, and the sockets
38. 27 an hundred sockets..a talent for a socket
38. 30 he made the sockets to the door of the ta.
38. 31 the sockets of the court round about, and
38. 31 the sockets of the court gate, and all the
39. 33 his bars, and his pillars, and his sockets
39. 40 his pillars, and his sockets, and the hang.
40. 18 fastened his sockets, and set up the boards
Num. 3. 36 the sockets thereof, and all the vessels th
3. 37 their sockets, and their pins, and their co.
4. 31 the pillars thereof, and the sockets there.
4. 32 their sockets, and their pins, and their co.
Song 5. 15 pillars of marble set upon sockets of fine

SO'-COH, SHO'-CHOH, SO'-CHOH, שׂוֹכֹה, שֹׂכֹה.
1. A city in the N.W. of the plain of Judah, near Adullam or Azekah.
Josh. 15. 35 Jarmuth, and Adullam, S., and Azekah
1 Sa. 17. 1 were gathered together at S., which (be.)
17. 1 pitched between S. and Azekah, in Ephes.
1 Ki. 4. 10 to him (pertained) S., and all the land of
2. Another city in the hill country of Judah, near Jattir.
Josh. 15. 48 in the mountains, Shamir, and Jattir..S.

SOD, be sodden, to—
1. *To boil, cook*, בָּשַׁל *bashal*, 3.
2 Ch. 35. 13 the (other) holy (offerings) sod they in pots
Lam. 4. 10 The hands of the pitiful women have sod.
2. *To be boiled, cooked*, בָּשַׁל *bashal*, 4.
Exod 12. 9 Eat not of it raw, nor sodden at all with
Lev. 6. 28 the earthen vessel wherein it is sodden
6. 28 if it be sodden in a brasen pot, it shall be
1 Sa. 2. 15 he will not have sodden flesh of thee, but
3. *Boiled, cooked*, בָּשֵׁל *bashel.*
Num. 6. 19 the priest shall take the sodden shoulder
4. *To (cause) to boil*, זוּד, זִיד *zid, zud*, 5.
Gen. 25. 29 Jacob sod pottage: and Esau came from

SODERING, soldering —
Joint, joining, דֶּבֶק *debeq.*
Isa. 41. 7 saying, It (is) ready for the sodering: and

SO'-DI, סוֹדִי *Jah determines.*
A Zebulonite, father of Gaddiel, one of the twelve spies sent out to view the land. B.C. 1492.
Num 13. 10 the tribe of Zebulun, Gaddiel the son of S.

SO'-DOM, SO-DO'-MA, סְדֹם *place of lime.* Σόδομα.
A city on the shore of the Salt Sea south of Engedi; destroyed in the days of Abraham and Lot along with Gomorrah, Admah, and Zeboim. B.C. 1900.
Gen 10. 19 as thou goest, unto S., and Gomorrah, and
13. 10 before the LORD destroyed S. and Gomor.
13. 12 Lot dwelt..and pitched (his) tent toward S.
13. 13 the men of S. (were) wicked and sinners
14. 2 (these) made war with Bera king of S., and
14. 8 there went out the king of S., and the king
14. 10 the kings of S. and Gomorrah fled, and fell
14. 11 they took all the goods of S. and Gomorrah
14. 12 Lot, Abram's brother's son who dwelt in S.
14. 17 the king of S. went out to meet him after
14. 21 the king of S. said unto Abram, Give me
14. 22 Abram said to the king of S., I have lift
18. 16 rose up from thence, and looked towards
18. 20 the cry of S. and Gomorrah is great, and
18. 22 And the men turned..and went toward S.
18. 26 If I find in S. fifty righteous within the ci.
19. 1 And there came two angels to S. at even
19. 1 Lot sat in the gate of S.: and Lot seeing
19. 4 the men of S., compassed the house round
19. 24 the LORD rained upon S. and upon Gom.
19. 28 he looked toward S. and Gomorrah, and
Deut 29. 23 like the overthrow of S., and Gomorrah
32. 32 their vine (is) of the vine of S., and of the
Isa. 1. 9 we should have been as S., (and) we should
1. 10 Hear the word of the LORD, ye rulers of S.
3. 9 they declare their sin as S., they hide (it)
13. 19 shall be as when God overthrew S. and G.
Jer. 23. 14 they are all of them unto me as S., and the
49. 18 As in the overthrow of S. and Gomorrah
50. 40 As God overthrew S. and Gomorrah and
Lam. 4. 6 than the punishment of the sin of S., (that
Eze. 16. 46 thy younger sister..(is) S. and her daugh.
16. 48 S. thy sister hath not done, she nor her
16. 49 this was the iniquity of thy sister S., pride
Eze. 16. 53 the captivity of S. and her daughters and
16. 55 S. and her daughters, shall return to their
16. 56 S. was not mentioned by thy mouth in the
Amos 4. 11 have overthrown..you, as God overthrew
Zeph. 2. 9 Moab shall be as S., and the children of
Matt 10. 15 shall be more tolerable for the land of S.
11. 23 if the mighty works..had been done in S.
11. 24 shall be more tolerable for the land of S.
Mark 6. 11 [It shall be more tolerable for S. and Go.]
Luke 10. 12 shall be more tolerable in that day for S.
17. 29 the same day that Lot went out of S. it
Rom. 9. 29 we had been as S., and been made like un.
2 Pe. 2. 6 turning the cities of S. and Gomorrah into
Jude 7 as S. and Gomorrah, and the cities about
Rev. 11. 8 great city, which spiritually is called S.

SODOMITE —
Separate, set apart, קָדֵשׁ *qadesh.*
Deut 23. 17 There shall be no..sodomite of the sons
1 Ki. 14. 24 And there were also sodomites in the land
15. 12 he took away the sodomites out of the l.
22. 46 the remnant of the sodomites, which re.
2 Ki. 23. 7 he brake down the houses of the sodomi.

SOEVER —
If, ἐάν *ean.*
Mark 6. 10 In what place soever ye enter into an ho.

SOFT, softly —
1. *Gently*, (לְ)אַט, *(le-)at.*
1 Ki. 21. 27 and lay in sackcloth, and went softly
Isa. 8. 6 the waters of Shiloah that go softly, and
2. *Gently*, לְאִטִּי *le-itti.*
Gen. 33. 14 I will lead on softly, according as the ca.
3. *Gentleness*, לְאַט *lat.*
Judg. 4. 21 went softly unto him, and smote the nail
4. *Gentleness*, לַט *lat.*
Ruth 3. 7 she came softly, and uncovered his feet
5. *Tender, soft, timid*, רַךְ *rak.*
Job 41. 3 will he speak soft (words) unto thee?
Prov. 15. 1 A soft answer turneth away wrath: but
25. 15 persuaded, and a soft tongue breaketh the
6. *Soft, delicate*, μαλακός *malakos.*
Matt 11. 8 A man clothed in soft raiment? Behold
11. 8 they that wear soft (clothing) are in kin.
Luke 7. 25 A man clothed in soft raiment? Behold

SOFT, softer, to be or make —
1. *To melt, soften*, מוּג *mug*, 3*a*.
Psa. 65. 10 thou makest it soft with showers; thou
2. *To be tender, soft*, רָכַךְ *rakak.*
Psa. 55. 21 his words were softer than oil, yet (were)
3. *To make tender*, רָכַךְ *rakak*, 5.
Job 23. 16 God maketh my heart soft, and the Alm.

SOIL —
A field, land, שָׂדֶה *sadeh.*
Eze. 17. 8 It was planted in a good soil by great wa.

SOJOURN (in), to —
1. *To sojourn*, גּוּר *gur.*
Gen. 12. 10 Abram went down into Egypt to sojourn
19. 9 This one (fellow) came in to sojourn, and
20. 1 Abraham journeyed..and sojourned in G.
21. 23 to the land wherein thou hast sojourned
21. 34 Abraham sojourned in the Philistines' la.
26. 3 Sojourn in this land, and I will be with t.
32. 4 I have sojourned with Laban, and stayed
35. 27 where Abraham and Isaac sojourned
47. 4 to sojourn in the land are we come; for
Exod. 3. 22 and of her that sojourneth in her house
12. 48 when a stranger shall sojourn with thee
12. 49 unto the stranger that sojourneth among
Lev. 16. 29 or a stranger that sojourneth among you
17. 8, 10, 13 the strangers that sojourn among
17. 12 any stranger that sojourneth among you
18. 26 nor any stranger that sojourneth among
19. 33 if a stranger sojourn with thee in your la.
20. 2 or of the strangers that sojourn in Israel
25. 6 for thy stranger that sojourneth with th.
25. 45 the strangers that do sojourn among you
Num. 9. 14 if a stranger shall sojourn among you, and
15. 14 if a stranger sojourn with you, or whoso.
15. 15, 16 for the stranger that sojourneth (with
15. 26, 29 the stranger that sojourneth among th.
19. 10 unto the stranger that sojourneth among
Deut 18. 6 if a Levite come from..where he sojourn.
26. 5 he went down into Egypt, and sojourned
Josh. 20. 9 the stranger that sojourneth among them
Judg 17. 7 who (was) a Levite, and he sojourned there
17. 8 to sojourn where he could find (a place)
17. 9 I go to sojourn where I may find (a place)
19. 1 there was a certain Levite sojourning on
19. 16 he sojourned in Gibeah: but the men of
Ruth 1. 1 went to sojourn in the country of Moab
2 Ki. 8. 1 sojourn wheresoever thou canst sojourn
8. 2 sojourned in the land of the Philistines se.
Ezra 1. 4 remaineth in any place where he sojourn.
Psa. 105. 23 and Jacob sojourned in the land of Ham
120. 5 Woe is me, that I sojourn in Mesech, (th.)
Isa. 23. 7 her own feet shall carry her afar..to sojo
52. 4 went down aforetime into Egypt to sojou.
Jer. 42. 15 enter into Egypt, and go to sojourn there
42. 17 set their faces to go into Egypt to sojourn
42. 22 the place whither ye desire..to sojourn
43. 2 to say, Go not into Egypt to sojourn there
44. 12, 14, 28 into the land of Egypt to sojourn
Lam. 4. 15 they said..They shall no more sojourn
Eze. 14. 7 or of the stranger that sojourneth in Israel

Eze. 47. 22 to the strangers that sojourn among you
47. 23 in what tribe the stranger sojourneth

2. *To sojourn, assemble self,* גּוּר *gur,* 7*a.*
1 Ki.17. 20 evil upon the widow with whom I sojourn

3. *Place of sojourn,* מָגוּר *magur.*
Eze. 20. 38 out of the country where they sojourn, and

4. *To dwell alongside, sojourn,* παροικέω *paroikeō.*
Heb. 11. 9 By faith he sojourned in the land of pro

5. *To be a sojourner,* εἰμὶ πάροικος *eimi paroikos.*
Acts 7. 6 That his seed should sojourn in a strange

SOJOURNER, sojourning —

1. *To sojourn,* גּוּר *gur.*
2 Sa. 4. 3 and were sojourners there until this day

2. *A sojourner,* גֵּר *ger.*
Lev. 25. 47 if a sojourner or stranger wax rich by thee

3. *A settler, dwelling,* מוֹשָׁב *moshab.*
Exod12. 40 the sojourning of the children of Israel

4. *A settler, dweller,* תּוֹשָׁב *toshab.*
Gen. 23. 4 I (am) a stranger and a sojourner with you
Lev. 22. 10 a sojourner of the priest, or an hired ser
25. 23 for ye (are) strangers and sojourners with
25. 35 (though he be) a stranger, or a sojourner
25. 40 as a sojourner, he shall be with thee (and)
25. 47 sell himself unto the stranger (or) sojou.
Num35. 15 for the stranger, and for the sojourner am.
1 Ch.29. 15 we (are) strangers before thee, and sojou.
Psa. 39. 12 I (am) a stranger with thee, (and) a sojo.

5. *A dwelling alongside,* παροικία *paroikia.*
1 Pe. 1. 17 pass the time of your sojourning (here) in

SOLACE selves, to —

To delight self, rejoice, עָלַס *alas,* 7.
Prov. 7. 18 Come..let us solace ourselves with loves

SOLD, to be —

1. *To come in with a price,* בּוֹא בִּמְחִיר *bo bi-mechir.*
Lam. 5. 4 water for money; our wood is sold unto

2. *To be sold,* מָכַר *makar,* 2.
Exod22. 3 if he have nothing, then he shall be sold
Lev. 25. 23 The land shall not be sold for ever: for
25. 34 the field of the suburbs..may not be sold
25. 39 if thy brother..be waxen poor, and be so
25. 42 my servants..they shall not be sold as bo
25. 48 After that he is sold he may be redeemed
25. 50 from the year that he was sold to him unto
27. 27 it shall be sold according to thy estimat
27. 28 no devoted thing..shall be sold or redee
Deut 15. 12 or an Hebrew woman, be sold unto thee
Neh. 5. 8 the Jews, which were sold unto the heat
5. 8 shall they be sold unto us? Then held they
Esth. 7. 4 we are sold, I and my people, to be dest
7. 4 if we had been sold for bond men and bo
Psa.105. 17 (even) Joseph, (who) was sold for a servant
Jer. 34. 14 an Hebrew, which hath been sold unto

3. *To sell self,* מָכַר *makar,* 7.
Deut28. 68 ye shall be sold unto your enemies for bo

4. *To sell, cause to pass over,* πιπράσκω *pipraskō.*
Matt 18. 25 his lord commanded him to be sold, and his
26. 9 ointment might have been sold for much
Mark14. 5 For it might have been sold for more than
John12. 5 Why was not this ointment sold for three
Acts 4. 34 the prices of the things that were sold
5. 4 after it was sold, was it not in thine own
Rom. 7. 14 spiritual: but I am carnal, sold under sin

5. *To sell,* πωλέω *pōleō.*
Matt 10. 29 Are not two sparrows sold for a farthing?
Luke12. 6 Are not five sparrows sold for two farth.?

SOLD, (that which is) —

Sale, thing sold, ware, מִמְכָּר *mimkar.*
Lev. 25. 25 shall he redeem that which his brother so
25. 28 that which is sold shall remain in the ha.
25. 29 within a whole year after it is sold
25. 33 the house that was sold, and the, Eze. 7. 13.

To be sold, πωλέομαι *pōleomai,* 1 Co. 10. 25.

SOLDIER, (fellow) —

1. *Son of the troop,* בֶּן־גְּדוּד *ben gedud.*
2 Ch.25 13 the soldiers of the army which Amaziah se

2. *Force,* חַיִל *chayil.*
Ezra 8. 22 to require of the king a band of soldiers

3. *To arm,* חָלַץ *chalats.*
Isa. 15. 4 the armed soldiers of Moab shall cry out

4. *Host,* צָבָא *tsaba.*
1 Ch.7. 4 bands of soldiers for war, six and thirty th.

5. *Military host,* στράτευμα *strateuma.*
Acts 23. 10 commanded the soldiers to go down, and

6. *To serve in the camp or host,* στρατεύω *strateuō.*
Luke 3. 14 the soldiers likewise demanded of him, sa.

7. *One serving as a soldier,* στρατιώτης *stratiōtēs.*
Matt. 8. 9 a man under authority, having soldiers un.
27. 27 the soldiers of the governor took Jesus
28. 12 they gave large money unto the soldiers
Mark15. 16 the soldiers led him away into the hall ca.
Luke 7. 8 I also am a man..having under me soldiers
23. 36 the soldiers also mocked him, coming to
John19. 2 the soldiers platted a crown of thorns, and
19. 23 the soldiers, when they had crucified Jes.
19. 23 and made four parts, to every soldier a
19. 24 These things therefore the soldiers did
19. 32 Then came the soldiers, and brake the le.
19. 34 one of the soldiers with a spear pierced his
Acts 10. 7 a devout soldier of them that waited on
12. 4 four quaternions of soldiers to keep him
12. 6 Peter was sleeping between two soldiers
12. 18 there was no small stir among the soldiers
21. 32 Who immediately took soldiers and cent.
21. 32 they saw the chief captain and the soldiers
21. 35 he was borne of the soldiers for the viole.
23. 23 Make ready two hundred soldiers to go to
23. 31 the soldiers, as it was commanded them
27. 31 said to the centurion and to the soldiers
27. 32 the soldiers cut off the ropes of the boat
27. 42 the soldiers' counsel was to kill the pris
28. 16 to dwell by himself with a soldier, 2 Ti. 2.3.

8. *Fellow soldier,* συστρατιώτης, Phil. 2. 25; Phm. 2.

SOLDIER, to choose to be a —

To collect a camp or host, στρατολογέω *stratologeō.*
2 Ti. 2. 4 him who hath chosen him to be a soldier

SOLE —

Palm (of hand), sole (of foot), כַּף *kaph.*
Gen. 8. 9 the dove found no rest for the sole of her
Deut11. 24 Every place whereon the soles of your fe
28. 35 from the sole of thy foot unto the top of
28. 56 to set the sole of her foot upon the grou.
28. 65 neither shall the sole of thy foot have re.
Josh. 1. 3 Every place that the sole of your foot sh.
3. 13 as soon as the soles of the feet of the pri.
4. 18 the soles of the priests' feet were lifted
2 Sa. 14. 25 from the sole of his foot even to the cro.
1 Ki. 5. 3 until the LORD put them under the soles
2 Ki. 19. 24 with the sole of my feet have I dried up
Job 2. 7 smote Job with sore boils from the sole of
Isa. 1. 6 From the sole of the foot even unto the
37. 25 with the sole of my feet have I dried up
60. 14 bow themselves down at the soles of thy
Eze. 1. 7 the sole of their feet (was) like the sole of
43. 7 the place of the soles of my feet, where I
Mal. 4. 3 they shall be ashes under the soles of yo.

SOLEMN (assembly, feast, meeting, day), solemnity —

1. *Festival,* חַג, חָג *chag.*
Psa. 81. 3 in the time appointed, on our solemn fe.
Isa. 30. 29 as in the night, (when) a holy solemnity
Nah. 1. 15 keep thy solemn feasts, perform thy vows
Mal. 2. 3 (even) the dung of your solemn feasts; and

2. *Appointed time, place, sign,* מוֹעֵד *moed.*
Num 10. 10 in your solemn days, and in the beginni.
15. 3 in your solemn feast, to make a sweet sa.
Deut31. 10 in the solemnity of the year of release, in
2 Ch 2. 4 on the solemn feasts of the LORD our God
Isa. 33. 20 Look upon Zion, the city of our solemnit.
Lam. 1. 4 because none come to the solemn feasts
2. 6 the LORD hath caused the solemn feasts
2. 7 a noise..as in the day of a solemn feast
2. 22 Thou hast called as in a solemn day my
Eze. 36. 38 as the flock..in her solemn feasts, so shall
45. 17 in the sabbaths, in all solemnities of the
46. 9 come before the LORD in the solemn fea.
46. 11 in the solemnities, the meat offering sh.
Hos. 2. 11 and her sabbaths, and all her solemn feasts
9. 5 What will ye do in the solemn day, and in
12. 9 dwell..as in the days of the solemn feasts
Zeph. 3. 18 I will gather (them)..for the solemn ass.

3. *Appointed times,* מוֹעֲדוֹת *moadoth.*
2 Ch. 8. 13 the new moons, and on the solemn feasts

4. *A restraint,* עֲצָרָה *atsarah.*
2 Ki. 10. 20 Jehu said, Proclaim a solemn assembly
Isa. 1. 13 (it is) iniquity, even the solemn meeting
Joel. 1. 14 call a solemn assembly, gather the elders
2. 15 sanctify a fast, call a solemn assembly

5. *A restraint,* עֲצֶרֶת *atsereth.*
Lev 23. 36 it (is) a solemn assembly; (and) ye shall do
Num29. 35 ye shall have a solemn assembly; ye shall
Deut 16. 8 the seventh day (shall be) a solemn asse
2 Ch. 7. 9 the eighth day they made a solemn assem
Neh. 8. 18 on the eighth day (was) a solemn assembly
Amos 5. 21 I will not smell in your solemn assemblies

SOLEMN feast, to keep a —

To keep a festival, חָגַג *chagag.*
Deut16. 15 shalt thou keep a solemn feast unto the

SOLEMNLY —

To (cause to) testify, עוּד *ud,* 5.
Gen. 43. 3 The man did solemnly protest unto us
1 Sa. 8. 9 protest solemnly unto them, and show

SOLITARY (place), solitarily —

1. *Alone, separate,* בָּדָד *badad.*
Lam. 1. 1 How doth the city sit solitary (that was)
Mic. 7. 14 which dwell solitarily (in) the wood, in

2. *Silent,* גַּלְמוּד *galmud.*
Job 3. 7 let that night be solitary; let no joyful
30. 3 For want and famine (they were) solitary

3. *Lonely, singly,* יָחִיד *yachid.*
Psa. 68. 6 God setteth the solitary in families: he

4. *Desolate place,* יְשִׁימוֹן *yeshimon.*
Psa.107. 4 They wandered in the wilderness in a so.

5. *A dry place,* צִיָּה *tsiyyah.*
Isa. 35. 1 the solitary place shall be glad for them

6. *Desert,* ἔρημος *erēmos.*
Mark 1. 35 departed into a solitary place, and there

SOLOMON, שְׁלֹמֹה *peace.* Σολομών.
The tenth son of David, and second by Bath-sheba, and the third king of Israel; born B.C. 1033, crowned 1015, died 975. He was crowned king at Gihon by the direction of his father when aged and infirm; offered sacrifices at Gibeon, chose wisdom in preference to all other things; judged wonderfully between two harlots; increased in power and wealth, had gold in abundance, and weapons of war, a throne of ivory, scientific knowledge of botany, etc.; congratulated by Hiram king of Tyre, prepared for building the temple, prayed at its dedication, sacrificed on that occasion, God appeared to him, warned him, covenanted with him; he built his own house, and the house of Lebanon for Pharaoh's daughter, appointed the courses of the priests, sent ships to Ophir, received the queen of Sheba, gave some cities to Hiram, had numerous wives and concubines, countenanced idolatry, and was threatened for it, opposed by Hadad the Edomite, and by Rezin the Syrian, and by Jeroboam an Ephrathite of Zereda; died, and was buried in the city of David, after a reign of forty years.

2 Sa. 5. 14 Shammuah, and Shobab, and Nathan..S.
12. 24 she bare a son, and he called his name S.
1 Ki. 1. 10 Benaiah, and the mighty men, and S. his
1. 11 spake unto Bath-sheba the mother of S.
1. 12 thine own life, and the life of thy son S.
1. 13, 17, 30 S. thy son shall reign after me, and
1. 19 but S. thy servant hath he not called
1. 21 I and my son S. shall be counted offenders
1. 26 the son of Jehoiada, and thy servant S.
1. 33 cause S. my son to ride upon mine own
1. 34 blow..the trumpet, and say, God save..S.
1. 37 even so be he with S., and make his throne
1. 38 caused S. to ride upon king David's mule
1. 39 Zadok the priest took..and anointed S.
1. 39 and all the people said, God save king S.
1. 43 Verily our Lord king David hath made S.
1. 46 also S. sitteth on the throne of the king.
1. 47 God make the name of S. better than thy
1. 50 Adonijah feared because of S., and arose
1. 51 And it was told S., saying, Behold
1. 51 Adonijah feareth king S.: for, lo, he hath
1. 51 Let king S. swear unto me to day that he
1. 52 S. said, If he will show himself a worthy
1. 53 king S. sent, and they brought him down
1. 53 came and bowed himself to king S.: and S.
2. 1 and he charged S. his son, saying
2. 12 Then sat S. upon the throne of David his
2. 13 came to Bath-sheba the mother of S.
2. 17 Speak, I pray thee, unto S. the king, for
2. 19 Bath-sheba therefore went unto king S.
2. 22 S. answered and said unto his mother
2. 23 S. sware by the LORD, saying, God do so
2. 25 S. sent by the hand of Benaiah the son of
2. 27 S. thrust out Abiathar from being priest
2. 29 it was told king S. that Joab was fled unto
2. 29 S. sent Benaiah the son of Jehoiada, say.
2. 41 it was told S. that Shimei had gone from
2. 45 S. (shall be) blessed, and the throne of D.
2. 46 kingdom was established in the hand of S.
3. 1 S. made affinity with Pharaoh king of E.
3. 3 S. loved the LORD, walking in the statutes
3. 4 a thousand burnt offerings did S. offer up.
3. 5 the LORD appeared to S. in a dream by
3. 6 S. said, Thou hast showed unto my serv.
3. 10 the speech pleased the LORD, that S. had
3. 15 S. awoke; and, behold, (it was) a dream
4. 1 So king S. was king over all Israel
4. 7 S. had twelve officers over all Israel, which
4. 11 which had Taphath the daughter of S. to
4. 15 he also took Basmath the daughter of S. to
4. 21 S. reigned over all kingdoms from the riv.
4. 21 they brought presents, and served S. all
4. 22 S.'s provision for one day was thirty mea.
4. 25 Israel dwelt safely..all the days of S.
4. 26 S. had forty thousand stalls of horses for
4. 27 those officers provided victual for king S.
4. 27 for all that came unto king S.'s table, ev.
4. 29 God gave S. wisdom and understanding
4. 30 S.'s wisdom excelled the wisdom of all the
4. 34 of all people to hear the wisdom of S.
5. 1 king of Tyre sent his servants unto S.; for
5. 2 And S. sent to Hiram, saying
5. 7 when Hiram heard the words of S., that
5. 8 Hiram sent to S., saying, I have conside.
5. 10 Hiram gave S. cedar trees and fir trees
5. 11 S. gave Hiram twenty thousand measures
5. 11 thus gave S. to Hiram year by year
5. 12 the LORD gave S. wisdom, as he promised
5. 12 there was peace between Hiram and S.
5. 13 S. raised a levy out of all Israel; and the
5. 15 S. had three score and ten thousand that
5. 16 the chief of S.'s officers which (were) over
5. 18 S.'s builders and Hiram's builders did hew
6. 1 in the fourth year of S.'s reign over Israel
6. 2 the house which king S. built for the Lo.
6. 11 the word of the LORD came to S., saying
6. 14 So S. built the house, and finished it
6. 21 S. overlaid the house within with pure go
7. 1 S. was building his own house thirteen
7. 8 S. made also an house for Pharaoh's dau.
7. 13 king S. sent and fetched Hiram out of T
7. 14 he came to king S., and wrought all his
7. 40 work that he made king S. for the house
7. 45 these vessels, which Hiram made..king S.
7. 47 S. left all the vessels (unweighed), because
7. 48 S. made all the vessels that (pertained) un.
7. 51 work that king S. made for the house of
7. 51 S. brought in the things which David his
8. 1 Then S. assembled..unto king S. in Jer.
8. 2 assembled themselves unto king S. at the
8. 5 king S., and all the congregation..(were)
8. 12 Then spake S., The LORD said that he wo
8. 22 And S. stood before the altar of the LORD
8. 54 when S. had made an end of praying all
8. 63 S. offered a sacrifice of peace offerings, wh.

1 Ki. 8. 65 And at that time S. held a feast, and all
9. 1 S. had finished the building of the house
9. 1 and all S.'s desire which he was pleased to
9. 2 That the LORD appeared to S. the second
9. 10 it came to pass..when S. had built the two
9. 11 Hiram..had furnished S. with cedar trees
9. 11 S. gave Hiram twenty cities in the land of
9. 12 Hiram came..to see the cities which S.
9. 15 the reason of the levy which king S. raised
9. 16 given it (for) a present..his daughter, S.'s
9. 17 S. built Gezer, and Beth-horon the nether
9. 19 all the cities of store that S. had, and cit.
9. 19 that which S. desired to build in Jerusal.
9. 21 upon those did S. levy a tribute of bond.
9. 22 of the children of Israel did S. make no
9. 23 the chief of the officers..(were) over S.'s
9. 25 three times in a year did S. offer burnt v.24.
9. 26 king S. made a navy of ships in Ezion-geber
9. 27 sent..his servants..with the servants of S.
9. 28 fetched..gold..and brought (it) to king S.
10. 1 the queen of Sheba heard of the fame of S.
10. 2 when she was come to S., she communed
10. 3 S. told her all her questions: there was
10. 4 the queen of Sheba had seen all S.'s wis.
10. 10 which the queen of Sheba gave to king S.
10. 13 S. gave unto the queen of Sheba all her des.
10. 13 (that) which S. gave her of..royal bounty
10. 14 Now the weight of gold that came to S. in
10. 16 king S. made two hundred targets (of) be.
10. 21 all king S.'s drinking vessels (were of) gold
10. 21 was nothing accounted of in the days of S.
10. 23 S. exceeded all the kings of the earth for
10. 24 all the earth sought to S., to hear his wi.
10. 26 S. gathered together chariots and horse.
10. 28 S. had horses brought out of Egypt, and
11. 1 S. loved many strange women, together
11. 2 the nations..S. clave unto these in love
11. 4 came to pass, when S. was old, (that) his
11. 5 S. went after Ashtoreth the goddess of the
11. 6 S. did evil in the sight of the LORD, and
11. 7 Then did S. build an high place for Che.
11. 9 the LORD was angry with S., because his
11. 11 the LORD said unto S., Forasmuch as this
11. 14 the LORD stirred up an adversary unto S.
11. 25 an adversary to Israel all the days of S.
11. 26 S.'s servant, whose mother's name (was)
11. 27 S. built Millo, (and) repaired the breaches
11. 28 S. seeing the young man that he was ind.
11. 31 rend the kingdom out of the hand of S.
11. 40 S. sought therefore to kill Jeroboam: and
11. 40 Jeroboam..in Egypt until the death of S.
11. 41 the rest of the acts of S., and all that he
11. 41 (are) they not written in the book..of S.?
11. 42 S. reigned in Jerusalem over all Israel
11. 43 S. slept with his fathers, and was buried
12. 2 he was fled from the presence of king S.
12. 6 old men, that stood before S. his father
12. 21 bring the kingdom again to..the son of S.
12. 23 Speak unto Rehoboam, the son of S., king
14. 21 Rehoboam the son of S. reigned in Judah
14. 26 took away all the shields of gold which S.
Ki. 21. 7 which the LORD said to David, and to S.
23. 13 the high places..which S. the king of Is.
24. 13 the vessels of gold which S. king of Israel
25. 16 the bases which S. had made for the house
1 Ch. 3. 5 Shimea, and Shobab, and Nathan, and S.
3. 10 S.'s son (was) Rehoboam, Abia his son, Asa
6. 10 in the temple that S. built in Jerusalem
6. 32 until S. had built the house of the LORD
14. 4 Shammua, and Shobab, Nathan, and S.
18. 8 S. made the brasen sea, and the pillars
22. 5 S. my son (is) young and tender, and the
22. 6 he called for S. his son, and charged him
22. 7 David said to S., My son, as for me, it was
22. 9 his name shall be S., and I will give peace
22. 17 all the princes of Israel to help S. his son
23. 1 David..made S. his son king over Israel
28. 5 he hath chosen S. my son to sit upon the
28. 6 he said unto me, S. thy son, he shall build
28. 9 S. my son, know thou the God of thy fat.
28. 11 David gave to S. his son the pattern of the
28. 20 David said to S. his son, Be strong and of
29. 1 S. my son, whom alone God hath chosen
29. 19 give unto S. my son a perfect heart, to ke.
29. 22 they made S. the son of David king the
29. 23 S. sat on the throne of the LORD as king
29. 24 princes..submitted themselves unto S.
29. 25 the LORD magnified S. exceedingly in the
29. 28 and S. his son reigned in his stead
Ch. 1. 1 S. the son of David was strengthened in
1. 2 S. spake unto all Israel, to the captains of
1. 3 S., and all the congregation with him
1. 5 and S. and the congregation sought unto
1. 6 S. went up thither to the brasen altar be.
1. 7 that night did God appear unto S., and sa.
1. 8 S. said unto God, Thou hast showed great
1. 11 God said to S., Because this was in thine
1. 13 S. came (from his journey) to the high pl.
1. 14 S. gathered chariots and horsemen: and
1. 16 S. had horses brought out of Egypt, and
2. 1 S. determined to build an house for the
2. 2 S. told out threescore and ten thousand
2. 3 S. sent to Huram the king of Tyre, saying
2. 11 answered in writing, which he sent to S.
2. 17 S. numbered all the strangers that (were)
3. 1 S. began to build the house of the LORD
3. 3 S. was instructed for the building of the
4. 11 the work that he was to make for king S.
4. 16 instruments, did Huram..make to king S.
4. 18 S. made all these vessels in great abund.
4. 19 S. made all the vessels that (were for) the
2 1 the work that S. made for the house of

2 Ch. 5. 1 S. brought in (all) the things that David
5. 2 S. assembled the elders of Israel, and all
5. 6 S., and all the congregation of Israel that
6. 1 Then said S., The LORD hath said that he
6. 13 S. had made a brasen scaffold, of five cub.
7. 1 when S. had made an end of praying, the
7. 5 S. offered a sacrifice of twenty and two th.
7. 7 S. hallowed the middle of the court that
7. 7 the brasen altar which S. had made was
7. 8 S. kept the feast seven days, and all Isr.
7. 10 LORD had showed unto David, and to S.
7. 11 S. finished the house of the LORD, and the
7. 11 all that came into S.'s heart to make in the
7. 12 the LORD appeared to S. by night, and said
8. 1 S. had built the house of the LORD, and
8. 2 cities which Huram had restored to S., S.
8. 3 S. went to Hamath-Zobah, and prevailed
8. 6 Baalath, and all the store cities that S. had
8. 6 all that S. desired to build in Jerusalem
8. 8 them did S. make to pay tribute until thi.
8. 9 of Israel did S. make no servants for his
8. 10 these (were) the chief of king S.'s officers
8. 11 S. brought up the daughter of P. out of the
8. 12 S. offered burnt offerings unto the LORD
8. 16 the work of S. was prepared unto the day
8. 17 Then went S. to Ezion-geber, and to Elo.
8. 18 they went with the servants of S. to Oph.
8. 18 talents..and brought (them) to king S.
9. 1 heard of the fame of S., she came to prove S
9. 1 when she was come to S., she communed
9. 2 And S. told her all her questions: and
9. 2 there was nothing hid from S. which he
9. 3 queen of Sheba had seen the wisdom of S.
9. 9 any such spice as the queen..gave king S.
9. 10 the servants of S., which brought gold fr.
9. 12 S. gave to the queen of Sheba all her de.
9. 13 the weight of gold that came to S. in
9. 14 the kings..brought gold and silver to S.
9. 15 king S. made two hundred targets (of) be.
9. 20 the drinking vessels of king S. (were of)
9. 20 was (not)..accounted of in the days of S.
9. 22 S. passed all the kings of the earth in ri.
9. 23 the kings..sought the presence of S., to
9. 25 S. had four thousand stalls for horses and
9. 28 they brought unto S. horses out of Egypt
9. 29 the rest of the acts of S., first and last
9. 30 S. reigned in Jerusalem over all Israel fo.
9. 31 S. slept with his fathers, and he was bur.
10. 2 he had fled from the presence of S. the ki.
10. 6 the old men that had stood before S. his
11. 3 Speak unto Rehoboam the son of S., king
11. 17 made Rehoboam the son of S. strong, th.
11. 17 they walked in the way of David and S.
12. 9 also the shields of gold which S. had ma.
13. 6 Nebat, the servant of S. the son of David
13. 7 against Rehoboam the son of S., when Re
30. 26 since the time of S. the son of David king
33. 7 which God had said to David and to S. his
35. 3 Put the holy ark in the house which S. the
35. 4 and according to the writing of S. his son
Neh. 12. 45 the commandment of David, (and) of S.
13. 26 Did not S. king of Israel sin by these th.?
Psa. 72. *title.* (A Psalm) for S.
127. *title.* A Song of degrees for S.
Prov. 1. 1 The proverbs of S. the son of David, kin<
10. 1 The proverbs of S. A wise son maketh
25. 1 These (are) also proverbs of S., which the
Song 1. 1 The song of songs, which (is) S.'s
1. 5 as the tents of Kedar, as the curtains o S.
3. 7 Behold his bed, which (is) S.'s; threescore
3. 9 S. made himself a chariot of the wood of
3. 11 behold king S. with the crown wherewith
8. 11 S. had a vineyard at Baal-hamon; he let
8. 12 thou, O S., (must have) a thousand, an
Jer. 52. 20 which king S. had made in the house of
Matt. 1. 6 the king begat S. of her (that had been the
1. 7 S. begat Roboam; and Roboam begat Ab
6. 29 S. in all his glory was not arrayed like one
12. 42 for she came..to hear the wisdom of S.
12. 42 and, behold, a greater than S. (is) here
Luke 11. 31 for she came..to hear the wisdom of S.
11. 31 and, behold, a greater than S. (is) here
12. 27 S. in all his glory was not arrayed like one
John 10. 23 Jesus walked in the temple in S.'s porch
Acts 3. 11 unto them in the porch that is called S.'s
5. 12 they were all with one accord in S.'s po ch
7. 47 But S. built him an house

SOLOMON'S servants, עַבְדֵי שְׁלֹמֹה *abede Shelomoh.*
Ezra 2. 55 The children of Solomon's servants
[So in 2. 58; Neh. 7. 57, 60; 11. 3.]

SOME (body, man, thing, sort, time, what) —

1. *One,* אֶחָד *echad.*
Gen. 37. 20 let us slay him, and cast him into some
1 Sa. 27. 5 let them give me a place in some town in
2 Sa. 17. 9 he is hid now in some pit, or in some (ot.)
17. 12 So shall we come upon him in some place
2 Ki. 2. 16 upon some mountain, or into some valley

2. *These,* אֵלֶּה *eleh.*
Josh. 8. 22 some on this side, and some on that side

3. *A (mortal) man,* אֱנוֹשׁ *enosh.*
Num 31. 3 Arm some of yourselves unto the war, and
Neh. 12. 44 at that time were some appointed over the

4. *A word, matter,* דָּבָר *dabar.*
Deut 24. 1 he hath found some uncleanness in her

5. *Anything,* מְאוּמָה *meumah.*
2 Ki. 5. 20 I will run after him, and take somewhat

6. *Little, few,* מְעַט *meat.*
2 Ch. 12. 7 but I will grant them some deliverance
Neh. 2. 12 I arose in the night, I and some few men

7. *End, extremity,* קְצָת, קָצֶה *qatseh, qetsath.*
Gen. 47. 2 he took some of his brethren, (even) five
Neh. 7. 70 some of the chief of the fathers gave unto

8. *Another, some,* ἄλλος *allos,* ἄλλοι *alloi.*
Matt 13. 5 Some fell upon stony places, where they
13. 7 some fell among thorns; and the thorns
16. 14 [some,] Elias; and others, Jeremias, or one
Mark 4. 5 some fell on stony ground, where it had not
4. 7 some fell among thorns, and the thorns
8. 28 some (say), Elias; and others, One of the
Luke 9. 19 some (say), Elias; and others (say) that one
John 7. 41 [some] said, Shall Christ come out of Gal.
9. 9 Some said, This is he; others (said), He
Acts 19. 32 Some therefore cried one thing, and
21. 34 some cried one thing..among the multit

9. *One, some,* ἕν *hen.*
Mark 4. 8 [some] thirty, and [some] sixty, and [some]
4. 20 [some] thirty fold, [some] sixty, and [some]

10. *Other, the other,* ἕτερος *heteros.*
Luke 8. 6 some fell upon a rock; and as soon as it
8. 7 some fell among thorns; and the thorns

11. *Some indeed,* ὁ μέν...ὁ δέ *ho men...ho de.*
Matt 13. 4 some [seeds] fell by the way side, and the
[13. 5, 8, 8, 8, 23, 23; 16. 14; Mr. 4. 4, 5; 12. 5, 5; Lu.
8. 5, 6; Jo. 7. 12; Ac. 17. 32; 19. 32 (2); 27. 44, 44; 28. 24, 24;
1 Co. 12. 38; Eph. 4. 11, 11; 2 Ti. 2. 20, 20; Jude 22, 23]

12. *In part,* ἀπὸ μέρους *apo merous.*
Rom 15. 15 written..boldly unto you in some sort
15. 24 if first I be somewhat filled with your (co.)

13. *Once, at some time or other,* ποτέ *pote.*
Eph. 2. 13 ye who sometimes were far off are made
5. 8 ye were sometimes darkness, but now (are
Col. 1. 21 you, that were sometime alienated, and
3. 7 In the which ye also walked sometime, wh.
Titus 3. 3 we ourselves also were sometimes foolish
1 Pe. 3. 20 Which sometime were disobedient, when

14. *A certain, some,* τις, τι *tis, ti.*
Matt 16. 28 There be some standing here which shall
27. 47 Some of them that stood there when they
28. 11 some of the watch came into the city, and
Mark 7. 2 they saw some of his disciples eat bread
9. 1 there be some of them that stand here, wh.
14. 4 there were some that had indignation wi.
14. 65 some began to spit on him, and to cover
15. 35 some of them that stood by, when they
Luke 7. 40 Simon, I have somewhat to say unto thee
8. 46 Somebody hath touched me: for I perce.
9. 7 it was said of some, that John was risen
9. 8 of some, that Elias had appeared; and of
9. 27 there be some standing here, which shall
11. 15 some of them said, He casteth out devils
11. 54 seeking to catch something out of his mo.
13. 1 There were present at that season some
19. 39 some of the Pharisees from among the mu.
21. 5 as some spake of the temple, how it was
23. 8 he hoped to have seen some miracle done
John 6. 64 But there are some of you that believe not
7. 25 Then said some of them of Jerusalem, Is
7. 44 And some of them would have taken him
9. 16 Therefore said some of the Pharisees, This
11. 37 some of them said, Could not this man
11. 46 some of them went their ways to the Ph.
13. 29 some (of them) thought, because Judas
13. 29 that he should give something to the poor
Acts 3. 5 expecting to receive something of them
5. 15 passing by might overshadow some of them
5. 36 Theudas, boasting himself to be somebody
8. 9 giving out that himself was some great one
8. 31 How can I, except some man should guide
8. 34 of whom..of himself, or of some other man?
11. 20 some of them were men of Cyprus and C.
15. 36 some days after, Paul said unto Barnabas
17. 4 some of them believed, and consorted with
17. 18 And some said, What will this babbler say
17. 21 but either to tell, or to hear some new th.
18. 23 after he had spent some time (there), he
23. 18 this young man..who hath something to
23. 20 as though they would enquire somewhat
25. 26 that, after..I might have somewhat to w.
27. 27 deemed that they drew near to some co.
Rom. 1. 11 that I may impart unto you some spiritual
1. 13 I might have some fruit among you also
3. 3 what if some did not believe? shall their
3. 8 some affirm that we say, Let us do evil, th.
5. 7 for a good man some would even dare to
11. 14 If by any means I..might save some of
11. 17 if some of the branches be broken off, and
1 Co. 4. 18 some are puffed up, as though I would
6. 11 such were some of you; but ye are washed
8. 7 some with conscience of the idol unto this
9. 22 that I might by all means save some
10. 7 Neither be ye idolaters, as (were) some of
10. 8 Neither let us commit fornication, as some
10. 9 Neither let us tempt Christ, as some of th.
10. 10 Neither murmur ye, as some of them also
15. 6 part remain..but some are fallen asleep
15. 12 how say some among you that there is no
15. 34 for some have not the knowledge of God
15. 35 some (man) will say, How are the dead
15. 37 it may chance of wheat, or of some other
2 Co. 3. 1 need we, as some (others), epistles of co.
10. 2 I think to be bold against some, which th.
10. 8 For though I should boast somewhat more
10. 12 or compare ourselves with some that co.

Gal. 1. 7 there be some that trouble you, and wo.
2. 6 of those who seemed to be somewhat, wh.
6. 3 if a man think himself to be something
Phil. 1. 15 Some indeed preach Christ..and some
2 Th. 3. 11 there are some which walk among you
1 Ti. 1. 3 that thou mightest charge some that they
1. 6 From which some having swerved have
1. 19 which some having put away, concerning
4. 1 in the latter times some shall depart from
5. 15 some are already turned aside after Satan
5. 24 Some men's sins are open..and some (men)
6. 10 which while some coveted after, they have
6. 21 Which some professing have erred conce.
2 Ti. 2. 18 already; and overthrow the faith of some
Heb. 3. 4 every house is builded by some (man); but
3. 16 some, when they had heard, did provoke
4. 6 it remaineth that some must enter there.
8. 3 that this man have somewhat also to offer
10. 25 Not forsaking..as the manner of some (is)
11. 40 God having provided some better thing
13. 2 some have entertained angels unawares
2 Pe. 3. 9 The Lord is not slack..as some men count
3. 16 in which are some things hard to be under.

[*See also* Befall, dark, few, lighter, reddish, sort, these.]

SON —

1. *Son, offspring,* בֵּן *ben.*

Gen. 4. 17 and called..after the name of his son, E.
4. 25 she bare a son, and called his name Seth
4. 26 Seth, to him also there was born a son; and
5. 4, 7, 10, 13, 16, 19, 22, 26, 30 begat sons and
5. 28 eighty and two years, and begat a son
6. 2 That the sons of God saw the daughters
6. 4 sons of God came in unto the daughters
6. 10 Noah begat three sons, Shem, Ham, and
6. 18 sons, and thy wife, and thy sons' wives wi.
7. 7 sons, and his wife, and his sons' wives wi.
7. 13 sons of Noah..and the three wives of his
8. 16 Go forth..thou..thy sons, and thy sons' w.
8. 18 his sons, and his wife, and his sons' wives
9. 1 God blessed Noah and his sons, and said
9. 8 God spake unto Noah, and to his sons wi.
9. 18 sons of Noah, that went forth of the ark
9. 19 These (are) the three sons of Noah: and
9. 24 knew what his younger son had done un.
10. 1 sons of Noah..unto them were sons born
10. 2 The sons of Japheth; Gomer, and Magog
10. 3 sons of Gomer; Ashkenaz, and Riphath
10. 4 sons of Javan; Elishah, and Tarshish, Ki.
10. 6 sons of Ham; Cush, and Mizraim, and P.
10. 7 sons of Cush..and the sons of Raamah, S.
10. 20 These (are) the sons of Ham, after their
10. 25 unto Eber were born two sons: the name
10. 29 Ophir, and .. all these (were) the sons of
10. 31 These (are) the sons of Shem, after their
10. 32 These (are) the families of the sons of N.
11. 11, 13, 15, 17, 19, 21, 23, 25 begat sons and d.
11. 31 Terah took Abram his son, and Lot the s.
11. 31 his son's son..his son Abram's wife
12. 5 Abram took..Lot his brother's son, and
14. 12 they took Lot, Abram's brother's son, who
16. 11 thou..shalt bear a son, and shalt call his
16. 15 bare Abram a son: and..called his son's
17. 16 bless her, and give thee a son also of her
17. 19 Sarah thy wife shall bear thee a son ind.
17. 23 Abraham took Ishmael his son, and all
17. 25 Ishmael his son (was) thirteen years old
17. 26 Abraham circumcised, and Ishmael his s.
18. 10 Sarah thy wife shall have a son. And S.
18. 14 At the time..Sarah shall have a son
19. 12 sons, and thy daughters, and whatsoever
19. 37 bare a son, and called his name Moab
19. 38 bare a son, and called his name Ben-am.
21. 2 bare Abraham a son in his old age, at the
21. 3 Abraham called the name of his son that
21. 4 Abraham circumcised his son Isaac being
21. 5 hundred years old when his son Isaac was
21. 7 for I have born (him) a son in his old age
21. 9 Sarah saw the son of Hagar the Egyptian
21. 10 Cast out this bond woman and her son
21. 10 son..shall not be heir with my son, (even)
21. 11 was very grievous..because of his son
21. 13 also of the son of the bond woman will I
22. 2 Take now thy son..whom thou lovest, and
22. 3 took..Isaac his son, and clave the wood
22. 6 laid (it) upon Isaac his son; and he took
22. 7 he said, Here (am) I, my son. And he sa.
22. 8 My son, God will provide himself a lamb
22. 9 bound Isaac his son, and laid him on the
22. 10 Abraham..took the knife to slay his son
22. 12, 16 hast not withheld thy son, thine only
22. 13 a burnt offering in the stead of his son
23. 3 Abraham..spake unto the sons of Heth
23. 8 entreat for me to Ephron the son of Zoh.
23. 11 in the presence of the sons of my people
23. 16 named in the audience of the sons of He.
23. 20 for a possession..by the sons of Heth
24. 3 shalt not take a wife unto my son of the
24. 4 shalt go..and take a wife unto my son I.
24. 5 must I needs bring thy son again unto the
24. 6 Beware thou that thou bring not my son
24. 7 shalt take a wife unto my son from thence
24. 8 oath: only bring not my son thither again
24. 15 who was born to Bethuel, son of Milcah
24. 24 daughter of Bethuel the son of Milcah, wh.
24. 36 Sarah my master's wife bare a son to my
24. 37 Thou shalt not take a wife to my son of
24. 38 shalt go..and take a wife unto my son
24. 40 thou shalt take a wife for my son of my
24. 44 hath appointed out for my master's son
24. 47 daughter of Bethuel, Nahor's son, whom
24. 48 my master's brother's daughter unto his

Gen. 24. 51 let her be thy master's son's wife, as the
25. 3 sons of Dedan were Asshurim, and Letus.
25. 4 sons of Midian; Ephah, and Epher, and
25. 6 But unto the sons of the concubines, wh.
25. 6 sent them away from Isaac his son, while
25. 9 his sons Isaac and Ishmael buried him in
25. 9 in the field of Ephron the son of Zohar the
25. 10 which Abraham purchased of the sons of
25. 11 God blessed his son Isaac: and Isaac dw.
25. 12 generations of Ishmael, Abraham's son, w.
25. 13 these (are) the names of the sons of Ishm.
25. 16 These (are) the sons of Ishmael, and these
25. 19 generations of Isaac, Abraham's son: Ab.
27. 1 his eldest son, and said unto him, My son
27. 5 heard when Isaac spake to Esau his son
27. 6 Rebekah spake unto Jacob her son, saying
27. 8, 43 Now therefore, my son, obey my voice
27. 13 Upon me (be) thy curse, my son: only ob.
27. 15 took goodly raiment of her eldest son E.
27. 15 and put them upon Jacob her younger son
27. 17 she gave..into the hand of her son Jacob
27. 18 said, Here (am) I; who (art) thou, my son?
27. 20 Isaac said unto his son, How (is it) that
27. 20 found (it) so quickly, my son? And he sa.
27. 21 my son, whether thou (be) my very son E.
27. 24 he said, (Art) thou my very son Esau? And
27. 25 will eat of my son's venison, that my soul
27. 26 said..Come near now, and kiss me, my son
27. 27 smell of my son (is) as the smell of a field
27. 29 let thy mother's sons bow down to thee
27. 31 Let my father arise, and eat of his son's v.
27. 32 he said, I (am) thy son, thy first born, Esau
27. 37 what shall I do now unto thee, my son?
27. 42 these words of Esau her elder son were
27. 42 she sent and called Jacob her younger son
28. 5 Laban, son of Bethuel the Syrian, the br.
28. 9 the daughter of Ishmael, Abraham's son
29. 5 Know ye Laban the son of Nahor? And
29. 12 told Rachel..that he (was) Rebekah's son
29. 13 heard the tidings of Jacob his sister's son
29. 32 bare a son, and she called his name Reu.
29. 33, 34, 35 she conceived again, and bare a son
29. 34 because I have born him three sons: th.
30. 5 Bilhah conceived, and bare Jacob a son
30. 6 hath given me a son: therefore called she
30. 7 conceived again, and bare Jacob a second s.
30. 10 And Zilpah, Leah's maid, bare Jacob a son
30. 12 Zilpah, Leah's maid, bare Jacob a second s.
30. 14 Give me, I pray thee, of thy son's mandr.
30. 15 wouldest thou take away my son's mand.
30. 15 lie with thee to night for thy son's man.
30. 16 have hired thee with my son's mandrakes
30. 17 she conceived, and bare Jacob the fifth son
30. 19 conceived..and bare Jacob the sixth son
30. 20 because I have born him six sons: and she
30. 23 she conceived, and bare a son; and said
30. 24 The LORD shall add to me another son
30. 35 and gave (them) into the hand of his sons
31. 1 he heard the words of Laban's sons, say.
31. 17 set his sons and his wives upon camels
31. 28 hast not suffered me to kiss my sons and
31. 55 kissed his sons and his daughters, and bl.
34. 2 when Shechem the son of Hamor the Hi.
34. 5 now his sons were with his cattle in the
34. 7 the sons of Jacob came out of the field
34. 8 The soul of my son Shechem longeth for
34. 13 the sons of Jacob answered Shechem and
34. 18 their words pleased..Shechem, Hamor's s.
34. 20 Shechem his son came unto the gate of the
34. 24 unto Shechem his son, hearkened all that
34. 25 two of the sons of Jacob, Simeon and Levi
34. 26 they slew Hamor and Shechem his son wi.
34. 27 The sons of Jacob came upon the slain, and
35. 5 they did not pursue after the sons of Ja.
35. 17 Fear not; thou shalt have this son also
35. 22 Now the sons of Jacob were twelve
35. 23 The sons of Leah; Reuben, Jacob's first
35. 24 The sons of Rachel; Joseph and Benjam.
35. 25 sons of Bilhah, Rachel's handmaid; Dan
35. 26 the sons of Zilpah, Leah's handmaid; Gad
35. 26 these (are) the sons of Jacob, which were
35. 29 and his sons Esau and Jacob buried him
36. 5 these (are) the sons of Esau, which were
36. 6 Esau took his wives, and his sons, and his
36. 10 the names of Esau's sons; Eliphaz the son
36. 10 Reuel the son of Bashemath the wife of E.
36. 11 the sons of Eliphaz were Teman, Omar, Z.
36. 12 And Timna was concubine to..Esau's son
36. 12 these (were) the sons of Adah, Esau's wife
36. 13 these (are) the sons of Reuel; Nahath, and
36. 13 these were the sons of Bashemath, Esau's
36. 14 these were the sons of Aholibamah the da.
36. 15 the sons of Esau: the sons of Eliphaz the
36. 16 the dukes..these (were) the sons of Adah
36. 17 these (are) the sons of Reuel, Esau's son
36. 17 these (are) the sons of Bashemath, Esau's
36. 18 these (are) the sons of Aholibamah, Esau's
36. 19 These (are) the sons of Esau, who (is) Edom
36. 20 These (are) the sons of Seir the Horite, w.
36. 32 And Bela the son of Beor reigned in Ed.
36. 33 Jobab the son of Zerah of Bozrah reigned
36. 35 the son of Bedad, who smote Midian in the
36. 38 Baal-hanan the son of Achbor reigned in
36. 39 Baal-hanan the son of Achbor died, and
37. 2 the sons of Bilhah, and with the sons of Z.
37. 3 because he (was) the son of his old age
37. 32 know now whether it (be) thy son's coat or
37. 33 (It is) my son's coat; an evil beast hath
37. 34 and mourned for his son many days
37. 35 all his sons and all his daughters rose up to
37. 35 I will go down into the grave unto my son
38. 3 she conceived, and bare a son, and he cal.

Gen. 38. 4 And she conceived again, and bare a son
38. 5 she yet again conceived, and bare a son
38. 11 Remain a widow..till Shelah my son be
38. 26 because that I gave her not to..my son
41. 50 unto Joseph were born two sons before the
42. 1 Jacob said unto his sons, Why do ye look
42. 5 the sons of Israel came to buy (corn) amo.
42. 11 We (are) all one man's sons: we (are) true
42. 13 the sons of one man in the land of Canaan
42. 32 We (be) twelve brethren, sons of our fat.
42. 37 Slay my two sons, if I bring him not to th.
42. 38 My son shall not go down with you; for
43. 29 his brother Benjamin, his mother's son
43. 29 God be gracious unto thee, my son
45. 9 Thus saith thy son Joseph, God hath ma.
45. 28 Joseph my son (is) yet alive: I will go and
46. 5 the sons of Israel carried Jacob their fat.
46. 7 sons, and his sons' sons..and his sons' da.
46. 8 Jacob and his sons: Reuben, Jacob's first
46. 9 the sons of Reuben; Hanoch, and Phallu
46. 10 the sons of Simeon; Jemuel, and Jamin
46. 10 Shaul the son of a Canaanitish woman
46. 11 the sons of Levi; Gershon, Kohath, and
46. 12 the sons of Judah; Er, and Onan, and S.
46. 12 the sons of Pharez were Hezron and Ha.
46. 13 the sons of Issachar; Tola, and Phuv.
46. 14 the sons of Zebulun; Sered, and Elon, and
46. 15 These (be) the sons of Leah, which she ba.
46. 15 the souls of his sons and his daughters
46. 16 the sons of Gad; Ziphion, and Haggi, Sh.
46. 17 the sons of Asher; Jimnah, and Ishuah
46. 17 the sons of Beriah; Heber, and Malchiel
46. 18 These (are) the sons of Zilpah, whom La.
46. 19 The sons of Rachel, Jacob's wife; Joseph
46. 21 the sons of Benjamin (were) Belah, and
46. 22 These (are) the sons of Rachel, which were
46. 23 And the sons of Dan; Hushim
46. 24 the sons of Naphtali; Jahzeel, and Guni
46. 25 These (are) the sons of Bilhah, which La.
46. 26 All the souls..besides Jacob's sons' wives
46. 27 the sons of Joseph, which were born him
47. 29 he called his son Joseph, and said unto
48. 1 he took with him his two sons, Manasseh
48. 2 Behold, thy son Joseph cometh unto thee
48. 5 thy two sons, Ephraim and Manasseh, wh.
48. 8 Israel beheld Joseph's sons, and said, Who
48. 9 They (are) my sons, whom God hath given
48. 19 I know (it), my son, I know (it): he also
49. 1 Jacob called unto his sons, and said, Ga.
49. 2 Gather..together, and hear, ye sons of J.
49. 9 from the prey, my son, thou art gone up
49. 33 had made an end of commanding his sons
50. 12 his sons did unto him according as he
50. 13 his sons carried him into the land of Ca.
50. 23 the children also of Machir the son of M.
Exod. 1. 16 if it (be) a son, then ye shall kill him, but
1. 22 Every son that is born ye shall cast into
2. 2 And the woman conceived, and bare a son
2. 10 she brought him..and he became her son
2. 22 she bare (him) a son, and he called his
3. 22 ye shall put (them) upon your sons, and
4. 20 Moses took his wife and his sons, and set
4. 22 Thus saith the LORD, Israel (is) my son
4. 23 Let my son go, that he may serve me
4. 23 behold, I will slay thy son, (even) thy first
4. 25 cut off the foreskin of her son, and cast
6. 14 The sons of Reuben the first born of Isr.
6. 15 the sons of Simeon; Jemuel, and Jamin
6. 15 Shaul the son of a Canaanitish woman
6. 16 these (are) the names of the sons of Levi
6. 17 The sons of Gershon; Libni and Shimi
6. 18 the sons of Kohath; Amram, and Izhar
6. 19 And the sons of Merari; Mahli and Mu.
6. 21 the sons of Izhar; Korah, and Nepheg
6. 22 the sons of Uzziel; Mishael, and Elzaph.
6. 24 the sons of Korah; Assir, and Elkanah
6. 25 Aaron's son, took him (one) of the daught.
10. 2 in the ears of thy son, and of thy son's son
10. 9 with our sons and with our daughters, wi.
12. 24 for an ordinance to thee and to thy sons
13. 8 thou shalt show thy son in that day, say.
13. 14 when thy son asketh thee in time to come
18. 3 her two sons; of which the name of the
18. 5 Moses' father in law, came with his sons
18. 6 and thy wife, and her two sons with her
20. 10 not do any work, thou, nor thy son, nor
21. 4 and she have born him sons or daughters
21. 9 if he have betrothed her unto his son, he
21. 31 Whether he have gored a son, or have g.
22. 29 the first born of thy sons shalt thou give
23. 12 the son of thy handmaid and the stranger
27. 21 his sons shall order it from evening to mo.
28. 1 Aaron thy brother, and his sons with him
28. 1 Eleazar and Ithamar, Aaron's sons
28. 4 for Aaron thy brother, and his sons, that
28. 40 for Aaron's sons thou shalt make coats
28. 41 Aaron thy brother, and his sons with him
28. 43 shall be upon Aaron, and upon his sons
29. 4 his sons thou shalt bring unto the door of
29. 8 thou shalt bring his sons, and put coats
29. 9 thou shalt gird..Aaron and his sons, and
29. 9 thou shalt consecrate Aaron and his sons
29. 10, 15, 19 his sons shall put their hands upon
29. 20 upon the tip of the right ear of his sons
29. 21 sons, and upon the garments of his sons
29. 21 his sons, and his sons' garments with him
29. 24 shalt put all..in the hands of his sons
29. 27 Aaron, and of (that) which (is) for his sons
29. 28 it shall be Aaron's and his sons' by a stat.
29. 29 garments of Aaron shall be his sons' after
29. 30 that son that is priest in his stead shall
29. 32 his sons shall eat the flesh of the ram

Exod. 29. 35 thus shalt thou do unto..his sons, accor.
29. 44 sanctify also both Aaron and his sons
30. 19 his sons shall wash their hands and their
30. 30 thou shalt anoint Aaron and his sons, and
31. 2 Bezaleel the son of Uri, the son of Hur
31. 6 I have given with him Aholiab the son of
31. 10 the garments of his sons, to minister in
32. 2 in the ears of your wives, of your sons, and
32. 26 the sons of Levi gathered themselves to.
32. 29 even every man upon his son, and upon
33. 11 the son of Nun, a young man, departed
34. 16 take of their daughters unto thy sons, and
34. 16 make thy sons go a whoring after their g.
34. 20 the first born of thy sons thou shalt re.
35. 19 the garments of his sons, to minister in
35. 30 Bezaleel the son of Uri, the son of Hur
35. 34 the son of Ahisamach, of the tribe of Dan
38. 21 by the hand of Ithamar, son to Aaron the
38. 22 Bezaleel the son of Uri, the son of Hur
38. 23 Aholiab, son of Ahisamach, of the tribe of
39. 27 made coats..for Aaron, and for his sons
39. 41 his sons' garments, to minister in the pr
40. 12 thou shalt bring Aaron and his sons unto
40. 14 thou shalt bring his sons, and clothe th.
40. 31 his sons washed their hands and their feet
Lev. 1. 5 Aaron's sons, shall bring the blood, and
1. 7 the sons of Aaron the priest shall put fire
1. 8 Aaron's sons, shall lay the parts, the he.
1. 11 Aaron's sons, shall sprinkle his blood ro.
2. 2 he shall bring it to Aaron's sons the pri.
2. 3 remnant..(shall be) Aaron's and his sons'
2. 10 that which is left..(shall be)..his sons' (it
3. 2 Aaron's sons the priests shall sprinkle the
3. 5 Aaron's sons shall burn it on the altar
3. 8 Aaron's sons shall sprinkle the blood th
3. 13 the sons of Aaron shall sprinkle the blood
6. 9 Command Aaron and his sons, saying, This
6. 14 the sons of Aaron shall offer it before the
6. 16 the remainder..shall Aaron and his sons
6. 20 the offering of Aaron, and of his sons, wh.
6. 22 the priest of his sons that is anointed in
6. 25 Speak unto Aaron and to his sons, saying
7. 10 shall all the sons of Aaron have, one (as
7. 31 the breast shall be Aaron's and his sons'
7. 33 He among the sons of Aaron that offereth
7. 34 unto Aaron the priest and unto his sons
7. 35 of Aaron, and of the anointing of his sons
8. 2 Take Aaron and his sons with him and
8. 6 Moses brought Aaron and his sons, and
8. 13 Moses brought Aaron's sons, and put co.
8. 14, 18, 22 his sons laid their hands upon the
8. 24 he brought Aaron's sons, and Moses put
8. 27 upon Aaron's hands, and upon his sons'
8. 30 upon his sons, and upon his sons' garme.
8. 30 his sons, and his sons' garments with him
8. 31 And Moses said unto Aaron and to his sons
8. 31 saying, Aaron and his sons shall eat it
8. 36 Aaron and his sons did all things which
9. 1 Moses called Aaron and his sons, and the
9. 9 the sons of Aaron brought the blood unto
9. 12, 18 Aaron's sons presented unto him the
10. 1 the sons of Aaron, took either of them his
10. 4 Mishael and Elzaphan, the sons of Uzziel
10. 6, 12 unto Eleazar and unto Ithamar, his s.
10. 9 Do not drink..thou, nor thy sons with th.
10. 13, 14 (is) thy due, and thy sons due, of the s.
10. 14 thou, and thy sons, and thy daughters w.
10. 15 it shall be thine, and thy sons' with thee
10. 16 Eleazar and Ithamar, the sons of Aaron
12. 6 when the days..are fulfilled, for a son, or
13. 2 he shall be brought..unto one of his sons
16. 1 after the death of the two sons of Aaron
17. 2 Speak unto Aaron, and unto his sons, and
18. 10 The nakedness of thy son's daughter, or
18. 15 thy daughter in law: she (is) thy son's
18. 17 neither shalt thou take her son's daught
21. 1 Speak unto the priests the sons of Aaron
21. 2 for his son, and for his daughter, and
21. 24 Moses told (it) unto Aaron..to his sons
22. 2, 18 Speak unto Aaron and to his sons, th.
24. 9 it shall be Aaron's and his sons'; and they
24. 10 son of an Israelitish woman..and this son
24. 11 the Israelitish woman's son blasphemed
25. 49 his uncle's son, may redeem him, or (any)
26. 29 ye shall eat the flesh of your sons, and th
Num. 1. 5 (the tribe of) Reuben; Elizur the son of
1. 6 Of Simeon; Shelumiel the son of Zurish
1. 7 Of Judah; Nashon the son of Amminadab
1. 8 Of Issachar; Nethaneel the son of Zuar
1. 9 Of Zebulun; Eliab the son of Helon
1. 10 of Ephraim; Elishama the son of Ammi
1. 10 of Manasseh; Gamaliel the son of Peda.
1. 11 Of Benjamin; Abidan the son of Gideoni
1. 12 Of Dan; Ahiezer the son of Ammishad.
1. 13 Of Asher; Pagiel the son of Ocran
1. 14 Of Gad; Eliasaph the son of Deuel
1. 15 Of Naphtali; Ahira the son of Enan
2. 3 the son of Amminadab (shall be) captain
2. 5 the son of Zuar (shall be) captain of..Iss.
2. 7 the son of Helon (shall be) captain of the
2. 10 the captain..(shall be) Elizur the son of
2. 12 the captain..(shall be) Shelumiel the son
2. 14 captain of the sons of Gad..Eliasaph..son
2. 18 and the captain of the sons of Ephraim
2. 18 (shall be) Elishama the son of Ammihud
2. 20 the captain..(shall be) Gamaliel the son
2. 22 and the captain of the sons of Benjamin
2. 22 (shall be) Abidan the son of Gideoni
2. 25 the captain..(shall be) Ahiezer the son of
2. 27 the captain..(shall be) Pagiel the son of
2. 29 the captain..(shall be) Ahira the son of
3. 2, 3 these (are) the names of the sons of A.

Num. 3. 9 thou shalt give the Levites..to his sons
3. 10 thou shalt appoint Aaron and his sons
3. 17 these were the sons of Levi by their na.
3. 18 these (are) the names of the sons of Gers.
3. 19 the sons of Kohath by their families; A.
3. 20 the sons of Merari by their families; Ma.
3. 24 the chief..(shall be) Eliasaph the son of
3. 25 the charge of the sons of Gershon in the
3. 29 The families of the sons of Kohath shall
3. 30 the chief..(shall be) Elizaphan the son of
3. 32 the son of Aaron the priest (shall be) chief
3. 35 the chief..(was) Zuriel the son of Abihael
3. 36 (under) the custody and charge of the sons
3. 38 his sons, keeping the charge of the sanct
3. 48 thou shalt give the money..to his sons
3. 51 Moses gave the money..to his sons, acco
4. 2 Take the sum of the sons of Kohath from
4. 2 among the sons of Levi, after their famil.
4. 4 This (shall be) the service of the sons of
4. 5 Aaron shall come, and his sons, and they
4. 15 when Aaron and his sons have made an
4. 15 the sons of Kohath shall come to bear (it)
4. 15 the burden of the sons of Kohath in the
4. 16 the office of Eleazar the son of Aaron the
4. 19 his sons shall go in, and appoint them ev.
4. 22 Take also the sum of the sons of Gershon
4. 27 At the appointment of Aaron and his sons
4. 27 the service of the sons of the Gershonites
4. 28 the service of the families of the sons of
4. 28, 33 under the hand of Ithamar the son of
4. 29 As for the sons of Merari, thou shalt nu.
4. 33, 42, 45 of the families of the sons of Mer
4. 34 numbered the sons of the Kohathites after
4. 38 those that were numbered of the sons of
4. 41 of the families of the sons of Gershon, of
6. 23 Speak unto Aaron, and unto his sons, say
7. 7 he gave unto the sons of Gershon, accor
7. 8 he gave unto the sons of Merari, according
7. 8 of Ithamar the son of Aaron the priest
7. 9 unto the sons of Kohath he gave none
7. 12, 17 Nashon the son of Amminadab
7. 18 Nethaneel the son of Zuar, prince of Issa.
7. 23 the offering of Nethaneel the son of Zuar
7. 24 Eliab the son of Helon, prince of the chi.
7. 29 this (was) the offering of Eliab the son of
7. 30 Elizur the son of Shedeur, prince of the
7. 35 the offering of Elizur the son of Shedeur
7. 36 Shelumiel the son of Zurishaddai, prince
7. 41 the offering of Shelumiel the son of Zuris.
7. 42 Eliasaph the son of Deuel, prince of the
7. 47 the offering of Eliasaph the son of Deuel
7. 48 Elishama the son of Ammihud, prince of
7. 53 the offering of Elishama the son of Amm.
7. 54 Gamaliel the son of Pedahzur, prince of
7. 59 the offering of Gamaliel the son of Ped.
7. 60 On the ninth day Abidan the son of Gid.
7. 65 the offering of Abidan the son of Gideoni
7. 66, 71 Ahiezer the son of Ammishaddai
7. 72 On the eleventh day Pagiel the son of Oc.
7. 77 the offering of Pagiel the son of Ocran
7. 78 On the twelfth day Ahira the son of Enan
7. 83 this (was) the offering of Ahira the son of
8. 13, 22 before Aaron, and before his sons
8. 19 (as) a gift to Aaron and to his sons from
10. 8 the sons of Aaron, the priests, shall blow
10. 14 over his host (was)..the son of
[So in v. 15, 16, 18, 19, 20, 22, 23, 24, 25, 26, 27.]
10. 17 the sons of Gershon and the sons of Mer
10. 29 Moses said unto Hobab, the son of Raguel
11. 28 Joshua the son of Nun, the servant of M.
13. 4 the tribe of Reuben, Shammua the son of
13. 5 the tribe of Simeon, Shaphat the son of
13. 6 the tribe of Judah, Caleb the son of Jep.
13. 7 the tribe of Issachar, Igal the son of Jos.
13. 8 the tribe of Ephraim, Oshea the son of N.
13. 9 the tribe of Benjamin, Palti the son of R.
13. 10 the tribe of Zebulun, Gaddiel the son of
13. 11 the tribe of Joseph..Gaddi the son of S.
13. 12 the tribe of Dan, Ammiel the son of Ge.
13. 13 the tribe of Asher, Sethur the son of M.
13. 14 the tribe of Naphtali, Nahbi the son of V.
13. 15 the tribe of Gad, Geuel the son of Machi
13. 16 Moses called Oshea the son of Nun, Je.
13. 33 we saw the giants, the sons of Anak, (wh.)
14. 6, 38 the son of Nun, and Caleb the son of
14. 30 the son of Jephunneh, and Joshua the son
16. 1 son of Izhar, the son of Kohath, the son
16. 1 Dathan and Abiram the sons of Eliab, and
16. 1 On the son of Peleth, sons of Reuben, took
16. 7 (ye take) too much upon you, ye sons of
16. 8 Moses said..Hear, I pray you, ye sons of
16. 10 all thy brethren the sons of Levi with th.
16. 12 to call Dathan and Abiram, the sons of E.
16. 27 their wives, and their sons, and their little
16. 37 Speak unto Eleazar the son of Aaron the
18. 1 Thou, and thy sons, and thy father's ho.
18. 1, 2, 7 thou and thy sons with thee shall
18. 8 have I given them..and to thy sons, by
18. 9 (shall be) most holy for thee and for thy s.
18. 11, 19 thy sons and to thy daughters with th.
20. 25 Take Aaron and Eleazar his son, and br.
20. 26, 28 and put them upon Eleazar his son
21. 29 he hath given his sons that escaped, and
21. 35 they smote him, and his sons, and all his
22. 2, 4, 10, 16 Balak the son of Zippor
22. 5 He sent..unto Baalam the son of Beor
23. 18 hearken unto me, thou son of Zippor
23. 19 neither the son of man, that he should re
24. 3, 15 Baalam the son of Beor hath said, and
25. 7, 11 the son of Eleazar, the son of Aaron
25. 14 Zimri, the son of Salu, a prince of a chief
26. 1 unto Eleazar the son of Aaron the priest

Num. 26. 8 And the sons of Pallu; Eliab
26. 9 the sons of Eliab; Nemuel, and Dathan
26. 12 The sons of Simeon after their families
26. 19 The sons of Judah (were) Er and Onan: and
26. 20 the sons of Judah after their families were
26. 21 the sons of Pharez were; of Hezron, the
26. 23 (Of) the sons of Issachar, after their fa.
26. 26 (Of) the sons of Zebulun after their fam.
26. 28 The sons of Joseph after their families
26. 29 Of the sons of Manasseh: of Machir, the
26. 30 These (are) the sons of Gilead: (of) Jeezer
26. 33 the son of Hepher had no sons, but dau.
26. 35 These (are) the sons of Ephraim after th.
26. 36 these (are) the sons of Shuthelah: of Eran
26. 37 These (are) the families of the sons of Ep.
26. 37 These (are) the sons of Joseph after their
26. 38 The sons of Benjamin after their families
26. 40 the sons of Bela were Ard and Naaman
26. 41 These (are) the sons of Benjamin after th.
26. 42 These (are) the sons of Dan after their fa.
26. 45 Of the sons of Beriah: of Heber, the fam.
26. 47 These (are) the families of the sons of A:
26. 48 (Of) the sons of Naphtali after their fam.
26. 65 the son of Jephunneh, and Joshua the son
27. 1 Zelophehad, the son of Hepher, the son
27. 1 the son of Machir, the son of Manasseh
27. 1 of the families of Manasseh the son of Jo.
27. 3 but died in his own sin, and had no sons
27. 4 be done away..because he hath no son?
27. 8 If a man die, and have no son, then ye sh.
27. 18 Take thee Joshua the son of Nun, a man
31. 6 Phinehas the son of Eleazar the priest, to
31. 8 Balaam also the son of Beor they slew wi.
32. 12 Save Caleb the son of Jephunneh the Ke.
32. 12 Joshua the son of Nun: for they have wh.
32. 28 Joshua the son of Nun, and the chief fat.
32. 33 unto half the tribe of Manasseh the son
32. 40 Moses gave Gilead unto Machir the son of
32. 41 Jair the son of Manasseh went and took
34. 17 Eleazar the priest, and Joshua the son of
34. 19 Of the tribe of Judah, Caleb the son of J.
34. 20 the children of Simeon, Shemuel the son
34. 21 Of the tribe of Benjamin, Elidad the son
34. 22 of the children of Dan, Bukki the son of
34. 23 the children of Manasseh, Hanniel the son
34. 24 children of Ephraim, Kemuel the son of S.
34. 25 children of Zebulun, Elizaphan the son of
34. 26 children of Issachar, Paltiel the son of A.
34. 27 children of Asher, Ahihud the son of She.
34. 28 children of Naphtali, Pedahel the son of
36. 1 the son of Machir, the son of Manasseh
36. 1 families of the sons of Joseph, came near
36. 3 if they be married to any of the sons of
36. 5 tribe of the sons of Joseph hath said well
36. 11 married unto their father's brother's sons
36. 12 families of the son's of Manasseh the son
Deut. 1. 28 we have seen the sons of the Anakims th.
1. 31 bare thee, as a man doth bear his son, in
1. 36 Save Caleb the son of Jephunneh; he sh.
1. 38 Joshua the son of Nun, which standeth
2. 33 smote him, and his sons, and all his peo
3. 14 Jair the son of Manasseh took all the cou.
4. 9 teach them thy sons, and thy sons' sons
5. 14 not do any work, thou, nor thy son, nor
6. 2 thou, and thy son, and thy son's son, all
6. 20 when thy son asketh thee in time to co.
6. 21 Then thou shalt say unto thy son, We we.
7. 3 daughter thou shalt not give unto his son
7. 3 his daughter shalt thou take unto thy son
7. 4 they will turn away thy son from following
8. 5 as a man chasteneth his son, (so) the Lo.
10. 6 Eleazar his son ministered in the priest's
11. 6 Abiram, the sons of Eliab, the son of Re.
12. 12 ye, and your sons, and your daughters, and
12. 18 son, and thy daughter, and thy man serv.
12. 31 for even their sons and their daughters th
13. 6 son of thy mother, or thy son, or thy dau.
16. 11, 14 shalt rejoice..thou, and thy son, and
18. 5 in the name of the LORD, him and his sons
18. 10 maketh his son or his daughter to pass
21. 5 priests the sons of Levi shall come near
21. 15 the first born son be hers that was hated
21. 16 when he maketh his sons to inherit (that)
21. 16 son of the beloved..before the son of the
21. 17 he shall acknowledge the son of the hated
21. 18 a man have a stubborn and rebellious son
21. 20 This our son (is) stubborn and rebellious
23. 4 hired against thee Balaam the son of Beor
23. 17 There shall be no..sodomite of the sons
28. 32 Thy sons and thy daughters (shall be) gi.
28. 41 Thou shalt beget sons and daughters, but
28. 53 flesh of thy sons and of thy daughters, wh.
28. 56 evil..toward her son, and toward her da.
31. 9 delivered it unto the priests the sons of L.
31. 23 gave Joshua the son of Nun a charge, and
32. 8 when he separated the sons of Adam, he
32. 19 because of the provoking of his sons and
32. 44 Moses came..he and Hoshea the son of N.
34. 9 Joshua the son of Nun was full of the sp.
Josh. 1. 1 the LORD spake unto Joshua the son of N.
2. 1 Joshua the son of Nun sent out of Shittim
2. 23 came to Joshua the son of Nun, and told
6. 6 Joshua the son of Nun called the priests
7. 1, 18 son of Carmi, the son of Zabdi, the son
7. 19 My son, give, I pray thee, glory to the LORD
7. 24 took Achan the son of Zerah, and the sil
7. 24 his sons, and his daughters, and his oxen
13. 22 Balaam also the son of Beor, the soothsa
13. 31 the children of Machir the son of Manas
14. 1 Eleazar the priest, and Joshua the son o
14. 6 Caleb the son of Jephunneh the Kenezite
14. 13 gave unto Caleb the son of Jephunneh H.

Josh 14. 14 inheritance of Caleb the son of Jephunneh
15. 6 went up to the stone of Bohan the son of R.
15. 8 border went up by the valley of the son
15. 13 unto Caleb the son of Jephunneh he gave
15. 14 Caleb drove thence the three sons of Anak
15. 17 Othniel the son of Kenez, the brother of
17. 2 male children of Manasseh the son of Jo.
17. 3 son of Hepher, the son of Gilead, the son
17. 3 son of Manasseh, had no sons, but daugh.
17. 4 before Joshua the son of Nun, and before
17. 6 his sons: and the rest of Manasseh's sons
18. 16 before the valley of the son of Hinnom
18. 17 descended to the stone of Bohan the son
19. 49 gave an inheritance to Joshua the son of
19. 51 which Eleazar the priest, and Joshua the
21. 1 unto Joshua the son of Nun, and unto the
21. 12 gave they to Caleb the son of Jephunneh
22. 13, 31, 32 Phinehas the son of Eleazar the pri.
22. 20 Did not Achan the son of Zerah commit a
24. 9 Then Balak the son of Zippor, king of M.
24. 9 sent and called Balaam the son of Beor to
24. 29 Joshua the son of Nun, the servant of the
24. 32 which Jacob bought of the sons of Hamor
24. 33 Eleazar the son of Aaron died; and they
24. 33 a hill (that pertained to) Phinehas his son
Judg. 1. 13 Othniel the son of Kenaz, Caleb's younger
1. 20 he expelled thence the three sons of Anak
2. 8 Joshua the son of Nun, the servant of the
3. 6 gave their daughters to their sons, and se.
3. 9 Othniel the son of Kenaz, Caleb's younger
3. 11 And Othniel the son of Kenaz died
3. 15 Ehud the son of Gera, a Benjamite, a m.
3. 31 Shamgar the son of Anath, which slew of
4. 6 she sent and called Barak the son of Abi.
4. 12 that Barak the son of Abinoam was gone
5. 1 Then sang Deborah and Barak the son of
5. 6 In the days of Shamgar the son of Anath
5. 12 lead thy captivity captive, thou son of A.
6. 11 his son Gideon threshed wheat by the wi.
6. 29 Gideon the son of Joash hath done this th.
6. 30 Bring out thy son, that he may die; bec.
7. 14 save the sword of Gideon the son of Joash
8. 13 Gideon the son of Joash returned from
8. 19 They (were) my brethren, (even) the sons
8. 22 thou and thy son, and thy son's son also
8. 23 I will not rule .neither shall my son rule
8. 29 Jerubbaal the son of Joash went and dwelt
8. 30 Gideon had threescore and ten sons of his
8. 31 she also bare him a son, whose name he
8. 32 Gideon the son of Joash died in a good
9. 1 Abimelech the son of Jerubbaal went to
9. 2 the sons of Jerubbaal, (which are) three.
9. 5 slew his brethren the sons of Jerubbaal
9. 5 Jotham the youngest son of Jerubbaal w.
9. 18 have slain his sons, threescore and ten pe.
9. 18 have made Abimelech, the son of his maid
9. 24 to the threescore and ten sons of Jerubb.
9. 26 Gaal the son of Ebed came with his bret.
9. 28 Gaal the son of Ebed said, Who (is) Abi.
9. 28 (Is) not (he) the son of Jerubbaal? and Z.
9. 30 heard the words of Gaal the son of Ebed
9. 31 Gaal the son of Ebed, and his brethren
9. 35 Gaal the son of Ebed went out, and stood
9. 57 the curse of Jotham the son of Jerubbaal
10. 1 Tola the son of Puah, the son of Dodo, a
10. 4 had thirty sons that rode on thirty asses
11. 1 Now Jephthah..(was) the son of an har.
11. 2 bare him sons: and his wife's sons grew
11. 2 for thou (art) the son of a strange woman
11. 25 any thing better than Balak the son of Z.
11. 34 beside her he had neither son nor daugh.
12. 9 he had thirty sons, and thirty daughters
12. 9 thirty daughters from abroad for his sons
12. 13 after him Abdon the son of Hillel, a Pir.
12. 14 he had forty sons and thirty nephews, th.
12. 15 Abdon the son of Hillel the Pirathonite
13. 3, 5, 7 thou shalt conceive, and bear a son
13. 24 the woman bare a son, and called his na.
17. 2 Blessed (be thou) of the LORD, my son
17. 3 dedicated the silver..for my son, to make
17. 5 consecrated one of his sons, who became
17. 11 and the young man was..as one of his sons
18. 30 the son of Gershom, the son of Manasseh
18. 30 his sons were priests to the tribe of Dan
19. 22 certain sons of Belial, beset the house ro.
20. 28 the son of Eleazar, the son of Aaron, stood
Ruth 1. 1 went..he, and his wife, and his two sons
1. 2 the name of his two sons Mahlon and Ch.
1. 3 died; and she was left, and her two sons
1. 11 (are) there yet (any more) sons in my wo.
1. 12 have an husband..and should also bear
4. 13 gave her conception, and she bare a son
4. 15 which is better to thee than seven sons
4. 17 gave it a name, saying, There is a son born
1 Sa. 1. 1 the son of Jeroham, the son of Elihu
1. 1 the son of Tohu, the son of Zuph; an Ep.
1. 3 the two sons of Eli, Hophni and Phinehas
1. 4 he gave..to all her sons and her daughters
1. 8 (am) I not better to thee than ten sons
1. 20 she bare a son, and called his name Sam.
1. 23 gave her son suck until she weaned him
2. 12 the sons of Eli (were) sons of Belial, they
2. 21 she conceived, and bare three sons and
2. 22 heard all that his sons did unto all Israel
2. 24 Nay, my sons; for (it is) no good report
2. 29 honourest thy sons above me, to make yo.
2. 34 that shall come upon thy two sons, on H.
3. 6 I called not, my son; lie down again
3. 13 his sons made themselves vile, and he
3. 16 called Samuel, and said, Samuel, my son
4. 4, 11 the two sons of Eli, Hophni and Phine.
4. 16 And he said, What is there done, my son?

1 Sa. 4. 17 thy two sons also, Hophni and Phinehas
4. 20 Fear not; for thou hast born a son. But
7. 1 sanctified Eleazar his son to keep the ark
8. 1 that he made his sons judges over Israel
8. 3 his sons walked not in his ways, but turn.
8. 5 thou art old, and thy sons walk not in thy
8. 11 He will take your sons, and appoint (them)
9. 1 son of Abiel, the son of Zeror, the son of
9. 1 the son of Aphiah, a Benjamite, a mighty
9. 2 he had a son, whose name (was) Saul, a
9. 3 Kish said to Saul his son, Take now one of
10. 2 saying, What shall I do for my son?
10. 11 What (is) this (that) is come unto the son
10. 21 and Saul the son of Kish was taken
12. 2 my sons (are) with you: and I have walked
13. 16 Saul, and Jonathan his son, and the peo.
13. 22 and with Jonathan his son was there fou.
14. 1 Jonathan the son of Saul said unto the
14. 3 Ahiah, the son of Ahitub, I-chabod's bro.
14. 3 the son of Phinehas, the son of Eli, the L.
14. 39 though it be in Jonathan my son, he shall
14. 40 Jonathan my son will be on the other side
14. 42 Cast (lots) between me and Jonat. my son
14. 49 the sons of Saul were Jonathan, and Ishui
14. 50 (was) Abner, the son of Ner, Saul's uncle
14. 51 the father of Abner (was) the son of Abi.
16. 1 have provided me a king among his sons
16. 5 he sanctified Jesse and his sons, and cal.
16. 10 Jesse made seven of his sons to pass bef.
16. 18 I have seen a son of Jesse the Beth-lehe.
16. 19 Send me David thy son, which (is) with
16. 20 and sent (them) by David his son unto S.
17. 12 D. (was) the son of that Ephrathite of Beth.
17. 12 whose name (was) Jesse; and he had eight
17. 13 the three eldest sons of Jesse went (and)
17. 13 the names of his three sons that went to
17. 17 Jesse said unto David his son, Take now
17. 55 Abner, whose son (is) this youth? And Ab.
17. 56 the king said, Enquire thou whose son the
17. 58 S. said to him, Whose son (art) thou, (thou)
17. 58 I (am) the son of thy servant Jesse the B.
19. 1 Saul spake to Jonathan his son, and to all
19. 2 Jonathan, Saul's son, delighted much in D.
20. 27 And Saul said unto Jonathan his son
20. 27 Wherefore cometh not the son of Jesse
20. 30 Thou son of the perverse rebellious (wo.)
20. 30 thou hast chosen the son of Jesse to thine
20. 31 as long as the son of Jesse liveth upon the
22. 7 will the son of Jesse give every one of you
22. 8 my son hath made a league with the son
22. 8 my son hath stirred up my servant again.
22. 9 I saw the son of Jesse coming to..the son
22. 11 to call Ahimelech the priest, the son of
22. 12 Saul said, Hear now, thou son of Ahitub
22. 13 conspired against me, thou and the son
22. 20 one of the sons of Ahimelech the son of
23. 6 Abiathar the son of Ahimelech fled to D.
23. 16 Jonathan, Saul's son, arose, and went to D.
24. 16 Saul said, (Is) this thy voice, my son D.?
25. 8 unto thy servants, and to thy son David
25. 10 Who (is) David? And who (is) the son of
25. 17 he (is such) a son of Belial, that (a man)
25. 44 to Phalti the son of Laish, which (was) of
26. 5 where Saul lay, and Abner the son of Ner
26. 6 Abishai the son of Zeruiah, brother to J.
26. 14 David cried..to Abner the son of Ner, sa.
26. 17 and said, (Is) this thy voice, my son Da.?
26. 21 return, my son David; for I will no more
26. 25 Blessed (be) thou, my son David: thou sh.
27. 2 unto Achish, the son of Maoch, king of G.
28. 19 to morrow (shalt) thou and thy sons (be)
30. 3 their sons, and their daughters, were ta.
30. 6 was grieved, every man for his sons and
30. 7 to Abiathar the priest, Ahimelech's son
30. 19 neither sons nor daughters, neither spoil
31. 2 followed hard upon Saul and upon his sons
31. 2 Abinadab, and Melchi-shua, Saul's sons
31. 6 Saul died, and his three sons, and his ar.
31. 7 and that Saul and his sons were dead, they
31. 8 they found Saul and his three sons fallen
31. 12 body of Saul and the bodies of his sons
2 Sa. 1. 4 Saul and Jonathan his son are dead also
1. 5 that Saul and Jonathan his son be dead
1. 12 for Saul, and for Jonathan his son, and
1. 13 I (am) the son of a stranger, an Amalek.
1. 17 over Saul and over Jonathan his son
2. 8 Abner the son of Ner, captain of Saul's
2. 8 took Ish-bosheth the son of Saul, and br.
2. 10 Saul's son, (was) forty years old, when he
2. 12 Abner the son of Ner..went out from M.
2. 12 the servants of Ish-bosheth the son of S.
2. 13 Joab the son of Zeruiah, and the servants
2. 15 which (pertained) to Ish-bosheth the son
2. 18 there were three sons of Zeruiah there, J.
3. 2 unto David were sons born in Hebron
3. 3 Absalom, the son of Maachah the daughter
3. 4 the fourth, Adonijah the son of Haggith
3. 4 and the fifth, Shephatiah the son of Abi.
3. 14 messengers to Ish-bosheth, Saul's son, say.
3. 15 took her..from Phaltiel the son of Laish
3. 23 Abner the son of Ner came to the king, and
3. 25 Thou knowest Abner the son of Ner, that
3. 28 from the blood of Abner the son of Ner
3. 37 not of the king to slay Abner the son of
3. 39 the sons of Zeruiah (be) too hard for me
4. 1 Saul's son heard that Abner was dead
4. 2 Saul's son had two men (that were) cap.
4. 2 the sons of Rimmon a Beerothite, of the
4. 4 Saul's son had a son (that was) lame of
4. 5 the sons of Rimmon a Beerothite, Rechab
4. 8 Ish-bosheth the son of Saul thine enemy
4. 9 and Baanah his brother, the sons of Rim.

2 Sa. 5. 13 there were yet sons and daughters born
6. 3 the sons of Abinadab, drave the new cart
7. 14 will be his father, and he shall be my son
8. 3 David smote also Hadadezer, the son of
8. 10 Toi sent Joram his son unto king David, to
8. 12 the spoil of Hadadezer, son of Rehob, king
8. 16 Joab the son of Zeruiah (was) over the
8. 16 Jehoshaphat the son of Ahilud (was) rec.
8. 17 the son of Ahitub, and Ahimelech the son
8. 18 Benaiah the son of Jehoiada (was over)
8. 18 and David's sons were chief rulers
9. 3 Jonathan hath yet a son, (which is) lame
9. 4 he (is) in the house of Machir, the son of
9. 5 the house of Machir, the son of Ammiel
9. 6 Mephibosheth, the son of Jonathan, the s.
9. 9 I have given unto thy master's son all
9. 10 thy sons, and thy servants, shall till the
9. 10 that thy master's son may have food to
9. 10 thy master's son shall eat bread alway at
9. 10 Ziba had fifteen sons and twenty servants
9. 11 eat at my table, as one of the king's sons
9. 12 Mephibosheth had a young son, whose
10. 1 and Hanum his son reigned in his stead
10. 2 show kindness unto Hanum the son of N.
11. 21 Who smote Abimelech the son of Jerub.
11. 27 she became his wife, and bare him a son
12. 24 she bare a son, and he called his name S.
13. 1 Absalom the son of David had a fair sister
13. 1 and Amnon the son of David loved her
13. 3 Jonadab, the son of Shimeah, David's br.
13. 4 Why (art) thou, (being) the king's son, le.
13. 23 and Absolom invited all the king's sons
13. 25 Nay, my son, let us not all now go, lest
13. 27 he let Amnon and all the king's sons go
13. 29 the king's sons arose, and every man gat
13. 30 Absalom hath slain all the king's sons
13. 32 slain all the young men the king's sons
13. 33 to think that all the king's sons are dead
13. 35 Behold, the king's sons come: as thy ser.
13. 36 the king's sons came, and lifted up their
13. 37 went to Talmai, the son of Ammihud, ki.
13. 37 And (David) mourned for his son every
14. 1 Joab the son of Zeruiah perceived that
14. 6 thy handmaid had two sons, and they two
14. 11 destroy..more, lest they destroy my son
14. 11 there shall not one hair of thy son fall to
14. 16 (that would) destroy me and my sons to.
14. 27 unto Absalom there were born three sons
15. 27 return into the city..and your two sons
15. 27 Ahimaaz thy son, and Jonathan the son
15. 36 (they have) there with them their two sons
16. 3 king said, And where (is) thy master's son?
16. 5 whose name (was) Shimei, the son of Gera
16. 8 kingdom into the hand of Absalom thy s.
16. 9 Then said Abishai the son of Zeruiah unto
16. 10 What have I to do with you, ye sons of Z.
16. 11 my son, which came forth of my bowels
16. 19 (should I)..in the presence of his son?
17. 25 Amasa (was) a man's son whose name (was)
17. 27 Shobi the son of Nahash of Rabbah of the
17. 27 Machir the son of Ammiel of Lo-debar
18. 2 under the hand of Abishai the son of Ze.
18. 12 put forth mine hand against the king's son
18. 18 I have no son to keep my name in reme.
18. 19 Then said Ahimaaz the son of Zadok, Let
18. 20 no tidings, because the king's son is dead
18. 22 Then said Ahimaaz the son of Zadok yet
18. 22 Wherefore wilt thou run, my son, seeing
18. 27 like the running of Ahimaaz the son of Z.
18. 33 O my son Absalom, my son, my son Abs.
18. 33 would God I had died..my son, my son
19. 2 heard..the king was grieved for his son
19. 4 my son Absalom, O Absalom, my son, my s.
19. 5 the lives of thy sons and of thy daughters
19. 16 Shimei the son of Gera, a Benjamite, wh.
19. 17 his fifteen sons and his twenty servants
19. 18 Shimei the son of Gera fell down before
19. 21 Abishai the son of Zeruiah answered and
19. 22 What have I to do with you, ye sons of Z.
19. 24 Mephibosheth the son of Saul came down
20. 1, 2, 6, 7, 10, 13, 21, 22 Sheba, the son of B.
20. 1 neither have we inheritance in the son of
20. 23 Benaiah the son of Jehoiada (was) over the
20. 24 Jehoshaphat the son of Ahilud (was) rec.
21. 6 Let seven men of his sons be delivered unto
21. 7 Mephibosheth, the son of Jonathan, the s.
21. 7 between David and Jonathan the son of S.
21. 8 the king took the two sons of Rizpah the
21. 8 the five sons of Michal the daughter of S.
21. 8 Adriel the son of Barzillai the Meholath.
21. 12, 13 and the bones of Jonathan his son
21. 14 the bones of Saul and Jonathan his son
21. 17 the son of Zeruiah succoured him, and
21. 19 where El-hanan the son of Jaare-oregim
21. 21 Jonathan the son of Shimeah, the brother
23. 1 David the son of Jesse said, and the man
23. 9 Eleazar the son of Dodo the Ahothite, (one)
23. 11 Shammah the son of Agee the Hararite
23. 18 the brother of Joab, the son of Zeruiah
23. 20 the son of Jehoiada, the son of a valiant
23. 22 These (things) did Benaiah the son of Je.
23. 24 Elhanan the son of Dodo of Beth-lehem
23. 26 Helez the Paltite, Ira the son of Ikkesh
23. 29 Heleb the son of Baanah, a Netophathite
23. 29 Ittai the son of Ribai out of Gibeah of the
23. 32 Eliahba the Shaalbonite, of the sons of J.
23. 33 Shammah the Hararite, Ahiam the son of
23. 34 the son of Ahasbai, the son of the Maach.
23. 34 Eliam the son of Ahithophel the Gilonite
23. 36 Igal the son of Nathan of Zobah, Bani the
23. 37 armour bearer to Joab the son of Zeruiah
1 Ki. 1. 5 Adonijah the son of Haggith exalted him.

1 Ki. 1. 7 he conferred with Joab the son of Zerui.
1. 8, 26, 32, 36, 38, 44 Benaiah the son of Jeh.
1. 9 called all his brethren the king's sons, and
1. 11 Adonijah the son of Haggith doth reign
1. 12 thine own life, and the life of thy son So.
1. 13, 17, 30 Assuredly Solomon thy son shall
1. 19 hath called all the sons of the king, and
1. 21 I and my son Solomon shall be counted
1. 25 hath called all the king's sons, and the ca.
1. 33 cause Solomon my son to ride upon mine
1. 42 Jonathan the son of Abiathar the priest
2. 1 and he charged Solomon his son, saying
2. 5 thou knowest also what Joab the son of
2. 5 the son of Ner, and unto Amasa the son
2. 7 show kindness unto the sons of Barzillai
2. 8 (thou hast) with thee Shimei the son of G.
2. 13 Adonijah the son of Haggith came to Ba.
2. 22 for Abiathar..and for Joab the son of Ze.
2. 25 sent by the hand of Benaiah the son of J.
2. 29 Solomon sent Benaiah the son of Jehoiada
2. 32 Abner the son of Ner, captain of the host
2. 32 Amasa the son of Jether, captain of the
2. 34 Benaiah the son of Jehoiada went up, and
2. 35 the king put Benaiah the son of Jehoiada
2. 39 ran away unto Achish son of Maachah ki.
2. 46 the king commanded Benaiah the son of
3. 6 thou hast given him a son to sit on his th.
3. 20 arose at midnight, and took my son from
3. 21 behold, it was not my son which I did be.
3. 22 living (is) my son, and the dead (is) thy s.
3. 22 the dead (is) thy son..the living (is) my s.
3. 23 This (is) my son that liveth, and thy son
3. 23 thy son (is) the dead, and my son (is) the
3. 26 her bowels yearned upon her son, and she
4. 2 Azariah the son of Zadok the priest
4. 3 Elihoreph and Ahiah, the sons of Shisha
4. 3 Jehoshaphat the son of Ahilud, the reco.
4. 4 Benaiah the son of Jehoiada (was) over the
4. 5 Azariah the son of Nathan (was) over the
4. 5 Zabud the son of Nathan (was) principal
4. 6 Adoniram the son of Abda (was) over the
4. 8 these (are) their names: The son of Hur
4. 9 The son of Dekar, in Makaz, and in Shaal.
4. 10 The son of Hesed, in Aruboth; to him
4. 11 The son of Abinadab, in all the region of
4. 12 Baana the son of Ahilud; (to him pertain.)
4. 13 The son of Geber, in Ramoth-gilead, to
4. 13 the towns of Jair the son of Manasseh
4. 14 Ahinadab the son of Iddo (had) Mahanaim
4. 16 Baanah the son of Hushai (was) in Asher
4. 17 Jehoshaphat the son of Paruah in Issac.
4. 18 Shimei the son of Elah in Benjamin
4. 19 Geber the son of Uri (was) in the country
4. 31 and Chalcol, and Darda, the sons of Ma.
5. 5 Thy son, whom I will set upon thy throne
5. 7 hath given unto David a wise son over this
7. 14 He (was) a widow's son of the tribe of N.
8. 19 thy son, that shall come forth out of thy
11. 12 I will rend it out of the hand of thy son
11. 13 will give one tribe to thy son for David
11. 20 bare him Genubath his son, whom Taha.
11. 20 Genubath was..among the sons of Phar.
11. 23 Rezon the son of Eliadah, which fled from
11. 26 Jeroboam the son of Nebat, an Ephrathite
11. 35 I will take the kingdom out of his son's
11. 36 unto his son will I give one tribe, that D.
11. 43 Rehoboam his son reigned in his stead
12. 2 Jeroboam the son of Nebat, who was yet
12. 15 spake by Ahijah..unto Jeroboam the son
12. 16 neither (have we) inheritance in the son
12. 21, 23 Rehoboam, the son of Solomon
12. 31 the people, which were not of the sons of
13. 11 his sons came and told him all the works
13. 12 his sons had seen what way the man of G.
13. 13 he said unto his sons, Saddle me the ass
13. 27 he spake to his sons, saying, Saddle me
13. 31 he spake to his sons, saying, When I am
14. 1 Abijah the son of Jeroboam fell sick
14. 5 cometh to ask a thing of thee for her son
14. 20 and Nadab his son reigned in his stead
14. 21 Rehoboam the son of Solomon reigned in
14. 31 And Abijam his son reigned in his stead
15. 1 of king Jeroboam the son of Nebat
15. 4 to set up his son after him, and to estab.
15. 8 and Asa his son reigned in his stead
15. 18 Ben-hadad, the son of Tabrimon, the son
15. 24 and Jehoshaphat his son reigned in his
15. 25 Nadab the son of Jeroboam began to reign
15. 27 Baasha the son of Ahijah, of the house of
15. 33 began Baasha the son of Ahijah to reign
16. 1 word of the LORD came to Jehu the son
16. 3 like the house of Jeroboam the son of N.
16. 6 and Elah his son reigned in his stead
16. 7 of the prophet Jehu the son of Hanani
16. 8 began Elah the son of Baasha to reign ov.
16. 13 sins of Baasha..and the sins of..his son
16. 21 the people followed Tibni the son of Gin.
16. 22 the people that followed Tibni the son of
16. 26 in all the way of Jeroboam the son of Ne.
16. 28 and Ahab his son reigned in his stead
16. 29 began Ahab the son of Omri to reign ov.
16. 29 Ahab the son of Omri reigned over Israel
16. 30 Ahab the son of Omri did evil in the sight
16. 31 in the sins of Jeroboam the son of Nebat
16. 34 which he spake by Joshua the son of Nun
17. 12 may go in and dress it for me and my son
17. 13 and after make for thee and for thy son
17. 17 the son of the woman, the mistress of the
17. 18 art thou come unto me..to slay my son?
17. 19 he said unto her, Give me thy son. And
17. 20 evil upon the widow..by slaying her son
17. 23 and Elijah said, See, thy son liveth

1 Ki. 18. 31 the number of the tribes of the sons of J.
19. 16 Jehu the son of Nimshi shalt thou anoint
19. 16 Elisha the son of Shaphat, of Abel-meholah
19. 19 found Elisha the son of Shaphat, who (w.)
20. 35 a certain man of the sons of the prophets
21. 10 set two men, sons of Belial, before him
21. 22 like the house of Jeroboam the son of N.
21. 22 like the house of Baasha the son of Ahij.
21. 29 in his son's days will I bring the evil upon
22. 8 Micaiah the son of Imlah, by whom we
22. 9 said, Hasten (hither) Micaiah the son of
22. 11 Zedekiah the son of Chenanah made him
22. 24 Zedekiah the son of Chenanah went near
22. 26 carry him back..to Joash the king's son
22. 40 Ahaziah his son reigned in his stead
22. 41 Jehoshaphat the son of Asa began to rei.
22. 49 Then said Ahaziah the son of Ahab unto
22. 50 and Jehoram his son reigned in his stead
22. 51 Ahaziah the son of Ahab began to reign
22. 52 in the way of Jeroboam the son of Nebat
2 Ki. 1. 17 Jehoram the son of Jehoshaphat king of
1. 17 Jehoram reigned..because he had no son
2. 3 the sons of the prophets that (were) at B.
2. 5 the sons of the prophets that (were) at J.
2. 7 fifty men of the sons of the prophets went
2. 15 the sons of the prophets which (were) to
3. 1 Jehoram the son of Ahab began to reign
3. 3 the sins of Jeroboam the son of Nebat
3. 11 Elisha the son of Shaphat, which poured
3. 27 he took his eldest son, that should have
4. 1 of the wives of the sons of the prophets
4. 4 shut the door upon thee and upon thy so.
4. 5 shut the door upon her and upon her sons
4. 6 she said unto her son, Bring me yet a ve.
4. 16 About this..thou shalt embrace a son
4. 17 bare a son at that season that Elisha had
4. 28 Did I desire a son of my lord? did I not
4. 36 when she was come..said, Take up thy son
4. 37 and took up her son, and went out
4. 38 the sons of the prophets (were) sitting be.
4. 38 seethe pottage for the sons of the prophets
5. 22 two young men of the sons of the proph.
6. 1 the sons of the prophets said unto Elisha
6. 28 Give thy son, that we may eat him to day
6. 28 and we will eat my son tomorrow
6. 29 we boiled my son, and did eat him: and
6. 29 Give thy son..and she hath hid her son
6. 31 if the head of Elisha the son of Shaphat
6. 32 See ye how this son of a murderer hath se.
8. 1, 5 the woman, whose son he had restored
8. 5 this (is) her son, whom Elisha restored to
8. 9 Thy son Ben-hadad king of Syria hath sent
8. 16 of Joram the son of Ahab king of Israel
8. 16 Jehoram the son of Jehoshaphat king of
8. 24 and Ahaziah his son reigned in his stead
8. 25 In the twelfth year of Joram the son of A.
8. 25 did Ahaziah the son of Jehoram king of J.
8. 28 he went with Joram the son of Ahab to the
8. 29 Ahaziah the son of Jehoram king of Judah
8. 29 to see Joram the son of Ahab in Jezreel
9. 2, 14 the son of Jehoshaphat, the son of Ni.
9. 9 like the house of Jeroboam the son of Ne.
9. 9 like the house of Baasha the son of Ahi.
9. 20 the driving of Jehu the son of Nimshi
9. 26 blood of Naboth, and the blood of his sons
9. 29 in the eleventh year of Joram the son of
10. 1 And Ahab had seventy sons in Samaria
10. 2 seeing your master's sons (are) with you
10. 3 the best and meetest of your master's sons
10. 6 the heads of the men your master's sons
10. 6 the king's sons, (being) seventy persons
10. 7 they took the king's sons, and slew seventy
10. 8 brought the heads of the king's sons
10. 15 he lighted on Jehonadab the son of Rechab
10. 23 Jehu went, and Jehonadab the son of Re.
10. 29 (from) the sins of Jeroboam the son of Ne.
10. 35 And Jehoahaz his son reigned in his stead
11. 1 the mother of Ahaziah saw that her son
11. 2 Jehosheba..took Joash the son of Ahaziah
11. 2 stole him from among the king's sons (wh.)
11. 4 took..and showed them the king's son
11. 12 he brought forth the king's son, and put
12. 21 the son of Shimeath, and Jehozabad the s.
12. 21 and Amaziah his son reigned in his stead
13. 1 Joash the son of Ahaziah king of Judah
13. 1 Jehoahaz the son of Jehu began to reign
13. 2, 11 the sins of Jeroboam the son of Neba.
13. 3 into the hand of Ben-hadad the son of H.
13. 9 and Joash his son reigned in his stead
13. 10 began Jehoash the son of Jehoahaz to reign
13. 24 Ben-hadad his son reigned in his stead
13. 25 Jehoash the son of Jehoahaz took again
13. 25 the hand of Ben-hadad the son of Hazael
14. 1 In the second year of Joash son of Jehoah.
14. 1 Amaziah the son of Joash king of Judah
14. 8 the son of Jehoahaz, son of Jehu, king of
14. 9 Give thy daughter to my son to wife, and
14. 13 the son of Jehoash, the son of Ahaziah, at
14. 16 and Jeroboam his son reigned in his stead
14. 17 Amaziah the son of Joash king of Judah
14. 17 of Jehoash, son of Jehoahaz king of Israel
14. 23 In the fifteenth year of Amaziah the son
14. 23 Jeroboam the son of Joash king of Israel
14. 24 the sins of Jeroboam the son of Nebat
14. 25 Jonah, the son of Amittai, the prophet
14. 27 by the hand of Jeroboam the son of Joash
14. 29 Zachariah his son reigned in his stead
15. 1 began Azariah son of Amaziah king of J.
15. 5 Jotham the king's son (was) over the house
15. 8 did Zachariah the son of Jeroboam reign
15. 9, 18, 24, 28 of Jeroboam the son of Nebat
15. 7 and Jotham his son reigned in his stead

2 Ki. 15. 10 Shallum the son of Jabesh conspired aga.
15. 12 Thy sons shall sit on the throne of Israel
15. 13 Shallum the son of Jabesh began to reign
15. 14 Menahem the son of Gadi went up from
15. 14 smote Shallum the son of Jabesh in Sam.
15. 17 began Menahem the son of Gadi to reign
15. 22 and Pekahiah his son reigned in his stead
15. 23 Pekahiah the son of Menahem began to
15. 25, 27, 30, 32, 37 Pekah the son of Remaliah
15. 30 Hoshea the son of Elah made a conspiracy
15. 30, 32 Jotham the son of Uzziah
15. 38 and Ahaz his son reigned in his stead
16. 1 In the seventeenth year of Pekah the son
16. 1 Ahaz the son of Jotham king of Judah
16. 3 made his son to pass through the fire, ac.
16. 5 Pekah son of Remaliah king of Israel came
16. 7 I (am) thy servant, and thy son; come up
16. 20 and Hezekiah his son reigned in his stead
17. 1 began Hoshea the son of Elah to reign in
17. 17 caused their sons and their daughters to
17. 21 they made Jeroboam the son of Nebat ki.
18. 1, 9 year of Hoshea son of Elah king of Isr.
18. 1 the son of Ahaz king of Judah began to re.
18. 18 there came out to them Eliakim the son
18. 18 Shebna the scribe, and Joah the son of A.
18. 26 Then said Eliakim the son of Hilkiah, and
18. 37 Eliakim the son of Hilkiah..and Joah the
19. 2 sent..to Isaiah the prophet, the son of A.
19. 20 Then Isaiah the son of Amoz sent to Hez.
19. 37 Adrammelech and Sharezer his sons smote
19. 37 Esarhaddon his son reigned in his stead
20. 1 prophet Isaiah the son of Amoz came to
20. 12 At that time Berodach-baladan, the son of
20. 18 of thy sons that shall issue from thee, wh.
20. 21 and Manasseh his son reigned in his stead.
21. 6 made his son pass through the fire, and ob.
21. 7 said to David, and to Solomon his son, In
21. 18 and Amon his son reigned in his stead
21. 24 people of the land made Josiah his son ki.
21. 26 and Josiah his son reigned in his stead
22. 3 sent Shaphan the son of Azaliah, the son
22. 12 son of Shaphan, and Achbor the son of M.
22. 14 the son of Tikvah, the son of Harhas, keep.
23. 10 that no man might make his son or his da.
23. 15 high place which Jeroboam the son of Ne.
23. 30 people of the land took Jehoahaz the son
23. 34 made Eliakim the son of Josiah king in the
24. 6 and Jehoiachin his son reigned in his ste.
25. 7 they slew the sons of Zedekiah before his
25. 22 made Gedaliah the son of Ahikam, the son
25. 23 even Ishmael the son of Nethaniah, and
25. 23 Johanan the son of Careah, and Seraiah the
25. 23 and Jaazaniah the son of a Maachathite
25. 25 Ishmael the son of Nethaniah, the son of
1 Ch. 1. 5 sons of Japheth; Gomer, and Magog, and
1. 6 sons of Gomer; Ashchenaz, and Riphath
1. 7 sons of Javan; Elishah, and Tarshish, Ki.
1. 8 sons of Ham; Cush, and Mizraim, Put, and
1. 9 sons of Cush..And the sons of Raamah
1. 17 sons of Shem; Elam, and Asshur, and A.
1. 19 unto Eber were born two sons: the name
1. 23 and Jobab. All these (were) the sons of
1. 28 The sons of Abraham; Isaac, and Ishmael
1. 31 and Kedemah. These are the sons of Is.
1. 32 Now the sons of Keturah, Abraham's co.
1. 32 And the sons of Jokshan; Sheba, and D.
1. 33 sons of Midian; Ephah..these (are) the s.
1. 34 Isaac. The sons of Isaac; Esau, and Isr.
1. 35 sons of Esau; Eliphaz, Reuel, and Jeush
1. 36 sons of Eliphaz; Teman, and Omar, Zep.
1. 37 sons of Reuel; Nahath, Zerah, Shammah
1. 38 sons of Seir; Lotan, and Shobal, and Zibe.
1. 39 sons of Lotan; Hori, and Homam: and
1. 40 sons of Shobal..And the sons of Zibeon
1. 41 sons of Anah; Dishon. And the sons of D.
1. 42 sons of Ezer..The sons of Dishan; Uz, and
1. 43 Bela the son of Beor: and the name of his
1. 44 Jobab the son of Zerah of Bozrah reigned
1. 46 Hadad the son of Bedad, which smote M.
1. 49 Baal-hanan the son of Achbor reigned in
2. 1 These (are) the sons of Israel; Reuben, S.
2. 3 sons of Judah; Er, and Onan, and Shelah
2. 4 and Zerah. All the sons of Judah (were)
2. 5 The sons of Pharez; Hezron, and Hamul
2. 6 sons of Zerah; Zimri, and Ethan, and H.
2. 7 sons of Carmi; Achar, the troubler of Is.
2. 8 And the sons of Ethan; Azariah
2. 9 The sons also of Hezron, that were born
2. 16 the sons of Zeruiah; Abishai, and Joab
2. 18 Caleb the son of Hezron begat (children)
2. 18 her sons are these; Jesher, and Shobab
2. 23 these (belonged to) the sons of Machir
2. 25 the sons of Jerahmeel the first born of H.
2. 27 the sons of Ram the first born of Jerah.
2. 28 the sons of Onam were Shammai, and J.
2. 28 the sons of Shammai; Nadab, and Abis.
2. 30 sons of Nadab; Seled, and Appaim: but
2. 31 the sons of Appaim; Ishi. And the sons
2. 32 the sons of Jada the brother of Shammai
2. 33 And the sons of Jonathan; Peleth, and Z.
2. 33 These were the sons of Jerahmeel
2. 34 Now Sheshan had no sons, but daughters
2. 42 the sons of Caleb the brother of Jerahm.
2. 42 the sons of Mareshah the father of Heb.
2. 43 the sons of Hebron; Korah, and Tappuah
2. 45 the son of Shammai (was) Maon: and M
2. 47 the sons of Jahdai; Regem, and Jotham
2. 50 These were the sons of Caleb the son of H.
2. 52 the father of Kirjath-jearim had sons; H.
2. 54 sons of Salma; Beth-lehem, and the Ne.
3. 1 these were the sons of David, which were
3. 2 Absalom the son of Maachah the daughter

1 Ch. 3. 2 the fourth, Adonijah the son of Haggith
3. 9 all the sons of David, besides the sons of
3. 10 Solomon's son (was) Rehoboam, Abia his s.
3. 10 Asa his son, Jehoshaphat his son
3. 11 his son, Ahaziah his son, Joash his son
3. 12 his son, Azariah his son, Jotham his son
3. 13 son, Hezekiah his son, Manasseh his son
3. 14 Amon his son, Josiah his son
3. 15 the sons of Josiah (were), the first born J.
3. 16 And the sons of Jehoiakim
3. 16 Jeconiah his son, Zedekiah his son
3. 17 sons of Jeconiah; Assir, Salathiel his son
3. 19 the sons of Pedaiah (were) Zerubbabel, and
3. 19 the sons of Zerubbabel; Meshullam, and
3. 21 the sons of Hananiah; Pelatiah, and Je.
3. 21 the sons of Rephaiah, the sons of Arnan
3. 21 the sons of Obadiah, the sons of Shechan.
3. 22 sons of Shechaniah; Shemaiah: and the
3. 23 the sons of Neariah; Elioenai, and Heze.
3. 24 the sons of Elioenai (were) Hodaiah, and
4. 1 The sons of Judah; Pharez, Hezron, and
4. 2 Reaiah the son of Shobal begat Jahath
4. 4 These (are) the sons of Hur, the firstborn
4. 6 These (were) the sons of Naarah
4. 7 the sons of Helah (were) Zereth, and Jez.
4. 8 the families of Aharhel the son of Harum
4. 13 the sons of Kenaz; Othniel, and Seraiah
4. 13 and the sons of Othniel; Hathath
4. 15 And the sons of Caleb the son of Jephun.
4. 15 Naam: and the sons of Elah, even Kenaz
4. 16 the sons of Jehaleleel; Ziph, and Ziphah
4. 17 the sons of Ezra (were) Jether, and Mered
4. 18 these (are) the sons of Bithiah the daugh.
4. 19 the sons of (his) wife Hodiah, the sister of
4. 20 the sons of Shimon (were) Amnon, and
4. 20 the sons of Ishi (were) Zoheth, and Ben.
4. 21 The sons of Shelah the son of Judah (we.)
4. 24 The sons of Simeon (were) Nemuel, and
4. 25 his son, Mibsam his son, Mishma his son
4. 26 And the sons of Mishma; Hamuel his son
4. 26 Zacchur his son, Shimei his son
4. 27 Shimei had sixteen sons and six daughters
4. 34 Jamlech, and Joshah the son of Amaziah
4. 35 And Joel, and Jehu the son of Josibiah
4. 35 the son of Seraiah, the son of Asiel
4. 37 son of Shiphi, the son of Allon, the son
4. 37 the son of Shimri, the son of Shemaiah
4. 42 (some) of them, (even) of the sons of Sim.
4. 42 and Rephaiah, and Uzziel, the sons of Is.
5. 1 the sons of Reuben, the first born of Isr.
5. 1 unto the sons of Joseph the son of Israel
5. 3 The sons, (I say), of Reuben the first born
5. 4 The sons of Joel; Shemaiah his son
5. 4 Gog his son, Shimei his son
5. 5 Micah his son, Reaia his son, Baal his son
5. 6 Beerah his son, whom Tilgath-pilneser ki.
5. 8 the son of Azaz, the son of Shema, the son
5. 14 Abihail the son of Huri, the son of Jaro.
5. 14 the son of Gilead, the son of Michael, the
5. 14 Jeshishai, the son of Jahdo, the son of B.
5. 15 Ahi the son of Abdiel, the son of Guni, ch.
5. 18 The sons of Reuben, and the Gadites, and
6. 1, 16 The sons of Levi; Gershon, Kohath
6. 2, 18 the sons of Kohath; Amram, Izhar, and
6. 3 The sons also of Aaron; Nadab, and Abi.
6. 17 these (be) the names of the sons of Gers.
6. 19 The sons of Merari; Mahli, and Mushi
6. 20 Libni his son, Jahath his son, Zimmah his s.
6. 21 Joah his son, Iddo his son
6. 21 Zerah his son, Jeaterai his son
6. 22 The sons of Kohath; Amminadab his son
6. 22 Korah his son, Assir his son
6. 23 his son, and Ebiasaph his son, and..his s.
6. 24 Tahath his son, Uriel his son
6. 24 Uzziah his son, and Shaul his son
6. 25 the sons of Elkanah; Amasai, and Ahim.
6. 26 (As for) Elkanah: the sons of Elkanah
6. 26 Zophai his son, and Nahath his son
6. 27 his son, Jeroham his son, Elkanah his son
6. 28 the sons of Samuel; the first born Vashni
6. 29 The sons of Merari; Mahli
6. 29 Libni his son, Shimei his son, Uzza his son
6. 30 his son, Haggiah his son, Asaiah his son
6. 33 of the sons of the Kohathites; Heman a
6. 33 singer, the son of Joel, the son of Shemuel
6. 34 The son of Elkanah, the son of Jeroham
6. 34 the son of Eliel, the son of Toah
6. 35 The son of Zuph, the son of Elkanah
6. 35 the son of Mahath, the son of Amasai
6. 36 The son of Elkanah, the son of Joel
6. 36 the son of Azariah, the son of Zephaniah
6. 37 The son of Tahath, the son of Assir
6. 37 the son of Ebiasaph, the son of Korah
6. 38 The son of Izhar, the son of Kohath
6. 38 the son of Levi, the son of Israel
6. 39 Asaph the son of Berachiah, the son of S.
6. 40 son of Michael, the son of Baaseiah, the s.
6. 41 The son of Ethni, the son of Zerah, the s.
6. 42 son of Ethan, the son of Zimmah, the son
6. 43 The son of Jahath..son of Gershom, the s.
6. 44 the sons of Merari (stood) on the left hand
6. 44 the son of Kishi, the son of Abdi, the son
6. 45 son of Hashabiah..son of Amaziah, the s.
6. 46 The son of Amzi, the son of Bani, the son
6. 47 The son of Mahli, the son of Mushi
6. 47 the son of Merari, the son of Levi
6. 49 his sons offered upon the altar of the bu.
6. 50 And these (are) the sons of Aaron; Elea.
6. 50 his son, Phinehas his son, Abishua his son
6. 51 his son, Uzzi his son, Zerahiah his son
6. 52 his son, Amariah his son, Ahitub his son
6. 53 Zadok his son, Ahimaaz his son

1 Ch. 6. 54 of the sons of Aaron, of the families of the
6. 56 they gave to Caleb the son of Jephunneh
6. 57 to the sons of Aaron they gave the cities
6. 61 unto the sons of Kohath, (which were) le.
6. 62 to the sons of Gershom, throughout their
6. 63 Unto the sons of Merari (were given) by
6. 66 (the residue) of the families of the sons
6. 70 the family of the remnant of the sons of
6. 71 Unto the sons of Gershom (were given)
7. 1 the sons of Issachar (were) Tola, and Puah
7. 2 the sons of Tola; Uzzi, and Rephaiah, and
7. 3 the sons of Uzzi; Izrahiah: and the sons
7. 4 soldiers..for they had many wives and sons
7. 7 the sons of Bela; Ezbon, and Uzzi, and
7. 8 the sons of Becher; Zemira, and Joash, and
7. 8 Alameth. All these (are) the sons of Bech.
7. 10 sons also of Jediael; Bilhan: and the sons
7. 11 All these the sons of Jediael, by the heads
7. 12 the children of Ir, (and) Hushim, the sons
7. 13 The sons of Naphtali; Jahziel, and Guni,
7. 13 Jezer, and Shallum, the sons of Bilhah
7. 14 The sons of Manasseh; Ashriel, whom she
7. 16 Maachah the wife of Machir bare a son
7. 16 his brother (was) Sheresh: and his sons
7. 17 And the sons of Ulam; Bedan. These (w.)
7. 17 sons of Gilead, the son of Machir, the son
7. 19 the sons of Shemidah were Ahian, and Sh.
7. 20 And the sons of Ephraim; Shuthelah
7. 20 and Bered his son, and Tahath his son
7. 20 and Eladah his son, and Tahath his son
7. 21 Zabad his son, and Shuthelah his son
7. 23 she conceived and bare a son, and he call.
7. 25 And Rephah (was) his son, also Resheph
7. 25 and Telah his son, and Tahan his son
7. 26 his son, Ammihud his son, Elishama his s.
7. 27 Non his son, Jehoshua his son
7. 29 the children of Joseph the son of Israel
7. 30 The sons of Asher; Imnah, and Isuah, and
7. 31 the sons of Beriah; Heber, and Malchiel
7. 33 the sons of Japhlet; Pasach, and Bimhal
7. 34 the sons of Shamer; Ahi, and Rohgah, Je.
7. 35 the sons of his brother Helem; Zophah, and
7. 36 The sons of Zophah; Suah, and Harnepher
7. 38 the sons of Jether; Jephunneh, and Pisp.
7. 39 the sons of Ulla; Arah, and Hanniel
8. 3 the sons of Bela were Addar, and Gera, and
8. 6 these (are) the sons of Ehud: these are
8. 10 These (were) his sons, heads of the fathers
8. 12 The sons of Elpaal; Eber, and Misham
8. 16 Michael, and Ispah, and Joha, the sons of
8. 18 and Jezliah, and Jobab, the sons of Elpaal
8. 21 Beraiah, and Shimrath, the sons of Shimhi
8. 25 Iphedeiah, and Penuel, the sons of Shas.
8. 27 Eliah, and Zichri, the sons of Jeroham
8. 30 his first born son Abdon, and Zur, and K.
8. 34 And the son of Jonathan (was) Merib-baal
8. 35 the sons of Micah (were) Pithon, and Me.
8. 37 (was) his son, Eleasah his son, Azel his son
8. 38 Azel had six sons, whose names (are) these
8. 38 and Hanan. All these (were) the sons of
8. 39 the sons of Eshek his brother (were) Ulam
8. 40 the sons of Ulam were mighty men of va.
8. 40 had many sons, and sons' sons, an hundred
8. 40 All these (are) of the sons of Benjamin
9. 4 Uthai the son of Ammihud, the son of O.
9. 4 the son of Imri, the son of Bani
9. 4 of the children of Pharez the son of Judah
9. 5 of the Shilonites; Asaiah..and his sons
9. 6 of the sons of Zerah; Jeuel and their bre.
9. 7 of the sons of Benjamin; Sallu the son of
9. 7 the son of Hodaviah, the son of Hasenuah
9. 8 the son of Jeroham, and Elah the son of U.
9. 8 the son of Michri, and Meshullam the son
9. 8 Shephathiah, the son of Reuel, the son of
9. 11 Azariah the son of Hilkiah, the son of Me.
9. 11 son of Zadok, the son of Meraioth, the son
9. 12 son of Jeroham, the son of Pashur, the son
9. 12 son of Adiel, the son of Jahzerah, the son
9. 12 the son of Meshillemith, the son of Immer
9. 14 Shemaiah the son of Hasshub, the son of
9. 14 the son of Hashabiah, of the sons of Mer.
9. 15 the son of Micah, the son of Zichri, the son
9. 16 son of Shemaiah, the son of Galal, the son
9. 16 Berechiah the son of Asa, the son of Elk.
9. 19 son of Kore, the son of Ebiasaph, the son
9. 20 Phinehas the son of Eleazar was the ruler
9. 21 Zechariah the son of Meshelemiah (was)
9. 30 (some) of the sons of the priests made the
9. 32 (other) of their brethren, of the sons of the
9. 36 his first born son Abdon, then Zur, and K.
9. 40 the son of Jonathan (was) Merib-baal: and
9. 41 the sons of Micah (were) Pithon, and Me.
9. 43 his son, Eleasah his son, Azel his son
9. 44 Azel had six sons, whose names (are) the.
9. 44 Obadiah, and Hanan. These (were) the s.
10. 2 Philistines followed hard..after his sons
10. 2 Abinadab, and Malchi-shua, the sons of
10. 6 Saul died, and his three sons, and all his
10. 7 and that Saul and his sons were dead, th.
10. 8 they found Saul and his sons fallen in m.
10. 12 took away..the bodies of his sons, and br.
10. 14 turned the kingdom unto David the son
11. 6 Joab the son of Zeruiah went first up, and
11. 12 after him (was) Eleazar the son of Dodo
11. 22 the son of Jehoiada, the son of a valiant
11. 24 These (things) did Benaiah the son of Je.
11. 26 Elhanan the son of Dodo of Beth-lehem
11. 28 Ira the son of Ikkesh the Tekoite, Abi-e.
11. 30 Heled the son of Baanah the Netophath.
11. 31 Ithai the son of Ribai of Gibeah, (that p.)
11. 34 The sons of Hashem the Gizonite
11. 34 Jonathan the son of Shage the Hararite

1 Ch. 11. 35 the son of Sacar..Eliphal the son of Ur
11. 37 Hezro the Carmelite, Naarai the son of
11. 38 the brother of Nathan, Mibhar the son of
11. 39 the armour bearer of Joab the son of Zer.
11. 41 Uriah the Hittite, Zabad the son of Ahl.
11. 42 Adina the son of Shiza the Reubenite, a
11. 43 Hanan the son of Maachah, and Joshap.
11. 44 and Jehiel the sons of Hothan the Aroer.
11. 45 Jediael the son of Shimri, and Joha his
11. 46 Jeribai and Joshaviah, the sons of Elnat.
12. 1 kept..close because of Saul the son of K.
12. 3 Ahiezer, then Joash, the sons of Shemaah
12. 3 Jeziel, and Pelet, the sons of Azmaveth
12. 7 Joelah, and Zebadiah, the sons of Jeroh.
12. 14 These (were) of the sons of Gad, captains
12. 18 Thine (are we), David..thou son of Jesse
14. 3 and David begat more sons and daughters
15. 5 Of the sons of Kohath; Uriel the chief
15. 6 Of the sons of Merari; Asaiah the chief
15. 7 Of the sons of Gershom; Joel the chief
15. 8 Of the sons of Elizaphan; Shemaiah the
15. 9 Of the sons of Hebron; Eliel the chief, and
15. 10 Of the sons of Uzziel; Amminadab the c.
15. 17 the Levites appointed Heman the son of
15. 17 of his brethren, Asaph the son of Berech.
15. 17 of the sons of Merari..Ethan the son of
16. 38 Obed-edom also the son of Jeduthun, and
16. 42 And the sons of Jeduthun (were) porters
17. 11 seed..which shall be of thy sons; and I
17. 13 I will be his father, and he shall be my s.
18. 10 He sent Hadoram his son to king David
18. 12 Moreover Abishai the son of Zeruiah slew
18. 15 son of Zeruiah..and Jehoshaphat the son
18. 16 son of Ahitub, and Abimelech the son of
18. 17 Benaiah the son of Jehoiada (was) over the
18. 17 the sons of David (were) chief about the
19. 1 Nahash..died, and his son reigned in his
19. 2 show kindness unto Hanun the son of N.
20. 5 Elhanan the son of Jair slew Lahmi the
20. 7 the son of Shimea, David's brother, slew
21. 20 and his four sons with him hid themselves
22. 5 Solomon my son (is) young and tender, and
22. 6 Then he called for Solomon his son, and
22. 7 My son, as for me, it was in my mind to
22. 9 son shall be born to thee, who shall be a
22. 10 he shall be my son, and I (will be) his fat.
22. 11 Now, my son, the LORD be with thee; and
22. 17 commanded..to help Solomon his son, (s.)
23. 1 he made Solomon his son king over Israel
23. 6 divided them into courses among the sons
23. 8 sons of Laadan; the chief (was) Jehiel, and
23. 9 sons of Shimei; Shelomith, and Haziel, and
23. 10 sons of Shimei..These four (were) the sons
23. 11 but Jeush and Beriah had not many sons
23. 12 sons of Kohath; Amram, Izhar, Hebron
23. 13 sons of Amram; Aaron and Moses: and
23. 13 he and his sons for ever, to burn incense
23. 14 his sons were named of the tribe of Levi
23. 15 The sons of Moses (were) Gershom and E.
23. 16 Of the sons of Gershom, Shebuel (was) the
23. 17 the sons of Eliezer (were) Rehabiah the ch.
23. 17 Eliezer had none other sons; but the sons
23. 18 Of the sons of Izhar; Shelomith the ch.
23. 19 Of the sons of Hebron; Jeriah the first
23. 20 Of the sons of Uzziel; Micah the first, and
23. 21 sons of Merari..sons of Mahli; Eleazar
23. 22 had no sons, but daughters: and..the sons
23. 23 sons of Mushi; Mahli, and Eder, and Jere.
23. 24 These (were) the sons of Levi after the h.
23. 28 Because their office (was) to wait on the s.
23. 32 charge of the sons of Aaron their brethren
24. 1 divisions of the sons of Aaron. The sons
24. 3 both Zadok of the sons of Eleazar, and A.
24. 3 of the sons of Ithamar, according to their
24. 4 more..of the sons..than of the sons of I.
24. 4 Among the sons of Eleazar (there were)
24. 4 eight among the sons of Ithamar, accor.
24. 5 the sons of Eleazar, and of the sons of I.
24. 6 Shemaiah the son of Nethaneel the scribe
24. 6 priest, and Ahimelech the son of Abiath.
24. 20 rest of the sons of Levi..Of the sons of A.
24. 20 Shubael: of the sons of Shubael; Jehde.
24. 21 of the sons of Rehabiah, the first (was) I.
24. 22 Shelomoth: of the sons of Shelomoth, J.
24. 23 sons (of Hebron); Jeriah (the first), Am.
24. 24 sons of Uzziel; Michah: of the sons of M.
24. 25 Isshiah: of the sons of Isshiah; Zechar.
24. 26 sons of Merari..sons of Jaaziah; Beno
24. 27 sons of Merari by Jaaziah; Beno, and S.
24. 28 Of Mahli (came) Eleazar, who had no sons
24. 29 Concerning Kish: the son of Kish (was) J.
24. 30 sons also of Mushi..These (were) the sons
24. 31 sons of Aaron in the presence of David the
25. 1 separated to the service of the sons of A.
25. 2 sons of Asaph..sons of Asaph, under the
25. 3 sons of Jeduthun; Gedaliah, and Zeri, and
25. 4 sons of Heman; Bukkiah, Mattaniah, U.
25. 5 sons of Heman..fourteen sons and three
25. 9 who with his brethren and sons (were) tw.
25. 10 (he), his sons, and his brethren, (were) tw.
[So in verse 11, 12, 13, 14, 15, 16, 17, 18, 19, 20, 21, 22, 23, 24, 25, 26, 27, 28, 29, 30, 31.]
26. 1 Meshelemiah the son of Kore, of the sons
26. 2 sons of Meshelemiah (were) Zechariah the
26. 4 Moreover the sons of Obed-edom (were) S.
26. 6 Also unto Shemaiah his son were sons bo.
26. 7 sons of Shemaiah; Othni, and Rephael, and
26. 8 sons of Obed-edom: they, and their sons
26. 9 Meshelemiah had sons and brethren, str.
26. 10 Also Hosah..had sons; Simri the chief
26. 11 the sons and brethren of Hosah (were) th.
26. 14 Then for Zechariah his son, a wise coun.

1 Ch.26. 15 To Obed-edom southward; and to his sons
26. 19 sons of Kore, and among the sons of M.
26. 21 sons of Laadan; the sons of the Gershonite
26. 22 sons of Jehieli; Zetham, and Joel his br.
26. 24 Shebuel the son of Gershom, the son of M.
26. 25 Rehabiah his son, and Jeshaiah his son
26. 25 his son..Zichri his son..Shelomith his son
26. 28 son of Kish..son of Ner..son of Zeruiah
26. 29 Chenaniah and his sons(were) for the out.
27. 2 Jashobeam the son of Zabdiel: and in his
27. 5 Benaiah the son of Jehoiada, a chief priest
27. 6 and in his course (was) Ammizabad his son
27. 7 Zebadiah his son after him: and in his co.
27. 9 Ira the son of Ikkesh the Tekoite: and in
27. 16 son of Zichri..Shephatiah the son of Ma.
27. 17 Of the Levites; Hashabiah the son of Ke.
27. 18 David: of Issachar; Omri the son of Mic.
27. 19 son of Obadiah..Jerimoth the son of Azriel
27. 20 son of Azaziah .Joel the son of Pedaiah
27. 21 the son of Zechariah..the son of Abner
27. 22 Of Dan; Azareel the son of Jeroham
27. 24 Joab the son of Zeruiah began to number
27. 25 over the king's treasures (was)..the son
27. 25 over the store houses..(was)..Jehon. the s.
27. 26 And over them..(was) Ezri the son of Che.
27. 29 over the herds..(was) Shaphat the son of
27. 32 son of Hachmoni (was) with the king's so.
27. 34 after Ahithophel (was) Jehoiada the son of
28. 1 possession of the king, and of his sons, wi.
28. 4 among the sons of my father he liked me
28. 5 of all my sons, for the LORD hath given me
28. 5 many sons, he hath chosen Solomon my s.
28. 6 Solomon thy son..chosen him (to be) my s.
28. 9 Solomon my son, know thou the God of
28. 11 Then David gave to Solomon his son the
28. 20 David said to Solomon his son, Be strong
29. 1 Solomon my son, whom alone God hath
29. 19 give unto Solomon my son a perfect heart
29. 22 made Solomon the son of David king the
29. 24 sons likewise of king David, submitted th.
29. 26 Thus David the son of Jesse reigned over
29. 28 and Solomon his son reigned in his stead
2 Ch. 1. 1 Solomon the son of David was strengthened
1. 5 Bezaleel the son of Uri, the son of Hur, had
2. 12 hath given to David the king a wise son
2. 14 son of a woman of the daughters of Dan
5. 12 Jeduthun, with their sons and their bre.
6. 9 son, which shall come forth out of thy loi.
9. 29 visions of Iddo .against Jeroboam the son
9. 31 and Rehoboam his son reigned in his ste
10. 2 when Jeroboam the son of Nebat, who
10. 15 which he spake..to Jeroboam the son of
10. 16 none inheritance in the son of Jesse: every
11. 3 Speak unto Rehoboam the son of Solomon
11. 14 Jeroboam and his sons had cast them off
11. 17 made Rehoboam the son of Solomon strong
11. 18 Jerimoth the son of David..Eliab the son
11. 21 begat twenty and eight sons, and three sc.
11. 22 Rehoboam made Abijah the son of Maach.
12. 16 and Abijah his son reigned in his stead
13. 5 to him and to his sons by a covenant of s.
13. 6 Jeroboam the son of Nebat, the servant
13. 6 Solomon the son of David, is risen up, and
13. 7 strengthened themselves against..the son
13. 8 kingdom..in the hand of the sons of Dav.
13. 9, 10 the sons of Aaron, and the Levites
13. 21 begat twenty and two sons, and sixteen
14. 1 Asa his son reigned in his stead. In his
15. 1 spirit of God came upon Azariah the son
17. 1 Jehoshaphat his son reigned in his stead
17. 16 next him (was) Amasiah the son of Zichri
18. 7 same (is) Micaiah the son of Imla. And
18 8 said, Fetch quickly Micaiah the son of Im
18. 10, 23 Zedekiah the son of Chenaanah
18. 25 carry him back..to Joash the king's son
19. 2 Jehu the son of Hanani the seer went out
19. 11 Zebadiah the son of Ishmael, the ruler of
20. 14 son of Zechariah, the son of Benaiah, the
20. 14 son of Mattaniah, a Levite of the sons of
20. 34 written in the book of Jehu the son of H.
20. 37 Then Eliezer the son of Dodavah of Mar.
21. 1 and Jehoram his son reigned in his stead
21. 2 sons of Jehoshaphat..all these (were) the s.
21. 7 promised to give a light..to his sons for
21. 17 sons also..there was never a son left him
21. 17 save Jehoahaz, the youngest of his sons
22. 1 made Ahaziah his youngest son king in his
22. 1 So Ahaziah the son of Jehoram king of Ju.
22. 5 went with Jehoram the son of Ahab king
22. 6 Azariah the son of Jehoram king of Judah
22. 6 went down to see Jehoram the son of Ah.
22. 7 against Jehu the son of Nimshi, whom the
22. 8 sons of the brethren of Ahaziah, that mi.
22. 9 he (is) the son of Jehoshaphat, who soug.
22. 10 mother of Ahaziah saw that her son was
22. 11 took Joash the son of Ahaziah, and stole
22. 11 from among the king's sons that were sl.
23. 1 the son of Jeroham, and Ishmael the son
23. 1 the son of Obed, and Maaseiah the son of
23. 1 and Elishaphat the son of Zichri, into
23. 3 he said unto them, Behold, the king's son
23. 3 as the LORD hath said of the sons of Dav.
23. 11 they brought out the king's son, and put
23. 11 Jehoiada and his sons anointed him, and
24. 3 And Jehoiada..begat sons and daughters
24. 7 the sons of Athaliah, that wicked woman
24. 20 Zechariah the son of Jehoiada the priest
24. 22 the king remembered not..but slew his s.
24. 25 for the blood of the sons of Jehoiada the
24. 26 Zabad the son of Shimeath an Ammonit.
24. 26 Jehozabad the son of Shimrith a Moabit.
24. 27 (concerning) his sons, and the greatness
2 Ch.24. 27 And Amaziah his son reigned in his stead
25. 17 Joash, the son of Jehoahaz, the son of J.
25. 18 saying, Give thy daughter to my son to
25. 23 the son of Joash, the son of Jehoahaz, at
25. 25 Amaziah the son of Joash king of Judah
25. 25 lived after the death of Joash, son of Je.
26. 18 the sons of Aaron, that are consecrated to
26. 21 Jotham his son (was) over the king's ho.
26. 22 did Isaiah the prophet, the son of Amoz
26. 23 and Jotham his son reigned in his stead
27. 9 and Ahaz his son reigned in his stead
28. 3 he burnt incense in the valley of the son
28. 6 the son of Remaliah slew in Judah an hu.
28. 7 Zichri..slew Maaseiah the king's son, and
28. 8 two hundred thousand, women, sons, and
28. 12 the son of Johanan, Berechiah the son of
28. 12 the son of Shallum, and Amasa the son of
28. 27 and Hezekiah his son reigned in his stead
29. 9 our sons and our daughters and our wives
29. 11 My sons, be not now negligent; for the
29. 12 Mahath the son of Amasai, and Joel the
29. 12 sons of the Kohathites: and of the sons
29. 12 Kish the son of Abdi, and Azariah the son
29. 12 Joah the son of Zimmah, and Eden the s.
29. 13 of the sons of Elizaphan; Shimri and Jeiel
29. 13 of the sons of Asaph; Zechariah and Mat.
29. 14 of the sons of Heman; Jehiel and Shimei
29. 14 of the sons of Jeduthun; Shemaiah and
29. 21 he commanded the priests the sons of A.
30. 26 since the time of Solomon the son of Da.
31. 14 Kore the son of Imnah the Levite, the p.
31. 18 their wives, and their sons, and their da.
31. 19 of the sons of Aaron the priests, (which
32. 20 the prophet Isaiah the son of Amoz, pray.
32. 32 the vision of Isaiah the prophet, the son
32. 33 of the sepulchres of the sons of David
32. 33 And Manasseh his son reigned in his stead
33. 6 through the fire in the valley of the son
33. 7 had said to David and to Solomon his son
33. 20 and Amon his son reigned in his stead
33. 25 people of the land made Josiah his son ki.
34. 8 he sent Shaphan the son of Azaliah, and
34. 8 and Joah the son of Joahaz the recorder
34. 12 Jahath and Obadiah..of the sons of Mer
34. 12 Zechariah and Meshullam, of the sons of
34. 20 the son of Shaphan, and Abdon the son of
34. 22 Shallum the son of Tikvath, the son of H.
35. 3 the house which Solomon the son of David
35. 4 according to..writing of Solomon his son
35. 14 the sons of Aaron (were busied) in offering
35. 14 and for the priests the sons of Aaron
35. 15 the singers the sons of Asaph (were) in th.
36. 1 took Jehoahaz the son of Josiah, and made
36. 8 and Jehoiachin his son reigned in his stead
36. 20 they were servants to him and his sons
Ezra 3. 2 Then stood up Jeshua the son of Jozadak
3. 2 Zerubbabel the son of Shealtiel, and his
3. 8 the son of Shealtiel, and Jeshua the son
3. 9 Then stood Jeshua (with) his sons and his
3. 9 Kadmiel and his sons, the sons of Judah
3. 9 the sons of Henadad, (with) their sons and
3. 10 the Levites, the sons of Asaph, with cym.
7. 1 son of Seraiah, the son of Azariah, the son
7. 2 son of Shallum, the son of Zadok, the son
7. 3 son of Amariah..son of Azariah, the son
7. 4 The son of Zerahiah, the son of Uzzi, the s.
7. 5 The son of Abishua, the son of Phinehas
7. 5 the son of Eleazar, the son of Aaron the
8. 2 Of the sons of Phinehas; Gershom
8. 2 of the sons of Ithamar, Daniel: of the sons
8. 3 the sons of Shechaniah; of the sons of Ph.
8. 4 Of the sons of Pahath-moab; Elihoenai
8. 4 the son of Zerahiah, and with him two h.
8. 5 Of the sons of Shechaniah; the son of Jah.
8. 6 Of the sons also of Adin; Ebed the son of
8. 7 of the sons of Elam; Jeshaiah the son of
8. 8 the sons of Shephatiah; Zebadiah the son
8. 9 Of the sons of Joab; Obadiah the son of J.
8. 10 of the sons of Shelomith; the son of Josi.
8. 11 the sons of Bebai; Zechariah the son of B.
8. 12 of the sons of Azgad; Johanan the son of
8. 13 of the last sons of Adonikam, whose nam.
8. 14 Of the sons also of Bigvai; Uthai, and Za.
8. 15 and found there none of the sons of Levi
8. 18 of the sons of Mahli, the son of Levi, the s.
8. 18 Sherebiah, with his sons and his brethren
8. 19 and with him Jeshaiah of the sons of
8. 19 Merari, his brethren, and their sons
8. 33 by the hand of Meremoth the son of Ur.
8. 33 with him (was) Eleazar the son of Phine.
8. 33 the son of Jeshua, and Noadiah the son
9. 2 taken of their daughters..for their sons
9. 12 give not your daughters unto their sons
9. 12 take their daughters unto your sons, nor
10. 2 the son of Jehiel, (one) of the sons of E.
10. 6 the chamber of Johanan the son of Elias.
10. 15 the son of Asahel and Jahaziah the son of
10. 18 among the sons of the priests there were
10. 18 of the sons of Jeshua the son of Jozadak
10. 20 of the sons of Immer; Hanani and Zebe.
10. 21 of the sons of Harim; Maaseiah, and E.
10. 22 of the sons of Pashur; Elioenai, Maaseiah
10. 25 of the sons of Parosh; Ramiah, and Jez.
10. 26 of the sons of Elam; Mattaniah, Zechar.
10. 27 of the sons of Zattu; Elioenai, Eliashib
10. 28 Of the sons also of Bebai; Jehohanan, H.
10. 29 of the sons of Bani; Meshullam, Malluch
10. 30 of the sons of Pahath-moab; Adna, and
10. 31 (of) the sons of Harim; Eliezer, Ishijah
10. 33 Of the sons of Hashum; Mattenai, Matt.
10. 34 Of the sons of Bani; Maadai, Amram, and
10. 43 Of the sons of Nebo; Jeiel, Mattithiah
Neh. 1. 1 The words of Nehemiah the son of Hach.
3. 2 next to them builded Zaccur the son of
3. 3 the fish gate did the sons of Hassenaah
3. 4, 21 Meremoth the son of Urijah, the son
3. 4 Meshullam the son of Berechiah, the son
3. 4 next unto them repaired Zadok the son of
3. 6 the son of Paseah, and Meshullam the son
3. 8 Next unto him repaired Uzziel the son of
3. 8 Hananiah the son of (one of) the apothe.
3. 9 the son of Hur, the ruler of the half part
3. 10 next unto them repaired Jedaiah the son
3. 10 next unto him repaired Hattush the son
3. 11 the son of Harim, and Hashub the son of
3. 12 Shallum the son of Halohesh, the ruler of
3. 14 Malchiah the son of Rechab, the ruler of
3. 15 Shallun the son of Col-hozeh, the ruler
3. 16 After him repaired Nehemiah the son of
3. 17 after him repaired..Rehum the son of B.
3. 18 Bavai the son of Henadad, the ruler of
3. 19 next to him repaired Ezer the son of Je.
3. 20 Baruch the son of Zabbai earnestly repa.
3. 23 Azariah the son of Maaseiah the son of
3. 24 After him repaired Binnui the son of H.
3. 25 Palal the son of Uzai, over against the tu.
3. 25 After him Pedaiah the son of Parosh
3. 29 After them repaired Zadok the son of I.
3. 29 Shemaiah the son of Shecaniah, the keep.
3. 30 son of Shelemiah, and Hanun the sixth son
3. 30 After him repaired Meshullam the son of
3. 31 repaired Malchiah the goldsmith's son un.
4. 14 fight for your brethren, your sons, and your
5. 2 We, our sons, and our daughters, (are) m.
5. 5 we bring into bondage our sons and our
6. 10 Shemaiah the son of Delaiah the son of M.
6. 18 the son of Arah; and his son Johanan
6. 18 the daughter of Meshullam the son of B.
8. 17 since the days of Jeshua the son of Nun
10. 1 Nehemiah, the Tirshatha, the son of Ha.
10. 9 the son of Azaniah, Binnui of the sons of
10. 28 their wives, their sons, and their daugh.
10. 30 nor take their daughters for our sons
10. 36 the first born of our sons, and of our cat.
10. 38 the son of Aaron shall be with the Levit.
11. 4 Athaiah the son of Uzziah, the son of Ze.
11. 4 the son of Amariah, the son of Shephat.
11. 4 the son of Mahaleel, of the children of P.
11. 5 Maaseiah the son of Baruch, the son of C.
11. 5 the son of Hazaiah, the son of Adaiah
11. 5 the son of Zechariah, the son of Shiloni
11. 6 the sons of Perez that dwelt at Jerusalem
11. 7 the sons of Benjamin; Sallu the son of M.
11. 7 son of Joed, the son of Pedaiah, the son
11. 7 son of Maaseiah..son of Ithiel, the son of
11. 9 And Joel the son of Zichri (was) their ov.
11. 9 the son of Senuah (was) second over the
11. 10 Of the priests: Jedaiah the son of Joiari
11. 11 the son of Hilkiah, the son of Meshullam
11. 11 son of Zadok, the son of Meraioth, the son
11. 12 Adaiah the son of Jeroham, the son of P.
11. 12 the son of Amzi, the son of Zechariah
11. 12 the son of Pashur, the son of Malchiah
11. 13 Amashai the son of Azareel, the son of A.
11. 13 the son of Meshillemoth, the son of Imm.
11. 14 Zabdiel, the son of (one of) the great men
11. 15 Shemaiah the son of Hashub, the son of A.
11. 15 the son of Hashabiah, the son of Bunni
11. 17 son of Micha, the son of Zabdi, the son of
11. 17 son of Shammua, the son of Galal, the son
11. 22 Uzzi the son of Bani, the son of Hashab.
11. 22 the son of Mattaniah, the son of Micha
11. 22 Of the sons of Asaph, the singers (were)
11. 24 And Pethahiah the son of Meshezabeel, of
11. 24 of the children of Zerah the son of Judah
12. 1 that went up with Zerubbabel the son of
12. 23 The sons of Levi, the chief of the fathers
12. 23 the days of Johanan the son of Eliashib
12. 24 Sherebiah, and Jeshua the son of Kadm.
12. 26 Joiakim the son of Jeshua, the son of Jo.
12. 28 the sons of the singers gathered themsel.
12. 35 (certain) of the priests' sons with trump.
12. 35 Zechariah the son of Jonathan, the son of
12. 35 the son of Mattaniah, the son of Michai.
12. 35 the son of Zaccur, the son of Asaph
12. 45 commandment of David, (and) of..his s.
13. 13 Hanan the son of Zaccur, the son of Mat.
13. 25 not give your daughters unto their sons
13. 25 nor take their daughters unto your sons
13. 28 (one) of the sons of Joiada, the son of E.
Esth. 2. 5 son of Jair, the son of Shimei, the son of
3. 1, 10 Haman the son of Hammedatha the
8. 5 Haman the son of Hammedatha the Ag.
9. 10 The ten sons of Haman the son of Ham.
9. 12 The Jews have slain..the ten sons of Ha.
9. 13 let Haman's ten sons be hanged upon the
9. 14 and they hanged Haman's ten sons
9. 24 Haman the son of Hammedatha the Aga.
9. 25 he and his sons should be hanged on the
Job 1. 2 there were born unto him seven sons and
1. 4 his sons went and feasted (in their) houses
1. 5 It may be that my sons have sinned, and
1. 6 the sons of God came to present themse.
1. 13 there was a day when his sons and his da.
1. 18 Thy sons and thy daughters (were) eating
2. 1 the sons of God came to present themsel.
14. 21 His sons come to honour, and he knoweth
25. 6 How much less..the son of man, (which
32. 2 the wrath of Elihu the son of Barachel the
32. 6 And Elihu the son of Barachel the Buzite
35. 8 thy righteousness (may profit) the son of
38. 7 and all the sons of God shouted for joy
38. 32 canst thou guide Arcturus with his sons?
42. 13 He had also seven sons and three daught.

Job 42. 16 saw his sons, and his sons' sons, (even) f.
Psa. 2. 7 Thou (art) my Son: this day have I bego.
3. *title.* when he fled from Absalom his son
4. 2 O ye sons of men, how long..my glory
8. 4 and the son of man, that thou visitest him
31. 19 that trust in thee before the sons of men
33. 13 The LORD..beholdeth all the sons of men
42. *title.* To the chief Musician..for the sons of
44. *title.* To the chief Musician for the sons of K.
45. *title.* To the chief Musician..for the sons of
46. *title.* To the chief Musician for the sons of
47. *title.* A psalm for the sons of Korah
48. *title.* A song (and) psalm for the sons of Korah
49. *title.* A psalm for the sons of Korah
50. 20 thou slanderest thine own mother's son
57. 4 the sons of men, whose teeth (are) spears
58. 1 do ye judge uprightly, O ye sons of men?
72. 1 and thy righteousness unto the king's son
72. 20 The prayers of David the son of Jesse are
77. 15 thy people, the sons of Jacob and Joseph
80. 17 the son of man (whom) thou madest strong
84. *title.* A psalm for the sons of Korah
85. *title.* A psalm for the sons of Korah
86. 16 give thy strength..and save the son of th.
87. *title.* A psalm (or) song for the sons of Korah
88. *title.* A psalm (or) song for the sons of Korah
89. 6 (who) among the sons of the mighty can be
89. 22 nor the son of wickedness afflict him
106. 37 they sacrificed their sons and their daug.
106. 38 the blood of their sons and of their daug.
116. 16 I (am) thy servant, (and) the son of thine
144. 3 (or) the son of man, that thou makest ac.
144. 12 That our sons (may be) as plants grown up
145. 12 To make known to the sons of men his mi.
146. 3 Put not your trust..in the son of man, in
Prov. 1. 1 The proverbs of Solomon the son of David
1. 8 My son, hear the instruction of thy father
1. 10 My son, if sinners entice thee, consent th.
1. 15 My son, walk not thou in the way with th.
2. 1 My son, if thou wilt receive my words, and
3. 1 My son, forget not my law; but let thine
3. 11 My son, despise not the chastening of the
3. 12 as a father the son (in whom) he delighteth
3. 21 My son, let not them depart from thine
4. 3 I was my father's son, tender and only
4. 10 Hear, O my son, and receive my sayings
4. 20 My son, attend to my words; incline thi.
5. 1 My son, attend unto my wisdom, (and) bow
5. 20 why wilt thou, my son, be ravished with a
6. 1 My son, if thou be surety for thy friend
6. 3 Do this now, my son, and deliver thyself
6. 20 My son, keep thy father's commandment
7. 1 My son, keep my words, and lay up my
8. 4 I call; and my voice (is) to the sons of
8. 31 and my delights (were) with the sons of
10. 1 A wise son maketh a glad father: but
10. 1 a foolish son (is) the heaviness of his mother
10. 5 He that gathereth in summer. a wise son
10. 5 he that sleepeth in harvest is a son that
13. 1 A wise son (heareth) his father's instruct.
13. 24 He that spareth his rod hateth his son
15. 20 wise son maketh a glad father: but a fool.
17. 2 wise servant shall have rule over a son that
17. 25 foolish son (is) a grief to his father, and
19. 13 foolish son (is) the calamity of his father
19. 18 Chasten thy son while there is hope, and
19. 26 He that wasteth (his) father. (is) a son th.
19. 27 Cease, my son, to hear the instruction (th)
23. 15 My son, if thine heart be wise, my heart
23. 19 Hear thou, my son, and be wise, and guide
23. 26 My son, give me thine heart, and let thine
24. 13 My son, eat thou honey, because (it is) go
24. 21 My son, fear thou the LORD and the king
27. 11 My son, be wise, and make my heart glad
28. 7 Whoso keepeth the law (is) a wise son: but
29. 17 Correct thy son, and he shall give thee rest
30. 1 words of Agur the son of Jakeh, (even) the
30. 4 what (is) his son's name, if thou canst tell?
Eccl. 1. 1 words of the Preacher, the son of David
1. 13 sore travail hath God given to the sons of
2. 3 see what (was) that good for the sons of
2. 8 I gat me..the delights of the sons of men
3. 10 travail which God hath given to the sons
3. 18 concerning the estate of the sons of men
3. 19 For that which befalleth the sons of men
5. 14 begetteth a son, and (there is) nothing in
8. 11 heart of the sons of men is fully set in th.
9. 3 heart of the sons of men is full of evil, and
9. 12 so (are) the sons of men snared in an evil
10. 17 when thy king (is) the son of nobles, and
12. 12 further, by these, my son, be admonished
Song 2. 3 so (is) my beloved among the sons. I sat
Isa. 1. 1 vision of Isaiah the son of Amoz, which he
2. 1 word that Isaiah the son of Amoz saw co
7. 1 days of Ahaz the son of Jotham, the son
7. 1 Pekah the son of Remaliah, king of Israel
7. 3 Go forth now..thou, and..thy son, at the
7. 4 Rezin with Syria, and of the son of Rem.
7. 5 Because Syria, Ephraim, and the son of
7. 6 set a king in the midst of it, (even) the son
7. 9 the head of Samaria (is) Remaliah's son. If
7. 14 virgin shall conceive, and bear a son, and
8. 2 Uriah the priest, and Zechariah the son
8. 3 conceived, and bare a son. Then said the
8. 6 and rejoice in Rezin and Remaliah's son
9. 6 For unto us a child is born, unto us a son
13. 1 burden of Babylon, which Isaiah the son
14. 12 O Lucifer, son of the morning! (how) art
19. 11 I (am) the son of the wise, the son of an.
20. 2 spake the LORD by Isaiah the son of Amoz
22. 20 will call my servant Eliakim the son of H.
36. 3 came forth unto him Eliakim, Hilkiah's s.

Isa. 36. 3 Shebna the scribe, and Joah, Asaph's son
36. 22 son of Hilkiah..and Joah the son of Asa.
37. 2 unto Isaiah the prophet, the son of Amoz
37. 21 Then Isaiah the son of Amoz sent unto H.
37. 38 his sons smote him with the sword; and
37. 38 and Esar-haddon his son reigned in his
38. 1 Isaiah the prophet, the son of Amoz, came
39. 1 the son of Baladan, king of Babylon, sent
39. 7 And of thy sons that shall issue from th.
43. 6 Keep not back: bring my sons from far
45. 11 things to come concerning my sons, and
49. 15 should not have compassion on the son of
49. 22 they shall bring thy sons in (their) arms
51. 12 of the son of man (which) shall be made
51. 18 none to guide her among all the sons (w.)
51. 18 taketh her by the hand of all the sons (th.)
51. 20 sons have fainted, they lie at the head of
52. 14 and his form more than the sons of men
56. 2 son of man (that) layeth hold on it; that
56. 3 Neither let the son of the stranger, that
56. 5 name better than of sons and of daughters
56. 6 Also the sons of the stranger, that join
57. 3 draw near hither, ye sons of the sorceress
60. 4 sons shall come from far, and thy daugh.
60. 9 bring thy sons from far, their silver and
60. 10 sons of strangers shall build up thy walls
60. 14 sons also of them that afflicted thee shall
61. 5 sons of the alien (shall be) your plowmen
62. 5 (so) shall thy sons marry thee; and (as)
62. 8 sons of the stranger shall not drink thy
Jer. 1. 1 words of Jeremiah the son of Hilkiah, of
1. 2 in the days of Josiah the son of Amon king
1. 3 days of Jehoiakim the son of Josiah king
1. 3 son of Josiah king of Judah, unto the car.
3. 24 their flocks and their herds, their sons
5. 17 sons and thy daughters should eat; they
6. 21 fathers and the sons together shall fall
7. 31 which (is) in the valley of the son of Hin.
7. 31 to burn their sons and their daughters
7. 32 no more be called..The valley of the son
11. 22 their sons and their daughters shall die
13. 14 even the fathers and the sons together
14. 16 wives, nor their sons, nor their daughters
15. 4 because of Manasseh the son of Hezekiah
16. 2 neither shalt thou have sons or daughters
16. 3 thus saith the LORD concerning the sons
19. 2 go forth unto the valley of the son of H.
19. 5 burn their sons with fire (for) burnt offer.
19. 6 no more be called..The valley of the son
19. 9 cause them to eat the flesh of their sons
20. 1 Now Pashur the son of Immer the priest
21. 1 son of Melchiah, and Zephaniah the son
22. 11 Shallum the son of Josiah king of Judah
22. 18 Jehoiakim the son of Josiah king of Jud.
22. 24 Coniah the son of Jehoiakim king of Jud.
24. 1 Jeconiah the son of Jehoiakim king of Ju.
25. 1 Jehoiakim the son of Josiah king of Jud.
25. 3 Josiah the son of Amon king of Judah, ev.
26. 1 Jehoiakim the son of Josiah king of Jud.
26. 20 Urijah the son of Shemaiah of Kirjath-j.
26. 22 Elnathan the son of Achbor, and (certain)
26. 24 the hand of Ahikam the son of Shaphan
27. 1 Jehoiakim the son of Josiah king of Jud.
27. 7 serve him, and his son, and his son's son
27. 20 Jeconiah the son of Jehoiakim king of J.
28. 1 Hananiah the son of Azur the prophet
28. 4 Jeconiah the son of Jehoiakim king of J.
29. 3 the son of Shaphan, and Gemariah the son
29. 6 Take ye wives, and beget sons and daug.
29. 6 take wives for your sons..they..bear sons
29. 21 son of Kolaiah, and of Zedekiah the son
29. 25 to Zephaniah the son of Maaseiah the pr.
31. 20 (Is) Ephraim my dear son? (is he) a plea.
32. 7 Hanameel the son of Shallum thine uncle
32. 8 mine uncle's son, came to me in the court
32. 9 the field of Hanameel, my uncle's son, th.
32. 12 Baruch the son of Neriah, the son of Ma.
32. 16 the purchase unto Baruch the son of Ne.
32. 19 open upon all the ways of the sons of men
32. 35 which (are) in the valley of the son of Hin.
32. 35 to cause their sons and their daughters to
33. 21 he should not have a son to reign upon his
35. 1 Jehoiakim the son of Josiah king of Jud.
35. 3 Jaazaniah the son of Jeremiah, the son of
35. 3 his brethren, and all his sons, and the wh.
35. 4 of the sons of Hanan, the son of Igdaliah
35. 4 the chamber of Maaseiah the son of Sha.
35. 5 I set before the sons of the house of the R.
35. 6, 8 Jonadab the son of Rechab our father
35. 6 drink no wine (neither) ye, nor your sons
35. 8 we, our wives, our sons, nor our daught.
35. 14 the son of Rechab, that he commanded
35. 16 the sons of Jonadab the son of Rechab ha.
35. 19 the son of Rechab shall not want a man
36. 1, 9 Jehoiakim the son of Josiah king of J.
36. 4 Jeremiah called Baruch the son of Neriah
36. 8 Baruch the son of Neriah did according
36. 10 the chamber of Gemariah the son of Sh.
36. 11 the son of Gemariah, the son of Shaphan
36. 12 son of Shemaiah, and Elnathan the son
36. 12 son of Achbor, and Gemariah the son of
36. 12 and Zedekiah the son of Hananiah
36. 14 the princes sent Jehudi the son of Neth.
36. 14 the son of Shelemiah, the son of Cushi
36. 14 Baruch the son of Neriah took the roll
36. 26 commanded Jerahmeel the son of Hamm.
36. 26 the son of Azriel, and Shelemiah the son
36. 32 gave it to Baruch the scribe, the son of N.
37. 1 And king Zedekiah the son of Josiah rei.
37. 1 instead of Coniah the son of Jehoiakim
37. 3 son of Shelemiah, and Zephaniah the son
37. 13 the son of Shelemiah, the son of Hananiah

Jer. 38. 1 son of Mattan, and Gedaliah the son of
38. 1 son of Shelemiah, and Pashur the son of
38. 6 the dungeon of Malchiah the son of Ham.
39. 6 the king of Babylon slew the sons of Zed.
39. 14 Gedaliah the son of Ahikam, the son of Sh.
40. 5, 9 the son of Ahikam, the son of Shaphan
40. 6 went Jeremiah unto Gedaliah the son of
40. 7 had made Gedaliah the son of Ahikam go.
40. 8 Ishmael the son of Nethaniah, and Joha.
40. 8 the sons of Kareah, and Seraiah the son of
40 8 and the sons of Ephai the Netophathite
40. 8 and Jezaniah the son of a Maachathite
40. 11 Gedaliah the son of Ahikam the son of Sh.
40. 13 the son of Kareah, and all the captains of
40. 14 Gedaliah the son of Ahikam believed them
40. 15 the son of Kareah spake to Gedaliah in
40. 15 I will slay Ishmael the son of Nethaniah
40. 16 son of Ahikam said unto Johanan the son
41. 1 the son of Nethaniah the son of Elishama
41. 2, 6, 10, 16, 18 Gedaliah the son of Ahikam
41. 2, 6, 7, 10, 11, 12, 15, 16, 18 Ishmael the son
41. 9 the son of Nethaniah filled it with (them
41. 11, 13, 14, 16 Johanan the son of Kareah
42. 1 the son of Kareah, and Jezaniah the son
42. 8 Then called he Johanan the son of Kareah
43. 2 Then spake Azariah the son of Hoshaiah
43. 2, 4, 5 the son of Kareah, and all the capt.
43. 3 the son of Neriah setteth thee on against
43. 6 the son of Ahikam, the son of Shaphan, and
43. 6 the prophet, and Baruch the son of Neriah
45. 1 prophet spake unto Baruch the son of N.
45. 1 in the fourth year of Jehoiakim the son
46. 2 in the fourth year of Jehoiakim the son
48. 46 for thy sons are taken captives, and thy
49. 1 Hath Israel no sons? hath he no heir?
49. 18 neither shall a son of man dwell in it
49. 33 no man abide there, nor (any) son of man
50. 40 neither shall any son of man dwell therein
51. 43 neither doth (any) son of man pass the.
51. 59 Seraiah the son of Neriah, the son of M.
52. 10 king of Babylon slew the sons of Zedekiah
Lam. 4. 2 precious sons of Zion, comparable to fine
Eze. 1. 3 Ezekiel the priest, the son of Buzi, in the
2. 1 Son of man, stand upon thy feet, and I
2. 3 Son of man, I send thee to the children of
2. 6 thou, son of man, be not afraid of them
2. 8 But thou, son of man, hear what I say un.
3. 1 Son of man, eat that thou findest; eat this
3. 3 Son of man, cause thy belly to eat, and
3. 4 Son of man, go, get thee unto the house
3. 10 Son of man, all my words that I shall sp.
3. 17 Son of man, I have made thee a watchman
3. 25 But thou, O son of man, behold, they sh.
4. 1 Thou also, son of man, take thee a tile
4. 16 Son of man, behold, I will break the staff
5. 1 thou, son of man, take thee a sharp knife
5. 10 Therefore the fathers shall eat the sons
5. 10 sons shall eat their fathers; and I will
6. 2 Son of man, set thy face toward the mo.
7. 2 son of man, thus saith the Lord GOD unto
8. 5 Son of man, lift up thine eyes now the way
8. 6 Son of man, seest thou what they do? (ev.)
8. 8 Son of man, dig now in the wall: and when
8. 11 stood Jaazaniah the son of Shaphan, with
8. 12 Son of man, hast thou seen what the an.
8. 15, 17 said..Hast thou seen (this), O son of
11. 1 among whom I saw Jaazaniah the son of
11. 1 Pelatiah the son of Benaiah, princes of
11. 2 Son of man, these (are) the men that dev
11. 4 prophesy against them, prophesy, O son
11. 13 that Pelatiah the son of Benaiah died
11. 15 Son of man, thy brethren, (even) thy bre.
12. 2 Son of man, thou dwellest in the midst of
12. 3 son of man, prepare thee stuff for remov.
12. 9 Son of man, hath not the house of Israel
12. 18 Son of man, eat thy bread with quaking
12. 22 Son of man, what (is) that proverb (that)
12. 27 Son of man behold, (they of) the house
13. 2 Son of man, prophesy against the proph.
13. 17 son of man set thy face against the dau.
14. 3 Son of man, these men have set up their
14. 13 Son of man when the land sinneth agai.
14. 16, 18 they shall deliver neither sons nor da.
14. 20 they shall deliver neither son nor daugh.
14. 22 that shall be brought forth, (both) sons
15. 2 Son of man, What is the vine tree more
16. 2 Son of man cause Jerusalem to know her
16. 20 thou hast taken thy sons and thy daugh.
17. 2 Son of man, put forth a riddle, and speak
18. 4 so also the soul of the son is mine: the soul
18. 10 If he beget a son (that is) a robber, a sh.
18. 14 (if) he beget a son, that seeth all his fat.
18. 19 doth not the son bear the iniquity of the
18. 19 the son hath done that which is lawful and
18. 20 The son shall not bear the iniquity of the
18. 20 the father bear the iniquity of the son
20. 3 Son of man, speak unto the elders of Isr
20. 4 Wilt thou judge them, son of man? wilt
20. 27 son of man, speak unto the house of Isr.
20. 31 when ye make your sons to pass through
20. 46 Son of man, set thy face toward the south
21. 2 Son of man, set thy face toward Jerusal.
21. 6 Sigh therefore, thou son of man, with the
21. 9 Son of man, prophesy, and say, Thus saith
21. 10 it contemneth the rod of my son, (as) ev.
21. 12 Cry and howl, son of man; for it shall be
21. 14 son of man, prophesy, and smite (thine)
21. 19 son of man, appoint thee two ways, that
21. 28 son of man, prophesy, and say, Thus saith
22. 2 son of man, wilt thou judge, wilt thou ju.
22. 18 Son of man, the house of Israel is to me
22. 24 Son of man, say unto her, Thou (art) the

Eze. 23. 2 Son of man, there were two women, the
23. 4 they were mine, and they bare sons and
23. 10 they took her sons and her daughters, and
23. 25 they shall take thy sons and thy daught.
23. 36 Son of man, wilt thou judge Aholah and
23. 37 have also caused their sons, whom they
23. 47 they shall slay their sons and their daug.
24. 2 Son of man, Write thee the name of the
24. 16 Son of man, behold, I take away from th.
24. 21 your sons and your daughters whom ye
24. 25 son of man, (shall it) not (be), in the day
24. 25 whereupon they set their minds, their sons
25. 2 Son of man, set thy face against the Am.
26. 2 Son of man, because that Tyrus hath said
27. 2 son of man, take up a lamentation for T.
28. 2 Son of man, say unto the prince of Tyrus
28. 12 Son of man, take up a lamentation upon
28. 21 Son of man, set thy face against Zidon, and
29. 2 Son of man, set thy face against Pharaoh
29. 18 Son of man, Nebuchadrezzar king of Bab.
30. 2 Son of man, prophesy and say, Thus saith
30. 21 Son of man, I have broken the arm of P.
31. 2 Son of man, speak unto Pharaoh king of
32. 2 Son of man, take up a lamentation for P.
32. 18 Son of man, wail for the multitude of Eg.
33. 2 Son of man, speak to the children of thy
33. 7 son of man, I have set thee a watchman
33. 10 son of man, speak unto the house of Isr.
33. 12 son of man, say unto the children of thy
33. 24 Son of man, they that inhabit those was.
33. 30 son of man, the children of thy people st.
34. 2 Son of man, prophesy against the sheph.
35. 2 Son of man, set thy face againt mount S.
36. 1 son of man, prophesy unto the mountains
36. 17 Son of man, when the house of Israel dw.
37. 3 he said unto me, Son of man, can these
37. 9 prophesy, son of man, and say to the wind
37. 11 Son of man, these bones are the whole ho.
37. 16 son of man, take thee one stick, and write
38. 2 Son of man, set thy face against Gog, the
38. 14 son of man, prophesy and say unto Gog
39. 1 son of man, prophesy against Gog, and
39. 17 thou son of man, thus saith the Lord GOD
40. 4 Son of man, behold with thine eyes, and
40. 46 these (are) the sons of Zadok among the
43. 7 Son of man, the place of my throne, and
43. 10 son of man, show the house to the house
43. 18 he said unto me, Son of man, thus saith
44. 5 Son of man, mark well, and behold with
44. 15 the sons of Zadok, that kept the charge
44. 25 for father, or for mother, or for son, or for
46. 16 the prince give a gift unto any of his sons
46. 16 the inheritance thereof shall be his son's
46. 17 his inheritance shall be his sons for them
46. 18 he shall give his sons inheritance out of his
47. 6 he said unto me, Son of man, hast thou se.
48. 11 the priests that are sanctified of the sons
Dan. 8. 17 he said unto me, Understand, O son of man
9. 1 In the first year of Darius the son of Ahas.
10. 16 (one) like the similitude of the sons of men
11. 10 his sons shall be stirred up, and shall as.
Hos. 1. 1 that came unto Hosea the son of Beeri
1. 1 in the days of Jeroboam the son of Joash
1. 3 which conceived, and bare him a son
1. 8 had weaned Lo-ruhamah, she..bare a son
1. 10 shall be said unto them, (Ye are) the sons
11. 1 I loved him, and called my son out of Eg.
13. 13 he (is) an unwise son; for he should not
Joel 1. 1 that came to Joel the son of Pethuel
1. 12 joy is withered away from the sons of men
2. 28 your sons and your daughters shall prop.
3. 8 I will sell your sons and your daughters
Amos 1. 1 in the days of Jeroboam the son of Joash
2. 11 I raised up of your sons for prophets, and
7. 14 no prophet, neither (was) I a prophet's son
7. 17 thy sons and thy daughters shall fall by the
Jon. 1. 1 came unto Jonah the son of Amittai
Mic. 5. 7 tarrieth not..nor waiteth for the sons of
6. 5 what Baalam the son of Beor answered him
7. 6 the son dishonoureth the father, the dau.
Zeph. 1. 1 Zephaniah the son of Cushi, the son of
1. 1 Gedaliah, the son of Amariah, the son of
1. 1 in the days of Josiah the son of Amon, ki.
Hag. 1. 1, 12, 14 Joshua the son of Josedech
1. 1, 12, 14 Zerubbabel the son of Shealtiel
2. 2 Speak now to Zerubbabel the son of She
2. 2 Joshua the son of Josedech, the high pri.
2. 4 be strong, O Joshua, son of Josedech, the
2. 23 O Zerubbabel, my servant, the son of Sh.
Zech. 1. 1, 7 Zechariah, the son of Barachiah, the son
6. 10 go into the house of Josiah the son of Z.
6. 11 Joshua the son of Josedech, the high pri.
6. 14 to Jedaiah, and to Hen the son of Zepha.
9. 13 raised up thy sons, O Zion, against thy sons
Mal. 1. 6 A son honoureth (his) father, and a serva.
3. 3 he shall purify the sons of Levi, and pur.
3. 6 therefore ye sons of Jacob are not consu.
3. 17 as a man spareth his own son that serveth

2. *A son, offspring,* בֵּן *ben.*
Ezra 6. 10 for the life of the king, and of his sons
7. 23 against the realm of the king and his sons
Dan. 5. 21 he was driven from the sons of men; and

3. *A son, offspring,* בַּר *bar.*
Psa. 2. 12 Kiss the Son, lest he be angry, and ye pe.
Prov. 31. 2 What, my son? and what, the son of my
31. 2 and what, the son of my vows

4. *A son, offspring,* בַּר *bar.*
Ezra 5. 1 Zechariah the son of Iddo, prophesied unto
5. 2 the son of Shealtiel, and Jeshua the son
6. 14 the prophet and Zechariah the son of Id.
Dan. 3. 25 the form of the fourth is like the Son of
5. 22 thou his son, O Belshazzar, hast not hum.
7. 13 (one) like the Son of man came with the

5. *Child, lad, produce,* יֶלֶד *yeled.*
Gen. 32. 22 two women servants, and his eleven sons
Ruth 1. 5 was left of her two sons and her husband
2 Ki. 4. 1 is come to take unto him my two sons to

6. *Child, lad, produce,* יָלִיד *yalid.*
2 Sa. 21. 16, 18 which (was) of the sons of the giant

7. *Continuator,* מָנוֹן *manon.*
Prov 29. 21 shall have him become (his) son at the le.

8. *Continuator, posterity,* נִין *nin.*
Gen. 21. 23 not deal falsely with me, nor with my son
Job 18. 19 He shall neither have son nor nephew am.
Isa. 14. 22 the name, and remnant, and son, and ne.

9. *Child, boy, servant,* παῖς *pais.*
John 4. 51 met him, and told (him), saying, Thy son
Acts 3. 13 God of Abraham..hath glorified his Son
3. 26 having raised up his Son Jesus, sent him

10. *Child, descendant,* τέκνον *teknon.*
Matt. 9. 2 said unto the sick of the palsy, Son, be of
21. 28 man had two sons; and he..said, Son, go
Mark 2. 5 said unto the sick of the palsy, Son, thy
13. 12 betray the brother..and the father the son
Luke 2. 48 mother said unto him, Son, why hast thou
15. 31 Son, thou art ever with me, and all that I
16. 25 Son, remember that thou in thy lifetime
John 1. 12 gave he power to become the sons of God
1 Co. 4. 14 not..to shame you, but, as my beloved s.
4. 17 Timotheus, who is my beloved son, and fa.
Phil. 2. 15 blameless and harmless, the sons of God
2. 22 as a son with the father, he hath served
1 Ti. 1. 2 Unto Timothy, (my) own son in the faith
1. 18 I commit unto thee, son Timothy, accord.
2 Ti. 1. 2 To Timothy, (my) dearly beloved son: G.
2. 1 Thou therefore, my son, be strong in the
Titus 1. 4 To Titus, (mine) own son after the common
Phil. 10 beseech thee for my son Onesimus, whom
1 Jo. 3. 1 that we should be called the sons of God
3. 2 Beloved, now are we the sons of God; and

11. *Son, descendant, offspring,* υἱός *huios.*
Matt. 1. 1 Jesus Christ, the son of David, the son of
1. 20 Joseph, thou son of David, fear not to take
1. 21 she shall bring forth a son, and thou shalt
1. 23 shall bring forth a son, and they shall call
1. 25 she had brought forth her first born son
2. 15 Out of Egypt have I called my son
3. 17 This is my beloved Son, in whom I am w.
4. 3 If thou be the Son of God, command that
4. 6 If thou be the Son of God, cast thyself do.
7. 9 what man is there of you, whom if his son
8. 20 Son of man hath not where to lay (his) he.
8. 29 What have we to do with thee..thou Son
9. 6 the Son of man hath power on earth to fo.
9. 27 saying, (Thou) son of David, have mercy
10. 23 Ye shall not have gone..till the Son of
10. 37 he that loveth son or daughter more than
11. 19 The Son of man came eating and drinking
11. 27 no man knoweth the Son, but the Father
11. 27 save the Son, and (he) to whomsoever the S.
12. 8 the Son of man is Lord even of the sab.
12. 23 and said, Is not this the son of David?
12. 32 whosoever speaketh a word against the Son
12. 40 so shall the Son of man be three days and
13. 37 He that soweth the good seed is the Son
13. 41 The Son of man shall send forth his angels
13. 55 Is not this the carpenter's son? is not his
14. 33 saying, Of a truth thou art the Son of God
15. 22 Have mercy on me, O Lord, (thou) son of
16. 13 Whom do men say that I the Son of man
16. 16 Thou art the Christ, the Son of the living
16. 27 the Son of man shall come in the glory of
16. 28 till they see the Son of man coming in his
17. 5 This is my beloved Son, in whom I am w.
17. 9 until the Son of man be risen again from
17. 12 Likewise shall also the Son of man suffer
17. 15 Lord, have mercy on my son: for he is lu.
17. 22 The Son of man shall be betrayed into the
18. 11 [the Son of man is come to save that wh.]
19. 28 when the Son of man shall sit in the thr.
20. 18 the Son of man shall be betrayed unto the
20. 20 mother of Zebedee's children with her s.
20. 21 Grant that these my two sons may sit, the
20. 28 the Son of man came not to be ministered
20. 30 Have mercy on us, O Lord, (thou) son of
20. 31 Have mercy on us, O Lord, (thou) son of
21. 9 cried, saying, Hosanna to the s. of David!
21. 15 and saying, Hosanna to the son of David
21. 37 son, saying, They will reverence my son
21. 38 when the husbandmen saw the son, they
22. 2 king, which made a marriage for his son
22. 42 whose son is he? They say..(The son) of
22. 45 If David..call him Lord, how is he his son?
23. 35 unto the blood of Zacharias son of Bara.
24. 27 so shall also the coming of the Son of man
24. 30 then shall appear the sign of the Son of
24. 30 they shall see the Son of man coming in
24. 37, 39 so shall also the coming of the Son of
24. 44 in such an hour as ye think not the Son
25. 13 [the day nor the hour wherein the Son of]
25. 31 When the Son of man shall come in his
26. 2 the Son of man is betrayed to be crucified
26. 24 The Son of man goeth as it is written of
26. 24 woe unto that man by whom the Son of
26. 37 he took with him Peter and the two sons
26. 45 the Son of man is betrayed into the hands
26. 63 whether thou be the Christ, the son of G.
Matt 26. 64 Hereafter shall ye see the Son of man si.
27. 40 If thou be the Son of God, come down fr.
27. 43 will have him: for he said, I am the Son
27. 54 saying, Truly this was the Son of God
28. 19 baptizing them in the name..of the Son, and
Mark 1. 1 the gospel of Jesus Christ, the Son of G.
1. 11 Thou art my beloved Son, in whom I am
2. 10 But that ye may know that the Son of man
2. 28 Therefore the Son of man is Lord also of
3. 11 cried, saying, Thou art the Son of God
3. 17 Boanerges, which is, The sons of thunder
3. 28 All sins shall be forgiven unto the sons of
5. 7 Jesus, (thou) Son of the most high God?
6. 3 Is not this the carpenter, the son of Mary
8. 31 that the Son of man must suffer many thin.
8. 38 of him also shall the Son of man be ash.
9. 7 saying, This is my beloved Son: hear him
9. 9 till the Son of man were risen from the de.
9. 12 how it is written of the Son of man, that
9. 17 have brought unto thee my son, which hath
9. 31 Son of man is delivered into the hands of
10. 33 Son of man shall be delivered unto the ch.
10. 35 James and John, the sons of Zebedee, co.
10. 45 For even the Son of man came not to be
10. 46 blind Bartimeus, the son of Timeus, sat
10. 47 Jesus, (thou) son of David, have mercy on
10. 48 (Thou) son of David, have mercy on me
12. 6 Having yet therefore one son, his well be.
12. 6 sent..saying, They will reverence my son
12. 35 How say the scribes that Christ is the son
12. 37 whence is he (then) his son? And the co.
13. 26 then shall they see the Son of man comi.
13. 32 knoweth no man..neither the Son, but the
14. 21 Son of man indeed goeth, as it is written
14. 21 woe to that man by whom the Son of man
14. 41 Son of man is betrayed into the hands of
14. 61 Art thou the Christ, the Son of the blessed?
14. 62 ye shall see the Son of man sitting on the
15. 39 he said, Truly this man was the Son of G.
Luke 1. 13 Elisabeth shall bear thee a son, and thou.
1. 31 bring forth a son, and shalt call his name
1. 32 shall be called the Son of the Highest: and
1. 35 born of thee shall be called the Son of G.
1. 36 she hath also conceived a son in her old
1. 57 be delivered; and she brought forth a son
2. 7 she brought forth her first born son, and
3. 2 word of God came unto John the son of
3. 22 Thou art my beloved Son; in thee I am we.
3. 23 the son of Joseph, which was (the son) of
4. 3 If thou be the Son of God, command this
4. 9 If thou be the Son of God, cast thyself
4. 22 And they said, Is not this Joseph's son?
4. 41 Thou art Christ, the Son of God. And he
5. 10 James and John, the sons of Zebedee, wh.
5. 24 But that ye may know that the Son of man
6. 5 That the Son of man is Lord also of the sa.
6. 22 cast out your name as evil, for the Son of
7. 12 dead man carried out, the only son of his
7. 34 The Son of man is come eating and drink.
8. 28 Jesus, (thou) Son of God most high? I be.
9. 22 Son of man, must suffer many things, and
9. 26 of him shall the Son of man be ashamed
9. 35 saying, This is my beloved Son: hear him
9. 38 look upon my son; for he is mine only ch.
9. 41 Jesus answering said..Bring thy son hit.
9. 44 for the Son of man shall be delivered into
9. 56 [For the Son of man is not come to destroy]
9. 58 Son of man hath not where to lay (his) he.
10. 6 if the son of peace be there, your peace
10. 22 no man knoweth who the Son is, but the
10. 22 but the Son, and (he) to whom the Son wi.
11. 11 If a son shall ask bread of any of you that
11. 19 by whom do your sons cast (them) out? th.
11. 30 so shall also the Son of man be to this ge.
12. 8 him shall the Son of man also confess be.
12. 10 shall speak a word against the Son of man
12. 40 the Son of man cometh at an hour when
12. 53 be divided against the son, and the son
15. 11 And he said, A certain man had two sons
15. 13 younger son gathered all together, and
15. 19, 21 no more worthy to be called thy son
15. 21 the son said unto him, Father, I have si.
15. 24 this my son was dead, and is alive again
15. 25 his elder son was in the field: and as he
15. 30 as soon as this thy son was come, which
17. 22 to see one of the days of the Son of man
17. 24 so shall also the Son of man be in his day
17. 26 so shall it be also in the days of the Son
17. 30 in the day when the Son of man is revealed
18. 8 when the Son of man cometh, shall he find
18. 31 all things..concerning the Son of man sh.
18. 38, 39 (thou) son of David, have mercy on me
19. 9 forsomuch as he also is a son of Abraham
19. 10 the Son of man is come to seek and to sa.
20. 13 I will send my beloved son: it may be
20. 41 How say they that Christ is David's son?
20. 44 calleth him Lord, how is he then his son?
21. 27 then shall they see the Son of man coming
21. 36 worthy..to stand before the Son of man
22. 22 the Son of man goeth, as it was determined
22. 48 betrayest thou the Son of man with a kiss
22. 69 Hereafter shall the Son of man sit on the
22. 70 Art thou then the Son of God? And he said
24. 7 The Son of man must be delivered into the
John 1. 18 the only begotten [Son], which is in the b.
1. 34 and bare record that this is the Son of God
1. 42 he said, Thou art Simon the son of Jona.
1. 45 Jesus of Nazareth the son of Joseph
1. 49 thou art the Son of God; thou art the ki.
1. 51 ascending and descending upon the Son
3. 13 (even) the Son of man which is in heaven
3. 14 even so must the Son of man be lifted up

John 3. 16 he gave his only begotten Son, that who.
3. 17 God sent not his Son into the world to co.
3. 18 in the name of the only begotten Son of
3. 35 The Father loveth the Son, and hath giv.
3. 36 He that believeth on the Son hath everl.
3. 36 he that believeth not the Son shall not see
4. 5 ground that Jacob gave to his son Joseph
4. 46 a certain nobleman, whose son was sick
4. 47 that he would come down, and heal his s.
4. 50 Jesus saith unto him, Go thy way; thy s.
4. 53 same hour..Jesus said unto him, Thy son
5. 19 The Son can do nothing of himself, but
5. 19 what..he doeth, these also doeth the Son
5. 20 the Father loveth the Son, and showeth
5. 21 even so the Son quickeneth whom he will
5. 22 committed all judgment unto the Son
5. 23 all (men) should honour the Son, even as
5. 23 He that honoureth not the Son honoureth
5. 25 the dead shall hear the voice of the Son of
5. 26 so hath he given to the Son to have life in
5. 27 judgment also, because he is the Son of
6. 27 which the Son of man shall give unto you
6. 40 every one which seeth the Son, and beli.
6. 42 Is not this Jesus, the son of Joseph, who.
6. 53 Except ye eat the flesh of the Son of man
6. 62 if ye shall see the Son of man ascend up
6. 69 [thou art that Christ, the Son of the living]
8. 28 When ye have lifted up the Son of man
8. 35 servant abideth not..(but) the Son abid.
8. 36 If the Son therefore shall make you free
9. 19 Is this your son, who ye say was born bli.
9. 20 We know that this is our son, and that he
9. 35 Dost thou believe on the Son of God?
10. 36 because I said, I am the Son of God
11. 4 that the Son of God might be glorified th.
11. 27 thou art the Christ, the Son of God, whi.
12. 23 The hour is come, that the Son of man sh.
12. 34 The Son of man..who is this Son of man?
13. 31 Now is the Son of man glorified, and God
14. 13 that the Father may be glorified in the Son
17. 1 glorify thy Son, that thy Son also may gl.
17. 12 none of them is lost, but the son of perd.
19. 7 because he made himself the Son of God
19. 26 he saith unto his mother..behold thy son
20. 31 that Jesus is the Christ, the Son of God
Acts 2. 17 your sons and your daughters shall prop.
4. 36 which is, being interpreted, The son of co.
7. 16 bought for a sum of money of the sons of
7. 21 took..and nourished him for her own son
7. 29 land of Madian, where he begat two sons
7. 56 the Son of man standing on the right hand
8. 37 [I believe that Jesus Christ is the Son of]
9. 20 preached Christ..that he is the Son of G.
13. 21 God gave unto them Saul the son of Cis, a
13. 33 Thou art my Son, this day have I begotten
16. 1 Timotheus, the son of a certain woman
19. 14 there were seven sons of (one) Sceva, a J.
23. 6 I am a Pharisee, the son of a Pharisee
23. 16 Paul's sister's son heard of their lying in
Rom. 1. 3 his son Jesus Christ our Lord, which was
1. 4 And declared (to be) the Son of God with
1. 9 whom I serve..in the gospel of his Son
5. 10 reconciled to God by the death of his Son
8. 3 God, sending his own Son in the likeness of
8. 14 by the spirit of God, they are the sons of
8. 19 waiteth for the manifestation of the sons
8. 29 (to be) conformed to the image of his Son
8. 32 He that spared not his own Son, but del.
9. 9 At this time..and Sara shall have a son
1 Co. 1. 9 called unto the fellowship of his Son Jesus
15. 28 then shall the Son also himself be subject
2 Co. 1. 19 the Son of God, Jesus Christ, who was pr.
6. 18 ye shall be my sons and daughters, saith
Gal. 1. 16 To reveal his Son in me, that I might pr.
2. 20 [I live by the faith of the Son of God, who]
4. 4 God sent forth his Son, made of a woman
4. 6 And because ye are sons, God hath sent
4. 6 the spirit of his Son into your hearts, cry.
4. 7 a servant, but a son; and if a son, then an
4. 22 it is written, that Abraham had two sons
4. 30 the bondwoman and her son: for the son
4. 30 bondwoman shall not be heir with the son
Eph. 3. 5 was not made known unto the sons of men
4. 13 and of the knowledge of the Son of God
Col. 1. 13 translated..into the kingdom of his..Son
1 Th. 1. 10 to wait for his Son from heaven, whom he
2 Th. 2. 3 that man of sin be revealed, the son of
Heb. 1. 2 spoken unto us by (his) Son, whom he hath
1. 5 Thou art my Son, this day have I begott.
1. 5 a Father, and he shall be to me a Son
1. 8 unto the Son (he saith), Thy throne, O God
2. 6 or the Son of man, that thou visitest him
2. 10 in bringing many sons unto glory, to ma.
3. 6 But Christ as a Son over his own house
4. 14 a great High Priest..Jesus the son of God
5. 5 Thou art my Son, today have I begotten
5. 8 Though he were a Son, yet learned he ob.
6. 6 they crucify to themselves the Son of God
7. 3 made like unto the Son of God; abideth
7. 5 they that are of [the sons of] Levi, who re.
7. 28 (maketh) the Son, who is consecrated for
10. 29 who hath trodden under foot the Son of
11. 21 By faith Jacob..blessed both the sons of
11. 24 refused to be called the son of Pharaoh's
12. 5 My son, despise not thou the chastening
12. 6 and scourgeth every son whom he receiv.
12. 7 with you as with sons; for what son is he
12. 8 then are ye bastards, and not sons
Jas. 2. 21 when he had offered Isaac his son upon
1 Pe. 5. 13 saluteth you; and (so doth) Marcus my s.
2 Pe. 1. 17 This is my beloved Son, in whom I am
1 Jo. 1. 3 with the Father, and with his Son Jesus
1 Jo. 1. 7 the blood of Jesus Christ his Son cleans.
2. 22 that denieth the Father and the Son
2. 23 Whosoever denieth the Son, the same ha.
2. 24 ye also shall continue in the Son, and in
3. 8 the Son of God was manifested, that he
3. 23 believe on the name of his Son Jesus Ch.
4. 9 God sent his only begotten Son into the
4. 10 sent his Son (to be) the propitiation for
4. 14 the Father sent the Son (to be) the Savio.
4. 15 shall confess that Jesus is the Son of God
5. 5 he that believeth that Jesus is the Son of
5. 9 of God which he hath testified of his S.
5. 10 He that believeth on the Son of God hath
5. 10 he believeth not the record..of his Son
5. 11 eternal life, and this life is in his Son
5. 12 He that hath the Son hath life; (and)
5. 12 he that hath not the Son of God hath not
5. [13,] 13 believe on the name of the Son of G.
5. 20 we know that the Son of God is come, and
5. 20 in him that is true, (even) in his Son Jes.
2 John 3 from the Lord Jesus Christ, the Son of the
9 he hath both the Father and the Son
Rev. 1. 13 (one) like unto the Son of man, clothed
2. 18 These things saith the Son of God, who
14. 14 (one) sat like unto the Son of man, having
21. 7 will be his God, and he shall be my son

SON, (in law, to be) —

1. *Son in law, bridegroom, husband,* חָתָן *chathan.*
Gen. 19. 12 Hast thou here any besides? son in law
19. 14 spake unto his sons in law, which married
19. 14 as one that mocked unto his sons in law
Judg 15. 6 Samson, the son in law of the Timnite
19. 5 damsel's father said unto his son in law
1 Sa. 18. 18 that I should be son in law to the king
22. 14 as David, which (is) the king's son in law
2 Ki. 8. 27 he (was) the son in law of the house of A.
Neh. 6. 18 he (was) the son in law of Shechaniah the
13. 28 (was) son in law to Sanballat the Horon.

2. *To be son in law,* חָתַן *chathan,* 7.
1 Sa. 18. 21 Thou shalt this day be my son in law in
18. 22 now therefore be the king's son in law
18. 23 (a) light (thing) to be a king's son in law
18. 26 pleased David..to be the king's son in law
18. 27 that he might be the king's son in law

SON of, to be the —

To be born, begotten, יָלַד *yalad,* 2.
1 Ch. 20. 6 and he also was the son of the giant

SON, only —

Only, single, יָחִיד *yachid.*
Gen. 22. 2 thine only (son) Isaac, whom thou lovest
Jer. 6. 26 make thee mourning, (as for) an only son
Zech 12. 10 as one mourneth for (his) only (son), and

SON'S son —

Son's son, successor, sprout, progeny, נֶכֶד *neked.*
Gen. 21. 23 wilt not deal falsely..with my son's son

SONG —

1. *A song of praise,* זָמִיר *zemir.*
Job 35. 10 God my maker, who giveth songs in the
Psa. 119. 54 Thy statutes have been my songs in the
Isa. 24. 16 we heard songs, (even) glory to the righ.

2. *A song of praise,* זִמְרָת *zimrath.*
Exod 15. 2 The LORD (is) my strength and song, and

3. *What is lifted up, burden,* מַשָּׂא *massa.*
1 Ch. 15. 22 (was) for song: he instructed about the so.
15. 27 the master of the song with the singers

4. *Song (accompanied by an instrument),* נְגִינָה *neginah.*
Job 30. 9 now am I their song; yea, I am their by.
Psa. 69. 12 and I (was) the song of the drunkards
77. 6 I call to remembrance my song in the ni.
Isa. 38. 20 we will sing my songs to the stringed ins.
Lam. 3. 14 a derision to all my people, (and) their so.

5. *A loud cry or song,* רֹן *ron.*
Psa. 32. 7 thou shalt compass me about with songs of

6. *A song,* שִׁיר *shir.*
Gen. 31. 27 with mirth, and with songs, with tabret
Judg. 5. 12 utter a song: arise, Barak, and lead thy ca.
1 Ki. 4. 32 and his songs were a thousand and five
1 Ch. 6. 31 whom David set over the service of song
25. 6 under the hands of their father for song
25. 7 that were instructed in the songs of the
2 Ch. 29. 27 the song of the LORD began (also) with the
Neh. 12. 46 songs of praise and thanksgiving unto G.
Psa. 28. 7 rejoiceth; and with my song will I praise
30. *title.* A Psalm (and) Song (at) the dedication
33. 3 Sing unto him a new song; play skilfully
40. 3 he hath put a new song in my mouth, (ev.)
42. 8 and in the night his song (shall be) with
45. 46. *title.* To the chief Musician..A Song
48. *title.* A Song (and) Psalm for the sons of
65. *title.* To the chief Musician, A Psalm..Song
66. *title.* To the chief Musician, A Song (or)
67. 75. 76. *title.* To the chief Musician..A..Song
68. *title.* To the chief Musician, A Psalm (or) S.
69. 30 I will praise the name of God with a song
83. *title.* A Song (or) Psalm of Asaph
87. 88. *title.* A Psalm (or) Song for the sons of K.
92. *title.* A Psalm (or) Song for the sabbath day
96. 1 O sing unto the LORD a new song; sing un.
98. 1 O sing unto the LORD a new song; for he
108. *title.* A Song (or) Psalm of David
120. 121 123. 125. 126. 128. 129. 130. 132. 134. *t.* A song
122. 124. 131. 133. *title.* A Song of degrees of David
137. 3 (saying), Sing us (one) of the songs of Zion
137. 4 How shall we sing the LORD'S song in a
Psa. 144. 9 I will sing a new song unto thee, O God
149. 1 Sing unto the LORD a new song, (and) his
Prov 25. 20 so (is) he that singeth songs to an heavy
Eccl. 7. 5 than for a man to hear the song of fools
Song 1. 1 The Song of songs, which (is) Solomon's
Isa. 23. 16 sing many songs, that thou mayest be re
24. 9 They shall not drink wine with a song
26. 1 In that day shall this song be sung in the
30. 29 Ye shall have a song, as in the night, (w.)
42. 10 Sing unto the LORD a new song, (and) his
Eze. 26. 13 I will cause the noise of thy songs to cease
33. 32 as a very lovely song of one that hath a pl.
Amos 5. 23 Take thou away..the noise of thy songs
8. 10 I will turn..your songs into lamentation

7. *A song,* שִׁירָה *shirah.*
Exod 15. 1 Then sang Moses..this song unto the LORD
Num 21. 17 Israel sang this song, Spring up, O well
Deut 31. 19 write ye this song for you, and teach it the
31. 19 that this song may be a witness for me
31. 21 this song shall testify against them as a
31. 22 Moses therefore wrote this song the same
31. 30 Moses spake..the words of this song, un.
32. 44 spake all the words of this song in the ears
2 Sa. 22. 1 David spake..the words of this song in
Psa. 18. *title.* unto the LORD the words of this song
Isa. 5. 1 a song of my beloved touching his viney.
Amos 8. 3 the songs of the temple shall be howlings

8. *Word or matter of a song,* דְּבַר שִׁיר *debar shir.*
Psa. 137. 3 For there they..required of us a song

9. *An ode,* ᾠδή *ōdē.*
Eph. 5. 19 in psalms and hymns and spiritual songs
Col. 3. 16 in psalms and hymns and spiritual songs
Rev. 5. 9 they sung a new song, saying, Thou art
14. 3 they sung as it were a new song before the
14. 3 no man could learn that song but the hu.
15. 3 they sing the song of Moses..and the song

SONS, adoption of —

The placing as a son, υἱοθεσία *huiothesia.*
Gal. 4. 5 we might receive the adoption of sons

SOON, sooner —

1. *Hastily, swiftly,* חִישׁ *chish.*
Psa. 90. 10 for it is soon cut off, and we fly away

2. *Hastily,* מַהֵר *maher.*
Deut. 4. 26 ye shall soon utterly perish from off the

3. *Haste,* מְהֵרָה *meherah.*
Psa. 37. 2 they shall soon be cut down like the grass

4. *A little,* מְעַט *meat.*
Job 32. 22 (in so doing) my Maker would soon take
Psa. 81. 14 I should soon have subdued their enemies

5. *Short,* קָצֵר *qatser.*
Prov. 14. 17 (He that is) soon angry dealeth foolishly

6. *To hasten,* מָהַר *mahar,* 3.
Psa. 106. 13 They soon forgot his works; they waited

7. *Along with the thing,* παραχρῆμα *parachrēma.*
Matt 21. 20 How soon is the fig tree withered away

8. *Quickly, speedily,* ταχέως *tacheōs.*
Gal. 1. 6 I marvel that ye are so soon removed from
2 Th. 2. 2 That ye be not soon shaken in mind, or be

9. *More swiftly, speedily,* τάχιον *tachion.*
Heb. 13. 19 that I may be restored to you the sooner

SOON, to be so —

To haste, מָהַר *mahar,* 3.
Exod 2. 18 How (is it that) ye are come so soon to day

SOON as, as —

1. *Appearance,* מַרְאֶה *mareh.*
Eze. 23. 16 as soon as she saw them with her eyes, she

2. *To become,* γίνομαι *ginomai.*
Acts 12. 18 as soon as it was day, there was no small
[*See* As, as soon as.]

SOOTHSAYER, soothsaying, (by) —

1. *To cut off or down, decree,* גְּזַר *gezar.*
Dan. 2. 27 the astrologers, the magicians, the sooth.
4. 7 Then came..the Chaldeans, and the soot.
5. 7 to bring..the Chaldeans, and the sooths.
5. 11 astrologers, Chaldeans, (and) soothsayers

2. *To observe the clouds,* עָנַן *anan,* 3a.
Isa. 2. 6 (and) are soothsayers like the Philistines
Mic. 5. 12 and thou shalt have no (more) soothsayers

3. *To divine, use divination,* קָסַם *qasam.*
Josh. 13. 22 Balaam also the son of Beor, the soothsa.

4. *To divine, use divination,* μαντεύομαι *manteuomai.*
Acts 16. 16 brought her masters..gain by soothsaying

SO-PA'-TER, Σώπατρος.

A believer from Berea, who accompanied Paul from Greece to Asia on his way to Syria; perhaps the same as *Sosipater.*
Acts 20. 4 there accompanied him into Asia, S. of B.

SOP, SOPE or SOAP —

1. *Soap,* בֹּרִית *borith.*
Jer. 2. 22 though thou wash..and take thee much s.
Mal. 3. 2 like a refiner's fire, and like fuller's soap

2. *A morsel,* ψωμίον *psōmion.*
John 13. 26 He it is to whom I shall give a sop, when I
13. 26 when he had dipped the sop, he gave (it)
13. 27 And after the sop Satan entered into him
13. 30 He then having received the sop went im.

SO-PHE'-RETH, הַסֹּפֶרֶת *learning.*
A servant of Solomon whose descendants returned with Zerubbabel. B.C. 536.
Ezra 2. 55 the children of S., the children of Peruda
Neh. 7. 57 the children of S., the children of Perida

SORCERER, sorceress, (to use) sorcerics —
1. *A wizard, sorcerer,* כַּשָּׁף *kashshaph.*
Jer. 27. 9 nor to your enchanters, nor to your sorc.
2. *To use witchcraft or sorcery,* כָּשַׁף *kashaph,* 3.
Exod. 7. 11 also called the wise men and the sorcerers
Dan. 2. 2 the astrologers, and the sorcerers, and the
Mal. 3. 5 a swift witness against the sorcerers, and
3. *Witchcrafts, sorceries,* כְּשָׁפִים *keshaphim.*
Isa. 47. 9 for the multitude of thy sorceries, (and)
47. 12 with the multitude of thy sorceries, whe.
4. *To observe the clouds,* עָנַן *anan,* 3a.
Isa. 57. 3 draw near hither, ye sons of the sorceress
5. *Magic,* μαγεία *mageia.*
Acts 8. 11 he had bewitched them with sorceries
6. *To use magic,* μαγεύω *mageuō.*
Acts 8. 9 used sorcery, and bewitched the people of
7. *A magician,* μάγος *magos.*
Acts 13. 6 they found a certain sorcerer, a false pro.
13. 8 Elymas the sorcerer for so is his name by
8. *Enchantment with drugs,* φαρμακεία *pharmakeia.*
Rev. 9. 21 nor of their [sorceries], nor of their forni.
18. 23 by thy sorceries were all nations deceived
9. *An enchanter with drugs,* φαρμακεύς *pharmakeus.*
Rev. 21. 8 [sorcerers,] and idolaters, and all liars, sh.
10. *An enchanter with drugs,* φαρμακός *pharmakos.*
Rev. 22. 15 without (are) dogs, and sorcerers and wh.

SORE, (to be full of sores, go, make, wax) —
1. *Hand,* יָד *yad.*
Psa. 77. 2 my sore ran in the night, and ceased not
2. *A great weeping,* בְּכִי גָדוֹל *beki gadol.*
Judg. 21. 2 and lifted up their voices, and wept sore
2 Sa. 13. 36 king also and all his servants wept very s.
2 Ki. 20. 3 I beseech thee..And Hezekiah wept sore
Isa. 38. 3 good in thy sight: and Hezekiah wept sore
3. *To be sick,* חָלָה *chalah.*
Eccl. 5. 13 There is a sore evil (which) I have seen
5. 16 this also (is) a sore evil, (that) in all points
4. *To be strong,* חָזַק *chazaq.*
Gen. 41. 56 the famine waxed sore in the land of Eg.
41. 57 because that the famine was (so) sore in
2 Ki. 3. 26 saw that the battle was too sore for him
Jer. 52. 6 the famine was sore in the city, so that
5. *Strong,* חָזָק *chazaq.*
1 Sa. 14. 52 there was sore war against the Philistines
1 Ki. 17. 17 his sickness was so sore, that there was
18. 2 And (there was) a sore famine in Samaria
6. *Slaughter,* טֶבַח *tebach.*
Eze. 21. 10 It is sharpened to make a sore slaughter
7. *To be pained,* כָּאַב *kaab.*
Gen. 34. 25 on the third day, when they were sore
8. *To cause pain, mar,* כָּאַב *kaab,* 5.
Job 5. 18 he maketh sore, and bindeth up; he wou.
9. *To be heavy, weighty,* כָּבֵד *kabed.*
Judg. 20. 34 the battle was sore: but they knew not th.
1 Sa. 31. 3 the battle went sore against Saul, and the
1 Ch. 10. 3 the battle went sore against Saul, and the
10. *Heavy, weighty,* כָּבֵד *kabed.*
Gen. 43. 1 And the famine (was) sore in the land
47. 4 the famine (is) sore in the land of Canaan
47. 13 the famine (was) very sore, so that the
50. 10 mourned with a great and very sore lam.
11. *Cause of anger, provocation, sadness,* כַּעַס *kaas.*
1 Sa. 1. 6 her adversary also provoked her sore, for
12. *Might, exceedingly,* מְאֹד *meod.*
Gen. 19. 9 they pressed sore upon the man, (even)
20. 8 told all..and the men were sore afraid
Exod. 14. 10 they were sore afraid: and the children of
Num. 22. 3 Moab was sore afraid of the people, beca.
Josh. 9. 24 we were sore afraid of our lives because
Judg. 10. 9 to fight..so that Israel was sore distressed
15. 18 he was sore athirst, and called on the L.
1 Sa. 17. 24 all the men of Israel..were sore afraid
21. 12 was sore afraid of Achish the king of Ga.
28. 15 I am sore distressed; for the Philistines
28. 20 Saul fell straightway..and was sore afraid
28. 21 the woman..saw that he was sore troub.
31. 3 and he was sore wounded of the archers
31. 4 would not; for he was sore afraid. Ther.
1 Ki. 17. 17 his sickness was so sore, that there was
1 Ch. 10. 4 would not; for he was sore afraid. So S.
2 Ch. 35. 23 Have me away; for I am sore wounded
Neh. 13. 8 it grieved me sore: therefore I cast forth
Psa. 6. 3 My soul is also sore vexed: but thou, O L.
6. 10 mine enemies be ashamed and sore vexed
38. 8 I am feeble and sore broken: I have ro.
Isa. 64. 9 Be not wroth very sore, O LORD, neither
64. 12 hold thy peace, and afflict us very sore?
Jer. 50. 12 Your mother shall be sore confounded
13. *Trespass, transgression,* מַעַל *maal.*
2 Ch. 28. 19 and transgressed sore against the LORD
14. *Stroke, plague,* נֶגַע *nega.*
Lev. 13. 42 in the bald head..a white reddish sore
Lev. 13. 43 (if) the rising of the sore (be) white redd.
2 Ch. 6. 28 whatsoever sore, or whatsoever sickness
6. 29 every one shall know his own sore and his
Psa. 38. 11 my friends stand aloof from my sore, and
15. *A smiting, blow, stroke,* מַכָּה *makkah.*
Isa. 1. 6 wounds, and bruises, and putrifying sores
16. *To be powerful, grievous,* מָרַץ *marats,* 2.
Mic. 2. 10 destroy (you), even with a sore destruct.
17. *With displeasure,* קֶצֶף *qetseph.*
Zech. 1. 2 The LORD hath been sore displeased with
1. 15 I am very sore displeased with the heath.
18. *To be sharp, hard,* קָשָׁה *qashah.*
1 Sa. 5. 7 his hand is sore upon us, and upon Dagon
19. *Sharp. hard,* קָשֶׁה *qasheh.*
2 Sa. 2. 17 And there was a very sore battle that day
Isa. 27. 1 the LORD with his sore and great and st.
20. *Weeping,* בָּכָה.
Ezra 10. 1 for the people wept very sore
21. *Evil,* רַע *ra.*
Deut. 6. 22 showed signs and wonders, great and sore
28. 35 with a sore botch that cannot be healed
28. 59 sore sickness, and of long continuance
2 Ch. 21. 19 so he died of sore diseases. And his peo.
Job 2. 7 smote Job with sore boils from the sole of
Psa. 71. 20 which hast showed me great and sore tr.
Eccl. 1. 13 this sore travail hath God given to the so.
4. 8 This (is) also vanity, yea, it (is) a sore tr.
Eze. 14. 21 when I send my four sore judgments upon
22. *Great, much, many,* שַׂגִּיא *saggi.*
Dan. 6. 14 the king..was sore displeased with him.
23. *Fear, fright, trembling,* שַׂעַר *saar.*
Eze. 27. 35 their kings shall be sore afraid, they shall
24. *Sufficient, coming up to,* ἱκανός *hikanos.*
Acts 20. 37 they all wept sore, and fell on Paul's neck
25. *To be ulcerated,* ἑλκόομαι *helkoomai.*
Luke 16. 20 which was laid at his gate, full of sores
26. *An ulcer,* ἕλκος *helkos.*
Luke 16. 21 moreover..dogs came and licked his sores
Rev. 16. 2 there fell a noisome and grievous sore v. 11
27. *Great fear,* φόβον μέγαν *phobon megan,* Lu. 2. 9.
28. *Evilly, wickedly,* κακῶς *kakōs.*
Matt 17. 15 he is lunatic, and sore vexed: for oftti.
29. *Very, very much, exceedingly,* λίαν *lian.*
Mark 6. 51 they were [sore] amazed in themselves be.
30. *Much, many,* πολύς *polus.*
Mark 9. 26 (the spirit) cried, and rent him sore, and
31. *Vehemently,* σφόδρα *sphodra.*
Matt 17. 6 they fell on their face, and were sore af.
32. *Worse,* χείρων *cheirōn.*
Heb. 10. 29 Of how much sorer punishment, suppose
[*See also* Afraid, amazed, break, broken, displeased displeasure, go, grieved, lie, pained, press, troubled very].

SO'-REK, שׂוֹרֵק *vineyard.*
A valley (and stream) between Askelon and Gaza, not far from Zorah: the stream was part of the boundary line between *Dan* and *Simeon.*
Judg 16. 4 he loved a woman in the valley of S., wh.

SORROW —
1. *Wo,* אֲבוֹי *aboy.*
Prov 23. 29 Who hath woe? who hath sorrow? who
2. *Vanity, iniquity,* אָוֶן *aven.*
Psa. 90. 10 yet (is) their strength labour and sorrow
3. *Lamentation,* אֲנִיָּה *aniyyah.*
Isa. 29. 2 and there shall be heaviness and sorrow
4. *Grief,* דְּאָבָה *deabah.*
Job 41. 22 and sorrow is turned into joy before
5. *Grief,* דְּאָבוֹן *deabon.*
Deut 28. 65 and failing of eyes, and sorrow of mind
6. *Sorrow, fear,* דְּאָגָה *deagah.*
Jer. 49. 23 (there is) sorrow on the sea; it cannot be
7. *Pang, cord,* חֵבֶל, חֶבֶל *chebel.*
2 Sa. 22. 6 The sorrows of hell compassed me about
Job 21. 17 (God) distributeth sorrows in his anger
39. 3 They bow..they cast out their sorrows
Psa. 18. 4 The sorrows of death compassed me, and
18. 5 The sorrows of hell compassed me about
116. 3 The sorrows of death compassed me, and
Isa. 13. 8 pangs and sorrows shall take hold of them
Jer. 13. 21 shall not sorrows take thee, as a woman
49. 24 sorrows have taken her, as a woman in
Hos. 13. 13 The sorrows of a travailing woman shall
8. *Pain,* חִיל *chil.*
Exod 15. 14 sorrow shall take hold on the inhabitants
9. *Pain,* חִילָה *chilah.*
Job 6. 10 yea, I would harden myself in sorrow: let
10. *Affliction,* יָגוֹן *yagon.*
Gen. 42. 38 my grey hairs with sorrow to the grave
44. 31 the grey hairs of thy servant..with sorr.
Esth. 9. 22 was turned unto them from sorrow to joy
Psa. 13. 2 I take counsel in my soul, (having) sorrow
107. 39 through oppression, affliction, and sorrow
116. 3 hold upon me; I found trouble and sorr.
Isa. 35. 10 and sorrow and sighing shall flee away
51. 11 (and) sorrow and mourning shall flee aw.
Jer. 8. 18 (When) I would comfort myself against so.
20. 18 out of the womb to see labour and sorrow
31. 13 and make them rejoice from their sorrow
Eze. 23. 33 filled with drunkenness and sorrow, with
11. *Pain,* כְּאֵב *keeb.*
Psa. 39. 2 I held my peace..and my sorrow was st.
Isa. 17. 11 in the day of grief and of desperate sorr.
65. 14 ye shall cry for sorrow of heart, and shall
12. *Sadness,* כַּעַס *kaas.*
Eccl. 7. 3 Sorrow (is) better than laughter: for by
11. 10 Therefore remove sorrow from thy heart
13. *Sadness,* כַּעַשׂ *kaas.*
Job 17. 7 Mine eye also is dim by reason of sorrow
14. *Blinding,* מְגִנָּה *meginnah.*
Lam. 3. 65 Give them sorrow of heart, thy curse unto
15. *Pain,* מַכְאוֹב *makob.*
Exod. 3. 7 heard their cry..for I know their sorrow
Psa. 32. 10 Many sorrows (shall be) to the wicked: but
38. 17 and my sorrow (is) continually before me
Eccl. 1. 18 increaseth knowledge increaseth sorrow
2. 23 all his days (are) sorrows, and his travail
Isa. 53. 3 a man of sorrows, and acquainted with
53. 4 borne our griefs, and carried our sorrows
Jer. 30. 15 thy sorrow (is) incurable for the multitude
45. 3 the LORD hath added grief to my sorrow
Lam. 1. 12 if there be any sorrow like unto my sorrow
1. 18 hear, I pray you..and behold my sorrow
16. *Grief,* מַעֲצֵבָה *maatsebah.*
Isa. 50. 11 ye that kindle a fire..lie down in sorrow
17. *Labour,* עָמָל *amal.*
Job 3. 10 it shut not up..nor hid sorrow from mine
Psa. 55. 10 mischief also and sorrow (are) in the mi.
18. *Grief,* עֶצֶב *etseb.*
Gen. 3. 16 in sorrow thou shalt bring forth children
Psa. 127. 2 to sit up late, to eat the bread of sorrows
Prov. 10. 22 it maketh rich, and he addeth no sorrow
19. *Grievous thing,* עֹצֶב *otseb.*
1 Ch. 4. 9 saying, because I bare him with sorrow
Isa. 14. 3 LORD shall give thee rest from thy sorrow
20. *Grievous thing,* עִצָּבוֹן *itstsabon.*
Gen. 3. 16 I will greatly multiply thy sorrow and thy
3. 17 in sorrow shalt thou eat (of) it all the days
21. *Grievous thing,* עַצֶּבֶת *atstsebeth.*
Job 9. 28 I am afraid of all my sorrows, I know th.
Psa. 16. 4 Their sorrows shall be multiplied (that)
Prov. 10. 10 that winketh with the eye causeth sorrow
15. 13 by sorrow of the heart the spirit is broken
22. *Pain, pang,* צִיר *tsir.*
Dan. 10. 16 by the vision my sorrows are turned upon
23. *Strait, close,* צַר, צָר *tsar.*
Isa. 5. 30 behold darkness (and) sorrow, and the li.
24. *Evil, bad,* רַע *ra.*
Gen. 44. 29 bring down my grey hairs with sorrow to
25. *Evil, badness,* רֹעַ *roa.*
Neh. 2. 2 this (is) nothing (else) but sorrow of heart
26. *Affliction, sorrow,* תּוּגָה *tugah.*
Prov. 17. 21 that begetteth a fool (doeth it) to his sor.
27. *Grief, sorrow, affliction,* λύπη *lupē.*
Luke 22. 45 disciples, he found them sleeping for sor.
John 16. 6 because I have said these..sorrow hath fi.
16. 20 but your sorrow shall be turned into joy
16. 21 woman when she is in travail hath sorrow
16. 22 ye now therefore have sorrow: but I will
2 Co. 2. 3 I should have sorrow from them of whom
2. 7 be swallowed up with overmuch sorrow
7. 10 godly sorrow worketh repentance to salv.
7. 10 the sorrow of the world worketh death
Phil. 2. 27 lest I should have sorrow upon sorrow
28. *Pain, torture, grief, sorrow,* ὀδύνη *odunē.*
Rom. 9. 2 That I have..continual sorrow in my he.
1 Ti. 6. 10 and pierced themselves..with many sor.
29. *Sorrow, grief, mourning,* πένθος *penthos.*
Rev. 18. 7 so much torment and sorrow give her
18. 7 am no widow, and shall see no sorrow
21. 4 no more death, neither sorrow, nor crying
30. *Labour, pain, sorrow,* ὠδίν *ōdin.*
Matt 24. 8 All these (are) the beginning of sorrows
Mark 13. 8 These (are) the beginnings of sorrows

SORROW, to (cause, have) —
1. *To be grieved, pained,* דָּאַב *daab.*
Jer. 31. 12 and they shall not sorrow any more at
2. *To be sorrowful, afraid,* דָּאַג *daag.*
1 Sa. 10. 2 sorroweth for you, saying, What shall I
3. *To cause pain, sorrow,* דּוּב *dub,* 5.
Lev. 26. 16 consume the eyes, and cause sorrow of he.
4. *To be pained,* חִיל, חוּל *chul, chil.*
Jer. 51. 29 the land shall tremble and sorrow: for ev.
5. *To begin,* חָלַל *chalal,* 5.
Hos. 8. 10 they shall sorrow a little for the burden
6. *To be angry, sad,* כָּעַס *kaas.*
Eccl. 5. 17 (he hath) much sorrow and wrath with his
7. *To grieve, make sad,* λυπέω *lupeō.*
2 Co. 7. 9 but that ye sorrowed to repentance: for
7. 11 this self same thing, that ye sorrowed af.
1 Th. 4. 13 that ye sorrow not, even as others which

8. *To be pained*, ὀδυνάομαι *odunaomai*.
Luke 2. 48 father and I have sought thee sorrowing
Acts 20. 38 Sorrowing most of all for the words which

SORROWFUL, (exceeding, less, very) —
1. *To be grieved, pained*, דָּאַב *daab*.
Jer. 31. 25 and I have replenished every sorrowful
2. *Sickness*, דְּוַי *devai*.
Job 6. 7 The things..(are) as my sorrowful meat
3. *To be afflicted*, יָגָה *yagah*, 2.
Zeph. 3. 18 I will gather (them that are) sorrowful
4. *To be pained*, כָּאַב *kaab*.
Psa. 69. 29 But I (am) poor and sorrowful: let thy sa.
5. *Sharp, hard*, קָשֶׁה *qasheh*.
1 Sa. 1. 15 I (am) a woman of a sorrowful spirit: I
6. *Less (or not) sorrowful*, ἀλυπότερος *alupoteros*.
Phil. 2. 28 and that I may be the less sorrowful
7. *To grieve, make sad*, λυπέω *lupeō*.
Matt 19. 22 he went away sorrowful · for he had great
2 Co. 6. 10 As sorrowful, yet alway rejoicing; as po.

SORROWFUL, to be —
1. *To be pained*, חִיל, חוּל *chul, chil*.
Zech. 9. 5 Gaza also (shall see it), and be very sorr.
2. *To be pained*, כָּאַב *kaab*.
Prov 14. 13 Even in laughter the heart is sorrowful
3. *To grieve, make sad*, λυπέω *lupeō*.
Matt 26. 22 they were exceeding sorrowful, and began
26. 37 and began to be sorrowful and very heavy
Mark 14. 19 they began to be sorrowful, and to say un
John 16. 20 ye shall be sorrowful, but your sorrow sh.
4. *Very or exceeding sorrowful*, περίλυπος *perilupos*.
Matt 26. 38 My soul is exceeding sorrowful, even unto
Mark 14. 34 My soul is exceeding sorrowful unto death
Luke 18. 23 when he heard this, he was very sorrow
18. 24 when Jesus saw [that he was very sorrow]

SORRY, exceeding, (to be or make) —
1. *To be sorrowful, afraid*, דָּאַג *daag*.
Psa. 38. 18 declare mine iniquity; I will be sorry for
2. *To be sick*, חָלָה *chalah*.
1 Sa. 22. 8 none of you that is sorry for me, or sho.
3. *To nod, bemoan*, נוּד *nud*.
Isa. 51. 19 who shall be sorry for thee? desolation, and
4. *To be grieved*, עָצַב *atsab*, 2.
Neh. 8. 10 neither be ye sorry; for the joy of the L.
5. *To grieve, make sad*, λυπέω *lupeō*.
Matt 14. 9 king was sorry: nevertheless for the oa.
17. 23 And they were exceeding sorry
18. 31 they were very sorry, and came and told
2 Co. 2. 2 For if I make you sorry, who is he then
2. 2 but the same which is made sorry by me?
7. 8 For though I made you sorry with a let.
7. 8 that the same epistle hath made you so.
7. 9 I rejoice, not that ye were made sorry, but
7. 9 for ye were made sorry after a godly ma.
6. *Very or exceeding sorrowful*, περίλυπος *perilupos*
Mark 6. 26 king was exceeding sorry; (yet) for his oa.

SORT, godly, this, what, some, all —
1. *Circle, age*, גִּיל *gil*.
Dan. 1. 10 than the children which (are) of your so.
2. *Word, matter*, דָּבָר *dabar*.
Neh. 6. 4 sent unto me four times after this sort; and
3. *Perfection*, מִכְלוֹל *miklol*.
Eze. 38. 4 all of them clothed with all sorts (of ar.)
4. *Perfect things*, מַכְלֻלִים *maklulim*.
Eze. 27. 24 These (were) thy merchants in all sorts
5. *Wing*, כָּנָף *kanaph*.
Gen. 7. 14 after his kind, every bird of every sort
Eze. 39. 4 unto the ravenous birds of every sort, and
6. *Mistress*, שִׁדָּה *shiddah*.
Eccl. 2. 8 musical instruments, and that of all sorts
7. *Partly, in part*, ἀπὸ μέρους *apo merous*.
Rom 15. 15 more boldly unto you in some sort, as pu.
8. *Worthily*, ἀξίως *axiōs*.
3 John 6 bring forward..after a godly sort, thou
9. *Of these*, ἐκ τούτων *ek toutōn*.
2 Ti. 3. 6 For of this sort are they which creep into
10. *Of what kind or sort*, ὁποῖος *hopoios*.
1 Co. 3. 13 try every man's work of what sort it is
[*See also* After this, baser, flies, garment, one, poorest, this, what.]

SO-SI-PA'-TER, Σωσίπατρος.
A kinsman of Paul, one whose salutation was sent to the church at Rome.
Rom 16. 21 Jason, and S., my kinsmen, salute you

SOS-THE'-NES, Σωσθένης.
1. The chief ruler of the synagogue at Corinth, who was beaten by the Hellenistic Greeks because of the tumult of the Jews when they brought Paul before Gallio in his second missionary journey into Greece.
Acts 18. 17 the Greeks took S., the chief ruler of the
2. A believer whom Paul unites with himself in addressing the Corinthian church.
1 Co. 1. 1 Paul, called (to be) an apostle..and S. (our)

SO'-TAI, סֹטַי, סוֹטַי *Jah is turning aside*.
One of Solomon's servants whose descendants returned with Zerubbabel. B.C. 536.
Ezra 2. 55 the children of S., the children of Sophe.
Neh. 7. 57 the children of S., the children of Sophe.

SOTTISH —
Thick headed, סָכָל *sakal*.
Jer. 4. 22 they (are) sottish children, and they have

SOUGHT (for, out or up), to be —
1. *To be sought, enquired after*, בָּעָה *baah*, 2.
Obad. 6. (how) are his hidden things sought up!
2. *To be sought, searched*, בָּקַשׁ *baqash*, 4.
Jer. 50. 20 the iniquity of Israel shall be sought for
Eze. 26. 21 though thou be sought for, yet shalt thou
3. *To seek, enquire, require*, דָּרַשׁ *darash*.
Psa 111. 2 sought out of all them that have pleasure
Isa. 62. 12 be called, Sought out, A city not forsaken
4. *To be sought, enquired after*, דָּרַשׁ *darash*, 2.
1 Ch. 26. 31 were sought for, and there were found am.
Isa. 65. 1 I am sought of (them that) asked not (for

SOUL —
1. *Willing, liberal or noble one*, נְדִיבָה *nedibah*.
Job 30. 15 they pursue my soul as the wind: and my
2. *Animal soul*, נֶפֶשׁ *nephesh*.
Gen. 2. 7 breathed..and man became a living soul
12. 5 the souls that they had gotten in Haran
12. 13 and my soul shall live because of thee
17. 14 that soul shall be cut off from his people
19. 20 (is) it not a little one? and my soul shall
27. 4 that my soul may bless thee before I die
27. 19 sit and eat of my venison, that thy soul
27. 25 eat of my son's venison, that my soul may
27. 31 eat of his son's venison, that thy soul may
34. 3 soul clave unto Dinah the daughter of J.
34. 8 soul of my son Shechem longeth for your
35. 18 came to pass, as her soul was in departing
42. 21 in that we saw the anguish of his soul, wh.
46. 15 all the souls of his sons and his daughters
46. 18 these she bare unto Jacob, (even) sixteen s.
46. 22 born to Jacob: all the souls (were) fourte.
46. 25 bare these unto Jacob: all the souls (were)
46. 26 All the souls that came..all the souls (w.)
46. 27 two souls: all the souls of the house of J.
49. 6 O my soul, come not thou into their secret
Exod. 1. 5 all the souls..were seventy souls: for Jo.
12. 4 according to the number of the souls: ev.
12. 15, 19 that soul shall be cut off from Israel
30. 12 give every man a ransom for his soul unto
30. 15, 16 to make an atonement for your souls
31. 14 that soul shall be cut off from among his
Lev. 4. 2 If a soul shall sin through ignorance aga.
5. 1 if a soul sin, and hear the voice of swear.
5. 2 Or if a soul touch any unclean thing, wh.
5. 4 Or if a soul swear, pronouncing with (his)
5. 15 If a soul commit a tresspass, and sin thr.
5. 17 if a soul sin, and commit any of these th.
6. 2 If a soul sin, and commit a tresspass ag.
7. 18 soul that eateth of it shall bear his iniqu.
7. 20 soul that eateth..even that soul shall be
7. 21 Moreover the soul..even that soul shall
7. 25 even the soul that eateth (it) shall be cut
7. 27 Whatsoever soul..even that soul shall be
16. 29 shall afflict your souls, and do no work at
16. 31 shall afflict your souls, by a statute for ev.
17. 10 I will even set my face against that soul
17. 11 to make an atonement for your souls: for
17. 11 (that) maketh an atonement for the soul
17. 12 No soul of you shall eat blood, neither s.
17. 15 every soul that eateth that which died (of
18. 29 even the souls that commit (them) shall be
19. 8 soul shall be cut off from among his peo.
20. 6 soul that turneth after such as have fam.
20. 6 I will even set my face against that soul
20. 25 shall not make your souls abominable by
22. 3 that soul shall be cut off from my prese.
22. 6 soul which hath touched any such shall
22. 11 But if the priest buy (any) soul with his
23. 27 ye shall afflict your souls, and offer an off.
23. 29 For whatsoever soul (it be) that shall not
23. 30 whatsoever soul..same soul will I destroy
23. 32 ye shall afflict your souls: in the ninth
26. 11 set my tabernacle..and my soul shall not
26. 15 or if your soul abhor my judgments, so
26. 30 your idols, and my soul shall abhor you
26. 43 because their soul abhorred my statutes
Num. 9. 13 even the same soul shall be cut off from
11. 6 But now our soul (is) dried away: (there
15. 27 if any soul sin through ignorance, then he
15. 28 atonement for the soul that sinneth ign.
15. 30 soul that doeth..that soul shall be cut off
15. 31 broken his commandment, that soul shall
16. 38 of these sinners against their own souls
19. 13 soul shall be cut off from Israel: because
19. 20 soul shall be cut off from among the con.
19. 22 soul that toucheth (it) shall be unclean
21. 4 soul of the people was much discouraged
21. 5 and our soul loatheth this light bread
29. 7 afflict your souls: ye shall not do any wo.
30. 2 swear an oath to bind his soul with a bo.
30. 4, 4, 5 wherewith she hath bound her soul
30. 6, 7, 8, 11 wherewith she bound her soul
30. 9 wherewith they have bound their souls
30. 10 bound her soul by a bond with an oath
30. 12 concerning the bond of her soul, shall not
30. 13 every binding oath to afflict the soul, her
31. 28 one soul of five hundred, (both) of the pe.

Num. 31. 50 to make an atonement for our souls be.
Deut. 4. 9 keep thy soul diligently, lest thou forget
4. 29 with all thy heart and with all thy soul
6. 5 love the LORD thy God with all..thy soul
10. 12 with all thy heart and with all thy soul
11. 13 with all your heart and with all your soul
11. 18 lay up these my words..in your soul, and
12. 15, 20, 21 whatsoever thy soul lusteth after
12. 20 because thy soul longeth to eat flesh, thou
13. 3 with all your heart and with all your soul
13. 6 thy friend, which (is) as thine own soul
14. 26 for whatsoever thy soul lusteth after, for
14. 26 strong drink, or for whatsoever thy soul
26. 16 with all thine heart, and with all thy soul
30. 2, 6, 10 all thine heart, and with all thy so.
Josh 10. 28, 30, 32, 35, 37, 37, 39 all the souls that (w.)
11. 11 they smote all the souls that (were) the.
22. 5 with all your heart, and with all your so.
23. 14 ye know..in all your souls, that not one
Judg. 5. 21 O my soul, thou hast trodden down str.
10. 16 his soul was grieved for the misery of I.
16. 16 (so) that his soul was vexed unto death
1 Sa. 1. 10 she (was) in bitterness of soul, and prayed
1. 15 have poured out my soul before the LORD
1. 26 Oh my lord, (as) thy soul liveth, my lord
2. 16 take (as much) as thy soul desireth; then
17. 55 (As) thy soul liveth, O king, I cannot tell
18. 1 soul of Jonathan was knit with the soul
18. 1 and Jonathan loved him as his own soul
18. 3 because he loved him as his own soul
20. 3 (as) the LORD liveth, and (as) thy soul li.
20. 4 Whatsoever thy soul desireth, I will even
20. 17 for he loved him as he loved his own soul
23. 20 according to all the desire of thy soul to
24. 11 against thee; yet thou huntest my soul
25. 26 (as) the LORD liveth, and (as) thy soul li.
25. 29 seek thy soul: but the soul of my lord s.
25. 29 souls of thine enemies, them shall he sl.
26. 21 because my soul was precious in thine ey.
30. 6 because the soul of all the people was gr.
2 Sa. 4. 9 hath redeemed my soul out of all adver.
5. 8 (that are) hated of David's soul, (he shall
11. 11 (as) thy soul liveth, I will not do this thi.
14. 19 (As) thy soul liveth, my lord the king, no.
1 Ki. 1. 29 that hath redeemed my soul out of all di.
2. 4 with all their heart and with all their soul
8. 48 return unto thee..with all their soul, in
11. 37 according to all that thy soul desireth, and
17. 21 let this child's soul come into him again
17. 22 soul of the child came into him again, and
2 Ki. 2. 2, 4, 6 (as) thy soul liveth, I will not leave
4. 27 her soul (is) vexed within her: and the L.
4. 30 (as) thy soul liveth, I will not leave thee
23. 3 with all (their) heart and all (their) soul
23. 25 with all his heart, and with all his soul
1 Ch. 22. 19 set your heart and your soul to seek the
2 Ch. 6. 38 with all their soul in the land of their ca.
15. 12 with all their heart, and with all their so.
34. 31 with all his soul, to perform the words of
Job 3. 20 misery, and life unto the bitter (in) soul
6. 7 The things (that) my soul refused to touch
7. 11 will complain in the bitterness of my soul
7. 15 So that my soul chooseth strangling, (and)
9. 21 would I not know my soul: I would desp.
10. 1 My soul is weary of my life: I will leave
10. 1 I will speak in the bitterness of my soul
12. 10 In whose hand (is) the soul of every living
14. 22 and his soul within him shall mourn
16. 4 if your soul were in my soul's stead, I co.
19. 2 How long will ye vex my soul, and break
21. 25 another dieth in the bitterness of his soul
23. 13 (what) his soul desireth, even (that) he do.
24. 12 soul of the wounded crieth out: yet God
27. 2 and the Almighty, (who) hath vexed my s.
27. 8 gained, when God taketh away his soul?
30. 16 now my soul is poured out upon me; the
30. 25 Did not I weep..was (not) my soul grieved
31. 30 to sin by wishing a curse to his soul
33. 18 He keepeth back his soul from the pit, and
33. 20 life abhorreth bread, and his soul dainty
33. 22 soul draweth near unto the grave, and his
33. 28 He will deliver his soul from going into
33. 30 To bring back his soul from the pit, to be
Psa. 3. 2 Many (there be) which say of my soul, (T.)
6. 3 My soul is also sore vexed: but thou, O L.
6. 4 Return, O LORD, deliver my soul: oh save
7. 2 Lest he tear my soul like a lion, rending
7. 5 Let the enemy persecute my soul, and ta.
11. 1 how say ye to my soul, Flee (as) a bird to
11. 5 him that loveth violence his soul hateth
13. 2 How long shall I take counsel in my soul
16. 10 For thou wilt not leave my soul in hell
17. 13 deliver my soul from the wicked, (which
19. 7 law..(is) perfect, converting the soul: the
22. 20 Deliver my soul from the sword; my da.
22. 29 and none can keep alive his own soul
23. 3 He restoreth my soul: he leadeth me in
24. 4 who hath not lifted up his soul from van.
25. 1 Unto thee, O LORD, do I lift up my soul
25. 13 His soul shall dwell at ease; and his seed
25. 20 O keep my soul, and deliver me: let me
26. 9 Gather not my soul with sinners, nor my
30. 3 thou hast brought up my soul from the gr.
31. 7 thou hast known my soul in adversities
31. 9 consumed with grief, (yea), my soul and
33. 19 To deliver their soul from death, and to
33. 20 Our soul waiteth for the LORD: he (is) our
34. 2 My soul shall make her boast in the LORD
34. 22 LORD redeemeth the soul of his servants
35. 3 say unto my soul, I (am) thy salvation
35. 4 put to shame that seek after my soul: let
35. 7 without cause they have digged for my s.

Psa. 35. 9 my soul shall be joyful in the LORD : it sh.
35. 12 evil for good, (to) the spoiling of my soul
35. 13 humbled my soul with fasting; and my
35. 17 rescue my soul from their destructions
40. 14 that seek after my soul to destroy it; let
41. 4 heal my soul; for I have sinned against
42. 1 so panteth my soul after thee, O God
42. 2 My soul thirsteth for God, for the living
42. 4 pour out my soul in me: for I had gone
42. 5, 11 Why art thou cast down, O my soul?
42. 6 my soul is cast down within me: theref.
43. 5 Why art thou cast down, O my soul? and
44. 25 For our soul is bowed down to the dust
49. 8 For the redemption of their soul (is) pre.
49. 15 God will redeem my soul from the power
49. 18 Though while he lived he blessed his so.
54. 3 oppressors seek after my soul: they have
54. 4 the LORD (is) with them that uphold my s.
55. 18 He hath delivered my soul in peace from
56. 6 mark my steps, when they wait for my so.
56. 13 For thou hast delivered my soul from de.
57. 1 for my soul trusteth in thee: yea, in the
57. 4 My soul (is) among lions; (and) I lie (ev.
57. 6 my soul is bowed down: they have digged
59. 3 they lie in wait for my soul: the mighty
62. 1 my soul waiteth upon God: from him (co.)
62. 5 My soul, wait thou only upon God; for my
63. 1 my soul thirsteth for thee, my flesh long.
63. 5 My soul shall be satisfied as (with) marr.
63. 8 My soul followeth hard after thee: thy ri.
63. 9 those (that) seek my soul, to destroy (it), sh.
66. 9 Which holdeth our soul in life, and suff.
66. 16 will declare what he hath done for my so.
69. 1 for the waters are come in unto (my) soul
69. 10 When I wept, (and chastened) my soul wi.
69. 18 Draw nigh unto my soul, (and) redeem it
70. 2 and confounded that seek after my soul
71. 10 they that lay wait for my soul take coun.
71. 13 consumed that are adversaries to my soul
71. 23 and my soul, which thou hast redeemed
72. 13 and shall save the souls of the needy
72. 14 He shall redeem their soul from deceit and
74. 19 deliver not the soul of thy turtle dove unto
77. 2 day of my trouble..my soul refused to be
78. 50 he spared not their soul from death, but
84. 2 My soul longeth, yea, even fainteth for the
86. 2 Preserve my soul, for I (am) holy: O thou
86. 4 Rejoice the soul of thy servant: for
86. 4 unto thee, O LORD, do I lift up my soul
86. 13 thou hast delivered my soul from the low.
86. 14 violent (men) have sought after my soul
88. 3 my soul is full of troubles, and my life dra.
88. 14 why castest thou off my soul? (why) hidest
89. 48 shall he deliver his soul from the hand of
94. 17 Unless the LORD (had been) my help, my s.
94. 19 within me thy comforts delight my soul
94. 21 gather themselves..against the soul of the
97. 10 he preserveth the souls of his saints; he
103. 1, 2, 22 Bless the LORD, O my soul; and all
104. 1 Bless the LORD, O my soul. O LORD my God
104. 35 Bless thou the LORD, O my soul. Praise
106. 15 he gave..but sent leanness into their soul
107. 5 Hungry and thirsty, their soul fainted in
107. 9 For he satisfieth the longing soul, and
107. 9 filleth the hungry soul with goodness
107. 18 Their soul abhorreth all manner of meat
107. 26 their soul is melted because of trouble
109. 20 of them that speak evil against my soul
109. 31 save (him) from those that condemn his
116. 4 O LORD, I beseech thee, deliver my soul
116. 7 Return unto thy rest, O my soul; for the
116. 8 thou hast delivered my soul from death
119. 20 My soul breaketh for the longing (that it
119. 25 My soul cleaveth unto the dust: quicken
119. 28 My soul melteth for heaviness: strengthen
119. 81 My soul fainteth for thy salvation: (but) I
119. 109 My soul (is) continually in my hand: yet
119. 129 wonderful: therefore doth my soul keep
119. 167 My soul hath kept thy testimonies; and
119. 175 Let my soul live, and it shall praise thee
120. 2 Deliver my soul, O LORD, from lying lips
120. 6 My soul hath long dwelt with him that ha.
121. 7 The LORD..he shall preserve thy soul
123. 4 Our soul is exceedingly filled with the sc.
124. 4 Then..the stream had gone over our soul
124. 5 the proud waters had gone over our soul
124. 7 Our soul is escaped as a bird out of the
130. 5 I wait for the LORD, my soul doth wait
130. 6 My soul (waiteth) for the LORD more than
131. 2 I have behaved..my soul (is) even as a w.
138. 3 strengthenedst me (with) strength in my s.
139. 14 and (that) my soul knoweth right well
141. 8 in thee is my trust; leave not my soul d.
142. 4 refuge failed me; no man cared for my so.
142. 7 Bring my soul out of prison, that I may
143. 3 the enemy hath persecuted my soul; he
143. 6 my soul (thirsteth) after thee, as a thirsty
143. 8 cause me to know..for I lift up my soul
143. 11 for thy righteousness' sake bring my soul
143. 12 and destroy all them that afflict my soul
146. 1 Praise ye..Praise the LORD, O my soul
Prov. 2. 10 and knowledge is pleasant unto thy soul
3. 22 So shall they be life unto thy soul, and gr.
6. 30 if he steal to satisfy his soul when he is hu
6. 32 he (that) doeth it destroyeth his own soul
8. 36 he that sinneth..wrongeth his own soul
10. 3 The LORD will not suffer the soul of the
11. 17 The merciful man doeth good to his..soul
11. 25 The liberal soul shall be made fat; and he
11. 30 and he that winneth souls (is) wise
13. 2 the soul of the transgressors (shall eat)
13. 4 The soul of the sluggard desireth, and (ha.)
Prov. 13. 4 the soul of the diligent shall be made fat
13. 19 desire accomplished is sweet to the soul
13. 25 eateth to the satisfying of his soul, but the
14. 25 A true witness delivereth souls: but a de.
15. 32 refuseth instruction despiseth his..soul
16. 17 that keepeth his way preserveth his soul
16. 24 sweet to the soul, and health to the bones
18. 7 A fool's..lips (are) the snare of his soul
19. 2 (that) the soul (be) without knowledge
19. 8 that getteth wisdom loveth his own soul
19. 15 and an idle soul shall suffer hunger
19. 16 He..keepeth his own soul; (but) he that
19. 18 and let not thy soul spare for his crying
20. 2 provoketh him..sinneth (against) his..so.
21. 10 The soul of the wicked desireth evil, his
21. 23 Whoso keepeth his mouth..keepeth his s.
22. 5 he that doth keep his soul shall be far fr.
22. 23 and spoil the soul of those that spoiled th.
22. 25 learn his ways, and get a snare to thy so.
23. 14 beat him..and shalt deliver his soul from
24. 12 he that keepeth thy soul, doth (not) he k.
24. 14 So (shall) the knowledge..(be) unto thy s.
25. 13 for he refresheth the soul of his masters
25. 25 (As) cold waters to a thirsty soul, so (is)
27. 7 The full soul loatheth an honey comb, but
27. 7 to the hungry soul every bitter thing is s.
29. 10 hate the upright..the just seek his soul
29. 17 yea, he shall give delight unto thy soul
29. 24 partner with a thief hateth his own soul
Eccl. 2. 24 (that) he should make his soul enjoy good
4. 8 For whom do I..bereave my soul of good?
6. 2 he wanteth nothing for his soul of all th.
6. 3 his soul be not filled with good, and also
7. 28 Which yet my soul seeketh, but I find not
Song 1. 7 Tell me, O thou whom my soul loveth, wh.
3. 1 I sought him whom my soul loveth: I so.
3. 2 I will seek him whom my soul loveth: I
3. 3 (I said), Saw ye him whom my soul loveth
3. 4 I found him whom my soul loveth: I he.
5. 6 my soul failed when he spake: I sought
6. 12 my soul made me (like) the chariots of A.
Isa. 1. 14 and your appointed feasts my soul hateth
3. 9 Woe unto their soul! for they have rew.
10. 18 of his fruitful field, both soul and body
26. 8 the desire of (our) soul (is) to thy name
26. 9 With my soul have I desired thee in the
29. 8 but he awaketh, and his soul is empty
29. 8 behold, (he is) faint, and his soul hath ap.
32. 6 to make empty the soul of the hungry
38. 15 go softly..in the bitterness of my soul
38. 17 thou hast in love to my soul (delivered
42. 1 Behold..mine elect, (in whom) my soul
44. 20 he cannot deliver his soul, nor say, (Is th.)
51. 23 which have said to thy soul, Bow down
53. 10 thou shalt make his soul an offering for
53. 11 He shall see of the travail of his soul, (and)
53. 12 he hath poured out his soul unto death
55. 2 and let your soul delight itself in fatness
55. 3 hear, and your soul shall live; and I will
58. 3 (wherefore) have we afflicted our soul, and
58. 5 Is it..a day for a man to afflict his soul?
58. 10 (if) thou draw out thy soul to the hungry
58. 10 And (if) thou..satisfy the afflicted soul
58. 11 satisfy thy soul in drought, and make fat
61. 10 my soul shall be joyful in my God, for he
66. 3 their soul delighteth in their abominati.
Jer. 2. 34 the blood of the souls of the poor innoc.
4. 10 whereas the sword reacheth unto the so.
4. 19 thou hast heard, O my soul, the sound of
4. 31 my soul is wearied because of murderers
5. 9, 29 shall not my soul be avenged on such
6. 8 lest my soul depart from thee; lest I m.
6. 16 walk therein, and..find rest for your so.
9. 9 shall not my soul be avenged on such a
12. 7 given the dearly beloved of my soul into
13. 17 my soul shall weep in secret places for (y.)
14. 19 hath thy soul loathed Zion? why hast th
18. 20 for they have digged a pit for my soul
20. 13 he hath delivered the soul of the poor fr.
26. 19 we procure great evil against our souls
31. 12 their soul shall be as a watered garden
31. 14 I will satiate the soul of the priests with
31. 25 For I have satiated the weary soul, and
31. 25 I have replenished every sorrowful soul
32. 41 my whole heart and with my whole soul
38. 16 (As) the LORD liveth, that made us this so.
38. 17 thy soul shall live, and this city shall not
38. 20 it shall be well unto thee, and thy soul
44. 7 commit ye (this)..evil against your souls
50. 19 his soul shall be satisfied upon mount E.
51. 6 Flee out..and deliver every man his soul
51. 45 deliver ye every man his soul from the fi.
Lam. 1. 11 their pleasant things..to relieve the soul
1. 16 comforter that should relieve my soul is
1. 19 sought their meat to relieve their souls
2. 12 their soul was poured out into their mot.
3. 17 thou hast removed my soul far off from
3. 20 My soul hath (them) still in remembrance
3. 24 The LORD (is) my portion, saith my soul
3. 25 The LORD (is) good..to the soul (that) see.
3. 58 thou hast pleaded the causes of my soul
Eze. 3. 19 die..but thou hast delivered thy soul
3. 21 live..also thou hast delivered thy soul
4. 14 my soul hath not been polluted; for from
7. 19 they shall not satisfy their souls, neither
13. 18 to hunt souls. Will ye hunt the souls of
13. 18 will ye save the souls alive (that come)
13. 19 to slay the souls that should not die, and
13. 19 to save the souls alive that should not li.
13. 20 wherewith ye there hunt the souls to make
13. 20 will let the souls go, (even) the souls that
14. 14 they should deliver (but) their own souls
Eze. 14. 20 they shall (but) deliver their own souls by
18. 4 all souls are mine; as the soul of the fa.
18. 4 so also the soul of the son is mine
18. 4, 20 the soul that sinneth, it shall die
18. 27 doeth..right, he shall save his soul alive
22. 25 they have devoured souls; they have ta.
22. 27 to shed blood, (and) to destroy souls, to
24. 21 and that which your soul pitieth; and yo.
33. 5 that taketh warning shall deliver his soul
33. 9 die..but thou hast delivered thy soul
Hos. 9. 4 their bread for their soul shall not come
Jon. 2. 5 The waters compassed me..(even) to the s.
2. 7 When my soul fainted within me I rem.
Mic. 6. 7 fruit of my body (for) the sin of my soul
7. 1 no cluster to eat: my soul desired the fir.
Hab. 2. 4 his soul (which) is lifted up is not upright
2. 10 and hast sinned (against) thy soul
Zech. 11. 8 my soul loathed them, and their soul also

3. *Breath*, נְשָׁמָה *neshamah.*
Isa. 57. 16 fail before me, and the souls (which) I ha.

4. *Animal soul*, ψυχή *psuchē.*
Matt 10. 28 body, but are not able to kill the soul
10. 28 which is able to destroy both soul and bo.
11. 29 and ye shall find rest unto your souls
12. 18 my beloved, in whom my soul is well ple.
16. 26 gain the..world, and lose his own soul
16. 26 or what shall a man give..for his soul?
22. 37 with all thy heart, and with all thy soul
26. 38 My soul is exceeding sorrowful, even unto
Mark 8. 36 gain the..world, and lose his own soul
8. 37 Or what shall a man give..for his soul?
12. 30 with all thy soul, and with all thy mind
12. 33 [with all the soul, and with all the strength]
14. 34 My soul is exceeding sorrowful unto death
Luke 1. 46 Mary said, My soul doth magnify the L.
2. 35 a sword shall pierce through thy own soul
10. 27 with all thy soul, and with all thy strength
12. 19 I will say to my soul, Soul, thou hast much
12. 20 this night thy soul shall be required of thee
21. 19 In your patience possess ye your souls
John 12. 27 Now is my soul troubled; and what shall
Acts 2. 27 thou wilt not leave my soul in hell, nei.
2. 31 [his soul] was not left in hell, neither his
2. 41 were added..about three thousand souls
2. 43 fear came upon every soul: and many wo.
3. 23 every soul, which will not hear that pro.
4. 32 multitude..of one heart and of one soul
7. 14 his kindred, threescore and fifteen souls
14. 22 Confirming the souls of the disciples, (and)
15. 24 subverting your souls, saying, (Ye must) be
27. 37 two hundred threescore and sixteen souls
Rom. 2. 9 anguish, upon every soul of man that do.
13. 1 Let every soul be subject unto the higher
1 Co. 15. 45 The first man Adam was made a living so.
2 Co. 1. 23 I call God for a record upon my soul, that
1 Th. 2. 8 but also our own souls, because ye were
5. 23 (I pray God) your whole spirit and soul
Heb. 4. 12 even to the dividing asunder of soul and
6. 19 we have as an anchor of the soul, both
10. 38 if (any man) draw back, my soul shall ha.
10. 39 them that believe to the saving of the so.
13. 17 they watch for your souls, as they that m.
Jas. 1. 21 word, which is able to save your souls
5. 20 shall save a soul from death, and shall hf.
1 Pe. 1. 9 your faith, (even) the salvation of (your) s.
1. 22 ye have purified your souls in obeying the
2. 11 fleshly lusts, which war against the soul
2. 25 the shepherd and bishop of your souls
3. 20 wherein few, that is, eight souls were sa.
4. 19 commit the keeping of their souls (to him)
2 Pe. 2. 8 vexed (his) righteous soul from day to day
2. 14 beguiling unstable souls: an heart they
3 John 2 be in health, even as thy soul prospereth
Rev. 6. 9 saw under the altar the souls of them th.
16. 3 and every living soul died in the sea
18. 13 and chariots, and slaves, and souls of men
18. 14 fruits that thy soul lusted after are depa.
20. 4 souls of them that were beheaded for the

SOUND, sounding, (high, joyful, solemn) —

1. *Meditation, utterance, mourning*, הֶגֶה *hegeh.*
Job 37. 2 Hear attentively..the sound (that) goeth

2. *Meditation*, הִגָּיוֹן *higgayon.*
Psa. 92. 3 upon the harp with a solemn sound

3. *Multitude, noise, store*, הָמוֹן *hamon.*
Isa. 63. 15 sounding of thy bowels and of thy merc

4. *Mouth*, פֶּה *peh.*
Amos 6. 5 That chant to the sound of the viol, (and)

5. *Voice*, קוֹל *qol.*
Exod 28. 35 sound shall be heard when he goeth in
Lev. 26. 36 the sound of a shaken leaf shall chase th.
Josh. 6. 5 when ye hear the sound of the trumpet
6. 20 when the people heard the sound of the
2 Sa. 5. 24 when thou hearest the sound of a going
6. 15 brought up the ark..with the sound of
15. 10 as ye hear the sound of the trumpet, then
1 Ki. 1. 40 the earth rent with the sound of them
1. 41 when Joab heard the sound of the trum.
14. 6 when Ahijah heard the sound of her feet
18. 41 for (there is) a sound of abundance of rain
2 Ki. 6. 32 (is) not the sound of his master's feet be.
1 Ch. 14. 15 when thou shalt hear a sound of going in
15. 28 with sound of the cornet, and with trum.
2 Ch. 5. 13 to make one sound to be heard in praising
Neh. 4. 20 In what place (therefore) ye hear the so.
Job 15. 21 A dreadful sound (is) in his ears: in pros.
21. 12 They..rejoice at the sound of the organ
39. 24 neither believeth he that (it is) the sound
Psa. 47. 5 the LORD with the sound of a trumpet

Psa. 77. 17 skies sent out a sound: thine arrows also
98. 6 With trumpets and sound of cornet make
Eccl.12. 4 when the sound of the grinding is low
Jer. 4. 19 hast heard..the sound of the trumpet, the
4. 21 see the standard, (and) hear the sound of
6. 17 Hearken to the sound of the trumpet. B.
8. 16 trembled at the sound of the neighing of
42. 14 hear the sound of the trumpet, nor have
50. 22 sound of battle (is) in the land, and of gr.
51. 54 sound of a cry (cometh) from Babylon, and
Eze. 10. 5 sound of the cherubim's wings was heard
26. 13 sound of thy harps shall be no more hea.
26. 15 Shall not the isles shake at the sound of
27. 28 suburbs shall shake at the sound of the
31. 16 made the nations to shake at the sound of
33. 4 Then whosoever heareth the sound of the
33. 5 heard the sound of the trumpet, and took
Amos 2. 2 Moab shall die..with the sound of the tr.

6. *Voice*, קָל *qal.*
Dan. 3. 5, 15 at what time ye hear the sound of the
3. 7 when all the people heard the sound of
3. 10 that every man that shall hear the sound

7. *Blowing*, תְּקַע *teqa.*
Psa.150. 3 Praise him with the sound of the trump.

8. *Shout, shouting*, תְּרוּעָה *teruah.*
2 Ch.13. 12 priests with sounding trumpets to cry al.
Psa. 89. 15 the people that know the joyful sound: th.
150. 5 praise him upon the high sounding cymb.

9. *Echo, resounding, shout, shouting*, הֵד *hed.*
Eze. 7. 7 not the sounding again of the mountains

10. *A sound, report, fame*, ἦχος *ēchos.*
Acts 2. 2 suddenly there came a sound from heav.
Heb. 12. 19 sound of a trumpet, and the voice of wo.

11. *A sound*, φθόγγος *phthoggos.*
Rom 10. 18 their sound went into all the earth, and
1 Co.14. 7 they give a distinction in the sounds, how

12. *A voice, sound*, φωνή *phōnē.*
Matt 24. 31 shall send his angels with a great sound
John 3. 8 hearest the sound thereof, but canst not
1 Co.14. 7 even things without life giving sound, wh.
14. 8 if the trumpet give an uncertain sound
Rev. 1. 15 and his voice as the sound of many wat.
9. 9 sound of their wings (was) as the sound
18. 22 sound of a millstone shall be heard no

SOUND, (perfect) soundness, (to be) safe and—

1. *Healing, yielding*, מַרְפֵּא *marpe.*
Prov 14. 30 A sound heart (is) the life of the flesh: but

2. *Soundness*, מְתֹם *methom.*
Psa. 38. 3 no soundness in my flesh because of thine
38. 7 and (there is) no soundness in my flesh
Isa. 1. 6 even unto the head (there is) no soundn.

3. *Perfect, whole, complete, plain*, תָּמִים *tamim.*
Psa.119. 80 Let my heart be sound in thy statutes, th.

4. *Sound, healthy*, ὑγιής *hugiēs.*
Titus 2. 8 Sound speech, that cannot be condemned

5. *To be sound, in health*, ὑγιαίνω *hugiainō.*
Luke 15. 27 because he hath received him safe and so.
1 Ti. 1. 10 any other thing that is contrary to sound
2 Ti. 1. 13 Hold fast the form of sound words, which
4. 3 when they will not endure sound doctrine
Titus 1. 9 he may be able by sound docrine both
1. 13 rebuke them..that they may be sound in
2. 1 the things which become sound doctrine
2. 2 temperate, sound in faith, in charity, in

6. *Perfect soundness*, ὁλοκληρία *holoklēria.*
Acts 3. 16 hath given him this perfect soundness in

SOUND (out), to —

1. *To roar, move, sound, make a noise*, הָמָה *hamah.*
Isa. 16. 11 my bowels shall sound like an harp for M.
Jer. 48. 36, 36 mine heart shall sound for Moab like

2. *To sound a trumpet*, חָצַר *chatsotser* [V.L. חצר, 5].
2 Ch. 5. 12 an hundred and twenty priests sounding
7. 6 the priests sounded trumpets before them
13. 14 and the priests sounded with the trumpets
29. 28 the singers sang, and the trumpeters sou.

3. *To search, investigate*, חָקַר *chaqar.*
1 Sa. 20. 12 when I have sounded my father about to.

4. *To cause to hear*, שָׁמַע *shamea*, 5.
1 Ch.15. 16 psalteries and harps and cymbals, soun.
15. 19 (were appointed) to sound with cymbals

5. *To blow*, תָּקַע *taqa.*
2 Ch.23. 13 the people..sounded with trumpets, also
Neh. 4. 18 he that sounded the trumpet (was) by me

6. *To sound out*, ἐξηχέομαι *exēcheomai.*
1 Th. 1. 8 from you sounded out the word of the L.

7. *To become*, γίνομαι *ginomai.*
Luke 1. 44 the voice of thy salutation sounded in m.

8. *To sound, roar*, ἠχέω *ēcheō.*
1 Co. 13. 1 I am become (as) sounding brass, or a ti.

9. *To blow or sound a trumpet*, σαλπίζω *salpizō.*
Rev. 8. 6 seven angels..prepared themselves to so.
8. 7 The first angel sounded, and there follow.
8. 8 the second angel sounded, and as it were
8. 10 the third angel sounded, and there fell a
8. 12 the fourth angel sounded, and the third
8. 13 of the trumpets..which are yet to sound
9. 1 the fifth angel sounded, and I saw a star
9. 13 the sixth angel sounded, and I heard a
Rev. 10. 7 in the days..when he shall begin to sound
11. 15 the seventh angel sounded; and there we.

SOUND an alarm or trumpet, to —

1. *To shout*, רוּעַ *rua*, 5.
Num 10. 7 shall blow, but ye shall not sound an al.
Joel 2. 1 and sound an alarm in my holy mountain

2. *To blow or sound a trumpet*, σαλπίζω *salpizō.*
Matt. 6. 2 do not sound a trumpet before thee, as
1 Co. 15. 52 the trumpet shall sound, and the dead

SOUND, to cause or make to —

1. *To cause to pass over*, עָבַר *abar*, 5.
Lev. 25. 9 cause the trumpet..to sound on the tenth
25. 9 shall ye make the trumpet sound throug.

2. *To cause to hear*, שָׁמַע *shamea*, 5.
1 Ch.16. 5 but Asaph made a sound with cymbals
16. 42 for those that should make a sound, and

SOUND, to —

To take soundings, use the sounding line, βολίζω.
Acts 27. 28 And sounded, and found (it) twenty fath.
27. 28 they sounded again, and found (it) fifteen

SOUND mind or wisdom —

1. *Substance, sound wisdom*, תּוּשִׁיָּה *tushiyyah.*
Prov. 2. 7 He layeth up sound wisdom for the righ.
3. 21 My son..keep sound wisdom and discre.
8. 14 Counsel (is) mine, and sound wisdom: I

2. *Soundness of mind, prudence*, σωφρονισμός *sōp.*
2 Ti. 1. 7 of power, and of love, and of a sound mi.

SOUR, (grape,) to be —

1. *Sour or unripe fruit*, בֹּסֶר *boser.*
Isa. 18. 5 and the sour grape is ripening in the flo.
Jer. 31. 29 The fathers have eaten a sour grape, and
31. 30 every man that eateth the sour grape, his
Eze. 18. 2 The fathers have eaten sour grapes, and

2. *To turn aside, degenerate*, סוּר *sur.*
Hos. 4. 18 Their drink is sour: they have committed

SOUTH (country, side, ward, west, wind) —

1. *The south country or wind*, דָּרוֹם *darom.*
Deut33. 23 possess thou the west and the south
Job 37. 17 he quieteth the earth by the south (wind)
Eccl. 1. 6 The wind goeth toward the south, and
11. 3 the tree fall toward the south, or toward
Eze. 20. 46 drop (thy word) toward the south, and p.
40. 24 After that he brought me toward the so.
40. 24 and, behold, a gate toward the south
40. 27 a gate in the inner court toward the so.
40. 27 measured from gate to gate toward the s.
40. 28 to the inner court by the south gate
40. 28 he measured the south gate according to
40. 44 and their prospect (was) toward the so.
40. 45 chamber, whose prospect (is) toward the s.
41. 11 another door toward the south: and the
42. 12 the chambers that (were) toward the so.
42. 13 the south chambers, which (are) before
42. 18 He measured the south side, five hundred

2. *Inner chamber*, חֶדֶר *cheder.*
Job 37. 9 Out of the south cometh the whirlwind

3. *Sea*, יָם *yam.*
Psa.107. 3 the west, from the north, and from the s.

4. *Right hand*, יָמִין *yamin.*
1 Sa. 23. 19 Hachilah, which (is) on the south of Je.
23. 24 Maon, in the plain on the south of Jes.
Psa. 89. 12 The north and the south thou hast cre.

5. *Pasture land, wilderness*, מִדְבָּר *midbar.*
Psa. 75. 6 east, nor from the west, nor from the so.

6. *Negeb, the south (country of Judah)*, נֶגֶב *negeb.*
Gen. 12. 9 journeyed, going on still toward the sou.
13. 1 Abram went up out of Egypt..into the so.
13. 3 he went on his journeys from the south
13. 14 northward, and southward, and eastward
20. 1 journeyed from thence toward the south
24. 62 Isaac came..for he dwelt in the south co.
28. 14 east, and to the north, and to the south
Exod26. 18 make..twenty boards on the south side
27. 9 for the south side..(there shall be) hang.
36. 23 made..twenty boards for the south side
38. 9 on the south side..the hangings of the
40. 24 on the side of the tabernacle southward
Num13. 17 Get you up this (way) southward, and go
13. 22 they ascended by the south, and came un.
13. 29 Amalekites dwell in the land of the south
21. 1 the Canaanite, which dwelt in the south
33. 40 which dwelt in the south of the land of
34. 3 your south quarter shall be from the w.
34. 3 your south border shall be the outmost
34. 4 your border shall turn from the south to
34. 4 shall be from the south to Kadesh-barnea
35. 5 the south side two thousand cubits, and
Deut. 1. 7 in the south, and by the seaside, to the land
34. 3 the south, and the plain of the valley of
Josh.10. 40 the country of the hills, and of the south
11. 2 of the plains south of Chinneroth, and in
11. 16 all the south country, and all the land of
12. 8 in the wilderness, and in the south country
15. 1 the wilderness of Zin southward (was) the
15. 2 their south border was from the shore of
15. 2 from the bay that looketh southward
15. 3 it went out to the south side to Maaleh.
15. 3 ascended up on the south side unto Kadesh.
15. 4 the sea; this shall be your south coast
15. 7 Adummim, which (is) on the south side
15. 8 went up..unto the south side of the Jebus.
Josh.15. 19 thou hast given me a south land; give me
15. 21 toward the coast of Edom southward
17. 9 the river Kanah, southward of the river
17. 10 Southward (it was) Ephraim's, and north.
18. 5 shall abide in their coast on the south
18. 13 the side of Luz, which (is) Beth-el south.
18. 13 the hill that (lieth) on the south side of
18. 14 compassed the corner of the sea southwa.
18. 14 that (lieth) before Beth-horn southward
18. 15 the south quarter (was) from the end of
18. 16 to the side of Jebusi on the south, and des.
18. 19 south end of Jordan: this (was) the south
19. 8 to Baalath-beer, Ramath of the south
19. 34 reacheth to Zebulun on the south side
Judg. 1. 9 in the mountain, and in the south, and in
1. 15 thou hast given me a south land, give me
1. 16 Judah, which (lieth) in the south of Arad
21. 19 (a place) which (is)..on the south of Leb.
1 Sa. 14. 5 the other southward over against Gibeah
20. 41 arose out of (a place) toward the south
27. 10 David said, Against the south of Judah
27. 10 and against the south of the Jerahmeelites
27. 10 and against the south of the Kenites
30. 1 the Amalekites had invaded the south, and
30. 14 We made an invasion (upon) the south of
30. 14 upon (the coast)..and upon the south of
30. 27 to (them) which (were) in south Ramoth
2 Sa. 24. 7 they went out to the south of Judah, (even)
1 Ki. 7. 25 three looking toward the south, and three
7. 39 the sea..eastward over against the south
1 Ch. 9. 24 toward the east, west, north, and south
26. 15 To Obed-edom southward; and to his sons
26. 17 northward four a day, southward four a
2 Ch. 4. 4 three looking toward the south, and three
4. 10 he set the sea..over against the south
28. 18 of the low country, and of the south of J.
Psa.126. 4 Turn again..as the streams in the south
Isa. 21. 1 As whirlwinds in the south pass through
30. 6 The burden of the beasts of the south: In.
Jer. 13. 19 The cities of the south shall be shut up
17. 26 and from the mountains, and from the so.
32. 44 take witnesses..in the cities of the south
33. 13 in the cities of the south, and in the land
Eze. 20. 46 prophesy against the forest of the south
20. 47 say to the forest of the south, Hear the wo.
20. 47 all faces from the south to the north shall
21. 4 against all flesh from the south to the no.
40. 2 (was) as the frame of a city on the south
46. 9 shall go out by the way of the south gate
46. 9 he that entereth by the way of the south
47. 1 the right side of the house, at the south
47. 19 the south side..from Tamar (even) to
47. 19 And (this is) the..side southward
48. 10 toward the south five and twenty thousa.
48. 16 the south side four thousand and five hu.
48. 17 toward the south two hundred and fifty
48. 28 at the south side southward, the border
48. 33 at the south side four thousand and five
Dan. 8. 4 westward, and northward, and southward
8. 9 toward the south, and toward the east
11. 5 the king of the south shall be strong, and
11. 6 the king's daughter of the south shall co.
11. 9 the king of the south shall come into (his)
11. 11 the king of the south shall be moved with
11. 14 stand up against the king of the south
11. 15 the arms of the south shall not withstand
11. 25 his courage against the king of the south
11. 25 the king of the south shall be stirred up to
11. 29 shall return, and come toward the south
11. 40 shall the king of the south push at him
Obad. 19 (they of) the south shall possess the mount
20 shall possess the cities of the south
Zech. 7. 7 when (men) inhabited the south and the pl.
14. 4 the north, and half of it toward the south
14. 10 from Geba to Rimmon south of Jerusalem

7. *South, the right hand*, תֵּימָן *teman.*
Exod26. 18 make..twenty boards on the..side south.
26. 35 side of the tabernacle toward the south
27. 9 southward (there shall be) hangings for
36. 23 made..twenty boards for the..side south.
38. 9 southward the hangings of the court (we.
Num. 2. 10 On the south side shall be the standard of
3. 29 on the side of the tabernacle southward
10. 6 the camps that lie on the south side shall
Deut. 3. 27 northward, and southward, and eastward
Josh.12. 3 and from the south, under Ashdoth-pisg.
13. 4 from the south, all the land of the Canaa.
15. 1 (was) the uttermost part of the south co.
Job 9. 9 Pleiades, and the chambers of the south
39. 26 (and) stretch her wings toward the south?
Psa. 78. 26 by his power he brought in the south wi.
Song. 4. 16 Awake, O north wind; and come, thou so.
Isa. 43. 6 I will say..to the south, Keep not back
Eze. 20. 46 set thy face toward the south, and drop
47. 19 southward..And (this is) the south side
48. 28 the border of Gad, at the..side southward
Zech. 6. 6 the grisled go forth toward the south co.
9. 14 and shall go with whirlwinds of the south

8. *The south west wind*, λίψ *lips.*
Acts 27. 12 lieth toward the south west and north w.

9. *Mid-day, the south*, μεσημβρία *mesēmbria.*
Acts 8. 26 go toward the south, unto the way that

10. *The south, south wind*, νότος *notos.*
Matt 12. 42 The queen of the south shall rise up in the
Luke11. 31 The queen of the south shall rise up in
12. 55 when (ye see) the south wind blow, ye say
13. 29 and from the north, and (from) the south
Acts 27. 13 when the south wind blew softly, suppos.
28. 13 after one day the south wind blew, and
Rev. 21. 13 on the south, three gates; and on the west

SOW —
A swine, boar, sow, ὗς *hus.*
2 Pe. 2. 22 the sow that was washed to her w.

SOW, be sown, sower, to —
1. *To sow,* זָרַע *zara.*
Gen. 26. 12 Isaac sowed in that land, and received in
47. 23 (here is) seed for you, and ye shall sow the
Exod23. 10 six years thou shalt sow thy land, and sh.
23. 16 the first fruits..which thou hast sown in
Lev. 19. 19 thou shalt not sow thy field with mingled
25. 3 Six years thou shalt sow thy field, and six
25. 4 thou shalt neither sow thy field, nor pru.
25. 11 ye shall now sow, neither reap that which
25. 20 we shall not sow, neither gather in our
25. 22 ye shall sow the eighth year, and eat (yet)
26. 16 ye shall sow your seed in vain, for your
Deut 11. 10 thou sowedst thy seed, and wateredst (it)
22. 9 Thou shalt not sow thy vineyard with di.
22. 9 the fruit of thy seed which thou hast sown
Judg. 6. 3 (so) it was, when Israel had sown, that
9. 45 beat down the city, and sowed it with sa.
2 Ki.19. 29 in the third year sow ye, and reap, and
Job 4. 8 they that plow iniquity, and sow wicked.
31. 8 let me sow, and let another eat; yea, let
Psa. 97. 11 Light (is) sown for the righteous, and gl.
107. 37 sow the fields, and plant vineyards, which
126. 5 They that sow in tears shall reap in joy
Prov 11. 18 to him that soweth righteousness (shall
22. 8 He that soweth iniquity shall reap vanity
Eccl. 11. 4 He that observeth the wind shall not sow
11. 6 In the morning sow thy seed, and in the
Isa. 28. 24 Doth the plowman plow all day to sow?
30. 23 that thou shalt sow the ground withal
32. 20 Blessed (are) ye that sow beside all wat
37. 30 in the third year sow ye, and reap, and
55. 10 that it may give seed to the sower, and
Jer. 2. 2 the wilderness, in a land (that was) not so.
4. 3 Break up your fallow ground, and sow
12. 13 They have sown wheat, but shall reap th.
31. 27 I will sow the house of Israel and the ho.
35. 7 Neither shall ye build house, nor sow se.
50. 16 Cut off the sower from Babylon, and him
Hos. 2. 23 And I will sow her unto me in the earth
8. 7 they have sown the wind, and they shall
10. 12 Sow to yourselves in righteousness, reap
Mic. 6. 15 Thou shalt sow, but thou shalt not reap
Hag. 1. 6 Ye have sown much, and bring in little
Zech.10. 9 I will sow them among the people: and

2. *To be sown,* זָרַע *zara,* 2.
Lev. 11. 37 fall upon any..seed which is to be sown
Deut21. 4 valley, which is neither eared nor sown
29. 23 it is not sown, nor beareth, nor any grass
Eze. 36. 9 will turn unto you, and ye shall be..sown
Nah. 1. 14 (that) no more of thy name be sown: out

3. *To be sown,* זָרַע *zara,* 4.
Isa. 40. 24 they shall not be sown; yea, their stock

4. *To draw out, scatter,* מָשַׁךְ *mashak.*
Amos 9. 13 the treader of grapes him that soweth se.

5. *To send,* שָׁלַח *shalach,* 3.
Prov. 6. 14 he deviseth mischief..he soweth discord
6. 19 he that soweth discord among brethren
16. 28 A froward man soweth strife; and a wh.

6. *To sow,* σπείρω *speirō.*
Matt. 6. 26 they sow not, neither do they reap, nor
13. 3 saying, Behold, a sower went forth to sow
13. 4 when he sowed, some (seeds) fell by the
13. 18 Hear ye therefore the parable of the sow.
13. 19 catcheth away that which was sown in
13. 24 a man which sowed good seed in his field
13. 25 his enemy came and [sowed] tares among
13. 27 didst not thou sow good seed in thy field
13. 31 which a man took, and sowed in his field
13. 37 He that soweth the good seed is the Son
13. 39 The enemy that sowed them is the devil
25. 24 reaping where thou hast not sown, and
25. 26 thou knewest that I reap where I sowed
Mark 4. 3 Behold, there went out a sower to sow
4. 4 as he sowed, some fell by the way side
4. 14 The sower soweth the word
4. 15 by the way side, where the word is sown
4. 15 taketh away the word that was sown in
4. 16 these are they likewise which are sown on
4. 18 these are they which are sown among th.
4. 20 these are they which are sown on good
4. 31 which, when it is sown in the earth, is le.
4. 32 But when it is sown, it groweth up, and
Luke 8. 5 A sower went out to sow his seed: and
8. 5 as he sowed, some fell by the way side
12. 24 Consider the ravens: for they neither sow
19. 21 and reapest that thou didst not sow
19. 22 taking..and reaping that I did not sow
John 4. 36 that both he that soweth and he that re.
4. 37 herein is that saying true, One soweth
1 Co. 9. 11 If we have sown unto you spiritual thin.
15. 36 that which thou sowest is not quickened
15. 37 that which thou sowest, thou sowest not
15. 42 It is sown in corruption; it is raised in
15. 43 It is sown in dishonour; it is raised in gl.
15. 43 it is sown in weakness; it is raised in po.
15. 44 It is sown a natural body; it is raised a
2 Co. 9. 6 He which soweth sparingly shall reap also
9. 6 he which soweth bountifully shall reap
9. 10 he that ministereth seed to the sower, bo.
Gal. 6. 7 whatsoever a man soweth, that shall he
6. 8 he that soweth to his flesh shall of the fle.
6. 8 he that soweth to the spirit shall of the
Jas. 3. 18 the fruit of righteousness is sown in peace

SOWING (time) —
1. *Seed,* זֶרַע *zera.*
Lev. 26. 5 the vintage shall reach unto the sowing t.
2. *Thing sown,* זֵרוּעַ *zerua.*
Lev. 11. 37 fall upon any sowing seed which is to be

SOWN thing —
1. *Thing sown,* זֵרוּעַ *zerua.*
Isa. 61. 11 causeth the things that are sown in it to
2. *Thing sown,* מִזְרָע *mizra.*
Isa. 19. 7 every thing sown by the brooks, shall wi.

SPACE —
1. *Border,* גְּבוּל *gebul.*
Eze. 40. 12 space also before the little chambers (was)
40. 12 and the space (was) one cubit on that side
2. *Days,* יוֹם *yom.*
Gen. 29. 14 he abode with him the space of a month
Lev. 25. 8 space of the seven sabbaths of years shall
Deut. 2. 14 space in which we came from Kadesh-bar.
3. *Fullness,* מְלֹא *male* (infin.).
Lev. 25. 30 if it be not redeemed within the space of
4. *Place, standing place,* מָקוֹם *maqom.*
1 Sa. 26. 13 stood on the top..a great space (being) be.
5. *Moment,* רֶגַע *rega.*
Ezra 9. 8 now for a little space grace hath been (sh.)
6. *Space, respite,* רֶוַח *revach.*
Gen. 32. 16 Pass over before me; and put a space bet.
7. *Distance,* רָחוֹק *rachoq.*
Josh. 3. 4 Yet there shall be a space between you and

SPACE, (for or by the, after or little) —
1. *From,* ἀπό *apo.*
Rev. 14. 20 by the space of a thousand (and) six hun.
2. *Short,* βραχύς *brachus.*
Acts 5. 34 to put the apostles forth a little space
3. *Interval, intervening time,* διάστημα *diastēma.*
Acts 5. 7 was about the space of three hours after
4. *To put apart, separate,* διΐστημι *diistēmi.*
Luke22. 59 about the space of one hour after, another
5. *Over, up to, against, for the purpose of,* ἐπί *epi.*
Acts 19. 8 spake boldly for the space of three months
19. 10 this continued by the space of two years
19. 34 with one voice about the space of two ho.
6. *Time, delay,* χρόνος *chronos.*
Acts 15. 33 after they had tarried (there) a space, they
Rev. 2. 21 gave her space to repent of her fornication

SPAIN, Σπανία.
The peninsula at the S.W. of Europe, 700 miles long and 500 broad; whether Paul ever visited it is uncertain. It was known to the ancient Greeks under the name of *Iberia*, and to the Romans by that of *Hispania*. In B.C. 237 Hamilcar the Carthagenian general established his authority in it; in 229 his son in law Hasdrubal founds Carthagena; in 221 Hannibal succeeds on the murder of his father; in 218 he takes Saguntun, and begins the second Punic war, in 212 Scipio is defeated; in 210 Scipio Africanus takes Carthagena; in 206 the Carthagenians finally expelled; in 205 it is divided into Hither and Further Spain; in 179 the Celtiberians revolt, but are suppressed; in 145 Viriathus defeats the Romans; in 140 he is murdered by them; in 133 they secure Central Spain; in 104 it is ravaged by Cimbrian invaders; in 77 Sertorius rises against Sylla; in 72 he is defeated and murdered; in 60 Julius Cæsar gains several victories; in 55 Pompey invested with its full government; in 27 Augustus divides it into three provinces; in 25 he subdued the N. tribes, the Cantabri and the Astures; in A.D. 251 Christianity is first introduced.
Rom 15. 24 Whensoever I take my journey into S.
15. 28 this fruit, I will come by you into S.

SPAN, (long, to) —
1. *A span,* זֶרֶת *zereth.*
Exod28. 16 span (shall be) the length thereof, and a s.
39. 9 span (was) the length thereof, and a span
1 Sa. 17. 4 whose height (was) six cubits and a span
Isa. 40. 12 meted out heaven with the span, and co.
Eze. 43. 13 edge thereof round about (shall be) a span
2. *To stretch out, swaddle, train up,* טָפַח *taphach,* 3.
Isa. 48. 13 my right hand hath spanned the heavens
3. *Stretching out, training,* טִפֻּחִים *tippuchim.*
Lam. 2. 20 eat their fruit, (and) children of a span long

SPARE, to — [*See* enough.]
1. *To shelter, spare,* חוּס *chus.*
1 Sa. 24. 10 spared thee; and I said, I will not put fo.
Neh. 13. 22 spare me according to the greatness of thy
Psa. 72. 13 He shall spare the poor and needy, and
Isa. 13. 18 have no pity..their eye shall not spare
Jer. 13. 14 I will not pity, nor spare, nor have mercy
21. 7 he shall not spare them, neither have pity
Eze. 5. 11 neither shall mine eye spare, neither will
7. 4 mine eye shall not spare thee, neither will
7. 9 mine eye shall not spare, neither will I
8. 18 mine eye shall not spare, neither will I
9. 5 let not your eye spare, neither have ye pity
9. 10 as for me also, mine eye shall not spare
20. 17 Nevertheless mine eye spared them from
24. 14 neither will I spare, neither will I repent
Joel 2. 17 Spare thy people, O LORD, and give not
Jonah4. 11 should not I spare Nineveh, that great ci
2. *To have pity, be mild, meek,* חָמַל *chamal.*
Deut 13. 8 neither shall thou spare, neither shalt th.
1 Sa. 15. 3 spare them not; but slay both man and
15. 9 Saul and the people spared Agag, and the
15. 15 for the people spared the best of the sheep
2 Sa. 12. 4 spared to take of his own flock, and of his
21. 7 But the king spared Mephibosheth, the
Job 6. 10 let him not spare; for I have not concealed
16. 13 doth not spare; he poureth out my gall up.
20. 13 spare it, and forsake it not, but keep it
27. 22 shall cast upon him, and not spare: he wo.
Prov. 6. 34 he will not spare in the day of vengeance
Isa. 9. 19 fuel of the fire: no man shall spare his br.
30. 14 he shall not spare: so that there shall not
Jer. 50. 14 spare no arrows: for she hath sinned aga.
51. 3 spare ye not her young men; destroy ye
Hab. 1. 17 not spare continually to slay the nations
Mal. 3. 17 will spare them, as a man spareth his own
3. *To keep back, withhold,* חָשַׂךְ *chasak.*
2 Ki. 5. 20 my master hath spared Naaman this Sy.
Job 30. 10 flee far from me, and spare not to spit in
Psa. 78. 50 he spared not their soul from death, but
Prov 13. 24 He that spareth his rod hateth his son]
17. 27 He that hath knowledge spareth his wo.
21. 26 but the righteous giveth and spareth not
Isa. 54. 2 spare not, lengthen thy cords, and stre.
58. 1 Cry aloud, spare not, lift up thy voice like
4. *To lift up,* נָשָׂא *nasa.*
Gen. 18. 24 wilt thou also destroy and not spare the
18. 26 then I will spare all the place for their
Prov 19. 18 and let not thy soul spare for his crying
5. *To send away, let go,* סָלַח *salach.*
Deut29. 20 LORD will not spare him, but then the an.
6. *To look dazzled, smear,* שָׁעָה *shaah,* 5.
Psa. 39. 13 spare me, that I may recover strength, be.
7. *To spare, forbear,* φείδομαι *pheidomai.*
Acts 20. 29 enter in among you, not sparing the flock
Rom. 8. 32 He that spared not his own Son, but de.
11. 21 spared not..(take heed) lest he also spare
1 Co. 7. 28 have trouble in the flesh: but I spare you
2 Co. 1. 23 to spare you I came not as yet unto Cor.
13. 2 that, if I come again, I will not spare
2 Pe. 2. 4 For if God spared not the angels that sin.
2. 5 And spared not the old world, but saved

SPARINGLY —
Sparingly, φειδομένως *pheidomenōs.*
2 Co. 9. 6 soweth sparingly shall reap also sparingly

SPARK —
1. *Son of the flame,* בֶּן־רֶשֶׁף *benresheph.*
Job 5. 7 born unto trouble, as the sparks fly upw.
2. *Sparks, darts, firebrands,* זִיקוֹת *ziqoth.*
Isa. 50. 11 that compass (yourselves) about with sp.
50. 11 walk..in the sparks (that) ye have kin.
3. *Spark, flame,* כִּידוֹד *kidod.*
Job 41. 19 Out of his mouth..sparks of fire leap out
4. *Spark,* נִיצוֹץ *nitsots.*
Isa. 1. 31 as tow, and the maker of it as a spark, and
5. *Spark, flame,* שְׁבִיב *shabib.*
Job 18. 5 and the spark of his fire shall not shine

SPARKLE, to —
To sparkle, נָצַץ *natsats.*
Eze. 1. 7 sparkled like the colour of burnished br.

SPARROW —
1. *Bird, fowl, sparrow,* צִפּוֹר *tsippor.*
Psa. 84. 3 Yea, the sparrow hath found an house
102. 7 am as a sparrow alone upon the house top
2. *A young sparrow,* στρουθίον *strouthion.*
Matt 10. 29 Are not two sparrows sold for a farthing?
10. 31 ye are of more value than many sparrows
Luke12. 6 Are not five sparrows sold for two farth.?
12. 7 ye are of more value than many sparrows

SPEAK, (against, of, often, to, with) — [*See* **SPOKEN.**]
1. *To say,* (*lift up the voice*), אָמַר *amar.*
Gen. 9. 8 spake unto Noah, and to his sons with h.
21. 22 captain of his host spake unto Abraham
22. 7 Isaac spake unto Abraham his father, and
27. 6 Rebekah spake unto Jacob her son, saying
31. 11 angel of God spake unto me in a dream
31. 29 God of your father spake unto me yester.
32. 4 Thus shall ye speak unto my lord Esau
34. 4 Shechem spake unto his father Hamor
39. 14 spake unto them, saying, See, he hath b.
42. 22 Spake I not unto you, saying, Do not sin
42. 37 Reuben spake unto his father, saying, Sl.
43. 3 Judah spake unto him, saying, The man
43. 27 old man of whom ye spake? (is) he yet
43. 29 younger brother, of whom ye spake unto
46. 2 God spake unto Israel in the visions of the
47. 5 Pharaoh spake unto Joseph, saying, Thy
Exod. 1. 15 king of Egypt spake to the Hebrew mid.
5. 10 spake to the people, saying, Thus saith
7. 8 the LORD spake unto Moses
So in 7. 19; 8. 1, 5; 12. 1; 31. 12; Num. 7. 4; 15. 37;
20. 12, 23; 21. 16; 26. 1; 27. 6; 31. 25.
15. 1 spake, saying, I will sing unto the LORD
16. 9 Moses spake unto Aaron, Say unto all the
19. 25 So Moses went down..and spake unto th.
32. 12 Wherefore should the Egyptians speak
32. 13 all this land that I have spoken of will I
35. 4 Moses spake unto all the congregation of
36. 5 spake unto Moses, saying, The people br.

Lev. 21. 1 Speak unto the priests the sons of Aaron
Num 12. 4 LORD spake suddenly unto Moses, and un.
14. 7 spake unto all the company of the childr.
14. 15 have heard the fame of thee will speak
16. 37 Speak unto Eleazar the son of Aaron the
17. 12 children of Israel spake unto Moses, say.
18. 20 spake unto Aaron, Thou shalt have no in.
20. 3 spake, saying, Would God that we had d.
32. 2 the children of Reuben came and spake
32. 25 the children of Reuben spake unto Moses
Deut. 1. 9 I spake unto you at that time, saying, I
2. 2 And the LORD spake unto me, saying
9. 4 Speak not thou in thine heart, after that
9. 13 the LORD spake unto me, saying, I have
28. 68 by the way whereof I spake unto thee, Th.
Josh. 1. 1 the LORD spake unto Joshua the son of N.
1. 12 to half the tribe of Manasseh, spake Josh.
3. 6 Joshua spake unto the priests, saying, T.
4. 1 that the LORD spake unto Joshua, saying
4. 15 And the LORD spake unto Joshua, saying
4. 21 he spake unto the children of Israel, say.
6. 8 it came to pass, when Joshua had spoken
7. 2 spake unto them, saying, Go up and view
9. 11 the inhabitants of our country spake to
17. 17 Joshua spake unto the house of Joseph
22. 8 he spake unto them, saying, Return with
22. 24 your children might speak unto our chil.
Judg. 8. 9 he spake also unto the men of Penuel, say.
15. 13 they spake unto him, saying, No; but we
17. 2 about which thou cursedst, and spakest
19. 22 spake to the master of the house, the old
1 Sa. 7. 3 Samuel spake unto all the house of Israel
9. 9 thus he spake, Come, and let us go to the
9. 17 Behold the man whom I spake to thee of!
10. 16 But of the matter.. whereof Samuel spake
17. 26 David spake to the men that stood by him
17. 30 he turned from him.. and spake after the
28. 12 the woman spake to Saul, saying, Why ha.
30. 6 the people spake of stoning him, because
2 Sa. 3. 18 the LORD hath spoken of David, saying, By
5. 1 Then came all the tribes.. and spake, say.
5. 6 which spake unto David, saying, Except
6. 22 the maid servants which thou hast spoken
14. 4 when the woman of Tekoah spake to the
17. 6 Absalom spake unto him, saying, Ahith.
20. 18 she spake, saying, They were wont to
24. 17 David spake unto the LORD, when he saw
1 Ki. 1. 11 Nathan spake unto Bath-sheba the mother
2. 17 Speak, I pray thee, unto Solomon the ki.
3. 26 Then spake the woman whose the living
8. 12 Then spake Solomon, The LORD said that
12. 10 Thus shalt thou speak unto this people th.
12. 23 Speak unto Rehoboam, the son of Solom.
13. 31 he spake to his sons, saying, When I am
20. 5 Thus speaketh Ben-hadad, saying, Altho.
20. 28 spake unto the king of Israel, and said, Th.
2 Ki. 9. 12 Thus and thus spake he to me, saying, Th.
17. 26 they spake to the king of Assyria, saying
18. 19 Speak ye now to Hezekiah, Thus saith the
19. 10 Thus shall ye speak to Hezekiah king of
1 Ch. 15. 16 David spake to the chief of the Levites to
2 Ch. 1. 2 Solomon spake unto all Israel, to the cap.
2. 15 the wine, which my lord hath spoken of
11. 3 Speak unto Rehoboam the son of Solomon
18. 19 one spake saying after this manner, and
32. 17 to speak against him, saying, As the gods
32. 24 he spake unto him, and he gave him a si.
35. 25 the singing women spake of Josiah in th.
Ezra 8. 22 we had spoken unto the king, saying, The
Neh. 2. 18 the king's words that he had spoken unto
6. 2 he spake before his brethren and the army
8. 1 they spake unto Ezra the scribe to bring
Esth. 3. 4 it came to pass, when they spake daily un.
4. 10 Esther spake unto Hatach, and gave him
5. 14 to morrow speak thou unto the king that
6. 4 to speak unto the king to hang Mordecai
Job 33. 8 thou hast spoken in mine hearing, and I
37. 20 If a man speak, surely he shall be swallo.
Psa. 29. 9 in his temple doth every one speak of (his)
33. 9 he spake, and it was (done); he comman.
41. 5 Mine enemies speak evil of me, When sh.
45. 1 I speak of the things which I have made
71. 10 mine enemies speak against me; and they
105. 31 He spake, and there came divers sorts of
105. 34 He spake, and the locusts came, and cat.
139. 20 they speak against thee wickedly, (and) th.
145. 6 (men) shall speak of the might of thy ter.
145. 11 They shall speak of the glory of thy king.
Isa. 8. 11 the LORD spake thus to me with a strong
8. 20 if they speak not according to this word
23. 4 the sea hath spoken, (even) the strength
31. 4 thus hath the LORD spoken unto me, Like
37. 10 Thus shall ye speak to Hezekiah king of
38. 15 he hath both spoken unto me, and himself
56. 3 Neither let the son of the stranger.. speak
Jer. 13. 12 thou shalt speak unto them this word, Th.
18. 11 speak to the men of Judah, and to the in.
26. 11 Then spake the priests and the prophets
26. 12 Then spake Jeremiah unto all the princes
26. 17 spake to all the assembly of the people, say.
26. 18 spake to all the people of Judah, saying
27. 9 your sorcerers, which speak unto you, sa.
27. 14 the words of the prophets that speak unto
28. 1 spake unto me in the house of the LORD, in
28. 2 Thus speaketh the LORD of hosts, the God
28. 11 Hananiah spake in the presence of all the
29. 24 (Thus) shalt thou also speak to Shemaiah
29. 25 Thus speaketh the LORD of hosts, the God
30. 2 Thus speaketh the LORD God of Israel, say.
34. 2 speak to Zedekiah king of Judah, and tell
39. 16 Go and speak to Ebed-melech the Ethio.
40. 15 Johanan the son of Kareah spake to Ged.

Jer. 43. 2 Then spake Azariah the son of Hoshaiah
48. 8 shall be destroyed, as the LORD hath spo.
Eze. 10. 2 he spake unto the man clothed with linen
11. 5 the spirit.. said unto me, Speak; Thus sa.
13. 7 have ye not spoken a lying divination, wh.
24. 21 Speak unto the house of Israel, Thus sai.
31. 2 speak unto Pharaoh king of Egypt, and to
33. 10 O thou son of man, speak unto the house
33. 10 Thus ye speak, saying, If our transgressi.
33. 24 they that inhabit those wastes.. speak, sa.
35. 12 thy blasphemies which thou hast spoken
37. 18 the children of thy people shall speak unto
39. 17 Speak unto every feathered fowl, and to
Dan. 1. 3 the king spake unto Ashpenaz the master
Amos 5. 14 shall be with you, as ye have spoken
Jon. 2. 10 the LORD spake unto the fish, and it vom.
Hag. 1. 2 Thus speaketh the LORD of hosts, saying
1. 13 Then spake Haggai the LORD's messenger
2. 2 Speak now to Zerubbabel the son of Shea.
2. 21 Speak to Zerubbabel, governor of Judah
Zech. 1. 21 he spake, saying, These (are) the horns
3. 4 he answered and spake unto those that
4. 4 I answered and spake to the angel that
4. 6 he answered and spake unto me, saying
6. 12 speak unto him, saying, Thus speaketh
7. 3 (And) to speak unto the priests which (w.)
7. 5 Speak unto all the people of the land, and
7. 9 Thus speaketh the LORD of hosts, saying

2. *To say*, אָמַר *amar*.
Dan. 2. 9 ye have prepared lying.. words to speak
3. 29 speak any thing amiss against the God of
4. 31 king Nebuchadnezzar, to thee it is spoken
6. 12 they came near, and spake before the ki.

3. *To speak wrongfully or rashly*, בָּטָה *batah*.
Prov 12. 18 There is that speaketh like the piercings

4. *To speak, (lead forth words)*, דָּבַר *dabar*.
Gen. 16. 13 called the name of the LORD that spake
Num 27. 7 The daughters of Zelophehad speak right
Deut. 5. 1 the statutes and judgments which I speak
Esth. 10. 3 seeking the wealth.. and speaking peace
Job 2. 13 they sat down.. and none spake a word un.
Psa. 5. 6 Thou shalt destroy them that speak leas.
15. 2 worketh righteousness, and speaketh the
28. 3 which speak peace to their neighbours, but
31. 18 which speak grievous things proudly and
51. 4 mightest be justified when thou speakest
58. 3 as soon as they be born, speaking lies
63. 11 the mouth of them that speak lies shall
109. 20 and of them that speak evil against my
Prov 16. 13 and they love him that speaketh right
Isa. 9. 17 every one (is) an hypocrite.. every mouth s.
33. 15 He that walketh righteously, and speak.
45. 19 I the LORD speak righteousness, I declare
Jer. 28. 7 that I speak in thine ears, and in the ears
38. 20 the voice of the LORD, which I speak unto
40. 16 Thou shalt not.. for thou speakest falsely
Dan. 10. 11 understand the words that I speak unto
Amos 5. 10 they abhor him that speaketh uprightly

5. *To speak (consult) together*, דָּבַר *dabar*, 2.
Psa. 119. 23 Princes also did sit (and) speak against me
Mal. 3. 13 What have we spoken (so much) against
3. 16 they that feared the LORD spake often one

6. *To speak*, דָּבַר *dabar*, 3.
Gen. 8. 15 And God spake unto Noah, saying
12. 4 Abraham departed, as the LORD had spo.
18. 19 upon Abraham that which he hath spok.
18. 27, 31 I have taken upon me to speak unto
18. 29 And he spake unto him yet again, and sa.
18. 30, 32 let not the LORD .. and I will speak

See also 19. 14, 21; 21. 1, 2; 23. 3, 13; 24. 7, 15, 30, 33, 45, 50, 51; 27. 5, 6; 28. 15; 29. 6; 31. 24, 29; 32. 19; 34. 3; 35. 15; 37. 4; 39. 10, 17, 19; 41. 9, 28; 42. 7, 14, 30; 44. 2, 6, 18; 45. 12; 49. 28; 50. 4, 4, 17, 21; Exod. 4. 10, 14, 15, 30, 30; 5. 23; 6. 2, 9, 10, 11, 12, 13, 27, 28, 29, 29; 7. 2, 2, 7, 9; 9. 12, 35; 10. 29; 11. 2; 12. 3; 13. 1; 14. 1, 2, 15; 16. 10, 11, 12; 19. 6, 8, 9, 19; 20. 1, 19, 19; 23. 22; 25. 1, 2; 28. 3; 29. 42; 30. 11, 17, 22, 31; 31. 1, 1, 13; 32. 34; 33. 11, 11, 17; 34. 32, 33, 34, 34, 35; 40. 1; Lev. 1. 1, 2; 4. 1, 2; 5. 14; 6. 1, 8, 19, 24, 25; 7. 22, 23, 28, 29; 8. 1; 9. 3; 10. 3, 8, 11, 12; 11. 1, 2; 12. 1, 2; 13. 1; 14. 1, 33; 15. 1, 2; 16. 1, 2; 17. 1, 2; 18. 1, 2; 19. 1, 2; 20. 1; 21. 16, 17; 22. 1, 2, 17, 18, 26; 23. 1, 2, 9, 10, 23, 24, 26, 33, 34; 24. 1, 13, 15, 23; 25. 1, 2; 27. 1, 2.

Num. 1. 1, 48; 2. 1; 3. 1, 5, 11, 14, 44; 4. 1, 17, 21; 5. 1, 4, 5, 6, 11, 12; 6. 1, 2, 22, 23; 7. 89, 89; 8. 1, 2, 5, 23; 9. 1, 4, 9, 10; 10. 1, 29; 11. 25; 12. 1, 2, 2, 6, 8, 8; 13. 1; 14. 17, 26, 28; 15. 1, 2, 17, 18, 22, 31, 38; 16. 5, 20, 23, 26, 36, 44; 17. 1, 2, 6; 18. 8, 25, 26; 19. 1, 2; 20. 7, 8; 21. 5, 7; 22. 7, 8, 35, 35, 38; 23. 2, 5, 12, 17, 19, 26; 24. 12, 13; 25. 10, 16; 26. 3, 52; 27. 8, 15; 28. 1; 30. 1; 31. 1, 3; 33. 50, 51; 34. 1, 16; 35. 1, 9, 10; 36. 1.

Deut. 1. 1, 1, 3, 6, 14, 43; 2. 1, 17; 3. 26; 4. 12, 15, 33, 45; 5. 22, 26, 27, 27, 28, 28, 28, 31; 6. 19; 9. 10; 10. 4; 11. 19; 13. 2, 5; 18. 17, 18, 19, 20, 20, 20, 21, 22, 22, 22; 20. 2, 5, 8, 9; 25. 8; 26. 19; 27. 9; 31. 1, 28, 30; 32. 1, 44, 45, 48; Josh. 4. 8, 10, 12; 9. 22; 10. 12; 14. 12; 17. 14; 20. 1, 2, 2; 21. 2, 45; 22. 15, 30; 23. 14; 24. 27; Judg. 2. 4; 6. 39; 8. 8; 9. 2, 3, 37; 13. 11; 15. 17; 19. 3, 30; 21. 13; Ruth 1. 18; 2. 13; 4. 1; 1 Sa. 1. 13, 16; 3. 9, 10, 12; 9. 21; 16. 4; 17. 23, 28, 31; 18. 1, 23, 24; 19. 1, 4; 20. 23, 26; 24. 16; 25. 9, 17, 24, 30, 40; 28. 17, 21; 2 Sa. 2. 27; 3. 19, 19, 27; 7. 7, 17, 19, 25, 29; 12. 18; 13. 13, 22, 36; 14. 3, 12, 15, 15, 18, 19; 17. 6, 6; 19. 7, 11, 29; 20. 16, 18; 22. 1; 23. 2, 3.

1 Ki. 1. 42; 2. 4, 18, 19, 23, 27; 3. 22; 4. 32, 33, 35; 5. 5; 6. 12; 8. 15, 20, 24, 26, 33; 12. 3, 7, 7, 9, 10, 10, 14, 15, 15; 13. 3, 11, 18, 26, 27; 14. 11, 18; 15. 29; 16. 12, 34; 17. 16; 21. 2, 4, 6, 19, 19, 23; 22. 13, 13, 14, 23, 24, 28, 38; 2 Ki. 1. 3, 9, 17; 2. 22; 5. 13; 6. 12; 7. 17, 18; 8. 1; 9. 36; 10. 10, 10, 17; 14. 25; 15. 12; 18. 26, 27, 28; 19. 21; 20. 9, 19; 21. 10, 19; 24. 2; 25. 28; 1 Ch. 17. 6, 15, 17, 23; 21. 9, 19; 2 Ch. 6. 4, 10, 15, 17; 10. 3, 7, 7, 9, 10, 10, 15; 18. 12, 12, 13, 22, 23, 27; 32. 6, 16, 19; 33. 10, 18; 34. 22; Neh. 9. 13; 13. 24, 24; Esth. 6. 10; 7. 9; 8. 3; Job 1. 16. 17, 18; 2. 10, 10; 7. 11; 9. 35; 10. 1; 11. 5; 13. 3, 7, 13. 22; 16. 4, 6; 18. 2; 19. 18; 21. 3, 3; 27. 4; 32. 7, 16, 20; 33. 2, 14, 31, 32; 34. 33, 35; 37. 20; 40. 5; 41. 3; 42. 4, 7, 7, 8; Psa. 2. 5; 12. 2, 2, 3; 17. 10; 18. 1; 34. 13; 35. 20; 38. 12; 39. 3; 40. 5; 41. 6; 49. 3; 50. 1, 7, 20; 52. 3, 58. 1; 60. 6; 62. 11; 66. 14; 73. 8, 8; 75. 5; 77. 4, 78. 19; 85. 8; 89. 19; 94. 4; 108. 7; 109. 2; 115. 5; 116. 10; 119. 46; 120. 7; 127. 5; 135. 16; 144. 8, 11; 145. 21; Prov. 2. 12; 8. 6; 21. 28; 23. 9, 16; Eccl. 3. 7. Song 5. 6; Isa. 1. 2, 20; 7. 10; 8. 5, 10; 16. 13, 14; 19. 18; 20. 2; 21. 17; 22. 15; 24. 3; 25. 8; 28. 11; 29. 4; 30. 10; 32. 4, 6, 7; 36. 11, 11, 12; 37. 22; 38. 7; 39. 8; 40. 2. 5, 27; 41. 1; 45. 19; 46. 11; 48. 15, 16; 52. 6; 58. 9, 13, 14; 59. 3, 4, 13; 63. 1; 65. 12, 24; 66. 4.

Jer. 1. 6, 7, 17; 3. 5; 4. 28; 5. 5, 14; 6. 10; 7. 13, 13, 22, 27; 8. 16; 9. 5, 5, 8, 8, 12, 22; 10. 1, 5; 11. 2; 12. 6; 13. 15; 14. 14; 18. 7, 9, 20; 19. 5; 20. 8, 9; 22. 1, 21; 23. 16, 21, 28, 35, 37; 25. 2, 3, 3; 26. 2, 2, 7, 8, 8, 15, 16; 27. 12, 13, 16; 29. 23; 30. 2, 4; 31. 20; 32. 4, 24; 34. 3, 6; 35. 2, 14, 14, 17; 36. 2, 2, 4; 37. 2; 38. 1, 4, 8; 43. 1, 2; 44. 16, 25; 45. 1; 46. 13; 50. 1; 51. 12, 62; 52. 32; Eze. 1. 28; 2. 1, 2, 7; 3. 1, 4, 10, 11, 18, 24, 27; 5. 13, 15, 17; 10. 5; 11. 25; 12. 25, 25, 28; 13. 7, 8; 14. 4, 9; 17. 21, 24; 20. 3, 27; 21. 32; 22. 14, 28; 23. 34; 24. 14, 18, 27; 26. 5, 14; 28. 10; 29. 3; 30. 12; 32. 21; 33. 2, 8, 30; 34. 24; 36. 5, 6, 36; 37. 14, 17, 19; 39. 5, 8; Dan. 2. 4; 8. 13, 13, 18; 9. 6, 12, 20, 21; 10. 11, 15, 16, 19, 19; 11. 27, 36; Hos. 2. 14; 7. 13; 10. 4; 12. 4, 10; 13. 1; Joel 3. 8; Amos 3. 1, 8; Obad. 18; Mic. 4. 4; 6. 12; Zeph. 3. 13; Zech. 2. 4; 6. 8; 8. 16; 9. 10; 10. 2; 13. 2.

7. *To speak (for self)*, דָּבַר *dabar*, 7.
Num. 7. 89 he heard the voice of one speaking unto
2 Sa. 14. 13 the king doth speak this thing as one wh.
Eze. 2. 2 that I heard him that spake unto me
43. 6 I heard (him) speaking unto me out of the

8. *To meditate, utter*, הָגָה *hagah*.
Psa. 35. 28 my tongue shall speak of thy righteousn.
37. 30 The mouth of the righteous speaketh wi.
115. 7 neither speak they through their throat
Prov. 8. 7 my mouth shall speak truth; and wicked

9. *Word, speech*, מִלָּה *millah*.
Job 36. 2 I will show thee that (I have) yet to speak

10. *To speak*, מָלַל *malal*.
Prov. 6. 13 he speaketh with his feet, he teacheth wi.

11. *To speak, (bring forth speech)*, מָלַל *malal*, 3.
Job 8. 2 How long wilt thou speak these (things)?

12. *To speak*, מְלַל *melal*, 3.
Dan. 7. 11 the great words which the horn spake
7. 20 a mouth that spake very great things wh.
7. 25 he shall speak (great) words against the

13. *To use similitudes*, מָשַׁל *mashal*.
Eze. 17. 2 and speak a parable unto the house of I.

14. *To use similitudes*, מָשַׁל *mashal*, 3.
Eze. 20. 49 they say of me, Doth he not speak para.?

15. *To affirm*, נְאֻם *naam*.
Prov. 30. 1 the man spake unto Ithiel, even unto It.

16. *To put or bring before*, נָגַד *nagad*, 5.
Job 17. 5 He that speaketh flattery to (his) friends

17. *To number, recount*, סָפַר *saphar*, 3.
Psa. 59. 12 and for cursing and lying (which) they s.
73. 15 If I say, I will speak thus; behold, I sh.

18. *To answer, respond, sing*, עָנָה *anah*.
Exod 23. 2 neither shalt thou speak in a cause to de.
Deut 26. 5 thou shalt speak and say before the LORD
27. 14 the Levites shall speak, and say unto all
Job 3. 2 And Job spake, and said
35. 1 Elihu spake moreover, and said
Psa. 119. 172 My tongue shall speak of thy word: for
Song 2. 10 My beloved spake, and said unto me, Rise
Isa. 14. 10 they shall speak, and say unto thee, Art

19. *To answer, respond*, עֲנָה *anah*.
Dan. 3. 9 They spake and said to the king Nebuch.
3. 14 Nebuchadnezzar spake and said unto them
3. 19 he spake, and commanded that they shou.
3. 24 spake, and said unto his counsellors, Did
3. 26 Nebuchadnezzar came near.. (and) spake
3. 28 Nebuchadnezzar spake, and said, Blessed
4. 19 The king spake, and said, Belteshazzar
4. 30 The king spake, and said, Is not this great
5. 7 the king spake, and said to the wise (men)
5. 10 the queen spake, and said, O king, live
5. 13 the king spake and said unto Daniel, (Art)
6. 16 the king spake and said unto Daniel, Thy
6. 20 the king spake and said to Daniel, O Da.
7. 2 Daniel spake, and said, I saw in my vision

20. *To breathe, break out or forth*, פּוּחַ *puach*, 5.
Prov. 6. 19 A false witness (that) speaketh lies, and he
12. 17 (He that) speaketh truth showeth forth
14. 25 but a deceitful (witness) speaketh lies
19. 5 and (he that) speaketh lies shall not esca.
19. 9 and (he that) speaketh lies shall perish
Hab. 2. 3 but at the end it shall speak, and not lie

21. *To converse, meditate*, שִׂיחַ *siach*.
Judg. 5. 10 Speak, ye that ride on white asses, ye
Job 12. 8 speak to the earth, and it shall teach thee
Psa. 69. 12 They that sit in the gate speak against
145. 5 I will speak of the glorious honour

23. *To speak against*, ἀντιλέγω *antilegō*.
John 19. 12 maketh himself a king speaketh against

Acts 13. 45 and spake [against] those things which
28. 19 when the Jews spake against (it), I was

24. *To lay out, reason,* διαλέγομαι *dialegomai.*
Heb. 12. 5 forgotten the exhortation which speaketh

25. *To speak, tell, declare,* εἶπον *eipon.*
Matt. 8. 8 speak the word only, and my servant shall
10. 27 What I tell you in darkness, (that) speak
12. 32 whosoever speaketh a word against the
12. 32 whosoever speaketh against the Holy Gh.
16. 11 I spake (it) not to you concerning bread
17. 13 the disciples understood that he spake
22. 1 Jesus answered and spake unto them ag.
Mark 1. 42 [as soon as he had spoken], immediately
3. 9 he spake to his disciples, that a small ship
9. 18 [I spake] to thy disciples that they should
12. 12 knew that he had spoken the parable ag.
12. 26 God spake unto him, saying, I (am) the God
14. 39 and prayed, and spake the same words
Luke 6. 26 Woe unto you when all men shall speak
6. 39 he spake a parable unto them: Can the
7. 39 he spake within himself, saying, This man
8. 4 when much people were gathered..he sp.
12. 3 whatsoever ye have spoken in darkness
12. 13 Master, speak to my brother, that he div.
12. 16 he spake a parable unto them, saying, The
14. 3 Jesus answering spake unto the lawyers
15. 3 And he spake this parable unto them, say.
18. 9 he spake this parable unto certain which
19. 11 he added and spake a parable, because he
19. 28 when he had thus spoken, he went before
20. 2 spake unto him, saying, Tell us, by what
20. 19 that he had spoken this parable against
21. 29 he spake to them a parable; Behold the
24. 40 [when he had thus spoken, he showed]
John 1. 15 This was he of whom I spake, He that
4. 50 the word that Jesus had spoken unto him
7. 39 this spake he of the spirit, which they
9. 6 When he had thus spoken, he spat on the
9. 22 These (words) spake his parents, because
10. 6 This parable spake Jesus unto them: but
10. 41 all things that John spake of this man
11. 43 when he thus had spoken, he cried with
11. 51 this spake he not of himself: but being
12. 38 That the saying of Esaias..which he spake
13. 28 knew for what intent he spake this unto
18. 1 When Jesus had spoken these words, he
18. 9 saying might be fulfilled which he spake
18. 16 and spake unto her that kept the door
18. 22 when he had thus spoken, one of the offi.
18. 32 That the saying of Jesus..which he spake
20. 18 (that) he had spoken these things unto
21. 19 This spake he, signifying by what death
21. 19 when he had spoken this, he saith unto
Acts 1. 9 when he had spoken these things, while
2. 29 let me freely speak unto you of the patr.
18. 9 Then spake the Lord to Paul in the night
19. 41 when he had thus spoken, he dismissed
20. 36 when he had thus spoken, he kneeled do.
21. 37 said unto the chief captain, May I speak
26. 30 [when he had thus spoken, the king rose]
27. 35 when he had thus spoken, he took bread
28. 25 departed, after that Paul had spoken one

26. *To say, speak, tell,* ἐρῶ, ἐρέω *erō, ereō.*
Luke 12. 10 whosoever shall speak a word against the
John 11. 13 Jesus spake of his death: but they thought
Acts 2. 16 this is that which was spoken by the pr.
8. 24 none of these things which ye have spoken
13. 40 lest that come upon you which is spoken
20. 38 Sorrowing..for the words which he spake
23. 5 Thou shalt not speak evil of the ruler of
Rom. 4. 18 according to that which was spoken, So
Heb. 4. 4 he spake in a certain place of the seventh

27. *To talk against,* καταλαλέω *katalaleō.*
1 Pe. 2. 12 they speak against you as evil doers, they

28. *To talk, speak, tell,* λαλέω *laleō.*
Matt. 9. 18 While he spake these things unto them
9. 33 when the devil was cast out, the dumb s.
10. 19 no thought how or what ye shall speak
10. 19 [shall be given you..what ye shall speak]
10. 20 For it is not ye that speak, but the Spirit
10. 20 spirit of your Father which speaketh in
12. 22 the blind and dumb both spake and saw
12. 34 how can ye, being evil, speak good things?
12. 34 for out of the..heart the mouth speaketh
12. 36 every idle word that men shall speak, they
12. 46 stood without, desiring to speak with him
12. 47 stand without, desiring to speak with thee
13. 3 spake many things unto them in parables
13. 10 Why speakest thou unto them in parables?
13. 13 Therefore speak I to them in parables, be.
13. 33 Another parable spake he unto them; The
13. 34 All these things spake Jesus unto the mu.
13. 34 without a parable spake he not unto them
14. 27 But straightway Jesus spake unto them
15. 31 wondered, when they saw the dumb to sp.
17. 5 While he yet spake, behold, a bright clo.
23. 1 Then spake Jesus to the multitude, and
26. 47 while he yet spake, lo, Judas, one of the
28. 18 Jesus came and spake unto them, saying
Mark 1. 34 suffered not the devils to speak, because
2. 7 Why doth this (man) thus speak blasph.?
4. 33 with many such parables spake he the wo.
4. 34 without a parable spake he not unto them
5. 35 While he yet spake, there came from the
5. 36 Jesus heard the word that was spoken, he
7. 35 the string..was loosed, and he spake pla.
7. 37 astonished, saying..maketh..dumb to sp.
8. 32 spake that saying openly. And Peter took
13. 11 take no thought..what ye shall speak, ne.
Mark 13. 11 whatsoever shall be given you..speak ye
13. 11 is not ye that speak, but the Holy Ghost
14. 9 (this) also..shall be spoken of for a me.
14. 43 immediately, while he yet spake, cometh
16. 17 [cast out devils; they shall speak with]
16. 19 [So then, after the Lord had spoken unto]
Luke 1. 19 am sent to speak unto thee, and to show
1. 20 thou shalt be dumb, and not able to speak
1. 22 when he came out, he could not speak un.
1. 55 As he spake to our fathers, to Abraham
1. 64 his tongue (loosed), and he spake, and pr.
1. 70 As he spake by the mouth of his holy pr.
2. 33 marvelled at those things which were sp.
2. 38 spake of him to all them that looked for
2. 50 understood not the saying which he spake
4. 41 rebuking (them), suffered them not to sp.
5. 4 Now when he had left speaking, he said
5. 21 Who is this which speaketh blasphemies?
6. 45 abundance of the heart his mouth speak.
7. 15 that was dead sat up, and began to speak
8. 49 While he yet spake, there cometh one from
9. 11 spake unto them of the kingdom of God
11. 14 the dumb spake; and the people wonde.
11. 37 as he spake, a certain Pharisee besought
12. 3 ye have spoken in the ear in closets shall
22. 47 while he yet spake, behold a multitude
22. 60 immediately, while he yet spake, the cock
24. 6 remember how he spake unto you when
24. 25 believe all that the prophets have spoken
24. 36 as they thus spake, Jesus himself stood in
24. 44 These (are) the words which I spake unto
John 1. 37 disciples heard him speak, and they foll.
3. 11 We speak that we do know, and testify
3. 31 of the earth is earthly, and speaketh of
3. 34 For he whom God had sent speaketh the
4. 26 saith unto her, I that speak unto thee am
6. 63 the words that I speak unto you, (they)
7. 13 Howbeit no man spake openly of him for
7. 17 whether it be of God, or (whether) I speak
7. 18 He that speaketh of himself seeketh his
7. 26 speaketh boldly, and they say nothing unto
7. 46 officers answered, Never man spake like
8. 12 Then spake Jesus again unto them, saying
8. 20 These words spake Jesus in the treasury
8. 28 as my Father hath taught me, I speak th.
8. 30 As he spake these words many believed
8. 38 speak that which I have seen with my F.
8. 44 When he speaketh a lie, he speaketh of
9. 21 he is of age; ask him: he shall speak for
9. 29 We know that God spake unto Moses: (as
10. 6 what things they were which he spake un.
12. 29 others said, An angel spake to him
12. 36 These things spake Jesus, and departed
12. 41 when he saw his glory, and spake of him
12. 48 word that I have spoken, the same shall
12. 49 For I have not spoken of myself; but the
12. 49 what I should say, and what I should sp.
12. 50 whatsoever I speak therefore..so I speak
14. 10 words that [I speak] unto you I speak not
14. 25 These things have I spoken unto you, be.
15. 3 clean through the word which I have sp.
15. 11 These things have I spoken unto you, that
15. 22 If I had not come and spoken unto them
16. 1, 25, 33 These things have I spoken unto you
16. 13 for he shall not speak of himself; but wh.
16. 13 he shall hear, (that) shall he speak: and
16. 25 These..have I spoken...I shall no more s.
16. 29 now speakest thou plainly, and speakest
17. 1 These words spake Jesus, and lifted up
17. 13 these things I speak in the world, that th.
18. 20 spake openly to the world; I ever taught
18. 23 If I have spoken evil, bear witness of the
19. 10 Speakest thou not unto me? knowest thou
Acts 2. 4 began to speak with other tongues, as the
2. 6 every man heard them speak in his own
2. 7 are not all these which speak Galileans!
2. 11 we do hear them speak in our tongues the
2. 31 spake of the resurrection of Christ, that
3. 21 which God hath spoken by the mouth of
3. 24 as many as have spoken, have likewise f.
4. 1 as they spake unto the people, the priests
4. 17 threaten them, that they speak henceforth
4. 20 For we cannot but speak the things which
4. 29 with all boldness they may speak thy word
4. 31 and they spake the word of God with bol.
5. 20 stand and speak in the temple to the pe.
5. 40 commanded that they should not speak in
6. 10 wisdom and the spirit by which he spake
6. 11 We have heard him speak blasphemous
6. 13 ceaseth not to speak blasphemous words
7. 6 God spake on this wise, That his seed sh.
7. 38 with the angel which spake to him in the
7. 44 speaking unto Moses, that he should make
8. 26 angel of the Lord spake unto Philip, say.
9. 27 declared..that he had spoken to him, and
9. 29 spake boldly in the name of the Lord Je.
10. 7 when the angel which spake unto Cornel.
10. 32 [who, when he cometh, shall speak unto]
10. 44 While Peter yet spake these words, the
10. 46 For they heard them speak with tongues
11. 15 began to speak, the Holy Ghost fell on th.
11. 20 spake unto the Grecians, preaching the
13. 46 word of God should first have been spoken
14. 1 so spake, that a great multitude both of
14. 9 The same heard Paul speak: who stedfa.
16. 13 and spake unto the women which resorted
16. 14 attended unto the things which were spo.
16. 32 they spake unto him the word of the Lord
17. 19 this new doctrine, whereof thou speakest
18. 9 Be not afraid, but speak, and hold not thy
18. 25 spake and taught diligently the things of
19. 6 they spake with tongues, and prophesied
Acts 20. 30 speaking perverse things, to draw away
21. 39 beseech thee, suffer me to speak unto the
22. 9 heard not the voice of him that spake to
23. 9 if a spirit or an angel hath spoken to him
26. 14 heard a voice [speaking] unto me, and say.
26. 26 the king..before whom also I speak freely
28. 21 neither any of the brethren..spake any
28. 25 Well spake the Holy Ghost by Esaias the
Rom. 7. 1 for I speak to them that know the law, how
15. 18 I will not dare to speak of any of those
1 Co. 2. 6 Howbeit we speak wisdom among them
2. 7 But we speak the wisdom of God in a my.
2. 13 Which things also we speak, not in the
3. 1 could not speak unto you as unto spirit.
12. 3 that no man speaking by the spirit of God
12. 30 do all speak with tongues? do all inter.?
13. 1 Though I speak with the tongues of men
13. 11 When I was a child, I spake as a child, I
14. 2 speaketh in an (unknown) tongue speaketh
14. 2 howbeit in the spirit he speaketh myster.
14. 3 But he that prophesieth speaketh unto
14. 4 He that speaketh in an (unknown) tongue
14. 5 I would that ye all spake with tongues
14. 5 he that prophesieth than he that speaketh
14. 6 speaking with tongues..except I shall sp.
14. 9 known what is spoken? for ye shall speak
14. 11 shall be unto him that speaketh a barbar.
14. 11 he that speaketh (shall be) a barbarian
14. 13 Wherefore let him that speaketh in an
14. 18 I thank my God, I speak with tongues mo.
14. 19 Yet in the church I had rather speak five
14. 21 With..other lips will I speak unto this
14. 23 all speak with tongues, and there come in
14. 27 If any man speak in an (unknown) tongue
14. 28 and let him speak to himself, and to God
14. 29 Let the prophets speak two or three, and
14. 34 for it is not permitted unto them to speak
14. 35 for it is a shame for women to speak in the
14. 39 and forbid not to speak with tongues
2 Co. 2. 17 in the sight of God speak we in Christ
4. 13 I believed, and therefore have I spoken
4. 13 we also believe, and therefore speak
7. 14 but as we spake all things to you in truth
11. 17 That which I speak, I speak (it) not after
11. 23 Are they ministers of Christ? I speak as
12. 19 we speak before God in Christ: but (we
13. 3 Since ye seek a proof of Christ speaking
Eph. 4. 25 speak every man truth with his neighbour
5. 19 Speaking to yourselves in psalms and hy.
6. 20 that therein I may speak boldly, as I ou.
Phil. 1. 14 much more bold to speak the word with.
Col. 4. 3 to speak the mystery of Christ, for which
4. 4 may make it manifest, as I ought to speak
1 Th. 1. 8 so that we need not to speak any thing
2. 2 we were bold in our God to speak unto
2. 4 even so we speak; not as pleasing men
2. 16 Forbidding us to speak to the Gentiles
1 Ti. 5. 13 speaking things which they ought not
Titus 2. 1 But speak thou the things which become
2. 15 These things speak, and exhort, and reb.
Heb. 1. 1 spake in time past unto the fathers by the
1. 2 Hath in these last days spoken unto us by
2. 2 if the word spoken by angels was stedfast
2. 3 which at the first began to be spoken by
2. 5 the world to come, whereof we speak
3. 5 those things which were to be spoken aft.
4. 8 then would he not afterward have spoken
6. 9 persuaded better..though we thus speak
7. 14 Moses spake nothing concerning priesth.
9. 19 when Moses had spoken every precept to
11. 4 and by it he, being dead, yet [speaketh]
12. 24 that speaketh better things than (that of)
12. 25 See that ye refuse not him that speaketh
13. 7 who have spoken unto you the word of G.
Jas. 1. 19 let every man be swift to hear, slow to sp.
2. 12 So speak ye, and so do, as they that shall
5. 10 the prophets, who have spoken in the na.
1 Pe. 3. 10 evil, and his lips that they speak no guile
4. 11 If any man speak, (let him speak) as the
2 Pe. 1. 21 holy men of God spake (as they were) mo.
3. 16 in all (his) epistles, speaking in them of th.
1 Jo. 4. 5 therefore speak they of the world, and the
2 Jo. 12 I trust to come unto you, and speak face
3 Jo. 14 shall shortly see thee, and we shall speak
Jude 15 which ungodly sinners have spoken agai.
16 their mouth speaketh great swelling (wo.)
Rev. 1. 12 I turned to see the voice that spake with
10. 8 the voice which I heard from heaven sp.
13. 5 a mouth speaking great things and blas.
13. 11 had two horns like a lamb, and he spake
13. 15 the image of the beast should both speak

29. *To lay out, say, speak,* λέγω *legō.*
Matt. 21. 45 they perceived that he spake of them
Mark 12. 1 he began [to speak] unto them by parab.
14. 31 [he spake] the more vehemently, If I sh.
14. 71 I know not this man of whom ye speak
Luke 5. 36 he spake also a parable unto them; No
7. 24 he began to speak unto the people concer.
9. 31 spake of his decease which he should acc.
9. 34 While he thus spake, there came a cloud
11. 27 as he spake these things, a certain woman
12. 41 speakest thou this parable unto us, or even
13. 6 He spake also this parable; A certain (m.)
18. 1 he spake a parable unto them (to this end)
18. 34 neither knew they the things which were s
20. 9 Then began he to speak to the people this
21. 5 as some spake of the temple, how it was
22. 65 many other things blasphemously spake
John 2. 21 But he spake of the temple of his body
6. 71 He spake of Judas Iscariot (the son) of S.
8. 26 [I speak] to the world those things which

John 8. 27 They understood not that he spake to th.
11. 13 they thought that he had spoken of tak.
11. 56 spake among themselves, as they stood in
13. 18 I speak not of you all: I know whom I
13. 22 disciples looked..doubting of whom he sp.
13. 24 ask who it should be of whom he spake
16. 29 disciples said..thou..speakest no proverb
Acts 1. 3 speaking of the things pertaining to the
2. 25 David speaketh concerning him, I foresaw
8. 6 heed unto those things which Philip sp.
8. 34 I pray thee, of whom speaketh the pro.?
13. 45 [those things which were spoken] by Paul
24. 10 governor had beckoned unto him to speak
26. 1 Thou art permitted to speak for thyself
27. 11 those things which were spoken by Paul
28. 24 some believed the things which were sp.
Rom. 3. 5 (Is) God unrighteous..I speak as a man
6. 19 I speak after the manner of men because
10. 6 righteousness which is of faith speaketh
11. 13 I speak to you Gentiles, inasmuch as I
1 Co. 1. 10 that ye all speak the same thing, and
6. 5 [I speak] to your shame. Is it so, that there
7. 6 I speak this by permission, (and) not of
7. 12 to the rest speak I, not the Lord: If any
7. 35 this I speak for your own profit; not that
10. 15 I speak as to wise men; judge ye what I
15. 34 some have not..[I speak] (this) to your sh.
2 Co. 6. 13 I speak as unto (my) children, be ye also
7. 3 I speak not (this) to condemn (you): for
8. 8 I speak not by commandment, but by oc.
11. 21 I speak as concerning reproach, as thou.
11. 21 whereinsoever any is bold, I speak fooli.
Gal. 3. 15 I speak after the manner of men; Though
Eph. 5. 12 it is a shame even to speak of those things
5. 32 I speak concerning Christ and the church
Phil. 4. 11 Not that I speak in respect of want: for
1 Ti. 2. 7 I speak the truth in Christ, (and) lie not
4. 1 the Spirit speaketh expressly, that in the
Heb. 7. 13 For he of whom these things are spoken
8. 1 of the things which we have spoken (this
9. 5 of which we cannot now speak particula.
Rev. 2. 24 have not known the depths..as they sp.

30. *To sound aloud, utter,* φθέγγομαι *phtheğgomai.*
Acts 4. 18 commanded them not to speak at all nor
2 Pe. 2. 16 the dumb ass speaking with man's voice
2. 18 when they speak great swelling (words) of

31. *To speak oracularly,* χρηματίζω *chrēmatizō.*
Heb. 12. 25 they escaped not who refused him that sp.

SPEAK, in season, not a word, unadvisedly, to cause to —

1. *To speak hastily, rashly,* בָּטָא *bata,* 3.
Psa. 106. 33 so that he spake unadvisedly with his lips

2. *To cause to speak, strengthen,* דָּבַב *dabab.*
Song 7. 9 causing..those that are asleep to speak

3. *To keep silent or deaf,* חָרַשׁ *charash,* 5.
2 Sa. 19. 10 why speak ye not a word of bringing th

4. *To speak in season, haste to support,* עוּת *uth.*
Isa. 50. 4 I should know how to speak a word in se.

SPEAK among, before, can, for one's self, forth, out, to —

1. *To sound up, back out,* ἀναφωνέω, *anaphōneō.*
Luke 1. 42 she spake out with a loud voice, and said

2. *To lay out for oneself,* ἀπολογέομαι *apologeomai.*
Acts 26. 24 as he thus spake for himself, Festus said

3. *To utter out,* ἀποφθέγγομαι *apophtheğgomai.*
Acts 26. 25 speak forth the words of truth and sober.

4. *To know, take cognizance of,* γινώσκω *ginōskō.*
Acts 21. 37 the chief captain..said, Canst thou speak

5. *To tell thoroughly,* καταγγέλλω *katağgelō.*
Rom. 1. 8 your faith is spoken of throughout the

6. *To speak or tell before,* προεῖπον *proeipon.*
Acts 1. 16 the Holy Ghost..spake before concerning

7. *To speak or tell before,* προερέω *proereō.*
2 Pe. 3. 2 the words which were spoken before by
Jude 17 the words which were spoken before of

8. *To talk with,* συλλαλέω *sullaleō.*
Luke 4. 36 they were all amazed, and spake among

SPEAK to, unto, with, to —

1. *To talk to,* προσλαλέω *proslaleō.*
Acts 13. 43 who, speaking to them, persuaded them
28. 20 called for you, to see (you,) and to speak w.

2. *To put to,* προστίθημι *prostithēmi.*
Heb. 12. 19 the word should not be spoken to them

3. *To sound to,* προσφωνέω *prosphōneō.*
Luke 23. 20 Pilate therefore..spake again to them
Acts 21. 40 he spake unto (them) in the Hebrew ton.
22. 2 when they heard that he spake in the H.

SPEAK blasphemy, boldly, evil, fair, to —

1. *To make the voice gracious,* חָנַן קוֹל *chanan* (3) *qol.*
Prov. 26. 25 When he speaketh fair, believe him not

2. *To speak freely,* παῤῥησιάζομαι *parrhēsiazomai.*
Acts 9. 29 he spake boldly in the name of the Lord
14. 3 therefore abode they speaking boldly in
18. 26 he began to speak boldly in the synagogue
19. 8 spake boldly for the space of three months
Eph. 6. 20 I may speak boldly, as I ought to speak

3. *To speak injuriously,* βλασφημέω *blasphēmeō.*
Matt 26. 65 He hath spoken blasphemy; what further
Rom 14. 16 Let not then your good be evil spoken of
1 Co. 10. 30 why am I evil spoken of for that which I
Titus 3. 2 To speak evil of no man, to be no brawl.
1 Pe. 4. 4 they think it strange..speaking evil of
1 Pe. 4. 14 [on their part he is evil spoken of, but on]
2 Pe. 2. 2 the way of truth shall be evil spoken of
2. 10 they are not afraid to speak evil of dign.
2. 12 speak evil of the things that they under.
Jude 8 despise dominion, and speak evil of dig.
10 they speak evil of those things which they

4. *To speak evil,* κακολογέω *kakologeō.*
Mark 9. 39 no man..that can lightly speak evil of me
Acts 19. 9 spake evil of that way before the multit.

5. *To speak against,* καταλαλέω *katalaleō.*
Jas. 4. 11 Speak not evil one of another, brethren
4. 11 He that speaketh evil of (his) brother
4. 11 speaketh evil of the law, and judgeth the
1 Pe. 2. 12 whereas they speak against you as evil
3. 16 whereas they speak evil of you as of evil

SPEAKING (lies, much, evil), speaker (chief) — *See* [evil.

1. *A word, speech,* מִלָּה *millah.*
Job 4. 2 who can withhold himself from speaking
32. 15 answered no more; they left off speaking

2. *To speak,* מָלַל *melal,* 3.
Dan. 7. 8 in this horn..a mouth speaking great th.

3. *Injurious speaking,* βλασφημία *blasphēmia.*
Eph. 4. 31 clamour, and evil speaking, be put away

4. *A talking against,* καταλαλία *katalalia.*
1 Pe. 2. 1 laying aside..envies, and all evil speakings

5. *Leader in discourse,* ἡγούμενος τοῦ λόγου [*hēgeo- mai*].
Acts 14. 12 because he was the chief speaker

6. *Much speech* or *discourse,* πολυλογία *polulogia.*
Matt. 6. 7 shall be heard for their much speaking

7. *Speaker of falsehood,* ψευδολόγος *pseudologos.*
1 Ti. 4. 2 Speaking lies in hypocrisy; having their

SPEARS, spearman —

1. *Spear, javelin,* חֲנִית *chanith.*
1 Sa. 13. 19 Lest the Hebrews make..swords or spears
13. 22 there was neither sword nor spear found
17. 7 the staff of his spear (was) like a weaver's
17. 7 his spear's head (weighed) six hundred
17. 45 Thou comest to me..with a spear, and
17. 47 the LORD saveth not with sword and sp.
21. 8 is there not here under thine hand spear
22. 6 Saul abode in Gibeah..having his spear
26. 7 his spear stuck in the ground at his bol.
26. 8 let me smite him..with the spear even to
26. 11 take thou now the spear that (is) at his
26. 12 David took the spear and the cruse of w.
26. 16 see where the king's spear (is), and the
26. 22 Behold the king's spear! and let one of
2 Sa. 1. 6 behold, Saul leaned upon his spear; and
2. 23 Abner with the hinder end of the spear
2. 23 that the spear came out behind him, and
21. 19 the staff of whose spear (was) like a wea.
23. 7 fenced with iron and the staff of a spear
23. 18 lifted up his spear against three hundred
23. 21 Egyptian had a spear in his hand; but he
23. 21 plucked the spear out of the Egyptian's
23. 21 and slew him with his own spear
2 Ki. 11. 10 did the priest give king David's spears
1 Ch. 11. 11 he lifted up his spear against three hun.
11. 20 for lifting up his spear against three hu.
11. 23 in the Egyptian's hand (was) a spear like
11. 23 plucked the spear out of the Egyptian's
11. 23 and slew him with his own spear
12. 34 with them with shield and spear thirty
20. 5 whose spear's staff (was) like a weaver's
2 Ch. 23. 9 priest delivered..spears, and bucklers
Job 39. 23 rattleth against him, the glittering spear
41. 26 the spear, the dart, nor the habergeon
Psa. 35. 3 Draw out also the spear, and stop (the w.)
46. 9 cutteth the spear in sunder; he burneth
57. 4 whose teeth (are) spears and arrows, and
Isa. 2. 4 they shall beat..their spears into prunn.
Mic. 4. 3 they shall beat..their spears into prunn.
Nah. 3. 3 the bright sword and the glittering spear
Hab. 3. 11 (and) at the shining of thy glittering spear

2. *Halbert, javelin,* כִּידוֹן *kidon.*
Josh. 8. 18 Stretch out the spear that (is) in thy hand
8. 18 Joshua stretched out the spear that (he
8. 26 wherewith he stretched out the spear, un.
Job 41. 29 he laugheth at the shaking of a spear
Jer. 6. 23 They shall lay hold on bow and spear

3. *Spear, harpoon,* צִלְצַל *tselatsal.*
Job 41. 7 Canst thou fill..his head with fish spears

4. *Spear, iron point of a lance,* קַיִן *qayin.*
2 Sa. 21. 16 weight of whose spear (weighed) three hu.

5. *A reed,* קָנֶה *qaneh.*
Psa. 68. 30 Rebuke the company of spearmen, the

6. *Javelin, spear, lance,* רֹמַח *romach.*
Judg. 5. 8 was there a shield or spear seen among
1 Ch. 12. 24 children..that bare shield and spear (we.)
2 Ch. 11. 12 in every several city (he put)..spears, and
14. 8 an army (of men) that bare targets and sp.
25. 5 choice (men)..that could handle spear
26. 14 Uzziah prepared for them..shields, and sp.
Neh. 4. 13 with their swords, their spears, and their
4. 16 other half of them held both the spears
4. 21 half of them held the spears from the ri.
Jer. 46. 4 furbish the spears, (and) put on the brig.
Eze. 39. 9 arrows, and the hand staves, and the sp.
Joel 3. 10 Beat your..prunning hooks into spears

7. *A spearman,* δεξιολάβος *dexiolabos.*
Acts 23. 23 Make ready..spearmen two hundred, at

8. *A spear head, lance,* λόγχη *loğchē.*
John 19. 34 one of the soldiers with a spear pierced

SPECIAL, specially —

1. *Peculiar treasure,* סְגֻלָּה *segullah.*
Deut 7. 6 hath chosen thee to be a special people

2. *Most of all, chiefly,* μάλιστα *malista.*
Acts 25. 26 brought him..specially before thee, O ki.
1 Ti. 4. 10 who is the Saviour of all men, specially
5. 8 provide not..specially for those of his own
Tit. 1. 10 deceivers, specially they of the circumci.
Phm. 16 specially to me, but how much more unto

3. *Not ordinary,* οὐ τὰς τυχούσας *ou tas tuchousas.*
Acts 19. 11 God wrought special miracles by the ha.

SPECKLED —

1. *Speckled,* נָקֹד *naqod.*
Gen. 30. 32 removing from thence all the speckled
30. 32 the spotted and speckled among the goa.
30. 33 every one that (is) not speckled and spot.
30. 35 she goats that were speckled and spotted
30. 39 brought forth cattle ringstraked, speckled
31. 8 said thus, The speckled shall be thy wages
31. 8 then all the cattle bare speckled: and if
31. 10, 12 the rams..ringstraked, speckled, and

2. *Spotted,* צָבוּעַ *tsabua.*
Jer. 12. 9 Mine heritage (is) unto me (as) a speckled

3. *Bay, speckled,* שָׂרֹק *saroq.*
Zech. 1. 8 behind him (were there) red horses, spe.

SPECTACLE —

Public spectacle or show, theatre, θέατρον *theatron.*
1 Co. 4. 9 we are made a spectacle unto the world

SPEECH, (boldness of, fair) —

1. *A saying, speech,* אֵמֶר *emer.*
Job 6. 26 Do ye imagine to reprove..the speeches
32. 14 neither will I answer him with your spe.

2. *A saying, speech,* אֹמֶר *omer.*
Psa. 19. 2 Day unto day uttereth speech, and night
19. 3 no speech nor language (where) their vo.

3. *A saying, speech,* אִמְרָה *imrah.*
Gen. 4. 23 hearken unto my speech: for I have slain
Deut 32. 2 my speech shall distil as the dew, as the
Psa. 17. 6 incline thine ear unto me, (and) hear my
Isa. 28. 23 Give ye ear..hearken, and hear my spee.
29. 4 thy speech shall be low out of the dust
29. 4 and thy speech shall whisper out of the
32. 9 hear my voice..give ear unto my speech

4. *A word,* דָּבָר *dabar.*
Gen. 11. 1 And the whole earth was of one..speech
Deut 22. 14 give occasions of speech against her, and
22. 17 hath given occasions of speech (against h.)
2 Sa. 14. 20 To fetch about this form of speech hath
19. 11 seeing the speech of all Israel is come to
1 Ki. 3. 10 speech pleased the LORD, that Solomon
Jer. 31. 23 As yet they shall use this speech in the

5. *A tumult,* הֲמֻלָּה *hamullah.*
Eze. 1. 24 the voice of speech, as the noise of an ho.

6. *What is received or taken, doctrine,* לֶקַח *leqach.*
Prov. 7. 21 With her much fair speech she caused him

7. *Speech, what is spoken,* מִדְבָּר *midbar.*
Song 4. 3 thy speech (is) comely: thy temples (are)

8. *A word,* מִלָּה *millah.*
Job 13. 17 Hear diligently my speech, and my decla.
15. 3 or with speeches wherewith he can do no
21. 2 Hear diligently my speech; and let this be
24. 25 make me a liar, and make my speech no.
29. 22 spake not again; and my speech dropped
33. 1 hear my speeches, and hearken to all my

9. *Mouth,* פֶּה *peh.*
Exod. 4. 10 but I (am) slow of speech, and of a slow to.

10. *Lip,* שָׂפָה *saphah.*
Job 12. 20 removeth away the speech of the trusty
Prov 17. 7 Excellent speech becometh not a fool, mu.
Isa. 33. 19 people of deeper speech than thou canst
Eze. 3. 5, 6 people of a strange speech and of an h.

11. *Hearing, what is heard,* שֵׁמַע *shema.*
Hab. 3. 2 O LORD, I have heard thy speech, (and) was

12. *Eulogy, fair talk,* εὐλογία *eulogia.*
Rom 16. 18 by good words and fair speeches deceive

13. *Talk,* λαλιά *lalia.*
Matt 26. 73 thou also art (one) of them; for thy speech
Mark 14. 70 thou art a Galilean, and thy speech agre.
John 8. 43 Why do ye not understand my speech?

14. *A word,* λόγος *logos.*
Acts 20. 7 and continued his speech until midnight
1 Co. 2. 1 came not with excellency of speech or of
2. 4 my speech and my preaching (was) not wi.
4. 19 not the speech of them which are puffed
2 Co. 10. 10 (his)..presence (is) weak, and (his) speech
11. 6 though (I be) rude in speech, yet not in k.
Col. 4. 6 Let your speech (be) alway with grace, se.
Titus 2. 8 Sound speech, that cannot be condemned

SPEECH of Lycaonia —

In the Lycaonic dialect, Λυκαονιστί *lukaonisti.*
Acts 14. 11 saying in the speech of Lycaonia, The gods

SPEECHLESS, (to be) —

1. *Without breath or speech,* ἐννεός *enneos,* ἐνεός.
Acts. 9. 7 the men..stood speechless, hearing a voi.

2. *Stricken, blunted, deaf, dumb*, κωφός *kōphos.*
Luke 1. 22 for he beckoned..and remained speechl.

3. *To muzzle, gag, silence*, φιμόω *phimoō.*
Matt22. 12 how camest thou in..And he was speech.

SPEED, speedily, speedy —

1. *Speedily*, אָסְפַּרְנָא *osparna.*
Ezra. 6. 12 made a decree; let it be done with speed
6. 13 according to that.. so they did speedily
7. 17 That thou mayest buy speedily with this
7. 21 shall require of you, it be done speedily
7. 26 let judgment be executed speedily upon

2. *To be hastened, troubled*, בָּהַל *bahal*, 2.
Zeph. 1. 18 he shall make even a speedy riddance of

3. *To go on*, הָלַךְ *halak.*
Zech. 8. 21 Let us go speedily to pray before the Lo.

4. *Hasting, hastily*, מַהֵר *maher.*
Psa. 69. 17 for I am in trouble: hear me speedily
79. 8 let thy tender mercies speedily prevent us
102. 2 in the day (when) I call answer me speed.
143. 7 Hear me speedily, O LORD; my spirit fail.

5. *Haste*, מְהֵרָה *meherah.*
Psa. 31. 2 deliver me speedily: be thou my strongr.
Eccl. 8. 11 Because sentence..is not executed speed.
Isa. 5. 26 behold, they shall come with speed swift.
58. 8 and thine health shall spring forth speed.
Joel 3. 4 speedily will I return your recompence u.

6. *To (make to) haste*, מָהַר *mahar*, 3
Gen. 44. 11 they speedily took down every man his

7. *To let escape*, מָלַט *malat*, 2.
1 Sa. 27. 1 I should speedily escape into the land of

8. *To pass over*, עָבַר *abar.*
2 Sa. 17. 16 speedily pass over; lest the king be swa.

9. *Most speedily*, τάχιστα *tachista.*
Acts 17. 15 commandment. to come to him with all s.

10. *In haste, speed, speedily*, ἐν τάχει *en tachei.*
Luke18. 8 I tell you he will avenge them speedily

SPEED, (to make) —

1. *To strengthen self*, אָמַץ *amats*, 7.
1Ki. 12. 18 Rehoboam made speed to get him up to
2 Ch.10. 18 Rehoboam made speed to get him up to

2. *To hasten*, מָהַר *mahar*, 3.
2 Sa. 15. 14 make speed to depart lest he overtake us
Isa. 5. 19 Let him make speed..hasten his work, th

3. *Haste*, מְהֵרָה *meherah.*
1 Sa. 20. 38 Jonathan cried after the lad, Make speed

4. *To find*, מָצָא *matsa.*
Judg. 5. 30 Have they not sped? have they (not) div.

SPEEDILY, to divide or give —

1. *To trouble, hasten*, בָּהַל *bahel*, 3.
Esth. 2. 9 speedily gave her her things for purifica.

2. *To cause to run*, רוּץ *ruts*, 5.
2 Ch.35. 13 divide (them) speedily among all the pe

SPEND, to —

1. *To separate, spend, destroy*, אָבַד *abad*, 3.
Prov29. 3 keepeth company with harlots spendeth

2. *To finish*, כָּלָה *kalah*, 3 [V.L. בלה, 3].
Job 21. 13 They spend their days in wealth, and in

3. *To complete, finish, consume*, כָּלָה *kalah*, 3.
Deut32. 23 heap mischiefs upon them; I will spend
Job 36. 11 they shall spend their days in prosperity
Psa. 90. 9 we spend our years as a tale (that is told
Isa. 49. 4 I have spent my strength for nought, and

4. *To do, make*, עָשָׂה *asah.*
Eccl. 6. 12 all the days of his vain life which he sp.

5. *To weigh out, pay, spend*, שָׁקַל *shaqal.*
Isa. 55. 2 Wherefore do ye spend money for (that

6. *To spend*, δαπανάω *dapanaō.*
Mark 5. 26 had spent all that she had, and was not.
Luke15. 14 when he had spent all, there arose a mi.
2 Co.12. 15 And I will very gladly spend..for you

7. *To do, make*, ποιέω *poieō.*
Acts 18. 23 after he had spent some time (there), he

8. *To take up besides*, προσαναλίσκω *prosanaliskō.*
Luke 8. 43 a woman..which had spent all her living

SPEND, more, time, up, to —

1. *To swallow up*, בָּלַע *bala*, 3.
Prov21. 20 treasure..but a foolish man spendeth it up

2. *To have a good or easy time*, εὐκαιρέω *eukaireō.*
Acts 17. 21 spent their time in nothing else, but eit.

3. *To spend besides*, προσδαπανάω *prosdapanaō.*
Luke10. 35 whatsoever thou spendest more, when I

4. *To rub (pass) time*, χρονοτριβέω *chronotribeō.*
Acts 20. 16 because he would not spend the time in

SPENT, (to be) far —

1. *To go away or about*, אָזַל *azal.*
1 Sa. 9. 7 the bread is spent in our vessels, and (th.

2. *To be completed, finished, consumed*, כָּלָה *kalah.*
Gen. 21. 15 the water was spent in the bottle, and
Job 7. 6 My days..are spent without hope
Psa. 31. 10 my life is spent with grief, and my years

3. *To subdue*, רָדַד *radad.*
Judg 19. 11 the day was far spent; and the servant

4. *To be perfect, finished, consumed*, תָּמַם *tamam.*
Gen. 47. 18 We will not hide..that our money is sp.
Lev. 26. 20 your strength shall be spent in vain
Jer. 37. 21 until all the bread in the city were spent

5. *To come through or over*, διαγίνομαι *diaginomai.*
Acts 27. 9 when much time was spent, and when sa.

6. *To expend*, ἐκδαπανάω *ekdapanaō.*
2 Co. 12. 15 And I will very gladly..be spent for you

7. *To bow down, recline*, κλίνω *klinō.*
Luke24. 29 toward evening..and the day is far spent

8. *To strike forward*, προκόπτω *prokoptō.*
Rom 13. 12 The night is far spent, the day is at hand

SPICE, spiced, spicery, (sweet) —

1. *Spice*, בָּשָׂם *basam.*
Song 5. 1 I have gathered my myrrh with my spice

2. *Spice*, בֶּשֶׂם *besem.*
Exod25. 6 spices for anointing oil, and for sweet in.
30. 23 Take thou also unto thee principal spices
35. 8 spices for anointing oil, and for the sweet
1 Ki. 10. 2 with camels that bare spices, and very mu.
10. 10 twenty talents of gold, and of spices very
10. 25 garments, and armour, and spices, horses
2 Ki. 20. 13 the gold, and the spices, and the precious
1 Ch. 9. 29 oil, and the frankincense, and the spices
9. 30 And (some)..made the ointment of the sp.
2 Ch. 9. 1 camels that bare spices, and gold in abu.
9. 9 twenty talents of gold, and of spices gr.
9. 24 raiment, harness, and spices, horses, and
32. 27 for precious stones, and for spices, and for
Song 4. 10 smell of thine ointments than all spices
4. 14 myrrh and aloes, with all the chief spices
4. 16 blow upon my garden, (that) the spices
8. 14 a young hart upon the mountains of spic.
Isa. 39. 2 the spices, and the precious ointment, and

3. *Spice*, בֹּשֶׂם *bosem.*
Exod35. 28 spice, and oil for the light, and for the
1 Ki. 10. 10 such abundance of spices as these which
2 Ch. 9. 9 neither was there any such spices as the
Song 5. 13 His cheeks (are) as a bed of spices, (as) sw
6. 2 into his garden, to the beds of spices, to
Eze. 27. 22 they occupied in thy fairs with..spices, and

4. *Spices, treasury*, נְכֹאת *nekoth.*
Gen. 37. 25 with their camels bearing spicery and ba.
43. 11 a little honey, spices, and myrrh, nuts, and

5. *Spices, perfume*, סַמִּים *sammim.*
Exod30. 34 Take unto thee sweet spices, stacte, and
30. 34 (these) sweet spices with pure frankince.
37. 29 pure incense of sweet spices, according to

6. *Compound, mixture, spice*, רֶקַח *reqach.*
Song 8. 2 I would cause thee to drink of spiced wi.

7. *Aroma, very fragrant*, ἄρωμα *arōma.*
Mark16. 1 had bought sweet spices, that they mig.
Luke23. 56 they returned, and prepared spices and
24. 1 bringing the spices which they had prep.
John19. 40 wound it in linen clothes with the spices

SPICE, spice merchant, to —

1. *To go to and fro, be a merchant*, רָכַל *rakal.*
1 Ki. 10. 15 of the traffic of the spice merchants, and

2. *To compound, spice*, רָקַח *raqach*, 5.
Eze. 24. 10 consume the flesh, and spice it well, and

SPIDER —

1. *A spider*, עַכָּבִישׁ *akkabish.*
Job 8. 14 and whose trust (shall be) a spider's web
Isa. 59. 5 They..weave the spider's web: he that

2. *Poisonous lizard, spider*, שְׂמָמִית *semamith.*
Prov 30. 28 The spider taketh hold with her hands, and

SPIED, to be —

To be seen, רָאָה *raah*, 2.
2 Ki. 23. 24 the abominations that were spied in the

SPIES —

1. *Spies, places or districts*, אֲתָרִים *atharim.*
Num21. 1 that Israel came by the way of the spies

2. *To use the feet, travel, traverse*, רָגַל *ragal*, 3.
Gen. 42. 9 Ye (are) spies; to see the nakedness of the
42. 11 we (are) true (men), thy servants are no sp.
42. 14 I spake unto you, saying, Ye (are) spies
42. 16 by the life of Pharaoh..ye (are) spies
42. 30 spake roughly to us, and took us for spies
42. 31 said..We (are) true (men); we are no sp.
42. 34 then shall I know that ye (are) no spies
Josh. 6. 23 young men that were spies went in, and
1 Sa. 26. 4 David therefore sent out spies, and und.
2 Sa. 15. 10 Absalom sent spies throughout all the tr.

3. *One sent in (to spy)*, ἐγκάθετος *egkathetos.*
Luke20. 20 sent forth spies, which should feign them.

4. *A spy*, κατάσκοπος *kataskopos.*
Heb. 11. 31 when she had received the spies with peace

SPIKENARD —

1. *Nard*, נֵרְדְּ *nerd.*
Song 1. 12 my spikenard sendeth forth the smell th.
4. 13 pleasant fruits; camphire, with spikenard
4. 14 Spikenard and saffron; calamus and cin.

2. *Genuine nard*, νάρδος πιστική *nardos pistikē.*
Mark14. 3 an alabaster box of ointment of spikenard
John 12. 3 a pound of ointment of spikenard, very

SPILL, be spilled or spilt, to —

1. *To be poured or spread out*, נָגַר *nagar*, 2.
2 Sa. 14. 14 as water spilt on the ground, which cann.

2. *To corrupt, destroy*, שָׁחַת *shachath*, 3.
Gen. 38. 9 he spilled (it) on the ground, lest that he

3. *To pour out*, ἐκχέω *ekcheō.*
Mark 2. 22 [the wine is spilled, and the bottles will]

4. *To pour out*, ἐκχύνω *ekchunō.*
Luke 5. 37 wine will burst the bottles, and be spilled

SPIN, to —

1. *To spin*, טָוָה *tavah.*
Exod35. 25 women that were wise hearted did spin
35. 26 stirred them up in wisdom spun goats'

2. *To spin*, νήθω *nēthō.*
Matt. 6. 28 the lilies..toil not, neither do they spin
Luke12. 27 the lilies..they toil not, they spin not

SPINDLE —

Spindle, distaff, כִּישׁוֹר *kishor.*
Prov31. 19 She layeth her hands to the spindle, and

SPIRIT —

1. *Breath*, נְשָׁמָה *neshamah.*
Job 26. 4 To whom..and whose spirit came from
Prov20. 27 The spirit of man (is) the candle of the L.

2. *Spirit, wind*, רוּחַ *ruach.*
Gen. 1. 2 the spirit of God moved upon the face of
6. 3 My spirit shall not always strive with m.
41. 8 his spirit was troubled; and he sent and
41. 38 Can we find..a man in whom the spirit of
45. 27 the spirit of Jacob their father revived
Exod. 6. 9 they hearkened not..for anguish of spirit
28. 3 whom I have filled with the spirit of wis.
31. 3 I have filled him with the spirit of God
35. 21 every one whom his spirit made willing
35. 31 he hath filled him with the spirit of God
Num. 5. 14 the spirit of jealousy come upon him, and
5. 14 if the spirit of jealousy come upon him
5. 30 when the spirit of jealousy cometh upon
11. 17 I will take of the spirit which (is) upon
11. 25 took of the spirit that (was) upon him, and
11. 25 when the spirit rested upon them, they
11. 26 the spirit rested upon them; and they
11. 29 that the LORD would put his spirit upon
14. 24 he had another spirit with him, and hath
16. 22 O God, the God of the spirits of all flesh
24. 2 and the spirit of God came upon him
27. 16 Let the LORD, the God of the spirits of
27. 18 son of Nun, a man in whom (is) the spirit
Deut. 2. 30 God hardened his spirit, and made his he.
34. 9 the son of Nun was full of the spirit of w.
Josh. 5. 1 neither was there spirit in them any mo.
Judg. 3. 10 the spirit of the LORD came upon him, and
6. 34 the spirit of the LORD came upon Gideon
9. 23 God sent an evil spirit between Abimele.
11. 29 spirit of the LORD came upon Jephthah
13. 25 spirit of the LORD began to move him at
14. 6 spirit of the LORD came mightily upon
14. 19 spirit of the LORD came upon him, and
15. 14 spirit of the LORD came mightily upon
15. 19 spirit came again, and he revived: where.
1 Sa. 1. 15 I (am) a woman of a sorrowful spirit: I
10. 6 spirit of the LORD will come upon thee
10. 10 spirit of God came upon him, and he pro.
11. 6 spirit of God came upon Saul when he he.
16. 13 spirit of LORD came upon David from that
16. 14 spirit of the LORD departed from Saul, and
16. 14 evil spirit from the LORD troubled him
16. 15 Behold now, an evil spirit from God tro.
16. 16 when the evil spirit from God is upon th.
16. 23 when the (evil) spirit from God was upon
16. 23 was well, and the evil spirit departed fr.
18. 10 the evil spirit from God came upon Saul
19. 9 the evil spirit from the LORD was upon
19. 20 the spirit of God was upon the messeng.
19. 23 the spirit of God was upon him also, and
30. 12 when he had eaten, his spirit came again
2 Sa. 23. 2 The spirit of the LORD spake by me, and
1 Ki. 10. 5 there was no more spirit in her
18. 12 the spirit of the LORD shall carry thee w.
21. 5 Why is thy spirit so sad, that thou eatest
22. 21 there came forth a spirit, and stood before
22. 22 I will be a lying spirit in the mouth of all
22. 23 the LORD hath put a lying spirit in the mo.
22. 24 Which way went the spirit of the LORD
2 Ki. 2. 9 let a double portion of thy spirit be upon
2. 15 they said, The spirit of Elijah doth rest on
2. 16 peradventure the spirit of the LORD hath
1 Ch. 5. 26 the God of Israel stirred up the spirit of
5. 26 the spirit of Tilgath-pilneser king of Ass.
12. 18 the spirit came upon Amasai, (who was)
28. 12 the pattern of all that he had by the spi.
2 Ch. 9. 4 there was no more spirit in her
15. 1 the spirit of God came upon Azariah the
18. 20 there came out a spirit, and stood before
18. 21 I will go out, and be a lying spirit in the
18. 22 the LORD hath put a lying spirit in the mo.
18. 23 Which way went the spirit of the LORD
20. 14 came the spirit of the LORD in the midst
21. 16 stirred up against Jehoram the spirit of
24. 20 the spirit of God came upon Zechariah the
36. 22 the LORD stirred up the spirit of Cyrus ki.
Ezra 1. 1 the LORD stirred up the spirit of Cyrus ki.
1. 5 with all (them) whose spirit God had rais.
Neh. 9. 20 Thou gavest also thy good spirit to instr.
9. 30 testifiedst against them by thy spirit in
Job 4. 15 a spirit passed before my face; the hair of
6. 4 the poison whereof drinketh up my spirit

Job 7. 11 I will speak in the anguish of my spirit
10. 12 thy visitation hath preserved my spirit
15. 13 thou turnest thy spirit against God, and
20. 3 the spirit of my understanding causeth me
21. 4 if (it were so), why should not my spirit
26. 13 By his spirit he hath garnished the heavens
27. 3 and the spirit of God (is) in my nostrils
32. 8 (there) is a spirit in man: and the inspirati.
32. 18 I am full of matter; the spirit within me
33. 4 The spirit of God hath made me, and the
34. 14 (if) he gather unto himself his spirit and
Psa. 31. 5 Into thine hand I commit my spirit: thou
32. 2 Blessed (is) the man..in whose spirit (the.
34. 18 and saveth such as be of a contrite spirit
51. 10 O God; and renew a right spirit within me
51. 11 Cast me not away..take not thy holy spi.
51. 12 and uphold me (with thy) free spirit
51. 17 The sacrifices of God (are) a broken spirit
76. 12 He shall cut off the spirit of princes (he
77. 3 I complained, and my spirit was overwh.
77. 6 and my spirit made diligent search
78. 8 and whose spirit was not stedfast with G
104. 4 Who maketh his angels spirits; his minis.
104. 30 Thou sendest forth thy spirit, they are cr.
106. 33 they provoked his spirit, so that he spake
139. 7 Whither shall I go from thy spirit? or wh.
142. 3 When my spirit was overwhelmed within
143. 4 Therefore is my spirit overwhelmed with
143. 7 Hear me speedily, O LORD; my spirit fail
143. 10 thou (art) my God: thy spirit (is) good
Prov 1. 23 I will pour out my spirit unto you, I will
11. 13 he that is of a faithful spirit concealeth
14 29 but (he that is) hasty of spirit exalteth fo.
15. 4 perverseness..(is) a breach in the spirit
15. 13 by sorrow of the heart the spirit is brok.
16. 2 but the LORD weigheth the spirits
16. 18 and an haughty spirit before a fall
16. 19 Better (it is to be) of an humble spirit wi.
16. 32 he that ruleth his spirit than he that ta.
17. 22 but a broken spirit drieth the bones
17. 27 of understanding is of an excellent spirit
18. 14 The spirit of a man will sustain his infir
18. 14 but a wounded spirit who can bear?
25. 28 He that (hath) no rule over his own spirit
29. 23 honour shall uphold the humble in spirit
Eccl. 1. 14 behold, all (is) vanity and vexation of sp
1. 17 perceived that this..is vexation of spirit
2. 11, 17, 26 vanity and vexation of spirit
3. 21 Who knoweth the spirit of man that go.
3. 21 the spirit of the beast that goeth downw.
4. 4 This (is) also vanity and vexation of spirit
4. 6 full (with) travail and vexation of spirit
4. 16 this also (is) vanity and vexation of spirit
6. 9 this (is) also vanity and vexation of spirit
7. 8 patient in spirit..the proud in spirit
7. 9 Be not hasty in thy spirit to be angry: for
8. 8 over the spirit, to retain the spirit
10. 4 If the spirit of the ruler rise up against
11. 5 knowest not..the way of the spirit, (nor)
12. 7 the spirit shall return unto God who gave
Isa. 4. 4 the spirit of judgment, and by the spirit
11. 2 the spirit of the LORD shall rest upon him
11. 2 the spirit of wisdom and understanding
11. 2 the spirit of counsel and might, the spirit
19. 3 the spirit of Egypt shall fail in the midst
19. 14 The LORD hath mingled a perverse spirit
26. 9 with my spirit within me will I seek thee
28. 6 a spirit of judgment to him that sitteth
29. 10 hath poured out upon you the spirit of
29. 24 They also that erred in spirit shall come
30. 1 cover with a covering, but not of my spi.
31. 3 and their horses flesh, and not spirit
32. 15 Until the spirit be poured upon us from
34. 16 it hath commanded, and his spirit it hath
38. 16 all these (things is) the life of my spirit
40. 7 because the spirit of the LORD bloweth up.
40. 13 Who hath directed the spirit of the LORD
42. 1 I have put my spirit upon him; he shall
42. 5 giveth..spirit to them that walk therein
44. 3 I will pour my spirit upon thy seed, and
48. 16 the Lord GOD, and his spirit, hath sent me
54. 6 as a woman forsaken, and grieved in spirit
57. 15 (that is) of a contrite and humble spirit
57. 15 to revive the spirit of the humble, and to
57. 16 the spirit should fail before me, and the
59. 19 the spirit of the LORD shall lift up a stan.
59. 21 My spirit that (is) upon thee, and my words
61. 1 The spirit of the Lord GOD (is) upon me
61. 3 the garment of praise for the spirit of he.
63. 10 they rebelled, and vexed his Holy Spirit
63. 11 where (is) he that put his Holy Spirit wi.
63. 14 the Spirit of the LORD caused him to rest
65. 14 and shall howl for vexation of spirit
66. 2 to (him that is) poor, and of a contrite sp.
Jer. 51. 11 the LORD hath raised up the spirit of the
Eze. 1. 12 whither..spirit was to go, they went; (and)
1. 20 Whithersoever the spirit was to go, they
1. 20 thither (was their) spirit to go; and the
1. 20, 21 the spirit of the living creature (was)
2. 2 the spirit entered into me when he spake
3. 12 the spirit took me up, and I heard behind
3. 14 the spirit lifted me up, and took me away
3. 14 and I went..in the heat of my spirit
3. 24 the spirit entered into me, and set me up.
8. 3 the spirit lifted me up between the earth
10. 17 the spirit of the living creature (was) in
11. 1 the spirit lifted me up, and brought me
11. 5 the spirit of the LORD fell upon me, and
11. 19 and I will put a new spirit within you
11. 24 Afterwards the spirit took me up, and br.
11. 24 in a vision by the spirit of God into Cha.
13. 3 prophets, that follow their own spirit, and

Eze. 18. 31 make you a new heart and a new spirit
21. 7 every spirit shall faint, and all knees shall
36. 26 and a new spirit will I put within you
36. 27 I will put my spirit within you, and cause
37. 1 carried me out in the spirit of the LORD, and
37. 14 shall put my spirit in you, and ye shall li.
39. 29 I have poured out my spirit upon the ho.
43. 5 the spirit took me up, and brought me into
Dan. 2. 1 his spirit was troubled, and his sleep brake
2. 3 my spirit was troubled to know the dream
Hos. 4. 12 the spirit of whoredoms hath caused (th)
5. 4 the spirit of whoredoms (is) in the midst
Joel 2. 28 I will pour out my spirit upon all flesh
2. 29 in those days will I pour out my spirit
Mic. 2. 7 is the spirit of the LORD straitened? (are)
2. 11 If a man walking in the spirit and falseh.
3. 8 I am full of power by the spirit of the L.
Hag. 1. 14 the LORD stirred up the spirit of Zerubb.
1. 14 the spirit of Joshua the son of Josedech
1. 14 the spirit of all the remnant of the people
2. 5 So my spirit remaineth among you: fear
Zech. 4. 6 Not by might, nor by power, but by my s.
6. 5 These (are) the four spirits of the heavens
6. 8 have quieted my spirit in the north cou.
7. 12 the LORD of hosts hath sent in his spirit
12. 1 and formeth the spirit of man within him
12. 10 the spirit of grace and of supplications
13. 2 and the unclean spirit to pass out of the
Mal. 2. 15 Yet had he the residue of the spirit. And
2. 15, 16 therefore take heed to your spirit

2. *Spirit, wind,* רוּחַ *ruach.*

Dan. 4. 8 and in whom (is) the spirit of the holy go.
4. 9 I know that the spirit of the holy gods (is)
4. 18 for the spirit of the holy gods (is) in thee
5. 11 in whom (is) the spirit of the holy gods
5. 12 Forasmuch as an excellent spirit, and kn.
5. 14 the spirit of the gods (is) in thee, and (th.)
6. 3 because an excellent spirit (was) in him
7. 15 I Daniel was grieved in my spirit in the

3. *Spirit,* πνεῦμα *pneuma.* [*See also* Holy].

Matt. 3. 16 he saw the spirit of God descending like
4. 1 Then was Jesus led up of the spirit into
5. 3 Blessed (are) the poor in spirit: for theirs
8. 16 he cast out the spirits with (his) word, and
10. 1 gave them power (against) unclean spirits
10. 20 the spirit of your Father which speaketh
12. 18 I will put my spirit upon him, and he sh.
12. 28 if I cast out devils by the spirit of God, th.
12. 43 When the unclean spirit is gone out of a
12. 45 taketh with himself seven other spirits
22. 43 How then doth David in spirit call him
26. 41 the spirit indeed (is) willing, but the flesh
Mark 1. 10 the spirit like a dove descending upon him
1. 12 the spirit driveth him into the wilderness
1. 23 there was..a man with an unclean spirit
1. 26 when the unclean spirit had torn him, and
1. 27 commandeth he even the unclean spirits
2. 8 Jesus perceived in his spirit that they so
3. 11 unclean spirits, when they saw him, fell
3. 30 they said, He hath an unclean spirit
5. 2 met him..a man with an unclean spirit
5. 8 Come out of the man, (thou) unclean spi.
5. 13 the unclean spirits went out, and entered
6. 7 and gave them power over unclean spi.
7. 25 whose young daughter had an unclean sp.
8. 12 he sighed deeply in his spirit, and saith
9. 17 brought..my son, which hath a dumb sp.
9. 20 the spirit tare him; and he fell on the
9. 25 he rebuked the foul spirit, saying unto
9. 25 (Thou) dumb and deaf spirit, I charge th.
14 38 The spirit truly (is) ready, but the flesh
Luke 1 17 he shall go before him in the spirit and
1 47 my spirit hath rejoiced in God my Sav.
1. 80 the child grew, and waxed strong in sp.
2. 27 And he came by the spirit into the temple
2. 40 the child grew, and waxed strong [in sp.]
4. 1 was led by the spirit into the wilderness
4. 14 Jesus returned in the power of the spirit
4. 18 The spirit of the LORD (is) upon me, bec.
4. 33 there was a man which had a spirit of an
4. 36 he commandeth the unclean spirits, and
6. 18 they that were vexed with unclean spirits
7. 21 cured many of..plagues, and of evil sp.
8. 2 which had been healed of evil spirits and
8. 29 he had commanded the unclean spirit to
8. 55 [her spirit came again, and she arose st.]
9. 39 a spirit taketh him, and he suddenly cr.
9. 42 Jesus rebuked the unclean spirit, and he.
9. 55 [Ye know not what manner of spirit ye are]
10. 20 rejoice not, that the spirits are subject
10. 21 In that hour Jesus rejoiced in spirit, and
11. 13 give the Holy Spirit to them that ask him
11. 24 When the unclean spirit is gone out of a
11. 26 taketh (to him) seven other spirits more
13. 11 there was a woman which had a spirit of
23. 46 into thy hands I commend my spirit
24. 37 and supposed that they had seen a spirit
24. 39 a spirit hath not flesh and bones, as ye see
John 1. 32 I saw the Spirit descending from heaven
1. 33 thou shalt see the Spirit descending, and
3. 5 Except a man be born..(of) the spirit, he
3. 6 that which is born of the spirit is spirit
3. 8 so is every one that is born of the spirit
3. 34 God giveth not the spirit by measure (unto
4. 23 shall worship the Father in spirit and in
4. 24 God (is) a Spirit: and they that worship
4. 24 must worship (him) in spirit and in truth
6. 63 It is the spirit that quickeneth; the flesh
6. 63 the words that I speak..(they) are spirit
7. 39 this spake he of the spirit, which they that
11. 33 he groaned in the spirit, and was troubled

John 13. 21 he was troubled in spirit, and testified
14. 17 (Even) the spirit of truth; whom the wo.
15. 26 I will send..the spirit of truth, which
16. 13 when he, the spirit of truth, is come, he
Acts 2. 4 began to speak..as the spirit gave them
2. 17 I will pour out of my spirit upon all flesh
2. 18 will pour out in those days of my spirit
5. 9 agreed together to tempt the spirit of the
5. 16 were vexed with unclean spirits: and th.
6. 10 they were not able to resist..the spirit by
7. 59 and saying, Lord Jesus, receive my spirit
8. 7 For unclean spirits, crying with loud voi.
8. 29 Then the spirit said unto Philip, Go near
8. 39 spirit of the Lord caught away Philip, th.
10. 19 spirit said unto him, Behold, three men
11. 12 spirit bade me go with them, nothing do.
11. 28 signified by the spirit that there should
16. 7 assayed to go into Bithynia: but the spi.
16. 16 damsel possessed with a spirit of divina.
16. 18 Paul..turned and said to the spirit, I co.
17. 16 spirit was stirred in him, when he saw the
18. 5 Paul was pressed [in the spirit,] and test.
18. 25 being fervent in the spirit, he spake and
19. 12 and the evil spirits went out of them
19. 13 to call over them which had evil spirits
19. 15 evil spirit answered and said, Jesus I kn.
19. 16 man in whom the evil spirit was leaped
19. 21 Paul purposed in the spirit, when he had
20. 22 go bound in the spirit unto Jerusalem, not
21. 4 who said to Paul through the spirit, that
23. 8 no resurrection, neither angel, nor spirit
23. 9 if a spirit or an angel hath spoken to him
Rom. 1. 4 according to the spirit of holiness, by the
1. 9 whom I serve with my spirit in the gospel
2. 29 in the spirit, (and) not in the letter, whose
7. 6 that we should serve in newness of spirit
8. 1 [walk not after the flesh, but after the sp.]
8. 2 For the law of the spirit of life in Christ
8. 4 walk not after the flesh, but after the sp.
8. 5 are after the spirit the things of the spir.
8. 9 in the spirit, if so be that the spirit of God
8. 9 if any man have not the spirit of Christ
8. 10 the spirit (is) life because of righteousness
8. 11 if the spirit of him that raised up Jesus
8. 11 quicken..by his spirit that dwelleth in you
8. 13 if ye through the spirit do mortify the de.
8. 14 as many as are led by the spirit of God
8. 15 ye have not received the spirit of bondage
8. 15 ye have received the spirit of adoption
8. 16 spirit..beareth witness with our spirit
8. 23 which have the first fruits of the spirit, ev.
8. 26 the spirit also helpeth our infirmities, for
8. 26 the spirit itself maketh intercession for
8. 27 knoweth what (is) the mind of the spirit
11. 8 God hath given them the spirit of slumber
12. 11 Not slothful in business; fervent in spirit
15. 19 wonders, by the power of the spirit of G.
15. 30 I beseech you..for the love of the spirit
1 Co. 2. 4 in demonstration of the spirit and of pow.
2. 10 revealed..by his spirit: for the spirit sea.
2. 11 save the spirit of man which is in him
2. 11 knoweth no man, but the spirit of God
2. 12 not the spirit of the world, but the spirit
2. 14 receiveth not the things of the spirit of G.
3. 16 and (that) the spirit of God dwelleth in
4. 21 shall I come..(in) the spirit of meekness
5. 3 as absent in body, but present in spirit
5. 4 my spirit, with the power of our Lord Je.
5. 5 that the spirit may be saved in the day of
6. 11 ye are justified..by the spirit of our God
6. 17 he..joined unto the Lord is one spirit
6. 20 [glorify God in your body, and in your sp.]
7. 34 may be holy both in body and in spirit
7. 40 I think also that I have the spirit of God
12. 3 no man speaking by the spirit of God ca.
12. 4 diversities of gifts, but the same spirit
12. 7 the manifestation of the spirit is given to
12. 8 to one is given by the spirit the word of
12. 8 the word of knowledge by the same spirit
12. 9 To another faith by the same spirit; to ano.
12. 9 the gifts of healing by the same spirit
12. 10 to another discerning of spirits; to another
12. 11 all these worketh..the self same spirit
12. 13 by one spirit are we all baptized into one
12. 13 been all made to drink into one spirit
14. 2 howbeit in the spirit he speaketh myster.
14. 14 my spirit prayeth, but my understanding
14. 15 I will pray with the spirit, and I will pray
14. 15 I will sing with the spirit, and I will sing
14. 16 when thou shalt bless with the spirit, how
14. 32 the spirits of the prophets are subject to
15. 45 last Adam (was made) a quickening spirit
16. 18 they have refreshed my spirit and yours
2 Co. 1. 22 given the earnest of the spirit in our hea.
2. 13 I had no rest in my spirit, because I found
3. 3 but with the spirit of the living God
3. 6 made us able ministers..of the spirit: for
3. 6 the letter killeth, but the spirit giveth li.
3. 8 shall not the ministration of the spirit be
3. 17 the Lord is that spirit: and where the sp.
3. 18 are changed..(even) as by the spirit of the
4. 13 We having the same spirit of faith, acco.
5. 5 given unto us the earnest of the spirit
7. 1 from all filthiness of the flesh and spirit
7. 13 because his spirit was refreshed by you
11. 4 (if) ye receive another spirit, which ye ha.
12. 18 walked we not in the same spirit? walked
Gal. 3. 2 Received ye the spirit by the works of the
3. 3 having begun in the spirit, are ye now ma.
3. 5 He..that ministereth to you the spirit
3. 14 we might receive the promise of the sp.
4. 6 God hath sent forth the spirit of his Son

Gal. 4. 29 him (that was born) after the spirit, even
5. 5 we through the spirit wait for the hope
5. 16 Walk in the spirit, and ye shall not fulfil
5. 17 lusteth against the spirit, and the spirit
5. 18 if ye be led of the spirit, ye are not und.
5. 22 the fruit of the spirit is love, joy, peace
5. 25 in the spirit, let us also walk in the spirit
6. 1 restore such an one in the spirit of meek.
6. 8 soweth to the spirit shall of the spirit re.
6. 18 the grace of our Lord..(be) with your sp.
Eph. 1. 13 ye were sealed with the Holy Spirit of pr.
1. 17 may give unto you the spirit of wisdom
2. 2 the spirit that now worketh in the child.
2. 18 we both have access by one spirit unto
2. 22 for an habitation of God through the sp.
3. 5 revealed unto his . prophets by the spirit
3. 16 strengthened with might by his spirit in
4. 3 to keep the unity of the spirit in the bond
4. 4 (There is) one body, and one spirit, even
4. 23 And be renewed in the spirit of your mi
4. 30 grieve not the Holy Spirit of God, where.
5. 9 the fruit of [the spirit] (is) in all goodness
5. 18 be not drunk..but be filled with the spi.
6. 17 the sword of the spirit, which is the word
6. 18 with all prayer and supplication in the sp.
Phil. 1. 19 and the supply of the spirit of Jesus Chr.
1. 27 that ye stand fast in one spirit, with one
2. 1 if any fellowship of the spirit, if any bow
3. 3 which worship God in the spirit, and rej.
Col. 1. 8 declared unto us your love in the spirit
2. 5 yet am I with you in the spirit, joying
1 Th. 4. 8 who hath also given unto us his Holy Sp
5. 19 Quench not the Spirit
5. 23 (I pray God) your whole spirit and soul
2 Th. 2. 2 neither by spirit, nor by word, nor by le.
2. 8 the Lord shall consume with the spirit of
2. 13 through sanctification of the spirit and
1 Ti. 3. 16 justified in the spirit, seen of angels, pr
4. 1 the spirit speaketh expressly, that in the
4. 1 giving heed to seducing spirits, and doc.
4. 12 in conversation, in charity, [in spirit], in
2 Ti. 1. 7 God hath not given us the spirit of fear
4. 22 The Lord Jesus Christ (be) with thy spirit
Phil. 25 The grace of our Lord..(be) with your sp
Heb. 1. 7 Who maketh his angels spirits, and his
1. 14 Are they not all ministering spirits, sent
4. 12 the dividing asunder of soul and spirit
9. 14 who through the eternal spirit offered hi.
10. 29 hath done despite unto the spirit of grace
12. 9 in subjection unto the Father of spirits, and
12. 23 and to the spirits of just men made perfe.
Jas. 2. 26 as the body without the spirit is dead, so
4. 5 The spirit that dwelleth in us lusteth to
1 Pe. 1. 2 through sanctification of the spirit, unto o.
1. 11 what manner of time, the spirit of Christ
1. 22 in obeying the truth [through the spirit]
3. 4 (the ornament) of a meek and quiet spirit
3. 18 put to death..but quickened by the spirit
3. 19 went and preached unto the spirits in pr.
4. 6 but live according to God in the spirit
4. 14 the spirit of glory and of God resteth up.
1 Jo. 3. 24 we know..by the spirit which he hath gi.
4. 1 believe not every spirit, but try the spirits
4. 2 know ye the spirit of God: Every spirit th.
4. 3 every spirit that confesseth not that Jes.
4. 6 the spirit of truth, and the spirit of error
4. 13 because he hath given us of his spirit
5. 6 spirit..beareth witness..because the spi.
5. 8 the spirit, and the water, and the blood
Jude 19 These be..sensual, having not the spirit
Rev. 1. 4 the seven spirits which are before his th.
1. 10 I was in the spirit on the Lord's day, and
2. 7, 11, 17, 29 let him hear what the spirit sa.
3. 1 he that hath the seven spirits of God, and
3. 6, 13, 22 let him hear what the spirit saith un.
4. 2 I was in the spirit: and, behold, a throne
4. 5 seven lamps..which are the seven spirits
5. 6 the seven spirits of God sent forth into
11. 11 the spirit of life from God entered into th.
14. 13 Yea, saith the spirit, that they may rest
16. 13 I saw three unclean spirits like frogs (come)
16. 14 they are the spirits of devils, working mi.
17. 3 he carried me away in the spirit into the
18. 2 the hold of every foul spirit, and a cage
19. 10 the testimony of Jesus is the spirit of pr.
21. 10 he carried me away in the spirit to a gre.
22. 17 And the spirit and the bride say, Come

4. *Phantasm, apparition,* φάντασμα *phantasma.*
Matt 14. 26 they were troubled, saying, It is a spirit
Mark 6. 49 they supposed it had been a spirit, and

SPIRITUAL (things), spiritually—

1. *Man of the spirit,* אִישׁ הָרוּחַ *ish ha-ruach.*
Hos. 9. 7 the spiritual man (is) mad, for the multi.

2. *Spirit,* πνεῦμα *pneuma.*
1 Co. 14. 12 ye are zealous of spiritual (gifts), seek that

3. *Spiritual,* πνευματικός *pneumatikos.*
Rom. 1. 11 may impart unto you some spiritual gift
7. 14 For we know that the law is spiritual: but
15. 27 been made partakers of their spiritual th.
1 Co. 2. 13 comparing spiritual things with spiritual
2. 15 he that is spiritual judgeth all thing, yet
3. 1 could not speak unto you as unto spiritual
9. 11 If we have sown unto you spiritual things
10. 3 And did all eat the same spiritual meat
10. 4 did all drink the same spiritual drink
10. 4 they drank of that spiritual rock that
12. 1 concerning spiritual (gifts), brethren, I
14. 1 desire spiritual gifts, but rather that ye
14. 37 If any man think himself..spiritual, let

1 Co. 15. 44 a natural body; it is raised a spiritual
15. 44 a natural body, and there is a spiritual
15. 46 that (was) not first which is spiritual, but
15. 46 and afterward that which is spiritual
Gal. 6. 1 ye which are spiritual restore such an one
Eph. 1. 3 who hath blessed us with all spiritual bl.
5. 19 in psalms and hymns and [spiritual] songs
6. 12 against spiritual wickedness in high (pl.)
Col. 1. 9 in all wisdom and spiritual understanding
3. 16 in psalms and hymns and spiritual songs
1 Pe. 2. 5 are built up a spiritual house, an holy pr.
2. 5 to offer up spiritual sacrifices, acceptable

4. *Spiritually,* πνευματικῶς *pneumatikōs.*
1 Co. 2. 14 because they are spiritually discerned
Rev. 11. 8 which spiritually is called Sodom and E.

SPIRITUALLY minded —

Minding of the spirit, φρόνημα τοῦ πνεύματος *phro.*
Rom. 8. 6 but to be spiritually minded (is) life and

SPIT (on or upon), spitting, spittle, to —

1. *To spit,* יָרַק *yaraq.*
Num 12. 14 If her father had but spit in her face, sh.
Deut 25. 9 spit in his face, and shall answer and

2. *Spittle, drivel,* רִיר *rir.*
1 Sa. 21. 13 and let his spittle fall down upon his bea.

3. *Spittle, spitting,* רֹק *roq.*
Job 7. 19 alone till I swallow down my spittle
30. 10 flee far from me, and spare not to spit in
Isa. 50. 6 I hid not my face from shame and spitting

4. *To spit,* רָקַק *raqaq.*
Lev. 15. 8 if he that hath the issue spit upon him

5. *To spit in or on,* ἐμπτύω *emptuō.*
Matt 26. 67 Then did they spit in his face, and buffe.
27. 30 they spit upon him, and took the reed, and
Mark 10. 34 shall scourge him, and shall spit upon
14. 65 some began to spit on him, and to cover
15. 19 did spit upon him, and bowing (their) kn.
Luke 18. 32 and spitefully entreated, and spitted on

6. *Spittle,* πτύσμα *ptusma.*
John 9. 6 made clay of the spittle, and he anointed

7. *To spit,* πτύω *ptuō.*
Mark 7. 33 put his fingers into his ears, and he spit
8. 23 when he had spit on his eyes, and Jn. 9. 6.

SPITE, entreat spitefully—

1. *Anger, provocation, sadness,* כַּעַס *kaas.*
Psa. 10. 14 thou beholdest mischief and spite, to re.

2. *To use despitefully,* ὑβρίζω, Matt. 22. 6; Lu. 18. 32.

SPOIL, spoiler, spoiling —

1. *Spoils, machinations,* אֲרֻבּוֹת *oraboth.*
Isa. 25. 11 bring down their pride..with the spoils

2. *Prey, spoil,* בַּז *baz* [V.L. error בז].
Eze. 25. 7 will deliver thee for a spoil to the heath.

3. *Prey, spoil,* בַּז *baz.*
Jer. 15. 13 thy treasures will I give to the spoil wit.
17. 3 I will give..thy treasures to the spoil, (and)
Eze. 26. 5 and it shall become a spoil to the nations

4. *Prey, spoil,* בִּזָּה *bizzah.*
2 Ch. 14. 14 they spoiled all the cities; for there was
25. 13 smote three thousand..and took much sp.
28. 14 left the captives and the spoil before the
Ezra 9. 7 to a spoil, and to confusion of face, as (it
Esth. 9. 10 but on the spoil laid they not their hand
Dan. 11. 33 and by flame, by captivity, and by spoil

5 *What is violently snatched away,* גְּזֵלָה *gezelah.*
Isa. 3. 14 the spoil of the poor (is) in your houses

6 *Armour,* חֲלִיצָה *chalitsah.*
Judg 14. 19 took their spoil, and gave change of gar

7. *Torn prey,* טֶרֶף *tereph.*
Job 29. 17 and plucked the spoil out of his teeth

8. *Spoil,* מְשִׁסָּה *meshissah* [V.L. משוסה].
Isa. 42. 24 Who gave Jacob for a spoil, and Israel to

9. *Spoil,* מְשִׁסָּה *meshissah.*
2 Ki. 21. 14 they shall become a prey and a spoil to all
Isa. 42. 22 they are..for a spoil, and none saith, Re.
Jer. 30. 16 they..shall be a spoil, and all that prey

10. *Destruction, spoiling,* שֹׁד *shod.*
Isa. 16. 4 the extortioner is at an end, the spoiler
22. 4 because of the spoiling of the daughter of
Jer. 6. 7 violence and spoil is heard in her; before
20. 8 I cried violence and spoil; because the
48. 3 A voice of crying..spoiling and great de.
Eze. 45. 9 remove violence and spoil, and execute
Hab. 1. 3 for spoiling and violence (are) before me
2. 17 the spoil of beasts, (which) made them afr.

11. *To destroy, spoil,* שָׁדַד *shadad.*
Isa. 16. 4 spoiler ceaseth, the oppressors are cons.
21. 2 dealeth treacherously, and the spoiler sp.
Jer. 6. 26 for the spoiler shall suddenly come upon
12. 12 spoilers are come upon all high places th.
15. 8 brought upon them..a spoiler at noond.
48. 8 spoiler shall come upon every city, and
48. 18 for the spoiler of Moab shall come upon
48. 32 spoiler is fallen upon thy summer fruits
51. 48 for the spoilers shall come unto her from
51. 53 from me shall spoilers come unto her, sa.
51. 56 Because the spoiler is come upon her, (ev.)

12. *To corrupt, destroy, mar,* שָׁחַת *shachath,* 5.
1 Sa. 13. 17 the spoilers came out of the camp of the
14. 15 the garrison, and the spoilers, they also

13. *To take spoil,* שָׁסָה *shasah.*
Judg. 2. 14 delivered them into the hands of spoilers
2 Ki. 17. 20 delivered them into the hand of spoilers

14. *To be bereaved,* שְׁכֹל *shakol.*
Psa. 35. 12 rewarded me evil for good, (to) the spoil.

15. *Spoil,* שָׁלָל *shalal.*
Gen. 49. 27 and at night he shall divide the spoil
Exod 15. 9 I will overtake, I will divide the spoil
Num 31. 11 they took all the spoil, and all the prey
31. 12 brought the captives..and the spoil, unto
Deut. 2. 35 and the spoil of the cities which we took
3. 7 the spoil of the cities, we took for a prey
13. 16 thou shalt gather all the spoil of it into
13. 16 shalt burn..all the spoil thereof every wh.
20. 14 all that is in the city, (even) all the spoil
20. 14 thou shalt eat the spoil of thine enemies
Josh. 7. 21 I saw among the spoils a goodly Babylo.
8. 2 only the spoil thereof, and the cattle th.
8. 27 the spoil of that city, Israel took for a pr.
11. 14 the spoil of these cities, and the cattle, the
22. 8 divide the spoil of your enemies with yo.
Judg. 5. 30 for the necks of (them that take) the sp.?
1 Sa. 14. 30 had eaten freely today of the spoil of th.
14. 32 the people flew upon the spoil, and took
15. 19 didst fly upon the spoil, and didst evil in
15. 21 the people took of the spoil, sheep and ox.
30. 16 the great spoil that they had taken out of
30. 19 neither spoil, nor any (thing) that they
30. 20 And David..said, This (is) David's spoil
30. 22 we will not give them (ought) of the spoil
30. 26 he sent of the spoil unto the elders of Ju.
30. 26 Behold a present for you of the spoil of
2 Sa. 3. 22 and brought in a great spoil with them
8. 12 of the spoil of Hadadezer, son of Rehob
12. 30 he brought forth the spoil of the city in
2 Ki. 3. 23 said..now therefore, Moab, to the spoil
1 Ch. 20. 2 he brought also exceeding much spoil out
26. 27 Out of the spoils won in battles did they
2 Ch. 14. 13 and they carried away very much spoil
15. 11 they offered..of the spoil (which) they had
20. 25 his people came to take away the spoil of
20. 25 were three days in gathering of the spoil
24. 23 sent all the spoil of them unto the king
28. 8 took..much spoil..and brought the spoil
28. 15 with the spoil clothed all that were naked
Esth. 3. 13 and (to take) the spoil of them for a prey
8. 11 and (to take) the spoil of them for a prey
Psa. 68. 12 she that tarried at home divided the spoil
119. 162 I rejoice..as one that findeth great spoil
Prov. 1. 13 we shall fill our houses with spoil
16. 19 than to divide the spoil with the proud
31. 11 so that he shall have no need of spoil
Isa. 8. 4 the spoil of Samaria shall be taken away
9. 3 as (men) rejoice when they divide the sp.
10. 6 to take the spoil, and to take the prey, and
33. 4 your spoil shall be gathered (like) the ga.
33. 23 then is the prey of a great spoil divided
53. 12 he shall divide the spoil with the strong
Jer. 49. 32 and the multitude of their cattle a spoil
50. 10 And Chaldea shall be a spoil: all that
Eze. 7. 21 and to the wicked of the earth for a spoil
29. 19 take her multitude, and take her spoil, and
38. 12 To take a spoil, and to take a prey; to turn
38. 13 Art thou come to take a spoil? hast thou
38. 13 take away cattle..to take a great spoil
Dan. 11. 24 scatter among them the prey, and spoil, and
Zech. 2. 9 and they shall be a spoil to their servants
14. 1 thy spoil shall be divided in the midst of

16. *Dedicated spoils,* ἀκροθίνιον *akrothinion.*
Heb. 7. 4 whom..Abraham gave the tenth of the sp.

17. *A snatching away,* ἁρπαγή *harpagē.*
Heb. 10. 34 took joyfully the spoiling of your goods

18. *What is stripped or carried off,* σκῦλον *skulon.*
Luke 11. 22 taketh from him..and divideth his spoils

SPOIL, (make or take), to —

1. *To take as spoil,* בָּזָא *baza.*
Isa. 18. 2, 7 nation..whose land the rivers have sp.

2. *To spoil, seize, plunder,* בָּזַז *bazaz.*
Gen. 34. 27 The sons of Jacob..spoiled the city, bec.
34. 29 and spoiled even all that (was) in the ho.
Num 31. 9 took the spoil of all their cattle, and all
31. 53 the men of war had taken spoil, every man
1 Sa. 14. 36 spoil them until the morning light, and
2 Ki. 7. 16 the people went out, and spoiled the te.
2 Ch. 14. 14 they spoiled all the cities; for there was
Psa. 109. 11 and let the stranger spoil his labour
Isa. 11. 14 they shall spoil them of the east together
Jer. 20. 5 their enemies, which shall spoil them, and
Nah. 2. 9 Take..the spoil of silver, take the spoil
Zeph. 2. 9 the residue of my people shall spoil them

3. *To snatch away,* גָּזַל *gazal.*
Psa. 35. 10 and the needy from him that spoileth him
Eze. 18. 7 hath spoiled none by violence, hath given
18. 12 hath spoiled by violence, hath not resto.
18. 16 neither hath spoiled by violence, (but) ha.
18. 18 spoiled his brother by violence, and did

4. *To destroy, injure,* חָבַל *chabal,* 3.
Song 2. 15 the foxes, the little foxes, that spoil the vi.

5. *To snatch away,* נָצַל *natsal,* 3.
Exod. 3. 22 borrow..and ye shall spoil the Egyptians
12. 36 lent unto them..and they spoiled the E.

6. *To strip off,* פָּשַׁט *pashat.*
Hos. 7. 1 (and) the troop of robbers spoileth with.
Nah. 3. 16 the canker worm spoileth, and fleeth aw.

7. *To strip off,* פָּשַׁט *pashat,* 3.
2 Sa. 23. 10 people returned after him only to spoil

8. *To spoil, deceive, fix,* קָבַע *qaba.*
Prov 22. 23 and spoil the soul of those that spoiled

9. *Destruction, spoiling,* שֹׁד *shod.*
Hos. 10. 14 as Shalman spoiled Beth-arbel in the day

10. *To destroy, spoil,* שָׁדַד *shadad.*
Isa. 21. 2 dealeth treacherously..and the spoiler sp.
33. 1 Woe to thee that spoilest, and thou (wast)
33. 1 when thou shalt cease to spoil, thou shalt
Jer. 5. 6 (and) a wolf of the evening shall spoil th.
25. 36 for the LORD hath spoiled their pasture
47. 4 to spoil..LORD will spoil the Philistines
49. 28 go up to Kedar, and spoil the men of the
51. 55 the LORD hath spoiled Babylon, and des.
Eze. 32. 12 they shall spoil the pomp of Egypt, and
Mic. 2. 4 We be utterly spoiled: he hath changed

11. *To destroy, spoil,* שָׁדַד *shadad,* 3.
Prov 24. 15 Lay not wait..spoil not his resting place

12. *To destroy, spoil,* שָׁדַד *shadad,* 3a.
Hos. 10. 2 break down their altars, he shall spoil th.

13. *To bereave,* שָׁכֹל *shakol,* 3.
Eze. 14. 15 they spoil it, so that it be desolate, that

14. *To spoil, take spoil,* שָׁלַל *shalal.*
Jer. 50. 10 all that spoil her shall be satisfied, saith
Eze. 26. 12 they shall make a spoil of thy riches, and
39. 10 they shall spoil those that spoiled them
Hab. 2. 8 Because thou hast spoiled many nations
2. 8 the remnant of the people shall spoil th.
Zech. 2. 8 sent me unto the nations which spoiled

15. *To take spoil,* שָׁסָה *shasah.*
Judg. 2. 16 out of the hand of those that spoiled them
1 Sa. 14. 48 out of the hands of them that spoiled th.
Psa. 44. 10 they which hate us spoil for themselves
Isa. 17. 14 This (is) the portion of them that spoil us
Jer. 30. 16 they that spoil thee..and all that prey up.
Hos. 13. 15 he shall spoil the treasure of all pleasant

16. *To take spoil,* שָׁסַס *shasas.*
Judg. 2. 14 into the hands of spoilers that spoiled th.
1 Sa. 17. 53 Israel returned..and they spoiled their
Psa. 89. 41 All that pass by the way spoil him: he is
Jer. 30. 16 that spoil thee shall be a spoil, and all th.

17. *To strip off, unclothe,* ἀπεκδύομαι *apekduomai.*
Col. 2. 15 having spoiled principalities and powers

18. *To snatch away thoroughly,* διαρπάζω *diarpazō.*
Matt 12. 29 how can one enter..and [spoil] his goods
12. 29 and then [he will spoil] his house
Mark 3. 27 No man can enter..and spoil his goods
3. 27 bind the..man; and then he will spoil

19. *To lead off as plunder,* συλαγωγέω *sulagōgeō.*
Col. 2. 8 lest any man spoil you through philosop.

SPOILED, (to be) —

1. *Prey, spoil,* בַּז *baz.*
Jer. 2. 14 a home born (slave)? why is he spoiled?
Eze. 23. 46 give them to be removed and spoiled

2. *To be spoiled,* בָּזַז *bazaz,* 2.
Isa. 24. 3 The land shall be utterly..spoiled: for
Amos 3. 11 saith the LORD..thy palaces shall be spo.

3. *To snatch violently away,* גָּזַל *gazal.*
Deut 28. 29 thou shalt be only oppressed and spoiled
Jer. 21. 12 deliver (him that is) spoiled out of the h.
22. 3 deliver the spoiled out of the hand of the

4. *Destruction, spoiling,* שֹׁד *shod.*
Amos 5. 9 That strengtheneth the spoiled against
5. 9 the spoiled shall come against the fortre.

5. *To destroy, spoil,* שָׁדַד *shadad.*
Isa. 33. 1 thou (wast) not spoiled; and dealest tre.
Jer. 4. 30 (when) thou (art) spoiled, what wilt thou

6. *To be destroyed, spoiled,* שָׁדַד *shadad,* 2.
Mic. 2. 4 We be utterly spoiled: he hath changed

7. *To be destroyed, spoiled,* שָׁדַד *shadad,* 4.
Jer. 4. 13 Woe unto us! for we are spoiled
4. 20 is spoiled: suddenly are my tents spoiled
9. 19 How are we spoiled! we are greatly conf.
10. 20 My tabernacle is spoiled, and all my co.
48. 1 Woe unto Nebo! for it is spoiled, Kiriat.
48. 15 Moab is spoiled, and gone up (out of) her
48. 20 tell ye it in Arnon, that Moab is spoiled
49. 3 Howl, O Heshbon, for Ai is spoiled: cry
49. 10 his seed is spoiled, and his brethren, and
Zech. 11. 2 Howl..because the mighty are spoiled
11. 3 glory is spoiled..pride of Jordan is spoiled

8. *To be destroyed, spoiled,* שָׁדַד *shadad,* 6.
Isa. 33. 1 thou shalt be spoiled; (and) when thou
Hos. 10. 14 all thy fortresses shall be spoiled, as Sh.

9. *Spoiled,* שׁוֹלָל *sholal.*
Job 12. 17 He leadeth counsellors away spoiled, and
12. 19 He leadeth princes away spoiled, and ov.

10. *To make self a spoil,* שָׁלַל *shalal,* 7a.
Psa. 76. 5 The stout hearted are spoiled, they have

11. *To take spoil,* שָׁסָה *shasah.*
Isa. 42. 22 this (is) a people robbed and spoiled, (th.

12. *To take spoil,* שָׁסַס *shasas,* 2.
Isa. 13. 16 their houses shall be spoiled, and their

SPOKEN (after, against, any more, for, of), to be—

1. *To be spoken of or for,* דָּבַר *dabar,* 4.
Psa. 87. 3 Glorious things are spoken of thee, O city
Song 8. 8 in the day when she shall be spoken for?

2. *A word,* דָּבָר *dabar.*
1 Ki. 18. 24 answered and said, It is well spoken
Job 32. 4 Elihu had waited till Job had spoken, be.

3. *Mouth,* פֶּה *peh.*
Obad. 12 neither shouldest thou have spoken pro.

4. *To tell again,* ἀναγγέλλω *anaggellō.*
Rom 15. 21 To whom he was not spoken of, they shall

5. *To be spoken against,* εἰμὶ ἀναντίῤῥητος *eimi an.*
Acts 19. 36 that these things cannot be spoken agai.

6. *To say or speak against,* ἀντιλέγω *antilegō.*
Luke 2. 34 for a sign which shall be spoken against
Acts 28. 22 know that everywhere it is spoken against

7. *To talk, speak,* λαλέω *laleō.*
Mark 5. 36 as Jesus heard the word that was spoken
14. 9 shall be spoken of for a memorial of her
Luke 2. 33 at those things which were spoken of him
Acts 13. 46 word of God should first have been spoken
16. 14 unto the things which were spoken of Pa.
1 Co. 14. 9 how shall it be known what is spoken? for
Heb. 2. 2 if the word spoken by angels was stedfast
2. 3 which at the first began to be spoken by
3. 5 those things which were to be spoken af.

8. *To lay out, say, speak,* λέγω *legō.*
Luke 18. 34 neither knew..the things which were sp.
Acts 13. 45 those things which were spoken by Paul
27. 11 those things which were spoken by Paul
28. 24 believed the things which were spoken
Heb. 7. 13 he of whom these things are spoken per.

9. *To utter,* ῥέω *rheō,* ἐρῶ *erō.*
Matt. 1. 22 which was spoken of the Lord by the pr.
2. 15 which was spoken of the Lord by the pr.
2. 17 that which was spoken by Jeremy the pr.
2. 23 might be fulfilled which was spoken by
3. 3 he that was spoken of by the prophet E.
4. 14 which was spoken by Esaias the prophet
8. 17 which was spoken by Esaias the prophet
12. 17 which was spoken by Esaias the prophet
13. 35 might be fulfilled which was spoken by
21. 4 might be fulfilled which was spoken by
22. 31 have ye not read that which was spoken
24. 15; 27. 9; 27. 35; Mark 13. 14.

10. *To tell thoroughly,* καταγγέλλω, Rom. 1. 8.

11. *To put unto,* προστίθημι, Heb. 12. 19.

SPOKES —

Spokes, felloes of a wheel, חִשֻּׁרִים *chishshurim.*
1 Ki. 7. 33 their felloes, and their spokes, (were) all

SPOKESMAN, to be a —

To speak, דָּבַר *dabar,* 3.
Exod. 4. 16 he shall be thy spokesman unto the people

SPONGE —

A spunge, σπόγγος *spoggos.*
Matt 27. 48 one of them ran and took a sponge, and
Mark 15. 36 one ran and filled a sponge full of vineg.
John 19. 29 they filled a sponge with vinegar, and put

SPOON —

A hollow object, dish, pan, כַּף *kaph.*
Exod. 25. 29 shalt make the dishes thereof, and the sp.
37. 16 his dishes, and his spoons, and his bowls
Num. 4. 7 the dishes and the spoons; and the bowls
7. 14 One spoon of ten (shekels) of gold, full of
7. 20 One spoon of gold of ten (shekels), full of
7. 26, 32, 38, 44, 50, 56, 62, 68, 74, 80 One golden s.
7. 84 twelve silver bowls, twelve spoons of gold
7. 86 The golden spoons (were) twelve, full of
7. 86 the gold of the spoons (was) an hundred
1 Ki. 7. 50 the basins, and the spoons, and the censers
2 Ki. 25. 14 the spoons, and all the vessels of brass wh.
2 Ch. 4. 22 and the spoons, and the censers, (of) pure
24. 14 and spoons, and vessels of gold and silver
Jer. 52. 18 the bowls, and the spoons, and all the ve.
52. 19 the candlesticks, and the spoons, and the

SPORT, (be in or make), sport self, to —

1. *To delight self,* עָנַג *anag,* 7.
Isa. 57. 4 Against whom do ye sport yourselves? ag.

2. *Laughter, derision, play,* שְׂחוֹק *sechoq.*
Prov 10. 23 (It is) as sport to a fool to do mischief: but

3. *To laugh, mock, play with,* צָחַק *tsachaq,* 3.
Gen. 26. 8 Isaac (was) sporting with Rebekah his wife
Judg 16. 25 he made them sport: and they set him be.

4. *To laugh, deride, play,* שָׂחַק *sachaq*
Judg. 16. 27 that beheld while Samson made sport

5. *To laugh, deride, play,* שָׂחַק *sachaq,* 3.
Judg. 16. 25 Call for Samson, that he may make us sp.
Prov. 26. 19 the man (that)..saith, Am not I in sport?

6. *To live in luxury,* ἐντρυφάω *entruphaō.*
2 Pe. 2. 13 sporting themselves with their own dece.

SPOT, (bright, freckled, without) —

1. *A freckled spot of leprosy,* בֹּהַק *bohaq.*
Lev. 13. 39 it (is) a freckled spot (that) groweth in the

2. *A freckled spot of leprosy,* בַּהֶרֶת *bahereth.*
Lev. 13. 2 a rising, a scab, or bright spot, and it be
13. 4 If the bright spot (be) white in the skin of
13. 19 there be a white rising, or a bright spot, wh.
13. 23 if the bright spot stay in his place, (and)
Lev. 13. 24 (flesh) that burneth have a white bright s.
13. 25 (if) the hair in the bright spot be turned
13. 26 (there be) no white hair in the bright spot
13. 28 if the bright spot stay in his place, (and)
13. 38 have..bright spots, (even) white bright sp.
13. 39 bright spots in the skin of their flesh (be)
14. 56 rising, and for a scab, and..a bright spot

3. *Spots,* חֲבַרְבֻּרוֹת *chabarburoth.*
Jer. 13. 23 change his skin, or the leopard his spots?

4. *Blemish,* מוּם *mum.*
Deut 32. 5 their spot (is) not..of his children: (they
Job 11. 15 shalt thou lift up thy face without spot
Song. 4. 7 Thou (art) all fair, my love; (there is) no s.

5. *Perfect, white, complete, plain,* תָּמִים *tamim.*
Num 19. 2 they bring thee a red heifer without spot
28. 3, 9 two lambs of the first year without spot
28. 11 seven lambs of the first year without spot
29. 17, 26 lambs of the first year, without spot

6. *Without blemish, unblemished,* ἄμωμος *amōmos.*
Heb. 9. 14 who..offered himself without spot to God

7. *Spotless, without spot,* ἄσπιλος *aspilos.*
1 Ti. 6. 14 keep this commandment without spot, un.
1 Pe. 1. 19 a lamb without blemish and without spot
2 Pe. 3. 14 may be found of him in peace, without sp.

8. *A sunken rock, defiled person,* σπιλάς *spilas.*
Jude 12 These are spots in your feasts of charity

9. *A spot, stain, blot,* σπῖλος *spilos.*
Eph. 5. 27 a glorious church, not having spot, or w.
2 Pe. 2. 13 Spots (they are) and blemishes, sporting

SPOT, be spotted, to —

1. *To be spotted,* טָלָא *tala.*
Gen. 30. 32 the speckled and spotted cattle, and all
30. 32 the spotted and speckled among the goats
30. 33 that (is) not speckled and spotted among
30. 35 goats that were ringstraked and spotted
30. 35 the she goats that were speckled and sp.
30. 39 brought forth cattle..speckled, and spot.

2. *To spot, stain, blot,* σπιλόω *spiloō.*
Jude 23 hating even the garment spotted by the

SPOUSE —

Spouse, bride, daughter in law, כַּלָּה *kallah.*
Song 4. 8 Come with me from Lebanon, (my) spouse
4. 9 ravished my heart, my sister, (my) spouse
4. 10 How fair is thy love, my sister, (my) sp.
4. 11 Thy lips, O (my) spouse, drop (as) the ho.
4. 12 A garden inclosed (is) my sister, (my) sp.
5. 1 I am come into my garden..(my) spouse
Hos. 4. 13 and your spouses shall commit adultery
4. 14 nor your spouses when they commit adu.

SPREAD, to —

1. *To scatter, winnow, spread,* זָרָה *zarah,* 3.
Mal. 2. 3 I will corrupt your seed, and spread dung

2. *To be scattered, winnowed, spread,* זָרָה *zarah,* 4.
Prov. 1. 17 in vain the net is spread in the sight of

3. *To go on,* יָלַךְ *yalak.*
2 Ch. 26. 8 his name spread abroad (even) to the ent.
Hos. 14. 6 His branches shall spread, and his beauty

4. *To go out or forth,* יָצָא *yatsa.*
2 Ch. 26. 15 his name spread far abroad; for he was

5. *To cause to go out or forth,* יָצָא *yatsa,* 5.
Isa. 58. 5 and to spread sackcloth and ashes (under

6. *To stretch out, incline,* נָטָה *natah.*
Gen. 33. 19 a field, where he had spread his tent, at
35. 21 Israel journeyed, and spread his tent bey.
Jer. 43. 10 he shall spread his royal pavilion over th.

7. *To (cause to) stretch out, incline,* נָטָה *natah,* 5.
2 Sa. 16. 22 they spread Absalom a tent upon the top
21. 10 took sackcloth, and spread it for her upon

8. *To break forth, finish,* פָּרַח *parach.*
Lev. 13. 57 it (is) a spreading (plague): thou shalt bu.

9. *To spread out, forth, abroad,* פָּרַשׂ *paras.*
Num. 4. 6 shall spread over (it) a cloth wholly of bl.
4. 7 they shall spread a cloth of blue, and put
4. 8 they shall spread upon them a cloth of sc.
4. 11 they shall spread a cloth of blue, and co.
4. 13 the altar, and spread a purple cloth the.
4. 14 they shall spread upon it a covering of ba.
Deut 22. 17 they shall spread the cloth before the el.
Judg. 8. 25 they spread a garment, and did cast the.
Ruth 3. 9 spread therefore thy skirt over thine ha.
2 Sa. 17. 19 the woman took and spread a covering
1 Ki. 8. 7 the cherubim spread forth (their) two wi.
2 Ki. 8. 15 dipped (it) in water, and spread (it) on his
19. 14 Hezekiah went..and spread it before the
Job 36. 30 he spreadeth his light upon it, and cove.
Psa. 105. 39 He spread a cloud for a covering, and fire
140. 5 have spread a net by the way side; they
Prov 29. 5 A man that flattereth his neighbour spr.
Isa. 19. 8 they that spread nets upon the waters sh.
33. 23 they could not spread the sail: then is the
37. 14 Hezekiah went..and spread it before the
Jer. 48. 40 fly as an eagle, and shall spread his win.
49. 22 fly as the eagle, and spread his wings ov.
Lam. 1. 10 The adversary hath spread out his hand
1. 13 he hath spread a net for my feet; he hath
Eze. 2. 10 he spread it before me: and it (was) wri.
12. 13 My net also will I spread upon him, and
16. 8 I spread my skirt over thee, and covered
17. 20 I will spread my net upon him, and he sh.
19. 8 the nations..spread their net over him: he
Hos. 7. 12 I will spread my net upon them; I will

10. *To spread out, forth, abroad,* פָּרַשׂ *paras,* 3.
Jer. 4. 31 (that) spreadeth her hands, (saying) Woe
Zech. 2. 6 I have spread you abroad as the four win.

11. *To spread out,* פַּרְשֵׁז *parshez.*
Job 26. 9 He holdeth back..(and) spreadeth his cl.

12. *To (be) spread,* פָּשָׂה *pasah.*
Lev. 13. 5, 6 (and) the plague spread not in the skin
13. 7 if the scab spread much abroad in the skin
13. 8 behold, the scab spreadeth in the skin, th.
13. 22 if it spread much abroad in the skin, then
13. 23, 28 bright spot stay in his place, (and) sp.
13. 32 (if) the scall spread not, and there be in
13. 35 if the scall spread much in the skin after
14. 48 the plague hath not spread in the house

13. *To spread out, subdue,* רָדַד *radad,* 5.
1 Ki. 6. 32 spread gold upon the cherubim, and upon

14. *To spread out, support,* רָפַד *raphad.*
Job 41. 30 he spreadeth sharp pointed things upon

15. *To spread out,* שָׁטַח *shatach.*
Num 11. 32 they spread (them) all abroad for thems
2 Sa. 17. 19 and spread ground corn thereon; and the
Jer. 8. 2 they shall spread them before the sun, and

16. *To be divulged, given throughout,* διανέμομαι.
Acts 4. 17 But that it spread no further among the

17. *To strew,* στρώννυμι *strōnnumi,* -νύω.
Matt 21. 8 a very great multitude spread their garm.
Mark 11. 8 [many spread their garments in the way]

18. *To strew under,* ὑποστρώννυμι *hupostrōnnumi.*
Luke 19. 36 as he went, they spread their clothes in the

SPREAD abroad, (forth, out, over, upon), to —

1. *Spreading,* מִשְׁטוֹחַ *mishtoach.*
Eze. 47. 10 they shall be a (place) to spread forth nets

2. *Spreading place,* מִשְׁטָח *mishtach.*
Eze. 26. 14 thou shalt be (a place) to spread nets up.

3. *To spread out,* מָתַח *mathach.*
Isa. 40. 22 spreadeth them out as a tent to dwell in

4. *To stretch out, incline,* נָטָה *natah.*
Job 9. 8 Which alone spreadeth out the heavens

5. *To break or burst forth,* פָּרַץ *parats.*
Gen. 28. 14 thou shalt spread abroad to the west, and

6. *To spread out,* פָּרַשׂ *paras.*
Exod. 9. 29 I will spread abroad my hands unto the
9. 33 and spread abroad his hands unto the Lo.
37. 9 the cherubim spread out (their) wings on
40. 19 he spread abroad the tent over the taber
Deut 32. 11 spreadeth abroad her wings, taketh them
1 Ki. 8. 22 and spread forth his hands toward heaven
8. 38 spread forth his hands toward this house
1 Ch. 28. 18 the cherubim, that spread out (their wi.)
2 Ch. 5. 8 the cherubim spread forth (their) wings
6. 12 And he stood..and spread forth his hands
6. 13 and spread forth his hands toward heaven
6. 29 shall spread forth his hands in this house
Ezra 9. 5 spread out my hands unto the LORD my
Job 36. 30 he spreadeth his light upon it, and
Eze. 32. 3 I will therefore spread out my net over

7. *To spread out,* פָּרַשׂ *paras,* 3.
Isa. 1. 15 when ye spread forth your hands, I will
25. 11 he shall spread forth his hands in the
25. 11 as he that swimmeth spreadeth forth (his
65. 2 I have spread out my hands all this day
Lam. 1. 17 Zion spreadeth forth her hands, and (th.

8. *To spread out or over,* רָקַע *raqa.*
2 Sa. 22. 43 stamp them..(and) did spread them abr.
Isa. 42. 5 he that spread forth the earth, and that
44. 24 that spreadeth abroad the earth by my s.

9. *To spread out or over,* רָקַע *raqa,* 3.
Isa. 40. 19 the goldsmith spreadeth it over with gold

10. *To (cause to) spread out or over,* רָקַע *raqa,* 5.
Job 37. 18 Hast thou with him spread out the sky

11. *To send,* שָׁלַח *shalach,* 3.
Jer. 17. 8 (that) spreadeth out her roots by the ri.

12. *To come or go out,* ἐξέρχομαι *exerchomai.*
Mark 1. 28 his fame spread abroad throughout all
1 Th. 1. 8 your faith to God ward is spread abroad

SPREAD abroad fame, to —

To make a fame abroad, διαφημίζω *diaphēmizō.*
Matt. 9. 31 spread abroad his fame in all that country

SPREAD into plates —

To be spread out or over, רָקַע *raqa,* 4.
Jer. 10. 9 Silver spread into plates is brought from

SPREAD selves abroad or forth, to —

1. *To (be) spread out,* נָטַשׁ *natash,* 2.
Judg 15. 9 the Philistines..spread themselves in L.
2 Sa. 5. 18 The Philistines also came and spread th.
5. 22 spread themselves in the valley of Reph.

2. *To spread self out, expose self,* עָרָה *arah,* 7.
Psa. 37. 35 spreading himself like a green bay tree

3. *To increase, scatter,* פּוּשׁ *push.*
Hab. 1. 8 their horsemen shall spread themselves

4. *To spread abroad or forth,* פָּרַשׂ *paras.*
2 Ch. 3. 13 wings of these cherubim spread thems. f.

5. *To strip off, rush,* פָּשַׁט *pashat.*
1 Ch. 14. 9 the Philistines came and spread themse.
14. 13 again spread themselves abroad in the

SPREAD (abroad, forth, out), to be —

1. *To be caused to go out or forth,* יָצָא *yatsa,* 6.
Isa. 14. 11 the worm is spread under thee, and the

2. *To be stretched out, inclined,* נָטָה *natah,* 2.
Num 24. 6 As the valleys are they spread forth, as

3. *To spread out,* נָטַשׁ *natash.*
1 Sa. 30. 16 (they were) spread abroad upon all the

4. *To pour out, spread,* נָסַךְ *nasak.*
Isa. 25. 7 the veil that is spread over all nations

5. *To be scattered,* פּוּץ *puts.*
Zech. 1. 17 My cities..shall yet be spread abroad

6. *To be or become scattered,* פּוּץ *puts,* 2.
Gen. 10. 18 families of the Canaanites spread abroad

7. *To spread out or forth,* פָּרַשׂ *paras.*
1 Ki. 8. 54 kneeling on his knees with his hands sp.
Hos. 5. 1 ye have been..a net spread upon Tabor
Joel 2. 2 as the morning spread upon the mounta.

8. *To spread out,* פָּשָׂה *pasah.*
Lev. 13. 27 if it be spread much abroad in the skin
13. 34 (if) the scall be not spread in the skin, nor
13. 36 if the scall be spread in the skin, the pr.
13. 51 if the plague be spread in the garment
13. 53 the plague be not spread in the garment
13. 55 and the plague be not spread; it (is) un.
14. 39 (if) the plague be spread in the walls of
14. 44 (if) the plague be spread in the house, it

9. *To open,* פָּתַח *pathach.*
Job 29. 19 My root (was) spread out by the waters

SPREADING, that which spreadest forth —

1. *Spreading,* מִפְרָשׂ *miphras.*
Job 36. 29 can (any) understand the spreadings of
Eze. 27. 7 that which thou spreadest forth to be

2. *A spreading, spreading place,* מִשְׁטָח *mishtach.*
Eze. 26. 5 It shall be (a place for) the spreading of

3. *To spread out,* סָרַח *sarach.*
Eze. 17. 6 it grew, and became a spreading vine of

SPRIG —

1. *Sprigs, shoots, twigs,* זַלְזַלִּים *zalzallim.*
Isa. 18. 5 he shall both cut off the sprigs with pru.

2. *Branch, leafy sapling,* פֹּארָה *porah.*
Eze 17. 6 brought..branches, and shot forth sprigs

SPRING, springing —

1. *Spring, stream, reveries,* אֲשֵׁדוֹת *ashedoth.*
Deut. 4. 49 all the plain..under the springs of Pis.
Josh 10. 40 smote all the country..of the springs, and
12. 8 in the plains, and in the springs, and in

2. *Billow, spring, wave,* גַּל *gal.*
Song 4. 12 A garden inclosed..a spring shut up, a

3. *Bowl, spring,* גֻּלָּה *gullah.*
Josh 15. 19 Give me a blessing..give me also springs
15. 19 the upper springs, and the nether springs
Judg. 1. 15 Give me a blessing..give me also springs
1. 15 the upper springs and the nether springs

4. *Living,* חַי *chai.*
Gen. 26. 19 and found there a well of springing water

5. *Fountain,* מַבּוּעַ *mabbua.*
Isa. 35. 7 and the thirsty land springs of water: in the
49. 10 by the springs of water shall he guide th.

6. *Outgoing, outlet,* מוֹצָא *motsa.*
2 Ki. 2. 21 he went forth unto the spring of the wa.
Psa. 107. 33 and the water springs into dry ground
107. 35 turneth..dry ground into water springs
Isa. 41. 18 I will make the..dry land springs of wa.
58. 11 like a spring of water, whose waters fail

7. *Fountain,* מַעְיָן *mayan.*
Psa. 87. 7 the singers..(shall be there): all my spr.
104. 10 He sendeth the springs into the valleys

8. *Source, fountain,* מָקוֹר *maqor.*
Prov 25. 26 a troubled fountain, and a corrupt spring
Jer. 51. 36 dry up her sea, and make her springs dry
Hos. 13. 15 his spring shall become dry, and his fou.

9. *A spring, depth,* נֶבֶךְ *nebek.*
Job 38. 16 Hast thou entered into the springs of the

10. *To go up,* עָלָה *alah.*
1 Sa. 9. 26 it came to pass, about the spring of the

11. *Shoot, plant, plantation,* צֶמַח *tsemach.*
Psa. 65. 10 thou blessest the springing thereof
Eze. 17. 9 shall wither in all the leaves of her spr.

SPRING (in, forth, out, up, with), to —

1. *To spring forth,* דָּשָׁא *dasha.*
Joel 2. 22 the pastures of the wilderness do spring

2. *To go out or forth,* יָצָא *yatsa.*
Deut. 8. 7 depths that spring out of valleys and hills
1 Ki. 4. 33 the hyssop that springeth out of the wall

3. *To go up,* עָלָה *alah.*
Num 21. 17 Israel sang this song, Spring up, O well

4. *To break forth, flourish,* פָּרַח *parach.*
Lev. 13. 42 it (is) a leprosy sprung up in his bald head
Psa. 92. 7 When the wicked spring as the grass, and
Hos. 10. 4 thus judgment springeth up as hemlock

5. *To shoot forth, sprout up,* צָמַח *tsamach.*
Gen. 41. 6 behold, seven thin ears..sprung up after
41. 23 behold, seven ears..sprung up after them
Job 5. 6 neither doth trouble spring out of the gr.
Psa. 85. 11 Truth shall spring out of the earth; and
Isa. 42. 9 before they spring forth I tell you of them
43. 19 it shall spring forth; shall ye not know
44. 4 they shall spring up (as) among the grass

6. *To cause to shoot forth,* צָמַח *tsamach,* 5.
Isa. 45. 8 and let righteousness spring up together
58. 8 and thine health shall spring forth speed.

7. *To leap up, bubble up,* ἅλλομαι *hallomai.*
John 4. 14 in him a well of water springing up into

8. *To go or come up,* ἀναβαίνω *anabainō.*
Matt 13. 7 the thorns sprung up and choked them
Mark 4. 8 did yield fruit that sprang up and incre.

9. *To rise, spring up,* ἀνατέλλω *anatellō.*
Matt. 4. 16 and to them which sat..light is sprung
Heb. 7. 14 evident that our Lord sprang out of Jud.

10. *To (cause to) bud, sprout up,* βλαστάνω *blastanō.*
Matt. 13. 26 when the blade was sprung up, and br.
Mark 4. 27 spring and grow up, he knoweth not how

11. *To produce, beget, bring forth,* γεννάω *gennaō.*
Heb. 11. 12 Therefore sprang there even of one, and

12. *To leap, rush or spring into,* εἰσπηδάω *eispēdaō.*
Acts 16. 29 Then he called for a light, and sprang in

13. *To rise or spring out,* ἐξανατέλλω *exanatellō.*
Matt 13. 5 sprung up, because they had no deepness
Mark 4. 5 immediately it sprang up, because it had

14. *To grow up together,* συμφύομαι *sumphuomai.*
Luke 8. 7 thorns sprang up with it, and choked it

15. *To spring up, sprout, produce,* φύω *phuō.*
Luke 8. 6 as soon as it was sprung up, it withered
8. 8 other fell on good ground, and sprang up
Heb. 12. 15 lest any root of bitterness springing up

SPRING, to begin to —

To go up, עָלָה *alah.*
Judg. 19. 25 when the day began to spring, they let her

SPRING forth, to cause to —

To cause to sprout or grow, צָמַח *tsamach,* 5.
Job 38. 27 and to cause the bud..to spring forth
Isa. 61. 11 causeth the things..in it to spring forth
61. 11 GOD will cause..praise to spring forth be.

SPRINGETH of the same, that which —

1. *After growth,* סָחִישׁ *sachish.*
2 Ki. 19. 29 eat..that which springeth of the same

2. *After growth,* שָׁחִיס *shachis.*
Isa. 37. 30 eat..that which springeth of the same

SPRINKLE, be sprinkled, to —

1. *To sprinkle, be sprinkled,* זָרַק *zaraq.*
Exod. 9. 8 let Moses sprinkle it toward the heaven
9. 10 and Moses sprinkled it up toward heaven
24. 6 half of the blood he sprinkled on the alt.
24. 8 Moses took the blood, and sprinkled (it)
29. 16 and sprinkle (it) round about upon the al.
29. 20 sprinkle the blood upon the altar round
Lev. 1. 5 sprinkle the blood round about upon the
1. 11 sprinkle his blood round about upon the
3. 2 the priests shall sprinkle the blood upon
3. 8 Aaron's sons shall sprinkle the blood the.
3. 13 the sons of Aaron shall sprinkle the blood
7. 2 the blood thereof shall he sprinkle round
7. 14 it shall be the priest's that sprinkleth the
8. 19, 24 Moses sprinkled the blood upon the al.
9. 12 which he sprinkled round about upon the
9. 18 which he sprinkled upon the altar round
17. 6 the priest shall sprinkle the blood upon
Num 18. 17 thou shalt sprinkle their blood upon the
2 Ki. 16. 13 sprinkled the blood of his peace offerings
16. 15 sprinkle upon it all the blood of the burnt
2 Ch. 29. 22 priests received the blood, and sprinkled
29. 22, 22 they sprinkled the blood upon the al.
30. 16 the priests sprinkled the blood, (which th.
35. 11 the priests sprinkled (the blood) from their
Job 2. 12 sprinkled dust upon their heads toward
Eze. 36. 25 Then will I sprinkle clean water upon you
43. 18 to offer burnt offerings..and to sprinkle

2. *To be sprinkled,* זָרַק *zaraq,* 4.
Num 19. 13 the water of separation was not sprinkled
19. 20 water of separation hath not been sprink.

3. *To be sprinkled,* נָזָה *nazah.*
Lev. 6. 27 when there is sprinkled of the blood the.
6. 27 wash that whereon it was sprinkled in the
2 Ki. 9. 33 (some) of her blood was sprinkled on the
Isa. 63. 3 their blood shall be sprinkled upon my

4. *To sprinkle,* נָזָה *nazah,* 5.
Exod 29. 21 sprinkle (it) upon Aaron, and upon his ga.
Lev. 4. 6 sprinkle of the blood seven times before
4. 17 sprinkle (it) seven times before the LORD
5. 9 he shall sprinkle of the blood of the sin
8. 11 he sprinkled thereof upon the altar seven
8. 30 sprinkled (it) upon Aaron, (and) upon his
14. 7 he shall sprinkle upon him that is to be
14. 16 shall sprinkle of the oil with his finger se.
14. 27 the priest shall sprinkle with his right fi.
14. 51 dip them in the blood..and sprinkle the
16. 14 sprinkle (it) with his finger upon the mer.
16. 14 before the mercy seat shall he sprinkle of
16. 15 sprinkle it upon the mercy seat, and bef.
16. 19 he shall sprinkle of the blood upon it wi.
Num. 8. 7 Sprinkle water of purifying upon them
19. 4 sprinkle of her blood directly before the
19. 18 sprinkle (it) upon the tent, and upon all
19. 19 the clean (person) shall sprinkle upon the

Num 19. 21 he that sprinkleth the water of separation
Isa. 52. 15 So shall he sprinkle many nations; the ki.

6. *To sprinkle, cleanse by sprinkling,* ῥαντίζω *rhan.*
Heb. 9. 13 the ashes of an heifer sprinkling the unc.
9. 19 sprinkled both the book, and all the peo.
9. 21 he sprinkled likewise with blood both the
10. 22 having our hearts sprinkled from an evil

SPRINKLING —
1. *A pouring on or over,* πρόσχυσις *proschusis.*
Heb. 11. 28 he kept the passover, and the sprinkling

2. *A sprinkling,* ῥαντισμός *rhantismos.*
Heb. 12. 24 the blood of sprinkling, that speaketh be.
1 Pe. 1. 2 unto obedience and sprinkling of the blo.

SPROUT, to —
To (cause to) pass on, change, substitute, חָלַף *chalaph.*
Job 14. 7 there is hope..that it will sprout again

SPUE (out), to —
1. *To vomit, spread out,* קוֹא *qo.*
Lev. 18. 28 as it spued out the nations that (were) be.

2. *To (cause to) vomit, spread out,* קוֹא *qo,* 5.
Lev. 18. 28 That the land spue not you out also, when
20. 22 do them: that the land..spue you not out

3. *To vomit,* קָיָה *qayah.*
Jer. 25. 27 Drink ye, and be drunken, and spue, and

4. *Shameful spewing, ignominy, shame,* קִיקָלוֹן *qiqalon.*
Hab. 2. 16 and shameful spewing (shall be) on thy

5. *To vomit,* ἐμέω *emeō.*
Rev. 3. 16 thou art luke warm..I will spue thee out

SPUN, that which they had —
Yarn, what is spun, מַטְוֶה *matveh.*
Exod 35. 25 brought that which they had spun, (both)

SPY (out), to —
1. *To see,* רָאָה *raah.*
Exod. 2. 11 he spied an Egyptian smiting an Hebrew
2 Ki. 6. 13 spy where he (is), that I may send and
9. 17 he spied the company of Jehu as he came
13. 21 as they were burying a man..they spied
23. 16 he spied the sepulchres that (were) there

2. *To use the feet, traverse,* רָגַל *ragal,* 3.
Num 21. 32 Moses sent to spy out Jaazer, and they
Josh. 2. 1 sent out of Shittim two men to spy secr.
6. 22 the two men that had spied out the coun.
6. 25 messengers which Joshua sent to spy out
Judg 18. 2 from Eshtaol, to spy out the land, and to
18. 14, 17 the five men that went to spy out the
2 Sa. 10. 3 to search the city, and to spy it out, and
1 Ch. 19. 3 and to overthrow, and to spy out the land

3. *To go about, trade, search, spy out,* תּוּר *tur.*
Num 13. 16 the men which Moses sent to spy out the
13. 17 Moses sent them to spy out the land of C.

4. *To spy,* κατασκοπέω *kataskopeō.*
Gal. 2. 4 who came in privily to spy out our liber.

SQUARE, squares, to be squared, (four) —
1. *To be four square,* רָבַע *raba.*
1 Ki. 7. 5 the doors and posts (were) square, with
Eze. 41. 21 The posts of the temple (were) squared
43. 16 twelve (cubits) long, twelve broad, square

2. *To be four square,* רָבַע *raba,* 4.
Eze. 45. 2 five hundred (in breadth), square round

3. *Fourth part, side, square,* רֶבַע *reba.*
Eze. 43. 16 twelve broad..in the four squares thereof
43. 17 fourteen broad in the four squares there

STABILITY —
Stability, אֱמוּנָה *emunah.*
Isa. 33. 6 knowledge shall be the stability of thy ti.

STABLE —
Habitation, fold, נָוֶה *naveh.*
Eze. 25. 5 I will make Rabbah a stable for camels

STABLE, to be —
To be prepared, established, right, כּוּן *kun,* 2.
1 Ch. 16. 30 the world also shall be stable, that it be

STABLISH, to —
1. *To prepare, establish,* כּוּן *kun,* 3a.
2 Sa. 7. 13 I will stablish the throne of his kingdom
1 Ch. 17. 12 and I will stablish his throne for ever
Hab. 2. 12 Woe to him that..stablisheth a city by

2. *To prepare, establish,* כּוּן *kun,* 5.
2 Ch. 17. 5 the LORD stablished the kingdom in his

3. *To set up, cause to stand, establish,* נָצַב *natsab,* 5.
1 Ch. 18. 3 he went to stablish his dominion by the

4. *To raise up, establish, confirm,* קוּם *qum,* 3.
Esth. 9. 21 To stablish (this) among them, that they

5. *To raise up, establish, confirm,* קוּם *qum,* 5.
2 Ch. 7. 18 Then will I stablish the throne of thy
Psa 119. 38 Stablish thy word unto thy servant, who

6. *To stand,* עָמַד *amad,* 5.
Psa. 148. 6 He hath also stablished them for ever and

7. *To confirm, establish,* βεβαιόω *bebaioō.*
2 Co. 1. 21 he which stablisheth us with you in Christ
Col. 2. 7 stablished in the faith, as ye have been

8. *To make firm, confirm,* στηρίζω *stērizō.*
Rom 16. 25 to him that is of power to stablish you
1 Th. 3. 13 he may stablish your hearts unblameable
2 Th. 2. 17 stablish you in every good word and work
2 Th. 3. 3 the Lord is faithful, who shall stablish
Jas. 5. 8 Be ye also patient; stablish your hearts
1 Pe. 5. 10 make you perfect, stablish, strengthen

STA'-CHYS, Στάχυς *ear of corn.*
A believer in Rome to whom Paul sends a salutation.
Rom. 16. 9 Salute Urbane our helper in Christ, and S.

STACK of corn —
A stack, shock or heap of corn, גָּדִישׁ *gadish.*
Exod. 22. 6 the stacks of corn, or the standing corn

STACTE —
A drop, stacte, an aromatic gum, נָטָף *nataph.*
Exod. 30. 34 Take unto thee sweet spices, stacte, and

STAFF, staves —
1. *Bar, branch, part, bough,* בַּד *bad.*
Exod. 25. 13 thou shalt make staves (of) shittim wood
25. 14 thou shalt put the staves into the rings by
25. 15 The staves shall be in the rings of the ark
25. 27 shall the rings be for places of the staves
25. 28 thou shalt make the staves (of) shittim
27. 6 thou shalt make staves for the altar, sta.
27. 7 And the staves shall be put into the rings
27. 7 the staves shall be upon the two sides of
30. 4 they shall be for places for the staves to
30. 5 thou shalt make the staves (of) shittim wo.
35. 12 The ark, and the staves thereof, (with)
35. 13 The table, and his staves, and all his ves.
35. 15 the incense altar, and his staves, and the
35. 16 his brasen grate, his staves, and all his ves.
37. 4, 15, 28 he made staves (of) shittim wood
37. 5 he put the staves into the rings by the si.
37. 14 the places for the staves to bear the table
37. 27 to be places for the staves to bear it wit.
38. 5 four rings..(to be) places for the staves
38. 6 he made the staves (of) shittim wood, and
38. 7 he put the staves into the rings on the si.
39. 35 The ark of the testimony, and the staves
39. 39 his grate of brass, his staves, and all his
40. 20 set the staves on the ark, and put the me.
Num. 4. 6 cloth..of blue, and shall put in the staves
4. 8 cover the same..and shall put in the stav.
4. 11 cover it..and shall put to the staves there.
4. 14 spread..a covering..and put to the staves
1 Ki. 8. 7 cherubim covered the ark and the staves
8. 8 the staves, that the ends of the staves we.
2 Ch. 5. 8 cherubim covered the ark and the staves
5. 9 And they drew out the staves (of the ark)
5. 9 the ends of the staves were seen from the

2. *An arrow, handle,* חֵץ *chets.*
1 Sa. 17. 7 the staff of his spear (was) like a weaver's

3. *A bar,* מוֹט *mot.*
Num 13. 23 and they bare it between two upon a staff

4. *A bar,* מוֹטָה *motah.*
1 Ch. 15. 15 bare the ark of God..with the staves the.

5. *A bar, rod, staff, tribe,* מַטֶּה *matteh.*
Gen. 38. 18 thy bracelets, and thy staff that (is) in thy
38. 25 these, the signet, and bracelets, and staff
Lev. 26. 26 when I have broken the staff of your bread
Psa. 105. 16 Moreover..he brake the whole staff of br.
Isa. 9. 4 the staff of his shoulder, the rod of his op.
10. 5 the staff in their hand is mine indignation
10. 15 as if the staff should lift up (itself, as if it
10. 24 shall lift up his staff against thee, after
14. 5 The LORD hath broken the staff of the wic.
28. 27 the fitches are beaten out with a staff, and
30. 32 every place where the grounded staff sha.
Jer. 48. 17 How is the strong staff broken, (and) the
Eze. 4. 16 I will break the staff of bread in Jerusalem
5. 16 famine..and will break your staff of bread
14. 13 will break the staff of the bread thereof
Hab. 3. 14 Thou didst strike through with his staves

6. *A rod, staff,* מַקֵּל *maqqel.*
Gen 32. 10 with my staff I passed over this Jordan
Exod 12. 11 your shoes on your feet, and your staff in
Num 22. 27 fell..and he smote the ass with a staff
1 Sa. 17. 40 he took his staff in his hand, and chose
17. 43 a dog, that thou comest to me with staves?
Eze. 39. 9 the arrows, and the hand staves, and the
Hos. 4. 12 their staff declareth unto them: for the
Zech. 11. 7 I took unto me two staves; the one I cal.
11. 10 I took my staff, (even) Beauty, and cut it
11. 14 I cut asunder mine other staff (even) Ba.

7. *A stay, support,* מַשְׁעֵנָה *mashenah.*
Isa. 3. 1 from Judah the stay and the staff, the wh.

8. *A stay, support,* מִשְׁעֶנֶת *misheneth.*
Exod 21. 19 rise again, and walk abroad upon his st.
Num 21. 18 princes digged the well..with their staves
Judg. 6. 21 the angel..put forth the end of the staff
2 Ki. 4. 29 Gird up thy loins, and take my staff in
4. 29 and lay my staff upon the face of the ch.
4. 31 and laid the staff upon the face of the ch.
18. 21 thou trustest upon the staff of this bruis.
Psa. 23. 4 thy rod and thy staff they comfort me
Isa. 36. 6 thou trustest in the staff of this broken
Eze. 29. 6 they have been a staff of reed to the ho.
Zech. 8. 4 every man with his staff in his hand for

9. *Wood, tree, stalk, staff,* עֵץ *ets.*
2 Sa. 21. 19 the staff of whose spear (was) like a weav.
23. 7 fenced with iron and the staff of a spear
1 Ch. 20. 5 whose spear's staff (was) like a weaver's

10. *A staff, distaff, circuit,* פֶּלֶךְ *pelek.*
2 Sa. 3. 29 a leper, or that leaneth on a staff, or that

11. *A reed, rod, sceptre, tribe,* שֵׁבֶט *shebet.*
2 Sa. 23. 21 he went down to him with a staff, and pl.
1 Ch. 11. 23 he went down to him with a staff, and pl.

12. *Wood, timber,* ξύλον *xulon.*
Matt 26. 47 a great multitude with swords and staves
26. 55 Are ye come..with swords and staves for
Mark 14. 43 a great multitude with swords and staves
14. 48 Are ye come..with swords and (with) sta.
Luke 22. 52 as against a thief, with swords and staves

13. *Staff, rod, sceptre,* ῥάβδος *rhabdos.*
Matt 10. 10 Nor scrip for (your) journey..nor yet st.
Mark. 6. 8 nothing for (their) journey, save a staff
Luke 9. 3 neither staves, nor scrip, neither bread
Heb. 11. 21 and worshipped..upon the top of his st.

STAGGER, to (make to) —
1. *To move, shake, stagger,* נוּעַ *nua.*
Psa. 107. 27 They reel to and fro, and stagger like a
Isa. 29. 9 they stagger, but not with strong drink

2. *To wander, go astray, err, be deceived,* תָּעָה *taah,* 2.
Isa. 19. 14 as a drunken (man) staggereth in his vo.

3. *To cause to wander, go astray,* תָּעָה *taah,* 5.
Job 12. 25 maketh them to stagger like (a) drunken

4. *To judge diversely, doubt,* διακρίνω *diakrinō.*
Rom. 4. 20 He staggered not at the promise of God

STAIN, to —
1. *To pollute, redeem, free,* גָּאַל *gaal.*
Job 3. 5 darkness and the shadow of death stain it

2. *To pollute,* גָּאַל *gaal,* 5.
Isa. 63. 3 my garments; and I will stain all my raime.

3. *To pierce, pollute, make common,* חָלַל *chalal,* 3.
Isa. 23. 9 to stain the pride of all glory, (and) to br.

STAIRS, (winding) —
1. *Winding stairs,* לוּלִים *lulim.*
1 Ki. 6. 8 they went up with winding stairs into the

2. *Rocky ascent, stair,* מַדְרֵגָה *madregah.*
Song 2. 14 my dove..in the secret (places) of the st.

3. *A going up, ascent, step,* מַעֲלָה *maalah.*
2 Ki. 9. 13 put (it) under him on the top of the stairs
Neh. 3. 15 stairs that go down from the city of Dav.
12. 37 went up by the stairs of the city of David
Eze. 40. 6 went up the stairs thereof, and measured
43. 17 and his stairs shall look toward the east

4. *A going up, ascent, stair,* מַעֲלֶה *maaleh.*
Neh. 9. 4 Then stood up upon the stairs, of the L.

5. *An ascent, going up,* ἀναβαθμός *anabathmos.*
Acts 21. 35 when he came upon the stairs, so it was
21. 40 Paul stood on the stairs, and beckoned

STAKE —
Pin, nail, stake, יָתֵד *yathed.*
Isa. 33. 20 not one of the stakes thereof shall ever
54. 2 lengthen thy cords..strengthen thy stak.

STALK —
1. *Wood, tree, stalk, staff,* עֵץ *ets.*
Josh. 2. 6 hid them with the stalks of flax, which she

2. *A stalk, standing corn,* קָמָה *qamah.*
Hos. 8. 7 it hath no stalk; the bud shall yield no

3. *A stalk, branch, cane, reed,* קָנֶה *qaneh.*
Gen. 41. 5 seven ears of corn came up upon one sta.
41. 22 seven ears came up in one stalk, full and

STALL, stalled —
1. *To fatten, be fattened,* אָבַס *abas.*
Prov 15. 17 than a stalled ox and hatred therewith

2. *Stalls,* אֻרְוֹת ,אֻרָיוֹת *uravoth, urayoth.*
1 Ki. 4. 26 Solomon had forty thousand stalls of ho.
2 Ch. 9. 25 Solomon had four thousand stalls for ho.
32. 28 stalls for all manner of beasts, and cotes

3. *A fattening stall,* מַרְבֵּק *marbeq.*
Amos 6. 4 and the calves out of the midst of the st.
Mal. 4. 2 ye shall..grow up as calves of the stall

4. *Stalls, cribs,* רְפָתִים *rephathim.*
Hab. 3. 17 and (there shall be) no herd in the stalls

5. *Eating place, manger, crib,* φάτνη *phatnē.*
Luke 13. 15 loose his ox or (his) ass from the stall, and

STAMMERER, stammering —
1. *To be scorned, stammering,* לָעַג *laag,* 2.
Isa. 33. 19 a stammering tongue, (that thou canst) not

2. *Scorning, stammering,* לַעַג *laeg.*
Isa. 28. 11 with stammering lips and another tongue

3. *Scorning, stammering,* עִלֵּג *illeg.*
Isa. 32. 4 the tongue of the stammerers shall be re.

STAMP (upon), stamping, to —
1. *To beat small or thin,* דָּקַק *daqaq,* 5.
2 Sa. 22. 43 I did stamp them as the mire of the street
2 Ki. 23. 6 stamped (it) small to powder, and cast the
23. 15 stamped (it) small to powder, and burned
2 Ch. 15. 16 Asa cut down her idol, and stamped (it)

2. *To beat down or out,* כָּתַת *kathath.*
Deut. 9. 21 burnt it with fire, and stamped it, (and) gr.

3. *To tread, trample down,* רָמַס *ramas.*
Dan. 8. 7 cast him down to the ground, and stamped
8. 10 cast down (some) of the host..and stamped

4. *To trample on,* רְפַס *rephas.*
Dan. 7. 7, 19 brake in pieces, and stamped the res.

5. *To spread out, stamp,* רָקַע *raqa.*
Eze. 6. 11 Smite with thine hand, and stamp with thy
25. 6 hast clapped (thine) hands, and stamped

6. *A stamping*, שְׁעָטָה *sheatah.*
Jer. 47. 3 the stamping of the hoofs of his strong

STANCH, to —
To set, place, ἵστημι *histēmi.*
Luke 8. 44 immediately her issue of blood stanched

STAND (before, by, fast, firm, forth, here, out), to —
1. *To be steady, faithful*, אָמַן *aman*, 2.
Psa. 89. 28 and my covenant shall stand fast with him

2. *To go out or forth*, יָצָא *yatsa.*
Psa. 73. 7 Their eyes stand out with fatness: they

3. *To set self up, station self*, יָצַב *yatsab*, 7.
Exod. 2. 4 his sister stood afar off, to wit what wou.
8. 20 Rise up early..and stand before Pharaoh
9. 13 stand before Pharaoh, and say unto him
19. 17 they stood at the nether part of the mou.
34. 5 stood with him there, and proclaimed the
Num 11. 16 that they may stand there with thee
22. 22 the angel of the LORD stood in the way
23. 3 Stand by thy burnt offering, and I will go
23. 15 Stand here by thy burnt offering, while I
1 Sa. 3. 10 the LORD came, and stood, and called as
10. 23 when he stood among the people, he was
12. 16 stand and see this great thing, which the
2 Sa. 18. 30 king said (unto him), Turn aside, (and) s.
23. 12 he stood in the midst of the ground, and
Job 38. 14 It is turned..they stand as a garment
Psa. 5. 5 The foolish shall not stand in thy sight
Prov 22. 29 stand before kings; he shall not stand be.
Jer. 46. 4 get up, ye horsemen, and stand forth wi.
46. 14 say ye, Stand fast, and prepare thee; for

4. *To be prepared, established*, כּוּן *kun*, 2.
Judg 16. 26 the pillars whereupon the house standeth
16. 29 middle pillars upon which the house sto.

5. *To draw nigh*, נָגַשׁ *nagash.*
Gen. 19. 9 they said, Stand back. And they said (ag.)

6. *To be set up*, נָצַב *natsab*, 2.
Gen. 18. 2 looked, and, lo, three men stood by him
24. 13 I stand (here) by the well of water; and
24. 43 I stand by the well of water; and it shall
28. 13 the LORD stood above it, and said, I (am)
45. 1 could not..before all them that stood by
Exod. 5. 20 they met Moses and Aaron, who stood in
7. 15 thou shalt stand by the river's brink aga.
17. 9 I will stand on the top of the hill with the
18. 14 the people stand by thee from morning un.
33. 8 the people rose up, and stood every man
33. 21 a place by me, and thou shalt stand upon
Num 16. 27 came out, and stood in the door of their
22. 34 I knew not that thou stoodest in the way
23. 6 he stood by his burnt sacrifice, he, and all
23. 17 he stood by his burnt offering, and the pr.
Deut 29. 10 Ye stand this day all of you before the Lo.
Judg 18. 16 six hundred men..stood by the entering
18. 17 the priest stood in the entering of the gate
1 Sa. 1. 26 I (am) the woman that stood by thee here
4. 20 the women that stood by her said unto her
22. 7 said unto his servants that stood about
22. 17 said unto the footmen that stood about
2 Sa. 13. 31 his servants stood by with their clothes
Psa. 45. 9 upon thy right hand did stand the queen
82. 1 God standeth in the congregation of the
Prov. 8. 2 She standeth in the top of high places, by
Lam. 2. 4 he stood with his right hand as an adver.
Amos 7. 7 the Lord stood upon a wall (made) by a

7. *To sustain, support*, סָמַךְ *samak.*
Psa. 111. 8 They stand fast for ever and ever, (and are)

8. *To stand, stand still or fast*, עָמַד *amad.*
Gen. 18. 8 he stood by them under the tree, and they
18. 22 but Abraham stood yet before the LORD
19. 27 to the place where he stood before the L.
24. 30 behold, he stood by the camels at the well
24. 31 wherefore standest thou without? for I
41. 1 Pharaoh dreamed: and, behold, he stood
41. 3 stood by the (other) kine upon the brink
41. 17 behold, I stood upon the bank of the riv.
41. 46 when he stood before Pharaoh king of Eg.
43. 15 went down to Egypt, and stood before J.
45. 1 there stood no man with him while Jose.
Exod. 3. 5 the place whereon thou standest (is) holy
9. 10 took ashes of the furnace, and stood before
9. 11 the magicians could not stand before Mo.
14. 19 pillar of the cloud..stood behind them
17. 6 I will stand before thee there upon the ro.
18. 13 the people stood by Moses from the mor.
20. 18 they removed, and stood afar off
20. 21 the people stood afar off: and Moses drew
32. 26 Moses stood in the gate of the camp, and
33. 9 the cloudy pillar descended, and stood (at)
33. 10 the people saw the cloudy pillar stand (at)
Lev. 9. 5 congregation drew near and stood before
18. 23 neither shall any woman stand before a b.
19. 16 neither shalt thou stand against the blood
Num. 1. 5 the names of the men that shall stand wi.
12. 5 stood (in) the door of the tabernacle, and
14. 14 (that) thy cloud standeth over them; and
16. 9 to stand before the congregation to min.
16. 18 stood in the door of the tabernacle of the
16. 48 he stood between the dead and the living
22. 24 the angel of the LORD stood in a path of
22. 26 the angel..stood in a narrow place, where
27. 2 they stood before Moses and before Eleazar
27. 21 he shall stand before Eleazar the priest
35. 12 until he stand before the congregation in
Deut. 1. 38 the son of Nun, which standeth before thee
4. 10 the day that thou stoodest before the LORD
4. 11 ye came near and stood under the mounta.

Deut. 5. 5 I stood between the LORD and you at that
5. 31 stand thou here by me, and I will speak
10. 8 to stand before the LORD to minister unto
17. 12 the priest that standeth to minister there
18. 5 to stand to minister in the name of the L.
18. 7 as all his brethren..(do), which stand there
19. 17 both the men..shall stand before the LORD
24. 11 Thou shalt stand abroad, and the man to
25. 8 (if) he stand (to it), and say, I like not to
27. 12 These shall stand upon mount Gerizim to
27. 13 these shall stand upon mount Ebal to cur.
29. 15 with (him) that standeth here with us th.
31. 15 the pillar of the cloud stood over the door
Josh. 3. 13 and they shall stand upon an heap
3. 16 the waters..stood (and) rose up upon an
3. 17 stood firm on dry ground in the midst
4. 10 the priests which bare the ark stood in the
5. 13 there stood a man over against him with
5. 15 for the place whereon thou standest (is)
8. 33 their judges, stood on this side the ark and
10. 8 there shall not a man of them stand befo.
20. 4 when he that doth flee..shall stand at the
20. 6 until he stand before the congregation for
20. 9 until he stood before the congregation
21. 44 there stood not a man of all their enemies
Judg. 2. 14 could not any longer stand before their en.
3. 19 all that stood by him went out from him
4. 20 he said unto her, Stand in the door of the
6. 31 Joash said unto all that stood against him
7. 21 they stood every man in his place round
9. 7 he went and stood in the top of mount G.
9. 35, 44 stood in the entering of the gate of the
20. 28 Phinehas..stood before it in those days
1 Sa. 6. 14 stood there, where (there was) a great sto.
6. 20 Who is able to stand before this holy LORD
9. 27 stand thou still a while, that I may show
16. 21 David came to Saul, and stood before him
16. 22 Let David, I pray thee, stand before me
17. 3 the Philistines stood on a mountain on
17. 3 Israel stood on a mountain on the other
17. 8 he stood and cried unto the armies of Is.
17. 26 David spake to the men that stood by him
17. 51 David ran, and stood upon the Philistine
19. 3 I will go out and stand beside my father
19. 20 Samuel standing (as) appointed over them
26. 13 stood on the top of an hill afar off, a great
2 Sa. 1. 9 Stand, I pray thee, upon me, and slay me
1. 10 I stood upon him, and slew him, because
2. 25 became one troop, and stood on the top of
15. 2 rose up early, and stood beside the way of
18. 4 the king stood by the gate side, and all
20. 11 one of Joab's men stood by him, and said
20. 15 cast up a bank..and it stood in the trench
1 Ki. 1. 2 let her stand before the king, and let her
1. 28 came into the king's presence, and stood
3. 15 he came to Jerusalem, and stood before
3. 16 Then came there two women..and stood b.
7. 25 It stood upon twelve oxen, three looking
8. 11 the priests could not stand to minister be.
8. 14 and all the congregation of Israel stood
8. 22 Solomon stood before the altar of the LORD
8. 55 he stood, and blessed all the congregation
10. 8 happy (are) these thy servants, which st.
10. 19 and two lions stood beside the stays
10. 20 twelve lions stood there on the one side
12. 6 the old men, that stood before Solomon
12. 8 with the young men..which stood before
13. 1 Jeroboam stood by the altar to burn inc.
13. 24 the ass stood by it, the lion also stood by
13. 25 and the lion standing by the carcase: and
13. 28 the ass and the lion standing by the carc.
17. 1 (As) the LORD..liveth, before whom I st.
18. 15 (As) the LORD..liveth, before whom I st.
19. 11 stand upon the mount before the LORD
19. 13 and stood in the entering in of the cave
22. 19 the host of heaven standing by him on his
22. 21 there came forth a spirit, and stood before
2 Ki. 2. 7 stood to view afar..and they two stood by
2. 13 went back, and stood by the bank of Jor.
3. 14 (As) the LORD..liveth, before whom I stand
3. 21 gathered all..and stood in the border
4. 12, 15 And when he had called her, she sto.
5. 9 and stood at the door of the house of El.
5. 11 He will surely come out to me, and stand
5. 15 returned..and came and stood before him
5. 16 (As) the LORD liveth, before whom I sta.
5. 25 But he went in, and stood before his ma.
6. 31 if the head of Elisha..shall stand on him
8. 9 came and stood before him, and said, Thy
9. 17 there stood a watchman on the tower in
10. 4 kings stood not..how then shall we stand?
10. 9 he went out, and stood, and said to all the
11. 11 the guard stood, every man with his wea.
11. 14 the king stood by a pillar, as the manner
18. 17 they came and stood by the conduit of the
18. 28 Rab-shakeh stood, and cried with a loud
23. 3 the king stood by a pillar, and made a co.
23. 3 and all the people stood to the covenant
1 Ch. 6. 39 his brother Asaph, who stood on his right
21. 1 Satan stood up against Israel, and provok.
21. 15 the angel of the LORD stood by the thre.
21. 16 saw the angel of the LORD stand between
23. 30 to stand every morning to thank and pra.
2 Ch. 3. 13 they stood on their feet, and their faces
4. 4 It stood on twelve oxen, three looking to.
5. 12 the Levites..stood at the east end of the
5. 14 the priests could not stand to minister
6. 3 and all the congregation of Israel stood
6. 12 he stood before the altar of the LORD in
6. 13 upon it he stood, and kneeled down upon
7. 6 sounded trumpets..and all Israel stood
9. 7 happy (are) these thy servants, which st.

2 Ch. 9. 18 and two lions standing by the stays
9. 19 twelve lions stood there on the one side
10. 6 the old men that had stood before Solom.
10. 8 with the young men..that stood before
18. 18 the host of heaven standing on his right
18. 20 there came out a spirit, and stood before
20. 5 Jehoshaphat stood in the congregation of
20. 9 we stand before this house, and in thy pr.
20. 13 Judah stood before the LORD, with their
20. 17 stand ye (still), and see the salvation of
20. 19 stood up to praise the LORD God of Israel
20. 20 Jehoshaphat stood and said, Hear me, O
20. 23 Moab stood up against the inhabitants of
23. 13 the king stood at his pillar at the enter.
29. 11 the LORD hath chosen you to stand before
29. 26 the Levites stood with the instruments
30. 16 they stood in their place after their man.
34. 31 the king stood in his place, and made a c.
35. 5 stand in the holy (place), according to the
35. 10 the priests stood in their place, and the
Ezra 3. 9 Then stood Jeshua (with) his sons and his
9. 15 we cannot stand before thee because of
10. 13 we are not able to stand without, neither
10. 14 Let now our rulers..stand, and let all th.
Neh. 7. 65 till there stood (up) a priest with Urim and
8. 4 the scribe stood upon a pulpit of wood
8. 4 beside him stood Mattithiah, and Shema
9. 2 stood and confessed their sins, and the in.
12. 40 So stood the two (companies of them that
Esth. 3. 4 whether Mordecai's matters would stand
5. 1 stood in the inner court of the king's ho.
5. 2 the king saw Esther the queen standing
6. 5 Behold, Haman standeth in the court. A.
7. 9 the gallows..standeth in the house of H.
8. 4 So Esther arose, and stood before the ki.
8. 11 to stand for their life, to destroy, to slay
9. 16 gathered themselves together, and stood
Job 8. 15 lean upon his house, but it shall not stand
Psa. 1. 1 nor standeth in the way of sinners, nor
10. 1 Why standest thou afar off, O LORD? (why)
26. 12 My foot standeth in an even place: in the
33. 9 For..he commanded, and it stood fast
33. 11 The counsel of the LORD standeth for ever
38. 11 friends stand aloof..kinsmen stand afar
76. 7 who may stand in thy sight when once th.
104. 6 the waters stood above the mountains
106. 23 had not Moses his chosen stood before him
109. 6 and let Satan stand at his right hand
109. 31 he shall stand at the right hand of the po.
122. 2 Our feet shall stand within thy gates, O J
130. 3 If thou..mark iniquities..who shall st.?
134. 1 by night stand in the house of the LORD
135. 2 Ye that stand in the house of the LORD
147. 17 casteth forth his ice..who can stand bef.
Prov 12. 7 but the house of the righteous shall stand
25. 6 and stand not in the place of great (men)
Eccl. 8. 3 stand not in an evil thing; for he doeth
Song 2. 9 he standeth behind our wall, he looketh
Isa. 3. 13 The LORD..standeth to judge the people
6. 2 Above it stood the seraphim: each one
11. 10 a root of Jesse, which shall stand for an
21. 8 I stand continually upon the watch tower
36. 2 he stood by the conduit of the upper pool
36. 13 Then Rabshakeh stood, and cried with a
46. 7 and set him in his place, and he standeth
47. 12 Stand now with thine enchantments, and
50. 8 who will contend with me? let us stand
59. 14 justice standeth afar off: for truth is fal.
61. 5 strangers shall stand and feed your flock.
Jer. 6. 16 Stand ye in the ways and see, and ask for
7. 2 Stand in the gate of the LORD's house, and
7. 10 come and stand before me in this house
14. 6 the wild asses did stand in the high place
15. 1 Though Moses and Samuel stood before
15. 19 If thou return..thou shalt stand before
17. 19 stand in the gate of the children of the
18. 20 I stood before thee to speak good for them
19. 14 he stood in the court of the LORD's house
23. 18 who hath stood in the counsel of the LORD
23. 22 if they had stood in my counsel, and had
26. 2 Stand in the court of the LORD's house, and
28. 5 the people that stood in the house of the
35. 19 shall not want a man to stand before me
36. 21 all the princes which stood beside the ki.
46. 15 they stood not, because the LORD did dr.
46. 21 they did not stand, because the day of
48. 19 inhabitant of Aroer, stand by the way, and
48. 45 They that fled stood under the shadow of
49. 19 that shepherd that will stand before me
50. 44 that shepherd that will stand before me
Eze. 1. 21 when those stood, (these) stood; and when
1. 24 when they stood, they let down their wi.
1. 25 when they stood, (and) had let down th.
2. 1 stand upon thy feet, and I will speak unto
3. 23 the glory of the LORD stood there, as the
8. 11 there stood before them seventy men of
8. 11 in the midst of them stood Jaazaniah the
9. 2 they went in, and stood beside the brasen
10. 3 the cherubim stood on the right side of
10. 6 then he went in, and stood beside the wh.
10. 17 When they stood, (these) stood; and when
10. 18 Then the glory..stood over the cherubim
10. 19 (every one) stood at the door of the east
11. 23 stood upon the mountain which (is) on the
13. 5 to stand in the battle in the day of the L.
17. 14 by keeping of his covenant it might stand
21. 21 the king of Babylon stood at the parting
22. 30 stand in the gap before me for the land
27. 29 shall come..they shall stand upon the la.
33. 26 Ye stand upon your sword, ye work abo.
40. 3 (there was) a man..and he stood in the ga.
43. 6 I heard (him)..and the man stood by me

Eze. 44. 11 they shall stand before them to minister
44. 15 they shall stand before me to offer unto
44. 24 in controversy they shall stand in judgm.
46. 2 shall stand by the post of the gate, and the
47. 10 the fishers shall stand upon it from En-g.
Dan. 1. 4 such as (had) ability in them to stand in
1. 5 at the end thereof they might stand bef.
1. 19 therefore stood they before the king
2. 2 So they came and stood before the king
8. 3 there stood before the river a ram which
8. 4 so that no beasts might stand before him
8. 6 which I had seen standing before the river
8. 7 no power in the ram to stand before him
8. 15 there stood before me as the appearance
10. 11 understand the words..and stand upright
10. 11 when he had spoken..I stood trembling
10. 16 said unto him that stood before me, O my
11. 6 neither shall he stand, nor his arm: but
11. 14 there shall many stand up against the ki.
11. 16 shall stand before him; and he shall stand
11. 17 she shall not stand (on his side), neither
11. 25 he shall not stand: for they shall forecast
11. 31 arms shall stand on his part, and they sh.
12. 1 stand up, the great prince which standeth
12. 5 there stood other two, the one on this si.
12. 13 and stand in thy lot at the end of the days
Hos. 10. 9 there they stood: the battle in Gibeah ag.
Amos 2. 15 Neither shall he stand that handleth the
Obad. 11 In the day that thou stoodest on the other
14 Neither shouldest thou have stood in the
Mic. 5. 4 he shall stand and feed in the strength of
Nah. 1. 6 Who can stand before his indignation?
2. 8 Stand, stand, (shall they cry); but none sh
Hab. 2. 1 I will stand upon my watch, and set me
3. 6 He stood, and measured the earth: he
Zech. 1. 8 he stood among the myrtle trees that (we)
1. 10 the man that stood among the myrtle tr
1. 11 the angel of the LORD that stood among
3. 1 the high priest standing before the angel
3. 1 Satan standing at his right hand to resist
3. 3 clothed with filthy garments, and stood
3. 4 spake unto those that stood before him
4. 14 that stand by the Lord of the whole earth
14. 4 his feet shall stand in that day upon the
14. 12 consume away while they stand upon th.
Mal. 3. 2 who shall stand when he appeareth? for

9. *To rise up, stand firm,* קוּם *qum.*
Lev. 27. 14 the priest shall estimate it, so shall it st
27. 17 according to thy estimation it shall stand
Num 30. 4, 11 shall stand, and every bond..shall st
30. 5 not any of her vows, or..bonds..shall st.
30. 7 shall stand, and her bonds..shall stand
30. 9 every vow of a widow..shall stand against
30. 12 shall not stand: her husband hath made
Josh. 7. 12 the children of Israel could not stand be
7. 13 thou canst not stand before thine enem.
1 Ch. 28. 2 the king stood up upon his feet, and said
Job 19. 25 he shall stand at the latter (day) upon the
Psa. 1. 5 the ungodly shall not stand in the judg.
24. 3 or who shall stand in his holy place?
Prov. 19. 21 the counsel of the LORD, that shall stand
Isa. 7. 7 It shall not stand, neither shall it come
8. 10 speak the word, and it shall not stand: for
14. 24 and as I have purposed, (so) shall it stand
28. 18 your agreement with hell shall not stand
32. 8 and by liberal things shall he stand
40. 8 but the word of our God shall stand for
46. 10 My counsel shall stand, and I will do all
Jer. 44. 28 shall know whose words shall stand, mi.
44. 29 my words shall surely stand against you

10. *To rise up, stand firm,* קוּם *qum.*
Dan. 2. 31 This great image..stood before thee, and
2. 44 consume all..and it shall stand for ever
3. 3 they stood before the image that Nebuc.
7. 10 ten thousand times ten thousand stood bef.
7. 16 I came near unto one of them that stood by

11. *To be or draw near,* קָרַב *qarab.*
Isa. 65. 5 Stand by thyself, come not near to me; for

12. *To set or place up,* ἀνίστημι *anistēmi.*
Acts 14. 10 Said with a loud voice, Stand..on thy feet

13. *To lift or raise up,* ἐγείρω *egeirō.*
Mark 3. 3 And he saith unto the man..[Stand] forth

14. *To set on, over, upon,* ἐφίστημι *ephistēmi.*
Luke 24. 4 two men stood by them in shining garm.
Acts 10. 17 had made enquiry..and stood before the
22. 13 Came unto me, and stood, and said unto
22. 20 I also was standing by, and consenting
23. 11 the Lord stood by him, and said, Be of go.

15. *To set, place,* ἵστημι *histēmi.*
Matt. 2. 9 it came and [stood] over where the young
6. 5 they love to pray standing in the synago.
12. 25 house divided against itself shall not stand
12. 26 how shall then his kingdom stand?
12. 46 (his) mother and his brethren stood with.
12. 47 thy mother and thy brethren stand with.
13. 2 and the whole multitude stood on the sh.
16. 28 There be some standing here which shall
20. 3 saw others standing idle in the market
20. 6 went out, and found others standing idle
20. 6 saith unto them, Why stand ye here all
24. 15 abomination of desolation..stand in the
26. 73 came unto (him) they that stood by, and
27. 11 Jesus stood before the governor: and the
27. 47 Some of them that stood there, when they
Mark 3. 24 a kingdom be divided..that..cannot stand
3. 25 against itself, that house cannot stand
3. 26 if Satan..be divided, he cannot [stand], but
3. 31 and, standing without, sent unto him, ca.
Mark 9. 1 there be some of them that stand here
11. 5 certain of them that stood there said un.
13. 14 abomination of desolation..standing wh.
Luke 1. 11 an angel of the Lord standing on the rig.
5. 1 pressed upon him to hear..he stood by
5. 2 saw two ships standing by the lake: but
6. 8 stand forth..And he arose and stood for.
6. 17 he came down with them, and stood in
7. 38 stood at his feet behind (him) weeping
8. 20 thy brethren stand without, desiring to
9. 27 there be some standing here, which shall
11. 18 be divided..how shall his kingdom stand?
13. 25 ye begin to stand without, and to knock
17. 12 men that were lepers, which stood afar
18. 11 The Pharisee stood and prayed thus with
18. 13 the publican, standing afar off, would not
18. 40 Jesus stood, and commanded him to be
19. 8 Zaccheus stood, and said unto the Lord
21. 36 accounted worthy..to stand before the Son
23. 10 scribes stood and vehemently accused him
23. 35 the people stood beholding. And the ru.
23. 49 his acquaintance..stood afar off, behold.
24. 36 Jesus himself stood in the midst of them
John 1. 26 there standeth one among you, whom ye
1. 35 the next day after, John stood, and two
3. 29 friend of the bridegroom, which standeth
6. 22 the people which stood on the other side
7. 37 Jesus stood and cried, saying, If any man
8. 9 [alone, and the woman standing in the m.]
11. 56 spake among themselves, as they stood in
12. 29 The people therefore that stood by, and
18. 5 Judas also, which betrayed him, stood wi.
18. 16 Peter stood at the door without. Then
18. 18 the servants and officers stood there, who
18. 18 Peter stood with them, and warmed him.
18. 25 And Simon Peter stood and warmed him.
19. 25 there stood by the cross of Jesus his mot.
20. 11 Mary stood without at the sepulchre we.
20. 14 saw Jesus standing, and knew not that it
20. 19 came Jesus and stood in the midst, and
20. 26 (Then) came Jesus..and stood in the mid.
21. 4 Jesus stood on the shore: but the discip.
Acts 1. 11 men of Galilee, why stand ye gazing up
3. 8 he leaping up stood, and walked, and en.
4. 14 the man which was healed standing with
5. 20 stand and speak in the temple to the pe.
5. 23 the keepers standing without before the
5. 25 the men whom ye put in prison are stan.
7. 33 the place where thou standest is holy gr.
7. 55 Jesus standing on the right hand of God
7. 56 the Son of man standing on the right ha.
9. 7 men which journeyed with him stood sp.
10. 30 a man stood before me in bright clothing
11. 13 an angel in his house, which stood and sa.
12. 14 ran in, and told how Peter stood before
16. 9 There stood a man of Macedonia, and pr.
17. 22 Paul stood in the midst of Mars' hill, and
21. 40 Paul stood on the stairs, and beckoned wi.
22. 25 Paul said unto the centurion that stood by
24. 20 any evil doing in me, while I stood before
24. 21 Except..that I cried standing among them
25. 10 I stand at Cesar's judgment seat, where
26. 6 I stand and am judged for the hope of the
26. 16 stand upon thy feet: for I have appeared
27. 21 Paul stood forth in the midst of them, and
Rom. 5. 2 access..into this grace wherein we stand
11. 20 they were broken off, and thou standest
1 Co. 7. 37 he that standeth stedfast in his heart, ha.
10. 12 let him that thinketh he standeth take h.
15. 1 ye have received, and wherein ye stand
2 Co. 1. 24 helpers of your joy: for by faith ye stand
Eph. 6. 11 that ye may be able to stand against the
6. 13 ye may be able..having done all, to stand
6. 14 Stand therefore, having your loins girt ab.
Col. 4. 12 that ye may stand perfect and complete
2 Ti. 2. 19 the foundation of God standeth sure, ha.
Heb. 10. 11 every priest standeth daily ministering
Jas. 2. 3 Stand thou there, or sit here under my fo.
5. 9 behold, the Judge standeth before the do.
1 Pe. 5. 12 the true grace of God wherein ye stand
Rev. 3. 20 I stand at the door and knock: if any man
5. 6 in the midst of the elders, stood a Lamb
6. 17 the great day..who shall be able to stand
7. 1 I saw four angels standing on the four co.
7. 9 stood before the throne, and before the
7. 11 the angels stood round about the throne
8. 2 I saw the seven angels which stood before
8. 3 another angel came and stood at the altar
10. 5 the angel which I saw stand upon the sea
10. 8 the angel which standeth upon the sea and
11. 1 [the angel stood, saying, Rise, and measu.]
11. 4 the two candlesticks standing before the
11. 11 the spirit..entered into them, and they
12. 4 the dragon stood before the woman which
13. 1 I stood upon the sand of the sea, and saw
14. 1 a Lamb stood on the mount Sion, and wi.
15. 2 stand on the sea of glass, having the harps
18. 10 Standing afar off for the fear of her torm.
18. 15 shall stand afar off for the fear of her to.
18. 17 and as many as trade by sea, stood afar
19. 17 I saw an angel standing in the sun; and
20. 12 the dead, small and great, stand before G.

16. *To remain,* μένω *menō.*
Rom. 9. 11 that the purpose of God..might stand, not

17. *To set alongside,* παρίστημι *paristēmi.*
Mark 14. 47 one of them that stood by drew a sword
14. 69 began to say to them that stood by, This
14. 70 they that stood by said again to Peter, Su.
15. 35 some of them that stood by, when they
15. 39 when the centurion, which stood over ag.
Luke 1. 19 I am Gabriel, that stand in the presence
19. 24 he said unto them that stood by, Take fr.
John 18. 22 one of the officers which stood by struck
19. 26 and the disciple standing by whom he lo.
Acts 1. 10 two men stood by them in white apparel
4. 10 by him doth this man stand here before
9. 39 the widows stood by him weeping, and sh.
23. 2 Ananias commanded them that stood by
23. 4 they that stood by said, Revilest thou G.
27. 23 there stood by me this night the angel of
Rom. 14. 10 we shall all stand before the judgment se.

18. *To set around,* περιΐστημι *periistēmi.*
John 11. 42 because of the people which stand by I said

19. *To stand firm,* στήκω *stēkō.*
Mark 11. 25 when ye stand praying, forgive, if ye have
Rom 14. 4 to his own master he standeth or falleth
1 Co. 16. 13 stand fast in the faith, quit you like men
Gal. 5. 1 Stand fast therefore in the liberty where.
Phil. 1. 27 that ye stand fast in one spirit, with one
4. 1 so stand fast in the Lord, (my) dearly belo.
1 Th. 3. 8 now we live, if ye stand fast in the Lord
2 Th. 2. 15 stand fast, and hold the traditions which

20. *To set together,* συνίστημι *sunistēmi.*
2 Pe. 3. 5 the earth standing out of the water and

21. *To be,* εἰμί *eimi.*
1 Co. 2. 5 That your faith should not stand in the

STAND over, round about, still, up, upright, with, to —

1. *To be silent, cease, stand still,* דָּמַם *damam.*
Josh 10. 12 Sun, stand thou still upon Gibeon; and
10. 13 the sun stood still, and the moon stayed

2. *To set self up,* יָצַב *yatsab,* 7.
Exod 14. 13 stand still, and see the salvation of the L.
1 Sa. 12. 7 stand still, that I may reason with you be.
Job 33. 5 set (thy words) in order before me, stand up
Psa. 94. 16 who will stand up for me against the wo.

3. *To be set up,* נָצַב *natsab,* 2.
Gen. 37. 7 lo, my sheaf arose, and also stood upright
Exod 15. 8 the floods stood upright as an heap, (and)
Isa. 3. 13 The LORD standeth up to plead, and..to
Zech. 11. 16 nor feed that that standeth still; but he

4. *To stand up or erect,* סָמַר *samar,* 3.
Job 4. 15 the hair of my flesh stood up

5. *To station self, stand upright,* עוּד *ud,* 7a.
Psa. 20. 8 fallen; but we are risen, and stand upri.

6. *To stand still,* עָמַד *amad.*
Exod 26. 15 make boards..(of) shittim wood stand. up.
36. 20 made boards..(of) shittim wood, stand. up.
Num. 9. 8 Stand still, and I will hear what the LORD
Josh. 3. 8 When ye are come..ye shall stand still in
3. 17 the priests..stood firm on dry ground in
10. 13 So the sun stood still in the midst of hea.
11. 13 (as for) the cities that stood still in their
23. 9 no man hath been able to stand before
1 Sa. 14. 9 we will stand still in our place, and will
2 Sa. 2. 23 as many as came to the place..stood still
2. 28 the people stood still, and pursued after
18. 30 And he turned aside, and stood still
20. 12 the man saw that all the people stood st.
20. 12 that every one that came by him stood st.
2 Ch. 24. 20 Zechariah..which stood above the people
Ezra 2. 63 till there stood up a priest with Urim and
Neh. 7. 3 while they stand by, let them shut the do.
8. 5 when he opened it, all the people stood up
12. 39 and they stood still in the prison gate
Esth. 7. 7 Haman stood up to make request for his
Job 4. 16 It stood still, but I could not discern the
29. 8 and the aged arose, (and) stood up
30. 20 I stand up, and thou regardest me (not)
32. 16 they spake not, but stood still, (and) an.
37. 14 stand still, and consider the wondrous wo.
Psa. 106. 30 Then stood up Phinehas, and executed j.
Prov 27. 4 Wrath (is) cruel..who (is) able to stand be.
Eccl. 4. 15 the second child that shall stand up in his
Isa. 44. 11 let them stand up; (yet) they shall fear
47. 13 Let now the astrologers..stand up and sa.
48. 13 (when) I call unto them, they stand up
Jer. 44. 15 the women that stood by, a great multit.
51. 50 Ye that have escaped..stand not still: re.
Eze. 31. 14 neither their trees stand up in their heig.
37. 10 they lived, and stood up upon their feet
Dan. 8. 22 stood up for it, four kingdoms shall stand u.
8. 23 king of fierce countenance..shall stand up
8. 25 he shall also stand up against the prince
11. 2 there shall stand up yet three kings in Pe.
11. 3 a mighty king shall stand up, that shall
11. 4 when he shall stand up, his kingdom sh.
11. 7 shall (one) stand up in his estate, which
11. 20 Then shall stand up in his estate a raiser
11. 21 in his estate shall stand up a vile person
Zech. 3. 5 And the angel of the LORD stood by
3. 7 places to walk among these that stand by
Hab. 3. 11 the sun (and) moon stood still in their

7. *To rise up, stand still,* קוּם *qum.*
Gen. 23. 3 Abraham stood up from before his dead
23. 7 Abraham stood up, and bowed himself to
Exod. 2. 17 Moses stood up and helped them, and wa.
2 Ki. 13. 21 touched the bones..he revived, and st. up.
2 Ch. 13. 4 Abijah stood up upon mount Zemaraim
28. 12 stood up against them that came from the
Ezra 3. 2 Then stood up Jeshua the son of Jozadak
10. 10 the priest stood up, and said unto them
Neh. 9. 3 they stood up in their place, and read in
9. 4 Then stood up upon the stairs, of the Le.
9. 5 Stand up (and) bless the LORD your God
Esth. 5. 9 that he stood not up, nor moved for him

Job 30. 28 I stood up, (and) I cried in the congrega.
Psa. 35. 2 Take hold of shield..and stand up for mi.
Isa. 27. 9 the groves and images shall not stand up
51. 17 stand up, O Jerusalem, which hast drunk

8. *To set or place up,* ἀνίστημι *anistēmi.*
Mark14. 60 the high priest stood up in the midst, and
Luke 4. 16 went into the synagogue..and stood up
10. 25 a certain lawyer stood up, and tempted
Acts 1. 15 Peter stood up in the midst of the discip.
5. 34 Then stood there up one in the council, a
10. 26 saying, Stand up; I myself also am a man
11. 28 there stood up one of them named Agab.
13. 16 Paul stood up, and beckoning with (his) ha.

9. *To set or place on,* ἐφίστημι *ephistēmi.*
Luke 4. 39 he stood over her, and rebuked the fever

10. *To set, place,* ἵστημι *histēmi.*
Matt20. 32 Jesus stood still, and called them, and
Mark10. 49 Jesus stood still, and commanded him to
Luke 7. 14 he came..and they that bare (him)s. still
Acts 2. 14 Peter, standing up with the eleven, lifted
8. 38 he commanded the chariot to stand still
25. 18 Against whom, when the accusers stood up

11. *To surround, encircle,* κυκλόω *kukloō.*
Acts 14. 20 as the disciples stood round about him, he

12. *To set alongside,* παρίστημι *paristēmi.*
Acts 4. 26 The kings of the earth stood up, and the
2 Ti. 4. 17 the Lord stood with me, and strengthened

13. *To set around,* περιΐστημι *periistēmi.*
Acts 25. 7 the Jews..stood round about, and laid ma.

14. *To be along with,* συμπαραγίνομαι *sumparagi.*
2 Ti. 4. 16 no man [stood with] me, but all (men) for.

15. *To set together,* συνίστημι *sunistēmi.*
Luke 9. 32 and the two men that stood with him

STAND, can, to be able to —
1. *To set self up,* יָצַב *yatsab,* 7.
Deut. 7. 24 there shall no man be able to stand before
9. 2 Who can stand before the children of An.
11. 25 There shall no man be able to stand before
Josh. 1. 5 There shall not any man be able to stand
Job 41. 10 who then is able to stand before me?
2. *To stand,* עָמַד *amad.*
Josh.23. 9 no man hath been able to stand before

STAND in awe or doubt, to —
1. *To fear, contract self,* גּוּר *gur.*
Psa. 33. 8 the inhabitants of the world stand in awe
2. *To have no passage through, doubt,* ἀπορέομαι.
Gal. 4. 20 to be present..for I stand in doubt of you

STAND, to cause, make or be made to —
1. *To set up, cause to stand, establish,* נָצַב *natsab,* 5.
Psa. 78. 13 and he made the waters to stand as an
2. *To cause to stand still or firm,* עָמַד *amad,* 5.
2 Ch.34. 32 he caused all that were present..to stand
Psa. 30. 7 hast made my mountain to stand strong
Eze. 29. 7 and madest all their loins to be at a stand
3. *To cause to rise up,* קוּם *qum,* 5.
Psa. 89. 43 hast not made him to stand in the battle
4. *To be caused to rise up,* קוּם *qum,* 6.
Dan. 7. 4 made stand upon the feet as a man, and
5. *To set, place,* ἵστημι *histēmi.*
Rom14. 4 shall..for God is able to make him stand

STANDARD, standard bearer, (to lift up a) —
1. *A banner or standard,* דֶּגֶל *degel.*
Num. 1. 52 every man by his own standard, through.
2. 2 shall pitch by his own standard, with the
2. 3 they of the standard of the camp of Jud.
2. 10 On the south side (shall be) the standard
2. 17 every man in his place by their standards
2. 18 On the west side (shall be) the standard
2. 25 The standard of the camp of Dan (shall
2. 31 They shall go hindmost with their stand.
2. 34 they pitched by their standards, and so
10. 14, 22, 25 the standard of the camp of the
10. 18 the standard of the camp of Reuben set
2. *To cause to flee, lift up an ensign,* נוּס *nus,* 3a.
Isa. 59. 19 the spirit of the LORD shall lift up a sta.
3. *Sign, ensign, banner, sail,* נֵס *nes.*
Isa. 49. 22 I will..set up my standard to the people
62. 10 Go through..lift up a standard for the
Jer. 4. 6 Set up the standard toward Zion: retire
4. 21 How long shall I see the standard, (and)
50. 2 set up a standard; publish, (and) conceal
51. 12 Set up the standard upon the walls of B.
51. 27 Set ye up a standard in the land, blow the
4. *To set up a standard,* נָסַס *nasas.*
Isa. 10. 18 shall be as when a standard bearer faint.

STANDING (corn, image, water) —
1. *Pool of water,* אֲגַם מַיִם [*agam*].
Psa.107. 35 turneth the wilderness into a standing wa.
114. 8 turned the rock (into) a standing water
2. *To set self up,* יָצַב *yatsab,* 7.
Zech. 6. 5 which go forth from standing before the L.
3. *Standing, station,* מַעֲמָד *moomad.*
Psa. 69. 2 in deep mire, where (there is) no standing
4. *Standing place or pillar,* מַצֵּבָה *matstsebah.*
Lev. 26. 1 neither rear you up a standing image, ne.
Mic. 5. 13 thy standing images out of the midst of

5. *To be set up,* נָצַב *natsab,* 2.
Num 22. 23, 31 the angel of the LORD standing in the
1 Sa. 22. 6 all his servants (were) standing about him
Amos 9. 1 I saw the Lord standing upon the altar
6. *Standing, station,* עֶמְדָּה *emdah.*
Mic. 1. 11 he shall receive of you his standing
7. *Standing corn, stalk,* קָמָה *qamah.*
Exod22. 6 the stacks of corn, or the standing corn
Deut23. 25 When thou comest into the standing co.
23. 25 a sickle unto thy neighbour's standing co.
Judg15. 5 he let (them) go into the standing corn
15. 5 the shocks, and also the standing corn, wi.
8. *A standing, standing up,* στάσις *stasis.*
Heb. 9. 8 as the first tabernacle was yet standing

STAR —
1. *A star,* כּוֹכָב *kokab.*
Gen. 1. 16 God made two great lights..the stars also
15. 5 tell the stars, if thou be able to number
22. 17 I will multiply thy seed as the stars of the
26. 4 make thy seed to multiply as the stars of
37. 9 and the eleven stars, made obeisance to
Exod32. 13 I will multiply your seed as the stars of
Num24. 17 there shall come a star out of Jacob, and
Deut. 1. 10 ye (are) this day as the stars of heaven for
4. 19 the sun, and the moon, and the stars, (ev.)
10. 22 God hath made thee as the stars of heav.
28. 62 ye were as the stars of heaven for multi.
Judg. 5. 20 the stars in their courses fought against S.
1 Ch.27. 23 would increase Israel like to the stars of
Neh. 4. 21 the rising of the morning till the stars ap.
9. 23 multipliedst thou as the stars of heaven
Job 3. 9 Let the stars of the twilight thereof be da.
9. 7 commandeth the sun..sealeth up the st.
22. 12 behold the height of the stars, how high
25. 5 yea, the stars are not pure in his sight
38. 7 the morning stars sang together, and all
Psa. 8. 3 the moon and the stars, which thou hast
136. 9 The moon and stars to rule by night
147. 4 He telleth the number of the stars; he
148. 3 sun and moon: praise him, all ye stars of
Eccl.12. 2 or the light, or the moon, or the stars, be
Isa. 13. 10 the stars of heaven and the constellations
14. 13 I will exalt my throne above the stars of
Jer. 31. 35 the ordinances of the moon and of the st.
Eze. 32. 7 cover the heaven, and make the stars th.
Dan. 8. 10 cast down..(some)..of the stars to the gr.
12. 3 turn many to righteousness as the stars for
Joel 2. 10 and the stars shall withdraw their shining
3. 15 the stars shall withdraw their shining
Amos 5. 26 the star of your god, which ye made to
Obad. 4 though thou set thy nest among the stars
Nah. 3. 16 multiplied thy merchants above the stars
2. *A star, luminous meteor,* ἀστήρ *astēr.*
Matt. 2. 2 we have seen his star in the east, and are
2. 7 enquired..diligently what time the star
2. 9 the star, which they saw in the east, went
2. 10 When they saw the star, they rejoiced wi.
24. 29 the stars shall fall from heaven, and the
Mark13. 25 the stars of heaven shall fall, and the po.
1 Co. 15. 41 the moon, and another glory of the stars
15. 41 (one) star differeth from (another) star in
Jude 13 wandering stars, to whom is reserved the
Rev. 1. 16 And he had in his right hand seven stars
1. 20 The mystery of the seven stars which thou
1. 20 The seven stars are the angels of the sev.
2. 1 he that holdeth the seven stars in his ri.
2. 28 And I will give him the morning star
3. 1 seven spirits of God, and the seven stars
6. 13 the stars of heaven fell unto the earth
8. 10 there fell a great star from heaven, burn.
8. 11 And the name of the star is called Worm.
8. 12 the moon, and the third part of the stars
9. 1 I saw a star fall from heaven unto the ea.
12. 1 upon her head a crown of twelve stars
12. 4 his tail drew the third part of the stars of
22. 16 offspring of David, (and) the..morning st.
3. *A constellation, star,* ἄστρον *astron.*
Luke21. 25 the sun, and in the moon, and in the stars
Acts 7. 43 tabernacle of Moloch, and the star of your
27. 20 neither sun nor stars in many days appea.
Heb. 11. 12 (so many) as the stars of the sky in mult.

STAR gazer, seven, day —
1. *A gazer on the stars,* חֹזֶה בַּכּוֹכָבִים [*chozeh*].
Isa. 47. 13 Let now the astrologers, the star gazers
2. *A group, the Pleiades,* כִּימָה *kimah.*
Amos 5. 8 (Seek him) that maketh the seven stars
3. *Light bearer, morning star,* φωσφόρος *phōsphoros.*
2 Pe. 1. 19 the day dawn, and the day star arise in

STARE, to —
To see, רָאָה *raah.*
Psa. 22. 17 tell all my bones: they look (and) stare up.

STATE, stately, station, (best) —
1. *Hand,* יָד *yad.*
Esth. 1. 7 wine in abundance, according to the state
2. 18 gave gifts, according to the state of the ki.
2. *Weight, honour,* כְּבוּדָּה *kebuddah.*
Eze. 23. 41 satest upon a stately bed, and a table pr.
3. *A base, station,* כֵּן *ken.*
Prov.28. 2 by a man of..knowledge the state (thereof)
4. *A standing, station,* מַעֲמָד *maamad.*
Isa. 22. 19 and from thy state shall he pull thee do.
5. *Station, standing place,* מַצָּב *matstsab.*
Isa. 22. 19 I will drive thee from thy station, and fr.

6. *Proper state or condition,* מַתְכֹּנֶת *mathkoneth.*
2 Ch.24. 13 they set the house of God in his state, and
7. *To be set up,* נָצַב *natsab,* 2.
Psa. 39. 5 every man at his best state (is) altogether
8. *Face,* פָּנִים *panim.*
Prov.27. 23 Be thou diligent to know the state of thy
9. *The things concerning or around,* τὰ περί *ta peri.*
Phil. 2. 19, 20 of good comfort when I know your st.
10. *The things against me,* τὰ κατ' ἐμέ, Col. 4. 7.

STATURE, (great) —
1. *Measure,* מִדִּין [? *middah*] [V. L. מָדוֹן].
2 Sa. 21. 20 a man of (great) stature, that had on ev.
2. *Measure, length,* מִדָּה *middah.*
Num13. 32 we saw in it..men of a great stature
1 Ch. 11. 23 he slew an Egyptian, a man of (great) st.
20. 6 a man of (great) stature, whose fingers
Isa. 45. 14 merchandise..of the Sabeans, men of sta.
3. *Upstanding, stature, height,* קוֹמָה *qomah.*
1 Sa. 16. 7 Look not..on the height of his stature, be.
Song 7. 7 thy stature is like to a palm tree, and thy
Isa. 10. 33 the high ones of stature (shall be) hewn
Eze. 13. 18 kerchiefs upon the head of every stature
17. 6 became a spreading vine of low stature
19. 11 her stature was exalted among the thick
31. 3 shadowing shroud, and of an high stature
4. *Greatness, length,* ἡλικία *hēlikia.*
Matt. 6. 27 Which..can add one cubit unto his stat.
Luke 2. 52 Jesus increased in wisdom and stature, and
12. 25 which of you..can add to his stature one
19. 3 could not..because he was little of statu.
Eph. 4. 13 measure of the stature of the fulness of

STATUTE —
1. *Decreed limit, portion, statute,* חֹק *choq.*
Exod15. 25 he made for them a statute and an ordin.
15. 26 If thou wilt..keep all his statutes, I will
18. 16 I do make (them) know the statutes of G.
29. 28 be Aaron's and his sons' by a statute for
30. 21 it shall be a statute for ever to them, (ev.)
Lev. 6. 18 (It shall be) a statute for ever in your ge.
6. 22 (it is) a statute for ever unto the LORD; it
7. 34 unto his sons by a statute for ever from
10. 11 the statutes which the LORD hath spoken
10. 15 and thy sons' with thee, by a statute for
24. 9 it (is) most holy..by a perpetual statute
26. 46 the statutes and judgments and laws wh.
Num18. 11, 19 thy daughters with thee, by a statute
30. 16 the statutes which the LORD commanded
Deut. 4. 1 hearken, O Israel, unto the statutes and
4. 5 I have taught you statutes and judgmen.
4. 6 nations, which shall hear all these statu.
4. 8 that hath statutes and judgments (so) ri.
4. 14 at that time to teach you statutes and ju.
4. 40 Thou shalt keep therefore his statutes, and
4. 45 These (are) the testimonies, and the stat.
5. 1 the statutes and judgments which I speak
5. 31 the statutes, and the judgments, which
6. 1, 20 the statutes, and the judgments, which
6. 17 his statutes, which he hath commanded
6. 24 commanded us to do all these statutes, to
7. 11 the statutes, and the judgments, which I
11. 32 the statutes and judgments which I set
12. 1 These (are) the statutes and judgments wh.
16. 12 thou shalt observe and do these statutes
17. 19 the words of this law and these statutes
26. 16 commanded thee to do these statutes and
26. 17 to keep his statutes, and his commandm.
27. 10 do his commandments and his statutes
Josh 24. 25 set them a statute and an ordinance in Sh.
1 Sa. 30. 25 he made it a statute and an ordinance for
1 Ki. 3. 14 to keep my statutes and my commandme.
8. 58 his statutes, and his judgments, which he
8. 61 to walk in his statutes, and to keep his
9. 4 (and) wilt keep my statutes and my judg.
2 Ki. 17. 15 they rejected his statutes, and his covena
17. 37 the statutes, and the ordinances, and the
1 Ch.22. 13 the statutes and judgments which the
29. 19 keep..thy testimonies, and thy statutes
2 Ch. 7. 17 shalt observe my statutes and my judgm.
19. 10 between law and commandment, statutes
33. 8 according to the whole law and the statut.
34. 31 to keep..his testimonies, and his statutes
Ezra 7. 10 to teach in Israel statutes and judgments
7. 11 commandments of the LORD, and of his s.
Neh. 1. 7 have not kept..the statutes, nor the judg.
9. 13 true laws, good statutes and commandm.
9. 14 commandedst them precepts, statutes, and
10. 29 do all..his judgments and his statutes
Psa. 50. 16 What hast thou..to declare my statutes
81. 4 this (was) a statute for Israel, (and) a law
105. 45 That they might observe his statutes, and
119. 5 my ways were directed to keep thy statu.
119. 8 I will keep thy statutes: O forsake me not
119. 12 Blessed (art) thou: O LORD, teach me thy s.
119. 23 thy servant did meditate in thy statutes
119. 26 thou heardest me: teach me thy statutes
119. 33 Teach me, O LORD, the way of thy statutes
119. 48 and I will meditate in thy statutes
119. 54 Thy statutes have been my songs in the
119. 64 is full of thy mercy: teach me thy statutes
119. 68 Thou (art) good..teach me thy statutes
119. 71 afflicted; that I might learn thy statutes
119. 80 Let my heart be sound in thy statutes, that
119. 83 (yet) do I not forget thy statutes
119. 112 to perform thy statutes alway, (even unto)
119. 117 I will have respect unto thy statutes co.
119. 118 trodden..them that err from thy statutes

Psa 119. 124 unto thy mercy, and teach me thy statu.
119. 135 to shine..and teach me thy statutes
119. 145 hear me, O LORD: I will keep thy statu.
119. 155 the wicked: for they seek not thy statu.
119. 171 when thou hast taught me thy statutes
147. 19 his statutes and his judgments unto Israel
Eze. 11. 12 ye have not walked in my statutes, neither
20. 18 Walk ye not in the statutes of your fath.
20. 25 I gave them also statutes (that were) not
36. 27 cause you to walk in my statutes, and ye
Zech. 1. 6 my statutes, which I commanded my ser
Mal. 4. 4 which I commanded..(with) the statutes

2. *Decreed limit, portion, statute,* חֻקָּה *chuqqah.*
Gen. 26. 5 my commandments, my statutes, and my
Exod 27. 21 (It shall be) a statute for ever unto their
28. 43 (It shall be) a statute for ever unto him
29. 9 shall be theirs for a perpetual statute
Lev. 3. 17 (It shall be) a perpetual statute for your
7. 36 a statute for ever throughout their gener.
10. 9 (it shall be) a statute for ever throughout
16. 29 (this) shall be a statute for ever unto you
16. 31 ye shall afflict your souls, by a statute for
16. 34 this shall be an everlasting statute unto
17. 7 This shall be a statute for ever unto them
18. 5, 26 Ye shall therefore keep my statutes
19. 19 Ye shall keep my statutes. Thou shalt not
19. 37 Therefore shall ye observe all my statutes
20. 8 And ye shall keep my statutes, and do th.
20. 22 Ye shall therefore keep all my statutes
23. 14, 21, 31, 41 (it shall be) a statute for ever
24. 3 (it shall be) a statute for ever in your ge.
25. 18 ye shall do my statutes, and keep my ju.
26. 3 If ye walk in my statutes, and keep my co
26. 15 if ye shall despise my statutes, or if your
26. 43 because their soul abhorred my statutes
Num 18. 23 (It shall be) a statute for ever throughout
19. 10 unto the stranger..for a statute for ever
19. 21 it shall be a perpetual statute unto them
27. 11 unto the children of Israel a statute of ju.
35. 29 these (things) shall be for a statute of ju.
Deut. 6. 2 to keep all his statutes, and his comman.
8. 11 his statutes, which I command thee this
10. 13 his statutes, which I command thee this
11. 1 keep his charge, and his statutes, and his
28. 15 his commandments and his statutes, wh.
28. 45 and his statutes which he commanded thee
30. 10 to keep his commandments and his statu.
30. 16 to keep his commandments, and his stat.
2 Sa. 22. 23 (as for) his statutes, I did not depart from
1 Ki. 2. 3 to keep his statutes, and his commandm.
3. 3 walking in the statutes of David his father
6. 12 if thou wilt walk in my statutes, and exe.
9. 6 my statutes which I have set before you
11. 11 not kept my covenant, and my statutes
11. 33 (to keep) my statutes and my judgments
11. 34 kept my commandments and my statutes
11. 38 to keep my statutes and my commandme.
2 Ki. 17. 8 walked in the statutes of the heathen, wh.
17. 13 keep my commandments (and) my statutes
17. 19 walked in the statutes of Israel which th.
17. 34 neither do they after their statutes, or af.
23. 3 his testimonies and his statutes with all
2 Ch. 7. 19 if ye turn away, and forsake my statutes
Psa 18. 22 and I did not put away his statutes from
89. 31 If they break my statutes, and keep not
119. 16 I will delight myself in thy statutes: I will
Jer. 44. 10, 23 nor walked in my law, nor in my stat.
Eze. 5. 6 my statutes more than the countries that
5. 6 have refused my judgments and my stat.
5. 7 have not walked in my statutes, neither
11. 20 That they may walk in my statutes, and
18. 9 Hath walked in my statutes, and hath ke.
18. 17 executed my judgments..walked in my st.
18 19 hath kept all my statutes, and hath done
18. 21 keep all my statutes, and do that which
20. 11 I gave them my statutes, and shewed th.
20. 13 they walked not in my statutes, and they
20. 16 walked not in my statutes, but polluted
20. 19 walk in my statutes, and keep my judg.
20. 21 they walked not in my statutes, neither
20. 24 had despised my statutes, and had pollu.
33. 15 walk in the statutes of life, without com.
37. 24 and observe my statutes, and do them
44. 24 they shall keep my laws and my statutes
Mic. 6. 16 the statutes of Omri are kept, and all the

3. *Appointments, charges, precepts,* פִּקּוּדִים *piqqudim.*
Psa. 19. 8 The statutes of the LORD (are) right, rej.

4. *Standing rule or custom,* קְיָם *qeyam.*
Dan. 6. 15 no decree nor statute which the king es.

STAY —
1. *Hand,* יָד *yad.*
1 Ki. 10. 19 (there were) stays on either side on the pl.
10. 19 and two lions stood beside the stays
2 Ch. 9. 18 and stays on each side of the sitting pla.
9. 18 and two lions standing by the stays

2. *Stay, support,* מַשְׁעֵן *mashen.*
Isa. 3. 1 doth take away..the stay and the staff

3. *Stay, support,* מִשְׁעָן *mishan.*
2 Sa. 22. 19 They prevented me..the LORD was my st.
Psa. 18. 18 They prevented me..the LORD was my st.
Isa. 3. 1 stay of bread, and the whole stay of wat.

4. *Corner, chief one,* פִּנָּה *pinnah.*
Isa. 19. 13 they that are) the stay of the tribes there

STAY (selves, there, up), to —
1. *To be behind, late,* אָחַר *achar.*
Gen. 32. 4 sojourned with Laban, and stayed there

2. *To take away,* הָגָה *hagah.*
Isa. 27. 8 he stayeth his rough wind in the day of the

3. *To (cause to) stay,* חוּל *chul,* 1, 5.
Gen. 8. 10 he stayed yet other seven days; and again
Lam. 4. 6 overthrown..and no hands stayed on her

4. *To wait with hope, stay,* יָחַל *yachal,* 2.
Gen. 8. 12 he stayed yet other seven days; and sent

5. *To tarry, linger, delay,* מָהַהּ *mahah,* 7a.
Isa. 29. 9 Stay yourselves, and wonder; cry ye out

6. *To smite, clap (the hand),* מְחָא *mecha,* 3.
Dan. 4. 35 none can stay his hand, or say unto him

7. *To be supported,* סָמַךְ *samak,* 2.
Isa. 48. 2 and stay themselves upon the God of Isr.

8. *To support,* סָמַךְ *samak,* 3.
Song 2. 5 Stay me with flagons, comfort me with

9. *To be grieved, solicitous,* עָגַן *agan,* 2.
Ruth 1. 13 would ye stay for them from having hus.

10. *To stand, stand still,* עָמַד *amad.*
Gen. 19. 17 look not behind thee, neither stay thou in
Exod. 9. 28 I will let you go, and ye shall stay no l.
Lev. 13. 23, 28 if the bright spot stay in his place, (and)
Deut. 10. 10 stayed in the mount, according to the first
Josh. 10. 13 the moon stayed, until the people had ave.
10. 19 stay ye not, (but) pursue after your ene.
1 Sa. 20. 38 Jonathan cried..Make speed, haste, stay
30. 9 where those that were left behind stayed
2 Sa. 17. 17 Jonathan and Ahimaaz stayed by En-rogel
2 Ki. 4. 6 (There is) not a vessel more. And the oils.
13. 18 Smite..and he smote thrice, and stayed
15. 20 turned back, and stayed not there in the
Jer. 4. 6 stay not; for I will bring evil from the no.
Hos. 13. 13 he should not stay long in (the place of)

11. *To keep back,* עָקַב *aqab,* 3.
Job 37. 4 he will not stay them when his voice is he.

12. *To make feeble, let go,* רָפָה *raphah,* 5.
1 Sa. 15. 16 Stay, and I will tell thee what the LORD
2 Sa. 24. 16 said to the angel..stay now thine hand
1 Ch. 21. 15 said to the angel..stay now thine hand

13. *To cause to lie down,* שָׁכַב *shakab,* 5.
Job 38. 37 or who can stay the bottles of heaven

14. *To cleave, rend, subdue,* שָׁסַע *shasa,* 3.
1 Sa. 24. 7 David stayed his servants with these words

15. *To be supported, to lean,* שָׁעַן *shaan,* 2.
Isa. 10. 20 shall no more again stay upon him that
10. 20 shall stay upon the LORD, the Holy One of
30. 12 and trust in oppression..and stay thereon
31. 1 stay on horses, and trust in chariots, be.
50. 10 let him trust..and stay upon his God

16. *To uphold, retain,* תָּמַךְ *tamak.*
Exod. 17. 12 Aaron and Hur stayed up his hands, the
Prov. 28. 17 shall flee to the pit; let no man stay him

17. *To hold on,* ἐπέχω *epechō.*
Acts 19. 22 but he himself stayed in Asia for a season

18. *To hold down or fast,* κατέχω *katechō.*
Luke 4. 42 came unto him, and stayed him, that he

STAY, stayed up, to be at a —
1. *To be set up, stayed,* יָצַג *yatsag,* 6.
Exod 10. 24 only let your flocks and your herds be st.

2. *To shut, be restrained,* כָּלָא *kala.*
Hag. 1. 10 is stayed from dew, and the earth is stay

3. *To be or become restrained,* כָּלָא *kala,* 2.
Eze. 31. 15 restrained the floods..waters were stayed

4. *To sustain, support,* סָמַךְ *samak.*
Isa. 26. 3 Thou wilt keep (him..whose) mind (is) st.

5. *To stand, stand still or fast,* עָמַד *amad.*
Lev. 13. 5 (if) the plague in his sight be at a stay, (and)
13. 37 if the scall be in his sight at a stay, and

6. *To be caused to stand,* עָמַד *amad,* 6.
1 Ki. 22. 35 the king was stayed up in his chariot ag.

7. *To be restrained,* עָצַר *atsar,* 2.
Num 16. 48 stood between..and the plague was stay.
16. 50 Aaron returned..the plague was stayed
25. 8 the plague was stayed from the children
2 Sa. 24. 21 the plague may be stayed from the peop.
24. 25 and the plague was stayed from Israel
1 Ch. 21. 22 the plague may be stayed from the people
Psa. 106. 30 judgment: and (so) the plague was stay.

8. *To set, put, place,* שִׁית *shith.*
Job 38. 11 and here shall thy proud waves be stay.?

STEAD (of), in —
1. *Under, in the stead of,* תַּחַת *tachath.*
Gen. 4. 25 appointed me another seed instead of A.
22. 13 for a burnt offering in the stead; Ex. 29. 30.

2. *In behalf of,* ὑπέρ *(gen.) huper.*
2 Co. 5. 20 we pray (you) in Christ's stead, be ye re.
Phm. 13 in thy stead he might have ministered un.

STEADY —
Faithfulness, stability, steadiness, אֱמוּנָה, *emunah.*
Exod 17. 12 his hands were steady until the going do.

STEAL (away, get by stealth), to —
1. *To steal, act furtively,* גָּנַב *ganab.*
Gen. 30. 33 the sheep, that shall be counted stolen
31. 19 Rachel had stolen the images that (were)
31. 20 Jacob stole away unawares to Laban the
31. 26 that thou hast stolen away unawares to
31. 27 flee away secretly, and steal away from
31. 30 (yet) wherefore hast thou stolen my gods?
31. 32 Jacob knew not that Rachel had stolen
31. 39 (whether) stolen by day, or stolen by nig.
44. 8 how then should we steal out of thy lord's
Exod 20. 15 Thou shalt not steal
21. 16 he that stealeth a man, and selleth him
22. 1 If a man shall steal an ox, or a sheep, and
Lev. 19. 11 Ye shall not steal, neither deal falsely, ne.
Deut. 5. 19 Neither shalt thou steal
24. 7 If a man be found stealing any of his br.
Josh. 7. 11 have also stolen, and dissembled also, and
2 Sa. 19. 41 Why have..men of Judah stolen thee aw.
15. 6 Absalom stole the hearts of the men of Is.
21. 12 which had stolen them from the street of
2 Ki. 11. 2 Jehosheba..stole him from among the ki.
2 Ch. 22. 11 Jehoshabeath..stole him from among the
Job 27. 20 a tempest stealeth him away in the night
Prov. 6. 30 (Men) do not despise a thief, if he steal to
9. 17 Stolen waters are sweet, and bread (eaten)
30. 9 lest I be poor, and steal, and take the na.
Jer. 7. 9 Will ye steal, murder, and commit adul.
23. 30 that steal my words every one from his n.
Hos. 4. 2 killing, and stealing, and committing ad.
Obad 5 would they not have stolen till they had
Zech. 5. 3 every one that stealeth shall be cut off

2. *To steal self away,* גָּנַב *ganab,* 7.
2 Sa. 19. 3 the people gat them by stealth that day
19. 3 as people being ashamed steal away when

3. *To steal,* κλέπτω *kleptō.*
Matt. 6. 19 where thieves break through and steal
6. 20 thieves do not break through nor steal
19. 18 Thou shalt not steal, Thou shalt not bear
27. 64 steal him away, and say unto the people
28. 13 came by night, and stole him (away) wh.
Mark 10. 19 Do not steal, Do not bear false witness
Luke 18. 20 Do not steal, Do not bear false witness
John 10. 10 The thief cometh not, but for to steal, and
Rom. 2. 21 a man should not steal, dost thou steal?
13. 9 Thou shalt not steal, Thou shalt not bear
Eph. 4. 28 Let him that stole steal no more, but rat.

STEDFAST, (to be) —
1. *To be faithful, steady,* אָמַן *aman,* 2.
Psa. 78. 8 and whose spirit was not stedfast with G.
78. 37 neither were they stedfast in his covena.

2. *To be cast, firm,* יָצַק *yatsaq,* 6.
Job 11. 15 yea, thou shalt be stedfast, and shalt not

3. *Standing, steady, established,* קַיָּם *qayyam.*
Dan. 6. 26 he (is) the living God, and stedfast for ever

4. *Firm, sure, stedfast,* βέβαιος *bebaios.*
2 Co. 1. 7 our hope of you (is) stedfast, knowing, that
Heb. 2. 2 if the word spoken by angels was stedfast
3. 14 the beginning of our confidence stedfast
6. 19 as an anchor of the soul, both sure and st

5. *Seated, stedfast, steady, settled,* ἑδραῖος *hedraios.*
1 Co. 7. 37 he that standeth [stedfast] in his heart
15. 58 be ye stedfast, unmoveable, always abou

6. *Standing, settled, stedfast,* στερεός *stereos.*
1 Pe. 5. 9 Whom resist stedfast in the faith, know.

STEDFASTLY, to behold, look up, set, be minded, —
1. *To strengthen self,* אָמַץ *amats,* 7.
Ruth 1. 18 she saw that she was stedfastly minded

2. *To place, set, put,* שִׂים *sum, sim.*
2 Ki. 8. 11 he settled his countenance stedfastly, un.

3. *To look intently,* ἀτενίζω *atenizō.*
Acts 1. 10 they looked stedfastly toward heaven as
6. 15 looking stedfastly on him, saw his face as
7. 55 looked up stedfastly into heaven, and saw
14. 9 who stedfastly beholding him, and perce.
2 Co. 3. 7, 13 the children of Israel could not stedf.

4. *To settle, make stedfast,* στηρίζω *stērizō.*
Luke 9. 51 he stedfastly set his face to go to Jerusa.

STEDFASTNESS —
1. *Stedfastness,* στερέωμα *stereōma.*
Col. 2. 5 and the stedfastness of your faith in Christ

2. *Stability, stedfastness,* στηριγμός *stērigmos.*
2 Pe. 3. 17 lest ye..fall from your own stedfastness

STEEL —
1. *Brass, copper,* נְחוּשָׁה *nechushah.*
2 Sa. 22. 35 so that a bow of steel is broken by mine
Job 20. 24 (and) the bow of steel shall strike him thr.
Psa. 18. 34 so that a bow of steel is broken by mine

2. *Brass, copper,* נְחֹשֶׁת *nechosheth.*
Jer 15. 12 Shall iron break the..iron and the steel?

STEEP (place) —
1. *Ascent, stairs,* מַדְרֵגָה *madregah.*
Eze. 38. 20 steep places shall fall, and every wall sh.

2. *A going down, descent, slope,* מוֹרָד *morad.*
Mic. 1. 4 waters (that are) poured down a steep pl.

3. *A steep place, precipice,* κρημνός *krēmnos.*
Matt. 8. 32 swine ran violently down a steep place
Mark 5. 13 the herd ran violently down a steep place
Luke 8. 33 the herd ran violently down a steep place

STEM —
Stick, stem, גֶּזַע *geza.*
Isa. 11. 1 a rod out of the stem of Jesse, and a bra.

STEP —

1. *A step*, אָשֻׁר *ashshur*.
Job 31. 7 If my step hath turned out of the way, and
Psa. 17. 11 They have now compassed us in our steps

2. *A step*, אָשֻׁר *ashur*.
Job 23. 11 My foot hath held his steps, his way have
Psa. 37. 31 in his heart; none of his steps shall slide
44. 18 neither have our steps declined from thy
73. 2 as for me..my steps had well nigh slipped

3. *A going*, הָלִיךְ *halik*.
Job 29. 6 I washed my steps with butter, and the

4. *A step, tread*, מִצְעָד *mitsad*.
Psa. 37. 23 The steps of a (good) man are ordered by
Dan. 11. 43 and the Ethiopians (shall be) at his steps

5. *Heel, footstep, trace, tract*, עָקֵב *aqeb*.
Psa. 56. 6 they mark my steps, when they wait for

6. *A movement, step, foot*, פַּעַם *paam*.
Psa. 57. 6 They have prepared a net for my steps
85. 13 and shall set (us) in the way of his steps
119. 133 Order my steps in thy word: and let not
Isa. 26. 6 feet of the poor,(and) the steps of the needy

7. *A step*, פֶּשַׂע *pesa*.
1 Sa. 20. 3 (there is) but a step between me and death

8. *A footstep*, צַעַד *tsaad*.
2 Sa. 22. 37 Thou hast enlarged my steps under me
Job 14. 16 thou numberest my steps: dost thou not
18. 7 The steps of his strength shall be straite.
31. 4 Doth not he see..and count all my steps?
31. 37 declare unto him the number of my steps
Psa. 18. 36 Thou hast enlarged my steps under me
Prov. 4. 12 When thou goest, thy steps shall not be
5. 5 Her feet go down to death; her steps take
16. 9 deviseth..but the LORD directeth his steps
Jer. 10. 23 (it is) not in man..to direct his steps
Lam 4. 18 They hunt our steps, that we cannot go in

9. *A going up, ascent*, מַעֲלָה *maalah*.
Exod 20. 26 Neither shalt thou go up by steps unto
1 Ki. 10. 19 The throne had six steps, and the top of
10. 20 twelve lions stood..upon the six steps
2 Ch. 9. 18 (there were) six steps to the throne, with
9. 19 twelve lions stood..upon the six steps
Eze. 40. 22 they went up unto it by seven steps; and
40. 26 (there were) seven steps to go up to it, and
40. 31, 34, 37 the going up to it (had) eight steps
40. 49 (he brought me) by the steps whereby th.

10. *Sole (of foot), trace, footprint*, ἴχνος *ichnos*.
Rom. 4. 12 who also walk in the steps of that faith of
2 Co. 12. 18 spirit? (walked we) not in the same steps?
1 Pe. 2. 21 example, that ye should follow his steps

STEP (down, in), to —

1. *To go into*, ἐμβαίνω *embainō*.
John 5. 4 [whosoever..stepped in was made whole]

2. *To go down*, καταβαίνω *katabainō*.
John 5. 7 while I am coming, another steppeth do.

STEPH-A'-NAS, Στεφανᾶς *crown*.
A believer whose household, as the first fruits of Achaia to the preaching of the gospel, Paul baptised, and whose coming with Fortunatus and Achaicus made him glad.
1 Co. 1. 16 I baptized also the household of S.: besi.
16. 15 ye know the house of S., that it is the first
16. 17 I am glad of the coming of S. and Fortun.

STE'-PHEN, Στέφανος *crown*.
One of the seven primitive disciples chosen to serve tables, a zealous Hellenist, and the first martyr in behalf of Christianity after the death of Christ himself, being stoned to death by the Jews. A.D. 33.
Acts 6. 5 they chose S., a man full of faith and of the
6. 8 S., full of faith and power, did great won.
6. 9 there arose certain..disputing with S.
7. 59 they stoned S., calling upon (God), and sa.
8. 2 devout men carried S. (to his burial), and
11. 19 upon the persecution that arose about S.
22. 20 when the blood of thy martyr S. was shed

STERN —

The stern, poop, πρύμνα *prumna*.
Acts 27. 29 they cast four anchors out of the stern, and

STEWARD, stewardship, (to be) —

1. *The man who is over*, הָאִישׁ אֲשֶׁר עַל *ha-ish asher al*.
Gen. 43. 19 they came near to the steward of Joseph's

2. *Who is over a house*, אֲשֶׁר עַל בַּיִת *asher al bayith*.
Gen. 44. 4 Joseph said unto his steward, Up, follow

3. *Son of acquisition*, בֶּן־מֶשֶׁק *ben mesheq*.
Gen. 15. 2 the steward of my house (is) this Eliezer

4. *Prince, head, chief, captain*, שַׂר *sar*.
1 Ch. 28. 1 the stewards over all the substance and

5. *One to whom a thing is committed*, ἐπίτροπος.
Matt 20. 8 lord of the vineyard saith unto his stewa.
Luke 8. 3 the wife of Chuza Herod's steward, and S.

6. *To be a house manager or steward*, οἰκονομέω.
Luke 16. 2 for thou mayest be no longer steward

7. *House management*, οἰκονομία *oikonomia*.
Luke 16. 2 give an account of thy stewardship, for
16. 3 lord taketh away from me the stewardship
16. 4 when I am put out of the stewardship, th.

8. *A house manager, steward*, οἰκονόμος *oikonomos*.
Luke 12. 42 Who then is that faithful and wise stew.
16. 1 a certain rich man which had a steward
16. 3 the steward said within himself, What sh.
Luke 16. 8 the lord commended the unjust steward
1 Co. 4. 1 the ministers of Christ, and stewards of
4. 2 it is required in stewards, that a man be
Titus 1. 7 a bishop must be blameless, as the stewa.
1 Pe. 4. 10 as good stewards of the manifold grace of

STICK —

1. *Wood, tree, stick*, עֵץ *ets*.
Num 15. 32 they found a man that gathered sticks up
15. 33 they that found him gathering sticks br.
1 Ki. 17. 10 widow woman (was) there gathering of st.
17. 12 I (am) gathering two sticks, that I may go
2 Ki. 6. 6 And he cut down a stick, and cast (it) in
Lam. 4. 8 it is withered, it is become like a stick
Eze. 37. 16 take thee one stick, and write upon it, For
37. 16 then take another stick, and write upon
37. 16 For Joseph, the stick of Ephraim, and (for)
37. 17 join them one to another into one stick
37. 19 I will take the stick of Joseph, which (is)
37. 19 the stick of Judah, and make them one st.
37. 20 the sticks whereon thou writest shall be

2. *A fagot*, φρύγανον *phruganon*.
Acts 28. 3 Paul had gathered a bundle of sticks, and

STICK, closer, fast, out, together, to cause to —

1. *To cleave to, adhere, pursue*, דָּבַק *dabaq*.
Psa. 119. 31 I have stuck unto thy testimonies: O L.
Eze. 29. 4 fish of thy rivers shall stick unto thy sca.

2. *To cause to cleave to*, דָּבַק *dabaq*, 5.
Eze. 29. 4 I will cause the fish of thy rivers to stick

3. *Cleaving to, adhering*, דָּבֵק *dabeq*.
Prov. 18. 24 a friend (that) sticketh closer than a bro.

4. *To become frozen, stick together*, לָכַד *lakad*, 7.
Job 41. 17 they stick together, that they cannot be

5. *To crush, stick in*, מָעַךְ *maak*.
1 Sa. 26. 7 his spear stuck in the ground at his bolster

6. *To go or come down*, נָחַת *nachath*, 2.
Psa. 38. 2 thine arrows stick fast in me, and thy hand

7. *To be high*, שָׁפָה *shaphah*, 4 [V.L. שׁפי].
Job 33. 21 his bones (that) were not seen stick out

8. *To support by a prop, stick fast*, ἐρείδω *ereidō*.
Acts 27. 41 the fore part stuck fast, and remained un.

STIFF, stiffen, to (make) —

1. *Old, removed*, עָתָק *athaq*.
Psa. 75. 5 Lift not up..speak (not with) a stiff neck

2. *Sharp, hard*, קָשֶׁה *qasheh*.
Deut 31. 27 For I know thy rebellion, and thy stiff ne.

3. *To make sharp or hard*, קָשָׁה *qashah*, 5.
Deut 10. 16 Circumcise..and be no more stiff necked
2 Ch. 30. 8 be ye not stiff necked, as your fathers
36. 13 he stiffened his neck, and hardened his
Jer. 17. 23 made their neck stiff, that they might not

STIFF HEARTED, stiff necked —

1. *Hard of heart*, חִזְקֵי לֵב [*chazeq*].
Eze. 2. 4 (they are) impudent children, and stiff he.

2. *Hard of neck*, קְשֵׁה עֹרֶף *qesheh oreph*.
Exod 32. 9 and, behold, it (is) a stiff necked people
33. 3 not go up..for thou (art) a stiff necked
33. 5 Ye (are) a stiff necked people: I will come
34. 9 go among us; for it (is) a stiff necked pe.
Deut 9. 6 for thou (art) a stiff necked people
9. 13 and, behold, it (is) a stiff necked people

3. *Hard necked*, σκληροτράχηλος *sklērotrachēlos*.
Acts 7. 51 Ye stiff necked and uncircumcised in he.

STILL —

1. *Silence, calm*, דְּמָמָה *demamah*.
1 Ki. 19. 12 a fire..and after the fire a still small voice

2. *Rest, place of rest*, מְנוּחָה *menuchah*.
Psa. 23. 2 he leadeth me beside the still waters

3. *To remove, journey*, נָסַע *nasa*.
Gen. 12. 9 Abram journeyed, going on still toward

4. *Still, yet, while, any more*, עוֹד *od*.
Lev. 13. 57 if it appear still in the garment, either in

5. *Still, yet*, ἔτι *eti*.
Rev. 22. 11 He that is unjust, let him be unjust still
22. 11 and he which is filthy, let him be filthy st.
22. 11 that is righteous, let him be righteous st.
22. 11 and he that is holy, let him be holy still

STILL, be still, to —

1. *To be silent, cease, stand still*, דָּמַם *damam*.
Exod 15. 16 they shall be (as) still as a stone; till thy
Psa. 4. 4 commune with your own heart..and be s.
Isa. 23. 2 Be still, ye inhabitants of the isle, thou
Jer. 47. 6 Put..thyself into thy scabbard..be still

2. *To still, silence*, הָסָה *hasah*, 5.
Num. 13. 30 Caleb stilled the people before Moses, and

3. *To keep or remain silent, deaf*, חָרַשׁ *charash*, 5.
Isa. 42. 14 I have been still, (and) refrained myself

4. *To be silent*, חָשָׁה *chashah*.
Psa. 107. 29 a calm, so that the waves thereof are still

5. *To keep silent*, חָשָׁה *chashah*, 5.
Judg. 18. 9 (are) ye still? be not slothful to go, (and) to
1 Ki. 22. 3 we (be) still, (and) take it not out of the
Neh. 8. 11 the Levites stilled all the people, saying

6. *Still, yet, while, any more*, עוֹד *od*.
Psa. 139. 18 when I awake, I am still with thee

7. *To cause to fall, let go*, רָפָה *raphah*, 5.
Psa. 46. 10 Be still, and know that I (am) God: I will

8. *To glorify, praise, restrain*, שָׁבַח *shabach*, 3.
Psa. 89. 9 the waves thereof arise, thou stillest them

9. *To glorify, praise, restrain*, שָׁבַח *shabach*, 5.
Psa. 65. 7 Which stilleth the noise of the seas, the

10. *To (cause to) keep sabbath*, שָׁבַת *shabath*, 5.
Psa. 8. 2 thou mightest still the enemy and the av.

11. *To give or keep quiet*, שָׁקַט *shaqat*.
Psa. 76. 8 judgment..the earth feared, and was still
83. 1 hold not thy peace, and be not still, O God

12. *To muzzle, gag*, φιμόω *phimoō*.
Mark 4. 39 and said unto the sea, Peace, be still
[*See also* Abide, keep, lie, sit, stand.]

STING, (to) —

1. *To sting, cut into*, פָּרַשׁ *parash*, 5.
Prov. 23. 32 it biteth like a serpent, and stingeth like

2. *A sting, goad, spur*, κέντρον *kentron*.
1 Co. 15. 55 O death, where (is) thy sting? O grave, wh.
15. 56 The sting of death (is) sin; and the strength
Rev. 9. 10 there were stings in their tails: and their

STINK, stinking savour, to make or cause a —

1. *A stink*, בְּאֹשׁ *beosh*.
Joel 2. 20 his stink shall come up, and his ill savour
Amos 4. 10 I have made the stink of your camps to
Isa. 34. 3 their stink shall come up out of their ca.

2. *To stink*, בָּאַשׁ *baash*.
Exod. 7. 18 the fish..shall die, and the river shall st.
7. 21 the river stank, and the Egyptians could
8. 14 together upon heaps; and the land stank
16. 20 it bred worms, and stank: and Moses was
Isa. 50. 2 their fish stinketh, because (there is) no

3. *To be stinking, abhorred*, בָּאַשׁ *baash*, 2.
2 Sa 10. 6 children of Ammon saw that they stank

4. *To cause to stink or be abhorred*, בָּאַשׁ *baash*, 5.
Gen. 34. 30 have troubled me to make me to stink am.
Exod 16. 24 it did not stink, neither was there any wo.
Psa. 38. 5 My wounds stink (and) are corrupt bec.
Eccl. 10. 1 Dead flies cause..a stinking savour

5. *Muck, dung, corruption*, מַק *maq*.
Isa. 3. 24 instead of sweet smell..shall be stink

6. *To give a smell, emit an odour*, ὄζω *ozō*.
John 11. 39 he stinketh: for he hath been (dead) four

STIR —

1. *Cry, crying, noise*, תְּשֻׁאוֹת *teshuoth*.
Isa. 22. 2 Thou that art full of stirs, a tumultuous

2. *A disturbance, stir, tumult*, τάραχος *tarachos*.
Acts 12. 18 there was no small stir among the soldi.
19. 23 there arose no small stir about that way

STIR up (self), be stirred (up), to —

1. *To stir up*, גָּרָה *garah*, 3.
Prov 15. 18 A wrathful man stirreth up strife: but
28. 25 He that is of a proud heart stirreth up st.
29. 22 An angry man stirreth up strife, and a fu.

2. *To stir self up*, גָּרָה *garah*, 7.
Dan. 11. 10 his sons shall be stirred up..and be stir.
11. 25 the king..shall be stirred up to battle

3. *To lift up*, נָשָׂא *nasa*.
Exod 35. 21 every one whose heart stirred him up, and
35. 26 women whose heart stirred them up in
36. 2 every one whose heart stirred him up to

4. *To move, persuade, remove*, סוּת *suth*, 5.
1 Sa. 26. 19 If the LORD have stirred thee up against
1 Ki. 21. 25 Ahab..whom Jezebel his wife stirred up

5. *To awake, stir up*, עוּר *ur*.
Job 41. 10 None (is so) fierce that dare stir him up

6. *To awake, lift up*, עוּר *ur*, 3a.
Psa. 80. 2 stir up thy strength, and come (and) save
Prov 10. 12 Hatred stirreth up strifes: but love cov.
Isa. 10. 26 the LORD of hosts shall stir up a scourge
14. 9 it stirreth up the dead for thee, (even) all

7. *To awake, stir up*, עוּר *ur*, 5.
Deut 32. 11 As an eagle stirreth up her nest, fluttereth
1 Ch. 5. 26 the God of Israel stirred up the spirit of
2 Ch. 21. 16 the LORD stirred up against Jehoram the
36. 22 the LORD stirred up the spirit of Cyrus ki.
Ezra 1. 1 the LORD stirred up the spirit of Cyrus ki.
Psa. 35. 23 Stir up thyself, and awake to my judgm.
78. 38 many a time..did not stir up all his wrath
Song 2. 7 that ye stir not up, nor awake (my) love
3. 5 that ye stir not up, nor awake (my) love
8. 4 that ye stir not up, nor awake (my) love
Isa. 13. 17 I will stir up the Medes against them, wh.
42. 13 he shall stir up jealousy like a man of war
Dan 11. 2 he shall stir up all against the realm of
11. 25 he shall stir up his power and his courage
Hag. 1. 14 the LORD stirred up the spirit of Zerubb.

8. *To awake or stir self up*, עוּר *ur*, 7a.
Job 17. 8 the innocent shall stir up himself against
Isa. 64. 7 that stirreth up himself to take hold of th.

9. *To be troubled, excited*, עָכַר *akar*, 2.
Psa. 39. 2 I held my peace..my sorrow was stirred

10. *To cause to go up*, עָלָה *alah*, 5.
Prov 15. 1 but grievous words stir up anger

11. *To cause to rise up, raise,* קוּם *qum,* 5.
Num 24. 9 lay down as a lion..who shall stir him up?
1 Sa. 22. 8 my son hath stirred up my servant against
1 Ki. 11. 14 the LORD stirred up an adversary unto Sol.
11. 23 God stirred him up (another) adversary

12. *To rekindle,* ἀναζωπυρέω *anazōpureō.*
2 Ti. 1. 6 that thou stir up the gift of God, which

13. *To shake or stir up,* ἀνασείω *anaseiō.*
Luke 23. 5 He stirreth up the people, teaching thro.

14. *To raise up thoroughly,* διεγείρω *diegeirō.*
2 Pe. 1. 13 to stir you up by putting (you) in remem.
3. 1 in (both) which I stir up your pure minds

15. *To raise up upon or over,* ἐπεγείρω *epegeirō.*
Acts 14. 2 the unbelieving Jews stirred up the Gent.

16. *To be sharpened beyond measure,* παροξύνομαι.
Acts 17. 16 his spirit was stirred in him, when he saw

17. *To excite beyond measure,* παροτρύνω *parotrunō.*
Acts 13. 50 the Jews stirred up the devout and honou.

18. *To shake, agitate, toss,* σαλεύω *saleuō.*
Acts 17. 13 they came thither also, and stirred up the

19. *To move together,* συγκινέω *sugkineō.*
Acts 6. 12 they stirred up the people, and the elders

20. *To pour together,* συγχέω *sugcheō.*
Acts 21. 27 stirred up all the people, and laid hands

STOCK, stocks —

1. *Increase, food, stock,* בּוּל *bul.*
Isa. 44. 19 shall I fall down to the stock of a tree?

2. *Stock, stem,* גֶּזַע *geza.*
Job 14. 8 and the stock thereof die in the ground
Isa. 40. 24 their stock shall not take root in the ear.

3. *Turning, stocks, pillory,* מַהְפֶּכֶת *mahpeketh.*
Jer. 20. 2 put him in the stocks that (were) in the
20. 3 brought forth Jeremiah out of the stocks

4. *Stocks, fetters,* סַד *sad.*
Job 13. 27 Thou puttest my feet also in the stocks
33. 11 He putteth my feet in the stocks, he mar.

5. *A tinkling ornament,* עֶכֶס *ekes.*
Prov. 7. 22 or as a fool to the correction of the stocks

6. *Wood, tree,* עֵץ *ets.*
Jer. 2. 27 Saying to a stock, Thou (art) my father
3. 9 adultery with stones and with stocks
10. 8 But..the stock (is) a doctrine of vanities
Hos. 4. 12 My people ask counsel at their stocks, and

7. *A root,* עֵקֶר *eqer.*
Lev. 25. 47 or to the stock of the stranger's family

8. *A neck, collar,* צִינֹק *tsinoq.*
Jer. 29. 26 put him in prison, and in the stocks

9. *Offspring, race, genus,* γένος *genos.*
Acts 13. 26 children of the stock of Abraham, and wh.
Phil. 3. 5 of the stock of Israel, (of) the tribe of Be.

10. *Wood, tree,* ξύλον *xulon.*
Acts 16. 24 and made their feet fast in the stocks

STOICKS, Στωϊκοί.

A sect of Greek philosophers who received their name from the *Stoa*, a porch at Athens, where *Zeno* taught. They were severe and lofty pantheists, and affected indifference in all circumstances. Zeno was born at Citium, a small town in the island of Cyprus, about B.C. 357, taught at Athens B.C. 299, and died B.C. 263.
Acts 17. 18 certain philosophers..of the S., encount.

STOLEN (away), to be —

1. *To be stolen,* גָּנַב *ganab,* 2.
Exod 22. 12 if it be stolen from him, he shall make re.

2. *To be stolen,* גֻּנַּב *ganab,* 4.
Gen. 40. 15 I was stolen away out of the land of the
Exod 22. 7 and it be stolen out of the man's house

STOMACH, stomacher —

1. *A festive garment, stomacher,* פְּתִיגִיל *pethigil.*
Isa. 3. 24 instead of a stomacher a girding of sack.

2. *Stomach* στόμαχος *stomachos.*
1 Ti. 5. 23 use a little wine for thy stomach's sake and

STONE, stony (ground, places), small —

1. *A stone,* אֶבֶן *eben.*
Gen. 2. 12 there (is) bdellium and the onyx stone
11. 3 they had brick for stone, and slime had
28. 11 he took of the stones of that place, and put
28. 18 took the stone that he had put (for) his
28. 22 this stone, which I have set (for) a pillar
29. 2 a great stone (was) upon the well's mouth
29. 3 they rolled the stone from the well's mo.
29. 3 put the stone again upon the well's mouth
29. 8 (till) they roll the stone from the well's
29. 10 rolled the stone from the well's mouth, and
31. 45 Jacob took a stone, and set it up (for) a
31. 46 Gather stones; and they took stones, and
35. 14 set up a pillar..(even) a pillar of stone
49. 24 from thence (is) the shepherd, the stone
Exod. 7. 19 in (vessels of) wood, and in (vessels of) st.
15. 5 they sank into the bottom as a stone
15. 16 they shall be (as) still as a stone; till thy
17. 12 they took a stone, and put (it) under him
20. 25 if thou wilt make me an altar of stone, thou
21. 18 one smite another with a stone, or with
24. 12 I will give thee tables of stone, and a law
25. 7 Onyx stones, and stones to be set in the
28. 9 thou shalt take two onyx stones, and gra.
28. 10 Six of their names on one stone, and (the
Exod 28. 10 six names of the rest on the other stone
28. 11 With the work of an engraver in stone
28. 11 shalt thou engrave the two stones with
28. 12 thou shalt put the two stones upon the
28. 12 stones of memorial unto the children of
28. 17 settings of stones, (even) four rows of st.
28. 21 the stones shall be with the names of the
31. 5 in cutting of stones, to set (them), and in
31. 18 tables of stone, written with the finger of G.
34. 1 Hew thee two tables of stone like unto
34. 4 he hewed two tables of stone like unto
34. 4 and took in his hand the two tables of st.
35. 9 onyx stones, and stones to be set for the
35. 27 the rulers brought onyx stones, and sto.
35. 33 in the cutting of stones, to set (them), and
39. 6 they wrought onyx stones inclosed in ouc.
39. 7 (they should be) stones for a memorial to
39. 10 they set in it four rows of stones: (the fir.)
39. 14 the stones (were) according to the names
Lev. 14. 40 command that they take away the stones
14. 42 And they shall take other stones, and
14. 42 put (them) in the place of those stones
14. 43 after that he hath taken away the stones
14. 45 he shall break down the house, the stones
20. 2 the people..shall stone him with stones
20. 27 they shall stone them with stones; their
24. 23 out of the camp, and stone him with st.
26. 1 neither shall ye set up (any) image of st.
Num 14. 10 congregation bade stone them with stones
15. 35 shall stone him with stones without the
15. 36 and stoned him with stones, and he died
35. 17 if he smite him with throwing a stone
35. 23 Or with any stone, wherewith a man may
Deut. 4. 13 he wrote them upon two tables of stone
4. 28 the work of men's hands, wood and stone
5. 22 he wrote them in two tables of stone, and
8. 9 a land whose stones (are) iron, and out of
9. 9 to receive the tables of stone, (even) the
9. 10 delivered unto me two tables of stone, wr.
9. 11 the LORD gave me the two tables of ston.
10. 1 Hew thee two tables of stone like unto the
10. 3 hewed two tables of stone like unto the
13. 10 thou shalt stone him with stones, that he
17. 5 shalt stone them with stones, till they die
21. 21 men of his city shall stone him with sto.
22. 21 men of her city shall stone her with sto.
22. 24 ye shall stone them with stones that they
27. 2 thou shalt set thee up great stones, and
27. 4 ye shall set up these stones, which I com.
27. 5 there shalt thou build..an altar of stones
27. 6 Thou shalt build the altar..of whole sto.
27. 8 thou shalt write upon the stones all the
28. 36 shalt thou serve other gods, wood and st.
28. 64 shalt serve other gods..(even) wood and st.
29. 17 their idols, wood and stone, silver and go.
Josh. 4. 3 Take you hence out..twelve stones; and
4. 5 take you up every man of you a stone up.
4. 6 saying, What (mean) ye by these stones?
4. 7 these stones shall be for a memorial unto
4. 8 took up twelve stones out of the midst of
4. 9 Joshua set up twelve stones in the midst
4. 20 those twelve stones, which they took out
4. 21 shall ask..What (mean) these stones?
7. 25 Israel stoned him with stones, and burned
7. 25 after they had stoned them with stones
7. 26 raised over him a great heap of stones un.
8. 29 raise thereon a great heap of stones, (that
8. 31 an altar of whole stones, over which no
8. 32 he wrote there upon the stones a copy of
10. 11 the LORD cast down great stones from he.
10. 18 Roll great stones upon the mouth of the
10. 27 laid great stones in the cave's mouth, (wh.)
15. 6 the border went up to the stone of Bohan
18. 17 descended to the stone of Bohan the son
24. 26 took a great stone, and set it up there
24. 27 this stone shall be a witness unto us; for
Judg. 9. 5, 18 threescore..ten persons, upon one st.
20. 16 every one could sling stones at an hair (b.)
1 Sa. 6. 14 stood there, where (there was) a great st.
6. 15 the Levites..put (them) on the great sto.
7. 12 Samuel took a stone, and set (it) between
14. 33 Ye have transgressed: roll a great stone
17. 40 chose him five smooth stones out of the
17. 49 took thence a stone, and slang (it), and s.
17. 49 the stone sunk into his forehead; and he
17. 50 David prevailed..with a stone, and smote
20. 19 go down..and shalt remain by the stone
25. 37 his heart died..and he became (as) a stone
2 Sa. 12. 30 a talent of gold with the precious stones
16. 6 he cast stones at David, and at all the se.
16. 13 cursed as he went, and threw stones at hi.
18. 17 laid a very great heap of stones upon him
20. 8 they (were) at the great stone which (is) in
1 Ki. 1. 9 Adonijah slew sheep..by the stone of Zo.
5. 17 great stones, costly stones, (and) hewed st.
5. 18 they prepared timber and stones to build
6. 7 was built of stone made ready before it
6. 18 all (was) cedar; there was no stone seen
7. 9 All these (were of) costly stones, accordi.
7. 10 foundation..costly stones, even great sto.
7. 10 stones of ten cubits, and stones of eight
7. 11 And above (were) costly stones, after the
8. 9 save the two tables of stone, which Moses
10. 2 and very much gold, and precious stones
10. 10 spices very great store, and precious ston.
10. 11 plenty of almug trees, and precious ston.
10. 27 made silver (to be) in Jerusalem as stones
12. 18 Israel stoned him with stones, that he died
15. 22 they took away the stones of Ramah, and
18. 31 Elijah took twelve stones, according to
18. 32 with the stones he built an altar in the
18. 38 the wood, and the stones, and the dust
1 Ki. 21. 13 and stoned him with stones, that he died
2 Ki. 3. 19 mar every good piece of land with stones
3. 25 cast every man his stone, and filled it
3. 25 in Kir-haraseth left they the stones there
12. 12 hewers of stone, and to buy..hewed stone
16. 17 and put it upon a pavement of stones
19. 18 the work of men's hands, wood and stone
22. 6 to buy timber and hewn stone to repair
1 Ch. 12. 2 in (hurling) stones and (shooting) arrows
20. 2 (there were) precious stones in it; and it
22. 2 he set masons to hew wrought stones to
22. 14 timber also and stone have I prepared
22. 15 hewers and workers of stone and timber
29. 2 onyx stones..glistering stones, and of di.
29. 2 precious stones, and marble stones in ab.
29. 8 they with whom (precious) stones were fo.
2 Ch. 1. 15 gold at Jerusalem (as plenteous) as stones
2. 14 in silver, in brass, in iron, in stone, and
3. 6 garnished the house with precious stones
9. 1 and gold in abundance, and precious sto.
9. 9 spices great abundance, and precious st.
9. 10 brought algum trees and precious stones
9. 27 made silver in Jerusalem as stones, and
10. 18 children of Israel stoned him with stones
16. 6 they carried away the stones of Ramah
24. 21 stoned him with stones at the command
26. 14 Uzziah prepared..slings (to cast) stones
26. 15 to shoot arrows and great stones withal
32. 27 for precious stones, and for spices, and
34. 11 to buy hewn stone, and timber for coup.
Neh. 4. 2 will they revive the stones out of the he.
4. 3 he shall even break down their stone wall
9. 11 thou threwest into the deeps, as a stone
Job 5. 23 thou shalt be in league with the stones of
6. 12 (Is) my strength the strength of stones?
8. 17 His roots..seeth the place of stones
14. 19 The waters wear the stones: thou washest
28. 2 and brass (is) molten (out of) the stone
28. 3 the stones of darkness, and the shadow of
28. 6 The stones of it (are) the place of sapphires
38. 6 Whereupon..or who laid the corner stone
38. 30 The waters are hid as (with) a stone, and
41. 24 His heart is as firm as a stone; yea as hard
41. 28 sling stones are turned with him into st.
Psa. 91. 12 lest thou dash thy foot against a stone
102. 14 thy servants take pleasure in her stones
118. 22 The stone (which) the builders refused is
Prov 17. 8 A gift (is as) a precious stone in the eyes
24. 31 the stone wall thereof was broken down
26. 8 As he that bindeth a stone in a sling, so
26. 27 he that rolleth a stone, it will return upon
27. 3 A stone (is) heavy, and the sand weighty
Eccl. 3. 5 to cast away stones..to gather stones to.
10. 9 Whoso removeth stones shall be hurt th.
Isa. 8. 14 for a stone of stumbling and for a rock of
14. 19 that go down to the stones of the pit
27. 9 the stones of the altar as chalk stones that
28. 16 for a foundation a stone, a tried stone, a
34. 11 the line of confusion, and the stones of
37. 19 the work of men's hands, wood and stone
54. 11 I will lay thy stones with fair colours, and
54. 12 and all thy borders of pleasant stones
60. 17 and for wood brass, and for stones iron
62. 10 gather out the stones; lift up a standard
Jer. 2. 27 Saying..to a stone, Thou hast brought me
3. 9 committed adultery with stones and with
43. 9 Take great stones in thine hand, and hide
43. 10 will set his throne upon these stones that
51. 26 a stone for a corner, nor a stone for foun.
51. 63 thou shalt bind a stone to it, and cast it
Lam. 3. 53 cut off my life..and cast a stone upon me
4. 1 the stones of the sanctuary are poured out
Eze. 1. 26 as the appearance of a sapphire stone
10. 1 over them as it were a sapphire stone, as
10. 9 appearance..the colour of a beryl stone
11. 19 I will take the stony heart out of their fl.
16. 40 they shall stone thee with stones, and th.
20. 32 as the heathen..to serve wood and stone
23. 47 the company shall stone them with stones
26. 12 they shall lay thy stones and thy timber
27. 22 and with all precious stones, and gold
28. 13 every precious stone (was) thy covering
28. 14 hast walked..in the midst of the stones
28. 16 destroy thee..from the midst of the stones
36. 26 I will take away the stony heart out of your
40. 42 the four tables (were) of hewn stone for the
Dan. 11. 38 and with precious stones, and pleasant th.
Mic. 1. 6 I will pour down the stones thereof into
Hab. 2. 11 the stone shall cry out of the wall, and the
2. 19 him that saith..to the dumb stone, Arise
Hag. 2. 15 a stone was laid upon a stone in the temple
Zech. 3. 9 behold the stone that I have laid before J.
3. 9 upon one stone (shall be) seven eyes, beho.
5. 4 with the timber thereof and the stones th.
9. 15 devour, and subdue with sling stones
9. 16 (they shall be as) the stones of a crown
12. 3 I make Jerusalem a burdensome stone for

2. *A stone,* אֶבֶן *eben.*
Ezra 5. 8 which is builded with great stones, and
6. 4 three rows of great stones, and a row of
Dan. 2. 34 Thou sawest till that a stone was cut out
2. 35 the stone that smote the image became a
2. 45 the stone was cut out of the mountain wi
5. 4 of brass, of iron, of wood, and of stone
5. 23 of brass, iron, wood, and stone; 6. 17.

2a. *By bruising,* דַּכָּה *dakkah.* Deut. 23. 1.

3. *A testicle,* אֶשֶׁךְ *eshek.*
Lev. 21. 20 scurvy, or scabbed, or hath his stones br.

4. *A rugged stone, cliff,* סֶלַע *sela.*
Psa. 137. 9 dasheth thy little ones against the stones
141. 6 judges..overthrown in stony places, they

5. *Fear, dread, thigh,* פַּחַד *pachad.*
Job 40. 17 the sinews of his stones are wrapped tog.

6. *A rock, sharp stone,* צוּר *tsur.*
Job 22. 24 (gold) of Ophir as the stones of the brooks

7. *Earthen ware, potsherd,* חֶרֶשׂ *cheres.*
Job 41. 30 Sharp stones (are) under him: he spread.

8. *A little round stone, kernel,* צְרוֹר *tseror.*
2 Sa. 17. 13 until there be not one small stone found

9. *A stone,* λίθος *lithos.*
Matt. 3. 9 God is able of these stones to raise up ch.
4. 3 command that these stones be made bread
4. 6 lest..thou dash thy foot against a stone
7. 9 son ask bread, will he give him a stone?
21. 42 The stone which the builders rejected, the
21. 44 [whosoever shall fall on this stone shall]
24. 2 There shall not be left here one stone up.an.
27. 60 he rolled a great stone to the door of the
27. 66 sealing the stone, and setting a watch
28. 2 came and rolled back the stone from the
Mark 5. 5 crying, and cutting himself with stones
12. 10 The stone which the builders rejected is
13. 1 see what manner of stones, and what bu.
13. 2 there shall not be left one stone upon an.
15. 46 rolled a stone unto the door of the sepul.
16. 3 Who shall roll us away the stone from the
16. 4 they saw that the stone was rolled away
Luke 3. 8 God is able of these stones to raise up ch.
4. 3 command this stone that it be made bread
4. 11 lest..thou dash thy foot against a stone
11. 11 shall ask bread..will he give him a stone?
19. 40 the stones would immediately cry out
19. 44 they shall not leave in thee one stone upon
20. 18 Whosoever shall fall upon that stone shall
20. 17 The stone which the builders rejected, the
21. 5 how it was adorned with goodly stones
21. 6 there shall not be left one stone upon an.
22. 41 was withdrawn from them about a stone's
24. 2 they found the stone rolled away from the
John 8. 7 [He that is without sin..cast a stone at]
8. 59 Then took they up stones to cast at him
10. 31 Then the Jews took up stones again to st.
11. 38 It was a cave, and a stone lay upon it
11. 39 Jesus said, Take ye away the stone Mar
11. 41 they took away the stone (from the place)
20. 1 seeth the stone taken away from the sep
Acts 4. 11 This is the stone which was set at nought
17. 29 like unto gold, or silver, or stone, graven
1 Co. 3. 12 gold, silver, precious stones, wood, hay
2 Co. 3. 7 if the ministration..engraven in stones
1 Pe. 2. 4 To whom coming, (as unto) a living stone
2. 5 Ye also, as lively stones, are built up a sp.
2. 6 I lay in Sion a chief corner stone, elect
2. 7 the stone which the builders disallowed
2. 8 a stone of stumbling, and a rock of offence
Rev. 4. 3 was to look upon like..a sardine stone
17. 4 decked with gold, and precious stones
18. 12 gold, and silver, and precious stones, and
18. 16 decked with gold, and precious stones
18. 21 mighty angel took up a stone like a great
21. 11 her light (was) like unto a st...a jasper s.
21. 19 garnished with all manner of precious st.
21. 11 even like a jasper stone, clear as crystal

10. *Stony, made of stone,* λίθινος *lithinos.*
John 2. 6 were set there six water pots of stone
2 Co. 3. 3 not in tables of stone, but in fleshy tables
Rev. 9. 20 of gold, and silver, and brass, and stone

11. *A (small) stone,* πέτρος *petros.*
John 1. 42 Cephas, which is, by interpretation, A st.

12. *Stony, full of small stones,* πετρώδης *petrōdēs.*
Matt 13. 5 Some fell upon stony places, where they
13. 20 he that received the seed into stony places
Mark 4. 16 they likewise which are sown on stony gr.
4. 5 some fell on stony ground, where it had

13. *A small pebble,* ψῆφος *psēphos.*
Rev. 2. 17 give him a white stone, and in the stone

[*See also* Adamant, corner, gravel, hail, head, hewn, mill, sharp, sling].

STONE, be stoned, to (cast) —

1. *To stone,* סָקַל *saqal.*
Exod. 8. 26 shall we sacrifice..will they not stone us?
17. 4 this people? they be almost ready to stone
Deut. 13. 10 And thou shalt stone him..that he die
17. 5 and shalt stone them..till they die
22. 21 and the men of her city shall stone her
22. 24 and ye shall stone them..that they die
Josh. 7. 25 after they had stoned them with stones
1 Sa. 30. 6 the people spake of stoning him, because
1 Ki. 21. 10 carry him out, and stone him, that he may
21. 13 they carried him forth..and stoned him

2. *To be stoned,* סָקַל *saqal,* 2.
Exod. 19. 13 but he shall surely be stoned, or shot th.
21. 28 the ox shall be surely stoned, and his flesh
21. 29 the ox shall be stoned, and his owner also
21. 32 thirty shekels..and the ox shall be stoned

3. *To be stoned,* סָקַל *saqal,* 4.
1 Ki. 21. 14 sent to Jezebel, saying, Naboth is stoned
21. 15 Jezebel heard that Naboth was stoned, and

4. *To collect or cast stones,* רָגַם *ragam.*
Lev. 20. 2 the people of the land shall stone him with
20. 27 they shall stone them..their blood (shall
24. 14 and let all the congregation stone him
24. 16 all the congregation shall certainly stone
24. 23 they should bring forth him..and stone
Num. 14. 10 But all the congregation bade stone them
15. 35 all the congregation shall stone him with
15. 36 brought him without the camp, and stoned
Deut. 21. 21 all the men of his city shall stone him with
Josh. 7. 25 all Israel stoned him..and burned them
1 Ki. 12. 18 and all Israel stoned him..that he died
2 Ch 10. 18 and the children of Israel stoned him wi.
24. 21 conspired against him, and stoned him
Eze. 16. 40 they shall stone thee..and thrust thee th.
23. 47 And the company shall stone them with

5. *To stone thoroughly,* καταλιθάζω *katalithazō.*
Luke 20. 6 the people will stone us: for they be per.

6. *To stone,* λιθάζω *lithazō.*
John 10. 31 the Jews took up stones again to stone
10. 32 for which of those works do ye stone me
10. 33 For a good work we stone thee not, but
11. 8 the Jews of late sought to stone thee, and
Acts 5. 26 feared..lest they should have been stoned
14. 19 having stoned Paul, drew (him) out of the
2 Co. 11. 25 once was I stoned, thrice I suffered ship.
Heb. 11. 37 They were stoned, they were sawn asun.

7. *To cast stones,* λιθοβολέω *lithoboleō.*
Matt 21. 35 beat one, and killed another, and stoned
23. 37 killest the prophets, and stonest them wh.
Mark 12. 4 and [at him they cast stones, and] woun.
Luke 13. 34 killest the prophets, and stonest them th.
John 8. 5 commanded us, that such should be stoned
Acts 7. 58 And cast (him) out of the city, and stoned
7. 59 they stoned Stephen, calling upon (God)
14. 5 to use (them) despitefully, and to stone
Heb. 12. 20 it shall be stoned, or thrust through with

STONE SQUARER —
Hebrew גִּבְלִי, *Giblite,* which see.
1 Ki. 5. 18 did hew (them), and the stone squarers

STOOD (firm), place where —
Station, standing place, מַצָּב *matstsab.*
Josh. 4. 3 the place where the priests' feet stood firm
4. 9 in the place where..the priests..stood

STOOD I, (where) —
My standing, עָמְדִי *[omed].*
Dan. 8. 17 he came near where I stood; and when he
11. 1 (even) I, stood to confirm and to strengthen

STOOL —

1. *Two children, (male and female),* אָבְנַיִם *obnayim.*
Exod. 1. 16 When ye..see (them) upon the stools, if

2. *A chair (of judge, king, or priest),* כִּסֵּא *kisse.*
2 Ki. 4. 10 a bed, and a table, and a stool, and a ca.

STOOP (down, make to), to —

1. *To bend or bow (the knee or leg),* כָּרַע *kara.*
Gen. 49. 9 he stooped down, he couched as a lion, and

2. *To bow (the head)* קָדַד *qadad.*
1 Sa. 24. 8 David stooped with his face to the earth
28. 14 he stooped with (his) face to the ground

3. *To stoop,* קָרַס *qaras.*
Isa. 46. 1 Bel boweth down, Nebo stoopeth; their
46. 2 They stoop, they bow down together; th.

4. *To cause to bow,* שָׁחָה *shachah,* 5.
Prov 12. 25 Heaviness in the heart..maketh it stoop

5. *To bow, be bowed,* שָׁחַח *shachach.*
Job 9. 13 the proud helpers do stoop under him

6. *To stoop, bend,* κύπτω *kuptō.*
Mark 1. 7 I am not worthy to stoop down and unl.
John 8. 6 [Jesus stooped down, and with (his) fing.]
8. 8 [he stooped down, and wrote on the gro.]

7. *To stoop or bend down,* παρακύπτω *parakuptō.*
Luke 24. 12 [stooping down, he beheld the linen clo.]
John 20. 5 he stooping down, (and looking in), saw
20. 11 she stooped down, (and looked) into the

STOOP for age, to —
Grey headed, old, dried up, יָשֵׁשׁ *yashesh.*
2 Ch. 36. 17 no compassion upon..him that st. for age

STOP, be stopped, to —

1. *To be narrow, shut, stop,* אָטַם *atam.*
Prov 21. 13 Whoso stoppeth his ears at the cry of the
Isa. 33. 15 that stoppeth his ears from hearing of bl.

2. *To make narrow, shut, stop,* אָטַם *atam,* 5.
Psa. 58. 4 (are) like the deaf adder (that) stoppeth

3. *To stop, muzzle,* חָסַם *chasam.*
Eze. 39. 11 and it shall stop the (noses) of the passe.

4. *To seal, seal up, stop,* חָתַם *chatham,* 5.
Lev. 15. 3 or his flesh be stopped from his issue, it

5. *To make heavy or weighty,* כָּבֵד *kabed,* 5.
Zech. 7. 11 stopped their ears, that they should not

6. *To shut in or up, close, refine,* סָגַר *sagar.*
Psa. 35. 3 stop (the way) against them that persec.

7. *To be stopped,* סָכַר *sakar,* 2.
Gen. 8. 2 the windows of heaven were stopped, and
Psa. 63. 11 but the mouth of them..shall be stopped

8. *To stop, hide,* סָתַם *satham.*
2 Ki. 3. 19 stop all wells of water, and mar every go.
3. 25 they stopped all the wells of water, and
2 Ch. 32. 3 to stop the waters of the fountains which
32. 4 who stopped all the fountains, and the br
32. 30 Hezekiah also stopped the upper water

9. *To be stopped,* סָתַם *satham,* 2.
Neh. 4. 7 the breaches began to be stopped, then

10. *To stop,* סָתַם *satham,* 3.
Gen. 26. 15 the Philistines had stopped them, and fi.
26. 18 the Philistines had stopped them after the

11. *To keep in, restrain, detain,* עָצַר *atsar.*
1 Ki. 18. 44 get thee down, that the rain stop thee not

12. *To shut, shut up,* קָפַץ *qaphats.*
Job 5. 16 the poor hath hope, and iniquity stopp.
Psa. 107. 42 and all iniquity shall stop her mouth

13. *To be caught, captured,* תָּפַשׂ *taphas,* 2.
Jer. 51. 32 passages are stopped, and the reeds they

14. *To hold together,* συνέχω *sunechō.*
Acts 7. 57 cried out with a loud voice, and stopped

15. *To hedge in, stop, restrain,* φράσσω *phrassō.*
Rom. 3. 19 that every mouth may be stopped, and all
2 Co. 11. 10 no man shall stop me of this boasting in
Heb. 11. 33 obtained promises, stopped the mouths

STORE, storehouse, (old) —

1. *Storehouses, barns,* אֲסָמִים *asamim.*
Deut 28. 8 the blessing upon thee in thy store hou.

2. *Treasure, treasury,* (בֵּית)אוֹצָר *(beth) otsar.*
1 Ch. 27. 25 over the storehouses in the fields, in the
2 Ch. 11. 11 put captains in them, and store of victu.
Psa. 33. 7 he layeth up the depth in storehouses
Mal. 3. 10 Bring ye all the tithes into the storeho.

3. *Multitude, store, noise,* הָמוֹן *hamon.*
1 Ch. 29. 16 all this store that we have prepared to
2 Ch. 31. 10 and that which is left (is) this great store

4. *Storehouse,* מַאֲבוּס *maabus.*
Jer. 50. 26 open her storehouses; cast her up as he.

5. *Stores, treasures,* מִסְכְּנוֹת *miskenoth.*
1 Ki. 9. 19 the cities of store that Solomon had, and
2 Ch. 8. 4 all the store cities, which he built in Ha.
8. 6 all the store cities that Solomon had, and
16. 4 Abel-maim, and all the store cities of Na.
17. 12 built in Judah castles and cities of store
32. 28 Storehouses also for the increase of corn

6. *Kneading trough,* מִשְׁאֶרֶת *mishereth.*
Deut. 28. 5 Blessed (shall be) thy basket and thy store
28. 17 Cursed (shall be) thy basket and thy store

7. *Deposit, store,* פִּקָּדוֹן *piqqadon.*
Gen. 41. 36 that food shall be for store to the landag.

8. *Prepared seat or place,* תְּכוּנָה *tekunah.*
Nah. 2. 9 (there is) none end of the store (and) glo.

9. *Much,* הַרְבֵּה *harbeh.*
1 Ki. 10. 10 of spices very great store, and precious st.
Neh. 5. 18 once in ten days store of all sorts of wine

10. *To be dried up, old,* יָשֵׁן *yashen,* 2.
Lev. 26. 10 ye shall eat old store, and bring forth the

11. *To treasure up,* θησαυρίζω *thēsaurizō.*
1 Co. 16. 2 let every one of you lay by him in store

12. *A cut off place, storehouse,* ταμεῖον *tameion.*
Luke 12. 24 which neither have store house nor barn

STORE up, keep or lay up in store, to —

1. *To treasure up,* אָצַר *atsar.*
2 Ki. 20. 17 which thy fathers have laid up in store un.
Isa. 39. 6 which thy fathers have laid up in store
Amos 3. 10 who store up violence and robbery in th.

2. *To store away,* ἀποθησαυρίζω *apothēsaurizō.*
1 Ti. 6. 19 Laying up in store for themselves a good

3. *To treasure up,* θησαυρίζω *thēsaurizō.*
2 Pe. 3. 7 by the same word are kept in store, rese.

STORIES —
A going up, ascent, מַעֲלָה *maalah.*
Amos 9. 6 (It is) he that buildeth his stories in the he.

STORK —
White goshawk, kite, stork, or heron, חֲסִידָה *chasidah.*
Lev. 11. 19 the stork, the heron, after her kind, and
Deut 14. 18 the stork, and the heron after her kind
Psa. 104. 17 (as for) the stork, the fir trees (are) her ho.
Jer. 8. 7 the stork in the heaven knoweth her app.
Zech. 5. 9 they had wings like the wings of a stork

STORM, stormy —

1. *Inundation, flood, storm,* זֶרֶם *zerem.*
Isa. 4. 6 and for a covert from storm and from ra.
25. 4 a refuge from the storm, a shadow from
25. 4 the blast of the terrible ones (is) as a sto.

2. *A hurricane,* סוּפָה *suphah.*
Job. 21. 18 and as chaff that the storm carrieth away
Psa. 83. 15 and make them afraid with thy storm
Isa. 29. 6 great noise, with storm and tempest, and

3. *To rush,* שָׂאָה *saah.*
Psa. 55. 8 hasten my escape from the windy storm

4. *Whirlwind,* סְעָרָה *searah.*
Psa. 107. 25 he commandeth, and raiseth the stormy
107. 29 He maketh the storm a calm, so that the
148. 8 snow, and vapour; stormy wind fulfilling
Eze. 13. 11 hailstones, shall fall; and a stormy wind
13. 13 I will even rend (it) with a stormy wind

5. *Wasting, desolation,* שׁוֹאָה *shoah.*
Eze. 38. 9 Thou shalt ascend and come like a storm

6. *Shower, tempest,* שַׂעַר *saar.*
Isa. 28. 2 a tempest of hail, (and) a destroying storm

7. *Shower, tempest,* שְׂעָרָה *searah.*
Nah. 1. 3 in the whirlwind and in the storm, and

8. *Violent storm, hurricane, whirlwind,* λαῖλαψ.
Mark 4. 37 there arose a great storm of wind, and the
Luke 8. 23 there came down a storm of wind on the

STORY —
Inquiry, investigation, מִדְרָשׁ *midrash.*
2 Ch.13. 22 (are) written in the story of the prophet
24. 27 written in the story of the book of the ki.

STOUT, stoutness, to be —
1. *Greatness,* גֹּדֶל *godel.*
Isa. 9. 9 that say in the pride and stoutness of he.
10. 12 I will punish the fruit of the stout heart
2. *To be strong, hard, severe,* חָזַק *chazaq.*
Mal. 3. 13 Your words have been stout against me
3. *Many, much, abundant, great,* רַב *rab.*
Dan. 7. 20 whose look (was) more stout than his fel.

STOUT HEARTED —
Mighty of heart, אַבִּיר לֵב *abbir leb.*
Psa. 76. 5 The stout hearted are spoiled, they have
Isa. 46. 12 Hearken unto me, ye stout hearted, that

STRAIGHT, (forward), straightway —
1. *Right, upright, straight,* יָשָׁר *yashar.*
Jer. 31. 9 walk by the rivers of waters in a straight
Eze. 1. 7 their feet (were) straight feet; and the so.
1. 23 their wings straight, the one toward the
2. *So, right, prepared,* כֵּן *ken.*
1 Sa 9. 13 ye shall straightway find him, before he
3. *To haste, hurry, speed,* מָהַר *mahar,* 3.
1 Sa. 28. 20 Saul fell straightway all along on the earth
4. *Uprightness, a plain,* מִישׁוֹר *mishor.*
Isa. 40. 4 the crooked shall be made straight, and
42. 16 I will make..crooked things straight
5. *From now, henceforth,* מֵעַתָּה *me-attah.*
Dan.10. 17 straightway there remained no strength in
6. *To beyond his face,* אֶל־עֵבֶר פָּנָיו [*el*].
Eze. 1. 9, 12 they went every one straight forward
10. 22 they went every one straight forward
7. *Suddenly,* פִּתְאֹם *pithom.*
Prov. 7. 22 He goeth after her straightway, as an ox
8. *From the same (moment),* ἐξαυτῆς *exautēs.*
Acts 23. 30 I sent [straightway] to thee, and gave co.
9. *Straightway,* εὐθέως *eutheōs.*
Matt. 4. 20 they straightway left (their) nets, and fo.
14. 22 straightway Jesus constrained his discip.
14. 27 [straightway] Jesus spake unto them, sa.
21. 2 straightway ye shall find an ass tied, and
21. 3 The Lord hath need..and [straightway] he
25 15 to every man..and straightway took his
27 48 straightway one of them ran, and took a
Mark 1. 10 [straightway] coming up out of the water
1. 18 straightway they forsook their nets, and
1. 20 [straightway] he called them: and they
1. 21 straightway on the sabbath day he enter.
2. 2 [straightway] many were gathered toget.
3. 6 [the Pharisees went forth, and [straight.]
5. 29 [straightway] the fountain of her blood
5. 42 And straightway the damsel arose, and
6. 25 she came in [straightway] with haste unto
6. 45 [straightway] he constrained his disciples
6. 54 when they were come..[straightway] they
7. 35 [straightway] his ears were opened, and
8. 10 [straightway] he entered into a ship with
9. 15 [straightway] all the people, when they
9. 20 when he saw him, [straightway] the spirit
9. 24 [straightway] the father of the child cried
11. 3 and [straightway] he will send him hith.
14. 45 he goeth [straightway] to him, and saith
15. 1 [straightway] in the morning the chief pr.
Luke 5. 39 No man also..[straightway] desireth new
12. 54 straightway ye say, There cometh a shower
14. 5 will not straightway pull him out on the
Acts 9. 20 straightway he preached Christ in the sy.
22. 29 straightway they departed from him wh.
Jas. 1. 24 straightway forgetteth what manner of m.
10. *Straight, upright, correct,* εὐθύς *euthus.*
Matt. 3. 3 Prepare ye..make his paths straight
3. 16 Jesus..went up straightway out of the wa.
Mark 1. 3 Prepare ye..make his paths straight
Luke 3. 4 Prepare ye..make his paths straight
3. 5 the crooked shall be made straight, and
John13. 32 God shall also..straightway glorify him
Acts 9. 11 go into the street which is called Straight
11. *Upright, erect, straight,* ὀρθός *orthos.*
Heb. 12. 13 make straight paths for your feet, lest th.
12. *Alongside of the thing,* παραχρῆμα *parachrēma.*
Luke 8. 55 spirit came again, and she arose straight.
Acts 5. 10 Then fell she down straightway at his fe.
16. 33 was baptized, he and all his, straightway

STRAIGHT course, (to come) with a —
To run straight, εὐθυδρομέω *euthudromeō.*
Acts 16. 11 we came with a straight course to Samo.
21. 1 we came with a straight course unto Coos

STRAIGHT, to bring, look, make —
1. *To go or make straight,* יָשַׁר *yashar,* 3.
2 Ch.32. 30 brought it straight down to the west side
Isa. 40. 3 make straight in the desert a highway for
45. 2 I will..make the crooked places straight
2. *To make straight,* יָשַׁר *yashar,* 5.
Psa. 5. 8 make thy way straight before my face
Prov. 4 25 let thine eye lids look straight before thee

3. *To be made straight or right,* תָּקַן *taqan.*
Eccl. 1. 15 (which is) crooked cannot be made strai.
4. *To make straight or right,* תָּקַן *taqan,* 3.
Eccl. 7. 13 who can make (that) straight which he hath
5. *To make straight or right again,* ἀνορθόω *anor.*
Luke13. 13 she was made straight, and glorified God
6. *To make straight or right,* εὐθύνω *euthunō.*
John 1. 23 Make straight the way of the Lord, as said

STRAIGHT way, to take the —
To be or go straight, יָשַׁר *yashar.*
1 Sa. 6. 12 the kine took the straight way to the way

STRAIN at, to —
To separate matter, strain out, filter, διϋλίζω *diulizō.*
Matt23. 24 (Ye) blind guides, which strain at a gnat

STRAIT, straitly, straitness —
1. *Straitness, anguish,* מוּצָק *mutsaq.*
Job 36. 16 broad place, where (there is) no straitne.
2. *Straitness, distress,* מָצוֹק *matsoq.*
Deut.28. 53, 55, 57 the straitness, wherewith thine
Jer. 19. 9 in the siege and straitness wherewith th.
3. *Strait, distressed person, place, or thing,* מֵצַר *metsar.*
Lam. 1. 3 persecutors overtook..between the straits
4. *To shut up or in, close,* סָגַר *sagar.*
Josh. 6. 1 Jericho was straitly shut up because of the
5. *Strait, close,* צַר, צָר *tsar.*
2 Ki. 6. 1 the place where we dwell..is too strait
Job 36. 16 removed thee out of the strait (into) a br.
Isa. 49. 20 The place (is) too strait for me: give place
6. *To ask, demand,* שָׁאַל *shaal.*
Gen. 43. 7 The man asked us straitly of our state, and
7. *To make to swear,* שָׁבַע *shaba,* 5.
Exod13. 19 he had straitly sworn the children of Isr.
1 Sa. 14. 28 Thy father straitly charged the people wi.
8. *With a threatening,* ἀπειλῇ *apeilē.*
Acts 4. 17 let us [straitly] threaten them, that they
9. *Much,* πολύς *polus.*
Mark 3. 12 he straitly charged them that they should
5. 43 he charged them straitly that no man sh.
10. *Strait, narrow, restrained,* στενός *stenos.*
Matt. 7. 13 Enter ye in at the strait gate: for wide
7. 14 strait (is) the gate, and narrow (is) the way
Luke13. 24 Strive to enter in at the strait gate, for m.

STRAIT, to be in —
1. *To be straitened, distressed,* יָצַר *yatsar.*
Job 20. 22 In the fulness..he shall be in straits: ev.
2. *To distress, be distressed,* צָרַר *tsarar.*
1 Sa. 13. 6 men of Israel saw that they were in a st.
2 Sa. 24. 14 I am in a great strait: let us fall now into
1 Ch.21. 13 I am in a great strait: let me fall now
3. *To hold together,* συνέχω *sunechō.*
Phil. 1. 23 I am in a strait betwixt two, having a d.

STRAITEN, be straitened, to —
1. *To be kept back, laid up,* אָצַל *atsal,* 2.
Eze. 42. 6 (the building) was straitened more than
2. *To be straitened, distressed,* יָצַר *yatsar.*
Job 18. 7 The steps of his strength shall be straite.
Prov. 4. 12 thy steps shall not be straitened; and wh.
3. *Straitness, anguish,* מוּצָק *mutsaq.*
Job 37. 10 and the breadth of the waters is straite.
4. *To lead forth,* נָחָה *nachah,* 5.
Job 12. 23 enlargeth the nations, and straiteneth th.
5. *To make strait, distress, oppress,* צוּק *tsuq,* 5.
Jer. 19. 9 they that seek their lives, shall straiten
6. *To be or make short, reap,* קָצַר *qatsar.*
Mic. 2. 7 is the spirit of the LORD straitened? (are)
7. *To hold together with,* συνέχω *sunechō.*
Luke12. 50 how am I straitened till it be accompli.
8. *To be straitened, constrained,* στενοχωρέομαι.
2 Co. 6. 12 straitened in us, but ye are straitened in

STRAITEST, most —
Most accurate, scrupulous, strict, ἀκριβέστατος.
Acts 26. 5 after the most straitest sect of our relig.

STRAKES, (hollow) —
1. *Peelings, stripings,* פְּצָלוֹת *petsaloth.*
Gen. 30. 37 pilled white strakes in them, and made
2. *Hollow places,* שְׁקַעֲרוּרֹת *sheqaaruroth.*
Lev. 14. 37 (if) the plague (be)..with hollow strakes

STRANGE (thing, woman), stranger —
1. *Another,* אַחֵר *acher.*
Judg.11. 2 for thou (art) the son of a strange woman
2. *A man, a sojourner,* אֱנוֹשׁ גֵּר *enosh ger.*
2 Ch. 2. 17 Solomon numbered all the strangers that
3. *Son of a stranger or foreigner,* בֶּן־נֵכָר *ben nekar.*
Gen. 17. 12 bought with money of any stranger, wh.
17. 27 the men..bought with money of the str.
Exod12. 43 There shall no stranger eat thereof
Lev. 22. 25 Neither from a stranger's hand shall ye
2 Sa. 22. 45 Strangers shall submit themselves unto
22. 46 Strangers shall fade away, and they shall
Neh. 9. 2 separated themselves from all strangers
Psa. 18. 44 the strangers shall submit themselves un.
18. 45 The strangers shall fade away, and be af.

Eze. 44. 7 have brought (into my sanctuary) strang.
44. 9 No stranger..of any stranger that (is) am.
4. *A man, an alien,* אִישׁ זָר *ish zar.*
Lev. 22. 12 daughter also be (married) unto a stran.
Num16. 40 no stranger, which (is) not of the seed of
Deut25. 5 shall not marry without unto a stranger
5. *A man, a stranger, or foreigner,* אִישׁ נָכְרִי *ish nokri.*
Deut17. 15 thou mayest not set a stranger over thee
Eccl. 6. 2 to eat thereof, but a stranger eateth it
6. *A man, a sojourner,* אִישׁ גֵּר *ish ger.*
2 Sa. 1. 13 I (am) the son of a stranger, an Amalekite
7. *To sojourn, draw up (self),* גּוּר *gur.*
1 Ch.16. 19 ye were but few, even a few, and strang.
2 Ch.15. 9 all Judah and Benjamin, and the strang.
Psa.105. 12 When they were..few, and strangers in it
Isa. 5. 17 waste places of the fat ones shall strang
Jer. 35. 7 may live..in the land where ye (be) stra
8. *A sojourner,* גֵּר *ger.*
Gen. 15. 13 thy seed shall be a stranger in a land (th.
23. 4 I (am) a stranger and a sojourner with you
Exod. 2. 22 for he said, I have been a stranger in a
12. 19 whether he be a stranger, or born in the
12. 48 when a stranger shall sojourn with thee
12. 49 unto the stranger that sojourneth among
20. 10 nor thy stranger that (is) within thy gates
22. 21 Thou shalt neither vex a stranger, nor op.
22. 21 for ye were strangers in the land of Egypt
23. 9 Also thou shalt not oppress a stranger: for
23. 9 of a stranger, seeing ye were strangers in
23. 12 son of thy handmaid and the stranger may
Lev. 16. 29 or a stranger that sojourneth among you
17. 8, 10, 13 or of the strangers which sojourn
17. 12 neither shall any stranger that sojourne.
17. 15 one of your own country, or a stranger, he
18. 26 nor any stranger that sojourneth among
19. 10 shalt leave them for the poor and stranger
19. 33 if a stranger sojourn with thee in your land
19. 34 the stranger that dwelleth with you shall
19. 34 for ye were strangers in the land of Egypt
20. 2 or of the strangers that sojourn in Israel
22. 18 of the house of Israel, or of the strangers
23. 22 thou shalt leave them unto..the stranger
24. 16 as well the stranger, as he that is born in
24. 22 one manner of law, as well for the stranger
25. 23 for ye (are) strangers and sojourners with
25. 35 (yea, though he be) a stranger, or a sojour.
25. 47 sell himself unto the stranger (or) sojourn.
25. 47 or to the stock of the stranger's family
Num. 9. 14 if a stranger shall sojourn among you, and
9. 14 both for the stranger, and for him that was
15. 14 if a stranger sojourn with you, or whoso.
15. 15, 16, 26, 29 the stranger that sojourneth
15. 15 as ye (are), so shall the stranger be before
15. 30 born in the land, or a stranger, the same
19. 10 unto the stranger that sojourneth among
35. 15 for the stranger, and for the sojourner am.
Deut. 1. 16 his brother, and the stranger (that is) with
5. 14 nor thy stranger that (is) within thy gates
10. 18 loveth the stranger, in giving him food
10. 19 Love..the stranger: for ye were strangers
14. 21 thou shalt give it unto the stranger that (is)
14. 29 the stranger, and the fatherless, and the
16. 11, 14, the stranger, and the fatherless, and
23. 7 because thou wast a stranger in his land
24. 14 thy strangers that (are) in thy land within
24. 17 not pervert the judgment of the stranger
24. 19, 20, 21 it shall be for the stranger, for the
26. 11 the Levite, and the stranger that (is) am.
26. 12 the stranger, the fatherless, and the wid.
26. 13 unto the stranger, to the fatherless, and
27. 19 perverteth the judgment of the stranger
28. 43 The stranger that (is) within thee shall
29. 11 and thy stranger that (is) in thy camp, fr.
31. 12 thy stranger that (is) within thy gates, th.
Josh. 8. 33 as well the stranger, as he that was born
8. 35 the strangers that were conversant amo.
20. 9 for the stranger that sojourneth among
1 Ch.22. 2 the strangers that (were) in the land of Is.
29. 15 we (are) strangers before thee, and sojou.
2 Ch.30. 25 the strangers that came out of the land
Job 31. 32 The stranger did not lodge in the street
Psa. 39. 12 I (am) a stranger with thee, (and) a sojo.
94. 6 They slay the widow and the stranger, and
119. 19 I (am) a stranger in the earth: hide not
146. 9 The LORD preserveth the strangers; he re.
Isa. 14. 1 the strangers shall be joined with them
Jer. 7. 6 (If) ye oppress not the stranger, the fath.
14. 8 why shouldest thou be as a stranger in
22. 3 do no violence to the stranger, the fathe.
Eze. 14. 7 or of the stranger that sojourneth in Isr.
22. 7 they dealt by oppression with the stran.
22. 29 they have oppressed the stranger wrong.
47. 22 to the strangers that sojourn among you
47. 23 in what tribe the stranger sojourneth, th.
Zech. 7. 10 oppress not the widow, nor..the stranger
Mal. 3. 5 that turn aside the stranger (from his rig.)
9. *A stranger, alien,* זָר *zar.*
Exod29. 33 a stranger shall not eat (thereof), because
30. 9 Ye shall offer no strange incense thereon
30. 33 whosoever putteth (any) of it upon a str.
Lev. 10. 1 offered strange fire before the LORD, which
22. 10 There shall no stranger eat (of) the holy
22. 13 but there shall no stranger eat thereof
Num. 1. 51 the stranger that cometh nigh shall be put
3. 4 they offered strange fire before the LORD
3. 10, 38 the stranger that cometh nigh shall be
[16. 40 no stranger, which (is) not of the seed of]
18. 4 and a stranger shall not come nigh unto

Num18. 7 the stranger that cometh nigh shall be
26. 61 when they offered strange fire before the
[Deut25. 5 shall not marry without unto a stranger]
Deut32. 16 provoked him to jealousy with strange
1 Ki. 3. 18 (there was) no stranger with us in the ho.
2 Ki. 19. 24 I have digged and drunk strange waters
Job 15. 19 and no stranger passed among them
19. 15 and my maids, count me for a stranger
Psa. 44. 20 or stretched out our hands to a strange
54. 3 strangers are risen up against me, and op.
81. 9 There shall no strange god be in thee; ne.
109. 11 catch all that he hath; and let the stran.
Prov. 2. 16 To deliver thee from the strange woman
5. 3 the lips of a strange woman drop (as) an
5. 10 Lest strangers be filled with thy wealth
5. 17 thine own, and not strangers' with thee
5. 20 ravished with a strange woman, and em.
6. 1 hast stricken thy hand with a stranger
7. 5 may keep thee from the strange woman
11. 15 He that is surety for a stranger shall sm.
14. 10 a stranger doth not intermeddle with his
20. 16 his garment that is surety (for) a 27. 13
22. 14 The mouth of strange women (is) a deep
23. 33 Thine eyes shall behold strange women
27. 13 Take his garment that is surety for a str.
Isa. 1. 7 strangers devour it in your presence, and
1. 7 (it is) desolate, as overthrown by strangers
17. 10 plant..and shalt set it with strange slips
25. 2 a palace of strangers to be no city; it sh.
25. 5 Thou shalt bring down the noise of stran.
28. 21 that he may do his work, his strange wo
29. 5 the multitude of thy strangers shall be li.
43. 12 when (there was) no strange (god) among
61. 5 strangers shall stand and feed your flocks
Jer. 2. 25 I have loved strangers, and after them wi
3. 13 hast scattered thy ways to the strangers
5. 19 so shall ye serve strangers in a land (that
30. 8 strangers shall no more serve themselves
51. 51 strangers are come into the sanctuaries of
Lam. 5. 2 Our inheritance is turned to strangers, our
Eze. 7. 21 give it into the hands of the strangers for
11. 9 deliver you into the hands of strangers
16. 32 (which) taketh strangers instead of her h.
28. 7 I will bring strangers upon thee, the ter.
28. 10 Thou shalt die..by the hand of strangers
30. 12 the land waste..by the hand of strangers
31. 12 strangers, the terrible of the nations, ha.
Hos. 5. 7 for they have begotten strange children
7. 9 Strangers have devoured his strength, and
8. 7 if so be it yield, the strangers shall swall.
8. 12 (but) they were counted as a strange thi
Joel 3. 17 there shall no strangers pass through her
Obad. 11 the strangers carried away captive his fo.

10. *To be an alien*, זוּר *zur*, 6.
Psa. 69. 8 I am become a stranger unto my brethren

11. *A stranger, one marked, a foreigner*, נֵכָר *nekar*.
Gen. 35. 2 Put away the strange gods that (are) am.
35. 4 they gave unto Jacob all the strange gods
Deut 31. 16 go a whoring after the gods of the stran.
32. 12 and (there was) no strange god with him
Josh.24. 20 If ye forsake the LORD, and serve strange
24. 23 put away, (said he), the strange gods wh
Judg 10. 16 they put away the strange gods from am.
1 Sa. 7. 3 put away the strange gods and Ashtaroth
2 Ch.14. 3 he took away the altars of the strange (g.)
33. 15 he took away the strange gods, and the
Neh. 13. 30 Thus cleansed I them from all strangers
Psa. 81. 9 shalt thou worship any strange god
137. 4 shall we sing the LORD'S song in a strange
144. 7, 11 from the hand of strange children
Isa. 56. 3 Neither let the son of the stranger, that
56. 6 the sons of the stranger, that join thems.
60. 10 the sons of strangers shall build up thy
62. 8 the sons of the stranger shall not drink
Jer. 5. 19 forsaken me, and served strange gods in
8. 19 they provoked me..with strange vanities
Dan. 11. 39 Thus shall he do..with a strange god, wh.
Mal. 2. 11 hath married the daughter of a strange

12. *A stranger or foreigner*, נֵכֶר *neker*.
Job 31. 3 a strange (punishment) to the workers of

13. *Strange, a stranger or foreigner*, נָכְרִי *nokri*.
Gen. 31. 15 Are we not counted of him strangers? for
Exod. 2. 22 for he said, I have been..in a strange la.
18. 3 said, I have been an alien in a strange la.
21. 8 to sell her unto a strange nation he shall
Deut 23. 20 Unto a stranger thou mayest lend upon
29. 22 the stranger that shall come from a far
Judg 19. 12 into the city of a stranger, that (is) not of
Ruth 2 10 knowledge of me, seeing I (am) a stranger
2 Sa. 15. 19 for thou (art) a stranger, and also an exi.
1 Ki. 8. 41 concerning a stranger, that (is) not of thy
8. 43 do according to all that the stranger cal.
11. 1 Solomon loved many strange women, tog.
11. 8 likewise did he for all his strange wives
2 Ch. 6. 32 concerning the stranger, which is not of
6. 33 do according to all that the stranger cal.
Ezra 10. 2 have taken strange wives of the people
10. 10 have taken strange wives, to increase the
10. 11 separate yourselves..from the strange wi.
10. 14 all them which have taken strange wives
10. 17 all the men that had taken strange wives
10. 18 there were found that had taken strange
10. 44 All these had taken strange wives: and
Neh. 13. 27 to transgress..in marrying strange wives
Prov. 2. 16 the stranger (which) flattereth with her
5. 10 and thy labours (be) in the house of a st.
5. 20 and embrace the bosom of a stranger
6. 24 flattery of the tongue of a strange woman
7. 5 the stranger (which) flattereth with her

Prov 20. 16 take a pledge of him for a strange woman
23. 27 and a strange woman (is) a narrow pit
27. 2 not thine own mouth; a stranger, and not
27. 13 take a pledge of him for a strange woman
Isa. 2. 6 please themselves in..children of strang.
28. 21 and bring to pass his act, his strange act
Jer. 2. 21 into the degenerate plant of a strange vi.
Zeph. 1. 8 all such as are clothed with strange app.

14. *Deep*, עָמֵק *ameq*.
Eze. 3. 5 (art) not sent to a people of a strange sp.
3. 6 Not to many people of a strange speech

15. *A settler*, תּוֹשָׁב *toshab*.
Lev. 25. 6 for thy stranger that sojourneth with th.
25. 45 the children of the strangers that do soj.
25. 47 if a sojourner or stranger wax rich by th.

16. *An alien*, זָר *zar*.
Prov 21. 8 The way of man (is) froward and strange

17. *Belonging to another race*, ἀλλογενής *allogenēs*.
Luke 17. 18 There are not found..save this stranger

18. *Belonging to another*, ἀλλότριος *allotrios*.
Matt 17. 25 of their own children, or of strangers?
17. 26 Peter saith unto him, Of strangers. Je.
John 10. 5 a stranger will they not follow, but will
10. 5 for they know not the voice of strangers
Acts 7. 6 That his seed should sojourn in a strange
Heb. 11. 9 he sojourned..as (in) a strange country

19. *To be among the people*, ἐπιδημέω *epidēmeō*.
Acts 2. 10 and strangers of Rome, Jews and prose.

20. *Without, outside*, ἔξω *exō*.
Acts 26. 11 I persecuted (them) even unto strange ci.

21. *Other, (not the same)*, ἕτερος *heteros*.
Jude 7 going after strange flesh, are set forth for

22. *To receive strangers, be strange*, ξενίζω *xenizō*.
Acts 17. 20 thou bringest certain strange things to

23. *Strange, stranger, foreigner*, ξένος *xenos*.
Matt 25. 35, 43 I was a stranger, and ye took me..in
25. 38 When saw we thee..a stranger, and took
25. 44 when saw we thee..a stranger, or naked
27. 7 the potter's field, to bury strangers in
Acts 17. 18 seemeth to be a setter forth of strange g.
17. 21 the Athenians and strangers which were
Eph. 2. 12 strangers from the covenants of promise
2. 19 ye are no more strangers and foreigners
Heb. 11. 13 confessed that they were strangers and
13. 9 Be not carried about with divers and str.
1 Pe. 4. 12 as though some strange thing happened
3 John 5 whatsoever thou doest..to strangers

24. *Paradoxical*, παράδοξος *paradoxos*.
Luke 5. 26 saying, We have seen strange things to d.

25. *One among the people, a stranger*, παρεπίδημος.
1 Pe. 1. 1 the strangers scattered throughout Pont.

26. *A sojourner, temporary resident*, πάροικος *par.*
Acts 7. 29 was a stranger in the land of Madian, wh.
1 Pe. 2. 11 I beseech (you) as strangers and pilgrims

STRANGE, to be, make self, think it —

1. *To be strange, estranged*, זוּר *zur*.
Job 19. 17 My breath is strange to my wife, though

2. *To make self strange*, הָכַר *hakar*, 5.
Job 19. 3 ashamed (that) ye make yourselves strange

3. *To make self strange*, נָכַר *nakar*, 7.
Gen. 42. 7 made himself strange unto them, and sp.

4. *To reckon or be strange*, ξενίζω *xenizō*.
1 Pe. 4. 4 they think it strange that ye run not with
4. 12 think it not strange concerning the fiery

STRANGELY, to behave self —

To make self marked, not to know, נָכַר *nakar*, 3.
Deut. 32. 27 adversaries..behave themselves strangely

STRANGER, to be, become, dwell as —

1. *To draw self up, sojourn*, גּוּר *gur*.
Exod. 6. 4 the land..wherein they were strangers

2. *A (place of) sojourn, dwelling*, מָגוּר *magur*.
Gen. 17. 8 the land wherein thou art a stranger, all
28. 4 the land wherein thou art a stranger
36. 7 the land wherein they were strangers could
37. 1 land wherein his father was a stranger

3. *One marked, strange*, נֹכֶר *noker*.
Obad. 12 in the day that he became a stranger

4. *To dwell alongside, sojourn*, παροικέω *paroikeō*.
Luke 24. 18 Art thou only a stranger in Jerusalem, and

5. *In the sojourning*, ἐν τῇ παροικίᾳ *en tē paroikia*.
Acts 13. 17 they dwelt as strangers in the land of Egypt

STRANGERS, to entertain, lodge —

1. *To receive strangers*, ξενοδοχέω *xenodocheō*.
1 Ti. 5. 10 if she have lodged strangers, if she have wa.

2. *Friendship for strangers*, φιλοξενία *philoxenia*.
Heb. 13. 2 Be not forgetful to entertain strangers

STRANGLE, strangled, strangling, to —

1. *To strangle, choke, suffocate*, חָנַק *chanaq*, 3.
Nah. 2. 12 strangled for his lionesses, and filled his

2. *Strangling*, מַחֲנָק *machanaq*.
Job 7. 15 my soul chooseth strangling, (and) death

3. *Strangled*, πνικτός *pniktos*.
Acts 15. 20 [and (from) things, strangled], and (from)
15. 29 from [things] strangled, and from fornic.
21. 25 from blood, and from [strangled], and from

STRAW —

1. *Straw*, מַתְבֵּן *mathben*.
Isa. 25. 10 even as straw is trodden down for the

2. *Straw*, תֶּבֶן *teben*.
Gen. 24. 25 We have both straw and provender enou.
24. 32 gave straw and provender for the camels
Exod. 5. 7 Ye shall no more give the people straw to
5. 7 let them go and gather straw for themsel.
5. 10 saith Pharaoh, I will not give you straw
5. 11 get you straw where ye can find it: yet not
5. 12 people..to gather stubble instead of straw
5. 13 Fulfil your works..as when there was str.
5. 16 There is no straw given unto thy servants
5. 18 there shall no straw be given you, yet sh.
Judg. 19. 19 there is both straw and provender for our
1 Ki. 4. 28 Barley also and straw for the horses and
Job 41. 27 He esteemeth iron as straw, (and) brass
Isa. 11. 7 and the lion shall eat straw like the ox
65. 25 and the lion shall eat straw like the bull.

STREAM —

1. *Stream, channel, tube, torrent*, אָפִיק *aphiq*.
Job 6. 15 (and) as the stream of brooks they pass aw.
Psa. 126. 4 Turn..our captivity..as the streams in the

2. *An outpouring*, אֶשֶׁד *eshed*.
Num. 21. 15 the stream of the brooks that goeth down

3. *A flood, brook*, יְאוֹר *yeor*.
Isa. 33. 21 a place of broad rivers (and) streams

4. *A stream, flowing*, יָבָל *yabal*.
Isa. 30. 25 streams of waters in the day of the great

5. *A river*, נָהָר *nahar*.
Exod. 7. 19 upon their streams, upon their rivers, and
8. 5 Stretch forth..thy rod over the streams

6. *A river*, נְהַר *nehar*.
Dan. 7. 10 A fiery stream issued and came forth fr.

7. *To flow*, נָזַל *nazal*.
Psa. 78. 16 He brought streams also out of the rock
Song 4. 15 of living waters, and streams from Leba

8. *A valley or brook*, נַחַל *nachal*.
Psa. 78. 20 the waters gushed out, and the streams
Isa. 11. 15 shall smite it in the seven streams, and
27. 12 from the channel of the river unto the st
30. 28 his breath, as an overflowing stream, sh.
30. 33 the breath of the LORD, like a stream of
34. 9 the streams thereof shall be turned into
35. 6 waters break out, and streams in the de.
57. 6 Among the smooth (stones) of the stream
66. 12 the glory of the Gentiles like a..stream
Amos 5. 24 and righteousness as a mighty stream

9. *A valley or brook*, נַחְלָה *nachlah*.
Psa. 124. 4 Then..the stream had gone over our soul

10. *A division, canal, track*, פֶּלֶג *peleg*.
Psa. 46. 4 the streams whereof shall make glad the

11. *A flowing river, torrent*, ποταμός *potamos*.
Luke 6. 48 the stream beat vehemently upon that ho.
6. 49 against which the stream did beat vehe.

STREET —

1. *Outside, without, street*, חוּץ *chuts*.
Josh. 2. 19 whosoever shall go out..into the street
2 Sa. 1. 20 publish (it) not in the streets of Askelon
22. 43 did stamp them as the mire of the street
1 Ki. 20. 34 thou shalt make streets for thee in Dam.
Job 31. 32 The stranger did not lodge in the street
Psa. 18. 42 did cast them out as the dirt in the stre.
144. 13 thousands and ten thousands in our streets
Isa. 5. 25 their carcases (were) torn in..the streets
10. 6 tread them..like the mire of the streets
15. 3 In their streets they shall gird themselves
24. 11 (There is) a crying for wine in the streets
42. 2 cause his voice to be heard in the street
51. 20 they lie at the head of all the streets, as
51. 23 thou hast laid thy body..as the street, to
Jer. 5. 1 Run ye to and fro through the streets of
7. 17 cities of Judah, and in the streets of Jer.
7. 34 from the streets of Jerusalem, the voice
11. 6 cities of Judah, and in the streets of Jer.
11. 13 (according to) the number of the streets of
14. 16 shall be cast out in the streets of Jerusa.
33. 10 the streets of Jerusalem, (that are) desol.
37. 21 a piece of bread out of the bakers' street
44. 6, 17, 21 and in the streets of Jerusalem
44. 9 in the land of Judah, and in the streets
51. 4 (that are) thrust through in her streets
Lam 2. 19 faint for hunger in the top of every street
2. 21 the old lie on the ground in the streets
4. 1 are poured out in the top of every street
4. 5 They..are desolate in the streets: (they
4. 8 they are not known in the streets: their
4. 14 have wandered (as) blind (men) in the st.
Eze. 7. 19 They shall cast their silver in the streets
11. 6 ye have filled the streets thereof with the
26. 11 shall he tread down all thy streets: he sh.
28. 23 For I will send..blood into her streets
Mic. 7. 10 trodden down as the mire of the streets
Nah. 2. 4 The chariots shall rage in the streets, th.
3. 10 were dashed..at the top of all the streets
Zeph. 3. 6 I made their streets waste, that none pa.
Zech. 9. 3 and fine gold as the mire of the streets
10. 5 tread down..in the mire of the streets in

2. *Face of the outside*, פְּנֵי חוּץ *pene chuts*.
Job 18. 17 and he shall have no name in the street

3. *A broad, wide place*, רְחוֹב *rechob*.
Gen. 19. 2 but we will abide in the street all night
Deut 13. 16 into the midst of the street thereof, and

Judg 19. 15 he sat him down in a street of the city
19. 17 he saw a wayfaring man in the street of
19. 20 old man said..lodge not in the street
2 Sa. 21. 12 which had stolen them from the street of
2 Ch. 29. 4 and gathered them..into the east street
32. 6 gathered them..in the street of the gate
Ezra 10. 9 the people sat in the street of the house
Neh. 8. 1 into the street that (was) before the wat.
8. 3 he read therein before the street that (was)
8. 16 in the courts..and in the street of the wa.
8. 16 and in the street of the gate of Ephraim
Esth. 4. 6 went forth to Mordecai unto the street of
6. 9, 11 on horseback through the street of the
Job 29. 7 (when) I prepared my seat in the street
Psa. 55. 11 deceit and guile depart not from her str.
144. 14 that (there be) no complaining in our str.
Prov. 1. 20 she uttereth her voice in the streets
5. 16 dispersed abroad, (and) rivers..in the st.
7. 12 Now (is she) without, now in the streets
22. 13 lion without, I shall be slain in the stree.
26. 13 a lion in the way; a lion (is) in the streets
Isa. 15. 3 in their streets, every one shall howl
59. 14 truth is fallen in the street, and equity
Jer. 9. 21 to cut off..the young men from the streets
48. 38 (There shall be) lamentation..in the str.
49. 26 her young men shall fall in her streets, and
50. 30 shall her young men fall in the streets, and
Lam. 2. 11 the sucklings swoon in the streets of the
2. 12 swooned as the wounded in the streets of
4. 18 we cannot go in our streets: our end is
Eze. 16. 24 hast made thee an high place in every st.
16. 31 and makest thine high place in every str.
Dan. 9. 25 the street shall be built again, and the
Amos 5. 16 Wailing (shall be) in all streets; and they
Zech. 8. 4 old women dwell in the streets of Jerusa.
8. 5 And the streets of the city shall be full of
8. 5 and girls playing in the streets thereof

4. *Street, place for walking in,* שׁוּק *shuq.*
Prov. 7. 8 Passing through the street near her corner
Eccl. 12. 4 the doors shall be shut in the streets, wh.
12. 5 and the mourners go about the streets
Song 3. 2 go about the city in the streets, and in the

5. *A public place of concourse,* ἀγορά *agora.*
Mark 6. 56 they laid the sick in the streets, and bes.

6. *A broad, wide, open street,* πλατεῖα *plateia.*
Matt. 6. 5 pray standing..in the corners of the str.
12. 19 neither..any man hear his voice in the st.
Luke 10. 10 go your ways out into the streets of the
13. 26 begin to say..thou hast taught in our st.
14. 21 Go out quickly into the streets and lanes
Acts 5. 15 they brought forth the sick into the streets
Rev. 11. 8 their dead bodies (shall lie) in the street
21. 21 street of the city (was) pure gold, as it we.
22. 2 In the midst of the street of it, and on ei.

7. *A narrow street, alley,* ῥύμη *rhumē.*
Matt. 6. 2 do in the synagogues and in the streets
Acts 9. 11 go into the street which is called Straight
12. 10 went out, and passed on through one str.

STRENGTH —

1. *Might, mighty one,* אוּל *ul.*
Psa. 73. 4 no bands in their death; but their stren.

2. *Strength, substance,* אוֹן *on.*
Gen. 49. 3 the beginning of my strength, the excell.
Deut 21. 17 he (is) the beginning of his strength: the
Job 18. 7 The steps of his strength shall be straite.
18. 12 His strength shall be hunger bitten, and
Psa. 78. 51 the chief of (their) strength in the taber.
105. 36 He smote..the chief of all their strength
Hos. 12. 3 and by his strength he had power with G.

3. *Might, power,* אֱיָל *eyal.*
Psa. 88. 4 I am as a man (that hath) no strength

4. *Might,* אֱיָלוּת *eyaluth.*
Psa. 22. 19 O LORD: O my strength, haste thee to help

5. *Perennial, strength,* אֵיתָן, אֵתָן *ethan.*
Gen. 49. 24 his bow abode in strength, and the arms
Exod 14. 27 the sea returned to his strength when the

6. *Strength, strong one,* אַמְצָה *amtsah.*
Zech 12. 5 inhabitants of Jerusalem (shall be) my st.

7. *Part, branch,* בַּד *bad.*
Job 18. 13 shall devour the strength of his skin: (even)
18. 13 first born of death shall devour his stren.

8. *Might, mighty deed,* גְּבוּרָה *geburah.*
Judg. 8. 21 Rise..for as the man (is, so is) his stren.
2 Ki. 18. 20 (I have) counsel and strength for the war
Job 12. 13 With him (is) wisdom and strength, he
39. 19 Hast thou given the horse strength? hast
Psa. 20. 6 with the saving strength of his right hand
54. 1 Save me..and judge me by thy strength
71. 16 I will go in the strength of the Lord GOD
80. 2 stir up thy strength, and come (and) save
90. 10 if by reason of strength (they be) foursc.
147. 10 He delighteth not in the strength of the
Prov. 8. 14 Counsel (is) mine, and..I have strength
Eccl. 9. 16 Wisdom (is) better than strength: never.
10. 17 thy princes eat in due season, for streng.
Isa. 28. 6 for strength to them that turn the battle
30. 15 and in confidence shall be your strength
36. 5 I say..(I have) counsel and strength for
63. 15 where (is) thy zeal and thy strength, the

9. *Flowing, wealth, strength, old age,* דֹּבֶא *dobe.*
Deut 33. 25 and as thy days, (so shall) thy strength (be)

10. *Arm, strength,* זְרוֹעַ *zeroa.*
Psa. 71. 18 I have showed thy strength unto (this) ge.

11. *Strength,* חֶזֶק *chezeq.*
Psa. 18. 1 I will love thee, O LORD, my strength

12. *Strong, strength,* חֹזֶק *chozeq.*
Exod 13. 3 by strength of hand the LORD brought you
13. 14, 16 By strength of hand the LORD brought
Amos 6. 13 not taken to us horns by our own strength
Hag. 2. 22 I will destroy the strength of the kingd.

13. *Strength,* חָזְקָה *chozqah.*
Dan. 11. 2 by his strength through his riches he shall

14. *Force, strength, army,* חַיִל *chayil.*
1 Sa. 2. 4 they that stumbled are girded with stren.
2 Sa. 22. 40 thou hast girded me with strength to bat.
Psa. 18. 32 (It is) God that girdeth me with strength
18. 39 thou hast girded me with strength unto
33. 17 neither shall he deliver (any) by his..str.
84. 7 They go from strength to strength; (every
Prov 31. 3 Give not thy strength unto women, nor
Eccl. 10. 10 then must he put to more strength: but
Isa. 5. 22 and men of strength to mingle strong dr.
Joel. 2. 22 fig tree and the vine do yield their stren.
Hab. 3. 19 The LORD God (is) my strength, and he wi.

15. *Strength, riches,* חֹסֶן *chosen.*
Isa. 33. 6 stability of thy times, (and) strength of sa.
Jer. 20. 5 I will deliver all the strength of this city

16. *Power,* כֹּחַ *koach.*
Gen. 4. 12 shall not henceforth yield..her strength
Lev. 26. 20 your strength shall be spent in vain: for
Josh. 14. 11 as my strength (was) then, even so (is) my
Judg 16. 5 see wherein his great strength (lieth), and
16. 6, 15 wherein thy great strength (lieth)
16. 9 brake the withs..so his strength was not
16. 17 my strength will go from me, and I shall
16. 19 began to afflict him, and his strength went
1 Sa. 2. 9 for by strength shall no man prevail
28. 20 there was no strength in him; for he had
28. 22 thou mayest have strength when thou go.
1 Ki. 19. 8 went in the strength of that meat forty
2 Ki. 19. 3 and (there is) not strength to bring forth
1 Ch. 26. 8 able men for strength for the service, (w.)
2 Ch. 13. 20 Neither did Jeroboam recover strength
Neh. 4. 10 The strength of the bearers of burdens is
Job 6. 11 What (is) my strength, that I should ho.
6. 12 (Is) my strength the strength of stones?
9. 4 (He is) wise in heart, and mighty in stre.
9. 19 If (I speak) of strength, lo, (he is) strong
30. 2 whereto (might) the strength of their ha.
36. 5 Behold..(he is) mighty in strength (and)
36. 19 (no), not gold, nor all the forces of stren.
39. 11 Wilt thou trust him, because his strength
39. 21 He paweth..and rejoiceth in his strength
40. 16 his strength (is) in his loins, and his force
Psa. 22. 15 My strength is dried up like a potsherd
31. 10 my strength faileth because of mine iniq.
33. 16 mighty man is not delivered by..strength
38. 10 My heart panteth, my strength faileth me
65. 6 Which by his strength setteth fast the
71. 9 forsake me not when my strength faileth
102. 23 He weakened my strength in the way: he
103. 20 his angels, that excel in strength, that do
Prov. 14. 4 much increase (is) by the strength of the
20. 29 The glory of young men (is) their strength
24. 5 yea, a man of knowledge increaseth stren.
24. 10 faint in the day of adversity, thy strength
Isa. 10. 13 By the strength of my hand I have done
37. 3 and (there is) not strength to bring forth
40. 9 lift up thy voice with strength; lift (it) up
40. 31 they..shall renew (their) strength; they
41. 1 let the people renew (their) strength: let
44. 12 and worketh it with the strength of his ar.
44. 12 yea, he is hungry, and his strength faileth
49. 4 I have spent my strength for nought, and
63. 1 travelling in the greatness of his strength
Lam. 1. 6 they are gone without strength before the
1. 14 he hath made my strength to fall; the Lo.
Dan. 10. 8 no strength in me..I retained no strength
10. 16 O my lord..I have retained no strength
10. 17 there remained no strength in me, neither
11. 15 neither (shall there be any) strength to wi
Hos. 7. 9 Strangers have devoured his strength, and

17. *A girdle,* מֵזִיחַ, מְזַח *meziach, mezach.*
Job. 12. 21 and weakeneth the strength of the mighty
Isa. 23. 10 Pass through..(there is) no more strength

18. *Strength, stronghold,* מָעוֹז *maoz.*
2 Sa. 22. 33 God (is) my strength (and) power: and he
Neh. 8. 10 for the joy of the LORD is your strength
Psa. 27. 1 the LORD (is) the strength of my life; of wh.
28. 8 and he (is) the saving strength of his ano.
31. 4 Pull me out of the net..thou (art) my str.
37. 39 (he is) their strength in the time of trouble
43. 2 thou (art) the God of my strength: why do.
52. 7 Lo..the man (that) made not God his str.
60. 7 Ephraim also (is) the strength of mine he.
108. 8 Ephraim also (is) the strength of mine he.
Prov. 10. 29 The way of the LORD (is) strength to the
Isa. 17. 10 not been mindful of the rock of thy stren.
23. 4 the sea hath spoken, (even) the strength
23. 14 Howl, ye ships..your strength is laid wa.
25. 4 a strength to the poor, a strength to the
27. 5 let him take hold of my strength, (that) he
30. 2 to strengthen themselves in the strength
30. 3 Therefore shall the strength of Pharaoh
Eze. 24. 25 when I take from them their strength, the
30. 15 I will pour my fury upon Sin, the strength
Dan. 11. 31 they shall pollute the sanctuary of stren.
Joel 3. 16 and the strength of the children of Israel
Nah. 3. 11 thou also shalt seek strength because of

19. *Standing, strength,* נִצְבָּה *nitsbah.*
Dan. 2. 41 there shall be in it of the strength of the

20. *Pre-eminence, prominence,* נֵצַח, נֶצַח *netsach.*
1 Sa. 15. 29 the strength of Israel will not lie nor repen
Lam. 3. 18 My strength and my hope is perished fro.
Isa. 63. 6 I will bring down their strength to the ea.

21. *Strength, might, hardness,* עֹז *oz.*
Exod 15. 2 The LORD (is) my strength and song, and
15. 13 thou hast guided (them) in thy strength
Judg. 5. 21 O my soul, thou hast trodden down streng.
1 Sa. 2. 10 he shall give strength unto his king, and
1 Ch. 16. 11 Seek the LORD and his strength, seek his
16. 27 strength and gladness (are) in his place
16. 28 give unto the LORD glory and strength
2 Ch. 6. 41 arise..thou, and the ark of thy strength
Job. 12. 16 With him (is) strength and wisdom: the
26. 2 savest thou the arm (that hath) no stren.
37. 6 likewise..to the great rain of his strength
41. 22 In his neck remaineth strength, and sor.
Psa. 8. 2 hast thou ordained strength because of
21. 1 The king shall joy in thy strength, O LORD
21. 13 Be thou exalted, LORD, in thine own stre.
28. 7 The LORD (is) my strength and my shield
28. 8 LORD (is) their strength, and he (is) the sa.
29. 1 give unto the LORD glory and strength
29. 11 The LORD will give strength unto his peo.
46. 1 God (is) our refuge and strength, a very
59. 9 (Because of) his strength will I wait upon
59. 17 Unto thee, O my strength, will I sing: for
62. 7 the rock of my strength, (and) my refuge
68. 28 Thy God hath commanded thy strength
68. 34 Ascribe ye strength..his strength (is) in
68. 35 he that giveth strength and power unto
74. 13 Thou didst divide the sea by thy strength
77. 14 thou hast declared thy strength among the
78. 61 delivered his strength into captivity, and
81. 1 Sing aloud unto God our strength: make
84. 5 Blessed (is) the man whose strength (is) in
86. 16 give thy strength unto thy servant, and
89. 17 thou (art) the glory of their strength; and
93. 1 the LORD is clothed with strength, (where.
96. 6 strength and beauty (are) in his sanctuary
96. 7 give unto the LORD glory and strength
99. 4 The king's strength also loveth judgment
105. 4 Seek the LORD and his strength; seek his
110. 2 The LORD shall send the rod of thy strength
118. 14 The LORD (is) my strength and song, and
132. 8 Arise..thou, and the ark of thy strength
138. 3 strengthenedst me (with) strength in my
140. 7 God the LORD, the strength of my salvat.
Prov 21. 22 casteth down the strength of the confid.
31. 17 She girdeth her loins with strength, and
31. 25 Strength and honour (are) her clothing
Isa. 12. 2 Jehovah (is) my strength and (my) song
45. 24 In the LORD have I righteousness and st.
49. 5 and my God shall be my strength
51. 9 awake! put on strength, O arm of the Lo.
52. 1 awake! put on thy strength, O Zion; put
62. 8 hath sworn..by the arm of his strength
Jer. 16. 19 my strength, and my fortress, and my re.
51. 53 she should fortify the height of her stre.
Eze. 24. 21 the excellency of your strength, the des.
30. 18 the pomp of her strength shall cease in
33. 28 and the pomp of her strength shall cease
Amos 3. 11 he shall bring down thy strength from
Mic. 5. 4 he shall stand and feed in the strength

22. *Strength,* עִזּוּז *ezuz.*
Psa. 78. 4 the praises of the LORD, and his strength
Isa. 42. 25 the fury of his anger, and the strength of

23. *Substance,* עֶצֶם *etsem.*
Job 21. 23 One dieth in his full strength, being wh.

24. *Substance,* עָצְמָה *otsmah.*
Isa. 40. 29 (them that have) no might he increaseth s.
Nah. 3. 9 Ethiopia and Egypt (were) her strength

25. *Breadth, pride, strength,* רַהַב *rahab.*
Isa. 30. 7 concerning this, Their strength (is) to sit

26. *Breadth, pride, strength,* רֹהַב *rohab.*
Psa. 90. 10 yet (is) their strength labour and sorrow

27. *High places or things,* תּוֹעָפוֹת *toaphoth.*
Num 23. 22 he hath as it were the strength of an un.
24. 8 he hath as it were the strength of an uni.
Psa. 95. 4 the deep places of the earth; the strength

28. *Strength, might,* תֹּקֶף *toqeph.*
Dan. 11. 17 set his face to enter with the strength of

29. *Strength, might,* תְּקֹף *teqoph.*
Dan. 2. 37 a kingdom, power, and strength, and gl

30. *Sharpness, firmness,* צוּר *tsur.*
Psa. 18. 2 my God, my strength, in whom I will tr
19. 14 acceptable in thy sight, O LORD, my str
73. 26 God (is) the strength of my heart, and m
144. 1 Blessed (be) the LORD my strength, which
Isa. 26. 4 for in the LORD..(is) everlasting strength

31. *A mound, heap,* תֵּל *tel.*
Josh. 11. 13 the cities that stood still in their strength

32. *Power, ability,* δύναμις *dunamis.*
1 Co. 15. 56 sting of death (is) sin; and the strength
2 Co. 1. 8 were pressed out of measure, above stre.
12. 9 for my strength is made perfect in weak.
Heb. 11. 11 Sara herself received strength to conce.
Rev. 1. 16 countenance (was) as the sun..in his str.
3. 8 thou hast a little strength and hast kept
12. 10 Now is come salvation, and strength, and

33. *Privilege, authority,* ἐξουσία *exousia.*
Rev. 17. 13 shall give their power and strength unto

34. *Force, strength,* ἰσχύς *ischus.*
Mark12. 30 with all thy mind, and with all thy stre.
12. 33 with all the soul, and with all the stren.
Luke10. 27 with all thy soul, and with all thy stren.
Rev. 5. 12 riches, and wisdom, and strength, and ho.

35. *Strength, power,* κράτος *kratos.*
Luke 1. 51 He hath showed strength with his arm

STRENGTH, to be of, draw with, give, receive —
1. *Fill hand with,* כִּלֵּא יָד בְּ *[male,* 3].
2 Ki. 9. 24 Jehu drew a bow with his full strength
2. *To brighten up, encourage,* בָּלַג *balag,* 5
Psa. 39. 13 O spare me, that I may recover strength
3. *To strengthen,* חָזַק *chazaq,* 3.
1 Ch.29. 12 to make great, and to give strength unto
4. *To have force, strength,* ἰσχύω *ischuō.*
Heb. 9. 17 it is of no strength at all while the testa.
5. *To make firm or strong,* στερεόω *stereoō.*
Acts 3. 7 his feet and ancle bones received strength

STRENGTH, without —
Without strength, ἀσθενής *asthenēs.*
Rom. 5. 6 when we were yet without strength, in d.

STRENGTHEN (self), be strengthened, to —
1. *To strengthen, harden,* אָמַץ *amats,* 3.
Deut. 3. 28 and encourage him, and strengthen him
2 Ch.24. 13 set the house..in his state, and strength.
Job 4. 4 and thou hast strengthened the feeble kn.
16. 5 I would strengthen you with my mouth
Psa. 89. 21 With whom..mine arm also shall streng.
Prov 31. 17 with strength, and strengtheneth her arms
Isa. 41. 10 I will strengthen thee ; yea, I will help
44. 14 and the oak, which he strengtheneth for
Amos 2. 14 the strong shall not strengthen his force
2. *To make strong or hard,* אָמַץ *amats,* 5.
Psa. 27. 14 be of good courage, and he shall strengt.
31. 24 Be of good courage, and he shall strengt.
3. *To strengthen self,* אָמַץ *amats,* 7.
2 Ch.13. 7 and have strengthened themselves against
4. *To brighten up, encourage,* בָּלַג *balag,* 5.
Amos 5. 9 That strengtheneth the spoiled against the
5. *To make mighty, strengthen,* גָּבַר *gabar,* 3.
Zech 10. 6 I will strengthen the house of Judah, and
10. 12 I will strengthen them in the LORD; and
6. *To show self mighty,* גָּבַר *gabar,* 7.
Job 15. 25 and strengtheneth himself against the A.
7. *To be strong, strengthen, harden,* חָזַק *chazaq.*
Judg. 7. 11 afterward shall thine hands be strength.
2 Sa. 2. 7 let your hands be strengthened, and be
2 Ch.28. 20 and distressed him but strengthened him
8. *To strengthen, harden,* חָזַק *chazaq,* 3.
Judg. 3. 12 the LORD strengthened Eglon, the king
16. 28 remember me, I pray thee, and strength.
1 Sa. 23. 16 Jonathan Saul's son arose..and strength.
1 Ch.29. 12 make great, and to give strength unto all
2 Ch.11. 17 So they strengthened the kingdom of Ju.
Ezra 1. 6 all they that (were) about them strength.
6. 22 to strengthen their hands in the work of
Neh. 2. 18 So they strengthened their hands for (th.)
6. 9 Now therefore, (O God), strengthen my h.
Job 4. 3 and thou hast strengthened the weak ha.
Psa.147. 13 he hath strengthened the bars of thy ga.
Isa. 22. 21 clothe him with thy robe, and strengthen
33. 23 they could not well strengthen their mast
35. 3 Strengthen ye the weak hands, and confi.
54. 2 lengthen thy cords, and strengthen thy
Jer. 23. 14 they strengthen also the hands of evil do.
Eze. 13. 22 strengthened the hands of the wicked, th.
30. 24 I will strengthen the arms of the king of
34. 4 The diseased have ye not strengthened
34. 16 and will strengthen that which was sick
Dan. 10. 18 the appearance of a man, and he streng.
10. 19 Let my lord speak ; for thou hast streng.
Hos. 7. 15 I have bound (and) strengthened their ar.
9. *To strengthen, do mightily,* חָזַק *chazaq,* 5.
2 Ch.26. 8 for he strengthened (himself) exceedingly
Eze. 16 49 neither did she strengthen the hand of the
30. 25 I will strengthen the arms of the king of
Dan. 11. 6 and he that strengthened her in (these) ti.
10. *To strengthen self,* חָזַק *chazaq,* 7.
Gen. 48. 2 Israel strengthened himself, and sat upon
1 Ki.20. 22 Go, strengthen thyself, and mark, and see
1 Ch.11. 10 who strengthened themselves with him in
2 Ch. 1. 1 Solomon the son of David was strengthe.
12. 13 So king Rehoboam strengthened himself
17. 1 reigned in his stead, and strengthened hi.
21. 4 strengthened himself, and slew all his br.
23. 1 Jehoiada strengthened himself, and took
25. 11 Amaziah strengthened himself, and led fo.
32. 5 Also he strengthened himself, and built
Ezra 7. 28 strengthened as the hand of the LORD my
Eze. 7. 13 strengthen himself in the iniquity of his
Dan. 10. 19 I was strengthened, and said, Let my lord
11. *Strength, hardness,* חָזְקָה *chozqah.*
2 Ch.12. 1 when Rehoboam..had strengthened him.
12. *A strength, stronghold,* מָעוֹז *maoz.*
Dan. 11. 1 stood to confirm and to strengthen him
13. *To support, refresh,* סָעַד *saad.*
Psa. 20. 2 Send thee help..and strengthen thee out
41. 3 LORD will strengthen him upon the bed
104. 15 and bread (which) strengtheneth man's he.
14. *To be or become or make strong,* עָזַז *azaz.*
Psa. 52. 7 (and) strengthened himself in his wicked.
68. 28 strengthen, O God, that which thou hast
Prov. 8. 28 he strengthened the fountains of the deep
Eccl. 7. 19 Wisdom strengtheneth the wise more than
Isa. 30. 2 to strengthen themselves in the strength
Dan. 11. 12 but he shall not be strengthened (by it)
15. *To raise up,* קוּם *qum,* 3.
Psa.119. 28 strengthen thou me according unto thy
16. *To puff up, strengthen,* רָהַב *rahab,* 5.
Psa.138. 3 strengthenedst me (with) strength in my
17. *To make powerful,* δυναμόω *dunamoō.*
Col. 1. 11 Strengthened with all might, according to
18. *To make powerful inwardly,* ἐνδυναμόω *endum.*
Phil. 4. 13 through Christ which strengtheneth me
2 Ti 4. 17 the Lord stood with me and strengthened
19. *To make strong inwardly,* ἐνισχύω *enischuō.*
Luke22. 43 [there appeared an angel .strengthening]
Acts 9. 19 when he had received meat, he was stren.
20. *To make firm besides,* ἐπιστηρίζω *epistērizō.*
Acts 18. 23 went over all..country..[strengthening]
21. *To strengthen, make strong,* κραταιόω *krataioō.*
Eph. 3. 16 to be strengthened with might by his
22. *To strengthen, make strong,* σθενόω *sthenoō.*
1 Pe. 5. 10 make you perfect, stablish, strengthen, se.
23. *To make firm, fix firmly,* στηρίζω *stērizō.*
Luke22. 32 when thou art converted, strengthen thy
Rev. 3. 2 Be watchful, and strengthen the things

STRETCH (beyond, forth, out), to —
1. *To draw or stretch out,* מָשַׁךְ *mashak.*
Hos. 7. 5 he stretched out his hand with scorners
2. *To stretch out, incline,* נָטָה *natah.*
Exod. 7. 5 when I stretch forth mine hand upon E.
7. 19 stretch out thine hand upon the waters
8. 5 Stretch forth thine hand with thy rod over
8. 6 stretched out his hand over the waters of
8. 16 Stretch out thy rod, and smite the dust
8. 17 for Aaron stretched out his hand with his
9. 22 Stretch forth thine hand toward heaven
9. 23 Moses stretched forth his rod toward he.
10. 12 Stretch out thine hand over the land of E.
10. 13 Moses stretched forth his rod over the la.
10. 21 Stretch out thine hand toward heaven, and
10. 22 Moses stretched forth his hand toward he.
14. 16, 26 stretch out thine hand over the sea
14. 21 Moses stretched out his hand over the sea
14. 27 Moses stretched forth his hand over the
15. 12 Thou stretchedst out thy right hand, the
Josh. 8. 18 Stretch out the spear..Joshua stretched o.
8. 19 ran as soon as he had stretched out his
8. 26 wherewith he stretched out the spear, un.
2 Ki. 21. 13 stretch over Jerusalem the line of Sama.
Job 15. 25 For he stretcheth out his hand against God
26. 7 He stretcheth out the north over the em.
38. 5 or who hath stretched the line upon it?
Psa.104. 2 who stretchest out the heavens like a cu.
Prov. 1. 24 I have stretched out my hand, and no man
Isa. 5. 25 and he hath stretched forth his hand
23. 11 He stretched out his hand over the sea, he
34. 11 shall stretch out upon it the line of conf.
40. 22 that stretcheth out the heavens as a cur.
42. 5 stretched them out; he that spread forth
44. 13 carpenter stretcheth out (his) rule, he ma.
44. 24 that stretcheth forth the heavens alone
45. 12 have stretched out the heavens, and all
51. 13 that hath stretched forth the heavens, and
Jer. 10. 12 hath stretched out the heavens by his di.
10. 20 none to stretch forth my tent any more
51. 15 stretched out the heaven by his underst.
51. 25 I will stretch out mine hand upon thee
Lam. 2. 8 he hath stretched out a line, he hath not
Eze. 6. 14 So will I stretch out my hand upon them
14. 9 will stretch out my hand upon him, and
14. 13 then will I stretch out mine hand upon it
16. 27 therefore I have stretched out my hand over
25. 7 therefore I will stretch out my hand upon
25. 13 will also stretch out mine hand upon Edom
25. 16 will stretch out mine hand upon the Phil.
30. 25 shall stretch it out upon the land of Egypt
35. 3 I will stretch out mine hand against thee
Zeph. 1. 4 will also stretch out mine hand upon Ju.
2. 13 will stretch out his hand against the nor.
Zech.12. 1 which stretcheth forth the heavens, and
3. *To (cause to) stretch out, incline,* נָטָה *natah,* 5.
Isa. 31. 3 When the LORD shall stretch out his hand
54. 2 let them stretch forth the curtains of th.
Jer. 6. 12 for I will stretch out my hand upon the
15. 6 therefore will I stretch out my hand aga.
4. *To spread out or forth,* פָּרַשׂ *paras.*
Exod25. 20 cherubims shall stretch forth (their) wings
1 Ki. 6. 27 stretched forth the wings of the cherubim
Job 11. 13 and stretch out thine hands toward him
39. 26 Doth the hawk..stretch her wings toward
Psa. 44. 20 stretched out our hands to a strange god
Prov31. 20 She stretcheth out her hand to the poor
5. *To spread out or forth,* פָּרַשׂ *paras,* 3.
Psa.143. 6 I stretch forth my hands unto thee: my
6. *To spread out or over,* רָקַע *raqa.*
Psa.136. 6 To him that stretched out the earth above
7. *To spread out,* שָׁטַח *shatach,* 3.
Psa. 88. 9 I have stretched out my hands unto thee
8. *To send,* שָׁלַח *shalach.*
Gen. 22. 10 Abraham stretched forth his hand, and
48. 14 Israel stretched out his right hand, and
Exod. 3. 20 I will stretch out my hand, and smite Eg.
9. 15 For now I will stretch out my hand, that
1 Sa. 24. 6 to stretch forth mine hand against him
26. 9 Destroy him not: for who can stretch forth
26. 11 LORD forbid that I should stretch forth
26. 23 would not stretch forth mine hand against
2 Sa. 1. 14 How wast thou not afraid to stretch forth
24. 16 when the angel stretched out his hand up.
Job 30. 24 Howbeit he will not stretch out (his) hand
Psa. 138. 7 thou shalt stretch forth thine hand again.
Eze. 10. 7 cherub stretched forth his hand from be.
Dan. 11. 42 He shall stretch forth his hand also upon
9. *To stretch out, expand,* ἐκπετάννυμι *ekpetannumi.*
Rom.10. 21 All day long I have stretched forth my ha.
10. *To extend, stretch out,* ἐκτείνω *ekteinō.*
Matt.12. 13 Stretch forth thine hand..stretched (it) fo.
12. 49 stretched forth his hand toward his disci.
14. 31 immediately Jesus stretched forth (his)
26. 51 one of them..stretched out (his) hand, and
Mark 3. 5 Stretch forth..And he stretched (it) out
Luke 6. 10 Stretch forth thy hand. And he did so
22. 53 ye stretched forth no hands against me
John 21. 18 thou shalt stretch forth thy hands, and
Acts 4. 30 By stretching forth thine hand to heal
26. 1 Paul stretched forth the hand, and answ.
11. *To cast over or upon,* ἐπιβάλλω *epiballō.*
Acts 12. 1 stretched forth (his) hands to vex certain
12. *To stretch over much,* ὑπερεκτείνω *huperekteinō.*
2 Co. 10. 14 For we stretch not ourselves beyond (our

STRETCH self, to —
1. *To stretch out, bow, prostrate,* גָּהַר *gahar.*
2 Ki. 4. 34 stretched himself upon the child, and the
4. 35 went up, and stretched himself upon him
2. *To measure or stretch self,* מָדַד *madad,* 7a.
1 Ki. 17. 21 stretched himself upon the child three ti.
3. *To spread out,* סָרַח *sarach.*
Amos 6. 4 stretch themselves upon their couches, and
6. 7 banquet of them that stretched themselve.
4. *To stretch self out,* שָׂרַע *sara,* 7.
Isa. 28. 20 shorter than that (a man) can stretch hims.

STRETCH out soon, to —
To cause to run, רוּץ *ruts,* 5.
Psa. 68. 31 Ethiopia shall soon stretch out her hands

STRETCHED out or forth, to be —
1. *To stretch out, incline,* נָטָה *natah.*
Exod. 6. 6 will redeem you with a stretched out arm
Deut. 4. 34 mighty hand, and by a stretched out arm
5. 15 a mighty hand and by a stretched out arm
7. 19 the mighty hand, and the stretched out
9. 29 mighty power and by thy stretched out
11. 2 his mighty hand, and his stretched out
1 Ki. 8. 42 strong hand, and of thy stretched out arm
2 Ki. 17. 36 with great power, and a stretched out arm
1 Ch.21. 16 drawn sword in his hand stretched out
2 Ch. 6. 32 thy mighty hand, and thy stretched out
Psa.136. 12 strong hand, and with a stretched out arm
Isa. 3. 16 walk with stretched forth necks, and wan.
5. 25 turned away, but his hand (is) stretched o.
9. 12, 17, 21 but his hand (is) stretched out still
10. 4 turned away, but his hand (is) stretched o.
14. 26 hand that is stretched out upon all the
14. 27 his hand (is) stretched out, and who shall
Jer. 32. 17 by thy great power, and stretched out arm
32. 21 with a stretched out arm, and with great
Eze. 1. 22 terrible crystal, stretched forth over their
20. 33, 34 with a stretched out arm, and with fu.
2. *To be stretched out, inclined,* נָטָה *natah,* 2.
Jer. 6. 4 shadows of the evening are stretched out
Zech. 1. 16 line shall be stretched forth upon Jerusa.
3. *To be spread out, left,* נָטַשׁ *natash,* 2.
Isa. 16. 8 branches are stretched out, they are gone
4. *To separate, part,* פָּרַד *parad.*
Eze. 1. 11 their wings (were) stretched upward; two

STRETCHING out —
Stretching out, מֻטּוֹת *muttoth.*
Isa. 8. 8 stretching out of his wings shall fill the

STREW, strow, to —
1. *To scatter, winnow, spread,* זָרָה *zarah.*
Exod32. 20 strawed (it) upon the water, and made the
2. *To sprinkle,* זָרַק *zaraq.*
2 Ch.34. 4 strowed (it) upon the graves of them that
3. *To scatter throughout,* διασκορπίζω *diaskorpizō.*
Matt25. 24 gathering where thou hast not strawed
25. 26 and gather where I have not strawed
4. *To strew,* στρώννυμι *strōnnumi.*
Matt21. 8 cut down branches..and strawed (them)
Mark11. 8 [branches off the trees, and strawed (th.)]

STRICKEN (through, to be) —
1. *To be pierced through,* דָּקַר *daqar,* 4.
Lam. 4. 9 stricken through for (want of) the fruits
2. *To touch, come upon, strike, plague,* נָגַע *naga.*
Isa. 53. 4 yet we did esteem him stricken, smitten
3. *Stroke, plague,* נֶגַע *nega.*
Isa. 53. 8 for the transgression..was he stricken

4. *To smite,* נָכָא *naka.*
Isa. 16. 7 every one shall howl..(they are) stricken
5. *To be smitten,* נָכָה *nakah,* 6.
Isa. 1. 5 Why should ye be stricken any more? ye

STRICKEN, to be (well) —
1. *To come or go in,* בּוֹא *bo.*
Gen. 18. 11 old (and) well stricken in age; (and) it ce.
24. 1 Abraham was old, (and) well stricken in
Josh 13. 1 Now Joshua was old (and) stricken in ye.
13. 1 Thou art old (and) stricken in years, and
23. 1 that Joshua waxed old (and) stricken in
23. 2 said unto them, I am old (and) stricken in
1 Ki. 1. 1 Now king David was old (and) stricken in
2. *To go forward,* προβαίνω *probainō.*
Luke 1. 7 they both were (now) well stricken in years
1. 18 an old man, and my wife well stricken in

STRIFE —
1. *Strife, plea, contention,* דִּין *din.*
Prov 22. 10 contention shall go out; yea, strife and
2. *Strife, contention,* מָדוֹן *madon.*
Psa. 80. 6 Thou makest us a strife unto our neighb.
Prov 15. 18 wrathful man stirreth up strife: but (he
16. 28 froward man soweth strife; and a whisp.
17. 14 beginning of strife (is as) when one letteth
26. 20 where (there is) no tale bearer, the strife
28. 25 He that is of a proud heart stirreth up st.
29. 22 An angry man stirreth up strife, and a fu.
3. *Strifes, contentions,* מְדָנִים *medanim.*
Prov 10. 12 Hatred stirreth up strifes: but love cove.
4. *A wringing out, debate,* מַצָּה *matstsah.*
Prov 17. 19 He loveth transgression that loveth strife
5. *Strife, contention,* מְרִיבָה *meribah.*
Gen. 13. 8 Let there be no strife, I pray thee, betw.
Num 27. 14 in the strife of the congregation, to sanc.
Psa. 106. 32 angered (him) also at the waters of strife
Eze. 47. 19 from Tamar (even) to the waters of strife
48. 28 even from Tamar (unto) the waters of st.
6. *Strife, pleading, cause,* רִיב *rib.*
Gen. 13. 7 there was a strife between the herdmen of
Deut. 1. 12 How can I myself alone bear..your strife
Judg 12. 2 I and my people were at great strife with
Psa. 31. 20 keep them secretly..from the strife of to.
55. 9 for I have seen violence and strife in the
Prov 15. 18 but (he that is) slow to anger appeaseth st.
17. 1 than an house full of sacrifices (with) st.
20. 3 an honour for a man to cease from strife
26. 17 meddleth with strife (belonging) not to
26. 21 so (is) a contentious man to kindle strife
30. 33 so the forcing of wrath bringeth forth st.
Isa. 58. 4 ye fast for strife and debate, and to smite
Jer. 15. 10 thou hast borne me a man of strife and a
Hab. 1. 3 there are (that) raise up strife and conte.
7. *Contradiction, controversy,* ἀντιλογία *antilogia.*
Heb. 6. 16 confirmation (is) to them an end of all st.
8. *Contention, strife, quarrel,* ἐριθεία *eritheia.*
2 Co. 12. 20 envyings, wraths, strifes, backbitings, wh.
Gal. 5. 20 emulations, wrath, strife, seditions, here.
Phil. 2. 3 (Let) nothing (be done) through strife or
Jas. 3. 14 But if ye have bitter envying and strife
3. 16 For where envying and strife (is), there
9. *Contention, strife, quarrel,* ἔρις *eris.*
Rom 13. 13 Let us walk honestly..not in strife and
1 Co. 3. 3 (there is) among you envying, and strife
Phil. 1. 15 preach Christ even of envy and strife, and
1 Ti. 6. 4 whereof cometh envy, strife, railings, ev.
10. *Fight, contention, battle,* μάχη *machē.*
2 Ti. 2. 23 avoid, knowing that they do gender stri.
11. *Love of contention or dispute,* φιλονεικία *philo.*
Luke 22. 24 there was also a strife among them, wh.

STRIFE (of words), at —
1. *To be at strife, judged,* דִּין *din,* 2.
2 Sa. 19. 9 all the people were at strife throughout
2. *A fighting about words,* λογομαχία *logomachia.*
1 Ti. 6. 4 doting about questions and strifes of wo

STRIKE (again, through), to —
1. *To pass on, through, or away,* חָלַף *chalaph.*
Judg. 5. 26 when she had pierced and stricken thro.
Job 20. 24 the bow of steel shall strike him through
2. *To smite, dash,* מָחַץ *machats.*
Psa. 110. 5 strike through kings in the day of his wr.
3. *To touch, come upon, strike, plague,* נָגַע *naga,* 5.
Exod 12. 22 strike the lintel and the two side posts
4. *To smite, plague,* נָגַף *nagaph.*
2 Sa. 12. 15 LORD struck the child that Uriah's wife
2 Ch. 13. 20 and the LORD struck him, and he died
5. *To wave, shake out,* נוּף *nuph,* 5.
2 Ki. 5. 11 strike his hand over the place, and reco.
6. *To smite,* נָכָה *nakah,* 5.
1 Sa. 2. 14 struck (it) into the pan, or kettle, or cal.
Prov 17. 26 to punish the just (is) not good, (nor) to s.
23. 35 They have stricken me..I was not sick; they
Jer. 5. 3 thou hast stricken them, but they have
7. *To pierce, define, mark out,* נָקַב *naqab.*
Hab. 3. 14 Thou didst strike through with his staves
8. *To give, put,* נָתַן *nathan.*
Exod 12. 7 strike (it) on the two side posts and on the
9. *To strike,* סָפַק *saphaq.*
Job 34. 26 striketh them as wicked men in the open
10. *To split, till, break forth,* פָּלַח *palach,* 3.
Prov. 7. 23 Till a dart strike through his liver; as a
11. *To change, repeat, do it again,* שָׁנָה *shanah.*
2 Sa. 20. 10 struck him not again; and he died. So J.
12. *To blow, strike, clap, thrust,* תָּקַע *taqa.*
Prov. 6. 1 thou hast stricken thy hand with a stran.
17. 18 man void of understanding striketh han.
22. 26 Be not thou (one) of them that strike ha.
13. *To be blown, struck,* תָּקַע *taqa,* 2.
Job 17. 3 who (is) he (that) will strike hands with
14. *To cast, throw,* βάλλω *ballō.*
Mark 14. 65 servants [did strike] him with the palms
15. *To give,* δίδωμι *didōmi.*
John 18. 22 struck Jesus with the palm of his hand
16. *To strike, smite, beat, sting,* παίω *paiō.*
Rev. 9. 5 torment of a scorpion, when he striketh
17. *To strike, smite,* πατάσσω *patassō.*
Matt 26. 51 struck a servant of the high priest, and
18. *To strike, smite,* τύπτω *tuptō.*
Luke 22. 64 [they struck him on the face, and asked]
19. *To loose, let go,* χαλάω *chalaō.*
Acts 27. 17 fearing lest they should fall..strake sail

STRIKER —
A striker, reviler, πλήκτης *plēktēs.*
1 Ti. 3. 3 Not given to wine, no striker, not greedy
Titus 1. 7 not given to wine, no striker, not given to

STRING, (ten stringed instrument) —
1. *A cord, string,* יֶתֶר *yether.*
Psa. 11. 2 they make ready their arrow upon the st.
2. *A cord, string,* מֵיתָר *methar.*
Psa. 21. 12 make ready (thine arrows) upon thy stri.
3. *Minnim, strings,* מִנִּים *minnim.*
Psa. 150. 4 praise him with stringed instruments and
4. *Ten stringed instrument,* עָשׂוֹר *asor.*
Psa. 33. 2 psaltery (and) an instrument of ten strings
92. 3 Upon an instrument of ten strings, and
144. 9 upon..an instrument of ten strings will
5. *Bond, chain, ligament,* δεσμός *desmos.*
Mark. 7. 35 string of his tongue was loosed, and he sp.

STRIP (off selves), to —
1. *To snatch off,* נָצַל *natsal,* 3.
2 Ch. 20. 25 jewels, which they stripped off for them.
2. *To snatch off from self,* נָצַל *natsal,* 7.
Exod 33. 6 stripped themselves of their ornaments by
3. *To strip off,* פָּשַׁט *pashat.*
1 Sa. 19. 24 stripped off his clothes also, and prophe.
Isa. 32. 11 strip you, and make you bare, and gird (s.)
4. *To strip off,* פָּשַׁט *pashat,* 3.
1 Sa. 31. 8 when the Philistines came to strip the sl.
1 Ch. 10. 8 when the Philistines came to strip the sl.
5. *To strip off,* פָּשַׁט *pashat,* 5.
Gen. 37. 23 that they stripped Joseph out of his coat
Num 20. 26 strip Aaron of his garments, and put them
20. 28 Moses stripped Aaron of his garments, and
1 Sa. 31. 9 stripped off his armour, and sent into the
1 Ch. 10. 9 when they had stripped him, they took his
Job 19. 9 He hath stripped me of my glory, and ta
22. 6 and stripped the naked of their clothing
Eze. 16. 39 they shall strip thee also of thy clothes
23. 26 They shall also strip thee out of thy clot
Hos. 2. 3 Lest I strip her naked, and set her as in
6. *To strip self,* פָּשַׁט *pashat,* 7.
1 Sa. 18. 4 Jonathan stripped himself of the robe that
7. *To put out, strip off,* ἐκδύω *ekduō.*
Matt 27. 28 [stripped] him, and put on him a scarlet

STRIP off raiment, to —
To put out, strip off, ἐκδύω *ekduō.*
Luke 10. 30 thieves, which stripped him of his raiment

STRIPE, stripes, to give —
1. *A bruise, bandage, scar,* חַבּוּרָה, חֲבוּרָה *chaburah.*
Exod 21. 25 burning, wound for wound, stripe for str
Isa. 53. 5 wounded..and with his stripes we are he.
2. *Stripes, beatings,* מַהֲלֻמּוֹת *mahalummoth.*
Prov 19. 29 prepared for scorners, and stripes for the
3. *A smiting, blow, stroke,* מַכָּה *makkah.*
Deut 25. 3 beat him above these with many stripes
Prov. 20. 30 so (do) stripes the inward parts of the be.
4. *A stroke, plague,* נֶגַע *nega.*
2 Sa. 7. 14 with the stripes of the children of men
Psa. 89. 32 will I visit..their iniquity with stripes
5. *To smite, strike,* נָכָה *nakah,* 5.
Deut 25. 3 Forty stripes he may give him, (and) not
Prov 17. 10 more..than a hundred stripes into a fool
6. *A wound, scar,* μώλωψ *mōlōps.*
1 Pe 2. 24 righteousness: by whose stripes ye were
7. *A stroke, stripe, plague,* πληγή *plēgē.*
Luke 12. 48 did commit things worthy of stripes, shall
Acts 16. 23 when they had laid many stripes upon th.
16. 33 washed (their) stripes; and was baptized
2 Co. 6. 5 In stripes, in imprisonments, in tumults
11. 23 in stripes above measure, in prisons more

STRIPLING —
A youth, עֶלֶם *elem.*
1 Sa. 17. 56 Enquire thou whose son the stripling (is)!

STRIPPED —
Stripped, barefoot, שׁוֹלָל *sholal* [V.L. שׁילל].
Mic. 1. 8 I will go stripped and naked: I will make

STRIVE (against, together for, with), to —
1. *To come forth with force,* גּוּחַ, גִּיחַ *guach, giach,* 5.
Dan. 7. 2 four winds of the heaven strove upon the
2. *To stir up self, strive,* גָּרָה *garah,* 7.
Jer. 50. 24 because thou hast striven against the Lo.
3. *To strive,* דּוּן *dun.*
Gen. 6. 3 My spirit shall not always strive with man
4. *One striving, contending,* יָרִיב *yarib.*
Psa. 35. 1 Plead..LORD, with them that strive with
5. *To strive,* נָצָה *natsah,* 2.
Exod 2. 13 two men of the Hebrews, strove together
21. 22 If men strive, and hurt a woman with ch.
Lev. 24. 10 this son..and a man of Israel strove tog.
Deut 25. 11 When men strive together one with ano.
2 Sa. 14. 6 they two strove together in the field, and
6. *To strive,* נָצָה *natsah,* 5.
Num 26. 9 strove against Moses, when they strove a.
Psa. 60. title. when he strove with Aram-naharaim
7. *To strive, oppress,* עָשַׂק *asaq,* 7.
Gen. 26. 20 because they strove with him
8. *To strive, plead,* רִיב *rib.*
Gen. 26. 20 herdmen of Gerar did strive with Isaac's
26. 21 strove for that also: and he called the na.
26. 22 for that they strove not: and he called the
Exod 21 18 if men strive together, and one smite ano.
Num 20. 13 because the children of Israel strove with
Deut 33. 8 whom thou didst strive at the waters of
Judg 11. 25 did he ever strive against Israel, or did
Job 33. 13 Why dost thou strive against him? for he
Prov. 3. 30 Strive not with a man without cause, if
25. 8 Go not forth hastily to strive, lest (thou
Isa. 41. 11 and they that strive with thee shall perish
45. 9 Woe unto him that striveth with his ma.
Hos. 4. 4 let no man strive, nor reprove another
9. *To strive, plead,* רִיב *rib,* 5.
Hos. 4. 4 people (are) as they that strive with the
10. *To agonize, contend,* ἀγωνίζομαι *agōnizomai.*
Luke 13. 24 Strive to enter in at the straight gate, for
1 Co. 9. 25 every man that striveth for the mastery
Col. 1. 29 striving according to his working, which
11. *To strive, contend, be a champion,* ἀθλέω *athleō.*
2 Tim 2. 5 if a man also strive..not..except he stri.
12. *Contend against,* ἀνταγωνίζομαι *antagōnizomai.*
Heb. 12. 4 Ye have not yet resisted blood, striving
13. *To fight thoroughly,* διαμάχομαι *diamachomai.*
Acts 23. 9 strove, saying, We find no evil in this man
14. *To contend, dispute,* ἐρίζω *erizō.*
Matt 12. 19 He shall not strive, nor cry; neither shall
15. *To fight,* μάχομαι *machomai.*
John 6. 52 Jews therefore strove among themselves
Acts 7. 26 showed himself unto them as they strove
2 Ti. 2. 24 servant of the Lord must not strive; but
16. *To agonize together,* συναγωνίζομαι *sunagōnizom.*
Rom 15. 30 strive together with me in (your) prayers
17. *To strive together,* συναθλέω *sunathleō.*
Phil. 1. 27 with one mind striving together for the
18. *To esteem as an honour,* φιλοτιμέομαι *philotim.*
Rom 15. 20 so have I strived to preach the gospel, not

STRIVINGS —
1. *Strife, pleading,* רִיב *rib.*
2 Sa. 22. 44 hast delivered me from the strivings of
Psa. 18. 43 Thou hast delivered me from the strivings
2. *A fight, fighting,* μάχη *machē.*
Titus 3. 9 But avoid..strivings about the law, for

STROKE, strokes —
1. *Hand,* יָד *yad.*
Job 23. 2 my stroke is heavier than my groaning
2. *Stroke, plague,* מַגֵּפָה *maggephah.*
Eze. 24. 16 take away..the desire of thine eyes w.a.s.
3. *Stripes, beatings,* מַהֲלֻמּוֹת *mahalummoth.*
Prov. 18. 6 contention, and his mouth calleth for st.
4. *A smiting,* מַחַץ *machats.*
Isa. 30. 26 and healeth the stroke of their wound
5. *A blow, stroke,* מַכָּה *makkah.*
Esth. 9. 5 smote all their enemies with the stroke
Isa. 14. 6 smote the people..with a continual stroke
6. *A stroke, plague,* נֶגַע *nega.*
Deut 17. 8 between stroke and stroke, (being) matt.
21. 5 by their word shall..every stroke be (tr.)
Psa. 39. 10 Remove thy stroke away from me: I am
7. *A sufficiency,* שֶׂפֶק *sepheq.*
Job 36. 18 lest he take thee away with (his) stroke

STRONG, (stronger one, man, most) —
1. *A mighty one,* אַבִּיר *abbir.*
Psa 22. 12 strong (bulls) of Bashan have beset me ro.
Jer. 8. 16 sound of the neighing of his strong ones
47. 3 stamping of the hoofs of his strong (hor.)

2. *Perennial, enduring,* אֵיתָן, אֵתָן *ethan.*
Num 24. 21 Strong is thy dwelling place, and thou
Job 33. 19 and the multitude of his bones with str.
Jer. 49. 19 come up..against the habitation of the st.
50. 44 come up..unto the habitation of the str.
Mic. 6. 2 Hear..ye strong foundations of the earth

3. *A mighty one, a god,* אֵל *el.*
Eze. 32. 21 The strong among the mighty shall speak

4. *Strong one,* אַמִּיץ *ammits.*
2 Sa. 15. 12 conspiracy was strong; for the people in.
Job 9. 19 If (I speak) of strength, lo, (he is) strong
Isa. 28. 2 the Lord hath a mighty and strong one
40. 26 for that (he is) strong in power; not one

5. *To cut off, fence,* בָּצַר *batsar.*
Neh. 9. 25 they took strong cities, and a fat land, and

6. *Mighty,* גִּבּוֹר *gibbor.*
1 Sa. 14. 52 when Saul saw any strong man, or any va.
2 Ki. 24. 16 all..strong..apt for war, even them the
Psa. 19. 5 (and) rejoiceth as a strong man to run a
Prov 30. 30 A lion..strongest among beasts, and tur.
Eccl. 9. 11 nor the battle to the strong, neither yet
Joel 3. 10 into spears: let the weak say, I (am) strong

7. *A bone,* גֶּרֶם *gerem.*
Gen. 49. 14 Issachar (is) a strong ass couching down

8. *Strong, hard,* חָזָק *chazaq.*
Exod. 6. 1 for with a strong hand shall he let them
6. 1 with a strong hand shall he drive them
10. 19 turned a mighty strong west wind, which
13. 9 for with a strong hand hath the LORD br.
Num 13. 18 whether they (be) strong or weak, few or
13. 31 We be not able..for they (are) stronger
20. 20 with much people, and with a strong ha.
Josh 14. 11 As yet I (am as) strong this day as (I was)
17. 18 drive out the Canaanites..though they (be)
Judg 18. 26 when Micah saw that they (were) too st.
1 Ki. 8. 42 For they shall hear..of thy strong hand
19. 11 strong wind rent the mountains, and br.
Neh. 1. 10 by thy great power, and by thy strong ha.
Job 37. 18 sky, (which is) strong, (and) as a molten
Psa. 35. 10 deliverest..from him that is too strong
136. 12 With a strong hand, and with a stretched
Isa. 27. 1 with his sore and great and strong sword
40. 10 Lord GOD will come with strong (hand)
Jer. 21. 5 with a strong arm, even in anger, and in
31. 11 from the hand of (him that was) stronger
32. 21 with a strong hand, and with a stretched
50. 34 Their Redeemer (is) strong; The LORD of
Eze. 3. 8 have made thy face strong against their
3. 8 thy forehead strong against their forehe.
26. 17 renowned city, which wast strong in the
30. 22 will break his arms, the strong, and that
34. 16 but I will destroy the fat and the strong
Amos 2. 14 strong shall not strengthen his force, ne.

9. *Strong, hard,* חָזֵק *chazeq.*
2 Sa. 3. 1 but David waxed stronger and stronger

10. *Strength, hardness,* חָזְקָה *chozqah.*
Isa. 8. 11 LORD spake thus to me with a strong ha.

11. *Force, might,* חַיִל *chayil.*
2 Ki. 2. 16 there be with thy servants fifty strong men
1 Ch. 26. 7 whose brethren (were) strong men, Elihu
26. 9 Meshelemiah had sons and brethren, str.
Eccl. 12. 3 strong men shall bow themselves, and the
Jer. 48. 14 We (are) mighty and strong men for the

12. *Strong, rich,* חָסִין *chasin.*
Psa. 89. 8 who (is) a strong LORD like unto thee? or

13. *Strength, riches,* חָסֹן *chason.*
Isa. 1. 31 strong shall be as tow, and the maker of
Amos 2. 9 strong as the oaks; yet I destroyed his

14. *Abundant, great, mighty, most,* כַּבִּיר *kabbir.*
Job 8. 2 the words of thy mouth (be like) a strong

15. *Fenced place,* מִבְצָר *mibtsar.*
Josh 19. 29 turneth to Ramah, and to the strong city
Psa. 108. 10 Who will bring me into the strong city?

16. *Strength, stronghold,* מָעוֹז *maoz.*
Psa. 31. 2 be thou my strong rock, for an house of
Isa. 17. 9 In that day shall his strong cities be as a
Dan. 11. 39 Thus shall he do in the most strong holds

17. *Siege, bulwark,* מָצוֹר *matsor.*
Psa. 31. 21 his marvellous kindness in a strong city
60. 9 Who will bring me (into) the strong city?

18. *Strong, fierce, impudent,* עַז *az.*
Exod 14. 21 caused the sea to go (back) by a strong
Num 13. 28 people (be) strong that dwell in the land
21. 24 border of the children of Ammon (was) st.
Judg 14. 14 and out of the strong came forth sweetn.
14. 18 what (is) stronger than a lion? And he said
2 Sa. 22. 18 He delivered me from my strong enemy
Psa. 18. 17 He delivered me from my strong enemy
Prov 21. 14 and a reward in the bosom strong wrath
30. 25 The ants (are) a people not strong, yet th.
Song 8. 6 for love (is) strong as death; jealousy (is)
Isa. 25. 3 Therefore shall the strong people glorify
Eze. 7. 24 will also make the pomp of the strong to
Amos 5. 9 strengtheneth the spoiled against the st.

19. *Strength, hardness,* עֹז *oz.*
Judg. 9. 51 But there was a strong tower within the
Psa. 30. 7 hast made my mountain to stand strong
61. 3 shelter for me, (and) a strong tower from
71. 7 unto many: but thou (art) my strong re.
89. 10 scattered thine enemies with thy strong
Prov 10. 15 The rich man's wealth (is) his strong city
14. 26 In the fear of the LORD (is) strong confid.
Prov. 18. 10 The name of the LORD (is) a strong tower
18. 11 The rich man's wealth (is) his strong city
18. 19 (is harder to be won) than a strong city
24. 5 A wise man (is) strong; yea, a man of kn.
Isa. 26. 1 We have a strong city; salvation will (G.)
Jer. 48. 17 How is the strong staff broken, (and) the
Eze. 19. 11 she had strong rods for the sceptres of th.
19. 12 her strong rods were broken and withered
19. 14 so that she hath no strong rod (to be) a sc.
26. 11 strong garrisons shall go down to the gr.

20. *Strong,* עִזּוּז *izzuz.*
Psa. 24. 8 LORD strong and mighty, the LORD mighty

21. *Substantial, bony,* עָצוּם *atsum.*
Josh 23. 9 hath driven out..great nations and strong
Psa. 10. 10 that the poor may fall by his strong ones
Prov. 7. 26 many strong (men) have been slain by her
Isa. 8. 7 strong and many, (even) the king of Ass.
53. 12 he shall divide the spoil with the strong
60. 22 a small one a strong nation: I the LORD
Joel 1. 6 strong, and without number, whose teeth
2. 2 a great people and a strong; there hath
2. 5 as a strong people set in battle array
2. 11 for (he is) strong that executeth his word
Mic. 4. 3 rebuke strong nations afar off; and they
4. 7 her that was cast far off a strong nation
Zech. 8. 22 many people and strong nations shall co.

22. *Substance, bone,* עֹצֶם *otsem.*
Job 30. 21 with thy strong hand thou opposest thys.

23. *Substantial, bony things,* עֲצֻמוֹת *atstsumoth.*
Isa. 41. 21 bring forth your strong (reasons), saith the

24. *Terrible,* עָרִיץ *arits.*
Prov 11. 16 retaineth honour; and strong (men) retain

25. *A rock, stone,* צוּר *tsur.*
Psa. 71. 3 Be thou my strong habitation, whereunto

26. *To bind, be strong,* קָשַׁר *qashar.*
Gen. 30. 42 feebler were Laban's, and the stronger J.

27. *To be bound, strong,* קָשַׁר *qashar,* 4.
Gen. 30. 41 whensoever the stronger cattle did con.

28. *Strong, mighty,* תַּקִּיף *taqqiph.*
Dan. 2. 40 the fourth kingdom shall be strong as iron
2. 42 kingdom shall be partly strong, and partly
7. 7 dreadful and terrible, and strong exceed.

29. *Able, powerful,* δυνατός *dunatos.*
Rom. 15. 1 We then that are strong ought to bear the
2 Co. 12. 10 for when I am weak, then am I strong
13. 9 glad when we are weak, and ye are strong

30. *Energy, inworking,* ἐνέργεια *energeia.*
2 Th. 2. 11 for this cause God shall send them strong

31. *Strong, robust,* ἰσχυρός *ischuros.*
Matt. 12. 29 Or else how can one enter into a strong
12. 29 except he first bind the strong man? and
Mark 3. 27 No man can enter into a strong man's ho.
3. 27 except he will first bind the strong man
Luke 11. 21 When a strong man armed keepeth his pa.
1 Co. 4. 10 we (are) weak, but ye (are) strong: ye (are)
Heb. 5. 7 offered up prayers..with strong crying
6. 18 we might have a strong consolation, who
1 Jo. 2. 14 written unto you..because ye are strong
Rev. 5. 2 saw a strong angel proclaiming with a lo.
18. 8 for strong (is) the Lord God who judgeth

32. *Stronger, more robust,* ἰσχυρότερος *ischuroteros.*
Luke 11. 22 when a stronger than he shall come upon
1 Co. 1. 25 the weakness of God is stronger than men
10. 22 Do we provoke the Lord..are we stronger

33. *Great,* μέγας *megas.*
Rev. 18. 2 [cried mightily with a strong voice, saying]

34. *Firm, standing,* στερεός *stereos.*
Heb. 5. 12 have need of milk, and not of strong me.
5. 14 But strong meat belongeth to them that

STRONG, stronger, to be, become, be made, be too —

1. *To be or become strong,* אָמֵץ *amats.*
Gen. 25. 23 people shall be stronger than (the other)
2 Sa. 22. 18 delivered me..for they were too strong
Psa. 18. 17 delivered me..for they were too strong
142. 6 deliver me..for they are stronger than I

2. *To be or become mighty,* גָּבַר *gabar.*
2 Sa. 1. 23 swifter than eagles, they were stronger th.

3. *To be or become strong, hard,* חָזַק *chazaq.*
Deut 11. 8 that ye may be strong, and go in and pos.
31. 6, 7, 23 Be strong, and of a good courage
Josh. 1. 6, 9, 18 Be strong and of a good courage
1. 7 Only be thou strong and very courageous
10. 25 be strong, and of good courage: for thus
Judg. 1. 28 it came to pass, when Israel was strong
2 Sa. 10. 11 If the Syrians be too strong for me, then
10. 11 children of Ammon be too strong for thee
13. 14 being stronger than she, forced her, and
16. 21 hands of all that (are) with thee be strong
1 Ki. 2. 2 be thou strong therefore, and show thys.
20. 23 were stronger than we; but let us fight
20. 23, 25 surely we shall be stronger than they
1 Ch. 19. 12 If the Syrians be too strong for me, then
19. 12 children of Ammon be too strong for thee
22. 13 be strong, and of good courage; dread not
28. 10 chosen thee to build an house..be strong
28. 20 Be strong and of good courage and do (it)
2 Ch. 15. 7 Be ye strong therefore, and let not your
25. 8 But if thou wilt go, do (it), be strong for the
26. 15 was marvellously helped, till he was stro.
32. 7 Be strong and courageous, be not afraid
Ezra 9. 12 that ye may be strong, and eat the good
Isa. 28. 22 lest your bands be made strong, for I have
Isa. 35. 4 Be strong, fear not: behold, your God will
Jer. 20. 7 thou art stronger than I, and hast preva.
Eze. 3. 14 but the hand of the LORD was strong upon
22. 14 can thine hands be strong, in the days that
Dan. 10. 19 peace (be) unto thee; be strong..be strong
11. 5 king of the south shall be strong, and (one)
11. 5 he shall be strong above him, and have
Hag. 2. 4 Yet now be strong..be strong, O Joshua
2. 4 be strong, all ye people of the land, saith
Zech. 8. 9 Let your hands be strong, ye that hear in
8. 13 fear not, (but) let your hands be strong

4. *To cause to be strong or hard,* חָזַק *chazaq,* 5.
Dan. 11. 32 people..shall be strong, and do (exploits)

5. *To strengthen self,* חָזַק *chazaq,* 7.
1 Sa. 4. 9 Be strong, and quit yourselves like men

6. *Strength,* חָזְקָה *chozqah.*
2 Ch. 26. 16 But when he was strong, his heart was

7. *To be or become or make strong,* עָזַז *azaz.*
Psa. 89. 13 strong is thy hand, (and) high is thy right

8. *To be substantial, bony,* עָצַם *atsam.*
Psa. 38. 19 mine enemies (are) lively, (and) they are s.
Isa. 31. 1 in horsemen, because they are very stro.
Dan. 8. 8 when he was strong, the great horn was
11. 23 and shall become strong with a small pe.

9. *To be moved, strengthened,* פָּזַז *pazaz.*
Gen. 49. 24 arms of his hands were made strong by

10. *To be or become high or strong,* שָׂגַב *sagab.*
Deut. 2. 36 there was not one city too strong for us

11. *To be or become strong,* תְּקֵף *teqeph.*
Dan. 4. 11 tree grew, and was strong, and the heig.
4. 20 which grew, and was strong, whose heig.
4. 22 thou..that art grown and become strong

12. *To make powerful inwardly,* ἐνδυναμόω *endun.*
Rom. 4. 20 but was strong in faith, giving glory to
Eph. 6. 10 be strong in the Lord, and in the power
Heb. 11. 34 out of weakness [were made strong], wa.
2 Ti. 2. 1 my son, be strong in the grace that is in

13. *To make strong, strengthen,* κραταιόω *krataioō.*
1 Co. 16. 13 Watch ye..quit you like men, be strong

STRONG, to wax, be waxen —

1. *To be or become strong or hard,* חָזַק *chazaq.*
Josh. 17. 13 the children of Israel were waxen strong

2. *To make strong, strengthen,* κραταιόω *krataioō.*
Luke 1. 80 child grew, and waxed strong in spirit, and
2. 40 child grew, and waxed strong in spirit, fi.

STRONG, stronger, to make, show self —

1. *To strengthen, harden,* אָמֵץ *amats,* 3.
2 Ch. 11. 17 made Rehoboam the son of Solomon str
Psa. 80. 15 branch (that) thou madest strong for thy.
80. 17 Son of man (whom) thou madest strong

2. *To be or become strong or hard,* חָזַק *chazaq.*
Eze. 30. 21 bind it, to make it strong to hold the sw.

3 *To strengthen, harden,* חָזַק *chazaq,* 3.
2 Ch. 11. 12 made them exceeding strong, having Ju.
Nah. 2. 1 make (thy) loins strong, fortify thy power

4. *To cause to be strong or hard,* חָזַק *chazaq,* 5.
2 Sa. 11. 25 make thy battle more strong against the
Jer. 51. 12 make the watch strong, set up the watch.
Nah. 3. 14 tread the mortar, make strong the brick

5. *To strengthen self,* חָזַק *chazaq,* 7.
2 Sa. 3. 6 Abner made himself strong for the house
2 Ch. 16. 9 to show himself strong in the behalf of

6. *To make mighty, bony,* עָצַם *atsam,* 5.
Psa. 105. 24 and made them stronger than their ene.

7. *To make firm,* στερεόω *stereoō.*
Acts 3. 16 hath made this man strong, whom ye s.

STRONG HOLD —

1. *Cut off or fenced place,* בִּצָּרוֹן *bitstsaron.*
Zech. 9. 12 Turn you to the strong hold, ye prison-

2. *Cut off or fenced place,* מִבְצָר *mibtsar.*
Num 13. 19 dwell in, whether in tents, or in strong h.
2 Sa. 24. 7 came to the strong hold of Tyre, and to all
2 Ki. 8. 12 their strong holds wilt thou set on fire, and
Psa. 89. 40 thou hast brought his strong holds to ruin
Jer. 48. 18 (and) he shall destroy thy strong holds
Lam. 2. 2 thrown down in his wrath the strong holds
2. 5 he hath destroyed his strong holds, and ha.
Dan. 11. 24 forecast his devices against the strong h.
Mic. 5. 11 and throw down all thy strong holds
Nah. 3. 12 All thy strong holds (shall be like) fig trees
3. 14 fortify thy strong holds: go into clay, and
Hab. 1. 10 they shall deride every strong hold; for

3. *A strong place, strong hold,* מָעוֹז *maoz.*
Isa. 23. 11 merchant (city), to destroy the strong ho.
Nah. 1. 7 LORD (is) good, a strong hold in the day of

4. *A fortress,* מְצַד *metsad.*
Judg. 6. 2 mountains, and caves, and strong holds
1 Sa. 23. 14 abode in the wilderness in strong holds
23. 19 David hide himself with us in strong holds
23. 29 And David..dwelt in strong holds at E.-g.
Jer. 48. 41 Kerioth is taken, and the strong holds are

5. *A fortress,* מְצוּדָה *metsudah.*
2 Sa. 5. 7 Nevertheless David took the strong hold

6. *Bulwark,* מָצוֹר *matsor.*
Zech. 9. 3 Tyrus did build herself a strong hold, and

7. *Bulwark,* מְצוּרָה *metsurah.*
2 Ch. 11. 11 fortified the strong holds, and put captains

8. *Cliff, rock,* סֶלַע *sela.*
Isa. 31. 9 he shall pass over to his strong hold for fe.
9. *High place,* עֹפֶל *ophel.*
Mic. 4. 8 stronghold of the daughter of Zion, unto
10. *A strong hold,* ὀχύρωμα *ochurōma.*
2 Co. 10. 4 mighty..to the pulling down of strong h.
STRONG pieces, place —
1. *Strong one, bar,* אָפִיק *aphiq.*
Job 40. 18 His bones (are as) strong pieces of brass
2. *A fortress,* מְצוּדָה *metsudah.*
Job 39. 28 dwelleth..upon the crag..the strong pl.
STRONGER and stronger, to be —
To add strength, יָסַף אֹמֶץ *yasaph, 5, omets.*
Job 17. 9 clean hands shall be stronger and stronger
STRUGGLE together, to —
To struggle together, רָצַץ *ratsats, 7a.*
Gen. 25. 22 children struggled together within her
STUBBLE —
1. *Stubble,* קַשׁ *qash.*
Exod. 5. 12 scattered..to gather stubble instead of st.
15. 7 thy wrath, (which) consumed them as st.
Job 13. 25 and wilt thou pursue the dry stubble?
41. 28 sling stones are turned with him into st.
41. 29 Darts are counted as stubble: he laugheth
Psa. 83. 13 make them like a wheel; as the stubble
Isa. 5. 24 Therefore as the fire devoureth the stub.
33. 11 ye shall bring forth stubble: your breath
40. 24 whirlwind shall take them away as stub.
41. 2 dust to his sword, (and) as driven stubble
47. 14 they shall be as stubble; the fire shall bu.
Jer. 13. 24 Therefore will I scatter them as the stub.
Joel 2. 5 flame of fire that devoureth the stubble
Obad. 18 house of Esau for stubble, and they shall
Nah. 1. 10 they shall be devoured as stubble fully
Mal. 4. 1 all that do wickedly, shall be stubble: and
2. *Straw,* תֶּבֶן *teben.*
Job 21. 18 They are as stubble before the wind, and
3. *Straw, stubble,* καλάμη *kalamē.*
1 Co. 3. 12 silver, precious stones, wood, hay, stub.
STUBBORN, stubbornness —
1. *To be refractory, stubborn,* סָרַר *sarar.*
Deut 21. 18 If a man have a stubborn and rebellious
21. 20 This our son (is) stubborn and rebellious
Psa. 78. 8 a stubborn and rebellious generation, a g.
Prov. 7. 11 She (is) loud and stubborn; her feet abide
2. *To press in, be stubborn,* פָּצַר *patsar, 5.*
1 Sa. 15. 23 stubbornness (is as) iniquity and idolatry
3. *Sharp, hard,* קָשֶׁה *qasheh.*
Judg 2. 19 they ceased not..from their stubborn way
4. *Sharpness, hardness,* קְשִׁי *qeshi.*
Deut. 9. 27 look not unto the stubbornness of this pe.
STUCK —
To crush, strike, מָעַךְ *maak.*
1 Sa. 26. 7 spear stuck in the ground at his bolster
STUDS —
Engraving, studs, נְקֻדּוֹת *nequddoth.*
Song 1. 11 will make thee borders of gold, with studs
STUDY, (to) —
1. *To meditate, utter, mutter,* הָגָה *hagah.*
Prov.15. 28 heart of the righteous studieth to answer
24. 2 For their heart studieth destruction, and
2. *Study,* לַהַג *lahag.*
Eccl.12. 12 and much study (is) a weariness of the fle.
3. *To use diligence, make speed,* σπουδάζω *spoudazō.*
2 Ti. 2. 15 Study to show thyself approved unto God
4. *To esteem as an honour,* φιλοτιμέομαι *philotimeo.*
1 Th. 4. 11 that ye study to be quiet, and to do your
STUFF —
1. *Vessel, instrument,* כְּלִי *keli.*
Gen. 31. 37 Whereas thou hast searched all my stuff
31. 37 hast thou found of all thy household stuff
45. 20 Also regard not your stuff; for the good
Exod22. 7 If a man shall deliver..money or stuff to
Josh. 7. 11 have put (it) even among their own stuff
1 Sa. 10. 22 Behold, he hath hid himself among the s.
25. 13 men; and two hundred abode by the stuff
30. 24 his part (be) that tarrieth by the stuff: th.
Neh. 13. 8 cast forth all the household stuff of Tobi.
Eze. 12. 3 prepare thee stuff for removing, and remo.
12. 4 bring forth thy stuff..as stuff for removi.
12. 7 brought forth my stuff by day, as stuff for
2. *Work,* מְלָאכָה *melakah.*
Exod36. 7 For the stuff they had was sufficient for
3. *Vessel, instrument,* σκεῦος *skeuos.*
Luke17. 31 his stuff in the house, let him not come
STUMBLE, to (cause to) —
1. *To stumble,* כָּשַׁל *kashal.*
Psa. 27. 2 to eat up my flesh, they stumbled and fell
Isa. 5. 27 None shall be weary nor stumble among
8. 15 many among them shall stumble, and fall
59. 10 we stumble at noon day as in the night, we
Jer. 46. 6 they shall stumble, and fall toward the no.
46. 12 mighty man hath stumbled against the
50. 32 most proud shall stumble and fall, and
Nah. 3. 3 corpses; they stumble upon their corpses

2. *To be stumbled,* כָּשַׁל *kashal, 2.*
1 Sa. 2. 4 they that stumbled are girded with stren.
Prov. 4. 12 when thou runnest, thou shalt not stumble
4. 19 they know not at what they stumble
24. 17 let not thine heart be glad when he stum.
Isa. 63. 13 That led them..(that) they should not st.
Jer. 20. 11 therefore my persecutors shall stumble
31. 9 way, wherein they shall not stumble; for
Dan. 11. 19 he shall stumble and fall, and not be found
Nah. 2. 5 they shall stumble in their walk; they sh.
3. *To cause to stumble,* כָּשַׁל *kashal, 5.*
Jer. 18. 15 have caused them to stumble in their wa.
Mal. 2. 8 ye have caused many to stumble at the
4. *To smite, plague,* נָגַף *nagaph.*
Prov. 3. 23 walk..safely, and thy foot shall not stu.
5. *To smite or plague self,* נָגַף *nagaph, 7.*
Jer. 13. 16 before your feet stumble upon the dark
6. *To stumble, smite together,* פּוּק *puq.*
Isa. 28. 7 they err in vision, they stumble (in) jud.
7. *To release, let go, throw down,* שָׁמַט *shamat.*
1 Ch. 13. 9 hand to hold the ark; for the oxen stum.
8. *To strike against,* προσκόπτω *proskoptō.*
John11. 9 If any man walk in the day, he stum. not
11. 10 if a man walk in the night, he stumbleth
Rom. 9. 32 for they stumbled at that stumbling stone
14. 21 whereby thy brother stumbleth, or is off.
1 Pe. 2. 8 which stumble at the word, being disobe.
9. *To stumble, fall,* πταίω *ptaiō.*
Rom.11. 11 Have they stumbled that they should fall
STUMBLING (block or stone) —
1. *Stumbling block,* מִכְשׁוֹל *mikshol.*
Lev. 19. 14 Thou shalt not..put a stumblingblock be.
Isa. 57. 14 take up the stumbling block out of the
Jer. 6. 21 I will lay stumbling blocks before this pe.
Eze. 3. 20 lay a stumbling block before him, he shall
7. 19 because it is the stumbling block of their
14. 3 put the stumbling block of their iniquity
14. 4, 7 putteth the stumbling block of his iniq.
2. *Stumbling block,* מַכְשֵׁלָה *makshelah.*
Zeph. 1. 3 and the stumbling blocks with the wicked
3. *A stroke, plague,* נֶגֶף *negeph.*
Isa. 8. 14 for a stone of stumbling and for a rock of
4. *A striking against, stumbling block,* πρόσκομμα.
Rom 14. 13 rather, that no man put a stumbling bl.
1 Co. 8. 9 liberty of yours become a stumbling block
1 Pe. 2. 8 a stone of stumbling, and a rock of offence
5. *Stone of stumbling,* λίθος τοῦ προσκόμματος.
Rom. 9. 32 for they stumbled at that stumbling stone
9. 33 lay in Zion a stumbling stone and rock of
6. *A trap, gin, stumbling block,* σκάνδαλον *skand.*
Rom11. 9 stumbling block, and a recompence unto
1 Co. 1. 23 crucified, unto the Jews a stumbling block
Rev. 2. 14 taught Balac to cast a stumbling block be.
STUMP —
Root, עִקָּר *iqqar.*
Dan. 4. 15 leave the stump of his roots in the earth
4. 23 yet leave the stump of the roots thereof
4. 26 commanded to leave the stump of the tree
SU'-AH, סוּחַ *riches, distinction.*
An Asherite, eldest son of Zophah. B.C. 1500.
1 Ch.7. 36 The sons of Zophah; S., and Harnepher
SUBDUE (unto, be subdued), to —
1. *To lead forth,* דָּבַר *dabar, 5.*
Psa. 18. 47 God that avengeth me, and subdueth the
47. 3 He shall subdue the people under us, and
2. *To make feeble,* חָשַׁל *chashal.*
Dan. 2. 40 iron breaketh in pieces and subdueth all
3. *To go down,* יָרַד *yarad.*
Deut20. 20 shalt build bulwarks..until it be subdued
4. *To subdue,* כָּבַשׁ *kabash.*
Gen. 1. 28 replenish the earth, and subdue it, and
Mic. 7. 19 he will subdue our iniquities; and thou
Zech. 9. 15 shall devour, and subdue with sling stones
5. *To be subdued,* כָּבַשׁ *kabash, 2.*
Num32. 22 land be subdued before the LORD; then
32. 29 land shall be subdued before you; then
Josh18. 1 And the land was subdued before them
1 Ch.22. 18 land is subdued before the LORD, and be.
6. *To subdue,* כָּבַשׁ *kabash, 3.*
2 Sa. 8. 11 dedicated of all nations which he subdued
7. *To be humbled,* כָּנַע *kana, 2.*
Judg 3. 30 So Moab was subdued that day under the
8. 28 Thus was Midian subdued before the chi.
11. 33 Thus the children of Ammon were subd.
1 Sa. 7. 13 So the Philistines were subdued, and they
1 Ch.20. 4 there arose war..and they were subdued
8. *To make humble,* כָּנַע *kana, 5.*
Judg. 4. 23 So God subdued on that day Jabin the ki.
2 Sa. 8. 1 smote the Philistines, and subdued them
1 Ch.17. 10 Moreover I will subdue all thine enemies
18. 1 smote the Philistines, and subdued them
Neh. 9. 24 subduedst before them the inhabitants of
Psa. 81. 14 I should soon have subdued their enemies
9. *To cause to bow or bend,* כָּרַע *kara, 5.*
2 Sa. 22. 40 them that rose up..hast thou subdued
Psa. 18. 39 thou hast subdued under me those that
10. *To subdue,* רָדַד *radad.*
Psa.144. 2 (he) in whom I trust; who subdueth my
Isa. 45. 1 whose right hand I have holden, to sub.

11. *To make low or humble,* שְׁפַל *shephal, 5.*
Dan. 7. 24 diverse from the first, and he shall subdue
12. *Contend against,* καταγωνίζομαι *katagōnizomai.*
Heb.11. 33 Who through faith subdued kingdoms, wr.
13. *To set in array under,* ὑποτάσσω *hupotassō.*
1 Co.15. 28 when all things shall be subdued unto him
Phil. 3. 21 whereby he is able even to subdue all th.
SUBJECT (to or unto, to be or make) —
1. *Held in, subject or liable to,* ἔνοχος *enochos.*
Heb. 2. 15 were all their lifetime subject to bondage
2. *To set in array under,* ὑποτάσσω *hupotassō.*
Luke 2. 51 was subject unto them: but his mother
10. 17 even the devils are subject unto us thro.
10. 20 rejoice not, that the spirits are subject u.
Rom. 8. 7 for it is not subject to the law of God, ne.
8. 20 For the creature was made subject to va.
13. 1 Let every soul be subject unto the higher
13. 5 Wherefore (ye) must needs be subject, not
1 Co.14. 32 spirits of the prophets are subject to the
15. 28 shall the Son also himself be subject unto
Eph. 5. 24 Therefore as the church is subject unto C.
Titus 3. 1 Put them in mind to be subject to princ.
1 Pe. 2. 18 Servants, (be) subject to (your) masters
3. 22 authorities and powers being made su. u.
5. 5 Yea, all (of you) [be subject] one to anot.
SUBJECT, to —
To set in array, ὑποτάσσω *hupotassō.*
Rom. 8. 20 by reason of him who hath subjected
SUBJECTION, (to be, bring, put, in, into, under) —
1. *To subdue,* כָּבַשׁ *kabash, 1,* [Jer. 34. 11. v L. 5].
Jer. 34. 11, 16 to return, and brought them into sub.
2. *To be humbled,* כָּנַע *kana, 2.*
Psa 106. 42 and they were brought into subjection un.
3. *To lead into servitude,* δουλαγωγέω *doulagōgeō.*
1 Co. 9. 27 bring (it) into subjection; lest that by any
4. *Subjection, submission,* ὑποταγή *hupotagē.*
2 Co. 9. 13 glorify God for your professed subjection
Gal. 2. 5 To whom we gave place by subjection, no
1 Ti. 2. 11 woman learn in silence with all subjection
3. 4 having his children in subjection with all
5. *To put in array under,* ὑποτάσσω *hupotassō.*
Heb. 2. 5 unto the angels hath he not put in subje.
2. 8 hast put all things in subjection under his
2. 8 For in that he put all in subjection under
12. 9 much rather be in subjection unto the Fa.
1 Pe. 3. 1 wives, (be) in subjection to your own hu.
3. 5 being in subjection unto their own husb.
SUBMIT (self, unto), to —
1. *To lie, feign,* כָּחַשׁ *kachash, 3.*
Psa. 18. 44 strangers shall submit themselves unto
66. 3 thine enemies submit themselves unto th.
81. 15 haters..should have submitted themsel. u
2. *To feign self obedient,* כָּחַשׁ *kachash, 7.*
2 Sa. 22. 45 Strangers shall submit themselves unto
3. *To give the hand,* נָתַן יָד *nathan yad.*
1 Ch.29. 24 submitted themselves unto Solomon the
4. *To humble self,* עָנָה *anah, 7.*
Gen. 16. 9 Return to thy mistress, and submit thys.
5. *To humble or stir up self,* רָפַס *raphas, 7*
Psa. 68. 30 submit himself with pieces of silver: scat.
6. *To yield under or submissively,* ὑπείκω *hupeikō.*
Heb. 13. 17 Obey them..and submit yourselves: for
7. *To set in array under,* ὑποτάσσω *hupotassō.*
Rom 10. 3 have not submitted themselves unto the
1 Co. 16. 16 That ye submit yourselves unto such, and
Eph. 5. 21 Submitting yourselves one to another in
5. 22 Wives, [submit yourselves unto] your own
Col. 3. 18 Wives, submit yourselves unto your own
Jas. 4. 7 Submit yourselves therefore to God. Res.
1 Pe. 2. 13 Submit yourselves to every ordinance of
5. 5 ye younger, submit yourselves unto the
SUBORN, to —
To cast under, suborn, ὑποβάλλω *hupoballō.*
Acts 6. 11 Then they suborned men, which said, We
SUBSCRIBE, to —
To write, כָּתַב *kathab.*
Isa. 44. 5 another shall subscribe (with) his hand un.
Jer. 32. 10 I subscribed the evidence, and sealed (it)
32. 12 witnesses that subscribed the book of the
32. 44 subscribe evidences, and seal (them), and
SUBSTANCE —
1. *Strength,* אוֹן *on.*
Hos.12. 8 I have found me out substance: (in) all my
2. *Mischief, calamity, desire,* הַוָּה *havvah.*
Prov 10. 3 casteth away the substance of the wicked
3. *Wealth, substance, sufficiency,* הוֹן *hon.*
Prov. 1. 13 We shall find all precious substance, we
3. 9 Honour the LORD with thy substance, and
6. 31 he shall give all the substance of his hou.
12. 27 the substance of a diligent man (is) prec.
28. 8 He that by usury..increaseth his substance
29. 3 keepeth company..spendeth (his) substa.
Song 8. 7 if a man would give all the substance of
4. *Force, might, wealth,* חַיִל *chayil.*
Deut33. 11 Bless, LORD, his substance, and accept the
Job 5. 5 the robber swalloweth up their substance
15. 29 shall not be rich, neither shall his subst.

Job 20. 18 according to (his) substance (shall) the re.
Jer. 15. 13 Thy substance and thy treasures will I
17. 3 I will give thy substance (and) all thy tr.
Obad. 13 nor have laid (hands) on their substance
Mic. 4. 13 consecrate..their substance unto the Lo.

5. *Stock, trunk,* מַצֶּבֶת *matstsebeth.*
Isa. 6. 13 as an oak, whose substance (is) in them
6. 13 the holy seed (shall be) the substance th.

6. *A living substance,* יְקוּם *yequm.*
Gen. 7. 4 every living substance that I have made
7. 23 every living substance was destroyed wh.
Deut 11. 6 swallowed them up..and all the substance

7. *Existence, substance,* יֵשׁ *yesh.*
Prov. 8. 21 cause those that love me to inherit subst.

8. *Power,* כֹּחַ *koach.*
Job 6. 22 or, Give a reward for me of your substance

9. *Acquisition, possession,* מִקְנֶה *miqneh.*
Job 1. 3 His substance also was seven thousand sh.
1. 10 and his substance is increased in the land

10. *Substance, bone,* עֹצֶם *otsem.*
Psa.139. 15 My substance was not hid from thee, wh.

11. *Standing substance,* קִים *qim.*
Job 22. 20 Whereas our substance is not cut down

12. *Acquisition, possession,* קִנְיָן *qinyan.*
Gen. 34. 23 their cattle and their substance and every
36. 6 all his beasts, and all his substance, which
Josh.14. 4 suburbs for their cattle and for their sub.
Psa. 105. 21 made him lord..and ruler of all his subs.

13. *What is gathered together, goods,* רְכוּשׁ *rekush.*
Gen. 12. 5 all their substance that they had gathered
13. 6 their substance was great, so that they co.
15. 14 shall they come out with great substance
1 Ch.27. 31 All these (were) the rulers of the substance
28. 1 stewards over all the substance and posse.
2 Ch.21. 17 carried away all the substance that was
31. 3 also the king's portion of his substance for
32. 29 for God hath given him substance very
35. 7 bullocks: these (were) of the king's subs.
Ezra 8. 21 for our little ones, and for all our substance
10. 8 all his substance should be forfeited, and

14. *Substance, wisdom,* תּוּשִׁיָּה *tushiyyah.*
Job 30. 22 ride (upon it), and dissolvest my substance

15. *Substance, being, essence,* οὐσία *ousia.*
Luke15. 13 there wasted his substance with riotous

16. *Substance, goods, property,* ὕπαρξις *huparxis.*
Heb. 10. 34 in heaven a better and an enduring subs.

17. *Things that are,* ὑπάρχοντα *huparchonta.*
Luke 8. 3 which ministered unto him of their subs.

18. *What stands under, substratum,* ὑπόστασις.
Heb. 11. 1 Now faith is the substance of things hop.

SUBSTANCE, being yet unperfect —
Embryo, גֹּלֶם *golem.*
Psa139. 16 did see my substance, yet being unperfect

SUBTIL, (to deal) subtilely, subtilty —
1. *Wise,* חָכָם *chakam.*
2 Sa. 13. 3 and Jonadab (was) a very subtil man

2. *Deceit,* מִרְמָה *mirmah.*
Gen. 27. 35 Thy brother came with subtilty, and hath

3. *To deceive self,* נָכַל *nakal,* 7.
Psa105. 25 turned their heart..to deal subtilely with

4. *To keep, watch, reserve, besiege,* נָצַר *natsar.*
Prov 7. 10 the attire of an harlot, and subtil of hea.

5. *Subtilty, crookedness,* עָקְבָה *oqbah.*
2 Ki. 10. 19 Jehu did (it) in subtilty, to the intent th.

6. *To be crafty, act craftily,* עָרַם *aram,* 5.
1 Sa. 23. 22 it is told me (that) he dealeth very subtil.

7. *Crafty, subtile,* עָרוּם *arum.*
Gen. 3. 1 serpent was more subtil than any beast of

8. *Craftiness, subtilty,* עָרְמָה *ormah.*
Prov. 1. 4 To give subtilty to the simple, to the yo.

9. *Deceit, fraud, guile,* δόλος *dolos.*
Matt26. 4 might take Jesus by subtilty, and kill (h.)
Acts 13. 10 O full of all subtilty and all mischief, (th.)

10. *Unscrupulousness, cunning,* πανουργία *panour.*
2 Co. 11. 3 serpent beguiled Eve through his subti.

SUBURB —
1. *Place for driving out cattle, suburb,* מִגְרָשׁ *migrash.*
Lev. 25. 34 field of the suburbs of their cities may not
Num 35. 2 unto the Levites suburbs for the cities ro.
35. 3 suburbs of them shall be for their cattle.
35. 4 suburbs of the cities, which ye shall give
35. 5 this shall be to them the suburbs of the
35. 7 cities: them (shall ye give) with their su.
Josh.14. 4 with their suburbs for their cattle and for
21. 2 cities..with the suburbs thereof for our
21. 3 children..gave..these cities and their su.
21. 8 gave..these cities with their suburbs, as
21. 11 gave them the city..with the suburbs th.
21. 13 with her suburbs..with her suburbs.
[So in verse 14, 15, 16, 17, 18, 19, 21, 22, 23, 24, 25, 26, 27, 28, 29, 30, 31, 32, 33, 34, 35, 38, 39, 41, 42.]
1 Ch. 5. 16 they dwelt..in all the suburbs of Sharon
6. 55 and the suburbs thereof round about it
6. 57 with her suburbs..with her suburbs
[So in verse 58, 59, 60, 64, 67, 68, 69, 70, 71, 72, 73, 74, 75, 76, 77, 78, 79, 80, 81].

1 Ch.13. 2 Levites (which are) in their cities (and) su.
2 Ch.11. 14 For the Levites left their suburbs, and th.
31. 19 (which were) in the fields of the suburbs
Eze. 27. 28 The suburbs shall shake at the sound of
45. 2 fifty cubits round about for the suburbs
48. 15 for the city, for dwelling, and for suburbs
48. 17 suburbs of the city shall be toward the

2. *Suburb, or open summer house,* פַּרְוָר *parvar.*
2 Ki. 23. 11 chamber..which (was) in the suburbs, and

SUBVERT, subverting, to —
1. *To deal or use perversely,* עָוַת *avath,* 3.
Lam. 3. 36 To subvert a man in his cause, the LORD

2. *To subvert, destroy,* ἀνασκευάζω *anaskeuazō.*
Acts 15. 24 subverting your souls, saying, (Ye must)

3. *To turn up, overturn,* ἀνατρέπω *anatrepō.*
Titus 1. 11 who subvert whole houses, teaching thi.

4. *To turn out of the way,* ἐκστρέφω *ekstrephō.*
Titus 3. 11 Knowing that he that is such is subverted

5. *A turning down or over, overthrow,* καταστροφή.
2 Ti. 2. 14 to no profit, (but) to the subverting of the

SUCCEED, to —
1. *To possess, take possession,* יָרַשׁ *yarash.*
Deut. 2. 12 but the children of Esau succeeded them
2. 21 they succeeded them, and dwelt in their
2. 22 succeeded them, and dwelt in their stead
12. 29 succeedest them, and dwellest in their la.
19. 1 succeedest them, and dwellest in their

2. *To rise up, stand still,* קוּם *qum.*
Deut 25. 6 shall succeed in the name of his brother

SUC'-COTH, סֻכֹּת, סֻכּוֹת *booths.*
1. A place E. of Jordan where Jacob went after Esau departed from him, now called *Sakut.*
Gen. 33. 17 Jacob journeyed to S., and built him an
33. 17 therefore the name of the place is called S.

2. The first station of Israel after leaving *Rameses* in Egypt.
Exod.12. 37 Israel journeyed from Rameses to S., ab.
13. 20 they took their journey from S., and enc.
Num33. 5 removed from Rameses, and pitched in S.
33. 6 they departed from S., and pitched in Et.

3. A place in Gad, near Beth-nimrah; perhaps the same as No. 1.
Josh.13. 27 Beth-aram, and Beth-nimrah, and S., and
Judg. 8. 5 he said unto the men of S., Give, I pray
8. 6 the princes of S. said, (Are) the hands of
8. 8 answered him as the men of S. had ans.
8. 14 caught a young man of the men of S., and
8. 14 he described unto him the princes of S.
8. 15 he came unto the men of S., and said, Be.
8. 16 and with them he taught the men of S.

4. A city in Ephraim, near Zarthan, now called *Sakut.*
1 Ki. 7. 46 in the clay ground between S. and Zarth.
2 Ch. 4. 17 in the clay ground between S. and Zered.
Psa. 60. 6 I will divide Shechem, and mete out..S.
108. 7 I will divide Shechem, and mete out..S

SUC-COTH BE'-NOTH, סֻכּוֹת בְּנוֹת *booths for the daug.*
A Babylonian god, mentioned along with Nergal, Ashema, Nibhaz, Tartah, Adrammelech, Annammelech, and other Assyrian gods.
2 Ki. 17. 30 the men of Babylon made S., and the men

SUCCOUR, succourer, to —
1. *To gird,* אָזַר *azar.*
2 Sa. 8. 5 when the Syrians..came to Succour Ha.
21. 17 Abishai the son of Zeruiah succoured him

2. *To gird,* אָזַר *azar* [V.L. 5]
2 Sa. 18. 3 better that thou succour us out of the ci.

3. *To come to the help of, aid, assist, help,* βοηθέω.
2 Co. 6. 2 in the day of salvation have I succoured
Heb. 2. 18 is able to succour them that are tempted

4. *One standing before, border, protector,* προστάτις.
Rom 16. 2 for she hath been a succourer of many, and

SUCH —
1. *These,* אֵלֶּה *eleh.*
Deut 25. 16 For all that do such things, (and) all that

2. *This,* דֵּן *den.*
Dan. 2. 10 asked such things at any magician, or as.

3. *That,* הַהוּא *ha-hu.*
1 Ki. 10. 10 there came no more such abundance of

4. *As they,* כָּהֵם *ka-hem.*
2 Ch. 9. 11 there were none such seen before in the

5. *As these,* כָּהֵנָּה *ka-henah.*
Gen. 41. 19 such as I never saw in all the land of Eg.
Job 23. 14 performeth..and many such (things are)

6. *This,* הַזֹּאת *haz-zoth.*
Deut 13. 14 such abomination is wrought among you

7. *This,* זֶה *zeh.*
Deut. 5. 29 O that there were such an heart in them

8. *This,* הַזֶּה *haz-zeh.*
2 Ki. 6. 9 Beware that thou pass not such a place

9. *Thus,* כֹּה *koh.*
Isa. 20. 6 Behold, such (is) our expectation, whither

10. *So,* כֵּן *ken.*
Exod 10. 14 before them there were no such locusts

11. *Such and such,* פְּלֹנִי אַלְמֹנִי *peloni almoni.*
1 Sa.21. 2 such and such a place; 2 Ki. 6. 8
Ruth 4. 1 Ho, such a one! turn aside,

12. *This, that, he, she, it,* ὅδε, τήνδε *hode, tende.*
Jas. 4. 13 tomorrow we will go into such a city, and

13. *These,* ταῦτα *tauta.*
1 Co. 6. 11 such were some of you; but ye are wash.

14. *Such as,* τοιόσδε *toiosde.*
2 Pe. 1. 17 when there came such a voice to him from

15. *Such as this,* τοιοῦτος *toioutos.*
Matt. 9. 8 God, which had given such power unto
18. 5 whoso shall receive one such little child
19. 14 for of such is the kingdom of heaven
Mark 4. 33 with many such parables spake he the wo.
6. 2 that even such mighty works are wrought
7. 8 [and many other such like things ye do]
7. 13 and many such like things do ye
9. 37 Whosoever shall receive one of such chi.
10. 14 forbid them not: for of such is the kingd.
13. 19 affliction, such as was not from the begin.
Luke18. 16 forbid them not: for of such is the kingd.
John 4. 23 for the Father seeketh such to worship
8. 5 [commanded us, that such should be sto.]
9. 16 can a man that is a sinner do such mirac.
Acts 16. 24 having received such a charge, thrust th.
21. 25 concluded that they observe no such thing
22. 22 Away with such a (fellow) from the earth
26. 29 were both almost and altogether such as
Rom.16. 18 For they that are such serve not our Lord
1 Co. 5. 1 such fornication as is not so much as na.
7. 15 a sister is not under bondage in such (cases)
7. 28 such shall have trouble in the flesh: but
11. 16 we have no such custom, neither the chur.
15. 48 As (is) the earthy, such (are) they also that
15. 48 as (is) the heavenly, such (are) they also
16. 16 That ye submit yourselves unto such, and
16. 18 therefore acknowledge ye them that are s.
2 Co. 2. 6 Sufficient to such a man (is) this punish.
3. 4 such trust have we through Christ to God
3. 12 Seeing then that we have such hope, we
10. 11 such (will we be) also in deed when we
11. 13 For such (are) false apostles, deceitful wo.
12. 3 knew such a man, whether in the body or
Gal. 5. 21 that they which do such things shall not
5. 23 Meekness, temperance: against such there
Phil. 2. 29 Receive..with all gladness; and hold such
2 Th. 3. 12 Now them that are such we command and
1 Ti. 6. 5 [gain is godliness: from such withdraw th.]
Titus 3. 11 Knowing that he that is such is subvert.
Heb. 7. 26 For such an high priest became us, (who
8. 1 We have such an high priest, who is set
12. 3 For consider him that endured such con.
13. 16 for with such sacrifices God is well pleased
Jas. 4. 16 rejoice in your boasting: all such rejoicing
3 John 8 We therefore ought to receive such, that

16. *To these,* τούτοις *toutois.*
Gal. 5. 21 drunkenness, revellings, and such like: of

17. *These,* τούτους *toutous.*
2 Ti. 3. 5 denying the power thereof: from such tu.

18. *Of these,* τούτων *toutōn.*
Acts 18. 15 I will not be a judge of s. 1 Th. 4. 6; Re. 20. 6

SUCH (a case, a time), in or at —
1. *Thus, according to this,* כָּכָה *kakah.*
Psa.144. 15 Happy (is that) people that is in such a ca.

2. *Now, so now,* כְּעֶנֶת *keeneth.*
Ezra 4. 10, 11 on this side the river, and at such a t.
7. 12 unto Ezra..perfect (peace), and at such at

3. *Now, so now,* כְּעֶת *keeth.*
Ezra 4. 17 beyond the river, Peace, and at such a ti.

SUCH a man, such a one —
1. *This,* זֶה *zeh.*
Job 14. 3 dost thou open thine eyes upon such an o.

2. *Any one, somebody,* δεῖνα *deina.*
Matt 26. 18 Go into the city to such a man, and say

3. *Such as this,* τοιοῦτος *toioutos.*
1 Co. 5. 5 To deliver such an one unto Satan for the
5. 11 extortioner; with such an one no not to
2 Co. 2. 7 lest perhaps such a one should be s. 6.
10. 11 Let such an one think this, that..as we are
12. 2 such an one caught up to the third heaven
12. 5 Of such an one will I glory: yet of myself
Gal. 6. 1 ye which are spiritual restore such an one
Phm. 9 being such an one as Paul the aged, and

SUCH and such things —
As these and as these, כָּהֵנָּה וְכָהֵנָּה [*ka-henah*].
2 Sa. 12. 8 have given unto thee such and such thi.

SUCH as —
1. *Such as,* כְּמוֹ *kemo.*
Neh. 6. 11 Should such a man as I flee? and who (is

2. *Such, such as,* οἷος *hoios.*
Matt 24. 21 such as was not since the beginning of the
Mark13. 19 affliction, such as was not from the begi.
2 Co. 10. 11 such as we are in word by letters when
12. 20 I shall not find you such as I would, and
12. 20 I shall be found unto you such as ye wo.
Rev. 16. 18 such as was not since men were upon the

3. *Of what kind or sort,* ὁποῖος *hopoios.*
Acts 26. 29 were both almost and altogether such as

4. *Who, whosoever, what, whatsoever,* ὅστις *hostis.*
Mark 4. 20 such as hear the word, and receive (it), and

5. *These, those,* οὗτοι *houtoi.*
Mark 4. 18 sown among thorns; such as hear the wo

SUCH deed, like, thing —
1. *They, these,* הֵן *hen.*
Eze. 18. 14 and considereth, and doeth not such like
2. *Like this,* כָּזֹאת *ka-zoth.*
Judg 19. 30 There was no such deed done nor seen fr.
3. *So,* כֵּן *ken.*
2 Sa. 13. 12 no such thing ought to be done in Israel
4. *These,* ταῦτα *tauta.*
John 7. 32 heard that the people murmured such th.
2 Pe. 3. 14 seeing that ye look for such things, be
5. *Of this kind or sort, such,* τοιοῦτος *toioutos.*
Luke 9. 9 but who is this of whom I hear such th.?
13. 2 sinners..because they suffered [such thi.?]
Acts 21. 25 written..that they observe no such thing
Rom. 1. 32 that they which commit such things are
2. 2 against them which commit such things
2. 3 that judgest them which do such things
Eph. 5. 27 not having spot, or wrinkle, or any such th.
Heb. 11. 14 For they that say such things de.Gal.5.21
6. *The things within,* τὰ ἐνόντα *ta enonta.*
Luke 11. 41 rather give alms of such things as ye have
7. *The things alongside,* τὰ πάροντα *ta paronta.*
Heb. 13. 5 content with such things as ye have: for

SUCHATHITES, שׂוּכָתִים.
A family of Scribes, dwelling at Jabez near Judah.
1 Ch. 2. 55 the Tirathites, the Shimeathites, (and) S.

SUCK (up, give, make), to —
1. *To wring or drain out,* מָצָה *matsah.*
Eze. 23. 34 Thou shalt even drink it and suck (it) out
2. *To suck,* יָנַק *yanaq.*
Deut 33. 19 they shall suck (of) the abundance of the
Job 3. 12 or why the breasts that I should suck?
20. 16 He shall suck the poison of asps: the vi.
Song 8. 1 that sucked the breasts of my mother!
Isa. 60. 16 suck the milk of the Gentiles, and shalt
66. 11 That ye may suck, and be satisfied with
66. 12 then shall ye suck, ye shall be borne upon
Joel 2. 16 children, and those that suck the breasts
3. *To suckle, give suck,* יָנַק *yanaq,* 5.
Gen. 21. 7 that Sarah should have given children su.?
Deut 32. 13 made him to suck honey out of the rock
1 Sa. 1. 23 gave her son suck until she weaned him
1 Ki. 3. 21 when I rose..to give my child suck, be.
Lam. 4. 3 they give suck to their young ones: the
4. *To gulph down, swallow,* עָלַע *ala,* 3.
Job 39. 30 Her young ones also suck up blood: and
5. *To suckle, give suck,* θηλάζω *thēlazō.*
Matt 24. 19 woe..to them that give suck, in those days
Mark 13. 17 woe..to them that give suck, in those da.
Luke 11. 27 and the paps which thou hast sucked
21. 23 woe..to them that give suck, in those da.
23. 29 and the paps which never [gave suck]

SUCKING (child), suckling —
1. *Fat, best,* חָלָב *chalab.*
1 Sa. 7. 9 Samuel took a sucking lamb, and offered
2. *To suck,* יָנַק *yanaq.*
Num 11. 12 as a nursing father beareth the sucking
Deut 32. 25 the suckling (also) with the man of grey
1 Sa. 15. 3 slay both..infant and suckling, ox and
22. 19 smote..sucklings, and oxen, and asses
Psa. 8. 2 Out of the mouth of babes and sucklings
Isa. 11. 8 sucking child shall play on the hole of
Jer. 44. 7 to cut off from you..child and suckling
Lam. 2. 11 the sucklings swoon in the streets of the
4. 4 tongue of the sucking child cleaveth to
3. *To suckle, give suck,* θηλάζω *thēlazō.*
Matt 21. 16 Out of the mouth of babes and sucklings

SUDDEN, (very suddenly, to make) —
1. *In a sudden, suddenly,* בְּפֶתַע פִּתְאֹם *be-petha pithom.*
Num. 6. 9 if any man die very suddenly by him, and
2. *Hasting,* מַהֵר *maher.*
Deut. 7. 4 kindled against you, and destroy thee su.
3. *To hasten,* מָהַר *mahar,* 3.
2 Sa. 15. 14 lest he overtake us suddenly, and bring
4. *Suddenly,* פִּתְאֹם *pithom.*
Num 12. 4 LORD spake suddenly unto Moses, and un.
Josh. 10. 9 Joshua therefore came unto them sudd.
11. 7 So Joshua came..against them..suddenly
2 Ch. 29. 36 rejoiced..for the thing was (done) sudde.
Job 5. 3 root: but suddenly I cursed his habitation
9. 23 If the scourge slay suddenly, he will la.
22. 10 round about thee, and sudden fear trou.
Psa. 64. 4 suddenly do they shoot at him, and fear
64. 7 God shall shoot..suddenly shall they be
Prov. 3. 25 Be not afraid of sudden fear, neither of
6. 15 Therefore shall his calamity come sudde.
24. 22 For their calamity shall rise suddenly, and
Eccl. 9. 12 evil time, when it falleth suddenly upon
Isa. 29. 5 yea, it shall be at an instant suddenly
30. 13 whose breaking cometh suddenly at an
47. 11 desolation shall come upon thee suddenly
48. 3 did (them) suddenly, and they came to
Jer. 4. 20 suddenly are my tents spoiled, (and) my
6. 26 for the spoiler shall suddenly come upon
15. 8 have caused (him) to fall upon it suddenly
18. 22 when thou shalt bring a troop suddenly
51. 8 Babylon is suddenly fallen and destroyed
Mal. 3. 1 shall suddenly come to his temple, even
5. *Any instant,* פֶּתַע *petha.*
Num 35. 22 But if he thrust him suddenly without
Prov. 6. 15 suddenly shall he be broken without rem.
29. 1 suddenly be destroyed, and that without
Hab. 2. 7 Shall they not rise up suddenly that sh.
6. *A moment, a rest,* רֶגַע *rega.*
Psa. 6. 10 let them return (and) be ashamed suddenly
7. *To cause to rest,* רָגַע *raga,* 5.
Jer. 49. 19 will suddenly make him run away from
50. 44 but I will make them suddenly run away
8. *Sudden, unexpected,* αἰφνίδιος *aiphnidios.*
1 Th. 5. 3 then sudden destruction cometh upon th.
9. *Suddenly, on a sudden,* ἄφνω *aphnō.*
Acts 2. 2 suddenly there came a sound from heav.
16. 26 suddenly there was a great earthquake
28. 6 swollen, or fallen down dead suddenly
10. *Suddenly, unexpectedly,* ἐξαίφνης *exaiphnēs.*
Mark 13. 36 Lest, coming suddenly, he find you sleep.
Luke 2. 13 suddenly there was with the angel a mul.
9. 39 spirit taketh him, and he suddenly crieth
Acts 9. 3 suddenly there shined round about him a
22. 6 suddenly there shone from heaven a gre.
11. *Unexpectedly, suddenly,* ἐξάπινα *exapina.*
Mark 9. 8 suddenly, when they had looked round
12. *Quickly, speedily,* ταχέως *tacheōs.*
1 Ti. 5. 22 Lay hands suddenly on no man, neither

SUE at the law, to —
To judge, sue at law, κρίνω *krinō.*
Matt. 5. 40 if any man will sue thee at the law, and

SUFFER, to —
1. *To be able, permit,* יָכֹל *yakol.*
Psa. 101. 5 him that hath..a proud heart will not I su.
2. *To give rest (peace), let alone,* נוּחַ *nuach,* 5.
Judg 16. 26 Suffer me that I may feel the pillars wh.
1 Ch. 16. 21 He suffered no man to do them wrong
Esth. 3. 8 (is) not for the king's profit to suffer them
Psa. 105. 14 He suffered no man to do them wrong; yea
Eccl. 5. 12 abundance of the rich will not suffer him
3. *To compass, wait,* כָּתַר *kathar,* 3.
Job 36. 2 Suffer me a little, and I will show thee th.
4. *To spread out, leave,* נָטַשׁ *natash.*
Gen. 31. 28 hast not suffered me to kiss my sons and
5. *To lift up,* נָשָׂא *nasa.*
Lev. 19. 17 rebuke thy neighbour, and not suffer sin
Job 21. 3 Suffer me that I may speak; and after th.
Psa. 88. 15 (while) I suffer thy terrors I am distract.
Prov 19. 19 A man of great wrath shall suffer punish.
Jer. 15. 15 know that for thy sake I have suffered re.
6. *To give,* נָתַן *nathan.*
Gen. 20. 6 therefore suffered I thee not to touch her
31. 7 but God suffered him not to hurt me
Exod 12. 23 will not suffer the destroyer to come in
Num 21. 23 Sihon would not suffer Israel to pass th.
Deut 18. 14 thy God hath not suffered thee so (to do)
Josh. 10. 19 suffer them not to enter into their cities
Judg. 1. 34 for they would not suffer them to come
3. 28 took the fords..and suffered not a man to
15. 1 but her father would not suffer him to go
1 Sa. 24. 7 and suffered them not to rise against Saul
2 Sa. 21. 10 suffered neither the birds of the air to rest
1 Ki. 15. 17 that he might not suffer any to go out or
Job 9. 18 He will not suffer me to take my breath
31. 30 Neither have I suffered my mouth to sin
Psa. 16. 10 neither wilt thou suffer thine holy one to
55. 22 shall never suffer the righteous to be mo.
66. 9 holdeth our soul in life, and suffereth not
121. 3 He will not suffer thy foot to be moved: he
Eccl. 5. 6 Suffer not thy mouth to cause thy flesh to
7. *To hold up,* ἀνέχομαι *anechomai.*
Matt 17. 17 perverse generation..how long shall I su.
Mark 9. 19 faithless generation..how long shall I su.
Luke 9. 41 perverse generation..how long shall I..su.
1 Co. 4. 12 we bless; being persecuted, we suffer it
2 Co. 11. 19 For ye suffer fools gladly, seeing ye (yo.)
11. 20 For ye suffer, if a man bring you into bo.
Heb. 13. 22 suffer the word of exhortation: for I have
8. *To send away, let go, permit,* ἀφίημι *aphiēmi.*
Matt. 3. 15 said unto him, Suffer..Then he suffered
19. 14 Jesus said, Suffer little children, and for.
23. 13 neither suffer ye them that are entering
Mark 1. 34 suffered not the devils to speak, because
5. 19 suffered him not, but saith unto him, Go
5. 37 suffered no man to follow him, save Peter
7. 12 suffer him no more to do ought for his fa.
10. 14 Suffer the little children to come unto me
11. 16 would not suffer that any man should ca.
Luke 8. 51 suffered no man to go in, save Peter and J.
12. 39 not have suffered his house to be broken
18. 16 Suffer little children to come unto me, and
Rev. 11. 9 shall not suffer their dead bodies to be put
9. *To give,* δίδωμι *didōmi.*
Acts 2. 27 neither wilt thou suffer thine holy one to
13. 35 Thou shalt not suffer thine holy one to see
10. *To permit, suffer, let fall,* ἐάω *eaō.*
Matt 24. 43 would not have suffered his house to be br.
Luke 4. 41 rebuking (them), suffered them not to spe.
22. 51 Jesus answered and said, Suffer ye thus
Acts 14. 16 Who in times past suffered all nations to
16. 7 assayed to go..but the spirit suffered them
19. 30 the people, the disciples suffered him not
28. 4 escaped the sea, yet vengeance suffereth
1 Co. 10. 13 who will not suffer you to be tempted abo.
Rev. 2. 20 because [thou sufferest] that woman Jeze.
11. *To turn over on, commit to,* ἐπιτρέπω *epitrepō.*
Matt. 8. 21 Lord, suffer me first to go and bury my fa.
8. 31 [suffer] us to go away into the herd of swine
19. 8 suffered you to put away your wives: but
Mark 10. 4 Moses suffered to write a bill of divorce.
Luke 8. 32 suffer them to enter..And he suffered th.
9. 59 Lord, suffer me first to go and bury my fat.
Acts 21. 39 beseech thee, suffer me to speak unto the
28. 16 but Paul was suffered to dwell by himself
1 Ti. 2. 12 suffer not a woman to teach nor to usurp
12. *Able to suffer,* παθητός *pathētos.*
Act. 26. 23 That Christ should suffer, (and) that he sh.
13. *To suffer, endure, experience,* πάσχω *paschō.*
Matt 16. 21 suffer many things of the elders and chief
17. 12 Likewise shall also the son of man suffer
27. 19 for I have suffered many things this day
Mark 5. 26 had suffered many things of many physic.
8. 31 that the son of man must suffer many th.
9. 12 that he must suffer many things, and be
Luke 9. 22 The son of man must suffer many things
13. 2 sinners..because they suffered such things
17. 25 But first must he suffer many things, and be
22. 15 to eat this passover with you before I su.
24. 26 Ought not Christ to have suffered these
24. 46 thus it behoved Christ to suffer, and to rise
Acts 3. 18 that Christ should suffer, he hath so ful.
9. 16 great things he must suffer for my name's
17. 3 Christ must needs have suffered, and risen
1 Co. 12. 26 whether one member suffer, all the mem.
2 Co. 1. 6 the same sufferings which we also suffer
Gal. 3. 4 Have ye suffered so many things in vain?
Phil. 1. 29 believe on him, but also to suffer for his
1 Th. 2. 14 for ye also have suffered like things of yo.
2 Th. 1. 5 kingdom of God, for which ye also suffer
2 Ti. 1. 12 For the which cause I also suffer these th.
Heb. 2. 18 For in that he himself hath suffered, being
5. 8 obedience by the things which he suffered
9. 26 For then must he often have suffered since
13. 12 Jesus also..suffered without the gate
1 Pe. 2. 19 if a man..endure grief, suffering wrongf.
2. 20 but if, when ye do well, and suffer (for it)
2. 21 because Christ also suffered for us, leaving
2. 23 when he suffered, he threatened not; but
3. 14 But and if ye suffer for righteousness' sake
3. 17 ye suffer for well doing, than for evil doing
3. 18 For Christ also hath once [suffered] for s.
4. 1 Christ hath suffered for us in the flesh, arm
4. 1 for he that hath suffered in the flesh hath
4. 15 But let none of you suffer as a murderer
4. 19 let them that suffer according to the will
5. 10 after that ye have suffered a while, make
Rev. 2. 10 none of those things which thou shalt su.
14. *To permit, let,* προσεάω *proseaō.*
Acts 27. 7 wind not suffering us, we sailed under C.
15. *To cover, endure, sustain, bear,* στέγω *stegō.*
1 Co. 9. 12 suffer all things, lest we should hinder the
16. *To hold up under,* ὑπέχω *hupechō.*
Jude 7 set forth for an example, suffering the ve.
17. *To remain under, sustain,* ὑπομένω *hupomenō.*
2 Ti. 2. 12 If we suffer, we shall also reign with (him)
[*See also* Adversity, affliction, bear, decrease, famish, hunger, lacking, live, manners, reproach, shipwreck, thirst, tribulation, trouble, wrong.]

SUFFER before, long, loss, need, with, to —
1. *To cause loss,* ζημιόω *zēmioō.*
1 Co. 3. 15 shall suffer loss: but he himself shall be
Phil. 3. 8 for whom I have suffered the loss of all th.
2. *To bear long,* μακροθυμέω *makrothumeō.*
1 Co. 13. 4 Charity suffereth long, (and) is kind; ch.
3. *To suffer before,* προπάσχω *propaschō.*
1 Th. 2. 2 But even after that we had suffered before
4. *To suffer with,* συμπάσχω *sumpaschō.*
Rom. 8. 17 if so be that we suffer with (him), that we
1 Co. 12. 26 all the members suffer with it; or one me.
5. *To be behind, lack,* ὑστερέω *hustereō.*
Phil. 4. 12 hungry, both to abound and to suffer need

SUFFER not, prosecution, shame, violence, to
1. *To dishonour,* ἀτιμάζω *atimazō.*
Acts 5. 41 counted worthy to suffer shame for his na.
2. *To be forced, urged vehemently,* βιάζομαι *biazomai*
Matt 11. 12 kingdom of heaven suffereth violence, and
3. *To run quickly, pursue,* διώκω *diōkō.*
Gal. 5. 11 why do I yet suffer persecution? then is
6. 12 only lest they should suffer persecution
2 Ti. 3. 12 all that will live godly..shall suffer pers.
4. *To hinder, restrain,* κωλύω *kōluō.*
Heb. 7. 23 because they were not suffered to contin.

SUFFERING —
Suffering, affection, πάθημα *pathēma.*
Rom. 8. 18 For I reckon that the sufferings of this pr.
2 Co. 1. 5 For as the sufferings of Christ abound in
1. 6 in the enduring of the same sufferings wh.
1. 7 that as ye are partakers of the sufferings
Phil. 3. 10 fellowship of his sufferings, being made
Col. 1. 24 Who now rejoice in my sufferings for you
Heb. 2. 9 suffering of death, crowned with glory and
2. 10 make the Captain..perfect through suff.
1 Pe. 1. 11 when it testified beforehand the sufferings
4. 13 as ye are partakers of Christ's sufferings
5. 1 witness of the sufferings of Christ, and

SUFFICE, be sufficed, to —

1. *To find for,* לְ מָצָא *matsa le.*
Num11. 22 the herds be slain for them, to suffice th.
11. 22 gathered together for them, to suffice th.
Judg 21. 14 and yet so they sufficed them not

2. *Many, much, enough,* רַב *rab.*
Deut. 3. 26 Let it suffice thee; speak no more unto
Eze. 44. 6 let it suffice you of all your abominations
45. 9 Let it suffice you, O princes of Israel: rem.

3. *Satisfied,* שָׂבֵעַ *sabea.*
Ruth 2. 14 and she did eat, and was sufficed, and le.

4. *Satiety,* שֹׂבַע *soba.*
Ruth 2. 18 that she had reserved after she was suffi.

5. *To suffice,* שָׂפַק *saphaq.*
1 Ki. 20. 10 dust of Samaria shall suffice for handfuls

6. *Sufficient,* ἀρκετός *arketos.*
1 Pe. 4. 3 For the time past of (our) life may suffice

7. *To suffice, satisfy,* ἀρκέω *arkeō.*
John14. 8 Lord, show us the Father, and it sufficeth

SUFFICIENCY, sufficient, sufficiently —

1. *Sufficiency,* דַּי *dai.*
Exod36. 7 For the stuff they had was sufficient for
Deut15. 8 shalt surely lend him sufficient for his ne.
Prov25. 16 eat so much as is sufficient for thee, lest
Isa. 40. 16 And Lebanon (is) not sufficient to burn
40. 16 beasts thereof sufficient for a burnt offer.

2. *For what sufficient,* לְמַדַּי [*dai*].
2 Ch. 30. 3 had not sanctified themselves sufficiently

3. *Sufficiency,* סֵפֶק *sepheq.*
Job 20. 22 In the fulness of his sufficiency he shall

4. *Many, much, enough,* רַב *rab.*
Deut33. 7 let his hands be sufficient for him; and be

5. *Satiety,* שָׂבְעָה *sobah.*
Isa. 23. 18 to eat sufficiently, and for durable cloth.

6. *Sufficient,* ἀρκετός *arketos.*
Matt. 6. 34 Sufficient unto the day (is) the evil there.

7. *To suffice, satisfy,* ἀρκέω *arkeō.*
John 6. 7 not sufficient for them, that every one of
2 Co. 12. 9 My grace is sufficient for thee; for my st.

8. *Self sufficiency,* αὐτάρκεια *autarkeia.*
2 Co. 9. 8 always having all sufficiency in all (things)

9. *Coming up to, sufficient,* ἱκανός *hikanos.*
2 Co. 2. 6 Sufficient to such a man (is) this punish.
2. 16 And who (is) sufficient for these things?
3. 5 Not that we are sufficient of ourselves

10. *Sufficiency,* ἱκανότης *hikanotēs.*
2 Co. 3. 5 of ourselves; but our sufficiency (is) of

SUIT, (to make) —

1. *To appease, weaken, smooth down,* חָלָה *chalah,* 3.
Job 11. 19 yea, many shall make suit unto thee

2. *Order, valuation, suit,* עֵרֶךְ *erek.*
Judg 17. 10 and a suit of apparel, and thy victuals. So

3. *Strife, pleading,* רִיב *rib.*
2 Sa. 15. 4 that every man which hath any suit or

SUKKIIMS, סֻכִּיִּים.
An African or Egyptian tribe, mentioned with the Lubim, and the Ethiopians; the Suchœ of Pliny. B.C. 29.
2 Ch. 12. 3 the Lubims, the S., and the Ethiopians

SUM (of money), to —

1. *Atonement, price, satisfaction,* כֹּפֶר *kopher.*
Exod 21. 30 If there be laid on him a sum of money

2. *Number, narration,* מִסְפָּר *mispar.*
2 Sa. 24. 9 Joab gave up the sum of the number of
1 Ch. 21. 5 Joab gave the sum of the number of the

3. *To inspect, lay a charge on,* פָּקַד *paqad.*
Exod 38. 21 This is the sum of the tabernacle, (even)

4. *Covering, exposition,* פָּרָשָׁה *parashah.*
Esth. 4. 7 sum of the money that Haman had prom.

5. *Head, sum,* רֹאשׁ *rosh.*
Exod 30. 12 When thou takest the sum of the childr.
Num 1. 2 Take ye the sum of all the congregation
1. 49 neither take the sum of them among the
4. 2 Take the sum of the sons of Kohath from
4. 22 Take also the sum of the sons of Gershon
26. 2 Take the sum of all the congregation of
31. 26 Take the sum of the prey that was taken
31. 49 Thy servants have taken the sum of the
Psa. 139. 17 O God! how great is the sum of them

6. *Head, sum,* רֵאשׁ *resh.*
Dan. 7. 1 wrote the dream, (and) told the sum of

7. *Measurement, standard,* תָּכְנִית *toknith.*
Eze. 28. 12 Thou sealest up the sum, full of wisdom

8. *To perfect, finish, consume,* תָּמַם *tamam,* 5.
2 Ki. 22. 4 that he may sum the silver which is bro.

9. *Sum, recapitulation,* κεφάλαιον *kephalaion.*
Acts 22. 28 With a great sum obtained I this freedom
Heb. 8. 1 (this is) the sum: We have such an high

10. *Honour, value,* τιμή *timē.*
Acts 7. 16 bought for a sum of money of the sons of

SUMMER, (fruit, house), to —

1. *A cooling,* מְקֵרָה *meqerah.*
Judg. 3. 20 he was sitting in a summer parlour, whi.
Judg. 3. 24 Surely he covereth his feet in his summer

2. *To pass the summer,* קוּץ *quts.*
Isa. 18. 6 fowls shall summer upon them, and all

3. *Summer,* קַיִט *qayit.*
Dan. 2. 35 became like the chaff of the summer thr.

4. *Summer, early fruit,* קַיִץ *qayits.*
Gen. 8. 22 summer and winter, and day and night
2 Sa. 16. 1 an hundred of summer fruits, and a bot.
16. 2 bread and summer fruit for the young men
Psa. 32. 4 moisture is turned into the drought of su.
74. 17 earth: thou hast made summer and wint.
Prov. 6. 8 Provideth her meat in the summer, (and)
10. 5 He that gathereth in summer (is) a
26. 1 As snow in summer, and as rain in harv.
30. 25 they prepare their meat in the summer
Isa. 16. 9 for the shouting for thy summer fruits
28. 4 as the hasty fruit before the summer; wh.
Jer. 8. 20 The harvest is past, the summer is ended
40. 10 gather ye wine, and summer fruits, and
40. 12 gathered wine and summer fruits very mu.
48. 32 spoiler is fallen upon thy summer fruits
Amos 3. 15 smite the winter house with the summer h.
8. 1 and behold a basket of summer fruit
8. 2 And I said, A basket of summer fruit
Mic. 7. 1 when they have gathered the summer fr.
Zech. 14. 8 in summer and in winter shall it be

5. *Summer,* θέρος *theros.*
Matt 24. 32 putteth forth leaves, ye know that sum.
Mark13. 28 putteth forth leaves, ye know that sum.
Luke21. 30 know..that summer is now nigh at hand

SUMPTUOUSLY —

Shining, brightly, λαμπρῶς *lamprōs.*
Luke16. 19 rich man, which..fared sumptuously

SUN —

1. *Light,* אוֹר *or.*
Job 31. 26 If I beheld the sun when it shined, or

2. *Heat,* חַמָּה *chammah.*
Job 30. 28 I went mourning without the sun: I sto.
Song 6. 10 fair as the moon, clear as the sun, (and)
Isa. 24. 23 sun ashamed, when the LORD of hosts shall
30. 26 light of the sun, and the light of the sun

3. *Itch, burning heat,* חֶרֶס *cheres.*
Judg. 8. 13 returned from battle before the sun (was
14. 18 on the seventh day before the sun went
Job 9. 7 Which commandeth the sun, and it riseth

4. *A ministrant, the sun,* שֶׁמֶשׁ *shemesh.*
Gen. 15. 12 when the sun was going down, a deep sl.
15. 17 sun went down, and it was dark, behold
19. 23 sun was risen upon the earth when Lot
28. 11 tarried there all night, because the sun
32. 31 as he passed over Penuel the sun rose upon
37. 9 behold, the sun..made obeisance to me
Exod16. 21 and when the sun waxed hot, it melted
17. 12 steady until the going down of the sun
22. 3 If the sun be risen upon him, (there shall
22. 26 unto him by that the sun goeth down
Lev. 22. 7 when the sun is down, he shall be clean
Num25. 4 hang them up..against the sun, that
Deut. 4. 19 when thou seest the sun, and the moon
11. 30 by the way where the sun goeth down
16. 6 at even, at the going down of the sun, at
17. 3 either the sun, or moon, or any of the host
23. 11 when the sun is down, he shall come into
24. 13 when the sun goeth down, that he may
24. 15 neither shall the sun go down upon it; for
33. 14 precious fruits (brought forth) by the sun
Josh. 1. 4 toward the going down of the sun, shall
8. 29 as soon as the sun was down, Joshua co.
10. 12 Sun, stand thou still upon Gibeon; and
10. 13 sun stood still..So the sun stood still in
10. 27 at the time of the going down of the sun
12. 1 toward the rising of the sun, from the ri.
Judg. 5. 31 (let) them that love him (be) as the sun
9. 33 as soon as the sun is up, thou shalt rise
19. 14 sun went down upon them (when they
1 Sa. 11. 9 Tomorrow, by (that time) the sun be hot
2 Sa. 2. 24 sun went down when they were come to
3. 35 taste bread, or ought else, till the sun be
12. 11 lie with thy wives in the sight of this sun
12. 12 thing before all Israel, and before the sun
23. 4 light of the morning (when) the sun riseth
1 Ki. 22. 36 about the going down of the sun, saying
2 Ki. 3. 22 sun shone upon the water, and the Moab.
23. 5 to the sun, and to the moon, and to the
23. 11 the kings of Judah had given to the sun
23. 11 and burned the chariots of the sun with
2 Ch. 18. 34 about the time of the sun going down he
Neh. 7. 3 Let not the gates..be opened until the sun
Job 8. 16 He (is) green before the sun, and his bra.
Psa. 19. 4 them hath he set a tabernacle for the sun
50. 1 from the rising of the sun unto the going
58. 8 a woman, (that) they may not see the sun
72. 5 They shall fear thee as long as the sun
72. 17 name shall be continued as long as the sun
74. 16 thou hast prepared the light and the sun
84. 11 For the LORD God (is) a sun and shield
89. 36 endure for ever, and his throne as the sun
104. 19 appointed the moon for seasons: the sun
104. 22 sun ariseth, they gather themselves toge.
113. 3 From the rising of the sun unto the going
121. 6 sun shall not smite thee by day, nor the
136. 8 sun to rule by day: for his mercy (endur.)
148. 3 Praise ye him, sun and moon: praise him
Eccl. 1. 3 his labour which he taketh under the sun
1. 5 sun also ariseth, and the sun goeth down
1. 9 and (there is) no new (thing) under the sun
Eccl. 1. 14 all the works that are done under the sun
2. 11 and (there was) no profit under the sun
2. 17 the work that is wrought under the sun
2. 18 labour which I had taken under the sun
2. 19 have showed myself wise under the sun
2. 20 all the labour which I took under the sun
2. 22 wherein he hath laboured under the sun?
3. 16 moreover I saw under the sun the place
4. 1 oppressions that are done under the sun
4. 3 the evil work that is done under the sun
4. 7 returned, and I saw vanity under the sun
4. 15 all the living which walk under the sun
5. 13 sore evil (which) I have seen under the sun
5. 18 his labour that he taketh under the sun
6. 1 an evil which I have seen under the sun
6. 5 Moreover he hath not seen the sun, nor
6. 12 what shall be after him under the sun?
7. 11 and..profit to them that see the sun
8. 9 every work that is done under the sun
8. 15 man hath no better thing under the sun
8. 15 life, which God giveth him under the sun
8. 17 find out the work..done under the sun
9. 3 all (things) that are done under the sun
9. 6 in any (thing) that is done under the sun
9. 9 which he hath given thee under the sun
9. 9 labour which thou takest under the sun
9. 11 returned, and saw under the sun, that
9. 13 wisdom have I seen also under the sun
10. 5 an evil (which) I have seen under the sun
11. 7 pleasant..for the eyes to behold the sun
12. 2 While the sun, or the light, or the moon
Song 1. 6 because the sun hath looked upon me: my
Isa. 13. 10 the sun shall be darkened in his going fo.
38. 8 which is gone down in the sun dial of A.
38. 8 So the sun returned ten degrees, by which
41. 25 from the rising of the sun shall he call up.
45. 6 may know from the rising of the sun, and
49. 10 neither shall the heat nor sun smite them
59. 19 and his glory from the rising of the sun
60. 19 The sun shall be no more thy light by day
60. 20 Thy sun shall no more go down; neither
Jer. 8. 2 they shall spread them before the sun, and
15. 9 her sun is gone down while (it was) yet d.
31. 35 which giveth the sun for a light by day
Eze. 8. 16 they worshipped the sun toward the east
32. 7 I will cover the sun with a cloud, and the
Joel. 2. 10 sun and the moon shall be dark, and the
2. 31 The sun shall be turned into darkness, and
3. 15 The sun and the moon shall be darkened
Dan. 6. 14 laboured till the going down of the sun to
Amos 8. 9 I will cause the sun to go down at noon
Jon. 4. 8 sun did arise..and the sun beat upon the
Hab. 3. 11 The sun (and) moon stood still in their
Mic. 3. 6 the sun shall go down over the prophets
Nah. 3. 17 when the sun ariseth they flee away, and
Mal. 1. 11 For from the rising of the sun, even unto
4. 2 unto you that fear my name shall the sun

5. *Sun, solar light,* ἥλιος *hēlios.*
Matt. 5. 45 for he maketh his sun to rise on the evil
13. 6 when the sun was up, they were scorched
13. 43 shall the righteous shine forth as the sun
17. 2 face did shine as the sun, and his raiment
24. 29 shall the sun be darkened, and the moon
Mark 1. 32 when the sun did set, they brought unto
4. 6 But when the sun was up, it was scorched
13. 24 sun shall be darkened, and the moon shall
16. 2 unto the sepulchre at the rising of the sun
Luke 4. 40 Now when the sun was setting, all they
21. 25 there shall be signs in the sun, and in the
23. 45 sun was darkened, and the veil of the te.
Acts 2. 20 The sun shall be turned into darkness, and
13. 11 be blind, not seeing the sun for a season
26. 13 brightness of the sun, shining round about
27. 20 when neither sun nor stars in many days
1 Co. 15. 41 one glory of the sun, and another glory of
Eph. 4. 26 let not the sun go down upon your wrath
Jas. 1. 11 For the sun is no sooner risen with a burn.
Rev. 1. 16 his countenance (was) as the sun shineth
6. 12 the sun became black as sackcloth of hair
7. 16 neither shall the sun light on them, nor
8. 12 and the third part of the sun was smitten
9. 2 sun and the air were darkened by reason
10. 1 face (was) as it were the sun, and his feet
12. 1 woman clothed with the sun, and the mo.
16. 8 angel poured out his vial upon the sun
19. 17 I saw an angel standing in the sun, and
21. 23 city had no need of the sun, neither of the
22. 5 need no candle, neither light of the sun

SUNRISING —

1. *Rising of the sun,* מִזְרַח שֶׁמֶשׁ *mizrach shemesh.*
Num 21. 11 the wilderness..toward the sunrising
Deut. 4. 41, 47 on this side Jordan, toward the sunris.
Josh. 1. 15 on this side Jordan toward the sunrising
13. 5 toward the sunrising, from Baal-gad un.
19. 12 toward the sunrising unto the border of
19. 27 turneth toward the sunrising to Beth-da.
19. 34 Judah upon Jordan toward the sunrising
Judg 20. 43 over against Gibeah toward the sunrising

2. *Rising,* מִזְרָח *mizrach.*
Num 34. 15 Jericho eastward, toward the sunrising

SUNDERED, to be —

To part, separate self, פָּרַד *parad,* 7.
Job 41. 17 stick together, that they cannot be sund.

SUNDRY times, at —

In many parts, πολυμερῶς *polumerōs.*
Heb. 1. 1 at sundry times and in divers manners sp.

SUNG, to be —
To be sung, שִׁיר *shir*, 6.
Isa. 26. 1 In that day shall this song be sung in the
SUNK, to be —
1. *To sink*, טָבַע *taba*.
Psa. 9. 15 heathen are sunk down in the pit (that)
Lam. 2. 9 Her gates are sunk into the ground; he
2. *To be sunk*, טָבַע *taba*, 6.
Jer. 38. 22 thy feet are sunk in the mire, (and) they
SUP (up), to —
1. *Desire, a crowd*, מְגַמָּה *megammah*.
Hab. 1. 9 their faces shall sup up(as) the east wind
2. *To sup, take evening meal*, δειπνέω *deipneō*.
Luke17. 8 Make ready wherewith I may sup, and g.
1 Co. 11. 25 also (he took) the cup, when he had sup.
Rev. 3. 20 will come in to him, and will sup with him
SUPERFLUOUS, superfluity, to have any thing —
1. *To be stretched out, superfluous*, שָׂרַע *sara*.
Lev. 21. 18 hath a flat nose, or any thing superfluous
22. 23 lamb that hath any thing superfluous or
2. *Abundance, superabundance*, περισσεία *perisseia*.
Jas. 1. 21 lay apart all filthiness and superfluity of
3. *Abundant, superfluous*, περισσός *perissos*.
2 Co. 9. 1 it is superfluous for me to write to you
SUPERSCRIPTION —
What is written upon or above, ἐπιγραφή *epigraphē*.
Matt 22. 20 Whose (is) this image and superscription
Mark12. 16 Whose (is) this image and superscription
15. 26 superscription of his accusation was wri.
Luke 20. 24 Whose image and superscription hath it?
23. 38 superscription also was written over him
SUPERSTITION, too superstitious —
1. *Much given to reverence*, δεισιδαιμονέστερος.
Acts 17. 22 perceive that in all things ye are too sup.
2. *Reverence of spirits*, δεισιδαιμονία *deisidaimonia*.
Acts 25. 19 questions against him of their own supe.
SUPPER —
1. *Supper, evening meal*, δεῖπνον *deipnon*
Mark 6. 21 Herod, on his birth day, made a supper to
Luke14. 12 When thou makest a dinner or a supper
14. 16 certain man made a great supper, and bade
14. 17 sent his servant at supper time to say to
14. 24 which were bidden shall taste of my sup.
John12. 2 There they made him a supper; and Martha
13. 2 supper being ended, the devil having now
13. 4 He riseth from supper, and laid aside his
21. 20 which also leaned on his breast at supper
1 Co. 11. 20 place, (this) is not to eat the Lord's supp.
11. 21 taketh before (other) his own supper: and
Rev. 19. 9 which are called unto the marriage supper
19. 17 Come..unto the supper of the great God
2. *To sup, take evening meal*, δειπνέω *deipneō*.
Luke22. 20 Likewise also the cup after supper, saying
SUPPLANT, to —
To take by the heel, supplant, trip up, עָקַב *aqab*.
Gen. 27. 36 for he hath supplanted me these two times
Jer. 9. 4 for every brother will utterly supplant, and
SUPPLE, to —
For cleansing (?), לְמִשְׁעִי *le-mishi*.
Eze. 16. 4 neither wast thou washed in water to su.
SUPPLIANT —
Suppliant, עָתַר *athar*.
Zeph. 3. 10 beyond the rivers of Ethiopia my suppli.
SUPPLICATION, (to make) —
1. *To smooth, appease*, חָלָה *chalah*, 3.
1 Sa. 13. 12 have not made supplication unto the Lo.
2. *To show self gracious, entreat grace*, חָנַן *chanan*, 7.
1 Ki. 8. 33 make supplication unto thee in this house
8. 47 make supplication unto thee in the land
8. 59 wherewith I have made supplication be.
9. 3 heard..thy supplication that thou hast
2 Ch. 6. 24 make supplication before thee in this ho.
Esth. 4. 8 to make supplication unto him, and to ma.
Job 8. 5 make thy supplication to the Almighty
9. 15 I would make supplication to my judge
Psa. 30. 8 and unto the LORD I made supplication
142. 1 with my voice..did I make my supplica.
Hos. 12. 4 made supplication unto him: he found
3. *To be gracious, to favour*, חָנַן *chanan*, 2.
Dan. 6. 11 praying and making supplication before
4. *To judge self, pray habitually*, פָּלַל *palal*, 7.
Isa. 45. 14 they shall make supplication unto thee
5. *Supplication for grace*, תְּחִנָּה *techinnah*.
1 Ki. 8. 28 have thou respect..to his supplication
8. 30 hearken thou to the supplication of thy
8. 38 What prayer and supplication soever be
8. 45 hear thou in heaven..their supplication
8. 49 hear thou their prayer and their supplic.
8. 52 thine eyes may be open unto the supplic.
8. 52 unto the supplication of thy people Isra.
8. 54 end of praying all this prayer and suppl.
9. 3 heard thy prayer and thy supplication th.
2 Ch. 6. 19 Have respect therefore..to his supplicat.
6. 29 what prayer (or) what supplication soever
6. 35, 39 Then hear thou..their supplication
33. 13 heard his supplication, and brought him
Psa. 6. 9 LORD hath heard my supplication; the L.
55. 1 and hide not thyself from my supplication
Psa.119. 170 my supplication come before thee, del.
Jer. 36. 7 It may be they will present their suppli.
37. 20 let my supplication..be accepted before
38. 26 presented my supplication before the ki.
42. 2 Let, we beseech thee, our supplication be
42. 9 sent me to present your supplication be.
Dan. 9. 20 presenting my supplication before the L.
6. *Supplications for grace*, תַּחֲנוּנוֹת *tachanunoth*.
Psa. 86. 6 and attend to the voice of my supplicat.
7. *Supplications for grace*, תַּחֲנוּנִים *tachanunim*.
2 Ch. 6. 21 Hearken therefore unto the supplications
Job 41. 3 Will he make many supplications unto
Psa. 28. 2 Hear the voice of my supplications when
28. 6 he hath heard the voice of my supplicat.
31. 22 thou heardest the voice of my supplicati.
116. 1 hath heard my voice(and)my supplications
130. 2 attentive to the voice of my supplications
140. 6 hear the voice of my supplications, O L.
143. 1 O LORD, give ear to my supplications: in
Jer. 3. 21 weeping (and) supplications of the child.
31. 9 with supplications will I lead them: I will
Dan. 9. 3 to seek by prayer and supplications, with
9. 17 hear..his supplications, and cause thy
9. 18 for we do not present our supplications
9. 23 At the beginning of thy supplications the
Zech 12. 10 the spirit of grace and of supplications
8. *Supplication, deprecation*, δέησις *deēsis*.
Acts 1. 14 with one accord in prayer [and supplica.]
Eph. 6. 18 Praying always with all prayer and sup.
6. 18 with all perseverance and supplication
Phil. 4. 6 in every thing by prayer and supplication
1 Ti. 2. 1 first of all, supplications, prayers, interc.
5. 5 continueth in supplications and prayers
9. *Supplication, suppliant branch*, ἱκετηρία *hiketē*.
Heb. 5. 7 when he had offered up prayers and sup.
SUPPLY, (to) —
1. *To make fully up*, ἀναπληρόω *anaplēroō*.
1 Co.16. 17 lacking on your part they have supplied
Phil. 2. 30 to supply your lack of service toward me
2. *A supply*, ἐπιχορηγία *epichorēgia*.
Eph. 4. 16 compacted by that which every joint su.
Phil. 1. 19 and the supply of the spirit of Jesus Ch.
3. *To make full*, πληρόω *plēroō*.
Phil. 4. 19 But my God shall supply all your need
4. *To make fully up toward*, προσαναπληρόω.
2 Co. 9. 12 not only supplieth the want of the saints
11. 9 lacking to me the brethren..supplied, and
SUPPORT, to —
1. *To hold over against*, ἀντέχομαι *antechomai*.
1 Th. 5. 14 support the weak, be patient toward all
2. *To take or receive over against*, ἀντιλαμβάνομαι.
Acts 20. 35 so labouring ye ought to support the weak
SUPPOSE, to —
1. *To say*, אָמַר *amar*.
2 Sa. 13. 32 Let not my lord suppose (that) they have
2. *To think*, δοκέω *dokeō*.
Mark 6. 49 supposed it had been a spirit, and cried
Luke12. 51 Suppose ye that I am come to give peace
13. 2 Suppose ye that these Galileans were si.
24. 37 and supposed that they had seen a spirit
John 20. 15 She, supposing him to be the gardener
Acts 27. 13 supposing that they had obtained (their)
Heb. 10. 29 Of how much sorer punishment, suppose
3. *To lead, think, account, esteem*, ἡγέομαι *hēgeomai*.
Phil. 2. 25 Yet I supposed it necessary to send to
4. *To reckon*, λογίζομαι *logizomai*.
2 Co.11. 5 For I suppose I was not a whit behind
1 Pe. 5. 12 as I suppose, I have written briefly, exh.
5. *To reckon as law*, νομίζω *nomizō*.
Matt 20. 10 when the first came, they supposed that
Luke 2. 44 supposing him to have been in the comp.
3. 23 being as was supposed the son of Joseph
Acts 7. 25 For he supposed his brethren would have
14. 19 drew (him) out of the city, supposing he
16. 27 supposing that the prisoners had been
21. 29 whom they supposed that Paul had broug.
1 Co. 7. 26 I suppose therefore that this is good for
1 Ti. 6. 5 supposing that gain is godliness: from such
6. *To suppose, be of opinion*, οἴομαι *oiomai*, οἶμαι.
John21. 25 suppose that even the world itself could
Phil. 1. 16 supposing to add affliction to my bonds
7. *To take or receive under, apprehend*, ὑπολαμβάνω.
Luke 7. 43 I suppose that (he) to whom he forgave
Acts 2. 15 For these are not drunken as ye suppose
8. *To think under, suspect*, ὑπονοέω *huponoeō*.
Acts 25. 18 none accusation of such things as I supp.
SUPREME —
To hold over or above, ὑπερέχω *huperechō*.
1 Pe. 2. 13 whether it be to the king, as supreme
SUR, סוּר *turning aside, entrance*.
A gate of the house (of the king or of the temple) in Jerusalem, called in 2 Ch. 23. 5 "gate of the foundation."
2 Ki. 11. 6 a third part (shall be) at the gate of S.
SURE, (more) —
1. *To be or become faithful, stedfast*, אָמַן *aman*, 2.
1 Sa. 2. 35 will build him a sure house, and he shall
25. 28 will certainly make my lord a sure house
1 Ki. 11. 38 build thee a sure house, as I built for D.
Psa. 19. 7 the testimony of the LORD (is) sure, making
111. 7 judgment: all his commandments (are) s.
Isa. 22. 23 I will fasten him (as) a nail in a sure pl.
22. 25 the nail that is fastened in the sure place
33. 16 shall be given him, his waters (shall be) s.
55. 3 covenant with you, (even) the sure mercies
2. *To remain faithful, stedfast*, אָמַן *aman*, 5.
Dan. 2. 45 certain, and the interpretation thereof su.
3. *Faithfulness, stedfastness*, אֲמָנָה *amanah*.
Neh. 9. 38 because of all this we make a sure (cove.)
4. *Truth, stedfastness*, אֱמֶת *emeth*.
Prov.11. 18 that soweth righteousness (shall be) a sure
5. *To be founded, laid as a foundation*, יָסַד *yasad*, 6.
Isa. 28. 16 a precious corner (stone), a sure foundat.
6. *Confidence, trust*, מִבְטָח *mibtach*.
Isa. 32. 18 in sure dwellings, and in quiet resting pl.
7. *Standing, abiding, established*, קַיָּם *qayyam*.
Dan. 4. 26 thy kingdom shall be sure unto thee, after
8. *To observe, watch, keep*, שָׁמַר *shamar*.
2 Sa. 23. 5 covenant, ordered in all (things), and sure
9. *Firm, secure, safe, certain*, ἀσφαλής *asphalēs*.
Heb. 6. 19 both sure and stedfast, and which enter.
10. *Firm, sure, stedfast*, βέβαιος *bebaios*.
Rom 4. 16 the promise might be sure to all the seed
2 Pe. 1. 10 make your calling and election sure: for
1. 19 We have also a more sure word of proph.
11. *Faithful, believing*, πιστός *pistos*.
Acts 13. 34 I will give you the sure mercies of David
12. *Firm, solid*, στερεός *stereos*.
2 Ti. 2. 19 the foundation of God standeth sure, har.
SURE, to be, make, or be made —
1. *To be faithful, stedfast*, אָמַן *aman*, 2.
Psa. 93. 5 Thy testimonies are very sure: holiness
2. *To lean on, trust, be confident*, בָּטַח *batach*.
Prov. 11. 15 and he that hateth suretiship is sure
3. *To be strong, hard*, חָזַק *chazaq*.
Deut.12. 23 Only be sure that thou eat not the blood
4. *To know*, יָדַע *yada*.
Exod. 3. 19 I am sure that the king of Egypt will not
Num.32. 23 and be sure your sin will find you out
1 Sa. 20. 7 be sure that evil is determined by him
2 Sa. 1. 10 because I was sure that he could not live
5. *To rise up, stand still*, קוּם *qum*.
Gen. 23. 17 the borders round about, were made sure
23. 20 field, and the cave..were made sure unto
6. *To enlarge, strengthen*, רָהַב *rahab*.
Prov. 6. 3 humble thyself, and make sure thy friend
7. *To make safe, secure*, ἀσφαλίζω *asphalizō*.
Matt.27. 64 that the sepulchre be made sure until the
27. 65 said..go your way, make (it) as sure as ye
27. 66 made the sepulchre sure, sealing the stone
8. *To know, take cognizance of*, γινώσκω *ginōskō*.
Luke10. 11 be ye sure of this, that the kingdom of G.
John 6. 69 we believe and are sure that thou art th.
9. *To see, know, be acquainted with*, οἶδα, *oida*.
Rom. 2. 2 But we are sure that the judg. Jo. 16. 30.
15. 29 am sure that, when I come unto you, I sh.
SURELY, of a surety —
1. *But, truly, yet*, אוּלָם *ulam*.
Job 13. 3 Surely I would speak to the Almighty, and
14. 18 surely the mountain falling cometh to no.
2. *Only*, אַךְ *ak*.
Gen. 9. 5 surely your blood of your lives will I re.
26. 9 Behold, of a surety she (is) thy wife; and
29. 14 Surely thou (art) my bone and my flesh
Prov.22. 16 he that giveth to the rich, (shall) surely
3. *Surely, but, yet*, אָכֵן *aken*.
Gen. 28. 16 Surely the LORD is in this place, and I kn.
Exod. 2. 14 feared, and said, Surely this thing is kn.
1 Sa. 15. 32 said, Surely the bitterness of death is pa.
1 Ki. 11. 2 surely they will turn away your heart af.
Isa. 40. 7 bloweth upon it: surely the people (is)
49. 4 surely my judgment (is) with the LORD
53. 4 Surely he hath borne our griefs and car.
Jer. 3. 20 Surely (as) a wife treacherously departe.
4. 10 surely thou hast greatly deceived this p.
4. *Truly, indeed*, אֻמְנָם *umnam*.
Gen. 18. 13 Shall I of a surety bear a child, which am
5. *Truly, indeed*, אָמְנָם *omnam*.
Job 34. 12 Yea, surely God will not do wickedly, ne.
6. *If not*, אִם לֹא *im lō*.
Num 14. 35 will surely do it unto all this evil congre.
1 Ki. 20. 23 and surely we shall be stronger than they
7. *Confidence, trust*, בֶּטַח *betach*.
Prov 10. 9 He that walketh uprightly walketh sure
8. *A son of*, בֶּן־ *ben*.
2 Sa. 12. 5 the man that hath done this ..shall surely
9. *To know, be acquainted with*, יָדַע *yada*.
Gen. 15. 13 Know of a surety that thy seed shall be
10. *That, because*, כִּי *ki*.
Gen. 29. 32 Surely the LORD hath looked upon my a.
11. *Therefore*, לָכֵן *la-ken*.
1 Sa. 28. 2 Surely thou shalt know what thy servant

12. *Only, surely, nevertheless,* רַק *raq.*
Gen. 20. 11 Surely the fear of God (is) not in this pl.

13. *Truly, really, certainly,* ἀληθῶς *alēthōs.*
Matt 26. 73 Surely thou also art (one) of them; for
Mark 14. 70 surely thou art (one) of them: for thou
John 17. 8 have known surely that I came out from
Acts 12. 11 Now I know of a surety, that the Lord ha.

14. *Indeed,* ἦ μήν *ē mēn.*
Heb. 6. 14 Saying, [Surely] blessing I will bless thee

15. *Verily, indeed, truly,* ναί *nai.*
Rev. 22. 20 saith, Surely I come quickly. Amen. Even

16. *By all means, entirely,* πάντως *pantōs.*
Luke 4. 23 Ye will surely say unto me this proverb

SURELY (believed), to be —
1. *To be or become faithful, stedfast,* אָמַן *aman,* 2.
Hos. 5. 9 I made known that which shall surely be
2. *To bear on fully,* πληροφορέω *plērophoreō.*
Luke 1. 1 things which are most surely believed am.

SURELY (no more, none, not) —
If, אִם *im.*
Num 14. 23 Surely they shall not see the land which
32. 11 Surely none of the men that came up out
Isa. 62. 8 Surely I will no more give thy corn (to be)

SURETISHIP, surety —
1. *Pledge, surety,* עֲרֻבָּה *arubbah.*
Prov 17. 18 becometh surety in the presence of his fr.
2. *To strike,* תָּקַע *taqa.* (partic.).
Prov 11. 15 and he that hateth suretiship is sure
3. *A bail, pledge, surety,* ἔγγυος *egguos.*
Heb. 7. 22 By so much was Jesus made a surety of a

SURETY, to be, become, put in —
1. *To be (become) surety,* עָרַב *arab.*
Gen. 43. 9 I will be surety for him; of my hand shalt
44. 32 For thy servant became surety for the lad
Job 17. 3 Lay down now, put me in a surety with
Psa. 119. 122 Be surety for thy servant for good: let
Prov. 6. 1 My son, if thou be surety for thy friend
11. 15 He that is surety for a stranger shall sm.
20. 16 garment that is surety (for); 22. 26; 27. 13
2. *Become surety by a pledge,* עָרַב עֲרֻבָּה [*arab*].
Prov. 17. 18 becometh surety in the presence of his

SURFEITING —
A headache, κραιπάλη *kraipalē.*
Luke 21. 34 hearts be overcharged with surfeiting, and

SURMISINGS—
A suspicion, surmise, ὑπόνοια *huponoia.*
1 Ti. 6. 4 whereof cometh envy..evil surmisings

SURNAME, (be surnamed,) to —
1. *To surname, give flattering titles,* כָּנָה *kanah,* 3.
Isa. 44. 5 surname (himself) by the name of Israel
45. 4 surnamed thee, though thou hast not kn.
2. *To call upon, be surnamed,* ἐπικαλέομαι *epikale.*
Matt 10. 3 Lebbæus, [whose surname was Thaddæus]
Luke 22. 3 Then entered Satan into Judas [surnam.]
Acts 1. 23 called Barsabas, who was surnamed Jus.
4. 36 Joses, who by the apostles was surnamed
10. 5 call for (one) Simon, whose surname is P.
10. 18 whether Simon, which was surnamed Pe.
10. 32 call hither Simon, whose surname is Pet.
11. 13 and call for Simon, whose surname is Pe.
12. 12 mother of John, whose surname was Ma.
12. 25 took with them John, whose surname was
15. 22 Judas [surnamed] Barsabas, and Silas, ch.
3. *To put a name upon,* ἐπιτίθημι ὄνομα [*epitithēmi*].
Mark 3. 16 And Simon he surnamed Peter
3. 17 surnamed them Boanerges, which is, The
4. *To call,* καλέω *kaleō.*
Acts 15. 37 take with them John, whose surname was

SURPRISE, be surprised, to —
1. *To lay hold,* אָחַז *achaz.*
Isa. 33. 14 fearfulness hath surprised the hypocrites
2. *To be caught, captured,* תָּפַשׂ *taphas,* 2.
Jer. 48. 41 strongholds are surprised, and the migh.
51. 41 the praise of the whole earth surprised!

SUSANCHITES, שׁוּשַׁנְכָיֵא.
The inhabitants of the city *Shushan* or *Susi*, or of the province *Susiana*, who were transplanted to Samaria by Shalmanezer.
Ezra 4. 9 the S., the Dehavites, (and) the Elamites

SU-SAN'-NA, Σουσάννα *lily.*
One of the women who ministered to Christ of their substance, and who followed him in his journeyings.
Luke 8. 3 S., and many others, which ministered

SU'-SI, סוּסִי *Jah is swift or rejoicing.*
A Manassite, father of Gaddi, one of the twelve men sent to spy out the land. B.C. 1492.
Num 13. 11 of the tribe of Manasseh, Gaddi..son of S.

SUSTAIN, to —
1. *To contain, sustain,* כּוּל *kul,* 3a.
1 Ki. 17. 9 commanded a widow woman there to s.
Neh. 9. 21 forty years didst thou sustain them in the
Psa. 55. 22 shall sustain thee: he shall never suffer
Prov. 18. 14 The spirit of a man will sustain his infir.
2. *To support,* סָמַךְ *samak.*
Gen. 27. 37 with corn and wine have I sustained him
Psa. 3. 5 slept; I awaked; for the LORD sustained
Isa. 59. 16 and his righteousness, it sustained him

SUSTENANCE, (to provide) —
1. *To contain, sustain,* כּוּל *kul,* 3a.
2 Sa. 19. 32 provided the king of sustenance while he
2. *Life preserver, sustenance, quickening,* מִחְיָה.
Judg. 6. 4 left no sustenance for Israel, neither sh.
3. *Food, sustenance,* χόρτασμα *chortasma.*
Acts 7. 11 affliction: and our fathers found no sust.

SWADDLE, to be swaddled, to —
1. *To be swaddled,* חָתַל *chathal,* 4, 6.
Eze. 16. 4 wast not salted at all, nor swaddled at all
2. *To stretch out, swaddle,* טָפַח *taphach,* 3.
Lam. 2. 22 those that I have swaddled and brought

SWADDLING band, to wrap in swaddling clothes —
1. *A swaddling band,* חֲתֻלָּה *chathullah.*
Job 38. 9 thick darkness a swaddling band for it
2. *To swaddle,* σπαργανόω *sparganoō.*
Luke 2. 7 wrapped him in swaddling clothes, and
2. 12 find the babe wrapped in swaddling clot.

SWALLOW —
1. *A swallow, wild pigeon,* דְּרוֹר *deror.*
Psa. 84. 3 found an house, and the swallow a nest
Prov 26. 2 as the swallow by flying, so the curse ca.
2. *A crane, swallow,* עָגוּר *agur.*
Isa. 38. 14 Like a crane (or) a swallow, so did I cha.
Jer. 8. 7 the crane and the swallow observe the ti.

SWALLOW (down, up), to —
1. *To swallow,* בָּלַע *bala.*
Exod 7. 12 but Aaron's rod swallowed up their rods
15. 12 thy right hand, the earth swallowed them
Num 16. 30 earth open her mouth, and swallow..up
16. 32 opened her mouth, and swallowed them up
16. 34 they said, Lest the earth swallow us up
26. 10 swallowed them up together with Korah
Deut 11. 6 swallowed them up, and their households
Job 7. 19 let me alone till I swallow down my spit.
20. 15 He hath swallowed down riches, and he
20. 18 he restore, and shall not swallow(it)down
Psa. 69. 15 neither let the deep swallow me up, and
106. 17 The earth opened and swallowed up Dat.
124. 3 Then they had swallowed us up quick, wh.
Prov. 1. 12 Let us swallow them up alive as the grave
Jer. 51. 34 he hath swallowed me up like a dragon
Hos. 8. 7 it yield, the strangers shall swallow it up
Jon. 1. 17 had prepared a great fish to swallow up
2. *To be swallowed,* בָּלַע *bala,* 2.
Isa. 28. 7 they are swallowed up of wine, they are
Hos. 8. 8 Israel is swallowed up: now shall they be
3. *To swallow,* בָּלַע *bala,* 3.
2 Sa. 20. 19 why wilt thou swallow up the inheritance
20. 20 far be it from me, that I should swallow u
Psa. 21. 9 LORD shall swallow them up in his wrath
35. 25 them not say, We have swallowed him up
Eccl. 10. 12 but the lips of a fool will swallow up him.
Isa. 25. 8 He will swallow up death in victory; and
49. 19 they that swallowed thee up shall be far
Lam. 2. 2 LORD hath swallowed up all the habitat.
2. 5 swallowed up Israel, he hath swallowed up
2. 16 We have swallowed (her) up; certainly
4. *To swallow up, run swiftly,* גָּמָא *gama,* 3.
Job 39. 24 He swalloweth the ground with fierceness
5. *To swallow up, be rash,* לוּעַ *lua.*
Obad. 16 shall swallow down, and they shall be as
6. *To pant, desire, swallow up,* שָׁאַף *shaaph.*
Job 5. 5 the robber swalloweth up their substance
Psa. 56. 1 for man would swallow me up; he fight.
56. 2 Mine enemies would daily swallow..up
57. 3 reproach of him that would swallow..up
Eze. 36. 3 swallowed you up on every side, that ye
Amos 8. 4 Hear this, O ye that swallow up the nee.
7. *To drink down, swallow up,* καταπίνω *katapinō.*
Matt 23. 24 which strain at a gnat, and swallow a ca.
Rev. 12. 16 swallowed up the flood which the dragon

SWALLOWED up, (to be) —
1. *To be swallowed up,* בָּלַע *bala,* 4.
2 Sa. 17. 16 lest the king be swallowed up, and all the
Job 37. 20 speak, surely he shall be swallowed up
2. *Swallowing up,* בֶּלַע *bela.*
Jer. 51. 44 that which he hath swallowed up: and the
3. *To swallow up, be rash,* לוּעַ *lua.*
Job 6. 3 therefore my words are swallowed up
4. *To drink down, swallow up,* καταπίνω *katapinō.*
1 Co. 15. 54 written, Death is swallowed up in victory
2 Co. 2. 7 perhaps such a one should be swallo. up
5. 4 that mortality might be swallowed up of

SWAN —
Chameleon, owl, תִּנְשֶׁמֶת *tinshemeth.*
Lev. 11. 18 the swan, and the pelican, and the gier
Deut 14. 16 little owl, and the great owl, and the sw.

SWARM —
1. *Company, swarm, congregation,* עֵדָה *edah.*
Judg 14. 8 swarm of bees and honey in the carcase
2. *A beetle, dog fly,* עָרֹב *arob.*
Exod 8. 21 I will send swarms (of flies) upon thee, and
8. 21 houses..shall be full of swarm (of flies)
Exod. 8. 22 that no swarms (of flies) shall be there, to
8. 24 there came a grievous swarm (of flies) into
8. 24 corrupted by reason of the swarm (of flies)
8. 29 entreat the LORD that the swarms (of fl.)
8. 31 he removed the swarms (of flies) from Ph.

SWEAR, (to cause or make) to —
1. *To appeal to God, take oath,* אָלָה *alah.*
Hos. 4. 2 By swearing, and lying, and killing, and
10. 4 swearing falsely in making a covenant
2. *To cause to appeal to God,* אָלָה *alah,* 5.
1 Ki. 8. 31 be laid upon him to cause him to swear
2 Ch. 6. 22 oath be laid upon him to make him swear
3. *To swear (in order to satisfy one),* שָׁבַע *shaba.*
Eze. 21. 23 to them that have sworn oaths: but he w.
4. *To be or become sworn, swear,* שָׁבַע *shaba,* 2.
Gen. 21. 23 therefore swear unto me here by God, that
21. 24 And Abraham said, I will swear
21. 31 because there they sware both of them
22. 16 By myself have I sworn, saith the LORD
24. 7 spake unto me, and that sware unto me
24. 9 and sware to him concerning that matter
25. 33 Swear to me this day; and he sware unto
26. 3 perform the oath which I sware unto A.
26. 31 rose up betimes..and sware one to anot.
31. 53 Jacob sware by the fear of his father Isa.
47. 31 Swear unto me. And he sware unto him
50. 24 which he sware to Abraham, to Isaac, and
Exod 13. 5 which he sware unto thy fathers to give
13. 11 sware unto thee and to thy fathers, and
32. 13 to whom thou swarest by thine own self
33. 1 land which I sware unto Abraham, to I.
Lev. 5. 4 Or if a soul swear, pronouncing with (his)
6. 3 sweareth falsely; in any of all these that
6. 5 Or all that about which he hath sworn fa.
19. 12 ye shall not swear by my name falsely
Num 11. 12 unto the land which thou swearest unto
14. 16 into the land which he sware unto them
14. 23 shall not see the land which I sware unto
30. 2 swear an oath to bind his soul with a bo.
32. 10 was kindled the same time, and he sware
32. 11 shall see the land which I sware unto A.
Deut. 1. 8 LORD sware unto your fathers, Abraham
1. 34 LORD heard the voice..and sware, saying
1. 35 land, which I sware to give unto your fa.
2. 14 among the host, as the LORD sware unto
4. 21 sware that I should not go over Jordan
4. 31 covenant of thy fathers which he sware
6. 10 which he sware unto thy fathers, to Abr.
6. 13 and serve him, and shalt swear by his na.
6. 18 good land which the LORD sware unto thy
6. 23 the land which he sware unto our fathers
7. 8 oath which he had sworn unto your fath.
7. 12 the mercy which he sware unto thy fath.
7. 13 land which he sware unto thy fathers to
8. 1 land which the LORD sware unto your fa.
8. 18 covenant which he sware unto thy fathers
9. 5 word which the LORD sware unto thy fat.
10. 11 land which I sware unto their fathers to
10. 20 shalt thou cleave, and swear by his name
11. 9, 21 land which the LORD sware unto your
13. 17 multiply thee, as he hath sworn unto thy
19. 8 enlarge thy coast, as he hath sworn unto
26. 3 country which the LORD sware unto our
26. 15 as thou swarest unto our fathers, a land
28. 9 as he hath sworn unto thee, if thou shalt
28. 11 land which the LORD sware unto thy fat.
29. 13 as he hath sworn unto thy fathers, to Ab.
30. 20 land which the LORD sware unto thy fath
31. 7 land which the LORD hath sworn unto th.
31. 20 the land which I sware unto their fathers
31. 21 brought them into the land which I sware
31. 23 into the land which I sware unto them
34. 4 This (is) the land which I sware unto Ab.
Josh. 1. 6 land which I sware unto their fathers to
2. 12 swear unto me by the LORD, since I have
5. 6 unto whom the LORD sware that he would
5. 6 land which the LORD sware unto their fa.
6. 22 bring out thence the woman..as ye sware
9. 15 princes of the congregation sware unto th.
9. 18 princes of the congregation had sworn un.
9. 19 We have sworn unto them by the LORD
9. 20 because of the oath which we sware unto
14. 9 Moses sware on that day, saying, Surely
21. 43 which he sware to give unto their fathers
21. 44 according to all that he sware unto their
Judg. 2. 1 unto the land which I sware unto your fa.
2. 15 as the LORD had sworn unto them: and
15. 12 Swear unto me, that ye will not fall upon
21. 1 men of Israel had sworn in Mizpeh, saying
21. 7 seeing we have sworn by the LORD that
21. 18 for the children of Israel have sworn, say.
1 Sa. 3. 14 therefore I have sworn unto the house of
19. 6 and Saul sware, (As) the LORD liveth, he
20. 3 David sware moreover, and said, Thy fa.
20. 42 forasmuch as we have sworn both of us in
24. 21 Swear now therefore unto me by the LORD
24. 22 David sware unto Saul. And Saul went
28. 10 Saul sware to her by the LORD, saying
30. 15 Swear unto me by God that thou wilt ne.
2 Sa. 3. 9 as the LORD hath sworn to David, even so
3. 35 David sware, saying, So do God to me, and
19. 7 for I swear by the LORD, if thou go not fo.
19. 23 Thou shalt not die. And the king sware
21. 2 the children of Israel had sworn unto them
21. 17 Then the men of David sware unto him
1 Ki. 1. 13 Didst not thou..swear unto thine handm.
1. 17 thou swarest by the LORD thy God unto
1. 29 the king sware and said..the LORD liveth
1. 30 as I sware unto thee by the LORD God of

1 Ki. 1. 51 Let king Solomon swear unto me to day
2. 8 I sware to him by the LORD, saying, I will
2. 23 Then king Solomon sware by the LORD
2 Ki.25. 24 Gedaliah sware to them, and to their men
2 Ch.15. 14 they sware unto the LORD with a loud vo.
15. 15 for they had sworn with all their heart
Ezra 10. 5 do according to this word. And they sware
Psa. 15. 4 sweareth to (his own) hurt, and changeth
24. 4 who hath not lifted up his soul..nor sworn
63. 11 every one that sweareth by him shall gl.
89. 3 I have sworn unto David my servant
89. 35 Once have I sworn by my holiness that I
89. 49 thou swarest unto David in thy truth?
95. 11 Unto whom I sware in my wrath, that th.
102. 8 they that are mad against me are sworn
110. 4 The LORD hath sworn, and will not repent
119. 106 I have sworn, and I will perform (it), that
132. 2 How he sware unto the LORD..vowed unto
132. 11 LORD hath sworn (in) truth unto David
Eccl. 9. 2 he that sweareth, as (he) that feareth an
Isa. 14. 24 LORD of hosts hath sworn, saying, Surely
19. 18 shall five cities in the land of Egypt..sw.
45. 23 I have sworn..That..every tongue shall sw.
48. 1 which swear by the name of the LORD
54. 9 I have sworn that..so have I sworn that
62. 8 LORD hath sworn by his right hand, and
65. 16 he that sweareth in the earth shall swear
Jer. 4. 2 thou shalt swear, The LORD liveth, in tr.
5. 2 they say, The LORD..surely they swear
5. 7 thy children have forsaken me, and sworn
7. 9 Will ye steal, murder..and swear falsely
11. 5 I may perform the oath which I have sw.
12. 16 to swear by my name..to swear by Baal
22. 5 I swear by myself, saith the LORD, that
32. 22 which thou didst swear to their fathers
38. 16 Zedekiah the king sware secretly unto Je.
40. 9 Gedaliah..sware unto them, and to their
44. 26 I have sworn by my great name, saith the
49. 13 I have sworn by myself, saith the LORD
51. 14 The LORD of hosts hath sworn by himself
Eze. 16. 8 I sware unto thee, and entered into a co.
21. 23 it shall be..to them that have sworn oaths
Dan. 12. 7 and sware by him that liveth for ever
Hos. 4. 15 neither go ye up to Beth-aven, nor swear
Amos 4. 2 The Lord GOD hath sworn by his holiness
6. 8 Lord GOD hath sworn by himself, saith
8. 7 LORD hath sworn by the excellency of J.
8. 14 They that swear by the sin of Samaria
Mic. 7. 20 which thou hast sworn unto our fathers
Zeph. 1. 5 that swear by the LORD, and that swear
Zech. 5. 3 every one that sweareth shall be cut off
5. 4 into the house of him that sweareth fal.

5. *A hand on the throne of Jah* (error), יָד עַל־כֵּס [*yad*].
Exod17. 16 For he said, Because the LORD hath sworn

6. *Master (possessor) of an oath*, בַּעַל שְׁבוּעָה [*baal*].
Neh. 6. 18 For (there were) many in Judah sworn

7. *To lift up (the hand)*, (יָד) נָשָׂא *nasa (yad)*.
Exod. 6. 8 the land, concerning the which I did swear
Num14. 30 which I sware to make you dwell therein
Neh. 9. 15 land which thou hadst sworn to give them
Isa. 3. 7 In that day shall he swear, saying, I will

8. *To cause to swear*, שָׁבַע *shaba*, 5.
Gen. 24. 3 I will make thee swear by the LORD, the
24. 37 my master made me swear, saying, Thou
50. 5 My father made me swear, saying, Lo, I
50. 6 Go..bury thy father..as he made thee sw.
Exod13. 19 he had straitly sworn the children of Is.
Josh. 2. 17, 20 oath which thou hast made us swear
23. 7 nor cause to swear..neither serve them
1 Sa. 20. 17 Jonathan caused David to swear again
1 Ki. 2. 42 Did I not make thee to swear by the LORD
2 Ch.36. 13 Nebuchadnezzar, who had made him sw.
Ezra 10. 5 Then arose Ezra, and made..Israel, to sw.
Neh.13. 25 I contended..and made them swear by G.

9. *To swear*, ὄμνυμι *omnumi*.
Matt. 5. 34 I say unto you, Swear not at all, neither
5. 36 Neither shalt thou swear by thy head, be.
23. 16 Whosoever shall swear..whosoever shall s.
23. 18 Whosoever shall swear..whosoever swea.
23. 20 Whoso..shall swear by the altar, sweareth
23. 21 whoso shall swear by the temple, swear.
23. 22 he that shall swear by heaven, sweareth
26. 74 Then began he to curse and to swear
Mark 6. 23 he sware unto her, Whatsoever thou shalt
14. 71 he began to curse and to swear..I know
Luke 1. 73 The oath which he sware to our father
Acts 2. 30 knowing that God had sworn with an oa.
7. 17 which God [had sworn] to Abraham, the
Heb. 3. 11 So I sware in my wrath, They shall not
3. 18 to whom sware he that they should not
4. 3 As I have sworn in my wrath, If they shall
6. 13 could swear by no greater, he sware by
6. 16 For men verily swear by the greater, and
7. 21 The Lord sware and will not repent, Thou
Jas. 5. 12 swear not, neither by heaven, neither by
Rev. 10. 6 sware by him that liveth for ever and ever

SWEARER, swearing —

1. *An appeal to God*, אָלָה *alah*.
Lev. 5. 1 sin, and hear the voice of swearing, and
Jer. 23. 10 for because of swearing the land mourn.

2. *To be sworn, swear*, שָׁבַע *shaba*, 2.
Mal. 3. 5 against false swearers, and against those

SWEAT, (anything that causeth) —

1. *Sweat*, זֵעָה *zeah*.
Gen. 3. 19 In the sweat of thy face shalt thou eat br.

2. *Sweat*, יֶזַע *yeza*.
Eze. 44. 18 gird..with any thing that causeth sweat

3. *Sweat*, ἱδρώς *hidrōs*.
Luke 22. 44 [sweat was as it were great drops of blood]

SWEEP, to be swept (away), sweeping —

1. *To sweep away*, גָּרַף *garaph*.
Judg. 5. 21 river of Kishon swept them away, that

2. *To sweep, daub*, טוּא *tu*, 3a.
Isa. 14. 23 will sweep it with the besom of destruct.

3. *To sweep away*, יָעָה *yaah*.
Isa. 28. 17 hail shall sweep away the refuge of lies

4. *To sweep away*, סָחַף *sachaph*.
Prov 28. 3 a sweeping rain which leaveth no food

5. *To be swept away*, סָחַף *sachaph*, 2.
Jer. 46. 15 Why are thy valiant (men) swept away?

6. *To sweep*, σαρόω *saroō*.
Matt 12. 44 he findeth (it) empty, swept, and garnis.
Luke 11. 25 when he cometh, he findeth (it) swept and
15. 8 sweep the house, and seek diligently till

SWEET, sweeter —

1. *Spice*, בֶּשֶׂם *besem*.
Exod 30. 23 of sweet cinnamon half so much, (even)

2. *Spice*, בֹּשֶׂם *bosem*.
Exod 30. 23 of sweet calamus two hundred and fifty

3. *Good*, טוֹב *tob*.
Jer. 6. 20 and the sweet cane from a far country?

4. *Sweet things*, מַמְתַּקִּים *mamtaqqim*.
Neh. 8. 10 eat the fat, and drink the sweet, and send
Song 5. 16 His mouth (is) most sweet; yea, he (is) al.

5. *Sweet*, מָתוֹק *mathoq*.
Judg. 14. 18 What (is) sweeter than honey? and what
Psa. 19. 10 sweeter also than honey, and the honey
Prov. 16. 24 sweet to the soul, and health to the bones
24. 13 the honeycomb, (which is) sweet to thy ta.
27. 7 the hungry soul every bitter thing is sweet
Eccl. 5. 12 The sleep of a labouring man (is) sweet
11. 7 Truly the light (is) sweet, and a pleasant
Song 2. 3 delight, and his fruit (was) sweet to my
Isa. 5. 20 put bitter for sweet, and sweet for bitter

6. *Rest, sweetness, sweet thing*, נִיחוֹחַ *nichoach*.
Gen. 8. 21 LORD smelled a sweet savour; and the Lo.
Exod29. 18, 41 a sweet savour, an offering made by
29. 25 for a sweet savour before the LORD: it (is)
Lev. 1. 9, 13, 17 of a sweet savour unto the LORD
2. 2, 9 offering made by fire, of a sweet savour
2. 12 not be burnt on the altar for a sweet sav.
3. 5 offering made by fire, of a sweet savour
3. 16 offering made by fire for a sweet savour
4. 31 burn (it) upon the altar for a sweet savour
6. 15 burn it upon the altar (for) a sweet savour
6. 21 shalt thou offer (for) a sweet savour unto
8. 21 it (was) a burnt sacrifice for a sweet sav.
8. 28 they (were) consecrations for a sweet sa.
17. 6 burn the fat for a sweet savour unto the
23. 13 made by fire unto the LORD (for) a sweet
23. 18 offering made by fire, of sweet savour unto
Num15. 3, 7, 10, 13, 14, 24 a sweet savour unto the
18. 17 for a sweet savour unto the LORD
28. 2 a sweet savour unto me, shall ye observe
28. 6, 13 a sweet savour, a sacrifice made by
28. 8, 24, 27 of a sweet savour unto the LORD
29. 2, 13, 36 a sweet savour unto the LORD
29. 6 for a sweet savour, a sacrifice made
29. 8 (for) a sweet savour, one young bullock
Eze. 6. 13 place where they did offer sweet savour
16. 19 even set it before them for a sweet savour
20. 28 there also they made their sweet savour
20. 41 I will accept you with your sweet savour

7. *Pleasant*, נָעִים *naim*.
2 Sa. 23. 1 David..the sweet Psalmist of Israel, said
Prov 23. 8 shalt thou vomit up, and loose thy sweet

8. *Spices, perfumes*, סַמִּים *sammim*.
Exod 25. 6 spices for anointing oil, and for sweet in.
30. 7 Aaron shall burn thereon sweet incense
30. 34 Take unto thee sweet spices..sweet spices
31. 11 the anointing oil, and sweet incense for
35. 8 for anointing oil, and for the sweet ince.
35. 15, 28 the anointing oil, and the sweet ince.
37. 29 he made..the pure incense of sweet spi.
39. 38 the anointing oil, and the sweet incense
40. 27 he burned sweet incense thereon; as the
Lev. 4. 7 upon the horns of the altar of sweet inc.
16. 12 his hands full of sweet incense beaten sm.
Num. 4. 16 the oil for the light, and the sweet incense
2 Ch. 2. 4 to burn before him sweet incense, and for
13. 11 burn..burnt sacrifices and sweet incense

9. *Sweet, sure*, עָרֵב *areb*.
Prov 20. 17 Bread of deceit (is) sweet to a man; but
Song 2. 14 sweet (is) thy voice, and thy countenance

10. *Compounds, perfumes*, מֶרְקָחִים *merqachim*.
Song 5. 13 His cheeks (are) as a bed of spices..sweet

11. *Sweet*, γλυκύς *glukus*.
Jas. 3. 11 send..at the same place sweet..and bitter?
Rev. 10. 9 it shall be in thy mouth sweet as honey
10. 10 it was in my mouth sweet as honey, and as

SWEET, to be, make, take —

1. *To make good, do well*, יָטַב *yatab*, 5.
Isa. 23. 16 make sweet melody, sing many songs, that

2. *To be sweet*, מָלַץ *malats*, 2.
Psa. 119. 103 How sweet are thy words unto my taste

3. *To be sweet*, מָתַק *mathaq*.
Exod 15. 25 when he..cast..the waters were made sw.
Job 21. 33 The clods of the valley shall be sweet unto
Prov. 9. 17 Stolen waters are sweet, and bread (eaten)

4. *To make sweet*, מָתַק *mathaq*, 5.
Job 20. 12 Though wickedness be sweet in his mouth
Psa. 55. 14 We took sweet counsel together..walked

5. *To be pleasant*, נָעֵם *naem*.
Psa. 141. 6 they shall hear my words; for they are sw.

6. *To be sweet or sure*, עָרֵב *areb*.
Psa. 104. 34 My meditation of him shall be sweet
Prov. 3. 24 shalt lie down, and thy sleep shall be sw.
13. 19 The desire accomplished is sweet to the
Jer. 6. 20 not acceptable, nor your sacrifices sweet
31. 26 I awaked..and my sleep was sweet unto

SWEET incense, odours, smell, smelling, savour, wine —

1. *Spice*, בֶּשֶׂם *besem*.
2 Ch. 16. 14 bed which was filled with sweet odours
Esth. 2. 12 six months with sweet odours, and with

2. *Incense*, קְטֹרֶת *qetoreth*.
Exod 31. 11 the anointing oil, and sweet incense for
Lev. 4. 7 upon the horns of the altar of sweet inc.

3. *To pass over, overpass*, עָבַר *abar*.
Song 5. 5 sweet smelling myrrh, upon the handles
5. 13 his lips..dropping sweet smelling myrrh

4. *A possession, mead, new wine*, תִּירוֹשׁ *tirosh*.
Mic. 6. 15 and sweet wine, but shalt not drink wine

5. *Sweet smell or odour*, εὐωδία *euōdia*.
2 Co. 2. 15 For we are unto God a sweet savour of Ch.
Eph. 5. 2 a sacrifice to God for a sweet smelling sa.
Phil. 4. 18 an odour of a sweet smell, a sacrifice acc.
[*See also* Odour, savour, smell, spices, wine].

SWEETLY, (to feed) —

1. *Upright things*, מֵישָׁרִים *mesharim*.
Song 7. 9 that goeth..sweetly, causing the lips of

2. *To be sweet*, מָתַק *mathaq*.
Job 24. 20 the worm shall feed sweetly on him, he

SWEETNESS —

1. *Sweet*, מָתוֹק *mathoq*.
Judg 14. 14 out of the strong came forth sweetness
Eze. 3. 3 it was in my mouth as honey for sweet.

2. *Sweetness*, מֶתֶק *metheq*.
Prov. 16. 21 the sweetness of the lips increaseth lear.
27. 9 the sweetness of a man's friend by hearty

3. *Sweetness*, מֹתֶק *motheq*.
Judg. 9. 11 Should I forsake my sweetness, and my

SWELL (out, to make), to —

1. *To be swelled out*, בָּעָה *baah*, 2.
Isa. 30. 13 a breach ready to fall, swelling out in a

2. *To swell*, בָּצֵק *batseq*.
Deut. 8. 4 neither did thy foot swell, these forty ye.
Neh. 9. 21 clothes waxed not old, and their feet sw

3. *To swell*, צָבָה *tsabah*.
Num. 5. 27 her belly shall swell, and her thigh shall

4. *To cause to swell*, צָבָה *tsabah*, 5.
Num. 5. 22 make (thy) belly to swell, and (thy) thigh

5. *Swelling*, צָבֶה *tsabeh*.
Num. 5. 21 make thy thigh to rot, and thy belly to sw.

SWELLING, (great) —

1. *Rising, excellency, pride*, גַּאֲוָה *gaavah*.
Psa. 46. 3 the mountains shake with the swelling

2. *Rising, excellency, pride*, גָּאוֹן *gaon*.
Jer. 12. 5 then how wilt thou do in the swelling of
49. 19 come up like a lion from the swelling of
50. 44 come up like a lion from the swelling of

3. *Over-swelling*, ὑπέρογκος *huperogkos*.
2 Pe. 2. 18 when they speak great swelling (words)
Jude 16 their mouth speaketh great swelling (wo.)

4. *A puffing up*, φυσίωσις *phusiōsis*.
2 Co. 12. 20 backbitings, whisperings, swellings, tum.

SWERVE, to —

To go irregularly, miss a mark, ἀστοχέω *astocheō*
1 Tim. 1. 6 From which some having swerved have

SWIFT, swifter, swiftly, to be —

1. *A reed, enmity*, אֵבֶה *ebeh*.
Job 9. 26 They are passed away as the swift ships

2. *Splendour, glitter*, יְעָף *yeaph*.
Dan. 9. 21 being caused to fly swiftly, touched me ab.

3. *To hasten*, מָהַר *mahar*, 3.
1 Ch. 12. 8 (were) as swift as the roes upon the mou.
Prov. 6. 18 feet that be swift in running to mischief
Mal. 3. 5 I will be a swift witness against the sorc.

4. *Haste*, מְהֵרָה *meherah*.
Psa. 147. 15 earth: his word runneth very swiftly

5. *Light, swift*, קַל *qal*.
Job 24. 18 He (is) swift as the waters; their portion
Eccl. 9. 11 race (is) not to the swift, nor the battle
Isa. 5. 26 behold, they shall come with speed swif.
18. 2 Go, ye swift messengers, to a nation sca.
19. 1 LORD rideth upon a swift cloud, and shall
30. 16 We will ride upon the swift; therefore sh.
Jer. 2. 23 a swift dromedary traversing her ways
46. 6 Let not the swift flee away, nor the mig.
Lam. 4. 19 Our persecutors are swifter than the ea.
Joel 3. 4 swiftly (and) speedily will I return your

Amos 2. 14 the flight shall perish from the swift, and
2. 15 swift of foot shall not deliver (himself), ne.

6. *To be light, swift,* קָלַל *qalal.*
2 Sa. 1. 23 they were swifter than eagles, they were
Job 7. 6 My days are swifter than a weaver's shu.
9. 25 Now my days are swifter than a post, they
Jer. 4. 13 whirlwind : his horses are swifter than ea.
Hab. 1. 8 Their horses also are swifter than the le.

7. *To be or become light, swift,* קָלַל *qalal,* 2.
Isa. 30. 16 shall they that pursue you be swift

8. *Sharp, swift, acute,* ὀξύς *oxus.*
Rom. 3. 15 Their feet (are) swift to shed blood

9. *Swift, speedy,* ταχινός *tachinos.*
2 Pe. 2. 1 bring upon themselves swift destruction

10. *Swift,* ταχύς *tachus.*
Jas. 1. 19 let every man be swift to hear, slow to sp.

SWIFT beast —

1. *Dromedaries,* כִּרְכָּרוֹת *kirkaroth.*
Isa. 66. 20 upon swift beasts, to my holy mountain

2. *A courser,* רֶכֶשׁ *rekesh.*
Mic. 1. 13 bind the chariot to the swift beast: she

SWIM (in or out, to make), to —

1. *To cause to flow, swim,* צוּף *tsuph,* 5.
2 Ki. 6. 6 cast (it) in thither; and the iron did swim

2. *Flowing, swimming,* צָפָה *tsaphah.*
Eze. 32. 6 water..the land wherein thou swimmest

3. *To swim,* שָׂחָה *sachah.*
Isa. 25. 11 swimmeth spreadeth forth (his hands) to sw.

4. *To cause to swim,* שָׂחָה *sachah,* 5.
Psa. 6. 6 all the night make I my bed to swim; I

5. *Swimming,* שָׂחוּ *sachu.*
Eze. 47. 5 waters to swim in, a river that could not

6. *To swim out, off, away,* ἐκκολυμβάω *ekkolumbaō.*
Acts 27. 42 lest any of them should swim out, and es.

7. *To swim,* κολυμβάω *kolumbaō.*
Acts 27. 43 commanded that they which could swim

SWINE —

1. *Sow, boar,* חֲזִיר *chazir.*
Lev. 11. 7 swine, though he divide the hoof, and be
Deut14. 8 swine, because it divideth the hoof, yet ch.
Prov11. 22 (As) a jewel of gold in a swine's snout, (so
Isa. 65. 4 which eat swine's flesh, and broth of ab.
66. 3 (as if he offered) swine's blood; he that
66. 17 eating swine's flesh, and the abomination

2. *A hog, pig,* χοῖρος *choiros.*
Matt. 7. 6 neither cast ye your pearls before swine
8. 30 there was..an herd of many swine feed.
8. 31 suffer us to go away into the herd of sw.
8. 32 they went into the herd of swine, and
8. 32 the whole herd [of swine] ran violently
Mark 5. 11 there was..a great herd of swine feeding
5. 12 Send us into the swine, that we may en.
5. 13 went out, and entered into the swine, and
5. 14 they that fed [the swine] fled, and told (it)
5. 16 told them..(also) concerning the swine
Luke 8. 32 there was there an herd of many swine fe.
8. 33 entered into the swine : and the herd ran
15. 15 and he sent him into his fields to feed sw.
15. 16 filled..with the husks that the swine did

SWOLLEN —

To be burning, enflamed, πίμπρημι *pimprēmi.*
Acts 28. 6 they looked when he should have swollen

SWOON to—

1. *To be or become feeble,* עָטַף *ataph,* 2.
Lam. 2. 11 children and the sucklings swoon in the

2. *To show self feeble,* עָטַף *ataph,* 7.
Lam. 2. 12 when they swooned as the wounded in

SWORD, (drawn, glittering) —

1. *Lightning, brightness,* בָּרָק *baraq.*
Job 20. 25 the glittering sword cometh out of his

2. *A sword, destroying weapon,* חֶרֶב *chereb.*
Gen. 3. 24 a flaming sword which turned every way
27. 40 by thy sword shalt thou live, and shalt
31. 26 daughters, as captives (taken) with the sw.
34. 25 took each man his sword, and came upon
34. 26 slew Hamor..with the edge of the sword
48. 22 hand of the Amorite with my sword and
Exod. 5. 3 said..lest he fall upon us..with the sw
5. 21 to put a sword in their hand to slay us
15. 9 will draw my sword, my hand shall destroy
17. 13 discomfited Amalek..the edge of the sw.
18. 4 and delivered me from the sword of Phar.
22. 24 kill you with the sword; and your wives
32. 27 Put every man his sword by his side, (and)
Lev. 26. 6 neither shall the sword go through your
26. 7 and they shall fall before you by the sword
26. 8 enemies shall fall before you by the sword
26. 25 I will bring a sword upon you, that shall
26. 33 will draw out a sword after you: and your
26. 36 they shall flee, as fleeing from a sword
26. 37 fall..as it were before a sword, when none
Num14. 3 to fall by the sword, that our wives and
14. 43 shall fall by the sword, because ye are tur.
19. 16 toucheth one that is slain with a sword in
20. 18 lest I come out against thee with the sword
21. 24 smote him with the edge of the sword, and
22. 23 standing in the way, and his sword drawn
22. 29 would there were a sword in mine hand

Num22. 31 his sword drawn in his hand: and he bow.
31. 8 the son of Beor they slew with the sword
Deut13. 15 smite..with the edge of the sword, destr.
13. 15 the cattle thereof, with the edge of the sw.
20. 13 smite every male..with the edge of the sw.
28. 22 an extreme burning, and with the sword
32. 25 The sword without, and terror within, sh.
32. 41 If I whet my glittering sword, and mine
32. 42 my sword shall devour flesh; (and that)
33. 29 and who (is) the sword of thy excellency
Josh. 5. 13 man over against him with his sword dr.
6. 21 destroyed..with the edge of the sword
8. 24 were all fallen on the edge of the sword
8. 24 and smote it with the edge of the sword
10. 11 the children of Israel slew with the sword
10. 28, 30, 32, 35, 37, 39 with the edge of the sw.
11. 10 smote the king thereof with the sword
11. 11 that (were) therein with the edge of the sw.
11. 12 smote them with..edge of the sword, (and)
11. 14 smote with the edge of the sword, until
13. 22 slay with the sword among them that we.
19. 47 smote it with the edge of the sword, and
24. 12 (but) not with thy sword, nor with thy bow
Judg. 1. 8 smitten it with the edge of the sword, and
1. 25 they smote the city with the edge of the
4. 15 discomfited..with the edge of the sword
4. 16 fell upon the edge of the sword; (and) th.
7. 14 This (is) nothing else save the sword of
7. 20 cried, The sword of the LORD, and of Gid.
7. 22 set every man's sword against his fellow
8. 10 and twenty thousand men that drew sword
8. 20 but the youth drew not his sword; for he
9. 54 Draw thy sword, and slay me, that men
18. 27 they smote them with the edge of the sw.
20. 2 hundred thousand footmen that drew sw.
20. 15 six thousand men that drew sword, besi.
20. 17 hundred thousand men that drew sword
20. 25, 35 men; all these drew the sword
20. 37 smote all the city with the edge of the sw.
20. 46 five thousand men that drew the sword
20. 48 and smote them with the edge of the sw.
21. 10 Go and smite..with the edge of the sword
1 Sa. 13. 19 Lest the Hebrews make (them) swords or
13. 22 there was neither sword nor spear found
14. 20 every man's sword was against his fellow
15. 8 all the people with the edge of the sword
15. 33 As thy sword hath made women childless
17. 39 David girded his sword upon his armour
17. 45 Thou comest to me with a sword, and with
17. 47 the LORD saveth not with sword and sp.
17. 50 (there was) no sword in the hand of David
17. 51 took his sword, and drew it out of the sh.
18. 4 even to his sword, and to his bow, and to
21. 8 not here under thine hand spear or sword?
21. 8 I have neither brought my sword nor my
21. 9 The sword of Goliath the Philistine, wh.
22. 10 gave him the sword of Goliath the Phili.
22. 13 thou hast given him bread, and a sword
22. 19 smote he with the edge of the sword. bo.
22. 19 asses, and sheep, with the edge of the sw.
25. 13 David said..Gird ye on every man his sw.
25. 13 And they girded on every man his sword
25. 13 David also girded on his sword: and th.
31. 4 Draw thy sword..Saul took a sword, and
31. 5 fell likewise upon his sword, and died wi.
2 Sa. 1. 12 because they were fallen by the sword
1. 22 and the sword of Saul returned not empty
2. 16 and (thrust) his sword in his fellow's side
2. 26 Shall the sword devour for ever? knowest
3. 29 that falleth on the sword, or that lacketh
11. 25 the sword devoureth one as well as anot.
12. 9 killed Uriah the Hittite with the sword
12. 9 slain him with the sword of the children
12. 10 sword shall never depart from thine house
15. 14 smite the city with the edge of the sword
18. 8 more people that day than the sword de.
20. 8 sword fastened upon his loins in the she.
20. 10 Amasa took no heed to the sword that
23. 10 hand clave unto the sword: and the Lo.
24. 9 valiant men that drew the sword; and the
1 Ki. 1. 51 he will not slay his servant with the sw.
2. 8 will not put thee to death with the sword
2. 32 slew them with the sword, my father Da.
3. 24 Bring me a sword..they brought a sword
19. 1 had slain all the prophets with the sword
19. 10, 14 slain thy prophets with the sword; and
19. 17 him that escapeth the sword of Hazael sh.
19. 17 him that escapeth from the sword of Je.
2 Ki. 3. 26 seven hundred men that drew swords, to
6. 22 thou hast taken captive with thy sword
8. 12 young men wilt thou slay with the sword
10. 25 smote them with the edge of the sword
11. 15 him that followeth her kill with the swo.
11. 20 slew Athaliah with the sword (beside) the
19. 7 cause him to fall by the sword in his own
19. 37 his sons smote him with the sword: and
1 Ch. 5. 18 men able to bear buckler and sword, and
10. 4 Draw thy sword..Saul took a sword, and
10. 5 he fell likewise on the sword, and died
21. 5 hundred thousand men that drew sword
21. 5 and ten thousand men that drew sword
21. 12 while that the sword of thine enemies ov.
21. 12 or else three days the sword of the LORD
21. 16 having a drawn sword in his hand stretc.
21. 27 put up his sword again into the sheath th.
21. 30 for he was afraid because of the sword of
2 Ch. 20. 9 evil cometh upon us, (as) the sword, jud.
21. 4 slew all his brethren with the sword, and
23. 14 let him be slain with the sword. For the
23. 21 they had slain Athaliah with the sword
29. 9 lo, our fathers have fallen by the sword
32. 21 they..slew him there with the sword

2 Ch. 36. 17 slew their young men with the sword in
36. 20 them that had escaped from the sword
Ezra 9. 7 to the sword, to captivity, and to a spoil
Neh. 4. 13 with their swords, their spears, and their
4. 18 every one had his sword girded by his side
Esth. 9. 5 Jews smote..with the stroke of the sword
Job 1. 15 slain the servants with the edge of the sw.
1. 17 slain the servants with the edge of the sw.
5. 15 But he saveth the poor from the sword, fr.
5. 20 and in war from the power of the sword
15. 22 darkness, and he is waited for of the sw.
19. 29 Be ye afraid of the sword: for wrath (br.)
19. 29 punishment of the sword, that ye may kn.
27. 14 children be multiplied, (it is) for the sword
39. 22 neither turneth he back from the sword
40. 19 he that made him can make his sword to
41. 26 The sword of him that layeth at him can.
Psa. 7. 12 If he turn not, he will whet his sword, he
17. 13 soul from the wicked, (which is) thy sw.
22. 20 Deliver my soul from the sword; my da.
37. 14 The wicked have drawn out the sword
37. 15 Their sword shall enter into their own he.
44. 3 got not the land..by their own sword, ne.
44. 6 not trust in my bow, neither shall my sw.
45. 3 Gird thy sword upon (thy) thigh, O (most)
57. 4 and arrows, and their tongue a sharp sw.
59. 7 swords (are) in their lips: for who, (say
63. 10 They shall fall by the sword; they shall
64. 3 Who whet their tongue like a sword, (and)
76. 3 the bow, the shield, and the sword, and
78. 62 gave his people over also unto the sword
78. 64 Their priests fell by the sword; and their
89. 43 hast also turned the edge of his sword, and
144. 10 who delivereth David..from the hurtful s.
149. 6 in their mouth, and a two edged sword
Prov. 5. 4 end is bitter..sharp as a two edged sword
12. 18 that speaketh like the piercings of a sw.
25. 18 (is) a maul, and a sword, and a sharp ar.
30. 14 a generation whose teeth (are as) swords
Song 3. 8 They all hold swords, (being) expert in
3. 8 every man (hath) his sword upon his th.
Isa. 1. 20 ye shall be devoured with the sword, for
2. 4 they shall beat their swords into plough.
2. 4 nation shall not lift up sword against na.
3. 25 Thy men shall fall by the sword, and thy
13. 15 joined (unto them) shall fall by the sword
14. 19 that are slain, thrust through with a sw.
21. 15 fled from the swords, from the drawn sw.
22. 2 thy slain (men are) not slain with the sw.
27. 1 with his sore and great and strong sword
31. 8 Then shall the Assyrian fall with the sw.
31. 8 the sword, not of a mean man, shall dev.
31. 8 he shall flee from the sword, and his yo.
34. 5 my sword shall be bathed in heaven, be.
34. 6 The sword of the LORD is filled with bl.
37. 7 I will cause him to fall by the sword in
37. 38 his sons smote him with the sword, and
41. 2 he gave (them) as the dust to his sword
49. 2 hath made my mouth like a sharp sword
51. 19 destruction, and the famine, and the sw.
65. 12 Therefore will I number you to the sw.
66. 16 by his sword, will the LORD plead with
Jer. 2. 30 your own sword hath devoured your pr.
4. 10 whereas the sword reacheth unto the so.
5. 12 neither shall we see sword nor famine
5. 17 impoverish thy fenced cities..with the sw.
6. 25 the sword of the enemy (and) fear (is) on
9. 16 I will send a sword after them, till I have
11. 22 the young men shall die by the sword, they
12. 12 the sword of the LORD shall devour from
14. 12 I will consume them by the sword, and by
14. 13 Ye shall not see the sword, neither shall
14. 15 Sword and famine shall not be in this la.
14. 15 By sword and famine shall those prophets
14. 16 out..because of the famine and the sword
14. 18 then behold the slain with the sword! and
15. 2 such as (are) for the sword, to the sword
15. 3 the sword to slay, and the dogs to tear, and
15. 9 residue of them will I deliver to the sword
16. 4 they shall be consumed by the sword, and
18. 21 pour out..(blood) by the force of the sw.
18. 21 (let) their young men (be) slain by the sw.
19. 7 I will cause them to fall by the sword be.
20. 4 they shall fall by the sword of their ene.
20. 4 carry them..and shall slay them with the
21. 7 from the pestilence, from the sword, and
21. 7 shall smite them with the edge of the sw.
21. 9 shall die by the sword, and by the famine
24. 10 I will send the sword, the famine, and the
25. 16 because of the sword that I will send am.
25. 27 because of the sword which I will send
25. 29 I will call for a sword upon all the inhab.
25. 31 will give them (that are) wicked to the sw.
26. 23 who slew him with the sword, and cast
27. 8 with the sword, and with the famine, and
27. 13 Why will ye die..by the sword, by the fa.
29. 17 I will send upon them the sword, the fa.
29. 18 I will persecute them with the sword, wi.
31. 2 The people (which were) left of the sword
32. 24 because of the sword, and of the famine
32. 36 by the sword, and by the famine, and by
33. 4 thrown down by the mounts..by the sw.
34. 4 saith the LORD..Thou shalt not die by..s.
34. 17 to the sword, to the pestilence, and to the
38. 2 shall die by the sword, by the famine, and
39. 18 thou shalt not fall by the sword, but thy
41. 2 smote Gedaliah..with the sword, and slew
42. 16 the sword, which ye feared, shall overtake
42. 17 they shall die by the sword, by the famine
42. 22 know certainly that ye shall die by the sw.
43. 11 such (as are) for the sword to the sword
44. 12 they shall (even) be consumed by the sw.

Jer. 44. 12 they shall die..by the sword and by the
44. 13 I have punished Jerusalem, by the sword
44. 18 have been consumed by the sword and by
44. 27 shall be consumed by the sword and by
44. 28 a small number that escape the sword
46. 10 the sword shall devour, and it shall be sa.
46. 14 the sword shall devour round about thee
46. 16 let us go again..from the oppressing sw.
47. 6 O thou sword of the LORD, how long (will
48. 2 thou shalt be cut down .the sword shall
48. 10 cursed (be) he that keepeth back his sword
49. 37 I will send the sword after them, till I have
50. 16 for fear of the oppressing sword they shall
50. 35 A sword (is) upon the Chaldeans, saith the
50. 36 A sword (is upon the liars; and they shall
50. 36 a sword (is) upon her mighty men and they
50. 37 A sword (is) upon their horses and upon
50. 37 a sword (is) upon her treasures; and they
51. 50 Ye that have escaped the sword go away
Lam. 1. 20 abroad the sword bereaveth, at home
2. 21 my young men are fallen by the sword
4. 9 (They that be) slain with the sword are be.
5. 9 because of the sword of the wilderness
Eze. 5. 2, 12 and I will draw out a sword after them
5. 12 a third part shall fall by the sword round
5. 17 I will bring the sword upon thee I the LORD
6. 3 I, (even) I, will bring a sword upon you
6. 8 (some) that shall escape the sword among
6. 11 they shall fall by the sword, by the famine
6. 12 and he that is near shall fall by the sword
7. 15 The sword (is) without, and the pestilence
7. 15 he that (is) in the field shall die with the sw
11. 8 feared the sword; and I will bring a sword
11. 10 Ye shall fall by the sword· I will judge you
12. 14 and I will draw out the sword after them
12. 16 will leave a few men of them from the sw.
14. 17 (if) I bring a sword and say, Sword, go
14. 21 the sword, and the famine, and the noiso.
16. 40 and thrust thee through with their swords
17. 21 his fugitives..shall fall by the sword and
21. 3 will draw forth my sword out of his shea.
21. 4 therefore shall my sword go forth out of
21. 5 I the LORD have drawn forth my sword out
21. 9 A sword, a sword is sharpened, and also
21. 11 this sword is sharpened, and it is furbished
21. 12 terrors by reason of the sword shall be up.
21. 14 let the sword be doubled..the sword of the
21. 14 it (is) the sword of the great (men that are)
21. 15 I have set the point of the sword against
21. 19 that the sword of the king of Babylon may
21. 20 that the sword may come to Rabbath of the
21. 28 The sword, the sword (is) drawn · for the
23. 10 took her sons .and slew her with the sword
23. 25 thy remnant shall fall by the sword, they
23. 47 dispatch them with their swords; they sh.
24. 21 whom ye have left shall fall by the sword
25. 13 and they of Dedan shall fall by the sword
26. 6 her daughters .shall be slain by the sword
26. 8 He shall slay with the sword thy daughters
26. 11 he shall slay thy people by the sword
28. 7 they shall draw their swords against the
28. 23 judged in the midst of her by the sword
29. 8 I will bring a sword upon thee, and cut
30. 4 the sword shall come upon Egypt, and gr.
30. 5 the men..shall fall with them by the sw.
30. 6 shall they fall in it by the sword saith the
30. 11 they shall draw their swords against Eg.
30. 17 young men of Aven .shall fall by the sw.
30. 21 bind it, to make it strong to hold the sw.
30. 22 I will cause the sword to fall out of his
30. 24 I will put my .sword in his hand: but I
30. 25 I shall put my sword into the hand of the
31. 17 unto (them that be) slain with the sword
31. 18 with (them that be) slain by the sword
32. 10 I shall brandish my sword before them
32. 11 The sword of the king of Babylon shall
32. 12 By the swords by the mighty will I cause
32. 20 midst of (them that are) slain by the sw.
32. 20 she is delivered to the sword: draw her
32. 21 they lie uncircumcised, slain by the swo.
32. 22, 23, 24 all of them slain, fallen by the sw.
32. 25, 26 all..uncircumcised, slain by the sword
32. 27 they have laid their swords under their
32. 28, 32 with (them that are) slain with the sw.
32. 29 laid by (them that were) slain by the sword
32. 30 with (them that be) slain by the sword
32. 31 Pharaoh and all his army slain by the sw.
32. 32 with (them that are) slain with the sword
33. 2 When I bring the sword upon a land, if
33. 3 when he seeth the sword come upon the
33. 4 if the sword come and take him away, his
33. 6 if the watchman see the sword come, and
33. 6 if the sword come and take (any) person
33. 26 Ye stand upon your sword, ye work abo.
33. 27 they..in the wastes shall fall by the swo.
35. 5 by the force of the sword in the time of
35. 8 shall they fall that are slain with the sw.
38. 4 great company ..all of them handling sw.
38. 8 the land (that is) brought back from the s.
38. 21 I will call for a sword against him throu.
38. 21 every man's sword shall be against his br.
39. 23 trespassed .so fell they all by the sword
Dan. 11. 33 they shall fall by the sword, and by flame
Hos. 1. 7 will not save them by bow, nor by sword
2. 18 I will break the bow and the sword and
7. 16 their princes shall fall by the sword for
11. 6 the sword shall abide on his cities, and
13. 16 they shall fall by the sword; their infants
Joel 3. 10 Beat your ploughshares into swords, and
Amos 1. 11 he did pursue his brother with the sword
4. 10 your young men have I slain with the sw.
7. 9 will rise against the house..with the sw.
Amos 7. 11 Jeroboam shall die by the sword, and Isr.
7. 17 thy daughters shall fall by the sword, and
9. 1 I will slay the last of them with the sword
9. 4 thence will I command the sword, and it
9. 10 All the sinners..shall die by the sword
Mic. 4. 3 they shall beat their swords into ploughsh.
4. 3 nation shall not lift up a sword against
5. 6 waste the land of Assyria with the sword
6. 14 thou deliverest will I give up to the sword
Nah. 2. 13 the sword shall devour thy young lions
3. 3 lifteth up both the bright sword and the
3. 15 the sword shall cut thee off, it shall eat
Zeph. 2. 12 Ye Ethiopians..(shall be) slain by my sw.
Hag. 2. 22 every one by the sword of his brother
Zech. 9. 13 made thee as the sword of a mighty man
11. 17 the sword (shall be) upon his arm, and
13. 7 Awake, O sword, against my shepherd

3. *Murder, murderous weapon*, רֶצַח *retsach.*
Psa. 42. 10 (As) with a sword in my bones, mine ene.

4. *Missile, dart, spear*, שֶׁלַח *shelach.*
Job 33. 18 and his life from perishing by the sword
36. 12 they shall perish by the sword, and they
Joel 2. 8 (when) they fall upon the sword, they

5. *Open swords*, פְּתִחוֹת *pethichoth.*
Psa. 55. 21 softer than oil, yet (were) they drawn sw.

6. *Fighting weapon, sword*, μάχαιρα *machaira.*
Matt 10. 34 I came not to send peace, but a sword
26. 47 a great multitude with swords and staves
26. 51 drew his sword, and struck a servant of
26. 52 Put up again thy sword into his place: for
26. 52 that take the sword shall perish with..s.
26. 55 as against a thief with swords and staves
Mark 14. 43 with him a great multitude with swords
14. 47 one of them that stood by drew a sword
14. 48 with swords and (with) staves to take me?
Luke 21. 24 they shall fall by the edge of the sword
22. 36 he that hath no sword, let him sell his g.
22. 38 they said, Lord, behold, here (are) two sw.
22. 49 Lord, shall we smite with the sword?
22. 52 come out, as against a thief, with swords
John 18. 10 Peter having a sword drew it, and smote
18. 11 Put up thy sword into the sheath: the
Acts 12. 2 killed..the brother of John with the sword
16. 27 he drew out his sword, and would have
Rom. 8. 35 or famine, or nakedness, or peril, or sw.?
13. 4 he beareth not the sword in vain: for he
Eph. 6. 17 the sword of the spirit, which is the word
Heb. 4. 12 sharper than any two edged sword, pier.
11. 34 escaped the edge of the sword, out of we.
11. 37 were tempted, were slain with the sword
Rev. 6. 4 there was given unto him a great sword
13. 10 with the sword..killed with the sword
13. 14 which had the wound by a sword, and did

7. *A brandishing weapon, sword, sabre*, ῥομφαία.
Luke 2. 35 a sword shall pierce through thy own so.
Rev. 1. 16 out of his mouth went a ..two edged sw.
2. 12 he which hath the sharp sword with two
2. 16 will fight against them with the sword of
6. 8 to kill with sword, and with hunger, and
19. 15 out of his mouth goeth a sharp sword, that
19. 21 the remnant were slain with the sword

SYCAMINE tree —
Sycamine, fig or mulberry tree, συκάμινος *sukami.*
Luke 17. 6 ye might say unto this sycamine tree, Be

SYCAMORE (fruit, tree) —
1. *A sycamine, fig or mulberry tree*, שִׁקְמָה *shiqmah.*
1 Ki. 10. 27 cedars made he (to be) as the sycamore
1 Ch. 27. 28 over the olive trees and the sycamore tr
2 Ch. 1. 15 cedar trees made he as the sycamore trees
9. 27 cedar trees made he as the sycamore trees
Psa. 78. 47 He destroyed..their sycamore trees with
Isa. 9. 10 the sycamores are cut down, but we will
Amos 7. 14 an herdman, and a gatherer of sycamore f.

2. *A sycamore, fig or mulberry tree*, συκομωραία.
Luke 19. 4 climbed up into a sycamore tree to see

SY'-CHAR, Συχάρ.
A city of Samaria, where Jesus met with a woman, and stayed two days teaching the people; perhaps *Asker*, whose ruins are on mount *Ebal.*
John 4. 5 a city of Samaria, which is called S., near

SY'-CHEM, Συχέμ.
A city (or person) in Samaria, called also *Shechem.*
Acts 7. 16 of the sons of Emmor (the father) of S.
7. 16, 16 carried over into S., and laid in the

SY-E'-NE, סְוֵנֵה.
A city in the S. of Egypt towards Ethiopia, as *Migdol* was toward the north of the land; now called *Asouan* or *Aswan.*
Eze. 29. 10 from the tower of S. even unto the bor.
30. 6 from the tower of S. shall they fall in it

SYNAGOGUE —
1. *Appointed place of meeting*, מוֹעֵד *moed.*
Psa. 74. 8 they have burnt up all the synagogues of

2. *Place where people are led together*, συναγωγή.
Matt 4. 23 teaching in their synagogues, and preach.
6. 2 as the hypocrites do in the synagogues
6. 5 love to pray standing in the synagogues
9. 35 teaching in their synagogues, and preach.
10. 17 they will scourge you in their synagogues
12. 9 departed thence, he went into their syn.
13. 54 he taught them in their synagogue, inso.
23. 6 And love..the chief seats in the synagog.
Matt 23. 34 (some)..shall ye scourge in your synago.
Mark 1. 21 he entered into the synagogue, and taught
1. 23 there was in their synagogue a man with
1. 29 when they were come out of the synago.
1. 39 he preached in their synagogues through
3. 1 And he entered again into the synagogue
6. 2 he began to teach in the synagogue, and
12. 39 the chief seats in the synagogues, and the
13. 9 and in the synagogues ye shall be beaten
Luke 4. 15 he taught in their synagogues, being glor.
4. 16 he went into the synagogue on the sabb.
4. 20 the eyes of all them that were in the syn.
4. 28 all they in the synagogue, when they he.
4. 33 in the synagogue there was a man which
4. 38 he arose out of the synagogue, and ente.
4. 44 he preached in the synagogues of Galilee
6. 6 he entered into the synagogue and taught
7. 5 he loveth our nation, and..built us a sy
8. 41 he was a ruler of the synagogue, and he
11. 43 ye love the uppermost seats in the syna.
12. 11 when they bring you unto the synagogues
13. 10 he was teaching in one of the synagogues
20. 46 the highest seats in the synagogues, and
21. 12 delivering..up to the synagogues, and into
John 6. 59 These things said he in the synagogue
18. 20 I ever taught in the synagogue, and in the
Acts 6. 9 Then there arose certain of the synagog.
9. 2 desired .letters to Damascus to the syn.
9. 20 straightway he preached Christ in the sy
13. 5 they preached the word of God in the sy
13. 14 went into the synagogue on the sabbath
13. 42 [when the Jews were gone out of the sy.]
14. 1 they went both together into the synag.
15. 21 being read in the synagogues every sab.
17. 1 came to Thessalonica, where was a syna.
17. 10 who..went into the synagogue of the Je.
17. 17 Therefore disputed he in the synagogue
18. 4 he reasoned in the synagogue every sab.
18. 7 whose house joined hard to the synagogue
18. 19 he himself entered into the synagogue, and
18. 26 he began to speak boldly in the synagogue
19. 8 he went into the synagogue, and spake
22. 19 I imprisoned and beat in every synagogue
24. 12 neither in the synagogues, nor in the city
26. 11 I punished them oft in every synagogue
Rev. 2. 9 are not, but (are) the synagogue of Satan
3. 9 I will make them of the synagogue of S.

SYNAGOGUE, (chief) ruler of —
Chief leader in the synagogue, ἀρχισυνάγωγος.
Mark 5. 22 one of the rulers of the synagogue, Jairus
5. 35 there came from the ruler of the synago.
5. 36 he saith unto the ruler of the synagogue
5. 38 to the house of the ruler of the synagogue
Luke 8. 49 from the ruler of the synagogue's [house]
13. 14 And the ruler of the synagogue answered
Acts 13. 15 the rulers of the synagogue sent unto th.
18. 8 Crispus, the chief ruler of the synagogue
18. 17 Sosthenes, the chief ruler of the synago.

SYNAGOGUE, put out of the —
One put away from the synagogue, ἀποσυνάγωγος.
John 9. 22 he should be put out of the synagogue
12. 42 they should be put out of the synagogue
16. 2 They shall put you out of the synagogues

SYN-TY'-CHE, Συντύχη.
A female believer in Philippi whom Paul beseeches along with Euodias to be of the same mind.
Phil. 4. 2 I beseech Euodias, and beseech S., that

SY-RA'-CUSE, Συρακουσαι
A city on the S E. corner of the island of Sicily, with a capacious harbour; birthplace of Archimedes, B.C. 250-212. It was the most ancient of the Greek colonies in the island, and founded by the Corinthians under Archias, B C. 734; in 648 the party called the Myletidae were expelled; in 486 also the oligarchy called Geomori or Gamori; in 478-467 Hieron patronises literature and the arts; in 414 it is besieged by the Athenians; in 394 it wars against Carthage; in 344, 60,000 immigrants introduced; in 275-216 Hieron II. makes a treaty with Rome; in 214-212 it is taken by the Romans; in 21 Augustus sends a Roman colony to revive it.
Acts 28. 12 landing at S., we tarried (there) three d.

SYRIA, אֲרָם *the high land.* Συρία.
The Hebrew *Aram*, is, strictly speaking, bounded by Amanus and Taurus on the N., by the Euphrates and the Arabian Desert on the E., by Palestine on the S., and by the Mediterranean near the mouth of the Orontes, and then by Phoenicia on the W.; this is about 300 miles from N. to S., and from 50 to 150 from E. to W., or an area of about 30,000 square miles—the size of Scotland. Its principal divisions were—Syria of Damascus, Syria of Zobah, the Plain of Aram, and Aram of the two Rivers (the Euphrates and the Tigris). The name *Syria* is evidently derived from the city *Tyre* (or Tzur), with which the ancient Greeks and Romans traded. In 1921 B.C. Abraham leaving Ur came to Haran; in 1857 his servant goes to get a wife for Isaac; in 1760 Jacob visits Laban; in 1452 Balaam is called to curse Israel; in 1040 David subdues Zobah and Damascus; in 975 these recover their independence; in 838-836 Joash or Jehoash obtained three important victories over Benhadad; in 740 Tiglath-pilezer defeats Rezin its last independent ruler, and reduces it to a dependency of Assyria; in 604 attacked by Pharaoh Necho it is captured by Nebuchadnezzar; in 333 it comes under Alexander the Great; in 323 Seleucus Nicator founds his dynasty; in 301 he founds Antioch as its capital; in 114 Antiochus Cyzicenus sets himself up at Damascus; in 65 the country becomes subject to

Rome; in 47 Julius Cæsar confirms the rights of many cities. In A.D. 6 Judea and Samaria are added to Syria; in 117 Hadrian fixes its E. boundary at the Euphrates; in 258 it is overrun by Sapor I. king of Persia; in 264 Odenathus delivers it; in 611 Chosroes II. destroys Antioch; in 614 he subdues Palestine; in 630 Mahommed takes some places in Syria; in 661 Damascus becomes its capital; in 762 Bagdad becomes the capital; in 868 the Tulonides dynasty set up; in 906 recovered by Caliph Moktofee; in 970 Fatimite dynasty set up, with Cairo for capital; in 1076 Syria invaded by the Turks; in 1096 Caliph Mostali dispossessed by the Crusaders; in 1099 the Christian kingdom of Jerusalem set up; in 1187 Saladin founds the Eyoobite dynasty; in 1250 it is partially destroyed by the revolt of the Baharite Mamlooks; in 1400 Tamerlane invades it; in 1516 Selim I. unites it to the Ottoman empire; in 1799 Bonaparte invades it from Egypt; in 1831 Ibrahim Pasha invades it; in 1841 it reverts to Turkey; in 1868 a general attack on the Maronites near Beyrout and Lebanon was made by the Druses, when 1200 persons were murdered: altogether about 12,000 persons lost their lives, 200 of whom were priests; 163 villages, 224 churches, and seven convents, were destroyed.

Judg 10. 6 the gods of S., and the gods of Zidon, and
2 Sa. 8. 6 David put garrisons in S. of Damascus
8. 12 Of S., and of Moab, and of the children
15. 8 vowed a vow while I abode at Geshur in S.
1 Ki 10. 29 for the kings of S., did they bring (them)
11. 25 he abhorred Israel, and reigned over S.
15. 18 Tabrimon, the son of Hezion, king of S.
19. 15 thou comest, anoint Hazael..king over S.
20. 1 the king of S. gathered all his host toge.
20. 20 the king of S. escaped on an horse with
20. 22 the king of S. will come up against thee
20. 23 the servants of the king of S. said unto
22. 1 three years without war between S. and
22. 3 take it not..of the hand of the king of S.?
22. 31 the king of S. commanded his thirty and
2 Ki. 5. 1 Naaman, captain of the host..of S., was
5. 1 the LORD had given deliverance unto S.
5. 5 the king of S. said, Go to, go, and I will
6. 8 the king of S. warred against Israel, and
6. 11 the king of S. was sore troubled for this
6. 23 the bands of S. came no more into the la.
6. 24 Ben-hadad king of S. gathered all his ho.
7. 5 to the uttermost part of the camp of S.
8. 7 Ben-hadad the king of S. was sick; and
8. 9 Ben-hadad king of S., hath sent me to th.
8. 13 showed..that thou (shalt be) king over S.
8. 28 the war against Hazael king of S. in Ram.
8. 29 when he fought against Hazael king of S.
9. 14 kept Ramoth. because of Hazael king of S.
9. 15 when he fought with Hazael king of S.
12. 17 Hazael king of S. went up, and fought
12. 18 Jehoash..sent (it) to Hazael king of S.
13. 3 into the hand of Hazael king of S., and
13. 4 because the king of S. oppressed them
13. 7 the king of S. had destroyed them, and
13. 17 and the arrow of deliverance from S.
13. 19 then hadst thou smitten S. till thou hadst
13. 19 whereas now thou shalt smite S. (but) th.
13. 22 Hazael king of S. oppressed Israel all the
13. 24 Hazael king of S. died; and Ben-hadad
15. 37 send against Judah Rezin the king of S.
16. 5 Rezin king of S. and Pekah son of Rem.
16. 6 Rezin king of S. recovered Elath to S., and
16. 7 save me out of the hand of the king of S.
1 Ch. 18. 6 David put (garrisons) in S. damascus, and
19. 6 out of Mesopotamia, and out of S.-maac.
2 Ch. 1. 17 so brought they..for the kings of S., by
16. 2 sent to Ben-hadad king of S., that dwelt
16. 7 thou hast relied on the king of S., and
16. 7 the host of the king of S. escaped out of
18. 10 With these thou shalt push S. until they
18. 30 the king of S. had commanded the cap.
20. 2 There cometh a..multitude..from..S.
22. 5 to war against Hazael king of S. at Ram.
22. 6 when he fought with Hazael king of S.
24. 23 (that) the host of S. came up against him
28. 5 delivered..into the hand of the king of S.
28. 23 the gods of the kings of S. help them, (th.)
Isa. 7. 1 the king of S., and Pekah the son of Re.
7. 2 saying, S. is confederate with Ephraim
7. 4 the fierce anger of Rezin with S., and of
7. 5 S.. Ephraim, and the son of Remaliah
7. 8 the head of S. (is) Damascus, and the head
17. 3 kingdom from Damascus..remnant of S.
Eze. 16. 57 of (thy) reproach of the daughters of S.
27. 16 S. (was) thy merchant by reason of the mu.
Hos. 12. 12 Jacob fled into the country of S., and Is.
Amos 1. 5 the people of S. shall go into captivity un.
Matt. 4. 24 his fame went throughout all S.: and they
Luke 2. 2 made when Cyrenius was governor of S.
Acts 15. 23 the Gentiles in Antioch and S. and Cil.
15. 41 he went through S. and Cilicia, confirm.
18. 18 sailed thence into S., and with him Pr.
20. 3 as he was about to sail into S., he pur.
21. 3 left it on the left hand, and sailed into S.
Gal. 1. 21 I came into the regions of S. and Cilicia

SYRIAC, SYRIAN, אֲרָמִית *aramith.*

The language used in Aram or Syria; substantially the same as *Chaldee.*

2 Ki. 18. 26 Speak..to thy servants in the S. language
Ezra 4. 7 in the S. tongue, and interpreted in the S.
Isa. 36. 11 Speak..unto thy servants in the S. langu.
Dan. 2. 4 Then spake the Chaldeans to the king in S.

SYRIAN, SYRIANS, אֲרַמִּי, אֲרַמִּים, אֲרָם.

The people of Aram or Syria.

Gen. 25. 20 of Bethuel the S...sister to Laban the S.
Gen. 28. 5 Laban, son of Bethuel the S., the brother
31. 20 Jacob stole away unawares to Laban the S.
31. 24 God came to Laban the S. in a dream by
Deut. 26. 5 A S. ready to perish (was) my father; and
2 Sa. 8. 5 the S. of Damascus came to succour Hada.
8. 5 David slew of the S. two and twenty tho.
8. 6 the S. became servants to David, (and) br.
8. 13 when he returned from smiting of the S.
10. 6 the S. of Beth-rehob, and the S. of Zoba
10. 8 the S. of Zoba, and of Rehob, and Ish-tob
10. 9 he..put (them) in array against the S.
10. 11 If the S. be too strong for me, then thou
10. 13 drew nigh..unto the battle against the S.
10. 14 children of Ammon saw that the S. were
10. 15 the S. saw that they were smitten before
10. 16 Hadarezer sent, and brought out the S.
10. 17 the S. set themselves in array against D.
10. 18 the S. fled before Israel; and David slew
10. 18 (men of) seven hundred chariots of the S.
10. 19 the S. feared to help the children of Am.
1 Ki. 20. 20 the S. fled and Israel pursued them; and
20. 21 the king..slew the S. with a great slaugh.
20. 26 Ben-hadad numbered the S., and went up
20. 27 but the S. filled the country
20. 28 the S. have said, The LORD (is) God of the
20. 29 Israel slew of the S. an hundred thousand
22. 11 With these shalt thou push the S., until
22. 35 stayed up in his chariot against the S.
2 Ki. 5. 2 the S. had gone out by companies, and had
5. 20 my master hath spared Naaman this S.
6. 9 Beware..for thither the S. are come down
7. 4 let us fall unto the host of the S.: if they
7. 5 they rose..to go unto the camp of the S.
7. 6 the LORD had made the host of the S. to
7. 10 We came to the camp of the S., and, beh.
7. 12 I will now show you what the S. have do.
7. 14 the king sent after the host of the S., sa.
7. 15 which the S. had cast away in their haste
7. 16 the people..spoiled the tents of the S.
8. 28 went with Joram..and the S. wounded J.
8. 29 wounds which the S. had given him at Ra.
9. 15 wounds which the S. had given him, when
13. 5 they went out from under the hand of..S.
13. 17 thou shalt smite the S. in Aphek, till thou
16. 6 the S. came to Elath, and dwelt there unto
24. 2 bands of the S., and bands of the Moabites
1 Ch. 18. 5 the S. of Damascus came to help Hadare.
18. 5 David slew of the S. two and twenty tho.
18. 6 the S. became David's servants, (and) bro.
19. 10 he..put (them) in array against the S.
19. 12 If the S. be too strong for me, then thou sh.
19. 14 Joab..drew nigh before the S. unto the ba.
19. 15 the children of Ammon saw that the S. we.
19. 16 the S. saw that they were put to the worse
19. 16 they sent messengers, and drew forth the S.
19. 17 put the battle in array against the S.
19. 18 But the S. fled before Israel
19. 18 David slew of the S. seven thousand (men
19. 19 neither would the S. help the children of A.
2 Ch. 18. 34 stayed..up in (his) chariot against the S.
22. 5 at Ramoth-gilead: and the S.'s smote J.
24. 24 the S. came with a small company of men
Isa. 9. 12 The S. before, and the Philistines behind
Jer. 35. 11 let us go..for fear of the army of the S.
Amos 9. 7 the Philistines from Caphtor, and the S.
Luke 4. 27 none of them was cleansed, saving..the S.

SY-RO-PHE-NI-CI-AN, *Συροφοίνισσα.*

Belonging to Phenicia (in Syria), on the N. of *Carmel.*

Mark 7. 26 The woman was a Greek, a S. by nation

T

TA-A'-NACH, תַּעְנָךְ, תַּעֲנָךְ *battlement.* **TANACH.**

A Levitical city on the W. of the Jordan in Manasseh or Issachar. On the slope of the western mountains that bound the plain of Jezreel over against Gilboa, and now called *Taanuk,* is a small village on the S. of *el-Lejjun.*

Josh 12. 21 The king of T., one; the king of Megiddo
17. 11 and the inhabitants of T. and her towns
21. 25 of the half tribe of Manasseh, T. with her
Judg. 1. 27 Neither..Beth-shean and her towns..T.
5. 19 then fought the kings of Canaan in T.
1 Ki. 4. 12 (to him pertained) T. and Megiddo, and
1 Ch. 7. 29 Beth-shean and her towns, T. and her to.

TA-A-NATH SHI'-LOH, תַּאֲנַת שִׁלֹה *circle of Shiloh.*

A city on the borders of Ephraim and Benjamin; now called *Tana,* between Shechem and the Jordan, and W. of Janohah.

Josh. 16. 6 the border went about eastward unto T.

TAB-BA'-OTH, טַבָּעוֹת *spots.*

One of the Nethinim whose descendants returned with Zerubbabel. B.C. 536.

Ezra 2. 43 children of Hasupha, the children of T.
Neh. 7. 46 children of Hashupha, the children of T.

TAB'-BATH, טַבַּת *extension.*

A city S. of Abel-meholah, in Issachar or Ephraim: *Tubukhet Fahil?*

Judg. 7. 22 to the border of Abel-meholah, unto T.

TA-BE'-AL, טָבְאַל *God is good.*

Father of one whom Syria and Ephraim sought to make king in Judah instead of Ahaz. B.C. 742.

Isa. 7. 6 and set a king in the midst..the son of T.

TA-BE'-EL, טָבְאֵל *God is good.*

An official in Samaria who wrote against the Jews to the king of Persia. B.C. 522.

Ezra 4. 7 wrote..T...unto Artaxerxes king of Per.

TABER, to —

To mince, trip daintily, תָּפַף *taphaph,* 3a.

Nah. 2. 7 her maids..tabering upon their breasts

TAB-ER'-AH, תַּבְעֵרָה *place of feeding.*

A place three days' journey N. of Sinai, where Israel was punished for murmuring.

Num 11. 3 And he called the name of the place T.
Deut. 9. 22 at T...ye provoked the LORD to wrath

TABERNACLE —

1. *A tent,* אֹהֶל *ohel.*

Exod. 26. 9 curtain in the fore front of the tabernacle
27. 21 the tabernacle of the congregation

[So in 28. 43; 29. 4, 10, 11, 30, 32, 42, 44; 30. 16, 18, 20, 26, 36; 31. 7; 33. 7, 7; 35. 21; 38. 8, 30; 40. 12; Lev. 1. 1, 3, 5; 3. 2, 8, 13; 4. 4, 5, 7, 7, 14. 16, 18, 18; 6. 16, 26, 30; 8. 3, 4, 31, 33, 35; 9. 5, 23; 10. 7, 9; 12. 6; 14. 11, 23; 15. 14, 29; 16. 7, 16, 17, 20, 23, 33; 17. 4, 5, 6, 9; 19. 21; 24. 3; Num. 1. 1; 2. 2, 17; 3. 7, 8, 25, 25, 38; 4. 3, 4, 15, 23, 25, 25, 28, 30, 31, 33, 35, 37, 39, 41, 43, 47; 6. 10, 13, 18; 7. 5, 89; 8. 9, 15, 19, 22, 24, 26; 10. 3; 11. 16; 12. 4, 5; 14. 10; 16. 18, 19, 42, 43, 50; 17. 4; 18. 4, 6, 21, 22, 23, 31; 19. 4; 20. 6; 25. 6; 27. 2; 31. 54; Deut. 31. 14, 14; Josh. 18. 1; 19. 51; 1 Sa. 2. 22; 1 Ki. 2. 30; 8. 4; 1 Ch. 6. 32; 9. 21; 23. 32; 2 Ch. 1. 3, 6, 13; 5. 5.]

Exod. 31. 7 and all the furniture of the tabernacle
33. 7 Moses took the tabernacle, and pitched
33. 8 when Moses went out unto the tabernacle
33. 8 until he was gone into the tabernacle
33. 9 as Moses entered into the tabernacle, the
33. 9 and stood (at) the door of the tabernacle
33. 10 cloudy pillar stand (at) the tabernacle door
33. 11 Joshua..departed not out of the tabern.
36. 37 he made an hanging for the tabernacle door
39. 38 and the hanging for the tabernacle door
Num. 9. 17 cloud was taken up from the tabernacle
11. 24 and set them round about the tabernacle
11. 26 but went not out unto the tabernacle
12. 10 the cloud departed from off the taberna.
17. 7 before the LORD in the tabernacle of wit.
17. 8 Moses went into the tabernacle of witness
18. 2 (minister) before the tabernacle of witness
18. 3 keep..the charge of all the tabernacle
18. 4 for all the service of the tabernacle
Deut 31. 15 stood over the door of the tabernacle
2 Sa. 6. 17 in the midst of the tabernacle that David
1 Ki. 1. 39 took an horn of oil out of the tabernacle
2. 28 Joab fled unto the tabernacle of the LORD
2. 29 that Joab was fled unto the tabernacle of
8. 4 holy vessels that (were) in the tabernacle
1 Ch. 9. 19 keepers of the gates of the tabernacle
9. 23 the house of the tabernacle, by wards
2 Ch. 5. 5 holy vessels that (were) in the tabernacle
24. 6 the collection..for the tabernacle of wit.
Job 5. 24 And thou shalt know that thy tabernacle
11. 14 let not wickedness dwell in thy taberna.
12. 6 The tabernacles of robbers prosper, and
15. 34 fire shall consume the tabernacles of bribe.
18. 6 The light shall be dark in his tabernacle
18. 14 shall be rooted out of his tabernacle
18. 15 It shall dwell in his tabernacle, because
19. 12 and encamp round about my tabernacle
20. 26 with him that is left in his tabernacle
22. 23 put away iniquity far from thy tabernac.
29. 4 when the secret of God (was) upon my ta.
31. 31 If the men of my tabernacle said not, Oh
Psa. 15. 1 LORD, who shall abide in thy tabernacle?
19. 4 In them hath he set a tabernacle for the
27. 5 in the secret of his tabernacle shall he
27. 6 offer in his tabernacle sacrifices of joy
61. 4 I will abide in thy tabernacle for ever
78. 51 (their) strength in the tabernacles of Ham
78. 67 Moreover he refused the tabernacle of J.
83. 6 The tabernacles of Edom, and the Ishm.
118. 15 in the tabernacles of the righteous
132. 3 Surely I will not come into the taberna.
Prov 14. 11 tabernacle of the upright shall flourish
Isa. 16. 5 in the tabernacle of David, judging, and
33. 20 a tabernacle (that) shall not be taken do.
Jer. 10. 20 My tabernacle is spoiled, and all my co.
Lam. 2. 4 in the tabernacle of the daughter of Zion
Eze. 41. 1 (which was) the breadth of the taberna.
Dan. 11. 45 he shall plant the tabernacles of his pal.
Hos. 9. 6 possess them thorns (shall be) in their tab.
12. 9 will yet make thee to dwell in tabernac.
Mal. 2. 12 the scholar, out of the tabernacles of Ja.

2. *Tabernacle, dwelling place,* מִשְׁכָּן *mishkan.*

Exod 25. 9 the pattern of the tabernacle, and the pa.
26. 1 thou shalt make the tabernacle (with) ten
26. 6 couple the curtains..it shall be one tab
26. 7 curtains..to be a covering upon the tab
26. 12 hang over the back side of the tabernacle
26. 13 it shall hang over the sides of the taber.
26. 15 thou shalt make boards for the taberna.
26. 17 make for all the boards of the tabernacle
26. 18 thou shalt make the boards for the tabe
26. 20 for the second side of the tabernacle, on
26. 22 for the sides of the tabernacle westward
26. 23 make for the corners of the tabernacle in
26. 26 the boards of the one side of the tabern.
26. 27 the boards of the other side of the taber.
26. 27 for the boards of the side of the taberna.
26. 30 thou shalt rear up the tabernacle accord.
26. 35 on the side of the tabernacle toward the
27. 9 thou shalt make the court of the tabern.
27. 19 the vessels of the tabernacle in all the se.

Exod35. 11 The tabernacle, his tent, and his covering
35. 15 the door at the entering in of the taberna.
35. 18 The pins of the tabernacle, and the pins
36. 8 them that wrought the work of the taber.
36. 13 fifty taches..so it became one tabernacle
36. 14 curtains..for the tent over the tabernacle
36. 20, 23 And he made boards for the tabernacle
36. 22 make for all the boards of the tabernacle
36. 25 for the other side of the tabernacle, (which
36. 27 for the sides of the tabernacle westward
36. 28 for the corners of the tabernacle in the two
36. 31 the boards of the one side of the tabern.
36. 32 the boards of the other side of the taber.
36. 32 five bars for the boards of the tabernacle
38. 20 the pins of the tabernacle, and of the co.
38. 21 the sum of the tabernacle, (even) of the t.
38. 31 the pins of the tabernacle, and all the pins
39. 32 Thus was all the work of the tabernacle
39. 33 they brought the tabernacle unto Moses
39. 40 the vessels of the service of the tabernacle
40. 2, 6, 29 the tabernacle of the tent of the co.
40. 5 put the hanging of the door to the taber.
40. 9 anoint the tabernacle, and all that (is) th.
40. 17 the second year..the tabernacle was rea.
40. 18 Moses reared up the tabernacle, and fast.
40. 19 he spread abroad the tent over the taber.
40. 21 he brought the ark into the tabernacle, and
40. 22 upon the side of the tabernacle northward
40. 24 the table, on the side of the tabernacle so.
40. 28 the hanging (at) the door of the tabernacle
40. 33 the court round about the tabernacle and
40. 34, 35 the glory of the LORD filled the taber.
40. 36 cloud was taken up from over the tabern.
40. 38 the cloud of the LORD (was) upon the ta.
Lev. 8. 10 anointed the tabernacle and all that (was)
15. 31 they defile my tabernacle that (is) among
17. 4 to offer..before the tabernacle of the Lo.
26. 11 I will set my tabernacle among you, and
Num. 1. 50 shalt appoint the Levites over the taber.
1. 50 they shall bear the tabernacle, and all the
1. 50 and shall encamp round about the taber.
1. 51 when the tabernacle setteth forward, the
1. 51 when the tabernacle is to be pitched, the
1. 53 Levites shall pitch round about the tab.
1. 53 Levites shall keep the charge of the tab.
3. 7, 8 to do the service of the tabernacle
3. 23 the Gershonites shall pitch behind the ta.
3. 25 the tabernacle, and the tent, the covering
3. 26 the court, which (is) by the tabernacle, and
3. 29 shall pitch on the side of the tabernacle
3. 35 shall pitch on the side of the tabernacle
3. 36 the boards of the tabernacle, and the bars
3. 38 those that encamp before the tabernacle
4. 16 the oversight of all the tabernacle, and
4. 25 they shall bear the curtains of the taber.
4. 26 gate of the court, which (is) by the taber.
4. 31 the boards of the tabernacle, and the bars
5. 17 the dust that is in the floor of the tabern.
7. 1 Moses had fully set up the tabernacle, and
7. 3 they brought them before the tabernacle
9. 15 the day that the tabernacle was reared up
9. 15 the cloud covered the tabernacle, (nam.)
9. 15 there was upon the tabernacle as it were
9. 18 as long as the cloud abode upon the tab.
9. 19 the cloud tarried long upon the taberna.
9. 20 the cloud was a few days upon the taber.
9. 22 the cloud tarried upon the tabernacle, re.
10. 11 the cloud was taken up from off the tab.
10. 17 the tabernacle was taken down; and the
10. 17 sons of Merari set forward, bearing the ta.
10. 21 (the other) did set up the tabernacle aga.
16. 9 to do the service of the tabernacle of the
16. 24, 27 the tabernacle of Korah, Dathan, and
17. 13 cometh any thing near unto the tabern.
19. 13 purifieth not himself, defileth the taber.
24. 5 How goodly are thy tabernacles, O Isra.!
31. 30, 47 the charge of the tabernacle of the L.
Josh.22. 19 the land..wherein the LORD'S tabernacle
22. 29 the altar..that (is) before his tabernacle
2 Sa. 7. 6 have walked in a tent and in a tabernacle
1 Ch. 6. 48 all manner of service of the tabernacle of
16. 39 before the tabernacle of the LORD, in the
17. 5 from tent to tent, and from (one) taberna.
21. 29 the tabernacle of the LORD, which Moses
23. 26 they shall no (more) carry the tabernacle
2 Ch. 1. 5 he put before the tabernacle of the LORD
Psa. 43. 3 unto thy holy hill, and to thy tabernacles
46. 4 the holy (place) of the tabernacles of the
78. 60 he forsook the tabernacle of Shiloh, the
84. 1 How amiable (are) thy tabernacles, O Lo.
132. 7 We will go into his tabernacles; we will
Eze. 37. 27 My tabernacle also shall be with them; yea

3. *A covering, covert, booth,* סֹךְ *sok.*
Psa. 76. 2 In Salem also is his tabernacle, and his

4. *A covering, covert, booth,* סֻכָּה *sukkah.*
Lev. 23. 34 (shall be) the feast of tabernacles (for) se.
Deut 16. 13 Thou shalt observe the feast of tabernacles
16. 16 the feast of weeks, and in the feast of ta.
31. 10 of the year of release, in the feast of tab.
2 Ch. 8. 13 feast of weeks, and in the feast of taber.
Ezra 3. 4 They kept also the feast of tabernacles
Job 36. 29 can (any) understand..the noise of his tab.
Isa. 4. 6 there shall be a tabernacle for a shadow
Amos 9. 11 that day will I raise up the tabernacle of
Zech 14. 16, 18, 19 to keep the feast of tabernacles

5. *Covering, covert, booth,* סִכּוּת *sikkuth.*
Amos 5. 26 ye have borne the tabernacle of your Mo.

6. *A covering, covert, booth,* שֹׂךְ *sok.*
Lam. 2. 6 he hath violently taken away his taberna.

7. *Tabernacle, dwelling place,* σκηνή *skēnē.*
Matt 17. 4 let us make here three tabernacles; one for
Mark 9. 5 let us make three tabernacles; one for th.
Luke 9. 33 let us make three tabernacles; one for th.
Acts 7. 43 ye took up the tabernacle of Moloch, and
7. 44 Our fathers had the tabernacle of witness
15. 16 will build again the tabernacle of David
Heb. 8. 2 the true tabernacle, which the Lord pitc.
8. 5 when he was about to make the tabernacle
9. 2 there was a tabernacle made; the first, wh.
9. 3 the tabernacle which is called the holiest
9. 6 the priests went always into the first tab.
9. 8 while as the first tabernacle was yet stan.
9. 11 by a greater and more perfect tabernacle
9. 21 the tabernacle and all the vessels of the
11. 9 dwelling in tabernacles with Isaac and Ja.
13. 10 no right to eat which serve the tabernacle
Rev. 13. 6 to blaspheme his name, and his tabernacle
15. 5 the temple of the tabernacle of the testi.
21. 3 the tabernacle of God (is) with men, and

8. *Tabernacle, dwelling place,* σκῆνος *skēnos.*
2 Co. 5. 1 if our earthly house of (this) tabernacle
5. 4 we that are in (this) tabernacle do groan

9. *Tabernacle, dwelling place,* σκήνωμα *skēnōma.*
Acts 7. 46 desired to find a tabernacle for the God
2 Pe. 1. 13 as long as I am in this tabernacle, to stir
1. 14 I must put off (this) my tabernacle, even

10. *A fixing up of tabernacles,* σκηνοπηγία *skēnop.*
John 7. 2 Now the Jews' feast of tabernacles was at

TA-BI'-THA, Ταβιθά *gazelle.*
A female in Joppa who was restored to life by the prayer of Peter; called also *Dorcas;* she was full of good deeds.
Acts 9. 36 there was..a certain disciple named T.
9. 40 and turning..to the body said, T., arise

TABLE, (at the) —

1. *Tablet, board,* לוּחַ *luach.*
Exod 24. 12 I will give thee tables of stone, and a law
31. 18 two tables of testimony, tables of stone
32. 15 the two tables of the testimony (were) in
32. 15 the tables (were) written on both their si.
32. 16 the tables (were) the work of God, and the
32. 16 the writing of God, graven upon the tab.
32. 19 he cast the tables out of his hands, and
34. 1 Hew thee two tables of stone like unto
34. 1 and I will write upon (these) tables the
34. 1 words that were in the first tables, which
34. 4 he hewed two tables of stone like unto the
34. 4 and took in his hand the two tables of st.
34. 28 He wrote upon the tables the words of the
34. 29 the two tables of testimony in Moses' ha.
Deut. 4. 13 and he wrote them upon two tables of st.
5. 22 he wrote them in two tables of stone, and
9. 9, 11 the tables of stone, (even) the tables
9. 10 LORD delivered unto me two tables of st.
9. 15 the two tables of the covenant (were) in
9. 17 I took the two tables, and cast them out
10. 1 Hew thee two tables of stone like unto the
10. 2 And I will write on the tables the words
10. 2 were in the first tables which thou brak.
10. 3 hewed two tables of stone like unto the
10. 3 went up..having the two tables in mine
10. 4 he wrote on the tables, according to the
10. 5 put the tables in the ark which I had made
1 Ki. 8. 9 nothing in the ark save the two tables of
2 Ch. 5. 10 nothing in the ark save the two tables wh.
Prov. 3. 3 write them upon the table of thine heart
7. 3 write them upon the table of thine heart
Isa. 30. 8 write it before them in a table, and note
Jer. 17. 1 (it is) graven upon the table of their heart
Hab. 2. 2 make (it) plain upon tables, that he may

2. *A circle, round table,* מֵסַב *mesab.*
Song 1. 12 While the king (sitteth) at his table, my

3. *A table,* שֻׁלְחָן *shulchan.*
Exod 25. 23 Thou shalt also make a table (of) shittim
25. 27 for places of the staves to bear the table
25. 28 overlay them with gold, that the table may
25. 30 thou shalt set upon the table showbread
26. 35 thou shalt set the table without the veil
26. 35 the candlestick over against the table on
26. 35 thou shalt put the table on the north side
30. 27 the table and all his vessels, and the can.
31. 8 the table and his furniture, and the pure
35. 13 The table, and his staves, and all his ves.
37. 10 And he made the table (of) shittim wood
37. 14 the places for the staves to bear the table
37. 15 overlaid them with gold, to bear the table
37. 16 the vessels which (were) upon the table
39. 36 The table, (and) all the vessels thereof, and
40. 4 thou shalt bring in the table, and set in
40. 22 he put the table in the tent of the congr.
40. 24 over against the table, on the side of the
Lev. 24. 6 six on a row, upon the pure table before
Num. 3. 31 the ark, and the table, and the candlestick
4. 7 upon the table of showbread they shall sp.
Judg. 1. 7 kings..gathered (their meat) under my ta.
1 Sa. 20. 29 therefore he cometh not unto the..table
20. 34 Jonathan arose from the table in fierce an.
2 Sa. 9. 7 thou shalt eat bread at my table contin.
9. 10 master's son shall eat bread..at my table
9. 11 he shall eat at my table, as one of the ki.
9. 13 for he did eat continually at the king's ta.
19. 28 among them that did eat at thine own ta.
1 Ki. 2. 7 let them be of those that eat at thy table
4. 27 all that came unto king Solomon's table
7. 48 the table of gold, whereupon the showbr.
10. 5 the meat of his table, and the sitting of
13. 20 it came to pass, as they sat at the table

1 Ki. 18. 19 four hundred, which eat at Jezebel's table
2 Ki. 4. 10 let us set for him there a bed, and a table
1 Ch. 28. 16 for the tables of showbread, for every ta.
28. 16 and (likewise) silver for the tables of silver
2 Ch. 4. 8 He made also ten tables, and placed (them)
4. 19 the tables whereon the showbread (was
9. 4 the meat of his table, and the sitting of
13. 11 also (set they in order) upon the pure ta.
29. 18 the showbread table, with all the vessels
Neh. 5. 17 (there were) at my table an hundred and
Job 36. 16 that which should be set on thy table (sh.)
Psa. 23. 5 Thou preparest a table before me in the
69. 22 Let their table become a snare before th.
78. 19 Can God furnish a table in the wilderness
128. 3 like olive plants round about thy table
Prov. 9. 2 wine; she hath also furnished her table
Isa. 21. 5 Prepare the table, watch in the watch-to.
28. 8 all tables are full of vomit (and) filthiness
65. 11 prepare a table for that troop, and that
Eze. 23. 41 a table prepared before it, whereupon th.
39. 20 ye shall be filled at my table with horses
40. 39 two tables on this side, and two tables on
40. 40 And at the side without..(were) two tab.
40. 40 and on the other side..(were) two tables
40. 41 Four tables..on this side, and four tables
40. 41 eight tables, whereupon they slew (their
40. 42 the four tables (were) of hewn stone for
40. 43 upon the tables (was) the flesh of the off.
41. 22 This (is) the table that (is) before the Lo.
44. 16 they shall come near to my table, to min.
Dan. 11. 27 they shall speak lies at one table; but it
Mal. 1. 7 ye say, The table of the LORD (is) contem.
1. 12 The table of the LORD (is) polluted; and

4. *To lie down or back, recline,* ἀνάκειμαι *anakeimai.*
John 13. 28 no man at the table knew for what intent

5. *A reclining couch or bed,* κλίνη *klinē.*
Mark 7. 4 the washing of..brazen vessels, and of ta.

6. *A broad slab or table,* πλάξ *plax.*
2 Co. 3. 3 not in tables of stone, but in fleshy tables
Heb. 9. 4 Aaron's rod that budded, and the tables

7. *A table (with four feet),* τράπεζα *trapeza.*
Matt 15. 27 crumbs which fall from their masters' ta.
21. 12 overthrew the tables of the money chang.
Mark 7. 28 the dogs under the table eat of the child.
11. 15 overthrew the tables of the money chan.
Luke 16. 21 crumbs which fell from the rich man's ta.
22. 21 betrayeth me (is) with me on the table
22. 30 That ye may eat and drink at my table in
John 2. 15 poured out..money, and overthrew the ta.
Acts 6. 2 leave the word of God, and serve tables
Rom. 11. 9 Let their table be made a snare, and a tr.
1 Co. 10. 21 of the Lord's table, and of the table of de.
Heb. 9. 2 the candlestick, and the table, and the sh.

TABLET, writing table —

1. *House of breath, scent-box,* בָּתֵּי נֶפֶשׁ *[beth].*
Isa. 3. 20 the head bands, and the tablets, and the

2. *Buckle, bracelet, necklace,* כּוּמָז *kumaz.*
Exod 35. 22 ear rings, and rings, and tablets, all jewe.
Num 31. 50 bracelets, rings, ear rings, and tablets, to

3. *A small writing tablet,* πινακίδιον *pinakidion.*
Luke 1. 63 he asked for a writing table, and wrote

TA'-BOR, תָּבוֹר *mountain height.*
1. An isolated mountain in Zebulun and Issachar between the plains of Jezreel and Scythopolis, in the midst of Galilee; now called *et Tur.*
Josh. 19. 22 the coast reacheth to T., and Shahazimah
Judg. 4. 6 Go and draw toward mount T., and take
4. 12 that Barak..was gone up to mount T.
4. 14 So Barak went down from mount T., and
8. 18 What manner of men..whom ye slew at T.?
Psa. 89. 12 T. and Hermon shall rejoice in thy name
Jer. 46. 18 Surely as T. (is) among the mountains
Hos. 5. 1 because ye have been..net spread upon T.
2. A plain or place in Benjamin S. of Bethel.
1 Sa. 10. 3 thou shalt come to the plain of T., and
3. A Levitical city in Zebulun, at the east.
1 Ch. 6. 77 Rimmon with her suburbs, T. with her

TABRET —

1. *Tabret, timbrel,* תֹּף *toph.*
Gen. 31. 27 with mirth, and with songs, with tabret
1 Sa. 10. 5 with a psaltery, and a tabret, and a pipe
18. 6 to meet king Saul, with tabrets, with joy
Isa. 5. 12 the tabret and pipe, and wine, are in their
24. 8 The mirth of tabrets ceaseth, the noise of
30. 32 (in) every place..(it) shall be with tabrets
Jer. 31. 4 shalt again be adorned with thy tabrets
Eze. 28. 13 the workmanship of thy tabrets and of thy

2. *Spittle (?),* תֹּפֶת *topheth.*
Job 17. 6 a byword..and aforetime I was as a tab.

TAB-RIM'-ON, טַבְרִמֹּן *Rimmon is good.*
Son of Hezion, and father of Benhadad king of Syria, in the days of Asa. B.C. 951.
1 Ki. 15. 18 Asa sent them to Ben-hadad, the son of T

TACHES —

Hoops, loops, קְרָסִים *qerasim.*
Exod 26. 6 And thou shalt make fifty taches of gold
26. 6 couple the curtains together with..taches
26. 11 make fifty taches of brass, and put the ta.
26. 33 shalt hang up the veil under the taches
35. 11 his tent, and his covering, his taches, and
36. 13 And he made fifty taches of gold, and
36. 13 coupled the curtains..with the taches: so
36. 18 he made fifty taches (of) brass to couple
39. 33 all his furniture, his taches, his boards

TACHMONITE, תַּחְכְּמֹנִי. See *Adino*.
An appellation of the first of David's valiant men; in 1 Chron. 11. 11 he is called "The son of Hachmoni," *i.e.* a Hachmonite. B.C. 1048.
2 Sa. 23. 8 The T. that sat in the seat, chief among

TACKLING —
1. *Rope, cord, line,* חֶבֶל *chebel.*
Isa. 33. 23 Thy tacklings are loosed; they could not
2. *Apparatus or furniture of a ship,* σκευή *skeuē.*
Acts 27. 19 cast out with our own hands the tackling

TAD'-MOR, תַּדְמֹר, (1 Ki. 9. 18, V.L. תמר).
A city rebuilt by Solomon, B.C. 1000, in the wilderness E. of Gilead, between Damascus and the Euphrates, at the foot of a range of chalky hills. About B.C. 333 its name was changed to Palmyra; in A.D. 130 it submitted to Hadrian; in 260 Odenathus defeated Sapor king of Persia here; in 266 his wife Zenobia took the title of Queen of the East; in 272-273 Aurelian besieged and took it; in 527 Justinian I. rebuilt it; in 1400 Tamerlane plundered it; in 1691 its ruins were discovered by some English merchants; in 1816 Forby and Mangles visited it. Its ruins cover several miles; it has an immense temple of the sun, and out of 390 columns 90 still remain; it lies on the great highway of traffic between Palestine and Thapsachus on the Euphrates.
1 Ki. 9. 18 Baalath, and T. in the wilderness, in the
2 Ch. 8. 4 he built T. in the wilderness, and all the

TA'-HAN, תַּחַן *graciousness.*
1. A son of Ephraim. B.C. 1600.
Num 26. 35 of T., the family of the Tahanites
2. A descendant of the same in the fourth generation. B.C. 1500.
1 Ch. 7. 25 Resheph, and Telah his son, and T. his son

TAHANITES, תַּחֲנִי.
The family of Tahan son of Ephraim.
Num 26. 35 Ephraim..of Tahan, the family of the T.

TA-HA-PA'-NES, TAH-PAN'-HES, תַּחְפַּנְחֵס.
A city in Egypt on the Nile, near Pelusium, on the S. extremity of Palestine; called in the LXX. *Taphne* or *Taphnai*, and by classical writers *Daphne*, and now *Tell Defenneh.* Thither many Jews fled from the Chaldeans, carrying with them by force Jeremiah and Baruch. See *Tehaphnehes.* (Jer. 2. 16, V.L. תחפנס.)
Jer. 2. 16 Noph and T. have broken the crown of thy
43. 7 So they came..thus came they (even) to T.
43. 8 Then came the word..unto Jeremiah in T.
43. 9 at the entry of Pharaoh's house in T., in
44. 1 all the Jews..which dwell..at T., and at
46. 14 Declare ye..and publish in Noph and in T.

TA'-HATH, תַּחַת *depression, humility.*
1. The twenty-seventh station of Israel from Egypt, and the eleventh from Sinai; between Makheloth and Tarah.
Num 33. 26 And they removed..and encamped at T.
33. 27 they departed from T., and pitched at
2. A Kohathite, son of Assir, and father of Uriel. B.C. 1480.
1 Ch. 6. 24 T. his son, Uriel his son, Uzziah his son
6. 37 The son of T., the son of Assir, the son of
3. Grandson of Shuthelah the son of Ephraim. B.C. 1600.
1 Ch. 7. 20 Bered his son, and T. his son, and Eladah
4. A grandson of the preceding.
1 Ch. 7. 20 and Eladah his son, and T. his son

TAH-PE'-NES, תַּחְפְּנֵיס.
Queen of Pharaoh king of Egypt in the days of Solomon. B.C. 1000. Her sister became wife of Hadad, a descendant of the kings of Syria and an adversary of Solomon.
1 Ki. 11. 19 he gave him to wife..the sister of T. the
11. 20 the sister of T. bare him Genubath his son
11. 20 whom T. weaned in Pharaoh's house and

TAH-RE'-A, תַּחְרֵעַ *flight.* See *Tarea.*
Son of Micah, grandson of Jonathan son of Saul. B.C. 1000.
1 Ch. 9. 41 the sons of Micah (were), Pithon and T.

TAH'-TIM HOD'-SHI, תַּחְתִּים חָדְשִׁי.
A district N. of Gilead, in the extremity of Bashan; mentioned with Dan-jaan and Sidon.
2 Sa. 24. 6 They came to Gilead, and to the land of T.

TAIL —
1. *Tail, rear,* זָנָב *zanab.*
Exod. 4. 4 Put forth thine hand..take it by the tail
Deut 28. 13 shall make thee the head, and not the ta.
28. 44 he shall be the head, and thou..the tail
Judg 15. 4 took fire brands, and turned tail to tail
15. 4 put a fire brand in..between two tails
Job 40. 17 He moveth his tail like a cedar: the sine.
Isa. 7. 4 neither be faint hearted for the two tails
9. 14 will cut off from Israel head and tail, br
9. 15 prophet that teacheth lies, he (is) the tail
19. 15 which the head or tail, branch or rush, may
2. *A tail,* οὐρά *oura.*
Rev. 9. 10 And they had tails like unto scorpions
9. 10 there were stings in their tails: and their
9. 19 their power is..in their tails: for their ta.
12. 4 his tail drew the third part of the stars of

TAKE (away, up), to —
1. *To cause to perish, destroy,* אָבַד *abad,* 5.
Jer. 25. 10 I will take from them the voice of mirth
2. *To lay hold,* אָחַז *achaz.*
Exod. 4. 4 Put forth thine hand, and take it by the
Judg 16. 3 took the doors of the gate of the city, and
16. 21 the Philistines took him, and put out his
20. 6 I took my concubine, and cut her in piec.
2 Sa. 20. 9 Joab took Amasa by the beard with the
Job 16. 12 he hath also taken (me) by my neck, and
18. 9 The gin shall take (him) by the heel, (and)
Psa. 137. 9 Happy (shall he be), that taketh and das.
Jer. 13. 21 shall not sorrows take thee, as a woman in
49. 24 sorrows have taken her, as a woman in tr.
3. *To gather,* אָסַף *asaph.*
Gen. 30. 23 and said, God hath taken away my repr.
Josh. 20. 4 they shall take him into the city unto th.
1 Sa. 14. 52 when Saul saw any strong man..he took
Psa. 27. 10 forsake me, then the LORD will take me
85. 3 Thou hast taken away all thy wrath: thou
104. 29 thou takest away their breath, they die
Isa. 4. 1 let us be called by thy name, to take aw.
Jer. 16. 5 I have taken away my peace from this pe.
4. *To keep back, lay up,* אָצַל *atsal.*
Num 11. 17 I will take of the spirit which (is) upon
5. *To keep back,* אָצַל *atsal,* 5.
Num 11. 25 took of the spirit that (was) upon him, and
6. *To cause to go or come in,* בּוֹא *bo,* 5.
Isa. 16. 3 Take counsel, execute judgment; make
7. *To spoil, prey, seize, plunder,* בָּזַז *bazaz.*
Deut 20. 14 the spoil thereof, shalt thou take unto
2 Ch. 20. 25 his people came to take away the spoil of
25. 13 smote three thousand of them, and took
28. 8 took also away much spoil from them, and
Isa. 10. 6 to take the prey, and to tread them down
33. 23 then is the prey..divided; the lame take
Eze. 29. 19 take her prey; and it shall be the wages
38. 12 to take a prey; to turn thine hand upon
38. 13 hast thou gathered thy company to take
8. *To burn, consume, feed, pasture,* בָּעַר *baar,* 3.
Deut 26. 14 neither have I taken away (ought) thereof
2 Sa. 4. 11 shall I not..take you away from the earth?
1 Ki. 14. 10 will take away the remnant of the house
14. 10 as a man taketh away dung, till it be all
21. 21 will take away thy posterity, and will cut
2 Ch. 19. 3 thou hast taken away the groves out of
9. *To cause to burn, consume,* בָּעַר *baar,* 5.
1 Ki. 16. 3 I will take away the posterity of Baasha
10. *To cast or take out,* גָּזָה *gazah.*
Psa. 71. 6 he that took me out of my mother's bow.
11. *To take violently away, rob, plunder,* גָּזַל *gazal.*
Psa. 69. 4 then I restored (that) which I took not
Isa. 10. 2 to take away the right from the poor of
12. *To cleave, adhere to, pursue,* דָּבַק *dabeq.*
Gen. 19. 19 I cannot escape..lest some evil take me
13. *To take away,* הָגָה *hagah.*
Prov 25. 4 Take away the dross from the silver, and
25. 5 Take away the wicked (from) before the
14. *To take or keep fast hold,* חָזַק *chazaq,* 5.
Deut 25. 11 putteth forth her hand, and taketh him
Judg 19. 25 the man took his concubine, and brought
2 Sa. 15. 5 he put forth his hand, and took him, and
2 Ch. 28. 15 took the captives, and with the spoil clo.
Prov 26. 17 (is like) one that taketh a dog by the ears
Isa. 41. 9 (Thou) whom I have taken from the ends
51. 18 neither (is there any) that taketh her by
Jer. 31. 32 I took them by the hand, to bring them
Mic. 4. 9 pangs have taken thee as a woman in tra.
15. *To draw out, away,* חָלַץ *chalats,* 3.
Lev. 14. 40 priest shall command that they take away
14. 43 after that he hath taken away the stones
16. *To make bare, draw up or out,* חָשַׂף *chasaph.*
Isa. 30. 14 or to take water (withal) out of the pit
17. *To take away, put,* חָתָה *chathah.*
Psa. 52. 5 he shall take thee away, and pluck thee
Prov. 6. 27 Can a man take fire in his bosom, and his
Isa. 30. 14 shall not be found..a sherd to take fire
18. *To snatch away, catch,* חָתַף *chathaph.*
Job 9. 12 he taketh away, who can hinder him? who
19. *To give,* יָהַב *yahab.*
Deut. 1. 13 Take you wise men, and understanding
20. *To cause to go on,* יָלַךְ *yalak,* 5.
Exod. 2. 9 Take this child away, and nurse it for me
21. *To sit down or still,* יָשַׁב *yashab,* 5.
Ezra 10. 2 have taken strange wives of the people of
10. 10 have taken strange wives, to increase the
10. 14 let all them which have taken strange wi.
10. 17 with all the men that had taken strange
10. 18 there were found that had taken strange
22. *To capture, take,* לָכַד *lakad.*
Num 21. 32 they took the villages thereof, and drove
32. 39 took it, and dispossessed the Amorite wh.
32. 41 went and took the small towns thereof
32. 42 Nobah went and took Kenath, and the
Deut. 2. 34 we took all his cities at that time, and
2. 35 Only..the spoil of the cities which we to.
3. 4 we took all his cities at that time, there
Josh. 6. 20 the people went..and they took the city
7. 14 the tribe which the LORD taketh shall
7. 14 the family which the LORD shall take sh.
7. 14 the household which the LORD shall take
7. 17 he took the family of the Zarhites: and he
8. 19 they entered into the city, and took it, and
8. 21 Israel saw that the ambush had taken the
10. 1 Joshua had taken Ai, and had utterly de.
Josh 10. 28 Joshua took Makkedah, and smote it wi.
10. 32 which took it on the second day, and sm.
10. 35 they took it on that day, and smote it with
10. 37 they took it, and smote it with the edge
10. 39 he took it, and the king thereof, and all
10. 42 these kings and their land did Joshua ta.
11. 10 took Hazar, and smote the king thereof
11. 12 the kings of them, did Joshua take, and
11. 17 all their kings he took, and smote them
15. 16 He that smiteth Kirjath-sepher, and tak.
15. 17 the son of Kenez, the brother of Caleb, to.
19. 47 took it, and smote it with the edge of the
Judg. 1. 8 had taken it, and smitten it with the ed.
1. 12 He that smiteth Kirjath-sepher, and tak.
1. 13 And Othniel..Caleb's younger brother, to
1. 18 Judah took Gaza with the coast thereof
3. 28 took the fords of Jordan toward Moab, and
7. 24 take before them the waters unto Beth-b.
7. 24 took the waters unto Beth-barah and Jo.
7. 25 they took two princes of the Midianites
8. 12 took the two kings of Midian, Zebah and
9. 45 he took the city, and slew the people that
9. 50 and encamped against Thebez, and took
12. 5 the Gileadites took the passages of Jordan
1 Sa. 14. 47 Saul took the kingdom over Israel, and
2 Sa. 5. 7 David took the strong hold of Zion: the
8. 4 David took from him a thousand (chariots)
12. 26 fought against Rabbah..and took the ro.
12. 27 I have fought against Rabbah, and have t.
12. 28 take it: lest I take the city, and it be ca
12. 29 to Rabbah, and fought against it, and took
1 Ki. 9. 16 Pharaoh..had gone up and taken Gezer
2 Ki. 12. 17 went up, and fought against Gath, and t.
17. 6 the king of Assyria took Samaria, and ca.,
18. 10 at the end of three years they took it; (ev.)
1 Ch. 11. 5 David took the castle of Zion, which (is)
18. 4 David took from him a thousand chariots
2 Ch. 12. 4 he took the fenced cities which (pertained)
13. 19 pursued after Jeroboam, and took cities
15. 8 out of the cities which he had taken from
17. 2 the cities..which Asa his father had tak.
28. 18 had taken Beth-shemesh, and Ajalon, and
32. 18 to trouble them, that they might take the
33. 11 which took Manasseh among the thorns
Neh. 9. 25 they took strong cities, and a fat land, and
Job 5. 13 He taketh the wise in their own craftiness
Prov. 5. 22 His own iniquities shall take the wicked
16. 32 he that ruleth his spirit than he that ta.
Isa. 20. 1 and fought against Ashdod, and took it
Jer. 18. 22 they have digged a pit to take me, and hid
32. 3, 28 king of Babylon, and he shall take it
32. 24 they are come unto the city to take it; and
34. 22 they shall fight against it, and take it, and
37. 8 fight against this city, and take it, and bu.
38. 3 king of Babylon's army, which shall take
Dan. 11. 15 cast up a mount, and take the most fen.
11. 18 After this shall he..take many: but a pr.
Amos 3. 4 will a young lion cry..if he have taken
3. 5 a snare..and have taken nothing at all?
Hab. 1. 10 for they shall heap dust, and take it
23. *To take, receive,* לָקַח *laqach.*
Gen. 2. 15 God took the man, and put him into the
2. 21 he took one of his ribs, and closed up the
2. 22 the rib, which the LORD God had taken
3. 6 she took of the fruit thereof, and did eat
3. 22 lest he put forth his hand, and take also
4. 19 Lamech took unto him two wives: the
5. 24 And Enoch..he (was) not; for God took
6. 2 they took them wives of all which they
6. 21 take thou unto thee of all food that is ea.
7. 2 Of every clean beast thou shalt take to th.
8. 9 he put forth his hand, and took her, and
8. 20 took of every clean beast, and of every cl.
9. 23 Japheth took a garment, and laid (it) up.
11. 29 Abram and Nahor took them wives: the
11. 31 Terah took Abram his son, and Lot the
12. 5 Abram took Sarai his wife, and Lot his
12. 19 so I might have taken her to me to wife
12. 19 therefore behold thy wife, take (her) and
14. 11 they took all the goods of Sodom and Go.
14. 12 they took Lot Abram's brother's son, who
14. 21 Give me the persons, and take the goods
14. 23 I will not take any thing that (is) thine
14. 24 Eshcol and Mamre; let them take their po.
15. 9 Take me an heifer of three years old, and
15. 10 he took unto him all these, and divided
16. 3 Abram's wife, took Hagar her maid, the
17. 23 Abraham took Ishmael his son, and all
18. 8 he took butter, and milk, and the calf wh.
19. 15 take thy wife, and thy two daughters, whi.
20. 2 Abimelech king of Gerar sent and took S.
20. 3 for the woman which thou hast taken
20. 14 Abimelech took sheep and oxen, and men.
21. 14 took bread and a bottle of water, and gave
21. 21 his mother took him a wife out of the land
21. 27 Abraham took sheep, and oxen, and gave
21. 30 (these) seven ewe lambs shalt thou take
22. 2 Take now thy son, thine only (son) Isaac
22. 3 took two of his young men with him, and
22. 6 Abraham took the wood of the burnt off.
22. 6 and he took the fire in his hand, and a kn.
22. 10 And Abraham..took the knife to slay his
22. 13 Abraham went and took the ram, and off.
23. 13 take (it) of me, and I will bury my dead
24. 3 thou shalt not take a wife unto my son of
24. 4 thou shalt go..and take a wife unto my
24. 7 The LORD God of heaven, which took me
24. 7 thou shalt take a wife unto my son from
24. 10 the servant took ten camels of the camels
24. 22 the man took a golden ear ring of half a sh.
24. 37 Thou shalt not take a wife to my son of

Gen. 24. 38 thou shalt go..and take a wife unto my son
24. 40 thou shalt take a wife for my son of my ki.
24. 48 had led me in the right way to take my
24. 51 Rebekah (is) before thee, take (her), and
24. 61 the servant took Rebekah, and went his
24. 65 therefore she took a veil, and covered her.
24. 67 and took Rebekah, and she became his
25. 1 Abraham took a wife, and her name (was)
25. 20 Isaac was forty years old when he took
26. 34 he took to wife Judith the daughter of
27. 15 Rebekah took goodly raiment of her eld.
27. 35 Thy brother..hath taken away thy bless.
27. 36 he took away my birthright; and, behold
27. 36 now he hath taken away my blessing
27. 46 if Jacob take a wife of the daughters of
28. 1, 6 Thou shalt not take a wife of the dau.
28. 2 take thee a wife from thence of the dau.
28. 6 sent him away..to take him a wife from
28. 9 took unto the wives which he had Maha.
28. 11 he took of the stones of that place, and
28. 18 took the stone that he had put (for) his
29. 23 he took Leah his daughter, and brought
30. 9 she took Zilpah her maid, and gave her
30. 15 (Is it) a small matter that thou hast taken
30. 15 and wouldest thou take away my son's
30. 37 Jacob took him rods of green poplar, and
31. 1 Jacob hath taken away all that (was) our
31. 23 he took his brethren with him, and purs.
31. 32 discern thou what (is) thine..and take (it)
31. 34 Rachel had taken the images, and put th.
31. 45 Jacob took a stone, and set it up (for) a
31. 46 and they took stones, and made an heap
31. 50 if thou shalt take (other) wives besides
32. 13 took of that which came to his hand a
32. 22 took his two wives, and his two women
32. 23 he took them, and sent them over the br.
33. 11 Take, I pray thee, my blessing..and he t.
34. 2 he took her, and lay with her, and defiled
34. 9 give your daughters unto us, and take our
34. 16 we will take your daughters to us, and
34. 17 then will we take our daughter, and we
34. 21 let us take their daughters to us for wi.
34. 25 Dinah's brethren, took each man his sw.
34. 26 took Dinah out of Shechem's house, and
34. 28 They took their sheep, and their oxen
36. 2 Esau took his wives of the daughters of
36. 6 Esau took his wives, and his sons, and his
37. 24 they took him, and cast him into a pit
37. 31 they took Joseph's coat, and killed a kid
38. 2 and he took her, and went in unto her
38. 6 Judah took a wife for Er his first born, wh.
38. 23 Let her take (it) to her, lest we be shamed
38. 28 the midwife took and bound upon his h.
39. 20 Joseph's master took him, and put him
40. 11 I took the grapes, and pressed them into
42. 24 took from them Simeon, and bound him
42. 33 take (food for) the famine of your house.
42. 36 Simeon (is) not, and ye will take Benjam.
43. 11 take of the best fruits in the land in your
43. 12 take double money in your hand, and the
43. 13 Take also your brother, and arise, go ag.
43. 15 the men took that present, and they took
43. 18 fall upon us, and take us for bond men
44. 29 if ye take this also from me, and mischief
45. 18 take your father, and your households, and
45. 19 take you wagons out of the land of Egypt
46. 6 they took their cattle, and their goods, wh.
47. 2 he took some of his brethren, (even) five
48. 1 he took with him his two sons, Manasseh
48. 13 Joseph took them both, Ephraim in his
48. 22 which I took out of the hand of the Am.
Exod. 2. 1 there went a man..and took (to wife) a d.
2. 3 she took for him an ark of bulrushes, and
2. 9 the woman took the child, and nursed it
4. 9 thou shalt take of the water of the river
4. 9 the water which thou takest out of the ri.
4. 17 thou shalt take this rod in thine hand, wh.
4. 20 Moses took his wife and his sons, and set
4. 20 and Moses took the rod of God in his ha.
4. 25 Zipporah took a sharp stone, and cut off
6. 7 I will take you to me for a people, and I
6. 20 Amram took him Jochebed his father's
6. 23 Aaron took him Elisheba, daughter of A.
6. 25 Aaron's son, took him (one) of the daugh.
7. 9 Take thy rod, and cast (it) before Pharaoh
7. 15 and the rod..shalt thou take in thine ha.
7. 19 Take thy rod, and stretch out thine hand
9. 8 Take to you handfuls of ashes of the fur.
9. 10 they took ashes of the furnace, and stood
10. 26 for thereof must we take to serve the Lo.
12. 3 they shall take to them every man a lamb
12. 4 take (it) according to the number of the
12. 5 ye shall take (it) out from the sheep, or
12. 7 they shall take of the blood, and strike
12. 21 take you a lamb according to your famil.
12. 22 ye shall take a bunch of hyssop, and dip
12. 32 take your flocks and your herds, as ye ha.
13. 19 Moses took the bones of Joseph with him
14. 6 made ready his chariot, and took his peo.
14. 7 he took six hundred chosen chariots, and
14. 11 hast thou taken us away to die in the wil.
15. 20 the sister of Aaron, took a timbrel in her
16. 16 take ye every man for (them) which (are)
16. 33 Take a pot, and put an omer full of man.
17. 5 and take with thee of the elders of Israel
17. 5 and thy rod..take in thine hand, and go
17. 12 they took a stone, and put (it) under him
18. 2, 12 And Jethro, Moses' father in law, took
21. 10 If he take him another (wife); her food
21. 14 thou shalt take him from mine altar, that
23. 8 thou shalt take no gift: for the gift blin.
24. 6 Moses took half of the blood, and put (it)

Exod 24. 7 he took the book of the covenant, and re.
24. 8 Moses took the blood, and sprinkled (it)
25. 2 of every man..ye shall take my offering
25. 3 this (is) the offering which ye shall take
28. 5 they shall take gold, and blue, and purple
28. 9 thou shalt take two onyx stones, and gra.
29. 1 Take one young bullock, and two rams
29. 5 thou shalt take the garments, and put up.
29. 7 Then shalt thou take the anointing oil
29. 12 thou shalt take of the blood of the bullo.
29. 13 thou shalt take all the fat that covereth
29. 15 Thou shalt also take one ram; and Aaron
29. 16 thou shalt take his blood, and sprinkle
29. 19 thou shalt take the other ram; and Aar.
29. 20 Then shalt thou kill the ram, and take of
29. 21 thou shalt take of the blood that (is) upon
29. 22 thou shalt take of the ram the fat, and the
29. 26 thou shalt take the breast of the ram of
29. 31 thou shalt take the ram of the consecrat.
30. 16 thou shalt take the atonement money of
30. 23 Take thou also unto thee principal spices
30. 34 Take unto thee sweet spices, stacte, and
32. 20 he took the calf which they had made, and
33. 7 Moses took the tabernacle, and pitched
34. 4 and took in his hand the two tables of st.
34. 16 thou take of their daughters unto thy so.
35. 5 Take ye from among you an offering unto
40. 9 thou shalt take the anointing oil, and an.
40. 20 he took and put the testimony into the
Lev. 4. 5 the priest that is anointed shall take of
4. 25, 30, 34 the priest shall take of the blood
7. 34 the heave shoulder have I taken of the ch.
8. 2 Take Aaron and his sons with him, and
8. 10 Moses took the anointing oil, and anoin.
8. 15 Moses took the blood, and put (it) upon
8. 16 he took all the fat that (was) upon the in.
8. 23 Moses took of the blood of it, and put (it)
8. 25 he took the fat, and the rump, and all the
8. 26 he took one unleavened cake, and a cake
8. 28 Moses took them from off their hands, and
8. 29 Moses took the breast, and waved it (for)
8. 30 Moses took of the anointing oil, and of the
9. 2 Take thee a young calf for a sin offering
9. 3 Take ye a kid of the goats for a sin offer.
9. 15 took the goat, which (was) the sin offeri.
10. 1 the sons of Aaron, took either of them his
10. 12 Take the meat offering that remaineth of
14. 4 Then shall the priest command to take
14. 6 he shall take it, and the cedar wood, and
14. 10 he shall take two he lambs without blem.
14. 12 the priest shall take one he lamb, and off.
14. 14, 15, 25 And the priest shall take (some) of
14. 21 he shall take one lamb (for) a trespass off.
14. 24 the priest shall take the lamb of the tresp.
14. 42 they shall take other stones, and put (them)
14. 42 he shall take other mortar, and shall pla.
14. 49 he shall take to cleanse the house two bi.
14. 51 he shall take the cedar wood, and the hy.
15. 14 he shall take to him two turtle doves, or
15. 29 she shall take unto her two turtles, or
16. 5 he shall take of the congregation of the
16. 7 he shall take the two goats, and present
16. 12 he shall take a censer full of burning coals
16. 14 he shall take of the blood of the bullock
16. 18 shall take of the blood of the bullock, and
18. 17 neither shalt thou take her son's daught.
18. 18 Neither shalt thou take a wife to her sister
20. 14 if a man take a wife and her mother, it (is)
20. 17 if a man shall take his sister, his father's
20. 21 if a man shall take his brother's wife, it
21. 7 They shall not take a wife (that is) a wh.
21. 7 neither shall they take a woman put aw.
21. 13 And he shall take a wife in her virginity
21. 14 A widow..an harlot, these shall he not ta.
21. 14 he shall take a virgin of his own people to
23. 40 ye shall take you on the first day the bo.
24. 5 thou shalt take fine flour, and bake twelve
25. 36 Take thou no usury of him, or increase
Num. 1. 17 Aaron took these men which are expressed
3. 12 I have taken the Levites from among the
3. 41 And thou shalt take the Levites for me
3. 45 Take the Levites instead of all the first
3. 47 Thou shalt even take five shekels a piece
3. 49 Moses took the redemption money of them
3. 50 Of the first born..took he the money, a th.
4. 9 they shall take a cloth of blue, and cover
4. 12 they shall take all the instruments of mi.
5. 17 the priest shall take holy water in an ea.
5. 17 the priest shall take, and put (it) into the
5. 25 the priest shall take the jealousy offering
6. 18 shall take the hair of the head of his sep.
6. 19 the priest shall take the sodden shoulder
7. 5 Take (it) of them, that they may be to do
7. 6 Moses took the wagons and the oxen, and
8. 6 Take the Levites from among the childr.
8. 8 let them take a young bullock, with his
8. 8 another young bullock shalt thou take for
8. 16 (instead of) the first born..have I taken
8. 18 I have taken the Levites for all the first
16. 1 On the son of Peleth, sons of Reuben, took
16. 6 Take you censers, Korah, and all his co.
16. 17 take every man his censer, and put incense
16. 18 they took every man his censer, and put
16. 39 the priest took the brasen censers, where.
16. 46 Take a censer, and put fire therein from
16. 47 Aaron took as Moses commanded, and ran
17. 2 take of every one of them a rod according
17. 9 they looked, and took every man his rod
18. 6 I have taken your brethren the Levites
18. 26 When ye take of the children of Israel the
19. 4 the priest shall take of her blood with his
19. 6 the priest shall take cedar wood, and hys.

Num 19. 17 they shall take of the ashes of the burnt
19. 18 a clean person shall take hyssop, and dip
20. 8 Take the rod, and gather thou the assem.
20. 9 Moses took the rod from before the LORD
20. 25 Take Aaron and Eleazar his son, and bring
21. 25 Israel took all these cities: and Israel dwe.
21. 26 taken all his land out of his hand, even un.
22. 41 Balak took Balaam, and brought him up
23. 11 I took thee to curse mine enemies, and
25. 4 Take all the heads of the people, and hang
25. 7 he rose up..and took a javelin in his hand
27. 18 Take thee Joshua the son of Nun, a man
27. 22 he took Joshua, and set him before Eleazar
31. 11 they took all the spoil, and all the prey
31. 29 Take (it) of their half, and give (it) unto
31. 30 thou shalt take one portion of fifty, of the
31. 47 Moses took one portion of fifty, (both) of
31. 51, 54 and Eleazar the priest took the gold of
34. 18 ye shall take one prince of every tribe, to
35. 31 ye shall take no satisfaction for the life of
35. 32 ye shall take no satisfaction for him that
Deut. 1. 15 I took the chief of your tribes, wise men
1. 23 I took twelve men of you, one of a tribe
1. 25 they took of the fruit of the land in their
3. 4 And we took all his cities at that time
3. 4 there was not a city which we took not
3. 8 we took at that time out of the hand of the
3. 14 the son of Manasseh took all the country
4. 20 the LORD hath taken you, and brought you
4. 34 hath God assayed to go (and) take him a
7. 3 nor his daughter shalt thou take unto thy
7. 25 nor take (it) unto thee, lest thou be snar.
9. 21 I took your sin, the calf which ye had made
10. 17 which regardeth not persons, nor taketh
15. 17 thou shalt take an awl, and thrust (it) thr
16. 19 shalt not respect persons, neither take a
20. 7 hath betrothed a wife, and hath not taken
20. 7 die in the battle, and another man take
21. 3 the elders of that city shall take an heifer
22. 6 thou shalt not take the dam with the you.
22. 7 let the dam go, and take the young to th.
22. 13 If any man take a wife, and go in unto
22. 14 I took this woman, and when I came to
22. 15 take and bring forth (the tokens of) the
22. 18 the elders of that city shall take that man
22. 30 A man shall not take his father's wife, nor
24. 1 When a man hath taken a wife, and ma.
24. 3 if the latter husband die, which took her
24. 4 may not take her again to be his wife, af.
24. 5 When a man hath taken a new wife, he
24. 5 shall cheer up his wife which he hath ta.
25. 5 shall go in unto her, and take her to him
25. 7 if the man like not to take his brother's
25. 8 (if) he stand (to it), and say, I like not to t.
26. 2 thou shalt take of the first of all the fruit
26. 4 the priest shall take the basket out of th.
27. 25 Cursed (be) he that taketh reward to slay
29. 8 we took their land, and gave it for an in.
31. 26 Take this book of the law, and put it in
32. 11 spreadeth abroad her wings, taketh them
Josh. 2. 4 the woman took the two men, and hid th.
3. 12 take you twelve men out of the tribes of I.
4. 2 Take you twelve men out of the people
4. 20 twelve stones, which they took out of Jo.
6. 18 when ye take of the accursed thing, and
7. 1 Achan..took of the accursed thing, and
7. 11 they have even taken of the accursed th.
7. 21 I coveted them, and took them; and, be.
7. 23 they took them out of the midst of the te.
7. 24 Joshua..took Achan the son of Zerah, and
8. 1 take all the people of war with thee, and
8. 12 he took about five thousand men, and set
9. 4 took old sacks upon their asses, and wine
9. 11 Take victuals with you for the journey, and
9. 14 the men took of their victuals, and asked
11. 16 Joshua took all that land, the hills, and
11. 19 save the Hivites..all (other) they took in
11. 23 Joshua took the whole land, according to
24. 3 I took your father Abraham from the ot.
24. 26 took a great stone, and set it up there un.
Judg. 3. 6 they took their daughters to be their wi.
3. 21 took the dagger from his right thigh, and
3. 25 they took a key, and opened (them), and
4. 6 take with thee ten thousand men of the
4. 21 Jael, Heber's wife, took a nail of the tent
5. 19 The kings came..they took no gain of mo.
6. 20 Take the flesh and the unleavened cakes
6. 25 Take thy father's young bullock, even the
6. 26 take the second bullock, and offer a burnt
6. 27 Gideon took ten men of his servants, and
7. 8 the people took victuals in their hand, and
8. 16 he took the elders of the city, and thorns
8. 21 took away the ornaments that (were) on
9. 43 he took the people, and divided them into
9. 48 Abimelech took an ax in his hand, and cut
11. 13 Israel took away my land, when they came
11. 15 Israel took not away the land of Moab, nor
13. 19 Manoah took a kid with a meat offering
14. 3 that thou goest to take a wife of the unc.
14. 8 after a time he returned to take her, and
14. 19 took their spoil, and gave change of gar.
15. 4 took firebrands, and turned tail to tail, and
15. 6 because he had taken his wife, and given
15. 15 put forth his hand and took it, and slew
16. 12 Delilah therefore took new ropes, and bo.
17. 2 behold, the silver (is) with me; I took it
17. 4 his mother took two hundred (shekels) of
18. 17 came in thither, (and) took the graven im.
18. 20 he took the ephod, and the teraphim, and
18. 24 Ye have taken away my gods which I ma.
18. 27 they took (the things) which Micah had
19. 1 who took to him a concubine out of Beth

Judg19. 28 the man took her (up) upon an ass, and the
19. 29 he took a knife, and laid hold on his con.
20. 10 we will take ten men of an hundred thro.
Ruth 4. 2 he took ten men of the elders of the city
4. 13 Boaz took Ruth, and she was his wife: and
4. 16 Naomi took the child, and laid it in her
1 Sa. 2. 14 all..brought up the priest took for hims.
2. 16 and (then) take (as much) as thy soul desi.
2. 16 give (it me) now: and if not, I will take
5. 1 the Philistines took the ark of God, and
5. 2 the Philistines took the ark of God, they
5. 3 they took Dagon, and set him in his place
6. 7 take two milch kine, on which there hath
6. 8 take the ark of the LORD, and lay it upon
6. 10 took two milch kine, and tied them to the
7. 9 Samuel took a sucking lamb, and offered
7. 12 Samuel took a stone, and set (it) between
7. 14 the cities which the Philistines had taken
8. 3 turned aside after lucre, and took bribes
8. 11 He will take your sons, and appoint (them)
8. 13 he will take your daughters (to be) confe.
8. 14 he will take your fields, and your vineyards
8. 16 he will take your men servants, and your
9. 3 Take now one of the servants with thee
9. 22 took Saul and his servant, and brought
10. 1 Samuel took a vial of oil, and poured (it)
11. 7 he took a yoke of oxen, and hewed them
12. 3 ox have I taken? or whose ass have I ta.?
12. 4 neither hast thou taken ought of any man's
14. 32 flew upon the spoil, and took sheep, and
15. 21 the people took of the spoil, sheep and ox.
16. 2 Take an heifer with thee, and say I am
16. 13 Samuel took the horn of oil, and anointed
16. 20 Jesse took an ass (laden) with bread, and
16. 23 David took an harp, and played with his
17. 17 Take now for thy brethren an ephah of
17. 18 look how thy brethren fare, and take th.
17. 40 he took his staff in his hand, and chose
17. 49 took thence a stone, and slang (it), and s.
17. 51 stood upon the Philistine, and took his sw.
17. 54 David took the head of the Philistine, and
17. 57 Abner took him, and brought him before
18. 2 Saul took him that day, and would let him
19. 13 Michal took an image, and laid (it) in the
19. 14 when Saul sent messengers to take David
19. 20 Saul sent messengers to take David: and
20. 21 the arrows (are) on this side of thee, take
21. 9 if thou wilt take that, take (it); for (there
24. 2 Saul took three thousand chosen men out
24. 11 yet thou huntest my soul to take it
25. 11 Shall I then take my bread, and my water
25. 18 Abigail made haste, and took two hundr.
25. 39 communed with Abigail, to take her to
25. 40 David sent us unto thee, to take thee to
25. 43 David also took Ahinoam of Jezreel; and
26. 11 take thou now the spear that (is) at his
26. 12 David took the spear and the cruse of wa.
27. 9 took away the sheep, and the oxen, and
28. 24 killed it, and took flour, and kneaded (it)
30. 16 the great spoil that they had taken out of
30. 19 nor any (thing) that they had taken to th.
30. 20 David took all the flocks and the herds
31. 4 Therefore Saul took a sword, and fell up.
31. 12 went all night, and took the body of Saul
31. 13 they took their bones, and buried (them)
2 Sa. 1. 10 I took the crown that (was) upon his head
2. 8 Abner .took Ish bosheth the son of Saul
2. 21 lay thee hold on one. and take thee his
3. 15 Ish-bosheth sent, and took her from (her)
4. 7 beheaded him, and took his head, and g.
4. 12 they took the head of Ish bosheth, and bu.
5. 13 David took (him) more concubines and
7. 8 I took thee from the sheep cote, from fo
8. 1 David took Metheg-ammah out of the ha.
8. 7 David took the shields of gold that were
8. 8 king David took exceeding much brass
10. 4 Hanun took David's servants, and shaved
11. 4 David sent messengers, and took her and
12. 4 he spared to take of his own flock, and of
12. 4 took the poor man's lamb, and dressed it
12. 9 hast taken his wife (to be) thy wife, and
12. 10 hast taken the wife of Uriah the Hittite
12. 11 I will take thy wives before thine eyes, and
12. 30 he took their king's crown from off his he.
13. 8 she took flour, and kneaded (it), and ma.
13. 9 she took a pan, and poured (them) out be.
13. 10 Tamar took the cakes which she had ma.
17. 19 the woman took and spread a covering
18. 14 he took three darts in his hand, and thr.
18. 17 they took Absalom, and cast him into a
18. 18 Absalom in his life time had taken and
19. 30 let him take all, forasmuch as my lord
20. 3 the king took the ten women (his) concu.
20. 6 take thou thy lord's servants, and pursue
21. 8 the king took the two sons of Rizpah the
21. 10 the daughter of Aiah took sackcloth, and
21. 12 David went and took the bones of Saul
22. 17 He sent from above, he took me; he drew
23. 6 because they cannot be taken with hands
24. 22 Let my lord the king take and offer up wh.
1 Ki. 1. 33 Take with you the servants of your lord
1. 39 the priest took an horn of oil out of the
3. 1 took Pharaoh's daughter, and brought her
3. 20 she arose at midnight, and took my son
4. 15 he also took Basmath the daughter of S.
7. 8 Pharaoh's daughter, whom he had taken
11. 18 they took men with them out of Paran
11. 31 he said to Jeroboam, Take thee ten pieces
11. 34 I will not take the whole kingdom out of
11. 35 I will take the kingdom out of his son's
11. 37 I will take thee, and thou shalt reign ac.
14. 3 take with thee ten loaves, and cracknels

1 Ki. 14. 26 he took away the treasures of the house
14. 26 he even took away all: and he took away
15. 18 Asa took all the silver and the gold (that
16. 31 he took to wife Jezebel, the daughter of
17. 19 he took him out of her bosom, and carr.
17. 23 Elijah took the child, and brought him
18. 4 Obadiah took an hundred prophets, and
18. 26 they took the bullock which was given
18. 31 Elijah took twelve stones, according to
19. 4 take away my life; for I (am) not better
19. 10, 14 and they seek my life, to take it away
19. 21 took a yoke of oxen, and slew them, and
20. 6 they shall put (it) in their hand, and take
20. 34 The cities which my father took from thy
22. 3 we (be) still, (and) take it not out of the
22. 26 Take Micaiah, and carry him back unto
2 Ki. 2. 3, 5 the LORD will take away thy master
2. 8 Elijah took his mantle, and wrapped (it)
2. 12 he took hold of his own clothes, and rent
2. 14 he took the mantle of Elijah that fell from
3. 26 he took with him seven hundred men that
3. 27 he took his eldest son, that should have
4. 1 the creditor is come to take unto him my
4. 29 Gird up thy loins, and take my staff in th.
5. 5 he departed, and took with him ten tale.
5. 15 therefore, I pray thee, take a blessing of
5. 16 And he urged him to take (it); but he re.
5. 20 I will run after him, and take somewhat
5. 23 And Naaman said, Be content, take two
5. 24 he took (them) from their hand, and besto.
6. 2 Let us go..and take thence every man a
6. 7 And he put out his hand, and took it
7. 13 Let (some) take, I pray thee, five of the
7. 14 They took therefore two chariot horses
8. 8 Take a present in thine hand, and go, meet
8. 9 Hazael went to meet him, and took a pr.
8. 15 he took a thick cloth, and dipped (it) in
9. 1 Gird up thy loins, and take this box of oil
9. 3 take the box of oil, and pour (it) on his
9. 13 they hasted, and took every man his gar.
9. 17 Take an horseman, and send to meet them
10. 6 take ye the heads of the men your master's
10. 7 they took the king's sons, and slew seventy
11. 2 Jehosheba..took Joash the son of Ahaziah
11. 9 they took every man his men that were
11. 19 he took the rulers over hundreds, and the
12. 5 Let the priests take (it) to them, every man
12. 9 the priest took a chest, and bored a hole
12. 18 Jehoash king of Judah took all the hall.
13. 15 Take bow and arrows: and he took unto
13. 18 And he said, Take the arrows: and he took
13. 25 the son of Jehoahaz took again out of the
13. 25 the cities which he had taken out of the
14. 14 he took all the gold and silver, and all the
14. 21 the people of Judah took Azariah, which
15. 29 took Ijon, and Abel-beth-maachah, and
16. 8 Ahaz took the silver and gold (that was)
18. 32 Until I come and take you away to a land
20. 7 Take a lump of figs. And they took and
20. 18 thy sons..shall they take away; and they
23. 16 sent, and took the bones out of the sepul.
23. 30 the people of the land took Jehoahaz the
23. 34 made Eliakim..king..and took Jehoahaz
24. 7 the king of Babylon had taken from the
24. 12 the king of Babylon took him in the eighth
25. 14 all the vessels of brass .took they away
25. 15 fire pans..the captain of the guard took
25. 18 the captain of the guard took Seraiah the
25. 19 he took an officer that was set over the men
25. 20 Nebuzar-adan..took these, and brought
1 Ch. 2. 19 Caleb took unto him Ephrath, which bare
2. 23 he took Geshur, and Aram, with the towns
4. 18 daughter of Pharaoh, which Mered took
7. 15 Machir took to wife (the sister) of Huppim
7. 21 they came down to take away their cattle
10. 4 So Saul took a sword, and fell upon it
14. 3 And David took more wives at Jerusalem
17. 7 I took thee from the sheep cote, (even) fr.
18. 1 subdued them, and took Gath and her to.
18. 7 David took the shields of gold that were
19. 4 Hanun took David's servants, and shaved
20. 2 David took the crown of their king from
21. 23 Take (it) to thee, and let my lord the king
2 Ch. 8. 18 took thence four hundred and fifty talents
11. 18 Rehoboam took him Mahalath the daugh.
11. 20 after her he took Maachah the daughter of
12. 9 took away the treasures of the house of
12. 9 the treasures of the king's house; he took
16. 6 Asa the king took all Judah; and they ca.
18. 25 Take ye Micaiah, and carry him back to
22. 11 Jehoshabeath..took Joash the son of Ah.
23. 1 strengthened himself, and took the capt.
23. 8 took every man his men that were to come
23. 20 he took the captains of hundreds, and the
26. 1 the people of Judah took Uzziah, who (was)
36. 1 the people of the land took Jehoahaz the
36. 4 Necho took Jehoahaz his brother, and ca.
Ezra 2. 61 which took a wife of the daughters of Ba.
Neh. 5. 2 we take up corn (for them), that we may
5. 15 had taken of them bread and wine, besi.
6. 18 Johanan had taken the daughter of Mes.
7. 63 which took (one) of the daughters of Bar.
10. 30 nor take their daughters for our sons
Esth. 2. 7 whom Mordecai..took for his own daugh.
2. 15 Mordecai, who had taken her for his da.
6. 10 Make haste, (and) take the apparel and
6. 11 Then took Haman the apparel and the ho.
Job 1. 15 the Sabeans fell (upon them), and took th
1. 21 the LORD gave, and the LORD hath take
2. 8 he took him a potsherd to scrape himself
5. 5 the hungry eateth up, and taketh it even
12. 20 taketh away the understanding of the ag.

Job 38. 20 That thou shouldest take it to the bound
40. 24 He taketh it with his eyes; (his) nose pie.
41. 4 wilt thou take him for a servant for ever?
42. 8 take unto you now seven bullocks and se.
Psa. 15. 5 nor taketh reward against the innocent
18. 16 He sent from above, he took me, he drew
31. 13 while..they devised to take away my life
50. 9 I will take no bullock out of thy house
51. 11 Cast me not away..take not thy Holy Sp.
78. 70 He chose David..and took him from the
109. 8 Let his days be few..let another take his
Prov. 1. 19 (which) taketh away the life of the own.
6. 25 neither let her take thee with her eyelids
7. 20 He hath taken a bag of money with him
17. 23 A wicked (man) taketh a gift out of the
20. 16 Take his garment that is surety (for) a st.
22. 27 why should he take away thy bed from
27. 13 Take his garment that is surety for a stra.
Isa. 6. 6 (which) he had taken with the tongs from
8. 1 Take thee a great roll, and write in it with
14. 2 the people shall take them, and bring th.
23. 16 Take an harp, go about the city, thou ha.
28. 19 the time that it goeth forth it shall take
36. 17 Until I come and take you away to a land
39. 7 thy sons..shall they take away; and they
44. 14 taketh the cypress and the oak, which he
44. 15 he will take thereof, and warm himself
47. 2 Take the millstones, and grind meal: un.
47. 3 I will take vengeance, and I will not me.
51. 22 I have taken out of thine hand the cup
57. 13 vanity shall take (them): but he that put.
66. 21 I will also take of them for priests, (and)
Jer 3. 14 I will take you one of a city, and two of
13. 4 Take the girdle that thou hast got, which
13. 6 go to Euphrates, and take the girdle from
13. 7 took the girdle from the place where I had
15. 15 take me not away in thy long suffering
16. 2 Thou shalt not take thee a wife, neither
20. 5 which shall spoil them, and take them
20. 10 and we shall take our revenge on him
25. 9 I will send and take all the families of the
25. 15 Take the wine cup of this fury at my na
25. 17 Then took I the cup at the LORD'S hand
25. 28 if they refuse to take the cup at thine ha.
27. 20 Nebuchadnezzar king of Babylon took not
28. 3 Nebuchadnezzar king of Babylon took aw.
28. 10 the prophet took the yoke from off the pr.
29. 6 Take ye wives, and beget sons and dau.
29. 6 take wives for your sons, and give your
32. 11 I took the evidence of the purchase, (both)
32. 14 Take these evidences, this evidence of the
33. 26 I will not take (any) of his seed (to be) ru.
35. 3 I took Jaazaniah the son of Jeremiah, the
36. 2 Take thee a roll of a book, and write th.
36. 14 Take in thine hand the roll wherein thou
36. 14 So Baruch. took the roll in his hand
36. 21 he took it out of Elishama the scribe's ch.
36. 26 to take Baruch the scribe, and Jeremiah
36. 28 Take thee again another roll, and write
36. 32 Then took Jeremiah another roll, and ga.
37. 17 Then Zedekiah the king sent, and took
38. 6 Then took they Jeremiah, and cast him
38. 10 Take from hence thirty men with thee
38. 11 Ebed melech took the men with him, and
38. 11 took thence old cast clouts and old rotten
38. 14 the king sent, and took Jeremiah the pr.
39. 5 when they had taken him, they brought
39. 12 Take him, and look well to him, and do
39. 14 they sent, and took Jeremiah out of the
40. 1 when he had taken him, being bound in
40. 2 the captain of the guard took Jeremiah
41. 12 they took all the men, and went to fight
41. 16 Then took Johanan the son of Kareah, and
43. 5 the captains of the forces, took all the re.
43. 9 Take great stones in thine hand, and hide
43. 10 I will send and take Nebuchadrezzar the
44. 12 I will take the remnant of Judah, that ha.
46. 11 take balm, O virgin, the daughter of Eg.
49. 29 their flocks shall they take away: they
51. 8 take balm for her pain, if so be she may
51. 26 they shall not take of thee a stone for a
52. 18 all the vessels of brass..took they away
52. 19 silver. took the captain of the guard aw.
52. 24 the captain of the guard took Seraiah the
52. 25 He took also out of the city an eunuch
52. 26 the captain of the guard took them, and
Eze. 3. 14 the spirit lifted me up, and took me aw.
4. 1 son of man take thee a tile, and lay it be.
4. 3 take thou unto thee an iron pan, and set
4. 9 Take thou also unto thee wheat, and ba.
5. 1 take thee a sharp knife, take thee a bar.
5. 1 take thee balances to weigh, and divide
5. 2 thou shalt take a third part, (and) smite
5. 3 Thou shalt also take thereof a few in nu.
5. 4 take of them again, and cast them into the
8. 3 put forth the form of an hand, and took
10. 6 Take fire from between the wheels, from
10. 7 clothed with linen; who took (it), and we.
15. 3 or will (men) take a pin of it to hang any
16. 16 of thy garments thou didst take, and de.
16. 17 Thou hast also taken thy fair jewels of
16. 18 tookest thy broidered garments, and cov.
16. 20 thou hast taken thy sons and thy daugh.
16. 32 (which) taketh strangers instead of her
16. 39 shall take thy fair jewels, and leave thee
17. 3 and took the highest branch of the cedar
17. 5 He took also of the seed of the land, and
17. 12 hath taken the king thereof, and the pri.
17. 13 And hath taken of the king's seed, and
17. 13 he hath also taken the mighty of the land
17. 22 I will also take of the highest branch of
18. 8 neither hath taken any increase, (that)

Eze. 18. 13 given forth upon usury, and hath taken
19. 5 she took another of her whelps, (and) ma.
22. 12 taken gifts to shed blood; thou hast tak.
22. 12 thou hast taken usury and increase, and
22. 16 thou shalt take thine inheritance in thy
22. 25 they have taken the treasure and precious
23. 10 they took her sons and her daughters, and
23. 25 they shall take thy sons and thy daughters
23. 26 They shall also..take away thy fair jew.
23. 29 shall take away all thy labour and shall
24. 5 Take the choice of the flock, and burn also
24. 16 I take away from thee the desire of thine
24. 25 the day when I take from them their str.
27. 5 they have taken cedars from Lebanon to
30. 4 they shall take away her multitude, and
33. 2 if the people of the land take a man of th.
33. 4 whosoever heareth..and taketh not war.
33. 4 if the sword come and take him away
33. 6 if the sword come and take (any) person
36. 24 I will take you from among the heathen
37. 16 take thee one stick, and write upon it, For
37. 16 take another stick, and write upon it, For
37. 19 I will take the stick of Joseph, which (is)
37. 21 I will take the children of Israel from am.
38. 13 silver and gold, to take away cattle and
43. 20 thou shalt take of the blood thereof, and
43. 21 Thou shalt take the bullock also of the
44. 22 Neither shall they take for their wives a
44. 22 they shall take maidens of the seed of the
45. 18 thou shalt take a young bullock without bl.
45. 19 the priest shall take of the blood of the
46. 18 the prince shall not take of the people's
Hos. 1. 2 take unto thee a wife of whoredoms and
1. 3 he went and took Gomer the daughter of
2. 9 take away my corn in the time thereof
4. 11 and wine and new wine take away the he.
11. 3 I taught Ephraim also to go, taking them
13. 11 I gave thee a king. and took (him) away
14. 2 Take with you words, and turn to the L.
Joel 3. 5 ye have taken my silver and my gold, and
Amos 5. 11 and ye take from him burdens of wheat
5. 12 they take a bribe and they turn aside the
6. 13 Have we not taken to us horns by our own
7. 15 the LORD took me as I followed the flock
9. 2 into hell, thence shall mine hand take th.
9. 3 I will search and take them out thence
Jon. 4. 3 take, I beseech thee, my life from me, for
Mic. 2. 9 from their children have ye taken away
Hag 2. 23 In that day..will I take thee, O Zerubb.
Zech. 6. 10 Take of (them of) the captivity, (even) of
6. 11 take silver and gold, and make crowns, and
11. 7 I took unto me two staves; the one I cal
11. 10 I took my staff, (even) Beauty, and cut it
11. 13 I took the thirty (pieces) of silver, and ca
11. 15 Take unto thee yet the instruments of a
14. 21 they that sacrifice shall come and take of

24. *To feel, touch,* מוּשׁ *mush*, 5
Exod 13. 22 He took not away the pillar of the cloud

25. *To lift up, lay on,* נָטַל *natal.*
Isa 40. 15 he taketh up the isles as a very little thing

26. *Separate self, cease* (?), סוּג [*sug*, 2; A.V. as from *nasag*]. Mic. 2. 6.

27. *To* (*cause to*) *remove,* נְסַק *nesaq*, 5
Dan. 3. 22 slew those men that took up Shadrach
6. 23 they should take Daniel up out of the den

28. *To take away, spoil,* נָצַל *natsal*, 5
Gen. 31 9 God hath taken away the cattle of your fa.
31. 16 the riches which God hath taken from our

29. *To lift up,* נָשָׂא *nasa.*
Gen. 27. 3 take, I pray thee, thy weapons, thy quiver
43 34 he took (and sent) messes unto them from
Exod 10 19 wind, which took away the locusts and
12 34 the people took their dough before it was
20. 7 Thou shalt not take the name of the LORD
20. 7 will not hold him guiltless that taketh his
30. 12 When thou takest the sum of the children
Num. 1. 2 Take ye the sum of all the congregation
1. 49 neither take the sum of them among the
3. 40 Number all the first born and take the
4. 2 Take the sum of the sons of Kohath from
4. 22 Take also the sum of the sons of Gershon
16. 15 I have not taken one ass from them, nei.
23. 7, 18 And he took up his parable, and said
24. 3, 15, 20, 21, 23 took up his parable, and said
26. 2 Take the sum of all the congregation of
31. 26 Take the sum of the prey that was taken
31. 49 Thy servants have taken the sum of the
Deut. 5. 11 Thou shalt not take the name of the LORD
5. 11 will not hold (him) guiltless that taketh
12. 26 thy vows, thou shalt take, and go unto
Josh. 3. 6 Take up the ark of the covenant, and pass
3. 6 they took up the ark of the covenant, and
4. 3 Take you hence out of the midst of Jord.
4. 8 took up twelve stones out of the midst of
6. 6 Take up the ark of the covenant, and let
6. 12 and the priests took up the ark of the L.
Judg. 9. 48 cut down a bough..and took it, and laid
16. 31 came down, and took him, and brought
21. 23 took (them) wives, according to their nu.
Ruth 1. 4 they took them wives of the women of M.
2. 18 she took (it) up, and went into the city
1 Sa. 17. 20 took, and went, as Jesse had commanded
17. 34 there came a lion and a bear, and took a
2 Sa. 2. 32 they took up Asahel, and buried him in
4. 4 his nurse took him up, and fled: and it c.
23. 16 and took (it) and brought (it) to David
1 Ki. 8. 3 the elders..came, and the priests took up
13. 29 the prophet took up the carcase of the man
15. 22 and they took away the stones of Ramah

2 Ki. 2. 16 the spirit of the LORD hath taken him up
4. 20 when he had taken him, and brought him
4. 36 when she was come in..he said, Take up
4. 37 bowed herself to the ground, and took up
9. 25 Take up, (and) cast him in the portion of
9. 26 take (and) cast him into the plat (of ground)
1 Ch. 10. 9 they took his head, and his armour, and
10. 12 took away the body of Saul, and the bodies
11. 18 and took (it), and brought (it) to David
21. 24 I will not take (that) which is thine for the
23. 22 their brethren the sons of Kish took them
27. 23 David took not the number of them from
2 Ch. 5. 4 the elders came; and the Levites took up
11. 21 he took eighteen wives, and threescore co.
24. 3 Jehoiada took for him two wives; and he
24. 11 came and emptied the chest, and took it
Ezra 9. 2 they have taken of their daughters for th.
9. 12 neither take their daughters unto your so.
10. 44 All these had taken strange wives: and
Neh. 2. 1 I took up the wine, and gave (it) unto the
13. 25 nor take their daughters unto your sons
Job 13. 14 Wherefore do I take my flesh in my teeth
21. 12 They take the timbrel and harp, and rej.
24. 10 and they take away the sheaf (from) the
31. 36 Surely I would take it upon my shoulder
32. 22 (so doing) my Maker would soon take me
Psa. 15. 3 nor taketh up a reproach against his nei.
16. 4 nor take up their names into my lips
50. 16 (that) thou shouldest take my covenant in
81. 2 Take a psalm, and bring hither the timb.
116. 13 I will take the cup of salvation, and call
139. 9 (If) I take the wings of the morning, (and)
139. 20 (and) thine enemies take (thy name) in vain
Eccl. 5. 15 shall take nothing of his labour, which he
5. 19 to take his portion, and to rejoice in his
Song 5. 7 the keepers of the walls took away my veil
Isa. 8. 4 the spoil of Samaria shall be taken away
14. 4 thou shalt take up this proverb against
38. 21 Let them take a lump of figs, and lay (it)
40. 24 the whirlwind shall take them away as st.
64. 6 and our iniquities..have taken us away
Jer. 7. 29 and take up a lamentation on high places
9. 10 For the mountains will I take up a weep.
9. 18 let them make haste, and take up a wail.
49. 29 they shall take to themselves their cur.
Lam. 5. 13 They took the young men to grind, and
Eze. 3. 12 the spirit took me up, and I heard behind
10. 7 took (thereof), and put (it) into the hands
11 24 the spirit took me up, and brought me in
19. 1 take thou up a lamentation for the prin.
26. 17 they shall take up a lamentation for thee
27. 2 son of man, take up a lamentation for T.
27. 32 they shall take up a lamentation for thee
28. 12 take up a lamentation upon the king of
29. 19 and he shall take her multitude, and
32. 2 take up a lamentation for Pharaoh king
39. 10 they shall take no wood out of the field
43. 5 the spirit took me up, and brought me
Dan. 1. 16 Melzar took away the portion of their m.
Hos. 1. 6 no more have mercy ..I will utterly take
5. 14 I will take away, and none shall rescue
14. 2 Take away all iniquity, and receive (us)
Amos 5. 1 Hear ye this word which I take up agai.
6. 10 a man's uncle shall take him up, and he
Jon. 1 12 Take me up, and cast me forth into the
1 15 they took up Jonah, and cast him forth
Mic. 2. 2 they covet..houses, and take (them) away
2 4 In that day shall (one) take up a parable
Hab 2. 6 Shall not all these take up a parable aga.
Mal. 2. 3 and (one) shall take you away with it

30. *To be lifted up,* נְשָׂא *nasa*, 2.
Dan 11 12 when he hath taken away the multitude

31. *To lift up,* נָשָׂא *nasa*, 3
Amos 4. 2 he will take you away with hooks, and

32. *To lift up,* נְשָׂא *nesa.*
Ezra 5. 15 Take these vessels, go, carry them into

33. *To cause to reach, attain, overtake,* נָשַׂג *nasag*, 5.
Psa. 7. 5 Let the enemy persecute my soul, and ta.

34. *To* (*cause to*) *turn aside, take away,* סוּר *sur*, 5.
Exod. 8. 8 Entreat the LORD, that he may take away
10. 17 that he may take away from me this de.
23. 25 I will take sickness away from the midst
33. 23 I will take away mine hand, and thou sh.
Lev. 3. 4, 10, 15 with the kidneys, it shall he take
4. 9 with the kidneys, it shall he take away
4. 31, 35 he shall take away all the fat thereof
7. 4 with the kidneys, it shall he take away
Num 21. 7 pray unto the LORD, that he take away the
Deut. 7. 15 the LORD will take away from thee all si.
Josh 7. 13 until ye take away the cursed thing from
1 Sa. 17. 26 and taketh away the reproach from Israel
17. 46 I will smite thee, and take thine head fr.
2 Sa. 5. 6 Except thou take away the blind and the
7. 15 as I took (it) from Saul, whom I put away
1 Ki. 2. 31 that thou mayest take away the innocent
20. 24 Take the kings away, every man out of his
20. 41 he hasted, and took the ashes away from
2 Ki. 6. 32 son of a murderer hath sent to take away
18. 22 whose altars Hezekiah hath taken away
23. 19 Josiah took away, and did to them accor.
1 Ch. 17. 13 and I will not take my mercy away from
17. 13 as I took (it) from (him) that was before
2 Ch. 14. 3 he took away the altars of the strange (go.)
14. 5 he took away out of all the cities of Judah
17. 6 he took away the high places and groves
30. 14 took away the altars that (were) in Jerus.
30. 14 the altars for incense took they away, and
32. 12 Hath not the same Hezekiah taken away
33. 15 he took away the strange gods, and the

2 Ch. 34. 33 Josiah took away all the abominations out
Esth. 3. 10 the king took his ring from his hand, and
4. 4 and to take away his sackcloth from him
Job 9. 34 Let him take his rod away from me, and
12. 24 He taketh away the heart of the chief of
19. 9 stripped me of my glory, and taken the
27. 2 (As) God liveth, (who) hath taken away
34. 5 and God hath taken away my judgment
Isa. 1. 25 purge away thy dross, and take away all
3. 1 the LORD of hosts, doth take away from
3. 18 the Lord will take away the bravery of
5. 5 I will take away the hedge thereof, and it
5. 23 take away the righteousness of the righte.
18. 5 and take away (and) cut down the branches
25. 8 the rebuke of his people shall he take aw.
27. 9 and this (is) all the fruit to take away his
36. 7 whose altars Hezekiah hath taken away
58. 9 If thou take away from the midst of thee
Jer. 4. 4 take away the foreskins of your heart, ye
5. 10 take away her battlements; for they (are)
Eze 11. 18 they shall take away all the detestable th.
11. 19 I will take the stony heart out of their fle.
16. 50 therefore I took them away as I saw (good)
23. 25 they shall take away thy nose and thine
36. 26 I will take away the stony heart out of
Dan. 11. 31 shall take away the daily (sacrifice), and
Hos. 2. 17 I will take away the names of Baalim out
Amos 5. 23 Take thou away from me the noise of thy
Zeph. 3. 11 I will take away out of the midst of thee
3. 15 The LORD hath taken away thy judgments
Zech. 3. 4 Take away the filthy garments from him
9. 7 I will take away his blood out of his mo.

35. *To* (*cause to*) *move, persuade, remove,* סוּת *suth*, 5.
Job 36. 18 (beware) lest he take thee away with (his)

36. *To cause to go or pass over,* עָבַר *abar*, 5.
2 Sa. 24. 10 take away the iniquity of thy servant; for
1 Ki. 15. 12 he took away the sodomites out of the
2 Ch. 35. 24 His servants therefore took him out of th.
Esth 8. 2 his ring, which he had taken from Haman
Job 7. 21 why dost thou not..take away mine iniq.

37. *To cause to pass away,* עָדָה *adah*, 5.
Prov 25. 20 (As) he that taketh away a garment in cold

38. *To cause to pass away or on,* עֲדָה *adah*, 5.
Dan. 5. 20 was deposed..and they took his glory fr.
7. 26 they shall take away his dominion, to co.

39. *To cause to go up,* עָלָה *alah*, 5.
1 Sa. 1. 24 she took him up with her, with three bu.
2 Ki. 2. 1 when the LORD would take up Eli.; 10.15.
Psa. 102. 24 take me not away in the midst of my days
Jer. 38. 10 take up Jeremiah; 38. 13 and took him up
Amos 3. 5 shall (one) take up a snare; Hab. 1. 15.

40. *To labour,* עָמַל *amal*; *labouring* עָמֵל *amel.*
Eccl. 1. 3, 2. 2, 5. 18; 2. 18, 9. 9.

41. *To do, make,* עָשָׂה *asah.*
Judg 11. 36 the LORD hath taken vengeance for thee
Isa. 30. 1 that take counsel, but not of me; and that

42. *To hunt,* צוּד *tsud.*
Gen. 27. 3 and take me (some) venison

43. *To accept, take, receive,* קָבַל *qabal*, 3.
Esth. 9. 27 The Jews ordained, and took upon them

44. *To accept, take, receive,* קְבַל *qebal*, 3.
Dan. 5. 31 Darius the Median took the kingdom, (be.)
7. 18 the saints of the Most High shall take the

45. *To gather, bring together, collect,* קָבַץ *qabats*, 3.
Isa. 13. 14 and as a sheep that no man taketh up

46. *To cause to draw near,* קָרַב *qarab*, 5.
Exod 28. 1 take thou unto thee Aaron thy brother

47. *To take down, cause to come down,* רָדָה *radah.*
Judg 14. 9 he took thereof in his hands, and went
14. 9 that he had taken the honey out of the

48. *To cause to be high, lift up,* רוּם *rum*, 5.
Lev. 2. 9 the priest shall take from the meat offer.
4. 19 shall take all his fat from him, and burn
6. 10 take up the ashes which the fire hath co.
6. 15 he shall take of it his handful, of the flour
Num 16. 37 that he take up the censers out of the bu.
Josh. 4. 5 take you up every man of you a stone up.
1 Sa. 9. 24 the cook took up the shoulder, and (that)
2 Ki. 2. 13 He took up also the mantle of Elijah that
6. 7 Therefore said he, Take (it) up to thee
Eze. 45. 9 take away your exactions from my people
Isa. 57. 14 take up the stumbling block out of the

49. *To take captive, capture,* שָׁבָה *shabah.*
Num 21. 1 he fought against Israel, and took (some)
Deut 21. 10 enemies..and thou hast taken them cap.
1 Ch. 5. 21 they took away their cattle; of their ca.

50. *A captive, captivity,* שְׁבִי *shebi.*
Amos 4. 10 have taken away your horses; and I have

51. *To cease, rest, keep sabbath,* שָׁבַת *shabath*, 5.
2 Ki. 23. 11 he took away the horses that the kings of

52. *To set, place, put,* שׂוּם, שִׂים *sum, sim.*
Judg. 4. 21 Heber's wife..took an hammer in her hand

53. *To set, place, put,* שִׁית *shith.*
Psa. 13. 2 How long shall I take counsel in my soul

54. *To be at rest, safe,* שָׁלָה *shalah.*
Job 27. 8 what (is) the hope..when God taketh aw.

55. *To catch, capture, keep hold, handle,* תָּפַשׂ *taphas.*
Num 31. 27 between them that took the war upon th.
Deut. 9. 17 I took the two tables, and cast them out
20. 19 When thou shalt besiege a city..to take

Josh. 8. 8 it shall be, when ye have taken the city
8. 23 the king of Ai they took alive, and brought
1 Sa. 15. 8 he took Agag the king of the Amalekites
23. 26 compassed..his men round about to take
1 Ki. 18. 40 Take the prophets of Baal; let not one of
18. 40 they took them; and Elijah brought them
20. 18 Whether they be..for peace, take them
20. 18 whether they be..for war, take them al.
2 Ki. 10. 14 he said, Take them alive. And they took
14. 7 took Selah by war, and called the name
14. 13 Jehoash king of Israel took Amaziah king
16. 9 went up against Damascus, and took it, and
18. 13 did Sennacherib..come up..and took th.
25. 6 they took the king, and brought him up to
2 Ch. 25. 23 the king of Israel took Amaziah king of J.
Psa. 71. 11 persecute and take him; for (there is) no.
Prov 30. 9 lest I be poor, and steal, and take the na.
Isa. 36. 1 defenced cities of Judah, and took them
Jer. 26. 8 the people took him, saying, Thou shalt
37. 13 took Jeremiah the prophet, saying, Thou
37. 14 Irijah took Jeremiah, and brought him to
40. 10 dwell in your cities that ye have taken
52. 9 they took the king, and carried him up un.
Eze. 14. 5 That I may take the house of Israel in th.

56. *To lift or take up or away*, αἴρω *airō.*

Matt. 9. 6 Arise, take up thy bed, and go unto thine
9. 16 that which is put in..taketh from the ga.
11. 29 Take my yoke upon you, and learn of me
14. 12 his disciples came, and took up the body
14. 20 they took up of the fragments that rema.
15. 37 they took up of the broken (meat) that
16. 24 let him deny himself, and take up his cr.
17. 27 cast an hook, and take up the fish that fi.
20. 14 Take (that) thine (is), and go thy way: I
22. 13 [take him away], and cast (him) into outer
24. 17 Let him..not come down to take any th.
24. 18 Neither let him..return back to take his
24. 39 until the flood came, and took them all
25. 28 Take therefore the talent from him, and
Mark 2. 9 or to say, Arise, and take up thy bed, and
2. 11 Arise, and take up thy bed, and go thy w.
2. 12 he arose, took up the bed, and went forth
2. 21 the new piece ..taketh away from the old
4. 15 taketh away the word that was sown in
6. 8 they should take nothing for (their) jour.
6. 29 they came and took up his corpse, v. 30.
6. 43 they took up twelve baskets full of the fr.
8. 8 they took up of the broken (meat) that
8. 19, 20 How many baskets full..took ye up?
8. 34 let him deny himself, and take up his cr.
10. 21 and come, [take up the cross], and follow
13. 15 neither enter (therein), to take anything
13. 16 not turn back again for to take up his ga
15. 24 casting lots..what every man should take
16. 18 [They shall take up serpents; and if they]
Luke 5. 24 Arise, and take up thy couch, and go
5. 25 he rose up before them, and took up that
6. 29 him that taketh away thy cloak forbid not
6. 30 of him that taketh away thy goods ask
8. 12 taketh away the word out of their hearts
9. 3 Take nothing for (your) journey, neither
9. 23 [let him deny himself, and take up his c]
11. 22 he taketh from him all his armour wherein
11. 52 ye have taken away the key of knowledge
17. 31 let him not come down to take it away
19. 21 thou takest up that thou layedst not do.
19. 22 taking up that I laid not down, and reap.
19. 24 Take from him the pound, and give (it) to
22. 36 he that hath a purse, let him take (it), and
John 1. 29 the Lamb of God, which taketh away the
2. 16 Take these things hence; make not my
5. 8 Jesus saith unto him, Rise, take up thy
5. 9 the man was made whole, and took up his
5. 11 the same said unto me, Take up thy bed
5. 12 What man is that which said..Take up
8. 59 Then took they up stones to cast at him
10. 18 No man taketh it from me, but I lay it do.
11. 39 Jesus said, Take ye away the stone.
11. 41 they took away the stone (from the place)
11. 48 the Romans shall come and take away bo.
15. 2 that beareth not fruit he taketh away
16. 22 and your joy no man taketh from you
17. 15 I pray not that thou shouldest take them
19. 38 besought Pilate that he might take away
19. 38 He came therefore, and took the body of
20. 2 They have taken away the Lord out of
20. 13 they have taken away my Lord, and I kn
20. 15 tell me where..and I will take him away
Acts 21. 11 he took Paul's girdle, and bound his own
27. 17 Which when they had taken up, they us.
1 Co. 6. 15 shall I then take the members of Christ
Col. 2. 14 took it out of the way, nailing it to his cr.
1 Jo. 3. 5 he was manifested to take away our sins
Rev. 18. 21 a mighty angel took up a stone like a gr.

57. *To lead up or back*, ἀνάγω *anagō.*

Luke 4. 5 the devil, taking him up into an high mo.

58. *To take up or off*, ἀναιρέω *anaireō.*

Acts 7. 21 Pharaoh's daughter took him up, and no.
Heb. 10. 9 He taketh away the first, that he may es.

59. *To take or receive up or back*, ἀναλαμβάνω.

Acts 7. 43 ye took up the tabernacle of Moloch, and
23. 31 took Paul, and brought (him) by night to
Eph. 6. 13 take unto you the whole armour of God
6. 16 taking the shield of faith, wherewith ye
2 Ti. 4. 11 Take Mark, and bring him with thee: for

60. *To lead away or off*, ἀπάγω *apagō.*

Acts 24. 7 [with great violence took (him) away out]

61. *To take away or off*, ἀφαιρέω *aphaireō.*

Luke 1. 25 to take away my reproach among men
Luke 16. 3 my lord taketh away from me the stewa.
Rom. 11. 27 this (is) my covenant..when I shall take
Heb. 10. 4 (it is) not possible that the blood..take
Rev. 22. 19 if any man shall take away from the wo.
22. 19 God shall take away his part out of the

62. *To bear up, take up*, βαστάζω *bastazō.*

John 10. 31 Then the Jews took up stones again to st.

63. *To receive*, δέχομαι *dechomai.*

Luke 2. 28 Then took he him up in his arms, and bles.
16. 6, 7 he said unto him Take thy bill, and
22. 17 he took the cup, and gave tha. Eph. 6. 17.

64*. *To give*, δίδωμι *didōmi*, 2 Th. 1. 8.

64. *To grasp in or with the fist*, δράσσομαι *drasso.*

1 Co. 3. 19 He taketh the wise in their own craftiness

65. *To lift or raise up*, ἐγείρω *egeirō.*

Acts 10. 26 Peter took him up, saying, Stand up; I m.

66. *To take hold upon*, ἐπιλαμβάνομαι *epilambanomai.*

Luke 9. 47 And Jesus..took a child, and set him by
14. 4 he took (him), and healed him, and let him
Acts 9. 27 Barnabas took him, and brought (him) to
17. 19 they took him, and brought him unto Ar.
18. 17 the Greeks took Sosthenes, the chief rul.
21. 30 they took Paul, and drew him out of the
21. 33 the chief captain came near, and took him

67. *To bear upon or against*, ἐπιφέρω *epipherō.*

Rom. 3. 5 (Is) God unrighteous who taketh vengea.

68. *To take down, apprehend*, καταλαμβάνω.

Mark 9. 18 wheresoever he taketh him, he teareth

69. *To hold down*, κατέχω *katechō.*

Luke 14. 9 thou begin with shame to take the lowest

70. *To lay or keep hold*, κρατέω *krateō.*

Matt 22. 6 the remnant took his servants, and entr.
26. 4 consulted that they might take Jesus by
26. 50 and laid hands on Jesus, and took him
Mark 9. 27 Jesus took him by the hand, and lifted
14. 1 the scribes sought how they might take
14. 44 that same is he; take him, and lead (him)
14. 46 they laid their hands on him, and took him
14. 49 I was daily with you..and ye took me not
Acts 24. 6 whom we took, and would have judged ac.

71. *To take, receive*, λαμβάνω *lambanō.*

Matt. 5. 40 take away thy coat, let him have (thy) cl.
8. 17 Himself took our infirmities, and bare
10. 38 [he that taketh] not his cross, and follow.
13. 31 which a man took, and sowed in his field
13. 33 which a woman took and hid in three me.
14. 19 took the five loaves, and the two fishes
15. 26 It is not meet to take the children's bread
15. 36 he took the seven loaves and the fishes
16. 5 disciples..they had forgotten to take br.
16. 7 saying, (It is) because we have taken no
16. 9, 10 and how many baskets ye took up?
17. 25 of whom do the kings of the earth take
17. 27 that take, and give unto them for me and
21. 35 the husbandmen took his servants, and
22. 15 took counsel how they might entangle
25. 1 ten virgins, which took their lamps, and
25. 3 they that were foolish took their lamps, and took no oil with
25. 4 the wise took oil in their vessels with th.
26. 26 Jesus took bread, and blessed (it), and b.
26. 26 gave (it) to the disciples, and said, Take
26. 27 he took the cup, and gave thanks, and g.
26. 52 they that take the sword shall perish with
27. 1 elders of the people took counsel against
27. 6 the chief priests took the silver pieces
27. 7 they took counsel, and bought with them
27. 9 they took the thirty pieces of silver, the
27. 24 he took water, and washed (his) hands
27. 30 they spit upon him, and took the reed
27. 48 one of them ran, and took a spunge, and
27. 59 when Joseph had taken the body, he wr
28. 12 when they were assembled..and had taken
28. 15 they took the money, and did as they w.
Mark 6. 41 when he had taken the five loaves and the
7. 27 it is not meet to take the childrens's bread
8. 6 he took the seven loaves, and gave thanks
8. 14 (the disciples) had forgotten to take bread
9. 36 he took a child, and set him in the midst
12. 8 they took him, and killed (him), and cast
12. 19 that his brother should take his wife, and
12. 20 the first took a wife, and dying left no s.
12. 21 the second took her, and died, neither
14. 22 Jesus took bread, and blessed, and brake
14. 22 gave to them, and said, Take, eat: this
14. 23 he took the cup, and when he had given
Luke 5. 5 toiled all the night, and have taken not.
6. 4 [did take] and eat the shewbread, and g.
9. 16 he took the five loaves and the two fishes
9. 39 a spirit taketh him, and he suddenly cri.
13. 19 grain of mustard seed, which a man took
13. 21 It is like leaven, which a woman took and
20. 28 his brother should take his wife, and raise
20. 29 the first took a wife, and died without ch.
20. 30 [the second took her to wife, and he died]
20. 31 the third took her: and in like manner
22. 17 and said. Take this and divide it among
22. 19 he took bread, and gave thanks, and brake
24. 30 he took bread, and blessed (it), and brake
24. 43 And he took (it), and did eat before them
John 6. 7 that every one of them may take a little
6. 11 Jesus took the loaves; and when he had
10. 17 I lay down my life, that I might take it
10. 18 and I have power to take it again
12. 3 Then took Mary a pound of ointment of
12. 13 Took branches of palm trees, and went
John 13. 4 laid aside his garments, and took a towel
13. 12 he had washed their feet, and had taken
16. 15 he shall take of mine, and shall show (it)
18. 31 Take ye him, and judge him according to
19. 1 Pilate therefore took Jesus, and scourged
19. 6 Take ye him, and crucify (him): for I find
19. 23 took his garments, and made four parts
19. 27 from that hour that disciple took her unto
19. 40 Then took they the body of Jesus, and
21. 13 Jesus then cometh, and taketh bread, and
Acts 1. 20 and, His bishopric let another take
1. 25 That he may take part of this ministry and
2. 23 Him..[ye have taken] and by wicked hands
9. 25 the disciples took him by night, and let
15. 14 to take out of them a people for his name
16. 3 took and circumcised him because of the
17. 9 when they had taken security of Jason
27. 35 he took bread, and gave thanks to God
28. 15 saw, he thanked God, and took courage
Rom. 7. 8, 11 sin, taking occasion by the command.
1 Co. 10. 13 There hath no temptation taken you but
11. 23 the Lord Jesus the (same) night..took b.
11. 24 [Take] eat: this is my body, which is br.
2 Co. 11. 8 I robbed other churches, taking wages
11. 20 if a man devour (you), if a man take (of
Phil. 2. 7 took upon him the form of a servant, and
Heb. 5. 1 every high priest taken from among men
5. 4 no man taketh this honour unto himself
9. 19 he took the blood of calves and of goats
Jas. 5. 10 Take, my brethren, the prophets, who
3 John 7 they went forth, taking nothing of the G.
Rev. 3. 11 hold that fast..that no man take thy cr.
5. 7 he came and took the book out of the ri.
5. 8 when he had taken the book, the four be
5. 9 Thou art worthy to take the book, and t
6. 4 (power) was given to him..to take peace
8. 5 the angel took the censer, and filled it
10. 8 take the little book which is open in the
10. 9 he said unto me, Take (it), and eat it up
10. 10 I took the little book out of the angel's ha.
11. 17 thou hast taken to thee thy great power
22. 17 whosoever will, let him take the water of

72. *To take along with*, μεταλαμβάνω *metalambanō.*

Acts 27. 33 Paul besought..all to take meat, saying

73. *To take alongside of*, παραλαμβάνω *paralambanō.*

Matt 2. 13, 20 Arise, and take the young child and his
2. 14, 21 took the young child and his mother
4. 5 the devil taketh him up into the holy city
4. 8 the devil taketh him up into an exceeding
12. 45 Then goeth he, and taketh with himself
17. 1 Jesus taketh Peter, James, and John his
18. 16 if he will not hear (thee, then) take with
20. 17 Jesus going up to Jerusalem took the tw.
27. 27 the soldiers of the governor took Jesus
Mark 4. 36 they took him even as he was in the ship
5. 40 he taketh the father and the mother of the
9. 2 Jesus taketh (with him) Peter, and James
10. 32 he took again the twelve, and began to
14. 33 he taketh with him Peter and James and
Luke 9. 10 he took them, and went aside privately
9. 28 he took Peter and John and James, and
11. 26 Then goeth he, and taketh (to him) seven
18. 31 Then he took (unto him) the twelve, and
John 19. 16 [And they took Jesus, and led (him) aw.]
Acts 15. 39 Barnabas took Mark, and sailed unto Cy.
16. 33 he took them the same hour of the night
21. 24 Them take, and purify thyself with them
21. 26 Then Paul took the men, and the next da
21. 32 Who immediately [took] soldiers and ce.
23. 18 he took him, and brought (him) to the ch.

74. *To bear alongside of*, παραφέρω *parapherō.*

Mark 14. 36 take away this cup from me: nevertheless

75. *To take away round about*, περιαιρέω *periaireō.*

Acts 27. 40 when they had taken up the anchors, th.
Heb. 10. 11 sacrifices, which can never take away si.

76. *To press, take or lay hold*, πιάζω *piazō.*

John 7. 30 they sought to take him: but no man laid
7. 32 the chief priests sent officers to take him
7. 44 some of them would have taken him; but
10. 39 they sought again to take him: but he es.
11. 57 he should show (it), that they might take
Acts 3. 7 he took him by the right hand, and lifted

77. *To do, make*, ποιέω *poieō.*

Mark 3. 6 [took] counsel with the Herodians against

78. *To receive besides*, προσδέχομαι *prosdechomai.*

Heb. 10. 34 took joyfully the spoiling of your goods

79. *To take besides*, προσλαμβάνω *proslambanō.*

Matt 16. 22 Peter took him, and began to rebuke him
Mark 8. 32 Peter took him, and began to rebuke him
Acts 27. 33 continued fasting, having taken nothing
27. 34 I pray you [to take] (some) meat; for this
27. 36 all of good cheer, and they also took (so)

80. *To take together*, συλλαμβάνω *sullambanō.*

Matt 26. 55 I sat daily with you teaching in the temp.
Mark 14. 48 with swords and (with) staves to take me?
Luke 5. 9 draught of the fishes which they had tak.
22. 54 Then took they him, and led (him), and
John 18. 12 officers of the Jews took Jesus, and bound
Acts 1. 16 which was guide to them that took Jesus
12. 3 he proceeded further to take Peter also

81. *To take together*, συναίρω *sunairō.*

Matt 18. 23 which would take account of his servants

[*See also* Accusation, advice, ashes, captive, care, counsel, courage, crafty, delight, ease, fill, hand, handful, heed, hold, hold on, hold upon, indignation, inheritance, journey, knowledge, much, notice, oath, oversight, part, pity, pleasure, pledge, possessions, provision, record, rest, route, spoil, straightway, sweet, tenth, thought, ties, throat, vengeance, violence, witness, wrong.]

TAKE away as with a whirlwind, to —

To whirl or be whirled away, שָׂעַר *saar.*
Psa. 58. 9 he shall take them away as with a whirl.

TAKE away (violently, by violence), to quite —

1. *To take violently away, rob, plunder,* גָּזַל *gazal.*
Gen. 21. 25 Abimelech's servants had violently taken a.
Lev. 6. 4 restore that which he took violently aw.
Deut 28. 31 thine ass (shall be) violently taken away
Job 20. 19 he hath violently taken away an house wh.
24. 2 they violently take away flocks, and feed
Mic. 2. 2 they covet fields, and take (them) by vio.

2. *To complete, finish, remove,* כָּלָה *kalah,* 3.
Num17. 10 thou shalt quite take away their murmu.

TAKE aside, back, to —

1. *To stretch out, cause to turn aside,* נָטָה *natah,* 5.
2 Sa. 3. 27 Joab took him aside in the gate, to speak

2. *To cause to turn back,* שׁוּב *shub,* 5.
2 Sa. 15. 20 return thou, and take back thy brethren

3. *To take off or away,* ἀπολαμβάνω *apolambanō.*
Mark 7. 33 he took him aside from the multitude, and

TAKE before or by, to —

1. *To take hold on,* ἐπιλαμβάνομαι *epilambanomai.*
Mark 8. 23 he took the blind man by the hand, and
Acts 23. 19 the chief captain took him by the hand
Heb. 8. 9 when I took them by the hand to lead th.

2. *To lay fast hold on,* κρατέω *krateō.*
Matt. 9. 25 he went in, and took her by the hand, and
Mark 1. 31 he came and took her by the hand, and li.
5. 41 he took the damsel by the hand, and said
Luke 8. 54 took her by the hand, and called, saying

3. *To take before,* προλαμβάνω *prolambanō.*
1 Co. 11. 21 every one taketh before (other) his own

TAKE by force, to —

1. *To take violently away,* גָּזַל *gazal.*
Gen. 31. 31 thou wouldest take by force thy daughters

2. *To snatch away,* ἁρπάζω *harpazō.*
Matt 11. 12 kingdom of heaven.. violent take it by fo.
John 6. 15 they would come and take him by force
Acts 23. 10 to take him by force from among them

TAKE down, for, forth, to —

1. *To cause to go down,* יָרַד *yarad,* 5.
Gen. 44. 11 they speedily took down every man his sa.
Num. 1. 51 the tabernacle. Levites shall take it do.
4. 5 they shall take down the covering veil, and
Josh. 8. 29 that they should take his carcase down fr.
10. 27 they took them down off the trees, and ca.
1 Sa. 6. 15 the Levites took down the ark of the Lo.
2 Ki. 16. 17 took down the sea from off the brasen oxen

2. *To cause to go out or forth,* יָצָא *yatsa,* 5.
Jer. 15. 19 if thou take forth the precious from the

3. *To cause to go forth,* נְפַק *nephaq,* 5.
Ezra 6. 5 Nebuchadnezzar took forth out of the te.

4. *To hold, have,* ἔχω *echō.*
Matt 21. 46 because they took him for a prophet

5. *To take down,* καθαιρέω *kathaireō.*
Mark 15. 36 whether Elias will come to take him down
15. 46 took him down, and wrapped him in the
Luke 23. 53 he took it down, and wrapped it in linen
Acts 13. 29 they took (him) down from the tree, and

TAKE heed (to), to —

1. *To be warned,* זְהַר *zehar.*
Ezra 4. 22 Take heed now that ye fail not to do this

2. *To see, look, perceive,* βλέπω *blepō*
Matt 24. 4 said unto them, Take heed that no man d.
Mark. 4. 24 Take heed what ye hear: with what mea
13. 5 began to say, Take heed lest any (man) de
13. 9 take heed to yourselves: for they shall de
13. 23 Take ye heed: behold, I have foretold you
13. 33 Take ye heed, watch and pray: for ye know
Luke 8. 18 Take heed therefore how ye hear: for wh.
21. 8 Take heed that ye be not deceived: for ma.
1 Co. 3. 10 let every man take heed how he buildeth
8. 9 take heed, lest by any means this liberty
10. 12 let him that thinketh he standeth take h
Gal. 5. 15 take heed that ye be not consumed one of
Col. 4. 17 Take heed to the ministry which thou hast
Heb. 3. 12 Take heed, brethren, lest there be in any

3. *To hold on or upon,* ἐπέχω *epechō*
1 Ti. 4. 16 Take heed unto thyself, and unto the do.

4. *To see, look, take heed,* ὁράω *horaō.*
Matt 16. 6 Take heed and beware of the leaven of the
18. 10 Take heed that ye despise not one of the.
Mark 8. 15 Take heed, beware of the leaven of the P
Luke 12. 15 Take heed, and beware of covetousness
Acts 22. 26 [Take heed] what thou doest; for this man

5. *To hold toward,* προσέχω *prosechō.*
Matt. 6. 1 Take heed that ye do not your alms before
Luke 17. 3 Take heed to yourselves: If thy brother
21. 34 take heed to yourselves, lest at any time
Acts 5. 35 Ye men of Israel, take heed to yourselves
20. 28 Take heed therefore unto yourselves, and
2 Pe. 1. 19 ye do well that ye take heed, as unto a li.

6. *To look at, view, observe,* σκοπέω *skopeō.*
Luke 11. 35 Take heed therefore that the light which

TAKE hold (of, on, upon), to —

1. *To lay or keep hold,* אָחַז *achaz.*
Gen. 25. 26 his hand took hold on Esau's heel; and his
Exod 15. 14 sorrow shall take hold on the inhabitants
15. 15 trembling shall take hold upon them; all
Deut. 32. 41 and mine hand take hold on judgment
2 Sa. 4. 10 I took hold of him, and slew him in Zikl.
6. 6 Uzzah put forth (his hand).. and took ho. of
Job 21. 6 and trembling taketh hold on my flesh
30. 16 the days of affliction have taken hold upon
38. 13 That it might take hold of the ends of the
Psa. 48. 6 Fear took hold upon them there, (and) p.
119. 53 Horror hath taken hold upon me because
Eccl. 7. 18 (It is) good that thou shouldest take hold o.
Song. 7. 8 I will take hold of the boughs thereof
Isa. 13. 8 sorrows shall take hold of them; they
21. 3 pangs have taken hold upon me, as the

2. *To cause to lay or keep hold,* חָזַק *chazaq,* 5.
2 Sa. 1. 11 David took hold on his clothes, and rent
13. 11 he took hold of her, and said unto her, C.
1 Ki. 9. 9 have taken hold upon other gods, and
2 Ki. 2. 12 he took hold of his own clothes, and rent
Psa. 35. 2 Take hold of shield and buckler, and stand
Isa. 4. 1 seven women shall take hold of one man
27. 5 let him take hold of my strength, (that)
56. 4 that please me, and take hold of my cov.
56. 6 every one that.. taketh hold of my cove.
64. 7 that stirreth up himself to take hold of
Jer. 6. 24 anguish hath taken hold of us, (and) pain
8. 21 astonishment hath taken hold on me
50. 43 anguish took hold of him, (and) pangs as
Zech. 8. 23 ten men shall take hold out of all langu.
8. 23 shall take hold of the skirt of him that is

3. *To find,* מָצָא *matsa.*
Psa. 119. 143 Trouble and anguish have taken hold on

4. *To separate self, flee,* הִסִּיג [*sug,* 5; A.V. as if from *nasag,* 5]. Mic. 6. 14.

5. *To cause to reach, attain, overtake,* נָשַׂג *nasag,* 5.
Job 27. 20 Terrors take hold on him as waters
Psa. 40. 12 mine iniquities have taken hold upon me
69. 24 let thy wrathful anger take hold of them
Prov. 2. 19 neither take they hold of the paths of life
Zech. 1. 6 did they not take hold of your fathers?

6. *To accept, take,* קָבַל *qabal,* 5.
Exod 26. 5 the loops may take hold one of another

7. *To hold, uphold, retain,* תָּמַךְ *tamak.*
Job 36. 17 judgment and justice take hold (on thee)
Prov. 5. 5 down to death; her steps take hold on

8. *To catch, capture, keep hold,* תָּפַשׂ *taphas.*
Isa. 3. 6 a man shall take hold of his brother, of
Eze. 29. 7 they took hold of thee by thy hand, thou

9. *To catch, capture, keep hold,* תָּפַשׂ *taphas,* 3.
Prov. 30. 28 The spider taketh hold with her hands

10. *To take hold of,* ἐπιλαμβάνομαι *epilambanomai.*
Luke 20. 20 that they might take hold of his words
20. 26 they could not take hold of his words be

TAKE in, into, to —

1. *To cause to go or come in,* בּוֹא *bo,* 5.
Judg 12. 9 took in thirty daughters from abroad for

2. *To gather,* אָסַף *asaph,* 3.
Judg 19. 15 (there was) no man that took them into

3. *To take up,* ἀναλαμβάνω *analambanō.*
Acts 20. 13 sailed unto As., there intending to take in
20. 14 when he met with us at As., we took him in

4. *To lead up,* συνάγω *sunagō.*
Matt 25. 35 I was a stranger, and ye took me in
25. 38 When saw we thee.. and took (thee) in
25. 43 I was a stranger, and ye took me not in

TAKE leave of, to —

1. *To arrange off,* ἀποτάσσομαι *apotassomai.*
Acts 18. 18 took his leave of the brethren, and sailed
2 Co. 2. 13 taking my leave of them, I went from th

2. *To draw together, embrace, salute,* ἀσπάζομαι.
Acts 21. 6 when [we had taken our leave one of] ano

TAKE off, from, on, out, to —

1. *To come or bring forth, draw up,* גִּיחַ, גּוּחַ *guach.*
Psa 22. 9 thou (art) he that took me out of the wo.

2. *To cause to go out or forth,* יָצָא *yatsa,* 5.
Exod. 4. 6 when he took it out, behold, his hand

3. *To cause to go or come forth,* נְפַק *nephaq,* 5.
Ezra 5. 14 which Nebuchadnezzar took out of the t.
5. 14 those did Cyrus the king take out of the
Dan. 5. 2 Nebuchadnezzar had taken out of the te.

4. *To cause to turn aside,* סוּר *sur,* 5.
Gen. 41. 42 Pharaoh took off his ring from his hand
Exod 14. 25 took off their chariot wheels, that they
34. 34 he took the veil off, until he came out
Lev. 3. 9 it shall he take off hard by the back bone
2 Sa. 16. 9 let me go over.. and take off his head
Esth. 8. 2 And the king took off his ring, which he

5. *To cause to go high,* רוּם *rum,* 5.
Lev. 4. 8 he shall take off from it all the fat of the
Eze. 21. 26 Remove the diadem, and take off the cr.

6. *To cause to turn back,* שׁוּב *shub,* 5.
Eze. 18. 17 (That) hath taken off his hand from the

7. *To cast out or forth,* ἐκβάλλω *ekballō.*
Luke 10. 35 he took out two pence, and gave (them)

8. *To put off, unclothe,* ἐκδύω *ekduō.*
Matt 27. 31 they took the robe off from him, and put
Mark 15. 20 they took off the purple from him, and

9. *To take on or upon,* ἐπιλαμβάνομαι *epilambano.*
Heb. 2. 16 he took not on (him the nature of) angels
2. 16 but he took on (him) the seed of Abraham

TAKE patiently, rest, ship, shipping, to —

1. *To lie down,* שָׁכַב *shakab.*
Job 11. 18 (and) thou shalt take thy rest in safety
30. 17 bones are pierced.. my sinews take no rest
Eccl. 2. 23 yea, his heart taketh not rest in the night

2. *To go in unto,* ἐμβαίνω εἰς *embainō eis.*
Matt 15. 39 he sent away the multitude, and [took] sh.
John 6. 24 they also took shipping, and came to Ca.

3. *To go up into,* ἐπιβαίνω εἰς *epibainō eis.*
Acts 21. 6 [we took] ship; and they returned home

4. *To remain under, sustain,* ὑπομένω *hupomenō.*
1 Pe. 2. 20 when ye be buffeted.. ye shall take it pati.
2. 20 if, when ye do well.. ye take it patiently

TAKE unto, upon, with, to, self, to—

1. *To begin, be pleased, desirous,* יָאַל *yaal,* 5.
Gen. 18. 27, 31 I have taken it upon me to speak unto

2. *To take in or on hand,* ἐπιχειρέω *epicheireō.*
Acts 19. 13 took upon them to call over them which

3. *To take alongside of,* παραλαμβάνω *paralambanō.*
Matt. 1. 20 fear not to take unto thee Mary thy wife
1. 24 Then Joseph.. took unto him his wife
26. 37 he took with him Peter and the two sons

4. *To take besides,* προσλαμβάνω *proslambanō.*
Acts 17. 5 took unto them certain lewd fellows of
18. 26 they took him unto (them), and expoun.

5. *To take along with,* συμπαραλαμβάνω *sumparal.*
Acts 12. 25 took with them John, whose sur. Gal. 2. 1.
15. 37 Barnabas determined to take with them
15. 38 Paul thought not good to take him with

6. *To take, receive,* λαμβάνω, Phil. 2. 7; Re. 11. 17.

TAKE in hand, to —

To take on or in hand, ἐπιχειρέω *epicheireō.*
Luke 1. 1 many have taken in hand to set forth in

TAKE up one's carriage —

To take up one's goods, ἀποσκευάζομαι.
Acts 21. 15 after those days [we took up our carriages]

TAKEN (away, from, off, up), to be —

1. *To be taken hold of,* אָחַז *achaz,* 2.
Eccl. 9. 12 as the fishes that are taken in an evil net

2. *To be gathered,* אָסַף *asaph,* 2.
Isa. 16. 10 gladness is taken away, and joy out of the
57. 1 merciful men (are) taken away, none co.
57. 1 the righteous is taken away from the evil
Jer. 48. 33 gladness is taken from the plentiful field
Hos. 4. 3 fishes of the sea also shall be taken away

3. *To be taken violently away,* גָּזַל *gazal,* 2.
Prov. 4. 16 their sleep is taken away, unless they ca.

4. *To be withdrawn, diminished,* גָּרַע *gara,* 2.
Num 36. 3 then shall their inheritance be taken fr.
36. 3 so shall it be taken from the lot of our in.
36. 4 so shall their inheritance be taken away

5. *To be captured, caught,* לָכַד *lakad,* 2.
Josh. 7. 15 he that is taken with the accursed thing

6. *To be taken, received, accepted,* לָקַח *laqach,* 2.
1 Sa. 4. 11 the ark of God was taken; and the two
4. 17 sons are dead, and the ark of God is ta.
4. 19 the tidings that the ark of God was taken
4. 21 because the ark of God was taken, and bec.
4. 22 glory is departed.. the ark of God is taken
21. 6 bread in the day when it was taken away
2 Ki. 2. 9 for thee, before I be taken away from thee.
Esth. 2. 16 Esther was taken unto king Ahasuerus
Eze 33. 6 he is taken away in his iniquity but his

7. *To be taken, received, accepted,* לָקַח *laqach,* 4.
Gen. 2. 23 Woman, because she was taken out of man
3. 19 the ground: for out of it wast thou taken
3. 23 to till the ground from whence he was ta.
Judg 17. 2 (shekels) of silver that were taken from th.
2 Ki. 2. 10 if thou see me (when I am) taken from
Isa. 52. 5 that my people is taken away for nought?
53. 8 He was taken from prison and from jud.
Jer. 29. 22 of them shall be taken up a curse by all
48. 46 thy sons are taken captives, and thy dau.

8. *To be taken, received, accepted,* לָקַח *laqach,* 6.
Gen. 12. 15 the woman was taken into Pharaoh's ho.
Job 28. 2 Iron is taken out of the earth, and brass
Isa. 49. 24 Shall the prey be taken from the mighty
49. 25 the captives of the mighty shall be taken a.
Eze. 15. 3 Shall wood be taken thereof to do any w.?

9. *To be taken up,* נְסַק *nesaq,* 6.
Dan. 6. 23 So Daniel was taken up out of the den

10. *To be snatched or taken away,* נָצַל *natsal,* 2.
Amos 3. 12 so shall the children of Israel be taken o.

11. *To be given,* נָתַן *nathan,* 6.
2 Sa. 18. 9 he was taken up between the heaven and

12. *To turn aside, be turned aside,* סוּר *sur.*
Exod 25. 15 The staves.. they shall not be taken from
1 Ki. 22. 43 the high places were not taken away, (for)
2 Ki. 14. 4 the high places were not taken away: as
2 Ch. 15. 17 the high places were not taken away out

2 Ch.20. 33 the high places were not taken away; for
Isa. 6. 7 thine iniquity is taken away, and thy sin
10. 27 his burden shall be taken away from off

13. *To be turned aside,* סוּר *sur,* 6.
1 Sa. 21. 6 shewbread, that was taken from before
Isa. 17. 1 Damascus is taken away from (being) a
Dan. 12. 11 the daily (sacrifice) shall be taken away

14. *To be gone up,* עָלָה *alah,* 2.
Exod 40. 36 the cloud was taken up from over the ta.
40. 37 But if the cloud were not taken up, then
40. 37 they journeyed not till..it was taken up
Num. 9. 17 when the cloud was taken up from the ta.
9. 21 (that) the cloud was taken up in the mo.
9. 21 or by night that the cloud was taken up
9. 22 but when it was taken up, they journeyed
10. 11 that the cloud was taken up from off the
Eze. 36. 3 and ye are taken up in the lips of talkers

15. *To be caused to go high,* רוּם *rum,* 6 [V.L. 5].
Dan. 8. 11 by him the daily (sacrifice) was taken away

16. *To be caused to go high,* רוּם *rum,* 6.
Lev. 4. 10 As it was taken off from the bullock of

17. *To be caught, captured,* תָּפַשׂ *taphas,* 2.
Num. 5. 13 (there be) no witness..neither she be ta
Psa. 10. 2 let them be taken in the devices that they
Jer. 34. 3 shalt surely be taken, and delivered into
38. 23 shalt be taken by the hand of the king
Eze. 12. 13 he shall be taken in my snare: and I will
17. 20 he shall be taken in my snare; and I will
19. 4 he was taken in their pit, and they brou
19. 8 spread their net over him: he was taken
21. 23 to remembrance, that they may be taken
21. 24 (I say)..ye shall be taken with the hand

18. *To lift up,* αἴρω *airō.*
Matt 13. 12 from him shall be taken away even that
21. 43 The kingdom of God shall be taken from
25. 29 shall be taken away even that which he
Mark 4. 25 from him shall be taken even that which
Luke 8. 18 from him shall be taken even that which
9. 17 there was taken up of fragments that re
19. 26 that he hath shall be taken away from
John 19. 31 and (that) they might be taken away
20. 1 seeth the stone taken away from the sep.
Acts 8. 33 his judgment was taken away: and who
8. 33 for his life is taken from the earth
20. 9 from the third loft, and was taken up d.

19. *To take up, take again,* ἀναλαμβάνω *analambanō.*
Acts 1. 2 Until the day in which he was taken up
1. 11 this same Jesus, which is taken up from
1. 22 that same day that he was taken up from

20. *To be taken off or away,* ἀπαίρομαι *apairomai.*
Matt. 9. 15 the bridegroom shall be taken from them
Mark 2. 20 the bridegroom shall be taken away from
Luke 5. 35 the bridegroom shall be taken away from

21. *To take off or away,* ἀφαιρέω *aphaireō.*
Luke 10. 42 which shall not be taken away from her

22. *To take out or forth,* ἐξαίρω *exairō.*
1 Co. 5. 2 that he..[might be taken away] from amo.

23. *To lift up,* ἐπαίρω *epairō.*
Acts 1. 9 while they beheld, he was taken up; and

24. *To take down, apprehend,* καταλαμβάνω *katal.*
John 8. 3 [brought unto him a woman taken in ad.]
8. 4 [this woman was taken in adultery, in the]

25. *To take alongside,* παραλαμβάνω *paralambanō*
Matt 24. 40, 41 the one shall be taken, and the other
Luke 17. 34, 35, [36] one shall be taken, and the other

26. *To take round about,* περιαιρέω *periaireō.*
Acts 27. 20 all hope..was then taken away
2 Co. 3. 16 Nevertheless..the veil shall be taken aw

27. *To use pressure, take hold on,* πιάζω *piazō*
Rev. 19. 20 the beast was taken, and with him the fa

28. *To take together,* συλλαμβάνω *sullambanō*
Acts 23. 27 This man was taken of the Jews and sh

29. *With a view to capture,* εἰς ἅλωσιν *eis halōsin*
2 Pe. 2. 12 brute beasts, made to be taken and des

30. *Not to uncover,* μὴ ἀνακαλύπτω *mē anakaluptō.*
2 Co. 3. 14 remaineth the same veil untaken away

31. *To make a very orphan,* ἀπορφανίζομαι *aporph.*
1 Th. 2. 17 being taken from you for a short time in

32. *To become,* γίνομαι *ginomai.*
2 Th. 2. 7 (will let), until he be taken out of the way

33. *To hold together,* συνέχω *sunechō.*
Matt. 4. 24 sick people that were taken with divers
Luke 4. 38 Simon's wife's mother was taken with a
8. 37 they were taken with great fear. And he

TAKEN away, to have—

To cause to pass away, take away, עֲדָה *adah,* 5.
Dan. 7. 12 they had their dominion taken away, yet

TAKEN, being —

Capture, לֶכֶד *leked.*
Prov. 3. 26 and shall keep thy foot from being taken

TAKEN down, out of (the way), to be —

1. *To be caused to go down,* יָרַד *yarad,* 6.
Num. 10. 17 the tabernacle was taken down; and the

2. *To cause to go forth,* נְפַק *nephaq,* 5.
Dan. 5. 3 the golden vessels that were taken out of

3. *To be taken down,* צָעַן *tsaan.*
Isa. 33. 20 a tabernacle (that) shall not be taken down

4. *To be shut up,* קָפַץ *qaphats,* 2.
Job 24. 24 they are taken out of the way as all (other)

TAKEN, (thing that was) —

1. *To withdraw, diminish,* גָּרַע *gara.*
Eccl. 3. 14 nothing..put to it, nor any thing taken

2. *Captive, captivity,* שְׁבִי *shebi.*
Num. 31. 26 the sum of the prey that was taken..of

TAKING —

1. *To take, receive,* לָקַח *laqach.*
Hos. 11. 3 taking them by their arms

2. *A taking, receiving,* מִקָּח *miqqach.*
2 Ch. 19. 7 nor respect of persons, nor taking of gifts

3. *To be caught, captured, handled,* תָּפַשׂ *taphas,* 2.
Jer. 50. 46 At the noise of the taking of Babylon the

TALE —

1. *A meditation, utterance,* הֶגֶה *hegeh.*
Psa. 90. 9 we spend our years as a tale (that is told)

2. *Number, narration,* מִסְפָּר *mispar.*
1 Ch. 9. 28 they should bring them in and out by tale

3. *Measure, proper quantity,* מַתְכֹּנֶת *mathkoneth.*
Exod. 5. 8 the tale of the bricks, which they did ma.

4. *A weight, measure,* תֹּכֶן *token.*
Exod. 5. 18 no straw..yet shall ye deliver the tale of b.

TALE bearer, —

1. *Talebearer, whisperer, busybody,* נִרְגָּן *nirgan.*
Prov 18. 8 The words of a tale bearer (are) as wounds
26. 20 where (there is) no tale bearer, the strife
26. 22 The words of a tale bearer (are) as wounds

2. *Slanderer,* רָכִיל *rakil.*
Lev. 19. 16 Thou shalt not go up and down (as) a t. b.
Prov 20. 19 He that goeth about (as) a tale bearer re.

3. *To go a slanderer,* הָלַךְ רָכִיל *halak rakil.*
Prov 11. 13 A tale bearer revealeth secrets: but he th.

TALENT, (weight of a) —

1. *A circuit, cake, talent,* כִּכָּר *kikkar.*
Exod 25. 39 (Of) a talent of pure gold shall he make it
37. 24 (Of) a talent of pure gold made he it, and
38. 24 twenty and nine talents, and seven hund.
38. 25 an hundred talents, and a thousand seven
38. 27 of the hundred talents of silver were cast
38. 27 the hundred talents, a talent for a socket
38. 29 the brass of the offering (was) seventy ta.
2 Sa. 12. 30 the weight whereof (was) a talent of gold
1 Ki. 9. 14 Hiram sent to the king six score talents
9. 28 gold, four hundred and twenty talents
10. 10 an hundred and twenty talents of gold, and
10. 14 six hundred threescore and six talents of
16. 24 he bought the hill..for two talents of sil.
20. 39 or else thou shalt pay a talent of silver
2 Ki. 5. 5 took with him ten talents of silver, and
5. 22 give them, I pray thee, a talent of silver
5. 23 Naaman said, Be content, take two talents
5. 23 he urged him, and bound two talents of
15. 19 Menahem gave Pul a thousand talents of
18. 14 talents of silver, and thirty talents of gold
23. 33 an hundred talents of silver, and a talent
1 Ch. 19. 6 children of Ammon sent a thousand tale.
20. 2 found it to weigh a talent of gold, and (th.
22. 14 an hundred thousand talents of gold, and
22. 14 a thousand thousand talents of silver; and
29. 4 three thousand talents of gold, of the gold
29. 4 seven thousand talents of refined silver, to
29. 7 five thousand talents and ten thousand dr.
29. 7 and of silver ten thousand talents, and
29. 7 of brass eighteen thousand talents
29. 7 and one hundred thousand talents of iron
2 Ch. 3. 8 fine gold, (amounting) to six hundred tal.
8. 18 took thence four hundred and fifty talents
9. 9 an hundred and twenty talents of gold, and
9. 13 six hundred and threescore and six talents
25. 6 He hired..for an hundred talents of silver
25. 9 what shall we do for the hundred talents
27. 5 an hundred talents of silver, and ten th
36. 3 an hundred talents of silver and a talent
Ezra 8. 26 six hundred and fifty talents of silver, and
8. 26 talents, (and) of gold an hundred talents
Esth. 3. 9 I will pay ten thousand talents of silver
Zech. 5. 7 behold, there was lifted up a talent of l.

2. *A circuit, cake, talent,* כִּכַּר *kikkar.*
Ezra 7. 22 Unto an hundred talents of silver, and to

3. *A talent, weight, balance,* τάλαντον *talanton.*
Matt 18. 24 one..which owed him ten thousand talents
25. 15 unto one he gave five talents, to another
25. 16 Then he that had received the five talents
25. 16 went..and made (them) other five [talents]
25. 20 And so he that had received five talents
25. 20 came and brought other five [talents], say.
25. 20 Lord, thou deliveredst unto me five tale.
25. 20 I have gained besides them five talents
25. 22 He also that had received two talents ca.
25. 22 Lord, thou deliveredst unto me two tale.
25. 22 I have gained two other talents besides
25. 24 he which had received the one talent ca.
25. 25 and went and hid thy talent in the earth
25. 28 Take therefore the talent from him, and
25. 28 give (it) unto him which hath ten talents

4. *Weighing a talent,* ταλαντιαῖος *talantiaios.*
Rev. 16. 21 (every stone) about the weight of a talent

TALES, to carry (idle) —

1. *Slanderer,* רָכִיל *rakil.*
Eze. 22. 9 In thee are men that carry tales to shed

2. *Idle or trifling talk,* λῆρος *lēros.*
Luke 24. 11 their words seemed to them as idle tales

TA-LI'-THA CU'-MI, Ταλιθὰ κοῦμι *(from Syriac).*
Mark 5. 41 said unto her, Talitha cumi..Damsel..ar.

TALK —

1. *Word, matter,* דָּבָר *dabar.*
Job 15. 3 Should he reason with unprofitable talk?
Prov. 14. 23 the talk of the lips (tendeth) only to pen.

2. *Mouth,* פֶּה *peh.*
Eccl. 10. 13 the end of his talk (is) mischievous mad.

3. *Lip,* שָׂפָה *saphah.*
Job 11. 2 and should a man full of talk be justified?

4. *Word, matter,* λόγος *logos.*
Matt 22. 15 how they might entangle him in (his) talk

TALK (with), to —

1. *To say, (lift up the voice),* אָמַר *amar.*
Gen. 4. 8 And Cain talked with Abel his brother

2. *To speak, (lead out words),* דָּבַר *dabar.*
Zech. 1. 9 the angel that talked with me said unto
1. 13 the LORD answered the angel that talked
1. 19 I said unto the angel that talked with me
2. 3 the angel that talked with me went forth
4. 1 the angel that talked with me came again
4. 4 spake to the angel that talked with me
4. 5 the angel that talked with me answered
5. 5 the angel that talked with me went forth
5. 10 Then said I to the angel that talked with
6. 4 said unto the angel that talked with me

3. *To be spoken, speak together,* דָּבַר *dabar,* 2.
Eze. 33. 30 children of thy people still are talking

4. *To speak,* דָּבַר *dabar,* 3.
Gen. 17. 3 Abram fell on his face: and God talked wi.
17. 22 he left off talking with him, and God went
35. 13 God went up from him..where he talked
35. 14 a pillar in the place where he talked with
45. 15 and after that his brethren talked with
Exod 20. 22 Ye have seen that I have talked with you
33. 9 stood (at) the door..and the LORD talked w.
34. 29 skin of his face shone while he talked with
34. 31 called unto them..and Moses talked with
Num 11. 17 I will come down and talk with thee the.
Deut. 5. 4 The LORD talked with you face to face in
5. 24 have seen this day that God doth talk with
6. 7 shalt talk of them when thou sittest in th.
Judg. 6. 17 show me a sign that thou talkest with me
14. 7 he went down and talked with the woman
1 Sa. 2. 3 Talk no more so exceeding proudly; let
14. 19 it came to pass, while Saul talked unto the
17. 23 as he talked with them, behold, there ca.
1 Ki. 1. 14 while thou yet talkest there with the king
1. 22 while she yet talked with the king, Nathan
2 Ki. 2. 11 as they still went on, and talked, that, be.
6. 33 while he yet talked with them, behold, the
8. 4 the king talked with Gehazi, the servant
18. 26 talk not with us in the Jews' language in
2 Ch. 25. 16 it came to pass, as he talked with him, th.
Esth. 6. 14 while they (were) yet talking with him
Job 13. 7 Will ye speak wickedly..and talk deceit.
Psa 37. 30 righteous..his tongue talketh of judgment
145. 11 They shall speak..and talk of thy power
Prov. 24. 2 heart studieth destruction..lips talk of
Jer. 12. 1 (yet) let me talk with thee of (thy) judg.
38. 25 if the princes hear that I have talked with
Eze. 3. 22 go forth..and I will there talk with thee
Dan. 9. 22 he informed (me), and talked with me, and
10. 17 can the servant of this my lord talk with

5. *To meditate, utter,* הָגָה *hagah.*
Psa. 71. 24 My tongue also shall talk of thy righteou.

6. *To number, recount,* סָפַר *saphar,* 3.
Psa. 69. 26 they talk to the grief of those whom thou

7. *To bow down, meditate,* שִׂיחַ *siach.*
1 Ch. 16. 9 sing psalms unto him, talk ye of all his
Psa. 77. 12 meditate also of all thy work, and talk
105. 2 sing psalms unto him: talk ye of all his
119. 27 so shall I talk of thy wondrous works
Prov. 6. 22 (when) thou awakest, it shall talk with

8. *To talk,* λαλέω *laleō.*
Matt 12. 46 While he yet talked to the people, behold
Mark 6. 50 he talked with them, and saith unto them
Luke 24. 32 while he talked with us by the way, and
John 4. 27 and marvelled that he talked with the wo.
4. 27 yet no man said..Why talkest thou with
9. 37 seen him, and it is he that talketh with
14. 30 I will not talk much with you: for the pr.
Acts 26. 31 they talked between themselves, saying
Rev. 4. 1 as it were of a trumpet talking with me
17. 1 talked with me, saying unto me, Come hi.
21. 9 talked with me, saying, Come hither, I
21. 15 he that talked with me had a golden reed

9. *To converse with,* ὁμιλέω *homileō.*
Luke 24. 14 they talked together of all these things
Acts 20. 11 talked a long while, even till break of day

10. *To talk together,* συλλαλέω *sullaleō.*
Matt 17. 3 there appeared..Moses and Elias talking
Mark 9. 4 appeared..they were talking with Jesus
Luke 9. 30 there talked with him two men, which we.

11. *To converse together,* συνομιλέω *sunomileō.*
Acts 10. 27 as he talked with him, he went in, and

TALKER, (vain) —

1. *Tongue,* לָשׁוֹן *lashon.*
Eze. 36. 3 ye are taken up in the lips of talkers, and

2. *A vain speaker*, ματαιολόγος *mataiologos.*
Titus 1. 10 there are many unruly and vain talkers

TALKING, (foolish) —

1. *A word, speech*, מִלָּה *millah.*
Job 29. 9 The princes refrained talking, and laid

2. *Meditation (talk) is to [him]*, שִׂיחַ לְ *siach le.*
1 Ki. 18. 27 either he is talking, or he is pursuing, or

3. *Foolish speaking*, μωρολογία *mōrologia.*
Eph. 5. 4 Neither filthiness, nor foolish talking, nor

TALL, taller —

1. *Height, stature*, קוֹמָה *qomah.*
2 Ki. 19. 23 will cut down the tall cedar trees thereof
Isa. 37. 24 I will cut down..tall cedars thereof, (and)

2. *To be high*, רוּם *rum.*
Deut. 1. 28 The people (is) greater and taller than we
2. 10 a people great, and many, and tall, as the
2. 21 A people great, and many, and tall; 9. 2.

TAMAH. *See* **THAMAH.**

TAL'-MAI, תַּלְמַי *bold, spirited.*
1. A son of Anak, in Hebron, in the days of Joshua. B.C. 1450.
Num 13. 22 where Ahiman, Sheshai, and T., the chil.
Josh 15. 14 Caleb drove thence..Ahiman, and T., the
Judg. 1. 10 they slew Sheshai, and Ahiman, and T.
2. A king of Geshur, father of Maacah one of David's wives. B.C. 1040.
2 Sa. 3. 3 Maacah the daughter of T., king of Geshur
13. 37 Absalom fled, and went to T., the son of
1 Ch. 3. 2 Maacah the daughter of T. king of Geshur

TAL'-MON, טַלְמוֹן, טַלְמֹן *oppressor, violent.*
A Levite in Jerusalem in the days of Ezra. B.C. 536-445.
1 Ch. 9. 17 the porters (were)..T., and Ahiman, and
Ezra 2. 42 children of T., the children of Akkub
Neh. 7. 45 children of T., the children of Akkub
11. 19 Akkub, T., and their brethren that kept
12. 25 T., Akkub..porters, keeping the ward at

TA'-MAR, תָּמָר *palm.*
1. Wife of Er the eldest son of Judah, and mother of Pharez and Zarah. B.C. 1670.
Gen. 38. 6 Judah took a wife for Er..whose name..T.
38. 11 Then said Judah to T. his daughter in law
38. 11 T. went and dwelt in her father's house
38. 13 it was told T., saying, Behold, thy father
38. 24 T. thy daughter in law hath played the ha.
Ruth 4. 12 of Pharez, whom T. bare unto Judah, of
1 Ch. 2. 4 T. his daughter in law bare him Pharez
2. Daughter of David violated by Amnon, and avenged by Absalom. B.C. 1022.
2 Sa. 13. 1 had a fair sister, whose name (was) T.
13. 2 Amnon..fell sick for his sister T.; for she
13. 4 I love T., my brother Absalom's sister
13. 5 let my sister T. come and give me meat
13. 6 Amnon said unto the king..let T. my sis.
13. 7 David sent home to T., saying, Go now to
13. 8 So T. went to her brother Amnon's house
13. 10 Amnon said unto T., Bring the meat into
13. 10 T. took the cakes which she had made, and
13. 19 And T. put ashes on her head, and rent
13. 20 So T. remained desolate in..Absalom's
13. 22 because he had forced his sister T.
13. 32 from the day that he forced his sister T.
1 Ch. 3. 9 beside the sons of the concubines, and T.
3. A daughter of Absalom. B.C. 1010.
2 Sa. 14. 27 and one daughter, whose name (was) T.
4. A city in the S. of Judah, near the Salt Sea; perhaps *En-gedi.*
Eze. 47. 19 from T...to the waters of strife (in) Kad.
48. 28 the border shall be even from T. (unto)

TAME, be tamed, to —
To tame, subdue, δαμάζω *damazō.*
Mark 5. 4 fetters broken..neither could..(man) ta.
Jas. 3. 7 is tamed, and hath been tamed of man.
3. 8 the tongue can no man tame; (it is) an

TAM-MUZ, תַּמּוּז.
A Syrian and Phœnician idol; the Greek Adonis.
Eze. 8. 14 behold, there sat women weeping for T.

TANACH. *See* **TAANACH.**

TAN-HU'-METH, תַּנְחֻמֶת *comfort.*
A Netophathite, whose son Seraiah was one of the captains whom Gedaliah tried to persuade to serve the Chaldeans. B.C. 620.
2 Ki. 25. 23 Seraiah the son of T. the Netophathite
Jer. 40. 8 Seraiah the son of T., and the sons of E.

TANNER —
A tanner, dresser of hides, βυρσεύς *burseus.*
Acts 9. 43 tarried..in Joppa with one Simon a tan.
10. 6 He lodgeth with one Simon a tanner, wh.
10. 32 lodged in the house of (one) Simon a tan.

TAPESTRY, coverings of —
Coverings, מַרְבַדִּים *marbaddim.*
Prov. 7. 16 decked my bed with coverings of tapestry
31. 22 She maketh herself coverings of tapestry

TA'-PHATH, טָפַת *ornament.*
A daughter of Solomon who became the wife of one of his officers. B.C. 1000.
1 Ki. 4. 11 which had T. the daughter of Solomon to

TAP-PU'-AH, תַּפּוּחַ *apple, hill place.*
1. A city in W. of Judah near Hebron, and now called *Teffuk.*
Josh. 12. 17 The king of T., one; the king of Hepher
15. 34 And Zanoah, and En-gannim, T., and E.
2. A city in Ephraim or Manasseh, now called *Atuf.*
Josh. 16. 8 The border went out from T. westward
17. 8 Manasseh had the land of T.: but T. on
3. A son of Hebron. B.C. 1500.
1 Ch. 2. 43 Korah, and T., and Rekem, and Shema

TA'-RAH, תֶּרַח *turning, duration, wandering.*
The twenty-third station of Israel from Egypt, and the twelfth from Sinai; between Tahath and Mithcah.
Num 33. 27 And they departed..and pitched at T.
33. 28 they removed from T., and pitched in M.

TAR-A'-LAH, תַּרְאֲלָה *power of God.*
A city in Benjamin, near Irpeel.
Josh. 18. 27 And Rekem, and Irpeel, and T.

TA-RE'-A, תַּאְרֵעַ *flight.* See *Tahrea.*
A son of Micah, grandson of Jonathan son of Saul. B.C. 1000.
1 Ch. 8. 35 the sons of Micah (were)..Melech, and T.

TARES —
Darnel, a weed like corn, ζιζάνιον *zizanion.*
Matt 13. 25 his enemy came and sowed tares among
13. 26 blade..sprung up..then appeared the ta.
13. 27 sow good seed..whence then hath it tares?
13. 29 lest, while ye gather up the tares, ye root
13. 30 Gather ye together first the tares, and bi.
13. 36 Declare unto us the parable of the tares
13. 38 the tares are the children of the wicked
13. 40 the tares are gathered and burned in the

TARGET —

1. *Halbert, javelin*, כִּידוֹן *kidon.*
1 Sa. 17. 6 and a target of brass between his shoul.

2. *Target, buckler*, צִנָּה *tsinnah.*
1 Ki. 10. 16 Solomon made two hundred targets (of)
10. 16 hundred (shekels) of gold went to one ta.
2 Ch. 9. 15 Solomon made two hundred targets (of)
9. 15 six hundred (shekels)..went to one target
14. 8 an army (of men) that bare targets and

TARPELITES, טַרְפְּלָיֵא.
An Assyrian tribe, in *Tapur*, E. of Elam, or in *Tarpet* in the Maeotic swamp; transported to Samaria by Shalmaneser. B.C. 678.
Ezra 4. 9 the T., the Apharsites, the Archevites, the

TARRY (all night, behind, for, long, longer), to —

1. *To be or keep behind, late*, אָחַר *achar*, 5.
2 Sa. 20. 5 he tarried longer than the set time which

2. *To keep behind, tarry*, אָחַר *achar*, 3.
Judg. 5. 28 cried..why tarry the wheels of his char.?
Psa. 40. 17 thou (art) my help..make no tarrying, O
70. 5 thou (art) my help..O LORD, make no ta.
Prov 23. 30 They that tarry long at the wine; they
Isa. 46. 13 my salvation shall not tarry: and I will
Hab. 2. 3 vision..will surely come, it will not tarry

3. *To cause to be long, prolong*, אָרַךְ *arak*, 5.
Num. 9. 19 when the cloud tarried long upon the ta.
9. 22 the cloud tarried upon the tabernacle, re.

4. *To be silent, cease, stand still*, דָּמַם *damam.*
1 Sa. 14. 9 Tarry until we come to you; then we will

5. *To stay*, חִיל, חוּל *chul, chil.*
Judg. 3. 25 they tarried till they were ashamed; and

6. *To wait earnestly*, חָכָה *chakah*, 3.
2 Ki. 7. 9 if we tarry till the morning light, some
9. 3 Then open the door and flee, and tarry

7. *To wait with hope, stay*, יָחַל *yachal*, 2.
1 Sa. 13. 8 he tarried seven days, according to the

8. *To cause to wait with hope*, יָחַל *yachal*, 5.
1 Sa. 10. 8 seven days shalt thou tarry, till I come
2 Sa. 18. 14 Then said Joab, I may not tarry thus wi.

9. *To be behind, late*, יָחַר *yachar.*
2 Sa. 20. 5 he tarried longer than the set time which

10. *To sit down or still*, יָשַׁב *yashab.*
Gen. 27. 44 tarry with him a few days, until thy br.
Exod 24. 14 Tarry ye here for us, until we come again
Lev. 14. 8 shall tarry abroad out of his tent seven
Num 22. 19 tarry ye also here this night, that I may
Judg. 6. 18 he said, I will tarry until thou come again
Ruth 2. 7 until now, that she tarried a little in the
1 Sa. 1. 23 Do what seemeth thee good; tarry until
14. 2 Saul tarried in the uttermost part of G.
30. 24 so (shall) his part (be) that tarrieth by the
2 Sa. 10. 5 Tarry at Jericho until your beards be gr.
11. 1 But David tarried still at Jerusalem
11. 12 Tarry here to day also, and to morrow I
15. 29 again to Jerusalem; and they tarried th.
2 Ki. 2. 2, 4, 6 Tarry here, I pray thee; for the LORD
2. 18 they came again to him, for he tarried at
14. 10 tarry at home; for why shouldest thou
1 Ch. 19. 5 Tarry at Jericho until your beards be gr.
20. 1 besieged Rabbah. But David tarried at J.

11. *To be prepared, established*, כּוּן *kun*, 2.
Psa. 101. 7 he that telleth lies shall not tarry in my

12. *To pass the night*, לִין, לוּן *lun, lin.*
Gen. 19. 2 tarry all night, and wash your feet, and
24. 54 they did eat and drink..and tarried all
28. 11 tarried there all night, because the sun
Gen. 31. 54 they did eat bread, and tarried all night
Judg 19. 6 tarry all night, and let thine heart be mer.
19. 9 I pray you tarry all night: behold, the
19. 10 the man would not tarry that night, but
Ruth 3. 13 Tarry this night, and it shall be in the m.
2 Sa. 19. 7 there will not tarry one with thee this ni.
Jer. 14. 8 man (that) turneth aside to tarry for a ni.

13. *To tarry, linger, delay*, מָהַהּ *mahah*, 7a.
Exod 12. 39 could not tarry, neither had they prepa.
Judg. 3. 26 Ehud escaped while they tarried, and pa.
19. 8 they tarried until afternoon, and they did
2 Sa. 15. 28 I will tarry in the plain of the wilderness
Hab. 2. 3 though it tarry, wait for it; because it will

14. *Dweller at home*, נָוָה *navah.*
Psa. 68. 12 she that tarried at home divided the sp.

15. *To stand, stand firm*, עָמַד *amad.*
Gen. 45. 9 Thus saith thy son..come down..tarry not
2 Sa. 15. 17 and tarried in a place that was far off

16. *To wait, expect*, קָוָה *qavah*, 3.
Mic. 5. 7 as the showers..that tarrieth not for man

17. *To hope, wait, look for*, שָׂבַר *sabar*, 3.
Ruth 1. 13 Would ye tarry for them till they were

18. *To be slow, to delay*, βραδύνω *bradunō.*
1 Ti. 3. 15 if I tarry long, that thou mayest know how

19. *To rub through, pass the time*, διατρίβω *diatribō.*
John 3. 22 there he tarried with them, and baptized
Acts 25. 6 when he had tarried among them more

20. *To remain on or upon*, ἐπιμένω *epimenō.*
Acts 10. 48 Then prayed they him to tarry certain da.
21. 4 finding disciples, we tarried there seven
21. 10 as we tarried (there) many days, there ca.
28. 12 landing at Syracuse, we tarried (there) th.
28. 14 were desired to tarry with them seven da.
1 Co. 16. 7 I trust to tarry a while with you, if the L.
16. 8 But I will tarry at Ephesus until Pentec.

21. *To sit or set down*, καθίζω *kathizō.*
Luke 24. 49 tarry ye in the city of Jerusalem, until yo

22. *To be about to, delay*, μέλλω *mellō.*
Acts 22. 16 why tarriest thou? arise, and be baptized

23. *To receive in*, ἐκδέχομαι *ekdechomai.*
1 Co. 11. 33 when ye come together to eat, tarry one

24. *To remain*, μένω *menō.*
Matt 26. 38 Then saith he..tarry ye here, and watch
Mark 14. 34 saith unto them..tarry ye here, and watch
Luke 24. 29 And he went in to tarry with them
John 4. 40 they besought him that he would tarry wi.
21. 22, 23 If I will that he tarry till I come, what
Acts 9. 43 he tarried many days in Joppa with one
18. 20 they desired (him) to tarry longer time wi.
20. 5 These going before tarried for us at Troas
20. 15 we arrived at Samos, and tarried at Trog.

25. *To do, make*, ποιέω *poieō.*
Acts 15. 33 after they had tarried (there) a space, they

26. *To look toward, expect*, προσδοκάω *prosdokaō.*
Acts 27. 33 that ye have tarried and continued fasting

27. *To remain toward*, προσμένω *prosmenō.*
Acts 18. 18 Paul (after this) tarried (there) yet a good

28. *To remain under, behind*, ὑπομένω *hupomenō.*
Luke 2. 43 the child Jesus tarried behind in Jerusa.

29. *To delay, defer, tarry*, χρονίζω *chronizō.*
Matt 25. 5 While the bridegroom tarried, they all sl.
Luke 1. 21 marvelled that he tarried so long in the
Heb. 10. 37 yet a little while, and he..will not tarry

TAR'-SHISH, THAR'-SHISH, תַּרְשִׁישׁ *hard.*
1. A son of Javan grandson of Noah; his descendants the *Tyrseni* in Western Italy.
Gen. 10. 4 the sons of Javan; Elishah, and T., Kitt.
1 Ch. 1. 7 the sons of Javan; Elishah, and T., Kitt.
2. Mighty ships fitted for long voyages.
1 Ki. 10. 22 For the king had at sea a navy of T. with
10. 22 once in three years came the navy of T.
22. 48 Jehoshaphat made ships of T. to go to O.
2 Ch. 9. 21 For the king's ships went to T. with the
Psa. 48. 7 Thou breakest the ships of T. with an east
Isa. 2. 16 upon all the ships of T., and upon all pl.
23. 1, 14 Howl, ye ships of T.
60. 9 ships of T. first, to bring thy sons from far
Eze. 27. 25 ships of T. did sing of thee in thy market
3. Son of Bilhan the grandson of Benjamin. B.C. 1600.
1 Ch. 7. 10 Chenaanah, and Zethan, and T., and Ah.
4. Tartessus in Spain; or Carthage in N. of Africa, or Ceylon in S. of India.
[2 Ch. 9. 21; 20. 36, 37; Ps. 72. 10; Isa. 23. 6, 10; 66. 19; Jer 10. 9; Eze. 27. 12; 38. 13; Jon. 1. 3, 3, 3; 4. 2.]
5. One of the seven princes of Persia who saw the king's face at pleasure. B.C. 520.
Esth. 1. 14 the next unto him (was)..T., Meres, Ma.

TARSUS, Ταρσός.
The birthplace of Paul the Apostle, and the capital of Cilicia in Asia Minor on the river Cydnus. It was a noted seat of philosophy and literature, ranking with Athens and Alexandria. Was made a free city by Augustus, being said to have been founded by Sardanapalus B.C. 820; in 401 it was taken and plundered by the younger Cyrus; in 333 it was taken by Alexander the Great; in 47 it sided with Cæsar against Pompey, and took the name of *Juliopolis.* It was seized by the Saracens in the early days of their empire, was taken from them in the second half of the tenth century, but restored; councils were held here in A.D. 431, 435, and 1177,

Acts 9. 11 enquire..for..Saul, of T.: for, behold, he pr.
9. 30 brought him..and sent him forth to T.
11. 25 Then departed Barnabas to T., for to seek
21. 39 Paul said, I am a man..a Jew of T...in C.
22. 3 I am verily a man..a Jew, born in T...in

TAR'-TAK, תַּרְתָּק *hero of darkness.*
A god worshipped by the Avites whom Shalmaneser removed to Samaria.
2 Ki. 17. 31 the Avites made Nibhaz and T., and the

TAR'-TAN, תַּרְתָּן.
An official of Sargon and of Sennacherib, kings of Assyria, sent to Hezekiah. B.C. 710.
2 Ki. 18. 17 the king of Assyria sent T., and Rabsaris
Isa. 20. 1 In the year that T. came unto Ashdod, wh.

TASK, taskmaster —
1. *A word, matter,* דָּבָר *dabar.*
Exod. 5. 13 Fulfil your works, (your) daily tasks, as
5. 19 shall not minish (ought)..of your daily ta.
2. *A statute, statutory work,* חֹק *choq.*
Exod. 5. 14 Wherefore have ye not fulfilled your task
3. *To exact,* נָגַשׂ *nagas.*
Exod. 3. 7 heard their cry by reason of their taskm.
5. 6 commanded the same day the taskmaste.
5. 10 the taskmasters of the people went out
5. 13 the taskmasters hasted (them), saying, F.
5. 14 which Pharaoh's taskmasters had set over
4. *Head or chief of the burden or levy,* שַׂר מַס *sar mas.*
Exod. 1. 11 they did set over them taskmasters to affl.

TASTE (to) —
1. *Palate, taste,* חֵךְ *chek.*
Job 6. 30 cannot my taste discern perverse things?
Psa. 119. 103 How sweet are thy words unto my taste!
Prov 24. 13 the honeycomb, (which is) sweet to thy ta.
Song 2. 3 I sat down..his fruit (was) sweet to my ta.
2. *Taste, reason,* טַעַם *taam.*
Exod 16. 31 the taste of it (was) like wafers (made) wi.
Num 11. 8 the taste of it was as the taste of fresh oil
Job 6. 6 or is there (any) taste in the white of an
Jer. 48. 11 his taste remained in him, and his scent
3. *To taste, perceive,* טָעַם *taam.*
1 Sa. 14. 24 So none of the people tasted (any) food
14. 29 enlightened, because I tasted a little of
14. 43 I did but taste a little honey with the end
2 Sa. 3. 35 if I taste bread, or ought else, till the sun
19. 35 can thy servant taste what I eat or what
Job 12. 11 Doth not..the mouth taste his meat?
34. 3 the ear trieth words, as the mouth tasteth
Psa. 34. 8 O taste and see that the LORD (is) good
Jon. 3. 7 Let neither man nor beast..taste any th.
4. *Taste,* טְעֵם *teem.*
Dan. 5. 2 Belshazzar, whiles he tasted the wine, c.
5. *To taste, experience,* γεύομαι *geuomai.*
Matt 16. 28 There be some..which shall not taste of
27. 34 when he had tasted (thereof), he would
Mark 9. 1 there be some..which shall not taste of
Luke 9. 27 there be some..which shall not taste of
14. 24 none..which were bidden shall taste of
John. 2. 9 When the ruler of the feast had tasted
8. 52 a man keep my saying, he shall never ta.
Col. 2. 21 Touch not; taste not; handle not
Heb. 2. 9 he by the grace of God should taste death
6. 4 have tasted of the heavenly gift, and were
6. 5 have tasted the good word of God, and
1 Pe. 2. 3 If so be ye have tasted that the Lord (is)

TAT'-NAI, תַּתְּנַי.
A governor of the king of Persia on the W. of the Jordan, in Samaria, who opposed the Jews, and wrote to Darius to stop the temple. B.C. 520.
Ezra 5. 3 At the same time came to them T., gov.
5. 6 The copy of the letter that T...sent unto
6. 6 Now..T...and your companions..be ye
6. 13 Then T...Shethar-boznai, and their com.

TATTLER —
A prater, tattler, φλύαρος *phluaros.*
1 Ti. 5. 13 not only idle, but tattlers also and busy.

TAUGHT, (to be) —
1. *To be chastised, instructed,* יָסַר *yasar,* 2.
Eze. 23. 48 that all women may be taught not to do
2. *To be taught,* לָמַד *lamad,* 4.
Isa. 29. 13 their fear toward me is taught by the pr.
Hos. 10. 11 Ephraim (is as) an heifer (that is) taught
3. *Taught, learned,* לִמּוּד *limmud.*
Isa. 54. 13 all thy children (shall be) taught of the
4. *Taught,* διδακτός *didaktos.*
John 6. 45 It is written..they shall be all taught of

TAUGHT, as hath been —
Teaching, doctrine, κατὰ διδαχὴν *kata didachēn.*
Titus 1. 9 Holding fast..as he hath been taught, that

TAUGHT of God —
God taught, θεοδίδακτος *theodidaktos.*
1 Th. 4. 9 ye yourselves are taught of God to love

TAUNT, taunting —
1. *Reviling,* גְּדוּפָה *geduphah.*
Eze. 5. 15 So it shall be a reproach and a taunt, an
2. *A moral, interpretation,* מְלִיצָה *melitsah.*
Hab. 2. 6 Shall not all these take up..a taunting pr.
3. *Sharp saying, byeword,* שְׁנִינָה *sheninah.*
Jer. 24. 9 (to be) a reproach and a proverb, a taunt

TAVERNS. *See* three.

TAX, be taxed, taxation —
1. *To set in array, value,* עָרַךְ *arak,* 5.
2 Ki. 23. 35 he taxed the land to give the money acc.
2. *Array, valuation,* עֵרֶךְ *erek.*
2 Ki. 23. 35 exacted..of every one according to his ta.
3. *A writing off, register,* ἀπογραφή *apographē.*
Luke 2. 2 this taxing was first made when Cyrenius
Acts 5. 37 rose up Judas..in the days of the taxing
4. *To write off, register,* ἀπογράφω *apographō.*
Luke 2. 1 a decree..that all the world should be ta.
2. 3 all went to be taxed, every one into his
2. 5 To be taxed with Mary his espoused wife

TEACH, to — [*See* **KEEP CATTLE.**]
1. *To teach,* אָלַף *alaph,* 3.
Job 33. 33 hold thy peace, and I shall teach thee wi.
35. 11 Who teacheth us more than the beasts of
2. *To cause to understand,* בִּין *bin,* 5.
2 Ch. 35. 3 said unto the Levites that taught all Isr.
Neh. 8. 9 the Levites that taught the people, said
3. *To speak,* דָּבַר *dabar,* 3.
Jer. 28. 16 thou hast taught rebellion against the L.
29. 32 he hath taught rebellion against the LORD
4. *To warn, cause to shine,* זָהַר *zahar,* 5.
Exod 18. 20 thou shalt teach them ordinances and la.
5. *To cause to know,* יָדַע *yada,* 5.
Deut. 4. 9 but teach them thy sons, and thy sons' so.
Judg. 8. 16 and with them he taught the men of Suc.
2 Ch. 23. 13 the singers..and such as taught to sing
Job 32. 7 and multitude of years should teach wis.
37. 19 Teach us what we shall say unto him; (for)
Psa. 90. 12 So teach (us) to number our days, that we
Prov. 9. 9 teach a just (man), and he will increase
Isa. 40. 13 or, (being) his counsellor, hath taught him?
6. *To cause to know,* יְדַע *yeda,* 5.
Ezra 7. 25 and teach ye them that know (them) not
7. *To chastise, instruct, teach,* יָסַר *yasar,* 3.
Prov 31. 1 the prophecy that his mother taught him
8. *To cast, show, direct, teach,* יָרָה *yarah,* 5.
Exod. 4. 12 I will be with thy mouth, and teach thee
4. 15 and will teach you what ye shall do
24. 12 commandments..that thou mayest teach
35. 34 he hath put in his heart that he may teach
Lev. 10. 11 that ye may teach the children of Israel
14. 57 To teach when (it is) unclean, and when
Deut 17. 11 sentence of the law which they shall teach
24. 8 all that the priests the Levites shall teach
33. 10 They shall teach Jacob thy judgments, and
Judg 13. 8 teach us what we shall do unto the child
1 Sa. 12. 23 I will teach you the good and the right
1 Ki. 8. 36 that thou teach them the good way wher.
2 Ki. 17. 27 let him teach them the manner of the God
17. 28 taught them how they should fear the L.
2 Ch. 6. 27 when thou hast taught them the good way
Job 6. 24 Teach me, and I will hold my tongue
8. 10 Shall not they teach thee, (and) tell thee
12. 7 ask now the beasts, and they shall teach
12. 8 speak to the earth, and it shall teach thee
27. 11 I will teach you by the hand of God: (that)
34. 32 (That which) I see not, teach thou me
36. 22 God exalteth by his power: who teacheth
Psa. 25. 8 therefore will he teach sinners in the way
25. 12 him shall he teach in the way (that) he sh.
27. 11 Teach me thy way, O LORD, and lead me
32. 8 I will instruct thee and teach thee in the
45. 4 thy right hand shall teach thee terrible
86. 11 Teach me thy way, O LORD; I will walk
119. 33 Teach me, O LORD, the way of thy statut.
119. 102 I have not departed..for thou hast tau.
Prov. 4. 4 He taught me also, and said unto me, Let
4. 11 I have taught thee in the way of wisdom
6. 13 he speaketh with his feet, he teacheth wi.
Isa. 2. 3 he will teach us of his ways, and we will
9. 15 the prophet that teacheth lies, he (is) the
28. 9 Whom shall he teach knowledge? and w.
28. 26 God doth instruct..(and) doth teach him
Eze. 44. 23 they shall teach my people (the difference)
Mic. 3. 11 the priests thereof teach for hire, and the
4. 2 he will teach us of his ways, and we will
Hab. 2. 19 to the dumb stone, Arise, it shall teach!
9. *To teach,* לָמַד *lamad,* 3.
Deut. 4. 1 and unto the judgments, which I teach
4. 5 I have taught you statutes and judgments
4. 10 and (that) they may teach their children
4. 14 commanded me at that time to teach you
5. 31 the judgments, which thou shalt teach
6. 1 the LORD your God commanded to teach
11. 19 ye shall teach them your children, speak,
20. 18 That they teach you not to do after all th.
31. 19 write ye this song for you, and teach it
31. 22 Moses therefore..taught it the children of
Judg. 3. 2 the children of Israel might know to tea.
2 Sa. 1. 18 he bade them teach the children of Judah
22. 35 He teacheth my hands to war; so that a
2 Ch. 17. 7 he sent to his princes..to teach in the ci.
17. 9 they taught in Judah, and (had) the book
17. 9 and went about..and taught the people
Ezra 7. 10 and to teach in Israel statutes and judg.
Job 21. 22 Shall (any) teach God knowledge? seeing
Psa. 18. 34 He teacheth my hands to war, so that a
25. 4 Show me thy ways, O LORD; teach me thy
25. 5 Lead me in thy truth, and teach me: for
Psa. 25. 9 and the meek will he teach his way
34. 11 hearken unto me; I will teach you the
51. 13 (Then) will I teach transgressors thy ways
60. *title.* To the chief Musician..to teach: when
71. 17 thou hast taught me from my youth: and
94. 10 he that teacheth man knowledge, (shall
94. 12 thou..LORD..teachest him out of thy law
119. 12, 26, 64, 68, 124, 135 teach me thy statutes
119. 66 Teach me good judgment and knowledge
119. 108 I beseech thee..teach me thy judgments
119. 171 when thou hast taught me thy statutes
132. 12 and my testimony that I shall teach them
143. 10 Teach me to do thy will; for thou (art) my
144. 1 which teacheth my hands to war, (and)
Eccl. 12. 9 the preacher was wise, he still taught the
Isa. 40. 14 taught him in the path of judgment, and
48. 17 the LORD thy God which teacheth thee to
Jer. 2. 33 therefore hast thou also taught the wic.
9. 5 they have taught their tongue to speak
9. 14 after Baalim, which their fathers taught
9. 20 teach your daughters wailing, and every
12. 16 as they taught my people to swear by B.
13. 21 thou hast taught them (to be) captains
31. 34 they shall teach no more every man his
32. 33 I taught them, rising up early and teach.
Dan. 1. 4 whom they might teach the learning and
10. *To cause to act wisely,* שָׂכַל *sakal,* 5.
2 Ch. 30. 22 the Levites that taught the good know.
Prov 16. 23 The heart of the wise teacheth his mouth
11. *Taught,* διδακτός *didaktos.*
1 Co. 2. 13 not in the words which man's wisdom te.
2. 13 but which the Holy Ghost teacheth; com.
12. *To teach,* διδάσκω *didaskō.*
Matt. 4. 23 teaching in their synagogues, and preach.
5. 2 he opened his mouth, and taught them
5. 19 Whosoever..shall teach men so, he shall
5. 19 whosoever shall do and teach (them), the
7. 29 he taught them as (one) having authority
9. 35 teaching in their synagogues, and preach.
11. 1 he departed thence, to teach and to preach
13. 54 he taught them in their synagogue, inso.
15. 9 teaching (for) doctrines the commandme.
21. 23 the elders..came unto him as he was te.
22. 16 thou art true, and teachest the way of
26. 55 I sat daily with you [teaching] in the te.
28. 15 took the money, and did as they were ta.
28. 20 Teaching them to observe all things wh.
Mark 1. 21 he entered into the synagogue, and tau.
1. 22 for he taught them as one that had auth.
2. 13 resorted unto him, and he taught them
4. 1 he began again to teach by the sea side
4. 2 he taught them many things by parables
6. 2 he began to teach in the synagogue: and
6. 6 he went round about the villages, teach.
6. 30 what they had done, and what they had t.
6. 34 and he began to teach them many things
7. 7 teaching (for) doctrines the commandm.
8. 31 he began to teach them, that the Son of
9. 31 he taught his disciples, and said unto th.
10. 1 and, as he was wont, he taught them ag.
11. 17 he taught, saying unto them, Is it not wr.
12. 14 for thou..teachest the way of God in tru.
12. 35 Jesus answered and said, while he taught
14. 49 I was daily with you..teaching, and ye
Luke 4. 15 he taught in their synagogues, being glo.
4. 31 and taught them on the sabbath days
5. 3 he sat down, and taught the people out
5. 17 on a certain day, as he was teaching, that
6. 6 he entered into the synagogue and taught
11. 1 teach us to pray, as John also taught his
12. 12 the Holy Ghost shall teach you in the same
13. 10 he was teaching in one of the synagogues
13. 22 teaching and journeying toward Jerusal.
13. 26 We have eaten..and thou hast taught in
19. 47 And he taught daily in the temple
20. 1 he taught the people in the temple, and
20. 21 thou sayest and teachest rightly, neither
20. 21 we know that thou..teachest the way of
21. 37 in the day time he was teaching in the te.
23. 5 He stirreth up the people, teaching thro.
John 6. 59 These things said he..as he taught in Ca.
7. 14 Jesus went up into the temple, and tau.
7. 28 Then cried Jesus in the temple, as he ta.
7. 35 will he go..among the Gentiles, and tea.
8. 2 [people came unto him; and he..taught]
8. 20 These words spake Jesus..as he taught in
8. 28 as my Father hath taught me, I speak th.
9. 34 born in sins, and dost thou teach us?
14. 26 he shall teach you all things, and bring
18. 20 I ever taught in the synagogue, and in the
Acts 1. 1 all that Jesus began both to do and teach
4. 2 Being grieved that they taught the peop.
4. 18 commanded them not to..teach in the na.
5. 21 they entered into the temple..and taught
5. 25 standing in the temple, and teaching the
5. 28 command you, that ye should not teach
5. 42 they ceased not to teach and preach Jesus
11. 26 they assembled..and taught much people
15. 1 certain men which came..taught the br.
15. 35 teaching and preaching the word of the
18. 11 he continued..teaching the word of God
18. 25 taught diligently the things of the Lord
20. 20 have taught you publicly, and from hou.
21. 21 thou teachest all the Jews which are among
21. 28 This is the man that teacheth all (men) ev.
28. 31 teaching those things which concern the
Rom. 2. 21 Thou..which teachest another, teachest
12. 7 Or ministry..or he that teacheth, on
1 Co. 4. 17 my ways..as I teach every where in every
11. 14 Doth not even nature itself teach you, that

Gal. 1. 12 neither was I taught (it), but by the rev.
Eph. 4. 21 ye have heard him, and have been taught
Col. 1. 28 warning every man, and teaching every
2. 7 stablished in the faith, as ye have been ta.
3. 16 teaching and admonishing one another in
2 Th. 2. 15 the traditions which ye have been taught
1 Ti. 2. 12 I suffer not a woman to teach, nor to us.
4. 11 These things command and teach
6. 2 do (them) service. These things teach and
2 Ti. 2. 2 faithful men, who shall be able to teach
Titus 1. 11 teaching things which they ought not, for
Heb. 5. 12 ye have need that one teach you again wh.
8. 11 they shall not teach every man his neigh.
1 Jo. 2. 27 and ye need not that any man teach you
2. 27 as the same anointing teacheth you of all
2. 27 even as it hath taught you, ye shall abide
Rev. 2. 14 who taught Balac to cast a stumbling bl.
Rev. 2. 20 to teach and to seduce my servants to ec.

13. *To tell down or thoroughly*, καταγγέλλω *katag.*
Acts 16. 21 teach customs, which are not lawful for

14. *To sound down, instruct orally*, κατηχέω *katēcheō.*
1 Co. 14. 19 that (by my voice) I might teach others
Gal. 6. 6 Let him that is taught in the word
6. 6 communicate unto him that teacheth in

15. *To be or make a disciple, teach*, μαθητεύω *math.*
Matt. 28. 19 Go ye therefore, and teach all nations, ba.
Acts 14. 21 when they had preached..and had taught

16. *To train, instruct*, παιδεύω *paideuō.*
Acts 22. 3 taught according to the perfect manner of
Titus 2. 12 Teaching us that, denying ungodliness and

TEACH diligently, to —

To sharpen, repeat, שָׁנַן *shanan*, 3.
Deut. 6. 7 thou shalt teach them diligently unto thy

TEACH other doctrine or otherwise, to —

To teach other or different things, ἑτεροδιδασκαλέω.
1 Ti. 1. 3 charge some that they teach no other doctr.
6. 3 If any man teach otherwise, and consent

TEACHER, teaching —

1. *To cause to understand*, בִּין *bin*, 5.
1 Ch. 25. 8 the small as the great, the teacher as the

2. *To cast, show, direct, teach*, יָרָה *yarah*, 5.
2 Ch. 15. 3 without a teaching priest, and without law
Prov. 5. 13 have not obeyed the voice of my teachers
Isa. 30. 20 yet shall not thy teachers be removed in.
30. 20 but thine eyes shall see thy teachers
Hab. 2. 18 the molten image, and a teacher of lies

3. *To interpret*, לוּץ *luts*, 5.
Isa. 43. 27 thy teachers have trangressed against me

4. *To teach*, לָמַד *lamad*, 3.
Psa. 119. 99 more understanding than all my teachers

5. *Teacher, instructor*, διδάσκαλος *didaskalos.*
John 3. 2 we know that thou art a teacher come fr.
Acts 13. 1 there were..certain prophets and teach.
Rom. 2. 20 a teacher of babes, which hast the form
1 Co. 12. 28 secondarily prophets, thirdly teachers, af.
12. 29 (are) all prophets? (are) all teachers? (are)
Eph. 4. 11 evangelists; and some, pastors and teac.
1 Ti. 2. 7 a teacher of the Gentiles in faith and ve.
2 Ti. 1. 11 an apostle, and a teacher of the Gentiles
4. 3 shall they heap to themselves teachers
Heb. 5. 12 when for the time ye ought to be teachers

6. *Teaching, instruction*, διδασκαλία *didaskalia.*
Rom 12. 7 (let us wait) on (our) ministering..on te.

TEACHER (of the law, of good things, false) —

1. *Teacher of good*, καλοδιδάσκαλος *kalodidaskalos.*
Titus 2. 3 not given to much wine, teachers of good t.

2. *Teacher of law*, νομοδιδάσκαλος *nomodidaskalos.*
1 Ti. 1. 7 Desiring to be teachers of the law: unde.

3. *A teacher of lies or falsehood*, ψευδοδιδάσκαλος.
2 Pe. 2. 1 there shall be false teachers among you

TEAR (in pieces, be torn), to —

1. *To cleave, rend, rip up, hatch*, בָּקַע *baqa*, 3.
2 Ki. 2. 24 and tare forty and two children of
Hos. 13. 8 devour them..the wild beast shall tear

2. *To take violently away*, גָּזַל *gazal.*
Mal. 1. 13 ye brought (that which was) torn, and the

3. *To tread down, thresh*, דּוּשׁ *dush.*
Judg 8. 7 I will tear your flesh with the thorns of

4. *To tear*, טָרַף *taraph.*
Deut 33. 20 teareth the arm with the crown of the he.
Job 16. 9 He teareth (me) in his wrath, who hateth
18. 4 He teareth himself in his anger: shall the
Psa. 7. 2 Lest he tear my soul like a lion, rending
50. 22 lest I tear (you) in pieces, and (there be)
Hos. 5. 14 I, even I, will tear and go away; I will
6. 1 he hath torn, and he will heal us; he hath
Amos. 1. 11 his anger did tear perpetually, and he kept
Mic. 5. 8 both treadeth down, and teareth in pieces
Nah 2. 12 The lion did tear in pieces enough for his

5. *To be torn*, טָרַף *taraph*, 2.
Exod 22. 13 If it be torn in pieces..let him bring it
Jer. 5. 6 every one that goeth..shall be torn in pie.

6. *To be torn*, טָרַף *taraph*, 4.
Gen. 44. 28 Surely he is torn in pieces; and I saw him

7. *To draw, tear*, סָחַב *sachab.*
Jer. 15. 3 the sword to slay, and the dogs to tear

8. *To deal out*, פָּרַס *paras.*
Jer. 16. 7 Neither shall (men) tear (themselves) for

9. *To break off, rend*, פָּרַק *paraq.*
Zec. 11. 16 of the fat, and tear their claws in pieces

10. *To rend away, cut off*, קָרַע *qara.*
2 Sa. 13. 31 the king arose, and tare his garments, and
Psa. 35. 15 the abjects..they did tear (me), and ceased
Eze. 13. 20 I will tear them from your arms, and will
13. 21 Your kerchiefs also will I tear, and deliver

11. *To break in pieces*, שָׁבַר *shabar.*
1 Ki. 13. 26 the lion, which had torn him, and slain
13. 28 had not eaten the carcase, nor torn the ass

12. *To break, burst, rend, tear*, ῥήγνυμι *rhēgnumi.*
Mark 9. 18 wheresoever he taketh him, he teareth

13. *To draw out and beat, tear, lacerate*, σπαράσσω.
Mark 1. 26 when the unclean spirit had torn him, and
9. 20 when he saw him..the spirit [tare] him
Luke 9. 39 it teareth him that he foameth again, and

14. *To tear or lacerate together*, συσπαράσσω *susp.*
Luke 9. 42 the devil threw him down, and tare (him)

TEARS, (with) —

1. *To weep*, בָּכָה *bakah.*
Esth. 8. 3 besought him with tears to put away the

2. *A tear*, דִּמְעָה *dimah.*
2 Ki. 20. 5 have heard thy prayer, I have seen thy te.
Psa. 6. 6 I am weary..I water my couch with myt.
39. 12 hold not thy peace at my tears: for I (am)
42. 3 My tears have been my meat day and ni.
56. 8 put thou my tears into thy bottle: (are
80. 5 Thou feedest them with the bread of tea.
80. 5 givest them tears to drink in great meas.
116. 8 mine eyes from tears, (and) my feet from
126. 5 They that sow in tears shall reap in joy
Eccl. 4. 1 behold the tears of (such as were) oppre.
Isa. 16. 9 I will water thee with my tears, O Hesh.
25. 8 the Lord GOD will wipe away tears from
38. 5 heard thy prayer, I have seen thy tears
Jer. 9. 1 and mine eyes a fountain of tears, that I
9. 18 that our eyes may run down with tears
13. 17 shall weep sore, and run down with tears
14. 17 Let mine eyes run down with tears night
31. 16 Refrain..thine eyes from tears: for thy
Lam. 1. 2 weepeth sore in the night, and her tears
2. 11 Mine eyes do fail with tears, my bowels
2. 18 let tears run down like a river day and
Eze. 24. 16 nor weep, neither shall thy tears run do.
Mal. 2. 13 covering the altar of the LORD with tea.

3. *A tear*, δάκρυ *dakru.*
Mark 9. 24 the father..cried out, and said [with tears]
Luke 7. 38 began to wash his feet with tears, and did
7. 44 she hath washed my feet with tears, and
Acts 20. 19 Serving the Lord..with many tears, and
20. 31 warn every one night and day with tears
2 Co. 2. 4 I wrote unto you with many tears, not th.
2 Ti. 1. 4 being mindful of thy tears, that I may be
Heb. 5. 7 supplications, with strong crying and te.
12. 17 though he sought it carefully with tears
Rev. 7. 17 God shall wipe away all tears from their
21. 4 God shall wipe away all tears from their

TEAT —

1. *Breast, teat*, דַּד *dad.*
Eze. 23. 3 there they bruised the teats of their virg.
23. 21 in bruising thy teats by the Egyptians for

2. *Breast, teat*, שַׁד *shad.*
Isa. 32. 12 They shall lament for the teats, for the

TE'-BAH, טֶבַח *thick, strong.*
A son of Nahor the brother of Abraham. B.C. 1860.
Gen. 22. 24 she bare also T., and Gaham, and Thah.

TE-BAL'-IAH, טְבַלְיָהוּ *Jah is protector.*
A son of Hosah, a Merarite, a gatekeeper for the tabernacle in the days of David. B.C. 1015.
1 Ch. 26. 11 Hilkiah the second, T. the third, Zechariah

TE'-BETH, טֵבֵת *winter.*
The tenth Jewish month, from the new moon of January till that of February.
Esth. 2. 16 the tenth month, which (is) the month T.

TEDIOUS unto, to be —

To cut in, interrupt, ἐγκόπτω *egkoptō.*
Acts 24. 4 that I be not further tedious unto thee

TEETH, (cheek, great, jaw) —

1. *Possessor of edges*, בַּעַל פִּיפִיּוֹת [*baal*].
Isa. 41. 15 sharp threshing instrument having teeth

2. *Jaw or great teeth*, מַלְתָּעוֹת *maltaoth.*
Psa. 58. 6 break out the great teeth of the young

3. *Jaw or great teeth*, מְתַלְּעוֹת *methalleoth.*
Prov. 30. 14 and their jaw teeth (as) knives, to devour
Joel 1. 6 he hath the cheek teeth of a great lion
[*See also* Tooth.]

TE-HAPH-NE'-HES, תְּחַפְנְחֵס.
Another form of *Tahpanhes.*
Eze. 30. 18 At T. also the day shall be darkened, wh.

TE-HIN'-NAH, תְּחִנָּה *entreaty.*
A son of Eshton, a descendant of Judah and father of Ir-na-hash. B.C. 1400.
1 Ch. 4. 12 and T. the father of Ir-nahash. These (are)

TEIL tree —

An oak, אֵלָה *elah.*
Isa. 6. 13 as a teil tree, and as an oak, whose sub.

TE'-KEL, תְּקֵל *weighed.*
Dan. 5. 25 this (is) the writing..Mene, Mene, T., U-.
5. 27 T.; Thou art weighed in the balances, and

TE-KO'-AH, TE-KO'-A, תְּקוֹעַ *firm, settlement.*
1. A city in Judah, six miles S.E. of Bethlehem, and twelve S. of Jerusalem, and now called *Tekua*; here dwelt the wise woman who interceded with David; also the prophet Amos.
2 Sa. 14. 2 Joab sent to T., and fetched thence a wise
14. 4 when the woman of T. spake to the king
14. 9 the woman of T. said unto the king, My
2 Ch. 11. 6 He built..Beth-lehem, and Etam, and T.
20. 20 went forth into the wilderness of T.
Jer. 6. 1 blow the trumpet in T., and set up a sign
Amos 1. 1 Amos, who was among the herdmen of T.

2. Family or possession of Asshur, a descendant of Hezron grandson of Judah.
1 Ch. 2. 24 Hezron's wife bare..Ashur the father of T.
4. 5 Ashur the father of T. had two wives, He.

TEKOITE, תְּקוֹעִי, תְּקֹעִי.
An inhabitant of the preceding city.
2 Sa. 23. 26 Helez..Ira the son of Ikkesh the T.
1 Ch. 11. 28 Ira the son of Ikkesh the T., Abi-ezer the
27. 9 sixth..(was) Ira the son of Ikkesh the T.
Neh. 3. 5 next unto them the T. repaired; but the
3. 27 After them the T. repaired another piece

TEL A'-BIB, תֵּל אָבִיב *hill of grass.*
A height on the river Chebar or Chaboras, where Ezekiel stayed with the Jewish exiles a week.
Eze. 3. 15 I came to them of the captivity at T., th.

TEL HA-RE'-SHA, (HARSHA) תֵּל חַרְשָׁא *hill of the magus.*
A height on the river Chebar or Chaboras, whence some Jewish exiles returned to Jerusalem. B.C. 536.
Ezra 2. 59 these (were) they which went up from..T
Neh. 7. 61 they which went up..from Tel-melah, T.

TEL ME'-LAH, תֵּל מֶלַח *hill of salt.*
A height on the river Chebar or Chaboras, whence some Jewish exiles returned who could not prove their genealogy.
Ezra 2. 59 these (were) they which went up from T.
Neh. 7. 61 these (were) they which went up..from T.

TE'-LAH, תֶּלַח *vigour.*
Father of Tahan, and a descendant of Ephraim through Beriah. B.C. 1640.
1 Ch. 7. 25 Resheph, and T. his son, and Tahan his

TE-LA'-IM, טְלָאִים *lambs.* See *Telem.*
A place in Judah, near Edom
1 Sa. 15. 4 Saul..numbered them in T., two hundred

TELASSAR. *See* **THELASSAR.**

TE'-LEM, טֶלֶם *a lamb.* See *Telaim.*
1. A city in Judah near Ziph or Bealoth.
Josh. 15. 24 Ziph, and T., and Bealoth
2. A gatekeeper of the sanctuary who returned from exile, and had married a strange wife. B.C. 445.
Ezra. 10. 24 of the porters; Shallum, and T., and Uri

TELL (out), to —

1. *To say, (lift up the voice,)*, אָמַר *amar.*
Gen. 22. 2 the mountains which I will tell thee of
22. 3 unto the place of which God had told him
22. 9 came to the place..God had told him of
26. 2 dwell in the land which I shall tell thee of
41. 24 I told (this) unto the magicians; but (th.)
48. 1 that (one) told Joseph, Behold, thy father
Exod. 5. 1 Aaron went in, and told Pharaoh, Thus
Num 14. 14 they will tell (it) to the inhabitants of th.
29. 40 Moses told the children of Israel accord.
Deut 17. 11 the judgment which they shall tell thee
32. 7 ask..thy elders, and they will tell thee
Judg 13. 6 the woman came and told her husband
1 Sa. 8. 10 Samuel told all the words of the LORD un.
23. 22 it is told me (that) he dealeth very subtl.
2 Sa. 7. 5 tell my servant David, Thus saith the L.
12. 18 how..if we tell him that the child is dead?
1 Ki. 14. 7 tell Jeroboam, Thus saith the LORD God
18. 8, 11, 14 go, tell thy lord, Behold, Elijah (is
20. 9 Tell my lord the king, All that thou didst
22. 18 Did I not tell thee that he would proph.
2 Ki. 6. 10 the place which the man of God told him
8. 14 He told me (that) thou shouldest surely
20. 5 tell Hezekiah the captain of my people
22. 15 Thus saith the LORD..Tell the man that
23. 17 the men of the city told him, (It is) the
1 Ch. 17. 4 tell David my servant, Thus saith the LORD
2 Ch. 18. 17 Did I not tell thee (that) he would not pr.
34. 23 Thus saith the LORD..Tell ye the man th.
Job 8. 10 Shall not they teach thee, (and) tell thee
34. 34 Let men of understanding tell me, and
Psa. 50. 12 If I were hungry, I would not tell thee
Isa. 6. 9 tell this people, Hear ye indeed, but und.
Jer. 15. 2 thou shalt tell them, Thus saith the LORD
28. 13 tell Hananiah, saying, Thus saith the LO.
34. 2 speak to Zedekiah king of Judah, and tell
35. 13 tell the men of Judah, and the inhabitan.
Eze. 3. 11 tell them, Thus saith the Lord GOD, whe.
12. 23 Tell them therefore, Thus saith the LORD
17. 12 tell (them), Behold, the king of Babylon

2. *To say*, אֲמַר *amar.*
Dan. 2. 4 tell thy servants the dream, and we will
2. 7 Let the king tell his servants the dream
2. 9 tell me the dream, and I shall know that
2. 36 we will tell the interpretation thereof be.
4. 7 I told the dream before them, but they did
4. 8 and before him I told the dream, (saying)
4. 9 tell me the visions of my dream that I h.
7. 1 he wrote the dream, (and) told the sum
7. 16 he told me, and made me know the inte.

3. *To uncover (the ear of)*, (אֹזֶן) גָּלָה, *galah (ozen)*.
1 Sa. 9. 15 the LORD had told Samuel in his ear a
1 Ch. 17. 25 thou, O my God, has told thy servant th.

4. *To speak, (lead forth words)*, דָּבַר *dabar*.
Psa. 101. 7 he that telleth lies shall not tarry in my

5. *To speak (lead forth words)*, דָּבַר *dabar*, 3.
Gen. 20. 8 called all his servants, and told all these
24. 33 I will not eat, until I have told mine err.
45. 27 they told him all the words of Joseph, wh.
Exod. 9. 1 Go in unto Pharaoh, and tell him, Thus
14. 12 (Is) not this the word that we did tell th.
Lev. 21. 24 Moses told (it) unto Aaron, and to his sons
Num 11. 24 Moses went out, and told the people the
14. 39 Moses told these sayings unto all the chi.
23. 26 Told not I thee, saying, All that the LORD
Judg 16. 10, 13 thou hast mocked me, and told me lies
20. 3 Then said the children of Israel, Tell (us)
1 Sa. 10. 25 Samuel told the people the manner of the
11. 4 told the tidings in the ears of the people
2 Sa. 11. 19 When thou hast made an end of telling
1 Ki. 13. 25 they came and told (it) in the city where
14. 2 the prophet, which told me that (I should
20. 11 Tell (him), Let not him that girdeth on (his
22. 16 I adjure thee that thou tell me nothing
2 Ki. 1. 7 came up to meet you, and told you these
1 Ch. 21. 10 Go and tell David, saying, Thus saith the
Psa. 41. 6 (when) he goeth abroad, he telleth (it)
Jer. 19. 2 proclaim there the words that I shall tell
Zech. 10. 2 have seen a lie, and have told false drea.

6. *To cause to know*, יָדַע *yada*, 5.
1 Sa. 6. 2 tell us wherewith we shall send it to his
Isa. 5. 5 I will tell you what I will do to my vine.

7. *To number, count, appoint*, מָנָה *manah*.
2 Ki. 12. 10 they put up in bags, and told the money (th.
Psa. 147. 4 He telleth the number of the stars; he ca.
Jer. 33. 13 under the hands of him that telleth (them)

8. *To put before, declare*, נָגַד *nagad*, 5.
Gen. 3. 11 Who told thee that thou (wast) naked?
9. 22 And Ham..told his two brethren without
12. 18 why didst thou not tell me that she (was)
14. 13 there came one that had escaped, and told
21. 26 neither didst thou tell me, neither yet he.
24. 23 Whose daughter (art) thou? tell me, I pray
24. 28 the damsel ran, and told (them of) her mo.
24. 49 tell me: and if not, tell me; that I may
26. 32 told him concerning the well which they
29. 12 Jacob told Rachel..and she ran and told
29. 15 Laban said..tell me, what (shall) thy wa.
31. 20 Jacob stole away..in that he told him not
31. 27 didst not tell me, that I might have sent
32. 5 I have sent to tell my lord, that I may find
32. 29 Jacob asked (him), and said, Tell (me), I
37. 5 Joseph dreamed a dream, and he told (it)
37. 16 tell me, I pray thee, where they feed (th.
42. 29 and told him all that befell unto them
43. 6 (as) to tell the man whether ye had yet a
43. 7 we told him according to the tenor of th.
44. 24 when we came..we told him the words of
45. 13 ye shall tell my father of all my glory in
45. 26 told him, saying, Joseph (is) yet alive, and
47. 1 Joseph came and told Pharaoh, and said
48. 2 (one) told Jacob, and said, Behold, thy son
49. 1 that I may tell you (that) which shall bef.
Exod. 4. 28 Moses told Aaron all the words of the L.
16. 22 the rulers of the congregation..told Moses
19. 3 Thus shalt thou..tell the children of Isr.
19. 9 Moses told the words of the people unto
Lev. 14. 35 he that owneth the house shall..tell the
Num 11. 27 there ran a young man, and told Moses
23. 3 whatsoever he showeth me I will tell thee
Josh. 7. 19 tell me now what thou hast done; hide
Judg. 9. 7 when they told (it) to Jotham, he went and
9. 42 the people went out..and they told Abi.
13. 6 asked..not..neither told he me his name
14. 2 he came up, and told his father and his
14. 6 he told not his father or his mother what
14. 9 he told not them that he had taken the ho.
14. 16 put forth a riddle..and hast not told (it)
14. 16 I have not told (it)..shall I tell (it) thee?
14. 17 he told her, because she lay sore upon him
14. 17 she told the riddle to the children of her
16. 6 Tell me, I pray thee, wherein thy great
16. 10 tell me, I pray thee, wherewith thou mi.
16. 13 tell me wherewith thou mightest be bound
16. 15 hast not told me wherein thy great stre.
16. 17 he told her all his heart, and said unto her
16. 18 Delilah saw that he had told her all his
Ruth 3. 4 and he will tell thee what thou shalt do
3. 16 she told her all that the man had done to
4. 4 tell me, that I may know: for (there is)
1 Sa. 3. 13 I have told him that I will judge his ho.
3. 18 Samuel told him every whit, and hid no.
4. 13 the man came into the city, and told (it)
4. 14 And the man came in hastily, and told Eli
9. 8 (that) will I give to the man of God to tell
9. 18 Tell me, I pray thee, where the seer's ho.
9. 19 and will tell thee all that (is) in thine he.
10. 15 Tell me, I pray thee, what Samuel said
10. 16 He told us plainly that the asses were fo.
10. 16 the matter of the kingdom..he told him
14. 1 let us go over..But he told not his father
14. 33 they told Saul, saying, Behold, the people
14. 43 Saul said to Jonathan, Tell me what thou
14. 43 Jonathan told him, and said, I did but ta.
15. 16 I will tell thee what the LORD hath said
18. 20 they told Saul, and the thing pleased him
18. 24 the servants of Saul told him, saying, On
1 Sa. 18. 26 when his servants told David these words
19. 2 Jonathan told David, saying, Saul my fa.
19. 3 and what I see, that I will tell thee
19. 11 David's wife, told him, saying, If thou sa.
19. 18 told him all that Saul had done to him
19. 21 when it was told Saul, he sent other
20. 9 if I knew..then would not I tell it thee
20. 10 Who shall tell me? or what (if) thy father
22. 22 I knew..that he would surely tell Saul
23. 1 they told David, saying, Behold, the Ph.
23. 11 O LORD God..I beseech thee, tell thy se.
23. 25 they told David: wherefore he came do.
24. 1 it was told him, saying, Behold, David (is)
25. 12 and came and told him all those sayings
25. 14 one of the young men told Abigail, Nab.
25. 19 But she told not her husband Nabal
25. 36 she told him nothing, less or more, until
25. 37 and his wife had told him these things, that
27. 11 Lest they should tell on us, saying, So did
2 Sa. 1. 4 How went the matter? I pray thee, tell
1. 5, 13 said unto the young man that told him
1. 6 the young man that told him, said, As I
1. 20 Tell (it) not in Gath, publish (it) not in the
2. 4 they told David, saying, (That) the men
3. 23 told Joab, saying, Abner the son of Ner
4. 10 When one told me, saying, Behold, Saul
7. 11 the LORD telleth thee that he will make
10. 5 When they told (it) unto David, he sent
11. 5 the woman conceived, and sent and told
11. 10 when they had told David, saying, Uriah
11. 18 Joab sent and told David all the things
12. 18 the servants of David feared to tell him
13. 4 he said unto him..wilt thou not tell me?
14. 33 So Joab came to the king, and told him
15. 31 (one) told David, saying, Ahithophel (is)
15. 35 thou shalt tell (it) to Zadok and Abiathar
17. 16 tell David, saying, Lodge not this night
17. 17 told them; and they went and told king
17. 18 a lad saw them, and told Absalom: but
17. 21 went and told king David, and said unto
18. 10 a certain man saw (it), and told Joab, and
18. 11 Joab said unto the man that told him, And
18. 21 Then said Joab to Cushi, Go tell the king
18. 25 And the watchman cried, and told the ki.
19. 8 they told unto all the people, saying, Be.
24. 13 Gad came to David, and told him, and said
1 Ki. 1. 20 that thou shouldest tell them who shall
1. 23 they told the king, saying, Behold Nathan
2. 39 they told Shimei, saying, Behold, thy se.
10. 3 And Solomon told her all her questions
10. 3 there was not (any) thing..he told her not
14. 3 he shall tell thee what shall become of the
18. 12 when I come and tell Ahab, and he cann.
18. 16 Obadiah went to meet Ahab, and told him
19. 1 Ahab told Jezebel all that Elijah had done
20. 17 they told him, saying, There are men come
2 Ki. 4. 2 What shall I do for thee? tell me, what
4. 7 Then she came and told the man of God
4. 27 hath hid (it) from me, and hath not told
4. 31 he went again to meet him, and told him
5. 4 (one) went in, and told his lord, saying
6. 12 Elisha..telleth the king of Israel the wo.
7. 9 we may go and tell the king's household
7. 10 they told them, saying, We came to the
7. 11 and they told (it) to the king's house wit.
7. 15 the messengers returned, and told the king
9. 12 And they said, (It is) false; tell us now
9. 15 let none go forth..to tell (it) in Jezreel
9. 18 the watchman told, saying, The messenger
9. 20 the watchman told, saying, He came even
9. 36 Wherefore they came again, and told him
10. 8 there came a messenger, and told him, sa.
18. 37 Then came Eliakim..and told him the wo.
1 Ch. 17. 10 I tell thee that the LORD will build thee
19. 5 there went (certain) and told David how
2 Ch. 9. 2 And Solomon told her all her questions
9. 2 there was nothing hid..which he told her
20. 2 there came some that told Jehoshaphat
34. 18 the scribe told the king, saying, Hilkiah
Neh. 2. 12 neither told I (any) man what my God had
2. 16 neither had I as yet told (it) to the Jews
2. 18 I told them of the hand of my God which
Esth. 2. 22 Mordecai, who told (it) unto Esther the
3. 4 they told Haman, to see whether Morde.
3. 4 for he had told them that he (was) a Jew
4. 4 and her chamberlains came and told (it)
4. 7 Mordecai told him of all that had happe.
4. 9 Hatach came and told Esther the words
4. 12 And they told to Mordecai Esther's words
6. 2 Mordecai had told of Bigthana and Ter.
8. 1 for Esther had told what he (was) unto
Job 1. 15, 16, 17, 19 I only am escaped alone to tell
12. 7 the fowls of the air, and they shall tell
15. 18 Which wise men have told from their fa.
Psa. 52. *title.* Doeg the Edomite came and told Saul
Eccl. 6. 12 who can tell a man what shall be after him
8. 7 for who can tell him when it shall be?
10. 14 what shall be after him, who can tell him?
10. 20 that which hath wings shall tell the mat.
Song 1. 7 Tell me, O thou whom my soul loveth, wh.
5. 8 I charge you..that ye tell him, that I (am)
Isa. 19. 12 let them tell thee now, and let them know
36. 22 Then came Eliakim..and told him the wo.
45. 21 Tell ye..(who) hath told it from that time?
Jer. 36. 16 We will surely tell the king of all these
36. 17 Tell us now, How didst thou write all th.
36. 20 and told all the words in the ears of the
38. 27 he told them according to all these words
48. 20 tell ye it in Arnon, that Moab is spoiled
Eze. 24. 19 Wilt thou not tell us what these (things
Jon. 1. 8 Tell us, we pray thee, for whose cause
1. 10 For the men knew..because he had told

9. *To number, write, cypher*, סָפַר *saphar*.
Gen. 15. 5 tell the stars, if thou be able to number
2 Ch. 2. 2 Solomon told out threescore and ten tho.
Psa. 48. 12 go round about her: tell the towers the.
56. 8 Thou tellest my wanderings: put thou my

10. *To number, recount*, סָפַר *saphar*, 3.
Gen. 24. 66 the servant told Isaac all things that he
29. 13 And he told Laban all these things
37. 9 he dreamed yet another dream, and told
37. 10 he told (it) to his father, and to his bret.
40. 8 (Do) not interpretations (belong) to G. tell
40. 9 the chief butler told his dream to Joseph
41. 8 Pharaoh told them his dream; but (there
41. 12 we told him, and he interpreted to us our
Exod 10. 2 that thou mayest tell in the ears of thy
18. 8 Moses told his father in law all that the L.
24. 3 Moses came and told the people all the
Num 13. 27 they told him, and said, We came unto
Josh. 2. 23 and told him all (things) that befell them
Judg. 6. 13 his miracles which our fathers told us of
7. 13 (there was) a man that told a dream unto
1 Sa. 11. 5 they told him the tidings of the men of
1 Ki. 13. 11 his sons came and told him all the works
13. 11 words..them they told also to their father
2 Ki. 8. 4 Tell me, I pray thee, all the great things
8. 5 as he was telling the king how he had re.
8. 6 when the king asked the woman, she told
Esth. 5. 11 Haman told them of the glory of his riches
6. 13 Haman told Zeresh his wife and all his fr.
Psa. 22. 17 I may tell all my bones: they look (and)
26. 7 That I may..tell of all thy wondrous wo.
44. 1 our fathers have told us, (what) work thou.
48. 13 that ye may tell (it) to the generation fo.
78. 3 we have heard..and our fathers have told
Jer. 23. 27 their dreams which they tell every man
23. 28 The prophet that hath a dream, let him t
23. 32 that prophesy false dreams..and do tell
Joel 1. 3 Tell ye your children of it, and (let) your

11. *To put in the mouth*, שׂוּם בְּפֶה.
Ezra 8. 17 I told them what they should say unto I.

12. *To cause to hear*, שָׁמַע *shamea*, 5.
Judg 13. 23 nor would, as at this time, have told us (su.
Isa. 42. 9 before they spring forth I tell you of them
44. 8 have not I told thee from that time, and
45. 21 hath told it from that time? (have) not I
48. 20 tell this, utter it (even) to the end of the

13. *To tell again*, ἀναγγέλλω *anaggellō*.
Mark 5. 14 [told] (it) in the city, and in the country
5. 19 [tell] them how great things the Lord hath
John 4. 25 when he is come, he will tell us all things
5. 15 [told] the Jews that it was Jesus which
Acts 16. 38 the serjeants [told] these words unto the
2 Co. 7. 7 he told us your earnest desire, your mo.

14. *To tell away or off*, ἀπαγγέλλω *apaggellō*.
Matt. 8. 33 told every thing, and what was befallen
14. 12 and buried it, and went and told Jesus
28. 9 [as they went to tell his disciples, behold]
28. 10 tell my brethren that they go into Galilee
Mark 6. 30 told him all things, both what they had
16. 10 [she went and told them that had been]
16. 13 [they went and told (it) unto the residue]
Luke 7. 22 tell John what things ye have seen and
8. 20 it was told him (by certain), which said
8. 34 went and told (it) in the city and in the
8. 36 They also which saw (it) told them by
9. 36 they kept (it) close, and told no man in
13. 1 There were..some that told him of the
18. 37 they told him, that Jesus of Nazareth pa.
24. 9 told all these things unto the eleven, and
John 4. 51 his servants met him, and [told] (him), sa.
20. 18 Mary Magdalene came and [told] the dis.
Acts 5. 22 found them not..returned and told
5. 25 Then came one and told them, saying, B.
12. 14 and told how Peter stood before the gate
15. 27 who shall also tell (you) the same things
16. 36 the keeper of the prison told this saying
22. 26 he went and told the chief captain, saying
23. 16 went and entered into the castle, and told
23. 17 for he hath a certain thing to tell him
23. 19 (him), What is this that thou hast to tell

15. *To lead through, relate*, διηγέομαι *diēgeomai*.
Mark 5. 16 they that saw (it) told them how it befell
9. 9 he charged them that they should tell no
Luke 9. 10 the apostles..told him all that they had
Heb. 11. 32 the time would fail me to tell of Gedeon, and

16. *To see, know, be acquainted with*, οἶδα, *oida*.
Matt 21. 27 they answered..and said, We cannot tell
Mark 11. 33 they answered and said..We cannot tell
Luke 20. 7 That they could not tell whence (it was)
John 3. 8 canst not tell whence it cometh, and whi.
8. 14 ye cannot tell whence I come, and whit.
16. 18 What is this..we cannot tell what he sa.
2 Co. 12. 2 whether in the body, I cannot tell..tell
12. 3 out of the body, [I cannot tell]: God kno.

17. *To talk out*, ἐκλαλέω *eklaleō*.
Acts 23. 22 tell no man that thou hast showed thes

18. *To lead out, bring forth*, ἐξηγέομαι *exēgeomai*.
Luke 24. 35 they told what things (were done) in the

19. *To speak, tell, say*, εἶπον *eipon*.
Matt. 8. 4 See thou tell no man; but go thy way, sh.
12. 48 answered and said unto him that [told]
16. 20 they should tell no man that he was Jesus
17. 9 Tell the vision to no man, until the Son
18. 17 if he shall neglect to hear them, tell (it)
21. 5 Tell ye the daughter of Sion, Behold, thy

Matt21. 24 will ask you one thing, which if ye tell me
22. 4 Tell them which are bidden, Behold, I ha.
22. 17 Tell us therefore, What thinkest thou? Is
24. 3 Tell us, when shall these things be? and
26. 63 that thou tell us whether thou be the Ch.
28. 7 tell his disciples that he is risen from the
28. 7 there shall ye see him: lo, I have told you
Mark 5. 33 and fell down..and told him all the truth
7. 36 he charged them that they [should tell]
8. 26 Neither go into the town, nor tell (it) to
9. 12 he answered and told them, Elias verily
13. 4 Tell us, when shall these things be? and
16. 7 tell his disciples and Peter that he goeth
Luke 5. 14 he charged him to tell no man: but go, and
7. 42 [Tell] me therefore, which of them will lo.
8. 56 he charged them that they should tell no
9. 21 commanded (them) [to tell] no man that
13. 32 tell that fox, Behold, I cast out devils, and
20. 2 Tell us, by what authority doest thou th.
22. 67 Saying, Art thou the Christ? tell us. And
22. 67 he said unto them, If I tell you, ye will
John 3. 12 If I have told you earthly things, and ye
3. 12 how shall ye believe, if I tell you (of) he.
4. 29 see a man which told me all things that
4. 39 which testified, He told me all that ever
9. 27 I have told you already, and ye did not
10. 24 said..If thou be the Christ, tell us plainly
10. 25 I told you, and ye believed not: the works
11. 46 and told them what things Jesus had done
14. 2 if (it were) not (so), I would have told you
16. 4 ye may remember that I told you of them
18. 8 Jesus answered, I have told you that I am
18. 34 Sayest thou this..or did others tell it thee
20. 15 tell me where thou hast laid him, and I
Acts 5. 8 Tell me whether ye sold the land for so mu.?

20. *To say, speak, tell,* ἐρέω *ereō.*
Matt21. 24 I in likewise will tell you by what autho.
Mark11. 29 I will tell you by what authority I do these
John14. 29 I have told you before it come to pass, th.
Rev. 17. 7 I will tell thee the mystery of the woman

21. *To talk,* λαλέω *laleō.*
Matt26. 13 (there) shall also this..be told for a me.
Luke 1. 45 those things which were told her from the
2. 17 the saying which was told them concern.
2. 18 those things which were told them by the
2. 20 had heard and seen, as it was told unto
John 8. 40 a man that hath told you the truth, which
16. 4 these things have I told you, that when
Acts 9. 6 it shall be told thee what thou must do
10. 6 [he shall tell thee what thou oughtest to]
11. 14 Who shall tell thee words, whereby thou
22. 10 it shall be told thee of all things which
27. 25 I believe..it shall be even as it was told

22. *To lay out, say, speak,* λέγω *legō.*
Matt10. 27 What I tell you in darkness, (that) speak
21. 27 Neither tell I you by what authority I do
Mark 1. 30 lay sick of a fever, and anon they tell him
8. 30 he charged them that they [should tell]
10. 32 began to tell them what things should ha.
11. 33 Neither do I tell you by what authority I do
Luke 4. 25 I tell you of a truth, many widows were
9. 27 I tell you of a truth, there be some stan.
10. 24 I tell you, that many prophets and kings
12. 51 to give peace on earth? I tell you, Nay
12. 59 I tell thee, thou shalt not depart thence
13. 3, 5 I tell you, Nay: but, except ye repent
13. 27 I tell you, I know you not whence ye are
17. 34 I tell you, in that night there shall be two
18. 8 I tell you that he will avenge them spee.
18. 14 I tell you, this man went down to his ho.
19. 40 I tell you that, if these should hold their
20. 8 Neither tell I you by what authority I do
22. 34 I tell thee, Peter, the cock shall not crow
24. 10 which told these things unto the apostles
John 8. 45 because I tell (you) the truth, ye believe me
12. 22 telleth Andrew..Andrew and Philip tell
13. 19 I tell you before it come, that, when it is
16. 7 I tell you the truth; It is expedient for
Acts 17. 21 but either to tell, or to hear some new thi.
22. 27 said unto him, Tell me, art thou a Roman
Gal. 4. 21 Tell me, ye that desire to be under the
Phil. 3. 18 I have told you often, and now tell you
2 Th. 2. 5 when I was yet with you, I told you these
Jude 18 they told you there should be mockers in

23. *To indicate, declare,* μηνύω *mēnuō.*
Acts 23. 30 it was told me how that the Jews laid wa.

TELL (a fault), in time past, to —

1. *To convict, convince,* ἐλέγχω *eleḡchō.*
Matt18. 15 go and tell him his fault between thee

2. *To say, speak or tell before,* προέπω *proepō.*
Gal. 5. 21 I have also told (you) in time past, that

TELL before or unto, to —

1. *To make thoroughly manifest,* διασαφέω *diasaph.*
Matt18. 31 came and told unto their lord all that was

2. *To say, speak or tell before,* προερέω *proereō.*
Matt24. 25 Behold, I have told you before
2 Co. 13. 2 I told you before, and foretell you, as if

3. *To lay out, say or speak before,* προλέγω *prolegō.*
Gal. 5. 21 of the which I tell you before, as I have
1 Th. 3. 4 we told you before that we should suffer

TELLING —

Number, narration, מִסְפָּר *mispar.*
Judg. 7. 15 when Gideon heard the telling of the dr.

TE'-MA, תֵּימָא, תֵּמָא *sun burnt.*

1. A son of Ishmael and his posterity at the Persian Gulf. B.C. 1840.
Gen. 25. 15 Hadar, and T., Jetur, Naphish, and Ked.
1 Ch. 1. 30 Mishma, and Dumah, Massa, Hadad..T.

2. A city or district on the N. of Arabia, near the desert of Syria; perhaps *Teyma,* on the Haj route.
Job 6. 19 The troops of T. looked, the companies of
Isa. 21. 14 The inhabitants..of T. brought water to
Jer. 25. 23 Dedan, and T., and Buz, and all..in the

TE'-MAN, TE-MA'-NI, תֵּימָן, תֵּימָנִי.

1. A son of Eliphaz son of Esau. B.C. 1700.
Gen. 36. 11 the sons of Eliphaz were T., Omar, Zepho
36. 15 duke T., duke Omar, duke Zepho, duke
1 Ch. 1. 36 The sons of Eliphaz; T., and Omar, Ze.

2. An Edomite chief. B.C. 1480.
Gen. 36. 42 Duke Kenaz, duke T., duke Mibzar
1 Ch. 1. 53 Duke Kenaz, duke T., duke Mibzar

3. A race and district in or at the N.E. of Edom.
Gen. 36. 34 Husham of the land of T. reigned in his
Jer. 49. 7 (Is) wisdom no more in T.? is counsel per.
49. 20 purposed against the inhabitants of T.
Eze. 25. 13 I will make it desolate from T.; and they
Amos 1. 12 I will send a fire upon T., which shall de.
Obad. 9 thy mighty (men), O T., shall be dismayed
Hab. 3. 3 God came from T., and the Holy One from

TEMANITE, תֵּימָנִי.

An inhabitant of Teman.
1 Ch. 1. 45 Husham..of the T. reigned in his stead
Job 2. 11 Eliphaz the T., and Bildad the Shuhite
4. 1 Then Eliphaz the T. answered and said
15. 1 Then answered Eliphaz the T., and said
22. 1 Then Eliphaz the T. answered and said
42. 7 the LORD said to Eliphaz the T., My wrath
42. 9 Eliphaz the T. and Bildad the Shuhite

TE-ME'-NI, תֵּימְנִי *fortunate.*

A son of Ashur, and descendant of Caleb son of Hur.
1 Ch. 4. 6 Ahuzam, and Hepher, and T., and Haah.

TEMPER, to —

1. *To mix, mingle,* בָּלַל *balal.*
Exod29. 2 cakes unleavened tempered with oil, and

2. *To sprinkle, temper,* רָסַס *rasas.*
Eze. 46. 14 the third part of an hin of oil, to temper

TEMPER, tempered (together), to (be) —

1. *To be salted, tempered,* מָלַח *malach,* 4.
Exod30. 35 shalt make it a perfume..tempered toge.

2. *To mix with, compound,* συγκεράννυμι *sugkeran.*
1 Co. 12. 24 God hath tempered the body together

TEMPERANCE, to be temperate —

1. *Self restraint, continence,* ἐγκράτεια *eḡkrateia.*
Acts 24. 25 he reasoned of righteousness, temperance
Gal. 5. 23 Meekness, temperance: against such th.
2 Pe. 1. 6 to knowledge temperance; and to temper.

2. *To be self restrained, continent,* ἐγκρατεύομαι.
1 Co. 9. 25 every man that striveth..is temperate in

3. *Self restrained, continent,* ἐγκρατής *eḡkratēs.*
Titus 1. 8 a lover of good men, sober, just, holy, te.

4. *Sound minded, prudent,* σώφρων *sōphrōn.*
Titus 2. 2 That the aged men be sober, grave, tem.

TEMPEST, (tossed with) —

1. *An inundation, flood, storm,* זֶרֶם *zerem.*
Isa. 28. 2 (which) as a tempest of hail (and) a des.
30. 30 a devouring fire, (with) scattering, and te
32. 2 an hiding place..and a covert from the te.

2. *Hurricane,* סוּפָה *suphah.*
Job 27. 20 a tempest stealeth him away in the night

3. *To be tossed about, tempestuous,* סָעַר *saar.*
Isa. 54. 11 O thou afflicted, tossed with tempest, (and)

4. *A whirlwind, tempest,* סַעַר *saar.*
Psa. 55. 8 I would hasten my escape from the..te.
83. 15 persecute them with thy tempest, and ma.
Amos 1. 14 with a tempest in the day of the whirlw.
Jon. 1. 4 there was a mighty tempest in the sea, so
1. 12 for my sake this great tempest (is) upon

5. *A whirlwind, tempest,* סְעָרָה *searah.*
Isa. 29. 6 with storm and tempest, and the flame of

6. *A wind,* רוּחַ *ruach.*
Psa. 11. 6 fire and brimstone, and an horrible tem.

7. *A tempest, whirlwind,* שְׂעָרָה *searah.*
Job 9. 17 he breaketh me with a tempest, and mul.

8. *A rushing, storm, tempest,* θύελλα *thuella.*
Heb. 12. 18 nor unto blackness, and darkness, and te.

9. *A violent storm,* λαῖλαψ *lailaps.*
2 Pe. 2. 17 clouds that are carried with a tempest; to

10. *A shaking, agitation,* σεισμός *seismos.*
Matt. 8. 24 there arose a great tempest in the sea, in.

11. *To be in a winter storm,* χειμάζομαι *cheimazom.*
Acts 27. 18 we being exceedingly tossed with a tem.

12. *Winter, a pouring storm,* χειμών *cheimōn.*
Acts 27. 20 no small tempest lay on (us), all hope th.

TEMPESTUOUS, (to be) —

1. *To be tossed about, be tempestuous,* סָעַר *saar.*
Jon. 1. 11, 13 for the sea wrought, and was tempes.

2. *To be tempestuous, frightful,* שָׂעַר *saar,* 2.
Psa. 50. 3 it shall be very tempestuous round about

3. *Smoking, violent, whirling,* τυφωνικός *tuphōnikos.*
Acts 27. 14 there arose against it a tempestuous wind

TEMPLE —

1. *House,* בַּיִת *bayith.*
2 Ki. 11. 10 shields, that (were) in the temple of the
11. 11 from the right corner of the temple to the
11. 11 the temple, (along) by the altar and the t
11. 13 she came to the people into the temple of
1 Ch. 6. 10 the temple that Solomon built in Jerusa.
10. 10 fastened his head in the temple of Dagon
2 Ch. 23. 10 of the temple to the left side of the tem.
23. 10 along by the altar and the temple, by the
35. 20 when Josiah had prepared the temple, N.

2. *Palace, temple,* הֵיכָל *hekal.*
1 Sa. 1. 9 sat upon a seat by a post of the temple of
3. 3 the lamp of God went out in the temple
2 Sa. 22. 7 he did hear my voice out of his temple, and
1 Ki. 6. 3 the porch before the temple of the house
6. 5 round about, (both) of the temple and of
6. 17 the temple before it, was forty cubits (lo.)
6. 33 also made he for the door of the temple
7. 21 set..the pillars in the porch of the temple
7. 50 the doors of the house, (to wit), of the te.
2 Ki. 18. 16 cut off (the gold from) the doors of the te.
23. 4 to bring forth out of the temple of the L.
24. 13 which Solomon..had made in the temple
2 Ch. 3. 17 he reared up the pillars before the temple
4. 7 set (them) in the temple, five on the right
4. 8 placed (them) in the temple, five on the
4. 22 the doors of the house of the temple, (we.
26. 16 went into the temple of the LORD to burn
27. 2 he entered not into the temple of the Lo.
29. 16 that they found in the temple of the Lo.
36. 7 and put them in his temple at Babylon
Ezra 3. 6 the foundation of the temple of the LORD
3. 10 builders laid the foundation of the temple
4. 1 builded the temple unto the LORD God of
Neh. 6. 10 Let us meet together..within the temple
6. 10 let us shut the doors of the temple: for
6. 11 would go into the temple to save his life
Psa. 5. 7 will I worship toward thy holy temple
11. 4 The LORD (is) in his holy temple, the Lo.
18. 6 he heard my voice out of his temple, and
27. 4 to behold..and to enquire in his temple
29. 9 in his temple doth every one speak of (his)
48. 9 We have thought..in the midst of thy te.
65. 4 goodness of thy house..of thy holy temple
68. 29 Because of thy temple at Jerusalem shall
79. 1 thy holy temple have they defiled; they
138. 2 I will worship toward thy holy temple, and
Isa. 6. 1 and lifted up, and his train filled the te.
44. 28 to the temple, Thy foundation shall be laid
66. 6 a voice from the temple, a voice of the L.
Jer. 7. 4 lying words, saying, The temple of the L.
7. 4 The temple of the LORD, The temple of
24. 1 baskets of figs (were) set before the temple
50. 28 to declare..the vengeance of his temple
51. 11 because it (is)..the vengeance of his tem.
Eze. 8. 16 the door of the temple of the LORD, betw.
8. 16 their backs toward the temple of the LORD
41. 1 he brought me to the temple, and meas.
41. 4 the breadth, twenty cubits, before the te.
41. 15 with the inner temple, and the porches of
41. 20 palm trees made, and (on) the wall of the t
41. 21 The posts of the temple (were) squared
41. 23 the temple and the sanctuary had two do.
41. 25 made on them, on the doors of the tem.
42. 8 before the temple (were) an hundred cu.
Hos. 8. 14 forgotten his Maker, and buildeth temp.
Joel 3. 5 have carried into your temples my goodly
Amos 8. 3 the songs of the temple shall be howlings
Jon. 2. 4 I will look again toward thy holy temple
2. 7 came in unto thee, into thine holy tem.
Mic. 1. 2 be witness against you..from his holy te
Hab. 2. 20 the LORD (is) in his holy temple: let all
Hag. 2. 15 was laid upon a stone in the temple of the
2. 18 the foundation of the LORD'S temple was
Zech. 6. 12 and he shall build the temple of the LORD
6. 13 he shall build the temple of the LORD; and
6. 14 a memorial in the temple of the LORD
6. 15 shall come and build in the temple of the
8. 9 the foundation..was laid, that the tem.
Mal. 3. 1 shall suddenly come to his temple, even

3. *Palace, temple,* הֵיכַל *hekal.*
Ezra 5. 14 Nebuchadnezzar took out of the temple
5. 14 brought them into the temple of Babylon
5. 14 those did Cyrus..take out of the temple
5. 15 carry them into the temple that (is) in J.
6. 5 Nebuchadnezzar took forth out of the te.
6. 5 brought again unto the temple which (is)
Dan. 5. 2 Nebuchadnezzar had taken out of the te.
5. 3 vessels that were taken out of the temple

4. *Sacred, priestly edifice, temple,* ἱερόν *hieron.*
Matt. 4. 5 setteth him on a pinnacle of the temple
12. 5 the priests in the temple profane the sa.
12. 6 in this place is (one) greater than the te.
21. 12 Jesus went into the temple of God, and
21. 12 bought in the temple, and overthrew the
21. 14 and the lame came to him in the temple
21. 15 the children crying in the temple, and sa.
21. 23 when he was come into the temple, the
24. 1 Jesus went out, and departed from the te.
24. 1 to show him the buildings of the temple.
26. 55 sat daily with you teaching in the temple
Mark11. 11 entered into Jerusalem, and into the te.
11. 15 Jesus went into the temple, and began to
11. 15 them that sold and bought in the temple
11. 16 should carry (any) vessel through the te.

Mark11. 27 as he was walking in the temple, there
12. 35 and said, while he taught in the temple
13. 1 as he went out of the temple, one of his
13. 3 And as he sat..over against the temple
14. 49 I was daily with you in the temple teach.
Luke 2. 27 And he came by the spirit into the temp.
2. 37 departed not from the temple, but served
2. 46 they found him in the temple, sitting in
4. 9 set him on a pinnacle of the temple, and
18. 10 Two men went up into the temple to pray
19. 45 he went into the temple, and began to ca.
19. 47 he taught daily in the temple. But the ch.
20. 1 he taught the people in the temple, and
21. 5 as some spake of the temple, how it was ad.
21. 37 the day time he was teaching in the tem.
21. 38 people came early..to him in the temple
22. 52 chief priests, and captains of the temple
22. 53 When I was daily with you in the temple
24. 53 were continually in the temple, praising
John 2. 14 found in the temple those that sold oxen
2. 15 he drove them all out of the temple, and
5. 14 Jesus findeth him in the temple, and said
7. 14 Jesus went up into the temple, and taught
7. 28 Then cried Jesus in the temple, as he ta.
8. 2 [he came again into the temple, and all]
8. 20 spake Jesus..as he taught in the temple
8. 59 went out of the temple, going through the
10. 23 Jesus walked in the temple, in Solomon's
11. 56 spake..as they stood in the temple, What
18. 20 in the temple, whither the Jews always
Acts 2. 46 continuing..with one accord in the temple
3. 1 went up together into the temple at the
3. 2 the gate of the temple which is called Be.
3. 2 alms of them that entered into the temple
3. 3 Peter and John about to go into the temple
3. 8 entered with them into the temple, walk.
3. 10 for alms at the Beautiful gate of the tem.
4. 1 the captain of the temple, and the Saddu.
5. 20 speak in the temple to the people all the
5. 21 they entered into the temple early in the
5. 24 the captain of the temple and the chief pr.
5. 25 men whom ye put in prison are..in the te.
5. 42 in the temple, and in every house, they
19. 27 the temple of the great goddess Diana sh.
21. 26 entered into the temple, to signify the ac.
21. 27 the Jews..when they saw him in the tem.
21. 28 brought Greeks also into the temple, and
21. 29 that Paul had brought into the temple
21. 30 took Paul, and drew him out of the temp.
22. 17 while I prayed in the temple, I was in a
24. 6 also hath gone about to profane the temp.
24. 12 they neither found me in the temple disp.
24. 18 certain Jews..found me purified in the te.
25. 8 neither against the temple, nor yet against
26. 21 the Jews caught me in the temple, and
1 Co. 9. 13 that they..live (of the things) of the tem.

5. *A dwelling place, inner sanctuary,* ναός *naos.*
Matt23. 16 Whosoever shall swear by the temple, it
23. 16 shall swear by the gold of the temple, he
23. 17 whether is greater, the gold, or the temple
23. 21 whoso shall swear by the temple, sweareth
23. 35 whom ye slew between the temple and
26. 61 I am able to destroy the temple of God
27. 5 he cast down the..silver in the temple
27. 40 Thou that destroyest the temple, and bu.
27. 51 the veil of the temple was rent in twain
Mark14. 58 I will destroy this temple that is made
15. 29 thou that destroyest the temple, and bu.
15. 38 the veil of the temple was rent in twain
Luke 1. 9 when he went into the temple of the Lord
1. 21 marvelled that he tarried..in the temple
1. 22 that he had seen a vision in the temple
23. 45 the veil of the temple was rent in the mi.
John 2. 19 Destroy this temple, and in three days I
2. 20 Forty and six years was this temple in b.
2. 21 But he spake of the temple of his body
Acts 7. 48 the Most High dwelleth not in [temples]
17. 24 dwelleth not in temples made with hands
1 Co. 3. 16 Know ye not that ye are the temple of God
3. 17 If any man defile the temple of God, him
3. 17 for the temple of God is holy, which..ye
6. 19 know ye not that your body is the temple
2 Co. 6. 16 what agreement hath the temple of God
6. 16 for ye are the temple of the living God
Eph. 2. 21 groweth unto an holy temple in the Lord
2 Th. 2. 4 so that he as God sitteth in the temple of
Rev. 3. 12 will I make a pillar in the temple of my
7. 15 and serve him day and night in his temple
11. 1 measure the temple of God, and the altar
11. 2 the court which is without the temple le.
11. 19 the temple of God was opened in heaven
11. 19 there was seen in his temple the ark of
14. [15], 17 another angel came out of the temple
15. 5 the temple of the tabernacle of the testi.
15. 6 the seven angels came out [of the temple]
15. 8 the temple was filled with smoke from the
15. 8 no man was able to enter into the temple
16. 1 I heard a great voice [out of the temple]
16 17 there came a great voice out of the temple
21. 22 I saw no temple therein: for the Lord
21. 22 God Almighty and the Lamb are the tem.

6. *House,* οἶκος *oikos.*
Luke11. 51 perished between the altar and the temple

TEMPLES —
The temples, upper cheeks, רַקָּה *raqqah.*
Judg. 4. 21 smote the nail into his temples, and fast.
4. 22 lay dead, and the nail (was) in his temples
5. 26 pierced and stricken through his temples
Song 4. 3 thy temples (are) like a piece of a pomeg.
6. 7 As a piece of a pomegranate (are) thy te.

TEMPORAL —
For a season or time, πρόσκαιρος *proskairos.*
2 Co. 4. 18 for the things which are seen (are) temp.

TEMPT, (not) to be tempted, to —
1. *To prove, try, test,* בָּחַן *bachan.*
Mal. 3. 15 (they that) tempt God are even delivered

2. *To try, prove,* נָסָה *nasah,* 3.
Gen. 22. 1 God did tempt Abraham, and said unto
Exod17. 2 Moses said..wherefore do ye tempt the
17. 7 they tempted the LORD, saying, Is the L.
Num14. 22 have tempted me now these ten times, and
Deut. 6. 16 Ye shall not tempt..as ye tempted (him)
Psa. 78. 18 they tempted God in their heart, by asking
78. 41 they turned back, and tempted God, and
78. 56 they tempted and provoked the most high
95. 9 your fathers tempted me, proved me, and
106. 14 lusted exceedingly..and tempted God in
Isa. 7. 12 I will not ask, neither will I tempt the L.

3. *Not to be tempted or tried,* ἀπείραστος *apeirastos.*
Jas. 1. 13 God cannot be tempted with evil, neither

4. *To try, prove exceedingly,* ἐκπειράζω *ekpeirazō.*
Matt. 4. 7 Thou shalt not tempt the Lord thy God
Luke 4. 12 Thou shalt not tempt the Lord thy God
10. 25 a certain lawyer stood up, and tempted
1 Co.10. 9 Neither let us tempt Christ, as some of

5. *To try, prove,* πειράζω *peirazō.*
Matt. 4. 1 Then was Jesus led..to be tempted of the
16. 1 the Sadducees came, and tempting desired
19. 3 The Pharisees also came unto him, temp.
22. 18 and said, Why tempt ye me, (ye) hypocr.?
22. 35 asked (him a question), tempting him, and
Mark 1. 13 he was there..forty days, tempted of Satan
8. 11 seeking of him a sign..tempting him
10. 2 And the Pharisees came to him..tempting
12. 15 Why tempt ye me? bring me a penny, that
Luke 4. 2 Being forty days tempted of the devil
11. 16 others, tempting (him), sought of him a
20. 23 [and said unto them, Why tempt ye me?]
John 8. 6 [This they said, tempting him, that they]
Acts 5. 9 ye have agreed together to tempt the sp.
15. 10 why tempt ye God, to put a yoke upon the
1 Co. 7. 5 that Satan tempt you not for your incon.
10. 9 as some of them also [tempted], and were
10. 13 who will not suffer you to be tempted ab.
Gal. 6. 1 considering thyself, lest thou also be tem.
1 Th. 3. 5 lest..the tempter have tempted you, and
Heb. 2. 18 that he himself hath suffered, being tem.
2. 18 he is able to succour them that are temp.
3. 9 your fathers tempted me, proved me, and
4. 15 was in all points [tempted] like as (we are
11. 37 they were sawn asunder, were tempted
Jas. 1. 13 Let no man say when he is tempted, I am t.
1. 13 God cannot..neither tempteth he any man
1. 14 every man is tempted, when he is drawn

TEMPTATION, tempter —
1. *A trying, trial,* מַסָּה *massah.*
Deut. 4. 34 by temptations, by signs, and by wonders
7. 19 The great temptations which thine eyes
29. 3 The great temptations which thine eyes
Psa. 95. 8 (in) the day of temptation in the wilder.

2. *Trial, proof,* πειρασμός *peirasmos.*
Matt. 6. 13 lead us not into temptation, but deliver
26. 41 and pray, that ye enter not into temptat.
Mark14. 38 Watch ye and pray, lest ye enter into te.
Luke 4. 13 when the devil had ended all the tempt.
8. 13 have no root..and in time of temptation
11. 4 lead us not into temptation, but deliver
22. 28 have continued with me in my temptati.
22. 40 Pray ye that ye enter not into temptation
22. 46 rise and pray, lest ye enter into temptation
Acts 20. 19 with many tears, and temptations, which
1 Co.10. 13 There hath no temptation taken you but
10. 13 will with the temptation also make a way
Gal. 4. 14 my temptation which was in my flesh ye
1 Ti. 6. 9 they that will be rich fall into temptation
Heb. 3. 8 in the day of temptation in the wilderness
Jas. 1. 2 count it all joy when ye fall into..tempt.
1. 12 Blessed (is) the man that endureth temp.
1 Pe. 1. 6 in heaviness through manifold temptati.
2 Pe. 2. 9 how to deliver the godly out of temptations
Rev. 3. 10 will keep thee from the hour of temptat.

3. *To try, prove,* πειράζω *peirazō.*
Matt. 4. 3 when the tempter came to him, he said
1 Th. 3. 5 sent to know..lest by some means the te.

TEN (strings, instrument of) —
1. *Ten, tenth, ten stringed instrument,* עָשׂוֹר *asor.*
Gen. 24. 55 Let the damsel abide..at the least ten
Psa. 33. 2 psaltery (and) an instrument of ten strings
92. 3 Upon an instrument of ten strings, and
144. 9 upon..an instrument of ten strings will

2. *Ten,* עֲשָׂרָה, עֶשֶׂר *eser, asarah.*
Gen. 5. 14 the days..were nine hundred and ten ye.
16. 3 Abram had dwelt ten years in the land of
18. 32 Peradventure ten shall be found there
18. 32 he said, I will not destroy (it) for ten's s.
24. 10 the servant took ten camels of the camels
24. 22 two bracelets for her hands of ten (shekels)
31. 7 deceived me, and changed my wages ten
31. 41 and thou hast changed my wages ten ti.
32. 15 ten bulls, twenty she asses, and ten foals
42. 3 Joseph's ten brethren went down to buy
45. 23 ten asses laden with the good things of E.
45. 23 ten she asses laden with corn and bread
50. 22 and Joseph lived an hundred and ten ye.
50. 26 Joseph died, (being) an hundred and ten

Exod18. 21, 25 rulers of fifties, and rulers of tens
26. 1 shalt make the tabernacle (with) ten cur.
26. 16 Ten cubits (shall be) the length of a board
27. 12 their pillars ten, and their sockets ten
34. 28 wrote upon the tables..the ten comman.
36. 8 every wise hearted man..made ten curt.
36. 21 The length of a board (was) ten cubits, and
38. 12 their pillars ten, and their sockets ten
Lev. 26. 26 ten women shall bake your bread in one
27. 5, 7 thy estimation..for the female ten sh.
Num. 7. 14 One spoon of ten (shekels) of gold, full of
7. 20 One spoon of gold of ten (shekels), full of
7. 26, 32, 38, 44, 50, 56 One golden spoon of ten
7. 62, 68, 74, 80 One golden spoon of ten (shekels)
7. 86 The golden spoons..(weighing) ten (sh.)
11. 19 Ye shall not eat one day..neither ten d.
11. 32 he that gathered least gathered ten hom.
14. 22 have tempted me now these ten times, and
29. 23 ten bullocks, two rams, (and) fourteen la.
Deut. 1. 15 captains over fifties, and captains over tens
4. 13 declared unto you his covenant..ten com.
10. 4 the first writing, the ten commandments
Josh.15. 57 Cain, Gibeah, and Timnah; ten cities with
17. 5 there fell ten portions to Manasseh, besi.
21. 5 out of the half tribe of Manasseh, ten cities
21. 26 All the cities (were) ten with their suburbs
22. 14 with him ten princes, of each chief house
24. 29 died, (being) an hundred and ten years
Judg. 1. 4 they slew of them in Bezek ten thousand
2. 8 died, (being) an hundred and ten years
3. 29 they slew of Moab..about ten thousand
4. 6 take with thee ten thousand men of the
4. 10 he went up with ten thousand men at his
4. 14 Barak went..and ten thousand men after
6. 27 Gideon took ten men of his servants, and
7. 3 and there remained ten thousand
12. 11 after him Elon..he judged Israel ten ye.
17. 10 I will give thee ten (shekels) of silver by
20. 10 we will take ten men of an hundred thr.
20. 34 there came against Gibeah ten thousand
Ruth 1. 4 and they dwelt there about ten years
4. 2 he took ten men of the elders of the city
1 Sa. 1. 8 (am) not I better to thee than ten sons?
15. 4 numbered them..ten thousand men of J.
17. 17 Take now..these ten loaves, and run to
17. 18 carry these ten cheeses unto the captain
25. 5 David sent out ten young men; and Dav.
25. 38 it came to pass about ten days (after), th.
2 Sa. 15. 16 the king left ten women, (which were) co.
18. 3 (thou art) worth ten thousand of us: the.
18. 11 I would have given thee ten (shekels) of
18. 15 ten young men that bare Joab's armour
19. 43 We have ten parts in the king, and we ha.
20. 3 the king took the ten women (his) concu.
1 Ki. 4. 23 Ten fat oxen, and twenty oxen out of the
5. 14 he sent them to Lebanon, ten thousand a
6. 3 ten cubits (was) the breadth thereof bef.
6. 23 two cherubim (of) olive tree, (each) ten cu.
6. 24 unto the uttermost part..(were) ten cub.
6. 25 the other cherub (was) ten cubits: both
6. 26 The height of the one cherub (was) ten cu.
7. 10 stones of ten cubits, and stones of eight
7. 23 ten cubits from the one brim to the other
7. 24 (there were) knops compassing it, ten in
7. 27 he made ten bases of brass; four cubits
7. 37 After this (manner) he made the ten bas.
7. 38 Then made he ten lavers of brass: one la.
7. 38 upon every one of the ten bases one laver
7. 43 the ten bases, and ten lavers on the bases
11. 31 he said to Jeroboam, Take thee ten piec.
11. 31 rend the kingdom..and will give ten tri.
11. 35 and will give it unto thee, (even) ten tri.
14. 3 take with thee ten loaves, and cracknels
2 Ki. 5. 5 he departed, and took with him ten tal.
5. 5 six thousand (pieces) of gold, and ten ch.
13. 7 ten chariots, and ten thousand footmen
14. 7 He slew of Edom..ten thousand, and to.
15. 17 Menahem..(reigned) ten years in Samaria
20. 9 go forward ten degrees, or go back ten de.
20. 10 for the shadow to go down ten degrees
20. 10 let the shadow return backward ten deg.
20. 11 he brought the shadow ten degrees back.
24. 14 ten thousand captives, and all the crafts.
25. 25 Ishmael..came, and ten men with him
1 Ch. 6. 61 the half (tribe) of Manasseh, by lot, ten
29. 7 of silver ten thousand talents, and of
2 Ch. 4. 1 twenty cubits the breadth..and ten cub.
4. 2 he made a molten sea of ten cubits from
4. 3 ten in a cubit, compassing the sea round
4. 6 He made also ten lavers, and put five on
4. 7 he made ten candlesticks of gold accordi.
4. 8 He made also ten tables, and placed (th.)
14. 1 In his days the land was quiet ten years
25. 11 smote of the children of Seir ten thousand
25. 12 (other) ten thousand (left) alive did the ch.
27. 5 ten thousand measures of wheat, and ten
30. 24 a thousand bullocks and ten thousand sh.
36. 9 he reigned three months and ten days in
Ezra 1. 10 silver basins..four hundred and ten, (and)
8. 12 and with him an hundred and ten males
8. 24 Sherebiah, Hashabiah, and ten of their
Neh. 4. 12 they said unto us ten times, From all pl.
5. 18 once in ten days store of all sorts of wine
11. 1 to bring one of ten to dwell in Jerusalem
Esth. 3. 9 I will pay ten thousand talents of silver
9. 10 The ten sons of Haman the son of Ham.
9. 12 The Jews have slain..the ten sons of Ha.
9. 13 let Haman's ten sons be hanged upon the
9. 14 decree was given..and they hanged Ha. t.
Job 19. 3 ten times have ye reproached me: ye are
Eccl. 7. 19 Wisdom strengtheneth..more than ten
Isa. 5. 10 ten acres of vineyard shall yield one bath

Isa. 38. 8 ten degrees backward..sun returned ten
Jer. 41. 1 ten men with him, came unto Gedaliah
41. 2 Then arose Ishmael..and the ten men th.
41. 8 ten men were found among them that sa.
42. 7 it came to pass after ten days that the wo.
Eze. 40. 11 And he measured the breadth..ten cubits
41. 2 the breadth of the door (was) ten cubits
42. 4 before the chambers (was) a walk of ten
45. 1 thousand (reeds), and the breadth..ten
45. 3 shalt thou measure..breadth of ten tho.
45. 5 the ten thousand of breadth, shall also the
45. 14 an homer of ten baths; for ten baths (are)
48. 9 twenty thousand in length, and of ten th.
48. 10 ten thousand in breadth, and toward
48. 10 the east ten thousand in breadth, and to
48. 13 twenty thousand in length, and ten thou.
48. 13 twenty thousand, and the breadth ten th.
48. 18 ten thousand eastward, and ten thousand
Dan. 1. 12 Prove thy servants, I beseech thee, ten
1. 14 So he consented..and proved them ten
1. 15 at the end of ten days their countenances
1. 20 he found them ten times better than all
Amos 5. 3 went forth (by) an hundred shall leave ten
6. 9 if there remain ten men in one house, that
Hag. 2. 16 heap of twenty (meas.), there were (but) ten
Zech. 5. 2 twenty cubits, and the breadth thereof t.
8. 23 ten men shall take hold out of all langu.

3. *Ten,* עֲשָׂרָא, עֲשַׂר *asar,*
Dan. 7. 7 behold a fourth beast..and it had ten ho.
7. 20 of the ten horns that (were) in his head
7. 24 ten horns out of this kingdom (are) ten

4. *Ten,* δέκα *deka.*
Matt 20. 24 when the ten heard (it), they were moved
25. 1 ten virgins, which took their lamps, and
25. 28 give (it) unto him which hath ten talents
Mark 10. 41 when the ten heard (it), they began to be
Luke 14. 31 whether he be able with ten thousand to
15. 8 what woman, having ten pieces of silver
17. 12 there met him ten men that were lepers
17. 17 Were there not ten cleansed? but where
19. 13 his ten servants, and delivered them ten
19. 16 Lord, thy pound hath gained ten pounds
19. 17 he said..have thou authority over ten ci.
19. 24 and give (it) to him that hath ten pounds
19. 25 they said unto him, Lord, he hath ten po.
Acts 25. 6 tarried among them more than ten days
Rev. 2. 10 ye shall have tribulation ten days: be thou
12. 3 having seven heads and ten horns, and se.
13. 1 ten horns, and upon his horns ten crowns
17. 3 beast..having seven heads and ten horns
17. 7 which hath the seven heads and ten horns
17. 12 the ten horns which thou sawest, are ten
17. 16 the ten horns which thou sawest upon the

TEN thousand —

1. *To become a myriad, ten thousand,* רְבַב *rabab,* 4.
Psa. 144. 13 bring forth thousands and ten thousands

2. *A myriad, ten thousand,* רְבָבָה *rebabah.*
Lev. 26. 8 an hundred of you shall put ten thousand
Deut 32. 30 How should..two put ten thousand to fli.
33. 2 and he came with ten thousands of saints
33. 17 they (are) the ten thousands of Ephraim
Judg 20. 10 we will take..a thousand out of ten tho.
1 Sa. 18. 7 slain his thousands, and David his ten th.
18. 8 They have ascribed unto David ten thou.
21. 11 slain his thousands, and David his ten th.
29. 5 slew his thousands, and David his ten th.
Psa. 3. 6 I will not be afraid of ten thousands of pe.
91. 7 A thousand shall fall..and ten thousand
Song 5. 10 My beloved (is)..the chiefest among ten t.
Mic. 6. 7 (or) with ten thousands of rivers of oil?

3. *A myriad, ten thousand,* רִבּוֹא, רִבּוֹ *ribbo.*
1 Ch. 29. 7 five thousand talents and ten thousand dr.
Dan. 11. 12 he shall cast down (many) ten thousands

4. *Ten thousand,* μυρίοι *murioi.*
Matt 18. 24 one was brought..which owed him ten th.
1 Co. 4. 15 though ye have ten thousand instructors
14. 19 than ten thousand words in an (unknown)

5. *Ten thousand,* μυριάς *murias.*
Jude 14 the Lord cometh with ten thousands

TEN thousand times ten thousand —

A myriad of myriads, רִבּוֹ רִבְּוָן [*ribbo*].
Dan. 7. 10 ten thousand times ten thousand stood be.

TENDER (one), tenderness —

1. *Tender, soft, timid,* רַךְ *rak.*
Gen. 18. 7 fetched a calf tender and good, and gave
29. 17 Leah (was) tender eyed; but Rachel was
33. 13 lord knoweth that the children (are) tender
Deut 28. 54 the man (that is) tender among you, and
28. 56 The tender and delicate woman among
1 Ch. 22. 5 my son (is) young and tender, and the ho.
29. 1 my son..(is yet) young and tender, and
Prov. 4. 3 I was my father's son, tender and only
Isa. 47. 1 thou shalt no more be called tender and
Eze. 17. 22 I will crop off from the top..a tender one

2. *Tenderness,* רֹךְ *rok.*
Deut 28. 56 would not..for delicateness and tender.

3. *Soft, tender,* ἁπαλός *hapalos.*
Matt 24. 32 When his branch is yet tender, and put.
Mark 13. 28 When her branch is yet tender, and put.

TENDER branch, hearted, mercy, plant —

1. *Suckling, tender branch or plant,* יוֹנֵק *yoneq.*
Isa. 53. 2 shall grow up before him as a tender p.

2. *Suckling, tender branch or plant,* יוֹנֶקֶת *yoneqeth.*
Job 14. 7 that the tender branch thereof will not

3. *Tender of heart,* רַךְ לֵבָב *rak lebab.*
2 Ch. 13. 7 Rehoboam was young and tender hearted

4. *Compassionate, merciful,* εὔσπλαγχνος *eusplagch.*
Eph. 4. 32 be ye kind one to another, tender hearted

5. *Pitiful,* οἰκτίρμων *oiktirmōn.*
Jas. 5. 11 the Lord is very pitiful, and of tender mer.

6. *Bowels of kindness,* σπλάγχνα ἐλέους [*splagchna*].
Luke 1. 78 Through the tender mercy of our God, wh.

TENON —

Hand, יָד *yad.*
Exod. 26. 17 Two tenons (shall there be) in one board
26. 19 sockets under one board for his two tenons
26. 19 sockets under another..for his two tenons
36. 22 One board had two tenons, equally distant
36. 24 sockets under one board for his two tenons
36. 24 sockets under another..for his two tenons

TENOR —

Mouth, פֶּה *peh.*
Gen. 43. 7 we told him according to the tenor of these
Exod. 34. 27 after the tenor of these words I have made

TENT —

1. *Tent,* אֹהֶל *ohel.*
Gen. 4. 20 he was the father of such as dwell in tents
9. 21 and he was uncovered within his tent
9. 27 and he shall dwell in the tents of Shem
12. 8 pitched his tent, (having) Beth-el on the w.
13. 3 unto the place where his tent had been
13. 5 Lot also..had flocks, and herds, and tents
18. 1 he sat in the tent door in the heat of the
18. 2 he ran to meet them from the tent door
18. 6 Abraham hastened into the tent unto Sa.
18. 9 Where (is) Sarah..he said, Behold, in the t.
18. 10 Sarah heard (it) in the tent door, which
24. 67 brought her into his mother Sarah's tent
25. 27 Jacob (was) a plain man, dwelling in tents
26. 25 builded an altar..and pitched his tent th.
31. 25 Jacob had pitched his tent in the mount
31. 33 went into Jacob's tent, and into Leah's t.
31. 33 into the two maid servants' tents; but he
31. 33 Leah's tent, and entered into Rachel's te.
31. 34 Laban searched all the tent, but found (th.)
33. 19 a field, where he had spread his tent, at
35. 21 and spread his tent beyond the tower of
Exod. 16. 16 take ye..for (them) which (are) in his te.
18. 7 (their) welfare; and they came into the tent
26. 11 couple the tent together, that it may be
26. 12 that remaineth of the curtains of the tent
26. 13 in the length of the curtains of the tent
26. 14 thou shalt make a covering for the tent
26. 36 make an hanging for the door of the tent
33. 8 stood every man (at) his tent door, and lo.
33. 10 and worshipped, every man (in) his tent
35. 11 his tent, and his covering, his taches, and
36. 14 made curtains of goats' (hair) for the tent
36. 18 fifty taches of brass to couple the tent to.
36. 19 he made a covering for the tent (of) rams'
39. 32 the tabernacle of the tent of the congreg.
39. 33 the tent, and all his furniture, his taches
39. 40 the tabernacle, for the tent of the congre.
40. 2, 6, 7, 22, 24, 26 the tent of the congregation
40. 19 he spread abroad the tent over the taber.
40. 19 put the covering of the tent above upon
40. 29, 30, 32, 34, 35 the tent of the congregation
Lev. 14. 8 shall tarry abroad out of his tent seven
Num. 3. 25 the tabernacle, and the tent, the covering
9. 15 the tabernacle, (namely), the tent of the
11. 10 weep..every man in the door of his tent
16. 26 Depart, I pray you, from the tents of th.
16. 27 stood in the door of their tents, and their
19. 14 when a man dieth in a tent: all that come
19. 14 into the tent, and all that (is) in the tent
19. 18 sprinkle (it) upon the tent, and upon all
24. 5 How goodly are thy tents, O Jacob! (and)
Deut. 1. 27 ye murmured in your tents, and said, Be.
5. 30 say to them, Get you into your tents again
11. 6 their tents, and all the substance that (was)
16. 7 turn in the morning, and go unto thy te.
33. 18 Rejoice, Zebulun..and, Issachar, in thy te.
Josh. 3. 14 the people removed from their tents, to
7. 21 hid in the earth, in the midst of my tent
7. 22 ran unto the tent..(it was) hid in his tent
7. 23 took them out of the midst of the tent, and
7. 24 his sheep, and his tent, and all that he had
22. 4 get you unto your tents, (and) unto the
22. 6 blessed them..and they went unto their t.
22. 7 Joshua sent them away also unto their te.
22. 8 Return with much riches unto your tents
Judg. 4. 11 pitched his tent unto the plain of Zaana.
4. 17 Sisera fled away on his feet to the tent of
4. 18 he had turned in unto her into the tent
4. 20 Stand in the door of the tent; and it shall
4. 21 Heber's wife, took a nail of the tent, and
5. 24 blessed shall she be above women in the t.
6. 5 came up with their cattle and their tents
7. 8 and he sent all..every man unto his tent
7. 13 came unto a tent, and smote it that it fell
7. 13 and overturned it, that the tent lay along
8. 11 them that dwelt in tents on the east of N.
20. 8 We will not any (of us) go to his tent, ne.
1 Sa. 4. 10 they fled every man into his tent: and
13. 2 the people he sent every man to his tent
17. 54 And David..put his armour in his tent
2 Sa. 7. 6 have walked in a tent and in a tabernacle
16. 22 they spread Absalom a tent upon the top
18. 17 and all Israel fled every one to his tent
2 Sa. 19. 8 for Israel had fled every man to his tent
20. 1 no part in David..every man to his tents
20. 22 retired from the city, every man to his tent
1 Ki. 8. 66 went unto their tents joyful and glad of
12. 16 to your tents, O Israel: now see to thine
12. 16 So Israel departed unto their tents
2 Ki. 7. 7 left their tents, and their horses, and their
7. 8 they went into one tent, and did eat and
7. 8 entered into another tent, and carried
7. 10 and asses tied, and the tents as they (we.)
8. 21 smote..and the people fled into their tents
13. 5 the children of Israel dwelt in their tents
14. 12 and they fled every man to their tents
1 Ch. 4. 41 smote their tents, and the habitations
5. 10 they dwelt in their tents throughout all
15. 1 prepared a place..and pitched for it a tent
16. 1 set it in the midst of the tent that David
17. 5 have gone from tent to tent, and from (one)
2 Ch. 1. 4 for he had pitched a tent for it at Jerusa.
7. 10 he sent the people away into their tents
10. 16 to your tents, O Israel..went to their tents
14. 15 They smote also the tents of cattle, and car.
25. 22 Judah..they fled every man to his tent
Psa. 69. 25 desolate; (and) let none dwell in their te.
78. 55 and made the tribes..to dwell in their te
78. 60 the tent (which) he placed among men
84. 10 than to dwell in the tents of wickedness
106. 25 murmured in their tents, (and) hearkened
120. 5 Woe (is) me..(that) I dwell in the tents of
Song 1. 5 as the tents of Kedar, as the curtains of
Isa. 38. 12 is removed from me as a shepherd's tent
40. 22 spreadeth them out as a tent to dwell in
54. 2 Enlarge the place of thy tent, and let them
Jer. 4. 20 suddenly are my tents spoiled, (and) my
6. 3 they shall pitch (their) tents against her
10. 20 (there is) none to stretch forth my tent
30. 18 bring again the captivity of Jacob's tents
35. 7 all your days ye shall dwell in tents; that
35. 10 we have dwelt in tents, and have obeyed
37. 10 should they rise up every man in his tent
49. 29 Their tents and their flocks shall they take
Hab. 3. 7 saw the tents of Cushan in affliction: (and)
Zech. 12. 7 The LORD also shall save the tents of Ju.

2. *Tabernacle, dwelling place,* מִשְׁכָּן *mishkan.*
Song 1. 8 feed thy kids beside the shepherds' tents

3. *Covering, booth,* סֻכָּה *sukkah.*
2 Sa. 11. 11 Israel, and Judah, abide in tents; and my

4. *Hollow place, belly,* קֻבָּה *qubbah.*
Num 25. 8 went after the man of Israel into the tent

TENTS, (to abide in) —

1. *To incline, encamp,* חָנָה *chanah.*
Num. 9. 20 they abode in their tents, and according
9. 22 children of Israel abode in their tents
Ezra 8. 15 there abode we in tents three days: and

2. *Camp,* מַחֲנֶה *machaneh.*
Num 13. 19 what cities (they be)..whether in tents, or
1 Sa. 17. 53 returned..and they spoiled their tents
2 Ki. 7. 16 people went out, and spoiled the tents
2 Ch. 31. 2 to praise in the gates of the tents of the
Zech. 14. 15 all the beasts that shall be in these tents

TENTH deal, part —

1. *A tenth part,* מַעֲשֵׂר *maaser.*
Num 18. 21 given the children of Levi all the tenth
18. 26 ye shall offer..a tenth (part) of the tithe
Eze. 45. 11 that the bath may contain the tenth part
45. 14 (ye shall offer) the tenth part of a bath

2. *Ten,* עָשׂוֹר *asor.*
Exod 12. 3 In the tenth (day) of this month they sh.
Lev. 16. 29 on the tenth (day) of the month, ye shall
23. 27 on the tenth (day) of this seventh month
25. 9 to sound on the tenth (day) of the seventh
Num 29. 7 ye shall have on the tenth (day) of this se.
Josh. 4. 19 came up out of Jordan on the tenth (day)
2 Ki. 25. 1 it came to pass..in the tenth (day) of the
Jer. 52. 4 it came to pass..in the tenth (day) of the
52. 12 in the fifth month, in the tenth (day) of
Eze. 20. 1 in the fifth (month), the tenth (day) of the
24. 1 in the tenth (day) of the month, the word
40. 1 in the tenth (day) of the month, in the fo.

3. *Tenth,* עֲשִׂירִי *asiri.*
Gen. 8. 5 until the tenth month: in the tenth (mo.)
Exod 16. 36 Now an omer (is) the tenth (part) of an ep.
Lev. 5. 11 bring for his offering the tenth part of an
6. 20 the tenth part of an ephah of fine flour
27. 32 concerning the tithe..the tenth shall be
Num. 5. 15 the tenth (part) of an ephah of barley meal
7. 66 On the tenth day Ahiezer the son of Am.
28. 5 a tenth (part) of an ephah of flour for a
Deut 23. 2 to his tenth generation shall he not enter
23. 3 to their tenth generation shall they not e.
2 Ki. 25. 1 the ninth year of his reign in the tenth m.
1 Ch. 12. 13 Jeremiah the tenth, Machbanai the elev.
24. 11 The ninth to Jeshuah, the tenth to Sheca.
25. 17 The tenth to Shimei, (he), his sons, and
27. 13 The tenth..for the tenth month (was) M.
Ezra 10. 16 sat down in the first day of the tenth mo.
Esth. 2. 16 the tenth month, which (is) the month T.
Isa. 6. 13 in it (shall be) a tenth, and (it) shall return
Jer. 32. 1 in the tenth year of Zedekiah king of Ju.
39. 1 in the tenth month, came Nebuchadrezzar
52. 4 ninth year of his reign in the tenth month
Eze. 24. 1 in the ninth year, in the tenth month, in
29. 1 In the tenth year, in the tenth (month), in
33. 21 in the tenth (month), in the fifth (day) of
45. 11 and the ephah the tenth part of an homer
Zech. 8. 19 the fast of the tenth, shall be to the house

4. *A tenth part,* עִשָּׂרוֹן *issaron.*
Exod29. 40 a tenth deal of flour mingled with the fo.
Lev. 14. 10 three tenth deals of fine flour (for) a meat
14. 21 one tenth deal of fine flour mingled with
23. 13 two tenth deals of fine flour mingled with
23. 17 bring..two wave loaves of two tenth deals
24. 5 bake twelve cakes..two tenth deals shall
Num15. 4 a tenth deal of flour mingled with the fo.
15. 6 two tenth deals of flour mingled with the
15. 9 three tenth deals of flour mingled with
28. 9 two tenth deals of flour (for) a meat offer.
28. 12 three tenth deals of flour (for) a meat off.
28. 12 two tenth deals of flour (for) a meat offer.
28. 13 a several tenth deal of flour mingled with
28. 20 three tenth deals..and two tenth deals
28. 21 A several tenth deal shalt thou offer for
28. 28 three tenth deals..two tenth deals unto
28. 29 A several tenth deal unto one lamb, thro.
29. 3 three tenth deals..(and) two tenth deals
29. 4 one tenth deal for one lamb, throughout
29. 9 three tenth deals..two tenth deals to one
29. 10 A several tenth deal for one lamb, throu.
29. 14 three tenth deals unto every bullock of the
29. 14 two tenth deals to each ram of the two ra.
29. 15 a several tenth deal to each lamb of the

5. *A tenth part,* δεκάτη *dekatē.*
Heb. 7. 2 To whom also Abraham gave a tenth part
7. 4 unto whom..Abraham gave the tenth of

6. *A tenth,* δέκατος *dekatos.*
John 1. 39 and abode..for it was about the tenth hour
Rev. 11. 13 the tenth part of the city fell, and in the
21. 20 the tenth, a chrysoprasus; the eleventh

TENTH, to give or take the —

1. *To receive a tenth,* עָשַׂר *asar.*
1 Sa. 8. 15 he will take the tenth of your seed, and
8. 17 He will take the tenth of your sheep: and

2. *To give a tenth,* עָשַׂר *asar,* 3.
Gen. 28. 22 I will surely give the tenth unto thee

TENTMAKER —

A tentmaker, σκηνοποιός *skēnopoios.*
Acts 18. 3 by their occupation they were tent mak.

TE'-RAH, תֶּרַח *turning, duration, wandering.*
Son of Nahor, and father of Abraham, Nahor, and Haran; he died in Haran aged 205 years. B.C. 2000.
Gen. 11. 24 lived nine and twenty years, and begat T.
11. 25 Nahor lived after he begat T. an hundred
11. 26 T. lived seventy years, and begat Abram
11. 27 these (are) the generations of T.: T. begat
11. 28 Haran died before his father T. in the la.
11. 31 T. took Abram his son, and Lot the son of
11. 32 the days of T. were two hundred..and T.
Josh 24. 2 T., the father of Abraham, and the fath.
1 Ch. 1. 26 Serug, Nahor, T.

TE-RA'-PHIM, תְּרָפִים *nourishers.*
A kind of household gods, probably in the human form.
Judg 17. 5 Micah..made an ephod, and teraphim
18. 14 ye know that there is in these houses..t.
18. 17 the five men..took..the teraphim, and
18. 18 these..fetched.. the teraphim, and the
18. 20 priest's heart was glad; and he took..the t.
Hos. 3. 4 the children of Israel shall abide..(wi.)t.

TE'-RESH, תֶּרֶשׁ *strictness, reverence.*
A chamberlain at the court of Persia that combined against Ahasuerus along with Bigthana, and was defeated by Mordecai discovering the plot. B.C. 510.
Esth. 2. 21 T...sought to lay hold on the king Ahas.
6. 2 Mordecai had told of Bigthana and T., two

TERMED, to be —

To be said, אָמַר *amar,* 2.
Isa. 62. 4 neither shall thy land any more be termed
62. 4 Thou shalt no more be termed Forsaken

TERRACE —

Highway, place raised up, מְסִלָּה *mesillah.*
2 Ch. 9. 11 the king made (of) the algum trees terra.

TERRESTRIAL —

Upon or belonging to the earth, ἐπίγειος *epigeios.*
1 Co 15. 40 also celestial bodies, and bodies terrestrial
15. 40 and the (glory) of the terrestrial (is) anot.

TERRIBLE (acts, things), terribleness —

1. *Terrible, awe-inspiring,* אָיֹם *ayom.*
Song 6. 4 comely as Jerusalem, terrible as (an army)
6. 10 clear as the sun, (and) terrible as (an ar.)
Hab. 1. 7 They (are) terrible and dreadful: their ju.

2. *Terror, awe, dread,* אֵימָה *emah.*
Job 39. 20 the glory of his nostrils (is) terrible
41. 14 Who can open..his teeth (are) terrible ro.

3. *Terrible, fearful,* אֵימְתָנִי *emthani.*
Dan. 7. 7 a fourth beast, dreadful and terrible, and

4. *To be afraid, terrible,* דְּחַל *dechal.*
Dan. 2. 31 stood before thee, and the form..(was) t.

5. *Horror, heat, wrath, raging,* זַלְעָפָה *zalaphah.*
Lam. 5. 10 skin was black..because of the terrible

6. *To be feared, reverenced,* יָרֵא *yare,* 2.
Exod34. 10 it (is) a terrible thing that I will do with
Deut. 1. 19 went through all that great and terrible
7. 21 God (is) among you, a mighty God and te.
8. 15 led thee through that great and terrible
10. 17 a great God, a mighty, and a terrible, wh.
10. 21 these great and terrible things which th.
Judg 13. 6 countenance of an angel of God, very te.
2 Sa. 7. 23 to do for you great things and terrible
1 Ch. 17. 21 to make thee a name of..terribleness, by
Neh. 1. 5 the great and terrible God, that keepeth
4. 14 the LORD, (which is) great and terrible
9. 32 the terrible God, who keepest covenant
Job 37. 22 out of the north: with God (is) terrible
Psa. 45. 4 thy right hand shall teach thee terrible t.
47. 2 the LORD most high (is) terrible; (he is)
65. 5 (By) terrible things in righteousness wilt
66. 3 Say unto God, How terrible (art thou in)
66. 5 (he is) terrible (in his) doing toward the
68. 35 O God, (thou art) terrible out of thy holy
76. 12 (he is) terrible to the kings of the earth
99. 3 Let them praise thy great and terrible
106. 22 Wondrous works..(and) terrible things
145. 6 shall speak of the might of thy terrible a.
Isa. 18. 2, 7 a people terrible from their beginning
21. 1 it cometh from the desert, from a terrible
64. 3 When thou didst terrible things (which)
Eze. 1. 22 (was) as the colour of the terrible crystal
Joel 2. 11 day of the LORD (is) great and very terr.
2. 31 before the great and the terrible day of the
Zeph. 2. 11 The LORD (will be) terrible unto them

7. *Fear, reverence,* מוֹרָא *mora.*
Deut 26. 8 with great terribleness, and with signs

8. *Terrible,* עָרִיץ *arits.*
Isa. 13. 11 will lay low the haughtiness of the terr.
25. 3 the city of the terrible nations shall fear
25. 4 the blast of the terrible ones (is) as a st.
25. 5 the branch of the terrible ones shall be br.
29. 5 the multitude of the terrible ones (shall be)
29. 20 the terrible one is brought to nought, and
49. 25 the prey of the terrible shall be delivered
Jer. 15. 21 redeem thee out of the hand of the terri.
20. 11 the LORD (is) with me as a mighty terrible
Eze. 28. 7 bring..upon thee, the terrible of the nat.
30. 11 the terrible of the nations, shall be brou.
31. 12 the terrible of the nations, have cut him
32. 12 the terrible of the nations, all of them

9. *A cause of terror,* תִּפְלֶצֶת *tiphletseth.*
Jer. 49. 16 Thy terribleness hath deceived thee, (and)

10. *Fearful, dreadful,* φοβερός *phoberos.*
Heb. 12. 21 so terrible was the sight, (that) Moses sa.

TERRIBLY, to shake —

To fear, be afraid, terrify, עָרַץ *arats.*
Isa. 2. 19, 21 when he ariseth to shake terribly the

TERRIFY, be terrified, to —

1. *To terrify, frighten,* בָּעַת *baath,* 3.
Job 3. 5 let the blackness of the day terrify it
7. 14 thou scarest me..and terrifiest me through
9. 34 Let him take..let not his fear terrify me

2. *To cause to break down, affright,* חָתַת *chathath,* 5.
Job 31. 34 did the contempt of families terrify me

3. *To fear, be afraid, terrified,* עָרַץ *arats.*
Deut. 20. 3 do not tremble, neither be ye terrified be.

4. *To terrify exceedingly,* ἐκφοβέω *ekphobeō.*
2 Co. 10. 9 That I may not seem as if I would terrify

5. *To be affrighted, terrified,* πτοέομαι *ptoeomai.*
Luke21. 9 when ye shall hear of wars..be not terri.
24. 37 they were terrified and affrighted, and su.

6. *To be affrighted, startled, terrified,* πτύρομαι.
Phil. 1. 28 And in nothing terrified by your adver.

TERROR —

1. *Terror,* אֵימָה *emah.*
Deut 32. 25 The sword without, and terror within, sh.
Josh. 2. 9 that your terror is fallen upon us, and th.
Job 20. 25 cometh out of his gall: terrors (are) upon
33. 7 my terror shall not make thee afraid, ne.
Psa. 55. 4 and the terrors of death are fallen upon
88. 15 (while) I suffer thy terrors I am distracted
Isa. 33. 18 Thine heart shall meditate terror. Where

2. *Trouble, haste,* בֶּהָלָה *behalah.*
Lev. 26. 16 I will even appoint over you terror, con.
Jer. 15. 8 caused (him) to fall..and terrors upon the

3. *A worn out or wasted thing,* בַּלָּהָה *ballahah.*
Job 18. 11 Terrors shall make him afraid on every si.
18. 14 and it shall bring him to the king of terr.
24. 17 (they are in) the terrors of the shadow of
27. 20 Terrors take hold on him as waters, a te.
30. 15 Terrors are turned upon me: they pursue
Psa. 73. 19 they are utterly consumed with terrors
Eze. 26. 21 I will make thee a terror, and thou (shalt
27. 36 thou shalt be a terror, and never (shalt
28. 19 thou shalt be a terror, and never (shalt)

4. *Terrors,* בִּעוּתִים *biuthim.*
Job 6. 4 the terrors of God do set themselves in ar.
Psa. 88. 16 goeth over me; thy terrors have cut me

5. *A cause of staggering,* חָגָּא *chogga.*
Isa. 19. 17 the land of Judah shall be a terror unto

6. *Terror, fright,* חִתָּה *chittah.*
Gen. 35. 5 the terror of God was upon the cities that

7. *Terror,* חִתִּית *chittith.*
Eze. 26. 17 which cause their terror (to be) on all th.
32. 23 which caused terror in the land of the li.
32. 24, 26 caused their terror in the land of the
32. 25 their terror was caused in the land of the
32. 27 (they were) the terror of the mighty in the
32. 30 with their terror they are ashamed of th.
32. 32 I have caused my terror in the land of the

8. *Fear,* מָגוֹר *magor.*
Jer. 20. 4 I will make thee a terror to thyself, and
Lam. 2. 22 hast called as in a solemn day my terrors

9. *To cast down,* מָגַר *magar.*
Eze. 21. 12 terrors by reason of the sword shall be up.

10. *Fear,* מוֹרָא *mora.*
Deut. 4. 34 by a stretched out arm, and by great ter.
34. 12 in all the great terror which Moses show.
Jer. 32. 21 a stretched out arm, and with great terr.

11. *Cause of terror or ruin,* מְחִתָּה *mechittah.*
Isa. 54. 14 from terror; for it shall not come near
Jer. 17. 17 Be not a terror unto me: thou (art) my

12. *Violence, terror,* מַעֲרָצָה *maaratsah.*
Isa. 10. 33 the LORD..shall lop the bough with terr.

13. *Fear, dread,* פַּחַד *pachad.*
Job 31. 23 destruction (from) God (was) a terror to
Psa. 91. 5 Thou shalt not be afraid for the terror by

14. *Fear,* φόβος *phobos.*
Rom 13. 3 rulers are not a terror to good works, but
2 Co. 5. 11 Knowing therefore the terror of the Lord
1 Pe. 3. 14 be not afraid of their terror, neither be

TER-TI'-US, Τέρτιος (*Latin, third*).
The person who wrote the Epistle to the Romans from Paul's dictation at Corinth, and thought to have been *Silas.*
Rom 16. 22 I T., who wrote (this) epistle salute you

TER-TUL'-LUS, Τέρτυλλος.
A (Roman) orator who went with the high priest and elders from Jerusalem to Cæsarea to accuse Paul before Felix the Roman governor. B.C. 60.
Acts 24. 1 and..a certain orator..T., who informed
24. 2 T. began to accuse (him), saying, Seeing

TESTAMENT —

Dispensation, full arrangement, διαθήκη *diathēkē.*
Matt 26. 28 this is my blood of the new testament, wh.
Mark14. 24 This is my blood of the new testament, w.
Luke22. 20 This cup (is) the new testament in my bl.
1 Co. 11. 25 This cup is the new testament in my blo.
2 Co. 3. 6 made us able ministers of the new testa.
3. 14 in the reading of the Old Testament, wh.
Heb. 7. 22 was Jesus made a surety of a better test.
9. 15 he is the mediator of the new testament
9. 15 transgressions..under the first testament
9. 16 where a testament (is), there must also of
9. 17 a testament (is) of force after men are de.
9. 20 This (is) the blood of the testament which
Rev. 11. 19 seen in his temple the ark of his testame.

TESTATOR —

To arrange fully, dispose, διατίθεμαι *diatithemai.*
Heb. 9. 16 there must..be the death of the testator
9. 17 of no strength..while the testator liveth

TESTIFY, (beforehand, unto), to be testified, to —

1. *To (cause to) testify, attest,* עוּד *ud,* 5.
Deut. 8. 19 I testify against you this day, that ye sh.
32. 46 the words which I testify among you this
2 Ki. 17. 13 the LORD testified against Israel and aga.
17. 15 his testimonies which he testified against
2 Ch.24. 19 they testified against them: but they wo.
Neh. 9. 26 slew thy prophets which testified against
9. 29 testifiedst against them, that thou migh.
9. 30 testifiedst against them by thy spirit in
9. 34 wherewith thou didst testify against them
13. 15 I testified (against them) in the day whe.
13. 21 I testified against them, and said unto th.
Psa. 50. 7 I will testify against thee: I (am) God
81. 8 Hear, O my people, and I will testify un.
Amos.3. 13 testify in the house of Jacob, saith the

2. *To be testified,* עוּד *ud,* 6.
Exod21. 29 it hath been testified to his owner, that

3. *To answer, respond,* עָנָה *anah.*
Num35. 30 one witness shall not testify against any
Deut 19. 16 to testify against him (that which is) wro.
19. 18 (and) hath testified falsely against his br.
31. 21 this song shall testify against them as a
Ruth 1. 21 the LORD hath testified against me, and
2 Sa. 1. 16 thy mouth hath testified against thee, sa.
Job 15. 6 yea, thine own lips testify against thee
Isa. 59. 12 our sins testify against us: for our trans.
Jer. 14. 7 though our iniquities testify against us
Hos. 5. 5 the pride of Israel doth testify to his face
7. 10 the pride of Israel testifieth to his face
Mic. 6. 3 wherein have I wearied thee? testify aga.

4. *To bear thorough witness,* διαμαρτύρομαι *diamar.*
Luke16. 28 that he may testify unto them, lest they
Acts 2. 40 with many other words did he testify and
8. 25 when they had testified and preached the
10. 42 to testify that it is he which was ordained
18. 5 testified to the Jews (that) Jesus (was) Ch.
20. 21 Testifying both to the Jews, and also to the
20. 24 to testify the gospel of the grace of God
23. 11 as thou hast testified of me in Jerusalem
28. 23 to whom he expounded and testified the
1 Th. 4. 6 we also have forewarned you and testified
Heb. 2. 6 one in a certain place testified, saying, Wh.

5. *To bear witness upon or besides,* ἐπιμαρτυρέω *epi.*
1 Pe. 5. 12 testifying that this is the true grace of God

6. *To bear witness,* μαρτυρέω *martureō.*
John 2. 25 needed not that any should testify of man
3. 11 We speak..and testify that we have seen
3. 32 what he hath seen and heard, that he tes.

John 4. 39 the woman, which testified, He told me all
4. 44 Jesus himself testified, that a prophet ha.
5. 39 and they are they which testify of me
7. 7 me it hateth, because I testify of it, that
13. 21 he was troubled in spirit, and testified, and
15. 26 the spirit of truth..shall testify of me
21. 24 This is the disciple which testifieth of th.
Acts 26. 5 if they would testify, that after the most
1 Co.15. 15 we have testified of God that he raised up
Heb. 7. 17 he testifieth, Thou (art) a priest for ever
11. 4 obtained witness..God testifying of his
1 Jo. 4. 14 we have seen and do testify that the Fath.
5. 9 the witness of God which he hath testified
3 John 3 the brethren came and testified of the tr.
Rev. 22. 16 I Jesus have sent mine angel to testify
22. 20 He which testifieth these things saith, Su.

7. *To bear witness*, μαρτύρομαι *marturomai.*
Gal. 5. 3 I testify again to every man that is circu.
Eph. 4. 17 I say therefore, and testify in the Lord

8. *The witness bearing*, τὸ μαρτύριον *to marturion.*
1 Ti. 2. 6 a ransom for all,[to be testified] in due time

9. *To bear witness before*, προμαρτύρομαι *promartur.*
1 Pe. 1. 11 it testified beforehand the sufferings of

10. *To bear witness together*, συμμαρτυρέω *summa.*
Rev. 22. 18 [I testify unto] every man that heareth the

TESTIMONY, (to give or have) —

1. *Witness, testimony*, עֵדָה *edah.*
Deut. 4. 45 These (are) the testimonies, and the stat.
6. 17 his testimonies, and his statutes, which he
6. 20 What (mean) the testimonies, and the st.
Psa. 25. 10 such as keep his covenant and his testim.
78. 56 provoked..God, and kept not his testim.
93. 5 Thy testimonies are very sure: holiness be.
99. 7 they kept his testimonies, and the ordin.
119. 2 Blessed (are) they that keep his testimo.
119. 22 Remove..reproach..I have kept thy test.
119. 24 Thy testimonies also (are) my delight, (and)
119. 46 I will speak of thy testimonies also before
119. 59 and turned my feet unto thy testimonies
119. 79 and those that have known thy testimon.
119. 95 waited for me..I will consider thy testi.
119. 119 puttest away all the wicked..love thy t.
119. 125 give me..that I may know thy testimon.
119. 138 Thy testimonies (that) thou hast comma.
119. 146 save me, and I shall keep thy testimonies
119. 152 Concerning thy testimonies, I have known
119. 167 My soul hath kept thy testimonies; and
119. 168 I have kept thy precepts and thy testim.
132. 12 my covenant and my testimony that I sh.

2. *Witness, testimony*, עֵדוּת *eduth.*
Exod16. 34 Aaron laid it up before the testimony, to
25. 16 thou shalt put into the ark the testimony
25. 21 in the ark thou shalt put the testimony th.
25. 22 cherubims..upon the ark of the testimony
26. 33 bring..within the veil the ark of the test.
26. 34 the ark of the testimony in the most holy
27. 21 without the veil, which (is) before the te.
30. 6 veil that (is) by the ark of the testimony
30. 6 before the mercy seat that (is) over the te.
30. 26 thou shalt anoint..the ark of the testim.
30. 36 put of it before the testimony in the tab.
31. 7 the ark of the testimony. and the mercy
31. 18 two tables of testimony, tables of stone
32. 15 the two tables of the testimony (were) in
34. 29 with the two tables of testimony in Moses'
38. 21 the sum..of the tabernacle of testimony
39. 35 The ark of the testimony. and the staves
40. 3 shalt put therein the ark of the testimony
40. 5 the incense before the ark of the testim.
40. 20 he took and put the testimony into the ark
40. 21 covered the ark of..testimony; as the L.
Lev. 16. 13 the mercy seat that (is) upon the testim.
24. 3 the veil of the testimony, in the taberna.
Num. 1. 50 the Levites over the tabernacle of testi.
1. 53 round about the tabernacle of testimony
1. 53 the charge of the tabernacle of testimony
4. 5 and cover the ark of testimony with it
7. 89 mercy seat that (was) upon the ark of te.
9. 15 tabernacle, (namely), the tent of the tes.
10. 11 up from off the tabernacle of the testim.
17. 4 the tabernacle..before the testimony, wh.
17. 10 Bring Aaron's rod again before the testi.
Josh. 4. 16 the priests that bear the ark of the testi.
1 Ki. 2. 3 to keep..his testimonies, as it is written
2 Ki. 11. 12 (gave him) the testimony: and they made
17. 15 his testimonies which he testified against
23. 3 his commandments and his testimonies
1 Ch.29. 19 to keep thy commandments, thy testimo.
2 Ch.23. 11 (gave him) the testimony, and made him
34. 31 to keep his commandments, and his test.
Neh. 9. 34 thy commandments, and thy testimonies
Psa. 19. 7 the testimony of the LORD (is) sure, mak.
78. 5 he established a testimony in Jacob, and
81. 5 This he ordained in Joseph (for) a testim.
119. 14 I have rejoiced in the way of thy testim.
119. 31 I have stuck unto thy testimonies: O LORD
119. 36 Incline my heart unto thy testimonies, and
119. 88 so shall I keep the testimony of thy mo.
119. 99 more understanding..for thy testimonies
119. 111 Thy testimonies have I taken as an her.
119. 129 Thy testimonies (are) wonderful: there.
119. 144 The righteousness of thy testimonies (is)
119. 157 (yet) do I not decline from thy testimo.
122. 4 the tribes go up..unto the testimony of Is.
Jer. 44. 23 nor in his statutes, nor in his testimonies

3. *Witness, testimony*, תְּעוּדָה *teudah.*
Ruth 4. 7 gave (it) to his neighbour..this (was) a te.
Isa. 8. 16 Bind up the testimony, seal the law am.
8. 20 to the testimony: if they speak not acco.

4. *To bear witness*, μαρτυρέω *martureō.*
Acts 13. 22 to whom also he gave testimony, and said
14. 3 which gave testimony unto the word of
Heb. 11. 5 before his translation he had this testim.

5. *Witness, testimony*, μαρτυρία *marturia.*
John 3. 32 testifieth; and no man receiveth his tes.
3. 33 He that hath received his testimony hath
5. 34 I receive not testimony from man: but
8. 17 written..that the testimony of two men
21. 24 and we know that his testimony is true
Acts 22. 18 they will not receive thy testimony con.
Rev. 1. 2 of the testimony of Jesus Christ, and of
1. 9 for the word of God, and for the testim.
6. 9 and for the testimony which they held
11. 7 when they shall have finished their testim.
12. 11 overcame him..by the word of their tes.
12. 17 and have the testimony of Jesus Christ
19. 10 thy brethren that have the testimony of
19. 10 the testimony of Jesus is the spirit of pr.

6. *Witness, testimony*, μαρτύριον *marturion.*
Matt. 8. 4 offer the gift..for a testimony unto them
10. 18 for a testimony against them and the Ge.
Mark 1. 44 offer..those things..for a testimony unto
6. 11 shake off the dust..for a testimony agai.
13. 9 brought before rulers..for a testimony
Luke 5. 14 as Moses commanded, for a testimony un.
9. 5 shake off the very dust..for a testimony
21. 13 And it shall turn to you for a testimony
1 Co. 1. 6 as the testimony of Christ was confirmed
2. 1 declaring unto you the [testimony] of God
2 Co. 1. 12 our rejoicing is this, the testimony of our
2 Th. 1. 10 our testimony among you was believed
2 Ti. 1. 8 Be not thou..ashamed of the testimony
Heb. 3. 5 for a testimony of those things which were
Rev. 15. 5 the temple of the tabernacle of the testi.

TETRARCH, (to be) —

1. *To be a tetrarch*, τετραρχέω *tetrarcheō.*
Luke 3. 1 Herod being tetrarch of Galilee, and his
3. 1 Philip tetrarch of Iturea and of the region
3. 1 and Lysanias the tetrarch of Abilene

2. *Chief or ruler of a fourth part*, τετράρχης *tetra.*
Matt14. 1 Herod the tetrarch heard of the fame of
Luke 3. 19 Herod the tetrarch, being reproved by him
9. 7 Herod the tetrarch heard of all that was
Acts 13. 1 had been brought up with Herod the tet.

THAD-DÆ'-US, Θαδδαῖος (*from Syr.* תְּדִי) *breast.*
One of the twelve apostles of Christ, and called also *Lebbeus:* perhaps the same as *Jude*, who wrote the Epistle.
Matt10. 3 James..and Lebbeus..[surname was T.]
Mark 3. 18 James..and T., and Simon the Canaanite

THA'-HASH, תַּחַשׁ *reddish.*
A son of Reumah concubine of Nahor, Abraham's brother. B.C. 1860.
Gen. 22. 24 she bare also Tebah, and Gaham, and T.

THA'-MAH, TA'-MAH, תָּמַח *combat.*
One of the Nethinim whose descendants returned with Zerubbabel. B.C. 536.
Ezra 2. 53 children of Sisera, the children of T.
Neh. 7. 55 children of Sisera, the children of T.

THA'-MAR, Θάμαρ (*from Heb.* תָּמָר) *a palm tree.*
An ancestor of Jesus. See *Tamar*.
Matt. 1. 3 Judas begat Phares and Zara of T.; and

THAN, (rather)—

1. *That, that which*, דִּי *di.*
Dan. 3. 19 seven times more than it was wont to be

2. *From*, מִן *min.*
Lev. 14. 37 which in sight (are) lower than the wall

3. *Upon, above*, עַל *al.*
Num. 3. 46 children of Israel, which are more than
Eccl. 5. 8 regardeth; and (there be) higher than they

4. *From above*, מֵעַל *meal.*
Eccl. 5. 8 for (he that is) higher than the highest

5. *Either, or; (after a comparative) than*, ἤ *ē.*
Matt10. 15 for the land of Sodom..than for that city
See also 11. 22, 24; 18. 8, 9, 13; 19. 24; 26. [53]; Mark 6. [11]; 9. 43, 45, 47; 10. 25; 15. 7; Luke 10. 12, 14; 16. 17; 17. 2; 18. 14, 25; John 3. 19; 4. 1; Acts 4. 19; 5. 29; 25. [6]; 27. 11; Rom. 13. 11; 1 Co. 7. 9; 9. 15; 14. 5, 19; 2 Co. 1. 13; Gal. 4. 27; 1 Ti. 1. 4; 2 Ti. 3. 4; Heb. 11. 25; 1 Pe. 3. 17; 2 Pe. 2. 21; 1 Jo. 4. 4.

6. *Or, than, truly*, ἤπερ *ēper.*
John 12. 43 they loved the praise of men more than

7. *To the side of, beyond*, παρά (acc.) *para.*
Luke 3. 13 Exact no more than that which is appoi.
1 Co. 3. 11 other foundation can no man lay than
Gal. 1. 8, 9 preach any other gospel unto you than
Heb. 1. 4 obtained a more excellent name than they
2. 7 Thou madest him a little lower than the
2. 9 Jesus, who was made a little lower than
3. 3 worthy of more glory than Moses; 12. 24.
9. 23 heavenly things..with better sacrifices t.
11. 4 offered..a more excellent sacrifice than

8. *But rather*, ἀλλ' ἤ *all' ē*, 2 Co. 1. 13.

9. *Beyond*, πλήν *plēn.*
Acts 15. 28 no greater burden than these necessary

10. *Above*, ὑπέρ (acc.) *huper.*
Luke16. 8 are in their generation wiser than the ch.
Heb. 4. 12 sharper than any two edged sword, pier.
[*See also* Conqueror, more, rather.]

THAN that —
But, כִּי *ki.*
1 Sa. 27. 1 (there is) nothing better for me than that

THANK, give thanks, to —

1. *To bless, declare blessed*, בָּרַךְ *barak*, 3.
2 Sa. 14. 22 and bowed himself, and thanked the king

2. *To confess, thank, praise*, יְדָא *yeda*, 5.
Dan. 2. 23 I thank thee, and praise thee, O thou God
6. 10 gave thanks before his God, as he did af.

3. *To confess, thank, praise*, יָדָה *yadah*, 5.
2 Sa. 22. 50 I will give thanks unto thee, O LORD, am.
1 Ch.16. 4 to thank and praise the LORD God of Isr.
16. 7 David delivered first (this psalm), to thank
16. 8 Give thanks unto the LORD, call upon his
16. 34 give thanks unto the LORD; for (he is) go.
16. 35 that we may give thanks to thy holy name
16. 41 to give thanks to the LORD, because his
23. 30 to stand every morning to thank and praise
25. 3 prophesied with a harp, to give thanks and
29. 13 we thank thee, and praise thy glorious na.
2 Ch. 5. 13 one sound to be heard in praising and th.
31. 2 to minister, and to give thanks, and to pr.
Ezra 3. 11 in praising and giving thanks unto the L.
Neh. 12. 24 to praise (and) to give thanks, according
Psa. 6. 5 in the grave who shall give thee thanks?
18. 49 Therefore will I give thanks unto thee, O
30. 4 give thanks at the remembrance of his
30. 12 O LORD my God, I will give thanks unto
35. 18 I will give thee thanks in the great cong.
75. 1 we give thanks, (unto thee) do we give th.
79. 13 we thy people..will give thee thanks for
92. 1 (It is a) good (thing) to give thanks unto
97. 12 give thanks at the remembrance of his ho.
105. 1 give thanks unto the LORD; call upon his
106. 1 give thanks unto the LORD; for (he is) go.
106. 47 to give thanks unto thy holy name, (and)
107. 1 give thanks unto the LORD, for (he is) go.
118. 1 give thanks unto the LORD; for (he is) go.
118. 29 give thanks unto the LORD; for (he is) go.
119. 62 At midnight I will rise to give thanks un.
122. 4 to give thanks unto the name of the LORD
136. 1 give thanks unto the LORD; for (he is) go.
136. 2 give thanks unto the God of gods: for his
136. 3 give thanks to the Lord of lords: for his
136. 26 give thanks unto the God of heaven: for
140. 13 the righteous shall give thanks unto thy

4. *To profess, confess, give glory to*, ἐξομολογέομαι.
Matt11. 25 I thank thee, O Father, Lord of heaven
Luke10. 21 I thank thee, O Father, Lord of heaven

5. *Grace, thanks*, χάρις *charis.*
Rom. 6. 17 But God be thanked, that ye were the

6. *To thank, be thankful*, εὐχαριστέω *eucharisteō.*
Matt.15. 36 took the seven loaves..and gave thanks
26. 27 he took the cup, and gave thanks, and ga.
Mark 8. 6 he took the seven loaves, and gave than.
14. 23 when he had given thanks, he gave (it) to
Luke17. 16 fell down on (his) face..giving him thanks
18. 11 I thank thee, that I am not as other men
22. 17 he took the cup, and gave thanks, and s.
22. 19 he took bread, and gave thanks, and bra.
John 6. 11 when he had given thanks, he distributed
6. 23 after that the Lord [had given thanks]
11. 41 Father, I thank thee that thou hast heard
Acts 27. 35 gave thanks to God in presence of them
28. 15 whom when Paul saw, he thanked God
Rom. 1. 8 I thank my God through Jesus Christ for
7. 25 [I thank] God through Jesus Christ our L.
14. 6 eateth to the Lord..he giveth God thanks
14. 6 he eateth not, and giveth God thanks
16. 4 unto whom not only I give thanks, but
1 Co. 1. 4 I thank my God always on your behalf
1. 14 I thank God that I baptized none of you
10. 30 spoken of for that for which I give thanks
11. 24 when he had given thanks, he brake (it)
14. 17 thou verily givest thanks well, but the
14. 18 I thank my God, I speak with tongues mo.
2 Co. 1. 11 thanks may be given by many on our be.
Eph. 1. 16 Cease not to give thanks for you, making
5. 20 Giving thanks always for all things unto
Phil. 1. 3 I thank my God upon every remembra.
Col. 1. 3 We give thanks to God and the Father of
1. 12 Giving thanks unto the Father, which ha.
3. 17 giving thanks to God and the Father by
1 Th. 1. 2 We give thanks to God always for you all
2. 13 For this cause also thank we God without
5. 18 In every thing give thanks: for this is the
2 Th. 1. 3 We are bound to thank God always for
2. 13 we are bound to give thanks alway to God
Phm. 4 I thank my God, making mention of thee
Rev. 11. 17 We give thee thanks, O Lord God Almig.

7. *To have grace, favour*, ἔχω χάριν *echō charin.*
Luke17. 9 Doth he thank that servant because he did
1 Ti. 1. 12 I thank Christ Jesus our Lord, who hath
2 Ti. 1. 3 I thank God, whom I serve from (my) for.

8. *To confess correspondingly*, ἀνθομολογέομαι.
Luke 2. 38 she coming in that instant gave thanks

9. *To confess, profess, say the same thing*, ὁμολογέω.
Heb. 13. 15 the fruit of (our) lips giving thanks to his

THANKFUL, (to be) —

1. *To thank, praise, confess*, יָדָה *yadah*, 5.
Psa.100. 4 be thankful unto him, (and) bless his name

2. *To thank, be thankful*, εὐχαριστέω *eucharisteō.*
Rom. 1. 21 they glorified (him) not..neither were tha.

3. *Thankful*, εὐχάριστος *eucharistos.*
Col. 3. 15 let the peace of God rule..be ye thankful

THANKS (giving, offering, worthy), thankfulness —

1. *Choir, choir of singing,* הֻיְּדוֹת *huyyedoth.*
Neh. 12. 8 Mattaniah, (which was) over the thanks.

2. *To thank, praise, confess,* יָדָה *yadah,* 5.
Neh. 11. 17 the principal to begin the thanksgiving
12. 46 songs of praise and thanksgiving unto G.

3. *Confession, thanksgiving, choir,* תּוֹדָה *todah.*
Lev. 7. 12 If he offer it for a thanksgiving, then he
7. 12 shall offer with the sacrifice of thanksg.
7. 13 with the sacrifice of thanksgiving of his
7. 15 sacrifice of his peace offerings for thanks
22. 29 when ye will offer a sacrifice of thanksg.
2 Ch. 29. 31 bring sacrifices and thank offerings into
29. 31 brought in sacrifices and thank offerings
33. 16 sacrificed..peace offerings and thank off.
Neh. 12. 27 with thanksgivings, and with singing, (wi.)
12. 31 great (companies of them that gave) tha.
12. 38 the other (company of them that gave) th.
12. 40 two (companies of them that gave) thanks
Psa. 26. 7 I may publish with the voice of thanksg.
50. 14 Offer unto God thanksgiving; and pay
69. 30 and will magnify him with thanksgiving
95. 2 Let us come before his presence with th.
100. 4 Enter into his gates with thanksgiving
107. 22 let them sacrifice the sacrifices of thanks.
116. 17 I will offer to thee the sacrifice of thanks.
147. 7 Sing unto the LORD with thanksgiving
Isa. 51. 3 gladness shall be found therein, thanks.
Jer. 30. 19 out of them shall proceed thanksgiving
Amos 4. 5 offer a sacrifice of thanksgiving with lea.
Jon. 2. 9 will sacrifice unto thee..with..thanksgiving

4. *Thanksgiving, thankfulness,* εὐχαριστία *euchar.*
Acts 24. 3 We accept (it) always..with all thankfu.
1 Co. 14. 16 how shall he..say Amen at thy giving oft
2 Co. 4. 15 might through the thanksgiving of many
9. 11 which causeth through us thanksgiving
9. 12 is abundant also by many thanksgivings
Eph. 5. 4 nor jesting..but rather giving of thanks
Phil. 4. 6 with thanksgiving let your requests be
Col. 2. 7 abounding therein with thanksgiving
4. 2 and watch in the same with thanksgiving
1 Th. 3. 9 what thanks can we render to God again
1 Ti. 2. 1 (and) giving of thanks, be made for all men
4. 3 created to be received with thanksgiving
4. 4 if it be received with thanksgiving
Rev. 4. 9 honour and thanks to him that sat on the
7. 12 glory, and wisdom, and thanksgiving, and

5. *Grace, favour,* χάρις *charis.*
Luke 6. 32, 33, 34 what thank have ye? for sinners
1 Co. 15. 57 thanks (be) to God, which giveth us the
2 Co. 2. 14 thanks (be) unto God, which always cau.
8. 16 thanks (be) to God, which put the same
9. 15 Thanks (be) unto God for his unspeakable
1 Pe. 2. 19 this (is) thankworthy, if a man for consc.

THA'-RA, Θάρα.
Hebrew Terah, father of Abraham. Luke 3. 34.

THARSHISH. *See* **TARSHISH.**

THAT (man, thing, same, may, could)—

1. *Concerning,* אֶל *el.*
1 Sa. 4. 19 she heard the tidings that the ark of God

2. *That, that which,* אֲשֶׁר *asher.*
Gen. 1. 31 God saw every thing that he had made, and
11. 7 that they may not understand one anoth.
Exod 20. 4 any likeness (of any thing) that (is) in he.
20. 4 or that (is) in the earth beneath, or that
Num. 6. 11 make an atonement for him, for that he

3. *So that, to the intent that,* לְמַעַן אֲשֶׁר *le-maan asher.*
Gen. 18. 19 I know him, that he will command his
Num 16. 40 that no stranger, which (is) not of the se.

4. *Which, that,* דִּי *di.*
Ezra 4. 11 This (is) the copy of the letter that they
4. 12 Be it known..that the Jews which came

5. *This, that,* דִּכֵּן *dikken.*
Dan. 7. 20 even (of) that horn that had eyes, and a

6. *He, it,* הוּא *hu.*
Gen. 2. 11 that (is) it which compasseth the whole
2. 19 whatsoever Adam called..that (was) the

7. *That (very),* הַהוּא *ha-hu.*
Gen. 19. 35 they made their father drink wine that

8. *She, it,* הִיא *hi.*
1 Ki. 3. 4 went to Gibeon..that (was) the great high

9. *That (very),* הַהִיא *ha-hi.*
Gen. 2. 12 the gold of that land (is) good: there (is)

10. *This or that (very),* הַלָּז *hallaz.*
2 Ki. 4. 25 man of God..said..Behold..that Shuna.
23. 17 Then he said, What title (is) that..I see?

11. *This,* זֹאת *zoth, f.*
Lev. 26. 44 yet for all that, when they be in the land

12. *This (very),* הַזֹּאת *haz-zoth.*
Gen. 43. 15 the men took that present, and they took

13. *This,* זֶה *zeh, m.*
Exod 13. 8 (This is done) because of that (which) the

14. *This (very),* הַזֶּה *haz-zeh.*
Gen. 24. 9 and sware to him concerning that matter

15. *This,* זוֹ *zo.*
Psa. 132. 12 and my testimony that I shall teach them

16. *This,* זוּ *zu.*
Psa. 10. 2 let them be taken in the devices that th.
17. 9 From the wicked that oppress me, (from)
31. 4 Pull me out of the net that they have laid

17. *That,* כִּי *ki.*
Gen. 1. 4 God saw the light, that (it was) good: and

18. *To the intent,* לְמַעַן *le-maan.*
Gen. 12. 13 that it may be well with me for thy sake

19. *In consequence, on account of,* בַּעֲבוּר *ba-abur.*
Gen. 21. 30 that they may be a witness unto me

20. *Until,* עַד *ad.*
Lev. 23. 14 until the selfsame day that ye have brou.

21. *This word,* הַדָּבָר הַזֶּה *had-dabar haz-zeh.*
Judg. 8. 3 anger was abated..when he had said that

22. *To the intent that,* יַעַן אֲשֶׁר *yaan asher.*
Eze. 12. 12 that he see not the ground with (his) eyes

23. *For this reason,* כָּל־קֳבֵל דְּנָה *kol qebel denah.*
Ezra 7. 17 That thou mayest buy speedily with this

24. *He, she, it,* αὐτός *autos.*
Luke 2. 38 she coming in that instant gave thanks li.

25. *If,* εἰ *ei.*
Mark 9. 42 that a millstone were hanged about hi
Luke 17. 2 that a millstone were hanged about his
Acts 26. 8 incredible with you, that God should ra.
26. 23 That Christ should suffer, (and) that he

26. *With a view to,* εἰς τό *eis to.*
1 Co. 9. 18 that I abuse not my power in the gospel
Eph. 1. 18 that ye may know what is the hope of his
Phil. 1. 10 That ye may approve things that are exc.
1 Th. 3. 10 praying exceedingly that we might see yo.
2 Th. 1. 5 that ye may be counted worthy of the ki.
2. 2 That ye be not soon shaken in mind, or
2. 6 ye know what withholdeth that he might
2. 11 strong delusion, that they should believe
Heb. 12. 10 that (we) might be partakers of his holin.
Jas. 1. 18 that we should be a kind of first fruits of
1 Pe. 3. 7 as being heirs. that your prayers be not
4. 2 That he no longer should live the rest of

27. *That, that very, he, she, it,* ἐκεῖνος *ekeinos.*
Matt. 7. 22 Many will say to me in that day, Lord
See also 7. 25, 27; 8. 28; 9. 22, 26, 31; 10. 14, 15; 11. 25; 12. 1, 45; 13. 44; 14. 1, 35; 17. 27; 18. [7, 27], 32; 22. 46; 24. 36, 46, 48, 50; 26. 24, 24, 29; 27. 8, 19, 63; Mark 3. 24, 25; 6. [11], 55; 7. 20; 13. 11, 24, 32; 14. 21, 21, 25; Luke 6. 23, 48, 49; 9. 5; 10. 12, 12, 31; 11. 26; 12. 43, 45, 46, 47; 14. [21]; 15. 14, 15; 17. [9], 31; 18. 3; 19. 4; 20. 18, 35; 21. 34; 22. 22; John 1. 39; 4. 39; 6. [22]; 11. 51, 53; 14. 20; 16. 23, 26; 18. 15; 19. 27, 31; 21. 3, 7, 23; Acts 1. 19; 3. 23; 8. 1, 8; 12. 1; 14. 21; 19. 16; 22. 11; Eph. 2. 12; 2 Th. 1. 10; 2 Ti. 1. 12, 18; 4. 8; Heb. 3. [10]; 4. 11; 8. 7; 11. 15; Jas. 1. 7; 4. 15; Rev. 16. [14].

28. *In the,* ἐν τῷ *en tō.*
Luke 1. 21 marvelled that he tarried so long in the

29. *By reason of, on account of,* ἕνεκα *(gen.) heneka.*
2 Co. 7. 12 that our care for you in the sight of God

30. *Either, or, than, verily,* ἤ *ē.*
Luke 22. 34 before that thou shalt thrice deny..thou
Acts 25. 16 before that he which is accused have the

31. *In order that, so that,* ἵνα *hina.*
Matt. 1. 22 that it might be fulfilled which was spok.
2. 15 that it might be fulfilled which was spok.
4. 3 command that these stones be made br.
4. 14 That it might be fulfilled which was
5. 29, 30 it is profitable for thee that one of thy
7. 1 Judge not, that ye be not judged
7. 12 ye would that men should do to you, do
8. 8 I am not worthy that thou shouldest come
9. 6 that ye may know that the Son of man
10. 25 It is enough for the disciple that he be
12. 10 they asked him..that they might accuse
12. 16 charged them that they should not make
14. 15 that they may go into the villages, and
14. 36 besought him that they might only touch
16. 20 Then charged he his disciples that they sh.
18. 6 it were better for him that a millstone we.
18. 14 that one of these little ones should perish
18. 16 that in the mouth of two or three witne.
19. 13 that he should put (his) hands on them
19. 16 what good thing shall I do, that I may
20. 21 Grant that these my two sons may sit
20. 33 They say unto him, Lord, that our eyes
21. 4 that it might be fulfilled which was sp.
23. 26 that the outside of them may be clean
24. 20 pray ye that your flight be not in the wi.
26. 4 consulted that they might take Jesus by
26. 41 Watch and pray, that ye enter not into te.
26. 56 that the scriptures of the prophets might
26. 63 that thou tell us whether thou be the Ch.
27. 20 persuaded the multitude that they shou.
27. 35 that it might be fulfilled which was spo.
28. 10 go tell my brethren that they go into G.
Mark 1. 38; 2. 10; 3. 2, 9, 12, 14, 14; 4. 12, 22; 5. 10, 12, 18, 43; 6. 8, 12, 25, 36, 56; 7. 9, 26, 36; 8. 30; 9. 9, 12, 18, 30; 10. 13, 17, 35, 37, 48, 51; 11. 16, 25; 12. 2, 15, 19; 13. 18; 14. 12, 35; 15. 11, 32; 16. 1.
Luke 1. 4, 43; 4. 3; 5. 24; 6. 7, 31; 7. 6, 36; 8. 10, 16, 31, 32; 9. 12, 45; 10. 40; 11. 33, 50, [54]; 12. 36; 14. 10, 23; 15. 29; 16. 4, 9, 24, 27; 17. 2; 18. 15, 39, 41; 19. 15; 20. 10, 14, 20, 28; 21. 36; 22. 8, 30, 32.
John 1. 7, 22, 31; 2. 25; 3. 15, 16, 17, 21; 4. 15, 36, 47; 5. 20, 23, 34, 40; 6. 5, 7, 12, 28, 29, 30, 39, 40, 50; 7. 3, 23; 8. [6]; 9. 2, 3, 22, 36, 39; 10. 10, 17, 38; 11. 4, 11, 16, 37, 42, 50, 52, 57; 12. 9, 10, 23, 36, 38, 40, 46; 13. 1, 15, 18, 19, 29, 34, 34; 14. 3, 13, 16, 29, 31; 15. 2, 8, 11, 12, 13, 16, 16, 17, 25; 16. 1, 2, 4, 7, 24, 30, 32, 33; 17. 1, [2], 3, 11, 12, 13, 15, 15, 19, 21, 21, 22, 23, 23, 24, 24, 26; 18. 9, [28], 32, 36, 37, 39; 19. 4, 24, 28, 31, 31, 35, 36, 38; 20. 31, 31.
Acts 2. 25; 4. 17; 5. 15; 8. 19; 9. 21; 19. 4; 21. 24; 22. 24; 23. 24; 24. 4.
Rom. 1. 11, 13; 3. 8, 19; 4. 16; 5. 20, 21; 6. 1, 4, 6; 7. 4, 13, 13; 8. 4, 17; 9. 11, 23; 11. 11, 19, 31, 32; 14. 9; 15. 4, 6, 16, 31, [31], 32; 16. 2; 1 Co. 1. 10, 31; 2. 5, 12; 3. 18; 4. 2, 3, 6, 6, 8; 5. 2, 5, 7; 7. 5, 5, 29, 34, 35; 9. [15], 15, 18, 19, 20, 20, 21, 22, 22, 23, 24; 10. 33; 11. 19, 32, 34; 12. 25; 14. 1, 5, 5, 12, 13, 19, 31; 15. 28; 16. 2, 6, 10, 11, 16; 2 Co. 1. 9, 11, 15, 17; 2. 4, 4, 5, 9; 4. 7, 10, 11, 15; 5. 4, 10, 12, 15, 21; 6. 3; 7. 9; 8. 6, 7, 9, 13, 14; 9. 3, 4, 5, 8; 10. 9; 11. 7, 12, 12, 16; 12. 8, 9; 13. 7, 7; Gal. 1. 16; 2. [4], 5, 9, 10, 16, 19; 3. 14, 14, 22, 24; 4. 5, 17; 6. 13; Eph. 1. 17; 2. 7, 10; 3. [16], 17, 19; 4. 10, 14, 28, 29; 5. 26, 27, 27, 33; 6. [3], 13, 19, 20, 21, 22; Phil. 1. 9, 10, 26, 27; 2. 2, 10, 15, 19, 28; 3. 8; Col. 1. 9, 18, 28; 2. 2; 4. 3, 4, 8, 12, 16, 16, 17; 1 Th. 2. 16; 4. 1, 12, 13; 5. 4, 10; 2 Th. 1. 11; 2. 12; 3. 1, 2, 12, 14; 1 Ti. 1. 3, 16, 18, 20; 2. 2; 3. 15; 4. 15; 5. 7, 16, 20, 21; 6. 1, 19; 2 Ti. 1. 4; 2. 4, 10; 3. 17; 4. 17; Titus 1. 5, 9, 13; 2. 4, 5, 8, 10, 12, 14; 3. 7, 8, 13, 14; Phm. 13, 14, 15.
Heb. 2. 14, 17; 4. 16; 5. 1; 6. 12, 18; 9. 25; 10. 9, 36; 11. 35, 40; 12. 27; 13. 12, 17, 19; Jas. 1. 4; 4. 3; 1 Pe. 1. 7; 2. 2, 12, 21, 24; 3. [1], 9, 16, 18; 4. 6, 11, 13; 5. 6; 2 Pe. 1. 4; 1 Jo. 1. 3, 4; 2. 1, 19, 27, 28; 3. 1, 8, 11, 23; 4. 9, 17, 21; 5. 3, 13, [13], 16, 20; 2 Jo. 5, 6, 6, 8, 12; 3 Jo. 8; Rev. 2. 10; 3. 11, 18, 18; 6. [4], [11]; 7. 1; 8. [3]; 9. 4, [5], 20; 11. 6; 12. 6, 14, 15; 13. 15, 15, 17; 14. [13], 13; 16. 12; 18. 4, 4; 19. 8, 15, 18; 20. 3; 22. 14.

32. *And,* καί *kai.*
Mark 9. 39 there is no man..that can lightly speak
Luke 5. 1 it came to pass, that, as the people pres.
8. 1 that he went throughout every city and
10. 38 that he entered into a certain village

33. *So that, to the end that,* ὅπως *hopōs.*
Matt. 2. 8 bring me word again, that I may come
See also v. 23; 5. 16, 45; 6. 2, 4, 5, 16, 18; 8. 17, [34]; 9. 38; 12. [17]; 13. 35; 23. 35; Mark 5. [23]; Luke 2. 35; 7. 3; 10. 2; 16. 28; John 11. 57; Acts 8. 15, 24; 9. 2, 12, 17; 15. 17; 23. 15, 20; 24. [26]; 25. 3, 26; Rom. 3. 4; 9. 17, 17; 1 Co. 1. 29; 2 Co. 8. 11, 14; Gal. 1. 4; 2 Th. 1. 12; Phm. 6; Heb. 2. 9; 9. 15; James 5. 16; 1 Pe. 2. 9.

34. *As much, as many,* ὅσος *hosos.*
Matt 13. 44 goeth and selleth all that he hath, and bu.
13. 46 went and sold all that he had, and bought
18. 25 his wife and children, and all that he had
Mark 12. 44 she of her want did cast in all that she
Luke 4. 40 they that had any sick with divers disea.
18. 12 I fast..I give tithes of all that I possess
18. 22 sell all that thou hast, and distribute un.
John 10. 41 all things that John spake of this man we.
16. 15 All things that the Father hath are mine

35. *Any one who,* ὅστις *hostis.*
Matt. 2. 6 a governor, that shall rule my people Is.
18. 28 took (him)..saying, Pay me [that] thou owe.
27. 62 the next day, that followed the day of the
Luke 7. 39 what manner of woman (this is) that tou.
John 8. 25 (the same) that I said unto you from the
Rom. 6. 2 How shall we, that are dead to sin, live
Rev. 1. 12 I turned to see the voice that spake with
17. 8 when they behold the beast [that] was, and

36. *When,* ὅταν *hotan.*
Mark 14. 25 day that I drink it new in the kingdom

37. *When,* ὅτε *hote.*
Mark 6. 21 when a convenient day was come, that H.

38. *Because, that,* ὅτι *hoti.*
Matt. 2. 16 Herod, when he saw that he was mocked
2. 22 when he heard that Archelaus did reign
See also 3. 9; 4. 12; 5. 17, 20, 21, 22, 23, 27, 28, 32, 33, 38, 43; 6. 29, 32; 8. 11, 27; 9. 6, 28; 10. 34; 11. 24; 12. 6, 36; 13. 17; 15. 12, 17; 16. 11, 12, 18, 20; 17. 10, 12, 13; 18. 10, 19; 19. 4, 23, 28; 20. 10. 25, 30; 21. 31, 45; 22. 16, 34; 23. 31; 24. 32, 33, 43, 47; 25. 24, 26; 26. 2, 21, 34, 53, 54; 27. 3, 18, 24, 63; 28. 5, 7.
Mark 2. 1, 8, 10, 16; 4. 38, 41; 5. 29; 6. [2], 14, 15, 15; 7. 18; 8. 31; 9. 1, 11, 13, 25; 10. 42, 47; 11. 3, 23, 24, 32; 12. 12, 14, 26, 28, 34, 35, 43; 13. 28, 29, 30; 14. 30; 15. 10, 39; 16. 4, 7, [11]; Luke 1. 22; 2. 49, 49; 3. 8; 4. 4; 5. 24; 6. [5]; 7. 4, 16, 16, 37, 43; 8. 47, 53; 9. 7, 8, 8, 19; 10. 11, 12, 20, 21, 24, 40; 11. 38; 12. 37, 39, 40, 44, 51; 13. 2, 4; 14. 24; 15. 7; 16. 25; 17. 15; 18. 8, 9, 11, 37; 19. 7, 22, 26, [40]; 20. 19, 21, 37; 21. 3, 20, 30, 31; 22. 37, 70; 23. 7; 24. 21, 39, 44.
John 1. 34; 2. 17, 18, 22, 25; 3. 2, 7, 19, 21, 28, 28, 33; 4. 1, 19, 20, 25, 27, 42, 44, 47, 53; 5. 6, 15, 32, 36, 42, 45; 6. 15, 22, 22, 24, 36, 46, 61, 65, 69; 7. 7, 26, 35, 42; 8. 17, 24, 24, 27, 28, 37, 48, 52, 54; 9. 8, 17, 18, 20, 20, 24, 25, 29, 30, 31, 32, 35; 10. 38; 11. 6, 13, 15, 20, 22, 24, 27, 31, 40, 41, 42, 42, 50, 56; 12. 6, 9, 12, 16, 34, 50; 13. 1, 3, 3, 19, 21, 29, 35; 14. 10, 11, 20, 22, 31; 15. 18; 16. 4, 15. 19, 20, 21, 26, 27, 30, 30; 17. 7, 8, 8, 21, 23, 25; 18. 8, 14, 37; 19. 4, 10, 21, 28, 35; 20. 9, 14, 18, 31; 21. 4, 7, 12, 15, 16, 17, 23, 24.
Acts 2. 29, 30, 31, 36; 3. 10, 17; 4. 10, 13, 13, 16; 5. 9, 41; 6. 14; 7. 6; 8. 14, 18; 9. 20, 22, 26, 27, 38; 10. 34, 42; 11. 1; 12. 9, 11; 13. 38; 14. 9, 22; 15. 5, 24; 16. 3, 10, 19, 38; 17. 3, 3, 13; 19. 25, 26, 26, 34; 20. 23, 23, 25, 26, 29, 31, 34, 38; 21. 21, 22, 24, 29, 31; 22. 2, 19, 29; 23. 5, 6, 22, 27, 34; 24. 11, 14, 26; 26. 5, 27; 27. 10, 25; 28. 1, 22, 28.
Rom. 1. 8, 13, 32; 2. 2, 3, 4; 3. 2, 19; 4. [9,] 21, 23; 5. 3; 6. 3, 6, 8, 9, 16, 17; 7. 14, 16, 18, 21; 8. 16, 18, 22, 28, 38; 9. 2, 30; 10. 2, 5, 9, 9; 11. 25; 13. 11; 14. 14; 15. 14, 29; 1 Co. 1. 5, 11, 12, 14, 15; 3. 16, 20; 4. [9]; 5. 6; 6. 2, 3, 9, 15, 16, 19; 7. 26; 8. 1, 4, 4; 9. 10, 13, 24; 10. [19,] 20; 11. 2, 3, 14, 17, 23; 12. 2, 3; 14. 23, 25, 37; 15. 4, 4, 5, 12, 12, 15, 27, 50,

58; 16. 15; 2 Co. 1. 7, 8, [10], 12, 14, 23; 2. 3; 3. 5; 4. 14; 5. 1, 6, 14, 19; 7. 3, 8, 9, 9, 16; 8. 9; 9. 2; 10. 7, 11; 11. 31; 12. 13. 19; 13. 2, 6, 6; Gal. 1. 6, 11, 23; 2. 7, 14, 16; 3. 7, 8, 11; 4. 15, 22; 5. 2, 3, 10, 21; Eph. 2. 11, 12; 4. 9; 5. 5; 6. 8, 9; Phil. 1. 6, 12, 17, 19, 20, 25, 27; 2. 11, 16, 22, 24, 26; 4. 10, 11, 15; Col. 3. 24; 4. 1, 13; 1 Th. 2. 1; 3. 3, 4, 6; 4. 14, 15; 5. 2; 2 Th. 2. 2, 4, 5; 3. 4, 10; 1 Ti. 1. 8, 9, 15; 4. 1; 2 Ti. 1. 5, 12, 15; 2. 23; 3. 1, 15; Tit. 3. 11; Phm. 21, 22.

Heb. 2. 6, 6; 3. 19; 7. 8, 14; 11. 6, 13, 14, 18, 19; Jas. 1. 3, 7; 2. 19, 20; 3. 1; 4. 4, 5; 5. 11, 20; 1 Pe. 1. 12; 2. 3; 3. 9; 2 Pe. 1. 14, 20; 3. 3, 5, 8; 1 Jo. 1. 5, 6, 8, 10; 2. 3, 5, 18, 18, 19, 21, 22, 29, 29; 3. 2, 5, 14, 15, 19, 24; 4. 3, 10, 10, 13, [14], 15; 5. 1, 2, 5, 11, 13, 14, 15, 15, 18, 19, 20; 2 Jo. 4; 3 Jo. 12; Rev. 2. 6, 23; 3. 1, 1, 9, 15, 17; 10. 6; 12. 12, 13.

39. *Toward, to the intent that,* πρός τό *pros to.*
2 Co. 3. 13 veil..that the children of Israel could not
Eph. 6. 11 that ye may be able to stand against the
2 Th. 3. 8 that we might not be chargeable to any
Jas. 3. 3 we put bits in the horses' mouths, [that]

40. *How,* πῶς *pōs.*
Eph. 5. 15 See then that ye walk circumspectly, not as

41. *These things,* ταῦτα *tauta.*
Mark 16. 12 After that he appeared in another form
Luke 12. 4 and after that have no more that they
Acts 7. 7 after t. shall they come, 13. 20; 1 Co. 6. 8.
Rev. 15. 5 after that I looked, and, behold, the temple
20. 3 after that he must be loosed a little season

42. *In these,* ταύταις *tautais.*
Luke 23. 7 who himself also was at Jerusalem at that

43. *To that,* ταύτῃ *tautē.*
Luke 13. 32 tell that fox, Behold, I cast out devils, and
17. 34 that night there shall be two (men) in one
Acts 16. 12 we were in that city abiding certain days

44. *That,* ταύτην *tautēn.*
Luke 23. 48 the people that came together to that si.

45. *This, that,* τοῦτο *touto.*
Mark 13. 11 that speak ye; for it is not ye..but the H.
Luke 9. 21 and commanded..to tell no man that thi.
John 3. [32]; 4. 18; 11. 7, 11; 14. 13; Rom. 1. 12; 7. [15], 15, 16, 19, 20; 10. 6, 7, 8; 13. 11; 1 Co. 6. 6; Gal. 6. 7; Eph. 2. 8; Phil. 1. 28; 1 Ti. 5. 4; Phm. 18; Heb. 13. 17.

46. *This, that,* τοῦτον *touton.*
John 19. 8 When Pilate therefore heard that saying
19. 13 When Pilate therefore heard that saying
Acts 2. 36 God hath made that same Jesus, whom ye
2 Th. 3. 14 note that man, and have no company wi.

47. *Of this, of that,* τούτου *toutou.*
John 6. 66 From that (time) many of his disciples
16. 19 Do ye enquire among yourselves of that I
Rom 11. 7 Israel hath not obtained that which he se.

48. *As, so that,* ὡς *hōs.*
Acts 28. 19 not that I had ought to 17. 22; Lu. 16. 1.
Rom. 1. 9 that without ceasing I make mention of
2 Ti. 1. 3 that without ceasing I have remembrance

49. *So that, as also,* ὥστε *hōste.*
John. 3. 16 God so loved the world, that he gave his
Acts 14. 1 that a great multitude both of the Jews and
15. 39 that they departed asunder one from the
Rom. 7. 6 that we should serve in newness of spirit
1 Co. 5. 1 that one...his father's wife, 1 Pe. 1. 21.

50. *From which,* ἀφ' ἧς *aph' hes,* Acts 20. 18.

[*See also* According to, after, all, as, because, before, but, except, for, he, how, in, oh, oh that, side, so, way.]

THAT, after —
Thus, οὕτως *houtōs.*
1 Co. 7. 7 one after this..and another after that

THAT ever —
As much, as many, ὅσος *hosos.*
John 4. 29 which told me all things [that ever] I did
4. 39 which testified, He told me [all that] ever
10. 8 All that ever came before me are thieves

THAT have —
1. *There is,* יֵשׁ *yesh.*
Isa. 43. 8 Bring forth the blind people that have eyes
2. *To them,* לָמוֹ *la-mo.*
Isa. 43. 8 Bring forth..the deaf that have ears

THAT he...again —
With, μετά *meta.*
Luke. 9. 39 it teareth him that he foameth again, and

THAT if —
If, הֵן *hen.*
Ezra 4. 13 Be it known..that if this city be builded
4. 16 if this city be builded (again), and the wa.

THAT is —
1. *To say,* אָמַר *amar.*
2 Sa. 3. 13 one thing I require of thee, that is, Thou
2. *That is,* τοῦτ' ἔστι *tout' esti.*
Acts 19. 4 believe on him..that is, on Christ Jesus
Rom. 7. 18 I know that in me that is, in my flesh, dw.
9. 8 That is, They which are the children of
10. 6 Who shall ascend into heaven? that is, to
10. 7 Who shall descend into the deep? that is
10. 8 that is, the word of faith, which we prea.
Phm. 12 therefore receive him that is mine own
Heb. 2. 14 him that had the power of death, that is
7. 5 that is, of their brethren, though they co.
11. 16 they desire a better (country), that is, an
13. 15 that is, the fruit of (our) lips giving tha.
1 Pe. 3. 20 wherein few, that is, eight souls were sa.

THAT is to say —
1. *Which is,* ὅ ἐστι *ho esti.*
Mark 7. 11 (It is) Corban, that is to say, a gift, by wh.
2. *That is,* τοῦτ' ἔστι *tout' esti.*
Matt 27. 46 Eli, Eli, lama sabachthani? that is to say
Mark 7. 2 defiled, that is to say, with unwashen ha.
Acts 1. 19 Aceldama, that is to say, The field of blood
Heb. 9. 11 not made with hands, that is to say, not
10. 20 through the veil, that is to say, his flesh

THAT...it —
He, it, הוּא *hu.*
Gen. 2. 11 that (is) it which compasseth the whole

THAT manner, on —
Thus, כָּכָה *be-koh.*
1 Ki. 22. 20 one said on this..another..on that man.

THAT...no or not, none, no one —
1. *If,* אִם *im.*
Gen. 14. 23 That I will not (take) from a thread even to
14. 23 that I will not take any thing that (is) th.
1 Sa. 24. 21 that thou wilt not cut off my seed after
2. *Not,* בַּל *bal.*
Isa. 14. 21 that they do not rise, nor possess the land
3. *In order not,* לְבִלְתִּי *le-bilti.*
Gen. 3. 11 I commanded..that thou shouldest not e.?
Exod. 8. 22 the land..that no swarms..shall be there
4. *Lest,* פֶּן *pen.*
Gen. 24. 6 Beware thou that thou bring not my son th.
5. *In order not, so as not,* ἵνα μή *hina mē.*
Matt. 7. 1 Judge not, that ye be not judged
26. 41 Watch and pray, that ye enter not into te.
John 3. 15, 16 That whosoever believeth..should not
4. 15 Sir, give me this water, that I thirst not
6. 50 that a man may eat thereof, and not die
7. 23 that the law of Moses should not be broken
11. 37 that even this man should not have died?
12. 46 that whosoever believeth..should not ab.
16. 1 These..have I spoken..that ye should not
18. 36 that I should not be delivered to the Jews
Acts 4. 17 that it spread no further among the peo.
24. 4 that I be not further tedious unto thee
1 Co. 2. 5 That your faith should not stand in the
4. 6 that ye might learn..that no one of you
7. 5 that Satan tempt you not for your incon.
11. 32 that we should not be condemned with
11. 34 that ye come not together unto condem.
12. 25 That there should be no schism in the bo.
16. 2 that there be no gatherings when I come
2 Co. 1. 9 that we should not trust in ourselves, but
2. 5 in part; that I may not overcharge you
6. 3 Giving no offence..that the ministry be
9. 4 we that we say not ye should be ashamed
10. 9 That I may not seem as if I would terrify
1 Th. 4. 13 that ye sorrow not, even as others which
1 Ti. 6. 1 that the name of God..be not blasphemed
Titus 2. 5 that the word of God be not blasphemed
3. 14 good works..that they be not unfruitful
Phm. 14 that thy benefit should not be as it were
Heb. 6. 12 That ye be not slothful, but followers of
11. 40 that they without us should not be made
1 Jo. 2. 1 these..write I unto you, that ye sin not
2 John 8 that we lose not those things which we
Rev. 7. 1 that the wind should not blow on the ea.
11. 6 that it rain not in the days of their prop.
18. 4 Come out..that ye be not partakers of
18. 4 and that ye receive not of her plagues
20. 3 that he should deceive the nations no more
6. *No, not,* μή *mē.*
Matt 18. 10 Take heed that ye despise not one 24. 6.
Mark 5. 7 I adjure thee..that thou torment me not
Luke 21. 8 Take heed that ye be not deceived: for
Gal. 5. 15 take heed that ye be not consumed one
2 Ti. 4. 16 (I pray God) that it may not He. 12. 25.
7. *Not any,* μήτις, Mt. 24. 4; 2 Co. 8. 20; 1 Th. 5. 15.

THAT same —
That, that very, he, she, it, ἐκεῖνος *ekeinos.*
Matt 10. 19 [it shall be given you in that same hour]
26. 55 In that same hour said Jesus to the mul.
John 11. 49 Caiaphas, being the high priest that same
18. 13 which was the high priest that same year

THAT (thing) which —
1. *That which,* אֲשֶׁר *asher.*
Gen. 14. 24 Save only that which the young Jos. 24. 5.
18. 17 Shall I hide from Abraham that thing wh.
27. 8 obey my voice according to that which I
2. *If any,* εἴ τις *ei tis,* Eph. 4. 29.
3. *What, that which,* מָה *mah.*
Ezra 6. 9 that which they have need of, both young

THAT time —
Then, τότε *tote.*
Matt. 4. 17 From that time Jesus began to preach, and
16. 21 From that time forth began Jesus to show
26. 16 from that time he sought opportunity to
Luke 16. 16 since that time the kingdom of God is pr.

THAT, (to this end) —
Toward, to the intent, πρός *pros.*
Luke 18. 1 spake a parable..(to this end), that men

THAT very —
That, that very, he, she, it, ἐκεῖνος *ekeinos.*
Matt 15. 28 daughter was made whole from that very
17. 18 and the child was cured from that very

THAT wherein —
That which, אֲשֶׁר *asher.*
Eccl. 3. 9 he that worketh in that wherein he labo.

THAT (which) one has —
Possessions, substance, property, ὑπάρχοντα *hupa.*
Matt 19. 21 sell that thou hast, and give to the poor
Luke 12. 33 Sell that ye have, and give 12. 44; 14. 33.

THAT then was—ὁ τότε *ho tote,* 2 Pe. 3. 6.

THAT way—δι' ἐκείνης *di' ekeinēs,* Luke 19. 4.

THE —
1. *These,* אִלֵּין *illen.*
Dan. 6. 2 that the princes might give accounts unto
2. *These,* ταῦτα *tauta.*
Gal. 2. 18 if I build again the things which I destr
5. 17 so that ye cannot do the things that ye
3. *This,* ταύτην *tautēn.*
Luke 24. 21 to day is the third day since these things

THE same —
These, οὗτοι *houtoi.*
Luke 20. 47 the same shall receive greater damnation
John 12. 21 The same came therefore to Philip, which
Gal. 3. 7 Know ye therefore..the same are the ch.

THE space of (for) —
Over, above, up to, for, ἐπί (acc.) *epi.*
Acts 19. 8 spake boldly for the space of three mon.
19. 10 this continued by the space of two years
19. 34 about the space of two hours cried out

THEATRE —
A public show or spectacle, θέατρον *theatron.*
Acts 19. 29 they rushed with one accord into the thea.
19. 31 would not adventure himself into the th.

THE'-BEZ, תֵּבֵץ *seen afar.*
A city in Ephraim, four hours N. of Shechem and thirteen miles S.W. of Beth-shean, now called *Tubaz,* where Abimelech was killed by a woman. B.C. 1236.
Judg. 9. 50 went..to T., and encamped against T. and
2 Sa. 11. 21 millstone upon him..that he died in T?

THEE, (as for) —
1. *Thou,* אַנְתְּ *ant* [V. L. אנתה].
Dan. 2. 29 As for thee, O king, thy thoughts came
2. *Thy hand,* יְדָךְ, יָדֶךָ [*yad*]. [*See* OCCASION SERVES]
1 Ki. 14. 3 take with thee ten loaves and cracknels
1 Sa. 16. 2 Take an heifer with thee, and say, I am
Jer. 38. 10 Take from hence thirty men with thee
Eze. 27. 21 they occupied with thee in lambs, and r.
3. *With thee,* לְוָתָךְ *levath-ak.*
Ezra 4. 12 the Jews which came up from thee to us
4. *In thine eyes,* בְּעֵינָךְ, בְּעֵינֶיךָ [*ayin*].
Gen. 16. 6 Abram said..do to her as it pleaseth thee
20. 15 Abimelech said..dwell where it pleaseth t
Josh. 9. 25 as it seemeth good and right unto thee to
Judg 10. 15 do..whatsoever seemeth good unto thee
1 Sa. 1. 23 Do what seemeth thee good; tarry until
14. 36 said, Do whatsoever seemeth good unto t.
14. 40 people said..Do what seemeth good unto t.
24. 4 do to him as it shall seem good unto thee
2 Sa. 19. 6 all we had died..it had pleased thee well
19. 37 do to him what shall seem good unto thee
19. 38 that which shall seem good unto thee
1 Ki. 21. 2 if it seem good to thee, I will give..money
Esth. 3. 11 do with them as it seemeth good to thee
Jer. 40. 4 If it seem good unto thee to come with
40. 4 if it seem ill unto thee to come with me
40. 4 whither it seemeth good..for thee to go
40. 5 it seemeth convenient unto thee
5. *Thy face,* פָּנֶיךָ *panim.*
Gen. 19. 21 I have accepted thee concerning this thing
Deut. 7. 23 God shall deliver them unto thee, and sh.
1 Sa. 29. 8 so long as I have been with thee unto this
1 Ki. 2. 17 Solomon the king..will not say thee nay
2. 20 Ask on, my mother; for I will not say thee
Job 11. 19 lie down..many shall make suit unto thee
6. *Her,* αὐτήν *autēn.*
Matt 23. 37 and stonest them which are sent unto thee
Luke 13. 34 and stonest them that are sent unto thee
7. *Thee,* σέ *se.*
Matt. 4. 6 in (their) hands they shall bear thee up
5. 25 lest at any time the adversary deliver thee
5. 25 the judge deliver [thee] to the officer, and
5. 29 if thy right eye offend thee, pluck it out
5. 30 if thy right hand offend thee, cut it off
5. 39 whosoever shall smite thee on thy right
5. 41 whosoever shall compel thee to go a mile
5. 42 Give to him that asketh thee, and from

See also 9. 22; 14. 28; 18. 8, 9, [15], 33; 20. 13; 25. 21, 23, 24, 37, 38, 39, 39, 44; 26. 35, 63, 68, 73; Mark 1. 24; 3. 32; 5. 7, 19, 31, 34; 9. 17, 43, 45, 47; 10. 49, 52; 14. 31; Luke 1. 19, 35; 2. 48; 4. 10, 11, 34; 6. 29, 30; 7. 7, 20, 50; 8. 20, 45, 48; 11. 27, 36; 12. 58, 58, 58; 13. 31; 14. 9, 10, 12, 18, 19; 16. 27; 17. [3], 4, [4], 19; 18. 42; 19. 21, 22, 43, 43, 43, 44; 22. 64; John 1. 48, 48, 50; 7. 20; 8. [10, 11]; 10. 33; 11. 8, 28; 13. 8; 16. 30; 17. 1, 3, 4, 11, 13, 25, 25; 18. 26, 35; 19. 10, 10; 21. 15, 16, 17, 18, 20, 22. 23.

Acts 5. 9; 7. 27, 34, 35; 9. 34; 10. 19, 22, 33; 11. 14; 13. 11, 33, 47; 18. 10; 21. 37; 22. 14, 19, 21; 23. 3, 18, 20, 30; 24. 4, [8], 25; 26. 3, 16, 17, 17, 24; Rom. 2. 4, 27; 4. 17; 9. 17; 11. 18, 22; 15. 3; 1 Co. 4. 7; 8. [10]; Phil. 4. 3; 1 Ti. 1. 3, 18; 3. 14; 2 Ti. 1. 4, 6; 3. 15; 4. 21; Titus 1. 5; 3. 12, 15; Phm. 10, 18, 23; Heb. 1. 5, 8; 2. 12; 5. 5; 6. 14, 14; 13. 5, 5; 2 Jo. 5, 13; 3 Jo. 14, 14; Rev. 3. [3], 3, 9, 10, 16; 15. [4].

8. *Of thyself*, σεαυτοῦ *seautou.*
2 Ti. 4. 11 Take Mark, and bring him with thee: for

9. *To thee*, σοί *soi.*
Matt. 2. 13 be thou there until I bring thee word: for
4. 9 All these things will I give thee, if thou
5. 26 Verily I say unto thee, Thou shalt by no
5. 29, 30 it is profitable for thee that one of thy
5. 40 if any man will sue thee at the law, and
6. 4 thy Father..himself shall reward thee op.
6. 6 and thy Father..shall reward thee openly
6. 18 and thy Father..shall reward thee openly
6. 23 If therefore the light that is in thee be
8. 13 as thou hast believed..be it done unto thee
8. 19 I will follow thee whithersoever thou go.
8. 29 What have we to do with thee, Jesus, thou
9. 2 be of good cheer, thy sins be forgiven [th.]
9. 5 to say, (Thy) sins be forgiven [thee]; or to
See also 11. 21, 21, 23, 24, 25; 12. 47; 14. 4; 15. 28; 16. 17, 18, 19, 22, 22; 17. 4; 18. 8, 9, 17, 22, [26], 29; 18. 32; 19. 27; 20. 14; 21. 5, 23; 25. 44; 26. 17, 33, 34, 35; Mark 1. 24; 2. [5, 9], 11; 5. 7, 19, 41; 6. 18, 22, 23; 9. 5, 25, 43, 45, 47; 10. 28, 51; 11. 28; 14. 30, 31, 36; Luke 1. 3, 13, 19, 35; 3. 22; 4. 6, 34; 5. 20, 23, 24; 7. 14, 40, 47; 8. 28, 39; 9. 33, 57, 61; 10. 13, 13, 21, 35; 11. 7, 35; 12. 59; 14. 9, 10, 10, 12, 14, 15, 29; 18. 11, 28, 41; 19. 43, 44, 44; 20. 2; 22. 11, 34; 23. 43; John 1. 50; 2. 4; 3. 3, 5, 7, 11; 4. 10, 10, 26; 5. 10, 12, 14; 6. 30; 9. 26; 11. 22, 40, 41; 13. 37, 38; 17. 5, 21; 18. 30, 34; 19. 11, 11; 21. 3, 18. Acts 3. 6; 7. 3; 8. 20, 22; 9. 5, 6, 17; 10. [6], 32, 33; 16. 18; 18. 10; 21. 23; 22. 10, 10; 23. 18; 24. 14; 26. 14, 16, 16; 27. 24; Rom. 9. 17; 13. 4; 15. 9; 2 Co. 6. 2; 12. 9; Gal. 3. 8; Eph. 5. 14; 6. 3; 1 Ti. 1. 18; 3. 14; 4. 14, 14; 6. 13; 2 Ti. 1. 5, 5, 6; 2. 7; Titus 1. 5; Phm. 8, 11, 11, 16, 19, 21; Heb. 8. 5; Jas. 2. 18; 2 Jo. 5; 3 Jo. 12, 14; Jude 9; Rev. 2. 5, 10, 16; 3. 18; 4. 1; 11. 17; 14. 15; 17. 1, 7; 18. 22, 22, 22, 23, 23; 21. 9.

10. *Of thee, thy, thine*, σοῦ *sou.*
Matt. 2. 6 out of thee shall come a governor, that sh.
3. 14 I have need to be baptized of thee, and
4. 6 shall give his angels charge concerning t.
See also 5. 23, 29, 30, 42; 6. 2; 11. 10; 12. 38; 17. 27; 18. 9, 15, 15, 16; 21. 19; 26. 62; 27. 13; Mark 1 [2]; 11. 14; 14. 60; 15. 4; Luke 1. 28, [35]; 4. 10; 7. 27; 8. 28; 9. 38; 12. 20; 15. 18; 16. 2; 22. 33; John 3. 26; 9. 37; 17. 7, 8; Acts 8. 34; 10. 22; 17. 32; 18. 10; 21. 21, 24, 39; 23. 21, 30, 35; 24. 2, 19; 25. 26; 26. 2, [3]; 27. 24; 28. 21, 21, 22; Rom. 10. 8; 11. 21; 1 Co. 12. 21; 2 Co. 6. 2; 1 Ti. 4. 16; 6. [21]; 2 Ti. 1. 3; Titus 2. 15; Phm. 4, 7, 20; 3 Jo. 3; Rev. 2. 4, &c.

THEFT —

1. *Theft, thing stolen*, גְּנֵבָה *genebah.*
Exod 22. 3 nothing, then he shall be sold for his th.
22. 4 If the theft be certainly found in his hand

2. *A theft*, κλέμμα *klemma.*
Rev. 9. 21 Neither repented they..of their thefts

3. *A theft*, κλοπή *klopē.*
Matt 15. 19 fornications, thefts, false witness, blasp.
Mark 7. 22 Thefts, covetousness, wickedness, deceit

THEIR, THEIRS —

1. *They*, הֵם *hem.*
Isa. 30. 7 concerning this, Their strength (is) to sit

2. *They*, הֵנָּה *henah.*
Lev. 18. 10 not uncover: for theirs (is) thine own na.

3. *He, they*, αὐτός *autos*, αὐτοί *autoi.*
Matt. 5. 3 Blessed (are) the poor in spirit: for theirs
5. 10 Blessed..for theirs is the kingdom of he.
Mark 12. 44 For all (they) did cast in of their abund.
1 Pe. 4. 14 on their part he is evil spoken of, but on

4. *Of self, selves*, αὑτοῦ *hautou.*
Matt. 2. 11 when they had opened their treasures, th.
3. 6 were baptized of him..confessing their
4. 21 mending their nets; and he called them
4. 22 immediately left the ship and their father
6. 2, 5, 16 I say unto you, They have their re.
6. 16 disfigure their faces, that they may app.
7. 6 lest they trample them under their feet
10. 17 they will scourge you in their synagogues
See also 11. 16; 13. 15, 43; 15. 2, 8, 27; 17. 6, 8; 18. 31; 21. 7; 22. 16; 23. 4, 5, 5, 5; 25. 1, 4, 7; 27. 39; Mark 1. 18, 20; 2. 6; 11. 7, 8; 14. 46; 15. 29; Luke 1. 66; 2. 8; 3. 15; 5. 15; 6. 17; 19. 36; 21. 1, 12; John 15. 22; Acts 5. 18; 7. 19, 39, 57, 58; 13. 50, 51; 14. 11, 14; 15. 26; 16. 19; 19. 18; 22. 22; 28. 27; Rom. 1. 21, 27, 27; 2. 15; 3. 13; Eph. 4. 17; 1 Th. 2. 16; Heb. 7. 5; 11. 35; 2 Pe. 3. 3, 16; Rev. 2. 22; 3. 4; 4. 4, 10; 6. 14; 7. 11, 14; 9. 4, 20, 21, 21, 21, 21; 11. 7, 11, 16, 16; 12. 11, 11; 14. 1, 2, 13; 16. 10, 11, 11, 11; 17. 17; 18. 19; 20. 4, 4; 21. 24.

5. *That, that very, he, she, it*, ἐκεῖνος *ekeinos.*
2 Co. 8. 14 for their want, that their abundance also
2 Ti. 3. 9 for their folly shall be manifest unto all

6. *Of self, selves*, ἑαυτοῦ *heautou.*
Matt. 8. 22 Follow me; and let the dead bury their
21. 8 very great multitude spread their garm.
25. 3 They that (were) foolish took [their] lamps
Luke 9. 60 Let the dead bury their dead: but go thou
12. 36 like unto men that wait for their lord, wh.
16. 8 children of this world are in their gener.
19. 35 they cast their garments upon the colt, and
22. 66 came together, and led him into their co.
23. 48 beholding..smote their breasts, and ret.
Eph. 5. 28 So ought men to love their wives..He that
1 Pe. 4. 19 commit the keeping of their souls (to him)
Jude 6 the angels which kept not their first estate
Rev. 10. 3 cried, seven thunders uttered their voices
10. 4 the seven thunders had uttered their vo.
17. 13 give their power and strength unto the be.

7. *One's own, proper, peculiar*, ἴδιος *idios.*
1 Co. 14. 35 let them ask their husbands at home: for
1 Ti. 4. 2 having their conscience seared with a hot

8. *Of them*, τούτων (*gen.*) *toutōn.*
Rom. 11. 30 now obtained mercy through their unbe.

THEIR own (selves) —

1. *Of self, selves*, αὑτοῦ *hautou.*
Mark 8. 3 send them away fasting to their own ho.
2 Pe. 2. 12 shall utterly perish in their own corrupt.
2. 13 sporting themselves with their own dece.

2. *Of ownself, selves*, ἑαυτοῦ *heautou.*
John 20. 10 disciples went away again unto their own
Rom. 16. 4 Who have for my life laid down their own
16. 18 serve not our Lord..but their own belly
2 Co. 8. 5 but first gave their own selves to the Lord
Eph. 5. 28 to love..wives as their own bodies. He th.
Phil. 2. 21 For all seek their own, not the things wh.
2 Th. 3. 12 with quietness they work, and eat their o.
Jude 13 foaming out their own shame; wandering
18 should walk after their own ungodly lusts

3. *One's own, proper, peculiar*, ἴδιος *idios.*
Acts 4. 23 went to their own company, and reported
Rom 10. 3 going about to establish their own right.
11. 24 be graffed into their own olive tree
Eph. 5. 24 wives (be) to their own husbands in every
1 Th. 2. 15 killed the Lord Jesus and their own pro.
1 Ti. 3. 12 ruling their children and their own hou.
6. 1 count their own masters worthy of all ho.
2 Ti. 4. 3 but after their own lusts shall they heap
Titus 2. 5 good, obedient to their own husbands, th.
2. 9 servants to be obedient unto their own
1 Pe. 3. 5 being in subjection unto their own hus.
Jude 6 but left their own habitation, he hath re.

THE-LAS'-AR, TE-LAS'-SAR, תְּלַאשַּׂר, תְּלַשָּׂר.
A city and district in Mesopotamia, inhabited by the children of Eden, and once subject to Assyria; perhaps *Theleda* or *Thelesa*, S.E. of Racca near Palmyra; or in Artemita in S. Assyria, N. of Babylonia; others say Resen, now called *Kalah Shergat.*
2 Ki. 19. 12 the children of Eden which (were) in T.?
Isa. 37. 12 the children of Eden which (were) in T.?

THEM —

1. *These*, אֵלֶּה *eleh.*
Eze. 4. 6 when thou hast accomplished them, lie

2. *They*, אִנּוּן *innin* [V.L. אנון].
Dan. 6. 24 cast..them, their children, and their wi.

3. *They, they themselves*, הֵם *hem.*
Gen. 14. 24 Eshcol, and Mamre; let them take their

4. *They, they themselves*, הֵמָּה *hemah.*
Judg 10. 14 let them deliver you in the time of your

5. *They, they themselves*, הִמּוֹ, הִמּוֹן *himo, himmon.*
Ezra 4. 23 and made them to cease by force and po.
5. 5 that they could not cause them to cease
5. 12 he gave them into the hand of Nebucha.
5. 14 brought them into the temple of Babylon
5. 15 carry them into the temple that (is) in J.
7. 17 offer them upon the altar of the house of
Dan. 2. 34 iron and clay, and brake them to pieces
2. 35 the wind carried them away, that no pl.

6. *In their eyes*, בְּעֵינֵיהֶם [*ayin*].
Josh 22. 30 when..the princes..heard..it pleased th.

7. *Their face*, פְּנֵיהֶם [*panim*].
Gen. 6. 13 earth is filled with violence through them

8. *To them*, αὐτοῖς *autois.*
Matt. 3. 7 said unto them, O generation of vipers

9. *Of self, selves*, αὑτοῦ *hautou.*
Mark 9. 16 he asked..What question ye with them?
Acts 13. 42 might be preached to them the next sab.
20. 30 things, to draw away disciples after them
Rev. 7. 14 made them white in the blood of the La.
9. 11 they had a king over them, (which is) the

10. *That, that very; he, she, it*, ἐκεῖνος *ekeinos.*
Matt 13. 11 given unto you..but to them it is not gi.
20. 4 said unto them, Go ye also into the vine.
Mark 4. 11 but unto them that are without, all (th.)
16. 13 [the residue: neither believed they them]
Luke 8. 32 suffer..to enter into them. And he suff.
John 10. 16 them also I must bring, and they shall
10. 35 If he called them gods unto whom the
Acts 18. 19 he came to Ephesus, and left them there
1 Co. 10. 11 Now all these things happened unto them
Heb. 4. 2 word preached did not profit them, not
6. 7 bringeth forth herbs meet for them by wh.

11. *Of ownself, selves*, ἑαυτοῦ *heautou.*
Matt 15. 30 having with them (those that were) lame
25. 3 took their lamps, and took no oil with th.
27. 35 They parted my garments among them
Mark 2. 19 as they have the bridegroom with them
8. 14 neither had they in the ship with them
John 19. 24 They parted my raiment among them, and
Acts 21. 23 have four men which have a vow on them
Rev. 4. 8 four beasts had each of them six wings

12. *And these*, κἀκεῖνοι *kakeinoi.*
Heb. 4. 2 For unto us..as well as unto them: but

13. *These*, ταῦτα *tauta.*
1 Co. 6. 13 shall destroy both it and them, Ro. 10. 4.

14. *In these*, ταύταις *tautais.*
Luke 13. 14 [in them] therefore come and be healed, and

15. *In these*, ἐν τούτοις *en toutois.*
1 Ti. 4. 15 give thyself wholly to them; that thy pr.

16. *These*, τούτους *toutous.*
Rom 8. 30 them he also called..them he, Acts 21. 24.
8. 30 whom he justified, them he also glorified
1 Co. 6. 4 set them to judge who are least esteemed
16. 3 them will I send to bring your liberality
Heb. 2. 15 deliver them who through fear of death

THEMSELVES —

1. *They, they themselves*, הֵם *hem.*
Exod 18. 26 every small matter they judged themselv.

2. *His hands*, יָדָיו [*yad*].
Eze. 43. 26 and they shall consecrate themselves

3. *Them, themselves*, ם, ־ם, *&c.*, a suff. of various forms.
1 Ki. 8 47 if they shall bethink themselves in the la.

4. *Their face*, פְּנֵיהֶם [*panim*].
Eze. 6. 9 they shall loathe themselves for the evils

5. *Their soul*, נַפְשָׁם [*nephesh*].
Esth. 9. 31 as they had decreed for themselves, and
Isa. 47. 14 they shall not deliver themselves from

6. *Of self, selves*, αὑτοῦ *hautou.*
Mark 1. 27 they questioned among themselves, sayi.
John 17. 13 might have my joy fulfilled in themselves

7. *Of ownself, selves*, ἑαυτοῦ *heautou.*
Matt. 9. 3 certain of the scribes said within themse.
14. 15 go into the villages, and buy themselves
16. 7 they reasoned among themselves, saying
19. 12 which have made themselves eunuchs for
21. 25 they reasoned with themselves, saying, If
21. 38 they said among themselves, This is the
Mark 2. 8, 11, 31; 4. 17; 6. 36, 51; 9. 8, 10; 10. 26; 11. 31; 12. 7; 14. 4; 16. 3; Luke 7. 30, 49; 18. 9; 20. 5, [14], 20; 22. 23; 23. [12]; John. 7. 35; 11. 55; 12. 19; Acts 23. 12, 21; 28. [29]; Rom. 1. [24], 27; 2. 14; 13. 2; 1 Co. 16. 15; 2 Co. 5. 15; 10. 12, 12, 12, 12; Eph. 4. 19; Phil 2. 3; 1 Ti. 2. 9; 3. 13; 6. 10, 19; 2 Ti. 4. 3; Heb. 6. 6; 1 Pe. 1. 12; 3. 5; 2 Pe. 2. 1; Jude 12, [19]; Rev. 6. 15; 8. [6.]

THEMSELVES, by —

Alone, μόνος *monos.*
Mark 9. 2 an high mountain apart by themselves
Luke 24. 12 beheld the linen clothes laid by themselves

THEN (not,) so —

1. *Then*, אֱדַיִן *edayin.*
Ezra 4. 9 Then (wrote) Rehum the chancellor, and
4. 24 Then ceased the work of the house of God
5. 2 Then rose up Zerubbabel the son of Shea.
5. 4 Then said we unto them after this manner
5. 5 then they returned answer by letter conc.
5. 9 Then asked we those elders, (and) said unto
5. 16 Then came the same Sheshbazzar, (and) la.
6. 1 Then Darius the king made a decree, and
6. 13 Then Tatnai, governor on this side the ri.
Dan. 2. 14, 15, 17, 19, 19, 25, 35, 46, 48; 3. 3, 13, 13, 19, 21, 24, 26, 26, 30; 4. 7, 19; 5. 3, 6, 8, 9, 13, 17, 24, 29; 6. 3, 4, 5, 6, 11, 12, 13, 14, 15, 16, 18, 19, 21, 23, 25; 7. 1, 11, 19.

2. *Or*, אוֹ *o.*
Eze. 21. 10 should we then make mirth? it contemneth

3. *Then*, אָז *az.*
Gen. 12. 6 And the Canaanite (was) then in the land
Exod 15. 15 Then the dukes of Edom shall be amazed
Eccl. 2. 15 it happeneth..to me; and why was I then

4. *Then*, אֲזַי *azai.*
Psa. 124. 3 Then they had swallowed us up quick, wh.
124. 4 Then the waters had overwhelmed us, the
124. 5 Then the proud waters had gone over our

5. *Also*, גַּם *gam.*
Jer. 33. 26 Then will I cast away the seed of Jacob

6. *That day*, הַיּוֹם *hay-yom.*
1 Sa. 22. 15 Did I then begin to enquire of God for h.?

7. *That, because, for*, כִּי *ki.*
Jer. 8. 22 why then is not the health of the daughter

8. *Indeed, in truth, then, therefore*, ἄρα *ara.*
Matt 12. 28 then the kingdom of God is come unto you
17. 26 Jesus saith unto him, Then are the chil.
19. 25 amazed, saying, Who then can be saved?
24. 45 Who then is a faithful and wise servant
Luke 12. 42 Who then is that faithful and wise steward
Acts 11. 18 Then hath God also to the Gentiles gran.
Rom. 7. 3 So then if, while (her) husband liveth, she
7. 21 I find then a law, that, when I would do
7. 25 So then with the mind I myself serve the
9. 16 So then (it is) not of him that willeth, nor
10. 17 So then faith (cometh) by hearing, and he.
14. 12 So then every one of us shall give account
1 Co. 5. 10 for then must ye needs go out of the wo.
15. 14 if Christ be not risen, then (is) our preac.
15. 18 Then they also which are fallen asleep in
2 Co. 5. 14 that if one died for all, then were all dead
Gal. 2. 21 if righteousness (come) by the law, then
3. 29 if ye (be) Christ's, then are ye Abraham's
4. 31 So then, brethren, we are not children of
5. 11 why do I yet suffer..then is the offence
Heb. 12. 8 without chastisement..then are ye bast.

9. *For*, γάρ *gar.*
Phil. 1. 18 What then? notwithstanding, every way

10. *But, now, then*, δέ *de.*
Acts 12. 3 Then were the days of unleavened bread
1 Co. 15. 13 if there be no resurrection..then is Christ
15. 16 if the dead rise not, then is not Christ ra.
Gal. 5. 16 I say then, Walk in the spirit, and ye

11. *If then, afterwards, furthermore*, εἶτα *eita.*
Mark 4. 28 first the blade, then the ear, after that the
Luke 8. 12 then cometh the devil, and taketh away

John19. 27 Then saith he to the disciple, Behold thy
20. 27 Then saith he to Thomas, Reach hither thy
1 Co.12. 28 after that miracles, then gifts of healings
15. 5 he was seen of Cephas, then of the twelve
15. 7 he was seen of James; then of all the ap.
15. 24 Then (cometh) the end, when he shall ha.
1 Ti. 2. 13 For Adam was first formed, then Eve
3. 10 then let them use the office of a deacon
Jas. 1. 15 Then, when lust hath conceived, it bring.

12. *Then, afterwards,* ἔπειτα *epeita.*
Mark 7. 5 [Then] the Pharisees and scribes asked him
Luke16. 7 Then said he to another, And how much
John11. 7 Then after that saith he to (his) disciples
Gal. 1. 18 Then after three years I went up to Jeru.
2. 1 Then fourteen years after I went up aga.
1 Th. 4. 17; Heb. 7. 27; Jas. 3. 17; 4. 14.

13. *And, also,* καί *kai,* Luke 19. 15; Jas. 2. 4.

14. *Neither,* οὐδέ *oude,* 1 Co. 15. 13, 16.

15. *As to the rest, henceforth,* λοιπόν *loipon.*
Acts 27. 20 hope that we should be saved was then

16. *Therefore, then, not so then,* οὐκοῦν *oukoun.*
John18. 37 said unto him, Art thou a king then? Je.

17. *Therefore, then, now,* οὖν *oun.*
Matt. 7. 11 If ye then, being evil, know how to give
12. 12 How much then is a man better than a
12. 26 he is divided..how shall then his kingd.
13. 27 didst not thou sow good seed..whence th.
13. 28 Wilt thou then that we go and gather th.
13. 56 Whence then hath this (man) all these
See also 17. 10; 19. 7; 21. 25; 22. 43, 45; 26. 54; 27. 22; Mark 3. [31]; 11. [31]; 15. 12; Luke 3. 7, 10; 6. [9]; 7. 31; 10. [37]; 11. 13; 12. 26; 13. [15]; 20. [5,] 17; 22. [36], 70; John 1. 21, [22], 25; 2. 18, 20; 3. 25; 4. 5, 9, 11, 28, [30], 45, 48, 52; 5. [4, 12], 19; 6. 5, 14, 21, 28, 30, [32], 34, 41, [42], 53, 67, [68]; 7. [6], 11 25, 28, 30, 33, 35, 45, [47]; 8. 12, 19, 21, 22, 25, 28, 31, [41], 48, 52, 57, 59; 9. [12], 15, 19, 24, [28]; 10. 7, 24, [31]; 11. 12, [14], 16, 17, 20, 21, 31, 32, 36, 41, 45, 47, 53, 56; 12. 1, 3, 4, 7, 28, 35; 13. 6, 14, [22], 27, 30; 16. 17; 18. 3, 6, 7, 10, 11, 12, 16, 17, 19, 27, [28], 29, [31], 33, 40; 19. 5, [10], 20, 21, 23, 32, 40; 20. 2, 6, 10, 19, 20, 21; 21. 5, 9, [13], 23.
Acts 2. 41; 9. 31; 10. 23; 11. 17; 17. 29; 19. 3, 36; 22. 29; 23. 31; Rom. 3. 1, 9, 27, 31; 4. 1, 9, 10; 5. 9; 6. 1, 15, 21; 7. 7, 13; 8. 31; 9. 14, 19, 30; 10. 14; 11. 1, 5, 7, 11, 19; 14. 16; 1 Co. 3. 5; 6. 4, 15; 9. 18; 10. 19; 14. 15, 26; 2 Co. 3. 12; Gal. 3. 19, 21; 4. 15; Eph. 5. 15; Col. 3. 1; 1 Th. 4. 1; 1 Ti. 3. 2; Heb. 2. 14; 4. 14; 9. 1; 1 Pe. 4. 1; 2 Pe. 3. 11.

18. *And, also,* τε *te.*
Acts 23. 5 Then said Paul, I wist not, brethren, that
27. 29 Then fearing lest we should have fallen up.

19. *Now truly, therefore, therefore now,* τοίνυν.
Jas. 2. 24 Ye see [then] how that by works a man is

20. *Then,* τότε *tote.*
Matt. 2. 7 Then Herod, when he had privily called
2. 16 Then Herod, when he saw that he was
2. 17 Then was fulfilled that which was spoken
3. 5 Then went out to him Jerusalem, and all
3. 13 Then cometh Jesus from Galilee to Jor.
3. 15 Suffer (it to be so)..Then he suffered him
4. 1 Then was Jesus led up of the spirit into
4. 5 Then the devil taketh him up into the ho.
4. 10 Then saith Jesus unto him, Get thee he.
4. 11 Then the devil leaveth him; and, behold
See also 5. 24; 7. 5, 23; 8. 26; 9. 6, 14, 15, 29, 37; 11. 20; 12. 13, 22, 29, 38, 44, 45; 13. 26, 36, 43; 15. 1, 12, 28; 16. 12, 20, 24, 27; 17. 13, 19; 18. 21, 32; 19. 13, 27; 20. 20; 21. 1; 22. 8, 13, 15, 21; 23. 1; 24. 9, 10, 14, 16, 21, 23, 30, 30, 40; 25. 1, 7, 31, 34, 37, 41, 44, 45; 26. 3, 14, 31, 36, 38, 45, 50, 52, 56, 65, 67, 74; 27. 3, 9, 13, 16, 26, 27, 38, 58; Mark 2. 20; 3. 27; 13. 14, 21, 26, 27; Luke 5. 35; 6. 42; 11. 26; 13. 26; 14. 10, 21; 21. 10, 20, 21, 27; 23. 30; 24. 45; John 2. [10]; 7. 10; 8. 28; 11. 14; 12. 16; 19. 1, 16; 20. 8; Acts 1. 12; 4. 8, 5. 26; 6. 11; 7. 4; 8. 17; 10. 46, 48; 13. 12; 15. 22; 17. 14; 21. 26, 33; 23. 3; 25. 12; 26. 1; 27. 32; 28. 1; Rom. 6. 21; 1 Co. 4. 5; 13. [10], 12, 12; 15. 28, 54; 2 Co. 12. 10; Gal. 4. 8, 29; 6. 4; Col. 3. 4; 1 Th. 5. 3; 2 Th. 2. 8; Heb. 10. 7, 9; 12. 26; 2 Pe. 3. 6.

THENCE, thenceforth, (from)—

1. *From there,* מֵהֵנָּה *me-henah.*
Jer. 5. 6 every one that goeth out thence shall be

2. *There,* שָׁם *sham.*
Gen. 11. 8 scattered them abroad from thence upon

3. *From there,* מִשָּׁם *mish-sham.*
Gen. 26. 17 Isaac departed thence, and pitched his

4. *There,* תַּם *tam.*
Ezra 6. 6 (therefore), Tatnai..be ye far from thence

5. *Yonder, hereafter,* הָלְאָה *haleah.*
Lev. 22. 27 from the eighth day and thenceforth it

6. *From thence,* ἐκεῖθεν *ekeithen.*
Matt. 5. 26 Thou shalt by no means come out thence
9. 27 when Jesus departed thence, two blind
11. 1 he departed thence, to teach and to pr.
12. 9 when he was departed thence, he went
13. 53 when Jesus had finished..he departed th.
14. 13 he departed thence by ship into a desert
15. 21 Then Jesus went thence, and departed
19. 15 laid (his) hands on them, and departed th.
Mark 1. 19 when he had gone a little farther [thence]
6. 11 when ye depart thence, shake off the dust
9. 30 they departed thence, and passed 10. 1.
Luke 9. 4 enter into, there abide, and thence depart
12. 59 thou shalt not depart thence, till thou

John 4. 43 he departed thence, and went into Gal.
11. 54; Acts 7. 4; 14. 26; 18. 7; 20. 15; 21. 1; 27. 4, 12; 28. 15.

7. *From this,* ἐκ τούτου *ek toutou,* John 19. 12.

8. *Whence,* ὅθεν *hothen,* Acts 28. 13.

9. *Yet, still, hitherto,* ἔτι *eti.*
Matt. 5. 13 it is thenceforth good for nothing, but to

THE-O-PHIL'-US, Θεόφιλος *loved by God.*
A nobleman for whose use the Evangelist Luke wrote his "Gospel" and the "Acts of the Apostles;" an early convert.
Luke 1. 3 to write unto thee in order..excellent T.
Acts 1. 1 The former treatise have I made, O T., of

THERE —

1. *There,* שָׁם *sham.*
Gen. 2. 8 there he put the man whom he had for.

2. *There,* תַּם *tam.*
Ezra 5. 17 treasure house, which (is) there at Baby.
6. 12 that hath caused his name to dwell there

3. *There, in that place,* αὐτοῦ *autou.*
Acts 15. 34 Notwithstanding it pleased S. to abide th.
18. 19 he came to Ephesus, and left them [there]
21. 4 finding disciples, we tarried there seven

4. *There, thither,* ἐκεῖ *ekei.*
Matt. 2. 13 be thou there until I bring thee word: for
2. 15 was there until the death of Herod: that
5. 23 there rememberest that thy brother hath
5. 24 Leave there thy gift before the altar, and
6. 21 where your treasure is, there will your he.
8. 12 there shall be weeping and gnashing of
10. 11 enquire who in it is worthy; and there
12. 45 they enter in and dwell there: and the
13. 42, 50 there shall be wailing and gnashing of
13. 58 he did not many mighty works there, be.
14. 23 when the evening was come, he was there
15. 29 went up into a mountain, and sat down th.
18. 20 where two or three are..there am I in the
See also 19. 2; 21. 17; 22. 11, 13; 24. 28, 51; 25. 30; 26. 71; 27. 36, 47, 55, 61; 28. 7, 10; Mark 1. [13], 35, 38; 2. 6; 3. 1; 5. 11; 6. 5, 10; 11. 5; 13. 21; 14. 15; 16. 7; Luke 2. 6; 6. 6; 8. 32; 9. 4; 10. 6; 11. 26; 12. 18, 34; 13. 28; 15. 13; 17. 21, 23; 22. 12; 23. 33; John 2. 1, 6, 12; 3. 22, 23; 4. 6, 40; 5. 5; 6. 3, 22, 24; 10. 40, 42; 11. 15, 31, 54; 12. 2, 9, 26; 19. 42; Acts 9. 33; 14. 7, [28]; 16. 1; 17. 14; 19. 21; 22. 10; 25. 9, 14, 20; 27. 6; Rom. 9. 26; 2 Co 3. [17]; Titus 3. 12; Heb. 7. 8; Jas. 2. 3; 3. 16; 4. 13; Rev. 2. 14; 12. 6; 21. 25; 22. [5].

5. *From thence,* ἐκεῖθεν *ekeithen.*
Acts 20. 13 there intending to take in Paul: for so had

6. *Thither, to that very place,* ἐκεῖσε *ekeise.*
Acts 21. 3 there the ship was to unlade her burden
22. 5 to bring them which were there bound

7. *In it,* ἐν αὐτῇ *en autē.*
Luke24. 18 the things which are come to pass there in
Acts 9. 38 disciples..heard that Peter was th. 20. 22.

8. *To lie, be laid,* κεῖμαι *keimai,* John 21. 9.

9. *Here,* ἐνθάδε *enthade.*
Acts 10. 18 and asked whether Simon..were lodged th.

10. *Here, thither,* ὧδε *hōde.*
Matt 24 23 any man shall say..here (is) Christ, or t.

THEREBY —

1. *In them, therein,* בָּהֵן *bahen.*
Jer. 51. 43 neither doth (any) son of man pass thereby

2. *Through it,* δι' αὐτῆς *di' autēs.*
John11. 4 the Son of man might be glorified thereby
Heb. 12. 11 unto them which are exercised thereby
12. 15 trouble (you), and thereby many be defiled

3. *Through this,* διὰ ταύτης *dia tautēs.*
Heb.13. 2 thereby some have entertained angels un.

4. *In it,* ἐν αὐτῷ *en autō.*
Eph. 2. 16 the cross, having slain the enmity thereby
1 Pe. 2. 2 desire..the word, that ye may grow ther.

THEREABOUT, thereat —

1. *Through it,* δι' αὐτῆς *di' autēs.*
Matt. 7. 13 and many there be which go in thereat

2. *Concerning this,* περὶ τούτου *peri toutou.*
Luke24. 4 as they were much perplexed thereabout

THEREFORE, and—

1. *Also,* גַּם *gam.*
1 Sa. 12. 16 therefore stand and see this great thing

2. *Therefore,* כָּל־קֳבֵל דִּי *kolqebel di.*
Dan. 2. 10 therefore (there is) no king, lord, nor ru.

3. *In this,* בְּזֹאת *ba-zoth.*
2 Ch.19. 2 therefore (is) wrath upon thee from before

4. *That, because,* כִּי *ki.*
Gen. 29. 32 now therefore my husband will love me

5. *Therefore,* לָהֵן *lahen.*
Dan. 2. 6 therefore show me the dream, and the int.
2. 9 therefore tell me the dream, and I shall

6. *Because of this,* עַל־דְּנָה *aldenah.*
Ezra 4. 14 therefore have we sent and certified the

7. *Therefore,* כָּל־קֳבֵל דְּנָה *kol qebel denah.*
Dan. 3. 7 Therefore at that time, when all the peo.
3. 22 Therefore because the king's commandm.

8. *But, except, unless,* ἀλλά *alla.*
Acts 10. 20 Arise therefore, and get thee down, and
2 Co. 8. 7 Therefore, as ye abound in every (thing
Eph. 5. 24 Therefore as the church is subject unto C.

9. *Indeed, in truth, then, therefore,* ἆρα, ἄρα *ara.*
Matt19. 27 followed thee; what shall we have theref.?
Rom. 8. 1 (There is) therefore now no condemnation
Gal. 2. 17 (is) [therefore] Christ the minister of sin?
3. 7 Know ye therefore that they which are of
Eph. 2. 19 therefore ye are no more strangers and
Heb. 4. 9 There remaineth therefore a rest to the pe.

10. *So then, now therefore,* ἄρα οὖν *ara oun.*
Rom. 5. 18 Therefore as by the offence of one (judg.
8. 12 Therefore, brethren, we are debtors, not
9. 18 Therefore hath he mercy on whom he will
14. 19 Let us therefore follow after the things
Gal. 6. 10 As we have therefore opportunity, let us
1 Th. 5. 6 Therefore let us not sleep, as (do) others
2 Th. 2. 15 Therefore, brethren, stand fast, and hold

11. *For,* γάρ *gar.*
Mark 8. 38 Whosoever therefore shall be ashamed of

12. *Truly, certainly, therefore,* δή *dē.*
1 Co. 6. 20 therefore glorify God in your body, and

13. *On account of which, wherefore,* διό *dio.*
Luke 1. 35 therefore also that holy thing which shall
Acts 10. 29 Therefore came I (unto you) without ga.
20. 31 Therefore watch, and remember, that by
Rom. 2. 1 Therefore thou art inexcusable, O man
4. 22 therefore it was imputed to him for rig.
2 Co. 4. 13 I believed, and therefore have I spoken
4. 13 we also believe, and therefore speak
12. 10 Therefore I take pleasure in infirmities
Heb. 11. 12 Therefore sprang there even of one 6. 1.

14. *Wherefore, because,* διότι *dioti.*
Rom. 3. 20 Therefore by the deeds of the law there

15. *Therefore, then, now,* οὖν *oun.*
Matt. 3. 8 Bring forth therefore fruits meet for rep.
See also 3. 10; 5. 19, 23, 48; 6. 2, 8, 9, 22, 23, 31, 34; 7. 12, 24; 9. 38; 10. 16, 26, 31, 32; 13. 18, 40; 18. 4, 26; 19. 6; 21. 40; 22. 9, 17, 21, 28; 23. 3, 20; 24. 15, 42; 25. 13, 27, 28; 27. 17, 64; 28. [19]; Mark 10. 9; 12. [6], 9, 23, 27, [37]; 13. 35; Luke 3. 8, 9; 4. 7; 6. [36]; 7. 42; 8. 18; 10. [2], 2, 40; 11. [34], 35, 36; 12. [7], 40; 13. 14; 15. [28]; 16. 11, 27; 19. 12; 20. 15, 29, 33, 34; 21. [8], 14, [36]; 23. 16, 20, 22; John 2. 22; 3. 29; 4. 1, 6, 33; 5. 10; 6. 13, 15, 24, 30, [43, 45], 52, 60; 7. 3, 40; 8. 13, 24, 36; 9. 7, 8, 10, 16, [41]; 10. [19, 39]; 11. 3, 6, 33, 38, 54; 12. 9, 17, 19, 21, [29], 50; 13. 24, [31]; 16. 18, 22; 18. 4, 8, 25, [31], 37, 39; 19. 1, [4], 6, 8, 13, 16, 24, 24, 26, 30, 31, 38, 42; 20. 3, 25; 21. 6, 7.
Acts 1. 6; 2. 30, 33, 36; 3. 19; 8. 4, 22; 10. 29, 32, 33, 33; 12. 5; 13. 38, 40; 14. 3; 15. [2], 10, 27; 16. [11], 36; 17. 12, 17, 20, 23; 19. 32; 20. [28]; 21. 22, 23; 23. 15; 25. 5, 17; 26. 22; 28. 20, 28; Rom. 2. 21, 26; 3. [28]; 5. 1; 6. 4, 12; 11. 22; 12. 1, [20]; 13. 7, 10, 12; 14. 8, 13; 15. 17, 28; 16. 19; 1 Co. 5. [7]; 6. 7; 7. 26; 8. 4; 10. 31; 11. 20; 14. 11, 23; 15. 11; 16. 11, 18; 2 Co. 1. 17; 5. 6, 11; 7. 1; 9. 5; 11. 15; 12. 9; Gal. 3. 5; 5. [1]; Eph. 4. 1, 17; 5. 1, 7; 6. 14; Phil. 2. 1, 23, 28, 29; 3. 15; Col. 2. 6, 16; 3. 5, 12; 1 Ti. 2. 1, 8; 5. 14; 2 Ti. 1. 8; 2. 1, [3], 21; 4. [1]; Phm. 17; Heb. 4. 1, 6, 11, 16; 7. 11; 9. 23; 10. 19, 35; 13. 15; Jas. 4. 4, 7, 17; 5. 7; 1 Pe. 2. 7; 4. 7; 5. 6; 2 Pe. 3. 17; 1 Jo. 2. [24]; 3 Jo. 8; Rev. 2. 5; 3. 3, 3, 19.

16. *Therefore truly, wherefore truly,* τοιγαροῦν.
1 Th. 4. 8 He therefore that despiseth, despiseth not

17. *Therefore now, truly now,* τοίνυν *toinun.*
Luke20. 25 Render therefore unto Cesar the things
1 Co. 9. 26 I therefore so run, not as uncertainly; so
Heb.13. 13 Let us go forth therefore unto him with.

18. *For this,* διὰ τοῦτο *dia touto.*
Matt.6. 25 Therefore I say unto you, Take no thought
See also 12. 27; 13. 13, 52; 14. 2; 18. 23; 21. 43; 23. [14]; 24. 44; Mark 6. 14; 11. 24; Luke 11. 19, 49; 12. 22; 14. 20; John 1. 31; 5. 16, 18; 6. 65; 7. 22; 8. 47; 9. 23; 10. 17; 12. 39; 13. 11; 15. 19; 16. 15; 19. 11; Acts 2. 26; Rom. 4. 16; 2 Co. 4. 1; 7. 13; 13. 10; 1 Th. 3. 7; 2 Ti. 2. 20; Phm. 15; Heb. 1. 9; 2. 1; 1 Jo. 3. 1; 4. 5; Rev. 7. 15; 12. 12; 18. 8.

19. *With a view to this,* εἰς τοῦτο *eis touto.*
Mark 1. 38 I may preach there also; for therefore
Luke 4. 43 I must preach..for [therefore] am I sent
1 Ti. 4. 10 therefore we both labour and suffer rep.

20. *So that, wherefore,* ὥστε *hōste.*
Mark 2. 28; Rom. 13. 2; 1 Co. 3. 21; 4. 5; 5. 8; 15. 58; 2 Co. 5. 17; Gal. 4. 16; Phil. 4. 1.

21. *Therefore, because,* ἀνθ' ὧν *anth' hōn,* Luke 12. 3.

22. *But,* δέ *de,* 1 Co. 7. 8.

23. *And, also,* καί *kai,* 2 Co. 8. 11.

24. *Because of this,* διὰ τοῦτο *dia touto.*
Matt. 6. 25; 12. 27; 13. 13, 52; 14. 2; 18. 23; 21. 43; 23. 14; 24. 44; Mr. 6. 14; 11. 24; 12. 24; Lu. 11. 19, 49, &c.

THEREIN, thereinto—

1. *In its midst,* בְּגַוַּהּ *[gav].*
Ezra 6. 2 and therein (was) a record thus written

2. *In them,* בָּהֶן *ba-hen.*
Lev. 10. 1 put fire therein, and put incense thereon
Num16. 7 put fire therein, and put incense in them
Jer. 4. 29 (be) forsaken, and not a man dwell ther.
48. 9 be desolate, without any to dwell therein

3. *In them,* בָּהֵנָּה *ba-henah.*
Lev. 6. 3 all these that a man doeth, sinning therein

4. *In its midst,* בְּקִרְבָּהּ *[gereb].*
Gen. 18. 24 for the fifty righteous that (are) therein?
Judg18. 7 saw the people that (were) therein, how

5. *There,* שָׁם *sham.*
Exod40. 3 thou shalt put therein the ark of the tes.

6. *In its midst,* בְּתוֹכָהּ [*tavek*].
Zech. 2. 4 the multitude of men and cattle therein

7. *With or in these,* τούτοις *toutois.*
2 Pe. 2. 20 they are again entangled therein, and ov.

8. *In this,* ἐν τούτῳ *en toutō.*
1 Co. 7. 24 let every man..therein abide with God
Phil. 1. 18 I therein do rejoice, yea, and will rejoice

9. *In it,* ἐν αὐτῇ *en autē.*
Luke10. 9 heal the sick that are therein; and say un.
19. 45 [began to cast out them that sold therein]
Acts 1. 20 let no man dwell therein: and, His bish.
14. 15 and the sea, and all things that are ther.
17. 24 that made the world and all things therein
Rom. 1. 17 therein is the righteousness of God revea.
6. 2 How shall we..live any longer therein?
Eph. 6. 20 that therein I may speak boldly, as I ou.
Col. 2. 7 abounding [therein] with thanksgiving
2 Pe. 3. 10 the works that are therein shall be burnt
Rev. 1. 3 keep those things which are written ther.
10. 6, 6, 6 and the things that therein are
11. 1 the altar, and them that worship therein
13. 12 the earth and them which dwell therein
21. 22 I saw no temple therein: for the Lord G.

10. *Into it,* εἰς αὐτήν *eis autēn.*
Mark10. 15 as a little child, he shall not enter therein
Luke18. 17 as a little child shall in no wise enter th.
21. 21 let not them that are in..enter thereinto
Heb. 4. 6 it remaineth that some must enter therein

11. *In which,* ἐν οἷς *en hois.*
Heb. 13. 9 them that have been occupied therein

THEREIN, all that is —
Its fulness, מְלֹאָהּ *melo-ah.*
Isa. 34. 1 let the earth hear, and all that is therein
42. 10 that go down to the sea, and all that is th.
Jer. 47. 2 overflow the land, and all that is therein
Eze. 12. 19 may be desolate from all that is therein
30. 12 make the land waste, and all that is the.
Amos 6. 8 deliver up the city, with all that is ther.
Mic. 1. 2 hearken, O earth, and all that therein is

THEREOF, thereon, thereout —
1. *On it,* עֲלוֹהִי [*al*].
Ezra 6. 11 being set up, let him be hanged thereon

2. *From thence,* מִשָּׁם *mish-sham.*
Lev. 2. 2 he shall take thereout his handful of the
1 Ki.17. 13 make me thereof a little cake first, and

3. *In it,* ἐν αὐτῇ *en autē.*
Matt 21. 19 he came to it, and found nothing thereon
Mark11. 13 he might find any thing thereon, Lu. 13. 6.

4. *Out of it,* ἐξ αὐτοῦ, Lu. 22. 16; Jo. 4. 12; 6. 50.

5. *Upon or above them,* ἐπάνω αὐτῶν (*or* αὐτοῦ).
Matt21. 7 ass..and they set (him) thereon, 23. 20, 22.

6. *Upon it,* ἐπ' αὐτό *ep'auto.*
John12. 14 when he had found a young ass, sat ther.
Rev. 6. 4 (power) was given to him that sat [thereon]

7. *Concerning it,* περὶ αὐτοῦ *peri autou.*
Matt 12. 36 they shall give account thereof in the d.

THEREUNTO, therewith —
1. *With a view to this very thing,* εἰς αὐτὸ τοῦτο.
Eph. 6. 18 watching [thereunto] with all perseverance

2. *With a view to this,* εἰς τοῦτο *eis touto.*
1 Th. 3. 3 yourselves know that we are appointed t.
1 Pe. 3. 9 knowing that ye are thereunto called, th.

3. *In it,* ἐν αὐτῇ *en autē.*
Jas. 3. 9 Therewith bless we God..and therewith

4. *Over or with these,* (ἐπὶ) τούτοις (*epi*) *toutois.*
1 Ti. 6. 8 having food and raiment let us therewith
3 John 10 not content therewith, neither doth he

THESE (things, matters) —
1. *These,* אֵל *el.*
Gen. 19. 8 unto these men do nothing: for therefore
26. 3 unto thy seed, I will give all these count.
26. 4 will give unto thy seed all these countries
Lev. 18. 27 all these abominations have the men of
Deut. 4. 42 that fleeing unto one of these cities he mi.
19. 11 smite..and fleeth unto one of these cities
1 Ch.20. 8 These were born unto the giant in Gath
Ezra 5. 15 Take these vessels, go, carry them into the

2. *These, those,* אֵלֶּה *eleh.*
Gen. 2. 4 These (are) the generations of the heavens
44. 6 and he spake unto them these same words
Lev. 18. 24 in any of these things; for in all these the
Jer. 10. 11 they shall perish..from under these heav.

3. *These, those,* אִלֵּין
Dan. 2. 40 as iron that breaketh all these, shall it bre.
2. 44 break in pieces and consume all these ki.
6. 6 these presidents and princes assembled to.
7. 17 These great beasts, which are four, (are)

4. *These, those,* אִלֵּךְ *illek.*
Ezra 4. 21 Give..commandment to cause these men
6. 8 ye shall do to the elders of these Jews for
6. 8 forthwith expences be given unto these
Dan. 3. 12 these men, O king, have not regarded
3. 13 they brought these men before the king
3. 21 these men were bound in their coats, their
3. 23 these three men, Shadrach, Meshach, and
3. 27 saw these men, upon whose bodies the fire
6. 5 Then said these men, We shall not find
6. 11 these men assembled, and found Daniel
6. 15 these men assembled unto the king, and

5. *These, those,* אִנּוּן *innun.*
Dan. 2. 44 in the days of these kings shall the God

6. *This,* דְּנָה *denah.*
Ezra 5. 9 Who commanded..to make up these walls?
5. 11 the house that was builded these many
Dan. 2. 28 visions of thy head upon thy bed, are th.

7. *He himself, the same,* הוּא *hu.*
Exod. 6. 26 These (are) that Aaron and Moses, to wh.

8. *They themselves, the same,* הֵם *hem.*
Exod. 6. 27 These (are) they which spake to Pharaoh
Lev. 16. 4 these (are) holy garments; therefore shall

9. *They themselves, the same,* הָהֵם *ha-hem.*
Deut 28. 65 among these nations shalt thou find no

10. *They themselves, the same,* הֵמָּה *hemha.*
1 Ch. 2. 55 These (are) the Kenites that came of He.
Eccl. 12. 12 further, by these, my son, be admonished

11. *They themselves, the same,* הָהֵמָּה *ha-hemah.*
Zech 14. 15 all the beasts that shall be in these tents

12. *They themselves,* הֵנָּה *henah.*
Num31. 16 these caused the children of Israel, thro.
Isa. 34. 16 no one of these shall fail, none shall want
Eze. 42. 5 the galleries were higher than these, than

13. *This, the same,* זֹאת *zoth.*
Lev. 11. 2 These (are) the beasts which ye shall eat
Judg13. 23 nor would..have told us (..things) as th.

14. *This, the same,* הַזֹּאת *haz zoth.*
Deut. 6. 25 if we observe to do all these commandm.

15. *This, the same,* זֶה *zeh.*
Gen. 27. 36 he hath supplanted me these two times

16. *This, the same,* הַזֶּה *haz-zeh.*
1 Sa. 17. 17 Take now..these ten loaves, and run to

17. *From,* מִן *min.*
Dan. 6. 2 over these three presidents, of whom Da.

18. *This, that, he, she, it, these,* τάδε, ὅδε *tade* (*hode*).
Rev. 2. 1 These things saith he that holdeth the se.
2. 8 These things saith the First and the Last
2. 12 These things saith he which hath the sh.
2. 18 These things saith the Son of God, who ha
3. 1 These things saith he that hath the seven
3. 7 These things saith he that is holy, he th.
3. 14 These things saith the Amen, the faithful

19. *These, those,* οὗτοι *houtoi.*
Matt. 4. 3 command that these stones be made bre.
20. 12 These last have wrought (but) one hour
20. 21 Grant that [these] my two sons may sit, the
21. 16 said unto him, Hearest thou what these
25. 46 these shall go away into everlasting pun.
26. 62 what (is it which) these witness against
Mark 4. 15, 16, [18, 20]; 12. 40; 14. 60; Luke 8. 13, 21; 13. 2; 19. 40; 21. 4; 26. 17, 44; John 6. 5; 17. 11, 25; Acts 1. 14; 2. 7, 15; 11. 12; 16. 17, 20; 17. 6, 7, 11; 20. 5; 24. 20; 25. 11; 27. 31; Rom. 2. [14]; 11. 24, 31; Col. 4. 11; 1 Ti. 3. 10; 2 Ti. 3. 8; Heb. 11. 13, 39; 2 Pe. 2. 12, 17; 1 Jo. 5. 7; Jude 8, 10, 12, 16, 19; Rev. 7. 13, 14; 11. 4, 6, 10; 14. 4, 4, 4; 17. 13, 14, 16; 19. 9; 21. 5; 22. 6.

20. *These,* αὗται *hautai.*
Luke21. 22 these be the days of vengeance, that all
Acts 20. 34 these hands have ministered unto my ne.
Gal. 4. 24 these are the two covenants; the one from

21. *These, those,* ταῦτα *tauta.*
Matt 10. 2 names of the twelve apostles are these
See also 11. 25; 13. 34, 51, 56; 15. 20; 19. 20; 21. 23, 24, 27; 23. 23, 23, 36; 24. 2, 3, 8, 33, 34; Mark 2. 8; 6. 2; 7. 23; 10. 20; 11. 28, 28, 29, 33; 13. 4, 4, 8, 29, 30; 16. [17]; Luke 1. 19, 20, 66; 2. 19, [51]; 4. 28; 5. 27; 7. 9; 8. 8; 10. 1, 21; 11. 27, 42, [53]; 12. 30, 31; 13. 17; 14. 6; 15. 26; 16. 14; 18. 21, [22]; 19. 11; 20. 2, 8; 21. 6, 7, 7, 9, 31, 36; 23. 31, 49; 24. 9, 10, 21, 26; John 1. 28; 2. 16, 18; 3. 2, 9, 10, 22; 5. 16, 19, 34; 6. 1, 59; 7. 1, 4; 8. 20, 28, 30; 9. 22, 40; 10. 21; 11. 11; 12. 16, 16, 16, 36, 41; 13. 17; 14. 25; 15. 11, 17, 21; 16. 1, 3, 4, 4, 6, 25, 33; 17. 1, 13; 18. 1; 19. 24, 36; 20. 18, 31; 21. 1, 24; Acts 1. 9; 5. [5], 11; 7. 1, 50, 54; 10. 44; 11. 18; 12. 17; 13. [42]; 14. 15, 18; 15. 17; 16. 38; 17. 8, 20; 18. 1; 19. 21; 21. 12; 23. 22; 24. 19, [22]; 28. [29]; Rom. 8. 31; 9. 8; 1 Co. 4. 6, 14; 9. 8, 15; 10. 6, 11; 12. 11; 13. 13; 2 Co. 2. 16; 13. 10; Gal. 5. 17; Eph. 5. 6; Phil. 4. 8; 2 Th. 2. 5; 1 Ti. 3. 14; 4. 6, 11, 15; 5. 7, 21; 6. 2, 11; 2 Ti. 1. 12; 2. 14; Titus 2. 15; 3. 8; Heb. 7. 13; Jas. 3. 10; 2 Pe. 1. 8, 9, 10; 1 Jo. 1. 4; 2. 1, 26; 5. 13; Rev. 7. [1]; 18. 1; 19. 1; 22. 8, 8, 16, [18], 20

22. *To these,* ταύταις *tautais.*
Matt 22. 40 On these two commandments hang all the
Luke24. 18 which are come to pass there in these days
John 5. 3 In these lay a great multitude of impot.
1 Th. 3. 3 no man should be moved by these afflict.
Rev. 9. 20 the men, which were not killed by these

23. *These,* ταύτας *tautas.*
Matt13. 53 when Jesus had finished these parables
Mark13. 2 Seest thou these great buildings? there sh.
Acts 3. 24 the prophets..have likewise foretold of t.
2 Co. 7. 1 Having therefore these promises, dearly
Heb. 9. 23 heavenly..with better sacrifices than th.
Rev. 16. 9 God, which hath power over these plagues

24. *To these,* τούτοις *toutois.*
Acts 4. 16 What shall we do to these men? 11. 27.
5. 35 what ye intend to do as touching these
Rom. 8. 37 in all these things we are more than con.
14. 18 he that in [these things] serveth Christ (is)
15. 23 now having no more place in these parts
1 Co. 12. 23 upon these we bestow more abundant ho.
Col. 3. 14 above all these things (put on) charity, wh.
1 Th. 4. 18 comfort one another with these words

Heb. 9. 23 patterns..should be purified with these
Jude 14 Enoch also..prophesied of these, saying

25. *These,* τούτους *toutous.*
Matt. 7. 24 whosoever heareth [these] sayings of mine
7. 26 every one that heareth these sayings of m.
7. 28 when Jesus had ended these sayings, the
10. 5 These twelve Jesus sent forth, and comm.
19. 1 when Jesus had finished these sayings he
26. 1 when Jesus had finished all these sayings
Mark 8. 4 whence can a man satisfy these men with
Luke 9. 28 eight days after these sayings, he took Pe.
9. 44 Let these sayings sink down into your ears
19. 15 he commanded these servants to be called
20 16 He shall come and destroy these husban.
John 10. 19 There was a division..for these sayings
18. 8 If therefore ye seek me, let these go their
Acts 2. 22 Ye men of Israel, hear these words; Jesus
5. 5 Ananias hearing these words fell v. 24.
10. 47 Can any man forbid water, that these sh.
19. 37 ye have brought hither these men, which

26. *Of these,* τούτων *toutōn.*
Matt. 3. 9 God is able of these stones to raise up ch.
5. 19 shall break one of these least commandm.
5. 37 whatsoever is more than these cometh of
6. 29 Solomon..was not arrayed like one of th.
6 32 after all these things do the Gentiles seek
10. 42 whosoever shall give to..one of these lit.
18. 6 whoso shall offend one of these little ones
18. 10 that ye despise not one of these little ones
18. 14 that one of these little ones should perish
25. 40 done (it) unto one of the least of these my
25. 45 ye did (it) not to one of the least of these
Mark 12. 31; Luke 3. 8; 7. 18; 10. 36; 12. 27, 30; 17. 2; 18. 34; 21. 12, 28; 24. 14, 48; John 1. 50; 5. 20; 7. [31]; 14. 12; 17. 20; 21. 15, 24; Acts 1. 21, 24; 5. 32, 36, 38; 14. 15; 15. [28]; 18. 17; 19. 36; 21. 38; 24. 8; 25. 9, 20; 26. 21, 26, 26, 29; 1 Co. 9. 15; 13. 13; 2 Ti. 2. 21; Titus 3. 8; Heb. 1. 2; 9. 6; 10. 18; 2 Pe. 1. 4, 12, 15; 3. 11, 16; Rev. 9. 18; 18. 15.

THESE many —
So great, so many, τοσοῦτος *tosoutos.*
Luke15. 29 these many years do I serve thee, neither

THESSALONIANS, Θεσσαλονικεῖς.
The inhabitants of Thessalonica.
Acts 20. 4 and of the T., Aristarchus and Secundus
1 Th. 1. 1 the church of the T...in God the Father
2 Th. 1. 1 unto the church of the T. in God our Fa.

THES-SA-LO-NI-CA, Θεσσαλονίκη.
A city of Macedonia on the shore of the Ægean Sea, at the head of the Gulf of *Salonika*, its modern name. Cassander called it Thessalonica after his wife, Philip's daughter. Under the Romans it was the capital of one of the four divisions of Macedonia, and the station of a Roman prætor and questor. In ancient times it was variously called *Emathia Helia*, and *Therma*; in B.C. 481 Xerxes rested here in his invasion of Greece; in 479 it was taken by Pausanius; in 421 by the Athenians; in 315 it was rebuilt; in 168 it surrendered to Rome; in 58 Cicero found refuge in it; in 42 it was made a free city; in A.D. 52–53 Paul addressed two Epistles to the Christians there; in the third century it was made a Roman colony; in 313 Diocletian's widow and daughter were beheaded here; in 390 its inhabitants were put to death for sedition by Theodosius the Great; in 479 Sabinianus defeated the Ostrogoths; in 904 the Saracen fleet attacked it; in 1185 the Normans of Sicily took it; in 1204 Boniface founded the Latin kingdom of Thessalonica; in 1222 Theodore Angelus became emperor; in 1234 it was united to the empire of Nicæa; in 1284 it was given up to Andronicus; in 1430 it was taken from the Venetians by Sultan Amurath II.
Acts 17. 11 These were more noble than those in T.
17. 13 the Jews of T. had knowledge that v. 1.
27. 2 Aristarchus, a Macedonian of T. being
Phil. 4. 16 in T. ye sent once and again unto my ne.
2 Ti. 4. 10 For Demas..is departed unto T.; Crescens

THEU'-DAS, Θευδᾶς.
A Jewish impostor, mentioned by Gamaliel before the Sanhedrim as having stirred up 400 men, who were destroyed with him.
Acts 5. 36 before these days rose up T., boasting

THEY, (but) —
1. *These,* אֵלֶּה *eleh.*
Isa. 28. 27 they also have erred through wine, and

2. *He himself, the same,* הוּא *hu.*
Exod. 1. 10 they join also unto our enemies, and fight

3. *They themselves,* הֵם *hem.*
Gen. 3. 7 knew that they (were) naked;..and..sewed
Eccl. 3. 18 might see that they themselves are beasts
Song 6. 5 Turn away thine eyes..they have overco.

4. *They themselves,* הֵמָּה *hemah.*
Gen. 7. 14 They, and every beast after his kind, and

5. *They themselves,* הֵנָּה *henah.*
Gen. 6. 2 saw the daughters of men that they (were)
Exod. 9. 32 were not smitten; for they (were) not gro.

6. *Their soul,* נַפְשָׁם [*nephesh*].
Job 36. 14 They die in youth, and their life (is) amo.

7. *He himself, the same,* αὐτός *autos.*
Matt. 5. 4 that mourn; for they shall be comforted
Mark16. 14 he appeared unto the eleven as they sat

8. *Of self, selves,* αὑτοῦ *hautou.*
Acts 27. 27 the shipmen deemed that they drew near

9. *Of own self, selves,* ἑαυτοῦ *heautou.*
Rev. 2. 9 which say they are Jews, and are not, but
3. 9 which say they are Jews, and are not, but
10. *That, that very, he,* ἐκεῖνος *ekeinos.*
Mark16. 20 [they went forth, and preached every wh.]
Luke 9. 34 feared as [they] entered into the cloud
John 5. 39 Search the Scriptures..they are..which te.
7. 45 they said unto them, Why have ye not br.
10. 6 but they understood not what things..we.
11. 13 they thought that he had spoken of tak.
20. 13 they say unto her, Woman, why weepest
Acts 10. 9 [they] went on their journey, and drew nigh
10. 10 while [they] made ready, he fell into a tr.
21. 6 we took ship; and they returned home
Rom 11. 23 they also, if they abide not still in unbe.
1 Co. 9. 25 they (do it) to obtain a corruptible crown
15. 11 whether (it were) I or they, so we pre.
Heb. 12. 25 if they escaped not who refused him that
11. *They also, even they,* κἀκεῖνοι *kakeinoi.*
Matt15. 18 come forth from the heart; and they de.
Mark16. 11 [they..had heard that he was alive, and]
16. 13 [they went and told (it) unto the residue]
Acts 15. 11 we believe..we shall be saved, even as th.
12. *These, those,* οὗτοι *houtoi.*
Luke 8. 14 that which fell among thorns are they
8. 15 that on the good ground are they, which
13. 4 think ye that [they] were sinners above all
John 18. 21 ask them which heard me..they know wh.
Acts 13. 4 [they,] being sent forth by the Holy Ghost
24. 15 which they themselves also allow, that
Rom. 8. 14 as many as are led by the spirit..they are
9. 6 For they (are) not all Israel which are of
1 Co. 16. 17 that which was lacking on your part [they]
Gal. 6. 12 they constrain you to be circumcised, only
13. *These,* ταῦτα *tauta.*
John 6. 9 two small fishes; but what are they, 10. 25.
14. *But they,* οἱ δέ *hoi de,* Matt. 9. 31.
15. *Of these,* τούτων *toutōn.*
Matt 11. 7 as they departed, Jesus began to say unto
THEY also, that, which —
1. *The men,* אֲנָשִׁים *anashim.*
Isa. 41. 11 they that strive with thee shall perish
41. 12 they that war against thee shall be as no.
2. *They also, even they,* κἀκεῖνοι *kakeinoi.*
John17. 24 Father, I will that they also, whom thou
1 Co. 10. 6 we should not lust after evil..as they also
3. *Those who,* αἵτινες, οἵτινες *haitines, hoitines.*
Matt.25. 3 [They that] (were) foolish took their lamps
Rev. 1. 7 every eye shall see him, and they (also)
THICK cloud. [*See* Cloud] —
Cloud of (thick) cloud, עַב הֶעָנָן *ab he-anan.*
Exod19. 9 I come unto thee in a thick cloud, that
THICKET, thickness, thick —
1. *Thick darkness, gloominess,* אֲפֵלָה *aphelah.*
Exod 10. 22 there was a thick darkness in all the land
2. *Heavy, weighty,* כָּבֵד *kabed.*
Exod 19. 16 a thick cloud upon the mount, and the
3. *Thicket, thickness,* סְבָךְ *sebak.*
Gen. 22. 13 behind (him) a ram caught in a thicket by
Isa. 9. 18 and shall kindle in the thickets of the fo.
10. 34 he shall cut down the thickets of the for.
4. *Thicket,* סְבֹךְ *sebok.*
Psa. 74. 5 had lifted up axes upon the thick trees
Jer. 4. 7 The lion is come up from his thicket, and
5. *Thorn, bramble, thicket,* חוֹחַ *choach.*
1 Sa. 13. 6 hide themselves in caves, and in thickets
6. *Thickness,* עָב *ab.* 1 Ki. 7. 6.
Jer. 4. 29 they shall go into thickets, and climb up
7. *Thickness,* עֳבִי *abi.*
Job 15. 26 upon the thick bosses of his bucklers
8. *Thickness,* עֳבִי *obi.*
1 Ki. 7. 26 it (was) an hand breadth thick, and the
2 Ch. 4. 5 the thickness of it (was) an hand breadth
Jer 52. 21 the thickness thereof (was) four fingers
9. *Thick, interwoven,* עָבֹת *aboth.*
Lev. 23. 40 the boughs of thick trees, and willows of
Neh. 8. 15 palm branches, and branches of thick tr.
Eze. 6. 13 under every thick oak, the place where
20. 28 every high hill, and all the thick trees
10. *Thick band, wreath, branch,* עֲבֹת *aboth.*
Eze. 19. 11 stature was exalted among the thick br.
31. 3 and his top was among the thick boughs
31. 10 he hath shot up his top among the thick
31. 14 shoot up their top among the thick bou.
11. *Sweet smell,* עָתָר *athar.*
Eze. 8. 11 and a thick cloud of incense went up
12. *Breadth, broad place,* רֹחַב *rochab.*
Eze. 41. 9 The thickness of the wall, which (was) for
41. 12 wall of the building (was) five cubits thick
42. 10 The chambers (were) in the thickness of
[*See also* Beam, bough, boughs, branch, clay, cloth, cloud, darkness, gathered, plank.]
THICK, to be thicker, be grown —
To be thick, עָבָה *abah.*
Deut32. 15 thou art waxen fat, thou art grown thick
1 Ki.12. 10 My little (finger) shall be thicker than
2 Ch.10. 10 My little (finger) shall be thicker than my
THIEF —
1. *A thief,* גַּנָּב *gannab.*
Exod. 22. 2 If a thief be found breaking up, and be sm.
Exod22. 7 if the thief be found, let him pay double
22. 8 If the thief be not found, then the master
Deut24. 7 that thief shall die; and thou shalt put
Job 24. 14 The murderer..in the night is as a thief
30. 5 they cried after them as (after) a thief
Psa. 50. 18 When thou sawest a thief, then thou con.
Prov. 6. 30 (Men) do not despise a thief, if he steal to
29. 24 Whoso is partner with a thief hateth his
Isa. 1. 23 Thy princes (are)..companions of thieves
Jer. 2. 26 As the thief is ashamed when he is found
48. 27 was he found among thieves? for since th.
49. 9 if thieves by night, they will destroy till
Hos. 7. 1 the thief cometh in, (and) the troop of ro.
Joel 2. 9 shall enter in at the windows like a thief
Obad. 5 If thieves came to thee, if robbers by ni.
Zech. 5. 4 it shall enter into the house of the thief
2. *A thief, robber,* κλέπτης *kleptēs.*
Matt. 6. 19 and where thieves break through and st.
6. 20 where thieves do not break through nor
24. 43 had known in what watch the thief would
Luke12. 33 where no thief approacheth, neither moth
12. 39 had known what hour the thief would co.
John10. 1 climbeth up some other way..is a thief and
10. 8 All that ever came before me are thieves
10. 10 The thief cometh not, but for to steal, and
12. 6 he was a thief, and had the bag, and bare
1 Co. 6. 10 Nor thieves, nor covetous, nor drunkards
1 Th. 5. 2 the day of the Lord so cometh as a thief
5. 4 that day should overtake you as a thief
1 Pe. 4. 15 let none of you suffer as a..thief, or (as)
2 Pe. 3. 10 the day of the Lord will come as a thief
Rev. 3. 3 I will come on thee as a thief, and thou
16. 15 Behold, I come as a thief. Blessed (is) he
3. *A robber, plunderer,* λῃστής *lēstēs.*
Matt.21. 13 My house..ye have made it a den of thie.
26. 55 Are ye come out as against a thief with
27. 38 Then were there two thieves crucified wi.
27. 44 The thieves also, which were crucified wi.
Mark11. 17 My house..ye have made it a den of thie.
14. 48 Are ye come out, as against a thief, with
15. 27 with him they crucify two thieves; the one
Luke10. 30 fell among thieves, which stripped him of
10. 36 unto him that fell among the thieves
19. 46 My house..ye have made it a den of thi.
22. 52 Be ye come out, as against a thief, with
THIGH —
1. *Thigh,* יָרֵךְ *yarek.*
Gen. 24. 2 Put, I pray thee, thy hand under my thigh
24. 9 the servant put his hand under the thigh
32. 25 he touched the hollow of his thigh; and
32. 25 hollow of Jacob's thigh was out of joint
32. 31 the sun rose..and he halted upon his th.
32. 32 which (is) upon the hollow of the thigh
32. 32 he touched the hollow of Jacob's thigh in
47. 29 put, I pray thee, thy hand under my thigh
Exod 28. 42 from the loins even unto the thighs they
Num. 5. 21 when the LORD doth make thy thigh to
5. 22 to make (thy) belly to swell, and (thy) thigh
5. 27 her belly shall swell, and her thigh shall
Judg. 3. 16 and he did gird it..upon his right thigh
3. 21 took the dagger from his right thigh, and
15. 8 he smote them hip and thigh with a great
Psa. 45. 3 Gird thy sword upon (thy) thigh, O (most)
Song 3. 8 every man (hath) his sword upon his thi.
7. 1 the joints of thy thighs (are) like jewels
Jer. 31. 19 I smote upon (my) thigh: I was ashamed
Eze. 21. 12 Cry..howl..smite therefore upon (thy) th.
24. 4 every good piece, the thigh, and the sho.
2. *Thigh,* יְרֵכָה *yarekah.*
Dan. 2. 32 his arms of silver, his belly and his thighs
3. *Leg,* שׁוֹק *shoq.*
Isa. 47. 2 make bare the leg, uncover the thigh, pass
4. *Thigh,* μηρός *mēros.*
Rev. 19. 16 hath on (his) vesture and on his thigh a
THIM-NA'-THAH, תִּמְנָתָה.
A city in Dan, near Elon or Ekron. See *Timnath.*
Josh 19. 43 And Elon, and T., and Ekron
THIN, (to be made) —
1. *To become lean, thin, poor, weak,* דָּלַל *dalal,* 2.
Isa. 17. 4 the glory of Jacob shall be made thin, and
2. *Lean, thin, small, dwarfish,* דַּק *daq.*
Gen. 41. 6 seven thin ears and blasted with the east
41. 7 the seven thin ears devoured the seven ra.
41. 23 seven ears, withered, thin, (and) blasted wi.
41. 24 the thin ears devoured the seven good ears
Lev. 13. 30 if..(there be) in it a yellow thin hair; then
3. *A slope, going down, descent,* מוֹרָד *morad.*
1 Ki. 7. 29 (were) certain additions made of thin wo.
4. *Lean, thin,* רַק *raq.*
Gen. 41. 27 the seven thin and ill favoured kine that
THINE (own) —
1. *Thy hand,* יָדְךָ *[yad].*
1 Ch.29. 14 all things (come) of thee, and of thine own
2. *Of own self, selves,* ἑαυτοῦ *heautou.*
1 Co.10. 29 Conscience, I say, not thine own, but of
3. *One's own, proper, peculiar,* ἴδιος *idios.*
Luke 6. 41 perceivest not the beam..in thine own eye
4. *To thee,* σοί *soi.*
Acts 5. 4 remained, was it not thine own, Jo.17.6,9.
5. *Thy, thine,* σός *sos.*
Matt. 7. 4 and, behold, a beam (is) in thine own eye
20. 14 Take (that) thine (is), and go thy way: I
25. 25 hid thy talent..thou hast (that is) thine
Luke 5. 33 disciples of John fast..thine eat and dr.
15. 31 thou art ever with me, and all..is thine
22. 42 nevertheless not my will, but thine, be do.
John17. 6 thine they were, and thou gavest them me
17. 9 which thou hast given me; for they are thi.
17. 10 all mine are thine, and thine are mine; and
18. 35 Thine own nation and the chief priests ha.
Acts 5. 4 after it was sold, was it not in thine own
6. *Of thee,* σοῦ *sou.*
Matt. 5. 25 Agree with thine adversary quickly whiles
5. 33 shalt perform unto the Lord thine oaths
5. 43 shalt love thy neighbour, and hate thine
6. 4 That thine alms may be in secret: and thy
6. 13 [thine is the kingdom, and the power, and]
6. 17 when thou fastest, anoint thine head, and
6. 22 if therefore thine eye be single, thy whole
6. 23 if thine eye be evil, thy whole body shall
7. 4 Let me pull out the mote out of thine eye
7. 4 and, behold, a beam (is) in thine own eye
7. 5 first cast out the beam out of thine own
9. 6 take up thy bed, and go unto thine house
12. 13 Stretch forth thine hand. And he stretc.
18. 9 if thine eye offend thee, pluck it out, and
20. 15 Is thine eye evil, because I am good?
22. 44 till I make thine enemies thy footstool
See also Mark 2. 11; 3. [5]; 9. 47; 12. 36; Luke 4. 7; 5. 24; 6. 42, 42, 42; 7. 44; 8. 39; 11. 34; 12. 58; 13. 12; 19. 22, [42], 4?; 20. 43; John 2. 17; 8. [10]; 9. [10], 17, 26; 17. 11; Acts ?. 27; 4. [30]; 5. 3, 4; 8. 22; 10. 31; 13. 35; 23 35; Rom. 10. 6, 9; 11. 3; 12. 20; 1 Ti. 5. [23]; Heb. 1. 10, 13; Rev. 3. 18.
THINE own self —
Of thyself, σεαυτοῦ *seautou.*
John17. 5 glorify thou me with thine own self with
Phm. 19 thou owest unto me even thine own self
THING —
1. *A saying, command,* אֹמֶר *omer.*
Job 22. 28 Thou shalt also decree a thing, and it sh.
2. *A word, matter, thing,* דָּבָר *dabar.*
Gen. 15. 1 After these things the word of the LORD
19. 21 accepted thee concerning this thing also
20. 8 Abimelech..told all these things in their
20. 10 What sawest thou, that..hast done this t.
21. 11 the thing was very grievous in Abraham's
21. 26 I wot not who hath done this thing; nei.
22. 1 it came to pass after these things that God
22. 16 because thou hast done this thing, and
22. 20 it came to pass after these things, that it
24. 28 told (them of) her mother's house these th.
24. 50 The thing proceedeth from the LORD: we
24. 66 the servant told Isaac all things that he
29. 13 And he told Laban all these things
30. 31 If thou wilt do this thing for me, I will
34. 14 We cannot do this thing, to give our sister
34. 19 the young man deferred not to do the th.
39. 7 it came to pass after these things, that his
40. 1 it came to pass after these things, (that) the
41. 28 This (is) the thing which I have spoken unto
41. 32 (it is) because the thing (is) established by
41. 37 the thing was good in the eyes of Pharaoh
44. 7 servants should do according to this thing
48. 1 it came to pass after these things, that
Exod. 1. 18 Why have ye done this thing, and have sa.
2. 14 feared, and said, Surely this thing is kno
2. 15 when Pharaoh heard this thing, he sought
9. 5 To morrow the LORD shall do this thing in
9. 6 the LORD did that thing on the morrow
12. 24 ye shall observe this thing for an ordina.
16. 16, 32 This (is) the thing which the LORD
18. 11 in the thing wherein they dealt proudly
18. 14 What (is) this thing that thou doest to the
18. 17 The thing that thou doest (is) not good
18. 18 this thing (is) too heavy for thee; thou art
18. 23 If thou shalt do this thing, and God com.
29. 1 this (is) the thing that thou shalt do unto
33. 17 I will do this thing also that thou hast sp.
35. 4 This (is) the thing which the LORD com
Lev. 4. 13 the thing be hid from the eyes of the ass.
5. 2 Or if a soul touch any unclean thing, wh.
8. 5 This (is) the thing which the LORD comm.
8. 36 his sons did all things which the LORD co.
9. 6 This (is) the thing which the LORD comm.
17. 2 This (is) the thing which the LORD hath
23. 37 drink offerings, every thing upon his day
Num18. 7 keep your priest's office for every thing of
30. 1 This (is) the thing which the LORD hath
31. 23 every thing that may abide the fire, ye sh.
32. 20 If ye will do this thing, if ye will go armed
36. 6 This (is) the thing which the LORD doth
Deut. 1. 14 The thing which thou hast spoken (is) good
1. 18 commanded you at that time all the things
1. 32 Yet in this thing ye did not believe the L.
4. 9 lest thou forget the things which thine
4. 30 and all these things are come upon thee
4. 32 as this great thing (is), or hath been heard
12. 32 What thing soever I command you, obse.
13. 14 (if it be) truth, (and) the thing certain
15. 10 because that for this thing the LORD thy
15. 15 therefore I command thee this thing to d.
17. 4 the thing certain, (that) such abomination
17. 5 which have committed that wicked thing
18. 22 if the thing follow not, nor come to pass
18. 22 that (is) the thing which the LORD hath
22. 20 But if this thing be true (and) the tokens
23. 9 then keep thee from every wicked thing
23. 14 that he see no unclean thing in thee, and
23. 19 usury of any thing that is lent upon usury
24. 18, 22 therefore I command thee to do this th.
30. 1 when all these things are come upon thee

Deut 32. 47 For it (is) not a vain thing for you; because
32. 47 through this thing ye shall prolong (your)
Josh. 4. 10 until every thing was finished that the L.
9. 24 were sore afraid..and have done this thi.
14. 6 Thou knowest the thing that the LORD sa.
21. 45 There failed not ought of any good thing
22. 24 done it for fear of (this) thing, saying, In
22. 33 thing pleased the children of Israel; and
23. 14 good things which the LORD your God sp.
23. 14 all are come to pass..not one thing hath
23. 15 (that) as all good things are come upon
23. 15 the LORD bring upon you all evil things
24. 29 came to pass after these things, that Josh.
Judg. 6. 29 Who hath done this thing? And when they
6. 29 the son of Joash hath done this thing
11. 37 Let this thing be done for me: let me alo.
18. 7 that might put (them) to shame in (any)t.
18. 10 place where (there is)no want of any thing
19. 19 thy servants: (there is)no want of any thin.
19. 24 but unto this man do not so vile a thing
20. 9 But now this (shall be) the thing which
21. 11 this (is) the thing that ye shall do, Ye sh.
Ruth 3. 18 until he have finished the thing this day
4. 7 for to confirm all things, a man plucked
1 Sa. 2. 23 Why do ye such things? for I hear of yo.
3. 11 will do a thing in Israel, at which both t.
3. 17 What (is) the thing that (the LORD) hath
3. 17 hide (any) thing from me of all the things
8. 6 But the thing displeased Samuel, 11. 18.
12. 16 therefore stand and see this great thing
14. 12 Come..and we will show you a thing. And
18. 20 they told Saul, and the thing pleased him
19. 7 and Jonathan showed him all those thin.
20. 2 why should my father hide this thing from
22. 15 Let not the king impute (any) thing unto
24. 6 forbid that I should do this thing unto
25. 37 his wife had told him these things, that
26. 16 This thing (is) not good that thou hast do.
28. 10 punishment happen to thee for this thing
28. 18 hath the LORD done this thing unto thee
Sa. 2. 6 requite..because ye have done this thing
3. 13 but one thing I require of thee, that is
11. 11 (as) thy soul liveth, I will not do this th.
11. 25 Let not this thing displease thee; for the
11. 27 But the thing that David had done displ.
12. 6 because he did this thing, and because
12. 12 but I will do this thing before all Israel
12. 21 What thing (is) this that thou hast done?
13. 20 he (is) thy brother; regard not this thing
13. 21 when king David heard of all these things
13. 33 let not my lord the king take the thing to
14. 13 the king doth speak this thing as one whi.
14. 15 I am come to speak of this thing unto my
14. 18 Hide not from me..the thing that I shall
14. 20 hath thy servant Joab done this thing: and
14. 21 Behold now, I have done this thing: go
15. 11 they went..and they knew not any thing
15. 35 what thing soever thou shalt hear out of
15. 36 by them ye shall send unto me every thi.
17. 19 spread a covering..and the thing was not
24. 3 doth my lord the king delight in this thi.
1 Ki. 1. 27 Is this thing done by my lord the king
3. 10 pleased..that Solomon had asked this th.
3. 11 Because thou hast asked this thing, and
11. 10 commanded him concerning this thing
12. 24 return..for this thing is from me. They
12. 30 this thing became a sin: for the people
13. 33 After this thing Jeroboam returned not
13. 34 this thing became sin unto the house of
14. 5 wife of Jeroboam cometh to ask a thing
14. 13 there is found (some) good thing toward
20. 9 I will do: but this thing I may not do. A.
20. 24 do this thing; Take the kings away, eve.
21. 1 came to pass after these things, (that) N
2 Ki. 5. 13 prophet had bid thee (do some) great thi.
5. 18 In this thing the LORD pardon thy servant
6. 11 the king..was sore troubled for this thing
7. 2 windows in heaven, might this thing be?
7. 19 windows in heaven, might such a thing
8. 13 a dog, that he should do this great thing?
11. 5 saying, This (is) the thing that ye shall do
17. 9 did secretly (those) things that (were) not
17. 11 wrought wicked things to provoke the L.
17. 12 said unto them, Ye shall not do this thi.
23. 17 proclaimed these things that thou hast
1 Ch. 4. 22 And (these are) ancient things
13. 4 the thing was right in the eyes of all the
17. 23 let the thing that thou hast spoken con.
21. 7 God was displeased with this thing; the.
21. 8 sinned..because I have done this thing
2 Ch. 11. 4 return every man..for this thing is done
12. 12 and also in Judah things went well
19. 3 there are good things found in thee, in th.
23. 4 This (is) the thing that ye shall do; A third
23. 19 none (which was) unclean in any thing sh.
29. 36 prepared the people: for the thing was
30. 4 the thing pleased the king and all the co.
32. 1 After these things, and the establishment
Ezra 9. 3 when I heard this thing, I rent my garm.
Neh. 2. 19 What (is) this thing that ye do? will ye re.
6. 8 There are no such things done as thou sa.
Esth. 2. 1 After these things, when the wrath of ki.
2. 4 the thing pleased the king; and he did so
2. 22 the thing was known to Mordecai, who
3. 1 After these things did king Ahasuerus pr.
5. 14 the thing pleased Haman; and he caused
8. 5 the thing (seem) right before the king, and
9. 20 Mordecai wrote these things, and sent le.
Job 4. 12 a thing was secretly brought to me, and
15. 11 is there any secret thing with thee?
Psa. 101. 3 I will set no wicked thing before mine
Eccl. 1. 8 All things (are) full of labour; man can.

Eccl. 1. 10 Is there (any) thing whereof it may be said
5. 2 be hasty to utter (any) thing before God
6. 11 there be many things that increase vanity
7. 8 Better (is) the end of a thing than the be.
8. 1 who knoweth the interpretation of a thi.
8. 3 stand not in an evil thing; for he doeth
8. 5 Whoso keepeth..shall feel no evil thing
Isa. 38. 7 the LORD will do this thing that he hath
42. 16 These things will I do unto them, and not
Jer. 7. 23 this thing commanded I them, saying, Ob.
20. 1 heard that Jeremiah prophesied these th.
22. 4 if ye do this thing indeed, then shall th.
26. 10 the princes of Judah heard these things
32. 27 I (am) the LORD..is there any thing too
33. 14 I will perform that good thing which I
38. 5 the king (is) not (he that) can do (any) th.
40. 3 therefore this thing is come upon you
40. 16 Thou shalt not do this thing; for thou sp.
42. 3 may show us..the thing that we may do
44. 4 do not this abominable thing that I hate
44. 17 certainly do whatsoever thing goeth forth
Eze. 11. 25 spake..all the things that the LORD had
14. 9 deceived when he hath spoken a thing, I
38. 10 at the same time shall things come into
Dan. 10. 1 thing was revealed..and the thing (was)
10. 1 understood the thing, and had understa.
Amos 6. 13 Ye which rejoice in a thing of nought, wh.
Zech. 8. 16 These (are) the things that ye shall do

3. *Vessel*, כְּלִי *keli.*
Lev. 13. 49, 52, 53, 57, 59 or in any thing of skin; it
13. 58 whatsoever thing of skin (it be), which
15. 4 every thing whereon he sitteth shall be
15. 6 he that sitteth on (any) thing whereon he
15. 22 whosoever toucheth any thing that she sat
15. 23 or on any thing whereon she sitteth, when
Num 35. 22 or have cast upon him any thing without

4. *Work*, מְלָאכָה *melakah.*
Lev. 13. 48 whether in a skin, or in any thing made
1 Sa. 15. 9 every thing (that was) vile and refuse, that

5. *A word, speech, matter*, מִלָּה *millah.*
Dan. 2. 5 The thing is gone from me: if ye will not
2. 8 because ye see the thing is gone from me
2. 10 nor ruler, (that) asked such things at any
2. 11 (it is) a rare thing that the king requireth
2. 15 Then Arioch made the thing known to Da.
2. 17 made the thing known to Hananiah, Mi.
4. 33 The same hour was the thing fulfilled upon
5. 15 could not show..interpretation of the th.
5. 26 This (is) the interpretation of the thing
6. 12 The thing (is) true, according to the law
7. 16 made me know the interpretation of the t.

6. *Animal soul*, נֶפֶשׁ *nephesh.*
Lev. 11. 10 of any living thing which (is) in the wat.
Eze. 47. 9 every thing that liveth, which moveth, wh.

7. *A loan, debt*, מַשָּׁאָה *mashshaah.*
Deut 24. 10 When thou dost lend thy brother any th.

7*a*. *Oppression*, עֹשֶׁק *osheq.* Lev. 6. 4.

8. *A word, matter, thing*, λόγος *logos.*
Matt 21. 24 I will also ask you one thing, which if ye
Luke 1. 4 know the certainty of those things, 20. 3.
Acts 5. 24 the chief priests heard these things, they

9. *A deed, doing, any thing done*, πρᾶγμα *pragma.*
Matt 18. 19 shall agree on earth as touching any thing
Luke 1. 1 a declaration of those things which are
Acts 5. 4 why hast thou conceived this thing in th.
Heb. 6. 18 That by two immutable things, in which
10. 1 not the very image of the things, 11. 1.

10. *Any thing*, τι *ti*, Acts 25. 26.

11. *Saying, matter*, ῥῆμα *rhēma.*
Luke 2. 15 see this thing which is come to pass, wh.
2. 19 Mary kept all these things, and pondered
Acts 5. 32 we are his witnesses of these things; and

12. *These*, αὐτά *auta.*
1 Pe. 1. 12 they did minister the things which are now

THINGS, these —

1. *These, these things*, ταῦτα *tauta.*
Matt. 1. 20 while he thought on these things, behold
4. 9 All these things will I give thee, if thou
6. 32 after all these things do the Gentiles seek
6. 33 and all these things shall be added unto
9. 18 While he spake these things unto them
11. 25 thou hast hid these things from the wise
13. 34 these things spake Jesus unto the multi.
13. 51 Have ye understood all these things? Th.
13. 56 Whence then hath this (man) all these th.?
19. 20 All these things have I kept from my yo.
21. 23 By what..doest thou these things? and
21. 24, 27 tell..by what authority I do these th.
23. 36 All these things shall come upon this ge.
24. 2 See ye not all these things? Verily I say
24. 3 when shall these things be? and what (sh.
24. 33 when ye shall see all these things, know
24. 34 shall not pass, till all these things be ful.
Mark 2. 8 Why reason ye these things in your he.?
6. 2 From whence hath this (man) these things?
11. 28 By what authority doest thou these thi.?
11. 28 gave thee this authority to do these thi.
11. 29, 33 tell..by what authority I do these th.
13. 4 when shall these things be? and what (sh.
13. 4 the sign when all these things shall be fu.
13. 29 when ye shall see these things come to
13. 30 shall not pass, till all these things be do.
Luke 1. 20 until the day that these things shall be
4. 28 when they heard these things, were filled
5. 27 after these things he went forth, and saw
7. 9 When Jesus heard these things, he mar.

Luke 8. 8 when he had said these things, he cried
10. 1 After these things the Lord appointed ot.
10. 21 thou hast hid these things from the wise
11. 27 as he spake these things, a certain woman
11. 53 [as he said these things unto them, the sc.]
12. 30 all these things do the nations of the wo.
12. 31 and all these things shall be added unto
13. 17 when he had said these things, all his ad.
14. 6 could not answer him again to these thi.
14. 15 one of them..with him heard these things
14. 21 servant came, and showed his lord these t.
15. 26 he called..and asked what these things
16. 14 the Pharisees also..heard all these things
18. 22 when Jesus heard [these things], he said
19. 11 as they heard these things, he added and
20. 2 by what authority doest thou these things
20. 8 tell..by what authority I do these things
21. 6 (As for) these things which ye behold, the
21. 7 Master, but when shall these things be?
21. 7 what sign (will there be) when these thi.
21. 9 these things must first come to pass; but
21. 31 when ye see these things come to pass
21. 36 worthy to escape all these things that sh.
23. 31 if they do these things in a green tree, wh.
23. 49 women..stood afar off, beholding these th.
24. 9 told all these things unto the eleven, and
24. 10 which told these things unto the apostles
24. 21 to day is the third day since these things
24. 26 Ought..Christ to have suffered these th.
John 1. 28 These things were done in Bethabara be
2. 16 Take these things hence; make not my
2. 18 sign..seeing that thou doest these things
3. 9 and said unto him, How can these things
3. 10 thou a master..knowest not these things
3. 22 After these things came Jesus and his di.
5. 16 he had done these things on the sabbath
5. 34 these things I say, that ye might be saved
6. 1 After these things Jesus went over the sea
6. 59 These things said he in the synagogue, as
7. 1 After these things Jesus walked in Galilee
7. 4 If thou do these things, show thyself to
8. 28 as my Father..taught..I speak these th.
11. 11 These things said he: and after that he
12. 16 These things understood not his disciples
12. 16 then remembered they that these things
12. 16 (that) they had done these things unto
12. 36 These things spake Jesus, and departed
12. 41 These things said Esaias, when he saw his
13. 17 If ye know these things, happy are ye if
14. 25 These things have I spoken unto you, be.
15. 11 These things have I spoken unto you, th.
15. 17 These things I command you, that ye lo.
15. 21 these things will they do unto you for my
16. 1 These things have I spoken unto you, that
16. 3 these things will they do unto you, because
16. 4 these things have I told you, that, when
16. 4 these things I said not unto you at the be.
16. 6 because I have said these things unto you
16. 25 These things have I spoken unto you in
16. 33 These things I have spoken unto you, that
17. 13 these things I speak in the world, that th.
19. 24 These things therefore the soldiers did
19. 36 these things were done, that the scripture
20. 18 (that) he had spoken these things unto her
21. 1 After these things Jesus showed himself
21. 24 the disciple which..wrote these things
Acts 1. 9 when he had spoken these things, while
5. 5 came on all them that heard [these things]
5. 11 and upon as many as heard these things
7. 1 Then said the high priest, Are these thi.
7. 50 Hath not my hand made all these things?
7. 54 When they heard these things, they were
11. 18 When they heard these things, they held
12. 17 Go show these things unto James, and to
14. 15 Sirs, why do ye these things? We also are
15. 17 saith the Lord, who doeth all these things
17. 8 they troubled..when they heard these th.
17. 20 would know therefore what these things
18. 1 After these things Paul departed from A.
19. 21 After these things were ended, Paul pur.
21. 12 when we heard these things, both we, and
23. 22 that thou hast showed these things to me
24. 9 also assented, saying that these things we.
24. 22 Felix heard [these things,] having more pe.
Rom. 8. 31 What shall we then say to these things?
1 Co. 4. 6 these things, brethren, I have in a figure
4. 14 I write not these things to shame you, but
9. 8 Say I these things as a man? or saith not
9. 15 neither have I written these things, that
10. 6 these things were our examples, to the in.
10. 11 these things happened unto them for en.
2 Co. 2. 16 And who (is) sufficient for these things?
13. 10 I write these things being absent, lest be.
Eph. 5. 6 because of these things cometh the wrath
Phil. 4. 8 if (there be) any praise, think on these th.
2 Th. 2. 5 I was yet with you, I told you these things
1 Ti. 3. 14 These things write I unto thee, hoping to
4. 6 If thou put..in remembrance of these th.
4. 11 These things command and teach
4. 15 Meditate upon these things, give thyself
5. 7 these things give in charge, that they may
5. 21 that thou observe these things without
6. 2 do (them) service..These things teach and
6. 11 flee these things; and follow after righte.
2 Ti. 1. 12 For the which cause I..suffer these things
2. 14 Of these things put (them) in remembra
Titus 2. 15 These things speak, and exhort, and rebu.
3. 8 These things are good and profitable unto
Heb. 7. 13 he of whom these things are spoken pe.
Jas. 3. 10 My brethren, these things ought not so to
2 Pe. 1. 8 if these things be in you, and abound, th.
1. 9 he that lacketh these things is blind, and

2 Pe. 1. 10 if ye do these things, ye shall never fall
1 Jo. 1. 4 these things write we unto you, that your
2. 1 these things write I unto you, that ye sin
5. 13 These things have I written unto you that
Rev. 7. 1 after [these things] I saw four angels stan.
18. 1 after these things I saw another angel co.
19. 1 after these things I heard a great voice of
22. 8 I John saw these things, and heard (them)
22. 8 the angel which showed me these things
22. 16 to testify unto you these things in the ch.
22. 18 If any man shall add unto [these things]
22. 20 He which testifieth these things saith, Su.

2. *Of these*, τούτων *toutōn*.
Matt. 6. 32 that ye have need of all these things
See also Luke 7. 18; 12. 30; 18. 34; 21. 28; 24. 14, 48; John 21. 24; Acts 19. 36; 24. 8; 25. 9; 26. 26, 26; 1 Co. 9. 15; Titus 3. 8; Heb. 9. 6; 2 Pe. 1. 12, 15; 3. 11, 16; Rev. 18. 15.

THINGS, the, such —
1. *These things*, ταῦτα *tauta*.
John 7. 32; Gal. 2. 18; 5. 17; 2 Pe. 3. 14.
2. *The, these*, τά *ta*, Matt. 6. 34; 16. 23. 22. 21, 21; Mr. 8. 33, 33; 12. 17, 17; Lu. 20. 25; Ro. 2. 14, &c.
[*See also* Any, certain, committed, creeping, draw, formed, high, holy, incredible, nought, one, what. *Also* All, base, boast of, to come, good, great, hoped for, move, those, weak.]

THING of nought —
Nought, אֱלִיל *elil*.
Jer. 14. 14 a thing of nought, and the deceit of their

THINGS that we have —
The things possessed, τὰ ἐνόντα *ta enonta*.
Luke 11. 41 rather give alms of such things as ye have

THINK (of, on), to—
1. *To say*, אָמַר *amar*.
Gen. 20. 11 I thought, Surely the fear of God (is) not
Num 24. 11 I thought to promote thee unto great ho.
Judg 15. 2 I verily thought that thou hadst utterly
Ruth 4. 4 I thought to advertise thee, saying, Buy
1 Sa. 20. 26 he thought, Something hath befallen him
2 Sa. 5. 6 thinking, David cannot come in hither
13. 33 to think that all the king's sons are dead
21. 16 he, being girded..thought to have slain
2 Ki. 5. 11 I thought, He will surely come out to me
2 Ch. 13. 8 ye think to withstand the kingdom of the
32. 1 encamped..and thought to win them for
Esth. 6. 6 Haman thought in his heart, To whom
Eccl. 8. 17 though a wise (man) think to know (it)
2. *To understand, consider*, בִּין *bin*, 7a.
Job 31. 1 why then should I think upon a maid?
3. *To speak*, דָּבַר *dabar*, 3.
Exod 32. 14 repented of the evil which he thought to
4. *To liken, think, devise*, דָּמָה *damah*, 3.
Num 33. 56 I shall do unto you, as I thought to do
Judg 20. 5 beset the house..(and) thought to have
Esth. 4. 13 Think not with thyself that thou shalt
Psa. 48. 9 We have thought of thy loving kindness
50. 21 thou thoughtest that I was altogether
Isa. 14. 24 as I have thought, so shall it come to pa.
5. *To devise, design*, זָמַם *zamam*.
Deut 19. 19 do unto him as he had thought to have
Zech. 1. 6 Like as the LORD of hosts thought to do
8. 14 I thought to punish you, when your fath.
8. 15 again have I thought in these days to do
6. *To think, reckon*, חָשַׁב *chashab*.
Gen. 38. 15 When Judah saw her, he thought her (to
50. 20 But as for you, ye thought evil against me
1 Sa. 1. 13 therefore Eli thought she had been drun.
18. 25 Saul thought to make David fall by the
2 Sa. 14. 13 Wherefore then hast thou thought such
Neh. 6. 2 But they thought to do me mischief
6. 6 thou and the Jews think to rebel: for wh.
Job 35. 2 Thinkest thou this to be right (that) thou
41. 32 (one) would think the deep (to be) hoary
Psa. 40. 17 the LORD thinketh upon me: thou (art)
Isa. 10. 7 meaneth not so, neither doth his heart th.
Jer. 18. 8 will repent of the evil that I thought to
23. 27 Which think to cause my people to forget
29. 11 I know the thoughts that I think toward
Eze. 38. 10 and thou shalt think an evil thought
Mal. 3. 16 that feared the LORD, and that thought
7. *To think, devise*, חָשַׁב *chashab*, 3.
Psa. 73. 16 When I thought to know this, it (was) too
119. 59 I thought on my ways, and turned my feet
8. *To hope, purpose*, סְבַר *sebar*.
Dan. 7. 25 he shall..think to change times and laws
9. *To think, purpose*, עֲשִׁת *ashith*.
Dan. 6. 3 the king thought to set him over the wh.
10. *To bethink self*, עֲשַׁת *ashath*, 7.
Jon. 1. 6 if so be that God will think upon us, that
11. *To judge, adjudge*, פָּלַל *palal*, 3.
Gen. 48. 11 I had not thought to see thy face; and, lo
12. *It was good before me*, שְׁפַר קֳדָם *shephar qodam*.
Dan. 4. 2 I thought it good to show the signs and
13. *To think, estimate*, שָׁעַר *shaar*.
Prov 23. 7 as he thinketh in his heart, so (is) he: Eat
14. *To see*, רָאָה *raah*.
2 Sa. 18. 27 Me thinketh the running of the foremost
15. *In the eyes of*, בְּעֵינֵי *beene*.
Num 36. 6 Let them marry to whom they think best

2 Sa. 4. 10 one told me..thinking to have brought go.
10. 3 Thinkest thou that David doth honour thy
13. 2 Amnon thought it hard for him to do any
19. 18 and to do what he thought good. And Sh.
1 Ch. 19. 3 Thinkest thou that David doth honour thy
Zech 11. 12 If ye think good, give (me) my price; and
16. *To reckon through, reason*, διαλογίζομαι *dialog*.
Luke 12. 17 he thought within himself, saying, What
17. *To think*, δοκέω *dokeō*.
Matt. 3. 9 think not to say within yourselves, We ha.
6. 7 they think that they shall be heard for th.
17. 25 What thinkest thou, Simon? of whom do
18. 12 How think ye? If a man have an hundred
21. 28 what think ye? A (certain) man had two so.
22. 17 What thinkest thou? Is it lawful to give
22. 42 Saying, What think ye of Christ? whose
24. 44 in such an hour as ye think not the Son
26. 53 Thinkest thou that I cannot now pray to
26. 66 What think ye? They answered and said
Luke 10. 36 Which now of these three, thinkest thou
12. 40 cometh at an hour when ye think not
13. 4 think ye that they were sinners above all
19. 11 they thought that the kingdom of God sh.
John 5. 39 for in them ye think ye have eternal life
5. 45 Do not think that I will accuse you to the
11. 13 they thought that he had spoken of taking
11. 56 What think ye, that he will not come to
13. 29 some (of them) thought, because Judas
16. 2 whosoever killeth you will think that he
Acts 12. 9 and wist not..but thought he saw a vision
26. 9 I verily thought with myself, that I ought
1 Co. 4. 9 I think that God hath set forth us the ap.
7. 40 and I think also that I have the Spirit of
8. 2 if any man think that he knoweth any th.
10. 12 let him that thinketh he standeth take
12. 23 those (members)..which we think to be
14. 37 If any man think himself to be a prophet
2 Co. 11. 16 Let no man think me a fool: if otherwise
12. 19 think ye that we excuse ourselves unto
Gal. 6. 3 if a man think himself to be something
Phil. 3. 4 If any other man thinketh that he hath
Jas. 4. 5 Do ye think that the Scripture saith in
18. *To bear or have in the mind*, ἐνθυμέομαι *enthu*.
Matt. 1. 20 while he thought on these things, behold
9. 4 Wherefore think ye evil in your hearts?
Acts 10. 19 While Peter thought on the vision, the S.
19. *To lead, account, esteem*, ἡγέομαι *hēgeomai*.
Acts 26. 2 I think myself happy, king Agrippa, bec.
2 Co. 9. 5 I thought it necessary to exhort the bret.
Phil. 2. 6 thought it not robbery to be equal with
2 Pe. 1. 13 I think it meet, as long as I am in this
20. *To judge*, κρίνω *krinō*.
Acts 26. 8 Why should it be thought a thing incred.
21. *To reckon*, λογίζομαι *logizomai*.
Rom. 2. 3 thinkest thou this, O man, that judgest
1 Co. 13. 5 is not easily provoked, thinketh no evil
13. 11 I understood as a child, I thought as a ch.
2 Co. 3. 5 sufficient of ourselves to think any thing
10. 2 think to be bold against some, which th.
10. 7 let him of himself think this again, that
10. 11 Let such an one think this, that, such as
12. 6 lest any man should think of me above th.
Phil. 4. 8 if (there be) any praise, think on these things
22. *To ponder, understand, conceive*, νοέω *noeō*.
Eph. 3. 20 abundantly above all that we ask or think
23. *To account, reckon in law*, νομίζω *nomizō*.
Matt. 5. 17 Think not that I am come to destroy the
10. 34 Think not that I am come to send peace
Acts 8. 20 thou hast thought that the gift of God may
17. 29 we ought not to think that the Godhead
1 Co. 7. 36 if any man think that he behaveth him.
24. *To be of opinion, think, suppose*, οἴομαι *oiomai*.
Jas. 1. 7 let not that man think that he shall rece.
25. *To ponder under, suspect, suppose*, ὑπονοέω.
Acts 13. 25 he said, Whom think ye that I am? I am
26. *To make to appear*, φαίνω *phainō*.
Mark 14. 64 Ye have heard the blasphemy: what think
27. *To be of opinion, set the affections on*, φρονέω.
Acts 28. 22 we desire to hear of thee what thou thi.
Rom. 12. 3 highly than he ought to think, but to think
1 Co. 4. 6 that ye might learn in us not [to think] (of
13. 11 I thought as a child; but when I became
Phil. 1. 7 as it is meet for me to think this of you

THINK evil, good, more highly, on, scorn, upon, to —
1. *To be mindful, remember*, זָכַר *zakar*.
Gen. 40. 14 think on me when it shall be well with
Neh. 5. 19 Think upon me, my God, for good, (accor).
6. 14 My God, think thou upon Tobiah and Sa.
2. *To devise, desire*, זָמַם *zamam*.
Prov. 30. 32 if thou hast thought evil, (lay) thine hand
3. *Be contemptible in...eyes*, בָּזָה בְּעֵינָיו [*bazah*] Est. 3. 6.
4. *To cast or throw upon*, ἐπιβάλλω *epiballō*.
Mark 14. 72 And when he thought thereon, he wept
4a. *Consider fitting*, ἀξιόω *axioō*. Acts 15. 38.
5. *To think well*, εὐδοκέω *eudokeō*.
1 Th. 3. 1 we thought it good to be left at Athens
6. *To think too highly*, ὑπερφρονέω *huperphroneō*.
Rom 12. 3 not to think..more highly than he ought

THIRD (part, rank, time, loft), thirdly —
1. *Three*, שָׁלֹשׁ, שְׁלוֹשָׁה *shalosh*,
Exod 19. 15 Be ready against the third day: come not
1 Ki. 15. 28, 33 in the third year of Asa king of Judah
2 Ki. 18. 1 in the third year of Hoshea son of Elah
1 Ch. 26. 11 Hilkiah the second, Tebaliah the third
2 Ch. 17. 7 in the third year of his reign he sent to
Esth. 1. 3 In the third year of his reign, he made a
Dan. 1. 1 In the third year of the reign of Jehoiakim
8. 1 In the third year of the reign of king Bel.
10. 1 In the third year of Cyrus king of Persia
2. *Third*, שְׁלִישִׁי *shelishi*.
Gen. 1. 13 evening and..morning were the third day
2. 14 the name of the third river (is) Hiddekel
6. 16 lower, second, and third..shalt thou make
22. 4 on the third day Abraham lifted up his eyes
31. 22 it was told Laban on the third day that
32. 19 so commanded he the second, and the th.
34. 25 it came to pass on the third day, when
40. 20 it came to pass the third day..Pharaoh's
42. 18 Joseph said unto them the third day, This
Exod 19. 1 In the third month, when the children of
19. 11 be ready against the third day: for the the
19. 16 it came to pass on the third day, in the
28. 19 the third row a ligure, an agate, and an
39. 12 the third row, a ligure, an agate, and an
Lev. 7. 17 the remainder..on the third day shall be
7. 18 if..the flesh..be eaten at all on the third
19. 6 if ought remain until the third day, it sh.
19. 7 if it be eaten at all on the third day, it (is)
Num. 2. 24 they shall go forward in the third rank
7. 24 On the third day Eliab the son of Helon
15. 6 mingled with the third..of an hin of oil
15. 7 thou shalt offer the third..of an hin of
19. 12 on the third day..but if..not..the third
19. 19 sprinkle upon the unclean on the third
28. 14 and the third (part) of an hin unto a ram
29. 20 on the third day eleven bullocks, two rams
31. 19 on the third day, and on the seventh day
Deut 23. 8 The children..in their third generation
26. 12 the tithes of thine increase the third year
Josh. 9. 17 and came unto their cities on the third
19. 10 the third lot came up for the children of
Judg 20. 30 Israel went up..on the third day, and put
1 Sa. 3. 8 LORD called Samuel again the third time
17. 13 and the third, Shammah
19. 21 Saul sent messengers again the third time
20. 5 that I may hide myself..unto the third
20. 12 about tomorrow any time, (or) the third
30. 1 it came to pass..on the third day, that the
2 Sa. 1. 2 It came even to pass on the third day, that
3. 3 the third, Absalom, the son of Maacah
18. 2 sent..a third part..a third part..a third
1 Ki. 3. 18 the third day after that I was delivered
6. 6 the third (was) seven cubits broad, for wi.
6. 8 went up..out of the middle into the third
12. 12 third day..saying, Come..again the third
18. 1 the word..came to Elijah in the third year
22. 2 it came to pass in the third year, that Je.
2 Ki. 1. 13 the third fifty..the third captain of fifty
11. 5 A third part of you that enter in on the
11. 6 a third part..a third part at the gate
19. 29 in the third year sow ye, and reap, and
20. 5 on the third day thou shalt go up unto the
20. 8 and that I shall go up..the third day?
1 Ch. 2. 13 Abinadab the second, and Shimma the th.
3. 2 The third, Absalom the son of Maachah
3. 15 the second Jehoiakim, the third Zedekiah
8. 1 Ashbel the second, and Aharah the third
8. 39 Jehush the second, and Eliphelet the third
12. 9 the first, Obadiah the second, Eliab the th.
23. 19 first, Amariah the second, Jahaziel the th.
24. 8 The third to Harim, the fourth to Seorim
24. 23 Jahaziel the third, Jekameam the fourth
25. 10 The third to Zaccur, (he), his sons, and
26. 2 Zebadiah the third, Jathniel the fourth
26. 4 Joah the third, and Sacar the fourth, and
26. 11 Hilkiah the second, Tebaliah the third
27. 5 The third captain of the host for the third
2 Ch. 10. 12 the third day..saying, Come..the third
15. 10 in the third month, in the fifteenth year
23. 4 A third part of you entering on the sabbath
23. 5 a third part..and a third part at the gate
27. 5 pay..both the second year and the third
31. 7 In the third month they began to lay the
Neh. 10. 32 with the third part of a shekel for the ser.
Esth. 5. 1 it came to pass on the third day, that Es.
8. 9 in the third month, that (is), the month
Job 42. 14 and the name of the third, Keren-happuch
Isa. 19. 24 In that day shall Israel be the third with
37. 30 in the third year sow ye, and reap, and pl.
Jer. 38. 14 into the third entry that (is) in the house
Eze. 5. 2, 12 a third part..a third part..a third part
10. 14 the third the face of a lion, and the fourth
21. 14 let the sword be doubled the third time
31. 1 in the eleventh year, in the third (month)
46. 14 the third part of an hin of oil, to temper
Hos. 6. 2 in the third day he will raise us up, and
Zech. 6. 3 in the third chariot white horses, and in
13. 8 it shall come to pass..the third shall be
13. 9 I will bring the third part through the
3. *Those of a third generation*, שִׁלֵּשִׁים *shilleshim*.
Gen. 50. 23 Joseph saw Ephraim's children of the th.
Exod 20. 5 upon the children unto the third and fo.
34. 7 upon the children's children, unto the th.
Num 14. 18 upon the children unto the third and fo.
Deut. 5. 9 upon the children unto the third and fou.
4. *Third*, תְּלִיתַי *telithai*.
Dan. 2. 39 another third kingdom of brass, which

5. *Three*, תְּלָת, תְּלָת *telath.*
Ezra 6. 15 this house was finished on the third day
Dan. 5. 16 and shalt be the third ruler in the kingd.
5. 29 he should be the third ruler in the king.

6. *Third*, תַּלְתִּי *talti.*
Dan. 5. 7 and shall be the third ruler in the kingd.

7. *Third*, τρίτον *triton.*
1 Co. 12. 28 thirdly teachers, after that miracles, then

8. *Third*, τρίτος *tritos.*
Matt 16. 21 be killed, and be raised again the third
17. 23 the third day he shall be raised again
20. 3 he went out about the third hour and saw
20. 19 crucify..and the third day he shall rise
22. 26 the second also, and the third, unto the
26. 44 went away again, and prayed [the third ti]
27. 64 sepulchre be made sure until the third
Mark 9. 31 after that he is killed, he shall rise the th.
10. 34 shall kill him: and [the third day] he shall
12. 21 neither left he any seed, and the third li.
14. 41 he cometh the third time, and saith unto
15. 25 it was the third hour, and they crucified
Luke 9. 22 and be slain, and be raised the third day
12. 38 if he shall come..in the third watch, and
13. 32 and the third (day) I shall be perfected
18. 33 and the third day he shall rise again
20. 12 again he sent a third: and they wounded
20. 31 the third took her; and in like manner the
23. 22 he said unto them the third time, Why
24. 7 and be crucified, and the third day rise
24. 21 to day is the third day since these things
24. 46 and to rise from the dead the third day
John 2. 1 the third day there was a marriage in Cana
21. 14 This is now the third time that Jesus sh.
21. 17 He saith unto him the third time, Simon
21. 17 he said unto him the third time, Lovest
Acts 2. 15 seeing it is (but) the third hour of the day
10. 40 Him God raised up the third day, and
23. 23 Make ready..at the third hour of the ni.
27. 19 the third (day) we cast out with our own
1 Co. 15. 4 he rose again the third day according to
2 Co. 12. 2 such an one caught up to the third heaven
12. 14 the third time I am ready to come to you
13. 1 This (is) the third (time) I am coming to
Rev. 4. 7 the third beast had a face as a man, and
6. 5 opened the third seal, I heard the third
8. 7 the third part of trees was burnt up, and
8. 8 and the third part of the sea became blo.
8. 9 the third part of the creatures which were
8. 9 and the third part of the ships were des.
8. 10 the third angel sounded, and there fell a
8. 10 it fell upon the third part of the rivers, and
8. 11 the third part of the waters became worm.
8. 12 the third part of the sun was smitten, and
8. 12 the third part of the moon, and the third
8. 12 the third part of them was darkened
8. 12 day shone not for a third part of it
9. 15 were loosed..to slay the third part of men
9. 18 By these three was the third part of men
11. 14 behold, the third woe cometh quickly
12. 4 his tail drew the third part of the stars of
14. 9 the third angel followed them, saying wi.
16. 4 the third angel poured out his vial upon
21. 19 the second, sapphire; the third, a chalce.

9. *Third story (of a building)*, τρίστεγον *tristegon.*
Acts 20. 9 fell down from the third loft, and was ta.

THIRD time, to do it a —
To do a thing a third time, שָׁלַשׁ *shalash*, 3.
1 Ki. 18. 34 Do (it) the third time..did (it) the third t.

THIRST, to (suffer) thirst —
1. *Thirst*, צָמָא *tsama.*
Exod 17. 3 to kill us and our children..with thirst?
Deut 28. 48 in hunger, and in thirst, and in nakedness
Judg 15. 18 now shall I die for thirst, and fall into the
2 Ch. 32. 11 to die by famine and by thirst, saying, The
Neh. 9. 15 broughtest forth water..for their thirst
9. 20 and gavest them water for their thirst
Psa. 69. 21 in my thirst they gave me vinegar to dr.
104. 11 They give drink..asses quench their thirst
Isa. 41. 17 their tongue faileth for thirst, I the LORD
50. 2 their fish stinketh..and dieth for thirst
Jer. 48. 18 come down from (thy) glory, and sit in th.
Lam. 4. 4 cleaveth to the roof of his mouth for thi.
Hos. 2. 3 like a dry land, and slay her with thirst
Amos 8. 11 not a famine of bread, nor a thirst for
8. 13 fair virgins and young men faint for thirst

2. *Thirsty*, צָמֵא *tsame.*
Deut 29. 19 though I walk..to add drunkenness to th.
Isa. 55. 1 Ho, every one that thirsteth, come ye to

3. *To thirst, be thirsty*, צָמֵא *tsame.*
Exod 17. 3 the people thirsted there for water; and
Job 24. 11 tread (their) wine presses, and suffer thi.
Psa. 42. 2 My soul thirsteth for God, for the living
63. 1 my soul thirsteth for thee, my flesh long.
Isa. 48. 21 they thirsted not (when) he led them thr.
49. 10 They shall not hunger nor thirst; neither

4. *Thirst*, צִמְאָה *tsimah.*
Jer. 2. 25 Withhold..thy throat from thirst: but th.

5. *Thirst*, צָמָה *tsamah.*
Isa. 5. 13 and their multitude dried up with thirst

6. *To thirst, be thirsty*, διψάω *dipsaō.*
Matt. 5. 6 Blessed (are) they which do..thirst after
John 4. 13 Whosoever drinketh of this water..thirst
4. 14 [drinketh of the water..shall never thirst]
4. 15 give me this water, that I thirst not, ne.
6. 35 he that believeth on me shall never thirst
John 7. 37 If any man thirst, let him come unto me
19. 28 After this, Jesus knowing..saith, I thirst
Rom 12. 20 if he thirst, give him drink: for in so do.
1 Co. 4. 11 we both hunger, and thirst, and are nak.
Rev. 7. 16 shall hunger no more, neither thirst any

7. *Thirst*, δίψος *dipsos.*
2 Co. 11. 27 in watchings often, in hunger and thirst

THIRSTY (land), to be thirsty —
1. *Weary, wearied*, עָיֵף *ayeph.*
Psa. 63. 1 longeth for thee in a dry and thirsty land
143. 6 my soul (thirsteth) after thee, as a thirsty
Prov 25. 25 (As) cold waters to a thirsty soul, so (is)

2. *Thirst*, צָמָא *tsama.*
Eze. 19. 13 she (is) planted..in a dry and thirsty gr.

3. *Thirsty*, צָמֵא *tsame.*
2 Sa. 17. 29 The people (is) hungry, and weary, and th.
Psa. 107. 5 Hungry and thirsty, their soul fainted in
Prov 25. 21 and if he be thirsty, give him water to dr.
Isa. 21. 14 brought water to him that was thirsty
29. 8 as when a thirsty (man) dreameth, and
32. 6 he will cause the drink of the thirsty to fail
44. 3 I will pour water upon him that is thirsty

4. *To thirst, be thirsty*, צָמֵא *tsame.*
Judg. 4. 19 Give me..a little water..for I am thirsty
Isa. 65. 13 servants shall drink, but ye shall be thir.

5. *Thirst, thirsty*, צִמָּאוֹן *tsimmaon.*
Isa. 35. 7 and the thirsty land springs of water: in

6. *To thirst, be thirsty*, διψάω *dipsaō.*
Matt 25. 35 I was thirsty, and ye gave me drink: I
25. 37 when saw we thee..thirsty, and gave (th.)
25. 42 I was thirsty, and ye gave me no drink

THIRTEEN, thirteenth —
Three (and) ten, שְׁלֹשָׁה עָשָׂר, שְׁלֹשׁ עֶשְׂרֵה *shelosh esreh.*
Gen. 14. 4 and in the thirteenth year they rebelled
17. 25 his son (was) thirteen years old when he
Num. 3. 43, 46 two hundred and threescore and thir.
29. 14 unto every bullock of the thirteen bullocks
Josh. 19. 6 Sharuhen; thirteen cities and their villa.
21. 4 of the tribe of Benjamin, thirteen cities
21. 6 and out of the half tribe..thirteen cities
21. 19 (were) thirteen cities with their suburbs
21. 33 according to their families (were) thirteen
1 Ki. 7. 1 was building his own house thirteen years
1 Ch. 6. 60 cities throughout their families (were) th.
6. 62 out of the tribe of Manasseh..thirteen ci.
24. 13 The thirteenth to Huppah, the fourteenth
25. 20 The thirteenth to Shubael, (he), his sons
Esth. 3. 12 on the thirteenth day of the first month
3. 13 in one day, (even) upon the thirteenth (day)
8. 12 upon the thirteenth (day) of the twelfth
9. 1 the month Adar, on the thirteenth day of
9. 17 On the thirteenth day of the month Adar
9. 18 assembled together on the thirteenth (d.)
Jer. 1. 2 word of the LORD came..in the thirteenth
25. 3 From the thirteenth year of Josiah the son
Eze. 40. 11 (and) the length of the gate, thirteen cu.

THIRTY, thirtyfold, thirtieth —
1. *Thirty*, שְׁלֹשִׁים *sheloshim.*
Gen. 5. 3 Adam lived an hundred and thirty years
5. 5 days..were nine hundred and thirty years
5. 16 lived..eight hundred and thirty years, and
6. 15 fifty cubits, and the height of it thirty cu.
11. 12 Arphaxad lived five and thirty years, and
11. 14 And Salah lived thirty years, and begat
11. 16 Eber lived four and thirty years, and be.
11. 17 Eber lived..four hundred and thirty years
11. 18 And Peleg lived thirty years, and begat
11. 20 And Reu lived two and thirty years
11. 22 Serug lived thirty years, and begat Nahor
18. 30 Peradventure there shall thirty be found
18. 30 he said, I will not do (it) if I find thirty
25. 17 an hundred and thirty and seven years
32. 15 Thirty milch camels with their colts, forty
41. 46 Joseph (was) thirty years old when he st.
46. 15 sons and his daughters (were) thirty and
47. 9 The days..(are) an hundred and thirty
Exod. 6. 16 (were) an hundred thirty and seven ye.
6. 18 the years..(were) an hundred thirty and
12. 40 sojourning..(was) four hundred and thirty
12. 41 the end of the four hundred and thirty
21. 32 he shall give unto their master thirty she.
26. 8 length of one curtain (shall be) thirty cub.
36. 15 The length of one curtain (was) thirty cub.
38. 24 seven hundred and thirty shekels, after
Lev. 12. 4 shall then continue..three and thirty days
27. 4 then thy estimation shall be thirty shek.
Num. 1. 35 thirty and two thousand and two hundred
1. 37 thirty and five thousand and four hundred
2. 21 thirty and two thousand and two hundred
2. 23 thirty and five thousand and four hundr.
4. 3, 23, 30, 35, 39, 43, 47 From thirty years old
4. 40 two thousand and six hundred and thirty
7. 13 the weight..(was) an hundred and thirty
So in verse 19, 25, 31, 37, 43, 49, 55, 61, 67, 73, 79, 85.
20. 29 they mourned for Aaron thirty days, (even)
26. 7 three thousand and seven hundred and
26. 37 thirty and two thousand and five hundred
26. 51 and a thousand seven hundred and thirty
31. 35 thirty and two thousand persons in all, of
31. 36 and thirty thousand and five hundred sh.
31. 38 the beeves (were) thirty and six thousand
31. 39 the asses (were) thirty thousand and five
31. 40 of which the LORD's tribute (was) thirty
31. 43 thirty thousand (and) seven thousand and
31. 44 And thirty and six thousand beeves
31. 45 And thirty thousand asses and five hund.
Deut. 2. 14 the space..(was) thirty and eight years
34. 8 And the children of Israel wept..thirty
Josh. 7. 5 men of Ai smote of them about thirty
8. 3 Joshua chose out thirty thousand mighty
12. 24 king of Tirzah, one: all the kings thirty
Judg 10. 4 he had thirty sons that rode on thirty
10. 4 they had thirty cities, which are called
12. 9 he had thirty sons, and thirty daughters
12. 9 took in thirty daughters from abroad for
12. 14 he had forty sons and thirty nephews, that
14. 11 they brought thirty companions to be with
14. 12, 13 thirty sheets and thirty change of ga.
14. 19 slew thirty men of them, and took their
20. 31 began to smite..about thirty men of Is.
20. 39 kill of the men of Israel about thirty pe.
1 Sa. 4. 10 there fell of Israel about thirty thousand
9. 22 were bidden, which (were) about thirty pe.
11. 8 and the men of Judah thirty thousand
13. 5 thirty thousand chariots, and six thousand
2 Sa. 5. 4 David (was) thirty years old when he be.
5. 5 he reigned thirty and three years over all
6. 1 all (the) chosen (men) of Israel, thirty tho.
23. 13 three of the thirty chief went down, and
23. 23 He was more honourable than the thirty
23. 24 the brother of Joab, (was) one of the th.
23. 39 Uriah the Hittite: thirty and seven in all
1 Ki. 2. 11 thirty and three years reigned he in Jer.
4. 22 Solomon's provision for one day was th.
5. 13 and the levy was thirty thousand men
6. 2 the house..the height thereof thirty cu.
7. 2 the height thereof thirty cubits, upon four
7. 6 the breadth thereof thirty cubits: and
7. 23 a line of thirty cubits did compass it rou.
16. 23 In the thirty and first year of Asa king of
16. 29 in the thirty and eighth year of Asa king
20. 1 (there were) thirty and two kings with him
20. 15 and they were two hundred and thirty two
20. 16 the thirty and two kings that helped him
22. 31 the king of Syria commanded his thirty
22. 42 Jehoshaphat (was) thirty and five years
2 Ki. 8. 17 Thirty and two years old was he when he
13. 10 In the thirty and seventh year of Joash
15. 8 In the thirty and eighth year of Azariah
15. 13 began to reign in the nine and thirtieth
15. 17 In the nine and thirtieth year of Azariah
18. 14 hundred talents of silver, and thirty tal.
22. 1 he reigned thirty and one years in Jerus.
25. 27 in the seven and thirtieth year of the cap.
1 Ch. 3. 4 in Jerusalem he reigned thirty and three
7. 4 soldiers for war, six and thirty thousand
7. 7 twenty and two thousand and thirty and
11. 15 Now three of the thirty captains went do.
11. 25 he was honourable among the thirty, but
11. 42 captain of the Reubenites, and thirty with
12. 4 mighty..among the thirty, and over the th.
12. 34 shield and spear thirty and seven thousand
15. 7 and his brethren an hundred and thirty
19. 7 So they hired thirty and two thousand ch.
23. 3 from the age of thirty years and upward
23. 3 their number..was thirty and eight thous.
27. 6 mighty (among) the thirty, and above the t.
29. 27 thirty and three (years) reigned he in Je.
2 Ch. 3. 15 made before the house two pillars of thirty
4. 2 line of thirty cubits did compass it round
15. 19 no (more) war unto the five and thirtieth
16. 1 In the six and thirtieth year of the reign
16. 12 Asa in the thirty and ninth year of his re.
20. 31 (He was) thirty and five years old when he
21. 5 Jehoram (was) thirty and two years old
21. 20 Thirty and two years old was he when he
24. 15 an hundred and thirty years old (was he)
34. 1 reigned in Jerusalem one and thirty yea.
35. 7 to the number of thirty thousand, and
Ezra 1. 9 number of them: thirty chargers of gold
1. 10 Thirty basins of gold, silver basins of a se.
2. 35 three thousand and six hundred and thi.
2. 42 porters..all an hundred thirty and nine
2. 65 seven thousand three hundred thirty and
2. 66 Their horses (were) seven hundred thirty
2. 67 Their camels, four hundred thirty and
Neh. 5. 14 even unto the two and thirtieth year of
7. 38 three thousand nine hundred and thirty
7. 45 children of Shobai, an hundred thirty and
7. 67 seven thousand three hundred thirty and
7. 68 Their horses, seven hundred thirty and
7. 69 camels, four hundred thirty and five; six
7. 70 five hundred and thirty priests' garments
13. 6 in the two and thirtieth year of Artaxerxes
Esth. 4. 11 to come in unto the king these thirty days
Jer. 38. 10 Take from hence thirty men with thee
52. 29 from Jerusalem eight hundred thirty and
52. 31 came to pass in the seven and thirtieth
Eze. 1. 1 Now it came to pass in the thirtieth year
40. 17 thirty chambers (were) upon the pavement
41. 6 one over another, and thirty in order; and
46. 22 of forty (cubits) long, and thirty broad
Dan. 12. 12 thousand three hundred and five and thi.
Zech. 11. 12 So they weighed for my price thirty (pie.)
11. 13 took the thirty (pieces) of silver, and cast

2. *Thirty*, תְּלָתִין *telathin.*
Dan. 6. 7 ask a petition of any god or man for thirty
6. 12 ask..of any god or man within thirty days

3. *Thirty*, τριάκοντα *triakonta.*
Matt 13. 8 hundred fold, some sixty fold, some thir.
13. 23 an hundred fold, some sixty, some thirty
26. 15 covenanted with him for thirty pieces of
27. 3 brought again the thirty pieces of silver
27. 9 And they took the thirty pieces of silver
Mark 4. 8 brought forth, some thirty, and some six.
4. 20 bring forth fruit, some thirty fold, some
Luke 3. 23 Jesus himself began to be about thirty ye.

John 5. 5 which had an infirmity thirty and eight
6. 19 rowed about fi.e and twenty or thirty fu.
Gal. 3. 17 which was four hundred and thirty years

THIS —

1. *These,* אֵלֶּה *eleh.*
Exod38. 21 This is the sum of the tabernacle, (even)

2. *This,* גֵּה *geh* (error for *zeh*).
Eze. 47. 13 This (shall be) the border whereby ye sh.

3. *This,* דָּא *da.*
Dan. 4. 30 Is not this great Babylon, that I have bu.
7. 8 in this horn (were) eyes like the eyes of

4. *This,* דָּךְ, דֵּךְ *dak, dek.*
Ezra 4. 13 if this city be builded, and the walls set
4. 15 know, that this city (is) a rebellious city
4. 15 for which cause was this city destroyed
4. 16 certify the king, that if this city be buil.
4. 19 it is found that this city of old time hath
4. 21 that this city be not builded, until (ano.)
5. 8 this work goeth fast on, and prospereth
5. 17 to build this house of God at Jerusalem
6. 7 Let the work of this house of God alone
6. 7 governor..build this house of God in his
6. 8 for the building of this house of God, th.
6. 12 destroy this house of God which (is) at J.

5. *This,* דִּכֵּן *dikken.*
Dan. 2. 31 This great image, whose brightness (was)

6. *This,* דֵּן *den.*
Ezra 4. 11 This (is) the copy of the letter that they
4. 16 by this means thou shalt have no portion
4. 22 Take heed now that ye fail not to do this
5. 3 build this house, and to make up this wall
5. 4 names of the men that make this building?
5. 5 returned answer by letter concerning this
5. 9 Who commanded you to build this house
5. 12 who destroyed this house, and carried the
5. 13 king Cyrus made a decree to build this
6. 11 whosoever shall alter this word, let timb.
6. 11 let his house be made a dunghill for this
6. 15 this house was finished on the third day
6. 16 kept the dedication of this house of God
6. 17 offered at the dedication of this house of
7. 17 thou mayest buy speedily with this money
7. 24 touching any of the..ministers of this ho.
Dan 2. 12 For this cause the king was angry and ve.
2. 18 would desire mercies..concerning this se.
2. 30 this secret is not revealed to me for (any)
2. 36 This,(is) the dream; and we will tell the
2. 47 seeing thou couldest reveal this secret
3. 16 we (are) not careful to answer thee in this
4. 18 This dream I king Nebuchadnezzar have
4. 24 This (is) the interpretation O king, and..the
5. 7 Whosoever shall read this writing, and sh.
5. 15 that they should read this writing, and
5. 22 not humbled..though thou knewest all th.
5. 24 sent from him; and this writing was wri.
5. 25 this (is) the writing that was written, M.
5. 26 This (is) the interpretation of the thing
6. 3 Then this Daniel was preferred above the
6. 5 shall not find any occasion against this D.
6. 28 So this Daniel prospered in the reign of D.
7. 6 After this I beheld, and lo another, like
7. 7 After this I saw in the night visions, and
7. 16 asked him the truth of all this. So he told

7. *He himself, the same,* הוּא *hu.*
Gen. 15. 2 steward of my house (is) this Eliezer of Da.

8. *He himself, the same,* הַהוּא *ha-hu.*
1 Sa. 1. 3 this man went up out of his city yearly to

9. *She, it, herself, itself, the same,* הִיא *hi.*
Josh 10. 13 (Is) not this written in the book of Jasher?
Jer. 29. 28 This (captivity is) long: build ye houses
Dan. 4. 24 this is the decree of the most high, which

10. *She herself, itself, the same,* הַהִיא *ha-hi.*
Num. 5. 31 and this woman shall bear her iniquity

11. *This, that,* הַלָּז *hallaz.*
Judg. 6. 20 lay (them) upon this rock, and pour out the
1 Sa. 17. 26 to the man that killeth this Philistine, and
Dan. 8. 16 make this (man) to understand the vision
Zech. 2. 4 Run, speak to this young man, saying, Je.

12. *This, that,* הַלָּזֶה *hallazeh.*
Gen. 24. 65 What man (is) this that walketh in the fi.
37. 19 said one to another, Behold this dreamer

13. *This, that,* הַלֵּזוּ *hallezu.*
Eze. 36. 35 This land that was desolate is become li.

14. *They themselves,* הֵמָּה *hemah.*
Num20. 13 This (is) the water of Meribah; because

15. *This, that,* זֹאת *zoth.*
Gen. 2. 23 This (is) now bone of my bones, and flesh
29. 27 we will give thee this also for the service
34. 15 But in this will we consent unto you: If
45. 23 to his father he sent after this (manner)
Exod 7. 23 neither did he set his heart to this also
1 Sa. 11. 2 On this (condition) will I make (a coven.)
2 Ch. 20. 17 Ye shall not (need) to fight in this (battle)
Job 37. 1 At this also my heart trembleth, and is
Isa. 27. 9 By this therefore shall the iniquity of J.
30. 7 therefore have I cried concerning this, T.
Jer. 5. 7 How shall I pardon thee for this? thy ch.
Eze. 21. 26 this (shall) not (be) the same: exalt him that

16. *This, that,* הַזֹּאת *haz-zoth.*
Gen. 12. 7 Unto thy seed will I give this land: and

17. *As this, thus,* כָּזֹאת *ka-zoth.*
Judg15. 7 Though ye have done this, yet will I be

18. *This,* זֶה *zeh.*
Gen. 5. 1 This (is) the book of the generations of A.
38. 21 they said, There was no harlot in this
41. 38 Can we find (such a one) as this (is), a man
1 Sa. 25. 21 in vain have I kept all that this (fellow)
Eccl. 6. 5 not seen the sun..this hath more rest th.

19. *This,* הַזֶּה *haz-zeh.*
Gen. 7. 1 thee have I seen righteous..in this gener.

20. *This,* זֹה *zoh.*
2 Ki. 6. 19 This (is) not the way, neither (is) this the
Eccl. 2. 24 This also I saw, that it (was) from the ha.
5. 16 this also (is) a sore evil, (that) in all poi.
5. 19 to rejoice in his labour; this (is) the gift
7. 23 All this have I proved by wisdom: I said
9. 13 This wisdom have I seen also under the
Eze. 40. 45 This chamber, whose prospect (is) toward

21. *This,* זוֹ *zo.*
Hos. 7. 16 This (shall be) their derision in the land

22. *This,* זוּ *zu.*
Psa. 12. 7 thou shalt preserve them from this gene.
62. 11 twice have I heard this, that power (belo.)
Isa. 43. 21 This people have I formed for myself; th.
Hab. 1. 11 offend, (imputing) this his power unto his

23. *Thus,* כֹּה *koh.*
2 Ch. 19. 10 warn them..this do, and ye shall not tr.
Lam. 2. 20 and consider to whom thou hast done th.

24. *So,* כֵּן *ken.*
Amos 4. 5 for this liketh you, O ye children of Israel

25. *This, it,* αὐτό *auto.*
John12. 7 against..my burying hath she kept this

26. *That, that very; he, she, it,* ἐκεῖνος *ekeinos.*
Matt24. 43 But know this, that if the goodman of

27. *This, that,* οὗτος *houtos.*
Matt. 3. 3 For this is he that was spoken of by the
Also in v. 17; 7. [12]; 8. 27; 9. 3; 11. 10; 12. 23, 24;
13. 19, 55; 14. 2; 15. 8; 17 5; 21. 10, 11, 38; 26. 61, 71;
27. 37, 47, 54; 28. 15; Mark 2. 7; 4. 41; 6. 3; 7. 6; 9. 7;
12. 7; 14. 69; Luke 1. 29, 36; 2. 34; 4. 22, 36; 5. 21; 7. 17, 27,
49; 8. 25; 9. 9, 35; 14. 30; 15. 24, 30, 32; 17. 18; 18. 11;
20. 14; 22. 59; 23. [38], 47, 52; John 1. 15, 30, 34; 2. 20; 4.
29, 42; 6. 14, 42, 50, 58, 60; 7. 25, 26, 31, 36, 40, 41, [46],
49; 9. 8, 9, 16, 19, 20, 24; 11. 47; 12. 34; 21. 23, 24; Acts
4. 11; 6. 13, 14; 7. 37, 38, 40; 9. 21, 22; 17. 3, 18; 18. 13;
19. 26; 21. 28; 22. 26; 26. 31, 32; 28. 4; Rom. 4. 9; 9. 9;
Heb. 3. 3; 7. 1; 2 Pe. 1. 17; 1 Jo. 5. 6, 20; 2 Jo. 7; Rev.
20. 14.

28. *This, that,* αὕτη *hautē.*
Matt13. 54 Whence..this wisdom, and (these) mighty
Also in 21. 42; 22. 20, 38; 24. 34; 26. 8; Mark 1. [27]; 8.
12; 12. 11, 16, [30, 31,] 43; 13. 30; 14. 4; Luke 2. 2; 4. 21;
8. 9, 11; 11. 29; 21. 3, 32; 22. 53; John 1. 19; 3. 19, 29;
8. [4]; 11. 4; 12. 30; 15. 12; 17. 3; Acts 5. [38]; 8. 32;
17. 19; 21. 11; Rom. 11. 27; 1 Co. 8. 9; 9. 3; 2 Co. 1.
12; 2. 6; 11. 10; Eph. 3. 8; Titus 1. 13; Heb. 8. 10; 10.16;
Jas. 1. 27; 3. 15; 1 Jo. 1. 5; 2. 25; 3. 11, 23; 5. 3, 4, 9,
11, 11, 14; 2 Jo. 6, 6; Rev. 20. 5.

29. *These things,* ταῦτα *tauta.*
Luke18. 23 when he heard this, he was very sorrow.
John 5. 1 After this there was a feast of the Jews
19. 38 after this, Joseph of Arimathea, being a
Acts 15. 16 After this I will return, and will build ag.
Rev. 4. 1 After this I looked, and, behold, a door
7. 9 After this I beheld, and, lo, a great mult.

30. *In this,* ταύτῃ *tautē.*
Matt.10. 23 when they persecute you in this city, flee
Also in 12. 45; 16. 18; 26. 31, 34; Mark 8. 12, 38; 14. [27],
30; Luke 11. 30; 12. 20; 13. 7; 16. 24; 17. 6; 19. 42; Acts 18.
10; 22. 3; 27. 23; 1 Co. 9. 12; 15. 19; 2 Co. 1. 15; 8. 7, 19,
20; 11. 17.

31. *This,* ταύτην *tautēn.*
Matt.11. 16 But whereunto shall I liken this generat.?
See also 15. [15]; 21. 23; 23. 36; Mark 4. 13; 10. 5; 11. 28;
12. 10; Luke 4. 6, 23; 7. 44; 12. 41; 13. 6, 16; 15. 3; 18. 5,
9; 20. 2, 9, 19; John 2. 11; 7. [8], 8; 10. 6, 18; 12. 27; Acts 1.
[16]; 3. 16; 7. 4, 60; 8. 19; 22. 4, 28; 23. 13; 27. 21; 28. 20,
20; Rom. 5. 2; 2 Co. 4. 1; 12. 13; 1 Ti. 1. 18; 2 Ti. 2. 19; 1
Pe. 5. 12; 2 Pe. 1. 18; 3. 1; 1 Jo. 3. 3; 4. 21; 2 Jo. 10; Rev.
2. 24; 12. 15.

32. *Of this,* ταύτης *tautēs.*
Matt.12. 41 men..shall rise in judgment with this ge.
See also v. 42; Luke 7. 31; 11. 31, 32, 50, 51; 17. 25; John 10.
16; 12. 27; 15. 13; Acts 1. 17, 25; 2. 6, 29, 40; 5. 20; 6. 3; 8.
22; Acts 10. 30; 13. 26; 19. 25, 40; 23. 1; 24. 21; 26. 22; 28.
22; 2 Co. 9. 12, 13; Heb. 9. 11; Rev. 22. 19.

33. *This,* τοῦτο *touto.*
Matt. 1. 22 Now all this was done, that it might be
See also 8. 9; 9. 28; 13. 28; 15. 11; 16. 22; 17. [21]; 18. 4;
19. 26; 21. 4; 24. 14; 26. 9, 12, 13, 26, 28, 39, 42, 56; 28. 14;
Mark 1. [27]; 5. 32; 9. 21, 29; 11. [3]; 14. [9], 22, 24, 36;
Luke 1. 18, 34, 43, 66; 2. 12, 15; 3. 20; 5. 6; 6. 3; 7. 4, 8;
9. 45, 48; 10. 11, 28; 12. 18, 39; 13. 8; 16. 2; 18. 34; 20. 17;
22. 15, 17, 19, 19, 20, 23, 37, 42; John 2. 12, 22; 4. 15, 54;
5. 28; 6. 6, 29, 39, 40, 61; 7. 39; 8. [6], 40; 11. 26, 51; 12.
5, 6, 18, 18, 27, 33; 13. 28; 16. 17, 18; 18. 34, 37, 37, 38;
19. 28; 20. 22; 21. 14, 19, 19; Acts 2. 12, 14, 16, 33; 4. 7,
22; 5. 4, 24, 38; 7. 60; 8. 34; 9. 21; 10. 16; 11. 10; 16.
18; 19. 10, 17, 27; 20. [29]; 21. 23; 24. 14; 26. 16, 26; 27.
34; Rom. 1. 12, 26; 2. 3; 6. 6; 9. 17; 11. 25; 13. 6, 6; 14. 9,
13; 15. 9, 28; 1 Co. 1. 12; 4. 17; 5. 2, 3; 7. 6, 26, 29, 35; 9.
17, [23]; 10. 28; 11. 10, 17, 24, 24, 25, 25, [26], 30; 15. 50, 53,
53, 54, 54; 2 Co. 2. 1, 3, 9; 4. 1; 7. 11; 8. 10, 20; 9. 6; 10. 7,
11; 13. 1, 9; Gal. 3. 2, 17; Eph. 4. 17; 5. 5, 32; 6. 1; Phil.
1. 6, 7, 9, 19, 22, 25; 2. 5, 15; Col. 1. 9; 2. 4; 3. 20; 1 Ti. 2.
13; 3. 5; 4. 3, 15; 5. 18; 2 Th. 2. 11; 3. 10; 1 Ti. 1. 9, 16;
2. 3; 4. 16; 2 Ti. 1. 15; 3. 1; Heb. 6. 3; 7. 27; 9. 8, 15,
20, 27; 13. 19; Jas. 4. 15; 1 Pe. 1. 25; 2. 19, 20; 4. 6;
2 Pe. 1. 5, 20; 3. 3, 5, 8; 1 Jo. 3. 8; 4. 3; Jude 4, [5];
Rev. 2. 6.

34. *To these,* τούτοις *toutois.*
Luke16. 26 beside all this, between us and you there
24. 21 beside all this, to day is the third day si.

35. *This,* τοῦτον *touton.*
Matt 19. 11 All..cannot receive [this] saying, save
See also 21. [44]; Mark 7. 29; 14. 58, 71; Luke 9. 14; 12. 56;
16. 28; 19. 14; 23. 2, 14, 18; John 2. 19; 6. 34, 58; 7. 27; 9.
29, 30; 18. 40; 19. 12, 20; Acts 2. 32; 3. 16; 5. 37; 6. 14;
7. 35; 21. 28; 23. 17, 18, 25, 27; 24. 5; 25. 24; 28. 26; Rom.
9. 9; 15. 28; 1 Co. 3. [12]; 11. 26, [27]; 2 Co. 4. 7; Heb. 8. 3.

36. *Of this,* τούτου *toutou.*
Matt 13. 15 For this people's heart is waxed gross, and
See also [22], [40]; 19. 5; 26. 29; 27. 24; Mark 4. [19];
10. 7; Luke 2. 17; 9. 45; 13. 16; 16. 8; 20. 34; John 4.
13; 6. 51; 8. 23; 10. 41; 11. 9; 12. [31], 31; 13. 1; 14.
[30]; 16. 11; 18. 17, 29, 36, 36; Acts 5. 28; 6. [13]; 9. 13;
13. 7, 23, 38; 15. 2, 6; 17. 32; 21. 28; 22. 22; 28. 9, 27;
Rom. 7. 24; 11. 7; 1 Co. 1. [20], 20; 2. 6, 6, 8; 3. 19; 5.
10; 7. 31; 2 Co. 4. 4; 12. 8; Eph. 2. 2; 3. 1, 14; 5. 31; 6.
12; Col. 1. 27; Titus 1. 5; Jas. 1. 26; 2. [5]; Rev. 22. 7,
9, 10, 18.

37. *These,* τούτους *toutous.*
Acts 16. 36 the keeper of the prison told [this] saying

38. *To this,* τούτῳ *toutō.*
Matt. 8. 9 I say to this..Go, and he goeth; and to
See also 12. 32; 13. 54, 56; 17. 20; 20. 14; 21. 21;
Mark 6. 2; 10. 30; 11. 23; Luke 1. 61, 4. 3; 10. 5, 20;
14. 9; 18. 30; 19. 9; 21. 23; 23. 4, 14; John 4. 20, 21, 27;
12. 25; 13. 35; 16. 30; 20. 30; Acts 1. 6; 3. 12; 4. 17;
5. 28; 7. 7, 29; 8. 21, 29; 15. 15; 23. 9; 24. 2, 10; Rom.
12. 2; 13. 9; 1 Co. 3. 18; 7. [31]; 11. 22; 14. 21; 2 Co.
3. 10; 5. 2; 9. 3; Gal. 6. 16; Heb. 4. 5; 1 Pe. 4. 16;
2 Pe. 1. 13; 1 Jo. 3. 10; 4. 9, 17; 5. 2; Rev. 22. 18, 19.
[*See also* After, cause, day, hour, means, place, once,
side, time, way, wise].

THIS man, woman, matter, thing, deed—

1. *This,* זֶה *zeh.*
2 Ki. 5. 7 God..that this man doth send unto me to

2. *This,* דֵּן *den.*
Ezra 5. 17 send..his pleasure..concerning this mat.

3. *This,* זֹאת *zoth.*
1 Ch.11. 19 God forbid it me, that I should do this th.

4. *Thus, as thus,* כָּכָה *kakah.*
Esth. 9. 26 which they had seen concerning this ma.

5. *At this,* τούτῳ *toutō.*
Acts 3. 12 Ye men of Israel, why marvel ye at this?

6. *This, he,* οὗτος *houtos.*
Mark15. 39 said, Truly this man was the son of God
Luke 7. 39; 14. 30; 15. 2; 18. 14; 22. 56; 23. 41; John
6. 52; 7. 15; 9. 2, 3, 33; 11. 37, 37; 21. 21; Acts 1. 18; 4.
10; 8. 10; 18. 25; Heb. 7. 4; 10. 12; Jas. 1. 25.

7. *This, she,* αὕτη *hautē*, Mt. 26. 13; Lu. 7. 45, 46, &c.

8. *This, she,* ταύτην *tautēn*, Luke 13. 16.

9. *This, she,* τοῦτο *touto*, Mark 5. 32; Lu. 22. 23, &c.

10. *This, she,* τούτῳ *toutō*, Luke 14. 9.

THIS fashion, manner, sort, time, wise —

1. *Thus,* כֹּה *koh.*
Num. 6. 23 On this wise ye shall bless the children of
1 Ki. 22. 20 one said on this manner, and another said

2. *Thus, so,* כְּנֵמָא *kenema.*
Ezra 4. 8 wrote..to Artaxerxes the king in this sort
5. 4 Then said we unto them after this manner

3. *Now,* νῦν *nun.*
Matt 24. 21 the beginning of the world to this time
Mark13. 19 God created unto this time, neither shall
Acts 24. 25 Go thy way for this time; when I have a
1 Co. 16. 12 his will was not at all to come at this time

4. *Thus, so,* οὕτως, οὕτω *houtōs, houtō.*
Matt. 1. 18 the birth of Jesus Christ was on this wise
Mark 2. 12 saying. We never saw it on this fashion
John21. 1 After these things..on this wise showed
Acts 7. 6 God spake on this wise, That his seed sh.
13. 34 he said on this wise, I will give you the
Rom 10. 6 which is of faith speaketh on this wise
Heb. 4. 4 For he spake..of the seventh..on this wise
Rev. 11. 5 will hurt them, he must in this manner

5. *Of these,* τούτων *toutōn.*
2 Ti. 3. 6 For of this sort are they which creep into

THIS place, side, way —

1. *Here, hither,* הֵנָּה *henah.*
Josh. 8. 20 and they had no power to flee this way or
Eze. 1. 23 every one..two, which covered on this side
Dan. 12. 5 one on this side of the bank of the river

2. *This,* זֶה *zeh.*
Exod26. 13 on this side and on that side, to cover it

3. *Thus,* כֹּה *koh.*
Exod. 2. 12 he looked this way and that way, and wh.
Num11. 31 as it were a day's journey on this side

4. *Here, hither,* ὧδε *hōde*
Matt12. 6 in this place is (one) greater than the te.
Luke 23. 5 beginning from Galilee to this place

THISTLE —

1. *Thistle, bramble,* דַּרְדַּר *dardar.*
Gen. 3. 18 Thorns also and thistles shall it bring fo.
Hos. 10. 8 the thistle shall come up on their altars

2. *Thorn, bramble, thicket,* חוֹחַ *choach.*
2 Ki. 14. 9 The thistle that (was) in Lebanon sent to
14. 9 there passed by..and trode down the thi.
2 Ch. 25. 18 The thistle that (was) in Lebanon sent to
25. 18 there passed by..and trode down the th.
Job 31. 40 Let thistles grow instead of wheat, and

3. *A thistle,* τρίβολος *tribolos.*
Matt. 7. 16 gather grapes of thorns, or figs of thistles?

THITHER, thitherward —

1. *Here, hither,* הֲלֹם *halom.*
1 Sa. 10. 22 further, if the man should yet come thi.

2. *Here, hither,* הֵנָּה *henah.*
Jer. 50. 5 they shall ask..with their faces thitherw.

3. *There,* שָׁם *sham.*
Deut. 1. 37 saying, Thou also shalt not go in thither

4. *There, thither,* ἐκεῖ *ekei.*
Matt. 2. 22 when he heard..he was afraid to go thit.
Mark 6. 33 many knew him, and ran afoot thither out
Luke 17. 37 thither will the eagles be gathered toget.
21. 2 a certain poor widow casting in thither
John 11. 8 sought to stone thee; and goest thou th.
18. 2 Jesus ofttimes resorted thither with his di.
18. 3 cometh thither with lanterns and torches
Acts 17. 13 they came thither also, and stirred up the
Rom 15. 24 to be brought on my way thitherward by

THO'-MAS, Θωμᾶς *twin.*
One of the twelve apostles of Jesus, and called also *Didymus;* he was zealous and inquisitive, yet at first incredulous at the report of the resurrection of Christ.
Matt 10. 3 T., and Matthew the publican; James
Mark 3. 18 Matthew, and T., and James the (son) of
Luke 6. 15 Matthew, and T., James the (son) of Al.
John 11. 16 Then said T., which is called Didymus, unto
14. 5 T. saith unto him, Lord, we know not wh.
20. 24 But T...was not with them when Jesus
20. 26 again his disciples were within, and T.
20. 27 Then saith he to T., Reach hither thy
20. 28 T. answered and said unto him, My Lord
20. 29 [T.,] because thou hast seen me, thou hast
21. 2 There were together Simon Peter, and T.
Acts 1. 13 John, and Andrew, Philip, and T., Barth.

THONGS —

A thong, strap, latchet, ἱμάς *himas.*
Acts 22. 25 as they bound him with thongs, Paul said

THORN, (of thorns) —

1. *A bramble,* אָטָד *atad.*
Psa. 58. 9 Before your pots can feel the thorns, he

2. *A brier,* חֵדֶק *chedeq.*
Prov 15. 19 way of the slothful..as an hedge of thorns

3. *Thorn, bramble, thicket,* חוֹחַ *choach.*
2 Ch. 33. 11 which took Manasseh among the thorns
Job 41. 2 or bore his jaw through with a thorn?
Prov 26. 9 (As) a thorn goeth up into the hand of a
Song 2. 2 As the lily among thorns, so (is) my love
Hos. 9. 6 For, lo..thorns (shall be) in their tabern.

4. *A thorn,* נַעֲצוּץ *naatsuts.*
Isa. 7. 19 and upon all thorns, and upon all bushes
55. 13 Instead of the thorn shall come up the fir

5. *A thorn, hook,* סִיר *sir.*
Eccl. 7. 6 For as the crackling of thorns under a pot
Isa. 34. 13 And thorns shall come up in her palaces
Hos. 2. 6 I will hedge up thy way with thorns, and
Nah. 1. 10 For while (they be) folden together (as) th.

6. *Briers, thorns,* סַלּוֹנִים *sallonim.*
Eze. 2. 6 though briers and thorns (be) with thee, and

7. *Thorn,* צֵן *tsen.*
Job 5. 5 taketh it even out of the thorns, and the
Prov 22. 5 Thorns..snares (are) in the way of the frow.

8. *Thorns,* צְנִינִים *tseninim.*
Num 33. 55 pricks in your eyes, and thorns in your si.
Josh 23. 13 scourges in your sides, and thorns in your

9. *A thorn,* קוֹץ *qots.*
Gen. 3. 18 Thorns also and thistles shall it bring fo.
Exod 22. 6 If fire break out, and catch in thorns, so
Judg. 8. 7 I will tear your flesh with the thorns of
8. 16 and thorns of the wilderness and briers
2 Sa. 23. 6 all of them as thorns thrust away, because
Psa. 118. 12 they are quenched as the fire of thorns
Isa. 32. 13 shall come up thorns (and) briers; yea
33. 12 thorns cut up shall they be burned in the
Jer. 4. 3 thus saith the LORD..sow not among th.
12. 13 They have sown wheat, but shall reap th.
Eze. 28. 24 nor..grieving thorn of all..round about
Hos. 10. 8 the thorn and the thistle shall come up

10. *Nettle, thorn,* קִמָּשׁוֹן *qimmashon.*
Prov 24. 31 And lo, it was all grown over with thorns

11. *A thorn,* שַׁיִת *shayith.*
5. 6 but there shall come up briers and thorns
7. 23 it shall (even) be for briers and thorns
7. 24 the land shall become briers and thorns
7. 25 there shall not come..the fear of..thorns
9. 18 it shall devour the briers and thorns, and
10. 17 burn and devour his thorns and his briers
27. 4 who would set the briers (and) thorns ag.

12. *A thorn, brier,* ἄκανθα *akantha.*
Matt. 7. 16 Do men gather grapes of thorns, or figs of
13. 7 some fell among thorns; and the thorns
13. 22 also that received seed among the thorns
27. 29 when they had platted a crown of thorns
Mark 4. 7 some fell among thorns, and the thorns
Mark 4. 18 these are they which are sown among th.
Luke 6. 44 For of thorns men do not gather figs, nor
8. 7 some fell among thorns; and the thorns
8. 14 that which fell among thorns are they, wh.
John 19. 2 soldiers platted a crown of thorns, and put
Heb. 6. 8 But that which beareth thorns and briers

13. *Thorny, made of thorns,* ἀκάνθινος *akanthinos.*
Mark 15. 17 platted a crown of thorns, and put it ab.
John 19. 5 wearing the crown of thorns, and the pu.

14. *A sharp stake, palisade,* σκόλοψ *skolops.*
2 Co. 12. 7 there was given to me a thorn in the flesh

THORN hedge —

A thorn hedge, מְסוּכָה *mesukah.*
Mic. 7. 4 most upright (is sharper) than a thorn he.

THOROUGHLY —

1. *To do good or well,* יָטַב *yatab,* 5.
2 Ki. 11. 18 his images brake they in pieces thoroug.

2. *To heal, repair,* רָפָא *rapha,* 3.
Exod 21. 19 and shall cause (him) to be thoroughly

THOSE (men, things) —

1. *These,* אֵל *el.*
Gen. 19. 25 he overthrew those cities, and all the pl.
Deut. 7. 22 LORD thy God will put out those nations

2. *These,* אֵלֶּה *eleh.*
Gen. 33. 5 Who (are) those with thee? And he said

3. *These,* אִלֵּךְ *illek.*
Ezra 5. 9 Then asked we those elders, (and) said un.
Dan. 3. 22 flame of the fire slew those men that took
6. 24 they brought those men which had accus.

4. *The men,* הָאֲנָשִׁים *ha-anashim.*
Num 14. 22 Because all those men which have seen
14. 37 Even those men that did bring up the evil

5. *He, he himself,* הַהוּא *ha-hu.*
1 Sa. 30. 20 they drave before those..cattle, and said

6. *They themselves,* הֵם *hem.*
Lev. 11. 27 that go on (all) four, those are unclean un.

7. *They themselves,* הָהֵם *ha-hem.*
Gen. 6. 4 There were giants in the earth in those

8. *They themselves,* הִמּוֹ, הִמּוֹן *himmo, himmon.*
Ezra 5. 14 those did Cyrus the king take out of the

9. *They themselves,* הֵנָּה *henah.*
1 Sa. 27. 8 for those..of old the inhabitants of the

10. *They themselves,* הָהֵנָּה *ha-henah.*
1 Sa. 17. 28 with whom hast thou left those few sheep

11. *Them,* αὐτούς *autous.*
Matt 21. 41 will miserably destroy those wicked men
John 17. 11 keep through thine own name those whom

12. *That, that very, he, she, it,* ἐκεῖνος *ekeinos.*
Matt. 3. 1 In those days came John the Baptist, pr.
See also 21. 40; 22. 7, 10; 24. 19, 22, 22, 29; 25. 7, 19;
Mark 1. 9; 2. 20; 7. [15]; 8. 1; 12. 7; 13. 17, 19, 24; Luke
2. 1; 4. 2; 5. 35; 9. 36; 12. 37, 38; 13. 4; 14. 24; 19. 27;
20. [1]; 21. 23; John 8. [10]; Acts 2. 18; 7. 41; 9. 37; 16. 3,
35; 20. 2; Rom. 6. 21; Heb. 8. 10; 10. 16; Rev. 9. 6.

13. *As much, as great,* ὅσος *hosos.*
Jude 10 But these speak evil of those things wh.

14. *These, those,* ταῦτα *tauta.*
John 8. 26 I speak to the world those things which
Acts 17. 11 searched..daily, whether those things we.
Phil. 3. 7 what things were gain to me, those I co.
4. 9 Those things, which ye have both learned

15. *In these, those,* ταύταις *tautais.*
Luke 1. 39 Mary arose in those days, and went into
6. 12 it came to pass in those days, that he went
Acts 1. 15 in those days Peter stood up in the midst
6. 1 in those days, when the number of the di.

16. *These, those,* ταύτας *tautas.*
Luke 1. 24 after those days his wife Elisabeth conce.
Acts 21. 15 after those days we took up our carriages

17. *In these,* τούτοις *toutois.*
Jude 10 in those things they corrupt themselves

18. *Of these,* τούτων *toutōn.*
Acts 18. 17 And Gallio cared for none of those things
Heb. 13. 11 the bodies of those beasts, whose blood is

THOU —

1. *Thou, thyself,* אַנְתְּ *ant.*
Ezra 7. 25 Thou, Ezra, after the wisdom of thy God
See also Dan. 2. 31, 37, 38; 3. 10; 4. 18, 18, 22; 5. 13, 18,
22, 23; 6. 16.

2. *Thou thyself,* אַתְּ *att.*
Gen. 24. 23 Whose daughter (art) thou? Tell me, I pr.
24. 60 and said unto her, Thou (art) our sister, be
39. 9 because thou (art) his wife: how then can

3. *Thou thyself,* אַתָּה *attah.*
Gen. 3. 14 thou (art) cursed above all cattle, and above
3. 19 for dust thou (art), and unto dust shalt
6. 18 thou, and thy sons, and thy wife, and thy

4. *Thee,* σέ *se.*
Matt 18. 33 Shouldest not thou also have had compas.
25. 27; Acts 8. 23; 9. 6; 10. [6]; 13. 47; 22. 14; 23. 11; 24. 4,
10; 26. 29; 27. 24; Rom. 3. 4; 1 Ti. 6. 14; Titus 3. 8; 3 Jo. 2.

5. *To thee,* σοί *soi.*
Matt. 17. 25 What thinkest thou, Simon? of whom do
See also 22. 16, 17; 27. 19; Mark 4. 38; 10. [21]; Luke 10.
36, 40; 14. 10, 14; 18. 22; Acts 8. 21; 26. 1.

6. *Of thee,* σοῦ *sou.*
Matt. 6. 3 when thou doest alms, let not thy left hand
19. 21 go..sell that thou hast, and give to the po.
Luke 14. 8 a more honourable man than thou Jo. 7. 3.
Acts 17. 19 this new doctrine, whereof thou speakest
24. 11 that thou mayest understand, that there

7. *Thou thyself,* σύ *su.*
Matt. 2. 6 thou, Bethlehem, (in) the land of Juda
See also 3. 14; 6. 6, 17; 11. 3, 23; 14. 28; 16. 16, 18; 26. 25,
39, 63, 64, 69, 73; 27. 4, 11, 11; Mark 1. 11; 3. 11; 8. 29; 14.
36, 61, 67, 68; 15. 2, 2; Luke 1. [28], 42, 76; 3. 22; 4. 7, 41;
7. 19, 20; 9. 60; 10. 15. 37; 15. 31; 16. 7, [25], 25; 17. 8; 19.
19, 42; 22. 32, 58, 67, 70; 23. 3, 3, 37, 39, 40; 24. 18; John 1.
19, 21, 21, 25, 42, 42, 49, 49; 2. 10, 20; 3. 2, 10, 26; 4. 9, 10,
12, 19; 6. 30, 69; 7. 52; 8. [5], 13, 25, 33, 48, 52, 53, [53]; 9.
17, 28, 34, 34, 35; 10. 24, 33; 11. 27, 42; 12. 34; 13. 6, 7; 14.
9; 17. 5, 8, 21, 21, 23, 23, 25; 18. 17, 25, 33, 34, 37, 37; 19.
9; 20. 15; 21. 12, 15, 16, 17, 17, 22; Acts 1. 24; 4. 24; 7. 28;
9. 5; 10. 15, 33; 11. 9, 14; 13. 33; 16. 31; 21. 38; 22. 8, 27;
23. 3, 21; 25. 10; 26. 15; Rom. 2. 3, 17; 9. 20; 11. 17, 18,
20, 22, 24; 14. 4, 10, 10, 32; 1 Co. 14. 17; 15. 36; Gal. 2. 14;
6. 1; 1 Ti. 6. 11; 2 Ti. 1. 18; 2. 1, [3]; 3. 10, 14; 4. 5, 15;
Titus 2. 1; Phm. [12]; Heb. 1. 5, 10, 11, 12; 5. 5, 6; 7. 17,
21; Jas. 2. 3, 3, 18, 19; 4. 12; 3 Jo. 3; Rev. 2. 15; 3. 17; 4.
11; 7. 14.

THOU thyself —

Thou thyself, σεαυτόν *seauton.*
Rom. 2. 19 art confident that thou thyself art a guide

THOUGH —

1. *If,* אִם *im.*
Judg. 13. 16 Though thou detain me, I will not eat of

2. *That,* אֲשֶׁר *asher.*
Zech. 10. 6 they shall be as though I had not cast th.

3. *Also,* גַּם *gam.*
Neh. 6. 1 though at that time I had not set up the

4. *If, though,* הֵן *hen.*
Job 13. 15 Though he slay me, yet will I trust in him

5. *That, because, though,* כִּי *ki.*
Deut. 29. 19 though I walk in the imagination of mine

6. *Though, if,* לוּ, לֹא *lu.*
2 Sa. 18. 12 Though I should receive a thousand (sh.)

7. *Therefore, because, although,* כָּל־קֳבֵל דִּי *kol qebel di.*
Dan. 5. 22 thou..hast not humbled thine heart, th.

8. *Through, during,* διά (gen.) *dia.*
Rom. 4. 11 the father of all them that believe, though

9. *If, though,* ἐάν *ean.*
Luke 16. 31 neither will they be persuaded, though
Acts 13. 41 which ye shall in no wise believe, though
Rom. 9. 27 Though the number of the children of Is.
1 Co. 4. 15 For though ye have ten thousand instruc.
9. 16 For though I preach the gospel, I have no.
13. 1 Though I speak with the tongues of men
13. 2 though I have (the gift of) prophecy, and
13. 2 though I have all faith, so that I could re.
13. 3 though I bestow all my goods to feed (the
13. 3 though I give my body to be burned, and
2 Co. 10. 8 For though I should boast somewhat more
12. 6 For though I would desire to glory, I shall
Gal. 1. 8 though we, or an angel from heaven, pre.
Jas. 2. 14 What (doth it) profit..though a man say

10. *Even if,* εἰ καί *ei kai.*
Matt 26. 33 [Though] all..shall be offended because of
Luke 11. 8 Though he will not rise and give him, be.
18. 4 Though I fear not God, nor regard man
2 Co. 4. 16 but though our outward man perish, yet
5. 16 though we have known Christ after the
7. 8 For though I made you sorry with a letter
7. 8 not repent, though I did repent: for I pe.
7. 8 made you sorry, though (it were) but for
7. 12 though I wrote unto you, (I did it) not
11. 6 But though (I be) rude in speech, yet not
12. 11 very chiefest apostles, though I be nothing
12. 15 [though] the more abundantly I love you
Col. 2. 5 For though I be absent in the flesh, yet am
Heb. 6. 9 accompany salvation, though we thus sp.

11. *If truly,* εἴπερ *eiper.*
1 Co. 8. 5 For though there be that are called gods

12. *And truly, although,* καίπερ *kaiper.*
Phil. 3. 4 Though I might also have confidence in
Heb. 5. 8 Though he were a Son, yet learned he ob.
7. 5 though they come out of the loins of Abrah.
12. 17 though he sought it carefully with tears
2 Pe. 1. 12 though ye know (them) and be established

13. *And though indeed,* καίτοιγε *kaitoige.*
John 4. 2 Though Jesus himself baptized not, but his
Acts 17. 27 [though] he be not far from every one of us

14. *Even if,* κἄν *kan.*
Matt 26. 35 Though I should die with thee, yet will I
John 8. 14 Though I bear record of myself, (yet) my
10. 38 though ye believe not me, believe, 11. 25.

15. *And, also, though,* καί *kai,* Luke 18. 7.

16. *Because, that,* ὅτι *hoti.*
Rom. 9. 6 Not as though the word of God hath taken
2 Co. 11. 21 I speak as concerning reproach, as though
Phil. 3. 12 Not as though I had already attained, eit.

17. *If,* εἰ *ei.*
2 Co. 13. 4 For [though] he was crucified through we.

THOUGH...but —

Yet, nevertheless, but, ὅμως *homōs.*
Gal. 3. 15 Though..but a man's covenant, yet (if it

THOUGHT —
1. *A word,* דָּבָר *dabar.*
Deut 15. 9 Beware that there be not a thought in thy
2. *Thought, conception, imagination,* הַרְהֹר *harhor.*
Dan. 4. 5 the thoughts upon my bed and the visions
3. *Thought, device,* זִמָּה *zimmah.*
Prov 24. 9 The thought of foolishness (is) sin, and
4. *A cutting, decree, resolution,* חֵקֶק *cheqeq.*
Judg. 5. 15 For the divisions of Reuben..great thou.
5. *Knowledge, mind,* מַדָּע, מַדַּע *madda.*
Eccl. 10. 20 Curse not the king, no not in thy thought
6. *Possession, inheritance,* מוֹרָשׁ *morash.*
Job 17. 11 my purposes are broken off..the thoughts
7. *Device, thoughtfulness,* מְזִמָּה *mezimmah.*
Job 42. 2 no thought can be withholden from thee
Psa. 10. 4 The wicked..God (is) not in all his thou.
Jer. 23. 20 till he have performed the thoughts of his
8. *Thought, device,* מַחֲשֶׁבֶת *machashebeth.*
Gen. 6. 5 every imagination of the thoughts of his
1 Ch. 28. 9 understandeth..imaginations of the tho.
29. 18 in the imagination of the thoughts of the
Job 21. 27 I know your thoughts, and the devices
Psa. 33. 11 the thoughts of his heart to all generati.
40. 5 thy thoughts (which are) to us ward: they
56. 5 all their thoughts (are) against me for evil
92. 5 how great are thy works! (and) thy tho.
94. 11 The LORD knoweth the thoughts of man
Prov 12. 5 The thoughts of the righteous (are) right
15. 26 The thoughts of the wicked (are) an abo.
16. 3 and thy thoughts shall be established
21. 5 The thoughts of the diligent (tend) only
Isa. 55. 7 the unrighteous man his thoughts: and
55. 8 my thoughts (are) not your thoughts, ne.
55. 9 and my thoughts than your thoughts
59. 7 their thoughts (are) thoughts of iniquity
65. 2 which walketh..after their own thoughts
66. 18 For I (know) their works and their thou.
Jer. 4. 14 how long shall thy vain thoughts lodge
6. 19 I will bring..(even) the fruit of their th.
29. 11 I know the thoughts that I think toward
29. 11 thoughts of peace, and not of evil, to give
Eze. 38. 10 and thou shalt think an evil thought
Mic. 4. 12 they know not the thoughts of the LORD
9. *Doubts, opinions,* סְעִפִּים *seaphim.*
Psa. 119. 113 I hate..thoughts: but thy law do I love
10. *Thoughts, purposes,* עֶשְׁתֹּנוֹת *eshtonoth.*
Psa. 146. 4 forth..in that very day his thoughts per.
11. *Thoughts, purposes,* עַשְׁתּוֹת *ashtoth.*
Job 12. 5 a lamp despised in the thought of him that
12. *Thought, will, desire,* רֵעַ *rea.*
Psa. 139. 2 thou understandest my thought afar off
139. 17 How precious also are thy thoughts unto
13. *Thought,* רַעְיוֹן *rayon.*
Dan. 2. 29 As for thee, O king, thy thoughts came
2. 30 thou mightest know the thoughts of thy
4. 19 was astonied..and his thoughts troubled
5. 6 his thoughts troubled him, so that the jo.
5. 10 let not thy thoughts trouble thee, nor let
14. *Meditation,* שֵׂחַ *seach.*
Amos 4. 13 and declareth unto man what (is) his tho.
15. *Doubts, opinions,* שְׂעִפִּים *seippim.*
Job 4. 13 In thoughts from the visions of the night
20. 2 Therefore do my thoughts cause me to an.
16. *Doubts, opinions,* שַׂרְעַפִּים *sarappim.*
Psa. 94. 19 In the multitude of my thoughts within
139. 23 heart: try me and know my thoughts
17. *Reasoning,* διαλογισμός *dialogismos.*
Matt 15. 19 For out of the heart proceed evil thoughts
Mark 7. 21 out of the heart of men, proceed evil th.
Luke 2. 35 thoughts of many hearts may be revealed
5. 22 But when Jesus perceived their thoughts
6. 8 But he knew their thoughts, and said to
9. 47 Jesus, perceiving the thought of their he.
24. 38 and why do thoughts arise in your hearts
1 Co. 3. 20 The Lord knoweth the thoughts of the
Jas. 2. 4 and are become judges of evil thoughts
18. *Thought, reflection,* διανόημα *dianoēma.*
Luke 11. 17 he, knowing their thoughts, said unto th.
19. *Reflection, thought,* ἐνθύμησις *enthumēsis.*
Matt. 9. 4 Jesus, knowing their thoughts, said, Wh.
12 25 Jesus knew their thoughts, and said unto
Heb. 4. 12 a discerner of the thoughts and intents
20. *Thought, contrivance, device,* ἐπίνοια *epinoia.*
Acts 8. 22 if perhaps the thought of thine heart may
21. *Computation, reckoning,* λογισμός *logismos.*
Rom. 2. 15 thoughts the mean while accusing or else
22. *A thought, contrivance, understanding,* νόημα.
2 Co. 10. 5 bringing into captivity every thought to

THOUGHT (beforehand), to take —
1. *To be sorrowful, afraid,* דָּאַג *daag.*
1 Sa. 9. 5 leave..the asses, and take thought for us
2. *To be over anxious, very careful,* μεριμνάω *meri.*
Matt. 6. 25 Take no thought for your life, what ye
6. 27 Which of you, by taking thought, can add
6. 28 why take ye thought for raiment? Consi.
6. 31 take no thought, saying, What shall we
6. 34 Take therefore no thought for the morrow
6. 34 morrow shall take thought for the things
Matt 10. 19 take no thought how or what ye shall sp.
Luke 12. 11 take ye no thought how or what thing ye
12. 22 Take no thought for your life, what ye
12. 25 which of you [with taking thought] can a.
12. 26 least, why take ye thought for the rest?
3. *To be very anxious beforehand,* προμεριμνάω.
Mark 13. 11 take no thought beforehand what ye sh.

THOUSAND —
1. *A thousand,* אֶלֶף *eleph.*
Gen. 20. 16 Behold, I have given thy brother a thou.
24. 60 be thou (the mother) of thousands of mil.
Exod 12. 37 about six hundred thousand on foot (that
18. 21 rulers of thousands, (and) rulers of hund.
18. 25 rulers of thousands, rulers of hundreds
20. 6 showing mercy unto thousands of them
32. 28 fell..that day about three thousand men
34. 7 Keeping mercy for thousands, forgiving
38. 25 thousand seven hundred and threescore
38. 26 hundred thousand and three thousand and
38. 28 of the thousand seven hundred seventy
38. 29 and two thousand and four hundred she.
Num. 1. 16 tribes of their fathers, heads of thousands
1. 21 forty and six thousand and five hundred
1. 23 fifty and nine thousand and three hundred
1. 25 forty and five thousand six hundred and
1. 27 threescore and fourteen thousand and six
1. 29 fifty and four thousand and four hundred
1. 31 fifty and seven thousand and four hundred
1. 33 (were) forty thousand and five hundred
1. 35 thirty and two thousand and two hundred
1. 37 thirty and five thousand and four hundred
1. 39 threescore and two thousand and seven
1. 41 forty and one thousand and five hundred
1. 43 fifty and three thousand and four hundred
1. 46 six hundred thousand and three thousand
2. 4 threescore and fourteen thousand and six
2. 6 fifty and four thousand and four hundred
2. 8 fifty and seven thousand and four hund.
2. 9 hundred thousand and fourscore thousand
2. 9 six thousand and four hundred, through.
2. 11 forty and six thousand and five hundred
2. 13 fifty and nine thousand and three hund.
2. 15 forty and five thousand and six hundred
2. 16 fifty and one thousand and four hundred
2. 19 (were) forty thousand and five hundred
2. 21 (were) thirty and two thousand and two
2. 23 thirty and five thousand and four hundr.
2. 24 hundred thousand and eight thousand
2. 26 threescore and two thousand and seven
2. 28 forty and one thousand and five hundred
2. 30 fifty and three thousand and four hundr.
2. 31 thousand and fifty and seven thousand
2. 32 six hundred thousand and three thousand
3. 22 (were) seven thousand and five hundred
3. 28 eight thousand and six hundred, keeping
3. 34 (were) six thousand and two hundred
3. 39 all the males..(were) twenty and two th.
3. 43 twenty and two thousand two hundred
3. 50 thousand three hundred and threescore
4. 36 were two thousand seven hundred and
4. 40 were two thousand and six hundred and
4. 44 Even those..were three thousand and two
4. 48 eight thousand and five hundred and fo.
7. 85 all the silver vessels (weighed) two thous.
10. 4 heads of the thousands of Israel, shall gat.
10. 36 Return..unto the many thousands of Is.
11. 21 The people..six hundred thousand foot.
16. 49 they that died..were fourteen thousand
25. 9 those that died..were twenty and four th.
26. 7 forty and three thousand and seven hun.
26. 14 twenty and two thousand and two hund.
26. 18 numbered of them, forty thousand and
26. 22 threescore and sixteen thousand and five
26. 25 threescore and four thousand and three
26. 27 threescore thousand and five hundred
26. 34 fifty and two thousand and seven hundred
26. 37 thirty and two thousand and five hundred
26. 41 forty and five thousand and six hundred
26. 43 threescore and four thousand and four hu.
26. 47 fifty and three thousand and four hund.
26. 50 forty and five thousand and four hundr.
26. 51 six hundred thousand and a thousand se.
26. 62 twenty and three thousand, all males from
31. 4 Of every tribe a thousand, throughout all
31. 5 were delivered out of the thousands of I.
31. 5 a thousand of (every) tribe, twelve thou.
31. 6 Moses sent them to the war, a thousand
31. 14 was wroth..(with) the captains over tho.
31. 32 the booty..was six hundred thousand and
31. 32 seventy thousand and five thousand sheep
31. 33 threescore and twelve thousand beeves
31. 34 And threescore and one thousand asses
31. 35 thirty and two thousand persons in all, of
31. 36 thousand and seven and thirty thousand
31. 38 beeves (were) thirty and six thousand; of
31. 39 asses (were) thirty thousand and five hu.
31. 40 persons (were) sixteen thousand, of which
31. 43 three hundred thousand and thirty thou.
31. 43 seven thousand and five hundred sheep
31. 44 And thirty and six thousand beeves
31. 45 And thirty thousand asses and five hund.
31. 46 And sixteen thousand persons
31. 48 officers which (were) over thousands of
31. 48 captains of thousands, and captains of h.
31. 52 of the captains of thousands, and of the
31. 52 was sixteen thousand seven hundred and
31. 54 took the gold of the captains of thousands
35. 4 and outward a thousand cubits round ab.
35. 5 on the east side two thousand cubits, and
35. 5 on the south side two thousand cubits, and
35. 5 on the west side two thousand cubits, and
Num. 35. 5 on the north side two thousand cubits
Deut. 1. 11 make you a thousand times so many more
1. 15 captains over thousands, and captains over
5. 10 showing mercy unto thousands of them
7. 9 keep his commandments, to a thousand
32. 30 chase a thousand, and two put ten thou
33. 17 and they (are) the thousands of Manasseh
Josh. 3. 4 about two thousand cubits by measure
4. 13 About forty thousand prepared for war
7. 3 let about two or three thousand men go
7. 4 of the people about three thousand men
8. 3 Joshua chose out thirty thousand mighty
8. 12 took about five thousand men, and set th.
8. 25 twelve thousand, (even) all the men of Ai
22. 14 house of their fathers among the thousa.
22. 21, 30 heads of the thousands of Israel
23. 10 One man of you shall chase a thousand
Judg. 1. 4 slew of them in Bezek ten thousand men
3. 29 they slew..about ten thousand men, all
4. 6 take with thee ten thousand men of the
4. 10 went up with ten thousand men at his fe.
4. 14 Barak went down..and ten thousand men
5. 8 spear seen among forty thousand in Israel?
7. 3 thousand; and there remained ten thous.
8. 10 their hosts with them, about fifteen tho.
8. 10 there fell an hundred and twenty thous.
8. 26 weight..was a thousand and seven hund.
9. 49 died also, about a thousand men and wo.
12. 6 and there fell..forty and two thousand
15. 11 Then three thousand men of Judah went
15. 15 took it, and slew a thousand men there.
15. 16 with the jaw of an ass have I slain a tho.
16. 27 upon the roof about three thousand men
20. 2 four hundred thousand footmen that drew
20. 10 we will take..an hundred of a thousand
20. 10 a thousand out of ten thousand, to fetch
20. 15 twenty and six thousand men that drew
20. 17 numbered four hundred thousand men
20. 21 that day twenty and two thousand men
20. 25 eighteen thousand men; all these drew
20. 34 came against Gibeah ten thousand chose
20. 35 twenty and five thousand and an hundred
20. 44 there fell of Benjamin eighteen thousand
20. 45 they gleaned of them..five thousand men
20. 45 pursued..and slew two thousand men of
20. 46 twenty and five thousand men that drew
21. 10 congregation sent thither twelve thousa.
1 Sa. 4. 2 slew of the army..about four thousand
4. 10 for there fell of Israel thirty thousand fo
6. 19 even he smote of the people fifty thousa.
8. 12 he will appoint him captains over thous.
10. 19 therefore present yourselves..by your th.
11. 8 three hundred thousand, and..thirty th.
11. 8 and the men of Judah thirty thousand
13. 2 Saul chose him three thousand (men) of Is.
13. 2 two thousand were with Saul..and a th.
13. 5 thirty thousand chariots, and six thous.
15. 4 thousand footmen, and ten thousand men
17. 5 weight of the coat (was) five thousand sh.
17. 18 ten cheeses unto the captain of (their) th.
18. 7 his thousands, and David his ten thous.
18. 8 and to me..(but) thousands: and
18. 13 and made him his captain over a thous.
21. 11 his thousands, and David his ten thous.
22. 7 make you all captains of thousands, and
23. 23 search him out throughout all the thous.
24. 2 Saul took three thousand chosen men out
25. 2 three thousand sheep, and a thousand go.
26. 2 having three thousand chosen men of I.
29. 2 passed on by hundreds and by thousands
29. 5 his thousands, and David his ten thous.
2 Sa. 6. 1 all (the) chosen (men) of Israel, thirty th.
8. 4 thousand (chariots)..and twenty thous.
8. 5 slew of the Syrians two and twenty thou.
8. 13 smiting of the S...(being) eighteen thou.
10. 6 Syrians of Zoba, twenty thousand foot.
10. 6 thousand men, and of Ish-tob twelve th.
10. 18 David slew..forty thousand horsemen
17. 1 Let me now choose out twelve thousand
18. 1 set captains of thousands and captains of
18. 3 but now (thou art) worth ten thousand of
18. 4 came out by hundreds, and by thousands
18. 7 great slaughter that day of twenty thous.
18. 12 Though I should receive a thousand (sh.)
19. 17 thousand men of Benjamin with him, and
24. 9 there were in Israel eight hundred tho.
24. 9 men of Judah (were) five hundred thous.
24. 15 even to Beersheba seventy thousand men
1 Ki. 3. 4 a thousand burnt offerings did Solomon
4. 26 forty thousand..and twelve thousand ho.
4. 32 And he spake three thousand proverbs
4. 32 and his songs were a thousand and five
5. 11 Solomon gave Hiram twenty thousand
5. 13 and the levy was thirty thousand men
5. 14 ten thousand a month by courses; a mo.
5. 15 Solomon had threescore and ten thous.
5. 15 fourscore thousand hewers in the mount.
5. 16 three thousand and three hundred, which
7. 26 of lilies: it contained two thousand bat.
8. 63 offered..two and twenty thousand oxen
8. 63 an hundred and twenty thousand sheep
10. 26 he had a thousand and four hundred ch.
10. 26 twelve thousand horsemen, whom he be.
12. 21 hundred and fourscore thousand chosen
19. 18 I have left (me) seven thousand in Israel
20. 15 the children of Israel, (being) seven thou.
20. 29 slew of the Syrians an hundred thousand
20. 30 fell upon twenty and seven thousand
2 Ki. 3. 4 thousand lambs, and an hundred thous.
5. 5 six thousand (pieces) of gold, and ten ch.
13. 7 ten thousand footmen; for the king of S.
14. 7 He slew of Edom..ten thousand, and took

2 Ki. 15. 19 Menahem gave Pul a thousand talents of
18. 23 I will deliver thee two thousand horses
19. 35 an hundred fourscore and five thousand
24. 14 ten thousand captives and all the crafts.
24. 16 seven thousand..and smiths a thousand
1 Ch. 5. 18 four and forty thousand seven hundred
5. 21 took..of their camels fifty thousand, and
5. 21 two hundred and fifty thousand, and of
5. 21 thousand, and of men an hundred thous.
7. 2 two and twenty thousand and six hun.
7. 4 six and thirty thousand (men): for they
7. 5 reckoned..fourscore and seven thousand
7. 7 twenty and two thousand and thirty and
7. 9 (was) twenty thousand and two hundred
7. 11 seventeen thousand and two hundred (so.)
7. 40 number..(was) twenty and six thousand
9. 13 thousand and seven hundred and three.
12. 14 hundred, and the greatest over a thous.
12. 20 captains of the thousands that (were) of
12. 24 six thousand and eight hundred, ready ar.
12. 25 Of the children of Simeon..seven thous.
12. 26 Of the children of Levi, four thousand and
12. 27 with him (were) three thousand and seven
12. 29 of the children of Benjamin..three thous.
12. 30 children of Ephraim twenty thousand and
12. 31 half tribe of Manasseh eighteen thousand
12. 33 fifty thousand, which could keep rank, (th.
12. 34 of Naphtali a thousand captains, and with
12. 34 shield and spear thirty and seven thous.
12. 35 twenty and eight thousand and six hund.
12. 36 such as went forth to battle..forty thous.
12. 37 the battle, an hundred and twenty thous.
13. 1 consulted with the captains of thousands
15. 25 captains over thousands, went to bring
16. 15 word (which) he commanded to a thous.
18. 4 David took from him a thousand chariots
18. 4 seven thousand horsemen, and twenty th.
18. 5 David slew..two and twenty thousand men
18. 12 slew..in the valley of Salt eighteen tho.
19. 6 the children of Ammon sent a thousand
19. 7 they hired thirty and two thousand char.
19. 18 seven thousand (men)..and forty thousand
21. 5 thousand thousand and an hundred tho.
21. 5 four hundred threescore and ten thousand
21. 14 and there fell of Israel seventy thousand
22. 14 an hundred thousand talents of gold
22. 14 and a thousand thousand talents of silver
23. 3 their number..was thirty and eight thou.
23. 4 twenty and four thousand (were) to set fo.
23. 4 and six thousand (were) officers and judges
23. 5 four thousand (were) porters, and four th.
26. 26 the captains over thousands and hundreds
26. 30 a thousand and seven hundred, (were) offi.
26. 32 two thousand and seven hundred chief fa.
27. 1 the chief fathers and captains of thousands
27. 1 every course (were) twenty and four tho.
27. 2 and in his course (were) twenty and four t.
[So in verse 5, 7, 8, 9, 10, 11, 12, 13, 14, 15.]
27. 4 in his course..(were) twenty and four tho.
28. 1 the captains over the thousands, and cap.
29. 4 three thousand talents of gold, of the gold
29. 4 seven thousand talents of refined silver
29. 6 the captains of thousands and of hundreds
29. 7 five thousand talents and ten thousand d.
29. 7 ten thousand talents..eighteen thousand
29. 7 and one hundred thousand talents of iron
29. 21 (even) a thousand bullocks, a thousand ra.
29. 21 a thousand lambs, with their drink offer.
2 Ch. 1. 2 the captains of thousands and of hundreds
1. 6 offered a thousand burnt offerings upon it
1. 14 he had a thousand and four hundred ch.
1. 14 twelve thous. horsemen, which he placed
2. 2 told out threescore and ten thousand men
2. 2 fourscore thousand to hew in the mount.
2. 2 three thousand and six hundred to oversee
2. 10 twenty thousand measures of beaten wh.
2. 10 and twenty thousand measures of barley
2. 10 thousand baths of wine, and twenty tho.
2. 17 fifty thousand and three thousand and six
2. 18 he set threescore and ten thousand of th.
2. 18 fourscore thousand (to be) hewers in the
2. 18 three thousand and six hundred overseers
4. 5 it received and held three thousand baths
7. 5 a sacrifice of twenty and two thousand ox.
7. 5 and an hundred and twenty thousand sh.
9. 25 Solomon had four thousand stalls for ho.
9. 25 and chariots, and twelve thousand horse.
11. 1 an hundred and fourscore thousand cho.
12. 3 chariots, and threescore thousand horse.
13. 3 (even) four hundred thousand chosen men
13. 3 eight hundred thousand chosen men, (be.)
13. 17 there fell down slain..five hundred thou.
14. 8 out of Judah three hundred thousand
14. 8 two hundred and fourscore thousand, all
14. 9 with an host of a thousand thousand, and
15. 11 seven hundred oxen and seven thousands.
17. 11 seven thousand and seven hundred rams
17. 11 seven thousand and seven hundred he go.
17. 14 of Judah, the captains of thousands; Ad.
17. 14 mighty men of valour three hundred tho.
17. 15 with him two hundred and fourscore tho.
17. 16 two hundred thousand mighty men of va.
17. 17 with him armed men..two hundred thou.
17. 18 an hundred and fourscore thousand ready
25. 5 made them captains over thousands, and
25. 5 found them three hundred thousand cho.
25. 6 He hired also an hundred thousand mig.
25. 11 smote of the children of Seir ten thousand
25. 12 (other) ten thousand (left) alive did the ch.
25. 13 smote three thousand of them, and took
26. 12 men of valour (were) two thousand and
26. 13 hundred thousand, and seven thousand

2 Ch. 27. 5 thousand measures of wheat, and ten th.
28. 6 an hundred and twenty thousand in one
28. 8 two hundred thousand, women, sons, and
29. 33 six hundred oxen and three thousand sh.
30. 24 a thousand bullocks and seven thousand
30. 24 a thousand bullocks and ten thousand sh.
35. 7 thirty thousand, and three thousand bul.
35. 8 two thousand and six hundred (small cat.)
35. 9 five thousand (small cattle), and five hun.
Ezra 1. 9 a thousand chargers of silver, nine and tw.
1. 10 Thirty basins..(and) other vessels a thou.
1. 11 vessels of gold and of silver (were) five th.
2. 3 two thousand an hundred seventy and two
2. 6 two thousand eight hundred and twelve
2. 7 a thousand two hundred fifty and four
2. 12 a thousand two hundred twenty and two
2. 14 children of Bigvai, two thousand fifty and
2. 31 a thousand two hundred fifty and four
2. 35 three thousand and six hundred and thirty
2. 37 The children of Immer, a thousand fifty
2. 38 a thousand two hundred forty and seven
2. 39 The children of Harim, a thousand and se.
2. 64 forty and two thousand three hundred
2. 65 seven thousand three hundred thirty and
2. 67 (their) asses, six thousand seven hundred
2. 69 one thousand drams of gold, and five tho.
8. 27 twenty basins of gold of a thousand drams
Neh. 3. 13 a thousand cubits on the wall unto the du.
7. 8 two thousand an hundred seventy and two
7. 11 two thousand and eight hundred (and) ei.
7. 12 a thousand two hundred fifty and four
7. 17 two thousand three hundred twenty and
7. 19 The children of Bigvai, two thousand th.
7. 34 a thousand two hundred fifty and four
7. 38 three thousand nine hundred and thirty
7. 40 The children of Immer, a thousand fifty
7. 41 a thousand two hundred forty and seven
7. 42 The children of Harim, a thousand and s.
7. 66 forty and two thousand three hundred and
7. 67 seven thousand three hundred thirty and
7. 69 six thousand seven hundred and twenty
7. 70 gave to the treasure a thousand drams of
7. 71 two thousand and two hundred pound of
7. 72 two thousand pound of silver, and three.
Esth. 3. 9 I will pay ten thousand talents of silver
9. 16 slew of their foes seventy and five thous.
Job 1. 3 seven thousand sheep, and three thousand
9. 3 he cannot answer him one of a thousand
33. 23 one among a thousand, to show unto man
42. 12 fourteen thousand sheep, and six thousa.
42. 12 a thousand yoke of oxen, and a thousand
Psa. 50. 10 (is) mine, (and) the cattle upon a thousand
60. *title*. smote..in the valley of Salt twelve th.
68. 17 The chariots of God (are)..thousands of a.
84. 10 a day in thy courts (is) better than a tho.
90. 4 a thousand years in thy sight (are but) as
91. 7 A thousand shall fall at thy side..at thy
105. 8 the word (which) he commanded to a th.
119. 72 (is) better unto me than thousands of gold
Eccl. 6. 6 though he live a thousand years twice (t.)
7. 28 one man among a thousand have I found
Song. 4. 4 whereon there hang a thousand bucklers
8. 11 every one..was to bring a thousand (pie.)
8. 12 thou, O Solomon, (must have) a thousand
Isa. 7. 23 a thousand vines at a thousand silverlings
30. 17 One thousand (shall flee) at the rebuke of
36. 8 I will give thee two thousand horses, if
37. 36 a hundred and fourscore and five thousa.
60. 22 A little one shall become a thousand, and
Jer. 32. 18 showest loving kindness unto thousands
52. 28 In the seventh year three thousand Jews
52. 30 all the persons..four thousand and six h.
Eze. 45. 1 the length of five and twenty thousand
45. 1 (reeds), and the breadth (shall be) ten th.
45. 3 thousand, and the breadth of ten thousa.
45. 5 twenty thousand of length, and the ten
45. 6 thousand broad, and five and twenty tho.
47. 3 he measured a thousand cubits, and he br.
47. 4, 4 he measured a thousand, and brought
47. 5 he measured a thousand; (and it was) a
48. 8 five and twenty thousand (reeds in) bread.
48. 9 thousand in length, and of ten thousand
48. 10 toward the north five and twenty thousa.
48. 10 toward the west ten thousand in breadth
48. 10 toward the east ten thousand in breadth
48. 10 toward the south five and twenty thous.
48. 13 thousand in length, and ten thousand in
48. 13 twenty thousand, and the breadth ten th.
48. 15 the five thousand (that are) left in the br.
48. 15 over against the five and twenty thousand
48. 16 the north side four thousand and five hu.
48. 16 the south side four thousand and five hu.
48. 16 on the east side four thousand and five h.
48. 16 the west side four thousand and five hun.
48. 18 ten thousand eastward, and ten thousand
48. 20 twenty thousand by five and twenty thou.
48. 21, 21 over against the five and twenty thou.
48. 30, 33 four thousand and five hundred
48. 32 at the east side four thousand and five h.
48. 34 At the west side four thousand and five
48. 35 (It was) round about eighteen thousand
Dan. 8. 14 Unto two thousand and three hundred da.
12. 11 (there shall be) a thousand two hundred
12. 12 cometh to the thousand three hundred
Amos 5. 3 The city that went out (by) a thousand
Mic. 5. 2 (though) thou be little among the thousa.
6. 7 Will the LORD be pleased with thousands

2. *A thousand*, אֲלַף, אֶלֶף *alaph, eleph.*
Dan. 5. 1 made a great feast to a thousand of his lo.
5. 1 and drank wine before the thousand
7. 10 thousand thousands ministered unto him

3. *Thousands*, χιλιάδες *chiliades.*
Luke 14. 31 whether he be able with ten thousand to
14. 31 cometh against him with twenty thousand
Acts 4. 4 number of the men was about five thous.
1 Co. 10. 8 fell in one day three and twenty thousand
Rev. 5. 11 number of them was..thousands of thou.
7. 4 an hundred (and) forty (and) four thous.
7. 5, 5, 5, 6, 6, 6, 7, 7, 7, 8, 8, 8 twelve thousand
11. 13 in the earthquake were slain..seven thou.
14. 1 an hundred forty (and) four thousand, ha.
14. 3 the hundred (and) forty (and) four thou.
21. 16 he measured the city..twelve thousand

4. *A thousand*, χίλιοι *chilioi.*
2 Pe. 3. 8 as a thousand years, and a thousand ye.
Rev. 11. 3 they shall prophesy a thousand two hun.
12. 6 they should feed her there a thousand two
14. 20 the space of a thousand (and) six hundred
20. 2 and Satan, and bound him a thousand ye.
20. 3 till the thousand years should be fulfilled
20. 4 and reigned with Christ a thousand years
20. 5 lived not again until the thousand years
20. 6 and shall reign with him a thousand years
20. 7 when the thousand years are expired, Sa.

5. *A myriad, ten thousand*, μυριάς *murias.*
Acts 21. 20 how many thousands of Jews there are

THOUSAND, fifty —
Five myriads, μυριάδας πέντε *muriadas pente.*
Acts 19. 19 and found (it) fifty thousand (pieces) of

THOUSAND, ten, five —
1. *A myriad, ten thousand*, μυριάς *murias.*
Jude 14 the Lord cometh with ten thousands
2. *A myriad, ten thousand*, μυρίοι *murioi.*
Matt. 18. 24; 1 Co. 4. 15; 14. 19.
3. *Five thousand*, πεντακισχίλιοι *pentakischilioi.*
Matt. 14. 21; 16. 9; Mr. 6. 44; 8. 19; Lu. 9. 14; Jo. 6. 10

THOUSANDS, to bring forth —
To bear thousands, אָלַף *alaph*, 5.
Psa. 144. 13 our sheep may bring forth thousands and

THREAD —
1. *A thread, cord*, חוּט *chut.*
Gen. 14. 23 I will not (take) from a thread even to a
Josh. 2. 18 thou shalt bind this line of scarlet thread
Judg. 16. 12 brake them from off his arms like a thr.
Song 4. 3 Thy lips (are) like a thread of scarlet, and
2. *Wire, ribbon, thread*, פָּתִיל *pathil.*
Judg. 16. 9 as a thread of tow is broken when it tou.

THREATEN (further, to) —
1. *To threaten, menace*, ἀπειλέω *apeileō.*
Acts 4. 17 let us straitly threaten them, that they
1 Pe. 2. 23 when he suffered, he threatened not; but
2. *To threaten further*, προσαπειλέομαι *prosapeile.*
Acts 4. 21 when they had further threatened them

THREATENING —
Threatening, menace, ἀπειλή *apeilē.*
Acts 4. 29 now, Lord, behold their threatenings: and
9. 1 Saul, yet breathing out threatenings and
Eph. 6. 9 do the same things..forbearing threaten

THREE —
1. *Three*, שְׁלֹשָׁה, שָׁלֹשׁ *shalosh, sheloshah.*
Gen. 5. 22 Enoch walked with God..three hundred
5. 23 the days of Enoch were three hundred si.
6. 10 Noah begat three sons, Shem, Ham, and
6. 15 The length of the ark (shall be) three hu.
7. 13 the three wives of his sons with them, into
9. 19 These (are) the three sons of Noah: and
9. 28 Noah lived after the flood three hundred
11. 13 Arphaxad lived..four hundred and three
11. 15 Salah lived..four hundred and three ye.
14. 14 armed his trained (servants)..three hun.
18. 2 looked, and, lo, three men stood by him
18. 6 Make ready quickly three measures of fi.
29. 2 there (were) three flocks of sheep lying by
29. 34 because I have born him three sons: th.
30. 36 he set three days' journey betwixt himself
38. 24 it came to pass, about three months after
40. 10 in the vine (were) three branches: and it
40. 12 Joseph said..The three branches (are) th.
40. 13, 19 Yet within three days shall Pharaoh
40. 16 behold, (I had) three white baskets on my
40. 18 Joseph answered..The three baskets (are)
42. 17 he put them altogether into ward three
43. 34 to Benjamin he gave three hundred (pi.)
46. 15 sons and his daughters..thirty and three
Exod. 2. 2 when she saw him..she hid him three mo.
3. 18 let us go, we beseech thee, three days' jo.
5. 3 let us go, we pray thee, three days' jour.
6. 18 (were) an hundred thirty and three years
7. 7 and Aaron fourscore and three years old
8. 27 We will go three days' journey into the
10. 22 darkness in all the land of Egypt three
10. 23 neither rose any from his place for three
15. 22 they went three days in the wilderness, and
21. 11 if he do not these three unto her, then
23. 14 Three times thou shalt keep a feast unto
23. 17 Three times in the year all thy males sh.
25. 32, 32 three branches of the candlestick out
25. 33 Three bowls made like unto almonds, (wi.)
25. 33 three bowls made like almonds in the ot.
27. 1 and the height thereof (shall be) three cu.
27. 14, 15 pillars three, and their sockets three
32. 28 there fell of the people..three thousand
37. 18, 18 three branches of the candlestick out
37. 19 Three bowls made after the fashion of al.

Exod37. 19 three bowls made like almonds in another
38. 1 (it was) foursquare; and three cubits the
38. 14, 15 pillars three, and their sockets three
38. 26 three thousand and five hundred and fifty
Lev. 12. 4 shall then continue..three and thirty days
14. 10 three tenth deals of fine flour (for) a meat
19. 23 three years shall it be as uncircumcised
25. 21 and it shall bring forth fruit for three ye.
27. 6 thy estimation (shall be) three shekels of
Num. 1. 23 fifty and nine thousand and three hund.
1. 43 fifty and three thousand and four hundr.
1. 46 three thousand and five hundred and fifty
2. 13 fifty and nine thousand and three hundred
2. 30 fifty and three thousand and four hundr.
2. 32 three thousand and five hundred and fifty
3. 50 a thousand three hundred and threescore
4. 44 were three thousand and two hundred
10. 33 they departed from the mount..three days'
10. 33 went before them in the three days' jour.
12. 4 Come out ye three..they three came out
15. 9 a meat offering of three tenth deals of fl.
22. 28 thou hast smitten me these three times
22. 32 hast thou smitten thine ass these three ti.
22. 33 saw me, and turned from me these three
24. 10 hast altogether blessed (them), these three
26. 7 forty and three thousand and seven hun.
26. 25 threescore and four thousand and three
26. 47 fifty and three thousand and four hundr.
26. 62 twenty and three thousand, all males from
28. 12 three tenth deals of flour (for) a meat off.
28. 20 three tenth deals shall ye offer for a bul.
28. 28 three tenth deals unto one bullock, two
29. 3 three tenth deals for a bullock, (and) two
29. 9 three tenth deals to a bullock, (and) two
29. 14 three tenth deals unto every bullock of
31. 36 three hundred thousand and seven and th.
31. 43 three hundred thousand and thirty thou.
33. 8 went three days' journey in the wildern.
33. 39 an hundred and twenty and three years
35. 14 three cities on this side Jordan, and three
Deut. 4. 41 Moses severed three cities on this side J.
14. 28 At the end of three years thou shalt bring
16. 16 Three times in a year shall all thy males
17. 6 At the mouth of two witnesses, or three
19. 2 Thou shalt separate three cities for thee
19. 7 Thou shalt separate three cities for thee
19. 9 add three cities more..beside these three
19. 15 at the mouth of three witnesses, shall the
Josh. 1. 11 within three days ye shall pass over this
2. 16 hide yourselves there three days, until the
2. 22 abode there three days, until the pursuers
3. 2 it came to pass after three days, that the
7. 3 let about two or three thousand men go up
7. 4 there went up..about three thousand men
9. 16 at the end of three days after they had ma.
15. 14 Caleb drove thence the three sons of Anak
17. 11 Megiddo and her towns, (even) three cou.
18. 4 Give out from among you three men for
21. 32 and Kartan with her suburbs; three cities
Judg. 1. 20 he expelled thence the three sons of Anak
7. 6 the number of them..were three hundred
7. 7 By the three hundred men that lapped
7. 8 and retained those three hundred men
7. 16 divided the three hundred men (into) three
7. 20 the three companies blew the trumpets
7. 22 the three hundred blew the trumpets, and
8. 4 he, and the three hundred men that (were)
9. 22 Abimelech had reigned three years over
9. 43 divided them into three companies, and
10. 2 he judged Israel twenty and three years
11. 26 While Israel dwelt..three hundred years?
14. 14 they could not in three days expound the
15. 4 Samson went and caught three hundred
15. 11 three thousand men of Judah went to the
16. 15 thou hast mocked me these three times
16. 27 about three thousand men and women
19. 4 he abode with him three days: so they did
1 Sa. 1. 24 took him up with her, with three bullocks
2. 13 with a flesh hook of three teeth in his ha.
2. 21 she conceived, and bare three sons and two
9. 20 as for thine asses that were lost three days
10. 3 there shall meet thee three men going up
10. 3 three kids, and another carrying three
11. 8 the children of Israel were three hundred
11. 11 Saul put the people in three companies
13. 2 Saul chose him three thousand (men) of Is.
13. 17 the spoilers came out..in three companies
17. 13 the three eldest sons of Jesse went (and)
17. 13 the names of his three sons that went to
17. 14 David (was) the youngest..the three eldest
20. 20 I will shoot three arrows on the side (th.)
20. 41 fell..to the ground, and bowed..three ti.
24. 2 Saul took three thousand chosen men out
25. 2 he had three thousand sheep, and a th.
26. 2 having three thousand chosen men of Isr.
30. 12 nor drunk (any) water, three days and th.
30. 13 my master left me, because three days ag.
31. 6 Saul died, and his three sons, and his ar.
31. 8 they found Saul and his three sons fallen
2 Sa. 2. 18 there were three sons of Zeruiah there, J.
2. 31 three hundred and threescore men died
5. 5 he reigned thirty and three years over all
6. 11 ark..continued in the house..three mon.
13. 38 went to Geshur, and was there three years
14. 27 unto Absalom there were born three sons
18. 14 he took three darts in his hand, and thr.
20. 4 Assemble me the men..within three days
21. 1 a famine in the days of David three years
21. 16 whose spear (weighed) three hundred (sh.)
23. 9 (one) of the three mighty men with David
23. 13 three of the thirty chief went down, and
23. 16 the three mighty men brake through the
2 Sa. 23. 17 These things did these three mighty men
23. 18 the son of Zeruiah, was chief among three
23. 18 he lifted up his spear against three hund.
23. 18 slew (them), and had the name among th.
23. 19 Was he not most honourable of three?
23. 19 howbeit he attained not unto the (first) th.
23. 22 and had the name among three mighty
23. 23 but he attained not to the (first) three
24. 12 I offer thee three (things); choose thee
24. 13 wilt thou flee three months before thine
24. 13 or that there be three days' pestilence in
1 Ki. 2. 11 thirty and three years reigned he in Jer.
2. 39 it came to pass at the end of three years
4. 32 he spake three thousand proverbs: and
5. 16 three thousand and three hundred, which
6. 36 he built the inner court with three rows
7. 4 And (there were) windows (in) three rows
7. 4, 5 light (was) against light (in) three ranks
7. 12 three rows of hewed stones, and a row of
7. 25 three looking toward the north, and three
7. 25 three looking toward the south, and three
7. 27 four cubits the breadth..and three cubits
9. 25 three times in a year did Solomon offer
10. 17 (he made) three hundred shields (of) bea.
10. 17 three pound of gold went to one shield
10. 22 once in three years came the navy of Th.
11. 3 princesses, and three hundred concubines
12. 5 Depart yet (for) three days, then come ag.
15. 2 Three years reigned he in Jerusalem: and
17. 21 stretched himself upon the child three t.
22. 1 they continued three years without war
2 Ki. 2. 17 and they sought three days, but found
3. 10, 13 hath called these three kings together
9. 32 there looked out to him two (or) three eu.
12. 6 in the three and twentieth year of king
13. 1 In the three and twentieth year of Joash
13. 25 three times did Joash beat him, and rec.
17. 5 went up to Samaria, and besieged it three
18. 10 And at the end of three years they took it
18. 14 three hundred talents of silver, and thirty
23. 31 Jehoahaz (was) twenty and three years
23. 31 and he reigned three months in Jerusalem
24. 1 Jehoiakim became his servant three years
24. 8 and he reigned in Jerusalem three months
25. 17 and the height of the chapiter three cub.
25. 18 took Seraiah..and the three keepers of
1 Ch. 2. 3 three were born unto him of the daughter
2. 16 Abishai, and Joab, and Asahel, three
2. 22 Jair, who had three and twenty cities in
3. 4 in Jerusalem he reigned thirty and three
3. 23 Elioenai, and Hezekiah, and Azrikam, thr.
7. 6 Bela, and Becher, and Jediael, three
10. 6 So Saul died, and his three sons, and all
11. 11 lifted up his spear against three hundred
11. 12 Ahohite, who (was one) of the three migh.
11. 15 Now three of the thirty captains went do.
11. 18 three brake through the host of the Phil.
11. 19 These things did these three mightiest
11. 20 chief of the three..a name among the th.
11. 20 for lifting up his spear against three hu.
11. 21 Of the three he was more honourable th.
11. 21, 25 attained not to the (first) three
11. 24 and had a name among the three might.
12. 27 with him (were) three thousand and seven
12. 29 of the children of Benjamin..three thou.
12. 39 there they were with David three days
13. 14 ark of God remained..three months. And
21. 10 Thus saith the LORD, I offer thee three
21. 12 Either three years' famine; or three mo.
21. 12 or else three days the sword of the LORD
23. 8 chief (was) Jehiel..Zetham, and Joel, th.
23. 9 Shelomith, and Haziel, and Haran, three
23. 23 Mahli, and Eder, and Jeremoth, three
24. 18 The three and twentieth to Delaiah, the
25. 5 gave to Heman fourteen sons and three
25. 30 The three and twentieth to Mahazioth
29. 4 three thousand talents of gold, of the gold
29. 27 thirty and three (years) reigned he in Je.
2 Ch. 2. 2 three thousand and six hundred to oversee
2. 17 fifty thousand and three thousand and six
2. 18 three thousand and six hundred overseers
4. 4 three looking toward the north, and three
4. 4 three looking toward the south, and three
4. 5 it received and held three thousand baths
6. 13 made a brasen scaffold, of..three cubits
7. 10 on the three and twentieth day of the se.
8. 13 three times in the year, (even) in the fea.
9. 16 three hundred shields (made he of) beaten
9. 16 three hundred (shekels) of gold went to
9. 21 every three years once came the ships of
10. 5 Come again unto me after three days.
11. 17 three years: for three years they walked
13. 2 He reigned three years in Jerusalem. His
14. 8 out of Judah three hundred thousand; and
14. 9 thousand thousand, and three hundred c.
17. 14 mighty men of valour three hundred th.
20. 25 they were three days in gathering of the
25. 5 found them three hundred thousand ch.
25. 13 smote three thousand of them, and took
26. 13 under their hand (was) an army three hu.
29. 33 six hundred oxen and three thousand sh.
31. 16 from three years old and upward, (even)
35. 7 thirty thousand, and three thousand bul.
35. 8 gave unto the priests..three hundred ox.
36. 2 Jehoahaz (was) twenty and three years old
36. 2 and he reigned three months in Jerusalem
36. 9 reigned three months and ten days in J.
Ezra 2. 4 children of Shephatiah, three hundred s.
2. 11 of Bebai, six hundred twenty and three
2. 17 of Bezai, three hundred twenty and three
2. 19 of Hashum, two hundred twenty and th.
2. 21 Beth-lehem, an hundred twenty and thr.
Ezra 2. 25 Beeroth, seven hundred and forty and th.
2. 28 and Ai, two hundred twenty and three
2. 32 children of Harim, three hundred and tw.
2. 34 children of Jericho, three hundred forty
2. 35 three thousand and six hundred and th.
2. 36 of Jeshua, nine hundred seventy and th.
2. 58 Nethinims..(were) three hundred ninety
2. 64 two thousand three hundred (and) three
2. 65 seven thousand three hundred thirty and
8. 5 son of Jahaziel, and with him three hun.
8. 15 and there abode we in tents three days
8. 32 came to Jerusalem, and abode there thr.
10. 8 whosoever would not come within three
10. 9 together unto Jerusalem within three da.
Neh. 2. 11 came to Jerusalem, and was there three
7. 9 children of Shephatiah, three hundred se.
7. 17 two thousand three hundred twenty and
7. 22 of Hashum, three hundred twenty and
7. 23 children of Bezai, three hundred twenty
7. 29 Beeroth, seven hundred forty and three
7. 32 men of..Ai, an hundred twenty and three
7. 35 children of Harim, three hundred and tw.
7. 36 children of Jericho, three hundred forty
7. 38 three thousand nine hundred and thirty
7. 39 The priests..nine hundred seventy and t.
7. 60 Nethinims..(were) three hundred ninety
7. 66 two thousand three hundred and threesc.
7. 67 of whom (there were) seven thousand th.
Esth. 4. 16 neither eat nor drink three days, night or
8. 9 on the three and twentieth (day) thereof
9. 15 slew three hundred men at Shushan; but
Job 1. 2 born unto him seven sons and three dau.
1. 3 His substance also was..three thousand
1. 4 sent and called for their three sisters, to
1. 17 Chaldeans made out three bands, and fell
2. 11 Now when Job's three friends heard of all
32. 1 So these three men ceased to answer Job
32. 3 Also against his three friends was his wr.
32. 5 answer in the mouth of (these) three men
42. 13 He had also seven sons and three daught.
Prov.30. 15 There are three (things that) are never s.
30. 18 There be three (things which) are too wo.
30. 21 For three (things) the earth is disquieted
30. 29 There be three (things) which go well, yea
Isa. 16. 14 Within three years, as the years of an hir.
17. 6 two (or) three berries in the top of the up.
20. 3 walked naked and barefoot three years (for)
Jer. 25. 3 that (is) the three and twentieth year, the
36. 23 when Jehudi had read three or four leav.
52. 24 second priest, and the three keepers of
52. 28 three thousand Jews, and three and twe.
52. 30 In the three and twentieth year of Neb.
Eze. 4. 5 three hundred and ninety days: so shalt
4. 9 three hundred and ninety days shalt thou
14. 14 Though these three men, Noah, Daniel
14. 16, 18 these three men (were) in it, (as) I live
40. 10, 21, three on this side, and three on that
40. 10 they three (were) of one measure: and the
40. 48 breadth of the gate (was) three cubits on
40. 48 and three cubits on that side
41. 6 side chambers (were) three, one over ano.
41. 16 galleries round about on their three sto.
41. 22 altar of wood (was) three cubits high, and
48. 31 three gates northward; one gate of Reu.
48. 32 at the east side..three gates; and one ga.
48. 33 three gates; one gate of Simeon, one gate
48. 34 three gates; one gate of Gad, one gate of
Dan. 1. 5 so nourishing them three years, that at
8. 14 Unto two thousand and three hundred d.
10. 2 I Daniel was mourning three full weeks
10. 3 anoint myself at all, till three whole wee.
11. 2 there shall stand up yet three kings in P.
12. 12 cometh to the thousand three hundred
Amos 1. 3, 6, 9, 11, 13 For three transgressions of
2. 1, 4, 6 saith the LORD, For three transgress.
4. 4 and bring..your tithes after three years
4. 7 when (there were) yet three months to the
4. 8 two (or) three cities wandered unto one
Jon. 1. 17 in the belly of the fish three days and th.
3. 3 was an exceeding great city of three days'
Zech 11. 8 Three shepherds also I cut off in one mo.

2. *Three, sheloshah* [V. L. שְׁלוֹשִׁים].
2 Sa. 23. 13 three of the thirty chief went down, and

3. *Third* שָׁלִישִׁי *shelishi.*
Eze. 42. 3 gallery against gallery in three (stories)

4. *To be threefold, three years old,* שָׁלַשׁ *shalash,* 4.
Eze. 42. 6 For they (were) in three (stories), but had

5. *Three,* תְּלָת *telath.*
Ezra 6. 4 three rows of great stones, and a row of
Dan. 3. 23 these three men, Shadrach, Meshach and
3. 24 Did not we cast three men bound into the
6. 2 over these three presidents, of whom Da.
6. 10 kneeled upon his knees three times a day
6. 13 but maketh his petition three times a day
7. 5 (it had) three ribs in the mouth of it bet.
7. 8 there were three of the first horns pluck.
7. 20 which came up, and before whom three
7. 24 be diverse..and he shall subdue three ki.

6. *Three,* τρεῖς *treis.*
Matt 12. 40 as Jonas was three days and three nights
12. 40 so shall the Son..be three days and three
13. 33 leaven, which a woman took and hid in th.
15. 32 because they continue with me now three d
17. 4 if thou wilt, let us make now three t.
18. 16 in the mouth of two or three witnesses
18. 20 where two or three are gathered together
26. 61 said, I am able..to build it in three days
27. 40 Thou that..buildest (it) in three days, save

Matt 27. 63 that deceiver said..After three days I will
Mark 8. 2 they have now been with me three days
8. 31 be killed, and after three days rise again
9. 5 let us make three tabernacles; one for th.
14. 58 within three days I will build another ma.
15. 29 that destroyest..and buildest (it) in three
Luke 1. 56 Mary abode with her about three months
2. 46 after three days they found him in the te.
4. 25 the heaven was shut up three years, and
9. 33 let us make three tabernacles; one for th.
10. 36 Which now of these three, thinkest thou
11. 5 say unto him, Friend, lend me three loa.
12. 52 three against two, and two against three
13. 7 these three years I come seeking fruit on
13. 21 took and hid in three measures of meal
John 2. 6 containing two or three firkins apiece
2. 19 Destroy this temple, and in three days I
2. 20 and wilt thou rear it up in three days?
21. 11 fishes, an hundred and fifty and three
Acts 5. 7 it was about the space of three hours af.
7. 20 nourished up in his father's house three
9. 9 he was three days without sight, and ne.
10. 19 said unto him, Behold, [three] men seek
11. 11 there were three men already come unto
17. 2 three sabbath days reasoned with them
19. 8 spake boldly for the space of three mon.
20. 3 (there) abode three months. And when
25. 1 after three days he ascended from Cesarea
28. 7 received us, and lodged us three days co.
28. 11 after three months we departed in a ship
28. 12 landing at Syracuse, we tarried (there) th.
28. 17 after three days Paul called the chief of
1 Co. 10. 8 fell in one day three and twenty thousand
13. 13 now abideth faith, hope, charity, these th.
14. 27 at the most (by) three, and (that) by cou.
14. 29 Let the prophets speak two or three, and
2 Co. 13. 1 In the mouth of two or three witnesses sh.
Gal. 1. 18 after three years I went up to Jerusalem
1 Ti. 5. 19 receive not. but before two or three wit.
Heb. 10. 28 died without mercy under two or three
Jas. 5. 17 by the space of three years and six mon.
1 Jo. 5. 7 there are three: [and these three are one]
5. 8 there are three..and these three agree in
Rev. 6. 6 and three measures of barley for a penny
8. 13 voices of the trumpet of the three angels
9. 18 By these three was the third part of men
11. 9 shall see their dead bodies three days and
11. 11 after three days and an half the spirit of
16. 13 I saw three unclean spirits like frogs (co.)
16. 19 the great city was divided into three pa.
21. 13 the east, three gates; on the north, three
21. 13 south, three gates; and on the west, three

THREE (hundred, thousand) —

1. *Three hundred*, τριακόσιοι *triakosioi.*
Mark 14. 5 sold for more than three hundred pence
John 12. 5 Why was not this..sold for three hundred

2. *Three thousand*, τρισχίλιοι *trischilioi.*
Acts 2. 41 there were added..about three thousand

THREE days, months, times, years old, space of—

1. *Third*, שְׁלִישִׁי *shelishi.*
Isa. 15. 5 an heifer of three years old: for by the m.
Jer. 48. 34 an heifer of three years old

2. *To be threefold, three years old*, שָׁלַשׁ *shalash*, 4.
Gen. 15. 9 Take me an heifer of three years old, and
15. 9 of three years old of three years old, and

3. *Third*, שִׁלְשׁוֹם *shilshom.*
1 Sa. 21. 5 kept from us about these three days, since

4. *Three months*, τρίμηνον *trimēnon.*
Heb. 11. 23 Moses..was hid three months of his par.

5. *Thrice*, τρίς *tris.*
Acts 11. 10 this was done three times, and all were

6. *Three years*, τριετία *trietia.*
Acts 20. 31 by the space of three years I ceased not

THREE days or parts, to stay or divide into —

To put into three, stay three days, שָׁלַשׁ *shalash*, 3.
Deut 19. 3 Thou shalt..divide the coasts..into three
1 Sa. 20. 19 And (when) thou hast stayed three days

THREE TAVERNS, Τρεῖς Ταβέρναι.

A place thirty-two miles S. of Rome, on the road which Paul travelled after he landed at Puteoli, and where some brethren met him.

Acts 28. 15 they came to meet us as far as..The T. T.

THREEFOLD —

To be threefold, שָׁלַשׁ *shalash*, 4.
Eccl. 4. 12 a threefold cord is not quickly broken

THREESCORE —

1. *Sixty*,* שִׁשִּׁים *shishshim.*
Gen. 25. 26 Isaac (was) threescore years old when she
46. 26 wives, all the souls (were) threescore and
Lev. 12. 5 shall continue..threescore and six days
Num. 1. 39 threescore and two thousand and seven
2. 26 threescore and two thousand and seven
3. 50 thousand three hundred and threescore
26. 25 threescore and four thousand and three
26. 27 threescore thousand and five hundred
26. 43 threescore and four thousand and four h.
31. 34 And threescore and one thousand asses
31. 39 of which the LORD's tribute (was) threes.
Deut. 3. 4 threescore cities, all the region of Argob
Josh 13. 30 which (are) in Bashan, threescore cities
2 Sa. 2. 31 three hundred and threescore men died
1 Ki. 4. 13 threescore great cities with walls and br.
4. 22 thirty measures of fine flour, and threes.
6. 2 length thereof (was) threescore cubits, and
1 Ki. 10. 14 six hundred threescore and six talents of
2 Ki. 25. 19 threescore men of the people of the land
1 Ch. 2. 21 whom he married when he (was) threesc.
2. 23 and the towns thereof, (even) threescore
5. 18 seven hundred and threescore, that went
9. 13 thousand and seven hundred and threes.
16. 38 with their brethren, threescore and eight
26. 8 (were) threescore and two of Obed-edom
2 Ch. 3. 3 length..(was) threescore cubits, and the
9. 13 six hundred and threescore and six talents
11. 21 threescore concubines; and begat..thre.
12. 3 chariots, and threescore thousand horse.
Ezra 2. 9 of Zaccai, seven hundred and threescore
2. 64 two thousand three hundred (and) three.
8. 10 with him an hundred and threescore males
8. 13 Shemaiah, and with them threescore ma.
Neh. 7. 14 of Zaccai, seven hundred and threescore
7. 18 of Adonikam six hundred threescore and
7. 19 of Bigvai two thousand threescore and
7. 66 two thousand three hundred and threes.
7. 72 and threescore and seven priests' garments
11. 6 four hundred threescore and eight valiant
Song 3. 7 threescore valiant men (are) about it, of
6. 8 There are threescore queens, and fourscore
Isa. 7. 8 within threescore and five years shall Ep.
Jer. 52. 25 threescore men of the people of the land
Eze. 40. 14 He made also posts of threescore cubits
Dan. 9. 25 seven weeks, and threescore and two we.
9. 26 after threescore and two weeks shall Me.

2. *Sixty*, שִׁתִּין *shittin.*
Ezra 6. 3 threescore cubits..breadth..threescore
Dan. 3. 1 whose height (was) threescore cubits, (and)
5. 31 (being) about threescore and two years old

3. *Sixty*, ἑξήκοντα *hexēkonta.*
Luke 24. 13 which was from Jerusalem..threescore f.
1 Ti. 5. 9 Let not a widow be taken..under threes.
Rev. 11. 3 a thousand two hundred (and) threescore
12. 6 a thousand two hundred (and) threescore
13. 18 his number (is) six hundred threescore (and)

THREESCORE and ten —

1. *Seventy*, שִׁבְעִים *shibim.*
Gen. 46. 27 the souls..which came..threescore and t.
50. 3 mourned for him threescore and ten days
Exod 15. 27 wells..and threescore and ten palm trees
Num 33. 9 in Elim (were)..threescore and ten palm t.
Deut 10. 22 down into Egypt with threescore and ten
Judg. 1. 7 Threescore and ten kings, having their t.
8. 30 Gideon had threescore and ten sons of his
9. 2 threescore and ten persons, reign over you
9. 4 they gave him threescore and ten (pieces)
9. 5, 18 threescore and ten persons, upon one
9. 24 to the threescore and ten sons of Jerubbaal
12. 14 that rode on threescore and ten ass colts
1 Sa. 6. 19 fifty thousand and threescore and ten men
1 Ki. 5. 15 Solomon had threescore and ten thousand
1 Ch. 21. 5 Judah (was) four hundred threescore and
2 Ch. 2. 2 Solomon told out threescore and ten tho.
2. 18 he set threescore and ten thousand of them
29. 32 was threescore and ten bullocks, an hun.
36. 21 kept sabbath, to fulfil threescore and ten
Psa. 90. 10 The days..(are) threescore years and ten
Zech. 1. 12 had indignation these threescore and ten

2. *Seventy*, ἑβδομήκοντα *hebdomēkonta.*
Acts 23. 23 Make ready..horsemen threescore and ten

THREESCORE thousand —

Six myriads, שֵׁשׁ רִבְּאוֹת *shesh ribboth.*
Ezra 2. 69 threescore and one thousand drams of go.

THREESCORE and fifteen —

1. *Seventy and five*, שִׁבְעִים וְחָמֵשׁ *shibim ve-chamesh.*
Gen. 25. 7 an hundred threescore and fifteen years
Exod 38. 25 seven hundred and threescore and fifteen
Num 31. 37 was six hundred and threescore and fifteen

2. *Seventy five*, ἑβδομήκοντα πέντε *hebdomēkonta pen.*
Acts 7. 14 all his kindred, threescore and fifteen so.

THREESCORE and fourteen —

Four and seventy, אַרְבָּעָה וְשִׁבְעִים *arbaah ve-shibim.*
Num. 1. 27 threescore and fourteen thousand and six
2. 4 threescore and fourteen thousand and six

THREESCORE and seventeen —

Seventy and seven, שִׁבְעִים וְשִׁבְעָה *shibim ve-shibah.*
Judg. 8. 14 elders thereof, (even) threescore and sev.

THREESCORE and sixteen —

1. *Six and seventy*, שִׁשָּׁה וְשִׁבְעִים *shishshah ve-shibim.*
Num 26. 22 threescore and sixteen thousand and five

2. *Seventy six*, ἑβδομήκοντα ἕξ *hebdomēkonta hex.*
Acts 27. 37 two hundred threescore and sixteen souls

THREESCORE and thirteen —

Three and seventy, שְׁלֹשָׁה וְשִׁבְעִים *sheloshah ve-shibim.*
Num. 3. 43, 46 two hundred and threescore and thir.

THREESCORE and twelve —

Two and seventy, שְׁנַיִם וְשִׁבְעִים *shenayim ve-shibim.*
Num 31. 33 threescore and twelve thousand beeves
31. 38 the LORD's tribute (was) threescore and t.

THRESH, be threshed, to —

1. *To tread down, thresh*, דּוּשׁ *dush.*
2 Ki. 13. 7 had made them like the dust by threshing
1 Ch. 21. 20 Now Ornan was threshing wheat
Isa. 28. 28 because he will not ever be threshing it
41. 15 thou shalt thresh the mountains, and beat
Amos 1. 3 because they have threshed Gilead with
Mic. 4. 13 Arise and thresh, O daughter of Zion: for
Hab. 3. 12 thou didst thresh the heathen in anger

2. *To be trodden down, threshed*, דּוּשׁ *dush*, 6.
Isa. 28. 27 For the fitches are not threshed with a

3. *To cause to go, tread*, דָּרַךְ *darak*, 5.
Jer. 51. 33 daughter of Babylon..(it is) time to thresh

4. *To beat out or off*, חָבַט *chabat.*
Judg. 6. 11 Gideon threshed wheat by the wine press

5. *To tread down, thresh*, ἀλοάω *aloaō.*
1 Co. 9. 10 that he that thresheth in hope should be

THRESHING (floor, instrument, place) —

1. *Threshing floors*, אִדְּרִין *idderin.*
Dan. 2. 35 like the chaff of the summer threshing fl.

2. *Threshing floor*, גֹּרֶן *goren.*
Gen. 50. 10 they came to the threshing floor of Atad
Num 15. 20 the heave offering of the threshing floor
18. 27 though (it were) the corn of the threshing f.
18. 30 as the increase of the threshing floor, and
Ruth 3. 2 he winnoweth barley..in the threshing fl.
1 Sa. 23. 1 fight..and they rob the threshing floors
2 Sa. 6. 6 when they came to Nachon's threshing fl.
24. 16 angel of the LORD was by the threshing pl.
24. 18 rear an altar..in the threshing floor of A.
24. 21 To buy the threshing floor of thee, to bu.
24. 24 David bought the threshing floor and the
1 Ch. 13. 9 when they came unto the threshing floor
21. 15 stood by the threshing floor of Ornan the
21. 18 in the threshing floor of Ornan the Jebu.
21. 21 went out of the threshing floor, and bowed
21. 22 Grant me the place of (this) threshing floor
21. 28 had answered him in the threshing floor
2 Ch. 3. 1 had prepared in the threshing floor of Or.
Jer. 51. 33 daughter of Babylon..like a threshing fl.

3. *Treading down, threshing*, דַּיִשׁ *dayish.*
Lev. 26. 5 your threshing shall reach unto the vin.

4. *A threshing roller*, חָרוּץ *charuts.*
Isa. 28. 27 not threshed with a threshing instrument
Amos 1. 3 have threshed Gilead with threshing in.

5. *What is trodden down or threshed*, מְדֻשָׁה *medushsh.*
Isa. 21. 10 O my threshing, and the corn of my floor

6. *A threshing instrument*, מוֹרַג *morag.*
2 Sa. 24. 22 behold..threshing instruments and (ot.)
1 Ch. 21. 23 the threshing instruments for wood, and
Isa. 41. 15 a new sharp threshing instrument having

THRESHOLD —

1. *Gatherings, store chambers*, אֲסֻפִּים *asuppim.*
Neh. 12. 25 keeping the ward at the thresholds of

2. *Threshold, entrance, space*, סַף *saph.*
Judg 19. 27 behold..her hands (were) upon the thres.
1 Ki. 14. 17 when she came to the threshold of the
Eze. 40. 6 measured the threshold of the gate, (wh.
40. 6 the other threshold (of the gate, which
40. 7 the threshold of the gate, by the porch
43. 8 setting of their threshold by my thresh.
Zeph. 2. 14 desolation (shall be) in the thresholds: for

3. *Threshold, sill*, מִפְתָּן *miphtan.*
1 Sa. 5. 4 his hands (were) cut off upon the thresh.
5. 5 tread on the threshold of Dagon in Ash.
Eze. 9. 3 was gone up..to the threshold of the ho.
10. 4 (and stood) over the threshold of the ho.
10. 18 departed from off the threshold of the
46. 2 he shall worship at the threshold of the
47. 1 waters issued out from under the thresh.
Zeph. 1. 9 punish all those that leap on the thresh.

THRICE —

1. *Three beats, times*, שָׁלוֹשׁ פְּעָמִים *shalosh peamim.*
Exod 34. 23 Thrice in the year shall all your men ch.
34. 24 appear before the LORD thy God thrice
2 Ki. 13. 18 Smite upon the ground: and he smote t.
13. 19 whereas now thou shalt smite. (but) th.

2. *Thrice*, τρίς *tris.*
Matt. 26. 34 before..cock crow, thou shalt deny me th.
26. 75 Before..cock crow, thou shalt deny me th.
Mark 14. 30 before the cock crow..shalt deny me th.
14. 72 Before the cock crow..shalt deny me th.
Luke 22. 34 thou shalt thrice deny that thou knowest
22. 61 Before the cock crow..shalt deny me th.
John 13. 38 not crow, till thou hast denied me thrice
Acts 10. 16 This was done thrice: and the vessel was
2 Co. 11. 25 Thrice was I beaten..thrice I suffered sh.
12. 8 For this thing I besought the Lord thrice

THROAT, (to take by the) —

1. *The throat, neck*, גָּרוֹן *garon.*
Psa. 5. 9 their throat (is) an open sepulchre; they
69. 3 I am weary of my crying; my throat is
115. 7 neither speak they through their throat
Jer. 2. 25 Withhold..thy throat from thirst: but

2. *Throat, gullet*, לֹעַ *loa.*
Prov 23. 2 put a knife to thy throat, if thou (be) a

3. *Throat, upper part of windpipe*, λάρυγξ *larugx.*
Rom. 3. 13 Their throat (is) an open sepulchre: with

4. *To press the throat*, πνίγω *pnigō.*
Matt. 18. 28 and took..by the throat, saying, Pay me

THRONE —

1. *Seat of king, judge or priest*, כִּסֵּא *kisse.*
Gen. 41. 40 only in the throne will I be greater than
Exod 11. 5 the first born..that sitteth upon his th.
12. 29 from the first born..that sat on his thr.
Deut. 17. 18 when he sitteth upon the throne of his
1 Sa. 2. 8 to make them inherit the throne of glory
2 Sa. 3. 10 to set up the throne of David over Israel
7. 13 I will stablish the throne of his kingdom

2 Sa. 7. 16 thy throne shall be established for ever
14. 9 and the king and his throne (be) guiltless
1 Ki. 1. 13, 17, 24, 30 he shall sit upon my throne
1. 20, 27 sit on the throne of my lord the king
1. 35 that he may come and sit upon my thro.
1. 37 make his throne greater than the throne
1. 46 Solomon sitteth on the throne of the kin.
1. 47 make his throne greater than thy throne
1. 48 hath given (one) to sit on my throne this
2. 4 there shall not fail..a man on the throne
2. 12 Then sat Solomon upon the throne of D.
2. 19 sat down on his throne, and caused a seat
2. 24 set me on the throne of David my father
2. 33 upon his house, and upon his throne, sh.
2. 45 the throne of David shall be established
3. 6 thou hast given him a son to sit on his th.
5. 5 Thy son, whom I will set upon thy throne
7. 7 he made a porch for the throne where he
8. 20 sit on the throne of Israel, as the LORD
8. 25 a man..to sit on the throne of Israel; so
9. 5 I will establish the throne of thy kingdom
9. 5 shall not fail thee a man upon the throne
10. 9 to set thee on the throne of Israel: beca.
10. 18 Moreover the king made a great throne
16. 11 as soon as he sat on his throne, (that) he
22. 10 sat each on his throne, having put on th.
22. 19 saw the LORD sitting on his throne, and
2 Ki. 10. 3 set (him) on his father's throne, and fight
10. 30 children..shall sit on the throne of Israel
11. 19 And he sat on the throne of the kings
13. 13 Jeroboam sat upon his throne: and Joash
15. 12 Thy sons shall sit on the throne of Israel
25. 28 set his throne above the throne of the ki.
1 Ch. 17. 12 and I will stablish his throne for ever
17. 14 throne shall be established for evermore
22. 10 will establish the throne of his kingdom
28. 5 chosen Solomon..to sit upon the throne
29. 23 Then Solomon sat on the throne of the L.
2 Ch. 6. 10 am set on the throne of Israel, as the Lo.
6. 16 not fail thee a man..to sit upon the thro.
7. 18 Then will I stablish the throne of thy kin.
9. 8 to set thee on his throne, (to be) king for
9. 17 Moreover the king made a great throne
9. 18 steps to the throne..fastened to the thr.
18. 9 sat either of them on his throne, clothed
18. 18 I saw the LORD sitting upon his throne
23. 20 set the king upon the throne of the king.
Neh. 3. 7 unto the throne of the governor on this
Esth. 1. 2 Ahasuerus sat on the throne of his king.
5. 1 king sat upon his royal throne in the ro.
Job 36. 7 but with kings (are they) on the throne
Psa. 9. 4 thou satest in the throne judging right
9. 7 hath prepared his throne for judgment
11. 4 the LORD'S throne (is) in heaven: his eyes
45. 6 Thy throne, O God, (is) for ever and ever
47. 8 God sitteth upon the throne of his holin.
89. 4 and build up thy throne to all generatio.
89. 14 the habitation of thy throne: mercy and
89. 29 and his throne as the days of heaven
89. 36 endure for ever, and his throne as the sun
89. 44 and cast his throne down to the ground
93. 2 Thy throne (is) established of old: thou
94. 20 Shall the throne of iniquity have fellows.
97. 2 judgment (are) the habitation of his thr.
103. 19 LORD hath prepared his throne in the he.
122. 5 thrones of judgment, the thrones of the
132. 11 fruit of thy body will I set upon thy throne
132. 12 children shall also sit upon thy throne for
Prov 16. 12 for the throne is established by righteous.
20. 8 A king that sitteth in the throne of jud.
20. 28 and his throne is upholden by mercy
25. 5 throne shall be established in righteous.
29. 14 his throne shall be established for ever
Isa. 6. 1 saw also the LORD sitting upon a throne
9. 7 upon the throne of David, and upon his
14. 9 it hath raised up from their thrones all
14. 13 I will exalt my throne above the stars of
16. 5 in mercy shall the throne be established
22. 23 he shall be for a glorious throne to his fa.
47. 1 no throne, O daughter of the Chaldeans
66. 1 The heaven (is) my throne, and the earth
Jer. 1. 15 they shall set every one his throne at the
3. 17 they shall call Jerusalem the throne of
13. 13 even the kings that sit upon David's throne
14. 21 do not disgrace the throne of thy glory
17. 12 A glorious high throne from the beginning
17. 25 kings and princes sitting upon the throne
22. 2 that sittest upon the throne of David, th.
22. 4 kings sitting upon the throne of David
22. 30 sitting upon the throne of David, and ru.
29. 16 king that sitteth upon the throne of David
33. 17 never want a man to sit upon the throne
33. 21 not have a son to reign upon his throne
36. 30 shall have none to sit upon the throne of
43. 10 will set his throne upon these stones that
49. 38 will set my throne in Elam, and will dest.
52. 32 set his throne above the throne of the kin.
Lam. 5. 19 thy throne from generation to generation
Eze. 1. 26 the likeness of a throne, as the appearance
1. 26 upon the likeness of the throne (was) the
10. 1 the appearance of the likeness of a throne
26. 16 shall come down from their thrones, and
43. 7 place of my throne, and the place of the
Jon. 3. 6 arose from his throne, and he laid his ro.
Hag. 2. 22 I will overthrow the throne of kingdoms
Zech. 6. 13 shall sit and rule upon his throne; and
6. 13 he shall be a priest upon his throne

2. *Seat, throne,* כִּסֵּה *kisseh.*
1 Ki. 10. 19 throne had six steps..the top of the thr.
Job 26. 9 He holdeth back the face of his throne

3. *Seat, throne,* כָּרְסֵא *korse.*
Dan. 5. 20 he was deposed from his kingly throne
7. 9 I beheld till the thrones were cast down
7. 9 his throne (was like) the fiery flame, (and)

4. *A judgment seat, tribunal,* βῆμα *bēma.*
Acts 12. 21 Herod..sat upon his throne, and made an

5. *Throne, seat,* θρόνος *thronos.*
Matt. 5. 34 neither by heaven; for it is God's throne
19. 28 when the Son of man shall sit in the thr.
19. 28 ye also shall sit upon twelve thrones, ju.
23. 22 sweareth by the throne of God, and by hi.
25. 31 then shall he sit upon the throne of his
Luke 1. 32 shall give unto him the throne of his fat.
22. 30 sit on thrones judging the twelves tribes
Acts 2. 30 he would raise up Christ to sit on his thro.
7. 49 Heaven (is) my throne, and earth (is) my fo.
Col. 1. 16 thrones, or dominions, or principalities
Heb. 1. 8 Thy throne, O God, (is) for ever and ever
4. 16 come boldly unto the throne of grace, that
8. 1 who is set on the right hand of the throne
12. 2 set down at the right hand of the throne
Rev. 1. 4 seven spirits which are before his throne
3. 21 will I grant to sit with me in my throne
3. 21 am set down with my Father in his throne
4. 2 throne was set.. and (one) sat on the thr.
4. 3 rainbow round about the throne, in sight
4. 4 round about the throne (were) four and
4. 5 out of the throne proceeded lightnings and
4. 5 lamps of fire burning before the throne
4. 6 before the throne (there was) a sea of glass
4. 6 midst of the throne, and round about the t.
4. 9 and thanks to him that sat on the throne
4. 10 fall down before him that sat on the thro.
4. 10 cast their crowns before the throne, sayi.
5. 1, 7 right hand of him that sat on the throne
5. 6 in the midst of the throne and of the four
5. 11 many angels round about the throne and
5. 13 unto him that sitteth upon the throne, and
6. 16 the face of him that sitteth on the throne
7. 9 [stood before the throne, and before the]
7. 10 to our God which sitteth upon the throne
7. 11 the angels stood round about the throne
7. 11 fell before the throne on their faces, and
7. 15 Therefore are they before the throne of
7. 15 he that sitteth on the throne shall dwell
7. 17 Lamb which is in the midst of the throne
8. 3 golden altar which was before the throne
12. 5 was caught up unto God, and (to) his thr.
14. 3 sung as it were a new song before the th.
14. 5 [they are without fault before the throne]
16. 17 came a great voice..from the throne, say.
19. 4 worshipped God that sat on the throne
19. 5 voice came out of the throne, saying, Pra.
20. 4 saw thrones, and they sat upon them, and
20. 11 saw a great white throne, and him that
21. 5 he that sat upon the throne said, Behold
22. 1 proceeding out of the throne of God and
22. 3 but the throne of God and of the Lamb sh.

THRONG —

1. *To squeeze, press,* θλίβω *thlibō.*
Mark 3. 9 should wait..lest they should throng him

2. *To press together,* συμπνίγω *sumpnigō.*
Luke 8. 42 But as he went the people thronged him

3. *To hold together,* συνέχω *sunechō.*
Luke 8. 45 the multitude throng thee and press (thee)

4 *To squeeze together,* συνθλίβω *sunthlibō.*
Mark 5. 24 much people followed him, and throng.
5. 31 Thou seest the multitude thronging thee

THROUGH (the midst of), throughout (every)—

1. *Unto,* אֶל *el.*
Num 25. 8 thrust..the man..and the woman throu.

2. *Into,* בְּמוֹ *bemo.*
Isa. 43. 2 when thou walkest through the fire, thou

3. *At, beside, through,* בְּעַד *bead.*
Josh. 2. 15 she let them down by a cord through the

4. *The way,* דֶּרֶךְ *derek.*
2 Sa. 4. 7 gat them away through the plain all nig.

5. *By the hand of, by means of,* בְּיַד *be-yad.*
Zech. 4. 12 What..two olive branches which through

6. *To shoot, cast,* יָרָה *yarah.*
Exod 19. 13 he shall surely be stoned, or shot through

7. *From,* מִן *min.*
Isa. 28. 7 the prophet have erred through strong dr.

8. *Over,* עַל *al.*
2 Ch. 20. 3 proclaimed a fast throughout all Judah
Jer. 52. 3 through the anger of the LORD it came to

9. *From the face of,* מִפְּנֵי *mip-pene.*
Gen. 6. 13 for the earth is filled with violence thro.

10. *In the heart of,* בְּקֶרֶב *be-qereb.*
Deut 29. 16 how we came through the nations which
Josh. 1. 11 Pass through the host, and command the
24. 17 among all the people through whom we

11. *In the midst of,* בְּתוֹךְ *[tavek].*
Exod 36. 33 he made the middle bar to shoot through
Num 33. 8 passed through the midst of the sea into
Neh. 9. 11 so that they went through the midst of
Eze. 9. 4 said unto him, Go through the midst of
9. 4 through the midst of Jerusalem, and set

12. *Up, through,* ἀνά *ana.*
Mark 7. 31 he came..through the midst of the coasts

13. *Through,* διά *(gen.) dia.*
Matt 12. 1 Jesus went on the sabbath day through the
12. 43 he walketh through dry places, seeking
19. 24 It is easier for a camel to go through the
Mark 2. 23 he went through the corn fields on the sa.
9. 30 they departed thence, and passed through
10. 25 It is easier for a camel to go through the
11. 16 any man should carry (any) vessel throu.
Luke 4. 30 he passing through the midst of them we.
5. 19 let him down through the tiling with (his)
6. 1 he went through the corn fields; and his
11. 24 he walketh through dry places, seeking re.
17. 1 but woe (unto him) through whom they
17. 11 he passed through the midst of Samaria
18. 25 it is easier for a camel to go through a ne.
John 1. 7 that all (men) through him might believe
3. 17 that the world through him might be sav.
4. 4 And he must needs go through Samaria
8. 59 went out of the temple, going through them.
17. 20 which shall believe on me through their
19. 23 coat was..woven from the top throughout
Acts 1. 2 after that he through the Holy Ghost had
8. 18 Simon saw that through laying on of the
9. 32 it came to pass, as Peter passed through.
10. 43 through his name whosoever believeth in
13. 38 through this man is preached unto you
13. 49 the word..was published throughout all
14. 22 we must through much tribulation enter
15. 11 we believe that through the grace of the
18. 27 helped them..which had believed throu.
20. 3 he purposed to return through Macedon.
21. 4 who said to Paul through the Spirit, that
Rom. 1. 8 I thank my God through Jesus Christ for
2. 23 through breaking the law dishonourest th.
3. 24 through the redemption that is in Christ
3. 25 through faith in his blood, to declare his
3. 30 shall justify..uncircumcision through fa.
3. 31 Do we then make void the law through fa.
4. 13 through the law, but through the righte.
5. 1 we have peace with God through our Lo.
5. 9 we shall be saved from wrath through him
5. 11 we also joy in God through our Lord Jes.
5. 21 so might grace reign through righteousn.
7. 25 I thank God through Jesus Christ our L.
8. 3 in that it was weak through the flesh, G.
8. 37 we are more than conquerors, through him
11. 36 For of him, and through him, and to him
12. 3 I say, through the grace given unto me
15. 4 we through patience and comfort of the
16. 27 To God only wise, (be) glory through Jesus
1 Co. 1. 1 called (to be) an apostle..through the will
4. 15 I have begotten you through the Gospel
10. 1 all our fathers..passed through the sea
13. 12 we see through a glass, darkly; but then
15. 57 which giveth us the victory through our
2 Co. 3. 4 such trust have we through Christ to God
4. 15 the abundant grace might through the
8. 18 whose praise (is) in the Gospel, through.
9. 11 which causeth through us thanksgiving
11. 33 through a window in a basket was I let
Gal. 2. 19 I through the law am dead to the law, that
3. 14 receive the promise of the Spirit through
4. 7 if a son, then an heir of God through Ch.
Eph. 1. 7 In whom we have redemption through his
2. 8 by grace are ye saved through faith; and
2. 18 through him we both have access by one
4. 6 who (is) above all, and through all, and
Phil. 1. 19 this shall turn to my salvation through
3. 9 that which is through the faith of Christ
Col. 1. 14 [In whom we have redemption through his]
1. 20 having made peace through the blood of
1. 22 In the body of his flesh through death, to
2. 8 lest any man spoil you through philosophy
2. 12 through the faith of the operation of God
2 Ti. 1. 10 life and immortality to light through the
3. 15 wise unto salvation through faith which
Titus 3. 6 Which he shed on us abundantly through
Phm. 22 I trust that through your prayers I shall
Heb. 2. 10 the Captain of their salvation perfect thr.
2. 14 through death he might destroy him that
6. 12 followers of them who through faith and
9. 14 who through the eternal spirit offered him.
10. 10 we are sanctified through the offering of
10. 20 a new and living way..through the veil, t.
11. 33 Who through faith subdued kingdoms
11. 39 having obtained a good report through fa.
13. 21 that which is well pleasing..through Jes.
1 Pe. 1. 5 kept by the power of God through faith un.
1. 22 obeying the truth [through the Spirit] unto
4. 11 that God..may be glorified through Jesus
2 Pe. 1. 3 through the knowledge of him that hath
1 Jo. 4. 9 into the world, that we might live through

14. *Through, on account of,* διά *(acc.) dia.*
Luke 1. 78 Through the tender mercy of our God
John 15. 3 ye are clean through the word which I ha.
Rom 2. 24 blasphemed among the Gentiles through
Gal. 4. 13 Ye know how through infirmity of the fl.
Eph. 4. 18 alienated from the life of God through the

15. *Into, to,* εἰς *eis.*
Matt. 4. 24 his fame went throughout all Syria: and
Mark 1. 28 his fame spread abroad throughout all the
1. 39 preached in their synagogues throughout
14. 9 this gospel shall be preached throughout
Acts 26. 20 [throughout] all the coasts of Judea, and
Eph. 3. 21 Unto him (be) glory..throughout all ages

16. *Out of,* ἐκ *ek,* ἐξ *ex.*
2 Co. 13. 4 though he was crucified through weakn.
Gal. 3. 8 God would justify the heathen through
Rev. 18. 3 through the abundance of her delicacies

17. *In, by, with, among,* ἐν *en.*
Matt. 9. 34 He casteth out devils through the prince
Luke 1. 65 these sayings were noised abroad throug.
7. 17 this rumour of him went forth throughout
7. 17 and [throughout] all the region round ab.
10. 17 the devils are subject unto us through thy
11. 15 He casteth out devils through Beelzebub
11. 18 ye say that I cast out devils through Be.
John17. 11 keep through thine own name those whom
17. 17 Sanctify them through thy truth: thy wo.
17. 19 they also might be sanctified through the
20. 31 that believing ye might have life through
Acts 4. 2 preached through Jesus the resurrection
Rom. 1. 8 your faith is spoken of throughout the wh.
1. 24 gave them up to uncleanness through the
3. 7 hath more abounded through my lie unto
3. 25 through the forbearance of God
6. 11 alive unto God through Jesus Christ our
6. 23 the gift of God (is) eternal life through Je.
9. 17 my name might be declared throughout
15. 13 abound in hope, through the power of the
15. 17 whereof I may glory through Jesus Christ
15. 19 Through mighty signs and wonders, by
2 Co. 11. 3 as the serpent beguiled Eve through his
Gal. 3. 14 come on the Gentiles through Jesus Chr.
5. 10 I have confidence in you through the L.
Eph. 2. 7 in (his) kindness toward us through Christ
2. 22 for an habitation of God through the spi.
Phil. 4. 7 keep your hearts and mind sthrough Chr.
2 Th. 2. 13 through sanctification of the spirit and
2. 16 consolation and good hope through gra.
Titus 1. 3 manifested his word through preaching
Heb. 13. 20 through the blood of the everlasting cov.
1 Pe. 1. 2 through sanctification of the spirit, unto
1. 6 in heaviness through manifold temptat.
2 Pe. 1. 1 through the righteousness of God and our
1. 2 Grace and peace be multiplied..through
1. 4 corruption that is in the world through
2. 3 through covetousness shall they with fei.
2. 18 they allure through the lusts of the flesh
2. 20 through the knowledge of the Lord and
Rev. 8. 13 heard an angel flying through the midst

18. *Upon, over,* ἐπί *(dat.) epi.*
Acts 3. 16 his name through faith in his name hath
1 Co. 8. 11 [through thy knowledge shall the weak b.]

19. *Upon, over,* ἐπί *(acc.) epi.*
Luke 4. 25 great famine was throughout all the land
Acts 11. 28 there should be great dearth throughout

20. *Down from, towards,* κατά *(gen) kata.*
Luke 4. 14 there went out a fame of him through all
23. 5 teaching throughout all Jewry, beginning
Acts 9. 31 Then had the churches rest throughout all
9. 42 it was known throughout all Joppa; and
10. 37 which was published throughout all Jud.

21. *Down to,* κατά *(acc.) kata.*
Luke 8. 1 he went throughout every city and village
8. 39 published throughout the whole city how
9. 6 they departed, and went through the to.
13. 22 he went through the cities and villages
Acts 3. 17 I wot that through ignorance ye did (it)
8. 1 they were all scattered abroad through.
24. 5 among all the Jews throughout the world
Phil. 2. 3 (Let) nothing (be done) through strife or

22. *All through,* δι᾽ ὅλου *di' holou.*
John19. 23 coat was..woven from the top throughout
See also Break, bring, dig, drop, go, march, number, pass, pierce, run, smite, stricken, strike, thrust, walk.

THROUGHLY —

1. *To do good or well,* יָטַב *yatab,* 5.
Jer. 7. 5 if ye throughly amend your ways and your

2. *To glean,* עָלַל *alal,* 3a.
Jer. 6. 9 They shall throughly glean the remnant

3. *To do,* עָשָׂה *asah.*
Jer. 7. 5 if ye throughly execute judgment betw.

4. *To cause to multiply, make abundant,* רָבָה *rabah,* 5.
Psa. 51. 2 Wash me throughly from mine iniquity

5. *To strive, plead,* רִיב *rib.*
Jer. 50. 34 he shall throughly plead their cause, that

6. *To weigh out, pay, spend,* שָׁקַל *shaqal.*
Job 6. 2 O that my grief were throughly weighed

7. *To burning,* לִשְׂרֵפָה *le-serephah.*
Gen. 11. 3 let us make brick, and burn them throu.

THROW (down), be thrown down, to —

1. *To break or throw down,* הָרַס *haras.*
Judg. 6. 25 throw down the altar of Baal that thy fa.
1 Ki.19. 10, 14 thrown down thine altars, and slain
Jer. 1. 10 and to throw down, to build, and to plant
31. 28 to throw down, and to destroy, and to
Lam. 2. 2 he hath thrown down in his wrath the st.
2. 17 he hath thrown down, and hath not pitied
Eze. 16. 39 they shall throw down thine eminent pl.
Mic. 5. 11 And I will..throw down all thy strongh.
Mal. 1. 4 They shall build, but I will throw down

2. *To be broken or thrown down,* הָרַס *haras,* 2.
Jer. 31. 40 it shall not be plucked up, nor thrown do.
50. 15 her walls are thrown down; for it (is) the
Eze. 38. 20 the mountains shall be thrown down, and

3. *To cause to fall,* נָפַל *naphal,* 5.
2 Sa. 20. 15 all..battered the wall, to throw it down

4. *To break down,* נָתַץ *nathats.*
Judg. 2. 2 ye shall throw down their altars: but ye
6. 32 because he hath thrown down his altar
Jer. 33. 4 which are thrown down by the mounts

5. *To be broken down,* נָתַץ *nathats,* 2.
Neh. 1. 6 and the rocks are thrown down by him

6. *To break down,* נָתַץ *nathats,* 3.
2 Ch.31. 1 threw down the high places and the altars

7. *To stone,* סָקַל *saqal,* 3.
2 Sa. 16. 13 Shimei..threw stones at him, and cast dust

8. *To throw down or forth, shoot,* רָמָה *ramah.*
Exod.15. 21 the horse and his rider hath he thrown

9. *To cast away, down, off, out,* שָׁלַךְ *shalak,* 5.
Neh. 9. 11 their persecutors thou threwest into the

10. *To be cast away, or out,* שָׁלַךְ *shalak,* 6.
2 Sa. 20. 21 his head shall be thrown to thee over the

11. *To release, let go, throw down,* שָׁמַט *shamat.*
2 Ki. 9. 33 Throw her down. So they threw her do.

12. *To cast, throw,* βάλλω *ballō.*
Mark12. 42 she threw in two mites, which make a fa.
Acts 22. 23 cast off (their) clothes, and threw dust into
Rev. 18. 21 shall that great city Babylon be thrown d.

13. *To loose down,* καταλύω *kataluō.*
Matt 24. 2 one stone..that shall not be thrown down
Mark13. 2 one stone..that shall not be thrown down
Luke21. 6 one stone..that shall not be thrown down

14. *To throw,* ῥίπτω *rhiptō.*
Luke 4. 35 when the devil had thrown him in the mi.

THROWING a stone, with —
With a stone of the hand, בְּאֶבֶן יָד *be-eben yad.*
Num.35. 17 if he smite him with throwing a stone

THRUST (away, down, out, self, through, together), to —

1. *To trouble, hasten,* בָּהַל *bahal,* 5.
2 Ch.26. 20 they thrust him out from thence, yea, hi.

2. *To thrust through,* בָּתַק *bathaq,* 3.
Eze. 16. 40 and thrust thee through with their swo.

3. *To drive away, cast out,* גָּרַשׁ *garash,* 3.
Exod11. 1 he shall surely thrust you out hence alto.
Deut 33. 27 he shall thrust out the enemy from be.
Judg. 9. 41 Zebul thrust out Gaal and his brethren
11. 2 thrust out Jephthah, and said unto him
1 Ki. 2. 27 Solomon thrust out Abiathar from being

4. *To thrust away or down,* דָּחָה *dachah.*
Psa. 118. 13 Thou hast thrust sore at me, that I mig.

5. *To thrust away,* דָּחַק *dachaq.*
Joel 2. 8 Neither shall one thrust another, they

6. *To pierce through,* דָּקַר *daqar.*
Num25. 8 he..thrust both of them through, the man
Judg. 9. 54 his young man thrust him through, and
1 Sa. 31. 4 Draw thy sword, and thrust me through
31. 4 lest these..come and thrust me through
1 Ch.10. 4 Draw thy sword, and thrust me through
Zech 13. 3 shall thrust him through when he proph.

7. *To thrust, away, forward, out,* הָדַף *hadaph.*
Num35. 20 if he thrust him of hatred, or hurl at him
35. 22 if he thrust him suddenly without enmi.
2 Ki. 4. 27 but Gehazi came near to thrust her away
Eze. 34. 21 ye have thrust with side and with shoul.

8. *To press, crush,* לָחַץ *lachats,* 2.
Num22. 25 the ass..thrust herself unto the wall, and

9. *To drive or force away,* נָדַח *nadach,* 5.
Deut 13. 5 to thrust thee out of the way which the
13. 10 to thrust thee away from the LORD thy

10. *To drive or thrust away,* נָדַף *nadaph.*
Job 32. 13 Lest ye should say..God thrusteth him d.

11. *To pick out,* נָקַר *naqar.*
1 Sa. 11. 2 that I may thrust out all your right eyes

12. *To give,* נָתַן *nathan.*
Deut 15. 17 thrust (it) through his ear unto the door

13. *To strike, clap, blow, thrust,* תָּקַע *taqa.*
Judg. 3. 21 Ehud..took..and thrust it into his belly
2 Sa. 18. 14 thrust them through the heart of Absal.

14. *To drive or push away,* ἀπωθέομαι *apōtheomai.*
Acts 7. 27 thrust him away, saying, Who made thee

15. *To cast, throw,* βάλλω *ballō.*
John20. 25 thrust my hand into his side, I will not
20. 27 thrust (it) into my side: and be not fait.
Acts 16. 24 Who..thrust them into the inner prison

16. *To cast out,* ἐκβάλλω *ekballō.*
Luke 4. 29 rose up, and thrust him out of the city
13. 28 in the kingdom of God, and you..thrust o.
Acts 16. 37 now do they thrust us out privily? nay

17. *To lead up upon, launch out,* ἐπανάγω *epanagō.*
Luke 5. 3 prayed him that he would thrust out a li.

THRUST from, in, to —

1. *To drive or push away,* ἀπωθέομαι *apōtheomai.*
Acts 7. 39 but thrust..from them, and in their hearts

2. *To cast, throw,* βάλλω *ballō.*
Rev. 14. 16 he that sat on the cloud thrust in his si.
14. 19 the angel thrust in his sickle into the ea.

3. *To push or drive out,* ἐξωθέω *exōtheō.*
Acts 27. 39 if it were possible, to thrust in the ship

4. *To send, put forth,* πέμπω *pempō.*
Rev. 14. 15 Thrust in thy sickle, and reap: for the
14. 18 Thrust in thy sharp sickle, and gather

THRUST away, down, out, through, together, to be —

1. *To be cast out,* גָּרַשׁ *garash,* 4.
Exod12. 39 they were thrust out of Egypt, and could

2. *To be pierced through,* דָּקַר *daqar,* 2.
Isa. 13. 15 Every one that is found shall be thrust t

3. *To be pierced through,* דָּקַר *daqar,* 4.
Jer. 51. 4 (they that are) thrust through in her st.

4. *To close, press, be closed,* זוּר *zur.*
Judg. 6. 38 he rose up early on the morrow, and thr.

5. *To be thrust through,* טָעַן *taan,* 4.
Isa. 14. 19 are slain, thrust through with a sword

6. *To be driven away,* נָדַד *nadad,* 6.
2 Sa. 23. 6 all of them as thorns thrust away, beca.

7. *To cause to come down,* καταβιβάζω *katabibazō.*
Luke10. 15 thou, Capernaum..shalt be thrust down

8. *To shoot through with an arrow,* κατατοξεύω.
Heb. 12. 20 [it shall be stoned, or thrust through with]

THUMB —

1. *Thumb, great toe,* בֹּהֶן *bohen.*
Exod29. 20 upon the thumb of their right hand, and
Lev. 8. 23 upon the thumb of his right hand, and up.
8. 24 and upon the thumbs of their right hands
14. 14, 17, 25, 28 upon the thumb of his right ha.

2. *Thumb (of the hand),* בֹּהֶן יָד *bohen yad.*
Judg 1. 6 and cut off his thumbs and his great toes
1. 7 their thumbs and their great toes cut

THUM'-MIM, תֻּמִּים *tummim, perfection.*
Symbolic figures in the high priest's breastplate.
Exod 28. 30 thou shalt put in the breastplate..the T.
Lev. 8. 8 also he put in the breastplate..the T.
Deut 33. 8 (Let) thy T. and thy Urim (be) with thy h.
Ezra 2. 63 stood up a priest with Urim and with T.
Neh. 7. 65 stood (up) a priest with Urim and T.

THUNDER (bolts), thundering —

1. *Voice,* קוֹל *qol.*
Exod 9. 23 LORD sent thunder and hail, and the fire
9. 28 there be no (more) mighty thunderings
9. 29 the thunder shall cease, neither shall th.
9. 33 the thunders and hail ceased, and the ra.
9. 34 and the hail and the thunders were ceas.
19. 16 there were thunders and lightnings, and
20. 18 the people saw the thunderings, and the
1 Sa. 7. 10 the LORD thundered with a great thunder
12. 17 he shall send thunder and rain; that ye
12. 18 the LORD sent thunder and rain that day
Job 28. 26 and a way for the lightning of the thund.
38. 25 or a way for the lightning of thunder

2. *Roaring, thunder,* רַעַם *raam.*
Job 26. 14 the thunder of his power who can unders
39. 25 the thunder of the captains, and the sho.
Psa. 77. 18 The voice of thy thunder (was) in the he.
81. 7 answered thee in the secret place of thu.
104. 7 at the voice of thy thunder they hasted
Isa. 29. 6 visited of the LORD of hosts with thunder

3. *Thunder, a waving mane,* רַעְמָה *ramah.*
Job 39. 19 hast thou clothed his neck with thunder

4. *Burning heat, coals, arrow,* רֶשֶׁף *resheph.*
Psa. 78. 48 He gave..their flocks to hot thunderbolts

5. *Thunder,* βροντή *brontē.*
Mark 3. 17 Boanerges, which is, The sons of thunder
Rev. 4. 5 out of the throne proceeded..thunderings
6. 1 I heard, as it were the noise of thunder
8. 5 voices, and thunderings, and lightnings
10. 3 when he had cried, seven thunders utter.
10. 4 when the seven thunders had uttered their
10. 4 those things which the seven thunders ut.
11. 19 lightnings, and voices, and thunderings
14. 2 I heard..as the voice of a great thunder
16. 18 there were voices, and thunders, and lig.
19. 6 as the voice of mighty thunderings, say.

THUNDER, to —

1. *To cause to roar, thunder,* רַעַם *raam,* 5.
1 Sa. 2. 10 out of heaven shall he thunder upon them
7. 10 but the LORD thundered with a great th.
2 Sa. 22. 14 The LORD thundered from heaven, and the
Job 37. 4 he thundereth with the voice of his excel.
37. 5 God thundereth marvellously with his vo.
40. 9 canst thou thunder with a voice like him
Psa. 18. 13 The LORD also thundered in the heavens
29. 3 the God of glory thundereth: the LORD

2. *Thunder came,* γέγονε βροντή *gegone brontē.*
John 12. 29 The people..said that it thundered

THUS —

1. *These,* אֵלֶּה *eleh.*
Num 10. 28 Thus (were) the journeyings of the child.

2. *This,* דְּנָה *denah.*
Ezra 5. 7 wherein was written thus; Unto Darius
Jer. 10. 11 Thus shall ye say unto them, The gods th.

3. *This,* זֹאת *zoth.*
Exod14. 11 wherefore hast thou dealt thus with us

4. *With this,* בְּזֹאת *be-zoth.*
Lev. 16. 3 Thus shall Aaron come into the holy (pl.)

5. *This,* זֶה *zeh.*
Gen. 25. 22 why (am) I thus? And she went to enq.

6. *Thus,* כֹּה *koh.*
Gen. 24. 30 saying, Thus spake the man unto me
Isa. 7. 7 Thus saith the Lord GOD, It shall not sta.

7. *As thus, thus,* כָּכָה *kakah.*
Exod12. 11 thus shall ye eat it..your loins girded

8. *Thus,* כְּמוֹ *kemo.*
Psa. 73. 15 If I say, I will speak thus: behold, I sh.

9. *So,* כֵּן *ken.*
Gen. 42. 25 Joseph commanded..thus did he unto th.

10. *Therefore,* עַל־כֵּן *al ken.*
Jer. 38. 4 for thus he weakeneth the hands of the

11. *So, thus,* כֵּן *ken.*
Ezra 5. 3 said thus unto them, Who hath comman.
6. 2 and therein (was) a record thus written
Dan. 2. 24 he went and said thus unto him, Destroy
2. 25 said thus unto him, I have found a man
4. 14 He cried aloud, and said thus, Hew down
6. 6 said thus unto him, King Darius, live for
7. 5 said thus unto it, Arise, devour much flesh
7. 23 Thus he said, The fourth beast shall be the

12. *Thus, so,* כְּנֵמָא *kenema.*
Ezra 5. 9 said unto them thus, Who commanded you
5. 11 thus they returned us answer, saying, We

13. *This thing,* הַדָּבָר הַזֶּה *had-dabar haz-zeh.*
Judg. 8. 1 Why hast thou served us thus, that thou

14. *According to these things,* κατὰ ταῦτα *kata ta.*
Luke 17. 30 Even thus shall it be in the day when the

15. *He she, it, thus,* ὅδε, τάδε *hode, tade.*
Acts 21. 11 Thus saith the Holy Ghost, So shall the

16. *Thus,* οὕτω, οὕτως *houtō, houtōs.*
Matt. 2. 5 In Bethlehem..for thus it is written by the
3. 15 for thus it becometh us to fulfil all right.
26. 54 scriptures be fulfilled, that thus it must
Mark 2. 7 Why doth this (man) thus speak blasph.?
Luke 1. 25 Thus hath the Lord dealt with me in the
2. 48 Son, why hast thou thus dealt with us?
19. 31 thus shall ye say unto him, Because the
24. 46 Thus it is written,[and thus it behoved] Ch.
John 4. 6 being wearied with (his) journey, sat thus
11. 48 If we let him thus alone, all (men) will be.
Rom. 9. 20 say..Why hast thou made me thus?
1 Co. 14. 25 [thus] are the secrets of his heart made ma.
Heb. 6. 9 accompany salvation, though we thus sp.
9. 6 Now when these things were thus ordained
Rev. 9. 17 thus I saw the horses in the vision, and
18. 21 Thus with violence shall that great city

17. *These things,* ταῦτα *tauta.*
Luke 9. 34 While he thus spake, there came a cloud
11. 45 Master, thus saying thou reproachest us
18. 11 Pharisee stood and prayed thus with him.
19. 28 when he had thus spoken, he went before
23. 46 and having said thus, he gave up the gh.
24. 36 as they thus spake, Jesus himself stood
John 9. 6 When he had thus spoken, he spat on the
11. 43 when he had thus spoken, he cried with
13. 21 When Jesus had thus said, he was troub.
18. 22 when he had thus spoken, one of the offi
20. 14 when she had thus said, she turned hers.
Acts 19. 41 when he had thus spoken, he dismissed
20. 36 when he had thus spoken, he kneeled do.
26. 24 as he thus spake for himself, Festus said
26. 30 [when he had thus spoken, the king rose]
27. 35 when he had thus spoken, he took bread
Rev. 16. 5 shalt be, because thou hast judged thus

18. *This,* τοῦτο *touto.*
Luke 24. 40 when he had thus spoken, he showed them
2 Co. 1. 17 When I therefore was thus minded, did
5. 14 because we thus judge, that if one died
Phil. 3. 15 as many as be perfect, be thus minded

19. *Of this,* τούτου *toutou.*
Luke 22. 51 Jesus answered and said, Suffer ye thus

THY (friends) —

1. *To thine own,* σεαυτῷ (*dat.*) *seautō.*
Acts 9. 34 arise, and make thy bed. And he arose

2. *To thee,* σοί *soi.*
Mark 5. 9 he asked him, What (is) thy name? And
Luke 8. 30 What is thy name? And he said, Legion
Heb. 11. 18 said, That in Isaac shall thy seed be cal.

3. *Thy, thine,* σός *sos.*
Matt. 7. 22 in thy name?..in thy name..in thy name
See also 13. 27; 24. 3; Mark 2. 18; 5. 19; 6. 30; John 4. 42; 17. 17; Acts 24. 2, 4; 1 Co. 8. 11; 14. 16; Phm. 14.

4. *Of thee, thy, thine,* σοῦ *sou.*
Matt. 1. 20 fear not to take unto thee Mary thy wife
See also 4. 6, 7, 10; 5. 23, 23, 24, 24, 24, 29, 29, 29, 30, 30, 30, 36, 39, 40, 43; 6. 3, 3, 4, 6, 6, 6, 6, 9, 10, 10, 17, 18, 18, 22, 23; 7. 3, 4, 5; 9. 2, 6, 14, 18, 22; 11. 10, 10, 26; 12. 2, 37, 37, 47, 47; 15. 2, [4,] 28; 17. 16; 18. 8, 8, 15, 15, 33; 19. [19,] 19; 20. [21,] 21; 21. 5; 22. 37, 37, 37, 37, 39, 44; 23. 37; 25. 21, 23, 25; 26. 42, 52, 73; Mark 1. 2. etc. etc.

THY-A-TI'-RA, Θυάτειρα.
A city of Lydia in Asia Minor, near the river Lycus, twenty seven miles N.W. of Sardis, and fifty six N.E. of Smyrna; once called *Pelopia* and *Euhippia*, now *Ak-Hissar* ("white castle"); it was famous for the art of dying purple; in A.D. 69 Christ sent a message to it through the apostle John, recorded in Rev. ii. 18–24; in 366 Valeus the Eastern emperor gained a victory over Procopius here.

Acts 16. 14 woman..seller of purple, of the city of T.
Rev. 1. 11 write in a book, and send..unto T., and
2. 18 unto the angel of the church in T. write
2. 24 unto you I say, and unto the rest in T.

THYINE (wood) —
Thya or thyine tree, θύϊνος *thuinos.*
Rev. 18. 12 The merchandise of..all thyine wood, and

THYSELF —

1. *Thy soul,* נַפְשְׁךָ *naphshek.*
Esth. 4. 13 Think not with thyself that thou shalt es.

2. *Oneself,* ἑαυτόν *heauton.*
Rom. 13. 9 Thou shalt love thy neighbour as [thyself]
Gal. 5. 14 Thou shalt love thy neighbour as [thyself]

3. *Of one's self,* ἑαυτοῦ *heautou.*
John 18. 34 Sayest thou this thing [of thyself], or did o.
Rom 13. 9 Thou shalt love thy neighbour as thyself
Gal. 5. 14 Thou shalt love thy neighbour as thyself

4. *Of own self,* σεαυτοῦ, σαυτοῦ *seautou, sautou.*
Matt. 4. 6 If thou be the Son of God, cast thyself do.
See also 8. 4; 19. 19; 22. [39]; 27. 40; Mark 1. 44; 12. 31; Luke 4. 9, 23; 5. 14; 10. 27; 23. 37, 39; John 1. 22; 7. 4; 8. 13, 53; 10. 33; 14. 22; 21. 18; Acts 16. 28; 26. 1; Rom. 2. 1, 5, 19, 21; 14. 22; Gal. 6. 1; 1 Ti. 4. 7, 16, 16; 5. 22; 2 Ti. 2. 15; Titus 2. 7; Jas. 2. 8.

TIBERIAS, Τιβεριάς.
A city on the W. side of the Sea of Galilee or Lake of Tiberias; it was built by Herod Antipas (who killed John the Baptist), and named by him in honour of the emperor Tiberius. It is noted for its hot springs; was destroyed by Vespasian, but quickly recovering it became the seat of a Rabbinical school till the fourth century, where the *Mishna*, the *Jerusalem Talmud*, and the *Masora* were composed. It is now called *Tabarieh* and was almost destroyed by an earthquake in A.D. 1837; it is, after Jerusalem, Hebron, and Safed, the fourth most holy city in Jewish estimation. According to Jerome, it is the Chinnereth of the Old Testament.

John 6. 1 sea of Galilee, which is (the sea) of T.
6. 23 there came other boats from T., nigh unto
21. 1 Jesus showed himself..at the sea of T.

TI-BE-RI'-US, Τιβέριος.
The stepson of Augustus, and third emperor of Rome, A.D. 14–37; surnamed Claudius Nero, and born B.C. 42.
Luke 3. 1 in the fifteenth year of the reign of T. Cæ.

TIB'-HATH, טִבְחַת *extension.*
A city in Aram Zobah which David spoiled along with Chun; comp. *Thaebata* in the N.W. of Mesopotamia, and *Thebetha*, S. of Nisibis.
1 Ch. 18. 8 Likewise from T., and from Chun, cities

TIB'-NI, תִּבְנִי *intelligent.*
The son of Ginath, whom some wished to be king after Zimri. B.C. 925.
1 Ki. 16. 21 half of the people followed T. the son of
16. 22 against the people that followed T... so T.

TID'-AL, תִּדְעָל *splendour, renown.*
A king of Goyim, confederate with Chedorlaomer, Amraphel, and Arioch, who invaded the cities of the plain in the days of Abraham. B.C. 1913.
Gen. 14. 1 Chedorlaomer king of Elam, and T. king
14. 9 T. king of nations, and Amraphel king of

TIDE —
Time, עֵת *eth.*
Josh. 8. 29 the king..he hanged on a tree until even.
2 Sa. 11. 2 it came to pass in an evening tide, that D.
Isa. 17. 14 behold at evening tide trouble; (and) be.
Jer. 20. 16 let him hear..the shouting at noon tide

TIDINGS, (reward for) —

1. *Tidings, good news, reward for,* בְּשׂוֹרָה *besorah.*
2 Sa. 4. 10 have given him a reward for his tidings
18. 20 Thou shalt not bear him tidings, but thou shalt
18. 22 seeing that thou hast no tidings ready?
18. 25 If he be alone, (there is) tidings in his mo.
18. 27 (is) a good man, and cometh with good ti.
2 Ki. 7. 9 this day (is) a day of good tidings, and we

2. *Word, matter, thing,* דָּבָר *dabar.*
Exod 33. 4 when the people heard these evil tidings
1 Sa. 11. 4 told the tidings in the ears of the people
11. 5 they told him the tidings of the men of Ja.
11. 6 came upon Saul when he heard those tid.

3. *What is heard, report, tidings,* שְׁמוּעָה *shemuah.*
1 Sa. 4. 19 when she heard the tidings that the ark
2 Sa. 4. 4 He was five years old when the tidings ca.
13. 30 tidings came to David, saying, Absalom
1 Ki. 2. 28 Then tidings came to Joab: for Joab had
Psa. 112. 7 He shall not be afraid of evil tidings: his
Jer. 49. 23 they have heard evil tidings: they are fa.
Eze. 21. 7 thou shalt answer, For the tidings, beca.
Dan. 11. 44 tidings out of the east and out of the no.

4. *Hearing, report, tidings,* שֵׁמַע *shema.*
Gen. 29. 13 when Laban heard the tidings of Jacob his
Jer. 37. 5 when the Chaldeans ..heard tidings of th.

5. *To let (good) tidings be proclaimed,* בָּשַׂר *basar,* 7.
2 Sa. 18. 31 Tidings, my lord the king: for the LORD

6. *A word, matter, thing,* λόγος *logos.*
Acts 11. 22 tidings of these things came unto the ears

7. *A saying, declaration, information,* φάσις *phasis.*
Acts 21. 31 tidings came unto the chief captain of the

TIDINGS, to bear, bring, carry —
To announce (good) tidings, בָּשַׂר *basar,* 3.
2 Sa. 18. 19 Let me now run and bear the king tidings
18. 20 thou shalt bear no tidings, because the
18. 20 but thou shalt bear tidings another day
18. 26 the king said, He also bringeth tidings
1 Ki. 1. 42 Come in; for thou..bringest good tidin.
1 Ch. 10. 9 to carry tidings unto their idols, and to
Jer. 20. 15 Cursed (be) the man who brought tidings

TIDINGS, to preach or bring good —
To announce (good) tidings, בָּשַׂר *basar,* 3.
2 Sa. 4. 10 thinking to have brought good tidings
Isa. 40. 9 O Zion, that bringest good tidings, get
40. 9 O Jerusalem, that bringest good tidings
41. 27 I will give..one that bringeth good tidi.
52. 7 the feet of him that bringeth good tidings
52. 7 that bringeth good tidings of good, that
61. 1 hath anointed me to preach good tidings
Nah. 1. 15 the feet of him that bringeth good tidings

TIE, to —

1. *To bind, direct,* אָסַר *asar.*
1 Sa. 6. 7 tie the kine to the cart, and bring their
6. 10 tied them to the cart, and shut up their
2 Ki. 7. 10 but horses tied, and asses tied, and the

2. *To give,* נָתַן *nathan.*
Exod 39. 31 they tied unto it a lace of blue, to fasten

3. *To tie, bind,* עָנַד *anad.*
Prov. 6. 21 Bind them..(and) tie them about thy ne.

4. *To tie, bind, oblige,* δέω *deō.*
Matt 21. 2 ye shall find an ass tied, and a colt with
Mark 11. 2 ye shall find a colt tied, whereon never
11. 4 found the colt tied by the door without
Luke 19. 30 ye shall find a colt tied, whereon yet ne.

TIG-LATH PIL-E'-SER, or **TIL-GATH PIL-NE'-SER,** תִּגְלַת פִּלְאֶסֶר or תִּלְגַת פִּלְנְאֶסֶר.
An Assyrian king who invaded Naphtali in the days of Pekah king of Israel He succeeded Pul, or more probably is Pul, conquered the N. of Palestine and Damascus, and carried off the people to Kir. B.C. 742.
2 Ki. 15. 29 In the days of Pekah..came T. king of A.
16. 7 Ahaz sent messengers to T. king of Assyr.
16. 10 Ahaz went to Damascus to meet T. king
1 Ch. 5. 6 Beerah his son, whom T., king of Assyria
5. 26 God..stirred up..the spirit of T. king of
2 Ch. 28. 20 T. king of Assyria came unto him, and

TIK'-VAH, TIK'-VATH, תִּקְוָה, תָּוקְהַת *strength.*
1. Father of Shallum, husband of Huldah the prophetess in the days of Josiah. B.C. 641.
2 Ki. 22. 14 Huldah..the wife of Shallum the son of T.
2 Ch. 34. 22 Huldah..the wife of Shallum the son of T.
2. Father of Jahaziah who was employed in taking account of those that had married strange wives. B.C. 445.
Ezra 10. 15 Jonathan..and Jahaziah the son of T.

TILE, tiling —

1. *Brick,* לְבֵנָה *lebenah.*
Eze. 4. 1 Thou also, son of man, take thee a tile

2. *Potter's clay, a tile,* κέραμος *keramos.*
Luke 5. 19 let him down through the tiling with (his)

TILL, until (the time) —

1. *Till, up to, during,* עַד *ad.*
Gen. 3. 19 shalt thou eat bread, till thou return unto
8. 5 the waters decreased continually until the
Ezra 4. 21 until (another) commandment shall be
5. 16 since that time even until now hath it be.
Dan. 2. 9 to speak before me, till the time be chan.
2. 34 Thou sawest till that a stone was cut out
4. 23 (let) his portion (be) with the beasts..till
4. 25 till thou know that the Most High ruleth
4. 32 until thou know that the Most High ruleth
4. 33 till his hairs were grown like eagles' (fea.)
5. 21 till he knew that the most high God ruled
6. 14 he laboured till the going down of the sun
7. 4 I beheld till the wings thereof were pluc.
7. 9 I beheld till the thrones were cast down
7. 11 I beheld (even) till the beast was slain
7. 22 Until the Ancient of days came, and jud.
7. 25 shall be given into his hand until a time

2. *Till that,* עַד כִּי *ad ki.*
Gen. 49. 10 from between his feet, until Shiloh come
2 Sa. 23. 10 smote the Philistines, until his hand was
2 Ch. 26. 15 he was marvellously helped, till he was

3. *Before,* לִפְנֵי *li-phene.*
2 Sa. 3. 35 if I taste bread, or ought else, till the sun

4. *Except, but when,* כִּי אִם *ki im.*
Ruth 3. 18 until thou know how the matter will fall

5. *Till that,* עַד אֲשֶׁר *ad asher.*
Gen. 27. 44 tarry..until thy brother's fury turn away
28. 15 for I will not leave thee, until I have do.

6. *Till, up to, within,* ἄχρι, ἄχρις *achri, achris.*
Matt 24. 38 until the day that Noe entered into the
See also Luke 1. 20; 17. 25; 21. 24; Acts 1. 2; 3. 21; 7. 18; 20. 11; 23. 1; Rom. 5. 13; 8. 22; 11. 25; 1 Co. 11. 26; 15. 25; 2 Co. 3. 14; Gal. 3. 19; 4. 2, 19; Phil. 1. 5, 6; Rev. 2. 25; 7. [3]; 15. 8; 17. 17; 20. 3.

7. *Till, up to,* ἄχρις οὗ *achris hou.*
Acts 7. 18; Ro. 11. 35; 1 Co. 11. 26; Ga. 3. 19; Re. 7. 3

8. *With a view to,* εἰς *eis.*
Eph. 1. 14 Which is the earnest..until the redempt.
Phil. 1. 10 sincere and without offence till the day

9. *Unto, up to,* ἕως *heōs.*
Matt. 1. 17 from David until the carrying away into
See also v. 25; 2. 9, 13, 15; 5. 18, 18, 26; 10. 11, 23; 11. 12, 13; 12. 20; 13. 33; 16. 28; 17. 9; 18. 21, 22, 22, [30, 34]; 22. 44; 23. 39; 24. 34, 39; 26. 29; 27. 64; Mark 6. 10; 9. 1; 12. 36; 14. 25; 15. 33; Luke 1. 80; 9. 27; 12. 50; 59; 13. 8, 21, 35; 15. 4, 8; 16. 16; 17. 8; 19. [13]; 20. 43; 21. 32; 22. 16; Luke 22. 18; 23. 44; 24. 49; John 2. 10; 9. 18; 13. 38; 21. 22, 23; Acts 2. 35; 8. 40; 13. 20; 21. 5; 26; 23. 12, 14, 21; 25. 21; 28. 23; 1 Co. 4. 5; 16. 8; 2 Th. 2. 7; 1 Ti. 4. 13; Heb. 1. 13; 10. 13; Jas. 5. 7; 2 Pe. 1. 19; 1 Jo. 2. 9; Rev. 6. 11; 20. 5.

10. *Unto, until,* μέχρι, μέχρις *mechri, mechris.*
Matt. 11. 23 it would have remained until this day
13. 30 Let both grow together until the harvest
28. 15 reported among the Jews until this day
Mark 13. 30 this generation shall not pass, till all th.
Acts 10. 30 Four days ago I was fasting until this ho.
20. 7 and continued his speech until midnight
Eph. 4. 13 Till we all come in the unity of the faith
1 Ti. 6. 14 until the appearing of our Lord Jesus C.
Heb. 9. 10 imposed (on them) until the time of ref.

11. *Except when,* εἰ μὴ ὅταν *ei mē hotan.*
Mark 9. 9 tell no man..till the Son of man were ri.

TILL, be tilled, to —
1. *To do service, labour, work,* עָבַד *abad.*
Gen. 2. 5 and (there was) not a man to till the gro.
3. 23 to till the ground from whence he was
4. 12 When thou tillest the ground, it shall not
2 Sa. 9. 10 thy servants, shall till the land for him
Prov 12. 11 He that tilleth his land shall be satisfied
28. 19 He that tilleth his land shall have plenty
Jer. 27. 11 and they shall till it, and dwell therein
2. *To be served, worked,* עָבַד *abad,* 2.
Eze. 36. 9 I will turn unto you, and ye shall be till.
36. 34 the desolate land shall be tilled, whereas

TILLAGE, tiller —
1. *Tillage, ground broken up,* נִיר *nir.*
Prov 13. 23 Much food (is in) the tillage of the poor
2. *To serve, labour, work,* עָבַד *abad.*
Gen. 4. 2 sheep, but Cain was a tiller of the ground
3. *Service, work,* עֲבֹדָה *abodah.*
1 Ch. 27. 26 that did the work of the field for tillage
Neh. 10. 37 have the tithes in all the cities of our til.

TI'-LON, תִּילוֹן ,תּוֹלוֹן *mockery, scorn.*
A son of Shimon, descended from Judah through Caleb son of Jephunneh. B.C. 1400.
1 Ch. 4. 20 the sons of Shimon (were) Amnon .. and T.

TIMBER —
1. *Wood, tree, timber,* אָע *a.*
Ezra 5. 8 timber is laid in the walls, and this work
6. 4 of great stones, and a row of new timber
6. 11 let timber be pulled down from his house
2. *Wood, tree, timber,* עֵץ *ets.*
Exod 31. 5 carving of timber, to work in all manner
Lev. 14. 45 the timber thereof, and all the morter of
1 Ki. 5. 6 any that can skill to hew timber like unto
5. 8 concerning timber of cedar, and..timber
5. 18 they prepared timber and stones to build
6. 10 they rested on the house with timber of c.
15. 22 the stones of Ramah, and the timber the.
2 Ki. 12. 12 to buy timber and hewed stone to repair
22. 6 to buy timber and hewn stone to repair
1 Ch. 14. 1 timber of cedars, with masons and carpen.
22. 14 timber also and stone have I prepared
22. 15 hewers and workers of stone and timber
2 Ch. 2. 8 thy servants can skill to cut timber in L.
2. 9 to prepare me timber in abundance: for
2. 10 I will give to..the hewers that cut timb.
2. 14 in timber, in purple, in blue, and in fine
16. 6 they carried away..the timber thereof
34. 11 to buy hewn stone, and timber for coupl.
Neh. 2. 8 he may give me timber to make beams for
Eze. 26. 12 they shall lay thy stones and thy timber
Hab. 2. 11 the beam out of the timber shall answer
Zech. 5. 4 shall consume it with the timber thereof

TIMBREL, (to play with) —
1. *Tabret, timbrel,* תֹּף *toph.*
Exod 15. 20 took a timbrel..with timbrels and with
Judg 11. 34 his daughter came out to meet him with t.
2 Sa. 6. 5 on timbrels, and on cornets, and on cym.
1 Ch. 13. 8 with timbrels, and with cymbals, and with
Job 21. 12 They take the timbrel and harp, and rej.
Psa. 81. 2 bring hither the timbrel, the pleasant ha.
149. 3 let them sing..with the timbrel and harp
150. 4 Praise him with the timbrel and dance
2. *To play on a timbrel or tabret,* תָּפַף *taphaph.*
Psa. 68. 25 among..the damsels playing with timb.

TIME, times, (due, this, at that) —
1. *Time, season,* זְמָן *zeman.*
Ezra 5. 3 At the same time came to them Tatnai
Neh. 2. 6 it pleased the king..and I set him a time
Esth. 9. 27 keep..according to their..time, every
9. 31 confirm these days of Purim in their tim.
Dan. 2. 16 desired..that he would give him time
3. 7 at that time, when all the people heard
3. 8 at that time certain Chaldeans came near
4. 36 At the same time my reason returned un.
6. 10 he kneeled upon his knees three times a day
6. 13 but maketh his petition three times a day
7. 22 the time came that the saints possessed
7. 25 he shall..think to change times and laws
2. *Hands,* יָדוֹת *[yad.]*
Gen. 43. 34 five times ; Dan. 1. 20, ten times
3. *Day, days,* יוֹם ,יָמִים *yom, yamim.*
Gen. 4. 3 in process of time it came to pass that C.
26. 8 when he had been there a long time, that
30. 33 my righteousness answer for me in time
38. 12 in process of time the daughter of Shuah
39. 11 it came to pass about this time, that (Jo.)
47. 29 time drew nigh that Israel must die, and
Exod 2. 23 it came to pass in process of time, that the
Num 13. 20 Now the time (was) the time of the first
20. 15 and we have dwelt in Egypt a long time
Num 32. 10 LORD'S anger was kindled the same time
Deut 10. 10 stayed..according to the first time, forty
20. 19 When thou shalt besiege a city a long ti.
Josh. 3. 15 overfloweth all his banks all the time of
11. 18 Joshua made war a long time with all th.
23. 1 a long time after that the LORD had given
Judg 14. 8 after a time he returned to take her, and
15. 1 it came to pass..in the time of wheat ha.
18. 31 all the time that the house of God was in
20. 15 were numbered at that time out of the ci.
1 Sa. 1. 4 when the time was that Elkanah offered
1. 20 when the time was come about after Ha.
3. 2 it came to pass at that time, when Eli (w.)
7. 2 the time was long; for it was twenty yea.
9. 13 get you up; for about this time ye shall
14. 18 the ark of God was at that time with the
18. 10 played with his hand, as at other times
2 Sa. 7. 6 since the time that I brought up the chil.
7. 11 since the time that I commanded judges
14. 2 be as a woman that had a long time mou.
23. 20 slew a lion in the midst of a pit in time of
1 Ki. 1. 6 had not displeased him at any time in say.
2. 26 I will not at this time put thee to death
8. 59 the cause of his people Israel at all times
11. 42 the time that Solomon reigned in Jerusa.
2 Ki. 3. 6 went out of Samaria the same time, and
10. 36 the time that Jehu reigned over Israel in
19. 25 (and) of ancient times that I have formed
1 Ch. 17. 10 since the time that I commanded judges
29. 27 the time that he reigned over Israel (was)
2 Ch. 15. 11 they offered unto the LORD the same time
30. 26 since the time of Solomon the son of David
Ezra 4. 15 moved sedition within the same of old ti.
4. 19 this city of old time hath made insurrect.
Neh. 4. 16 it came to pass from that time forth, (th.)
5. 14 from the time that I was appointed to be
9. 32 since the time of the kings of Assyria un.
12. 44 at that time were some appointed over the
Job 15. 32 It shall be accomplished before his time
Psa. 27. 5 in the time of trouble he shall hide me in
41. 1 the LORD will deliver him in time of tro.
44. 1 (what) work thou didst..in the times of
56. 3 What time I am afraid, I will trust in thee
Prov 25. 13 As the cold of snow in the time of harvest
25. 19 Confidence in an unfaithful man in time
31. 25 and she shall rejoice in time to come
Isa. 30. 8 that it may be for the time to come for ev.
37. 26 of ancient times, that I have formed it?
Jer. 39. 10 and gave them vineyards..at the same ti.
Lam. 5. 20 Wherefore..forsake us so long time?
Eze. 38. 10 at the same time shall things come into
38. 17 of whom I have spoken in old time by my
38. 18 it shall come to pass at the same time wh.
4. *An appointed time or season,* מוֹעֵד *moed.*
Exod 34. 18 in the time of the month Abib: for in the
1 Sa. 9. 24 unto this time hath it been kept for thee
Dan. 12. 7 that (it shall be) for a time, times, and
5. *Numbers, times,* מֹנִים *monim.*
Gen. 31. 7 your father..changed my wages ten times
31. 41 and thou hast changed my wages ten times
6. *An appointed time or season,* עִדָּן *iddan.*
Dan. 2. 8 I know..that ye would gain the time, be.
2. 9 to speak before me, till the time be chan.
2. 21 he changeth the times and the seasons, he
3. 5 at what time ye hear the sound of the co.
3. 15 if ye be ready that at what time ye hear
4. 16 changed..and let seven times pass over
4. 23 (let) his portion (be)..till seven times pass
4. 25, 32 seven times shall pass over thee,
7. 12 yet their lives were prolonged for a..time
7. 25 time and times and the dividing of time
7. *Time,* עֵת *eth.*
Gen. 18. 10 return unto thee according to the time of
18. 14 I will return..according to the time of life
21. 22 it came to pass at that time, that Abime.
24. 11 at the time of the evening, (even) the time
29. 7 neither (is it) time that the cattle should
31. 10 it came to pass at the time that the cattle
38. 1 it came to pass at that time, that Judah
38. 27 it came to pass, in the time of her travail
Exod 9. 18 about this time I will cause it to rain a ve.
Lev. 15. 25 many days out of the time of her separat.
16. 2 that he come not at all times into the ho.
Num 22. 4 the son of Zippor (was) king..at that time
23. 23 according to this time it shall be said of
Deut. 1. 9 I spake unto you at that time, saying, I
1. 16 I charged your judges at that time, say.
1. 18 I commanded you at that time all the th.
2. 34 we took all his cities at that time, and
3. 4 we took all his cities at that time, there
3. 8 we took at that time out of the hand of
3. 12 this land, (which) we possessed at that ti.
3. 18 I commanded you at that time, saying
3. 21 I commanded Joshua at that time, saying
3. 23 I besought the LORD at that time, saying
4. 14 the LORD commanded me at that time to
5. 5 between the LORD and you at that time
9. 20 and I prayed for Aaron also the same ti.
10. 1 At that time the LORD said unto me, Hew
10. 8 At that time the LORD separated the tribe
32. 35 their foot shall slide in (due) time: for the
Josh. 5. 2 At that time the LORD said unto Joshua
6. 26 Joshua adjured (them) at that time, say.
10. 27 it came to pass at the time of the going
11 6 to morrow, about this time, will I deliver
11. 10 Joshua at that time turned back, and to.
11. 21 at that time came Joshua, and cut off the
Judg. 3. 29 they slew of Moab at that time about ten
4. 4 a prophetess..judged Israel at that time
Judg 10. 14 let them deliver you in the time of your
11. 26 did ye not recover (them) within that ti.
12. 6 there fell at that time of the Ephraimites
13. 23 nor would as at this time have told us (s.
14. 4 at that time the Philistines had dominion
21. 14 Benjamin came again at that time; and
21. 22 ye did not give unto them at this time
21. 24 Israel departed thence at that time, every
Ruth 2. 14 At meal time come thou hither, and eat
1 Sa. 4. 20 about the time of her death the women
9. 16 about this time, I will send thee a man
18. 19 it came to pass at the time when Merab
20. 12 about tomorrow any time, (or) the third
2 Sa. 11. 1 at the time when kings go forth (to bat.)
24. 15 from the morning even to the time appo.
1 Ki. 8. 65 at that time Solomon held a feast, and all
11. 29 it came to pass at that time when Jerobo.
14. 1 At that time Abijah the son of Jeroboam
15. 23 in the time of his old age he was diseased
19. 2 if I make not..by to morrow about this t.
20 6 I will send..to morrow about this time
2 Ki. 4. 16 About this season, according to the time
4. 17 bare a son..according to the time of life
5. 26 (Is it) a time to receive money, and to re.
7. 1 To morrow, about this time, (shall) a meas.
7. 18 shall be to morrow about this time in the
8. 22 Then Libnah revolted at the same time
10. 6 come..to Jezreel by tomorrow this time
16. 6 At that time Rezin king of Syria recov.
18. 16 At that time did Hezekiah cut off (the go.
20. 12 At that time Berodach-baladan, the son
24. 10 At that time the servants of Nebuchadn.
1 Ch. 9. 25 to come after seven days from time to ti.
12. 22 at (that) time day by day there came to D.
12. 32 men) that had understanding of the times
20. 1 at the time that kings go out (to battle)
21. 28 At that time when David saw that the L.
29. 30 the times that went over him, and over
2 Ch. 7. 8 at the same time Solomon kept the feast
13. 18 were brought under at that time, and the
15. 5 in those times (there was) no peace to him
16. 7 at that time Hanani the seer came to Asa
16. 10 Asa oppressed..the people the same time
18. 34 about the time of the sun going down he
21. 10 The same time (also) did Libnah revolt
25. 27 after the time that Amaziah did turn aw.
28. 16 At that time did king Ahaz send unto the
28. 22 in the time of his distress did he trespass
30. 3 they could not keep it at that time, beca.
35. 17 Israel..kept the passover at that time, and
Ezra 8. 34 all the weight was written at that time
10. 13 (it is) a time of much rain, and we are not
10. 14 let all them..come at appointed times
Neh. 4. 22 at the same time said I unto the people
6. 1 at that time I had not set up the doors
9. 27 in the time of their trouble, when they
9. 28 many times didst thou deliver them acco.
10. 34 to bring (it)..at times appointed year by
13. 21 From that time forth came they no (mo.)
13. 31 for the wood offering, at times appointed
Esth. 1. 13 said to the wise men, which knew the ti.
4. 14 if thou..holdest thy peace at this time
4. 14 art come to the kingdom for (such) a time
8. 9 called at that time in the third month, th
Job 22. 16 Which were cut down out of time, whose
24. 1 seeing times are not hidden from the Al.
38. 23 I have reserved against the time of trou
39. 1 Knowest thou the time when the wild go
39. 2 knowest thou the time when they bring
Psa. 4. 7 more than in the time (that) their corn
9. 9 The LORD also will be..a refuge in times
10. 1 (why) hidest thou (thyself) in times of tr.?
21. 9 make them as a fiery oven in the time of
31. 15 My times (are) in thy hand: deliver me fr.
32. 6 pray unto thee in a time when thou may.
34. 1 I will bless the LORD at all times: his pr.
37. 19 They shall not be ashamed in the evil ti.
37. 39 (he is) their strength in the time of trou.
62. 8 Trust in him at all times; ye people, pour
69. 13 my prayer (is..in) an acceptable time
71. 9 Cast me not off in the time of old age; for
81. 15 their time should have endured for ever
102. 13 for the time to favour her, yea, the set
105. 19 Until the time that his word came: the
106. 3 he that doeth righteousness at all times
119. 20 (it hath) unto thy judgments at all times
119. 126 (It is) time for (thee), LORD, to work, (for)
Prov. 5. 19 let her breasts satisfy thee at all times; and
17. 17 A friend loveth at all times, and a brother
Eccl. 3. 1 a time to every purpose under the heaven
3. 2 A time to be born, and a time to die; a time
3. 2 a time to pluck up (that which is) planted
3. 3 A time to kill, and a time to heal; a time
3. 3 to break down, and a time to build up
3. 4 A time to weep, and a time to laugh
3. 4 a time to mourn, and a time to dance
3. 5 A time to cast away stones, and a time to
3. 5 a time to embrace, and a time to refrain
3. 6 A time to get, and a time to lose; a time
3. 6 to keep, and a time to cast away
3. 7 A time to rend, and a time to sew
3. 7 a time to keep silence, and a time to spe.
3. 8 A time to love, and a time to hate
3. 8 a time of war, and a time of peace
3. 11 hath made every (thing) beautiful in his t.
3. 17 (there is) a time there for every purpose
7. 17 why shouldest thou die before thy time?
8. 5 a wise man's heart discerneth both time
8. 6 to every purpose there is time and judg.
8. 9 (there is) a time wherein one man ruleth
9. 11 but time and chance happeneth to them all
9. 12 man also knoweth not his time: as the fi

Eccl. 9. 12 the sons of men snared in an evil time, wh.
Song 2. 12 the time of the singing (of birds) is come
Isa. 13. 22 her time (is) near to come, and her days
18. 7 In that time shall the present be brought
20. 2 At the same time spake the LORD by Isa.
33. 2 our salvation also in the time of trouble
33. 6 the stability of thy times, (and) strength
39. 1 At that time Merodach-baladan, the son
48. 16 from the time that it was, there (am) I: and
49. 8 In an acceptable time have I heard thee
60. 22 I the LORD will hasten it in his time
Jer. 2. 27 in the time of their trouble they will say
2. 28 if they can save thee in the time of thy tr.
3. 17 At that time they shall call Jerusalem the
4. 11 At that time shall it be said to this people
6. 15 at the time (that) I visit them they shall
8. 1 At that time, saith the LORD, they shall
8. 7 the crane and the swallow observe the ti.
8. 12 in the time of their visitation they shall
8. 15 for a time of health, and behold trouble
10. 15 in the time of their visitation they shall
11. 12 shall not save them at all in the time of
11. 14 I will not hear (them) in the time that th.
14. 8 the saviour thereof in time of trouble, why
14. 19 for the time of healing, and behold trouble
15. 11 in the time of evil, and in the time of affl.
18. 23 deal (thus) with them in the time of thine
27. 7 shall serve him..until the very time of his
30. 7 it (is) even the time of Jacob's trouble
31. 1 At the same time, saith the LORD, will I
33. 15 at that time, will I cause the branch of ri.
46. 21 calamity was come..(and) the time of th.
49. 8 I will bring the calamity..the time (that)
50. 4 in that time, saith the LORD, the children
50. 16 that handleth the sickle in the time of ha.
50. 20 in that time, saith the LORD, the iniquity
50. 27 their day is come, the time of their visit.
50. 31 thy day is come, the time (that) I will vi.
51. 6 this (is) the time of the LORD'S vengeance
51. 18 in the time of their visitation they shall
51 33 like a threshing floor, (it is) time to thresh
51. 33 and the time of her harvest shall come
Eze. 4. 10 twenty shekels a day: from time to time
4. 11 from time to time shalt thou drink
7. 7 the time is come, the day of trouble (is)
7. 12 The time is come, the day draweth near
12. 27 he prophesieth of the times (that are) far
16. 8 thy time (was) the time of love; and I sp.
16. 57 at the time of (thy) reproach of the daug.
22. 3 sheddeth blood..that her time may come
27. 34 In the time (when) thou shalt be broken
30. 3 a cloudy day; it shall be the time of the
35. 5 in the time of their calamity, in the time
Dan. 8. 17 for at the time of the end (shall be) the vi.
9. 21 touched me about the time of the evening
9. 25 street shall be built..in troublous times
11. 6 and he that strengthened her in (these) ti.
11. 14 in those times there shall many stand up
11. 24 shall forecast his devices..for a time
11. 35 to make..white. to the time of the end
11. 40 at the time of the end shall the king of
12. 1 at that time shall Michael stand up, the
12. 1 there shall be a time of trouble, such as
12. 1 to that same time: and at that time thy
12. 4 seal the book, (even) to the time of the end
12. 9 closed up and sealed till the time of the
12. 11 from the time (that) the daily (sacrifice)
Hos. 2. 9 take away my corn in the time thereof
10. 12 (it is) time to seek the LORD, till he come
Joel 3. 1 in that time, when I shall bring again the
Amos 5. 13 silence in that time..it (is) an evil time
Mic. 2. 3 neither shall ye go haughtily: for this ti.
3. 4 hide his face from them at that time, as
5. 3 until the time (that) she which travaileth
Zeph. 1. 12 it shall come to pass at that time, (that) I
3. 19 at that time I will undo all that afflict
3. 20 At that time will I bring you (again), even
3. 20 in the time that I gather you: for I will
Hag. 1. 2 The time is not come, the time that the
1. 4 (Is it) time for you, O ye, to dwell in your
Zech. 10. 1 Ask ye of the LORD rain in the time of
14. 7 it shall come to pass, (that) at evening ti.

8. *Beat, step,* פַּעַם *paam.*
Gen. 33. 3 bowed himself to the ground seven times
Exod 8. 32 Pharaoh hardened his heart at this time
9. 14 I will at this time send all my plagues up.
23. 17 Three times in the year all thy males sh.
Lev. 4. 6 sprinkle of the blood seven times before
4. 17 sprinkle (it) seven times before the LORD
8. 11 he sprinkled..upon the altar seven times
14. 7 he shall sprinkle upon him..seven times
14. 16 shall sprinkle of the oil ..seven times bef.
14. 27 shall sprinkle..the oil..seven times before
14. 51 And he shall..sprinkle the house seven ti.
16. 14, 19 sprinkle of the blood..seven times
25. 8 thou shalt number..seven times seven ye.
Num 14. 22 have tempted me now these ten times
19. 4 and sprinkle of her blood..seven times
24. 10 altogether blessed (them) these three times
Deut 1. 11 make you a thousand times so many more
9. 19 the LORD hearkened unto me at that time
10. 10 the LORD hearkened unto me at that time
16. 16 Three times in a year shall all thy males
Josh. 6. 4 ye shall compass the city seven times, and
6. 15 compassed the city..seven times: only on
6. 15 that day they compassed the city seven ti.
6. 16 it came to pass at the seventh time, when
10. 42 their land did Joshua take at one time
Judg 16. 15 thou hast mocked me these three times
1 Sa. 20. 41 fell on his face..and bowed..three times
2 Sa. 17. 7 The counsel..(is) not good at this time

2 Sa. 23. 8 eight hundred, whom he slew at one time
1 Ki. 9. 25 three times in a year did Solomon offer
17. 21 he stretched himself..three times, and
18. 43 And he said, Go again seven times
22. 16 How many times shall I adjure thee that
2 Ki. 4. 35 the child sneezed seven times, and the
5. 10 wash in Jordan seven times, and thy flesh
5. 14 dipped himself seven times in Jordan, ac.
13. 19 shouldest have smitten five or six times
13. 25 three times did Joash beat him, and rec.
1 Ch. 11. 11 three hundred, slain (by him) at one time
21. 3 make his people an hundred times so ma.
2 Ch. 8. 13 on the solemn feasts, three times in the
18. 15 How many times shall I adjure thee that
Neh. 4. 12 they said unto us ten times, From all pl.
6. 4 they sent unto me four times after this
6. 5 Then sent Sanballat..the fifth time with
Job 19. 3 These ten times have ye reproached me, ye
Psa. 106. 43 Many times did he deliver them; but th.

9. *Foot, feet,* רֶגֶל, רְגָלִים *regel,*
Exod 23. 14 Three times thou shalt keep a feast unto
Num 22. 28 thou hast smitten me these three times
22. 32 Wherefore hast thou smitten..three times
22. 33 the ass..turned from me these three times

10. *Number of the days,* מִסְפַּר הַיָּמִים *mispar hay-yamim.*
1 Sa. 27. 7 the time that David dwelt in the country
2 Sa. 2. 11 the time that David was king in Hebron

11. *A generation,* γενεά *genea.*
Acts 14. 16 Who in times past suffered all nations to
15. 21 Moses of old time hath in every city them

12. *A day, period,* ἡμέρα *hēmera.*
Luke 9. 51 when the time was come that he should
21. 37 in the day time he was teaching in the te.
23. 7 who..also was at Jerusalem at that time
Acts 8. 1 at that time there was a great persecution

13. *A fixed time or season,* καιρός *kairos.*
Matt. 8. 29 come hither to torment us before the ti.?
11. 25 At that time Jesus answered and said, I
12. 1 At that time Jesus went on the sabbath
13. 30 in the time of harvest I will say to the re.
14. 1 At that time Herod the tetrarch heard of
16. 3 can ye not (discern) the signs of the times?
21. 34 when the time of the fruit drew near, he
26. 18 My time is at hand; I will keep the pass.
Mark 1. 15 The time is fulfilled, and the kingdom of
10. 30 receive an hundred fold now in this time
11. 13 he found nothing but leaves; for the time
13. 33 Take ye heed..ye know not when the time
Luke 8. 13 no root..and in time of temptation fall
12. 56 how is it that ye do not discern this time?
18. 30 receive manifold more in this present ti.
19. 44 thou knewest not the time of thy visitation
21. 8 the time draweth near: go ye not theref.
21. 24 until the times of the Gentiles be fulfilled
John 7. 6 My time is not yet come: but your time
7. 8 I go not up..for my time is not yet full
Acts 3. 19 when the times of refreshing shall come
7. 20 In which time Moses was born, and was
12. 1 about that time Herod the king stretched
17. 26 hath determined the times before appoin.
19. 23 the same time there arose no small stir ab.
Rom. 3. 26 To declare..at this time his righteousness
8. 18 the sufferings of this present time (are) not
9. 9 At this time will I come, and
11. 5 at this present time also there is a remn.
13. 11 And that, knowing the time, that now (it
1 Co. 4. 5 judge nothing before the time, until the
7. 5 except (it be) with consent for a time, th.
7. 29 the time (is) short: it remaineth, that both
2 Co. 6. 2 I have heard thee in a time accepted, and
6. 2 behold, now (is) the accepted time; behold
8. 14 at this time your abundance (may be a s.)
Gal. 4. 10 Ye observe days, and months, and times
Eph. 1. 10 the dispensation of the fulness of times
2. 12 at that time ye were without Christ, being
5. 16 Redeeming the time, because the days are
Col. 4. 5 Walk in wisdom..redeeming the time
1 Th. 2. 17 being taken from you for a short time in
2 Th. 2. 6 that he might be revealed in his time
1 Ti. 2. 6 a ransom for all, to be testified in due ti.
4. 1 in the latter times some shall depart fr.
6. 15 in his times he shall show, (who is) the bl.
2 Ti. 3. 1 in the last days perilous times shall come
4. 3 the time will come when they will not en.
4. 6 and the time of my departure is at hand
Titus 1. 3 hath in due times manifested his word th.
Heb. 9. 9 Which (was) a figure for the time then pr.
9. 10 imposed (on them) until the time of refor.
1 Pe. 1. 5 ready to be revealed in the last time
1. 11 Searching what, or what manner of time
4. 17 the time (is come) that judgment must be.
Rev. 1. 3 keep those things..for the time (is) at hand
11. 18 thy wrath is come, and the time of the de.
12. 12 he knoweth that he hath but a short time
12. 14 a time, and times, and half a time 22. 10.

14. *Now,* νῦν, Mt. 24. 21; Mr. 13. 19; 1 Co. 16. 12.

15. *Time,* χρόνος *chronos.*
Matt. 2. 7 enquired of them diligently what time the
2. 16 according to the time which he had dilig.
25. 19 After a long time the lord of those serva.
Luke 1. 57 Elisabeth's full time came that she should
4. 5 showed unto him all..in a moment of ti.
8. 27 which had devils long time, and ware no
20. 9 went into a far country for a long time
John 5. 6 knew that he had been now a long time
14. 9 Have I been so long time with you, and
Acts 1. 6 wilt thou at this time restore again the ki.
1. 7 It is not for you to know the times or the

Acts 1. 21 have companied with us all the time that
3. 21 the heaven must receive until the times
7. 17 the time of the promise drew nigh, which
8. 11 because that of long time he had bewitched
13. 18 about the time of forty years suffered he
14. 3 Long time therefore abode they speaking
14. 28 there they abode long time with the dis.
17. 30 the times of this ignorance God winked at
18. 20 they desired (him) to tarry longer time wi.
18. 23 after he had spent some time (there), he
27. 9 when much time was spent, and when sa.
Gal. 4. 4 when the fulness of the time was come
1 Th. 5. 1 of the times and the seasons, brethren, ye
Heb. 4. 7 To day, after so long a time; as it is said
5. 12 when for the time ye ought to be teachers
11. 32 the time would fail me to tell of Gedeon
1 Pe. 1. 17 pass the time of your sojourning (here) in
1. 20 but was manifest in these last times for
4. 2 he no longer should live the rest of (his)t
4. 3 the time past of (our) life may suffice; 5. 6
Jude 18 there should be mockers in the last time
Rev. 10. 6 sware..that there should be time no lon.

16. *An hour, time, season,* ὥρα *hōra.*
Matt. 14. 15 This is a desert place, and the time is now
18. 1 At the same [time] came the disciples unto
Mark 6. 35 This is a desert place, and now the time
Luke 1. 10 were praying without at the time of inc.
14. 17 sent his servant at supper time to say to
John 16. 2 the time cometh, that whosoever killeth
16. 4 that, when the time shall come, ye may
16. 25 the time cometh, when I shall no more
1 Jo. 2. 18 Little children, it is the last time: and as
2. 18 whereby we know that it is the last time
Rev. 14. 15 the time is come for thee to reap; for the
See also About, ancient, appoint, appointed, before, beforetime, beyond, born, beyond, by, come, convenient, day, due, ear ring, endure, fifth, first, former, high, in, long, many, old, past, second, set, seventh, short, sowing, spend, such, that, third, this.

TIME, appointed, set, second, at any —

1. *To go forth,* יָצָא *yatsa* (adv. inf.).
Num 35. 26 if the slayer shall at any time come with

2. *Festival of the new moon,* כֶּסֶה *keseh.*
Psa. 81. 3 in the new moon, in the time appointed

3. *Appointed time,* מוֹעֵד *moed.*
Gen. 17. 21 Sarah shall bear unto thee at this set time
18. 14 At the time appointed I will return unto
21. 2 at the set time of which God had spoken
Exod. 9. 5 the LORD appointed a set time, saying, To
23. 15 in the time appointed of the month Abib
1 Sa. 13. 8 according to the set time that Samuel (had
20. 35 Jonathan went out..at the time appoint.
2 Sa. 20. 5 he tarried longer than the set time which
Psa. 102. 13 yea, the set time, is come
Jer. 8. 7 the stork..knoweth her appointed times
46. 17 Pharaoh..hath passed the time appointed
Dan. 8. 19 for at the time appointed the end (shall
11. 27 yet the end (shall be) at the time appoin.
11. 29 At the time appointed he shall return, and
11. 35 because (it is) yet for a time appointed
Hab. 2. 3 the vision (is) yet for an appointed time

4. *Appointed time,* מוֹעָד *moad.*
Isa. 14. 31 and none..alone in his appointed times

5. *Indefinite time,* עוֹלָם (מִ) *(me-) olam.*
Lev. 25. 32 houses..may the Levites redeem at any ti.
Isa. 42. 14 I have long time holden my peace; I have

6. *Beat, step,* פַּעַם *paam.*
Gen. 43. 10 surely..we had returned this second time
Nah. 1. 9 affliction shall not rise up the second time

7. *Host, warfare, service,* צָבָא *tsaba.* [Dan. 10. 1.]
Job 7. 1 (Is there) not an appointed time to man
14. 14 All the days of my appointed time will I

8. *A second time,* δεύτερον *deuteron.*
John 3. 4 can he enter the second time into his mo.
21. 16 He saith to him again the second time, S.
2 Co. 13. 2 foretell you, as if..present, the second ti.

9. *Of a second time,* ἐκ δευτέρου *ek deuterou.*
Matt 26. 42 He went away again the second time, and
Mark 14. 72 the second time the cock crew. And Pet.
Acts 10. 15 the voice (spake)..again the second time
Heb. 9. 28 unto them..shall he appear the second ti.

10. *At some time or other, once,* ποτέ *pote.*
1 Co. 9. 7 Who goeth a warfare any time at his own
1 Th. 2. 5 neither at any time used we flattering wo.
Heb. 1. 5 unto which..said he at any time, Thou
1. 13 to which of the angels said he at any time
2. 1 lest at any time we should let (them) slip

11. *A time or day appointed before,* προθεσμία.
Gal. 4. 2 under tutors..until the time appointed

12. *Ever yet, at any time,* πώποτε *pōpote.*
John 1. 18 No man hath seen God at any time, the
5. 37 have neither heard his voice at any time
1 Jo. 4. 12 No man hath seen God at any time. If we

TIME of need, of a long, in —

1. *Of old time, anciently,* ἔκπαλαι *ekpalai.*
2 Pe. 2. 3 whose judgment now of a long time ling.

2. *Seasonable, timely, opportune,* εὔκαιρος *eukairos.*
Heb. 4. 16 we may..find grace to help in time of need

TIME, loss of, process of —

1. *From days,* מִיָּמִים *miy-yamim.*
Judg 11. 4 it came to pass in process of time, that
2 Ch. 21. 19 in process of time, after the end of two

2. *Cessation, rest,* שֶׁבֶת *shebeth.*
Exod21. 19 only he shall pay (for) the loss of his time

TIME, to come, old, past —
1. *Behind, backwards,* אָחוֹר *achor.*
Isa. 42. 23 will hearken, and hear for the time to co.

2. *Yesterday, in time past,* אֶתְמוֹל *ethmol.*
1 Sa. 19. 7 he was in his presence, as in times past
2 Sa. 5. 2 in time past, when Saul was king over us

3. *Indefinite time,* עוֹלָם *olam.*
Josh.24. 2 on the other side of the flood in old time
Eccl. 1. 10 it hath been already of old time, which
Eze. 26. 20 bring thee..with the people of old time

4. *Formerly, before,* לְפָנִים *le-phanim.*
1 Ch. 9. 20 Phinehas..the ruler over them in time p.
Deut. 2. 10 The Emims dwelt therein in times past

5. *Yesterday, third day,* תְּמוֹל שִׁלְשׁוֹם *temol shilshom.*
Exod21. 29 if the ox were wont to push..in time past
21. 36 that the ox hath used to push in time past
Deut 4. 42 unawares, and hated him not in times pa.
19. 4 neighbour..whom he hated not in time p.
19. 6 inasmuch as he hated him not in time p.
1 Sa. 19. 7 and he was in his presence, as in times p.
2 Sa. 3. 17 Ye sought for David in times past (to be)
5. 2 in time past, when Saul was king over us
1 Ch. 11. 2 in time past, even when Saul was king, th.

6. *Time before, to morrow,* מָחָר *machar.*
Exod13. 14 when thy son asketh thee in time to come
Deut. 6. 20 when thy son asketh thee in time to come
Josh. 4. 6 children ask (their fathers) in time to co.
4. 21 shall ask their fathers in time to come
22. 24 In time to come your children might sp.
22. 27 not say to our children in time to come
22. 28 or to our generations in time to come

7. *At some time or other, once,* ποτέ *pote.*
Rom11. 30 as ye in times past have not believed God
Gal. 1. 13 ye..heard of my conversation in time past
1. 23 he which persecuted us in times past now
Eph. 2. 2 Wherein in time past ye walked according
2. 3; 2. 11; Phm. 11; 1 Pe. 2. 10; 3. 5; 2 Pe. 1. 21.

8. *What is about to be,* τὸ μέλλον *mellon,* 1 Ti. 6. 19.

9. *Of old,* πάλαι *palai,* Heb. 1. 1.

TIME (or season), for a —
For a season, πρόσκαιρος, Mt. 13. 21 ; Mark 4. 17.

TIME, at which, that, this, what —
1. *Then,* אֱדַיִן *edayin.*
Ezra 5. 16 since that time even until now hath it

2. *Then,* אָז *az.*
1 Ch.20. 4 at which time Sibbechai the Hushathite

3. *Time,* עֵת *eth.*
2 Ch.24. 11 at what time the chest was brought unto
Job 6. 17 What time they wax warm, they vanish
39. 18 What time she lifteth up herself on high

4. *Now,* עַתָּה *attah.*
Isa. 48. 6 showed thee new things from this time
Psa 115. 18 from this time forth and for evermore

5. *Beat, step,* פַּעַם *paam.*
Gen. 29. 34 this time will my husband be joined unto
Exod 9. 27 I have sinned this time: the LORD (is) rig.

TIMES, as at other —
1. *As day by day,* כְּיוֹם בְּיוֹם *ke-yom be-yom.*
1 Sa. 18. 10 D. played with his hand, as at other times

2. *As step by step,* כְּפַעַם בְּפַעַם *ke-phaam be-phaam.*
Num24. 1 he went not, as at other times, to seek
Judg16. 20 I will go out, as at other times before, and
20. 30 and put themselves..as at other times
20. 31 began to smite..as at other times, in the hi.
1 Sa. 3. 10 called as at other times, Samuel, Samuel
20. 25 king sat upon his seat, as at other times

TIMES, two —
Two steps, פַּעֲמַיִם *[paam].*
Gen. 27. 36 for he hath supplanted me these two times

TI-MÆ'-US, Τιμαῖος.
Father of Bartimeus, a blind man who received his sight from Jesus at Jericho.
Mark10. 46 the son of T., sat by the highway side

TIM'-NA, TIM'-NAH, תִּמְנָע, *restraining.*
1. Concubine of Eliphaz son of Esau. B.C. 1700.
Gen. 36. 12 T. was concubine to Eliphaz, Esau's son
2. Daughter of Seir the Horite, and sister of Lotan. B.C. 1700.
Gen. 36. 22 and Hemam; and Lotan's sister (was) T.
1 Ch. 1. 39 and Hemam: and T. (was) Lotan's sister
3. A chief of Edom descended from Esau. B.C. 1500.
Gen. 36. 40 duke T., duke Alvah, duke Jetheth
1 Ch. 1. 51 duke T., duke Aliah, duke Jetheth
4. A son of Eliphaz son of Esau. B.C. 1700.
1 Ch. 1. 36 Gatam, Kenaz, and T., and Amalek

TIM'-NAH, תִּמְנָה *allotment.*
A city in Judah between Ekron and Beth-shemesh; now called *Tibneh.*
Josh 15. 10 the border compassed..and passed on to T.
15. 57 Cain, Gibeah, and T.; ten cities with their
2 Ch.28. 18 The Philistines..had taken..T. with the

TIM'-NATH, תִּמְנָה.
1. A city in Judah, now called *Tibneh,* two miles W. of Beth-shemesh.
Gen. 38. 12 Judah was comforted, and went..to T.
Gen. 38. 13 Behold thy father in law goeth up to T.
38. 14 open place, which (is) by the way to T.
2. A city in Dan, near Philistia. See *Thimnathah.*
Judg14. 1 Samson went..to T., and saw ...in T.
14. 2 I have seen a woman in T. of the daugh.
14. 5 to T., and came to the vineyards of T.

TIM-NATH HE'-RES, תִּמְנַת־חֶרֶס.
The portion allotted to Joshua in Mount Ephraim, N.E. side of the hill of Gaash, now called *Tibneh,* six miles W. of *Jifneh.*
Judg. 2. 9 they buried him..in T., in the mount of

TIM'-NATH SE'-RAH, תִּמְנַת־סֶרַח.
The same as the preceding.
Josh 19. 50 they gave..the city which he asked..T.
24. 30 they buried him..in T., which (is) in mo.

TIMNITE, תִּמְנִי. *An inhabitant of Timnath.*
Judg15. 6 answered, Samson, the son in law of the T.

TI'-MON, Τίμων *honourable.*
One of the seven who were appointed to serve tables in the early church.
Acts 6. 5 Nicanor, and T., and Parmenas, and N.

TI-MO-THE'-US, TI-MO-THY, Τιμόθεος *honoured of God.*
A young man of Lystra, son of Eunice a Jewess, by a Greek father; Paul circumcised him, took him as his companion in travel, and addressed two Epistles to him.
Acts 16. 1 a certain disciple was there, named T.
17. 14 but Silas and T. abode there still
17. 15 receiving a commandment unto..T. for
18. 5 when Silas and T. were come from Mac.
19. 22 So he sent into Macedonia..T. and Eras.
20. 4 and Gaius of Derbe, and T.; and of Asia
Rom16. 21 T. my work fellow, and Lucius..salute you
1 Co. 4. 17 For this cause have I sent unto you T.
16. 10 Now if T. come, see that he may be with
2 Co. 1. 1 Paul..and T. (our) brother, unto the chu.
1. 19 who was preached among you by..T., was
Phil. 1. 1 Paul and T., the servants of Jesus Christ
2. 19 But I trust in the Lord Jesus to send T.
Col. 1. 1 Paul, an apostle of Jesus Christ..and T.
1 Th. 1. 1 Paul, and Silvanus, and T., unto the ch.
3. 2 And sent T., our brother, and minister of
3. 6 when T. came from you unto us, and br.
2 Th. 1. 1 Paul, and Silvanus, and T., unto the chu.
1 Ti. 1. 2 Unto T., (my) own son in the faith: Grace
1. 18 This charge I commit unto thee, son T.
6. 20 O T., keep that which is committed to thy
2 Ti. 1. 2 To T...dearly beloved son: Grace, mercy
Phm. 1 Paul..and T. (our) brother, unto Philem.
Heb. 13. 23 Know ye that..brother T. is set at liberty

TIN —
Tin, lead alloy, בְּדִיל *bedil.*
Num31. 22 the brass, the iron, the tin, and the lead
Isa. 1. 25 purge..thy dross, and take away all thy tin
Eze. 22. 18 they (are) brass, and tin, and iron, and
22. 20 (As) they gather silver..and tin, into
27. 12 with silver, iron, tin, and lead, they tra.

TINGLE, to —
To quiver, tingle, צָלַל *tsalal,* 5, 2.
1 Sa. 3. 11 ears of every one that heareth it shall ti.
2 Ki. 21. 12 whosoever heareth..his ears shall tingle
Jer. 19. 3 whosoever heareth, his ears shall tingle

TINKLE, make a tinkling, to —
1. *To make a tinkling,* עָכַס *akas,* 3.
Isa. 3. 16 walking..making a tinkling with their fe.

2. *To clash, clank, cry aloud,* ἀλαλάζω *alalazō.*
1 Co. 13. 1 (as) sounding brass, or a tinkling cymbal

TIP —
1. *Tip (of ear),* תְּנוּךְ *tenuk.*
Exod29. 20 tip of the right ear..tip of the right ear
Lev. 8. 23 put (it) upon the tip of Aaron's right ear
8. 24 put of the blood upon the tip of their rig.
14. 14 priest shall put (it) upon the tip of the ri.
14. 17 shall the priest put upon the tip of the ri.
14. 25 put (it) upon the tip of the right ear of him
14. 28 upon the tip of the right ear of him that

2. *Point, tip,* ἄκρον *akron.*
Luke16. 24 that he may dip the tip of his finger in w.

TIPH'-SAH, תִּפְסַח *passage, ford.*
1. The city *Thapsacus* on the W. bank of the Euphrates; from the time of Seleucus Nicator it was also called *Amphipolis.*
1 Ki. 4. 24 For he had dominion..from T. even to A.
2. A city in Judah, on the Jordan; perhaps *Tappuah.*
2 Ki.15. 16 Then Menahem smote T., and all that

TI'-RAS, תִּירָס.
A son of Japheth and his posterity in Thracia. B.C. 2300.
Gen. 10. 2 sons of Japheth..Tubal..Meshech, and T.
1 Ch. 1. 5 sons of Japheth..Tubal..Meshech, and T.

TIRATHITES, תִּרְעָתִי. *A family or race of scribes.*
1 Ch. 2. 55 the T., the Shimeathites, (and) Suchathi.

TIRE, (round tires like the moon) —
1. *Beauty, ornament, head dress,* פְּאֵר *peer.*
Eze. 24. 17 bind the tire of thine head upon thee, and
24. 23 your tires..upon your heads, and your sh.

2. *Moon shaped ornaments,* שַׂהֲרֹנִים *saharonim.*
Isa. 3. 18 cauls, and..round tires like the moon

TIRE, to —
To make good or well, יָטַב *yatab,* 5.
2 Ki. 9. 30 tired her head, and looked out at a win.

TIR-HA'-KAH, תִּרְהָקָה.
A king of Ethiopia and Thebais, same as *Tarakos,* the third and last king of the twentieth dynasty, and successor of Sevechus; he was contemporary with Hezekiah. B.C. 726.
2 Ki.19. 9 when he heard say of T. king of Ethiopia
Isa. 37. 9 he heard say concerning T. king of Ethi.

TIR-HA'-NAH, תִּרְחֲנָה *kindness.*
A son of Caleb son of Hezron, through Maacah his concubine. B.C. 1440.
1 Ch. 2. 48 Caleb's concubine, bare Sheber, and T.

TIR'-IA, תִּירְיָא *foundation.*
A son of Jehaleleel, a descendant of Judah through Caleb son of Jephunneh. B.C. 1400.
1 Ch. 4. 16 sons of Jehaleleel..Ziphah, T., and Asa.

TIR-SHA'-THA, הַתִּרְשָׁתָא *the fear, the reverence.*
A title given to Zerubbabel and Nehemiah as governors of Judah under the king of Persia. B.C. 536-445.
Ezra 2. 63 the T. said unto them, that they should
Neh. 7. 65 the T. said unto them, that they should
7. 70 The T. gave to the treasure a thousand
8. 9 Nehemiah, which (is) the T...said unto
10. 1 those that sealed (were) Nehemiah, the T.

TIR'-ZAH, תִּרְצָה *delight.*
1. The youngest daughter of Zelophehad. B.C. 1452.
Num26. 33 Mahlah, and Noah, Hoglah, Milcah, and T.
27. 1 M...Noah, and Hoglah, and Milcah, and T.
36. 11 For Mahlah, T., and Hoglah..were mar.
Josh 17. 3 Mahlah, and Noah, Hoglah, Milcah, and T.
2. A city in Ephraim, or Manasseh; perhaps *Tersa,* three hours E. of Samaria; or *Taluza,* six miles N.E. of Nablus.
Josh 12. 24 The king of T., one: all the kings thirty
1 Ki. 14. 17 Jeroboam's wife..departed, and came to T.
15. 21 left off building of Ramah, and dwelt in T.
15. 33 began Baasha..to reign over..Israel in T.
16. 6 with his fathers, and was buried in T.
16. 8 began Elah..to reign over Israel in T.
16. 9 as he was in T., drinking himself drunk
16. 9 house of Arza, steward of (his) house in T.
16. 15 did Zimri reign seven days in T.
16. 17 O...and all Israel with him..besieged T.
16. 23 Omri to reign..six years reigned he in T.
2 Ki.15. 14 Menahem the son of Gadi went up from T.
15. 16 Menahem smote..coasts thereof from T.
Song 6. 4 Thou (art) beautiful, O my love, as T., co.

TISHBITE, הַתִּשְׁבִּי.
An inhabitant of *Tisbeh* or *Tesheb,* supposed to have been in Naphtali, or in Gilead. B.C. 897.
1 Ki. 17. 1 Elijah the T...(was) of the inhabitants of
21. 17, 28 word of..LORD came to Elijah the T.
2 Ki. 1. 3 angel of the LORD said to Elijah the T.
1. 8 And he said, It (is) Elijah the T.
9. 36 which he spake by his servant E. the T.

TITHE, to give, have, pay, receive, take tithes, to —
1. *To give a tenth,* עָשַׂר *asar,* 3.
Deut 14. 22 Thou shalt truly tithe all the increase of
Neh. 10. 37 that the same Levites might have the ti.

2. *To give a tenth,* עָשַׂר *asar,* 5.
Neh. 10. 38 the Levites, when the Levites take tithes

3. *To give away a tenth,* ἀποδεκατόω *apodekatoō.*
Matt23. 23 ye pay tithe of mint and anise and cum.
Luke11. 42 ye tithe mint and rue, and all manner of
18. 12 I fast twice in the week, I give tithes of
Heb. 7. 5 to take tithes of the people according to

4. *To give a tenth,* δεκατόω *dekatoō.*
Heb. 7. 6 received tithes of Abraham, and blessed
7. 9 Levi..who receiveth..payed tithes in A.

TITHES, tithing —
1. *A tenth,* מַעֲשֵׂר *maaser.*
Gen. 14. 20 into thy hand. And he gave him tithes of
Lev. 27. 30 the tithe of the land, (whether) of the seed
27. 31 if a man will..redeem (ought) of his tith.
27. 32 concerning the tithe of the herd, or of the
Num 18. 24 the tithes of the children of Israel, which
18. 26 take of the children of Israel the tithes
18. 26 shall offer up..a tenth (part) of the tithe
18. 28 offer an heave offering..of all your tithes
Deut 12. 6 your sacrifices, and your tithes, and he.
12. 11 your sacrifices, your tithes, and the heave
12. 17 Thou mayest not eat..the tithe of thy corn
14. 23 the tithe of thy corn, of thy wine, and of
14. 28 thou shalt bring forth all the tithe of th.
26. 12 tithes of..the third year..the year of tit.
2 Ch.31. 5 the tithe of all (things) brought they in
31. 6 the tithe of oxen and sheep, and the tithe
31. 12 brought in the offerings and the tithes and
Neh. 10. 37 the tithes of our ground unto the Levites
10. 38 Levites shall bring..the tithe of the tith.
12. 44 for the first fruits, and for the tithes, to
13. 5, 12 the tithes of the corn, the new wine
Amos 4. 4 bring your sacrifices..(and) your tithes
Mal. 3. 8 Wherein have we robbed thee? In tithes
3. 10 Bring ye all the tithes into the storehouse

2. *To give a tenth,* עָשַׂר *asar,* 5.
Deut 26. 12 When thou hast made an end of tithing

3. *A tenth (part),* δεκάτη *dekatē.*
Heb. 7. 8 here men that die receive tithes, but the.
7. 9 Levi also, who receiveth tithes, payed..in

TITLE —

1. *A sign, monument,* צִיּוּן *tsiyyun.*
2 Ki. 23. 17 Then he said, What title (is) that that I

2. *A title,* (*Lat. titulus*), τίτλος *titlos.*
John 19. 19 Pilate wrote a title, and put (it) on the cr.
19. 20 This title then read many of the Jews, for

TITTLE —

A horn, (*ornamental curl of Heb. letters*), κεραία.
Matt. 5. 18 one jot or one tittle shall in no wise pass
Luke 16. 17 to pass, than one tittle of the law to fail

TI'-TUS, Τίτος.

A Greek disciple who accompanied Paul in several of his journeys, was sent by him to Dalmatia, and left in Crete to settle the churches. A.D. 65.

2 Co. 2. 13 I had no rest..because I found not T. my
7. 6 God..comforted us by the coming of T.
7. 13 the more joyed we for the joy of T.
7. 14 so our boasting, which I (made) before T.
8. 6 Insomuch that we desired T., that as he
8. 16 put the same..care into the heart of T.
8. 23 Whether (any do enquire) of T., (he is) my
12. 18 I desired T., and with (him) I sent: ..T.
Gal. 2. 1 I went up again to Jerusalem..and took T.
2. 3 But neither T...was compelled to be cir.
2 Ti. 4. 10 Crescens to Galatia, T. into Dalmatia
Titus 1. 4 To T., (mine) own son after the common

TIZITE, תִּיצִי.

Patronymic of Joha one of David's valiant men. B.C. 1048.

1 Ch. 11. 45 of Shimri, and Joha his brother, the T.

TO, unto, (even)—

1. *Unto, to, toward,* אֶל *el.*
Gen. 1. 9 Let the waters..be gathered together unto
14. 7 they returned, and came to En-mishpat

2. *With a view to,* לְמוֹ *lemo.*
Job 38. 40 When they..abide in the covert to lie in

3 *From, than,* מִן *min.*
Dan. 2. 39 shall arise another kingdom inferior to th.

4. *In order that, so that,* לְמַעַן *le-maan.*
Gen. 50. 20 God meant..to bring..as (it is) this day

5. *In order that,* בַּעֲבוּר *bo-abur.*
2 Sa. 10. 3 hath not David..sent..to search the city

6. *In order that,* לְבַעֲבוּר *le-ba-abur.*
Exod 20. 20 God is come to prove you, and that his f.
2 Sa. 14. 20 To fetch about this form of speech hath

7. *Till, unto, up to,* עַד *ad.*
Ezra 4. 24 So it ceased unto the second year of the
7. 22 Unto an hundred talents of silver, and to
7. 22 to an hundred baths of wine, and to an
Dan. 4. 17 to the intent that the living may know th.
6. 26 his dominion (shall be even) unto the end
7. 13 came to the Ancient of days, and they b.
7. 26 consume and..destroy (it) unto the end

8. *On, upon,* עַל *al.*
Gen. 18. 5 for therefore are ye come to your servant
Ezra 4. 11 they sent unto him. (even) unto Artaxer.
4. 12 that the Jews which came up from thee to
4. 17 sent the king an answer unto Rehum the
4. 18 letter which ye sent unto us hath been pl.
4. 23 they went up in haste..unto the Jews, and
See also 5. 1, 1, 3, 6, 7, 17, 17; 7 18. 18; Dan. 2. 24; 4. 27, 34, 36, 36; 6. 6, 15; 7. 16.

9. *With,* עִם *im.*
Gen. 24. 12 show kindness unto my master Abraham
Ezra 6. 8 what ye shall do to the elders of these Je.
Dan. 6. 21 Then said Daniel unto the king, O king

10. *From with,* מֵעִם *me-im.*
Gen. 44. 32 thy servant became surety for the lad unto

11. *At the mouth of,* לְפִי [*le-peh*].
Prov 27 21 (As) the fining pot..so (is) a man to his praise

12. *Before,* לִפְנֵי *li-phene.*
Gen. 27. 20 Because the LORD thy God brought (it) to

13. *At the hand of,* עַל־יַד *al-yad.*
2 Ch. 17. 15 next to him was Jehohanan the captain

14. *To meet,* לִקְרַאת inf. of *qara.*
Isa. 21. 14 brought water to him that was thirsty

15. *Until, unto, within,* ἄχρι, ἄχρις *achri, achris.*
Acts 2. 29 and his sepulchre is with us unto this day
13. 6 when they had gone through the isle unto
22. 4 persecuted this way unto the death, bind.
22. 22 they gave him audience unto this word
26. 22 I continue unto this present day, witnessing both
1 Co. 4. 11 Even unto this present hour we both hun.
2 Co. 10. 13 us, a measure to reach even unto you
Heb. 6. 11 the full assurance of hope unto the end
Rev. 2. 10 be thou faithful unto death, and I will gi.
2. 26 keepeth my works unto the end, to him
12. 11 they loved not their lives unto the death
14. 20 blood came out..even unto the horse br.
18. 5 For her sins have reached unto heaven

16. *Through,* διά (*gen.*) *dia.*
2 Pe. 1. 3 him that hath called us [to] glory and vir.

17. *Into, to,* εἰς *eis.*
Matt. 2. 1 there came wise men from the east to Je.
2. 8 he sent them to Bethlehem, and said, Go
See also 3. 11; 17. 13, 14; 8. 18, 34; 9. 6, 7, [13]; 10. 17, 21, 22; 12. 20; 13. [52]; 14. 22; 15. 24; 16. 5, 21; 17. 24, 27; 20. 17, 18; 21. 1, 1; 22. 3, 4, 5, [5], 9; 23. 34; 24. 9, 13; 25. 1, 6, 10; 26. 2, 3, 8, 36; 27. 7, 33; Mark 2. [17]; 4. 35; 5. 1, 19, 21, 38; 6. 41, 45; 7. 30, 54; 8. 3, 13, 22; 9. 33; 10. 32, 33, 46; 11. 1, 1, 11, 15, 27; 13. 9, 12, 13, 14; 14. 8, 32; 15. 41; Luke 1. 23, 26, 50, 56; 2. 4, 22, 32, 39, 41, [42], 45, 51; 4. 9, 16, 26, 31; 5. 17, 24, 25, 32; 7. 10; 8. 22, 39; 9. 16, 51, 53, 56; 10. 7, 30, 34; 11. 24; 14. 8, 31; 15. 17; 16. 27, 34; 18. 14, 31, 35; 19. 28, 29; 21. 12, 21; 22. 33, 39; 24. 5, 13, 20, 28, 33, [50], 52; John 1. 11; 2. 2, 12, 13, 13; 4. 5, 8, 36, 45; 5. 1, 24, 29, 29; 6. 27; 7. 8, 8, 10, 35, [53]; 8. [1], 26; 9. 11; 11. 31, 38, 54, 55, 56; 12. 1, 12, 12, 13, 25, 27; 13. 1; 16. 32; 17. 1; 18. 28; 19. 27; 20. 1, 3, 4, 8.
Acts 1. 12, 25; 4. 3, 30; 5. [16], 21, 36; 6. 12; 8. 3, 5, 25, 26, 27, 40; 9. 2, 2, [26], 30, 30; 10. 5, 8, 32; 11. 2; 13. 18, 20, 22, 25, 26, 27; 12. 10, 19; 13. 4, 4, 13, 14, 22, 31, 34, 46, 47, 48, 51; 14. 6, 20, 21, 24, 26; 15. 2, 4, 22, 30, 38, 39; 16. 1, 8, 11, 11, 12, 16; 17. 1, 5, 10, 20; 18. 1, 6, 19, 22, 24; 19. 1, 3, 3, 21, 27; 20. 6, [13], 14, 15, 17, 22, 38; 21. 1, 1, 1, 2, 4, 7, 8, 12, 15, 17; 22. 5, 5, 7, 17, 21; 23. 31, 32, 33; 24. 17; 25. 1, 3, 6, 9, 13, 16, 20, 21; 26. 7, 11, 12, 14, 17, 18; 27. 5, 8, 12, 40; 28. 6, 13, 13, 15, 16.
Rom. 1. 1, 16, 17, 24, 26, 28; 2. 4; 3. 7, 22, 25; 5. 15, 16, 16, 18, 18, 21; 6. [16], 16, 16, 19, 19, 22; 7. 5, 10, 10; 8. 15; 9. 21, 21, 22, 23, 31; 10. 10, 10, 12, 18; 11. 36; 12. 3, 10; 13. [4], 14; 14. 1; 15. 7, 25; 16. 5, 19, 19, 26; 1 Co. 1. 9; 2. 7; 4. 6; 8. 10; 10. 2, 31; 11. 22, 33, 34; 14. 8, 36; 16. 3, 15; 2 Co. 1. 23; 2. 4, 12, 16, 16; 3. 13, 18; 4. 11, 15; 7. 3, 9, 10; 8. 2, 4, 24; 9. 1, 5, 8, 11, 13, 13, 13; 10. 5, 14; 12. 1; 13. 10, 10; Gal. 1. 6, 17, 17, 18; 2. 1, 8, 9, 9, 11; 3. 23, 24; 4. 24; 6. 8, 8; Eph. 1. 5, 5, 6, 14, 15; 2. 21; 4. 13, 13, 16, 19, 30, 32; 6. 18; Phil. 1. 11, 12, 19, 23; 2. 11; 3. 11, 16; 4. [16], 17; Col. 1. 4, 6, 10, 11, 12, 20, 29; 2. 2, 2, 22; 3. 9, 15; 4. 11; 1 Th. 1. [5]; 2. 9, 12, 16, 16; 3. 2, 3, 5; 4. 9, 15, 17; 5. 9, 9; 2 Th. 2. 13, 14; 3. 9; 1 Ti. 1. 6; 2. 4, 7; 4. 3; 5. 24; 6. 12, 17; 2 Ti. 1. 11; 2. [14], 20, 20, 21, 21, 25; 3. 7, 15; 4. 10, 10, 10, 12, 18; Titus 3. 12; Heb. 1. 14; 2. 3, 10, 17; 4. 16; 6. 6, 8; 7. 25, 25; 8. 3; 9. 14, 26, 28, 28; 10. 19, 24, 39, 39; 11. 7, 11, 26; 12. 2; 13. 21; Jas. 1. 19, 19, 19; 2. 2; 4. 9, 9; 1 Pe. 1, 2, 3, 4, 5, 7, 10, 22, 25; 2. 8, 21; 3. 9, 12; 4. 4, 7, 9, 10; 5. 10; 2 Pe. 2. 4, 9, 12, 22; 3. 9; 1 Jo. 3. 14; 3 John 5, [5]; Jude 4, 6, 21; Rev. 1. 11, 11, 11, 11, 11, 11, 11; 6. 13; 9. 1, 7, 9; 10. 5; 11. 6, 12; 12. 4, 13; 13. 3; 16. 14; 19. 9, 17; 20. 8.

18. *In, among,* ἐν *en.*
Matt 17. 12 have done unto him whatsoever they lis.
Luke 1. 17 the disobedient to the wisdom of the just
John 13. 35 are my disciples, if ye have love one to an.
Acts 12. 11 when Peter was come to himself, he said
26. 20 showed first unto them of Damascus, and
Rom. 5. 21 That as sin hath reigned unto death, even
1 Co. 7. 15 bondage..but God hath called us to peace
9. 15 that it should be so done unto me: for (it
14. 11 that speaketh (shall be) a barbarian unto
2 Co. 4. 3 if our gospel be hid, it is hid to them that
5. 19 hath committed unto us the word of rec.
8. 7 (in) your love to us, (see) that ye abound
Col. 1. 23 was preached to every creature which is
1 Th. 4. 7 God hath not called..but unto holiness
5. 23 unto the coming of our Lord Jesus Christ
1 Ti. 3. 16 preached unto the Gentiles, believed on
2 Pe. 1. 5 add to your faith virtue; and to virtue
1. 6 to knowledge..to temperance..and to pa.
1. 7 to godliness brotherly kindness; and to
1 Jo. 4. 16 and believed the love that God hath to us

19. *Before,* ἐνώπιον *enōpion.*
Luke 24. 11 their words seemed to them as idle tales

20. *Out of* ἐκ *ek.*
Matt 28. 14 if this come to the governor's ears, we will
Luke 23. 7 that he belonged unto Herod's jurisdiction

21. *On, upon,* ἐπί (*gen.*) *epi.*
John 21. 11 drew the net [to] land full of great fishes
Acts 10. 11 vessel descending..and let down to the ea.

22. *Upon, over,* ἐπί (*dat.*) *epi.*
Matt. 9. 16 No man putteth a piece of new cloth unto
Gal. 5. 13 ye have been called unto liberty; only
Eph. 2. 10 created in Christ Jesus unto good works
1 Th. 4. 7 For God hath not called us unto unclean.
2 Ti. 2. 14 strive..(but) to the subverting of the he.

23. *Upon, about, for, up to,* ἐπί (*acc.*) *epi.*
Matt. 3. 7 when he saw many..come to his baptism
3. 13 Then cometh Jesus from Galilee to Jord.
5. 23 if thou bring thy gift to the altar, and th.
6. 27 Which of you..can add one cubit unto his
12. 28 then the kingdom of God is come unto you
13. 48 when it was full, they drew to shore, and
21. 19 he came to it, and found nothing thereon
27. 27 gathered unto him the whole band (of so.
Mark 5. 21 much people gathered unto him: and he
11 13 when he came to it, he found nothing but
15. 22 they bring him unto the place Golgotha
15. 46 rolled a stone unto the door of the sepul.
16. 2 they came unto the sepulchre at the risi.
Luke 1. 16 And many..shall he turn to the Lord th.
1. 17 to turn the hearts of the fathers to the ch.
5. 11 when they had brought their ships to la.
6. 35 for he is kind unto the unthankful and
8. 27 when he went forth to land, there met
9. 62 No man, having put his hand to the plo.
10. 6 if not, it shall turn to you again
10. 11 the kingdom of God is come nigh [unto]
12. 11 when they bring you unto the synagogues
12. 25 which of you..can add to his stature one
12. 58 When thou goest with thine adversary to
17. 4 seven times in a day turn again [to] thee
19. 5 when Jesus came to the place, he looked
22. 44 [great drops of blood falling down to the]
22. 52 and the elders, which were come to him
23. 1 the whole multitude..led him unto Pilate
23. 33 when they were come to the place which
Luke 23. 48 the people that came together to that sig.
24. 1 they came unto the sepulchre, bringing
24. 12 Then arose Peter, and ran [unto] the sepul.
24. 24 certain of them..went to the sepulchre, and
John 6. 16 his disciples went down unto the sea
19. 33 when they came to Jesus, and saw that
Acts 8. 26 unto the way that goeth down from Jer.
8. 32 He was led as a sheep to the slaughter
8. 36 they came unto a certain water, and the
9. 4 he fell to the earth, and heard a voice say.
9. 21 he might bring them bound unto the ch.
9. 35 all that dwelt at Lydda..turned to the L.
10. 11 a certain vessel descending [unto] him, as
11. 11 there were three men already come unto
11. 21 and a great number..turned unto the L.
12. 10 they came unto the iron gate that leadeth
12. 12 he came to the house of Mary the mother
14. 13 brought oxen and garland's unto the gates
14. 15 turn from these vanities unto the living
15. 19 trouble not them which..are turned to G.
16. 19 drew (them) into the market place unto
17. 6 drew Jason and certain brethren unto the
17. 14 sent away Paul, to go as it were to the sea
17. 19 brought him unto Areopagus, saying, May
18. 12 and brought him to the judgment seat
19. 12 from his body were brought unto the sick
20. 13 And we went before to ship, and sailed
21. 32 took soldiers..and ran down unto them
24. 8 [Commanding his accusers to come unto]
25. 12 Hast thou appealed..? unto Cesar shalt
26. 18 (from) the power of Satan unto God, that
26. 20 that they should repent and turn to God
27. 43 cast (themselves)..(into the sea), and get to
27. 44 it came to pass, that they escaped..to la.
Gal. 4. 9 how turn ye again to the weak and begg.
2 Th. 2. 1 and (by) our gathering together unto him
2 Ti. 2. 16 they will increase unto more ungodliness
4. 4 turn away (their) ears..turned unto fab.
Heb. 6. 1 let us go on unto perfection; not laying
Jas. 2. 3 ye have respect to him that weareth the
1 Pe. 2. 25 are now returned unto the Shepherd and
2 Pe. 2. 22 The dog (is) turned to his own vomit ag.
Rev. 16. 14 (which) go forth unto the kings of the ea.
21. 10 he carried me..to a great and high mou.
22. 14 that they may have right to the tree of
22. 18 God shall add unto him the plagues that

24. *Unto, up to, hitherto,* ἕως *heōs.*
Matt. 1. 17 from Abraham to David..and..unto Chr.
11. 23 Capernaum, which art exalted unto hea.
20. 8 hire, beginning from the last unto the first
22. 26 Likewise the second also..unto the seve.
23. 35 from the blood of righteous Abel unto the
24. 21 since the beginning of the world to this
24. 27 as the lightning..shineth even unto the
24. 31 from one end of heaven to the other
26. 38 My soul is exceeding sorrowful, even unto
26. 58 followed him afar off unto the high priest
27. 8 was called, The field of blood, unto this
27. 45 darkness over all the land unto the ninth
27. 51 was rent in twain from the top to the bo.
28. 20 I am with you alway, (even) unto the end
Mark 6. 23 will give (it) thee, unto the half of my ki.
13. 19 creation which God created unto this time
13. 27 from the uttermost part of the earth to
14. 34 My soul is exceeding sorrowful unto death
15. 38 was rent in twain from the top to the bo.
Luke 2. 15 Let us now go even unto Beth-lehem, and
4. 29 led him unto the brow of the hill whereon
4. 42 came unto him, and stayed him, that he
10. 15 exalted to heaven, shall be thrust down to
11. 51 blood of Abel, unto the blood of Zachar.
John 8. 9 [beginning at the eldest, (even) unto the]
Acts 1. 8 and unto the uttermost part of the earth
1. 22 unto that same day that he was taken up
7. 45 face of our fathers, unto the days of Da.
8. 10 all gave heed, from the least to the grea.
9. 38 that he would not delay to come to them
13. 47 be for salvation unto the ends of the earth
17. 15 brought him unto Athens: and receiving
23. 23 go to Cesarea, and horsemen threescore
26. 11 I persecuted (them) even unto strange ci.
Rom 11. 8 that they should not hear, unto this day
1 Co. 1. 8 Who shall confirm you unto the end, (that
4. 13 the offscouring of all things unto this day
8. 7 unto this hour eat (it) as a thing offered
15. 6 the greater part remain unto this present
2 Co. 1. 13 trust ye shall acknowledge even to the end
3. 15 But even unto this day, when Moses is re.
12. 2 such an one caught up to the third heaven
Heb. 8. 11 shall know me, from the least to the gre.
Jas. 5. 7 Be patient..unto the coming of the Lord

25. *In order that, so that,* ἵνα *hina.*
Matt 26. 16 from that time he sought opportunity to
27. 26 scourged Jesus, he delivered (him) to be
27. 32 him they compelled to bear his cross
Mark 4. 21 Is a candle brought to be put under a bu.
4. 21 under a bed? and not to be set on a can.
6. 41 to set before them; and the two fishes di.
7. 32 they beseech him to put his hand upon
8. 6 gave..to set before (them); and they did
8. 22 bring a blind man..and besought him to
9. 22 cast him into the fire..to destroy him
11. 28 who gave thee this authority to do these
12. 13 And they send..to catch him in (his) wo.
13. 34 and commanded the porter to watch
14. 10 Judas Iscariot..went..to betray him
15. 15 Pilate..delivered Jesus..to be crucified
15. 20 clothes on him, and led him out to cruc.
15. 21 they compel one Simon..to bear his cross
Luke 6. 34 sinners also lend..to receive as much ag.
9. 40 I besought thy disciples to cast him out

Luke19. 4 climbed up into a sycamore tree to see
John 1. 7 The same came for a witness, to bear wit.
1. 8 but (was sent) to bear witness of that li.
1. 19 sent priests..to ask him, Who art thou?
1. 27 whose shoe's latchet I am not worthy to
3. 17 sent not his Son into the world to conde.
4. 8 his disciples were gone away..to buy me.
4. 34 My meat is to do the will of him that sent
5. 7 I have no man..to put me into the pool
5. 36 which the Father hath given me to finish
6. 15 take him by force, to make him a king, he
6. 38 not to do mine own will, but the will of
7. 32 the chief priests sent officers to take him
8. 56 Your father Abraham rejoiced to see my
8. 59 Then took they up stones to cast at him
10. 31 the Jews took up stones again to stone
11. 19 to comfort them concerning their brother
11. 31 She goeth unto the grave to weep there
11. 53 they took counsel together for to put him
11. 55 went..before the passover, to purify th.
12. 20 Greeks among them that came up to wo.
12. 47 came not to judge the world, but to save
13. 2 now put into the heart of Judas..to betray
17. 4 finished the work..thou gavest me to do
19. 16 Then delivered he him..to be crucified
Acts 16. 30 and said, Sirs, what must I do to be saved
16. 36 The magistrates have sent to let you go
27. 42 soldiers' counsel was to kill the prisoners
1 Co. 1. 27 [foolish things of the world to confound]
1. 27 to confound the things which are mighty
1. 28 (yea), and things which are not, to bring
9. 25 they (do it) to obtain a corruptible crown
13. 3 though I give my body [to] be burned, and
16. 12 greatly desired him to come unto you with
16. 12 but his will was not at all to come at this
2 Co. 12. 7 messenger of Satan to buffet me, lest I
Gal. 4. 5 To redeem them that were under the law
Phil. 2. 30 to supply your lack of service toward me
2 Th. 3. 9 Not because we have not power, but to
1 Jo. 1. 9 he is faithful and just to forgive us (our)
3. 5 know that he was manifested to take away
3 John 4 I have no greater joy than to hear that
Rev. 2. 21 gave her space to repent of her fornicat.
3. 9 I will make them [to] come and worship
6. 2 he went forth conquering, and to conquer
8. 6 seven angels..prepared themselves to so.
13. 12 causeth the earth..to worship the first be.
13. 16 to receive a mark in their right hand, or
21. 15 had a golden reed to measure the city, and
21. 23 city had no need of the sun..to shine in

26. *Down to,* κατά *(acc.) kata.*
Acts 16. 7 After they were come to Mysia, they ass.
20. 20 taught you publicly, and from house to
25. 16 have the accusers face to face, and have
Rom 14. 22 Hast thou faith? have (it) to thyself bef.
2 Co. 8. 3 For to (their) power, I bear record, yea
Gal. 2. 11 I withstood him to the face, because he
Phil. 1. 12 things (which happened) unto me have

27. *With,* μετά *(gen.) meta.*
Luke 1. 72 perform the mercy (promised) to our fat.
Rev. 10. 8 voice..spake unto me again, and said, Go

28. *Unto, until,* μέχρι, μέχρις *mechri, mechris.*
Rom. 5. 14 Nevertheless death reigned from Adam
15. 19 round about unto Illyricum, I have fully
Phil. 2. 8 became obedient unto death, even the
2. 30 he was nigh unto death, not regarding his
2 Ti. 2. 9 Wherein I suffer trouble..unto bonds, but
Heb. 3. 6 [rejoicing of the hope firm unto the end]
3. 14 beginning of our confidence stedfast unto
12. 4 Ye have not yet resisted unto blood, stri.

29. *How, to the end that,* ὅπως *hopōs.*
Matt 26. 59 sought false witness..to put him to death
Luke 11. 37 a certain Pharisee besought him to dine
Acts 9. 24 watched the gates day and night to kill
23. 23 Make ready two hundred soldiers to go

30. *Toward,* πρός *(acc.) pros.*
Matt. 2. 12 that they should not return to Herod, th.
3. 5 Then went out to him Jerusalem, and all
3. 10 the axe is laid unto the root of the
3. 13 cometh Jesus..unto John, to be baptized
3. 14 baptized of thee, and comest thou to me?
3. 15 Jesus answering said unto [him], Suffer
5. 28 whosoever looketh on a woman to lust
6. 1 do not your alms before men, to be seen
7. 15 which come to you in sheep's clothing
10. 6 But go rather to the lost sheep of the h.
10. 13 not worthy, let your peace return to you
11. 28 Come unto me, all (ye) that labour and
13. 2 multitudes were gathered together unto
13. 30 and bind them in bundles to burn them
14. 25 Jesus went unto them, walking on the sea
14. 28 if it be thou, bid me come unto thee on
14. 29 he walked on the water..to Jesus
17. 14 when they were come to the multitude, th.
19. 14 forbid them not, to come unto me; for of
21. 1 when they..were come..unto the mount
21. 32 John came unto you in the way of right.
21. 34 he sent his servants to the husbandmen
21. 37 last of all he sent unto them his son, say.
23. 34 I send unto you prophets, and wise men
23. 37 stonest them which are sent unto thee
25. 9 go ye rather to them that sell, and buy for
25. 36 I was in prison, and ye came unto me
25. 39 when saw we thee sick..and came unto
26. 14 one of the twelve..went unto the chief pr.
26. 18 Go into the city to such a man, and say un.
26. 40 he cometh unto the disciples, and findeth
26. 45 Then cometh he to his disciples, and saith
26. 57 led (him) away to Caiaphas the high priest

Matt27. 4 they said, What (is that) to us? see thou
27. 14 he answered him to never a word; insom.
27. 19 his wife sent unto him, saying, Have thou
27. 62 and Pharisees came together unto Pilate
Mark 1. 5, 32, 40, 45; 2. 3, 13; 3. [7], 8, 13, 31; 4. 1, 41; 5. 15, 19; 6. 25, 30, 33, 45, 48, 51; 7. 1, [31]; 9. 14, 17, 19, 20; 10. 1, [7], 14, 50; 11. 7, 27; 12. 2, 4, 6, 13; 18; 13. 22; 14. 10, 35; 15. 43; Luke 1. 13, 18, 19, 27, 28, 34, 43, 55, 61, 73, 80; 2. 15, 20, 34, 48, 49; 3. 9, 12, 13, [14]; 4. 21, 23, 26, 26, 40, 43; 5. 10, 22, 31, 33, 34, 36; 6. 9, 47; 7. 3, 4, 6, 7, 19, 20, 20, 24, 40, 44, 50; 8. 4, 19, [21], 22, 25, 35; 9. 3, 13, 14, 23, 33, 43, 50, 57, 59, [62]; 10. 2, 23, 26, 29; 11. 1, 5, 5, 6, 39, [53]; 12. 1, 15, 16, 22, 41, 41, 58; 13. 7, 23, 34; 14. 3, 6, 7, 7, 23, 25, 26, 28; 15. 3, 18, 20, 22; 16. 1, 26, 26, 30; 17. 1, 22 18. 3, [7], 9, 16, 31, 40; 19. 5, 8, 9, 13, 33, 35, 39, 43; 20. 2, 3, 9, 10, 23, 41; 21. 38; 22. 15, 45, 52, 70; 23. 4, 7, 14, 15, 22, 28; 24. 5, 10, 17, 17, 18, 25, 32, 44; John 1. 29, 42, 47; 2. 3; 3. 2, 4, 20, 21, 26, 26; 4. 15, 30, 33, 35, 40, 47, 48, 49; 5. 33, 40, 45; 6. 5, 5, 17, 28, 34, 35, 37, 37 44, 45, 65, 68; 7. 3, 33, 37, 45, 50, 50; 8. [2, 3, 7], 31, 57; 9. 13; 10. 35, 41; 11. 3, 4, 15, 19, 21, 29, 45, 46; 12. 32; 13. 1, 3, 6; 14. 3, 6, 12, 18, 23, 28, 28; 16. 5, 7, 7, 10, [16], 17, 28; 17. 11, 13; 18. 13, 24, 29, 38; 19. 39; 20. 2, 2, 10, 17, 17, 17; 21. 22, 23.
Acts 1. 7; 2. [7], 12, 29, 37, 38; 3. 11, 12, [22], 22, 25; 4. 1, 8, 19, 23, 23, 24; 5. 9, 35; 7. 3, [31]; 8. 14, 20, 24, 26; 9. 2, [6], 10, 11, 15, 27, 32, 38, 40; 10. 3, 13, 15, [21,] 21, 28, 33; 11. 3, 11, 20, 30; 12. 5, 8, 15, 20, 21; 13. 15, 31, 32, 36; 14. 11; 15. 2, 7, 25, 33, 36; 16. 36, 37; 17. 2, 15, 15; 18. 6, 14, 21; 19. 2, 2, [3], 31; 20. 6, 18; 21. 11, 18, 37, 39; 22. 1, 5, 8, 10, 13, 15, 21, 25; 23. 3, [15], 17, 18, 18, 22, 24, 30; 25. 16, 21, 22; 26. 1, [6], 9, 14, 28; 27. 3, 12; 28. 8, 17, 21, 23, 25, 26, 30; Rom. 1. 10, 13; 3. 26; 8. 31; 10. 1, 21, 21; 15. 2, 22, 23, [24], 29, 30, 32; 1 Co. 2, 1; 4. 18, 19, 21; 6. 5; 12. 2, 7; 13. 12; 14. 6, 12, 26; 15. 34; 16. 5, 11, 12; 2 Co. 1. 15, 16, 20; 2. 1; 3. 1, 16; 4. 2, 6; 5. 12; 6. 11; 7. 3, 12; 8. 17, 19; 10. 4; 11. 8; 12. 14, 17; 13. 1, 7; Gal. 1. 17; 6. 10, 10; Eph. 2. 18; 3. 14; 4. 14, 29; 5. [31]; 6. 9, 22; Phil. 1. 26; 2. 25; 4. 6; Col. 2. 23; 4. 8, 10; 1 Th. 1. 9, 9; 2. 1, 2, 18; 3. 6, 11; 1 Ti. 3. 14; 4. 7. 8; 2 Ti. 2. 24; 3. 17; 4. 9; Titus 1. 16; 3. 1, 2, 12, 12; Heb. 1. 8, 13; 2. 17; 5. 1, 5, 7, 14; 6. 11; 7. 21; 9. 13, 20; 13. 13; Jas. 4. [5]; 1 Pe. 2. 4; 3. 15; 4. 12; 2 Pe. 1. 3; 3. 16; 1 Jo. 5. 16, 16, 16, 17; 2 Jo. 10, 12, 12; 3 Jo. 14; Rev. 3. 20; 10. 9; 12. 5, 12; 21. [9]; 22. [18].

31. *Above, beyond,* ὑπέρ *(acc.) huper.*
2 Co. 12. 13 what is it wherein ye were inferior to

32. *As,* ὡς *hōs.*
Rom. 9. 29 we had been..made like unto Gomorrha

33. *So as,* ὥστε *hōste.*
Matt 10. 1 he gave them power..to cast them out, and
27. 1 elders..took counsel against Jesus to put
Luke 9. 52 entered into a village..[to] make ready for

See also About, according, add, attendance, bring, call, chargeable, cleave, come, communicate, conformed, contrary, day, end, even, for, go, like, nail, put, run, shut, speak.

TO and fro —

1. *Here, hither,* הֵנָּה *henah.*
2 Ki. 4. 35 returned, and walked in the house to and f.

2. *Going and returning,* יָצֹא וְשׁוֹב *[yatsa].*
Gen. 8. 7 which went forth to and fro, until the waters

3. *To move, shake, stagger, wander,* נוּעַ *nua.*
Isa. 24. 20 The earth shall reel to and fro like a dru.

See also Driven, go, reel, removing, run, running, toss, tossed, tossings, walk.

TO day —

1. *The day, to day,* הַיּוֹם *hay-yom.*
Gen. 30. 32 I will pass through all thy flock to day
Exod. 2. 18 How (is it)..ye are come so soon to day
5. 14 making brick both yesterday and to day
14. 13 see the salvation..he will show to you to day
14. 13 the Egyptians whom ye have seen to day
16. 25 And Moses said, Eat that to day; for to day
16. 25 to day (is) a sabbath unto the LORD: to day
32. 29 Consecrate yourselves to day to the LORD
Deut 29. 13 That he may establish thee to day for a peo.
Josh. 22. 18 (seeing) ye rebel to day against the LORD
1 Sa. 4. 3 Wherefore hath the LORD smitten us to d.
4. 16 the man said..I fled to day out of the ar.
9. 12 haste now, for he came to day to the city
9. 12 (there is) a sacrifice of the people to day in
9. 19 ye shall eat with me to day; and to morrow
10. 2 When thou art departed from me to day
11. 13 to day the LORD hath wrought salvation
12. 17 (Is it) not wheat harvest to day? I will call
20. 27 cometh not the son of Jesse to meat..to d.
24. 10 that the LORD had delivered thee to day
26. 23 delivered thee into (my) hand to day, but
27. 10 said, Whither have ye made a road to day?
2 Sa. 11. 12 Tarry here to day also, and to morrow I
14. 22 To day thy servant knoweth that I have
16. 3 To day shall the house of Israel restore me
1 Ki. 8. 28 thy servant prayeth before thee to day
2 Ki. 4. 23 Wherefore wilt thou go to him to day? (it
6. 28 we may eat him to day, and we will eat my
Job 23. 2 to day (is) my complaint bitter: my stroke
Psa. 95. 7 he (is) our God..To day if ye will hear his

2. *To day, this day,* σήμερον *sēmeron.*
Matt. 6. 30 the grass of the field, which to day is, and
16. 3 foul weather to day; for the sky is red and
21. 28 said, Son, go work to day in my vineyard
Luke 5. 26 saying, We have seen strange things to d.
12. 28 the grass, which is to day in the field, and
13. 32 I cast out devils, and I do cures to day and
13. 33 I must walk to day and to morrow, and the
19. 5 Zaccheus..to day I must abide at thy ho.
23. 43 To day shalt thou be with me in paradise

Luke24. 21 beside all this, [to day] is the third day
Heb. 3. 7 saith, To day if ye will hear his voice
3. 13 But exhort..while it is called To day; lest
3. 15 To day if ye will hear his voice, harden
4. 7 To day..To day if ye will hear his voice
5. 5 Thou art my Son, to day have I begotten
13. 8 same yesterday, and to day, and for ever
Jas. 4. 13 To day or to morrow we will go into such a

TO morrow —

1. *Time before, to morrow,* מָחָר *machar.*
Exod. 8. 10 And he said, To morrow. And he said
8. 23 a division..to morrow shall this sign be
8. 29 (flies) may depart..from his people, to mo.
9. 5 To morrow the LORD shall do this thing in
9. 18 to morrow about this time I will cause it
10. 4 to morrow will I bring the locusts into thy
16. 23 To morrow (is) the rest of the holy sabbath
17. 9 to morrow I will stand on the top of the
19. 10 sanctify them to day and to morrow, and
32. 5 and said, To morrow (is) a feast to the L.
Num 11. 18 Sanctify yourselves against to morrow, and
14. 25 To morrow turn you, and get you into the
16. 7 put incense in them before the LORD to m.
16. 16 thou, and they, and Aaron, to morrow
Josh. 3. 5 for to morrow the LORD will do wonders
7. 13 Sanctify yourselves against to morrow: for
11. 6 to morrow, about this time, will I deliver
22. 18 to morrow he will be wroth with the wh.
Judg 19. 9 to morrow get you early on your way, that
20. 28 to morrow I will deliver them into thine h.
1 Sa. 9. 16 To morrow, about this time, I will send
11. 9 To morrow, by (that time) the sun be hot
11. 10 To morrow we will come out unto you, and
19. 11 save not thy life to night, to morrow thou
20. 5 to morrow (is) the new moon, and I should
20. 12 have sounded my father about to morrow
20. 18 To morrow (is) the new moon: and thou
28. 19 to morrow (shalt) thou and thy sons (be)
2 Sa. 11. 12 Tarry ye here to day also, and to morrow
1 Ki. 19. 2 as the life of one of them by to morrow
20. 6 send my servants unto thee to morrow ab.
2 Ki. 6. 28 woman said..we will eat my son to morr.
7. 1 To morrow, about this time, (shall) a me.
7. 18 shall be to morrow about this time in the
10. 6 come to me to Jezreel by to morrow this
2 Ch. 20. 16 To morrow go ye down against them, be.
20. 17 to morrow go out against them: for the
Esth. 5. 8 I will do to morrow as the king hath said
5. 12 to morrow am I invited unto her also with
9. 13 to morrow also according unto this day's
Prov. 3. 28 Say not..to morrow I will give; when thou
27. 1 Boast not thyself of to morrow; for thou
Isa. 22. 13 let us eat and drink; for to morrow we sh.
56. 12 to morrow shall be as this day, (and) much

2. *To morrow,* αὔριον *aurion.*
Matt. 6. 30 which to day is, and to morrow is cast into
Luke 12. 28 and to morrow is cast into the oven, how
13. 32 I do cures to day and to morrow, and the
13. 33 I must walk to day, and to morrow, and
Acts 23. 15 he bring him down unto you [to morrow]
23. 20 thou wouldest bring down Paul to morrow
25. 22 To morrow, said he, thou shalt hear him
1 Co. 15. 32 let us eat and drink; for to morrow we die
Jas. 4. 13 to morrow we will go into such a city, and

TO the end or intent —

1. *With a view to,* εἰς *eis.*
Acts 7. 19 cast out their young children, to the end
Rom. 1. 11 may impart..to the end ye may be estab.
4. 16 to the end the promise might be sure to
1 Co. 10. 6 to the intent we should not lust after evil
1 Th. 3. 13 To the end he may stablish your hearts

2. *In order that, so that,* ἵνα *hina.*
John 11. 15 And I am glad..to the intent ye may be.
Eph. 3. 10 To the intent that now unto the princip.

TO wit —

As, how, ὡς *hōs.*
2 Co. 5. 19 To wit, that God was in Christ reconcil-

TO (God or you) ward —

Toward, πρός *(acc.) pros.*
2 Co. 1. 12 world, and more abundantly to youward
3. 4 trust have we through Christ to Godward
1 Th. 1. 8 your faith to Godward is spread abroad

TO'-AH, תּוֹחַ *depression, humility.*
Father of Eliel, and grandfather of Jeroham the grandfather of Samuel the prophet; called also *Nahath* in ver. 26; and *Tohu* in 1 Sa. 1. 1. B.C. 1230.
1 Ch. 6. 34 Jeroham, the son of Eliel, the son of T.

TOB, טוֹב *fruitful, good.*
A district in Syria N.E. of Gilead, to which Jephthah fled, and which sent out mercenary troops, 2 Sa. 10. 6; Macc. 5. 13.
Judg 11. 3 Then Jephthah..dwelt in the land of T.
11. 5 elders..went to fetch Jephthah out of..T.

TOB ADO-NI'-JAH, טוֹב אֲדוֹנִיָּה *the Lord Jah is good.*
A Levite sent by Jehoshaphat to teach the people in the cities of Judah. B.C. 913
2 Ch. 17. 8 Adonijah, and Tobijah, and T., Levites

TO-BI'-AH, TOB-I'-JAH, טוֹבִיָּהוּ, טֹבִיָּה, טוֹבִיָּה *Jah is good.*
1. A Levite sent by Jehoshaphat to teach the people in the cities of Judah. B.C. 913.
2 Ch. 17. 8 Adonijah, and T., and Tob-adonijah, Lev.
2. A person whose descendants returning from exile were unable to prove their genealogy. B.C. 445.
Ezra 2. 60 children of Delaiah, the children of T.
Neh. 7. 62 children of Delaiah, the children of T.

3. An Ammonite who opposed Nehemiah. B.C. 445.
Neh. 2. 10 When..T. the servant, the Ammonite, he.
2. 19 But when Sanballat..and T...heard (it)
4. 3 Now T. the Ammonite (was) by him, and
4. 7 T...heard that the walls of Jerusalem we.
6. 1 T...heard that I had builded the wall
6. 12 for T. and Sanballat had hired him
6. 14 My God, think thou upon T...that would
6. 17 sent..letters unto T...(the letters) of T.
6. 19 (And) T. sent letters to put me in fear
13. 4 Eliashib the priest..(was) allied unto T.
13. 7 the evil that Eliashib did for T., in prep.
13. 8 I cast forth all the household stuff of T.

4. A chief man whose posterity returned from exile. B.C. 519.
Zech. 6. 10 T., and..Jedaiah, which are come from
6. 14 the crowns shall be to Helem, and to T.

TO'-CHEN, תֹּכֶן *establishment.*
A city in Simeon, near Rimmon (or Remnon); omitted in Josh. 19. 7.
1 Ch. 4. 32 And their villages (were)..T., and Ashan

TOE (great) —
1. *Thumb, great toe,* בֹּהֶן *bohen.*
Exod 29. 20 and upon the great toe of their right foot
Lev. 8. 23 and upon the great toe of his right foot
8. 24 and upon the great toes of their right feet
14. 14, 17, 25, 28 upon the great toe of his right
2. *Finger,* אֶצְבַּע *etsba.*
2 Sa. 21. 20 six fingers, and on every foot six toes
1 Ch. 20. 6 fingers and toes (were) four and twenty
3. *Fingers, toes,* אֶצְבְּעָן *etsbean.*
Dan. 2. 41 whereas thou sawest the feet and toes, part
2. 42 the toes of the feet (were) part of iron, and
4. *Toes* or *thumbs of the feet,* בְּהֹנוֹת רַגְלַיִם [*bohen*].
Judg. 1. 6 and cut off his thumbs and his great toes
1. 7 their thumbs and their great toes cut off

TO-GAR'-MAH, תֹּגַרְמָה, תּוֹגַרְמָה.
A son of Gomer, son of Japheth, in the N. of Armenia. B.C. 2200.
Gen. 10. 3 And the sons of Gomer..Riphath, and T.
1 Ch. 1. 6 And the sons of Gomer..Riphath, and T.
Eze. 27. 14 They of the house of T. traded in thy fa
38. 6 the house of T of the north quarters, and

TOGETHER —
1. *As one,* כְּאֶחָד *ke-echad.*
Ezra 2. 64 The whole congregation together (was) fo.
3. 9 sons of Judah, together, to set forward
6. 20 priests and the Levites were purified tog.
Neh. 7. 66 The whole congregation together (was) fo.
Isa. 65. 25 The wolf and the lamb shall feed together
2. *Each to its fellow,* אִשָּׁה אֶל־אֲחֹתָהּ [*ishshah*].
Exod 26 6 couple the curtains together with the ta.
3. *As one,* כַּחֲדָה *ka-chadah.*
Dan. 2. 35 broken in pieces together, and became like
4. *Together,* יַחַד, יַחְדָּו *yachad, yachdav.*
Gen. 13. 6 might dwell together..could not dwell tog.
22. 6, 8 they went both of them together
22. 19 they rose up and went together to Beer-s.
36. 7 more than that they might dwell together
Exod 19. 8 all the people answered together, and said
26. 24 they shall be coupled together above the
36. 29 coupled together at the head thereof, to
Deut 22. 10 not plow with an ox and an ass together
22. 11 divers sorts, (as) of woollen and linen tog.
25. 5 If brethren dwell together, and one of th.
25. 11 When men strive together one with ano.
33. 5 the tribes of Israel were gathered together
33. 17 with them he shall push the people toge.
Josh. 9. 2 they gathered themselves together, to fight
11. 5 they came and pitched together at the
Judg. 6. 33 children of the east were gathered toget.
19. 6 did eat and drink both of them together
1 Sa. 11. 11 so that two of them were not left together
17. 10 give me a man, that we may fight together
31. 6 and all his men, that same day together
2 Sa. 2. 13 met together by the pool of Gibeon: and
2. 16 so they fell down together: wherefore th.
10. 15 Israel, they gathered themselves together
12. 3 it grew up together with him, and with his
14. 16 destroy me and my son together out of the
21. 9 they fell (all) seven together, and were put
1 Ki. 3. 18 we (were) together; (there was) no stran.
1 Ch. 10. 6 Saul died..and all his house died together
Ezra 4. 3 but we ourselves together will build unto
Neh. 4. 8 conspired all of them together to come
6. 2 Come, let us meet together in (some one
6. 7 Come..and let us take counsel together
Job 2. 11 they had made an appointment together
3. 18 prisoners rest together; they hear not the
6. 2 my calamity laid in the balances together
9. 32 (and) we should come together in judgm.
10. 8 and fashioned me together round about
16. 10 they have gathered themselves together
17. 16 when (our) rest together (is) in the dust
19. 12 His troops come together, and raise up th.
24. 4 poor of the earth hide themselves together
34. 15 All flesh shall perish together, and man
38. 7 When the morning stars sang together, and
40. 13 Hide them in the dust together; (and) bi.
Psa. 2. 2 rulers take counsel together, against the
14. 3 they are (all) together become filthy; (th.
31. 13 while they took counsel together against
34. 3 magnify..and let us exalt his name toge.
35. 26 brought to confusion together that rejoice
Psa. 37. 38 transgressors shall be destroyed together
40. 14 be ashamed and confounded together that
41. 7 All that hate me whisper together against
48. 4 For, lo, the kings..passed by together
49. 2 Both low and high, rich and poor, together
55. 14 We took sweet counsel together, (and) wa.
71. 10 they that lay wait..take counsel together
74. 8 Let us destroy them together: they have
83. 5 For they have consulted together with one
88. 17 water; they compassed me about together
98. 8 (their) hands: let the hills be joyful toge.
102. 22 When the people are gathered together
122. 3 builded as a city that is compact together
133. 1 pleasant (it is) for brethren to dwell toge.
Isa. 1. 28 destruction..of the sinners (shall be) tog.
1. 31 they shall both burn together, and none
9. 21 they together (shall be) against Judah
11. 6 the young lion and the fatling together
11. 7 their young ones shall lie down together
11. 14 they shall spoil them of the east together
18. 6 They shall be left together unto the fowls
22. 3 All thy rulers are fled together, they are
22. 3 all that are found in thee are bound toget.
27. 4 I would burn them together
31. 3 fall down, and they all shall fail together
40. 5 all flesh shall see (it) together: for the
41. 1 let us come near together to judgment
41. 19 (and) the pine, and the box tree together
41. 20 know, and consider, and understand tog
41. 23 we may be dismayed, and behold (it) toge.
43. 9 Let all the nations be gathered together
43. 17 they shall lie down together, they shall
43. 26 let us plead together: declare thou, that
44. 11 they shall fear..they shall be ashamed to
45. 8 let righteousness spring up together, I the
45. 16 they shall go to confusion together (that
45. 20 draw near together, ye (that are) escaped
45. 21 let them take counsel together. who hath
46. 2 They stoop, they bow down together, they
48. 13 (when) I call unto them, they stand up tog.
50. 8 let us stand together: who (is) mine adv.
52. 8 with the voice together shall they sing
52. 9 sing together, ye waste places of Jerusal.
60. 13 the pine tree, and the box together, to bea.
65. 7 the iniquities of your fathers together, sa
66. 17 shall be consumed together, saith the LORD
Jer. 3. 18 they shall come together out of the land
6. 11 upon the assembly of young men together
6. 12 others, (with their) fields and wives togeth.
6. 21 the fathers and the sons together shall fall
13. 14 will dash..the fathers and the sons toge.
31. 8 and her that travaileth with child togeth.
31. 13 rejoice..both young men and old togeth.
31. 24 and in all the cities thereof together
41. 1 there they did eat bread together in Miz.
46. 12 stumbled..they are fallen both together
46. 21 turned back, (and) are fled away together
48. 7 (with) his priests and his princes together
49. 3 (and) his priests and his princes together
50. 4 they and the children of Judah together
50. 33 the children of Judah (were) oppressed to.
51. 38 They shall roar together like lions; they
Lam. 2. 8 rampart and the wall..languished toget.
Hos. 1. 11 the children of Israel be gathered toget.
11. 8 is turned..my repentings are kindled to.
Amos 1. 15 he and his princes together, saith the Lo.
3. 3 Can two walk together, except they be ag.
Mic. 2. 12 I will put them together as the sheep of
Zech. 10. 4 Out of him came..every oppressor toget.
5. *Couple, team, yoke, together,* צֶמֶד *tsemed.*
2 Ki. 9. 25 when I and thou rode together after Ah.
6. *A gathering,* אֲסֵפָה *asephah.*
Isa. 24. 22 And they shall be gathered together
7. *Of one another,* ἀλλήλων *allēlōn.*
1 Th. 5. 11 Wherefore comfort yourselves together
8. *Toward each other,* πρὸς ἀλλήλους *pros allēlous.*
Luke 24. 14 they talked together of all these things
9. *Together with,* ἅμα *hama.*
Rom. 3. 12 they are together become unprofitable
1 Th. 4. 17 shall be caught up together with them in
5. 10 died for us, that .we should live together
10. *Together, upon or about the same,* ἐπὶ τὸ αὐτό.
Matt 22. 34 the Pharisees..were gathered together
Luke 17. 35 Two (women) shall be grinding together
Acts 1. 15 the number of names together were
2. 44 all that believed were together and had
3. 1 Peter and John went up together into the
4. 26 the rulers were gathered together against
1 Co. 7. 5 come together again, that Satan tempt you
11. *Together, down to the same,* κατὰ τὸ αὐτό.
Acts 14. 1 they went both together into the synag
12. *With one another,* μετ' ἀλλήλων *met' allēlōn.*
Luke 23. 12 Pilate and Herod were made friends tog.
13. *Together,* ὁμοῦ *homou.*
John 4. 36 and he that reapeth may rejoice together
20. 4 So they ran both together: and the other
21. 2 There were together Simon Peter, and T.

See also Agree, assemble, assembled, assembling, band, bow, bring, builded, call, called, cleave fast, come, comforted, consult, counsel, coupled, flow, folden, follower, framed, gather, gathered, gathering, glorified, grow, join, joined, knit, meet, met, planted, put, raise up, reason, rise up, rolled, run, shake, shut up, smite, sow, stick, strive, struggle, take, temper, tempered, travail in pain, thrust, whisper, work, wrap, wrapped, yoke. *Also* sing together by course, gather together in one. Together with, *see* elected, labour, quicken, sit.

TO'-HU, תֹּחוּ *humility, depression.*
A Kohathite, ancestor of Samuel; called *Nahadh* in 1 Ch. 6. 26, and *Toah* in 1 Ch. 6. 34. B.C. 1230.
1 Sa. 1. 1 Elihu, the son of T., the son of Zuph

TO'-I, TO'-U, תֹּעִי, תֹּעוּ *error, wandering.*
A king of Hamath in the days of David. B.C. 1040.
2 Sa. 8. 9 T...heard that David had smitten all the
8. 10 Then T. sent Joram his son unto king D.
8. 10 fought..for Hadadezer had wars with T.
1 Ch. 18. 9 T...heard how David had smitten all the
18. 10 fought..for Hadarezer had war with T.

TOIL, (to) —
1. *Labour,* עָמָל *amal.*
Gen. 41. 51 God..hath made me forget all my toil, and
2. *Grievous thing, labour,* עִצָּבוֹן *itstsabon.*
Gen. 5. 29 concerning our work and toil of our hands
3. *To try,* βασανίζω *basanizō.*
Mark 6. 48 he saw them toiling in rowing; for the
4. *To labour, be weary, fatigued,* κοπιάω *kopiaō.*
Matt. 6. 28 Consider the lilies..they toil not, neither
Luke 5. 5 we have toiled all the night, and have ta.
12. 27 [they toil not, they spin not; and yet I say]

TOKEN (evident, manifest) —
1. *A sign, token,* אוֹת *oth.*
Gen. 9. 12, 17 This (is) the token of the covenant wh.
9. 13 be for a token of a covenant between me
17. 11 it shall be a token of the covenant betw.
Exod. 3. 12 a token unto thee that I have sent thee
12. 13 blood shall be to you for a token upon the
13. 16 it shall be for a token upon thine hand
Num 17. 10 to be kept for a token against the rebels
Josh. 2. 12 show kindness, and give me a true token
Job 21. 29 the way? and do ye not know their tokens
Psa. 65. 8 They also..are afraid at thy tokens: thou
86. 17 Show me a token for good; that they wh.
135. 9 sent tokens and wonders into the midst
Isa. 44. 25 That frustrateth the tokens of the liars
2. *Proof, manifest token,* ἔνδειγμα *endeigma.*
2 Th. 1. 5 a manifest token of the righteous judgm.
3. *A showing in, indication,* ἔνδειξις *endeixis.*
Phil. 1. 28 is to them an evident token of perdition
4. *A sign, signal, mark,* σημεῖον *sēmeion.*
2 Th. 3. 17 mine own hand, which is the token in ev.
5. *A joint sign, signal,* σύσσημον *sussēmon.*
Mark 14. 44 had given them a token, saying, Whomso.

TO'-LA, תּוֹלָע *warm, crimson.*
1. A son of Issachar. B.C. 1690.
Gen. 46. 13 And the sons of Issachar; T., and Phuv.
Num 26. 23 (of) T., the family of the Tolaites: of Pua
1 Ch. 7. 1 the sons of Issachar (were) T., and Puah
7. 2 the sons of T.; Uzzi, and Rephaiah, and
7. 2 heads of their father's house..of T.
2. A judge of Israel, of the tribe of Issachar. B.C. 1206-1183.
Judg 10. 1 there arose to defend Israel, T. the son of

TO'-LAD, תּוֹלָד *begetter.*
A city in Simeon near Ezem; same of *El-tolad* in Josh. 15. 30.
1 Ch. 4. 29 And at Bilhah, and at Ezem, and at T.

TOLAITES, הַתּוֹלָעִי.
Family of Tola son of Issachar.
Num. 26. 23 (of) Tola, the family of the T.: of Pua, the

TOLD, to be —
1. *To be said,* אָמַר *amar,* 2.
Josh. 2. 2 it was told the king of Jericho, saying
Dan. 8. 26 And the vision..which was told (is) true
2. *To be put before, declared,* נָגַר *nagad,* 6.
Gen. 22. 20 it was told Abraham, saying, Behold, Mi.
27. 42 words of Esau her elder son were told to
31. 22 it was told Laban on the third day that J.
38. 13 it was told Tamar, saying, Behold, thy fa.
38. 24 it was told Judah, saying, Tamar thy da.
Exod 14. 5 it was told the king of Egypt that the pe.
Deut. 17. 4 it be told thee, and thou hast heard (of it)
Josh. 9. 24 Because it was certainly told thy servants
10. 17 it was told Joshua, saying, The five kings
Judg. 9. 25 they robbed all..and it was told Abimel.
9. 47 it was told Abimelech, that all the men
1 Sa. 15. 12 it was told Samuel, saying, Saul came to
19. 19 was told Saul, saying, Behold, David (is)
23. 7, 13 And it was told Saul that David was
27. 4 it was told Saul that David was fled to G.
2 Sa. 6. 12 it was told king David, saying, The LORD
10. 17 when it was told David, he gathered all
19. 1 it was told Joab, Behold, the king weepeth
21. 11 it was told David what Rizpah the daug.
1 Ki. 1. 51 it was told Solomon, saying, Behold, Ad.
2. 29 it was told king Solomon that Joab was
2. 41 it was told Solomon that Shimei had gone
10. 7 the half was not told me: thy wisdom and
18. 13 Was it not told my lord what I did when
2 Ki. 6. 13 it was told him, saying, Behold, (he is) in
8. 7 it was told him, saying, The man of God
1 Ch. 19. 17 it was told David; and he gathered all Is.
2 Ch. 9. 6 the one half..was not told me: (for) thou
Isa. 7. 2 it was told the house of David, saying, S.
40. 21 hath it not been told you from the begin.

3. *To be numbered, recounted,* סָפַר *saphar,* 2.
1 Ki. 8. 5 that could not be told nor numbered for
2 Ch. 5. 6 which could not be told nor numbered

4. *To be numbered, recounted,* סָפַר *saphar,* 4.
Job 37. 20 Shall it be told him that I speak? if a man
Isa. 52. 15 which had not been told them shall they
Hab. 1. 5 ye will not believe, though it be told (y.)

5. *To be weighed,* תָּכַן *takan,* 4.
2 Ki. 12. 11 they gave the money, being told, into the h.

TOLERABLE, more —
More tolerable, ἀνεκτότερον *anektoteron.*
Matt 10. 15 It shall be more tolerable for the land of
11. 22 It shall be more tolerable for Tyre and S.
11. 24 it shall be more tolerable for the land of
Mark 6. 11 [It shall be more tolerable for Sodom and]
Luke 10. 12 it shall be more tolerable in that day for
10. 14 it shall be more tolerable for Tyre and S.

TOLL —
1. *Measured thing, tribute, toll,* מִדָּה *middah.*
Ezra 4. 20 toll, and tribute, and custom, was paid
2. *Measured thing, tribute, toll,* מִנְדָּה *mindah.*
Ezra 4. 13 will they not pay toll, tribute, and custom
7. 24 it shall not be lawful to impose toll, tribute

TOMB —
1. *A stack, heap, tomb,* גָּדִישׁ *gadish.*
Job 21. 32 the grave, and shall remain in the tomb
2. *A monument, tomb,* μνῆμα *mnēma.*
Mark 5. 5 he was in the mountains, and in the tom.
Luke 8. 27 neither abode in. .house, but in the tombs
3. *A monument, tomb,* μνημεῖον *mnēmeion.*
Matt. 8. 28 coming out of the tombs, exceeding fierce
27. 60 laid it in his own new tomb, which he had
Mark 5. 2 there met him out of the tombs a man wi.
5. 3 Who had (his) dwelling among the [tombs]
6. 29 took up his corpse, and laid it in a tomb
4. *A burying place, sepulchre,* τάφος *taphos.*
Matt 23. 29 ye build the tombs of the prophets, and

TONGS —
1. *Tongs, snuffers,* מַלְקָחַיִם *malqachayim.*
Exod 25. 38 the tongs thereof, and the snuff dishes th.
Num. 4. 9 his tongs, and his snuff dishes, and all the
2. *Tongs, snuffers,* מֶלְקָחַיִם *melqachayim.*
1 Ki. 7. 49 the flowers, and the lamps, and the tongs
2 Ch. 4. 21 the tongs, (made he of), gold, (and) that
Isa. 6. 6 (which) he had taken with the tongs from
3. *Axe, tongs,* מַעֲצָד *maatsad.*
Isa. 44. 12 The smith with the tongs both worketh

TONGUE —
1. *Tongue, language,* לָשׁוֹן *lashon.*
Gen. 10. 5 every one after his tongue, after their fa.
10. 20 after their families, after their tongues
10. 31 after their families, after their tongues
Exod 4. 10 I (am) slow of speech, and of a slow ton.
11. 7 against any. .shall not a dog move his to.
Deut 28. 49 a nation whose tongue thou shalt not un.
Josh. 10. 21 none moved his tongue against any of the
Judg. 7. 5 Every one that lappeth. .with his tongue
2 Sa. 23. 2 spake by me, and his word (was) in my t.
Job 5. 21 be hid from the scourge of the tongue
6. 30 Is there iniquity in my tongue? cannot my
15. 5 and thou choosest the tongue of the craf.
20. 12 (though) he hide it under his tongue
20. 16 suck the poison. .the viper's tongue shall
27. 4 not speak wickedness, nor my tongue ut.
29. 10 their tongue cleaved to the roof of their
33. 2 Behold. .my tongue hath spoken in my
41. 1 his tongue with a cord (which) thou lett.
Psa. 5. 9 sepulchre; they flatter with their tongue
10. 7 under his tongue (is) mischief and vanity
12. 3 LORD shall cut off. . the tongue that spea
12. 4 Who have said, With our tongue will we
15. 3 (He that) backbiteth not with his tongue
22. 15 my tongue cleaveth to my jaws, and thou
31. 20 keep them. .from the strife of tongues
34. 13 Keep thy tongue from evil, and thy lips
35. 28 my tongue shall speak of thy righteousn.
37. 30 speaketh wisdom, and his tongue talketh
39. 1 take heed. .that I sin not with my tongue
39. 3 fire burned: (then) spake I with my tong.
45. 1 my tongue (is) the pen of a ready writer
50. 19 givest thy mouth to evil, and thy tongue
51. 14 my tongue shall sing aloud of thy righteo.
52. 2 Thy tongue deviseth mischiefs, like a sh.
52. 4 lovest all devouring words. .deceitful to.
55. 9 Destroy, O LORD, (and) divide their tong.
57. 4 and arrows, and their tongue a sharp sw.
64. 3 Who whet their tongue like a sword, (and)
64. 8 they shall make their own tongue to fall
66. 17 I cried. .he was extolled with my tongue
68. 23 (and) the tongue of thy dogs in the same
71. 24 My tongue also shall talk of thy righteo.
73. 9 and their tongue walketh through the ea.
78. 36 and they lied unto him with their tongues
109. 2 spoken against me with a lying tongue
119. 172 My tongue shall speak of thy word: for
120. 2 Deliver my soul. .from a deceitful tongue
120. 3 what shall be done. .thou false tongue?
126. 2 filled with laughter, and our tongue with
137. 6 let my tongue cleave to the roof of my mo.
139. 4 (there is) not a word in my tongue, (but)
140. 3 They have sharpened their tongues like a
Prov. 6. 17 A proud look, a lying tongue, and hands
6. 24 the flattery of the tongue of a strange wo.
Prov 10. 20 The tongue of the just (is as) choice silver
10. 31 but the froward tongue shall be cut out
12. 18 but the tongue of the wise (is) health
12. 19 but a lying tongue (is) but for a moment
15. 2 The tongue of the wise useth knowledge
15. 4 A wholesome tongue (is) a tree of life, but
16. 1 the answer of the tongue, (is) from the L.
17. 4 (and) a liar giveth ear to a naughty tongue
17. 20 he that hath a perverse tongue falleth in.
18. 21 Death and life. .in the power of the tong.
21. 6 The getting of treasures by a lying tongue
21. 23 Whoso keepeth. .his tongue keepeth his
25. 15 and a soft tongue breaketh the bone
25. 23 an angry countenance a backbiting tongue
26. 28 A lying tongue hateth (those that are) affl.
28. 23 than he that flattereth with the tongue
31. 26 and in her tongue (is) the law of kindness
Song 4. 11 honey and milk (are) under thy tongue
Isa. 3. 8 their tongue and their doings (are) again.
11. 15 the LORD shall utterly destroy the tongue
28. 11 For with. .another tongue will he speak
30. 27 full of indignation, and his tongue as a
32. 4 the tongue of the stammerers shall be re.
33. 19 a stammering tongue, that thou canst not
35. 6 Then shall. .the tongue of the dumb sing
41. 17 (there is) none, and their tongue faileth
45. 23 every knee shall bow, every tongue shall
50. 4 GOD hath given me the tongue of the lea.
54. 17 every tongue (that) shall rise against thee
57. 4 against whom. .draw out the tongue? (are)
59. 3 your tongue hath muttered perverseness
66. 18 I will gather all nations and tongues; and
Jer. 9. 3 they bend their tongues (like) their bow
9. 5 they have taught their tongue to speak
9. 8 Their tongue (is as) an arrow shot out, it
18. 18 let us smite him with the tongue, and let
23. 31 the prophets, that use their tongues, and
Lam. 4. 4 The tongue of the sucking child cleaveth
Eze. 3. 26 I will make thy tongue cleave to the roof
Dan. 1. 4 the learning and the tongue of the Chal.
Hos. 7. 16 shall fall. .for the rage of their tongue
Mic. 6. 12 their tongue (is) deceitful in their mouth
Zeph. 3. 13 neither shall a deceitful tongue be found
Zech 14. 12 their tongue shall consume away in their

2. *A tongue, language,* γλῶσσα *glōssa.*
Mark 7. 33 took him. .and he spit, and touched his to.
7. 35 the string of his tongue was loosed, and
16. 17 [cast out devils. .speak with new tongues]
Luke 1. 64 his tongue (loosed), and he spake, and pr.
16. 24 and cool my tongue; for I am tormented
Acts 2. 3 there appeared unto them cloven tongues
2. 4 began to speak with other tongues, as the
2. 11 we do hear them speak in our tongues
2. 26 my tongue was glad; moreover also my
10. 46 they heard them speak with tongues, and
19. 6 and they spake with tongues, and proph.
Rom. 3. 13 with their tongues they have used deceit
14. 11 and every tongue shall confess to God
1 Co. 12. 10 to another (divers) kinds of tongues; to
12. 10 to another the interpretation of tongues
12. 28 helps, governments, diversities of tongues
12. 30 do all speak with tongues? do all interp.
13. 1 Though I speak with the tongues of men
13. 8 whether (there be) tongues, they shall ce.
14. 2 he that speaketh in an (unknown) tongue
14. 4 He that speaketh in an (unknown) tongue
14. 5 I would that ye all spake with tongues, but
14. 5 greater. than he that speaketh with tong.
14. 6 if I come unto you speaking with tongues
14. 9 except ye utter by the tongue words easy
14. 13 let him that speaketh in an (unknown) to.
14. 14 if I pray in an (unknown) tongue, my sp.
14. 18 I speak with tongues more than ye all
14. 19 ten thousand words in an (unknown) ton.
14. 22 tongues are for a sign, not to them that
14. 23 all speak with tongues, and there come
14. 26 hath a doctrine, hath a tongue, hath a re.
14. 27 If any man speak in an (unknown) tongue
14. 39 and forbid not to speak with tongues
Phil. 2. 11 every tongue should confess that Jesus
Jas. 1. 26 If any man. .bridleth not his tongue, but
3. 5 the tongue is a little member, and boast.
3. 6 And the tongue (is) a fire, a world of ini.
3. 6 so is the tongue among our members, that
3. 8 the tongue can no man tame; (it is) an
1 Pe. 3. 10 let him refrain his tongue from evil, and
1 Jo. 3. 18 let us not love in word, neither in tongue
Rev. 5. 9 out of every kindred, and tongue, and pe.
7. 9 kindreds, and people, and tongues, stood
10. 11 many peoples, and nations, and tongues
11. 9 they of the people, and kindreds, and to.
13. 7 over all kindreds, and tongues, and nati.
14. 6 nation, and kindred, and tongue, and pe.
16. 10 and they gnawed their tongues for pain
17. 15 and multitudes, and nations, and tongues

3. *Dialect,* διάλεκτος *dialektos.*
Acts 1. 19 as that field is called in their proper ton.
2. 8 hear we every man in our own tongue, wh.
21. 40 he spake unto (them) in the Hebrew ton.
22. 2 heard that he spake in the Hebrew tong.
26. 14 saying in the Hebrew tongue, Saul, Saul

TONGUES, (other, Hebrew)—
1. *One of another or different tongue,* ἑτερόγλωσσος.
1 Co. 14. 21 With. .other tongues and other lips will

2. *Hebraically, in the Hebrew,* Ἑβραϊστί *hebraisti.*
John 5. 2 which is called in the Hebrew tongue B.
Rev. 9. 11 whose name in the Hebrew tongue (is)
16. 16 into a place called in the Hebrew tongue

TONGUE, to hold the —
1. *To still, silence,* הָסָה *hasah,* 3.
Amos 6. 10 Hold thy tongue; for we may not make
2. *To keep or remain silent,* חָרַשׁ *charash,* 5.
Esth. 7. 4 if we had been sold. .I had held my ton.
Job 6. 24 Teach me, and I will hold my tongue, and
13. 19 if I hold my tongue, I shall give up the
Hab. 1. 13 holdest thy tongue when the wicked de.

TOO —
[*See* Far, hard, heavy, high, much, strong, superstitious].

TOO much —
Sufficiency, דַּי *dai.*
Esth. 1. 18 Thus. .too much contempt and wrath

TOOK in hunting, that which he —
Hunting, provision, venison, צַיִד *tsayid.*
Prov 12. 27 roasteth not that which he took in hunt.

TOOL —
1. *Destroying weapon, sword, axe,* חֶרֶב *chereb.*
Exod 20. 25 if thou lift up thy tool upon it, thou hast
2. *Vessel,* כְּלִי *keli.*
1 Ki. 6. 7 nor ax (nor) any tool of iron heard in the

TOOTH, teeth —
1. *A tooth,* שֵׁן *shen.*
Gen. 49. 12 His eyes. .red with wine, and his teeth wh.
Exod 21. 24 Eye for eye, tooth for tooth, hand for
21. 27 tooth, or his maid servant's tooth; he sh.
21. 27 shall let him go free for his tooth's sake
Lev. 24. 20 eye for eye, tooth for tooth: as he hath
Num 11. 33 the flesh (was) yet between their teeth
Deut. 19. 21 tooth for tooth, hand for hand, foot for
32. 24 will also send the teeth of beasts upon them
1 Sa. 2. 13 with a flesh hook of three teeth in his ha.
Job 4. 10 and the teeth of the young lions, are bro.
13. 14 Wherefore do I take my flesh in my teeth
16. 9 he gnasheth upon me with his teeth, mine
19. 20 and I am escaped with the skin of my tee.
29. 17 and plucked the spoil out of his teeth
41. 14 his face? his teeth (are) terrible round ab.
Psa. 3. 7 thou hast broken the teeth of the ungodly
35. 16 they gnashed upon me with their teeth
37. 12 and gnasheth upon him with his teeth
57. 4 whose teeth (are) spears and arrows, and
58. 6 Break their teeth, O God, in their mouth
112. 10 shall gnash with his teeth, and melt away
124. 6 hath not given us (as) a prey to their teeth
Prov. 10. 26 As vinegar to the teeth, and as smoke to
25. 19 (is like) a broken tooth, and a foot out of
30. 14 a generation whose teeth (are as) swords
Song. 4. 2 Thy teeth. .like a flock. .shorn, which ca.
6. 6 Thy teeth (are) as a flock of sheep which
Jer. 31. 29 and the children's teeth are set on edge
31. 30 eateth the sour grape, his teeth shall be
Lam. 2. 16 they hiss and gnash the teeth: they say
3. 16 He hath also broken my teeth with gravel
Eze. 18. 2 and the children's teeth are set on edge?
Dan. 7. 5 three ribs. .between the teeth of it, and
7. 7 fourth beast. .and it had great iron teeth
7. 19 whose teeth (were of) iron, and his nails
Joel 1. 6 whose teeth (are) the teeth of a lion, and
Amos 4. 6 I also have given you cleanness of teeth
Mic. 3. 5 that bite with their teeth, and cry, Peace
Zech. 9. 7 his abominations from between his teeth
2. *A tooth,* ὀδούς *odous.*
Matt 5. 38 His eye for an eye, and a tooth for a tooth
8. 12 there shall be weeping and gnashing of te.
13. 42, 50 shall be wailing and gnashing of teeth
22. 13 there shall be weeping and gnashing of te.
24. 51 there shall be weeping and gnashing of te.
25. 30 there shall be weeping and gnashing of te.
Mark 9. 18 gnasheth with his teeth, and pineth away
Luke 13. 28 There shall be weeping and gnashing of te.
Acts 7. 54 and they gnashed on him with (their) teeth
Rev. 9. 8 and their teeth were as (the teeth) of lions

TOP —
1. *Roof, top, pinnacle,* גַּג *gag.*
Exod. 30. 3 the top thereof, and the sides thereof ro
37. 26 the top of it, and the sides thereof roun
Judg. 9. 51 and gat them up to the top of the tower
2 Ki. 23. 12 altars that (were) on the top of the uppe
3. *Bone, substance,* גֶּרֶם *gerem.*
2 Ki. 9. 13 put (it) under him on the top of the stairs
3. *A cleft,* סְעִיף *seiph.*
Judg. 15. 8 he went down and dwelt in the top of the
15. 11 went to the top of the rock Etam, and sa.
Isa. 2. 21 into the tops of the ragged rocks, for fear
4. *Clear or dry place,* צְחִיחַ *tsechiach.*
Eze. 24. 7 blood. .she set it upon the top of a rock
24. 8 I have set her blood upon the top of a ro.
26. 4 I will also. .make her like the top of a ro.
26. 14 I will make thee like the top of a rock
5. *Foliage, highest branch,* צַמֶּרֶת *tsammereth.*
Eze. 31. 3 and his top was among the thick boughs
31. 10 hath shot up his top among the thick bo.
31. 14 neither shoot up their top among the th.
6. *Head, top,* רֹאשׁ *rosh.*
Gen. 8. 5 first (day) of the month, were the tops of
11. 4 build us a city, and a tower whose top (may
28. 12 top of it reached to heaven: and behold
28. 18 a pillar, and poured oil upon the top of
Exod 17. 9 I will stand on the top of the hill with the
17. 10 Aaron, and Hur, went up to the top of the
19. 20 upon mount Sinai, on the top of the mo.

Exod19. 20 LORD called Moses (up) to the top of the
24. 17 devouring fire on the top of the mount in
28. 32 there shall be an hole in the top of it, in
34. 2 present thyself there to me in the top of
Num.14. 40 gat them up into the top of the mountain
14. 44 they presumed to go up unto the hill top
20. 28 Aaron died there in the top of the mount
21. 20 to the top of Pisgah, which looketh toward
23. 9 For from the top of the rocks I see him
23. 14 the field of Zophim, to the top of Pisgah
23. 28 Balak brought Balaam unto the top of P.
Deut. 3. 27 Get thee up into the top of Pisgah, and
34. 1 to the top of Pisgah, that (is) over against
Josh.15. 8 the border went up to the top of the mo.
15. 9 border was drawn from the top of the hill
Judg. 6. 26 build an altar..upon the top of this rock
9. 7 stood in the top of mount Gerizim, and li.
9. 25 set liers in wait for him in the top of the
9. 36 there came people down from the top of
16. 3 carried them up to the top of an hill, that
1 Sa. 26. 13 stood on the top of an hill afar off, a great
2 Sa. 2. 25 became one troop, and stood on the top of
5. 24 sound of a going in the tops of the mulb.
15. 32 (when) David was come to the top..where
16. 1 when David was a little past the top (of
1 Ki. 7. 16 to set upon the tops of the pillars: the he.
7. 17, 19 chapiters which (were) upon the top of
7. 18 cover the chapiters that (were) upon the t.
7. 22 upon the top of the pillars (was) lily work
7. 35 in the top of the base..on the top of the
7. 41 chapiters that (were) on the top of the two
7. 41 chapiters which (were) upon the top of the
10. 19 the top of the throne (was) round behind
18. 42 and Elijah went up to the top of Carmel
2 Ki. 1. 9 and, behold, he sat on the top of an hill
1 Ch.14. 15 of going in the tops of the mulberry trees
2 Ch. 3. 15 chapiter that (was) on the top of each of
4. 12, 12 chapiters which (were) on the top of
25. 12 brought them unto the top of the rock
25. 12 cast them down from the top of the rock
Esth. 5. 2 Esther drew near, and touched the top of
Job 24. 24 and cut off as the tops of the ears of corn
Psa. 72. 16 an handful..upon the top of the mountains
Prov. 8. 2 She standeth in the top of high places, by
23. 34 or as he that lieth upon the top of a mast
Song 4. 8 look from the top of Amana, from the top
Isa. 2. 2 be established in the top of the mountains
17. 6 two (or) three berries in the top of the up.
30. 17 as a beacon upon the top of a mountain
42. 11 let them shout from the top of the moun.
Lam. 2. 19 that faint for hunger in the top of every
4. 1 are poured out in the top of every street
Eze. 6. 13 in all the tops of the mountains, and under
17. 4 He cropped off the top of his young twigs
17. 22 will crop off from the top of his young tw.
43. 12 Upon the top of the mountain the whole
Hos. 4. 13 They sacrifice upon the tops of the moun.
Joel. 2. 5 Like the noise of chariots on the tops of
Amos 1. 2 mourn, and the top of Carmel shall wither
9. 3 though they hide themselves in the top
Mic. 4. 1 shall be established in the top of the mo.
Nah. 3. 10 were dashed in pieces at the top of all the
Zech. 4. 2 with a bowl upon the top of it, and his se.
4. 2 seven lamps, which (are) upon the top th.

7. *A point, tip,* ἄκρον *akron.*
Heb. 11. 21 and worshipped..upon the top of his staff

8. *From above, top, upper part,* ἄνωθεν *anōthen.*
Matt27. 51 was rent in twain from the top to the bo.
Mark15. 38 rent in twain from the top to the bottom
John19. 23 without seam, woven from the top throu.

TOP of head or house —

1. *Roof, top, pinnacle,* גַּג *gag.*
1 Sa. 9. 25 communed with Saul upon the top of the h.
9. 26 Samuel called Saul to the top of the house
2 Sa. 16. 22 spread..a tent upon the top of the house
Isa. 15. 3 on the tops of their houses, and in their

2. *Top or crown of the head, pate,* קָדְקֹד *qodqod.*
Deut28. 35 from .thy foot unto the top of thy head
33. 16 and upon the top of the head of him (that

TOPAZ —

1. *Topaz, emerald,* פִּטְדָה *pitedah.*
Exod28. 17 a sardius, a topaz, and a carbuncle: (this
39. 10 a sardius, a topaz, and a carbuncle: this
Job 28. 19 The topaz of Ethiopia shall not equal it
Eze. 28. 13 topaz, and the diamond, the beryl, the on.

2. *Topaz, (gem of a yellowish green colour),* τοπάζιον.
Rev. 21. 20 the eighth, beryl; the ninth, a topaz; the

TO'-PHEL, תֹּפֶל *mortar.*
A place in the wilderness of Sinai over against Paran; now called *Tufileh,* S. E. of Salt Sea.
Deut. 1. 1 between Paran, and T., and Laban, and

TOPH'-ET, תָּפְתֶּה *altar.*
A place in the valley of Hinnom where sacrifices were offered and the dead bodies buried or consumed.
Isa. 30. 33 T. (is) ordained of old; yea, for the king

TO'-PHETH, TO'-PHET, תֹּפֶת, הַתֹּפֶת.
The same as the preceding.
2 Ki.23. 10 he defiled T., which (is) in the valley of
Jer. 7. 31 And they have built the high places of T.
7. 32 Therefore..it shall no more be called T.
7. 32 they shall bury in T., till there be no pl.
19. 6 that this place shall no more be called T.
19. 11 they shall bury (them) in T., till (there be)
19. 12 Thus will I..(even) make this city as T.
Jer. 19. 13 house..shall be defiled as the place of T.
19. 14 Then came Jeremiah from T., whither the

TORCH —

1. *A torch, flame,* לַפִּיד *lappid.*
Nah. 2. 3 with flaming torches in the day of his pr.
Zech.12. 6 will I make..like a torch of fire in a sheaf

2. *A torch, flashing fire,* פְּלָדָה *peladah.*
Nah. 2. 4 they shall seem like torches, they shall

3. *A lamp, torch, shining light,* λαμπάς *lampas.*
John 18. 3 with lanterns, and torches, and weapons

TORMENT, tormentor —

1. *A trial, testing, torment,* βασανισμός *basanismos.*
Rev. 9. 5 their torment..as the torment of a scorp.
14. 11 the smoke of their torment ascendeth up
18. 7 so much torment and sorrow give her, for
18. 10 Standing afar off for the fear of her torm.
18. 15 stand afar off for the fear of her torment

2. *One who tries or tests, inquisitor,* βασανιστής.
Matt18. 34 delivered him to the tormentors, till he

3. *A test, trial, inquisition, torment,* βάσανος *basanos.*
Matt. 4. 24 were taken with divers diseases and torm.
Luke16. 23 lifted up his eyes, being in torments, and
16. 28 lest they also come into this place of tor.

4. *A pruning, restraining, restraint,* κόλασις.
1 Jo. 4. 18 casteth out fear: because fear hath torm.

TORMENT, be tormented, to —

1. *To try, test, torment,* βασανίζω *basanizō.*
Matt. 8. 6 sick of the palsy, grievously tormented
8. 29 art thou come hither to torment us before
Mark 5. 7 adjure thee by God, that thou torment me
Luke 8. 28 cried out..I beseech thee, torment me not
Rev. 9. 5 that they should be tormented five months
11. 10 because these two prophets tormented th.
14. 10 he shall be tormented with fire and brim.
20. 10 shall be tormented day and night for ever

2. *Having or suffering evil, ill used,* κακουχούμενος.
Heb. 11. 37 wandered..being destitute, afflicted, tor.

3. *To be pained,* ὀδυνάομαι *odunaomai.*
Luke16. 24 have mercy..I am tormented in this flame
16. 25 he is comforted, and thou art tormented

TORN (in pieces, of or with beasts) —

1. *Something torn,* טְרֵפָה *terephah.*
Gen. 31. 39 That which was torn..I brought not unto
Exod22. 13 shall not make good that which was torn
22. 31 eat (any) flesh (that is) torn of beasts in
Lev. 7. 24 fat of that which is torn with beasts, may
17. 15 torn (with beasts, whether it be) one of
22. 8 That which dieth of itself, or is torn (with
Eze. 4. 14 which dieth of itself, or is torn in pieces
44. 31 dead of itself, or torn, whether it be fowl

2. *Filth, sweepings, scrapings,* סוּחָה *suchah.*
Isa. 5. 25 their carcases..torn in the midst of the

TORN in pieces, to be —

1. *To be torn,* טָרַף *taraph,* 2.
Exod22. 13 If it be torn in pieces..let him bring it
Jer. 5. 6 that goeth out thence shall be torn in pi.

2. *To be torn,* טָרַף *taraph,* 4.
Gen. 44. 28 I said, Surely he is torn in pieces, and I

TORTOISE —

Tortoise, a species of Lybian lizard, צָב *tsab.*
Lev. 11. 29 the weasel, and the mouse, and the tort.

TORTURED, to be —

To be beaten with clubs, bastinaded, τυμπανίζομαι.
Heb.11. 35 were tortured, not accepting deliverance

TOSS (self), be tossed, to —

1. *To shake self,* גָּעַשׁ *gaash,* 7.
Jer. 5. 22 though the waves thereof toss themselves

2. *A wrapping,* צְנֵפָה *tsenephah.*
Isa. 22. 18 He will surely violently turn and toss th.

3. *To try, test, toss,* βασανίζω *basanizō.*
Matt14. 24 tossed with winds: for the wind was con.

4. *To be agitated,* ῥιπίζομαι *rhipizomai.*
Jas. 1. 6 a wave..driven with the wind, and tossed

TOSSED to and fro, up and down, to be —

1. *To be driven away,* נָדַף *nadaph,* 2.
Prov 21. 6 a vanity tossed to and fro of them that se.

2. *To be shaken,* נָעַר *naar,* 2.
Psa.109. 23 I am tossed up and down as the locust

3. *To be tossed, agitated,* κλυδωνίζομαι *kludōnizom.*
Eph. 4. 14 be no more children, tossed to and fro, and

TOSSINGS to and fro —

Movings, tossings, נְדֻדִים *nedudim.*
Job 7. 4 I am full of tossings to and fro unto the

TOTTER, to —

To thrust away, down, over, דָּחָה *dachah.*
Psa. 62. 3 ye shall be..as a bowing wall..a tottering

TOU. *See* TOI.

TOUCH, be touched, to —

1. *To touch, come upon, plague,* נָגַע *naga.*
Gen. 3. 3 Ye shall not eat..neither shall ye touch
20. 6 therefore suffered I thee not to touch her
26. 11 He that toucheth this man or his wife sh.
26. 29 as we have not touched thee, and as we
32. 25 he touched the hollow of his thigh, 32.32.
Exod 19. 12 or touch the border..whosoever toucheth
19. 13 There shall not an hand touch it, but he
29. 37 whatsoever toucheth the altar shall be holy
30. 29 whatsoever toucheth them shall be holy
Lev. 5. 2 if a soul touch any unclean thing, whether
5. 3 if he touch the uncleanness of man, what.
6. 18 every one that toucheth them shall be ho.
6. 27 Whatsoever shall touch the flesh thereof
7. 19 the flesh that toucheth any unclean (th.)
7. 21 the soul that shall touch any unclean (th.)
11. 8 their carcase shall ye not touch, they (are)
11. 24 whosoever toucheth the carcase of them
11. 26 every one that toucheth them shall be un.
11. 27 whoso toucheth their carcase shall be un.
11. 31 whosoever doth touch them, when they
11. 36 that which toucheth their carcase shall be
11. 39 he that toucheth the carcase thereof shall
12. 4 she shall touch no hallowed thing, nor co.
15. 5 whosoever toucheth his bed shall wash his
15. 7 he that toucheth the flesh of him that hath
15. 10 whosoever toucheth any thing that was
15. 11 whomsoever he toucheth that hath the is.
15. 12 the vessel of earth that he toucheth which
15. 19 whosoever toucheth her shall be unclean
15. 21 whosoever toucheth her bed shall wash his
15. 22 whosoever toucheth any thing that she sat
15. 23 when he toucheth it, he shall be unclean
15. 27 whosoever toucheth those things shall be
22. 4 whoso toucheth any thing (that is) uncl.
22. 5 whosoever toucheth any creeping thing
22. 6 The soul which hath touched any such sh.
Num. 4. 15 they shall not touch (any) holy thing, lest
16. 26 touch nothing of theirs, lest ye be consu.
19. 11 He that toucheth the dead body of any
19. 13 Whosoever toucheth the dead body of any
19. 16 whosoever toucheth one that is slain with
19. 18 him that touched a bone, or one slain, or
19. 21 he that toucheth the water of separation
19. 22 whatsoever the unclean (person) toucheth
19. 22 the soul that toucheth (it) shall be uncle.
31. 19 whosoever hath touched any slain, purify
Deut 14. 8 not eat of their flesh, nor touch their dead
Josh. 9. 19 now therefore we may not touch them
Judg. 6. 21 touched the flesh and the unleavened ca.
Ruth 2. 9 the young men that they shall not touch
1 Sa. 10. 26 a band of men, whose hearts God had to.
2 Sa. 14. 10 and he shall not touch thee any more
23. 7 the man (that) shall touch them must be
1 Ki. 6. 27 the wing of the one touched the (one) wall
6. 27 touched the other..touched one another
19. 5 an angel touched him, and said unto him
19. 7 and touched him, and said unto him, Ar.
2 Ki.13. 21 the man was let down, and touched the
1 Ch.16. 22 Touch not mine anointed, and do my pro.
Esth. 5. 2 Esther drew near, and touched the top
Job 1. 11 put forth thine hand now, and touch all
2. 5 put forth thine hand now, and touch his
4. 5 it toucheth thee, and thou art troubled
5. 19 in seven there shall no evil touch thee
6. 7 The things (that) my soul refused to touch
19. 21 for the hand of God hath touched me
Psa.104. 32 he toucheth the hills, and they smoke
105. 15 Touch not mine anointed, and do my pr
144. 5 touch the mountains, and they shall sm.
Prov. 6. 29 whosoever toucheth her shall not be inn.
Isa. 6. 7 this hath touched thy lips; and thine in.
52. 11 go ye out from thence, touch no unclean
Jer. 12. 14 that touch the inheritance which I have
Lam. 4. 14 so that men could not touch their garment
4. 15 (it is) unclean; depart, depart, touch not
Eze. 17. 10 wither when the east wind toucheth it?
Dan. 8. 5 came from the west..and touched not the
8. 18 but he touched me, and set me upright
9. 21 Gabriel..touched me about the time of
10. 10 an hand touched me, which set me upon
10. 16 (one) like..the sons of men touched my
10. 18 there came again and touched me (one)
Hos. 4. 2 they break out, and blood toucheth blood
Amos 9. 5 the LORD..(is) he that toucheth the land
Hag. 2. 12 with his skirt do touch bread, or pottage
2. 13 If (one that is) unclean..touch any of th.
Zech. 2. 8 he that toucheth you toucheth the apple

2. *To (cause to) touch,* נָגַע *naga,* 5.
Jer. 1. 9 LORD put forth his hand, and touched my

3. *To kiss, touch,* נָשַׁק *nashaq,* 5.
Eze. 3. 13 the noise of the wings..that touched one

4. *To smell, refresh, touch,* רוּחַ *ruach,* 5.
Judg16. 9 as a thread..is broken when it toucheth

5. *To touch, hold on, embrace,* ἅπτομαι *haptomai.*
Matt.8. 3 Jesus put forth (his) hand, and touched
8. 15 he touched her hand, and the fever left
9. 20 came behind (him), and touched the hem
9. 21 If I may but touch his garment, I shall
9. 29 Then touched he their eyes, saying, Acc.
14. 36 that they might only touch the hem of his
14. 36 as many as touched were made perfectly
17. 7 Jesus came and touched them, and said
20. 34 had compassion (on them), and touched
Mark 1. 41 put forth (his) hand, and touched him, and
3. 10 they pressed upon him for to touch him
5. 27 came in the press behind, and touched
5. 28 If I may but touch his clothes, I shall be
5. 30 turned..and said, Who touched my clo.?
5. 31 thronging thee, and sayest thou, Who to.
6. 56 besought him that they might touch if it
6. 56 as many as touched him were made whole
7. 33 and he spit, and touched his tongue
8. 22 bring a blind man..and besought him to t.
10. 13 brought young children..that he should t.

Luke 5. 13 he put forth (his) hand, and touched him
6. 19 the whole multitude sought to touch him
7. 14 he came and touched the bier: and they that
7. 39 what manner of woman (this is) that t.
8. 44 and touched the border of his garment
8. 45 Jesus said, Who touched me? When all
8. 45 [press (thee), and sayest thou, Who touch.]
8. 46 Somebody hath touched me: for I perce.
8. 47 for what cause she had touched him, and
18. 15 brought..infants, that he would touch th.
22. 51 And he touched his ear, and healed him
John20. 17 Touch me not; for I am not yet ascended
1 Co. 7. 1 good for a man not to touch a woman
2 Co. 6. 17 touch not the unclean (thing); and I will
Col. 2. 21 Touch not; taste not; handle not
1 Jo. 5. 18 and that wicked one toucheth him not

6. *To touch, arrive at, come to,* θίγω *thigō.*
Heb.11. 28 kept the passover..lest he..should touch
12. 20 if so much as a beast touch the mountain

7. *To lead down to (land),* κατάγω *katagō.*
Acts 27. 3 And the next (day) we touched at Sidon

8. *To touch, touch lightly,* προσψαύω *prospsauō.*
Luke11. 46 ye yourselves touch not the burdens with

9. *To feel, handle, grope after,* ψηλαφάω *psēlaphaō.*
Heb.12. 18 the mount that might be touched, and

TOUCHED with the feeling of, to be —
To feel with, συμπαθέω *sumpatheō.*
Heb. 4. 15 cannot be touched with the feeling of our

TOUCHING, (as) —
1. *Unto, concerning, in reference to,* אֶל *el.*
Jer. 22. 11 For thus saith the LORD touching Shallum
2. *On, over, concerning,* עַל *al.*
Jer. 1. 16 I will utter my judgments..touching all
3. *Upon, over,* ἐπί *(acc.) epi.*
2 Th. 3. 4 we have confidence in the Lord touching
4. *Down to,* κατά *(acc.) kata.*
Rom 11. 28 as touching the election..beloved for the
Phil. 3. 5 Hebrews; as touching the law, a Pharis.
3. 6 touching the righteousness which is in
5. *Concerning,* περί *(gen.) peri.*
Acts 24. 21 Touching the resurrection of the dead I
26. 2 answer for myself..touching all the thin.
Col. 4. 10 touching whom ye received commandme.

TOW —
1. *Tow, refuse of flax,* נְעֹרֶת *neoreth.*
Judg 16. 9 as a thread of tow is broken when it tou.
Isa. 1. 31 the strong shall be as tow, and the maker
2. *Flax,* פִּשְׁתָּה *pishtah.*
Isa. 43. 17 they are extinct, they are quenched as tow

TOWARD —
1. *Unto, toward,* אֶל *el.*
Gen. 30. 40 toward the ring straked, and all the bro.
2. *At the side of,* אֵצֶל *etsel.*
1 Sa. 20. 41 David arose out of (a place) toward the
3. *The way of,* דֶּרֶךְ *derek.*
1 Ki. 8. 44 shall pray unto the LORD toward the city
8. 48 pray unto thee toward their land which
18. 43 Go up now, look toward the sea. And
2 Ki.25. 4 and (the king) went the way toward the
2 Ch. 6. 34 they pray unto thee toward this city wh.
6. 38 pray toward their land, which thou gav.
Eze. 20. 46 Son of man, set thy face toward the south
40. 6 unto the gate which looketh toward the
40. 20 outward court that looked toward the no.
40. 22 measure of the gate that looketh toward
40. 24 toward the south..a gate toward the so.
40. 27 a gate in the inner court toward the south
40. 27 measured..toward the south an hundred
40. 32 brought me into the inner court toward
40. 44 and their prospect (was) toward the south
40. 44 one..(having) the prospect toward the no
40. 45, 46 chamber, whose prospect (is) toward
41. 11 one door toward the north, and another
41. 12 at the end toward the west (was) seventy
42. 1 brought me forth..the way toward the n.
42. 7 toward the outer court on the fore part
42. 10 the wall of the court toward the east, over
42. 11 the chambers which (were) toward the
42. 12 doors of the chambers that (were) toward
42. 12 directly before the wall toward the east
42. 15 toward the gate whose prospect (is) towa.
43. 1 (even) the gate that looketh toward the
43. 4 way of the gate whose prospect (is) toward
4. *Over against,* מוּל *mul.*
Exod18. 19 Be thou for the people to God ward, that
28. 27 toward the fore part thereof, over against
39. 20 toward the fore part of it, over against
5. *Before,* נֶגֶד *neged.*
Dan. 6. 10 his windows being open..toward Jerusa.
6. *Unto, up to,* עַד *ad.*
Gen. 13. 12 and Lot..pitched (his) tent toward Sodom
7. *With,* עִם *im.*
Dan. 4. 2 that the high God hath wrought toward
8. *On the face of,* עַל־פְּנֵי *al-pene.*
Gen. 18. 16 the men rose up..and looked toward Sod.
19. 28 toward Sodom and Gomorrah, and toward
Num21. 20 Pisgah, which looketh toward Jeshimon
23. 28 top of Peor, that looketh toward Jeshim.
2 Sa. 15. 23 passed over, toward the way of the wild.
9. *To, unto, toward,* εἰς *eis.*
Matt28. 1 as it began to dawn toward the first (day)
Luke12. 21 layeth up treasure..and is not rich towa.
13. 22 teaching and journeying toward Jerusal.
John 6. 17 went over the sea toward Capernaum. And
Acts 1. 10 while they looked stedfastly toward hea.
20. 21 repentance toward God, and faith toward
24. 15 have hope toward God, which they them.
27. 40 hoised up the mainsail..and made towa.
28. 14 desired to tarry..so we went toward Rome
Rom. 1. 27 burned in their lust one toward another
5. 8 But God commendeth his love toward us
12. 16 (Be) of the same mind one toward 14. 19.
2 Co. 1. 16 of you to be brought on my way toward.
2. 8 that ye would confirm (your) love toward
7. 15 inward affection is more abundant towa.
9. 8 able to make all grace abound toward you
10. 1 myself..being absent am bold toward you
13. 4 live with him by the power of God toward
Gal. 2. 8 same was mighty in me toward the Gent.
Eph. 1. 8 Wherein he hath abounded toward us in
1 Th. 3. 12 in love one toward another, and toward
4. 10 indeed ye do it toward all the brethren
2 Th. 1. 3 charity of every one of you all toward ea.
Phm. 5 faith, which thou hast..toward all saints
Heb. 6. 10 love, which ye have showed toward his
1 Pe. 3. 21 the answer of a good conscience toward
2 Pe. 3. 9 in long suffering [to] us ward, not willing
10. *In, among,* ἐν *en.*
Luke 2. 14 and on earth peace, good will toward men
Rom.15. 5 like minded one toward another according
1 Jo. 4. 9 was manifested the love of God toward
11. *Upon, over,* ἐπί *(dat.) epi.*
Mark 6. 34 and was moved with compassion [toward]
12. *Upon, over, up to,* ἐπί *(acc.) epi.*
Matt12. 49 he stretched forth his hand toward his d.
14. 14 and was moved with compassion toward
Rom.11. 22 but toward thee, goodness, if thou conti.
1 Co. 7. 36 behaveth himself uncomely toward his vi.
Eph. 2. 7 in (his) kindness toward us through Christ
Heb. 6. 1 from dead works, and of faith toward G.
13. *Down to,* κατά *(acc.) kata.*
Acts 8. 26 Arise, and go toward the south, unto
27. 12 lieth toward the south west and north we.
Phil. 3. 14 I press toward the mark for the prize of
14. *Toward,* πρός *(acc.) pros.*
Luke24. 29 Abide with us; for it is toward evening
Acts 24. 16 always a conscience void of offence towa.
2 Co. 1. 12 conversation..more abundantly to you wa.
1. 18 our word toward you was not yea and nay
3. 4 And such trust have we..to God ward
7. 4 Great (is) my boldness of speech toward
Phil. 2. 30 to supply your lack of service toward me
Col. 4. 5 Walk in wisdom toward them that are wi.
1 Th. 1. 8 your faith to God ward is spread abroad
4. 12 That ye may walk honestly toward them
5. 14 support the weak, be patient toward all
Phm. 5 faith, which thou hast [toward] the Lord
1 Jo. 3. 21 (then) have we confidence toward God
15. *Over, for, in behalf of,* ὑπέρ *(gen.) huper.*
2 Co. 7. 7 when he told..your fervent mind toward

TOWEL —
Linen towel, (Lat. linteum), λέντιον *lention.*
John13 4 He riseth from supper..and took a towel
13. 5 to wipe..with the towel wherewith he

TOWER, (high) —
1. *A watch tower,* בַּחוֹן *bachon.*
Jer. 6. 27 I have set thee..a tower..a fortress am.
2. *A watch tower,* בַּחוּן *bachun.*
Isa. 23. 13 they set up the towers thereof; they rais.
3. *A watch tower,* בַּחַן *bachan.*
Isa. 32. 14 the forts and towers shall be for dens fo.
4. *Tower,* מִגְדּוֹל *migdol* [V.L. מגדיל].
2 Sa. 22. 51 the tower of salvation for his king, and
5. *A great tower,* מִגְדָּל *migdal.*
Gen. 11. 4 Go to, let us build us a city, and a tower
11. 5 LORD came down to see . . the tower
35. 21 spread his tent beyond the tower of Edar
Judg. 8. 9 When I come. I will break down this to.
8. 17 beat down the tower of Penuel, and slew
9. 46, 47, 49 all the men of the tower of Shech.
9. 51 there was a strong tower within the city
9. 51 and gat them up to the top of the tower
9. 52 unto the tower..the door of the tower
2 Ki. 9. 17 there stood a watchman on the tower in
17. 9 from the tower of the watchmen to the
18. 8 from the tower of the watchmen to the
2 Ch.14. 7 walls and towers, gates and bars, (while)
26. 9 Moreover Uzziah built towers in Jerusal.
26. 10 Also he built towers in the desert, and
26. 15 to be on the towers and upon the bulwark
27. 4 in the forests he built castles and towers
32. 5 raised (it) up to the towers, and another
Neh. 3. 1 unto the tower of Meah .unto the tower
3. 11 repaired the other piece, and the tower of
3. 25 tower which lieth out from the king's hi.
3. 26 toward the east, and the tower that lieth
3. 27 over against the great tower that lieth out
12. 38 from beyond the tower of the furnaces
12. 39 the tower of Hananeel, and the tower of
Psa. 48. 12 go round about her: tell the towers the.
61. 3 a shelter..(and) a strong tower from the
Prov 18. 10 The name of the LORD (is) a strong tower
Song 4. 4 Thy neck (is) like the tower of David buil.
Song 7. 4 as a tower of ivory..thy nose (is) as the to.
8. 10 I (am) a wall, and my breasts like towers
Isa. 2. 15 upon every high tower, and upon every
5. 2 built a tower in the midst of it, and also
30. 25 the great slaughter, when the towers fall
33. 18 where (is) he that counted the towers?
Jer. 31. 38 from the tower of Hananeel unto the gate
Eze. 26. 4 shall destroy..and break down her towers
26. 9 with his axes he shall break down thy to.
27. 11 and the Gammadims were in thy towers
Mic. 4. 8 thou, O tower of the flock, the strong hold
Zech 14. 10 (from) the tower of Hananeel unto the ki.
6. *A great tower,* מִגְדּוֹל *migdol.*
2 Sa. 22. 51 (He is) the tower of salvation for his king
Eze. 29. 10 from the tower of Syene even unto the bo.
30. 6 from the tower of Syene shall they fall in
7. *Bulwark,* מָצוֹר *matsor.*
Hab. 2. 1 I will..set me up on the tower, and will wa
8. *High place,* עֹפֶל *ophel.*
2 Ki. 5. 24 And when he came to the tower, he took
9. *Corner,* פִּנָּה *pinnah.*
Zeph. 1. 16 A day of..alarm..against the high towers
3. 6 I have cut off the nations: their tower
10. *High place, tower,* מִשְׂגָּב *misgab.*
2 Sa. 22. 3 my high tower, and my refuge, my savi.
Psa. 18. 2 horn of my salvation, (and) my high tow.
144. 2 my high tower, and my deliverer; my sh.
11. *A tower, castle,* πύργος *purgos.*
Matt21.33 digged a winepress in it, and built a tow.
Mark12. 1 built a tower, and let it out to husband.
Luke13. 4 those eighteen, upon whom the tower in
14. 28 which of you, intending to build a tower

TOWER OF DAVID, מִגְדַּל דָּוִד *migdal David.*
Part of the castle in Zion.
Song. 4. 4 Thy neck (is) like the tower of David buil.

TOWER OF EDAR, מִגְדַּל עֵדֶר *migdal Eder.*
Between Bethlehem and Hebron.
Gen. 35. 21 spread his tent beyond the tower of Edar

TOWER OF THE FLOCK, מִגְדַּל עֵדֶר *migdal Eder.*
Same as the preceding, or in Zion.
Mic. 4. 8 O tower of the flock..unto thee shall it co.

TOWER OF THE FURNACES, מִגְדַּל הַתַּנּוּרִים *migdal hattannurim.*
On the wall of Jerusalem, near the valley gate.
Neh. 3. 11 Hashub..repaired..the tower of the fur.
12. 38 from beyond the tower of the furnaces even

TOWER OF HANANEEL, מִגְדַּל חֲנַנְאֵל *migdal Hananeel.*
On the wall of Jerusalem, near the sheep gate.
Neh. 3. 1 they sanctified it..unto the tower of Han.
12. 39 And from above..the tower of Hananeel
Jer. 31. 38 from the tower of Hananeel unto the gate
Zech.14. 10 the tower of Hananeel unto the king's wine

TOWER OF LEBANON, מִגְדַּל הַלְּבָנוֹן *migdal hal-leban.*
On the E. of Lebanon.
Song. 7. 4 thy nose (is) as the tower of Lebanon whi.

TOWER OF MEAH, מִגְדַּל הַמֵּאָה *migdal ham-meah.*
On the wall of Jerusalem, between the sheep gate and the tower of Hananeel.
Neh. 3. 1 even unto the tower of Meah they sancti.
12. 39 from above..the tower of Meah, even unto

TOWER OF PENUEL, מִגְדַּל פְּנוּאֵל *migdal Penuel.*
In Penuel, a city of Gilead.
Judg. 8. 17 he beat down the tower of Penuel, and

TOWER OF SHECHEM, מִגְדַּל שְׁכֶם *migdal Shechem.*
In Shechem, a city of Ephraim.
Judg. 9. 46 the men of the tower of Shechem heard
9. 47, 49 that all the men of the tower of Shec.

TOWER OF SYENE, מִגְדַּל סְוֵנֵה *migdal Seveneh.*
In Syene, a city in the S. of Egypt.
Eze. 29. 10 from the tower of Syene even unto the bo.
30. 6 from the tower of Syene shall they fall in

TOWN, (small, without walls) —
1. *Daughter,* בַּת *bath.*
Josh 15. 45 Ekron, with her towns and her villages
15. 47, 47 with her towns and her villages
17. 11, 11, 11, 11, 11 and her towns, and the
17. 16 of Beth-shean and her towns, and..of the
Judg 11. 26 Heshbon and her towns..Aroer and her t.
1 Ch. 2. 23 and the towns thereof..threescore cities
7. 28 Beth-el and the towns..towns..towns..t.
8. 12 built Ono and Lod, with the towns there.
2 Ch.13. 19, 19, 19 with the towns thereof
2. *Hamlets,* חַוּוֹת *chavvoth.*
Num32. 41 went and took the small towns thereof
Josh 13. 30 the towns of Jair, which (are) in Bashan
1 Ki. 4. 13 to him (pertained) the towns of Jair the
1 Ch. 2. 23 took Geshur, and Aram, with the towns
3. *Court, village,* חָצֵר *chatser.*
Gen. 25. 16 their names, by their towns, and by their
4. *A city, (place of stir),* עִיר *ir.*
Deut. 3. 5 cities..besides unwalled towns a great ma.
1 Sa. 16. 4 the elders of the town trembled at his co.
23. 7 by entering into a town that hath gates
27. 5 let them give me a place in some town in
Esth. 9. 19 Jews..that dwelt in the unwalled towns
Jer. 19. 15 bring upon this city and upon all her to.
Hab. 2. 12 Woe to him that buildeth a town with

5. *A city (with walls)*, קִיר *qir.*
Josh. 2. 15 her house (was) upon the town wall, and
6. *Open villages*, פְּרָזוֹת *perazoth.*
Zech. 2. 4 shall be inhabited (as) towns without wa.
7. *A town (without walls)*, κώμη *kōmē.*
Matt 10. 11 into whatsoever city or town ye shall en.
Mark 8. 23 by the hand, and led him out of the town
8. 26 Neither go into..town, nor tell..in the to.
8. 27 Jesus went..into the towns of Cesarea P.
Luke 5. 17 which were come out of every town of G.
9. 6 went through the towns, preaching the
9. 12 they may go into the towns and country
John 7. 42 out of the town of Bethlehem, where Da.
11. 1 Bethany, the town of Mary and her sister
11. 30 Jesus was not yet come into the town, but
8. *A small town or village*, κωμόπολις *kōmopolis.*
Mark 1. 38 Let us go into the next towns, that I may

TOWN clerk —
A writer, scribe, clerk, γραμματεύς *grammateus.*
Acts 19. 35 when the town clerk had appeased the p.

TRA-CHO-NI'-TIS, Τραχωνῖτις.
A small rocky part of the tetrarchy of Philip, on the E. of the Jordan, having the Arabian desert on the E. and Auranitis and Gaulonitis on the S.W., and extending from the territory of Damascus on the N. to near Bostra on the S.; now called *Lejah*, anciently *Argob*, and is nearly in the centre of ancient Bashan.
Luke 3. 1 Philip tetrarch..of the region of T., and

TRADE, (is about, is to feed)—
1. *To be men of*, הָיוּ אַנְשֵׁי [*hayah*].
Gen. 46. 32 for their trade hath been to feed cattle
46. 34 Thy servants' trade hath been about cat.
2. *To give*, נָתַן *nathan.*
Eze. 27. 12 with silver..and lead, they traded in thy
27. 13 they traded the persons of men and ves.
27. 14 They of the house of Togarmah traded in
27. 17 they traded in thy market wheat of Min.
3. *To go about, trade*, סָחַר *sachar.*
Gen. 34. 10 dwell and trade ye therein, and get you
34. 21 let them dwell in the land, and trade th.
4. *To work, toil, labour*, ἐργάζομαι *ergazomai.*
Matt 25. 16 went and traded with the same, and made
Rev. 18. 17 as many as trade by sea, stood afar off

TRADITION — [*See* FATHERS.]
A giving over, handing down, παράδοσις *paradosis.*
Matt 15. 2 Why do thy disciples transgress the trad.
15. 3 Why do ye also transgress..by your trad.
15. 6 commandment..of none effect by your tr.
Mark 7. 3 eat not, holding the tradition of the elders
7. 5 according to the tradition of the elders
7. 8 ye hold the tradition of men, (as) the wa.
7. 9 reject..that ye may keep your own tradi.
7. 13 of none effect through your tradition, wh.
Gal. 1. 14 more exceedingly zealous of the traditions
Col. 2. 8 after the tradition of men, after the rudi.
2 Th. 2. 15 hold the traditions which ye have been
3. 6 not after the tradition which he received

TRAITOR —
One who gives over, forth, or up, προδότης *prodotēs.*
Luke 6. 16 and Judas Iscariot, which also was the tr
2 Ti. 3. 4 Traitors..high minded, lovers of pleasures

TRAFFIC or TRAFFICK, trafficker —
1. *A pedlar, hawker, a Canaanite*, כְּנַעַן *kenaan*
Isa. 23. 8 whose traffickers (are) the honourable of
Eze. 17. 4 cropped off..and carried it into a land of t.
2. *Traffic*, מִסְחָר *mischar.*
1 Ki. 10. 15 of the merchantmen, and of the traffic
3. *To go about, trade*, סָחַר *sachar.*
Gen. 42. 34 deliver you..and ye shall traffic in the land
4. *Merchandise, traffic*, רְכֻלָּה *rekullah.*
Eze. 28. 5 By thy great wisdom..by thy traffic hast
28. 18 hast defiled..by the iniquity of thy traffic

TRAIN —
1. *Force*, חַיִל *chayil.*
1 Ki. 10. 2 came to Jerusalem with a very great train
2. *Hem, skirt, train*, שׁוּל *shul.*
Isa. 6. 1 the LORD sitting..and his train filled the

TRAIN up, trained, to —
1. *Trained, instructed*, חָנִיךְ *chanik.*
Gen. 14. 14 when Abram heard..he armed his trained
2. *To train, dedicate, give instruction*, חָנַךְ *chanak.*
Prov 22. 6 Train up a child in the way he should go

TRAMPLE (under foot), to —
1. *To tread or trample down*, רָמַס *ramas.*
Psa. 91. 13 the dragon shalt thou trample under feet
Isa. 63. 3 I will..trample them in my fury; and their
2. *To tread or trample down*, καταπατέω *katapateō.*
Matt 7. 6 lest they trample them under their feet

TRANCE —
Ecstasy, trance, a standing out, ἔκστασις *ekstasis.*
Acts 10. 10 while they made ready, he fell into a tra.
11. 5 in a trance I saw a vision, A certain vessel
22. 17 I prayed in the temple, I was in a trance

TRANQUILLITY —
Rest, ease, security, שְׁלֵוָה *shelevah.*
Dan. 4. 27 may be a lengthening of thy tranquillity

TRANSFER in a figure, to —
To transfer in a figure, μετασχηματίζω *metaschēma.*
1 Co. 4. 6 I have in a figure transferred to myself

TRANSFIGURED, to be —
To be transformed, μεταμορφόομαι *metamorphoom.*
Matt 17. 2 was transfigured before them; and his face
Mark 9. 2 taketh..and he was transfigured before them

TRANSFORM self, be transformed, to —
1. *To be transformed*, μεταμορφόομαι *metamorphoo.*
Rom 12. 2 be ye transformed by the renewing of yo.
2. *To transfer in a figure*, μετασχηματίζω *metaschē.*
2 Co. 11. 13 transforming themselves into the apostles
11. 14 Satan himself is transformed into an angel
11. 15 if his ministers also be transformed as

TRANSGRESS (the law), to —
1. *To deal treacherously, deceive*, בָּגַד *bagad.*
1 Sa. 14. 33 Ye have transgressed: roll a great stone
Psa. 25. 3 let them be ashamed which transgress wi.
Hab. 2. 5 he transgresseth by wine, (he is) a proud
2. *To trespass*, מָעַל *maal.*
1 Ch. 2. 7 Achar..transgressed in the thing accursed
5. 25 they transgressed against the God of their
2 Ch. 12. 2 because they had transgressed against the
26. 16 for he transgressed against the LORD his
28. 19 made Judah naked, and transgressed sore
36. 14 people transgressed very much after all
Ezra 10. 10 Ye have transgressed, and have taken st.
Neh. 1. 8 (If) ye transgress, I will scatter you abro.
13. 27 transgress against our God in marrying
Prov 16. 10 his mouth transgresseth not in judgment
3. *To pass over*, עָבַר *abar* [V.L. עָבַד *abad*].
Jer. 2. 20 and thou saidst, I will not transgress
4. *To pass over*, עָבַר *abar.*
Num 14. 41 Wherefore now do ye transgress the com.
Deut 26. 13 have not transgressed thy commandments
Josh. 7. 11 they have also transgressed my covenant
7. 15 because he hath transgressed the covenant
23. 16 When ye have transgressed the covenant
Judg. 2. 20 this people hath transgressed my coven.
1 Sa. 15. 24 I have transgressed the commandment of
2 Ki. 18. 12 transgressed his covenant, (and) all that
2 Ch. 24. 20 Why transgress ye the commandments of
Esth. 3. 3 Why transgressest thou the king's comm.
Psa. 17. 3 purposed (that) my mouth shall not tran.
Isa. 24. 5 they have transgressed the laws, changed
Jer. 34. 18 I will give the men that have transgressed
Dan. 9. 11 all Israel have transgressed thy law, even
Hos. 6. 7 they, like men, have transgressed the co.
8. 1 because they have transgressed my cove.
5. *To step over, transgress, rebel, revolt*, פָּשַׁע *pasha.*
1 Ki. 8. 50 wherein they have transgressed against
Ezra 10. 13 we are many that have transgressed in
Prov 28. 21 for a piece of bread (that) man will tran.
Isa. 43. 27 thy teachers have transgressed against
66. 24 the men that have transgressed against
Jer. 2. 8 the pastors also transgressed against me
2. 29 ye all have transgressed against me, saith
3. 13 thou hast transgressed against the LORD
33. 8 whereby they have transgressed against
Lam. 3. 42 We have transgressed and have rebelled
Eze. 2. 3 they and their fathers have transgressed
18. 31 Cast away..all..whereby ye have transg.
20. 38 I will purge out..them that transgress ag.
Hos. 7. 13 because they have transgressed against
Amos 4. 4 Come to Bethel, and transgress; at Gilgal
Zeph. 3. 11 wherein thou hast transgressed against
6. *To go beyond, transgress, trespass*, παραβαίνω.
Matt 15. 2 Why do thy disciples transgress the trad.
15. 3 Why do ye also transgress the command.
2 John 9 Whosoever [transgresseth], and abideth
7. *A transgressor, trespasser*, παραβάτης *parabatēs.*
Rom. 2. 27 by..circumcision dost transgress the law?
8. *To come or go over, or beyond*, παρέρχομαι *parer.*
Luke 15. 29 neither transgressed I at any time thy co.
9. *To do lawlessness*, ποιέω ἀνομίαν *poieō anomian.*
1 Jo. 3. 4 Whosoever committeth sin transgresseth

TRANSGRESS, to make to —
To cause to go over, עָבַר *abar*, 5.
1 Sa. 2. 24 ye make the LORD'S people to transgress

TRANSGRESSING, transgression, transgressor —
1. *To deal treacherously, deceive*, בָּגַד *bagad.*
Psa. 59. 5 be not merciful to any wicked transgress.
119. 158 I beheld the transgressors, and was grie.
Prov. 2. 22 the transgressors shall be rooted out of
11. 3 the perverseness of transgressors shall d.
11. 6 transgressors shall be taken in (their own)
13. 2 but the soul of the transgressors..violence
13. 15 but the way of transgressors (is) hard
21. 18 a ransom for the righteous, and the tran.
22. 12 he overthroweth the words of the transg.
23. 28 and increaseth the transgressors among
2. *Trespass*, מַעַל *maal.*
Josh. 22. 22 or if in transgression against the LORD
1 Ch. 9. 1 were carried away..for their transgression
10. 13 Saul died for his transgression which he
2 Ch. 29. 19 Ahaz..did cast away in his transgression
Ezra 9. 4 the transgression of those that had been
10. 6 he mourned because of the transgression
3. *To go over*, עָבַר *abar.*
Deut 17. 2 wrought wickedness..in transgressing his
Prov 26. 10 The great (God)..rewardeth transgressors
4. *To step over, transgress, rebel, revolt*, פָּשַׁע *pasha.*
Psa. 37. 38 the transgressors shall be destroyed tog.
51. 13 (Then) will I teach transgressors thy ways
Isa. 1. 28 the destruction of the transgressors and
46. 8 bring (it) again to mind, O ye transgress.
48. 8 wast called a transgressor from the womb
53. 12 he was numbered with the transgressors
53. 12 and made intercession for the transgres.
59. 13 In transgressing and lying against the L.
Dan. 8. 23 the transgressors are come to the full, a
Hos. 14. 9 but the transgressors shall fall therein
Amos 4. 4 at Gilgal multiply transgression; and br.
5. *Transgression, rebellion*, פֶּשַׁע *pesha.*
Exod 23. 21 for he will not pardon your transgressions
34. 7 forgiving iniquity and transgression and
Lev. 16. 16 because of their transgressions in all their
16. 21 all their transgressions in all their sins
Num 14. 18 forgiving iniquity and transgression, and
Josh 24. 19 he will not forgive your transgressions
1 Sa. 24. 11 (there is) neither evil nor transgression in
1 Ki. 8. 50 all their transgressions wherein they have
Job 7. 21 why dost thou not pardon my transgress.
8. 4 he have cast them away for their transg.
13. 23 make me to know my transgression and
14. 17 My transgression (is) sealed up in a bag
31. 33 If I covered my transgressions as Adam
33. 9 I am clean without transgression, I (am)
34. 6 my wound (is) incurable without transg.
35. 6 (if) thy transgressions be multiplied, what
36. 9 their transgressions that they have exce.
Psa. 5. 10 in the multitude of their transgressions
19. 13 I shall be innocent from the great transg.
25. 7 Remember not..my transgressions, acc.
32. 1 Blessed (is he whose) transgression (is) fo.
32. 5 I will confess my transgressions unto the
36. 1 The transgression of the wicked saith wi.
39. 8 Deliver me from all my transgressions
51. 1 Have mercy upon me..blot out my trans.
51. 3 I acknowledge my transgressions: and
59. 3 not (for) my transgression, nor (for) my sin
65. 3 (as for) our transgressions, thou shalt pu.
89. 32 Then will I visit their transgression with
103. 12 (so) far hath he removed our transgressions
107. 17 Fools, because of their transgression and
Prov 12. 13 The wicked is snared by the transgression
17. 9 He that covereth a transgression seeketh
17. 19 He loveth transgression that loveth strife
19. 11 (it is) his glory to pass over a transgress.
28. 2 For the transgression of a land many (are)
28. 24 Whoso..saith, (It is) no transgression, the
29. 6 In the transgression of an evil man (there)
29. 16 When the wicked are multiplied, transg.
29. 22 a furious man aboundeth in transgression
Isa. 24. 20 transgression thereof shall be heavy upon
43. 25 he that blotteth out thy transgressions
44. 22 I have blotted out..thy transgressions
50. 1 for your transgressions is your mother
53. 5 But he (was) wounded for our transgress.
53. 8 for the transgression of my people was he
57. 4 children of transgression, a seed of false.
58. 1 show my people their transgression, and
59. 12 our transgressions are multiplied..our
59. 20 unto them that turn from transgression
Jer. 5. 6 because their transgressions are many
Lam. 1. 5 afflicted her for the multitude of her tra.
1. 14 The yoke of my transgressions is bound
1. 22 done unto me for all my transgressions
Eze. 14. 11 polluted any more with all their transgr.
18. 22 All his transgressions that he hath com.
18. 28 turneth away from all his transgressions
18. 30 Repent, and turn..from all your transg.
18. 31 Cast away from you all your transgressi.
21. 24 in that your transgressions are discovered
33. 10 If our transgressions and our sins (be)
33. 12 deliver him in the day of his transgression
37. 23 nor with any of their transgressions, but
39. 24 according to their transgressions, have I
Dan. 8. 12 the daily (sacrifice) by reason of transgr.
8. 13 transgression of desolation, to give both
9. 24 finish the transgression, and to make an
Amos 1. 3, 6, 9, 11, 13 For three transgressions..and
2. 1, 4, 6 For three transgressions..and for fo.
3. 14 day that I shall visit the transgressions
5. 12 For I know your manifold transgressions
Mic 1. 5 For the transgression..What (is) the tra.
1. 13 for the transgressions of Israel were found
3. 8 to declare unto Jacob his transgression
6. 7 shall I give my first born (for) my transg.
7. 18 passeth by the transgression of the remn.
6. *Lawless*, ἄνομος *anomos.*
Mark 15. 28 he was numbered with the transgressors
Luke 22. 37 he was reckoned among the transgressors
7. *Transgression, trespass*, παράβασις *parabasis.*
Rom. 4. 15 for where no law is..no transgression
5. 14 after the similitude of Adam's transgres.
Gal. 3. 19 It was added because of transgressions
1 Ti. 2. 14 woman being deceived was in the transg.
Heb. 2. 2 every transgression and disobedience rec.
9. 15 for the redemption of the transgressions
8. *Transgressor, trespass*, παραβάτης *parabatēs.*
Gal. 2. 18 if I build again..I make myself a transg.
Jas. 2. 9 are convinced of the law as transgressors
2. 11 thou art become a transgressor of the law

TRANSGRESSION of the law, to fall by —
1. *Lawlessness*, ἀνομία *anomia.*
1 Jo. 3. 4 for sin is the transgression of the law

2. *To transgress, trespass,* παραβαίνω *parabainō.*
Acts 1. 25 from which Judas by transgression fell

TRANSLATE, translation, to —

1. *To cause to pass over,* עָבַר *abar,* 5.
2 Sa. 3. 10 To translate the kingdom from the house

2. *A putting over, translation,* μετάθεσις *metathesis.*
Heb. 11. 5 before his translation he had this testim.

3. *To put over, translate,* μεθίστημι *methistēmi.*
Col. 1. 13 translated (us) into the kingdom of his

4. *To transpose, translate,* μετατίθημι *metatithēmi.*
Heb. 11. 5 Enoch was translated..God had transla.

TRANSPARENT —

Appearing through, transparent, διαφανής *diaph.*
Rev. 21. 21 (was) pure gold, as it were transparent

TRAP —

1. *Snare,* מוֹקֵשׁ *moqesh.*
Josh. 23. 13 they shall be snares and traps unto you
Psa. 69. 22 for (their) welfare, (let it become) a trap

2. *Trap,* מַלְכֹּדֶת *malkodeth.*
Job 18. 10 The snare (is) laid for him..and a trap

3. *Corruption, destruction, trap,* מַשְׁחִית *mashchith.*
Jer. 5. 26 wicked..they set a trap, they catch men

4. *Hunting, trap, snare,* θήρα *thēra.*
Rom. 11. 9 Let their table be made a snare, and a trap

TRAVAIL or TRAVEL —

1. *To bear, bring forth,* יָלַד *yalad.*
Gen. 38. 27 it came to pass, in the time of her travail
Jer. 13. 21 sorrows take thee, as a woman in travail?

2. *Labour, toil,* עָמָל *amal.*
Eccl. 4. 4 I considered all travail, and every right
4. 6 than both the hands full (with) travail
Isa. 53. 11 He shall see of the travail of his soul

3. *Business, travail,* עִנְיָן *inyan.*
Eccl. 1. 13 this sore travail hath God given to the
2. 23 his days (are) sorrows, and his travail gr.
2. 26 but to the sinner he giveth travail, to ga.
3. 10 I have seen the travail which God hath
4. 8 (is) also vanity, yea, it (is) a sore travail
5. 14 But those riches perish by evil travail

4. *Weariness, travail,* תְּלָאָה *telaah.*
Exod. 18. 8 all the travail that had come upon them
Num. 20. 14 Thou knowest all the travail that hath
Lam. 3. 5 and compassed (me) with gall and travail

6. *Toil, labour, weariness,* μόχθος *mochthos.*
1 Th. 2. 9 remember, brethren, our labour and tra.
2 Th. 3. 8 wrought with labour and travail night

7. *Pain, labour, sorrow,* ὠδίν *ōdin.*
1 Th. 5. 3 cometh..as travail upon a woman with

TRAVAIL (in or with pain together), to —

1. *To travail in birth,* חָבַל *chabal,* 3.
Psa. 7. 14 he travaileth with iniquity, and hath co.

2. *To be pained, bring forth,* חוּל, חִיל *chul, chil.*
Isa. 23. 4 I travail not, nor bring forth children
54. 1 thou (that) didst not travail with child
66. 7 Before she travailed, she brought forth
66. 8 for as soon as Zion travailed, she brought

3. *To be pained,* חוּל *chul,* 7a.
Job 15. 20 The wicked man travaileth with pain all

4. *To bear, bring forth,* יָלַד *yalad.*
Gen. 35. 16 and Rachel travailed, and she had hard
38. 28 it came to pass, when she travailed, that
1 Sa. 4. 19 she bowed herself and travailed; for her
Mic. 5. 3 until the time (that) she which travaileth

5. *To be in pain,* ὠδίνω *ōdinō.*
Gal. 4. 27 break forth and cry, thou that travailest

6. *To feel pain together, travail,* συνωδίνω *sunōdinō.*
Rom. 8. 22 groaneth and travaileth in pain together

TRAVAIL, (in birth), to be in —

1. *To bring forth,* τίκτω *tiktō.*
John 16. 21 A woman when she is in travail hath sor.

2. *To be in pain,* ὠδίνω *ōdinō.*
Gal. 4. 19 of whom I travail in birth again until C.
Rev. 12. 2 being with child cried, travailing in birth

TRAVAIL, woman in, travailing woman —

1. *To be sick, weak,* חָלָה *chalah.*
Jer. 4. 31 I have heard a voice as of a woman in tr.

2. *To bear, bring forth,* יָלַד *yalad.*
Psa. 48. 6 Fear took hold..as of a woman in travail
Isa. 13. 8 be in pain as a woman that travaileth, th.
21. 3 as the pangs of a woman that travaileth
42. 14 will I cry like a travailing woman; I will
Jer. 6. 24 hath taken hold..as of a woman in travail
22. 23 upon thee, the pain as of a woman in tra.
30. 6 see whether a man doth travail with ch.?
30. 6 hands on his loins, as a woman in travail
31. 8 and her that travaileth with child together
49. 24 sorrows have taken her as of a woman in t.
50. 43 (and) pangs as of a woman in travail
Hos. 13. 13 sorrows of a travailing woman shall come
Mic. 4. 9 pangs have taken thee as a woman in tr.
4. 10 Be in pain..like a woman in travail, for

TRAVEL, companions in —

Fellow absentee, or traveller, συνέκδημος *sunekdēmos.*
Acts 19. 29 having caught..Paul's companions in tr.

TRAVEL (with, into a far country) to —

1. *To go on, walk,* הָלַךְ *halak,* 3.
Prov. 6. 11 So shall thy poverty come as one that tr.

2. *To go up and down,* הָלַךְ *halak,* 7.
Prov. 24. 34 So shall..poverty come (as) one that tra.

3. *To be from home, absent,* ἀποδημέω *apodēmeō.*
Matt. 25. 14 For..as a man travelling into a far coun.

4. *To come or go through,* διέρχομαι *dierchomai.*
Acts 11. 19 travelled as far as Phenice, and Cyprus

5. *Fellow absentee or traveller,* συνέκδημος *sunek.*
2 Co. 8. 19 chosen of the churches to travel with us

TRAVELLER, travelling (company) —

1. *To travel, go on one's way,* אָרַח *arach.*
Isa. 21. 13 O ye travelling companies of Dedanim

2. *Traveller, wayfarer,* אֹרַח *orach.*
Job 31. 32 (but) I opened my doors to the traveller

3. *To go on the path,* הָלַךְ נְתִיבָה *halak nethibah.*
Judg. 5. 6 the travellers walked through by ways

4. *A traveller, one going on,* הֵלֶךְ *helek.*
2 Sa. 12. 4 there came a traveller unto the rich man

5. *To wander, lay down,* צָעָה *tsaah.*
Isa. 63. 1 travelling in the greatness of his strength

TRAVERSING —

To traverse, wound about, שָׂרַךְ *sarak,* 3.
Jer. 2. 23 a swift dromedary traversing her ways

TREACHEROUS (dealer, man) —

1. *To deal treacherously, deceive,* בָּגַד *bagad.*
Isa. 21. 2 the treacherous dealer dealeth treachero.
24. 16 the treacherous dealers..the treacherous
Jer. 3. 8 yet her treacherous sister Judah feared
3. 11 justified herself more than treacherous J.
9. 2 adulterers, an assembly of treacherous m.

2. *Treacheries,* בֹּגְדוֹת *bogedoth.*
Zeph. 3. 4 Her prophets (are) light..treacherous pe.

3. *Treacherous,* בָּגוֹד *bagod.*
Jer. 3. 7 And her treacherous sister Judah saw (it)
3. 10 yet for all this her treacherous sister Ju.

TREACHEROUSLY, to deal or depart —

To deal treacherously, deceive, בָּגַד *bagad.*
Judg. 9. 23 the men of Shechem dealt treacherously
Isa. 21. 2 dealer dealeth treacherously, and the sp.
24. 16 dealt treacherously..dealt very treacher.
33. 1 dealest treacherously, and they dealt not t.
33. 1 shalt make an end to deal treacherously
33. 1 they shall deal treacherously with thee
48. 8 knew that thou wouldest deal very treac.
Jer. 3. 20 Surely (as) a wife treacherously departeth
3. 20 so have ye dealt treacherously with me
5. 11 have dealt very treacherously against me
12. 1 are all they happy that deal very treache.
12. 6 even they have dealt treacherously with
Lam. 1. 2 all her friends have dealt treacherously
Hos. 5. 7 They have dealt treacherously against the
6. 7 there have they dealt treacherously agai.
Hab. 1. 13 lookest..upon them that deal treachero.
Mal. 2. 10 why do we deal treacherously every man
2. 11 Judah hath dealt treacherously, and an
2. 14 against whom thou hast dealt treachero.
2. 15 let none deal treacherously against the
2. 16 take heed..that ye deal not treacherously

TREACHERY —

Deceit, מִרְמָה *mirmah.*
2 Ki. 9. 23 Joram..said to Ahaziah..treachery, . Aha.

TREAD (down, out, under, upon), to —

1. *To tread down,* בּוּס *bus.*
Psa. 44. 5 through thy name will we tread them un.
60. 12 he (it is that) shall tread down our enem.
108. 13 he (it is that) shall tread down our enem.
Isa. 14. 25 upon my mountains tread him under foot
63. 6 I will tread down the people in mine an.
Zech. 10. 5 which tread down (their enemies) in the

3. *To tread down,* בּוּס *bus,* 3a.
Isa. 63. 18 our adversaries have trodden down thy s.
Jer. 12. 10 they have trodden my portion under foot

4. *To tread on,* בָּשַׁס *bashas,* 3a.
Amos 5. 11 Forasmuch therefore as your treading (is)

5. *To tread down, thresh,* דּוּשׁ *dush.*
Hos. 10. 11 And Ephraim..loveth to tread out (the
Dan. 7. 23 and shall tread it down, and break it in

6. *To tread, thresh,* דִּישׁ *dish.*
Deut. 25. 4 not muzzle the ox when he treadeth out

7. *To tread on, proceed,* דָּרַךְ *darak.*
Deut. 1. 36 give the land that he hath trodden upon
11. 24 Every place whereon..your feet shall tre.
11. 25 upon all the land that ye shall tread upon
33. 29 and thou shalt tread upon their high pla.
Josh. 1. 3 Every place..your foot shall tread upon
14. 9 the land whereon thy feet have trodden
Judg. 5. 21 O my soul, thou hast trodden down stre.
9. 27 trode (the grapes), and made merry, and
20. 43 trode them down with ease over against
1 Sa. 5. 5 tread on the threshhold of Dagon in Ash.
Job 9. 8 and treadeth upon the waves of the sea
22. 15 the old way which wicked men have trod.
24. 11 tread (their) wine presses, and suffer thi.
Psa. 91. 13 Thou shalt tread upon the lion and adder
Isa. 16. 10 treaders shall tread out no wine in (their)
63. 2 garments like him that treadeth in the wi.
63. 3 I have trodden..I will tread them in mi.
Jer. 25. 30 he shall give a shout, as they that tread
48. 33 none shall tread with shouting; (their) sh.
Lam. 1. 15 hath trodden the virgin, the daughter of
Amos 4. 13 treadeth upon the high places of the earth
Mic. 1. 3 and tread upon the high places of the ea.
5. 5 when he shall tread in our palaces, then
5. 6 and when he treadeth within our borders
6. 15 thou shalt tread the olives, but thou shalt

8. *To cause to tread on or proceed,* דָּרַךְ *darak,* 5.
Judg. 20. 43 trode them down with ease over against
Job 28. 8 The lion's whelps have not trodden it, nor

9. *To tread on,* הָדַךְ *hadak.*
Job 40. 12 and tread down the wicked in their place

10. *To tread down,* סָלָה *salah.*
Psa. 119. 118 Thou hast trodden down all them that

11. *To tread down,* עָסַס *asas.*
Mal. 4. 3 ye shall tread down the wicked; for they

12. *To tread, trample down,* רָמַס *ramas.*
2 Ki. 7. 17, 20 the people trode upon him in the gate
9. 33 threw her down..and he trode her under
14. 9 passed by a wild beast..and trode down
2 Ch. 25. 18 passed by a wild beast..and trode down
Psa. 7. 5 let him tread down my life upon the earth
Isa. 1. 12 required this at your hand, to tread my
26. 6 The foot shall tread it down, (even) the
41. 25 (upon) mortar, and as the potter treadeth
Eze. 26. 11 With the hoofs..shall he tread down all
34. 18 but ye must tread down with your feet
Mic. 5. 8 who, if he go through, both treadeth do.
Nah. 3. 14 tread the mortar, make strong the brick

13. *To make a treading,* שׂוּם מִרְמָס *sum mirmas.*
Isa. 10. 6 to tread them down like the mire of the

14. *To tread or trample down,* καταπατέω *katapateō.*
Luke 12. 1 insomuch that they trode 8. 5. Mt 5. 13

15. *To tread, trample,* πατέω *pateō.*
Luke 10. 19 I give unto you power to tread on serpents
Rev. 19. 15 he treadeth the wine press of the fierceness

TREAD out the corn, under foot, to —

1. *To tread down or out,* סָלָה *salah,* 3.
Lam. 1. 15 LORD hath trodden under foot all my migh.

2. *To tread down or out,* ἀλοάω *aloaō.*
1 Co. 9. 9 muzzle..the ox that treadeth out the corn
1 Ti. 5. 18 not muzzle the ox that treadeth out the c.

3. *To tread or trample down,* καταπατέω *katapateō.*
Heb. 10. 29 who hath trodden under foot the Son of G.

4. *To tread, trample,* πατέω *pateō.*
Rev. 11. 2 the holy city shall they tread under foot

TREADER, treading (down) —

1. *To tread on, proceed, go on the way,* דָּרַךְ *darak.*
Neh. 13. 15 treading wine presses on the sabbath, and
Isa. 16. 10 the treaders shall tread out no wine in
Amos 9. 13 the treader of grapes him that soweth se.

2. *Treading down,* מְבוּסָה *mebusah.*
Isa. 22. 5 a day of trouble, and of treading down

3. *A treading,* מִרְמָס *mirmas.*
Isa. 7. 25 it shall be..for the treading of lesser cat.

TREASON —

A bond, conspiracy, קֶשֶׁר *qesher.*
1 Ki. 16. 20 the rest of the acts of Zimri, and his tre.
2 Ki. 11. 14 rent her clothes, and cried, Treason, treas.
2 Ch. 23. 13 rent her clothes, and said, Treason, treason

TREASURE, (hid) —

1. *A treasure, thing laid up,* אוֹצָר *otsar.*
Deut. 28. 12 LORD shall open unto thee his good trea.
32. 34 (Is) not this..sealed up among my treas.
1 Ki. 7. 51 did he put among the treasures of the ho.
14. 26 he took away the treasures of the house
14. 26 and the treasures of the king's house, he
15. 18 (that were) left in the treasures of the ho.
15. 18 and the treasures of the king's house, and
2 Ki. 12. 18 the gold (that was) found in the treasures
14. 14 in the treasures of the king's house, and
16. 8 gold (that was) found..in the treasures of
18. 15 found..in the treasures of the king's hou.
20. 13 and all that was found in his treasures
20. 15 there is nothing among my treasures that
24. 13 he carried out thence all the treasures of
24. 13 and the treasures of the king's house, and
1 Ch. 26. 20 Ahijah (was) over the treasures of the ho.
26. 20 and over the treasures of the dedicated
26. 22 (which were) over the treasures of the ho.
26. 24 the son of Moses, (was) ruler of the treas.
26. 26 over all the treasures of the dedicated th.
27. 25 over the king's treasures (was) Azmaveth
29. 8 gave (them) to the treasure of the house
2 Ch. 5. 1 put he among the treasures of the house
8. 15 concerning any matter, or concerning..t.
12. 9 took away the treasures of the house of
12. 9 and the treasures of the king's house; he
16. 2 out of the treasures of the house of the L.
25. 24 the treasures of the king's house, the hosta.
36. 18 the treasures of the house of the LORD, and
36. 18 the treasures of the king, and of his pri.
Ezra 2. 69 gave after their ability unto the treasure
Neh. 7. 70 The Tirshatha gave to the treasure a th.
7. 71 gave to the treasure of the work twenty
Neh. 10. 38 to the chambers, into the treasure house
12. 44 appointed over the chambers for the treas.

Job 38. 22 Hast thou entered into the treasures of the
38. 22 or hast thou seen the treasures of the hail
Prov. 8. 21 substance; and I will fill their treasures
10. 2 Treasures of wickedness profit nothing
15. 16 than great treasure, and trouble therewith
21. 6 The getting of treasures by a lying tongue
21. 20 (There is) treasure to be desired and oil
Isa. 2. 7 neither (is there any) end of their treasu.
30. 6 their treasures upon the bunches of cam.
33. 6 the fear of the LORD (is) his treasure
39. 2 and all that was found in his treasures
39. 4 there is nothing among my treasures that
45. 3 I will give thee the treasures of darkness
Jer. 10. 13 bringeth forth the wind out of his treasu.
15. 13 thy treasures will I give to the spoil wit.
17. 3 I will give thy substance (and) all thy tre.
20. 5 the treasures of the kings of Judah will I
48. 7 trusted in thy works and in thy treasures
49. 4 that trusted in her treasures, (saying), Who
50. 37 a sword (is) upon her treasures; and they
51. 13 O thou..abundant in treasures, thine end
51. 16 bringeth forth the wind out of his treasu.
Eze. 28. 4 gotten gold and silver into thy treasures
Dan. 1. 2 brought the vessels into the treasure ho.
Hos. 13. 15 he shall spoil the treasure of all pleasant
Mic. 6. 10 Are there yet the treasures of wickedness

2. *Treasures*, גִּנְזִין *ginzin.*
Ezra 5. 17 let there be search made in the king's tr.
6. 1 the house of the rolls, where the treasures
7. 20 bestow (it) out of the king's treasure ho.

3. *Strength, riches*, חֹסֶן *chosen.*
Prov 15. 6 In the house of the righteous (is) much tr.
Eze. 22. 25 they have taken the treasure and precious

4. *Hidden or secret thing*, מַטְמוֹן *matmon.*
Gen. 43. 23 God..hath given you treasure in your sa.
Job 3. 21 and dig for it more than for hid treasures
Prov. 2. 4 and searchest for her as (for) hid treasur
Jer. 41. 8 we have treasures in the field, of wheat

5. *Treasures*, מִכְמַנִּים *mikmannim.*
Dan. 11. 43 he shall have power over the treasures of

6. *Treasures, stores*, מִסְכְּנוֹת *miskenoth.*
Exod. 1. 11 And they built for Pharaoh treasure cit.

7. *Ready, prepared*, עָתוּד *athud* [V.L. עתיד].
Isa. 10. 13 I..have robbed their treasures, and I ha.

8. *To cover*, שָׂפַן *saphan.*
Deut 33. 19 they shall suck..treasures hid in the sand

9. *Treasury, treasure*, θησαυρός *thēsauros.*
Matt. 2. 11 when they had opened their treasures, th.
6. 19 Lay not up for yourselves treasures upon
6. 20 lay up for yourselves treasures in heaven
6. 21 where your treasure is, there will your he.
12. 35 A good man, out of the good treasure of
12. 35 an evil man, out of the evil treasure, bri.
13. 44 the kingdom of heaven is like unto treas.
13. 52 which bringeth forth out of his treasure
19. 21 thou shalt have treasure in heaven; and
Mark 10. 21 thou shalt have treasure in heaven, and
Luke 6. 45 A good man out of the good treasure of
6. 45 [an evil man out of the evil treasure of his]
12. 33 a treasure in the heavens that faileth not
12. 34 where your treasure is, there will your he.
18. 22 and thou shalt have treasure in heaven
2 Co. 4. 7 we have this treasure in earthen vessels
Col. 2. 3 In whom are hid all the treasures of wis.
Heb. 11. 26 greater riches than the treasures in Egy

10. *Treasure, (from the Persian)*, γάζα *gaza.*
Acts 8. 27 who had the charge of all her treasure

TREASURE (lay up, heap together, be treasured), to —

1. *To be treasured up*, אָצַר *atsar*, 2.
Isa. 23. 18 it shall not be treasured nor laid up, for

2. *To treasure up*, θησαυρίζω *thēsaurizō.*
Luke 12. 21 So (is) he that layeth up treasure for him.
Rom. 2. 5 treasurest up unto thyself wrath against
Jas. 5. 3 Ye have heaped treasure together for the

TREASURER (to make) —

1. *To treasure up*, אָצַר *atsar.*
Neh. 13. 13 And I made treasurers over the treasuries

2. *Treasures*, גְּדָבְרִין *gedaberin.*
Dan. 3. 2, 3 the treasurers, the counsellors, the she.

3. *Treasurer*, גִּזְבָּר *gizbar.*
Ezra 1. 8 by the hand of Mithredath the treasurer
7. 21 do make a decree to all the treasurers

4. *To profit, be useful*, סָכַן *sakan.*
Isa. 22. 15 Go, get thee unto this treasurer..unto S.

TREASURY —

1. *Treasure, treasury*, אוֹצָר *otsar.*
Josh. 6. 19 they shall come into the treasury of the L.
6. 24 they put into the treasury of the house of
1 Ch. 9. 26 over the chambers and treasuries of the
28. 12 of the treasuries of the house of God, and
28. 12 of the treasuries of the dedicated things
2 Ch. 32. 27 he made himself treasuries for silver, and
Neh. 13. 12 the new wine, and the oil, unto the trea.
13. 13 I made treasurers over the treasuries, S.
Psa. 135. 7 he bringeth the wind out of his treasuries
Jer. 38. 11 the house of the king under the treasury

2. *Treasuries*, גְּנָזִים *genazim.*
Esth. 3. 9 silver..to bring (it) into the king's treas.
4. 7 had promised to pay to the king's treasu.

3. *Treasury*, גַּנְזַךְ *ganzak.*
1 Ch. 28. 11 the pattern..of the treasuries thereof, and

4. *Treasury*, γαζοφυλάκιον *gazophulakion.*
Mark 12. 41 over against the treasury..into the trea.
12. 43 than all they which have cast into the tr.
Luke 21. 1 saw..rich men casting..gifts into the tre.
John 8. 20 These words spake Jesus in the treasury

5. *Place of offerings*, κορβανᾶς *korbanas, Heb.* קָרְבָּן.
Matt. 27. 6 not lawful for to put them into the treas.

TREATISE —

A word, discourse, λόγος *logos.*
Acts 1. 1 The former treatise have I made, O Theo.

TREE —

1. *Trees, mighty ones*, אֵילִים *elim.*
Isa. 61. 3 that they might be called trees of righte.
Eze. 31. 14 neither their trees stand up in their height

2. *A tree*, אִילָן *ilan.*
Dan. 4. 10 behold a tree in the midst of the earth, and
4. 11 tree grew, and was strong, and the height
4. 14 Hew down the tree, and cut off his branc.
4. 20 tree that thou sawest, which grew, and
4. 23 Hew the tree down, and destroy it; yet
4. 26 commanded to leave the stump of the tr.

3. *A tamarisk, grove*, אֶשֶׁל *eshel.*
1 Sa. 22. 6 now Saul abode in Gibeah under a tree in
31. 13 buried (them) under a tree in Jabesh, and

4. *A tree, wood, timber, stick*, עֵץ *ets.*
Gen. 1. 11 the fruit tree yielding fruit after his kind
1. 12 tree yielding fruit, whose seed (was) in it.
1. 29 tree, in the which (is) the fruit of a tree
2. 9 to grow every tree..the tree of life also
2. 9 and the tree of knowledge of good and evil
2. 16 Of every tree of the garden thou mayest
2. 17 But of the tree of the knowledge of good
3. 1 Ye shall not eat of every tree of the gard.
3. 2 We may eat of the fruit of the trees of the
3. 3 But of the fruit of the tree which (is) in the
3. 6 saw that the tree (was)..a tree to be des.
3. 8 hid themselves..amongst the trees of the
3. 11 Hast thou eaten of the tree, whereof I co.
3. 12 woman..gave me of the tree, and I did eat
3. 17 hast eaten of the tree, of which I comma.
3. 22 take also of the tree of life, and eat, and
3. 24 every way, to keep the way of the tree of
18. 4 I pray you..rest yourselves under the tr.
18. 8 stood by them under the tree, and they
23. 17 and all the trees that (were) in the field
40. 19 shall hang thee on a tree; and the birds
Exod. 9. 25 And the hail..brake every tree of the field
10. 5 shall eat every tree which groweth for you
10. 15 they did eat..all the fruit of the trees wh.
10. 15 remained not any green thing in the trees
15. 25 showed him a tree, (which) when he had
Lev. 19. 23 shall have planted all manner of trees for
23. 40 boughs of goodly trees..boughs of thick tr.
26. 4 the trees of the field shall yield their fru.
26. 20 neither shall the trees of the land yield
27. 30 all the tithe..of the fruit of the tree, (is)
Deut. 12. 2 upon the hills, and under every green tr.
16. 21 shalt not plant thee a grove of any trees
19. 5 fetcheth a stroke..to cut down the tree
20. 19 not destroy the trees..for the tree of the
20. 20 trees which..(be) not trees for meat, thou
21. 22 put to death, and thou hang him on a tree
21. 23 shall not remain all night upon the tree
22. 6 to be before thee in the way in any tree
28. 42 All thy trees and fruit of thy land shall
Josh. 8. 29 king of Ai he hanged on a tree until even.
8. 29 should take his carcase down from the tree
10. 26 trees: and they..hanging upon the trees
10. 27 they took them down off the trees, and
Judg. 9. 8 The trees went forth (on a time) to anoint
9. 10 trees said to the fig tree, Come thou, (and)
9. 11 and go to be promoted over the trees?
9. 12 Then said the trees unto the vine, Come
9. 14 Then said all the trees unto the bramble
9. 15 bramble said unto the trees, If in truth ye
9. 48 cut down a bough from the trees, and to.
2 Sa. 5. 11 and cedar trees, and carpenters, and ma.
1 Ki. 4. 33 spake of trees..spake also of beasts, and
5. 10 gave Solomon cedar trees and fir trees, (ac.)
6. 23 two cherubim (of) olive tree, (each) ten cu.
6. 31 he made doors (of) olive tree: the lintel
6. 32 The two doors also (were of) olive tree
6. 33 the door of the temple posts (of) olive tr.
6. 34 two doors (were of) fir tree: the two leaves
9. 11 furnished..with cedar trees and fir trees
10. 11 brought..great plenty of almug trees, and
10. 12 king made of the almug trees pillars for
10. 12 there came no such almug trees, nor were
14. 23 every high hill, and under every green tr.
2 Ki. 3. 19 shall fell every good tree, and stop all we.
3. 25 felled all the good trees: only in Kir-har.
16. 4 on the hills, and under every green tree
17. 10 set them up images..under every green t.
1 Ch. 16. 33 Then shall the trees of the wood sing out
22. 4 Also cedar trees in abundance: for the Z.
2 Ch. 2. 8 Send me also cedar trees..out of Lebanon
3. 5 the greater house he ceiled with fir tree
9. 10 brought algum trees and precious stones
9. 11 the king made (of) the algum trees terra.
28. 4 on the hills, and under every green tree
Ezra 3. 7 to bring cedar trees from Lebanon to the
Neh. 8. 15 branches of thick trees, to make booths
9. 25 olive yards, and fruit trees in abundance
10. 35 the first fruits of all fruit of all trees, ye.
10. 37 the fruit of all manner of trees, of wine
Esth. 2. 23 they were both hanged on a tree: and it
Job 14. 7 there is hope of a tree, if it be cut down
Job 19. 10 and mine hope hath he removed like a tr.
24. 20 and wickedness shall be broken as a tree
Psa. 1. 3 he shall be like a tree planted by the riv.
74. 5 he had lifted up axes upon the thick trees
96. 12 then shall all the trees of the wood rejo.
104. 16 The trees of the LORD are full (of sap); the
105. 33 smote their vines..and brake the trees of
148. 9 and all hills; fruitful trees, and all cedars
Prov. 3. 18 She (is) a tree of life to them that lay ho.
11. 30 The fruit of the righteous (is) a tree of li.
13. 12 but..the desire cometh, (it is) a tree of li.
15. 4 A wholesome tongue (is) a tree of life: but
Eccl. 2. 5 I planted trees in them of all (kinds of) fr.
2. 6 water..the wood that bringeth forth tre.
11. 3 if the tree fall toward the south, or tow.
11. 3 in the place where the tree falleth, there
Song 2. 3 As the apple..among the trees of the wo.
4. 14 cinnamon, with all trees of frankincense
Isa. 7. 2 as the trees of the wood are moved with
10. 19 the rest of the trees of his forest shall be
40. 20 He that (is) so..chooseth a tree (that) will
41. 19 I will plant..the myrtle, and the oil tree
44. 14 for himself among the trees of the forest
44. 19 shall I fall down to the stock of a tree?
44. 23 break forth..O forest, and every tree th.
55. 12 the trees of the field shall clap (their) ha.
56. 3 neither..say, Behold, I (am) a dry tree
57. 5 Enflaming yourselves..under every..tree
65. 22 as the days of a tree (are) the days of my
Jer. 2. 20 under every green tree thou wanderest
3. 6 she is gone up..under every green tree
3. 13 ways to the strangers under every green t.
7. 20 upon the trees of the field, and upon the
10. 3 (one) cutteth a tree out of the forest the
11. 19 Let us destroy the tree with the fruit th.
17. 2 their groves by the green trees upon the
17. 8 he shall be as a tree planted by the waters
Eze. 6. 13 under every green tree, and under every
15. 2 What is the vine tree more than any tree
15. 2 a branch which is among the trees of the
15. 6 As the vine tree among the trees of the
17. 24 the trees of the field shall know that I the
17. 24 the high tree, have exalted the low tree
17. 24 dried up the green tree..made the dry tr.
20. 28 every high hill, and all the thick trees
20. 47 devour every green tree..and every dry t.
21. 10 contemneth the rod of my son, (as) every t.
31. 4 sent out her little rivers unto all the tre.
31. 5 was exalted above all the trees of the fie.
31. 8 nor any tree in the garden of God was like
31. 9 the trees of Eden, that (were) in the gar.
31. 14 To the end that none of all the trees by
31. 15 all the trees of the field fainted for him
31. 16 the trees of Eden, the choice and best of
31. 18 and in greatness among the trees of Eden
31. 18 be brought down with the trees of Eden
34. 27 the tree of the field shall yield her fruit
36. 30 I will multiply the fruit of the tree, and
47. 7 many trees on the one side and on the ot.
47. 12 shall grow all trees for meat, whose leaf
Joel 1. 12 (even) all the trees of the field, are with.
1. 19 the flame hath burnt all the trees of the
2. 22 Be not afraid..for the tree beareth her fr.
Hag. 2. 19 and the olive tree, hath not brought forth

5. *A tree*, עֵצָה *etsah.*
Jer. 6. 6 Hew ye down trees, and cast a mount ag.

6. *A tree*, δένδρον *dendron.*
Matt. 3. 10 laid unto the root of the trees..every tree
7. 17 good tree..good fruit; but a corrupt tree
7. 18 A good tree cannot..neither (can) a corr. t.
7. 19 Every tree that bringeth not forth good
12. 33 make the tree..make the tree..for the tree
13. 32 it is the greatest..and becometh a tree, so
21. 8 others cut down branches from the trees
Mark 8. 24 looked up, and said, I see men as trees
11. 8 others cut down branches off [the trees]
Luke 3. 9 unto the root of the trees: every tree th.
6. 43 a good tree..neither doth a corrupt tree
6. 44 every tree is known by his own fruit. For
13. 19 it grew, and waxed a great tree; and the
21. 29 he spake..Behold the fig..and all the tr.
Jude 12 trees whose fruit withereth, without fr.
Rev. 7. 1 that the wind should not blow..on any tr.
7. 3 Hurt not the earth, neither..the trees
8. 7 the third part of trees was burnt up, and
9. 4 neither any green thing, neither any tree

7. *Wood, timber, tree*, ξύλον *xulon.*
Luke 23. 31 if they do these things in a green tree, wh.
Acts 5. 30 Jesus, whom ye slew and hanged on a tree
10. 39 whom they slew and hanged on a tree
13. 29 they took (him) down from the tree, and
Gal. 3. 13 Cursed (is) every one that hangeth on a tr.
1 Pe. 2. 24 Who his own self bare our sins..on the tr.
Rev. 2. 7 will I give to eat of the tree of life, which
22. 2 In the midst..(was there) the tree of life
22. 2 the leaves of the tree (were) for the heal.
22. 14 that they may have right to the tree of

See also **Almond, apple, bay, box, cedar, chestnut, figs, fir, juniper, mulberry, myrtle, olive, palm, pine, pomegranate, shittah, sycamore, vine, willow.**

TREES (of lign aloes), shady —

1. *Aloes, aloe trees*, אֲהָלִים *ahalim.*
Num 24. 6 as the trees of lign aloes, which the LORD

2. *Shades, shady trees*, צֶאֱלִים *tseelim.*
Job 40. 21 He lieth under the shady trees, in the co.
40. 22 The shady trees cover him (with) their sh.

TREMBLE, (to make to, come trembling), to —

1. *To tremble, move,* זוּעַ *zua.*
Eccl.12. 3 when the keepers of the house shall tre.
Dan. 5. 19 all people..trembled and feared before
6. 26 that..men tremble and fear before the

2. *To be pained,* חִיל, חוּל *chul, chil.*
Psa.114. 7 Tremble, thou earth, at the presence of

3. *To pain,* חִיל, חוּל *chul, chil,* 5.
Psa. 97. 4 His lightnings..the earth saw, and tre.
Jer. 5. 22 will ye not tremble at my presence, wh.
Hab. 3. 10 The mountains saw thee..they trembled

4. *To make haste,* חָפַז *chaphaz.*
Deut20. 3 do not tremble, neither be ye terrified

6. *To tremble, trouble,* חָרַד *charad.*
Gen. 27. 33 Isaac trembled very exceedingly, and said
Exod19. 16 the people that (was) in the camp trem.
1 Sa. 13. 7 and all the people followed him trembling
14. 15 the spoilers, they also trembled, and the
16. 4 the elders of the town trembled at his co.
28. 5 he was afraid, and his heart greatly trem.
Job 37. 1 At this also my heart trembleth, and is
Isa. 32. 11 Tremble, ye women that are at ease; be
Eze. 26. 16 shall tremble at (every) moment, and be
26. 18 Now shall the isles tremble in the day of
32. 10 they shall tremble at (every) moment, ev.
Hos. 11. 10 the children shall tremble from the west
11. 11 They shall tremble as a bird out of Egypt

5. *Trembling, troubling self,* חָרֵד *chared.*
1 Sa. 4. 13 for his heart trembled for the ark of God
Ezra 9. 4 every one that trembled at the words of
10. 3 of those that tremble at the commandment
Isa. 66. 2 poor, and of a contrite spirit, and tremb.
66. 5 Hear the word of the LORD, ye that trem.

7. *To stand up, tremble,* סָמַר *samar.*
Psa.119. 120 My flesh trembleth for fear of thee, and

8. *To show self trembling,* פָּלַץ *palats,* 7.
Job 9. 6 shaketh the earth..the pillars thereof tr.

9. *To be angry, troubled, to tremble,* רָגַז *ragaz.*
Deut. 2. 25 shall hear report of thee, and shall trem.
Psa. 77. 18 lightnings lightened the world..earth tr.
99. 1 The LORD reigneth; let the people trem.
Isa. 5. 25 the hills did tremble, and their carcases
64. 2 the nations may tremble at thy presence
Jer. 33. 9 they shall fear and tremble for all the go.
Joel 2. 1 let all the inhabitants of the land tremb.
Amos 8. 8 Shall not the land tremble for this, and
Hab. 3. 7 curtains of the land of Midian did tremb.
3. 16 When I heard, my belly trembled; my
3. 16 I trembled in myself, that I might rest

10. *To cause to tremble or be angry,* רָגַז *ragaz,* 5.
Isa. 14. 16 (Is) this the man that made..earth to tr.

11. *To tremble,* רוּף *ruph,* 3a.
Job 26. 11 The pillars of heaven tremble and are as.

12. *To tremble,* רְעַד *raad.*
Psa.104. 32 He looketh on the earth, and it trembleth

13. *To (cause to) tremble,* רְעַד *raad,* 5.
Ezra 10. 9 all the people sat..trembling because of
Dan. 10. 11 had spoken this word unto me, I stood tr.

14. *To shake, tremble,* רָעַשׁ *raash.*
Judg. 5. 4 the earth trembled, and the heavens dro.
2 Sa. 22. 8 Then the earth shook and trembled, the
Psa. 18. 7 Then the earth shook and trembled, the
Jer. 4. 24 they trembled, and all the hills moved lig.
8. 16 whole land trembled at the sound of the
10. 10 at his wrath the earth shall tremble, and
51. 29 land shall tremble and sorrow: for every
Joel 2. 10 heavens shall tremble: the sun and the m.

15. *To cause to shake or tremble,* רָעַשׁ *raash,* 5.
Psa. 60. 2 Thou hast made the earth to tremble

16. *To become afraid,* γίνομαι ἔμφοβος *ginomai em.*
Acts 24. 25 as he reasoned..Felix trembled, and an.

17. *To become trembling, frightened,* γίνομαι ἔντρομος
Acts 7. 32 Then Moses trembled, and durst not be.
16. 29 came trembling, and fell down before

18. *Trembling or fear had,* εἶχε τρόμος *eiche tromos.*
Mark16. 8 they..fled..for they trembled and were

19. *To tremble, fear, be afraid,* τρέμω *tremō.*
Mark 5. 33 the woman fearing and trembling, know.
Luke 8. 47 came trembling, and falling down before
Acts 9. 6 [he, trembling and astonished, said, Lord]

20. *To shudder, have the hair on end,* φρίσσω.
Jas. 2. 19 the devils also believe and tremble

TREMBLING, trembled —

1. *A trembling, fear, trouble,* חֲרָדָה *charadah.*
1 Sa.14. 15 there was trembling..a very great tremb.
Jer. 30. 5 We have heard a voice of trembling, of
Eze. 26. 16 they shall clothe themselves with trem.

2. *A trembling, horror, fright,* פַּלָּצוּת *pallatsuth.*
Job 21. 6 and trembling taketh hold on my flesh

3. *Trembling,* רַגָּז *raggaz.*
Deut.28. 65 shall give thee there a trembling heart

4. *A trembling, trouble, anger, rage,* רָגְזָה *rogzah.*
Eze. 12. 18 drink thy water with trembling and with

5. *A trembling,* רַעַד *raad.*
Exod15. 15 men..trembling shall take hold upon th.
Psa. 55. 5 Fearfulness and trembling are come upon

6. *A trembling,* רְעָדָה *readah.*
Job 4. 14 Fear came upon me, and trembling, whi.
Psa. 2. 11 Serve the LORD..and rejoice with tremb.

7. *A reeling,* רַעַל *raal.*
Zech12. 2 I will make Jerusalem a cup of trembling

8. *A reeling, trembling,* תַּרְעֵלָה *tarelah.*
Isa. 51. 17 thou hast drunken..of the cup of tremb.
51. 22 taken out of thine hand the cup of trem.

9. *A trembling,* רֶתֶת *retheth.*
Hos.13. 1 When Ephraim spake trembling, he exal.

10. *A trembling, fear,* τρόμος *tromos.*
1 Co. 2. 3 I was with you..in fear, and in much tr.
2 Co. 7. 15 how with fear and trembling ye received
Eph. 6. 5 be obedient to..with fear and trembling
Phil. 2. 12 work out your..with fear and trembling

TRENCH —

1. *A bulwark,* חֵל, חֵיל *chel.*
2 Sa.20. 15 they cast up a bank..and it stood in the tr.

2. *A round rampart,* מַעְגָּל *magal.*
1 Sa.26. 5 Saul lay in the trench, and the people pi.
26. 7 Saul lay sleeping within the trench, and

3. *A round rampart,* מַעְגָּלָה *magalah.*
1 Sa.17. 20 he came to the trench, as the host was

4. *A trench, conduit,* תְּעָלָה *tealah.*
1 Ki.18. 32 he made a trench about the altar, as great
18. 35 and he filled the trench also with water
18. 38 licked up the water that (was) in the tre.

5. *A stake of wood, palisade, rampart,* χάραξ *charax.*
Luke19. 43 thine enemies shall cast a trench about

TRESPASS, (offering, cause of,) trespassing —

1. *Guilty, guilt offering,* אָשָׁם *asham.*
Lev. 5. 6 he shall bring his trespass offering unto
5. 7 he shall bring for his trespass, which he
5. 15 bring for his trespass..a trespass offering
5. 16 with the ram of the trespass offering, and
5. 18 he shall bring a ram..for a trespass offe.
5. 19 It (is) a trespass offering: he hath certa.
6. 6 bring his trespass offering..for a tres. offe.
6. 17 the sin offering, and as the trespass offer.
7. 1, 37 this (is) the law of..the trespass offe.
7. 2 the place where they kill the..trespass o.
7. 5 shall burn them..it (is) a trespass offering
7. 7 As the sin offering..so..the trespass off.
14. 12 he lamb, and offer him for a trespass off.
14. 13 (so is) the trespass offering: it (is) most
14. 14, 17, 25, 28 the blood of the trespass offer.
14. 21 shall take one lamb (for) a trespass offer.
14. 24, 25 the lamb of the trespass offering, and
19. 21 trespass offering..a ram for a trespass off.
19. 22 with the ram of the trespass offering bef.
Num. 5. 7 he shall recompense his trespass with the
5. 8 the trespass..let the trespass be recomp.
6. 12 a lamb of the first year for a trespass off.
18. 9 every trespass offering of theirs, which
1 Sa. 6. 3 in any wise return him a trespass offering
6. 4 What..the trespass offering that we shall
6. 8 which ye return him (for) a trespass offe.
6. 17 returned (for) a trespass offering unto the
2 Ki. 12. 16 The trespass money and sin money was
Psa. 68. 21 such an one as goeth on still in his tresp.
Eze. 40. 39 slay..the sin offering and the trespass off.
42. 13 lay..the sin offering and the trespass off.
44. 29 eat..the sin offering and the trespass off.

2. *Guilt, (cause of, or offering for),* אַשְׁמָה *ashmah.*
Lev. 6. 5 appertaineth, in the day of his trespass off.
6. 7 any thing of all that he hath done in tres.
22. 16 suffer them to bear the iniquity of trespass
1 Ch.21. 3 why will he be a cause of trespass to Is.?
2 Ch.24. 18 and wrath came..for this their trespass
28. 13 and to our trespass: for our trespass is gr.
33. 23 but Amon trespassed more and more
Ezra. 9. 6 our trespass is grown up unto the heavens
9. 7 in a great trespass unto this day; and for
9. 13 for our great trespass, seeing that thou our
9. 15 we (are) before thee in our trespasses, for
10. 10 have transgressed..to increase the tresp.
10. 19 offered) a ram of the flock for their tresp.

3. *A transgression, trespass,* מַעַל *maal.*
Lev. 5. 15 If a soul commit a trespass, and sin thro.
6. 2 If a soul sin, and commit a trespass aga.
26. 40 with their trespass which they trespassed
Num. 5. 6 to do a trespass against the LORD, and th.
5. 12 go aside, and commit a trespass against
5. 27 and have done trespass against her husb.
31. 16 to commit trespass against the LORD in
Josh. 7. 1 children of Israel committed a trespass in
22. 16 What trespass (is) this that ye have com.
22. 20 Did not Achan..commit a trespass in the
22. 31 because ye have not committed this tres.
2 Ch.33. 19 all his sins, and his trespass, and the pl.
Ezra 9. 2 and rulers hath been chief in this trespass
Eze. 15. 8 because they have committed a trespass
17. 20 plead with him there for his trespass that
18. 24 in his trespass that he hath trespassed, and
20. 27 that they have committed a trespass aga.
39. 26 all their trespasses whereby they have tr.
Dan. 9. 7 because of their trespass that they have tr.

4. *To transgress, trespass,* מָעַל *maal.*
Eze. 14. 13 when the land sinneth..by trespassing gr.

5. *Transgression, stepping aside,* פֶּשַׁע *pesha.*
Gen. 31. 36 What (is) my trespass? what (is) my sin
50. 17 Forgive..the trespass..forgive the trespass
Exod22. 9 For all manner of trespass, (whether it be)
1 Sa. 25. 28 forgive the trespass of thine handmaid, for

6. *A trespass, falling aside,* παράπτωμα *paraptōma.*
Matt. 6. 14 if ye forgive men their trespasses, your
6. 15 if..not..[their trespasses], neither..your t.
18. 35 ye from your hearts forgive not..[their tr.]
Mark11. 25 your Father..may forgive you your tresp.
11. 26 [neither will your Father..forgive your tr.]
2 Co. 5. 19 not imputing their trespasses unto them
Eph. 2. 1 you..who were dead in trespasses and si.
Col. 2. 13 quickened..having forgiven you all tres.

TRESPASS, to —

1. *To be or become guilty,* אָשַׁם *asham.*
Lev. 5. 19 he hath certainly trespassed against the
Num. 5. 7 unto (him) against whom he hath trespa.
2 Ch.19. 10 even warn them that they trespass not ag.
19. 10 brethren: this do, and ye shall not tresp.

2. *To sin, err, miss the mark,* חָטָא *chata.*
1 Ki. 8. 31 If any man trespass against his neighbour

3. *To transgress, trespass,* מָעַל *maal.*
Lev. 26. 40 which they trespassed against me, and th.
Deut32. 51 Because ye trespassed against me among
2 Ch.26. 18 go out of the sanctuary; for thou hast tr.
28. 22 in the time of his distress did he trespass
29. 6 For our fathers have trespassed, and done
30. 7 your brethren, which trespassed against
Ezra 10. 2 We have trespassed against our God, and
Eze. 14. 13 the land sinneth against me by trespassing
17. 20 trespass that he hath trespassed against
18. 24 in his trespass that he hath trespassed, and
39. 23 because they trespassed against me, there.
39. 26 whereby they have trespassed against me
Dan. 9. 7 because..that they have trespassed agai.

4. *To miss the mark, not attain,* ἁμαρτάνω *hamar.*
Matt18. 15 if thy brother shall trespass against thee
Luke17. 3 If thy brother trespass against thee, reb.
17. 4 if he trespass against thee seven times in

TRIAL, (fiery) —

1. *To be tried, proved, tested,* בָּחַן *bachan,* 4.
Eze. 21. 13 Because (it is) a trial, and what if (the s.)

2. *A trial, proving, testing,* מַסָּה *massah.*
Job 9. 23 he will laugh at the trial of the innocent

3. *A trial, proof,* δοκιμή *dokimē.*
2 Co. 8. 2 How that in a great trial of affliction the

4. *A trial, test,* δοκίμιον *dokimion.*
1 Pe. 1. 7 That the trial of your faith, being much

5. *A piercing through, experience,* πεῖρα *peira*
Heb. 11. 36 others had trial of..mockings and scour.

6. *A burning, trial by fire,* πύρωσις *purōsis.*
1 Pe. 4. 12 concerning the fiery trial which is to try

TRIBE —

1. *Rod, staff, tribe,* מַטֶּה *matteh.*
Exod31. 2 Uri, the son of Hur, of the tribe of Judah
31. 6 the son of Ahisamach, of the tribe of Dan
35. 30 Uri, the son of Hur, of the tribe of Judah
35. 34 the son of Ahisamach, of the tribe of Dan
38. 22 the son of Hur, of the tribe of Judah, ma.
38. 23 Aholiab, son of Ahisamach, of the tribe
Lev. 24. 11 the daughter of Dibri, of the tribe of Dan
Num. 1. 4 there shall be a man of every tribe, every
1. 16 princes of the tribes of their fathers, hea.
1. 21, 23, 25, 27, 29, 31, 33, 35, 37, 39, 41, 43 tribe
1. 47 the Levites after the tribe of their fathers
1. 49 thou shalt not number the tribe of Levi
2. 5 next unto him (shall be) the tribe of Issa.
2. 7 the tribe of Zebulun: and Eliab the son
2. 12 those which pitch by him..the tribe of S.
2. 14 Then the tribe of Gad: and the captain
2. 20 by him (shall be) the tribe of Manasseh
2. 22 Then the tribe of Benjamin: and the ca.
2. 27 those that encamp..(shall be) the tribe of
2. 29 the tribe of Naphtali: and the captain of
3. 6 Bring the tribe of Levi near, and present
7. 2 princes..who (were) the princes of the tr.
7. 12 the son of Amminadab, of the tribe of J.
10. 15, 16, 19, 20, 23, 24, 26, 27 the tribe of the
13. 2 of every tribe of their fathers shall ye se.
13. 4, 5, 6, 7, 8, 9, 10, 11, 12, 13, 14, 15 of the tri.
18. 2 And thy brethren also of the tribe of Levi.
26. 55 according to the names of the tribes of th.
30. 1 spake unto the heads of the tribes conce.
31. 4 every tribe..throughout all the tribes of
31. 5 a thousand of (every) tribe, twelve thou.
31. 6 Moses sent..a thousand of (every) tribe
32. 28 the chief fathers of the tribes of the chil.
33. 54 according to the tribes of your fathers ye
34. 13 unto the nine tribes, and to the half tribe
34. 14 For the tribe of the children of Reuben
34. 14 the tribe of the children of Gad according
34. 14 half the tribe of Manasseh have received
34. 15 The two tribes and the half tribe have re.
34. 18 ye shall take one prince of every tribe, to
34. 19, 20, 21, 22, 23, 24, 25, 26, 27, 28 of the tribe
36. 3 the inheritance of the tribe whereunto
36. 4 be put unto the inheritance of the tribe
36. 4 from the inheritance of the tribe of our fat.
36. 5 The tribe of the sons of Joseph hath said
36. 6 only to the family of the tribe of their fa.
36. 7 the inheritance..remove from tribe to tri.
36. 7 the inheritance of the tribe of his fathers
36. 8 that possesseth an inheritance in any tri.
36. 8 unto one of the family of the tribe of her
36. 9 remove from (one) tribe to another tribe
36. 9 every one of the tribes of the children of
36. 12 their inheritance remained in the tribe of
Josh. 7. 1, 18 the son of Zerah, of the tribe of Judah

Josh.13. 15 Moses gave unto the tribe of the children
13. 24 Moses gave (inheritance) unto the tribe of
13. 29 Moses gave (inheritance) unto the half tri.
14. 1 the heads of the fathers of the tribes of
14. 2 for the nine tribes, and (for) the half tribe
14. 3 two tribes and an half tribe on the other
14. 4 For the children of Joseph were two tribes
15. 1, 20, 21 of the tribe of the children of
16. 8 This (is) the inheritance of the tribe of the
17. 1 There was also a lot for the tribe of Man.
18. 11, 21 the tribe of the children of Benjamin
19. 1, 8 the tribe of the children of Simeon ac.
19. 23, 24, 31, 39, 40, 48, 51 the tribe of the chil.
20. 8 upon the plain out of the tribe of Reuben
20. 8 Ramoth in Gilead out of the tribe of Gad
20. 8 Golan in Bashan out of the tribe of Mana.
21. 1 unto the heads of the fathers of the tribes
21. 4 the tribe of Judah, and out of the tribe
21. 4 out of the tribe of Benjamin, thirteen ci.
21. 5 the tribe of Ephraim, and out of the tribe
21. 5 out of the half tribe of Manasseh, ten cities
21. 6 the tribe of Issachar, and out of the tribe
21. 6 tribe of Naphtali, and out of the half tribe
21. 7 the tribe of Reuben, and out of the tribe
21. 7 out of the tribe of Zebulun, twelve cities
21. 9 they gave out of the tribe of the children
21. 9 out of the tribe of the children of Simeon
21. 17 out of the tribe of Benjamin, Gibeon with
21. 20 the cities of their lot out of the tribe of
21. 23 out of the tribe of Dan, Eltekeh with her
21. 25 out of the half tribe of Manasseh, Taana.
21. 27 out of the (other) half tribe of Manasseh
21. 28 out of the tribe of Issachar, Kishon with
21. 30 out of the tribe of Asher, Mishal with her
21. 32 out of the tribe of Naphtali, Kedesh in
21. 34 out of the tribe of Zebulun, Jokneam with
21. 38 out of the tribe of Gad, Ramoth in Gilead
22. 1 Then Joshua called..the half tribe of M.
22. 14 a prince throughout all the tribes of Isr.
1 Ki. 7. 14 He (was) a widow's son of the tribe of N.
8. 1 Solomon assembled..the heads of the tr.
1 Ch. 6. 60 out of the tribe of Benjamin; Geba with
6. 61 family of that tribe..out of the half tribe
6. 62 the tribe of Issachar, and out of the tribe
6. 62 the tribe of Naphtali, and out of the tri.
6. 63 the tribe of Reuben, and out of the tribe
6. 63 out of the tribe of Zebulun, twelve cities
6. 65 they gave by lot out of the tribe of the
6. 65 out of the tribe of the children of Simeon
6. 65 out of the tribe of the children of Benja.
6. 66 had cities of their coasts out of the tribe
6. 70 out of the half tribe of Manasseh; Aner
6. 71 out of the family of the half tribe of Mana.
6. 72 out of the tribe of Issachar; Kedesh with
6. 74 out of the tribe of Asher; Mashal with her
6. 76 out of the tribe of Naphtali; Kedesh in
6. 77 out of the tribe of Zebulun, Rimmon with
6. 78 out of the tribe of Reuben, Bezer in the
6. 80 out of the tribe of Gad; Ramoth in Gilead
12. 31 of the half tribe of Manasseh eighteen th.
2 Ch. 5. 2 Solomon assembled..the heads of the tr.
Hab. 3. 9 to the oaths of the tribes, (even thy) word

2. *A rod, sceptre, tribe,* שֵׁבֶט, שֵׁבֶט *shebet.*
Gen. 49. 16 shall judge his people, as one of the tribes
49. 28 these (are) the twelve tribes of Israel: and
Exod 24. 4 according to the twelve tribes of Israel
28. 21 shall they be according to..twelve tribes
39. 14 his name, according to the twelve tribes
Num. 4. 18 Cut ye not off the tribe of the families of
18. 2 the tribe of thy father, bring thou with
24. 2 Israel abiding..according to their tribes
32. 33 unto half the tribe of Manasseh the son
36. 3 the sons of the (other) tribes of the child.
Deut. 1. 13 Take..wise men..known among your tri.
1. 15 I took the chief of your tribes, wise men
1. 15 captains..and officers among your tribes
1. 23 I took twelve men of you, one of a tribe
3. 13 gave I unto the half tribe of Manasseh
5. 23 all the heads of your tribes, and your elders
10. 8 the LORD separated the tribe of Levi, to
12. 5 out of all your tribes to put his name th.
12. 14 the LORD shall choose in one of thy tribes
16. 18 thy God giveth thee, throughout thy tri.
18. 1 the tribe of Levi, shall have no part nor
18. 5 God hath chosen him out of all thy tribes
29. 8 inheritance..to the half tribe of Manass.
29. 10 your captains of your tribes, your elders
29. 18 Lest there should be..family, or tribe, wh.
29. 21 shall separate him..out of all the tribes
31. 28 Gather unto me all the elders of your tri.
33. 5 the tribes of Israel were gathered toget.
Josh. 1. 12 to half the tribe of Manasseh, spake Jos.
3. 12 of the tribes of Israel, out of every tribe
4. 2 Take you twelve men..out of every tribe
4. 4 whom he had prepared..out of every tri.
4. 5, 8, according unto the number of the tri.
4. 12 half the tribe of Manasseh, passed over ar.
7. 14 shall be brought according to your tribes
7. 14 the tribe which the LORD taketh shall co.
7. 16 by their tribes, and the tribe of Judah was
11. 23 according to their divisions by their tribes
12. 6 the Gadites, and the half tribe of Manas.
12. 7 which Joshua gave unto the tribes of Is.
13. 7 unto the nine tribes and the half tribe of
13. 14 Only unto the tribe of Levi he gave none
13. 29 gave (inheritance) unto the half tribe of
13. 33 But unto the tribe of Levi Moses gave not
18. 2 seven tribes, which had not yet received
18. 4 Give out..three men for (each) tribe: and
18. 7 half the tribe of Manasseh, have received
21. 16 suburbs; nine cities out of those two trib.

Josh.22. 7 Now to the..half of the tribe of Manasseh
22. 9, 10, 11, 13, 15, 21 the half tribe of Manass.
23. 4 to be an inheritance for your tribes, from
24. 1 Joshua gathered all the tribes of Israel
Judg 18. 1 in those days the tribe of the Danites so.
18. 1 had not fallen unto them among the trib.
18. 19 that thou be a priest unto a tribe and a f.
18. 30 were priests to the tribe of Dan until the
20. 2 chief..of all the tribes of Israel, presented
20. 10 throughout all the tribes of Israel, and
20. 12 tribes of Israel sent men through all the
21. 3 there should be to day one tribe lacking
21. 5 Who (is there) among all the tribes of Is.
21. 6 There is one tribe cut off from Israel this
21. 8 What one (is there) of the tribes of Israel
21. 15 LORD had made a breach in the tribes of
21. 17 that a tribe be not destroyed out of Israel
21. 24 every man to his tribe and to his family
1 Sa. 2. 28 did I choose him out of all the tribes of
9. 21 a Benjamite, of the smallest of the tribes
9. 21 least of all the families of the tribe of Be.
10. 19 before the LORD by your tribes, and by
10. 20 when Samuel had caused all the tribes of
10. 20 come near, the tribe of Benjamin was ta.
10. 21 When he had caused the tribe of Benjam.
15. 17 (wast) thou not..the head of the tribes of
2 Sa. 5. 1 Then came all the tribes of Israel to Dav.
7. 7 spake I a word with any of the tribes of
15. 2 Thy servant (is) of one of the tribes of Is.
15. 10 sent spies throughout all the tribes of Is.
19. 9 were at strife throughout all the tribes of
20. 14 he went through all the tribes of Israel
24. 2 Go now through all the tribes of Israel
1 Ki. 8. 16 I chose no city out of all the tribes of Is.
11. 13 will give one tribe to thy son for David
11. 31 Behold, I will..give ten tribes to thee
11. 32 he shall have one tribe for my servant D.
11. 32 which I have chosen out of all the tribes
11. 35 and will give it unto thee, (even) ten tribes
11. 36 unto his son will I give one tribe, that D.
12. 20 there was none that followed..but the tr.
12. 21 with the tribe of Benjamin, an hundred
14. 21 the LORD did choose out of all the tribes
18. 31 according to the number of the tribes of
2 Ki. 17. 18 there was none left but the tribe of Judah
21. 7 which I have chosen out of all tribes of I.
1 Ch. 5. 18, 26 the Gadites, and the half tribe of Ma.
5. 23 the children of the half tribe of Manass.
12. 37 of the half tribe of Manasseh, with all man.
23. 14 his sons were named of the tribe of Levi
26. 32 the Gadites, and the half tribe of Manas.
27. 16 Furthermore over the tribes of Israel, the
27. 20 of the half tribe of Manasseh; Joel the son
27. 22 These (were) the princes of the tribes of Is.
28. 1 the princes of the tribes, and the captains
29. 6 and princes of the tribes of Israel, and the
2 Ch. 6. 5 I chose no city among all the tribes of Is.
11. 16 after them out of all the tribes of Israel
12. 13 the LORD had chosen out of all the tribes
33. 7 which I have chosen before all the tribes
Psa. 78. 55 made the tribes of Israel to dwell in their
78. 67 Moreover he..chose not the tribe of Eph.
78. 68 chose the tribe of Judah, the mount Zion
105. 37 not one feeble (person) among their tri.
122. 4 Whither the tribes go up, the tribes of
Isa. 19. 13 (they that are) the stay of the tribes the.
49. 6 to raise up the tribes of Jacob, and to re.
63. 17 Return for thy servants' sake, the tribes
Eze. 37. 19 I will take..the tribes of Israel his fellows
45. 8 shall they give..according to their tribes
47. 13 according to the twelve tribes of Israel
47. 21 divide this land..according to the tribes
47. 22 inheritance with you among the tribes of
47. 23 in what tribe the stranger sojourneth th.
48. 1 Now these (are) the names of the tribes
48. 19 shall serve it out of all the tribes of Isra.
48. 23 As for the rest of the tribes, from the east
48. 29 ye shall divide by lot unto the tribes of Is.
48. 31 (shall be) after the names of the tribes of
Hos. 5. 9 among the tribes of Israel have I made
Zech. 9. 1 the eyes of man, as of all the tribes of I.

3. *A rod, staff, tribe,* שֵׁבֶט *shebat.*
Ezra 6. 17 according to the number of the tribes of

4. *A tribe,* φυλή *phulē.*
Matt 19. 28 shall sit..judging the twelve tribes of Is.
24. 30 then shall all the tribes of the earth mo.
Luke 2. 36 the daughter of Phanuel, of the tribe of
22. 30 sit on thrones judging the twelve tribes of
Acts 13. 21 Saul the son of Cis, a man of the tribe of
Rom. 11. 1 of the seed of Abraham, (of) the tribe of
Phil. 3. 5 of the stock of Israel, (of) the tribe of Be.
Heb. 7. 13 pertaineth to another tribe, of which no
7. 14 of which tribe Moses spake nothing con.
Jas. 1. 1 to the twelve tribes which are scattered
Rev. 5. 5 the lion of the tribe of Juda, the root of
7. 4 forty (and) four thousand of all the tribes
7. 5, 5, 5, 6, 6, 6, 7, 7, 7, 8, 8, 8 of the tribe of
21. 12 of the twelve tribes of the children of Is.

TRIBES, twelve —
The twelve tribes, δωδεκάφυλον *dōdekaphulon.*
Acts 26. 7 Unto which..our twelve tribes, instantly

TRIBULATION, (to suffer) —
1. *Straitness, distress,* צַר *tsar.*
Deut. 4. 30 When thou art in tribulation, and all th.

2. *Straitness, distress,* צָרָה *tsarah.*
Judg. 10. 14 let them deliver you in the time of..trib.
1 Sa. 10. 19 out of all your adversities and your tribu.
26. 24 let him deliver me out of all tribulation

3. *To press, squeeze, afflict,* θλίβω *thlibō.*
1 Th. 3. 4 we told you..that we should suffer tribu.

4. *Pressure, affliction,* θλῖψις *thlipsis.*
Matt. 13. 21 for when tribulation or persecution arise.
24. 21 For then shall be great tribulation, such
24. 29 Immediately after the tribulation of those
Mark 13. 24 in those days, after that tribulation, the
John 16. 33 In the world ye shall have tribulation, but
Acts 14. 22 we must through much tribulation enter
Rom. 2. 9 Tribulation and anguish, upon every soul
5. 3 we glory in tribulations also: knowing...t.
8. 35 tribulation, or distress, or persecution, or
12. 12 Rejoicing in hope; patient in tribulation
2 Co. 1. 4 Who comforteth us in all our tribulation
7. 4 am exceeding joyful in all our tribulation
Eph. 3. 13 desire that ye faint not at my tribulations
2 Th. 1. 4 in all your persecutions and tribulations
1. 6 recompense tribulation to them that tro.
Rev. 1. 9 your brother, and companion in tribulat.
2. 9 know thy works, and tribulation, and po.
2. 10 ye shall have tribulation ten days: be thou
2. 22 I will cast..them..into great tribulation
7. 14 are they which came out of great tribula

TRIBUTE, tributary —
1. *Custom, tribute,* בְּלוֹ *belo.*
Ezra 4. 13 will they not pay toll, tribute, and custom
4. 20 toll, tribute, and custom, was paid unto
7. 24 to impose toll, tribute, or custom, upon

2. *A measured thing, tribute, toll,* מִדָּה *middah.*
Ezra 6. 8 of the tribute beyond the river, 4. 20.
Neh. 5. 4 We have borrowed money for the king's tr.

3. *A tribute,* מֶכֶס *mekes.*
Num 31. 28 levy a tribute unto the LORD of the men
31. 37 tribute of the sheep was six hundred and
31. 38, 39, 40 of which the LORD'S tribute (was)
31. 41 Moses gave the tribute..unto Eleazar the

4. *Tribute, burden, levy,* מַס *mas.*
Gen. 49. 15 bowed..and became a servant unto tri.
Deut 20. 11 people..found therein shall be tributaries
Josh 16. 10 but the Canaanites..serve under tribute
17. 13 that they put the Canaanites to tribute
Judg. 1. 28 that they put the Canaanites to tribute
1. 30 dwelt among them, and became tributar.
1. 33 the inhabitants..became tributaries unto
1. 35 prevailed, so that they became tributaries
2 Sa. 20. 24 Adoram (was) over the tribute; and Je.
1 Ki. 4. 6 Adoniram the son of Abda (was) over the tr.
9. 21 upon those did Solomon levy a tribute of
12. 18 sent Adoram, who (was) over the tribute
2 Ch. 8. 8 them did Solomon make to pay tribute until
10. 18 sent Hadoram that (was) over the tribute
Esth 10. 1 king Ahasuerus laid a tribute upon the
Prov 12. 24 but the slothful shall be under tribute
Lam. 1. 1 princess..(how) is she become tributary

5. *Burden, tribute,* מִסָּה *missah.*
Deut 16. 10 with a tribute of a freewill offering of

6. *A burden, tribute,* מַשָּׂא *massa.*
2 Ch. 17. 11 brought Jehoshaphat presents and tribute

7. *Fine, punishment, confiscation,* עֹנֶשׁ *onesh.*
2 Ki. 23. 33 put the land to a tribute of an hundred

8. *A double drachma,* (i.e. 15 *pence*), δίδραχμον.
Matt 17. 24 they that received tribute..came to Peter
17. 24 said, Doth not your master pay tribute?

9. *A census, tax,* (*Lat. census*), κῆνσος *kēnsos.*
Matt 17. 25 of whom do..kings of the earth take..t.?
22. 17 Is it lawful to give tribute unto Cesar, or
22. 19 Show me the tribute money. And they br.
Mark 12. 14 Is it lawful to give tribute to Cesar, or

10. *A tribute, tax, burden,* φόρος *phoros.*
Luke 20. 22 Is it lawful for us to give tribute unto C.
23. 2 forbidding to give tribute to Cesar, say.
Rom 13. 6 for this cause pay ye tribute also: for th.
13. 7 tribute to whom tribute..custom to whom

TRICKLE down, to —
To be poured or spread out, נָגַר *nagar,* 2.
Lam. 3. 49 Mine eye trickleth down, and ceaseth not

TRIED, (to be) —
1. *Trial, proof, test,* בֹּחַן *bochan.*
Isa. 28. 16 I lay in Zion for a foundation..a tried st.
2. *To be tested,* בָּחַן *bachan,* 2.
Job 34. 36 My desire..Job may be tried unto the end
3. *To be refined, tried, purified,* צָרַף *tsaraph,* 2.
Dan. 12. 10 shall be purified, and made white, and tr.
4. *Approved, tried, tested,* δόκιμος *dokimos.*
Jas. 1. 12 for when he is tried, he shall receive the

TRIM, to —
1. *To make good, do well,* יָטַב *yatab,* 5.
Jer. 2. 33 Why trimmest thou thy way to seek love?
2. *To do, make,* עָשָׂה *asah.*
2 Sa. 19. 24 trimmed his beard, nor washed his clothes
3. *To adorn, trim, set in order,* κοσμέω *kosmeō.*
Matt 25. 7 Then all those virgins arose, and trimmed

TRIUMPH, triumphing —
1. *Loud cry, singing,* רִנָּה *rinnah.*
Psa. 47. 1 shout unto God with the voice of triumph
2. *Singing,* רְנָנָה *renanah.*
Job 20. 5 That the triumphing of the wicked (is)

TRIUMPH (over, to cause to), to —

1. *To triumph, rise,* גָּאָה *gaah.*
Exod15. 1, 21 he hath triumphed gloriously, the ho.

2. *To rejoice, exult,* עָלַז *alaz.*
2 Sa. 1. 20 the daughters of the uncircumcised triu.
Psa. 94. 3 LORD..how long shall the wicked trium.?

3. *To rejoice, exult,* עָלַץ *alats.*
Psa. 25. 2 God..let not mine enemies triumph over

4. *To shout,* רוּעַ *rua,* 5.
Psa. 41. 11 mine enemy doth not triumph over me

5. *To shout,* רוּעַ *rua,* 7*a.*
Psa. 60. 8 Philistia, triumph thou because of me
108. 9 over Edom..over Philistia will I triumph

6. *To sing, cry aloud,* רָנַן *ranan,* 3.
Psa. 92. 4 I will triumph in the works of thy hands

7. *To glorify self,* שָׁבַח *shabach,* 7.
Psa.106. 47 to give thanks..to triumph in thy praise

8. *To lead in triumph, cause to triumph,* θριαμβεύω.
2 Co. 2. 14 which always causeth us to triumph in
Col. 2. 15 he made a show..triumphing over them

TRO'-AS, Τρωάς.
Strictly Alexandria-Troas, a seaport of Phrygia Minor, in Mysia, on the shores of the Archipelago, a little S.W. of the Hellespont, twenty five miles N. of Asso, and a little S. of ancient Troy; now called *Eski-Stamboul.*
Acts 16. 8 they passing by Mysia came down to T.
16. 11 loosing from T., we came..to Samothra.
20. 5 These going before tarried for us at T.
20. 6 And we..came unto them to T. in five da.
2 Co. 2. 12 when I came to T. to (preach) Christ's go.
2 Ti. 4. 13 The cloke that I left at T. with Carpus

TRODDEN (down), to be —

1. *To be trodden down,* דּוּשׁ *dush,* 2.
Isa. 25. 10 as straw is trodden down for the dunghill
25. 10 shall be trodden down under him

2. *A treading down,* מְבוּסָה *mebusah.*
Isa. 18. 2 to..a nation meted out and trodden down

3. *A treading,* מִרְמָס *mirmas.*
Isa. 5. 5 And now go to..it shall be trodden down
28. 18 scourge shall pass..ye shall be trod. down
Mic. 7. 10 be trodden down as the mire of the street

4. *To be trodden,* רָמַס *ramas,* 2.
Isa. 28. 3 The crown of pride..shall be trodden un.

TRODDEN under foot, (to be) —

1. *A trodden down thing,* מְבוּסָה *mebusah.*
Isa. 18. 7 a nation meted out and trodden under f.

2. *A treading,* מִרְמָס *mirmas.*
Dan. 8. 13 to give..the host to be trodden under foot

TRO-GYL-LI'-UM, Τρωγύλλιον.
A city and promontory at the foot of Mount Mycale, in Caria (the S.W. province of Asia Minor), nearly opposite to Samos, and not far from Miletus.
Acts 20. 15 [we arrived at Samos, and tarried at T., and]

TROOP (of robbers) —

1. *A troop, band,* אֲגֻדָּה *aguddah.*
2 Sa. 2. 25 the children of Benjamin..became one tr.
Amos 9. 6 and hath founded his troop in the earth

2. *Wayfarer, traveller,* אֹרַח *orach.*
Job 6. 19 The troops of Tema looked, the compan.

3. *A troop, invading force,* גַּד *gad.*
Gen. 30. 11 Leah said, A troop cometh: and she cal.
Isa. 65. 11 that prepare a table for that troop, and

4. *A troop, invading force,* גְּדוּד *gedud.*
Gen. 49. 19 Gad, a troop shall overcome him: but he
1 Sa. 30. 8 Shall I pursue after this troop? shall I
2 Sa. 3. 22 Joab came from..a troop, and brought in
22. 30 For by thee I have run through a troop
Job 19. 12 His troops come together, and raise up th.
Psa. 18. 29 For by thee I have run through a troop
Jer. 18. 22 when thou shalt bring a troop suddenly
Hos. 6. 9 And as troops of robbers wait for a man
7. 1 the troop of robbers spoileth without
Mic. 5. 1 O daughter of troops: he hath laid siege

5. *Company,* חַיָּה *chayyah.*
2 Sa. 23. 11 were gathered together into a troop, wh.
23. 13 the troop of the Philistines pitched in the
[*See* Gather self in troops.]

TRO-PHI'-MUS, Τρόφιμος.
A believer in Ephesus who accompanied Paul to Jerusalem when he returned from Greece.
Acts 20. 4 there accompanied him..Tychicus and T.
21. 29 they had seen..in the city T. an Ephes.
2 Ti. 4. 20 but T. have I left at Miletum sick

TROUBLE, troubling —

1. *Trouble,* בֶּהָלָה *behalah.*
Psa. 78. 33 consume in vanity, and their years in t.
Isa. 65. 23 They shall not..bring forth for trouble

2. *Terror, worn out thing,* בַּלָּהָה *ballahah.*
Isa. 17. 14 behold at evening tide trouble..before the

3. *Terror,* בְּעָתָה *beathah.*
Jer. 8. 15 for a time of health, and behold trouble
14. 19 for the time of healing, and behold trouble

4. *Trembling,* זועה *zevaah* [V.L. זַעֲוָה *zaavah*].
2 Ch.29. 8 he hath delivered them to trouble, to

5. *Burden, pressure,* טֹרַח *torach.*
Isa. 1. 14 they are a trouble unto me; I am weary

6. *Trouble, destruction,* מְהוּמָה *mehumah.*
Prov 15. 16 than great treasure, and trouble therew.
Isa. 22. 5 day of trouble, and of treading down, and
Eze. 7. 7 the day of trouble (is) near, and not the so.

7. *Labour, toil,* עָמָל *amal.*
Job 5. 6 neither doth trouble spring out of the gr.
5. 7 man is born unto trouble, as the sparks fly
Psa. 73. 5 They (are) not in trouble (as other) men

8. *Affliction, cry,* עֳנִי *oni.*
1 Ch.22. 14 in my trouble I have prepared for the
Psa. 9. 13 Have mercy upon me..consider my tro.
31. 7 thou hast considered my trouble, thou

9. *Straitness, distress,* צַר, צָר *tsar.*
2 Ch.15. 4 when they in their trouble did turn unto
Job 15. 24 Trouble and anguish shall make him
38. 23 have reserved against the time of trouble
Psa. 32. 7 thou shalt preserve me from trouble, th.
59. 16 defence and refuge in the day of my tro.
60. 11 Give us help from trouble: for vain (is)
66. 14 mouth hath spoken, when I was in trou.
102. 2 I am in trouble; incline thine ear unto
107. 6, 13 cried unto the LORD in their trouble
107. 19, 28 They cry unto the LORD in their trou.
108. 12 Give us help from trouble: for vain (is)
119. 143 Trouble and anguish have taken hold on
Isa. 26. 16 LORD, in trouble have they visited thee

10. *Straitness, distress,* צָרָה *tsarah.*
Deut 31. 17 many evils and troubles shall befall them
31. 21 many evils and troubles are befallen them
2 Ki. 19. 3 This day (is) a day of trouble, and of reb.
Neh. 9. 27 in the time of their trouble, when they
Job 5. 19 He shall deliver thee in six troubles; yea
27. 9 Will God hear his cry when trouble com.
Psa. 9. 9 also will be..a refuge in times of trouble
10. 1 (why) hidest thou (thyself) in times of tr.?
20. 1 LORD hear thee in the day of trouble, the
22. 11 Be not far from me, for trouble (is) near
25. 17 The troubles of my heart are enlarged, O
25. 22 Redeem Israel, O God, out of all his tro.
34. 6 the LORD..saved him out of all his trou.
34. 17 and delivereth them out of all their tro.
37. 39 (he is) their strength in the time of trou.
46. 1 God (is)..a very present help in trouble
50. 15 And call upon me in the day of trouble
54. 7 For he hath delivered me out of all trou.
71. 20 which hast showed me great and sore tr.
77. 2 In the day of my trouble I sought the L.
78. 49 wrath, and indignation, and trouble, by
81. 7 Thou calledst in trouble, and I delivered
86. 7 In the day of my trouble I will call upon
91. 15 I (will be) with him in trouble; I will de.
116. 3 gat hold upon me: I found trouble and
138. 7 Though I walk in the midst of trouble, th.
142. 2 before him; I showed before him my tr.
143. 11 for thy..sake bring my soul out of trou.
Prov 11. 8 The righteous is delivered out of trouble
12. 13 but the just shall come out of trouble
21. 23 keepeth his mouth..keepeth..from troub.
25. 19 Confidence..in time of trouble (is like) a
Isa. 8. 22 behold trouble and darkness, dimness of
30. 6 Into the land of trouble and anguish, fr.
33. 2 our salvation also in the time of trouble
37. 3 This day (is) a day of trouble, and of re.
46. 7 not answer, nor save him out of his trou.
65. 16 because the former troubles are forgotten
Jer. 14. 8 Saviour thereof in time of trouble, why
30. 7 it (is) even the time of Jacob's trouble
Dan. 12. 1 there shall be a time of trouble, such as
Nah. 1. 7 strong hold in the day of trouble, and he
Hab. 3. 16 that I might rest in the day of trouble
Zeph. 1. 15 a day of wrath, a day of trouble and dis.

11. *Trembling, trouble, anger,* רֹגֶז *rogez.*
Job 3. 17 There the wicked cease (from) troubling
3. 26 neither was I quiet; yet trouble came
14. 1 Man..(is) of few days, and full of trouble

12. *Evil,* רַע *ra.*
Psa. 27. 5 in the time of trouble he shall hide me
41. 1 the LORD will deliver him in time of tro.
88. 3 For my soul is full of troubles, and my
107. 26 their soul is melted because of trouble
Jer. 2. 27 but in the time of their trouble they will
2. 28 if they can save thee in the time of thy t.
11. 12 save them at all in the time of their tro.
11. 14 time that they cry unto me for their tro.
51. 2 for in the day of trouble they shall be ag.
Lam. 1. 21 mine enemies have heard of my trouble

13. *Travail, weariness,* תְּלָאָה *telaah.*
Neh. 9. 32 let not all the trouble seem little before

14. *Pressure, affliction,* θλῖψις *thlipsis.*
1 Co. 7. 28 Nevertheless such shall have trouble in
2 Co. 1. 4 to comfort them which are in any trouble
1. 8 have you ignorant of our trouble which

15. *Trembling, agitation, disturbance,* ταραχή *tar.*
Mark13. 8 and there shall be famines [and troubles]
John 5. 4 after the troubling of the water stepped in

TROUBLE, self, exceedingly, to make or suffer —

1. *To press, compel,* אָנַס *anas.*
Dan. 4. 9 because I know..no secret troubleth thee

2. *To trouble, hasten,* בָּהַל *bahel,* 3.
2 Ch.32. 18 to affright them, and to trouble them, that
Ezra 4. 4 weakened..and troubled them in build.
Job 22. 10 snares..and sudden fear troubleth thee
Dan. 11. 44 tidings..out of the north shall trouble him

3. *To trouble, hasten,* בְּהַל *bahel,* 5.
Job 23. 16 God maketh..the Almighty troubleth me

4. *To trouble, hasten,* בְּהַל *behal,* 3.
Dan 4. 5 and the visions of my head troubled me
4. 19 astonied..and his thoughts troubled him
4. 19 Belteshazzar, let not the dream..trouble
5. 6 his thoughts troubled him, so that the jo.
5. 10 let not thy thoughts trouble thee, nor let
7. 15 and the visions of my head troubled me
7. 28 my cogitations much troubled me, and

5. *To trouble,* בָּהַל *bahal,* 3 [V.L. בלה].
Ezra 4. 4 weakened..and troubled them in building

6. *To affright, terrify,* בָּעַת *baath,* 3.
1 Sa. 16. 14 an evil spirit from the LORD troubled him
16. 15 an evil spirit from God troubleth thee

7. *To trouble, make muddy,* דָּלַח *dalach.*
Eze. 32. 2 thou..troubledst the waters with thy feet
32. 13 foot of man trouble..hoofs of beasts tro.

8. *To trouble, crush, destroy,* הָמַם *hamam.*
Exod14. 24 looked..and troubled the host of the Eg.

9. *To trouble,* עָכַר *akar.*
Gen. 34. 30 Ye have troubled me to make me to stink
Josh. 6. 18 when ye..make the camp..a curse, and tr.
7. 25 Why hast thou troubled us?..LORD shall t.
Judg11. 35 and thou art one of them that trouble me
1 Sa. 14. 29 My father hath troubled the land: see
1 Ki. 18. 17 said..(Art) thou he that troubleth Israel?
18. 18 I have not troubled Israel; but thou, and
Prov 11. 17 (he that is) cruel troubleth his own flesh
11. 29 He that troubleth his own house shall in.
15. 27 He that is greedy of gain troubleth his

10. *Straitness, distress,* צַר, צָר *tsar.*
Psa. 3. 1 LORD, how are they increased that trou.
13. 4 that trouble me rejoice when I am moved

11. *To do wickedly,* רָשַׁע *rasha,* 5.
Job 34. 29 When..quietness, who then can make tr.?

12. *To set up, excite,* ἀναστατόω *anastatoō.*
Gal. 5. 12 I would they were..cut off which trouble

13. *To disturb exceedingly,* ἐκταράσσω *ektarassō.*
Acts 16. 20 These men, being Jews, do exceedingly tr.

14. *To excite tumult in,* ἐνοχλέω *enochleō.*
Heb. 12. 15 lest..root of bitterness springing up tro.

15. *To press, squeeze, afflict,* θλίβω *thlibō.*
2 Th. 1. 6 recompense tribulation to them that tro.

16. *To be disturbed,* θορυβέομαι *thorubeomai.*
Acts 20. 10 Trouble not yourselves; for his life is in

17. *To suffer evil,* κακοπαθέω *kakopatheō.*
2 Ti. 2. 9 Wherein I suffer trouble, as an evil doer

18. *To hold out or give vexation,* παρέχω κόπον.
Matt26. 10 Why trouble ye the woman? for she hath
Mark14. 6 Let her alone; why trouble ye her? she
Luke11. 7 Trouble me not: the door is now shut, and
18. 5 Yet because this widow troubleth me, I
Gal. 6. 17 From henceforth let no man trouble me

19. *To excite tumult besides,* παρενοχλέω *parenochleō.*
Acts 15. 19 Wherefore my sentence is, that we troub.

20. *To flay, trouble, harass,* σκύλλω *skullō.*
Mark 5. 35 why troublest thou the Master any furt.?
Luke 7. 6 trouble not thyself; for I am not worthy
8. 49 Thy daughter is dead; trouble not the M.

21. *To trouble, disturb, agitate,* ταράσσω *tarassō.*
John 5. 4 [an angel went down..and troubled the]
Acts 15. 24 have troubled you with words, subverting
17. 8 they troubled the people and the rulers of
Gal. 1. 7 there be some that trouble you, and wo.
5. 10 he that troubleth you shall bear his judg.

TROUBLE, (to be) in —

1. *Sharp or hard of the day,* קְשֵׁה־יוֹם [*qasheh*].
Job 30. 25 Did not I weep for him that was in trou.

2. *To press, distress, be distressed,* צָרַר *tsarar.*
Psa. 31. 9 LORD have mercy upon me..for I am in tr.
69. 17 hide not thy face..I am in trouble: hear

TROUBLED, to be (sore) —

1. *To be troubled, hastened,* בָּהַל *bahel,* 2.
Gen. 45. 3 could not answer..for they were troubled
1 Sa. 28. 21 saw that he was sore troubled, and said
2 Sa. 4. 1 feeble, and all the Israelites were troubled
Job 4. 5 it toucheth thee, and thou art troubled
23. 15 Therefore am I troubled at his presence
Psa. 30. 7 thou didst hide thy face, (and) I was tro.
48. 5 they were troubled, (and) hasted away
83. 17 Let them be confounded and troubled for
90. 7 anger, and by thy wrath are we troubled
104. 29 Thou hidest thy face, they are troubled
Eze. 7. 27 the people of the land shall be troubled
26. 18 isles that (are) in the sea shall be troubled

2. *To be troubled, hastened,* בְּהַל *behal,* 2.
Dan. 5. 9 Then was king Belshazzar greatly troub.

3. *To be shaken,* גָּעַשׁ *gaash,* 4.
Job 34. 20 the people shall be troubled at midnight

4. *To be cast out, troubled,* גָּרַשׁ *garash,* 2.
Isa. 57. 20 the wicked (are) like the troubled sea, w.

5. *To roar, move, sound, make a noise,* הָמָה *hamah.*
Psa. 77. 3 I remembered God, and was troubled; I
Jer. 31. 20 therefore my bowels are troubled for him

6. *To daub, be troubled, adulterated,* חָמַר *chamar.*
Psa. 46. 3 the waters thereof roar (and) be troubled

7. *To be foul,* חָמַר *chamar,* 3b.
Lam. 1. 20 my bowels are troubled; mine heart is
2. 11 my bowels are troubled, my liver is pou.

8. *To become bent down, perverse,* עָוָה *avah,* 2.
Psa. 38. 6 I am troubled; I am bowed down greatly

9. *To be troubled, excited,* עָכַר *akar,* 2.
Prov 15. 6 but in the revenues of the wicked is tro.

10. *To be humbled, afflicted,* עָנָה *anah.*
Zech. 10. 2 they were troubled, because..no sheph.

11. *To be moved, troubled,* פָּעַם *paam,* 2.
Gen. 41. 8 it came to pass..that his spirit was trou.
Psa. 77. 4 I am so troubled that I cannot speak
Dan. 2. 3 my spirit was troubled to know the dream

12. *To move self,* פָּעַם *paam,* 7.
Dan. 2. 1 dreams, wherewith his spirit was troubled

13. *To be or become shortened, grieved,* קָצַר *qatser.*
Job 21. 4 why should not my spirit be troubled?

14. *To be angry, troubled,* רָגַז *ragaz.*
Psa. 77. 16 were afraid: the depths also were troub.
Isa. 32. 10 Many days and years shall ye be troubled
32. 11 be troubled, ye careless ones; strip you

15. *To be fouled, troubled,* רָפַשׂ *raphas,* 2.
Prov 25. 26 a troubled fountain, and a corrupt spring

16. *To be tempestuous, tossed about,* סָעַר *saar,* 2.
2 Ki. 6. 11 heart of the king of Syria was sore troub.

17. *To be troubled, roar,* רָעַם *raam.*
Eze. 27. 35 they shall be troubled in..countenance

18. *To trouble thoroughly,* διαταράττω *diatarattō.*
Luke 1. 29 when she saw (him), she was troubled at

19. *To press, squeeze, afflict,* θλίβω *thlibō.*
2 Co. 4. 8 troubled on every side, yet not distressed
7. 5 we were troubled on every side; without
2 Th. 1. 7 And to you who are troubled rest with us

20. *To be tumultuous,* θροέομαι *throeomai.*
Matt 24. 6 see that ye be not troubled: for all..mu.
Mark 13. 7 when ye shall hear of wars..be ye not tr.
2 Th. 2. 2 ye be not soon shaken in mind, or be tr.

21. *To trouble, disturb, agitate,* ταράσσω *tarassō.*
Matt. 2. 3 he was troubled, and all Jerusalem with
14. 26 they were troubled, saying, It is a spirit
Mark 6. 50 For they all saw him, and were troubled
Luke 1. 12 when Zacharias saw (him), he was troub.
24. 38 he said unto them, Why are ye troubled?
John 5. 7 have no man, when the water is troubled
12. 27 Now is my soul troubled; and what shall
13. 21 he was troubled in spirit, and testified, and
14. 1 Let not your heart be troubled, ye believe
14. 27 Let not your heart be troubled, neither
1 Pe. 3. 14 afraid of their terror, neither be troubled

22. *To trouble self,* ταράσσειν ἑαυτόν *tarassein heaut.*
John 11. 33 he groaned in the spirit, and was troubled

23. *To be in a tumult, tumultuous,* τυρβάζομαι *tur.*
Luke 10. 41 thou art careful and [troubled] about many

TROUBLER, troublous —

1 *To trouble,* עָכַר *akar.*
1 Ch. 2. 7 Achar, the troubler of Israel, who trans.

2. *Distress,* צוֹק *tsoq.*
Dan. 9. 25 the street shall be built..in troublous ti.

TROUGH —

1. *Trough, gutter,* רַהַט *rahat.*
Exod. 2. 16 filled the troughs to water their father's

2. *Watering trough,* שֹׁקֶת *shoqeth.*
Gen. 24. 20 she..emptied her pitcher into the trough
30. 38 in the gutters in the watering troughs wh

TROW, to —

To think, δοκέω *dokeō.*
Luke 17. 9 Doth he thank that servant..[I trow not]

TRUCE BREAKERS —

Implacable, irreconcileable, ἄσπονδος *aspondos.*
2 Ti. 3. 3 Without natural affection, truce breakers

TRUE, truly, in or of a truth, it is —

1. *Truly, yet, but,* אוּלָם *ulam.*
Gen. 48. 19 truly his younger brother shall be greater
Num 14. 21 But (as) truly (as) I live, all the earth sh.
1 Sa. 20. 3 but truly, (as) the LORD liveth, and (as)
Mic. 3. 8 But truly I am full of power by the spirit

2. *Only,* אַךְ *ak.*
Jer. 10. 19 Truly this (is) a grief, and I must bear it

3. *Surely, but, yet,* אָכֵן *aken.*
Jer. 3. 23 Truly in vain..truly in the LORD our God

4. *But rather,* כִּי אִם *ki im.*
1 Sa. 21. 5 Of a truth women..kept from us about th.

5. *If not,* אִם לֹא *im lo.*
Num 14. 28 (As truly as) I live, saith the LORD, as ye
Isa. 5. 9 Of a truth, many houses shall be desolate

6. *Stability, faithfulness,* אֱמוּנָה *emunah.*
Psa. 33. 4 For the word..and all his works..in truth
Prov 12. 22 the LORD..they that deal truly (are) his

7. *Surely, truly,* אָמְנָם *omnam.*
Ruth 3. 12 now it is true that I (am thy) near kins.
2 Ki. 19. 17 Of a truth, LORD, the kings of Assyria
Job 9. 2 I know (it is) so of a truth: but how sho.
36. 4 For truly my words (shall) not (be) false
Isa. 37. 18 Of a truth, LORD, the kings of Assyria

8. *Truth, faithfulness,* אֱמֶת *emeth.*
Gen. 24. 49 now if ye will deal kindly and truly with
47. 29 deal kindly and truly with me; bury me
Deut. 17. 4 behold, (it be) true, (and) the thing cert.
22. 20 But if this thing be true, (and the tokens
Josh. 2. 12 show kindness..and give me a true token
2. 14 that we will deal kindly and truly with
Judg. 9. 16 if ye have done truly and sincerely, in
9. 19 If ye then have dealt truly and sincerely
2 Sa. 7. 28 thy words be true, and thou hast promised
1 Ki. 10. 6 It was a true report that I heard in mine
22. 16 tell me nothing but (that which is) true
2 Ch. 9. 5 a true report which I heard in mine own
15. 3 Israel (hath been) without the true God
Neh. 9. 13 gavest them right judgments, and true
Psa. 19. 9 judgments of the LORD (are) true (and)
119. 160 Thy word (is) true (from) the beginning
Prov 14. 25 A true witness delivereth souls: but a de.
Jer. 10. 10 But the LORD (is) the true God, he (is) the
26. 15 for of a truth the LORD hath sent me unto
28. 9 known, that the LORD hath truly sent him
42. 5 The LORD be a true and faithful witness
Eze. 18. 8 hath executed true judgment between
18. 9 and hath kept my judgments, to deal truly
Dan. 8. 26 vision .which was told (is) true: where.
10. 1 thing (was) true, but the time appointed
Zech. 7. 9 Execute true judgment, and show mercy

9. *Set up, certain, certainty,* יַצִּיב *yatstsib.*
Dan. 3. 24 They answered and said unto the king, True
6. 12 king answered and said, The thing (is) true

10. *That, because,* כִּי *ki.*
Josh. 2. 24 Truly the LORD hath delivered into our

11. *Right, established,* כֵּנִים *kenim.*
Gen. 42. 11 we (are) true (men), thy servants are no
42. 19 If ye (be) true (men), let one of your br.
42. 31 we said..We (are) true (men); we are no
42. 33 Hereby shall I know that ye (are) true
42. 34 ye (are) no spies, but (that) ye (are) true

12. *Truth, laid plan,* צְדָא *tseda.*
Dan. 3. 14 true, O Shadrach, Meshach, and Abed-nego

13. *To tithe,* עָשַׂר *asar,* 3.
Deut. 14. 22 Thou shalt truly tithe all the increase of

14. *Upon* (*or of*) *truth,* (ἐπ') ἀληθείας (*epi*) *alētheı.*
Luke 20. 21 thou..teachest the way of God truly

15. *True, genuine, honest, sincere,* ἀληθής *alēthēs.*
Matt 22. 16 we know that thou art true, and teachest
Mark 12. 14 we know that thou art true, and carest for
John 3. 33 He..hath set to his seal that God is true
4. 18 not thy husband: in that saidst thou truly
5. 31 witness of myself, my witness is not true
5. 32 witness which he witnesseth of me is true
7. 18 same is true, and no unrighteousness is in
8. 13 Pharisees therefore said..record is not tr.
8. 14 my record is true: for I know whence I ca.
8. 16 yet if I judge, my judgment is [true], for
8. 17 that the testimony of two men is true
8. 26 but he that sent me is true; and I speak to
10. 41 things that John spake of this man were t.
19. 35 and he knoweth that he saith true, that ye
21. 24 and we know that his testimony is true
Acts 12. 9 wist not that it was true which was done
Rom. 3. 4 yea, let God be true, but every man a liar
2 Co. 6. 8 good report: as deceivers, and (yet) true
Phil. 4. 8 whatsoever things are true, whatsoever
Titus 1. 13 This witness is true. Wherefore rebuke
1 Pe. 5. 12 testifying that this is the true grace of God
2 Pe. 2. 22 happened according to the true proverb
1 Jo. 2. 8 which thing is true in him and in you, be.
3 John 12 record; and ye know that our record is tr.

16. *True, real, sincere, veracious,* ἀληθινός *alēthinos.*
Luke 16. 11 who will commit to your trust the true
John 1. 9 was the true light, which lighteth every
4. 23 when the true worshippers shall worship
4. 37 herein is that saying true, One soweth, and
6. 32 my Father giveth you the true bread from
7. 28 he that sent me is true, whom ye know not
15. 1 I am the true vine, and my Father is the
17. 3 they might know thee the only true God
19. 35 bare record, and his record is true: and
1 Th. 1. 9 from idols to serve the living and true G.
Heb. 8. 2 minister of the sanctuary, and of the true
9. 24 hands, (which are) the figures of the true
10. 22 Let us draw near with a true heart, in full
1 Jo. 2. 8 darkness is past, and the true light now
5. 20 that is true; and we are in him that is true
5. 20 This is the true God, and eternal life
Rev. 3. 7 he that is true, he that hath the key of
3. 14 saith the Amen, the faithful and true wi.
6. 10 holy and true, dost thou not judge and
15. 3 just and true (are) thy ways, thou king of
16. 7 Lord God Almighty, true and righteous
19. 2 For true and righteous (are) his judgments
19. 9 saith unto me, These are the true sayings
19. 11 sat upon him .called Faithful and True
21. 5 Write; for these words are true and fai.
22. 6 These sayings (are) faithful and true, and

17. *Truly, really, certainly,* ἀληθῶς *alēthōs.*
Matt 14. 33 saying, Of a truth thou art the Son of God
27. 54 feared greatly, saying, Truly this was the
Mark 15. 39 said, Truly this man was the Son of God
Luke 9. 27 But I tell you of a truth, There be some
12. 44 Of a truth I say unto you, that he will ma.
21. 3 Of a truth I say unto you, that this poor
John 6. 14 This is of a truth that prophet that should
7. 40 Many..said, Of a truth this is the prophet
1 Th. 2. 13 but, as it is in truth, the word of God, wh.

18. *In deed, in truth, then, therefore,* ἄρα *ara.*
Luke 11. 48 Truly ye bear witness that ye allow the

19. *Genuine, legitimate,* γνήσιος *gnēsios.*
Phil. 4. 3 I entreat thee also, true yoke fellow, help

20. *Truly, indeed,* μέν *men.*
Matt. 9. 37 The harvest truly (is) plenteous, but the
17. 11 Elias truly shall first come, and restore all
Mark 14. 38 spirit truly (is) ready, but the flesh (is) we.
Luke 10. 2 harvest truly (is) great, but the labourers
22. 22 truly the Son of man goeth, as it was de.
Acts 1. 5 For John truly baptized with water; but
3. 22 For Moses truly said unto the fathers, A
5. 23 prison [truly] found we shut with all saf.
2 Co. 12. 12 Truly the signs of an apostle were wrought
Heb. 7. 23 they truly were many priests, because th.
11. 15 truly, if they had been mindful of that

21. *Therefore,* μὲν οὖν *men oun.*
John 20. 30 many other signs truly did Jesus in the

22. *Actually,* ὄντως *ontōs.*
1 Co. 14. 25 and report that God is in you of a truth

23. *Steady, faithful,* πιστός *pistos.*
2 Co. 1. 18 But..God (is) true, our word toward you
1 Ti. 3. 1 This (is) a true saying, If a man desire the

TRUMP, trumpet, trumpeter — [See SOUND.]

1. *To blow a trumpet,* חֲצֹצֵר *chatsotser* [V. L. חצר, 3].
2 Ch. 5. 13 It came even to pass, as the trumpeters

2. *Trumpet,* חֲצֹצְרָה *chatsotserah.*
Num 10. 2 Make thee two trumpets of silver; of a
10. 8 priests, shall blow with the trumpets: and
10. 9 ye shall blow an alarm with the trumpets
10. 10 ye shall blow with the trumpets over your
31. 6 and the trumpets to blow in his hand
2 Ki. 11. 14 the princes and the trumpeters by the ki.
11. 14 the land rejoiced, and blew with trumpets
12. 13 snuffers, basins, trumpets, any vessels of
1 Ch. 13. 8 timbrels, and with cymbals, and with tru.
15. 24 did blow with the trumpets before the ark
15. 28 with trumpets, and with cymbals, making
16. 6 with trumpets continually before the ark
16. 42 with trumpets and cymbals for those that
2 Ch. 5. 12 with them..priests sounding with trump.
5. 13 lifted up (their) voice with the trumpets
13. 12 priests with sounding trumpets to cry al.
13. 14 and the priests sounded with the trumpets
15. 14 with shouting, and with trumpets, and
20. 28 harps and trumpets unto the house of the
23. 13 sounded with trumpets, also the singers
23. 13 and the princes and the trumpets by the
29. 26 Levites stood..priests with the trumpets
29. 27 song..began (also) with the trumpets, and
29. 28 singers sang, and the trumpeters sounded
Ezra 3. 10 the priests in their apparel with trumpets
Neh. 12. 35 (certain) of the priests' sons with trumpets
12. 41 Zechariah, (and) Hananiah, with trumpets
Psa. 98. 6 With trumpets and sound of cornet make
Hos. 5. 8 Blow ye..the trumpet in Ramah: cry al.

3. *Jubilee, cornet, ram's horn,* יוֹבֵל *yobel.*
Exod 19. 13 when the trumpet soundeth long, they

4. *Trumpet,* שׁוֹפָר *shophar.*
Exod 19. 16 the voice of the trumpet exceeding loud
19. 19 when the voice of the trumpet sounded
20. 18 noise of the trumpet, and the mountain
Lev. 25. 9 Then shalt thou cause the trumpet of the
25. 9 make the trumpet sound throughout all
Josh. 6. 4 before the ark seven trumpets of rams'
6. 4 the priests shall blow with the trumpets
6. 5 when ye hear the sound of the trumpet
6. 6 let seven priests bear seven trumpets of
6. 8 seven priests bearing the seven trumpets
6. 8 blew with the trumpets: and the ark of
6. 9 the priests that blew with the trumpets
6. 9 going on, and blowing with the trumpets
6. 13 seven priests bearing seven trumpets of
6. 13 blew with the trumpets..blowing with..tr.
6. 16 when the priests blew with the trumpets
6. 20 blew with the trumpets: and it came to
6. 20 people heard the sound of the trumpet
Judg. 3. 27 that he blew a trumpet in the mountain
6. 34 blew a trumpet; and Abi-ezer was gathe.
7. 8 took victuals in their hand, and their tru.
7. 16 he put a trumpet in every man's hand
7. 18 blow with a trumpet..blow ye the trum.
7. 19 blew the trumpets, and brake the pitchers
7. 20 blew the trumpets..and the trumpets in
7. 22 three hundred blew the trumpets, and the
1 Sa. 13. 3 blew the trumpet throughout all the land
2 Sa. 2. 28 So Joab blew a trumpet, and all the people
6. 15 shouting, and with the sound of the tru.
15. 10 soon as ye hear the sound of the trumpet
18. 16 Joab blew the trumpet, and the people re.
20. 1 blew a trumpet, and said, We have no
20. 22 blew a trumpet, and they retired from the
1 Ki. 1. 34 blow ye with the trumpet, and say, God
1. 39 blew the trumpet; and all the people
1. 41 when Joab heard the sound of the trum.
2 Ki. 9. 13 blew with trumpets, saying, Jehu is king
Neh. 4. 18 he that sounded the trumpet (was) by me
4. 20 what place..ye hear the sound of the tr.
Job 39. 24 believeth he that (it is) the sound of the tr.
39. 25 He saith among the trumpets, Ha, ha! and
Psa. 47. 5 shout, the LORD with the sound of a trum.
81. 3 Blow up the trumpet in the new moon, in
150. 3 Praise him with the sound of the trumpet
Isa. 18. 3 and when he bloweth a trumpet, hear ye
27. 13 great trumpet shall be blown, and they
58. 1 lift up thy voice like a trumpet, and show

Jer. 4. 5 Blow ye the trumpet in the land: cry, gat.
4. 19 the sound of the trumpet, the alarm of
4. 21 standard, (and) hear the sound of the tru.
6. 1 blow the trumpet in Tekoa, and set up a
6. 17 Hearken to the sound of the trumpet. But
42. 14 nor hear the sound of the trumpet, nor
51. 27 blow the trumpet among the nations, pr.
Eze. 33. 3 he blow the trumpet, and warn the people
33. 4 whosoever heareth the sound of the tru.
33. 5 He heard the sound of the trumpet, and
33. 6 blow not the trumpet, and the people be
Hos. 8. 1 (Set) the trumpet to thy mouth. (He shall
Joel 2. 1 Blow ye the trumpet in Zion, and sound
2. 15 Blow the trumpet in Zion, sanctify a fast
Amos 2. 2 shall die..with the sound of the trumpet
3. 6 Shall a trumpet be blown in the city and
Zeph. 1. 16 A day of the trumpet and alarm against
Zech. 9. 14 GOD shall blow the trumpet, and shall go

5. *A trumpet,* תָּקוֹעַ *taqoa.*
Eze. 7. 14 They have blown the trumpet, even to m.

6. *A trumpet,* σάλπιγξ *salpigx.*
Matt24. 31 his angels with a great sound of a trump.
1 Co.14. 8 if the trumpet give an uncertain sound
15. 52 In a moment..at the last trump: for the t.
1 Th. 4. 16 the archangel, and with the trump of God
Heb. 12. 19 the sound of a trumpet, and the voice of
Rev. 1. 10 heard..a great voice, as of a trumpet
4. 1 as it were of a trumpet talking with me
8. 2 and to them were given seven trumpets
8. 6 the seven angels which had the seven tru.
8. 13 by reason of the other voices of the trum.
9. 14 Saying to..sixth angel which had the tru.

7. *A trumpeter,* σαλπιστής *salpistēs.*
Rev. 18. 22 voice of harpers..musicians..trumpeters

TRUST —

1. *Refuge, trust,* חָסוּת *chasuth.*
Isa. 30. 3 therefore shall the..trust in the shadow

2. *Confidence, trust,* מִבְטָח *mibtach.*
Job 8. 14 and whose trust (shall be) a spider's web
Psa. 40. 4 that man that maketh the LORD his trust
71. 5 O Lord GOD..my trust from my youth
Prov.22. 19 That thy trust may be in the LORD, I have

3. *A refuge,* מַחְסֶה *machseh.*
Psa. 73. 28 I have put my trust in the Lord GOD, that

4. *Trust, confidence,* πεποίθησις *pepoithēsis.*
2 Co. 3. 4 such trust have we through Christ to God

TRUST, to (ommit to, first, make to, put in, have) —

1. *To remain stedfast, give credence,* אָמַן *aman,* 5.
Judg11. 20 Sihon trusted not Israel to pass through
Job 4. 18 Behold, he put no trust in his servants
15. 15 Behold, he putteth no trust in his saints
15. 31 Let not him that is deceived trust in van.
Mic. 7. 5 Trust ye not in a friend, put ye not conf.

2. *To lean on, trust, be confident,* בָּטַח *batach.*
Deut28. 52 thy..walls come down, wherein thou tru.
Judg20. 36 they trusted unto the liers in wait which
2 Ki.18. 5 He trusted in the Lord GOD of Israel; so
18. 19 What confidence (is) this wherein thou tr.
18. 20 on whom dost thou trust, that thou rebe.
18. 21 thou trustest upon the staff of this bruised
18. 21 so (is) Pharaoh..unto all that trust in him
18. 22 if ye say unto me, We trust in the LORD
18. 24 put thy trust on Egypt for chariots and
19. 10 Let not thy God in whom thou trustest
1 Ch. 5. 20 entreated..because they put their trust
2 Ch.32. 10 Whereon do ye trust, that ye abide in the
Job 39. 11 Wilt thou trust him, because his strength
40. 23 he trusteth that he can draw up Jordan
Psa. 4. 5 Offer..and put your trust in the LORD
9. 10 they that know thy name will put their t.
13. 5 I have trusted in thy mercy; my heart
21. 7 the king trusteth in the LORD; and thro.
22. 4 Our fathers trusted in thee; they trusted
22. 5 they trusted in thee, and were not confo.
25. 2 O my God, I trust in thee: let me not be
26. 1 Judge me..I have trusted also in the LORD
28. 7 my heart trusted in him, and I am helped
31. 6 I have hated them..but I trust in the Lo.
31. 14 I trusted in thee, O LORD: I said, Thou
32. 10 he that trusteth in the LORD, mercy shall
33. 21 because we have trusted in his holy name
37. 3 Trust in the LORD, and do good; so shalt
37. 5 trust also in him, and he shall bring (it)
40. 3 many shall see (it)..and shall trust in the
41. 9 mine own familiar friend, in whom I trus.
44. 6 I will not trust in my bow, neither shall
49. 6 They that trust in their wealth, and boast
52. 7 trusted in the abundance of his riches
52. 8 I trust in the mercy of God for ever and
55. 23 shall not live..but I will trust in thee
56. 3 What time I am afraid, I will trust in thee
56. 4 in God I have put my trust; I will not fe.
56. 11 In God have I put my trust: I will not be
62. 8 Trust in him at all times; ye people, pour
62. 10 Trust not in oppression, and become not
78. 22 they believed not in God, and trusted not
84. 12 blessed (is) the man that trusteth in thee
86. 2 save thy servant that trusteth in thee
91. 2 my fortress: my God; in him will I trust
112. 7 his heart is fixed, trusting in the LORD
115. 8 (so is) every one that trusteth in them
115. 9 O Israel, trust thou in the LORD: he (is) th.
115. 10 O house of Aaron, trust in the LORD: he
115. 11 Ye that fear the LORD, trust in the LORD
119. 42 wherewith to answer..for I trust in thy
125. 1 They that trust in the LORD (shall be) as
Psa.135. 18 (so is) every one that trusteth in them
143. 8 Cause me to hear..for in thee do I trust
146. 3 Put not your trust in princes, (nor) in the
Prov. 3. 5 Trust in the LORD with all thine heart; and
11. 28 He that trusteth in his riches shall fall: but
16. 20 whoso trusteth in the LORD, happy (is) he
28. 25 he that putteth his trust in the LORD shall
28. 26 He that trusteth in his own heart is a fool
29. 25 whoso putteth his trust in the LORD shall
31. 11 The heart of her husband doth..trust in
Isa. 12. 2 I will trust, and not be afraid: for the L.
26. 3 wilt keep (him)..because he trusteth in th.
26. 4 Trust ye in the LORD for ever: for in the
30. 12 trust in oppression and perverseness, and
31. 1 stay on horses, and trust in chariots, bec.
36. 4 What confidence (is) this wherein thou tr.?
36. 5 on whom dost thou trust, that thou rebe.
36. 6 thou trustest in the staff of this broken re.
36. 6 so (is) Pharaoh..to all that trust in him
36. 7 if thou say to me, We trust in the LORD
36. 9 put thy trust on Egypt for chariots and for
37. 10 Let not thy God in whom thou trustest de.
42. 17 they shall be greatly ashamed, that trust
47. 10 thou hast trusted in thy wickedness: thou
50. 10 let him trust in the name of the LORD, and
59. 4 they trust in vanity, and speak lies; they
Jer. 5. 17 thy fenced cities, wherein thou trustedst
7. 4 Trust ye not in lying words, saying, The
7. 8 ye trust in lying words, that cannot profit
7. 14 will I do unto (this) house..wherein ye tr.
9. 4 Take ye heed..and trust ye not in any br.
12. 5 (if) in the land of peace, (wherein) thou tr.
13. 25 thou hast forgotten me, and trusted in fa.
17. 5 Cursed (be) the man that trusteth in man
17. 7 Blessed (is) the man that trusteth in the
39. 18 because thou hast put thy trust in me, sa.
46. 25 even Pharaoh, and (all) them that trust
48. 7 thou hast trusted in thy works and in thy
49. 4 that trusted in her treasures, (saying), Who
49. 11 I will preserve..and let thy widows trust
Eze. 16. 15 thou didst trust in thine own beauty, and
33. 13 if he trust to his own righteousness, and
Hos. 10. 13 because thou didst trust in thy way, in the
Amos 6. 1 Woe to them (that)..trust in the mount.
Hab. 2. 18 that the maker of his work trusteth ther.
Zeph. 3. 2 she trusted not in the LORD; she drew not

3. *To cause to trust, be confident,* בָּטַח *batach,* 5.
2 Ki.18. 30 Neither let Hezekiah make you trust in
Isa. 36. 15 Neither let Hezekiah make you trust in
Jer. 28. 15 thou makest this people to trust in a lie
29. 31 Shemaiah..caused you to trust in a lie

4. *To roll on, devolve,* גָּלַל *galal.*
Psa. 22. 8 He trusted on the LORD (that) he would

5. *To stay self,* חִיל ,חוּל *chul, chil,* 3a.
Job 35. 14 judgment (is) before him; therefore trust

6. *To take refuge, trust,* חָסָה *chasah.*
Deut32. 37 Where..their gods..rock in whom they tr.
Judg. 9. 15 come..put your trust in my shadow, and
Ruth 2. 12 under whose wings thou art come to trust
2 Sa. 22. 3 The God of my rock; in him will I trust
22. 31 he (is) a buckler to all them that trust in
Psa. 2. 12 Blessed (are) all they that put their trust
5. 11 let all those that put their trust in thee
7. 1 O LORD..in thee do I put my trust: save
11. 1 In the LORD put I my trust: how say ye
16. 1 Preserve me..in thee do I put my trust
17. 7 hand them which put their trust (in thee)
18. 2 my strength, in whom I will trust; my bu.
18. 30 he (is) a buckler to all those that trust in
25. 20 let me not be ashamed, for I put my trust
31. 1 In thee, O LORD, do I put my trust; let
31. 19 thou hast wrought for them that trust in
34. 8 blessed (is) the man (that) trusteth in him
34. 22 none of them that trust in him shall be de.
36. 7 the children of men put their trust under
37. 40 and save them, because they trust in him
57. 1 my soul trusteth in thee: yea, in the sha.
61. 4 I will abide..I will trust in the covert of
64. 10 The righteous..shall trust in him; and all
71. 1 In thee, O LORD, do I put my trust; let
91. 4 under his wings shalt thou trust: his truth
118. 8, 9 (It is) better to trust in the LORD than
141. 8 in thee is my trust; leave not my soul de.
144. 2 my shield, and (he) in whom I trust; who
Prov30. 5 a shield unto them that put their trust in
Isa. 14. 32 and the poor of his people shall trust in
30. 2 go down..to trust in the shadow of Egypt?
57. 13 he that putteth his trust in me, shall pos.
Nah. 1. 7 and he knoweth them that trust in him
Zeph. 3. 12 they shall trust in the name of the LORD

7. *To (make to) wait with hope,* יָחַל *yachal,* 3.
Job 13. 15 Though he slay me, yet will I trust in him
Isa. 51. 5 the isles..on mine arm shall they trust

8. *To trust one's self on,* רָחַץ *rechats,* 7.
Dan. 3. 28 delivered his servants that trusted in him

9. *To hope,* ἐλπίζω *elpizō.*
Matt12. 21 And in his name shall the Gentiles trust
Luke24. 21 we trusted that it had been he which sh.
John 5. 45 there is (one)..(even) Moses, in whom ye tr.
Rom.15. 12 Esaias saith..in him shall the Gentiles tr.
15. 24 I trust to see you in my journey, and to
1 Co. 16. 7 I trust to tarry a while with you, if the
2 Co. 1. 10 in whom we trust that he will yet deliver
1. 13 I trust ye shall acknowledge even to the
5. 11 I trust also are made manifest in your co.
13. 6 I trust that ye shall know that we are not
Phil. 2. 19 I trust in the Lord Jesus to send Timoth.
1 Ti. 4. 10 we trust in the living God, who is the
5. 5 trusteth in God, and continueth in supp.
6. 17 nor trust in uncertain riches, but in the
Phm. 22 I trust that through your prayers I shall
1 Pe. 3. 5 the holy women also, who trusted in God
2 John 12 I trust to come unto you, and speak face
3 John 14 I trust I shall shortly see thee, and we sh.

10. *To persuade,* πείθω *peithō.*
Matt27. 43 He trusted in God; let him deliver him
Mark10. 24 how hard is it for them that trust in riches
Luke11. 22 he taketh..his armour wherein he trusted
18. 9 certain which trusted in themselves that
2 Co. 1. 9 should not trust in ourselves, but in God
10. 7 If any man trust to himself that he is Ch.
Phil. 2. 24 I trust in the Lord that I also myself sh.
3. 4 that he hath whereof he might trust in
Heb. 2. 13 And again, I will put my trust in him. And
13. 18 we trust we have a good conscience, in all

11. *To trust, have confidence, believe,* πιστεύω *piste.*
Luke16. 11 who will commit to your trust the true
1 Th. 2. 4 allowed..to be put in trust with 1 Ti.1.11

12. *To hope first or before others,* προελπίζω *proel.*
Eph. 1. 12 be to the praise of his glory, who first trust.

TRUSTY —

To be steady, אָמַן *aman,* 2.
Job 12. 20 He removeth away the speech of the tru.

TRUTH, (of a) —

1. *Stedfastness,* אֵמֻן *emun.*
Isa. 26. 2 that the..nation which keepeth the truth

2. *Stedfastness, stability,* אֱמוּנָה *emunah.*
Deut.32. 4 a God of truth, and without iniquity, just
Psa. 89. 49 thou swarest unto David in thy truth?
96. 13 he shall judge..the people with his truth
98. 3 hath remembered his mercy and his truth
100. 5 and his truth (endureth) to all generations
119. 30 I have chosen the way of truth; thy judg.
Prov.12. 17 (He that) speaketh truth sheweth forth ri.
Isa. 59. 4 None calleth..nor (any) pleadeth for truth
Jer. 5. 1 if there be (any)..that seeketh the truth
5. 3 O LORD, (are) not thine eyes upon the tr.?
7. 28 truth is perished, and is cut off from their
9. 3 they are not valiant for the truth upon the

3. *Amen, so it is, so be it,* אָמֵן *amen.*
Isa. 65. 16 in the God of truth..by the God of truth

4. *Stedfast,* אֹמֶן *omen.*
Isa. 25. 1 counsels of old (are) faithfulness (and) tr.

5. *Stedfastness, truth,* אֱמֶת *emeth.*
Gen. 24. 27 left destitute..of his mercy and his truth
32. 10 I am not worthy..of all the truth, which
42. 16 proved, whether (there be any) truth in
Exod18. 21 such as fear God, men of truth, hating co.
34. 6 and abundant in goodness and truth
Deut.13. 14 (if it be) truth, and the thing certain, (th.)
Josh.24. 14 and serve him in sincerity and in truth
Judg. 9. 15 If in truth ye anoint me king over you
1 Sa. 12. 24 and serve him in truth with all your he.
2 Sa. 2. 6 now the LORD show kindness and truth
15. 20 return thou..mercy and truth (be) with
1 Ki. 2. 4 to walk before me in truth with all their
3. 6 he walked before thee in truth, and in ri.
17. 24 the word of the LORD in thy mouth (is) tr.
2 Ki.20. 3 I have walked before thee in truth and
20. 19 (Is it) not (good), if peace and truth be in
2 Ch. 18. 15 that thou say nothing but the truth to me
31. 20 wrought..good and right and truth before
Esth. 9. 30 he sent..(with) words of peace and truth
Psa. 15. 2 He that..speaketh the truth in his heart
25. 5 Lead me in thy truth, and teach me, for
25. 10 the paths of the LORD (are) mercy and tr.
26. 3 and I have walked in thy truth
30. 9 dust praise thee? shall it declare thy truth?
31. 5 thou hast redeemed me, O Lord GOD of t.
40. 10 I have not concealed..thy truth from the
40. 11 let thy lovingkindness and thy truth con.
43. 3 O send out thy light and thy truth: let
45. 4 because of truth and meekness (and) rig.
51. 6 thou desirest truth in the inward parts
54. 5 mine enemies: cut them off in thy truth
57. 3 God shall send forth his mercy and his tr.
57. 10 unto the heavens, and thy truth unto the
61. 7 prepare mercy and truth, which may pre.
69. 13 O God..hear me, in the truth of thy salv.
71. 22 I will also praise..thy truth, O my God
85. 10 Mercy and truth are met together; right.
85. 11 Truth shall spring out of the earth; and
86. 11 I will walk in thy truth: unite my heart
86. 15 (art) a God..plenteous in mercy and truth
89. 14 mercy and truth shall go before thy face
91. 4 his truth (shall be thy) shield and buckler
108. 4 and thy truth (reacheth) unto the clouds
111. 8 (and are) done in truth and uprightness
115. 1 for thy mercy, (and) for thy truth's sake
117. 2 and the truth of the LORD (endureth) for
119. 43 take not the word of truth utterly out of
119. 142 Thy righteousness..thy law (is) the truth
119. 151 and all thy commandments are truth
132. 11 The LORD hath sworn (in) truth unto Da.
138. 2 for thy loving kindness and for thy truth
145. 18 nigh..to all that call upon him in truth
146. 6 Which made heaven..which keepeth tru.
Prov. 3. 3 Let not mercy and truth forsake thee, bind
8. 7 my mouth shall speak truth; and wicked.
12. 19 The lip of truth shall be established for
14. 22 mercy and truth (shall be) to them that de.
16. 6 By mercy and truth iniquity is purged
20. 28 Mercy and truth preserve the king; and

Prov 22. 21 know the certainty of the words of truth
22. 21 mightest answer the words of truth to th.
23. 23 Buy the truth, and sell (it) not; (also) wi.
Eccl. 12. 10 (that which was) written (was)..words of t.
Isa. 10. 20 stay upon..the Holy One of Israel, in truth
16. 5 he shall sit upon it in truth in the tabern.
38. 3 I have walked before thee in truth and
38. 18 they that go..cannot hope for thy truth
38. 19 to the children shall make known thy tr.
39. 8 there shall be peace and truth in my days
42. 3 he shall bring forth judgment unto truth
43. 9 or let them hear, and say, (It is) truth
48. 1 (but) not in truth, nor in righteousness
59. 14 truth is fallen in the street, and equity
59. 15 Yea, truth faileth; and he (that) depart.
61. 8 I will direct their work in truth, and I
Jer. 4. 2 The LORD liveth, in truth, in judgment
9. 5 will deceive..and will not speak the truth
33. 6 reveal..the abundance of peace and truth
Dan. 8. 12 it cast down the truth to the ground; and
9. 13 we might turn..and understand thy truth
10. 21 which is noted in the scripture of truth
11. 2 now will I show thee the truth. Behold
Hos. 4. 1 (there is) no truth, nor mercy, nor knowl.
Mic. 7. 20 Thou wilt perform the truth to Jacob,(and)
Zech. 8. 3 Jerusalem shall be called, A city of truth
8. 8 I will be their God, in truth and in right.
8. 16 Speak ye every man the truth to his neig.
8. 16 execute the judgment of truth and peace
8. 19 cheerful feasts; therefore love the truth
Mal. 2. 6 The law of truth was in his mouth, and

6. *To be set up, certain, true,* יְצַב *yetseb,* 3.
Dan. 7. 19 I would know the truth of the fourth be.

7. *Set up, certain, true,* יַצִּיב *yatstsib.*
Dan. 7. 16 I came..and asked him the truth of all

8. *Truth,* קְשֹׁט *qeshot.*
Dan. 4. 37 king of heaven, all whose works (are) truth
2. 47 Of a truth (it is), that your God (is) a God

9. *Truth,* קֹשֶׁט *qoshet.*
Psa. 60. 4 that it may be displayed because of the t.

10. *Truth,* קֹשְׁט *qosht.*
Prov 22. 21 know the certainty of the words of truth

11. *Truth,* ἀλήθεια *alētheia.*
Matt 22. 16 teachest the way of God in truth, neither
Mark 5. 33 came and fell..and told him all the truth
12. 14 but teachest the way of God in truth
12. 32 thou hast said the truth; for there is one
Luke 4. 25 I tell you of a truth, many widows were
22. 59 Of a truth this (fellow) also was with him
John 1. 14 beheld his glory..full of grace and truth
1. 17 (but) grace and truth came by Jesus Chr
3. 21 he that doeth truth cometh to the light
4. 23 worship the Father in spirit and in truth
4. 24 they..must worship..in spirit and in tr.
5. 33 John, and he bare witness unto the truth
8. 32 shall know the truth, and the truth shall
8. 40 a man that hath told you the truth, wh.
8. 44 not in the truth, because there is no tru.
8. 45 because I tell (you) the truth, ye believe
8. 46 if I say the truth, why do ye not believe
14. 6 I am the way, and the truth, and the life, no
14. 17 (Even) the spirit of truth; whom the wor.
15. 26 the spirit of truth, which proceedeth from
16. 7 I tell you the truth; It is expedient for
16. 13 Howbeit when he, the spirit of truth, is
16. 13 he will guide you into all truth: for he
17. 17 Sanctify..thy truth: thy word is truth
17. 19 also might be sanctified through the truth
18. 37 that I should bear witness unto the truth
18. 37 Every one that is of the truth heareth my
18. 38 Pilate saith unto him, What is truth? And
Acts 4. 27 For of a truth against thy holy child Jes.
10. 34 Of a truth I perceive that God is no resp.
26. 25 speak forth the words of truth and sober.
Rom. 1. 18 who hold the truth in unrighteousness
1. 25 Who changed the truth of God into a lie
2. 2 the judgment of God is according to truth
2. 8 unto them that..do not obey the truth
2. 20 which hast the form of knowledge..truth
3. 7 if the truth of God hath more abounded
9. 1 I say the truth in Christ, I lie not, my c.
15. 8 minister of the circumcision for the truth
1 Co. 5. 8 the unleavened (bread) of sincerity and tr.
13. 6 Rejoiceth not in iniquity, but..in the tr.
2 Co. 4. 2 by manifestation of the truth commending
6. 7 By the word of truth, by the power of G.
7. 14 as we spake all things to you in truth, ev.
7. 14 which (I made) before Titus, is found a tr.
11. 10 As the truth of Christ is in me, no man
12. 6 I will say the truth: but (now) I forbear
13. 8 nothing against the truth, but for the trut.
Gal. 2. 5 that the truth of the Gospel might conti.
2. 14 walked not..according to the truth of the
3. 1 [that ye should not obey the truth, before]
5. 7 that ye should not obey the truth
Eph. 1. 13 after that ye heard the word of truth, the
4. 21 have been taught by him, as the truth is
4. 25 speak every man truth with his neighbour
5. 9 all goodness and righteousness and truth
6. 14 having your loins girt about with truth
Phil. 1. 18 whether in pretence, or in truth, Christ
Col. 1. 5 ye heard before in the word of the truth
1. 6 heard..and knew the grace of God in tru.
2 Th. 2. 10 because they received not..love of the t.
2. 12 might be damned who believed not the tr.
2. 13 chosen you..through..belief of the truth
1 Ti. 2. 4 to come unto the knowledge of the truth
1 Ti. 2. 7 I speak the truth in Christ, (and) lie not
3. 15 church..pillar and ground of the truth
4. 3 them which believe and know the truth
6. 5 disputings of men..destitute of the truth
2 Ti. 2. 15 workman..rightly dividing the word of t.
2. 18 Who concerning the truth have erred, sa.
2. 25 repentance to..acknowledging of the tru.
3. 7 able to come to the knowledge of the tru.
3. 8 so do these also resist the truth: men of
4. 4 shall turn away (their) ears from the tru.
Titus 1. 1 the acknowledging of the truth which is
1. 14 fables..of men, that turn from the truth
Heb. 10. 26 have received the knowledge of the truth
Jas. 1. 18 begat he us with the word of truth, that
3. 14 glory not, and lie not against the truth
5. 19 if any of you do err from the truth, and
1 Pe. 1. 22 in obeying the truth through the spirit
2 Pe. 1. 12 and be established in the present truth
2. 2 by reason of whom the way of truth shall
1 Jo. 1. 6 walk in darkness, we..do not the truth
1. 8 we deceive ourselves, and the truth is not
2. 4 He that saith..is a liar, and the truth is
2. 21 not written..because ye know not the tr.
2. 21 ye know it, and that no lie is of the truth
3. 18 let us not love in word..but..in truth
3. 19 we know that we are of the truth, and sh.
4. 6 Hereby know we the spirit of truth, and
5. 6 beareth witness, because the spirit is tr.
2 John 1 her children, whom I love in the truth
1 also all they that have known the truth
2 For the truth's sake, which dwelleth in
3 Grace be with you..in truth and love
4 I found of thy children walking in truth, as
3 John 1 well beloved Gaius, whom I love in the tr.
3 testified of the truth..walkest in the tru.
4 to hear that my children walk in truth
8 we might be fellow helpers to..tr. v. 12.

12. *Indeed,* ὄντως *ontōs,* 1 Co. 14. 25.

13. *True, genuine, honest, sincere,* ἀληθής *alēthēs.*
1 Jo. 2. 27 is truth, and is no lie, and even as it hath

14. *Verily, indeed, truly,* ναί *nai.*
Matt 15. 27 Truth, Lord: yet the dogs eat of the cru.

TRUTH, to tell or speak the —
To speak truly, or the truth, ἀληθεύω *alētheuō.*
Gal. 4. 16 your enemy, because I tell you the truth
Eph. 4. 15 speaking the truth in love, may grow up

TRY, be tried, to —
1. *To try, prove, test,* בָּחַן *bachan.*
1 Ch. 29. 17 I know also, my God, that thou triest the
Job 7. 18 visit him every morning, (and) try him ev.
12. 11 Doth not the ear try words? and the mo.
23. 10 he hath tried me, I shall come forth as
34. 3 For the ear trieth words, as the mouth ta.
Psa. 7. 9 the righteous God trieth the hearts and
11. 4 behold, his eyelids try, the children of men
11. 5 LORD trieth the righteous; but the wicked
139. 23 Search me..try me, and know my thoughts
Prov. 17. 3 for gold: but the LORD trieth the hearts
Jer. 6. 27 that thou mayest know and try their way
9. 7 I will melt them, and try them, for how
11. 20 that triest the reins and the heart, let me
12. 3 hast seen me, and tried mine heart toward
17. 10 try the reins, even to give every man acc.
20. 12 LORD of hosts, that triest the righteous
Zech. 13. 9 will try them as gold is tried, they shall

2. *To search, investigate,* חָקַר *chaqar.*
Lam. 3. 40 Let us search and try our ways, and turn

3. *To try, prove,* נָסָה *nasah,* 3.
2 Ch. 32. 31 God left him, to try him, that he might

4. *To refine, try, purify,* צָרַף *tsaraph.*
Judg 7. 4 bring them down..and I will try them for
Psa. 17. 3 thou hast tried me, (and) shalt find nothi.
26. 2 Examine me..try my reins and my heart
66. 10 thou, O God..hast tried us, as silver is tr.
105. 19 word came: the word of the LORD tried
Dan. 11. 35 to try them, and to purge, and to make

5. *To try, assay, prove,* δοκιμάζω *dokimazō.*
1 Co. 3. 13 the fire shall try every man's work of what
1 Th. 2. 4 pleasing..God, which trieth our hearts
1 Pe. 1. 7 of your faith..though it be tried with fire
1 Jo. 4. 1 try the spirits whether they are of God

6. *To try, tempt, pierce through,* πειράζω *peirazō.*
Heb. 11. 17 By faith Abraham, when he was tried, off.
Rev. 2. 2 thou hast tried them which say they are
2. 10 cast..you into prison, that ye may be tr.
3. 10 come..to try them that dwell upon the ea.

7. *For a trial, proving, temptation,* πρὸς πειρασμόν.
1 Pe. 4. 12 concerning the fiery trial which is to try

8. *To be set on fire,* πυρόομαι *puroomai.*
Rev. 3. 18 I counsel thee to buy of me gold tried in

TRYING —
A proof, test, δοκίμιον *dokimion.*
Jas. 1. 3 the trying of your faith worketh patience

TRY-PHE'-NA, Τρύφαινα.
A female in Rome, to whom Paul sends a salutation.
Rom 16. 12 Salute T. and Tryphosa, who labour in the

TRY-PHO'-SA, Τρυφῶσα.
A female in Rome, to whom Paul sends a salutation.
Rom 16. 12 Salute Tryphena and T., who labour in the

TU'-BAL, תּוּבַל, תֻּבַל.
1. A son of Japheth. B.C. 2300.
Gen. 10. 2 and Javan, and T., and Meshech, and Tiras
1 Ch. 1. 5 and Javan, and T., and Meshech, and Tiras
2. The Tibarenes, S. of Black Sea, and W. of Colchis, whence they went to Spain, Sicily, &c.
Isa. 66. 19 I will send those that escape..(to) T. and
Eze. 27. 13 Javan, T., and Meshech, they (were) thy
32. 26 There (is) Meshech, T., and all her mult.
38. 2, 3 Gog, the chief prince of Meshech and T.
39. 1 Gog, the chief prince of Meshech and T.

TU-BAL CA'-IN, תּוּבַל קַיִן.
Son of Zillah, one of Lamech's wives, and sister of Naamah, of the race of Cain. B.C. 3800.
Gen. 4. 22 T., an instructor..and the sister of T.

TUMBLE, to —
To turn self, tumble, הָפַךְ *haphak,* 7.
Judg. 7. 13 a cake of barley bread tumbled into the

TUMULT, (to make a), tumultuous —
1. *Sons of desolation, wasting, noise,* בְּנֵי שָׁאוֹן [*ben*].
Jer. 48. 45 crown of the head of the tumultuous ones
2. *To roar, move, sound, make a noise,* הָמָה *hamah.*
Psa. 83. 2 For, lo, thine enemies make a tumult
Isa. 22. 2 Thou that art full of stirs, a tumultuous
3. *Multitude, noise, stone,* הָמוֹן *hamon.*
1 Sa. 4. 14 What (meaneth) the noise of this tumult?
2 Sa. 18. 29 I saw a great tumult, but I knew not wh.
Psa. 65. 7 Which stilleth the noise..and the tumult
Isa. 33. 3 At the noise of the tumult the people fled
4. *Tumult,* הֲמֻלָּה *hamullah.*
Jer. 11. 16 with the noise of a great tumult he hath
5. *Trouble, destruction,* מְהוּמָה *mehumah.*
Amos 3. 9 and behold the great tumults in the midst
Zech 14. 13 a great tumult from the LORD shall be
6. *Desolation, wasting, noise,* שָׁאוֹן *shaon.*
Psa. 74. 23 the tumult of those that rise up against
Isa. 13. 4 a tumultuous noise of the kingdoms of
Hos. 10. 14 Therefore shall a tumult arise among thy
Amos 2. 2 Moab shall die with tumult, with shout.
7. *At ease, quiet, insolent,* שַׁאֲנָן *shaanan.*
2 Ki. 19. 28 Because thy rage against me and thy tu.
Isa. 37. 29 Because thy rage against me, and thy tu.
8. *Instability,* ἀκαταστασία *akatastasia.*
2 Co. 6. 5 In stripes, in imprisonments, in tumults
12. 20 backbitings, whisperings, swellings, tum.
9. *A tumult, tumultuous assembly,* θόρυβος *thorubos.*
Matt 27. 24 When Pilate saw that..rather a tumult
Mark 5. 38 seeth the tumult, and them that wept
Acts 21. 34 could not know the certainty for the tum.
24. 18 neither with multitude, nor with tumult

TURN, turning —
1. *Corner, angle, turning,* מִקְצֹעַ *miqtsoa.*
2 Ch. 26. 9 Uzziah built towers..at the turning (of
Neh. 3. 19, 20, 24, 25 the turning (of the wall)
2. *To be turned round about,* סָבַב *sabab,* 6.
Eze. 41. 24 the doors had two leaves..two turning
3. *To turn back,* שׁוּב *shub.*
2 Ch. 36. 13 hardened his heart from turning unto
4. *Turn, row, garland,* תּוֹר *tor.*
Esth. 2. 12 when every maid's turn was come to go
2. 15 when the turn of Esther, the daughter of
5. *A turning,* τροπή *tropē.*
Jas. 1. 17 no variableness, neither shadow of turn.

TURN (to, unto, back), be turned, to —
1. *To exult,* דּוּץ *duts.*
Job 41. 22 and sorrow is turned into joy before him
2. *To turn, be turned, overturn,* הָפַךְ *haphak.*
Exod 10. 19 the LORD turned a mighty strong west wi.
Lev. 13. 3 the hair in the plague is turned white, and
13. 4 hair thereof be not turned white; then
13. 10 it have turned the hair white, and (there
13. 13 plague: it is all turned white: he (is) cl.
13. 20 hair thereof be turned white; the priest
Deut 23. 5 turned the curse into a blessing unto thee
Josh. 7. 8 when Israel turneth their backs before
1 Sa. 25. 12 So David's young men turned their way
1 Ki. 22. 34 Turn thine hand, and carry me out of the
2 Ki. 9. 23 Joram turned his hands, and fled, and sa.
21. 13 wiping (it), and turning (it) upside down
2 Ch. 9. 12 So she turned, and went away to her own
18. 33 Turn thine hand, that thou mayest carry
Neh. 13. 2 howbeit our God turned the curse into a
Psa. 30. 11 Thou hast turned for me my mourning into
66. 6 He turned the sea into dry (land): they
78. 44 had turned their rivers into blood; and
105. 25 He turned their heart to hate his people
105. 29 He turned their waters into blood, and
114. 8 Which turned the rock (into) a standing
Jer. 31. 13 for I will turn their mourning into joy
Lam. 3. 3 he turneth his hand (against me) all the
Amos 5. 7 Ye who turn judgment to wormwood, and
5. 8 turneth the shadow of death into the mo.
6. 12 for ye have turned judgment into gall, and
8. 10 I will turn your feasts into mourning, and
Zeph. 3. 9 For then will I turn to the people a pure
Hos. 7. 8 Ephraim..Ephraim is a cake not turned
3. *To be turned, overturned,* הָפַךְ *haphak,* 2.
Exod 7. 15 the rod which was turned to a serpent
7. 17 smite..and they shall be turned to blood

Exod. 7. 20 waters that (were) in the river were turned
14. 5 heart of Pharaoh..was turned against the
Lev. 13. 17 the plague be turned into white; then the
13. 25 (if) the hair in the bright spot be turned
1 Sa. 10. 6 and shalt be turned into another man
Esth. 9. 22 month which was turned unto them from
Job 19. 19 they whom I loved are turned against me
20. 14 his meat in his bowels is turned..the gall
41. 28 sling stones are turned with him into st.
Psa. 32. 4 my moisture is turned into the drought
Isa. 34. 9 streams thereof shall be turned into pitch
63. 10 therefore he was turned to be their enemy
Jer. 2. 21 how then art thou turned into the degen.
30. 6 and all faces are turned into paleness?
Lam. 1. 20 mine heart is turned within me, for I ha.
5. 2 Our inheritance is turned to strangers, our
5. 15 ceased; our dance is turned into mourn.
Eze. 4. 8 thou shalt not turn thee from one side to
Dan. 10. 8 for my comeliness was turned in me into
10. 16 by the vision my sorrows are turned upon
Hos. 11. 8 Mine heart is turned within me, my rep.
Joel 2. 31 The sun shall be turned into darkness, and

4. *To be turned, overturned,* הָפַךְ *haphak*, 6.
Job 30. 15 Terrors are turned upon me, they pursue

5. *To turn or overturn self,* הָפַךְ *haphak*, 7.
Job 37. 12 it is turned round about by his counsels
38. 14 It is turned as clay (to) the seal; and they

6. *To incline, stretch out, turn aside,* נָטָה *natah.*
Gen. 38. 1 Judah..turned in to a certain Adullamite
38. 16 he turned unto her by the way, and said
Num 20. 17 we will not turn to the right hand nor to
20. 21 wherefore Israel turned away from him
21. 22 we will not turn into the fields, or into
22. 26 no way to turn either to the right hand
22. 33 the ass saw me, and turned from me th.
22. 33 unless she had turned from me, surely
1 Sa. 14. 7 Do all that (is) in thine heart: turn thee
2 Sa. 2. 19 turned not to the right hand nor to the
1 Ki. 2. 28 had turned after Adonijah, though he tu.
11. 9 because his heart was turned from the L.
Job 31. 7 If my step hath turned out of the way, and
Prov. 4. 27 Turn not to the right hand nor to the left

7. *To stretch out, turn aside, incline,* נָטָה *natah*, 5.
Num 22. 23 Balaam smote the ass, to turn her into
Job 24. 4 They turn the needy out of the way, the
Prov 21. 1 he turneth it whithersoever he will
Isa. 30. 11 turn aside out of the path, cause the Holy

8. *To give,* נָתַן *nathan.*
Deut 14. 25 Then shalt thou turn (it) into money, and
2 Ch. 29. 6 For our fathers have..turned (their) bac.

9. *To go, turn, or bring round about,* סָבַב *sabab.*
1 Sa. 22. 17 Turn, and slay the priests of the LORD
22. 18 Turn thou, and fall upon the priests
2 Ki. 9. 18, 19 What hast thou to do with peace? turn
Song 2. 17 turn, my beloved, and be thou like a roe

10. *To be, go, turn or bring round about,* סָבַב *sabab*, 2.
Num 34. 4 your border shall turn from the south to
1 Sa. 17. 30 he turned from him toward another, and
22. 18 Doeg the Edomite turned, and he fell upon
2 Sa. 14. 24 Let him turn to his own house, and let him
Prov 26. 14 (As) the door turneth upon his hinges, so
Jer. 6. 12 their houses shall be turned unto others
Eze. 1. 9 they turned not when they went; they
1. 12, 17 (and) they turned not when they went
10. 11, 11 they turned not as they went
10. 16 wheels also turned not from beside them
26. 2 she is turned unto me; I shall be repleni
Hab. 2. 16 shall be turned unto thee, and shameful
Zech. 14. 10 All the land shall be turned as a plain fr.

11. *To go, turn or bring round about,* סָבַב *sabab*, 5.
Judg 18. 23 they turned their faces, and said unto M.
1 Ki. 8. 14 king turned his face about, and blessed
18. 37 thou hast turned their heart back again
2 Ki. 16. 18 turned he from the house of the LORD for
20. 2 Then he turned his face to the wall, and
23. 34 turned his name to Jehoiakim, and took
1 Ch. 10. 14 turned the kingdom unto David the son
12. 23 came..to turn the kingdom of Saul to him
2 Ch. 6. 3 king turned his face, and blessed the wh.
35. 22 Josiah would not turn his face from him
36. 4 turned his name to Jehoiakim. And Ne.
Ezra 6. 22 turned the heart of the king of Assyria
Isa. 38. 2 Then Hezekiah turned his face toward the
Eze. 7. 22 My face will I turn also from them, and

12. *To be turned back,* סוּג *sug*, 2.
Psa. 35. 4 let them be turned back and brought to
44. 18 Our heart is not turned back, neither have
70. 2 let them be turned backward, and put to
129. 5 Let them all be..turned back that hate Z.
Isa. 42. 17 they shall be turned back, they shall

13. *To turn (or be turned) aside,* סוּר *sur.*
Deut. 2. 27 I will neither turn unto the right hand nor
Josh. 1. 7 turn not from it (to) the right hand or (to)
Judg. 2. 17 they turned quickly out of the way which
20. 8 neither will we any (of us) turn into his
2 Ki. 4. 11 he turned into the chamber, and lay th.
2 Ch. 20. 10 turned from them, and destroyed them

14. *To face, front,* פָּנָה *panah.*
Gen. 24. 49 that I may turn to the right hand, or to
Exod. 7. 23 Pharaoh turned and went into his house
10. 6 turned himself, and went out from Phar.
32. 15 Moses turned, and went down from the
Lev. 19. 4 Turn ye not unto idols, nor make to you.
20. 6 soul that turneth after such as have fam.
Num 14. 25 turn you, and get you into the wilderne.
21. 33 turned, and went up by the way of Bash.

Deut. 1. 7 Turn you, and take your journey, and go
1. 24 they turned and went up into the moun.
1. 40 turn you, and take your journey into the
2. 1 Then we turned, and took our journey
2. 3 Ye have compassed..turn you northward
2. 8 we turned and passed by the way of the
3. 1 Then we turned, and went up the way to
9. 15 So I turned, and came down from the mo.
10. 5 turned myself, and came down from the
16. 7 thou shalt turn in the morning, and go
31. 18 in that they are turned unto other gods
31. 20 then will they turn unto other gods, and
Josh. 7. 12 turned (their) backs before their enemies
Judg 18. 21 So they turned and departed, and put the
18. 26 he turned and went back unto his house
20. 42 Therefore they turned (their backs) before
20. 45 they turned and fled toward the wildern.
20. 47 six hundred men turned and fled to the
1 Sa. 13. 17 one company turned unto the way (that
13. 18 another company turned the way (to) B.
13. 18 another company turned (to) the way of
1 Ki. 10. 13 so she turned, and went to her own cou.
17. 3 Get thee hence, and turn thee eastward
2 Ki. 2. 24 turned back, and looked on them, and
5. 12 So he turned, and went away in a rage
Job 5. 1 and to which of the saints wilt thou turn
Psa. 25. 16 Turn thee unto me, and have mercy upon
69. 16 turn unto me according to the multitude
86. 16 O turn unto me, and have mercy upon me
Prov 17. 8 whithersoever it turneth, it prospereth
Eccl. 2. 12 And I turned myself to behold wisdom
Isa. 13. 14 they shall every man turn to his own pe.
53. 6 we have turned every one to his own way
Jer. 2. 27 for they have turned (their) back unto me
32. 33 they have turned unto me the back, and
50. 16 they shall turn every one to his people, and
Eze. 17. 6 whose branches turned toward him, and
36. 9 will turn unto you, and ye shall be tilled

15. *To (cause to) face, or turn the face,* פָּנָה *panah*, 5.
Judg 15. 4 turned tail to tail, and put a firebrand in
1 Sa. 10. 9 he had turned his back to go from Samu.
Jer. 48. 39 how hath Moab turned the back with sh.

16. *To set, place, put,* שׂוּם, שִׂים *sum, sim.*
Psa. 107. 33 He turneth rivers into a wilderness, and
107. 35 He turneth the wilderness into a standing
Isa. 21. 4 the night..hath he turned into fear unto

17. *To turn aside,* שָׂטָה *satah.*
Prov. 4. 15 Avoid it, pass not by it, turn from it

18. *To turn back,* שׁוּב *shub* 1, 5.
Exod. 4. 7 behold, it was turned again as his..flesh
14. 2 Speak..that they turn and encamp before
32. 12 Turn from thy fierce wrath, and repent of
Deut. 4. 30 if thou turn to the LORD thy God
13. 17 that the LORD may turn from the fierce.
30. 3 God will turn thy captivity, and have co.
30. 10 if thou turn unto the LORD thy God with
Josh. 7. 26 the LORD turned from the fierceness of his
19. 12 turned from Sarid eastward toward the
19. 27 turneth toward the sun rising to Beth-da.
19. 29 the coast turneth to Ramah, and to the
19. 29 the coast turneth to Hosah; and the out.
19. 34 the coast turneth westward to Aznoth ta.
22. 23 we have built us an altar to turn from
22. 29 turn this day from following the LORD, to
24. 20 he will turn and do you hurt, and consu.
1 Ki. 8. 33 shall turn again to thee, and confess thy
8. 35 turn from their sin, when thou afflictest
9. 6 if ye shall at all turn from following me
22. 33 that they turned back from pursuing him
2 Ki. 17. 13 Turn ye from your evil ways, and keep
23. 25 that turned to the LORD with all his heart
23. 26 the LORD turned not from the fierceness
24. 1 then he turned and rebelled against him
2 Ch. 6. 26 turn from their sin, when thou dost afflict
6. 37 turn and pray unto thee in the land of th.
7. 14 seek my face, and turn from their wicked
12. 12 the wrath of the LORD turned from him
15. 4 they in their trouble did turn unto the L.
36. 13 hardened his heart from turning unto the
Ezra 10. 14 until the fierce wrath..be turned from us
Neh. 1. 9 (if) ye turn unto me, and keep my comm.
4. 4 turn their reproach upon their own head
9. 26 testified against them to turn them to th.
9. 35 neither turned they from their wicked wo.
Job 15. 13 That thou turnest thy spirit against God
23. 13 he (is) in one (mind), and who can turn
Job 42. 10 LORD turned the captivity of Job, when
Psa. 7. 12 If he turn not, he will whet his sword: he
9. 17 The wicked shall be turned into hell. (and)
22. 27 the ends of the world shall..turn unto
56. 9 then shall mine enemies turn back: this
81. 14 turned my hand against their adversaries
85. 3 thou hast turned..from the fierceness of
85. 4 Turn us, O God of our salvation, and ca.
89. 43 Thou hast also turned the edge of his
90. 3 Thou turnest man to destruction, and sa.
119. 59 and turned my feet unto thy testimonies
119. 79 Let those that fear thee turn unto me, and
132. 11 he will not turn from it; Of the fruit of
Prov. 1. 23 Turn you at my reproof: behold, I will
Isa. 1. 25 I will turn my hand upon thee, and pur.
9. 13 the people turneth not unto him that sm.
23. 17 she shall turn to her hire, and shall com.
28. 6 for strength to them that turn the battle
29. 17 Lebanon shall be turned into a fruitful
31. 6 Turn ye unto (him from) whom the child.
44. 25 turneth wise (men) backward, and maketh
59. 20 unto them that turn from transgression
Jer. 2. 35 surely his anger shall turn from me: beh.
3. 7 Turn thou unto me: but she returned not

Jer. 3. 10 Judah hath not turned unto me with her
3. 14 Turn, O backsliding children, saith the
8. 4 saith the LORD..shall he turn away and
8. 6 every one turned to his course, as the ho.
18. 8 If that nation..turn from their evil, I will
23. 22 they should have turned them from their
26. 3 If so be they will hearken, and turn every
31. 18 I shall be turned; for thou (art) the LORD
31. 19 Surely after that I was turned, I repented
34. 11 But afterward they turned, and caused the
34. 15 ye were now turned, and had done right
34. 16 ye turned, and polluted my name, and ca.
44. 5 nor inclined their ear to turn from their
Lam. 1. 13 he hath turned me back; he hath made
3. 3 Surely against me is he turned..all the day
5. 21 Turn thou us..and we shall be turned
Eze. 3. 19 he turn not from his wickedness, nor from
3. 20 When a righteous (man) doth turn from
14. 6 Repent, and turn..from your idols, and
18. 21 if the wicked will turn from all his sins
18. 30 Repent, and turn..from all your transg.
18. 32 I have no pleasure..wherefore turn..and
33. 9 to turn from it; if he do not turn from his
33. 11 but that the wicked turn from his way
33. 11 turn ye, turn ye from your evil ways, for
33. 12 in the day that he turneth from his wick.
33. 14 if he turn from his sin, and do that which
33. 18 When the righteous turneth from his rig.
33. 19 if the wicked turn from his wickedness
38. 12 to turn thine hand upon the desolate pl.
Dan. 9. 13 we might turn from our iniquities, and
11. 18 After this shall he turn his face unto the
11. 19 he shall turn his face toward the fort of
Hos. 5. 4 will not frame their doings to turn unto
12. 6 turn thou to thy God: keep mercy and ju.
14. 2 Take with you words, and turn to the L.
Joel 2. 12 Turn ye (even) to me with all your heart
2. 13 rend your heart..and turn unto the LORD
Amos 1. 8 and I will turn mine hand against Ekron
Jon. 3. 8 let them turn every one from his evil way
3. 9 Who can tell (if) God will turn and repent
3. 10 saw..that they turned from their evil way
Zech. 1. 3 Turn ye unto me..and I will turn unto
1. 4 Turn ye now from your evil ways, and
5. 1 Then I turned, and lifted up mine eyes
6. 1 And I turned, and lifted up mine eyes, and
9. 12 Turn you to the strong hold, ye prisoners
13. 7 will turn mine hand upon the little ones
Mal. 4. 6 he shall turn the heart of the fathers to

19. *To look, glance, be dazzled,* שָׁעָה *shaah.*
Job 14. 6 Turn from him, that he may rest, till he

20. *To pervert, turn, make crooked,* עָוָה *avah*, 3.
Isa. 24. 1 maketh it waste, and turneth it upside

21. *To come or go away or off,* ἀποβαίνω *apobainō.*
Luke 21. 13 And it shall turn to you for a testimony
Phil. 1. 19 I know that this shall turn to my salvat.

22. *To become,* γίνομαι *ginomai.*
John 16. 20 but your sorrow shall be turned into joy

23. *To be turned out,* ἐκτρέπομαι *ektrepomai.*
2 Ti. 4. 4 from the truth, and shall be turned unto fa.

24. *To turn over, upon, unto,* ἐπιστρέφω *epistrephō.*
Luke 1. 16 many of the children of Israel shall he tu.
1. 17 to turn the hearts of the fathers to the
Acts 9. 35 all that dwelt in Lydda..turned to the L
9. 40 turning..to the body said, Tabitha, arise
11. 21 number believed, and turned unto the L.
14. 15 preach unto you that ye should turn from
15. 19 from among the Gentiles are turned
16. 18 turned and said to the spirit, I command
26. 18 to turn (them) from darkness to light, and
26. 20 that they should repent and turn to God
2 Co. 3. 16 Nevertheless when it shall turn to the L.
Gal. 4. 9 how turned ye again to the weak and begg.
1 Th. 1. 9 how ye turned to God from idols to serve
2 Pe. 2. 21 [turn from the holy commandment deliv.]
Rev. 1. 12 I turned..And being turned I saw seven

25. *To turn afterward or over,* μεταστρέφω *metas.*
Acts 2. 20 The sun shall be turned into darkness, and
Jas. 4. 9 let your laughter be turned to mourning

26. *To put or place with or apart,* μετατίθημι *meta.*
Jude 4 turning the grace of our God into lascivi.

27. *To turn,* στρέφω *strephō.*
Matt. 5. 39 shall smite thee on thy right cheek, turn
16. 23 he turned, and said unto Peter, Get thee
Luke 7. 44 he turned to the woman, and said unto S.
9. 55 he turned, and rebuked them, and said, Ye
10. 23 [he turned him unto (his) disciples, and]
14. 25 and he turned, and said unto them
22. 61 the Lord turned, and looked upon Peter
23. 28 Jesus, turning unto them said, Daughters
John 1. 38 Then Jesus turned, and saw them follow.
Acts 7. 42 God turned, and gave them up to worship
13. 46 everlasting life, lo, we turn to the Genti.
Rev. 11. 6 have power over waters to turn them to

28. *To turn under, by degrees,* ὑποστρέφω *hupostre.*
Luke 17. 15 turned back, and with a loud voice glorified

TURN, be turned about, to —

1. *To go, turn or bring round about,* סָבַב *sabab.*
Eccl. 1. 6 The wind..turneth about unto the north
Eze. 42. 19 He turned about to the west side, (and) me.

2. *To be turned round about,* סָבַב *sabab*, 2.
Gen. 42. 24 he turned himself about from them, and
1 Sa. 15. 27 And as Samuel turned about to go away
1 Ki. 2. 15 the kingdom is turned about, and is bec.

3. *To be turned round about,* סָבַב *sabab,* 6.
Isa. 28. 27 neither is a cart wheel turned about upon

4. *To turn over, upon, toward,* ἐπιστρέφω *epistrephō.*
Matt. 9. 22 Jesus [turned him about]; and when he
Mark 5. 30 turned him about in the press, and said
8. 33 when he had turned about, and looked on
John 21. 20 Then Peter, turning about, seeth the dis.

5. *To lead along with, after, back, away,* μετάγω.
Jas. 3. 3 bits..and we turn about their whole body
3. 4 yet are they turned about with a very sm.

6. *To turn, change,* στρέφω *strephō.*
Luke 7. 9 he marvelled at him, and turned him ab.

TURN again, to—

1. *To turn, be turned,* הָפַךְ *haphak.*
Judg 20. 41 when the men of Israel turned again, the
2 Ki. 5. 26 when the man turned again from his char.

2. *To turn back,* שׁוּב *shub* (in Psa. 80 *shub,* 5).
Exod 33. 11 he turned again into the camp: but his
Lev. 13. 16 Or if the raw flesh turn again, and be ch.
Num 33. 7 turned again unto Pi-hahiroth, which (is)
Josh. 8. 21 they turned again, and slew the men of
Judg. 3. 19 he himself turned again from the quar.
8. 33 the children of Israel turned again, and
11. 8 Therefore we turn again to thee now, that
20. 48 men of Israel turned again upon the ch.
Ruth 1. 11 Turn again, my daughters; why will ye
1. 12 Turn again, my daughters, go (your way)
1 Sa. 15. 25 turn again with me, that I may worship
15. 30 turn again with me, that I may worship
15. 31 So Samuel turned again after Saul, and
2 Sa. 22. 38 turned not again until I had consumed
1 Ki. 12. 27 then shall the heart of this people turn a.
13. 9 nor turn again by the same way that thou
13. 17 nor turn again to go by the way that thou
2 Ki. 1. 6 Go, turn again unto the king that sent you
20. 5 Turn again, and tell Hezekiah the captain
2 Ch. 18. 32 they turned back again from pursuing him
30. 6 turn again unto the LORD God of Abrah.
30. 9 For if ye turn again unto the LORD, your
Job 34. 15 perish together, and man shall turn aga.
Psa. 18. 37 neither did I turn again till they were co.
80. 3, 7. 19 Turn us again..cause thy face to
85. 8 to his saints: but let them not turn aga.
104. 9 that they turn not again to cover the ea.
126. 1 When the Lord turned again the captivity
126. 4 Turn again our captivity, O LORD, as the
Eccl. 3. 20 are of the dust, and all turn to dust ag.
Jer. 25. 5 Turn ye again now every one from his evil
31. 21 turn again, O virgin of Israel, turn again
Lam. 3. 40 search and try our ways, and turn again
Eze. 8. 6, 13, 15 turn thee yet again, (and) thou sh.
Mic. 7. 19 He will turn again, he will have compas.
Zech 10. 9 live with their children, and turn again

3. *To bend back or up,* ἀνακάμπτω *anakamptō.*
Luke 10. 6 shall rest..if not, it shall turn to you ag.

4. *To turn over, upon, toward,* ἐπιστρέφω *epistre.*
Mark 13. 16 let him that is in the field not turn..again
Luke 17. 4 and seven times in a day turn again to thee
2 Pe. 2. 22 The dog (is) turned to his own vomit ag.

5. *To turn,* στρέφω *strephō.*
Matt. 7. 6 lest they trample them..and turn again

6. *To turn under, by degrees,* ὑποστρέφω *hupostre.*
Luke 2. 45 they turned back again to Jerusalem, se.

TURN (be turned) aside, to —

1. *To turn, be turned, overturned,* הָפַךְ *haphak,* 2.
Psa. 78. 57 they were turned aside like a deceitful

2. *To turn aside, lay hold of,* לָפַת *laphath,* 2.
Job 6. 18 The paths of their way are turned aside

3. *To stretch out, turn aside or away,* נָטָה *natah.*
Num 22. 23 the ass turned aside out of the way, and
1 Sa. 8. 3 turned aside after lucre, and took bribes
2 Sa. 2. 21 Turn thee aside to thy right hand or to
Jer. 14. 8 as a wayfaring man (that) turneth aside
To stretch out, turn aside or away, נָטָה *natah,* 5.
Psa. 125. 5 As for such as turn aside unto their croo.
Isa. 10. 2 To turn aside the needy from judgment
29. 21 turn aside the just for a thing of nought
30. 11 Get you out of the way, turn aside out of
44. 20 a deceived heart hath turned him aside
Lam. 3. 35 To turn aside the right of a man before
Amos 2. 7 That pant..and turn aside the way of the
5. 12 and they turn aside the poor in the gate
Mal. 3. 5 that turn aside the stranger..and fear not

5. *To go, turn, bring round about,* סָבַב *sabab.*
2 Sa. 18. 30 And the king said..Turn aside..stand he.

6. *To be brought or turned round about,* סָבַב *sabab,* 2.
2 Sa. 18. 30 And he turned aside, and stood still

7. *To turn or be turned aside,* סוּר *sur.*
Exod. 3. 3 I will now turn aside, and see this great
3. 4 when the LORD saw that he turned aside
32. 8 They have turned aside quickly out of the
Deut. 5. 32 ye shall not turn aside to the right hand
9. 12 they are quickly turned aside out of the
9. 16 ye had turned aside quickly out of the way
11. 16 ye turn aside, and serve other gods, and
11. 28 turn aside out of the way which I comm.
17. 20 turn not aside from the commandment
31. 29 turn aside from the way which I have co.
Josh 23. 6 turn not aside therefrom (to) the right ha.
Judg 14. 8 he turned aside to see the carcase of the
19. 12 We will not turn aside hither into the city
19. 15 they turned aside thither, to go in (and)
Ruth 4. 1 turn aside..And he turned aside, and sat
1 Sa. 6. 12 turned not aside (to) the right hand or (to)
12. 20 yet turn not aside from following the Lo.
12. 21 turn ye not aside: for (then should ye go)
2 Sa. 2. 21 Asahel would not turn aside from follow.
2. 22 Turn thee aside from following me: whe.
2. 23 Howbeit he refused to turn aside: wher.
1 Ki. 15. 5 turned not aside from any (thing) that he
20. 39 turned aside, and brought a man unto me
22. 32 And they turned aside to fight against him
22. 43 he turned not aside from it, doing (that
2 Ki. 22. 2 turned not aside to the right hand or to

8. *To turn aside,* סוּר *sur,* 3a.
Lam. 3. 11 He hath turned aside my ways, and pulled

9. *Those turning aside,* סֵטִים *setim.*
Psa. 101. 3 I hate the work of them that turn aside

10. *To cover, wrap up, veil,* עָטָה *atah.*
Song 1. 7 as one that turneth aside by the flocks of

11. *To turn the face, front, look,* פָּנָה *panah.*
Song 6. 1 whither is thy beloved turned aside? that

12. *To turn aside,* שׂוּט *sut.*
Psa. 40. 4 not the proud, nor such as turn aside to

13. *To give space again, withdraw,* ἀναχωρέω *ana.*
Matt. 2. 22 he turned aside into the parts of Galilee

14. *To be turned out or off,* ἐκτρέπομαι *ektrepomai.*
1 Ti. 1. 6 some having swerved have turned aside
5. 15 some are already turned aside after Satan

TURN (be turned) away, to —

1. *To stretch out, turn aside, incline,* נָטָה *natah,* 5.
1 Ki. 11. 2 they will turn away your heart after their
11. 3 and his wives turned away his heart
11. 4 his wives turned away his heart after ot.
Jer. 5. 25 Your iniquities have turned away these (th.

2. *To be caused to remove,* נָסַג *nasag,* 6.
Isa. 59. 14 judgment is turned away backward, and

3. *To cause to go, turn, or bring round,* סָבַב *sabab,* 5.
1 Ki. 21. 4 turned away his face, and would eat no br.
1 Ch. 14. 14 Go not up after them; turn away from th.
2 Ch. 29. 6 have forsaken him, and have turned away
Song 6. 5 Turn away thine eyes from me, for they

4. *To be turned back,* סוּג *sug,* 2.
Isa. 50. 5 not rebellious, neither turned away back
Jer. 38. 22 thy feet are sunk..are turned away back
46. 5 have I seen them dismayed..turned away

5. *To turn aside,* סוּר *sur.*
2 Ch. 25. 27 after the time that Amaziah did turn away

6. *To cause to turn aside,* סוּר *sur,* 5.
Deut. 7. 4 they will turn away thy son from following
17. 17 that his heart turn not away: neither sh.
2 Ch. 30. 9 will not turn away (his) face from you, if
Psa. 66. 20 Blessed (be) God, which hath not turned a.
Prov 28. 9 He that turneth away his ear from hearing

7. *A turning aside,* סָרָה *sarah.*
Deut 13. 5 he hath spoken to turn (you) away from the

8. *To cause to pass over,* עָבַר *abar,* 5.
Psa. 119. 37 Turn away mine eyes from beholding
119. 39 Turn away my reproach which I fear, for

9. *To turn the face,* פָּנָה *panah.*
Deut 29. 18 whose heart turneth away this day from
30. 17 if thine heart turn away, so that thou wilt

10. *To turn back,* שׁוּב *shub.*
Gen. 27. 44 tarry..until thy brother's fury turn away
27. 45 Until thy brother's anger turn away from
Num 14. 43 because ye are turned away from the Lo.
25. 4 fierce anger..may be turned away from Is.
32. 15 if ye turn away from after him, he will
Deut 23. 14 see no unclean thing..and turn away fr.
Josh. 22. 16 to turn away this day from following the
22. 18 that ye must turn away this day from fol.
2 Ch. 7. 19 if ye turn away, and forsake my statutes
29. 10 his fierce wrath may turn away from us
30. 8 fierceness of his wrath may turn away fr.
Prov 25. 10 to shame, and thine infamy turn not away
30. 30 A lion, (which)..turneth not away for any
Isa. 5. 25 his anger is not turned away, but his ha.
9. 12, 17, 21 his anger is not turned away, but
10. 4 his anger is not turned away, but his ha.
12. 1 thine anger is turned away, and thou co.
Jer. 3. 19 My father; and shalt not turn away from
29. 14 I will turn away your captivity, and I will
32. 40 I will not turn away from them, to do th.
50. 6 they have turned them away (on) the mo.
Eze. 18. 24 when the righteous turneth away from his
18. 26 When a righteous (man) turneth away fr.
18. 27 when the wicked (man) turneth away fr.
18. 28 turneth away from all his transgressions
Dan. 9. 16 let thine anger..be turned away from thy
Hos. 14. 4 for mine anger is turned away from him
Jon. 3. 9 repent, and turn away from his fierce an.
Nah. 2. 2 LORD hath turned away the excellency of
Zeph. 2. 7 shall visit them, and turn away their cap.

11. *To cause to turn back,* שׁוּב *shub,* 5.
Num 25. 11 hath turned my wrath away from the ch.
2 Ki. 18. 24 How then wilt thou turn away the face
2 Ch. 6. 42 turn not away the face of thine anointed
Psa. 78. 38 many a time turned he his anger away, and
106. 23 to turn away his wrath, lest he should de.
132. 10 turn not away the face of thine anointed
Prov 15. 1 A soft answer turneth away wrath: but
24. 18 Lest the LORD..turn away his wrath from
29. 8 into a snare: but wise (men) turn away
Isa. 36. 9 How then wilt thou turn away the face of
58. 13 If thou turn away thy foot from the sab.
Jer. 2. 24 in her occasion who can turn her away?
18. 20 (and) to turn away thy wrath from them
Lam. 2. 14 discovered thine iniquity, to turn away
Eze. 14. 6 turn away your faces from all your abom.
Amos 1. 3, 6, 9, 11, 13 I will not turn away (the pu.)
2. 1, 4, 6, I will not turn away (the punishment)
Mal. 2. 6 and did turn many away from iniquity

12. *To turn or bring back,* שׁוּב *shub,* 3a.
Jer. 50. 6 they have turned them away (on) the mo.

13. *To turn off or away,* ἀποστρέφω *apostrephō.*
Matt. 5. 42 would borrow of thee turn not thou away
Acts 3. 26 in turning away every one of you from his
Rom 11. 26 and shall turn away ungodliness from Ja.
2 Ti. 1. 15 all they which are in Asia be turned away
4. 4 they shall turn away (their) ears from the
Heb. 12. 25 if we turn away from him that (speaketh)

14. *To be turned off or away,* ἀποτρέπομαι *apotrepo.*
2 Ti. 3. 5 denying the power..from such turn away

15. *To turn thoroughly or diversely,* διαστρέφω *dia.*
Acts 13. 8 seeking to turn away the deputy from the

16. *To set or put away,* μεθίστημι *methistēmi.*
Acts 19. 26 Paul hath persuaded and turned away m.

TURN, (be turned) back, back again, backward, to —

1. *To turn, be turned,* הָפַךְ *haphak.*
Psa. 78. 9 The children of Ephraim..turned back in
Josh. 8. 20 the people..turned back upon their purs.

2. *To cause to go round about,* סָבַב *sabab,* 5.
Jer. 21 4 I will turn back the weapons of war that

3. *To be turned back,* סוּג *sug,* 2.
Psa. 78. 57 turned back, and dealt unfaithfully like
Zeph. 1. 6 them that are turned back from the LORD

4. *To turn aside,* סוּר *sur.*
Job 34. 27 Because they turned back from him, and

5. *To cause to turn the face,* פָּנָה *panah,* 5.
Jer. 46. 21 they also are turned back..are fled away

6. *To be caused to turn the face,* פָּנָה *panah,* 6.
Jer. 49. 8 Flee ye, turn back, dwell deep, O inhabi.

7. *To turn back,* שׂוּג *sug,* 2.
2 Sa. 1. 22 the bow of Jonathan turned not back, and

8. *To turn back,* שׁוּב *shub.*
Deut 23. 13 turn back and cover that which cometh
Josh. 11. 10 Joshua at that time turned back, and to.
1 Sa. 15. 11 for he has turned back from following me
2 Sa. 19. 37 Let thy servant..turn back again, that I
2 Ki. 1. 5 when the messengers turned back unto
1. 5 said unto them, Why are ye now turned
15. 20 so the king of Assyria turned back, and
1 Ch. 21. 20 Ornan turned back, and saw the angel
2 Ch. 18. 32 they turned back again from pursuing
Neh. 2. 15 turned back, and entered by the gate of
Job 39. 22 neither turneth he back from the sword
Psa. 9. 3 When mine enemies are turned back, th.
70. 3 Let them be turned back for a reward of
78. 41 they turned back, and tempted God, and
Jer. 4. 8 anger of the LORD is not turned back from
4. 28 not repent, neither will I turn back from
11. 10 They are turned back to the iniquities of
Lam. 1. 8 yea, she sinneth, and turneth backward
Zeph. 3. 20 when I turn back your captivity before

9. *To turn or bring back,* שׁוּב *shub,* 3a.
Eze. 38. 4 I will turn thee back, and put hooks into
39. 2 I will turn thee back, and leave but the

10. *To cause to turn back,* שׁוּב *shub,* 5.
2 Ki. 19. 28 I will turn thee back by the way by which
Isa. 14. 27 stretched out, and who shall turn it back
37. 29 I will turn thee back by the way by which
Jer. 6. 9 turn back thine hand as a grape gatherer

11. *To turn,* στρέφω *strephō.*
Acts 7. 39 in their hearts turned back again into Eg.

12. *To turn by degrees, quietly,* ὑποστρέφω *hupostr.*
Luke 2. 45 they turned back again to Jerusalem, se.

TURN every way, face, far away, to —

1. *To turn self,* הָפַךְ *haphak,* 7.
Gen. 3. 24 a flaming sword which turned every way

2. *To cast off or away,* זָנַח *zanach,* 5.
Isa. 19. 6 they shall turn the rivers far away..the

3. *To turn the face, look,* פָּנָה *panah.*
Gen. 18. 22 the men turned their faces from thence

TURN from, upside down, to —

1. *To bend, twist,* עָוַת *avath,* 3. Psa. 146. 9.

1 a. *Overturn the surface of,* עִוָּה פָנֶיהָ [*avah,* 3]. Is. 24. 1

2. *To turn back,* שׁוּב *shub.*
Isa. 59. 20 unto them that turn from transgression

3. *To turn away or off,* ἀποστρέφω *apostrephō.*
Titus 1. 14 commandments of men, that turn from

4. *To set up, excite,* ἀναστατόω *anastatoō.*
Acts 17. 6 These that..turned the world upside do.

TURN in, over, violently, to —

1. *To turn over, be perverse,* יָרַט *yarat.*
Job 16. 11 God hath..turned me over into the hands

2. *To turn aside,* סוּר *sur.*
Gen. 19. 2 turn in, I pray you, into your servants' h.
19. 3 turned in unto him, and entered into his
Judg. 4. 18 Turn in, my lord, turn in to me; fear not
4. 18 when he had turned in unto her into the
18. 3 turned in thither, and said unto him, W.
18. 15 turned thitherward, and came to the ho.
19. 11 let us turn in into this city of the Jebusi.
2 Ki. 4. 8 as oft as he passed by, he turned in thith.
4. 10 when he cometh..he shall turn in thither
Prov. 9. 4, 16 Whoso (is) simple, let him turn in hi.

3. *To wrap round,* צָנַף *tsanaph.*
Isa. 22. 18 He will surely violently turn and toss thee?

TURN self (about or again), to —

1. *To be turned,* לָפַת *laphath,* 2.
Ruth 3. 8 that the man was afraid, and turned him.

2. *To go, or turn round about,* סָבַב *sabab.*
Gen. 42. 24 he turned himself about from them, and

3. *To turn the face,* פָּנָה *panah.*
1 Sa. 14. 47 whithersoever he turned himself, he vex.
1 Ki. 2. 3 prosper..whithersoever thou turnest thy.
2 Ki. 23. 16 as Josiah turned himself, he spied the se.

4. *To cause to turn the face,* פָּנָה *panah,* 5.
Jer. 49. 24 Damascus is waxed feeble..turneth hers.

5. *To turn back, bring back,* שׁוּב *shub,* 3a.
Psa. 60. 1 been displeased; O turn thyself to us ag.

6. *To turn,* στρέφω *strephō.*
John 20. 14 she had thus said, she turned herself ba.
20. 16 She turned herself, and saith unto him

TURN to flight, to —

To incline, put to flight, κλίνω *klinō.*
Heb. 11. 34 turned to flight the armies of the aliens

TURN, to cause or make to —

To cause to turn back, שׁוּב *shub,* 5.
Psa. 44. 10 Thou makest us to turn back from the e.
Dan. 11. 18 reproach..he shall cause (it) to turn upon

TURNED to the contrary, up, to be —

To be turned, הָפַךְ *haphak,* 2.
Esth. 9. 1 though it was turned to the contrary
Job 28. 5 and under it is turned up as it were fire

TURNING away —

1. *Turning back,* מְשׁוּבָה *meshubah.*
Prov. 1. 32 the turning away of the simple shall slay

2. *To turn or bring back,* שׁוּב *shub,* 3a.
Mic. 2. 4 turning away he hath divided our fields

TURNING of things upside down —

To turn, הָפַךְ *haphak.*
Isa. 29. 16 Surely your turning of things upside do.

See also Ashes, foolishness, left, right, right hand, righteousness, way.

TURTLE (dove) —

1. *A turtle dove,* תּוֹר *tor.*
Gen. 15. 9 and a turtle dove, and a young pigeon
Lev. 1. 14 shall bring his offering of turtle doves, or
5. 7 he shall bring..two turtle doves, or two
5. 11 if he be not able to bring two turtle dov.
12. 6 she shall bring..a turtle dove, for a sin
12. 8 she shall bring two turtle doves, or two
14. 22 two turtle doves, or two young pigeons
14. 30 he shall offer the one of the turtle doves
15. 14 he shall take to him two turtle doves, or
15. 29 she shall take unto her two turtles, or two
Num. 6. 10 he shall bring two turtles, or two young
Psa. 74. 19 deliver not the soul of thy turtle dove un.
Song 2. 12 the voice of the turtle is heard in our la.
Jer. 8. 7 the turtle and the crane and the swallow

2. *A turtle dove,* τρυγών *trugōn.*
Luke 2. 24 A pair of turtle doves, or two young pig.

TUTOR —

One on whom a thing is devolved, ἐπίτροπος *epitro.*
Gal. 4. 2 is under tutors and governors until the

TWAIN, twice —

1. *Two,* שְׁנַיִם *shenayim.*
1 Sa. 18. 21 be my son in law in (the one of) the tw.
2 Ki. 4. 33 shut the door upon them twain, and pra.
Isa. 6. 2 six wings; with twain he covered his face
6. 2 with twain he covered his feet, and with t.
Jer. 34. 18 they cut the calf in twain, and passed be.
Eze. 21. 19 both twain shall come forth out of one

2. *Two,* δύο, *duo.*
Matt. 5. 41 compel thee to go a mile, go with him tw.
19. 5 shall cleave..they twain shall be one fle.
19. 6 Wherefore they are no more twain, but
21. 31 Whether of them twain did the will of
27. 21 Whether of the twain will ye that I rele.
27. 51 the veil of the temple was rent in twain
Mark 10. 8 they twain..they are no more twain, but
15. 38 the veil of the temple was rent in twain
Eph. 2. 15 to make in himself of twain one new man

TWELFTH, twelve —

1. *Two (and) ten,* שְׁנֵים עָשָׂר *shenem asar.*
Gen. 5. 8 days of Seth were nine hundred and tw.
14. 4 Twelve years they served Chedorlaomer
17. 20 twelve princes shall he beget, and I will
25. 16 twelve princes according to their nations
35. 22 it came to pass..the sons of Jacob were tw.
42. 13 Thy servants (are) twelve brethren, the
42. 32 We (be) twelve brethren, sons of our fat.
Gen. 49. 28 these (are) the twelve tribes of Israel: and
Exod 15. 27 they came to Elim, where (were) twelve
24. 4 twelve pillars, according to the twelve tr.
28. 21 the stones shall be..twelve, according to
28. 21 shall they be according to the twelve tr.
39. 14 the stones (were)..twelve, according to
39. 14 every one..according to the twelve tribes
Lev. 24. 5 take fine flour, and bake twelve cakes th.
Num. 1. 44 and the princes of Israel, (being) twelve
7. 3 brought..six covered wagons, and twelve
7. 78 On the twelfth day Ahira the son of Enan
7. 84 twelve chargers..twelve silver bowls, tw.
7. 86 The golden spoons (were) twelve, full of
7. 87 oxen..(were) twelve bullocks..rams twe.
7. 87 the lambs of the first year twelve, with
7. 87 kids of the goats for sin offering twelve
17. 2 take of every one of them..twelve rods
17. 6 according to their fathers' houses..twel.
29. 17 (ye shall offer) twelve young bullocks, two
31. 5 a thousand of (every) tribe, twelve thou.
33. 9 in Elim (were) twelve fountains of water
Deut. 1. 23 I took twelve men of you, one of a tribe
Josh. 3. 12 take you twelve men out of the tribes of
4. 2 Take you twelve men out of the people
4. 3 Take you..out of the place..twelve ston.
4. 4 Joshua called the twelve men, whom he
4. 8 took up twelve stones out of the midst of
4. 9 Joshua set up twelve stones in the midst
4. 20 those twelve stones, which they took out
8. 25 all that fell that day..(were) twelve tho.
18. 24 and Gaba, twelve cities with their villag.
19. 15 Beth-lehem: twelve cities with their vil.
21. 7 out of the tribe of Zebulun, twelve cities
21. 40 the cities..were (by) their lot twelves cit.
Judg 19. 29 divided her..into twelve pieces, and sent
21. 10 the congregation sent thither twelve tho.
2 Sa. 2. 15 there arose..twelve of Benjamin..and tw.
10. 6 sent and hired..of Ish-tob twelve thousa.
17. 1 Let me now choose out twelve thousand
1 Ki. 4. 7 Solomon had twelve officers over all Isr.
4. 26 Solomon had..twelve thousand horsemen
7. 15 a line of twelve cubits did compass either
7. 25 It stood upon twelve oxen, three looking
7. 44 one sea, and twelve oxen under the sea
10. 20 twelve lions stood there on the one side
10. 26 chariots, and twelve thousand horsemen
11. 30 Ahijah caught..and rent it (in) twelve
16. 23 began Omri to reign over Israel, twelve
18. 31 Elijah took twelve stones, according to
19. 19 twelve yoke (of oxen)..he with the twel.
2 Ki. 3. 1 Jehoram..the son of Ahab..reigned twe.
8. 25 In the twelfth year of Joram the son of Ah.
17. 1 In the twelfth year of Ahaz king of Judah
21. 1 Manasseh (was) twelve years old when he
1 Ch. 6. 63 out of the tribe of Zebulun, twelve cities
9. 22 chosen to be porters..two hundred and t.
15. 10 and his brethren an hundred and twelve
24. 12 The eleventh to Eliashib, the twelfth to
25. 9 who with his brethren and sons (were) tw.
25. 10 his sons, and his brethren, (were) twelve
[So in verse 11, 12, 13, 14, 15, 16, 17, 18, 19, 20, 21, 22, 23, 24, 25, 26, 27, 28, 29, 30, 31.]
25. 19 The twelfth to Hashabiah, (he), his sons
27. 15 The twelfth (captain) for the twelfth mo.
2 Ch. 1. 14 four hundred chariots, and twelve thous.
4. 4 It stood upon twelve oxen, three looking
4. 15 One sea, and twelve oxen under it
9. 19 twelve lions stood there on the one side
9. 25 Solomon had..twelve thousand horsemen
33. 1 Manasseh was twelve years old when he
34. 3 in the twelfth year he began to purge Ju.
Ezra 2. 6 two thousand eight hundred and twelve
2. 18 The children of Jorah, an hundred and t.
8. 24 I separated twelve of the chief priests, S.
8. 31 we departed..on the twelfth (day) of the
8. 35 twelve bullocks for all Israel, ninety and
8. 35 seventy and seven lambs, twelve he goats
Neh. 5. 14 twelve years, I and my brethren have not
7. 24 children of Hariph, an hundred and twel.
Esth. 2. 12 after that she had been twelve months
3. 7 in the twelfth year of king Ahasuerus, th.
3. 7 from month to month, (to) the twelfth
3. 13 upon the thirteenth (day) of the twelfth
8. 12 upon the thirteenth (day) of the twelfth
9. 1 in the twelfth month, that (is), the month
Psa. 60. *title.* smote of Edom in the valley..twelve
Jer. 52. 20 twelve brasen bulls that (were) under the
52. 21 a fillet of twelve cubits did compass it
52. 31 in the twelfth month, in the five and tw.
Eze. 29. 1 in the twelfth (day) of the month, the wo.
32. 1 in the twelfth year, in the twelfth month
32. 17 It came to pass also in the twelfth year
33. 21 it came to pass in the twelfth year of our
43. 16 altar (shall be) twelve (cubits) long, twel.
47. 13 inherit the land, according to the twelve tr.

2. *Two (and) ten,* תְּרֵי עֲשַׂר *tere asar.*
Ezra 6. 17 for a sin offering for all Israel, twelve he
Dan. 4. 29 At the end of twelve months he walked

3. *Ten (and) two,* δεκαδύο *dekaduo.*
Acts 19. 7 And all the men were about [twelve]
24. 11 there are yet but [twelve] days since I we.

4. *Two (and) ten,* δώδεκα *dōdeka.*
Matt. 9. 20 was diseased with an issue of blood twe.
10. 1 he had called unto (him) his twelve disc.
10. 2 the names of the twelve apostles are these
10. 5 These twelve Jesus sent forth, and comm.
11. 1 an end of commanding his twelve discip.
14. 20 took up of the fragments..twelve baskets
19. 28 upon twelve thrones, judging the twelve
20. 17 took the twelve disciples apart in the way
Matt 26. 14 one of the twelve, called Judas Iscariot
26. 20 even was come, he sat down with the tw.
26. 47 Judas, one of the twelve, came, and with
26. 53 give me more than twelve legions of ang.
Mark 3. 14 he ordained twelve, that they should be
4. 10 they that were about him with the twelve
5. 25 which had an issue of blood twelve years
5. 42 for she was (of the age) of twelve years
6. 7 he called (unto him) the twelve, and began
6. 43 they took up twelve baskets full of the fr.
8. 19 how many..took ye up? They say..Twelve
9. 35 he sat down, and called the twelve, and
10. 32 he took again the twelve, and began to tell
11. 11 he went out unto Bethany with the twelve
14. 10 Judas Iscariot, one of the twelve, went
14. 17 And in the evening he cometh with the tw.
14. 20 (It is) one of the twelve, that dippeth with
14. 43 cometh Judas, one of the twelve, and with
Luke 2. 42 when he was twelve years old, they went
6. 13 of them he chose twelve, whom also he
8. 1 he went..and the twelve (were) with him
8. 42 he had one only daughter, about twelve
8. 43 a woman, having an issue of blood twelve
9. 1 he called his twelve disciples together, and
9. 12 then came the twelve, and said unto him
9. 17 and there was taken up..twelve baskets
18. 31 he took (unto him) the twelve, and said
22. 3 Iscariot, being of the number of the twelve
22. 14 he sat down, and the [twelve] apostles wi.
22. 30 sit on thrones judging the twelve tribes of
22. 47 Judas, one of the twelve, went before them
John 6. 13 filled twelve baskets with the fragments
6. 67 Then said Jesus unto the twelve, Will ye
6. 70 Have not I chosen you twelve, and one of
6. 71 for he it was..being one of the twelve
11. 9 Are there not twelve hours in the day?
20. 24 Thomas, one of the twelve, called Didymus
Acts 6. 2 the twelve called the multitude of the di.
7. 8 Isaac begat Jacob; and Jacob..the twelve
1 Co. 15. 5 he was seen of Cephas, then of the twelve
Jas. 1. 1 to the twelve tribes that are scattered ab.
Rev. 7. 5, 5, 5, 6, 6, 6, 7, 7, 7, 8, 8, 8 sealed twelve th.
12. 1 and upon her head a crown of twelve stars
21. 12 twelve gates..[twelve angels]..twelve trib.
21. 14 the wall of the city had twelve foundati.
21. 14 in them the names of the twelve apostles
21. 16 he measured the city..twelve thousand
21. 21 the twelve gates (were) twelve pearls, ev.
22. 2 the tree of life, which bare twelve (manner

5. *Twelfth,* δωδέκατος *dōdekatos.*
Rev. 21. 20 the eleventh, a jacinth, the twelfth, an am.

TWELVE tribes —

Twelve tribes, δωδεκάφυλον *dōdekaphulon.*
Acts 26. 7 Unto which..our twelve tribes, instantly

TWENTIETH, twenty —

1. *Twenty,* עֶשְׂרִים *esrim.*
Gen. 6. 3 his days shall be an hundred and twenty
8. 14 on the seven and twentieth day of the mo.
11. 24 Nahor lived nine and twenty years, and
18. 31 Peradventure there shall be twenty found
18. 31 said, I will not destroy (it) for twenty's sa.
23. 1 an hundred and seven and twenty years
31. 38 This twenty years (have I been) with thee
31. 41 Thus have I been twenty years in thy ho.
32. 14 Two hundred she goats, and twenty he go.
32. 14 two hundred ewes, and twenty rams
32. 15 forty kine, and ten bulls, twenty she asses
37. 28 sold Joseph..for twenty (pieces) of silver
Exod. 12. 18 until the one and twentieth day of the mo.
26. 2 The length..(shall be) eight and twenty
26. 18 twenty boards on the south side southw.
26. 19 forty sockets of silver under the twenty
26. 20 the north side, (there shall be) twenty bo.
27. 10 twenty pillars thereof, and their twenty
27. 11 twenty pillars and their twenty sockets
27. 16 an hanging of twenty cubits, (of) blue, and
30. 13 a shekel (is) twenty gerahs: an half shekel
30. 14 Every one..from twenty years old and ab.
36. 9 The length of one curtain (was) twenty
36. 23 twenty boards for the south side southw.
36. 24 forty sockets..he made under the twenty
36. 25 for the other side..he made twenty boar.
38. 10 (were) twenty, and their brasen sockets t.
38. 11 twenty, and their sockets of brass twenty
38. 18 twenty cubits (was) the length, and the
38. 24 twenty and nine talents, and seven hund.
38. 26 from twenty years old and upwards, for
Lev. 27. 3 from twenty years old even unto sixty ye.
27. 5 from five years old even unto twenty years
27. 5 thy estimation shall be..twenty shekels
27. 25 the shekel of the sanctuary: twenty ger.
Num. 1. 3 From twenty years old and upward
[So in verse 18, 20, 22, 24, 26, 28, 30, 32, 34, 36, 38, 40, 42, 45.]
3. 39 all the males..(were) twenty and two tho.
3. 43 twenty and two thousand two hundred
3. 47 the shekel of the sanctuary..(is) twenty
7. 86 the gold..(was) an hundred and twenty
7. 88 twenty and four bullocks, the rams sixty
8. 24 from twenty and five years old and upw.
10. 11 on the twentieth (day) of the second mon.
11. 19 five days, neither ten days, nor twenty
14. 29 from twenty years old and upward, which
18. 16 the shekel of the sanctuary..(is) twenty
25. 9 those that died..were twenty and four
26. 2, 4 from twenty years old and upward
26. 14 twenty and two thousand and two hund.
26. 62 twenty and three thousand, all males from
32. 11 Surely none..from twenty years old and

Num 33. 39 Aaron (was) an hundred and twenty and
Deut31. 2 I (am) an hundred and twenty years old
34. 7 Moses (was) an hundred and twenty years
Josh.15. 32 all the cities..twenty and nine, with their
19. 30 twenty and two cities with their villages
Judg. 4. 3 twenty years he mightily oppressed the
7. 3 there returned of the people twenty and
8. 10 an hundred and twenty thousand men th.
10. 2 he judged Israel twenty and three years
10. 3 and judged Israel twenty and two years
11. 33 till thou come to Minnith, (even) twenty
15. 20 And he judged Israel ..twenty years
16. 31 buried him..he judged Israel twenty ye.
20. 15 twenty and six thousand men that drew
20. 21 destroyed..that day twenty and two tho.
20. 35 destroyed..twenty and five thousand and
20. 46 twenty and five thousand men that drew
1 Sa. 7. 2 the time was long; for it was twenty ye.
14. 14 that first slaughter..was about twenty
2 Sa. 3. 20 Abner came to David..and twenty men
8. 4 seven hundred horsemen, and twenty th.
8. 5 David slew of the Syrians two and twenty
9. 10 Now Ziba had fifteen sons and twenty ser.
10. 6 the Syrians of Zoba, twenty thousand fo.
18. 7 a great slaughter that day of twenty tho.
19. 17 his fifteen sons and his twenty servants
21. 20 on every foot six toes, four and twenty in
24. 8 at the end of nine months and twenty da.
1 Ki. 4. 23 Ten fat oxen, and twenty oxen out of the
5. 11 twenty thousand measures..and twenty
6. 2 the breadth thereof twenty (cubits), and
6. 3 twenty cubits (was) the length thereof
6. 16 he built twenty cubits on the sides of the
6. 20 twenty cubits in length, and twenty cub.
6. 20 and twenty cubits in the height thereof
8. 63 twenty thousand..and an hundred and
9. 10 it came to pass at the end of twenty years
9. 11 Solomon gave Hiram twenty cities in the
9. 28 gold, four hundred and twenty talents
10. 10 an hundred and twenty talents of gold
14. 20 the days..(were) two and twenty years: and
15. 9 in the twentieth year of Jeroboam king of
15. 33 to reign over all Israel..twenty and four
16. 8 In the twenty and sixth year of Asa king
16. 10, 15 in the twenty and seventh year of
16. 29 reigned over Israel in Samaria twenty and
20. 30 a wall fell upon twenty and seven thous.
22. 42 he reigned twenty and five years in Jeru.
2 Ki. 4. 42 twenty loaves of barley, and full ears of
8. 26 Two and twenty years old (was) Ahaziah
10. 36 Jehu reigned over Israel..twenty and ei.
12. 6 in the three and twentieth year of king
13. 1 In the three and twentieth year of Joash
14. 2 He was twenty and five years old when he
14. 2 reigned twenty and nine years in Jerusa.
15. 1 In the twenty and seventh year of Jerob.
15. 27 the son of Remaliah..(reigned) twenty
15. 30 in the twentieth year of Jotham the son
15. 33 Five and twenty years old was he when
16. 2 Twenty years old (was) Ahaz when he be.
18. 2 Twenty and five years old was he when he
18. 2 he reigned twenty and nine years in Jer.
21. 19 Amon (was) twenty and two years old wh.
23. 31 Jehoahaz (was) twenty and three years
23. 36 Jehoiakim (was) twenty and five years old
24. 18 Zedekiah (was) twenty and one years old
25. 27 on the seven and twentieth (day) of the mo.
1 Ch. 2. 22 Jair, who had three and twenty cities in
7. 2 two and twenty thousand and six hundred
7. 7 twenty and two thousand and thirty and
7. 9 the number..(was) twenty thousand and
7. 40 the number..(was) twenty and six thousa.
12. 28 of his father's house twenty and two cap.
12. 30 of the children of Ephraim twenty thous.
12. 35 twenty and eight thousand and six hund.
12. 37 on the other side..an hundred and twenty
15. 5 and his brethren an hundred and twenty
15. 6 and his brethren two hundred and twenty
18. 4 David took from him..twenty thousand
18. 5 slew of the Syrians two and twenty thou.
20. 6 whose fingers and toes (were) four and tw.
23. 4 twenty and four thousand (were) to set
23. 24 from the age of twenty years and upward
23. 27 (were) numbered from twenty years old
24. 16 nineteenth to Pethahiah, the twentieth to
24. 17 The one and twentieth..the two and tw.
24. 18 The three and twentieth..the four and tw.
25. 27 The twentieth to Eliathah, (he), his sons
25. 28 The one and twentieth to Hothir, (he), his
25. 29 The two and twentieth to Gidalti, (he), his
25. 30 The three and twentieth to Mahazioth
25. 31 The four and twentieth to Romamti-ezer
27. 1 of every course were twenty and four th.
27. 2 in his course (were) twenty and four tho.
So in v. 5, 7, 8, 9, 10, 11, 12, 13, 14, 15.
27. 4 in his course likewise (were) twenty and
27. 23 took not the number of them from twenty
2 Ch. 2. 10, 10 twenty thousand..and twenty thousa.
3. 3 three score cubits, and the breadth twenty
3. 4 twenty cubits, and..an hundred and tw.
3. 8 twenty cubits, and the breadth..twenty
3. 11 the wings of the cherubim (were) twenty
3. 13 spread themselves forth twenty cubits
4. 1 twenty cubits the length thereof, and tw.
5. 12 an hundred and twenty priests sounding
7. 5 Solomon offered a sacrifice of twenty and
7. 5 and an hundred and twenty thousand sh.
7. 10 on the three and twentieth day of the se.
8. 1 it came to pass at the end of twenty yea.
9. 9 gave the king an hundred and twenty tal.
11. 21 begat twenty and eight sons, and threes.
13. 21 begat twenty and two sons, and sixteen
2 Ch.20. 31 he reigned twenty and five years in Jeru.
25. 1 Amaziah (was) twenty and five years old
25. 1 he reigned twenty and nine years in Jer.
25. 5 numbered them from twenty years old
27. 1 Jotham (was) twenty and five years old w.
27. 8 He was five and twenty years old when
28. 1 Ahaz (was) twenty years old when he began
28. 6 slew in Judah an hundred and twenty th.
29. 1 to reign (when he was) five and twenty
29. 1 he reigned nine and twenty years in Jer.
31. 17 the Levites from twenty years old and up.
33. 21 Amon (was) two and twenty years old wh.
36. 2 Jehoahaz (was) twenty and three years
36. 5 Jehoiakim (was) twenty and five years old
36. 11 Zedekiah (was) one and twenty years old
Ezra 1. 9 chargers of silver, nine and twenty knives
2. 11 The children of Bebai, six hundred twenty
2. 12 a thousand two hundred twenty and two
2. 17 children of Bezai, three hundred twenty
2. 19 children of Hashum, two hundred twenty
2. 21 of Beth-lehem, an hundred twenty and
2. 23 The men of Anathoth, an hundred twen.
2. 26 children of Ramah..six hundred twenty
2. 27 The men of Michmas, an hundred twenty
2. 28 The men of Beth-el..two hundred twenty
2. 32 of Harim, three hundred and twenty
2. 33 The children of Lod..seven hundred twe.
2. 41 the children of Asaph, an hundred twen.
2. 67 six thousand seven hundred and twenty
3. 8 Levites, from twenty years old and upw.
8. 11 the sons of Bebai, and with him twenty
8. 19 Merari, his brethren, and their sons, tw.
8. 20 two hundred and twenty Nethinims, all
8. 27 twenty basins of gold of a thousand dra
10. 9 the ninth month, and the twentieth (day)
Neh. 1. 1 in the month Chisleu, in the twentieth ye.
2. 1 in the twentieth year of Artaxerxes the ki.
5. 14 from the twentieth year even unto the
6. 15 the wall was finished in the twenty and
7. 16 The children of Bebai, six hundred twen.
7. 17 two thousand three hundred twenty and
7. 22 children of Hashum, three hundred twe.
7. 23 children of Bezai, three hundred twenty
7. 27 The men of Anathoth, an hundred twenty
7. 30 The men of Ramah..six hundred twenty
7. 31 men of Michmas, an hundred and twenty
7. 32 The men of Beth-el..an hundred twenty
7. 35 of Harim, three hundred and twenty
7. 37 The children of Lod..seven hundred twe.
7. 69 six thousand seven hundred and twenty
9. 1 in the twenty and fourth day of this mo.
11. 8 after him Gabbai..nine hundred twenty
11. 12 their brethren..(were) eight hundred tw.
11. 14 their brethren..an hundred twenty and
Esth. 1. 1 an hundred and seven and twenty provi.
8. 9 the month Sivan, on the three and twen.
8. 9 an hundred twenty and seven provinces
9. 30 sent the letters..to the hundred twenty
Jer. 25. 3 unto this day, that (is) the three and twe.
52. 1 Zedekiah (was) one and twenty years old
52. 28 three thousand Jews, and three and twe.
52. 30 In the three and twentieth year of Nebu.
52. 31 in the five and twentieth (day) of the mo.
Eze. 4. 10 (shall be) by weight, twenty shekels a day
8. 16 five and twenty men, with their backs to.
11. 1 at the door of the gate five and twenty
29. 17 it came to pass in the seven and twentieth
40. 1 In the five and twentieth year of our cap.
40. 13 the breadth (was) five and twenty cubits
40. 21, 25 the breadth five and twenty cubits
40. 29, 30, 33 five and twenty cubits
40. 36 and the breadth five and twenty cubits
40. 49 The length of the porch (was) twenty cu.
41. 2 forty cubits, and the breadth, twenty cu.
41. 4 twenty cubits, and the breadth, twenty
41. 10 the wideness of twenty cubits round abo.
42. 3 Over against the twenty (cubits) which
45. 1 the length of five and twenty thousand
45. 3 measure the length of five and twenty th.
45. 5 five and twenty thousand..for twenty ch.
45. 6 five and twenty thousand long, over agai.
45. 12 twenty gerahs: twenty shekels, five and
48. 8 five and twenty thousand (reeds in) brea.
48. 9 five and twenty thousand in length, and
48. 10, 10 five and twenty thousand in length
48. 13 the Levites (shall have) five and twenty
48. 13 the length (shall be) five and twenty tho.
48. 15 over against the five and twenty thousa.
48. 20 twenty thousand by five and twenty tho.
48. 21, 21 over against the five and twenty tho.
Dan. 10. 4 in the four and twentieth day of the first
10. 13 the prince .withstood me one and twenty
Hag. 1. 15 In the four and twentieth day of the six
2. 1 in the one and twentieth (day) of the mo.
2. 10 In the four and twentieth (day) of the ni.
2. 16 when (one) came to an heap of twenty (me.)
2. 16 to draw out fifty..there were (but) twenty
2. 18 from the four and twentieth day of the
2. 20 in the four and twentieth day of the mo.
Zech. 1. 7 Upon the four and twentieth (day) of the
5. 2 the length thereof (is) twenty cubits, and

2. *Twenty*, עֶשְׂרִין *esrin.*
Dan. 6. 1 an hundred and twenty princes, which sh.

3. *Twenty*, εἴκοσι *eikosi.*
Luke14. 31 that cometh against him with twenty th.
John 6. 19 when they had rowed about five and twe.
Acts 1. 15 together were about an hundred and tw.
27. 28 sounded, and found (it) twenty fathoms
1 Co. 10. 8 fell in one day three and twenty thousand
Rev. 4. 4 round about..(were) four and twenty se.
4. 4 four and twenty elders sitting, clothed in
4. 10 The four and twenty elders fall down bef.
5. 8 four (and) twenty elders fell down before
5. 14 the [four (and) twenty] elders fell down
11. 16 the four and twenty elders which sat be.
19. 4 the four and twenty elders, and the four

TWENTY thousand —
Two myriads, שְׁתֵּי רִבּוֹא ,רִבֹּתַיִם *shete ribbo, ribbothayim.*
Neh. 7. 71, 72 twenty thousand drams of gold, and
Psa. 68. 17 The chariots of God (are) twenty thousa.

TWICE (as much) —
1. *A beat, step*, פַּעַם *paam.*
Gen. 41. 32 for that the dream was doubled..twice
Num20. 11 and with his rod he smote the rock twice
1 Sa. 18. 11 David avoided out of his presence twice
1 Ki. 11. 9 God..which had appeared unto him twice
Eccl. 6. 6 though he live a thousand years twice (to.)

2. *Two*, שְׁנַיִם *shenayim.*
2 Ki. 6. 10 saved himself there, not once nor twice
Neh.13. 20 lodged without Jerusalem once or twice
Job 33. 14 God speaketh once, yea twice, (yet man)
40. 5 spoken; but I will not answer: yea, twice
Psa. 62. 11 twice have I heard this, that power (be.)
Eccl. 6. 6 [though he live a thousand years twice (to.)]

3. *Second, double, copy, college*, מִשְׁנֶה *mishneh.*
Exod16. 5 it shall be twice as much as they gather
16. 22 on the sixth day they gathered twice as m.
Job 42. 10 LORD gave Job twice as much as he had

4. *Twice*, δίς *dis.*
Mark14. 30, 72 before the cock crow twice, thou shalt
Luke18. 12 I fast twice in the week, I give tithes of
Jude 12 trees..twice dead, plucked up by the ro.

TWIG, young —
1. *Suckling*, יוֹנֶקֶת *yoneqeth.*
Eze. 17. 22 I will crop off from..his young twigs a te.

2. *Sucklings*, יְנִיקוֹת *yeniqoth.*
Eze. 17. 4 He cropped off the top of his young twigs

TWILIGHT —
1. *Twilight*, נֶשֶׁף *nesheph.*
1 Sa. 30. 17 David smote them from the twilight even
2 Ki. 7. 5 they rose up in the twilight, to go unto
7. 7 they arose, and fled in the twilight, and
Job 3. 9 Let the stars of the twilight thereof be
24. 15 The eye also..waiteth for the twilight, sa.
Prov. 7. 9 In the twilight, in the evening, in the bl.

2. *Darkness*, עֲלָטָה *alatah.*
Eze. 12. 6 In their sight..carry (it) forth in the tw.
12. 7 I brought (it) forth in the twilight..I bare
12. 12 shall bear upon (his) shoulder in the twi.

TWINED —
To be twined, שָׁזַר *shazar*, 6.
Exod26. 1 ten curtains (of) fine twined linen, and
26. 31, 36 purple, and scarlet, and fine twined
27. 9 hangings for the court (of) fine twined li.
27. 16 fine twined linen, wrought with needle
27. 18 the height five cubits (of) fine twined lin.
28. 6 and fine twined linen, with cunning work
28. 8 purple, and scarlet, and fine twined linen.
28. 15 and (of) fine twined linen, shalt thou ma.
36. 8 made ten curtains (of) fine twined linen
36. 35 purple, and scarlet, and fine twined linen
36. 37 scarlet, and fine twined linen, of needlew.
38. 9 the hangings..(were of) fine twined linen
38. 16 All the hangings..(were) of fine twined li.
38. 18 purple, and scarlet, and fine twined linen
39. 2, 5, 8 purple, and scarlet, and fine twined
39. 24 and purple, and scarlet, (and) twined (li.)
39. 28 and linen breeches (of) fine twined linen
39. 29 a girdle (of) fine twined linen, and blue

TWINS, (to bear) —
1. *To bear twins*, תָּאַם *taam*, 5.
Song 4. 2 whereof every one bear twins, and none
6. 6 whereof every one beareth twins, and (th.

2. *Twins*, תְּאוֹמִים *teomim.*
Gen. 25. 24 when her days..were fulfilled, behold..tw.
38. 27 it came to pass..twins (were) in her womb
Song 4. 5 like two young roes that are twins, which
7. 3 two breasts..like two young roes..twins

TWINKLING —
A sudden motion, twinkling, ῥιπή *rhipē.*
1 Co. 15. 52 In a moment, in the [twinkling] of an eye

TWO (apiece)—
1. *A pair, yoke*, צֶמֶד *tsemed.*
2 Ki. 5. 17 two mules' bur.; Judg. 19. 10 two asses sad.

2. *Two damsels*, רַחֲמָתַיִם *rachamathayim.*
Judg. 5. 30 to every man a damsel (or) two; to Sisera

3. *Two*, שְׁנַיִם *shenayim.*
Gen. 1. 16 God made two great lights; the greater
4. 19 Lamech took unto him two wives: the na.
5. 18 Jared lived an hundred sixty and two ye.
5. 20 were nine hundred sixty and two years
5. 26 lived..seven hundred eighty and two ye.
5. 28 Lamech lived an hundred eighty and two
6. 19 two of every (sort) shalt thou bring into
6. 20 two of every (sort) shall come unto thee
7. 2 of beasts that (are) not clean by two, the
7. 9 There went in two and two unto Noah into
7. 15 two and two of all flesh, wherein (is) the
9. 22 saw the nakedness..told his two brethren
10. 25 unto Eber were born two sons: the name
11. 20 Reu lived two and thirty years, and begat

Gen. 19. 1 there came two angels to Sodom at even
19. 8 I have two daughters which have not kn.
19. 15 take thy wife, and thy two daughters, wh.
19. 16 upon the hand of his two daughters; the
19. 30 dwelt in the mountain, and his two dau.
19. 30 he dwelt in a cave, he and his two daug.
22. 3 took two of his young men with him, and
24. 22 two bracelets for her hands of ten (shek.)
25. 23 Two nations (are) in thy womb, and two
27. 9 fetch me from thence two good kids of the
29. 16 Laban had two daughters: the name of
31. 33 Laban went..into the two maid servants'
31. 41 I served thee fourteen years for thy two
32. 7 he divided the people..into two bands
32. 10 I passed over..now I am become two ba.
32. 22 rose up that night, and took his two wiv.
32. 22 two women servants, and his eleven sons
33. 1 unto Rachel, and unto the two hand ma.
34. 25 two of the sons of Jacob, Simeon and Levi
40. 2 Pharaoh was wroth against two (of) his
41. 50 unto Joseph were born two sons before
42. 37 Slay my two sons, if I bring him not to
44. 27 Ye know that my wife bare me two (sons)
46. 27 the sons of Joseph..(were) two souls, all
48. 1 he took with him his two sons, Manasseh
48. 5 now thy two sons, Ephraim and Manasseh
Exod. 2. 13 behold, two men of the Hebrews strove
4. 9 if they will not believe also these two sig.
12. 7 strike (it) on the two side posts and on the
12. 22 strike the lintel and the two side posts wi.
12. 23 blood upon the lintel, and upon the two
16. 22 they gathered twice as much bread, two
18. 3 her two sons; of which the name of the one
18. 6 and thy wife, and her two sons with her
25. 12 two rings..in the one side of it, and two
25. 18 make two cherubim..in the two ends of
25. 19 make the cherubim on the two ends ther.
25. 22 the two cherubim which (are) upon the ark
25. 35, 35, 35 a knop under two branches of the
26. 17 Two tenons (shall there be) in one board
26. 19, 19 two sockets under..board for his two
26. 21 two sockets under one board, and two so.
26. 23 two boards shalt thou make for the corn.
26. 24 thus..they shall be for the two corners
26. 25 two sockets under one board, and two soc.
27. 7 the staves shall be upon the two sides of
28. 7 two shoulder pieces..joined at the two ed.
28. 9 thou shalt take two onyx stones, and gra.
28. 11 shalt thou engrave the two stones with
28. 12 thou shalt put the two stones upon the sh.
28. 12 bear their names..upon his two shoulders
28. 14 two chains (of) pure gold at the ends; (of)
28. 23 two rings of gold, and shalt put the two
28. 24 two wreathen (chains) of gold in the two
28. 25 two ends of the two wreathen..in the two
28. 26 thou shalt make two rings of gold, and
28. 26 thou shalt put them upon the two ends
28. 27 two (other) rings of gold thou shalt make
28. 27 shalt put them on the two sides of the ep.
29. 1 Take one young bullock, and two rams wi.
29. 3 bring..with the bullock and the two rams
29. 13, 22 the two kidneys, and the fat that (is)
29. 38 two lambs of the first year day by day co.
30. 4 two golden rings shalt thou make to it
30. 4 by the two corners thereof, upon the two
31. 18 two tables of testimony, tables of stone
32. 15 the two tables of testimony (were) in his
34. 1 Hew thee two tables of stone like unto the
34. 4 he hewed two tables of stone like unto the
34. 4 and took in his hand the two tables of st.
34. 29 the two tables of testimony in Moses' ha.
36. 22 One board had two tenons, equally dista.
36. 24 two sockets under one board for his two
36. 24 two sockets under another..for his two te.
36. 26 two sockets under one board, and two so.
36. 28 two boards made he for the corners of the
36. 30 their sockets..under every board two so.
37. 3 two rings upon the one side of it, and two
37. 7 two cherubim..on the two ends of the m.
37. 8 made he the cherubim on the two ends th.
37. 21, 21, 21 a knop under two branches of the
37. 27 two rings of gold..by the two corners of
39. 4 by the two edges was it coupled together
39. 16 made two ouches (of) gold, and two gold
39. 16 put the two rings in the two ends of the
39. 17 two wreathen chains of gold in the two
39. 18 the two ends of the two wreathen chains
39. 18 they fastened in the two ouches, and put
39. 19 two rings of gold, and put (them) on the
39. 20 two (other) golden rings..on the two sides
Lev. 3. 4, 10, 15 the two kidneys, and the fat that
4. 9 the two kidneys, and the fat that (is) upon
5. 7, 11 two turtle doves, or two young pigeons
7. 4 the two kidneys, and the fat that (is) on
8. 2 two rams, and a basket of unleavened br.
8. 16, 25 the caul (above) the liver, and the two
12. 8 she shall bring two turtles, or two young
14. 4 two birds alive (and) clean, and cedar wo.
14. 10 he shall take two he lambs without blemish
14. 22 two turtle doves, or two young pigeons
14. 49 two birds, and cedar wood, and scarlet
15. 14 take to him two turtle doves, or two yo.
15. 29 take unto her two turtles, or two young
16. 1 after the death of the two sons of Aaron
16. 5 two kids of the goats for a sin offering, and
16. 7 he shall take the two goats, and present
16. 8 Aaron shall cast lots upon the two goats
23. 13 two tenth deals of fine flour mingled with
23. 17 bring two wave loaves of two tenth deals
23. 18 offer..one young bullock, and two rams
23. 19 two lambs of the first year for a sacrifice
23. 20 (for) a wave offering..with the two lambs

Lev. 24. 5 bake..two tenth deals shall be in one cake
24. 6 thou shalt set them in two rows, six on a
Num. 1. 35 Manasseh, (were) thirty and two thousand
1. 39 threescore and two thousand and seven
2. 21 those that were numbered..thirty and two
2. 26 threescore and two thousand and seven
3. 39 all the males..(were) twenty and two th.
3. 43 those that were numbered..twenty and t.
6. 10 bring two turtles, or two young pigeons
7. 3 a wagon for two of the princes, and for
7. 7 Two wagons and four oxen he gave unto
7. 17, 23 two oxen, five rams, five he goats, five
So in verse 29, 35, 41, 47, 53, 59, 65, 71, 77, 83.
7. 89 speaking..from between the two cherub.
10. 2 Make thee two trumpets of silver; of a
11. 26 there remained two (of the) men in the ca.
13. 23 and they bare it between two upon a staff
15. 6 two tenth deals of flour mingled with the
22. 22 he was riding..and his two servants (were)
26. 14 These (are) the families..twenty and two
26. 34 fifty and two thousand and seven hundred
26. 37 thirty and two thousand and five hundred
28. 3, 9 two lambs of the first year without spot
28. 9, 12 two tenth deals of flour (for) a meat off.
28. 11, 19, 27 two young bullocks, and one ram
28. 20 three..for a bullock, and two tenth deals
28. 28 their meat offering..two tenth deals unto
29. 3 for a bullock, (and) two tenth deals for a
29. 9 to a bullock, (and) two tenth deals to one
29. 13, 17, 20, 23, 26, 29, 32 two rams..fourteen l.
29. 14 two tenth deals to each ram of the two ra.
31. 35 thirty and two thousand persons in all, of
31. 40 the LORD'S tribute (was) thirty and two p.
34. 15 The two tribes and the half tribe have
35. 6 to them ye shall add forty and two cities
Deut. 3. 8 took at that time out of the hand of the two
3. 21 your God hath done unto these two kings
4. 13 and he wrote them upon two tables of st.
4. 47 two kings of the Amorites, which (were)
5. 22 he wrote them in two tables of stone, and
9. 10 the LORD delivered unto me two tables of
9. 11 the LORD gave me the two tables of stone
9. 15 two tables of the covenant (were) in my
9. 17 two tables, and cast them out of my two
10. 1 Hew thee two tables of stone like unto the
10. 3 hewed two tables of stone like unto the
10. 3 went up..having the two tables in mine
14. 6 cleaveth the cleft unto two claws, (and)
17. 6 At the mouth of two witnesses, or three
19. 15 at the mouth of two witnesses, or at the
21. 15 If a man have two wives, one beloved, and
32. 30 How should..two put ten thousand to fli.
Josh. 2. 1 sent out of Shittim two men to spy secret.
2. 4 the woman took the two men, and hid th.
2. 10 what ye did unto the two kings of the A.
2. 23 So the two men returned, and descended
6. 22 Joshua had said unto the two men that
9. 10 all that he did to the two kings of the Am.
14. 3 Moses had given the inheritance of two tr.
14. 4 For the children of Joseph were two trib.
15. 60 Rabbah; two cities with their villages
19. 30 twenty and two cities with their villages
21. 16 suburbs, nine cities out of those two tribes
21. 25 Gath-rimmon with her suburbs; two cit.
21. 27 and Beeshterah with her suburbs; two c.
24. 12 drave them out..the two kings of the A.
Judg. 3. 16 made him a dagger which had two edges
7. 3 there returned..twenty and two thousand
7. 25 they took two princes of the Midianites
8. 12 took the two kings of Midian, Zebah and
9. 44 the two (other) companies ran upon all
10. 3 and judged Israel twenty and two years
11. 37 let me alone two months, that I may go
11. 38 he sent her away (for) two months: and
11. 39 it came to pass, at the end of two months
12. 6 fell at that time..forty and two thousand
15. 4 put a firebrand, in the midst between two
15. 13 they bound him with two new cords, and
16. 3 took the doors..and the two posts, and
16. 28 avenged of the Philistines for my two ey.
16. 29 Samson took hold of the two middle pill.
20. 21 destroyed..twenty and two thousand men
Ruth. 1. 1 sojourn..he, and his wife, and his two sons
1. 2 the name of his two sons Mahlon and Ch.
1. 3 died; and she was left, and her two sons
1. 5 the woman was left of her two sons and
1. 7 she went..and her two daughters in law
1. 8 Naomi said unto her two daughters in law
1. 19 they two went until they came to Beth-l.
4. 11 which two did build the house of Israel
1 Sa. 1. 2 he had two wives; the name of the one was
1. 3 the two sons of Eli, Hophni and Phinehas
2. 21 conceived, and bare three sons and two
2. 34 that shall come upon thy two sons, on H.
4. 4, 11 the two sons of Eli, Hophni and Phin.
4. 17 thy two sons also, Hophni and Phinehas
6. 7 take two milch kine, on which there hath
6. 10 took two milch kine, and tied them to
10. 2 thou shalt find two men by Rachel's sepul.
10. 4 will salute thee, and give thee two (loaves)
11. 11 so that two of them were not left together
13. 1 when he had reigned two years over Isr.
14. 49 the names of the two daughters (were th.)
23. 18 they two made a covenant before the Lo.
25. 18 and..two bottles..of wine, and five sheep
27. 3 David with his two wives, Ahinoam the
28. 8 he went, and two men with him, and they
30. 5 David's two wives were taken captives
30. 12 a cake of figs, and two clusters of raisins
30. 18 David recovered..and rescued his two wiv.
2 Sa. 1. 1 and David had abode two days in Ziklag
2. 2 David went up thither, and his two wives

2 Sa. 2. 10 Ish-bosheth, Saul's son..reigned two years
4. 2 Saul's son had two men (that were) capta.
8. 2 with two lines measured he to put to death
8. 5 David slew of the Syrians two and twenty
12. 1 There were two men in one city; the one
14. 6 had two sons, and they two strove together
15. 27 return into the city, and your two sons wi.
15. 36 (they have) there with them their two sons
18. 24 David sat between the two gates: and the
21. 8 the king took the two sons of Rizpah the
23. 20 he slew two lion like men of Moab: he we.
1 Ki. 2. 5 what he did to the two captains of the ho.
2. 32 who fell upon two men more righteous
2. 39 two of the servants of Shimei ran away
3. 16 Then came there two women (that were)
3. 18 (there was) no stranger..save we two in
3. 25 Divide the living child in two, and give
5. 12 there was peace..and they two made a le.
5. 14 a month they were in Lebanon, (and) two
6. 23 within the oracle he made two cherubim
6. 32 The two doors also (were of) olive tree, and
6. 34 the two doors (were of) fir tree: the two l.
6. 34 the two leaves of the other door (were) fo.
7. 15 he cast two pillars of brass, of eighteen
7. 16 he made two chapiters (of) molten brass
7. 18 he made the pillars, and two rows round
7. 20 the chapiters upon the two pillars (had po.)
7. 24 the knops (were) cast in two rows when it
7. 41 The two pillars, and the..bowls of the ch.
7. 41 the top of the two pillars; and the two net
7. 41 to cover the two bowls of the chapiters
7. 42 for the two net works, (even) two rows of
7. 42 to cover the two bowls of the chapiters
8. 9 the two tables of stone, which Moses put
8. 63 two and twenty thousand oxen, and an hu.
9. 10 Solomon had built the two houses, the ho.
10. 19 (there were) stays..and two lions stood b.
11. 29 and they two (were) alone in the field
12. 28 the king took counsel, and made two cal.
14. 20 the days..(were) two and twenty years
16. 29 the son of Omri reigned..twenty and two
17. 12 I (am) gathering two sticks, that I may go
18. 21 How long halt ye between two opinions?
18. 23 Let them therefore give us two bullocks
20. 1 (there were) thirty and two kings with him
20. 15 they were..hundred and thirty two, and
20. 16 the thirty and two kings that helped him
20. 27 Israel pitched before them like two little
21. 10 set two men, sons of Belial, before him, to
21. 13 there came in two men, children of Belial
22. 31 commanded his thirty and two captains
2 Ki. 1. 14 burnt up the two captains of the former
2. 6 I will not leave thee. And they two went
2. 7 stood to view afar off: and they two stood
2. 8 so that they two went over on dry ground
2. 12 he took hold..and rent them in two piec.
2. 24 there came forth two she bears out of the
2. 24 and tare forty and two children of them
4. 1 is come to take unto him my two sons to
5. 22 two young men of the sons of the proph.
5. 22 a talent of silver, and two changes of gar.
5. 23 in two bags, with two changes..upon two
7. 14 They took therefore two chariot horses
8. 17 Thirty and two years old was he when he
8. 26 Two and twenty years old (was) Ahaziah
9. 32 there looked out to him two (or) three eu.
10. 4 Behold, two kings stood not before him
10. 8 Lay ye them in two heaps at the entering
10. 14 slew them at the pit..two and forty men
11. 7 two parts of all you that go forth on the
15. 2 he reigned two and fifty years in Jerusa.
15. 27 In the two and fiftieth year of Azariah ki.
17. 16 made them molten images, (even) two ca.
21. 5 in the two courts of the house of the Lo
21. 19 Amon (was) twenty and two years old wh.
21. 19 and he reigned two years in Jerusalem
23. 12 in the two courts of the house of the LORD
25. 16 The two pillars, one sea, and the bases
1 Ch. 1. 19 unto Eber were born two sons: the name
4. 5 the father of Tekoa had two wives, Helah
7. 2 two and twenty thousand and six hundr.
7. 7 twenty and two thousand and thirty and
11. 21 he was more honourable than the two, for
11. 22 he slew two lion like men of Moab, also
12. 28 of his father's house twenty and two cap.
18. 5 slew of the Syrians two and twenty thou.
19. 7 they hired thirty and two thousand char.
24. 17 The one and twentieth to Jachin, the two
25. 29 The two and twentieth to Gidalti, (he), his
26. 8 (were) threescore and two of Obed-edom
26. 17 four a day..and toward Asuppim two..two
26. 18 four at the causeway..two at Parbar
2 Ch. 3. 10 he made two cherubim of image work, and
3. 15 he made before the house two pillars of
4. 3 Two rows of oxen (were) cast, when it was
4. 12 the two pillars, and the pommels, and the
4. 12 the top of the two pillars, and the two w.
4. 12 to cover the two pommels of the chapiters
4. 13 pomegrantes on the two wreaths; two ro.
4. 13 to cover the two pommels of the chapiters
5. 10 nothing in the ark save the two tables wh.
7. 5 offered a sacrifice of twenty and two tho.
9. 18 stays on each side..and two lions standing
13. 21 begat twenty and two sons, and sixteen
21. 5 Jehoram (was) thirty and two years old
21. 19 after the end of two years, his bowels fell
21. 20 Thirty and two years old was he when he
22. 2 Forty and two years old (was) Ahaziah wh.
24. 3 Jehoiada took for him two wives; and he
26. 3 he reigned fifty and two years in Jerusal.
33. 5 in the two courts of the house of the LORD
33. 21 Amon (was) two and twenty years old wh.

2 Ch.33. 21 began to reign, and reigned two years in J.
Ezra 2. 3 thousand an hundred seventy and two
2. 4 Shephatiah, three hundred seventy and t.
2. 10 children of B., six hundred forty and two
2. 12 a thousand..hundred twenty and two
2. 24 The children of Azmaveth, forty and two
2. 27 of Michmas, an hundred twenty and two
2. 29 The children of Nebo, fifty and two
2. 37 children of Immer, a thousand fifty and t.
2. 58 Nethinims..three hundred ninety and two
2. 60 The children..six hundred fifty and two
8. 27 two vessels of fine copper, precious as gold
10. 13 neither (is this) a work of one day or two
Neh. 5. 14 even unto the two and thirtieth year of
6. 15 wall was finished..in fifty and two days
7. 8 thousand an hundred seventy and two
7. 9 Shephatiah, three hundred seventy and t.
7. 10 The children..six hundred fifty and two
7. 17 thousand three hundred twenty and two
7. 28 The men of Beth-azmaveth, forty and two
7. 31 Michmas, an hundred and twenty and two
7. 33 The men of the other Nebo, fifty and two
7. 40 children of Immer, a thousand fifty and t.
7. 60 Nethinims..three hundred ninety and two
7. 62 The children..six hundred forty and two
11. 12 brethren..eight hundred twenty and two
11. 13 his brethren..hundred forty and two: and
11. 19 their brethren..an hundred seventy and t.
12. 31 Then I..appointed two great (companies
12. 40 So stood the two (companies of them that
13. 6 in the two and thirtieth year of Artaxer.
Esth. 2. 21 two of the king's chamberlains, Bigthan
6. 2 two of the king's chamberlains, the keep.
9. 27 they would keep these two days according
Job 13. 20 do not two (things) unto me; then will
42. 7 against thee, and against thy two friends
Prov 30. 7 Two (things) have I required of thee; de.
30. 15 The horse leach hath two daughters, (cr.)
Eccl. 4. 9 Two (are) better than one; because they
4. 11 if two lie together, then they have heat
4. 12 if one prevail against him, two shall with.
Song 4. 5 Thy two breasts (are) like two young roes
7. 3 Thy two breasts (are) like two young roes
Isa. 7. 4 neither be faint hearted for the two tails
7. 21 a man shall nourish a young cow and two
17. 6 two (or) three berries in the top of the up.
47. 9 these two (things) shall come to thee in
51. 19 These two (things) are come unto thee: who
Jer. 2. 13 my people have committed two evils, th.
3. 14 I will take you one of a city, and two of a
24. 1 two baskets of figs (were) set before the
33. 24 The two families which the LORD hath ch.
52. 20 The two pillars, one sea, and twelve bra.
52. 29 eight hundred thirty and two persons
Eze. 1. 11 two..(were) joined one to another, and two
1. 23 every one had two..and every one had two
21. 19 appoint thee two ways, that the sword of
21. 21 stood..at the head of the two ways, to use
23. 2 there were two women, the daughters of
35. 10 These two nations and these two countries
37. 22 and they shall be no more two nations
37. 22 neither shall they be divided into two king.
40. 9 the posts thereof, two cubits; and the po.
40. 39 two tables on this side, and two tables on
40. 40 And at the side without..(were) two tab.
40. 40 at the porch of the gate, (were) two tables
41. 3 measured the post of the door two cubits
41. 18 made with cherubim..(every) cherub had
41. 22 the length thereof two cubits; and the co.
41. 23 the temple and the sanctuary had two do.
41. 24 the doors had two leaves (apiece), two tu.
41. 24 two (leaves) for the one door, and two le.
43. 14 (even) to the lower settle (shall be) two cu.
Dan. 8. 7 and smote the ram, and brake his two ho
9. 25 seven weeks, and threescore and two we
9. 26 after threescore and two weeks shall Me.
12. 5 there stood other two, the one on this side
Hos. 10. 10 shall bind themselves in their two furrows
Amos 3. 3 Can two walk together, except they be ag.
3. 12 taketh out of the mouth of the lion two
4. 8 two (or) three cities wandered unto one ci
Zech. 4. 3 two olive trees by it, one upon the right
4. 11 What (are) these two olive trees upon the
4. 12 two olive branches which through the two
4. 14 These (are) the two anointed ones, that st
5. 9 there came out two women, and the wind
6. 1 four chariots out from between two mou
11. 7 I took unto me two staves; the one I ca
13. 8 two parts therein shall be cut off (and) die

4. *Two*, תְּרֵין *teren*.
Dan. 5. 31 Darius..about threescore and two years

5. *Two*, δύο *duo*.
Matt. 4. 18 Jesus, walking..saw two brethren, Simon
4. 21 he saw other two brethren, James (the son)
6. 24 No man can serve two masters: for either
8. 28 there met him two possessed with devils
9. 27 two blind men followed him, crying, and
10. 10 neither two coats, neither shoes, nor yet
10. 29 Are not two sparrows sold for a farthing?
11. 2 when John had heard..he sent [two of] his
14. 17 We have here but five loaves, and two fis.
14. 19 took the five loaves, and the two fishes, and
18. 8 than having two hands or two feet to be
18. 9 rather than having two eyes to be cast into
18. 16 or two more, that in the mouth of two or
18. 19 if two of you shall agree on earth as tou.
18. 20 where two or three are gathered together
20. 21 Grant that these my two sons may sit, the
20. 24 moved with indignation against the two
20. 30 two blind men sitting by the way side, w.
Matt 21. 1 drew nigh..then sent Jesus two disciples
21. 28 A (certain) man had two sons; and he came
22. 40 On these two commandments hang all the
24. 40 Then shall two be in the field; the one sh.
24. 41 Two (women shall be) grinding at the mill
25. 15 one he gave five talents, to another two
25. 17 (had received) two, he also gained other two
25. 22 He also that had received two talents ca.
25. 22 Lord, thou deliveredst unto me two tale.
25. 22 I have gained two other talents besides th.
26. 2 Ye know that after two days is (the feast
26. 37 he took with him Peter and the two sons
26. 60 At the last came two false witnesses
27. 38 Then were there two thieves crucified wi.
Mark 6. 7 began to send them forth by two and two
6. 9 shod with sandals; and not put on two co.
6. 38 when they knew, they say, Five, and two
6. 41 had taken the five loaves and the two fis.
6. 41 the two fishes divided he among them all
9. 43 than having two hands to go into hell, in.
9. 45 than having two feet to be cast into hell
9. 47 than having two eyes to be cast into hell
11. 1 when they came..he sendeth forth two of
12. 42 she threw in two mites, which make a fa.
14. 1 After two days was (the feast of) the pas.
14. 13 he sendeth forth two of his disciples, and
15. 27 with him they crucify two thieves; the one
16. 12 [he appeared in another form unto two of]
Luke 2. 24 A pair of turtle doves, or two young pig.
3. 11 He that hath two coats, let him impart to
5. 2 saw two ships standing by the lake: but
7. 19 John calling (unto him) two of his disci.
7. 41 a certain creditor which had two debtors
9. 3 neither money; neither have two coats ap.
9. 13 no more but five loaves and two fishes
9. 16 he took the five loaves and the two fishes
9. 30 there talked with him two men, which we.
9. 32 they saw..the two men that stood with
10. 1 sent them two and two (lit. two apiece)
10. 35 he took out two pence, and gave (them)
12. 6 Are not five sparrows sold for two farth.?
12. 52 divided, three against two, and two agai.
15. 11 And he said, A certain man had two sons
16. 13 No servant can serve two masters: for ei.
17. 34 in that night there shall be two (men) in
17. 35 Two (women) shall be grinding together
17. 36 Two (men) shall be in the field; the one
18. 10 Two men went up into the temple to pray
19. 29 when he was come..he sent two of his d.
21. 2 a certain poor widow casting in..two mi.
22. 38 they said, Lord, behold, here (are) two sw.
23. 32 there were also two others, malefactors
24. 4 two men stood by them in shining garm.
24. 13 two of them went that same day to a vil.
John 1. 35 the next day after, John stood, and two
1. 37 the two disciples heard him speak, and
1. 40 One of the two which heard him (speak)
2. 6 containing two or three firkins apiece
4. 40 besought him..and he abode there two
4. 43 after two days he departed thence, and
6. 9 hath five barley loaves, and two small fish.
8. 17 that the testimony of two men is true
11. 6 he abode two days still in the same place
19. 18 they crucified him, and two other with
20. 12 seeth two angels in white sitting, the one
21. 2 the (sons) of Zebedee, and two other of
Acts 1. 10 two men stood by them in white apparel
1. 23 they appointed two, Joseph called Barsa.
1. 24 show whether of these two thou hast ch.
7. 29 the land of Madian, where he begat two
9. 38 they sent unto him [two] men, desiring
10. 7 he called two of his household servants
12. 6 between two soldiers, bound with two
19. 10 this continued by the space of two years
19. 22 he sent into Macedonia two of them that
19. 34 all..about the space of two hours cried
21. 33 commanded (him) to be bound with two
23. 23 he called unto (him) two centurions, sa.
1 Co. 6. 16 for two, saith he, shall be one flesh
14. 27 (let it be) by two, or at the most (by) thr.
14. 29 Let the prophets speak two or three, and
2 Co.13. 1 In the mouth of two or three witnesses
Gal. 4. 22 it is written, that Abraham had two sons
4. 24 these are the two covenants; the one from
Eph. 5. 31 joined unto his wife, and they two shall
Phil. 1. 23 I am in a strait betwixt two, having a de.
1 Ti. 5. 19 receive not an accusation, but before two
Heb. 6. 18 That by two immutable things, in which
10. 28 died without mercy under two or three
Rev. 9. 12 behold, there come two woes more here.
9. 16 the horsemen (were) two hundred thous.
11. 2 they tread under foot forty (and) two mo.
11. 3 I will give (power) unto my two witnes.
11. 4 the two olive trees, and the two candles.
11. 10 these two prophets tormented them that
12. 14 to the woman were given two wings of a
13. 5 power..to continue forty (and) two mon.
13. 11 he had two horns like a lamb, and he sp.

TWO hundred, two thousand —

1. *Two hundred*, διακόσιοι *diakosioi*.
Mark 6. 37 Shall we go and buy two hundred penny.
John 6. 7 Two hundred pennyworth of bread is not
21. 8 not far from land, but as it were two hun.
Acts 23. 23 two hundred soldiers..spearmen two hu.
27. 37 two hundred threescore and sixteen sou.
Rev. 11. 3 a thousand two hundred..threescore days
12. 6 a thousand two hundred..threescore da.

2. *Two thousand*, δισχίλιοι *dischilioi*.
Mark 5. 13 the herd..they were about two thousand

TWO parts, two edged —

1. *Half, middle, part*, חֲצִי *chatsi*.
1 Ki. 16. 21 Then were the people..divided into two p.

2. *Mouth*, פֶּה *peh*.
Prov. 5. 4 her end is..sharp as a two edged sword

3. *Edges*, פִּיפִיּוֹת [*peh*].
Psa. 149. 6 and a two edged sword in their hand

4. *Double edged*, δίστομος *distomos*.
Heb. 4. 12 sharper than any two edged sword, pierc.
Rev. 1. 16 out of his mouth went a sharp two edged
2. 12 which hath the sharp sword with two ed.

TWOFOLD more —

Doubly, twice as much, διπλότερον *diploteron*.
Matt 23. 15 ye make him twofold more the child of

TY-CHI'-CUS, Τυχικός *fortunate*.

A believer in Asia Minor, who accompanied Paul to Jerusalem, when he left Greece, and was sent by him first to Ephesus, and then to Colosse.

Acts 20. 4 there accompanied him..T. and Trophim.
Eph. 6. 21 T...shall make known to you all things
Col. 4. 7 All my state shall T. declare unto you
2 Ti. 4. 12 And T. have I sent to Ephesus
Titus 3. 12 I shall send Artemas unto thee, or T.

TY-RAN'-NUS, Τύραννος.

A person in Ephesus, in whose school Paul disputed daily for two years.

Acts 19. 9 disputing daily in the school of one T.

TYRE, TYRUS, צוֹר, צֹר *rock*, Τύρος.

A city in the centre of Phœnicia, on the coast of the Mediterranean Sea, five miles S. of the Leontes River, and midway between Accho and Sidon, and three miles W. of Raamah. Said to have been founded B.C. 2750; in 1443 it was assigned to the tribe of Asher, but was never occupied by them; in 1210 it received many fugitives from Sidon; in 1014 Hiram its king helped Solomon in his great works; in 721–716 it successfully resisted Shalmaneser king of Assyria; in 585–572 it did the same to Nebuchadnezzar king of Babylon, when the inhabitants founded insular Tyre, which in 332 was taken by Alexander the Great (after a siege of seven months), by his constructing a mole connecting it with the mainland; in 315 it was taken by Antigonus of Syria after a siege of fifteen months; in 248 it was treacherously surrendered to Antiochus the Great by Theodotus, lieutenant of Ptolemy Philopater; in A.D. 1124 it was taken by the Crusaders from the Saracens, after a siege of five and a half months, when a third of it was assigned to Venice; in 1187 it successfully resisted Saladin; in 1391 it was taken by the Turks; in 1766 the Metâwila, a sect of the Shiites, settled at it, and established a trade in grain and tobacco; in 1841 it was taken by the allied fleet. Councils were held here, A.D. 335 and 518. Eze. 27. 1-32 contains a glowing account of its ancient riches and extensive traffic, from Spain to India, including Greece, Cyprus, Egypt, Palestine, Syria, Arabia, and Persia, in gold, silver, iron, lead, tin, copper; wheat, cereals, honey, oil, balm; wools and linen fabrics; ivory and ebony; jewellery, and dyes of all kinds. It has now about 4000 of a population. Jos. 19. 29.

2 Sa. 5. 11 Hiram king of T. sent messengers to Da.
24. 7 came to the strong hold of T., and to all
1 Ki. 5. 1 Hiram king of T. sent his servants unto
7. 13 Solomon sent..fetched Hiram out of T.
9. 11 the king of T. had furnished Solomon wi.
9. 12 Hiram came out from T. to see the cities
1 Ch.14. 1 Hiram king of T. sent messengers to David
2 Ch. 2. 3 Solomon sent to Huram the king of T., sa.
2. 11 Huram the king of T. answered in writing
Psa. 45. 12 the daughter of T. (shall be there) with a
83. 7 the Philistines with the inhabitants of T.
87. 4 behold Philistia, and T., with Ethiopia
Isa. 23. 1 burden of T. Howl, ye ships of Tarshish
23. 5 shall they be..pained at the report of T.
23. 8 Who hath taken this counsel against T.
23. 15 that T. shall be forgotten seventy years
23. 15 after the end of seventy years shall T. sing
23. 17 the LORD will visit T., and she shall turn
Jer. 25. 22 all the kings of T., and all the kings of Z.
27. 3 send them..to the king of T...by the ha.
47. 4 to cut off from T. and Zidon every helper
Eze. 26. 2 T. hath said..Aha she is broken (that was)
26. 3 Behold, I (am) against thee, O T., and wi.
26. 4 they shall destroy the walls of T., and br.
26. 7 I will bring upon T. Nebuchadrezzar king
26. 15 Thus saith the Lord GOD to T.; Shall not
27 2 son of man, take up a lamentation for T.
27. 3 say unto T., O thou that art situate at the
27. 3 O T., thou hast said, I (am) of perfect be.
27. 8 thy wise (men), O T...were thy pilots
27. 32 What (city is) like T., like the destroyed
28. 2 Son of man, say unto the prince of T., Th.
28. 12 take up a lamentation upon the king of T.
29. 18 N...caused his army to serve..against T.
29. 18 yet had he no wages, nor his army, for T.
Hos. 9. 13 Ephraim, as I saw T., (is) planted in a pl.
Joel 3. 4 Yea..what have ye to do with me, O T.
Amos 1. 9 For three transgressions of T...I will not
1. 10 But I will send a fire on the wall of T.
Zech. 9. 2 Hamath also shall border thereby; T., and
9. 3 And T. did build herself a strong hold
1 Ki. 7. 14 his father (was) a man of T., a worker in
1 Ch.22. 4 they of T., brought much cedar wood to D.
2 Ch. 2. 14 his father (was) a man of T., skilful to wo.
Ezra 3. 7 They gave..meat..drink..to them of T.
Neh. 13. 16 There dwelt men of T. also therein, which
Matt 11. 21 if the mighty works..had been done in T.

Matt11. 22 It shall be more tolerable for T. and Sidon
15. 21 Jesus..departed into the coasts of T. and
Mark 3. 8 they about T. and Sidon..came unto him
7. 24 he arose, and went into the borders of T.
7. 31 departing from the coasts of T...he came
Luke 6. 17 people..from the sea coast of T...came to
10. 13 if the mighty works had been done in T.
10. 14 But it shall be more tolerable for T. and
Acts 12. 20 H. was highly displeased with them of T.
21. 3 we..sailed into Syria, and landed at T.
21. 7 when we had finished (our) course from T.

U

UC'-AL, אֻכָל or אֻכָּל.
A person unknown, mentioned along with *Ithiel.*
Prov.30. 1 the man spake unto Ithiel, even unto..U.

U'-EL, אוּאֵל.
A son of Bani, that had taken a strange wife during the exile. B.C. 445.
Ezra 10. 34 the sons of Bani; Maadai, Amram, and U.

UL'-AI, אוּלַי.
A river surrounding Susa, falling into the Euphrates below its junction with the Tigris; called by the Greeks Eulæus or Choaspes; and now *Kerah*, or *Kerkhah.*
Dan. 8. 2 and I saw..and I was by the river of U.
8. 16 heard a..voice between (the banks of) U.

U'-LAM, אוּלָם *solitary.*
1. A son of Sheresh, grandson of Manasseh. B.C. 1400.
1 Ch. 7. 16 and his sons (were) U. and Rakem
7. 17 And the sons of U.; Bedan. These (were)
2. A son of Eshek, a Benjamite, of the family of Saul. B.C. 840.
1 Ch. 8. 39 the sons of Eshek his brother (were) U
8. 40 the sons of U. were mighty men of valour

UL'-LA, עֻלָּא *burden.*
An Asherite, father of Arah, and Haniel and Rezia. B.C. 1452.
1 Ch. 7. 39 the sons of Ulla Arah, and Haniel, and

UM'-MAH, עֻמָּה *union, kindred*
A city in Asher, near Aphek or Rehob; now called *Alma*, near *Ras Nakhura*
Josh.19. 30 U. also, and Aphek, and Rehob: twenty

UNACCUSTOMED —
Not taught, לֹא לֻמָּד [*lamad*, 4].
Jer 31. 18 I was chastised, as a bullock unaccustom.

UNAWARES (at) —
1. *Without knowledge,* בִּבְלִי דַעַת *bi-beli daath.*
Deut. 4. 42 which should kill his neighbour unawares
2. *Not to know,* לֹא יָדַע *lo yada.*
Psa. 35. 8 Let destruction come upon him at unaw.
3. *The heart,* לֵב, לֵבָב *leb, lebab.*
Gen. 31. 20 Jacob stole away unawares to Laban the
31. 26 that thou hast stolen away unawares to
4. *Error, ignorance,* בִּשְׁגָגָה *bi-shegagah.*
Num35. 11 flee..which killeth any person at unawa.
35. 15 that killeth any person unawares may
Josh.20. 3 That..slayer that killeth. person unawa.
20. 9 that whosoever killeth..person at unawa.
5. *Unforseen, unexpected,* αἰφνίδιος *aiphnidios.*
Luke21. 34 and (so) that day come upon you unawa.
6. *To be or lie hid, concealed,* λανθάνω *lanthanō.*
Heb. 13. 2 some have entertained angels unawares

UNBELIEF —
1. *Unbelief, disobedience,* ἀπείθεια *apeitheia.*
Rom 11. 30 have now obtained mercy through..unb.
11. 32 For God hath concluded them all in unb.
Heb. 4. 6 and they..entered not in because of unb.
4. 11 lest any..fall after the..example of unb.
2. *Unbelief, distrust,* ἀπιστία *apistia.*
Matt13. 58 not many..works there, because of..unb.
17. 20 Because of your [unbelief]: for verily I
Mark 6. 6 And he marvelled because of their unbe.
9. 24 Lord, I believe; help thou mine unbelief
16. 14 [upbraided them with their unbelief and]
Rom. 3. 3 shall their unbelief make the faith of God
4. 20 He staggered not..through unbelief; but
11. 20 because of unbelief they were broken off
11. 23 they also, if they abide not still in unbelief
1 Ti. 1. 13 because I did (it) ignorantly in unbelief
Heb. 3. 12 lest there be..an evil heart of unbelief
3. 19 they could not enter in because of unbel.

UNBELIEVER, unbelieving —
1. *To disbelieve, disobey,* ἀπειθέω *apeitheō.*
Acts 14. 2 the unbelieving Jews stirred up the Gen.
2. *Disbelieving, disobedient,* ἄπιστος *apistos.*
Luke12. 46 will appoint him his portion with the un.
1 Co. 6. 6 to law..and that before the unbelievers
7. 14 the unbelieving husband is sanctified by
7. 14 the unbelieving wife is sanctified by the
7. 15 if the unbelieving depart, let him depart
14. 23 (those that are) unlearned, or unbelievers
2 Co. 6. 14 Be ye not unequally yoked..with unbeliev.
Titus 1. 15 unto them that are..unbelieving (is) not.
Rev. 21. 8 the fearful, and unbelieving, and the ab.

UNBLAMEABLE, unblameably —
1. *Blameless, unblameable,* ἄμεμπτος *amemptos.*
1 Th. 2. 10 how holily and justly and unblameably
3. 13 the end he may establish your hearts un.
2. *Unblemished, without blemish,* ἄμωμος *amōmos.*
Col. 1. 22 to present you holy and unblameable and

UNCERTAIN, uncertainly —
1. *Not manifest, uncertain,* ἄδηλος *adēlos.*
1 Co. 9. 26 I therefore so run, not as uncertainly, so
14. 8 For if the trumpet give an uncertain so.
2. *Uncertainty,* ἀδηλότης *adēlotēs.*
1 Ti. 6. 17 nor trust in uncertain riches, but in the

UNCHANGEABLE —
Not passing over, unchanging, ἀπαράβατος *apara.*
Heb. 7. 24 this (man)..hath an unchangeable priest.

UNCIRCUMCISED (be, person) —
1. *One uncircumcised,* עָרֵל *arel.*
Gen. 17. 14 the uncircumcised man child, whose fle.
Exod. 6. 12 hear me, who (am) of uncircumcised lips?
6. 30 I (am) of uncircumcised lips, and how sh.
12. 48 no uncircumcised person shall eat thereof
Lev. 19. 23 three years shall it be as uncircumcised
26. 41 if then their uncircumcised hearts be hu.
Josh. 5. 7 they were uncircumcised, because they
Judg14. 3 thou goest to take a wife of the uncircu.
15. 18 and fall into the hand of the uncircumci.
1 Sa. 14. 6 go over unto the garrison of these unc.
17. 26 who (is) this uncircumcised Philistine, th.
17. 36 this uncircumcised Philistine shall be as
31. 4 lest these uncircumcised come and thrust
2 Sa. 1. 20 lest the daughters of the uncircumcised
1 Ch.10. 4 lest these uncircumcised come and abuse
Isa. 52. 1 there shall no more come..the uncircum.
Jer. 6. 10 their ear (is) uncircumcised, and they ca.
9. 26 for all (these) nations (are) uncircumcised
9. 26 the house of Israel (are) uncircumcised
Eze. 28. 10 Thou shalt die the deaths of the uncircu.
31. 18 thou shalt lie in the midst of the uncirc.
32. 19 and be thou laid with the uncircumcised
32. 21 they lie uncircumcised, slain by the sword
32. 24 which are gone down uncircumcised into
32. 25, 26 all of them uncircumcised, slain by the
32. 27 the mighty (that are) fallen of the uncir.
32. 28 be broken in the midst of the uncircum.
32. 29 they shall lie with the uncircumcised, and
32. 30 they lie uncircumcised with (them that be)
32. 32 in the midst of the uncircumcised with
44. 7, 9 uncircumcised in heart, and uncircum.
2. *Uncircumcision,* עָרְלָה *orlah.*
Jer. 9. 25 that I will punish all..with the uncircu.
2a. *To him a foreskin,* לוֹ עָרְלָה *lo orlah.* Gen. 34. 14.
3. *Uncircumcised,* ἀπερίτμητος *aperitmētos.*
Acts 7. 51 Ye stiff necked and uncircumcised in he.
4. *To have uncircumcision,* ἔχω ἀκροβυστίαν.
Acts 11. 3 Saying, Thou wentest in to men uncircu.
5. *In the uncircumcision,* ἐν τῇ ἀκροβυστίᾳ.
Rom. 4. 11 of the faith which (he had yet) being un.
4. 12 (he had) being (yet) uncircumcised

UNCIRCUMCISED, to become or count —
1. *To remove(?) (or leave) its foreskin,* עָרֵל עָרְלָתוֹ [*arel*].
Lev. 19. 23 ye shall count the fruit thereof as uncir.
2. *To become uncircumcised,* ἐπισπάομαι *epispaomai.*
1 Co. 7. 18 let him not become uncircumcised. Is any

UNCIRCUMCISION —
Uncircumcision, ἀκροβυστία *akrobustia.*
Rom. 2. 25 thy circumcision is made uncircumcision
2. 26 if the uncircumcision keep the righteous.
2. 26 shall not his uncircumcision be counted
2. 27 shall not his uncircumcision which is by
3. 30 justify the..uncircumcision through faith
4. 9 (Cometh) this..upon the uncircumcision
4. 10 when he was in circumcision, or in uncir.
4. 10 Not in circumcision, but in uncircumcis.
1 Co. 7. 18 Is any called in uncircumcision? let him
7. 19 uncircumcision is nothing, but the keep.
Gal. 2. 7 the gospel of the uncircumcision was co.
5. 6 neither circumcision..nor uncircumcision
6. 15 nor uncircumcision, but a new creature
Eph. 2. 11 who are called uncircumcision by that wh.
Col. 2. 13 being dead in your sins and the uncircu.
3. 11 circumcison nor uncircumcision, Barbar.

UNCLE —
Beloved, uncle, relation, דּוֹד *dod.*
Lev. 10. 4 Moses called..the sons of Uzziel the un.
20. 20 he hath uncovered his uncle's nakedness
25. 49 Either his uncle, or his uncle's son, may
1 Sa. 10. 14 Saul's uncle said unto him and to his ser.
10. 15 Saul's uncle said, Tell me, I pray thee
10. 16 Saul said unto his uncle, He told us plain.
14. 50 (was) Abner, the son of Ner, Saul's uncle
1 Ch.27. 32 David's uncle, was a counsellor, a wise man
Esth. 2. 7 he brought up Hadassah..his uncle's da.
2. 15 the daughter of Abihail the uncle of Mor.
Jer. 32. 7 Hanameel the son of Shallum thine uncle
32. 8 Hanameel, mine uncle's son, came to me
32. 9 I bought the field of Hanameel, my unc.
32. 12 in the sight of Hanameel mine uncle's
Amos 6. 10 a man's uncle shall take him up, and he

UNCLEAN (thing), uncleanness (some) —
1. *A thing offensive,* עֶרְוַת דָּבָר [*ervah*].
Deut24. 1 because he hath found some uncleanness
2. *Unclean, defiled,* טָמֵא *tame.*
Lev. 5. 2 touch any unclean thing..an unclean be.?
5. 2 unclean cattle, or..unclean creeping th.
5. 2 (if) it be hidden..he also shall be unclean
7. 19 the flesh that toucheth any unclean (th.)
7. 21 the soul that shall touch any unclean (th.)
7. 21 unclean beast, or any abominable unclean
10. 10 put difference..between unclean and cl.
11. 4, 5, 6 he cheweth the cud..he (is) unclean
11. 7 he cheweth not the cud; he (is) unclean
11. 8 shall ye not touch; they (are) unclean to
11. 26 (The carcases) of every beast..(are) uncl.
11. 27 that go on (all) four, those (are) unclean
11. 28 wash his clothes..they (are) unclean unto
11. 29 These also (shall be) unclean unto you am.
11. 31 These (are) unclean to you among all that
11. 35 they (are) unclean, and shall be unclean
11. 38 fall thereon, it (shall be) unclean unto you
11. 47 To make a difference between the unclean
13. 11 shall not shut him up; for he (is) unclean
13. 15 (for) the raw flesh (is) unclean; it (is) a le.
13. 36 the priest shall not seek..he (is) unclean
13. 44 He is a leprous man, he (is) unclean, the
13. 45 And the leper..shall cry, Unclean, uncl.
13. 46 he (is) unclean: he shall dwell alone, wit.
13. 51 plague (is) a fretting leprosy; it (is) uncl.
13. 55 it (is) unclean; thou shalt burn it in the
14. 40 they shall cast them into an unclean pla.
14. 41 pour out the dust..into an unclean place
14. 44 a fretting leprosy in the house: it (is) un.
14. 45 carry them forth..into an unclean place
14. 57 To teach when (it is) unclean, and when
15. 2 (because of) his issue he (is) unclean
15. 25 all the days..she (shall be) unclean
15. 26 whatsoever she sitteth upon shall be un.
15. 33 of him that lieth with her that is unclean
20. 25 between clean..and unclean, and betwe.
22. 4 whoso toucheth any thing (that is) uncle.
27. 11 if (it be) any unclean beast, of which they
27. 27 if (it be) of an unclean beast, then he shall
Num. 9. 10 If any man of you..shall be unclean by
18. 15 the firstling of unclean beasts shalt thou
19. 13 he shall be unclean; his uncleanness (is)
19. 15 vessel, which hath no covering..(is) unc.
19. 17 for an unclean (person) they shall take of
19. 19 shall sprinkle upon the unclean on the thi.
19. 20 hath defiled the sanctuary..he (is) uncle.
19. 22 whatsoever the unclean (person) toucheth
Deut12. 15 the unclean and the clean may eat there.
12. 22 the unclean and the clean shall eat (of) th.
14. 7 they chew the cud..they (are) unclean un.
14. 8 yet cheweth not the cud, it (is) unclean
14. 10 ye may not eat; it (is) unclean unto you
14. 19 every creeping thing..(is) unclean unto
15. 22 the unclean and the clean (person) shall
26. 14 neither have I taken away..for (any) un.
Josh.22. 19 if the land of your possession (be) unclean
Judg13. 4 drink not wine..and eat not any unclean
2 Ch.23. 19 none (which was) unclean in any thing
Job 14. 4 Who can bring a clean (thing) out of an un.
Eccl. 9. 2 to the clean, and to the unclean; to him
Isa. 6. 5 because I (am) a man of unclean lips, and
6. 5 dwell in the midst of a people of unclean
35. 8 the unclean shall not pass over it; but it
52. 1 no more come into thee..the unclean
52. 11 go ye out from thence, touch no unclean
64. 6 we are all as an unclean (thing), and all our
Lam. 4. 15 Depart ye; (it is) unclean; depart, depart
Eze. 22. 26 showed (difference) between the unclean
44. 23 cause them to discern between the unclean
Hos. 9. 3 they shall eat unclean (things) in Assyria
Hag. 2. 13 If (one that is) unclean by a dead body to.
2. 14 and that which they offer there (is) uncl.
3. *To make or declare unclean,* טָמֵא *tame,* 3.
Lev. 20. 25 which I have separated from you as uncl.
4. *Uncleanness, defilement,* טֻמְאָה *tumah.*
Lev. 5. 3 the uncleanness of man, whatsoever unc.
7. 20 having his uncleanness upon him, even
7. 21 any unclean (thing, as) the uncleanness
14. 19 him that is to be cleansed from his uncl.
15. 3 this shall be his uncleanness in his issue
15. 3 be stopped from his issue, it (is) his uncl.
15. 25 the days of the issue of her uncleanness
15. 26 And..as the uncleanness of her separation
15. 30 atonement..for the issue of her unclean.
15. 31 uncleanness; that they die not in their un.
16. 16 uncleanness..in the midst of their uncle.
16. 19 hallow it from the uncleanness of the ch.
18. 19 as long as she is put apart for her uncle.
22. 3 having his uncleanness upon him, that so.
22. 5 or a man..whatsoever uncleanness he ha.
Num. 5. 19 if thou hast not gone aside to uncleanness
19. 13 he shall be..his uncleanness (is) yet upon
Judg13. 7 neither eat any unclean (thing): for the ch.
13. 14 neither let her..eat any unclean (thing)
2 Sa. 11. 4 she was purified from her uncleanness: and
2 Ch.29. 16 brought out all the uncleanness that they
Ezra 9. 11 which have filled it..with their unclean.
Eze. 36. 17 as the uncleanness of a removed woman
36. 29 I will also save you from all your unclea.
39. 24 According to their uncleanness, and acc.
Zech.13. 2 and the unclean spirit to pass out of the
5. *Separation, impurity,* נִדָּה *niddah.*
Lev. 20. 21 it (is) an unclean thing; he hath uncover
Ezra 9. 11 is an unclean land with the filthiness of
Zech.13. 1 a fountain opened..for sin and for uncle.
6. *Nakedness, disgracefulness,* עֶרְוָה *ervah.*
Deut.23. 14 that he see no unclean thing in thee, an

7. *Separate, consecrated,* קָדֵשׁ *qadesh.*
Job 36. 14 They die..and their life (is) among the un.

8. *An accident,* קָרֶה *qareh.*
Deut.23. 10 by reason of uncleanness that chanceth

9. *Uncleanness, impurity,* ἀκαθαρσία *akatharsia.*
Matt 23. 27 full of dead..bones, and of all uncleanness
Rom. 1. 24 God also gave them up to uncleanness th.
6. 19 yielded your members servants to unclea.
2 Co.12. 21 have not repented of the uncleanness, and
Gal. 5. 19 Adultery, fornication, uncleanness, lasci.
Eph. 4. 19 to work all uncleanness with greediness
5. 3 all uncleanness, or covetousness, let it not
Col. 3. 5 uncleanness, inordinate affection, evil co.
1 Th. 2. 3 our exhortation (was) not..of uncleanness
4. 7 God hath not called us unto uncleanness

10. *Unclean, impure,* ἀκάθαρτος *akathartos.*
Matt.10. 1 he gave them power (against) unclean sp.
12. 43 When the unclean spirit is gone out of a
Mark 1. 23 in their synagogue a man with an unclean
1. 26 when the unclean spirit had torn him, and
1. 27 commandeth he even the unclean spirits
3. 11 unclean spirits, when they saw him, fell
3. 30 Because they said, He hath an unclean sp.
5. 2 met him..a man with an unclean spirit
5. 8 Come out of the man, (thou) unclean spi.
5. 13 the unclean spirits went out, and entered
6. 7 and gave them power over unclean spirits
7. 25 whose young daughter had an unclean sp.
Luke 4. 33 a man which had a spirit of an unclean
4. 36 he commandeth the unclean spirits, and
6. 18 they that were vexed with unclean spirits
8. 29 he had commanded the unclean spirit to
9. 42 Jesus rebuked the unclean spirit, and he.
11. 24 When the unclean spirit is gone out of a
Acts 5. 16 them which were vexed with unclean sp.
8. 7 unclean spirits, crying with a loud voice
10. 14 never eaten any thing that is..unclean
10. 28 I should not call any man common or un.
11. 8 nothing common or unclean hath at any
1 Co. 7. 14 else were your children unclean, but now
2 Co. 6. 17 touch not the unclean (thing); and I will
Eph. 5. 5 no whoremonger, nor unclean person, nor
Rev. 16. 13 I saw three unclean spirits like frogs (come)
18. 2 a cage of every unclean and hateful bird

11. *Common, profane, polluted,* κοινός *koinos.*
Rom. 14. 14 I know..that..nothing unclean of itself
14. 14 any thing to be unclean, to him (it is) un.

12. *To make common, profane, pollute,* κοινόω.
Heb. 9. 13 For if the blood..sprinkling the unclean

13. *Pollution, defilement,* μιασμός *miasmos.*
2 Pe. 2. 10 that walk after the flesh in the lust of un.

UNCLEAN, to (be made), make self, pronounce —

1. *Unclean, defiled,* טָמֵא *tame.*
Lev. 11. 24, 27, 31, 32, 39 unclean until the even
11. 25, 28, 40, 40 be unclean until the even
11. 26 every one that toucheth..shall be unclean
11. 32 whatsoever (any)..doth fall, it shall be un.
11. 33 whatsoever (is) in it shall be unclean, and
11. 34 (that) on which (such)..cometh shall be u.
11. 34 drunk..in every (such) vessel shall be un.
11. 35 every (thing)..shall be unclean, (whether
11. 36 that which toucheth..shall be unclean
12. 2 she shall be unclean seven days, according
12 2 for her infirmity shall she be unclean
12. 5 she shall be unclean two weeks, as in her
13 14 raw flesh appeareth..he shall be unclean
14. 36 that all that (is) in..be not made unclean
14. 46 he that goeth..shall be unclean until the
15. 4 Every bed whereon he lieth..is unclean
15. 4 whereon he sitteth shall be unclean
15. 5, 6, 7, 8, 10, 10, 11, 16 be unclean until the
15. 9 what saddle..he rideth..shall be unclean
15. 18, 21, 22, 27 be unclean until the even
15. 24 he shall be unclean seven days; and all
15. 24 the bed whereon he lieth shall be unclean
15. 27 whosoever toucheth those..shall be uncl.
17. 15 bathe (himself) in water, and be unclean
22. 5 whereby he may be made unclean, or
22. 6 which hath touched any such shall be un.
Num 19. 7 the priest shall be unclean until the even
19. 8 he that burneth her..shall be unclean un.
19. 10 shall wash his clothes, and be unclean un.
19. 11 He that toucheth..shall be unclean seven
19. 14 all that (is) in the tent, shall be unclean
19. 16 whosoever toucheth..a grave, shall be un.
19. 20 the man that shall be unclean, and shall
19. 21 he that toucheth..shall be unclean until
19. 22 shall be unclean..shall be unclean until
Hag. 2. 13 shall it be unclean..It shall be unclean

2. *To make or declare unclean, defile,* טָמֵא *tame,* 3.
Lev. 13. 3 priest shall look..and pronounce him un.
13. 8, 11 the priest shall pronounce him unclean
13. 15 the priest shall..pronounce him to be un.
13. 20, 22, 25, 27, 30 priest shall pronounce..un.
13. 44 the priest shall pronounce him..unclean
13. 59 This (is) the law..to pronounce it unclean

3. *To defile self, make self unclean,* טָמֵא *tame,* 7.
Lev. 11. 24 for these ye shall be unclean: whosoever
11. 43 neither shall ye make yourselves unclean
Num. 6. 7 He shall not make himself unclean for

UNCLEANNESS, to take—

To be unclean, טָמֵא *tame.*
Lev. 22. 5 or a man of whom he may take unclean.

UNCLE'S wife —

Beloved, uncle's wife, דּוֹדָה *dodah.*
Lev. 20. 20 if a man shall lie with his uncle's wife, he

UNCLOTHED —

To lead out, unclothe, ἐκδύω *ekduō.*
2 Co. 5. 4 not for that we would be unclothed, but

UNCOMELY (parts) —

Unseemly, ἀσχήμων *aschēmōn.*
1 Co. 12. 23 our uncomely (parts) have more abundant

UNCONDEMNED —

Uncondemned, not judged down, ἀκατάκριτος *aka.*
Acts 16. 37 They have beaten us openly uncondemned
22. 25 a man that is a Roman, and uncondemned?

UNCORRUPTIBLE, uncorruptness —

1. *Incorruption,* ἀδιαφθορία *adiaphthoria.*
Titus 2. 7 in doctrine..[uncorruptness], gravity, sinc.

2. *Incorruptible, incorrupted,* ἄφθαρτος *aphthartos.*
Rom. 1. 23 changed the glory of the uncorruptible

UNCOVER, (self, be uncovered), to —

1. *To be removed, uncovered, revealed,* גָּלָה *galah,* 2.
2 Sa. 6. 20 uncovered himself..as one..uncovereth
Isa. 47. 3 Thy nakedness shall be uncovered, yea

2. *To remove, uncover, reveal,* גָּלָה *galah,* 3.
Lev. 18. 6 to uncover..nakedness: I (am) the LORD
18. 7 shalt thou not uncover..thou shalt not un.
So in v. 8, 9, 10, 11, 12, 13, 14, 15, 15, 16, 17.
18. 17 to uncover her nakedness..they (are) her
18. 18 to uncover her nakedness, besides the ot.
18. 19 to uncover her nakedness as long as she
20. 11 hath uncovered his father's nakedness
20. 17 he hath uncovered his sister's nakedness
20. 18 shall uncover her..she hath uncovered
20. 19 thou shalt not uncover the nakedness of
20. 20, 21 he hath uncovered his..nakedness
Deut 27. 20 because he uncovereth his father's skirt
Ruth 3. 4 and uncover his feet, and lay thee down
3. 7 and uncovered his feet, and laid her do.
Isa. 47. 2 uncover thy locks..uncover the thigh
Jer. 49. 10 I have uncovered his secret places, and

3. *To uncover or reveal self,* גָּלָה *galah,* 7.
Gen. 9. 21 and he was uncovered within his tent

4. *To make bare, or draw out,* חָשַׂף *chasaph.*
Isa. 20. 4 with..buttocks uncovered, to the shame
Eze. 4. 7 thine arm..uncovered, and thou shalt

5. *To make bare,* עָרָה *arah,* 3.
Isa. 22. 6 Elam bare the quiver..Kir uncovered the
Zeph. 2. 14 desolation..he shall uncover the cedar

6. *To make bare,* עָרָה *arah,* 5.
Lev. 20. 19 he uncovereth his near kin: they shall

7. *To free, keep or make bare,* פָּרַע *para.*
Lev. 10. 6 Uncover not your heads, neither rend yo.
21. 10 shall not uncover his head, nor rend his
Num. 5. 18 the priest shall..uncover the woman's he.

8. *Uncovered, unveiled,* ἀκατακάλυπτος *akatakalup.*
1 Co.11. 5 or prophesieth with (her) head uncovered
11. 13 comely that a woman pray unto God un.

9. *To uncover, unroof,* ἀποστεγάζω *apostegazō.*
Mark 2. 4 they uncovered the roof where he was

UNCTION —

Anointing, unction, χρίσμα *chrisma.*
1 Jo. 2. 20 ye have an unction from the Holy One

UNDEFILED —

1. *Perfect, finished, plain,* תָּם *tam.*
Song 5. 2 my sister, my love, my dove, my undefiled
6. 9 My dove, my undefiled is (but) one; she

2. *Perfect, whole, complete,* תָּמִים *tamim.*
Psa.119. 1 Blessed (are) the undefiled in the way, who

3. *Undefiled, unpolluted, immaculate,* ἀμίαντος.
Heb. 7. 26 holy, harmless, undefiled, separate from
13. 4 Marriage (is) honourable..the bed undefi.
Jas. 1. 27 Pure religion and undefiled before God
1 Pe. 1. 4 To an inheritance incorruptible, and und.

UNDER, underneath —

1. *Unto,* אֶל *el.*
2 Sa. 2. 23 smote him under the fifth (rib), that the

2. *Beneath, below,* מַטָּה *mattah.*
Exod 28. 27 the two sides of the ephod underneath
39. 20 on the two sides of the ephod underneath
1 Ch.27. 23 took not..from twenty years old and un.

3. *Under, beneath,* תְּחוֹת *techoth.*
Jer. 10. 11 they shall perish..from under these hea.
Dan. 4. 12 the beasts of the field had shadow under
4. 21 under which the beasts of the fields dwe.
7. 27 the greatness of the kingdom under the

4. *Under, beneath,* תַּחַת *tachath.*
Gen. 1. 7 under the firmament from the waters wh.
6. 17 flood..to destroy all flesh..from under
7. 19 all the high hills that (were) under the
Dan. 4. 14 let the beasts get away from under it

5. *Unto the place of, under,* אֶל־תַּחַת *el tachath.*
Jer. 3. 6 upon every high mountain and under

6. *Under, beneath,* לְמִתַּחַת *le-mit-tachath.*
1 Ki. 7. 32 And under the borders (were) four whe.

7. *In, among, with, by,* ἐν *en.*
Matt. 7. 6 lest they trample them under their feet
Rom. 3. 19 it saith to them who are under the law

8. *On, upon, over,* ἐπί (*dat.*) *epi.*
Heb. 7. 11 for [under] it the people received the law
9. 15 of the transgressions..under the first tes
10. 28 died without mercy under two or three

9. *Down beneath, below, under,* κατωτέρω *katōterō.*
Matt. 2. 16 slew all..from two years old and under

10. *Under,* ὑπό (*acc.*) *hupo.*
Matt. 5. 15 Neither do men..put it under a bushel
8. 8 not worthy that thou shouldest come un.
8. 9 man under authority, having soldiers un.
23. 37 even as a hen gathereth her chickens un.
Mark 4. 21 to be put under a bushel, or under a bed?
4. 32 the fowls of the air may lodge under the
Luke 7. 6 not worthy that thou shouldest enter un.
7. 8 For I also am a man set under authority
7. 8 having under me soldiers; and I say un.
11. 33 neither under a bushel, but on a candle.
13. 34 as a hen..her brood under (her) wings
17. 24 under heaven..unto the other (part) und.
John 1. 48 when thou wast under the fig tree, I saw
Acts 2. 5 devout men out of every nation under
4. 12 there is none other name under heaven
Rom. 3. 9 before proved..that they are all under sin
3. 13 the poison of asps (is) under their lips
6. 14, 15 are not under the law, but under grace
7. 14 spiritual: but I am carnal, sold under sin
16. 20 the God of peace shall bruise Satan under
1 Co. 9. 20 them that are under the law, as under the
9. 20 that I might gain them that are under the
10. 1 all our fathers were under the cloud, and
15. 25 till he hath put all enemies under his feet
15. 27 For he hath put all things under his feet
Gal. 3. 10 as many..are under the curse: for it is
3. 22 the scripture hath concluded all under sin
3. 23 we were kept under the law, shut up unto
3. 25 we are no longer under a schoolmaster
4. 2 But is under tutors and governors until
4. 3 were in bondage under the elements of
4. 4 made of a woman, made under the law
4. 5 To redeem them that were under the law
4. 21 Tell me, ye that desire to be under the law
5. 18 led by the spirit, ye are not under the law
Eph. 1. 22 hath put all (things) under his feet, and
Col. 1. 23 to every creature which is under heaven
1 Ti. 6 1 Let as many servants as are under the yo.
Jas. 2 3 Stand thou there, or sit here under my
1 Pe. 5. 6 Humble yourselves therefore under the
Jude 6 under darkness, unto the judgment of the

11. *Underneath,* ὑποκάτω *hupokatō.*
Mark 6. 11 shake off the dust under your feet for a
7. 28 the dogs under the table eat of the chil.
Luke 8. 16 No man..putteth (it) under a bed, but
John 1. 50 I said unto thee, I saw thee under the fig
Heb. 2. 8 put all things in subjection under his feet
Rev. 5. 3 no man in heaven..neither under the ea.
5. 13 on the earth, and under the earth, and
6. 9 I saw under the altar the souls of them
12. 1 the moon under her feet, and upon her

12. *Smaller, inferior, younger,* ἐλάσσων *elassōn.*
1 Ti. 5. 9 be taken into the number under threescore

[*See also* Bondage, brought, curse, earth. foot, keep, obedience, persecution, put, run, sail, tread, trodden.]

UNDER the law —

In or under law, ἔννομος *ennomos.*
1 Co. 9. 21 not without law to God, but under the law

UNDERGIRD, to —

To undergird, ὑποζώννυμι *hupozōnnumi.*
Acts 27. 17 they used helps, undergirding the ship

UNDERSETTER —

Shoulder, corner, side, כָּתֵף *katheph.*
1 Ki. 7. 30 had undersetters..undersetters molten, at
7. 30 under the laver (were) undersetters molten
7. 34 four undersetters..the undersetters (we.)

UNDERSTAND, to (cause, give or make to) —

1. *To understand, consider,* בִּין *bin.*
Neh. 8. 8 and caused..to understand the reading
13. 7 understood of the evil that Eliashib did
Job 13. 1 mine ear hath heard and understood it
15. 9 (what) understandest thou, which (is) not
23. 5 and understand what he would say unto
32. 9 neither do the aged understand judgment
36. 29 can (any) understand the spreadings of the
42. 3 therefore have I uttered that I understood
Psa. 19. 12 Who can understand (his) errors? cleanse
49. 20 Man (that is) in honour, and understand.
73. 17 Until I went..(then) understood I their
82. 5 They know not, neither will they unders.
92. 6 knoweth not; neither doth a fool unders.
94. 8 Understand, ye brutish among the people
139. 2 thou understandest my thought afar off
Prov. 2. 5 Then shalt thou understand the fear of the
2. 9 Then shalt thou understand righteousness
19. 25 reprove..(and) he will understand know.
20. 24 how can a man then understand his own
28. 5 Evil men understand not judgment: but
28. 5 they that seek the LORD understand all
29. 19 though he understand he will not answer
Isa. 6. 9 Hear ye indeed, but understand not; and
6. 10 hear with their ears, and understand with
28. 9 whom shall he make to understand doct.
32. 4 The heart also of the rash shall understand
43. 10 believe me, and understand that I (am) he

Isa. 44. 18 They have not known nor understand, for
Jer. 9. 12 Who (is) the wise man, that may unders.
Dan. 9. 2 I Daniel understood by books the number
9. 23 understand the matter, and consider the
10. 1 and he understood the thing, and had
12. 8 I heard, but I understood not: then said
12. 10 understand; but the wise shall understand
Hos. 4. 14 the people (that) doth not understand shall
14. 9 Who (is) wise, and he shall understand th.

2. *To have understanding, be intelligent,* בִּין *bin,* **2.**
Prov 14. 6 knowledge (is) easy unto him that underst.

3. *To cause to understand, attend,* בִּין *bin,* **5.**
1 Ch. 28. 9 understandeth all the imaginations of the
Neh. 8. 3 read..before.. those that could understa.
8. 7 caused the people to understand the law
8. 12 they had understood the words that were
Job 6. 24 cause me to understand wherein I have
28. 23 God understandeth the way thereof, and
Psa. 119. 27 Make me to understand the way of thy
Prov. 1. 6 To understand a proverb, and the interp.
8. 5 O ye simple, understand wisdom; and, ye
8. 9 They (are) all plain to him that underst.
14. 8 The wisdom of the prudent (is) to under.
Isa. 28. 19 it shall be a vexation only (to) understand
40. 21 have ye not understood from the founda.
56. 11 they (are) shepherds (that) cannot under.
Dan. 8. 16 make this (man) to understand the vision
8. 17 Understand, O son of man; for at the time
8. 27 I was astonished..but none understood
10. 11 understand the words that I speak unto
10. 12 set thine heart to understand, and to ch.
10. 14 I am come to make thee understand what
Mic. 4. 12 they know not..neither understand they

4. *To understand, consider,* בִּין *bin,* **7a.**
Job 26. 14 the thunder of his power who can unders.
Psa. 107. 43 they shall understand the loving kindness
119. 100 I understand more than the ancients, be.

5. *Understanding,* בִּינָה *binah.*
Isa. 33. 19 tongue, (that thou canst) not understand

6. *To know, be acquainted with,* יָדַע *yada.*
Num 16. 30 ye shall understand that these men have
9. 3 Understand therefore this day, that the
Deut 9. 6 Understand therefore, that the LORD thy
1 Sa. 4. 6 they understood that the ark of the LORD
26. 4 understood that Saul was come in very de.
2 Sa. 3. 37 all Israel, understood that day, that it was
Psa. 81. 5 I heard a language (that) I understood not

7. *To (cause to act) wisely,* שָׂכַל *sakal,* **5.**
Deut 32. 29 (that) they understood this, (that) they
1 Ch. 28. 19 the LORD made me understand in writing
Neh. 8. 13 even to understand the words of the law
Psa. 14. 2 to see if there were any that did underst.
53. 2 to see if there were (any) that did under.
106. 7 Our fathers understood not thy wonders
Isa. 41. 20 consider, and understand together, that
44. 18 their hearts, that they cannot understand
Jer. 9. 24 that he understandeth and knoweth me
Dan. 9. 13 turn from our iniquities, and understand
9. 25 Know therefore and understand..from the
11. 33 they that understand among the people

8. *To hear, hearken,* שָׁמַע *shamea.*
Gen. 11. 7 that they may not understand one anot.
41. 15 thou canst understand a dream to interpr.
42. 23 they knew not that Joseph understood (th.)
Deut. 28. 49 whose tongue thou shalt not understand
2 Ki. 18. 26 the Syrian language; for we understand
Isa. 36. 11 the Syrian language; for we understand
Jer. 5. 15 neither understandest what they say
Eze. 3. 6 whose words thou canst not understand

9. *To hear, hearken,* ἀκούω *akouō.*
1 Co 14. 2 speaketh not unto men..for no man unde.

10. *To know, be cognizant of,* γινώσκω *ginōskō.*
Matt 26. 10 When Jesus understood (it), he said unto
John 8. 27 They understood not that he spake to them
8. 43 Why do ye not understand my speech?
10. 6 they understood not what things they we.
12. 16 These things understood not his disciples
Acts 8. 30 said, Understandest thou what thou read!
24. 11 Because [that thou mayest understand],
Phil. 1. 12 But I would ye should understand, breth.

11. *To make known,* γνωρίζω *gnōrizō.*
1 Co. 12. 3 I give you to understand, that no man

12. *To see, know, be acquainted with,* εἴδω *eidō.*
1 Co. 13. 2 understand all mysteries, and all knowled.
14. 16 he understandeth not what thou sayest?

13. *To know about, be acquainted with,* ἐπίσταμαι.
Mark 14. 68 neither understand I what thou sayest

14. *To learn,* μανθάνω *mathanō.*
Acts 23. 27 came..having understood that he was a

15. *To ponder, think, understand,* νοέω *noeō.*
Matt 15. 17 Do not ye yet understand, that whatsoever
16. 9 Do ye not yet understand, neither remem.
16. 11 How is it that ye do not understand that
24. 15 Daniel ..whoso readeth, let him underst.
Mark 13. 14 Daniel ..let him that readeth understand
John 12. 40 nor understand with (their) heart, and be
Rom. 1. 20 being understood by the things that are
Eph. 3. 4 when ye read, ye may understand my kn.
1 Ti. 1. 7 understanding neither what they say, nor
Heb. 11. 3 Through faith we understand that the w.

16. *To learn by enquiry,* πυνθάνομαι *punthanomai.*
Acts 23. 34 when he understood that (he was) of Cil.

17. *To send together, consider, understand,* συνίημι.
Matt 13. 13 hearing, they hear not; neither do they
13. 14 ye shall hear, and shall not understand
13. 15 should understand with (their) heart, and
13. 19 When any one heareth..and understand.
13. 23 he that heareth the word, and understa.
13. 51 Jesus saith..Have ye understood all the.
15. 10 said unto them, Hear, and understand
16. 12 Then understood they how that he bade
17. 13 the disciples understood that he spake
Mark 4. 12 hearing they may hear, and not underst.
7. 14 Hearken..every one (of you), and under.
8. 17 perceive ye not yet, neither understand?
8. 21 How is it that ye do not understand?
Luke 2. 50 they understood not the saying which he
8. 10 and hearing they might not understand
18. 34 they understood none of these things, and
24. 45 that they might understand the Scriptu.
Acts 7. 25 have understood ..but they understood
28. 26 Hearing ye shall hear, and shall not und.
28. 27 hear with (their) ears, and understand wi.
Rom. 3. 11 There is none that understandeth, there
15. 21 they that have not heard shall understand
Eph. 5. 17 understanding what the will of the Lord

18. *To set the mind or affections on,* φρονέω *phroneō.*
1 Co. 13. 11 When I was a child..I understood as a c.

UNDERSTAND not, to —
Not to know, to be ignorant, ἀγνοέω *agnoeō.*
Mark 9. 32 they understood not that saying, and we.
Luke 9. 45 they understood not this saying, and it
2 Pe. 2. 12 speak evil of..things..they understand n.

UNDERSTANDING, (man of) —

1. *To be intelligent, have understanding,* בִּין *bin,* **2.**
Deut. 1. 13 Take you wise men, and understanding
4. 6 nation (is) a wise and understanding peo.
1 Ki. 3. 12 given..a wise and an understanding he.
Prov. 1. 5 a man of understanding shall attain unto
8. 5 fools, be ye of an understanding heart
17. 28 (and) he..(is esteemed) a man of unders.
Eccl. 9. 11 nor yet riches to men of understanding

2. *To cause to understand,* בִּין *bin,* **5.**
1 Ki. 3. 11 but hast asked for thyself understanding
Ezra 8. 16 Then sent I for..men of understanding
Neh. 8. 2 all that could hear with understanding
10. 28 having knowledge, and having understa.
Prov 28. 2 by a man of understanding (and) knowl.
Dan. 1. 4 cunning in knowledge, and understanding
8. 23 a king..understanding dark sentences, sh.

3. *Understanding, intelligence,* בִּינָה *binah.*
Deut. 4. 6 this (is) your wisdom and your understan.
1 Ch. 12. 32 (men) that had understanding of the times
22. 12 the LORD give thee wisdom and underst.
2 Ch. 2. 12 endued with prudence and understanding
2. 13 a cunning man, endued with understand.
Job 20. 3 the spirit of my understanding causeth
28. 12, 20 where (is) the place of understanding?
28. 28 and to depart from evil (is) understanding
34. 16 If now..understanding, hear this; hear.
38. 4 declare, if thou hast understanding?
38. 36 who hath given understanding to the he.
39. 17 neither hath he imparted to her unders.
Prov. 1. 2 to perceive the words of understanding
3. 5 and lean not unto thine own understand.
4. 1 Hear..and attend to know understanding
4. 5 get understanding: forget (it) not; neit.
4. 7 and with all thy getting get understanding
7. 4 and call understanding (thy) kinswoman
8. 14 Counsel (is) mine..I (am) understanding
9. 6 and live; and go in the way of understan.
9. 10 the knowledge of the holy (is) understan.
16. 16 to get understanding rather to be chosen
23. 23 wisdom, and instruction, and understan.
30. 2 and have not the understanding of a man
Isa. 11. 2 the spirit of wisdom and understanding
27. 11 it (is) a people of no understanding, there.
29. 14 the understanding of their prudent (men)
29. 24 that erred in spirit shall come to under.
Dan. 1. 20 in all matters of wisdom (and) understa.
9. 22 come..to give thee skill and understand.
10. 1 and had understanding of the vision

4. *Taste, perception,* טַעַם *taam.*
Job 12. 20 taketh away the understanding of the ag.

5. *Heart,* לֵב *leb.*
Prov. 6. 32 whoso committeth adultery..lacketh un.
7. 7 beheld..a young man void of understan.
9. 4, 16 (as for) him that wanteth understan.
10. 13 a rod (is) for..him that is void of under.
12. 11 he that followeth..(is) void of understan.
15. 32 he that heareth reproof getteth underst.
17. 18 A man void of understanding striketh
24. 30 the vineyard of the man void of underst.
Jer. 5. 21 O foolish people, and without understan.

6. *Heart,* לֵבָב *lebab.*
Job 12. 3 But I have understanding as well as you
34. 10 hearken unto me, ye men of understand.
34. 34 Let men of understanding tell me, and let

7. *Knowledge,* מַנְדַּע *manda.*
Dan. 4. 34 mine understanding returned unto me

8. *To cause to act wisely,* שָׂכַל *sakal,* **5.**
Psa. 47. 7 sing ye praises with understanding
Prov. 21. 16 man that wandereth out of the way of un.
Jer. 3. 15 shall feed you with knowledge and unde.
Dan. 11. 35 (some) of them of understanding shall fall

9. *Understanding, wisdom, meaning,* שֶׂכֶל, שֵׂכֶל *sekel.*
1 Sa. 25. 3 a woman of good understanding, and of
Ezra 8. 18 they brought us a man of understanding
Job 17. 4 thou hast hid their heart from understa.
Psa. 111. 10 a good understanding have all they that
Prov. 3. 4 So shalt thou find favour and good unde.
13. 15 Good understanding giveth favour: but
16. 22 Understanding (is) a well spring of life un.

10. *Understanding,* שָׂכְלְתָנוּ *soklethanu.*
Dan. 5. 11 light and understanding: and wisdom, like
5. 12 an excellent spirit, and knowledge, and un.
5. 14 light and understanding and excellent

11. *To hear, hearken,* שָׁמַע *shamea.*
1 Ki. 3. 9 Give..thy servant an understanding hea.

12. *Understanding,* תְּבוּן *tabun.*
Hos. 13. 2 idols according to their own understand.

13. *Understanding,* תְּבוּנָה *tebunah.*
Exod 31. 3 in understanding, and in knowledge, and
35. 31 with the spirit of God, in wisdom, in un.
36. 1 in whom the LORD put wisdom and unde.
Deut 32. 28 neither (is there any understanding) in
1 Ki. 4. 29 God gave Solomon wisdom and understa.
7. 14 he was filled with wisdom and understa.
Job 12. 12 wisdom; and in length of days understa.
12. 13 he hath counsel and understanding
26. 12 by his understanding he smiteth through
Psa. 49. 3 meditation of my heart (shall be) of und.
147. 5 Great (is) our Lord..his understanding
Prov. 2. 2 (and) apply thine heart to understanding
2. 3 liftest up thy voice for understanding
2. 6 out of his mouth (cometh)..understand.
2. 11 preserve thee, understanding shall keep
3. 13 and the man (that) getteth understanding
3. 19 by understanding hath he established the
5. 1 (and) bow thine ear to my understanding
8. 1 and understanding put forth her voice?
10. 23 but a man of understanding hath wisdom
11. 12 a man of understanding holdeth his pea.
14. 29 (He that is) slow to wrath (is) of great un.
15. 21 a man of understanding walketh uprigh.
17. 27 a man of understanding is of an excellent
18. 2 A fool hath no delight in understanding
19. 8 he that keepeth understanding shall find
20. 5 a man of understanding will draw it out
21. 30 (There is) no wisdom nor understanding
24. 3 and by understanding it is established
28. 16 The prince that wanteth understanding
Isa. 40. 14 showed to him the way of understanding
40. 28 (there is) no searching of his understand.
44. 19 neither (is there) knowledge nor underst.
Jer. 51. 15 hath stretched out the heaven by his un.
Eze. 28. 4 With thy wisdom and with thine unders.
Hos. 13. 2 idols according to their own understand.
Obad. 7 (their is) none understanding in him
8 and understanding out of the mount of E.

14. *Understanding,* תּוּבְנָה *tubnah.*
Job 26. 12 by his understanding he smiteth through

15. *Whole mind, intellect, understanding,* διάνοια.
Eph. 1. 18 The eyes of your [understanding] being
4. 18 Having the understanding darkened
1 Jo. 5. 20 the Son..hath given us an understanding

16. *Mind, understanding,* νοῦς *nous.*
Luke 24. 45 Then opened he their understanding, th.
1 Co. 14. 14 my spirit prayeth, but my understanding
14. 15 I will pray with the understanding also
14. 15 I will sing with the understanding also
14. 19 rather speak five words with my underst.
Phil. 4. 7 the peace..which passeth all understand.
Rev. 13. 18 Let him that hath understanding count

17. *A sending together, intelligence,* σύνεσις *sunesis.*
Mark 12. 33 with all the understanding, and with all
Luke 2. 47 were astonished at his understanding and
1 Co. 1. 19 will bring to nothing the understanding
Col. 1. 9 in all wisdom and spiritual understanding
2. 2 riches of the full assurance of understand.
2 Ti. 2. 7 the Lord give thee understanding in all

18. *Heart, mind, understanding,* φρήν *phrēn.*
1 Co. 14. 20 not children in understanding..in under.

UNDERSTANDING, without —
Not sent together, unintelligent, ἀσύνετος *asunetos.*
Matt 15. 16 Are ye also yet without understanding
Mark 7. 18 Are ye so without understanding also?
Rom. 1. 31 Without understanding, covenant breakers

UNDERSTANDING, to be of, get, give, have perfect—

1. *To be intelligent,* בִּין *bin,* **2.**
Prov 10. 13 In the lips of him that hath understand.
14. 33 resteth in the heart of him that hath un.
15. 14 The heart of him that hath understanding
19. 25 and reprove one that hath understanding
Jer. 4. 22 my people..they have none understand.

2. *To cause to understand,* בִּין *bin,* **5.**
2 Ch. 26. 5 who had understanding in the visions of
Job 32. 8 the Almighty giveth them understanding
Psa. 32. 9 (which) have no understanding, whose
119. 34, 73, 125, 144, 169 Give me understanding
119. 130 it giveth understanding unto the simple
Prov. 8. 5 and, ye fools, be ye of an understanding
17. 24 Wisdom (is) before him that hath under.
28. 11 the poor that hath understanding search.
Isa. 29. 16 say of him..He had no understanding
Dan. 1. 17 Daniel had understanding in all visions

3. *To understand, consider, attend,* בִּין *bin,* **7a.**
Psa. 119. 104 Through thy precepts I get understand.

4. *To cause to act wisely,* שָׂכַל *sakal,* 5.
Psa.119. 99 I have more understanding than all my
Dan. 11. 35 (some) of them of understanding shall f

5. *To follow alongside of,* παρακολουθέω *parakolou.*
Luke 1. 3 having had perfect understanding of all

UNDERSTANDING, to make of quick —
To refresh, רוּחַ *ruach,* 5.
Isa. 11. 3 shall make him of quick understanding in

UNDERSTOOD, easy or hard, to be —
1. *Hard to be understood,* δυσνόητος *dusnoētos.*
2 Pe. 3. 16 in which are some things hard to be und.

2. *Easily noted,* εὔσημος *eusēmos.*
1 Co.14. 9 by the tongue words easy to be understo.

UNDERTAKE, to —
1. *To mix, traffic, negotiate, pledge,* עָרַב *arab.*
Isa. 38. 14 O LORD, I am oppressed: undertake for

2. *To accept, take, receive, undertake,* קָבַל *qabal,* 3.
Esth. 9. 23 the Jews undertook to do as they had be.

UNDO, be or leave undone, to —
1. *To be parted, lost, separated,* אָבַד *abad.*
Num21. 29 thou art undone, O people of Chemosh

2. *To be cut off, dumb,* דָּמָה *damah,* 2.
Isa. 6. 5 Then said I, Woe (is) me! for I am undone

3. *To move, loose, shake off,* נָתַר *nathar,* 5.
Isa. 58. 6 to undo the heavy burdens, and to let the

4. *To turn aside,* סוּר *sur,* 5.
Josh 11. 15 he left nothing undone of all that the Lo.

5. *To do, make,* עָשָׂה *asah.*
Zeph. 3. 19 at that time I will undo all that afflict th.

UNDRESSED, vine —
Separated thing or person, נָזִיר *nazir.*
Lev. 25. 5 neither gather the grapes of thy vine un.
25. 11 nor gather..in it of thy vine undressed

UNEQUAL —
Not to be weighed or pondered, לֹא תָּכַן *lo thakan,* 2.
Eze. 18. 25, 29 house of Israel..are not your ways un.?

UNFAITHFUL man, to deal unfaithfully —
To deal treacherously, deceive, בָּגַד *bagad.*
Psa. 78. 57 But turned back, and dealt unfaithfully
Prov25. 19 Confidence in an unfaithful man in time

UNFEIGNED —
Undisguised, unfeigned, ἀνυπόκριτος *anupokritos.*
2 Co. 6. 6 by kindness, by the holy ghost, by love un
1 Ti. 1. 5 (of) a good conscience, and (of) faith unf.
2 Ti. 1. 5 When I call to remembrance the unfeign.
1 Pe. 1. 22 obeying..unto unfeigned love of the bre.

UNFRUITFUL —
Unfruitful, without fruit, ἄκαρπος *akarpos.*
Matt13. 22 choke the word, and he becometh unfru.
Mark 4. 19 choke the word, and it becometh unfrui.
1 Co. 14. 14 prayeth, but my understanding is unfru.
Eph. 5. 11 have no fellowship with the unfruitful
Titus 3. 14 good works..that they be not unfruitful
2 Pe. 1. 8 ye shall) neither (be) barren nor unfruit.

UNGIRD, to —
To open up, פָּתַח *pathach,* 3.
Gen. 24. 32 he ungirded his camels, and gave straw

UNGODLINESS —
Irreverence, impiety, ἀσέβεια *asebeia.*
Rom. 1. 18 against all ungodliness and unrighteous.
1. 26 shall turn away ungodliness from Jacob
2 Ti. 2. 16 for they will increase unto more ungodli.
Titus 2. 12 Teaching us, that denying ungodliness

UNGODLY (men) —
1. *Belial, worthless, without value,* בְּלִיַּעַל *beliyyaal.*
2 Sa. 22. 5 the floods of ungodly men made me afra.
Psa. 18. 4 the floods of ungodly men made me afra.
Prov 16. 27 An ungodly man diggeth up evil, and in
19. 28 An ungodly witness scorneth judgment

2. *Unkind, not pious,* לֹא חָסִיד *lo chasid.*
Psa. 43. 1 plead my cause against an ungodly nation

3. *Perverse,* עֲוִיל *avil.*
Job 16. 11 God hath delivered me to the ungodly

4. *Wrong, wicked,* רָשָׁע *rasha.*
2 Ch.19. 2 Shouldest thou help the ungodly, and lo.
Job 34. 18 (Is it fit) to say..to princes, (Ye are) un.
Psa. 1. 1 walketh not in the counsel of the ungod.
1. 4 The ungodly (are) not so: but (are) like
1. 5 the ungodly shall not stand in the judg.
1. 6 but the way of the ungodly shall perish
3. 7 thou hast broken the teeth of the ungod.
73. 12 these (are) the ungodly, who prosper in

5. *Irreverence, impiety,* ἀσέβεια *asebeia.*
Jude 15 of all their ungodly deeds which they ha.
18 should walk after their own ungodly lu.

6. *Irreverent, impious,* ἀσεβής *asebēs.*
Rom. 4. 5 believeth on him that justifieth the ung.
5. 6 in due time Christ died for the ungodly
1 Ti. 1. 9 for the ungodly and for sinners, for unh.
1 Pe. 4. 18 where shall the ungodly and the sinner
2 Pe. 2. 5 the flood upon the world of the ungodly
3. 7 judgment and perdition of ungodly men
Jude 4 ungodly men, turning the grace of our God
15 all that are ungodly.. which [ungodly] si.

UNGODLY, commit or live, to —
To be or act irreverently, ἀσεβέω *asebeō.*
2 Pe. 2. 6 ensample unto those that..should live un.
Jude 15 deeds which they have ungodly commit.

UNHOLY —
1. *Pierced, common,* חֹל *chol.*
Lev. 10. 10 between holy and unholy, and between un.

2. *Unholy, unkind,* ἀνόσιος *anosios.*
1 Ti. 1. 9 for unholy and profane, for murderers of
2 Ti. 3. 2 disobedient to parents, unthankful, unh.

3. *Common,* κοινός *koinos.*
Heb. 10. 29 counted the blood of the covenant..unh.

UNICORN —
A reem, buffalo, wild ox, roaring animal, רְאֵם *reem.*
Num23. 22 he hath as it were the strength of an un.
24. 8 hath as it were the strength of an unico.
Deut 33. 17 and his horns (are like) the horns of uni.
Job 39. 9 Will the unicorn be willing to serve thee
39. 10 Canst thou bind the unicorn with his ba.
Psa. 22. 21 heard me from the horns of the unicorns
29. 6 Lebanon and Sirion like a young unicorn
92. 10 shalt thou exalt like (the horn of) an unic.
Isa. 34. 7 the unicorns shall come down with them

UNITE, be united, to —
1. *To be united,* יָחַד *yachad.*
Gen. 49. 6 unto their assembly..be not thou united

2. *To unite,* יָחַד *yachad,* 3.
Psa. 86. 11 O LORD..unite my heart to fear thy name

UNITY, (together in) —
1. *At one, together,* יַחַד *yachad.*
Psa.133. 1 good..for brethren to dwell together in un.

2. *Unity,* ἑνότης *henotēs.*
Eph. 4. 3 Endeavouring to keep the unity of the sp.
4. 13 Till we all come in the unity of the faith

UNJUST (gain), to be unjust —
1. *Iniquity, vanity,* אָוֶן *aven.*
Prov 11. 7 and the hope of unjust (men) perisheth

2. *Perverse,* עַוָּל *avval.*
Zeph. 3. 5 not do iniquity..the unjust knoweth no

3. *Perverseness, perversity,* עָוֶל, עֶוֶל *avel, evel.*
Prov.29. 27 An unjust man (is) an abomination to the

4. *Perverseness, perversity,* עַוְלָה *avlah.*
Psa. 43. 1 deliver me from the deceitful and unjust

5. *Increase, usury,* תַּרְבִּית *tarbith.*
Prov 28. 8 He that by usury and unjust gain increa.

6. *Injustice, unrighteousness,* ἀδικία *adikia.*
Luke16. 8 the Lord commended the unjust steward
18. 6 the Lord saith, Hear what the unjust ju.

7. *To be unjust, unrighteous,* ἀδικέω *adikeō.*
Rev. 22. 11 He that is unjust, let him be unjust still

8. *Unjust, unrighteous,* ἄδικος *adikos.*
Matt 5. 45 sendeth rain on the just and on the unj.
Luke16. 10 he that is unjust in the least is unjust also
18. 11 extortioners, unjust, adulterers, or even
Acts24. 15 a resurrection..of the just and unjust
1 Co. 6. 1 go to law before the unjust, and not bef.
1 Pe 3. 18 suffered for sins, the just for the unjust
2 Pe. 2. 9 to reserve the unjust unto the day of ju.

UNJUSTLY, (to deal) —
1. *To do perversely,* עָוַל *aval,* 3.
Isa. 26. 10 in the land of uprightness will he deal un.

2. *Perverseness, perversity,* עָוֶל, עֶוֶל *avel, evel.*
Psa 82. 2 How long will ye judge unjustly, and ac.

UNKNOWN —
1. *Not to know, to be ignorant,* ἀγνοέω *agnoeō.*
2 Co 6. 9 As unknown, and..yet known; as dying
Gal. 1. 22 was unknown by face unto the churches

2 *Unknown,* ἄγνωστος *agnōstos.*
Acts 17. 23 with this inscription, To the unknown G.

UNLADE, to —
To put away a load or burden, ἀποφορτίζομαι.
Acts 21 3 there the ship was to unlade her burden

UNLAWFUL (thing) —
1. *Unlawful, not appointed,* ἀθέμιτος *athemitos.*
Acts 10. 28 Ye know how that it is an unlawful thing

2. *Lawless, unlawful,* ἄνομος *anomos.*
2 Pe. 2. 8 vexed..from day to day with..unlawful d.

UNLEARNED, (to be) —
1. *Untaught, illiterate,* ἀγράμματος *agrammatos.*
Acts 4. 13 perceived that they were unlearned and

2. *Untaught, unlearned,* ἀμαθής *amathēs.*
2 Pe. 3. 16 which they that are unlearned and unst.

3. *Uninstructed, uneducated,* ἀπαίδευτος *apaideutos.*
2 Ti. 2. 23 foolish and unlearned questions avoid

4. *A private person,* ἰδιώτης *idiōtēs.*
1 Co.14. 16 shall he that occupieth the room of the un.
14. 23 there come in..unlearned, or unbelievers
14. 24 one that believeth not, or..unlearned, he

UNLEAVENED (bread, cakes) —
1. *Unleavened cake, food,* מַצָּה *matstsah.*
Gen. 19. 3 did bake unleavened bread, and they did
Exod12. 8 roast with fire and unleavened bread; (and)
Exod12. 15 Seven days shall ye eat unleavened bread
12. 17 ye shall observe (the feast of) unleavened
12. 18 ye shall eat unleavened bread, until the
12. 20 in..habitations shall ye eat unleavened
12. 39 they baked unleavened cakes of the dough
13. 6 Seven days thou shalt eat unleavened bread
13. 7 Unleavened bread shall be eaten seven
23. 15 unleavened bread..eat unleavened bread
29. 2 unleavened bread, and cakes unleavened
29. 23 the basket of the unleavened bread that
34. 18 unleavened bread..eat unleavened bread
Lev. 2. 4 unleavened cakes..or unleavened wafers
2. 5 it shall be (of) fine flour unleavened, min.
6. 16 with unleavened bread shall it be eaten
7. 12 unleavened cakes..and unleavened wafers
8. 2 rams, and a basket of unleavened bread
8. 26 unleavened bread..one unleavened cake
23. 6 unleavened bread..must eat unleavened
Num 6. 15 unleavened bread..wafers of unleavened
6. 17 offer..with the basket of unleavened bread
6. 19 one unleavened cake..one unleavened wa.
9. 11 eat it with unleavened bread and bitter
28. 17 seven days shall unleavened bread be eat.
Deut 16. 3 seven days shalt thou eat unleavened br.
16. 8 Six days thou shalt eat unleavened bread
16. 16 in the feast of unleavened bread, and in
Josh. 5. 11 unleavened cakes, and parched (corn) in
Judg. 6. 19 and unleavened cakes of an ephah of flour
20, 21, 21. the flesh and the unleavened cakes
1 Sa. 28. 24 and did bake unleavened bread thereof
2 Ki.23. 9 they did eat of the unleavened bread am.
1 Ch.23. 29 for the unleavened cakes, and for (that wh.
2 Ch. 8. 13 in the feast of unleavened bread, and in
30. 13 to keep the feast of unleavened bread in
30. 21 kept the feast of unleavened bread seven
35. 17 and the feast of unleavened bread seven
Ezra 6. 22 kept the feast of unleavened bread seven
Eze. 45. 21 seven days; unleavened bread shall be

2. *Unleavened cake or food,* ἄζυμος *azumos.*
Matt26. 17 the first (day) of the (feast of) unleavened
Mark14. 1 the passover, and of unleavened bread
14. 12 the first day of unleavened bread, when
Luke22. 1 the feast of unleavened bread drew nigh
22. 7 Then came the day of unleavened bread
Acts 12. 3 Then were the days of unleavened bread
20. 6 after the days of unleavened bread, and
1 Co. 5. 7 ye may be a new lump, as ye are unleav.
5. 8 with the unleavened (bread) of sincerity

UNLESS —
1. *Unless,* אוּלַי, אֻלַי *ulai.*
Num 22. 33 unless she had turned from me, surely now

2. *But rather, except,* כִּי אִם *ki im.*
Lev. 22. 6 not eat..unless he wash his flesh with wa.

3. *Unless, if not,* לוּלֵי, לוּלֵא *lule.*
2 Sa. 2. 27 unless thou hadst spoken, surely then in
Psa 27. 13 unless I had believed to see the goodness
94. 17 Unless the LORD (had been) my help, my

4. *Unless,* ἐκτὸς εἰ μή *ektos ei mē.*
1 Co.15. 2 are saved..unless ye have believed in va.

UNLOOSE, to —
To loose, λύω *luō.*
Mark 1. 7 I am not worthy to stoop down and unl.
Luke 3. 16 of whose shoes I am not worthy to unloose
John 1. 27 shoe's latchet I am not worthy to unloose

UNMARRIED —
Unwedded, not wedded, ἄγαμος *agamos.*
1 Co. 7. 8 I say therefore to the unmarried and wi.
7. 11 if she depart, let her remain unmarried
7. 32 He that is unmarried careth for the thi.
7. 34 The unmarried woman careth for the th.

UNMERCIFUL —
Unmerciful, without kindness, ἀνελεήμων *aneleē.*
Rom. 1. 31 without natural affection, implacable, un.

UNMINDFUL —
To leave, forget, שָׁיָה *shayah.*
Deut32. 18 Of the Rock..thou art unmindful, and h.

UNMOVEABLE —
1. *Unmoved, immoveable,* ἀμετακίνητος *ametakinē.*
1 Co.15. 58 be ye stedfast, unmoveable, always abo.

2. *Unshaken, unmoveable,* ἀσάλευτος *asaleutos.*
Acts 27. 41 the forepart stuck fast, and remained un.

UN'-NI, עֻנִּי *answering is with Jah* [Neh. V.L. ענו].
1. A Levite over the choral services in the tabernacle in the days of David. B.C. 1015.
1 Ch.15. 18 Shemiramoth, and Jehiel, and U., Eliab
15. 20 Shemiramoth, and Jehiel, and U., and E.
2. A Levite who returned with Zerubbabel. B.C. 536.
Neh. 12. 9 Also Bakbukiah and U., their brethren

UNOCCUPIED, to be —
To cease, leave off, forbear, חָדַל *chadal.*
Judg. 5. 6 in the days of Jael, the highways were un.

UNPREPARED —
Unprepared, ἀπαρασκεύαστος *aparaskeuastos.*
2 Co. 9. 4 come with me, and find you unprepared

UNPROFITABLE, (to be, become) —
1. *Not to profit, be useful,* לֹא סָכַן *lo sakan.*
Job. 15. 3 Should he reason with unprofitable talk?

2. *Unprofitable, hurtful,* ἀλυσιτελής *alusitelēs.*
Heb. 13. 17 joy, and not with grief; for that (is) un.

3. *Unprofitable*, ἀνωφελής *anōphelēs*.
Titus 3. 9 questions..for they are unprofitable and

4. *Useless, worthless*, ἀχρεῖος *achreios*.
Matt 25. 30 cast ye the unprofitable servant into ou.
Luke 17 10 We are unprofitable servants: we have

5. *To become useless, worthless*, ἀχρειόομαι *achreioom*.
Rom. 3. 12 they are together become unprofitable

6. *Useless, worthless*, ἄχρηστος *achrēstos*.
Phm. 11 Which in time past was to thee unprofit.

UNPROFITABLENESS —
Unprofitable, useless, hurtful, ἀνωφελής *anōphelēs*.
Heb 7. 18 for the weakness and unprofitableness th.

UNPUNISHED, to be or leave —
1. *To be or become innocent, free*, נָקָה *naqah*, 2.
Prov. 11. 21 the wicked shall not be unpunished: but
16. 5 (join) in hand, he shall not be unpunished
17. 5 glad at calamities shall not be unpunished
19. 5, 9 A false witness shall not be unpunished
Jer. 25. 29 utterly unpunished? Ye shall not be un.
49. 12 go unpunished? thou shalt not go unpunis.

2. *To make or declare innocent, free*, נָקָה *naqah*, 3.
Jer. 30. 11 will not leave thee altogether unpunished
46. 28 yet will I not leave thee wholly unpunis.

UNQUENCHABLE—
Unquenchable, unquenched, ἄσβεστος *asbestos*.
Matt. 3. 12 he will burn up the chaff with unquenc.
Luke 3. 17 the chaff he will burn with fire unquenc.

UNREASONABLE —
1. *Irrational, unreasonable*, ἄλογος *alogos*.
Acts 25. 27 it seemeth to me unreasonable to send a

2. *Unsuitable, improper*, ἄτοπος *atopos*.
2 Th. 3. 2 that we may be delivered from unreason.

UNREBUKEABLE —
Irreprehensible, not to be caught, ἀνεπίληπτος.
1 Ti. 6. 14 unrebukeable, until the appearing of our

UNREPROVEABLE —
Not to be called in, unchallengeable, ἀνέγκλητος.
Col. 1. 22 holy and unblameable and unreproveable

UNRIGHTEOUS, unrighteously, unrighteousness —
1. *Iniquity, vanity*, אָוֶן *aven*.
Isa. 10. 1 Woe unto them that decree unrighteous.
55. 7 Let the wicked..and the unrighteous man

2. *Violence*, חָמָס *chamas*.
Exod 23. 1 put not thine hand..to be an unrighteous

3. *To do perversely*, עָוַל *aval*, 3.
Psa. 71. 4 Deliver me..out of the hand of the unri.

4. *Perverse*, עַוָּל *avval*.
Job 27. 7 he that riseth up against me as the unri.

5. *Perverseness, perversity*, עָוֶל, עֶוֶל *avel, evel*.
Lev. 19. 15, 35 Ye shall do no unrighteousness in jud.
Deut. 25. 16 all that do unrighteously, (are) an abom.

6. *Perverseness, perversity*, עַוְלָה [*avlah*] [V.L. עלתה].
Psa. 92. 15 LORD..(there is) no unrighteousness in h.

7. *Not justice, not righteousness*, לֹא צֶדֶק *lo tsedeq*.
Jer. 22. 13 Woe unto him that buildeth..by unrigh.

8. *Injustice, unrighteousness*, ἀδικία *adikia*.
Luke 16. 9 Make..friends of the mammon of unrigh.
John 7. 18 the same is true, and no unrighteousness
Rom. 1. 18 unrighteousness..the truth in unrighteo.
1. 29 Being filled with all unrighteousness, for.
2. 8 obey unrighteousness, indignation and
3. 5 if our unrighteousness commend the rig.
6. 13 your members (as) instruments of unrigh.
9. 14 (Is there) unrighteousness with God? God
2 Th. 2. 10 with all deceivableness of unrighteousne.
2. 12 believed not..but had pleasure in unright.
Heb. 8. 12 I will be merciful to their unrighteousn.
2 Pe. 2. 13 shall receive the reward of unrighteous.
2. 15 who loved the wages of unrighteousness
1 Jo. 1. 9 and to cleanse us from all unrighteousn.
5. 17 All unrighteousness is sin; and there is a

9. *Unjust, unrighteous*, ἄδικος *adikos*.
Luke 16. 11 If..ye have not been faithful in the unri.
Rom. 3. 5 (Is) God unrighteous who taketh venge.?
1 Co. 6. 9 Know ye not that the unrighteous shall
Heb. 6. 10 God (is) not unrighteous to forget your w.

10. *Lawlessness*, ἀνομία *anomia*.
2 Co. 6. 14 fellowship hath righteousness with unri.

UNRIPE grape —
Unripe fruit, בֹּסֶר *beser*.
Job 15. 33 He shall shake off his unripe grape as the

UNRULY —
1. *Unrestrained*, ἀκατάσχετος *akataschetos*.
Jas. 3. 8 the tongue..an [unruly] evil, full of dea.

2. *Not in array, not obedient*, ἀνυπότακτος *anupot*.
Titus 1. 6 faithful children, not accused of riot, or u.
1. 10 there are many unruly and vain talkers

3. *Not in array, disarranged*, ἄτακτος *ataktos*.
1 Th 5. 14 warn them that are unruly, comfort the

UNSATIABLE —
Without satiety, בִּלְתִּי שָׂבְעָה *bilti sobah*.
Eze. 16. 28 played the whore..because thou wast un.

UNSAVOURY, (to shew self) —
1. *To show self a wrestler*, פָּתַל *pathal*, 7.
2 Sa. 22. 27 the froward thou wilt show thyself unsa.

2. *Insipid, untempered*, תָּפֵל *taphel*.
Job 6. 6 Can that which is unsavoury be eaten wi.

UNSEARCHABLE —
1. *There is no searching*, אֵין חֵקֶר *en cheqer*.
Job. 5. 9 Which doeth great things and unsearch.
Psa. 145. 3 Great (is) the LORD..his greatness (is) un.
Prov 25. 3 earth..and the heart of kings (is) unsearc.

2. *Not searched out*, ἀνεξερεύνητος *anexereunētos*.
Rom. 11. 33 how unsearchable (are) his judgments, and

3. *Not traced out*, ἀνεξιχνίαστος *anexichniastos*.
Eph. 3. 8 preach..the unsearchable riches of Chr.

UNSEEMLY, (that which is)—[See BEHAVE SELF.]
Unseemliness, ἀσχημοσύνη *aschemosune*.
Rom. 1. 27 men with men working that which is un.

UNSHOD, being —
Barefoot, unshod, יָחֵף *yacheph*.
Jer. 2. 25 Withhold thy foot from being unshod, and

UNSKILFUL —
Inexperienced, unskilful, ἄπειρος *apeiros*.
Heb. 5. 13 every one that useth milk (is) unskilful

UNSPEAKABLE —
1. *Not led out, inexpressible*, ἀνεκδιήγητος *anekdi.*
2 Co. 9. 15 Thanks (be) unto God for his unspeakab.

2. *Not told out, unspeakable*, ἀνεκλάλητος *aneklalē*.
1 Pe. 1. 8 ye rejoice with joy unspeakable and full

3. *Not uttered, unutterable*, ἄῤῥητος *arrhētos*.
2 Co. 12. 4 heard unspeakable words, which it is not

UNSPOTTED —
Unspotted, ἄσπιλος *aspilos*.
Jas. 1. 27 to keep himself unspotted from the world

UNSTABLE —
1. *Instability, uncertainty*, פַּחַז *pachaz*.
Gen. 49. 4 Unstable as water, thou shalt not excel

2. *Unstable, unsettled*, ἀκατάστατος *akatastatos*.
Jas. 1. 8 A double minded man (is) unstable in

3. *Unconfirmed, unsteady*, ἀστήρικτος *astēriktos*.
2 Pe. 2. 14 eyes full of adultery..beguiling unstable
3. 16 they that are unlearned and unstable wr.

UNSTOPPED, to be —
To be opened, פָּתַח *pathach*, 2.
Isa. 35. 5 and the ears of the deaf shall be unstop.

UNTAKEN away —
Not uncovered, μὴ ἀνακαλυπτόμενον *mē anakalupto.*
2 Co. 3. 14 remaineth the same veil untaken away

UNTEMPERED —
Insipid, untempered, תָּפֵל *taphel*.
Eze. 13. 10 and, lo, others daubed it with untemper.
13. 11 Say unto them which daub (it) with untem.
13. 14 the wall that ye have daubed with unte.
13. 15 upon them that have daubed it with unt.
22. 28 her prophets have daubed them with un.

UNTHANKFUL —
Ungrateful, unthankful, ἀχάριστος *acharistos*.
Luke 6. 35 he is kind unto the unthankful and..the
2 Ti. 3. 2 disobedient to parents, unthankful, unh.

UNTIL—See TILL.

UNTIMELY birth, figs —
1. *A fallen thing, untimely birth*, נֵפֶל, נֶפֶל *nephel*.
Job 3. 16 Or as an hidden untimely birth I had
Psa. 58. 8 (like) the untimely birth of a woman, (th.)
Eccl. 6. 3 (that) an untimely birth (is) better than he

2. *An untimely fig*, ὄλυνθος *olunthos*.
Rev. 6. 13 as a fig tree casteth her untimely figs, wh.

UNTO —See TO.

UNTOWARD —
Crooked, perverse, untoward, σκολιός *skolios*.
Acts 2. 40 Save yourselves from this untoward gene.

UNWALLED (town, village) —
1. *Open villages*, פְּרָזוֹת *perazoth*.
Esth. 9. 19 the Jews..that dwelt in the unwalled to.
Eze. 38. 11 I will go up to the land of unwalled vill.

2. *Inhabitant of an open village*, פְּרָזִי *perazi*.
Deut. 3. 5 besides unwalled towns a great many

UNWASHEN —
Unwashed, ἄνιπτος *aniptos*.
Matt 15. 20 to eat with unwashen hands defileth not
Mark 7. 2 with defiled that is to say, with unwashen
7. 5 walk not..but eat bread with [unwashen]

UNWISE —
1. *Not wise, unwise*, לֹא חָכָם *lo chakam*.
Deut. 32. 6 O foolish people and unwise? (is) not he
Hos. 13. 13 he (is) an unwise son; for he should not

2. *Thoughtless, inconsiderate*, ἀνόητος *anoētos*.
Rom. 1. 14 I am debtor..to the wise and to the unw.

3. *Without a mind or common sense*, ἄφρων *aphrōn*.
Eph. 5. 17 be ye not unwise, but understanding what

UNWITTINGLY —
1. *Without knowledge*, בִּבְלִי דַעַת *bi-beli daath*.
Josh. 20. 3 that killeth..person unawares (and) un.
20. 5 because he smote his neighbour unwitti.

2. *In error*, בִּשְׁגָגָה *bi-shegagah*.
Lev. 22. 14 if a man eat (of) the holy thing unwittin

UNWORTHILY, unworthy —
1. *Unworthy*, ἀνάξιος *anaxios*.
1 Co. 6. 2 unworthy to judge the smallest matter

2. *Unworthily*, ἀναξίως *anaxiōs*.
1 Co. 11. 27 and drink (this) cup of the Lord, unworthily
11. 29 For he that eateth and drinketh [unwort.]

3. *Not worthy*, οὐκ ἄξιος *ouk axios*.
Acts 13. 46 judge yourselves unworthy of everlasting

UP, up to —
1. *Up, over, after*, בְּעַד *bead*.
1 Sa. 1. 6 because the LORD had shut up her womb

2. *Above, upward, onward*, לְמַעְלָה *le-malah*.
Psa. 74. 5 was famous according as he had lifted up

3. *Upward, above*, ἄνω *anō*.
John 11. 41 Jesus lifted up (his) eyes, and said, Father
Heb. 12. 15 lest any root of bitterness springing up tr.

4. *Up to, unto, until*, ἕως *heōs*.
John 2. 7 And they filled them up to the brim

[*See also* Arise, arms, ascend, banners, bear, beforehand, bind, borne, bound, break, breaking, bring, bringer, broken, brought, build, burn, burned, carry, cast, casting, caught, cheer, climb, close, closed, come, cut, deliver, devour, draw, dried, drink, driven, dry, early, eat, ensign, fence, fetch, fill, fold, from, gather, gathered, gaze, get, gird, give, given, giving, go, going, grow, grown, hang, heap, heaved, hedge, help, hold, laid, lay, lead, leap, lick, lift, lift self, lifted, lifter, lifting, look, made, make, mound, mounting, nourish, offer, order, pluck, plucked, pulled, put, raise, raised, reach, rear, reared, receive, rip, rise, risen, rising, root, rooted, rouse, set, sew, shoot, shut, sit, snuff, sought, spring, springeth, stand, stayed, stir, store, suck, sup, swallow, swallowed, take, taken, train, turned, vomit, wake, walled, wrap, wrapped, yield.]

UP, to be —
1. *To rise, burst forth*, זָרַח *zarach*.
Judg. 9. 33 in the morning, as soon as the sun is up

2. *To rise up, stand still*, קוּם *qum*.
Gen. 19. 14 Up, get you out of this place; for the LO.
44. 4 Up, follow after the men; and when thou
Exod 32. 1 Up, make us gods, which shall go before
Josh. 7. 13 Up, sanctify the people, and say, Sanctify
Judg 4. 14 Up; for this (is) the day in which the LO.
8. 20 Up, (and) slay them: but the youth drew
9. 32 Now therefore up by night, thou and the
19. 28 he said unto her, Up, and let us be going
1 Sa. 9. 26 saying, Up, that I may send thee away
2 Sa. 24. 11 For when David was up in the morning

3. *To rise up*, ἀνατέλλω *anatellō*.
Matt 13. 6 when the sun was up, they were scorched
Mark 4. 6 when the sun was up, it was scorched, and

UPBRAID, to —
1. *To reproach, expose*, חָרַף *charaph*, 3.
Judg. 8. 15 Zalmunna, with whom ye did upbraid

2. *To upbraid, reproach, revile*, ὀνειδίζω *oneidizō*.
Matt 11. 20 Then began he to upbraid the cities whe.
Mark 16. 14 [upbraided them with their unbelief and]
Jas. 1. 5 God, that giveth to all..liberally, and up.

U PHAR'-SIN, וּפַרְסִין *and divided*.
Dan. 5. 25 this (is) the writing..Mene, Mene, Tekel, U.

U-PHAZ, אוּפָז.
A place in S. Arabia; or a corruption of *Ophir*.
Jer. 10. 9 Silver..is brought..and gold from U.
Dan. 10. 5 whose loins..girded with fine gold of U.

UPHOLD, be upholden, to —
1. *To sustain, support, lean*, סָמַךְ *samak*.
Psa. 37. 17 but the LORD upholdeth the righteous
37. 24 for the LORD upholdeth his hand
51. 12 Restore..and uphold me (with thy) free S.
54. 4 the LORD (is) with them that uphold my
119. 116 Uphold me according unto thy word, that
145. 14 The LORD upholdeth all that fall, and
Isa. 63. 5 I wondered that (there was) none to uph.
63. 5 therefore mine own arm..it upheld me
Eze. 30. 6 They also that uphold Egypt shall fall, and

2. *To support, refresh*, סָעַד *saad*.
Prov 20. 28 the king..his throne is upholden by mercy

3. *To rise up, stand still*, קוּם *qum*.
Job 4. 4 Thy words have upholden him that was fa.

4. *To hold up, retain*, תָּמַךְ *tamak*.
Psa. 41. 12 as for me, thou upholdest me in mine int.
63. 8 My soul..thy right hand upholdeth me
Prov 29. 23 honour shall uphold the humble in spirit
Isa. 41. 10 I will uphold thee with the right hand of
42. 1 Behold my servant, whom I uphold, mine

5. *To bear, carry*, φέρω *pherō*.
Heb. 1. 3 upholding all things by the word of his

UPON —
1. *Unto*, אֶל *el*.
Gen. 22. 12 Lay not thine hand upon the lad, neither

2. *Behind, after*, בְּעַד *bead*.
Judg. 3. 22 the fat closed upon the blade, so that he
2 Ki. 4. 4 shut the door upon thee and upon thy son
4. 5 shut the door upon her and upon her sons

3. *To*, לְמוֹ *lemo*.
Job 40. 4 Behold..I will lay my hand upon my mo.

4. *From*, מִן *min.*
Ezra 7. 26 let judgment be executed speedily upon
5. *Above*, מִמַּעַל *mim-maal.*
Gen. 22. 9 and laid him on the altar upon the wood
Jer. 43. 10 will set his throne upon these stones that
Dan. 12. 6, 7 which (was) upon the waters of the ri.
6. *On, upon, above, over*, עַל *al.*
Gen. 1. 2 darkness (was) upon the face of the deep
1. 2 spirit of God moved upon the face of the
7. *From on, from above*, מֵעַל *me-al.*
Gen. 40. 17 birds did eat them out of the basket upon
Ezra 5. 5 the eye of their God was upon the elders
7. 17 offer them upon the altar of the house of
7. 24 not be lawful to impose toll..upon them
Dan. 2. 10 There is not a man upon the earth that can
2. 28 the visions of thy head upon thy bed, are
2. 29 thy thoughts came (into thy mind) upon
2. 34 stone..which smote the image upon his fe.
2. 46 Nebuchadnezzar fell upon his face, and wo.
4. 5 the thoughts upon my bed and the visions
4. 13 I saw in the visions of my head upon my
4. 24 which is come upon my lord the king
4. 28 All this came upon the king Nebuchadn.
4. 33 The same hour was the thing fulfilled upon
5. 5 upon the plaster of the wall of the king's
6. 17 a stone was brought, and laid upon the
7. 1 a dream and visions of his head upon his
7. 4 made stand upon the feet as a man, and
7. 6 which had upon the back of it four wings
8. *With*, עִמָּד *immad.*
Job 10. 17 and increasest thine indignation upon me
9. *On the face of*, עַל־פְּנֵי *al pene.*
Lev. 16. 14 sprinkle (it) with his finger upon the me.
10. *From*, ἀπό *apo.*
Acts 11. 19 scattered abroad upon the persecution th
11. *In regard to, with a view to, toward, at*, εἰς *eis.*
Matt 26. 10 she hath wrought a good work upon me
27. 30 they spit upon him, and took the reed, and
Mark 13. 3 as he sat upon the mount of Olives, over
Luke 8. 43 which had spent all her living [upon] ph.
18. 13 smote [upon] his breast, saying, God be me.
Acts 3. 4 Peter, fastening his eyes upon him with
11. 6 Upon the which when I had fastened mine
22. 13 And the same hour I looked up upon him
27. 26 we must be cast upon a certain island
27. 29 fearing lest we should have fallen [upon]
Rom. 5. 12 death passed upon all men, for that all
5. 18 (judgment came) upon all men to conde.
5. 18 (the free gift came) upon all men unto ju.
13. 6 attending continually upon this very th.
1 Co. 10. 11 upon whom the ends of the world are co.
15. 10 his grace which (was bestowed) upon me
2 Co. 1. 11 that for the gift (bestowed) upon us by
Gal. 4. 11 lest I have bestowed upon you labour in
Rev. 8. 7 they were cast upon the earth: and the
9. 3 there came out of the smoke locusts upon
16. 1 pour..the vials of the wrath of God upon
16. 2 grievous sore [upon] the men which had
16. 3 the second angel poured out his vial upon
16. 4 out his vial upon the rivers and upon
12. *In, during, among*, ἐν *en.*
Matt 12. 2 that which is not lawful to do upon the
Luke 21. 23 distress in the land, and wrath [upon] this
Acts 20. 7 upon the first..of the week, when the di.
Jas. 4. 3 Ye ask..that ye may consume (it) upon
13. *Above, upon, over*, ἐπάνω *epanō.*
Matt 23. 18 whosoever sweareth by the gift..upon it
28. 2 and rolled back the stone..and sat upon
Rev. 20. 3 shut him up, and set a seal upon him, that
14. *On, upon*, ἐπί (*gen.*) *epi.*
Matt. 6. 19 Lay not up for yourselves treasures upon
See also 10. 27; 23. 9, 35; 24. 3; 25. 31; Mark 6. 48, 49; 7. 30; Luke 5. 24; 12. 3; 17. 31; 21. 25; Jo. 19. 31; Acts 12. 21; Rom. 9. 28; Col. 3. 5; Heb. 6. 7; Rev. 3. 10, 10; 5. 7, 13; 7. 10; 10. 1, 5, 5, 8, 8; 11. 10; 12. 1; 13. 1, 8; 16. 18; 17. 1; 18. 24; 19. 21; 21. 5.
15. *On, upon, over*, ἐπί (*dat.*) *epi.*
Matt 16. 18 and upon this rock I will build my church
See also Mark 6. 39; 11. 7; 13. 2; Luke 19. 44; 21. 6; John 4. 27; 11. 38; Acts 8. 16; Eph. 2. 20; 4. 26; Phil. 1. 3; 2. 17, 27; Heb. 8. 6; Rev. 19. 14.
16. *On, upon, over, up to*, ἐπί (*acc.*) *epi.*
Matt. 3. 16 descending like a dove, and lighting upon
See also 7. 24, 25, 26; 9. 18; 10. 13; 11. 29; 12. 18; 13. 5; 19. 28; 21. 5; 23. 35, 36; 24. 2; 27. 29, [35]; Mark 1. [10]; 8. 25; 10. 16; 15. 24; Luke 1. 12, 35; 2. 25, 40; 3. 22; 4. 18; 5. 19, 36; 6. 48, [49]; 8. 6; 9. 38; 10. 6; 11. 20; 13. 4; 19. 35; 19. 43; 20. 18; 21. 34; 24. 49; John 1. 32, 33, 51; 9. 15; 18. 4; Acts 1. 8, 26; 2. 3, 17; 4. 33; 5. 11, 11, 28; 7. 57; 8. 24; 10. 9; 13. 11, [40]; 15. 10, 17; 18. 6; 21. 35; 26. 16; Rom. 2. 9; 3. [22]; 4. 9; 15. 20; 1 Co. 3. 12; 2 Co. 1. 23; 3. 15; 12. 9; Gal. 6. 16; Eph. 5. 6; 1 Th. 2. 16; Heb. 11. 21; Jas. 2. 21; 1 Pe. 4. 14; 5. 7; Rev. 1. 17; 2. 24; 3. 3, 12; 4. 4; 8. 3, 10, 10; 10. 2; 11. 11, 11, 16; 12. 3; 13. 1, 1; 14. 14; 16. [2], 8, 10, 12, 21; 17. 3, 5, [16]; 19. 11; 20. 4, 4.
17. *Down from, against, toward*, κατά (*gen.*) *kata.*
Jude 15 To execute judgment upon all, and to co.
18. *Down to, over against*, κατά (*acc.*) *kata.*
1 Co. 16. 2 Upon the first..of the week let every one
19. *With*, μετά (*gen.*) *meta.*
Luke 1. 58 how the Lord had showed..mercy upon

[*See also* Attend, beat, bestow, blow, bring, burn, burn incense, build, call, cast, clothed, come, compassion, fall, get hold, grew, hold, lay, light, look, mercy, pity, press, put, rained, rest, run, seize, sit, spread, spit, stamp, take, think, tread, wait, waiting.]

UPPER, (room or chamber), uppermost —
1. *Upper*, עִלִּי *illi.*
Josh 15. 19 he gave her the upper springs, and the ne.
Judg. 1. 15 gave her the upper springs and the nether
2. *Upper, uppermost, highest*, עֶלְיוֹן *elyon.*
Gen. 40. 17 in the uppermost basket..of all manner
Josh 16. 5 Ataroth-adar, unto Beth-horon the upper
2 Ki. 18. 17 stood by the conduit of the upper pool
1 Ch. 7. 24 Beth-horon the nether, and the upper, and
2 Ch. 8. 5 he built Beth-horon the upper, and Beth.
32. 30 Hezekiah also stopped the upper water
Isa. 7. 3 at the end of the conduit of the upper po.
36. 2 stood by the conduit of the upper pool
Eze. 42. 5 the upper chambers (were) shorter, for
3. *Upper chamber, above the ground*, ἀνώγεον *anōg.*
Mark 14. 15 he shall show you a large upper room fu.
Luke 22. 12 he shall show you a large upper room fu.
4. *Above, higher*, ἀνωτερικός *anōterikos.*
Acts 19. 1 Paul having passed through the upper co.
5. *An upper chamber*, ὑπερῷον *huperōon.*
Acts 1. 13 they went up into an upper room, where
9. 37 had washed, they laid..in an upper cham.
9. 39 they brought him into the upper chamber
20. 8 there were many lights in the upper cha.
[*See also* Chamber, doorpost, lintel, lip, millstone, room, seat.]

UPRIGHT (most), uprightly, uprightness —
1. *Upright*, יָשָׁר *yashar.*
1 Sa. 29. 6 the LORD liveth, thou hast been upright
2 Ch. 29. 34 the Levites (were) more upright in heart
Job 1. 1 that man was perfect and upright, and one
1. 8 a perfect and an upright man, one that
2. 3 a perfect and an upright man, one that
8. 6 If thou (wert) pure and upright, surely
17. 8 Upright (men) shall be astonied at this, and
Psa. 7. 10 defence (is) of God, which saveth the up.
11. 2 they may privily shoot at the upright in
11. 7 his countenance doth behold the upright
25. 8 Good and upright (is) the LORD: therefore
32. 11 shout for joy, all (ye that are) upright in
33. 1 Rejoice..praise is comely for the upright
36. 10 thy righteousness to the upright in heart
37. 14 to slay such as be of upright conversation
37. 37 Mark the perfect (man), and behold the u.
49. 14 the upright shall have dominion over th.
64. 10 and all the upright in heart shall glory
92. 15 To show that the LORD (is) upright, (he
94. 15 and all the upright in heart shall follow
97. 11 Light (is) sown..and gladness for the up.
111. 1 in the assembly of the upright, and (in)
111. 8 (and are) done in truth and uprightness
112. 2 the generation of the upright shall be bl.
112. 4 Unto the upright there ariseth light in the
119. 137 Righteous (art) thou, O LORD, and upri.
125. 4 to (them that are) upright in their heart
140. 13 the upright shall dwell in thy presence
Prov. 2. 21 the upright shall dwell in the land, and
11. 3 The integrity of the upright shall guide
11. 6 The righteousness of the upright shall de.
11. 11 By the blessing of the upright the city is
12. 6 the mouth of the upright shall deliver th.
14. 11 the tabernacle of the upright shall flour.
15. 8 but the prayer of the upright (is) his del.
16. 17 The highway of the upright (is) to depart
21. 18 and the transgressor for the upright
21. 29 (as for) the upright, he directeth his way
29. 27 (he that is) upright in the way (is) abomi.
Eccl. 7. 29 God hath made man upright; but they
Isa. 26. 7 thou, most upright, dost weigh the path
Dan. 11. 17 to enter..and upright ones with him
Mic. 2. 7 do good to him that walketh uprightly
7. 2 (there is) none upright among men: they
7. 4 the most upright (is sharper) than a thorn
2. *Uprightness*, יֹשֶׁר *yosher.*
Deut. 9. 5 Not..for the uprightness of thine heart
1 Ki. 9. 4 in integrity of heart, and in uprightness
1 Ch. 29. 17 that thou..hast pleasure in uprightness
Job 33. 3 My words (shall be of) the uprightness of
33. 23 one..to show unto man his uprightness
Psa. 25. 21 Let integrity and uprightness preserve
119. 7 I will praise thee with uprightness of he.
Prov. 2. 13 Who leave the paths of uprightness, to
14. 2 He that walketh in his uprightness fear.
Eccl. 12. 10 (that which was) written (was) upright
3. *Uprightness*, יְשָׁרָה *yishrah.*
1 Ki. 3. 6 walked..in uprightness of heart with thee
4. *Uprightness*, מִישׁוֹר *mishor.*
Psa. 143. 10 God..lead me into the land of uprightn.
5. *Uprightness*, מֵישָׁרִים *mesharim.*
1 Ch. 29. 17 triest the heart, and hast pleasure in up.
Psa. 9. 8 shall minister..to the people in upright.
58. 1 do ye judge uprightly, O ye sons of men?
75. 2 I shall receive..I will judge uprightly
Song. 1. 4 we will remember thy love..the upright
Isa. 26. 7 The way of the just (is) uprightness
33. 15 walketh righteously, and speaketh uprig.
6. *Straightforward*, נָכֹחַ *nakoach.*
Isa. 26. 10 in the land of uprightness will he deal
57. 2 He shall enter..walking (in) his upright.

7. *In my place*, עַל־עָמְדִי [*omed*].
Dan. 8. 18 sleep..but he touched me, and set me up.
10. 11 understand the words..stand upright, for
8. *Upright, erect*, קוֹמְמִיּוּת *qomemiyyuth.*
Lev. 26. 13 broken the..yoke, and made you go upri.
9. *Stiffness, beaten work*, מִקְשָׁה *miqshah.*
Jer. 10. 5 They (are) upright as the palm tree, but
10. *Perfect, plain*, תָּם *tam.*
Prov. 29. 10 The blood thirsty hate the upright, but
11. *Perfection, integrity*, תֹּם *tom.*
Job 4. 6 thy hope, and the uprightness of thy ways
Prov. 2. 7 a buckler to them that walk uprightly
10. 9 He that walketh uprightly walketh surely
10. 29 way of the LORD (is) strength to the upri.
13. 6 Righteousness keepeth (him that is) upr.
28. 6 Better..the poor that walketh in his upr.
12. *Perfect, complete, plain*, תָּמִים *tamim.*
2 Sa. 22. 24 I was also upright before him, and have
22. 26 with the upright man thou wilt show th.
Job 12. 4 the just upright (man is) laughed to scorn
Psa. 15. 2 He that walketh uprightly, and worketh
18. 23 I was also upright before him, and I kept
18. 25 with an upright man. wilt show thyself
37. 18 The LORD knoweth the days of the upri.
84. 11 withhold from them that walk uprightly
Prov. 11. 20 (such as are) upright in their way (are)
28. 10 the upright shall have good (things) in po.
28. 18 Whoso walketh uprightly shall be saved
Amos 5. 10 they abhor him that speaketh uprightly
13. *To make right or straight*, יָשַׁר *yashar*, 3.
Prov. 15. 21 a man of understanding walketh uprightly
14. *Upright, erect, straight*, ὀρθός *orthos.*
Acts 14. 10 Said with a loud voice, Stand upright on

UPRIGHT, to be or show one self —
1. *To be upright*, יָשַׁר *yashar.*
Hab. 2. 4 his soul (which) is lifted up is not upright
2. *To be perfect*, תָּמַם *tamam.*
Psa. 19. 13 then shall I be upright, and I shall be in
3. *To show self perfect*, תָּמַם *tamam*, 7.
2 Sa. 22. 26 with..man thou wilt show thyself uprig
Psa. 18. 25 with..man thou wilt show thyself upright

UPRISING —
To rise up, stand still, קוּם *qum.*
Psa. 139. 2 Thou knowest..mine up rising, thou und.

UPROAR, to be in, make, set on an —
1. *To roar, make a noise*, הָמָה *hamah.*
1 Ki. 1. 41 (this) noise of the city being in an uproar
2. *To set up, excite*, ἀναστατόω *anastatoō.*
Acts 21. 38 which before these days madest an uproar
3. *Tumult, tumultuous assembly*, θόρυβος *thorubos.*
Matt. 26. 5 lest there be an uproar among the peop.
Mark 14. 2 Not..lest there be an uproar of the people
Acts 20. 1 after the uproar was ceased, Paul called
4. *To be tumultuous*, θορυβέομαι *thorubeomai.*
Acts 17. 5 set all the city on an uproar, and assaulted
5. *To pour out or mix together*, συγχύνω *sugchunō.*
Acts 21. 31 came..that all Jerusalem was in an uproar
6. *Standing up, upstanding*, στάσις *stasis.*
Acts 19. 40 called in question for this day's uproar

UPSIDE (down) —
On the face of it, עַל־פָּנֶיהָ [*al*].
2 Ki. 21. 13 wiping (it), and turning (it) upside down
[*See* Turn.]

UPWARD —
1. *To cause to go up high*, גָּבַהּ *gabah*, 5.
Job 5. 7 born unto trouble, as the sparks fly upw.
2. *Above, from above, upward*, לְמַעְלָה, מִלְמַעְלָה *le-malah.*
Gen. 7. 20 Fifteen cubits upward did the waters pr.
Exod 38. 26 numbered, from twenty years old and up.
Num. 1. 3 From twenty years old and upward, all that
So in verse 18, 20, 22, 24, 26, 28, 30, 32, 34, 36, 38, 40, 42, 45.
3. 15, 22, 28, 34, 39, 40, 43 month old and upward
4. 3, 23, 30, 35, 39, 43, 47 years old and upward
8. 24 from twenty and five years old and upwa.
14. 29 from twenty years old and upward, which
26. 2, 4 from twenty years old and upward
26. 62 all males from a month old and upward
32. 11 none..from twenty years old and upward
Judg. 1. 36 to Akrabbim, from the rock, and upward
1 Sa. 9. 2 from his shoulders and upward (he was)
10. 23 higher..from his shoulders and upward
2 Ki. 3. 21 able to put on armour, and upward and
1 Ch. 23. 3 from the age of thirty years and upward
23. 24 from the age of twenty years and upward
2 Ch. 31. 16 from three years old and upward, (even)
31. 17 Levites from twenty years old and upwa.
Ezra 3. 8 Levites, from twenty years old and upwa.
Eccl. 3. 21 the spirit of man that goeth upward, and
Isa. 8. 21 and curse their king..and look upward
37. 31 take root downward, and bear fruit upw.
Eze. 1. 11 their wings (were) stretched upward, two
1. 27 from the appearance of his loins even up.
8. 2 from his loins even upward, as the appea.
41. 7 still upward..went still upward..upward
43. 15 from the altar and upward (shall be) four
Hag. 2. 15 consider from this day and upward, from
2. 18 Consider now from this day and upward
3. *High place, on high*, מָרוֹם *marom.*
Isa. 38. 14 mine eyes fail (with looking) upward, O

UR, אור *light, brightness.*

1. A city or district in N. Mesopotamia; perhaps *Mugheir*, six miles W. of the Euphrates, midway between Babylon and the Persian Gulf. (*Orfa? Warkah?*).

Gen. 11. 28 And Haran died..in U. of the Chaldees
11. 31 they went forth with them from U. of the
15. 7 LORD..brought thee out of U. of the Ch.
Neh. 9. 7 God..broughtest him forth out of U. of

2. Father of Eliphal, one of David's valiant men. B.C. 1070.

1 Ch. 11. 35 Sacar the Hararite, Eliphal the son of U.

UR'-BANE, Οὐρβανός. (Latin, *Urbanus.*)

A believer in Rome to whom Paul sends a salutation.

Rom 16. 9 Salute U. our helper in Christ, and Stac.

URGE, be urgent, to —

1. *To urge,* אָלַץ *alats*, 3.
Judg 16. 16 urged him..that his soul was vexed unto

2. *To be strong, firm,* חָזַק *chazaq.*
Exod 12. 33 the Egyptians were urgent upon the peo.

3. *To be urgent,* חָצַף *chatsaph*, 5.
Dan. 3. 22 because the king's commandment was urg.

4. *To press,* פָּצַר *patsar.*
Gen. 33. 11 Take, I pray thee..And he urged him, and
Judg 19. 7 rose up to depart, his father in law urged
2 Ki. 2. 17 when they urged him till he was ashamed
5. 16 he urged him to take (it): but he refused

5. *To break, spread, burst forth, down, in,* פָּרַץ *parats.*
2 Ki. 5. 23 he urged him, and bound two talents of

6. *To hold in,* ἐνέχω *enechō.*
Luke 11. 53 the Pharisees began to urge (him) vehem.

UR'-I, אוּרִי, אֻרִי *enlightened.*

1. Son of Hur, and father of Bezaleel, who was filled with the spirit of wisdom to prepare the tabernacle. B.C. 1525.

Exod 31. 2 See, I have called..the son of U., the son
35. 30 LORD hath called..the son of U., the son
38. 22 Bezaleel the son of U...made all that the
1 Ch. 2. 20 And Hur begat U., and U. begat Bezaleel
2 Ch. 1. 5 brasen altar, that..the son of U...had ma.

2. Father of Geber, one of Solomon's officers in Gilead. B.C. 1040.

1 Ki. 4. 19 Geber the son of U. (was) in the country

3. A gatekeeper that had taken a strange wife during the exile. B.C. 445.

Ezra 10. 24 the porters; Shallum, and Telem, and U.

U-RI'-AH, U-RI'-JAH, אוּרִיָּה, אוּרִיָּהוּ *Jah is light.*

1. A Hittite, husband of Bath-sheba, and one of David's valiant men. B.C. 1048.

2 Sa. 11. 3 (Is) not this Bath-sheba..the wife of U.
11. 6 Send me U...And Joab sent U. to David
11. 7 when U. was come unto him, David dem.
11. 8 David said to U., Go down to thy house
11. 8 And U. departed out of the king's house
11. 9 But U. slept at the door of the king's ho.
11. 10 saying, U. went not down unto his house
11. 10 David said unto U., Camest thou not from
11. 11 U. said unto David, The ark, and Israel
11. 12 David said to U., Tarry here to day also
11. 12 So U. abode in Jerusalem that day, and
11. 14 David wrote..and sent..by the hand of U.
11. 15 Set ye U. in the forefront of the hottest
11. 16 he assigned U. unto a place where he kn.
11. 17 there fell (some)..and U. the Hittite died
11. 21, 24 Thy servant U. the Hittite is dead also
11. 26 the wife of U. heard that U. her husband
12. 9 thou hast killed U. the Hittite with the
12. 10 thou..hast taken the wife of U...to be thy
12. 15 the LORD struck the child that U.'s wife
23. 39 U. the Hittite: thirty and seven in all
1 Ki. 15. 5 save only in the matter of U. the Hittite
1 Ch. 11. 41 U. the Hittite, Zabad the son of Ahlai

2. A priest in Jerusalem, who built an altar according to the pattern sent him by king Ahaz. B.C. 740.

2 Ki. 16. 10 Ahaz sent to U. the priest the fashion of
16. 11 U. the priest built an altar according to
16. 11 so U. the priest made (it) against king A.
16. 15 king Ahaz commanded U. the priest, sa.
16. 16 Thus did U. the priest, according to all

3. A priest, father of Meremoth, who rebuilt part of the wall of Jerusalem at the instance of Nehemiah. B.C. 445.

Ezra 8. 33 by the hand of Meremoth the son of U.
Neh. 3. 4, 21 them repaired Meremoth the son of U.

4. A priest, Levite, or ruler who stood beside Ezra when he read the book of the law to the people. B.C. 470.

Neh. 8. 4 beside him stood..U., and Hilkiah, and

5. A priest whom Isaiah took as a witness. B.C. 740.

Isa. 8. 2 I took unto me..U. the priest, and Zech.

6. A prophet, son of Shemaiah, whom Jehoiakim sent for into Egypt and slew him. B.C. 609.

Jer. 26. 20 U...prophesied against this city and ag.
26 21 when U. heard it, he was afraid, and fled
26. 23 they fetched forth U. out of Egypt, and

U-RI'-AS, Οὐρίας. See *Uriah.*

The husband of Bath-sheba, Solomon's mother.

Matt. 1. 6 and David..begat Solomon of her..of U.

U-RI'-EL, אוּרִיאֵל *God is light.*

1. A Kohathite, son of Tahath. B.C. 1460.

1 Ch. 6. 24 Tahath his son, U. his son Uzziah his son
1 Ch. 15. 5 U. the chief, and his brethren an hundr.
15. 11 David called..for the Levites, for U., As.

2. Father of Michaiah, one of Rehoboam's wives; a Gibeathite. B.C. 1010.

2 Ch. 13. 2 Michaiah the daughter of U. of Gibeah

U'-RIM, אוּרִים *lights.*

Mentioned along with *Thummim*, as something in the high priest's breastplate that gave an oracular response.

Exod 28. 30 thou shalt put in the breastplate..the U.
Lev. 8. 8 he put in the breastplate the U. and the
Num 27. 21 after the judgment of U. before the LORD
Deut. 33. 8 (Let) thy Thummim and thy U. (be) with
1 Sa. 28. 6 LORD answered him not, neither..by U. nor
Ezra 2. 63 till there stood up a priest with U. and
Neh. 7. 65 till there stood (up) a priest with U. and

US —

1. *We, we ourselves,* אֲנַחְנוּ *anachnu.*
Deut. 5. 3 (even) us, who (are) all..here alive this
Neh. 4. 23 none of us put off our clothes..every one

2. *Into our hand,* בְּיָדֵנוּ *be-yad-enu.*
Exod 10. 25 Thou must give us also sacrifices and bu.

3. *Our eye,* עֵינֵנוּ *en-enu.*
2 Sa. 20. 6 lest..get him fenced cities, and escape us

4. *Us,* ἡμᾶς *hēmas.*
Matt. 6. 13 lead us not into temptation, but deliver us
See also 8. [25], 29, 31; 9. 27; 13. 56; 17. 4; 20. 7, 30, 31; 27. 4, 25; Mark 1. 24; 5. 12; 6. 3; 9. 5, 22; Luke 1. 71, 78; 4. 34; 7. 20; 9. 33; 11. 1, 4, [4], 45; 12. 41; 16. 26; 17. 13; 19. 14; 20. 6; 23. 30, 30, 39; 24. 22; John 1. 22; 9. 34; Acts 1. 21; 3. 4; 5. 28; 7. [27], 40; 11. 15; 14. 11; 16. 10, 15, 37, 37, 37; 20. 5; 21. 5, 11, 17; 27. 6, 7; 28. 2, 7, 10; Rom. 4. 24; 5. 8; 8. 18, 35, 37, 39; 9. 24; 15. [7]; 16. [6]; 1 Co. 4. 1, 9; 6. 14; 7. [15]; 8. 8; 2 Co. 1. 4, 5, 10, 11, 14, 21, 21, 22; 2. 14; 3. 6; 4. 14; 5. 5, 14, 18; 7. 2, 6; 8. 20; 10. 2; Gal. 1. 4, 23; 2. 4; 3. 13; 5. 1; Eph. 1. 3, 4, 5, 6, 8, 19; 2. 4, 7; 5. [2]; Phil. 3. 17; Col. 1. 12, 13; 1 Th. 1. 10; 2. [15], 16, 18; 3. 6, 6; 4. 7, [8]; 5. 9; 2 Th. 2. 16; 3. 7, 9; 2 Ti. 1. 9; 2. 12; Titus 2. 12, 14; 3. 5, 6, 15; Heb 2. 3; Jas. 1. 18; 1 Pe. 1. 3; 3. [18, 21]; 5. [10]; 2 Pe. 1. 3; 3. [9]; 1 Jo. 1. 7, 9; 3. 1; 4. 10, 11, 19; 3 Jo. 9, 10; Rev. 1. 5, 5, [6]; 5. [9, 10]; 6. 16, 16.

5. *We, we ourselves,* ἡμεῖς *hēmeis.*
John 11. 16 Let us also go, that we may die He. 12. 1.

6. *To us,* ἡμῖν *hēmin.*
Matt. 3. 15 thus it becometh us to fulfil all righteou.
See also 6. 11, 12; 8. [31]; 13. 36; 15. 15; 20. 12; 21. 25; 22. 17, 25; 24. 3; 25. 8, 9, 11; 26. 63, 68; Mark 9. 22, [38, 38]; 10. 35, 37; 12. 19; 13. 4; 14. 15; 16. 3; Luke 1. 1, 2, 69, 74; 2. 15, 48; 7. 5, 16; 10. 11, 17; 11. 3, 4, 4; 13. 25; 20. 2, [22], 28; 22. 8, 67; 23. 18; 24. 24, [32], 32, 32; John 1. 14; 2. 18; 4. 12, 25; 6. 34, 52; 8. [5]; 10. 24; 11. [50]; 14. 8, 8, 22; 16. 17; 17. 21; 18. 31; Acts 1. 17, 21, 22; 2. 29; 3. 12; 6. 14; 7. 38, 40; 10. 41, 42; 11. 13, 17; 13. [33], 47; 14. [17]; 15. 7, 8, 25, 28; 16. 9, 16, 17, [17], 21; 20. 14; 21. 16, 18; 25. 24; 27. 2; 28. 2, 15; Rom. 5. 5; 8. 4, 32; 9. 29; 12. 6; 1 Co. 1. 18, 30; 2. 10, 12; 4. 6; 8. 6; 15. 57; 2 Co. 1. [8]; 4. 12, 17; 5. 5, 18, 19; 6. 12; 7. 7; 10. [8], 13; Eph. 1. 9; 3. 20; Col. 1. 8; 2. 14; 4. 3; 1 Th. 2. 8; 3. 6; 1 Ti. 6. 17; 2 Ti. 1. 7, 9, 14; Heb. 1. 2; 7. 26; 10. 15, 20; 12. 1; Jas. 3. 3; 4. 5; 1 Pe. 1. [12]; 2. [21]; 4. [3]; 2 Pe. 1. 1, 3, 4; 1 Jo. 1. 2, 8, 9, 10; 2. 25; 3. 1, [23], 24, 24; 4. 9, 12, 12, 13, 13, 16; 5. 11, 20; 2 Jo. 2.

7. *Of us,* ἡμῶν *hēmōn.*
Matt. 1. 23 which being interpreted is, God with us
See also Matt. 15. 23; Mark 9. [40]; Luke 9. 49, [50, 50]; 16. 26; 24. 29; Acts 1. 22; 7. 40; 15. 9, 24; 17. 27; 24. 4; 28. 15; Rom. 4. 16; 5. 8; 8. [26], 31, 31, 32, 34; 14. 7, 12; 15. 2; 1 Co. 4. 8; 5. [7]; 2 Co. 1. 11, 19, 20; 2. 14; 3. 3; 4. 7; 5. 20, 21; 7. 9; 8. 4, 19, 19, 20; 9. 11; Gal. 3. 13; 4. 26; Eph. 4. 7; 5. [2]; Col. 2. 14; 4. 3; 1 Th. 1. 6, 9; 2. 13; 3. 6; 4. 1; 5. 10, 25; 2 Th. 1. 7; 2. 2; 3. 1, 6; Titus 2. 14; Heb. 6. 20; 9. 24; 11. 40, 40; 13. 18; 1 Pe. 2. [21]; 4. [1], 17; 2 Pe. 3. [2]; 1 Jo. 1. 3; 2. 19, 19, 19, 19, 19; 3. 16, 20, 21; 4. 6, 6; 5. [14], 15; 2 John 2.

8. *Our soul,* τὴν ψυχὴν ἡμῶν *tēn psuchēn hēmōn.*
John 10. 24 How long dost thou make us to doubt?

USE (be used, to), using —

1. *To say,* אָמַר *amar.*
Jer. 31. 23 As yet they shall use this speech in the

2. *To speak,* דָּבַר *dabar*, 3.
Prov. 18. 23 The poor useth entreaties; but the rich

3. *Work, occupation,* מְלָאכָה *melakah.*
Lev. 7. 24 and the fat..may be..in any other use

4. *Taught,* לִמּוּד *limmud.*
Jer. 2. 24 A wild ass used to the wilderness, (that)

5. *To take, receive,* לָקַח *laqach.*
Jer. 23. 31 that use their tongues, and say, He saith

6. *To speak proverbially,* מָשַׁל *mashal.*
Eze. 18. 2 What mean ye, that ye use this proverb
18 3 ye shall not have..any more to use this

7. *To do, make,* עָשָׂה *asah.*
Eze. 35. 11 which thou hast used out of thy hatred

8. *To be done, made,* עָשָׂה *asah*, 2.
Lev. 7. 24 and the fat..may be used in any other

9. *Service,* עֲבוֹדָה *abodah.*
1 Ch. 28. 15 according to the use of every candlestick

10. *To oppress,* עָשַׁק *ashaq.*
Eze. 22. 29 The people of the land have used oppre.

11. *To divine, use divination,* קָסַם *qasam.*
Deut 18. 10 that useth divination, (or) an observer of
2 Ki. 17. 17 they..used divination and enchantments
Eze. 21. 21 the king of Babylon stood..to use divina.

12. *Judgment,* מִשְׁפָּט *mishpat.*
Psa. 119 132 as thou usest to do unto those that love

13. *To turn up,* ἀναστρέφω *anastrephō.*
Heb. 10. 33 companions of them that were so used

14. *Use, consumption by use,* ἀπόχρησις *apochrēsis.*
Col. 2. 22 Which are all to perish with the using

15. *To come in or with,* γίνομαι ἐν *ginomai en.*
1 Th. 2. 5 For neither at any time used we flattering

16. *Habit, use,* ἕξις *hexis.*
Heb. 5. 14 those who by reason of use have their se.

17. *To have,* ἔχω *echō.*
1 Pe. 2. 16 As free, and not using..liberty for a clo

18. *To be,* εἰμί *eimi.*
Mark 2. 18 the disciples..of the Pharisees used to f

19. *To hold with,* μετέχω *metechō.*
Heb. 5. 13 every one that useth milk (is) unskilful

19*a*. *Practise,* πράσσω *prassō.* Acts 19. 19.

20. *To use, make use of,* χράομαι *chraomai.*
Acts 27. 17 Which, when they had taken up, they us.
1 Co. 7. 21 if thou mayest be made free, use; 7. 31.
9. 12 Nevertheless we have not used this pow.
9. 15 But I have used none of these things
2 Co. 1. 17 When I..was thus minded, did I use lig.?
3. 12 Seeing..we have such hope, we use great
13. 10 lest being present I should use sharpness
1 Ti. 1. 8 the law (is) good, if a man use it lawfully
5. 23 use a little wine for thy stomach's sake

21. *Necessary business, use, need,* χρεία *chreia.*
Eph. 4. 29 that which is good to the use of edifying
Titus 3. 14 maintain good works for necessary uses

22. *Use, manner of using,* χρῆσις *chrēsis.*
Rom. 1. 26 did change the natural use into that v. 27.

23. *To practise,* πράσσω *prassō*, Acts 19. 19.

USE deceit, despitefully, to —

1. *To deceive,* δολιόω *dolioō.*
Rom. 3. 13 with their tongues they have used deceit

2. *To injure, harass, criminate,* ἐπηρεάζω *epēreazō.*
Matt. 5. 44 which despitefully use you, and persecute
Luke 6. 28 pray for them which despitefully use you

3. *To insult, injure,* ὑβρίζω *hubrizō.*
Acts 14. 5 to use..despitefully, and to stone them
[*See also* Aright, arts, enchantment, hospitality, many, proverb, right hand, service, sorcery.]

USURP authority over, to —

To exercise power of one's self, αὐθεντέω *authenteō.*
1 Ti. 2. 12 not to usurp authority over the man, but

USURY, to give, lend on, take, be lent upon —

1. *To exact,* נָשָׁא *nasha.*
Isa. 24. 2 as with..so with the giver of usury to him

2. *An exaction,* מַשָּׁא *mashsha.*
Neh. 5. 7 Ye exact usury, every one of his brother
5. 10 I pray you, let us leave off this usury

3. *To exact,* נָשָׁה *nashah.*
Exod 22. 25 thou shalt not be to him as an usurer
Isa. 24. 2 as with the taker of usury, so with the gi.
Jer. 15. 10 neither lent on usury, nor..lent..me on u.

4. *To bite, lend on usury,* נָשַׁךְ *nashak.*
Deut 23. 19 of any thing that is lent upon usury

5. *To (cause to) bite, lend on usury,* נָשַׁךְ *nashak*, 5.
Deut 23. 19 Thou shalt not lend upon usury to thy
23. 20 Unto a stranger thou mayest lend upon us.
23. 20 thy brother thou shalt not lend upon us.

6. *Biting, usury,* נֶשֶׁךְ *neshek.*
Exod 22. 25 neither shalt thou lay upon him usury
Lev. 25. 36 Take thou no usury of him, or increase
25. 37 Thou shalt not give him..upon usury, nor
Deut 23. 19 usury of money, usury of victuals, usury
Psa. 15. 5 putteth not out his money to usury, nor
Prov. 28. 8 He that by usury and unjust gain increa.
Eze. 18. 8 He (that) hath not given forth upon usu.
18. 13 Hath given forth upon usury, and hath t.
18. 17 hath not received usury nor increase, hath
22. 12 thou hast taken usury and increase, and

7. *Offspring, usury,* τόκος *tokos.*
Matt 25. 27 I should have received mine own with u.
Luke 19. 23 I might have required mine own with u.?

U'-THAI, עוּתַי *Jah is help.*

1. Son of Ammihud, a descendant of Pharez, son of Judah, dwelling in Jerusalem. B.C. 536.

1 Ch. 9. 4 U. the son of Ammihud, the son of Omri

2. A chief man, of the sons of Bigvai, that returned from exile with Ezra in the time of Artaxerxes. B.C. 457.

Ezra 8. 14 Of the sons also of Bigvai; U., and Zabb.

UTMOST (border, part), uttermost —

1. *Behind, last, furthest,* אַחֲרוֹן *acharon.*
Deut 11. 24 unto the uttermost sea, shall your border
34. 2 the land of Judah, unto the utmost sea
Joel 2. 20 his hinder part toward the utmost sea

2. *Latter end, furthest part,* אַחֲרִית *acharith.*
Psa. 139. 9 dwell in the uttermost parts of the sea

3. *End, cessation,* אֶפֶס *ephes.*
Psa. 2. 8 uttermost parts of the earth..thy posses.

4. *Wing*, כָּנָף *kanaph*.
Isa. 24. 16 From the uttermost part of the earth have

5. *End, extremity*, קֵץ *qets*.
Jer. 50. 26 Come against her from the utmost border

6. *End, extremity*, קָצָה *qatsah*.
1 Ki. 6. 24 the uttermost part..unto..uttermost part

7. *End, extremity*, קָצֶה *qatseh*.
Num 11. 1 consumed..in the uttermost parts of the
20. 16 Kadesh, a city in the uttermost of thy bo.
22. 36 border of Arnon, which (is) in the utmost
22. 41 he might see the utmost..of the people
23. 13 Thou shalt see but the utmost part of th.
34. 3 your south border shall be the utmost co.
Deut 30. 4 be driven out unto the utmost..of heaven
Josh. 15. 1 Zin southward (was) the uttermost part
15. 5 the sea at the uttermost part of Jordan
15. 21 the uttermost cities of the tribe of the ch.
1 Sa. 14. 2 Saul tarried in the uttermost part of Gib.
2 Ki. 7. 5 when they were come to the uttermost
7. 8 when these lepers came to the uttermost
Neh. 1. 9 cast out unto the uttermost part of the
Isa. 7. 18 the fly that (is) in the uttermost part of

8. *Extreme, outward*, קִיצוֹן *qitson*.
Exod 26. 4 shalt thou make in the uttermost edge of
36. 11 likewise be made in the uttermost side of
36. 17 he made fifty loops upon the uttermost

9. *End, extremity*, קְצָת *qetsath*.
Psa. 65. 8 They also that dwell in the uttermost pa.

10. *To cut off or asunder*, קָצַץ *qatsats*.
Jer. 9. 26 all..in the utmost corners, that dwell in
25. 23 and Buz, and all..in the utmost corners
49. 32 I will scatter..them..in the utmost corn

11. *Last, most distant, extreme*, ἔσχατος *eschatos*.
Matt. 5. 26 come out..till thou hast paid the utterm.
Acts 1. 8 and unto the uttermost part of the earth

12. *The things down to*, τὰ κατά *ta kata*.
Acts 24. 22 I will know the uttermost of your matter

13. *Perfect, complete*, παντελής *pantelēs*.
Heb. 7. 25 to save them to the uttermost that come

14. *Bound, limit, end*, πέρας *peras*.
Matt 12. 42 she came from the uttermost parts of the
Luke 11. 31 she came from the utmost parts of the

15. *End, event, consequence*, τέλος *telos*.
1 Th. 2. 16 wrath is come upon them to the utterm.

16. *Point, extremity*, ἄκρον (acc.) *akron*.
Mark 13. 27 the uttermost part..to the uttermost pa.

UTTER, outer, utterly — [*See* **OUTER.**]

1. *To gather*, אָסַף *asaph*.
Zeph. 1. 2 I will utterly consume all..from off the

2. *Drought, heat, waste, destruction*, חֹרֶב *choreb*.
Eze. 29. 10 I will make the land of Egypt utterly wa.

3. *To devote (to God or to destruction)*, חָרַם *charam*, 5.
Deut. 7. 2 thou shalt smite them..utterly destroy
20. 17 But thou shalt utterly destroy them

4. *Complete, completely*, כָּלִיל *kalil*.
Isa. 2. 18 And the idols he shall utterly abolish

5. *Might, very, exceedingly*, מְאֹד *meod*.
Psa. 119. 8 I will keep thy statutes..forsake..not ut.
119. 43 take not the word of truth utterly out of

6. *Corruption, destruction*, מַשְׁחִית *mashchith*.
Eze. 9. 6 Slay utterly old (and) young, both maids

7. *Baldness*, קָרְחָה *qorchah*.
Eze. 27. 31 they shall make themselves utterly bald

8. *Wholly*, ὅλως *holōs*.
1 Co. 6. 7 there is utterly a fault among you, beca.

UTTER (abundantly), be uttered, to —

1. *To teach*, אָלַף *alaph*, 3.
Job 15. 5 thy mouth uttereth thine iniquity, and

2. *To say*, אָמַר *amar*.
Prov. 1. 21 in the city she uttereth her words, (saying)

3. *To speak*, דָּבַר *dabar*.
Mic. 7. 3 he uttereth his mischievous desire: so th.

4. *To speak*, דָּבַר *dabar*, 3.
Judg. 5. 12 Awake, awake, Deborah..utter a song, ar.
11. 11 Jephthah uttered all his words before the
Prov 23. 33 thine heart shall utter perverse things
Isa. 32. 6 to utter error against the LORD, to make
Jer. 1. 16 I will utter my judgments against them

5. *To meditate, mutter, utter*, הָגָה *hagah*.
Job 27. 4 shall not speak..nor my tongue utter de.

6. *To meditate, utter, mutter*, הָגָה *hagah*, 3a.
Isa. 59. 13 conceiving and uttering from the heart

7. *To cause to go forth*, יָצָא *yatsa*, 5.
Neh. 6. 19 Also they..uttered my words to him
Job 8. 10 Shall not they..utter words out of their
Prov 10. 18 and he that uttereth a slander, (is) a fool
29. 11 A fool uttereth all his mind: but a wise
Eccl. 5. 2 and let not thine heart be hasty to utter
Isa. 48. 20 tell this, utter it..to the end of the earth

8. *To speak, say*, מָלַל *malal*, 3.
Job 33. 3 and my lips shall utter knowledge clearly
Psa. 106. 2 Who can utter the mighty acts of the Lo.

9. *To use similitudes*, מָשַׁל *mashal*.
Eze. 24. 3 utter a parable unto the rebellious house

10. *To utter, send forth, belch out*, נָבַע *naba*, 5.
Psa. 19. 2 Day unto day uttereth speech, and night
78. 2 I will open my mouth..I will utter dark
94. 4 shall they utter (and) speak hard things?
119. 171 My lips shall utter praise, when thou h.
145. 7 They shall abundantly utter the memory

11. *To cause to go before, bring forward*, נָגַד *nagad*, 5.
Lev. 5. 1 if he do not utter (it), then he shall bear
Josh 2. 14 Our life for your's, if ye utter not this our
2. 20 if thou utter this our business, then we
Job 26. 4 To whom hast thou uttered words? and
42. 3 therefore have I uttered that I understood

12. *To give*, נָתַן *nathan*.
2 Sa. 22. 14 The LORD..the Most High uttered his vo.
Psa. 46. 6 he uttered his voice, the earth melted
Prov. 1. 20 Wisdom..uttereth her voice in the streets
Jer. 10. 13 When he uttereth his voice..a multitude
25. 30 and utter his voice from his holy habita.
48. 34 unto Jahaz. have they uttered their voice
51. 16 When he uttereth (his) voice..a multitude
Joel 2. 11 the LORD shall utter his voice before his
3. 16 The LORD also shall..utter his voice from
Amos 1. 2 The LORD will..utter his voice from Jer.
Hab. 3. 10 the deep uttered his voice..lifted up his

13. *To be given*, נָתַן *nathan*, 2.
Jer. 51. 55 her waves..a noise of their voice is uttered

14. *To answer, respond*, עָנָה *anah*.
Job 15. 2 Should a wise man utter vain knowledge

15. *To breathe forth, utter*, פּוּחַ *puach*, 5.
Prov 14. 5 will not lie..a false witness will utter lies

16. *To open, gape, free, utter*, פָּצָה *patsah*.
Psa. 66. 14 Which my lips have uttered, and my mo.

17. *To give*, δίδωμι *didōmi*.
1 Co. 14. 9 except ye utter by the tongue words easy

18. *To belch out, utter copiously*, ἐρεύγομαι *ereugo*.
Matt 13. 35 I will utter things which have been kept

19. *To talk*, λαλέω *laleō*.
2 Co. 12. 4 which it is not lawful for a man to utter
Rev. 10. 3 when he had cried, seven thunders uttered
10. 4 when the seven thunders had uttered th.
10. 4 things which the seven thunders uttered

20. *To lay out, say*, λέγω *legō*.
Heb. 5. 11 many things to say, and hard to be uttered

UTTER destruction —
Devotion, ban, חֵרֶם, חֵרֶם *cherem*.
1 Ki. 20. 42 a man whom I appointed to utter des.
Zech 14. 11 there shall be no more utter destruction

UTTERANCE —

1. *To speak sententiously*, ἀποφθέγγομαι *apophtheg*.
Acts 2. 4 speak..as the spirit gave them utterance

2. *A word, discourse*, λόγος *logos*.
1 Co. 1. 5 ye are enriched by him, in all utterance
2 Co. 8. 7; Eph. 6. 19 Col. 4. 3.

UTTERED, aught out of, (that which is) —
Thing uttered wrongfully or rashly, מִבְטָא *mibta*.
Num 30. 6 when she vowed, or uttered aught out of
30. 8 and that which she uttered with her lips

UTTERED, which cannot be —
Unspeakable, unutterable, ἀλάλητος *alalētos*.
Rom. 8. 26 with groanings which cannot be uttered

UTTERLY —

1. *To be ended*, סוּף *suph*. Psa. 73. 19.
2. *Desolation*, שְׁמָמָה *shemamah*. Isa. 6. 11.

[*See also* Burn, cast down, consume, destroy, destroyed, perish slay, take.]

UZ, עוּץ *firmness*.

1. A son of Aram, son of Shem. B.C. 2200.
Gen. 10. 23 the children of Aram; U., and Hul, and
1 Ch. 1. 17 sons of Shem..U., and Hul, and Gether

2. A son of Dishon, of the family of Seir, and ancestor of the Horim. B.C. 1700.
Gen. 36. 28 children of Dishan (are) these; U., and A.
1 Ch. 1. 42 The sons of Dishan; U., and Aran

3. A region at the S. of Edom and W. of the great Arabian desert which runs into Chaldea.
Job 1. 1 There was a man in the land of U., whose
Jer. 25. 20 all the kings of the land of U., and all the
Lam. 4. 21 O daughter of Edom, that dwellest in..U.

U'-ZAI, אוּזַי *hoped for*.
Father of Palal who repaired part of the wall of Jerusalem. B.C. 445.
Neh. 3. 25 Palal the son of U., over against the tur.

U'-ZAL, אוּזָל.
The sixth son of Joktan, of the family of Shem, who settled in S. Arabia, in Zanaa, where the kings of Yemen dwelt. Comp. Eze. 27. 19. B.C. 2200.
Gen. 10. 27 And Hadoram, and U., and Diklah
1 Ch. 1. 21 Hadoram also, and U., and Diklah

UZ'-ZA, UZ'-ZAH, עֻזָּא, עֻזָּה *strength*.
1. A son of Abinadab who died for touching the ark. B.C. 1042.
2 Sa. 6. 3 and U. and Ahio..drave the new cart
6. 6 U. put forth (his hand) to the ark of God
6. 7 anger of the LORD was kindled against U.
6. 8 because the LORD..made a breach upon U.
1 Ch. 13. 7 and U. and Ahio drave the cart
1 Ch. 13. 9 U. put forth his hand to hold the ark
13. 10 anger of the LORD was kindled against U.
13. 11 because the LORD..made a breach upon U.

2. A person in whose garden Manasseh and Amon, kings of Judah, were buried.
2 Ki. 21. 18 Manasseh..was buried..in the garden..U.
21. 26 buried in his sepulchre in..garden of U.

3. Son of Shimei, a Merarite.
1 Ch. 6. 29 Libni his son, Shimei his son, U. his son

4. A Benjamite, brother of Alihud. B.C. 1400.
1 Ch. 8. 7 he removed them, and begat U. and Ahi.

5. Ancestor of a family of the Nethinim that returned with Zerubbabel. B.C. 536.
Ezra 2. 49 children of U., the children of Paseah
Neh. 7. 51 children of U., the children of Phaseah

UZ-ZEN-SHE'-RAH, אֻזֵּן שֶׁאֱרָה *point, top of Sherah*.
A city in Ephraim, near the two Beth-horons; now called *Beit Sira*.
1 Ch. 7. 24 his daughter (was) Sherah, who built..U.

UZ'-ZI, עֻזִּי *Jah is strong*.
1. A son of Bukki and father of Zerahiah, a descendant of Phinehas grandson of Aaron. B.C. 1350.
1 Ch. 6. 5 Abishua begat Bukki, and Bukki begat U.
6. 6 U. begat Zerahiah, and Zerahiah begat
6. 51 Bukki his son, U. his son, Zerahiah his so
Ezra 7. 4 The son of Zerahiah, the son of U., the

2. Grandson of Issachar, and father of Izrahiah. B.C. 1600.
1 Ch. 7. 2 And the sons of Tola: U., and Rephaiah
7. 3 the sons of U.; Izrahiah: and the sons of

3. Son of Bela, son of Benjamin. B.C. 1600.
1 Ch. 7. 7 sons of Bela; Ezbon, and U., and Uzziel

4. Father of Elah, a Benjamite, whose descendants dwelt in Jerusalem after the exile. B.C 445.
1 Ch. 9. 8 And Ibneiah..and Elah the son of U.

5. An overseer of the Levites in Jerusalem after the exile. B.C. 445.
Neh. 11. 22 The overseer also..(was) U. the son of B.

6. A priest of the family of Jedaiah in the days of Joiakim, grandson of Jozadah. B.C. 500.
Neh. 12. 19 And of Joiarib, Mattenai; of Jedaiah, U.
12. 42 U., and Jehohanan, and Malchijah, and

UZ-ZI'-A, עֻזִּיָּא *Jah is strong*.
An Ashterathite, one of David's valiant men. B.C. 1048.
1 Ch. 11. 44 U. the Ashterathite, Shama and Jehiel

UZ-ZI'-AH, עֻזִּיָּה, עֻזִּיָּהוּ *Jah is strong*.
1. Son of Amaziah and father of Jotham, kings of Judah: called also Azariah. B.C. 810-758.
2 Ki. 15. 13 in the nine and thirtieth year of U. king
15. 30 twentieth year of Jotham the son of U.
15. 32 began Jotham the son of U. king of Jud.
15. 34 he did according to all that..U. had done
2 Ch. 26. 1 Then all the people of Judah took U., who
26. 3 Sixteen years old (was) U. when he began
26. 8 the Ammonites gave gifts to U.: and his
26. 9 U. built towers in Jerusalem at the corner
26. 11 Moreover U. had an host of fighting men
26. 14 U. prepared for them throughout all the
26. 18 And they withstood U. the king, and said
26. 18 (It appertaineth) not unto thee, U., to bu.
26. 19 Then U. was wroth, and (had) a censer in
26. 21 U...was a leper unto the day of his death
26. 22 the rest of the acts of U...did Isaiah..wr.
26. 23 U. slept with his fathers, and they buried
27. 2 according to all that his father U. did
Isa. 1. 1 vision..which he saw..in the days of U.
6. 1 In the year that king U. died I saw also
7. 1 Ahaz the son of Jotham, the son of U.
Hos. 1. 1 in the days of U., Jotham, Ahaz, (and) H.
Amos 1. 1 which he saw..in the days of U. king of
Zech 14. 5 from..the earthquake in the days of U

2. Son of Uriel, a Kohathite. B.C. 1100.
1 Ch. 6. 24 Tahath his son, Uriel his son, U. his son

3. Father of Jehonathan, keeper of the storehouses in the days of David. B.C. 1060.
1 Ch. 27. 25 over the storehouses..(was)..the son of U.

4. A priest that had taken a strange wife. B.C. 445.
Ezra 10. 21 Elijah, and Shemaiah, and Jehiel, and U.

5. Father of Athaiah who dwelt in Jerusalem after the exile. B.C. 445.
Neh. 11. 4 Athaiah the son of U., the son of Zecha.

UZ-ZI'-EL, עֻזִּיאֵל *God is strong*.
1. A son of Kohath, son of Levi. B.C. 1600.
Exod. 6. 18 And the sons of Kohath..Hebron, and U.
6. 22 the sons of U.; Mishael, and Elzaphan
Lev. 10. 4 Moses called..the sons of U. the uncle of
Num. 3. 19 And the sons of Kohath..Hebron, and U.
3. 30 chief..(shall be) Elizaphan the son of U.
1 Ch. 6. 2, 18 sons of Kohath (were)..Hebron, and U.
15. 10 Of the sons of U.; Amminadab the chief
23. 12 sons of Kohath..Izhar, Hebron, and U.
23. 20 Of the sons of U.; Micah the first, and J.
24. 24 the sons of U.; Michah: of the sons of M.

2. A Simeonite, son of Ishi, who with Pelatiah and Neariah and Rephaiah and five hundred men went to Mount Seir, and smote the Amalekites, and dwelt there. B.C. 715.
1 Ch. 4. 42 Neariah, and Rephaiah, and U., the sons

8. A son of Bela, son of Benjamin. B.C. 1600.
1 Ch. 7. 7 the sons of Bela; Ezbon, and Uzzi, and U.

4. A son of Heman, set by David over the service of song. B.C. 1015.
1 Ch.25. 4 Mattaniah, U., Shebuel, and Jerimoth

5. A Levite who helped to cleanse the temple in the days of Hezekiah. B.C. 724.
2 Ch.29. 14 the sons of Jeduthun; Shemariah, and U.

6. Son of Hashaiah, a goldsmith who repaired part of the wall of Jerusalem. B.C. 445.
Neh. 3. 8 Next unto him repaired U. the son of H.

UZZIELITES, עָזִּיאֵלִי.
The family of Uzziel son of Kohath.
Num. 3. 27 of Kohath (was)..the family of the U.
1 Ch.26. 23 the Izharites, the Hebronites, (and) the U.

V

VAGABOND, (to be a) —
1. *To move, wander, bemoan,* נוּד *nud.*
Gen. 4. 12 a fugitive and a vagabond shalt thou be in
4. 14 I shall be a fugitive and a vagabond in the
2. *To move, shake, stagger, wander,* נוּעַ *nua.*
Psa 109. 10 Let his children be continually vagabonds
3. *To come or go round about,* περιέρχομαι *perierc.*
Acts 19. 13 certain of the vagabond Jews, exorcists

VAIL, veil —
1. *A covering,* מִטְפַּחַת *mitpachath.*
Ruth 3. 15 Bring the veil (thou hast) upon thee, and
2. *A veil,* מַסְוֶה *masveh.*
Exod34. 33 Moses had done speaking..he put a veil
34. 34 But..he took the veil off, until he came
34. 35 Moses put the veil upon his face again, un.
3. *A covering,* מַסֵּכָה *massekah.*
Isa. 25. 7 and the veil that is spread over all nations
4. *Separation, curtain,* פָּרֹכֶת *paroketh.*
Exod26. 31 thou shalt make a veil (of) blue, and pur.
26. 33 thou shalt hang up the veil .and the veil
26. 33 bring in thither within the veil the ark of
26. 35 thou shalt set the table without the veil
27. 21 without the veil. which is before the test.
30. 6 thou shalt put it before the veil that (is)
35. 12 the mercy seat, and the veil of the coveri.
36. 35 he made a veil (of) blue, and purple. and
38. 27 of silver were cast..the sockets of the veil
39. 34 the covering..and the veil of the covering
40. 3 And thou shalt. cover the ark with the ve.
40. 21 set up the veil of the covering, and cove.
40. 22 And he put the table..without the veil
40. 26 he put the golden altar .before the veil
Lev. 4. 6 sprinkle. .before the veil of the sanctuary
4. 17 sprinkle (it) seven times. .before the veil
16. 2 into the holy (place) within the veil before
16. 12 take a censer and bring (it) within the v.
16. 15 bring his blood within the veil, and do
21. 23 Only he shall not go in unto the veil, nor
24. 3 Without the veil of the testimony, in the
Num. 4. 5 they shall take down the covering veil
18. 7 keep your priest s office..within the veil
2 Ch. 3. 14 he made the veil (of) blue, and purple, and
5. *A veil, wrapping,* צָעִיף *tsaiph.*
Gen. 24. 65 therefore she took a veil, and covered he
38. 14 covered her with a veil, and wrapped he
38. 19 went away and laid by her veil from her
6. *A veil,* רְדִיד *radid.*
Song 5. 7 the keepers of the walls took away my v.
Isa. 3. 23 the fine linen, and the hoods, and the veils
7. *A covering, veil,* κάλυμμα *kalumma.*
2 Co. 3. 13 not as Moses, (which) put a veil over his
3. 14 for until this day remaineth the same veil
3. 15 when Moses is read, the veil is upon their
3. 16 when it shall turn to the Lord, the veil
8. *An extension, large veil,* καταπέτασμα *katapeta.*
Matt27. 51 the veil of the temple was rent in twain
Mark15. 38 the veil of the temple was rent in twain
Luke23. 45 the veil of the temple was rent in the mi.
Heb. 6. 19 which entereth unto that within the veil
9. 3 after the second veil, the tabernacle which
10. 20 through the veil, that is to say, his flesh

VAIN (babbling, fellow, glory, men, thing, in) vainly —
1. *Iniquity, vanity,* אָוֶן *aven.*
Jer. 4. 14 shall thy vain thoughts lodge within thee
2. *Vanity,* הֶבֶל *hebel.*
Job 9. 29 (If) I be wicked, why then labour I in vain?
21. 34 How then comfort ye me in vain, seeing
35. 16 doth Job open his mouth in vain; he mu.
Psa. 39. 6 surely they are disquieted in vain: he he.
Prov.31. 30 Favour (is) deceitful, and beauty (is) vain
Eccl. 6. 12 all the days of his vain life which he spe.
Isa. 30. 7 the Egyptians shall help in vain, and to
49. 4 I have spent my strength..and in vain
Jer. 10. 3 the customs of the people (are) vain, for
Lam. 4. 17 our eyes as yet failed for our vain help
Zech.10. 2 they comfort in vain: therefore they went
3. *Gratis, for nought,* חִנָּם *chinnam.*
Prov. 1. 17 Surely in vain the net is spread in the si.
Eze. 6. 10 I have not said in vain that I would do
4. *To be hollow,* נָבַב *nabab.*
Job 11. 12 For vain man would be wise, though man
5. *Wind,* רוּחַ *ruach.*
Job 15. 2 Should a wise man utter vain knowledge
16. 3 Shall vain words have an end? or what em.
6. *Empty, vain, vanity,* רִיק *riq.*
Lev. 26. 16 ye shall sow your seed in vain, for your
26. 20 And your strength shall be spent in vain
Job 39. 16 She is hardened..her labour is in vain wi.
Psa. 2. 1 Why do the..people imagine a vain thing?
73. 13 Verily I have cleansed my heart (in) vain
Isa. 49. 4 I have laboured in vain, I have spent my
65. 23 They shall not labour in vain, nor bring
Jer. 51. 58 the people shall labour in vain, and the
7. *Empty. vain, vanity,* רֵק ,רִיק *req.*
Deut.32. 47 For it (is) not a vain thing for you; because
Judg. 9. 4 wherewith Abimelech hired light and vain
11. 3 there were gathered vain men to Jephthah
2 Sa. 6. 20 as one of the vain fellows shamelessly un.
2 Ch.13. 7 there are gathered unto him vain men, the
Prov.12. 11 he that followeth vain (persons is) void of
28. 19 he that followeth after vain (persons) sh.
8. *Emptily, vainly, for nought,* רֵיקָם *reqam.*
Jer. 50. 9 their arrows..none shall return in vain
9. *Vanity, falsehood,* שָׁוְא *shav.*
Exod20. 7 Thou shalt not take the name of..God in v.
20. 7 not..guiltless that taketh his name in vain
Deut. 5. 11 shalt not take the name of..God in vain
5. 11 not..guiltless that taketh his name in vain
Job 11. 11 he knoweth vain men: he seeth wickedn.
Psa. 26. 4 I have not sat with vain persons, neither
60. 11 Give us help..for vain (is) the help of man
89. 47 wherefore hast thou made all men in vain
108. 12 Give us help..for vain (is) the help of man
127. 1 Except..the LORD build they labour in vain
127. 1 keep..the watchman waketh (but) in vain
127. 2 (It is) vain for you to rise up early, to sit
139. 20 thine enemies take (thy name) in vain
Isa. 1. 13 Bring no more vain oblations; incense is
Jer. 2. 30 In vain have I smitten your children, th.
4. 30 in vain shalt thou make thyself fair; (thy)
6. 29 the founder melteth in vain; for the wic.
46. 11 in vain shalt thou use many medicines
Lam. 2. 14 Thy prophets have seen vain and foolish
Eze. 12. 24 there shall be no more any vain nor flatt.
13. 7 Have ye not seen a vain vision, and have
Mal. 3. 14 Ye have said, It (is) vain to serve God; and
10. *Falsehood, lie,* שֶׁקֶר *sheqer.*
Exod.5. 9 the men..let them not regard vain words
1 Sa. 25. 21 Surely in vain have I kept all that this
Psa. 33. 17 An horse (is) a vain thing for safety: nei.
Jer. 3. 23 Truly in vain..from the hills..the multi.
8. 8 in vain made he (it); the pen..(is) in vain
11. *Ruin, vacancy, vanity,* תֹּהוּ *tohu.*
1 Sa. 12. 21 after vain (things)..for they (are) vain
Isa. 45. 18 he created it not in vain, he formed it to
45. 19 I said not..Seek ye me in vain: I the Lo.
12. *Lip,* שָׂפָה *saphah.*
Isa. 36. 5 vain words, I (have) counsel and strength
13. *Freely,* δωρεάν *dōrean.*
Gal. 2. 21 if..by the law, then Christ is dead in vain
14. *Easily, at random,* εἰκῆ *eikē.*
Rom.13. 4 he beareth not the sword in vain; for he
1 Co. 15. 2 unto you, unless ye have believed in vain
Gal. 3. 4 Have ye suffered..in vain? if..yet in vain?
4. 11 I have bestowed upon you labour in vain
Col. 2. 18 man..vainly puffed up by his fleshly mind
15. *Vainly, emptily,* κενῶς *kenōs.*
Jas. 4. 5 Do ye think..the scripture saith in vain
16. *Vain, empty,* κενός *kenos.*
Acts 4. 25 Why did..the people imagine vain things?
1 Co.15. 10 grace..(bestowed) upon me was not in va.
15. 14 preaching vain, and your faith (is) also vain
15. 58 ye know that your labour is not in vain
2 Co. 6. 1 ye receive not the grace of God in vain
Gal. 2. 2 lest by any means I should run .in vain
Eph. 5. 6 Let no man deceive you with vain words
Phil. 2. 16 not run in vain, neither laboured in vain
Col. 2. 8 spoil you through philosophy and vain de.
1 Th. 2. 1 yourselves..know..that it was not in vain
3. 5 tempted you, and our labour be in vain
Jas. 2. 20 wilt thou know, O vain man, that faith
17. *Vain, empty sound,* κενοφωνία *kenophōnia.*
1 Ti. 6. 20 avoiding profane .vain babblings, and
2 Ti. 2. 16 But shun profane. .vain babblings; for
18. *Vain, unprofitable, useless,* μάταιος *mataios.*
1 Co. 3. 20 the thoughts of the wise, that they are va.
15. 17 if Christ be not raised, your faith (is) vain
Titus 3. 9 strivings..for they are unprofitable and va.
Jas. 1. 26 but deceiveth. .this man's religion is vain
1 Pe. 1. 18 redeemed. .from your vain conversation
19. *In vain,* μάτην *matēn.*
Matt 15. 9 But in vain they do worship me, teaching
Mark 7. 7 Howbeit in vain do they worship me, tea.

VAIN, to be (in), become, make —
1. *To be or become vain,* הָבַל *habal.*
2 Ki.17. 15 they followed vanity, and became vain
Job 27. 12 why then are ye thus altogether vain?
Psa. 62. 10 become not vain in robbery: if riches in.
Jer. 2. 5 that they are gone. .and are become vain?
2. *To make vain,* הָבַל *habal,* 5.
Jer. 23. 16 they make you vain: they speak a vision
3. *To be found false, a liar,* כָּזַב *kazab,* 2.
Job 41. 9 Behold, the hope of him is in vain: shall
4. *To empty, make vain,* κενόω *kenoō.*
2 Co. 9. 3 lest our boasting of you should be in vain
5. *To be or become vain,* ματαιόομαι *mataioomai.*
Rom. 1. 21 became vain in their imaginations, and

VAIN glory, (desirous of) —
1. *Vain glory,* κενοδοξία *kenodoxia.*
Phil. 2. 3 nothing..through strife or vain glory; but
2. *Vain glorious,* κενόδοξος *kenodoxos.*
Gal. 5. 26 Let us not be desirous of vain glory, pro.

VA-JE-ZA'-THA, וַיְזָתָא *born of Ized.*
The tenth son of Haman the Agagite in the days of Esther and Ahasuerus. B.C. 510.
Esth. 9. 9 Parmashta, and Arisai, and Aridai, and V.

VALE, VALLEY, OR DALE —
1. *Biqah,* בִּקְעָה *a cleft place, valley.*

Valley of Jericho, בִּקְעַת יְרֵחוֹ.
Between Jericho and the Salt Sea.
Deut.34. 3 the plain of the valley of Jericho, the city

Valley of Lebanon, בִּקְעַת הַלְּבָנוֹן. *W. of Hermon.*
Josh.11. 17 unto Baal-gad in the valley of Lebanon

Valley of Megiddo, בִּקְעַת מְגִדּוֹ.
Through which the Kishon flows, in Issachar or Manasseh.
2 Ch.35. 22 Josiah..came to fight in the valley of M.
Zech.12. 11 mourning of Hadadri. in the valley of M.

Valley of Mizpeh, בִּקְעַת מִצְפֶּה. *In Dan.*
Josh.11. 8 Israel..chased them..unto the valley of M.

2. *Emeq,* עֵמֶק *a deep difficult place.*

Valley of Achor, עֵמֶק עָכוֹר. *Near Jericho.*
Josh. 7. 24 they brought them into the valley of A.
7. 26 that place was called, The valley of A. to
15. 7 the border went up..from the valley of A.
Isa. 65. 10 the valley of A. a place for the herds to lie
Hos. 2. 15 I will give..the valley of A. for a door of h.

Valley of Ajalon, עֵמֶק אַיָּלוֹן. *In Dan.*
Josh.10. 12 stand..thou, Moon, in the valley of A.

Valley of Baca, עֵמֶק הַבָּכָא. *Near Jerusalem.*
Psa. 84. 6 passing through the valley of B. make it

Valley of Berachah, עֵמֶק בְּרָכָה. *West of Tekoa.*
2 Ch.20. 26 assembled themselves in the valley of Be.
20. 26 was called, The valley of B., unto this day

Valley of Decision, עֵמֶק הֶחָרוּץ. *At Jerusalem.*
Joel 3. 14 Multitudes, multitudes in the valley of D.
3. 14 the day of the LORD..in the valley of D.

Valley of Elah, עֵמֶק הָאֵלָה. *Near Shocah.*
1 Sa. 17. 2 and the men..pitched by the valley of E.
17. 19 the men of Israel, (were) in the valley of E.
21. 9 whom thou slewest in the valley of E. beh.

Valley of the Giants, עֵמֶק רְפָאִים. *S. of Jerusalem.*
See the *valley of Rephaim* (below.)
Josh.15. 8 which (is) at the end of the valley of the gi.
18. 16 which (is) in the valley of the giants on

Valley of Gibeon, עֵמֶק בְּגִבְעוֹן. *In Benjamin.*
Isa. 28. 21 shall be wroth as (in) the valley of G. that

Valley of Hebron, עֵמֶק חֶבְרוֹן. *S. of Judah.*
Gen. 37. 14 So he sent him out of the vale of H., and he

Valley of Jehoshaphat, עֵמֶק יְהוֹשָׁפָט.
Between Jerusalem and the mount of Olives.
Joel 3. 2 I..will bring them..into the valley of J.
3. 12 Let..heathen..come up to the valley of J.

Valley of Jezreel, עֵמֶק יִזְרְעֶאל. *In Issachar.*
Josh.17. 16 and (they) who (are) of the valley of J.
Judg. 6. 33 the Amalekites..pitched in the valley of J.
Hos. 1. 5 I will break the bow..in the valley of J.

Valley of Keziz, עֵמֶק קְצִיץ. *In Benjamin.*
Josh.18. 21 the cities..Jericho..and the valley of K.

Valley of the King, or the King's Dale, עֵמֶק הַמֶּלֶךְ.
The S. part of the valley of Jehoshaphat.
Gen. 14. 17 at the valley of Shaveh..the king's dale
2 Sa. 18. 18 reared..a pillar, which (is) in the king's dale

Valley of Rephaim, עֵמֶק רְפָאִים.
N. part of the valley of Hinnom, on the W. of Jerusalem.
2 Sa. 5. 18, 22 spread themselves in the valley of R.
23. 13 of the Philistines pitched in the valley of R.
1 Ch.11. 15 Philistines encamped in the valley of R.
14. 9 and spread themselves in the valley of R.
Isa. 17. 5 he that gathereth ears in the valley of R.

Valley of Shaveh, עֵמֶק שָׁוֵה.
See the King's Dale.
Gen. 14. 17 at the valley of Shaveh..the king's dale

Valley of Siddim, עֵמֶק הַשִּׂדִּים. *S.W. of Salt Sea.*
Gen. 14. 3 were joined together in the vale of S.
14. 8 joined battle with them in the vale of S.
14. 10 the vale of S. (was full) of slimepits, and the

Valley of Succoth, עֵמֶק סֻכּוֹת. *In Gad.*
Psa. 60. 6 I will divide..and mete out the valley of S.
108. 7 I will divide..and mete out the valley of S.

3. *Ge,* גֵּי, גֵּיא *a low, flat place.*

Valley of Charasim, גֵּיא חֲרָשִׁים. *In Judah.*
1 Ch. 4. 14 begat Joab, the father of the valley of C.

Valley of Craftsmen, גֵּיא חֲרָשִׁים. *Same as preceding.*
Neh. 11. 35 Lod, and Ono, the valley of Craftsmen

Valley of Hamon-Gog, גֵּיא הֲמוֹן גּוֹג.
E. of Chinnereth. See the *Valley of the Passengers.*
Eze. 39. 11 they shall call (it), The valley of H. G.
39. 15 buriers have buried it in the valley of H. G.

Valley of Hinnom, גֵּי הִנֹּם. *S. of Jerusalem.*
Josh. 15. 8 mountain..(lieth) before the valley of H.
18. 16 the border..descended to the valley of H.
Neh. 11. 30 dwelt from Beer-sheba to the valley of H.

Valley of Jiphthah-el, גֵּי יִפְתַּח־אֵל *N. E. of Zebulun.*
Josh. 19. 14 outgoings thereof are in the valley of J.
19. 27 reacheth..to the valley of J. toward the n.

Valley of the Mountains, גֵּיא־הָרַי. *Near Jerusalem.*
Zech. 14. 5 ye shall flee (to) the valley of the mount.
14. 5 the valley of the mountains shall reach

Valley of the Passengers, גֵּי הָעֹבְרִים.
In E. of Chinnereth. *See Valley of Hamon-Gog.*
Eze. 39. 11 the valley of the passengers on the east

Valley of Salt, גֵּיא מֶלַח. *S. end of Salt Sea.*
2 Sa. 8. 13 smiting of the Syrians in the valley of salt
2 Ki. 14. 7 He slew of Edom in the valley of salt ten
1 Ch. 18. 12 Abishai..slew..in the valley of salt eigh.
2 Ch. 25. 11 And Amaziah..went to the valley of salt
Psa. 60. *title.* smote of Edom in the valley of salt tw.

Valley of Slaughter, גֵּיא הַהֲרֵגָה. *A symbolic name.*
Jer. 7. 32 it shall..be called..the valley of slaugh.
19. 6 place shall..be called..The valley of sla.

Valley of the Son of Hinnom, גֵּי בֶן־הִנֹּם.
See the *Valley of Hinnom.*
Josh. 15. 8 the border..by the valley of the son of H.
18. 16 (lieth) before the valley of the son of H.
2 Ki. 23. 10 (is) in the valley of the children of H.
2 Ch. 28. 3 he burnt..in the valley of the son of H.
33. 6 the fire in the valley of the son of H.
Jer. 7. 31 which (is) in the valley of the son of H.
7. 32 be called..the valley of the son of H.
19. 2 go forth unto the valley of the son of H.
19. 6 nor, The valley of the son of H., but the
32. 35 which (are) in the valley of the son of H.

Valley of Vision, גֵּיא חִזָּיוֹן.
A symbolic name for the lower part of Jerusalem.
Isa. 22. 1 The burden of the valley of Vision. What
22. 5 a day of trouble..in the valley of Vision

Valley of Zeboim, גֵּי הַצְּבֹעִים. *In Benjamin.*
1 Sa. 13. 18 border that looketh to the valley of Z.

Valley of Zephathah, גֵּיא צְפָתָה. *In Simeon.*
2 Ch. 14. 10 set the battle in array in the valley of Z.

4. *Nachal,* נַחַל *a ravine, gorge, watercourse.*

Valley of Eschol, נַחַל אֶשְׁכּוֹל. *S. of Judah.*
Num 32. 9 when they went up unto the valley of E.
Deut. 1. 24 And they..came unto the valley of E., and

Valley of Gerar, נַחַל גְּרָר. *S. W. of Palestine.*
Gen. 26. 17 Isaac..pitched his tent in the valley of G.

Valley of Shittim, נַחַל הַשִּׁטִּים. *Valley of the Acacias.*
Joel 3. 18 a fountain..shall water the valley of S.

Valley of Sorek, נַחַל שׂוֹרֵק. *In Dan.*
Judg. 16. 4 that he loved a woman in the valley of S.

Valley of Zared, נַחַל זֶרֶד. *E. of Salt Sea.*
Num 21. 12 removed, and pitched in the valley of Z.

5. *Shephelah,* שְׁפֵלָה *a low, flat place.*
The low country generally, from Joppa southward to the river of Egypt.
Deut. 1. 7 Turn you..and go..unto all..in the vale
Josh 10. 40 Joshua smote all the country..of the vale
11. 16 So Joshua took all that land..and the va.
11. 16 the mountain of Israel, and the valley of

VALE, valley —

1. *A cleft, vale,* בִּקְעָה *biqah.*
Deut. 8. 7 depths that spring out of valleys and hi.
11. 11 the land..(is) a land of hills and valleys
Psa. 104. 8 they go down by the valleys unto the pl.
Isa. 41. 18 and fountains in the midst of the valleys
63. 14 As a beast goeth down into the valley
Eze. 37. 1 set me down in the midst of the valley
37. 2 (there were) very many in the open vall.
See also Deut. 34. 3; Josh. 11. 8, 17; 12. 7; 2 Ch. 35. 22; Zech. 12. 11.

2. *Valley, low plain, a gorge,* גַּיְא *gay.*
Num 21. 20 from Bamoth (in) the valley, that (is) in
Deut. 3. 29 we abode in the valley over against Beth.
4. 46 in the valley over against Beth-peor, in
34. 6 he buried him in the valley in the land
Josh. 8. 11 (there was) a valley between them and Ai
1 Sa. 17. 3 and (there was) a valley between them
17. 52 until thou come to the valley, and to the
2 Ki. 2. 16 upon some mountain, or into some valley
1 Ch. 4. 39 they went..unto the east side of the vall.
2 Ch 26. 9 at the corner gate, and at the valley gate
Neh. 2. 13 I went..by the gate of the valley, even
2. 15 entered by the gate of the valley, and (so)
3. 13 The valley gate repaired Hanun, and the
Psa. 23. 4 though I walk through the valley of the
Isa. 28. 1 which (are) on the head of the fat valleys
28. 4 which (is) on the head of the fat valley
40. 4 Every valley shall be exalted, and every
Jer. 2. 23 See thy way in the valley, know what th.
Eze. 6. 3 to the hills, to the rivers, and to the val.
7. 16 on the mountains like doves of the valley
31. 12 in all the valleys his branches are fallen
32. 5 And I will..fill the valleys with thy heig.
35. 8 in thy valleys, and in all thy rivers, shall
36. 4, 6 to the hills, to the rivers, and to the va.
Mic. 1. 6 pour down the stones thereof into the va.
Zech. 14. 4 (and there shall be) a very great valley
See also Josh. 15. 8, 8; 18. 16, 16; 19. 14, 27; 1 Sa. 13. 18; 2 Sa. 8. 13; 2 Ki. 14. 7; 23. 10; 1 Ch. 4. 14; 18. 12; 2 Ch. 14. 10; 25. 11; 28. 3; 33. 6; Neh. 11. 30, 35; Psa. 60; Isa. 22. 1, 5; Jer. 7. 31, 32, 32; 19. 2, 6, 6; 32. 35; Eze. 39. 11, 11, 15; Zech. 14. 5, 5.

3. *A vale with a brook, a ravine,* נַחַל *nachal.*
Gen. 26. 19 Isaac's servants digged in the valley, and
Num 24. 6 As the valleys are they spread forth, as
Deut. 3. 16 even unto the river Arnon half the valley
21. 4 bring down the heifer unto a rough vall.
21. 4 strike off the heifer's neck..in the valley
21. 6 the heifer that is beheaded in the valley
1 Sa. 15. 5 And Saul came..and laid wait in the va.
2 Ki. 3. 16 he said..Make this valley full of ditches
3. 17 yet that valley shall be filled with water
2 Ch. 33. 14 on the west side of Gihon, in the valley
Job 21. 33 The clods of the valley shall be sweet unto
30. 6 to dwell in the cliffs of the valleys..caves
Psa. 104. 10 He sendeth the springs into the valleys
Prov 30. 17 the ravens of the valley shall pick it out
Song 6. 11 I went down..to see the fruits of the val.
Isa. 7. 19 shall rest all of them in the desolate val.
57. 5 slaying the children in the valleys under
See also Gen. 26. 17; Num. 21. 12; 32. 9; Deut. 1. 24; Judg. 16. 4.

4. *A deep or difficult place,* עֵמֶק *emeq.*
Num 14. 25 the A. and the Canaanites dwell in the va.
Josh. 8. 13 went that night into the midst of the va.
13. 19 Zareth-shahar in the mount of the valley
13. 27 in the valley, Beth-aram, and Beth-nimrah
17. 16 all..that dwell in the land of the valley
Judg. 1. 19 not drive out the inhabitants of the valley
1. 34 not suffer them to come down to the val.
5. 15 Barak: he was sent on foot into the valley
7. 1 were..by the hill of Moreh, in the valley
7. 8 host of Midian was beneath him in the va.
7. 12 lay along in the valley like grasshoppers
18. 28 and it was in the valley..by Beth-rehob
1 Sa. 6. 13 reaping their wheat harvest in the valley
31. 7 that (were) on the other side of the valley
1 Ki. 20. 28 he (is) not God of the valleys, therefore
1 Ch. 10. 7 when all the men of Israel..in the valley
12. 15 they put to flight all (them) of the valleys
14. 13 again spread themselves abroad in the va.
27. 29 over the herds (that were) in the valleys
Job 39. 10 or will he harrow the valleys after thee?
39. 21 He paweth in the valley, and rejoiceth
Psa. 65. 13 valleys also are covered over with corn
Song 2. 1 I (am) the rose of S...the lily of the valleys
Isa. 22. 7 thy choicest valleys shall be full of char.
Jer. 21. 13 O inhabitant of the valley..rock of the pl.
31. 40 the whole valley of the dead bodies, and
47. 5 A. is cut off (with) the remnant of their va.
48. 8 the valley also shall perish, and the plain
49. 4 gloriest thou in thy valleys, thy flowing va.
Mic. 1. 4 the valleys shall be cleft, as wax before the
See also Gen. 14. 3, 8, 10, 17; 37. 14; Josh. 7. 24, 26; 10. 12; 15. 7, 8; 17. 16; 18. 16, 21; Judg. 6. 33; 1 Sa. 17. 2, 19; 21. 9; 2 Sa. 5. 18, 22; 23. 13; 1 Ch. 11. 15; 14. 9; 2 Ch. 20. 26, 26; Psa. 60. 6; 84. 6; 108. 7; Isa. 17. 5; 28. 21; 65. 10; Hos. 1. 5; 2. 15; Joel 3. 2, 12, 14, 14.

5. *Low land, plain, slope or flat,* שְׁפֵלָה *shephelah.*
Josh. 9. 1 in the hills, and in the valleys, and in all
10. 40 the hills, and of the south, and of the va.
11. 2 in the valley, and in the borders of Dor
11. 16 took all..the valley..the valley of the sa.
12. 8 In the mountains, and in the valleys, and
15. 33 in the valley, Eshtaol, and Zoreah, and As.
Judg. 1. 9 that dwelt..in the south, and in the valley
1 Ki. 10. 27 the sycamore trees that (are) in the vale
2 Ch. 1. 15 as the sycamore trees that (are) in the vale
Jer. 32. 44 in the cities of the valley, and in the cit.
33. 13 in the cities of the vale, and in the cities

6. *A precipice, precipitous valley,* φάραγξ *pharagx.*
Luke 3. 5 Every valley shall be filled, and every m.

VALIANT, (man, one, to be) valiantest, valour —

1. *A mighty one,* אַבִּיר *abbir.*
Jer. 46. 15 Why are thy valiant..swept away? they

2. *A hero,* אֶרְאֵל *erel.*
Isa. 33. 7 Behold, their valiant ones shall cry with.

3. *A son of force or might,* בֶּן־חַיִל *ben chayil.*
Judg 21. 10 sent..twelve thousand of the valiantest
1 Sa. 18. 17 only be thou valiant for me, and fight the
2 Sa. 2. 7 now..be strengthened, and be ye valiant
13. 28 fear not..be courageous, and be valiant
17. 10 he also (that is) valiant, whose heart (is)
1 Ch. 5. 18 of valiant men, men able to bear buckler
2 Ch. 28. 6 an hundred and twenty thousand..valiant

4. *A mighty man,* גִּבּוֹר *gibbor.*
1 Ch. 7. 2 valiant men of might in their generations
7. 5 valiant men of might, reckoned in all by
11. 26 Also the valiant men of the armies (were)
2 Ch. 13. 3 with an army of valiant men of war..four
Song 3. 7 threescore valiant men..of the valiant of

5. *To be mighty,* גָּבַר *gabar.*
Jer. 9. 3 they are not valiant for the truth upon

6. *Force, strength,* חַיִל *chayil.*
Josh. 1. 14 ye shall pass..all the mighty men of val.
Josh. 6. 2 the king thereof..the mighty men of val.
8. 3 chose..thirty thousand mighty men of va.
10. 7 Joshua..and all the mighty men of valour
Judg. 3. 29 ten thousand men..and all men of valour
6. 12 The LORD (is) with thee; thou..man of va.
11. 1 Jephthah the G. was a mighty man of va.
18. 2 five men from their coasts, men of valour
20. 44 eighteen thousand men: all..men of valo.
20. 46 twenty and five thousand..all..men of val.
1 Sa. 14. 52 when Saul saw any strong..or valiant man
16. 18 a mighty valiant man, and a man of war
31. 12 All the valiant men arose, and went all
2 Sa. 11. 16 a place where he knew that valiant men
17. 10 (they) which (be) with him (are) valiant m.
23. 20 Benaiah..son of a valiant man, of Kabzeel
24. 9 eight hundred thousand valiant men that
1 Ki. 1. 42 thou (art) a valiant man, and bringest go.
11. 28 Jeroboam (was) a mighty man of valour
2 Ki. 5. 1 Naaman..was also a mighty man in valo.
24. 14 the princes, and all the mighty men of va.
1 Ch. 5. 24 mighty men of valour, famous men..he.
7. 7 the sons of Bela..mighty men of valour
7. 9 the number of them..mighty men of val.
7. 11 mighty men of valour..seventeen thous.
7. 40 mighty men of valour..chief of the prin.
8. 40 were mighty men of valour, archers, and
10. 12 They arose, all the valiant men, and took
11. 22 Benaiah..son of a valiant man of Kabzeel
12. 21 mighty men of valour, and were captains
12. 25 of the children of S., mighty men of val.
12. 28 Zadok, a young man mighty of valour, and
12. 30 mighty men of valour, famous throughout
26. 6 ruled..for they (were) mighty men of val.
26. 30 Hashabiah and his brethren, men of val.
26. 31 mighty men of valour at Jazar of Gilead
26. 32 his brethren, men of valour..two thousand
28. 1 assembled..all the valiant men, unto Je.
2 Ch. 13. 3 chosen men, (being) mighty men of valour
14. 8 army..all these (were) mighty men of va.
17. 13 and the men of war, mighty men of valo.
17. 14 with him mighty men of valour three hu.
17. 16 two hundred thousand mighty men of va.
17. 17 Eliada a mighty man of valour, and with
25. 6 He hired..mighty men of valour out of
26. 12 of the fathers of the mighty men of valo.
26. 17 fourscore priests of the LORD..valiant men
32. 21 which cut off all the mighty men of valo.
Neh. 11. 6 four hundred threescore and eight valia.
11. 14 their brethren, mighty men of valour, an
Nah. 2. 3 the valiant men (are) in scarlet, the char.

7. *Abundant, great, mighty,* כַּבִּיר *kabbir.*
Isa. 10. 13 I have put down the inhabitants like a va.

8. *Strong, stout,* ἰσχυρός *ischuros.*
Heb. 11. 34 waxed valiant in fight, turned to flight

VALIANTLY, (to behave self) —

1. *To strengthen self, show self strong,* חָזַק *chazaq,* 7.
1 Ch. 19. 13 let us behave ourselves valiantly for our

2. *Force, strength,* חַיִל *chayil.*
Num 24. 18 his enemies: and Israel shall do valiantly
Psa. 60. 12 Through God we shall do valiantly: for he
108. 13 Through God we shall do valiantly: for he
118. 15, 16 the right hand of the LORD doeth val.

VALUE, (be of more), be valued, to —

1. *Nought, an idol,* אֱלִיל *elil.*
Job 13. 4 forgers..ye (are) all physicians of no value

2. *To be weighed,* סָלָה *salah,* 4.
Job 28. 16 It cannot be valued with the gold of Op.
28. 19 neither shall it be valued with pure gold

3. *To value, set in array,* עָרַךְ *arak,* 5.
Lev. 27. 8 shall value him..shall the priest value h.
27. 12 the priest shall value it, whether it be g.

4. *Array, valuation,* עֵרֶךְ *erek.*
Lev. 27. 12 as thou valuest it..the priest, so shall it

5. *To carry different ways, excel,* διαφέρω *diapherō.*
Matt 10. 31 ye are of more value than many sparrows
Luke 12. 7 ye are of more value than many sparrows

6. *To honour,* τιμάω *timaō.*
Matt 27. 9 that was valued, whom they..did value

VAN'-IAH וַנְיָה *Jah is praise.*
One of the sons of Bani that had taken a strange wife. B.C. 456.
Ezra 10. 36 V., Meremoth, Eliashib

VANISH (away, out of sight), be vanished, to —

1. *To go on,* הָלַךְ *yalak.*
Job 7. 9 the cloud is consumed, and vanisheth aw.

2. *To vanish,* מָלַח *malach,* 2.
Isa. 51. 6 the heavens shall vanish away like smoke

3. *To be spread out,* סָרַח *sarach,* 2.
Jer. 49. 7 Concerning Edom..is their wisdom vani.?

4. *To be cut off,* צָמַת *tsamath,* 2.
Job 6. 17 What time they wax warm, they vanish

5. *To disappear, vanish,* ἀφανίζομαι *aphanizomai.*
Jas. 4. 14 appeareth for a little..and..vanisheth a.

6. *To become invisible,* γίνομαι ἄφαντος *gin. aphantos.*
Luke 24. 31 they knew him; and he vanished out of s

7. *A disappearing, vanishing,* ἀφανισμός *aphanism.*
Heb. 8. 13 which..waxeth old (is) ready to vanish a.

8. *To make idle, inactive, useless,* καταργέω *katar.*
1 Co. 13. 8 whether..knowledge, it shall vanish aw.

VANITY, vanities —
1. *Iniquity, vanity,* אָוֶן *aven.*
Job 15. 35 They..bring forth vanity, and their belly
Psa. 10. 7 under his tongue (is) mischief and vanity
Prov22. 8 that soweth iniquity shall reap vanity
Isa. 41. 29 Behold, they (are) all vanity; their works
58. 9 the putting forth of the finger, and..van.
Zech.10. 2 the idols have spoken vanity, and the di.

2. *Vanity,* הֲבֵל *habel.*
Eccl. 1. 2 Vanity..saith the Preacher..vanity..all
12. 8 Vanity..saith the Preacher; all (is)

3. *Vanity,* הֶבֶל *hebel.*
Deut32. 21 provoked me to anger with their vanities
1 Ki.16. 13 in provoking the LORD..with their vanit.
16. 26 to provoke the LORD..with their vanities
2 Ki.17. 15 they followed vanity, and became vain
Job 7. 16 let me alone; for my days (are) vanity
Psa. 31. 6 I have hated them that regard lying van.
39. 5 man at his best state (is) altogether van.
39. 11 like a moth; surely every man (is) vanity
62. 9 Surely men of low degree (are) vanity,(and)
62. 9 they (are) altogether (lighter) than vanity
78. 33 their days did he consume in vanity, and
94. 11 knoweth the thoughts..that they (are) va.
144. 4 Man is like to vanity: his days (are) as a
Prov13. 11 Wealth (gotten) by vanity shall be dimin.
21. 6 The getting of treasures..(is) a vanity to.
Eccl. 1. 2 vanities..vanities; all (is) vanity
1. 14 behold, all (is) vanity and vexation of sp.
2. 1 enjoy pleasure,.behold, this also (is) van.
2. 11 all (was) vanity and vexation of spirit, and
2. 15 I said in my heart, that this also (is) van.
2. 17 for all (is) vanity and vexation of spirit
2. 19 wise under the sun. This (is) also vanity
2. 21 This also (is) vanity and a great evil
2. 23 heart taketh not rest..This is also vanity
2. 26 This also (is) vanity and vexation of spirit
3. 19 a man hath no pre-eminence..all (is) va.
4. 4 This (is) also vanity and vexation of spirit
4. 7 I returned, and I saw vanity under the
4. 8 This (is) also vanity, yea, it (is) a sore tr.
4. 16 this also (is) vanity and vexation of spirit
5. 7 in..words (there are) also divers vanities
5. 10 not be satisfied..This (is) also vanity
6. 2 this (is) vanity, and it (is) an evil disease
6. 4 he cometh in with vanity, and departeth
6. 9 this (is) also vanity and vexation of spirit
6. 11 there be many things that increase vanity
7. 6 the laughter of the fool. This also (is) va.
7. 15 All..have I seen in the days of my vanity
8. 10 they were forgotten..This (is) also vanity
8. 14 There is a vanity which is done upon the
8. 14 according to the work..this also (is) van.
9. 9 the days..of thy vanity..the days of thy v.
11. 8 shall be many. All that cometh (is) vanity
11. 10 evil..for childhood and youth (are) vanity
12. 8 vanities, saith the Preacher; all (is) vanity
Isa. 57. 13 vanity shall take (them): but he that pu.
Jer. 2. 5 have walked after vanity, and are become
8. 19 graven images, (and) with strange vanitie.
10. 8 foolish; the stock (is) a doctrine of vanities
10. 15 They (are) vanity, (and) the work of erro.
14. 22 Are there (any) among the vanities of the
16. 19 our fathers have inherited lies, vanity, and
51. 18 They (are) vanity, the work of errors: in
Jon. 2. 8 They that observe lying vanities forsake

4. *Empty, vain, vanity,* רִיק *riq.*
Psa. 4. 2 will ye love vanity?..seek after leasing?
Hab. 2. 13 shall weary themselves for very vanity

5. *Vanity,* שָׁוְא [V.L. שָׁו] *shav.*
Job 15. 31 Let not him that is deceived trust in va.

6. *Vanity,* שָׁוְא *shav.*
Job. 7. 3 So am I made to possess months of vanity
15. 31 trust in vanity; for vanity shall be his re.
31. 5 If I have walked with vanity, or if my fo.
35. 13 God will not hear vanity; neither will the
Psa. 12. 2 They speak vanity every one with his ne.
24. 4 who hath not lifted up his soul unto vanity
41. 6 if he come to see (me), he speaketh vanity
119. 37 Turn away mine eyes from beholding van.
144. 8 Whose mouth speaketh vanity, v. 11
Prov.30. 8 Remove far from me vanity and lies, give
Isa. 5. 18 that draw iniquity with cords of vanity
30. 28 to sift the nations with the sieve of vanity
Jer. 18. 15 they have burnt incense to vanity, and th.
Eze. 13. 6 They have seen vanity and lying divinati.
13. 8 ye have spoken vanity, and seen lies, the.
13. 9 shall be upon the prophets that see vanity
13. 23 ye shall see no more vanity, nor divine
21. 29 Whiles they see vanity unto thee, whiles
22. 28 seeing vanity, and divining lies unto them
Hos. 12. 11 surely they are vanity: they sacrifice bull.

7. *Ruin, vacancy, vanity,* תֹּהוּ *tohu.*
Isa. 40. 17 counted to him less than nothing, and va.
40. 23 he maketh the judges of the earth as van.
44. 9 they that make a graven image (are)..van.
59. 4 they trust in vanity, and speak lies; they

8. *Vain, unprofitable, useless,* μάταιον *mataion.*
Acts 14. 15 that ye should turn from these vanities

9. *Vanity, uselessness,* ματαιότης *mataiotēs.*
Rom. 8. 20 the creature was made subject to vanity
Eph. 4. 17 walk not as other Gentiles walk, in the va.
2 Pe. 2. 18 when they speak great swelling..of vanity

VAPOUR —
1. *Vapour,* אֵד *ed.*
Job 36. 27 they pour down rain according to the va.

2. *What is lifted up, cloud, vapour,* נָשִׂיא *nasi.*
Psa.135. 7 He causeth the vapours to ascend from the
Jer. 10. 13 he causeth the vapours to ascend from the
51. 16 he causeth the vapours to ascend from the

3. *To go up,* עָלָה *alah.*
Job 36. 33 the cattle also concerning the vapour

4. *Smoke, vapour,* קִיטוֹר *qitor.*
Psa.148. 8 Fire, and hail; snow, and vapour; stormy

5. *Breath, vapour, smoke,* ἀτμίς *atmis.*
Acts 2. 19 signs..blood, and fire, and vapour of sm.
Jas. 4. 14 It is even a vapour, that appeareth for

VARIABLENESS —
Change, variableness, παραλλαγή *parallagē.*
Jas. 1. 17 no variableness, neither shadow of turn.

VARIANCE, (to set at) —
1. *To make two, divide into two,* διχάζω *dichazō.*
Matt10. 35 For I am come to set a man at variance

2. *Contention, strife, quarrel,* ἔρις *eris.*
Gal. 5. 20 Idolatry, witchcraft, hatred, variance, em.

VASH'-NI, וַשְׁנִי *Jah is strong.*
First born of Samuel the prophet; perhaps the same with Joel in Ch. 6. 33. B.C. 1070.
1 Ch. 6. 28 the sons of Samuel; the firstborn V., and

VASH'-TI, וַשְׁתִּי.
A queen whom Ahasuerus repudiated, and whom Esther succeeded. B.C. 519.
Esth. 1. 9 V. the queen made a feast for the women
1. 11 To bring V. the queen before the king wi.
1. 12 the queen V. refused to come at the kin.
1. 15 What shall we do unto the queen V. acc
1. 16 V. the queen hath not done wrong to the
1. 17 The king..commanded V. the queen to be
1. 19 That V. come no more before king Ahas.
2. 1 he remembered V., and what she had do.
2. 4 let the maiden..be queen instead of V.
2. 17 so that he..made her queen instead of V.

VAUNT self, to —
1. *To beautify self,* פָּאַר *paar,* 7.
Judg. 7. 2 lest Israel vaunt themselves against me

2. *To vaunt, boast, brag self,* περπερεύομαι *perper.*
1 Co. 13. 4 charity vaunteth not itself, is not puffed

VEHEMENT, (desire) —
1. *Cutting, still, sultry,* חֲרִישִׁי *charishi.*
Jon. 4. 8 that God prepared a vehement east wind

2. *Great desire,* ἐπιπόθησις *epipothēsis.*
2 Co. 7. 11 (what) vehement desire, yea..zeal, yea..re.

VEHEMENTLY, (to beat) —
1. *Terribly,* δεινῶς *deinōs.*
Luke11. 53 the Pharisees began to urge..vehemently

2. *Abundantly,* ἐκ περισσοῦ *ek perissou.*
Mark14. 31 he spake the more [vehemently], If I should

3. *Intensely, strenuously,* εὐτόνως *eutonōs.*
Luke23. 10 the chief priests and scribes stood and ve.

4. *To break or dash toward,* προσρήγνυμι *prosrēg.*
Luke 6. 48 the stream beat vehemently upon that ho.
6. 49 against which the stream did beat vehem.

VEIN — [**VEIL.** *See* VAIL.]
Outgoing, outlet, מוֹצָא *motsa.*
Job 28. 1 Surely there is a vein for the silver, and

VENGEANCE, (to take, be taken) —
1. *To avenge, take vengeance,* נָקַם *naqam.*
Psa. 99. 8 thou tookest vengeance of their inventions
Nah. 1. 2 LORD will take vengeance on his adversa.

2. *To be avenged,* נָקַם *naqam,* 2.
Jer. 50. 15 take vengeance upon her; as she hath done

3. *To be avenged,* נָקַם *naqam,* 6.
Gen. 4. 15 vengeance shall be taken on him sevenfo.

4. *Vengeance,* נָקָם *naqam.*
Deut32. 35 To me (belongeth) vengeance and recom.
32. 41 I will render vengeance to mine enemies
32. 43 will render vengeance to his adversaries
Psa. 58. 10 shall rejoice when he seeth the vengeance
Prov. 6. 34 he will not spare in the day of vengeance
Isa. 34. 8 (it is) the day of the LORD'S vengeance,(and)
35. 4 God will come (with) vengeance,(even) God
47. 3 I will take vengeance, and I will not meet
59. 17 he put on the garments of vengeance (for)
61. 2 To proclaim..the day of vengeance of our
63. 4 the day of vengeance (is) in mine heart
Eze. 24. 8 cause fury to come up to take vengeance
25. 12 hath dealt against..Judah by taking ven.
25. 15 have taken vengeance with a despiteful
Mic. 5. 15 I will execute vengeance in anger and fury

5. *Vengeance,* נְקָמָה *neqamah.*
Judg 11. 36 forasmuch as the LORD hath taken venge.
Psa. 94. 1, 1 God, to whom vengeance belongeth
149. 7 To execute vengeance upon the heathen
Jer. 11. 20 let me see thy vengeance on them: for un.
20. 12 let me see thy vengeance on them; for un.
46. 10 this (is) the day..a day of vengeance, that
50. 15 for it (is) the vengeance of the LORD: take
50. 28 the vengeance of the LORD our God, the
51. 6 this (is) the time of the LORD'S vengeance
51. 11 the vengeance of the LORD, the vengeance
51. 36 plead thy cause, and take vengeance for
Lam. 3. 60 Thou hast seen all their vengeance (and)
Eze. 25. 14 I will lay my vengeance upon Edom by
Eze. 25. 14 they shall know my vengeance, saith the
25. 17 I will execute great vengeance upon them
25. 17 when I shall lay my vengeance upon them

6. *Justice, vengeance,* δίκη *dikē.*
Acts 28. 4 whom..vengeance suffereth not to live
Jude 7 Sodom..suffering the vengeance of eternal

7. *Full vengeance,* ἐκδίκησις *ekdikēsis.*
Luke21. 22 these be the days of vengeance, that all
Rom.12. 19 Vengeance (is) mine; I will repay, saith
2 Th. 1. 8 In flaming fire taking vengeance on them
Heb. 10. 30 Vengeance..I will recompense, saith the

8. *Anger, wrath,* ὀργή *orgē.*
Rom. 3. 5 (Is) God unrighteous who taketh vengea.

VENISON —
1. *Hunting, venison,* צַיִד *tsayid.*
Gen. 25. 28 loved Esau, because he did eat of (his) v.
27. 5 Esau went to the field to hunt (for) venison
27. 7 Bring me venison, and make me savoury
27. 19 arise, I pray thee, sit and eat of my venison
27. 25 Bring..and I will eat of my son's venison
27. 31 Let my father..eat of his son's venison, th.
27. 33 where (is) he that hath taken venison, and

2. *Hunting, venison,* צֵידָה *tsedah.*
Gen. 27. 3 go out to the field, and take me..venison

VENOM —
Venom, poisonous herb, רֹאשׁ *rosh.*
Deut32. 33 Their wine (is)..the cruel venom of asps

VENT, to have —
To be opened, פָּתַח *pathach,* 2.
Job 32. 19 my belly (is) as wine (which) hath no vent

VENTURE, at a —
Perfection, simplicity, תֹּם *tom.*
1 Ki.22. 34 And a..man drew a bow at a venture, and
2 Ch.18. 33 And a..man drew a bow at a venture, and

VERIFIED, to be —
To be or become stedfast, אָמַן *aman,* 2.
Gen. 42. 20 so shall your words be verified, and ye sh.
1 Ki. 8. 26 let thy word, I pray thee, be verified, wh.
2 Ch. 6. 17 let thy word be verified, which thou hast

VERILY, verity —
1. *But, verily,* אֲבָל *abal.*
Gen.42. 21 We (are) verily guilty concerning our bro.
1 Ki. 1. 43 Verily our lord king David hath made S.
2 Ki. 4. 14 Verily she hath no child, and her husband

2. *Only,* אַךְ *ak.*
Exod31. 13 Verily my sabbaths ye shall keep: for it

3. *Surely,* אָכֵן *aken.*
Psa. 66. 19 verily God hath heard..he hath attended
Isa. 45. 15 Verily thou (art) a God that hidest thyself

4. *If not,* אִם לֹא *im lo.*
Jer. 15. 11 Verily it shall be well with thy remnant

5. *Stedfastness, stability,* אֱמוּנָה *emunah.*
Psa. 37. 3 Trust in the LORD..verily thou shalt be fed

6. *To say,* אָמַר *amar.*
Judg15. 2 I verily thought that thou hadst utterly

7. *Truth, stedfastness,* אֱמֶת *emeth.*
Psa.111. 7 The works of his hands (are) verity and ju.

8. *To acquire, get, set up,* קָנָה *qanah.*
1 Ch.21. 24 but I will verily buy it for the full price

9. *Truth, reality, certainty,* ἀλήθεια *alētheia.*
1 Ti. 2. 7 teacher of the Gentiles in faith and verity

10. *Truly, really, certainly,* ἀληθῶς *alēthōs.*
1 Jo. 2. 5 whoso keepeth his word, in him verily is

11. *Amen, so be it, so it is,* ἀμήν *amēn.*
Matt. 5. 18 verily I say unto you, Till heaven and ea
5. 26 Verily I say unto thee, Thou shalt by no
6. 2, 5, 16 Verily I say unto you, They have
See also 8. 10; 10. 15, 23, 42; 11. 11; 13. 17; 16. 28; 17. 20; 18, 3, 13, 18; 19. 23, 28; 21. 21, 31; 23. 36; 24. 2, 34, 47; 25. 12, 40, 45; 26. 13, 21, 34; Mark 3. 28; 6. [11]; 8. 12; 9. 1, 41; 10. 15, 29; 11. 23; 12. 43; 13. 30; 14. 9, 18, 25, 30; Luke 4. 24; 12. 37; 13. [35]; 18. 17, 29; 21. 32; 23. 43; John 1. 51, 51; 3. 3, 3, 5, 5, 11, 11; 5. 19, 19, 24, 24, 25, 25; 6. 26, 26, 32, 32, 47, 47, 53, 53; 8. 34, 34, 51, 51, 58, 58; 10. 1, 1, 7, 7; 12. 24, 24; 13. 16, 16, 20, 20, 21, 21, 38, 38; 14. 12, 12; 16. 20, 20, 23, 23; 21. 18, 18.

12. *For,* γάρ *gar.*
Acts 16. 37 do they thrust us out privily? nay verily
Rom 15. 27 It hath pleased them verily; and their de.

13. *Truly,* δήπου *dēpou.*
Heb. 2. 16 For verily he took not on..angels; but he

14. *Truly, indeed,* μέν (δέ) *men (de).*
Mark 9. 12 Elias [verily] cometh first, and restoreth
Acts 19. 4 John [verily] baptized with the baptism
22. 3 I am [verily] a man..a Jew, born in Tarsus
Rom. 2. 25 For circumcision verily profiteth, if thou
1 Co. 5. 3 For I verily, as absent in body, but pres.
14. 17 For thou verily givest thanks well, but
Heb. 3. 5 Moses verily (was) faithful in all his house
6. 16 For men [verily] swear by the greater, and
7. 5 verily they that are of the sons of Levi
7. 18 For there is verily a disannulling of the
9. 1 verily the first..had also ordinances of
12. 10 For they verily for a few days chastened
1 Pe. 1. 20 Who verily was foreordained before the

15. *Verily, indeed, truly,* ναί *nai.*
Luke 11. 51 verily I say unto you, It shall be required
16. *Really, actually,* ὄντως *ontōs.*
Gal. 3. 21 verily righteousness should have been by
17. *Therefore,* μὲν οὖν *men oun.*
Acts 26. 9 I verily thought with myself, that I ought

VERMILION —
Red lead, red ochre, red colour, שָׁשַׁר *shashar.*
Jer. 22. 14 cieled with cedar, and painted with ver.
Eze. 23. 14 images of..Chaldeans pourtrayed with ve.

VERY (much, sore) —
1. *To deal treacherously, deceive,* בָּגַד *bagad.*
Isa. 48. 8 I knew that thou wouldest deal very tre.
2. *(With) treachery,* בֶּגֶד *beged.*
Isa. 24. 16 treacherous dealers have dealt very trea.
Jer. 12. 1 are all they happy that deal very treach.
3. *Great,* גָּדוֹל *gadol.*
Gen. 27. 33 Isaac trembled very exceed.; Zech. 1. 15.
4. *Sufficient,* דַּי *dai.*
Hab. 2. 13 shall labour in the very fire..for very vanity
5. *This,* זֶה *zeh.*
Gen. 27. 21 whether thou (be) my very son Esau or
6. *Might, very,* מְאֹד *meod.*
Gen. 1. 31 God saw every thing..and, behold..very
4. 5 Cain was very wroth, and his countenance
12. 14 beheld the woman, that she (was) very fair
13. 2 Abram (was) very rich in cattle, in silver
18. 20 and because their sin is very grievous
21. 11 the thing was very grievous in Abraham's
24. 16 the damsel (was) very fair to look upon, a
26. 13 and grew until he became very great
34. 7 they were very wroth, because he had wr.
41. 19 seven other kine..poor and very ill favo.
41. 31 not be known..it (shall be) very grievous
41. 49 gathered corn as the sand of the sea, very
47. 13 the famine (was) very sore, so that the la.
50. 9 horsemen: and it was a very great comp.
50. 10 they mourned with a great and very sore
Exod. 1. 20 the people multiplied, and waxed very mi.
9. 3 (there shall be) a very grievous murrain
9. 18 I will cause it to rain a very grievous hail
9. 24 fire mingled with the hail, very grievous
10. 14 very grievous (were they); before them th.
11. 3 Moses (was) very great in the land of Eg.
12. 38 and flocks and herds, (even) very much
Num. 11. 33 the LORD smote the people with a very
12. 3 Moses (was) very meek, above all the men
13. 28 and the cities (are) walled, (and) very gr.
16. 15 Moses was very wroth, and said unto the
22. 17 I will promote thee unto very great hon.
32. 1 the children of Gad had a very great mul.
Deut. 9. 20 the LORD was very angry with Aaron to ha.
20. 15 all the cities (which are) very far off from
28. 54 the man (that is) tender..and very delic.
30. 14 the word (is) very nigh unto thee, in thy
Josh. 1. 7 be thou strong and very courageous, that
3. 16 rose up upon an heap very far from the ci.
8. 4 go not very far from the city, but be ye
9. 9 From a very far country thy servants are
9. 13 are become old by reason of the very long
9. 22 We (are) very far from you; when ye dw.
10. 20 slaying them with a very great slaughter
11. 4 went..with horses and chariots very many
13. 1 there remaineth yet very much land to be
22. 8 with very much cattle..with very much
23. 6 Be ye therefore very courageous to keep
Judg. 3. 17 unto Eglon..and Eglon (was) a very fat man
11. 33 he smote them..with a very great slaugh.
13. 6 and his countenance (was)..very terrible
18. 9 for we have seen the land..it (is) very go.
Ruth 1. 20 the Almighty hath dealt very bitterly wi.
1 Sa. 2. 17 the sin of the young men was very great
2. 22 Eli was very old, and heard all that his so.
4. 10 there was a very great slaughter; for th
5. 9 was against the city with a very great de.
5. 11 the hand of God was very heavy there
14. 20 (and there was) a very great discomfiture
14. 31 to Aijalon: and the people were very fai.
18. 8 Saul was very wroth, and the saying dis.
18. 15 Saul saw that he behaved himself very wi.
19. 4 works (have been) to thee ward very good
25. 2 the man (was) very great, and he had three
25. 15 the men (were) very good unto us, and we
2 Sa. 1. 26 very pleasant hast thou been unto me, thy
2. 17 there was a very sore battle that day: and
3. 8 Then was Abner very wroth for the words
11. 2 the woman (was) very beautiful to look up.
13. 3 and Jonadab (was) a very subtil man
13. 21 when king David heard..he was very wr.
13. 36 king also and all his servants wept very so.
18. 17 laid a very great heap of stones upon him
19. 32 Barzillai was a very aged man, (even) fou.
19. 32 had provided..for he (was) a very great
24. 10 take away the iniquity..I have done very
1 Ki. 1. 4 the damsel (was) very fair, and cherished
1. 6 he also (was a) very goodly (man); and (his
1. 15 the king was very old; and Abishag the
10. 2 she came to Jerusalem with a very great
10. 2 with camels that bare spices, and very mu.
10. 10 of spices very great store, and precious
21. 26 he did very abominably in following idols
2 Ki. 14. 26 the LORD saw..(that it was) very bitter
17. 18 the LORD was very angry with Israel, and
21. 16 Manasseh shed innocent blood very much
1 Ch. 18. 8 brought David very much brass, wherew.
21. 8 do away the iniquity..I have done very foo
1 Ch. 21. 13 let me fall now..for very great (are) his m.
2 Ch. 7. 8 all Israel with him, a very great congreg.
9. 1 with a very great company, and camels th.
14. 13 and they carried away very much spoil
16. 8 a huge host, with very many chariots and
24. 24 the LORD delivered a very great host into
30. 13 there assembled..a very great congregat.
32. 29 God had given him substance very much
33. 14 raised it up a very great height, and put
Ezra 10. 1 a very great congregation of men and wo.
Neh. 2. 2 this (is) nothing..I was very sore afraid
4. 7 to be stopped, then they were very wro.
5. 6 I was very angry when I heard their cry
8. 17 And there was very great gladness
Esth. 1. 12 therefore was the king very wroth, and his
Job 1. 3 five hundred she asses, and a very great
2. 13 for they saw that (his) grief was very great
Psa. 46. 1 God (is)..a very present help in trouble
50. 3 it shall be very tempestuous round about h.
79. 8 prevent us; for we are brought very low
92. 5 O LORD..thy thoughts are very deep
93. 5 Thy testimonies are very sure: holiness
104. 1 O LORD my God, thou art very great, thou
119. 138 testimonies..(are) righteous and very fa.
119. 140 Thy word (is) very pure: therefore thy s.
142. 6 Attend unto my cry; for I am brought ve.
Isa 16. 6 he (is) very proud: (even) of his haughti.
31. 1 horsemen, because they are very strong
47. 6 upon the ancient hast thou very heavily
52. 13 be exalted and extolled, and be very high
64. 9 Be not wroth very sore, O LORD, neither
64. 12 hold thy peace, and afflict us very sore?
Jer. 2. 12 be horribly afraid, be ye very desolate, sa.
14. 17 with a great breach, with a very grievous
18. 13 the virgin of Israel hath done a very hor.
24. 2 One basket (had) very good figs, (even) li.
24. 2 the other basket (had) very naughty figs
24. 3 the good figs, very good; and the evil, ve.
40. 12 gathered wine and summer fruits very mu.
Eze. 27. 25 made very glorious in the midst of the seas
37. 2 (there were) very many..(they were) very
40. 2 set me upon a very high mountain, by wh.
47. 7 at the bank..(were) very many trees on
47. 9 there shall be a very great multitude of fi.
Joel 2. 11 his camp (is) very great: for (he is) strong
2. 11 the day of the LORD (is) great and very te.
Zech. 9. 2 Tyrus, and Zidon, though it be very wise
9. 5 Gaza also (shall see it), and be very sorr.
14. 4 (and there shall be) a very great valley
7. *Unto might,* עַד־מְאֹד, עַד־לִמְאֹד *ad (le-)meod.*
1 Sa. 25. 36 merry within him, for he (was) very drunk
2 Ch. 16. 14 they made a very great burning for him
Psa. 119. 107 I am afflicted very much: quicken me, O
Lam. 5. 22 But thou..thou art very wroth against
Dan. 8. 8 Therefore the he goat waxed very great
11. 25 shall be stirred up to battle with a very
8. *Little, small, few,* מִזְעָר *mizar.*
Isa. 10. 25 For yet a very little while, and the indig.
16. 14 and the remnant very small (and) feeble
29. 17 (Is) it not yet a very little while, and Le.
9. *Upward,* מַעְלָה, לְמַעְלָה *(le-)malah.*
Deut 28. 43 The stranger shall get up above thee very
1 Ch. 23. 17 but the sons of Rehabiah were very many
10. *Bone, substance,* עֶצֶם *etsem.*
Josh. 10. 27 stones in the cave's mouth..until this very
Eze. 2. 3 transgressed against me..unto this very
11. *In an instant,* בְּפֶתַע *be-petha.*
Num. 6. 9 if any man die very suddenly by him, and
12. *Loathsome* or *only* (?), קַט *qat* (prob. error).
Eze. 16. 47 but, as..a very little (thing), thou wast co.
13. *Wall, side, roof,* קִיר *qir.*
Jer. 4. 19 my bowels! I am pained at my very heart
14. *Great, much, many, very,* שַׂגִּיא *saggi.*
Dan. 2. 12 For this cause the king was very angry and very
15. *Truly, really, certainly,* ἀληθῶς *alēthōs.*
John 7. 26 Do the rulers know..this is the [very] Ch.
16. *He (she, it) himself,* αὐτός *autos.*
Rom 13. 6 attending continually upon this very thi.
1 Th. 5. 23 the very God of peace sanctify you wholly
Heb. 10. 1 not the very image of the things, can ne.
17. *And, also, even,* καί *kai.*
Luke 9. 5 shake off the [very] dust from your feet
18. *Very,* λίαν *lian,* or βαθέως *batheos.*
Mark 16. 2 And very early in the morning, Lu. 24. 1.
19. *Vehemently, impetuously,* σφόδρα *sphodra.*
Matt 18. 31 they were very sorry, and came and told
Mark 16. 4 stone was rolled away: for it was very gr.
Luke 18. 23 he was..sorrowful, for he was very rich
20. *Above,* ὑπέρ *huper.*
1 Th. 5. 13 to esteem them very highly in love for

[*See also* Act, aged men, attentive, bold, costly, dark, diligently, early, fair, far off, frowardness, fruitful, great, great things, heavy, high, little, lovely, low, much, old, pitiful, precious, rainy, small, sorrowful, that, well, wickedness.]

VERY chiefest, deed, great, many, small, well —
1. *But, truly, yet,* אוּלָם *ulam.*
Exod 9. 16 in very deed for this..have I raised thee
1 Sa. 25. 34 in very deed..the LORD God of Israel liv.
2. *Truly, indeed,* אָמְנָם *umnam.*
2 Ch. 6. 18 will God in very deed dwell with men on
3. *(Of) God,* אֱלֹהִים *elohim.*
1 Sa. 14. 15 trembling..it was a very great trembling
4. *Abundance, multitude, greatness,* רֹב *rob.*
Zech 8. 4 and every man with his staff..for very age
5. *Better,* κάλλιον *kallion.*
Acts 25. 10 done no wrong, as thou very well know.
6. *More, greater, more excellent,* πλείων, πλεῖστος.
Matt 21. 8 a very great multitude spread their gar.
2 Co. 9. 2 and your zeal hath provoked very many
7. *Very chiefest, exceedingly,* ὑπὲρ λίαν *huper lian.*
2 Co. 11. 5 I was not a whit behind the very chiefest
12. 11 in nothing am I behind the very chiefest

VERY deed, small —
1. *To beat small,* דָּקַק *daqaq,* 5.
Exod 30. 36 thou shalt beat..of it very small, and
2. *To be found, prepared, established,* כּוּן *kun,* 2.
1 Sa. 26. 4 understood that Saul was come in very

VESSEL —
1. *Vessel, instrument,* כְּלִי *keli.*
Gen. 43. 11 take of the..fruits in the land in your ve.
Exod 25. 39 shall he make it, with all these vessels
27. 3 all the vessels thereof thou shalt make
27. 19 All the vessels of the tabernacle in all the
30. 27 vessels, and the candlestick and his vess.
30. 28 the altar of burnt offering with all his ve.
35. 13 The table, and his staves, and all his ve.
35. 16 and all his vessels, the laver and his foo
37. 16 he made the vessels which (were) upon
37. 24 of pure gold made he it, and all the vess.
38. 3 he made all the vessels..all the vessels
38. 30 therewith he made..all the vessels of the
39. 36 The table..all the vessels thereof, and the
39. 37 all the vessels thereof, and the oil for li.
39. 39 and all his vessels, the laver and his foot
39. 40 all the vessels of the service of the tabe.
40. 9 thou shalt take..and anoint..all the ves
40. 10 thou shalt anoint the altar..all his ves.
Lev. 6. 28 the earthen vessel wherein it is sodden
8. 11 anointed the altar and all his vessels, both
11. 32 any vessel of wood..whatsoever vessel (it
11. 33 every earthen vessel whereinto (any) of th.
11. 34 drink that may be drunk in every..vessel
14. 5 in an earthen vessel over running water
14. 50 in an earthen vessel over running water
15. 12 the vessel of earth..every vessel of wood
Num. 1. 50 over all the vessels thereof..all the vess.
3. 31 the vessels of the sanctuary wherewith
3. 36 all the vessels thereof, and all that serve.
4. 9 all the oil vessels thereof, wherewith they
4. 10 they shall put it and all the vessels ther.
4. 14 all the vessels thereof..all the vessels of
4. 15 of covering..all the vessels of the sanctuary
4. 16 in the sanctuary, and in the vessels ther.
5. 17 shall take holy water in an earthen vessel
7. 1 both the altar and all the vessels thereof
7. 85 all the silver vessels..two thousand and
18. 3 only they shall not come nigh the vessels
19. 15 every open vessel, which hath no covering
19. 17 running water shall be put thereto in a v.
19. 18 upon all the vessels, and upon the persons
Deut 23. 24 but thou shalt not put (any) in thy vessel
Josh. 6. 19, 24 the silver, and gold, and vessels
Ruth 2. 9 when thou art athirst, go unto the vessels
1 Sa. 9. 7 for the bread is spent in our vessels, and
21. 5 the vessels of the young men are holy, and
21. 5 though it were sanctified this day in the v.
2 Sa. 8. 10 vessels of silver..vessels of gold..vessels
17. 28 Brought beds, and basins, and earthen v.
1 Ki. 7. 45 all these vessels, which Hiram made to
7. 47 Solomon left all the vessels..because they
7. 48 And Solomon made all the vessels that
7. 51 the silver, and the gold, and the vessels
8. 4 all the holy vessels that (were) in the tab.
10. 21 drinking vessels..all the vessels of the ho.
10. 25 vessels of silver, and vessels of gold and
15. 15 he brought in..silver, and gold, and vessels
17. 10 Fetch me..a little water in a vessel, that
2 Ki. 4. 3 Go, borrow thee vessels..empty vessels
4. 4 and shalt pour out into all those vessels
4. 6 it came to pass, when the vessels were full
4. 6 she said unto her son, Bring me yet a ves.
4. 6 And he said unto her..not a vessel more
7. 15 all the way (was) full of garments and ves.
12. 13 any vessels of gold, or vessels of silver, of
14. 14 all the vessels..found in the house of the
23. 4 to bring forth..all the vessels that were
24. 13 cut in pieces all the vessels of gold which
25. 14 all the vessels of brass wherewith they
25. 16 the brass of all these vessels was without
1 Ch. 9. 28 had the charge of the ministering vessels
9. 29 to oversee the vessels, and all the instru.
18. 8 and the pillars, and the vessels of brass
18. 10 all manner of vessels of gold and silver
22. 19 to bring..the holy vessels of God, into the
23. 26 nor any vessels of it for the service there.
28. 13 for all the vessels of service in the house
2 Ch. 4. 18 Solomon made all these vessels in great
4. 19 And Solomon made all the vessels that
5. 5 all the holy vessels that (were) in the tab.
9. 20 the drinking vessels..all the vessels of the
9. 24 brought..vessels of silver, and vessels of
15. 18 had dedicated, silver, and gold, and vess.
24. 14 whereof were made vessels for the house
24. 14 vessels to minister..vessels of gold and

2 Ch.25. 24 all the vessels that were found in the ho.
28. 24 the vessels..and cut in pieces the vessels
29. 18 with all the vessels..all the vessels there.
29. 19 all the vessels, which king Ahaz in his
36. 7 N. also carried off the vessels of the hou.
36. 10 brought him to B., with the goodly vesse.
36. 18 all the vessels of the house of God, great
36. 19 and destroyed all the goodly vessels the.
Ezra 1. 6 strengthened their hands with vessels of
1. 7 the king brought forth the vessels of the
1. 10 silver basons..(and) other vessels a thou.
1. 11 the vessels of gold and of silver (were) five
8. 25 the silver, and the gold, and the vessels
8. 26 silver vessels an hundred talents, (and) of
8. 27 two vessels of fine copper, precious as go.
8. 28 Ye (are) holy unto the LORD; the vessels
8. 30 the silver, and the gold, and the vessels
8. 33 the silver and the gold and the vessels w.
Neh. 10. 39 where (are) the vessels of the sanctuary
13. 5 the vessels, and the tithes of the corn, the
13. 9 thither brought I again the vessels of the
Esth. 1. 7 in vessels of gold, the vessels being dive.
Psa. 2. 9 dash them in pieces like a potter's vessel
31. 12 I am forgotten..I am like a broken vess.
Prov 25. 4 there shall come forth a vessel for the fi.
Isa. 18. 2 in vessels of bulrushes upon the waters
22. 24 vessels of small quantity, from the vessels
22. 24 of cups,even to all the vessels of flagons
52. 11 be ye clean, that bear the vessels of the
65. 4 of abominable (things is in) their vessels
66. 20 bring an offering in a clean vessel into
Jer. 14. 3 they returned with their vessels empty
18. 4 the vessel that he made of clay was mar.
18. 4 he made it again another vessel, as seem.
19. 11 as (one) breaketh a potter's vessel, that
22. 28 (is he) a vessel wherein (is) no pleasure?
25. 34 and ye shall fall like a pleasant vessel
27. 16 the vessels of the LORD'S house shall now
27. 18 the vessels which are left in the house of
27. 19 concerning the residue of the vessels that
27. 21 concerning the vessels that remain (in) the
28. 3 the vessels of the LORD'S house that Ne.
28. 6 to bring again the vessels of the LORD'S
32. 14 put them in an earthen vessel, that they
40. 10 put (them) in your vessels, and dwell in
48. 11 not been emptied from vessel to vessel
48. 12 shall empty his vessels, and break their
48. 38 I have broken Moab like a vessel wherein
49. 29 their curtains, and all their vessels, and
51. 34 he hath made me an empty vessel, he ha.
52. 18 all the vessels of brass wherewith they
52. 20 the brass of all these vessels was without
Eze. 4. 9 put them in one vessel, and make thee
15. 3 will (men) take a pin..to hang any vessel
27. 13 they traded the persons of men and ves.
Dan. 1. 2 with part of the vessels of the house of God
1. 2 he brought the vessels into the treasure
11. 8 with their precious vessels of silver and
Hos. 8. 8 Israel..as a vessel wherein (is) no pleas.
13. 15 shall spoil the treasure of all pleasant ve.

2. *A vessel, utensil,* מָאן *man.*
Ezra 5. 14 the vessels also of gold and silver of the
5. 15 Take these vessels, go, carry them into the
6. 5 let the golden and silver vessels of the ho.
7. 19 The vessels also that are given thee for the
Dan. 5. 2 to bring the golden and silver vessels wh.
5. 3 Then they brought the golden vessels
5. 23 they have brought the vessels of his ho.

3. *A bottle,* נֶבֶל, נֵבֶל *nebel.*
Isa. 30. 14 as the breaking of the potter's vessel that

4. *A vessel, utensil,* ἀγγεῖον *aggeion.*
Matt 13. 48 gathered the good into [vessels], but cast
25. 4 the wise took oil in their vessels with th.

5. *A vessel, utensil, instrument,* σκεῦος *skeuos.*
Mark 11. 16 that any man should carry (any) vessel
Luke 8. 16 covereth it with a vessel, or putteth (it)
John 19. 29 Now there was set a vessel full of vinegar
Acts 9. 15 he is a chosen vessel unto me, to bear my
10. 11 a certain vessel descending unto him, as
10. 16 the vessel was received up again into he.
11. 5 A certain vessel descend, as it had been
Rom. 9. 21 to make one vessel unto honour, and an.
9. 22 the vessels of wrath fitted to destruction
9. 23 the riches of his glory on the vessels of
2 Co. 4. 7 we have this treasure in earthen vessels
1 Th. 4. 4 how to possess his vessel in sanctification
2 Ti. 2. 20 there are not only vessels of gold and of
2. 21 he shall be a vessel unto honour, sancti.
Heb. 9. 21 the tabernacle and all the vessels of the
1 Pe. 3. 7 giving honour..as unto the weaker vessel
Rev. 2. 27 as the vessels of a potter shall they be br.
18. 12 vessels of ivory, and all manner vessels of

VESTMENT, vestry, vesture —

1. *Cloak, garment, covering,* בֶּגֶד *beged.*
Gen. 41. 42 arrayed him in vestures of fine linen, and

2. *A covering,* כְּסוּת *kesuth.*
Deut 22. 12 fringes upon the four quarters of thy ve.

3. *Clothing, dress, attire,* לְבוּשׁ *lebush.*
2 Ki. 10. 22 Bring forth vestments for all the worship.
Psa. 22. 18 They part..and cast lots upon my vesture
102. 26 as a vesture shalt thou change them, and

4. *Clothing,* מַלְבּוּשׁ *malbush.*
2 Ki. 10. 22 And he brought them forth vestments

5. *Wardrobe, vestry,* מֶלְתָּחָה *meltachah.*
2 Ki. 10. 22 he said unto him that (was) over the ves.

6. *What is put on, garment, mantle,* ἱμάτιον *hima.*
Rev. 19. 13 he (was) clothed with a vesture dipped in
19. 16 he hath on (his) vesture, and on his thigh

7. *Dress, raiment, apparel,* ἱματισμός *himatismos.*
Matt 27. 35 [and upon my vesture did they cast lots]
John 19. 24 and for my vesture they did cast lots

8. *What is thrown round one,* περιβόλαιον *peribol.*
Heb. 1. 12 as a vesture shalt thou fold them up, and

VEX (self), be vexed (with a devil), to—

1. *To be troubled, hastened,* בָּהַל *bahel,* 2.
Psa. 6. 2 O LORD, heal me; for my bones are vexed
6. 3 My soul is also sore vexed: but thou, O L.
6. 10 Let all mine enemies be..sore vexed: let

2. *To trouble, hasten,* בָּהַל *bahel,* 3.
Psa. 2. 5 shall he..vex them in his sore displeasure

3. *To thrust away,* דָּחַק *dachaq.*
Judg. 2. 18 of them that oppressed them and vexed

4. *To trouble, crush, destroy,* הָמַם *hamam.*
2 Ch. 15. 6 for God did vex them with all adversity

5. *To make to tremble, shake,* זוּעַ *zua,* 3a.
Hab. 2. 7 Shall they not..awake that shall vex thee

6. *To afflict, grieve,* יָגָה *yagah,* 5.
Job 19. 2 How long will ye vex my soul, and break

7. *To press, thrust out,* יָנָה *yanah,* 5.
Exod 22. 21 Thou shalt neither vex a stranger nor op.
Lev. 19. 33 And if a stranger..ye shall not vex him
Eze. 22. 7 in thee have they vexed the fatherless and
22. 29 have vexed the poor and needy; yea, they

8. *To be distressed, straitened,* יָצַר *yatsar.*
2 Sa. 13. 2 Amnon was so vexed, that he fell sick for

9. *To be angry, sad,* כָּעַס *kaas.*
Eze. 32. 9 I will also vex the hearts of many people

10. *To be bitter,* מָרַר *marar.*
2 Ki. 4. 27 Let her alone; for her soul is vexed with

11. *To cause to be bitter,* מָרַר *marar,* 5.
Job 27. 2 the Almighty, (who) hath vexed my soul

12. *To grieve, wrest, take pains, labour,* עָצַב *atsab,* 3.
Isa. 63. 10 they rebelled, and vexed his holy Spirit

13. *To do evil,* עָשָׂה רַע *asah ra.*
2 Sa. 12. 18 how will he then vex himself, if we tell

14. *To bind up, distress, be distressed,* צָרַר *tsarar.*
Lev. 18. 18 to vex (her), to uncover her nakedness
Num 25. 17 Vex the Midianites, and smite them
25. 18 For they vex you with their wiles where.
33. 55 shall vex you in the land wherein ye dw.
Isa. 11. 13 not envy Judah, and Judah shall not vex

15. *To cause to be distressed,* צָרַר *tsarar,* 5.
Neh. 9. 27 into the hand of their enemies, who vex.

16. *To cause to be vexed, wearied,* קוּץ *quts,* 5.
Isa. 7. 6 Let us go up against Judah, and vex it

17. *To be or become short or grieved,* קָצַר *qatser.*
Judg. 16. 16 it came to pass..his soul was vexed unto

18. *To cause evil, treat ill,* רָעַע *raa,* 5.
Num 20. 15 the Egyptians vexed us and our fathers

19. *To crush,* רָעַץ *raats.*
Judg. 10. 8 they vexed and oppressed the children

20. *To do wickedly, vex,* רָשַׁע *rasha,* 5.
1 Sa. 14. 47 whithersoever he turned himself, he ve.

21. *To try, test,* βασανίζω *basanizō.*
2 Pe. 2. 8 [vexed (his) righteous soul from day to]

22. *To do evil,* κακόω *kakoō.*
Acts 12. 1 king stretched forth (his) hands to vex

23. *To have or act as a demon,* δαιμονίζομαι *daim.*
Matt 15. 22 my daughter is grievously vexed with a

24. *To be worn down,* καταπονέομαι *kataponeomai.*
2 Pe. 2. 7 delivered just Lot, vexed with the filthy

25. *To be crowded, harassed,* ὀχλέομαι *ochleomai.*
Luke 6. 18 [they that were vexed] with unclean spi.
Acts 5. 16 them which were vexed with unclean sp.

26. *To experience, suffer, endure,* πάσχω *paschō.*
Matt 17. 15 he is lunatic, and sore [vexed]: for oft ti.

VEXATION, vexed —

1. *Trembling,* זַעֲוָה *zevaah.*
Isa. 28. 19 it shall be a vexation only (to) understa.

2. *Trouble, destruction,* מְהוּמָה *mehumah.*
Deut 28. 20 LORD shall send upon thee cursing, vexa.
2 Ch. 15. 5 great vexations..upon all the inhabitants
Eze. 22. 5 thee, (which art) infamous..much vexed

3. *Sadness, wrong, vexation,* רְעוּת *reuth.*
Eccl. 1. 14 behold, all (is) vanity and vexation of sp.
2. 11 all (was) vanity and vexation of spirit, and
2. 17 for all (is) vanity and vexation of spirit
2. 26 This also (is) vanity and vexation of spir.
4. 4 This (is) also vanity and vexation of spir.
4. 6 full (with) travail and vexation of spirit
6. 9 this (is) also vanity and vexation of spirit

4. *Sadness, wrong, vexation,* רַעְיוֹן *rayon.*
Eccl. 1. 17 I perceived, that this also is vexation of
2. 22 what hath man..of the vexation of his h.
4. 16 Surely this also (is) vanity and vexation

5. *A breaking, breach, destruction,* שֶׁבֶר, שֵׁבֶר *sheber.*
Isa. 65. 14 but ye..shall howl for vexation of spirit

VIAL —

1. *A vial, cruet, flask,* פַּךְ *pak.*
1 Sa. 10. 1 Then Samuel took a vial of oil, and pour.

2. *A vial, bowl, basin,* φιάλη *phialē.*
Rev. 5. 8 golden vials full of odours, which are the
15. 7 seven golden vials full of the wrath of G.
16. 1 pour out the vials of the wrath of God up.
16. 2 went and poured out his vial upon the ea.
16. 3, 4, 8, 10, 12 angel poured out his vial up.
16. 17 the seventh angel poured out his vial into
17. 1 the seven angels which had the seven vi.
21. 9 the seven angels, which had the seven vi.

VICTORY, (to get) —

1. *To give ease or security,* יָשַׁע *yasha,* 5.
Psa. 98. 1 his holy arm, hath gotten him the victory

2. *Prominence, pre-eminence,* נֵצַח, נֶצַח *netsach.*
1 Ch. 29. 11 the glory, and the victory, and the majes
Isa. 25. 8 He will swallow up death in victory, and the

3. *Ease, security,* תְּשׁוּעָה *teshuah.*
2 Sa. 19. 2 the victory that day was..into mourning
23. 10 the LORD wrought a great victory that day
23. 12 and the LORD wrought a great victory

4. *To get victory, be invincible, conquer,* νικάω *nikaō*
Rev. 15. 2 them that had gotten the victory over the

5. *Victory,* νίκη *nikē.*
1 Jo. 5. 4 this is the victory that overcometh the wo.

6. *Victory,* νῖκος *nikos.*
Matt 12. 20 till he send forth judgment unto victory
1 Co. 15. 54 saying..Death is swallowed up in victory
15. 55 O death..O grave, where (is) thy victory?
15. 57 God, which giveth us the victory through

VICTUALS, (to provide) —

1. *Eating, food,* אֹכֶל *okel.*
Gen. 14. 11 took..all their victuals, and went their w.
Lev. 25. 37 Thou shalt not..lend him thy victuals for
Deut 23. 19 usury of victuals, usury of any thing that

2. *Usual allowance or diet,* אֲרֻחָה *aruchah.*
Jer. 40. 5 gave..victuals, and a reward, and let him

3. *Eating, food,* מַאֲכָל *maakal.*
2 Ch. 11. 11 and store of victuals, and of oil and wine

4. *Food,* מָזוֹן *mazon.*
2 Ch. 11. 23 and he gave them victual in abundance

5. *Quickening, sustenance,* מִחְיָה *michyah.*
Judg 17. 10 I will give..a suit of apparel, and thy vi.

6. *To contain, provide, nourish, sustain,* כּוּל *kul,* 3a.
1 Ki. 4. 7 which provided victuals for the king and
4. 27 those officers provided victuals for king S.

7. *Bread, food,* לֶחֶם *lechem.*
1 Ki. 11. 18 appointed him victuals, and gave him la.
Jer. 44. 17 had we plenty of victuals, and were well

8. *Hunting, venison,* צַיִד *tsayid.*
Josh 9. 14 the men took of their victuals, and asked
Neh. 13. 15 testified..in the day wherein they sold vic.

9. *Hunting, venison,* צֵידָה *tsedah.*
Exod 12. 39 neither had they prepared..any victual
Josh. 1. 11 Prepare you victuals; for within three days
9. 11 Take victuals with you for the journey
Judg. 7. 8 So the people took victuals in their hand
20. 10 to fetch victual for the people, that they
1 Sa. 22. 10 gave him victuals, and gave him the sword

10. *Ground corn, victuals,* שֶׁבֶר *sheber.*
Neh. 10. 31 bring ware or any victuals on the sabbath

11. *Eating, food,* βρῶμα *brōma.*
Matt 14. 15 may go into the villages, and buy. victu.

12. *Corn, provisions,* ἐπισιτισμός *episitismos.*
Luke 9. 12 they may go into the towns..and get vict.

VIEW, to —

1. *To understand, consider,* בִּין *bin,* 1, 5.
Ezra 8. 15 I viewed the people and the priests, and

2. *From before,* מִנֶּגֶד *min-neged.*
2 Ki. 2. 7 fifty men..went, and stood to view afar off

3. *To see,* רָאָה *raah.*
Josh. 2. 1 saying, Go, view the land, even Jericho

4. *To travel on foot, traverse,* רָגַל *ragal,* 3.
Josh. 7. 2 Go up and view..And the men..viewed A.

5. *To view,* שָׂבַר בְּ *sabar be* [V.L. שָׁבַר בְּ].
Neh. 2. 13 And I..viewed the walls of Jerusalem
2. 15 Then went I up..and viewed the wall, and

VIGILANT, (to be) —

To be vigilant, wakeful, γρηγορέω *grēgoreō.*
1 Pe. 5. 8 Be sober, be vigilant; because your adver.

VILE, (person), vilest —

1. *To be despised, despicable,* בָּזָה *bazah,* 2.
Dan. 11. 21 in his estate shall stand up a vile person

2. *Vileness, depression,* זֻלּוּת *zulluth.*
Psa. 12. 8 The wicked walk..when the vilest men

3. *To be gluttonous, vile, lightly esteemed,* זָלַל *zalal.*
Jer. 15. 19 if thou take..the precious from the vile
Lam. 1. 11 see..and consider, for I am become vile

4. *To fade, wear away, be empty, foolish,* נָבֵל *nabel.*
Isa. 32. 5 The vile person shall be no more called l.
32. 6 For the vile person will speak villany, and

5. *Emptiness, folly,* נְבָלָה *nebalah.*
Judg. 19. 24 but unto this man do not so vile a thing

6. *What is despised,* נִמְבְזָה *nemibzah.*
1 Sa. 15. 9 vile and refuse, that they destroyed utte.
7. *Vile,* שֹׁעָר *shoar.*
Jer. 29. 17 will make them like vile figs, that cannot
8. *Dishonour,* ἀτιμία *atimia.*
Rom. 1. 26 For this..God gave them up unto vile aff.
9. *Filthy, dirty,* ῥυπαρός *rhuparos.*
Jas. 2. 2 if there come..in also a poor man in vile
10. *Low estate, humiliation, abasement,* ταπείνωσις.
Phil. 3. 21 Who shall change our vile body, that it

VILE, to be (more, reputed, viler) —
1. *To be defiled,* טָמָה *tamah,* 2.
Job 18. 3 Wherefore are we reputed vile in your si.
2. *To be pained, vile,* כָּאָה *kaah,* 2.
Job 30. 8 children of base men; they were viler than
3. *To be light, lightly esteemed,* קָלַל *qalal.*
Job 40. 4 Behold, I am vile; what shall I answer
Nah. 1. 14 I will make thy grave; for thou art vile
4. *To be or become light, lightly esteemed,* קָלַל *qalal,* 2.
2 Sa. 6. 22 I will yet be more vile than thus, and will be

VILE, to make or seem —
1. *To dishonour,* נָבַל *nabel,* 3.
Nah. 3. 6 I will..make thee vile, and will set thee
2. *To be lightly esteemed,* קָלָה *qalah,* 2.
Deut. 25. 3 then thy brother should seem vile unto
3. *To lightly esteem,* קָלַל *qalal,* 3.
1 Sa. 3. 13 because his sons made themselves vile

VILELY cast away, to be —
To become loathsome, cast away, גָּעַל *gaal,* 2.
2 Sa. 1. 21 for there the shield..is vilely cast away

VILLAGE —
1. *Daughter,* בַּת *bath.*
Num. 21. 25 in Heshbon, and in all the villages thereof
21. 32 they took the villages thereof, and drove
32. 42 took Kenath, and the villages thereof, and
2 Ch. 28. 18 with the villages..the villages..the villa.
Neh. 11. 25 the villages thereof..the villages thereof
11. 27 at Beer-sheba, and (in) the villages thereof
11. 30 at Azekah, and (in) the villages thereof
11. 28 at Mekonah, and in the villages thereof
11. 31 and Aija, and Beth-el, and (in) their vill.
2. *Court, village,* חָצֵר *chatser.*
Exod. 8. 13 died out of the houses, out of the villages
Lev. 25. 31 But the houses of the villages which have
Josh 13. 23 inheritance..the cities and the villages
13. 28 inheritance..the cities and their villages
15. 32 cities..twenty and nine, with their villa.
15. 36 Sharaim..fourteen cities with their villa.
15. 41 Gederoth..sixteen cities with their villa.
15. 44 Mareshah; nine cities with their villages
15. 45 Ekron, with her towns and her villages
15. 46 all that (lay) near Ashdod, with their vi.
15. 47 towns and her villages..towns and her vil.
15. 51, 54, 57, 59, 60, 62 cities with their villages
16. 9 separate..all the cities with their villages
18. 24 Gaba; twelve cities with their villages
18. 28 Zelah..fourteen cities with their villages
19. 6 Sharuhen; thirteen cities and their villag.
19. 7 Ashan; four cities and their villages
19. 8 all the villages that (were) round about
19. 15, 16, 22, 30, 31, 38 cities with their villages
19. 23, 39 inheritance..the cities and their villa.
19. 48 inheritance..these cities with their villa.
21. 12 the fields of the city, and the villages th.
1 Ch. 4. 32 their villages (were) Etam, and Ain, Rim.
4. 33 all their villages that (were) round about
6. 56 the fields of the city, and the villages th.
9. 16 dwelt in the villages of the Netophathites
9. 22 reckoned by their genealogy in their vill.
9. 25 their brethren..in their villages, (were) to
Neh. 11. 25 for the villages and (in) the villages the
11. 30 Zanoah, Adullam, and (in) their villages
12. 28 gathered themselves..from the villages
12. 29 builded them villages round about Jeru.
Psa. 10. 8 He sitteth in..lurking places of the vill.
Isa. 42. 11 the villages..Kedar doth inhabit: let the
3. *Hamlet, village,* כְּפִיר *kephir.*
Neh. 6. 2 let us meet together in..the villages in
4. *Hamlet, village,* כָּפָר *kaphar.*
1 Ch. 27. 25 in the cities, and in the villages, and in
Song 7. 11 Come, my beloved..let us lodge in the vi.
5. *Hamlet, village,* כֹּפֶר *kopher.*
1 Sa. 6. 18 of fenced cities, and of country villages
6. *Open village (?),* פְּרָז *paraz.*
Hab. 3. 14 Thou didst strike..the head of his villag.
7. *Open village (?),* פְּרָזוֹן *perazon.*
Judg. 5. 7 the villages ceased, they ceased in Israel
5. 11 the righteous acts..of his villages in Isr.
8. *Villagers,* פְּרָזִים [V.L. פרוזים] *perazim.*
Esth. 9. 19 the Jews of the villages, that dwelt in the
9. *A village,* κώμη *kōmē.*
Matt. 9. 35 Jesus went about all the cities and villa.
14. 15 that they may go into the villages, and buy
21. 2 Go into the village over against you, and
Mark 6. 6 he went round about the villages, teach.
6. 36 that they may go..into the villages, and
6. 56 whithersoever he entered, into villages
11. 2 Go your way into the village over against
Luke 8. 1 he went throughout every city and villa.
Luke 9. 52 entered into a village of the Samaritans
9. 56 And they went to another village
10. 38 he entered into a certain village, and a c.
13. 22 he went through the cities and villages
17. 12 as he entered into a certain village, there
19. 30 Go ye into the village over against (you)
24. 13 two of them went that same day to a vil.
24. 28 they drew nigh unto the village whither
Acts 8. 25 preached the gospel in many villages of

VILLANY —
Emptiness, folly, נְבָלָה *nebalah.*
Isa. 32. 6 For the vile person will speak villany
Jer. 29. 23 Because they have committed villany in

VINE (branch, choice, cluster, noble, tree) —
1. *A vine,* גֶּפֶן *gephen.*
Gen. 40. 9 In my dream, behold, a vine..before me
40. 10 in the vine (were) three branches, and it
49. 11 Binding his foal unto the vine, and his
Num 20. 5 no place of seed, or of figs, or of vines, or
Deut. 8. 8 A land of wheat, and barley, and vines, and
32. 32 For their vine (is) of the vine of Sodom
Judg. 9. 12 Then said the trees unto the vine, Come
9. 13 the vine said unto them, Should I leave
13. 14 may not eat of any..that cometh of the v.
1 Ki. 4. 25 every man under his vine and under his
2 Ki. 4. 39 found a wild vine, and gathered thereof
18. 31 eat ye every man of his own vine, and ev.
Job 15. 33 shall shake off his unripe grape as the vi.
Psa. 78. 47 He destroyed their vines with hail, and
80. 8 Thou hast brought a vine out of Egypt
80. 14 look down..and behold, and visit this vi.
105. 33 He smote their vines also and their fig tr.
128. 3 Thy wife..as a fruitful vine by the sides
Song 2. 13 the vines..the tender grape give a..smell
6. 11 went..to see whether the vine flourished
7. 8 breasts shall be as clusters of the vine
7. 12 let us see if the vine flourish..the tender
Isa. 7. 23 a thousand vines at a thousand silverlings
16. 8 the fields of Heshbon languish..the vine
16. 9 Therefore I will bewail..the vine of Sib.
24. 7 The new wine mourneth, the vine langu.
32. 12 They shall lament..for the fruitful vine
34. 4 fall..as the leaf falleth off from the vine
36. 16 eat ye every one of his vine, and every one
Jer. 2. 21 the degenerate plant of a strange vine
5. 17 they shall eat up thy vines and thy fig tr.
6. 9 shall..glean the remnant of I. as a vine
8. 13 no grapes on the vine, nor figs on the fig
48. 32 O vine of Sibmah, I will weep for thee wi.
Eze. 15. 2 What is the vine tree more than any tree
15. 6 As the vine tree among the trees of the
17. 6 became a spreading vine of low stature
17. 6 so it became a vine, and brought forth
17. 7 this vine did bend her roots toward him
17. 8 planted..that it might be a goodly vine
19. 10 Thy mother (is) like a vine in thy blood
Hos. 2. 12 I will destroy her vines and her fig trees
10. 1 Israel (is) an empty vine, he bringeth fo.
14. 7 they shall..grow as the vine: the scent
Joel 1. 7 He hath laid my vine waste, and barked
1. 12 The vine is dried up, and the fig tree lan.
2. 22 the fig tree and the vine do yield their s.
Mic. 4. 4 they shall sit every man under his vine and
Hab. 3. 17 neither..fruit..in the vines; the labour of
Hag. 2. 19 as yet the vine, and the fig tree, and the
Zech. 3. 10 call..under the vine and under the fig tr.
8. 12 the vine shall give her fruit, and the gro.
Mal. 3. 11 neither shall your vine cast her fruit be.
2. *Branch, slip,* זְמוֹרָה *zemorah.*
Nah. 2. 2 the emptiers have..marred their vine br.
3. *Wine-vine,* גֶּפֶן הַיַּיִן *gephen hay-yayin.*
Num. 6. 4 nothing that is made of the vine tree
Judg 13. 14 eat of any (thing) that cometh of the vine
4. *An enclosed place, olive or vineyard,* כֶּרֶם *kerem.*
Song 2. 15 foxes, that spoil the vines: for our vines
Jer. 31. 5 Thou shalt yet plant vines upon the mo.
5. *A choice or intertwining vine,* שֹׂרֵק *soreq.*
Isa. 5. 2 planted it with the choicest vine, and bu.
Jer. 2. 21 I had planted thee a noble vine, wholly
6. *A choice or intertwining vine,* שֹׂרֵקָה *soreqah.*
Gen. 49. 11 and his ass's colt unto the choice vine
7. *A vine, vine fruit,* ἄμπελος *ampelos.*
Matt 26. 29 I will not drink..of this fruit of the vine
Mark 14. 25 I will drink no more of the fruit of the v.
Luke 22. 18 I will not drink of the fruit of the vine
John 15. 1 I am the true vine, and my Father is the
15. 4 cannot bear..except it abide in the vine
15. 5 I am the vine, ye (are) the branches
Jas. 3. 12 Can the fig..bear olive berries? either a v.
Rev. 14. 19 gathered the vine of the earth, and cast
8. *Clusters of the vineyard,* βότρυας τῆς ἀμπέλου.
Rev. 14. 18 gather the clusters of the vine of the ea.

VINE undressed, vine dressers, dresser of vineyard —
1. *Vineyard dressers,* כֹּרְמִים *koremim.*
2 Ki. 25. 12 left of the poor of the land..vine dressers.
2 Ch. 26. 10 vine dressers in the mountains, and in C.
Isa. 61. 5 and the sons of the alien..your vine dre.
Jer. 52. 16 left..of the poor of the land for vine dre.
Joel 1. 11 howl, O ye vine dressers, for the wheat
2. *Separated,* נָזִיר *nazir.*
Lev. 25. 5 neither gather..grapes of thy vine undr.
25. 11 nor gather..in it of thy vine undressed
3. *A vine dresser,* ἀμπελουργός *ampelourgos.*
Luke 13. 7 Then said he unto the dresser of his vin.

VINEGAR —
1. *Vinegar, sour or unripe grapes,* חֹמֶץ *chomets.*
Num 6. 3 no vinegar of wine, or vinegar of strong
Ruth 2. 14 come thou..and dip thy morsel in the vi.
Psa. 69. 21 in my thirst they gave me vinegar to dri.
Prov 10. 26 As vinegar to the teeth, and as smoke to
25. 20 vinegar upon nitre, so (is) he that singeth
2. *Vinegar,* ὄξος *oxos.*
Matt 27. 34 They gave him [vinegar] to drink mingled
27. 48 took a sponge, and filled (it) with vinegar
Mark 15. 36 one ran and filled a sponge full of vinegar
Luke 23. 36 coming to him, and offering him vinegar
John 19. 29 vessel..of vinegar..filled a sponge with v.
19. 30 When Jesus..had received the vinegar

VINEYARD, (Plain of the) — אָבֵל כְּרָמִים.
On the E. of the Jordan; perhaps *Beit-el-Kerm,* N. of Kerak.
Judg 11. 33 he smote them..unto the plain of the vi.

VINEYARD, (increase of the, dresser of the) —
1. *A shoot, plant, stock,* כַּנָּה *kannah.*
Psa. 80. 15 the vineyard, which thy right hand hath
2. *An enclosed place, olive or vineyard,* כֶּרֶם *kerem.*
Gen. 9. 20 Noah began..and he planted a vineyard
Exod 22. 5 or vineyard..of the best of his own viney.
23. 11 In like manner..deal with thy vineyard
Lev. 19. 10 And thou shalt not glean thy vineyard
19. 10 neither shalt thou gather..of thy vineya.
25. 3 six years thou shalt prune thy vineyard
25. 4 sow thy field, nor prune thy vineyard
Num 16. 14 given us inheritance of fields and vineyards
20. 17 we will not pass..through the vineyards
21. 22 we will not turn..into the vineyards, we
22. 24 the angel..stood in a path of the vineyards
Deut. 6. 11 vineyards and olive trees, which thou pl.
20. 6 what man..that hath planted a vineyard
22. 9 Thou shalt not sow thy vineyard with di.
22. 9 and the fruit of thy vineyard, be defiled
23. 24 thou comest into thy neighbour's vineya.
24. 21 thou gatherest the grapes of thy vineyard
28. 30 thou shalt plant a vineyard, and shalt not
28. 39 Thou shalt plant vineyards, and dress (th.)
Josh. 24. 13 of the vineyards and oliveyards which ye
Judg 9. 27 gathered their vineyards, and trode (the
11. 33 unto the plain of the vineyards, with a
14. 5 and came to the vineyards of Timnath
15. 5 the standing corn, with the vineyards (and)
21. 20 saying, Go and lie in wait in the vineyards
21. 21 come ye out of the vineyards, and catch
1 Sa. 8. 14 he will take your fields, and your vineya.
8. 15 he will take the tenth..of your vineyards
22. 7 give every one of you fields and vineyards
1 Ki. 21. 1 Naboth the Jezreelite had a vineyard, wh.
21. 2 Give me thy vineyard, that I may have it
21. 2 I will give thee for it a better vineyard
21. 6 Give me thy vineyard for money, or else
21. 6 I will give thee (another) vineyard for it
21. 6 answered, I will not give thee my vineya.
21. 7 I will give thee the vineyard of Naboth
21. 15 take possession of the vineyard of Naboth
21. 16 Ahab rose up to go down to the vineyard
21. 18 (he is) in the vineyard of Naboth, whither
2 Ki. 5. 26 vineyards, and sheep, and oxen, and men
18. 32 a land of bread and vineyards, a land of
19. 29 plant vineyards, and eat the fruits there.
1 Ch. 27. 27 the vineyards..the increase of the viney.
Neh. 5. 3 We have mortgaged our lands, vineyards
5. 4 (and that upon) our lands and vineyards
5. 5 other men have our lands and vineyards
5. 11 Restore, I pray you..their vineyards, th.
9. 25 vineyards, and oliveyards, and fruit trees
Job 24. 18 he beholdeth not the way of the vineyar.
Psa. 107. 37 sow the fields, and plant vineyards, which
Prov. 24. 30 I went..by the vineyard of the man void
31. 16 with the fruit..she planteth a vineyard
Eccl. 2. 4 I builded me houses; I planted me vine.
Song 1. 6 keeper of the vineyards..mine own vine.
1. 14 a cluster of camphire in the vineyards of
7. 12 Let us get up early to the vineyards; let
8. 11 Solomon had a vineyard..let out the vin.
8. 12 My vineyard, which (is) mine, (is) before
Isa. 1. 8 as a cottage in a vineyard, as a lodge in a
3. 14 ye have eaten up the vineyard; the spoil
5. 1 touching his vineyard..hath a vineyard
5. 3 judge..betwixt me and my vineyard
5. 4 could have been done more to my vineya.
5. 5 I will tell you what I will do to my viney.
5. 7 the vineyard of the LORD of hosts (is) the
5. 10 ten acres of vineyard shall yield one bath
16. 10 in the vineyards there shall be no singing
27. 2 sing ye unto her, A vineyard of red wine
36. 17 a land of corn..of bread and vineyards
37. 30 plant vineyards, and eat the fruit thereof
65. 21 they shall plant vineyards, and eat the fr.
Jer. 12. 10 Many pastors have destroyed my vineyard
32. 15 vineyards shall be possessed again in this
35. 7 sow seed, nor plant vineyard, nor have
35. 9 neither have we vineyard, nor field, nor
39. 10 gave them vineyards and fields at the same
Eze. 28. 26 shall build houses, and plant vineyards
Hos. 2. 15 I will give her her vineyards from thence
Amos 4. 9 your vineyards and your fig trees and your
5. 11 ye have planted pleasant vineyards, but ye
5. 17 in all vineyards (shall be) wailing: for I
9. 14 they shall plant vineyards, and drink the
Mic. 1. 6 make Samaria..as plantings of a vineyard
Zeph. 1. 13 they shall plant vineyards, but not drink
3. *A vineyard,* ἀμπελών *ampelōn.*
Matt 20. 1 went..to hire labourers into his vineyard

Matt 20. 2 had agreed..he sent them into his viney.
20. 4 Go ye also into the vineyard, and whatso.
20. 7 Go ye also into the vineyard, and whatso
20. 8 the lord of the vineyard saith unto his st.
21. 28 said Son, go work to day in my vineyard
21. 33 planted a vineyard, and hedged it round
21. 39 cast (him) out of the vineyard, and slew
21. 40 the lord therefore of the vineyard cometh
21. 41 will let out (his) vineyard unto other hus.
Mark12. 1 A (certain) man planted a vineyard, and
12. 2 might receive..the fruit of the vineyard
12. 8 killed (him), and cast him out of the vine.
12. 9 What shall..the lord of the vineyard do?
12. 9 come..and will give the vineyard unto
Luke13. 6 (man) had a fig tree planted in his viney.
20. 9 A certain (man) planted a vineyard, and let
20. 10 they should give him of the fruit of the vi.
20. 13 Then said the lord of the vineyard, What
20. 15 So they cast him out of the vineyard, and
20. 15 What..shall the lord of the vineyard do
20. 16 He shall..give the vineyard to others
1 Co. 9. 7 who planteth a vineyard, and eateth not

4. *Vineyard-worker, ἀμπελουργός ampelourgos.*
Luke13. 7 Then said he unto the dresser of his viney.

VINTAGE —

1. *Reaping, harvest,* בָּצִיר *batsir.*
Lev. 26. 5 shall reach unto the vintage, and the vin.
Judg. 8. 2 the gleaning..better than the vintage of
Isa. 24. 13 as the gleaning grapes when the vintage
32. 10 the vintage shall fail, the gathering shall
Jer. 48. 32 upon thy summer fruits and upon thy vi.
Mic. 7. 1 I am..as the grape gleanings of the vintage

2. *Cutting, harvest,* בָּצִיר *batsir* [V.L. בצור].
Zech 11. 2 for the forest of the vintage is come down

3. *Olive or vineyard,* כֶּרֶם *kerem.*
Job 24. 6 and they gather the vintage of the wicked

VIOL —

A lyre, נֶבֶל, נֵבֶל *nebel.*
Isa. 5. 12 the harp and the viol, the tabret and pipe
14. 11 to the grave, (and) the noise of thy viols
Amos 5. 23 for I will not hear the melody of thy viols
6. 5 That chant to the sound of the viol, (and)

VIOLATE, to —

To use violence, חָמַס *chamas.*
Eze. 22. 26 Her priests have violated my law, and ha.

VIOLENCE, (against or done), taken away by —

1. *What is snatched away,* גָּזֵל *gazel.*
Lev. 6. 2 or in a thing taken away by violence, or
2. *What is snatched away,* גְּזֵל *gezel.*
Eze. 18. 18 because he..spoiled his brother by viol.

3. *What is snatched away,* גְּזֵלָה *gezelah.*
Eze. 18. 7 hath spoiled none by violence, hath given
18. 12 hath spoiled by violence, hath not resto.
18. 16 neither hath spoiled by violence, (but) h.

4. *Violence,* חָמָס *chamas.*
Gen. 6. 11 corrupt..and the earth was filled with vio.
6. 13 the earth is filled with violence through
2 Sa. 22. 3 my saviour, thou savest me from violence
Psa. 11. 5 him that loveth violence his soul hateth
55. 9 for I have seen violence and strife in the
58. 2 ye weigh the violence of your hands in
72. 14 redeem their soul from deceit and violen.
73. 6 Therefore..violence covereth them (as) a
Prov. 4. 17 For they..drink the wine of violence
10. 6, 11 violence covereth the mouth of the
13. 2 soul of the transgressors (shall eat) viole.
Isa 53. 9 he had done no violence, neither (was any)
59. 6 and the act of violence (is) in their hands
60. 18 Violence shall no more be heard in thy
Jer. 6. 7 violence and spoil is heard in her; before
20. 8 I cried violence and spoil; because the
51. 35 The violence done to me and to my flesh
51. 46 violence in the land, ruler against ruler
Eze. 7. 11 Violence is risen up into a rod of wicked.
7. 23 crimes, and the city is full of violence
8. 17 they have filled the land with violence
12. 19 because of the violence of all them that
28. 16 have filled the midst of thee with violen.
45. 9 remove violence and spoil, and execute
Joel 3. 19 for the violence (against) the children of
Amos 3. 10 who store up violence and robbery in th.
6. 3 cause the seat of violence to come near
Obad. 10 For (thy) violence against thy brother J.
Jon. 3. 8 from the violence that (is) in their hands
Mic. 6. 12 the rich men thereof are full of violence
Hab. 1. 2 cry out unto thee (of) violence, and thou
1. 3 for spoiling and violence (are) before me
1. 9 They shall come all for violence: their
2. 8 (for) the violence of the land, of the city
2. 17 the violence of Lebanon shall cover thee
2. 17 the violence of the land, of the city, and
Zeph. 1. 9 fill their masters' houses with violence and
Mal. 2. 16 (one) covereth violence with his garment

5. *A running, course, oppression,* מְרוּצָה *merutsah.*
Jer. 22. 17 for oppression, and for violence, to do (it)

6. *Force, violence, βία bia.*
Acts 5. 26 went..and brought them without violen.
21. 35 he was borne of the soldiers for the viol.
24. 7 [with great violence took..away out of]
27. 41 the hinder part was broken with the vio.

7. *Power, δύναμις dunamis.*
Heb. 11. 34 Quenched the violence of fire, escaped

8. *A rushing, impetuosity, ὅρμημα hormēma.*
Rev. 18. 21 Thus with violence shall that great city

VIOLENCE, to do, suffer, take by —

1. *To snatch away,* גָּזַל *gazal.*
Mic. 2. 2 they covet fields, and take..by violence

2. *To use violence,* חָמַס *chamas.*
Jer. 22. 3 do no violence to the stranger, the fath.
Zeph. 3. 4 her priests..have done violence to the

3. *To oppress, use oppression,* עָשַׁק *ashaq.*
Prov28. 17 A man that doeth violence to the blood

4. *To be forced or urged, βιάζομαι biazomai.*
Matt.11. 12 the kingdom of heaven suffereth violence

5. *To shake thoroughly, διασείω diaseiō.*
Luke 3. 14 Do violence to no man, neither accuse..fa.

VIOLENT (dealing, perverting) —

1. *What is snatched away,* גֵּזֶל *gezel.*
Eccl. 5. 8 If thou seest..violent perverting of judg.

2. *Violence,* חָמָס *chamas.*
2 Sa. 22. 49 thou hast delivered me from the violent
Psa. 7. 16 his violent dealing shall come down upon
18. 48 thou hast delivered me from the violent
140. 1, 4 O LORD..preserve me from the violent
140. 11 evil shall hunt the violent man to overth.
Prov.16. 29 A violent man enticeth his neighbour, and

3. *Terrible,* עָרִיץ *arits.*
Psa. 86. 14 the assemblies of violent (men) have sou.

4. *Forcible, violent, βιαστής biastēs.*
Matt.11. 12 the kingdom of heaven..the violent take

VIOLENTLY, to take away —

1. *To snatch away,* גָּזַל *gazal.*
Gen. 21. 25 which A.'s servants had violently taken a.
Deut.28. 31 thine ass..violently taken away from be.
Job 20. 19 he hath violently taken away an house
24. 2 they violently take away flocks, and feed

2. *To take violently,* חָמַס *chamas.*
Lam. 2. 6 he hath violently taken away his tabern.

VIPER —

1. *A viper,* אֶפְעֶה *epheh.*
Job 20. 16 He shall suck the poison of asps: the vip.
Isa. 30. 6 whence..the viper and fiery flying serpent
59. 5 which is crushed breaketh out into a vip.

2. *A female viper, ἔχιδνα echidna.*
Matt. 3. 7 generation of vipers, who hath warned you
12. 34 generation of vipers, how can ye, being
23. 33 serpents..generation of vipers, how can
Luke 3. 7 generation of vipers, who hath warned
Acts 28. 3 there came a viper out of the heat, and fas.

VIRGIN, virginity —

1. *Separation, virginity, virgin,* בְּתוּלָה *bethulah.*
Gen. 24. 16 a virgin, neither had any man known her
Exod 22. 17 pay money according to the dowry of vir.
Lev. 21. 3 for his sister a virgin, that is nigh unto
21. 14 he shall take a virgin of his own people
Deut 22. 19 hath brought up an evil name upon a vir.
22. 23 If a damsel..a virgin be betrothed unto
22. 28 If a man find a damsel..a virgin, which
32. 25 destroy both the young man and the vir.
Judg.21. 12 they found..four hundred young virgins
2 Sa. 13. 2 for his sister Tamar; for she (was) a virgin
13. 18 were the king's daughters..virgins appa.
1 Ki. 1. 2 sought for my lord the king a young virg.
2 Ki. 19. 21 The virgin, the daughter of Zion, hath de.
Esth. 2. 2 Let there be fair young virgins sought for
2. 3 may gather together all the fair young vi.
2. 17 favour in his sight more than all the vir.
2. 19 when the virgins were gathered together
Psa. 45. 14 the virgins her companions that follow
Isa. 23. 4 nourish up young men..bring up virgins
23. 12 O thou oppressed virgin, daughter of Zi.
37. 22 The virgin, the daughter of Zion, hath de.
47. 1 O virgin daughter of Babylon, sit on the
62. 5 For (as) a young man marrieth a virgin
Jer. 14. 17 for the virgin daughter of my people is
18. 13 the virgin of Israel hath done a very hor.
31. 4 Again..thou shalt be built, O virgin of Is.
31. 13 Then shall the virgin rejoice in the dance
31. 21 O virgin of Israel, turn again to these thy
46. 11 Go up into Gilead, and take balm, O vir.
Lam. 1. 4 her priests sigh, her virgins are afflicted
1. 15 LORD hath trodden the virgin, the daugh.
1. 18 my virgins and my young men are gone
2. 10 the virgins of Jerusalem hang down their
2. 13 that I may comfort thee, O virgin daugh.
2. 21 my virgins and my young men are fallen
Joel 1. 8 Lament like a virgin girded with sackcl.
Amos 5. 2 The virgin of Israel is fallen; she shall no
8. 13 In that day shall the fair virgins and yo.

2. *(Tokens of) virginity,* בְּתוּלִים *bethulim.*
Lev. 21. 13 And he shall take a wife in her virginity
Deut22. 15 take and bring forth..the damsel's virgi.
22. 17 and yet these..my daughter's virginity
22. 20 if..virginity be not found for the damsel
Judg.11. 37 and bewail my virginity, I and my fellows
11. 38 bewailed her virginity upon the mountains
Eze. 23. 3 there they bruised the teats of their virg.
23. 8 they bruised the breasts of her virginity

3. *Concealment, unmarried female,* עַלְמָה *almah.*
Gen. 24. 43 that when the virgin cometh forth to dr.
Song 1. 3 ointment..therefore do the virgins love t.
6. 8 fourscore concubines, and virgins without
Isa. 7. 14 a virgin shall conceive, and bear a son, and

4. *State of seclusion, virginity, παρθενία parthenia.*
Luke 2. 36 had lived..seven years from her virginity

5. *A virgin, one put aside, παρθένος parthenos.*
Matt. 1. 23 Behold, a virgin shall be with child, and
25. 1 be likened unto ten virgins, which took
25. 7 Then all those virgins arose, and trimmed
25. 11 Afterward came also the other virgins
Luke 1. 27 To a virgin espoused..and the virgin's na.
Acts 21. 9 the same man had four daughters, virgins
1 Co. 7. 25 concerning virgins I have no commandm.
7. 28 and if a virgin marry, she hath not sinned
7. 34 difference (also) between a wife and [a vi.]
7. 36 he behaveth..uncomely toward his virgin
7. 37 so decreed..that he will keep his virgin
2 Co. 11. 2 I may present (you as) a chaste virgin to
Rev. 14. 4 defiled with women; for they are virgins

VIRTUE, virtuous, virtuously —

1. *Force, strength (of mind or body),* חַיִל *chayil.*
Ruth 3. 11 doth know that thou (art) a virtuous wo.
Prov.12. 4 A virtuous woman (is) a crown to her hu.
31. 10 Who can find a virtuous woman? for her
31. 29 Many daughters have done virtuously, but

2. *Force, strength (of mind or body), ἀρετή aretē.*
Phil. 4. 8 if..any virtue, and if..any praise, think
2 Pe. 1. 3 him that hath called us to glory and vir.
1. 5 add to your faith virtue: and to virtue k.

3. *Power, δύναμις dunamis.*
Mark 5. 30 knowing in himself that virtue had gone
Luke 6. 19 there went virtue out of him, and healed
8. 46 for I perceive that virtue is gone out of

VISAGE, visible —

1. *Face, lineaments,* אַנְפִּין *anpin.*
Dan. 3. 19 the form of his visage was changed agai.

2. *Appearance, sight,* מַרְאֶה *mareh.*
Isa. 52. 14 his visage was so marred more than any

3. *Form,* תֹּאַר *toar.*
Lam. 4. 8 Their visage is blacker than a coal; they

4. *What may be seen, visible, ὁρατός horatos.*
Col. 1. 16 all things..visible and invisible, whether

VISION —

1. *Vision, aspect,* חֵזוּ *chezev.*
Dan. 2. 19 was..revealed unto Daniel in a night vis.
2. 28 Thy dream, and the visions of thy head
4. 5 and the visions of my head troubled me
4. 9 tell me the visions of my dream that I ha.
4. 10 Thus..the visions of mine head in my bed
4. 13 I saw in the visions of my head upon my
7. 1 Daniel had a dream and visions of his he.
7. 2 I saw in my vision by night, and behold
7. 7 After this I saw in the night visions, and
7. 13 I saw in the night visions, and, behold
7. 15 and the visions of my head troubled me

2. *Vision,* חָזוֹן *chazon.*
1 Sa. 3. 1 And the word..was precious..no open vi.
1 Ch.17. 15 according to all this vision, so did Nathan
2 Ch.32. 32 they (are) written in the vision of Isaiah
Psa. 89. 19 thou speakest in vision to thy Holy One
Prov 29. 18 Where (there is) no vision, the people pe.
Isa. 1. 1 The vision of Isaiah the son of Amoz, wh.
29. 7 even all..shall be as a dream of a night v.
Jer. 14. 14 they prophesy unto you a false vision and
23. 16 they speak a vision of their own heart
Lam. 2. 9 her prophets also find no vision from the
Eze. 7. 13 the vision (is) touching the whole multit.
7. 26 then shall they seek a vision of the prop.
12. 22 The days are prolonged, and every vision
12. 23 are at hand, and the effect of every vision
12. 24 there shall be no more any vain vision nor
12. 27 The vision that he seeth (is) for many da.
13. 16 which see visions of peace for her, and
Dan. 1. 17 Daniel had understanding in all visions
8. 1 a vision appeared unto me, (even unto) me
8. 2 I saw in a vision..I saw in a vision, and
8. 13 How long (shall be) the vision (concerning)
8. 15 I Daniel, had seen the vision, and sought
8. 17 at the time of the end (shall be) the vision
8. 26 wherefore shut thou up the vision, for it
9. 21 whom I had seen in the vision at the be.
9. 24 to seal up the vision and prophecy, and
10. 14 in the latter days: for yet the vision (is)
11. 14 exalt themselves to establish the vision
Hos. 12. 10 I have multiplied visions, and used sim.
Obad. 1 The vision of Obadiah. Thus saith the L.
Mic. 3. 6 ye shall not have a vision; and it shall be
Nah. 1. 1 The book of the vision of Nahum the Elk.
Hab. 2. 2 Write the vision, and make (it) plain up.
2. 3 the vision (is) yet for an appointed time

3. *Vision,* חָזוֹת *chazoth.*
2 Ch. 9. 29 written..in the visions of Iddo the seer

4. *Vision,* חָזוּת *chazuth.*
Isa. 21. 2 A grievous vision is declared unto me
29. 11 the vision of all is become unto you as the

5. *Vision,* חִזָּיוֹן *chizzayon.*
2 Sa. 7. 17 according to all this vision, so did Nath.
Job 4. 13 In thoughts from the visions of the night
7. 14 Then thou..terrifiest me through visions
20. 8 be chased away as a vision of the night
33. 15 In a dream, in a vision of the night, wh.
Isa. 22. 1 The burden of the valley of vision. What
22. 5 Lord GOD of hosts in the valley of vision
Joel 2. 28 afterward..your young men shall see vi.
Zech 13. 4 shall be ashamed every one of his vision

6. *Vision*, מַחֲזֶה *machazeh*.
Gen. 15. 1 of the LORD came unto Abram in a vision
Num 24. 4, 16 He..which saw the vision of the Alm.
Eze. 13. 7 Have ye not seen a vain vision, and have

7. *Appearance, sight*, מַרְאָה *marah*.
Gen. 46. 2 God spake unto Israel in the visions of the
Num 12. 6 will make myself known unto him in a v.
1 Sa. 3. 15 And Samuel feared to show Eli the vision
Eze. 1. 1 the heavens were opened, and I saw vis.
8. 3 brought me in the visions of God to Jeru.
40. 2 In the visions of God brought he me into
43. 3 and the visions (were) like..that I saw by
Dan. 10. 7 And I Daniel alone saw the vision, for the
10. 7 men that were with me saw not the vision
10. 8 I was left alone, and saw this great vision
10. 16 by the vision my sorrows are turned up.

8. *Appearance, sight*, מַרְאֶה *mareh*.
Eze. 8. 4 according to the vision that I saw in the
11. 24 brought me in a vision by the spirit of God
11. 24 the vision that I had seen went up from
43. 3 according to the appearance of the vision
43. 3 the vision that I saw..like the vision that
Dan. 8. 16 make this (man) to understand the vision
8. 26 the vision of the evening and the morning
8. 27 I was astonished at the vision, but none
9. 23 therefore understand..and consider the v.
10. 1 and had understanding of the vision

9. *Seeing, vision*, רֹאֶה *roeh*.
Isa. 28. 7 they err in vision, they stumble (in) judg.

10. *To see*, רָאָה *raah*.
2 Ch. 26. 5 who had understanding in the visions of

11. *A sight, apparition, vision*, ὀπτασία *optasia*.
Luke 1. 22 they perceived that he had seen a vision
24. 23 that they had also seen a vision of angels
Acts 26. 19 was not disobedient unto the heavenly v.
2 Co. 12. 1 I will come to visions and revelations of

12. *A sight, vision*, ὅραμα *horama*.
Matt 17. 9 Tell the vision to no man, until the Son
Acts 9. 10 to him said the Lord in a vision, Ananias
9. 12 hath seen [in a vision] a man named Ana.
10. 3 He saw in a vision evidently, about the
10. 17 Peter doubted in himself what this vision
10. 19 While Peter thought on the vision, the
11. 5 in a trance I saw a vision, A certain vess.
12. 9 and wist not..but thought he saw a vision
16. 9 a vision appeared to Paul in the night
16. 10 after he had seen the vision, immediately
18. 9 Then spake the Lord..by a vision, Be not

13. *Act of seeing, sight, vision*, ὅρασις *horasis*.
Acts 2. 17 your young men shall see visions, and
Rev. 9. 17 thus I saw the horses in the vision, and

VISIT, be visited, to —

1. *To look over, or after, inspect*, פָּקַד *paqad*.
Gen. 21. 1 LORD visited Sarah as he had said, and the
50. 24 God will surely visit you, and bring you
50. 25 God will surely visit you, and ye shall ca.
Exod. 3. 16 I have surely visited you, and (seen) that
4. 31 they heard that the LORD had visited the
13. 19 God will surely visit you; and ye shall
20. 5 visiting the iniquity of the fathers upon
32. 34 in the day when I visit I will visit their sin
34. 7 visiting the iniquity of the fathers upon
Lev. 18. 25 therefore I do visit the iniquity thereof
Num 14. 18 visiting the iniquity of the fathers upon
Deut. 5. 9 visiting the iniquity of the fathers upon
Judg 15. 1 that Samson visited his wife with a kid
Ruth 1. 6 the LORD had visited his people in giving
1 Sa. 2. 21 the LORD visited Hannah, so that she co.
Job 5. 24 thou shalt visit thy habitation, and shalt
7. 18 thou shouldest visit him every morning
31. 14 when he visiteth, what shall I answer him
35. 15 he hath visited in his anger; yet he kno.
Psa. 8. 4 and the son of man, that thou visitest him
17. 3 thou hast visited (me) in the night; thou
59. 5 O LORD..awake to visit all the heathen
65. 9 Thou visitest the earth, and waterest it
80. 14 Return..and behold, and visit this vine
89. 32 Then will I visit their transgression with
106. 4 O LORD..visit me with thy salvation
Isa. 23. 17 LORD will visit Tyre, and she shall turn
26. 14 therefore hast thou visited and destroyed
26. 16 LORD, in trouble have they visited thee
Jer. 3. 16 neither shall they visit (it), neither shall
5. 9, 29 Shall I not visit for these (things)? sa.
6. 15 at the time..I visit them they shall be ca.
9. 9 Shall I not visit them for these (things)?
14. 10 remember their iniquity, and visit their
15. 15 remember me, and visit me, and revenge
23. 2 Ye..have not visited them..I will visit upon
27. 22 there shall they be until the day..I visit
29. 10 after seventy years..I will visit you, and
32. 5 there shall he be until I visit him, saith
49. 8 I will bring..the time..I will visit him
50. 31 thy day is come, the time..I will visit thee
Lam. 4. 22 he will visit thine iniquity, O daughter of
Hos. 2. 13 I will visit upon her the days of Baalim
8. 13 remember their iniquity, and visit their
9. 9 remember their iniquity, he will visit their
Amos 3. 14 That in the day that I shall visit the tra.
3. 14 I will also visit the altars of Beth-el
Zeph. 2. 7 for the LORD their God shall visit them
Zech 10. 3 for the LORD of hosts hath visited his fl.
11. 16 shall not visit those that be cut off, neit.

2. *To be inspected, missed*, פָּקַד *paqad*, 2.
Num 16. 29 or if they be visited after the visitation of
Prov 19. 23 abide..he shall not be visited with evil
Isa. 24. 22 and after many days shall they be visited
29. 6 Thou shalt be visited of the LORD of hosts
Eze. 38. 8 After many days thou shalt be visited

3. *To be inspected, missed*, פָּקַד *paqad*, 6.
Jer. 6. 6 Jerusalem: this (is) the city to be visited

4. *To be inspected, looked over*, ἐπισκέπτομαι *episk.*
Matt 25. 36 I was sick, and ye visited me: I was in pr.
25. 43 sick, and in prison, and ye visited me not
Luke 1. 68 he hath visited and redeemed his people
1. 78 the dayspring from on high hath visited
7. 16 saying..That God hath visited his people
Acts 7. 23 to visit his brethren the children of Israel
15. 14 how God at the first did visit the Gentiles
15. 36 Let us go again and visit our brethren in
Heb. 2. 6 or the son of man, that thou visitest him
Jas. 1. 27 To visit the fatherless and widows in the.

VISITATION —

1. *Inspection, a looking after*, פְּקֻדָּה *pequddah*.
Num 16. 29 or if they be visited after the visitation of
Job 10. 12 thy visitation hath preserved my spirit
Isa. 10. 3 what will ye do in the day of visitation
Jer. 8. 12 in the time of their visitation they shall
10. 15 in the time of their visitation they shall
11. 23 for I will bring evil..the year of their vi.
23. 12 for I will bring evil..the year of their vis.
46. 21 because the day..the time of their visita.
48. 44 for I will bring..the year of their visitat.
50. 27 their day is come, the time of their visit.
51. 18 in the time of their visitation they shall
Hos. 9. 7 The days of visitation are come, the days
Mic. 7. 4 the day of thy watchmen..thy visitation

2. *Inspection, a looking over*, ἐπισκοπή *episkopē*.
Luke 19. 44 thou knewest not the time of thy visitation
1 Pe. 2. 12 may..glorify God in the day of visitation

VOCATION —

A calling, κλῆσις *klēsis*.
Eph. 4. 1 walk worthy of the vocation wherewith ye

VOICE —

1. *A voice, sound*, קוֹל *qol*.
Gen. 3. 8 they heard the voice of the LORD God wa.
3. 10 I heard thy voice in the garden, and I was
3. 17 Because thou hast hearkened unto the vo.
4. 10 the voice of thy brother's blood crieth unto
4. 23 Adah and Zillah, hear my voice, ye wives
16. 2 And Abram hearkened to the voice of Sa.
21. 12 hearken unto her voice; for in Isaac shall
21. 16 And she sat..and lift up her voice, and
21. 17 God heard..the voice of the lad where
22. 18 And..because thou hast obeyed my voice
26. 5 Because that Abraham obeyed my voice
27. 8 obey my voice according to that which I
27. 13 only obey my voice, and go fetch me (th.)
27. 22 The voice (is) Jacob's voice, but the hands
27. 38 And Esau lifted up his voice, and wept
27. 43 Now therefore, my son, obey my voice
29. 11 Jacob kissed Rachel, and lifted up his vo.
30. 6 God..hath also heard my voice, and hath
39. 14 he came in..and I cried with a loud voice
39. 15 when he heard that I lifted up my voice
39. 18 it came to pass, as I lifted up my voice
Exod. 3. 18 they shall hearken to thy voice, and thou
4. 1 believe me, nor hearken unto my voice
4. 8 the voice of the first..the voice of the la.
4. 9 if they will not..hearken unto thy voice
5. 2 that I should obey his voice to let Israel
15. 26 If thou wilt diligently hearken to the vo
18. 19 Hearken now unto my voice, I will give
18. 24 So Moses hearkened to the voice of his fa.
19. 5 if ye will obey my voice indeed, and keep
19. 16 the voice of the trumpet exceeding loud
19. 19 when the voice of the trumpet sounded
19. 19 Moses spake, and God answered..by a v.
23. 21 Beware of him, and obey his voice, prov.
23. 22 if thou shalt indeed obey his voice, and
24. 3 all the people answered with one voice
32. 18 the voice of (them that) shout..the voice
Lev. 5. 1 if a soul sin, and hear the voice of swear.
Num. 7. 89 he heard the voice of one speaking unto
14. 1 all the congregation lifted up their voice
14. 22 those men..have not hearkened to my v.
20. 16 he heard our voice, and sent an angel, and
21. 3 the LORD hearkened to the voice of Isra.
Deut. 1. 34 the LORD heard the voice of your words
1. 45 the LORD would not hearken to your vo.
4. 12 heard the voice of the words..only..a vo.
4. 30 if thou..shalt be obedient unto his voice
4. 33 Did..people hear the voice of God speak.
4. 36 he made thee to hear his voice, that he
5. 22 of..the thick darkness, with a great voi.
5. 23 when ye heard the voice out of the midst
5. 24 we have heard his voice out of the midst
5. 25 if we hear the voice of the LORD our God
5. 26 that hath heard the voice of the living God
5. 28 the voice of your words..the voice of the
8. 20 ye would not be obedient unto the voice
9. 23 believed him not, nor hearkened to his vo.
13. 4 keep his commandments, and obey his vo.
13. 18 When thou shalt hearken to the voice of
15. 5 if thou carefully hearken unto the voice
18. 16 Let me not hear again the voice of the
21. 18 obey the voice of his father, or the voice
21. 20 he will not obey our voice..a glutton and
26. 7 LORD heard our voice, and looked on our
26. 14 I have hearkened to the voice of the LORD
26. 17 to keep..and to hearken unto his voice
27. 10 Thou shalt therefore obey the voice of the
27. 14 say unto all the men of I. with a loud
Deut 28. 1 shalt hearken diligently unto the voice
28. 2 if thou shalt hearken unto the voice of the
28. 15 if thou wilt not hearken unto the voice
28. 45 unto the voice of the LORD thy God
28. 62 thou wouldest not obey the voice of the
30. 2 shalt return..and shalt obey his voice
30. 8 thou shalt return, and obey the voice of
30. 10 If thou shalt hearken unto the voice of
30. 20 that thou mayest obey his voice, and that
33. 7 Hear, LORD, the voice of Judah, and bri.
Josh. 5. 6 they obeyed not the voice of the LORD
6. 10 shall not..make any noise with your voi.
10. 14 that the LORD hearkened unto the voice
22. 2 Ye..have obeyed my voice in all that I
24. 24 The LORD our God..his voice will we ob.
Judg. 2. 2 ye have not obeyed my voice: why have
2. 4 the people lifted up their voice, and wept
2. 20 and have not hearkened unto my voice
6. 10 fear not..but ye have not obeyed my vo.
9. 7 lifted up his voice and cried, and said
13. 9 God hearkened to the voice of Manoah
18. 3 they knew the voice of the young man the
18. 25 Let not thy voice be heard among us, lest
20. 13 would not hearken to the voice of their
21. 2 and lifted up their voices, and wept sore
Ruth 1. 9 and they lifted up their voice, and wept
1. 14 they lifted up their voice, and wept again
1 Sa. 1. 13 her lips moved, but her voice was not he.
2. 25 they hearkened not unto the voice of their
8. 7 Hearken unto the voice of the people in
8. 9 Now therefore hearken unto their voice
8. 19 the people refused to obey the voice of S.
8. 22 Hearken unto their voice, and make them
11. 4 the people lifted up their voices, and we.
12. 1 I have hearkened unto your voice in all
12. 14 If ye will fear the LORD..and obey his v.
12. 15 if ye will not obey the voice of the LORD
15. 1 hearken thou unto the voice of the words
15. 19 Wherefore..didst thou not obey the voi.
15. 20 Yea, I have obeyed the voice of the LORD
15. 22 as in obeying the voice of the LORD?
15. 24 I feared the people, and obeyed their vo.
19. 6 Saul hearkened unto the voice of Jonath.
24. 16 (Is) this thy voice..S. lifted up his voice
25. 35 I have hearkened to thy voice, and have
26. 17 And Saul knew David's voice, and said
26. 17 (Is) this thy voice..(It is) my voice, my l.
28. 12 saw Samuel, she cried with a loud voice
28. 18 Because thou obeyedst not the voice of
28. 21 thine handmaid hath obeyed thy voice, and
28. 22 hearken thou also unto the voice of thine
28. 23 hearkened unto their voice. So he arose
30. 4 the people..lifted up their voice and we.
2 Sa. 3. 32 the king lifted up his voice, and wept at
12. 18 and he would not hearken unto our voice
13. 14 he would not hearken unto her voice, but
13. 36 king's sons came, and lifted up their vo.
15. 23 all the country wept with a loud voice, and
19. 4 the king cried with a loud voice, O my
19. 35 Can I hear any more the voice of singing
22. 7 he did hear my voice out of his temple
22. 14 The LORD..the most High uttered his vo.
1 Ki. 8. 55 blessed..the congregation..with a loud v.
17. 22 LORD heard the voice of Elijah, and the
18. 26 (there was) no voice, nor any that answ.
18. 29 neither voice, nor any to answer, nor any
19. 12 and after the fire a still small voice
19. 13 a voice..said, What doest thou here, Eli.?
20. 25 he hearkened unto their voice, and did so
20. 36 thou hast not obeyed the voice of the L.
2 Ki. 4. 31 but..neither voice nor hearing: wheref.
7. 10 no man there, neither voice of man, but
10. 6 If ye..will hearken unto my voice, take
18. 12 Because they obeyed not the voice of the
18. 28 Rab-shakeh stood, and cried with a loud
19. 22 against whom hast thou exalted (thy) v.?
1 Ch. 15. 16 sounding, by lifting up the voice with joy
2 Ch. 5. 13 when they lifted up (their) voice with the
15. 14 they sware unto the LORD with a loud vo.
20. 19 to praise the LORD..with a loud voice on
30. 27 their voice was heard, and their prayer
32. 18 Then they cried with a loud voice in the
Ezra 3. 12 many..ancient men..wept with a loud vo.
10. 12 answered and said with a loud voice, As
Neh. 9. 4 cried with a loud voice unto the LORD th.
Job 2. 12 knew him not, they lifted up their voice
3. 18 prisoners..hear not the voice of the opp.
4. 10 the voice of the fierce lion, and the teeth
4. 16 It stood still..and I heard a voice, (saying)
9. 16 not believe..had hearkened unto my voi.
30. 31 my organ into the voice of them that weep
33. 8 and I have heard the voice of (thy) words
34. 16 hear this; hearken to the voice of my wo.
37. 2 Hear attentively the noise of his voice, and
37. 4 After it a voice..the voice of his excellen.
37. 4 not stay them when his voice is heard
37. 5 God thundereth marvellously with his vo.
38. 34 Canst thou lift up thy voice to the clouds
40. 9 canst thou thunder with a voice like him?
Psa. 3. 4 I cried unto the LORD with my voice, and
5. 2 Hearken unto the voice of my cry, my ki.
5. 3 My voice shalt thou hear in the morning
6. 8 LORD hath heard the voice of my weeping
18. 6 he heard my voice out of his temple,
18. 13 The LORD..the Highest gave his voice
19. 3 no speech nor language..their voice is not
26. 7 That I may publish with the voice of th.
27. 7 Hear, O LORD, (when) I cry with my voi.
28. 2 Hear the voice of my supplications when
28. 6 he hath heard the voice of my supplicat
29. 3, 4, 4, 5, 7, 8, 9 The voice of the LORD (is)
31. 22 thou heardest the voice of my supplicat.

Psa. 42. 4 with the voice of joy and praise, with a
44. 16 For the voice of him that reproacheth and
46. 6 he uttered his voice, the earth melted
47. 1 shout unto God with the voice of triumph
55. 3 Because of the voice of the enemy, beca.
55. 17 will I pray..and he shall hear my voice
58. 5 Which will not hearken to the voice of ch.
64. 1 Hear my voice, O God, in my prayer
66. 8 make the voice of his praise to be heard
66. 19 he hath attended to the voice of my pra.
68. 33 he doth send out his voice..a mighty vo.
74. 23 Forget not the voice of thine enemies, the
77. 1 I cried unto God with my voice. my voi.
77. 18 The voice of thy thunder (was) in the he.
81. 11 my people would not hearken to my voice
86. 6 Give ear..attend to the voice of my sup.
93. 3 The floods..floods have lifted up their v.
95. 7 To day if ye will hear his voice
98. 5 Sing unto the LORD with..the voice of a
102. 5 By reason of the voice of my groaning my
103. 20 hearkening unto the voice of his word
104. 7 at the voice of thy thunder they hasted
106. 25 hearkened not unto the voice of the LORD
116. 1 because he hath heard my voice..my su.
118. 15 The voice of rejoicing and salvation (is)
119. 149 Hear my voice according unto thy lo.
130. 2 LORD, hear my voice; let thine ears be at
130. 2 attentive to the voice of my supplications
140. 6 hear the voice of my supplications, O L.
141. 1 give ear unto my voice, when I cry unto
142. 1 I cried..with my voice; with my voice unto
Prov. 1. 20 Wisdom crieth..she uttereth her voice
2. 3 (and) liftest up thy voice for understand
5. 13 have not obeyed the voice of my teachers
8. 1 and understanding put forth her voice
8. 4 I call; and my voice (is) to the sons of man
27. 14 that blesseth his friend with a loud voice
Eccl. 5. 3 a fool's voice (is known) by the multitude
5. 6 wherefore should God be angry at thy vo.
10. 20 a bird of the air shall carry the voice, and
12. 4 he shall rise up at the voice of the bird
Song 2. 8 The voice of my beloved! behold, he co.
2. 12 the voice of the turtle is heard in our la
2. 14 let me hear thy voice .sweet (is) thy voice
5. 2 (it is) the voice of my beloved that knoc
8. 13 the companions hearken to thy voice: ca.
Isa. 6. 4 the posts of the door moved at the voice
6. 8 I heard the voice of the LORD, saying. Wh.
10. 30 Lift up thy voice, O daughter of Gallim, ca.
13. 2 exalt the voice unto them, shake the hand
15. 4 their voice shall be heard (even) unto Ja
24. 14 They shall lift up their voice, they shall
28. 23 Give ye ear, and hear my voice; hearken
29. 4 thy voice shall be, as of one that hath a fa.
30. 19 will be very gracious..at the voice of thy
30. 30 the LORD shall cause his glorious voice to
30. 31 through the voice of the LORD shall the A.
31. 4 (he) will not be afraid of their voice, nor
32. 9 hear my voice, ye careless daughters; give
36. 13 cried with a loud voice in the Jews' lan.
37. 23 against whom hast thou exalted (thy) vo.
40. 3 The voice of him that crieth in the wild.
40. 6 The voice said, Cry And he said, What
40. 9 lift up thy voice with strength; lift (it)
42. 2 nor cause his voice to be heard in the st.
48. 20 with a voice of singing declare ye, tell this
50. 10 that obeyeth the voice of his servant, that
51. 3 thanksgiving, and the voice of melody
52. 8 shall lift up the voice; with the voice to.
58. 1 lift up thy voice like a trumpet, and show
58. 4 to make your voice to be heard on high
65. 19 the voice of weeping..nor the voice of cr
66. 6 A voice of noise..a voice from..a voice of
Jer. 3. 13 ye have not obeyed my voice, saith the L
3. 21 A voice was heard upon the high places
3. 25 have not obeyed the voice of the LORD our
4. 15 a voice declareth from Dan, and publis
4. 16 give out their voice against the cities of
4. 31 I have heard a voice..the voice of the da.
6. 23 their voice roareth like the sea, and they
7. 23 Obey my voice, and I will be your God, and
7. 28 a nation that obeyeth not the voice of the
7. 34 the voice of mirth, and the voice of glad
7. 34 the voice of the bridegroom. and the voi.
8. 19 Behold the voice of the cry of the daught.
9. 10 neither can (men) hear the voice of the ca.
9. 13 have not obeyed my voice, neither walked
9. 19 a voice of wailing is heard out of Zion, Ho.
10. 13 When he uttereth his voice, (there is) a mu.
11. 4 Obey my voice, and do them, according
11. 7 and protesting, saying, Obey my voice
16. 9 the voice of mirth, and the voice of glad
16. 9 the voice of the bridegroom, and the voi.
18. 10 that it obey not my voice, then I will re.
18. 19 hearken to the voice of them that conte.
22. 20 lift up thy voice in Bashan, and cry from
22. 21 thy manner .thou obeyedst not my voice
25. 10 the voice of mirth, and the voice of glad.
25. 10 the voice of the bridegroom, and the voi.
25. 30 utter his voice from his holy habitation
25. 36 A voice of the cry of the shepherds, and
26. 13 and obey the voice of the LORD your God
30. 5 We have heard a voice of trembling, of
30. 19 and the voice of them that make merry
31. 15 A voice was heard in Ramah, lamentation
31. 16 Refrain thy voice from weeping, and thi.
32. 23 they obeyed not thy voice, neither walked
33. 11 The voice of joy, and the voice of gladness
33. 11 the voice of the bridegroom, and the voice
33. 11 the voice of them that shall say, Praise
35. 8 Thus have we obeyed the voice of Jonad.
38. 20 Obey, I beseech thee, the voice of the LORD
Jer. 40. 3 have not obeyed his voice, therefore this
42. 6 obey the voice..the voice of the LORD our
42. 13 neither obey the voice of the LORD your
42. 21 ye have not obeyed the voice of the LORD
43. 4 the people, obeyed not the voice of the L.
43. 7 for they obeyed not the voice of the LORD
44. 23 have not obeyed the voice of the LORD
46. 22 The voice thereof shall go like a serpent
48. 3 A voice of crying (shall be) from Horona.
48. 34 unto Jahaz, have they uttered their voice
50. 28 The voice of them that flee and escape
50. 42 their voice shall roar like the sea, and th.
51. 16 When he uttereth (his) voice, (there is) a
51. 55 had destroyed out of her the great voice
51. 55 her waves..a noise of their voice is uttered
Lam. 3. 56 Thou hast heard my voice; hide not thine
Eze. 1. 24 as the voice of the Almighty, the voice of
1. 25 there was a voice from the firmament that
1. 28 and I heard a voice of one that spake
3. 12 I heard behind me a voice of a great rus.
8. 18 though they cry..with a loud voice, (yet)
9. 1 He cried also..with a loud voice, saying
10. 5 as the voice of the Almighty God when
11. 13 cried with a loud voice, and said, Ah Lord
19. 9 his voice should no more be heard upon
21. 22 to lift up the voice with shouting, to app.
23. 42 a voice of a multitude being at ease (was)
27. 30 shall cause their voice to be heard against
33. 32 song of one that hath a pleasant voice
43. 2 and his voice (was) like a noise of many
Dan. 8. 16 I heard a man's voice between (the banks)
9. 10 Neither have we obeyed the voice of the
9. 11 that they might not obey thy voice, the.
9. 14 (is) righteous..for we obeyed not his voice
10. 6 the voice of his words like the voice of a
10. 9 Yet heard I the voice..the voice of his
Joel 2. 11 the LORD shall utter his voice before his
3. 16 The LORD also shall..utter his voice from
Amos 1. 2 LORD will..utter his voice from Jerusalem
Jon. 2. 2 cried I, (and) thou heardest my voice
2. 9 I will sacrifice unto thee with the voice
Mic. 6. 1 contend thou..let the hills hear thy voice
6. 9 The LORD'S voice crieth unto the city, and
Nah. 2. 7 maids shall lead (her) as with the voice of
2. 13 the voice of thy messengers shall no more
Hab. 3. 10 the deep uttered his voice, (and) lifted up
3. 16 my lips quivered at the voice:
Zeph. 1. 14 (even) the voice of the day of the LORD
2. 14 (their) voice shall sing in the windows; de.
3. 2 She obeyed not the voice; she received not
Hag. 1. 12 obeyed the voice of the LORD their God
Zech. 6. 15 if ye will diligently obey the voice of the
11. 3 (There is)..a voice of the roaring of young

2. *A voice, sound,* קָל *qal.*
Dan. 4. 31 there fell a voice from heaven..O king N.
6. 20 cried with a lamentable voice unto Daniel
7. 11 I beheld then because of the voice of the

3. *A voice, sound,* φωνή *phōnē.*
Matt. 2. 18 In Rama was there a voice heard, lamen.
3. 3 The voice of one crying in the wilderness
3. 17 And lo a voice from heaven, saying, Th.
12. 19 neither shall any man hear his voice in
17. 5 behold a voice out of the cloud, which sa.
27. 46 Jesus cried with a loud voice, saying, Eli!
27. 50 when he had cried again with a loud voice
Mark 1. 3 The voice of one crying in the wilderness
1. 11 there came a voice from heaven, (saying)
1. 26 had torn him, and cried with a loud voice
5. 7 cried with a loud voice, and said, What
9. 7 a voice came out of the cloud, saying, Th.
15. 34 Jesus cried with a loud voice, saying, Eloi
15. 37 Jesus cried with a loud voice, and gave up
Luke 1. 42 she spake out with a loud [voice], and said
1. 44 as soon as the voice of thy salutation so.
3. 4 The voice of one crying in the wilderness
3. 22 a voice came from heaven, which said, Th.
4. 33 a man which..cried out with a loud voice
8. 28 and with a loud voice said, What have I to
9. 35 there came a voice out of the cloud saying
9. 36 when the voice was past, Jesus was found
11. 27 a certain woman. lifted up her voice, and
17. 13 they lifted up (their) voices and said, Je
17. 15 turned back, and with a loud voice glori
19. 37 praise God with a loud voice for all the
23. 23 they were instant with loud voices requi
23. 23 the voices of them and of the chief priests
23. 46 when Jesus had cried with a loud voice
John 1. 23 I (am) the voice of one crying in the wil
3. 29 rejoiceth..because of..bridegroom's voice
5. 25 the dead shall hear the voice of the Son of
5. 28 all..in the graves shall hear his voice
5. 37 Ye have neither heard his voice at any ti.
10. 3 the sheep hear his voice: and he calleth
10. 4 sheep follow him: for they know his voice
10. 5 for they know not the voice of strangers
10. 16 they shall hear my voice; and there shall
10. 27 My sheep hear my voice, and I know them
11. 43 he cried with a loud voice, Lazarus, come
12. 28 Then came there a voice from heaven, (sa.)
12. 30 This voice came not because of me, but
18. 37 Every one .of the truth heareth my voice
Acts 2. 14 lifted up his voice, and said unto them
4. 24 they lifted up their voice to God with one
7. 31 the voice of the Lord came unto him
7. 57 they cried out with a loud voice, and sto
7. 60 cried with a loud voice, Lord, lay not this
8. 7 unclean spirits, crying with a loud voice
9. 4 heard a voice saying unto him, Saul, Saul
9. 7 stood speechless, hearing a voice, but se.
10. 13 there came a voice to him, Rise, Peter
10. 15 the voice (spake) unto him again the sec.
Acts 11. 7 I heard a voice saying unto me, Arise, P.
11. 9 the voice answered me again from heaven
12. 14 when she knew Peter's voice, she opened
12. 22 (It is) the voice of a god, and not of a man
13. 27 nor yet the voices of the Prophets which
14. 10 Said with a loud voice, Stand upright on
14. 11 they lifted up their voices, saying in the
16. 28 Paul cried with a loud voice, saying, Do
19. 34 all with one voice about the space of two
22. 7 heard a voice saying unto me, Saul, Saul
22. 9 they heard not the voice of him that spa.
22. 14 and shouldest hear the voice of his mouth
22. 22 (then) lifted up their voices, and said, A.
24. 21 Except it be for this one voice, that I cried
26. 14 I heard a voice speaking unto me, and sa.
26. 24 Festus said with a loud voice, Paul, thou
1 Co. 14. 10 There are, it may be, so many kinds of vo.
14. 11 if I know not the meaning of the voice, I
Gal. 4. 20 I desire..to change my voice; for I stand
1 Th. 4. 16 with the voice of the archangel, and with
Heb. 3. 7, 15 To day if ye will hear his voice
4. 7 To day if ye will hear his voice, harden
12. 19 the sound of a trumpet, and the voice of
12. 26 Whose voice then shook the earth, but
2 Pe. 1. 17 when there came such a voice to him from
1. 18 this voice which came from heaven we he.
2. 16 the dumb ass speaking with man's voice
Rev. 1. 10 heard behind me a great voice, as of a tr.
1. 12 I turned to see the voice that spake with
1. 15 and his voice as the sound of many waters.
3. 20 if any man hear my voice, and open the
4. 1 the first voice which I heard (was) as it
4. 5 lightnings and thunderings and voices
5. 2 angel proclaiming with a loud voice
5. 11 I heard the voice of many angels round
5. 12 Saying with a loud voice, Worthy is the
6. 6 I heard a voice in the midst of the four
6. 7 I heard [the voice of] the fourth beast say
6. 10 they cried with a loud voice, saying, How
7. 2 he cried with a loud voice to the four an.
7. 10 cried with a loud voice, saying, Salvation
8. 5 there were voices, and thunderings, and
8. 13 saying with a loud voice, Woe, woe, woe
8. 13 by reason of the other voices of the trum.
9. 13 I heard a voice from the four horns of the
10. 3 cried with a loud voice, as (when) a lion
10. 3 cried, seven thunders uttered their voices.
10. 4 seven thunders had uttered [their voices]
10. 4 I heard a voice from heaven saying unto
10. 7 in the days of the voice of the seventh an.
10. 8 the voice which I heard from heaven spa.
11. 12 they heard a great voice from heaven say.
11. 15 there were great voices in heaven, saying
11. 19 there were lightnings and voices, and th.
12. 10 I heard a loud voice saying in heaven, N.
14. 2 I heard a voice from heaven, as the voice
14. 2 as the voice..I heard the voice of harpers.
14. 7 Saying with a loud voice, Fear God, and
14. 9 saying with a loud voice, If any man wo.
14. 13 I heard a voice from heaven saying unto
14. 15 crying with a loud voice to him that sat
16. 1 I heard a great voice out of the temple
16. 17 there came a great voice out of the tem.
16. 18 there were voices, and thunders, and lig.
18. 2 [he cried mightily with a strong voice, say.]
18. 4 I heard another voice from heaven, saying
18. 22 the voice of harpers, and musicians, and
18. 23 the voice of the bridegroom and of the br.
19. 1 I heard a great voice of much people in
19. 5 a voice came out of the throne, saying, P.
19. 6 the voice..as the voice..and as the voice
19. 17 he cried with a loud voice, saying to all
21. 3 I heard a great voice out of heaven, say.

4. *A small pebble, vote,* ψῆφος *psēphos.*
Acts 26. 10 they were put to death, I gave my voice

VOID, (place, to be or make) —

1. *To be parted, lost,* אָבַד *abad.*
Deut. 32. 28 For they (are) a nation void of counsel

2. *Emptiness,* בֹּהוּ *bohu.*
Gen. 1. 2 And the earth was without form, and void
Jer. 4. 23 I beheld the earth..without form and vo.

3. *To empty, make void,* בָּקַק *baqaq.*
Jer. 19. 7 I will make void the counsel of Judah and

4. *Threshing floor, forum,* גֹּרֶן *goren.*
1 Ki. 22. 10 in a void place in the entrance of the gate
2 Ch. 18. 9 in a void place at the entering in of the

5. *Lacking,* חָסֵר *chaser.*
Prov. 7. 7 beheld..a young man void of understan
10. 13 a rod (is) for the back of him that is void
11. 12 He that is void of wisdom despiseth his n.
12. 11 he that followeth vain..is void of under.
17. 18 A man void of understanding striketh h.
24. 30 by the vineyard of the man void of unde.

6. *Emptiness,* מְבוּקָה *mebuqah.*
Nah. 2. 10 She is empty, and void, and waste; and

7. *To reject,* נָאַר *naar,* 3.
Psa. 89. 39 Thou hast made void the covenant of thy

8. *To break, make void,* פָּרַר *parar,* 5.
Num. 30. 12 if her husband hath..made them void on
30. 12 her husband hath made them void, and
30. 13 may establish it. or..may make it void
30. 15 if he shall any ways make them void aft.
Psa. 119. 126 to work ..they have made void thy law

9. *Emptily, vainly, without care,* רֵיקָם *reqam.*
Isa. 55. 11 it shall not return unto me void, but it

10. *To make thoroughly useless or idle*, καταργέω.
Rom. 3. 31 Do we then make void the law through f.

11. *To make vain, useless*, κενόω *kenoō*.
Rom. 4. 14 faith is made void, and the promise made
1 Co. 9. 15 any man should make my glorying void

VOLUME —

1. *A roll, volume*, מְגִלָּה *megillah*.
Psa. 40. 7 in the volume of the book (it is) written

2. *Head of a pillar, a scroll rolled up*, κεφαλίς.
Heb. 10. 7 in the volume of the book it is written of

VOLUNTARY (offering, will), voluntarily —

1. *Willing or liberal offering*, נְדָבָה *nedabah*.
Lev. 7. 16 if the sacrifice of his offering (be)..a v. of.
Eze. 46. 12 prepare a voluntary burnt offering, or..v.

2. *Good will or pleasure*, רָצוֹן *ratson*.
Lev. 1. 3 he shall offer it of his own voluntary will

VOMIT (out, up, up again, to) —

1. *Vomit, thing vomited*, קֵא *qe*.
Prov 26. 11 As a dog returneth to his vomit..a fool

2. *To (cause to) vomit, spread out*, קוֹא *qo*, 5.
Lev. 18. 25 land itself vomiteth out her inhabitants
Job 20. 15 he shall vomit them up again: God shall
Prov 23. 8 The morsel..shalt thou vomit up, and lo.
25. 16 lest thou be filled therewith, and vomit
Jon. 2. 10 and it vomited out Jonah upon the dry

3. *Vomit*, קִיא *qi*.
Isa. 19. 14 as a drunken (man) staggereth in his vo.
28. 8 For all tables are full of vomit..filthiness
Jer. 48. 26 Moab also shall wallow in his vomit, and

4. *Vomit*, ἐξέραμα *exerama*.
2 Pe. 2. 22 The dog (is) turned to his own vomit ag.

VOPH'-SI, וָפְסִי *rich*.
Father of Nahbi of the tribe of Naphtali; one of those sent to spy out the land. B.C. 1515.
Num 13. 14 the tribe of Naphtali, Nahbi the son of V.

VOW, (vowed, to)—

1. *To vow*, נָדַר *nadar*.
Gen. 28. 20 Jacob vowed..saying, If God will be with
31. 13 the God of Beth-el..where thou vowedst
Lev. 27. 8 according to his ability that vowed shall
Num. 6. 2 to vow..to separate..unto the LORD
6. 21 Nazarite who hath vowed..which he vo.
21. 2 Israel vowed..unto the LORD, and said
30. 2 If a man vow..unto the LORD, or swear
30. 3 If a woman also vow..unto the LORD, and
30. 10 if she vowed in her husband's house, or
Deut 12. 11 shall ye bring all..which ye vow unto the
12. 17 nor any..which thou vowest, nor thy fr.
23. 21 When thou shalt vow..unto the LORD
23. 22 if thou shalt forbear to vow, it shall be
23. 23 as thou hast vowed unto the LORD thy
Judg 11. 30 Jephthah vowed..unto the LORD, and sa.
11. 39 did..(according) to..which he had vowed
1 Sa. 1. 11 she vowed..and said, O LORD of hosts, if
2 Sa. 15. 7 let me go and pay..which I have vowed
15. 8 For thy servant vowed..while I abode at
Psa. 76. 11 Vow, and pay unto the LORD your God
132. 2 How he..vowed unto the mighty..of Jac.
Eccl. 5. 4 When thou vowest .pay that..hast vow.
5. 5 Better (is it) that thou shouldest not vow
5. 5 than that thou shouldest vow and not pay
Isa. 19. 21 they shall vow..unto the LORD, and per.
Jer. 44. 25 We will surely perform..that we have vo.
Jon. 2. 9 I will pay..that I have vowed. Salvation
Mal. 1. 14 which hath in his flock a male, and vow.

2. *A vow*, נֶדֶר, נֵדֶר *neder*.
Gen. 28. 20 a vow, saying, If God will be with me
31. 13 a vow unto me: now arise, get thee out
Lev. 7. 16 if the sacrifice of his offering (be) a vow
22. 18 that will offer oblation for all his vows
22. 21 to accomplish (his) vow, or a free will of.
22. 23 but for a vow it shall not be accepted
23. 38 beside all your vows, and beside all your
27. 2 When a man shall make a singular vow
Num. 6. 2 a vow of a Nazarite, to separate..unto the
6. 5 All the days of the vow of his separation
6. 21 according to the vow..so he must do after
15. 3, 8 a sacrifice in performing a vow, or
21. 2 a vow unto the LORD, and said, If thou
29. 39 beside your vows, and your free will off.
30. 2 a vow unto the LORD, or swear an oath
30. 3 a vow unto the LORD, and bind .by a bo.
30. 4 hear her vow..all her vows shall stand
30. 5 not any of her vows, or of her bonds where.
30. 6 if she had at all an husband when she vo.
30. 7 then her vows shall stand, and her bonds
30. 8 then he shall make her vow which she
30. 9 every vow of a widow, or of her that is
30. 11 all her vows shall stand, and every bond
30. 12 concerning her vows, or concerning the
30. 13 Every vow, and every binding oath to
30. 14 he establisheth all her vows, or all her bo.
Deut 12. 6 your vows, and your free will offerings, and
12. 11 and all your choice vows..unto the LORD
12. 17 Thou mayest not eat..any of thy vows
12. 26 Only thy holy things..and thy vows, thou
23. 18 into the house of the LORD..for any vow
23. 21 a vow unto the LORD thy God, thou shalt
Judg 11. 30 a vow unto the LORD, and said, If thou sh.
11. 39 who did with her (according) to his vow
1 Sa. 1. 11 a vow, and said, O LORD of hosts, if thou
1. 21 to offer..the yearly sacrifice, and his vow
2 Sa. 15. 7 I pray thee, let me go and pay my vow
15. 8 a vow while I abode at Geshur in Syria
Job 22. 27 shall hear thee..thou shalt pay thy vows
Psa. 22. 25 I will pay my vows before them that fear
50. 14 and pay thy vows unto the Most High
56. 12 Thy vows (are) upon me, O God, I will re.
61. 5 For thou, O God, hast heard my vows, th.
61. 8 sing..that I may daily perform my vows
65. 1 and unto thee shall the vow be performed
66. 13 I will go into..I will pay thee my vows
116. 14, 18 I will pay my vows unto the LORD now
Prov. 7. 14 peace offerings..this day..I paid my vows
20. 25 (It is) a snare..after vows to make enquiry
31. 2 What, my son?..and what, the son of my v.
Eccl. 5. 4 When..a vow unto God, defer not to pay
Isa. 19. 21 yea..a vow unto the LORD, and perform
Jer. 44. 25 We will surely perform our vows that we
44. 25 ye will..accomplish your vows..your vows
Jon. 1. 16 offered..unto the LORD, and made vows
Nah. 1. 15 keep thy solemn feasts, perform thy vows

3. *A vow*, εὐχή *euchē*.
Acts 18. 18 having shorn (his) head..for he had a vow
21. 23 We have four men which have a vow on

VOYAGE —

Sailing, πλόος *ploos*.
Acts 27. 10 I perceive that this voyage will be with

VULTURE —

1. *A kite, vulture*, אַיָּה *ayyah*.
Job 28. 7 path..which the vulture's eye hath not se.

2. *A vulture*, דָּאָה *daah*.
Lev. 11. 14 the vulture, and the kite after his kind

3. *A vulture*, דַּיָּה *dayyah*.
Deut 14. 13 the glede, and the kite, and the vulture
Isa. 34. 15 there shall the vultures also be gathered

W

WAFER —

1. *A cake*, צַפִּיחִת *tsappichith*.
Exod 16. 31 the taste of it..like wafers..with honey

2. *Thin cake, wafer*, רָקִיק *raqiq*.
Exod 29. 2 and wafers unleavened anointed with oil
29. 23 one wafer out of the basket of the unlea.
Lev. 2. 4 or unleavened wafers anointed with oil
7. 12 unleavened wafers anointed with oil, and
8. 26 took..a cake of oiled bread, and one wafer
Num. 6. 15 wafers of unleavened bread anointed with
6. 19 the priest shall take..one unleavened wa.

WAG, to —

1. *To cause to move*, נוּד *nud*, 5.
Jer. 18. 16 one..shall be astonished, and wag his head

2. *To cause to move, shake*, נוּעַ *nua*, 5.
Lam. 2. 15 they hiss and wag their head at the daugh.
Zeph. 2. 15 every one..shall hiss, (and) wag his hand

3. *To move, agitate, shake*, κινέω *kineō*.
Matt 27. 39 they..reviled him, wagging their heads
Mark 15. 29 they..railed on him, wagging their heads

WAGES, (without) —

1. *Hire, wages*, מַשְׂכֹּרֶת *maskoreth*.
Gen. 29. 15 said..tell me, what (shall) thy wages (be)?
31. 7 your father hath..changed my wages ten
31. 41 and thou hast changed my wages ten tim.

2. *Gratis, in vain, for nought*, חִנָּם *chinnam*.
Jer. 22. 13 useth his neighbour's service without wa.

3. *Work, wage*, פְּעֻלָּה *peullah*.
Lev. 19. 13 the wages of him that is hired shall not

4. *To hire self out*, שָׂכַר *sakar*, 7.
Hag. 1. 6 he that earneth wages, earneth wages (to

5. *Hire, reward, wage*, שָׂכָר *sakar*.
Gen. 30. 28 Appoint me thy wages, and I will give (it)
31. 8 If he said..The speckled shall be thy wag.
Exod. 2. 9 nurse it for me, and I will give. thy wag.
Eze. 29. 18 yet had he no wages, nor his army, for
29. 19 Egypt..it shall be the wages for his army
Mal. 3. 5 that oppress the hireling in (his) wages

6. *Hire, reward*, μισθός *misthos*.
John 4. 36 he that reapeth receiveth wages, and ga.
2 Pet. 2. 15 who loved the wages of unrighteousness

7. *A soldier's rations, allowance*, ὀψώνιον *opsōnion*.
Luke 3. 14 And he said..be content with your wag.
Rom. 6. 23 the wages of sin (is) death; but the gift
2 Co. 11. 8 I robbed other churches, taking wages

WAGON —

1. *Wagon, cart, chariot*, עֲגָלָה *agalah*.
Gen. 45. 19 take you wagons out of the land of Egypt
45. 21 Joseph gave them wagons, according to
45. 27 when he saw the wagons which Joseph
46. 5 in the wagons which Pharaoh had sent to
Num. 7. 3 six covered wagons..a wagon for two of
7. 6 Moses took the wagons and the oxen, and
7. 7, 8 wagons and..oxen he gave unto the sons

2. *Rider, chariot*, רֶכֶב *rekeb*.
Eze. 23. 24 come..with chariots, wagons, and wheels

WAIL, wailing, to —

1. *A smiting or beating of the breast*, מִסְפֵּד *misped*.
Esth. 4. 3 great mourning..and weeping, and wail.
Eze. 27. 31 with bitterness of heart..bitter wailing
Amos 5. 16 Wailing..and they shall call..to wailing
5. 17 in all vineyards..wailing: for I will pass
Mic. 1. 8 I will make a wailing like the dragons, and

2. *Wailing*, נֹהַּ *noah*.
Eze. 7. 11 neither (shall there be) wailing for them

3. *To wail*, נָהָה *nahah*.
Eze. 32. 18 Son of man, wail for the multitude of Eg.

4. *A wailing*, נְהִי *nehi*.
Jer. 9. 10 For the mountains will I take up..waili.
9. 18 let them make haste, and take up a wail.
9. 19 For a voice of wailing is heard out of Zion
9. 20 teach your daughters wailing, and every

5. *Wailing*, נִי *ni*.
Eze. 27. 32 in their wailing they shall take up a lam.

6. *To smite or beat the breast*, סָפַד *saphad*.
Mic. 1. 8 I will wail and howl, I will go stripped

7. *To cry aloud, yell*, ἀλαλάζω *alalazō*.
Mark 5. 38 seeth..them that wept and wailed greatly

8. *Wailing, lamentation*, κλαυθμός *klauthmos*.
Matt 13. 42, 50 shall be wailing and gnashing of teeth

9. *To cut, smite or beat the breast*, κόπτομαι *koptomai*.
Rev. 1. 7 all kindreds of the earth shall wail beca.

10. *To sorrow, mourn, grieve*, πενθέω *pentheō*.
Rev. 18. 15 shall stand afar off..weeping and wailing
18. 19 and cried, weeping and wailing, saying

WAIT at, for, on, upon, continually, to —

1. *Silence*, דּוּמִיָּה *dumiyyah*.
Psa. 62. 1 Truly my soul waiteth upon God: from
65. 1 Praise waiteth for thee, O God, in

2. *To be silent, cease, stand still*, דָּמַם *damam*.
Psa. 62. 5 My soul, wait thou only upon God, for

3. *To wait earnestly*, חָכָה *chakah*.
Isa. 30. 18 blessed (are) all they that wait for him

4. *To wait earnestly*, חָכָה *chakah*, 3.
Job 32. 4 Now Elihu had waited till Job had spoken
Psa. 33. 20 Our soul waiteth for the LORD: he (is) our
106. 13 They soon forgat his works; they waited
Isa. 8. 17 I will wait upon the LORD, that hideth his
30. 18 therefore will the LORD wait, that he may
64. 4 he hath prepared for him that waiteth
Dan. 12. 12 Blessed (is) he that waiteth, and cometh
Hos. 6. 9 And as troops of robbers wait for a man
Hab. 2. 3 though it tarry, wait for it; because it will
Zeph. 3. 8 Therefore wait ye upon me, saith the Lo.

5. *At the hand of*, לְיַד *le-yad*.
1 Ch. 23. 28 their office (was) to wait on the sons of A.

6. *To wait with hope, stay*, יָחַל *yachal*, 2.
Eze. 19. 5 Now when she saw that she had waited

7. *To (make to) wait with hope*, יָחַל *yachal*, 3.
Job 14. 14 the days of my appointed time will I wait
29. 21 gave ear, and waited, and kept silence at
29. 23 they waited for me as for the rain, and th.
30. 26 when I waited for light, there came dark.
Psa. 69. 3 mine eyes fail while I wait for my God
Isa. 42. 4 He shall not fail..isles shall wait for his
Mic. 5. 7 tarrieth not..nor waiteth for the sons of

8. *To (cause to) wait with hope*, יָחַל *yachal*, 5.
2 Ki. 6. 33 what should I wait for the LORD any lon
Job 32. 11 I waited for your words; I gave ear to yo.
32. 16 When I had waited, for they spake not
Mic. 7. 7 I will wait for the God of my salvation

9. *To stand still or fast*, עָמַד *amad*.
1 Ki. 20. 38 So the prophet departed, and waited for
1 Ch. 6. 32 they waited on their office according to
6. 33 these (are) they that waited with their ch.
2 Ch. 7. 6 And the priests waited on their offices
Neh. 12. 44 Judah rejoiced..for the Levites that wa.

10. *To serve the host*, צָבָא *tsaba*.
Num. 8. 24 they shall go in to wait upon the service

11. *The service of the host*, צָבָא *tsaba*.
Num. 8. 25 they shall cease waiting upon the service

12. *To watch, look out*, צָפָה *tsaphah*.
Job 15. 22 He believeth not that..he is waited for of

13. *To wait, expect, look for, hope*, קָוָה *qavah*.
Psa. 25. 3 Yea, let none that wait on thee be asha.
37. 9 those that wait upon the LORD, they shall
69. 6 Let not them that wait on thee, O Lord
Isa. 40. 31 they that wait upon the LORD shall renew
49. 23 they shall not be ashamed that wait for
Lam. 3. 25 The LORD (is) good unto them that wait

14. *To wait, expect*, קָוָה *qavah*, 3.
Gen. 49. 18 I have waited for thy salvation, O LORD
Job 6. 19 the companies of Sheba waited for them
17. 13 If I wait, the grave (is) mine house, I have
Psa. 25. 5 Lead me..on thee do I wait all the day
25. 21 Let integrity..preserve me; for I wait on
27. 14 Wait on the LORD..wait, I say, on the
37. 34 Wait on the LORD, and keep his way, and
39. 7 now, Lord, what wait I for? my hope (is)
40. 1 I waited patiently for the Lord; and he
52. 9 I will wait on thy name; for (it is) good
56. 6 they mark my steps, when they wait for
119. 95 The wicked have waited for me to destroy
130. 5 I wait for the LORD, my soul doth wait, and
Prov. 20. 22 wait on the LORD, and he shall save thee
Isa. 25. 9 we have waited for him..we have waited
26. 8 Yea, in the way..have we waited for thee
33. 2 be gracious unto us; we have waited for

Isa. 51. 5 isles shall wait upon me, and on mine arm
59. 9 we wait for light, but behold obscurity
60. 9 Surely the isles shall wait for me, and the
Jer. 14. 22 we will wait upon thee; for thou hast m.
Hos. 12. 6 keep mercy and judgment, and wait on

15. *To hope, wait, look for*, שָׂבַר *sabar*, 3.
Psa.104. 27 These wait all upon thee, that thou may.
145. 15 The eyes of all wait upon thee: and thou

16. *To observe, watch, take heed*, שָׁמַר *shamar*.
Num. 3. 10 and they shall wait on their priest's office
2 Ch. 5. 11 for all the priests..did not..wait by cour.
Job 24. 15 the eye also of the adulterer waiteth for
Psa. 59. 9 (Because of) his strength will I wait upon
Prov. 8. 34 watching daily at my gates, waiting at
27. 18 he that waiteth on his master shall be h.
Zech.11. 11 the poor of the flock that waited upon me

17. *To serve, minister*, שָׁרַת *sharath*, 3.
2 Ch.17. 19 These waited on the king, beside (those)

18. *To remain up or back*, ἀναμένω *anamenō*.
1 Th. 1. 10 to wait for his Son from heaven,

19. *To wait long for, expect earnestly*, ἀπεκδέχομαι.
Rom. 8. 19 waiteth for the manifestation of the sons
8. 23 waiting for the adoption..the redemption
8. 25 But if we hope..we with patience wait for
1 Co. 1. 7 waiting for the coming of our Lord Jesus
Gal. 5. 5 we through the spirit wait for the hope of

20. *To wait long, expect earnestly*, ἐκδέχομαι *ekdec*.
John 5. 3 lay ..[waiting for the moving of the wat.]
Acts 17. 16 Now while Paul waited for them at Ath.
Jas. 5. 7 the husbandman waiteth for the precious
1 Pe. 3. 20 [when once the longsuffering] of God [wa.]

21. *To remain around*, περιμένω *perimenō*.
Acts 1. 4 but wait for the promise of the Father

22. *To wait on or towards*, προσδέχομαι *prosdecho*.
Mark15. 43 which also waited for the kingdom of God
Luke 2. 25 man..waiting for the consolation of Isr.
12. 36 ye yourselves like unto men that wait for
23. 51 who also himself waited for the kingdom

23. *To look to or toward*, προσδοκάω *prosdokaō*.
Luke 1. 21 the people waited for Zacharias, and ma.
8. 40 received him: for they were all waiting
Acts 10. 24 Cornelius waited for them, and had called

24. *To sit by or near, attend to or on*, προσεδρεύω.
1 Co. 9. 13 they which [wait at] the altar are partak.

25. *To persevere on*, προσκαρτερέω *proskartereō*.
Mark 3. 9 that a small ship should wait on him, be.
Acts 10. 7 a devout soldier of them that waited on

WAIT carefully, patiently, quietly, to —

1. *Silently*, דּוּמָם *dumam*.
Lam. 3. 26 should both hope and quietly wait for the

2. *To stay*, חִיל, חוּל *chul, chil*.
Mic. 1. 12 the inhabitant of Maroth waited carefully

3. *To stay self*, חִיל, חוּל *chul, chil*, 7a.
Psa. 37. 7 Rest in the LORD, and wait patiently for
[*See also* Patient.]

WAIT, (lying in, that lay) —

1. *A lying in wait*, אֶרֶב *ereb*.
Job 38. 40 When they..abide in the covert to lie in w.

2. *A lying in wait, ambush*, אֹרֶב *oreb*.
Jer. 9. 8 peaceably..but in heart he layeth his wa.

3. *A lying in wait, (men or place)*, מַאֲרָב *maarab*.
Judg. 9. 35 Abimelech rose up..from lying in wait

4. *To observe, watch*, שָׁמַר *shamar*.
Psa. 71 10 they that lay wait for my soul take coun.

[*See also* Lay, laying, lie in, lier in, liers, lying, lying in.]

WAKE (up, waken, be wakened), to —

1. *To awake or stir up*, עוּר *ur*.
Song 5. 2 I sleep, but my heart waketh..the voice

2. *To be awaked or roused up*, עוּר *ur*, 2.
Joel 3. 12 Let the heathen be wakened, and come
Zech. 4. 1 as a man that is wakened out of his sleep

3. *To awake up*, עוּר *ur*, 5.
Isa. 50. 4 he wakeneth..he wakeneth mine ear to
Joel 3. 9 Prepare war, wake up the mighty men
Zech. 4. 1 the angel..came again, and waked me, as

4. *To awake, rise, be early*, קוּץ *quts*, 5.
Jer. 51. 39, 57 sleep a perpetual sleep, and not wake

5. *Watches, eye lids*, שְׁמֻרוֹת *shemuroth*.
Psa. 77. 4 Thou holdest mine eyes waking: I am so

6. *To watch*, שָׁקַד *shaqad*.
Psa.127. 1 except the LORD keep..the watchman wa.

7. *To be vigilant, wakeful*, γρηγορέω *grēgoreō*.
1 Th. 5. 10 Who died for us, that, whether we wake

WALK —

1. *A going, company*, הֲלִיכָה *halikah*.
Nah. 2. 5 they shall stumble in their walk; they

2. *A walk, journey*, מַהֲלָךְ *mahalak*.
Eze. 42. 4 before the chambers (was) a walk of ten cu.

WALK (about, in, orderly, through, uprightly), to —

1. *To go on the way, tread*, דָּרַךְ *darak*.
Hab. 3. 15 Thou didst walk through the sea with th.

2. *To go on*, הָלַךְ *halak*.
Gen. 24. 65 What man (is) this that walketh in the fi.
Exod. 2. 5 maidens walked along by the river's side
14. 29 the children of Israel walked upon dry
Lev. 26. 23 if ye will not be reformed..but will walk
26. 24 Then will I also walk contrary unto you
26. 27 if ye will not..hearken unto me, but walk
26. 28 Then I will walk contrary unto you also
26. 40 confess..they have walked contrary unto
Deut. 8. 19 if thou..walk after other gods, and serve
28. 9 if thou shalt keep..and walk in his ways
Josh. 5. 6 the children of Israel walked forty years
Judg 2. 17 out of the way..their fathers walked in
5. 10 Speak..ye that sit in judgment, and walk
1 Sa. 8. 3 his sons walked not in his ways, but tur.
8. 5 thou art old, and thy sons walk not in thy
2 Sa. 2. 29 walked all that night through the plain
1 Ki. 2. 42 on the day..thou walkest abroad anywh.
3. 6 according as he walked before thee in tr.
3. 14 in my ways..as thy father David did walk
8. 23 that walk before thee with all their heart
8. 25 before me as thou hast walked before me
9. 4 if thou wilt..as David thy father walked
11. 33 Because that they..have not walked in my
11. 38 if thou wilt hearken unto..and wilt walk
2 Ki. 13. 6 departed not from the sins..(but) walked
13. 11 he departed not..(but) he walked therein
21. 21 in all the way that his father walked in
21. 22 and walked not in the way of the LORD
1 Ch.17. 8 with thee whithersoever thou hast walked
2 Ch. 6. 14 that walk before thee with all their heart
6. 16 in my law, as thou hast walked before me
7. 17 if thou wilt..as David thy father walked
11. 17 for three years they walked in the way of
17. 3 he walked in the first ways of his father
17. 4 walked in his commandments, and not af.
21. 12 Because thou hast not walked in the ways
22. 3 He also walked in the ways of the house
22. 5 He walked also after their counsel, and
Job 31. 5 If I have walked with vanity, or if my foot
31. 7 If..mine heart walked after mine eyes
31. 26 If I beheld..the moon walking (in) brig.
Psa. 1. 1 Blessed (is) the man that walketh not in
15. 2 He that walketh uprightly, and worketh
26. 1 Judge me..for I have walked in mine in.
73. 9 their tongue walketh through the earth
84. 11 will he withhold from them that walk
91. 6 for the pestilence (that) walketh in dark.
101. 6 he that walketh in a perfect way, he shall
119. 1 undefiled..who walk in the law of the L.
119. 3 They also do no iniquity: they walk in his
128. 1 that feareth the LORD: that walketh in
Prov. 2. 7 (he is) a buckler to them that walk upri.
6. 12 A naughty person, a wicked man, walketh
10. 9 He that walketh uprightly..he that perv.
13. 20 He that walketh with wise (men) shall be
14. 2 He that walketh in his uprightness fear.
19. 1 Better (is) the poor that walketh in his
28. 6 Better (is) the poor that walketh in his up.
28. 18 Whoso walketh uprightly shall be saved
28. 26 Whoso walketh wisely, he shall be deliv.
Eccl. 2. 14 the fool walketh in darkness: and I my.
6. 8 what hath the poor, that knoweth to walk
10. 3 when he that is a fool walketh by the way
10. 7 I have seen..princes walking as servants
Isa. 3. 16 walking and mincing (as) they go, and mak.
9. 2 The people that walked in darkness have
20. 2 And he did so, walking naked and baref.
20. 3 Like as my servant Isaiah hath walked na.
30. 2 That walk to go down into Egypt, and ha.
33. 15 He that walketh righteously, and speake.
35. 9 No lion shall be..the redeemed shall walk
42. 5 that giveth..spirit to them that walk th.
42. 24 they would not walk in his ways, neither
50. 10 that walketh (in) darkness, and hath no
57. 2 they shall rest..walking (in) his uprightn.
65. 2 a rebellious people, which walketh in a w.
Jer. 2. 8 and walked after (things that) do not pr.
6. 28 They (are) all grievous revolters; walking
7. 9 Will ye..walk after other gods whom ye
7. 23 walk ye in all the ways that I have comm.
8. 2 the host..after whom they have walked
9. 4 every neighbour will walk with slanders
9. 13 have not obeyed my voice neither walked
10. 23 not in man that walketh to direct his ste.
13. 10 which walk in the imagination of their he.
16. 12 ye walk every one after the imagination
23. 14 prophets..commit adultery, and walk in
23. 17 they say unto every one that walketh after
32. 23 they obeyed not thy voice, neither walked
44. 10 neither have they feared, nor walked in
44. 23 nor walked in his law, nor in his statutes
Eze. 5. 6 my statutes, they have not walked in th.
5. 7 have not walked in my statutes, neither
11. 12 ye have not walked in my statutes, neit.
11. 21 whose heart walketh after the heart of
16. 47 Yet hast thou not walked after their ways
18. 17 hath executed my judgments, hath walked
20. 13 they walked not in my statutes, and they
20. 16 Because they..walked not in my statutes
20. 21 they walked not in my statutes, neither ke.
23. 31 Thou hast walked in the way of thy sister
33. 15 give again that he hath robbed, walk in
Hos. 5. 11 he willingly walked after the commandm.
Amos 2. 4 after the which their fathers have walked
Mic. 2. 7 my words do good to him that walketh up.
2. 11 If a man walking in the spirit and falseh.
Nah. 2. 11 where the lion, (even) the old lion, walked
Zeph. 1. 17 that they shall walk like blind men, bec.
Mal. 2. 6 he walked with me in peace and equity
3. 14 that we have walked mournfully before

3. *To go on*, הָלַךְ *halak*, 3.
Psa. 55. 14 walked unto the house of God in company
Psa. 81. 13 O that..Israel had walked in my ways
86. 11 I will walk in thy truth: unite my heart
89. 15 they shall walk..in the light of thy count.
115. 7 feet have they, but they walk not, neither
142. 3 In the way wherein I walked have they
Eccl. 4. 15 I considered all the living which walk un.
11. 9 walk in the ways of thine heart, and in
Isa. 59. 9 for brightness, (but) we walk in darkness
Lam. 5. 18 which is desolate, the foxes walk upon it
Eze. 18. 9 Hath walked in my statutes, and hath k.
Psa.104. 3 who walketh upon the wings of the

4. *To go on*, הֲלַךְ *halak*, 3.
Dan. 4. 29 walked in the palace of the kingdom of Ba.

5. *To cause to go on*, הֲלַךְ *halak*, 5.
Dan. 3. 25 walking in the midst of the fire, and they
4. 37 those that walk in pride he is able to abase

6. *To go on*, יָלַךְ *yalak*.
Exod16. 4 whether they will walk in my law, or no
18. 20 show them the way wherein they must w.
Lev. 18. 3 neither shall ye walk in their ordinances
18. 4 keep mine ordinances, to walk therein
20. 23 ye shall not walk in the manners of the
26. 3 If ye walk in my statutes, and keep my
26. 21 if ye walk contrary unto me, and will not
26. 41 I also have walked contrary unto them
Deut. 2. 7 he knoweth thy walking through this gr.
5. 33 Ye shall walk in all the ways which the
6. 7 when thou walkest by the way, and when
8. 6 Keep..to walk in his ways, and to fear
10. 12 but to fear the LORD thy God, to walk in
11. 19 speaking of them..when thou walkest by
11. 22 to walk in all his ways, and to cleave unto
13. 4 Ye shall walk after the LORD your God
13. 5 which..thy God commanded thee to walk
19. 9 to love the LORD thy God, and to walk
26. 17 to be thy God, and to walk in his ways
29. 19 though I walk in the imagination of mine
30. 16 to walk in his ways, and to keep his com.
Josh.22. 5 to walk in all his ways, and to keep his c.
Judg. 2. 22 they will keep the way of the LORD to wa.
5. 6 the travellers walked through byways
11. 16 Israel..walked through the wilderness
1 Ki. 2. 3 to walk in his ways, to keep his statutes
2. 4 to walk before me in truth with all their
3. 3 walking in the statutes of David his father
3. 14 if thou wilt walk in my ways, to keep my
6. 12 if thou wilt walk in my statutes..to walk
8. 25 take heed to their way, that they walk be.
8. 36 the good way wherein they should walk
8. 58 may incline our hearts unto him, to walk
8. 61 to walk in his statutes, and to keep his c.
9. 4 if thou wilt walk before me, as David thy
15. 3 he walked in all the sins of his father, wh.
15. 26, 34 walked in the way of..and in his sin
16. 2 thou hast walked in the way of Jeroboam
16. 19 sins..in walking in the way of Jeroboam
16. 26 he walked in all the way of Jeroboam
16. 31 to walk in the sins of Jeroboam the son
22. 43 he walked in all the ways of Asa his fath.
22. 52 walked in the way of his father, and in
2 Ki. 4. 35 he returned, and walked in the house to
8. 18 he walked in the way of the kings of Isr.
8. 27 he walked in the way of the house of Ah.
10. 31 Jehu took no heed to walk in the law of
16. 3 he walked in the way of the kings of Israel
17. 8 walked in the statutes of the heathen, wh.
17. 19 walked in the statutes of Israel which th.
17. 22 the children of Israel walked in all the
21. 21 he walked in all the way that his father
22. 2 walked in all the way of David his father
23. 3 to walk after the LORD, and to keep his
2 Ch. 6. 16 take heed to their way, to walk in my law
6. 27 the good way wherein they should walk
6. 31 to walk in thy ways, so long as they live
7. 17 if thou wilt walk before me, as David thy
20. 32 he walked in the way of Asa his father
21. 6 he walked in the way of the kings of Isr.
21. 13 hast walked in the way of the kings of Is.
28. 2 he walked in the ways of the kings of Is.
34. 2 walked in the ways of David his father
34. 31 to walk after the LORD, and to keep his
Neh. 5. 9 ought ye not to walk in the fear of our
10. 29 to walk in God's law, which was given by
Job 29. 3 When..by his light I walked (through)
34. 8 Which goeth..and walketh with wicked
Psa. 23. 4 though I walk through the valley of the
26. 11 But as for me, I will walk in mine integ.
78. 10 They kept not..and refused to walk in
81. 12 I gave them up..they walked in their own
89. 30 If his children..walk not in my judgment
138. 7 Though I walk in the midst of trouble
143. 8 cause me to know..wherein I should walk
Prov. 1. 15 My son, walk not thou in the way with
2. 13 Who leave..to walk in the ways of dark.
2. 20 That thou mayest walk in the way
3. 23 Then shalt thou walk in thy way safely
10. 9 walketh surely; but he that perverteth
15. 21 a man of understanding walketh uprigh.
Isa. 2. 3 he will teach us..and we will walk in his
2. 5 come..let us walk in the light of the Lo.
3. 16 walk with stretched forth necks, and wa.
8. 11 that I should not walk in the way of this
30. 21 This (is) the way, walk ye in it, when ye
40. 31 they that wait..shall walk, and not faint
43. 2 when thou walkest through the fire, thou
50. 11 walk in the light of your fire, and in the
Jer. 2. 5 that they..have walked after vanity, and
3. 17 neither shall they walk any more after the
3. 18 In those days the house of Judah shall w.
6. 16 walk therein..But they said, We will not

Jer. 6. 25 Go not forth into the field, nor walk by
7. 6 neither walk after other gods to your hurt
7. 24 walked in the counsels..in the imaginat.
9. 14 have walked after the imagination of
11. 8 walked every one in the imagination of
13. 10 and walk after other gods, to serve them
16. 11 have walked after other gods, and have
18. 12 we will walk after our own devices, and
18. 15 they have caused them to stumble..to wa.
26. 4 If ye will not hearken to me, to walk
42. 3 show us the way wherein we may walk, and
Eze. 11. 20 That they may walk in my statutes, and
20. 18 Walk ye not in the statutes of your fathers
20. 19 walk in my statutes, and keep my judgm.
36. 27 I will..cause you to walk in my statutes
37. 24 they shall also walk in my judgments
Dan. 9. 10 to walk in his law which he set before us
Hos. 11. 10 They shall walk after the LORD: he shall
14. 9 the just shall walk in them: but the tran.
Joel 2. 8 they shall walk every one in his path, and
Amos 3. 3 Can two walk together, except they be a.
Mic. 4. 2 we will walk in his paths: for the law sh.
4. 5 all people will walk..and we will walk in
6. 8 require of thee..but..to walk humbly with
6. 16 ye walk in their counsels; that I should
Zech. 3. 7 If thou wilt walk in my ways, and if thou

7. *To be or go round about*, סָבַב *sabab.*
Psa. 48. 12 Walk about Zion, and go round about her

8. *To walk about among*, ἐμπεριπατέω *emperipateō.*
2 Co. 6. 16 hath said, I will dwell in them, and walk

9. *To come or go through*, διέρχομαι *dierchomai.*
Matt 12. 43 he walketh through dry places, seeking re.
Luke 11. 24 he walketh through dry places, seeking re.

10. *To step rightly*, ὀρθοποδέω *orthopodeō.*
Gal. 2. 14 when I saw that they walked not uprightly

11. *To walk around*, περιπατέω *peripateō.*
Matt. 4. 18 Jesus, walking by the sea of Galilee, saw
9. 5 whether is easier..to say, Arise, and walk?
11. 5 the lame walk, the lepers are cleansed, and
14. 25 Jesus went unto them, walking on the sea
14. 26 when the disciples saw him walking on the
14. 29 Peter..walked on the water, to go to Jesus
15. 31 wondered, when they saw..the lame to w.
Mark 1. 16 Now as [he walked] by the sea of Galilee
2. 9 Arise, and take up thy bed, and walk?
5. 42 straightway the damsel arose, and walked
6. 48 cometh unto them, walking upon the sea
6. 49 when they saw him walking upon the sea
7. 5 Why walk not thy disciples according to
8. 24 looked..and said, I see men as trees, walk.
11. 27 as he was walking in the temple, there co.
16. 12 [as they walked, and went into the coun.]
Luke 5. 23 Whether is easier, to say..Rise up and w.?
7. 22 tell..how that the blind see, the lame wa.
11. 44 the men that walk over.. are not aware
20. 46 scribes, which desire to walk in long robes
24. 17 these that ye have ..as ye walk, and are s.?
John 1. 36 looking upon Jesus as he walked, he saith
5. 8 Jesus saith..Rise, take up thy bed, and w.
5. 9 immediately..took up his bed, and walked
5. 11 the same said..Take up thy bed, and walk
5. 12 What man ..said..Take up thy bed, and w.?
6. 19 they see Jesus walking on the sea, and dr.
6. 66 went back, and walked no more with him
7. 1 walked in Galilee: for he would not walk
8. 12 he that followeth me shall not walk in da.
10. 23 Jesus walked in the temple, in Solomon's
11. 9 If any man walk in the day, he stumbleth
11. 10 if any man walk in the night, he stumbleth
11. 54 Jesus therefore walked no more openly
12. 35 Walk while ye have the light, lest darkn.
12. 35 he that walketh in darkness knoweth not
21. 18 When thou wast young ..thou walkedst
Acts 3. 6 In the name of Jesus Christ ..rise up..walk
3. 8 he leaping up stood, and walked, walking
3. 9 all the people saw him walking and prais.
3. 12 as though ..we had made this man to wa.?
14. 8 sat a certain man..who never had walked
14. 10 Stand upright ..And he leaped and walked
21. 21 ought not to circumcise ..neither to walk
Rom. 6. 4 so we also should walk in newness of life
8. [1], 4 who walk not after the flesh, but after
13. 13 Let us walk honestly, as in the day, not
14. 15 grieved..now walkest thou not charitably
1 Co. 3. 3 For.. are ye not carnal, and walk as men?
7. 17 as the Lord hath called ..so let him walk
2 Co. 4. 2 not walking in craftiness, nor handling
5. 7 For we walk by faith, not by sight
10. 2 think..as if we walked according to the fl.
10. 3 though we walk in the flesh, we do not
12. 18 (walked we) not in the same spirit?..not in
Gal. 5. 16 Walk in the spirit, and ye shall not fulfil
Eph. 2. 2 Wherein in time past ye walked according
2. 10 ordained that we should walk in them
4. 1 I..beseech you that ye walk worthy of the
4. 17 henceforth walk not as other Gentiles walk
5. 2 walk in love, as Christ also hath loved us
5. 8 but now..light in the Lord..walk as ch.
5. 15 See then that ye walk circumspectly, not
Phil. 3. 17 mark them which walk so as ye have us
3. 18 For many walk, of whom I have told you
Col. 1. 10 That ye might walk worthy of the Lord
2. 6 As ye have..received Christ..walk ye in
3. 7 In the which ye also walked sometime
4. 5 Walk in wisdom toward them that are wi.
1 Th. 2. 12 That ye would walk worthy of God, who
4. 1 how ye ought to walk and to please God
4. 12 That ye may walk honestly toward them
2 Th. 3. 6 withdraw..from every brother that walk.
2 Th. 3. 11 there are some which walk among you di.
1 Pe. 5. 8 as a roaring lion, walketh about, seeking
1 Jo. 1. 6 If we say..and walk in darkness, we lie
1. 7 if we walk in the light, as he is in the lig.
2. 6 ought..also so to walk, even as he walked
2. 11 walketh in darkness, and knoweth not wh.
2 John 4 that I found of thy children walking in
6 this is love, that we walk after his comm.
6 That, as ye have heard..ye should walk
3 John 3 truth..even as thou walkest in the truth
4 than to hear that my children walk in tr.
Rev. 2. 1 who walketh in the midst of the seven
3. 4 they shall walk with me in white: for th.
9. 20 which neither can see, nor hear, nor walk
16. 15 lest he walk naked, and they see his sha.
21. 24 nations..saved shall walk in the light of

12. *To pass over or through*, πορεύομαι *poreuomai.*
Luke 1. 6 walking in all the commandments and or.
13. 33 I must walk to day, and to morrow, and the
Acts 9. 31 walking in the fear of the Lord, and in the
14. 16 suffered all nations to walk in their own
1 Pe. 4. 3 when we walked in lasciviousness, lusts
2 Pe. 2. 10 chiefly them that walk after the flesh in
3. 3 there shall come..scoffers, walking after
Jude 16 complainers, walking after their own lusts
18 who should walk after their own ungodly

13. *To walk, proceed or step in order*, στοιχέω *stoicheō.*
Acts 21. 24 thou thyself also walkest orderly, and ke.
Rom. 4. 12 who also walk in the steps of that faith
Gal. 5. 25 If we live in the spirit, let us also walk
6. 16 as many as walk according to this rule
Phil. 3. 16 let us walk by the same rule, let us mind

WALK abroad, on, to and fro, up and down, to —
To go on habitually or up and down, הָלַךְ *halak*, 7.
Gen. 3. 8 walking in the garden in the cool of the
5. 22 Enoch walked with God after he begat
5. 24 Enoch walked with God: and he (was) not
6. 9 Noah was a just man..Noah walked with
13. 17 walk through the land, in the length of
17. 1 said..walk before me, and be thou perf.
24. 40 LORD, before whom I walk, will send his
48. 15 God, before whom my fathers..did walk
Exod 21. 19 If he rise again, and walk abroad upon
Lev. 26. 12 I will walk among you, and will be your
Deut 23. 14 the LORD thy God walketh in the midst
Josh. 18. 8 Go and walk through the land, and descr.
1 Sa. 2. 30 thy house..should walk before me for ever
2. 35 he shall walk before mine anointed for e.
12. 2 the king walketh before you..I have wa.
2 Sa. 7. 6 have walked in a tent and in a tabernacle
7. 7 In all (the places) wherein I have walked
11. 2 walked upon the roof of the king's house
2 Ki. 20. 3 remember now how I have walked before
1 Ch. 17. 6 Wheresoever I have walked with all Israel
Esth. 2. 11 Mordecai walked every day before the co
Job 1. 7 From going..and from walking up and
2. 2 From going..and from walking up and
18. 8 he is cast..and he walketh upon a snare
22. 14 and he walketh in the circuit of heaven
38. 16 hast thou walked in the search of the de.
Psa. 12. 8 The wicked walk on every side, when the
26. 3 (is) before mine eyes; and I have walked
39. 6 Surely every man walketh in a vain show
56. 13 that I may walk before God in the light
82. 5 neither will they understand; they walk
101. 2 I will walk within my house with a perf.
116. 9 I will walk before the LORD in the land
119. 45 I will walk at liberty: for I seek thy pre.
Prov 20. 7 The just ..walketh in his integrity: his ch.
Isa. 38. 3 how I have walked before thee in truth
Eze. 28. 14 thou hast walked up and down in the mi.
Zech. 1. 10 sent to walk to and fro through the earth
1. 11 We have walked to and fro through the
6. 7 they might walk to and fro through the
6. 7 Get you hence, walk to and fro through
6. 7 they walked to and fro through the earth
10. 12 they shall walk up and down in his name

WALK, to cause or make to —
1. *To cause to tread*, דָּרַךְ *darak*, 5
Hab. 3. 19 he will make me to walk upon mine high

2. *To cause to go on*, יָלַךְ *yalak*, 5.
Eze. 36. 12 Yea, I will cause men to walk upon you
Jer. 31. 9 I will cause them to walk by the rivers

WALK, places to —
To cause to go on, הָלַךְ *halak*, 5.
Zech. 3. 7 I will give..places to walk among these

WALL (walled up, to be) —
1. *A wall*, אֻשַּׁרְנָא *ushsharna.*
Ezra 5. 3 hath commanded..to make up this wall?
5. 9 commanded you..to make up these walls?

2. *To cut off, fence*, בָּצַר *batsar.*
Num 13. 28 and the cities (are) walled, (and) very gr.
Deut. 1. 28 the cities (are) great and walled up to h.

3. *A wall, hedge*, גָּדֵר *gader.*
Num 22. 24 a wall..on this side, and a wall on that si.
Ezra 9. 9 to give us a wall in Judah and in Jerusa.
Isa. 5. 5 break down the wall thereof, and it shall
Eze. 42. 7 the wall that (was) without over against
Hos. 2. 6 make a wall, that she shall not find her p.
Mic. 7. 11 the day that thy walls are to be built..that

4. *Wall, hedge*, גָּדֵר *geder.*
Prov 24. 31 the stone wall thereof was broken down
Eze. 42. 10 in the thickness of the wall of the court

5. *Wall, hedge*, גְּדֵרָה *gederah.*
Eze. 42. 12 the way directly before the wall toward

6. *Bulwark*, חֵיל, חֵל *chel.*
1 Ki. 21. 23 dogs shall eat Jezebel by the wall of Jez.
Psa. 122. 7 Peace be within thy walls..prosperity w.

7. *Outside, a wall*, חַיִץ *chayits.*
Eze. 13. 10 one built up a wall, and, lo, others daub.

8. *A wall, enclosure*, חוֹמָה *chomah.*
Exod 14. 22, 29 the waters (were) a wall unto them on
Lev. 25. 29 if a man sell a dwelling house in a walled
25. 30 the house that (is) in the walled city shall
25. 31 houses of the villages which have no wall
Deut. 3. 5 these cities (were) fenced with high walls
28. 52 until thy high and fenced walls come do.
Josh. 2. 15 the town wall, and she dwelt upon the w.
6. 5 the wall of the city shall fall down flat, and
6. 20 the wall fell down flat, so that the people
1 Sa. 25. 16 They were a wall unto us, both by night
31. 10 they fastened his body to the wall of Beth.
31. 12 took the body..from the wall of Beth-sh.
2 Sa. 11. 20 knew ye not that they..shoot from the w.?
11. 21 did not a woman cast..from the wall, that
11. 21 why went ye nigh the wall? then say thou
11. 24 the shooters shot from off the wall upon
18. 24 to the roof over the gate unto the wall
20. 15 all..battered the wall, to throw it down
20. 21 head shall be thrown to thee over the wall
1 Ki. 3. 1 and the wall of Jerusalem round about
4. 13 threescore great cities with walls and br.
9. 15 to build..the wall of Jerusalem, and Ha.
20. 30 a wall fell upon twenty and seven thous.
2 Ki. 3. 27 offered him..a burnt offering upon the w.
6. 26 as the king..was passing by upon the wall
6. 30 he passed by upon the wall, and the peo.
14. 13 brake down the wall of Jerusalem from
18. 26 in the ears of the people that..on the wall
18. 27 sent me..to the men which sit on the wall
25. 4 by the way of the gate between two walls
25. 10 brake down the walls of Jerusalem round
Ch. 8. 5 fenced cities, with walls, gates, and bars
14. 7 Let us build these cities, and make..walls
25. 23 brake down the wall of Jerusalem from
26. 6 wall of Gath..wall of Jabneh..wall of As.
27. 3 and on the wall of Ophel ..he built much
32. 5 built up all the wall that was broken, and
32. 5 and another wall without, and repaired
32. 18 people of Jerusalem that (were) on the wall
33. 14 after this he built a wall without the city
36. 19 brake down the wall of Jerusalem, and
Neh. 1. 3 the wall of Jerusalem also (is) broken do.
2. 8 for the wall of the city, and for the house
2. 13 went out..and viewed the walls of Jerus.
2. 15 Then went I up..and viewed the wall, and
2. 17 let us build up the wall of Jerusalem, that
3. 8 they fortified Jerusalem unto the broad w.
3. 13 a thousand cubits on the wall unto the
3. 15 the wall of the pool of Siloah by the king's
3. 27 another piece..even unto the wall of Op.
4. 1 when Sanballat heard..we builded the w.
4. 3 a fox..shall..break down their stone wall
4. 6 So built we the wall; and all the wall was
4. 7 heard that the walls of Jerusalem were
4. 10 so that we are not able to build the wall
4. 13 set I in the lower places behind the wall
4. 15 returned all of us to the wall, every one
4. 17 They which builded on the wall, and they
4. 19 separated upon the wall, one far from an.
5. 16 also I continued in the work of this wall
6. 1 Sanballat..heard that I had builded the w.
6. 6 for which cause thou buildest the wall, th.
6. 15 So the wall was finished in the twenty and
7. 1 when the wall was built, and I had set up
12. 27 at the dedication of the wall of Jerusalem
12. 30 purified the people..the gates, and the wall
12. 31 the princes of Judah upon the wall
12. 31 went on the right hand upon the wall to.
12. 37 at the going up of the wall, above the ho.
12. 38 half of the people upon the wall, from be.
12. 38 tower of the furnaces even to the broad w.
13. 21 Why lodge ye about the wall? if ye do(so)
Psa. 51. 18 Do good ..build thou the walls of Jerusa.
55. 10 Day and night they go ..upon the walls
Prov 18. 11 his strong city, and as an high wall in his
25. 28 a city (that is)..(and) without walls
Song 5. 7 keepers of the walls took away my veil fr.
8. 9 If she (be) a wall, we will build upon her
8. 10 I (am) a wall, and my breasts like towers
Isa. 2. 15 every high tower..upon every fenced w
22. 10 houses..broken down to fortify the wall
22. 11 Ye made also a ditch between the two w.
25. 12 fortress of the high fort of thy walls shall
26. 1 salvation will (God) appoint (for) walls
30. 13 swelling out in a high wall, whose break.
36. 11 the ears of the people that (are) on the w.
36. 12 to the men that sit upon the wall
49. 16 I have graven thee..thy walls (are) cont.
56. 5 within my walls a place and a name better
60. 10 the sons of strangers shall build up thy w.
60. 18 shalt call thy walls Salvation, and thy ga.
62. 6 I have set watchmen upon thy walls, O J.
Jer. 1. 15 against all the walls thereof round about
1. 18 brasen walls against the whole land, aga.
15. 20 make thee unto this people a fenced..wall
21. 4 which besiege you without the walls, and
39. 4 by the gate betwixt the two walls: and he
39. 8 the Chaldeans..brake down the walls of
49. 27 I will kindle a fire in the wall of Damas.
50. 15 foundations are fallen, her walls are thr.
51. 12 Set up the standard upon the walls of B.
51. 44 will punish Bel..the wall of Babylon sh.
51. 58 The broad walls of Babylon shall be utt.
52. 7 by the way of the gate between the two w.

Jer. 52. 14 brake down all the walls of Jerusalem ro.
Lam. 2. 7 he hath given up..the walls of her palaces
2. 8 LORD hath purposed to destroy the wall
2. 8 therefore he made the rampart and the w.
2. 18 O wall of the daughter of Zion, let tears
Eze. 26. 4 they shall destroy the walls of Tyrus, and
26. 9 he shall set engines of war against thy wa.
26. 10 thy walls shall shake at the noise of the
26. 12 break down thy walls, and destroy thy
27. 11, 11 upon thy walls round about
38. 11 all of them dwelling without walls, and
38. 20 shall fall, and every wall shall fall to the
40. 5 behold a wall on the outside of the house
42. 20 it had a wall round about, five hundred
Joel 2. 7 they shall climb the wall like men of war
2. 9 they shall run upon the wall, they shall
Amos 1. 7, 10 will send a fire on the wall..which sh.
1. 14 But I will kindle a fire in the wall of Ra.
7. 7 Lord stood upon a wall (made) by a plumb
Nah. 2. 5 they shall make haste to the wall thereof
3. 8 whose rampart (was) the sea, (and) her w.
Zech. 2. 5 For I..will be unto her a wall of fire round

9. *A rampart*, חָרוּץ *charuts.*
Dan. 9. 25 street shall be built again, and the wall

10. *A wall*, כֹּתֶל *kothel.*
Song 2. 9 he standeth behind our wall, he looketh

11. *A wall*, כְּתַל *kethal.*
Ezra 5. 8 timber is laid in the walls, and this work
Dan. 5. 5 upon the plaster of the wall of the king's

12. *A wall, beam (of roof and floor)*, קִיר *qir.*
Lev. 14. 37 (if) the plague (be) in the walls of the ho.
14. 37 which in sight (are) lower than the wall
14. 39 behold, (if) the plague be spread in the w.
Num 22. 25 the ass..thrust herself unto the wall, and
22. 25 crushed Balaam's foot against the wall
35. 4 from the wall of the city and outward a
1 Sa. 18. 11 he said, I will smite David even to the wall
19. 10 Saul sought to smite David even to the w.
19. 10 smote the javelin into the wall: and Da.
20. 25 king sat..upon a seat by the wall: and
25. 22 if I leave..any that pisseth against the w.
25. 34 been left..any that pisseth against the w.
1 Ki. 4. 33 the hyssop that springeth out of the wall
6. 5 against the wall..the walls of the house
6. 6 should not be fastened in the walls of the
6. 15 built the walls of the house within with
6. 15 both the floor of the house and the walls
6. 16 both the floor and the walls with boards
6. 27 that the wing of the one touched the..w.
6. 27 wing of the other cherub touched the..w.
6. 29 he carved all the walls of the house round
14. 10 cut off..him that pisseth against the wall
16. 11 left him not one that pisseth against a wall
21. 21 cut off..him that pisseth against the wa.
2 Ki. 4. 10 a little chamber, I pray thee, on the wa.
9. 8 cut off..him that pisseth against the wa.
9. 33 of her blood was sprinkled on the wall
20. 2 Then he turned his face to the wall, and
1 Ch. 29. 4 refined silver, to overlay the walls of the
2 Ch. 3. 7 He overlaid..the walls thereof, and the
3. 7 gold; and graved cherubim on the walls
3. 11, 12 five cubits, reaching to the wall of the
Psa. 62. 3 as a bowing wall (shall ye be, and as) a
Isa. 22. 5 breaking down the walls, and of crying to
25. 4 terrible ones (is) as a storm (against) the w.
38. 2 Hezekiah turned his face toward the wall
59. 10 We grope for the wall like the blind, and
Eze. 4. 3 set it (for) a wall of iron between thee and
8. 7 when I looked, behold, a hole in the wall
8. 8 Son of man, dig now in the wall: and
8. 8 when I had digged in the wall, behold, a
8. 10 idols..pourtrayed upon the wall round
12. 5 Dig thou through the wall in their sight
12. 7 in the even I digged through the wall wi.
12. 12 shall dig through the wall to carry out
13. 12 when the wall is fallen, shall it not be sa.
13. 14 So will I break down the wall that ye ha.
13. 15 will I accomplish my wrath upon the wa.
13. 15 wall (is) no (more), neither they that
23. 14 she saw men pourtrayed upon the wall
33. 30 still are talking against thee by the walls
41. 5 After he measured the wall of the house
41. 6 entered into the wall which (was) of the
41. 6 but they had not hold in the wall of the
41. 9 thickness of the wall, which (was) for the
41. 12 wall of the building (was) five cubits
41. 13 with the walls thereof, an hundred cubits
41. 17 by all the wall round about, within and
41. 20 palm trees made, and (on) the wall of the
41. 22 the length thereof, and the walls thereof
41. 25 trees, like as (were) made upon the walls
43. 8 post by my posts, and on the wall betwe.
Amos 5. 19 leaned his hand on the wall, and a serp.
Hab. 2. 11 For the stone shall cry out of the wall

13. *A wall*, שׁוּר *shur.*
Gen. 49. 22 bough..(whose) branches run over the wall
2 Sa. 22. 30 troops..by..God have I leaped over a wa.
Ezra 4. 12 have set up the walls (thereof), and join.
4. 13 if this city be builded, and the walls set
4. 16 city be builded (again), and the walls th.
Job 24. 11 make oil within their walls, (and) tread
Psa. 18. 29 and by my God have I leaped over a wall

14. *A prince, ox*, שׁוֹר *shor.*
Gen. 49. 6 in their self will they digged down a wall

15. *Walls*, שָׁרוֹת *sharoth.*
Jer. 5. 10 Go ye up upon her walls, and destroy, but

16. *An outer wall*, τεῖχος *teichos.*
Acts 9. 25 disciples..let him down by the wall in a
2 Co. 11. 33 a window..was I let down by the wall
Heb. 11. 30 By faith the walls of Jericho fell down
Rev. 21. 12 had a wall great and high, (and) had tw.
21. 14 wall of the city had twelve foundations
21. 15 and the gates thereof, and the wall ther.
21. 17 measured the wall thereof, an hundred
21. 18 building of the wall of it was of jasper
21. 19 foundations of the wall of the city (were)

17. *An inner wall*, τοῖχος *toichos.*
Acts 23. 3 God shall smite thee, (thou) whited wall

WALLOW (self), to —

1. *To roll self*, גָּלַל *galal, 7a.*
2 Sa. 20. 12 Amasa wallowed in blood in the midst of

2. *To reel, totter to and fro*, סָפַק *saphaq.*
Jer. 48. 26 Moab shall wallow in his vomit, and he

3. *To roll self, press self on*, פָּלַשׁ *palash, 7.*
Jer. 6. 26 wallow thyself in ashes; make thee mou.
25. 34 wallow yourselves (in the ashes), ye prin.
Eze. 27. 30 they shall wallow themselves in the ash.

4. *To roll, wallow*, κυλίομαι *kuliomai.*
Mark 9. 20 and he fell on the ground, and wallowed

5. *A rolling, wallowing*, κύλισμα *kulisma.*
2 Pe. 2. 22 sow that was washed to her wallowing in

WANDER (about, abroad, up and down), to —

1. *To go on*, הָלַךְ *halak.*
Josh. 14. 10 while (the children of) Israel wandered
Eccl. 6. 9 Better (is) the..than the wandering of the

2. *To flee away, move, wander*, נָדַד *nadad.*
Job 15. 23 He wandered abroad for bread, (saying)
Prov 27. 8 As a bird that wandereth from her nest
27. 8 (is) a man that wandereth from his place
Isa. 16. 3 hide the outcasts; bewray not him that wa.
Jer. 49. 5 and none shall gather up him that wand.

3. *To move, shake, stagger, wander*, נוּעַ *nua.*
Jer. 14. 10 Thus have they loved to wander, they have
Lam. 4. 14 They have wandered (as) blind (men) in
4. 15 when they fled away and wandered, they
Amos 4. 8 So two (or) three cities wandered unto one
8. 12 they shall wander from sea to sea, and fr.

4. *To cause to move, shake, wander*, נוּעַ *nua, 5.*
Psa. 59. 15 Let them wander up and down for meat

5. *To wander, cast down, depress*, צָעָה *tsaah.*
Jer. 2. 20 under every green tree thou wanderest

6. *To feed*, רָעָה *raah.*
Num 14. 33 your children shall wander in the wilder.

7. *To err, go astray*, שָׁגָה *shagah.*
Eze. 34. 6 My sheep wandered through all the mou.

8. *To err, wander, go astray*, תָּעָה *taah.*
Gen. 21. 14 and wandered in the wilderness of Beer.
37. 15 behold, (he was) wandering in the field
Job 38. 41 young ones cry unto God, they wander for
Psa. 107. 4 They wandered in the wilderness in a sol.
Prov 21. 16 The man that wandereth out of the way
Isa. 16. 8 wandered (through) the wilderness, her
47. 15 they shall wander every one to his quart.

9. *To go or come around*, περιέρχομαι *perierchomai.*
1 Ti. 5. 13 learn (to be) idle, wandering about from
Heb. 11. 37 they wandered about in sheep skins and

10. *To lead astray*, πλανάω *planaō.*
Heb. 11. 38 they wandered in deserts, and (in) moun.

WANDER, to cause, let or make to —

1. *To cause to wander*, נוּעַ *nua, 5.*
Num 32. 13 made them wander in the wilderness forty

2. *To make to bend, or wander*, צָעָה *tsaah, 3.*
Jer. 48. 12 that shall cause him to wander

3. *To cause to err, or go astray*, שָׁגָה *shagah, 5.*
Deut 27. 18 (be) he that maketh the blind to wander
Psa. 119. 10 let me not wander from thy commandm.

4. *To cause to err, wander, go astray*, תָּעָה *taah, 5.*
Gen. 20. 13 when God caused me to wander from my
Job 12. 24 causeth them to wander in a wilderness
Psa. 107. 40 causeth them to wander in the wilderness

WANDERER, wandering —

1. *To flee away, move, wander*, נָדַד *nadad.*
Isa. 16. 2 as a wandering bird cast out of the nest
Hos. 9. 17 they shall be wanderers among the nations

2. *To move, flee, wander, bemoan*, נוּד *nud.*
Prov 26. 2 As the bird by wandering, as the swallow

3. *A moving or wandering about*, נוֹד *nod.*
Psa. 56. 8 Thou tellest my wanderings: put thou my

4. *To bend, wander*, צָעָה *tsaah.*
Jer. 48. 12 I will send unto him wanderers, that shall

5. *Wandering*, πλανήτης *planētēs.*
Jude 13 wandering stars, to whom is reserved the

WANT, (for, in want of, to) —

1. *End, cessation*, אֶפֶס *ephes.*
Prov. 14. 28 but in the want of people (is) the destru.

2. *Without, in not (having)*, בְּלֹא *be-lo.*
Prov 13. 23 there is..destroyed for want of judgment

3. *To cease*, חָדַל *chadal.*
Prov 10. 19 In the multitude of words there wanteth

4. *Lacking*, חָסֵר *chaser.*
Prov. 9. 4, 16 him that wanteth understanding, she
Prov 10. 21 feed many: but fools die for want of wis.
28. 16 prince that wanteth understanding (is)
Eccl. 6. 2 so that he wanteth nothing for his soul of

5. *To lack, be lacking*, חָסֵר *chaser.*
Deut 15. 8 sufficient for his need, (in that)..he want.
Psa. 23. 1 The LORD (is) my shepherd, I shall not w.
34. 10 they that seek the LORD shall not want
Prov 13. 25 but the belly of the wicked shall want
Song 7. 2 navel (is like) a round goblet, (which) w.
Jer. 44. 18 we have wanted all (things), and have be.
Eze. 4. 17 That they may want bread and water, and

6. *Lack*, חֶסֶר *cheser.*
Job 30. 3 For want and famine (they were) solitary

7. *Lack*, חֹסֶר *choser.*
Deut 28. 48 in thirst, and in nakedness, and in want
28. 57 for she shall eat them for want of all (th.)
Amos 4. 6 have given you..want of bread in all yo.

8. *Lack*, מַחְסוֹר *machsor.*
Judg 18. 10 place where (there is) no want of any th.
19. 19 there is bread and..no want of any thing
19. 20 howsoever (let) all thy wants (lie) upon
Psa. 34. 9 fear the LORD..for (there is) no want to
Prov. 6. 11 come as one that travelleth, and thy wa.
21. 5 but of every one (that is) hasty, only to wa.
22. 16 giveth to the rich, (shall) surely (come) to w.
24. 34 come (as) one that travelleth, and thy wa.

9. *To be cut off*, כָּרַת *karath, 2.*
Jer. 33. 17 David shall never want a man to sit upon
33. 18 Neither shall the priests the Levites want
35. 19 shall not want a man to stand before me

10. *To look into, after or over, miss*, פָּקַד *paqad.*
Isa. 34. 16 none shall want her mate: for my mouth

11. *What is behind, want, deficiency*, ὑστέρημα.
2 Co. 8. 14 abundance (may be a supply) for their wa.
8. 14 abundance also may be (a supply) for..wa.
9. 12 not only supplieth the want of the saints

12. *A being behind, want, deficiency*, ὑστέρησις.
Mark 12. 44 but she of her want did cast in all that
Phil. 4. 11 Not that I speak in respect of want: for

13. *Necessary business, necessity, need, use*, χρεία.
Phil. 2. 25 messenger, and..that ministered to my w.

14. *To be behind, inferior, in want*, ὑστερέω *huster.*
John 2. 3 when they wanted wine, the mother of J
2 Co. 11. 9 when I was present with you, and wanted

WANT, to be in; (to be) wanting —

1. *Lacking*, חַסִּיר *chassir.*
Dan. 5. 27 Thou art weighed..and art found want

2. *Lack, want*, חֶסְרוֹן *chesron.*
Eccl. 1. 15 that which is wanting cannot be numbe.

3. *To be looked after, inspected, missed*, פָּקַד *paqad, 2.*
2 Ki. 10. 19 none be wanting..whosoever shall be w.

4. *To be behind, inferior*, ὑστερέω *hustereō.*
Luke 15. 14 a mighty famine..and he began to be in w.

5. *To leave, fail, be wanting*, λείπω *leipō.*
Titus 1. 5 set in order the things that are wanting
3. 13 diligently, that nothing be wanting unto
Jas. 1. 4 may be perfect and entire, wanting noth.

WANTON (against, to begin to wax), wantonness —

1. *To glance round, ogle, look much*, שָׂקַר *saqar, 3.*
Isa. 3. 16 walk with stretched forth necks, and wa.

2. *Lasciviousness, lewdness*, ἀσέλγεια *aselgeia.*
Rom 13. 13 not in chambering and wantonness, not
2 Pe. 2. 18 they allure through..wantonness, those

3. *To grow very wanton*, καταστρηνιάζω *katastrēnia.*
1 Ti. 5. 11 they have begun to wax wanton against

WAR, (against, men of to make, to) —

1. *Force, army*, חַיִל *chayil.*
Deut. 3. 18 pass over..all (that are) meet for the war
2 Ch. 33. 14 put captains of war in all the fenced cit.

2. *To fight, devour one another*, לָחַם *lacham, 2.*
Deut 20. 19 in making war against it to take it, thou
Josh. 10. 5 encamped before Gibeon, and made war
24. 9 warred against Israel, and sent and call.
Judg 11. 4 children of Ammon made war against Is.
11. 5 when the children of Ammon made war a.
11. 27 but thou doest me wrong to war against
1 Sa. 28. 15 for the Philistines make war against me
1 Ki. 14. 19 how he warred, and how he reigned, be.
20. 1 and he went up..and warred against it
22. 45 his might that he showed, and how he wa.
2 Ki. 6. 8 Then the king of Syria warred against Is.
14. 28 how he warred, and how he recovered D.
19. 8 found the king of Assyria warring against
2 Ch. 17. 10 so that they made no war against Jehosh.
26. 6 went forth and warred against the Phili.
Isa. 37. 8 found the king of Assyria warring against
37. 9 He is come forth to make war with thee
Jer. 21. 2 king of Babylon maketh war against us

3. *Fighting*, לָחֶם *lachem.*
Judg. 5. 8 They chose new gods; then (was) war in

4. *A fighting, war, battle*, מִלְחָמָה *milchamah.*
Gen. 14. 2 made war with Bera king of Sodom, and
Exod. 1. 10 when there falleth out any war, they join
13. 17 people repent when they see war, and th..
15. 3 The LORD (is) a man of war: the LORD (is)
17. 16 war with Amalek from generation to gen.
32. 17 said..(There is) a noise of war in the ca.
Num 10. 9 if ye go to war in your land against the
21. 14 Wherefore it is said in the book of the w.
31. 27 between them that took the war upon th.

Num 31. 28 tribute..of the men of war which went
31. 49 taken the sum of the men of war which
32. 6 Shall your brethren go to war, and shall
32. 20 if ye will go armed before the LORD to war
Deut. 1. 41 girded on every man his weapons of war
2. 14 generation of the men of war were wasted
2. 16 when all the men of war were consumed
4. 34 and by war, and by a mighty hand, and
20. 12 but will make war against thee, then thou
20. 20 against the city that maketh war with
21. 10 When thou goest forth to war against th.
Josh. 5. 4 all the men of war, died in the wilderness
5. 6 till all the people (that were) men of war
6. 3 shall compass the city, all (ye) men of war
8. 1 take all the people of war with thee, and
8. 3 So Joshua arose, and all the people of war
8. 11 all the people..of war that (were) with
10. 7 all the people of war with him, and all the
10. 24 said unto the captains of the men of war
11. 7 So Joshua came, and all the people of war
11. 18 Joshua made war a long time with all th.
11. 23 by their tribes..the land rested from war
14. 11 even so (is) my strength now, for war, bo.
14. 15 Anakims. And the land had rest from war
17. 1 because he was a man of war, therefore
Judg. 3. 1 as many..as had not known all the wars
3. 2 might know to teach them war, at the le.
3. 10 he judged Israel, and went out to war: and
18. 11 hun. men appointed with weapons of war
18. 16 men appointed with their weapons of war
18. 17 men .. appointed with weapons of war
20. 17 drew sword: all these (were) men of war
21. 22 reserved not to each man his wife in the w.
1 Sa. 8. 12 to make his instruments of war, and inst.
14. 52 there was sore war against the Philistines
16. 18 mighty valiant man, and a man of war, and
17. 33 a youth, and he a man of war from his yo.
18. 5 Saul set him over the men of war; and he
19. 8 there was war again: and David went out
23. 8 Saul called all the people together to war
2 Sa. 1. 27 How are..the weapons of war perished!
3. 1 Now there was long war between the ho.
3. 6 while there was war between the house of
8. 10 for Hadadezer had wars with Toi. And (J.)
11. 7 how the people did, and how the war pr.
11. 18 David all the things concerning the war
11. 19 an end of telling the matters of the war
17. 8 thy father (is) a man of war, and will not
21. 15 Moreover the Philistines had yet war ag.
22. 35 He teacheth my hands to war; so that a
1 Ki. 2. 5 whom he slew, and shed the blood of war
2. 5 put the blood of war upon his girdle that
5. 3 for the wars which were about him on ev.
9. 22 but they (were) men of war, and his serva.
14. 30 there was war between Rehoboam and Je.
15. 6 there was war between Rehoboam and Je.
15. 7 there was war between Abijam and Jero.
15. 16, 32 there was war between Asa and Baas.
20. 18 whether they be come out for war, take
22. 1 they continued three years without war
2 Ki. 8. 28 with Joram the son of Ahab to the war ag.
13. 25 out of the hand of Jehoahaz .. by war
14. 7 took Selah by war, and called the name
16. 5 Then Rezin .. came up to Jerusalem to w
18. 20 (I have) counsel and strength for the war
24. 16 all (that were) strong (and) apt for war
25. 4 all the men of war (fled) by night by the
25. 19 that was set over the men of war
1 Ch. 5. 10 in the days of Saul they made war with
5. 18 and to shoot with bow, and skilful in war
5. 19 they made war with the Hagarites, with
5. 22 there fell..many slain, because the war
7. 4 bands of soldiers for war, six and thirty
12. 1 among the mighty men, helpers of the war
12. 33 expert in war, with all instruments of war
12. 35 of the Danites expert in war twenty and
12. 36 such as went forth to battle, expert in war
12. 38 All these men of war, that could keep ra.
18. 10 for Hadarezer had war with Tou; and..all
20. 4 that there arose war at Gezer with the Ph.
20. 5 there was war again with the Philistines
20. 6 yet again there was war at Gath, where
22. 8 hast made great wars: thou shalt not bu.
28. 3 because thou (hast been) a man of war, and
2 Ch. 6. 34 If thy people go out to war against their
8. 9 but they (were) men of war, and chief of
12. 15 wars between Rehoboam and Jeroboam
13. 2 there was war between Abijah and Jero.
13. 3 array with an army of valiant men of war
14. 6 land had rest, and he had no war in those
15. 19 there was no (more) war unto the five and
16. 9 therefore..henceforth thou shalt have wars
17. 13 men of war, mighty men of valour, (were)
18. 3 answered..(we will be) with thee in the w.
22. 5 went with Jehoram..to war against
26. 13 that made war with mighty power, to help
27. 7 rest of the acts of Jotham, and all his wars
32. 6 set captains of war over the people, and
35. 21 against the house wherewith I have war
Job 5. 20 and in war from the power of the sword
38. 23 reserved..against the day of battle and w.?
Psa. 18. 34 He teacheth my hands to war, so that a
27. 3 though war should rise against me, in this
46. 9 He maketh wars to cease unto the end of
120. 7 peace: but when I speak, they (are) for
140. 2 continually are they gathered..(for) war
144. 1 which teacheth my hands to war, (and)
Prov 20. 18 counsel; and with good advice make war
24. 6 by wise counsel thou shalt make thy war
Eccl. 3. 8 time to hate; a time of war, and a time
8. 8 (there is) no discharge in (that) war, nei.
Song 3. 8 They all hold swords. (being) expert in war

Isa. 2. 4 neither shall they learn war any more
3. 2 The mighty man, and the man of war
3. 25 by the sword, and thy mighty in the war
7. 1 went up toward Jerusalem to war against
21. 15 bow, and from the grievousness of war
36. 5 counsel and strength for war: now, on
41. 12 they that war against thee shall be as no.
42. 13 he shall stir up jealousy like a man of war
Jer. 4. 19 the sound of the trumpet, the alarm of w.
6. 4 Prepare ye war against her; arise, and let
6. 23 set in array as men for war, against thee
21. 4 I will turn back the weapons of war that
28. 8 prophesied..of war, and of evil, and of
38. 4 weakeneth the hands of the men of war
39. 4 saw them, and all the men of war, then
41. 3 were found there, (and) the men of war
41. 16 mighty men of war, and the women, and
42. 14 where we shall see no war, nor hear the
48. 14 (are) mighty and strong men for the war?
49. 2 that I will cause an alarm of war to be
49. 26 all the men of war shall be cut off in that
50. 30 all her men of war shall be cut off in that
51. 20 (art) my battle ax (and) weapons of war
51. 32 burned with fire, and the men of war are
52. 7 all the men of war fled, and went forth
52. 25 which had the charge of the men of war
Eze. 17. 17 make for him in the war, by casting up
27. 10 thy men of war: they hanged the shield
27. 27 all thy men of war, that (are) in thee, and
32. 27 down to hell with their weapons of war
39. 20 and with all men of war, saith the Lord
Dan. 9. 26 unto the end of the war desolations are
Joel 2. 7 they shall climb the wall like men of war
3. 9 Prepare war..let all the men of war draw
Mic. 2. 8 pass by securely as men averse from war
3. 5 mouths, they even prepare war against
4. 3 neither shall they learn war any more

5. *To assemble, serve the host,* צָבָא *tsaba.*
Num 31. 7 they warred against the Midianites, as the
31. 42 Moses divided from the men that warred

6. *A host, assembly, warfare, service,* צָבָא *tsaba.*
Num. 1. 3 all that are able to go forth to war in Isr.
1. 20 all that were able to go forth to war
So in verse 22, 24, 26, 28, 30, 32, 34, 36, 38, 40, 42, 45.
26. 2 all that are able to go to war in Israel
31. 3 Arm some of yourselves unto the war, and
31. 4 tribes of Israel, shall ye send to the war
31. 5 of (every) tribe, twelve thousand armed
31. 6 Moses sent them to the war, a thousand
31. 6 son of Eleazar the priest, to the war, with
31. 21 said unto the men of war which went to
31. 32 rest of the prey which the men of war had
31. 36 portion of them that went out to war
31. 53 men of war had taken spoil, every man
32. 27 pass over, every man armed for war, bef.
Deut 24. 5 he shall not go out to war, neither shall
Josh. 4. 13 About forty thousand prepared for war
22. 12 together at Shiloh, to go up to war agai.
1 Ch. 5. 18 four and forty thousand seven..to the w.
7. 11 hundred (soldiers), fit to go out for war
7. 40 them that were apt to the war (and) to ba.
12. 8 men of war (fit) for the battle, that could
12. 23 bands (that were) ready armed to the war
12. 24 (were) six thousand..ready armed to..w.
12. 25 mighty men of valour for the war, seven
12. 37 with all manner of instruments of war for
2 Ch. 17. 18 fourscore thousand ready prepared..war
25. 5 to go forth to war, that could handle spe.
26. 11 that went out to war by bands, according
28. 12 stood up against them that came from..w.
Job 10. 17 upon me; changes and war (are) against

7. *Before, over against, battering ram,* קָבָל *qobel.*
Eze. 26. 9 he shall set engines of war against thy

8. *A drawing near, conflict, war,* קְרָב *qerab.*
Psa. 55. 21 war (was) in his heart: his words were s.
68. 30 scatter thou the people (that) delight in
144. 1 which teacheth my hands to war, (and)
Eccl. 9. 18 Wisdom (is) better than weapons of war
Dan. 7. 21 same horn made war with the saints, and

9. *To war against,* ἀντιστρατεύομαι *antistrateuom.*
Rom. 7. 23 another law in my members, warring ag.

10. *War, battle, strife, contention,* πόλεμος *polemos.*
Matt 24. 6 ye shall hear of wars and rumours of wars
Mark 13. 7 ye shall hear of wars and rumours of wars
Luke 14. 31 what king, going to make war against an.
21. 9 when ye shall hear of wars and commoti.
Jas. 4. 1 From whence..wars and fightings among
Rev. 11. 7 beast..shall make war against them, and
12. 7 there was war in heaven: Michael and
12. 17 went to make war with the remnant of her
13. 7 [it was given unto him to make war with]
19. 19 gathered together to make war against

11. *To wage war, fight,* πολεμέω *polemeō.*
Jas. 4. 2 ye fight and war, yet ye have not, because
Rev. 13. 4 the beast? who is able to make war with
17. 14 These shall make war with the Lamb, and
19. 11 in righteousn. he doth judge and make w.

12. *Warlike force, army,* στράτευμα *strateuma.*
Luke 23. 11 Herod with his men of war set him at no.

13. *To war, wage war,* στρατεύομαι *strateuomai.*
2 Co. 10. 3 though we walk in the flesh, we do not w.
1 Ti. 1. 18 that thou by them mightest war a good
2 Ti. 2. 4 No man that warreth entangleth himself
Jas. 4. 1 of your lusts that war in your members
1 Pe. 2. 11 abstain from fleshly lusts, which war agai.

WARD —

1. *A ward, guard, charge,* מִשְׁמָר *mishmar.*
Gen. 40. 3 he put them in ward in the house of the
40. 4 and they continued a season in ward
40. 7 with him in the ward of his lord's house
41. 10 put me in ward in the captain of the gua.
42. 17 he put them all together into ward three
Lev. 24. 12 they put him in ward, that the mind of
Num 15. 34 they put him in ward, because it was not
1 Ch. 26. 16 causeway of the going up, ward against w.
Neh. 12. 24 to give thanks..ward over against ward
12. 25 keeping the ward at the thresholds of the

2. *A ward, charge, guard,* מִשְׁמֶרֶת *mishmereth.*
1 Ch. 9. 23 the house of the tabernacle, by wards
12. 29 greatest part of them had kept the ward
25. 8 they cast lots, ward against (ward), as w.
26. 12 wards one against another, to minister in
Neh. 12. 45 kept the ward of their God, and the ward
13. 30 appointed the wards of the priests and the
Isa. 21. 8 day time, and I am set in my ward whole

3. *House of ward,* בֵּית מִשְׁמֶרֶת *beth mishmereth.*
2 Sa. 20. 3 put them in ward, and fed them, but went

4. *A prison,* סוּגַר *sugar.*
Eze. 19. 9 they put him in ward in chains, and brou.

5. *Inspection, supervision,* פְּקִדֻת *peqiduth.*
Jer. 37. 13 captain of the ward (was) there, whose

6. *A guarding, guard, ward,* φυλακή *phulakē.*
Acts 12. 10 they were past the first and the second w.

WARDROBE —

Cloaks, garments, coverings, בְּגָדִים *begadim.*
2 Ki. 22. 14 son of Harhas, keeper of the wardrobe, n.
2 Ch. 34. 22 son of Hasrah, keeper of the wardrobe, n.

WARE, to be—

To be conscious of, know together, σύνοιδα *sunoida.*
Acts 14. 6 They were ware of (it), and fled unto Ly.

WARE, wares—

1. *Vessel, utensil, instrument,* כְּלִי *keli.*
Jon. 1. 5 cast forth the wares that (were) in the sh.

2. *Thing for sale, price,* מֶכֶר *meker.*
Neh. 13. 16 which brought fish, and all manner of w.

3. *Sale, thing for sale,* מִמְכָּר *mimkar.*
Neh. 13. 20 sellers of all kind of ware, lodged without

4. *Wares, what are brought,* מַקָּחוֹת *maqqachoth.*
Neh. 10. 31 people of the land bring ware or any vic.

5. *Merchandise,* כִּנְעָה *kinah.*
Jer. 10. 17 Gather up thy wares out of the land, O

6. *Traffic, exchange, remnant,* עִזָּבוֹן *izzabon.*
Eze. 27. 33 When thy wares went forth out of the se.

7. *Work,* מַעֲשֶׂה *maaseh.*
Eze. 27. 16 by reason of the multitude of the wares

WARFARE, (to go a) —

1. *A host,* צָבָא *tsaba.*
1 Sa. 28. 1 gathered their armies t.for warf. Isa. 40. 2.

2. *Warfare, military service,* στρατεία *strateia.*
2 Co. 10. 4 For the weapons of our warfare (are) not
1 Ti. 1. 18 that thou by them mightest war a good w.

3. *To wage war,* στρατεύομαι *strateuomai.*
1 Co. 9. 7 Who goeth a warfare any time at his own

WARM (at, self, to) —

1. *Hot, warm,* חַם *chom.*
Job 37. 17 How thy garments (are) warm, when he

2. *To be or become bold or warm,* חָמַם *chamam.*
Isa. 44. 15 for he will take thereof, and warm him.
44. 16 yea, he warmeth (himself), and saith, Aha
47. 14 (there shall) not (be) a coal to warm at

3. *To warm,* חָמַם *chamam,* 3.
Job 39. 14 leaveth her eggs in the earth, and warm.

4. *To heat, warm,* θερμαίνω *thermainō.*
Mark 14. 54 sat with the servants, and warmed him
14. 67 when she saw Peter warming himself, she
John 18. 18 warmed themselves: and Peter..warm h
18. 25 And Simon Peter stood and warmed him

WARM, to be, wax, be warmed —

1. *Heat, warmth,* חֹם *chom.*
Hag. 1. 6 ye clothe you, but there is none warm, and

2. *To heat, warm,* חָמַם *chamam.*
2 Ki. 4. 34 child, and the flesh of the child wax.
Isa. 44. 16 and saith, Aha, I am warm, I have seen

3. *To heat or warm self,* חָמַם *chamam,* 7.
Job 31. 20 (if) he were (not) warmed with the fleece

4. *To be hot, warm,* יָחַם *yacham.*
Eccl. 4. 11 they have heat; but how can one be warm?

5. *To be heated, warmed,* θερμαίνομαι *thermainomai.*
Jas. 2. 16 Depart in peace, be (ye) warmed and fill.

WARN, be warned, give warning, to —

1. *To be warned, take or receive warning,* זָהַר *zahar,* 2.
Psa. 19. 11 Moreover by them is thy servant warned
Eze. 3. 21 he shall surely live, because he is warned
33. 4 heareth the sound..and taketh not warn.
33. 5 heard the sound..and took not warning
33. 5 he that taketh warning shall deliver his
33. 6 blow not..and the people be not warned

2. *To warn, (cause to) shine,* זָהַר *zahar,* 5.
2 Ki. 6. 10 which the man of God told him and war

2 Ch. 19. 10 ye shall even warn them that they tresp.
Eze. 3. 17 hear the word..and give them warning
3. 18 givest him not warning..speakest to warn
3. 19 Yet if thou warn the wicked, and he turn
3. 20 because thou hast not given him warning
3. 21 if thou warn the righteous (man), that the
33. 3 he blow the trumpet, and warn the people
33. 7 hear the word at my mouth, and warn th.
33. 8 if thou dost not speak to warn the wicked
33. 9 if thou warn the wicked of his way to turn

3. *To cause to testify, protest,* עוּד *ud*, 5.
Jer. 6. 10 To whom shall I speak, and give warning

4. *To put in before the mind, warn,* νουθετέω *noutheteō*.
Acts 20. 31 I ceased not to warn every one night and
1 Co. 4. 14 shame you, but, as my beloved sons, I wa.
Col. 1. 28 warning every man, and teaching every
1 Th. 5. 14 warn them that are unruly, comfort the

5. *To show secretly, partly,* ὑποδείκνυμι *hupodeikn.*
Matt. 3. 7 who hath warned you to flee from the wr.
Luke 3. 7 who hath warned you to flee from the wr.

WARNED of God, to be —

To warn by an oracle, χρηματίζω *chrēmatizō.*
Matt. 2. 12 being warned of God in a dream that they
2. 22 being warned of God in a dream, he turned
Acts 10. 22 Cornelius..was warned from God by an
Heb. 11. 7 By faith Noah, being warned of God of th.

WARP —

Web, woven stuff, warp, שְׁתִי *shethi.*
Lev. 13. 48 Whether (it be) in the warp, or woof, of li.
13. 49, 51, 53, 57 either in the warp, or in the w.
13. 52 whether warp or woof, in woollen or in li.
13. 56 out of the skin, or out of the warp, or out
13. 58 either warp or woof, or whatsoever thing
13. 59 either in the warp, or woof, or any thing

WARRIOR, (to be a) —

1. *To do war or battle,* עָשָׂה מִלְחָמָה *asah milchamah.*
1 Ki. 12. 21 chosen men, which were warriors, to fight
2 Ch. 11. 1 chosen (men), which were warriors, to fl.

2. *To equip, shoe or prepare self,* סָאַן *saan.*
Isa. 9. 5 For every battle of the warrior (is) with

WASH (away, self, throughly, be washed), to —

1. *To cast out, purge, force away,* דּוּחַ *duach,* 5.
2 Ch. 4. 6 such things as they offered..they washed
Eze. 40. 38 gates, where they washed the burnt offer.

2. *To wash,* כָּבַס *kabas,* 3.
Gen. 49. 11 washed his garments in wine, and his cl.
Exod 19. 10 said unto Moses..let them wash their cl.
19. 14 sanctified the people; and they washed th.
Lev. 6. 27 thou shalt wash that whereon it was spri.
11. 25, 28, 40, 40 wash his clothes, and be unclean
13. 6, 34 and he shall wash his clothes, and be cl.
13. 54 Then the priest shall command that they
13. 58 the garment..which thou shalt wash, if
14. 8 he that is to be cleansed shall wash his cl.
14. 9 and he shall wash his clothes, also he sh.
14. 47 shall wash his clothes..shall wash his cl.
15. 5, 6, 7, 8, 10, 11, 13, 21, 22, 27 wash his clothes
16. 26, 28 wash his clothes, and bathe his flesh in
17. 15 both wash his clothes, and bathe (himself)
17. 16 But if he wash (them) not, nor bathe his
Num. 8. 7 wash their clothes, and (so) make themse.
8. 21 were purified, and they washed their clo.
19. 7 Then the priest shall wash his clothes, and
19. 8 wash his clothes in water, and bathe his fl.
19. 10 wash his clothes, and be unclean until the
19. 19 wash his clothes, and bathe himself in wa.
19. 21 he that sprinkleth..shall wash his clothes
31. 24 ye shall wash your clothes on the seventh
2 Sa. 19. 24 nor trimmed his beard, nor washed his cl.
Psa. 51. 2 Wash me throughly from mine iniquity
51. 7 Purge me with hyssop..wash me, and I
Jer. 2. 22 For though thou wash thee with nitre, and
4. 14 wash thine heart from wickedness, that

3. *To be washed,* כָּבַס *kabas,* 4.
Lev. 13. 58 then it shall be washed the second time
15. 17 shall be washed with water, and be uncl.

4. *To wash self,* כָּבַס *kabas,* 7.
Lev. 13. 55 look on the plague, after that it is washed

5. *To wash, bathe,* רָחַץ *rachats.*
Gen. 18. 4 wash your feet, and rest yourselves under
19. 2 tarry all night, and wash your feet, and
24. 32 water to wash his feet, and the men's feet
43. 24 gave (them) water, and they washed their
43. 31 washed his face, and went out, and refr.
Exod. 2. 5 daughter of Pharaoh came down to wash
29. 4 congregation..shalt wash them with wa.
29. 17 wash the inwards of him, and his legs, and
30. 18 and his foot (also of) brass, to wash (wi.)
30. 19 shall wash their hands and their feet th.
30. 20 they shall wash with water, that they die
30. 21 So they shall wash their hands and their
40. 12 bring Aaron and his sons..and wash them
40. 30 and the altar, and put water there, to wa.
40. 31 Moses and Aaron and his sons washed th.
40. 32 they washed; as the LORD commanded M.
Lev. 1. 9 inwards and his legs shall he wash in wa.
1. 13 But he shall wash the inwards and the legs
8. 6 brought Aaron and his sons, and washed
8. 21 he washed the inwards and the legs in wa.
9. 14 he did wash the inwards and the legs, and
14. 8 shave off all his hair, and wash himself in
14. 9 also he shall wash his flesh in water, and
15 16 then he shall wash all his flesh in water
16. 4 therefore shall he wash his flesh in water
16. 24 he shall wash his flesh with water in the
22. 6 not eat..unless he wash his flesh with wa.

Deut 21. 6 shall wash their hands over the heifer th.
23. 11 he shall wash (himself) with water, and
Judg 19. 21 they washed their feet, and did eat and
Ruth 3. 3 Wash thyself therefore, and anoint thee
1 Sa. 25. 41 servant to wash the feet of the servants
2 Sa. 11. 2 from the roof he saw a woman washing
11. 8 Go down to thy house, and wash thy feet
12. 20 David arose from the earth, and washed
1 Ki. 22. 38 they washed his armour; according unto
2 Ki. 5. 10 Go and wash in Jordan seven times, and
5. 12 may I not wash in them, and be clean?
5. 13 when he saith to thee, Wash, and be clean
2 Ch. 4. 6 lavers..to wash in..the sea..to wash in
Job 29. 6 When I washed my steps with butter, and
Psa. 26. 6 I will wash mine hands in innocency: so
58. 10 shall wash his feet in the blood of the wi.
73. 13 cleansed my heart (in) vain, and washed
Song 5. 3 I have washed my feet; how shall I defile
5. 12 rivers of waters, washed with milk, (and)
Isa. 1. 16 Wash you, make you clean; put away the
4. 4 When the Lord shall have washed away
Eze. 16. 9 Then washed I thee with water; yea, I
23. 40 for whom thou didst wash thyself, paint.

6. *To be washed, bathed,* רָחַץ *rachats,* 4.
Prov 30. 12 a generation..not washed from their filt.
Eze. 16. 4 neither wast thou washed in water to su.

7. *To wash or bathe self,* רָחַץ *rachats,* 7.
Job 9. 30 If I wash myself with snow water, and

8. *To overflow, rinse, wash away,* שָׁטַף *shataph.*
1 Ki. 22. 38 washed the chariot in the pool of Samaria
Job 14. 19 thou washest away the things which grow
Eze. 16. 9 I throughly washed away thy blood from

9. *To wash off or away,* ἀπολούω *apolouō.*
Acts 22. 16 wash away thy sins, calling on the name
1 Co. 6. 11 but ye are washed, but ye are sanctified

10. *To wash off or fully,* ἀπονίπτομαι *aponiptomai.*
Matt. 27. 24 washed (his) hands before the multitude

11. *To wash or rinse off or away,* ἀποπλύνω *apop.*
Luke 5. 2 were gone out of them, and [were wash.]

12. *To baptize, pour out (water),* βαπτίζω *baptizō.*
Mark 7. 4 except they wash, they eat not. And ma
Luke 11. 38 marvelled that he had not first washed

13. *To wet, send rain,* βρέχω *brechō.*
Luke 7. 38 began to wash his feet with tears, and did
7. 44 but she hath washed my feet with tears

14. *To wash, cleanse, bathe,* λούω *louō.*
John 13. 10 He that is washed needeth not save to
Acts 9. 37 whom when they had washed, they laid
16. 33 took them..and washed (their) stripes
Heb. 10. 22 having..our bodies washed with pure wa.
2 Pe. 2. 22 sow that was washed to her wallowing in
Rev. 1. 5 and washed us from our sins in his own

15. *To wash or wet (the hands or feet),* νίπτω *niptō.*
Matt. 6. 17 But thou, when thou fastest..wash thy
15. 2 they wash not their hands when they eat
Mark 7. 3 all the Jews, except they wash (their) h.
John 9. 7 Go, [wash]..He went..and washed, and
9. 11 wash: and I went and washed, and I rec.
9. 15 He put clay upon mine eyes, and I washed
13. 5 began to wash the disciples' feet, and to
13. 6 saith unto him, Lord, dost thou wash my
13. 8 Thou shalt never wash my feet..If I wash
13. 10 He..needeth not save to wash (his) feet
13. 12 So after he had washed their feet, and had
13. 14 washed your feet, ye also ought to wash
1 Ti. 5. 10 if she have washed the saints' feet, if she

16. *To wash clean,* πλύνω *plunō.*
Rev. 7. 14 have washed their robes, and made them

WASHING, washpot —

1. *To wash self,* כָּבַס *kabas,* 7.
Lev. 13. 56 plague (be) somewhat dark after the wa.

2. *The waters,* הַמַּיִם *ham-mayim.*
Neh. 4. 23 every one put them off for washing

3. *Pot for washing or bathing,* סִיר רַחַץ *sir rachats.*
Psa. 60. 8 Moab (is) my washpot; over Edom will I
108. 9 Moab (is) my washpot; over Edom will I

4. *Washing, bathing,* רַחְצָה *rachtsah.*
Song 6. 6 flock of sheep which go up from the wash.
4. 2 a flock..which came up from the washing

5. *Washing, pouring on (of water),* βαπτισμός.
Mark 7. 4 washing of cups, and pots, brasen vessels
7. 8 [washing of pots and cups: and many ot.]
Heb. 9. 10 only in meats and drinks, and divers wa.

6. *A laver, bath, washing vessel,* λουτρόν *loutron.*
Eph. 5. 26 cleanse it with the washing of water by
Titus 3. 5 by the washing of regeneration, and ren.

WASTE (place), wasteness, waster, wasting, wasted —

1. *To be wasted,* בָּלַק *balaq,* 4.
Nah. 2. 10 She is empty, and void, and waste; and

2. *Waste, desolation,* בָּתָה *bathah.*
Isa. 5. 6 I will lay it waste: it shall not be pruned

3. *Dry, waste,* חָרֵב *chareb.*
Neh. 2. 3 place of my fathers' sepulchres, (lieth) w.
2. 17 how Jerusalem (lieth) waste, and the ga.
Eze. 36. 35 and the waste and desolate and ruined
36. 38 so shall the waste cities be filled with flo.
Hag. 1. 4 in your cieled houses, and this house (lie)
1. 9 Because of mine house that (is) waste, and

4. *Drought, waste,* חֹרֶב *choreb.*
Isa. 61. 4 they shall repair the waste cities, the de.

5. *A waste, place of drought,* חָרְבָּה *chorbah.*
Lev. 26. 31 I will make your cities waste, and bring
26. 33 land shall be desolate, and your cities wa.
Isa. 5. 17 the waste places of the fat ones shall str.
49. 19 For thy waste and thy desolate places, and
51. 3 he will comfort all her waste places; and
52. 9 sing together, ye waste places of Jerusal.
58. 12 shall build the old waste places: thou sh.
61. 4 they shall build the old wastes, they shall
Jer. 44. 6 they are wasted (and) desolate, as at this
49. 13 the cities thereof shall be perpetual was.
Eze. 5. 14 Moreover I will make thee waste, and a
29. 9 the land of Egypt shall be desolate and wa.
29. 10 will make the land of Egypt utterly waste
33. 24 they that inhabit those wastes of the land
33. 27 surely they that (are) in the wastes shall
35. 4 I will lay thy cities waste, and thou shalt
36. 4 to the desolate wastes, and to the cities
36. 10 cities shall be inhabited, and the wastes
36. 33 dwell in the cities, and the wastes shall
38. 8 mountains..which have been always wa.

6. *A waste, desolation,* מְשׁוֹאָה *meshoah.*
Job 30. 3 wilderness in former time desolate and w.
38. 27 To satisfy the desolate and waste (ground)

7. *A waste, desolation,* שׁוֹאָה *shoah.*
Zeph. 1. 15 a day of wasteness and desolation, a day

8. *Destruction, spoiling,* שֹׁד *shod.*
Isa. 59. 7 wasting and destruction (are) in their pa.
60. 18 wasting nor destruction within thy bord.

9. *To corrupt, destroy,* שָׁחַת *shachath,* 5.
Prov 18. 9 is brother to him that is a great waster
Isa. 54. 16 and I have created the waster to destroy

10. *Desolation, astonishment,* שַׁמָּה *shammah.*
Jer. 2. 15 they made his land waste: his cities are
46. 19 Noph shall be waste and desolate without
Joel 1. 7 He hath laid my vine waste, and barked

11. *To be or become astonished,* שָׁמֵם *shamem,* 2.
Amos 9. 14 they shall build the waste cities, and in.

12. *Astonishment, desolation,* שְׁמָמָה *shemamah.*
Mal. 1. 3 laid his mountains and his heritage waste

13. *Ruin, vacancy, vanity,* תֹּהוּ *tohu.*
Deut 32. 10 He found him..in the waste howling wil.

14. *Destruction, loss, losing away,* ἀπώλεια *apōleia.*
Matt 26. 8 saying, To what purpose (is) this waste?
Mark 14. 4 Why was this waste of the ointment ma.?

WASTE (away, laid be laid, lay, lie, make), to —

1. *To wear out, make old,* בָּלָה *balah,* 3.
1 Ch. 17. 9 neither..waste them any more, as at the

2. *To waste,* בָּלַק *balaq.*
Isa. 24. 1 maketh the earth empty..maketh it waste

3. *To burn, consume,* בָּעַר *baar,* 3.
Num 24. 22 the Kenite shall be wasted, until Asshur

4. *To weaken, become weak,* חָלַשׁ *chalash.*
Job 14. 10 man dieth, and wasteth away: yea, man

5. *To be or dry up, waste,* חָרֵב *chareb.*
Isa. 19. 5 and the river shall be wasted and dried up
34. 10 generation to generation it shall lie waste
60. 12 yea, (those) nations shall be utterly wasted
Jer. 50. 21 waste and utterly destroy after them, sa.
Eze. 6. 6 shall be laid waste..altars may be laid w.
12. 20 the cities..inhabited shall be laid waste
Amos 7. 9 the sanctuaries of Israel shall be laid wa.

6. *To cause to dry up, lay waste,* חָרַב *chareb,* 5.
Isa. 37. 18 the kings of Assyria have laid waste all
42. 15 I will make waste mountains and hills, and
49. 17 they that made thee waste shall go forth
Eze. 19. 7 he laid waste their cities; and the land
Zeph. 3. 6 I made their streets waste, that none pa.

7. *To be dried up, laid waste,* חָרֵב *chareb,* 6.
Eze. 26. 2 I shall be replenished..she is laid waste
29. 12 her cities among the cities..laid waste sh.

8. *A place of drought, destruction,* חָרְבָּה *chorbah.*
Isa. 64. 11 and all our pleasant things are laid waste
Jer. 27. 17 wherefore should this city be laid waste

9. *To be completed, consumed,* כָּלָה *kalah.*
1 Ki. 17. 14 The barrel of meal shall not waste, neither
17. 16 the barrel of meal wasted not, neither did

10. *To brouse, crop off,* כִּרְסֵם *kirsem.*
Psa. 80. 13 The boar out of the wood doth waste it, and

11. *To feed, eat up, consume,* רָעָה *raah.*
Mic. 5. 6 they shall waste the land of Assyria with

12. *To lay waste, desolate,* שָׁאָה *shaah,* 5.
2 Ki. 19. 25 that thou shouldest be to lay waste fenc.
Isa. 37. 26 shouldest be to lay waste defenced cities

13. *To destroy, spoil,* שָׁדַד *shadad,* 3.
Prov. 19. 26 He that wasteth (his) father, (and) chase.

14. *A spoiler, causing howling,* תּוֹלָל *tolal.*
Psa. 137. 3 they that wasted us (required of us) mirth

15. *To destroy, spoil,* שׁוּד *shud.*
Psa. 91. 6 for the destruction (that) wasteth at noon

16. *To corrupt, act corruptly,* שָׁחַת *shachath,* 5.
1 Ch. 20. 1 and wasted the country of the children of

17. *To be astonished, desolate,* שָׁמֵם *shamem,* 2.
Isa. 33. 8 The highways lie waste, the wayfaring

18. *To astonish, desolate,* שָׁמֵם *shamem,* 5.
Num 21. 30 we have laid them waste even unto Noph.
Psa. 79. 7 For they have devoured Jacob, and laid w.
Eze. 30. 12 I will make the land waste, and all that

19. *To scatter abroad, disperse,* διασκορπίζω *diaskor.*
Luke15. 13 there wasted his substance with riotous li.
16. 1 accused unto him that he had wasted his

20. *To lay waste,* πορθέω *portheō.*
Gal. 1. 13 I persecuted the church of God, and was.

WASTED, to be —

1. *To be dried up, waste,* חָרֵב *chareb.*
Isa. 19. 5 fail from the sea, and the river shall be w.
60. 12 yea, (those) nations shall be utterly was.

2. *To be waste, desolate,* שָׁאָה *shaah.*
Isa. 6. 11 Until the cities be wasted without inhab.

3. *To be destroyed, spoiled,* שָׁדַד *shadad,* 4.
Isa. 15. 1 Ar of Moab is laid waste, (and) brought
15. 1 because in the night Kir of Moab is laid w.
23. 1 for it is laid waste, so that there is no ho.
23. 14 Howl, ye ships..your strength is laid wa.
Joel 1. 10 The field is wasted..the corn is wasted
Nah. 3. 7 Nineveh is laid waste: who will bemoan

4. *To be perfected, consumed,* תָּמַם *tamam.*
Num. 14. 33 until your carcases be wasted in the wild.
Deut. 2. 14 were wasted out from among the host, as

WATCH, watchtower, watching —

1. *Watch, guard,* אַשְׁמֻרָה, אַשְׁמוּרָה *ashmurah.*
Exod 14. 24 in the morning watch the LORD looked
Judg. 7. 19 came..in the beginning of the middle wat.
1 Sa. 11. 11 into the midst of the host in the morning w.
Psa. 63. 6 When I..meditate on thee in the (night) w.
90. 4 as yesterday when it is past, and (as) a wa.
119. 148 Mine eyes prevent the (night) watches
Lam. 2. 19 in the beginning of the watches pour out

2. *A watch tower,* מִצְפֶּה *mitspeh.*
Isa. 21. 8 I stand continually upon the watch tower
2 Ch. 20. 24 when Judah came toward the watch tower

3. *A watch, guard, charge, ward,* מִשְׁמָר *mishmar.*
Neh. 4. 9 set a watch against them day and night
7. 3 every one in his watch, and every one (to
Job 7. 12 or a whale, that thou settest a watch over
Jer. 51. 12 Set up..make the watch strong, set up the

4. *A watch, guard, charge,* מִשְׁמֶרֶת *mishmereth.*
2 Ki. 11. 5 even be keepers of the watch of the king's
11. 6 so shall ye keep the watch of the house
11. 7 they shall keep the watch of the house of
2 Ch. 23. 6 but all the people shall keep the watch of
Neh. 7. 3 appoint watches of the inhabitants of Je
12. 9 brethren, (were) over against them in the w
Hab. 2. 1 I will stand upon my watch, and set me

5. *A looking out, watching,* צְפִיָּה *tsephiyyah.*
Lam. 4. 17 in our watching..for a nation (that) could

6. *A watch tower, place of outlook,* צָפִית *tsaphith.*
Isa. 21. 5 in the watch tower, eat, drink: arise, ye pr.

7. *A watch, guard,* שְׁמֻרָה *shomrah.*
Psa. 141. 3 Set a watch, O LORD, before my mouth

8. *To watch, be awake,* שָׁקַד *shaqad.*
Prov. 8. 34 watching daily at my gates, waiting at the

9. *A guard of soldiers* (*Lat. custodia*), κουστωδία.
Matt. 27. 65 Ye have a watch: go your way, make (it) as
27. 66 went..sealing the stone, and setting a wa.
28. 11 some of the watch came into the city, and

10. *A guarding, time of watching,* φυλακή *phulakē.*
Matt 14. 25 in the fourth watch of the night Jesus
24. 43 had known in what watch the thief would
Mark 6. 48 about the fourth watch of the night he
Luke 2. 8 shepherds..keeping watch over their floc.
12. 38 in the second [watch, or come] in the th. w.

11. *Watchfulness, wakefulness,* ἀγρυπνία *agrupnia.*
2 Co. 6. 5 in tumults, in labours, in watchings, in fa.
11. 27 in watchings often, in hunger and thirst

WATCH (for), keep the; be watchful, to —

1. *To look out, watch,* צָפָה *tsaphah.*
Gen. 31. 49 The LORD watch between me and thee, wh.
2 Sa. 13. 34 young man that kept the watch lifted up
Psa. 37. 32 The wicked watcheth the righteous, and
Isa. 21. 5 Prepare the table, watch..arise, ye prin.

2. *To look out, watch,* צָפָה *tsaphah,* 3.
1 Sa. 4. 13 Eli sat upon a seat by the wayside watch
Lam. 4. 17 we have watched for a nation (that) could
Nah. 2. 1 keep the munition, watch the way, make
Hab. 2. 1 will watch to see what he will say unto

3. *To awake, rise,* קִיץ *quts,* 5.
Eze. 7. 6 the end is come: it watcheth for thee

4. *To observe, watch, take heed,* שָׁמַר *shamar.*
Judg. 7. 19 and they had but newly set the watch
1 Sa. 19. 11 to watch him, and to slay him in the mo.
Job 14. 16 numberest my steps: dost thou not wat.
Psa. 59. *title.* Saul sent, and they watched the house
130. 6, 6 than they that watch for the morning
Jer. 20. 10 All my familiars watched for my halting

5. *To watch, awake,* שָׁקַד *shaqad.*
Ezra 8. 29 Watch ye, and keep (them), until ye wei.
Psa. 102. 7 I watch, and am as a sparrow alone upon
Prov. 8. 34 watching daily at my gates, waiting at
Isa. 29. 20 and all that watch for iniquity are cut off
Jer. 5. 6 a leopard shall watch over their cities, ev.
31. 28 like as I have watched..so will I watch
44. 27 I will watch over them for evil, and not
Dan. 9. 14 Therefore hath the LORD watched upon

6. *To watch, keep guard, be wakeful,* ἀγρυπνέω.
Mark 13. 33 Take ye heed, watch and pray: for ye kn.
Luke 21. 36 Watch ye therefore, and pray always, th.
Eph. 6. 18 watching thereunto with all perseverance
Heb. 13. 17 for they watch for your souls, as they th.

7. *To watch, be awake, vigilant,* γρηγορέω *grēgoreō.*
Matt 24. 42 Watch therefore; for ye know not what
24. 43 he would have watched, and would not
25. 13 Watch therefore; for ye know neither the
26. 38 Then saith he..tarry ye here, and watch
26. 40 What! could ye not watch with me one
26. 41 Watch and pray, that ye enter not into
Mark 13. 34 left..and commanded the porter to watch
13. 35 Watch ye therefore; for ye know not wh.
13. 37 what I say unto you I say unto all, Watch
14. 34 saith unto them..tarry ye here, and wat.
14. 37 sleepest thou? couldest thou not watch
14. 38 Watch ye and pray, lest ye enter into te.
Luke 12. 37 the lord when he cometh shall find watc.
12. 39 he would have watched, and not have su.
Acts 20. 31 Therefore watch, and remember, that by
1 Co. 16. 13 Watch ye, stand fast in the faith, quit you
Col. 4. 2 Continue in prayer, and watch in the sa.
1 Th. 5. 6 let us not sleep..but let us watch and be
Rev. 3. 2 Be watchful, and strengthen the things
3. 3 If therefore thou shalt not watch, I will
16. 15 Blessed (is) he that watcheth, and keep.

8. *To be sober, watchful,* νήφω *nēphō.*
2 Ti. 4. 5 But watch thou in all things, endure affl.
1 Pe. 4. 7 be ye therefore sober, and watch unto pr.

9. *To watch alongside of, or narrowly,* παρατηρέω.
Mark 3. 2 they watched him, whether he would heal
Luke 6. 7 Pharisees watched him, whether he wou.
14. 1 as he went into the house..they watched
20. 20 they watched (him), and sent forth spies
Acts 9. 24 watched the gates day and night to kill

10. *To keep watch, preserve, guard,* τηρέω *tēreō.*
Matt 27. 36 And sitting down they watched him there
27. 54 they that were with him watching Jesus

WATCHER, watchman —

1. *To keep, watch, preserve, besiege,* נָצַר *natsar.*
2 Ki. 17. 9 from the tower of the watchmen to th
18. 8 from the tower of the watchmen to the
Jer. 4. 16 watchers come from a far country, and
31. 6 watchmen upon the mount Ephraim sh

2. *A watcher,* עִיר *ir.*
Dan. 4. 13 watcher and an holy one came down from
4. 17 This matter (is) by the decree of the wat.
4. 23 whereas the king saw a watcher and an

3. *To look out, watch,* צָפָה *tsaphah.*
1 Sa. 14. 16 watchmen of Saul in Gibeah of Benjamin
2 Sa. 18. 24 watchman went up to the roof over the
18. 25 watchman cried, and told the king. And
18. 26 watchman saw another..and the watch.
18. 27 watchman said, Me thinketh the running
2 Ki. 9. 17 there stood a watchman on the tower in
9. 18 watchman told, saying, The messenger
9. 20 watchman told, saying, He came even unto
Isa. 52. 8 watchmen shall lift up the voice; with
56. 10 His watchmen (are) blind: they are all
Jer. 6. 17 Also I set watchmen over you, (saying), He.
Eze. 3. 17 have made thee a watchman unto the ho.
33. 2 take a man..and set him for their watch.
33. 6 if the watchman see the sword come, and
33. 6 his blood will I require at the watchma.
33. 7 have set thee a watchman unto the house
Hos. 9. 8 watchman of Ephraim (was) with my God

4. *To look out, watch,* צָפָה *tsaphah,* 3.
Isa. 21. 6 Go, set a watchman, let him declare what
Mic. 7. 4 day of thy watchmen (and) thy visitation

5. *To observe, watch, take heed,* שָׁמַר *shamar.*
Psa. 127. 1 except the LORD keep the city, the watc.
Song 3. 3 The watchmen that go about the city fo.
5. 7 The watchmen that went about the city
Isa. 21. 11 Watchman, what of the night? Watchman
21. 12 watchman said, The morning cometh, and
62. 6 I have set watchmen upon thy walls, O J.
Jer. 51. 12 set up the watchmen, prepare the ambu.

WATER —

1. *Waters, water,* מַיִם *mayim.*
Gen. 1. 2 spirit of God moved on the face of the w.
1. 6 midst of the waters..let it divide the w.
1. 7 divided the waters..from the waters wh.
1. 9 Let the waters under the heaven be gath.
1. 10 gathering together of the waters called
1. 20 Let the waters bring forth abundantly the
1. 21 which the waters brought forth abundan.
1. 22 fill the waters in the seas, and let fowl mu.
6. 17 I, do bring a flood of waters upon the ea.
7. 6 hundred years old when the flood of wat.
7. 7 into the ark, because of the waters of the
7. 10 that the waters of the flood were upon the
7. 17 waters increased, and bare up the ark, and
7. 18 waters prevailed, and were increased gr.
7. 18 and the ark went upon the face of the wa.
7. 19 waters prevailed exceedingly upon the ea.
7. 20 Fifteen cubits upward did the waters pr.
7. 24 waters prevailed upon the earth an hund.
8. 1 to pass over the earth, and the waters as.
8. 3 the waters returned..the waters were ab.
8. 5 waters decreased continually until the te.
8. 7, 13 the waters were dried up from off the
8. 8 to see if the waters were abated from off
8. 9 for the waters (were) on the face of the
8. 11 so Noah knew that the waters were abated
9. 11 flesh be cut off any more by the waters of
Gen. 9. 15 waters shall no more become a flood to de.
16. 7 found her by a fountain of water in the wi.
18. 4 Let a little water, I pray you, be fetched
21. 14 took bread and a bottle of water, and gave
21. 15 water was spent in the bottle, and she ca.
21. 19 a well of water..filled the bottle with wa.
21. 25 repro. Abimelech because of a well of wa.
24. 11 kneel down..by a well of water at the time
24. 13 Behold, I stand (here) by the well of wa.
24. 13 the daughters..come out to draw water
24. 17 Let me, I pray thee, drink a little water
24. 32 water to wash his feet, and the men's feet
24. 43 Behold, I stand by the well of water; and
24. 43 Give me, I pray thee, a little water of thy
26. 18 Isaac digged again the wells of water wh.
26. 19 and found there a well of springing water
26. 20 The water (is) ours: and he called the na.
26. 32 and said unto him, We have found water
37. 24 the pit (was) empty, (there was) no water
43. 24 gave (them) water, and they washed their
49. 4 Unstable as water, thou shalt not excel
Exod. 2. 10 said, Because I drew him out of the water
4. 9 take of the water..and the water which
7. 15 he goeth out unto the water; and thou sh.
7. 17 smite..upon the waters which (are) in the
7. 18, 21 Egyptians..to drink of the water of the
7. 19 the waters of Egypt..all their pools of wa.
7. 20 smote the waters..and all the waters that
7. 24 water..they could not drink of the water
8. 6 stretched out his hand over the waters of
8. 20 lo, he cometh forth to the water; and say
12. 9 nor sodden at all with water, but roast
14. 21 made the sea dry (land) and the waters
14. 22, 29 the waters (were) a wall unto them on
14. 26 that the waters may come again upon the
14. 28 the waters returned, and covered the ch.
15. 8 with the blast of thy nostrils the waters
15. 10 they sank as lead in the mighty waters
15. 19 the LORD brought again the waters of the
15. 22 they went three days..and found no wat.
15. 23 they could not drink of the waters of Ma.
15. 25 had cast into the waters, the waters were
15. 27 twelve wells of water..there by the waters
17. 1 (there was) no water for the people to dr.
17. 2 and said, Give us water that we may drink
17. 3 the people thirsted there for water, and
17. 6 there shall come water out of it, that the
20. 4 or that (is) in the water under the earth
23. 25 he shall bless thy bread, and thy water
29. 4 shalt bring..and shalt wash them with w.
30. 18 a laver..and thou shalt put water therein
30. 20 they shall wash with water, that they die
32. 20 strawed (it) upon the water, and made the
34. 28 he did neither eat bread, nor drink water
40. 7 set the laver..and shalt put water therein
40. 12 thou shalt bring..and wash them with wa.
40. 30 he set the laver..and put water there, to
Lev. 1. 9 But his inwards..shall he wash in water
1. 13 wash the inwards and the legs with water
6. 28 shall be both scoured, and rinsed in water
8. 6 Moses brought..and washed them with w.
8. 21 washed the inwards and the legs in water
11. 9 in the waters..fins and scales in the waters
11. 10 in the waters..which (is) in the waters
11. 12 Whatsoever hath no fins..in the waters
11. 32 it must be put into water, and it shall be
11. 34 (that) on which (such) water cometh shall
11. 36 or pit, (wherein there is) plenty of water
11. 38 if (any) water be put upon the seed, and
11. 46 living creature that moveth in the waters
14. 5, 50 an earthen vessel over running water
14. 6 that (was) killed over the running water
14. 8 wash himself in water, that he may be
14. 9 he shall wash his flesh in water, and he
14. 51 dip them..in the running water, and spri.
14. 52 cleanse the house..with the running wa.
15. 5, 6, 7, 8, 10, 11, 21, 22, 27 bathe..in water
15. 11 hath not rinsed his hands in water, he
15. 12 every vessel..shall be rinsed in water
15. 13 bathe his flesh in running water, and sh.
15. 16 he shall wash all his flesh in water, and
15. 17 every skin..shall be washed with water
15. 18 they shall (both) bathe themselves in wa.
16. 4 therefore shall he wash his flesh in water
16. 24 he shall wash his flesh with water in the
16. 26 bathe his flesh in water, and afterward
16. 28 bathe his flesh in water, and afterward he
17. 15 bathe (himself) in water, and be unclean
22. 6 unclean..unless he wash his flesh with wa.
Num. 5. 17 take holy water..put (it) into the water
5. 18 have in his hand the bitter water that ca.
5. 19 be thou free from this bitter water that
5. 22 this water that causeth the curse shall go
5. 23 shall blot (them) out with the bitter wa.
5. 24 to drink the bitter water..the water that
5. 26 shall cause the woman to drink the water
5. 27 to drink the water..the water that caus.
8. 7 Sprinkle water of purifying upon them
19. 7 he shall bathe his flesh in water, and aft.
19. 8 in water, and bathe his flesh in water, and
19. 9 it shall be kept..for a water of separation
19. 13 the water of separation was not sprinkled
19. 17 running water shall be put thereto in a
19. 18 take hyssop, and dip (it) in the water, and
19. 19 bathe himself in water, and shall be clean
19. 20 the water of separation hath not been sp.
19. 21 sprinkleth the water..the water of sepa.
20. 2 there was no water for the congregation
20. 5 no place of seed..neither (is) there any wa.
20. 8 give forth his water..water out of the ro.
20. 10 must we fetch you water out of this rock?
20. 11 the water came out abundantly, and the

Num 20. 13 This (is) the water of Meribah; because
20. 17 neither will we drink (of) the water of the
20. 19 if I and my cattle drink of thy water, th.
20. 24 because ye rebelled..at the water of Me.
21. 5 no bread, neither (is there any) water and
21. 16 Gather the people..I will give them wat.
21. 22 we will not drink (of) the waters of the
24. 6 as gardens..as cedar trees beside the wa.
24. 7 He shall pour the water..in many waters
27. 14 sanctify me at the water..the water of M.
31. 23 purified with the water..through the wa.
33. 9 in Elim (were) twelve fountains of water
33. 14 Rephidim, where was no water for the pe.
Deut. 2. 6 ye shall also buy water of them for money
2. 28 give me water for money, that I may dri.
4. 18 the likeness of any fish that (is) in the wa.
5. 8 or that (is) in the waters beneath the earth
8. 7 a land of brooks of water, of fountains
8. 15 no water; who brought thee forth water
9. 9 I neither did eat bread nor drink water
9. 18 I did neither eat bread nor drink water
10. 7 from Gudgodah..a land of rivers of wat.
11. 4 he made the water of the Red sea to over.
11. 11 (and) drinketh water of the rain of heaven
12. 16 ye shall pour it upon the earth as water
12. 24 thou shalt pour it upon the earth as water
14. 9 ye shall eat of all that (are) in the waters
15. 23 shalt pour it upon the ground as water
23. 4 met you not with bread and with water
23. 11 he shall wash (himself) with water; and
29. 11 the hewer..unto the drawer of thy water
32. 51 ye trespassed..at the waters of Meribah
33. 8 thou didst strive at the waters of Meribah
Josh. 2. 10 heard how the LORD dried up the water
3. 8 ye are come to the brink of the water of
3. 13 the soles..shall rest in the waters of Jordan
3. 13 waters..shall be cut off (from) the waters
3. 15 feet..were dipped in the brim of the wa.
3. 16 the waters which came down from above
4. 7, 7 the waters of Jordan were cut off
4. 18 the waters of Jordan returned unto their
4. 23 God dried up the waters of Jordan from
5. 1 the LORD had dried up the waters of Jo.
7. 5 hearts of the people melted..as water
9. 21, 23, 27 hewers of wood and drawers of w.
11. 5 pitched together at the waters of Merom
11. 7 Joshua came..against them by the waters
15. 7 the border passed toward the waters of
15. 9 unto the fountain of the water of Nepht.
15. 19 answered..give me also springs of water
16. 1 from Jordan by Jericho unto the water
18. 15 went out to the well of waters of Nepht.
Judg. 1. 15 she said..give me also springs of water
4. 19 Give me, I pray thee, a little water to dr.
5. 4 dropped, the clouds also dropped water
5. 19 then fought the kings..by the waters of
5. 25 He asked water, (and) she gave (him) mi.
6. 38 dew out of the fleece, a bowl full of water
7. 4 bring them down unto the water, and I w.
7. 5 unto the water..lappeth of the water wi.
7. 6 bowed down upon their knees to drink w.
7. 24, 24 the waters unto Beth-barah and Jord.
15. 19 an hollow place..there came water ther.
1 Sa. 7. 6 drew water, and poured (it) out before the
9. 11 young maidens going out to draw water
25. 11 Shall I then take my bread, and my water
26. 11 take thou..the cruse of water, and let us
26. 12 took the spear and the cruse of water fr.
26. 16 and the cruse of water that (was) at his
30. 11 did eat; and they made him drink water
30. 12 eaten no bread, nor drunk (any) water, th.
2 Sa. 5. 20 hath broken forth..as the breach of wa.
12. 27 fought..and have taken the city of waters
14. 14 we must needs die, and (are) as water sp.
17. 20 They be gone over the brook of water
17. 21 pass quickly over the water: for thus hath
21. 10 until water dropped upon them out of he.
22. 12 dark waters, (and) thick clouds of the sk.
22. 17 took me; he drew me out of many waters
23. 15 one would give me drink of the water of
23. 16 drew water out of the well of Beth-lehem
1 Ki. 13. 8, 16 neither will I eat bread nor drink wa.
13. 9 Eat no bread, nor drink water, nor turn
13. 17 Thou shalt eat no bread nor drink water
13. 18 that he may eat bread and drink water
13. 19 did eat bread in his house, and drank wa.
13. 22 drunk water in the place..drink no water
14. 15 smite..as a reed is shaken in the water
17. 10 Fetch me, I pray thee, a little water in a
18. 4 hid..and fed them with bread and water
18. 5 Go..unto all fountains of water, and unto
18. 13 how I..fed them with bread and water
18. 33 Fill four barrels with water, and pour (it)
18. 35 water ran round about..also with water
18. 38 licked up the water that (was) in the tre.
19. 6 (there was)..a cruse of water at his head
22. 27 feed him..with water of affliction, until
2 Ki. 2. 8 smote the waters, and they were divided
2. 14 smote the waters..had smitten the wat.
2. 19 the water (is) naught, and the ground bar.
2. 21 spring of the waters..healed these waters
2. 22 the waters were healed unto this day, ac.
3. 9 there was no water for the host, and for
3. 11 which poured water on the hands of Elijah
3. 17 that valley shall be filled with water, that
3. 19 stop all wells of water, and mar every good
3. 20 there came water..was filled with water
3. 22 sun shone upon the water..saw the water
3. 25 they stopped all the wells of water, and
5. 12 Abana and Pharpar..better than all the w.
6. 5 the ax head fell into the water: and he
6. 22 Set bread and water before them, that they

2 Ki. 8. 15 dipped (it) in water, and spread (it) on his
18. 31 drink ye every one the waters of his ciste.
19. 24 I have digged and drunk strange waters
20. 20 how he made a pool..and brought water
1 Ch. 11. 17 one would give me drink of the water of
11. 18 drew water out of the well of Beth-lehem
14. 11 broken..like the breaking forth of waters
2 Ch. 18. 26 feed him..with water of affliction, until I
32. 3 to stop the waters of the fountains which
32. 4 Why should the kings..find much water?
Ezra 10. 6 he did eat no bread, nor drink water: for
Neh. 3. 26 unto (the place) over against the water
8. 1, 3 the street that (was) before the water
8. 16 in the street of the water gate, and in the
9. 11 threwest..as a stone into the mighty wate.
9. 15 broughtest forth water for them out of
9. 20 and gavest them water for their thirst
12. 37 above the house..unto the water gate ea.
13. 2 met not..Israel with bread and with water
Job 3. 24 my roarings are poured out like the water
5. 10 Who giveth rain..and sendeth waters up.
8. 11 can the rush..the flag grow without water?
9. 30 If I wash myself with snow water, and
11. 16 (and) remember (it) as waters that (pass)
12. 15 he withholdeth the waters, and they dry
14. 9 through the scent of water it will bud, and
14. 11 (As) the waters fail from the sea, and the
14. 19 The waters wear the stones: thou washe.
15. 16 man, which drinketh iniquity like water
22. 7 Thou hast not given water to the weary
22. 11 and abundance of waters cover thee
24. 18 He (is) swift as the waters; their portion
24. 19 Drought and heat consume the snow wat.
26. 5 Dead (things) are formed..under the wat.
26. 8 He bindeth up the waters in his thick
26. 10 He hath compassed the waters with bou.
27. 20 Terrors take hold on him as waters, a te.
28. 25 and he weigheth the waters by measure
29. 19 My root (was) spread out by the waters
34. 7 Job, (who) drinketh up scorning like wa.?
36. 27 he maketh small the drops of water: they
37. 10 and the breadth of the waters is straitened
38. 30 The waters are hid as (with) a stone, and
38. 34 that abundance of waters may cover thee
Psa. 1. 3 like a tree planted by the rivers of water
18. 11 dark waters (and) thick clouds of the skies
18. 15 the channels of waters were seen, and the
18. 16 took me, he drew me out of many waters
22. 14 I am poured out like water, and all my bo.
23. 2 he leadeth me beside the still waters
29. 3 (is) upon the waters..(is) upon many wa.
32. 6 in the floods of great waters they shall
33. 7 He gathereth the waters of the sea toget.
42. 1 As the hart panteth after the water broo.
46. 3 (Though) the waters thereof roar (and) be
58. 7 Let them melt away as waters (which) run
63. 1 a dry and thirsty land, where no water is
65. 9 the river of God, (which) is full of water
66. 12 we went through fire and through water
69. 1 for the waters are come in unto (my) soul
69. 2 I am come into deep waters, where the
69. 14 be delivered..out of the deep waters
73. 10 waters of a full (cup) are wrung out to
74. 13 thou brakest the heads..in the waters
77. 16 The waters saw thee, O God, the waters
77. 17 The clouds poured out water; the skies
77. 19 thy path in the great waters, and thy fo.
78. 13 he made the waters to stand as an heap
78. 16 caused waters to run down like rivers
78. 20 he smote the rock, that the waters gush.
79. 3 Their blood have they shed like water
81. 7 I proved thee at the waters of Meribah
88. 17 They came round about me daily like wa.
93. 4 (is) mightier than the noise of many wat.
104. 3 Who layeth the beams..in the waters
104. 6 the waters stood above the mountains
105. 29 He turned their waters into blood, and
105. 41 He opened the rock, and the waters gush.
106. 11 the waters covered their enemies; there
106. 32 They angered (him) also at the waters of
107. 23 They..that do business in great waters
107. 35 turneth the wilderness into a standing w.
109. 18 let it come into his bowels like water, and
114. 8 water, the flint into a fountain of waters
119. 136 Rivers of water run down mine eyes, be.
124. 4 the waters had overwhelmed us, the stre.
124. 5 Then the proud waters had gone over our
136. 6 stretched out the earth above the waters
144. 7 deliver me out of great waters, from the
147. 18 he causeth his wind to blow, (and) the wa.
148. 4 ye waters that (be) above the heavens
Prov. 5. 15 Drink waters out of thine own cistern, and
5. 16 dispersed abroad, (and) rivers of waters
8. 24 (were) no fountains abounding with water
8. 29 the waters should not pass his command.
9. 17 Stolen waters are sweet, and bread (eaten)
17. 14 of strife (is as) when one letteth out water
18. 4 The words..(are as) deep waters, (and) the
20. 5 Counsel in the heart..(like) deep water
21. 1 king's heart (is)..(as) the rivers of water
25. 21 if he be thirsty, give him water to drink
25. 25 (As) cold waters to a thirsty soul, so (is) good
27. 19 As in water face (answereth) to face, so the
30. 4 who hath bound the waters in a garment?
30. 16 the earth (that) is not filled with water
Eccl. 2. 6 I made me pools of water, to water there.
11. 1 Cast thy bread upon the waters: for thou
Song 4. 15 a well of living waters, and streams from
5. 12 (eyes) of doves by the rivers of waters
8. 7 Many waters cannot quench love, neither
Isa. 1. 22 become dross, thy wine mixed with water
1. 30 and as a garden that hath no water

Isa. 3. 1 stay of bread, and the whole stay of water
8. 6 this people refuseth the waters of Shiloah
8. 7 the Lord bringeth up upon them the wat.
11. 9 the earth shall be full..as the waters co.
12. 3 with joy shall ye draw water out of the
14. 23 I will also make it..pools of water, and
15. 6 the waters of Nimrim shall be desolate
15. 9 the waters of Dimon shall be full of blood
17. 12, 13 like the rushing of..waters
18. 2 in vessels of bulrushes upon the waters
19. 5 the waters shall fail from the sea, and the
19. 8 they that spread nets upon the waters sh.
21. 14 The inhabitants..brought water to him t.
22. 9 ye gathered together the waters of the lo.
22. 11 between the two walls for the water of
23. 3 by great waters the seed of Sihor, the ha.
28. 2 as a flood of mighty waters overflowing
28. 17 the waters shall overflow the hiding place
30. 14 a sherd..to take water (withal) out of the
30. 20 the bread of adversity, and the water of
30. 25 streams of waters in the day of the great
32. 2 as rivers of water in a dry place; as the
32. 20 Blessed (are) ye that sow beside all waters
33. 16 bread shall be given him, his waters (sha.
35. 6 in the wilderness shall waters break out
35. 7 and the thirsty land springs of water
36. 16 drink ye every one the waters of his own
37. 25 I have digged, and drunk water; and wi.
40. 12 Who hath measured the waters in the ho.
41. 17 (When) the poor and needy seek water, and
41. 18 make the wilderness a pool of water, and
41. 18 I will make..the dry land springs of water
43. 2 When thou passest through the waters, I
43. 16 which maketh..a path in the mighty wa.
43. 20 I give waters in the wilderness, (and) riv.
44. 3 I will pour water upon him that is thirsty
44. 12 strength faileth: he drinketh no water, and
48. 1 are come forth out of the waters of Judah
48. 21 he caused the waters..waters gushed out
49. 10 by the springs of water shall he guide th.
50. 2 fish stinketh, because (there is) no water
51. 10 which hath dried the sea, the waters of
54. 9 this (is as) the waters..the waters of Noah
55. 1 come ye to the waters, and he that hath
57. 20 the troubled sea..whose waters cast up
58. 11 and like a spring..whose waters fail not
63. 12 dividing the water before them, to make
64. 2 the fire causeth the waters to boil, to make
Jer. 2. 13 living waters..that can hold no water
2. 18 to drink the waters..the waters of the ri.
6. 7 As a fountain casteth out her waters, so
8. 14 put us to silence, and given us water of
9. 1 O that my head were waters, and mine
9. 15 I will feed..and give them water of gall
9. 18 that..our eyelids gush out with waters
10. 13 a multitude of waters in the heavens, and
13. 1 get thee a linen girdle..put it not in wa.
14. 3 have sent their little ones to the waters
14. 3 they came to the pits, (and) found no wa.
15. 18 wilt thou be..as a liar..waters (that) fail
17. 8 he shall be as a tree planted by the waters
17. 13 have forsaken..the fountain of living wa.
18. 14 shall the cold flowing waters that come
23. 15 I will..make them drink the waters of g.
31. 9 I will cause them to walk by..waters in
38. 6 in the dungeon..no water, but mire: so
41. 12 found him by the great waters..in Gibeon
46. 7 this..whose waters are moved as the ri.?
46. 8 and (his) waters are moved like the rivers
47. 2 Behold, waters rise up out of the north
48. 34 the waters also of Nimrim shall be desol.
50. 38 A drought (is) upon her waters; and they
51. 13 O thou that dwellest upon many waters
51. 16 a multitude of waters in the heavens
51. 55 when her waves do roar like great waters
Lam. 1. 16 mine eye runneth down with water, bec.
2. 19 pour out thine heart like water before the
3. 48 Mine eye runneth down with..water for
3. 54 Waters flowed over mine head..I said
5. 4 We have drunken our water for money
Eze. 1. 24 like the noise of great waters, as the voi.
4. 11 Thou shalt drink also water by measure
4. 16 they shall drink water by measure, and
4. 17 That they may want bread and water, and
7. 17 hands..all knees shall be weak (as) water
12. 18 drink thy water with trembling and with
12. 19 drink their water with astonishment, that
16. 4 neither wast thou washed in water to su
16. 9 Then washed I thee with water; yea, I
17. 5 placed (it) by great waters..set it..a wil.
17. 8 It was planted in a good soil by great wa.
19. 10 by the waters..by reason of many waters
21. 7 all knees shall be weak (as) water: behold
24. 3 Set on a pot..and also pour water into it
26. 12 shall lay..thy dust in the midst of the wa.
26. 19 when I shall bring up the deep..great wa
27. 26 rowers have brought thee into great wat
27. 34 broken by the seas in the depths of the wa.
31. 4 The waters made him great, the deep set
31. 5 because of the multitude of waters, when
31. 7 Thus was he fair..his root was by great w.
31. 14 that none of all the trees by the waters
31. 14 neither their trees..all that drink water
31. 15 the great waters were stayed; and I caus.
31. 16 all the trees..all that drink water, shall
32. 2 thou..troubledst the waters with thy fe.
32. 13 I will destroy..from beside the great wa.
32. 14 Then will I make their waters deep, and
34. 18 and to have drunk of the deep waters
36. 25 Then will I sprinkle clean water upon you
43. 2 his voice (was) like a noise of many wat.
47. 1 waters issued out..the waters came down

Eze. 47. 2 behold, there ran out waters on the right
47. 3, 4 brought me through the waters: the w.
47. 4 brought me through; the waters (were) to
47. 5 the waters were risen, waters to swim in
47. 8 These waters..the waters shall be healed
47. 9 because these waters shall come thither
47. 12 their waters they issued out of the sanct.
47. 19 from Tamar..to the waters of strife (in)
48. 28 from Tamar (unto) the waters of strife (in)
Dan. 1. 12 let them give us pulse to eat, and water
12. 6, 7 which (was) upon the waters of the ri.
Hos. 2. 5 lovers, that give..my bread and my wa.
5. 10 will pour out my wrath upon them..wat.
10. 7 king is cut off as the foam upon the wat.
Joel 1. 20 the rivers of waters are dried up, and the
3. 18 the rivers of Judah shall flow with waters
Amos 4. 8 three..wandered unto one city, to drink w.
5. 8 that calleth for the waters of the sea, and
5. 24 let judgment run down as waters, and ri.
8. 11 not..a thirst for water, but of hearing
9. 6 he that calleth for the waters of the sea
Jon. 2. 5 waters compassed me about..to the soul
3. 7 Let neither man nor beast..drink water
Mic. 1. 4 as the waters..poured down a steep pla.
Nah. 2. 8 But Nineveh (is) of old like a pool of wa.
3. 8 that was situate among the rivers..water
3. 14 Draw thee waters for the siege, fortify thy
Hab. 2. 14 shall be filled..as the waters cover the
3. 10 the overflowing of the water passed by
3. 15 through the sea..the heap of great wate.
Zech. 9. 11 sent..out of the pit wherein (is) no wat.
14. 8 living waters shall go out from Jerusalem

2. *A flowing, flood, torrent,* ποταμός *potamos.*
2 Co. 11. 26 journeyings often..perils of waters..perils

3. *Water,* ὕδωρ *hudōr.*
Matt. 3. 11 I indeed baptize you with water unto re.
3. 16 Jesus..went up straightway out of the wa.
8. 32 into the sea, and perished in the waters
14. 28 Lord..bid me come unto thee on the wa.
14. 29 Peter..walked on the water, to go to Jes.
17. 15 falleth into the fire, and oft into the water
27. 24 Pilate..took water, and washed (his) hands
Mark 1. 8 I indeed have baptized you with water
1. 10 straightway coming up out of the water
9. 22 cast him into the fire, and into the waters
9. 41 whosoever shall give you a cup of water
14. 13 meet you a man bearing a pitcher of water
Luke 3. 16 saying..I indeed baptize you with water
7. 44 I entered..thou gavest me no water for
8. 24 rebuked the wind..the raging of the water
8. 25 he commandeth even the winds and water
16. 24 that he may dip the tip of his finger in wa.
22. 10 a man meet you, bearing a pitcher of wa.
John 1. 26 I baptize with water: but there standeth
1. 31 therefore am I come baptizing with water
1. 33 but he that sent me to baptize with water
2. 7 Jesus saith unto them, Fill..pots with wa.
2. 9 had tasted the water that was made wine
2. 9 the servants which drew the water knew
3. 5 Except a man be born of water and (of)
3. 23 John..because there was much water th.
4. 7 There cometh a woman of S. to draw wa.
4. 10 and he would have given thee living water
4. 11 whence then hast thou that living water
4. 13 Whosoever drinketh of this water shall th.
4. 14 But whosoever drinketh of the water that
4. 14 [water]..shall be in him a well of water
4. 15 Sir, give me this water, that I thirst not
4. 46 Cana of Galilee, where he made the water
5. 3 lay..[waiting for the moving of the water]
5. 4 [an angel went down..and troubled the w.]
5. 4 [then first after the troubling of the water]
5. 7 I have no man, when the water is troubled
7. 38 out of his belly shall flow rivers of..water
13. 5 he poureth water into a bason, and began
19. 34 forthwith came there out blood and water
Acts 1. 5 John truly baptized with water; but ye
8. 36 as they went..they came unto a certain wa.
8. 36 and the eunuch said, See, (here is) water
8. 38 they went down both into the water, both
8. 39 when they were come up out of the water
10. 47 Can any man forbid water, that these sh.
11. 16 John indeed baptized with water; but ye
Eph. 5. 26 cleanse it with the washing of water by
Heb. 9. 19 he took..water, and scarlet wool, and hy.
10. 22 having..our bodies washed with pure wa.
Jas. 3. 12 so (can) no fountain both yield salt water
1 Pe. 3. 20 few, that is, eight souls, were saved by wa.
2 Pe. 3. 5 standing out of the water and in the wat.
3. 6 the world..being overflowed with water
1 Jo. 5. 6 This is he that came by water and blood
5. 6 not by water only, but by water and blood
5. 8 the spirit, and the water, and the blood
Rev. 1. 15 and his voice as the sound of many waters
7. 17 lead them unto living fountains of water
8. 10 and it fell..upon the fountains of waters
8. 11 the third part of the waters became wor.
8. 11 many men died of the waters, because
11. 6 have power over waters to turn them to
12. 15 the serpent cast out of his mouth water as
14. 2 I heard a voice from heaven..of many wat.
14. 7 that made..the fountains of waters
16. 4 poured..the rivers and fountains of w.
16. 5 And I heard the angel of the waters say
16. 12 the water thereof was dried up, that the
17. 1 the great whore that sitteth upon many w.
17. 15 The waters which thou sawest, where the
19. 6 as the voice of many waters, and as the
21. 6 of the fountain of the water of life freely
22. 1 he showed me a pure river of water of life
22. 17 whosoever will, let him take the water of

WATER, with or without —

1. *With water of,* בְּמֵי *[be-mayim]* [V.L. בְּמוֹ *bemo*].
Job 9. 30 If I wash myself with snow water, and

2. *Without water, waterless,* ἄνυδρος *anudros.*
2 Pe. 2. 17 These are wells without water, clouds
Jude 12 clouds (they are) without water, carried

WATER, (abundantly), be watered, to —

1. *A sprinkling or fertilizing shower,* זַרְזִיף *zarziph.*
Psa. 72. 6 the mown grass; as showers (that) water

2. *To cause to shoot or pour forth,* יָרָא *yara,* 5.
Prov. 11. 25 The liberal soul..shall be watered also

3. *To melt, waste,* מָסָה *masah,* 5.
Psa. 6. 6 make I my bed to swim; I water my co.

4. *To fill, be filled, satisfied, watered,* רָוָה *ravah,* 3.
Psa. 65. 10 Thou waterest the ridges thereof abund.
Isa. 16. 9 I will water thee with my tears, O Hesh.

5. *To fill, satisfy, water,* רָוָה *ravah,* 5.
Prov. 11. 25 The liberal soul..he that watereth shall
Isa. 55. 10 returneth not thither, but watereth the ear.

6. *To water, give to drink,* שׁוּק *shuq,* 3a.
Psa. 65. 9 Thou visitest the earth, and waterest it

7. *To water, give or cause to drink,* שָׁקָה *shaqah,* 5.
Gen. 2. 6 and watered the whole face of the ground
2. 10 a river went out of Eden to water the ga.
29. 2 for out of that well they watered the flo.
29. 3 watered the sheep, and put the stone ag.
29. 7 water ye the sheep, and go (and) feed (th.)
29. 8 they roll the stone..then we water the sh.
29. 10 watered the flock of Laban his mother's br.
Exod 2. 16 filled the troughs to water their father's
2. 17 Moses stood up and helped them, and w.
2. 19 drew (water) enough for us, and watered
Deut 11. 10 wateredst (it) with thy foot, as a garden
Psa. 104. 13 He watereth the hills from his chambers
Eccl. 2. 6 to water therewith the wood that bringe.
Isa. 27. 3 I the LORD do keep it; I will water it ev.
Eze. 17. 7 might water it by the furrows of her pla.
32. 6 I will also water with thy blood the land
Joel 3. 18 a fountain..shall water the valley of Shi.

8. *To water, give to drink,* ποτίζω *potizō.*
Luke 13. 15 from the stall, and lead (him) away to w.
1 Co. 3. 6 I have planted, Apollos watered; but God
3. 7 planteth any thing, neither he that wate.
3. 8 Now he that planteth and he that water.

WATER, to drink —

To drink water, ὑδροποτέω *hudropoteō.*
1 Ti. 5. 23 Drink no longer water, but use a little w.

WATER course, flood, spout, spring —

1. *Flowing of waters,* יִבְלֵי מַיִם *[yabal].*
Isa. 44. 4 spring..as willows by the water courses

2. *Outlet of water,* מוֹצָא מַיִם *motsa mayim.*
2 Ch. 32. 30 Hezekiah also stopped the upper water c.
Psa. 107. 33 He turneth..water springs into dry gro.
107. 35 He turneth..dry ground into water spri.
Isa. 41. 18 I will make..the dry land springs of wa.
58. 11 thou shalt be like..a spring of water, wh.

3. *A gutter, canal, conduit,* צִנּוֹר *tsinnor.*
Psa. 42. 7 unto deep at the noise of thy water spouts

4. *Stream or flood of water,* שִׁבֹּלֶת מַיִם *shibboleth mayim.*
Psa. 69. 15 Let not the waterflood overflow me, nei.

5. *A trench, conduit,* תְּעָלָה *tealah.*
Job 38. 25 Who hath divided a water course for the

WATERED, watering, well —

1. *Water, of waters,* מַיִם *mayim.*
Gen. 30. 38 in the gutters in the watering troughs wh.

2. *Watering,* מַשְׁקֶה *mashqeh.*
Gen. 13. 10 it (was) well watered every where, before

3. *Full, satiated,* רָוֶה *raveh.*
Isa. 58. 11 thou shalt be like a watered garden, and
Jer. 31. 12 their soul shall be as a watered garden

4. *Watering,* רִי *ri.*
Job 37. 11 Also by watering he wearieth the thick cl.

WATERPOT —

A water vessel, ὑδρία *hudria.*
John 2. 6 there were set there six waterpots of stone
2. 7 Jesus saith..Fill the waterpots with water
4. 28 The woman then left her waterpot, and

WATERS OF MEROM, מֵי מֵרוֹם.
A lake ten miles N. of the Sea of Chinnereth, and now called *el-Huleh,* through which the Jordan flows in its passage southward.
Josh 11. 5 came and pitched..at the waters of M.
11. 7 came..against them by the waters of M.

WATERS OF STRIFE, מֵי מְרִיבָה. See *Meribah.*
Eze. 47. 19 from Tamar (even) to the waters of strife
48. 28 from Tamar (unto) the waters of strife (in)

WAVE —

1. *High place, height,* בָּמָה *bamah.*
Job 9. 8 and treadeth upon the waves of the sea

2. *Rolling thing, billow, wave,* גַּל *gal.*
Job 38. 11 and here shall thy proud waves be stayed
Psa. 65. 7 the noise of their waves, and the tumult
89. 9 when the waves thereof arise, thou still.
107. 25 stormy wind, which lifteth up the waves
107. 29 a calm, so that the waves thereof are still
Isa. 48. 18 thy righteousness as the waves of the sea
Isa. 51. 15 that divided the sea, whose waves roared
Jer. 5. 22 though the waves thereof toss themselves
31. 35 divideth the sea when the waves thereof
51. 42 covered with the multitude of the waves
51. 55 when her waves do roar like great waters
Eze. 26. 3 as the sea causeth his waves to come up
Jon. 2. 3 thy billows and thy waves passed over me
Zech 10. 11 shall smite the waves in the sea, and all

3. *A breaker,* דֳּכִי *doki.*
Psa. 93. 3 their voice; the floods lift up their waves

4. *A breaker,* מִשְׁבָּר *mishbar.*
2 Sa. 22. 5 When the waves of death compassed me
Psa. 42. 7 thy waves and thy billows are gone over
88. 7 thou hast afflicted (me) with all thy wav.
93. 4 (is) mightier..(than) the mighty waves of

5. *A washing, surging,* κλύδων *kludōn.*
Jas. 1. 6 he that wavereth is like a wave of the sea

6. *A wave, billow,* κῦμα *kuma.*
Matt. 8. 24 that the ship was covered with the waves
14. 24 in the midst of the sea, tossed with waves
Mark 4. 37 the waves beat into the ship, so that it
Acts 27. 41 was broken with the violence [of the wa.]
Jude 13 Raging waves of the sea, foaming out th.

7. *Shaking, agitation,* σάλος *salos.*
Luke 21. 25 perplexity; the sea and the waves roaring

WAVE, be waved, waver, to —

1. *To wave, shake,* נוּף *nuph,* 5.
Exod 29. 24 shalt wave them (for) a..offering before
29. 26 and wave it (for) a..offering before the L.
Lev. 7. 30 bring, that the breast may be waved (for)
8. 27 waved them (for) a..offering before the L.
8. 29 Moses took the breast, and waved it (for)
9. 21 and the right shoulder Aaron waved (for)
10. 15 to wave (it for) a..offering before the L.
14. 12 wave them (for) a..offering before the L.
14. 24 the priest shall wave them (for) a..offer.
23. 11 wave the sheaf..the priest shall wave it
23. 12 ye shall offer that day when ye wave the
23. 20 the priest shall wave them with the bread
Num. 5. 25 shall wave the offering before the LORD
6. 20 the priest shall wave them (for) a..offer.

2. *To be waved,* נוּף *nuph,* 6.
Exod 29. 27 which is waved, and which is heaved up

3. *Wave offering, shaking,* תְּנוּפָה *tenuphah.*
Lev. 14. 21 he shall take one lamb..to be waved, to

4. *To judge diversely, hesitatingly,* διακρίνω *diakrinō.*
Jas. 1. 6 nothing wavering. For he that wavereth

WAVE (offering), without wavering —

1. *Wave offering, shaking,* תְּנוּפָה *tenuphah.*
Exod 29. 24 them (for) a wave offering before the Lo.
29. 26 wave it (for) a wave offering before the L.
29. 27 sanctify the breast of the wave offering
Lev. 7. 30 the breast may be..(for) a wave offering
7. 34 the wave breast and the heave shoulder
8. 27, 29 (for) a wave offering before the LORD
9. 21 Aaron waved (for) a wave offering before
10. 14 the wave breast and heave shoulder shall
10. 15 the wave breast..a wave offering before
14. 12, 24 (for) a wave offering before the LORD
23. 15 ye brought the sheaf of the wave offering
23. 17 Ye shall bring..two wave loaves of two
23. 20 (for) a wave offering before the LORD, with
Num. 6. 20 a wave offering..with the wave breast
18. 11 with all the wave offerings of the children
18. 18 as the wave breast and as the right shou.

2. *Without inclining or bending,* ἀκλινής *aklinēs.*
Heb. 10. 23 hold fast the profession..without waver.

WAX —

Wax, דּוֹנַג *donag.*
Psa. 22. 14 my heart is like wax; it is melted in the
68. 2 as wax melteth before the fire..let the wi.
97. 5 The hills melted like wax at the presence
Mic. 1. 4 shall be cleft, as wax before the fire, (and)

WAX (louder, old, strong, warm, short), to —

1. *To go on, proceed,* הָלַךְ, יָלַךְ *yalak, halak.*
2 Sa. 3. 1 David waxed..the house of Saul waxed
1 Ch. 11. 9 David waxed greater and greater: for the
2 Ch. 17. 12 And Jehoshaphat waxed great exceeding.
Esth. 9. 4 this man Mordecai waxed greater and gr.

2. *To be or become aged,* זָקֵן *zaqen.*
Josh. 23. 1 that Joshua waxed old (and) stricken in a.
2 Ch. 24. 15 Jehoiada waxed old, and was full of days

3. *To become aged,* זָקֵן *zaqen,* 5.
Job 14. 8 Though the root thereof wax old in the

4. *To be melted, to flow,* זָרַב *zarab,* 4.
Job 6. 17 What time they wax warm, they vanish

5. *Strong, hard, loud,* חָזֵק *chazeq.*
Exod 19. 19 when the voice..waxed louder and louder

6. *To reap, shorten,* קָצַר *qatsar.*
Num 11. 23 Is the LORD's hand waxed short? thou sh.

7. *To become aged,* γηράσκω *gēraskō.*
Heb. 8. 13 Now that which decayeth and waxeth old

8. *To become,* γίνομαι *ginomai.*
Luke 13. 19 and it grew, and waxed a great tree
Heb. 11. 34 waxed valiant in fight, turned to flight the

9. *To strike forward, advance,* προκόπτω *prokoptō.*
2 Ti. 3. 13 evil men and seducers shall wax worse and

10. *To strengthen, make strong,* κραταιόω *krataioō.*
Luke 1. 80 the child grew, and waxed strong in spirit
2. 40 the child grew, and waxed strong in spirit
[*See also* Bold, cold, confident, dim, faint, fat, feeble, great, gross, hot, lean, mighty, old, pale, rich, sore, strong, wanton, warm.]

WAY —

1. *Customary or ordinary path or way,* אֹרַח *orach.*
Job 16. 22 then I shall go the way..I shall not retu.
19. 8 He hath fenced up my way that I cannot
22. 15 Hast thou marked the old way which wi.
30. 12 they raise up against me the ways of their
34. 11 cause. .man to find according to (his) ways
Psa. 44. 18 neither have . . declined from thy way
119. 9 Where withal shall . . man cleanse his way
119. 15 meditate. .and have respect unto thy w.
119. 101 I have refrained my feet from every. .w.
119. 104 Through thy precepts..I hate every fa..w.
119. 128 (to be) right; (and) I hate every false way
142. 3 in the way wherein I walked have they
Prov. 1. 19 So (are) the ways of every one that is gr
2. 15 Whose ways (are) crooked, and (they) fr.
4. 14 the wicked, and go not in the way of evil
8. 20 I lead in the way of righteousness, in the
9. 15 call passengers who go right on their ways
10. 17 He (is in) the way of life that keepeth in
12. 28 In the way of righteousness (is) life, and
15. 10 grievous unto him that forsaketh the way
15. 19 but the way of the righteous (is) made pl.
15. 24 The way of life (is) above to the wise, that
17. 23 taketh a gift..to pervert the ways of jud.
22. 25 Lest thou learn his ways, and get a snare
Isa. 26. 7 The way of the just (is) uprightness · thou
26. 8 in the way of thy judgments, O LORD. have
30. 11 Get you out of the way, turn aside out of
41. 3 by the way..he had not gone with his feet

2. *Customary path or way,* אָרְחָא *orcha.*
Dan. 4. 37 whose works (are) truth, and his ways ju.
5. 23 the God..whose (are) all thy ways, hast

3. *Earth, land, ground,* אֶרֶץ *erets.*
Gen. 35. 16 there was but a little way to
48. 7 but a little way to come unto Ephrath
2 Ki. 5. 19 Go..So he departed from him a little way

4. *To go or come in,* בּוֹא *bo.*
Gen. 24. 62 Isaac came from the way of the well La.

5. *Trodden path or way,* דֶּרֶךְ *derek.*
Gen. 3. 24 flaming sword..to keep the way of the
6. 12 all flesh had corrupted his way upon the
16. 7 found her..by the fountain in the way to
18. 19 they shall keep the way of the LORD, to
19. 2 ye shall rise up early, and go on your w.
24. 27 I..in the way, the LORD led me to the ho.
24. 40 his angel with thee, and prosper thy way
24. 42 if now thou do prosper my way which I
24. 48 which had led me in the right way to take
24. 56 seeing the LORD hath prospered my way
28. 20 If God..will keep me in this way that I
32. 1 Jacob went on his way, and the angels of
33. 16 Esau returned that day on his way unto S.
35. 3 and was with me in the way which I went
35. 19 Rachel died, and was buried in the way
38. 14 sat in an open place, which (is) by the way
38. 16 he turned unto her by the way, and said
42. 25 and to give them provision for the way
42. 38 if mischief befall him by the way in the
45. 21 Joseph..gave them provision for the way
45. 23 bread and meat for his father by the way
45. 24 said..See that ye fall not out by the way
48. 7 R. died..in the land of Canaan in the way
48. 7 I buried her there in the way of Ephrath
49. 17 Dan shall be a serpent by the way, an ad.
Exod. 4. 24 it came to pass by the way in the inn, that
13. 17 God led them not..the way of the land
13. 18 the way of the wilderness of the Red sea
13. 21 went before them. .to lead them the way
18. 8 all. .that had come upon them by the way
18. 20 shalt show them the way wherein they
23. 20 I send an angel. .to keep thee in the way
32. 8 They have turned aside. .out of the way
33. 3 I will not. .lest I consume thee in the w.
33. 13 show me now thy way, that I may know
Lev. 26. 22 I will..send wild beasts..and your..ways
Num. 14. 25 the wilderness by the way of the Red sea
20. 17 we will go by the king's (high) way, we
21. 1 that Israel came by the way of the spies
21. 4 way of the Red sea..because of the way
21. 22 we will go along by the king's (high) way
21. 33 they turned, and went up by the way of
22. 22 the angel of the LORD stood in the way for
22. 23, 31 angel of the LORD standing in the way
22. 23 the ass turned aside out of the way, and
22. 23 smote the ass, to turn her into the way
22. 26 where (was) no way to turn either to the
22. 32 because (thy) way is perverse before me
22. 34 that thou stoodest in the way against me
24. 25 Balaam rose up..Balak also went his way
Deut. 1. 2 from Horeb by the way of Mount Seir unto
1. 19 which ye saw by the way of the mountain
1. 22 bring us word again by what way we must
1. 31 in all the way that ye went, until ye came
1. 33 went in the way..by what way ye should
1. 40 take your journey..by the way of the Red
2. 1 took our journey..by the way of the Red
2. 8 through the way..passed by the way of
3. 1 we turned, and went up the way to Bash.
5. 33 Ye shall walk in all the ways which the
6. 7 when thou walkest by the way, and when
8. 2 thou shalt remember all the way which

Deut. 8. 6 to walk in his ways, and to fear him
9. 12 quickly turned aside out of the way which
9. 16 turned aside quickly out of the way which
10. 12 to walk in all his ways, and to love him
11. 19 when thou walkest by the way, when
11. 22 to walk in all his ways, and to cleave unto
11. 28 turn aside out of the way which I command
11. 30 by the way where the sun goeth down, in
13. 5 to thrust thee out of the way which the L.
14. 24 if the way be too long for thee, so that th.
17. 16 shall henceforth return no more that way
19. 3 Thou shalt prepare thee a way, and divide
19. 6 overtake him, because the way is long, and
19. 9 to love..and to walk ever in his ways
22. 4 not see..his ox fall down by the way
22. 6 chance to be before thee in the way in any
23. 4 met you not..with water in the way
24. 9 LORD thy God did unto Miriam by the way
25. 17 Remember what Amalek did..by the way
25. 18 he met thee by the way, and smote the
26. 17 to walk in his ways, and to keep his stat.
27. 18 maketh the blind to wander out of the w.
28. 7 one way, and flee before thee seven ways
28. 9 thou shalt keep. .and walk in his ways
28. 25 go out one way. .and flee seven ways before
28. 29 thou shalt not prosper in thy ways: and
28. 68 by the way whereof I spake unto thee, T.
30. 16 to walk in his ways, and to keep his com.
31. 29 turn aside from the way which I have co.
32. 4 his work (is) perfect; for all his ways (are)
Josh. 1. 8 thou shalt make thy way prosperous, and
2. 7 the men pursued after them the way to
2. 16 and afterward may ye go your way
2. 22 pursuers sought (them)..all the way, but
3. 4 know the way..have not passed (this) wa.
5. 4, 5 in the wilderness by the way as they
5. 7 had not circumcised them by the way
8. 15 and fled by the way of the wilderness
10. 10 chased them along the way that goeth up
12. 3 the salt sea on the east, the way to Beth.
22. 5 to walk in all his ways, and to keep his
23. 14 this day I (am) going the way of all the
24. 17 preserved us in all the way wherein we
Judg. 2. 17 they turned quickly out of the way which
2. 19 they ceased not..from their stubborn way
2. 22 whether they will keep the way of the Lo.
5. 10 sit in judgment, and walk by the way
8. 11 Gideon went up by the way of them that
9. 25 robbed all that came along that way by
18. 5 we may know whether our way which we
18. 6 before the LORD (is) your way wherein ye
18. 26 And the children of Dan went their way
19. 9 get you early on your way, that thou ma.
19. 27 opened the doors..to go his way; and, be.
20. 42 they turned. .unto the way of the wildern.
Ruth 1. 7 they went on the way to return unto the
1 Sa. 1. 18 the woman went her way, and did eat
6. 9 if it goeth up by the way of his own coast
6. 12 the kine took the straight way to the way
8. 3 his sons walked not in his ways, but turn.
8. 5 thy sons walk not in thy ways: now make
9. 6 he can show us our way that we should
9. 8 give to the man of God to tell us our way
12. 23 will teach you the good and the right wa.
13. 17 one company turned unto the way..unto
13. 18 turned the way (to) B...turned (to) the w.
15. 2 Amalek..how he laid..for him in the way
15. 20 have gone the way which the LORD sent
17. 52 wounded..fell down by the way to Shaa.
18. 14 D. behaved himself wisely in all his ways
24. 3 he came to the sheep cotes by the way
24. 7 But Saul rose up..and went on (his) way
25. 12 David's young men turned their way, and
26. 3 which (is) before Jeshimon, by the way
26. 25 David went on his way, and Saul returned
28. 22 have strength when thou goest on thy way
30. 2 but carried..away, and went on their way
2 Sa. 2. 24 by the way of the wilderness of Gibeon
13. 30 it came to pass, while they were in the w.
13. 34 by the way of the hill side behind him
15. 2 Absalom..stood beside the way of the gate
15. 23 the people passed over, toward the way of
16. 13 And as David and his men went by the w.
18. 23 Ahimaaz ran by the way of the plain, and
22. 22 For I have kept the ways of the LORD
22. 31 God, his way (is) perfect; the word of the
22. 33 God (is) my strength..he maketh my way
1 Ki. 1. 49 all..rose up, and went every man his way
2. 2 I go the way of all the earth: be thou str.
2. 3 to walk in his ways, to keep his statutes
2. 4 If thy children take heed to their way, to
3. 14 if thou wilt walk in my ways, to keep
8. 25 that thy children take heed to their way
8. 32 condemning the wicked, to bring his w.
8. 36 that thou teach them the good way whe.
8. 39 give to every man according to his ways
8. 58 to walk in all his ways, and to keep his
11. 29 Ahijah the Shilonite found him in the w.
11. 33 and have not walked in my ways, to do
11. 38 wilt walk in my ways, and do..right in
13. 9 nor turn again by the same way that thou
13. 10 he went another way..not by the way
13. 12 What way went he?..had seen what way
13. 17 nor turn again to go by the way that thou
13. 24 a lion met him by the way, and slew him
13. 24 his carcase (was) cast in the way, and the
13. 25 saw the carcase cast in the way, and the
13. 26 that brought him back from the way hea.
13. 28 he went and found his carcase cast in the w.
13. 33 Jeroboam returned not from his evil way
15. 26 walked in the way of his father, and in
15. 34 walked in the way of Jeroboam, and in

1 Ki. 16. 2 thou hast walked in the way of Jeroboam
16. 19 in walking in the way of Jeroboam, and
16. 26 he walked in all the way of Jeroboam the
18. 6 went one way..Obadiah went another w.
18. 7 as Obadiah was in the way, behold, Eli.
19. 15 Go, return on thy way to the wilderness
20. 38 and waited for the king by the way, and
22. 43 he walked in all the ways of Asa his fath.
22. 52 walked in the way of his father, and in
22. 52 the way of his mother, and in the way of
2 Ki. 2. 23 as he was going up by the way, there came
3. 8 Which way..he answered, The way thro.
3. 20 there came water by the way of Edom
6. 19 This (is) not the way, neither (is) this the
7. 15 all the way (was) full of garments and ve.
8. 18, 27 And he walked in the way of the
9. 27 Ahaziah..fled by the way of the garden
10. 12 he (was) at the shearing house in the way
11. 16 and she went by the way by the which
11. 19 came by the way of the gate of the guard
16. 3 he walked in the way of the kings of Isr.
17. 13 Turn ye from your evil ways, and keep
19. 28 I will turn thee back by the way by wh.
19. 33 By the way that he came, by the same
21. 21 he walked in all the way that his father
21. 22 and walked not in the way of the LORD
22. 2 walked in all the way of David his father
25. 4 by the way of the gate between two walls
25. 4 (the king) went the way toward the plain
2 Ch. 6. 16 that thy children take heed to their way
6. 23 recompensing his way upon his own head
6. 27 when thou hast taught them the good way
6. 30 unto every man according unto all his w.
6. 31 to walk in thy ways, so long as they live
6. 34 go..by the way that thou shalt send th.
7. 14 If my people..turn from their wicked w.
11. 17 for three years they walked in the way of
13. 22 the rest of the acts of Abijah, and his w.
17. 3 he walked in the first ways of his father
17. 6 his heart was lifted up in the ways of the
18. 23 Which way went the spirit of the LORD
20. 32 he walked in the way of Asa his father
21. 6 he walked in the way of the kings of I.
21. 12 not walked in the ways..nor in the ways
21. 13 hast walked in the way of the kings of Is.
22. 3 He also walked in the ways of the house
27. 6 he prepared his ways before the LORD his
27. 7 all his wars, and his ways, lo, they (are)
28. 2 he walked in the ways of the kings of Is.
28. 26 the rest of his acts and of all his ways
34. 2 walked in the ways of David his father
Ezra 8. 21 to seek of him a right way for us, and for
8. 22 to help us against the enemy in the way
8. 31 and of such as lay in wait by the way
Neh. 9. 12 to give them light in the way wherein th.
9. 19 lead them in the way..the way wherein
Job 3. 23 (Why is light given) to a man whose way
4. 6 thy hope, and the uprightness of thy wa.
6. 18 The paths of their way are turned aside
8. 19 this (is) the joy of his way, and out of the
12. 24 in a wilderness (where there is) no way
13. 15 I will maintain mine own ways before him
17. 9 The righteous also shall hold on his way
19. 12 raise up their way against me, and encamp
21. 14 we desire not the knowledge of thy ways
21. 29 Have ye not asked them..by the way? and
21. 31 Who shall declare his way to his face? and
22. 3 that thou makest thy ways perfect?
22. 28 and the light shall shine upon thy ways
23. 10 he knoweth the way that I take: (when)
23. 11 My foot hath held his steps, his way have
24. 4 They turn the needy out of the way: the
24. 13 they know not the ways thereof, nor abide
24. 18 he beholdeth not the way of the vineyards
24. 23 resteth, yet his eyes (are) upon their ways
26. 14 these (are) parts of his ways; but how li.
28. 23 God understandeth the way thereof, and
28. 26 and a way for the lightning of the thun.
29. 25 I chose out their way, and sat chief, and
31. 4 Doth not he see my ways, and count all
31. 7 If my step hath turned out of the way
34. 21 his eyes (are) upon the ways of man, and
34. 27 and would not consider any of his ways
36. 23 Who hath enjoined him his way? or who
38. 19 Where (is) the way (where) light dwelle.?
38. 24 By what way is the light parted, (which)
38. 25 or a way for the lightning of thunder
40. 19 He (is) the chief of the ways of God: he th.
Psa. 1. 1 nor standeth in the way of sinners, nor
1. 6 the way of the righteous: but the way of
2. 12 ye perish (from) the way, when his wrath
5. 8 make thy way straight before my face
10. 5 His ways are always grievous; thy judg.
18. 21 I have kept the ways of the LORD, and ha.
18. 30 (As for) God, his way (is) perfect: the word
18. 32 (It is) God that..maketh my way perfect
25. 4 Show me thy ways, O LORD; teach me thy
25. 8 therefore will he teach..in the way
25. 9 and the meek will he teach his way
25. 12 him shall he teach in the way (that) he sh.
27. 11 Teach me thy way, O LORD, and lead me
32. 8 teach thee in the way which thou shalt go
35. 6 Let their way be dark and slippery: and
36. 4 he setteth himself in a way (that is) not
37. 5 Commit thy way unto the LORD; trust also
37. 7 because of him who prospereth in his way
37. 23 a (good) man..he delighteth in his way
37. 34 Wait on the LORD, and keep his way, and
39. 1 I will take heed to my ways, that I sin not
49. 13 This their way (is) their folly: yet their
51. 13 Then will I teach transgressors thy ways
67. 2 That thy way may be known upon

Psa. 77. 13 Thy way, O God, (is) in the sanctuary: who
77. 19 Thy way (is) in the sea, and thy path in the
80. 12 all they which pass by the way do pluck
81. 13 Oh that..Israel had walked in my ways
85. 13 and shall set (us) in the way of his steps
86. 11 Teach me thy way, O LORD; I will walk
89. 41 All that pass by the way spoil him: he is
91. 11 charge over thee, to keep thee in..thy ways
95. 10 do err..they have not known my ways
101. 2 will behave myself wisely in a perfect way
101. 6 he that walketh in a perfect way, he shall
102. 23 He weakened my strength in the way; he
103. 7 He made known his ways unto Moses, his
107. 4 wandered in..wilderness in a solitary way
107. 7 he led them forth by the right way, that
107. 40 in the wilderness, where (there is) no way
110. 7 He shall drink of the brook in the way, the
119. 1 Blessed (are) the undefiled in the way, who
119. 3 also do no iniquity: they walk in his ways
119. 5 O that my ways were directed to keep thy
119. 14 I have rejoiced in the way of thy testim.
119. 26 I have declared my ways, and thou heard.
119. 27 Make me to understand the way of thy pr.
119. 29 Remove from me the way of lying; and
119. 30 I have chosen the way of truth; thy jud.
119. 32 I will run the way of thy commandments
119. 33 Teach me, O LORD, the way of thy statutes
119. 37 vanity; (and) quicken thou me in thy w.
119. 59 I thought on my ways, and turned my fe.
119. 168 testimonies; for all my ways (are) before
128. 1 that feareth, that walketh in his ways
138. 5 they shall sing in the ways of the LORD
139. 3 Thou..art acquainted (with) all my ways
139. 24 any) wicked way..lead me in the way ev.
143. 8 cause me to know the way wherein I should
145. 17 The LORD (is) righteous in all his ways, and
146. 9 the way of the wicked he turneth upside
Prov. 1. 15 My son, walk not thou in the way with
1. 31 they eat of the fruit of their own way, and
2. 8 He keepeth..and preserveth the way of
2. 12 To deliver thee from the way of the evil
2. 13 Who leave..to walk in the ways of darkn.
2. 20 That thou mayest walk in the way of good
3. 6 In all thy ways acknowledge him, and he
3. 17 Her ways (are) ways of pleasantness, and
3. 23 Then shalt thou walk in thy way safely
3. 31 Envy thou not..and choose none of his w.
4. 11 I have taught thee in the way of wisdom
4. 14 Enter not..go not into the way of evil (men)
4. 19 The way of the wicked (is) as darkness, th.
4. 26 Ponder..and let all thy ways be established
5. 8 Remove thy way far from her, and come
5. 21 the ways of man (are) before the eyes of
6. 6 Go to the ant..consider her ways, and be
6. 23 reproofs of instruction (are) the way of life
7. 8 Passing..he went the way to her house
7. 25 Let not thine heart decline to her ways, go
7. 27 Her house (is) the way to hell, going down
8. 2 She standeth..by the way in the places of
8. 13 the evil way, and the froward mouth, do I
8. 22 possessed me in the beginning of his way
8. 32 for blessed (are they that) keep my ways
9. 6 Forsake the foolish, and live; and go in..w.
10. 9 he that perverteth his ways shall be kno.
10. 29 The way of the LORD (is) strength to the
11. 5 righteousness..shall direct his way, but
11. 20 (such as are) upright in (their) way (are)
12. 15 The way of a fool (is) right in his own ey.
12. 26 but the way of the wicked seduceth them
13. 6 keepeth (him that is) upright in the way
13. 15 giveth favour: but the way of transgressors
14. 2 (he that is) perverse in his ways despiseth
14. 8 wisdom..(is) to understand his way, but
14. 12 There is a way..the end..the ways of death
14. 14 The backslider..filled with his own ways
15. 9 The way of the wicked (is) an abomination
15. 19 The way of the slothful..the way of the ri.
16. 2 All the ways of a man (are) clean in his
16. 7 When a man's ways please the LORD, he
16. 9 A man's heart deviseth his way: but the
16. 17 he that keepeth his way preserveth his soul
16. 25 There is a way..the end..the ways of death
16. 29 leadeth him into the way (that is) not go.
16. 31 (if) it be found in the way of righteousness
19. 3 The foolishness of man perverteth his way
19. 16 (but) he that despiseth his ways shall die
20. 24 can a man then understand his own way?
21. 2 Every way of a man (is) right in his own
21. 8 The way of man (is) froward and strange
21. 16 The man that wandereth out of the way
21. 29 (as for) the upright, he directeth his way
22. 5 Thorns (and) snares are in the way of the
22. 6 Train up a child in the way he should go
23. 19 be wise, and guide thine heart in the way
23. 26 My son..let thine eyes observe my ways
26. 13 (There is) a lion in the way; a lion (is) in
28. 6 than (he that is) perverse (in his) ways, th.
28. 10 the righteous to go astray in an evil way
28. 18 (he that is) perverse (in his) ways shall fa.
29. 27 (he that is) upright in the way (is) abomin.
30. 19 The way of an eagle..the way of a serpent
30. 19 the way of a ship..the way of a man with
30. 20 Such (is) the way of an adulterous woman
31. 3 nor thy ways to that which destroyeth ki.
Eccl. 10. 3 when he that is a fool walketh by the way
11. 5 As thou knowest not what (is) the way of
11. 9 walk in the ways of thine heart, and in
12. 5 fears (shall be) in the way, and the almond.
Isa. 2. 3 he will teach us of his ways, and we will
3. 12 cause (thee) to err, and destroy the way
8. 11 that I should not walk in the way of this
9. 1 did more grievously afflict (her by) the way

Isa. 15. 5 in the way of Horonaim they shall raise
30. 11 Get you out of the way, turn aside out of
30. 21 This (is) the way, walk ye in it, when ye
35. 8 a way, and it shall be called the way of
37. 29 I will turn thee back by the way by which
37. 34 By the way that he came, by the same sh.
40. 3 Prepare ye the way of the LORD, make st.
40. 14 showed to him the way of understanding
40. 27 My way is hid from the LORD, and my ju.
42. 16 I will bring the blind by a way (that) they
42. 24 they would not walk in his ways, neither
43. 16 Thus saith the LORD, which maketh a way
43. 19 I will even make a way in the wilderness
45. 13 I will direct all his ways: he shall build
48. 15 I have spoken..he shall make his way pr.
48. 17 which leadeth thee by the way..thou sh.
49. 9 They shall feed in the ways, and their pa.
49. 11 I will make all my mountains a way, and
51. 10 that hath made the depth of the sea a w.
53. 6 we have turned every one to his own way
55. 7 Let the wicked forsake his way, and the
55. 8 neither (are) your ways my ways, saith
55. 9 so are my ways higher than your ways, and
56. 11 they all look to their own way, every one
57. 10 art wearied in the greatness of thy way
57. 14 prepare the way..take up..out of the w.
57. 17 went on frowardly in the way of his heart
57. 18 I have seen his ways, and will heal him
58. 2 delight to know my ways, as a nation that
58. 13 not doing thine own ways, nor finding
59. 8 The way of peace they know not, and (th.
62. 10 prepare ye the way of the people; cast up
63. 17 why hast thou made us to err from thy w.
64. 5 (those that) remember thee in thy ways
65. 2 rebellious people, which walketh in a way
66. 3 they have chosen their own ways, and th.
Jer. 2. 17 forsaken..when he led thee by the way?
2. 18 in the way of Egypt..in the way of Assy.
2. 23 thy way..a dromedary traversing her ways
2. 33 Why trimmest thou thy way to seek love?
2. 33 wherefore hast thou also taught..thy wa.?
2. 36 Why gaddest thou about..to change thy w.?
3. 2 in the ways hast thou sat for them, as the
3. 13 hast scattered thy ways to the strangers
3. 21 they have perverted their way..they have
4. 18 Thy way and thy doings have procured
5. 4 for they know not the way of the LORD
5. 5 they have known the way of the LORD
6. 16 Stand ye in the ways..the good way, and
6. 25 Go not forth..nor walk by the way, for
6. 27 that thou mayest know and try their way
7. 3 Amend your ways and your doings, and
7. 5 For if ye throughly amend your ways and
7. 23 walk ye in all the ways that I have com.
10. 2 Learn not the way of the heathen, and be
10. 23 I know that the way of man (is) not in
12. 1 Wherefore doth the way of the wicked pr.?
12. 16 if they will diligently learn the ways of
15. 7 (since) they return not from their ways
16. 17 For mine eyes (are) upon all their ways
17. 10 to give every man according to his ways
18. 11 from his evil way, and make your ways
18. 15 to stumble in their ways..a way not cast
21. 8 set..the way of life, and the way of death
23. 12 Wherefore their way shall be unto them
23. 22 have turned them from their evil way, and
25. 5 Turn ye again..every one from his evil w.
26. 3 and turn every man from his evil way
26. 13 Therefore now amend your ways and your
28. 11 And the prophet Jeremiah went his way
31. 9 by the rivers of waters in a straight way
31. 21 set thine heart..the way (which) thou we.
32. 19 upon all the ways..according to his ways
32. 39 I will give them one heart, and one way
35. 15 Return ye..every man from his evil way
36. 3 may return every man from his evil way
36. 7 will return every one from his evil way
39. 4 the way of the King's garden..the way
42. 3 That the LORD..may show us the way wh
48. 19 O inhabitants of Aroer, stand by the way
50. 5 They shall ask the way to Zion with their
52. 7 the way of the gate..the way of the plain
Lam. 1. 4 The ways of Zion do mourn, because none
3. 9 He hath inclosed my ways with hewn st.
3. 11 He hath turned aside my ways, and pull.
3. 40 Let us search and try our ways, and turn
Eze. 3. 18 to warn the wicked from his wicked way
3. 19 his wickedness, nor from his wicked way
7. 3, 8 will judge thee according to thy ways
7. 4 I will recompense thy ways upon thee
7. 9 recompense thee according to thy ways
7. 27 I will do unto them after their way, and
8. 5 lift up thine eyes now the way toward the
8. 5 I lifted up mine eyes the way toward the
9. 2 six men came..the way of the higher gate
9. 10 I will recompense their way upon their he.
11. 21 I will recompense their way upon their
13. 22 he should not return from his wicked w.
14. 22 and ye shall see their way and their doings
14. 23 when ye see their ways and their doings
16. 25 thy high place at every head of the way
16. 27 daughters..which are ashamed of thy..w.
16. 31 eminent place in the head of every way
16. 43 I also will recompense thy way upon (th.
16. 47 Yet hast thou not walked after their ways
16. 47 corrupted more than they in all thy ways
16. 61 Then thou shalt remember thy ways, and
18. 23 not that he should return from his ways
18. 25, 29 The way of the Lord is not equal
18. 25, 29 Is not my way equal? are not your w.
18. 30 every one according to his ways, saith the
20. 43 there shall ye remember your ways, and

Eze. 20. 44 not according to your wicked ways, nor
21. 19 two ways..at the head of the way to the
21. 20 Appoint a way, that the sword may come
21. 21 of the way, at the head of the two ways
22. 31 their own way have I recompensed upon
23. 13 I saw that she was defiled..both one way
23. 31 Thou hast walked in the way of thy sister
24. 14 according to thy ways, and according to
28. 15 Thou (was) perfect in thy ways from the
33. 8 not speak to warn the wicked from his w.
33. 9 if thou warn the wicked of his way to tu.
33. 9 if he do not turn from his way, he shall
33. 11 turn from his way..from your evil ways
33. 17, 20 the way of the Lord is not equal
33. 17 but, as for them, their way is not equal
33. 20 I will judge you every one after his ways
36. 17 defiled it by their own way..their way was
36. 19 according to their way and according to
36. 31 Then shall ye remember your own evil w.
36. 32 be ashamed and confounded for your..w.
42. 1 the utter court, the way toward the north
42. 4 ten cubits breadth inward, a way of one c.
42. 11 the way before them (was) like the appear.
42. 12 a door in the head of the way..the way di.
43. 2 the glory..came from the way of the east
43. 4 the glory of the LORD came..by the way
44. 1 Then he brought me back the way of the
44. 3 he shall enter by the way of the porch of
44. 3 and shall go out by the way of the same
44. 4 Then brought he me the way of the north
46. 2 the prince shall enter by the way of the
46. 8 by the way of the porch..by the way th.
46. 9 the way of the north..the way of the so.
46. 9 the way of the south..the way of the no.
46. 9 he shall not return by the way of the gate
47. 2 the way of the gate..the way without unto
47. 2 the utter gate by the way that looketh ea.
47. 15 from the great sea, the way of Hethlon, as
48. 1 From the north end to the coast of the way
Hos. 2. 6 I will hedge up thy way with thorns, and
4. 9 I will punish them for their ways, and re.
6. 9 company of priests murder in the way by
9. 8 a snare of a fowler in all his ways..hatred
10. 13 thou didst trust in thy way, in the multi
12. 2 and will punish Jacob according to his w.
13. 7 as a leopard by the way will I observe (th.)
14. 9 the ways of the LORD (are) right, and the
Joel 2. 7 they shall march every one on his ways
Amos 2. 7 That pant..and turn aside the way of the
Jon. 3. 8 let them turn every one from his evil way
3. 10 saw..that they turned from their evil w.
Mic. 4. 2 he will teach us of his ways, and we will
Nah. 1. 3 LORD..his way in the whirlwind and in
2. 1 Keep the munition, watch the way, make
Hag. 1. 5 thus saith the LORD..Consider your ways
Zech. 1. 4 Turn ye now from your evil ways..your e.
1. 6 according to our ways, and according to
3. 7 If thou wilt walk in my ways, and if thou
Mal. 2. 8 But ye are departed out of the way, ye have
2. 9 according as ye have not kept my ways
3. 1 and he shall prepare the way before me

6. *A going, walk,* הֲלִיכָה *halikah* [V.L. Prov. הילכה].
Prov 31. 27 She looketh well to the ways of her house
Hab. 3. 6 the perpetual hills did bow: his ways (are)

7. *A track, course,* מַעְגָּלָה *magalah.*
Prov. 5. 6 her ways are moveable..thou canst not k.

8. *A trodden path or way,* נָתִיב *nathib.*
Job 18. 10 The snare is laid for him..in the way
Psa. 78. 50 He made a way to his anger; he spared

9. *Midst, middle,* μέσον, μέσος *meson, mesos.*
Col. 2. 14 took it out of the way, nailing it to his c
2 Th. 2. 7 letteth..until he be taken out of the way

10. *Way, road, journey, custom,* ὁδός *hodos.*
Matt. 2. 12 departed into their..country another w.
3. 3 Prepare ye the way of the Lord, make his
4. 15 the way of the sea, beyond Jordan, Galilee
5. 25 Agree..whiles thou art in the way with
7. 13 for wide (is) the gate, and broad (is) the w.
7. 14 strait (is) the gate, and narrow (is) the w.
8. 28 so that no man might pass by that way
10. 5 Go not into the way of the Gentiles, and
11. 10 which shall prepare thy way before thee
13. 4 when he sowed, some..fell by the way
13. 19 This is he which received seed by the way
15. 32 away fasting, lest they faint in the way
20. 17 took the twelve disciples apart in the way
20. 30 two blind men, sitting by the way side
21. 8 spread..in the way..strawed..in the way
21. 19 when he saw a fig tree in the way, he ca.
21. 32 For John came unto you in the way of ri.
22. 16 that thou..teachest the way of God in tr.
Mark 1. 2 which shall prepare thy way before thee
1. 3 Prepare ye the way of the Lord, make his
4. 4 as he sowed, some fell by the way side
4. 15 these are they by the way side, where the
8. 3 If I send them..they will faint by the way
8. 27 by the way he asked his disciples, saying
9. 33 What was it that ye disputed..by the w.?
9. 34 for [by the way] they had disputed among
10. 17 And when he was gone forth into the way
10. 32 they were in the way going up to Jerusa.
10. 52 immediately he..followed Jesus in the way
11. 8 spread..in the way..[strawed..in the w.]
12. 14 that thou..teachest the ways of God in t.
Luke 1. 76 thou shalt go before..to prepare his way
1. 79 to guide our feet into the way of peace
3. 4 Prepare ye the way of the Lord, make
3. 5 the rough ways (shall be) made smooth
7. 27 which shall prepare thy way before thee

Luke 8. 5 as he sowed, some fell by the way side
8. 12 Those by the way side are they that hear
9. 57 it came to pass. .as they went in the way
10. 4 nor shoes; and salute no man by the w.
10. 31 there came down a certain priest that w.
12. 58 in the way, give diligence that thou may.
18. 35 a certain blind man sat by the way side
19. 36 And. .they spread their clothes in the w.
20. 21 that thou. .teachest the way of God truly
24. 32 while he talked with us by the way, and
24. 35 they told what things (were done) in. .w.
John 1. 23 Make straight the way of the Lord, as sa.
14. 4 whither I go ye know, and the way ye kn.
14. 5 know not. .and how can we know the way
14. 6 I am the way, the truth, and the life
Acts 2. 28 Thou hast made known to me the ways
8. 26 unto the way that goeth down from Jer.
8. 36 as they went on (their) way, they came
8. 39 the eunuch. .went on his way rejoicing
9. 2 if he found any of this way, whether they
9. 17 Jesus, that appeared unto thee in the way
9. 27 how he had seen the Lord in the way, and
13. 10 wilt thou not cease to pervert the. .ways
14. 16 suffered all nations to walk in their. .wa.
16. 17 which show unto us the way of salvation
18. 25 This man was instructed in the way of
18. 26 expounded unto him the way of God mo
19. 9 spake evil of that way before the multit.
19. 23 there arose no small stir about that way
22. 4 And I persecuted this way unto the death
24. 14 that after the way which they call heresy
24. 22 having. .perfect knowledge of (that) way
25. 3 And. .laying wait in the way to kill him
26. 13 I saw in the way a light from heaven, ab.
Rom. 3. 16 Destruction and misery (are) in their wa
3. 17 the way of peace have they not known
11. 33 unsearchable. .and his ways past finding
1 Co. 4. 17 remembrance of my ways which be in Ch.
12. 31 yet show I unto you a more excellent way
1 Th. 3. 11 Now. .Jesus Christ, direct our way unto
Heb. 3. 10 I. .said. .they have not known my ways
9. 8 that the way into the holiest of all was
10. 20 By a new and living way, which he hath
Jas. 1. 8 a double minded man. .unstable in. .his w.
2. 25 when she. .had sent (them) out another w.
5. 20 the sinner from the error of his way shall
2 Pe. 2. 2 by reason of whom the way of truth shall
2. 15 Which have forsaken the right way, and
2. 15 are gone astray, following the way of Ba.
2. 21 better. .not to have known the way of right
Jude 11 for they have gone in the way of Cain, and
Rev. 15. 3 just and true (are) thy ways, thou king of
16. 12 that the way of the kings of the east mig.

11. *A passing along, passage,* πάροδος *parodos.*
1 Co. 16. 7 For I will not see you now by the way

12. *A passage, passage way,* πορεία *poreia.*
Jas. 1. 11 shall the rich man fade away in his ways

13. *A turn,* τρόπος *tropos.*
Rom. 3. 2 Much every way: chiefly, because that
Phil. 1. 18 notwithstanding, every way, whether in

[*See also* Bring, bring on, broad, flee, go, other, pernicious, straight, taken out, this, turn every, which.]

WAY and that way, this —
Thus and thus, כֹּה וָכֹה *koh va-koh.*
Exod. 2. 12 he looked this way and that way, and wh.

WAY (off), to be a good or great —
1. *To be or put far off,* רָחַק *rachaq,* 5.
Judg 18. 22 when they were a good way from the ho.
Gen. 21. 16 sat. .down over against (him) a good way off
2. *Far off,* πόῤῥω *porrhō.*
Luke 14. 32 while the other is yet a great way off, he
3. *Far off,* μακράν *makran.*
Matt. 8. 30 there was a good way off from them an he.
Luke 15. 20 when he was yet a great way off, his father

WAY to escape or flee —
1. *Flight, place of flight,* מָנוֹס *manos.*
Jer. 25. 35 the shepherds shall have no way to flee, nor
2. *A way or passage out,* ἔκβασις *ekbasis.*
1 Co. 10. 13 with the temptation. .make a way to esc.

WAY, to be or turn out of the —
1. *To err, wander, go astray,* תָּעָה *taah.*
Isa. 28. 7 are out of the way. .are out of the way
2. *To be turned out or aside,* ἐκτρέπομαι *ektrepomai.*
Heb. 12. 13 which is lame be turned out of the way
3. *To make to err or wander,* πλανάω *planaō.*
Heb. 5. 2 and on them that are out of the way

WAY (of), by or in the —
1. *To meet,* קָרָא *qara.*
Exod. 5. 20 Moses and Aaron, who stood in the way
2. *In,* ἐν *en.*
2 Pe. 3. 1 I stir up your pure minds by way of rem.

WAY, to be or go on the —
To remove, journey, נָסַע *nasa.*
Jer. 4. 7 the destroyer of the Gentiles is on his way
Zech 10. 2 they went their way as a flock, they were

WAYFARING man —
1. *To use the customary path,* אָרַח *arach.*
Judg 19. 17 he saw a wayfaring man in the street of
2 Sa. 12. 4 to dress for the wayfaring man that was
Jer. 9. 2 a lodging place of wayfaring men, that I
14. 8 as a wayfaring man (that) turneth aside
2. *To go on in the way,* הָלַךְ דֶּרֶךְ *halak derek.*
Isa. 35. 8 the wayfaring men, though fools, shall not
3. *To go or pass over the path,* עָבַר אֹרַח *abar orach.*
Isa. 33. 8 the wayfaring man ceaseth: he hath bro.

WAYMARK, wayside —
1. *Way or trodden path,* דֶּרֶךְ *derek.*
Gen 38. 21 Where (is) the harlot. .by the way side?
2. *The (hand or) side of the way,* יַד דֶּרֶךְ *yad derek.*
1 Sa. 4. 13 Eli sat upon a seat by the way side watch.
3. *The (hand or) side of the track,* יַד מַעְגָּל *yad magal.*
Psa. 140. 5 they have spread a net by the way side, they
4. *Sign, monument,* צִיּוּן *tsiyyun.*
Jer. 31. 21 Set thee up waymarks, make thee high he.

WE —
1. *We, we ourselves,* אָנוּ *anu.*
Jer. 42. 6 the LORD our God, to whom we send thee
2. *We, we ourselves,* אֲנַחְנָא, אֲנַחְנָה *anachna.*
Ezra 4. 16 We certify the king, that if this city be b.
5. 11 We are the servants of the God of heaven
Dan. 3. 16 we (are) not careful to answer thee in this
3. 17 God whom we serve is able to deliver us
3. *We, we ourselves,* אֲנַחְנוּ *anachnu.*
Gen. 19. 13 we will destroy this place, because the cry
2 Ch. 20. 12 neither know we what to do: but our eyes
Jer. 26. 19 Thus might we procure great evil against
4. *I, I myself,* אֲנִי *ani.*
2 Sa. 19. 43 we have also more (right) in David than
5. *We, we ourselves,* נַחְנוּ *nachnu.*
Gen. 42. 11 We (are) all one man's sons. .true (men), thy
Exod 16. 7 what (are) we, that ye murmur against us
16. 8 what (are) we? your murmurings (are) not
Num 32. 32 We will pass over armed before the LORD
2 Sa. 17. 12 we will light upon him as the dew falleth
Lam. 3. 42 We have transgressed and have rebelled
6. *Us,* ἡμᾶς *(acc.) hēmas.*
Acts 4. 12 given among men whereby we must be sa.
6. 2 It is not reason that we should leave the
14. 22 we must through much tribulation enter
21. 1 that after we were gotten from them, and
21. 5 And when we had accomplished those days
27. 1 when it was determined that we should
27. 20 all hope that we should be saved was then
27. 26 Howbeit we must be cast upon a certain
Rom. 3. 8 as some affirm that we say, Let us do evil
6. 6 that henceforth we should not serve sin
7. 6 that [we] should serve in newness of spi.
1 Co. 10. 6 to the intent we should not lust after evil
2 Co. 1. 4 that we may be able to comfort them
1. 8 insomuch that we despaired even of life
5. 10 For we must all appear before the judg.
8. 4 Praying us with much entreaty that [we]
8. 6 Insomuch that we desired Titus, that as
Eph. 1. 4 that we should be holy and without blame
1. 12 That we should be to the praise of his gl.
2. 5 Even when we were dead in sins, hath qu.
1 Th. 1. 8 so that we need not to speak any thing
2 Th. 1. 4 So that we ourselves glory in you in the
Heb. 2. 1 Therefore we ought to give the more ear.
13. 6 So that we may boldly say, The Lord (is)
Jas. 1. 18 that we should be a kind of first fruits
7. *We, we ourselves,* ἡμεῖς *(pl.) hēmeis.*
Matt. 6. 12 forgive us our debts, as we forgive our d.
9. 14 Why do we and the Pharisees fast oft, but
17. 19 and said, Why could not we cast him out?
19. 27 Behold, we have forsaken all, and followed
28. 14 if this come to the governor's ears, we will

See also Mark 9. 28; 10. 28; 14. 58; Luke 3. 14; 9. 13; 18. 18; 23. 41; 24. 21; John 1. 16; 4. 22; 6. 42, 69; 7. 35; 8. 41, 48; 9. 21, 24, 28, 29, 40; 12. 34; 17. 11, 22; 19. 7; 21. 3; Acts 2. 8, 32; 3. 15; 4. 9, 20; 5. 32; 6. 4; 10. 33, 39, 47; 13. 32; 14. 15; 15. 10; 20. 6, 13; 21. 7, 12, 25; 23. 15; 24. 8; 28. 21; Rom. 6. 4; 8. [23]; 15. 1; 1 Co. 1. 23; 2. 12, 16; 4. 8, 10, 10, 10; 8. 6, 6; 9. 11, 11, 12, 25; 11. 16; 12. 13; 15. 30, 52; 2 Co. 1. 6; 3. 18; 4. 11, 13; 5. 16, 21; 9. 4; 10. 7, 13; 11. 12, 21; 13. 4, 6, 7, 7, 9; Gal. 1. 8; 2. 9, 15, 16; 4. 3, [28]; 5. 5; Eph. 2. 3; Phil. 3. 3; Col. 1. 9, 28; 1 Th. 2. 13, 17; 3. 6, 12; 4. 15, 17; 5. 8; 2 Th. 2. 13; Titus 3. 5; Heb. 2. 3; 3. 6; 10. 39; 12. 25; 2 Pe. 1. 18; 1 Jo. 3. 14, 16; 4. 6, 10, 11, 14, 16, 17, 19; 3 Jo. 8, 12.

8. *To us,* ἡμῖν *(dat. pl.) hēmin.*
Matt. 8. 29 What have we to do with thee, Jesus, th.
15. 33 Whence should we have so much bread
19. 27 said unto him. .what shall we have there.?
Mark 1. 24 what have we to do with thee, thou Jesus
Luke 4. 34 what have we to do with thee. .Jesus of N.
9. 13 We have no more but five loaves and two
Acts 21. 23 We have four men which have a vow
28. 22 we know that every where it is spoken ag.
Eph. 6. 12 For [we] wrestle not against flesh and bl.
Heb. 4. 13 unto the eyes of him with whom we have
5. 11 of whom we have many things to say, and
12. 1 Wherefore seeing we also are compassed
Jas. 5. 17 was a man subject to like passions as we
9. *Of us, our,* ἡμῶν *(gen. pl.) hēmōn.*
Matt. 28. 13 His disciples. .stole him. .while we slept
Acts 16. 16 it came to pass. .as we went to prayer, a
21. 10 as [we] tarried. .many days, there came do.
21. 17 when we were come to Jerusalem, the br.
26. 14 when we were all fallen to the earth, I he.
27. 18 we being exceedingly tossed with a temp.
27. 27 as we were driven up and down in Adria
Rom. 5. 6 For when we were yet without strength
5. 8 while we were yet sinners Christ died for
2 Co. 4. 18 While we look not at the things which are
7. 5 For, when we were come into Macedonia
Heb. 10. 26 For if we sin wilfully. .there remaineth no

WE ourselves —
We, we ourselves, ἡμεῖς *hēmeis.*
Titus 3. 3 For we ourselves also were sometimes fool.

WEAK (thing), weaker, weakness —
1. *To be weak,* אָמַל *amal.*
Eze. 16. 30 How weak is thine heart, saith the Lord
2. *Weak,* אֻמְלַל *umlal.*
Psa. 6. 2 Have mercy upon me, O LORD; for I (am) w.
3. *Lean, poor, weak,* דַּל *dal.*
2 Sa. 3. 1 house of Saul waxed weaker and weaker
4. *Weak, overcome,* חַלָּשׁ *challash.*
Joel 3. 10 into spears: let the weak say, I (am) str.
5. *Tender, soft, timid,* רַךְ *rak.*
2 Sa. 3. 39 I (am) this day weak, though anointed ki.
6. *Feeble, remiss,* רָפֶה *rapheh.*
Num. 13. 18 whether they (be) strong or weak, few or
2 Sa. 17. 2 I will come upon him while he (is). .weak
Job 4. 3 and thou hast strengthened the weak ha.
Isa. 35. 3 Strengthen ye the weak hands, and confi.
7. *Unable, not able,* ἀδύνατος *adunatos.*
Rom 15. 1 ought to bear the infirmities of the weak
8. *To be without strength,* ἀσθενέω *astheneō.*
Acts 20. 35 so labouring ye ought to support the weak
1 Co. 8. 11 through thy knowledge shall the weak br
8. 12 But when ye. .wound their weak conscie.
9. *Without strength,* ἀσθενής *asthenēs.*
Matt 26. 41 spirit. .(is) willing, but the flesh (is) weak
Mark 14. 38 spirit. .(is) ready, but the flesh (is) weak
1 Co. 1. 25 the weakness of God is stronger than men
1. 27 [God hath chosen the weak things of the]
4. 10 we (are) weak, but ye (are) strong: ye (are)
8. 7 and their conscience being weak is defiled
8. 10 shall not the conscience of him which is w.
9. 22 the weak. .as weak. .might gain the weak
11. 30 For this cause many (are) weak and sickly
2 Co. 10. 10 bodily presence (is) weak, and (his) speech
Gal. 4. 9 how turn ye again to the weak and begg.
1 Th. 5. 14 support the weak, be patient toward all
Heb. 7. 18 for the weakness and unprofitableness th.
10. *With less strength,* ἀσθενέστερος *asthenesteros.*
1 Pe. 3. 7 honour unto the wife, as unto the weaker
11. *Strengthlessness,* ἀσθένεια *astheneia.*
1 Co. 2. 3 I was with you in weakness, and in fear
15. 43 it is sown in weakness; it is raised in po.
2 Co. 12. 9 my strength is made perfect in weakness
13. 4 though he was crucified through weakness
Heb. 11 34 out of weakness were made strong, waxed

WEAK, to be, become, be made, be weakened —
1. *To be weak,* חָלָה *chalah.*
Judg 16. 7, 11 then shall I be weak, and be as anot.
16. 17 I shall become weak, and be like any
2. *To become weak,* חָלָה *chalah,* 4.
Isa. 14. 10 Art thou also become weak as we? art
3. *To weaken, overcome, be weak,* חָלַשׁ *chalash.*
Isa. 14. 12 cut down. .which didst weaken the nations
4. *To go on, proceed,* יָלַךְ *yalak.*
Eze. 7. 17 All hands shall be feeble, and all. .weak
21. 7 cometh. all knees shall be weak (as) wat.
5. *To stumble,* כָּשַׁל *kashal.*
Psa. 109. 24 My knees are weak through fasting, and
6. *To humble, afflict,* עָנָה *anah,* 3.
Psa. 102. 23 He weakened my strength in the way, he
7. *Feeble, remiss,* רָפֶה *rapheh.*
2 Ch. 15. 7 Be ye strong. .let not your hands be weak
Neh. 6. 9 Their hands shall be weakened from the
8. *To enfeeble, made to fall,* רָפָה *raphah,* 3.
Ezra 4. 4 Then the people of the land weakened the
Job 12. 21 and weakeneth the strength of the mighty
Jer. 38. 4 thus he weakeneth the hands of the men
9. *To be without strength,* ἀσθενέω *astheneō.*
Rom. 4. 19 being not weak in faith, he considered not
8. 3 in that it was weak through the flesh, God
14. 1 Him that is weak in the faith receive ye
14. 2 may eat all things: another, who is weak
14. 21 stumbleth, [or is offended, or is made w.]
1 Co. 8. 9 a stumbling block [to them that are weak]
2 Co. 11. 21 I speak. .as though we had been weak
11. 29 Who is weak, and I am not weak? who
12. 10 for when I am weak, then am I strong
13. 3 which to you ward is not weak, but is
13. 4 For we also are weak in him, but we shall
13. 9 we are glad when we are weak, and ye are

WEALTH, wealthy —
1. *Wealth, substance, sufficiency,* הוֹן *hon.*
Psa. 112. 3 Wealth and riches (shall be) in his house
Prov 10. 15 The rich man's wealth (is) his strong city
13. 11 Wealth (gotten) by vanity shall be dimin.
18. 11 The rich man's wealth (is) his strong city
19. 4 Wealth maketh many friends: but the
2. *Force, might, strength,* חַיִל *chayil.*
Gen. 34. 29 all their wealth, and all their little ones
Deut. 8. 17 My power. .hath gotten me this wealth
8. 18 he that giveth thee power to get wealth
Ruth 2. 1 a mighty man of wealth, of the family of
2 Ki. 15. 20 exacted. .of all the mighty men of wealth

Job 31. 25 If I rejoiced because my wealth (was) great
Psa. 49. 6 They that trust in their wealth, and boast
49. 10 men die..and leave their wealth to others
Prov 13. 22 the wealth of the sinner (is) laid up for the
Zech. 14. 14 the wealth of all the heathen round about

3. *Good, good thing,* טוֹב *tob.*
Ezra 9. 12 nor seek their peace or their wealth for
Esth. 10. 3 seeking the wealth of his people, and spe.
Job 21. 13 They spend their days in wealth, and in

4. *Power,* כֹּחַ *koach.*
Prov. 5. 10 Lest strangers be filled with thy wealth

5. *Wealth, riches, things laid up,* נְכָסִים *nekasim.*
2 Ch. 1. 11 thou hast not asked riches, wealth, or ho.
1. 12 I will give thee riches, and wealth, and
Eccl. 5. 19 to whom God hath given riches and wea.
6. 2 to whom God hath given riches, wealth

6. *Fulness, satiety,* רְוָיָה *revayah.*
Psa. 66. 12 thou broughtest us out into a wealthy (pl.)

7. *At ease, at rest, safe,* שְׁלֵיו, שָׁלֵו *shalev.*
Jer. 49. 31 get you up unto the wealthy nation, that

8. *Prosperity, affluence,* εὐπορία *euporia.*
Acts 19. 25 know that by this craft we have our wea.

WEAN, weaned child, be weaned, to —

1. *To complete, ripen, wean,* גָּמַל *gamal.*
1 Sa. 1. 23 until thou have weaned..until she weaned
1. 24 when she had weaned him, she took him
1 Ki. 11. 20 whom Tahpenes weaned in Pharaoh's hou.
Psa. 131. 2 as a child that is weaned..a weaned child
Isa. 11. 8 the weaned child shall put his hand on the
28. 9 (them that are) weaned from..milk, (and)
Hos. 1. 8 when she had weaned Lo-ruhamah, she

2. *To be completed, ripened, weaned,* גָּמַל *gamal,* 2
Gen. 21. 8 grew, and was weaned..Isaac was weaned
1 Sa. 1. 22 (will not go up) until the child be weaned

WEAPON —

1. *A pointed weapon, or staff,* אָזֵן *azen.*
Deut 23. 13 thou shalt have a paddle upon thy weap.

2. *A vessel, utensil, instrument,* כְּלִי *keli.*
Gen. 27. 3 take, I pray thee, thy weapons, thy quiver
Num 35. 18 (if) he smite him with an hand weapon
Deut. 1. 41 ye had girded on every man his weapons
Judg 18. 11 six hundred men appointed with weapons
18. 16 men appointed with their weapons of war
18. 17 men (that were) appointed with weapons
1 Sa. 21. 8 brought my sword nor my weapons with
2 Sa. 1. 27 the mighty fallen, and the weapons of w
2 Ki. 11. 8 every man with his weapons in his hand
2 Ch. 23. 7 every man with his weapons in his hand
Eccl. 9. 18 Wisdom (is) better than weapons of war
Isa. 13. 5 the weapons of his indignation, to destroy
54. 17 No weapon that is formed against thee
Jer. 21. 4 I will turn back the weapons of war that
22. 7 I will prepare..every one with his weap
50. 25 hath brought forth the weapons of his in.
51. 20 Thou (art) my battle ax (and) weapons of
Eze. 9. 1 every man (with) his destroying weapon in
9. 2 every man a slaughter weapon in his ha.
32. 27 are gone down to hell with their weapons

3. *Armour,* נֶשֶׁק, נֵשֶׁק *nesheq.*
Job 20. 24 He shall flee from the iron weapon, (and)
Eze. 39. 9 shall set on fire and burn the weapons
39. 10 for they shall burn the weapons with fire

4. *A missile, dart,* שֶׁלַח *shelach.*
2 Ch. 23. 10 every man having his weapon in his hand
Neh. 4. 17 and with the other (hand) held a weapon

5. *Arms, instruments,* ὅπλα *hopla.*
John 18. 3 cometh thither with..torches and weapons
2 Co. 10. 4 the weapons of our warfare (are) not car

WEAR, (away, out, clothes),

1. *To wear out, trouble,* בְּלָא *bela,* 3.
Dan. 7. 25 shall wear out the saints of the Most Hi.

2. *To clothe, put on clothing,* לְבַשׁ *labash.*
Deut 22. 11 Thou shalt not wear a garment of divers
Esth. 6. 8 be brought which the king (useth) to we.
Isa. 4. 1 We will eat our own bread, and wear our
Zech. 13. 4 neither shall they wear a rough garment

3. *To fade, wear away, be empty, foolish,* נָבֵל *nabel.*
Exod 18. 18 Thou wilt surely wear away, both thou

4. *To lift or take up, bear or carry away,* נָשָׂא *nasa.*
1 Sa. 2. 28 to burn incense, to wear an ephod before
14. 3 the LORD'S priest in Shiloh, wearing an
22. 18 slew..persons that did wear a linen eph.

5. *To beat or wear away,* שָׁחַק *shachaq.*
Job 14. 19 The waters wear the stones, thou washest

6. *To be or become clothed,* ἐνδιδύσκομαι *endidusko.*
Luke 8. 27 which had devils long time, and ware no c.

7. *To incline, decline,* κλίνω *klinō.*
Luke 9. 12 when the day began to wear away, then

8. *A putting around,* περίθεσις *perithesis.*
1 Pe. 3. 3 wearing of gold, or of putting on of app.

9. *To bear, wear,* φορέω *phoreō.*
Matt 11. 8 they that wear soft (clothing) are in kin.
John 19. 5 Then came Jesus forth, wearing the cro.
Jas. 2. 3 ye have respect to him that weareth the

WEARIED, weary (self), to be, make —

1. *To press, make heavy,* טָרַח *tarach,* 5.
Job 37. 11 Also by watering he wearieth the thick

2. *To labour, be wearied, fatigued,* יָגַע *yaga.*
2 Sa. 23. 10 until his hand was weary, and his hand
Psa. 6. 6 I am weary with my groaning; all the
69. 3 I am weary of my crying; my throat is d.
Isa. 40. 28 the creator..fainteth not, neither is wea.
40. 30 Even the youths shall faint and be weary
40. 31 they that wait..shall run, and not be we.
43. 22 but thou hast been weary of me, O Israel
57. 10 Thou art wearied in the greatness of thy

3. *To make to labour, make weary,* יָגַע *yaga,* 3
Eccl. 10. 15 foolish wearieth every one of them

4. *To cause to labour, weary, be wearied,* יָגַע *yaga,* 5.
Isa. 43. 23 I have not..wearied thee with incense
43. 24 thou hast wearied me with thine iniquit.
Mal. 2. 17 Ye have wearied the LORD with your wo.
2. 17 yet ye say, Wherein have we wearied (h.)?

5. *To be or become faint, tired,* יָעֵף *yaaph.*
Jer. 2. 24 all they that seek her will not weary the.
51. 58 people shall labour..and they shall be we.
51. 64 they shall be weary. Thus far (are) the
Hab. 2. 13 shall weary themselves for very vanity?

6. *To be weary,* לָאָה *laah.*
Gen. 19. 11 they wearied themselves to find the door

7. *To be or become weary,* לָאָה *laah,* 2.
Psa. 68. 9 confirm thine inheritance, when it was we.
Isa. 1. 14 are a trouble unto me; I am weary to be.
16. 12 when it is seen that Moab is weary on the
47. 13 Thou art wearied in the multitude of thy
Jer. 6. 11 I am weary with holding in: I will pour
9. 5 they..weary themselves to commit iniqu.
15. 6 will I..destroy thee; I am weary with re.
20. 9 I was weary with forbearing, and I could

8. *To cause to weary,* לָאָה *laah,* 5.
Job 16. 7 now he hath made me weary: thou hast
Isa. 7. 13 small..to weary men, but will ye weary
Jer. 12. 5 If thou hast run..and they have wearied
Eze. 24. 12 She hath wearied (herself) with lies, and
Mic. 6. 3 wherein have I wearied thee? testify ag.

9. *To be faint,* עָיֵף *ayeph.*
Jer. 4. 31 my soul is wearied because of murderers

10. *To be vexed or weary,* קוּץ *quts.*
Gen. 27. 46 I am weary of my life because of the da.
Prov. 3. 11 My son..neither be weary of his correct.

11. *Satisfied, satiated,* שָׂבֵעַ *sabea.*
Prov. 25. 17 lest he be weary of thee, and..hate thee

12. *To faint, despond, be greatly harassed,* ἐκκακέω.
Gal. 6. 9 let us not be weary in well doing, for in
2 Th. 3. 13 ye, brethren, be not weary in well doing

13. *To labour, be fatigued,* κάμνω *kamnō.*
Heb. 12 3 lest ye be wearied and faint in your minds

14. *To labour, be weary or fatigued,* κοπιάω *kopiaō.*
John 4. 6 therefore, being wearied with (his) journey

15. *To force under, beat down, weary out,* ὑπωπιάζω.
Luke 18. 5 lest by her continual coming she weary me

WEARINESS, wearisome, weary, (what a) —

1. *Wearied (exhausted) of strength,* יְגִיעַ כֹּחַ *[yagia]*
Job 3. 17 There the wicked cease..there the weary

2. *Labour, weariness,* יְגִעָה *yegiah.*
Eccl. 12. 12 and much study (is) a weariness of the fle.

3. *Faint, weary, tired,* יָעֵף *yaeph.*
Judg. 8. 15 should give bread unto thy men..weary
Isa. 50. 4 how to speak a word in season to..weary

4. *What a weariness,* מַה־תְּלָאָה *mat-telaah.*
Mal. 1. 13 Ye said also, Behold, what a weariness

5. *To loathe, be weary,* נָקַט *naqat.*
Job 10. 1 My soul is weary of my life: I will leave

6. *To be weary,* עוּף *uph.*
Judg. 4. 21 smote..for he was fast asleep and weary

7. *Faint, weary, tired,* עָיֵף *ayeph.*
2 Sa. 16. 14 the people that (were) with him, came we.
17. 29 The people (is) hungry, and weary, and
Job 22. 7 Thou hast not given water to the weary
Isa. 5. 27 None shall be weary nor stumble among
28. 12 This (is) the rest..ye may cause the wea.
32. 2 as the shadow of a great rock in a weary
46. 1 (they are) a burden to the weary (beast)
Jer. 31. 25 I have satiated the weary soul, and I ha.

8. *Labour, perverseness, misery,* עָמָל *amal.*
Job 7. 3 wearisome nights are appointed to me

9. *Weary, labouring,* יָגֵעַ *yagea.*
Deut. 25. 18 and smote..when thou (wast) faint and we.
2 Sa. 17. 2 I will come upon him while he (is) weary

10. *A beating, toil, trouble, vexation,* κόπος *kopos.*
2 Co. 11. 27 In weariness and painfulness, in watchings

WEASEL —

A weasel, mole, חֹלֶד *choled.*
Lev. 11. 29 the weasel, and the mouse, and the tort.

WEATHER (fair, foul) —

1. *Golden brightness,* זָהָב *zahab.*
Job 37. 22 Fair weather cometh out of the north

2. *A day of,* יוֹם *yom.*
Prov. 25. 20 that taketh away a garment in cold wea.

3. *Good or fine heavens or sky,* εὐδία *eudia.*
Matt 16. 2 When it is evening, ye say..fair weather

4. *Winter weather, storm,* χειμών *cheimōn.*
Matt 16. 3 And in the morning..foul weather to day

WEAVE, weaver, weaver's shuttle, to —

1. *To weave, plait,* אָרַג *arag.*
Exod 28. 32 it shall have a binding of woven work ro.
35. 35 to work all manner of work of the..wea.
39. 22 he made the robe of the ephod..woven wo.
39. 27 they made coats (of) fine linen..woven w.
Judg 16. 13 If thou weavest the seven locks of my he.
1 Sa. 17. 7 the staff of his spear..like a weaver's beam
2 Sa. 21. 19 the staff of whose spear (was) like a wea.
2 Ki. 23. 7 the women wove hangings for the grove
1 Ch. 11. 23 a spear like a weaver's beam; and he went
20. 5 whose spear staff..like a weaver's beam
Isa. 19. 9 that weave net works shall be confounded
38. 12 I have cut off like a weaver my life, he
59. 5 They hatch cockatrice' eggs, and weave

2. *Web, weaving machine,* אֶרֶג *ereg.*
Job 7. 6 My days are swifter than a weaver's shut.

WEB —

1. *House,* בַּיִת *bayith.*
Job 8. 14 and whose trust (shall be) a spider's web

2. *Web,* מַסֶּכֶת *masseketh.*
Judg 16. 13 If thou weavest the seven locks with..the w.
16. 14 with the pin of the beam, and with the w.

3. *Beams, webs,* קוּרִים *qurim.*
Isa. 59. 5 They hatch..and weave the spider's web
59. 6 Their webs shall not become garments

WEDDING —

A rejoicing, wedding feast, γάμος *gamos.*
Matt 22. 3 to call them that were bidden to the wed.
22. 8 The wedding is ready, but they which w.
22. 10 the wedding was furnished with guests
22. 11 a man which had not on a wedding garm.
22. 12 how camest thou in..not having a wed.
Luke 12. 36 lord, when he will return from the wed.
14. 8 When thou art bidden of any..to a wed.

WEDGE —

A tongue, לָשׁוֹן *lashon.*
Josh. 7. 21 a wedge of gold of fifty shekels weight
7. 24 the wedge of gold, and his sons, Isa. 13. 12

WEDLOCK, women that break —

To commit adultery, נָאַף *naaph.*
Eze. 16. 38 judge thee, as women that break wedlock

WEED —

A weed, סוּף *suph.*
Jon. 2. 5 the weeds were wrapped about my head

WEEK —

1. *A seven, a week,* שָׁבוּעַ *shabua.*
Gen. 29. 27 Fulfil her week, and we will give thee this
29. 28 And Jacob did so, and fulfilled her week
Exod 34. 22 thou shalt observe the feast of weeks, of
Lev. 12. 5 she shall be unclean two weeks, as in her
Num 28. 26 after your weeks..ye shall have an holy co.
Deut 16. 9 Seven weeks shalt thou number unto thee
16. 9 begin to number the seven weeks from
16. 10 thou shalt keep the feast of weeks unto
16. 16 in the feast of weeks, and in the feast of
2 Ch. 8. 13 in the feast of weeks, and in the feast of
Jer. 5. 24 he reserveth unto us the appointed weeks
Dan. 9. 24 Seventy weeks are determined upon thy
9. 25 seven weeks, and threescore and two we.
9. 26 after threescore and two weeks shall Mes.
9. 27 for one week: and in the midst of the we.
10. 2 I Daniel was mourning three full weeks
10. 3 I ate no..bread..till three whole weeks

2. *A week, (from sabbath to sabbath),* σάββατα.
Matt 28. 1 dawn toward the first (day) of the week
Mark 16. 2 the first (day) of the week, they came unto
Luke 24. 1 upon the first (day) of the week, very early
John 20. 1 The first (day) of the week cometh Mary M.
20. 19 same day..being the first (day) of the we.
Acts 20. 7 upon the first (day) of the week, when the
1 Co. 16. 2 Upon the first (day) of the week let every

3. *A week, (from sabbath to sabbath),* σάββατον.
Mark 16. 9 [was risen early the first (day) of the week]
Luke 18. 12 I fast twice in the week, I give tithes of

WEEP (abundantly) to, weeping (continual) —

1. *To weep,* בָּכָה *bakah.*
Gen. 21. 16 And she sat over against (him)..and wept
23. 2 Abraham came to mourn..and to weep for
27. 38 And Esau lifted up his voice, and wept
29. 11 And Jacob..lifted up his voice, and wept
33. 4 And Esau ran to meet him..and they wept
37. 35 mourning. Thus his father wept for him
42. 24 turned himself about from them, and we.
43. 30 he sought (where) to weep..and wept there
45. 14 and wept; and Benjamin wept upon his
45. 15 he kissed all his brethren, and wept upon
46. 29 he fell on his neck, and wept on his neck
50. 1 Joseph fell upon his father's face, and we.
50. 17 Joseph wept when they spake unto him
Exod. 2. 6 saw the child: and, behold, the babe we.
Num 11. 4 the children of Israel also wept again, and
11. 10 Moses heard the people weep throughout
11. 13 they weep unto me, saying, Give us flesh
11. 18 ye have wept in the ears of the LORD, say.
11. 20 have wept before him, saying, Why came
14. 1 cried; and the people wept that night
25. 6 who (were) weeping (before) the door of the
Deut. 1. 45 ye returned and wept before the LORD; but
34. 8 the children of Israel wept for Moses in

Judg. 2. 4 the people lifted up their voice, and wept
14. 16 Samson's wife wept before him, and said
14. 17 she wept before him the seven days, while
20. 23 the children of Israel went up and wept
20. 26 came unto the house of God, and wept, and
21. 2 and lifted up their voices, and wept sore
Ruth 1. 9 and they lifted up their voice, and wept
1. 14 they lifted up their voice, and wept again
1 Sa. 1. 7 she provoked her; therefore she wept, and
1. 8 why weepest thou? and why eatest thou
1. 10 and prayed unto the LORD, and wept sore
11. 4 the people lifted up their voices, and wept
11. 5 What (aileth) the people that they weep?
20. 41 they kissed one another, and wept one with
24. 16 And Saul lifted up his voice, and wept
30. 4 wept, until they had no more power to we.
2 Sa. 1. 12 they mourned and wept, and fasted until
1. 24 Ye daughters of Israel, weep over Saul
3. 16 her husband went with her along weeping
3. 32 wept at the grave..all the people wept
3. 34 And all the people wept again over him
12. 21 Thou didst fast and weep for the child (wh.
12. 22 I fasted and wept: for I said, Who can tell
13. 36 the king's sons..wept..his servants wept
15. 23 the country wept with a loud voice, and
15. 30 wept as he went..weeping as they went up
18. 33 and went up to the chamber..and wept
19. 1 the king weepeth and mourneth for Abs.
2 Ki. 8. 11 was ashamed: and the man of God wept
8. 12 Hazael said, Why weepeth my lord? And
13. 14 wept over his face, and said, O my father
20. 3 O LORD, remember..And Hezekiah wept
22. 19 hast rent thy clothes, and wept before me
2 Ch. 34. 27 didst rend thy clothes, and weep before
Ezra 3. 12 many of the priests..wept with a loud vo.
10. 1 confessed, weeping..people wept very sore
Neh. 1. 4 I sat down and wept, and mourned (cer.)
8. 9 nor weep For all the people wept, when
Job 2. 12 they lifted up their voice, and wept; and
27. 15 in death; and his widows shall not weep
30. 25 Did not I weep for him that was in trou.
30. 31 organ into the voice of them that weep
Psa. 69. 10 I wept, (and chastened) my soul with fa
126. 6 He that goeth forth and weepeth, bearing
137. 1 yea, we wept, when we remembered Zion
Eccl. 3. 4 A time to weep, and a time to laugh; a t.
Isa. 30. 19 thou shalt weep no more: he will be very
33. 7 the ambassadors of peace shall weep bit.
38. 3 Remember now, O LORD..Hezekiah wept
Jer. 9. 1 that I might weep day and night for the
13. 17 my soul shall weep in secret places for
22. 10 Weep ye not..(but) weep sore for him th.
41. 6 to meet them, weeping all along as he we.
48. 32 O vine of Sibmah, I will weep for thee wi.
50. 4 going and weeping: they shall go, and se.
Lam. 1. 2 She weepeth sore in the night, and her te.
1. 16 For these (things) I weep; mine eye, mi.
Eze. 24. 16 neither shalt thou mourn nor weep, nei.
24. 23 ye shall not mourn nor weep; but ye sh.
27. 31 they shall weep for thee with bitternes
Hos. 12. 4 he wept, and made supplication unto him
Joel 1. 5 Awake, ye drunkards, and weep; and howl
2. 17 Let the priests..weep between the porch
Mic. 1. 10 Declare ye (it) not at Gath, weep ye not
Zech. 7. 3 Should I weep in the fifth month, separ.

2. *To weep*, בָּכָה *bakah*, 3
Jer. 31. 15 Rahel weeping for her children, refused
Eze. 8. 14 behold, there sat women weeping for Ta.

3. *Weeping*, בְּכִי *beki*.
Deut 34. 8 the days of weeping (and) mourning for
Ezra 3. 13 from the noise of the weeping of the peo
Esth. 4. 3 (there was) great mourning..and weeping
Job 16. 16 My face is foul with weeping, and on my
Psa. 6. 8 the LORD hath heard the voice of my we.
30. 5 weeping may endure for a night, but joy
102. 9 For I have..mingled my drink with wee.
Isa. 15. 2 He is gone up to Bajith..to weep: Moab
15. 5 by the mounting up of Luhith with weep.
16. 9 I will bewail with the weeping of Jazer
22. 12 did the Lord GOD of hosts call to weeping
65. 19 the voice of weeping shall be no more he.
Jer. 3. 21 weeping (and) supplications of the child.
9. 10 For the mountains will I take up a weep.
31. 9 They shall come with weeping, and with
31. 15 A voice was heard in Ramah..bitter we.
31. 16 Refrain thy voice from weeping, and thi.
48. 32 O vine of Sibmah..with the weeping of
Joel 2. 12 (even) to me..with weeping; Mal. 2. 13.

3a. *Weeping with weeping* (? error), בְּכִי בְּבְכִי [*beki*].
Jer. 48. 5 continual weeping shall go up

3b. *To go down with weeping*, יָרַד בִּבְכִי [*yarad*] Is. 15. 3.

4. *To shed tears*, דָּמַע *dama*.
Jer. 13. 17 and mine eye shall weep sore, and run

5. *To give the voice in weeping*, נָתַן אֶת־קוֹל בִּבְכִי [*nathan*].
Gen. 45. 2 he wept aloud: and the Egyptians and the

6. *To shed tears*, δακρύω *dakruō*.
John 11. 35 Jesus wept

7. *To break forth, wail*, κλαίω *klaiō*.
Matt. 2. 18 Rachel weeping (for) her children, and wo.
26. 75 And he went out, and wept bitterly
Mark 5. 38 and them that wept and wailed greatly
5. 39 Why make ye this ado, and weep? the da.
14. 72 And when he thought thereon, [he wept]
16. 10 [and told them..as they mourned and w.]
Luke 6. 21 Blessed (are ye) that weep now: for ye
6. 25 Woe unto you..ye shall mourn and weep
7. 13 had compassion on her, and said..Weep
7. 32 have mourned to you, and ye have not we.
Luke 7. 38 stood at his feet behind (him) weeping
8. 52 all wept..but he said, Weep not; she is
19. 41 when he was come near, he..wept over
22. 62 And Peter went out, and wept bitterly
23. 28 weep not for me, but weep for yourselves
John 11. 31 She goeth unto the grave to weep there
11. 33 saw her weeping, and the Jews also weep.
16. 20 ye shall weep and lament, but the world
20. 11 Mary stood without at the sepulchre we.
20. 11 and as she wept, she stooped down..into
20. 13 they say unto her, Woman, why weepest
20. 15 Jesus saith unto her, Woman, why weep.
Acts 9. 39 the widows stood by him weeping, and
21. 13 What mean ye to weep and to break mine
Rom 12. 15 and weep with them that weep
1 Co. 7. 30 And they that weep, as though they wept
Phil. 3. 18 told you often, and now tell you even we.
Jas. 4. 9 Be afflicted, and mourn, and weep: let
5. 1 weep and howl for your miseries that sh.
Rev. 5. 4 I wept much, because no man was found
5. 5 one of the elders saith unto me, Weep not
18. 11 the merchants of the earth shall weep
18. 15 shall stand afar off..weeping and wailing
18. 19 and cried, weeping and wailing, saying

8. *A breaking forth, wailing*, κλαυθμός *klauthmos*.
Matt. 2. 18 lamentation, and weeping, and great mo.
8. 12 there shall be weeping and gnashing of te.
So in 22. 13; 24. 51; 25. 30; Luke 13. 28.

9. *There came a wailing*, κλαυθμὸς ἐγένετο *klauth.*
Acts 20. 37 they all wept sore and fell on Paul's neck

WEIGH, be weighed, to —

1. *To ponder*, פָּלַס *palas*, 3.
Psa. 58. 2 ye weigh the violence of your hands in
Isa. 26. 7 thou, most upright, dost weigh the path

2. *To weigh*, שָׁקַל *shaqal*.
Gen. 23. 16 Abraham weighed to Ephron the silver
2 Sa. 14. 26 he weighed the hair of his head at two hu.
Ezra 8. 25 weighed unto them the silver and the go.
8. 26 I even weighed unto their hand six hun.
8. 29 until ye weigh..before the chief of the
Job 31. 6 Let me be weighed in an even balance
Isa. 40. 12 Who hath..weighed the mountains in sca.
46. 6 They..weigh silver in the balance, (and)
Jer. 32. 9 weighed him the money, (even) seventeen
32. 10 and weighed (him) the money in the bala.
Zech. 11. 12 they weighed for my price thirty (pieces)

3. *To be weighed*, שָׁקַל *shaqal*, 2.
Ezra 8. 33 on the fourth day was the silver..weighed
Job 6. 2 O that my grief were throughly weighed
28. 15 neither shall silver be weighed (for) the

4. *To weigh, ponder*, תָּכַן *takan*.
Prov. 16. 2 (are) clean..but the LORD weigheth the sp.

5. *To be weighed, pondered*, תָּכַן *takan*, 2.
1 Sa. 2. 3 for the LORD..by him actions are weigh.

6. *To weigh, ponder*, תָּכַן *takan*, 3.
Job 28. 25 and he weigheth the waters by measure

7. *To weigh*, תְּקַל *teqal*.
Dan. 5. 27 Thou art weighed in the balances, and art

WEIGHT, weighty, weightier, (full) —

1. *A stone*, אֶבֶן *eben*.
Lev. 19. 36 just weights, a just ephah, and a just hin
Deut 25. 13 shalt not have in thy bag divers weights, a
25. 15 thou shalt have a perfect and just weight
2 Sa. 14. 26 two hundred shekels after the king's we.
Prov 11. 1 the LORD: but a just weight (is) his deli.
16. 11 all the weights of the bag, (are) his work
20. 10 Divers weights, (and) divers measures, both
20. 23 Divers weights (are) an abomination unto
Mic. 6. 11 and with the bag of deceitful weights
Zech. 5. 8 he cast the weight of lead upon the mouth

2. *A weight, burden*, נֵטֶל *netel*.
Prov 27. 3 A stone (is) heavy, and the sand weighty

3. *Balance, beam of scales*, פֶּלֶס *peles*.
Prov 16. 11 A just weight and balance (are) the LOR.

4. *A weight, weighing*, מִשְׁקוֹל *mishqol*.
Eze. 4. 10 which thou shalt eat (shall be) by weight

5. *A weight, weighing*, מִשְׁקָל *mishqal*.
Gen. 24. 22 half a shekel weight..ten (shekels) weight
43. 21 and, behold..our money in full weight
Lev. 19. 35 do no unrighteousness..in weight, or in
26. 26 deliver (you) your bread again by weight
Num. 7. 13 the weight thereof (was) an hundred and
So in verse 19, 25, 37, 49, 61, 67, 73, 79.
7. 31, 43, 55 of the weight of an hundred and
Josh. 7. 21 a wedge of gold of fifty shekels weight
Judg. 8. 26 the weight of the golden ear rings that he
1 Sa. 17. 5 the weight of the coat (was) five thousand
2 Sa. 12. 30 the weight whereof (was) a talent of gold
21. 16 the weight of whose spear..in weight
1 Ki. 7. 47 neither was the weight of the brass found
10. 14 the weight of gold that came to Solomon
2 Ki. 25. 16 the brass of all..was without weight
1 Ch. 20. 2 found it to weigh a talent of gold, and
21. 25 six hundred shekels of gold by weight
22. 3 and brass in abundance without weight
22. 14 of brass and iron without weight; for it
28. 14 gold by weight..silver by weight, for all
28. 15 Even the weight..by weight for every ca.
28. 15 for the candlesticks of silver by weight
28. 16 by weight (he gave) gold for the tables of
28. 17 by weight..by weight for every basin of
28. 18 for the altar of incense refined gold by we.
2 Ch. 3. 9 weight of the nails (was) fifty shekels of
2 Ch. 4. 18 for the weight of the brass could not be
9. 13 Now the weight of gold that came to Sol.
Ezra 8. 30 So took the priests and the Levites the w.
8. 34 by weight of every one: and all the weight
Job 28. 25 To make the weight for the winds; and
Jer. 52. 20 brass of all these vessels was without we.
Eze. 4. 16 they shall eat bread by weight, and with
5. 1 take thee balances to weigh, and divide

6. *A weight, burden*, βάρος *baros*.
2 Co. 4. 17 more exceeding (and) eternal weight of

7. *Weighty, heavy*, βαρύς *barus*.
2 Co. 10. 10 For (his) letters, say they, (are) weighty

8. *Weightier, heavier*, βαρύτερος *baruteros*.
Matt 23. 23 have omitted the weightier (matters) of

9. *Tumour, swelling, encumbering weight*, ὄγκος.
Heb. 12. 1 let us lay aside every weight, and the sin

WELFARE —

1. *Good, goodness, prosperity, welfare*, טוֹב *tob*.
Neh. 2. 10 there was come a man to seek the welfare

2. *Ease, security*, יְשׁוּעָה *yeshuah*.
Job 30. 15 pursue my soul as the wind: and my we.

3. *Peace, completeness*, שָׁלוֹם *shalom*.
Gen. 43. 27 he asked them of (their) welfare, and said
Exod 18. 7 they asked each other of (their) welfare
1 Ch. 18. 10 to enquire of his welfare, and to congrat.
Psa. 69. 22 (that which should have been) for (their) w.
Jer. 38. 4 for this man seeketh not the welfare of

WELL —

1. *A well, cistern, pit*, בְּאֵר *beer*.
Gen. 16. 14 Wherefore the well was called Beer-lahai-r
21. 19 God opened her eyes, and she saw a well
21. 25 reproved Abimelech because of a well of
21. 30 witness unto me, that I have digged this w.
24. 11 kneel down without the city by a well of
24. 20 ran again unto the well to draw (water)
26. 15 For all the wells which his father's servants
26. 18 Isaac digged again the wells of water wh.
26. 19 and found there a well of springing water
26. 20 called the name of the well Esek; because
26. 21 they digged another well, and strove for
26. 22 remov. from thence, and digged another w.
26. 25 and there Isaac's servants digged a well
26. 32 told him concerning the well which they
29. 2 behold a well in the field, and, lo, there
29. 2 for out of that well they watered the flocks
29. 2 and a great stone (was) upon the well's mo.
29. 3, 10 rolled the stone from the well's mouth
29. 3 put the stone again upon the well's mouth
29. 8 they roll the stone from the well's mouth
Exod. 2. 15 But Moses fled..and he sat down by a well
Num 20. 17 neither will we drink (of) the water of the w.
21. 16 that (is) the well whereof the LORD spake
21. 17 Then Israel sang this song, Spring up, O w.
21. 18 princes digged the well, the nobles of the
21. 22 we will not drink (of) the waters of the we.
2 Sa. 17. 18 which had a well in his court; whither th.
17. 19 took and spread a covering over the well's
17. 21 they came up out of the well, and went
Prov. 5. 15 Drink..running waters out..thine own we.
Song. 4. 15 A fountain of gardens, a well of living wat.

2. *A well, cistern, pit*, בּוֹר *bor*.
Deut. 6. 11 wells digged, which thou diggedst not, vin.
1 Sa. 19. 22 came to a great well that (is) in Sechu
2 Sa. 3. 26 which brought him again from the well
23. 15 would give me drink of the water of the
23. 16 drew water out of the well of Beth-lehem
1 Ch. 11. 17 would give me drink of the water of the we.
11. 18 drew water out of the well of Beth-lehem
2 Ch. 26. 10 digged many wells: for he had much cattle
Neh. 9. 25 wells digged, vineyards, and oliveyards

3. *Fountain*, מַעְיָן *mayan*.
Josh 18. 15 and went out to the well of waters of Ne.
2 Ki. 3. 19 stop all wells of water, and mar every good
3. 25 stopped all the wells of water, and felled
Psa. 84. 6 passing through the valley..make it a well
Isa. 12. 3 with joy shall ye draw water out of the w.

4. *Source, spring*, מָקוֹר *maqor*.
Prov 10. 11 The mouth of a righteous (man is) a well

5. *Eye, fountain*, עַיִן *ayin*.
Gen. 24. 13 I stand (here) by the well of water; and
24. 16 she went down to the well, and filled her
24. 29 Laban ran out unto the man, unto the well
24. 30 behold, he stood by the camels at the well
24. 42 I came this day unto the well, and said
24. 43 I stand by the well of water; and it shall
24. 45 went down unto the well, and drew (wa.)
49. 22 fruitful bough by a well, (whose) branches
Exod 15. 27 where (were) twelve wells of water, and
Neh. 2. 13 even before the dragon well, and to the

6. *A fountain, spring, well, running*, πηγή *pēgē*.
John 4. 6 Now Jacob's well was there. Jesus ther.
4. sat thus on the well: (and) it was about
4. 14 shall be in him a well of water springing
2 Pe. 2. 17 These are wells without water, clouds that

7. *A well, pit, dungeon*, φρέαρ *phrear*.
John 4. 11 hast nothing to draw with, and the well
4. 12 Jacob, which gave us the well, and drank

WELL, (full) —

1. *Good, excellent*, טוֹב *tob*.
Judg. 9. 16 if ye have dealt well with Jerubbaal and
Ruth 3. 13 perform..thee the part of a kinsman, we.
1 Sa. 9. 10 Then said Saul to his servant, Well said
20. 7 If he say thus, (It is) well; thy servant

1 Sa.24. 18 showed this..how that thou hast dealt w.
24. 19 his enemy, will he let him go well away?
2 Sa. 3. 13 he said, Well; I will make a league with
1 Ki. 2. 18 Well; I will speak for thee unto the king
18. 24 the people answered and said, It is well
2 Ch.12. 12 and also in Judah things went well
Psa.119. 65 Thou hast dealt well with thy servant, O
128. 2 happy (shalt) thou (be), and (it shall be) w.
Eccl. 8. 12 yet surely I know that it shall be well with
8. 13 But it shall not be well with the wicked
Isa. 3. 10 ye to the righteous that (it shall be) well
Jer. 15. 11 Verily it shall be well with thy remnant
22. 15 do judgment..(and) then (it was) well with
22. 16 then (it was) well (with him: was) not this
44. 17 had we plenty of victuals, and were well
Dan. 1. 4 Children in whom (was) no blemish..well

2. *To do good or well*, טוֹב *tob*, 5.
Prov 30. 29 There be three (things) which go well, yea

3. *Fair, beauteous*, יָפֶה *yapheh.*
Gen. 29. 17 but Rachel was beautiful and well favour.
39. 6 And Joseph was..goodly..and well favo.
41. 2 seven well favoured kine and fat fleshed
41. 4 did eat up the seven well favoured and fat
41. 18 fat fleshed, and well favoured; and they

4. *Right*, כֵּן *ken.*
Exod 10. 29 Thou hast spoken well, I will see thy face
Isa. 33. 23 they could not well strengthen their mast

5. *Might, exceedingly*, מְאֹד *meod.*
Psa. 78. 29 So they did eat, and were well filled: for

6. *Peace, completeness*, שָׁלוֹם *shalom.*
Gen. 29. 6 (Is) he well? And they said, (He is) well
43. 27 (Is) your father well, the old man of whom
2 Ki. 4. 23 nor sabbath. And she said, (It shall be) w.
4. 26 (Is it) well with thee? (is it) well with thy
4. 26 (is it) well with the child..(It is) well
5. 21 he lighted down..and said, (Is) all well?
5. 22 And he said, All (is) well. My master hath
9. 11 said unto him, (Is) all well? wherefore

7. *To set the heart*, שִׁית לֵב *shith leb.*
Psa. 48. 13 Mark ye well her bulwarks, consider her
Prov 27. 23 Be thou diligent..look well to thy herds
Eze. 44. 5 Son of man, mark well..mark well the

8. *Work*, מַעֲשֶׂה *maaseh.*
Isa. 3. 24 instead of well set hair baldness; and in.

9. *With perfume or spices*, מֶרְקָחָה *merqachah*
Eze. 24. 10 consume the flesh, and spice it well, and

10. *Well, happily, rightly, well done*, εὖ *eu.*
Luke 19. 17 said unto him, [Well], thou good servant
Acts 15. 29 which if ye keep yourselves, ye shall do w.
Eph. 6. 3 That it may be well with thee, and thou

11. *Good, excellent*, ἀγαθός *agathos.*
Rom. 2. 7 To them who by patient continuance in

12. *Beautiful, good, excellent, benevolent*, καλός.
Gal. 6. 9 let us not be weary in well doing: for in

13. *Well, rightly, truly*, καλῶς *kalōs.*
Matt 12. 12 Wherefore it is lawful to do well on the
15. 7 hypocrites, well did Esaias prophesy of you
Mark 7. 6 Well hath Esaias prophesied of you 7. 9.
7. 37 He hath done all things well: he maketh
12. 28 perceiving that he had answered them w.
12. 32 scribe said unto him, Well, Master, thou
Luke 6. 26 Woe to you when all men shall speak well
20. 39 scribes answering said, Master, thou hast w.
John 4. 17 Jesus said unto her, Thou hast well said
8. 48 Say we not well that thou art a Samaritan
13. 13 Ye call me Master and Lord; and ye say w.
18. 23 but if well, why smitest thou me?
Acts 10. 33 and thou hast well done that thou art co.
28. 25 Well spake the Holy Ghost by Esaias the
Rom.11. 20 Well; because of unbelief they were broken
1 Co. 7. 37 he that standeth stedfast..doeth well
7. 38 he that giveth (her) in marriage doeth well
14. 17 For thou verily givest thanks well, but
2 Co. 11. 4 which ye have not accepted, ye might w.
Gal. 4. 17 They zealously affect you, (but) not well
5. 7 Ye did run well; who did hinder you that
Phil. 4. 14 Notwithstanding ye have well done that
1 Ti. 3. 4 One that ruleth well his own house, having
3. 12 ruling their children and..houses well
3. 13 they that have used the office of a deacon w.
5. 17 Let the elders that rule well be counted
Jas. 2. 8 love thy neighbour as thyself, ye do well
2. 19 thou doest well: the devils also believe, and
2 Pe. 1. 19 whereunto ye do well that ye take heed
3 John 6 if thou bring forward..thou shalt do well

[*See also* Doing, drink, full, know, look, mark, play, please, pleased, reported, stricken, very.]

WELL, to be, can, deal, do, doing, entreat, go, with —

1. *Goodness*, טוּב *tub.*
Prov.11. 10 When it goeth well with the righteous, the

2. [*Be*] *for good*, לְטוֹב *le tob.*
Jer. 15. 11 Verily it shall be well with thy remnant

3. *To be good, well, glad*, טוֹב *tob.*
Num.11. 18 shall give us flesh to eat? for (it was) well
Deut. 5. 33 that ye may live, and (that it may be) well
15. 16 and thine house, because he is well with
19. 13 blood from Israel, that it may go well with
1 Sa. 16. 16 play with his hand, and thou shalt be well
16. 23 so Saul was refreshed, and was well, and

4. *To do good or well*, טוֹב *tob*, 5.
1 Ki. 8. 18 thou didst well that it was in thine heart
2 Ki. 10. 30 said..Because thou hast done well in ex.
2 Ch. 6. 8 thou didst well in that it was in thine he.

5. *To be or become good, well, right*, יָטַב *yatab.*
Gen. 12. 13 that it may be well with me for thy sake
40. 14 But think on me when it shall be well wi.
Deut. 4. 40 that it may go well with thee, and with
5. 16 that it may go well with thee, in the land
5. 29 that it might be well with them, and with
6. 3 that it may be well with thee, and that
6. 18 that it may be well with thee, and that
12. 25, 28 that it may go well with thee, and wi.
22. 7 that it may be well with thee, and (that)
Ruth 3. 1 shall I not seek..that it may be well with
2 Ki. 25. 24 serve the king..and it shall be well with
Jer. 7. 23 commanded you, that it may be well unto
38. 20 so it shall be well unto thee, and thy soul
40. 9 serve the king..and it shall be well with
42. 6 that it may be well with us, when we obey

6. *To do good or well*, יָטַב *yatab*, 5.
Gen. 4. 7 If thou doest well, shalt thou not be acc.
4. 7 if thou doest not well, sin lieth at the do.
12. 16 he entreated Abram well for her sake: and
32. 9 to thy kindred, and I will deal well with
Exod. 1. 20 Therefore God dealt well with the midw.
Deut. 5. 28 they have well said all that they have sp.
18. 17 They have well (spoken that) which they
1 Sa. 16. 17 Provide me now a man that can play well
25. 31 when the LORD shall have dealt well with
Psa. 49. 18 praise thee, when thou doest well to thy.
Isa. 1. 17 Learn to do well; seek judgment, relieve
Jer. 1. 12 Thou hast well seen: for I will hasten my
Jon. 4. 4 Then said the LORD, Doest thou well to
4. 9 Doest thou well to be angry for the gourd?
4. 9 he said, I do well to be angry, (even) unto
Zech. 8. 15 have I thought in these days to do well

7. *A boiling*, רֶתַח *rethach.*
Eze. 24. 5 make it boil well, and let them seethe the

8. *Peace, completion*, שָׁלוֹם *shalom.*
Gen. 37. 14 whether it be well with thy brethren and
2 Sa. 18. 28 called, and said unto the king, All is well

9. *To do good or well*, ἀγαθοποιέω *agathopoieō.*
1 Pe. 2. 15 that with well doing ye may put to silence
2. 20 but if, when ye do well and suffer (for it)
3. 6 daughters ye are as long as ye do well, and
3. 17 better..that ye suffer for well doing, than

10. *Good or well doer, benefactor*, ἀγαθοποιός *agath.*
1 Pe. 2. 14 and for the praise of them that do well

11. *Good or well doing, beneficence*, ἀγαθοποιΐα.
1 Pe. 4. 19 the keeping of their souls (to him) in w.d.

12. *To make sound, heal, cure*, σώζω *sōzō.*
John 11. 12 said..Lord, if he sleep, he shall do well

13. *To do well or good*, καλοποιέω *kalopoieō.*
2 Th. 3. 13 But ye, brethren, be not weary in well do.

WELL done, nigh, known —

1. *As nothing*, כְּאַיִן *ke-ayin.*
Psa. 73. 2 almost gone; my steps had well nigh sli.

2. *Well, happily, rightly, well done!* εὖ *eu.*
Matt 25. 21 Well done, (thou) good and faithful serv.
25. 23 said unto him, Well done, good and fait.

3. *To know thoroughly*, ἐπιγινώσκω *epiginōskō.*
2 Co. 6. 9 As unknown, and (yet) well known; as

WELL beloved, favoured, pleasing, spring —

1. *Beloved*, דּוֹד *dod.*
Song 1. 13 A bundle of myrrh (is) my well beloved

2. *Beloved*, יָדִיד *yadid.*
Isa. 5. 1 Now will I sing to my well beloved a song
5. 1 My well beloved hath a vineyard in a very

3. *The good of grace*, טוֹבַת חֵן [*tob chen*].
Nah. 3. 4 multitude of the whoredoms of the well f.

4. *Source, spring*, מָקוֹר *maqor.*
Prov 16. 22 Understanding (is) a well spring of life un.
18. 4 the well spring of wisdom (as) a flowing

5. *Loveable, beloved*, ἀγαπητός *agapētos.*
Mark 12. 6 Having yet therefore one son, his well be.
Rom. 16. 5 Salute my well beloved Epænetus, who
3 John 1 The elder unto the well beloved Gaius

6. *Well pleasing*, εὐάρεστος *euarestos.*
Phil. 4. 18 a sacrifice acceptable, well pleasing to God
Col. 3. 20 obey..for this is well pleasing unto the L.
Heb. 13. 21 working in you that which is well pleasing

WEN —

A flowing, festering, suppurating sore, יַבֶּל *yabbal.*
Lev. 22. 22 Blind..broken, or maimed, or having a w.

WENCH —

Maid servant, שִׁפְחָה *shiphchah.*
2 Sa. 17. 17 a wench went and told them; and they we.

WERE, there —

There is, there are, יֵשׁ *yesh.*
Num 22. 29 I would there were a sword in mine hand
Neh. 5. 2 For there were that said, We, our sons
5. 3 also there were that said, We have mort.
5. 4 There were also that said, We have borr.
Psa. 14. 2 to see if there were any that did unders.
53. 2 to see if there were (any) that did under.

WERE it not that —

If not, unless, לוּלֵי *lule.*
Deut 32. 27 Were it not that I feared the wrath of the
2 Ki. 3. 14 surely, were it not that I regard the pre.

WEST (side), wester, westward —

1. *The sea* (*being the W. border of Caanan*), יָם *yam.*
Gen. 12. 8 pitched his tent, (having) Beth-el on the w.
13. 14 look from the place where thou art..we.
28. 14 thou shalt spread abroad to the west, and
Exod 10. 19 the LORD turned a mighty strong west w.
26. 22 for the sides of the tabernacle westward
26. 27 of the tabernacle for the two sides west.
27. 12 breadth of the court on the west side (sh.
36. 27 for the sides of the tabernacle westward
36. 32 of the tabernacle for the sides westward
38. 12 for the west side (were) hangings of fifty
Num. 2. 18 On the west side (shall be) the standard of
3. 23 shall pitch behind the tabernacle westw.
34. 6 western border..this shall be your west
35. 5 on the west side two thousand cubits, and
Deut. 3. 27 lift up thine eyes westward, and northw.
33. 23 possess thou the west and the south
Josh. 5. 1 which (were) on the side of Jordan west.
8. 9 between Beth-el and Ai, on the west side
8. 12 set them to lie..on the west side of the c.
8. 13 their liers in wait on the west of the city
11. 2 valley, and in the borders of Dor on the w.
11. 3 the Canaanite on the east and on the we.
12. 7 smote on this side Jordan on the west, fr.
15. 8 that (lieth) before the valley of Hinnom
15. 10 border compassed from Baalah westward
15. 12 west border (was) to the great sea, and the
16. 3 goeth down westward to the coast of Japh.
16. 8 border went out from Tappuah westward
18. 12 and went up through the mountains west.
18. 14 children of Judah: this (was) the west qu.
18. 15 the border went out on the west, and went
19. 26 reacheth to Carmel westward, and to Sh.
19. 34 coast turneth westward to Aznoth-tabor
19. 34 reacheth to Asher on the west side, and
22. 7 their brethren on this side Jordan westw.
1 Ki. 7. 25 three looking toward the west, and three
1 Ch. 9. 24 porters, toward the east, west, north, and
2 Ch. 4. 4 three looking toward the west, and three
Isa. 11. 14 shoulders of the Philistines toward the we.
49. 12 these from the north and from the west
Eze. 41. 12 the building..at the end toward the west
42. 19 He turned about to the west side, (and)
45. 7 from the west side westward, and from
45. 7 from the west border unto the east border
46. 19 there (was) a place on the two sides west.
47. 20 The west side..This (is) the west side
48. 1 for these are his sides east (and) west, a
48. 2 from the east side unto the west side
So in verse 4, 5, 8, 23, 24, 25, 26, 27.
48. 3, 6, 7 from the east side even unto the w.
48. 10 toward the west ten thousand in breadth
48. 16 the west side four thousand and five hun.
48. 17 and toward the west two hundred and fifty
48. 18 ten thousand westward: and it shall be
48. 21 westward over against the five and twenty
48. 21 toward the west border, over against the
48. 34 At the west side four thousand and five
Dan. 8. 4 I saw the ram pushing westward, and no.
Hos. 11. 10 then the children shall tremble from the w
Zech 14. 4 cleave in the midst thereof toward..the w.

2. *Going in of the sun*, מְבוֹא הַשֶּׁמֶשׁ [*mabo*].
Josh. 23. 4 have cut off, even unto the great sea we.
Zech. 8. 7 from the east country, and from the west

3. *Sun setting*, מַעֲרָב *maarab.*
1 Ch. 7. 28 westward Gezer, with the towns thereof
12. 15 (both) toward the east and toward the w.
26. 16 westward, with the gate Shallecheth, by
26. 18 At Parbar westward, four at the causew.
26. 30 them of Israel on this side Jordan westw.
2 Ch. 32. 30 brought it straight down to the west side
33. 14 on the west side of Gihon, in the valley
Psa. 75. 6 neither from the east, nor from the west
103. 12 As far as the east is from the west, (so)
107. 3 from the east, and from the west, from
Isa. 43. 5 from the east, and gather thee from the w.
59. 19 fear the name of the LORD from the west
Dan. 8. 5 an he goat came from the west, on the

4. *Place of darkness, sun setting*, מַעֲרָבָה *maarabah.*
Isa. 45. 6 from the rising of the sun, and from the w.

5. *Sinking or setting* (*of the sun*), δυσμή *dusmē.*
Matt. 8. 11 many shall come from the east and west
24. 27 shineth even unto the west; so shall also
Luke 12. 54 When ye see a cloud rise out of the west
13. 29 shall come from the east, and (from) the w.
Rev. 21. 13 on the south, three gates; and on the west

WET, (to be) —

1. *To wet, moisten*, צְבַע *tseba*, 3.
Dan. 4. 25 they shall wet thee with the dew of hea.

2. *To be wet, moistened*, צְבַע *tseba*, 4.
Dan. 4. 15, 23 let it be wet with the dew of heaven
4. 33 his body was wet with the dew of heaven
5. 21 and his body was wet with the dew of

3. *To be wet*, רָטַב *ratab.*
Job 24. 8 They are wet with the showers of the mo.

WHALE —

1. *A great sea monster*, תַּנִּים *tannim.*
Eze. 32. 2 thou (art) as a whale in the seas; and thou

2. *A great sea monster*, תַּנִּין *tannin.*
Gen. 1. 21 God created great whales, and every liv.
Job 7. 12 (Am) I a sea, or a whale, that thou settest

3. *A great sea monster*, κῆτος *kētos.*
Matt 12. 40 three days and three nights in the whale's

WHAT (thing) —

1. *Where this?* אֵי זֶה *e zeh.*
1 Ki. 13. 12 their father said unto them, What way
Job 38. 24 By what way is the light parted, (which)

2. *How? how,* אֵיךְ *ek.*
2 Ch. 10. 6 What counsel give ye (me) to return ans.

3. *Also,* גַּם *gam.*
Job 2. 10 What! shall we receive good at the hand

4. *A word, matter, thing,* דָּבָר *dabar.*
Ezra 8. 17 and I told them what they should say un.

5. *What that (is),* מָא דִי *ma di.*
Ezra 6. 8 Moreover I make a decree what ye shall

6. *What? what,* מָה *mah.*
Gen. 20. 10 What sawest thou, that thou hast done
1 Sa. 19. 3 and what I see, that I will tell thee
Lam. 2. 13 What thing shall I take to witness for th.

7. *As or like what, how much,* כַּמָּה *kam-mah.*
Zech. 2. 2 what (is) the breadth thereof, and what (is)

8. *For what? why? wherefore?* לָמָּה *la-mah.*
Gen. 33. 15 said, What needeth it? let me find grace

9. *What?* מֶה *meh.*
Gen. 4. 10 What hast thou done? the voice of thy br.

10. *What?* מָה *mah.*
Dan. 2. 22 knoweth what (is) in the darkness, and
2. 28 maketh known . . what shall be in the lat.
2. 29 upon thy bed what should come to pass
2. 29 maketh known to thee what shall come
2. 45 made known to the king what shall come
4. 35 stay his hand, or say unto him, What do.

11. *Who?* מִי *mi.*
Gen. 24. 65 What man (is) this that walketh in the

12. *What?* מָן *man.*
Ezra 5. 4 What are the names of the men that ma.

13. *For,* γάρ *gar.*
1 Co. 11. 22 What! have ye not houses to eat and to

14. *Such as, such,* οἷος *hoios.*
2 Ti. 3. 11 what persecutions I endured: but out of

15. *As much, as great, how much, how great,* ὅσα *hosa.*
Mark 6. 30 both what they had done, and what they
11. 24 What things [soever] ye desire, when ye pr.
Acts 15. 12 declaring what miracles and wonders God
Rom. 3. 19 Now we know that what things soever the
Jude 10 but what they know naturally, as brute

16. *Whosoever, whatsoever,* ὅστις *hostis.*
Phil. 3. 7 But what things were gain to me, those I

17. *Thus, in like manner, so, accordingly,* οὕτως.
Matt 26. 40 What! could ye not watch with me one

18. *Of what sort or kind?* ποῖος *poios.*
Matt 21. 23 By what authority doest thou these things?
21. 24 I in likewise will tell you by what autho.
21. 27 Neither tell I you by what authority I do
24. 42 for ye know not what hour your Lord do
24. 43 had known in what watch the thief wou.
Mark 4. 30 with [what] comparison shall we compare
11. 28 By what authority doest thou these thi.?
11. 29 tell you by what authority I do these th.
11. 33 Neither do I tell you by what authority
Luke 5. 19 when they could not find by what (way)
6. 32, 33, 34 what thank have ye? for sinners
12. 39 had known what hour the thief would co.
20. 2 Tell us, by what authority doest thou th.
20. 8 Neither tell I you by what authority I do
24. 19 said unto them, What things? And they
John 12. 33 This he said, signifying what death he sh.
18. 32 he spake, signifying what death he should
21. 19 signifying by what death he should glor.
Acts 4. 7 By what power, or by what name, have ye
7. 49 what house will ye build me? saith the L.
23. 34 he asked of what province he was. And
Rom. 3. 27 By what law? of works? Nay; but by the
1 Co. 15. 35; Jas. 4. 14; 1 Pe. 2. 20; Rev. 3. 3.

19. *What word,* τίνι λόγῳ *tini logō,* 1 Co. 15. 2.
20. *The things concerning,* τὰ πρός, Acts 23. 30.

21. *How much? how great?* πόσος *posos.*
2 Co. 7. 11 what carefulness it wrought in you, yea

22. *Of what kind or sort? how great?* ποταπός.
Mark 13. 1 saith unto him, Master, see . . what build.

23. *Either, or truly, verily,* ἤ *ē.*
1 Co. 6. 16 [What !] know ye not that he which is jo.
6. 19 What! know ye not that your body is the
14. 36 What! came the word of God out from

24. *Who? what?* τίς, τί *tis, ti.*
Matt. 5. 46 For if ye love them which love you, what
5. 47 what do ye more (than others)? do not even
6. 3 let not thy left hand know what thy right
6. 25 what ye shall eat, or [what ye shall] drink
6. 25 nor yet for your body, what ye shall put
6. 31 What shall we eat, or what shall we drink
7. 9 Or what man is there of you, whom if his
8. 29 What have we to do with thee, Jesus, thou
9. 13 But go ye and learn what (that) meaneth
10. 19 take no thought how or what ye shall speak
10. 19 [given you in that same hour what ye sh.]
11. 7 What went ye out into the wilderness to
11. 8, 9 But what went ye out for to see? A
12. 3 Have ye not read what David did, when
12. 7 But if ye had known what (this) meaneth
12. 11 What man shall there be among you that
16. 26 what is a man profited . . or what shall a
Matt 17. 25 What thinkest thou, Simon? of whom do
19. 16 what good things shall I do, that I may
19. 20 The young man saith . . what lack I yet?
19. 27 Behold . . what shall we have therefore?
20. 21 said unto her, What wilt thou? She saith
20. 22 answered and said, Ye know not what ye
20. 32 and said, What will ye that I shall do unto
21. 16 Hearest thou what these say? And Jesus
21. 28 But what think ye? A (certain) man had
21. 40 what will he do unto those husbandmen?
22. 17 Tell us therefore, What thinkest thou? Is
22. 42 Saying, What think ye of Christ? whose
24. 3 what (shall be) the sign of thy coming, and
26. 8 had indignation, saying, To what purpose
26. 15 What will ye give me, and I will deliver
26. 62 what (is it which) these witness against
26. 65 what further need have we of witnesses?
26. 66 What think ye? They answered and said
26. 70 denied . . saying, I know not what thou sa.
27. 4 they said, What (is that) to us? see thou
27. 22 What shall I do then with Jesus which is
27. 23 said, Why, what evil hath he done? But
Mark 1. 24, 27, [27]; 2. 25; 4. 24, 41; 5. 7, 9, 14; 6. 2, 24;
8. 36, 37; 9. 6, 10, 16, 33; 10. 3, 17, 36, 38, 51; 11. 5; 12. 9; 13.
4, 11; 14. 36, 36, 40, 60, 63, 64, 68; 15. 12, 14, 24; Luke 1. 66;
3. 10, 12, 14; 4. 34, 36; 5. 22; 6. 11; 7. 24, 25, 26, 31; 8. 9, 25, 28,
30; 9. 25; 10. 25, 26; 12. 11, 11, 17, 22, 22, 29, 29, 49; 13. 18;
14. 31; 15. 4, 8, 26; 16. 3, 4; 18. 6, 18, 36, 41; 19. 48; 20. 13, 15,
17; 21. 7; 22. 71; 23. 22, 31, [34]; John 1. 21, 22, 38; 2. 4, 18,
25; 4. 27; 5. 12; 6. 6, 9, 28, 30, 30; 7. 36, 51; 8. [5]; 9. 17, 26;
10. 6; 11. 47, 56; 12. 27, 49, 49; 13. 12, 28; 15. 15; 16. 17, 18,
18; 18. 21, 29, 35, 38; 21. 21, 22, 23; Acts 2. 12, 37; 4. 9, 16; 5.
35; 7. 40, 49; 8. 36; 9. [6, 6]; 10. 4, [6], 17, 21, 29; 11. 17; 12.
18; 16. 30; 17. 18, 19, 20; 19. 3, 35; 21. 13, 22, 33; 22. 10, 26;
23. 19; Rom. 3. 1, 1, 3, 5, 9; 4. 1, 3; 6. 1, 15, 21; 7. 7; 8. 26, 27,
31; 9. 14, 30; 10. 8; 11. 2, 4, 7, 15; 12. 2; 1 Co. 2. 11; 4. 7, 21;
5. 12; 7. 16; 9. 18; 10. 19; 11. 22; 14. 6, 15, 16; 15. 29, 32; 2
Co. 6. 14, 14, 15, 15, 16; 12. 13; Gal. 4. 30; Eph. 1. 18, 18,
19; 3. 9, 18; 4. 9; 5. 10, 17; Phil. 1. 18, 22; Col. 1. 27; 1 Th. 2.
19; 3. 9; 4. 2; Heb. 2. 6; 7. 11; 11. 32; 12. 7; 13. 6; Jas. 2. 14,
16; 1 Pe. 1. 11; 4. 17; 1 Jo. 3. 2; Rev. 2. 7, 11, 17, 29; 3. 6, 13,
22; 7. 13; 18. 18.

WHAT manner or sort of (men) —

1. *Where? how? when?* אֵיפֹה *ephoh.*
Judg. 8. 18 What manner of men (were they) whom

2. *Indeed, in truth, then, therefore,* τίς ἄρα *tis ara.*
Mark 4. 41 What manner of man is this, that even the
Luke 1. 66 saying, What manner of child shall this
8. 25 What manner of man is this! for he com.

3. *Such as, such,* οἷος *hoios.*
Luke 9. 55 [Ye know not what manner of spirit ye]
1 Th. 1. 5 as ye know what manner of men we were

4. *Of what kind or sort?* ὁποῖος *hopoios.*
1 Co. 3. 13 shall try every man's work of what sort it
1 Th. 1. 9 what manner of entering in we had unto
Jas. 1. 24 straightway forgetteth what manner of

5. *Of what sort or kind,* ποῖος *pois.*
1 Pe. 1. 11 Searching what, or what manner of time

6. *Of what sort or kind? how great?* ποταπός *potapos.*
Matt. 8. 27 What manner of man is this, that even
Mark 13. 1 Master, see what manner of stones and
Luke 1. 29 cast in her mind what manner of salutat.
7. 39 would have known who and what manner
2 Pe. 3. 11 what manner of (persons) ought ye to be
1 Jo. 3. 1 Behold what manner of love the Father

7. *Who? what?* τίς *tis.*
Luke 24. 17 What manner of communications (are)

WHAT end, good, purpose, what man soever —

1. *A man,* אִישׁ אִישׁ *ish ish.*
Lev. 17. 3 What man soever (there be) of the house
22. 4 What man soever of the seed of Aaron

2. *What?* מָה *mah.*
Gen. 27. 46 said to Isaac . . what good shall my life do
Isa. 1. 11 To what purpose (is) the multitude of your
Amos 5. 18 to what end (is) it for you? the day of the

WHAT place, soever, in —

Where, whether, where, whereas, ὅπου *hopou.*
Mark 6. 10 [In what place] soever ye enter into an h.

WHATSOEVER (things) —

1. *A man,* אִישׁ אִישׁ *ish ish.*
Lev. 17. 8, 10 Whatsoever man . . of the house of Isr.
17. 13 whatsoever man . of the children of Israel
22. 18 Whatsoever (he be) of the house of Israel

2. *All,* כֹּל *kol.*
Gen. 8. 19 whatsoever creepeth upon the earth, after

3. *All that,* כָּל־דִּי *kol di.*
Ezra 7. 21 whatsoever Ezra the priest, the scribe of
7. 23 Whatsoever is commanded by the God of

4. *Every vessel,* כָּל־הַכְּלִי *kol hak-keli.*
Lev. 15. 26 whatsoever she sitteth upon shall be un.

5. *What, that which,* מָה דִי *mah di.*
Ezra 7. 18 whatsoever shall seem good to thee, and

6. *Whatsoever,* ὃ ἐάν *ho ean.*
Matt 14. 7 promised with an oath to give her [what.]
15. 5 by whatsoever thou mightest be profited
16. 19 [whatsoever] thou shalt bind on earth sh.
16. 19 [whatsoever] thou shalt loose on earth sh.
20. 4, [7] Go ye also into the vineyard, and what.
Mark 6. 22 Ask of me whatsoever thou wilt, and I will
6. 23 Whatsoever thou shalt ask of me, I will
7. 11 by whatsoever thou mightest be profited
10. 35 that thou shouldest do for us whatsoever
Mark 11. 23 come to pass; he shall have [whatsoever]
13. 11 but whatsoever shall be given you in that
Gal. 6. 7 for [whatsoever] a man soweth, that shall
1 Jo. 3. 22 and whatsoever we ask, we receive of him, be.
3 John 5 Beloved, thou doest faithfully whatsoever

7. *Whatsoever,* ὃ ἐάν τι *ho ean ti.*
Eph. 6. 8 Knowing that [whatsoever] good thing

8. *Of what kind or sort?* ὁποῖοι ποτε, *hopoioi pote.*
Gal. 2. 6 seemed to be somewhat, whatsoever they

9. *As many as,* ὅσα *(neut. pl.) hosa.*
Matt. 17. 12 but have done unto him whatsoever they
28. 20 Teaching them to observe all things what.
Mark 9. 13 they have done unto him whatsoever they
10. 21 sell whatsoever thou hast, and give to the
Luke 4. 23 whatsoever we have heard done in Cape.
12. 3 whatsoever ye have spoken in darkness
John 15. 14 Ye are my friends, if ye do [whatsoever]
17. 7 they have known that all things whatso.
Acts 4. 28 For to do whatsoever thy hand and thy
Rom. 15. 4 For whatsoever things were written afore.
Phil. 4. 8 whatsoever things are true, whatsoever
4. 8 whatsoever things (are) just, whatsoever
4. 8 whatsoever things (are) lovely, whatsoever

10. *As many as,* ὅσα ἄν *(neut. pl.) hosa an.*
Matt. 7. 12 all things whatsoever ye would that men
21. 22 all things, [whatsoever] ye shall ask in pr.
23. 3 All therefore [whatsoever] they bid you
John 11. 22 whatsoever thou wilt ask of God, God will
16. 13 but [whatsoever] he shall hear, (that) shall
16. 23 [Whatsoever] ye shall ask the Father in
Acts 3. 22 him shall ye hear in all things wh. Ro. 3. 19.

11. *As many as,* ὅσα ἐάν *hosa (neut. pl.) ean.*
Matt. 18. 18 [Whatsoever] ye shall bind . . whatsoever

12. *Whatsoever,* ὅ τι ἄν *(neut.) ho ti an.*
Luke 10. 35 whatsoever thou spendest more, when I
John 2. 5 mother saith unto the servants, Whatso.
14. 13 whatsoever ye shall ask in my name, that
15. 16 whatsoever ye shall ask of the Father in

13. *Whatsoever,* πᾶν ὅ τι ἄν *(neut.) pan ho ti an.*
Col. 3. 17 whatsoever ye do in word or deed, (do)
3. 23 whatsoever ye do, do (it) heartily, as to

14. *All, whatsoever,* πᾶν *(neut.) pan.*
Matt 15. 17 whatsoever entereth in at the mouth go.
Mark 7. 18 whatsoever thing from without entereth
Rom. 14. 23 not of faith: for whatsoever (is) not of fa.
1 Co. 10. 25 Whatsoever is sold in the shambles, (that)
10. 27 whatsoever is set before you eat, asking
Eph. 5. 13 for whatsoever doth make manifest is li.
1 Jo. 5. 4 For whatsoever is born of God, Rev. 18. 22

15. *Whatsoever,* ᾧ δήποτε *hō dēpote,* John 5. 4.
16. *Whatsoever,* τί *(neut.) ti.*
1 Co. 10. 31 or whatsoever ye do, do all to the glory of

WHEAT, wheaten —

1. *Corn, grain,* בַּר *bar.*
Jer. 23. 28 What (is) the chaff to the wheat? saith the
Joel 2. 24 floors shall be full of wheat, and the fats
Amos 5. 11 ye take from him burdens of wheat: ye
8. 5 we may set forth wheat, making the eph.
8. 6 That we may . . sell the refuse of the wh.?

2. *Corn,* דָּגָן *dagan.*
Num 18. 12 all the best of the wine, and of the wheat
Jer. 31. 12 for wheat, and for wine, and for oil, and

3. *Wheat,* חִטָּה *chittah.*
Gen. 30. 14 Reuben went in the days of wheat harv.
Exod. 9. 32 But the wheat and the rie were not smi.
29. 2 (of) wheaten flour shalt thou make them
34. 22 of the first fruits of wheat harvest, and
Deut. 8. 8 A land of wheat, and barley, and vines
32. 14 and goats, with the fat of kidneys of wh.
Judg. 6. 11 his son Gideon threshed wheat by the w.
15. 1 a while after, in the time of wheat harvest
Ruth 2. 23 unto the end of barley harvest and of w.
1 Sa. 6. 13 (were) reaping their wheat harvest in the
12. 17 (Is it) not wheat harvest to day? I will
2 Sa. 4. 6 (as though) they would have fetched wh.
17. 28 wheat, and barley, and flour, and parched
1 Ki. 5. 11 twenty thousand measures of wheat (for
1 Ch. 21. 20 hid . Now Ornan was threshing wheat
21. 23 and the wheat for the meat offering, I gi.
2 Ch. 2. 10 twenty thousand measures of beaten w.
2. 15 Now therefore the wheat, and the barl.
27. 5 ten thousand measures of wheat, and t.
Job 31. 40 Let thistles grow instead of wheat, and
Psa. 81. 16 fed them also with the finest of the whe.
147. 14 (and) filleth thee with the finest of the
Song 7. 2 thy belly (is like) an heap of wheat set
Isa. 28. 25 cast in the principal wheat, and the app
Jer. 12. 13 They have sown wheat, but shall reap th
41. 8 for we have treasures in the field, of whe
Eze. 4. 9 Take thou also unto thee wheat, and ba.
27. 17 they traded in thy market wheat of Min.
45. 13 sixth part of an ephah of an homer of w.
Joel 1. 11 Be ye ashamed . . for the wheat and for the

4. *Wheat, grain,* חִנְטִין *chintin.*
Ezra 6. 9 burnt offerings of the God of heaven, wh.
7. 22 to an hundred measures of wheat, and to

5. *Ground corn, wheat, grits,* רִיפוֹת *riphoth.*
Prov 27. 22 bray a fool in a mortar among wheat with

6. *Sifted wheat or corn,* σῖτος *sitos.*
Matt. 3. 12 gather his wheat into the garner, but he
13. 25 enemy came and sowed tares among the w
13. 29 lest . . ye root up also the wheat with them
13. 30 bind them . . but gather the wheat into my

Luke 3. 17 will gather the wheat into his garner; but
16. 7 And he said, An hundred measures of w.
22. 31 (to have) you, that he may sift you as w.
John12. 24 Except a corn of wheat fall into the gro.
Acts 27. 38 lightened the ship, and cast out the whe.
1 Co.15. 37 it may chance of wheat, or of some other
Rev. 6. 6 A measure of wheat for a penny, and th.
18. 13 fine flour, and wheat, and beasts, and sh.

WHEEL —

1. *Turnings, wheels,* אָבְנַיִם *obnayim.*
Jer. 18. 3 behold, he wrought a work on the wheels

2. *A wheel,* אוֹפָן *ophan.*
Exod14. 25 took off their chariot wheels, that they
1 Ki. 7. 30 every base had four brasen wheels, and
7. 32 four wheels, and the axletrees of the wh
7. 32 height of a wheel (was) a cubit and half
1 Ki. 7. 33 the work of the wheels. a chariot wheel
Prov 20. 26 a wise king .bringeth the wheel over th.
Isa. 28. 27 neither is a cart wheel turned about upon
Eze. 1. 15 behold one wheel upon the earth by the
1. 16 The appearance of the wheels and their
1. 16 as it were a wheel in the middle of a wheel
1. 19 the wheels went by them..the wheels were
1. 20, 21 the wheels were lifted up..in the wh.
3. 13 the noise of the wheels over against them
10. 6 he went in, and stood beside the wheels
10. 9 the four wheels by the cherubim, one wh.
10. 9 another wheel..the appearance of the wh
10. 10 a wheel had been in the midst of a wheel
10. 12 the wheels..(even) the wheels that they
10. 13 As for the wheels, it was cried unto them
10. 16 the wheels went by them..the same wh.
10. 19 when they went out, the wheels also (we.)
11. 22 lift up their wings, and the wheels beside
Nah. 3. 2 the noise of the rattling of the wheels, and

3. *A rolling thing, wheel,* גַּלְגַּל *galgal.*
Psa 83. 13 make them like a wheel; as the stubble
Eccl. 12. 6 bowl..or the wheel broken at the cistern
Isa 5. 28 counted like flint, and their wheels like
Jer. 47. 3 (at) the rumbling of his wheels, the fath.
Eze. 10. 2 Go in between the wheels, (even) under
10. 6 Take fire from between the wheels, from
10. 13 cried unto them in my hearing, O wheel
23. 24 they shall come against thee with..wheels
26. 10 shall shake at the noise..of the wheels, and
Dan. 7. 9 (was like) the fiery flame, (and) his wheels

4. *A rolling thing, wheel,* גִּלְגַּל *gilgal.*
Isa. 28. 28 nor break (it with) the wheel of his cart

5. *Beat, step,* פַּעַם *paam.*
Judg. 5. 28 cried..why tarry the wheels of his chariots?

WHELP —

1. *A son,* בֵּן *ben.*
Job 4. 11 the stout lion's whelps are scattered abro.
28. 8 The lion's whelps have not trodden it, nor

2. *A whelp,* גּוֹר *gor.*
Jer. 51. 38 They shall roar together like lions, they
Nah. 2. 12 did tear in pieces enough for his whelps

3. *A whelp,* גּוּר *gur.*
Gen. 49. 9 Judah (is) a lion's whelp: from the prey
Deut 33. 22 Dan is a lion's whelp: he shall leap from
Eze. 19. 2 she nourished her whelps among young
19. 3 she brought up one of her whelps: it bec.
19. 5 she took another of her whelps, (and) made
Nah. 2. 11 the old lion walked, (and) the lion's whelp

WHEN —

1. *After,* אַחַר *achar.*
Gen. 24. 36 bare a son to my master when she was

2. *If,* אִם *im.*
Gen. 38. 9 when he went in unto his brother's wife

3. *That, in that,* אֲשֶׁר *asher.*
Gen. 6. 4 when the sons of God came in unto the da.

4. *When as,* כַּאֲשֶׁר *ka-asher.*
Gen. 12. 11 when he was come near to enter into Eg

5. *From that (time)* מִדֵּי *mid-de.*
1 Sa. 1. 7 when she went up to the house of the Lo.
1 Ki. 14. 28 when the king went into the house of the
2 Ch.12. 11 when the king entered into the house of

6. *As that,* כְּדֵי *ke-di.*
Dan. 3. 7 when all the people heard the sound of

7. *In the day,* בְּיוֹם *be-yom.*
Lev. 13. 14 when raw flesh appeareth in him, he shall
14. 57 To teach when (it is) unclean, and when
Deut21. 16 when he maketh his sons to inherit (that)
2 Sa. 21. 12 when the Philistines had slain Saul in Gil.
Eze. 38. 18 when Gog shall come against the land of
Zech.14. 3 fight against those nations, as when he fo.

8. *When,* כִּי *ki.*
Gen. 4. 12 When thou tillest the ground, it shall not

9. *As,* כְּמוֹ *kemo.*
Gen. 19. 15 when the morning arose, then the angels

10. *From (the time) that,* מִן דִּי *min di.*
Ezra 4. 23 Now when the copy of king Artaxerxes'

11. *When?* מָתַי *mathai.*
Gen. 30. 30 when shall I provide for mine own house

12. *For when?* לְמָתַי *le-mathai.*
Exod. 8. 9 when shall I entreat for thee, and for thy

13. *During,* עַד *ad.*
Psa. 71. 18 Now also when I am old and grey headed

14. *While yet,* בְּעוֹד *be-od.*
Gen. 48. 7 when yet (there was) but a little way to

15. *In or at the time,* בְּעֵת *be-eth,* לְעֵת *le-eth.*
1 Ki. 11. 4 when Solomon was old, (that) his wives
2 Ch.20. 22 when they began to sing and to praise, the
29. 27 when the burnt offering began, the song
Jer. 2. 17 forsaken the LORD thy God, when he led
Eze. 21. 25 whose day is come, when iniquity (shall
21. 29 whose day is come, when their iniquity

16. *If,* ἐάν *ean.*
1 Co. 14. 16 when thou shalt bless with the spirit, how
1 Jo. 3. 2 when he shall appear. we shall be like him

17. *After that, when,* ἐπάν *epan.*
Matt. 2. 8 when ye have found (him), bring me word
Luke11. 22 But when a stronger than he shall come
11. 34 when (thine eye) is evil, thy body also (is)

18. *Since, when, after that,* ἐπεί *epei.*
Luke 7. 1 Now [when] he had ended all his sayings

19. *When,* ἡνίκα *hēnika.*
2 Co. 3. 15 when Moses is read, the veil is upon their
3. 16 Nevertheless when it shall turn to the L.

20. *According as,* καθώς *kathōs.*
Acts 7. 17 But when the time of the promise drew

21. *After,* μετά *(acc.) meta.*
Acts 7. 4 when his father was dead, he removed
1 Co. 11. 25 After the same manner..when he had

22. *When,* ὁπότε *hopote.*
Luke 6. 3 what David did, [when] himself was an

23. *So that,* ὅπως *hopōs.*
Acts 3. 19 when the times of refreshing shall come

24. *Whenever,* ὅταν *hotan.*
Matt. 5. 11 Blessed are ye when (men) shall revile you
See also 6. 2, 5, 6, 16; 9. 15; 10. 19, 23; 12. 43; 13. 32;
15. 2; 19. 28; 21. 40; 23. 15; 24. 15, 32, 33; 25. 31; 26.
29; Mark 2. 20; 3. 11; 4. 15, 16, 29, 31, 32; 8. 38; 11. 25;
12. [23], 25; 13. 4, 7, 11, 14, 28, 29; Luke 5. 35; 6. 22, 22, 26;
8. 13; 9. 26; 11. 2, 21, 24, 34, 36; 12. 11, 54, 55; 13. 28,
14. 8, 10, 10, 12, 13; 16. 4, 9; 17. 10; 21. 7, 9, 20, 30, 31; 23. 42;
John 2. 10; 4. 25; 5. 7; 7. 27, 31; 8. 28, 44; 10. 4; 13.
19; 14. 29; 15. 26; 16. 4, 13, 21; 21. 18; Acts 23. 35; 24.
22; Rom. 2. 14; 11. 27; 1 Co. 13. 10; 14. 26; 15. 24, 24,
27, 28, 54; 16. 2, 3, 5, 12; 2 Co. 10. 6; 12. 10; 13. 9; Col.
3. 4; 4. 16; 1 Th. 5. 3; 2 Th. 1. 10; 1 Ti. 5. 11; Titus 3.
12; Heb. 1. 6; Jas. 1. 2; 1 Jo. 2. [28]; 5. 2; Rev. 4. 9;
9. 5; 10. 7; 11. 7; 17. 10; 18. 9; 20. 7.

25. *When,* ὅτε *hote.*
Matt. 7. 28 when Jesus had ended these sayings, the
See also 9. 25; 11. 1; 12. 3; 13. 26, 48, 53; 17. [25]; 19.
1; 21. 1, 34; 26. 1; Mark 1. 32; 2. 25; 4. 10; 7. 17; 8. 19,
20; 11. 1, [19]; 14. 12; 15. 20, 41; Luke 2. 21, 22, 42; 4. 25;
6. 13; 13. [35]; 17. 22; 22. 14, 35; 23. 33; John 1. 19; 2. 22; 4.
21, 23, 45; 5. 25; 6. 24; 9. 4, [14]; 12. 16, [17], [41]; 13. 31; 16.
25; 19. 6, 8, 23, 30; 20. 24; 21. 15, 18; Acts 1. 13; 8. 12, 39;
11. 2; 12. 6; 21. 5, 35; 22. 20; 27. 39; 28. 16; Rom. 2. [16];
6. 20; 7. 5; 13. 11; 1 Co. 13. 11, 11; Gal. 1. 15; 2. 11, 12, 14;
4. 3, 4; Phil. 4. 15; Col. 3. 7; 1 Th. 3. 4; 2 Th. 3. 10; 2 Ti.
4. 3; Heb. 7. 10; 1 Pe. 3. 20; Jude [9]; Rev. 1. 17; 5. 8; 6.
1, 3, 5, 7, 9, 12; 8. [1]; 10. 3, 4; 12. 13; 22. 8.

26. *Where,* οὗ *hou.*
Heb. 3. 9 When your fathers tempted me, proved

27. *When?* πότε *pote.*
Matt.24. 3 Tell us, when shall these things be? and
25. 37, 44 saying, Lord, when saw we thee an hu.
25. 38 When saw we thee a stranger, and took
25. 39 when saw we thee sick, or in prison, and
Mark13. 4 Tell us, when shall these things be? and
13. 33 watch and pray: for ye know not when
13. 35 for ye know not when the master of the
Luke12. 36 lord, when he will return from the wedd.
17. 20 demanded..when the kingdom of God sh.
21. 7 saying, Master, but when shall these things
John 6. 25 said..Rabbi, when camest thou hither?

28. *Once, at some time or other,* ποτέ *pote.*
Luke 22. 32 when thou art converted, strengthen thy

29. *As, when,* ὡς *hōs.*
Luke 1. 41 when Elisabeth heard the salutation of
2. 39 when they had performed all things acco.
4. 25 when great famine was throughout all the
5. 4 Now when he had left speaking, he said
7. 12 Now when he came nigh to the gate of the
11. 1 when he ceased, one of his disciples said
12. 58 When thou goest with thine adversary to
19. 5 when Jesus came to the place, he looked
19. 29 when he was come nigh to Bethphage and
19. 41 when he was come near, he beheld the ci.
20. 37 when he calleth the Lord the God of Abr.
John 2. 9 When the ruler of the feast had tasted
2. 23 Now when he was in Jerusalem at the pa.
4. 1 When therefore the Lord knew how the
4. 40 So when the Samaritans were come unto
6. 12 When they were filled, he said unto his di.
6. 16 when even was (now) come, his disciples
7. 10 when his brethren were gone up, then we.
8. 7 [So when they continued asking him, he]
11. 6 When he had heard therefore that he was
11. 32 Then when Mary was come where Jesus
11. 33 When Jesus therefore saw her weeping, and
19. 33 But when they came to Jesus, and saw
Acts 5. 24 Now when the high priest and the captain
7. 23 when he was full forty years old, it came
10. 7 when the angel which spake unto Cornel.
13. 29 when they had fulfilled all that was written
14. 5 when there was an assault made both of

Acts 16. 15 when she was baptized, and her househo.
17. 13 when the Jews of Thessalonica had know.
18. 5 when Silas and Timotheus were come from
19. 9 when divers were hardened, and believed
20. 14 when he met with us at Assos, we took
20. 18 when they were come to him, he said unto
21. 12 when we heard these things, both we, and
21. 27 when the seven days were almost ended
22. 11 when I could not see for the glory of that
25. 14 when they had been there many days, Fest.
27. 1 when it was determined that we should
27. 27 But when the fourteenth night was come
28. 4 when the barbarians saw the (venomous)
1 Co. 11. 34 And the rest will I set in order when I co.

30. *In the,* ἐν τῷ *en tō.*
Matt.13. 4 when he sowed, some (seeds) fell by the
27. 12 when he was accused of the chief priests
Luke 2. 27 when the parents brought in the child J.
3. 21 Now when all the people were baptized
5. 12 when he was in a certain city, behold a
8. 40 when Jesus was returned, the people (gl.)
9. 36 when the voice was past, Jesus was found
9. 51 when the time was come that he should
10. 35 whatsoever thou spendest more, when I
19. 15 when he was returned, having received
Acts 2. 1 when the day of Pentecost was fully come
Rom. 3. 4 and mightest overcome when thou art ju.
Gal. 4. 18 and not only when I am present with you
1 Pe. 4. 13 when his glory shall be revealed, ye may

31. *In which, the,* ἐν ᾗ, ἐν τῇ *en hē, en tē.*
Luke22. 7 day of unleavened bread, when the pass.
John 4. 52 Then enquired he of them the hour when
Acts 13. 17 exalted the people when they, 2 Th. 1. 7

32. *And, also,* καί *kai,* Acts 5. 7; Heb. 8. 8.

WHENCE? (from) —

1. *From whence?* אֵי מִזֶּה *e miz-zeh.*
Gen. 16. 8 whence camest thou? and whither wilt th.

2. *Whence?* מֵאַיִן *me-ayin.*
Gen. 29. 4 My brethren, whence (be) ye? And they sa.
42. 7 said unto them, Whence come ye? And they
Num 11. 13 Whence should I have flesh to give unto
Josh. 2. 4 There came men unto me, but I wist not
9. 8 said unto them, Who (are) ye? and from w.
Judg17. 9 Micah said unto him, Whence comest thou?
19. 17 Whither goest thou? and whence comest
2 Ki. 5. 25 Elisha said unto him, Whence (comest th.)
6. 27 whence shall I help thee? out of the barn
20. 14 What said these men? and from whence
Job 1. 7 LORD said unto Satan, Whence comest th.?
28. 20 whence then cometh wisdom? and where
Psa.121. 1 unto the hills, from whence cometh my he.
Isa. 39. 3 What said these men? and from whence
Jon. 1. 8 whence comest thou? what (is) thy count.
Nah. 3. 7 who will bemoan her? whence shall I seek

3. *Whence,* ὅθεν *hothen.*
Matt 12. 44 I will return into my house from whence
Luke11. 24 I will return unto my house whence I ca.
Acts 14. 26 from whence they had been re. He. 11.19.

4. *Where,* οὗ *hou,* Phil. 3. 20.

5. *Whence? how?* πόθεν *pothen.*
Matt13. 27 sow good seed in thy field? from whence
See also v. 54, 56; 15. 33; 21. 25; Mark 6. 2; 8. 4; 12.
37; Luke 1. 43; 13. 25, 27; 20. 7; John 1. 48; 2. 9; 3. 8;
4. 11; 6. 5; 7. 27, 27, 28; 8. 14, 14; 9. 29, 30; 19. 9; Jas.
4. 1; Rev. 2. 5; 7. 13.

WHENSOEVER —

1. *Whensoever,* ὅταν *hotan.*
Mark14. 7 whensoever ye will ye may do them good

2. *Whensoever,* ὡς ἐάν *hōs ean.*
Rom 15. 24 [Whensoever] I take my journey into Sp.

WHERE —

1. *Where?* אֵי *e.*
Gen. 3. 9 God called unto Adam..Where (art) thou?
4. 9 said unto Cain, Where (is) Abel thy bro.?
Job 20. 7 they which have seen him shall say, Wh.
Isa. 19. 12 Where (are) they?..let them tell thee now

2. *Where?* אֵי זֶה *e zeh.*
1 Sa. 9. 18 Tell me, I pray thee, where the seer's ho.
Job 28. 12 and where (is) the place of understanding?

3. *Where?* אַיֵּה *ayyeh.*
Gen. 18. 9 Where (is) Sarah thy wife? And he said
Jer. 37. 19 Where (are) now your prophets which pr.

4. *How, how?* אֵיכָה *ekah.*
Song 1. 7 Tell me..where thou feedest, where thou

5. *How, how?* אֵיכֹה *ekoh.*
2 Ki. 6. 13 Go and spy where he (is), that I may send

6. *Whence?* מֵאַיִן *me-ayin.*
Job 28. 12 But where shall wisdom be found? and wh.

7. *Where?* אֵיפֹה *ephoh.*
Gen. 37. 16 tell me, I pray thee, where they feed (th.
Ruth 2. 19 Where hast thou gleaned to day? and wh
1 Sa. 19. 22 asked and said, Where (are) Samuel and
2 Sa. 9. 4 king said unto him, Where (is) he? And
Job 4. 7 Remember..where were the righteous cut
38. 4 Where wast thou when I laid the found.
Isa. 49. 21 I was left alone; these, where (had) they
Jer. 3. 2 see where thou hast not been lien with: in
36. 19 Go, hide thee..and let no man know wh.

8. *Unto,* אֶל *el.*
Lev. 4. 12 clean place, where the ashes are poured

9. *Whither?* אָנָה *anah.*
1 Ki. 6. 6 man of God said, Where fell it? And he

10. *Where?* אֵפוֹא ,אֵפוֹ *epho.*
Gen. 27. 33 where (is) he that hath taken venison, and
Job 9. 24 judges thereof; if not, where, (and) who
Isa. 19. 12 where (are) thy wise (men)?. let them tell
Hos. 13. 10 where (is any other) that may save thee in

11. *In (the place) that, where,* בַּאֲשֶׁר *ba-asher.*
Judg 5. 27 where he bowed, there he fell down dead

12. *Whence,* מֵאֲשֶׁר *me-asher.*
Exod. 5. 11 Go ye, get you straw where ye can find it

13. *Where, whither,* אֲשֶׁר שָׁם *asher sham.*
Gen. 2. 11 the whole land of Havilah, where (there

14. *A hand, part,* יָד *yad.*
Isa. 57. 8 thou lovedst their bed where thou sawest

15. *Whither,* תַּמָּה *[tam].*
Ezra 6. 1 where the treasures were laid up in Bab.

16. *In which,* ἐν ᾧ *en hō.*
Acts 4. 31 place was shaken where they were assem.
7. 33 for the place [where] thou standest is ho.
11. 11 already come unto the house where I was
15. 36 where we have preached the word of the

17. *Down to,* κατά (acc.) *kata.*
Luke 10. 33 Samaritan, as he journeyed, came where

18. *Whence,* ὅθεν *hothen.*
Matt 25. 24 and gathering where thou hast not straw.
25. 26 and gather where I have not strawed

19. *Where,* ὅπου *hopou.*
Matt. 6. 19 where moth and rust doth corrupt and wh.
6. 20 where neither moth nor rust doth corrupt
6. 20 where thieves do not break through
6. 21 For where your treasure is, there will
13. 5 Some fell upon stony places, where they
25. 24 reaping where thou hast not sown, and
25. 26 thou knewest that I reap where I sowed
26. 57 where the scribes and the elders were as.
28. 6 Come, see the place where the Lord lay
Mark 2. 4 they uncovered the roof where he was
4. 5 some fell on stony ground, where it had
4. 15 these are they by the way side, where the
5. 40 and entereth in where the damsel was
6. 55 those that were sick, where they heard he
9. [44, 46], 48 Where their worm dieth not, and
13. 14 see the abomination..standing where it
14. 14 where I shall eat the passover with my
16. 6 he is not here: behold the place where
Luke 12. 33 where no thief approacheth, neither moth
12. 34 For where your treasure is, there will yo.
22. 11 where I shall eat the passover with my
John 1. 28 in Bethabara beyond Jordan, where John
3. 8 The wind bloweth where it listeth, and
4. 20 Jerusalem is the place where men ought
4. 46 Jesus came again into Cana of Galilee, w.
6. 23 unto the place where they did eat bread
6. 62 see the Son of man ascend up where he
7. 34, 36 and where I am, (thither) ye cannot
7. 42 out of the town of Beth-lehem, where D.
10. 40 into the place where John at first bapti.
11. 30 but was in that place where Martha met
11. 32 Then when Mary was come where Jesus
12. 1 Bethany, where Lazarus was which had
12. 26 and where I am, there shall also my ser.
14. 3 myself; that where I am, (there) ye may
17. 24 whom thou hast given me be with me w.
18. 1 brook Cedron, where was a garden, into
19. 18 Where they crucified him, and two other
19. 20 for the place where Jesus was crucified
19. 41 Now in the place where he was crucified
20. 12 at the feet, where the body of Jesus had
20. 19 when the doors were shut where the dis.
Acts 17. 1 came to Thessalonica, where was a syna.
Rom 15. 20 preach the gospel, not where Christ was
Col. 3. 11 Where there is neither Greek nor Jew, ci.
Heb. 9. 16 For where a testament (is), there must
10. 18 Now where remission of these (is, there
Jas. 3. 16 For where envying and strife (is), there
Rev. 2. 13 (even) where Satan's seat (is): and thou
2. 13 was slain among you, where Satan dwell.
11. 8 and Egypt, where also our Lord was cru.
12. 6 wilderness, where she hath a place prep.
12. 14 [where] she is nourished for a time, 20. 10

20. *Where...there,* ὅπου ἐκεῖ, Mr. 6. 55; Re. 12. 14.

21. *Where,* οὗ *hou.*
Matt. 2. 9 till it came and stood over where the yo.
18. 20 For where two or three are gathered to.
28. 16 into a mountain where Jesus had appoi.
Luke 4. 16 came to Nazareth, where he had been br.
4. 17 he found the place where it was written
22. 10 follow him into the house [where] he en.
John 11. 41 [took away the stone (from the place) wh].
Acts 1. 13 into an upper room, where abode both P.
2. 2 it filled all the house where they were si.
7. 29 stranger in the land of Madian, where he
12. 12 where many were gathered together pra.
16. 13 river side, where prayer was wont to be
20. 6 came unto them to Troas in five days; wh.
20. 8 upper chamber, where they were gathered
25. 10 judgment seat, where I ought to be jud.
28. 14 Where we found brethren, and were de.
Rom. 4. 15 for where no law is, (there is) no transg.
5. 20 But where sin abounded, grace did much
9. 26 in the place where it was said unto them
2 Co. 3. 17 where the Spirit of the Lord (is), there
Col. 3. 1 where Christ sitteth on the right hand of
Rev. 17. 15 where the whore sitteth, are peoples, and

22 *Where?* ποῦ *pou.*
Matt. 2. 2 Where is he that is born King of the Jews?
2. 4 he demanded of them where Christ shou.
8. 20 but the Son of man hath not where to lay
26. 17 Where wilt thou that we prepare for thee
Mark 14. 12 Where wilt thou that we go and prepare
14. 14 The Master saith, Where is the guest ch.
15. 47 (the mother) of Joses beheld where he was
Luke 8. 25 Where is your faith? And they being afr.
9. 58 but the Son of man hath not where to lay
12. 17 because I have no room where to bestow
17. 17 Were there not ten cleansed? but where
17. 37 they answered and said unto him, Where
22. 9 said unto him, Where wilt thou that we
22. 11 The Master saith.. Where is the guest ch.
John 1. 38 being interpreted, Master, where dwell.
1. 39 They came and saw where he dwelt, and
7. 11 sought him at the feast, and said, Where
8. 10 [Woman, where are those thine accusers?]
8. 19 Then said they unto him, Where is thy
9. 12 Then said they unto him, Where is he?
11. 34 Where have ye laid him? They said unto
11. 57 that, if any man knew where he were, he
20. 2, 13 know not where they have laid him
20. 15 tell me where thou hast laid him, and I
Rom. 3. 27 Where (is) boasting then? It is excluded
1 Co. 1. 20 Where (is) the wise? where (is) the scribe?
1. 20 where is the disputer of this world? hath
12. 17 where (were) the hearing.. where (were)
12. 19 they were all one member, where (were)
15. 55 where (is) thy sting?.. where (is) thy vi.?
1 Pe. 4. 18 where shall the ungodly and the sinner
2 Pe. 3. 4 Where is the promise of his coming? for
Rev. 2. 13 where thou dwellest, (even).. Satan's seat

23. *What?* τίς *tis.*
Gal. 4. 15 [Where] is then the blessedness ye spake

24. *Place,* τόπος *topos.*
1 Ti. 2. 8 I will therefore that men pray every wh.

WHERE no —

In not, in the cessation of, בְּאֶפֶס *be-ephes.*
Prov 26. 20 Where no wood is, (there) the fire goeth

WHEREAS —

1. *If, since,* אִם *im.*
Job 22. 20 Whereas our substance is not cut down

2. *For,* כִּי *ki.*
Gen. 31. 37 Whereas thou hast searched all my stuff

3. *Now,* עַתָּה *attah.*
2 Ch. 10. 11 For whereas my father put a heavy yoke

4. *Under, instead of,* תַּחַת *tachath.*
Isa. 60. 15 Whereas thou hast been forsaken and ha.

5. *Because that,* יַעַן אֲשֶׁר *yaan asher.*
1 Ki. 8. 18 Whereas it was in thine heart to build an

6. *In that which,* ἐν ᾧ *en hō.*
1 Pe. 2. 12 whereas they speak against you as evil do.
3. 16 whereas they speak evil of you, as of evil

7. *Where, whereas,* ὅπου *hopou.*
1 Co. 3. 3 for whereas (there is) among you envying
2 Pe. 2. 11 Whereas angels which are greater in po.

8. *Whoever,* ὅστις *hostis.*
Jas. 4. 14 Whereas ye know not what (shall be) on

WHEREBY —

1. *In, with, or by what?* בַּמָּה *bam-mah.*
Gen. 15. 8 whereby shall I know that I shall inherit

2. *Whereby (?),* מִנִּי *minni (? error for minnim).*
Psa. 45. 8 palaces, whereby they have made thee g.

3. *Through which,* δι' ἧς *di' hēs.*
Heb. 12. 28 whereby we may serve God acceptably
2 Pe. 1. 4 Whereby are given unto us exceeding gr.
3. 6 Whereby the world that then was, being

4. *In which,* ἐν ᾧ, ἐν οἷς *en hō, en hois.*
Luke 1. 78 whereby the dayspring from on high hath
Acts 4. 12 none other name.. whereby we must be
11. 14 whereby thou and all thy house shall be
Rom. 8. 15 Spirit of adoption..whereby we cry, Abba
14. 21 whereby thy brother stumbleth, Ep. 4. 30

* *By which,* πρὸς ὅ *pros ho,* Eph. 3. 4.

5. *Down to or by what thing?* κατὰ τί (acc.) *kata ti.*
Luke 1. 18 Whereby shall I know this? for I am an

6. *Whence,* ὅθεν *hothen.*
1 Jo. 2. 18 whereby we know that it is the last time

7. *Concerning which,* περὶ οὗ *peri (gen.) hou.*
Acts 19. 40 there being no cause whereby we may give

WHEREFORE —

1. *But, truly, yet,* אוּלָם *ulam.*
Job 33. 1 Wherefore, Job, I pray thee, hear my sp.

2. *Therefore,* לָהֵן *la-hen.*
Dan. 4. 27 Wherefore, O king, let my counsel be ac

3. *Wherefore, wherefore?* מַדּוּעַ *maddua.*
Gen. 26. 27 Wherefore come ye to me, seeing ye hate
Isa. 5. 4 wherefore, when I looked that it should

4. *For what, wherefore?* לָמָּה *la-mah.*
Gen. 18. 13 Wherefore did Sarah laugh, saying, Shall

5. *Concerning what?* עַל־מָה *al mah.*
Mal. 2. 14 Yet ye say, Wherefore? Because the LORD

6. *For this reason, because,* כָּל־קֳבֵל דְּנָה *kol qebel denah.*
Dan. 3. 8 Wherefore at that time certain Chaldeans
6. 9 Wherefore king Darius signed the writing

7. *Surely only,* כִּי אַךְ *ki ak.*
2 Ki. 5. 7 wherefore consider, I pray you, and see

8. *Therefore,* עַל־כֵּן *al ken.*
Gen. 10. 9 wherefore it is said, Even as Nimrod the

9. *Therefore,* לָכֵן *la-ken.*
Exod. 6. 6 Wherefore say unto the children of Israel

10. *Under or instead of what?* תַּחַת מָה *tachath meh.*
Jer. 5. 19 Wherefore doeth the LORD our God all th.

11. *In deed, in truth, then, therefore,* ἄρα *ara.*
2 Co. 7. 12 Wherefore, though I wrote unto you, I

12. *Then truly, therefore,* ἄραγε *arage.*
Matt. 7. 20 Wherefore by their fruits ye shall know

13. *Because of what?* διὰ τί *diati.*
Luke 19. 23 Wherefore then gavest not thou my money
Rom. 9. 32 Wherefore? Because (they sought it) not
2 Co. 11. 11 Wherefore? because I love you not? God
Rev. 17. 7 Wherefore didst thou marvel? I will tell

14. *On account of which,* διό *dio.*
Matt. 27. 8 Wherefore that field was called, The field
Luke 7. 7 Wherefore neither thought I myself wort.
Acts 13. 35 [Wherefore] he saith also in another (psalm)
15. 19 Wherefore my sentence is, that we trouble
20. 26 Wherefore I take you to record this day
24. 26 wherefore he sent for him the oftener, and
25. 26 Wherefore I have brought him forth bef.
26. 3 wherefore I beseech thee to hear me pat.
27. 25 Wherefore, sirs, be of good cheer: for I
27. 34 Wherefore I pray you to take (some) m.
Rom. 1. 24 Wherefore God also gave them up to un.
13. 5 Wherefore (ye) must needs be subject, not
15. 7 Wherefore receive ye one another as Ch.
1 Co. 12. 3 Wherefore I give you to understand, that
2 Co. 2. 8 Wherefore I beseech you that ye would
5. 9 Wherefore we labour, that, whether pres.
6. 17 Wherefore come out from among them
Eph. 2. 11 Wherefore remember, that ye (being) in
3. 13 Wherefore I desire that ye faint not at
4. 8 Wherefore he saith, When he ascended
4. 25 Wherefore, putting away lying, speak ev.
5. 14 Wherefore he saith, Awake thou that sl.
Phil. 2. 9 Wherefore God also hath highly exalted
1 Th. 2. 18 [Wherefore] we would have come unto you
3. 1 Wherefore, when we could no longer for.
5. 11 Wherefore comfort yourselves together
Phm. 8 Wherefore, though I might be much bold
Heb. 3. 7 Wherefore as the Holy Ghost saith, To d.
3. 10 Wherefore I was grieved with that gene.
10. 5 Wherefore, when he cometh into the wo.
11. 16 wherefore God is not ashamed to be called
12. 12 Wherefore lift up the hands which hang
12. 28 Wherefore, we receiving a kingdom which
13. 12 Wherefore Jesus also, that he might sa.
Jas. 1. 21 Wherefore lay apart all filthiness and su.
4. 6 Wherefore he saith, God resisteth the pr.
1 Pe. 1. 13 Wherefore gird up the loins of your mind
2. 6 [Wherefore] also it is contained in the
2 Pe. 1. 10 Wherefore the rather, brethren, give
1. 12 Wherefore I will not be negligent to put
3. 14 Wherefore, beloved, seeing that ye look

15. *Wherefore truly,* διόπερ *dioper.*
1 Co. 8. 13 Wherefore, if meat make my brother to
10. 14 Wherefore, my dearly beloved, flee from
14. 13 [Wherefore] let him that speaketh in an

16. *Wherefore? why?* ἵνα τί *hina ti.*
Matt. 9. 4 said, Wherefore think ye evil in your hea.

17. *Whence,* ὅθεν *hothen.*
Heb. 2. 17 Wherefore in all things it behoved him
3. 1 Wherefore, holy brethren, partakers of
7. 25 Wherefore he is able also to save them to
8. 3 wherefore (it is) of necessity that this man

18. *Therefore, then,* οὖν *oun.*
Matt 24. 26 Wherefore, if they shall say unto you, B.
Acts 1. 21 Wherefore of these men which have com.
6. 3 [Wherefore] brethren, look ye out among
1 Co. 4. 16 Wherefore I beseech you, be ye followers
2 Co. 8. 24 Wherefore show ye to them, and before
Col. 2. 20 [Wherefore], if ye be dead with Christ fr.
1 Pe. 2. 1 Wherefore, laying aside all malice, and

19. *What?* τί *ti.*
John 9. 27 wherefore would ye hear (it) again? will
Acts 22. 30 known the certainty wherefore he was ac.
Gal. 3. 19 Wherefore then (serveth) the law? It was

20. *On account of what?* τίνος ἕνεκεν *tinos heneken.*
Acts 19. 32 knew not wherefore they were come tog.

21. *On account of what?* χάριν τίνος *charin tinos.*
1 Jo. 3. 12 wherefore slew he him? because his own

22. *On account of, or because of this,* διὰ τοῦτο.
Matt 12. 31 Wherefore I say unto you, All manner of
23. 34 Wherefore, behold, I send unto you pro.
Rom. 5. 12 Wherefore, as by one man sin entered in.
Eph. 1. 15 Wherefore I also, after I heard of your fa.
5. 17 Wherefore be ye not unwise, but unders.
6. 13 Wherefore take unto you the whole arm.
3 John 10 Wherefore, if I come, I will re. 2 Ti. 1. 6

23. *Because of which,* δι' ἣν *di' hēn,* (αἰτίαν).
Acts 10. 21 what (is) the cause wherefore ye are co.?
22. 24; 23. 28; 2 Ti. 1. 6; Titus 1. 13.

24. *Upon what,* ἐφ' ᾧ *eph' hō,* Matt. 26. 50.

25. *For what,* οὗ χάριν *hou charin,* Luke 7. 47.

26. *Wherefore (therefore) truly,* τοιγαροῦν *toigaroun.*
Heb. 12. 1 Wherefore, seeing we also are compassed

2 *. So that,* ὥστε *hōste.*
Matt 12. 12 Wherefore it is lawful to do well on the

Matt19. 6 Wherefore they are no more twain, but
23. 31 Wherefore ye be witnesses unto yoursel.
Rom. 7. 4 Wherefore, my brethren, ye also are bec.
7. 12 Wherefore the law (is) holy, and the co.
1 Co.10. 12 Wherefore let him that thinketh he stan.
11. 27 Wherefore whosoever shall eat this bread
11. 33 Wherefore, my brethren, when ye come
14. 22 Wherefore tongues are for a sign, not to
14. 39 Wherefore, brethren, covet to prophesy
2 Co. 5. 16 Wherefore henceforth know we no man
Gal. 3. 24 Wherefore the law was our schoolmaster
4. 7 Wherefore thou art no more a servant, but
Phil. 2. 12 Wherefore, my beloved, as ye have alwa.
1 Th. 4. 18 Wherefore comfort one another with th.
Jas. 1. 19 [Wherefore], my beloved brethren, let ev.
1 Pe. 4. 19 Wherefore let them that suffer according

28. *With a view to what? εἰς τί eis ti (neut.)*
Matt 14. 31 O thou of little faith, wherefore didst th.

29. *Indeed then, μὲν οὖν men oun.*
Acts 19. 38 Wherefore if Demetrius, and the craftsmen

30. *With a view to which, εἰς ὅ eis ho.*
2 Th. 1. 11 Wherefore also we pray always for you, th.

WHEREIN, whereinto, whereinsoever —

1. *In that which, בַּאֲשֶׁר ba-asher.*
Eccl. 3. 9 What profit hath he that worketh in that w.

2. *In which, lit. which in it, אֲשֶׁר בּוֹ asher bo.*
Gen. 7. 15 two and two of all flesh, wherein (is) the

3. *Which there, where, אֲשֶׁר שָׁם asher sham.*
Deut.12. 2 shall utterly destroy all the places where.

4. *In the midst of, בְּגַו be-gav.*
Ezra 5. 7 They sent a letter unto him, wherein was

5. *In them, in which, אֲשֶׁר בָּהֶן asher ba-hen.*
Deut.28. 52 wherein thou trustedst, throughout all

6. *In them, in which, אֲשֶׁר בָּהֵנָּה asher ba-henah.*
Jer. 5. 17 they shall impoverish thy fenced cities, wh.

7. *This, which, זוּ zu.*
Psa. 142. 3 In the way wherein I walked have they
143. 8 cause me to know the way wherein I sh.

8. *In what, בַּמָּה bam-mah.*
1 Sa. 14. 38 know and see wherein this sin hath been

9. *In the midst of which, אֲשֶׁר בְּתוֹכָהּ asher be-tok-ah.*
Num.35. 34 land which ye shall inhabit, wherein I

10. *Unto whose midst, אֲשֶׁר אֶל־תּוֹכוֹ asher el tok-o.*
Lev. 11. 33 every earthen vessel whereinto (any) of

11. *On account of which, δι' ἣν di' hēn.*
2 Pe. 3. 12 wherein the heavens being on fire shall be

12. *With a view to which, εἰς ὅ eis ho.*
John 6. 22 save that one whereinto his disciples were
Acts 7. 4 removed him into this land, wherein ye
1 Pe. 3. 20 wherein few, that is, eight souls were sa.
5. 12 this is the true grace of God wherein ye

13. *In which, ἐν αἷς, ἐν ᾗ, ἐν τῷ, ἐν ᾧ, en hais, en hē.*
Matt.11. 20 began he to upbraid the cities wherein
25. 13 [know neither the day nor the hour whe.]
John19. 41 new sepulchre, wherein was never man
Acts 2. 8 every man in our own tongue, wherein we
10. 12 Wherein were all manner of four footed
Rom. 2. 1 for wherein thou judgest another, thou co.
5. 2 access by faith into this grace wherein we
7. 6 that being dead wherein we were held, th.
1 Co. 7. 20 Let every man abide in the same calling w.
7. 24 let every man, wherein he is called, the.
15. 1 which also ye have received, and wherein
2 Co. 11. 12 wherein they glory they may be found ev.
Eph. 1. 6 [wherein] he hath made us accepted in the
2. 2 Wherein in time past ye walked according
5. 18 be not drunk with wine, wherein is excess
Col. 2. 12; 2 Ti. 2. 9; Heb. 6. 17; 9. 2; 9. 4; 1 Pe. 1. 6; 4. 4; 2 Pe. 3. 13; Rev. 2. 13; 18. 19.

14. *Upon which, ἐφ' ᾧ eph hō,* Lu. 11. 22; Phil. 4. 10

15. *Whereinsoever, ἐν ᾧ ἂν en hō an.*
2 Co. 11 21 Howbeit whereinsoever any is bold, I sp.

16. *Concerning which, περὶ ὧν peri hōn.*
Luke 1. 4 those things, wherein thou hast been in.

17. *Where, whither, οὗ hou.*
Luke23. 53 sepulchre that was hewn in stone, where.

WHEREOF, whereon, whereupon —

1. *Which, of which, אֲשֶׁר asher.*
Num. 5. 3 defile not their camps, in the midst whe.

2. *On which, lit. which on it, אֲשֶׁר עָלָיו asher al-av.*
Exod. 3. 5 for the place whereon thou standest (is)

3. *Concerning which, περὶ ἧς or ὧν peri hēs or hōn.*
Acts 24. 13 Neither can they prove the things whereof
1 Co. 7. 1 Now concerning the things whereof ye
Heb. 2. 5 in subjection the world to come, whereof

4. *Among which things, ἐν οἷς (neu. pl.) en hois.*
Acts 24. 18 Whereupon certain Jews from Asia found
26. 12 Whereupon, as I went to Damascus with

5. *Whence, ὅθεν hothen.*
Matt.14. 7 Whereupon he promised with an oath to
Acts 26. 19 Whereupon O king Agrippa, I was not
Heb. 9. 18 Whereupon neither the first (testament)

6. *Out of which, ἐξ οὗ, or ὧν,* 1 Ti. 6. 4; He. 13. 10

7. *Upon which, ἐφ' οὗ eph hou,* Luke 4. 29.

8. *Upon which, ἐφ' ᾧ eph hō,* Lu. 5. 25; Ro. 6. 21.

9. *Upon which, ἐφ' ὃν hon,* Mr. 11. 2; Lu. 19. 30.

10. *Which, ὃς hos,* Acts 2. 32; 3. 15.

11. *Concerning what things, περὶ τίνων peri tinōn.*
1 Ti. 1. 7 neither what they say, nor whereof they

WHERESOEVER —

1. *In (the place) which, בַּאֲשֶׁר ba-asher.*
2 Ki. 8. 1 sojourn wheresoever thou canst sojourn

2. *In every (place) that, בְּכָל־דִּי be-kol di.*
Dan. 2. 38 wheresoever the children of men dwell

3. *Where, ὅπου hopou.*
Luke17. 37 Wheresoever the body (is), thither will the

4. *Wherever, ὅπου ἂν hopou an.*
Mark 9. 18 wheresoever he taketh him, he teareth
14. 9 [Wheresoever] this gospel shall be preach.

5. *Wheresoever, ὅπου ἐάν hopou ean.*
Matt 24. 28 For wheresoever the carcase is, there will
26. 13 Wheresoever this gospel shall be preached
Mark14. 14 [wheresoever] he shall go in, say ye to the

WHERETO, whereunto —

1. *For what, wherefore? לָמָּה la-mah.*
Job 30. 2 whereto (might) the strength of their ha.

2. *With a view to which, εἰς ὅ eis ho.*
Phil. 3. 16 whereto we have already attained, let us
Col. 1. 29 Whereunto I also labour, striving accord.
2 Th. 2. 14 Whereunto he called you by our gospel
1 Ti. 2. 7 Whereunto I am ordained a preacher, and
6. 12 whereunto thou art also called, and hast
2 Ti. 1. 11 Whereunto I am appointed a preacher
1 Pe. 2. 8 being disobedient; whereunto also they

3. *To what? τίνι tini.*
Matt 11. 16 But whereunto shall I liken this genera.?
Mark 4. 30 [Whereunto] shall we liken the kingdom
Luke 7. 31 Whereunto then shall I liken the men of
13. 18 what is the kingdom of God like? and wh.
13. 20 Whereunto shall I liken the kingdom of

4. *What, τί ti.*
Acts 5. 24 they doubted of them whereunto this wo.

WHEREWITH, wherewithal, wherewith soever —

1. *Which, with which, אֲשֶׁר asher.*
Gen. 27. 41 because of the blessing wherewith his fa.

2. *A word, דָּבָר dabar.*
Psa.119. 42 So shall I have wherewith to answer him

3. *With what? בַּמָּה bam-mah.*
Judg. 6. 15 Oh my Lord, wherewith shall I save Israel?

4. *In, with or by which, ἐν ᾧ en hō.*
Eph. 6. 16 wherewith ye shall be able to quench all
Heb. 10. 29 wherewith he was sanctified, an unholy

5. *As much or as many as, ὅσας ἂν hosas an.*
Mark 3. 28 blasphemies [wherewith soever] they sh.

6. *What? τί ti.*
Matt. 6. 31 What shall we drink? or, Wherewithal
Luke17. 8 Make ready wherewith I may sup, and

7. *In, with or by what? ἐν τίνι en tini.*
Matt. 5. 13 if the salt have lost his savour, wherewith
Mark 9. 50 if the salt have lost his saltness, wherew.
Luke14. 34 if the salt have lost his savour, wherewith

WHET, to —

1. *To sharpen, instruct, לָטַשׁ latash.*
Psa. 7. 12 If he turn not, he will whet his sword; he

2. *To roll, devolve, trust, קָלַל qalal, 3a.*
Eccl. 10. 10 If the iron be blunt, and he do not whet

3. *To sharpen, repeat, שָׁנַן shanan.*
Deut32. 41 If I whet my glittering sword, and mine
Psa. 64. 3 Who whet their tongue like a sword, (and)

WHETHER, (any, yet, or, not) —

1. *Or, whether, אוֹ o.*
Exod21. 31 Whether he have gored a son, or have go.
Lev. 5. 1 whether he hath seen or known (of it); if

2. *Where? אֵי זֶה e zeh.*
Eccl. 11. 6 for thou knowest not whether shall pro.

3. *If, אִם im.*
Exod19. 13 whether (it be) beast or man, it shall not

4. *Between, בֵּין ben.*
Lev. 27. 12 priest shall value it, whether it be good
2 Ch.14. 11 whether with many, or with them that

5. *Whether, or, הֵן hen.*
Ezra 7. 17 whether it be (so), that a decree was made
7. 26 whether (it be) unto death, or to banish.

6. *That, כִּי ki.*
Job 34. 33 whether thou refuse, or whether thou ch.

7. *Even from, לְמִן le-min.*
2 Ch.15. 13 whether small or great, whether man or

8. *Whether yet? הַעוֹד ha-od.*
Exod 4. 18 return..and see whether they be yet alive

9. *If not, אִם לֹא im lo.*
Exod22. 8 whether he have put his hand unto his ne.

10. *If, ἐάν τε ean te.*
Rom 14 8 whether we live..[whether] we die..whe.

11. *If, εἰ ei.*
Matt.26. 63 tell us whether thou be the Christ, the
27. 49 let us see whether Elias will come to save
Mark 3. 2 whether he would heal him on the sabba.
15. 36 let us see whether Elias will come to take
Luke 6. 7 watched him, whether he would heal on
14. 28 counteth the cost, whether he have (suffi.)
14. 31 consulteth whether he be able with ten th.
23. 6 he asked whether the man were a Galile.
John 9. 25 Whether he be a sinner (or no), I know
Acts 4. 19 Whether it be right in the sight of God
5. 8 Tell me whether ye sold the land for so
10. 18 asked whether Simon, which was surna.
17. 11 searched the scriptures daily, whether th.
19. 2 We have not so much as heard whether
25. 20 I asked (him) whether he would go to Je.
1 Co. 1. 16 besides, I know not whether I baptized
7. 16 whether thou shalt save (thy) husband?
2 Co. 2. 9 that I might know the proof of you, whe.
13. 5 Examine yourselves, whether ye, 1 Jo. 4. 1

12. *The one which, ἕνα ὃν hena hon,* Acts 1. 24.

13. *If anything, whatever, whichever, εἴτε eite.*
Rom 12. 6 grace that is given unto us, whether pro.
1 Co. 3. 22 Whether Paul, or Apollos, or Cephas, or
8. 5 whether in heaven or in earth, as there
10. 31 Whether therefore ye eat, or drink, or w.
12. 13 whether (we be) Jews or Gentiles, wheth.
12. 26 [whether] one member suffer, all the me.
13. 8 whether (there be) prophecies, they shall
13. 8 whether (there be) knowledge, it shall va.
14. 7 whether pipe or harp, except they give a
15. 11 Therefore whether (it were) I or they, so
2 Co. 1. 6 whether we be afflicted..whether we be co.
5. 9 whether present or absent, we may be ac.
5. 10 according to that he hath done, whether
5. 13 whether we be beside ourselves..or whe.
8. 23 Whether (any do enquire) of Titus, (he is)
12. 2 whether in the body, I cannot tell; or wh.
12. 3 whether in the body, or out of the body
Eph. 6. 8 the same shall he receive of the Lord, wh.
Phil. 1. 18 whether in pretence, or in truth, Christ
1. 20 in my body, whether (it be) by life, or by
1. 27 whether I come and see you, or else be
Col. 1. 16 whether (they be) thrones, or dominions
1. 20 whether (they be) things in earth, or thi.
1 Th. 5. 10 whether we wake or sleep, we should li.
2 Th. 2. 15 traditions which ye have been taught, w.
1 Pe. 2. 13 whether it be to the king, as supreme

14. *Whether, indeed, ἤτοι ētoi.*
Rom. 6. 16 whether of sin unto death, or of obedience

15. *Lest at any time, whether, if perhaps, μήποτε.*
Luke 3. 15 mused..whether he were the Christ, or not

16. *Whether? πότερον poteron.*
John 7. 17 shall know of the doctrine, whether it be

17. *Both, τε καί te kai.*
Acts 9. 2 whether they were men or women, he mig.

18. *What? τί ti.*
Matt. 9. 5 For whether is easier, to say, (Thy) sins
21. 31 Whether of them twain did the will of (h.)
23. 17, 19 (Ye) fools, and blind! for whether is
27. 21 Whether of the twain will ye that I rele.
Mark 2. 9 Whether is it easier to say to the sick of
Luke 5. 23 Whether is easier, to say, Thy sins be for.
22. 27 For whether (is) greater, he that sitteth

WHICH (thing, the, on) —

1. *Where? אֵי e.*
2 Ch.18. 23 Which way went the spirit of the LORD

2. *These, אֵלֶּה el eh.*
1 Ch.23. 4 Of which, twenty and four thousand (we.)

3. *And I myself, וַאֲנִי va-ani.*
Gen. 18. 13 Shall I of a surety bear a child, which am

4. *And I myself, וְאָנֹכִי ve-anoki.*
Gen. 18. 27 I have taken upon me..which (am but)

5. *Which, אֲשֶׁר asher.*
Gen. 1. 7 from the waters which (were) above the

6. *Which, דִּי di.*
Ezra 4. 12 that the Jews which came up from thee

7. *This, דְּנָה denah.*
Ezra 4. 15 for which cause was this city destroyed

8. *He, it, that, הוּא hu.*
Gen. 14. 17 at the valley of Shaveh, which (is) the ki.

9. *That itself, הַהוּא ha-hu.*
Deut. 3. 13 all Bashan, which was called the land of

10. *They, הֵם hem.*
Deut. 2. 11 Which also were accounted giants, as the

11. *Which they, אֲשֶׁר הֵן asher hen.*
Gen. 19. 29 when he overthrew the cities in the which

12. *This, זֶה zeh.*
Psa.104. 8 unto the place which thou hast founded

13. *This, זוּ zu.*
Exod 15. 13 Thou..hast led forth the people which
15. 16 till the people pass over, which thou hast
Psa. 9. 15 in the net which they hid is their own fo.
32. 8 and teach thee in the way which thou sh.

14. *Who, who? מִי mi.*
Judg.20. 18 Which of us shall go up first to the battle

15. *He, it, αὐτός autos.*
Rev. 17. 9 seven mountains, on which the woman si.

16. *Such as, such, οἷος hoios.*
Phil. 1. 30 Having the same conflict which ye saw
2 Ti. 3. 11 Persecutions, afflictions, which came un.

17. *As much, as great, ὅσος hosos.*
John21. 25 there are also many other things which J.
Acts 9. 39 showing the coats and garments which

18. *Whosoever, whatsoever,* ὅστις *hostis.*
Matt. 7. 15 Beware of false prophets, which come to
7. 24 will liken him unto a wise man, which bu.
7. 26 foolish man, which built his house upon
13. 52 an householder, which bringeth forth out
16. 28 There be some standing here which shall
19. 12 which were so born..which were made
19. 12 which have made themselves eunuchs for
20. 1 an householder, which went out early in
21. 33 a certain householder, which planted a vi
21. 41 other husbandmen, which shall render
22. 2 a certain king, which made a marriage for
23. 27 whited sepulchres, which indeed appear
25. 1 virgins, which took their lamps, and went
27. 55 many women..which followed Jesus from
Mark 9. 1 which shall not taste of death, till they
12. 18 Sadducees, which say there is no resurre.
Luke 1. 20 my words, which shall be fulfilled in their
2. 4 the city of David, which is called Beth-le.
2. 10 good tidings of great joy, which shall be
7. 37 a woman in the city, which was a sinner
8. 3 Susanna, and many others, which minist
8. 15 they, which in an honest and good heart
8. 26 at the country of the Gadarenes, which is
8. 43 a woman..which had spent all her living
9. 30 there talked with him two men, which w.
10. 42 Mary hath chosen that good part, which
12. 1 the leaven of the Pharisees, which is hyp.
15. 7 just persons, which need no repentance
23. 55 the women also, which came with him
John 8. 53 greater than our father Abraham, which
21. 25 the which, if they should be written every
Acts 10. 47 that these should not be baptized, which
11. 20 men of Cyprus and Cyrene, which, when
11. 28 which came to pass in the days of Claud.
12. 10 iron gate..which opened to them of his
16. 12 Philippi, which is the chief city of that
16. 16 a certain damsel..which brought her ma.
16. 17 servants of the most high God, which sh.
23. 21 forty men, which have bound themselves
Rom. 2. 15 Which show the work of the law written
16. 12 [Salute the beloved Persis, which laboured]
1 Co. 3. 17 the temple of God is holy, which..ye are
6. 20 [in your body, and in your spirit, which]
7. 13 the woman which hath an husband that
2 Co. 3. 14 remaineth the same veil..which..is done
9. 11 bountifulness, which causeth through us
Gal. 4. 24 Which things are an allegory..which is A.
4. 26 Jerusalem..which is the mother of us all
5. 19 the works of the flesh are manifest, which
Eph. 1. 23 Which is his body, the fulness of him that
3. 13 my tribulations for you, which is your gl.
6. 2 which is the first commandment with pr.
Phm. 1. 28 which is to them an evident token of per.
4. 3 help those women which laboured with
Col. 2. 23 Which things have indeed a show of wisd.
3. 5 evil..and covetousness, [which] is idolatry
3. 14 charity, [which] is the bond of perfectness
4. 11 fellow workers..which have been a com.
1 Ti. 1. 4 which minister questions rather than god.
3. 15 which is the church of the living God, the
6. 9 which drown men in destruction and perd.
2 Ti. 1. 5 which dwelt first in thy grandmother Lo.
Heb. 2. 3 which at the first began to be spoken by
8. 6 which was established upon better prom.
9. 2 a tabernacle..which is called the sanctuary
9. 9 Which (was) a figure for the time then pr.
10. 8 burnt offerings..which are offered by the
10. 11 sacrifices, which can never take away sin
10. 35 which hath great recompence of reward
12. 5 the exhortation which speaketh unto you
1 Pe. 2. 11 abstain from fleshy lusts, which war aga.
1 Jo. 1. 2 that eternal life which was with the Father
Rev. 1. 7 shall see him, and they (also) which pierc.
2. 24 which have not known the depths of Sat.
9. 4 those men which have not the seal of God
11. 8; 12. 13; 17. 12; 19. 2; 20. 4.

19. *Upon which,* ὅπου...ἐπ' αὐτῶν, Rev. 17. 9.

20. *Which,* ὅ *ho,* Acts 11. 30; 26. 10; Gal. 2. 10
Col. 2. 17, 22; 2 Ti. 1. 6; Rev. 21. 8.

21. *Whosoever, whatsoever,* ὅστις ἄν *hostis an.*
Acts 3. 23 every soul, which will not hear that proph.

22. *This,* αὕτη *hautē.*
Acts 8. 26 from Jerusalem unto Gaza, which is desert

23. *Of what sort or kind?* ποῖος *poios.*
Matt 19. 18 He saith unto him, Which? Jesus said, Th.
22. 36 which (is) the great commandment in the
Mark 12. 28 asked him, Which is the first commandm.
John 10. 32 for which of those works do ye stone me?

24. *Who? which?* τίς *tis.*
Matt. 6. 27 Which of you, by taking thought, can add
Luke 7. 42 Tell me..which of them will love him mo.
9. 46 there arose a reasoning..which of them
10. 36 Which now of these three, thinkest thou
11. 5 Which of you shall have a friend, and sh.
12. 25 which of you with taking thought can add
14. 5 Which of you shall have an ass or an
14. 28 which of you, intending to build a tower
17. 7 which of you, having a servant plowing
22. 23 which of them it was that should do this
22. 24 which of them should be accounted the
John 8. 46 Which of you convinceth me of sin? And
21. 20 Lord, which is he that betrayeth thee?
Acts 7. 52 Which of the prophets have not your fat.
Heb. 1. 5, 13 unto which of the angels said he at any
5. 12 teach you again which (be) the first princ.

25. *To those which are,* ταῖς *tais.*
Jas. 1. 1 to the twelve tribes which are scattered

WHICH is or make —

1. *He, it, that,* הוּא *hu.*
Gen. 14. 3 the vale of Siddim, which is the salt sea

2. *She, it, that,* הִיא *hi.*
Gen. 14. 2 war with..the king of Bela, which is Zoar

3. *Which is,* ὅ ἐστιν *ho estin.*
Mark 3. 17 Boanerges, which is, The sons of thunder
12. 42 she threw in two mites, which make a fa.
Eph. 6. 17 the sword of the spirit, which is the word
Col. 1. 24 for his body's sake, which is the church
Heb. 7. 2 also king of Salem, which is, king of pea.
Rev. 21. 8 burneth with fire..which is the second de.

WHICH hath, way —

1. *Where?* אֵי זֶה *e zeh.*
1 Ki. 22. 24 Which way went the spirit of the LORD

2. *There is, there are,* יֵשׁ *yesh.*
Mal. 1. 14 the deceiver, which hath in his flock a

WHILE, a little, that, the, within a, yet, whiles —

1. *If,* אִם *im.*
1 Sa. 20. 14 thou shalt not only while yet I live show

2. *From the day, the days,* מִיּוֹם, יָמִים *miy-yom, yamim.*
1 Sa. 7. 2 it came to pass, while the ark abode in K.
25. 7 neither..ought missing..all the while th.
25. 16 all the while we were with them keeping
1 Ki. 17. 7 it came to pass after a while, that the br.

3. *Because,* כִּי *ki.*
Deut 19. 6 pursue the slayer, while his heart is hot

4. *Till,* עַד *ad.*
Exod 33. 22 will cover thee with my hand while I pass

5. *While,* עוֹד *od.*
Gen. 29. 9 while he yet spake with them, Rachel ca.
2 Sa. 3. 35 to cause David to eat meat while it was

6. *In yet, while yet,* בְּעוֹד *be-od.*
Job 27. 3 All the while my breath (is) in me, and the
Psa 104. 33 I will sing praise to my God while I have

7. *When,* כַּאֲשֶׁר *ka-asher.*
Neh. 6. 3 why should the work cease, whilst I leave

8. *A little,* מִצְעָר *mitsar.*
Isa. 63. 18 The people..possessed (it) but a little while

9. *Until which,* ἄχρι οὗ *achri hou.*
Acts 27. 33 while the day was coming on, Paul besou.

10. *Until which,* ἄχρις οὗ *achris hou.*
Heb. 3. 13 exhort one another daily, while it is called

11. *In, during,* ἐν τῷ *en tō.*
Matt 13. 25 while men slept, his enemy came and so.
Mark 2. 19 fast while the bridegroom is with them?
Luke 1. 8 while he executed the priest's office before
5. 34 fast while the bridegroom is with them?
24. 15 while they communed (together) and rea.
24. 51 it came to pass, while he blessed them, he
John 5. 7 while I am coming, another steppeth do.
Acts 19. 1 while Apollos was at Corinth, Paul having
Heb. 3. 15 While it is said, To day if ye will hear his

12. *Unto, up to,* ἕως *heōs.*
Matt 14. 22 to go..while he sent the multitudes away
26. 36 Sit ye here, while I go and pray yonder
Mark 6. 45 to go to the other side..while he sent aw.
14. 32 saith to his disciples, Sit ye here, while I
John 9. 4 I must work the works..while it is day
12. 35 Walk [while] ye have the light, lest dark.
12. 36 [While] ye have light, believe in the light

13. *A day, time,* ἡμέρα *hēmera.*
Acts 15. 7 ye know how that a good while ago God
18. 18 Paul..tarried (there) yet a good while, and

14. *As much, as great,* μικρὸν ὅσον ὅσον *mikron.*
Heb. 10. 37 yet a little while, and he that shall come

15. *Until, while,* ἕως ὅτου *heōs hotou.*
Matt. 5. 25 Agree..whiles thou art in the way with

16. *Whenever,* ὅταν *hotan.*
1 Co. 3. 4 while one saith, I am of Paul; and anot.

17. *When,* ὅτε *hote.*
John 17. 12 While I was with them in the world, I ke.
Heb. 9. 17 it is of no strength at all while the testa.

18. *A season,* καιρός *kairos.*
Luke 8. 13 which for a while believe, and in time of

19. *Little, small, short,* μικρόν *mikron.*
Matt 26. 73 after a while came unto (him) they that

20. *A little, in a small degree,* ὀλίγον *oligon.*
Mark 6. 31 Come ye yourselves..and rest a while, for
1 Pe. 5. 10 after that ye have suffered a while, make

21. *A time,* χρόνος *chronos.*
Luke 18. 4 he would not for a while: but afterward
John 7. 33 Yet a little while am I with you and (th.)
12. 35 Yet a little while is the light 1 Co. 16. 7.

22. *As,* ὡς *hōs.*
Luke 24. 32 while he talked with us..and while he op.
Acts 1. 10 while they looked stedfastly toward hea.
10. 17 while Peter doubted in himself what this

23. *A certain time,* χρόνον τινά *chronon tina.*
1 Co. 16. 7 I trust to tarry a while with you, if the

WHILE ago, to come, any while, a great —

1. *Far off,* רָחוֹק *rachoq.*
2 Sa. 7. 19 hast spoken..for a great while to come

2. *Long ago, formerly, anciently,* πάλαι *palai.*
Mark 15. 44 asked..whether he had been [any while]
Luke 10. 13 they had a great while ago repented, sit.

3. *For a season,* πρόσκαιρος *proskairos.*
Matt 13. 21 hath he not root..but dureth for a while

WHIP —

A scourge, whip, rod, שׁוֹט *shot.*
1 Ki. 12. 11 my father hath chastised you with whips
12. 14 my father (also) chastised you with whips
2 Ch. 10. 11, 14 my father chastised you with whips
Prov. 26. 3 A whip for the horse, a bridle for the ass
Nah. 3. 2 The noise of a whip, and the noise of the

WHIRL (about,) to —

To go round (and) go on, סָבַב הָלַךְ *sabab halak.*
Eccl. 1. 6 The wind..it whirleth about continually

WHIRLWIND (to come out as, drive or scatter with a) —

1. *A hurricane,* סוּפָה *suphah.*
Job 37. 9 Out of the south cometh the whirlwind
Prov. 1. 27 your destruction cometh as a whirlwind
10. 25 As the whirlwind passeth, so (is) the wic.
Isa. 5. 28 like flint, and their wheels like a whirlw.
17. 13 like a rolling thing before the whirlwind
21. 1 As whirlwinds in the south pass through
66. 15 LORD will come..with his chariots like a w.
Jer. 4. 13 his chariots..as a whirlwind: his horses
Hos. 8. 7 they shall reap the whirlwind: it hath no
Amos 1. 14 with a tempest in the day of the whirlw.
Nah. 1. 3 way in the whirlwind and in the storm

2. *To be tossed about, tempestuous,* סָעַר *saar.*
Hab. 3. 14 they came out as a whirlwind to scatter

3. *To toss about,* סָעַר *saar,* 3.
Zech. 7. 14 I scattered them with a whirlwind among

4. *To be tossed about, tempestuous,* סָעַר *saar,* 4.
Hos. 13. 3 as the chaff..is driven with the whirlwi.

5. *A whirlwind,* סַעַר *saar.*
Jer. 23. 19 a grievous whirlwind; it shall fall grievo.
25. 32 a great whirlwind shall be raised up from
30. 23 a continuing whirlwind; it shall fall with

6. *A whirlwind,* סְעָרָה *searah.*
2 Ki. 2. 1 would take up Elijah into heaven by a wh.
2. 11 Elijah went up by a whirlwind into heav.
Job 38. 1 Then the LORD answered Job out of the w.
40. 6 Then answered the L...Job out of the wh.
Isa. 40. 24 the whirlwind shall take them away as st.
41. 16 wind shall carry them away, and the whi.
Jer. 23. 19 a whirlwind of the LORD is gone forth in
30. 23 the whirlwind of the LORD goeth forth
Zech. 9. 14 LORD..shall go with whirlwinds of the so.

7. *A whirling wind,* רוּחַ סְעָרָה *ruach searah.*
Eze. 1. 4 I looked, and behold, a whirlwind came

8. *To be whirled away,* שָׂעַר *saar.*
Psa. 58. 9 he shall take them away as with a whirl.

9. *To show self tempestuous,* שָׂעַר *saar,* 7.
Dan. 11. 40 shall come against him like a whirlwind

WHISPER (together), whisperer, whispering, to —

1. *To show self a whisperer,* לָחַשׁ *lachash,* 7.
2 Sa. 12. 19 when David saw that his servants whisp.
Psa. 41. 7 All that hate me whisper together against

2. *To chatter, whisper,* צָפַף *tsaphaph,* 3a.
Isa. 29. 4 thy speech shall whisper out of the dust

3. *Talebearer, whisperer, busybody,* נִרְגָּן *nirgan.*
Prov. 16. 28 and a whisperer separateth chief friends

4. *A whispering, muttering,* ψιθυρισμός *psithurismos.*
2 Co. 12. 20 backbitings, whisperings, swellings, tum.

5. *A whisperer, detractor,* ψιθυριστής *psithuristēs.*
Rom. 1. 29 full of..debate, deceit, malignity: whisp.

WHIT, (not a) —

1. *A word, matter, thing,* דָּבָר *dabar.*
1 Sa. 3. 18 Samuel told him every whit, and hid no.

2. *Complete, completely,* כָּלִיל *kalil.*
Deut. 13. 16 shalt burn..all the spoil thereof every wh.

3. *No one,* μηδείς *mēdeis.*
2 Co. 11. 5 I suppose I was not a whit behind the very
[*See* Every whit.]

WHITE, (linen, of an egg) —

1. *Fine linen, byssus,* בּוּץ *buts.*
2 Ch. 5. 12 arrayed in white linen, having cymbals

2. *Whiteness, mother of pearl,* דַּר *dar.*
Esth. 1. 6 a pavement of red, and blue, and white

3. *White,* חִוָּר *chivvar.*
Dan. 7. 9 whose garment (was) white as snow, and

4. *Whiteness,* חוּר *chur.*
Esth. 1. 6 white, green, and blue..fastened with co.
8. 15 in royal apparel of blue and white, and

5. *White bread,* חֹרִי *chori.*
Gen. 40. 16 and behold..three white baskets on my

6. *White,* לָבָן *laban.*
Gen. 30. 35 every one that had..white in it, and all
30. 37 pilled white strakes..and made the white
Exod 16. 31 it (was) like coriander seed, white, and
Lev. 13. 3 and..the hair in the plague is turned wh.
13. 4 If the bright spot (be) white in the skin
13. 4 and the hair thereof be not turned white
13. 10 behold, (if) the rising (be) white in the skin

Lev. 13. 10 and it have turned the hair white, and
13. 13 plague: it is all turned white: he (is) clean
13. 16 Or if the raw flesh ..be changed unto wh.
13. 17 behold, (if) the plague be turned into wh.
13. 19 a white rising, or a bright spot, white
13. 20 behold. .the hair thereof be turned white
13. 21 But if. .no white hairs therein, and (if) it
13. 24 a white bright spot, somewhat reddish, or
13. 25 (if) the hair in the bright spot be turned w.
13. 26 But if..no white hair in the bright spot
13. 38 If a man also or a woman have..white
13. 39 (if) the bright spots..(be) darkish white
13. 42 if there be in the bald head..a white re.
13. 43 (if) the rising of the sore (be) white redd.
Eccl. 9. 8 Let thy garments be always white; and
Zech. 1. 8 behind him..red horses, speckled, and w.
6. 3 in the third chariot white horses, and in
6. 6 black horses..the white go forth after th.

7. *White*, לָבָן [*laban*].
Gen. 49. 12 His eyes. .red with wine..his teeth white

8. *Clear, dry*, צַח *tsach*.
Song 5. 10 My beloved (is) white and ruddy, the ch.

9. *Whiteness*, צָחַר *tsachar*.
Eze. 27. 18 Damascus (was) thy merchant in. .white

10. *White*, צָחֹר *tsachor*.
Judg. 5. 10 Speak, ye that ride on white asses, ye th.

11. *Spittle, drivel, albumen*, רִיר *rir*.
Job 6. 6 or is there..taste in the white of an egg?

12. *Shining, bright, resplendent*, λαμπρός *lampros*.
Rev. 15. 6 angels..clothed in pure and white linen
19. 8 be arrayed in fine linen, clean and white

13. *White*, λευκός *leukos*.
Matt. 5. 36 thou canst not make one hair white or bl.
17. 2 his face did shine..his raiment was white
28. 3 like lightning, and his raiment white as
Mark 9. 3 his raiment became shining exceeding w
16. 5 young man..clothed in a long white gar.
Luke 9. 29 and his raiment (was) white..glistering
John 4. 35 look on the fields; for they are white alr.
20. 12 seeth two angels in white sitting, the one
Acts 1. 10 two men stood by them in white apparel
Rev. 1. 14 hairs (were) white like wool, as white as
2. 17 will give him a white stone, and in the st.
3. 4 they shall walk with me in white: for th.
3. 5 the same shall be clothed in white raime.
3. 18 white raiment, that thou mayest be cloth.
4. 4 I saw..elders sitting, clothed in white ra.
6. 2 I saw, and behold a white horse: and he
6. 11 white robes were given unto every one of
7. 9 with white robes, and palms in their ha.
7. 13 What are these which are arrayed in wh.
14. 14 I looked, and behold a white cloud, and
19. 11 I saw heaven opened, and behold a white
19. 14 white horses, clothed in fine linen, white
20. 11 I saw a great white throne, and him that

WHITE, to be as, be made, make, whited —

1. *To make white*, לָבַן *laban*, 5.
Isa. 1. 18 Though..as scarlet, they shall be as white
Dan. 11. 35 and to purge, and to make (them) white
Joel 1. 7 fig tree..the branches thereof are made w.

2. *To become or show self white*, לָבַן *laban*, 7.
Dan. 12. 10 Many shall be purified, and made white

3. *To make white, whiten*, κονιάω *koniaō*.
Matt 23. 27 ye are like unto whited sepulchres, which
Acts 23. 3 God shall smite thee, (thou) whited wall

4. *To make white, whiten*, λευκαίνω *leukainō*.
Mark 9. 3 so as no fuller on earth can white them
Rev. 7. 14 made them white in the blood of the La.

WHITER, to be —

1. *To make white, whiten*, לָבַן *laban*, 5.
Psa. 51. 7 wash me, and I shall be whiter than snow

2. *To be clear, white*, צָחַח *tsachach*.
Lam. 4. 7 they were whiter than milk, they were

WHITHER, whithersoever —

1. *Unto, toward*, אֶל *el*.
Jer. 40. 4 whither it seemeth good and convenient

2. *Whither?* אָן *an*.
1 Sa. 10. 14 Saul's uncle said unto him..Whither we

3. *Whither?* אָנָה *anah*.
Gen. 37. 30 The child (is) not; and I, whither shall I
Eze. 21. 16 Go thee..whithersoever thy face (is) set

4. *Which*, אֲשֶׁר *asher*.
Gen. 28. 15 will keep thee in all (places) whither thou

5. *In (the place) which*, בַּאֲשֶׁר *ba-asher*.
1 Sa. 23. 13 departed..and went whithersoever they

6. *Unto every (place) which*, אֶל־כָּל־אֲשֶׁר *el kol asher*.
Josh. 1. 16 whithersoever thou sendest us we will go

7. *And there*, וְשָׁם *ve-sham*.
2 Sa. 17. 18 well in his court; whither they went down

8. *Because there*, שֶׁשָּׁם *shesh-sham*.
Psa. 122. 4 Whither the tribes go up, the tribes of the

9. *In the way which*, בַּדֶּרֶךְ אֲשֶׁר *bad-derek asher*.
1 Ki. 8. 44 whithersoever thou shalt send them, and

10. *The place which*, מְקוֹם אֲשֶׁר *meqom asher*.
Esth. 4. 3 whithersoever the king's commandment

11. *Where, whither*, ὅπου *hopou*.
John 8. 21 I go my way..whither I go, ye cannot co.
8. 22 he saith, Whither I go, ye cannot come
John 13. 33 I said..Whither I go, ye cannot come
13. 36 Whither I go, thou canst not follow me
14. 4 whither I go ye know, and the way ye kn.
18. 20 the temple, whither the Jews always res.
21. 18 whither thou wouldest..carry (thee) wh.
Heb. 6. 20 Whither the forerunner is for us entered

12. *Wheresoever, whithersoever*, ὅπου ἄν *hopou an*.
Mark 6. 56 whithersoever he entered, into villages
Luke 9. 57 I will follow thee [whithersoever] thou
Jas. 3. 4 turned..whithersoever the governor list.
Rev. 14. 4 they which follow the Lamb whithersoe.

13. *Wheresoever, whithersoever*, ὅπου ἐάν *hopou ean*.
Matt. 8. 19 I will follow thee whithersoever thou go.

14. *Where, whither*, οὗ *hou*.
Luke 10. 1 into every city..whither he himself would
24. 28 they drew nigh unto the village whither

15. *Whithersoever*, οὗ ἐάν *hou ean*.
1 Co. 16. 6 bring me on my journey whithersoever I

16. *Where? whither?* ποῦ *pou*.
John 3. 8 tell whence it cometh, and whither it go.
7. 35 Whither will he go, that we shall not find
8. 14 I know whence I came, and whither I go
8. 14 tell whence I come, or whither I go
12. 35 in darkness knoweth not whither he goeth
13. 36 Peter said unto him, Lord, whither goest
14. 5 we know not whither thou goest; and how
16. 5 none of..asketh me, Whither goest thou
Heb. 11. 8 he went out, not knowing wh. 1 Jo. 2. 11

17. *Toward which*, εἰς ἥν *eis hēn*, John 6. 21.

WHO —

1. *These*, אֵלֶּה *el eh*.
Deut. 5. 3 (even) us, who (are) all of us here alive

2. *And I myself*, וַאֲנִי *va-ani*.
Exod. 6. 12 hear me, who (am) of uncircumcised lips

3. *Which, that*, אֲשֶׁר *asher*.
Gen. 24. 15 Rebekah came out, who was born to Be.

4. *He*, הוּא *hu*.
Gen. 36. 1 the generations of Esau, who (is) Edom

5. *They*, הֵם *hem*.
2 Ki. 4. 5 her sons, who brought (the vessels) to her

6. *They*, הֵמָּה *hemah*.
1 Ch. 8. 13 who drove away the inhabitants of Gath

7. *Who, who?* מִי *mi*.
Gen. 3. 11 he said, Who told thee that thou (wast)

8. *Who?* מַן *man*.
Ezra 5. 3 Who hath commanded you to build this
5. 9 Who commanded you to build this house
Dan. 3. 15 who (is) that God that shall deliver you

9. *As much, as many*, ὅσοι *hosoi*.
Heb. 2. 15 deliver them who through fear of death

10. *Whosoever, whatsoever*, ὅστις *hostis*.
Mark 15. 7 who had committed murder in the insur.
Luke 23. 19 Who for a certain sedition made in the ci.
Acts 7. 53 Who have received the law by the dispo.
8. 15 Who, when they were come down, prayed
10. 41 who did eat and drink with him after he
13. 31 who are his witnesses unto the people
13. 43 who, speaking to them, persuaded them
17. 10 who coming (thither) went into the syna.
21. 4 who said to Paul through the spirit, that
23. 33 Who, when they came to Cesarea, and de
24. 1 who informed the governor against Paul
28. 18 Who, when they had examined me, would
Rom. 1. 25 Who changed the truth of God into a lie
1. 32 Who knowing the judgment of God, that
9. 4 Who are Israelites; to whom (pertaineth)
11. 4 who have not bowed the knee to (the im.)
16. 4 Who have for my life laid down their own
16. 6 Greet Mary, who bestowed much labour
16. 7 fellow prisoners, who are of note among
2 Co. 8. 10 who have begun before, not only to do, but
Gal. 2. 4 who came in privily to spy out our liberty
Eph. 4. 19 Who being past feeling have given them.
Phil. 2. 20 who will naturally care for your state
2 Th. 1. 9 Who shall be punished with everlasting
2 Ti. 2. 2 men, who shall be able to teach others also
2. 18 Who concerning the truth have erred, say.
Titus 1. 11 who subvert whole houses, teaching things
Heb. 8. 5 Who serve unto the example and shadow
13. 7 who have spoken unto you the word of G.
2 Pe. 2. 1 who privily shall bring in damnable here.

11. *This, that*, οὗτος *houtos*.
Acts 13. 7 who called for Barnabas and Saul, and de.

12. *Who? what?* τίς *tis*.
Matt. 3. 7 who hath warned you to flee from the wr.
See also 10. 11; 12. 48; 18. 1; 19. 25; 21. 10, 23; 24. 45; 26. 68; Mark 1. 24; 2. 7; 3. 33; 5. 30, 31; 9. 34; 10. 26; 11. 28; 16. 3; Luke 4. 34; 5. 21, 21; 7. 39, 49; 8. 45, [45]; 9. 9; 10. 22, 22, 29; 12. 14, 42; 16. 11, 12; 18. 26; 19. 3; 20. 2; 22. 64; John 1. 19, 22; 4. 10; 5. 13; 6. 60, 64, 64; 7. 20; 8. 25; 9. 2, 21, 36; 12. 34, 38; 13. 24, 25; Acts 7. 27, 35; 8. 33; 9. 5; 19. 15; 21. 33; 22. 8; 26. 15; Rom. 7. 24; 8. 31, 33; 8. 34, 35; 9. 19, 20; 10. 6, 7, 16; 11. 34, 34, 35; 14. 4; 1 Co. 2. 16; 3. 5; 4. 7; 9. 7, 7, 7; 14. 8; 2 Co. 2. 2, 16; 11. 29, 29; Gal. 3. 1; 5. 7; Jas. 3. 13; 4. 12; 1 Pe. 3. 13; 1 Jo. 2. 22; Rev. 5. 2; 6. 17; 13. 4, 4; 15. 4.

WHOLE, (piece, the) —

1. *Days, of days*, יָמִים *yamim*.
Num 11. 20 even a whole month, until it come out at
11. 21 said, I will give them flesh..a whole mo.
Judg 19. 2 his concubine..was there four whole mo.
Dan. 10. 3 anoint..till three whole weeks were fulfi

2. *All, the whole, entire*, כֹּל *kol*.
Exod 12. 6 the whole assembly of the congregation
Isa. 3. 1 the whole stay of bread, and the whole
Dan. 2. 35 the stone that smote..filled the whole ea.
2. 48 made him ruler over the whole province
6. 1 princes, which should be over the whole
6. 3 the king thought to set him over the wh.
7. 23 shall devour the whole earth, and shall
7. 27 the kingdom under the whole, Zech. 4. 10

3. *Beaten work*, מִקְשָׁה *miqshah*.
Num 10. 2 trumpets of silver; of a whole piece shalt

4. *Finished, perfect, whole*, שָׁלֵם *shalem*.
Deut 27. 6 Thou shalt build the altar..of whole stone
Josh. 8. 31 an altar of whole stones, over which no
Amos 1. 6 they carried away captive the whole cap.
1. 9 they delivered up the whole captivity to

5. *Perfect, whole, complete, plain*, תָּמִים *tamim*.
Lev. 3. 9 the fat thereof..the whole rump, it shall
Josh 10. 13 hasted not to go down about a whole day
Prov. 1. 12 Let us swallow them up..whole, as those

6. *To be perfect, finished, consumed*, תָּמַם *tamam*.
Lev. 25. 29 he may redeem it within a whole year af.

7. *All, universally, the whole*, ἅπας *hapas*.
Luke 8. 37 Then the whole multitude of the country
19. 37 the whole multitude of the disciples began
23. 1 the whole multitude of them arose, and

8. *Inheriting the whole, entire, perfect*, ὁλόκληρος.
1 Th. 5. 23 (I pray God) your whole spirit and soul and

9. *All, the whole, entire*, ὅλος *holos*.
Matt. 5. 29, 30 thy whole body should be cast into hell
6. 22, 23 if..thine eye be single, thy whole body
13. 33 hid in three measures of meal, till the wh.
16. 26 what..if he shall gain the whole world
26. 13 Wheresoever..shall be preached in the wh.
27. 27 and gathered unto him the whole band of
Mark 6. 55 ran through that whole region round ab.
8. 36 what..if he shall gain the whole world
14. 9 shall be preached throughout the whole
15. 1 with the elders and scribes and the whole
15. 16 the soldiers..call together the whole ba.
15. 33 there was darkness over the whole land
Luke 8. 39 published throughout the whole city how
9. 25 what..if he gain the whole world, and lo.
11. 34 when thine eye is single, thy whole body
11. 36 If thy whole body therefore (be) full of li.
11. 36 the whole shall be full of light, as when
13. 21 took and hid..till the whole was leavened
John 4. 53 and himself believed, and his whole hou.
11. 50 expedient..that the whole nation perish
Acts 11. 26 it came to pass, that a whole year they
15. 22 apostles and elders, with the whole church
19. 29 the [whole] city was filled with confusion
28. 30 Paul dwelt two whole years in his own
Rom. 1. 8 faith is spoken of throughout the whole
16. 23 Gaius mine host, and of the whole church
1 Co. 5. 6 that a little leaven leaveneth the whole
12. 17 If the whole body..if the whole (were) he.
14. 23 If therefore the whole church be come to.
Gal. 5. 3 testify..he is a debtor to do the whole law
5. 9 A little leaven leaveneth the whole lump
Titus 1. 11 who subvert whole houses, teaching thi.
Jas. 2. 10 whosoever shall keep the whole law, and
3. 2 perfect..able also to bridle the whole bo.
3. 3 Behold..we turn about their whole body
3. 6 it defileth the whole body, and setteth on
1 Jo. 2. 2 not for ours only, but also for..the whole
5. 19 we know..the whole world lieth in wick.
Rev. 12. 9 that old serpent..which deceiveth the wh.
16. 14 unto the kings of the earth and of the wh.

10. *All, every, the whole*, πᾶς *pas*.
Matt. 8. 32 the whole herd of swine ran violently do.
8. 34 behold, the whole city came out to meet
13. 2 the whole multitude stood on the shore
Mark 4. 1 the whole multitude was by the sea on the
Luke 1. 10 the whole multitude of the people were
6. 19 the whole multitude sought to touch him
21. 35 that dwell on the face of the whole earth
Acts 6. 5 the saying pleased the whole multitude
13. 44 came almost the whole city together to
Rom. 8. 22 we know that the whole creation groaneth
Eph. 3. 15 Of whom the whole family in heaven and
4. 16 From whom the whole body fitly joined

WHOLE, wholesome —

1. *Healing*, מַרְפֵּא *marpe*.
Prov 15. 4 A wholesome tongue (is) a tree of life, but

2. *To be sound, well, in health*, ὑγιαίνω *hugiainō*.
Luke 7. 10 found the servant whole that had been sick
1 Ti. 6. 3 If any man..consent not to wholesome

3. *Sound, whole, wholesome*, ὑγιής *hugiēs*.
Matt 12. 13 it was restored whole, like as the other
15. 31 when they saw..the maimed to be whole
Mark 3. 5 his hand was restored [whole as the other]
5. 34 go in peace, and be whole of thy plague
Luke 6. 10 [his hand was restored whole as the other]
John 5. 4 [was made whole of whatsoever disease]
5. 6 saith unto him, Wilt thou be made whole?
5. 9 immediately the man was made whole, and
5. 11 He that made me whole, the same said
5. 14 thou art made whole: sin no more, lest
5. 15 that it was Jesus which had made him wh.
7. 23 I have made a man every whit whole on
Acts 4. 10 by him doth this man stand here..whole

WHOLE, to be, make, be made, (perfectly) —

1. *To live, be alive, revive,* חָיָה *chayah.*
Josh. 5. 8 they abode..in the camp till they were w.

2. *To heal,* רָפָא *rapha.*
Job 5. 18 he woundeth, and his hands make whole

3. *To be healed,* רָפָא *rapha,* 2.
Jer 19. 11 vessel, that cannot be made whole again

4. *To make thoroughly sound,* διασώζω *diasōzō.*
Matt 14. 36 many as touched were made perfectly w.

5. *To heal, cure,* ἰάομαι *iaomai.*
Matt 15. 28 her daughter was made whole from that
Acts 9. 34 Æneas, Jesus Christ maketh thee whole

6. *To be strong,* ἰσχύω *ischuō.*
Matt. 9. 12 They that be whole need not a physician
Mark 2. 17 They that are whole have no need of the p.

7. *To make sound,* σώζω *sōzō.*
Matt. 9. 21 If I..but touch his garment, I shall be w.
9. 22 Daughter..thy faith hath made thee wh.
9. 22 the woman was made whole from that hour
Mark 5. 28 If I..touch but his clothes, I shall be w.
5. 34 Daughter, thy faith hath made thee whole
6. 56 as many as touched him were made whole
10. 52 Go thy way; thy faith hath made thee w.
Luke 8. 48 thy faith hath made thee whole; go in p.
8. 50 believe only, and she shall be made whole
17. 19 Go thy way: thy faith hath made thee w.
Acts 4. 9 examined..by what means he is made wh.

8. *To be sound, well, in health,* ὑγιαίνω *hugiainō.*
Luke 5. 31 They that are whole need not a physician

WHOLE burnt offering or sacrifice —
Whole burnt offering, כָּלִיל *kalil.*
Deut 33. 10 and whole burnt sacrifice upon thine al.
Psa. 51. 19 with burnt offering, and whole burnt off.

WHOLLY, to have or give —

1. *A whole burnt offering,* כָּלִיל *kalil.*
Lev. 6. 22 a statute for ever..it shall be wholly bu.
6. 23 every meat offering..shall be wholly burnt
Num. 4. 6 shall spread over (it) a cloth wholly of blue
1 Sa. 7. 9 offered..a burnt offering wholly unto the

2. *To fill in or up,* מָלֵא *male,* 3.
Num 32. 11 because they have not wholly followed
32. 12 for they have wholly followed the LORD
Deut. 1. 36 because he hath wholly followed the Lo.
Josh. 14. 8 but I wholly followed the LORD my God
14. 9 thou hast wholly followed the LORD my
14. 14 he wholly followed the LORD God of Israel

3. *To declare or regard as innocent,* נָקָה *naqah,* 3.
Jer. 46. 28 yet will I not leave thee wholly unpunis.

4. *To separate, sanctify,* קָדַשׁ *qadesh,* 5.
Judg 17. 3 I had wholly dedicated the silver unto the

5. *To put, set, place,* שׂוּם, שִׂים *sum, sim.*
Jer. 42. 15 If ye wholly set your faces to enter into

6. *Completenesses,* שְׁלוֹמִים (? error) [*shalom*].
Jer. 13. 19 Judah..shall be wholly carried away ca.

7. *All, the complete whole,* ὁλοτελής *holotelēs.*
1 Th. 5. 23 very God of peace sanctify you wholly

8. *To be in,* εἰμὶ ἐν *eimi en.*
1 Ti. 4. 15 give thyself wholly to them; that thy pr.

WHOM, whomsoever —

1. *These,* אֵלֶּה *eleh.*
Ezra 2. 65 their servants and their maids, of whom

2. *That, which,* אֲשֶׁר *asher.*
Gen. 2. 8 there he put the man whom he had formed
31. 32 With whomsoever thou findest thy gods
Exod. 6. 5 Israel, whom the Egyptians keep in bon.
35. 21 and every one whom his spirit made wil.

3. *That,* דִּי *di.*
Ezra 4. 10 the rest of the nations whom the great and

4. *Who,* אֲשֶׁר הֵמָּה *asher hemah.*
Exod 36. 1 in whom the LORD put wisdom and und.
1 Ch. 9. 22 whom David and Samuel the seer did or.

5. *Who,* אֲשֶׁר הֵן *asher hen.*
Gen. 30. 26 for whom I have served thee, and let me

6. *This,* זוּ *zu.*
Isa. 42. 24 LORD, he against whom we have sinned

7. As No. 3.
Dan. 3. 12 Jews whom thou hast set over the affairs

8. *For, that,* כִּי *ki.*
Gen. 4. 25 another seed instead of Abel, whom Cain

9. *Who?* מִי *mi.*
Josh 24. 15 choose you this day whom ye will serve

10. *Who, who? what, what?* מַן *man.*
Dan. 4. 17, 25, 32 giveth it to whomsoever he will

11. *Whom, that,* מַן דִּי *man di.*
Dan. 5. 21 he appointeth over it whomsoever he wi.

12. *Who if,* ὃς ἐάν *hos ean.*
Matt 11. 27 (he) to whomsoever the Son will reveal
Luke 4. 6 and to whomsoever I will I give it
1 Co. 16. 3 whomsoever ye shall approve by (your) le.

13. *All or every one who,* πᾶς ὃς *pas hos.*
Luke 12. 48 unto whomsoever much is given, of him

14. *If any one,* ἐάν τις *ean tis.*
John 13. 20 He that receiveth [whomsoever] I send

15. *Who, which, what?* τί, τίς *ti, tis.*
Matt 12. 27 by whom do your children cast (them)
16. 13 Whom do men say that I the Son of man
16. 15 He saith unto them, But whom say ye
17. 25 of whom do the kings of the earth take
27. 17 Whom will ye that I release unto you?
Mark 8. 27 saying unto them, Whom do men say th.
8. 29 he saith unto them, But whom say ye th.
Luke 6. 47 doeth them, I will show you to whom he
9. 18 saying, Whom say the people that I am?
9. 20 He said unto them, But whom say ye th.
11. 19 if I..cast out devils, by whom do your so.
12. 5 But I will forewarn you whom ye shall f.
John 6. 68 Lord, to whom shall we go? thou hast the
8. 53 the prophets are dead: whom makest th.
12. 38 to whom hath the arm of the Lord been
13. 22 looked one on another, doubting of whom
18. 4 went forth, and said unto them, Whom
18. 7 Then asked he them again, Whom seek
20. 15 why weepest thou? whom seekest thou?
Acts 8. 34 of whom speaketh the prophet this? of
13. 25 Whom think ye that I am? I am not (he)
2 Ti. 3. 14; Heb. 3. 17; 3. 18; 1 Pe. 5. 8.

16. *Who, whom,* ὅς, οὗ *hos, hou,* Heb. 5. 11.

17. *Whomsoever,* ὅσπερ *hosper,* Mark 15. 6.

WHORE, whoremonger, whorish —

1. *To commit fornication,* זָנָה *zanah.*
Lev. 21. 7 They shall not take a wife (that is) a wh.
Deut 23. 18 Thou shalt not bring the hire of a whore
Prov. 6. 26 For by means of a whorish woman (a man
23. 27 a whore (is) a deep ditch; and a strange w.
Isa. 57. 3 the seed of the adulterer and the whore
Eze. 6. 9 I am broken with their whorish heart, wh.
16. 30 the work of an imperious whorish woman
16. 33 They give gifts to all whores; but thou
Hos. 4. 14 themselves are separated with whores, and

2. *Separated, consecrated (to an idol),* קְדֵשָׁה *qedeshah.*
Deut. 23. 17 There shall be no whore of the daughters

3. *Fornicatress,* πόρνη *pornē.*
Rev. 17. 1 the judgment of the great whore that si.
17. 15 which thou sawest, where the whore sit.
17. 16 these shall hate the whore, and shall ma.
19. 2 he hath judged the great whore, which

4. *A fornicator,* πόρνος *pornos.*
Eph. 5. 5 no whoremonger, nor unclean person, nor
1 Ti. 1. 10 For whoremongers, for them that defile
Heb. 13. 4 whoremongers and adulterers God will
Rev. 21. 8 whoremongers, and sorcerers, and idola.
22. 15 whoremongers, and murderers, and idol.

5. *Fornicatress,* אִשָּׁה זוֹנָה [*zanah*]. Jer. 3. 3.

WHORE, to cause to be a, play the —
To commit fornication, זָנָה *zanah.*
Lev. 19. 29 daughters to cause her to be a wh.; 21. 9
Deut 22. 21 to play the whore in her father's house
Judg 19. 2 his concubine played the whore against
Eze. 16. 28 Thou hast played the whore also with the
Lev. 19. 29 thy daughters to cause her to be a whore

WHOREDOM, (to commit or fall to) —

1. *To commit fornication,* זָנָה *zanah.*
Lev. 19. 29 lest the land fall to whoredom, and the
20. 5 to commit whoredom with Molech, from
Num 25. 1 the people began to commit whoredom wi.
Eze. 16. 17 and didst commit whoredom with them
20. 30 commit ye whoredom after their abomin.
23. 3 committed whoredoms..committed who.
Hos. 1. 2 the land hath committed great whoredom
4. 13 your daughters shall commit whoredom
4. 14 your daughters when they commit whor.

2. *To commit fornication,* זָנָה *zanah,* 4.
Eze. 16. 34 none followeth thee to commit whoredoms

3. *To cause or lead to fornication,* זָנָה *zanah,* 5.
2 Ch. 21. 13 like to the whoredoms of the house of A.
Hos. 4. 10 they shall commit whoredom, and shall
4. 18 they have committed whoredom continu.
5. 3 thou committest whoredom, (and) Israel

4. *Fornications,* זְנוּנִים *zenunim.*
Gen. 38. 24 behold, she (is) with child by whoredom
2 Ki. 9. 22 so long as the whoredoms of thy mother
Eze. 23. 11 more than her sister in (her) whoredoms
23. 29 the nakedness of thy whoredoms shall be
Hos. 1. 2 whoredoms and children of whoredoms
2. 2 let her therefore put away her whoredoms
2. 4 for they (be) the children of whoredoms
4. 12 the spirit of whoredoms hath caused (them)
5. 4 the spirit of whoredoms (is) in the midst
Nah. 3. 4 of the whoredoms..through her whored.

5. *Fornication,* זְנוּת *zenuth.*
Num 14. 33 your children shall..bear your whoredo.
Jer. 3. 2 polluted the land with thy whoredoms
3. 9 it came to pass through..her whoredom
13. 27 I have seen..the lewdness of thy whored.
Eze. 23. 27 thy whoredom (brought) from the land of
43. 7 by their whoredom, nor by the carcases of
43. 9 let them put away their whoredom, and
Hos. 4. 11 Whoredom and wine and new wine take
6. 10 there (is) the whoredom of Ephraim, Isr.

6. *Fornication,* תַּזְנוּת *taznuth.*
Eze. 16. 20 (Is this) of thy whoredoms a small matter
16. 22 in all thine abominations and thy whore.
16. 25 Thou hast..multiplied thy whoredoms
16. 26 hast increased thy whoredoms, to provoke
16. 33 may come unto thee..for thy whoredom
16. 34 the contrary is in thee..in thy whoredoms
Eze. 16. 36 discovered through thy whoredoms with
23. 7 she committed her whoredoms with them
23. 8 her whoredoms..poured their whoredom
23. 11 in her whoredoms more than her sister in
23. 14 she increased her whoredoms: for when
23. 17 they defiled her with their whoredom, and
23. 18 she discovered her whoredoms, and disc.
23. 19 she multiplied her whoredoms, in calling
23. 29 both thy lewdness and thy whoredoms
23. 35 therefore bear thou also..thy whoredoms
23. 43 Will they now commit whoredoms with

WHORING, (to make or use) to go a —

1. *To commit fornication,* זָנָה *zanah.*
Exod 34. 15 they go a whoring after their gods, and
34. 16 their daughters go a whoring after their
Lev. 17. 7 after whom they have gone a whoring
20. 5 cut him off, and all that go a whoring after
20. 6 after wizards, to go a whoring after them
Num 15. 39 eyes, after which ye use to go a whoring
Deut 31. 16 go a whoring after the gods of the strang.
Judg. 2. 17 they went a whoring after other gods, and
8. 27 all Israel went thither a whoring after it
8. 33 Israel turned again, and went a whoring
1 Ch. 5. 25 went a whoring after the gods of the peo.
Psa. 73. 27 destroyed all them that go a whoring from
106. 39 went a whoring with their own inventions
Eze. 6. 9 their eyes, which go a whoring after their
23. 30 because thou hast gone a whoring after
Hos. 4. 12 they have gone a whoring from under th.
9. 1 thou hast gone a whoring from thy God

2. *To cause or lead to fornication,* זָנָה *zanah,* 5.
Exod 34. 16 make thy sons go a whoring after their

WHOSE (soever) —

1. *Which,* אֲשֶׁר *asher.*
Gen. 1. 11 whose seed (is) in itself, upon the earth
Exod 35. 29 whose heart made them willing to bring

2. *Which,* דִּי *di.*
Ezra 7. 15 the God..whose habitation (is) in Jerusa.

3. *Who,* מִי *mi.*
Gen. 24. 23 Whose daughter (art) thou? tell me, I pray

4. *Who, of whom?* τίς, τίνος *(gen. or dat.) tis, tinos.*
Matt 22. 20 Whose (is) this image and superscription?
22. 28 whose wife shall she be of the seven? for
22. 42 What think ye of Christ? whose son is he?
Mark 12. 16 Whose (is) this image and superscription?
12. 23 whose wife shall she be of them? for the
Luke 12. 20 whose shall those things be which thou
20. 24 Whose image and superscription hath it?
20. 33 in the resurrection whose wife of them
John 19. 24 Let us not rend it, but cast lots for it, wh.

5. *Whose,* ἄν τινων *an tinōn.*
John 20. 23 [Whose soever] sins ye remit, they are re.
20. 23 [whose soever]..ye retain, they are retained

WHOSO, whosoever —

1. *(Every) man (that),* אִישׁ, אִישׁ אֲשֶׁר (כָּל) *(kol) ish (asher).*
Exod 30. 33 Whosoever compoundeth..like it, or who
30. 38 Whosoever shall make like unto that, to
Lev. 19. 20 whosoever lieth carnally with a woman
21. 17 Whosoever..of thy seed in their generat.
22. 3 Whosoever..of all your seed among your
22. 5 Or whosoever toucheth any creeping thi.
22. 21 whosoever offereth a sacrifice of peace
24. 15 Whosoever curseth his God shall bear his
Deut 18. 19 whosoever will not hearken unto my wo.
Josh. 1. 18 Whosoever..doth rebel against thy comm.
Prov 25. 14 Whoso boasteth himself of a false gift (is)

2. *Every one,* כֹּל *kol.*
Exod 35. 5 whosoever (is) of a willing heart, let him
Ezra 6. 11 whosoever shall alter this word, let timb.
7. 26 whosoever will not do the law of thy God
Dan. 5. 7 Whosoever shall read this writing, and sh.
6. 7 whosoever shall ask a petition of any god

3. *Who, who?* מִי *mi.*
Isa. 54. 15 whosoever shall gather together against

4. *If any one,* εἴ τις *ei tis.*
Rev. 14. 11 whosoever receiveth the mark of his na.
20. 15 whosoever was not found written in the

5. *As many as,* ὅσοι ἄν *hosoi an.*
Mark 6. 11 [whosoever shall not receive you, nor]
Luke 9. 5 whosoever will not receive you, when ye

6. *Whoever, whosoever,* ὅστις *hostis.*
Matt. 5. 39 whosoever shall smite thee on thy right
5. 41 whosoever shall compel thee to go a mile
13. 12 Whosoever hath..but whosoever hath not
18. 4 Whosoever therefore shall humble himself
23. 12 whosoever shall exalt himself shall be ab.
Mark 8. 34 [Whosoever] will come after me, let him
Luke 14. 27 whosoever doth not bear his cross, and co.
Gal. 5. 4 whosoever of you are justified by the law
Jas. 2. 10 whosoever shall keep the whole law, and

7. *Whosoever,* ὅστις ἄν *hostis an.*
Matt 10. 33 [whosoever] shall deny me before men
12. 50 whosoever shall do the will of my Father
Gal. 5. 10 shall bear his judgment, whosoever he

8. *Every one that,* πᾶς ὁ or ὃς *pas ho or hos.*
Matt. 5. 22 whosoever is angry with his brother with
5. 28 whosoever looketh on a woman to lust
Luke 6. 47 Whosoever cometh to me, and heareth
12. 8 Whosoever shall confess me before men
12. 10 whosoever shall speak a word against the
14. 11 whosoever exalteth himself shall be aba.
14. 33 whosoever he be of you that forsaketh not
16. 18 Whosoever putteth away..[whosoever] m.

Luke20. 18 Whosoever shall fall upon that stone shall
John 3. 15, 16 whosoever believeth in him should not
4. 13 Whosoever drinketh of this water shall th
8. 34 Whosoever committeth sin is the servant
11. 26 whosoever liveth and believeth in me sh.
12. 46 whosoever believeth on me should not ab.
16. 2 whosoever killeth you will think that he
19. 12 whosoever maketh himself a king speak.
Acts 2. 21 whosoever shall call on the name of the
10. 43 whosoever believeth in him shall receive
Rom. 2. 1 thou art inexcusable..whosoever thou art
9. 33 [whosoever] believeth on him shall not be
10. 11 Whosoever believeth on him shall not be
10. 13 whosoever shall call upon the name of the
1 Jo. 2. 23 Whosoever denieth the Son, the same hath
3. 4 Whosoever committeth sin transgresseth
3. 6 Whosoever abideth..whosoever sinneth
3. 9 Whosoever is born of God doth not com.
3. 10 whosoever doeth not righteousness is not
3. 15 Whosoever hateth his brother is a murd.
5. 1 Whosoever believeth that Jesus is the Ch.
5. 18 whosoever is born of God sinneth not, but
2 Jo. 9 whosoever transgresseth, and
Rev. 22. 15 and whosoever loveth and maketh a lie

9. *Every one who*, πᾶς ὅστις *pas hostis*.
Matt. 7. 24 whosoever heareth these sayings of mine
10. 32 Whosoever therefore shall confess me be.

WHOSOEVER would (or heareth) —

1. *He who is willing, or desirous*, הֶחָפֵץ *he-chaphets*.
1 Ki. 13. 33 whosoever would, he consecrated him, and

2. *To hear, hearken*, שָׁמֵעַ *shamea*.
2 Sa. 17. 9 whosoever heareth it will say, There is a
Eze. 33. 4 whosoever heareth the sound of the tru.

WHY, (for) —

1. *Wherefore, wherefore?* מַדּוּעַ *maddua*.
Exod. 1. 18 Why have ye done this thing, and have
3. 3 I will now turn aside, and see..why the
Jer. 2. 14 (Is) Israel a servant?..why is he spoiled?

2. *What?* מָה *mah*.
Judg. 8. 1 Why hast thou served us thus, that thou

3. *Why?* לָמָה *la-mah*.
Gen. 27. 45 why should I be deprived also of you both

4. *For why?* שַׁלָּמָה *shal-la-mah*.
Song 1. 7 why should I be as one that turneth aside

5. *What?* מֶה *meh*.
Josh. 7. 25 Joshua said, Why hast thou troubled us?
Ezra 4. 22 why should damage grow to the hurt of the
7. 23 why should there be wrath against the re

6. *On account of what?* עַל־מָה *al mah*.
Dan. 2. 15 Why (is) the decree (so) hasty from the king?

7. *Because of what?* יַעַן מֶה *yaan meh*.
Hag. 1. 9 Why? saith the LORD of hosts. Because of

8. *For*, γάρ *gar*.
Matt27. 23 the governor said, Why, what evil hath
Mark15. 14 Pilate said unto them, Why, what evil ha.
Luke23. 22 he said unto them the third time, Why
John 9. 30 Why herein is a marvellous thing, that ye

9. *Because of what? why?* διὰ τί *diati*.
Matt. 9. 11 Why eateth your Master with publicans
9. 14 Why do we and the Pharisees fast oft, but
13. 10 Why speakest thou unto them in parab.?
15. 2 Why do thy disciples trangress the tradi.
15. 3 Why do ye also transgress the command.
17. 19 and said, Why could not we cast him out?
21. 25 he will say..Why did ye not then believe
Mark 2. 18 Why do the disciples of John and of the
7. 5 Why walk not thy disciples according to
11. 31 he will say, Why then did ye not believe
Luke 5. 30 Why do ye eat and drink with publicans
5. 33 [Why do] the disciples of John fast often
19. 31 if any man ask you, Why do ye loose (h.)?
20. 5 he will say, Why then believed ye him not?
24. 38 and why do thoughts arise in your hearts?
John 7. 45 they said..Why have ye not brought him?
8. 43 Why do ye not understand my speech?
8. 46 if I say the truth, why do ye not believe
12. 5 Why was not this ointment sold for three
13. 37 said..Lord, why cannot I follow thee now?
Acts 5. 3 why hath Satan filled thine heart to lie to
1 Co. 6. 7 Why do ye not rather take wrong? why

10. *Wherefore? why?* ἱνατί *hinati*.
Matt27. 46 My God, my God, why hast thou forsaken
Luke13. 7 cut it down; why cumbereth it the gro.?
Acts 4. 25 Why did the heathen rage, and the peo.
7. 26 Sirs, ye are brethren; why do ye wrong
1 Co.10. 29 for why is my liberty judged of another

11. *That*, ὅτι *hoti*.
Mark 9. 11 Why say the scribes that Elias must first
9. 28 asked..[Why] could not we cast him out?

12. *Why?* τί (*neut.*) *ti*.
Matt. 6. 28 why take ye thought for raiment? Consi.
7. 3 why beholdest thou the mote that is in
8. 26 Why are ye fearful, O ye of little faith?
16. 8 why reason ye among yourselves, because
17. 10 Why then say the scribes that Elias must
19. 7 Why did Moses then command to give a
19. 17 Why callest thou me good?..none good
20. 6 saith..Why stand ye here all the day idle?
22. 18 Jesus..said, Why tempt ye me..hypocr.?
26. 10 Why trouble ye the woman? for she hath
Mark 2. 7 Why doth this..thus speak blasphemies?
2. 8 Why reason ye these things in your hearts?
2. 24 why do they on the sabbath day that wh.
Mark 4. 40 Why are ye so fearful? how is it that ye
5. 35 why troublest thou the Master any furt.?
5. 39 Why make ye this ado, and weep? the da.
8. 12 Why doth this generation seek after a sign?
8. 17 Why reason ye because ye have no bread?
10. 18 Why callest thou me good?..none good
11. 3 if any man say unto you, Why do ye this?
12. 15 Why tempt ye me? bring me a penny, that
14. 4 Why was this waste of the ointment made?
14. 6 why trouble ye her? she hath wrought a
15. 34 My God, my God, why hast thou forsaken
Luke 2. 48 Son, why hast thou thus dealt with us?
6. 2 Why do ye that which is not lawful to do
6. 41 why beholdest thou the mote that is in
6. 46 why call ye me, Lord, Lord, and do not
12. 26 If ye then be not able..why take ye tho.
12. 57 why even of yourselves judge ye not wh.
18. 19 Why callest thou me good? none (is) good
19. 33 the owners..said..Why loose ye the colt?
20. 23 [and said unto them, Why tempt ye me?]
22. 46 Why sleep ye? rise and pray, lest ye enter
24. 5 Why seek ye the living among the dead?
24. 38 he said unto them, Why are ye troubled?
John 1. 25 Why baptizest thou then, if thou be not
4. 27 yet no man said..Why talkest thou with
7. 19 Did not Moses..Why go ye about to kill
10. 20 He hath a devil, and is mad; why hear ye
18. 21 Why askest thou me? ask them which he.
18. 23 If I have spoken..well, why smitest thou
20. 13 they say unto her, Woman, why weepest
20. 15 Jesus saith unto her, Woman, why weep.
Acts 1. 11 said..why stand ye gazing up into heaven?
3. 12 why marvel ye at this? or why look ye so
5. 4 why hast thou conceived this thing in th.
9. 4 saying..Saul, Saul, why persecutest thou
14. 15 Sirs, why do ye these things? We also are
15. 10 Now therefore why tempt ye God, to put
22. 7 saying..Saul, Saul, why persecutest thou
22. 16 why tarriest thou? arise, and be baptized
26. 8 Why should it be thought a thing incred.
26. 14 saying..Saul, Saul, why persecutest thou
Rom. 3. 7 why yet am I also judged as a sinner?
8. 24 what a man seeth, why doth he yet hope
9. 19 Why doth he yet find fault? for who hath
9. 20 say to him..Why hast thou made me thus?
14. 10 why dost thou judge thy brother? or why
1 Co. 4. 7 why dost thou glory, as if thou hadst not
10. 29 for why is my liberty judged of another
10. 30 why am I evil spoken of for that for wh.
15. 29 why are they then baptized for the dead?
15. 30 And why stand we in jeopardy every hour?
Gal. 2. 14 [why] compellest thou the Gentiles to li.
5. 11 why do I yet suffer persecution? then is
Col. 2. 20 why, as..living in the world, are ye subje.

13. *With a view to what?* εἰς τί *eis ti*.
Mark14. 4 Why was this waste of the ointment ma.?
15. 34 My God, my God, why hast thou forsaken

WICKED (doer, man, one, thing, woman, more) —

1. *Iniquity, vanity*, אָוֶן *aven*.
Job 22. 15 the old way which wicked men have tro.?
34. 36 tried..because of..answers for wicked m.
Psa. 59. 5 be not merciful to any wicked transgres.
101. 8 that I may cut off all wicked doers from
Prov. 6. 12 A naughty person, a wicked man, walketh
6. 18 An heart that deviseth wicked imaginati.

2. *Worthless, without utility*, בְּלִיַּעַל *beliyyaal*.
Deut15. 9 that there be not a thought in thy wicked
Job 34. 18 to say to a king..wicked..to princes..un.?
Psa.101. 3 I will set no wicked thing before mine ey.
Nah. 1. 11 There is..come out of thee..a wicked co.
1. 15 the wicked shall no more pass through th.

3. *Disgrace, shame*, חֶסֶד *chesed*.
Lev. 20. 17 it (is) a wicked thing; and they shall be

4. *Wickedness, wicked woman*, מִרְשַׁעַת *mirshaath*.
2 Ch.24. 7 the sons of Athaliah, that wicked woman

5. *Perverse*, עַוָּל *avval*.
Job 18. 21 Surely such (are) the dwellings of the wic.
29. 17 I brake the jaws of the wicked, and plu.
31. 3 (Is) not destruction to the wicked? and a

6. *Perverseness, perversity*, עַוְלָה *avlah*.
2 Sa. 3. 34 as a man falleth before wicked men..fel.

7. *Labouring, perverse, miserable*, עָמֵל *amel*.
Job 20. 22 every hand of the wicked shall come upon

8. *A grievous thing*, עֹצֶב *otseb*.
Psa.139. 24 see if..wicked way in me, and lead me in

9. *Evil*, רַע *ra*.
Gen. 13. 13 the men of Sodom (were) wicked and sin.
38. 7 Er, Judah's first born, was wicked in the
Deut17. 5 which have committed that wicked thing
23. 9 then keep thee from every wicked thing
1 Sa. 30. 22 Then answered all the wicked men and
2 Ki.17. 11 wrought wicked things to provoke the L.
2 Ch. 7. 14 If my people..turn from their wicked wa.
Neh. 9. 35 neither turned they from their wicked
Esth. 9. 25 he commanded by letters, that his wicked
Job 21. 30 That the wicked is reserved to the day of
Esth. 7. 6 The adversary and enemy (is) this wicked
Psa.101. 4 I will not know a wicked (person)
Prov. 2. 14 Who..delight in the frowardness of the wi.
11. 21 hand..in hand, the wicked shall not be
12. 13 The wicked is snared by the transgression
15. 26 The thoughts of the wicked (are) an abo.
26. 23 Burning lips and a wicked heart (are like)
Jer. 2. 33 therefore hast thou..taught the wicked
5. 28 yea, they overpass the deeds of the wicked
Jer. 6. 29 the founder melteth in vain; for the wic.
15. 21 I will deliver..out of the hand of the wi.
Eze. 8. 9 Go in, and behold the wicked abominations
11. 2 these (are) the men that..give wicked co.
13. 22 strengthened the hands of the wicked, that
20. 44 not according to your wicked ways, nor
30. 12 sell the land into the hand of the wicked

10. *To do or suffer evil, treat ill*, רָעַע *raa*, 5.
Psa. 22. 16 the assembly of the wicked have enclosed
27. 2 When the wicked..mine enemies and my
64. 2 Hide me from the..counsel of the wicked
92. 11 mine ears shall hear..of the wicked that
Prov.17. 4 A wicked doer giveth heed to false lips

11. *Wrong, wicked*, רָשָׁע *rasha*.
Gen. 18. 23 Wilt thou..destroy..righteous with the w.
18. 25 far..to slay the righteous with the wicked
18. 25 that the righteous should be as the wicked
Exod. 9. 27 LORD (is) righteous..and my people (are) w.
23. 1 put not thine hand with the wicked to be an
23. 7 Keep thee far..I will not justify the wicked
Num16. 26 from the tents of these wicked men, and
Deut25. 1 justify the righteous, and condemn the w.
25. 2 if the wicked man (be) worthy to be beaten
1 Sa. 2. 9 the wicked shall be silent in darkness, for
24. 13 Wickedness proceedeth from the wicked
2 Sa. 4. 11 How much more, when wicked men have
1 Ki. 8. 32 condemning the wicked, to bring his way
2 Ch. 6. 23 requiting the wicked, by recompensing
Job 3. 17 There the wicked cease (from) troubling
8. 22 the dwelling place of the wicked shall come
9. 22 He destroyeth the perfect and the wicked
9. 24 earth is given into the hand of the wicked
10. 3 and shine upon the counsel of the wicked?
11. 20 the eyes of the wicked shall fail, and they
15. 20 The wicked man travaileth with pain all
16. 11 turned me over into the hand of the wic.
18. 5 the light of the wicked shall be put out
20. 5 That the triumphing of the wicked (is) sh.
20. 29 This (is) the portion of a wicked man from
21. 7 Wherefore do the wicked live, become old
21. 16 the counsel of the wicked is far from me
21. 17 How oft is the candle of the wicked put
21. 28 where (are) the dwelling places of the wi.?
22. 18 but the counsel of the wicked is far from
24. 6 and they gather the vintage of the wicked
27. 7 Let mine enemy be as the wicked, and he
27. 13 This (is) the portion of a wicked man with
34. 26 He striketh them as wicked men in the
36. 6 He preserveth not the life of the wicked
36. 17 hast fulfilled the judgment of the wicked
38. 13 that the wicked might be shaken out of it
38. 15 from the wicked their light is withholden
40. 12 and tread down the wicked in their place
Psa. 7. 9 let the wickedness of the wicked come to
9. 5 thou hast destroyed the wicked, thou hast
9. 16 the wicked is snared in the work of his
9. 17 The wicked shall be turned into hell, (and)
10. 2 The wicked in (his) pride doth persecute
10. 3 the wicked boasteth of his heart's desire
10. 4 The wicked, through the pride of his cou.
10. 13 Wherefore doth the wicked contemn God
10. 15 Break thou the arm of the wicked and the
11. 2 the wicked bend (their) bow, they make
11. 5 the wicked and him that loveth violence
11. 6 Upon the wicked he shall rain snares, fire
12. 8 The wicked walk on every side, when the
17. 9 From the wicked that oppress me, (from) m.
17. 13 deliver my soul from the wicked, (which
26. 5 hated..and will not sit with the wicked
28. 3 Draw me not away with the wicked, and
31. 17 let the wicked be ashamed, (and) let them
32. 10 Many sorrows (shall be) to the wicked, but
34. 21 Evil shall slay the wicked; and they that
36. 1 The transgression of the wicked saith wit.
36. 11 let not the hand of the wicked remove me
37. 10 a little while, and the wicked (shall) not
37. 12 The wicked plotteth against the just, and
37. 14 The wicked have drawn out the sword, and
37. 16 better than the riches of many wicked
37. 17 the arms of the wicked shall be broken
37. 20 the wicked shall perish, and the enemies
37. 21 The wicked borroweth, and payeth not
37. 28 but the seed of the wicked shall be cut
37. 32 The wicked watcheth the righteous, and
37. 34 when the wicked are cut off, thou shalt
37. 35 I have seen the wicked in great power, and
37. 38 the end of the wicked shall be cut off
37. 40 he shall deliver them from the wicked
39. 1 I will keep my mouth..while the wicked
50. 16 unto the wicked God saith, What hast th.
55. 3 because of the oppression of the wicked
58. 3 The wicked are estranged from the womb
58. 10 wash his feet in the blood of the wicked
68. 2 let the wicked perish at the presence of
71. 4 Deliver..out of the hand of the wicked
73. 3 (when) I saw the prosperity of the wicked
75. 4 and to the wicked, Lift not up the horn
75. 8 the wicked of the earth shall wring (them)
75. 10 the horns of the wicked also will I cut off
82. 2 and accept the persons of the wicked?
82. 4 rid (them) out of the hand of the wicked
91. 8 behold and see the reward of the wicked
92. 7 When the wicked spring as the grass, and
94. 3 the wicked, how long shall the wicked tr.
94. 13 until the pit be digged for the wicked
97. 10 delivereth..out of the hand of the wicked
101. 8 I will early destroy all the wicked of the
104. 35 Let the sinners..let the wicked be no m.
106. 18 was kindled..the flame burnt up the wi.
109. 2 the mouth of the wicked and the mouth

Psa. 109. 6 Set thou a wicked man over him; and let
112. 10 The wicked shall see (it)..the wicked sh.
119. 53 because of the wicked that forsake
119. 61 The bands of the wicked have robbed me
119. 95 The wicked have waited for me to destroy
119. 110 The wicked have laid a snare for me, yet
119. 119 Thou puttest away all the wicked of the
119. 155 Salvation (is) far from the wicked: for th.
129. 4 he hath cut asunder the cords of the wic.
139. 19 Surely thou wilt slay the wicked, O God
140. 4 Keep me..from the hands of the wicked
140. 8 Grant not, O LORD, the desires of the wi.
141. 10 Let the wicked fall into their own nets
145. 20 the LORD..all the wicked will he destroy
146. 9 the way of the wicked he turneth upside
147. 6 he casteth the wicked down to the ground
Prov. 2. 22 the wicked shall be cut off from the earth
3. 25 neither of the desolation of the wicked
3. 33 The curse..(is) in the house of the wicked
4. 14 Enter not into the path of the wicked, and
4. 19 The way of the wicked (is) as darkness, th.
5. 22 His own iniquities shall take the wicked
9. 7 he that rebuketh a wicked (man getteth)
10. 3 casteth away the substance of the wicked
10. 6 violence covereth the mouth of the wick.
10. 7 but the name of the wicked shall rot
10. 16 (tendeth) to life: the fruit of the wicked
10. 20 the heart of the wicked (is) little worth
10. 24 The fear of the wicked, it shall come up.
10. 25 As the whirlwind passeth, so (is) the wic.
10. 27 the years of the wicked shall be shorten.
10. 28 the expectation of the wicked shall perish
10. 30 the wicked shall not inhabit the earth
10. 32 mouth of the wicked (speaketh) froward.
11. 5 but the wicked shall fall by his own wick.
11. 7 When a wicked man dieth, (his) expecta.
11. 8 is delivered..the wicked cometh in his
11. 10 when the wicked perish, (there is) shout.
11. 11 overthrown by the mouth of the wicked
11. 18 The wicked worketh a deceitful work, but
11. 23 (but) the expectation of the wicked (is) wr.
11. 31 much more the wicked and the sinner
12. 5 (but) the counsels of the wicked (are) de.
12. 6 The words of the wicked (are) to lie in wa.
12. 7 The wicked are overthrown, and (are) not
12. 10 the tender mercies of the wicked (are) cr.
12. 12 The wicked desireth the net of evil (men)
12. 21 but the wicked shall be filled with misc.
12. 26 but the way of the wicked seduceth them
13. 5 a wicked (man) is loathsome, and cometh
13. 9 the lamp of the wicked shall be put out
13. 17 A wicked messenger falleth into mischief
13. 25 but the belly of the wicked shall want
14. 11 The house of the wicked shall be overth.
14. 19 the wicked at the gates of the righteous
14. 32 The wicked is driven away in his wicked.
15. 6 in the revenues of the wicked is trouble
15. 8 The sacrifice of the wicked (is) an abom.
15. 9 The way of the wicked (is) an abominat.
15. 28 the mouth of the wicked poureth out ev.
15. 29 The LORD (is) far from the wicked, but he
16. 4 yea, even the wicked for the day of evil
17. 15 He that justifieth the wicked, and he th.
17. 23 A wicked (man) taketh a gift out of the
18. 3 When the wicked cometh, (then) cometh
18. 5 good to accept the person of the wicked
19. 28 the mouth of the wicked devoureth iniq.
20. 26 A wise king scattereth the wicked, and
21. 4 (and) the plowing of the wicked, (is) sin
21. 7 The robbery of the wicked shall destroy
21. 10 The soul of the wicked desireth evil, his
21. 12 of the wicked..(God) overthroweth the w.
21. 18 The wicked (shall be) a ransom for the
21. 27 The sacrifice of the wicked (is) abominat.
21. 29 A wicked man hardeneth his face, but
24. 15 Lay not wait, O wicked (man), against the
24. 16 but the wicked shall fall into mischief
24. 19 neither be thou envious at the wicked
24. 20 the candle of the wicked shall be put out
24. 24 He that saith unto the wicked, Thou (art)
25. 5 Take away the wicked (from) before the
25. 26 falling down before the wicked (is as) a tr.
28. 1 The wicked flee when no man pursueth
28. 4 They that forsake the law praise the wi.
28. 12 but when the wicked rise, a man is hidd.
28. 15 (so is) a wicked ruler over the poor peop.
28. 28 When the wicked rise, men hide themselv.
29. 2 when the wicked beareth rule, the people
29. 7 (but) the wicked regardeth not to know
29. 12 hearken to lies, all his servants (are) wic.
29. 16 When the wicked are multiplied, transg.
29. 27 and (he)..(is) abomination to the wicked
Eccl. 3. 17 shall judge the righteous and the wicked
7. 15 there is a wicked (man) that prolongeth
8. 10 I saw the wicked buried, who had come
8. 13 it shall not be well with the wicked, nei.
8. 14 work of the wicked..there be wicked (m.)
9. 2 (there is) one event..to the wicked; to the
Isa. 3. 11 Woe unto the wicked! (it shall be) ill (wi.)
5. 23 Which justify the wicked for reward, and
11. 4 with the breath..shall he slay the wicked
13. 11 I will punish..the wicked for their iniq.
14. 5 hath broken the staff of the wicked, (and)
26. 10 Let favour be showed to the wicked, (yet)
48. 22 no peace, saith the LORD, unto the wick.
53. 9 he made his grave with the wicked, and
55. 7 Let the wicked forsake his way, and the
57. 20 the wicked (are) like the troubled sea
57. 21 no peace, saith my God, to the wicked
Jer. 5. 26 among my people are found wicked (m.)
12. 1 Wherefore doth the way of the wicked
23. 19 shall fall..upon the head of the wicked

Jer. 25. 31 he will give them (that are) wicked to the
30. 23 fall with pain upon the head of the wic.
Eze. 3. 18 When I say unto the wicked, Thou shalt
3. 18 to warn the wicked from his wicked way
3. 18 the same wicked (man) shall die in his
3. 19 warn the wicked..from his wicked way
7. 21 and to the wicked of the earth for a spoil
13. 22 strengthened the hands of the wicked
18. 20 the wickedness of the wicked shall be upon
18. 21 if the wicked will turn from all his sins
18. 23 Have I any pleasure..that the wicked sh.
18. 24 the abominations that the wicked (man)
18. 27 when the wicked (man) turneth away fr.
21. 3, 4 cut off..the righteous and the wicked
21. 25 thou, profane wicked prince of Israel, w.
21. 29 the wicked, whose day is come, when th.
33. 8 When I say unto the wicked, O wicked
33. 8 warn the wicked from his way, that wic.
33. 9 if thou warn the wicked of his way to tu
33. 11 the wicked; but that the wicked turn fr.
33. 12 as for the wickedness of the wicked, he
33. 14 when I say unto the wicked, Thou shalt
33. 15 (If) the wicked restore the pledge, give
33. 19 if the wicked turn from his wickedness
Dan. 12. 10 the wicked shall do wickedly..the wicked
Mic. 6. 10 wickedness in the house of the wicked
Hab. 1. 4 the wicked doth compass about the righ.
1. 13 holdest thy tongue when the wicked de.
3. 13 out of the house of the wicked, by discov.
Zeph. 1. 3 and the stumbling blocks with the wick.
Mal. 3. 18 between the righteous and the wicked, be.
4. 3 ye shall tread down the wicked; for they

2. *Wrong, wickedness*, רֶשַׁע *resha.*
Job 34. 8 Which goeth..and walketh with wicked m.
Psa. 125. 3 the rod of the wicked shall not rest upon
141. 4 to practise wicked works with men that
Mic. 6. 11 Shall I count (them) pure with the wicked

13. *Unsettled, lawless*, ἄθεσμος *athesmos.*
2 Pe. 2. 7 with the filthy conversation of the wick.
3. 17 led away with the error of the wicked

14. *Lawless, without law*, ἄνομος *anomos.*
Acts 2. 23 and by wicked hands have crucified and
2 Th. 2. 8 then shall that wicked be revealed, whom

15. *Evil*, κακός *kakos.*
Matt 21. 41 He will miserably destroy those wicked m.

16. *Bad, malignant, miserable*, πονηρός *ponēros.*
Matt 12. 45 Even so shall it be also unto this wicked
13. 19 then cometh the wicked (one), and catch.
13. 38 the tares are the children of the wicked
13. 49 and sever the wicked from among the just
16. 4 A wicked and adulterous generation se.
18. 32 O thou wicked servant, I forgave thee all
25. 26 (Thou) wicked and slothful servant, thou
Luke 19. 22 will I judge thee, (thou) wicked servant
Acts 18. 14 a matter of wrong or wicked lewdness, O
1 Co. 5. 13 Therefore put away..that wicked person
Eph. 6. 16 to quench all the fiery darts of the wick.
Col. 1. 21 enemies in (your) mind by wicked works
2 Th. 3. 2 delivered from unreasonable and wick. m.
1 Jo. 2. 13, 14 ye have overcome the wicked one
3. 12 Cain, (who) was of that wicked one, and
5. 18 and that wicked one toucheth him not

17. *More malignant, miserable*, πονηρότερος *ponēr.*
Matt 12. 45 seven other spirits more wicked than hi.
Luke 11. 26 seven other spirits more wicked than hi.

WICKED, to be (desperately) —

1. *To be sickly, mortal, incurable*, אָנַשׁ *anash.*
Jer. 17. 9 The heart (is)..desperately wicked: who

2. *To do wrong, wickedly*, רָשַׁע *rasha.*
Job 9. 29 (If) I be wicked, why then labour I in vain
10. 7 Thou knowest that I am not wicked; and
10. 15 If I be wicked, woe unto me; and (if) I be
Eccl. 7. 17 Be not overmuch wicked, neither be thou

WICKED device, mind —

1. *Wicked thought or device*, זִמָּה *zimmah.*
Prov 21. 27 (when) he bringeth it with a wicked mind?
Isa. 32. 7 he deviseth wicked devices to destroy the

2. *To devise, design*, זָמַם *zamam.*
Psa. 140. 8 further not his wicked device, (lest) they

3. *A wicked thought, or device*, מְזִמָּה *mezimmah.*
Psa. 37. 7 the man who bringeth wicked devices to
Prov 12. 2 a man of wicked devices will he condemn
14. 17 and a man of wicked devices is hated

WICKEDLY, (to deal, depart, do) —

1. *A wicked thought or device*, מְזִמָּה *mezimmah.*
Psa. 139. 20 For they speak against thee wickedly

2. *To pervert, make crooked*, עָוָה *avah*, 5.
2 Sa. 24. 17 I have sinned, and I have done wickedly

3. *Perversity*, עַוְלָה *avlah.*
Job 13. 7 Will ye speak wickedly for God? and talk

4. *Evil, bad*, רַע *ra.*
Deut. 9. 18 in doing wickedly in the sight of the Lo.
Psa. 73. 8 They are corrupt, and speak wickedly

5. *To do or suffer evil, treat ill*, רָעַע *raa*, 5.
Gen. 19. 7 said, I pray you, brethren, do not so wic.
Judg 19. 23 I pray you, do not..wickedly; seeing th.
1 Sa. 12. 25 if ye shall still do wickedly, ye shall be
2 Ki. 21. 11 hath done wickedly above all that the A.
Psa. 74. 3 the enemy hath done wickedly in the sa.

6. *To do wrong or wickedly*, רָשַׁע *rasha.*
2 Sa. 22. 22 have not wickedly departed from my God
2 Ch. 6. 37 we have done amiss, and have dealt wic.

Psa. 18. 21 have not wickedly departed from my God
Dan. 9. 15 we have sinned, we have done wickedly

7. *To do wrong or wickedly*, רָשַׁע *rasha*, 5.
2 Ch. 20. 35 Ahaziah king of Israel, who did very wic.
22. 3 his mother was his counsellor to do wick.
Neh. 9. 33 thou hast done right, but we have done w.
Job 34. 12 Surely God will not do wickedly, neither
Psa. 106. 6 have committed iniquity, we have done w.
Dan. 9. 5 committed iniquity, and have done wick.
11. 32 such as do wickedly against the covenant
12. 10 the wicked shall do wickedly, and none

8. *Wickedness*, רִשְׁעָה *rishah.*
Mal. 4. 1 all the proud, yea, and all that do wickedly

WICKEDNESS, (to commit, very) —

1. *Iniquity, vanity*, אָוֶן *aven.*
Job 11. 11 he knoweth vain men: he seeth wickedn.
Prov 30. 20 and saith, I have done no wickedness

2. *Mischief, calamity*, הַוָּה *havvah.*
Psa. 5. 9 their inward part (is) very wickedness
52. 7 strengthened himself in his wickedness
55. 11 Wickedness (is) in the midst thereof, dec.

3. *A wicked thought or device*, זִמָּה *zimmah.*
Lev. 18. 17 they (are) her near kinswomen: it (is) wi.
19. 29 lest..the land become full of wickedness
20. 14 it (is) wickedness..that there be no wick.

4. *Perverseness, perversity*, עַוְלָה *avlah.*
2 Sa. 7. 10 neither shall the children of wickedness
1 Ch. 17. 9 neither shall the children of wickedness
Job 11. 14 let not wickedness dwell in thy tabernac.
24. 20 and wickedness shall be broken as a tree
27. 4 My lips shall not speak wickedness, nor
Psa. 89. 22 nor exact upon him; nor the son of wick.

5. *Perverseness, perversity*, עֹלָה *olah.*
Psa. 58. 2 in heart ye work wickedness; ye weigh

6. *Labour, toil, misery*, עָמָל *amal.*
Job 4. 8 they that plow iniquity, and sow wicked.

7. *Evil, bad*, רַע *ra.*
Gen. 6. 5 GOD saw that the wickedness of man (was)
39. 9 how then can I do this great wickedness
Deut 13. 11 shall do no more any such wickedness as
17. 2 that hath wrought wickedness in the sig.
Judg. 9. 56 God rendered the wickedness of Abimel.
20. 3 said..Tell (us), how was this wickedness?
20. 12 What wickedness (is) this that is done
1 Sa. 12. 17 ye may perceive and see that your wick.
12. 20 ye have done all this wickedness: yet tu.
25. 39 for the LORD hath returned the wickedn.
2 Sa. 3. 39 reward the doer of evil acc. to his wick.
1 Ki. 1. 52 if wickedness shall be found in him, he
2. 44 all the wickedness..return thy wickedn.
21. 25 Ahab, which did sell himself to work wi.
2 Ki. 21. 6 he wrought much wickedness in the sight
Job 20. 12 Though wickedness be sweet in his mouth
22. 5 (Is) not thy wickedness great? and thine
Psa. 7. 9 O let the wickedness of the wicked come
55. 15 wickedness (is) in their dwellings..among
94. 23 shall cut them off in their own wickedn.
107. 34 the wickedness of them that dwell there.
Prov 14. 32 The wicked is driven away in his wicked.
21. 12 overthroweth the wicked for..wickedness
26. 26 his wickedness shall be showed before the
Eccl. 7. 15 that prolongeth (his life) in his wickedn.
Isa. 47. 10 For thou hast trusted in thy wickedness
Jer. 1. 16 touching all their wickedness, who have
2. 19 Thine own wickedness shall correct thee
3. 2 with thy whoredoms and with thy wicked.
4. 14 O Jerusalem, wash thine heart from wic.
4. 18 this (is) thy wickedness, because it is bitt.
6. 7 As a fountain..so she casteth out her wi.
7. 12 see what I did to it for the wickedness of
8. 6 no man repented him of his wickedness
12. 4 the wickedness of them that dwell therein
14. 16 for I will pour their wickedness upon them
22. 22 be ashamed and confounded for all thy w.
23. 11 in my house have I found their wickedness
23. 14 that none doth return from his wickedness
Jer. 33. 5 for all whose wickedness I have hid my f.
44. 3 Because of their wickedness which they
44. 5 inclined their ear to turn from their wic.
44. 9 the wickedness of your fathers, and the
44. 9 the wickedness of their wives, and your
44. 9 wickedness, and the wickedness of your
Lam. 1. 22 Let all their wickedness come before thee
Eze. 16. 23 it came to pass, after all thy wickedness
16. 57 Before thy wickedness was discovered, as
Hos. 7. 1 the iniquity of Ephraim..and the wicked.
7. 2 they consider not..I remember all their w.
7. 3 They make the king glad with their wick.
9. 15 All their wickedness (is) in Gilgal; for th.
10. 15 do unto you because of your great wicke.
Joel. 3. 13 Put ye in the sickle..for their wickedness
Jon. 1. 2 for their wickedness is come up before me
Nah. 3. 19 for upon whom hath not thy wickedness

8. *Evil, badness, sadness*, רֹעַ *roa.*
Deut 28. 20 because of the wickedness of thy doings
Psa. 28. 4 according to the wickedness of their end.
Hos. 9. 15 for the wickedness of their doings I will

9. *To do wickedly or wrong*, רָשַׁע *rasha.*
1 Ki. 8. 47 We have sinned..we have committed wic.

10. *Wickedness, wrong*, רֶשַׁע *resha.*
Deut. 9. 27 look not..to their wickedness, nor to their
1 Sa. 24. 13 wickedness proceedeth from the wicked
Job 34. 10 Far be it from God..wickedness; and (fro.)
35. 8 Thy wickedness (may hurt) a man as thou

Psa. 5. 4 (art) not a God that hath pleasure in wic.
10. 15 seek out his wickedness (till) thou find .
45. 7 Thou lovest righteousness, and hatest wi.
84. 10 than to dwell in the tents of wickedness
Prov. 4. 17 For they eat the bread of wickedness, and
8. 7 wickedness (is) an abomination to my lips
10. 2 Treasures of wickedness profit nothing
12. 3 A man shall not be established by wicked.
16. 12 an abomination to kings to commit wick.
Eccl. 3. 16 the place of judgment..wickedness (was)
7. 25 to know the wickedness of folly, even of
8. 8 neither shall wickedness deliver those th.
Isa. 58. 4 and to smite with the fist of wickedness
58. 6 to loose the bands of wickedness, to undo
Jer. 14. 20 We acknowledge, O LORD, our wickedness
Eze. 3. 19 and he turn not from his wickedness, nor
7. 11 Violence is risen up into a rod of wicked.
31. 11 I have driven him out for his wickedness
33. 12 in the day that he turneth from his wick.
Hos. 10. 13 Ye have ploughed wickedness, ye have re.
Mic. 6. 10 Are there yet the treasures of wickedness

11. *Wrong, wickedness*, רִשְׁעָה *rishah*.
Deut. 9. 4, 5 but for the wickedness of these nations
Prov. 11. 5 but the wicked shall fall by his own wic.
13. 6 but wickedness overthroweth the sinner
Isa. 9. 18 For wickedness burneth as the fire, it sh.
Eze. 5. 6 she hath changed my judgments into wi.
18. 20 the wickedness of the wicked shall be upon
18. 27 when the wicked..turneth away from his
33. 12 as for the wickedness of the wicked, he
33. 19 But if the wicked turn from his wickedn.
Zech. 5. 8 he said, This (is) wickedness. And he cast
Mal. 1. 4 they shall call them The border of w. 3, 15.

12. *Out of place*, ἄτοπος *atopos*, Acts 25. 5.

13. *Evil, badness, wickedness*, κακία *kakia*.
Acts 8. 22 Repent therefore of this thy wickedness

14. *Malignity, evil*, πονηρία *ponēria*.
Matt 22. 18 Jesus perceived their wickedness, and said
Mark 7. 22 Thefts, covetousness, wickedness, deceit
Luke 11. 39 inward part is full of ravening and wicked.
Rom. 1. 29 Being filled with all unrighteousness..wi.
1 Co. 5. 8 neither with the leaven of malice and w.
Eph. 6. 12 For we wrestle..against spiritual wicke.

15. *Malignant, evil*, πονηρός *ponēros*.
1 Jo. 5. 19 we know that..the whole world lieth in w.

16. *In this (man)*, τούτῳ *toutō*.
Acts 25. 5 accuse this man, if there be any (wicked)

WIDE, wideness, to make or open —

1. *Companionship, society*, חֶבֶר *cheber*.
Prov. 21. 9 than with a brawling woman in a w..de
25. 24 than with a brawling woman..in a wide

2. *Wide of hands*, (יָדַיִם) רְחַב [*rachab*].
1 Ch. 4. 40 they found fat pasture..and the land ..w.
Psa. 104. 25 this great and wide sea, wherein (are) thi
Job 30. 14 They came..as a wide breaking in..in the

3. *Measure, stature*, מִדָּה *middah*.
Jer. 22. 14 That saith, I will build me a wide house

4. *To open*, פָּתַח *pathach*.
Deut 15. 8, 11 thou shalt open thine hand wide unto
Nah. 3. 13 the gates of thy land shall be set wide open

5. *To make wide, broad*, רָחַב *rachab*, 5.
Psa. 35. 21 Yea, they opened their mouth wide agai.
81. 10 open thy mouth wide and I will fill it
Isa. 57. 4 against whom make ye a wide mouth, (and)

6. *Breadth, broad place*, רֹחַב *rochab*.
Eze. 41. 10 between the chambers (was) the wideness

7. *Wide, broad, ample*, πλατύς *platus*.
Matt. 7. 13 Enter ye in at the strait gate, for wide

WIDOW, widowhood —

1. *Widowhood, silence*, אַלְמֹן *almon*.
Isa. 47. 9 in one day, the loss of children, and wid.

2. *Widow, silent one*, אַלְמָנָה *almanah*.
Gen. 38. 11 Remain a widow at thy father's house, till
Exod 22. 22 Ye shall not afflict any widow, or father.
22. 24 your wives shall be widows, and your ch.
Lev. 21. 14 A widow, or a divorced woman, or profane
22. 13 if the priest's daughter be a widow, or di
Num 30. 9 every vow of a widow, and of her that is
Deut 10. 18 He doth execute the judgment of the..wi.
14. 29 stranger, and the fatherless, and the wi
16. 11, 14 stranger, and..fatherless, and the wi.
24. 17 Thou shalt not..take a widow's raiment
24. 19, 20, 21 for the fatherless, and for the wi.
26. 12 the stranger, the fatherless, and the wid.
26. 13 stranger, to the fatherless, and to the wi.
27. 19 that perverteth the judgment of the..w.
2 Sa. 14. 5 she answered, I (am) indeed a widow wo.
1 Ki. 7. 14 He (was) a widow's son of the tribe of N.
11. 26 whose mother's name (was) Zeruah, a wi.
17. 9 I have commanded a widow woman there
17. 10 the widow woman (was) there gathering
17. 20 hast thou also brought evil upon the wid.
Job 22. 9 Thou hast sent widows away empty, and
24. 3 They drive away..they take the widow's
24. 21 beareth not, and doeth not good to the w.
27. 15 shall be buried in death; and his widows
29. 13 caused the widow's heart to sing for joy
31. 16 have caused the eyes of the widow to fail
Psa. 68. 5 a judge of the widows, (is) God in his holy
78. 64 and their widows made no lamentation
94. 6 They slay the widow and the stranger, and
109. 9 his children be fatherless..his wife a wi.
146. 9 The LORD..relieveth the fatherless and w.
Prov 15. 25 but he will establish the border of the w.
Isa. 1. 17 judge the fatherless, plead for the widow
1. 23 neither doth the cause of the widow come
9. 17 neither shall have mercy on..their..wido.
10. 2 that widows may be their prey, and (that)
47. 8 I shall not sit..a widow, neither shall I
Jer. 7. 6 (If) ye oppress not the stranger..the wid.
15. 8 Their widows are increased to me above
18. 21 be bereaved of their children, and (be) w.
22. 3 do no violence to the stranger..nor the w.
49. 11 I will preserve..and let thy widows trust
Lam. 1. 1 (how) is she become as a widow, she (that
5. 3 We are orphans..our mothers (are) as w.
Eze. 22. 7 they vexed the fatherless and the widow
22. 25 they have made her many widows in the
44. 22 Neither..a widow..or a widow that had
Zech. 7. 10 oppress not the widow, nor the fatherless
Mal. 3. 5 oppress the hireling in..wages, the wid.

3. *Widowhood, silence*, אַלְמָנוּת *almanuth*.
Gen. 38. 14 she put her widow's garments off from her
38. 19 and put on the garments of her widowh.
2 Sa. 20. 3 unto the day of their death, living in wi.
Isa. 54. 4 shalt..remember the reproach of thy wi.

A widow, one bereaved, χήρα *chēra*.
Matt 23. 14 [Woe unto..hypocrites, for ye devour w.]
Mark 12. 40 Which devour widows' houses, and for a
12. 42 there came a certain poor widow, and she
12. 43 Verily I say unto you, That this poor wi.
Luke 2. 37 she (was) a widow of about fourscore and
4. 25 But I tell you of a truth, many widows
4. 26 was Elias sent..save..a woman..a widow
7. 12 only son of his mother, and she was a w.
18. 3 there was a widow in that city, and she
18. 5 Yet because this widow troubleth me, I
20. 47 Which devour widows' houses, and for a
21. 2 he saw also a certain poor widow casting
21. 3 Of a truth I say unto you..this poor wid.
Acts 6. 1 because their widows were neglected in
9. 39 all the widows stood by him weeping, and
9. 41 when he had called the saints and widows
1 Co. 7. 8 I say therefore to the unmarried and wi.
1 Ti. 5. 3 Honour widows that are widows indeed
5. 4 But if any widow have children or neph.
5. 5 Now she that is a widow indeed, and de.
5. 9 Let not a widow be taken into the numb.
5. 11 But the younger widows refuse: for when
5. 16 If any man..that believeth have widows
5. 16 that it may relieve them that are widows
Jas. 1. 27 To visit the fatherless and widows in th.
Rev. 18. 7 I sit a queen, and am no widow, and sha.

WIFE, wives —

Woman, a wife, female, אִשָּׁה *ishshah*.
Gen. 2. 24 Therefore shall a man..cleave unto his w.
2. 25 they were both naked, the man and his w.
3. 8 Adam and his wife hid themselves from
3. 17 hast hearkened unto the voice of thy wife
3. 20 Adam called his wife's name Eve; because
3. 21 Unto Adam also and to his wife did the
4. 1 Adam knew Eve his wife; and she conce.
4. 17 Cain knew his wife; and she conceived
4. 25 Adam knew his wife again; and she bare
6. 18 thou, and thy sons, and thy wife, and thy
7. 7 Noah went in, and his sons, and his wife
7. 13 the sons of Noah, and Noah's wife, and the
8. 16 thou, and thy wife, and thy sons, and thy
8. 18 Noah went forth, and his sons, and his w.
11. 29 took..wives..Abram's wife..Nahor's wife
11. 31 Terah took Abram..son Abram's wife, and
12. 5 Abram took Sarai his wife, and Lot his b.
12. 11 he said unto Sarai his wife, Behold now
12. 12 the Egyptians..shall say, This (is) his w.
12. 17 plagues because of Sarai, Abram's wife
12. 18 why didst thou not tell..she (was) thy w.?
12. 19 her..to wife: now therefore behold thy w.
12. 20 they sent him away, and his wife, and all
13. 1 he, and his wife and all that he had, and
16. 1 Sarai, Abram's wife, bare him no children
16. 3 Abram's wife..gave her to be his wife
17. 15 As for Sarai thy wife, thou shalt not call
17. 19 Sarah thy wife shall bear thee a son ind.
18. 9 they said unto him, Where (is) Sarah thy w.
18. 10 and, lo, Sarah thy wife shall have a son
19. 15 Arise, take thy wife, and thy two daughters
19. 16 men laid hold..upon the hand of his wife
19. 26 his wife looked back from behind him
20. 2 Abraham said of Sarah his wife, She (is)
20. 7 restore the man (his) wife; for he (is) a pr
20. 11 and they will slay me for my wife's sake
20. 12 yet..my sister..and she became my wife
20. 14 Abimelech. restored him Sarah his wife
20. 17 God healed Abimelech, and his wife, and
20. 18 closed up..because of Sarah, Abraham's w.
21. 21 his mother took him a wife out of the land
23. 19 Abraham buried Sarah his wife in the ca.
24. 3 that thou shalt not take a wife unto my
24. 4 shalt go..to my kindred, and take a wife
24. 7 thou shalt take a wife unto my son from
24. 15 Milcah, the wife of Nahor, Abraham's br.
24. 36 Sarah my master's wife bare a son to my
24. 37 Thou shalt not take a wife to my son of
24. 38 thou shalt go..and take a wife unto my son
24. 40 thou shalt take a wife for my son of my
24. 51 Rebekah..let her be thy master's son's w.
24. 67 took Rebekah, and she became his wife
25. 1 again Abraham took a wife, and her name
25. 10 was Abraham buried, and Sarah his wife
25. 20 Isaac was..when he took Rebekah to wife
25. 21 entreated..for his wife..and..his wife con.
26. 7 the men of the place asked..of his wife, and
26. 7 for he feared to say, (She is) my wife, lest
26. 8 Isaac (was) sporting with Rebekah his w.
Gen. 26. 9 said, Behold, of a surety she (is) thy wife
26. 10 one..might lightly have lien with thy wife
26. 11 He that toucheth this man or his wife sh.
26. 34 E. was forty years old when he took to w.
27. 46 if Jacob take a wife of the daughters of
28. 1, 6 Thou shalt not take a wife of the dau.
28. 2 take thee a wife from thence of the daug.
28. 6 Isaac.. sent him away..to take him a wife
28. 9 took unto the wives..Mahalath..to..wife
29. 21 Give..my wife, for my days are fulfilled
29. 28 he gave him Rachel his daughter to wife
30. 4 she gave him Bilhah her handmaid to wife
30. 9 she took Zilpah..and gave her Jacob to w.
34. 4 spake..saying, Get me this damsel to wife
34. 8 saying..I pray you give her him to wife
34. 12 ask..dowry..but give me the damsel to w.
36. 10 Adah the wife of Esau..B. the wife of Es.
36. 12 these (were) the sons of Adah, Esau's wife
36. 13, 17 the sons of Bashemath, Esau's wife
36. 14 Anah the daughter of Zibeon, Esau's wife
36. 18 wife..the daughter of Anah, Esau's wife
36. 39 his wife's name (was) Mehetabel, the da.
38. 6 Judah took a wife for Er his first born
38. 8 Go in unto thy brother's wife, and marry
38. 9 when he went in unto his brother's wife
38. 12 the daughter of Shuah, Judah's wife, died
38. 14 and she was not given unto him to wife
39. 7 his master's wife cast her eyes upon Joseph
39. 8 refused, and said unto his master's wife
39. 9 but thee, because thou (art) his wife
39. 19 his master heard the words of his wife, wh.
41. 45 he gave him to wife Asenath the daughter
44. 27 Ye know that my wife bare me two (sons)
46. 19 The sons of Rachel, Jacob's wife; Joseph
49. 31 Sarah his wife..Isaac and Rebekah his w.
Exod. 4. 20 Moses took his wife and his sons, and set
6. 20 Amram took..his father's sister to wife
6. 23 Aaron took him Elisheba..to wife
6. 25 (one) of the daughters of Putiel to wife
18. 2 Jethro..took Zipporah, Moses' wife, after
18. 5 Jethro..came with his sons and his wife
18. 6 and thy wife, and her two sons with her
19. 15 Be ready..come not at (your) wives
20. 17 thou shalt not covet thy neighbour's wife
21. 3 if he were married, then his wife shall go
21. 4 given him a wife..the wife and her chil.
21. 5 I love my master, my wife, and my child.
22. 16 he shall surely endow her to be his wife
Lev. 18. 8 The nakedness of thy father's wife shalt
18. 11 The nakedness of thy father's wife's dau.
18. 14 thou shalt not approach to his wife, she
18. 15 she (is) thy son's wife; thou shalt not unc.
18. 16 the nakedness of thy brother's wife: it (is)
18. 18 Neither shalt thou take a wife to her sist.
18. 20 not lie carnally with thy neighbour's wife
20. 10 (another) man's wife..his neighbour's wife
20. 11 the man that lieth with his father's wife
20. 14 if a man take a wife and her mother, it
20. 21 if a man shall take his brother's wife, it
21. 7 They shall not take a wife (that is) a who.
21. 13 And he shall take a wife in her virginity
21. 14 but he shall take a virgin..to wife
Num. 5. 12 If any man's wife go aside, and commit
5. 14 jealous of his wife..jealous of his wife
5. 15 Then shall the man bring his wife unto
5. 29 when a wife goeth aside (to another) ins
5. 30 he be jealous over his wife, and shall set
26. 59 the name of Amram's wife (was) Jochebed
30. 16 between a man and his wife, between the
36. 8 shall be wife unto one of the family of the
Deut. 5. 21 shalt thou desire thy neighbour's wife, ne.
13. 6 thy daughter, or the wife of thy bosom, or
20. 7 what man..hath betrothed a wife, and ha.
21. 11 that thou wouldest have her to thy wife
21. 13 her husband, and she shall be thy wife
22. 13 If any man take a wife, and go in unto her
22. 16 I gave my daughter unto this man to wife
22. 19 she shall be his wife; he may not put her
22. 24 he hath humbled his neighbour's wife
22. 29 she shall be his wife; because he hath hu.
22. 30 A man shall not take his father's wife, nor
24. 1 When a man hath taken a wife, and mar.
24. 3 husband die, which took her (to be) his w.
24. 4 may not take her again to be his wife, af.
24. 5 hath taken a new wife..cheer up his wife
25. 5 wife of the dead..take her..to wife
25. 11 the wife of the one draweth near for to de.
27. 20 Cursed..that lieth with his father's wife
28. 30 Thou shalt betroth a wife, and another m.
28. 54 toward the wife of his bosom, and toward
Josh 15. 16 to him will I give Achsah..to wife
15. 17 gave him Achsah his daughter to wife
Judg. 1. 12 to him will I give Achsah..to wife
1. 13 gave him Achsah his daughter to wife
4. 4 the wife of Lapidoth, she judged Israel at
4. 17 to the tent of Jael the wife of Heber the
4. 21 Jael, Heber's wife, took a nail of the tent
5. 24 Blessed above women shall Jael the wife
11. 2 Gilead's wife bare him sons: and his wif
13. 2 and his wife (was) barren, and bare not
13. 11 Manoah arose, and went after his wife, and
13. 19 and Manoah and his wife looked on
13. 20 Manoah and his wife looked on (it), and
13. 21 angel..did no more appear..to his wife
13. 22 Manoah said unto his wife, We shall sur.
13. 23 his wife said unto him, If the LORD were
14. 2 now therefore get her for me to wife
14. 3 thou goest to take a wife of the uncircu
14. 15 they said unto Samson's wife, Entice thy
14. 16 Samson's wife wept before him, and said
14. 20 Samson's wife was (given) to his compan
15. 1 visited his wife..will go in to my wife

Judg 15. 6 he had taken his wife, and given her to
21. 1 give his daughter unto Benjamin to wife
21. 18 Cursed (be) he that giveth a wife to Benj.
21. 21 catch you every man his wife of the dau.
21. 22 we reserved not to each man his wife in
Ruth 1. 1 went to sojourn..he, and his wife, and his
1. 2 the name of his wife Naomi, and the na.
4. 5 Ruth the Moabitess, the wife of the dead
4. 10 the wife of Mahlon..to be my wife, to ra.
4. 13 Boaz took Ruth, and she was his wife, and
1 Sa. 1. 4 he gave to Peninnah his wife, and to all
1. 19 Elkanah knew Hannah his wife; and the
2. 20 Eli blessed Elkanah and his wife, and said
4. 19 Phinehas' wife, was with child, (near) to be
14. 50 the name of Saul's wife (was) Ahinoam
18. 17 her will I give thee to wife; only be thou
18. 19 given unto Adriel the Meholathite to wi.
18. 27 Saul gave him Michal his daughter to wi.
19. 11 David's wife, told him, saying, If thou s.
25. 3 Nabal, and the name of his wife Abigail
25. 14 one of the young men told..Nabal's wife
25. 37 his wife had told him these things, that
25. 39 David sent..to take her to him to wife
25. 40 David sent..to take thee to him to wife
25. 42 she went after..and became his wife
25. 44 Saul had given..David's wife, to Phalti
27. 3 and Abigail the Carmelitess, Nabal's wife
30. 5 Abigail the wife of Nabal the Carmelite
30. 22 save to every man his wife and his child.
2 Sa. 2. 2 and Abigail, Nabal's wife, the Carmelite
3. 3 Chileab, of Abigail the wife of Nabal the
3. 5 the sixth, Ithream, by Eglah, David's wife
3. 14 Deliver (me) my wife Michal, which I es.
11. 3 (Is) not this Bath-sheba..the wife of Uri.
11. 11 and to drink, and to lie with my wife
11. 26 the wife of Uriah heard that Uriah her
11. 27 she became his wife, and bare him a son
12. 9 hast taken his wife (to be) thy wife, and
12. 10 the wife of Uriah the Hittite to be thy w.
12. 15 the child that Uriah's wife bare unto Da.
12. 24 David comforted Bath-sheba his wife, and
1 Ki. 2. 17 give me Abishag the Shunammite to wife
2. 21 be given to Adonijah thy brother to wife
4. 11 had..the daughter of Solomon to wife
4. 15 Basmath the daughter of Solomon to wife
9. 16 a present unto his daughter, Solomon's w.
11. 19 gave him to wife the sister of his own w.
14. 2 said to his wife..the wife of Jeroboam, and
14. 4 Jeroboam's wife did so, and arose, and
14. 5 the wife of Jeroboam cometh to ask a th.
14. 6 Come in, thou wife of Jeroboam; why fe.
14. 17 Jeroboam's wife arose, and departed, and
16. 31 he took to wife Jezebel, the daughter of
21. 5 his wife came to him, and said unto him
21. 7 his wife said unto him, Dost thou now go.
21. 25 Ahab..whom Jezebel his wife stirred up
2 Ki. 5. 2 and she waited on Naaman's wife
8. 18 the daughter of Ahab was his wife: and
14. 9 Give thy daughter to my son to wife: and
22. 14 the prophetess, the wife of Shallum the
1 Ch. 1. 50 his wife's name (was) Mehetabel, the da.
2. 18 Caleb..begat (children) of Azubah (his)w.
2. 24 Hezron's wife, bare him Ashur the father
2. 26 Jerahmeel had also another wife, whose
2. 29 the name of the wife of Abishur (was) A.
2. 35 Sheshan..his daughter to Jarha..to wife
3. 3 the sixth, Ithream, by Eglah his wife
4. 18 his wife Jehudijah bare Jered the father
4. 19 the sons of (his) wife Hodiah, the sister of
7. 15 Machir took to wife (the sister) of Hupp.
7. 16 the wife of Machir bare a son, and she ca.
7. 23 he went in to his wife, she conceived and
8. 9 begat of Hodesh his wife, Jobab, and Zi.
8. 29 the father of Gibeon; whose wife's name
9. 35 Jehiel, whose wife's name (was)
2 Ch 8. 11 My wife shall not dwell in the house of
11. 18 Rehoboam took him Mahalath..to wife
21. 6 he had the daughter of Ahab to wife, and
22. 11 the wife of Jehoiada. hid him from Ath
25. 18 Give thy daughter to my son to wife, and
34. 22 went to Huldah the prophetess, the wife
Ezra 2. 61 which took a wife of the daughters of B.
Neh. 7. 63 which took (one) of the daughters..to w.
Esth. 5. 10 called for his friends, and Zeresh his wi.
5. 14 Then said Zeresh his wife and all his fri.
6. 13 told Zeresh his wife..Zeresh his wife
Job 2. 9 Then said his wife unto him, Dost thou
19. 17 My breath is strange to my wife, though
31. 10 let my wife grind unto another, and let
Psa. 109. 9 children be fatherless, and his wife a wi.
128. 3 Thy wife (shall be) as a fruitful vine by
Prov. 5. 18 and rejoice with the wife of thy youth
6. 29 he that goeth in to his neighbour's wife
18. 22 (Whoso) findeth a wife findeth a good
19. 13 the contentions of a wife (are) a continual
19. 14 and a prudent wife (is) from the LORD
Eccl. 9. 9 Live joyfully with the wife whom thou lo.
Isa. 54. 6 a wife of youth, when thou wast refused
Jer. 3. 1 If a man put away his wife, and she go
3. 20 (as) a wife treacherously departeth from
5. 8 one neighed after his neighbour's wife
6. 11 the husband with the wife shall be taken
16. 2 Thou shalt not take thee a wife, neither
Eze. 16. 32 (as) a wife that committeth adultery, (w.)
18. 6 neither hath defiled his neighbour's wife
18. 11 but even..defiled his neighbour's wife
18. 15 hath not defiled his neighbour's wife
22. 11 abomination with his neighbour's wife
24. 18 at even my wife died: and I did in the mo.
33. 26 ye defile every one his neighbour's wife
Hos. 1. 2 take unto thee a wife of whoredoms and
2. 2 she (is) not my wife, neither (am) I her h.
Hos. 12. 12 Israel served for a wife, and for a wife he
Amos 7. 17 Thy wife shall be an harlot in the city, and
Mal. 2. 14 the wife of thy youth..the wife of thy co.
2. 15 deal treacherously against the wife of his

2. *A wife, queen,* שֵׁגַל *shegal.*
Dan. 5. 2, 3 his princes, his wives, and his concub.
5. 23 thy wives, and thy concubines, have drunk

3. *Lady, mistress, married woman,* בְּעֻלָה [*baal*].
Gen. 20. 3 for the woman..for she (is) a man's wife

4. *Women, wives,* נָשִׁים *nashim.*
Gen. 4. 19 Lamech took unto him two wives: the na.
4. 23 said unto his wives..ye wives of Lamech
6. 2 they took them wives of all which they
6. 18 thy sons..and thy sons' wives with thee
7. 7 Noah went in..his sons' wives with him
7. 13 the three wives of his sons with them, into
8. 16 and thy sons, and thy sons' wives with thee
8. 18 Noah went..and his sons' wives with him
11. 29 Abram and Nahor took them wives, the
28. 9 took unto the wives which he had Maha.
30. 26 Give (me) my wives and my children, for
31. 17 set his sons and his wives upon camels
31. 50 shalt take (other) wives beside my daug.
32. 22 took his two wives, and his two women
34. 21 let us take their daughters to us for wives
34. 29 their wives took they captive, and spoiled
36. 2 Esau took his wives of the daughters of C.
36. 6 Esau took his wives, and his sons, and his
37. 2 with the sons of Zilpah, his father's wives
45. 19 take you wagons..for your wives, and bri.
46. 5 their wives, in the wagons which Pharaoh
46. 26 besides Jacob's sons' wives, all the souls
Exod 22. 24 your wives shall be widows, and your chi.
32. 2 golden ear rings..in the ears of your wives
Num 14. 3 that our wives and our children should be
16. 27 their wives, and their sons, and their little
32. 26 Our little ones, our wives, our flocks, and
Deut. 3. 19 your wives, and your little ones, and your
17. 17 Neither shall he multiply wives to himself
21. 15 If a man have two wives, one beloved, and
29. 11 Your little ones, your wives, and thy str.
Josh. 1. 14 Your wives, your little ones, and your ca.
Judg. 3. 6 they took their daughters to be their wi.
8. 30 threescore and ten..he had many wives
21. 14 they gave them wives which they had sa.
21. 16 How shall we do for wives for them that
21. 18 we may not give them wives of our daug.
21. 23 took (them) wives, according to their nu.
Ruth 1. 4 they took them wives of the women of M.
1 Sa. 1. 2 he had two wives; the name of the one
25. 43 they were also both of them his wives
27. 3 David with his two wives, Ahinoam the
30. 3 their wives, and their sons..were taken
30. 5 David's two wives were taken captives, Ah.
30. 18 and David rescued his two wives
2 Sa. 2. 2 David went up thither, and his two wives
5. 13 David took (him) more..wives out of Jer.
12. 8 I gave thee..thy master's wives into thy
12. 11 take thy wives..shall lie with thy wives
19. 5 the lives of thy wives, and the lives of thy
1 Ki. 11. 3 seven hundred wives..his wives turned
11. 4 his wives turned away his heart after ot.
11. 8 likewise did he for all his strange wives
20. 3 thy wives also and thy children..the go.
20. 5 Thou shalt deliver me thy..wives, and thy
20. 7 he sent unto me for my wives, and for my
2 Ki. 4. 1 there cried a certain woman of the wives
24. 15 he carried away..the king's wives, and
1 Ch. 4. 5 Ashur the father of Tekoa had two wives
7. 4 with them..for they had many wives and
8. 8 Shaharaim..Hushim and Baara (were) h.w.
14. 3 David took more wives at Jerusalem, and
2 Ch. 11. 21 loved..above all his wives..eighteen wiv.
11. 23 dispersed..And he desired many wives
13. 21 Abijah waxed mighty, and married..wiv.
20. 13 Judah..with their little ones, their wives
21. 14 will the LORD smite..thy wives, and all
21. 17 carried away..his sons also, and his wives
24. 3 Jehoiada took for him two wives, and he
29. 9 and our wives (are) in captivity for this
31. 18 genealogy of all their little ones, their w.
Ezra 10. 2 We have..taken strange wives of the pe.
10. 3 make a covenant..to put away all the w.
10. 10 Ye have..taken strange wives, to increase
10. 11 separate yourselves..from the strange w.
10. 14 let all them which have taken strange w.
10. 17 all the men that had taken strange wives
10. 18 there were found that had taken strange w
10. 19 that they would put away their wives, and
10. 44 had taken strange wives..(some)..had w.
Neh. 4. 14 your sons, and your daughters, your wives
5. 1 a great cry of the people, and of their wi
10. 28 their wives, their sons, and their daught.
12. 43 the wives also and the children rejoiced
13. 23 Jews (that) had married wives of Ashdod
13. 27 to transgress..in marrying strange wives
Esth. 1. 20 all the wives shall give to their husbands
Isa. 13. 16 their houses shall be spoiled, and their w.
Jer. 6. 12 (with their) fields and wives together, for
8. 10 Therefore will I give their wives unto ot.
14. 16 them, their wives, nor their sons, nor th.
18. 21 let their wives be bereaved of their chil.
29. 6 Take ye wives, and..take wives for your
29. 23 adultery with their neighbours' wives and
35. 8 to drink no wine all our days, we, our w.
38. 23 So they shall bring out all thy wives and
44. 9 the wickedness of their wives..of your w.
44. 15 all the men which knew that their wives
44. 25 Ye and your wives have both spoken with
Eze. 44. 22 Neither..they take for their wives a wid.
Zech. 12. 12, 12, 13, 13, 14 and their wives apart

5. *Women, wives,* נָשִׁין *nashin.*
Dan. 6. 24 cast..them, their children, and their wi.

6. *Belonging to a woman,* γυναικεῖος *gunaikeios.*
1 Pe. 3. 7 giving honour unto the wife, as unto the

7. *A woman, wife,* γυνή *gunē.*
Matt. 1. 20 fear not to take unto thee Mary thy wife
1. 24 Joseph, being raised..took unto him his w.
5. 31, 32 whosoever shall put away his wife
14. 3 Herodias' sake, his brother Philip's wife
18. 25 commanded him to be sold, and his wife
19. 3 Is it lawful for a man to put away his wife
19. 5 For this..shall a man..cleave to his wife
19. 8 Moses..suffered you to put away your w.
19. 9 whosoever shall put away his wife, exce.
19. 10 If the case of the man be so with (his) w.
19. 29 every one that hath forsaken..[wife], or
22. 24 his brother shall marry his wife, and raise
22. 25 deceased, and, having no issue, left his w.
22. 28 whose wife shall she be of the seven? for
27. 19 When he was set down..his wife sent unto
Mark 6. 17 for Herodias' sake, his brother Philip's w.
6. 18 It is not lawful..to have thy brother's w.
10. 2 Is it lawful for a man to put away (his) w.?
10. 7 For this..shall a man..cleave to his wife
10. 11 Whosoever shall put away his wife, and
10. 29 There is no man that hath left..[wife], or
12. 19 If a man's brother die, and leave (his) w.
12. 19 his brother should take his wife, and raise
12. 20 the first took a wife, and dying left no seed
12. 23 whose wife..for the seven had her to wife?
Luke 1. 5 his wife (was) of the daughters of Aaron
1. 13 thy wife Elisabeth shall bear thee a son
1. 18 I am an old man, and my wife well stric.
1. 24 after those days his wife Elisabeth conc.
2. 5 To be taxed with Mary his espoused [wife]
3. 19 for Herodias his brother Philip's wife, and
8. 3 Joanna the wife of Chuza Herod's steward
14. 20 I have married a wife, and..I cannot come
14. 26 any..come to me, and hate not his..wife
16. 18 Whosoever putteth away his wife, and ma.
17. 32 Remember Lot's wife
18. 29 There is no man that hath left..wife, or
20. 28 die, having a wife..should take his wife
20. 29 the first took a wife, and died without ch.
20. 30 [the second took her to wife, and he died]
20. 33 wife..is she? for seven had her to wife
Acts 5. 1 a certain man..with Sapphira his wife
5. 2 kept back..of the price, his wife also be.
5. 7 his wife, not knowing what was done, ca.
18. 2 a certain Jew named Aquila..with his w.
21. 5 they all brought us on our way, with wives
24. 24 when Felix came with his wife Drusilla
1 Co. 5. 1 that one should have his father's wife
7. 2 let every man have his own wife, and let
7. 3 render unto the wife..likewise also the w.
7. 4 The wife hath not power of her own body
7. 4 not power of his own body, but the wife
7. 10 Let not the wife depart from (her) husband
7. 11 let not the husband put away (his) wife
7. 12 If any brother hath a wife that believeth
7. 14 sanctified by the wife, and the..wife is
7. 16 wife..whether thou shalt save (thy) wife?
7. 27 Art thou bound unto a wife? seek not to
7. 27 Art thou loosed from a wife? seek..a wi.
7. 29 that both they that have wives be as tho.
7. 33 married careth..how he may please..wi.
7. 34 There is a difference..between a wife and
7. 39 The wife is bound by the law as long as
9. 5 Have we not power to lead about..a wife
Eph. 5. 22 Wives, submit yourselves unto your
5. 23 For the husband is the head of the wife
5. 24 so (let) the wives (be) to their own husb.
5. 25 Husbands, love your wives, even as Chr.
5. 28 So ought men to love their wives as their
5. 28 He that loveth his wife loveth himself
5. 31 shall be joined unto his wife, and they
5. 33 let every one..so love his wife even as
5. 33 the wife..that she reverence (her) husband
Col. 3. 18 Wives, submit yourselves unto your own
3. 19 Husbands, love (your) wives, and be not
1 Ti. 3. 2 bishop..must be..the husband of one w.
3. 11 Even so (must their) wives (be) grave, not
3. 12 the deacons be the husbands of one wife
5. 9 a widow..having been the wife of one man
Titus 1. 6 the husband of one wife, having faithful
1 Pe. 3. 1 wives..by the conversation of the wives
Rev. 19. 7 the Lamb..his wife hath made herself re.
21. 9 I will show thee the bride, the Lamb's wife

[*See also* Brother's wife, married wife, uncle's wife.]

WIFE'S mother —

A wife's mother, πενθερά *penthera.*
Matt. 8. 14 he saw his wife's mother laid, and sick of
Mark 1. 30 Simon's wife's mother lay sick of a fever
Luke 4. 38 Simon's wife's mother was taken with a

WIVES' (old) —

Belonging to an old woman, γραώδης *graōdēs.*
1 Ti. 4. 7 refuse profane and old wives' fables, and

WILD —

1. *A wild ass, free,* פֶּרֶא *pere.*
Gen. 16. 12 he will be a wild man; his hand..against

2. *Level place, field, land,* שָׂדֶה *sadeh.*
Lev. 26. 22 I will also send wild beasts among you, whi.
2 Sa. 2. 18 and Asahel..light of foot as a wild roe
2 Ki. 4. 39 found a wild vine, and gathered..wild go.

2 Ki. 14. 9 there passed by a wild beast that (was) in
2 Ch.25. 18 there passed by a wild beast that (was) in
Job 39. 15 forgetteth..that the wild beast may break
Hos. 13. 8 I will meet them..the wild beast shall te.

3. *Belonging to the field,* ἄγριος *agrios.*
Matt. 3. 4 John..his meat was locusts and wild honey
Mark 1. 6 John..he did eat locusts and wild honey

[*See also* Ass, beast, bull, goats, grapes, olive tree, ox.]

WILD beast (of the desert or islands), goat—

1. *Inhabitants of islands (sea shores),* אִיִּים *iyyim.*
Isa. 13. 22 the wild beasts of the islands shall cry
34. 14 the wild beasts of the islands, and the satyr
Jer. 50. 39 with the wild beasts of the islands

2. *Wild goat or roe,* אַקּוֹ *aqqo.*
Deut 14. 5 The hart, and the roebuck..and the wild g.

3. *Wild beast,* זִיז *ziz.*
Psa. 50. 11 and the wild beasts of the field (are) mine
80. 13 the wild beast of the field doth devour it

4. *Inhabitants of the dry places,* צִיִּים *tsiyyim.*
Isa. 13. 21 wild beasts of the desert shall lie there
34. 14 The wild beasts of the desert shall also
Jer. 50. 39 Therefore the wild beasts of the desert

WILDERNESS —

1. *A wilderness, pasture land,* אֶרֶץ מִדְבָּר *erets midbar.*
Prov 21. 19 better to dwell in the wilderness, than wi.

2. *Jeshimon, a desolate place,* יְשִׁימוֹן *yeshimon.*
Deut 32. 10 found him..in the waste howling wilde.
Psa. 68. 7 when thou didst march through the wil.

3. *A wilderness desert, pasture land,* מִדְבָּר *midbar.*
Gen. 14. 6 unto El-paran, which (is) by the wildern.
16. 7 found her by a fountain of water in the w.
21. 14 departed, and wandered in the wilderness
21. 20 dwelt in the wilderness, and became an
21. 21 And he dwelt in the wilderness of Paran
36. 24 Anah that found the mules in the wilde.
37. 22 cast him into this pit that (is) in the wil.
Exod. 3. 18 three days' journey into the wilderness
4. 27 into the wilderness to meet Moses. And
5. 1 may hold a feast unto me in the wildern.
7. 16 that they may serve me in the wilderness
8. 27 will go three days' journey into the wild.
8. 28 sacrifice to the LORD your God in the wi.
13. 18 the way of the wilderness of the Red sea
13. 20 encamped in Etham, in the edge of the w.
14. 3 They (are) entangled in the land, the wi.
14. 11 hast thou taken us away to die in the wi.
14. 12 than that we should die in the wilderness
15. 22 into the wilderness..three days in the w
16. 1 came unto the wilderness of Sin, which
16. 2 murmured against Moses..in the wilder.
16. 3 ye have brought us forth into this wilde.
16. 10 that they looked toward the wilderness
16. 14 upon the face of the wilderness (there lay)
16. 32 bread wherewith I have fed you in the w.
17. 1 journeyed from the wilderness of Sin, after
18. 5 came with his sons..into the wilderness
19. 1 same day came they (into) the wilderness
19 2 had pitched in the wilderness: and there
Lev. 7. 38 to offer their oblations..in the wilderness
16. 10 let him go for a scape goat into the wild.
16. 21 by the hand of a fit man into the wilder.
16. 22 and he shall let go the goat in the wilde
Num 1. 1 spake unto Moses in the wilderness of S
1. 19 so he numbered them in the wilderness
3. 4 offered strange fire. in the wilderness of
3. 14 LORD spake unto Moses in the wilderness
9. 1 LORD spake unto Moses in the wilderness
9. 5 in the wilderness of Sinai: according to
10. 12 their journeys out of the wilderness of S
10. 12 the cloud rested in the wilderness of Par.
10. 31 knowest how we are to encamp in the w.
12. 16 people..pitched in the wilderness of Par.
13. 3 sent them from the wilderness of Paran
13. 21 searched the land from the wilderness of
13. 26 unto the wilderness of Paran, to Kadesh
14. 2 or would God we had died in this wilder
14. 16 therefore he hath slain them in the wild.
14. 22 my miracles which I did. in the wilder.
14. 25 get you into the wilderness by the way of
14. 29 Your carcases shall fall in this wilderness
14. 32 your carcases, they shall fall in this wild.
14. 33 your children shall wander in the wilder
14. 33 until your carcases be wasted in the wil.
14. 35 in this wilderness they shall be consumed
15. 32 while the children of Israel were in the w.
16. 13 to kill us in the wilderness, except thou
20. 4 congregation of the LORD into this wild.
21. 5 brought..out of Egypt to die in the wi.?
21. 11 in the wilderness which (is) before Moab
21. 13 which (is) in the wilderness that cometh
21. 18 And from the wilderness (they went) to
21. 23 and went out against Israel into the wil.
24. 1 but he set his face toward the wilderness
26. 64 they numbered the children..in the wild.
26. 65 They shall surely die in the wilderness
27. 3 Our father died in the wilderness, and he
27. 14 water of Meribah in Kadesh in the wild.
32. 13 made them wander in the wilderness forty
32. 15 he will yet again leave them in the wild.
33. 6 pitched in Etham..in the edge of the w.
33. 8 through the midst of the sea into the w.
33. 8 went three days' journey in the wilderness
33. 11 removed..and encamped in the wilderness
33. 12 took their journey out of the wilderness
33. 15 departed..and pitched in the wilderness
33. 36 pitched in the wilderness of Zin, which
34 3 south quarter shall be from the wildern.

Deut. 1. 1 all Israel on this side Jordan in the wild.
1. 19 through all that great and terrible wilde.
1. 31 in the wilderness, where thou hast seen
1. 40 take your journey into the wilderness by
2. 1 took our journey into the wilderness by
2. 7 knoweth thy walking through this great w.
2. 8 passed by the way of the wilderness of Mo.
2. 26 sent messengers out of the wilderness of
4. 43 Bezer in the wilderness, in the plain cou.
8. 2 God led thee these forty years in the wil.
8. 15 led thee through that great..terrible wil.
8. 16 Who fed thee in the wilderness with ma.
9. 7 provokedst the LORD..to wrath in the wil.
9. 28 brought them out to slay them in the wi.
11. 5 what he did unto you in the wilderness
11. 24 from the wilderness and Lebanon, from
29. 5 I have led you forty years in the wildern.
32. 51 waters of Meribah-Kadesh, in the wilder.
Josh. 1. 4 From the wilderness and this Lebanon, ev.
5. 4 died in the wilderness by the way, after
5. 5 all the people (that were) born in the wil.
5. 6 walked forty years in the wilderness, till
8. 15 before them, and fled by the way of the w.
8. 20 people that fled to the wilderness turned
8. 24 in the wilderness wherein they chased them
12. 8 and in the wilderness, and in the south
14. 10 wandered in the wilderness: and now, lo
15. 1 to the border of Edom the wilderness of
15. 61 In the wilderness, Beth-arabah, Middin
16. 1 to the wilderness that goeth up from Jer.
18. 12 goings out thereof were at the wilderness
20. 8 they assigned Bezer in the wilderness upon
24. 7 and ye dwelt in the wilderness a long sea.
Judg. 1. 16 with the children of Judah into the wild.
8. 7 tear your flesh with the thorns of the wi.
8. 16 thorns of the wilderness and briers, and
11. 16 walked through the wilderness unto the
11. 18 Then they went along through the wilde.
11. 22 and from the wilderness even unto Jord.
20. 42 unto the way of the wilderness; but the
20. 45 turned and fled toward the wilderness un.
20. 47 turned and fled to the wilderness unto the
1 Sa. 4. 8 that smote the Egyptians..in the wildern.
13. 18 to the valley of Zeboim toward the wilde.
17. 28 hast thou left those few sheep in the wil.
23. 14 David abode in the wilderness in strong
23. 14 remained in a mountain in the wilderness
23. 15 David (was) in the wilderness of Ziph in
23. 24 David and his men (were) in the wilderness
23. 25 came down into a rock, and abode in the w.
23. 25 pursued after David in the wilderness of
24. 1 Behold, David (is) in the wilderness of E.
25. 1 and went down to the wilderness of Paran
25. 4 David heard in the wilderness that Nabal
25. 14 David sent messengers out of the wildern.
25. 21 kept all that this (fellow) hath in the wil.
26. 2 Saul arose, and went down to the wilder.
26. 2 with him, to seek David in the wilderness
26. 3 but David abode in the wilderness; and he
26. 3 that Saul came after him into the wilder.
2 Sa. 2. 24 before Giah by the way of the wilderness
15. 23 passed over, toward the way of the wild.
15. 28 See, I will tarry in the plain of the wild.
16. 2 such as be faint in the wilderness may dr.
17. 16 Lodge not this night in the plains of the
17. 29 hungry, and weary, and thirsty, in the wi.
1 Ki. 2. 34 he was buried in his own house in the wi.
9. 18 Baalath, and Tadmor in the wilderness
19. 4 he himself went a day's journey into the w.
19. 15 return on thy way to the wilderness of D.
2 Ki. 3. 8 The way through the wilderness of Edom
1 Ch. 5. 9 unto the entering in of the wilderness from
6. 78 Bezer in the wilderness with her suburbs
12. 8 into the hold to the wilderness men of m.
21. 29 which Moses made in the wilderness, and
2 Ch. 1. 3 servant of the LORD had made in the wil.
8. 4 built Tadmor in the wilderness, and all
20. 16 end of the brook, before the wilderness
20. 20 went forth into the wilderness of Tekoa
20. 24 came toward the watch tower in the w..
24. 9 servant of God (laid) upon Israel in the w.
Neh. 9. 19 forsookest them not in the wilderness, the
9. 21 forty years didst..sustain them in the wi.
Job 1. 19 there came a great wind from the wilder.
38. 26 (on) the wilderness, wherein (there is) no
Psa. 29. 8 wilderness; the LORD shaketh the wilder.
55. 7 wander far off, (and) remain in the wild.
63. *title.* Psalm of David, when he was in the wi.
65. 12 They drop (upon) the pastures of the wi.
78. 15 He clave the rocks in the wilderness, and
78. 19 said, Can God furnish a table in the wild.?
78. 40 How oft did they provoke him in the wi.
78. 52 and guided them in the wilderness like a
95. 8 as (in) the day of temptation in the wild.
102. 6 I am like a pelican of the wilderness, I
106. 9 through the depths, as through the wild.
106. 14 lusted exceedingly in the wilderness, and
106. 26 against them, to overthrow them in the w.
107. 4 They wandered in the wilderness in a sol.
107. 33 He turneth rivers into a wilderness, and
107. 35 He turneth the wilderness into a standing
136. 16 him which led his people through the w.
Prov. 21. 19 better to dwell in the wilderness, than w.
Song 3. 6 Who (is) this that cometh out of the wil.
8. 5 Who (is) this that cometh up from the w.
Isa. 14. 17 made the world as a wilderness, and des.
16. 1 ruler of the land from Sela to the wilde.
16. 8 they wandered (through) the wilderness
27. 10 habitation forsaken, and left like a wild.
32. 15 wilderness be a fruitful field, and the fr.
32. 16 Then judgment shall dwell in the wilder.
35. 1 The wilderness and the solitary place sh.

Isa. 35. 6 for in the wilderness shall waters break
40. 3 The voice of him that crieth in the wild.
41. 18 I will make the wilderness a pool of wa.
41. 19 I will plant in the wilderness the cedar
42. 11 Let the wilderness and the cities thereof
43. 19 I will even make a way in the wilderness
43. 20 because I give waters in the wilderness
50. 2 I dry up the sea, I make the rivers a wild.
51. 3 will make her wilderness like Eden, and
63. 13 through the deep, as an horse in the wil.
64. 10 holy cities are a wilderness, Zion is a wi.
Jer. 2. 2 when thou wentest after me in the wild.
2. 6 led us through the wilderness, through a
2. 24 A wild ass used to the wilderness, (that) sn.
2. 31 Have I been a wilderness unto Israel? a
3. 2 sat for them, as the Arabian in the wilde.
4. 11 A dry wind of the high places in the wild.
4. 26 fruitful place (was) a wilderness, and all
9. 2 Oh that I had in the wilderness a lodging
9. 10 for the habitations of the wilderness a la.
9. 12 land perisheth (and) is burnt up like a w.
9. 26 utmost corners, that dwell in the wilder.
12. 10 made my pleasant portion a desolate wil.
12. 12 come upon all high places through the w.
13. 24 that passeth away by the wind of the wil.
17. 6 inhabit the parched places in the wilder.
22. 6 surely I will make thee a wilderness, (and)
23. 10 pleasant places of the wilderness are dri.
31. 2 the people..found grace in the wilderness
48. 6 Flee..and be like the heath in the wilder
50. 12 hindermost of the nations (shall be) a wi
Lam. 4. 3 cruel, like the ostriches in the wilderness
4. 19 mountains, they laid wait for us in the w
5. 9 our lives because of the sword of the wil
Eze. 6. 14 more desolate than the wilderness toward
19. 13 now she (is) planted in the wilderness, in
20. 10 Wherefore I..brought them into the wil.
20. 13 rebelled against me in the wilderness, the.
20. 13 pour out my fury upon them in the wild.
20. 15 lifted up my hand unto them in the wild.
20. 17 did I make an end of them in the wilder.
20. 18 But I said unto their children in the wil.
20. 21 my anger against them in the wilderness
20. 23 lifted up mine hand..in the wilderness, th.
20. 35 I will bring you into the wilderness of the
20. 36 I pleaded with your fathers in the wilde.
23. 42 brought Sabeans from the wilderness, wh.
29. 5 I will leave thee (thrown) into the wilder.
34. 25 and they shall dwell safely in the wilder.
Hos. 2. 3 make her as a wilderness, and set her like
2. 14 bring her into the wilderness, and speak
9. 10 I found Israel like grapes in the wildern.
13. 5 I did know thee in the wilderness, in the
13. 15 of the LORD shall come up from the wild.
Joel 1. 19, 20 hath devoured the pastures of the wi.
2. 3 behind them a desolate wilderness; yea
2. 22 for the pastures of the wilderness do spr.
3. 19 Edom shall be a desolate wilderness, for
Amos 2. 10 led you forty years through the wilderness
5. 25 sacrifices and offerings in the wilderness
Zeph. 2. 13 Nineveh a desolation, (and) dry like a wi.
Mal. 1. 3 heritage waste for the dragons of the wil.

4. *A plain, obscure or unknown place,* עֲרָבָה *arabah.*
Job 24. 5 wilderness (yieldeth) food for them (and)
39. 6 Whose house I have made the wilderness
Isa. 33. 9 Sharon is like a wilderness; and Bashan
Jer. 51. 43 Her cities are a desolation..and a wilder.
Amos 6. 14 entering in..unto the river of the wilder.

5. *A dry place,* צִיָּה *tsiyyah.*
Job 30. 3 fleeing into the wilderness in former time
Psa. 78. 17 by provoking the Most High in the wild.

6. *Ruin, desert,* תֹּהוּ *tohu.*
Job 12. 24 causeth them to wander in a wilderness
Psa. 107. 40 causeth them to wander in the wilderness

7. *A desert, desolate place,* ἐρημία *erēmia.*
Matt 15. 33 we have so much bread in the wilderness
Mark 8. 4 these (men) with bread here in the wild.?
2 Co. 11. 26 perils in the wilderness, (in) perils in the

8. *Deserted, desolate (place),* ἔρημος *erēmos.*
Matt. 3. 1 John the Baptist, preaching in the wild.
3. 3 The voice of one crying in the wilderness
4. 1 Jesus led up of the spirit into the wilder.
11. 7 What went ye out into the wilderness to
Mark 1. 3 voice of one crying in the wilderness, Pr.
1. 4 John did baptize in the wilderness, and
1. 12 the spirit driveth him into the wilderness
1. 13 he was there in the wilderness forty days
Luke 3. 2 unto John the son of Zacharias in the wi.
3. 4 The voice of one crying in the wilderness
4. 1 was led by the spirit into the wilderness
5. 16 he withdrew himself into the wilderness
7. 24 What went ye out into the wilderness for
8. 29 and was driven of the devil into the wil.
15. 4 not leave the ninety and nine in the wil.
John 1. 23 I (am) the voice of one crying in the wil.
3. 14 as Moses lifted up the serpent in the wil.
6. 49 Your fathers did eat manna in the wilde.
11. 54 thence unto a country near to the wilde.
Acts 7. 30 there appeared to him in the wilderness
7. 36 in the Red sea, and in the wilderness forty
7. 38 is he that was in the church in the wilde.
7. 42 (by the space of) forty years in the wild.
7. 44 had the tabernacle of witness in the wil.
13. 18 suffered he their manners in the wildern.
21. 38 leddest out into the wilderness four thou.
1 Co. 10. 5 for they were overthrown in the wilder.
Heb. 3. 8 in the day of temptation in the wildern.
3. 17 sinned, whose carcases fell in the wilder.
Rev. 12. 6 woman fled into the wilderness, where

Rev. 12. 14 that she might fly into the wilderness
17. 3 carried me away in the spirit into the w.

WILDERNESS, that dwell in, inhabiting the —
Inhabitants of the dry places, צִיִּים *tsiyyim.*
Psa. 72. 9 They that dwell in the wilderness shall
74. 14 meat to the people inhabiting the wilder.
Isa. 23. 13 founded it for them that dwell in the wi.

Wilderness of Beer-Sheba, מִדְבַּר בְּאֵר שָׁבַע.
At the S. of Simeon.
Gen. 21. 14 she..wandered in the wilderness of Beer-s.

Wilderness of Beth-Aven, מִדְבַּר בֵּית אָוֶן.
At the E. of Bethel and N. of Benjamin.
Josh 18. 12 goings out..were at the wilderness of B. A.

Wilderness of Damascus, מִדְבַּר דַּמֶּשֶׂק.
Near Damascus, in Syria.
1 Ki. 19. 15 return on thy way to the wilderness of D.

Wilderness of Edom, מִדְבַּר אֱדוֹם.
At the S. end and E. side of Salt sea.
2 Ki. 3. 8 The way through the wilderness of E.

Wilderness of En-gedi, מִדְבַּר עֵין גֶּדִי.
At the W. of Salt Sea, in Judah.
1 Sa. 24. 1 Behold, David (is) in the wilderness of E.

Wilderness of Etham or of Red Sea, מִדְבַּר יַם סוּף *or* מִדְבַּר אֵתָם.
At the E. side of W. Gulf of Red Sea.
Exod 13. 18 the way of the wilderness of the Red Sea
Num 33. 8 three days' journey in the wilderness of E.

Wilderness of Gibeon, מִדְבַּר גִּבְעוֹן.
At the W. of Gibeon in Benjamin.
2 Sa. 2. 24 hills..by the way of the wilderness of G.

Wilderness of Jeruel, מִדְבַּר יְרוּאֵל.
At the S. of Judah.
2 Ch. 20. 16 ye shall find..before the wilderness of J.

Wilderness of Judah, מִדְבַּר יְהוּדָה.
On the extreme S. of Judah.
Judg. 1. 16 into the wilderness of J., which (lieth) in the
Psa. 63. *title.* when he was in the wilderness of J.

Wilderness of Kadesh, מִדְבַּר קָדֵשׁ.
Near Kadesh-barnea.
Psa. 29. 8 the LORD shaketh the wilderness of K.

Wilderness of Kedemoth, מִדְבַּר קְדֵמוֹת.
On the E. of Salt Sea, and N. of Arnon.
Deut. 2. 26 messengers out of the wilderness of Ked.

Wilderness of Maon, מִדְבַּר מָעוֹן.
On the S.W. of Salt Sea.
1 Sa. 23. 24 his men (were) in the wilderness of M., in
23. 25 wherefore he..abode in the wilderness of M.
23. 25 pursued after David in the wilderness of M.

Wilderness of Moab, מִדְבַּר מוֹאָב.
On the E. of Salt Sea.
Deut. 2. 8 passed by the way of the wilderness of M.

Wilderness of Paran, מִדְבַּר פָּארָן.
At the S. of Kadesh-barnea.
Gen. 21. 21 And he dwelt in the wilderness of P., and
Num. 10. 12 and the cloud rested in the wilderness of P.
12. 16 the people..pitched in the wilderness of P.
13. 3 Moses..sent them from the wilderness of P.
13. 26 went and came..unto the wilderness of P.
1 Sa. 25. 1 David..went down to the wilderness of P.

Wilderness of Shur, מִדְבַּר שׁוּר.
On the E. side of W. Gulf of Red Sea.
Exod. 15. 22 they went out into the wilderness of S.

Wilderness of Sin, מִדְבַּר סִין. *N. W. of Sinai.*
Exod 16. 1 they..came unto the wilderness of S., which
17. 1 Israel journeyed from the wilderness of S.
Num 33. 11 they..encamped in the wilderness of S.
33. 12 took their journey out of the wilder. of S.

Wilderness of Sinai, מִדְבַּר סִינַי. *N. of Sinai.*
Exod 19. 1 same day came they (into) the wilder. of S.
19. 2 they..were come (to) the desert of S., and
Lev. 7. 38 to offer..unto the LORD, in the wild. of S.
Num. 1. 1 the LORD spake..in the wilderness of Sin.
1. 19 he numbered them in the wilderness of S.
3. 4 Nadab and Abihu died..in the wilder. of S.
3. 14 the LORD spake..in the wilderness of Sin.
9. 1 the LORD spake..in the wilderness of Sin.
9. 5 kept the passover..in the wilderness of Sin.
10. 12 took their journey out of the wilder. of S.
26. 64 numbered..Israel in the wilderness of S.
33. 15 And they..pitched in the wilderness of S.
33. 16 And they removed from the desert of Sin.

Wilderness of Zin, מִדְבַּר צִן. *S. of Salt Sea.*
Num. 13. 21 from the wilderness of Z. unto Rehob, as
20. 1 Then came..Israel..into the desert of Z.
27. 14 For ye rebelled..in the desert of Z.
27. 14 water of Meribah..in the wilderness of Z.
33. 36 And they..pitched in the wilderness of Z.
34. 3 from the wilderness of Z. along by the co.
Deut. 32. 51 ye trespassed against me..in the wild. of Z.
Josh 15. 1 the wilderness of Z. southward (was) the

Wilderness of Ziph, מִדְבַּר זִיף.
Between Hebron and the Salt Sea.
1 Sa. 23. 14 David..remained..in the wilderness of Z.
23. 15 David (was) in the wilderness of Z. in a
26. 2 Saul..went down to the wilderness of Z.
26. 2 to seek David in the wilderness of Z.

WILE, wilily —
1. *Fraud, deceit,* נֵכֶל *nekel.*
Num 25. 18 For they vex you with their wiles, where.

2. *With craftiness, subtilty,* בְּעָרְמָה *be-ormah.*
Josh. 9. 4 They did work wilily, and went and made

3. *A method, artifice, cunning, fraud,* μεθοδεία -δία
Eph. 6. 11 ye may be able to stand against the wiles

WILFULLY —
Willingly, voluntarily, ἑκουσίως *hekousiōs.*
Heb. 10. 26 For if we sin wilfully after that we have

WILL, (would), be willing —
1. *Soul, desire,* נֶפֶשׁ *nephesh.*
Psa. 27. 12 Deliver me not over unto the will of mine
41. 2 wilt not deliver him unto the will of his
Eze. 16. 27 delivered thee unto the will of them that

2. *To will or wish,* צְבָא *tseba.*
Dan. 4. 35 doeth according to his will in the army of

3. *Thought, desire, will,* רְעוּת *reuth.*
Ezra 7. 18 with..the gold, that do after the will of

4. *Goodwill, good pleasure,* רָצוֹן *ratson.*
Gen. 49. 6 and in their self will they digged down a
Lev. 1. 3 he shall offer it of his own voluntary will
19. 5 the LORD, ye shall offer it at your own w.
22. 19 at your own will a male without blemish
22. 29 offer a sacrifice..offer (it) at your own w.
Neh. 9. 24 that they might do with them as they wo.
Esth. 9. 5 did what they would unto those that ha.
Psa. 40. 8 I delight to do thy will, O my God, yea
143. 10 Teach me to do thy will; for thou (art)
Dan. 8. 4 but he did according to his will, and be.
11. 3 great dominion, and do according to his w.
11. 16 shall do according to his own will, and
11. 36 And the king shall do according to his w.

5. *Counsel, purpose,* βουλή *boulē.*
Acts 13. 36 had served his own generation by the w.

6. *Counsel, purpose,* βούλημα *boulēma.*
Rom. 9. 19 find fault? for who hath resisted his will?

7. *Mind, judgment, decision,* γνώμη *gnōmē.*
Rev. 17. 17 G. hath put in their hearts to fulfil his w.

8. *Will, wish,* θέλημα *thelēma.*
Matt. 6. 10 Thy will be done in earth, as (it is) in he.
7. 21 doeth the will of my Father which is in
12. 50 For whosoever shall do the will of my Fa.
18. 14 Even so it is not the will of your Father
21. 31 Whether of them twain did the will of (his)
26. 42 may not pass..except I drink it, thy will
Mark 3. 35 For whosoever shall do the will of God
Luke 11. 2 [Thy will be done, as in heaven, so in ea.]
12. 47 that servant, which knew his lord's will
12. 47 neither did according to his will, shall be
22. 42 nevertheless not my will, but thine, be
23. 25 desired; but he delivered Jesus to their w.
John 1. 13 nor of the will of the flesh, nor of the will
4. 34 My meat is to do the will of him that sent
5. 30 seek not mine own will, but the will of the
6. 38 not to do mine own will, but the will of
6. 39 this is the Father's will which hath sent
6. 40 this is the will of him that sent me, that
7. 17 If any..do his will, he shall know of the
9. 31 be a worshipper of God, and doeth his w.
Acts 13. 22 a man..which shall fulfil all my will
21. 14 we ceased, saying, The will of the Lord
22. 14 that thou shouldest know his will, and
Rom. 1. 10 might have a prosperous journey by the w.
2. 18 knowest (his) will, and approvest the things
12. 2 good, and acceptable, and perfect will of
15. 32 That I may come to you with joy by the w.
1 Co. 1. 1 apostle of Jesus Christ through the will of
7. 37 hath power over his own will, and hath so
16. 12 but his will was not at all to come at this
2 Co. 1. 1 apostle of Jesus Christ by the will of God
8. 5 to the Lord, and unto us by the will of G.
Gal. 1. 4 according to the will of God and our Fat.
Eph. 1. 1 apostle of Jesus Christ by the will of God
1. 5 according to the good pleasure of his will
1. 9 made known unto us the mystery of his w.
1. 11 all things after the counsel of his own w.
5. 17 but understanding what the will of the L.
6. 6 but as the servants of Christ, doing the w.
Col. 1. 1 apostle of Jesus Christ by the will of God
1. 9 be filled with the knowledge of his will
4. 12 stand perfect and complete in all the will
1 Th. 4. 3 For this is the will of God, (even) your sa.
5. 18 for this is the will of God in Christ Jesus
2 Ti. 1. 1 apostle of Jesus Christ by the will of God
2. 26 who are taken captive by him at his will
Heb. 10. 7 Then said I, Lo, I come..to do thy will
10. 9 Then said he, Lo, I come to do thy will
10. 10 By the which will we are sanctified thro.
10. 36 after ye have done the will of God, ye mi.
13. 21 perfect in every good work to do his will
1 Pe. 2. 15 For so is the will of God, that with well
3. 17 For (it is) better, if the will of God be so
4. 2 the flesh to the lusts of men, but to the w.
4. 3 suffice us to have wrought [the will] of the
4. 19 let them that suffer according to the will
2 Pe. 1. 21 prophecy came not in old time by the will
1 Jo. 2. 17 he that doeth the will of God abideth for
5. 14 that if we ask anything according to his w.

9. *Will, wish, inclination,* θέλησις *thelēsis.*
Heb. 2. 4 divers miracles..according to his own w.?
[*See also* Good, own, self, voluntary.]

WILL (be or make) willing, willingly, to —
1. *To be willing,* אָבָה *abah.*
Gen. 24. 5 Peradventure the woman will not be wil.
24. 8 if the woman will not be willing to follow
Exod 10. 27 hardened Pharaoh's heart, and he would
Lev. 26. 21 if ye walk contrary to me, and will not he.
Deut. 1. 26 Notwithstanding ye would not go up, but
2. 30 But Sihon king of Heshbon would not let
10. 10 time also, (and) the LORD would not dest.
23. 5 Nevertheless the LORD thy God would not
25. 7 he will not perform the duty of my husb.
29. 20 LORD will not spare him, but then the an.
Josh. 24. 10 But I would not hearken unto Balaam, the.
Judg 11. 17 unto the king of Moab: but he would not
19. 10 But the man would not tarry that night
19. 25 But the men would not hearken to him, so
20. 13 would not hearken to the voice of their
1 Sa. 15. 9 would not utterly destroy them: but every
22. 17 servants of the king would not put forth
26. 23 would not stretch forth mine hand agai.
31. 4 But his armour bearer would not; for he
2 Sa. 2. 21 But Asahel would not turn aside from fo.
6. 10 So David would not remove the ark of the
12. 17 but he would not, neither did he eat bre.
13. 14 Howbeit he would not hearken unto her
13. 16 But he would not hearken unto her
13. 25 howbeit he would not go, but blessed him
14. 29 but he would not come to him: and when
14. 29 again the second time, he would not come
23. 16 nevertheless he would not drink thereof
23. 17 therefore he would not drink it. These
1 Ki. 22. 49 Let my servants go..but Jehoshaphat wo.
2 Ki. 8. 19 Yet the LORD would not destroy Judah
13. 23 would not destroy them, neither cast he
24. 4 innocent blood, which the LORD would
1 Ch. 10. 4 But his armour bearer would not; for he
11. 18 but David would not drink (of) it, but po.
11. 19 Therefore he would not drink it. These
19. 19 neither would the Syrians help the child.
2 Ch. 21. 7 Howbeit the LORD would not destroy the
Job 39. 9 Will the unicorn be willing to serve thee
Psa. 81. 11 But my people..Israel would none of me
Prov. 1. 25 all my counsel, and would none of my re.
1. 30 They would none of my counsel; they de.
Isa. 1. 19 If ye be willing and obedient, ye shall eat
28. 12 this (is) the refreshing: yet they would
30. 9 children (that) will not hear the law of
30. 15 shall be your strength; and ye would not
42. 24 for they would not walk in his ways, nei.
Eze. 3. 7 the house of Israel will not hearken unto
3. 7 they will not hearken unto me; for all the
20. 8 rebelled against me, and would not hear.

2. *I will be,* אֱהִי *[hayah].*
Hos. 13. 10 I will be thy king: where (is any other)
13. 14 O death, I will be thy plagues..I will be

3. *To have delight, please, desire,* חָפֵץ *chaphets.*
Ruth 3. 13 if he will not do the part of a kinsman to
1 Sa. 2. 25 hearkened not..because the LORD would
Job 9. 3 If he will contend with him, he cannot
Prov 21. 1 water: he turneth it whithersoever he w.

4. *One delighting, will, desirous,* חָפֵץ *chaphets.*
1 Ki. 13. 33 whosoever would, he consecrated him, and
1 Ch. 28. 9 serve him..with a willing mind; for the

5. *Delight, pleasure, business,* חֵפֶץ *chephets.*
Prov 31. 13 seeketh wool and flax, and worketh will.

6. *To be pleased, desirous,* יָאַל *yaal,* 5.
Josh 17. 12 but the Canaanites would dwell in that
Judg. 1. 27 but the Canaanites would dwell in that
1. 35 But the Amorites would dwell in mount
Hos. 5. 11 because he willingly walked after the co.

7. *To know, be acquainted with,* יָדַע *yada.*
Eccl. 4. 13 foolish king, who will no more be admo.

8. *From his heart,* מִלִּבּוֹ *[leb].*
Lam. 3. 33 For he doth not afflict willingly nor grieve

9. *To offer willingly, make willing,* נָדַב *nadab.*
Exod 25. 2 of every man that giveth it willingly with
35. 21 every one whom his spirit made willing
35. 29 whose heart made them willing to bring, for

10. *To offer (self) willingly,* נָדַב *nadab,* 7.
1 Ch. 29. 5 who (then) is willing to consecrate his se.

11. *Willing offering or guilt,* נְדָבָה *nedabah.*
2 Ch. 35. 8 his princes gave willingly unto the people
Psa. 110. 3 Thy people (shall be) willing in the day of

12. *Willing, noble, liberal,* נָדִיב *nadib.*
Exod 35. 5 whosoever (is) of a willing heart, let him
35. 22 both men and women, as many as were w.
1 Ch. 28. 21 every willing skilful man, for any manner

13. *Soul, desire,* נֶפֶשׁ *nephesh.*
Deut 21. 14 then thou shalt let her go whither she will

14. *To wish, will,* צְבָא *tseba.*
Dan. 4. 17, 25, 32 and giveth it to whomsoever he will
5. 21 he appointeth over it whomsoever he will

15. *To give,* נָתַן *nathan.*
Judg. 8. 25 And they answered, We will willingly give

16. *To wish, will,* βούλομαι *boulomai.*
Matt 11. 27 and (he) to whomsoever the Son [will] re.
Mark 15. 15 Pilate, willing to content the people, rel.
Luke 10. 22 but the Son, and (he) to whom the Son w.
22. 42 Saying, Father, if thou be willing, remove
John 18. 39 will ye therefore that I release unto you
Acts 18. 15 look ye (to it); for I will be no judge of such
27. 43 But the centurion, willing to save Paul
1 Co. 12. 11 dividing to every man severally as he will
1 Ti. 2. 8 I will therefore that men pray everywhere

1 Ti. 5. 14 I will therefore that the younger women
6. 9 But they that will be rich fall into temp.
Titus 3. 8 these things I will that thou affirm const.
Heb. 6. 17 willing more abundantly to show unto the
Jas. 4. 4 whosoever therefore will be a friend of
2 Pe. 3. 9 not willing that any should perish, but
Jude 5 I will therefore put you in remembrance

17. *To become, happen,* γίνομαι *ginomai.*
Acts 20. 16 because he would not spend the time in

18. *To think well, be pleased,* εὐδοκέω *eudokeō.*
2 Co. 5. 8 willing rather to be absent from the body
1 Th. 2. 8 we were willing to have imparted unto

19. *Willingly, voluntarily,* κατὰ ἑκούσιον *kata hekous.*
Phm. 14 not be as it were of necessity, but willing.

20. *Willingly, voluntarily,* ἑκουσίως *hekousiōs.*
1 Pe. 5. 2 not by constraint, but willingly; not for

21. *Willing, voluntary,* ἑκοῦσα *hekousa.*
Rom. 8. 20 was made subject to vanity, not willing.
1 Co. 9. 17 For if I do this thing willingly, I have a

22. *To wish, will, mean,* θέλω *thelō.*
Matt. 1. 19 willing to make her a public example, was
5. 40 if any man will sue thee at the law, and
8. 2 Lord, if thou wilt, thou canst make me cl.
8. 3 touched him, saying, I will; be thou clean
9. 13 I will have mercy and not sacrifice: for I
11. 14 if ye will receive (it), this is Elias, which
13. 28 Wilt thou then that we go and gather th.
15. 28 be it unto thee even as thou wilt. And her
15. 32 will not send them away fasting, lest they
16. 24 If any (man) will come after me, let him
16. 25 For whosoever will save his life shall lose
17. 4 if thou wilt, let us make here three taber.
19. 17 but if thou wilt enter into life, keep the
19. 21 If thou wilt be perfect, go (and) sell that
20. 14 I will give unto this last even as unto th.
20. 15 Is it not lawful for me to do what I will
20. 21 said unto her, What wilt thou? She saith
20. 26 whosoever will be great among you, let
20. 27 whosoever will be chief among you, let
20. 32 and said, What will ye that I shall do unto
21. 29 said, I will not: but afterward he repen.
23. 4 will not move them with one of their fin.
26. 15 and said..What will ye give me, and I
26. 17 Where wilt thou that we prepare for thee
26. 39 nevertheless not as I will, but as thou (w.)
27. 17 Whom will ye that I release unto you? B.
27. 43 let him deliver him now, if he will have
Mark 1. 40 saying unto him, If thou wilt, thou canst
1. 41 touched him, and saith unto him, I will
6. 22 Ask of me whatsoever thou wilt, and I
6. 25 I will that thou give me by and by in a ch.
8. 34 Whosoever will come after me, let him de.
8. 35 For whosoever will save his life shall lose
10. 43 whosoever will be great among you, shall
10. 44 whosoever of you will be the chiefest, sh.
10. 51 What wilt thou that I should do unto th.?
14. 7 whensoever ye will ye may do them good
14. 12 Where wilt thou that we go and prepare
14. 36 nevertheless not what I will, but what th.
15. 9 Will ye that I release unto you the King
15. 12 What [will ye then that] I shall do (unto
Luke 4. 6 delivered unto me; and to whomsoever I w.
5. 12 Lord, if thou wilt, thou canst make me
5. 13 touched him, saying, I will; be thou clean
9. 23 If any (man) will come after me, let him
9. 24 For whosoever will save his life shall lose
9. 54 Lord, wilt thou that we command fire to
10. 29 But he, willing to justify himself, said
12. 49 and what will I, if it be already kindled?
13. 31 Get thee out, and depart hence: for H. will
18. 41 What wilt thou that I shall do unto thee?
19. 14 We will not have this (man) to reign over
22. 9 said unto him, Where wilt thou that we
23. 20 Pilate therefore, willing to release Jesus
John 5. 6 he saith unto him, Wilt thou be made wh.?
5. 21 even so the Son quickeneth whom he w.
5. 35 ye were willing for a season to rejoice in
5. 40 ye will not come to me, that ye might ha.
6. 21 Then they willingly received him
6. 67 Then said Jesus unto the twelve, Will ye
7. 17 If any man will do his will, he shall know
8. 44 the lusts of your father ye will do. He
9. 27 wherefore would ye hear (it) again? will
15. 7 ye shall ask what ye will, and it shall be
17. 24 I will that they also whom thou hast giv.
21. 22 If I will that he tarry till I come, what
21. 23 If I will that he tarry till I come, what (is
Acts 7. 28 Wilt thou kill me, as thou diddest the E.
9. 6 [Lord, what wilt thou have me to do? And]
17. 18 What will this babbler say? other some
18. 21 but I..return again unto you, if God will
24. 27 Felix, willing to show the Jews a pleasure
25. 9 willing to do..pleasure..said, Wilt thou
Rom. 7. 18 for to will is present with me; but (how)
9. 16 So then (it is) not of him that willeth, nor
9. 18 on whom he will (have mercy)..whom he
9. 22 if God, willing to show (his) wrath, and
13. 3 Wilt thou then not be afraid of the pow.?
1 Co. 4. 19 But I..come to you shortly, if the Lord w.
4. 21 What will ye? shall I come unto you with
7. 36 let him do what he will, he sinneth not
7. 39 at liberty to be married to whom she will
14. 35 if they will learn any thing, let them ask
16. 7 For I will not see you now by the way, but
2 Co. 8. 11 that as (there was) a readiness to will, so
Phil. 2. 13 For it is God which worketh in you both
1 Ti. 2. 4 Who will have all men to be saved, and to
5. 11 to wax wanton against Christ, they will
2 Ti. 3. 12 all that will live godly in Christ Jesus sh.
Heb. 13. 18 good conscience, in all things willing to
Jas. 2. 20 But wilt thou know, O vain man, that fa.
4. 15 If the Lord will, we shall live, and do this
2 Pe. 3. 5 For this they willingly are ignorant of
3 John 13 but I will not with ink and pen write unto
Rev. 11. 5, 5 And if any man will hurt them
11. 6 to smite the earth..as often as they will
22. 17 whosoever will, let him take the water of

23. *To be about to,* μέλλω *mellō.*
Matt. 2. 13 Herod will seek the young child to dest.
John 7. 35 Whither will he go..will he go unto the
14. 22; Acts 17. 31; 27. 10; Rev. 3. 16.

24. *Forwardly,* προθύμως *prothumōs,* 1 Pe. 5. 2.

25. *Yieldingly,* ἑκών *hekōn,* Ro. 8. 20; 1 Co. 9. 17

26. *Forward, prompt, ready,* πρόθυμος *prothumos.*
Matt 26. 41 the spirit indeed (is) willing, but the flesh
[*See also* Would.]

WILL worship —
Worship springing from self will, ἐθελοθρησκεία.
Col. 2. 23 a show of wisdom in will worship and hu.

WILL, against the, of his own —
1. *Not willing, unwilling,* ἄκων *akōn.*
1 Co. 9. 17 but if against my will, a dispensation..is
2. *To will, wish,* βουλόμαι *boulomai.*
Jas. 1. 18 Of his own will begat he us with the word

WILLING of...self —
Choosing of one's self, αὐθαίρετος *authairetos.*
2 Co. 8. 3 beyond..power, (they were) willing of th.

WILLING mind, offering —
1. *Willing offering, gift, or mind,* נְדָבָה *nedabah.*
Exod 35. 29 children of Israel brought a willing offe.
2. *Forwardness, promptitude, readiness,* προθυμία.
2 Co. 8. 12 For if there be first a willing mind, (it is)

WILLOW (tree) —
1. *A willow, salix tree,* עֲרָבִים *arabim.*
Lev. 23. 40 boughs of thick trees, and willows of the
Job 40. 22 the willows of the brook compass him ab.
Psa. 137. 2 We hanged our harps upon the willows
Isa. 15. 7 they carry away to the brook of the will.
44. 4 among the grass, as willows by the water
2. *A water willow, osier,* צַפְצָפָה *tsaphtsaphah.*
Eze. 17. 5 by great waters,(and) set it (as) a willow tree

WIMPLE —
A wide covering, mantle, מִטְפַּחַת *mitpachath.*
Isa. 3. 22 mantles, and the wimples, and the crisp.

WIN, be won, to —
1. *To cleave, rend,* בָּקַע *baqa.*
2 Ch. 32. 1 encamped..and thought to win them for
2. *To take, receive,* לָקַח *laqach.*
Prov 11. 30 a tree of life; and he that winneth souls
3. *To gain,* κερδαίνω *kerdainō.*
Phil. 3. 8 do count them (but) dung, that I may w.
1 Pe. 3. 1 they also may without the word be won

WIND, windy —
1. *Wind,* רוּחַ *ruach.*
Gen. 8. 1 God made a wind to pass over the earth
Exod 10. 13 brought an east wind..the east wind br.
10. 19 turned a mighty strong west wind, which
14. 21 the sea to go (back) by a strong east wind
15. 10 Thou didst blow with thy wind, the sea
Num 11. 31 there went forth a wind from the LORD
2 Sa. 22. 11 and he was seen upon the wings of the w.
1 Ki. 18. 45 the heaven was black with clouds and wi.
19. 11 a great and strong wind rent the mount.
19. 11 not in the wind: and after the wind an
2 Ki. 3. 17 Ye shall not see wind, neither shall ye
Job 1. 19 there came a great wind from the wilder.
6. 26 speeches of one that is desperate..as wi.
7. 7 remember that my life (is) wind: mine
8. 2 words of thy mouth (be like) a strong wi
15. 2 knowledge..fill his belly with the..wind
21. 18 They are as stubble before the wind, and
28. 25 To make the weight for the winds, and
30. 15 they pursue my soul as the wind, and my
30. 22 Thou liftest me up to the wind; thou ca.
37. 21 but the wind passeth, and cleanseth them
Psa. 1. 4 like the chaff which the wind driveth aw.
18. 10 yea, he did fly upon the wings of the wi.
18. 42 beat them small as the dust before the w.
35. 5 Let them be as chaff before the wind, and
48. 7 breakest the ships of Tarshish..an east w.
78. 39 wind that passeth away, and cometh not
83. 13 a wheel; as the stubble before the wind
103. 16 For the wind passeth over it, and it is go.
104. 3 who walketh upon the wings of the wind
107. 25 raiseth the stormy wind, which lifteth up
135. 7 he bringeth the wind out of his treasuries
147. 18 causeth his wind to blow, (and) the wate.
148. 8 and vapours; stormy wind fulfilling his
Prov 11. 29 troubleth his..house shall inherit the wi.
25. 14 Whoso boasteth..(is like) clouds and wi.
25. 23 north wind driveth away rain; so (doth)
27. 16 Whosoever hideth her hideth the wind
30. 4 who hath gathered the wind in his fists?
Eccl. 1. 6 wind goeth toward the south..and the w.
5. 16 profit hath he that..laboured for the wind
11. 4 He that observeth the wind shall not sow
Isa. 7. 2 trees of the wood are moved with the wi
11. 15 with his mighty wind shall he shake his
Isa. 17. 13 the chaff of the mountains before the w.
26. 18 we have as it were brought forth wind
27. 8 stayeth his rough wind in the day of the
32. 2 shall be as an hiding place from the wind
41. 16 Thou shalt fan them, and the wind shall
41. 29 their molten images (are) wind and confu.
57. 13 but the wind shall carry them all away
64. 6 iniquities, like the wind, have taken us
Jer. 2. 24 snuffeth up the wind at her pleasure, in
4. 11 A dry wind of the high places in the wil.
4. 12 full wind from those (places) shall come
5. 13 prophets shall become wind, and the wo.
10. 13 bringeth forth the wind out of his treas.
13. 24 stubble that passeth away by the wind of
14. 6 they snuffed up the wind like dragons
18. 17 I will scatter them as with an east wind
22. 22 wind shall eat up all thy pastors, and thy
49. 32 will scatter into all winds them (that are)
49. 36 upon Elam will I bring the four winds
49. 36 and will scatter them toward all those w.
51. 1 raise up against Babylon..a destroying w.
51. 16 and bringeth forth the wind out of his
Eze. 5. 2 third part thou shalt scatter in the wind
5. 10 remnant of thee..scatter into all the w.
5. 12 I will scatter a third part into all the wi.
12. 14 will scatter toward every wind all that
13. 11 great hailstones, shall fall; and a stormy w.
13. 13 I will even rend (it) with a stormy wind
17. 10 utterly wither when the east wind touch.
17. 21 that remain shall be scattered toward all w
19. 12 east wind dried up her fruit; her strong
27. 26 east wind hath broken thee in the midst
37. 9 Prophesy unto the wind..and say to the w.
37. 9 Come from the four winds, O breath, and
Dan. 2. 35 wind carried them away, that no place
7. 2 four winds of the heaven strove upon the
8. 8 four notable ones, toward the four winds
11. 4 shall be divided toward the four winds
Hos. 4. 19 The wind hath bound her up in her wings
8. 7 For they have sown the wind, and they
12. 1 Ephraim feedeth on wind, and followeth
13. 15 wind shall come, the wind of the LORD shall
Amos 4. 13 createth the wind, and declareth unto man
Jon. 1. 4 LORD sent out a great wind into the sea
4. 8 God prepared a vehement east wind, and
Zech. 2. 6 I have spread you abroad as the four win.
5. 9 wind (was) in their wings; for they had

2. *Wind,* ἄνεμος *anemos.*
Matt. 7. 25, 27 winds blew, and beat upon that house
8. 26 Then he arose, and rebuked the winds
8. 27 What manner of man..that even the w.
11. 7 went..to see? A reed shaken with the w.?
14. 24 tossed with waves: for the wind was con.
14. 30 when he saw the wind boisterous, he was
14. 32 when they were come into the ship, the w.
24. 31 gather together his elect from the four wi.
Mark 4. 37 there arose a great storm of wind, and the
4. 39 rebuked the wind..And the wind ceased
4. 41 What manner of man is this, that even..w.
6. 48 for the wind was contrary unto them: and
6. 51 went up unto them into the ship; and..w.
13. 27 gather together his elect from the four wi.
Luke 7. 24 went..to see? A reed shaken with the wi.?
8. 23 there came down a storm of wind on the
8. 24 rebuked the wind and the raging of the wa.
8. 25 for he commandeth even the winds and
John 6. 18 sea arose, by reason of a great wind that
Acts 27. 4 sailed under Cyprus, because the winds
27. 7 wind not suffering us, we sailed under C.
27. 14 there arose against it a tempestuous wind
27. 15 caught, and could not bear up into the w.
Eph. 4. 14 carried about with every wind of doctrine
Jas. 3. 4 driven of fierce winds, yet are they turned
Jude 12 carried about of winds; trees whose fruit
Rev. 6. 13 fig tree..she is shaken of a mighty wind
7. 1 four winds of the earth, that the wind sh.

3. *Spirit,* πνεῦμα *pneuma.*
John 3. 8 wind bloweth where it listeth, and thou
4. *To blow, breathe,* πνέω *pneō.*
Acts 27. 40 hoised up the mainsail to the wind, and
5. *Wind,* πνοή *pnoē.*
Acts 2. 2 a sound..as of a rushing mighty wind, and

WIND, (about), or up, to be driven with the —
1. *To be or go round about,* סָבַב *sabab,* 2.
Eze. 41. 7 a winding about still upward to the side
2. *A winding about, circuit,* מוּסָב *musab.*
Eze. 41. 7 for the winding about of the house went
3. *To bind, tie,* δέω *deō.*
John 19. 40 wound it in linen clothes with the spices
4. *To swathe, wrap together,* συστέλλω *sustellō.*
Acts 5. 6 young men arose, wound him up, and ca.
5. *To be driven by the wind,* ἀνεμίζομαι *anemizomai.*
Jas. 1. 6 like a wave of the sea driven with the wi.

WINDOW —
1. *A window, woven work,* אֲרֻבָּה *arubbah.*
Gen. 7. 11 broken up, and the windows of heaven
8. 2 fountains also of the deep and the wind.
2 Ki. 7. 2, 19 the LORD would make windows in he.
Eccl. 12. 3 those that look out of the windows be d.
Isa. 24. 18 for the windows from on high are open, and
60. 8 as a cloud, and as the doves to their wi.?
Mal. 3. 10 if I will not open you the windows of he.
2. *A window, perforated place,* חַלּוֹן *challon.*
Gen. 8. 6 Noah opened the window of the ark which
26. 8 looked out at a window, and saw, and, be

Josh. 2. 15 let them down by a cord through the wi.
2. 18 bind this line of scarlet thread in the wi.
2. 21 and she bound the scarlet line in the wi.
Judg. 5. 28 mother of Sisera looked out at a window
1 Sa. 19. 12 So Michal let David down through a wi.
2 Sa. 6. 16 looked through a window, and saw king
1 Ki. 6. 4 for the house he made windows of narrow
2 Ki. 9. 30 and tired her head, and looked out at a w.
9. 32 lifted up his face to the window, and said
13. 17 Open the window eastward:
1 Ch. 15. 29 looking out at a window, saw king David
Prov. 7. 6 For at the window of my house I looked
Song 2. 9 looketh forth at the windows, showing
Jer. 9. 21 For death is come up into our windows
22. 14 cutteth him out windows; and (it is) ciel.
Eze. 40. 16 narrow windows..windows (were) round
40. 22 their windows, and their arches, and their
40. 25 windows in it..like those windows: the
40. 29 windows in it and in the arches thereof
40. 33 windows therein, and in the arches thereof
40. 36 windows to it round about: the length
41. 16 narrow windows..up to the windows..and
41. 26 narrow windows and palm trees on the
Joel 2. 9 they shall enter in at the windows like a
Zeph. 2. 14 voice shall sing in the windows; desolat.

3. *Windows*, כַּוִּין *kavvin.*
Dan. 6. 10 his windows being open in his chamber

4. *Bright object*, צֹהַר *tsohar.*
Gen. 6. 16 A window shalt thou make to the ark, and

5. *Suns, battlements (?)*, שְׁמָשׁוֹת [*shemesh*].
Isa. 54. 12 I will make thy windows of agates, and

6. *An outlook*, שֶׁקֶף *sheqeph.*
1 Ki. 7. 5 doors and posts (were) square, with the w.

7. *Outlooks*, שְׁקֻפִים *shequphim.*
1 Ki. 7. 4 windows (in) three rows, and light (was)

8. *A little door or window*, θυρίς *thuris.*
Acts 20. 9 there sat in a window a certain young man
2 Co. 11. 33 through a window in a basket was I let

WINDY —
Wind, רוּחַ *ruach.*
Psa. 55. 8 would hasten my escape from the windy

WINE, (mixed, new, red, strong, sweet, on the lees) —

1. *A thick, sticky syrup*, חֶמֶר *chemer.*
Isa. 27. 2 In that day sing ye..A vineyard of red w.

2. *A thick, sticky (mixed) syrup*, חֲמַר *chamar.*
Ezra 6. 9 wheat, salt, wine, and oil, according to
7. 22 to an hundred baths of wine, and to an
Dan. 5. 1 Belshazzar..drank wine before the thou.
5. 2 Belshazzar, whiles he tasted the wine, co.
5. 4 They drank wine, and praised the gods of
5. 23 thy concubines, have drunk wine in them

3. *What is pressed out, grape juice*, יַיִן *yayin.*
Gen. 9. 21 he drank of the wine, and was drunken
9. 24 Noah awoke from his wine, and knew what
14. 18 Melchizedek..brought forth bread and w.
19. 32 Come, let us make our father drink wine
19. 33, 35 they made their father drink wine that
19. 34 let us make him drink wine this night also
27. 25 and he brought him wine, and he drank
49. 11 he washed his garments in wine, and his
49. 12 His eyes (shall be) red with wine, and his
Exod 29. 40 fourth part of an hin of wine..a drink off.
Lev. 10. 9 Do not drink wine nor strong drink, thou
23. 13 the drink offering thereof..of wine, the
Num. 6. 3 He shall separate (himself) from wine and
6. 3 shall drink no vinegar of wine, or vinegar
6. 20 and after that the Nazarite may drink w.
15. 5 fourth..of an hin of wine for a drink off.
15. 7 thou shalt offer the third..of an hin of w.
15. 10 for a drink offering half an hin of wine
28. 14 offerings shall be half an hin of wine unto
Deut 14. 26 thou shalt bestow that money..for wine
28. 39 but shalt neither drink (of) the wine, nor
29. 6 neither have ye drunk wine or strong dri.
32. 33 Their wine (is) the poison of dragons, and
32. 38 Which..drank the wine of their drink offe.?
Josh. 9. 4 took old sacks upon their asses, and wine
9. 13 these bottles of wine which we filled (were)
Judg 13. 4 drink not wine nor strong drink, and eat
13. 7 and now drink no wine nor strong drink
13. 14 neither let her drink wine or strong drink
19. 19 there is bread and wine also for me, and
1 Sa. 1. 14 Eli said unto her..put away thy wine from
1. 15 I have drunk neither wine nor strong dr.
1. 24 one ephah of flour, and a bottle of wine
10. 3 meet..another carrying a bottle of wine
16. 20 with bread, and a bottle of wine, and a
25. 18 two bottles of wine, and five sheep ready
25. 37 when the wine was gone out of Nabal, and
2 Sa. 13. 28 when Amnon's heart is merry with wine
16. 1 hundred of summer fruits..a bottle of wi.
16. 2 the wine, that such as be faint in the wi.
1 Ch. 9. 29 fine flour, and the wine, and the oil, and
12. 40 wine, and oil, and oxen, and sheep abund.
27. 27 over.. the wine cellars (was) Zabdi the
2 Ch. 2. 10 twenty thousand baths of wine, and twe.
2. 15 the barley, the oil, and the wine, which
11. 11 put..store of victual, and of oil and wine
Neh. 2. 1 wine..before him: and I took up the wi.
5. 15 had taken of them bread and wine, beside
5. 18 once in ten days store of all sorts of wine
13. 15 as also wine, grapes, and figs, and all..bu.
Esth. 1. 7 royal wine in abundance, according to the
1. 10 the heart of the king was merry with wine
5. 6 the king said..at the banquet of wine, What
7. 2 the king said..at the banquet of wine, What
Esth. 7. 7 arising from the banquet of wine in his wr.
7. 8 returned..into the place of..banquet of w.
Job 1. 13, 18 eating and drinking wine in their elder
32. 19 Behold, my belly (is) as wine (which) hath
Psa. 60. 3 thou hast made us to drink the wine of
75. 8 a cup, and the wine is red; it is full of m.
78. 65 like a..man that shouteth by reason of wi.
104. 15 wine (that) maketh glad the heart of man
Prov. 4. 17 eat the bread..and drink the wine of vio.
9. 2 she hath mingled her wine; she hath also
9. 5 come..drink of the wine..I have mingled
20. 1 Wine (is) a mocker, strong drink (is) raging
21. 17 he that loveth wine and oil shall not be
23. 30 They that tarry long at the wine; they
23. 31 Look not thou upon the wine when it is
31. 4 not for kings to drink wine, nor for prin.
31. 6 Give..wine unto those that be of heavy
Eccl. 2. 3 I sought in..heart to give myself unto w.
9. 7 Go..and drink thy wine with a merry he.
10. 19 A feast is..for laughter, and wine maketh
Song 1. 2 Let him kiss me..love (is) better than wi.
1. 4 we will remember thy love more than wi.
4. 10 how much better is thy love than wine
5. 1 I have drunk my wine with my milk: eat
7. 9 the roof of thy mouth like the best wine
8. 2 of spiced wine of the juice of my pomeg.
Isa. 5. 11 continue until night, (till) wine inflame
5. 12 tabret and pipe, and wine, are in their
5. 22 Woe unto..mighty to drink wine, and
16. 10 the treaders shall tread out no wine in
22. 13 killing sheep, eating flesh..drinking wine
24. 9 They shall not drink wine with a song
24. 11 a crying for wine in the streets; all joy
28. 1 valleys of them that are overcome with wine
28. 7 they also have erred through wine, and
28. 7 they are swallowed up of wine, they are
29. 9 they are drunken, but not with wine; they
51. 21 thou afflicted..drunken, but not with w.
55. 1 buy wine and milk without money, and
56. 12 Come ye..I will fetch wine, and we will
Jer. 13. 12, 12 Every bottle shall be filled with wine
23. 9 I am..like a man whom wine hath over
25. 15 Take the wine cup of this fury at my hand
35. 2 bring them..and give them wine to drink
35. 5 pots full of wine..and I said..Drink ye w.
35. 6 will drink no wine..Ye shall drink no wi.
35. 8 to drink no wine all our days, we, our wi.
35. 14 he commanded his sons not to drink wine
40. 10 gather ye wine, and summer fruits, and
40. 12 gathered wine and summer fruits very
48. 33 I have caused wine to fail from the wine.
51. 7 the nations have drunken of her wine
Lam. 2. 12 to their mothers, Where (is) corn and w.?
Eze. 27. 18 Damascus (was) thy merchant..in the wine
44. 21 Neither shall any priest drink wine when
Dan. 1. 5 of the king's meat, and of the wine which
1. 8 would not defile himself..with the wine
1. 16 took away..the wine that they should dr.
10. 3 neither came flesh nor wine in my mouth
Hos. 4. 11 Whoredom and wine..take away the he.
7. 5 princes have made..sick with bottles of w.
9. 4 They shall not offer wine (offerings) to the
14. 7 the scent thereof..as the wine of Leban.
Joel 1. 5 howl, all ye drinkers of wine, because of
3. 3 sold a girl for wine, that they might drink
Amos 2. 8 they drink the wine of the condemned (in)
2. 12 ye gave the Nazarites wine to drink, and
5. 11 vineyards, but ye shall not drink wine of
6. 6 That drink wine in bowls, and anoint th.
9. 14 shall plant vineyards, and drink the wine
Mic. 2. 11 I will prophesy unto thee of wine and of
6. 15 thou shalt tread..but shalt not drink wi.
Hab. 2. 5 Yea also, because he transgresseth by wi.
Zeph. 1. 13 plant vineyards, but not drink the wine
Hag. 2. 12 with his skirt do touch..wine, or oil, or
Zech. 9. 15 shall drink..make a noise as through wi.
10. 7 their heart shall rejoice as through wine

4. *A vat or trough*, יֶקֶב *yeqeb.*
Deut 16. 13 after that thou hast gathered in..thy wi.

5. *Any thing mixed*, מִמְסָךְ *mimsak.*
Prov 23. 30 They that tarry..that go to seek mixed w.

6. *Any thing sucked in or up*, סֹבֶא *sobe.*
Isa. 1. 22 Thy silver is become dross, thy wine mix.

7. *A (ripe or round) grape, grape cake*, עֵנָב *enab.*
Hos. 3. 1 look to other gods, and love flagons of wi.

8. *Any thing pressed on, mead*, עָסִיס *asis.*
Isa. 49. 26 they shall be drunken..as with sweet wi.
Joel 1. 5 howl, all ye drinkers..because of..new w.
3. 18 the mountains shall drop down new wine
Amos 9. 13 the mountains shall drop sweet wine, and

9. *What satiates, pleases*, שֵׁכָר *shekar.*
Num 28. 7 cause the strong wine to be poured unto

10. *What is preserved, sediment*, שְׁמָרִים *shemarim.*
Isa. 25. 6 wines on the lees..wines on the lees well

11. *What is possessed, mead, new wine*, תִּירוֹשׁ *tirosh.*
Gen. 27. 28 God give thee..plenty of corn and wine
27. 37 with corn and wine have I sustained him
Num 18. 12 all the best of the wine, and of the wheat
Deut. 7. 13 he will also bless..thy corn, and thy wine
11. 14 mayest gather in thy corn, and thy wine
12. 17 Thou mayest not eat..the tithe..of thy wi.
14. 23 the tithe..of thy wine, and of thine oil
18. 4 The first fruit..of thy corn, of thy wine
28. 51 shall not leave thee..corn, wine, or oil
33. 28 fountain..upon a land of corn and wine
Judg. 9. 13 Should I leave my wine, which cheereth
2 Ki. 18. 32 a land of corn and wine, a land of bread
2 Ch. 31. 5 brought in abundance..first fruits of..w.
32. 28 for the increase of corn, and wine, and
Neh. 5. 11 of the corn, the wine, and the oil, that ye
10. 37 fruit of all manner of trees, of wine, and
10. 39 the offering of the corn, of the new wine
13. 5 tithes of the corn, the new wine, and the
13. 12 brought all Judah the tithe of..the new w.
Psa. 4. 7 time..their corn and their wine increased
Prov. 3. 10 thy presses shall burst out with new wine
Isa. 24. 7 The new wine mourneth, the vine langui.
36. 17 a land of corn and wine, a land of bread
62. 8 sons of..stranger shall not drink thy wine
65. 8 As the new wine is found in the cluster
Jer. 31. 12 for wheat, and for wine, and for oil, and
Hos. 2. 8 she did not know..I gave her corn, and w.
2. 9 take away..my wine in the season thereof
2. 22 the earth shall hear the corn, and the wine
4. 11 Whoredom..and new wine take away the
7. 14 they assemble themselves for corn and w.
9. 2 shall not feed them, and the new wine
Joel 1. 10 new wine is dried up, the oil languisheth
2. 19 I will send you corn, and wine, and oil
2. 24 the fats shall overflow with wine and oil
Mic. 6. 15 shalt not anoint..with oil; and sweet wine
Hag. 1. 11 I called for a drought..upon the new wine
Zech. 9. 17 Corn shall make..cheerful, and new wine

12. *Sweet or new wine*, γλεῦκος *gleukos.*
Acts 2. 13 mocking said, These men are full of new w.

13. *Wine, grape juice*, οἶνος *oinos.*
Matt. 9. 17 Neither..put new wine..else..the wine ru.
9. 17 but they put new wine into new bottles
Mark 2. 22 no man putteth new wine..else the new w.
2. 22 the wine is spilled..[but new wine must]
15. 23 they gave him to drink wine mingled with
Luke 1. 15 shall drink neither wine nor strong drink
5. 37 no man putteth new wine..else the new w.
5. 38 But new wine must be put into new bott.
7. 33 neither eating bread nor drinking [wine]
10. 34 bound..wounds, pouring in oil and wine
John 2. 3 they wanted wine..saith..They have no wi.
2. 9 had tasted the water that was made wine
2. 10 at the beginning doth set forth good wine
2. 10 thou hast kept the good wine until now
4. 46 of Galilee, where he made the water wine
Rom 14. 21 good neither to eat flesh, nor to drink wi.
Eph. 5. 18 be not drunk with wine, wherein is excess
1 Ti. 3. 8 not given to much wine, not greedy of fil.
5. 23 Drink no longer water, but use a little wi.
Titus 2. 3 not given to much wine, teachers of good
Rev. 6. 6 and (see) thou hurt not the oil and the wi.
14. 8 she made all nations drink of the wine of
14. 10 The same shall drink of the wine of the
16. 19 to give unto her the cup of the wine of the
17. 2 made drunk with the wine of her fornica.
18. 3 For all nations have drunk [of the wine]
18. 13 frankincense, and wine, and oil, and fine
19. 15 he treadeth the wine press of the fiercen.

WINE bibber —

1. *Wine sucker*, סֹבֵא יַיִן *sobe yayin.*
Prov 23. 20 Be not among wine bibbers; among riot.

2. *Wine drinker*, οἰνοπότης *oinopotēs.*
Matt 11. 19 Behold a man gluttonous, and a wine bib.
Luke 7. 34 Behold a gluttonous man and a wine bib.

WINE fat, wine press —

1. *A trough, wine or wheat press*, גַּת *gath.*
Judg. 6. 11 Gideon threshed wheat by the wine press
Neh. 13. 15 treading wine presses on the sabbath, and
Isa. 63. 2 and..like him that treadeth in the wine fat
Lam. 1. 15 hath trodden the virgin..(as) in a wine pr

2. *A vat or trough*, יֶקֶב *yeqeb.*
Num 18. 27 as though..the fulness of the wine press
18. 30 counted..as the increase of the wine press
Deut 15. 14 shalt furnish him..out of thy wine press
Judg. 7. 25 Zeeb they slew at the wine press of Zeeb
2 Ki. 6. 27 out of the barn floor, or out of the wine p.?
Job 24. 11 (and) tread..wine presses, and suffer thirst
Isa. 5. 2 also made a wine press therein: and he lo.
Jer. 48. 33 I have caused..to fail from the wine pre.
Hos. 9. 2 The floor and the wine press shall not feed
Zech 14. 10 tower of Hananeel unto the king's wine p.

3. *A vat or trough*, פּוּרָה *purah.*
Isa. 63. 3 I have trodden the wine press alone, and

4. *A vat or wine press*, ληνός *lēnos.*
Matt 21. 33 hedged it round about, and digged a wine
Rev. 14. 19 cast (it) into the great wine press of the
14. 20 the wine press was trodden without the
14. 20 blood came out of the wine press, even

5. *Press of the vine*, ληνὸς τοῦ οἴνου *lēnos tou oinou.*
Rev. 19. 15 he treadeth the wine press of the fiercen.

6. *An under vat*, ὑπολήνιον *hupolēnion.*
Mark 12. 1 digged..the wine fat, and built a tower

WINE, excess of, given to —

1. *An overflowing of wine*, οἰνοφλυγία *oinophlugia.*
1 Pe. 4. 3 excess of wine, revellings, banquetings

2. *One alongside of wine*, πάροινος *paroinos.*
1 Ti. 3. 3 Not given to wine, no striker, not greedy
Titus 1. 7 not given to wine, no striker, not given to

WING, (winged) —

1. *A wing, (from its strength)*, אֵבֶר *eber.*
Psa. 55. 6 Oh that I had wings like a dove! (for th.)
Isa. 40. 31 they shall mount up with wings as eagles

2. *A wing, (from its strength)*, אֶבְרָה *ebrah.*
Deut32. 11 taketh them, beareth them on her wings
Job 39. 13 or wings and feathers unto the ostrich?

3. *A wing, (from its arched appearance)*, גַּף *gaph.*
Dan. 7. 4 had eagle's wings; I beheld till the wings
7. 6 which had upon the back of it four wings

4. *A wing, (as covering and protecting)*, כָּנָף *kanaph.*
Gen. 1. 21 every winged fowl after his kind: and God
Exod19. 4 bare you on eagle's wings, and brought you
25. 20 cherubim shall stretch forth (their) wings
25. 20 covering the mercy seat with their wings
37. 9 cherubim spread out (their) wings on high
37. 9 covered with their wings over the mercy
Lev. 1. 17 he shall cleave it with the wings thereof
Deut. 4. 17 likeness of any winged fowl that flieth in
32. 11 spreadeth abroad her wings, taketh them
Ruth 2. 12 under whose wings thou art come to trust
2 Sa. 22. 11 and he was seen upon the wings of the wi.
1 Ki. 6. 24 one wing of the cherub..other wing of the
6. 24 from the uttermost part of the one wing
6. 27 stretched forth the wings..that the wing
6. 27 wing of the other cherub touched the ot.
6. 27 their wings touched one another in the
8. 6 even) under the wings of the cherubim
8. 7 cherubim spread forth (their) two wings
2 Ch. 3. 11 wings of the cherubim (were) twenty cu.
3. 11 one wing..and the other wing..five cub.
3. 11 reaching to the wing of the other cherub
3. 12 wing of the other cherub (was) five cubits
3. 12 other wing..joining to the wing of the ot.
3. 13 wings of these cherubim spread themsel.
5. 7 even) under the wings of the cherubim
5. 8 cherubim spread forth (their) wings over
Job 39. 13 (Gavest thou) the goodly wings unto the
39. 26 by thy wisdom, (and) stretch her wings to.
Psa. 17. 8 hide me under the shadow of thy wings
18. 10 yea, he did fly upon the wings of the wind
36. 7 put their trust under the shadow of thy w.
57. 1 in the shadow of thy wings will I make
61. 4 ever: I will trust in the covert of thy wi.
63. 7 therefore in the shadow of thy wings will
68. 13 wings of a dove covered with silver, and
91. 4 under his wings shalt thou trust: his tr.
104. 3 who walketh upon the wings of the wind
139. 9 (If) I take the wings of the morning, (and)
Prov 23. 5 for (riches) certainly make themselves wi.
Eccl. 10. 20 that which hath wings shall tell the mat.
Isa. 6. 2 each one had six wings; with twain he co.
8. 8 stretching out of his wings shall fill the
10. 14 there was none that moved the wing, or
18. 1 Woe to the land shadowing with wings
Jer. 48. 40 fly as an eagle, and shall spread his wings
49. 22 fly as the eagle, and spread his wings over
Eze. 1. 6 had four faces, and every one had four wi.
1. 8 hands of a man under their wings on th.
1. 8 and they four had their faces and their w.
1. 9 Their wings (were) joined one to another
1. 11 their wings (were) stretched upward, two
1. 23 under the firmament (were) their wings
1. 24 heard the noise of their wings, like the no.
1. 24 when they stood, they let down their wi.
1. 25 when they stood, (and)..let down their w.
3. 13 the noise of the wings of the living creat.
10. 5 the sound of the cherubim's wings was
10. 8 the form of a man's hand under their w.
10. 12 their hands, and their wings, and the w.
10. 16 when the cherubim lifted up their wings
10. 19 cherubim lifted up their wings, and mou.
10. 21 four faces apiece..every one had four wi.
10. 21 the hands of a man (was) under their wi.
11. 22 Then did the cherubim lift up their wings
17. 3 A great eagle with great wings, long win.
17. 7 another great eagle with great wings and
17. 23 and under it shall dwell all fowl of every w.
Hos. 4. 19 The wind hath bound her up in her wings
Zech. 5. 9 two women, and the wind (was) in their w.
5. 9 for they had wings like the wings of a st.
Mal. 4. 2 arise with healing in his wings; and ye sh.

5. *A wing, (from its feathers), flower*, צִיץ *tsits.*
Jer. 48. 9 Give wings unto Moab, that it may flee

6. *A wing, (from its power of flying)*, πτέρυξ.
Matt23. 37 a hen gathereth her chickens under (her) w.
Luke13. 34 hen (doth gather) her brood under (her) w.
Rev. 4. 8 four beasts had each of them six wings
9. 9 sound of their wings (was) as the sound
12. 14 to the woman were given two wings of a

WINK (at), to —

1. *To move, wink*, קָרַץ *qarats.*
Psa. 35. 19 wink with the eye that hate me without
Prov. 6. 13 He winketh with his eyes, he speaketh wi.
10. 10 He that winketh with the eye causeth sor.

2. *To wink at, roll, move to and fro*, רָזַם *razam.*
Job 15. 12 heart carry..and what do thy eyes wink a.

3. *To overlook, connive at*, ὑπερείδω *hupereidō.*
Acts 17. 30 the times of this ignorance God winked a.

WINNOW, to —

To scatter, winnow, spread, זָרָה *zarah.*
Ruth 3. 2 he winnoweth barley to night in the thr.
Isa. 30. 24 which hath been winnowed with the sho.

WINTER, (in, to) —

1. *Winter or autumn, youth or maturity*, חֹרֶף *choreph.*
Gen. 8. 22 summer and winter, and day and night
Psa. 74. 17 the earth: thou hast made summer and
Jer. 36. 22 Now the king sat in the winterhouse, in
Amos 3. 15 will smite the winterhouse with the sum.
Zech.14. 8 hinder sea: in summer and in winter sh.

2. *To pass the winter or autumn*, חָרַף *charaph.*
Isa. 18. 6 the beasts of the earth shall winter upon

3. *Winter or autumn*, סְתָו, סְתָיו *sethav.*
Song 2. 11 For, lo, the winter is past, the rain is over

4. *A wintering at, passing the winter*, παραχειμασία.
Acts 27. 12 haven was not commodious to winter in

5. *To pass the winter at or near*, παραχειμάζω *pa.*
Acts 27. 12 if by any means they might attain..to wi.
28. 11 ship of Alexandria, which had wintered
1 Co. 16. 6 winter with you, that ye may bring me
Titus 3. 12 for I have determined there to winter

6. *Winter, storm, tempest*, χειμών *cheimōn.*
Matt24. 20 pray ye that your flight be not in the wi.
Mark13. 18 pray ye that your flight be not in the wi.
John 10. 22 the feast of the dedication, and it was w.
2 Ti. 4. 21 Do thy diligence to come before winter

WIPE (away, off, out), be wiped, to —

1. *To wipe away, blot out*, מָחָה *machah.*
2 Ki. 21. 13 wipe Jerusalem as (a man) wipeth a dish
Prov.30. 20 she eateth, and wipeth her mouth, and
Isa. 25. 8 GOD will wipe away tears from off all fa.

2. *To be wiped away, blotted out*, מָחָה *machah*, 2.
Prov. 6. 33 and his reproach shall not be wiped away

3. *To (cause to) wipe away, blot out*, מָחָה *machah*, 5.
Neh. 13. 14 wipe not out my good deeds that I have

4. *To wipe away or off*, ἀπομάσσω *apomassō.*
Luke10. 11 which cleaveth on us, we do wipe off ag.

5. *To wipe out*, ἐκμάσσω *ekmassō.*
Luke 7. 38 did wipe (them) with the hairs of her head
7. 44 and wiped (them) with the hairs of her
John 11. 2 wiped his feet with her hair, whose brot.
12. 3 anointed the feet of Jesus, and wiped his
13. 5 to wipe (them) with the towel wherewith

6. *To smear out*, ἐξαλείφω *exaleiphō.*
Rev. 7. 17 God shall wipe away all tears from their
21. 4 God shall wipe away all tears from their

WIRE —

Wire, ribbon, thread, פְּתִיל *pathil.*
Exod39. 3 cut (it into) wires, to work (it) in the blue

WISDOM, (to teach) —

1. *Understanding, intelligence*, בִּינָה *binah.*
Job 39. 26 Doth the hawk fly by thy wisdom, (and)
Prov 23. 4 not to be rich; cease from thine own wi.

2. *To make wise, teach*, חָכַם *chakam*, 3.
Psa.105. 22 at his pleasure, and teach his senators w.

3. *Wisdom, skill*, חָכְמָה *chokmah.*
Exod28. 3 whom I have filled with the spirit of wi.
31. 3 filled him..in wisdom, and in understan.
31. 6 in the hearts of all..I have put wisdom
35. 26 women whose heart stirred them up in w.
35. 31 filled him..in wisdom, in understanding
35. 35 Them hath he filled with wisdom of heart
36. 1 in whom the LORD put wisdom and und.
36. 2 in whose heart the LORD had put wisdom
Deut. 4. 6 this (is) your wisdom and your understa.
34. 9 Joshua..was full of the spirit of wisdom
2 Sa. 14. 20 according to the wisdom of an angel of God
20. 22 woman went unto all the people in her w.
1 Ki. 2. 6 Do therefore according to thy wisdom, and
3. 28 for they saw that the wisdom of God (was)
4. 29 God gave Solomon wisdom and understa.
4. 30 Solomon's wisdom excelled the wisdom
4. 34 wisdom..which had heard of his wisdom
5. 12 LORD gave Solomon wisdom, as he prom.
7. 14 he was filled with wisdom and understa.
10. 4 the queen..had seen all Solomon's wisd.
10. 6 a true report that I heard..of thy wisdom
10. 7 thy wisdom and prosperity exceedeth the
10. 8 Happy (are) thy men..that hear thy wis.
10. 23 Solomon exceeded..for riches and for w.
10. 24 all the earth sought..to hear his wisdom
11. 41 Solomon, and all that he did, and his wi.
2 Ch. 1. 10 Give me now wisdom and knowledge, that
1. 11 hast asked wisdom and knowledge for th.
1. 12 Wisdom and knowledge (is) granted unto
9. 3 queen..had seen the wisdom of Solomon
9. 5 a true report which I heard..of thy wis.
9. 6 the one half of the greatness of thy wisd.
9. 7 Happy (are) thy men..which..hear thy w.
9. 22 king Solomon passed all..in riches and w.
9. 23 all..sought..Solomon, to hear his wisdom
Ezra 7. 25 after the wisdom of thy God that (is) in th.
Job 4. 21 go away? they die, even without wisdom
11. 6 that he would show thee the secrets of w.
12. 2 No doubt..ye (are) the people, and wisd.
12. 12 With the ancient (is) wisdom; and in len.
12. 13 With him (is) wisdom and strength, he ha.
13. 5 hold your peace, and it should be your w.
15. 8 and dost thou restrain wisdom to thyself?
26. 3 How hast thou counselled..no wisdom?
28. 12 where shall wisdom be found? and where
28. 18 for the price of wisdom (is) above rubies
28. 20 Whence then cometh wisdom? and where
28. 28 Behold, the fear of the Lord, that (is) w.
32. 7 and multitude of years should teach wi.
32. 13 Lest ye..say, We have found out wisdom
33. 33 hold thy peace, and I shall teach thee w.
38. 36 Who can number the clouds in wisdom
38. 37 Who hath put wisdom in the inward parts?
39. 17 God hath deprived her of wisdom, neither
Psa. 37. 30 The mouth of the righteous speaketh wi.
51. 6 Behold..thou shalt make me to know w.
Psa. 90. 12 that we may apply (our) hearts unto wis
104. 24 LORD..in wisdom hast thou made them
111. 10 fear of the LORD (is) the beginning of w.
Prov. 1. 2 To know wisdom and instruction, to per.
1. 7 (but) fools despise wisdom and instruction
2. 2 So that thou incline thine ear unto wisdom
2. 6 For the LORD giveth wisdom: out of his
2. 10 When wisdom entereth into thine heart
3. 13 Happy (is) the man (that) findeth wisdom
3. 19 LORD by wisdom hath founded the earth
4. 5 Get wisdom, get understanding; forget
4. 7 Wisdom (is) the principal thing..get wis.
4. 11 I have taught thee in the way of wisdom
5. 1 My son, attend unto my wisdom..bow th.
7. 4 Say unto wisdom, Thou (art) my sister, and
8. 1 Doth not wisdom cry? and understanding
8. 11 For wisdom (is) better than rubies, and all
8. 12 I wisdom dwell with prudence, and find
9. 10 The fear..(is) the beginning of wisdom
10. 13 In the lips of him..wisdom is found
10. 23 a man of understanding hath wisdom
10. 31 mouth of the just bringeth forth wisdom
11. 2 cometh shame: but with the lowly (is) w.
13. 10 but with the well advised (is) wisdom
14. 6 A scorner seeketh wisdom, and findeth
14. 8 The wisdom of the prudent (is) to under.
14. 33 Wisdom resteth in the heart of him that
15. 33 The fear..(is) the instruction of wisdom
16. 16 How much better (is it) to get wisdom
17. 16 a price in the hand of a fool to get wisdom
17. 24 Wisdom (is) before him that hath under.
18. 4 the well spring of wisdom (as) a flowing
21. 30 (There is) no wisdom nor understanding
23. 23 Buy the truth, and sell (it) not; (also) wi.
24. 3 Through wisdom is an house builded, and
24. 14 So (shall) the knowledge of wisdom (be)
29. 3 Whoso loveth wisdom rejoiceth his father
29. 15 The rod and reproof give wisdom, but a
30. 3 I neither learned wisdom, nor have the
31. 26 She openeth her mouth with wisdom, and
Eccl. 1. 13 to seek and search out by wisdom conce.
1. 16 gotten more wisdom..experience of wis.
1. 17 I gave my heart to know wisdom, and to
1. 18 in much wisdom (is) much grief; and he
2. 3 yet acquainting mine heart with wisdom
2. 9 I was great..my wisdom remained with
2. 12 I turned myself to behold wisdom, and
2. 13 I saw that wisdom excelleth folly, as far
2. 21 there is a man whose labour (is) in wisdom
2. 26 (God) giveth to a man that (is) good..wis.
7. 11 Wisdom (is) good with an inheritance; and
7. 12 wisdom (is) a defence..wisdom giveth life
7. 19 Wisdom strengtheneth the wise more than
7. 23 All this have I proved by wisdom: I said
7. 25 to seek out wisdom, and the reason (of
8. 1 a man's wisdom maketh his face to shine
8. 16 I applied mine heart to know wisdom, and
9. 10 there is no..wisdom, in the grave, whith.
9. 13 This wisdom have I seen also under the
9. 15 and he by his wisdom delivered the city
9. 16 Wisdom (is) better than strength: never.
9. 16 the poor man's wisdom (is) despised, and his
9. 18 Wisdom (is) better than weapons of war
10. 1 him that is in reputation for wisdom (and)
10. 10 put to more strength: but wisdom (is) pr.
Isa. 10. 13 I have done (it), and by my wisdom, for
11. 2 the spirit of wisdom and understanding
29. 14 the wisdom of their wise (men) shall per.
33. 6 wisdom and knowledge shall be the stabi.
47. 10 Thy wisdom and thy knowledge, it hath
Jer. 8. 9 rejected..and what wisdom (is) in them
9. 23 Let not the wise (man) glory in his wisdom
10. 12 hath established the world by his wisdom
49. 7 (Is) wisdom no more..is counsel perished
49. 7 concerning Edom..is their wisdom vanis.?
51. 15 hath established the world by his wisdom
Eze. 28. 4 With thy wisdom and with thine unders.
28. 5 By thy great wisdom (and) by thy traffic ha.
28. 7 swords against the beauty of thy wisdom
28. 12 Thou sealest up the sum, full of wisdom
28. 17 thou hast corrupted thy wisdom by reason
Dan. 1. 4 skilful in all wisdom, and cunning in kn.
1. 17 and skill in all learning and wisdom
1. 20 in all matters of wisdom (and) understand.
2. 20 Blessed be the name of God..for wisdom
2. 21 he giveth wisdom unto the wise, and kno.
2. 23 who hast given me wisdom and might, and
2. 30 secret is not revealed to me for (any) wisd.
5. 11 understanding and wisdom, like the wisd.
5. 14 understanding and excellent wisdom is fo.

4. *Wisdom, skill*, חָכְמוֹת *chokmoth.*
Psa. 49. 3 My mouth shall speak of wisdom; and the
Prov. 1. 20 Wisdom crieth without; she uttereth her
9. 1 Wisdom hath builded her house, she hath
24. 7 Wisdom (is) too high for a fool, he openeth

5. *Taste, reason, discretion*, טְעֵם *teem.*
Dan. 2. 14 Daniel answered with counsel and wisdom

6. *Heart*, לֵב *leb.*
Job 36. 5 God (is)..mighty in strength (and) wisdom
Prov 10. 21 feed many: but fools die for want of wis.
11. 12 He that is void of wisdom despiseth his
15. 21 Folly (is) joy to (him that is) destitute of w.
19. 8 He that getteth wisdom loveth his own
Eccl. 10. 3 his wisdom faileth (him), and he saith to

7. *Craftiness, subtilty, prudence*, עָרְמָה *ormah.*
Prov. 8. 5 O ye simple, understand wisdom; and, ye

8. *To become wise or intelligent*, שָׂכַל *sakal*, 5.
Job 34. 35 knowledge, and his words (were) without w
Prov. 1. 3 To receive the instruction of wisdom, jus.

9. *Understanding, wisdom, meaning,* שֶׂכֶל *sekel.*
1 Ch.22. 12 Only the LORD give thee wisdom and un.
Prov 12. 8 shall be commended according to his wi.
23. 9 for he will despise the wisdom of thy wo.

10. *Understanding, skilfulness, reason,* תְּבוּנָה *tebunah*
Psa.136. 5 To him that by wisdom made the heavens

11. *Substance, wisdom,* תּוּשִׁיָּה *tushiyyah.*
Job 6. 13 and is wisdom driven quite from me?
12. 16 With him (is) strength and wisdom: the
Prov 18. 1 seeketh (and) intermeddleth with all wis.
Mic. 6. 9 (the man of) wisdom shall see thy name

12. *Thoughtfulness,* φρόνησις *phronēsis.*
Luke 1. 17 and the disobedient to the wisdom of the

13. *Wisdom, skill,* σοφία *sophia.*
Matt 11. 19 sinners. But wisdom is justified of her ch.
12. 42 to hear the wisdom of Solomon: and, be.
13. 54 Whence hath this (man) this wisdom, and
Mark 6. 2 what wisdom (is) this which is given unto
Luke 2. 40 waxed strong in spirit, filled with wisdom
2. 52 Jesus increased in wisdom and stature, and
7. 35 But wisdom is justified of all her children
11. 31 she came..to hear the wisdom of Solomon
11. 49 Therefore also said the wisdom of God, I
21. 15 I will give you a mouth and wisdom, wh.
Acts 6. 3 seven men..full of the Holy Ghost and wi.
6. 10 they were not able to resist the wisdom
7. 10 gave him favour and wisdom in the sight
7. 22 Moses was learned in all the wisdom of the
Rom 11. 33 both of the wisdom and knowledge of G.
1 Co. 1. 17 not with wisdom of words, lest the cross
1. 19 I will destroy the wisdom of the wise, and
1. 20 hath not God made foolish the wisdom of
1. 21 in the wisdom of God the world by wisd.
1. 22 a sign, and the Greeks seek after wisdom
1. 24 Christ the power of God, and the wisdom
1. 30 Jesus, who of God is made unto us wisd.
2. 1 came not with excellency of speech or of w.
2. 4 not with enticing words of man's wisdom
2. 5 your faith should not stand in the wisdom
2. 6 we speak wisdom..yet not the wisdom of
2. 7 we speak the wisdom of God in a mystery
2. 13 not in the words which man's wisdom te.
3. 19 For the wisdom of this world is foolishness
12. 8 For to one is given..the word of wisdom
2 Co. 1. 12 not with fleshly wisdom, but by the grace
Eph. 1. 8 he hath abounded toward us in all wisdom
1. 17 may give unto you the spirit of wisdom and
3. 10 might be known..the manifold wisdom of
Col. 1. 9 with the knowledge of his will in all wis.
1. 28 and teaching every man in all wisdom
2. 3 In whom are hid all the treasures of wis.
2. 23 Which things have indeed a show of wis.
3. 16 Let the word..dwell in you richly in all w.
4. 5 Walk in wisdom toward them that are
Jas. 1. 5 If any of you lack wisdom, let him ask of
3. 13 show..his works with meekness of wisdom
3. 15 This wisdom descendeth not from above
3. 17 the wisdom that is from above is first pure
2 Pe. 3. 15 Paul also, according to the wisdom given
Rev. 5. 12 to receive power, and riches, and wisdom
7. 12 Blessing, and glory, and wisdom, and th.
13. 18 Here is wisdom. Let him that hath under.
17. 9 And here (is) the mind that hath wisdom

WISDOM, sound —
Substance, wisdom, תּוּשִׁיָּה *tushiyyah.*
Prov. 2. 7 He layeth up sound wisdom for the righ.
3. 21 My son..keep sound wisdom and discre.
8. 14 Counsel (is) mine, and sound wisdom, I (am)

WISE (hearted, man, woman) —
1. *To cause to understand, give intelligence,* בִּין *bin,* 5.
1 Ch.27. 32 was a counsellor, a wise man, and a scribe
Prov 17. 10 reproof entereth more into a wise man th.
28. 7 Whoso keepeth the law (is) a wise son: but

2. *Wise, skilful,* חַכִּים *chakkim.*
Dan. 2. 12 commanded to destroy all the wise (men)
2. 13 decree went forth that the wise (men) sh.
2. 14 which was gone forth to slay the wise (m.)
2. 18 perish with the rest of the wise (men) of
2. 21 he giveth wisdom unto the wise, and kn.
2. 24 king had ordained to destroy the wise (m.)
2. 24 Destroy not the wise (men) of Babylon: br.
2. 27 cannot the wise (men)..show unto the ki.
2. 48 chief of the governors over all the wise (m.)
4. 6 made I a decree to bring in all the wise (m.)
4. 18 forasmuch as all the wise (men) of my k.
5. 7 king spake, and said to the wise (men) of
5. 8 Then came in all the king's wise (men)
5. 15 now the wise (men), the astrologers, have

3. *Wise, skilful,* חָכָם *chakam.*
Gen. 41. 8 sent and called for all..the wise men th.
41. 33 Pharaoh look out a man discreet and wise
41. 39 (there is) none so discreet and wise as thou
Exod. 7. 11 Pharaoh also called the wise men and the
28. 3 shalt speak unto all (that are) wise hear.
31. 6 in the hearts of all that are wise hearted
35. 10 every wise hearted among you shall come
35. 25 the women that were wise hearted did sp.
36. 1, 2 Aholiab, and every wise hearted man
36. 4 the wise men, that wrought all the work
36. 8 every wise hearted man among them that
Deut. 1. 13 Take you wise men, and understanding
1. 15 I took the chief of your tribes, wise men
4. 6 nation (is) a wise and understanding peo.
16. 19 a gift doth blind the eyes of the wise, and
Judg. 5. 29 Her wise ladies answered her, yea, she re.
2 Sa. 14 2 fetched thence a wise woman, and said un.
2 Sa. 14. 20 my lord (is) wise, according to the wisdom
20. 16 Then cried a wise woman out of the city
1 Ki. 2. 9 thou (art) a wise man, and knowest what
3. 12 I have given thee a wise and an understa.
5. 7 which hath given unto David a wise son
2 Ch. 2. 12 hath given to David the king a wise son
Esth. 1. 13 the king said to the wise men, which knew
6. 13 Then said his wise men and Zeresh his
Job 5. 13 He taketh the wise in their own craftiness
9. 4 (He is) wise in heart, and mighty in stren.
15. 2 Should a wise man utter vain knowledge
15. 18 Which wise men have told from their fat.
17. 10 I cannot find (one) wise (man) among you
34. 2 Hear my words, O ye wise (men); and give
34. 34 and let a wise man hearken unto me
37. 24 he respecteth not any (that are) wise of
Psa. 49. 10 he seeth (that) wise men die, likewise the
107. 43 Whoso (is) wise, and will observe these
Prov. 1. 5 A wise (man) will hear, and will increase
1. 6 the words of the wise, and their dark sa.
3. 7 Be not wise in thine own eyes: fear the
3. 35 The wise shall inherit glory: but shame
9. 8 rebuke a wise man, and he will love thee
9. 9 Give (instruction) to a wise (man), and he
10. 1 A wise son maketh a glad father: but a
10. 8 The wise in heart will receive command.
10. 14 Wise (men) lay up knowledge: but the
11. 29 the fool (shall be) servant to the wise of
11. 30 and he that winneth souls (is) wise
12. 15 he that hearkeneth unto counsel (is) wise
12. 18 but the tongue of the wise (is) health
13. 1 A wise son (heareth) his father's instruc.
13. 14 The law of the wise (is) a fountain of life
13. 20 He that walketh with wise (men) shall be
14. 3 but the lips of the wise shall preserve th.
14. 16 A wise (man) feareth, and departeth from
14. 24 The crown of the wise (is) their riches
15. 2 The tongue of the wise useth knowledge
15. 7 The lips of the wise disperse knowledge
15. 12 neither will he go unto the wise
15. 20 A wise son maketh a glad father: but a
15. 31 The ear that..abideth among the wise
16. 14 wrath of a king..a wise man will pacify
16. 21 The wise in heart shall be called prudent
16. 23 The heart of the wise teacheth his mouth
17. 28 when he holdeth his peace, is counted w.
18. 15 and the ear of the wise seeketh knowled.
20. 26 A wise king scattereth the wicked, and
21. 11 when the wise is instructed, he receiveth
21. 20 treasure..and oil in the dwelling of the wise
21. 22 A wise (man) scaleth the city of the mig.
22. 17 hear the words of the wise, and apply th.
23. 24 he that begetteth a wise (child) shall have
24. 5 A wise man (is) strong; yea, a man of k.
24. 23 These (things) also (belong) to the wise
25. 12 (so is) a wise reprover upon an obedient
26. 5 Answer a fool..lest he be wise in his own
26. 12 Seest thou a man wise in his own conceit?
26. 16 The sluggard (is) wiser in his own conce.
28. 11 The rich man (is) wise in his own conceit
29. 8 into a snare: but wise (men) turn away
29. 9 (If) a wise man contendeth with a foolish
29. 11 but a wise (man) keepeth it in till afterw.
30. 24 four (things)..but they (are) exceeding w.
Eccl. 2. 14 The wise man's eyes (are) in his head, but
2. 16 remembrance of the wise..the wise (man)
2. 19 who knoweth whether he shall be a wise
4. 13 Better (is) a poor and a wise child than
6. 8 what hath the wise more than the fool?
7. 4 The heart of the wise (is) in the house of
7. 5 better to hear the rebuke of the wise, than
7. 7 oppression maketh a wise man mad, and
7. 19 Wisdom strengtheneth the wise more th.
8. 1 Who (is) as the wise (man)? and who kn.
8. 5 a wise man's heart discerneth both time
8. 17 though a wise (man) think to know (it)
9. 1 the wise, and their works, (are) in the ha.
9. 11 neither yet bread to the wise, nor yet ri.
9. 15 there was found in it a poor wise man
9. 17 The words of wise (men are) heard in qu.
10. 2 A wise man's heart (is) at his right hand
10. 12 The words of a wise man's mouth (are)
12. 9 moreover, because the Preacher was wise
12. 11 The words of the wise (are) as goads, and
Isa. 5. 21 Woe unto..wise in their own eyes, and
19. 11 of the wise counsellors..the son of the w.
19. 12 Where (are) they? where (are)..wise (m.?)
29. 14 the wisdom of their wise (men) shall per.
31. 2 Yet he also (is) wise, and will bring evil
44. 25 that turneth wise (men) backward, and
Jer. 4. 22 they (are) wise to do evil, but to do good
8. 8 How do ye say, We (are) wise, and the law
8. 9 The wise (men) are ashamed, they are di.
9. 12 Who (is) the wise man, that may unders.
9. 23 Let not the wise (man) glory in his wisd.
10. 7 among all the wise (men) of the nations
18. 18 nor counsel from the wise, nor the word
50. 35 upon her princes, and upon her wise (m.)
51. 57 I will make drunk..her wise (men), her
Eze. 27. 8 thy wise (men), O Tyrus, (that) were in th.
27. 9 The ancients of Gebal and the wise (men)
Hos. 14. 9 Who (is) wise, and he shall understand
Obad. 8 even destroy the wise (men) out of Edom

4. *Wise,* חָכְמוֹת [*chakam*].
Prov. 14. 1 Every wise woman buildeth her house

5. *Open, seeing,* פִּקֵּחַ *piqqeach.*
Exod 23. 8 for the gift blindeth the wise, and perv.

6. *To cause to understand,* שָׂכַל *sakal,* 5.
Job 22. 2 as he that is wise may be profitable unto
Prov. 10. 5 He that gathereth in summer (is) a wise
Prov 10. 19 sin; but he that refraineth his lips (is) wise
14. 35 The king's favour (is) toward a wise serv.
15. 24 The way of life (is) above to the wise, that
17. 2 A wise servant shall have rule over a son
Dan. 12. 3 they that be wise shall shine as the brig.
12. 10 wicked shall understand; but the wise sh.

7. *Understanding, wisdom,* שֶׂכֶל *sekel.*
1 Ch.26. 14 Then for Zechariah his son, a wise coun.

8. *Magian, (a Persian astronomer or priest),* μάγος.
Matt 2. 1 there came wise men from the east to Je.
2. 7 when he had privily called the wise men
2. 16 he saw that he was mocked of the wise m.
2. 16 he had diligently enquired of the wise men

9. *Wise, skilful,* σοφός *sophos.*
Matt 11. 25 thou hast hid these things from the wise
23. 34 I send unto you prophets, and wise men
Luke 10. 21 these things from the wise and prudent
Rom. 1. 14 I am debtor..both to the wise and to the
1. 22 Professing themselves to be wise, they be.
16. 19 I would have you wise unto that which is
16. 27 To God only wise, (be) glory through Jes.
1 Co. 1. 19 I will destroy the wisdom of the wise, and
1. 20 Where (is) the wise? where (is) the scribe?
1. 26 not many wise men after the flesh, not
1. 27 [chosen the foolish..to confound the wise]
3. 10 as a wise master builder, I have laid the
3. 18 If any man among you seemeth to be w.
3. 18 let him become a fool, that he may be wise
3. 19 He taketh the wise in their own craftiness
3. 20 The Lord knoweth the thoughts of the w.
6. 5 Is it so, that there is not a wise man am.
Eph. 5. 15 walk circumspectly, not as fools, but as w.
1 Ti. 1. 17 unto the king eternal..the only [wise] G.
Jas. 3. 13 Who (is) a wise man and endued with kn.
Jude 25 To the only [wise] God our Saviour, (be) g.

10. *Mindful, prudent, provident,* φρόνιμος *phronimos*
Matt. 7. 24 I will liken him unto a wise man, which
10. 16 be ye therefore wise as serpents, and ha.
24. 45 Who then is a faithful and wise servant
25. 2 And five of them were wise, and five (we.)
25. 4 But the wise took oil in their vessels with
25. 8 foolish said unto the wise, Give us of your
25. 9 But the wise answered, saying, (Not so)
Luke 12. 42 Who then is that faithful and wise stew.
Rom 11. 25 lest ye should be wise in your own conc.
12. 16 low estate. Be not wise in your own con.
1 Co. 4. 10 We (are) fools for Christ's sake, but..wise
10. 15 I speak as to wise men; judge ye what I
2 Co. 11. 19 Ye suffer fools gladly, seeing ye..are wise

WISE, in any, in no, or on this —
1. *To reason, reprove, decide,* יָכַח *yakach,* 5.
Lev. 19. 17 thou shalt in any wise rebuke thy neigh.

2. *To afflict, humble,* עָנָה *anah,* 3.
Exod 22. 23 If thou afflict them in any wise, and they

3. *Thus, so, accordingly,* οὕτω, οὕτως *houtō, houtōs.*
Matt. 1. 18 Now the birth of Jesus Christ was on this w.
John 21. 1 at the sea of Tiberias; and on this wise sh.
Acts 7. 6 God spake on this wise, That his seed sh.
13. 34 said on this wise, I will give you the sure
Rom. 10. 6 speaketh on this wise, Say not in thine he.
Heb. 4. 4 For he spake..on this wise, And God did

4. *Not completely, not at all,* μὴ εἰς τὸ παντελές.
Luke 13. 11 was bowed together, and could in no wise

5. *Not at all,* οὐ πάντως *ou pantōs.*
Rom. 3. 9 No, in no wise: for we have before proved

WISE, to be, make, show self —
1. *To be or become wise, act wisely,* חָכַם *chakam.*
Deut. 32. 29 Oh that they were wise, (that) they unde.
1 Ki. 4. 31 For he was wiser than all men; than Ethan
Job 32. 9 Great men are not (always) wise; neither
Prov. 6. 6 thou sluggard; consider her ways..be w.
8. 33 Hear instruction, and be wise, and refuse
9. 9 and he will be yet wiser; teach a just (man)
9. 12 If thou be wise, thou shalt be wise for th.
13. 20 He that walketh with wise (men) shall be
19. 20 that thou mayest be wise in thy latter end
20. 1 and whosoever is deceived thereby is n. w.
21. 11 the scorner is punished, the simple is m. w.
23. 15 My son, if thine heart be wise, my heart
23. 19 Hear thou, my son, and be wise, and guide
27. 11 My son, be wise, and make my heart glad
Eccl. 2. 15 why was I then more wise? Then I said in
2. 19 wherein I have showed myself wise under
7. 23 I said, I will be wise; but it (was) far from
Zech. 9. 2 Tyrus, and Zidon, though it be very wise

2. *To make wise,* חָכַם *chakam,* 5.
Psa. 19. 7 testimony of the LORD (is) sure, making w.

3. *To show self wise,* חָכַם *chakam,* 7.
Eccl. 7. 16 neither make thyself over wise: why sho.

4. *To take heart, be bold,* לָבַב *labab,* 2.
Job 11. 12 For vain man would be wise, though man

5. *To cause to act wisely,* שָׂכַל *sakal,* 5.
Gen. 3. 6 a tree to be desired to make (one) wise
Psa. 2. 10 Be wise now therefore, O ye kings, be
36. 3 he hath left off to be wise, (and) to do good
94. 8 the people: and (ye) fools, when will..w.?

6. *To make wise,* σοφίζω *sophizō.*
2 Ti. 3. 15 which are able to make thee wise unto sa.

7. *To send together, consider,* συνίημι *suniēmi.*
2 Co. 10. 12 and comparing themselves..are not wise

WISELY, to behave self, consider, deal —
1. *To understand, attend to,* בִּין *bin.*
2 Ch. 11. 23 he dealt wisely, and dispersed of all his

2. *To show self wise*, חָכַם *chakam*, 7.
Exod. 1. 10 Come on, let us deal wisely with them; lest

3. *To act wisely*, שָׂכַל *sakal*.
1 Sa. 18. 30 David behaved himself more wisely than

4. *To act wisely, or to understand*, שָׂכַל *sakal*, 5.
1 Sa. 18. 5 David went out..(and) behaved himself wi.
18. 14 David behaved himself wisely in all his w.
18. 15 saw that he behaved himself very wisely
Psa. 64. 9 for they shall wisely consider of his doing
101. 2 I will behave myself wisely in a perfect
Prov. 21. 12 The righteous (man) wisely considereth

WISELY, (never so) —

1. *To be made wise*, חָכַם *chakam*, 4.
Psa. 58. 5 voice of charmers, charming never so wis.

2. *Wisdom*, חָכְמָה *chokmah*.
Prov. 28. 26 but whoso walketh wisely, he shall be de.
Eccl. 7. 10 thou dost not enquire wisely concerning

3. *To cause to act wisely or understand*, שָׂכַל *sakal*, 5.
Prov. 16. 20 He that handleth a matter wisely shall

4. *Mindfully, prudently, providently*, φρονίμως.
Luke 16. 8 because he had done wisely: for the chil.

WISER, (to make) —

1. *To make wise*, חָכַם *chakam*, 3.
Job 35. 11 and maketh us wiser than the fowls of he.?
Psa. 119. 98 Thou..hast made me wiser than mine en.

2. *Wiser than*, חָכָם מִן *chakam min*.
Eze. 28. 3 Behold, thou (art) wiser than Daniel; the.

3. *Wiser, more skilful*, σοφώτερον *sophōteron*.
1 Co. 1. 25 Because the foolishness of God is wiser

4. *More mindful, prudent*, φρονιμώτερος *phronim*.
Luke 16. 8 in their generation wiser than the child.

WISH, wishing —

1. *Willing, desirous, delighting*, חָפֵץ *chaphets*.
Psa. 40. 14 driven backward and put to shame that w.

2. *Mouth, speech*, פֶּה *peh*.
Job 33. 6 I (am) according to thy wish in God's ste.

3. *To ask, demand*, שָׁאַל *shaal*.
Job 31. 30 have I suffered my mouth to sin by wish.
Jon. 4. 8 that he fainted, and wished in himself to

4. *Imagery, imagination*, מַשְׂכִּית *maskith*.
Psa. 73. 7 they have more than heart could wish

5. *To wish, desire, solicit*, εὔχομαι *euchomai*.
Acts 27. 29 cast four anchors out of the stern, and w.
Rom. 9. 3 For I could wish that myself were accur.
2 Co. 13. 9 and this also we wish, (even) your perfe.
3 John 2 I wish above all things that thou mayest

WIST, wit, (do to wit,) to —

1. *Wisdom*, חָכְמָה *chokmah*.
Psa. 107. 27 like a drunken man, and are at their wit's

2. *To know, be acquainted with*, יָדַע *yada*.
Gen. 24. 21 to wit whether the LORD had made his
Exod. 2. 4 his sister stood afar off, to wit what wou.
16. 15 It (is) manna: for they wist not what it
34. 29 Moses wist not that the skin of his face
Lev. 5. 17 though he wist (it) not, yet is he guilty
5. 18 his ignorance wherein he erred and wist
Josh. 2. 4 There came men unto me, but I wist not
8. 14 but he wist not that (there were) liers in
Judg 16. 20 wist not that the LORD was departed from

3. *To know, be acquainted with, see*, οἶδα *oida*.
Mark 9. 6 For he wist not what to say: for they we.
14. 40 heavy, neither wist they what to answer
Luke 2. 49 wist ye not that I must be about my Fat.
John 5. 13 he that was healed wist not who it was
Acts 12. 9 wist not that it was true which was done
23. 5 I wist not, brethren, that he was the high

4. *As, how*, ὡς *hōs*.
2 Co. 5. 19 To wit, that God was in Christ, reconcil.

5. *To make known*, γνωρίζω *gnōrizō*.
2 Co. 8. 1 we do you to wit of the grace of God bes.
[*See also* Wot.]

WITCH, (to use) witchcraft —

1. *To use witchcraft or sorcery*, כָּשַׁף *kashaph*, 3.
Exod 22. 18 Thou shalt not suffer a witch to live
Deut 18. 10 observer of times, or an enchanter, or a w.
2 Ch. 33. 6 used witchcraft, and dealt with a familiar

2. *Witchcrafts, sorceries*, כְּשָׁפִים *keshaphim*.
2 Ki. 9. 22 whoredoms..and her witchcrafts (are so)
Mic. 5. 12 I will cut off witchcrafts out of thine ha.
Nah. 3. 4 well favoured harlot, the mistress of wi.
3. 4 selleth nations..through her witchcrafts

3. *Divination, oath*, קֶסֶם *qesem*.
1 Sa. 15. 23 For rebellion (is as) the sin of witchcraft

4. *A charm, remedy*, φαρμακεία *pharmakeia*.
Gal. 5. 20 Idolatry, witchcraft, hatred, variance, em.

WITH —

1. *After*, אַחַר *achar*.
Lev. 20. 5 that go..to commit whoredom with Molech

2. *Unto*, אֶל *el*.
Gen. 4. 8 And Cain talked with Abel his brother

3. *Also*, אַף *aph*.
Deut 33. 20 teareth the arm with the crown of the

4. *Near*, אֵצֶל *etsel*.
Gen. 39. 15 he left his garment with me, and fled, and
39. 18 he left his garment with me, and fled out
Dan. 10. 13 I remained there with the kings of Persia

5. *With*, אֵת *eth*.
Gen. 5. 22 Enoch walked with God after he begat M.
6. 13 behold, I will destroy them with the earth
13. 5 Lot also, which went with Abram, had
14. 2 made war with Bera..and with Birsha ki.
Josh 14. 12 if so be the LORD (will be) with me, then
Eze. 3. 27 when I speak with thee, I will open thy

6. *With, in*, בְּמוֹ *bemo*.
Job 9. 30 If I wash myself with snow water, and
16. 5 I would strengthen you with my mouth
19. 16 my servant..I entreated him with my m.

7. *Also*, גַּם *gam*.
2 Ch. 20. 13 all Judah stood before the LORD, with

8. *Over against*, מוּל *mul*.
Mic. 2. 8 ye pull off the robe with the garment from

9. *From*, מִן *min*.
Gen. 25. 30 Feed me, I pray thee, with that same red

10. *Against, besides, in addition to*, עַל *al*.
Gen. 33. 11 God hath dealt graciously with me, and
Dan. 6. 14 the king..was sore displeased with hims.

11. *With*, עִם *im*.
Gen. 18. 23 Wilt thou..destroy the righteous with the
Ezra 5. 2 and with them..the prophets of God he.
7. 13 I make a decree, that all..go with thee
7. 16 with the free will offering of the people
Dan. 2. 11 the gods, whose dwelling is not with flesh
2. 18 should not perish with the rest of the wi.
2. 22 he knoweth..and the light dwelleth with
2. 43 not cleave..as iron is not mixed with clay
4. 15, 23 and (let) his portion (be) with the
4. 25, 32 and thy dwelling (shall be) with the be.
5. 21 and his dwelling (was) with the wild asses
7. 13 (one) like the son of man came with the
7. 21 the same horn made war with the saints

12. *With, by*, עִמָּד *immad*.
Gen. 3. 12 The woman whom thou gavest..with me

13. *And before them*, וְלִפְנֵיהֶם [*panim*].
1 Sa. 10. 5 with a psaltery, and a tabret, and a pipe

14. *Under, beneath*, תַּחַת *tachath*.
Psa. 66. 17 I cried..he was extolled with my tongue

15. *In the hand*, בְּיַד *be-yad*.
Gen. 44. 16 and (he) also with whom the cup is found
Josh. 9. 11 Take victuals with you for the journey

16. *In the midst of*, בְּתוֹךְ *be-thok*.
Exod. 9. 24 there was hail, and fire mingled with the

17. *Together with*, ἅμα *hama*.
Matt 13. 29 lest..ye root up also the wheat with them

18. *From*, ἀπό *apo*.
Luke 14. 18 they all with one (consent) began to make
15. 16 he would fain have filled his belly with
16. 21 desiring to be fed with the crumbs which
Acts 20. 9 he sunk down with sleep, and fell down

19. *Through, by*, διά (*gen.*) *dia*.
Mark 16. 20 [confirming the word with signs following]
Acts 8. 20 the gift of God may be purchased with
15. 32 exhorted the brethren with many words
19. 26 they be no gods which are made with ha.
20. 28 which he hath purchased with his own
Rom 14. 20 evil for that man who eateth with 8. 25.
1 Co. 14. 19 I had rather speak five words [with] my
2 Co. 2. 4 I wrote unto you with many tears; not
Eph. 6. 18 Praying always with all prayer and supp.
1 Ti. 2. 10 But, which becometh women..with good
Heb. 12. 1 let us run with patience the race that is
13. 12 that he might sanctify the people with his
1 Pe. 1. 7 that perisheth, though it be tried with fire
2 John 12 I would not..with paper and ink, but I
3 John 13 I will not with ink and pen write unto

20. *Through, on account of*, διά (*acc*) *dia*.
Rom 14. 15 But if thy brother be grieved with..meat

21. *With a view to*, εἰς *eis*.
Eph. 3. 19 might be filled with all the fulness of God

22. *Out of*, ἐκ *ek*.
Matt 27. 7 bought with them the potter's field, to
Mark 12. 30 with all thy heart, and with all thy soul
12. 30 with all thy mind, and with all thy stren.
12. 33 with all the heart, and with all the und.
12. 33 with all the soul, [and with all the stren.]
Luke 10. 27 with all thy heart, and [with] all thy soul
10. 27 [with] all thy strength, and [with] all thy
John 4. 6 therefore being wearied with (his) jo. 12. 3.
Acts 1. 18 this man purchased a field with the rew.
8. 37 [If thou believest with all thine heart, th.]
1 Co. 7. 5 except..with consent for a time, that ye
1 Pe. 1. 22 love one another with a pure heart ferv.
Rev. 8. 5 took the censer, and filled it with fire of
17. 2 made drunk with the wine of her fornica.
17. 6 with the blood of the saints, and with the
18. 1 and the earth was lightened with his glory
19. 21 all the fowls were filled with their flesh

23. *In, among, by, with*, ἐν *en*.
Matt. 3. 11 baptize you with water..baptize you with
7. 2 with what judgment..with what measure
20. 15 Is it not lawful..to do what I will with
22. 37 with all thy..with all thy..with all thy
25. 16 went and traded with the same, and made
26. 52 they that take the sword shall perish with
Mark 1. [8, 8], 23; 4. 24, 30; 5. 2; 9. 1, 50; Luke 1. 51;
3. 16; 4. 32, 36; 8. 15; 11. 20; 14. 31; 21. 25, 34; 22. 49; John
1. 26, 31, 33, 33; Acts 1. 5; 2. 29, 46; 5. 23; 11. 16, 26;
Rom. 1. 4, 9, 12, 27; 9. 22; 10. 9; 12. 8, 8, 8, 21; 15. 32;
16. 16; 1 Co. 1. 17; 2. 4; 4. 21; 5. 8, 8, 8; 10. 5; 14. 21; 16.
14, 20; 2 Co. 1. 12; 7. 8; 13. 12; Eph. [illegible]; Col. 1. 11; 2.
4, 7; 3. 16, 22; 4. 2, 6; 1 Th. 2. 2, 17; 4. 16, 16, 16, 18; 5.
26; 2 Th. 1. 11; 2. 9, 10; 3. 8; 1 Ti. 2. 9, 11; 5. 2; 2 Ti. 1.
3; 4. 2; Heb. 9. 22, 25; 11. 37; Jas. 1. 21; 2. 1; 3. 13; 1 Pe.
1. [12]; 2. 18; 3. 2; 5. 14; 2 Pe. 2. 7, 13, 16; Jude 14, 23,
24; Rev. 2. 16, 23, 27; 6. 8, 8, 8; 9. 19; 12. 5; 13. 10, 10;
14. 2, [7], 9, 10, 15; 16. 8; 17. 16; 18. 8, [16]; 19. 2, 15, 15,
20, 20, 21.

24. *On, upon, over*, ἐπί (*dat.*) *epi*.
Matt. 18. 26, 29 have patience with me, and I will pay
Luke 18. 7 avenge..though he bear long with them?
Acts 21. 24 Them take..and be at charges with them
28. 14 were desired to tarry [with] them seven da.
Rev. 12. 17 the dragon was wroth [with] the woman

25. *Upon, over, for*, ἐπί (*acc.*) *epi*.
Heb. 8. 8 with the house of Israel, and with the ho.

26. *Down to, in, by, according to*, κατά (*acc*) *kata*.
Mark 1. 27 for with authority commandeth he even
1 Co. 2. 1 came not with excellency of speech or of
Eph. 6. 6 Not with eyeservice as men pleasers, but

27. *With, in common with*, μετά (*gen.*) *meta*.
Matt. 1. 23 which, being interpreted, is, God with us
2. 3 he was troubled, and all Jerusalem with
2. 11 they saw the young child with Mary his
4. 21 in a ship with Zebedee their father, men.
5. 25 whiles thou art in the way with him, lest
5. 41 compel thee to go a mile, go with him tw.
8. 11 shall sit down with Abraham, and Isaac
9. 11 Why eateth your Master with publicans
9. 15 as long as the bridegroom is with them
See also 12. 3, 4, 30, 30, 41, 42, 45; 13. 20; 14. 7; 15. 30; 16.
27; 17. 3, 17; 18. 16; 19. 10; 20. 2, 20; 21. 2; 22. 16; 24. 30,
31, 49, 51; 25. 3, 4, 10, 19, 31; 26. 11, 18, 20, 23, 29, 36, 38,
40, 47, 47, 51, 55, 58, 69, 71, 72; 27. 34, 41, 54; 28. 8, 12, 20;
Mark 1. 13, 20, 29, 36; 2. 16, 16, 19, [19], 25; 3. 5, 6, 7, 14;
4. 16, 36; 5. 18, 24, 40; 6. 25, 50; 8. 10, 14, 38; 9. 8, [24];
10. 30; 11. 11; 13. 26; 14. 7, 14, 17, 18, 20, 33, 43, 43, 48, 54,
67; 15. 17, [28], 31; 16. [10]; Luke 1. 28, 39, 66; 2. 36, 51;
5. 29, 31, 34; 6. 3, 4, 17; 7. 36; 8. 13, [45]; 9. 49; 10. 17;
11. 7, 23, 23, 31, 32; 12. 13, 46, 58; 13. 1; 14. 9, 31; 15. 29,
30, 31; 17. 15, 20; 21. 27; 22. 11, 15, 21, 28, 33, 52, 53, 59;
23. 43; 24. 29, 30, 52; John 3. 2, 22, 26; 4. 27, 27; 6. 3, 66;
7. 33; 8. 29; 9. 37, 40; 11. 16, 31, 54; 12. 8, 17, [35]; 13. 8,
[18,] 33; 14. 9, 16, 30; 15. 27; 16. 4, 32; 17. 12, 24; 18. 2, 3, 5,
[18], 26; 19. 18, 40; 20. 7, 24, 26; Ac. 1. [4,] 26; 2. 28; 4. 29,
31; 7. 9, 38, 45; 9. 19, 28, 39; 10. 38; 11. 21; 13. 17; 14. 23,
27; 15. 4, 35; 17. 11; 18. 10; 20. 18, 19, [24], 31, 34; 24. 1,
3, [7], 18, 18; 25. 12, 23; 26. 12; 27. 10, 24; 28. 31; Rom. 12.
15, 15, 18; 15. 10, 33; 16. 20, [24]; 1 Co. 6. 6, 7; 7. 12, 13;
16. 11, 12, 23, 24; 2 Co. 6. 15, 16; 7. 15; 8. 4, 18; 13. 11, 14;
Gal. 2. 1, 12; 4. 25, 30; 6. 18; Eph. 4. 2, 2, 25; 6. 5, 7, 23,
24; Phil. 1. 4; 2. 12, 29; 4. 3, 6, 9, 23; Col. 1. 11; 4. 18;
1 Th. 1. 6; 3. 13; 5. 28; 2 Th. 1. 7, 7; 3. 12, 16, 18; 1 Ti. 1.
14; 2. 9, 15; 3. 4; 4. 3, 4, 14; 6. 6, 21; 2 Ti. 2. 10, 22; 4. 11,
11, 22, [22]; Titus 2. 15; 3. 15, 15; Phm. 25; Heb. 5. 7; 7.
21; 9. 19; 10. 22; 11. 9, 31; 12. 14, 17, 28; 13. 17, 23, 25;
1 Pe. 3. 15; 1 Jo. 1. 3, 3, 3, 6, 7; 2. 19; 2 Jo. 2, 3; Rev. 1.
7. 12; 2. 22; 3. 4, 20, 20, 21, 21; 4. 1; 6. [8]; 9. 8; 12. 9,
17; 13. 4, [7]; 14. 1, 4; 17. 1, 2, 12, 14, 14; 18. 3, 9;
19. 20; 20. 4, [6]; 21. 3, 3, 3, 9, 15; 22. 12, 21.

28. *Along side of, with, among*, παρά (*dat.*) *para*.
Matt 19. 26 With men this is impossible; but with G.
21. 25 they reasoned [with] themselves, saying
22. 25 there were with us seven brethren: and
Mark 10. 27 With men..but not with God: [for with]
Luke 1. 30 Fear not..thou hast found favour with G.
1. 37 with God nothing shall be impossible
2. 52 Jesus increased..in favour with God and
11. 37 Pharisee besought him to dine with him
18. 27 impossible with men are possible with God
19. 7 he was gone to be guest with a man that
John 1. 39 They came..and abode with him that day
4. 40 besought him that he would tarry with
8. 38 seen with my Father..seen with your fa.
14. 17 he dwelleth with you, and shall be in you
14. 23 come unto him, and make our abode with
14. 25 have I spoken..being..present with you
17. 5 with thine own self..with thee before the
Acts 9. 43 he tarried many days in Joppa with one
10. 6 He lodgeth with one Simon a tanner, wh
18. 3 of the same craft, he abode with them, and
18. 20 they desired (him) to tarry longer time [w.]
21. 7 we..saluted the brethren, and abode with
21. 8 entered into the house..and abode with
21. 16 an old disciple, with whom we should lo.
26. 8 Why..incredible with you, that God sho.
Rom. 2. 11 For there is no respect of persons with God
9. 14 unrighteousness with God? God forbid
1 Co. 3. 19 the wisdom of this world is foolishness
7. 24 every man, wherein he is called..abide w.
2 Co. 1. 17 that with me there should be yea yea, and
Eph. 6. 9 neither is there respect of persons with
2 Th. 1. 6 Seeing..a righteous thing with God to re.
2 Ti. 4. 13 The cloak that I left at Troas with Carpus
Jas. 1. 17 Father of lights, with whom is no variabl.
1 Pe. 2. 20 ye take it patiently, this (is) acceptable
2 Pe. 3. 8 one day (is) with the Lord as a thousand

29. *About, concerning*, περί (*gen.*) *peri*.
Mark 10. 41 they began to be much displeased with

30. *The things concerning me*, τὰ περὶ ἐμέ *ta peri*.
Phil. 2. 23 so soon as I shall see how it will go with

31. *Toward, by, near*, πρός (*acc.*) *pros*.
Matt 13. 56 And his sisters, are they not all with us?
26. 55 I sat daily [with] you teaching in the tem.
Mark 6. 3 are not his sisters here with us? And they
9. 10 they kept that saying with themselves, qu.
9. 16 asked the scribes, What question ye with
9. 19 O faithless..how long shall I be with you?

Mark 11. 31 they reasoned with themselves, saying, If
14. 49 I was daily with you in the temple teac.
Luke 6. 11 communed one with another what they
9. 41 how long shall I be with you, and suffer
18. 11 The Pharisee stood and prayed thus with
20. 5 they reasoned with themselves saying, If
John 1. 1 the Word was with God, and the Word
1. 2 The same was in the beginning with God
Acts 2. 47 Praising God, and having favour with all
3. 25 of the covenant which God made with our
11. 2 they..of the circumcision contended with
15. 2 had..dissension and disputation with th.
17. 17 disputed he..with them that met with him
24. 12 they neither found me..disputing with
Rom. 5. 1 we have peace with God through our Lord
8. 18 with the glory which shall be revealed in
1 Co. 2. 3 I was with you in weakness, and in fear
16. 6 that I will abide, yea, and winter with
16. 7 I trust to tarry a while with you, if the
16. 10 see that he may be with you without fear
2 Co. 5. 8 We are..willing..to be present with the
6. 14 what communion hath light with darkn.
6. 15 what concord hath Christ with Belial? or
11. 9 when I was present with you, and wanted
Gal. 1. 18 to see Peter, and abode with him fifteen
2. 5 that the truth..might continue with you
4. 18 and not only when I am present with you
4. 20 I desire to be present with you now, and
1 Th. 3. 4 when we were with you, we told you bef.
2 Th. 2. 5 when I was yet with you, I told you these
3. 1 word..may..be glorified, even as..with
3. 10 For even when we were with you, this we
Phm. 13 Whom I would have retained with me, th.
Heb. 4. 13 unto the eyes of him with whom we have
10. 16 This (is) the covenant that I will make w.
1 Jo. 1. 2 that eternal life which was with the Father
2. 1 we have an advocate with the Father, J.

32. *With, along with,* σύν *sun.*
Matt 25. 27 I should have received mine own with us.
26. 35 Though I should die with thee, yet will I
27. 38 Then were there two thieves crucified w.
Mark 2. 26 and gave also to them which were with
4. 10 they that were about him with the twelve
8. 34 when he had called the people..with his
9. 4 there appeared unto them Elias with M.
15. 27 with him they crucify two thieves; the
See also Luke 1. 56; 2. 5, 13; 5. 9, 19; 7. 6, 12; 8. 1, 38; 9. 32; 19. 23; 20. 1; 22. 14, 56; 23. 11, 32, [35]; 24. [1], 10, 24, 29, 33, 44; John 18. 1; 21. 3; Acts 1. 14, [14, 17], 22; 2. 14; 3. 4, 8; 4. 13, 14, 27; 5. 1, 17, 21, 26; 8. 20, 31; 10. 2, 20, 23; 13. 7; 14. 4, 4, 5, 13, 20, 28; 15. 22, 22, 25; 16. 3; 17. 34; 18. 8, 18; 19. 38; 20. 36; 21. 5, 16, 18, 24, 26, 29; 22. 9; 23. 15, 27, 32; 24. 24; 25. 23; 26. 13; 27. 2; 28. 16; Rom. 6. 8; 8. 32; 16. 14, 15; 1 Co. 1. 2; 5. 4; 10. 13; 11. 32; 15. 10; 16. 4, 19; 2 Co. 1. 1, 21; 4. 14; 8. [19]; 9. 4; 13. 4; Gal. 1. 2; 2. 3; 3. 9; 5. 24; Eph. 3. 18; 4. 31; Phil. 1. 1, 23; 2. 22; 4. 21; Col. 2. 5, 13, 20; 3. 3, 4, 9; 4. 9; 1 Th. 4. 14, 17, 17; 5. 10; Jas. 1. 11; 2 Pe. 1. 18.

33. *From under, by, from,* ὑπό *(gen.) hupo.*
Matt. 8. 24 that the ship was covered with the waves
11. 7 went..to see? A reed shaken with the w.
14. 24 tossed with waves: for the wind was co.
Luke 6. 18 they that were vexed [with] unclean spi.
7. 24 went..to see? A reed shaken with the w.?
8. 14 are choked with cares, and riches, and pl
21. 20 ye shall see Jerusalem compassed with
Acts 5. 16 them which were vexed with unclean sp.
17. 25 Neither is worshipped with men's hands
27. 41 was broken with the violence of the wav.
Jas. 3. 4; 2 Pe. 2. 7; 2. 17; Rev. 6. 8.

34. *To you,* ὑμῖν *humin,* Jo. 14. 27; Acts 14. 15.

35. *To have,* ἔχω *echō,* Acts 27. 39.

[*See also* Abide, abounding, accord, affliction, agree, away, be, bear, beasts, bound, brought, buried, charge, child, cieled, clothe, clothed, cloud, come, commune, communicate, company, compare, compassed, compassion, confer, consent, consort, consume continue, crucify, deal, drink, dwellers, entangle, feast, feed, filled, friendship, go, gird, indignation, labour, lie, lien, lieth, lying, meddle, meddled, meet, mixed, occupy, pleased, reason, rejoice, rise, run, satisfied satisfy, send, sit, sit at meat, smite, speak, speed, spring up, stand, suffer, take, take away, talk, travel, work, young.]

WITH child —
Having in the womb, ἐν γαστρὶ ἔχουσα *en gastri.*
Matt. 1. 18 she was found with child of the Holy Gh.
1. 23 a virgin shall be with child, and shall br.
24. 19 woe unto them that are with child, and
Mark 13. 17 woe to them that are with child, and to
Luke 21. 23 woe unto them that are with child, and
1 Th. 5. 3 cometh..as travail upon a woman with c.
Rev. 12. 2 she being with child cried, travailing in

WITHAL —
1. *With them,* בָּהֵמָּה *ba-hemah.*
Exod 30. 4 be for places for the staves to bear it wi.

2. *With them,* בָּהֵן *ba-hen.*
Exod 25. 29 shalt make..bowls thereof, to cover with
37. 16 his covers to cover withal, (of) pure gold
Lev. 11. 21 which have legs..to leap withal upon the

3. *Together,* יַחַד יַחְדָּו *yachad, yachdav.*
Psa. 141. 10 into their own nets, whilst that I withal
Prov 22. 18 For..they shall withal be fitted in thy lips

4. *With,* עִם *im.*
1 Sa. 16. 12 Now he (was) ruddy..withal of a beauti.

5. *Together with,* ἅμα *hama.*
Col. 4. 3 Withal praying also for us, that God wo.

1 Ti. 5. 13 withal they learn (to be) idle, wa. Phm. 22

6. *And, also,* καὶ *kai,* Acts 25. 27; 1 Ti. 5. 13.

WITHDRAW (far, self), to —
1. *To gather up or together,* אָסַף *asaph.*
1 Sa. 14. 19 Saul said unto the priest, Withdraw thine
Joel 2. 10 and the stars shall withdraw their shini.
3. 15 and the stars shall withdraw their shini.

2. *To be gathered up or together,* אָסַף *asaph,* 2.
Isa. 60. 20 neither shall thy moon withdraw itself

3. *To diminish, withdraw,* גָּרַע *gara.*
Job 36. 7 He withdraweth not his eyes from the ri.

4. *To arm, withdraw, draw away,* חָלַץ *chalats.*
Hos. 5. 6 LORD..hath withdrawn himself from them

5. *To withdraw,* חָמַק *chamaq.*
Song 5. 6 but my beloved had withdrawn himself

6. *To cause to rest,* נוּחַ *nuach,* 5.
Eccl. 7. 18 yea, also from this withdraw not thine ha.

7. *To make rare or precious,* יָקַר *yaqar,* 5.
Prov 25. 17 Withdraw thy foot from thy neighbour's

8. *To drive or force away,* נָדַח *nadach,* 5.
Deut 13. 13 have withdrawn the inhabitants of their

9. *To give a refractory shoulder,* נָתַן כָּתֵף סוֹרֶרֶת *[nathan].*
Neh. 9. 29 withdrew the shoulder, and hardened the.

10. *To (cause to) turn aside,* סוּר *sur,* 5.
Job 33. 17 that he may withdraw man (from his) pur.

11. *To put far off,* רָחַק *rachaq,* 5.
Job 13. 21 Withdraw thine hand far from me, and

12. *To cause to turn back,* שׁוּב *shub,* 5.
Job 9. 13 (If) God will not withdraw his anger, the
Psa. 74. 11 Why withdrawest thou thy hand, even thy
Lam. 2. 8 he hath not withdrawn his hand from de.
Eze. 18. 8 hath withdrawn his hand from iniquity
20. 22 I withdrew mine hand, and wrought for

13. *To give place again, withdraw,* ἀναχωρέω.
Matt. 12. 15 when Jesus knew..he withdrew himself
Mark 3. 7 Jesus withdrew himself with his disciples

14. *To draw away,* ἀποσπάω *apospaō.*
Luke 22. 41 he was withdrawn from them about a sto.

15. *To set, put or place away,* ἀφίστημι *aphistēmi.*
1 Ti. 6. 5 [corrupt minds..from such withdraw th.]

16. *To withdraw self, avoid, beware of,* στέλλομαι.
2 Th. 3. 6 that ye withdraw yourselves from every

17. *To send under, withdraw,* ὑποστέλλω *hupostellō.*
Gal 2. 12 withdrew and separated himself, fearing

18. *To give place under, secretly, quietly,* ὑποχωρέω.
Luke 5. 16 withdrew himself into the wilderness, and

WITHER, be withered (away), to —
1. *To be dry, dried up,* יָבֵשׁ *yabesh.*
Job 8. 12 Whilst..not cut down, it withereth bef.
Psa. 90. 6 in the evening it is cut down, and wither.
102. 4 My heart is smitten, and withered like gr.
102. 11 My days (are) like a shadow..I am with.
129. 6 grass..which withereth afore it groweth
Isa. 15. 6 the nay is withered away, the grass faileth
19. 7 every thing sown by the brooks, shall wi.
27. 11 When the boughs thereof are withered, th.
40. 7, 8 The grass withereth, the flower fadeth
40. 24 they shall wither, and the whirlwind sha.
Jer. 12. 4 How long shall..the herbs of..field wither
Lam. 4. 8 their skin..it is withered, it is become like
Eze. 17. 9 shall he not..cut off the fruit..that it wi.?
17. 9 it shall wither in all the leaves of her sp.
17. 10 shall it not utterly wither..it shall wither
19. 12 her strong rods were broken and withered
Joel 1. 12 all the trees of the field are withered, bec.
1. 17 barns are broken down..corn is withered
Amos 1. 2 And he said..the top of Carmel shall wit.
4. 7 the piece whereupon it rained not withered
Jon. 4. 7 a worm..smote the gourd that it withered

2. *To (cause to) dry up,* יָבֵשׁ *yabesh,* 5.
Joel 1. 12 joy is withered away from the sons of men
1. 17 broken down; for the corn is withered

3. *To fade, wear away,* נָבֵל *nabel.*
Psa. 1. 3 his leaf also shall not wither; and what.
37. 2 cut down..and wither as the green herb

4. *To be hard, dry, withered, lean,* צָנַם *tsanam.*
Gen. 41. 23 And, behold, seven ears, withered, thin

5. *To wither, pine, be weak,* קָמַל *qamal.*
Isa. 19. 6 dried up: the reeds and flags shall wither

6. *To dry up, wither,* ξηραίνω *xērainō.*
Matt 13. 6 because they had no root; they withered a.
21. 19 And presently the fig tree withered away
21. 20 How soon is the fig tree withered away
Mark 3. 1 there was a man there which had a with.
3. 3 he saith unto the man [which had the wi.]
4. 6 and because it had no root, it withered
11. 21 fig tree which thou cursedst is with. away
Luke 8. 6 as soon as it was sprung up, it withered
John 15. 6 he is cast forth as a branch, and is with.
Jas. 1. 11 risen with a burning heat, but it withereth
1 Pe. 1. 24 The grass withereth, and the flower thereof

7. *Dry, withered,* ξηρός *xēros.*
Matt 12. 10 there was a man which had (his) hand wi.
Luke 6. 6 a man whose right hand was withered
6. 8 said to the man which had the withered
John 5. 3 of impotent folk, of blind, halt, withered

WITHERETH, whose fruit —
Withering autumnal fruit, φθινοπωρινός *phthinop.*
Jude 12 trees whose fruit withereth, without fruit

WITHHOLD (self), be withholden, to —
1. *To be cut off,* בָּצַר *batsar,* 2.
Job 42. 2 no thought can be withholden from thee

2. *To take a pledge, bind on,* חָבַל *chabal.*
Eze. 18. 16 hath not withholden the pledge, neither

3. *To keep back, withhold,* חָשַׂךְ *chasak.*
Gen. 20. 6 I also withheld thee from sinning against
22. 12, 16 hast not withheld thy son, thine only
Prov. 11. 24 (there is) that withholdeth more than is

4. *To cause to rest,* נוּחַ *nuach,* 5.
Eccl. 11. 6 in the evening withhold not thine hand

5. *To shut, restrain,* כָּלָא *kala.*
Gen. 23. 6 none of us shall withhold from thee his se.
Psa. 40. 11 Withhold not thou thy tender mercies from

6. *To withhold, keep back,* מָנַע *mana.*
Gen. 30. 2 who hath withheld from thee the fruit of
1 Sa. 25. 26 the LORD hath withholden thee from com.
2 Sa. 13. 13 for he will not withhold me from thee
Neh. 9. 20 withheldest not thy manna from their mo.
Job 22. 7 thou hast withholden bread from the hu.
31. 16 If I have withheld the poor from (their) de.
Psa. 21. 2 hast not withholden the request of his lips
84. 11 no good (thing) will he withhold from them
Prov. 3. 27 Withhold not good from them to whom
11. 26 He that withholdeth corn, the people shall
23. 13 Withhold not correction from the child
Eccl. 2. 10 I withheld not my heart from any joy, for
Jer. 2. 25 Withhold thy foot from being unshod, and
5. 25 your sins have withholden good (things) fr.
Amos 4. 7 I have withholden the rain from you, when

7. *To be withheld, kept back,* מָנַע *mana,* 2.
Job 38. 15 and from the wicked their light is withho.
Jer. 3. 3 the showers have been withholden, and
Joel 1. 13 the drink offering is withholden from the

8. *To keep in, restrain, detain, retain,* עָצַר *atsar.*
Job 4. 2 who can withhold himself from speaking
12. 15 he withholdeth the waters, and they dry

9. *To hold down or fast,* κατέχω *katechō.*
2 Th. 2. 6 ye know what withholdeth that he might

WITHIN (me, self, thee, from)—
1. *Unto,* אֶל *el.*
Lev. 26. 25 when ye are gathered together within yo.

2. *Between,* בֵּין *ben.*
Job 24. 11 (Which) make oil within their walls, (and)

3. *In the belly,* בְּבֶטֶן *be-beten.* Prov. 22. 18.

3a. *Within me (of my belly),* בְּטְנִי *[beten].* Job 32. 18.

4. *From within,* מִבַּיִת *mib-bayith.*
Gen. 6. 14 shalt pitch it within and without with pi.
39. 11 none of the men of the house there with.
Exod 25. 11 within and without shalt thou overlay it
26. 33 thou mayest bring in thither within the
37. 2 he overlaid it with pure gold within and
Lev. 14. 41 cause the house to be scraped within round
16. 2 into the holy (place) within the veil before
16. 12 take a censer..and bring (it) within the
16. 15 bring his blood within the veil, and do
Num 18. 7 every thing of the altar, and within the
1 Ki. 6. 15 he built the walls of the house within wi.
6. 16 he even built (them) for it within, (even)
7. 8 his house..(had) another court within the
7. 9 sawed with saws, within and without, ev.
7. 31 the mouth of it within the chapiter and
2 Ki. 6. 30 behold, (he had) sackcloth within upon his
Eze. 1. 27 the appearance of fire round about with.
7. 15 and the pestilence and the famine within
40. 7 by the porch of the gate within, (was) one
40. 8 measured..the porch of the gate within
40. 43 within (were) hooks, an hand broad, faste.
41. 9 place of the side chambers that (were) wit.
44. 17 in the gates of the inner court, and within

5. *From behind, from through,* מִבַּעַד *mib-bead.*
Song 4. 1 thou (hast) doves' eyes within thy locks
4. 3 a piece of a pomegranate within thy locks
6. 7 As a piece of a pomegranate..within thy

6. *From inner chambers,* מֵחֲדָרִים *me-chadarim.*
Deut. 32. 25 The sword without, and terror within, sh.

7. *In the bosom,* בְּחֵיק *be-cheq.*
Job 19. 27 (though) my reins be consumed within me

8. *During, until,* עַד *ad.*
Dan. 6. 12 shall ask (a petition)..within thirty days

9. *With,* עִמָּד *immad.*
Job 6. 4 the arrows of the Almighty (are) within

10. *(On the) face,* פָּנִים *panim.*
Eze. 2. 10 and it (was) written within and without

11. *Within, inner part,* פְּנִים *penim.*
Lev. 10. 18 the blood of it was not brought in wit..n
1 Ki. 6. 18 the cedar of the house within (was) carv.
6. 19 the oracle he prepared in the house with.
6. 21 Solomon overlaid the house within with
6. 29 palm trees and open flowers, within and
6. 30 he overlaid with gold, within and without
2 Ki. 7. 11 and they told (it) to the king's house wit.
2 Ch. 3. 4 And he overlaid it within with pure gold
Psa. 45. 13 The king's daughter (is) all glorious with.
Eze. 40. 16 to their posts within the gate round abo.

12. *Inner part, within,* פְּנִימִי *penimi.*
Eze. 41. 17 by all the wall round about, within and
13. *In the heart, midst, centre of,* בְּקֶרֶב *be-qereb.*
Gen. 18. 12 Sarah laughed within herself, saying, Af.
25. 22 the children struggled together within
Deut 28. 43 The stranger that (is) within thee shall get
1 Sa. 25. 37 his heart died within him, and he became
Job 20. 14 (Yet) his meat..(is) the gall of asps within
Psa. 36. 1 transgression of the wicked saith within
39. 3 My heart was hot within me; while I was
51. 10 Create..and renew a right spirit within
55. 4 My heart is sore pained within me, and
94. 19 In the multitude of my thoughts within
101. 2 I will walk within my house with a perf.
101. 7 that worketh deceit shall not dwell within
103. 1 all that is within me, (bless) his holy na
109. 22 I (am) poor..my heart is wounded within
147. 13 he hath blessed thy children within thee
Prov 26. 24 He that hateth..layeth up deceit within
Isa. 26. 9 with my spirit within me will I seek thee
63. 11 where (is) he that put his Holy Spirit wi.
Jer. 4. 14 long shall thy vain thoughts lodge within
23. 9 Mine heart within me is broken because
Lam. 1. 20 mine heart is turned within me; for I ha.
Eze. 11. 19 I will put a new spirit within you; and I
36. 26 a new spirit will I put within you; and I
36. 27 I will put my spirit within you, and cause
Zeph. 3. 3 Her princes within her (are) roaring lions
Zech. 12. 1 and formeth the spirit of man within him
14. *In the midst of,* בְּתוֹךְ *be-thok.*
Gen. 9. 21 and he was uncovered within his tent
18. 24 Peradventure there be fifty righteous wi.
18. 26 If I find in Sodom fifty righteous within
Deut 23. 10 he shall not come within the camp
Josh. 19. 1 their inheritance was within the inherit.
19. 9 had their inheritance within the inherit.
21. 41 All the cities of the Levites within the p.
Judg. 7. 16 empty pitchers, and lamps within the pi.
9. 51 there was a strong tower within the city
2 Sa. 7. 2 the ark of God dwelleth within curtains
1 Ki. 6. 27 he set the cherubim within the inner hou.
Neh. 4. 22 Let every one with his servant lodge wit.
6. 10 Let us meet together..within the temple
Job 20. 13 forsake it not, but keep it still within his
Psa. 40. 8 I delight to do thy will..thy law (is) within
40. 10 I have not hid thy righteousness within
143. 4 Therefore..my heart within me is desol.
Eze. 3. 24 said unto me, Go, shut thyself within thine
12. 24 nor flattering divination within the house
15. *Through, during,* διά *(gen.) dia.*
Mark 14. 58 within three days I will build another
16. *In, among,* ἐν *en.*
Matt. 3. 9 think not to say within yourselves, We
9. 3 certain of the scribes said within themse.
9. 21 she said within herself, If I may but to.
Mark 2. 8 that they so reasoned within themselves
Luke 3. 8 begin not to say within yourselves, We
7. 39 he spake within himself, saying, This m.
7. 49 began to say within themselves, Who is
12. 17 he thought within himself, saying, What
16. 3 the steward said within himself, What
18. 4 afterward he said within himself, Though
19. 44 lay thee even..and thy children within
24. 32 Did not our heart burn within us, while
Rom. 8. 23 even we ourselves groan within ourselves
17. *Within,* ἐντός *entos.*
Matt 23. 26 cleanse first that..within the cup and pl.
Luke 17. 21 behold, the kingdom of God is within you
18. *Into, in, within,* ἔσω *esō.*
John 20. 26 after eight days, again his disciples were w.
Acts 5. 23 when we had opened, we found no man wi.
1 Co. 5. 12 For..do not ye judge them that are within?
19. *From within,* ἔσωθεν *esōthen.*
Matt 23. 25 within they are full of extortion and exc.
23. 27 but are within full of dead (men's) bones
23. 28 within ye are full of hypocrisy and iniqu.
Mark 7. 21 For from within, out of the heart of men
7. 23 All these evil things come from within
Luke 11. 7 And he from within shall answer and say
11. 40 did not he..make that which is within
2 Co. 7. 5 without (were) fightings, within (were)
Rev. 4. 8 the four beasts..(were) full of eyes within
5. 1 I saw..a book written within and on the
20. *Inner, interior,* ἐσώτερος *esōteros.*
Heb. 6. 19 which entereth into that within the veil
21. *Toward, among,* πρός *(acc.) pros.*
Mark 14. 4 there were some that had indignation wi.

WITHOUT, (from)—
1. *Behind,* אָחוֹר *achor.*
Eze. 2. 10 and it (was) written within and without
2. *There is not,* אַיִן *ayin.*
Gen. 41. 49 until he left numbering: for (it was) wit.
3. *In cessation of,* בְּאֶפֶס *be-ephes.*
Job 7. 6 than a weaver's shuttle, and are spent w.
Dan. 8. 25 stand up..but he shall be broken without
4. *Unto from the place of,* אֶל־מִבֵּית *el-mib-beth.*
2 Ki. 11. 15 said..Have her forth without the ranges
5. *Without,* בְּלִי *beli.*
Job 8. 11 Can the rush..can the flag grow without
6. *In not, without,* בִּבְלִי *bi-beli.*
Job 35. 16 he multiplieth words without knowledge
7. *So as not, without,* לִבְלִי *li-beli.*
Job 41. 33 there is not his like, who is made without
8. *Except, without, save, besides,* בִּלְעֲדֵי *bilade.*
Gen. 41. 44 I (am) Pharaoh, and without thee shall
2 Ki. 18. 25 Am I..come up without the LORD against
Isa. 36. 10 am I..come up without the LORD against
Jer. 44. 19 did we make her cakes..without our men?
9. *Without, save, not, besides,* בִּלְתִּי *bilti.*
Isa. 10. 4 Without me they shall bow down under
Dan. 11. 18 without his own reproach he shall cause
10. *So as not,* לְבִלְתִּי *le-bilti.*
Judg. 2. 23 LORD left those nations, without driving
11. *Outside, without,* חוּץ *chuts.*
Gen. 6. 14 shalt pitch it within and without with pi.
9. 22 Ham..saw..and told his two brethren w.
19. 16 they brought him forth, and set him wit.
24. 11 he made his camels to kneel down with.
24. 31 Come in..wherefore standest thou with.?
Exod 25. 11 within and without shalt thou overlay it
26. 35 thou shalt set the table without the veil
27. 21 In the tabernacle..without the veil, wh.
29. 14 shalt thou burn with fire without the ca.
33. 7 pitched it without the camp..without the
37. 2 overlaid it with pure gold within and wi.
40. 22 he put the table in the tent..without the
Lev. 4. 12 the whole bullock shall he carry forth wi.
4. 21 he shall carry forth the bullock without
6. 11 carry forth the ashes without the camp
8. 17 the bullock..he burnt with fire without
9. 11 the hide he burnt with fire without the
13. 46 without the camp (shall) his habitation
14. 40 cast them into an unclean place without
14. 41 pour out the dust that they scrape off wi.
16. 27 shall (one) carry forth without the camp
24. 3 Without the veil of the testimony, in the
24. 14 Bring forth him that hath cursed without
Num. 5. 3 without the camp shall ye put them that
5. 4 Israel did so, and put them out without
15. 35 shall stone him with stones without the
15. 36 all the congregation brought him without
19. 3 that he may bring her forth without the
19. 9 lay..up without the camp in a clean place
31. 13 went forth to meet them without the ca.
31. 19 And do ye abide without the camp seven
35. 5 ye shall measure from without the city on
35. 27 And the revenger of blood find him with.
Deut 23. 12 Thou shalt have a place also without the
25. 5 the wife of the dead shall not marry wit.
32. 25 The sword without, and terror within, sh.
Josh. 6. 23 and left them without the camp of Israel
1 Ki. 6. 6 for without (in the wall) of the house he
7. 9 sawed with saws, within and without, even
8. 8 they were not seen without: and there
2 Ki. 10. 24 Jehu appointed fourscore men without
23. 4 he burned them without Jerusalem, in the
23. 6 he brought out the grove..without Jeru.
2 Ch. 5. 9 the ends of the staves..were not seen wi.
24. 8 set it without at the gate of the house of
32. 3 waters of the fountains which (were) wit.
32. 5 built..all the wall..and another wall wi.
Ezra 10. 13 we are not able to stand without, neither
Neh. 13. 20 lodged without Jerusalem once or twice
Psa. 31. 11 they that did see me without fled from me
Prov. 1. 20 Wisdom crieth without; she uttereth her
7. 12 Now..without, now in the street, and li.
22. 13 a lion without, I shall be slain in the str.
24. 27 Prepare thy work without, and make it
Song 8. 1 I should find thee without, I would kiss
Isa. 33. 7 Behold, their valiant ones shall cry with.
Jer. 9. 21 entered..to cut off the children from wi.
21. 4 which besiege you without the walls, and
Eze. 7. 15 The sword (is) without, and the pestilence
40. 19 unto the fore front of the inner court wi.
40. 40 at the side without, as one goeth up to the
40. 44 without the inner gate (were) the chamb.
41. 9 which (was) for the side chamber without
41. 17 even unto the inner house, and without
41. 25 planks upon the face of the porch without
42. 7 the wall that (was) without over against
43. 21 he shall burn it..without the sanctuary
46. 2 by the way of the porch of (that) gate w.
47. 2 led me about the way without unto the
Hos. 7. 1 (and) the troop of robbers spoileth without
12. *Outward, without,* חִיצוֹן *chitson.*
1 Ki. 6. 29 the walls of the house..within and with.
6. 30 the floor of the house..within and without
2 Ki. 16. 18 the king's entry without, turned he from
2 Ch. 33. 14 Now after this he built a wall without the
Eze. 41. 17 all the wall round about, within and wit.
13. *Baldness in the front,* גַּבַּחַת *gabbachath.*
Lev. 13. 55 inward, (whether) it (be) bare within or w.
14. *That (is) not,* דִּי־לָא *di la.*
Ezra 7. 22 baths of oil, and salt without prescribing
15. *Not,* לֹא *lo.*
2 Sa. 23. 4 a morning without clouds; (as) the tend.
2 Ki. 25. 16 brass of all these vessels was without we.
16. *In not, without,* בְּלֹא *be-lo.*
Num 35. 22 if he thrust him suddenly without enmity
Job 8. 11 Can the rush grow up without mire? can
17. *So that not, without,* לְלֹא *le-lo.*
2 Ch. 15. 3 without..true God..without..priest..w.
Job 26. 2 How hast thou helped (him that is) with.
18. *Without, away from,* ἄνευ *aneu.*
Matt 10. 29 of them shall not fall on the ground wit.
1 Pe. 3. 1 they also may without the word be won
4. 9 Use hospitality one to another without
19. *In the absence of,* ἄτερ *ater.*
Luke 22. 35 When I sent you without purse, and scrip.
20. *Out of,* ἐκ *ek.*
Jas. 2. 18 show me thy faith without thy works, and
21. *Outside, without, except, besides,* ἐκτός *ektos.*
1 Co. 6. 18 Every sin that a man doeth is without the
22. *Outside, without,* ἔξω *exō.*
Matt 12. 46 (his) mother and his brethren stood with.
12. 47 thy mother and thy brethren stand with.
26. 69 Now Peter sat without in the palace, and
Mark 1. 45 but was without in desert places; and they
3. 31 and, standing without, sent unto him
3. 32 thy mother and thy brethren without seek
4. 11 but unto them that are without, all (these)
11. 4 found the colt tied by the door without
Luke 1. 10 the whole multitude..were praying with.
13. 25 ye begin to stand without, and to 8. 20.
John 18. 16 But Peter stood at the door without
20. 11 Mary stood [without] at the sepulchre we.
Acts 5. 23 the keepers standing [without] before the
1 Co. 5. 12 have I to do to judge them..that are wi.?
5. 13 But them that are without God judgeth
Col. 4. 5 Walk in wisdom toward them that are wi.
1 Th. 4. 12 walk honestly toward them that are wit.
Heb. 13. 11 the bodies..are burnt without the camp
13. 12 Wherefore Jesus..suffered without the g.
13. 13 Let us go forth..unto him without the ca.
Rev. 14. 20 the wine press was trodden without the
22. 15 For [without] (are) dogs, and sorcerers, and
23. *From without, externally,* ἔξωθεν *exōthen.*
Mark 7. 15 There is nothing from without a man
7. 18 whatsoever thing from without entereth
Luke 11. 40 did not he that made that which is with.
2 Co. 7. 5 without (were) fightings, within (were) fe.
1 Ti. 3. 7 have a good report of them which are wi.
Rev. 11. 2 the court [which is without] the temple
24. *Not with,* οὐ μετά *(gen.) ou meta.*
Acts 5. 26 the captain..brought them without viole.
25. *Not,* μή *mē.*
Acts 9. 9 he was three days without sight, and ne.
26. *Outside, except, without,* παρεκτός *parektos.*
2 Co. 11. 28 Besides those things that are without, that
27. *Apart, apart from,* χωρίς *chōris.*
Matt 13. 34 without a parable spake he not unto them.
Mark 4. 34 without a parable spake he not unto them
Luke 6. 49 is like a man that without a foundation
John 1. 3 without him was not any thing made that
15. 5 I am the vine..without me ye can do not.
Rom. 3. 21 the righteousness of God without the law
3. 28 a man is justified by faith without the d.
4. 6 unto whom God imputeth righteousness w.
7. 8 For without the law sin (was) dead
7. 9 For I was alive without the law once, but
10. 14 how shall they hear without a preacher?
1 Co. 4. 8 ye have reigned as kings without us, and
11. 11 neither is the man without the woman
11. 11 neither the woman without the man
Eph. 2. 12 That at that time ye were without Christ
Phil. 2. 14 Do all things without murmurings and
1 Ti. 2. 8 lifting up holy hands, without wrath and
5. 21 that thou observe these things without pr.
Phm. 14 But without thy mind would I do nothing
Heb. 4. 15 but was in all points tempted..without sin
7. 7 without..contradiction, the less is blessed
7. 20 And inasmuch as not without an oath
7. 21 For those priests were made without an
9. 7 priest alone once every year, not without
9. 18 neither the first..was dedicated without
9. 22 without shedding of blood is no remission
9. 28 the second time without sin unto salvat.
10. 28 He that despised Moses' law died without
11. 6 But without faith (it is) impossible to pl.
11. 40 that they without us should not be made
12. 8 if ye be without chastisement, whereof all
12. 14 holiness, without which no man shall see
Jas. 2. 20 thou know, O vain man, that faith without
2. 26 For as the body without the spirit is dead
2. 26 so faith without works is dead also

[*See also* Affection, blame, blemish, cause, care, ceasing, charge, children, come, controversy, coast covetousness, descent, dissimulation, destruction, doubt, effect, end, excuse, fail, father, fear, form, from, fruit, gainsaying, god, hands, honour, hypocrisy, leaven, life, measure, mercy, mixture, mother, offence, partiality rebuke, repentance, signification, sin, spot, strength towns, understanding, wages, water, wavering, witness.]

WITHOUT cause, any delay, a seam (to be) —
1. *In cessation of,* בְּאֶפֶס *be-ephes.*
Isa. 52. 4 Assyrian oppressed them without cause
2. *To turn aside,* סוּר *sur.*
Prov 11. 22 a fair woman which is without discretion
3. *To make no delay,* ἀναβολὴν μηδεμίαν ποιέω.
Acts 25. 17 without any delay on the morrow I sat on
4. *Without a seam,* ἄρραφος *arrhaphos.*
John 19. 23 the coat was without seam; woven from

WITHS —
A cord, string, יֶתֶר *yether.*
Judg 16. 7 If they bind me with seven green withs
16. 8 seven green withs which had not been
16. 9 he brake the withs, as a thread of tow is

WITHSTAND, to —
1. *To strengthen self,* חָזַק *chazaq,* 7.
2 Ch. 13. 7 when Rehoboam..could not withstand th.
13. 8 ye think to withstand the kingdom of th.

2. *To set up self, withstand,* יָצַב *yatsab,* 7.
2 Ch.20. 6 so that none is able to withstand thee

3. *To stand against* or *before,*(נֶגֶד, לִפְנֵי) עָמַד עַל [*amad*].
2 Ch.26. 18 they withstood Uzziah the king, and said
Esth. 9. 2 no man could withstand them ; for the
Eccl. 4. 12 if one prevail..two shall withstand him
Dan. 10. 13 prince of the kingdom of Persia withstood
11. 15 shall not withstand..strength to withsta.

4. *One opposing, an opponent,* שָׂטָן *satan.*
Num.22. 32 I went out to withstand thee, because (thy)

5. *To set or place against,* ἀνθίστημι *anthistēmi.*
Acts 13. 8 Elymas..withstood them, seeking to turn
Gal. 2. 11 I withstood him to the face, because he
Eph. 6. 13 that ye may be able to withstand in the
2 Ti. 3. 8 as Jannes and Jambres withstood Moses
4. 15 for he hath greatly withstood our words

6. *To hinder, withhold, forbid,* κωλύω *kōluō.*
Acts 11. 17 what was I, that I could withstand God

WITNESS, (false, without) —

1. *Witness,* עֵד *ed.*
Gen. 31. 44 let it be for a witness between me and th.
31. 48 This heap (is) a witness between me and
31. 50 see, God (is) witness betwixt me and thee
31. 52 This heap (be) witness, and this pillar
Exod20. 16 Thou shalt not bear false witness against
22. 13 let him bring it (for) witness, (and) he sh.
23. 1 the wicked to be an unrighteous witness
Lev. 5. 1 (is) a witness, whether he hath seen or kno.
Num. 5. 13 (there be) no witness against her, neither
35. 30 the mouth of witnesses: but one witness
Deut. 5. 20 Neither shalt thou bear false witness aga.
17. 6 two witnesses, or three witnesses, shall he
17. 6 at the mouth of one witness he shall not
17. 7 The hands of the witnesses shall be first up.
19. 15 One witness..two witnesses..three witn.
19. 16 If a false witness rise up against any man
19. 18 behold, (if) the witness (be) a false witness
31. 19 that this song may be a witness for me
31. 21 song shall testify against them as a witn.
31. 26 it may be there for a witness against thee
Josh.22. 27 it (may be) a witness between us and you
22. 28 but it (is) a witness between us and you
22. 34 it (shall be) a witness between us that the
24. 22 Ye (are) witnesses..(We are) witnesses
Ruth 4. 9 Ye (are) witnesses this day, that I have bo.
4. 10 to raise up the name..ye (are) witnesses
4. 11 and the elders, said, (We are) witnesses
1 Sa. 12. 5 The LORD (is) witness..his anointed (is) w.
12. 5 And they answered, (He is) witness
Job 10. 17 Thou renewest thy witnesses against me
16. 8 wrinkles, (which) is a witness (against me)
16. 19 my witness (is) in heaven, and my record
Psa. 27. 12 false witnesses are risen up against me, and
35. 11 False witnesses did rise up: they laid to
89. 37 be established..(as) a faithful witness in
Prov. 6. 19 A false witness (that) speaketh lies, and
12. 17 showeth..righteousness: but a false wit.
14. 5 witness will not lie: but a false witness
14. 25 A true witness delivereth souls: but a de.
19. 5, 9 A false witness shall not be unpunished
19. 28 An ungodly witness scorneth judgment
21. 28 A false witness shall perish: but the man
24. 28 Be not a witness against thy neighbour wi.
25. 18 A man that beareth false witness against
Isa. 8. 2 I took unto me faithful witnesses to rec.
19. 20 it shall be for a sign and for a witness unto
43. 9 let them bring forth their witnesses, that
43. 10, 12 Ye (are) my witnesses, saith the LORD
44. 8 have declared (it)? ye (are) even my witn.
44. 9 they (are) their own witnesses; they see
55. 4 I have given him (for) a witness to the pe.
Jer. 29. 23 I know, and (am) a witness, saith the LORD
32. 10 took witnesses, and weighed (him) the mo.
32. 12 in the presence of the witnesses that sub.
32. 25 Buy thee the field..and take witnesses
32. 44 seal (them), and take witnesses in the land
42. 5 The LORD be a true and faithful witness
Mic. 1. 2 let the Lord GOD be witness against you
Mal. 3. 5 I will be a swift witness against the sorc.

2. *Witness,* עֵדָה *edah.*
Gen. 21. 30 they may be a witness unto me, that I ha.
31. 52 and (this) pillar (be) witness, that I will
Josh.24. 27 Behold, this stone shall be a witness un.
24. 27 it shall be therefore a witness unto you

3. *Witness, testimony,* עֵדוּת *eduth.*
Num17. 7 Moses laid up..in the tabernacle of witness
17. 8 Moses went into the tabernacle of witness
18. 2 (minister) before the tabernacle of witness
2 Ch.24. 6 collection..for the tabernacle of witness

4. *To hear, hearken,* שָׁמַע *shamea.*
Judg11. 10 The LORD be witness between us, if we do

5. *Witness, martyr,* μάρτυς *martus.*
Matt18. 16 in the mouth of two or three witnesses
26. 65 what further need have we of witnesses?
Mark14. 63 saith, What need we any further witnes.
Luke24. 48 And ye are witnesses of these things
Acts 1. 8 ye shall be witnesses unto me both in Je.
1. 22 must one be ordained to be a witness with
2. 32 God raised up, whereof we all are witne.
3. 15 raised from the dead; whereof we are wi.
5. 32 we are his witnesses of these things, and
6. 13 set up false witnesses, which said, This
7. 58 the witnesses laid down their clothes at
10. 39 we are witnesses of all things which he
10. 41 Not to all the people, but unto witnesses
13. 31 who are his witnesses unto the people
Acts 22. 15 thou shalt be his witness unto all men of
26. 16 to make thee a minister and a witness bo.
Rom. 1. 9 God is my witness, whom I serve with my
2 Co. 13. 1 In the mouth of two or three witnesses
1 Th. 2. 5 nor a cloak of covetousness; God (is) wit.
2. 10 Ye (are) witnesses, and God (also), how
1 Ti. 5. 19 receive not..but before two or three wit.
6. 12 a good profession before many witnesses
2 Ti. 2. 2 hast heard of me among many witnesses
Heb. 10. 28 without mercy under two or three witne.
12. 1 compassed..with so great a cloud of wit.
1 Pe. 5. 1 and a witness of the sufferings of Christ
Rev. 1. 5 Jesus Christ, (who is) the faithful witness
3. 14 the faithful and true witness, the beginn.
11. 3 I will give (power) unto my two witnesses

6. *Witness, testimony,* μαρτυρία *marturia.*
Mark14. 55 the council sought for witness against J.
14. 56 but their witness agreed not together
14. 59 neither so did their witness agree toget.
Luke22. 71 What need we any further witness? for
John 1. 7 The same came for a witness, to bear
3. 11 have seen: and ye receive not our witness
5. 31 I bear..of myself, my witness is not true
5. 32 and I know that the witness which he
5. 36 I have greater witness than (that) of John
Titus 1. 13 This witness is true. Wherefore rebuke
1 Jo. 5. 9 receive the witness of men, the witness
5. 9 this is the witness of God which he hath
5. 10 He that believeth..hath the witness in
Rev. 20. 4 them that were beheaded for the witness

7. *Witness, testimony,* μαρτύριον *marturion.*
Matt24. 14 preached in all the world for a witness
Acts 4. 33 with great power gave the apostles witne.
7. 44 Our fathers had the tabernacle of witness
Jas. 5. 3 the rust of them shall be a witness again.

8. *Without a witness, not testified to,* ἀμάρτυρος.
Acts 14. 17 he left not himself without witness, in that

9. *A false or lying witness,* ψευδομάρτυρ *pseudom.*
Matt26. 60 [many false witnesses..two false witnes.]
1 Co. 15. 15 and we are found false witnesses of God

10. *False or lying testimony,* ψευδομαρτυρία.
Matt15. 19 fornications, thefts, false witness, blasph.
26. 59 the council, sought false witness against

WITNESS, (to be, bear, call to, give, take to), obtain—

1. *Testify for,* הֵעִיד [*ud* 5; V.L. *ud* 1].
Lam. 2. 13 What thing shall I take to witness for thee

2. *To cause to bear witness,* עוּד *ud,* 5.
Deut. 4. 26 I call heaven and earth to witness again.
1 Ki. 21. 10 set two men..before him, to bear witness
21. 13 the men of Belial witnessed against him
Job 29. 11 when the eye saw (me), it gave witness to
Mal. 2. 14 the LORD hath been witness between th.

3. *To respond, answer,* עָנָה *anah.*
1 Sa. 12. 3 witness against me before the LORD, and
Isa. 3. 9 show of their countenance doth witness

3*a*. *Answer witness,* עָנָה עֵד *anah ed.*
Exod. 20. 14 ; Job 16. 8 ; Prov. 25. 18.

4. *To be a witness, bear testimony,* μαρτυρέω *mart.*
Matt23. 31 ye be witnesses unto yourselves, that ye
Luke 4. 22 all bare him witness, and wondered at
11. 48 Truly [ye bear witness] that ye allow the
John 1. 7 came..to bear witness of the Light, that
1. 8 but (was sent) to bear witness of that Li.
1. 15 John bare witness of him, and cried, say.
3. 26 he..to whom thou barest witness, behold
3. 28 Ye yourselves bear me witness, that I sa.
5. 31 If I bear witness of myself, my..is not
5. 32 There is another that beareth witness of
5. 32 I know that the witness which he witne.
5. 33 Ye sent unto John, and he bare witness
5. 36 same works that I do, bear witness of me
5. 37 the Father himself..hath borne witness
8. 18 I am one that bear witness of myself, and
8. 18 the Father that sent me beareth witness
10. 25 the works that I do..they bear witness of
15. 27 ye also shall bear witness, because ye ha.
18. 23 If I have spoken evil, bear witness of the
18. 37 that I should bear witness unto the truth
Acts 10. 43 To him give all the prophets witness, th.
15. 8 God, which knoweth the hearts, bare..wi.
22. 5 As also the high priest doth bear me wit.
23. 11 so must thou bear witness also at Rome
26. 22 witnessing both to small and great, saying
Rom. 3. 21 being witnessed by the Law and the Pro.
1 Ti. 6. 13 who before Pontius Pilate witnessed a go.
Heb. 7. 8 he..of whom it is witnessed that he live.
10. 15 the Holy Ghost also is a witness to us, for
11. 4 by which he obtained witness that he was
1 Jo. 1. 2 we have seen..and bear witness, and sho.
5. 6 And it is the spirit that beareth witness
5. 8 [there are three that bear witness in earth]
3 John 6 Which have borne witness of thy charity

5. *To bear thorough witness,* διαμαρτύρομαι *diamar.*
Acts 20. 23 Save that the Holy Ghost witnesseth in

WITNESS, against, also, with, to bear —

1. *To bear witness against,* καταμαρτυρέω *katamar.*
Matt26. 62 what (is it which) these witness against
27. 13 how many things they witness against
Mark14. 60 what (is it which) these witness against
15. 4 how many things [they witness against]

2. *To bear witness with,* συμμαρτυρέω *summartureō.*
Rom. 2. 15 their conscience also bearing witness, and
8. 16 The spirit itself beareth witness with our
9. 1 my conscience also bearing me witness in

3. *To bear witness with,* συνεπιμαρτυρέω *sunepimar.*
Heb. 2. 4 God also bearing..witness, both with signs

WITNESS, to bear false —

To bear a false or lying witness, ψευδομαρτυρέω.
Matt19. 18 He saith..thou shalt not bear false witne.
Mark10. 19 Do not steal, Do not bear false witness, De.
14. 56 For many bare false witness against him
14. 57 there arose certain, and bare false witness
Luke18. 20 Do not steal, Do not bare false witness
Rom 13. 9 this..[thou shalt not bare false witness]

WITTINGLY, to guide —

To act wisely, intelligently, שָׂכַל *sakal,* 3.
Gen. 48. 14 guiding his hands wittingly : for Manass.

WIZARD —

A knowing one, a wizard, יִדְּעֹנִי *yiddeoni.*
Lev. 19. 31 neither seek after wizards, to be defiled by
20. 6 the soul that turneth after..wizards, to go
20. 27 hath a familiar spirit, or that is a wizard
Deut 18. 11 Or a charmer..or a wizard..or a necrom.
1 Sa. 28. 3 Saul had put away..the wizards, out of the
28. 9 how he hath cut off..the wizards, out of
2 Ki.21. 6 and dealt with familiar spirits and wizar.
23. 24 familiar spirits, and the wizards, and the
2 Ch.33. 6 dealt with a familiar spirit, and with wiz.
Isa. 8. 19 Seek..unto wizards that peep and that m.
19. 3 they shall seek to the idols, and..wizards

WOE (worth), woeful —

1. *O! (interj. of sorrow)* אוֹי *oy.*
Num21. 29 Woe to thee Moab ! thou art undone, O
1 Sa. 4. 7 Woe unto us ! for there hath not been such
4. 8 Woe unto us ! who shall deliver us out of
Prov.23. 29 Who hath woe? who hath sorrow? who hath
Isa. 3. 9 Woe unto their soul, for they have reward.
3. 11 Woe unto the wicked ! (it shall be) ill (with
6. 5 Woe (is) me ! for I am undone ; because
24. 16 My leanness, my leanness, woe unto me
Jer. 4. 13 Behold..Woe unto us ! for we are spoiled
4. 31 Woe (is) me now, for my soul is wearied, be.
6. 4 Woe unto us ! for the day goeth away, for
10. 19 Woe is me for my hurt ! my wound is griev.
13. 27 Woe unto thee, O Jerusalem ! wilt thou
15. 10 Woe is me, my mother, that thou hast
45. 3 Woe is me now ! for the LORD hath added
48. 46 Woe be unto thee, O Moab ! the people of
Lam. 5. 16 The crown is fallen..woe unto us, that we
Eze. 16. 23 woe, woe unto thee ! saith the Lord GOD
24. 6 Woe to the bloody city, to the pot whose
24. 9 Woe to the bloody city! I will even make
Hos. 7. 13 Woe unto them ! for they have fled from
9. 12 woe also to them when I depart from th.

2. *O! oyah! (interj. of sorrow),* אוֹיָה *oyah.*
Psa.120. 5 Woe is me, that I sojourn in Mesech, (that)

3. *O! (interj. of sorrow),* אִי *i.*
Eccl. 4. 10 woe to him (that is) alone when he falleth
10. 16 Woe to thee, O land, when thy king (is) a

4. *O! (interj. of sorrow),* אַלְלַי *alelai.*
Job 10. 15 If I be wicked, woe unto me ; and (if) I
Mic. 7. 1 Woe is me ! for I am as when they have

5. *Ha! (interj. of sorrow),* הָהּ *hah.*
Eze. 30. 2 Thus saith the Lord..Woe worth the day!

6. *Ho! (int. of exhortation, warning, sorrow),* הוֹי *hoy.*
Isa. 5. 8 Woe unto them that join house to house
5. 11 Woe unto them that rise up early in the
5. 18 Woe unto them that draw iniquity with
5. 20 Woe unto them that call evil good, and
5. 21 Woe unto (them that are) wise in their
5. 22 Woe unto (them that are) mighty to drink
10. 1 Woe unto them that decree unrighteous
17. 12 Woe to the multitude of many people
18. 1 Woe to the land shadowing with wings
28. 1 Woe to the crown of pride, to the drunk.
29. 1 Woe to Ariel, to Ariel, the city (where)
29. 15 Woe unto them that seek deep to hide
30. 1 Woe to the rebellious children, saith the
31. 1 Woe to them that go down to Egypt for
33. 1 Woe to thee that spoilest, and thou (wast)
45. 9 Woe unto him that striveth with his
45. 10 Woe unto him that saith unto (his) father
Jer. 22. 13 Woe unto him that buildeth his house by
23. 1 Woe be unto the pastors that destroy and
48. 1 Woe unto Nebo, for it is spoiled, Kiriath.
50. 27 woe unto them! for their day is come, the
Eze. 13. 3 Woe unto the foolish prophets, that fo.
13. 18 Woe to the (women) that sew pillows to
34. 2 Woe (be) to the shepherds of Israel that
Amos 5. 18 Woe unto you that desire the day of the
6. 1 Woe to them (that are) at ease in Zion
Mic. 2. 1 Woe to them that devise iniquity, and w.
Nah. 3. 1 Woe to the bloody city! it is all full of
Hab. 2. 6 Woe to him that increaseth (that which
2. 9 Woe to him that coveteth an evil coveto.
2. 12 Woe to him that buildeth a town with b.
2. 15 Woe unto him that giveth his neighbour
2. 19 Woe unto him that saith to the wood, Aw.
Zeph. 2. 5 Woe unto the inhabitants of the sea coast
3. 1 Woe to her that is filthy and polluted, to
Zech.11. 17 Woe to the idol shepherd that leaveth the

7. *He! (interj. of sorrow),* הִי *hi.*
Eze. 2. 10 lamentations, and mourning, and woe

8. *To be sickly, mortal, incurable,* אָנַשׁ *anash.*
Jer. 17. 16 neither have I desired the woeful day, th.

9. *Wo, (interj. of sorrow),* οὐαί *ouai.*
Matt 11. 21 Woe unto thee, Chorazin ! woe unto thee
18. 7 Woe unto the world because of offences !
18. 7 woe to that man by whom the offence co.

Matt 23. 13, [14], 15, 23, 25, 27, 29 woe unto you, scrib.
23. 16 Woe unto you..blind guides, which say
24. 19 woe unto them that are with child, and
26. 24 woe unto that man by whom the Son of
Mark 13. 17 woe to them that are with child, and to
14. 21 woe to that man by whom the Son of man
Luke 6. 24 woe unto you that are rich! for ye have
6. 25 Woe unto you that..Woe unto you that
6. 26 Woe unto you when all men shall speak
10. 13 Woe unto thee Chorazin! woe unto thee
11. 42, 43 woe unto you, Pharisees! for ye
11. 44 Woe unto you, scribes and Pharisees, hyp.
11. 46 Woe unto you also..lawyers! for ye lade
11. 47 Woe unto you! for ye build the sepulch.
11. 52 Woe unto you, lawyers! for ye have taken
17. 1 but woe (unto him) through whom they
21. 23 woe unto them that are with child, and
22. 22 woe unto that man by whom he is betray.
1 Co. 9. 16 woe is unto me, if I preach not the gospel
Jude 11 Woe unto them! for they have gone in the
Rev. 8. 13 Woe, woe, woe to the inhabiters of the
9. 12 One woe is past..there come two woes
11. 14 The second woe is past..the third woe co.
12. 12 Woe to the inhabiters of the earth and of

WOLF —

1. *A wolf or jackal*, זְאֵב *zeeb.*
Gen. 49. 27 Benjamin shall ravin (as) a wolf: in the
Isa. 11. 6 The wolf also shall dwell with the lamb
65. 25 The wolf and the lamb shall feed together
Jer. 5. 6 a wolf of the evenings shall spoil them
Eze. 22. 27 Her princes..like wolves ravening the
Hab. 1. 8 and are more fierce than the evening wo.
Zeph. 3. 3 her judges (are) evening wolves; they gn.

2. *A wolf*, λύκος *lukos.*
Matt. 7. 15 but inwardly they are ravening wolves
10. 16 I send you..as sheep in the midst of wo.
Luke 10. 3 I send you forth as lambs among wolves
John 10. 12 seeth the wolf coming..and the wolf ca.
Acts 20. 29 shall grievous wolves enter in among you

WOMAN, (silly, every, this) —

1. *A woman, wife*, אִשָּׁה *ishshah.*
Gen. 2. 22 the rib..made he a woman, and brought
2. 23 she shall be called Woman, because she
3. 1 the serpent..said unto the woman, Yea
3. 2 the woman said unto the serpent, We may
3. 4 the serpent said unto the woman, Ye sh.
3. 6 when the woman saw that the tree (was)
3. 12 The woman whom thou gavest..with me
3. 13 said unto the woman..And the woman
3. 15 I will put enmity between thee and the w.
3. 16 Unto the woman he said, I will greatly
12. 11 I know that thou (art) a fair woman to
12. 14 the Egyptians beheld the woman, that she
12. 15 the woman was taken into Pharaoh's ho.
20. 3 a dead man, for the woman which thou
24. 5, 8 the woman will not be willing to follow
24. 39 Peradventure the woman will not follow
24. 44 (let) the same (be) the woman whom the L.
38. 20 sent..to receive (his) pledge from the wo.
Exod. 2. 2 the woman conceived, and bare a son, and
2. 9 And the woman took the child, and nur.
3. 22 every woman shall borrow of her neigh.
11. 2 and let..every woman of her neighbour
21. 22 If men strive, and hurt a woman with ch.
21. 22 as the woman's husband will lay upon him
21. 28 If an ox gore a man or a woman, that they
21. 29 but that he hath killed a man or a woman
35. 25 all the women that were wise hearted did
35. 29 every man and woman, whose heart made
36. 6 Let neither man nor woman make any
Lev. 12. 2 If a woman have conceived seed, and born
13. 29 If a man or woman have a plague upon
13. 38 If a man also or a woman have in the skin
15. 18 The woman also with whom man shall lie
15. 19 if a woman have an issue, (and) her issue
15. 25 if a woman have an issue of her blood
18. 17 Thou shalt not uncover..a woman and
18. 19 thou shalt not approach unto a woman
18. 22 Thou shalt not lie..as with woman kind
18. 23 neither shall any woman stand before a
19. 20 whosoever lieth carnally with a woman
20. 13 If a man also lie..as he lieth with a wo.
20. 16 if a woman approach..kill the woman and
20. 18 if a man shall lie with a woman having
20. 27 A man also or woman that hath a famil.
21. 7 neither shall they take a woman put away
24. 10 the son of an Israelitish woman, whose
24. 11 the Israelitish woman's son blasphemed
Num. 5. 6 When a man or woman shall commit any
5. 18 shall set the woman..and uncover the w.
5. 19 And the priest shall..say unto the woman
5. 21 shall charge the woman..say unto the w.
5. 22 And the woman shall say, Amen,
5. 24 he shall cause the woman to drink the bi.
5. 25 take the jealousy offering out of the wom.
5. 26 shall cause the woman to drink the water
5. 27 the woman shall be a curse among her pe.
5. 28 if the woman be not defiled, but be clean
5. 30 and shall set the woman before the LORD
5. 31 guiltless..this woman shall bear her ini.
6. 2 When either man or woman shall separate
12. 1 of the Ethiopian woman..an Ethiopian w.
25. 8 and thrust..the woman through her belly
25. 15 the name of the Midianitish woman that
30. 3 If a woman also vow a vow unto the LORD
31. 17 kill every woman that hath known man
Deut 17. 2 If there be found among you..man or wo.
17. 5 man or that woman..that man or that wo.
21. 11 seest among the captives a beautiful wo.
22. 5 The woman shall not wear that which per.
Deut 22. 5 neither shall a man put on a woman's gar.
22. 14 I took this woman, and when I came to
22. 22 If a man be found lying with a woman
22. 22 man that lay with the woman, and the wo.
29. 18 Lest there should be among you..woman
Josh. 2. 4 the woman took the two men, and hid th.
6. 21 destroyed..both man and woman, young
6. 22 bring out thence the woman, and all that
8. 25 all that fell that day, both of men and w.
Judg. 4. 9 shall sell Sisera into the hand of a woman
9. 49 died also, about a thousand men and wo.
9. 53 a certain woman cast a piece of a millstone
9. 54 that men say not of me, A woman slew him
11. 2 for thou (art) the son of a strange woman
13. 3 the angel..appeared unto the woman, and
13. 6 Then the woman came and told her husb.
13. 9 the angel of God came again unto the wo.
13. 10 the woman made haste, and ran, and sh.
13. 11 thou the man that spakest unto the woman
13. 13 Of all that I said unto the woman let her
13. 24 the woman bare a son, and called his na.
14. 1 Samson went down to Timnath..saw a w.
14. 2 I have seen a woman in Timnath of the
14. 3 never a woman among the daughters of thy
14. 7 And he went down and talked with the w.
14. 10 So his father went down unto the woman
16. 4 he loved a woman in the valley of Sorek
16. 27 roof about three thousand men and wo.
19. 26 Then came the woman in the dawning of
19. 27 the woman his concubine was fallen down
20. 4 the Levite, the husband of the woman th.
21. 11 destroy..every woman that hath lain by
21. 16 seeing the women are destroyed out of B.
Ruth 1. 5 the woman was left of her two sons and
3. 8 it came to pass at midnight..a woman lay
3. 11 doth know that thou (art) a virtuous wo.
3. 14 Let it not be known that a woman came
4. 11 LORD make the woman that is come into
1 Sa. 1. 15 I (am) a woman of a sorrowful spirit: I
1. 18 So the woman went her way, and did eat
1. 23 So the woman abode, and gave her son su.
1. 26 I (am) the woman that stood by thee here
2. 20 LORD give thee seed of this woman, for the
15. 3 slay both man and woman, infant and su.
21. 4 have kept themselves at least from women
21. 5 Of a truth women..kept from us about th.
22. 19 Nob..smote he..both men and women
25. 3 Abigail..a woman of good understanding
27. 9 David..left neither man nor woman alive
27. 11 David saved neither man nor woman alive
28. 7 Seek me a woman..a woman that hath a
28. 8 they came to the woman by night, and he
28. 9 the woman said unto him, Behold, thou
28. 11 Then said the woman, Whom shall I bri.
28. 12 when the woman saw..the woman spake
28. 13 the woman said unto Saul, I saw gods asc.
28. 21 the woman came unto Saul, and saw that
28 23 But his servants, together with the woman
28. 24 the woman had a fat calf in the house, and
2 Sa. 3. 8 thou chargest me..concerning this woman
6. 19 he dealt..as well to the women as men, to
11. 2 he saw a woman..and the woman (was)
11. 3 David sent and enquired after the woman
11. 5 the woman conceived, and sent and told
11. 21 did not a woman cast a piece of a millstone
14. 2 a wise woman..and said..be as a woman
14. 4 when the woman of Tekoah spake to the
14. 5 I (am) indeed a widow woman, and mine
14. 8 the king said unto the woman, Go to thine
14. 9 the woman of Tekoah said unto the king
14. 12 Then the woman said, Let thine handm.
14. 13 the woman said, Wherefore then hast th.
14. 18 said unto the woman..And the woman sa.
14. 19 the woman answered and said..thy soul
14. 27 Tamar..was a woman of a fair countenan.
17. 19 the woman took and spread a covering ov.
17. 20 came to the woman..And the woman said
20. 16 Then cried a wise woman out of the city
20. 17 when he was come near unto her, the wo.
20. 21 the woman said unto Joab, Behold, his he.
20. 22 Then the woman went unto all the people
1 Ki. 3. 17 the one woman said..I and this woman dw.
3. 18 it came to pass the third day..this woman
3. 19 this woman's child died in the night, be.
3. 22 the other woman said, Nay; but the liv.
3. 26 Then spake the woman whose the living
11. 26 whose mother's name..Zeruah, a widow w.
17. 9 I have commanded a widow woman there
17. 10 the widow woman (was) there gathering
17. 17 the son of the woman, the mistress of the
17. 24 the woman said unto Elijah, Now by this
2 Ki. 4. 1 there cried a certain woman of the wives
4. 8 passed to Shunem, where (was) a great w.
4. 17 the woman conceived, and bare a son at
6. 26 there cried a woman unto him, saying
6. 28 This woman said unto me, Give thy son
6. 30 when the king heard the words of the w.
8. 1 Then spake Elisha unto the woman, wh.
8. 2 the woman arose, and did after the say.
8. 3 the woman returned out of the land of
8. 5 behold, the woman..this (is) the woman
8. 6 when the king asked the woman, she told
1 Ch. 16. 3 he dealt to every one..both man and wo.
2 Ch. 2. 14 The son of a woman of the daughters of
15. 13 whether small or great, whether man or w.
Neh. 8. 2 before the congregation..of men and wo.
Esth. 4. 11 know..whosoever, whether man or wom.
Job 14. 1 Man..born of a woman (is) of few days
15. 14 What (is) man..born of a woman, that
25. 4 or how can he be clean..born of a woman?
31. 9 If mine heart have been deceived by a w.
Psa. 58. 8 the untimely birth of a woman..they may
Prov. 2. 16 To deliver thee from the strange woman
6. 24 To keep thee from the evil woman, from
6. 26 For by means of a whorish woman (a man
6. 32 whoso committeth adultery with a woman
7. 5 they may keep thee from the strange wo.
7. 10 there met him a woman..the attire of an
9. 13 A foolish woman (is) clamorous..simple
11. 16 A gracious woman retaineth honour, and
11. 22 a fair woman which is without discretion
12. 4 A virtuous woman (is) a crown to her hu.
21. 9 than with a brawling woman in a wide h.
21. 19 than with a contentious and an angry w.
25. 24 than with a brawling woman and in a w.
27. 15 continual dropping..and a contentious w.
30. 20 Such (is) the way of an adulterous woman
31. 10 Who can find a virtuous woman? for her
31. 30 a woman (that) feareth the LORD, she sh.
Eccl. 7. 26 I find more bitter than death the woman
7. 28 a woman among all these have I not found
Isa. 45. 10 Woe unto him that saith..to the woman
49. 15 Can a woman forget her sucking child, th.
54. 6 For the LORD hath called thee as a wom.
Jer. 13. 21 shall not sorrows take thee, as a woman
44. 7 to cut off from you man and woman, child
48. 41 shall be as the heart of a woman in her p.
49. 22 shall..be as the heart of a woman in her
51. 22 With thee..I break in pieces man and wo.
Eze. 16. 30 the work of an imperious whorish woman
18. 6 neither hath come near to a menstruous w.
23. 44 as they go in unto a woman..the lewd wo.
Hos. 3. 1 Go yet, love a woman beloved of (her) friend
Zech. 5. 7 this (is) a woman that sitteth in the midst

2. *A female*, נְקֵבָה *neqebah.*
Lev. 15. 33 of the man, and of the woman, and of him
Num 31. 15 said..Have ye saved all the women alive?
Jer. 31. 22 created a new thing..A woman shall com.

3. *Women*, נָשִׁים *nashim.*
Gen. 18. 11 it ceased to be..after the manner of wo.
31. 35 for the custom of women (is) upon me
Exod. 1. 19 the Hebrew..are not as the Egyptian wo.
15. 20 the women went out after her with tim.
35. 22 they came, both men and women, as many
35. 26 the women whose heart stirred them up
Lev. 26. 26 ten women shall bake your bread in one
Num 31. 9 the children of Israel took (all) the women
31. 18 all the women children, that have not k.
31. 35 women that had not known man by lying
Deut. 2. 34 destroyed the men, and the women, and
3. 6 utterly destroying the men, women, and
20. 14 the women, and the little ones, and the
31. 12 Gather the people..men, and women, and
Josh. 8. 35 with the women, and the little ones, and
Judg. 5. 24 Blessed above women..above women in
9. 51 thither fled all the men and women, and
16. 27 the house was full of men and women, and
21. 10 inhabitants..with the women and the ch.
21. 14 which they had saved alive of the women
Ruth 4. 14 the women said unto Naomi, Blessed (be)
1 Sa. 2. 22 they lay with the women that assembled
15. 33 made women childless..childless among w.
18. 6 the women came out of all cities of Israel
18. 7 the women answered (one another) as they
30. 2 had taken the women captives that (were)
2 Sa. 1. 26 wonderful, passing the love of women
15. 16 the king left ten women, (which were) co.
20. 3 the king took the ten women (his) concu.
1 Ki. 3. 16 Then came there two women (that were)
11. 1 Solomon loved many strange women, tog.
2 Ki. 23. 7 where the women wove hangings for the
2 Ch. 28. 8 two hundred thousand, women, sons, and
Ezra 10. 1 congregation of men and women and ch.
Neh. 8. 3 before the men and the women, and those
13. 26 even him did outlandish women cause to
Esth. 1. 9 the queen made a feast for the women
1. 17 shall come abroad unto all women, so that
2. 3 the house of the women..keeper of the w.
2. 8 the custody of Hegai, keeper of the wom.
2. 9 the best (place) of the house of the women
2. 11 before the court of the women's house, to
2. 12 (other) things for the purifying of the w.
2. 13 go with her out of the house of the women
2. 14 she returned into the..house of the wom.
2. 15 Hegai..the keeper of the women, appoi.
3. 13 young and old, little children and women
8. 11 assault them, (both) little ones and wom.
Job 42. 15 in all the land were no women found (so)
Prov 14. 1 Every wise woman buildeth her house: b.
31. 3 Give not thy strength unto women, nor thy
Song 1. 8 O thou fairest among women, go thy way
5. 9 O thou fairest among women? what (is)
6. 1 Whither..O thou fairest among women?
Isa. 3. 12 children (are) their oppressors, and women
4. 1 seven women shall take hold of one man
19. 16 that day shall Egypt be like unto women
27. 11 the women come, (and) set them on fire
32. 9 Rise up, ye women that are at ease; hear
Jer. 7. 18 the women knead (their) dough, to make
9. 20 hear the word of the LORD, O ye women
38. 22 the women that are left in the king of J.
40. 7 had committed unto him men, and women
41. 16 the women, and the children, and the eu.
43. 6 women, and children, and the king's da.
44. 15 all the women that stood by, a great mu.
44. 20 to the women, and to all the people whi.
44. 24 Jeremiah said..to all the women, Hear
50. 37 they shall become as women: a sword is
51. 30 they became as women: they have burned
Lam. 2. 20 Shall the women eat their fruit, (and) chil.
4. 10 The hands of the pitiful women have so
5. 11 They ravished the women in Zion, (and)

Eze. 8. 14 there sat women weeping for Tammuz
9. 6 both maids, and little children, and wo.
16. 34 the contrary is in thee from (other) wom.
16. 41 upon thee in the sight of many women
23. 2 there were two women, the daughters of
23. 10 she became famous among women, for
23. 48 that all women may be taught not to do
Dan. 11. 17 he shall give him the daughter of women
11. 37 nor the desire of women, nor regard any
Mic. 2. 9 The women of my people have ye cast out
Nah. 3. 13 thy people in the midst of thee (are) wom.
Zech. 5. 9 there came out two women, and the wind
14. 2 the houses rifled, and the women ravished

4. *A woman, wife,* γυνή *gunē.*
Matt. 5. 28 whosoever looketh on a woman to lust af.
9. 20 a woman, which was diseased with an iss.
9. 22 the woman was made whole from that ho.
11. 11 Among them that are born of women the.
13. 33 is like unto leaven, which a woman took a.
14. 21 about five thousand men, beside women
15. 22 a woman of Canaan came out of the same
15. 28 said unto her, O woman, great (is) thy fa.
15. 38 four thousand men, beside women and ch.
22. 27 And last of all the woman died also
26. 7 There came unto him a woman having an
26. 10 said unto them, Why trouble ye the wo.?
27. 55 many women were there, beholding afar
28. 5 the angel answered and said unto the wo.
Mark 5. 25 a certain woman, which had an issue of
5. 33 the woman, fearing and trembling, know.
7. 25 a..woman, whose young daughter had an
7. 26 The woman was a Greek, a Syrophenician
10. 12 if [a woman] shall put away her husband
12. 22 and left no seed: last of all the woman died
14. 3 there came a woman having an alabaster
15. 40 There were also women looking on afar off
Luke 1. [28], 42 blessed (art) thou among women!
4. 26 sent, save unto..a woman (that was) a wi.
7. 28 Among those that are born of women th.
7. 37 behold, a woman in the city, which was
7. 39 who and what manner of woman (this is)
7. 44 turned to the woman..Seest thou this w.
7. 50 he said to the woman, Thy faith hath sa.
8. 2 certain women, which had been healed
8. 43 a woman, having an issue of blood twelve
8. 47 when the woman saw that she was not hid
10. 38 a certain woman named Martha received
11. 27 a certain woman of the company lifted up
13. 11 there was a woman which had a spirit of
13. 12 Woman, thou art loosed from thine infir.
13. 21 It is like leaven, which a woman took and
15. 8 what woman, having ten pieces of silver
20. 32 Last of all the woman died also
22. 57 denied him, saying, Woman, I know him
23. 27 great company of people, and of women
23. 49 the women that followed him from Gali.
23. 55 the women also, which came with him
24. 22 certain women also of our company made
24. 24 found (it) even so as the women had said
John 2. 4 Woman, what have I to do with thee?
4. 7 There cometh a woman of Samaria to draw
4. 9 Then saith the woman of Samaria unto him
4. 9 askest drink of me, which am a woman of
4. 11 The woman saith unto him, Sir, thou hast
4. 15 The woman saith unto him, Sir, give me th.
4. 17 The woman answered and said, I have no
4. 19 The woman saith unto him, Sir, I perceive
4. 21 Woman, believe me, the hour cometh, wh.
4. 25 The woman saith unto him, I know that
4. 27 marvelled that he talked with the woman
4. 28 The woman then left her water pot, and
4. 39 believed..for the saying of the woman
4. 42 said unto the woman, Now we believe, not
8. 3 [brought unto him a woman taken in ad.]
8. 4 [this woman was taken in adultery, in]
8. 9 [and the woman standing in the midst]
8. 10 [saw none but the woman, he said..Wo.]
16. 21 A woman when she is in travail hath so.
19. 26 he saith unto his mother, Woman, behold
20. 13, 15 unto her, Woman, why weepest thou?
Acts 1. 14 in prayer and supplication, with the wo.
5. 14 added..multitudes both of men and wom.
8. 3 Saul..haling men and women, committed
8. 12 they were baptized, both men and women
9. 2 if he found..whether they were men or w.
13. 50 stirred up the devout and honourable w.
16. 1 of a certain woman, which was a Jewess
16. 13 we sat down, and spake unto the women
16. 14 a certain woman named Lydia, a seller of
17. 4 believed..of the chief women not a few
17. 12 also of honourable women which were G.
17. 34 a woman named Damaris, and others with
22. 4 delivering into prisons both men and wo.
Rom. 7. 2 For the woman which hath an husband
1 Co. 7. 1 (It is) good for a man not to touch a wo.
7. 13 the woman which hath an husband that
11. 3 the head of the woman (is) the man, and
11. 5 every woman that prayeth or prophesieth
11. 6 if the woman be not covered, let her also
11. 6 if it be a shame for a woman to be shorn
11. 7 but the woman is the glory of the man
11. 8 the man is not of the woman; but the w.
11. 9 Neither..created for..woman, but the w.
11. 10 For this cause ought the woman to have
11. 11 man without the woman, neither the wo.
11. 12 For as the woman..even so..by the wom.
11. 13 is it comely that a woman pray unto God
11. 15 if a woman have long hair, it is a glory to
14. 34 Let your women keep silence in the chu.
14. 35 it is a shame for women to speak in the
Gal. 4. 4 God sent forth his Son, made of a woman
1 Ti. 2. 9 In like manner also, that women adorn t.
2. 10 which becometh women professing godl.
2. 11 Let the woman learn in silence with all
2. 12 I suffer not a woman to teach, nor to us.
2. 14 the woman being deceived was in the tr.
Heb. 11. 35 Women received their dead raised to life
1 Pe. 3. 5 in the old time the holy women also, who
Rev. 2. 20 because thou sufferest that woman Jeze.
9. 8 they had hair as the hair of women, and
12. 1 a woman clothed with the sun, and the
12. 4 the dragon stood before the woman which
12. 6 the woman fled into the wilderness, where
12. 13 he persecuted the woman which brought
12. 14 to the woman were given two wings of a
12. 15 cast out..water as a flood after the wom.
12. 16 the earth helped the woman: and the ea.
12. 17 the dragon was wroth with the woman, and
14. 4 These..which were not defiled with wom.
17. 3 I saw a woman sit upon a scarlet coloured
17. 4 the woman was arrayed in purple and sc.
17. 6 I saw the woman drunken with the blood
17. 7 I will tell thee the mystery of the woman
17. 9 are seven mountains on which the woman
17. 18 the woman which thou sawest is that gr.

5. *This one,* αὕτη *hautē.*
Matt 26. 13 shall also this, that this woman hath done
Luke 7. 45 this woman since the time I came in hath
7. 46 this woman hath anointed my feet with
Acts 9. 36 this woman was full of good works and

6. *Each or every one,* ἑκάστη *hekastē.*
1 Co. 7. 2 let every woman have her own husband

7. *A female,* θήλεια *thēleia.*
Rom. 1. 26 even their women did change the natural
1. 27 the men, leaving the natural use of the w.

8. *A little silly woman,* γυναικάριον *gunaikarion.*
2 Ti. 3. 6 lead captive silly women laden with sins

WOMAN servant —
Maid servant, שִׁפְחָה *shiphchah.*
Gen. 20. 14 oxen, and men servants, and women serv.
32. 5 I have..men servants, and women serv.
32. 22 took his two wives, and his two women s.

WOMB —
1. *Belly, womb, body,* בֶּטֶן *beten.*
Gen. 25. 23 Two nations (are) in thy womb, and two
25. 24 And..behold, (there were) twins in her w.
30. 2 withheld from thee the fruit of the womb?
38. 27 it came to pass..twins (were) in her womb
Deut. 7. 13 he will also bless the fruit of thy womb
Judg 13. 5, 7 be a Nazarite to God from the womb
16. 17 a Nazarite unto God from my mother's wo.
Job 1. 21 Naked came I out of my mother's womb
3. 10 it shut not up the doors of my..womb
10. 19 I should have been carried from the wo.
31. 15 Did not he that made me in the womb
31. 18 I have guided her from my mother's wo.
38. 29 Out of whose womb came the ice? and
Psa. 22. 9 thou (art) he that took me out of the wo.
71. 6 By thee have I been holden up from the w.
127. 3 Lo..the fruit of the womb (is his) reward
139. 13 thou hast covered me in my mother's w.
Prov 31. 2 What, my son? and what, the son of my w.?
Eccl. 5. 15 As he came forth of his mother's womb
11. 5 how the bones..in the womb of her that
Isa. 13. 18 shall have no pity on the fruit of the wo.
44. 2 made thee, and formed thee from the w.
44. 24 and he that formed thee from the womb
48. 8 wast called a transgressor from the womb
49. 1 LORD hath called me from the womb
49. 5 the LORD that formed me from the womb
49. 15 not have compassion on the son of her w.?
Hos. 9. 11 from the birth, and from the womb, and
9. 16 yet will I slay..the beloved..of their wo.
12. 3 He took his brother by the heel in the w.

2. *Bowels,* מֵעִים *meim.*
Ruth 1. 11 Turn again..(are) there yet..sons in my w.

3. *A womb, female,* רַחַם *racham.*
Gen. 49. 25 blessings of the breasts and of the womb
Prov 30. 16 The grave; and the barren womb; the e.
Isa. 46. 3 which are borne..carried from the womb
Eze. 20. 26 pass through..all that openeth the womb

4. *A womb, female,* רֶחֶם *rechem.*
Gen. 20. 18 LORD had fast closed up all the wombs
29. 31 when the LORD saw..he opened her womb
30. 22 God hearkened to her, and opened her w.
Exod 13. 2 Sanctify..whatsoever openeth the womb
Num. 8. 16 they..instead of such as open every womb
12. 12 when he cometh out of his mother's womb
1 Sa. 1. 5, 6 the LORD had shut up her womb
Job 3. 11 Why died I not from the womb?.. did I
10. 18 hast thou brought me forth out of the w.?
24. 20 The womb shall forget him: the worm
31. 15 and did not one fashion us in the womb?
38. 8 brake forth..it had issued out of the wo.?
Psa. 22. 10 I was cast upon thee from the womb, th.
58. 3 The wicked are estranged from the womb
110. 3 in the beauties of holiness from the womb
Jer. 1. 5 before thou camest forth out of the womb
20. 17 slew me not from the womb..and her wo.
20. 18 Wherefore came I forth out of the womb
Hos. 9. 14 give them a miscarrying womb and dry b.

5. *Belly, womb,* γαστήρ *gastēr.*
Luke 1. 31 thou shalt conceive in thy womb, and br.

6. *Belly, womb, hollow place,* κοιλία *koilia.*
Matt 19. 12 which were so born from (their) mother's w.
Luke 1. 15 shall be filled..even from his mother's w.
1. 41 it came to pass..the babe leaped in her w.
1. 42 and said..blessed (is) the fruit of thy womb
1. 44 lo..the babe leaped in my womb for joy.
2. 21 named..before he was conceived in the w.
11. 27 Blessed (is) the womb that bare thee, and
23. 29 Blessed..the wombs that never bare, and
John 3. 4 can he enter..into his mother's womb, and
Acts 3. 2 a certain man, lame from his mother's w.
14. 8 being a cripple from his mother's womb
Gal. 1. 15 who separated me from my mother's womb

7. *A womb, matrix,* μήτρα *mētra.*
Luke 2. 23 Every male that openeth the womb shall
Rom. 4. 19 neither yet the deadness of Sarah's w.

WONDER, (great), wondered at —
1. *Wonder, miracle,* מוֹפֵת *mopheth.*
Exod. 4. 21 see that thou do all those wonders before
7. 3 I will..multiply my signs and my wonders
11. 9 that my wonders may be multiplied in the
11. 10 Moses and Aaron did all these wonders be.
Deut. 4. 34 to go..take him a nation..by wonders, and
6. 22 LORD showed signs and wonders, great and
7. 19 the signs, and the wonders, and the mighty
13. 1 If..a prophet..giveth thee a sign or a wo.
13. 2 And the sign or the wonder come to pass
26. 8 the LORD brought us forth..with wonders
28. 46 they shall be upon thee for..a wonder, and
34. 11 In all the signs and the wonders which the
1 Ch. 16. 12 Remember his marvellous works..his wo.
2 Ch. 32. 31 who sent unto him to enquire of the won.
Neh. 9. 10 showedst signs and wonders upon Phara.
Psa. 71. 7 I am as a wonder unto many: but thou
78. 43 How he had wrought..his wonders in the
105. 5 Remember his marvellous works..his wo.
105. 27 They showed his..wonders in the land of
135. 9 (Who) sent tokens and wonders into them..
Isa. 8. 18 I and the children..(are)..for wonders in
20. 3 Isaiah hath walked..a sign and wonder
Jer. 32. 20 Which hast set signs and wonders in the
32. 21 hast brought forth thy people..with wo.
Joel 2. 30 I will show wonders in the heavens and
Zech. 3. 8 men wondered at: for, behold, I will bring

2. *To show self wonderful or singular,* פָּלָא *pala,* 2.
Exod. 3. 20 I will..smite Egypt with all my wonders
Josh. 3. 5 to morrow the LORD will do wonders amo.
Neh. 9. 17 neither were mindful of thy wonders that
Job 9. 10 Which doeth great things..and wonders
Psa. 78. 11 forgat his works, and his wonders that he
96. 3 Declare..his wonders among all people
106. 7 Our fathers understood not thy wonders
107. 24 These see the works of the LORD..his wo.
136. 4 To him who alone doeth great wonders

3. *A wonder, singular thing,* פֶּלֶא *pele.*
Exod 15. 11 Who (is) like unto thee, O LORD..doing w.
Psa. 77. 11 surely I will remember thy wonders of old
77. 14 Thou (art) the God that doest wonders, th.
88. 10 Wilt thou show wonders to the dead? shall
88. 12 Shall thy wonders be known in the dark?
89. 5 the heavens shall praise thy wonders, O
Isa. 29. 14 I will..do..a marvellous work and a wo.
Dan. 12. 6 (one) said..How long..the end of these w.?

4. *Miracle, wonder,* תְּמַהּ *temah.*
Dan. 4. 2 I thought it good to show..the wonders
4. 3 how mighty..his wonders! his kingdom
6. 27 he worketh signs and wonders in heaven

5. *Astonishment, amazement,* θάμβος *thambos.*
Acts 3. 10 they were filled with wonder and amaze

6. *A sign,* σημεῖον *sēmeion.*
Rev. 12. 1 And there appeared a great wonder in he.
12. 3 there appeared another wonder in heaven
13. 13 And he doeth great wonders, so that he

7. *A prodigy, wonder,* τέρας *teras.*
Matt 24. 24 false Christs..shall show..signs and won
Mark 13. 22 false Christs..shall show signs and wond.
John 4. 48 Except ye see signs and wonders, ye will
Acts 2. 19 I will show wonders in heaven above, and
2. 22 a man approved of God..by miracles and w.
2. 43 many wonders and signs were done by the
4. 30 that signs and wonders may be done by
5. 12 were many signs and wonders wrought
6. 8 Stephen..did great wonders and miracles
7. 36 after that he had showed wonders and si.
14. 3 granted signs and wonders to be done by
15. 12 declaring what miracles and wonders God
Rom. 15. 19 Through mighty signs and wonders, by the
2 Co. 12. 12 in signs, and wonders, and mighty deeds
2 Th. 2. 9 with all power, and signs, and lying won.
Heb. 2. 4 God..bearing..witness..with signs..wo.

WONDER, greatly, wondering, to —
1. *To show self astonished,* שָׁמֵם *shamem,* 7a.
Isa. 59. 16 he saw that..no man, and wondered
63. 5 I wondered that..none to uphold: there

2. *To be astonished, wonder,* תָּמַהּ *tamah.*
Isa. 29. 9 Stay yourselves, and wonder; cry ye out
Jer. 4. 9 be astonished, and the prophets shall wo.

3. *To show self astonished,* תָּמַהּ *tamah,* 7.
Hab. 1. 5 Behold ye..regard, and wonder marvell.

4. *Greatly astonished or amazed,* ἔκθαμβος *ektham.*
Acts 3. 11 the people ran together..greatly wonder.

5. *To put out, startle, perplex,* ἐξίστημι *existēmi.*
Acts 8. 13 Simon..continued with Philip, and won.

6. *To be astonished, amazed,* θαυμάζω *thaumazō.*
Matt 15. 31 Insomuch that the multitude wondered
Mark 6. 51 amazed..beyond measure, [and wonder.]
Luke 2. 18 all they that heard (it) wondered at those

Luke 4. 22 all bare him witness, and wondered at
8. 25 they being afraid, wondered, saying one
9. 43 while they wondered every one at al th.
11. 14 the dumb spake; and the people wonde.
24. 12 [wondering in himself at that which was]
24. 41 while they..believed not for joy, and wo.
Acts 7. 31 When Moses saw..he wondered at the s.
13. 41 Behold, ye despisers, and wonder, and pe.
Rev. 13. 3 and all the world wondered after the be.
17. 6 when I saw her, I wondered with great
17. 8 and they that dwell on the earth shall w.

WONDERFUL thing, work, to be or make —

1. *To be or become wonderful, singular,* פָּלָא *pala,* 2.
2 Sa. 1. 26 thy love to me was wonderful, passing
Job 42. 3 too wonderful for me, which I knew not
Psa. 40. 5 Many, O LORD..God..thy wonderful wo.
78. 4 and his wonderful works that he hath do.
107. 8, 15, 21, 31 his wonderful works to the ch.
111. 4 He hath made his wonderful works to be
Prov 30. 18 There be three..are too wonderful for me

2. *To make wonderful, singular,* פָּלָא *pala,* 5.
Deut 28. 59 Then the LORD will make thy plagues w.
2 Ch. 2. 9 for the house..(shall be) wonderful great
Isa. 28. 29 LORD of hosts; (which) is wonderful in c.

3. *Any thing wonderful or singular,* פֶּלֶא *pele.*
Psa. 119. 129 Thy testimonies (are) wonderful: there.
Isa. 9. 6 and his name shall be called Wonderful
25. 1 I will praise..for thou hast done wonder.

4. *Wonderful, singular,* פְּלִאי *pili.*
Psa. 139. 6 knowledge is too wonderful for me; it is

5. *Astonishment, amazement,* שַׁמָּה *shammah.*
Jer. 5. 30 A wonderful and horrible thing is com.

6. *Wonderful,* θαυμάσιος *thaumasios.*
Matt 21. 15 saw the wonderful things that he did, and

7. *Great doings or deeds,* μεγαλεῖα *megaleia.*
Acts 2. 11 we do hear them speak..the wonderful

WONDERFULLY (made, to be) —

1. *To be or become wonderful or singular,* פָּלָא *pala,* 2.
Dan. 8. 24 he shall destroy wonderfully, and shall p.

2. *Any thing wonderful or singular,* פֶּלֶא *pele.*
Lam. 1. 9 therefore she came down wonderfully

3. *To be or become wonderful,* פָּלָה *palah,* 2.
Psa. 139. 14 for I am fearfully (and) wonderfully made

WONDERING —

To show self astonished, שָׁאָה *shaah,* 7.
Gen. 24. 21 the man wondering at her held his peace

WONDROUS things, works, wondrously —

1. *A wonderful or singular thing,* מִפְלָאָה *miphlaah.*
Job 37. 16 the wondrous works of him which is perfect

2. *To be or become wonderful,* פָּלָא *pala,* 2.
1 Ch. 16. 9 Sing..talk ye of all his wondrous works
Job 37. 14 stand still, and consider the wondrous w.
Psa. 26. 7 That I may..tell of all thy wondrous wo.
71. 17 hitherto have I declared thy wondrous w.
72. 18 LORD God..who only doeth wondrous th.
75. 1 thy name (is) near thy wondrous works
78. 32 and believed not for his wondrous works
86. 10 For thou (art) great, and doest wondrous
105. 2 Sing..talk ye of all his wondrous works
106. 22 Wondrous works in the land of Ham, (and)
119. 18 that I may behold wondrous things out of
119. 27 so shall I talk of thy wondrous works
145. 5 I will speak..of thy majesty, and..w w.
Jer. 21. 2 deal..according to all his wondrous wor.

3. *To make wonderful or singular,* פָּלָא *pala,* 5.
Judg 13. 19 did wondrously; and Manoah and his wi
Joel 2. 26 God, that hath dealt wondrously with

WONT (to be) —

1. *To speak,* דָּבַר *dabar,* 3.
2 Sa. 20. 18 They were wont to speak in old time, say

2. *Seen,* חֲזָה *chazah.*
Dan. 3. 19 one seven times more than it was wont to

3. *To accustom,* סָכַן *sakan,* 5.
Num 22. 30 said..was I ever wont to do so unto thee?

4. *To be customary,* ἔθω *ethō,* εἴωθα *eiōtha.*
Matt 27. 15 at (that) feast the governor was wont to
Mark 10. 1 and, as he was wont, he taught them ag.

5. *According to custom,* κατὰ τὸ ἔθος *kata to ethos.*
Luke 22. 39 he came out, and went, as he was wont

6. *To make or reckon legal or customary,* νομίζω.
Acts 16. 13 river side, where prayer was wont to be

WOOD, (of) —

1. *Wood, a tree,* אָע *a.*
Dan. 5. 4, 23 praised the gods of..wood, and of sto.

2. *A bough, forest,* חֹרֶשׁ *choresh.*
1 Sa. 23. 15 (was) in the wilderness of Ziph in a wood
23. 16 arose, and went to David into the wood
23. 18 David abode in the wood, and Jonathan
23. 19 Doth not David hide himself..in the wood

3. *A forest, wood,* יַעַר *yaar.*
Deut 19. 5 As when a man goeth into the wood with
Josh. 17. 15 get thee up to the wood..and cut down
17. 18 mountain shall be thine: for it (is) a wood
1 Sa. 14. 25 And all (they of) the land came to a wood
14. 26 when the people were come into the wood
2 Sa. 18. 6 and the battle was in the wood of Ephra.
18. 8 the wood devoured more people that day
18. 17 and cast him into a great pit in the wood
2 Ki. 2. 24 there came..two she bears out of the wo.
1 Ch. 16. 33 Then shall the trees of the wood sing out
Psa. 80. 13 The boar out of the wood doth waste it
83. 14 As the fire burneth a wood, and as the fl.
96. 12 then shall all the trees of the wood rejoice
132. 6 we found it in the fields of the wood
Eccl. 2. 6 to water therewith the wood that bring.
Song 2. 3 apple tree among the trees of the wood
Isa. 7. 2 as the trees of the wood are moved with
Mic. 7. 14 which dwell solitarily (in) the wood, in

4. *Woods, forests,* יְעָרִים [V. L. יערים] [*yaar*].
Eze. 34. 25 dwell safely..and sleep in the woods

5. *A tree, wood,* עֵץ *ets.*
Gen. 6. 14 Make thee an ark of gopher wood; rooms
22. 3 clave the wood for the burnt offering, and
22. 6 Abraham took the wood of the burnt off.
22. 7 Behold the fire and the wood; but where
22. 9 laid the wood in order..upon the wood
Exod 7. 19 both in (vessels of) wood, and in (vessels
25. 5 and badgers' skins, and shittim wood
25. 10 they shall make an ark (of) shittim wood
25. 13 thou shalt make staves (of) shittim wood
25. 23 shalt also make a table (of) shittim wood
25. 28 shalt make the staves (of) shittim wood
26. 15 shalt make boards..(of) shittim wood st.
26. 26 thou shalt make bars (of) shittim wood
27. 1 shalt make an altar of shittim wood, five
27. 6 staves for the altar, staves (of) shittim w.
30. 1 (of) shittim wood shalt thou make it
30. 5 thou shalt make the staves (of) shittim w.
35. 7 and badgers' skins, and shittim wood
35. 24 with whom was found shittim wood, for
35. 33 in carving of wood, to make any manner
36. 20 he made boards..(of) shittim wood, stan.
36. 31 he made bars of shittim wood; five for the
37. 1 made the ark (of) shittim wood: two cub.
37. 4 he made staves (of) shittim wood, and ov.
37. 10 he made the table (of) shittim wood, two
37. 15, 28 he made the staves (of) shittim wood
37. 25 made the incense altar (of) shittim wood
38. 1 he made the altar..of shittim wood, five
38. 6 he made the staves (of) shittim wood, and
Lev. 1. 7 and lay the wood in order upon the fire
1. 8 the fat in order upon the wood that (is)
1. 12 shall lay them in order on the wood that
1. 17 burn it upon the altar, upon the wood th.
3. 5 which (is) upon the wood that (is) on the
4. 12 and burn him on the wood with fire
6. 12 the priest shall burn wood on it every mo.
11. 32 whether..any vessel of wood, or raiment
14. 4 and cedar wood, and scarlet, and hyssop
14. 6 he shall take it, and the cedar wood, and
14. 49 two birds, and cedar wood, and scarlet
14. 51 he shall take the cedar wood, and the hy.
14. 52 cleanse the house..with the cedar wood
15. 12 every vessel of wood shall be rinsed in wa.
Num 13. 20 the land..whether there be wood therein
19. 6 the priest shall take cedar wood, and hy.
31. 20 of goats' (hair), and all things made of w.
35. 18 he smite him with an hand weapon of wo.
Deut. 4. 28 serve gods, the work of men's hands, wood
10. 1 Hew thee..and make thee an ark of wood
10. 3 I made an ark (of) shittim wood, and he.
19. 5 goeth..with his neighbour to hew wood
28. 36 there shalt thou serve other gods, wood
28. 64 there shalt thou serve other gods..wood and
29. 11 from the hewer of thy wood unto the dra.
29. 17 ye have seen..their idols, wood and stone
Josh. 9. 21, 23, 27 hewers of wood and drawers of wa.
Judg. 6. 26 offer a burnt sacrifice with the wood of the
1 Sa. 6. 14 they clave the wood of the cart, and offe.
2 Sa. 6. 5 manner of (instruments made of) fir wood
24. 22 behold..instruments of the oxen for wood
1 Ki. 6. 15 he covered (them) on the inside with wood
18. 23 and lay (it) on wood..and lay (it) on wood
18. 33 he put the wood in order, and cut the bu.
18. 33 laid (him) on the wood, and said, Fill four
18. 33 pour (it) on the..sacrifice, and on the wo.
18. 38 consumed the burnt sacrifice, and the wo.
2 Ki. 6. 4 they came to Jordan, they cut down wood
19. 18 no gods, but the work of men's hand, wo.
1 Ch. 21. 23 I give..the threshing instruments for wo.
22. 4 they of Tyre, brought much cedar wood
29. 2 I have prepared..wood for (things) of wo.
2 Ch. 2. 16 we will cut wood out of Lebanon, as much
Neh. 8. 4 Ezra the scribe stood upon a pulpit of w.
10. 34 for the wood offering, to bring (it) into the
13. 31 for the wood offering, at times appointed
Job 41. 27 esteemeth..as straw..brass as rotten wood
Prov 26. 20 Where no wood is..the fire goth out, so
26. 21 (As) coals..to burning coals, and wood to
Eccl. 10. 9 he that cleaveth wood shall be endange.
Song 3. 9 Solomon made himself a chariot of the w.
Isa. 10. 15 as if the staff should lift up..no wood
30. 33 the pile thereof (is) fire and much wood
37. 19 no gods, but the work of men's hands, w.
45. 20 have no knowledge that set up the wood
60. 17 For brass I will bring gold..and for wood
Jer. 5. 14 I will make..this people wood, and it sh.
7. 18 The children gather wood, and the fath.
28. 13 Thou hast broken the yokes of wood, but
46. 22 and come..with axes, as hewers of wood
Lam. 5. 4 have drunken..for money; our wood is s.
5. 13 and the children fell under the wood
Eze. 15. 3 Shall wood be taken thereof to do any w.
20. 32 We will be as the heathen..to serve wood
24. 10 Heap on wood, kindle the fire, consume
39. 10 So that they shall take no wood out of the
41. 16 cieled with wood round about, and from
41. 22 The altar of wood..and the walls..wood
Hab. 2. 19 Woe unto him that saith to the wood
Hag. 1. 8 Go up to the mountain, and bring wood
Zech 12. 6 like an hearth of fire among the wood, and

6. *Wooden, made of wood,* ξύλινος *xulinos.*
2 Ti. 2. 20 not only vessels of gold..but also of wood
Rev. 9. 20 they should not worship..idols..of wood

7. *Wood, tree,* ξύλον *xulon.*
1 Co. 3. 12 any man build upon this foundation..wo.
Rev. 18. 12 thyine wood..vessels of most precious wo.

WOOF —

Mixture, woof, עֵרֶב *ereb.*
Lev. 13. 48 Whether..in the warp, or woof, of linen
13. 49, 51, 53, 57, 59 in the warp, or in the woof
13. 52 whether warp or woof, in woollen or in li.
13. 56 rend..out of the warp, or out of the woof
13. 58 the garment, either warp or woof, or wh.

WOOL, woollen —

1. *Wool,* עֲמַר *amar.*
Dan. 7. 9 and the hair of his head like the pure wo.

2. *Wool,* צֶמֶר *tsemer.*
Lev. 13. 47 a woollen garment, or a linen garment
13. 48 in the warp, or woof, of linen, or of wool.
13. 52 in woollen or in linen, or any thing of
13. 59 in a garment of woollen or linen, either
Deut 22. 11 Thou shalt not wear a garment..of woo.
Judg. 6. 37 I will put a fleece of wool in the floor
2 Ki. 3. 4 an hundred thousand rams, with the w.
Psa. 147. 16 He giveth snow like wool: he scattereth
Prov 31. 13 She seeketh wool and flax, and worketh
Isa. 1. 18 though..like crimson, they shall be as w.
51. 8 and the worm shall eat them like wool
Eze. 27. 18 riches..the wine of Helbon, and white w.
34. 3 Ye eat the fat..ye clothe you with the w.
44. 17 no wool shall come upon them whiles they
Hos. 2. 5 will go after my lovers, that give..my w.
2. 9 and will recover my wool and my flax

3. *A mixed cloth of wool and linen,* שַׁעַטְנֵז *shaatnez.*
Lev. 19. 19 neither shall a garment..woollen come

4. *Wool,* ἔριον *erion.*
Heb. 9. 19 he took the blood..and scarlet wool, and
Rev. 1. 14 His head and..hairs..white like wool, as

WORD —

1. *A saying, speech,* אֵמֶר *emer.*
Gen. 49. 21 Naphtali..let loose; he giveth goodly w.
Num 24. 4, 16 He hath said, which heard the words
Deut 32. 1 and hear, O earth, the words of my mouth
Josh 24. 27 this stone..hath heard all the words of
Job 6. 10 I have not concealed the words of the H.
6. 25 How forcible are right words! but what
8. 2 and..the words of thy mouth..a strong
22. 22 Receive..lay up his words in thine heart
23. 12 I have esteemed the words of his mouth
32. 12 convinced Job, (or) that answered his w.
33. 3 My words..the uprightness of my heart
34. 37 and multiplieth his words against God
Psa. 5. 1 Give ear to my words, O LORD; consider
19. 14 Let the words of my mouth, and the me.
54. 2 Hear..give ear to the words of my mouth
78. 1 incline your ears to the words of my mo.
107. 11 Because they rebelled against the words
138. 4 when they hear the words of thy mouth
141. 6 they shall hear my words: for they are
Prov. 1. 2 to perceive the words of understanding
1. 21 She crieth..in the city she uttereth her w.
2. 1 My son, if thou wilt receive my words, and
2. 16 stranger (which) flattereth with her words
5. 7 and depart not from the words of my mo.
6. 2 snared with the words..the words of thy
7. 1 My son, keep my words, and lay up my
7. 5 stranger (which) flattereth with her words
7. 24 Hearken..attend to the words of my mo.
8. 8 All the words of my mouth (are) in righ.
15. 26 (the words) of the pure (are) pleasant w.
16. 24 Pleasant words (are as) an honey comb
17. 27 He that hath knowledge spareth his words
19. 7 he pursueth (them with) words..they are
19. 27 instruction..to err from the words of kn.
22. 21 know..words of truth..answer the words
23. 12 Apply..thine ears to the words of know.
Isa. 32. 7 to destroy the poor with lying words, even
41. 26 (there is) none that heareth your words
Hos. 6. 5 I have slain them by the words of my m.

2. *A saying, speech,* אֹמֶר *omer.*
Psa. 68. 11 The Lord gave the word; great (was) the
Hab. 3. 9 the oaths of the tribes, (even thy) word

3. *A saying, speech,* אֶמְרָה *emrah.*
Lam. 2. 17 he hath fulfilled his word that he had co.

A saying, speech, אִמְרָה *imrah.*
Deut 33. 9 they have observed thy word, and kept
2 Sa. 22. 31 the word of the LORD (is) tried; he (is) a
Psa. 12. 6 The words of the LORD (are) pure words
18. 30 the word of the LORD is tried; he (is) a
105. 19 the word of the LORD tried him
119. 11 Thy word have I hid in mine heart, that
119. 38 Stablish thy word unto thy servant, who
119. 41 Let thy mercies come..according to thy w.
119. 50 This (is) my comfort..thy word hath qu.
119. 58 be merciful unto me according to thy w.
119. 67 I went astray: but now have I kept thy w.
119. 76 according to thy word unto thy servant
119. 82 Mine eyes fail for thy word, saying, When
119. 103 How sweet are thy words unto my taste
119. 116 Uphold me according to thy word that
119. 123 Mine eyes fail..for the word of thy rig.
119. 133 Order my steps in thy word: and let not

Psa.119. 140 Thy word (is) very pure; therefore thy
119. 148 prevent..that I might meditate in thy wo.
119. 154 deliver..quicken me according to thy w.
119. 158 was grieved; because they kept not thy w.
119. 162 I rejoice at thy word, as one that findeth
119. 170 deliver me according to thy word
119. 172 My tongue shall speak of thy word, for
138. 2 thou hast magnified thy word above all
Prov.30. 5 Every word of God (is) pure: he (is) a sh.
Isa. 5. 24 despised the word of the Holy One of Isr.

5. *A word, matter, thing,* דָּבָר *dabar.*

Gen. 15. 1 After these things the word of the LORD
15. 4 the word of the LORD (came) unto him, say.
24. 30 when he heard the words of Rebekah his
24. 52 when Abraham's servant heard their wo.
27. 34 when Esau heard the words of his father
27. 42 these words of Esau her elder son were told
30. 34 I would it might be according to thy wo.
31. 1 he heard the words of Laban's sons, saying
34. 18 their words pleased Hamor, and Shechem
37. 8 And they hated him..for his words
37. 14 Go, I pray thee..bring me word again
39. 17 spake unto him according to these words
39. 19 when his master heard the words of his
42. 16 that your words may be proved, whether
42. 20 so shall your words be verified, and ye sh.
43. 7 told..according to the tenor of these wo.
44. 2 he did according to the word that Joseph
44. 6 and he spake unto them these same words
44. 7 Wherefore saith my lord these words? God
44. 10 also (let) it (be) according unto your words
44. 18 let thy servant, I pray thee, speak a word
44. 24 when we came..we told him the words of
45. 27 they told him all the words of Joseph, wh.
Exod. 4. 15 thou shalt speak unto him, and put words
4. 28 Moses told Aaron all the words of the L.
4. 30 Aaron spake all the words which the Lo.
5. 9 and let them not regard vain words
8. 10 (Be it) according to thy word; that thou
8. 13 the LORD did according to the word of M.
9. 20 He that feared the word of the LORD am.
9. 21 he that regarded not the word of the LORD
12. 35 did according to the word of Moses
14. 12 (Is) not this the word that we did tell thee
19. 6 These (are) the words which thou shalt sp.
19. 7 laid before their faces all these words wh.
19. 8 Moses returned the words of the people
19. 9 Moses told the words of the people unto
20. 1 And God spake all these words, saying
23. 8 and perverteth the words of the righteo.
24. 3 all the words..the words which the LORD
24. 4 Moses wrote all the words of the LORD
24. 8 made with you concerning all these wor.
32. 28 the children..did according to the word
34. 1 I will write upon (these) tables the words
34. 27 Write thou these words..these words I
34. 28 He wrote upon the tables the words of the
35. 1 These (are) the words which the LORD ha.
Lev. 10. 7 they did according to the word of Moses
Num 11. 23 thou shalt see now whether my word sh.
11. 24 told the people the words of the LORD, and
12. 6 he said, Hear now my words: If there be
13. 26 brought back word unto them, and unto
14. 20 I have pardoned, according to thy word
15. 31 he hath despised the word of the LORD
16. 31 made an end of speaking all these words
22. 7 and spake unto him the words of Balak
22. 8 I will bring you word again, as the LORD
22. 20 the word which I shall say unto thee, th.
22. 35 the word that I shall speak unto thee, th.
22. 38 the word that God putteth in my mouth
23. 5 the LORD put a word in Balaam's mouth
23. 16 put a word in his mouth, and said, Go ag.
30. 2 he shall not break his word, he shall do
Deut. 1. 1 These (be) the words which Moses spake
1. 22 bring us word again by what way we mu.
1. 25 brought us word again, and said, (It is) a
1. 34 the LORD heard the voice of your words
2. 26 I sent messengers..with words of peace
4. 2 Ye shall not add unto the word which I
4. 10 I will make them hear my words, that
4. 12 ye heard the voice of the words, but saw
4. 36 thou heardest his words out of the midst
5. 5 I stood..to show you the word of the Lo.
5. 22 These words the LORD spake unto all your
5. 28 the voice of your words..the words of th.
6. 6 these words, which I command thee this
9. 5 that he may perform the word which the
9. 10 the words which the LORD spake with you
10. 2 I will write on the tables the words that
11. 18 Therefore shall ye lay up these my words
12. 28 hear all these words which I command
13. 3 Thou shalt not hearken unto the words
16. 19 and pervert the words of the righteous
17. 19 to keep all the words of this law and these
18. 18 will put my words in his mouth, and he
18. 19 whosoever will not hearken unto my wo.
18. 20 which shall presume to speak a word in
18. 21 How shall we know the word which the
27. 3 thou shalt write upon them all the words
27. 8 write upon the stones all the words of th.
27. 26 that confirmeth not (all) the words of this
28. 14 shalt not go aside from any of the words
28. 58 will not observe to do all the words of th.
29. 1 These (are) the words of the covenant w.
29. 9 Keep therefore the words of this covena.
29. 19 when he heareth the words of this curse
29. 20 that (we) may do all the words of this law
30. 14 the word (is) very nigh unto thee, in thy
31. 1 Moses went and spake these words unto
31. 12 and observe to do all the words of this

Deut 31. 24 Moses had made an end of writing the w.
31. 28 that I may speak these words in their ears
31. 30 Moses spake..the words of this song, un.
32. 44 Moses came and spake all the words of
32. 45 made an end of speaking all these words
32. 46 the words which I testify among you this
32. 46 to observe to do all the words of this law
Josh. 1. 13 Remember the word which Moses the se.
1. 18 will not hearken unto thy words in all th.
2. 21 she said, According unto your words, so
3. 9 and hear the words of the LORD your God
6. 10 neither shall (any) word proceed out of
8. 27 according unto the word of the LORD wh.
8. 34 he read all the words of the law, the ble.
8. 35 There was not a word of all that Moses
14. 7 I brought him word again as (it was) in m.
14. 10 the LORD spake this word unto Moses
22. 30 heard..words that the children of Reuben
22. 32 returned..and brought them word again
24. 26 Joshua wrote these words in the book of
Judg. 2. 4 angel of the LORD spake these words unto
9. 3 his mother's brethren spake..these words
9. 30 when Zebul..heard the words of Gaal the
11. 10 if we do not so according to thy words
11. 11 Jephthah uttered all his words before the
11. 28 hearkened not unto the words of Jephth.
13. 12 Manoah said, Now let thy words come to
16. 16 she pressed him daily with her words, and
1 Sa. 1. 23 tarry..only the LORD establish his word
3. 1 the word of the LORD was precious in th.
3. 7 neither was the word of the LORD yet re.
3. 19 did let none of his words fall to the gro.
3. 21 the LORD revealed himself..by the word
4. 1 the word of Samuel came to all Israel
8. 10 Samuel told all the words of the LORD un.
8. 21 Samuel heard all the words of the people
9. 27 that I may show thee the word of God
15. 1 hearken thou unto the voice of the words
15. 10 Then came the word of the LORD unto S.
15. 23 thou hast rejected the word of the LORD
15. 24 for I have transgressed..thy words, beca.
15. 26 thou hast rejected the word of the LORD
17. 11 Israel heard those words of the Philistine
17. 23 and spake according to the same words
17. 31 when the words were heard which David
18. 23 Saul's servants spake those words in the
18. 26 when his servants told David these words
21. 12 David laid up these words in his heart
24. 7 David stayed his servants with these wo.
24. 9 Wherefore hearest thou men's words, say.
24. 16 had made an end of speaking these words
25. 9 according to all those words in the name
25. 24 and hear the words of thine handmaid
26. 19 let my lord the king hear the words of his
28. 20 was sore afraid, because of the words of
28. 21 have hearkened unto thy words which th.
2 Sa. 3. 8 Then was Abner very wroth for the words
3. 11 he could not answer Abner a word again
7. 4 the word of the LORD came to Nathan, sa.
7. 7 spake I a word with any of the tribes of
7. 17 According to all these words, and accor.
7. 21 For thy word's sake, and according to thine
7. 25 the word that thou hast spoken concern.
7. 28 thou (art) that God, and thy words be tr.
14. 3 So Joab put the words in her mouth
14. 12 I pray thee, speak (one) word unto my lord
14. 17 The word of my lord the king shall now
14. 19 he put all these words in the mouth of th.
15. 28 until there come word from you to certify
19. 43 the words..were fiercer than the words
20. 17 she said unto him, Hear the words of thi.
22. 1 spake unto the LORD the words of this so.
23. 1 these (be) the last words of David. David
24. 4 the king's word prevailed against Joab
24. 11 the word of the LORD came unto the pro.
1 Ki. 1. 14 come in after thee, and confirm thy words
2. 4 the LORD may continue his word which he
2. 23 if Adonijah have not spoken this word
2. 27 that he might fulfil the word of the LORD
2. 30 Benaiah brought the king word again, say.
2. 42 saidst..The word..I have heard (is) good
3. 12 I have done according to thy words; lo, I
5. 7 when Hiram heard the words of Solomon
6. 11 the word of the LORD came to Solomon
6. 12 then will I perform my word with thee
8. 20 the LORD hath performed his word that
8. 26 let thy word, I pray thee, be verified, wh.
8. 56 there hath not failed one word of all his
8. 59 let these my words, wherewith I have ma.
10. 7 I believed not the words, until I came
12. 7 If thou wilt..speak good words to them
12. 22 the word of God came unto Shemaiah the
12. 24 to the word of the LORD..to the word of
13. 1 there came a man of God..by the word of
13. 2 he cried against the altar in the word of
13. 5 which the man..had given by the word of
13. 9 For so was it charged me by the word of
13. 11 the words which he had spoken unto the
13. 17 For it was said to me by the word of the
13. 18 an angel spake unto me by the word of the
13. 20 the word of the LORD came unto the pro.
13. 26 according to the word of the LORD
13. 32 For the saying which he cried by the wo.
14. 18 according to the word of the LORD, which
16. 1 Then the word of the LORD came to Jehu
16. 7 came the word of the LORD against Baasha
16. 12, 34 according to the word of the LORD, wh.
17. 1 there shall not..but according to my wo.
17. 2, 8 the word of the LORD came unto him
17. 5, 16 according to the word of the LORD
17. 24 I know..that the word of the LORD in my
18. 1 the word of the LORD came to Elijah in

2 Ki. 18. 21 And the people answered him not a word
18. 31 unto whom the word of the LORD came
18. 36 I have done all these things at thy word
19. 9 the word of the LORD (came) to him, and
20. 9 departed and brought him word again
20. 35 said unto his neighbour in the word of the
21. 4 heavy and displeased because of the word
21. 17, 28 the word of the LORD came to Elijah
21. 27 came to pass, when Ahab heard those w.
22. 5 Enquire..at the word of the LORD to day
22. 13 Behold, now, the words of the prophets
22. 13 let thy word..be like the word of one of t.
22. 19 Hear thou therefore the word of the LORD
22. 38 according unto the word of the LORD wh.
2 Ki. 1. 7 What manner of man..told you these wo.?
1. 16 no God in Israel to enquire of his word?
1. 17 So he died according to the word of the
3. 12 said, The word of the LORD is with him
4. 44 left..according to the word of the LORD
6. 12 telleth the king of Israel the words that
6. 18 smote..with blindness according to the w.
6. 30 came to pass, when the king heard the w.
7. 1 Then Elisha said, Hear ye the word of
7. 16 So..according to the word of the LORD
9. 26 cast..according to the word of the LORD
9. 36 he said, This (is) the word of the LORD
10. 10 there shall fall..nothing of the word of
14. 25 according to the word of the LORD God
15. 12 This (was) the word of the LORD which he
18. 20 Thou sayest, but (they are but) vain words
18. 27 sent me..to thee, to speak these words
18. 28 Hear the word of the great king, the king
18. 36 the people answered him not a word, for
18. 37 and told him the words of Rab-shakeh
19. 4 hear all the words..will reprove the words
19. 6 Be not afraid of the words which thou
19. 16 hear the words of Sennacherib, which
19. 21 This (is) the word that the LORD hath sp.
20. 4 the word of the LORD came to him, saying
20. 16 Isaiah said unto Hezekiah, Hear the word
20. 19 Good (is) the word of the LORD which thou
22. 9 Shaphan..brought the king word again
22. 11 when the king had heard the words of the
22. 13 the words of this book..words of this book
22. 16 all the words of the book which the king
22. 18 touching the words which thou hast heard
22. 20 And they brought the king word again
23. 2 he read in their ears all the words of the
23. 3 to perform the words of this covenant that
23. 16 took..according to the word..these words
23. 24 that he might perform the words of the
24. 2 according to the word of the LORD, which
1 Ch. 10. 13 against the word of the LORD, which he
11. 3, 10 according to the word of the LORD
15. 15 commanded according to the word of the
16. 15 the word which he commanded to a thous.
17. 3 the word of God came to Nathan, saying
17. 6 spake I a word to any of the judges of Is.
17. 15 According to all these words, and accor.
21. 4 the king's word prevailed against Joab
21. 6 the king's word was abominable to Joab
21. 12 advise thyself what word I shall bring
22. 8 the word of the LORD came to me, saying
23. 27 by the last words of David the Levites
25. 5 in the words of God, to lift up the horn
2 Ch. 6. 10 The LORD therefore hath performed his
6. 17 let thy word be verified, which thou hast
9. 6 I believed not their words, until I came
10. 7 please them, and speak good words to
10. 15 the LORD might perform his word, which
11. 2 the word of the LORD came to Shemaiah
11. 4 they obeyed the words of the LORD, and
12. 7 the word of the LORD came to Shemaiah
15. 8 when Asa heard these words, and the pr.
18. 4 Enquire, I pray thee, at the word of the
18. 12 the words of the prophets..let thy word
18. 18 hear the word of the LORD; I saw the L.
29. 15 by the words of the LORD, to cleanse the
29. 30 sing praise unto the LORD with the words
30. 12 to do the commandment..by the word of
32. 8 people rested themselves upon the words
33. 18 the words of the seers that spake to him
34. 16 brought the king word back again, say.
34. 19 when the king had heard the words of
34. 21 the words of the book..the word of the
34. 26 (concerning) the words which thou hast
34. 27 thou heardest his words against this place
34. 28 So they brought the king word again
34. 30 he read in their ears all the words of the
34. 31 to perform the words of the covenant wh.
35. 6 (they) may do according to the word of
35. 22 hearkened not unto the words of Necho
36. 16 despised his words, and misused his pro.
36. 21 To fulfil the word of the LORD by the m.
36. 22 the word of the LORD (spoken) by the mo.
Ezra 1. 1 the word of the LORD by the mouth of J.
7. 11 a scribe of the words of the command.
9. 4 every one that trembled at the words of
10. 5 they should do according to this word
Neh. 1. 1 The words of Nehemiah the son of Hach.
1. 4 it came to pass, when I heard these words
1. 8 the word that thou commandedst
2. 18 the king's words that he had spoken unto
5. 6 when I heard their cry and these words
6. 6 be their king, according to these words
6. 7 be reported..according to these words
6. 19 they reported..and uttered my words to
8. 9 people wept, when they heard the words
8. 12 they had understood the words that were
8. 13 even to understand the words of the law
9. 8 performed thy words; for thou (art) righ.
Esth. 1. 21 the king did according to the word of Mo.

Esth. 4. 9 Hatach came and told Esther the words
4. 12 And they told to Mordecai Esther's wo.
7. 8 As the word went out of the king's mou.
9. 26 for all the words of this letter, and (of
9. 30 sent the letters..(with) words of peace and
Job 2. 13 they sat down. .and none spake a word
6. 3 therefore my words are swallowed up
9. 14 choose out my words (to reason) with him
11. 2 Should not the multitude of words be an.
16. 3 Shall vain words have an end? or what
29. 22 After my words they spake not again, and
31. 40 The words of Job are ended
32. 11 I waited for your words; I gave ear to
33. 1 I pray thee. .hearken to all my words
34. 35 and his words (were) without wisdom
42. 7 after the LORD had spoken these words
Psa. 7. *title.* sang unto the LORD, concerning the w.
17. 4 by the word of thy lips I have kept (me
18. *title.* who spake unto the LORD the words of
22. 1 (why art thou so) far. .(from) the words of
33. 4 the word of the LORD (is) right; and all
33. 6 By the word of the LORD were the heave.
36. 3 The words of his mouth (are) iniquity and
50. 17 Seeing thou. .castest my words behind th.
52. 4 Thou lovest all devouring words, O thou
55. 21 his words were softer than oil, yet (were)
56. 4 In God I will praise his word: in God I
56. 5 Every day they wrest my words: all their
56. 10 I praise (his) word. .I praise (his) word
59. 12 the sin of their (mouth) and the words of
64. 3 (to shoot) their arrows, (even) bitter wo.
103. 20 hearkening unto the voice of his word
105. 8 the word (which) he commanded to a th.
105. 19 Until the time that his word came; the
105. 28 and they rebelled not against his word
106. 12 Then believed they his words; they sang
106. 24 they despised..they believed not his wo.
107. 20 He sent his word, and healed them, and
109. 3 They compassed me about..with words of
119. 9 By taking heed..according to thy word
119. 16 I will delight..I will not forget thy word
119. 17 Deal..(that) I may live, and keep thy w.
119. 25 quicken thou me according to thy word
119. 28 strengthen thou me according unto thy w.
119. 42 have..to answer..for I trust in thy word
119. 43 take not the word of truth utterly out of
119. 49 Remember the word unto thy servant
119. 57 I have said that I would keep thy words
119. 65 Thou hast dealt..according unto thy wo.
119. 74 be glad..because I have hoped in thy w.
119. 81 My soul fainteth..(but) I hope in thy w.
119. 89 For ever..thy word is settled in heaven
119. 101 have refrained..that I might keep thy w.
119. 105 Thy word (is) a lamp unto my feet, and
119. 107 quicken me, O LORD, according to thy w.
119. 114 Thou (art). .my shield: I hope in thy w.
119. 130 The entrance of thy words giveth light
119. 139 mine enemies have forgotten thy words
119. 147 I prevented. .cried: I hoped in thy word
119. 160 Thy word (is) true (from) the beginning
119. 161 my heart standeth in awe of thy word
119. 169 give. .understanding according to thy w.
130. 5 I wait for the LORD. .and in his word do
147. 15 He sendeth forth. .his word runneth very
147. 18 He sendeth out his word and melteth th.
147. 19 He showeth his word unto Jacob, his sta.
148. 8 Fire and. .stormy wind fulfilling his word
Prov. 1. 6 the words of the wise, and their dark sa.
1. 23 I will make known my words unto you
4. 4 Let thine heart retain my words; keep my
4. 20 My son, attend to my words; incline thi.
10. 19 In the multitude of words there wanteth
12. 6 The words of the wicked (are) to lie in w.
12. 25 Heaviness..maketh it stoop; but a good w.
13. 13 Whoso despiseth the word shall be destr.
14. 15 The simple believeth every word: but the
15. 1 soft answer turneth. .wrath. .grievous w.
15. 23 and a word. .in due season, how good (is it)
18. 4 The words of a man's mouth (are as) deep
18. 8 The words of a talebearer (are) as wounds
22. 12 he overthroweth the words of the transg.
22. 17 Bow down thine ear, and hear the words
23. 8 shalt thou vomit up, and lose thy sweet w.
25. 11 A word fitly spoken (is like) apples of
26. 22 The words of a talebearer (are) as wounds
29. 19 A servant will not be corrected by words
29. 20 Seest thou a man. .hasty in his words?
30. 1 The words of Agur the son of Jakeh, (even)
30. 6 Add thou not unto his word, lest he rep.
31. 1 The words of king Lemuel, the prophecy
Eccl. 1. 1 The words of the Preacher, the son of D.
5. 2 God (is) in heaven. .let thy words be few
5. 3 and a fool's voice. .by multitude of words
5. 7 in the multitude of dreams and many w.
7. 21 Also take no heed unto all words that are
8. 4 Where the word of a king (is, there is) po.
9. 16 the poor man. .his words are not heard
9. 17 The words of wise (men are) heard in qu.
10. 12 The words of a wise man's mouth are gr.
10. 13 The beginning of the words of his mouth
10. 14 A fool also is full of words; a man cannot
12. 10 sought. .acceptable words. .words of truth
12. 11 The words of the wise (are) as goads, and
Isa. 1. 10 Hear the word of the LORD, ye
2. 1 The word that Isaiah the son of Amoz saw
2. 3 and the word of the LORD from Jerusalem
8. 10 speak the word, and it shall not stand: for
8. 20 if they speak not according to this word
9. 8 The Lord sent a word into Jacob, and it
16. 13 This (is) the word that the LORD hath sp.
24. 3 spoiled; for the LORD hath spoken this w.
28. 13 But the word of the LORD was
Isa. 28. 14 Wherefore hear the word of the LORD, ye
29. 11 the vision of all is become. .as the words
29. 18 in that day shall the deaf hear the words
29. 21 That make a man an offender for a word
30. 12 Because ye despise this word, and trust
30. 21 thine ears shall hear a word behind thee
31. 2 Yet he also. .will not call back his words
36. 5 I say. .but (they are but) vain words, I
36. 12 Hath. .sent me. .to speak these words?
36. 13 Hear ye the words of the great king, the
36. 21 But they..answered him not a word: for
36. 22 came. .and told him the words of Rabsh.
37. 4 will hear the words. .will reprove the w.
37. 6 Be not afraid of the words that thou hast
37. 17 and hear all the words of Sennacherib
37. 22 This (is) the word which the LORD hath
38. 4 Then came the word of the LORD to Isaiah
39. 5 Then said Isaiah. .Hear the word of the
39. 8 Good (is) the word of the LORD which th.
40. 8 the word of our God shall stand for ever
41. 28 no..counsellor..could answer a word
44. 26 That confirmeth the word of his servant
45. 23 the word is gone out of my mouth (in) right.
50. 4 I should know how to speak a word in se.
51. 16 I have put my words in thy mouth, and
55. 11 So shall my word be that goeth forth out
58. 13 nor finding..nor speaking (thine own) wo.
59. 13 uttering from the heart words of falsehood
59. 21 my words which I have put in thy mouth
66. 2 contrite spirit, and trembleth at my word
66. 5 Hear the word..that tremble at his word
Jer. 1. 1 The words of Jeremiah the son of Hilkiah
1. 2 the word of the LORD came
So in v. 4, 11, 13; 2. 1; 11. 1; 13. 3, 8; 16. 1; 18. 5; 24.
4; 28. 12; 32. 6; 33. 1, 19, 23; 34. 12; 36. 27; 39. 15; 49.
34; Eze. 1. 3; 3. 16; 6. 1; 7. 1; 11. 14; 12. 1, 17, 21, 26;
13. 1; 14. 2, 12; 15. 1; 16. 1; 17. 1; 18. 1; 20. 45; 21. 1,
8, 18; 22. 1, 17, 23; 23. 1; 24. 1, 15, 20; 25. 1; 26. 1; 27.
1; 28. 1, 11, 20; 29. 1, 17; 30. 1, 20; 31. 1; 32. 1, 17; 33.
1, 23; 34. 1; 35. 1; 36. 16; 37. 15; 38. 1; Jon. 1. 1; 3. 1;
Hag. 2. 20; Zech. 4. 8; 6. 9; 7. 1, 8.
Jer. 1. 9 Behold, I have put my words in thy mou.
1. 12 for I will hasten my word to perform it
2. 4 Hear ye the word of the LORD, O house of
2. 31 O generation, see ye the word of the LORD
3. 12 proclaim these words toward the north
5. 14 saith..Because ye speak this word, behold
5. 14 I will make my words in thy mouth fire
6. 10 the word of the LORD is unto them a rep.
6. 19 they have not hearkened unto my words
7. 1 The word that came to Jeremiah from the
7. 2 proclaim there this word..Hear the word
7. 4 Trust ye not in lying words, saying, The
7. 8 ye trust in lying words, that cannot profit
7. 27 thou shalt speak all these words unto th.
8. 9 they have rejected the word of the LORD
9. 20 Yet hear the word..the word of his mouth
10. 1 Hear ye the word which the LORD speak.
11. 1 The word that came to Jeremiah from the
11. 2, 6 Hear ye the words of this covenant, and
11. 3 the man that obeyeth not the words of th.
11. 6 Proclaim all these words in the cities of
11. 8 bring upon them all the words of this co.
11. 10 forefathers, which refused to hear my wo.
13. 2 I got a girdle, according to the word of
13. 10 which refuse to hear my words, which w.
13. 12 thou shalt speak unto them this word, Th.
14. 17 thou shalt say this word unto them; Let
15. 16 Thy words were found..thy word was un.
16. 10 thou shalt show this people all these wo.
17. 15 Where (is) the word of the LORD? let it
17. 20 Hear ye the word of the LORD, ye kings of
18. 1 The word which came to Jeremiah from
18. 2 there I will cause thee to hear my words
18. 18 word from the prophet..any of his words
19. 2 proclaim there the words that I shall tell
19. 3 Hear ye the word of the LORD, O kings of
19. 15 that they might not hear my words
20. 8 the word of the LORD was made a reproach
21. 1 The word which came unto Jeremiah from
21. 11 touching the house. .(say), Hear ye the w.
22. 1 Go down..and speak there this word
22. 2 Hear the word of the LORD, O king of Ju.
22. 5 if ye will not hear these words, I swear by
22. 29 earth, earth, hear the word of the LORD
23. 9 and because of the words of his holiness
23. 16 Hearken not unto the words of the prop.
23. 18 heard his word? who hath marked his w.
23. 22 had caused my people to hear my words
23. 28 hath my word, let him speak my word fa.
23. 29 (Is) not my word like as a fire? saith the
23. 30 that steal my words every one from his
23. 36 every man's word..the words of the living
23. 38 Because ye say this word, The burden of
25. 1 The word that came to Jeremiah concer.
25. 3 the word of the LORD hath come unto me
25. 8 Because ye have not heard my words
25. 13 I will bring upon that land all my words
25. 30 prophesy thou against them all these wo.
26. 1 came this word from the LORD, saying
26. 2 speak..all the words..diminish not a word
26. 5 To hearken to the words of my servants
26. 7 heard Jeremiah speaking these words in
26. 12 to prophesy..all the words that ye have
26. 15 sent me..to speak all these words in your
26. 20 according to all the words of Jeremiah
26. 21 all the princes, heard his words, the king
27. 1 came this word unto Jeremiah from the
27. 12 I spake..according to all these words, sa.
27. 14 hearken not unto the words of the proph.
27. 16 Hearken not to the words of your proph.
27. 18 if the word of the LORD be with them, let
Jer. 28. 6 the LORD perform thy words which thou
28. 7 hear thou now this word that I speak in
28. 9 the word of the prophet shall come to pa.
29. 1 these (are) the words of the letter that
29. 10 perform my good word toward you, in ca.
29. 19 they have not hearkened to my words, sa.
29. 20 Hear ye therefore the word of the LORD
29. 23 have spoken lying words in my name, wh.
29. 30 Then came the word of the LORD unto Je.
30. 1 The word that came to Jeremiah from the
30. 2 Write thee all the words that I have spo.
30. 4 these (are) the words that the LORD spake
31. 10 Hear the word of the LORD, O ye nations
32. 1 The word that came to Jeremiah from the
32. 8 according to the word..the word of the
32. 26 Then came the word of the LORD unto Jer.
34. 1 The word which came unto Jeremiah from
34. 4 hear the word of the LORD, O Zedekiah
34. 5 for I have pronounced the word, saith the
34. 6 the prophet spake all these words unto
34. 8 (This is) the word that came unto Jerem.
34. 18 which have not performed the words of
35. 1 The word which came unto Jeremiah from
35. 12 Then came the word of the LORD unto Jer.
35. 13 receive instruction to hearken to my words
35. 14 The words of Jonadab the son of Rechab
36. 1 this word came unto Jeremiah from the
36. 2 write therein all the words that I have sp.
36. 4 Baruch wrote..all the words of the LORD
36. 6 read in the roll..the words of the LORD
36. 8 reading in the book the words of the LORD
36. 10 Then read Baruch in the book the words
36. 13 Michaiah declared unto them all the wo.
36. 16 had heard all the words..all these words
36. 17 How didst thou write all these words at
36. 18 He pronounced all these words unto me
36. 20 told all the words in the ears of the king
36. 24 of his servants that heard all these words
36. 27 the words which Baruch wrote at the mo.
36. 28 write in it all the former words that were
36. 32 the words of the book..many like words
37. 2 did hearken unto the words of the LORD
37. 6 Then came the word of the LORD unto
37. 17 and said, Is there (any) word from the Lo.
38. 1 heard the words that Jeremiah had spoken
38. 4 weakeneth..hands..in speaking such w.
38. 21 this (is) the word that the LORD hath sh.
38. 24 Let no man know of these words, and th.
38. 27 he told them according to all these words
39. 16 I will bring my words upon this city for
40. 1 The word that came to Jeremiah from
42. 4 I will pray..according to your words, and
42. 15 hear the word of the LORD, ye remnant of
43. 1 the words of the LORD..all these words
43. 8 Then came the word of the LORD unto J.
44. 1 The word that came to Jeremiah concer.
44. 16 As for the word that thou hast spoken un.
44. 24 Hear the word of the LORD, all Judah th.
44. 26 hear ye the word of the LORD, all Judah
44. 28 shall know whose words shall stand, mine
44. 29 ye may know that my words shall surely
45. 1 The word..he had written these words in
46. 1 The word of the LORD which came to Je.
46. 13 The word that the LORD spake to Jerem.
47. 1 The word of the LORD that came to Jere.
50. 1 The word that the LORD spake against B.
51. 59 The word which Jeremiah the prophet co.
51. 60 these words (that are) written against Ba.
51. 61 and shalt see, and shalt read all these w.
51. 64 Thus far (are) the words of Jeremiah
Eze. 2. 6 afraid of their words..afraid of their wo.
2. 7 thou shalt speak my words unto them
3. 4 go..and speak with my words unto them
3. 6 whose words thou canst not understand
3. 10 all my words that I shall speak unto thee
3. 17 hear the word at my mouth, and give th.
6. 3 mountains of Israel, hear the word of the
12. 8 in the morning came the word of the Lo.
12. 17, 21, 26 the word of the LORD came to me
12. 25 and the word..will I say the word, and
12. 28 none of my words..the word which I ha.
13. 2 say thou..Hear ye the word of the LORD
13. 6 hope that they would confirm the word
16. 35 O harlot, hear the word of the LORD
20. 2 Then came the word of the LORD unto me
20. 47 Hear the word of the LORD; Thus saith
25. 3 Hear the word of the Lord GOD, Thus sa.
33. 7 thou shalt hear the word at my mouth, and
33. 30 hear what is the word that cometh forth
33. 31 they hear thy words, but they will not do
33. 32 they hear thy words, but they do them
34. 7, 9 ye shepherds, hear the word of the Lo.
35. 13 have multiplied your words against me
36. 1, 4 mountains of Israel, hear the word of
37. 4 O ye dry bones, hear the word of the Lo.
Dan. 9. 2 the word of the LORD came to Jeremiah
9. 12 he hath confirmed his words, which he sp.
10. 6 the voice of his words like the voice of a
10. 9 the voice of his words..voice of his words
10. 11 understand the words. .spoken this word
10. 12 words were heard. .I am come for thy w.
10. 15 when he had spoken such words unto me
12. 4 O Daniel, shut up the words, and seal the
12. 9 the words (are) closed up and sealed till
Hos. 1. 1 The word of the LORD that came unto H.
4. 1 Hear the word of the LORD, ye children
10. 4 They have spoken words, swearing falsely
14. 2 Take with you words, and turn to the L.
Joel 1. 1 The word of the LORD that came to Joel
2. 11 for (he is) strong that executeth his word
Amos 1. 1 The words of Amos, who was among the
3. 1 Hear this word that the LORD hath spoken

Amos 4. 1 Hear this word, ye kine of Bashan, that
5. 1 Hear ye this word which I take up again.
7. 10 the land is not able to bear all his words
7. 16 hear thou the word of the LORD: Thou
8. 11 a famine..of hearing the words of the LORD
8. 12 run to and fro to seek the word of the L.
Jon. 3. 3 went..according to the word of the LORD
3. 6 word came unto the king of Nineveh, and
Mic. 1. 1 The word of the LORD that came to Micah
2. 7 do not my words do good to him that wa.
4. 2 and the word of the LORD from Jerusalem
Zeph. 1. 1 The word of the LORD which came unto
2. 5 the word of the LORD (is) against you, O
Hag. 1. 1 came the word of the LORD by Haggai
1. 3 Then came the word of the LORD by Hag.
1. 12 the words of Haggai the prophet, as the
2. 1 came the word of the LORD by the proph.
2. 5 (According to) the word that I covenanted
2. 10 came the word of the LORD by Haggai the
Zech. 1. 1, 7 came the word of the LORD unto Zech.
1. 6 my words and my statutes, which I com.
1. 13 (with) good words (and) comfortable wo.
4. 6 This (is) the word of the LORD unto Zeru.
7. 4 Then came the word of the LORD of hos.
7. 7 (Should ye) not (hear) the words which
7. 12 the words which the LORD of hosts hath
8. 1 the word of the LORD of hosts came (to
8. 9 ye that hear in these days these words
8. 18 the word of the LORD of hosts came unto
9. 1 The burden of the word of the LORD in
11. 11 knew that it (was) the word of the LORD
12. 1 The burden of the word of the LORD for
Mal. 1. 1 The burden of the word of the LORD to
2. 17 Ye have wearied the LORD with your wo
3. 13 Your words have been stout against me

6. *Words, speeches, utterances,* דִּבְּרוֹת *dabbereth.*
Deut 33. 3 and they..shall receive of thy words

7. *A saying, speech,* מַאֲמַר *memar.*
Dan. 4. 17 the demand by the word of the holy ones

8. *A word, speech, matter,* מִלָּה *millah.*
2 Sa. 23. 2 The spirit..spake by me, and his word
Job 4. 4 Thy words have upholden him that was
6. 26 Do ye imagine to reprove words, and the
8. 10 tell thee, and utter words out of their he.
12. 11 Doth not the ear try words? and the mo.
15. 13 and lettest (such) words go out of thy m.
16. 4 I could heap up words against you, and
18. 2 How long..(ere) ye make an end of words
19. 2 will ye..break me in pieces with words?
19. 23 O that my words were now written! oh
23. 5 I would know the words (which) he wou.
26. 4 To whom hast thou uttered words? and
32. 14 he hath not directed (his) words against
33. 8 I have heard the voice of (thy) words, (say.)
34. 2 Hear my words, O ye wise (men), and gi.
34. 3 the ear trieth words, as the mouth tasteth
34. 16 hear this; hearken to the voice of my w.
35. 16 he multiplieth words without knowledge
36. 4 my words (shall) not (be) false: he that
38. 2 (is) this that darkeneth counsel by words
Psa. 19. 4 and their words to the end of the world
139. 4 (there is) not a word in my tongue, (but)
Prov 23. 9 for he will despise the wisdom of thy wo.
Dan. 2. 9 have prepared lying and corrupt words
3. 28 have changed the king's word, and yield.
4. 31 While the word (was) in the king's mouth
5. 10 by reason of the words of the king and
6. 14 the king, when he heard (these) words
7. 11 the voice of the great words which the
7. 25 he shall speak (great) words against the

9. *Mouth,* פֶּה *peh.*
Gen. 41. 40 according unto thy word shall all my peo.
Num. 3. 16 numbered them, according to the word
3. 51 to his sons, according to the word of the
4. 45 according to the word of the LORD by the
20. 24 ye rebelled against my word at the water
22. 18 I cannot go beyond the word of the LORD
27. 21 at his word..they go out, and at his wo.
36. 5 according to the word of the LORD, say.
Deut 21. 5 by their word shall every controversy and
34. 5 died..according to the word of the LORD
Josh. 19. 50 According to the word of the LORD, they
22. 9 according to the word of the LORD by the
1 Ki. 13. 26 who was disobedient unto the word of the
1 Ch. 12. 23 turn the kingdom..according to the word

10. *Matter, sentence,* פִּתְגָם *pithgam.*
Ezra 6. 11 whosoever shall alter this word, let tim.

11. *A word, speech, matter, reason,* λόγος *logos.*
Matt. 8. 8 speak the word only, and my servant sh.
8. 16 he cast out the spirits with (his) word
10. 14 whosoever shall not..hear your words
12. 32 whosoever speaketh a word against the
12. 37 by thy words thou..by thy words thou
13. 19 When any one heareth the word of the
13. 20 the same is he that heareth the word, and
13. 21 or persecution ariseth because of the wo.
13. 22 heareth the word..choke the word, and
13. 23 that received..is he that heareth the wo.
15. 23 he answered her not a word. And his
22. 46 And no man was able to answer him a w.
24. 35 Heaven and earth shall pass..but my w
26. 44 and prayed the third time..the same wo.
Mark 2. 2 straightway..he preached the word unto
4. 14 The sower soweth the word
4. 15 where the word is..taketh away the word
4. 16 who, when they have heard the word, im.
4. 17 when..persecution ariseth for the word's
4. 18 And these are they..such as hear the wo.
4. 19 choke the word, and it becometh unfruit.
4. 20 such as hear the word, and receive (it)
4. 33 with many such parables spake he the w.
5. 36 As soon as Jesus heard the word that
7. 13 Making the word of God of none effect
8. 38 Whosoever..shall be ashamed..of my w.
10. 24 the disciples were astonished at his wor.
12. 13 send..Herodians, to catch him in (his) w.
13. 31 Heaven and earth shall pass..but my wo.
14. 39 again he..prayed, and spake the same w.
16. 20 [confirming the word with signs following]
Luke 1. 2 eye witnesses, and ministers of the word
1. 20 because thou believest not my words, wh.
3. 4 As it is written in the book of the words
4. 22 wondered at the gracious words which
4. 32 were astonished..for his word was with
4. 36 What a word (is) this! for with authority
5. 1 people pressed upon him to hear the wo.
7. 7 say in a word, and my servant shall be he.
8. 11 the parable is this: The seed is the word
8. 12 taketh away the word out of their hearts
8. 13 which, when they hear, receive the word
8. 15 having heard the word, keep (it), and br.
8. 21 are these which hear the word of God
9. 26 whosoever shall be ashamed..of [my w.]
10. 39 which..sat at Jesus'..and heard his wor.
11. 28 blessed (are) they that hear the word of
12. 10 whosoever shall speak a word against
20. 20 that they might take hold of his words
21. 33 Heaven and earth shall pass..but my w.
22. 61 Peter remembered the word of the Lord
23. 9 Then he questioned with him in many w.
24. 19 Jesus..a prophet mighty in deed and wo.
24. 44 These (are) the words which I spake unto
John 1. 1 In the beginning was the Word, and the
1. 1 Word was with God, and the Word was
1. 14 the Word was made flesh, and dwelt amo.
2. 22 believed..the word which Jesus had said
4. 41 many more believed because of his own w.
4. 50 the man believed the word that Jesus had
5. 24 He that heareth my word, and believeth
5. 38 ye have not his word abiding in you, for
8. 31 If ye continue in my word, (then) are ye
8. 37 ye seek to kill me, because my word hath
8. 43 Why..(even) because ye cannot hear my w.
10. 35 If he called them gods unto whom the w.
12. 48 the word that I have spoken, the same
14. 23 If a man love me, he will keep my words
14. 24 the word which ye hear is not mine, but
15. 3 Now ye are clean through the word whi.
15. 20 Remember the word that I said unto you
15. 25 that the word might be fulfilled that is
17. 6 thine they were..they have kept thy wo.
17. 14 I have given them thy word; and the wo.
17. 17 Sanctify them through thy truth; thy wo.
17. 20 which shall believe on me through their w.
Acts 2. 22 Ye men of Israel, hear these words: Jesus
2. 40 with many other words did he testify and
2. 41 Then they that gladly received his word
4. 4 Howbeit many of them which heard the w.
4. 29 with all boldness they may speak thy wo.
4. 31 they spake the word of God with boldness
5. 5 Ananias hearing these words fell down
6. 2 It is not reason..we should leave the wo.
6. 4 give ourselves..to the ministry of the wo.
6. 7 the word of God increased; and the num.
7. 22 Moses..was mighty in words and in deeds
8. 4 they..went every where preaching the w.
8. 14 heard that Samaria had received the word
8. 25 when they..testified and preached the w.
10. 36 The word which (God) sent unto the chi.
10. 44 Holy Ghost fell on all..which heard the w.
11. 1 Gentiles had also received the word of G.
11. 19 preaching the word to none but unto the
12. 24 But the word of God grew and multiplied
13. 5 they preached the word of God in the sy.
13. 7 Sergius..desired to hear the word of God
13. 15 if ye have any word of exhortation for the
13. 26 to you is the word of this salvation sent
13. 44 whole city together to hear the word of G.
13. 46 It was necessary that the word of God sh.
13. 48 they were glad, and glorified the word of
13. 49 the word of the Lord was published
14. 3 Lord, which gave testimony unto the w.
14. 25 when they had preached the word in Pe.
15. 7 by my mouth should hear the word of the
15. 15 And to this agree the words of the proph.
15. 24 that certain..have troubled you with wo.
15. 32 exhorted the brethren with many words
15. 35 teaching and preaching the word of the
15. 36 where we have preached the word of the
16. 6 forbidden..to preach the word in Asia
16. 32 they spake unto him the word of the Lo.
17. 11 in that they received the word with all re.
17. 13 when the Jews..had knowledge that the w.
18. 11 teaching the word of God among them
18. 15 But if it be a question of words and nam.
19. 10 they which dwelt in Asia heard the word
19. 20 So mightily grew the word of God and pr.
20. 32 I commend you to God, and to the word
20. 35 to remember the words of the Lord Jesus
20. 38 Sorrowing most of all for the words which
22. 22 they gave him audience unto this word
Rom. 9. 6 Not as though the word of God
9. 9 For this (is) the word of promise, At this
15. 18 to make the Gentiles obedient, by word
1 Co. 1. 17 not with wisdom of words, lest the cross
2. 4 not with enticing [words of] man's wisd.
2. 13 not in the words which man's wisdom te.
4. 20 For the kingdom of God (is) not in word
12. 8 the word of wisdom..the word of knowle.
1 Co. 14. 9 except ye utter by the tongue words easy
14. 19 rather..five words..than ten thousand w.
14. 36 What? came the word of God out from
2 Co. 1. 18 But..God (is) true, our word toward you
2. 17 we are not as many, which corrupt the w.
4. 2 nor handling the word of God deceitfully
5. 19 hath committed unto us the word of rec.
6. 7 By the word of truth, by the power of G.
10. 11 such as we are in word by letters when
Gal. 5. 14 For all the law is fulfilled in one word
6. 6 Let him that is taught in the word com.
Eph. 1. 13 after that ye heard the word of truth, the
5. 6 Let no man deceive you with vain words
Phil. 1. 14 are much more bold to speak the word
2. 16 Holding forth the word of life, that I may
Col. 1. 5 whereof ye heard before in the word of
1. 25 is given to me for you, to fulfil the word
3. 16 Let the word of Christ dwell in you richly
3. 17 And whatsoever ye do in word or deed
1 Th. 1. 5 For our gospel came not unto you in word
1. 6 having received the word in much afflict.
1. 8 For from you sounded forth the word of
2. 5 neither at any time used we flattering w.
2. 13 the word of God..word of men..word of
4. 15 For this we say unto you by the word of
4. 18 Wherefore comfort one another with..w.
2 Th. 2. 2 be troubled, neither by spirit, nor by w.
2. 15 which ye have been taught, whether by w.
2. 17 stablish you in every good word and work
3. 1 pray for us, that the word of the Lord
3. 14 if any man obey not our word by this ep.
1 Ti. 4. 5 it is sanctified by the word of God and p.
4. 6 nourished up in the words of faith and of
4. 12 be thou an example of..believers, in word
5. 17 especially they who labour in the word
6. 3 consent not to wholesome words, (even)
2 Ti 1. 13 Hold fast the form of sound words, which
2. 9 I suffer..but the word of God is not bou.
2. 15 a workman..rightly dividing the word of
2. 17 And their word will eat as doth a canker
4. 2 Preach the word; be instant in season, out
4. 15 for he hath greatly withstood our words
Titus 1. 3 But hath in due times manifested his wo.
1. 9 Holding fast the faithful word as he hath
2. 5 that the word of God be not blasphemed
Heb. 2. 2 For if the word spoken by angels was st.
4. 2 but the word preached did not profit them
4. 12 For the word of God (is) quick, and pow.
5. 13 (is) unskilful in the word of righteousness
7. 28 but the word of the oath, which was since
12. 19 that the word should not be spoken to th.
13. 7 who have spoken unto you the word of God
13. 22 suffer the word of exhortation, for I have
Jas. 1. 18 Of his own will begat he us with the word
1. 21 receive with meekness the ingrafted word
1. 22 But be ye doers of the word, and not he.
1. 23 For if any be a hearer of the word, and not
3. 2 If any man offend not in word, the same
1 Pe. 1. 23 Being born again..by the word of God
2. 8 which stumble at the word, being disobe.
3. 1 obey not the word..may without the word
2 Pe. 1. 19 We have also a more sure word of proph.
2. 3 shall they with feigned words make mer.
3. 5 by the word of God the heavens were of
3. 7 by the same word are kept in store, reser.
1 Jo. 1. 1 hands have handled, of the word of life
1. 10 we make him a liar, and his word is not
2. 5 But whoso keepeth his word, in him verily
2. 7 The old commandment is the word which
2. 14 because ye are strong, and the word of G.
3. 18 let us not love in word, neither in tongue
5. 7 [the Father, the Word, and the Holy Gh.]
3 John 10 prating against us with malicious words
Rev. 1. 2 Who bare record of the word of God, and
1. 3 they that hear the words of this prophecy
1. 9 for the word of God, and for the testimony
3. 8 kept my word, and hast not denied my na.
3. 10 Because thou hast kept the word of my p.
6. 9 souls of them that were slain for the word
12. 11 overcame..by the word of their testimony
19. 13 and his name is called, The Word of God
20. 4 that were beheaded..for the word of God
21. 5 Write: for these words are true and faith.
22. 18 testify unto every man that heareth the w.
22. 19 if any man shall take away from the words

12. *A saying, speech, matter, thing,* ῥῆμα *rhēma.*
Matt. 4. 4 not live by bread alone, but by every wo.
12. 36 That every idle word that men shall speak
18. 16 that..in the mouth of..witnesses every w.
26. 75 Peter remembered the word of Jesus, wh.
27. 14 And he answered him to never a word
Mark 14. 72 Peter called to mind the word that Jesus
Luke 1. 38 said..be it unto me according to thy word
2. 29 lettest thou..depart..according to thy w.
3. 2 the word of God came unto John the son
4. 4 [not live by bread alone, but by every w.]
5. 5 nevertheless at thy word I will let down
20. 26 they could not take hold of his words be.
24. 8 And they remembered his words
24. 11 their words seemed to them as idle tales
John 3. 34 he whom God hath sent speaketh the wo.
5. 47 believe not..how shall ye believe my wo.?
6. 63 the words that I speak unto you..are sp.
6. 68 Lord..thou hast the words of eternal life
8. 20 These words spake Jesus in the treasury
8. 47 He that is of God heareth God's words
10. 21 These are not the words of him that hath
12. 47 if any man hear my words, and believe
12. 48 He that..receiveth not my words, hath
14. 10 the words that I speak unto you I speak
15. 7 If ye abide in me, and my words abide in

John17. 8 For I have given unto them the words wh.
Acts 2. 14 be this known unto you..hearken to my w.
5. 20 speak..to the people all the words of this
6. 11 We have heard him speak blasphemous w.
6. 13 blasphemous words against this holy place
10. 22 to send for thee..and to hear words of thee
10. 37 That word..ye know, which was published
10. 44 While Peter yet spake these words, the
11. 14 Who shall tell thee words, whereby thou
11. 16 Then remembered I the word of the Lord
13. 42 the Gentiles besought that these words
16. 38 the serjeants told these words unto the
26. 25 but speak forth the words of truth and
28. 25 departed, after..Paul had spoken one wo.
Rom.10. 8 The word is nigh thee..the word of faith
10. 17 faith..by hearing, and hearing by the wo.
10. 18 and their words unto the ends of the wo
2 Co.12. 4 How that he..heard unspeakable words
13. 1 In the mouth of..witnesses shall every w.
Eph. 5. 26 it with the washing of water by the word
6. 17 the sword of the spirit, which is the word
Heb. 1. 3 upholding all things by the word of his
6. 5 have tasted the good word of God, and
11. 3 that the worlds were framed by the word
12. 19 sound of a trumpet, and the voice of words
1 Pe. 1. 25 the word of the Lord..this is the word wh.
2 Pe. 3. 2 That ye may be mindful of the words which
Jude 17 remember ye the words which were spok.
Rev. 17. 17 until [the words] of God shall be fulfilled

WORDS, of the word, a few —
1. *Logical, reasonable, verbal*, λογικός *logikos.*
1 Pe. 2. 2 babes, desire the sincere milk of the word
2. *Concisely, briefly*, συντόμως *suntomōs.*
Acts 24. 4 pray..hear us of thy clemency a few words
WORD (again), to bring or strive about words —
1. *To tell off, away, again*, ἀπαγγέλλω *apaggellō.*
Matt. 2. 8 bring me word again, that I may come and
28. 8 and did run to bring his disciples word
2. *To say, speak*, εἶπον *eipon.*
Matt. 2. 13 and be thou there until I bring thee word
3. *To fight about words*, λογομαχέω *logomacheō.*
2 Ti. 2. 14 that they strive not about words to no pr.
4. *A fighting about words*, λογομαχία *logomachia.*
1 Ti. 6. 4 doting about questions and strifes of wo.
WORK (effectual) working, workmanship —
1. *A word, matter, thing*, דָּבָר *dabar.*
1 Ch.16. 37 continually, as every day's work required
Psa.145. 5 of thy majesty, and of thy wondrous wo.
2. *Labour*, יְגִיעַ *yagia.*
Job 10. 3 that thou shouldest despise the work of
3. *Hand, power*, יָד *yad.*
Exod 14. 31 Israel saw that great work which the L.
4. *Formation, frame*, יֵצֶר *yetser.*
Hab. 2. 18 that the maker of his work trusteth the.
5. *Work*, מְלָאכָה *melakah.*
Gen. 2. 2 God ended his work..all his work which
2. 3 in it he had rested from all his work wh.
Exod12. 16 no manner of work shall be done in them
20. 9 Six days shalt thou..do all thy work
20. 10 thou shalt not do any work, thou, nor thy
31. 3 spirit..in all manner of workmanship
31. 5 to work in all manner of workmanship
31. 14 for whosoever doeth (any) work therein
31. 15 Six days may work be done; but in the
31. 15 whosoever doeth (any) work in the sabbath
35. 2 Six days shall work be done, but on the
35. 2 whosoever doeth work therein shall be
35. 21 brought the LORD'S offering to the work
35. 24 every man with whom was found..any w.
35. 29 for all manner of work which the LORD
35. 31 the spirit..in all manner of workmanship
35. 33 And..to make any manner of cunning w.
35. 35 manner of work..of them that do any w.
36. 1 to know how to work all manner of work
36. 2 stirred him up to come unto the work to
36. 3 had brought for the work of the service
36. 4 the wise men, that wrought all the work
36. 4 came every man from his work which they
36. 5 for the service of the work which the L.
36. 6 Let neither man nor woman make..work
36. 7 the stuff..was sufficient for all the work
36. 8 among them that wrought the work of the
38. 24 for the work in all the work of the holy
39. 43 Moses did look upon all the work, and
40. 33 court gate. So Moses finished the work
Lev. 11. 32 whatsoever vessel..wherein (any) work
13. 51 be spread..in any work that is made of
16. 29 ye shall afflict your souls, and do no work
23. 3 Six days shall work be done: but the se.
23. 3 the seventh day..ye shall do no work (th.)
23. 7, 8, 21, 25, 35, 36 ye shall do no servile wo.
23. 28 ye shall do no work in that same day, for
23. 30 whatsoever soul..doeth any work in that
23. 31 Ye shall do no manner of work..a statute
Num. 4. 3 to do the work in the tabernacle of the
28. 18 ye shall do no manner of servile work (th.)
28. 25, 26 ye shall do no servile work
29. 1, 12, 35 ye shall do no servile work
29. 7 afflict your souls: ye shall not do any w.
Deut. 5. 13 Six days thou shalt labour, and do..work
5. 14 thou shalt not do any work, thou, nor thy
16. 8 a solemn assembly..thou shalt do no w.
1 Sa. 8. 16 will take..your asses, and put..to his w.
1 Ki. 5. 16 over the work..over the people..in the w.
7. 14 all works in brass..and wrought..his w.
1 Ki. 7. 22 And..so was the work of the pillars fini.
7. 40 Hiram made an end of doing all the work
7. 51 So was ended all the work that king Sol.
9. 23 over S.'s work..over the people..in the w.
2 Ki. 12. 11 into the hands of them that did the work
22. 5 doers of the work..to the doers of the w.
22. 9 into the hand of them that do the work
1 Ch. 4. 23 they dwelt with the king for his work
6. 49 for all the work of the (place) most holy
9. 13 very able men for the work of the service
9. 19 over the work of the service, keepers of
9. 33 they were employed in..work day and ni.
22. 15 cunning men for every manner of work
23. 4 to set forward the work of the house of the
23. 24 that did the work for the service of the ho.
27. 26 over them that did the work of the field
28. 13 and for all the work of the service of the
28. 19 LORD made me understand..all the works
28. 20 until thou hast finished all the work for
28. 21 with thee for all manner of workmanship
29. 1 the work (is) great: for the palace (is) not
29. 5 for all manner of work..by the hands of
29. 6 with the rulers of the king's work, offered
2 Ch. 4. 11 Huram finished the work that he was to
5. 1 Thus all the work that Solomon made for
8. 9 Solomon make no servants for his work
8. 16 all the work of Solomon was prepared unto
16. 5 he left off building..and let his work cea.
24. 12 gave it to such as did the work of the ser.
24. 13 So the workmen wrought, and the work
29. 34 the Levites did help them, till the work
34. 12 the men did the work faithfully, and the
34. 13 overseers of all that wrought the work in
Ezra 2. 69 They gave..unto the treasure of the work
3. 8 to set forward the work of the house of
6. 22 to strengthen their hands in the work of
10. 13 neither (is this) a work of one day or two
Neh. 2. 16 neither..told (it)..the rest that did the w.
4. 11 and slay them, and cause the work to ce.
4. 15 we returned all..every one unto his work
4. 16 half of my servants wrought in the work
4. 17 with one of his hands wrought in work
4. 19 The work (is) great and large, and we are
4. 21 So we laboured in the work: and half of
5. 16 also I continued in the work of this wall
5. 16 my servants..gathered thither unto the w.
6. 3 I (am) doing a great work..should the w.
6. 9 hands shall be weakened from the work
6. 16 they perceived that this work was wrought
7. 70, 71 chief of the fathers gave unto the..wo.
10. 33 (for) all the work of the house of our God
11. 12 their brethren that did the work of the
13. 10 Levites and the singers, that did the work
Psa. 73. 28 my trust..that I may declare all thy works
Prov18. 9 He..that is slothful in his work is brother
24. 27 Prepare thy work without, and make it fit
Jer. 17. 22 neither do ye any work; but hallow ye the
17. 24 but hallow the sabbath day, to do no wo.
18. 3 behold, he wrought a work on the wheels
48. 10 Cursed (be) he that doeth the work of the
50. 25 this (is) the work of the Lord GOD of hosts
Eze. 15. 3 Shall wood be taken thereof to do any w.?
15. 4 is cast into the fire..Is it meet for..work?
15. 5 when it was whole, it was meet for no w.
15. 5 shall it be meet yet for..work, when the
28. 13 the workmanship of thy tabrets and of thy
Hag. 1. 14 they came and did work in the house of
6. *Deed, act, doing*, מַעְבָד *mabad.*
Job 34. 25 Therefore he knoweth their works, and he
Dan. 4. 37 all whose works (are) truth, and his ways
7. *An act, deed*, מַעֲלָל *maalal.*
Neh. 9. 35 neither turned they from their wicked w.
Psa. 77. 11 I will remember the works of the LORD
78. 7 That they might..not forget the works of
8. *Deed, doing, act, work*, מַעֲשֶׂה *maaseh.*
Gen. 5. 29 concerning our work and toil of our hands
Exod. 5. 4 do ye..let the people from their works?
5. 13 Fulfil your works..daily tasks, as when
18. 20 show them..the work that they must do
23. 12 Six days thou shalt do thy work, and on
23. 24 nor serve them, nor do after their works
24. 10 under his feet as it were a paved work
26. 1 cherubim of cunning work shalt thou m.
26. 31 and fine twined linen, of cunning work
28. 6 and fine twined linen, with cunning work
28. 8 shall be of the same, according to the w.
28. 11 With the work of an engraver in stone
28. 14 wreathen work shalt thou make them, and
28. 15 with cunning work; after the work of the
28. 22 chains at the ends (of) wreathen work (of)
28. 32 it shall have a binding of woven work ro.
32. 16 the tables..the work of God, and the wr.
34. 10 all the people..shall see the work of the
36. 8 cherubim of cunning work made he them
36. 35 cherubim made he it of cunning work
37. 29 according to the work of the apothecary
39. 3 and in the fine linen, (with) cunning work
39. 5 the same, according to the work thereof
39. 8 cunning work, like the work of the ephod
39. 15 chains at the ends, (of) wreathen work (of)
39. 22 made the robe of the ephod (of) woven w.
39. 27 made coats (of) fine linen, (of) woven work
39. 29 blue, and purple, and scarlet, (of) needlew.
Num. 8. 4 this work of the candlestick..beaten gold
16. 28 the LORD hath sent me to do all these wo.
31. 20 all work of goat's (hair), and all things ma.
Deut. 2. 7 God hath blessed thee in all the works of
3. 24 what God..can do according to thy works
4. 28 ye shall serve gods, the work of men's ha.
14. 29 God may bless thee in all the work of thi.
Deut15. 10 God shall bless thee in all thy works, and
16. 15 God shall bless thee..in all the works of
24. 19 God may bless thee in all the work of th.
27. 15 the work of the hands of the craftsman
28. 12 and to bless all the work of thine hand
30. 9 will make thee plenteous in every work
31. 29 to provoke him to anger through the wo.
Josh.24. 31 which had known all the works of the Lo.
Judg. 2. 7 had seen all the great works of the LORD
2. 10 knew not the LORD, nor yet the works wh.
19. 16 there came an old man from his work out
1 Sa. 8. 8 According to all the works which they ha.
19. 4 his works (have been) to thee ward very
1 Ki. 7. 8 another court..(which) was of the like w.
7. 17 checker work, and wreaths of chain work
7. 19 the chapiters..(were) of lily work in the
7. 22 upon the top of the pillars (was) lily work
7. 28 the work of the bases (was) on this (man.)
7. 29 (were) certain additions made of thin wo.
7. 31 (after) the work of the base, a cubit and
7. 33 the work of the wheels (was) like the wo.
13. 11 sons came and told him all the works that
16. 7 in provoking him to anger with the work
2 Ki.16. 10 according to all the workmanship thereof
19. 18 the work of men's hands, wood and stone
22. 17 provoke me to anger with all the works
1 Ch. 23. 28 the work of the service of the house of
2 Ch. 3. 10 he made two cherubim of image work, and
4. 5 the brim of it like the work of the brim
20. 37 the LORD hath broken thy works. And the
31. 21 in every work that he began in the servi.
32. 19 (which were) the work of the hands of m.
32. 30 And Hezekiah prospered in all his works
34. 25 provoke me to anger with all the works
Neh. 6. 14 think thou..according to these their wo.
Job 1. 10 Thou hast blessed the work of his hands
14. 15 thou wilt have a desire to the work of th.
34. 19 for they all (are) the work of his hands?
37. 7 sealeth..that all men may know his work
Psa. 8. 3 I consider thy heavens, the work of thy
8. 6 to have dominion over the works of thy
19. 1 and the firmament showeth his handy wo.
28. 4 give them after the work of their hands
33. 4 right; and all his works (are done) in tru.
33. 15 fashioneth..he considereth all their work
62. 12 renderest to every man according to his w
66. 3 How terrible (art thou in) thy works! thr.
86. 8 neither (are there)..like unto thy works
90. 17 establish thou the work..the work of
92. 4 I will triumph in the works of thy hands
92. 5 O LORD, how great are thy works! (and)
102. 25 and the heavens (are) the work of thy ha.
103. 22 Bless the LORD, all his works in all places
104. 13 is satisfied with the fruit of thy works
104. 24 O LORD, how manifold are thy works! in
104. 31 the LORD shall rejoice in his works
106. 13 They soon forgat his works; they waited
106. 35 were mingled..and learned their works
106. 39 Thus were they defiled with their..works
107. 22 let them..declare his works with rejoicing
107. 24 These see the works of the LORD, and his
111. 2 The works of the LORD (are) great, sought
111. 6 showed his people the power of his works
111. 7 The works of his hands (are) verity and
115. 4 Their idols (are) silver and gold, the work
118. 17 but live, and declare the works of the L.
135. 15 silver and gold, the work of men's hands
138. 8 forsake not the works of thine own hands
139. 14 marvellous (are) thy works; and (that) my
143. 5 I meditate..I muse on the work of thy ha.
145. 4 One generation shall praise thy works to
145. 9 his tender mercies (are) over all his works
145. 10 All thy works shall praise thee, O LORD
145. 17 The LORD (is) righteous..in all his works
Prov16. 3 Commit thy works unto the LORD, and
16. 11 all the weights of the bag (are) his work
31. 31 let her own works praise her in the gates
Eccl. 1. 14 I have seen all the works that are done
2. 4 I made me great works; I builded me ho.
2. 11 Then I looked on all the works that my
2. 17 the work that is wrought under the sun
3. 11 so that no man can find out the work that
3. 17 time..for every purpose and for every w.
3. 22 that a man should rejoice in his own wo.
4. 3 who hath not seen the evil work that is
4. 4 I considered all travail, and every right w.
5. 6 wherefore should God..destroy the work
7. 13 Consider the work of God; for who can ma.
8. 9 applied my heart unto every work that is
8. 11 Because sentence against an evil work is
8. 14 according to the work..according to the w.
8. 17 Then I beheld all the work of God, that
8. 17 a man cannot find out the work that is
9. 7 Go thy way..God now accepteth thy wo.
9. 10 no work, nor device, nor knowledge, nor
11. 5 even so thou knowest not the works of God
12. 14 God shall bring every work into judgment
Song 7. 1 the work of the hands of a cunning wor.
Isa. 2. 8 they worship the work of their own hands
5. 19 Let him make speed, (and) hasten his work
10. 12 the LORD hath performed his whole work
17. 8 he shall not look to the altars, the work
19. 14 have caused Egypt to err in every work th.
19. 15 Neither shall there be..work for Egypt
19. 25 Blessed (be)..Assyria the work of my ha.
26. 12 for thou hast wrought all our works in us
28. 21 that he may do his work, his strange work
29. 15 their works are in the dark and they say
29. 16 for shall the work say of him that made
29. 23 when he seeth his children, the work of
32. 17 the work of righteousness shall be peace
37. 19 no gods, but the work of men's hands, wo.

Isa. 41. 29 they (are) all vanity; their works (are) no.
54. 16 bringeth forth an instrument for his work
57. 12 I will declare..thy works; for they shall
59. 6 with their works: their works (are) works
60. 21 the work of my hands, that I may be glo.
64. 8 But now..we all (are) the work of thy ha.
65. 22 mine elect shall long enjoy the work of
66. 18 For I (know) their works and their thou.
Jer. 1. 16 worshipped the works of their own hands
7. 13 because ye have done all these works, sa.
10. 3 (the work of the hands of the workman)
10. 9 work of the workman..the work of cunn.
10. 15 They (are) vanity..the work of errors: in
25. 6, 7 provoke me..with the works of your
25. 14 according to the works of their own hands
32. 30 provoked me..with the work of their ha.
44. 8 provoke me..with the works of your hands
48. 7 For because thou hast trusted in thy wo.
51. 10 let us declare in Zion the work of the Lo.
51. 18 They (are) vanity, the work of errors: in
Lam. 3. 64 Render..according to the work of their
4. 2 esteemed..the work of the hands of the
Eze. 1. 16 their work (was) like..their work (was) as
6. 6 cut down, and your works may be abolish.
16. 30 the work of an imperious whorish woman
46. 1 The gate..shall be shut the six working
Dan. 9. 14 righteous in all his works which he doeth
Hos. 13. 2 idols..all of it the work of the craftsmen
14. 3 neither will we say any more to the work
Amos 8. 7 Surely I will never forget any of their wo.
Jon. 3. 10 God saw their works, that they turned fr.
Mic. 5. 13 thou shalt no more worship the work of
6. 16 and all the works of the house of Ahab
Hag. 2. 14 so (is) every work of their hands; and that

9. *Work, doing, act,* מִפְעָל *miphal.*
Prov. 8. 22 The LORD possessed me..before his works

10. *Work, doing, act,* מִפְעָלָה *miphalah.*
Psa. 46. 8 Come, behold the works of the LORD, wh.
66. 5 Come, and see the works of God: (he is)

11. *A deed, doing, service,* עֲבַד *abad.*
Eccl. 9. 1 righteous, and the wise, and their works

12. *Service, deed,* עֲבֹדָה *abodah.*
Exod. 5. 9 Let there more work be laid upon the men
5. 11 yet not ought of your work shall be dim.
39. 32 Thus was all the work of the tabernacle
39. 42 so the children of Israel made all the wo.
Num. 4. 30 to do the work of the tabernacle of the co.
4. 35, 39, 43 for the work in the tabernacle of
Neh. 3. 5 nobles put not their necks to the work

13. *Service, deed,* עֲבִידָה *abidah.*
Ezra 4. 24 Then ceased the work of the house of God
5. 8 work goeth fast on, and prospereth in th.
6. 7 Let the work of this house of God alone

14. *Act, action,* עֲלִילָה *alilah.*
Psa. 14. 1 they have done abominable works; (the.
78. 11 forgat his works, and his wonders that he
141. 4 practise wicked works with men that wo.

15. *Act, action,* עֲלִילִיָּה *aliliyyah.*
Jer. 32. 19 Great in counsel, and mighty in work: for

16. *Work, deed, doing,* פֹּעַל *poal.*
Deut 32. 4 his work (is) perfect; for all his ways (are)
33. 11 LORD, his substance, and accept the work
Ruth 2. 12 LORD recompense thy work, and a full re.
Job 7. 2 hireling looketh for(the reward of) his w.
24. 5 (as) wild asses..go they forth to their w.
34. 11 For the work of a man shall he render un.
36. 9 Then he showeth them their work, and
36. 24 Remember that thou magnify his work
Psa. 9. 16 the wicked is snared in the work of his
44. 1 (what) work thou didst in their days, in
64. 9 men shall fear, and shall declare the work
77. 12 I will meditate also of all thy work, and
90. 16 Let thy work appear unto thy servants, and
92. 4 hast made me glad through thy work: I
95. 9 tempted me, proved me, and saw my wo.
104. 23 Man goeth forth unto his work and to his
111. 3 His work(is) honourable and glorious; and
143. 5 meditate on all thy works; I muse on the
Prov 20. 11 whether his work (be) pure, and whether
21. 8 strange: but (as for) the pure, his work
24. 12 render to (every) man according to his w.
24. 29 will render to the man according to his w.
Isa. 5. 12 but they regard not the work of the LORD
41. 24 Behold, ye (are) of nothing, and your w.
45. 9 What makest thou? or thy work, He hath
45. 11 concerning..work of my hands, command
Jer. 22. 13 without wages..giveth him not for his w.
50. 29 recompense her according to her work
Hab. 1. 5 for(I) will work a work in your days, (wh.)
3. 2 revive thy work in the midst of the years

17. *Work, deed, doing,* פְּעֻלָּה *peullah.*
2 Ch. 15. 7 let not your hands be weak: for your w.
Psa. 17. 4 Concerning the works of men, by the wo.
28. 5 Because they regard not the works of the
Prov 11. 18 The wicked worketh a deceitful work: but
Isa. 40. 10 his reward (is) with him, and his work
49. 4 judgment (is) with the LORD, and my wo.
61. 8 will direct their work in truth, and I will
62. 11 his reward (is) with him, and his work be.
65. 7 therefore will I measure their former w.
Jer. 31. 16 for thy work shall be rewarded, saith the

18. *Substance, wisdom,* תּוּשִׁיָּה *tushiyyah.*
Isa. 28. 29 wonderful in counsel, (and) excellent in w.

19. *Energy, in working,* ἐνέργεια *energeia.*
Eph. 1. 19 according to the working of his mighty
Eph. 3. 7 given unto me by the effectual working of
4. 16 according to the effectual working in the
Phil. 3. 21 according to the working whereby he is
Col. 1. 29 striving according to his working, which
2 Th. 2. 9 whose coming is after the working of Sa.

20. *An energy, inworking,* ἐνέργημα *energēma.*
1 Co. 12. 10 To another the working of miracles; to

21. *Work, business, gain,* ἐργασία *ergasia.*
Eph. 4. 19 unto lasciviousness, to work all unclean.

22. *Work, deed, business,* ἔργον *ergon.*
Matt. 5. 16 they may see your good works, and glorify
11. 2 when John had heard in the prison the w.
23. 3 but do not ye after their works: for they
23. 5 But all their works they do for to be seen
26. 10 for she hath wrought a good work upon
Mark 13. 34 to every man his work, and commanded
14. 6 Jesus said..she hath wrought a good w.
John 4. 34 saith unto them, My meat..finish his w.
5. 20 will show him greater works than these
5. 36 for the works..the same works that I do
6. 28 shall we do that we might work the works
6. 29 This is the work of God, that ye believe
7. 3 that thy disciples also may see the works
7. 7 because I testify of it, that the works th.
7. 21 said unto them, I have done one work, and
8. 39 Abraham's children, ye would do the wo.
9. 3 but that the works of God should be made
9. 4 I must work the works of him that sent
10. 25 works that I do in my Father's name, they
10. 32 Many good works have I showed you from
10. 32 for which of those works do ye stone me?
10. 33 for a good work we stone thee not; but
10. 37 If I do not the works of my Father, beli.
10. 38 though ye believe not me, believe the w.
14. 10 that dwelleth in me, he doeth the works
14. 11 or else believe me for the very work's sa.
14. 12 works that I do shall he do also; and gr.
15. 24 If I had not done among them the works
17. 4 have finished the work which thou gavest
Acts 5. 38 for if this counsel or this work be of men
7. 41 and rejoiced in the works of their own ha.
9. 36 this woman was full of good works and
13. 2 for the work whereunto I have called th.
13. 41 a work in your days, [a work] which ye sh.
14. 26 recommended to..grace of God for the w.
15. 18 [Known unto God are all his works from]
15. 38 who..went not with them to the work
26. 20 repent, and turn to God, and do works m.
Rom. 2. 15 Which show the work of the law written
3. 27 It is excluded. By what law? of works?
4. 2 For if Abraham were justified by works
4. 6 God imputeth righteousness without wo.
9. 11 according to election might stand..works
9. 32 not by faith, but as it were by the works
11. 6 no more of works..[But if (it be) of works]
11. 6 [no more grace; otherwise work is no m.]
13. 3 For rulers are not a terror to good works
13. 12 let us therefore cast off the works of dar.
14. 20 For meat destroy not the work of God. A.
1 Co. 3. 13 Every man's work..try every man's work
3. 14 If any man's work abide which he hath
3. 15 If any man's work shall be burnt, he sh.
9. 1 Christ our Lord? are not ye my work in
15. 58 always abounding in the work of the Lord
16. 10 for he worketh the work of the Lord, as
2 Co. 9. 8 (things), may abound to every good work
11. 15 whose end shall be according to their w.
Gal. 2. 16 works of the law..works of the law..works
3. 2 Received ye the spirit by the works of the
3. 5 by the works of the law, or by the hearing
3. 10 For as many as are of the works of the law
5. 19 Now the works of the flesh are manifest
6. 4 But let every man prove his own work, and
Eph. 2. 9 Not of works, lest any man should boast
2. 10 created in Christ Jesus unto good works
4. 12 for the work of the ministry, for the edi.
5. 11 have no fellowship with the unfruitful w.
Phil. 1. 6 that he which hath begun a good work in
2. 30 Because for the work of Christ he was ni.
Col. 1. 10 being fruitful in every good work, and in.
1. 21 enemies in (your) mind by wicked works
1 Th. 1. 3 Remembering without ceasing your work
5. 13 esteem them very highly..for their work's
2 Th. 1. 11 goodness, and the work of faith with po.
2. 17 stablish you in every good word and work
1 Ti. 2. 10 women professing godliness with good wo.
3. 1 If a man desire..he desireth a good work
5. 10 Well reported of for good works; if she h.
5. 10 have diligently followed every good work
5. 25 Likewise also the good works (of some)
6. 18 that they may be rich in good works, re.
2 Ti. 1. 9 not according to our works, but according
2. 21 (and) prepared unto every good work
3. 17 throughly furnished unto all good works
4. 5 do the work of an evangelist, make full
4. 14 the Lord reward him according to his w.
4. 18 Lord shall deliver me from every evil w.
Titus 1. 16 in works they deny..unto every good w.
2. 7 showing thyself a pattern of good works
2. 14 a peculiar people, zealous of good works
3. 1 magistrates, to be ready to every good w.
3. 5 Not by works of righteousness which we
3. 8 might be careful to maintain good works
3. 14 let ours also learn to maintain good works
Heb. 1. 10 and the heavens are the works of thine
2. 7 [and didst set him over the works of thy]
3. 9 tempted me, proved me, and saw my wo.
4. 3 works were finished from the foundation
4. 4 God did rest the seventh day from..works
4. 10 he also hath ceased from his own works
Heb. 6. 1 the foundation of repentance from dead w.
6. 10 God (is) not unrighteous to forget your w.
9. 14 purge your conscience from dead works
10. 24 to provoke unto love and to good works
13. 21 Make you perfect in every good work to
Jas. 1. 4 But let patience have (her) perfect work
1. 25 a forgetful hearer, but a doer of the work
2. 14 a man say he hath faith, and have not w.?
2. 17 Even so faith, if it hath not works, is de.
2. 18 works: show me thy faith without thy w.
2. 18 and I will show thee my faith by my wo.
2. 20 wilt thou know..that faith without works
2. 21 was not Abraham..justified by works, w.
2. 22 Seest thou how faith wrought with his w.
2. 22 Seest thou how..by works was faith ma.
2. 24 Ye see then how that by works a man is
2. 25 was not Rahab the harlot justified by w.
2. 26 spirit is dead, so faith without works is
3. 13 show out of a good conversation his wor.
1 Pe. 1. 17 judgeth according to every man's work
2. 12 they may by (your) good works, which th.
2 Pe. 3. 10 earth also and the works that are therein
1 Jo. 3. 8 that he might destroy the works of the
3. 12 because his own works were evil, and his
Rev. 2. 2 know thy works, and thy labour, and thy
2. 5 do the first works; or else I will come un.
2. 9 know thy [works, and] tribulation, and
2. 13 [I know thy works, and where thou dwel.]
2. 19 I know [thy works]..and thy works; and
2. 23 unto every one of you according to your w.
2. 26 keepeth my works unto the end, to him
3. 1 I know thy works, that thou hast a name
3. 2 for I have not found thy works perfect
3. 8 I know thy works: behold, I have set be.
3. 15 I know thy works, that thou art neither
9. 20 yet repented not of the works of their h.
14. 13 rest from their labours, and their works
15. 3 Great and marvellous (are) thy works, L.
18. 6 doub. unto her double according to her w.
20. 12 written in the books, according to their w.
20. 13 judged every man according to their wo.
22. 12 to give every man according as his work

23. *A word, matter,* λόγος *logos.*
Rom. 9. 28 For he will finish the work, and cut (it)
9. 28 because a short work will the Lord make

24. *Any thing done, affair,* πρᾶγμα *pragma.*
Jas. 3. 16 strife (is), there (is) confusion..evil work

25. *A work, action,* πρᾶξις *praxis.*
Matt 16. 27 shall reward every man according to his w.

26. *Any thing made, workmanship,* ποίημα *poiēma.*
Eph. 2. 10 For we are his workmanship, created in

[*See also* Beaten, broidered, carved, cedar, cunning, curious, handy, marvellous, mighty, needle, net, wonderful, wondrous, wreathen.]

WORK, be wrought, to —

1. *To go on, proceed,* הָלַךְ *halak.*
Jon. 1. 11, 13 for the sea wrought, and was tempe

2. *To do,* עָבַד *abad.*
Exod. 5. 18 Go therefore now (and) work: for there
34. 21 Six days thou shalt work; but on the se.
Deut 15. 19 thou shalt do no work with the firstling
Isa. 19. 9 Moreover, they that work in fine flax, and

3. *To do,* עֲבַד *abad.*
Dan. 4. 2 wonders that the high God hath wrought
6. 27 worketh signs and wonders in heaven and

4. *To cause to go up,* עָלָה *alah,* 5.
2 Ch. 3. 14 and fine linen, and wrought cherubim th.

5. *To do repeatedly,* עָלַל *alal,* 7.
Exod 10. 2 what things I have wrought in Egypt, and

6. *To do,* עָשָׂה *asah.*
Gen. 34. 7 because he had wrought folly in Israel, in
Exod 31. 4 To devise cunning works, to work in gold
31. 5 to work in all manner of workmanship
35. 32 to work in gold, and in silver, and in br.
35. 35 to work all manner of work of the engra.
36. 1 Then wrought Bezaleel and Aholiab, and
36. 1 to know how to work all manner of work
36. 4 wise men, that wrought all the work of
36. 8 them that wrought the work of the tabe.
39. 3 to work (it) in the blue, and in the purple
39. 6 they wrought onyx stones inclosed in ou.
Lev. 20. 12 they have wrought confusion; their blo.
Deut 17. 2 that hath wrought wickedness in the sight
22. 21 because she hath wrought folly in Israel
31. 18 for all the evils which they shall have w.
Josh. 7. 15 and because he hath wrought folly in Is.
9. 4 They did work wilily, and went and made
Judg 20. 10 all the folly that they have wrought in I.
Ruth 2. 19 where wroughtest thou? blessed be he
2. 19 with whom she had wrought..with whom
1 Sa. 11. 13 to day the LORD hath wrought salvation
14. 6 it may be that the LORD will work for us
14. 45 Shall Jonathan die, who hath wrought
14. 45 for he hath wrought with God this day
19. 5 the LORD wrought a great salvation for
2 Sa. 18. 13 Otherwise I should have wrought falseh.
23. 10 and the LORD wrought a great victory th.
23. 12 slew the Philistines: and the LORD wro.
1 Ki. 5. 16 which ruled over the people that wrought
7. 14 understanding, and cunning to work all w
7. 14 to king Solomon, and wrought all his wo.
9. 23 which bare rule over the people that wr.
16. 25 But Omri wrought evil in the eyes of the
21. 20 thyself to work evil in the sight of the L.
21. 25 which did sell himself to work wickedness

2 Ki. 3. 2 he wrought evil in the sight of the LORD
12. 11 builders that wrought upon the house of
17. 11 wrought wicked things to provoke the L.
21. 6 wrought much wickedness in the sight of
2 Ch. 2. 7 me now therefore a man cunning to work
2. 14 skilful to work in gold, and in silver, in
21. 6 wrought (that which was) evil in the..L.
24. 13 So the workmen wrought, and the work
31. 20 wrought (that which was) good and right
33. 6 wrought much evil in the sight of the L.
34. 10 workmen..wrought in the house of the L
34. 13 overseers of all that wrought the work in
Neh. 4. 6 thereof: for the people had a mind to w.
4. 16 the half of my servants wrought in the w.
4. 17 with one of his hands wrought in the w.
9. 18 brought thee up out of Egypt, and had w.
9. 26 and they wrought great provocations
Job 12. 9 that the hand of the LORD hath wrought
23. 9 On the left hand, where he doth work, but
Psa. 52. 2 mischiefs: like a sharp razor, working de.
101. 3 hate the work of them that turn aside, (it)
101. 7 He that worketh deceit shall not dwell
119. 126 (It is) time for (thee), LORD, to work, (for)
Prov 11. 18 The wicked worketh a deceitful work, but
26. 28 and a flattering mouth worketh ruin
31. 13 seeketh wool and flax, and worketh will.
Eccl. 2. 11 on all the works that my hands had wro.
3. 9 What profit hath he that worketh in that
Isa. 26. 18 have not wrought any deliverance in the
32. 6 his heart will work iniquity, to practise
64. 5 Thou meetest him that rejoiceth and wo.
Jer. 11. 15 she hath wrought lewdness with many, and
18. 3 behold, he wrought a work on the wheels
Eze. 20. 9, 14, 22 I wrought for my name's sake, that
20. 44 when I have wrought with you for my na.
29. 20 because they wrought for me, saith the L.
33. 26 Ye stand upon your sword, ye work abo.
Dan. 11. 23 after the league..with him he shall work
Hag. 2. 4 work: for I (am) with you, saith the Lo.
Mal. 3. 15 yea, they that work wickedness are set up

7. *To act, work, make, do,* פָּעַל *paal.*
Num 23. 23 said..of Israel, What hath God wrought!
Job 33. 29 all these (things) worketh God oftentimes
36. 23 or who can say, Thou hast wrought iniq.
Psa. 15. 2 worketh righteousness, and speaketh the
31. 19 thou hast wrought for them that trust in
58. 2 Yea, in heart ye work wickedness; ye w.
68. 28 strengthen..that which thou hast wrought
74. 12 working salvation in the midst of the ea.
141. 4 practise wicked works with men that w.
Isa. 26. 12 for thou also hast wrought all our; 31. 2.
41. 4 Who hath wrought and done (it), calling
43. 13 none that can deliver..I will work, and
44. 12 smith with the tongs both worketh in the
44. 12 worketh it with the strength of his arms
Hos. 6. 8 Gilead (is) a city of them that work iniq.
Mic. 2. 1 devise iniquity, and work evil upon their
Hab. 1. 5 (I) will work a work in your days, (which)
Zeph. 2. 3 ye meek of the earth, which have wrought

8. *To set, put, place,* שׂוּם, שִׂים *sum, sim.*
Psa. 78. 43 How he had wrought his signs in Egypt

9. *To work in,* ἐνεργέω *energeō.*
Rom. 7. 5 did work in our members to bring forth
1 Co. 12. 6 but it is the same God which worketh all
12. 11 But all these worketh that one and the
2 Co. 4. 12 So then death worketh in us, but life in
Gal. 3. 5 He therefore that..worketh miracles am.
5. 6 uncircumcision; but faith which worketh by
Eph. 1. 11 purpose of him who worketh all things
1. 20 Which he wrought in Christ, when he ra.
2. 2 spirit that now worketh in the children
3. 20 according to the power that worketh in
Phil. 2. 13 For it is God which worketh in you both
Col. 1. 29 working, which worketh in me mightily
2 Th. 2. 7 For the mystery of iniquity doth already w.

10. *To work, toil, labour,* ἐργάζομαι *ergazomai.*
Matt. 7. 23 knew you, depart from me, ye that work
21. 28 and said, Son, go work to day in my vine.
26. 10 for she hath wrought a good work upon
Mark 14. 6 why trouble ye her? she hath wrought a
Luke 13. 14 six days in which men ought to work, in
John 3. 21 made manifest, that they are wrought in
5. 17 My Father worketh hitherto, and I work
6. 28 What shall we do, that we might work
6. 30 What..showest thou..what dost thou wo.
9. 4 I must work the works of him that sent
9. 4 day: the night cometh, when no..can w.
Acts 10. 35 he that feareth him, and worketh righte.
13. 41 for I work a work in your days, a work
18. 3 he abode with them, and wrought: for by
Rom. 2. 10 to every man that worketh good, to the
4. 4 Now to him that worketh is the reward
4. 5 But to him that worketh not, but believ.
13. 10 Love worketh no ill to his neighbour, the.
1 Co. 4. 12 labour, working with our own hands:
9. 6 have not we power to forbear working?
16. 10 for he worketh the work of the Lord, as I
Eph. 4. 28 working with (his) hands the thing which
1 Th. 4. 11 work with your own hands, as we comm.
2 Th. 3. 8 wrought with labour and travail night
3. 10 if any would not work, neither should he
3. 11 disorderly, working not at all, but are
3. 12 with quietness they work, and eat their
Heb. 11. 33 wrought righteousness, obtained promises
2 John 8 lose not those things which we have wrou.

11. *To work down, thoroughly,* κατεργάζομαι.
Rom. 1. 27 men with men working that which is
4. 15 Because the law worketh wrath: for wh.
5. 3 knowing that tribulation worketh patien.
Rom. 7. 8 wrought in me all manner of concupisce.
7. 13 working death in me by that which is go.
15. 18 those things which Christ hath not wrou.
2 Co. 4. 17 worketh for us a far more exceeding (and)
5. 5 Now he that hath wrought us for the self
7. 10 For godly sorrow [worketh] repentance
7. 10 but the sorrow of the world worketh de.
7. 11 what carefulness it wrought in you, yea
12. 12 Truly the signs of an apostle were wrou.
Jas. 1. 3 that the trying of your faith worketh pa.
1. 20 For the wrath of man [worketh] not the
1 Pe. 4. 3 may suffice us to have wrought the will

12. *To do, make,* ποιέω *poieō.*
Matt 20. 12 Saying, These last have wrought (but) one
Acts 15. 12 God had wrought among the Gentiles by
19. 11 God wrought special miracles by the hand
21. 19 what things God had wrought among the
Heb. 13. 21 working in you that which is well pleasing
Rev. 16. 14 working miracles, (which) go forth unto
19. 20 false prophet that wrought miracles bef.
21. 27 neither (whatsoever) worketh abomination

WORK, to set a, have much —

1. *To cause to do, or serve,* עָבַד *abad,* 5.
2 Ch. 2. 18 hundred overseers to set the people a w.

2. *To prevail with difficulty,* μόλις ἰσχύω *molis isc.*
Acts 27. 16 we had much work to come by the boat

WORK effectually in, wonderfully —

1. *To do repeatedly,* עָלַל *alal,* 7.
1 Sa. 6. 6 when he had wrought wonderfully among

2. *To work in,* ἐνεργέω *energeō.*
Gal. 2. 8 For he that wrought effectually in Peter
1 Th. 2. 13 which effectually worketh also in you th.

WORK out, together, with, to —

1. *To work down, against, thoroughly,* κατεργάζομαι.
Phil. 2. 12 work out your own salvation with fear and

2. *To work with,* συνεργέω *sunergeō.*
Mark 16. 20 the Lord working with (them), and confi.
Rom. 8. 28 know that all things work together for go.
Jas. 2. 22 Seest thou how faith wrought with his w.

WORKER, workfellow, workman, fellow —

1. *To grave, plough, work,* חָרַשׁ *charash.*
1 Ki. 7. 14 his father (was) a man of Tyre, a worker

2. *Graver, artificer, worker,* חָרָשׁ *charash.*
1 Ch. 22. 15 hewers and workers of stone and timber
Isa. 40. 20 seeketh unto him a cunning workman to
44. 11 and the workmen they (are) of men: let
Jer. 10. 3 work of the hands of the workman with
10. 9 work of the workman, and of the hands
Hos. 8. 6 workman made it, therefore it (is) not G.

3. *Men of work,* אַנְשֵׁי מְלָאכָה *aneshe melakah.*
1 Ch. 25. 1 the number of the workmen according to

4. *To do work,* עָשָׂה מְלָאכָה *asah melakah.*
2 Ki. 12. 14 But they gave that to the workmen, and
12. 15 delivered the money to be bestowed on w.
1 Ch. 22. 15 Moreover (there are) workmen with thee
2 Ch. 24. 13 So the workmen wrought, and the work
34. 10 they put (it) in the hand of the workmen
34. 10 gave it to the workmen that wrought in
34. 17 the overseers, and to the hand of the wo.
Ezra 3. 9 to set forward the workmen in the house

4a. *Workers,* עָשָׂה *asah.* Psa. 37. 1.

5. *To act, work, do, make,* פָּעַל *paal.*
Job 31. 3 strange (punishment) to the workers of
34. 8 Which goeth in company with the work.
34. 22 where the workers of iniquity may hide
Psa. 5. 5 in thy sight: thou hatest all workers of
6. 8 Depart from me, all ye workers of iniquity
14. 4 Have all the workers of iniquity no kno.?
28. 3 with the workers of iniquity, which speak
36. 12 There are the workers of iniquity fallen
53. 4 Have the workers of iniquity no knowl.?
59. 2 Deliver me from the workers of iniquity
64. 2 from the insurrection of the workers of
92. 7 when all the workers of iniquity do flour.
92. 9 all the workers of iniquity shall be scatt.
94. 4 all the workers of iniquity boast themse.
94. 16 who will stand up for me against the w.
125. 5 lead them forth with the workers of iniq.
141. 9 Keep me from..the gins of the workers
Prov 10. 29 destruction (shall be) to the workers of in.
21. 15 but destruction (shall be) to the workers

6. *Labouring, toiling,* עָמֵל *amel.*
Judg. 5. 26 put..her right hand to the workmen's ha.

7. *Worker, workman,* ἐργάτης *ergatēs.*
Matt 10. 10 for the workman is worthy of his meat
Luke 13. 27 depart from me, all (ye) workers of iniq.
Acts 19. 25 Whom he called together with the work.
2 Co. 11. 13 deceitful workers, transforming themsel.
Phil. 3. 2 Beware of dogs, beware of evil workers
2 Ti. 2. 15 a workman that needeth not to be asha.

8. *Fellow or joint worker,* συνεργός *sunergos.*
Rom 16. 21 Timotheus my work fellow, and Col. 4. 11

WORKER together, of miracles —

1. *Power,* δύναμις *dunamis.*
1 Co. 12. 29 (are) all teachers? (are) all workers of mi.

2. *To work with or together,* συνεργέω *sunergeō.*
2 Co. 6. 1 We then, (as) workers together (with him)

WORKS, mighty, wonderful —

1. *Power,* δύναμις *dunamis.*
Matt. 7. 22 in thy name done many wonderful wo.?
11. 20 wherein most of his mighty works were
Matt 11. 21 for if the mighty works which were done
11. 23 for if the mighty works, which have been
13. 54 Whence hath this (man)..these mighty w.?
13. 58 he did not many mighty works there bec.
14. 2 therefore mighty works do show forth
Mark 6. 2 that even such mighty works are wrought
6. 5 he could there do no mighty work, save
6. 14 therefore mighty works do show forth th.
Luke 10. 13 for if the mighty works had been done in
19. 37 for all the mighty works that they had se.

2. *Great doings or deeds,* μεγαλεῖα *megaleia.*
Acts 2. 11 speak in our tongues the wonderful works

WORLD —

1. *Land, earth,* אֶרֶץ *erets.*
Psa. 22. 27 All the ends of the world shall remember
Isa. 23. 17 fornication with all the kingdoms of the w.
62. 11 hath proclaimed unto the end of the world
Jer. 25. 26 all the kingdoms of the world, which (are)

2. *Cessation,* חֶדֶל *chedel.*
Isa. 38. 11 no more with the inhabitants of the world

3. *Lifetime, age,* חֶלֶד *cheled.*
Psa. 17. 14 from men of the world, (which have) their
49. 1 give ear, all (ye) inhabitants of the world

4. *Indefinite time, or its love,* עוֹלָם *olam.*
Psa. 73. 12 these (are) the ungodly, who prosper in t. w.
Eccl. 3. 11 also he hath set the world in their heart

5. *Fruit bearing or habitable earth,* תֵּבֵל *tebel.*
1 Sa. 2. 8 the LORD'S, and he hath set the world up.
2 Sa. 22. 16 foundations of the world were discovered
1 Ch. 16. 30 world also shall be stable, that it be not
Job 18. 18 into darkness, and chased out of the wor.
34. 13 or who hath disposed the whole world?
37. 12 commandeth them upon the face of the
Psa. 9. 8 he shall judge the world in righteousness
18. 15 foundations of the world were discovered
19. 4 their words to the end of the world. In th.
24. 1 the world, and they that dwell therein
33. 8 let all the inhabitants of the world stand
50. 12 for the world (is) mine, and the fulness th.
77. 18 lightnings lightened the world: the earth
89. 11 the world and the fulness thereof thou ha.
90. 2 or ever thou hadst formed the..world, ev.
93. 1 world also is stablished, that it cannot
96. 10 world also shall be establishad that it sh.
96. 13 he shall judge the world with righteousn.
97. 4 His lightnings enlightened the world: the
98. 7 the world, and they that dwell therein
98. 9 with righteousness shall he judge the wo.
Prov. 8. 26 nor the highest part of the dust of the wo.
Isa. 13. 11 I will punish the world for (their) evil
14. 17 made the world as a wilderness, and des.
14. 21 nor fill the face of the world with cities
18. 3 All ye inhabitants of the world, and dwe.
24. 4 the world languisheth (and) fadeth away
26. 9 inhabitants of the world will learn right.
26. 18 neither have the inhabitants of the world
27. 6 blossom and bud, and fill the face of the w.
34. 1 the world, and all things that come forth
Jer. 10. 12 he hath established the world by his wis.
51. 15 he hath established the world by his wisd.
Lam. 4. 12 all the inhabitants of the world, would
Nah. 1. 5 yea, the world, and all that dwell therein

6. *Age, indefinite time, dispensation,* αἰών *aiōn.*
Matt 12. 32 neither in this world, neither in the (wor).
13. 22 care of this world, and the deceitfulness
13. 39 the harvest is the end of the world; and
13. 40 so shall it be in the end of this world
13. 49 So shall it be at the end of the world: the
24. 3 sign of thy coming, and of the end of the w.
28. 20 with you alway..unto the end of the wor.
Mark 4. 19 cares of this world, and the deceitfulness
10. 30 persecutions; and in the world to come
Luke 16. 8 children of this world are in their genera.
18. 30 and in the world to come life everlasting
20. 34 children of this world marry, and are given
20. 35 accounted worthy to obtain that world
Rom 12. 2 be not conformed to this world, but be ye
1 Co. 1. 20 where (is) the disputer of this world? hath
2. 6 of this world, nor of the princes of this w.
2. 8 Which none of the princes of this world
3. 18 seemeth to be wise in this world, let him
2 Co. 4. 4 In whom the god of this world hath blin.
Gal. 1. 4 might deliver us from this present evil w.
Eph. 1. 21 not only in this world, but also in that wh.
6. 12 against..rulers of the darkness of this [w.]
1 Ti. 6. 17 Charge them that are rich in this world
2 Ti. 4. 10 forsaken me, having loved this present w.
Titus 2. 12 should live soberly..in this present world
Heb. 1. 2 all things, by whom also he made the wo.
6. 5 word of God, and the powers of the world
11. 3 Through faith we understand that the wo.

7. *Ages, dispensations,* αἰώνων *(gen. pl.) aiōnōn.*
1 Co. 2. 7 which God ordained before the world unto
10. 11 upon whom the ends of the world are
Heb. 9. 26 but now once in the end of the world

8. *Land, earth,* γῆ *gē.*
Rev. 13. 3 and all the world wondered after the be.

9. *Arrangement, beauty, world,* κόσμος *kosmos.*
Matt. 4. 8 showeth him all the kingdoms of the wor.
5. 14 Ye are the light of the world. A city that
13. 35 kept secret from the foundation [of the w.]
13. 38 The field is the world; the good seed are
16. 26 if he shall gain the whole world, and lose
18. 7 Woe unto the world because of offences!
24. 21 as was not since the beginning of the wo.
25. 34 prepared..from the foundation of the wo.

Matt.26. 13 this gospel shall be preached..whole wor.
Mark 8. 36 if he shall gain the whole world, and lose
14. 9 be preached throughout the whole world
16. 15 [Go ye into all the world, and preach the]
Luke 9. 25 if he gain the whole world, and lose him.
11. 50 was shed from the foundation of the world
12. 30 these things do the nations of the world
John 1. 9 lighteth every man that cometh into the w.
1. 10 He was in the world, and the world was
1. 10 made by him, and the world knew him not
1. 29 which taketh away the sin of the world
3. 16 For God so loved the world, that he gave
3. 17 God sent not his Son into the world to co.
3. 17 the world; but that the world through
3. 19 light is come into the world, and men lo.
4. 42 is indeed the Christ, the Saviour of the w.
6. 14 Prophet that should come into the world
6. 33 from heaven, and giveth life unto the w.
6. 51 which I will give for the life of the world
7. 4 do these things, show thyself to the world
7. 7 The world cannot hate you; but me it ha.
8. 12 I am the light of the world: he that foll.
8. 23 ye are of this world; I am not of this wo.
8. 26 speak to the world those things which I
9. 5 am in the world, I am the light of the w.
9. 39 For judgment I am come into this world
10. 36 whom the Father..sent into the world
11. 9 because he seeth the light of this world
11. 27 the Christ..which should come into the w.
12. 19 prevail nothing? behold, the world is gone
12. 25 he that hateth his life in this world shall
12. 31 Now is the judgment of this world: now
12. 31 shall the prince of this world be cast out
12. 46 I am come a light into the world, that w.
12. 47 not to judge the world, but to save the w.
13. 1 should depart out of this world unto the
13. 1 having loved his own which were in the w.
14. 17 whom the world cannot receive, because
14. 19 little while, and the world seeth me no
14. 22 wilt manifest thyself..not unto the world?
14. 27 not as the world giveth, give I unto you
14. 30 for the prince of [this] world cometh, and
14. 31 But that the world may know that I love
15. 18 If the world hate you, ye know that it ha.
15. 19 If ye were of the world, the world would
15. 19 but because ye are not of the world, but
15. 19 out of the world, therefore the world ha.
16. 8 when he is come, he will reprove the wo.
16. 11 Of judgment, because the prince of this w.
16. 20 ye shall weep and lament, but the world
16. 21 for joy that a man is born into the world
16. 28 come into the world: again, I leave the w.
16. 33 In the world ye shall have tribulation: but
16. 33 be of good cheer; I have overcome the w.
17. 5 glory which I had with thee before the w.
17. 6 men which thou gavest me out of the wo.
17. 9 I pray not for the world, but for them
17. 11 more in the world, but these are in the w.
17. 12 While I was with them [in the world] I
17. 13 these things I speak in the world, that
17. 14 world hath hated them, because they are
17. 14, 16 the world, even as I am not of the w.
17. 15 thou shouldest take them out of the world
17. 18 As thou hast sent me into the world, even
17. 18 so have I also sent them into the world
17. 21 the world may believe that thou hast sent
17. 23 the world may know that thou hast sent
17. 24 lovedst me before the foundation of the w.
17. 25 righteous Father, the world hath not kn.
18. 20 answered him, I spake openly to the wo.
18. 36 answered, My kingdom is not of this wo.
18. 36 If my kingdom were of this world, then
18. 37 for this cause came I into the world, that
21. 25 suppose that even the world itself could
Acts 17. 24 God that made the world and all things
Rom. 1. 8 is spoken of throughout the whole world
1. 20 from the creation of the world are clearly
3. 6 forbid: for..how shall God judge the w.
3. 19 and all the world may become guilty be.
4. 13 promise, that he should be the heir of..w.
5. 12 as by one man sin entered into the world
5. 13 For until the law sin was in the world: but
11. 12 if the fall of them (be) the riches of the w.
11. 15 casting away..the reconciling of the wo.
1 Co. 1. 20 God made foolish the wisdom of this wo.
1. 21 the world by wisdom knew not God, it
1. 27 hath chosen the foolish things of the w.
1. 27 [hath chosen the weak things of the world]
1. 28 base things of the world, and things which
2. 12 we have received, not the spirit of the w.
3. 19 For the wisdom of this world is foolishness
3. 22 Paul, or Apollos, or Cephas, or the world
4. 9 for we are made a spectacle unto the w.
4. 13 we are made as the filth of the world, (and
5. 10 altogether with the fornicators of this w.
5. 10 for then must ye needs go out of the wo.
6. 2 judge the world? and if the world shall
7. 31 they that use this world, as not abusing
7. 31 for the fashion of this world passeth away
7. 33 careth for the things that are of the world
7. 34 careth for the things of the world, how
8. 4 we know that an idol (is) nothing in the w.
11. 32 we should not be condemned with the w.
14. 10 so many kinds of voices in the world, and
2 Co. 1. 12 we have had our conversation in the world
5. 19 reconciling the world unto himself, not
7. 10 but the sorrow of the world worketh de.
Gal. 4. 3 in bondage under the elements of the w.
6. 14 world is crucified unto me, and I..the w.
Eph. 1. 4 before the foundation of the world, that
2. 2 walked according to the course of this w.
2. 12 having no hope. without God in the world
Phil. 2. 15 among whom ye shine as lights in the w.
Col. 1. 6 is come unto you, as (it is) in all the world
2. 8 after the rudiments of the world, and not
2. 20 dead..from the rudiments of the world
2. 20 though living in the world, are ye subject
1 Ti. 1. 15 Christ Jesus came into the world to save
3. 16 believed on in the world, received up into
6. 7 For we brought nothing into (this) world
Heb. 4. 3 finished from the foundation of the world
9. 26 suffered since the foundation of the world
10. 5 when he cometh into the world, he saith
11. 7 by the which he condemned the world
11. 38 Of whom the world was not worthy: they
Jas. 1. 27 to keep himself unspotted from the world
2. 5 Hath not God chosen the poor of [this] w.
3. 6 the tongue (is) a fire, a world of iniquity
4. 4 know ye not that the friendship of the w.
4. 4 will be a friend of the world is the enemy
1 Pe. 1. 20 before the foundation of the world, but
5. 9 in your brethren that are in the world
2 Pe. 1. 4 escaped the corruption that is in the wo.
2. 5 spared not the old world, but saved Noah
2. 5 bringing in the flood upon the world of
2. 20 escaped the pollutions of the world, thr.
3. 6 Whereby the world that then was, being
1 Jo. 2. 2 but also for (the sins of) the whole world
2. 15 world, neither the things..in the world
2. 15 If any man love the world, the love of the
2. 16 For all that (is) in the world..is of the w.
2. 17 world, passeth away, and the lust thereof
3. 1 world knoweth us not, because it knew
3. 13 Marvel not my brethren, if the world hate
3. 17 But whoso hath this world's good, and se.
4. 1 false prophets are gone out into the world
4. 3 and even now already is it in the world
4. 4 that is in you, than he that is in the wo.
4. 5 They are of the world: therefore speak th.
4. 5 of the world, and the world heareth them
4. 9 God sent his only begotten Son into the w.
4. 14 Father..Son (to be) the Saviour of the w.
4. 17 because as he is, so are we in this world
5. 4 is born of God overcometh the world: and
5. 4 this is the victory that overcometh the w.
5. 5 Who is he that overcometh the world, but
5. 19 that we are of God, and the whole world
2 John 7 many deceivers are entered into the world
Rev. 11. 15 The kingdoms of this world are become
13. 8 Lamb slain from the foundation of the w.
17. 8 from the foundation of the world, when

10. *Habitable earth or land*, οἰκουμένη *oikoumenē*.
Matt 24. 14 preached in all the world for a witness
Luke 2. 1 a decree..that all the world should be ta.
4. 5 showed..him all the kingdoms of the w.
Acts 11. 28 be great dearth throughout all the world
17. 6 These that have turned the world upside
17. 31 in the which he will judge the world in
19. 27 whom all Asia and the world worshippeth
24. 5 among all the Jews throughout the world
Rom 10. 18 and their words unto the ends of the wo.
Heb. 1. 6 bringeth in the first begotten into the w.
2. 5 hath he not put in subjection the world
Rev. 3. 10 which shall come upon all the world, to
12. 9 Satan, which deceiveth the whole world
16. 14 kings of the earth and of the whole world

WORLD, (standeth, beginning of the, without end) —
1. *Unto ages of duration*, עַד־עָלְמֵי עַד *ad oleme ad.*
Isa. 45. 17 be ashamed nor confounded world witho.

2. *From the age*, מֵעוֹלָם *me-olam.*
Isa. 64. 4 For since the beginning of the world (men)

3. *From the age*, ἀπ' αἰῶνος *ap' aiōnos.*
Luke 1. 70 prophets, which have been since the wo.
Acts 3. 21 all his holy prophets [since the world b.]
15. 18 all his works from the beginning of the w.
Eph. 3. 9 which from the beginning of the world

4. *To the age*, εἰς τὸν αἰῶνα *eis ton aiōna.*
1 Co. 8. 13 I will eat no flesh while the world stand.

5. *Of the age of the ages*, τοῦ αἰῶνος τῶν αἰώνων.
Eph. 3. 21 throughout all ages, [world without end]

6. *Of or from the age*, ἐκ τοῦ αἰῶνος *ek tou aiōnos.*
John 9. 32 Since the world began was it not heard th.

7. *From the ancient ages*, χρόνοις αἰωνίοις.
Rom. 16. 25 which was kept secret since the world be.

8. *Before the times of the ages*, πρὸ χρόνων αἰωνίων.
2 Ti. 1. 9 given us in Christ Jesus before the world b.
Titus 1. 2 which God..promised before the world be.

WORLDLY —
Belonging to the world, worldly, κοσμικός *kosmikos.*
Titus 2. 12 denying ungodliness and worldly lusts, we
Heb. 9. 1 ordinances of divine service, and a worldly

WORM, eaten of worms —
1. *To be afraid, creep*, זָחַל *zachal.*
Mic. 7. 17 move out of their holes like worms of the

2. *A moth, wood louse*, סָס *sas.*
Isa. 51. 8 worm shall eat them like wool: but my ri.

3. *A worm*, רִמָּה *rimmah.*
Exod 16. 24 did not stink, neither was there any wor.
Job 7. 5 My flesh is clothed with worms and clods
17. 14 to the worm, (Thou art) my mother, and
21. 26 lie down alike in the dust, and the worms
24. 20 worm shall feed sweetly on him; he shall
25. 6 How much less man, (that is) a worm; and
Isa. 14. 11 the worm is spread under thee, and the

4. *A coccus worm*, תּוֹלַעַת, תּוֹלֵעָה *toleah, tolaath.*
Deut. 28. 39 nor gather (the grapes); for the worms sh.
Job 25. 6 and the son of man, (which is) a worm
Psa. 22. 6 But I (am) a worm, and no man; a reproach
Isa. 14. 11 spread under thee, and the worms cover
41. 14 Fear not, thou worm Jacob, (and) ye men
66. 24 for their worm shall not die, neither shall
Jon. 4. 7 But God prepared a worm when the mor.

5. *Worm*, תּוֹלָע *tola.*
Exod. 16. 20 it bred worms, and stank: and Moses was

6. *A worm, maggot*, σκώληξ *skōlēx.*
Mark 9. [44, 46], 48 Where their worm dieth not, and

7. *Eaten by worms*, σκωληκόβρωτος *skōlēkobrōtos.*
Acts 12. 23 he was eaten of worms, and gave up the

WORMWOOD —
1. *Wormwood*, לַעֲנָה *laanah.*
Deut 29. 18 be..a root that beareth gall and wormwood
Prov. 5. 4 But her end is bitter as wormwood, sharp
Jer. 9. 15 feed them, (even) this people, with worm.
23. 15 Behold, I will feed them with wormwood
Lam. 3. 15 he hath made me drunken with wormwo.
3. 19 Remembering..the wormwood and the g.
Amos 5. 7 Ye who turn judgment to wormwood, and

2. *Wormwood, undrinkable*, ἄψινθος *apsinthos.*
Rev. 8. 11 the name of the star is called wormwood
8. 11 third part of the waters became wormwood

WORSE (thing, to be, deal, do, be put to the) —
1. *To be smitten*, נָגַף *nagaph*, 2.
2 Ki. 14. 12 Judah was put to the worse before Israel
1 Ch. 19. 16, 19 saw that they were put to the worse,
2 Ch. 6. 24 if thy people Israel be put to the worse
25. 22 Judah was put to the worse before Israel

2. *To be evil*, רָעַע *raa.*
2 Sa. 19. 7 that will be worse unto thee than all the

3. *To do evil, treat ill*, רָעַע *raa*, 5.
Gen. 19. 9 now will we deal worse with thee than
1 Ki. 16. 25 and did worse than all that (were) before
Jer. 7. 26 hardened their neck: they did worse than
16. 12 ye have done worse than your fathers, for

4. *Evil*, רַע *ra.*
2 Ch. 33. 9 made Judah..to do worse than the heat.
Eze. 7. 24 Wherefore I will bring the worst of the

5. *Smaller, inferior, younger*, ἐλάσσων *elassōn.*
John 2. 10 then that which is worse: (but) thou hast

6. *Less, inferior, worse*, ἥττων *hēttōn.*
1 Co. 11. 17 together..for the better, but for the worse

7. *Worse, inferior*, χείρων *cheirōn.*
Matt. 9. 16 from the garment, and the rent is made w.
12. 45 the last (state) of that man is worse than
27. 64 so the last error shall be worse than the
Mark 2. 21 away from the old, and the rent is made w.
5. 26 was nothing bettered, but rather grew w.
Luke 11. 26 the last (state) of that man is worse than
John 5. 14 sin no more, lest a worse thing come unto
1 Ti. 5. 8 hath denied the faith, and is worse than
2 Ti. 3. 13 men and seducers shall wax worse and w.
2 Pe. 2. 20 latter end is worse with them than the b.

8. *To be behind, inferior*, ὑστερέω *hustereō.*
1 Co. 8. 8 [neither, if we eat not, are we the worse]

WORSE liking —
To be displeasing, זָעַף *zaaph.*
Dan. 1. 10 Why should he see your faces worse lik.

WORSHIP, worshipper, worshipping, to —
1. *To bow down, do obeisance*, סְגִד *segad.*
Dan. 2. 46 worshipped Daniel, and commanded that
3. 5 ye fall down and worship the golden im.
3. 6 whoso falleth not down and worshippeth
3. 7 fell down (and) worshipped the golden im.
3. 10 shall fall down and worship the golden
3. 11 whoso falleth not down and worshippeth
3. 12 nor worship the golden image which thou
3. 14 nor worship the golden image which I ha
3. 15 worship the image..but if ye worship not
3. 18 worship the golden image which thou h.
3. 28 nor worship any god, except their own G.

2. *To make an idol*, עָצַב *atsab*, 5.
Jer. 44. 19 did we make her cakes to worship her, an[d]

3. *To do, serve*, עָבַד *abad.*
2 Ki. 10. 19 that he might destroy the worshippers of
10. 21 all the worshippers of Baal came, so that
10. 22 Bring forth vestments for all the worship.
10. 23 said unto the worshippers of Baal, Search
10. 23 servants of the LORD, but the worshippers

4. *To bow self down*, שָׁחָה *shachah*, 7a.
Gen. 22. 5 I and the lad will go yonder and worship
24. 26, 48 bowed down..and worshipped the L.
24. 52 heard their words, he worshipped the L.
Exod. 4. 31 then they bowed their heads and worshi.
12. 27 And the people bowed the head and wor.
24. 1 Come up unto the LORD..and worship ye
32. 8 have worshipped it, and have sacrificed
33. 10 all the people rose up, and worshipped
34. 8 bowed his head toward the earth, and w.
34. 14 For thou shalt worship no other god, for
Deut. 4. 19 shouldest be driven to worship them, and
8. 19 serve them, and worship them, I testify
11. 16 turn aside, and serve other gods, and wo.
17. 3 hath gone and served other gods, and w.
26. 10 set it before the LORD thy God, and wor.

Deut 29. 26 served other gods, and worshipped them
30. 17 shalt be drawn away, and worship other
Josh. 5. 14 did worship, and said unto him, What
Judg. 7. 15 worshipped, and returned into the host
1 Sa. 1. 3 to worship and to sacrifice unto the LORD
1. 19 worshipped before the LORD, and return.
1. 28 And he worshipped the LORD there
15. 25, 30 turn again with me, that I may worsh.
15. 31 turned again after Saul; and Saul worsh.
2 Sa. 12. 20 came into the house of the LORD, and w.
15. 32 top (of the mount), where he worshipped
1 Ki. 9. 6 but go and serve other gods and worship
9. 9 worshipped them, and served them; there.
11. 33 have worshipped Ashtoreth the goddess
16. 31 and went and served Baal, and worship.
22. 53 For he served Baal, and worshipped him
2 Ki. 5. 18 goeth into the house of Rimmon to wor.
17. 16 worshipped all the host of heaven, and
17. 36 him shall ye worship, and to him shall ye
18. 22 Ye shall worship before this altar in Jer.
19. 37 as he was worshipping in the house of
21. 3 worshipped all the host of heaven, and
21. 21 served the idols..and worshipped them
1 Ch. 16. 29 worship the LORD in the beauty of holin.
29. 20 bowed down their heads, and worshipped
2 Ch. 7. 3 worshipped, and praised the LORD, (say.)
7. 19 shall go and serve other gods, and wors.
7. 22 worshipped them, and served them: the.
20. 18 fell before the LORD, worshipping the L.
29. 28 all the congregation worshipped, and the
29. 29 king and all that were present..worship.
29. 30 and they bowed their heads and worship.
32. 12 Ye shall worship before one altar, and
33. 3 worshipped all the host of heaven, and
Neh. 8. 6 worshipped the LORD with (their) faces
9. 3 fourth part they confessed, and worship.
9. 6 and the host of heaven worshippeth thee
Job 1. 20 and fell down upon the ground, and wor.
Psa. 5. 7 in thy fear will I worship toward thy holy
22. 27 all the kindreds of the nations shall wor.
22. 29 fat upon earth shall eat and worship, all
29. 2 worship the LORD in the beauty of holin.
45. 11 for he (is) thy LORD; and worship thou
66. 4 All the earth shall worship thee, and sh.
81. 9 neither shalt thou worship any strange
86. 9 All nations..shall come and worship be.
95. 6 O come, let us worship and bow down, let
96. 9 O worship the LORD in the beauty of hol.
97. 7 boast themselves of idols: worship him
99. 5 Exalt ye the LORD our God, and worship
99. 9 Exalt the LORD our God, and worship at
106. 19 They made a calf in Horeb, and worship.
132. 7 will go into his tabernacles; we will wo.
138. 2 I will worship toward thy holy temple
Isa. 2. 8 they worship the work of their own han.
2. 20 which they made..for himself to worship
27. 13 worship the LORD in the holy mount at
36. 7 said to Judah..Ye shall worship before
37. 38 as he was worshipping in the house of N.
44. 15 yea, he maketh a god, and worshippeth
44. 17 he falleth down unto it, and worshippeth
46. 6 it a god: they fall down, yea, they wors.
49. 7 princes also shall worship, because of the
66. 23 shall all flesh come to worship before me
Jer. 1. 16 and worshipped the works of their own
7. 2 enter in at these gates to worship the L.
8. 2 whom they have worshipped: they shall
13. 10 to serve them, and to worship them, sha.
16. 11 have worshipped them, and have forsak.
22. 9 and worshipped other gods, and served
25. 6 to worship them, and provoke me not to
26. 2 which come to worship in the LORD'S ho.
Eze. 8. 16 and they worshipped the sun toward the
46. 2 he shall worship at the threshhold of the
46. 3 Likewise the people of the land shall wo.
46. 9 he that entereth in..to worship shall go
Mic. 5. 13 shalt no more worship the work of thine
Zeph. 1. 5 them that worship..and them that wors.
2. 11 shall worship him, every one from his pl.
Zech. 14. 16 go up from year to year to worship the
14. 17 whoso will not come..to worship the king

5. *Glory, esteem,* δόξα *doxa.*
Luke 14. 10 shalt thou have worship in the presence

6. *To be reverential, pious,* εὐσεβέω *eusebeō.*
Acts 17. 23 Whom therefore ye ignorantly worship

7. *To serve, cure, heal,* θεραπεύω *therapeuō.*
Acts 17. 25 Neither is worshipped with men's hands

8. *Religious observance,* θρησκεία *thrēskeia.*
Col. 2. 18 in a voluntary humility and worshipping

9. *To worship publicly,* λατρεύω *latreuō.*
Acts 7. 42 Then God turned, and gave them up to w.
24. 14 so worship I the God of my fathers, beli.
Phil. 3. 3 which worship God in the spirit, and re.
Heb. 10. 2 because that the worshippers once purg.

10. *A temple sweeper,* νεωκόρος *neōkoros.*
Acts 19. 35 city of the Ephesians is a worshipper of

11. *To kiss (the hand) toward,* προσκυνέω *proskun.*
Matt. 2. 2 star in the east, and are come to worship
2. 8 me word again, that I may come and wo.
2. 11 fell down and worshipped him: and wh.
4. 9 give thee, if thou wilt fall down and wor.
4. 10 Thou shalt worship the Lord thy God, and
8. 2 there came a leper and worshipped him
9. 18 there came a certain ruler, and worship.
14. 33 worshipped him, saying, Of a truth thou
15. 25 Then came she and worshipped him, say.
18. 26 worshipped him, saying, Lord, have pati.
20. 20 worshipping (him), and desiring a certain
Matt 28. 9 came and held him by the feet, and wors.
28. 17 when they saw him, they worshipped him
Mark 5. 6 saw Jesus afar off, he ran and worshipped
15. 19 and bowing (their) knees worshipped him
Luke 4. 7 If thou therefore wilt worship me, all sh.
4. 8 Thou shalt worship the Lord thy God, and
24. 52 [worshipped him, and returned to Jerus.]
John 4. 20 Our fathers worshipped in this mountain
4. 20 is the place where men ought to worship
4. 21 nor yet at Jerusalem, worship the Father
4. 22 Ye worship..we know what we worship
4. 23 shall worship the Father in spirit and in
4. 23 for the Father seeketh such to worship
4. 24 they that worship him must worship (him)
9. 38 said, Lord, I believe. And he worshipped
12. 20 Greeks..that came up to worship at the
Acts 7. 43 figures which ye made to worship them
8. 27 and had come to Jerusalem for to worsh.
10. 25 fell down at his feet, and worshipped (h.)
24. 11 since I went up to Jerusalem for to wor.
1 Co. 14. 25 falling down on (his) face he will worship
Heb. 1. 6 And let all the angels of God worship him
11. 21 worshipped, (leaning) upon the top of his
Rev. 3. 9 will make them to come and worship be.
4. 10 worship him that liveth for ever and ever
5. 14 fell down and worshipped him that liveth
7. 11 fell before the throne..and worshipped
9. 20 that they should not worship devils, and
11. 1 and the altar, and them that worship th.
11. 16 fell upon their faces, and worshipped God
13. 4 worshipped the dragon which gave power
13. 4 and they worshipped the beast; saying
13. 8 all that dwell upon the earth shall worsh.
13. 12 causeth..to worship the first beast, whose
13. 15 cause that as many as would not worship
14. 7 worship him that made heaven, and earth
14. 9 If any man worship the beast and the im.
14. 11 they have no rest..who worship the beast
15. 4 for all nations shall come and worship be.
16. 2 and (upon) them which worshipped his
19. 4 fell down and worshipped God that sat on
19. 10 I fell at his feet to worship him. And he
19. 10 worship God: for the testimony of Jesus
19. 20 deceived..them that worshipped his im.
20. 4 which had not worshipped the beast, ne.
22. 8 fell down to worship before the feet of the
22. 9 keep the sayings of this book: worship G.

12. *A worshipper,* προσκυνητής *proskunētēs.*
John 4. 23 now is, when the true worshippers shall

13. *To venerate, reckon venerable,* σεβάζομαι *sebazo.*
Rom. 1. 25 worshipped and served the creature more

14. *To venerate,* σέβομαι *sebomai.*
Matt 15. 9 But in vain they do worship me, teaching
Mark 7. 7 Howbeit in vain do they worship me, te.
Acts 16. 14 a certain woman..which worshipped God
18. 7 that worshipped God, whose house joined
18. 13 persuadeth men to worship God contrary
19. 27 whom all Asia and the world worshippeth

15. *An object of veneration,* σέβασμα *sebasma.*
2 Th. 2. 4 all that is called God, or that is worship.

WORSHIPPER of God —

One who venerates God, θεοσεβής *theosebēs.*
John 9. 31 if any man be a worshipper of God, and

WORTH, (as is) —

1. *As, like,* כְּמוֹ *kemo.*
2 Sa. 18. 3 but now (thou art) worth ten thousand

2. *Price, hire,* מְחִיר *mechir.*
1 Ki. 21. 2 I will give thee the worth of it in money

3. *Number, amount,* מִכְסָה *miksah.*
Lev. 27. 23 priest shall reckon unto him the worth of

4. *Full,* מָלֵא *male.*
Gen. 23. 9 for as much money as it is worth he shall

5. *Hire, wage, price, reward, fare,* שָׂכָר *sakar.*
Deut 15. 18 for he hath been worth a double hired

WORTHY, worthily, worthies —

1. *Honourable,* אַדִּיר *addir.*
Nah. 2. 5 He shall recount his worthies: they shall

2. *A man,* אִישׁ *ish.*
1 Ki. 2. 26 for thou (art) worthy of death: but I will

3. *(Of) faces,* אַפַּיִם *[aph].*
1 Sa. 1. 5 But unto Hannah he gave a worthy port.

4. *A son of,* בֶּן *ben.*
Deut 25. 2 if the wicked man (be) worthy to be beat.
1 Sa. 26. 16 ye (are) worthy to die, because ye have

5. *(With) strength or might,* חַיִל *chayil.*
Ruth 4. 11 do thou worthily in Ephratah, and be

6. *A son of strength,* בֶּן־חַיִל *ben chayil.*
1 Ki. 1. 52 If he will show himself a worthy man, th.

7. *Judgment,* מִשְׁפָּט *mishpat.*
Deut 19. 6 whereas he (was) not worthy of death, in.
21. 22 if a man have committed a sin worthy of
Jer. 26. 11 This man (is) worthy to die; for he hath
26. 16 This man (is) not worthy to die: for he

8. *Worthy, deserving, merited,* ἄξιος *axios.*
Matt 10. 10 for the workman is worthy of his meat
10. 11 enquire who in it is worthy; and there
10. 13 if the house be worthy..if it be not worthy
10. 37 is not worthy of me..is not worthy of me
10. 38 taketh not his cross..is not worthy of me
22. 8 but they which were bidden were not w.
Luke 3. 8 Bring forth therefore fruits worthy of re.
7. 4 That he was worthy for whom he should
Luke 10. 7 for the labourer is worthy of his hire. Go
12. 48 knew not, and did commit things worthy
15. 19 am no more worthy to be called thy son
15. 21 and am no more worthy to be called thy
23. 15 lo, nothing worthy of death is done unto
John 1. 27 whose shoe's latchet I am not worthy to
Acts 13. 25 whose shoes of (his) feet I am not worthy
23. 29 nothing laid to his charge worthy of death
25. 11 or have committed any thing worthy of
25. 25 found that he had commited nothing wor.
26. 31 doeth nothing worthy of death or of bonds
Rom. 1. 32 which commit such things are worthy of
8. 18 sufferings of this present time (are) not w.
1 Ti. 1. 15 This (is) a faithful saying, and worthy of
4. 9 This (is) a faithful saying, and worthy of
5. 18 And, The labourer (is) worthy of his rewa.
6. 1 count their own masters worthy of all ho.
Heb. 11. 38 Of whom the world was not worthy: they
Rev. 3. 4 walk with me in white: for they are wor.
4. 11 Thou art worthy, O LORD, to receive glory
5. 2 Who is worthy to open the book, and to
5. 4 because no man was found worthy to open
5. 9 Thou art worthy to take the book, and to
5. 12 Worthy is the Lamb that was slain to
16. 6 given them blood to drink; for they are w.

9. *Worthily,* ἀξίως *axiōs.*
Eph. 4. 1 beseech you that ye walk worthy of the v.
Col. 1. 10 That ye might walk worthy of the Lord
1 Th. 2. 12 That ye would walk worthy of God, who

10. *Sufficient,* ἱκανός *hikanos.*
Matt. 3. 11 whose shoes I am not worthy to bear: he
8. 8 I am not worthy that thou shouldest come
Mark 1. 7 latchet of whose shoes I am not worthy
Luke 3. 16 latchet of whose shoes I am not worthy
7. 6 for I am not worthy that thou shouldest

11. *Beautiful, good, excellent,* καλός *kalos.*
Jas. 2. 7 Do not they blaspheme that worthy name

WORTHY, to be (not, count, think) —

1. *To be little, small, young,* קָטֹן *qaton.*
Gen. 32. 10 I am not worthy of the least of all the

2. *To reckon worthy,* ἀξιόω *axioō.*
Luke 7. 7 Wherefore neither thought I myself wor.
2 Th. 1. 11 that our God would count you worthy of
1 Ti. 5. 17 Let the elders that rule well be counted w.
Heb. 3. 3 For this (man) was counted worthy of mo.
10. 29 shall he be thought worthy, who hath tr.

3. *To be reckoned very worthy,* καταξιόομαι *kataxio.*
Luke 20. 35 But they which shall be accounted worthy
21. 36 that [ye may be accounted worthy] to esc.
Acts 5. 41 rejoicing that they were counted worthy
2 Th. 1. 5 that ye may be counted worthy of the ki.

WORTHY deeds, very —

A very right or straightforward action, κατόρθωμα.
Acts 24. 2 very worthy deeds are done unto this na.

WOT, to —

1. *To know, be acquainted with,* יָדַע *yada.*
Gen. 21. 26 I wot not who hath done this thing: neit.
39. 8 my master wotteth not what (is) with me
44. 15 wot ye not that such a man as I can cert.
Exod. 32. 1, 23 we wot not what is become of him
Num. 22. 6 for I wot that he whom thou blessest (is)
Josh. 2. 5 whither the men went I wot not: pursue

2. *To see, know, be acquainted with,* οἶδα *oida.*
Acts 3. 17 I wot that through ignorance ye did (it)
7. 40 we wot not what is become of him
Rom. 11. 2 Wot ye not what the scripture saith of E.?

3. *To make known,* γνωρίζω *gnōrizō.*
Phil. 1. 22 my labour: yet what I shall choose I wot

WOULD (to God, have it) —

1. *O that,* אַחְלַי *achale.*
2 Ki. 5. 3 Would God my lord (were) with the pro.

2. *Willing, desiring, delighting,* חָפֵץ *chaphets.*
1 Sa. 2. 25 their father, because the LORD would slay

3. *To desire,* יָאַל *yaal,* 5.
Josh. 17. 12 but the Canaanites would dwell in that
Judg. 1. 27 but the Canaanites would dwell in that la.
1. 35 But the Amorites would dwell in mount

4. *To will, wish,* צְבָא *tseba.*
Dan. 5. 19, 19, 19, 19 and whom he would he
7. 19 Then I would know the truth of the fourth

5. *There is, there are,* יֵשׁ *yesh.*
2 Ki. 4. 13 wouldest thou be spoken for to the king

6. *O that, if,* לוּ *lu.*
Gen. 30. 34 I would it might be according to thy word
Num 14. 2 Would God that we had died..or would G.
20. 3 Would God that we had died when our
22. 29 I would there were a sword in mine hand
Josh. 7. 7 would to God we had been content, and

7. *Our soul or desire,* נַפְשֵׁנוּ *[nephesh].*
Psa. 35. 25 Ah! so would we have it: let them not say

8. *Who doth (or will) give?* מִי יִתֵּן *mi yitten.*
Exod 16. 3 Would to God we had died by the hand of
Num 11. 29 Would God that all the LORD'S people w.
Deut 28. 67 Would God it were even..Would God it
Judg. 9. 29 would to God this people were under my
2 Sa. 18. 33 would God I had died for thee, O Absalom

9. *To become, come to pass,* γίνομαι *ginomai.*
Acts 20. 16 because he would not spend the time in

10. *To will, wish,* θέλω *thelō.*
Matt. 2. 18 would not be comforted, because they are
5. 42 from him that would borrow of thee turn

Matt. 7. 12 whatsoever ye would that men should do
12. 38 saying, Master, we would see a sign from
14. 5 when he would have put him to death, he
18. 23 king, which would take account of his se.
18. 30 he would not; but went and cast him into
22. 3 bidden to the wedding: and they would
23. 37 how often would I have gathered..ye w.
27. 15 unto the people a prisoner, whom they w.
27. 34 when he had tasted (thereof), he would
Mark 3. 13 calleth (unto him) whom he would: and
6. 19 [would have] killed him; but she could
6. 26 for their sakes which sat with him, he w.
6. 48 walking upon the sea, and would have pa.
7. 24 would have no man know (it): but he co.
9. 30 and he would not that any man should k.
10. 35 would that thou shouldest do for us wha.
10. 36 said unto them, What would ye that I sh.
Luke 1. 62 made signs to his father, how he would
6. 31 as ye would that men should do to you, do
13. 34 how often would I..and ye would not!
15. 28 he was angry, and would not go in; there.
16. 26 so that they which would pass from hence
18. 4 would not for a while: but afterward he
18. 13 would not lift up so much as (his) eyes un.
19. 27 which would not that I should reign over
John 1. 43 The day following Jesus would go forth
6. 11 likewise of the fishes as much as they wo.
7. 1 for he would not walk in Jewry, because
7. 44 some of them would have taken him; but
9. 27 wherefore would ye hear (it) again? will
12. 21 desired him, saying, Sir, we would see J.
21. 18 walkedst whither thou wouldest: but w.
21. 18 and carry (thee) whither thou wouldest
Acts 7. 39 To whom our fathers would not obey, but
10. 10 he became very hungry, and would have
14. 13 would have done sacrifice with the people
16. 3 Him would Paul have to go forth with him
19. 33 would have made his defence unto the pe.
24. 6 whom we took, and would have judged
26. 5 if they would testify, that after the most
Rom. 1. 13 Now I would not have you ignorant, bre.
7. 15 for what I would, that do I not; but wh.
7. 16 If then I do that which I would not, I co.
7. 19 would I do not: but the evil which I wo.
7. 20 Now if I do that I would not, it is no more
7. 21 when I would do good, evil is present w.
11. 25 For I would not, brethren, that ye should
16. 19 yet I would have you wise unto that whi.
1 Co. 7. 7 For I would that all men were even as I
7. 32 But I would have you without carefulness
10. 1 I would not that ye should be ignorant
10. 20 would not that ye should have fellowship
11. 3 But I would have you know, that the he.
12. 1 concerning spiritual (gifts), brethren, I w.
14. 5 I would that ye all spake with tongues
2 Co. 1. 8 For we would not, brethren, have you ig.
5. 4 not for that we would be unclothed, but
12. 20 when I come, I shall not find you..as I w.
12. 20 shall be found unto you such as ye would
Gal. 1. 7 some that trouble you, and would pervert
3. 2 This only would I learn of you, Received
4. 17 they would exclude you, that ye might aff.
5. 17 that ye cannot do the things that ye wou.
Col. 1. 27 To whom God would make known what
2. 1 For I would that ye knew what great co.
1 Th. 2. 18 Wherefore we would have come unto you
4. 13 But I would not have you to be ignorant
2 Th. 3. 10 if any would not work, neither should he
Phm. 14 But without thy mind would I do nothing
Heb. 10. 5 Sacrifice and offering thou wouldest not
10. 8 thou wouldest not, neither hadst, 12. 17

11. *According to*, κατά (acc.) *kata*, Acts 18. 14.

12. *To wish, desire, solicit*, εὔχομαι *euchomai*.
Acts 26. 29 I would to God, that not only thou, but

13. *To be about to*, μέλλω *mellō*.
Luke 10. 1 every city and place whither he himself w
John 6. 6 him: for he himself knew what he would
6. 15 Jesus therefore perceived that they would
Acts 12. 6 when Herod would have brought him forth
16. 27 would have killed himself, supposing that
23. 15 as though ye would enquire something
23. 20 as though they would enquire somewhat
25. 4 and that he himself would depart shortly
27. 30 under colour as though they would have

14. *I wish, would*, ὄφελον *ophelon*.
1 Co. 4. 8 I would to God ye did reign, that we also
2 Co. 11. 1 Would to God ye could bear with me a lit.
Gal. 5. 12 I would they were even cut off which tro.
Rev. 3. 15 neither cold nor hot; I would thou wert

WOUND, wounding —

1. *Bruise, bandage, scar*, חַבּוּרָה *chabburah*.
Psa. 38. 5 My wounds stink (and) are corrupt beca.

2. *An arrow, handle*, חֵץ *chets*.
Job 34. 6 my wound (is) incurable without transgr.

3. *To wound self*, לָהַם *laham*, 7.
Prov. 18. 8 The words of a talebearer (are) as wounds
26. 22 The words of a talebearer (are) as wounds

4. *A wound, binding*, מָזוֹר *mazor*.
Hos. 5. 13 Judah..his wound..cure you of your wou.
Obad. 7 have laid a wound under thee: (there is)

5. *A smiting, stroke, blow*, מַכָּה *makkah*.
1 Ki. 22. 35 the blood ran out of the wound into the
2 Ki. 8. 29 went back to be healed..of the wounds
9. 15 to be healed in Jezreel of the wounds wh.
2 Ch. 22. 6 because of the wounds which were given
Isa. 30. 26 people, and healeth the stroke of their w.
Jer. 6. 7 before me continually (is) grief and wou.
Jer. 10. 19 Woe is me for my hurt! my wound is
15. 18 Why is my pain perpetual, and my wound
30. 12 bruise (is) incurable, (and) thy wound (is)
30. 14 for I have wounded thee with the wound
30. 17 I will heal thee of thy wounds, saith the
Mic. 1. 9 For her wound (is) incurable; for it is come
Nah. 3. 19 healing of thy bruise: thy wound is griev.
Zech. 13. 6 What (are) these wounds in thine hands

6. *A stroke, plague*, נֶגַע *nega*.
Prov. 6. 33 A wound and dishonour shall he get, and

7. *A grievous thing, labour*, עַצֶּבֶת *atstsebeth*.
Psa. 147. 3 broken in heart, and bindeth up their wo.

8. *A wound, wounding*, פֶּצַע *petsa*.
Gen. 4. 23 for I have slain a man to my wounding
Exod 21. 25 Burning for burning, wound for wound
Job 9. 17 and multiplieth my wounds without cau.
Prov. 20. 30 The blueness of a wound cleanseth away
23. 29 who hath wounds without cause? who ha.
27. 6 Faithful (are) the wounds of a friend: but
Isa. 1. 6 wounds, and bruises, and putrifying sores

9. *A stroke, stripe, wound*, πληγή *plēgē*.
Rev. 13. 3 his deadly wound was healed: and all the
13. 12 the first beast, whose deadly wound was
13. 14 which had the wound by a sword, and did

10. *A wound*, τραῦμα *trauma*.
Luke 10. 34 bound up his wounds, pouring in oil and

WOUND, be (deadly) wounded, to —

1. *To cut off*, בָּצַע *batsa*.
Joel 2. 8 fall upon the sword, they shall not be wo.

2. *Wounded, bruised*, פְּצוּעַ [*patsa*].
Deut. 23. 1 He that is wounded in the stones, or hath

3. *To be pierced through*, דָּקַר *daqar*, 4.
Jer. 37. 10 there remained (but) wounded men among

4. *To be pained*, חִיל, חוּל *chul, chil*.
1 Sa. 31. 3 hit him; and he was sore wounded of the
1 Ch. 10. 3 hit him, and he was wounded of the arc.

5. *To pierce*, חָלַל *chalal*.
Psa. 109. 22 poor and needy, and my heart is wounded

6. *To pierce*, חָלַל *chalal*, 3a.
Isa. 51. 9 (Art) thou not it that hath..wounded the

7. *To be pierced*, חָלַל *chalal*, 4.
Isa. 53. 5 But he (was) wounded for our transgress.

8. *Pierced*, חָלָל *chalal*.
Judg. 9. 40 many were overthrown (and) wounded
1 Sa. 17. 52 wounded of the Philistines fell down by
Job 24. 12 soul of the wounded crieth out: yet God
Psa. 69. 26 to the grief of those whom thou hast wo.
Prov. 7. 26 For she hath cast down many wounded
Jer. 51. 52 through all her land the wounded shall
Lam. 2. 12 when they swooned as the wounded in
Eze. 26. 15 when the wounded cry, when the slaug.
28. 23 wounded shall be judged in the midst of
30. 24 with the groanings of a deadly wounded

9. *To be or become sick or pierced*, חָלָה *chalah*, 6.
1 Ki. 22. 34 carry me out of the host; for I am woun.
2 Ch. 18. 33 carry me out of the host; for I am woun.
35. 23 said..Have me away: for I am sore wou.

10. *To smite, dash*, מָחַץ *machats*.
Deut 32. 39 I kill, and I make alive; I wound, and I
2 Sa. 22. 39 I have consumed them, and wounded th.
Job 5. 18 maketh sore, and bindeth up; he wound.
Psa. 18. 38 I have wounded them, that they were not
68. 21 But God shall wound the head of his ene.
110. 6 he shall wound the heads over many cou.
Hab. 3. 13 Thou woundedst the head out of the ho.

11. *Smitten*, נָכֵא *nake*.
Prov. 18. 14 infirmity: but a wounded spirit who can

12. *To smite, strike forth*, נָכָה *nakah*, 5.
2 Ki. 8. 28 Ramoth-gilead; and the Syrians wounded
Jer. 30. 14 for I have wounded thee with the wound

13. *To be smitten*, נָכָה *nakah*, 6.
Zech. 13. 6 with which I was wounded (in) the house

14. *A smiting, blow, stroke*, מַכָּה *makkah*.
Psa. 64. 7 an arrow; suddenly shall they be wounded

15. *To wound*, פָּצַע *patsa*.
Deut 23. 1 He that is wounded in the stones, or hath
1 Ki. 20. 37 man smote him, so that in smiting he wo.
Song 5. 7 they smote me, they wounded me; the k.

16. *To put stripes on*, ἐπιτίθημι πληγάς *epitithēmi*.
Luke 10. 30 wounded (him), and departed, leaving

17. *To kill, slay*, σφάττω *sphattō*.
Rev. 13. 3 I saw one of his heads as it were wounded

18. *To wound, lacerate*, τραυματίζω *traumatizō*.
Luke 20. 12 and they wounded him also, and cast (h.)
Acts 19. 16 they fled out of that house naked and w.

19. *To strike, smite*, τύπτω *tuptō*.
1 Co. 8. 12 wound their weak conscience, ye sin aga.

WOVEN —

Woven, ὑφαντός *huphantos*.
John 19. 23 now the coat was without seam, woven

WRAP (in self, together, up) to —

1. *To wrap together*, גָּלַם *galam*.
2 Ki. 2. 8 Elijah took his mantle, and wrapped (it)

2. *To wrap up*, לוּט *lut*, 5.
1 Ki. 19. 13 that he wrapped his face in his mantle

3. *To gather, heap up*, כָּנַס *kanas*, 7.
Isa. 28. 20 narrower than that he can wrap himself

4. *To wrap up, hide, confirm*, עָבַת *abath*, 3.
Mic. 7. 3 his mischievous desire; so they wrap it up

5. *To cover or wrap self up*, עָלַף *alaph*, 7.
Gen. 38. 14 covered her with a veil, and wrapped he.

6. *To roll up in*, ἐνειλέω *eneileō*.
Mark 15. 46 took him down, and wrapped him in the

7. *To roll or wrap up or in*, ἐντυλίττω *entulittō*.
Matt. 27. 59 taken the body, he wrapped it in a clean
Luke 23. 53 he took it down, and wrapped it in linen
John 20. 7 but wrapped together in a place by itself

WRAPPED (about, together, up), to be —

1. *To bind, bind up, gird*, חָבַשׁ *chabash*.
Jon. 2. 5 about, the weeds were wrapped about my

2. *To wrap up*, לוּט *lut*.
1 Sa. 21. 9 it (is here) wrapped in a cloth behind the

3. *Covered*, מָעַט *maot*.
Eze. 21. 15 made bright, (it is) wrapped up for the sl.

4. *To be folded, wrapped together*, סָבַךְ *sabak*, 4.
Job 8. 17 His roots are wrapped about the heap

5. *To be wrapped together*, שָׂרַג *sarag*, 4.
Job 40. 17 the sinews of his stones are wrapped tog.

WRATH, (fierce), wrathful —

1. *Face, anger, temper*, אַף *aph*.
Gen. 39. 19 came to pass..that his wrath was kindled
Exod 22. 24 my wrath shall wax hot, and I will kill
32. 10 let me alone, that my wrath may wax hot
32. 11 why doth thy wrath wax hot against thy
32. 12 Turn from thy fierce wrath, and repent
Num 11. 33 wrath of the LORD was kindled against the
Deut 11. 17 LORD'S wrath be kindled against you, and
1 Sa. 28. 18 nor executedst his fierce wrath upon Am.
2 Ki. 23. 26 not from the fierceness of his great wrath
2 Ch. 12. 12 wrath of the LORD turned from him, that
28. 11 for the fierce wrath of the LORD (is) upon
28. 13 trespass is great, and (there is) fierce w.
29. 10 that his fierce wrath may turn away from
30. 8 that the fierceness of his wrath may turn
Ezra 8. 22 his wrath (is) against all them that forsa.
10. 14 until the fierce wrath of our God for this
Job 14. 13 wouldest keep me secret, until thy wrath
16. 9 He teareth (me) in his wrath, who hateth
19. 11 He hath also kindled his wrath against
20. 23 shall cast the fury of his wrath upon him
20. 28 goods) shall flow away in the day of his w.
32. 2 Then was kindled the wrath of Elihu the
32. 2 against Job was his wrath kindled, beca.
32. 3 Also against his three friends was his w.
32. 5 no answer..then his wrath was kindled
36. 13 But the hypocrites in heart heap up wra.
40. 11 Cast abroad the rage of thy wrath: and
42. 7 My wrath is kindled against thee, and
Psa. 2. 5 Then shall he speak unto them in his wr.
2. 12 when his wrath is kindled but a little. Bl.
21. 9 the LORD shall swallow them up in his w.
55. 3 cast iniquity upon me, and in wrath they
78. 31 The wrath of God came upon them, and
95. 11 Unto whom I sware in my wrath, that th.
106. 40 Therefore was the wrath of the LORD kin.
110. 5 strike through kings in the day of his w.
124. 3 when their wrath was kindled against us
138. 7 stretch forth thine hand against the wra.
Prov 14. 29 (He that is) slow to wrath (is) of great un.
24. 18 displease him, and he turn away his wra.
29. 8 a snare: but wise (men) turn away wrath
30. 33 so the forcing of wrath bringeth forth st.

2. *Wrath, rage, raging*, זַעַף *zaaph*.
Prov 19. 12 The king's wrath (is) as the roaring of a

3. *Heat, fury*, חֵמָה *chemah*.
Num 25. 11 hath turned my wrath away from the ch.
Deut 29. 23 overthrew in his anger, and in his wrath
29. 28 LORD rooted them out..in wrath, and in
2 Sa. 11. 20 if so be that the king's wrath arise, and
2 Ki. 22. 13 for great (is) the wrath of the LORD that
22. 17 therefore my wrath shall be kindled aga.
2 Ch. 12. 7 my wrath shall not be poured out upon
34. 21 for great (is) the wrath of the LORD that
34. 25 therefore my wrath shall be poured out
36. 16 until the wrath of the LORD arose against
Esth. 2. 1 when the wrath of king Ahasuerus was
3. 5 reverence, then was Haman full of wrath
7. 7 arising from the banquet of wine in his w.
7. 10 Mordecai. Then was the king's wrath pa.
Job 19. 29 wrath (bringeth) the punishments of the
21. 20 and he shall drink of the wrath of the A.
36. 18 Because (there is) wrath, (beware) lest he
Psa. 37. 8 Cease from anger, and forsake wrath
59. 13 Consume (them) in wrath, consume (them)
76. 10 Surely the wrath of man shall praise thee
76. 10 the remainder of wrath shalt thou restrain
78. 38 anger away, and did not stir up all his w.
79. 6 Pour out thy wrath upon the heathen th.
88. 7 Thy wrath lieth hard upon me, and thou
89. 46 thou hide thyself for ever? shall thy wr.
90. 7 consumed by thine anger, and by thy w.
106. 23 to turn away his wrath; lest he should
Prov 15. 1 A soft answer turneth away wrath: but
15. 18 A wrathful man stirreth up strife: but
16. 14 The wrath of a king (is as) messengers of
19. 19 A man of great wrath shall suffer punish.
21. 14 and a reward in the bosom strong wrath
27. 4 Wrath (is) cruel, and anger (is) outrage.
Jer. 18. 20 (and) to turn away thy wrath from them
Eze. 13. 15 Thus will I accomplish my wrath upon

4. *Fierceness, heat, wrath,* חָרוֹן *charon.*
Exod15. 7 thou sentest forth thy wrath, (which) co.
Neh.13. 18 ye bring more wrath upon Israel by pro.
Psa. 58. 9 with a whirlwind, both living..in (his) w.
69. 24 and let thy wrathful anger take hold of
88. 16 Thy fierce wrath goeth over me; thy ter.
Eze. 7. 12, 14 wrath (is) upon all the multitude the.
5. *Anger, provocation, sadness,* כַּעַס *kaas.*
Deut32. 27 Were it not that I feared the wrath of the
Prov12. 16 A fool's wrath is presently known: but a
27. 3 but a fool's wrath (is) heavier than them
6. *Anger, provocation, sadness,* כַּעַשׂ *kaas.*
Job 5. 2 For wrath killeth the foolish man, and
7. *Transgression, wrath,* עֶבְרָה *ebrah.*
Gen.49. 7 Cursed (be)..their wrath, for it was cruel
Job 21. 30 they shall be brought forth to the day of w.
Psa. 78. 49 cast upon them the fierceness of his..wr.
85. 3 Thou hast taken away all thy wrath: thou
90. 9 For all our days are passed away in thy w.
90. 11 even according to thy fear, (so is) thy wr.
Prov11. 4 Riches profit not in the day of wrath: but
11. 23 (but) the expectation of the wicked (is) w.
14. 35 his wrath is (against) him that causeth sh.
21. 24 scorner (is) his name who dealeth in..w.
Isa. 9. 19 Through the wrath of the LORD of hosts
10. 6 against the people of my wrath will I give
13. 9 cruel both with wrath and fierce anger
13. 13 shall remove out of her place, in the wra.
14. 6 He who smote the people in wrath with
16. 6 haughtiness, and his pride, and his wrath
Jer. 7. 29 and forsaken the generation of his wrath
48. 30 I know his wrath, saith the LORD; but
Lam. 2. 2 he hath thrown down in his wrath the
3. 1 hath seen affliction by the rod of his wra.
Eze. 7. 19 deliver them in the day of the wrath of
21. 31 blow against thee in the fire of my wrath
22. 21 blow upon you in the fire of my wrath
22. 31 consumed them with the fire of my wrath
38. 19 in the fire of my wrath have I spoken, Su.
Hos. 5. 10 I will pour out my wrath upon them like
13. 11 I gave..and took (him) away in my wrath
Amos 1. 11 his anger did tear..and he kept his wrath
Hab. 3. 8 (was) thy wrath against the sea, that thou
Zeph. 1. 15 That day (is) a day of wrath, a day of tro.
1. 18 deliver them in the day of the LORD's w.
8. *To be wroth,* קְצַף *qetsaph.*
Ezra 7. 23 why should there be wrath against the re.
9. *Wrath,* קְצַף *qetseph.*
Num. 1. 53 there be no wrath upon the congregation
16. 46 there is wrath gone out from the LORD
18. 5 that there be no wrath any more upon
Josh. 9. 20 let them live, lest wrath be upon us, bec.
22. 20 wrath fell on all the congregation of Isra.
1 Ch.27. 24 because there fell wrath for it against Is.
2 Ch.19. 2 therefore (is) wrath upon thee from before
19. 10 (so) wrath come upon you, and upon your
24. 18 wrath came upon Judah and Jerusalem
29. 8 the wrath of the LORD was upon Judah
32. 25 there was wrath upon him, and upon Ju.
32. 26 the wrath of the LORD came not upon th.
Esth. 1. 18 Thus (shall there arise) too much..wrath
Psa. 38. 1 LORD, rebuke me not in thy wrath, neit.
102. 10 Because of thine indignation and thy wr.
Eccl. 5. 17 (he hath) much sorrow and wrath with
Isa. 54. 8 In a little wrath I hid my face from thee
60. 10 in my wrath I smote thee, but in my fav
Jer. 10. 10 at his wrath the earth shall tremble, and
21. 5 in anger, and in fury, and in great wrath
32. 37 whither I have driven them..in great w.
50. 13 Because of the wrath of the LORD it shall
Zech. 7. 12 therefore came a great wrath from the L.
10. *Anger, trembling, trouble,* רֹגֶז *rogez.*
Hab. 3. 2 O LORD..in wrath remember mercy
11. *Mind, wrath,* θυμός *thumos.*
Luke 4. 28 when they heard..were filled with wrath
Acts 19. 28 they were full of wrath, and cried out, sa.
2 Co.12. 20 lest (there be) debates, envyings, wraths
Gal. 5. 20 emulations, wrath, strife, seditions, heres.
Eph. 4. 31 Let all bitterness, and wrath, and anger
Col. 3. 8 put off all these; anger, wrath, malice
Heb.11. 27 he forsook Egypt, not fearing the wrath
Rev.12. 12 having great wrath, because he knoweth
14. 8 drink of the wine of [the wrath of] her
14. 10 shall drink of the wine of the wrath of
14. 19 into the great wine press of the wrath of
15. 1 for in them is filled up the wrath of God
15. 7 seven golden vials full of the wrath of God
16. 1 pour out the vials of the wrath of God upon
18. 3 have drunk of the wine of the wrath of her
12. *Anger, wrath,* ὀργή *orgē.*
Matt. 3. 7 who hath warned you to flee from the wra.
Luke 3. 7 who hath warned you to flee from the wr.
21. 23 for there shall be..wrath upon this people
John 3. 36 but the wrath of God abideth on him
Rom. 1. 18 the wrath of God is revealed from heaven
2. 5 wrath against the day of wrath and reve.
2. 8 obey unrighteousness, indignation and w.
4. 15 Because the law worketh wrath: for where
5. 9 we shall be saved from wrath through him
9. 22 willing to show his wrath..vessels of wra.
12. 19 Dearly beloved..give place unto wrath
13. 4 a revenger to (execute) [wrath] upon him
13. 5 not only for wrath, but also for conscience
Eph. 2. 3 were by nature the children of wrath, even
5. 6 because of these things cometh the wrath
Col. 3. 6 the wrath of God cometh on the children
1 Th. 1. 10 which delivered us from the wrath to co.
1 Th. 2. 16 the wrath is come upon them to the utte.
5. 9 God hath not appointed us to wrath, but
1 Ti. 2. 8 lifting up holy hands, without wrath and
Heb. 3. 11 I sware in my wrath, They shall not enter
4. 3 I have sworn in my wrath, If they shall
Jas. 1. 19 swift to hear, slow to speak, slow to wrath
1. 20 the wrath of man worketh not the righte.
Rev. 6. 16 and hide us..from the wrath of the lamb
6. 17 the great day of his wrath is come, and w.
11. 18 thy wrath is come, and the time of the de.
16. 19 of the wine of the fierceness of his wrath
19. 15 the fierceness and wrath of Almighty God
13. *A provoking to anger,* παροργισμός *parorgismos.*
Eph. 4. 26 let not the sun go down upon your wrath

WRATH, to provoke to, to come, be wroth —
1. *To be wroth,* קָצַף *qatsaph.*
Gen. 40. 2 Pharaoh was wroth against two (of) his offi.
41. 10 Pharaoh was wroth with his servants, and
Exod16. 20 it bred worms..and Moses was wroth with
Lev. 10. 6 lest ye die, and lest wrath come upon all
Num16. 22 will thou be wroth with all the congreg.
31. 14 Moses was wroth with the officers of the
Deut. 1. 34 the LORD heard the voice..and was wroth
9. 19 the LORD was wroth against you to dest.
Josh.22. 18 he will be wroth with the whole congreg.
1 Sa. 29. 4 the princes of the Philistines were wroth
2 Ki. 5. 11 Naaman was wroth, and went away, and
13. 19 the man of God was wroth with him, and
Esth. 1. 12 therefore was the king very wroth, and
2. 21 Bigthan and Teresh..were wroth, and so.
Isa. 47. 6 I was wroth with my people, I have poll.
54. 9 I would not be wroth with thee, nor reb.
57. 16 neither will I be always wroth: for the sp.
57. 17 was I wroth..and was wroth, and he we.
64. 5 thou art wroth; for we have sinned: in th.
64. 9 Be not wroth very sore, O LORD, neither
Jer. 37. 15 the princes were wroth with Jeremiah
Lam. 5. 22 rejected us; thou art very wroth against
2. *To cause wrath,* קָצַף *qatsaph,* 5.
Deut. 9. 7 provokedst the LORD thy God to wrath in
9. 8 ye provoked the LORD to wrath, so that
9. 22 at Massah..ye provoked the LORD to wr.
Zech. 8.14 when your fathers provoked me to wrath
3. *To cause to tremble or be angry,* רְגַז *regaz,* 5.
Ezra 5. 12 provoked the God of heaven unto wrath
4. *To be wroth, sad, morose,* זָעַף *zaaph.*
2 Ch.26. 19 Uzziah was wroth, and (had) a censer in his
26. 19 and while he was wroth with the priests
5. *To be heated, wroth,* חָרָה *charah.*
Gen. 4. 5 Cain was very wroth, and his countenance
4. 6 Why art thou wroth? and why is thy cou.
31. 36 Jacob was wroth, and chode with Laban
34. 7 they were very wroth, because he had w.
Num16. 15 Moses was very wroth, and said unto the
1 Sa. 18. 8 Saul was very wroth, and the saying disp.
20. 7 if he be very wroth, (then) be sure that
2 Sa. 3. 8 Then was Abner very wroth for the words
13. 21 when king David heard..he was very wr.
22. 8 moved and shook, because he was wroth
Neh. 4. 1 he was wroth, and took great indignation
4. 7 to be stopped, then they were very wroth
Psa. 18. 7 and were shaken, because he was wroth
6. *To be angry, sad,* כָּעַס *kaas.*
2 Ch.16. 10 Asa was wroth with the seer, and put him
7. *To show self wroth,* עָבַר *abar,* 7.
Deut. 3. 26 the LORD was wroth with me for your sa.
Psa. 78. 21 Therefore the LORD heard..and was wroth
78. 59 When God heard..he was wroth, and gr.
78. 62 He gave his people over..and was wroth
89. 38 thou hast been wroth with thine anointed
8. *To be angry, tremble,* רָגַז *ragaz.*
Isa. 28. 21 he shall be wroth as (in) the valley of Gi.
9. *To be or become angry,* ὀργίζομαι *orgizomai.*
Matt.18. 34 his lord was wroth, and delivered him to
22. 7 But when the king heard..he was wroth
Rev. 12. 17 the dragon was wroth with the woman, and
10. *To anger beyond measure,* παροργίζω *parorgizō.*
Eph. 6. 4 fathers, provoke not your children to wr.
11. *To be wroth,* θυμόομαι *thumoomai.*
Matt. 2. 16 Herod..was exceeding wroth, and sent

WREATH, wreathen (work), to be wreathed —
1. *Fringes, wreathes,* גְּדִלִים *gedilim.*
1 Ki. 7. 17 wreaths of chain work, for the chapiters
2. *Thick band, wreath, branch,* עֲבֹת *aboth.*
Exod.28. 14 chains..(of) wreathen work..the wreathen
28. 22 chains..(of) wreathen work (of) pure gold
28. 24 And thou shalt put the two wreathen
28. 25 two ends of the two wreathen (chains) th.
39. 15 chains..(of) wreathen work (of) pure gold
39. 17 they put the two wreathen chains of gold
39. 18 the two ends of the two wreathen chains
3. *Net or wreathed work, lattice,* שְׂבָכָה *sebakah.*
2 Ki.25. 17 the wreathen work..with wreathen work
2 Ch. 4. 12 two wreaths to cover the two pommels of
4. 13 on the two wreaths..rows..on each wre.
4. *To wrap self together,* שָׂרַג *sarag,* 7.
Lam. 1. 14 they are wreathed, (and) come up upon

WREST —
1. *To stretch out, turn aside or away,* נָטָה *natah,* 5.
Exod 23. 2 speak in a cause to decline after many to w.
23. 6 Thou shalt not wrest the judgment of thy
Deut 16. 19 Thou shalt not wrest judgment; thou sh.
2. *To take pains, grieve, wrest,* עָצַב *atsab,* 3.
Psa. 56. 5 Every day they wrest my words: all their
3. *To distort, pervert,* στρεβλόω *strebloō.*
2 Pe. 3. 16 they that are unlearned and unstable wr.

WRESTLE, wrestlings, to —
1. *To wrestle, clasp round,* אָבַק *abaq,* 2.
Gen. 32. 24 there wrestled a man with him until the
32. 25 thigh was out of joint as he wrestled with
2. *Wrestlings,* נַפְתּוּלִים *naphtulim.*
Gen. 30. 8 And Rachel said, With great wrestlings ha.
3. *To wrestle,* פָּתַל *pathal,* 2.
Gen. 30. 8 have I wrestled with my sister, and I ha.
4. *The wrestling is,* ἡ πάλη ἐστιν *hē palē estin.*
Eph. 6. 12 For we wrestle not against flesh and blood

WRETCHED, wretchedness —
1. *Evil, bad,* רַע *ra.*
Num.11. 15 and let me not see my wretchedness
2. *Miserable, wretched,* ταλαίπωρος *talaipōros.*
Rom. 7. 24 O wretched man that I am! who shall de.
Rev. 3. 17 knowest not that thou art wretched, and

WRING (off, out,) wringing, to —
1. *Wringing out, forcing, churning,* מִיץ *mits.*
Prov.30. 33 The wringing of the nose bringeth forth
2. *To wring off, break,* מָלַק *malaq.*
Lev. 1. 15 wring off his head, and burn (it) on the
5. 8 wring off his head from his neck, but sh.
3. *To wring out, drain out,* מָצָה *matsah.*
Judg. 6. 38 wringed the dew out of the fleece, a bowl
Psa. 75. 8 the wicked of the earth shall wring (th.)
Isa. 51. 17 drunken the dregs..(and) wrung (them) o.
4. *To be wrung or drained out,* מָצָה *matsah,* 2.
Lev. 1. 15 blood thereof shall be wrung out at the si.
5. 9 rest of the blood shall be wrung out at the
Psa. 73. 10 waters of a full (cup) are wrung out to th.

WRINKLE, to fill with wrinkles —
1. *To lay hold on, wrinkle,* קָמַט *qamat.*
Job 16. 8 thou hast filled me with wrinkles, (which)
2. *A wrinkle,* ῥυτίς *rhutis.*
Eph. 5. 27 not having spot, or wrinkle, or any such

WRITE (afore, unto, up), to —
1. *To write, inscribe, describe,* כָּתַב *kathab.*
Exod.17. 14 Write this (for) a memorial in a book, and
24. 4 Moses wrote all the words of the LORD
24. 12 and commandments which I have written
32. 32 blot..out of thy book which thou hast w.
34. 1 will write upon (these) tables the words
34. 27 Write thou these words: for after the te.
34. 28 wrote upon the tables the words of the
39. 30 wrote upon it a writing, (like to) the eng.
Num 5. 23 the priest shall write these curses in a bo.
17. 2 write thou every man's name upon his rod
17. 3 shalt write Aaron's name upon the rod of
33. 2 Moses wrote their goings out according
Deut. 4. 13 and he wrote them upon two tables of st.
5. 22 wrote them in two tables of stone, and
6. 9 thou shalt write them upon the posts of
10. 2 I will write on the tables the words that
10. 4 wrote on the tables according to the first
11. 20 thou shalt write them upon the door po.
17. 18 he shall write him a copy of this law in a
24. 1 then let him write her a bill of divorcem.
24. 3 write her a bill of divorcement, and giveth
27. 3 shalt write upon them all the words of
27. 8 thou shalt write upon..stones all the wo.
31. 9 Moses wrote this law, and delivered it
31. 19 Now therefore write ye this song for you
31. 22 Moses therefore wrote this song the same
Josh. 8. 32 wrote there..a copy..which he wrote in
24. 26 Joshua wrote these words in the book of
1 Sa. 10. 25 wrote (it) in a book, and laid (it) up before
2 Sa. 11. 14 wrote a letter to Joab, and sent (it) by
11. 15 wrote in the letter, saying, Set ye Uriah
1 Ki.21. 8 So she wrote letters in Ahab's name, and
21. 9 she wrote in the letters, saying, Proclaim
2 Ki.10. 1 Jehu wrote letters, and sent to Samaria
10. 6 Then he wrote a letter the second time to
17. 37 commandment, which he wrote for you
1 Ch. 24. 6 wrote them before the king, and the pri.
2 Ch.26. 22 Isaiah the prophet, the son of Amoz, wr.
30. 1 wrote letters also to Ephraim and Manas.
32. 17 He wrote also letters to rail on the LORD
Ezra 4. 6 wrote they (unto him) an accusation aga
4. 7 wrote Bishlam..written in the Syrian to
Neh. 9. 38 we make a sure (covenant), and write (it),
Esth. 8. 5 which he wrote to destroy the Jews which
8. 8 Write ye also for the Jews, as it liketh
8. 10 wrote in the king Ahasuerus' name, and
9. 20 Mordecai wrote these things, and sent le.
9. 23 and as Mordecai had written unto them
9. 29 wrote with all authority, to confirm this
Job 13. 26 For thou writest bitter things against me
31. 35 and (that) mine adversary had written a
Psa. 87. 6 LORD shall count, when he writeth up the
Prov. 3. 3 write them upon the table of thine heart
7. 3 Bind them upon thy fingers, write them
22. 20 Have not I written to thee excellent thi.
Isa. 8. 1 write in it with a man's pen concerning
10. 19 shall be few, that a child may write them
30. 8 write it before them in a table, and note
Jer. 22. 30 Write ye this man childless, a man (that)
30. 2 Write thee all the words that I have spo.
31. 33 write it in their hearts, and will be their

Jer. 36. 2 write therein all the words that I have
36. 4 Baruch wrote from the mouth of Jerem.
36. 6 which thou hast written from my mouth
36. 17 How didst thou write all these words at
36. 18 and I wrote (them) with ink in the book
36. 27 words which Baruch wrote at the mouth
36. 28 write in it all the former words that were
36. 29 Why hast thou written therein, saying
36. 32 who wrote therein, from the mouth of J.
45. 1 when he had written these words in a bo.
51. 60 So Jeremiah wrote in a book all the evil
Eze. 24. 2 Write thee the name of the day, (even) of
37. 16 write upon it..write upon it, For Joseph
37. 20 sticks whereon thou writest shall be in th.
43. 11 write (it) in their sight, that they may ke.
Hos. 8. 12 I have written to him the great things of
Hab. 2. 2 Write the vision, and make (it) plain up.

2. *To write, prescribe,* כָּתַב *kathab,* 3.
Isa. 10. 1 write grievousness (which) they have pres.

3. *To write,* כְּתַב *kethab.*
Ezra 4. 8 wrote a letter against Jerusalem to Arta.
5. 10 write the names of the men that (were)
Dan. 5. 5 wrote over against the candlestick upon
5. 5 the king saw the part of the hand that w.
6. 25 Then king Darius wrote unto all people
7. 1 then he wrote the dream, (and) told the

4. *To write, inscribe,* γράφω *graphō.*
Mark 10. 4 Moses suffered to write a bill of divorce.
10. 5 For the hardness of your heart he wrote
12. 19 Moses wrote unto us, If a man's brother
Luke 1. 3 write unto thee in order, most excellent
1. 63 asked..and wrote, saying, His name is John
16. 6 thy bill, and sit down quickly, and write
16. 7 said unto him, Take thy bill, and write fo.
20. 28 Moses wrote unto us, If any man's brother
John 1. 45 found him of whom Moses..did write, Je.
5. 46 ye would have believed me; for he wrote
8. 6 [with (his) finger wrote on the ground, (as)]
8. 8 [again he stooped down, and wrote on the]
19. 19 Pilate wrote a title, and put (it) on the cr.
19. 21 Write not, The king of the Jews; but that
19. 22 answered, What I have written I have wr.
21. 24 wrote these things; and we know that his
Acts 15. 23 they wrote (letters) by them after this m.
18. 27 brethren wrote, exhorting the disciples to
23. 25 And he wrote a letter after this manner
25. 26 Of whom I have no certain thing to write
25. 26 that after..I might have somewhat to wr.
Rom 15. 15 I have written the more boldly unto you
16. 22 I Tertius, who wrote (this) epistle, salute
1 Co. 4. 14 I write not these things to shame you, but
5. 9 wrote unto you in an epistle not to comp.
5. 11 I have written unto you not to keep com.
7. 1 concerning the things whereof ye wrote
9. 15 neither have I written these things, that
14. 37 that the things that I write unto you are
2 Co. 1. 13 For we write none other things unto you
2. 3 I wrote this same unto you, lest, when I
2. 4 I wrote unto you with many tears; not
2. 9 For to this end also did I write, that I mi.
7. 12 Wherefore, though I wrote unto you, (I
9. 1 saints, it is superfluous for me to write to
13. 2 being absent now [I write] to them which
13. 10 Therefore I write these things being abs.
Gal. 1. 20 Now the things which I write unto you
6. 11 Ye see how large a letter I have written
Phil. 3. 1 To write the same things to you, to me
1 Th. 4. 9 need not that I write unto you; for ye yo.
5. 1 ye have no need that I write unto you
2 Th. 3. 17 which is the token in every epistle..I wr.
1 Ti. 3. 14 These things write I unto thee, hoping to
Phm. 19 I Paul have written (it) with mine own h.
21 wrote unto thee, knowing that thou wilt
1 Pe. 5. 12 I have written briefly, exhorting and tes.
2 Pe. 3. 1 second epistle, beloved, I now write unto
3. 15 as..Paul also..hath written unto you
1 Jo. 1. 4 these things write we unto you, that your
2. 1 these things write I unto you, that ye sin
2. 7 I write no new commandment unto you
2. 8 a new commandment I write unto you, wh.
2. 12 I write unto you, little children, because
2. 13 I write unto you..I write unto you..I wr.
2. 14 I have written unto you, fathers, because
2. 14 I have written unto you, young men, be.
2. 21 I have not written unto you because ye
2. 26 These..have I written unto you concern.
2 John 5 not as though I wrote a new commandm.
12 Having many things to write unto you, I
3 John 9 I wrote unto the church: but Diotrephes
13 to write, but I will not with ink and pen w.
Jude 3 when I gave all diligence to write unto you
3 it was needful for me to write unto you
Rev. 1. 11 What thou seest, write in a book, and send
1. 19 Write the things which thou hast seen, and
2. 1 Unto the angel of the church of Ephesus w.
2. 8, 18 unto the angel of the church..write
2. 12 to the angel of the church in Pergamos w.
3. 1, 14 unto the angel of the church..write
3. 7 write; These things saith he that is holy
3. 12 I will write upon him the name of my G.
10. 4 I was about to write: and I heard a voice
10. 4 Seal up these things..and write them not
14. 13 voice from heaven saying unto me, Write
19. 9 Write, Blessed (are) they which are called
21. 5 said unto me, Write: for these words are

5. *To write upon or over,* ἐπιγράφω *epigraphō.*
Heb. 8. 10 write them in their hearts; and I will be
10. 16 hearts, and in their minds will I write th.

6. *To send to, or upon,* ἐπιστέλλω *epistellō.*
Acts 15. 20 But that we write unto them, that they
21. 25 [we have written] (and) concluded that

WRITE a letter unto, to —
To send to, ἐπιστέλλω *epistellō.*
Heb. 13. 22 I have written a letter unto you in few

WRITER, writing —
1. *To write,* כָּתַב *kathab.*
Deut 31. 24 Moses had made an end of writing the w.

2. *To write,* כְּתַב *kethab.*
Dan. 5. 7 Whosoever shall read this writing, and sh.
5. 8 but they could not read the writing, nor
5. 15 that they should read this writing, and m
5. 16 now if thou canst read the writing, and
5. 17 yet I will read the writing unto the king
5. 24 sent from him; and this writing was wri.
5. 25 this (is) the writing that was written, Me.
6. 8 sign the writing, that it be not changed
6. 9 Wherefore king Darius signed the writing
6. 10 when Daniel knew that the writing was

3. *A writing, register,* כְּתַב *kethab.*
1 Ch. 28. 19 made me understand in writing by (his) h.
2 Ch. 2. 11 Huram the king of Tyre answered in wri.
35. 4 according to the writing of David king of
Ezra 4. 7 and the writing of the letter (was) written
Esth. 1. 22 every province according to the writing
3. 12 every province according to the writing
3. 14 The copy of the writing, for a command.
4. 8 Also he gave him the copy of the writing
8. 8 the writing which is written in the king's
8. 9 every province according to the writing
8. 9 and to the Jews according to their writing
8. 13 The copy of the writing for a command.
9. 27 keep these two days according to their w.
Eze. 13. 9 neither shall they be written in the writ.

4. *A writing,* מִכְתָּב *miktab.*
Exod 32. 16 and the writing (was) the writing of God
39. 30 wrote upon it a writing, (like to) the eng.
Deut 10. 4 according to the first writing, the ten co.
2 Ch. 21. 12 there came a writing to him from Elijah
35. 4 and according to the writing of Solomon
36. 22 made a proclamation..in writing, saying
Ezra 1. 1 made a proclamation..in writing, saying
Isa. 38. 9 The writing of Hezekiah king of Judah

5. *To number, write, cypher,* סָפַר *saphar.*
Judg 5. 14 and..they that handle the pen of the wr.
Psa. 45. 1 I speak..my tongue (is)..of a ready wri.
Eze. 9. 2 one man..with a writer's inkhorn by his
9. 3 which (had) the writer's inkhorn by his

6. *A little book, roll, scroll,* βιβλίον *biblion.*
Matt 19. 7 Why did Moses then command to give a w.

7. *A letter, character, any thing written,* γράμμα.
John 5. 47 But if ye believe not his writings, how

8. *To write, inscribe,* γράφω *graphō.*
John 19. 19 writing was, Jesus of Nazareth the king

WRITING table —
A small writing table, πινακίδιον *pinakidion.*
Luke 1. 63 he asked for a writing table, and wrote

WRITTEN, (aforetime, in, over, on), to be —
1. *To write,* כָּתַב *kathab.*
Exod 31. 18 tables of stone, written with the finger of
32. 15 the tables (were) written on both their
32. 15 one side and on the other (were) they w.
Num 11. 26 they (were) of them that were written, but
Deut. 9. 10 written with the finger of God: and on th.
28. 58 words of this law that are written in this
28. 61 which (is) not written in the book of this
29. 20 all the curses that are written in this book
29. 21 curses of the covenant that are written
29. 27 bring upon it all the curses that are wri.
30. 10 statutes (which are) written in this book
Josh. 1. 8 observe to do according to all that is wri.
8. 31 as it is written in the book of the law of M.
8. 34 according to all that is written in the book
10. 13 (Is) not this written in the book of Jasher?
23. 6 to keep and to do all that is written in the
2 Sa. 1. 18 behold, (it is) written in the book of Jas.
1 Ki. 2. 3 as it is written in the law of Moses, that
11. 41 (are) they not written in the book of the
14. 19 written in the book of the chronicles of
So in verse 29; 15. 7, 23, 31; 16. 5, 14, 20, 27; 22. 39, 45;
2 Ki. 1. 18; 8. 23; 10. 34; 12. 19; 13. 8, 12; 14. 15, 28; 15.
6, 11, 15, 21, 26, 31, 36; 16. 19; 20. 20; 21. 17, 25; 23. 28;
24. 5; 1 Ch. 9. 1; 29. 29; 2 Ch. 9. 29; 12. 15; 16. 11; 20.
34; 25. 26; 27. 7; 28. 26; 34. 24; 35. 12, 27; 36. 8; Esth.
10. 2.
2 Ki. 14. 6 according to that which is written in the
22. 13 to do according unto all that which is w.
23. 3 words of this covenant that were written
23. 21 as (it is) written in the book of this cove.
23. 24 the words of the law which were written
1 Ch. 4. 41 these written by name came in the days
16. 40 according to all that is written in the law
2 Ch. 13. 22 (are) written in the story of the prophet I.
23. 18 as (it is) written in the law of Moses, with
24. 27 written in the story of the book of the ki.
25. 4 written in the law in the book of Moses
30. 5 of a long (time in such sort) as it was writ.
30. 18 eat the passover otherwise than it was w.
31. 3 as (it is) written in the law of the LORD
32. 32 they (are) written in the vision of Isaiah
33. 19 they (are) written among the sayings of
34. 21 to do after all that is written in this book
34. 31 words of the covenant which are written
2 Ch. 35. 12 as (it is) written in the book of Moses, and
35. 25 behold, they (are) written in the Lamen.
35. 26 according to (that which was) written in
Ezra 3. 2 as (it is) written in the law of Moses the
3. 4 as (it is) written, and (offered) the daily
4. 7 was written in the Syrian tongue, and in.
Neh. 6. 6 Wherein (was) written, It is reported am.
7. 5 came up at the first, and found written
8. 14 they found written in the law which the
8. 15 of thick trees, to make booths, as it is w.
10. 34 burn upon the altar..as (it is) written in the
10. 36 as (it is) written in the law, and the first.
12. 23 written in the book of the chronicles, even
13. 1 found written, that the Ammonite and the
Esth. 6. 2 found written, that Mordecai had told
Psa. 40. 7 in the volume of the book (it is) written
149. 9 To execute upon them the judgment wr.
Eccl. 12. 10 (that which was) written (was) upright
Isa. 4. 3 every one that is written among the living
65. 6 Behold, (it is) written before me; I will
Jer. 17. 1 The sin of Judah (is) written with a pen
25. 13 all that is written in this book, which Je.
51. 60 all these words that are written against
Eze. 2. 10 written within and without: and..writt.
Dan. 9. 11 written in the law of Moses the servant
9. 13 As (it is) written in the law of Moses, all
12. 1 every one that shall be found written in.

2. *To be written,* כָּתַב *kathab,* 2.
Ezra 8. 34 and all the weight was written at that ti.
Esth. 1. 19 let it be written among the laws of the
2. 23 it was written in the book of the chronic.
3. 9 let it be written that they may be destro.
3. 12 there was written, according to all that
3. 12 in the name of king Ahasuerus was it wr.
8. 5 let it be written to reverse the letters de.
8. 8 for the writing which is written in the
8. 9 it was written according to all that Mor.
9. 32 matters of Purim; and it was written in
Job 19. 23 Oh that my words were now written! oh
Psa. 69. 28 book of the living, and not be written wi.
102. 18 This shall be written for the generation
139. 16 and in thy book all (my members) were w.
Jer. 17. 13 they that depart from me shall be writt.
Eze. 13. 9 neither shall they be written in the writ
Mal. 3. 16 book of remembrance was written before

3. *A writing,* כְּתַב *kethab.*
Ezra 6. 18 at Jerusalem; as it is written in the book

4. *To write,* כְּתַב *kethab.*
Ezra 5. 7 sent a letter unto him, wherein was wri.
6. 2 found..a roll, and therein..thus written

5. *To note down, sign,* רְשַׁם *resham.*
Dan. 5. 24 sent from him; and this writing was wr.
5. 25 this (is) the writing that was written, M.

6. *To write off, enrol,* ἀπογράφω *apographō.*
Heb. 12. 23 church of the first born, which are writ.

7. *Written, inscribed,* γραπτός *graptos.*
Rom. 2. 15 show the work of the law written in their

8. *To be written,* γράφομαι *graphomai.*
Matt. 2. 5 In Beth-lehem of Judea: for thus it is w.
4. 4 It is written, Man shall not live by bread
4. 6 for it is written, He shall give his angels
4. 7 It is written again, Thou shalt not tempt
4. 10 for it is written, Thou shalt worship the
11. 10 For this is (he), of whom it is written, Be.
21. 13 It is written, My house shall be called the
26. 24 Son of man goeth as it is written of him
26. 31 for it is written, I will smite the shepherd
27. 37 set up over his head his accusation writ.
Mark 1. 2 As it is written in the prophets, Behold
7. 6 as it is written, This people honoureth me
9. 12 how it is written of the Son of man, that
9. 13 whatsoever they listed, as it is written of
11. 17 Is it not written, My house shall be called
14. 21 Son of man indeed goeth, as it is written
14. 27 for it is written, I will smite the shepherd
Luke 2. 23 As it is written in the law of the Lord, Ev.
3. 4 As it is written in the book of the words
4. 4 It is written, That man shall not live by
4. 8 for it is written, Thou shalt worship the
4. 10 For it is written, He shall give his angels
4. 17 he found the place where it was written
7. 27 This is (he) of whom it is written, Behold
10. 20 rejoice, because your names [are written]
10. 26 What is written in the law? how readest
18. 31 all things that are written by the proph.
19. 46 It is written, My house is the house of pr.
20. 17 What is this then that is written, The st.
21. 22 all things which are written may be ful.
22. 37 this that is written must yet be accomp.
23. 38 superscription also [was written] over him
24. 44 which were written in the law of Moses
24. 46 Thus it is written, and thus it behoved
John 2. 17 his disciples remembered that it was wr.
6. 31 as it is written, He gave them bread from
6. 45 It is written in the prophets. And they
8. 17 It is also written in your law; that the
10. 34 Is it not written in your law, I said, Ye
12. 14 found a young ass, sat thereon; as it is w.
12. 16 rememb. they that these things were wr.
15. 25 word might be fulfilled that is written in
19. 20 it was written in Hebrew, (and) Greek
20. 30 other signs..which are not written in this
20. 31 But these are written, that ye might bel.
21. 25 if they should be written every one, I su.
21. 25 could not contain the books that should
Acts 1. 20 For it is written in the book of Psalms
7. 42 as it is written in the book of the proph.
13. 29 when they had fulfilled all that was writ.

Acts 13. 33 as it is also written in the second psalm
15. 15 the words of the prophets; as it is writt.
23. 5 for it is written, Thou shalt not speak
24. 14 believing all things which are written in
Rom. 1. 17 as it is written, The just shall live by fai.
2. 24 among the Gentiles through you, as it is w.
3. 4 as it is written, That thou mightest be
3. 10 As it is written, There is none righteous
4. 17 As it is written, I have made thee a fath.
4. 23 Now it was not written for his sake alone
8. 36 As it is written, For thy sake we are kill.
9. 13 As it is written, Jacob have I loved, but
9. 33 As it is written, Behold, I lay in Sion a
10. 15 as it is written, How beautiful are the fe.
11. 8 According as it is written, God hath given
11. 26 as it is written, There shall come out of
12. 19 for it is written, Vengeance (is) mine, I
14. 11 For it is written, (As) I live, saith the L.
15. 3 as it is written, The reproaches of them
15. 9 as it is written, For this cause I will con.
15. 21 But as it is written, To whom he was not
1 Co. 1. 19 For it is written, I will destroy the wisd.
1. 31 That, according as it is written, He that
2. 9 But as it is written, Eye hath not seen
3. 19 For it is written, He taketh the wise in
4. 6 to think (of men) above that which is wr.
9. 9 For it is written in the law of Moses, Thou
9. 10 For our sakes, no doubt, (this) is written
10. 7 as it is written, The people sat down to
10. 11 they are written for our admonition, upon
14. 21 In the law it is written, With (men of)
15. 45 so it is written, The first man Adam was
15. 54 the saying that is written, Death is swal.
2 Co. 4. 13 same spirit of faith, according as it is w.
8. 15 As it is written, He that (had gathered)
9. 9 As it is written, He hath dispersed abroad
Gal. 3. 10 for it is written, Cursed (is) every one that
3. 10 all things which are written in the book
3. 13 for it is written, Cursed (is) every one th.
4. 22 For it is written, that Abraham had two
4. 27 For it is written; Rejoice, (thou) barren
Heb. 10. 7 in the volume of the book it is written of
1 Pe. 1. 16 Because it is written, Be ye holy; for I am
Rev. 1. 3 keep those things which are written ther.
2. 17 in the stone a new name written, which
5. 1 a book written within and on the back
13. 8 whose names are not written in the book
14. 1 having his Father's name written in their
17. 5 upon her forehead (was) a name written
17. 8 whose names were not written in the book
19. 12 name written that no man knew but he
19. 16 on his thigh a name written, King of kings
20. 12 written in the books, according to their
20. 15 whosoever was not found written in the
21. 27 They which are written in the Lamb's bo
22. 18 add unto him the plagues that are written
22. 19 (from) the things which are written in this

9. *To write in*, ἐγγράφω *eggraphō*.
2 Co. 3. 2 Ye are our epistle written in our hearts
3. 3 written not with ink, but with the spirit

10. *In letters*, ἐν γράμμασιν *en grammasin*.
2 Co. 3. 7 if the ministration of death, written (and

11. *To write upon or over*, ἐπιγράφω *epigraphō*.
Mark 15. 26 superscription of his accusation was writ.
Rev. 21. 12 names written thereon, which are (the na.

12. *To write before or publicly*, προγράφω *prographō*.
Rom 15. 4 things were written aforetime were writ.
Eph. 3. 3 made known..as I wrote afore in few wor.

WRONG (matter of), wrongfully —

1. *Violence*, חָמָס *chamas*.
Gen. 16. 5 My wrong (be) upon thee: I have given my
1 Ch. 12. 17 seeing (there is) no wrong in mine hands
Job 19. 7 I cry out of wrong, but I am not heard: I

2. *No judgment*, לֹא מִשְׁפָּט *lo mishpat*.
Jer. 22. 13 him that buildeth..his chambers by wrong
Eze. 22. 29 they have oppressed the stranger wrongf.

3. *A turning aside*, סָרָה *sarah*.
Deut. 19. 16 to testify against him (that which is) wr.

4. *An overthrow*, עַוָּתָה *avvathah*.
Lam. 3. 59 O LORD, thou hast seen my wrong: judge

5. *To be wrong, crooked*, עָקַל *aqal*, 4.
Hab. 1. 4 therefore wrong judgment proceedeth

6. *Evil, bad*, רַע *ra*.
Judg 11. 27 but thou doest me wrong to war against

7 *Falsehood, falsely*, שֶׁקֶר *sheqer*.
Psa. 35. 19 Let not them..wrongfully rejoice over
38. 19 they that hate me wrongfully are multip.
69. 4 destroy me, (being) mine enemies wrong.
119. 86 they persecute me wrongfully; help thou

8. *An act of injustice*, ἀδίκημα *adikēma*.
Acts 18. 14 If it were a matter of wrong or wicked le.

9. *Injustice, unrighteousness*, ἀδικία *adikia*.
2 Co. 12. 13 not burdensome to you? forgive me this w.

10. *Unjustly, unrighteously*, ἀδίκως *adikōs*.
1 Pe. 2. 19 for conscience toward God..suffering wr.

WRONG, to (go, suffer, take) —

1. *To do violence*, חָמַס *chamas*.
Prov. 8. 36 But he that sinneth against me wrongeth

2. *To oppress, cause oppression*, יָנָה *yanah*, 5.
Jer. 22. 3 do no wrong, do no violence to the stran.

3. *To do perversely*, עָוָה *avah*.
Esth. 1. 16 Vashti the queen hath not done wrong to

4. *To press on, oppress*, עָשַׁק *ashaq*.
1 Ch. 16. 21 He suffered no man to do them wrong; yea
Psa. 105. 14 He suffered no man to do them wrong; yea

5. *To do wickedly, or wrong*, רָשַׁע *rasha*.
Exod. 2. 13 said to him that did the wrong, Wherefore

6. *To do injustice, or unrighteousness*, ἀδικέω.
Matt. 20. 13 Friend, I do thee no wrong: didst not th.
Acts 7. 24 seeing one (of them) suffer wrong, he de.
7. 26 Sirs, ye are brethren; why do ye wrong one
7. 27 But he that did his neighbour wrong thrust
25. 10 to the Jews have I done no wrong, as th.
1 Co. 6. 7 Why do ye not rather take wrong? why do
6. 8 Nay, ye do wrong, and defraud, and that
2 Co. 7. 2 we have wronged no man, we have corru.
7. 12 not for his cause that had done the wrong
7. 12 nor for his cause that suffered wrong, but
Col. 3. 25 But he that doeth wrong shall receive for
3. 25 wrong which he hath done: and there is
Phm. 18 If he hath wronged thee, or oweth (thee)

WRONGFULLY, to imagine —

To do violence, חָמַס *chamas*.
Job 21. 27 devices (which) ye wrongfully imagine ag.

WROUGHT, (to be) — [*See* Work.]

1. *Hewn work*, גָּזִית *gazith*.
1 Ch. 22. 2 set masons to hew wrought stones to build

2. *Work*, מַעֲשֶׂה *maaseh*.
1 Ki. 7. 26 brim thereof was wrought like the brim

3. *Settings, brocade*, מִשְׁבְּצוֹת *mishbetsoth*.
Psa. 45. 13 glorious within; her clothing (is) of wrou.

4. *Service*, עֲבֹדָה *abodah*.
1 Ch. 4. 21 families of the house of them that wrought

5. *To be served, tilled*, עָבַד *abad*, 4.
Deut. 21. 3 heifer, which hath not been wrought wi.

6. *Artificer, graver, carver*, חָרָשׁ *charash*.
2 Ch. 24. 12 also such as wrought iron and brass to m.

7. *To be done*, עָשָׂה *asah*, 2.
Deut. 13. 14 (that) such abomination is wrought among
17. 4 (that) such abomination is wrought in Is.
Neh. 6. 16 perceived that this work was wrought of
Eccl. 2. 17 because the work that is wrought under

8. *To do*, עָשָׂה *asah*.
Exod 36. 1 Then wrought Bezaleel and Aholiab, and
36. 4 wrought all the work of the sanctuary, ca
36. 8 man among them that wrought the work
39. 6 they wrought onyx stones inclosed in ou.
Lev. 20. 12 They have wrought confusion; their blood
Deut 22. 21 because she hath wrought folly in Israel
Josh. 7. 15 and because he hath wrought folly in Isr.
Ruth 2. 19 where wroughtest thou? blessed be he th.
2. 19 showed her..with whom she had wrought
2. 19 man's name with whom I wrought to day
1 Sa. 11. 13 for to day the LORD hath wrought salvation
14. 45 who hath wrought this great salvation in
14. 45 for he hath wrought with God this day
19. 5 the LORD wrought a great salvation for
2 Sa. 18. 13 I should have wrought falsehood against
23. 10, 12 and the LORD wrought a great victory
1 Ki. 5. 16 ruled..the people that wrought in the w.
7. 14 came to king Solomon, and wrought all
16. 25 But Omri wrought evil in the eyes of the
2 Ki. 3. 2 And he wrought evil in the sight of the
12. 11 builders that wrought upon the house of
17. 11 wrought wicked things to provoke the Lo.
21. 6 wrought much wickedness in the sight of
2 Ch. 21. 6 wrought (that which was) evil in the
24. 13 So the workmen wrought, and the work
31. 20 wrought (that which was) good and right
33. 6 wrought much evil in the sight of the L.
34. 10 workmen that wrought in the house of
34. 13 overseers of all that wrought the work in
Neh. 4. 16 the half of my servants wrought in the w.
4. 17 with one of his hands wrought in the wo
Isa. 26. 18 we have not wrought any deliverance in
Jer. 11. 15 she hath wrought lewdness with many
18. 3 behold, he wrought a work on the wheels
Eze. 20. 9, 14, 22 I wrought for my name's sake, that
20. 44 when I have wrought with you for my na.

9. *To become*, γίνομαι *ginomai*.
Mark 6. 2 such mighty works are wrought, Ac. 5. 12

10. *To be wrought out*, κατεργάζομαι, 2 Co. 12. 12.

WRUNG—*See* Wring.

Y

YE —

1. *Ye, ye yourselves*, אַנְתּוּן *antun*.
Dan. 2. 8 of certainty that ye would gain the time

2. *Ye, ye yourselves*, אַתֶּם *attem*.
Gen. 29. 4 said to them, My brethren whence (be) ye
42. 9 Ye (are) spies; to see the nakedness of the
42. 19 If ye (be) true (men)..go..carry corn for

3. *Ye, ye yourselves*, אַתֵּן, אַתֵּנָה *atten, attenah*.
Gen. 31. 6 ye know that with all my power I have
Eze. 13. 11 and ye, O great hailstones, shall fall, and
13. 20 wherewith ye there hunt the souls to ma.
34. 31 ye my flock, the flock of my pasture, (are)

4. *They, they themselves*, הֵמָּה *hemah*.
Zeph 2. 12 Ethiopians also, ye (shall be) slain by my

5. *Faces*, פָּנִים *panim*.
Gen. 40. 7 Wherefore look ye (so) sadly to day?

6. *You, ye*, ὑμᾶς (acc.) *humas*.
Matt. 6. 8 For your Father knoweth..before ye ask
John 3. 7 Marvel not that I said unto thee, Ye mu.
Acts 14. 15 preach unto you that ye should turn from
17. 22 perceive that in all things ye are too sup.
19. 36 ye ought to be quiet, and to do nothing
Rom. 1. 11 spiritual gift, to the end ye may be esta.
7. 4 dead..that ye should be married to anot.
11. 25 that ye should be ignorant of this myste.
12. 2 that ye may prove what (is) that g. 15. 13.
1 Co. 1. 7 So that ye come behind in no gift: 10. 1.
10. 13 a way to escape, that [ye] may be able to
10. 20 would not that ye should have fellowship
14. 5 I would that ye all spake with tongues
2 Co. 2. 7 So that contrariwise ye (ought) rather to
6. 1 also that ye receive not the grace 13. 7.
7. 11 For behold this self same thing, that [ye]
Eph. 4. 17 that ye henceforth walk not as ot. 1. 18.
4. 22 That ye put off, concerning the former co.
6. 11 that ye may be able to stand against the
Phil. 1. 7 of the gospel, ye all are partakers of my
1. 10 That ye may approve things that are exc.
1. 12 But I would ye should understand, bret.
Col. 1. 10 That [ye] might walk worthy of the Lord
2. 1 For I would that ye knew what great co.
4. 6 Know how ye ought to answer every man
1 Th. 1. 7 So that ye were ensamples to all that be.
2. 12 That ye would walk worthy of God, who
4. 1 have received of us how ye ought to walk
4. 3 that ye should abstain from fornication
2 Th. 1. 5 that ye may be counted worthy of the
2 2 That ye be not soon shaken in mind, or be
3. 6 That ye withdraw yourselves from every
Jas. 2. 7 that worthy name by the which ye are ca.
4. 2 desire..yet..have not, because ye ask not
4. 15 For that ye (ought) to say, If the Lord will
2 Pe. 1. 15 endeavour that ye may be able after my
3. 11 what manner of (persons) ought ye to be
Jude 5 though [ye] once knew this, how that the

7. *Ye, ye yourselves*, ὑμεῖς *humeis*.
Matt. 5. 13 Ye are the salt of the earth: but if the
5. 14 Ye are the light of the world. A city that
5. 48 Be ye therefore perfect, even as your Fa.
6. 9 After this manner therefore pray ye: Our
6. 26 Father feedeth them. Are ye not much
7. 11 If ye then, being evil, know how to give
7. 12 that men should do to you, do ye even so
9. 4 Wherefore think [ye] evil in your heart?
10. 20 For it is not ye that speak, but the Spirit
10. 31 ye are of more value than many sparrows
See also 13. 18; 14. 16; 15. 3, 5, 16; 16. 15; 19. 28, [28]; 20. 4, 7; 21. 13, 32; 23. 8, 8, 13, 28, 32; 24. 33, 44; 26. 31; 27. 24; 28. 5; Mark 6. 31, 37; 7. 11, 18; 8. 29; 11. 17, [26]; 12. [27]; 13. 11, 23, 29; Luke 6. [31]; 9. 13, 20; 9. [55]; 10. 23, 24; 11. 13, 39, 48; 12. 24, 29, 36, 40; 16. 15; 17. 10; 19. 46; 21. 31; 22. 26, 28, 70; 24. 48, 49; John 1. 26; 3. 28; 4. 20, 22, 32, 35, 38, 38; 5. 20, 33, 34, 35, 38, 39, 44, 45; 6. 67; 7. 8, 28, 34, 36, 47; 8. 14, 15, 21, 22, 23, 23, 31, 38, 41, 44, 46, 47, 49, 54; 9. 19, 27, 30; 10. 26, 36; 11. 49; 13. 10, 13, 14, 15, 33, 34; 14. 3, 17, 19, 19, [20], 20; 15. 3, 4, 5, 14, 16, 16, 27; 16. 20, 20, 22, 27; 18. 31; 19. 6, 35; Acts 1. 5; 2. 15, 33, 36; 3. 13, 14, 25; 4. 7, 10; 5. 30; 7. 4, [26], 51, 51, 52; 8. 24; 10. 28, 37; 11. 16; 15. 7; 19. 15; 20. 18, 25; 22. 3; 23. 15; 27. 31; Rom. 1. 6; 6. 11; 7. 4; 8. 9; 9. 26; 11. 30; 16. 17; 1 Co. 1. 30; 3. 17, 23; 4. 10, 10, 10; 5. 2, 12; 6. 8; 9. 1, 2; 10. 15; 12. 27; 14. 9, 12; 16. 1, 6, 16; 2 Co. 1. 14; 3. 2; 6. 13, [16], 18; 8. 9; 9. 4; 11. 7; 12. 11; 13. 7, 9; Gal. 3. 28, 29; 4. 12; 5. 13; 6. 1; Eph. 1. 13; 2. 11, 13, 22; 4. 20; 5. 33; 6. 21; Phil. 2. 18; 4. 15, 15; Col. 3. 4, 7, 8, 13; 4. 1, 16; 1 Th. 1. 6; 2. 10, 14, 14, 19, 20; 3. 8; 4. 9; 5. 4, 5; 2 Th. 1. 12; 3. 13; Jas. 2. 6; 5. 8; 1 Pe. 2. 9; 2 Pe. 3. 17; 1 Jo. 1. 3; 2. 20, 24; 4. 4; Jude 17, 20.

8. *To you*, ὑμῖν (*dat.*) *humin*.
Matt 18. 12 How think ye? If a man have an hundr.
21. 28 But what think ye? A (certain), 22. 42.
26. 66 What think ye? They answered and said
Mark 14. 64 the blasphemy; what think ye? 11. 24.
Luke 6. 32 them which love you, what thank have ye
6. 33 which do good to you, what thank have ye
6. 34 whom..hope to receive, what thank have ye
John 11. 56 What think ye, that he will not 18. 39.
Acts 5. 9 How is it that ye have agreed together to
13. 15 if ye have any word of exhort. 2 Co. 8. 13.

9. *Of you, your, yours*, ὑμῶν (*gen.*) *humōn*.
Luke 12. 33 Sell that ye have, and give alms; provide
22. 10 when ye are entered into the city, there
1 Co. 5. 4 when ye are gathered together, and my
11. 18 first of all, when ye come together in the
11. 20 When ye come together therefore into one
Gal. 4. 15 Where is then the blessedness ye spake of?
1 Pe. 4. 4 Wherein they think it strange that ye run

YE will —

There is, there are, יֵשׁ *yesh*.
Gen. 24. 49 now if ye will deal kindly and truly with

YE yourselves —

Ye yourselves, ὑμεῖς *humeis*.
Luke 12. 36 ye yourselves like unto men that wait for

YEA (doubtless, rather, though) —

1. *Also, even, but, yea, though*, אַף *aph*.
Deut 33. 3 Yea, he loved the people; all his saints

2. *Also, (is it true) that*, אַף כִּי *aph ki*.
Gen. 3. 1 Yea, hath God said, Ye shall not eat of

3. *If, though*, אִלּוּ *illu*.
Eccl. 6. 6 Yea, though he live a thousand years tw.

4. *Even, also, yea, yet,* גַּם *gam.*
Gen. 20. 6 Yea, I know that thou didst Gen. 27. 33
Neh. 5. 15 yea, even their servants bare rule over the

5. *That,* כִּי *ki.*
Isa. 5. 10 Yea, ten acres of vineyard shall yield one

6. *But, except, unless,* ἀλλά *alla.*
Luke 24. 22 Yea, and certain women also of our comp.
John 16. 2 yea, the time cometh, that whosoever ki.
Rom. 3. 31 through faith? God forbid: yea, we esta.
1 Co. 4. 3 or of man's judgment: yea, I judge not
2 Co. 7. 11 yea, (what) clearing of yourselves, yea
7. 11 yea, (what) fear, yea, (what) vehement de.
7. 11 yea, (what) revenge! In all (things) ye
Gal. 4. 17 yea, they would exclude you, that ye mi.
Phil. 1. 18 and I therein do rejoice, yea, and will re.
2. 17 Yea, and if I be offered upon the sacrifice
3. 8 [Yea] doubtless, and I count all things
Jas. 2. 18 Yea, a man may say, Thou hast faith, and

7. *Or, either, even,* ἤ *ē.*
1 Co. 16. 6 it may be that I will abide, yea, and win.

8. *Indeed then, yea rather, yea verily,* μενοῦνγε.
Luke 11. 28 Yea rather, blessed (are) they that hear
Phil. 3. 8 yea doubtless, and I count all things (but)

9. *Verily, indeed, truly, pray,* ναί *nai.*
Matt. 5. 37 But let your communication be, Yea, yea
9. 28 Believe ye.. They said unto him, Yea, Lo.
11. 9 yea, I say unto you, and more than a pr.
13. 51 all these things? They say unto him, Yea
21. 16 Jesus saith unto them, Yea; have ye nev
Luke 7. 26 Yea, I say unto you, and much more than
12. 5 power to cast into hell; yea, I say unto
John 11. 27 She saith unto him, Yea, Lord: I believe
21. 15, 16 Yea, Lord: thou knowest that I love
Acts 5. 8 Tell me.. And she said, Yea, for so much
22. 27 Tell me, art thou a Roman? He said, Yea
2 Co. 1. 17 that with me there should be yea yea, and
1. 18 our word toward you was not yea and nay
1. 19 was not yea and nay, but in him was yea
1. 20 all the promises of God in him (are) yea
Phm. 20 Yea, brother, let me have joy of thee in
Jas. 5. 12 but let your yea be yea; and (your) nay
Rev. 14. 13 Yea, saith the spirit, that they may rest

YEAR, yearly —

1. *Days,* יָמִים *yamim.*
Exod 13. 10 this ordinance in his season from year to y
Lev. 25. 29 then.. (within) a full year may he redeem
Num. 9. 22 two days, or a month, or a year, that the
Josh. 13. 1 Now Joshua was old (and) stricken in ye.
13. 1 Thou art old (and) stricken in years, and
Judg 11. 40 daughters of Israel went yearly to lament
17. 10 give thee ten (shekels) of silver by the ye.
21. 19 (there is) a feast of the LORD in Shiloh ye.
1 Sa. 1. 3 this man went up out of his city yearly
1. 21 went up to offer unto the LORD the year.
2. 19 brought (it) to him from year to year, wh.
2. 19 with her husband to offer the yearly sac.
20. 6 (there is) a yearly sacrifice there for all
27. 7 time that David dwelt.. was a full year
2 Sa. 14. 26 it was at every year's end that he polled
1 Ki. 1. 1 king David was old (and) stricken in years
Amos 4. 4 and bring.. your tithes after three years

2. *A year, a repetition,* שְׁנָה *shenah.*
Ezra 4. 24 So it ceased unto the second year of the
5. 11 the house that was builded these many y
5. 13 But in the first year of Cyrus the king of
6. 3 In the first year of Cyrus the king, (the
6. 15 which was in the sixth year of the reign
Dan. 5. 31 (being) about threescore and two years
7. 1 In the first year of Belshazzar king of B.

3. *A year, a repetition,* שָׁנָה *shanah.*
Gen. 1. 14 let them be.. for seasons, and for.. years
5. 3 Adam lived an hundred and thirty years
5. 4 days of Adam.. were eight hundred years
5. 5 days.. were nine hundred and thirty yea.
5. 6 Seth lived an hundred and five years, and
5. 7 eight hundred and seven years, and begat
5. 8 were nine hundred and twelve years: and
5. 9 And Enos lived ninety years, and begat
5. 10 eight hundred and fifteen years, and beg.
5. 11 of Enos were nine hundred and five years
5. 12 Cainan lived seventy years, and begat M.
5. 13 eight hundred and forty years, and begat
5. 14 were nine hundred and ten years: and he
5. 15 Mahalaleel lived sixty and five years, and
5. 16 eight hundred and thirty years, and beg.
5. 17 were eight hundred ninety and five years
5. 18 Jared lived an hundred sixty and two ye.
5. 19 after he begat Enoch eight hundred years
5. 20 nine hundred sixty and two years; and b.
5. 21 Enoch lived sixty and five years, and beg.
5. 22 he begat Methuselah three hundred years
5. 23 days.. were three hundred sixty and five y.
5. 25 lived an hundred eighty and seven years
5. 26 lived.. seven hundred eighty and two ye.
5. 27 were nine hundred sixty and nine years
5. 28 Lamech lived an hundred eighty.. two y.
5. 30 five hundred ninety and five years, and
5. 31 were seven hundred seventy and seven ye.
5. 32 Noah was five hundred years old: and
6. 3 his days shall be an hundred and twenty
7. 6 Noah (was) six hundred years old when
7. 11 In the six hundredth year of Noah's life
8. 13 in the six hundredth and first year, in the
9. 28 after the flood three hundred and fifty y.
9. 29 days of Noah were nine hundred and fifty
11. 10 years old, and begat Arphaxad two years

Gen. 11. 11 five hundred years, and begat sons and
11. 12 Arphaxad lived five and thirty years
11. 13, 15 four hundred and three years, and be.
11. 14 And Salah lived thirty years, and begat
11. 16 Eber lived four and thirty years, and be.
11. 17 four hundred and thirty years, and begat
11. 18 And Peleg lived thirty years, and begat
11. 19 two hundred and nine years, and begat
11. 20 Reu lived two and thirty years, and beg.
11. 21 two hundred and seven years, and begat
11. 22 And Serug lived thirty years, and begat
11. 23 two hundred years, and begat sons and
11. 24 Nahor lived nine and twenty years, and
11. 25 an hundred and nineteen years, and beg.
11. 26 Terah lived seventy years, and begat A.
11. 32 days of Terah were two hundred and five
12. 4 Abram (was) seventy and five years old
14. 4 Twelve years.. in the thirteenth year they
14. 5 in the fourteenth year came Chedorlaom.
15. 13 they shall afflict them four hundred years
16. 3 after Abram had dwelt ten years in the
16. 16 Abram (was) fourscore and six years old
17. 1 when Abram was ninety years old and
17. 17 be born unto him that is an hundred ye.
17. 17 and shall Sarah, that is ninety years old
17. 21 unto thee at this set time in the next ye.
17. 24 Abraham (was) ninety years old and nine
17. 25 Ishmael his son (was) thirteen years old
21. 5 hundred years old when his son Isaac was
23. 1 Sarah was an hundred and seven and tw.
23. 1 (these were) the years of the life of Sarah
25. 7 these (are) the days of the years of Abra.
25. 7 lived, an hundred threescore and fifteen y.
25. 17 these (are) the years of the life of Ishmael
25. 17 hundred and thirty and seven years: and
25. 20 Isaac was forty years old when he took
25. 26 Isaac (was) threescore years old when she
26. 12 received in the same year an hundredfold
26. 34 Esau was forty years old when he took
29. 18 I will serve thee seven years for Rachel
29. 20 Jacob served seven years for Rachel, and
29. 27 thou shalt serve with me yet seven other y.
29. 30 and served with him yet seven other ye.
31. 38 This twenty years (have) I (been) with
31. 41 Thus have I been twenty years in thy ho.
31. 41 served thee fourteen years.. and six ye.
35. 28 days.. were an hundred and fourscore y.
37. 2 Joseph, (being) seventeen years old, was
41. 1 it came to pass at the end of two full ye.
41. 26 years; and the seven good ears (are) sev. y.
41. 27 that came up after them (are) seven ye.
41. 27 with the east wind, shall be seven years
41. 29 there come seven years of great plenty
41. 30 there shall arise after them seven years
41. 34 the fifth part.. in the seven plenteous ye.
41. 35 let them gather all the food of.. good ye.
41. 36 for store to the land against the seven y.
41. 46 Joseph (was) thirty years old when he st.
41. 47 in the seven plenteous years the earth
41. 48 he gathered up all the food of the seven y.
41. 50 born two sons before the years of famine
41. 53 seven years of plenteousness that was in
41. 54 seven years of dearth began to come, acc.
45. 6 For these two years.. five years, in the
45. 11 for yet (there are) five years of famine
47. 9 The days of the years of my pilgrimage
47. 9 years: few and evil have the days of the y.
47. 9 have not attained unto the days of the y.
47. 17 with bread for all their cattle for that year
47. 18 When that year was ended, they came
47. 18 the second year, and said unto him, We
47. 28 lived in the land of Egypt seventeen ye.
47. 28 age.. was an hundred forty and seven ye.
50. 22 and Joseph lived an hundred and ten ye.
50. 26 Joseph died, (being) an hundred and ten ye.
Exod. 6. 16 years.. (were) an hundred.. and seven ye.
6. 18 years.. (were) an hundred thirty and thr.
6. 20 years.. an hundred and thirty and seven y.
7. 7 And Moses (was) fourscore years old, and
7. 7 fourscore and three years old, when they
12. 2 it (shall be) the first month of the year to
12. 5 be without blemish, a male of the first y.
12. 40 sojourning.. (was) four.. and thirty years
12. 41 end of the four hundred and thirty years
16. 35 children of Israel did eat manna forty yea.
21. 2 six years he shall serve; and in the seve.
23. 10 six years thou shalt sow thy land, and sh.
23. 14 thou shalt keep a feast unto me in the ye.
23. 16 in the end of the year, when thou hast ga.
23. 17 Three times in the year all thy males sh.
23. 29 drive them out from before thee in one year
29. 38 two lambs of the first year day by day co.
30. 10 atonement upon the horns of it once in a
30. 10 once in the year shall he make atonement
30. 14 from twenty years old and above, shall
34. 22 and the feast of ingathering at the year's
34. 23 Thrice in the year shall your men children
34. 24 appear before the LORD.. thrice in the ye.
38. 26 from twenty years old and upward, for six
40. 17 in the first month in the second year, on
Lev. 9. 3 a calf and a lamb, (both) of the first year
12. 6 she shall bring a lamb of the first year for
14. 10 one ewe lamb of the first year without bl.
16. 34 to make an atonement.. once a year. And
19. 23 three years shall it be as uncircumcised
19. 24 in the fourth year all the fruit thereof sh.
19. 25 in the fifth year shall ye eat of the fruit
23. 12 of the first year for a burnt offering unto
23. 18 seven lambs without blemish of the first y.
23. 19 two lambs of the first year for a sacrifice
23. 41 a feast unto the LORD seven days in the y.
25. 3 Six years thou shalt sow thy field, and six

Lev. 25. 4 But in the seventh year shall be a sabbath
25. 5 undressed: (for) it is a year of rest unto
25. 8 sabbaths of years.. seven times seven ye.
25. 8 years shall be unto thee forty and nine y.
25. 10 ye shall hallow the fiftieth year, and pro.
25. 11 A jubilee shall that fiftieth year be unto
25. 13 In the year of this jubilee ye shall return
25. 15 According to the number of years after the
25. 15 according unto the number of years of the
25. 16 According to the multitude of years thou
25. 16 according to the fewness of years thou sh.
25. 20 What shall we eat the seventh year? beh.
25. 21 my blessing upon you in the sixth year
25. 21 and it shall bring forth fruit for three ye
25. 22 year, and eat.. of old fruit until the n. y.
25. 27 Then let him count the years of the sale
25. 28 hand of him that hath bought it until the y.
25. 29 whole year after it is sold; (within) a full
25. 30 not redeemed within the space of a full y.
25. 40 (and) shall serve thee unto the year of ju.
25. 50 from the year.. unto the year of jubilee
25. 50 shall be according unto the number of ye.
25. 51 If (there be) yet many years (behind), acc.
25. 52 if there remain but few years unto the ye.
25. 52 according unto his years shall he give him
25. 53 as a yearly hired servant shall he be with
25. 54 then he shall go out in the year of jubilee
27. 3 from twenty years old even unto sixty ye.
27. 5 from five years old even unto twenty yea.
27. 6 from a month old even unto five years old
27. 7 if (it be) from sixty years old and above
27. 17 If he sanctify his field from the year of ju.
27. 18 years that remain, even unto the year of
27. 23 thy estimation, (even) unto the year of the
27. 24 In the year of the jubilee the field shall
Num. 1. 1 in the second year after they were come
1. 3 From twenty years old and upward
So in v. 18, 20, 22, 24, 26, 28, 30, 32, 34, 36, 38, 40, 42, 45.
4. 3 thirty years old and upward even until
So in v. 23, 30, 35, 39, 43, 47.
6. 12 bring a lamb of the first year for a trespass
6. 14 one he lamb of the first year without ble.
6. 14 one ewe lamb of the first year without ble.
7. 15 one lamb of the first year, for a burnt
So in v. 21, 27, 33, 39, 45, 51, 57, 63, 69, 75, 81.
7. 17 five lambs of the first year: This (was) the
So in v. 23, 29, 35, 41, 47, 53, 59, 65, 71, 77, 83.
7. 87 the lambs of the first year twelve, with
7. 88 he goats sixty, the lambs of the first year
8. 24 from twenty and five years old and upw.
8. 25 from the age of fifty years they shall cease
9. 1 in the first month of the second year after
10. 11 second month, in the second year, that th.
13. 22 Now Hebron was built seven years before
14. 29 whole number, from twenty years old and
14. 33 shall wander in the wilderness forty years
14. 34 each day for a year.. (even) forty years
15. 27 then he shall bring a she goat of the first y
26. 2, 4 from twenty years old and upward
28. 3, 9, 11 lambs of the first year without spot
28. 14 every month throughout the months of the
28. 19 seven lambs of the first year: they shall
28. 27 ye shall offer.. seven lambs of the first y.
29. 2 seven lambs of the first year, without bl.
29. 8 seven lambs of the first year; they shall
29. 13, 17, 20, 23, 26, 29, 32 lambs of the first ye.
29. 36 seven lambs of the first year, without bl.
32. 11 from twenty years old and upward, shall
32. 13 wander in the wilderness forty years, un.
33. 38 died there, in the fortieth year after the
33. 39 an hundred and twenty and three years
Deut. 1. 3 came to pass in the fortieth year, in the
2. 7 these forty years the LORD thy God (hath
2. 14 thirty and eight years; until all the gen.
8. 2 God led thee these forty years in the wil.
8. 4 neither did thy foot swell, these forty ye.
11. 12 of the year even unto the end of the year
14. 22 that the field bringeth forth year by year
14. 28 At the end of three years thou shalt bring
14. 28 all the tithe of thine increase the same ye.
15. 1 At the end of (every) seven years thou sh.
15. 9 The seventh.. year of release, is at hand
15. 12 serve thee six years, then in the seventh y.
15. 18 in serving thee six years: and the LORD
15. 20 year by year in the place which the LORD
16. 16 Three times in a year shall all thy males
24. 5 he shall be free at home one year, and sh.
26. 12 the tithes of thine increase the third year
29. 5 I have led you forty years in the wilder.
31. 2 I (am) an hundred and twenty years old
31. 10 seven years, in the solemnity of the year
32. 7 consider the years of many generations
34. 7 Moses (was) an hundred and twenty years
Josh. 5. 6 For the children of Israel walked forty y.
5. 12 eat of the fruit of the land of Canaan that y.
14. 7 Forty years old (was) I when Moses the se.
14. 10 kept me alive.. these forty and five years
14. 10 I (am) this day fourscore and five years
24. 29 died, (being) an hundred and ten years old
Judg. 2. 8 died, (being) an hundred and ten years old
3. 8 children.. served Chushan-ris. eight years
3. 11 land had rest forty years. And Othniel the
3. 14 served Eglon the king of Moab eighteen y.
3. 30 And the land had rest fourscore years
4. 3 twenty years he mightily oppressed the
5. 31 his might. And the land had rest forty y.
6. 1 them into the hand of Midian seven years
6. 25 even the second bullock of seven years old
8. 28 country was in quietness forty years in the
9. 22 When Abimelech had reigned three years
10. 2 judged Israel twenty and three years, and
10. 3 arose.. and judged Israel twenty.. two y.

Judg 10. 8 that year they vexed and oppressed the
10. 8 eighteen years, all the children of Israel
11. 26 by the coasts of Arnon, three hundred y.
11. 40 went..to lament..four days in a year
12. 7 Jephthah judged Israel six years. Then
12. 9 for his sons: and he judged Israel seven y.
12. 11 judged Israel; and he judged Israel ten y.
12. 14 ten ass colts: and he judged Israel eight y.
13. 1 into the hands of the Philistines forty ye.
15. 20 in the days of the Philistines twenty years
16. 31 his father: and he judged Israel twenty y.
Ruth 1. 4 Ruth: and they dwelt there about ten ye.
1 Sa. 1. 7 he did so year by year, when she went up
4. 15 Now Eli was ninety and eight years old
4. 18 died..And he had judged Israel forty ye.
7. 2 the time was long; for it was twenty years
7. 16 went from year to year in circuit to Beth.
13. 1 one year; and when he had reigned two y.
29. 3 hath been with me these days, or these y.
2 Sa. 2. 10 forty years old..and reigned two years
2. 11 the time..was seven years and six months
4. 4 He was five years old when the tidings
5. 4 thirty years old..(and) he reigned forty y.
5. 5 reigned over Judah seven years and six
5. 5 in Jerusalem he reigned thirty and three
11. 1 came to pass, after the year was expired
13. 23 came to pass after two full years, that A.
13. 38 and went to Geshur, and was there three y.
14. 28 So Absalom dwelt two full years in Jeru.
15. 7 came to pass after forty years, that Abs.
19. 32 was a very aged man, (even) fourscore y.
19. 35 I (am) this day fourscore years old; (and)
21. 1 three years, year after year; and David
24. 13 Shall seven years of famine come unto
1 Ki. 2. 11 forty years: seven years reigned he in H.
2. 11 thirty and three years reigned he in Jer.
2. 39 came to pass at the end of three years, th.
4. 7 each man his month in a year made pro.
5. 11 thus gave Solomon to Hiram year by year
6. 1 in the four hundred and eightieth year af.
6. 1 in the fourth year of Solomon's reign ov.
6. 37 In the fourth year was the foundation of
6. 38 in the eleventh year..So was he seven ye.
7. 1 was building his own house thirteen years
9. 10 came to pass at the end of twenty years
9. 25 three times in a year did Solomon offer
10. 14 gold that came to Solomon in one year
10. 22 once in three years came the navy of Tar.
10. 25 spices, horses, and mules, a rate year by
11. 42 the time that Solomon reigned..forty ye.
14. 20 two and twenty years: and he slept with
14. 21 Rehoboam (was) forty and one years old
14. 21 reigned seventeen years in Jerusalem, the
14. 25 came to pass, in the fifth year of king Re.
15. 1 Now in the eighteenth year of king Jer.
15. 2 Three years reigned he in Jerusalem, and
15. 9 in the twentieth year of Jeroboam king of
15. 10 forty and one years reigned he in Jerus.
15. 25 second year..and reigned over Israel two
15. 28 Even in the third year of Asa king of Ju.
15. 33 In the third year of Asa king of Judah be.
15. 33 son of Ahijah to reign..twenty and four y.
16. 8 In the twenty and sixth year of Asa king
16. 8 to reign over Israel in Tirzah, two years
16. 10 twenty and seventh year of Asa king of J.
16. 15 In the twenty and seventh year of Asa ki.
16. 23 In the thirty and first year of Asa king of
16. 23 twelve years: six years reigned he in Tir.
16. 29 in the thirty and eighth year of Asa king
16. 29 reigned over Israel..twenty and two yea.
17. 1 there shall not be dew nor rain these yea.
18. 1 came to Elijah in the third year, saying
20. 22 for at the return of the year the king of S.
20. 26 it came to pass at the return of the year
22. 1 continued three years without war betw.
22. 2 came to pass in the third year, that Jeh.
22. 41 to reign over Judah in the fourth year of
22. 42 Jehoshaphat (was) thirty and five years
22. 42 he reigned twenty and five years in Jeru.
22. 51 over Israel in Samaria the seventeenth ye
22. 51 of Judah, and reigned two years over Is.
2 Ki. 1. 17 in the second year of Jehoram the son of
3. 1 over Israel in Samaria the eighteenth ye.
3. 1 king of Judah, and reigned twelve years
8. 1 it shall also come upon the land seven ye.
8. 2 woman..sojourned in the land..seven ye.
8. 3 it came to pass at the seven years' end
8. 16 in the fifth year of Joram the son of Ahab
8. 17 Thirty and two years old..reigned eight y.
8. 25 In the twelfth year of Joram the son of A.
8. 26 Two and twenty years old..reigned one y.
9. 29 in the eleventh year of Joram the son of
10. 36 And the time..(was) twenty and eight ye.
11. 3 with her hid in the house of the LORD six y.
11. 4 seventh year Jehoiada sent and fetched
11. 21 Seven years old (was) Jehoash when he be.
12. 1 In the seventh year of Jehu, Jehoash be.
12. 1 forty years reigned he in Jerusalem. And
12. 6 in the three and twentieth year of king J.
13. 1 In the three and twentieth year of Joash
13. 1 Isr. in Samaria, (and reigned) seventeen y.
13. 10 In the thirty and seventh year of Joash
13. 10 in Samaria (and reigned) sixteen years
13. 20 invaded the land at the coming in of the y.
14. 1 In the second year of Joash son of Jehoa.
14. 2 He was twenty and five years old when
14. 2 reigned twenty and nine years in Jerusa.
14. 17 son of Jehoahaz king of Israel, fifteen ye.
14. 21 sixteen years old, and made him king in
14. 23 In the fifteenth year of Amaziah the son
14. 23 in Samaria, (and reigned) forty and one ye.
15. 1 In the twenty and seventh year of

2 Ki. 15. 2 Sixteen years old was he when he began
15. 2 and he reigned two and fifty years in Jer.
15. 8 In the thirty and eighth year of Azariah
15. 13 began to reign in the nine and thirtieth y.
15. 17 In the nine and thirtieth year of Azariah
15. 17 reign over Israel, (and reigned) ten years
15. 23 In the fiftieth year of Azariah king of Ju.
15. 23 Israel in Samaria, (and reigned) two yea.
15. 27 In the two and fiftieth year of Azariah ki.
15. 27 over Israel in Samaria..twenty years
15. 30 reigned in his stead, in the twentieth ye.
15. 32 In the second year of Pekah the son of R.
15. 33 Five and twenty years old was he when
15. 33 reigned sixteen years in Jerusalem. And
16. 1 In the seventeenth year of Pekah the son
16. 2 Twenty years old was Ahaz when he beg.
16. 2 reigned sixteen years in Jerusalem, and
17. 1 In the twelfth year of Ahaz king of Judah
17. 1 Elah to reign in Samaria over Israel nine y.
17. 4 no present..as (he had done) year by year
17. 5 went..to Samaria, and besieged it three y.
17. 6 In the ninth year of Hoshea the king of A.
18. 1 in the third year of Hoshea son of Elah
18. 2 Twenty and five years old was he when he
18. 2 he reigned twenty and nine years in Jer.
18. 9 fourth year..which was the seventh year
18. 10 at the end of three years..in the sixth ye.
18. 10 that (is) the ninth year of Hoshea king of
18. 13 Now in the fourteenth year of king Hez.
19. 29 eat this year..in the second year that wh.
19. 29 in the third year sow ye, and reap, and
20. 6 I will add unto thy days fifteen years, and
21. 1 Manasseh (was) twelve years old when he
21. 1 reigned fifty and five years in Jerusalem
21. 19 Amon (was) twenty and two years old when
21. 19 reigned two years in Jerusalem. And his
22. 1 Josiah (was) eight years old when he beg.
22. 1 he reigned thirty and one years in Jerus.
22. 3 came to pass in the eighteenth year of king
23. 23 But in the eighteenth year of king Josiah
23. 31 Jehoahaz (was) twenty and three years old
23. 36 Jehoiakim (was) twenty and five years old
23. 36 and he reigned eleven years in Jerusalem
24. 1 and Jehoiakim became his servant three y.
24. 8 Jehoiachin (was) eighteen years old when
24. 12 king of Babylon took him in the eighth y.
24. 18 Zedekiah (was) twenty and one years old
24. 18 reigned eleven years in Jerusalem. And
25. 1 came to pass in the ninth year of his reign
25. 2 city was besieged unto the eleventh year
25. 8 which (is) the nineteenth year of king Ne.
25. 27 came to pass in the seven and thirtieth y.
25. 27 in the year that he began to reign, did lift
1 Ch. 2. 21 he married when he (was) threescore ye.
3. 4 there he reigned seven years and six mo.
3. 4 Jerusalem he reigned thirty and three y.
20. 1 came to pass, that after the year was ex.
21. 12 Either three years famine; or three mon.
23. 3 numbered from the age of thirty years and
23. 24 from the age of twenty years and upward
23. 27 numbered from twenty years old and ab.
26. 31 In the fortieth year of the reign of David
27. 1 throughout all the months of the year, of
27. 23 number of them from twenty years old
29. 27 time..(was) forty years; seven years reig.
2 Ch. 3. 2 second month, in the fourth year of his
8. 1 it came to pass at the end of twenty years
8. 13 three times in the year, (even) in the fe.
9. 13 gold that came to Solomon in one year was
9. 21 every three years once came the ships of
9. 24 spices, horses..mules, a rate year by year
9. 30 reigned in Jerusalem over..Israel forty y.
11. 17 three years: for three years they walked
12. 2 in the fifth year of king Rehoboam, Shis.
12. 13 Rehoboam (was) one and forty years old
12. 13 reigned seventeen years in Jerusalem, the
13. 1 Now in the eighteenth year of king Jero.
13. 2 He reigned three years in Jerusalem. His
14. 1 In his days the land was quiet ten years
14. 6 land had rest..he had no war in those ye.
15. 10 month, in the fifteenth year of the reign
15. 19 no (more) war unto the five and thirtieth y.
16. 1 In the six and thirtieth year of the reign
16. 12 Asa in the thirty and ninth year of his re.
16. 13 died in the one and fortieth year of his
17. 7 Also in the third year of his reign he sent
18. 2 after (certain) years he went down to A.
20. 31 thirty and five years old when he began
20. 31 he reigned twenty and five years in Jeru.
21. 5 Jehoram (was) thirty and two years old
21. 5 to reign, and he reigned eight years in J.
21. 20 thirty and two years old was he when he
21. 20 and he reigned in Jerusalem eight years
22. 2 Forty and two years old (was) Ahaziah when
22. 2 he reigned one year in Jerusalem. His m.
22. 12 with them hid in the house of God six y.
23. 1 in the seventh year Jehoiada strengthen.
24. 1 Joash (was) seven years old when he be.
24. 1 reigned forty years in Jerusalem. His mo.
24. 5 the house of your God from year to year
24. 15 hundred and thirty years old (was he) wh.
24. 23 came to pass at the end of the year, (that)
25. 1 Amaziah (was) twenty and five years old
25. 1 reigned twenty and nine years in Jerusa.
25. 5 numbered them from twenty years old and
25. 25 lived after the death of Joash..fifteen y.
26. 1 who (was) sixteen years old, and made
26. 3 Sixteen years old (was) Uzziah when he
26. 3 he reigned fifty and two years in Jerusa.
27. 1 Jotham (was) twenty and five years old
27. 1 and he reigned sixteen years in Jerusalem
27. 5 children of Ammon gave him the same y.

2 Ch. 27. 5 pay unto him, both the second year and
27. 8 He was five and twenty years old when he
27. 8 to reign, and reigned sixteen years in Je.
28. 1 Ahaz (was) twenty years old when he be.
28. 1 reigned sixteen years in Jerusalem, but
29. 1 five and twenty years old, and he reigned
29. 1 nine and twenty years in Jerusalem. And
29. 3 He, in the first year of his reign, in the
31. 16 from three years old and upward, (even)
31. 17 from twenty years old and upward, in th.
33. 1 Manasseh (was) twelve years old when he
33. 1 and he reigned fifty and five years in Jer.
33. 21 Amon (was) two and twenty years old wh.
33. 21 began to reign, and reigned two years in
34. 1 Josiah (was) eight years old when he beg.
34. 1 he reigned in Jerusalem one and thirty y.
34. 3 For in the eighth year of his reign, while
34. 3 in the twelfth year he began to purge Ju.
34. 8 Now in the eighteenth year of his reign
35. 19 In the eighteenth year of the reign of Jo.
36. 2 Jehoahaz (was) twenty and three years old
36. 5 Jehoiakim (was) twenty and five years old
36. 5 reigned eleven years in Jerusalem, and
36. 9 Jehoiachin (was) eight years old when he
36. 10 when the year was expired, king Nebuch.
36. 11 Zedekiah (was) one and twenty years old
36. 11 to reign, and reigned eleven years in Jer.
36. 21 sabbath, to fulfil threescore and ten years
36. 22 Now in the first year of Cyrus king of Pe.
Ezra 1. 1 Now in the first year of Cyrus king of Pe.
3. 8 Now in the second year of their coming
3. 8 from twenty years old and upward, to set
7. 7 in the seventh year of Artaxerxes the king
7. 8 month, which (was) in the seventh year of
Neh. 1. 1 in the twentieth year, as I was in Shushan
2. 1 in the twentieth year of Artaxerxes the k.
5. 14 year even unto the two and thirtieth year
5. 14 twelve years, I and my brethren have not
9. 21 Yea, forty years didst thou sustain them
9. 30 Yet many years didst thou forbear them
10. 31 we would leave the seventh year, and the
10. 32 to charge ourselves yearly with the third
10. 34 at times appointed year by year, to burn
10. 35 fruit of all trees, year by year, unto the ho.
13. 6 for in the two and thirtieth year of Arta.
Esth. 1. 3 In the third year of his reign he made a
2. 16 month Tebeth, in the seventh year of his
3. 7 in the twelfth year of king Ahasuerus, they
9. 21 and the fifteenth day of the same, yearly
9. 27 acc. to their (appointed) time, every year
Job 3. 6 let it not be joined unto the days of the ye.
10. 5 days as the days of man? (are) thy years
15. 20 the number of years is hidden to the op.
16. 22 When a few years are come, then I shall
32. 7 and multitude of years should teach wis.
36. 11 spend their days in prosperity, and their y.
36. 26 neither can the number of his years be se.
42. 16 this lived Job an hundred and forty years
Psa. 31. 10 For my life is spent with grief, and my y.
61. 6 prolong the king's life; (and) his years as
65. 11 Thou crownest the year with thy goodness
77. 5 I have considered the days of old, the ye.
77. 10 the years of the right hand of the
78. 33 consume in vanity, and their years in tr.
90. 4 For a thousand years in thy sight (are but)
90. 9 we spend our years as a tale (that is told)
90. 10 The days of our years are threescore years
90. 10 by reason of strength (they be) fourscore y
90. 15 (and) the years (wherein) we have seen evil
95. 10 Forty years long was I grieved with (this)
102. 24 thy years (are) throughout all generations
102. 27 (art) the same, and thy years shall have
Prov. 4. 10 sayings; and the years of thy life shall be
5. 9 Lest thou give..thy years unto the cruel
9. 11 and the years of thy life shall be increased
10. 27 but the years of the wicked shall be sho.
Eccl. 6. 3 so that the days of his years be many, and
6. 6 though he live a thousand years twice (t.)
11. 8 But if a man live many years, (and) rejo.
12. 1 years draw nigh, when thou shalt say, I
Isa. 6. 1 In the year that king Uzziah died I saw
7. 8 within threescore and five years shall Ep.
14. 28 In the year that king Ahaz died was this
16. 14 Within three years, as the years of an hir.
20. 1 In the year that Tartan came unto Ashdod
20. 3 walked naked and barefoot three years
21. 16 Within a year, according to the years of
23. 15 Tyre shall be forgotten seventy years, acc.
23. 15, 17 after the end of seventy years
29. 1 add ye year to year; let them kill sacrifi.
32. 10 Many days and years shall be troubled, ye
34. 8 year of recompences for the controversy
36. 1 Now it came to pass in the fourteenth ye.
37. 30 Ye shall eat (this) year such as groweth
37. 30 the second year..and in the third year
38. 5 behold, I will add unto thy days..years
38. 10 I am deprived of the residue of my years
38. 15 I shall go softly all my years in the bitter.
61. 2 To proclaim the acceptable year of the
63. 4 mine heart, and the year of my redeemed
65. 20 for the child shall die an hundred years
65. 20 sinner, (being) an hundred years old, sh.
Jer. 1. 2 king of Judah, in the thirteenth year of
1. 3 unto the end of the eleventh year of Zed.
11. 23 men of Anathoth, (even) the year of their
17. 8 shall not be careful in the year of drought
23. 12 evil upon them, (even) the year of their
25. 1 fourth year of Jehoiakim the son of Jos.
25. 1 first year of Nebuchadrezzar king of Bab.
25. 3 From the thirteenth year of Josiah the
25. 3 that is the three and twentieth year the
25. 11 shall serve the king of Babylon seventy y

Jer 25. 12 when seventy years are accomplished, (that)
28. 1 came to pass the same year, in the begin.
28. 1 in the fourth year, (and) in the fifth mon.
28. 3 Within two full years will I bring again
28. 11 nations within the space of two full years
28. 16 this year thou shalt die, because thou ha.
28. 17 So Hananiah the prophet died the same y.
29. 10 That after seventy years be accomplished
32. 1 in the tenth year of Zedekiah king of Ju.
32. 1 which (was) the eighteenth year of Nebuc.
34. 14 At the end of seven years let ye go every
34. 14 when he hath served thee six years, thou
36. 1 in the fourth year of Jehoiakim the son
36. 9 came to pass in the fifth year of Jehoiakim
39. 1 In the ninth year of Zedekiah king of Ju.
39. 2 in the eleventh year of Zedekiah, in the
45. 1 in the fourth year of Jehoiakim the son
46. 2 smote in the fourth year of Jehoiakim
48. 44 upon Moab, the year of their visitation
51. 46 rumour shall both come (one) year, and
51. 46 in (another) year (shall come) a rumour
51. 59 into Babylon in the fourth year of his re.
52. 1 Zedekiah was one and twenty years old
52. 1 and he reigned eleven years in Jerusalem
52. 4 it came to pass in the ninth year of his re.
52. 5 So the city was besieged unto the..year
52. 12 which was the nineteenth year of Nebuc.
52. 28 In the seventh year three thousand Jews
52. 29 In the eighteenth year of Nebuchadrezzar
52. 30 In the three and twentieth year of Nebu.
52. 31 in the seven and thirtieth year of the ca.
52. 31 king of Babylon in the (first) year of his
Eze 1. 1 Now it came to pass in the thirtieth year
1. 2 which (was) the fifth year of king Jehoia.
4. 5 I have laid upon thee the years of their
4. 6 I have appointed thee each day for a ye.
8. 1 came to pass in the sixth year, in the six.
20. 1 came to pass in the seventh year, in the
22. 4 art come (even) unto thy years; therefore
24. 1 Again, in the ninth year, in the tenth m.
26. 1 came to pass in the eleventh year, in the
29. 1 In the tenth year, in the tenth (month)
29. 11 neither shall it be inhabited forty years
29. 12 laid waste shall be desolate forty years
29. 13 At the end of forty years will I gather the
29. 17 came to pass in the seven and twentieth y.
30. 20 came to pass in the eleventh year, in the
31. 1 came to pass in the eleventh year, in the
32. 1 came to pass in the twelfth year, in the
32. 17 It came to pass also in the twelfth year
33. 21 came to pass in the twelfth year of our
38. 8 in the latter years thou shalt come into
38. 17 prophesied in those days (many) years
39. 9 and they shall burn them with fire..years
40. 1 In the five and twentieth year of our cap.
40. 1 in the beginning of the year..fourteenth
46. 13 a lamb of the first year without blemish
46. 17 then it shall be his (to) the year of liberty
Dan. 1. 1 In the third year of the reign of Jehoiakim
1. 5 so nourishing them three years, that at
1. 21 Daniel continued (even) unto the first year
2. 1 in the second year of the reign of Nebuc.
8. 1 In the third year of the reign of king Be.
9. 1 In the first year of Darius the son of Ah.
9. 2 In the first year of his reign, I Daniel un.
9. 2 by books the number of the years, where.
9. 2 would accomplish seventy years in the
10. 1 In the third year of Cyrus king of Persia
11. 1 Also I, in the first year of Darius the M.
11. 6 in the end of years they shall join them.
11. 8 continue (more) years than the king of
11. 13 certainly come after certain years with
Joel 2. 2 after it, (even) to the years of many gen.
2. 25 will restore to you the years that the lo.
Amos 1. 1 king of Israel, two years before the eart.
2. 10 led you forty years through the wilderness
5. 25 and offerings in the wilderness forty years
Mic. 6. 6 with burnt offerings, with calves of a ye.
Hab. 3. 2 years, in the midst of the years make kn.
Hag. 1. 1, 15 In the second year of Darius the king
2. 10 in the second year of Darius, came the w.
Zech. 1. 1 In the eighth month, in the second year
1. 7 in the second year of Darius, came the
1. 12 indignation these threescore and ten ye.
7. 1 came to pass in the fourth year of king D.
7. 3 myself, as I have done these so many y.?
7. 5 even those seventy years, did ye at all
14. 16 even go up from year to year to worship
Mal. 3. 4 as in the days of old, and as in former y.

4. *A year, repetition, revolution,* ἐνιαυτός *eniautos.*
Luke 4. 19 To preach the acceptable year of the Lo.
John 11. 49 Caiaphas, being the high priest that..year
11. 51 but being high priest that year, he prop.
18. 13 which was the high priest that same yea.
Acts 11. 26 that a whole year they assembled thems.
18. 11 continued (there) a year and six months
Gal. 4. 10 observe days, and months, and times, and
Heb. 9. 7 (went) the high priest alone once every y.
9. 25 entereth into the holy place every year
10. 1 which they offered year by year continu.
10. 3 remembrance again (made) of sin every y.
Jas. 4. 13 continue there a year, and buy and sell
5. 17 rained not..by the space of three years
Rev. 9. 15 were prepared for..a year, for to slay the

5. *A year,* ἔτος *etos.*
Matt. 9. 20 diseased with an issue of blood twelve y.
Mark 5. 25 which had an issue of blood twelve years
5. 42 for she was (of the age) of twelve years
Luke 2. 36 had lived with an husband seven years
2. 37 widow of about fourscore and four years
2. 41 went to Jerusalem every year at the feast
Luke 2. 42 when he was twelve years old, they went
3. 1 Now in the fifteenth year of the reign of
3. 23 Jesus himself began to be about thirty y.
4. 25 when the heaven was shut up three years
8. 42 only daughter, about twelve years of age
8. 43 woman, having an issue of blood twelve y.
12. 19 hast much goods laid up for many years
13. 7 these three years I come seeking fruit on
13. 8 let it alone this year also, till I shall dig
13. 11 had a spirit of infirmity eighteen years
13. 16 Satan hath bound, lo, these eighteen years
15. 29 Lo, these many years do I serve thee
John 2. 20 Forty and six years was this temple in bu.
5. 5 which had an infirmity thirty and eight y.
8. 57 Thou art not yet fifty years old, and hast
Acts 4. 22 For the man was above forty years old
7. 6 and entreat (them) evil four hundred yea.
7. 30 when forty years were expired, there ap.
7. 36 wonders..in the wilderness forty years
7. 42 (by the space of) forty year in the wilder.?
9. 33 which had kept his bed eight years, and
13. 20 the space of four hundred and fifty years
13. 21 tribe of Benjamin, by the space of forty y.
19. 10 this continued by the space of two years
24. 10 know that thou hast been of many years
24. 17 Now after many years I came to bring
Rom. 15. 23 having a great desire these many years
2 Co. 12. 2 knew a man in Christ above fourteen ye.
Gal. 1. 18 Then after three years I went up to Jer.
2. 1 Then fourteen years after I went up
3. 17 which was four hundred and thirty years
1 Ti. 5. 9 into the number under threescore years
Heb. 1. 12 Thou art the same, and thy years shall
3. 9 proved me, and saw my works forty years
3. 17 But with whom was he grieved forty yea.
2 Pe. 3. 8 as a thousand years, and a thousand years
Rev. 20. 2 and Satan, and bound him a thousand y.
20. 3 till the thousand years should be fulfilled
20. 4 and reigned with Christ a thousand years
20. 5 lived not again until the thousand years
20. 6 and shall reign with him a thousand yea.
20. 7 when the thousand years are expired, Sa.

6. *Days,* ἡμέραι *hēmerai.*
Luke 1. 7 they both were (now) well stricken in ye.
1. 18 old man, and my wife well stricken in ye.

YEAR ago, two years (old) —

1. *Two years old,* διετής *dietēs.*
Matt. 2. 16 from two years old and under, according

2. *Space of two years,* διετία *dietia.*
Acts 24. 27 But after two years Porcius Festus came
28. 30 Paul dwelt two whole years in his own

3. *From last year,* ἀπὸ πέρυσι *apo perusi.*
2 Co. 8. 10 only to do, but also to be forward a year a.
9. 2 that Achaia was ready a year ago; and

YEARS, to be come to —

To become great, γίνομαι μέγας *ginomai megas.*
Heb. 11. 24 By faith Moses, when he was come to ye.

YEARN, to —

To be burning, yearning, כָּמַר *kamar,* 2.
Gen. 43. 30 for his bowels did yearn upon his brother
1 Ki. 3. 26 for her bowels yearned upon her son, and

YELL, to —

1. *To growl, shake,* נָעַר *naar.*
Jer. 51. 38 roar together like lions; they shall yell

2. *To give forth the voice,* נָתַן קוֹל *nathan qol.*
Jer. 2. 15 The young lions roared upon him, (and) y.

YELLOW —

1. *Green or yellow,* יְרַקְרַק *yeraqraq.*
Psa. 68. 13 with silver, and her feathers with yellow

2. *Shining,* צָהֹב *tsahob.*
Lev. 13. 30 in it a yellow thin hair; then the priest
13. 32 there be in it no yellow hair, and the sc.
13. 36 priest shall not seek for yellow hair; he

YES (verily) —

1. *Indeed then, yea, yea ver[ily],* μενοῦνγε *menounge.*
Rom 10. 18 Yes verily, the[ir] sound went into all the

2. *Verily, indeed, truly, pray,* ναί *nai.*
Matt 17. 25 He saith, Yes. And when he was come
Mark 7. 28 Yes, Lord; yet the dogs under the table
Rom. 3. 29 not also of the Gentiles? Yes, of the Gen.

YESTERDAY, yesternight —

1. *Yesternight, former time,* אֶמֶשׁ *emesh.*
Gen. 19. 34 I lay yesternight with my father: let us
31. 29 God of your father spake unto me yester.
31. 42 of my hands, and rebuked (thee) yestern.
2 Ki. 9. 26 Surely I have seen yesterday the blood of

2. *Yesterday, former time,* אֶתְמוֹל ,אֶתְמוֹל *ethmol.*
Psa. 90. 4 thousand years in thy sight..as yester.

3. *Yesterday, third day,* תְּמוֹל שִׁלְשֹׁם *temol shilshom.*
Exod. 5. 14 in making brick both yesterday and to day
1 Sa. 20. 27 cometh not..neither yesterday nor to day?
2 Sa. 15. 20 Whereas thou camest (but) yesterday, sh.
Job 8. 9 For we (are but of) yesterday, and know

4. *Yesterday, yesternight,* χθές *chthes* ἐχθές.
John 4. 52 Yesterday at the seventh hour the fever
Acts 7. 28 kill me, as thou diddest the Egyptian y.?
Heb. 13. 8 Jesus Christ the same yesterday, and to

YET (as but so, within) more and more, to be —

1. *Then,* אָז *az.*
Job 9. 31 Yet shalt thou plunge me in the ditch, and

2. *Only,* אַךְ *ak.*
Gen. 18. 32 will speak yet but this once: Peradven.
27. 30 Jacob was yet scarce gone out from the
Num 22. 20 but yet the word which I shall say unto

3. *But,* כִּי אִם *ki im.*
Judg 15. 7 yet will I be avenged of you, and after

4. *To say,* אָמַר *amar.*
Eze. 28. 9 Wilt thou yet say before him that slayeth

5. *But, certainly,* בְּרַם *beram.*
Dan. 4. 23 yet leave the stump of the roots thereof
5. 17 yet I will read the writing unto the king

6. *To (cause to) add, increase, continue,* יָסַף *yasaph,* 5.
Exod. 9. 34 sinned yet more, and hardened his heart
1 Sa. 18. 29 Saul was yet the more afraid of David, and
2 Ki. 19. 30 And the remnant..shall yet again take
Psa. 71. 14 hope continually, and will yet praise thee

7. *That, but,* כִּי *ki.*
Exod. 5. 11 yet not ought of your work shall be dim.

8. *Unto, up to, during,* עַד *ad.*
Lev. 26. 18 if ye will not yet for all this hearken unto

9. *Till now, hitherto,* עַד עַתָּה *ad attah.*
2 Ki. 13. 23 neither cast he them from his p. as yet

10. *Yet, hitherto,* עֲדֶנָה ,עֲדֶן *aden, adennah.*
Eccl. 4. 2 dead, more than the living which are yet
4. 3 than both they which hath not yet been

11. *Again, yet, while, any more,* עוֹד *od.*
Gen. 7. 4 For yet seven days, and I will cause it to
18. 22 but Abraham stood yet before the LORD
29. 9 while he yet spake with them, Rachel ca.
40. 13 Yet within three days shall Pharaoh lift
Exod 4. 18 Let me go..and see whether they be yet
2 Ki. 14. 4 as yet the people did sacrifice and burnt in.

12. *Unto here, hitherto,* עַד הֵנָּה *ad henah.*
Gen. 15. 16 for the iniquity of the Amorites (is) not y.

13. *Only, sure, nevertheless,* רַק *raq.*
2 Ki. 14. 3 yet not like David his father: he did acc.
2 Ch. 6. 16 yet so that thy children take heed to th.

14. *Up to this point, still,* ἀκμήν *akmēn.*
Matt. 15. 16 Jesus said, Are ye also yet without und.?

15. *But, except, unless,* ἀλλά *alla.*
Mark 14. 29 Although all shall be offended, yet (will)
1 Co. 4. 4 know nothing by myself; yet am I not he.
4. 15 yet (have ye) not many fathers: for in Ch.
9. 2 yet doubtless I am to you: for the seal of
14. 19 Yet in the church I had rather speak five
2 Co. 4. 8 troubled on every side, yet not distressed
4. 16 yet the inward (man) is renewed day by
5. 16 yet now henceforth know we (him) no more
11. 6 though (I be) rude in speech, yet not in
13. 4 yet he liveth by the power of God. For we
Col. 2. 5 For though I be absent in the flesh, yet

16. *For,* γάρ *gar.*
Matt 15. 27 yet the dogs eat of the crumbs which fall
Mark 7. 28 [yet] the dogs under the table eat of the ch.
Rom. 5. 7 yet peradventure for a good man some

17. *Verily, truly,* γέ *ge.*
Luke 11. 8 yet because of his importunity he will rise
18. 5 Yet because this widow troubleth me, I

18. *Still, yet, hitherto,* ἔτι *eti.*
Matt 12. 46 While he yet talked to the people, behold
17. 5 While he yet spake, behold, a bright cloud
19. 20 kept from my youth up: what lack I yet
26. 47 while he yet spake, lo, Judas, one of the
27. 63 said while he was yet alive, After three
Mark 5. 35 While he yet spake, there came from the
8. 17 understand? have ye your heart [yet] hard.
12. 6 Having yet therefore one son, his well be.
14. 43 while he yet spake, cometh Judas, one of
Luke 8. 49 While he yet spake, there cometh one fr.
9. 42 as he was yet a coming, the devil threw
14. 22 as thou hast commanded, and yet there
14. 32 while the other is yet a great way off, he
15. 20 when he was yet a great way off, his fat.
18. 22 Yet lackest thou one thing: sell all that
22. 37 this that is written must [yet] be accompl.
22. 47 while he yet spake, behold a multitude
22. 60 immediately, while he yet spake, the cock
24. 6 how he spake unto you when he was yet
24. 41 while they yet believed not for joy, and
24. 44 while I was yet with you, that all things
John 4. 35 There are [yet] four months, and (then) c.
7. 33 Yet a little while am I with you, and (th.)
12. 35 said unto them, Yet a little while is the
13. 33 yet a little while I am with you. Ye sh.
14. 19 Yet a little while, and the world seeth
16. 12 I have yet many things to say unto you
20. 1 while it was yet dark, unto the sepulchre
Acts 9. 1 Saul, yet breathing out threatenings and
10. 44 While Peter yet spake these words, the
18. 18 Paul (after this) tarried (there) yet a good
Rom. 3. 7 why yet am I also judged as a sinner?
5. 6 For when we were yet without strength
5. 8 while we were yet sinners, Christ died for
9. 19 Why doth he yet find fault, for who hath
1 Co. 3. 2 not able (to bear it), neither [yet] now are
3. 3 For ye are yet carnal: for whereas (there
12. 31 and yet show I unto you a more excellent
15. 17 your faith (is) vain; ye are yet in your sins
2 Co. 1. 10 in whom we trust that he will [yet] deliver
Gal. 1. 10 for if I yet pleased men, I should not be
2. 20 yet not I, but Christ liveth in me: and the
5. 11 if I yet preach circumcision, why do I yet

Phil. 1. 9 that your love may abound yet more and
2 Th. 2. 5 when I was yet with you, I told you these
Heb. 7. 10 For he was yet in the loins of his father
7. 15 it is yet far more evident: for that after
9. 8 while as the first tabernacle was yet stan.
10. 37 For yet a little while, and he that shall
11. 4; 12. 26; 12. 27; Rev. 6. 11.

19. *Or,* ἢ ē, Acts 24. 11.

20. *And, also,* καί *kai,* Lu. 3. 20; Jo. 8. 16; Ga. 3. 4.

21. *Now, already,* ἤδη *ēdē.*
Matt 24. 32 When his branch is yet tender, and putt.
Mark 13. 28 When her branch is yet tender, and putt.

22. *Yet even,* κἄν *kan.*
2 Co. 11. 16 if otherwise, yet as a fool receive me, that

23. *To be about to,* μέλλω *mellō.*
Rev. 8. 13 trumpet of the three angels, which are yet

24. *Truly, indeed,* μέντοι *mentoi.*
John 4. 27 yet no man said, What seekest thou? or
20. 5 saw the linen clothes lying; yet went he

25. *Not more,* οὐ πλείους *ou pleious.*
Acts 24. 11 There are [yet] but twelve days since I went

YET (nor, not) never, as —

1. *No one at any time,* οὐδείς πώποτε *oudeis pōpote.*
Luke 19. 30 shall find a colt tied, where on yet never

2. *Not yet,* οὐδέπω *oudepō.*
John 7. 39 for the Holy Ghost was not [yet] (given), be.
19. 41 new sepulchre, wherein was never man yet
20. 9 For as yet they knew not the scripture, t..
1 Co. 8. 2 he knoweth nothing [yet] as he ought to k.

3. *Not yet, no more, no longer,* οὐκέτι *ouketi.*
Mark 15. 5 But Jesus yet answered nothing; so that
2 Co. 1. 23 that to spare you I came not as yet unto
Gal. 2. 20 yet not I, but Christ liveth in me: and the

4. *And not, neither, nor,* οὔτε *oute.*
Luke 14. 35 It is neither fit for the land, nor yet for
John 4. 21 neither in this mountain, nor yet at Jeru.
Acts 19. 37 neither robbers of churches, nor yet blas.
25. 8 nor yet against Cesar, have I offended any
Rev. 9. 20 [yet] repented not of the works of their ha.

YIELD, unto, to (cause to) —

1. *To do, ripen,* גָּמַל *gamal.*
Num 17. 8 and bloomed blossoms, and yielded almo.

2. *To sow,* זָרַע *zara.*
Gen. 1. 29 in the which (is) the fruit of a tree yielding

3. *To (cause to) sow,* זָרַע *zara,* 5.
Gen. 1. 11 the herb yielding seed (and) the fruit tree
1. 12 herb yielding seed after his kind, and the

4. *To give,* יְהַב *yehab.*
Dan. 3. 28 yielded their bodies, that they might not

5. *To (cause to) add, increase,* יָסַף *yasaph,* 5.
Lev. 19. 25 that it may yield unto you the increase th.

6. *To (cause to) turn aside, incline,* נָטָה *natah,* 5.
Prov. 7. 21 she caused him to yield, with the flatter.

7. *To lift up,* נָשָׂא *nasa.*
Eze. 36. 8 yield your fruit to my people of Israel, for

8. *To do, make,* עָשָׂה *asah.*
Gen. 1. 11 herb yielding seed..fruit tree yielding fr.
1. 12 herb yielding seed..the tree yielding fruit
Psa. 107. 37 plant vineyards, which may yield fruits
Isa. 5. 10 Yea, ten acres of vineyard shall yield one
5. 10 and the seed of an homer shall yield an
Jer. 17. 8 drought, neither shall cease from yield.
Hos. 8. 7 bud shall yield no meal: if so be it yield

9. *To give,* נָתַן *nathan.*
Gen. 4. 12 it shall not henceforth yield unto thee
49. 20 bread (shall be) fat, and he shall yield ro.
Lev. 25. 19 land shall yield her fruit, and ye shall eat
26. 4 land shall yield..trees of the field shall yi.
26. 20 for your land shall not yield her increase
26. 20 neither shall the trees of the land yield
Deut 11. 17 that the land yield not her fruit; and
Psa. 67. 6 shall the earth yield her increase; (and)
85. 12 and our land shall yield her increase
Prov 12. 12 but the root of the righteous yieldeth (fr.)
Eze. 34. 27 yield her fruit, and the earth shall yield
Joel 2. 22 the fig tree and the vine do yield their st.

10. *To give the hand,* נָתַן יָד *nathan yad.*
2 Ch. 30. 8 yield yourselves unto the LORD, and enter

11. *To cause to be many, multiply,* רָבָה *rabah,* 5.
Neh 9. 37 it yieldeth much increase unto the kings

12. *Healing,* מַרְפֵּא *marpe.*
Eccl. 10. 4 leave not thy place; for yielding pacifieth

13. *To give off, away, or back,* ἀποδίδωμι *apodidōmi.*
Heb. 12. 11 afterward it yieldeth the peaceable fruit
Rev. 22. 2 yielded her fruit every month: and the

14. *To give,* δίδωμι *didōmi.*
Mark 4. 7 thorns grew up, and choked it, and it yi.
4. 8 did yield fruit that sprang up and incre.

15. *To set or place alongside,* παριστάνω *paristanō.*
Rom. 6. 13 Neither yield ye your members (as) instr.
6. 16 Know ye not, that to whom ye yield you.

16. *To set or place alongside,* παρίστημι *paristēmi.*
Rom. 6. 13 but yield yourselves unto God, as those
6. 19 as ye have yielded..even so now yield yo.

17. *To persuade,* πείθω *peithō.*
Acts 23. 21 But do not thou yield unto them; for th.

18. *To do, make,* ποιέω *poieō.*
Jas. 3. 12 so (can) no fountain both yield salt water

YIELD up (the ghost) —

1. *To send away,* ἀφίημι *aphiēmi.*
Matt 27. 50 cried..with a loud voice, yielded up the

2. *To breathe out,* ἐκψύχω *ekpsuchō.*
Acts 5. 10 yielded up the ghost: and the young men

YOKE (of oxen), yokefellow —

1. *A bar,* מוֹט *mot.*
Nah. 1. 13 For now will I break his yoke from off thee

2. *A bar,* מוֹטָה *motah.*
Isa. 58. 6 go free, and that ye break every yoke?
58. 9 take away from the midst of thee the yoke
Jer. 27. 2 Make thee bonds and yokes, and put them
28. 10 Then Hananiah the prophet took the yoke
28. 12 Hananiah the prophet had broken the yo.
28. 13 saith the LORD, Thou hast broken the yo.
28. 13 but thou shalt make for them yokes of iron
Eze. 30. 18 when I shall break there the yokes of E.

3. *A yoke,* עֹל, עֹל *ol.*
Gen. 27. 40 thou shalt break his yoke from off thy neck
Lev. 26. 13 have broken the bands of your yoke, and
Num 19. 2 no blemish, (and) upon which never came
Deut 21. 3 heifer..which hath not drawn in the yoke
28. 48 he shall put a yoke of iron upon thy neck
1 Sa. 6. 7 kine, on which there hath come no yoke
1 Ki. 12. 4 Thy father made our yoke grievous: now
12. 4 heavy yoke which he put upon us, lighter
12. 9 Make the yoke which thy father did put
12. 10 Thy father made our yoke heavy, but m.
12. 11 my father did lade you with a heavy yoke
12. 11 will add to your yoke: my father hath
12. 14 yoke heavy, and I will add to your yoke
2 Ch. 10. 4 made our yoke grievous..yoke that he put
10. 9 Ease somewhat the yoke that thy father
10. 10 Thy father made our yoke heavy, but m.
10. 11 yoke upon you, I will put more to your y.
10. 14 My father made your yoke heavy, but I
Isa. 9. 4 For thou hast broken the yoke of his bur.
10. 27 his yoke from off thy neck, and the yoke
14. 25 then shall his yoke depart from off them
47. 6 ancient hast thou very heavily laid thy y.
Jer. 2. 20 For of old time I have broken thy yoke
5. 5 these have altogether broken the yoke
27. 8, 11, 12 under the yoke of the king of Bab.
28. 2 I have broken the yoke of the king of Ba.
28. 4 for I will break the yoke of the king of B.
28. 11 Even so will I break the yoke of Nebuch.
28. 14 I have put a yoke of iron upon the neck
30. 8 I will break his yoke from off thy neck, and
Lam. 1. 14 The yoke of my transgressions is bound
3. 27 good for a man that he bear the yoke in
Eze. 34. 27 when I have broken the bands of their yo.
Hos. 11. 4 was to them as they that take off the yoke

4. *A couple, team, yoke of oxen,* צֶמֶד *tsemed.*
1 Sa. 11. 7 he took a yoke of oxen, and hewed them
14. 14 were an half acre of land, (which) a yoke
1 Ki. 19. 19 who (was) plowing (with) twelve yoke (of
19. 21 returned back from him, and took a yoke
Job 1. 3 five hundred yoke of oxen, and five hun.
42. 12 thousand yoke of oxen, and a thousand
Jer. 51. 23 the husbandman and his yoke of oxen, and

5. *A yoke, pair,* ζεῦγος *zeugos.*
Luke 14. 19 I have bought five yoke of oxen, and I go

6. *A yoke, beam, balance,* ζυγός *zugos.*
Matt 11. 29 Take my yoke upon you, and learn of me
11. 30 For my yoke (is) easy, and my burden is
Acts 15. 10 why tempt ye God, to put a yoke upon the
Gal. 5. 1 be not entangled again with the yoke of b.
1 Ti. 6. 1 as many servants as are under the yoke co.

7. *A yoke fellow,* σύζυγος *suzugos.*
Phil. 4. 3 I entreat thee also, true yokefellow, help

YOKE together unequally with, to —

To be yoked with one of another kind, ἑτεροζυγέω.
2 Co. 6. 14 Be ye not unequally yoked together with

YONDER (place) —

1. *Yonder, beyond, henceforth,* הָלְאָה *haleah.*
Num. 16. 37 scatter thou the fire yonder; for they are

2. *Thus, so, here, now,* כֹּה *koh.*
Num. 23. 15 Stand here..while I meet (the LORD) yon.

3. *Unto thus, up to yonder,* עַד כֹּה *ad koh.*
Gen. 22. 5 I and the lad will go yonder and worship

4. *There, thither,* ἐκεῖ *ekei.*
Matt. 17. 20 say..Remove hence to yonder place, and
26. 36 Sit ye here, while I go and pray yonder

YOU —

1. *You, you yourselves,* אַתֵּן, אַתֵּנָה *atten, attenah.*
Eze. 34. 17 (as for) you, O my flock, thus saith the L.

2. *To you, you, therefore,* לָכֵן *la-ken.*
Zech. 11. 7 I will feed the flock of slaughter, (even) y.

3. *Your eyes,* עֵינֵיכֶם *[ayin].*
Josh. 24. 15 if it seem evil unto you to serve the LORD

4. *Your face,* פְּנֵיכֶם *[panim].*
Josh 2. 9, 11 the inhabitants..faint because of you
2. 10 the LORD dried up the water..for you
2. 11 our hearts did melt..because of you; for the

5. *Of yourselves,* ἑαυτῶν *(gen.) heautōn.*
Matt. 26. 11 For ye have the poor always with you; but
Mark 14. 7 For ye have the poor with you always, and
John 12. 8 poor..ye have with you; 5. 42; 6. 53.

6. *You,* ὑμᾶς *(acc.) humas.*
Matt. 3. 11 indeed baptize you..he shall baptize you
4. 19 Follow me, and I will make you fishers
5. 11 Blessed are ye when (men) shall revile you
5. 44 [curse you..hate you..use you. perse. y.]
5. 46 For if ye love them which love you, what
See also 6. 30; 7. 6, 15, 23; 10. 13, 14, 16, 17, 17, 19, 23, 40; 11. 28, 29; 12. 28; 21. 24, 31, 32; 23. 34, 35; 24. 4, 9, 9; 25. 12; 26. 32, [55]; 28. 7, 14; Mark 1. 8, 8, 17; 6. 11; 9. 19, 41; 11. 29; 13. 5, 9, 11, 36; 14. 28, 49; 16. 7; Luke 3. 16, 16; 6. 9, 22, 22, 26, 27, 28, 32, 33; 9. 5, 41; 10. 3, 6, 8, 9, 10, [11,] 16, 19; 11. 20; 12. 11, 12, 14, 28; 13. 25, [27,] 28; 16. 9, 26; 19. 31; 20. 3; 21. 12, 34; 22. 31, 35; 23. [15]; 24. 44, 49; John 4. 38; 5. 42; 6. 61, 70; 7. 7; 8. 32, 36; 12. 35; 13. 34; 14. 3, 18, 18, 26, 28; 15. 9, 12, 15, 15, 16, 16, 18, 19, 19, 20; 16. 2, 2, 7, 7, 13, 22, 27; 20. 21; Acts 1. 8; 2. 22, 29; 3. 22, 26; 7. 43; 13. 32, [40]; 15. 24, 25; 18. 21; 19. 13; 20. 20, 28, 29, 32; 22. 1; 23. 15; 27. 22, 34; 28. 20; Rom. 1. 10. 11, 13, 13; 2. 24; 10. 19, 19; 12. 1, [14]; 15. 13, 15, 22, 23, [24,] 24, 29, 30, 32; 16. 16, 17, 19, 21, 22, 23, 23, 25; 1 Co. 1. 8, 10; 2. 1, 3; 3. 2; 4. 14, 15, 16, 17, 18, 19, 21; 7. 5, 32; 10. 13, 13, 27; 11. 2, 3, 14, 22; 12. 1; 14. 6, 6, 36; 16. 5, 6, 7, 7, 10, 12, 15, 19, 19, 20; 2 Co. 1. 8, 12, 15, 16, 18; 2. 1, 2, 3, 4, 5, 8; 3. 1; 6. 11, 17; 7. 4, 8, 8, 12, 15; 8. 6, 17, 22, 23; 9. 4, 5, 8, 14; 10. 1, 1, 9, 14; 11. 2, 2, 6, 9, 11, 20, 20; 12. 14, 14, 15, 16, 16, 17, 17, 18, 20, 21; 13. 1, 3, 4, 13; Gal. 1. 6, 7, 9; 2. 5; 3. 1; 4. 11, 11, 17, [17,] 18, 20; 5. 2, 7, 8, 10, 10, 12; 6. 12, 13; Eph. 2. 1; 3. 2; 4. 1; 5. 6; 6. 22; Phil. 1. 7, 8, 24, 26, 27; 2. 25, 26; 4. 21, 22; Col. 1. 6, 21, 22, 25; 2. 4, 8, 13, 16, 18; 4. 6, 8, 10, 10, 12, 14; 1 Th. 1. 5, 9; 2. 1, 2, 9, 11, 12, 18; 3. 2, [2,] 4, 5, 6, 11, 12, 12; 4. 1, 10, 13; 5. 4, 12, 12, 14, 18, 23, 24, 27; 2 Th. 1. 6, 10, 11; 2. 1, 3, 5, 13, 14, [17]; 3. 1, 3, 4, 10; Heb. 5. 12; 9. 20; 13. 21, 22, 23, 24; Jas. 2. 6; 4. 10; 1 Pe. 1. [4,] 10, 12, 15, 20, 25; 2. 9; 3. 13, 15; 4. 14; 5. 6, [10,] 13; 2 Pe. 1. 12, 13; 2. 3; 1 Jo. 2. 26, 27, 27, 27; 3. 7, 13; 2 Jo. 10, 12; Jude 5, [24]; Rev. 2. 24; 12. 12.

7. *You, you yourselves,* ὑμεῖς *humeis.*
Eph. 5. 33 Nevertheless let every one of you in part.

8. *To you,* ὑμῖν *(dat.) humin.*
Matt. 3. 7 who hath warned you to flee from the wr.
3. 9 for I say unto you, that God is able of th.
5. 18 For verily I say unto you, Till heaven and
5. 20 For I say unto you, That except your ri.
5. 22, 28, 32 But I say unto you, That whosoe.
5. 34 But I say unto you, Swear not at all; nei.
5. 39 But I say unto you, That ye resist not ev.
5. 44 But I say unto you, Love your enemies
See also 6. 2, 5, 11, 16, 25, 29, 33; 7. 2, 7, 7, 12; 8. 10, 11; 9. 29; 10. 15, [19,] 20, 23, 27, 42; 11. 9, 11, 17, [17,] 21, 22, 22, 24; 12. 6, 31, 36; 13. 11, 17; 16. 11, 28; 17. 12, 20, 20; 18. 3, 10, 13, 18, 19, 35; 19. 8, 9, 23, 24, 28; 20. 4, 26, 26, 27, 32; 21. 3, 21, 24, 27, 31, 43; 22. 31; 23. 3, 13, [14,] 15, 16, 23, 25, 27, 29, 36, 38, 39; 24. 2, 23, 25, 26, 34, 47; 25. 9, 12, 34, 40, 45; 26. 13, 15, 21, 29, 64; 27. 17, 21; 28. 7, 20; Mark 3. 28; 4. 11, [24,] 24; 6. [11]; 8. 12; 9. 1, 13, 41; 10. 3, 5, 15, 29, 36, 43, 43; 11. 3, 23, 24, 25, 29, 33; 12. 43; 13. 11, 21, 23, 30, 37; 14. 9, 13, 15, 18, 25; 15. 9; 16. 7; Luke 2. 10, 11, 12; 3. 7, 8, 13; 4. 24, 25; 6. 24, 25, [25, 26,] 27, [28,] 31, 38, 38, 47; 7. 9, 26, 28, [32,] 32; 8. 10; 9. 27, 48; 10. 8, 11, 12, 13, 14, 19, 20, 24; 11. 8, 9, 9, 9, 41, 42, 43, 44, 46, 47, 51, 52; 12. 4, 5, 5, 8, 22, 27, 31, 32, 37, 44, 51; 13. 3, 5, 24, 25, 27, 35, 35; 14. 24; 15. 7, 10; 16. 9, 11, 12; 17. 6, 10, 23, 34; 18. 8, 14, 17, 29; 19. 26, 40; 20. 8; 21. 3, 13, 15, 32; 22. 10, 12, 16, 18, 26, 29, 37, 67; 24. 6, [36, 44]; John 1. 51; 2. 5; 3. 12, 12; 4. 35; 5. 19, 24, 25, 38; 6. 26, 27, 32, 32, 32, 36, 47, 53, 63, 65; 7. 19, 22; 8. 24, 25, 34, 37, 40, 51, 58; 9. 27; 10. 1, 7, 25, [26,] 32; 12. 24; 13. 12, 15, 15, 16, 19, 20, 21, 33, 34; 14. 2, 2, 3, 10, 12, 16, 17, 17, 20, 25, 26, 27, 27, 27, 28, 29; 15. 3, 4, 7, 7, 14, 15, 16, 17, 20, 21, 26; 16. 1, [3,] 4, 4, 4 6, 7, 7, 12, 13, 14, 15, 20, 23, 23, 25, 25, 25, 26, 33; 18. 8, 39, 39; 19. 4; 20. 19, 21, 26; Acts 2. 14, 39; 3. 14, 20, 22, 26; 4. 10; 5. 28, 38; 7. 37; 13. 26, 26, 34, 38, 38, 41, 46; 14. 15; 15. 28; 17. 3, 23; 20. 20, 26, 27, [32,] 35; 22. 25; 25. 5; 26. 8; 28. 28; Rom. 1. 7, 11, 12, 13, 15; 8. 9, 10, 11, 11; 11. 13; 12. 3; 15. 5, 15, [32]; 16. 1, 19; 1 Co. 1. 3, 4, 6, 10, 11; 2. 1, 2; 3. 1, 3, 16, 18; 4. 8, 17; 5. 1, 9, 11; 6. 2, 5, 7, 19; 7. 35; 9. 2, 11; 10. 27, 28; 11. 2, 18, 19, 19, 22, 23, 30; 12. 3, 31; 14. 6, 25, 37; 15. 1, 1, 2, 3, 12, 51; 2 Co. 1. 2, 13, 19, 21; 2. [3,] 4; 4. 12, 14; 5. 12, 12, 13; 6. 18; 7. 7, 11, 12, 14, 16; 8. 1, 10; 9. 1, 14; 10. 1, 15; 11. 7, 9; 12. 12, 19, 20; 13. 3, 5; Gal. 1. 3, 8, 8, 11, 20; 3. [1,] 5, 5; 4. 13, 15, 16, 19, 20; 5. 2, 21; 6. 11; Eph. 1. 2, 17; 2. 17; 3. 16; 4. [6, 32]; 5. 3; 6. 21; Phil. 1. 2, 6, 25, [28,] 29; 2. 5, 13, 17, 19; 3. 1, 1, 15, 18; Col. 1. 2, 5, 6, 27; 2. 5, [13]; 3. 13, 16; 4. 7, 9, 16; 1 Th. 1. 1, 5; 2. 8, 10, 13; 3. 4, 7; 4. 2, 6, 9, 11, 15; 5. 1, 12; 2 Th. 1. 2, 4, 7, 12; 2. 5; 3. [4,] 6, 7, 9, 10, 11, 16; Phm. 3, [6,] 22; Heb. 12. 5, 7; 13. 7, 17, 19, 21, 22; Jas 1. [26]; 3. 13; 4. 1, 8; 5. 3, 6, 13, 14, 19; 1 Pe. 1. 2, 12, 13; 2. 7; 3. 15; 4. 12, 12; 5. 1, 2, 12, 14; 2 Pe. 1. 2, 8, 11, 16; 2. 1, 13; 3. 1, 15; 1 Jo. 1. 2, 3, [4,] 5; 2. 1, 7, [8,] 8, 12, 12, 13, 13, 13, 14, 14, 14, 21, 24, 24, 26, 27; 4. 4; 5. 13; 2 Jo. 12; Jude 2, 3, 3, 18; Rev. 1. 4; 2. 13, 23, 24; 18. [6]; 22. 16.

9. *Of you,* ὑμῶν *(gen.) humōn.*
Matt. 5. 11 shall say all manner of evil against you
5. 12 persecuted..prophets which were bef. y.
6. 27 Which of you, by taking thought, can add
See also 7. 9; 12. 11; 15. 7; 17. 17, 17; 21. 2, 43; 23. 11; 26. 21, 29; 28. 20; Mark 6. 11; 7. 6; 9. 19; 11. 2; 14. 18; Luke 9. 41; 10. 16; 11. 5; 12. 25; 14. 28, 33; 15. 4; 16. 26; 17. 7, 21; 21. 16; 22. 15, 19, 20, 27, 53; 23. 14; John 1. 26; 5. 45, 45; 6. 64, 70; 7. 19, 33; 8. [7,] 26, 46, [55]; 12. [35]; 13. 18, 21, 33; 14. 9, 16, 30; 15. 18; 16. 4, 5, 22, 26; Acts 1. 7; 2. 22, 38; 3. 16; 4. 10, 11, 19; 6. 3; 18. 14; 20. 18; 24. 21; 25. 26; 27. 22, 34; Rom. 1. 8, 9, 12; 6. 14; 12. 18; 15. 14, 24, 28, 33; 16. 2, 20, [24]; 1 Co. 1. 11, 12, 13, 14; 4. 3; 5. 2; 6. 1; 7. 28; 9. 12; 11. 24; 12. 21; 14. 26, 36; 16. 2, 23, 24; 2 Co. 1. 7, 16, 16, 23; 2. 3, 9; 3.

1; 7. 4, [12,] 13, 14, 15; 8. 16; 9. 2, 3, 14; 10. 13, 14, 16; 11. 8; 12. 11, 13, [14,] 15; 13. 11, 14; Gal. 3. 2; 4. 12; Eph. 1. 16, 16; 3. 1, 13; 4. 32; Phil. 1. 3, 4, 7; 4. 9, 18, 23; Col. 1. 3, [7,] 9, 24; 2. 1; 4. 9, 12, 12, 13, 18; 1 Th. 1. 2, 2, 8; 2. 6, 7, 8, 9, 11, 17; 3. 6, 9; 4. 4; 5. 12, 23, 28; 2 Th. 1. 3, 3, 11; 2. 13; 3. 8, 16, 18; 2 Ti. 4. [22]; Titus 2. [8]; 3. 15; Heb. 3. 12, 13; 4. 1; 6. 9, 11; 13. 7, 17, 24, 25; Jas. 1. 5; 2. 6, 16; 4. 7; 5. 4; 1 Pe. 2. 12; 3. [16]; 4. 15; 5. 7; 2 Jo. [3]; Rev. 2. 10; 18. 20; 22. 21.

10. *Your souls*, ψυχῶν ὑμῶν *psuchōn humōn*.
2 Co. 12. 15 I will..gladly spend and be spent for you

YOUNG (children, maiden, man, one, woman), younger—

1. *Brood, young birds*, אֶפְרֹחִים *ephrochim*.
Deut. 22. 6 young ones..and the dam sitting upon the
Job. 39. 30 Her young ones also suck up blood: and
Psa. 84. 3 where she may lay her young..thine altar

2. *Choice, young, unmarried man*, בָּחוּר *bachur*.
Deut 32. 25 shall destroy both the young man and the
Judg 14. 10 there a feast; for so used the young men
Ruth 3. 10 as thou followedst not young men, wheth.
1 Sa. 8. 16 he will take. your goodliest young men
9. 2 Saul, a choice young man, and a goodly
2 Ki. 8. 12 their young men wilt thou slay with the
2 Ch. 36. 17 who slew their young men with the sword
36. 17 had no compassion upon young man or
Psa. 78. 63 fire consumed their young men: and their
148. 12 Both young men and maidens; old men
Prov. 20. 29 glory of young men (is) their strength
Eccl 11. 9 Rejoice, O young man, in thy youth, and
Isa. 9. 17 the LORD shall have no joy in their young
23. 4 neither do I nourish up young men, (nor)
31. 8 flee from the sword, and his young men
40. 30 faint and be weary, and the young men
62. 5 For (as) a young man marrieth a virgin
Jer. 6. 11 and upon the assembly of young men tog.
9. 21 children from without, (and) the young
11. 22 young men shall die by the sword; their
15. 8 against the mother of the young men a
18. 21 their young men (be) slain by the sword
31. 13 rejoice in the dance, both young men and
48. 15 chosen young men are gone down to the
49. 26 Therefore her young men shall fall in
50. 30 Therefore shall her young men fall in the
51. 3 spare ye not her young men; destroy ye
51. 22 will I break in pieces the young man and
Lam. 1. 15 assembly against me to crush my young
1. 18 virgins and my young men are gone into
2. 21 my young men are fallen by the sword
5. 13 They took the young men to grind, and
5. 14 ceased from the gate, the young men from
Eze. 9. 6 Slay utterly old (and) young, both maids
23. 6, 12, 23 all of them desirable young men
30. 17 The young men of Aven and of Pi-beseth
Joel 2. 28 dream dreams, your young men shall see
Amos 2. 11 I raised up..of your young men for Naz.
4. 10 your young men have I slain with the sw.
8. 13 the fair virgins and young men faint for
Zech. 9. 17 Corn shall make the young men cheerful

3. *Choice young unmarried men*, בַּחֻרִים *bechurim*.
Num 11. 28 (one) of his young men, answered and said

4. *A son of*, בֶּן־ *ben*.
Lev. 1. 14 his offering of turtle doves, or of young
4. 3 young bullock without blemish unto the
4. 14 congregation shall offer a young bullock
5. 7 two turtle doves, or two young pigeons
5. 11 bring two turtle doves, or two young pig.
9. 2 Take thee a young calf for a sin offering
12. 6 young pigeon, or a turtle dove, for a sin
12. 8 she shall bring two turtles, or two young
14. 22 two turtle doves, or two young pigeons
14. 30 one of the turtle doves, or of the young
15. 14 two turtle doves, or two young pigeons
15. 29 take unto her two turtles, or two young
16. 3 with a young bullock for a sin offering, and
22. 28 ye shall not kill it and her young both in
23. 18 one young bullock, and two rams: they
Num. 6. 10 shall bring two turtles, or two young pig.
7. 15 One young bullock, one ram, one lamb of
So in 21, 27, 33, 39, 45, 51, 57, 63, 69, 75, 81.
8. 8 take a young bullock..and another young
15. 24 congregation shall offer one young bull.
28. 11, 19, 27 two young bullocks, and one ram
29. 2, 8 one young bullock, one ram, (and) sev.
29. 13 thirteen young bullocks, two rams, (and)
29. 17 twelve young bullocks, two rams, fourte.
Deut 22. 6 thou shalt not take the dam with the yo.
22. 7 let the dam go, and take the young to th.
Ezra 6. 9 both young bullocks, and rams, and lam.
Esth. 8. 10 riders on mules, camels, (and) young dr.
Job 39. 4 Their young ones are in good liking, they
39. 16 She is hardened against her young ones, as
Psa. 29. 6 Lebanon and Sirion like a young unicorn
147. 9 to the beast his food, (and) to the young
Prov 30. 17 pick it out, and the young eagles shall eat
Jer. 31. 12 for the young of the flock and of the herd
Eze. 43. 19 thou shalt give..a young bullock for a sin
43. 23 thou shalt offer a young bullock without
43. 25 they shall also prepare a young bullock
45. 18 shalt take a young bullock without blem.
46. 6 a young bullock without blemish, and six

5. *A young bird*, גּוֹזָל *gozal*.
Gen. 15. 9 Take me..a turtle dove, and a young pi.
Deut 32. 11 stirreth up her nest, fluttereth over her y.

6. *A lion's whelp*, גּוּר *gur*.
Lam. 4. 3 they give suck to their young ones: the

7. *Little for days*, צְעִיר לְיָמִים *tsair le-yamim*.
Job 30. 1 But now (they that are) younger than I
32. 6 said I (am) young, and ye (are) very old

8. *Child, young of man or beast*, יֶלֶד *yeled*.
Gen. 4. 23 slain a man to my wounding, and a young
1 Ki. 12. 8 consulted with the young men that were
12. 10 young men that were grown up with him
12. 14 after the counsel of the young men, say.
2 Ch. 10. 8 took counsel with the young men that we.
10. 10 young men that were brought up with him
10. 14 after the advice of the young men, saying
Job 38. 41 when his young ones cry unto God, they
39. 3 they bring forth their young ones, they
Isa. 11. 7 their young ones shall lie down together

9. *A whelp or young lion*, כְּפִיר *kephir*.
Judg 14. 5 behold, a young lion roared against him

10. *Young person*, lit. *growing*, נַעַר *naar*.
Gen. 14. 24 Save only that which the young men have
18. 7 gave (it) unto a young man; and he hast.
19. 4 both old and young, all the people from
22. 3 took two of his young men with him, and
22. 5 Abraham said unto his young men, Abide
22. 19 So Abraham returned unto his young men
34. 19 the young man deferred not to do the th.
41. 12 a young man, an Hebrew, servant to the
Exod 10. 9 We will go with our young and with our
24. 5 sent young men of the children of Israel
33. 11 young man, departed not out of the tabe.
Num 11. 27 there ran a young man, and told Moses
Deut 28. 50 which shall not..shew favour to the you.
Josh. 6. 21 young and old, and ox, and sheep, and
6. 23 young men that were spies went in, and
Judg. 8. 14 caught a young man of the men of Succ.
9. 54 Then he called hastily unto the young
9. 54 his young man thrust him through, and
17. 7 there was a young man out of Beth-lehem
17. 11 the young man was unto him as one of
17. 12 young man became his priest, and was in
18. 3 they knew the voice of the young man the
18. 15 came to the house of the young man the
19. 19 for the young man (which is) with thy se.
Ruth 2. 9 have I not charged the young men that
2. 9 drink of (that) which the young men have
2. 15 Boaz commanded his young men, saying
2. 21 Thou shalt keep fast by my young men
1 Sa. 1. 24 The LORD in Shiloh: and the child (was) y.
2. 17 Wherefore the sin of the young men was
9. 11 said unto the young man that bare his ar.
14. 6 Jonathan said to the young man that bare
17. 58 Whose son (art) thou, (thou) young man?
21. 4 if the young men have kept themselves
21. 5 and the vessels of the young men are holy
25. 5 young men, and David said unto the yo.
25. 8 Ask thy young men, and they will show
25. 8 Wherefore let the young men find favour
25. 9 when David's young men came, they spake
25. 12 So David's young men turned their way
25. 14 one of the young men told Abigail, Nab.
25. 25 but I thine handmaid saw not the young
25. 27 let it even be given unto the young men
26. 22 let one of the young men come over and
30. 13 I (am) a young man of Egypt, servant to
30. 17 save four hundred young men, which rode
2 Sa. 1. 5 David said unto the young man that told
1. 6 young man that told him said, As I hap.
1. 13 David said unto the young man that told
1. 15 David called one of the young men, and
2. 14 Let the young men now arise and play be.
2. 21 lay thee hold on one of the young men
4. 12 David commanded his young men, and
13. 32 they have slain all the young men the ki.
13. 34 young man that kept the watch lifted up
14. 21 go therefore, bring the young man Absalom
16. 2 bread and summer fruit for the young men
18. 5 gently for my sake with the young man
18. 12 Beware that none (touch) the young man
18. 15 ten young men that bare Joab's armour
18. 29, 32 Is the young man Absalom safe? And
18. 32 answered, The enemies..be as (that) yo. m.
1 Ki. 11. 28 Solomon seeing the young man that he
20. 14, 15, 17, 19 young men of the princes of the
2 Ki. 4. 22 Send me, I pray thee, one of the young
5. 22 two young men of the sons of the prophets
6. 17 LORD opened the eyes of the young man
9. 4 So the young man, (even) the young man
1 Ch. 12. 28 Zadok a young man mighty of valour, and
22. 5 Solomon my son (is) young and tender
29. 1 Solomon..(is yet) young and tender, and
2 Ch. 13. 7 when Rehoboam was young and tender
34. 3 while he was yet young, he began to seek
Esth. 3. 13 both young and old, little children and
Job 1. 19 it fell upon the young men, and they are
29. 8 The young men saw me, and hid themse.
Psa. 37. 25 I have been young, and (now) am old, yet
119. 9 Wherewithal shall a young man cleanse
Prov. 1. 4 to the young man knowledge and discre.
7. 7 among the youths, a young man void of
Isa. 13. 18 bows also shall dash the young to pieces
20. 4 young and old, naked and barefoot, even
40. 30 be weary, and the young men shall utte.
Jer. 51. 22 will I break in pieces old and young
Lam. 2. 21 The young and the old lie on the ground in
Zech. 2. 4 Run, speak to this young man, saying, Je.
11. 16 neither shall seek the young one, nor he.

11. *A young female*, נַעֲרָה *naarah*.
Judg 21. 12 four hundred young virgins, that had kn.
Ruth 4. 12 the LORD shall give thee of this young w.
1 Sa. 9. 11 found young maidens going out to draw
1 Ki. 1. 2 Let there be sought for my lord..a young
Esth. 2. 2 Let there be fair young virgins sought
2. 3 gather together all the fair young virgins

12. *A young person*, lit. *hidden or growing*, עֶלֶם *elem*.
1 Sa. 20. 22 But if I say thus to the young man,

13. *A young roe*, עֹפֶר *opher*.
Song 2. 9 My beloved is like a roe or a young hart
2. 17 be thou like a roe or a young hart upon
4. 5 Thy two breasts (are) like two young roes
7. 3 Thy two breasts (are) like two young roes
8. 14 be thou like to a roe or to a young hart

14. *Small*, צָעִיר *tsair*.
Gen. 19. 31, 34 the first born said unto the younger
19. 35 younger arose, and lay with him, and he
19. 38 younger, she also bare a son, and called
25. 23 people; and the elder shall serve the you.
29. 26 to give the younger before the first born.
43. 33 youngest according to his youth, and the
48. 14 who (was) the younger, and his left hand
Josh. 6. 26 his youngest (son) shall he set up the gates
1 Ki. 16. 34 set up the gates thereof in his youngest

15. *Little*, קָטָן *qatan*.
Gen. 9. 24 knew what his younger son had done unto
27. 15 and put them upon Jacob her younger son
27. 42 she sent and called Jacob her younger son
29. 16 and the name of the younger (was) Rachel
29. 18 seven years for Rachel thy younger daug.
Judg 15. 2 (is) not her younger sister fairer than she?
1 Sa. 14. 49 Merab, and the name of the younger Mic.
16. 11 There remaineth yet the youngest, and
17. 14 David (was) the youngest: and the three
2 Sa. 9. 12 Mephibosheth had a young son, whose na
1 Ch. 24. 31 fathers over against their younger brethr
Eze. 16. 46 thy younger sister, that dwelleth at thy
16. 61 receive thy sisters, thine elder and thy y.

16. *Little*, קָטֹן *qaton*.
Gen. 42. 13, 32 the youngest (is) this day with our fa.
42. 15 go forth hence, except your youngest bro.
42. 20 But bring your youngest brother unto me
42. 34 bring your youngest brother unto me, then
43. 29 this your younger brother, of whom ye sp.
44. 2 in the sack's mouth of the youngest, and
44. 12 left at the youngest: and the cup was fo.
44. 23 Except your youngest brother come down
44. 26 if our youngest brother be with us, then
44. 26 except our youngest brother (be) with us
48. 19 but truly his younger brother shall be gr.
Judg. 1. 13 son of Kenaz, Caleb's younger brother, to
3. 9 Othniel the son of Kenaz, Caleb's younger
9. 5 youngest son of Jerubbaal was left; for
2 Ch. 21. 17 save Jehoahaz the youngest of his sons
22. 1 his youngest son king in his stead: for the

17. *A seed, progeny*, שִׁלְיָה *shilyah*.
Deut 28. 57 toward her young one that cometh out fr.

18. *A babe, infant, child*, βρέφος *brephos*.
Acts 7. 19 so that they cast out their young children

19. *Smaller, inferior*, ἐλάσσων *elassōn*.
Rom. 9. 12 said unto her, The elder shall serve the yo.

20. *A young person*, νεανίας *neanias*.
Acts 7. 58 laid down their clothes at a young man's
20. 9 there sat in a window a certain young man
23. 17 Bring this young man unto the chief cap.
23. 18 prayed me to bring this [young man] unto
23. 22 So the chief captain..let the [young man]

21. *A young man in the prime of life*, νεανίσκος.
Matt. 19. 20 young man saith unto him, All these thi.
19. 22 But when the young man heard that saying
Mark 14. 51 there followed him a certain young man
14. 51 cast about (his) naked (body); and [the y.]
16. 5 they saw a young man sitting on the right
Luke 7. 14 And he said, Young man, I say unto thee
Acts 2. 17 your young men shall see visions, and yo.
5. 10 young men came in, and found her dead
1 Jo. 2. 13 I write unto you, young men, because ye
2. 14 I have written unto you, young men, be.

22. *New, young*, νέος *neos*, νεώτερος *neōteros*.
Luke 15. 12 younger of them said to (his) father, Fat.
15. 13 younger son gathered all together, and to.
22. 26 greatest among you, let him be as the yo.
1 Ti. 5. 1 as a father, (and) the younger men as br.
5. 2 The elder women as mothers; the younger
5. 11 But the younger widows refuse: for when
5. 14 I will therefore that the younger women
Titus 2. 4 That they may teach the young women to
1 Pe. 5. 5 Likewise, ye younger, submit yourselves

23. *A young bird, chicken*, νεοσσός *neossos*, νοσσός.
Luke 2. 24 A pair of turtle doves, or two young pig.

24. *Newer, younger*, νεώτερος *neōteros*.
John 21. 18 When thou wast young, thou girdest thy.
Acts 5. 6 young men arose, wound him up, and ca.
Titus 2. 6 Young men likewise exhort to be sober

25. *A child, boy, servant*, παῖς *pais*.
Acts 20. 12 brought the young man alive, and were

YOUNG, with —
To give suck, עוּל *ul*.
Gen. 33. 13 flocks and herds with young (are) with me
Isa. 40. 11 shall gently lead those that are with young

[*See also* Ass, asses, bring forth, bullock, calf, cast, child, daughter, ewes, lion, man, pigeon, roe, twigs.]

YOUR, your own (business), yourselves —

1. *Your hand*, יֶדְכֶם [*yad*].
2 Ch. 29. 31 ye have consecrated yourselves unto the

2. [*In*] *your eyes*, עֵינֵיכֶם [*ayin*].
Gen. 45. 5 be not grieved nor angry with yourselves

3. *Animal soul*, נֶפֶשׁ *nephesh*.
Lev. 11. 43 Ye shall not make yourselves abominable
Josh. 23. 11 Take good heed therefore unto yourselves
Jer. 37. 9 Deceive not yourselves, saying, The cha.

4. *Of selves,* ἑαυτοῦ *heautou.*
Matt. 3. 9 think not to say within yourselves, We
16. 8 why reason ye among yourselves, because
23. 31 Wherefore ye be witnesses unto yourselv.
25. 9 rather to them that sell, and buy for yo.
Mark 9. 33 What was it that ye disputed [among yo.]
9. 50 Have salt in yourselves, and have peace
13. 9 But take heed to yourselves: for they sh.
Luke 3. 8 begin not to say within yourselves, We
12. 33 provide yourselves bags which wax not
12. 57 why even of yourselves judge ye not what
16. 9 Make to yourselves friends of the mammon
16. 15 Ye are they which justify yourselves bef.
17. 3 Take heed to yourselves: If thy brother
17. 14 he said unto them, Go show yourselves un.
21. 34 take heed to yourselves, lest at any 21. 30.
22. 17 Take this, and divide (it) [among yourselv.]
23. 28 weep for yourselves, and for your childr.
Acts 5. 35 take heed to yourselves what ye intend to
13. 46 judge yourselves unworthy of everlasting
15. 29 from which if ye keep yourselves, ye shall
20. 28 Take heed therefore unto yourselves, and
Rom. 6. 11 reckon ye also yourselves to be dead ind.
6. 13 yield yourselves unto God, as those that
6. 16 to whom ye yield yourselves serv. 11. 25.
12. 19 avenge not yourselves, but (rather) give pl.
2 Co. 7. 11 ye have approved yourselves to 1 Co. 6. 19.
13. 5 Examine yourselves, whether ye be in the
13. 5 prove your own selves: Know ye not your
Eph. 5. 19 Speaking to yourselves in psalms v. 25.
1 Th. 5. 13 (And) be at peace among [yourselves]
Heb. 10. 34 knowing in yourselves that ye have in he.
Jas. 2. 4 Are ye not then partial in yoursel. 1. 22.
1 Pe. 4. 8 have fervent charity among yourselves
1 Jo. 5. 21 Little children, keep [yourselves] from id
2 John 8 Look to yourselves, that we lose not those
Jude 20 building up yourselves on your most holy
21 Keep yourselves in the love of God, look.

5. *One's own, private, peculiar,* ἴδιος *idios.*
Col. 3. 18 Wives, submit yourselves unto [your own]
1 Th. 2. 14 have suffered like things of your own co.
4. 11 to do your own business..with [your own]

6. *You,* ὑμᾶς *(acc.) humas.*
John 14. 26 bring all things to your remembrance, wh
Acts 18. 15 if it be a question of words..and (of) your
24. 22 I will know the uttermost of your matter
Rom 11. 28 (they are) enemies for your sakes: but as
1 Co. 4. 6 for your sakes; that ye might learn in us
2 Co. 2. 10 for your sakes (forgave I it) in the person
4. 15 For all things (are) for your sakes, that the
8. 9 yet for your sakes he became poor, that
Eph. 1. 15 I also, after I heard of your faith in the
1 Th. 3. 9 all the joy wherewith we joy for your sa.
1 Pe. 4. 14 [evil spoken of, but on your part he is]

7. *Your, yours, your own,* ὑμέτερος *humeteros.*
Luke 6. 20 Blessed (be ye) poor; for yours is the ki.
16. 12 who shall give you that which is your own
John 7. 6 My time is not yet come; but your time
8. 17 It is also written in your law, that the te
15. 20 have kept my saying, they will keep your
Acts 27. 34 pray you to take .. for this is for your
Rom 11. 31 through your mercy they also may obtai
1 Co. 15. 31 I protest by your rejoicing which I have
2 Co. 8. 8 and to prove the sincerity of your love
Gal. 6. 13 circumcised, that they may glory in your

8. *To you,* ὑμῖν *(dat.) humin.*
Matt. 6. 19 Lay not up for yourselves treasures upon
6. 20 But lay up for yourselves treasures in he.
Luke 16. 11 who will commit to your trust the true
21. 15 which all your adversaries shall not be
Rom 16. 19 I am glad therefore on your behalf, but
1 Co. 6. 5 I speak to your shame Is it so, that there
11. 13 Judge in yourselves: is it comely that a
15. 34 knowledge of God: I speak (this) to your
2 Co. 5. 13 or whether we be sober, (it is) for your

9. *Of you, your,* ὑμῶν *(gen.) humōn.*
Matt. 5. 12 be exceeding glad; for great (is) your rew.
5. 16 Let your light so shine before men, that
5. 16 see your good works, and glorify your fa.
5. 20 say unto you, That except your righteou.
5. 37 But let your communication be,
5. 44 Love your enemies, bless them that curse
5. 45 That ye may be the children of your Fat.
5. 47 if ye salute your brethren only, what do
5. 48 Be ye therefore perfect, even as your Fat.

See also 6. 1, 1, 8, 14, 15, [21, 21], 25, 25, 26, 32; 7. 6, 11, 11; 9. 4, 11, 29; 10. 9, 13, 13, 14, 14, 20, 29, 30; 11. 29; 12. 27, 27; 13. 16, [16]; 15. 3, 6; 17. 20, 24; 18. [14], 35; 19. 8, 8; 20. 26, 27; 23. 8, 9, 9, [10], 11, 15, 32, 34, 38; 24. 20, 42; 25. 8; Mark 2. 8; 6. 11; 7. 9, 13; 8. 17; 10. 5, 43; 11. 25, 25, [26, 26]; 13. [18]; Luke 3. 14; 4. 21; 5. 4, 22; 6. 22, 23, 24, 27, 35, 35, 36, 38; 8. 25; 9. 5, 44; 10. 6, 11, 20; 11. 13, 19, 19, 39, 46, 47, 48; 12. 7, [22], 30, 32, 34, 34, 35; 13. 35; 16. 15; 21. 14, 18, 19, 28, 28, 34; 22. 53; 23. 28; 24. 38; John 4. 35; 6. 49, [58]; 8. 21, 24, 24, [38], 41, 42, 44, [54], 56; 9. 19, 41; 10. 34; 13. 14; 14. 1, 27; 15. 11, 16; 16. 6, 20, 22, 22, 24; 18. 31; 19. 14, 15; 20. 17, 17; Acts 2. 17, 17, 17, 17, 39; 3. 17, 19, 22, 22; 5. 28; 7. 37, [37, 43], 51, 52; 13. 41; 15. 24; 17. 23; 18. 6; 19. 37; 20. 30; Rom. 1. 8; 6. 12, 13, 13, 19, 19, 19, 22; 8. 11; 12. 1, 1, [2]; 14. 16; 15. 24; 16. 19, 20; 1 Co. 1. 4, 26; 2. 5; 3. 21, 22; 5. 6, 13; 6. 15, 19, 20, [20]; 7. 5, 14, 35; 8. 9; 9. 11; 14. [34]; 15. 14, 17, 17, 58; 16. 3, 14, [17], 18; 2 Co. 1. 6, 6, 14, 24, 24; 4. 5; 5. 11; 6. 12; 7. 7, 7, 7, [13]; 8. 7, 14, 14, [19], 24, 24; 9. 2, 2, 5, 10, 10, 13; 10. 6, 8, 15; 11. 3; 12. 14, 19; 13. 9; Gal. 4. [6], 15, 16; 6. 18; Eph. 1. 13, 18; 2. 8; 3. 13, 17; 4. 4, 23, 26, 29; 5. 19; 6. 1, 4, 5, [9], 14, 22; Phil. 1. 5, 9, 19, 25, 26, 27; 2. 17, 19, 20, 25, 30; 4. 5, 6, 7, 17, 19; Col. 1. 4, 8; 2. 5, 5, 13; 3. 3, 5, 8, 15, 16, 21; 4. 6, 8, [8]; 1 Th. 1. 4, 8; 2. 17; 3. 2, 5, 6, 7, 10, 10, 13; 4. 3, 11; 2 Th. 1. 3, 4, 4; 2. 17; 3. 5; Phm. 22, 25; Heb. 3. 8, 9, 15; 4. 7; 6. 10; 9. [14]; 10. 34, 35; 12. 3, 13; 13. 17; Jas. 1. 3, 21; 2. 2; 3. 14; 4. 1, 3, 9, 14, 16; 5. 1, 2, 2, 3, 3, 4, 5, 8, 12; 1 Pe. 1. 7, [9], 13, 14, 17, 18, 21, 22; 2. 12, 25; 3. 2, 7, 15, 16; 5. 7, 8, 9; 2 Pe. 1. 5, 10, 19; 3. 1; 1 Jo. 1. [4]; Jude 12, 20; Rev. 1. 9; 2. 23; 22. [21].

YOUTH, youthful —

1. *Youth,* בְּחוּרוֹת *bechuroth.*
Eccl. 11. 9 O young man..in the days of thy youth
12. 1 in the days of thy youth, while the evil

2. *A son of,* בֶּן־ *ben.*
Prov. 7. 7 discerned among the youths, a young man

3. *Youth, maturity,* חֹרֶף *choreph.*
Job 29. 4 As I was in the days of my youth, when

4. *Youth, childhood,* יַלְדוּת *yalduth.*
Psa. 110. 3 the morning: thou hast the dew of thy y.
Eccl. 11. 9 Rejoice, O young man, in thy youth, and

5. *Youth,* נְעוּרוֹת *neuroth.*
Jer. 32. 30 have only done evil before me from their y.

6. *Youth,* נְעוּרִים *neurim.*
Gen. 8. 21 (is) evil from his youth; neither will I ag.
46. 34 hath been about cattle from our youth ev.
Lev. 22. 13 unto her father's house, as in her youth
Num 30. 3 (being) in her father's house in her youth
30. 16 (being yet) in her youth in her father's ho.
1 Sa. 17. 33 a youth, and he a man of war from his
2 Sa. 19. 7 evil that befell thee from thy youth until
1 Ki. 18. 12 I thy servant fear the LORD from my you.
Job 13. 26 makest me to possess..iniquities of my y.
31. 18 For from my youth he was brought up wi.
Psa. 25. 7 Remember not the sins of my youth, nor
71. 5 Lord GOD: (thou art) my trust from my y.
71. 17 O God, thou hast taught me from my yo.
103. 5 (so that) thy youth is renewed like the ea.
127. 4 As arrows..so (are) children of the youth
129. 1. 2 Many a time..afflicted me from my yo.
144. 12 (may be) as plants grown up in their you.
Prov. 2. 17 Which forsaketh the guide of her youth
5. 18 blessed..rejoice with the wife of thy youth
Isa. 47. 12 wherein thou hast laboured from thy yo.
47. 15 (even) thy merchants, from thy youth, they
54. 6 a wife of youth, when thou wast refused
Jer. 2. 2 I remember thee, the kindness of thy yo.
3. 4 My father, thou (art) the guide of my yo.
3. 24 the labour of our fathers from our youth
3. 25 from our youth even unto this day, and
22. 21 this (hath been) thy manner from thy yo.
31. 19 because I did bear the reproach of my yo.
48. 11 Moab hath been at ease from his youth
Lam. 3. 27 for a man that he bear the yoke in his yo.
Eze. 4. 14 for from my youth up, even till now, ha.
16. 22, 43 not remembered the days of thy youth
16. 60 covenant with thee in the days of thy yo.
23. 3 they committed whoredoms in their you
23. 8 for in her youth they lay with her, and
23. 19 calling to remembrance the days of her y.
23. 21 lewdness of thy youth, in bruising thy
23. 21 by the Egyptians for the paps of thy yo.
Hos. 2. 15 shall sing there, as in the days of her yo.
Joel 1. 8 sackcloth for the husband of her youth
Zech. 13. 5 man taught me to keep cattle from my y.
Mal. 2. 14 between thee and the wife of thy youth
2. 15 treacherously against the wife of his yo.

7. *A young person,* נַעַר *naar.*
Judg 8. 20 but the youth..because he (was) yet a y.
1 Sa. 17. 33 for thou..a youth, and he a man of war
17. 42 for he was..a youth, and ruddy, and of a
17. 55 he said..Abner, whose son (is) this youth?

8. *Youth,* נֹעַר *noar.*
Job 36. 14 They die in youth, and their life (is) am.
Psa. 88. 15 afflicted and ready to die from (my) youth

9. *Youth,* עֲלוּמִים *alumim.*
Job 20. 11 His bones are full (of the sin) of his youth
33. 25 he shall return to the days of his youth
Psa. 89. 45 The days of his youth hast thou shorten.
Isa. 54. 4 for thou shalt forget the shame of thy yo.

10. *A brood,* פִּרְחָה *pirchah.*
Job 30. 12 Upon (my) right (hand) rise the youth, th.

11. *Littleness, youth,* צְעִירָה *tseirah.*
Gen. 43. 33 youngest according to his youth: and the

12. *Dawn, youth,* שַׁחֲרוּת *shacharuth.*
Eccl. 11. 10 thy flesh: for childhood and youth (are)

13. *Youth,* νεότης *neotēs.*
Matt 19. 20 All these things have I kept [from my yo.]
Mark 10. 20 all these have I observed from my youth
Luke 18. 21 said, All these have I kept from my youth
Acts 26. 4 My manner of life from my youth, which
1 Ti. 4. 12 Let no man despise thy youth; but be th.

14. *Youthful,* νεωτερικός *neōterikos.*
2 Ti. 2. 22 Flee also youthful lusts: but follow righ.

Z

ZA-A-NA'-IM, צַעֲנַנִּים [V.L. בצענים], *double migratory tent.*
A plain (or oak) near Kedesh, in Naphtali. See *Zaanannim.*
Judg. 4. 11 and pitched his tent unto the plain of Z.

ZA-A'-NAN, צַאֲנָן *rich in flocks.* See *Zenan.*
A city in Judah or Benjamin.
Mic. 1. 11 the inhabitant of Z. came not forth in the

ZA-A-NAN'-NIM, צַעֲנַנִּים. Same as *Zaanaim.*
Josh. 19. 33 their coast was..from Allon to Z., and A.

ZA-A'-VAN, ZA'-VAN, זַעֲוָן *causing fear.*
A son of Ezer, son of Seir the Horite. B.C. 1700.
Gen 36. 27 children of Ezer (are) these; Bilhan, and Z.
1 Ch. 1. 42 sons of Ezer; Bilhan, and Z., (and) Jakan

ZA'-BAD, זָבָד *endower.*
1. A son of Nathan, a descendant of Jerahmeel, grandson of Pharez son of Judah. B.C. 1380.
1 Ch. 2. 36 Attai begat Nathan, and Nathan begat Z.
2. 37 Z. begat Ephlal, and Ephlal begat Obed
2. Son of Tahath, and father of Shuthelah, an Ephraimite. B.C. 1650.
1 Ch. 7. 21 And Z. his son, and Shuthelah his son
3. A son of Alai, one of David's valiant men. B.C. 1048.
1 Ch. 11. 41 Uriah the Hittite, Z. the son of Ahlai
4. The son of Shimeath, an Ammonitess, who joined with Jehozabad in slaying Joash king of Judah. B.C. 839.
2 Ch. 24. 26 Z. the son of Shimeath an Ammonitess
5. One of the sons of Zattu that had taken a strange wife. B.C. 445.
Ezra 10. 27 Mattaniah, and Jeremoth, and Z., and A.
6. One of the sons of Hashum that had done the same.
Ezra 10. 33 Of the sons of Hashum..Z., Eliphelet, Je.
7. One of the sons of Nebo that had done the same.
Ezra 10. 43 Of the sons of Nebo..Z., Zebina,

ZAB'-BAI, זַבַּי *roving about, pure.*
1. One of the sons of Bebai that had taken a strange wife. B.C. 445.
Ezra 10. 28 Of the sons also of Bebai..Z., (and) Ath.
2. Father of Baruch who helped to repair the wall of Jerusalem after the exile. B.C. 445.
Neh. 3. 20 After him Baruch the son of Z. earnestly

ZAB'-BUD, זַבּוּד [V.L. זכור], *well remembered, endowed.*
One of the sons of Bigvai who returned from exile with Ezra. B.C. 457.
Ezra 8. 14 Of the sons also of Bigvai; Uthai, and Z.

ZAB'-DI, זַבְדִּי *Jah is endower.*
1. Father of Carmi father of Achan. B.C. 1500.
Josh. 7. 1 Achan, the son of Carmi, the son of Z., the
7. 17 and he brought the family..Z. was taken
7. 18 Achan, the son of Carmi, the son of Z., the
2. A Benjamite, son of Shimhi. B.C. 1300.
1 Ch. 8. 19 And Jakim, and Zichri, and Z.
3. One of David's storekeepers, a Shiphmite from Shepham in Judah. B.C. 1015.
1 Ch. 27. 27 the increase of the vineyards..(was) Z.
4. A Levite, father of Micha, and grandfather of Mattaniah who led the thanksgiving in prayer in the days of Nehemiah. B.C. 445.
Neh. 11. 17 Mattaniah the son of Micha, the son of Z.

ZAB-DI'-EL, זַבְדִּיאֵל *God is endower.*
1. Father of Jashobeam, one of David's captains. B.C. 1070.
1 Ch 27. 2 Over the first..Jashobeam the son of Z.
2. An overseer of the priests in Jerusalem. B.C. 445.
Neh. 11. 14 their overseer (was) Z., the son of (one of)

ZA'-BUD, זָבוּד *endowed.*
Son of Nathan, and friend of Solomon, and his principal officer. B.C. 1000.
1 Ki. 4. 5 Z. the son of Nathan (was) principal offi.

ZA-BU'-LON, Ζαβουλών. See *Zebulun.*
Matt. 4. 13 Capernaum..is..in the borders of Z. and
4. 15 The land of Z., and the land of Nephtha.
Rev. 7. 8 Of the tribe of Z. (were) sealed twelve th.

ZAC'-CAI, זַכַּי *pure.*
One whose descendants returned from exile with Zerubbabel. B.C. 536.
Ezra 2. 9 children of Z., seven hundred and three.
Neh. 7. 14 children of Z., seven hundred and three.

ZAC'-CHÆUS, Ζακχαῖος, *from Heb.* זַכַּי *pure.*
A chief taxgatherer whom Jesus called on when passing through Jericho.
Luke 19. 2 And, behold, (there was) a man named Z.
19. 5 Jesus..said unto him, Z., make haste, and
19. 8 And Z. stood, and said unto the Lord

ZAC'-CUR, ZAC'-CHUR, זַכּוּר *well remembered.*
1. A Reubenite, father of Shammuah, one of those sent by Moses to spy the land. B.C. 1515.
Num 13. 4 the tribe of Reuben, Shammua..son of Z.
2. A Simeonite, son of Hamuel, and father of Shimei who had sixteen sons and six daughters. B.C. 1170.
1 Ch. 4. 26 Hamuel his son, Z. his son, Shimei his son
3. A Merarite. B.C. 1015.
1 Ch. 24. 27 Beno, and Shoham, and Z., and Ibri
4. A son of Asaph, and father of Michaiah, set over the service of song by David. B.C. 1015.
1 Ch. 25. 2 Of the sons of Asaph; Z., and Joseph, and
25. 10 The third to Z., (he), his sons, and his br.
Neh. 12. 35 Michaiah, the son of Z., the son of Asaph
5. A son of Imri, who rebuilt part of the wall of Jerusalem after Nehemiah came from Shushan. B.C. 445.
Neh. 3. 2 next to them builded Z. the son of Imri

6. A Levite that with Nehemiah sealed the covenant. B.C. 445.

Neh. 10. 12 Z., Sherebiah, Shebaniah

7. Father of Hanan whom Nehemiah made one of the treasurers of the Lord's house. B.C. 445.

Neh. 13. 13 next to them (was) Hanan the son of Z.

ZA-CHAR'-IAH, זְכַרְיָה, זְכַרְיָהוּ *Jah is renowned.*

1. Son of Jeroboam II., king of Israel. B.C. 773.

2 Ki. 14. 29 and Z. his son reigned in his stead
15. 8 did Z. the son of Jeroboam reign over Is.
15. 11 And the rest of the acts of Z., behold, th.

2. Father of Abi or Abijah, wife of Ahaz and mother of Hezekiah kings of Judah. B.C. 750. See *Zechariah.*

2 Ki. 18. 2 mother's name..Abi, the daughter of Z.
2 Ch. 29. 1 mother's name..Abijah..daughter of Z.

ZA-CHA-RI'-AS, Ζαχαρίας. See *Zechariah.*

1. The son of Barachias (or Jehoiada, 2 Ch. 24. 20-22) whom the Jews stoned for rebuking them. B.C. 840.

Matt 23. 35 Z. son of Barachias, whom ye slew be.
Luke 11. 51 the blood of Abel unto the blood of Z.

2. A priest of the course of Abia (the eighth), father of John the Baptist.

Luke 1. 5 a certain priest named Z., of the course of
1. 12 when Z. saw..he was troubled, and fear
1. 13 the angel said unto him, Fear not, Z., for
1. 18 Z. said unto the angel, Whereby shall I
1. 21 the people waited for Z., and marvelled
1. 40 entered into the house of Z., and saluted
1. 67 his father Z. was filled with the Holy Gh.
3. 2 word of God came unto John the son of Z.

3. The name proposed to be given to John the Baptist by his friends.

Luke 1. 59 they called him Z., after the name of his

ZA'-CHER, זֶכֶר *fame.*

A son of Jeiel father of Gibeon, a Benjamite; called Zechariah in 1 Ch. 9. 37. B.C. 1180.

1 Ch. 8. 31 And Gedor, and Ahio, and Z.

ZA'-DOK, צָדוֹק *righteous.*

1. Son of Ahitub, and father of Ahimaaz, a priest in the days of David. B.C. 1015.

2 Sa. 8 17 Z. the son of Ahitub, and Ahimelech the
15. 24 lo Z. also..bearing the ark of the covena.
15 25 the king said unto Z., Carry back the ark
15. 27 The king said also unto Z. the priest, (Art
15. 29 Z. therefore and Abiathar carried the ark
15. 35 (hast thou) not there with thee Z. and Abi.
15. 35 thou shalt tell (it) to Z. and Abiathar the
15. 36 Ahimaaz, Z.'s (son), and Jonathan, Abiat.
17. 15 Then said Hushai unto Z. and to Abiath.
18. 19, 22 Then said Ahimaaz the son of Z.
18. 27 like the running of Ahimaaz the son of Z.
19. 11 king David sent to Z. and to Abiathar the
20. 25 and Z. and Abiathar (were) the priests
1 Ki. 1. 8 Z. the priest, and Benaiah..were not with
1. 26 and Z. the priest..hath he not called
1. 32 king David said, Call me Z. the priest,
1. 34 let Z...anoint him there king over Israel
1. 38 So Z. the priest..caused Solomon to ride
1. 39 Z. the priest took an horn of oil out of the
1. 44 the king hath sent with him Z. the priest
1. 45 Z. the priest..anointed him king in Gihon
2. 35 Z...did the king put in the room of Abia.
4. 2 princes which he had; Azariah the son of Z.
4. 4 and Z. and Abiathar (were) the priests
1 Ch. 6. 8 Ahitub begat Z., and Z. begat Ahimaaz
6. 53 Z. his son, Ahimaaz his son
15. 11 David called for Z. and Abiathar the pri.
16. 39 Z the priest, and his brethren the priests
18. 16 Z. the son of Ahitub, and Abimelech..(w.)
24. 3 David distributed them, both Z. of the
24. 6 Shemaiah..wrote them before..Z. the pr.
24. 31 likewise cast lots..in the presence of..Z.
27. 17 the son of Kemuel: of the Aaronites, Z.
29. 22 And they made..Z. (to be) priest
2 Ch. 31. 10 Azariah the chief priest of the house of Z.
Ezra 7. 2 The son of Shallum, the son of Z., the
Eze. 40. 46 these (are) the sons of Z. among the sons
43. 19 give..the Levites that be of the seed of Z.
44. 15 the sons of Z., that kept the charge of my
48. 11 priests that are sanctified of..sons of Z.

2. Father of Jerusha, wife of Uzziah and mother of Jotham kings of Judah.

2 Ki. 15. 33 mother's name..Jerusha..daughter of Z.
2 Ch. 27. 1 mother's name..Jerushah..daughter of Z.

3. Son of Ahitub, grandson of Azariah, high priest in Solomon's temple.

1 Ch. 6. 12 And Ahitub begat Z., and Z. begat Shall.
9. 11 Hilkiah..son of Meshullam, the son of Z.

4. A young man mighty of valour, that came to David to Hebron to help him.

1 Ch. 12. 28 And Z., a young man mighty of valour

5. The son of Baana who repaired a portion of the wall of Jerusalem. B.C. 445.

Neh. 3. 4 next unto them repaired Z. the son of B.

6. A priest, son of Immer, that did the same.

Neh. 3. 29 After them repaired Z. the son of Immer

7. A person that with Nehemiah sealed the covenant. B.C. 445.

Neh. 10. 21 Meshezabeel, Z., Jaddua

8. A son of Meraioth, ancestor of one of the priests that dwelt in Jerusalem. B.C. 740.

Neh. 11. 11 Meshullam, the son of Z., the son of Me.

9. A scribe whom Nehemiah put in charge over the treasuries of the Lord's house. B.C. 445.

Neh. 13. 13 And I made treasurers..Z. the scribe, and

ZA'-HAM, זַהַם *fatness.*

A son of Rehoboam, son of Solomon. B.C. 960.

2 Ch. 11. 19 Which bare..children..Shamariah, and Z.

ZA'-IR, צָעִיר *little.*

A city or place in Edom; or perhaps a scribe's mistake for *Seir.*

2 Ki. 8. 21 Joram went over to Z., and all the chariots

ZA'-LAPH, צָלָף *purification.*

Father of Hanun who repaired a part of the wall of Jerusalem after the exile. B.C. 445.

Neh. 3. 30 After him repaired..Hanun the..son of Z.

ZAL'-MON, SAL'-MON, צַלְמוֹן *terrace, ascent.*

1. A hill near Ebal or Shechem in Samaria.

Judg. 9. 48 Abimelech gat him up to mount Z., he and
Psa. 68. 14 it was (white) as snow in S.

2. An Ahohite, one of David's valiant men. It is *Ilai* in 1 Ch. 9. 29. B.C. 1048.

2 Sa. 23. 28 Z. the Ahohite, Maharai the Netophath.

ZAL-MO'-NAH, צַלְמֹנָה *terrace, ascent.*

The thirty-fourth station of Israel from Egypt, the twenty-third from Sinai, and the third from Ezion-geber; near the S. of the Salt Sea.

Num. 33. 41 And they departed..and pitched in Z.
33. 42 they departed from Z., and pitched in P.

ZAL-MUN'-NA, צַלְמֻנָּע *withdrawn from protection.*

A king of Midian defeated and slain by Gideon. B.C. 1249.

Judg. 8. 5 I am pursuing after Zebah and Z., kings
8. 6, 15 (Are) the hands of Zebah and Z. now
8. 7 when the LORD hath delivered..Z. into
8. 10 Now Zebah and Z. (were) in Karkor, and
8. 12 when Zebah and Z. fled, he pursued after
8. 12 and took..Zebah and Z., and discomfited
8. 15 Behold Zebah and Z., with whom ye did
8. 18 Then said he unto Zebah and Z., What
8. 21 Then Zebah and Z. said, Rise thou, and
8. 21 Gideon arose, and slew Zebah and Z., and
Psa. 83. 11 Make..all their princes as Zebah and as Z.

ZAM-ZUM'-MIM, זַמְזֻמִּים *powerful, vigorous.*

A tribe of the Rephaim dwelling in the region afterwards occupied by the Ammonites; called *Zuzim* in Gen. 14. 5.

Deut. 2. 20 giants..therein..Ammonites call them Z.

ZA-NO'-AH, זָנוֹחַ *broken district.*

1. A city in W. of the plain of Judah; near Adullam and Dan; now called *Zanua,* on the *Wady Ismail.*

Josh 15. 34 And Z., and En-gannim, Tappuah, and E.
Neh. 3. 13 The valley gate repaired..the inhabit. of Z.
11. 30 Z., Adullam, and (in) their villages, at L.

2. A city on the E. of the hill country of Judah, near Jezreel or Yokdeam; now *Januta,* ten miles S. of Hebron.

Josh. 15. 56 And Jezreel, and Jokdeam, and Z.

3. One of the family of Caleb son of Jephunneh.

1 Ch. 4. 18 his wife..bare..Jekuthiel the father of Z.

ZAPH-NATH PAA'-NEAH, צָפְנַת פַּעְנֵחַ *saviour of world.*

Name given to Joseph by Pharaoh. B.C. 1745-1635.

Gen. 41. 45 Pharaoh called Joseph's name Z., and he

ZA'-PHON, צָפוֹן *concealed.*

A city in Gad, a little E. of Sea of Galilee, near Succoth or Beth-nimrah; called *Shophan* in Num. 32. 35.

Josh. 13. 27 in the valley..and Succoth, and Z., the

ZA'-RA, Ζαρά. See *Zarah.*

The son of Judah and Thamar. B.C. 1700.

Matt. 1. 3 And Judas begat Phares and Z. of Thamar

ZA'-RAH, ZE'-RAH, זֶרַח, זָרַח *sprout.*

A son of Judah by his daughter in law Tamar. B.C. 1700.

Gen. 38. 30 his brother..and his name was called Z.
46. 12 And the sons of Judah..Pharez, and Z.
Num 26. 20 of Z., the family of the Zarhites
Josh. 7. 1, 18 Zabdi, the son of Z., of the tribe of Ju.
7. 24 Joshua..took Achan the son of Z., and the
22. 20 Did not Achan the son of Z. commit a tr.
1 Ch. 2. 4 Tamar his daughter in law bare him..Z.
2. 6 the sons of Z.; Zimri, and Ethan, and H.
9. 6 of the sons of Z.; Jeuel, and their breth.
Neh. 11. 24 of the children of Z. the son of Judah

ZA-RE'-AH, צָרְעָה *stinging, wasp.* See *Zorah.*

A city in the plain of Judah near Dan: now called *Zarah* or *Surah,* two and a half miles N. of Beth-shemesh.

Neh. 11 29 at En-rimmon, and at Z., and at Jarmuth

ZAREATHITES, צָרְעָתִי.

Family of Shobal, a descendant of Caleb son of Hur; the same as the Zorathites in 1 Ch. 4. 2.

1 Ch. 2. 53 of them came the Z., and the Eshtaulites

ZA'-RED, ZE'-RED, זֶרֶד, זָרֶד *willow bush.*

A brook (and valley) running into the Salt Sea; the boundary line between Moab and Edom: it is called the "brook of the willows" in Isa. 15. 7; and the "river of the wilderness," in Amos 6. 14; perhaps the *Wady el-Ahsy.*

Num 21. 12 removed, and pitched in the valley of Z.
Deut. 2. 13 over..Z.: and we went over the brook Z.
2. 14 space..until we were..over the brook Z.

ZA-RE'-PHATH, צָרְפַת *place of refining.*

A city of the Phoenicians, between Tyre and Sidon, where Elijah lodged with a widow; in Luke 4. 26 it is called *Sarepta,* and now *Surafend.*

1 Ki. 17. 9 Arise, get thee to Z.. and dwell there, be.
17. 10 So he arose and went to Z. And when he
Obad. 20 that of the Canaanites, (even) unto Z.; and

ZA-RE'-TAN, ZARTANAH, ZARTHAN, צָרְתָן *cooling.*

A city or district in Ephraim or Manasseh, near Beth-shean and Succoth: here the waters of Jordan rose in a heap. See *Zereda, Zeredathah, Zererath.*

Josh. 3. 16 far from the city Adam, that (is) beside Z.
1 Ki. 4. 12 Beth-shean, which (is) by Z. beneath Jez.
7. 46 the clay ground between Succoth and Z.

ZA-RETH SHA'-HAR, צֶרֶת הַשַּׁחַר *light of the dawn.*

A city in Reuben, S. of Heshbon, and three miles S. of the mouth of the Zerka Ma'in; now called *Zara.*

Josh 13. 19 Sibmah, and Z. in the mount of the valley

ZARHITES, זַרְחִי.

1. The family of Zerah a Simeonite.

Num 26. 13 Of Zerah, the family of the Z.

2. The family of Zarah or Zerah, son of Judah.

Num 26. 20 of Zerah, the family of the Z.
Josh. 7. 17 and he took the family of the Z.
7. 17 he brought the family of the Z. man by m.
1 Ch. 27. 11 eighth..Sibbecai the Hushathite, of the Z.
27. 13 Maharai the Netophathite, of the Z.; and

ZAT'-TU, ZAT'-THU, זַתּוּא *lovely, pleasant.*

1. One whose descendants returned with Zerubbabel. B.C. 536.

Ezra 2. 8 children of Z., nine hundred forty and five
10. 27 of the sons of Z.; Elioenai, Eliashib, Mat.
Neh. 7. 13 children of Z., eight hundred forty and five

2. One who sealed with Nehemiah the covenant. B.C. 445.

Neh. 10. 14 Parosh, Pahathmoab, Elam, Z., Bani

ZA'-ZA, זָזָא *projection.*

A son of Jonathan, and descendant of Jerahmeel great grandson of Judah. B.C. 1340.

1 Ch. 2. 33 And the sons of Jonathan; Peleth, and Z.

ZEAL, (to be) zealous, to zealously affect —

1. *To be or make zealous,* קָנָא *qana,* 3.

Num 25. 11 while he was zealous for my sake among
25. 13 because he was zealous for his God, and
2 Sa. 21. 2 sought to slay them in his zeal to the ch.

2. *Zeal,* קִנְאָה *qinah.*

2 Ki. 10. 16 Come with me, and see my zeal for the L.
19. 31 the zeal of the LORD (of hosts) shall do
Psa. 69. 9 For the zeal of thine house hath eaten me
119. 139 My zeal hath consumed me; because mi.
Isa. 9. 7 The zeal of the LORD of hosts will perform
37. 32 the zeal of the LORD of hosts shall do this
59. 17 (for) clothing, and was clad with zeal
63. 15 where (is) thy zeal and thy strength, the s.
Eze. 5. 13 that I the LORD have spoken (it) in my ze.

3. *Zeal,* ζῆλος *zēlos.*

John 2. 17 The zeal of thine house hath eaten me up
Rom 10. 2 bear them record that they have a zeal of
2 Co. 7. 11 yea, (what) zeal, yea, what revenge. In all
9. 2 ago; and your zeal hath provoked very
Phil. 3. 6 Concerning zeal, persecuting the church
Col. 4. 13 bear him record, that he hath a great [z.]

4. *A zealot, zealous,* ζηλωτής *zēlōtēs.*

Acts 21. 20 which believe; and they are all zealous
22. 3 was zealous toward God, as ye all are this
1 Co. 14. 12 forasmuch as ye are zealous of spiritual
Gal. 1. 14 being more exceedingly zealous of the tr.
Titus 2. 14 purify unto himself a peculiar people, ze.

5. *To be zealous for,* ζηλόω *zēloō.*

Gal. 4. 17 They zealously affect you, (but) not well
4. 18 But (it is) good to be zealously affected
Rev. 3. 19 I rebuke, and chasten: [be zealous] there.

ZE-BAD'-IAH, זְבַדְיָה, זְבַדְיָהוּ *Jah is endower.*

1. Grandson of Elpael, a Benjamite. B.C. 1300.

1 Ch. 8. 15 And Z., and Arad, and Ader

2. A son of Elpael. B.C. 1280.

1 Ch. 8. 17 Z., and Meshullam, and Hezeki, and Heb.

3. One who joined David at Ziklag. B.C. 1058.

1 Ch. 12. 7 Joelah, and Z., the sons of Jeroham of G.

4. A Kohathite, son of Meshelemiah, a gatekeeper of the tabernacle in the days of David. B.C. 1015.

1 Ch. 26. 2 Jediael the second, Z. the third, Jathniel

5. A son of Asahel son of Zeruiah. B.C. 1025.

1 Ch. 27. 7 The fourth..Asahel..and Z. his son after

6. A Levite sent by Jehoshaphat to teach the people in the cities of Judah. B.C. 912.

2 Ch. 17. 8 with them..Levites, (even)..Z., and Azahel

7. Son of Ishmael, and ruler of the house of Judah in the days of Jehoshaphat. B.C. 912.

2 Ch. 19. 11 Z. the son of Ishmael..for all the king's

8. Son of Shephaniah, and head of a family which returned with Ezra in the days of Artaxerxes. B.C. 457.

Ezra 8. 8 Z. the son of Michael, and with him four.

9. A priest that had taken a strange wife during the exile. B.C. 445.

Ezra 10. 20 And of the sons of Immer; Hanani, and Z.

ZE'-BAH, זֶבַח *slaughter, sacrifice.*
A king of Midian defeated and slain by Gideon. B.C. 1249.
Judg. 8. 5 I am pursuing after Z. and Zalmunna, ki.
8. 6, 15 (Are) the hands of Z. and Zalmunna
8. 7 LORD hath delivered Z. and Zalmunna
8. 10 Now Z. and Zalmunna (were) in Karkor
8. 12 when Z. and Zalmunna fled, he pursued
8. 12 and took..Z. and Zalmunna, and discom.
8. 15 Behold Z. and Zalmunna, with whom ye
8. 18 Then said he unto Z. and Zalmunna
8. 21 Then Z. and Zalmunna said, Rise thou
8. 21 And Gideon arose, and slew Z. and Zalm.
Psa. 83. 11 Make..all their princes as Z., and as Zal.

ZE-BA'-IM, צְבָיִם *gazelles.*
Place unknown; perhaps *Zeboim;* the residence of Pochereth whose descendants returned from exile with Zerubbabel. B.C. 536.
Ezra 2. 57 children of Pochereth of Z., the children
Neh. 7. 59 children of Pochereth of Z., the children

ZE-BE'-DEE, Ζεβεδαῖος (*from Heb.* זְבַדְיָה) *Jah is gift.*
Husband of Salome, and father of James and John, two of the apostles of Jesus; a fisherman by trade.
Matt. 4. 21 he saw..James..of Z., and John his brot.
4. 21 in a ship with Z. their father, mending
10. 2 James (the son) of Z., and John his broth.
20. 20 Then came to him the mother of Z.'s chi.
26. 37 took with him Peter and the..sons of Z.
27. 56 Among which was..the mother of Z.'s ch.
Mark 1. 19 he saw James the (son) of Z., and John his
1. 20 they left their father Z. in the ship with
3. 17 James the (son) of Z., and John the brot.
10. 35 James and John, the sons of Z., come unto
Luke 5. 10 the sons of Z...were partners with Simon
John 21. 2 There were together..the (sons) of Z., and

ZE-BI'-NA, זְבִינָא *purchase.*
One of the sons of Nebo that had taken a strange wife during the exile. B.C. 445.
Ezra 10. 43 the sons of Nebo; Jeiel, Mattithiah..Z.

ZE-BO'-IM, ZEBOIIM, צְבֹיִם [V.L. צבים, צביים, צבאים].
One of the five cities in the valley of Siddim, and destroyed with Sodom and Gomorrah. B.C. 1898.
Gen. 10. 19 as thou goest, unto..Admah, and Z., even
14. 2 made war with..Shemeber king of Z., and
14. 8 And there went out..the king of Z., and
Deut 29. 23 and Z., which the LORD overthrew in his
Hos. 11. 8 shall I set thee as Z.? mine heart is turned

ZE-BO'-IM, צְבֹעִים *wild place.*
A city and valley in Benjamin sloping eastward to the Jordan plain; perhaps the *Shug ed Dubba'* or *Wady Abu-l-Dda-baa.*
1 Sa. 13. 18 border that looketh to the valley of Z. to.
Neh. 11. 34 Hadid, Z., Neballat

ZE-BU'-DAH, זְבוּדָּה *endowed.*
Daughter of Pedaiah of Rumah, wife of Josiah and mother of Eliakim (or Jehoiakim) kings of Judah. B.C. 640.
2 Ki. 23. 36 And his mother's name (was) Z...of Rum.

ZE'-BUL, זְבֻל *gift, dwelling.*
An officer of Abimelech and governor of Shechem. B.C. 1206.
Judg. 9. 28 (is) not..Z. his officer? Serve the men of
9. 30 Z...heard the words of Gaal the son of
9. 36 when Gaal saw the people, he said to Z.
9. 36 Z. said unto him, Thou seest the shadow
9. 38 Then said Z. unto him, Where (is) now
9. 41 and Z. thrust out Gaal and his brethren

ZEBULONITES זְבוּלֹנִי.
The descendants of Zebulun.
Num 26. 27 These (are) the families of the Z. accord.
Judg 12. 11 And after him Elon, a Z., judged Israel
12. 12 And Elon the Z. died, and was buried in

ZE-BU'-LUN, זְבוּלֻן, זְבוּלוּן, זְבֻלוּן *dwelling.*
1. Tenth son of Jacob, and sixth of Leah. B.C. 1740.
Gen. 30. 20 I have..sons; and..called his name Z.
35. 23 Levi, and Judah, and Issachar, and Z.
46. 14 the sons of Z.; Sered, and Elon, and Jah.
49. 13 Z. shall dwell at the haven of the sea
Exod. 1. 3 Issachar, Z., and Benjamin
1 Ch. 2. 1 Simeon, Levi..Judah, Issachar, and Z.

2. His posterity.
Num. 1. 9 Of Z.; Eliab the son of Helon
1. 30 Of the children of Z...all that were able
1. 31 Those that were numbered..of..tribe of Z.
2. 7 tribe of Z...captain of the children of Z.
7. 24 Eliab..prince of the children of Z., (did
10. 16 over the host..of Z...Eliab the son of H.
13. 10 Of the tribe of Z., Gaddiel the son of Sodi
26. 26 (Of) the sons of Z. after their families
34. 25 prince of the tribe of the children of Z.
Deut 27. 13 Reuben, Gad, and Asher, and Z., Dan, and
33. 18 of Z. he said, Rejoice, Z., in thy going out
Josh. 19. 10 third lot came up for the children of Z.
19. 16 the inheritance of the children of Z. acc.
19. 27 reacheth to Z., and to the valley of Jiph.
19. 34 the coast..reacheth to Z. on the south
21. 7 Merari..(had)..out of the tribe of Z., twelve
21. 34 out of the tribe of Z., Jokneam with her
Judg. 1. 30 Neither did Z. drive out the inhabitants
4. 6 take with thee..men..of the children of Z.
4. 10 Barak called Z. and Naphtali to Kedesh
5. 14 out of Z. they that handle the pen of the
5. 18 Z...a people (that) jeoparded their lives
6. 35 he sent messengers..unto Z., and unto Na.
Judg 12. 12 was buried in Aijalon in the country of Z.
1 Ch. 6. 63 and out of the tribe of Z., twelve cities
6. 77 out of the tribe of Z., Rimmon with her
12. 33 Of Z., such as went forth to battle, expert
12. 40 they that were nigh..unto..Z...brought
27. 19 Of Z., Ishmaiah the son of Obadiah
2 Ch. 30. 10 So the posts passed..even unto Z.; but they
30. 11 Nevertheless divers..of Z. humbled them.
30. 18 many of..Z., had not cleansed themselves
Psa. 68. 27 the princes of Z...the princes of Naphtali
Isa. 9. 1 he lightly afflicted the land of Z. and the
Eze. 48. 26 And by the border of Issachar..Z. a (por.)
48. 27 And by the border of Z...Gad a (portion)
48. 33 Simeon, one gate of Issachar, one..of Z.
The following localities were in the territory of Zebulun:—Ajalon, Bethlehem, Cabul, Chisloth-tabor, Dabareh or Daberath, Dabasheth, Dimnah, Gath (or Gittah), Hepher, Hannathon, Hepher, Idalah, Ittah-kazin, Japhia, Jiphtah-el, Jokneam, Kartah, Kattah, Kitron, Maralah, Nahalol, Neah, Remmon-methoar, Rimmon, Sarid, Shimron, Tabor, &c.

ZE-CHAR'-IAH, זְכַרְיָהוּ, זְכַרְיָה *Jah is renowned.*
1. A chief Reubenite when the genealogy was reckoned. B.C. 740.
1 Ch. 5. 7 his brethren..(were)..chief, Jeiel, and Z.
2. A Levite, son of Meshelemiah, a gatekeeper of the tabernacle in the days of David. B.C. 1015.
1 Ch. 9. 21 Z. the son of Meshelemiah (was) porter
26. 2 the sons of Meshelemiah..Z. the first born
26. 14 for Z. his son, a wise counsellor, they cast
3. A Benjamite, in Gibeon; called *Zacher* in 1 Ch. 8. 31. B.C. 1180.
1 Ch. 9. 37 And Gedor, and Ahio, and Z., and Mikl.
4. A Levite set over the service of song in the days of David. B.C. 1015.
1 Ch. 15. 18 Z., Ben, and Jaaziel, and Shemiramoth
15. 20 Z., and Aziel, and Shemiramoth, and Je.
16. 5 Asaph the chief, and next to him Z., Je.
5. A priest in the tabernacle, at the same time.
1 Ch. 15. 24 Z., and Benaiah, and Eliezer, the priests
6. A Kohathite, son of Isshiah, at the same time.
1 Ch. 24. 25 Isshiah; of the sons of Isshiah; Z.
7. A Merarite, son of Hosah, a gatekeeper of the tabernacle at the same time.
1 Ch. 26. 11 Hilkiah the second, Tebaliah the third, Z.
8. Father of Iddo, the chief of the half tribe of Manasseh E. of Jordan in the days of David. B.C. 1040.
1 Ch. 27. 21 of Manasseh in Gilead, Iddo the son of Z.
9. A prince whom Jehoshaphat sent to teach the people in the cities of Judah. B.C. 913.
2 Ch. 17. 7 he sent to..Z...to teach in the cities of J.
10. A Levite, father of Jehaziel who encouraged Jehoshaphat's army against Moab. B.C. 896.
2 Ch. 20. 14 Then upon Jehaziel the son of Z...came
11. Third son of Jehoshaphat. B.C. 880.
2 Ch. 21. 2 he had brethren the sons of..Z., and Az.
12. Son of Jehoiada the priest, and stoned for rebuking the people. B.C. 840.
2 Ch. 24. 20 the Spirit of God came upon Z. the son
13. A person having understanding in the visions of God in the days of Uzziah. B.C. 810.
2 Ch. 26. 5 he sought God in the days of Z., who had
14. A Levite, son of Asaph, who helped to cleanse the temple in the days of Hezekiah. B.C. 726.
2 Ch. 29. 13 of the sons of Asaph; Z., and Mattaniah
15. A Kohathite, one of the overseers of the repairs of the temple in the days of Josiah. B.C. 624.
2 Ch. 34. 12 Z. and Meshullam, of the sons of the Koh.
16. A prince of Judah in the days of Josiah. B.C. 624.
2 Ch. 35. 8 Hilkiah and Z. and Jehiel, rulers of the
17. A prophet in Judah, whose Book still remains. B.C. 520.
Ezra 5. 1 Z. the son of Iddo, prophesied unto the J.
6. 14 Z. the son of Iddo: and they builded, and
Zech. 1. 1, 7 came the word of the LORD unto Z., the
7. 1 word of the LORD came unto Z. in the
7. 8 word of the LORD came unto Z., saying
18. A chief man that returned with Ezra. B.C. 457.
Ezra 8. 3 of the sons of Pharosh; Z.: and with him
19. Another that did the same. B.C. 457.
Ezra 8. 11 Z. the son of Bebai, and with him twenty
8. 16 Then sent I for..Z., and for Meshullam
20. One that had taken a strange wife.
Ezra 10. 26 Mattaniah, Z., and Jehiel, and Abdi, and
21. A prince that stood beside Ezra. B.C. 457.
Neh. 8. 4 Hashum, and Hashbadana, Z., (and) Mes.
22. A descendant of Pharez, some of whose descendants dwelt in Jerusalem. B.C. 457.
Neh. 11. 4 Z., the son of Amariah, the son of Shepha.
23. Another, whose descendants dwelt in Jerusalem.
Neh. 11. 5 son of Joiarib, the son of Z., the son of Sh.
24. A priest, some of whose descendants dwelt in Jerusalem.
Neh 11. 12 son of Amzi, the son of Z., the son of Pa.
25. A priest in the time of Joiakim son of Jeshua.
Neh. 12. 16 Of Iddo, Z.; of Ginnethon, Meshullam
26. A priest of the family of Asaph, who officiated in the ceremony of purifying the walls of Jerusalem. B.C. 457.
Neh. 12. 35 Z. the son of Jonathan, the son of Shem
12. 41 Michaiah, Elioenai, Z., (and) Hananiah
27. One whom Isaiah took as a witness; perhaps the same as No. 13.
Isa. 8. 2 Uriah the priest, and Z. the son of Jeber.

ZE'-DAD, צְדָדָה *sloping place.*
A place in the N. of Palestine, near Hamath; perhaps *Sadad* between Hums and Baalbec, now in ruins. The *Sept.* and Vulg. read *Zeradah.*
Num 34. 8 goings forth of the border shall be to Z.
Eze. 47. 15 the way of Hethlon, as men go to Z.

ZE-DE-KI'-AH, צִדְקִיָּהוּ, צִדְקִיָּה *Jah is might.*
1. A false prophet, son of Chenaanah, who encouraged Ahab to attack the Syrians at Ramoth-Gilead. B.C. 897.
1 Ki. 22. 11 Z...made him horns of iron: and he said
22. 24 Z...went near, and smote Micaiah on the
2 Ch. 18. 10 Z...made him horns of iron, and said
18. 23 Z...came near, and smote Micaiah upon
2. The name given by Nebuchadnezzar to Mattaniah whom he made king instead of Jehoiachin. B.C. 588.
2 Ki. 24. 17 And the king..changed his name to Z.
24. 18 Z. (was) twenty and one years old when
24. 20 Z. rebelled against the king of Babylon
25. 2 was besieged unto the eleventh year of..Z.
25. 7 they slew the sons of Z. before his eyes
25. 7 they..put out the eyes of Z., and bound
1 Ch. 3. 15 the sons of Josiah (were)..Z...Shallum
2 Ch. 36. 10 N. sent..and made Z...king over Judah
36. 11 Z. (was) one and twenty years old when
Jer. 1. 3 unto the end of the eleventh year of Z. the
21. 1 when king Z. sent unto him Pashur the
21. 3 Then said Jerem...Thus shall ye say to Z.
21. 7 I will deliver Z. king of Judah, and his se.
24. 8 So will I give Z. the king of Judah, and
27. 3 messengers which come..unto Z. king of
27. 12 I spake also to Z. king of Judah according
28. 1 in the beginning of the reign of Z. king of
29. 3 whom Z. king of Judah sent unto Babylon
32. 1 word that came..in the tenth year of Z.
32. 3 For Z. king of Judah had shut him up
32. 4 Z. king of Judah shall not escape out of
32. 5 he shall lead Z. to Babylon, and there sh.
34. 2 Go and speak to Z. king of Judah, and tell
34. 4 Yet hear the word of the LORD, O Z. king
34. 6 Jeremiah..spake all these words unto Z.
34. 8 Z. had made a covenant with all the peo.
34. 21 Z...and his princes, will I give into the ha.
37. 1 Z. the son of Josiah reigned instead of Co.
37. 3 Z. the king sent Jehucal..to the prophet
37. 17 Then Z. the king sent, and took him out
37. 18 Moreover Jeremiah said unto king Z.
37. 21 Z...commanded that they should commit
38. 5 Z. the king said, Behold, he (is) in your
38. 14 Then Z. the king sent, and took Jeremiah
38. 15 Jeremiah said unto Z., If I declare (it) un.
38. 16 So Z. the king sware secretly unto Jerem.
38. 17 Then said Jeremiah unto Z., Thus saith
38. 19 Z. the king said unto Jeremiah, I am af.
38. 24 Then said Z. unto Jeremiah, Let no man
39. 1 In the ninth year of Z. king of Judah, in
39. 2 in the eleventh year of Z...the city was
39. 4 when Z. the king of Judah saw them, and
39. 5 the Chaldean's army..overtook Z. in the
39. 6 the king of Babylon slew the sons of Z.
39. 7 Moreover he put out Z.'s eyes, and bound
44. 30 as I gave Z. king of Judah into the hand
49. 34 in the beginning of the reign of Z. king of
51. 59 when he went with Z. the king of Judah
52. 1 Z. (was) one and twenty years old when
52. 3 Z. rebelled against the king of Babylon
52. 5 was besieged unto the eleventh year of..Z.
52. 8 the Chaldeans..overtook Z. in the plains
52. 10 the king of Babylon slew the sons of Z.
52. 11 he put out the eyes of Z...and put him in
3. Grandson of Jehoiakim. B.C. 530.
1 Ch. 3. 16 sons of Jehoiakim; Jeconiah his son, Z.
4. A false prophet, son of Maaseiah.
Jer. 29. 21 Thus saith the LORD..of Z. the son of M.
29. 22 The LORD make thee like Z. and like Ahab
5. A prince of Judah, son of Hananiah, in the days of Jehoiakim. B.C. 600.
Jer. 36. 12 Z. the son of Hananiah, and all the princes

ZE'-EB, זְאֵב *wolf.*
A prince of Midian defeated and slain by Gideon. B.C. 1249.
Judg. 7. 25 And they took two princes..Oreb and Z.
7. 25 and Z. they slew at the winepress of Z.
7. 25 they..brought the heads of Oreb and Z. to
8. 3 God..delivered into your hands..Oreb..Z.
Psa. 83. 11 Make their nobles like Oreb, and like Z.

ZE'-LAH, צֵלַע *slope.*
A city in Benjamin (near Eleph or Jebusi), where Saul and his sons were buried. B.C. 1056.
Josh 18. 28 And Z., Eleph, and Jebusi, which (is) Jeru.
2 Sa. 21. 14 the bones of Saul..buried they..in Z., in

ZE'-LEK, צֶלֶק *split, rent.*
An Ammonite, one of David's valiant men. B.C. 1048.
2 Sa. 23. 37 Z. the Ammonite, Nahari the Beerothite
1 Ch. 11. 39 Z. the Ammonite, Naharai the Berothite

ZE-LOPH-E'-HAD, צְלָפְחָד.
Grandson of Gilead, son of Manasseh. B.C. 1492.
Num 26. 33 Z. the son of Hepher had no sons, but da.

Num 26. 33 names of the daughters of Z. (were) Mah.
27. 1 Then came the daughters of Z., the son
27. 7 The daughters of Z. speak right: thou sh.
36. 2 to give the inheritance of Z.. unto his da.
36. 6 command concerning.. daughters of Z.
36. 10 commanded.. so did the daughters of Z.
36. 11 Milcah, and Noah, the daughters of Z.
Josh. 17. 3 Z., the son of Hepher.. had no sons, but
1 Ch. 7. 15 and the name of the second (was) Z.; and Z.

ZE-LO'-TES, Ζηλωτής *zealous*. See *Simon*.
A surname of Simon, one of the twelve apostles, elsewhere called the *Canaanite* by mistake for *Cananite*, or Kananite.
Luke 6. 15 James.. of Alpheus, and Simon called Z.
Acts 1. 13 James (the son) of Alpheus, and Simon Z.

ZEL'-ZAH, צֶלְצַח *sun protection*.
A city in Benjamin on the border.
1 Sa. 10. 2 then thou shalt find two men.. at Z., and

ZE-MA-RA'-IM, צְמָרַיִם *double mount forest*.
1. A city in the N. of Benjamin, near Bethel; now called *Sumrah*, five miles N. of Jericho.
Josh. 18. 22 And Beth-arabah, and Z., and Beth-el
2. A part of Ephraim.
2 Ch. 13. 4 Abijah stood up upon mount Z., which (is)

ZE-MA-RITE, צְמָרִי.
A tribe at the Eleutherus, at the W. foot of Lebanon, where there are still ruins called *Sumra*.
Gen. 10. 18 the Arvadite, and the Z., and the Hama.
1 Ch. 1. 16 the Arvadite, and the Z., and the Hama

ZE-MI'-RA, זְמִירָה *song*.
A son of Becher, son of Benjamin. B.C. 1630.
1 Ch. 7. 8 the sons of Becher; Z., and Joash, and E.

ZE'-NAN, צְנָן *rich in flocks*.
A city in Judah, E of Askelon; same as *Zaanan*.
Josh. 15. 37 Z., and Hadashah, and Migdal-gad

ZE'-NAS, Ζηνᾶς.
A believer who was a "lawyer," or one skilled in the law of Moses, whom Paul desired Titus to bring or send to him with Apollos to Nicopolis, whither Paul proposed going to winter.
Titus 3. 13 Bring Z. the lawyer and Apollos on their

ZE-PHAN'-IAH, צְפַנְיָה, צְפַנְיָהוּ *Jah is darkness*.
1. The "second" priest whom the captain of the king of Babylon's guard took with him to Riblah after he had plundered Jerusalem. B.C. 598.
2 Ki. 25. 18 the captain of the guard took.. Z. the se.
Jer. 21. 1 Zedekiah sent unto him.. Z. the son of M.
29. 25 Because thou hast sent letters.. to Z., the
29. 29 Z... read this letter in the ears of Jerem.
37. 3 the king sent.. Z. the son of Maaseiah the
52. 24 the captain of the guard took.. Z. the se.
2. A Kohathite, ancestor of the prophet Samuel. B.C. 1460.
1 Ch. 6. 36 Joel, the son of Azariah, the son of Z.
3. Son of Cushi, a prophet in the days of Josiah, whose Book of Prophecies still remain. B.C. 640-609
Zeph. 1. 1 The word of the LORD which came unto Z.
4. Son of Josiah the priest who dwelt in Jerusalem when Darius gave a decree to rebuild the temple. B.C. 550.
Zech. 6. 10 go into the house of Josiah the son of Z.
6. 14 the crowns shall be.. to Hen the son of Z.

ZE'-PHATH, צְפַת *mountain watch*.
A city in Simeon, at the S. border of Edom and in Judah, called also *Hormah*; now called *Sebaita*; twenty-four miles N. of Kadesh.
Judg. 1. 17 slew the Canaanites that inhabited Z.

ZE-PHA'-THAH, צְפָתָה.
A valley in the W. of Judah, near Mareshah; perhaps the same as the preceding.
2 Ch. 14. 10 set the battle in array in the valley of Z.

ZE'-PHO, ZE'-PHI, צְפוֹ, צְפִי *watch*.
A son of Eliphaz, son of Esau. B.C. 1650.
Gen. 36. 11 sons of Eliphaz were Teman.. Z., and G
36. 15 duke Teman, duke Omar, duke Z., duke
1 Ch. 1. 36 Teman, and Omar, Z., and Gatam, Kenaz

ZE'-PHON, צְפוֹן *dark, wintry*.
A Gadite. B.C. 1680.
Num 26. 15 of Z., the family of the Zephonites

ZEPHONITES, הַצְּפוֹנִי.
The descendants of Zephon.
Num 26. 15 of Zephon, the family of the Z

ZER, צֵר *rock*.
A city in Naphtali, near the lake of Genesareth.
Josh. 19. 35 the fenced cities (are) Ziddim, Z., and H.

ZE'-RAH, ZA'-RAH, זֶרַח, זָרַח *sprout*.
1. A son of Reuel, son of Esau. B.C. 1700.
Gen. 36. 13 these.. the sons of Reuel; Nahath, and Z.
36. 17 duke Nahath, duke Z., duke Shammah
1 Ch. 1. 37 The sons of Reuel; Nahath, Z., Shammah
2. Father of Jobab, second of the early kings of Edom. B.C. 1670.
Gen. 36. 33 Jobab the son of Z. of Bozrah reigned in
1 Ch. 1. 44 Jobab the son of Z. of Bozrah reigned in
3. A son of Judah by his daughter in law Tamar. B.C. 1700.
Gen. 38. 30 And.. his brother.. his name was called Z.
Num 26. 20 of Z., the family of the Zarhites
Josh. 7. 1, 18 Zabdi, the son of Z., of the tribe of J.
7. 24 Joshua.. took Achan the son of Z., and
22. 20 Did not Achan the son of Z. commit a tr.
1 Ch. 2. 4 Tamar his daughter in law bare him.. Z.
2. 6 the sons of Z.; Zimri, and Ethan, and H.
9. 6 of the sons of Z.; Jeuel, and their breth.
Neh. 11. 24 of the children of Z. the son of Judah
4. A son of Simeon. B.C. 1700.
Num 26. 13 Of Z., the family of the Zarhites: of Shaul
1 Ch. 4. 24 The sons of Simeon.. Jarib, Z., (and) Sha.
5. A Gershonite. B.C. 1250.
1 Ch. 6. 21 Joah his son, Iddo his son, Z. his son
6. Father of Ethni, a Levite. B.C. 1250.
1 Ch. 6. 41 The son of Ethni, the son of Z., the son of
7. A king of Ethiopia, who warred with Asa. B.C. 941.
2 Ch. 14. 9 there came out against them Z. the Ethiop.

ZE-RAH'-IAH, זְרַחְיָה *Jah is appearing*.
1. A descendant of Phinehas, an ancestor of Ezra. B.C. 1116.
1 Ch. 6. 6 Uzzi begat Z., and Z. begat Meraioth
6. 51 Bukki his son, Uzzi his son, Z. his son
Ezra 7. 4 son of Z., the son of Uzzi, the son of Bu.
2. Father of Elihoenai (a descendant of Pahath Moab) who returned with Ezra. B.C. 480. Ezra 8. 4.

ZERED. *See* ZARED.

ZE-RE'-DA, הַצְּרֵדָה *the fortress; town*.
A city or district on N. of Mount Ephraim, but in Manasseh, and birthplace of Jeroboam; same as *Zererath, Zaretan, Zarthan*, and *Zartanah*.
1 Ki. 11. 26 J. the son of Nebat, an Ephrathite of Z.

ZE-RE-DA'-THAH, צְרֵדָתָה.
In Manasseh, near Succoth.
2 Ch. 4. 17 the clay ground between Succoth and Z.

ZE-RE'-RATH, צְרֵרָתָה.
A district in Manasseh, near Abelmeholah and Beth-shittah.
Judg. 7. 22 and the host fled to Beth-shittah in Z.

ZE'-RESH, זֶרֶשׁ.
Wife of Haman the Agagite, enemy of the Jews in the days of Ahasuerus and Esther. B.C. 510.
Esth. 5. 10 sent and called for his friends, and Z. his
5. 14 Then said Z. his wife and all his friends
6. 13 And Haman told Z. his wife and all his fr.
6. 13 Then said his wise men and Z. his wife

ZE'-RETH, צֶרֶת *splendour, brightness*.
A son of Helah son of Ashur, descendant of Judah, through Caleb son of Hur. B.C. 1470.
1 Ch. 4. 7 the sons of Helah (were) Z., and Jezoar

ZE'-RI, צְרִי *balm*.
A son of Jeduthun set over the service of song in the days of David. B.C. 1015.
1 Ch. 25. 3 sons of Jeduthun; Gedaliah, and Z., and

ZE'-ROR, צְרוֹר *bundle*.
Father of Abiel a Benjamite, and ancestor of Saul the first king of Israel. B.C. 1160.
1 Sa. 9. 1 Kish, the son of Abiel, the son of Zeror, the

ZE-RU'-AH, צְרוּעָה *full breasted*.
A widow, mother of Jeroboam first king of the ten tribes of Israel. B.C. 1000.
1 Ki. 11. 26 whose mother's name (was) Z., a widow w.

ZE-RUB-BA'-BEL, זְרֻבָּבֶל *shoot of Babylon*.
A descendant of Salathiel or Shealtiel grandson of Jehoiakim king of Judah; he led back the first band of exiles. B.C. 536.
1 Ch. 3. 19 the sons of Pedaiah (were) Z., and Shimei
3. 19 the sons of Z.; Meshullam, and Hananiah
Ezra 2. 2 Which came with Z.: Jeshua, Nehemiah
3. 2 Then stood up.. Z. the son of Shealtiel, and
3. 8 in the second year.. began Z. the son of
4. 2 they came to Z., and to the chief of the
4. 3 Z... said unto them, Ye have nothing to
5. 2 Then rose up Z., the son of Shealtiel, and
Neh. 7. 7 Who came with Z., Jeshua, Nehemiah
12. 1 these.. the priests.. that went up with Z.
12. 47 all Israel in the days of Z.,.. gave the po.
Hag. 1. 1 came the word of the LORD.. unto Z. the
1. 12 Then Z... with all the.. people, obeyed the
1. 14 And the LORD stirred up the spirit of Z.
2. 2 Speak now to Z. the son of Shealtiel, gover.
2. 4 Yet now be strong, O Z., saith the LORD
2. 21 Speak to Z., governor of Judah, saying
2. 23 In that day.. will I take thee, O Z., my se.
Zech. 4. 6 This (is) the word of the LORD unto Z., sa.
4. 7 before Z. (thou shalt become) a plain: and
4. 9 The hands of Z. have laid the foundation
4. 10 shall see the plummet in the hand of Z.

ZE-RU'-IAH, צְרוּיָה *balm*.
A daughter of Jesse father of David, whose three sons were officers over David's army, viz., Joab, Abishai, and Asahel. B.C. 1070.
1 Sa. 26. 6 Then answered David.. Abishai.. son of Z.
2 Sa. 2. 13 And Joab the son of Z... went out, and
2. 18 there were three sons of Z. there, Joab
3. 39 these men the sons of Z. (be) too hard for
8. 16 Joab the son of Z. (was) over the host
14. 1 Now Joab the son of Z. perceived that the
16. 9 Then said Abishai the son of Z. unto the
16. 10 What have I to do with you, ye sons of Z.?
17. 25 daughter of Nahash, sister to Z., Joab's mo.
2 Sa. 18. 2 under the hand of Abishai the son of Z.
19. 21 Abishai the son of Z. answered and said
19. 22 What have I to do with you, ye sons of Z.
21. 17 But Abishai the son of Z. succoured him
23. 18 the son of Z., was chief among three; and
23. 37 Zelek.. armour bearer to Joab the son of Z.
1 Ki. 1. 7 he conferred with Joab the son of Z., and
2. 5 thou knowest also what Joab the son of Z.
2. 22 even for him.. and for Joab the son of Z.
1 Ch. 2. 16 Whose sisters (were) Z... And the sons of Z.
11. 6 Joab the son of Z. went first up, and was
11. 39 the armour bearer of Joab the son of Z.
18. 12 the son of Z. slew of the Edomites.. eigh.
18. 15 And Joab the son of Z. (was) over the ho.
26. 28 all that.. Joab the son of Z., had dedicat.
27. 24 Joab the son of Z. began to number, but

ZE'-THAM, זֵתָם *shining*.
A son or grandson of Laadan Gershonite. B.C. 1015.
1 Ch. 23. 8 the chief (was) Jehiel, and Z., and Joel
26. 22 sons of Jehieli; Z., and Joel his brother

ZE'-THAN, זֵיתָן *shining*.
A son of Bilhan, grandson of Benjamin. B.C. 1600.
1 Ch. 7. 10 Chenaanah, and Z., and Tharshish, and

ZE'-THAR, זֵתַר *sacrifice*.
One of the seven chamberlains of the king of Persia that saw the king's face at pleasure. B.C. 519.
Esth. 1. 10 Z... served in the presence of Ahasuerus

ZI'-A, זִיעַ *terrified*.
A Gadite, head of a family. B.C. 1070.
1 Ch. 5. 13 Sheba, and Jorai, and Jachan, and Z., and

ZI'-BA, צִיבָא *plantation*.
A servant of Saul who served Mephibosheth, and afterwards obtained half of his property from David by ascribing treachery to his master. B.C. 1025.
2 Sa. 9. 2 (there was).. a servant, whose name (was) Z.
9. 2 (Art) thou Z.? And he said, Thy servant
9. 3 Z. said unto the king, Jonathan hath yet a
9. 4 Z. said unto the king, Behold, he (is) in
9. 9 Then the king called to Z., Saul's servant
9. 10 Z. had fifteen sons and twenty servants
9. 11 Then said Z. unto the king, According to
9. 12 all that dwelt in the house of Z. (were) se.
16. 1 Z. the servant of Mephibosheth met him
16. 2 the king said unto Z., What meanest th.
16. 2 Z. said, The asses (be) for the king's hous.
16. 3 Z. said unto the king, Behold, he abideth
16. 4 Then said the king to Z., Behold, thine
16. 4 Z. said, I humbly beseech thee (that) I
19. 17 Z. the servant of the house of Saul, and
19. 29 I have said, Thou and Z. divide the land

ZI-BE'-ON, צִבְעוֹן *wild robber*.
1. A Hivite, grandfather of Adah one of Esau's wives. B.C. 1800.
Gen. 36. 2 the daughter of Anah the daughter of Z.
36. 14 the daughter of Anah the daughter of Z.
2. A son of Seir the Horite. B.C. 1800.
Gen. 36. 20 Lotan, and Shobal, and Z., and Anah
36. 24 these (are) the children of Z.; both Ajah
36. 24 found.. as he fed the asses of Z. his father
36. 29 duke Lotan, duke Shobal, duke Z., duke
1 Ch. 1. 38 sons of Seir; Lotan, and Shobal, and Z.
1. 40 And the sons of Z., Aiah, and Anah

ZIB'-IA, צִבְיָא *gazelle*.
A Benjamite, son of Hodesh. B.C. 1320.
1 Ch. 8. 9 he begat of Hodesh his wife, Jobab, and Z.

ZIB'-IAH, צִבְיָה.
The wife of Ahaziah and mother of Jehoash or Joash, kings of Judah; from the city of Beer-sheba. B.C. 890.
2 Ki. 12. 1 his mother's name (was) Z. of Beer-sheba
2 Ch. 24. 1 His mother's name also (was) Z. of Beer-s.

ZICH'-RI, זִכְרִי *renowned*.
1. A son of Izhar, grandson of Levi. B.C. 1490.
Exod. 6. 21 sons of Izhar; Korah, and Nepheg, and Z.
2. A Benjamite of the family of Shimhi. B.C. 1300.
1 Ch. 8. 19 And Jakim, and Z., and Zabdi
3. A Benjamite, son of Shishak. B.C. 1300.
1 Ch. 8. 23 And Abdon, and Z., and Hanan
4. A Benjamite, son of Jeroham. B.C. 1300.
1 Ch. 8. 27 Jaresiah, and Eliah, and Z., the sons of J.
5. A Levite, son of Asaph. B.C. 500.
1 Ch. 9. 15 Mattaniah the son of Micah, the son of Z.
6. A descendant of Eliezer, son of Moses, in the days of David. B.C. 1040.
1 Ch. 26. 25 Joram his son, and Z. his son, and Shelo.
7. Father of Eliezer, a chief Reubenite in the days of David. B.C. 1040.
1 Ch. 27. 16 ruler of the Reubenites.. the son of Z.
8. Father of Amaziah, a captain of Jehoshaphat. B.C. 960.
2 Ch. 17. 16 And next him (was) Amasiah the son of Z.
9. Father of Elishaphat, a captain of hundreds, who helped Jehoiada the priest to make Joash king of Israel. B.C. 900.
2 Ch. 23. 1 Jehoiada.. took.. Elishaphat the son of Z.
10. An Ephraimite, a mighty man of valour, that slew the son of Ahaz king of Judah. B.C. 741.
2 Ch. 28. 7 Z., a mighty man of Ephraim, slew Maase.
11. Father of Joel, overseer of the Benjamites in Jerusalem after the exile. B.C. 470.
Neh. 11. 9 Joel the son of Z. (was) their overseer

12. A priest of the sons of Abijah in the days of Nehemiah. B.C. 445.
Neh. 12. 17 of Abijah, Z.; of Miniamin, of Moadiah, Pi.

ZID'-DIM, הַצִּדִּים *the mountain sides.*
A fenced city in Naphtali; now called *Hattin.*
Josh. 19. 35 the fenced cities (are) Z., Zer, and Ham.

ZID-KI'-JAH, צִדְקִיָּה *Jah is might.*
A chief prince of the Jews that with Nehemiah sealed the covenant. B.C. 445. See *Zedekiah.*
Neh. 10. 1 those that sealed (were) Nehemiah..Z.

ZI'-DON, SIDON, צִידֹן, צִדֹן *fortress.*
1. Eldest son of Canaan, son of Ham. B.C. 2200.
Gen. 10. 15 Canaan begat S. his first born, and Heth
1 Ch. 1. 13 Canaan begat S. his first born, and Heth.
2. A city in Asher, now called *Saida;* its authority extended S. to Carmel and Dor, and E. towards Damascus.
Gen. 10. 19 the border of the Canaanites was from S.
49. 13 shall dwell..his border (shall be) unto Z.
Josh 11. 8 smote them, and chased them unto great Z.
19. 28 and Hammon, and Kanah..unto great Z.
Judg. 1. 31 Neither did Asher drive out..inhab. of Z.
10. 6 children of Israel..served..the gods of Z.
18. 28 no deliverer, because it (was) far from Z.
2 Sa. 24. 6 they came to Dan-jaan, and about to Z.
1 Ki. 17. 9 Arise, get thee to Zarephath, which..to Z.
Ezra 3. 7 They gave..meat, and drink..unto..Z.
Isa. 23. 2 thou whom the merchants of Z...have re.
23. 4 Be thou ashamed, O Z.: for the sea hath
23. 12 Thou shalt no more rejoice..daughter..Z.
Jer. 25. 22 all the kings of Tyrus..all the kings of Z.
27. 3 send them..to the king of Z., by the hand
47. 4 to cut off from Tyrus and Z. every helper
Eze. 27. 8 The inhabitants of Z. and Arvad were thy
28. 21 set thy face against Z., and prophesy aga.
28. 22 Behold, I (am) against thee, O Z.; and I
Joel 3. 4 what have ye to do with me, O Tyre, and Z.
Zech. 9. 2 Hamath also shall border thereby..and Z.

ZIDONIANS, SIDONIANS, צִדֹנִים, צִידֹנִין, צִדֹנִי, צִדֹנִית
The inhabitants of the preceding city and state.
Judg 10. 12 The Z. also..did oppress you; and ye cr.
18. 7 dwelt careless, after the manner of the Z.
18. 7 they (were) far from the Z., and had no
1 Ki. 11. 1 Moabites, Ammonites, Edomites, Z., (and)
11. 5, 33 Ashtoreth the goddess of the Z.
16. 31 Jezebel the daughter of Ethbaal..the Z.
2 Ki. 23. 13 for Ashtoreth the abomination of the S.
1 Ch. 22. 4 the Z...brought much cedar wood to Da.
Eze. 32. 30 all the Z., which are gone down with the

ZIF, זִו *blossom or flower month.*
The second month of the Hebrew year; from the new moon of May to that of June.
1 Ki. 6. 1 in the month Z., which (is) the second mo.
6. 37 was the foundation..laid, in the month Z.

ZI'-HA, צִיחָא.
1. One of the Nethinim, whose descendants returned with Zerubbabel. B.C. 536.
Ezra 2. 43 The Nethinims: the children of Z., the c.
Neh. 7. 46 The Nethinims: the children of Z., the c.
2. A ruler of the Nethinim in Jerusalem. B.C. 536.
Neh. 11. 21 and Z. and Gispa (were) over the Nethin.

ZIK'-LAG, צִקְלַג, צִיקְלַג *winding, bending.*
A city in the S. of Judah, afterwards given to Simeon.
Josh 15. 31 And Z., and Madmannah, and Sansannah
19. 5 And Z., and Beth-marcaboth, and Hazar.
1 Sa. 27. 6 Then Achish gave him Z. that day
27. 6 wherefore Z. pertaineth unto the kings of
30. 1 when David and his men were come to Z.
30. 1 Amalekites..invaded..Z., and smitten Z.
30. 14 We made an invasion..and we burnt Z.
30. 26 when David came to Z., he sent of the sp.
2 Sa. 1. 1 and David had abode two days in Z.
4. 10 I took hold of him, and slew him in Z.
1 Ch. 4. 30 And at Bethuel, and at Hormah, and at Z.
12. 1 these (are) they that came to David to Z.
12. 20 As he went to Z., there fell to him of M.
Neh. 11. 28 at Z., and Mekonah, and in the villages

ZIL'-LAH, צִלָּה *protection, screen.*
One of the wives of Lamech, son of Methusael of the family of Cain. B.C. 3874.
Gen. 4. 19 one..Adah, and the name of the other Z.
4. 22 Z., she also bare Tubal-cain, an instructer
4. 23 Lamech said unto his wives Adah and Z.

ZIL'-PAH, זִלְפָּה *myrrh dropping.*
Handmaid of Leah, eldest daughter of Laban. B.C. 1730.
Gen. 29. 24 Laban gave unto his daughter Leah Z. his
30. 9 she took Z. her maid, and gave her Jacob
30. 10, 12 And Z., Leah's maid, bare Jacob a
35. 26 And the sons of Z., Leah's handmaid; Gad
37. 2 and the lad (was)..with the sons of Z.
46. 18 These (are) the sons of Z., whom Laban

ZIL'-THAI, צִלְּתַי.
1. A Benjamite, son of Shimhi. B.C. 1300.
1 Ch. 8. 20 And Elienai, and Z., and Eliel
2. A captain of Manasseh who joined David in Ziklag. B.C. 1058.
1 Ch. 12. 20 Elihu, and Z., captains of the thousands

ZIM'-MAH, זִמָּה *counsel, consideration.*
1. A son of Jahath, grandson of Gershom son of Levi. B.C. 1370.
1 Ch. 6. 20 Libni his son, Jahath his son, Z. his son
2. A Gershonite in the fourth or fifth degree. B.C. 1600.
1 Ch. 6. 42 The son of Ethan, the son of Z., the son
3. A Gershonite, father of Joah who assisted in cleansing the temple in the days of Hezekiah. B.C. 726.
2 Ch. 29. 12 of the Gershonites; Joah the son of Z., and

ZIM'-RAN, זִמְרָן *celebrated.*
A son of Abraham by Keturah. B.C. 1800.
Gen. 25. 2 And she bare him Z., and Jokshan, and
1 Ch. 1. 32 she bare Z., and Jokshan, and Medan, and

ZIM'-RI, זִמְרִי *celebrated.*
1. Son of a chief Simeonite, slain along with Cozbi a Midianitess, by Phinehas son of Aaron. B.C. 1452.
Num 25. 14 Now the name of the Israelite..(was) Z.
2. A captain who slew Elah, and was himself slain by Omri. B.C. 929.
1 Ki. 16. 9 And his servant Z...conspired against him
16. 10 Z. went in and smote him, and killed him
16. 12 Thus did Z. destroy all the house of Baa.
16. 15 did Z. reign seven days in Tirzah. And the
16. 16 Z. hath conspired, and hath also slain the
16. 18 it came to pass, when Z. saw that the city
16. 20 the rest of the acts of Z...(are) they not
2 Ki. 9. 31 she said, (Had) Z. peace, who slew his mas.
3. A son of Zerah, son of Judah. B.C. 1600.
1 Ch. 2. 6 the sons of Zerah; Z., and Ethan, and H
4. A Benjamite. B.C. 940.
1 Ch. 8. 36 Jehoadah begat Alemeth..and Z.; and Z.
9. 42 Jarah begat Alemeth, and..Z., and Z. be.
5. An unknown place.
Jer. 25. 25 all the kings of Z., and all the kings of E.

ZIN, צִן *low land.*
A desert on the S. of Judah, and W. of the S. end of Salt Sea.
Num 13. 21 they..searched..the wilderness of Z. un.
20. 1 Then came..Israel..into the desert of Z.
27. 14 in the desert of Z.,..in the wilderness of Z
33. 36 And they..pitched in the wilderness of Z.
34. 3 your south quarter shall be from..Z. along
34. 4 And your border shall..pass on to Z.: and
Deut 32. 51 ye trespassed..in the wilderness of Z.
Josh. 15. 1 the wilderness of Z...(was) the uttermost
15. 3 And it went out..and passed along to Z.

ZI'-NA, זִינָא.
A son of Shimei, Gershonite; in ver. 11 it is *Zizah.* B.C. 1015.
1 Ch. 23. 10 the sons of Shimei (were) Jahath, Z., and

ZI'-ON, צִיּוֹן *fortress.* See *Sion.*
The S.W. hill of Jerusalem, the older and higher part of the city; it is often called the city of David.
2 Sa. 5. 7 Nevertheless D. took the stronghold of Z.
1 Ki. 8. 1 they might bring up the ark..out of..Z.
2 Ki. 19. 21 The virgin, the daughter of Z., hath despi.
19. 31 and they that escape out of mount Z.
1 Ch. 11. 5 Nevertheless David took the castle of Z.
2 Ch. 5. 2 assembled..to bring up the ark..out of..Z.
Psa. 2. 6 Yet..set my king upon my holy hill of Z.
9. 11 Sing..to the LORD, which dwelleth in Z.
9. 14 in the gates of the daughter of Z.: I will
14. 7 salvation of Israel (were come) out of Z.
20. 2 Send..help..and strengthen thee out of Z.
48. 2 the joy of the whole earth, (is) mount Z.
48. 11 Let mount Z. rejoice, let the daughters of
48. 12 Walk about Z., and go round about her
50. 2 Out of Z., the perfection of beauty, God
51. 18 Do good in thy good pleasure unto Z.: bu.
53. 6 salvation of Israel (were come) out of Z.!
65. 1 Praise waiteth for thee, O God, in S.: and
69. 35 For God will save Z., and will build the
74. 2 Remember..this mount Z., wherein thou
76. 2 tabernacle, and his dwelling place in Z.
78. 68 chose the tribe of Judah, the mount Z.
84. 7 (every one of them) in Z. appeareth before
87. 2 LORD loveth the gates of Z. more than all
87. 5 of Z. it shall be said, This and that man
97. 8 Z. heard, and was glad; and the daughters
99. 2 LORD (is) great in Z.; and he (is) high ab.
102. 13 Thou shalt arise, (and) have mercy upon Z.
102. 16 When the LORD shall build up Z., he sha.
102. 21 To declare the name of the LORD in Z.
110. 2 shall send the rod of thy strength out of Z.
125. 1 trust in the LORD (shall be) as mount Z.
126. 1 the LORD turned..the captivity of Z.
128. 5 LORD shall bless thee out of Z.: and thou
129. 5 Let them all be confounded..that hate Z.
132. 13 the LORD hath chosen Z.; he hath desired
133. 3 that descended upon the mountains of Z.
134. 3 LORD that made heaven..bless..out of Z.
135. 21 Blessed be the LORD out of Z., which dw.
137. 1 yea, we wept, when we remembered Z.
137. 3 (saying), Sing us (one) of the songs of Z.
146. 10 LORD shall reign for ever..thy God, O Z.
147. 12 Praise the LORD, O Jerusalem..God, O Z.
149. 2 let the children of Z. be joyful in their k.
Song 3. 11 Go forth, O ye daughters of Z., and beho.
Isa. 1. 8 And the daughter of Z. is left as a cottage
1. 27 Z. shall be redeemed with judgment, and
2. 3 for out of Z. shall go forth the law, and
3. 16 Because the daughters of Z. are haughty
3. 17 the LORD will smite..the daughters of Z.
4. 3 (he that is) left in Z...shall be called holy
4. 4 washed..the filth of the daughters of Z.
4. 5 LORD will create upon..mount Z...a cl.
8. 18 LO. of hosts, which dwelleth in mount Z.
10. 12 L...performed his..work upon mount Z.
Isa. 10. 24 O my people that dwellest in Z., be not
10. 32 he shall shake his hand (against) the..Z.
12. 6 Cry out and shout, thou inhabitant of Z.
14. 32 the LORD hath founded Z., and the poor
16. 1 unto the mount of the daughter of Z.
18. 7 be brought..to the place of..the mount Z.
24. 23 LORD of hosts shall reign in mount Z.
28. 16 Behold, I lay in Z. for a foundation a st.
29. 8 multitude of..nations..fight against..Z.
30. 19 the people shall dwell in Z. at Jerusalem
31. 4 shall the LORD of hosts..fight for mount Z.
31. 9 saith the LORD, whose fire (is) in Z., and
33. 5 he hath filled Z. with judgment and righ
33. 14 The sinners in Z. are afraid; fearfulness
33. 20 Look upon Z., the city of our solemnities
34. 8 of recompences for the controversy of Z.
35. 10 ransomed of the LORD shall..come to Z.
37. 22 The virgin, the daughter of Z., hath des.
37. 32 and they that escape out of mount Z.
40. 9 O Z...get thee up into the high mountain
41. 27 The first (shall say) to Z., Behold, behold
46. 13 I will place salvation in Z. for Israel my
49. 14 But Z. said, The LORD hath forsaken me
51. 3 the LORD shall comfort Z.: he will comf.
51. 11 redeemed of..LORD shall..come..unto Z.
51. 16 that I may..say unto Z., Thou (art) my p.
52. 1 Awake, awake; put on thy strength, O Z
52. 2 thyself from the bands..daughter of Z.
52. 7 that saith unto Z., Thy God reigneth!
52. 8 see..when the LORD shall bring again Z.
59. 20 the Redeemer shall come to Z., and unto
60. 14 The city of the LORD, The Z. of the Holy
61. 3 To appoint unto them that mourn in Z.
62. 1 For Z.'s sake will I not hold my peace, and
62. 11 Say ye to the daughter of Z...thy salvat.
64. 10 Z. is a wilderness, Jerusalem a desolation
66. 8 as soon as Z. travailed, she brought forth
Jer. 3. 14 two of a family..I will bring you to Z.
4. 6 Set up the standard toward Z.: retire, stay
4. 31 the voice of the daughter of Z., (that) be.
6. 2 I have likened the daughter of Z. to a co.
6. 23 they ride upon horses..O daughter of Z.
8. 19 (Is) not the LORD in Z.? (is) not her king
9. 19 For a voice of wailing is heard out of Z.
14. 19 hath thy soul loathed Z.? why hast thou
26. 18 Z. shall be plowed (like) a field, and Jeru.
30. 17 This (is) Z., whom no man seeketh after
31. 6 let us go up to Z. unto the LORD our God
31. 12 shall come and sing in the height of Z.
50. 5 They shall ask the way to Z., with their fa.
50. 28 to declare in Z. the vengeance of the LORD
51. 10 let us declare in Z. the work of the LORD
51. 24 evil that they have done in Z. in your si
51. 35 violence..(be) upon Babylon, shall..Z. say
Lam. 1. 4 The ways of Z. do mourn, because none
1. 6 from the daughter of Z. all her beauty is
1. 17 Z. spreadeth forth her hands, (and) there
2. 1 Lord covered the daughter of Z. with a
2. 4 in the tabernacle of the daughter of Z.
2. 6 caused the..sabbaths to be forgotten in Z.
2. 8 hath purposed to destroy the wall..of Z.
2. 10 The elders of the daughter of Z. sit upon
2. 13 what shall I equal to thee..daughter of Z.?
[*See also* 2. 18; 4. 2, 11, 22; 5. 11, 18.]
Joel 2. 1 Blow ye the trumpet in Z., and sound an
2. 15 Blow the trumpet in Z., sanctify a fast
2. 23 Be glad then, ye children of Z., and rejo.
2. 32 in mount Z...shall be deliverance, as the
3. 16 LORD also shall roar out of Z., and utter
3. 17 I (am) the LORD your God dwelling in Z.
3. 21 will cleanse..for the LORD dwelleth in Z.
Amos 1. 2 And he said, The LORD will roar from Z.
6. 1 Woe to them (that are) at ease in Z., and
Obad. 17 But upon mount Z. shall be deliverance
21 saviours shall come upon mount Z. to ju
Mic. 1. 13 beginning of..sin to the daughter of Z.
3. 10 They build up Z. with blood, and Jerusa.
3. 12 Therefore shall Z...be plowed (as) a field
4. 2 the law shall go forth of Z., and the word
4. 7 LORD shall reign over them in mount Z.
4. 8 thou..the stronghold of the daughter of Z.
4. 10 labour to bring forth, O daughter of Z.
4. 11 Let her be defiled..let our eye look upon Z.
4. 13 Arise and thresh, O daughter of Z.: for I
Zeph. 3. 14 Sing, O daughter of Z.; shout, O Israel
3. 16 (and to) Z., Let not thine hands be slack
Zech. 1. 14 I am jealous for Jerusalem and for Z. with
1. 17 the LORD shall yet comfort Z., and shall
2. 7 Deliver thyself, O Z., that dwellest (with)
2. 10 Sing and rejoice, O daughter of Z.; for, lo
8. 2 I was jealous for Z. with great jealousy
8. 3 saith the LORD; I am returned unto Z.
9. 9 Rejoice greatly, O daughter of Z.; shout
9. 13 When I have..raised up thy sons, O Z., ag.

ZI'-OR, צִיעֹר *smallness.*
A city in Judah, near Hebron; now called *Sair.*
Josh 15. 54 Kirjath-arba, which (is) Hebron, and Z.

ZIPH, זִיף *refining place.*
1. A city in the S.E. of Judah.
Josh. 15. 24 Z., and Telem, and Bealoth
1 Sa. 23. 14 David abode..in a mountain in the w. of Z.
23. 15 David (was) in the wilderness of Z. in a
23. 24 And they arose, and went to Z. before S.
26. 2 Saul..went down to the wilderness of Z
26. 2 to seek David in the wilderness of Z.
2 Ch. 11. 8 And Gath, and Mareshah, and Z.
2. Another in Judah, near Carmel or Juttah; now called *Ziph.*
Josh. 15. 55 Maon, Carmel, and Z., and Juttah

3. A patronymic of a grandson of Caleb son of Hezron. B.C. 1500.

1 Ch. 2. 42 his first born, which (was) the father of Z.

4. A son of Jehaleleel. B.C. 1380.

1 Ch. 4. 16 Z., and Ziphah, Tiria, and Asareel

ZI'-PHAH, זִיפָה *lent.*
A son of Jehaleleel, a descendant of Caleb son of Jephunneh. B.C. 1380.

1 Ch. 4. 16 Ziph, and Z., Tiria, and Asareel

ZIPH'-ION, צִפְיוֹן *looking out, serpent, dark.*
A son of Gad, called *Zephon* in Num. 26. 15. B.C. 1680.

Gen. 46. 16 the sons of Gad; Z., and Haggi, Shuni

ZIPHITES, זִיפִים, זִפִים.
The inhabitants of Ziph.

1 Sa. 23. 19 Then came up the Z. to Saul to Gibeah
26. 1 And the Z. came unto Saul to Gibeah
Psa. 54. *title.* when the Z. came and said to Saul

ZIPH'-RON, זִפְרֹן *beautiful top.*
A place at the N. of Palestine.

Num. 34. 9 the border shall go on to Z., and the go.

ZIP'-POR, צִפּוֹר *sparrow, bird.*
Father of Balak king of Moab, who hired Balaam to curse Israel. B.C. 1490.

Num. 22. 2 the son of Z. saw all that Israel had done
22. 4 Balak the son of Z. (was) king of the Moa.
22. 10 Balak the son of Z... hath sent unto me
22. 16 Thus saith Balak the son of Z., Let n th.
23. 18 Rise.. hearken unto me, thou son of Z.
Josh. 24. 9 Balak the son of Z... warred against Isra.
Judg. 11. 25 thou anything better than.. the son of Z.

ZIP-PO'-RAH, צִפֹּרָה *little bird.*
The wife of Moses and daughter of Reuel, Jethro *or* Jether, priest of Midian. B.C. 1500.

Exod. 2. 21 and he gave Moses Z. his daughter
4. 25 Z. took a sharp stone, and cut off the fo.
18. 2 Then Jethro, Moses' father in law, took Z.

ZITH'-RI, סִתְרִי *Jah is protection.*
A son of Uzziel, son of Kohath. B.C. 1530.

Exod. 6. 22 And the sons of Uzziel.. Elzaphan, and Z.

ZIZ, צִיץ *protection.*
A place in S.E. of Judah, near which Jehoshaphat defeated the Moabites and Ammonites. *Husasah? Ain-Jidy?*

2 Ch. 20. 16 behold, they come up by the cliff of Z.

ZI'-ZA, ZI'-ZAH, זִיזָא, זִיזָה *shining, brightness.*
1. A Simeonite, son of Ziphi. B.C. 800.

1 Ch. 4. 37 And Z. the son of Shiphi, the son of Allon

2. A Gershonite, son of Shimei; in verse 10 it is *Zina.* B.C. 1015.

1 Ch. 23. 11 Jahath was the chief, and Z. the second

3. A son of Rehoboam, and grandson of Solomon. B.C. 960.

2 Ch. 11. 20 which bare him Abijah, and Attai.. Z.

ZO'-AN, צֹעַן.
The capital of Egypt on the E. bank of the Tanitic arm of the Nile, the seat of a dynasty in the days of Psammetichus, quoted by Manetho as the twenty-first and twenty-third, built seven years after Hebron; now called *San*, a small village by the lake *Menzeleh.*

Num 13. 22 Hebron was built seven years before Z. in
Psa. 78. 12 Marvellous things did he.. (in).. field of Z.
78. 43 How he.. wrought.. wonders in the.. of Z.
Isa. 19. 11 Surely the princes of Z. (are) fools, the
19. 13 The princes of Z. are become fools, the
30. 4 his princes were at Z., and his ambassad.
Eze. 30. 14 I.. will set fire in Z., and will execute jud.

ZO'-AR, צֹעַר, צוֹעַר *little.*
A small city (once called *Bela*) at the S.E. corner of Salt Sea, afterwards reckoned to Moab, into which Lot and his two daughters fled when Sodom was destroyed; now called *Ziara.*

Gen. 13. 10 the land of Egypt, as thou comest unto Z.
14. 2 and the king of Bela, which is Z.
14. 8 and the king of Bela, the same (is) Z.
19. 22 Therefore the name of the city was.. Z.
19. 23 sun was risen.. when Lot entered into Z.
19. 30 Lot went up out of Z., and dwelt in the
19. 30 he feared to dwell in Z.: and he dwelt in
Deut 34. 3 the plain of the valley of Jericho.. unto Z.
Isa. 15. 5 his fugitives (shall flee) unto Z., an heifer
Jer. 48. 34 they uttered their voice, from Z... unto H.

ZO'-BAH, ZO'-BA, צוֹבָה, צֹבָה, צוֹבָא.
A district and kingdom in Syria, N.E. of Damascus and S. of Hamath, or the land between the Orontes and the Euphrates.

1 Sa. 14. 47 So Saul.. fought against.. the kings of Z.
2 Sa. 8. 3 David smote.. the son of Rehob, king of Z.
8. 5 Syrians.. came to succour Hadadezer.. Z.
8. 12 spoil of Hadadezer, son of Rehob, ki. of Z.
10. 6 children of Ammon.. hired.. Syrians of Z.
10. 8 and the Syrians of Z., and of Rehob, and
23. 36 Igal the son of Nathan of Z., Bani the G.
1 Ki. 11. 23 which fled from his lord Hadadezer.. of Z.
1 Ch. 18. 3 And David smote Hadarezer king of Z.
18. 5 Syrians.. came to.. Hadarezer king of Z.
18. 9 smitten all the host of Hadarezer king of Z.
19. 6 and out of Syria-maachah, and out of Z.
2 Ch. 8. 3 Solomon went to Hamath-z., and prevail.
Psa. 60. *title.* when he strove with.. Aram Z. when Jo.

ZO-BE'-BAH, הַצֹּבֵבָה *the affable.*
A daughter of Coz, a descendant of Judah through Caleb son of Hur. B.C. 1430.

1 Ch. 4. 8 Coz begat Anub, and Z., and the families

ZO'-HAR, צֹחַר *nobility, distinction.*
1. Father of Ephron the Hittite, from whom Abraham purchased the cave of Machpelah. B.C. 1880.

Gen. 23. 8 and entreat for me to Ephron the son of Z.
25. 9 in the field of Ephron the son of Z. the H.

2. A son of Simeon, second son of Judah. B.C. 1690.

Gen. 46. 10 Jamin, and Ohad, and Jachin, and Z., and
Exod. 6. 15 Jamin, and Ohad, and Jachin, and Z., and

ZO-HE'-LETH, זֹחֶלֶת *serpent.*
A stone near En-rogel, S.E. of Jerusalem.

1 Ki. 1. 9 Adonijah slew sheep.. by the stone of Z.

ZO'-HETH, זוֹחֵת *corpulent, strong.*
A son of Ishi, descendant from Judah through Caleb son of Jephunneh. B.C. 1400.

1 Ch. 4. 20 and the sons of Ishi (were) Z., and Ben-Z.

ZO'-PHAH, צוֹפַח *watch.*
A son of Helem, grandson of Beriah son of Asher. B.C. 1570.

1 Ch. 7. 35 the sons of his brother Helem; Z., and
7. 36 The sons of Z.; Suah, and Harnepher, and

ZO'-PHAI, צוֹפַי *watcher.*
A son of Elkanah, father of Samuel the prophet; called Zuph in 1 Sa. 1. 1, and Ziph in 1 Ch. 6. 35. B.C. 1120.

1 Ch. 6. 26 sons of Elkanah; Z. his son, and Nahath

ZO'-PHAR, צוֹפַר *hairy, rough.*
A Naamathite, and friend of Job; probably from Edom. B.C. 1520.

Job 2. 11 Bildad the Shuhite, and Z. the Naamath.
11. 1 Then answered Z. the Naamathite, and
20. 1 Then answered Z. the Naamathite, and
42. 9 Bildad the Shuhite.. Z. the Naamathite

ZO'-PHIM, צֹפִים *watchers.*
1. A place on the top of Pisgah to which Balak brought Balaam. B.C. 1452.

Num 23. 14 And he brought him into the field of Z.

2. A city on Mount Ephraim, the birthplace of Samuel; generally called *Rama.*

1 Sa. 1. 1 Now there was a certain man of R. Z.

ZO'-RAH, ZAREAH, ZOREAH, צָרְעָה *prominent, wasp.*
A city in W. of Judah, reckoned to Dan, near Eshtaol; now called *Surah*, near *Wady Surar.* See *Zareathites.*

Josh 15. 33 in the valley, Eshtaol, and Z., and Ashnah
19. 41 And the coast of their inheritance was Z.
Judg 13. 2 And there was a certain man of Z., of the
13. 25 in the camp of Dan between Z. and Esht.
16. 31 his brethren.. buried him between Z. and
18. 2 children of Dan sent.. five men.. from Z.
18. 8 And they came unto their brethren to Z.
18. 11 there went.. out of Z... six hundred men
2 Ch. 11. 10 And Z., and Aijalon, and Hebron, which
Neh. 11. 29 And at En-rimmon, and at Z., and at Ja

ZORATHITES, צָרְעָתִי.
A family sprung from Shobal son of Judah; or the *Zareathites* of 1 Ch. 2. 53.

1 Ch. 4. 2 These (are) the families of the Z.

ZORITES, צָרְעִי.
A family of Judah, of the posterity of Salma.

1 Ch. 2. 54 and half of the Manahethites the Z.

ZO-RO-BA'-BEL, Ζοροβάβελ. See *Zerubbabel.*
An ancestor of Jesus.

Matt. 1. 12 begat Salathiel; and Salathiel begat Z.
1. 13 Z. begat Abiud; and Abiud begat Eliak.
Luke 3. 27 Rhesa, which was (the son) of Z., which

ZU'-AR צוּעָר *little.*
Father of Nethaneel, a chief of Issachar, chosen to aid Moses to number the people. B.C. 1520.

Num. 1. 8 Of Issachar; Nethaneel the son of Z.
2. 5 and Nethaneel the son of Z. (shall be) ca.
7. 18 On the second day Nethaneel the son of Z.
7. 23 the offering of Nethaneel the son of Z.
10. 15 over the host.. Nethaneel the son of Z.

ZUPH, צוּף *honey comb.* See *Zophai.*
1. A Kohathite, ancestor of Samuel the prophet. B.C. 1280.

1 Sa. 1. 1 Elihu, the son of Tohu, the son of Z., an
1 Ch. 6. 35 The son of Z., the son of Elkanah, the son

2. A district N.W. of Jerusalem. See *Ramathaim-Zophim.*

1 Sa. 9. 5 when they were come to the land of Z.

ZUR, צוּר *rock.*
1. A prince of Midian, and father of Cozbi who was slain by Phinehas. B.C. 1480.

Num. 25. 15 woman.. (was) Cozbi, the daughter of Z.
31. 8 Evi, and Rekem, and Z., and Hur, and R.
Josh. 13. 21 Evi, and Rekem, and Z., and Hur, and R.

2. A Benjamite, brother of Ner the grandfather of Saul the first king of Israel. B.C. 1250.

1 Ch. 8. 30 his first born son Abdon, and Z., and Kish
9. 36 his first born son Abdon, then Z., and K.

ZUR-I'-EL, צוּרִיאֵל *God is a rock.*
A Merarite, son of Abihail, and head of the families. B.C. 1490.

Num. 3. 35 And the chief.. (was) Z. the son of Abih

ZU-RI-SHAD'-DAI, צוּרִישַׁדַּי *the Almighty is a rock.*
Father of Shelumiel, a chief of Simeon, chosen to aid Moses to number the people. B.C. 1510.

Num. 1. 6 Of Simeon; Shelumiel the son of Z.
2. 12 captain.. (shall be) Shelumiel.. son of Z.
7. 36 On the fifth day Shelumiel the son of Z.
7. 41 the offering of Shelumiel the son of Z.
10. 19 over the host.. Shelumiel the son of Z.

ZU'-ZIMS, זוּזִים *prominent, strong, giant.*
A primitive race in the country afterwards possessed by the children of Ammon.

Gen. 14. 5 the Z. in Ham, and the Emims in Shaveh

INDEX-LEXICON TO THE OLD TESTAMENT.

EXPLANATORY NOTE.—Regarding these index-lexicons, see reviser's preface. They are dictionaries and indexes to parallel passages. They show all the meanings of the original Greek, Hebrew, and Aramaic words in the Bible, and the number of times each occurs in our English version. Rare words, occurring once or twice, and, therefore, often of doubtful meaning, may be recognised by means of this record, and the large numbers are sometimes a useful guide to the most literal meaning of a word. Whenever the translation is clearly not literal it is marked by * or † (see below). Meanings of frequent occurrence are sometimes marked *freq.*, and in a few unimportant cases the number is entirely omitted. The index-lexicons are also, particularly, a means of finding all, or most, of the passages where the same original word is used in the Bible. The concordance already places together under each English word the passages which belong to the same original. The index, by giving all the meanings of that original, shows what English words in the concordance must be turned up to find other passages where it is used. It will be found that the best index of such parallels must also be a lexicon. In the case of a Hebrew verb, for instance, it should be noticed that the only exact parallels to a Hiph. are Hiph. meanings, to a Piel, Piel meanings, etc. The verb has generally different meanings, according as it is a Hiph. or one of the other verb forms (indicated in the concordance by the Nos. 1-7 ; see general preface). Words in italic capitals are Aramaic, not Hebrew. Aramaic words identical with Hebrew have not always been printed separately.

A אָע
timber 3
wood 2.

AB[1] אָב
father *freq.*
*chief 3
*principal 1.
†fatherless (en[1] ab) 1; forefather (*with* rishon) 1; patrimony (al[2] *with plur. of* ab) 1.

AB[2] אֵב
desire 1.

AB[3] עָב
clay 1
cloud 23
thick beam 1
thick cloud 7
thicket 1.
†thick plank (*with* ets) 1.

AB אַב
father 9.

ABABUOTH אֲבַעְבֻּעֹת *f. pl.*
blains 2.

ABAD[1] אבד
be broken 1
be destroyed 4
be lost 8
be perished 12
be ready to perish 4
be undone 1
be void of 1
fail 2
perish 79
*not have 1
Inf. destruction 1
Adv. inf. surely 2
utterly 1
PIEL cause to perish 2
destroy 33
lose 1
make to perish 2
spend 1
*be destroyed 1
Adv. inf. utterly 1
HIPH. cause to perish 1
destroy 24
*take 1.
†KAL, lose (*with* min) 1
See manos.

ABAD[2] עבד
be servants 1
become servants 1
bring to pass 1
do 14
do service 3
do work 1
dress 2
ear 1
execute 1
keep 1
labour 2
serve 14
serve self 1
till 6
work 3
Partic. labouring man 1
servant 3
tiller 2
worshipper 5
NIPH. be eared 1
be served 1
be tilled 2
PUAL be made serve 1
be wrought 1
HIPH. cause to serve 3
keep in bondage 1
make to serve 3
set a work 1
HOPH. serve 4.
†KAL, *with* be: compel to serve 1, make to serve 1, use service 1, *be bondmen 1. *Partic.* bond service (*with* mas) 1. *See* ish.

ABAD[3] עֲבַד
work 1.

ABAD[1] אבד
perish 1
HAPH. destroy 4
*perish 1
HOPH. be destroyed 1.

ABAD[2] עבד
do 10
keep 1
make 5
move 1
work 2
HITHP. be cut 1
be done 3
be executed 1
be made 2
go on 1.

ABAD[3] עֲבַד
servant 7.

ABADDON אֲבַדּוֹן
destruction 6.

ABAH[1] אבה
be willing 4
consent 3
rest content 1
will 46.

ABAH[2] עבה
be grown thick 1
be thick[er] 2.

ABAK אבך
HITHP. mount up 1.

ABAL[1] אבל
lament 1
mourn 17.
HIPH. cause a mourning 1
make to lament 1
HITHP. feign self a mourner 1
lament 1
mourn 17.

ABAL[2] אֲבָל
but 4
indeed 2
nevertheless 2
verily 3.

ABAQ[1] אָבָק
dust 4
powder 1
small dust 1.

ABAQ[2] אבק
NIPH. wrestle 2.

ABAQAH אֲבָקָה *f.*
powder 1.

ABAR[1] אבר
HIPH. fly 1

ABAR[2] עבר
be altered 1
be come over 5
be delivered 1
be gone 2
be gone over 1
be overpast 2
be passed 2
be passed over 6
be past 9
come 7
come on 1
come over 3
enter 1
escape 1
fail 2
get over 1
go 24
go away 1
go beyond 2
go by 3
go forth 2
go his way 1
go in 1
go on 6
go over 51
go through 9
have more 1
overcome 1
overpass 1
overrun 2
pass 83
pass along 8
pass away 10
pass away from 1
pass beyond 1
pass by 35
pass on 19
pass out 1
pass over 81
pass through 21
perish 2
transgress 19
Partic. current 1
passage 1
passenger 4
passing 6
sweet-smelling 1
transgressing 1
transgressor 1
Adv. inf. speedily 1
NIPH. be passed over 1
PIEL gender 1
make a partition 1
HIPH. alienate 1
bring 3
bring over 4
bring through 1
carry over 3
cause to pass 16
cause to sound 1
conduct 1
conduct over 1
convey over 1
do away 1
have away 1
lay away 1
let pass 2
make go 2
make pass 12
make pass by 1
make proclamation 1
make sound 1
make transgress 1
pass 1
put away 4
remove 1
send over 2
set apart 1
take 2
take away 3
translate 1
turn away 2
*beyond 1
Adv. inf. at all 1
HITHP. be wroth 5
meddle 1
provoke to anger 1
rage 1
†KAL, *be charged (*with* al[2]) 1. *Partic.* passenger (*with* derek) 1; wayfarer (*with* orach) 1; wayfaring man (*with* orach) 1. HIPH. cause to be proclaimed (*with* qol) 1; proclaim (*with* qol) 1; shave (*with* taar) 1.
Partic. raiser of taxes (*with* noges) 1.

ABAR עֲבַר
beyond 7
this side 7.

ABARAH עֲבָרָה *f.*
ferry boat 1.

ABAS אבס
Partic. fatted 1
stalled 1.

ABASH עבש
be rotten 1.

ABAT עבט
borrow 1
fetch [a pledge] 1
PIEL break [ranks] 1
HIPH. lend 2
Adv. inf. surely 1.

ABATH עבת
wrap up 1.

ABATTICHIM אֲבַטִּחִים *pl.*
melons 1.

ABBIR אַבִּיר
angel 1
bull 4
chiefest 1
mighty 3
mighty one 1
strong 2
strong one 1
valiant 2.
†stout-hearted (*with* leb) 2.

ABDUTH עַבְדוּת *f.*
bondage 3.

ABEDAH אֲבֵדָה *f.*
lost thing 1
that which was lost 1.

ABEL[1] אָבֵל
mourner 2
mourning 2
one that mourneth 1
that mourn 1
them that mourn 1
*to mourn 1.

ABEL[2] אָבֵל *f.*
plain 1.

ABEDAN (אָבְדָן) אַבְדָן
destruction 2.

ABI עֳבִי
thick 1.

ABIB אָבִיב
ear 1
green ears of corn 1.

ABIDAH עֲבִידָה *f.*
affairs 2
service 1
work 8.

ABIR אָבִיר
mighty 6.

ABIYONAH אֲבִיּוֹנָה *f.*
desire 1.

ABNET אַבְנֵט
girdle 9.

ABODAH עֲבוֹדָה *f.*
act 2
bondage 8
effect 1
labour 1
ministry 1
office 1
service 112
servitude 2
them that wrought 1
those that serve 1
tillage 2
use 1
work 6
*ministering 1
*servile 11.
†bond servant (*with* ebed) 1. *Repeated*: all manner of service 1, any manner of service 1, every kind of service 1.

ABOT עֲבוֹט
pledge 4.

ABOTH[1] עָבֹת
thick 4

ABOTH[2] עֲבֹת
band 4
cord 5
rope 3
thick bough 3
thick branch 2
wreathen chain 2
*wreathen 6.

ABOY אֲבוֹי
sorrow 1.

ABREK אַבְרֵךְ
bow the knee 1.

ABTIT עַבְטִיט
thick clay 1.

ABUDDAH עֲבֻדָּה *f.*
household 1
store of servants 1.

ABUR[1] עָבוּר
old corn 2.

ABUR[2] *See* BA-ABUR.

ACH[1] אָח
another 24
brother *freq.*
kindred 1
like 1
other 2
*brotherly 1.

ACH[2] אָח
ah 1
alas 1

ACH[3] אָח *f.*
hearth 3.

ACHAD[1] = ECHAD.

ACHAD[2] אחד
HITHP. go one way or other 1.

ACHALAI אַחֲלַי
would God 1.

ACHALE אַחֲלֵי
O that 1.

ACHAR[1] אחר
stay there 1
tarry longer 1
PIEL be late 1
be slack 2
continue 1
defer 3
delay 1
hinder 1
tarry 6.

ACHAR[2] (**ACHARE**) אַחַר (אַחֲרֵי)
after 408
after that 26
afterward 29
at 1
backside 1
behind 49
beside 2
by 1
following after 1
following 23
forasmuch as 1
hereafter 1
hinder end 1
posterity 4
pursuing 2
remnant 1
*follow 18
*since 1
*when 1.
†again (*lit.* behind thee) 1; forasmuch as (*with* asher) 2; seeing that (*with* asher) 1. *With* ken: after that, after this, afterward, following thenceforth, etc. *See* arak[1], bo, halak, hayah, me, radaph, yalak, zanah.

ACHARE אַחֲרֵי
after 1.
†thereafter (with *denah*) 2.

ACHARITH אַחֲרִית *f.*
end 21
last (*n.*) 2
last end 4
last of them 1
latter end 8
latter time 1
length 1
posterity 3
remnant 1
residue 1
reward 2
*hindermost 1
*last (*adj.*) 3
*latter 11
*uttermost 1.

ACHARITH אַחֲרִית *f.*
*latter 2

ACHARON אַחֲרוֹן
after 5
afterward 1
following 1
hinder 1
hindermost 1
hindmost 1
last 20
latter 8
rearward 1
to come 9
utmost 2
uttermost 1.
†ba-acharonah: afterward 1, afterwards 1.

ACHASHDARPENAYYA אֲחַשְׁדַּרְפְּנַיָּא *pl.*
princes 9.

ACHASHDARPENIM אֲחַשְׁדַּרְפְּנִים *pl.*
lieutenants 4.

ACHASHTERANIM אֲחַשְׁתְּרָנִים *pl.*
camels 2.

ACHATH = ECHAD.

ACHAVAH אַחֲוָה *f.*
brotherhood 1.

ACHAVAYAH אַחֲוָיָה *f.*
shewing 1.

ACHAZ אחז
bar 1
catch 2
catch hold 1
come upon 1
fasten 2
handle 1
hold 11
lay hold 3
rest 1
surprise 1

* Inexact translations, *e.g.*, of a noun by a verb or adjective, of an active by a passive.
† Cases where two or more words in the original are translated by one word or by a phrase.

take 15
take hold 15
Pass. pt. portion 2
NIPH. be caught 1
be possessed 1
be taken 1
get possessions 1
have possession 2
take possessions 1
PIEL hold back 1
HOPH. be fastened 1.
†KAL, be affrighted (*with* saar) 1.

ACHER אַחֵר
another 54
another man 2
following 1
next 2
other 103
other man 1
strange 1

ACHIDAN אֲחִידָן *pl.*
hard sentences 1.

ACHLAMAH אַחְלָמָה *f.*
amethyst 2.

ACHOR אָחוֹר
afterwards 1
back 12
back part 1
backside 2
backward 10
behind 4
hinder part 3
time to come 1
without 1.
†back (le-achor) 2; backward (le-achor) 1; behind (me-achor) 1; hereafter (le-achor) 1

ACHORANNITH אֲחֹרַנִּית *f.*
back again 1
backward 6.

ACHOTH אָחוֹת *f.*
another 6
other 1
sister *freq.*
†*See* ishshah.

ACHU אָחוּ
flag 1
meadow 2.

ACHUZZAH אֲחֻזָּה *f.*
possession 66.

ACHVAH אַחְוָה *f.*
declaration 1.

AD[1] עַד (עֲדֵי)
even to
for
into
so long as
so that
till
toward
until, etc.
†as yet (*with* attah[2], *with* ken); hither (*with* henah); hitherto (*with* halom, *with* henah, *with* koh); how long (*with* mathai); past (*with* ayin[1]); perish for ever (ade obed) 2; since (*with* henah); thus far (*with* henah); till (*with* ki); until (*with* ki); world without end (*with* alam (*pl.*) *and* ad[2]); yet (*with* henah). Ad meod: greatly 1, sore 1, very 4, very much 1.

AD[2] עַד
eternity 1
ever 42
everlasting 2
evermore 1
old 1
perpetually 1.
†*See* ad[1].

AD[3] עַד
prey 3.

AD עַד
for
till
to
until
unto, etc.
†hitherto (with *kah*).

ADA. *See ADAH.*

ADAB אדב
HIPH. grieve 1.

ADAH[1] עדה
adorn 1
be adorned 1
be decked 1
deck 2
deck self 3.

ADAH[2] עדה
pass by 1
HIPH. take away 1.

ADAH עדה (עדא)
alter (*intr.*) 1
be departed 1
pass 1
pass away 1
APH. have . . . taken away 1
remove 1
take 1
take away 1.

ADAM[1] אָדָם
another 1
low 1
man *freq.*
man of low degree 1
mean man 3
person 8.
†hypocrite (*with* chaneph[2]) 1. *See* ben[2], rob.

ADAM[2] אדם
be ruddy 1
PUAL be dyed red 5
be red 1
be made red 1
HIPH. be red 1
HITHP. be red 1.

ADAMAH אֲדָמָה *f.*
country 1
earth 53
ground 43
husbandry 1
land 125.
†*See* ish[1].

ADAMDAM אֲדַמְדָּם
reddish 4
somewhat reddish 2

ADAN עדן
HITHP. delight selves 1.

ADANIM עֲדָנִים *pl.*
delicates 1
delights 1
pleasures 1.

ADAPH עדף
Part. odd number 1
overplus 1
that (which) remaineth 4
that were over and above 2
which are more 1
HIPH. have over 1.

ADAR[1] אדר
NIPH. become glorious 1
Partic. glorious 1
HIPH. make honourable 1.

ADAR[2] עדר
NIPH. be lacking 1
fail 4
lack 1
PIEL lack 1.

ADAR[3] עדר
keep rank 2
NIPH. be digged 2.

ADARGAZERAIYA אֲדַרְגָּזְרַיָּא *pl.*
judges 2.

ADARKONIM אֲדַרְכֹּנִים *pl.*
drams 2.

ADASHIM עֲדָשִׁים *pl.*
lentiles 4.

ADDERETH אַדֶּרֶת *f.*
garment 4
glory 2
mantle 5
robe 1
*goodly 1.

ADDIR אַדִּיר
excellent 4
famous 2
gallant 1
glorious 1
goodly 1
lordly 1
mightier 1
mighty 4
mighty one 1
noble 7
principal 3
worthy 1.

ADE = **AD**[1]

ADEN עֲדֶן
yet 1.

ADENNAH עֲדֶנָּה
yet 1.

ADI עֲדִי
mouth 2
ornament 11
*excellent 1.

ADIN עָדִין
given to pleasures 1.

ADMONI אַדְמֹנִי
red 1
ruddy 2.

ADOM אָדוֹם
red 7
ruddy 1.

ADON אָדוֹן
lord *freq.*
master *freq.*
owner 1
sir 1.

ADONAI אֲדֹנָי
Lord *freq.*
my Lord 1.

ADRAZDA אַדְרַזְדָּא
diligently 1.

AGAB עגב
dote 6.
Partic. lover 1.

AGABAH עֲגָבָה *f.*
inordinate love 1.

AGABIM עֲגָבִים *pl.*
much love 1
*very lovely 1.

AGALAH עֲגָלָה *f.*
cart 15
chariot 1
wagon 9.

AGAM[1] אֲגַם (אֲגָם)
pond 3
pool 4
reed 1.
†standing water (*with* mayim) 2.

AGAM[2] עגם
be grieved 1.

AGAN עגן
NIPH. stay 1.

AGAPPIM אֲגַפִּים *pl.*
bands 7.

AGAR אגר
gather 3.

AGARTELIM אֲגַרְטְלִים *pl.*
chargers 2.

AGGAN אַגָּן
bason 1
cup 1
goblet 1.

AGIL עָגִיל
earrings 2.

AGMON אַגְמוֹן
bulrush 1
caldron 1
hook 1
rush 2.

AGOL עָגוֹל
round 6.

AGORAH אֲגוֹרָה *f.*
†piece of silver (*with* keseph) 1.

AGUDDAH אֲגֻדָּה *f.*
bunch 1
burden 1
troop 1.

AGUR עָגוּר
swallow 2.

AHAB אהב
like 1
love *freq.*
Partic. friend 11
lover 4
Pass. pt. beloved 5
Inf. in love 1
NIPH. *pt.* lovely 1
PIEL *pt.* lover 14
friend 1.

AHABAH אַהֲבָה *f.*
love 30.

AHABIM אֲהָבִים *pl.*
lovers 1
*loving 1

AHAH אֲהָהּ
ah 8
alas 7.

AHAL[1] אהל
pitch a tent 1
remove a tent 1
PIEL pitch a tent 1.

AHAL[2] אהל
HIPH. shine 1.

AHALIM (AHALOTH) (אֲהָלוֹת) אֲהָלִים *pl.*
aloes 3
trees of lign aloes 1.

AHEB = **AHAB.**

AK אַךְ
at least
but
certainly
howbeit
nevertheless
only
save
surely
truly
yet, etc.

AKAL אכל
burn up 1
consume 26
devour 101
devour up 1
dine 1
eat 566
eat up 19
feed 2
*be devoured 2
Partic. devourer 1
eater 3
Inf. food 1
meat 4
Adv. inf. at all 1
freely 2
in [no] wise 1
indeed 1
in plenty 1
quite 1
NIPH. be consumed 2
be devoured 5
be eaten 36
*eat 1
Adv. inf. at all 2
PIEL consume 1
PUAL be consumed 3
be devoured 2
HIPH cause to eat 3
feed 12
give to eat 1
lay meat 1
*consume 1.

AKAL אכל
devour 4
eat 1.
†accuse (with *qaretsin*) 2.

AKAPH אכף
crave 1.

AKAR עכר
trouble 12
NIPH. be stirred 1
Partic. trouble 1.

AKAS עכס
PIEL make a tinkling 1.

AKBAR עַכְבָּר
mouse 6.

AKEN אָכֵן
but
certainly
nevertheless
surely
truly
verily.

AKILAH אֲכִילָה *f.*
meat 1.

AKKABISH עַכָּבִישׁ
spider 2.

AKSHUB עַכְשׁוּב
adder 1.

AKZAB אַכְזָב
liar 1
lie 1.

AKZAR אַכְזָר
cruel 3
fierce 1.

AKZARI אַכְזָרִי
cruel 7
cruel one 1.

AKZERIYUTH אַכְזְרִיּוּת *f.*
*cruel 1.

AL[1] אַל
nay
not.
†neither, never, no, none, nor, etc.

AL[2] עַל
above
against
beside
concerning
on
over
upon, etc.
†according to (al pene) 2; as (*with* panim) 1; because (*with* dabar asher) 2; because of (*with* dabar 4, *with* odoth 5) 9; concerning (*with* dabar 3, with odoth 2) 5; for (*with* dabar) 1; fitly (*with pl.* (*dual*) *of* ophen) 1; have charge of ([hayah] al) 1; in (*with* panim 3, *with* peh 1) 4; near (*with* vad) 2; throughout (al pene) 1; toward (*with* pene) 5; upon (*with* pene) 1; upside down (*with* panim, *and pron.*) 1. *With* ken: because, for which cause, therefore, thus, wherefore, etc. *See* eber[2], ke, leb, lebab, male, me-al, panim.

AL[3] עַל (עָל)
above 3
most High 2
on high 1.

AL[1] אַל
not 3
†nor (*ve-al*) 1.

AL[2] עַל
about
against
concerning
on
over
to
unto
upon
with, etc.
†therefore (with *denah*) 1; thereon (*with pronoun*); why (with *mah*).

ALA עלע
PIEL suck up 1.

ALA עֲלַע
rib 1.

ALACH אלח
NIPH. become filthy 3.

ALAH[1] אלה
curse 1
swear 2
HIPH. adjure 1
cause to swear 1
make to swear 1.

ALAH[2] אָלָה
curse 14
cursing 4
execration 2
oath 14
swearing 1.

ALAH[3] אלה
lament 1.

ALAH[4] עלה
arise (up) 5
ascend (up, into) 17
be burnt 1
be come up 23
be cut off 1
be gone away 1
be gone up 17
be grown over 1
be laid 1
be offered 1
be put 1
begin to spring 1
break 1
climb (up) 5
come (in) 20
come up 140
depart 1
fall 2
get up 24
go 8
go away 1
go up 302
grow (up) 3
increase 4
leap 2
mount up 4
rise (up) 9
scale 1
shoot forth 1
spring up 1
*offer 1
Partic. vapour 1
Inf. breaking 1
dawning 1
offering 2
shooting up 1
spring 1
Adv. inf. at once 1
surely 1
NIPH. be broken up 1
be brought up 1
be exalted 2
be gone up 1
be taken up 9
depart 1
get up 2
go up 1
HIPH. bring 11
bring up 92
carry up 7
cast up 2
cause to ascend 3
cause to burn 2
cause to come up 8
chew 9
fetch up 3
levy 1
lift up 2
light 6
make come up 4
make go up 1
make pay 1
make rise up 1
offer (up) 77
prefer 1
put (on) 2
raise (up) 3
restore 1
set (up) 3
stir up 1
take away 1
take up 7
work 1
HOPH. be brought up 1
be mentioned 1
be offered 1
HITHP. lift self up 1.
†KAL, excel (*with* al[2]) 1. *See* arukah.

ALAH עֲלָה *f.*
burnt offering 1.

ALAL[1] עלל
POEL affect 1
do 3
glean 5
Partic. children 1
Adv. inf. throughly 1
POAL be done 1
HITHPA. abuse 3
mock 2
work 1
work wonderfully 1
HITHPO. practise 1.

ALAL[2] עלל
POEL defile 1

ALAL עלל
come 1
come in 1
go (in) 3
HAPH. bring in 4
*be brought 1
HOPH. be brought in 1.

ALAM[1] אלם
NIPH. be dumb 7
be put to silence 1
become dumb 1
PIEL bind 1.

ALAM[2] עלם
Pass.part. secret 1
NIPH. be hid 8
be hidden 1
Partic. dissembler 1
secret thing 1
HIPH. blind 1
hide 8
Adv. inf. any ways 1
HITHP. be hid 1
hide self 5.

ALAM עָלַם
ever 13
everlasting 4
old 2
†never (*la le-alemin*) 1.

ALAPH[1] אלף
learn 1
PIEL teach 2
utter 1.

ALAPH[2] אָלַף
HIPH. bring forth thousands 2.

* Inexact translations, *e.g.*, of a noun by a verb or adjective, of an active by a passive.
† Cases where two or more words in the original are translated by one word or by a phrase.

ALAPH[3] עלף
PUAL faint 1
Partic. overlaid 1
HITHP. faint 2
wrap self 1.

ALAPH אֲלַף (אֶלֶף)
thousand 3.

ALAS עלס
rejoice 1
NIPH. *pt.* *goodly 1
HITHP. solace self 1.

ALATAH עֲלָטָה *f.*
twilight 3
*dark 1.

ALATS[1] אלץ
PIEL urge 1.

ALATS[2] עלץ
be joyful 1
rejoice 6
triumph 1.

ALAZ עלז
be joyful 2
greatly rejoice 1
rejoice 11
triumph 2.

ALEH עָלֶה
branch 6
leaf 12.

ALELAI אַלְלַי
woe 2.

ALEMA = ***ALAM.***

ALEZ עָלֵז
that rejoiceth 1.

ALGUMMIM אַלְגּוּמִּים *pl.*
algum trees 3.

ALIL עֲלִיל
furnace 1.

ALILAH עֲלִילָה *f.*
act 1
action 1
deed 2
doing 14
invention 1
occasion 2
work 3.

ALILIYAH עֲלִילִיָּה *f.*
work 1.

ALITSUTH עֲלִיצוּת *f.*
rejoicing 1.

ALIYAH עֲלִיָּה *f.*
ascent 1
chamber 8
going up 2
loft 1
parlour 1
upper chamber 4.

ALLAH אַלָּה *f.*
oak 1.

ALLIZ עַלִּיז
joyous 3.
rejoicing 1
that rejoice 2
them that rejoice 2.

ALLON אַלּוֹן
oak 8.

ALLUPH אַלּוּף (אלף)
captain 1
chief friend 2
duke 57
friend 1
governor 3
guide 4
ox 2.

ALMAH עַלְמָה *f.*
damsel 1
maid 2
virgin 4.

ALMAN אַלְמָן
forsaken 1.

ALMANAH אַלְמָנָה *f.*
widow 53

ALMANOTH אַלְמָנוֹת *pl.*
desolate houses 1
desolate palaces 1

ALMANUTH אַלְמָנוּת *f.*
widow 1
widowhood 5.

ALMON אַלְמוֹן
widowhood 1.

ALMONI אַלְמֹנִי
†*See* peloni.

ALMUGGIM אַלְמֻגִּים *pl.*
almug trees 3.

ALQUM אַלְקוּם
no rising up 1.

ALU אֲלוּ
behold 5.

ALUMIM עֲלוּמִים *pl.*
youth 4.

ALUMMAH אֲלֻמָּה *f.*
sheaf 5.

ALUQAH עֲלוּקָה *f.*
horseleach 1.

ALVAH עַלְוָה *f.*
iniquity 1.

ALYAH אַלְיָה *f.*
rump 5.

AM עַם
folk 2
men 1
nation 17
people 1835.
†*Repeated*: every people 4. *See* ben[2].

AM עַם
people 15.

AMAD עמד
abide 4
abide behind 1
arise 2
be 1
be at a stay 1
be employed 1
be present 1
cease 1
continue 6
dwell 1
endure 8
leave 2
remain 8
stand (by, fast, firm, still, up) *freq.*
stay 15
tarry 2
wait 5
withstand 2
HIPH. appoint 12
cause to stand 1
confirm 2
establish 5
make 2
make stand 1
make be at a stand 1
ordain 1
place 1
present 4
present self 1
raise (up) 2
repair 1
set (forth, over, up) 46
settle 1
stablish 1
stay 1
HOPH. be presented 1
be stayed up 1.
†serve (*with* li-phene) 2; withstand (*with prepos.*) 4.

AMAH אָמָה *f.*
bondmaid 2
bondwoman 4
handmaid 23
maid 8
maid-servant 19.

AMAL[1] אמל
Pass.part. weak 1
PULAL be waxed feeble 1
languish 14.

AMAL[2] עמל
labour 8
take [labour] 3.

AMAL[3] עָמָל
grievance 1
grievousness 1
iniquity 1
labour 25
mischief 9
misery 4
pain 2
perverseness 1
sorrow 2
toil 1
travail 3
trouble 2
wickedness 1
*miserable 1
*painful 1
*wearisome 1.

AMAM עמם
hide 2
HOPH. become dim 1.

AMAN[1] אמן
bring up 3
Partic. bringer up 1
faithful 3
nurse 2
nursing father 1
NIPH. be established 7
be faithful 17
be of long continuance 2
be nursed 1
be steadfast 2
be verified 3
stand fast 1
Partic. sure 10
that which shall surely 1
trusty 1.
HIPH. believe 45
have assurance 1
put trust 2
trust 3.
†NIPH. fail (*with* lo *prefixed*) 1.

AMAN[2] אמן
HIPH. turn to the right 1.

AMAN[3] אָמָן
cunning workman 1.

AMAN אֲמַן
HAPH. believe 1
Pass. pt. faithful 1
sure 1.

AMANAH אֲמָנָה *f.*
certain portion 1
*sure 1.

AMAQ עמק
be deep 1
HIPH. be profound 1
make deep 1
seek deep 1
*deep 2
*deeply 1
*in the depth 1.
†HIPH. *with* sarah[1]: revolt deeply 1.

AMAR[1] אמר (אָמַר)
answer 98
appoint 3
bid 13
call 2
certify 1
challenge 1
charge 1
command 29
commune 1
consider 1
declare 1
demand 1
desire 2
determine 1
give commandment 1
intend 3
name 3
promise 6
publish 1
purpose 2
report 2
require 1
say *freq.*
speak 168
speak against 1
speak of 11
suppose 1
talk 2
tell 41
think 14
use [speech] 1
utter 1
*be answered 1
*be reported 1
*be said 5
*be told 1
*commandment 1
*that is 1
Adv. inf. expressly 1
indeed 1
plainly 1
still 1
verily 1
yet 1
NIPH. be called 5
be said 13
be termed 2
be told 2
*call 1
HIPH. avouch 2
HITHP. boast self 1.

AMAR[2] עמר
PIEL bind sheaves 1
HITHP. make merchandise 2.

AMAR[1] אמר
command 12
declare 1
say 45
speak 4
tell 9.

AMAR[2] עֲמַר
wool 1.

AMAS עמס (*once* עמשׂ)
bear 1
burden self with 1
lade 2
load 1
load heavy 1
Part. laded 1
HIPH. lade 1
put 1.

AMATS אמץ
be courageous 2
be of good courage 9
be strong (stronger) 4
prevail 1.
PIEL confirm 1
establish 1
fortify 1
harden 2
increase 1
make obstinate 1
make strong 3
strengthen 9
HIPH. strengthen 2
HITHP. be steadfastly minded 1
make speed 2
strengthen self 2.

AMEL עָמֵל
that laboureth 4
that is in misery 1
wicked 1
workman 1
*take [labour] 2.

AMELAL אֲמֵלָל
feeble 1.

AMEN אָמֵן
amen 27
so be it 1
truth 2.

AMEQ עָמֵק
deeper 1
depth 1
strange 2.

AMIQ עַמִּיק
deep 1.

AMIR[1] אָמִיר
bough 1
branch 1.

AMIR[2] עָמִיר
handful 1
sheaf 3.

AMITH עָמִית
another 2
fellow †
neighbour 9.

AMMAH אַמָּה *f.*
cubit 242
measure 1
post 1.

AMMIN אַמִּין *pl.*
cubits 4.

AMMITS אַמִּיץ (אמץ)
mighty 1
strong 3
strong one 1.
†courageous (*with* leb) 1.

AMMUD עַמּוּד
pillar 109.
†apiece (*with* echad) 1; either of them (*with* sheni) 1.

AMON אָמוֹן
multitude 2
one brought up 1
populous 1.

AMOQ עָמֹק
deep 14
deep things (*pl.*) 1.
†*Repeated*; exceeding deep 1.

AMTACHATH אַמְתַּחַת *f.*
sack 15.

AMTSAH אַמְצָה *f.*
strength 1.

AMUTSTSIM אֲמֻצִּים *pl.*
bay 2.

AN אָן (אָנָה ; אָנָה)
where?
whither?
whithersoever, etc.
† any whither (*repeated*); how long (ad[1] an).

ANA אֲנָא (אֲנָה)
as for me 2
I 14.

ANACH אנח
NIPH. groan 1
mourn 1
sigh 10.

ANACHAH אֲנָחָה *f.*
groaning 4
mourning 1
sigh 1
sighing 5.

ANACHNA אֲנַחְנָא (אֲנַחְנָה)
we 4.

ANACHNU אֲנַחְנוּ
ourselves
us
we.

ANAD ענד
bind 1
tie 1.

ANAG ענג
PUAL *pt.* delicate 1
HITHP. be delighted 1
delight selves 5
have delight 1
sport selves 12
Inf. delicateness 1.

ANAH (ANA) אָנָּה (אָנָּא)
I beseech thee 7
I pray thee 2
Oh, O 3
we beseech thee 1.

ANAH[1] אנה
lament 1
mourn 1.

ANAH[2] אנה
PIEL deliver 1
PUAL befall 1
happen 1.
HITHP. seek a quarrel 1.

ANAH[3] = **AN.**

ANAH[4] ענה
answer 234
bear witness 1
bear [witness] 2
cause to answer 1
cry 2
give answer 1
give a shout 1
give account 1
hear 41
lift up 1
make answer 5
say unto 1
shout 1
sing 5
sing together by course 1
speak 8
testify 12
utter 1
witness 2
Partic. scholar 1
NIPH. answer 2
be answered 1
be heard 2
PIEL sing 2
HIPH. answer 1.

ANAH[5] ענה
abase self 1
be afflicted 2
be brought low 1
be exercised 2
be troubled 1
*afflict 1
Inf. gentleness 1
NIPH. be afflicted 3
humble self 1
PIEL afflict 37
deal hardly with 1
defile 1
force 5
humble 10
hurt 1
ravish 1
weaken 1
Adv. inf. in any wise 1
PUAL be afflicted 4
Inf. afflictions 1
HIPH. afflict 2
HITHP. afflict self 1
be afflicted 2
chasten self 1
submit self 1.

ANAH[1] *See Ana.*

ANAH[2] ענה
answer 16
speak 14.

ANAH[3] ענה
Partic. poor 1.

ANAK אֲנָךְ
plumbline 4.

ANAN[1] אנן
HITHPO. complain 2.

ANAN[2] ענן
PIEL bring [a cloud] 1
POEL observe times 5
Partic. enchanter 1
soothsayer 2
sorceress 1.

ANAN[3] עָנָן
cloud 81
*cloudy 6
*thick 1.

ANAN עֲנָן
cloud 1.

ANANAH עֲנָנָה *f.*
cloud 1.

ANAPH[1] אנף
be angry 7
be displeased 1
HITHP. be angry 6.

ANAPH[2] עָנָף
bough 3
branch 4.

ANAPH עֲנַף
bough 1
branch 3.

ANAPHAH אֲנָפָה *f.*
heron 2.

ANAQ[1] אנק
cry 1
groan 1
NIPH. cry 2.

ANAQ[2] ענק
compass about as a chain 1
HIPH. furnish 1
Adv. inf. liberally 1.

ANAQ[3] עָנָק
chain 3.

ANAQAH אֲנָקָה *f.*
crying out 1
ferret 1
groaning 1
sighing 2.

ANAS אנס
compel 1

ANAS אנס
trouble 1.

ANASH[1] אנשׁ
Pass. pt. desperate 1
desperately wicked 1
incurable 1
woeful 1
NIPH. be very sick 1.

ANASH[2] ענשׁ
amerce 1
condemn 2
punish 1
*be punished 1
Adv. inf. surely 1
NIPH. be punished 3.

ANASH עֲנָשׁ
confiscation 1.

ANASHIM אֲנָשִׁים
(*plur. of* ish *or* enosh)
certain 11
certain men 1
divers 1
fellows 1
husbands 3
men 480
people 1
persons 2
servants 1
some 1
some of them 1
them that 1
they that 2
those 2
*in the flower of their age 1.
†blood-thirsty (*with* dam) 1; chapmen (*with part. of* tur) 1; counsellors (*with* etsah[2]) 1; famished (*with* raob) 1; famous (*with* shem) 1; friends (*with* shalom)

* Inexact translations, *e.g.*, of a noun by a verb or adjective, of an active by a passive.
† Cases where two or more words in the original are translated by one word or by a phrase.

1; merchantmen (*with part. of* tur) 1; shipmen (*with pl of* oni) 1; workmen (*with* melaka) 1. *See* hayah, yarah.

ANAW עָנָו (עָנִיו)
humble 5
lowly 2
meek 13
poor 1.

ANAVAH עֲנָוָה *f.*
gentleness 1
humility 3
meekness 1.

ANEH = AN.

ANEPH עָנֵף
full of branches 1

ANESHE = ANASHIM.

ANI [1] אֲנִי
I
me
myself, etc.
†which (va-ani); who (va-ani).

ANI [2] עָנִי
afflicted 15
lowly 1
poor 59.

ANIYYAH אֲנִיָּה *f.*
lamentation 1
sorrow 1.

ANOG עָנֹג
delicate 3.

ANOKI אָנֹכִי
as for me
I, etc.
†which (ve-anoki).

ANPIN אַנְפִּין *pl.*
face 1
visage 1.

ANT אַנְתְּ
as for thee 1
thou 14.

ANTUN אַנְתּוּן
ye 1.

ANU אֲנוּ
we 1.

ANVAH עַנְוָה *f.*
gentleness 1
meekness 1.

APH [1] אַף
also
and
and furthermore
and yet
but
even
how much less
moreover
therefore also
yea, etc.
†although (*with* ki) 1; how much less (*with* ki lo) 1; how much more (*with* ki) 1; how much rather then (*with* ki) 1; yea (*with* ki) 1.

APH [2] אַף
anger 171
countenance 1
face 22
forehead 1
nose 12
nostril 13
snout 1
wrath 42
*angry 4
*worthy (*dual*) 1.
†before (be-aph) 1. *See* erek, orek.

APH אַף
also 4.

APHAD אפד
bind 1
gird 1.

APHAH אָפָה
bake 10
Partic. baker 11
NIPH. be baken 3.
†*See* maakal.

APHAL עפל
PUAL be lifted up 1
HIPH. presume 1

APHAPH אפף
compass 5.

APHAPPIM עַפְעַפַּיִם *pl.*
dawning 1
eyelids 9.

APHAR [1] עָפָר
ashes 2
dust 91
earth 8
ground 1
mortar 1
powder 3
rubbish 1.

APHAR [2] עפר
PIEL cast [dust] 1.

APHAQ אפק
HITHP. be restrained 1
force self 1
refrain self 5.

APHEL אָפֵל
very dark 1.

APHELAH אֲפֵלָה *f.*
darkness 6
dark night 1
gloominess 2
*thick 1.

APHER אֵפֶר
ashes 2.

APHES אפס
be at an end 1
be brought to nought 1
be clean gone 1
fail 2.

APHILOTH אֲפִילֹת *f. pl*
not grown up 1.

APHIQ אָפִיק
brook 1
channel 3
river 10
stream 2
*mighty 1
*strong pieces (*pl.*) 1.
†scales (*pl. with* magen) 1.

APHSI = EPHES.

APHUDDAH אֲפֻדָּה *f.*
ephod 2
ornament 1.

APPEDEN אַפֶּדֶן
palace 1.

APPETHOM אַפְּתֹם
revenue 1.

APPIRYON אַפִּרְיוֹן
chariot 1.

AQAB עקב
supplant 2
take by the heel 1
Adv. inf. utterly 1
PIEL stay 1.

AQAD עקד
bind 1.

AQAH עָקָה *f.*
oppression 1.

AQAL עקל
Pual pt wrong 1.

AQALLATHON עֲקַלָּתוֹן
crooked 1.

AQALQAL עֲקַלְקַלּוֹת *f. pl.*
crooked ways 1.
†*See* orach.

AQAR [1] עקר
pluck up 1
NIPH. be rooted up 1
PIEL dig down 1
hough 4.

AQAR [2] עָקָר
barren 9
barren woman 1
female barren 1
male barren 1.

AQAR עקר
HITHP. be plucked up by the roots 1.

AQASH עקשׁ
prove perverse 1.
NIPH. *pt.* that is perverse 1.
PIEL make crooked 1.
pervert 1.

AQEB עָקֵב
footstep 3
heel 7
lier in wait 1
step 1
*at the last 1.
†horsehoof (*with* sus) 1.

AQOB עָקֹב
crooked 1
deceitful 1
polluted 1.

AQOD עָקֹד
ring-straked 7.

AQQO אַקּוֹ
wild goat 1.

AQRAB עַקְרָב
scorpion 6.

AR עָר
city 4
enemy 2.

AR עָר
enemy 1.

ARA אֲרַע *f.*
earth 20
*inferior 1.

ARAB [1] ארב
lay wait 8
lie in ambush 1
lie in wait 15
Partic ambush 5
lier in ambush 1
lier in wait 7
man lying in wait 1.
PIEL *pt.* ambushment 1
lier in wait 1
HIPH. lay wait 1.

ARAB [2] ערב
become surety for 1
be surety 6
engage 1
mortgage 1
occupy 1
put in surety 1
undertake 1
Partic. occupier 1
them that are surety 1
HITHP. be mingled 1
give pledges 2
intermeddle 1
meddle with 2
mingle selves 1.
†become surety (*with* arubbah) 1.

ARAB [3] ערב
be pleasant 1
be pleasing 1
be sweet 5
take pleasure 1.

ARAB [4] ערב
be darkened 1
Inf. toward evening 1
Hiph. inf. evening 1.

ARAB ערב
Pael pt. mixed 2
HITHPA. be mixed 1
mingle selves 1.

ARABAH עֲרָבָה *f.*
champaign 1
desert 9
plain 42
wilderness 5
*evening 1
*heaven 1.

ARABIM עֲרָבִים *pl.*
willows 6.

ARACH ארח
go 1
Partic. company 1
travelling company 1
wayfaring 1
wayfaring man 3.

ARAD עָרָד
wild ass 1.

ARAG [1] ארג
weave 3
Partic. they that weave 1
weaver 6
woven 3.

ARAG [2] ערג
cry 1
pant 2.

ARAH [1] ארה
gather 1
pluck 1.

ARAH [2] ערה
NIPH. be poured 1
PIEL discover 2
empty 2
leave destitute 1
rase 2
uncover 2
HIPH. discover 1
pour out 1
uncover 1
HITHP. make self naked 1
spread self 1.

ARAK [1] ארך
become long 1
be long 1
be prolonged 1
HIPH. be lengthened 1
be long 1
be prolonged 4
defer 2
draw out 3
lengthen 2
make long 1
prolong 13
tarry 1
tarry long 1.
†outlive (*with* yamim achar[2]) 1; overlive (*with* yamim achar[2]) 1.

ARAK [2] ערך
be compared 1
compare 2
direct 2
equal 2
esteem 1
furnish 2
handle 1
join [battle] 1
lay in order 6
ordain 2
order 8
prepare 5
put in array 7
put in order 1
put selves in array 6
put the battle in array 1
reckon up in order 1
set in array 8
set in order 5
set selves in array 3
set selves in array against 1
Partic. expert in 3
HIPH. estimate 2
tax 1
value 3.
†set in order (*with* erek[2]) 1.

ARAK ארך
Partic. meet 1.

ARAM [1] ארם
Adv. inf. very 1
HIPH. be prudent 1
beware 1
deal subtilly 1.
†take crafty counsel (*with* sod) 1.

ARAM [2] ערם
NIPH. be gathered together 1.

ARAPH [1] ערף
drop 1
drop down 1.

ARAPH [2] ערף
behead 1
break down 1
break neck 2
cut off neck 1
strike off neck 1.

ARAPHEL עֲרָפֶל
dark cloud 1
darkness 3
gross darkness 2
thick darkness 8
dark 1.

ARAQ ערק
Partic. fleeing 1
sinews 1.

ARAR [1] ארר
curse 54
Adv. inf. bitterly 1
NIPH. be cursed 1
PIEL cause the curse 6
curse 1
HOPH. be cursed 1.

ARAR [2] עַרְעָר
destitute 1.

ARAR [3] עֲרֹעֵר
heath 1.

ARAR [4] ערר
make bare 1
POEL raise up 1
Pilp. adv. inf. utterly 1
HITHP. be broken 1.

ARAS ארשׂ
PIEL betroth 5
espouse 1
PUAL be betrothed 5.

ARATS ערץ
be affrighted 1
be afraid 2
be terrified 1
break 1
dread 1
fear 1
oppress 1
prevail 1
shake terribly 2
NIPH. be feared 1
HIPH. be afraid 1
fear 1
Partic. dread 1.

ARBA אַרְבַּע
four.
†fourteen (*with* asar); fourteenth (*with* asar).

ARBA אַרְבַּע
four 8.

ARBAIM אַרְבָּעִים *pl.*
forty.

ARBATAYIM אַרְבַּעְתַּיִם *du.*
fourfold 1.

ARBAYIM. *Dual of* **EREB** [2]

ARBEH אַרְבֶּה
grasshopper 4
locust 20.

AREB עָרֵב
sweet 2.

AREKAH אֲרֻכָה *f.*
lengthening 1.
†be prolonged (with Peil of *yehab*) 1.

AREL [1]
NIPH. let (one's) foreskin be uncovered 1
†KAL, count as uncircumcised (*with* orlah) 1.

AREL [2] עָרֵל
uncircumcised 34
uncircumcised person 1.

AREMAH עֲרֵמָה *f.*
heap 8
heap of corn 1
sheaf 1.

ARESHETH אֲרֶשֶׁת *f.*
request 1.

ARGAMAN אַרְגָּמָן
purple 36.

ARGAZ אַרְגַּז
coffer 3.

ARGEVAN אַרְגְּוָן
purple 1.

ARGEVANA אַרְגְּוָנָא
scarlet 3

ARI (אַרְיֵה) אֲרִי
lion 78
*pierce 1.
†*See* kephir.

ARIEL אֲרִיאֵל
altar 2
lion like men 2.

ARIPHIM עֲרִיפִים *pl.*
heavens 1.

ARIRI עֲרִירִי
childless 4.

ARISAH עֲרִיסָה *f.*
dough 4.

ARITH אַרְעִית *f.*
bottom 1.

ARITS עָרִיץ
in great power 1
mighty 1
oppressor 3
strong 1
terrible 13
violent 1.

ARKUBAH אַרְכֻּבָה *f.*
knee 1.

ARMON [1] אַרְמוֹן
castle 1
palace 31.

ARMON [2] עַרְמוֹן
chestnut tree 2.

ARNEBETH אַרְנֶבֶת *f.*
hare 2.

AROB עָרֹב
divers sorts of flies 2
swarm of flies 3
swarms of flies 4.

AROD עָרוֹד
wild ass 1.

AROER עֲרוֹעֵר
heath 1.

AROK אָרֹךְ
long 2
longer 1.

AROM עָרֹם
naked 16.

ARON אָרוֹן
ark 195
chest 6
coffin 1.

AROTH עָרוֹת *f. pl.*
paper reeds 1.

ARQA אַרְקָא *f.*
earth 1.

ARU אֲרוּ
behold 4
lo 1.

ARUBBAH [1] אֲרֻבָּה *f.*
chimney 1
window 8.

ARUBBAH [2] עֲרֻבָּה *f.*
pledge 1.
†*See* arab[2].

ARUCHAH אֲרֻחָה *f.*
allowance 2
diet 2
dinner 1
victuals 2.

ARUGAH עֲרוּגָה *f.*
bed 2
furrow 2.

ARUKAH אֲרוּכָה *f.*
health 4.
†be made up (*with* alah[4]) 1; be perfected (*with* alah[4]) 1.

ARUKKAH = AROK.

ARUM עָרוּם
crafty 2
prudent 8
subtil 1.

ARUTS עָרוּץ
cliffs 1.

ARUZIM אֲרֻזִים *pl.*
made of cedar 1.

ARVAH עַרְוָה *f.*
dishonour 1.

ARYEH = ARI.

ARYEH אַרְיֵה *f.*
lion 10.

ARZAH אַרְזָה *f.*
cedar work 1.

ASAB עֲשַׂב
grass 5.

ASAH עשׂה
accomplish 2
advance 1
appoint 2
bear 4
bestow 5
bring forth 10
bring to pass 4
bruise 1
cause 1
cause to be made 1
commit 45
deal 50
deal with 2
deck 1
do 1292
dress 11
effect 1
execute 47
exercise 1
fashion 1
fit 1
fulfil 4
gather 1
get 13
give 1
go about 1
govern 1
hold [feast] 1
keep 43
labour 3
maintain 7
make 631
make up 1
make ready 2
observe 4
occupy 1
offer 47
ordain 5
pare 1
perform 18
practise 4
prepare 36
procure 4
provide 2
put 1
requite 1
sacrifice 3

*** Inexact translations, *e.g.*, of a noun by a verb or adjective, of an active by a passive.**
† Cases where two or more words in the original are translated by one word or by a phrase.

set 3
shew 44
spend 1
take [counsel, vengeance] 2
trim 1
undo 1
use 1
work 79
yield 10
*be done 6
*be made 9
*sin 1
Partic. apt 1
busy 1
those that have the charge 1
worker 1
Pass. pt. done 1
made 8
ready dressed 1
that which is done 1
Inf. very 1
Adv. inf. certainly 2
great things 1
indeed 1
surely 4
thoroughly 1
NIPH. become 1
be committed 3
be done 54
be dressed 1
be executed 1
be followed 1
be given 1
be holden 2
be kept 3
be made 12
be meet 2
be occupied 1
be offered 2
be performed 2
be prepared 2
be put in execution 1
be used 1
be wrought 4
come to pass 1
Inf. they shall make 1
PIEL bruise 2
PUAL be made 1.

†be at agreement (*with* chozeh) 1; displease (*with* ra be-ayin[3]) 1; do great things (*with* gadal) 4; feast (*with* mishteh) 1; furnish to go (*with* keli) 1; grant (*with* im) 1; hinder (*with* thoah le) 1; journey (*with* derek) 1; serve (*with* dabar[2] le) 1; utterly consume (*with* kalah[2]) 1; vex self (*with* ra) 1. *Part.* fighting man (*with* milchamah) 1; industrious (*with* melakah) 1; officer (*with* melakah) 1; warrior (*with* milchamah) 2; workman (*with* melakah) 8. *See* kalah, pala.

ASAMIM אֲסָמִים *pl.*
barns 1
storehouses 2.

ASAPH אסף
assemble 9
be rearward 1
bring 2
destroy 1
fetch 1
gather 43
gather in 8
gather together 17
gather up 1
lose 1
put all together 1
recover 4
take 2
take away 5
take up 1
withdraw 3
Pass. pt. consumed 1
Adv. inf. surely 2
utterly 1
NIPH. assemble 1
assemble selves 3
assemble selves together 1
be assembled 3
be brought 4
be brought together 1
be gathered 23
be gathered together 13
be gathered up again 1
be gotten 1
be received 1
be taken 1
be taken away 4
gather selves 3
gather selves together 14
gather together 3
get him 1
put up self 1
withdraw self 1
Adv. inf. generally 1
PIEL gather 2
receive 1
take into 1
Partic. rereward 4
PUAL be gathered 4
be gathered together 1
HITHP. be gathered together 1.

ASAPHSUPH אֲסַפְסֻף
mixt multitude 1.

ASAQ עשׂק
HITHP. strive 1.

ASAR[1] אסר
bind 41
bind selves 1
gird 2
harness 1
make ready 4
order 1
prepare 1
put in bands 1
set in array 1
tie 4
Pass. pt. held 1
prisoner 2
*prison (*adj.*) 2
Adv. inf. fast 2
NIPH. be bound 4
be kept 1
PUAL be bound 2.

ASAR[2] עֶשֶׂר
[ten *or* tenth.]

ASAR[3] עשׂר
take the tenth 2.
PIEL give the tenth 1
have tithes 1
tithe 1
Adv. inf. surely 1
truly 1
HIPH. take tithes 1
Inf. tithing 1.

ASAR עֲשַׂר
ten 4.

†See teren.

ASARAH = ESER.

ASAS עסס
tread down 1.

ASEPHAH אֲסֵפָה *f.*
*together 1.

ASH עָשׁ
moth 7.

ASHAM[1] אשׁם (אָשֵׁם)
acknowledge offence 1
be desolate 3
be found faulty 1
be found guilty 1
be guilty 11
be made desolate 1
become desolate 1
become guilty 1
hold one's self guilty 1
offend 6
trespass 4
Adv. inf. certainly 1
greatly 1
NIPH. be made desolate 1
HIPH. destroy 1.

ASHAM[2] אָשָׁם
guiltiness 1
offering for sin 1
sin 1
trespass 7
trespass offering 35.

ASHAN[1] עשׁן
be angry 1
be on a smoke 1
smoke 4.

ASHAN[2] עָשָׁן
smoke 24
smoking 1

ASHAQ עשׁק
deceive 1
defraud 3
do violence 1
do wrong 2
drink up 1
get deceitfully 1
oppress 22
use [oppression] 1
Partic. oppressor 4
Pual pt. oppressed 1.

ASHAR[1] אשׁר
go 1
PIEL go 1
guide 1
lead 1
relieve 1
Partic. leader 1
PUAL be led 1.

ASHAR[2] אשׁר
PIEL bless 2
call blessed 4
call happy 1.
PUAL be blessed 1
be happy 1.

ASHAR[3] עשׁר
become rich 1
be rich 1.
HIPH. be rich 5
enrich 3
make rich 5
wax rich 1
HITHP. make self rich 1.

ASHATH עשׁת
shine 1.
HITHP. think 1.

ASHEDOTH אֲשֵׁדוֹת *f. pl.*
springs 3.

ASHEM[1] = ASHAM[1].

ASHEM[2] אָשֵׁם
guilty 2
one which is faulty 1.

ASHEN עָשֵׁן
smoking 2.

ASHER אֲשֶׁר
as
because
for
so that
that
that thing which
that wherein
that which
when
where
wherewith
which
whither
who
whom
whomsoever
whose, etc.

†because, everyone, for as much as, from whence, how, howsoever, steward (*with* al[2] bayith) 1, that, until, whatsoever, where, whereas, wherein, whereof, whereon, whithersoever, whosoever, why, etc. *See* achar[2], ba-asher, ka-asher, maqom, me-asher.

ASHERAH אֲשֵׁרָה *f.*
grove 40.

ASHERE אַשְׁרֵי *pl.*
blessed 27
happy 18.

ASHESH עשׁשׁ
be consumed 3.

ASHIR עָשִׁיר
rich 17
rich man 6.

ASHISH אָשִׁשׁ
foundation 1.

ASHISHAH אֲשִׁישָׁה *f.*
flagon 4.

ASHITH עֶשְׁית
think 1.

ASHMAH אַשְׁמָה *f.*
cause of trespass 1
sin 4
trespass 11
trespassing 2
trespass offering 1*

†offend (*with* al[2]) 1. *See* rabah.

ASHMANNIM אַשְׁמַנִּים *pl.*
desolate places 1.

ASHMURAH אַשְׁמוּרָה *f.*
watch 7.

ASHOQ עָשׁוֹק
oppressor 1.

ASHOTH עָשׁוֹת
bright 1.

ASHPAH אַשְׁפָּה
quiver 6.

ASHPOTH (ASHPATH) אַשְׁפֹּת
dung 4
dung hill 3.

ASHSHAPH אָשַּׁף
astrologer 6.

ASHSHAPHIM אַשָּׁפִים *pl.*
astrologers 2.

ASHSHUR אַשֻּׁר *f.*
step 2.

ASHTAROTH עַשְׁתָּרוֹת *f. pl.*
flocks 4.

ASHTE ASAR עַשְׁתֵּי עָשָׂר
eleven 6
eleventh 16.

ASHTOTH עַשְׁתּוֹת *f. pl.*
thought 1.

ASHUQIM עֲשׁוּקִים *pl.*
oppressed 1
oppressions 2.

ASHUR אַשּׁוּר *f.*
going 3
step 4.

ASIPH אָסִיף
ingathering 2.

ASIR אָסִיר
bound 1
prisoner 10
those which are bound (*pl.*) 1.

ASIRI עֲשִׂירִי
tenth 23
tenth part 6.

ASIS עָסִיס
juice 1
new wine 2
sweet wine 2.

ASON אָסוֹן
mischief 5.

ASOR עָשׂוֹר
instrument of ten strings 3
ten 1
tenth 12.

ASOTH *inf. of* **ASAH.**

ASRAH = ASAR.

ASSIR אַסִּיר
prisoner 3.

ASUK אָסוּךְ
pot 1.

ASUPPIM אֲסֻפִּים *pl.*
thresholds 1.

ASSUPPOTH אֲסֻפּוֹת *f. pl.*
assemblies 1.

AT אַט
softly 1.

†gently (le-at) 1; secret (la-at) 1; softly (le-at) 1.

ATAD אָטָד
bramble 3
thorn 1.

ATAH עטה
array self 1
be clad 1
be covered 1
cover 7
cover selves 1
fill 1
put a covering 1
put on 1
turn aside 1
Adv. inf. surely 1.
HIPH. cover 1.

ATALLEPH עֲטַלֵּף
bat 3.

ATAM אטם
shut 1
stop 2
Pass. pt. narrow 4.
HIPH. stop 1

ATAPH עטף
be covered over 1
be overwhelmed 2
cover 1
fail 1
faint 1
hide self 1
Pass. pt. feebler 1.
NIPH. swoon 1.
HIPH. be feeble 1.
HITHP. be overwhelmed 3
faint 2
swoon 1.

ATAR[1] אטר
shut 1.

ATAR[2] עטר
compass 2.
PIEL crown 4
Hiph. pt. crowning 1.

ATARAH עֲטָרָה *f.*
crown 23.

ATHA אתא (אתה)
be come 1
come 14
come upon 1
Partic. things that are coming 1
things to come 2.
HIPH. bring 1
come 1.

ATHA אתא (אתה)
be come 1
come 6.
HAPH. bring 7.
HOPH. be brought 1
*bring 1.

ATHAD עתד
PIEL make fit 1.
HITHP. be ready to become 1.

ATHAH = ATHA.

ATHAH = ATHA.

ATHAM עתם
NIPH. be darkened 1.

ATHAQ[1] עתק
become old 1
be removed 2
wax old 1.
HIPH. copy out 1
leave off 1
remove 3.

ATHAQ[2] עָתָק
stiff 1
As noun arrogancy 1
grievous things 1
hard things 1.

ATHAR[1] עתר
intreat 4
pray 1.
NIPH. be intreated 8.
HIPH. intreat 6
make prayer 1.

ATHAR[2] עתר
Niph. pt. deceitful 1.
HIPH. multiply 1.

ATHAR[3] עָתָר
suppliant 1
thick 1.

ATHAR אֲתַר
place 5.

†after (be-athar) 3.

ATHARIM אֲתָרִים *pl.*
spies 1.

ATHEQ עָתֵק
durable 1.

ATHERETH עֲתֶרֶת *f.*
abundance 1.

ATHID עָתִיד
ready 4
things that shall come (*pl.*) 1.

ATHID עֲתִיד
ready 1.

ATHIN אַתִּין *pl.*
signs 3.

ATHIQ עָתִיק
durable 1.

ATHON אָתוֹן *f.*
ass 28
she ass 6.

ATHUD עַתּוּד
treasure 1.

ATIN עֲטִינִים *pl.*
breasts 1.

ATISHAH עֲטִישָׁה *f.*
neesing 1.

ATSAB[1] עצב
displease 1
grieve 2.
NIPH. be grieved 5
be hurt 1
be sorry 1.
PIEL make 1
vex 1
wrest 1
HIPH. grieve 1
worship 1
HITHP. be grieved 1
it grieved 1.

ATSAB[2] עָצָב
idol 16
image 1.

ATSAB עצב
Partic. lamentable 1.

ATSAH עצה
shut 1.

ATSAL[1] אצל
keep 1
reserve 1
take 1
NIPH. be straitened 1
HIPH. take 1.

ATSAL[2] עצל
NIPH. be slothful 1

ATSAM עצם
be great 1
be increased 4
be mightier 1
be mighty 2
be more 2
be strong 3
become strong 1
shut 1
wax mighty 1
PIEL break bones 1
close 1
HIPH. make stronger 1.

ATSAR[1] אצר
lay up in store 2
make treasurer 1
store up 1
NIPH. be treasured 1.

ATSAR[2] עצר
be able 1
close up 2
detain 2
keep self close 1
keep still 1
prevail 1
recover 1
refrain 1
reign over 1
restrain 1
retain 3
shut 1
shut up 3
slack 1
stop 1
withhold 1
withhold self 1
Pass. pt. fast 1
kept 1
shut up 10
NIPH. be shut up 2
be stayed 7
Partic. detained 1

†be able (*with* koach) 2.

ATSARAH עֲצָרָה *f.*
solemn assembly 3
solemn meeting 1.

ATSEB עָצֵב
labour 1.

ATSEH עָצֶה
backbone 1.

ATSEL עָצֵל
slothful 8
sluggard 6.

ATSERETH עֲצֶרֶת *f.*
assembly 1
solemn assembly 6

ATSILIM אֲצִילִים *pl.*
chief men 1
nobles 1

ATSLAH עַצְלָה *f.*
slothfulness 2.

ATSLUTH עַצְלוּת *f.*
idleness 1.

ATSTSEBETH עַצֶּבֶת *f.*
sorrow 4
wound 1

* Inexact translations, *e.g.*, of a noun by a verb or adjective, of an active by a passive.
† Cases where two or more words in the original are translated by one word or by a phrase.

ATSTSIL אָצִיל
great 1.
†armhole (*with* yad) 2
ATSTSUMOTH עַצְמוֹת *f. pl.*
strong *reasons* 1.
ATSUM עָצוּם
great 1
mighty 15
much 1
strong 12
strong one 1
†feeble (lo atsum) 1.
ATT אַתְּ *f.*
thou *freq.*
ATTAH [1] אַתָּה
thou *freq.*
ATTAH [2] עַתָּה
now
whereas
etc.
†*See* ad[3], me-attah.
ATTEM אַתֶּם
ye *freq.*
ATTEN אַתֵּן (אַתֵּנָה)
ye 4
you 1.
ATTIQ [1] אַתִּיק
gallery 5.
ATTIQ [2] עַתִּיק
ancient 1
drawn 1.
ATTIQ עַתִּיק
ancient 3.
ATTUD עַתּוּד
chief one 1
goat 8
he goat 18
ram 2.
ATTUN אַתּוּן
furnace 10.
AVAH [1] אוה
desire 9
long 1
lust after 1
HITHP. be desirous 1
covet 2
desire 6
greatly desire 1
long 2
lust 3
point out 1.
AVAH [2] עוה
commit iniquity 1
do wrong 1.
NIPH. be bowed down 1
be perverse 2
be troubled 1
PIEL make crooked 1
HIPH. commit iniquity 3
do amiss 1
do perversely 2
do wickedly 1
pervert 2.
†PIEL turn upside down (*with* panim) 1
AVAL עול
PIEL deal unjustly 1
Partic. unrighteous 1.
AVAR עור
blind 2
put out 3
AVATH עות
PIEL deal perversely 1
falsify 1
make crooked 1
overthrow 1
pervert 2
subvert 1
turn upside down 1
Pual pt. that which is crooked.
HITHP. bow selves 1.
AVAYYAH עַוָּיָה *f.*
iniquity 1.
AVEL עָוֶל (עֶוֶל)
iniquity 1
unrighteousness 2
*unjust 1
*unjustly 1
*unrighteously 1.
AVEN אָוֶן
affliction 3
evil 1
idol 1
iniquity 47
mischief 3
mourning 1
nought 1
sorrow 1
vanity 6
wickedness 5
*false 1
*mourners 1
*unjust 1
*unrighteous 1
*vain 1
*wicked 2.
AVEROTH אֻוֵרוֹת *f. pl.*
cotes 1.
AVIL [1] עֲוִיל
ungodly 1.
AVIL [2] עֲוִיל
little one 1
young child 1.
AVLAH עַוְלָה *f.*
iniquity 18
perverseness 1
unrighteousness 1
wickedness 6
*unjust 1
*wicked 1
*wickedly 1.
AVON עָוֹן
fault 2
iniquity 218
mischief 1
punishment 6
punishment of iniquity 4
sin 1.
AVVAH [1] אַוָּה *f.*
desire 3
pleasure 1
*lust after 3.
AVVAH [2] עַוָּה *f.*
†*See* sum.
AVVAL עַוָּל
unjust 1
unrighteous 1
wicked 3.
AVVATHAH עַוָּתָה *f.*
wrong 1.
AVVERETH עַוֶּרֶת *f.*
*blind 1.
AYAB איב
Partic. enemy 281
foe 2.
AYAM עָיָם
mighty 1.
AYEPH [1] עָיֵף
be wearied 1.
AYEPH [2] עָיֵף
faint 6
thirsty 3
weary 8.
AYIL אַיִל
lintel 1
post 21
ram 153.
AYIN [1] (=EN) אַיִן
are not
be gone 2
be no
be without
come to nought
fail
is never
none 2
nor 2
nor anything
nothing
nothing can be
shall neither be
shall never
was no
was not
were nowhere
etc.
†could not recover [themselves] (*with* michyah) 1; except [he] be (ve-ayin); in abundance (le-en-mispar); more than (le-en); none escaped (en peletah) 1; nothing shall offend (*with* mikshol le) 1; well nigh (ke-ayin). *See* ab[1], ad[3], cheqer, in, marpe, mispar.
AYIN [2]. *See* **ME-AYIN.**

AYIN [3] (=EN) עַיִן *c.*
colour 11
conceit 4
eye 497
eyesight 2
face 9
fountain 11
resemblance 1
sight 217
well 10
*affliction 1
Dual countenance 1
knowledge 1
look 3
looks 3
outward appearance 1
presence 8
†before (be-en) 8; me (*with poss. adj.*); openly (ba-enayim) 1; regard (*with* chus) 1; think (be-enayim) 7. *See* asah, bazah, gabboth, hayah, mareh, pethach, shach, sum, tob,[2] yashar, yatab, yera.
AYIN עַיִן *f.*
eye 5.
AYIR עַיִר
ass colt 2
colt 2
foal 2
young ass 2.
AYIT עַיִט
bird 2
fowl 4
ravenous bird 1
*ravenous 1.
AYOM אָיֹם
terrible 3.
AYYAH אַיָּה *f.*
kite 2
vulture 1
AYYAL אַיָּל *c.*
hart 8.
†*See* opher.
AYYALAH אַיָּלָה *f.*
hind 8.
AYYEH אַיֵּה
where?
AYYELETH אַיֶּלֶת *f.*
hind 2.
AZ [1] אָז
at which time
for
now
then
yet.
†*See* me-az.
AZ [2] עַז
fierce 4
mighty 3
strong 13
*roughly 1.
†greedy (*with* nephesh) 1.
AZ [3] עֹז (=עוֹז)
power 1.
AZA אזא (אזה)
heat 1
*be heated 1
Pass. pt. hot 1.
AZAB עזב
commit self 1
fail (*tr.*) 2
forsake 123
fortify 2
leave 67
leave destitute 1
leave off 4
refuse 1
*help 2
Adv. inf. surely 1
NIPH. be forsaken 6
be left 3
PUAL be left 2.
AZAD אזד
be gone 2.
AZAI אֱזַי
then 3.
AZAL אזל
be gone 2
be spent 1
fail 1
gad about 1
PUAL go to and fro 1.
AZAL אזל
go 6
go up 1.

AZAN אזן
PIEL give good heed 1
HIPH. give ear 32
hear 2
hearken unto 6
perceive by the ear 1.
AZAQ עזק
PIEL fence 1.
AZAR [1] אזר
be girded 2
bind about 1
gird up 3
NIPH. be girded 1
PIEL compass about 1
gird 2
gird with 3
HITHP. gird self 3.
AZAR [2] עזר
help 72
succour 3
NIPH. be helped 3
be holpen 1
HIPH. help 6.
AZARAH עֲזָרָה *f.*
court 3
settle 6.
AZAZ עזז
be strengthened 1
be strong 1
prevail 3
strengthen selves 2
*strengthen 3
HIPH. harden 1
*impudent 1.
AZAZEL עֲזָאזֵל
scapegoat 4.
AZEN אָזֵן
weapon 1.
AZIQQIM אֲזִקִּים *pl.*
chains 2.
AZKARAH אַזְכָּרָה *f.*
memorial 7.
AZUBAH עֲזוּבָה *f.*
forsaking 1.

B

BA=BE.
BA-ABUR בַּעֲבוּר
because of
for sake of
that, etc.
BAAH בעה
cause to boil 1
enquire 2
NIPH. be sought up 1
swell out 1.
BAAL [1] בעל
be husband 3
be married 1
have dominion 1
have dominion over 1
marry 4
Pass. pt. married 1
married wife 1
wife 1
NIPH. be married 2.
BAAL [2] בַּעַל
captain 1
chief man 1
husband 11
lord 2
man 26
master 5
owner 14
person 1
*great 1
*having 2
*he that hath 3
*man given to 1
*one that is given to 1
*one to whom is due 1
*one who has to do 1
*that had 1
*that which hath 1
*they 1.
†adversary (*with* mishpat) 1; archer (*with* chets) 1; babbler (*with* lashon) 1; bird (*with* kanaph) 1; confederate (*with* berith) 1; creditor (*with* mashsheh yad) 1; dreamer (*with* chalom) 1; furious (*with* chemah[3]) 1; hairy (*with* sear) 1; horseman (*with* parash) 1; married (*with* ishshah) 1; sworn (*with* shebuah) 1.
BAALAH בַּעֲלָה *f.*
mistress 2
*that hath 2.
BAAR [1] באר
PIEL declare 1
make plain 1
Inf. plainly 1.
BAAR [2] בער
be burned 2
be kindled 6
burn 26
burn up 1
heat 1
kindle 1
PIEL bring away 1
burn 9
eat 1
eat up 2
feed 1
kindle 4
put away 13
set on fire 1
take away 7
take out 1
waste 1
PUAL burn 1
HIPH. burn 3
burn up 1
cause to be eaten 1
kindle 1
take away 1.
†HIPH. set on fire (*with* esh le) 1.
BAAR [3] בַּעַר
brutish 3
brutish person 1
foolish 1.
BAAR [4] בער
be brutish 3
NIPH. be brutish 2
become brutish 2.
BAASH באש
stink 5
NIPH. be abhorred 1
be had in abomination 1
stink 1
HIPH. be loathsome 1
cause a stinking savour 1
make to abhor 1
make to be abhorred 2
make to stink 1
stink 4
Adv. inf. utterly 1
HITHP. make selves odious 1.
BA-ASHER בַּאֲשֶׁר
because
for
where
wherein
wheresoever
whithersoever, etc.
BAAT בעט
kick 2.
BAATH בעת
NIPH. be afraid 3
PIEL affright 1
make afraid 7
terrify 3
trouble 2.
BABAH בָּבָה *f.*
apple [of the eye] 1.
BACHAL בחל
abhor 1.
BACHAN [1] בחן
examine 1
prove 5
tempt 1
try 17
*be tried 1
NIPH. be proved 2
be tried 1
PUAL be a trial 1.
BACHAN [2] בַּחַן
tower 1.
BACHAR בחר
appoint 1
be rather 1
choose 152
choose out 5
require 1
Pass. pt. choice 2
excellent 1
NIPH. be chosen 3
Partic. acceptable 1
choice 3.
BACHIR בָּחִיר
chosen 7
chosen one 1
elect 4
*choose 1
BACHON בָּחוֹן
tower 1.
BACHUN בָּחוּן
tower 1.
BACHUR בָּחוּר
choice young man 1
chosen 1
young 1
young man 42.
BAD [1] בַּדִּים *pl.*
bars 1
branches 4
parts 1
staves 36
strength 2.
BAD [2] בַּד (*only* לְבַד)
†alone, apart, beside, by selves, except, of each a like, only, etc.
BAD [3] בַּד
liar 2
lie 3.
BAD [4] בַּד
linen 23
BADA ברא
devise 1
feign 1
BADAD [1] בדד
Partic. alone 3.
BADAD [2] בָּדָד
alone 7
desolate 1
only 1
solitarily 1
solitary 2.
BADAL [1] בדל
NIPH. be separated 3
separate selves 7.
HIPH. divide 7
divide asunder 2
make a difference 1
make a separation 1
put difference 3
separate 15
sever 2
sever out 1
Adv. inf. utterly 1.
BADAL [2] בָּדָל
piece 1.
BADAQ בדק
repair 1.
BAGAD בגד
deal deceitfully 2
deal treacherously 23
deal unfaithfully 1
offend 1
transgress 3
treacherously depart 1
Partic. transgressor 10
treacherous 2
treacherous dealer 2
treacherous man 1
unfaithful man 1
Adv. inf. very 2
BAGOD בָּגוֹד
treacherous 2
BAHAL בהל (בָּהַל)
be affrighted 1
be afraid 2
be amazed 2
be dismayed 2
be hasty 1
be troubled 12
be vexed 3
haste 1
Partic. speedy 1.
PIEL be hasty 1
be rash 1
give speedily 1
make afraid 1

* Inexact translations, *e.g.*, of a noun by a verb or adjective, of an active by a passive.
† Cases where two or more words in the original are translated by one word or by a phrase.

make haste 1
trouble 4
vex 1.
PUAL be hastened 1
be gotten hastily 1.
HIPH. haste 1
thrust out 1
trouble 1.
BAHAT בַּהַט
red marble 1.
BAHEL = BAHAL.
BAHERETH בַּהֶרֶת *f.*
bright spot 12.
BAHIR בָּהִיר
bright 1.
BAKA בָּכָא
mulberry tree 4.
BAKAH בכה
bewail 5
complain 1
make lamentation 1
mourn 2
weep 97
*with tears 1
Adv. inf. at all 1
more 1
sore 3
PIEL weep 2.
BAKAR בכר
PIEL bring forth new fruit 1
make firstborn 1.
PUAL be firstling 1.
HIPH. bring forth first child 1.
BAKKURAH בִּכּוּרָה *f.*
*first ripe 1.
BAL בַּל
not
*none, etc.
†*With* ve: neither, nor.
BAL בַּל
heart 1.
BALA בלע
devour 2
eat up 1
swallow 1
swallow down 3
swallow up 13
NIPH. be swallowed up 1.
PIEL cover 1
destroy 8
devour 2
spend up 1
swallow up 11.
PUAL be destroyed 1
be swallowed up 2.
HITHP. be at end 1.
BALADE (בִּלְעֲדֵי) בִּלְעֲדֵי
beside 7
not 1
not in 1
save 4
without 4.
BALAG בלג
HIPH. comfort 1
recover strength 1
strengthen 2
take comfort 1.
BALAH בלה
become old 1
consume 1
wax old 9.
PIEL consume 1
enjoy long 1
make old 1
waste 1.
BALAL [1] בלל
be anointed 1
confound 2
temper 1
Pass. pt. mingled 37
HITHP. mix self 1.
BALAL [2] בלל
give provender 1
BALAL [3] בלל (=NABEL)
HIPH. fade 1.
BALAM בלם
be held in 1.
BALAQ בלק
make waste 1.
PUAL be waste 1.

BALAS בלס
Partic. gatherer 1.
BALEH בָּלֶה
old 5.
BALLAHAH בַּלָּהָה *f.*
terror 9
trouble 1.
BAMAH בָּמָה *f.*
height 1
high place 101
wave 1.
BANAH בנה
begin to build 1
build 328
build up 11
make 3
repair 2
set up 1
Adv. inf. surely 1.
NIPH. be built 25
be built up 2
be set up 1
have children 1
obtain children 1.
BANIM = BEN [2] *pl.*
BAQA בקע
break into 1
break through 2
cleave 5
divide 4
hatch 1
rend 1
rip up 1
win 1.
NIPH. be broken in pieces 1
be broken up 4
be divided 1
be ready to burst 1
be rent 2
be rent asunder 1
break forth 1
break out 1
cleave (*intr.*) 1
cleave asunder (*intr.*) 1.
PIEL cleave 4
cut out 1
hatch 1
rend 2
rip up 2
tear 2.
PUAL be made breach 2
be ripped up 1
Partic. rent 1.
HIPH. break through 1
make a breach 1
HOPH. be broken up.
HITHP. be cleft 1
be rent 1.
BAQAQ בקק
empty out 1
make empty 1
make void 1
Partic. empty 1
emptier 1.
NIPH. be emptied 1
fail 1
Adv. inf. utterly 1
POLEL empty 1.
BAQAR [1] בקר
enquire 2
make enquiry 1
search 1
seek 1
seek out 2.
BAQAR [2] בָּקָר
beeve 7
bull 1
cow 1
great cattle 1
herd 44
kine 2
ox 3
oxen 75.
†*See* ben,[2] egel, eglah, par.
BAQASH בקש
PIEL ask 2
beg 1
beseech 2
desire 1
enquire after 1
enquire of 2
get 1
make request 3
procure 1
request 1
require 14
seek 193.

PUAL be sought for 2
inquisition be made 1.
BAQBUQ בַּקְבֻּק
bottle 2
cruse 1.
BAQQARAH בַּקָּרָה *f.*
*seek out 1.
BAQQASHAH בַּקָּשָׁה *f.*
request 9.
BAR [1] בַּר
son 4.
BAR [2] בַּר
choice 1
clean 3
clear 1
pure 2.
BAR [3] (בָּר) בַּר
corn 9
wheat 5.
BAR [1] בַּר
son 7.
*old 1
BAR [2] בַּר
field 8.
BARA ברא
create 33
make 2
Partic. Creator 3.
NIPH. be created 9
be done 1.
PIEL choose 2
cut down 2
dispatch 2.
HIPH. make selves fat 1.
BARACH ברח
be fled 5
flee 46
flee away 3
make haste 1
run away 1
shoot 1.
HIPH. chase 1
chase away 1
drive away 1
make to flee 1
put to flight 1
reach 1.
BARAD [1] ברד
hail (*vb.*) 1.
BARAD [2] בָּרָד
hail 27.
†*See* eben.
BARAH ברה
choose 1
eat 3.
Piel inf. meat 1.
HIPH. cause to eat 1
give [meat] 1.
BARAK ברך
kneel 1
kneel down 1
Pass. pt. blessed 72
Adv. inf. still 1.
NIPH. be blessed 3.
PIEL bless 211
congratulate 1
praise 1
salute 5
thank 1
*be praised 1
*blaspheme 2
*curse 4
Adv. inf. abundantly 1
altogether 1
at all 1
greatly 1
indeed 1
PUAL be blessed 13
HIPH. make to kneel down 1
HITHP. be blessed 3
bless self 4.
BARAQ [1] ברק
cast forth 1.
BARAQ [2] בָּרָק
glittering sword 1
lightning 14
*bright 2
*glitter 1
*glittering 4.
BARAR ברר
manifest 1
purge out 1
Pass. pt. choice 2
chosen 2
polished 1
pure 1
*clearly 1.
NIPH. be clean 1
Partic. pure 2.

PIEL purge 1.
HIPH. cleanse 1
make bright 1.
HITHP. be purified 1
shew self pure 2.
BARBURIM בַּרְבֻּרִים *pl.*
fowl 1.
BAREQATH בָּרְקַת *f.*
carbuncle 1.
BAREQETH בָּרֶקֶת *f.*
carbuncle 2.
BARI בָּרִיא
fat 1
fatter 1
firm 1
plenteous 1
rank 2.
†fatfleshed (*with* basar[2]) 2.
BARIACH בָּרִיחַ
crooked 1
nobles (*pl.*) 1
piercing 1.
BAROD בָּרֹד
grisled 4.
BARQANIM בַּרְקָנִים *pl.*
briers 2.
BARUTH בָּרוּת *f.*
meat 1.
BARZEL בַּרְזֶל
ax head 1
head 1
iron 73.
†*See* charash.
BASAM בָּשָׂם
spice 1.
BASAR [1] בשׂר
PIEL bear tidings 3
bring good tidings 3
bring tidings 3
carry tidings 1
preach 1
preach good tidings 1
publish 2
shew forth 3
Partic. he that bringeth good tidings 3
messenger 1
one that bringeth good tidings 1
those that published 1.
HITHP. *tidings 1.
BASAR [2] בָּשָׂר
body 2
flesh 256
kin 2
skin 1
†mankind (*with* ish) 1; myself (*with poss. adj.*) 1; nakedness (*with* ervah) 1. *See* bari, daq, raq, sheer.
BASHAL בשׁל
be ripe 1
seethe 1.
PIEL bake 2
boil 6
roast 2
seethe (sod) 11.
PUAL be sodden 4
NIPH. bring forth ripe 1
BASHAS בשׁס .
POEL tread 1.
BASHEL בָּשֵׁל
sodden 1
*at all 1.
BATA (בטה) בטא
speak 1
PIEL pronounce 2
speak unadvisedly 1.
BATACH בטח
be bold 1
be confident 2
be secure 1
be sure 1
hope 1
put confidence 4
put trust 11
trust 87
trust safely 1
Partic. careless 1
careless one 1
careless woman 1
secure 3.
HIPH. cause to trust 1
make to hope 1
make to trust 3.
BATAH = BATA.

BATAL בטל
cease 1.
BATH [1] בַּת *f.*
apple [of the eye] 1
branch 1
company 1
daughter 529
town 32
village 12
*of 3
*old 1
†owl (*with* yaanah) 8. *See* ishon.
BATH [2] בַּת *c.*
bath 12.
BATH בַּת
bath 2.
BATHAH בָּתָה *f.*
waste 1.
BATHAQ בתק
PIEL thrust through 1
BATHAR בתר
divide 1
PIEL divide 1.
BATSA בצע
be wounded 2
cut 1
gain 1
get [gain] 1
Partic. covetous 1
him that coveteth 1
given to [covetousness] 2
greedy of [gain] 2
PIEL cut off 2
finish 1
fulfil 1
gain greedily 1
perform 1.
BATSAR בצר
cut off 1
gather 9
Partic. grape gatherer 3
Pass. pt. defenced 5
fenced 16
mighty things (*pl.*) 1
strong 1
walled 1
walled up 1
NIPH. be restrained 1
be withholden 1
PIEL fortify 2.
BATSEQ [1] בָּצֵק
swell 2.
BATSEQ [2] בָּצֵק
dough 4
flour 1.
BATSIR בָּצִיר
vintage 8.
BATSTSORETH בַּצֹּרֶת *f.*
dearth 1
drought 1.
BATTOTH בַּתּוֹת *f. pl.*
*desolate 1.
BATTUCHOTH בַּטֻּחוֹת *f. pl.*
secure 1.
BAU בָּעוּ *f.*
petition.
BAYIR בַּיִר [V. L.] *f.*
fountain 1.
BAYITH בַּיִת
court 1
door 1
family 5
hangings (*pl.*) 1
home 25
house *freq.*
household *freq.*
inside 1
inward 7
palace 1
place 16
temple 11
web 1
*as would contain 1
†dungeon (*with* bor) 2; prison (*with* esur 1, kele 6, kelu 2, pequddah 1, sohar 8, surim 1) 19; shearing house (*with* eqed 1, *with* eqed *and pt. of* raah 1) 2; storehouse (*with* otsar) 1; tablet (*with* nephesh) 1; treasure-house (*with* otsar) 1; ward (*with* mishmereth) 1; winterhouse (*with* choreph) 2; within (mib-bayith) 23. *See* asher, el,[1] yalid, yeled.

BAYITH בַּיִת
house 44.
BAZ בַּז
booty 1
prey 18
spoil 4
*spoiled 2
BAZA בזא
spoil 1.
BAZAH בזה
despise 27
disdain 1
Pass. pt. despised 4
Niph. pt. contemned 1
contemptible 3
despised 4
vile person 1
HIPH. despise 1.
†think scorn (*with* ayin[3]) 1.
BAZAQ בָּזָק
flash of lightning 1.
BAZAR בזר
scatter 1
PIEL scatter 1.
BAZAZ בזז
catch 1
gather 1
make a prey 1
prey upon 1
rob 5
spoil 9
take 7
take away 2
take for a prey 5
take spoil 4
Partic. robber 1
Inf. prey 2
NIPH. be spoiled 2
Adv. inf. utterly 1
PUAL be robbed 1
BAZOH בָּזֹה
*despise 1.
BE בְּ
against
among
for
in
on
with, etc.
†among (be-ben, be-de 1); for that (be-sha; *Gen.* 6, 3) 1; in (be-de) 2; without (*with* lo). Be-yad; because of 2, by 43, in 1, of 1, through 1, to 1. *See* ba-abur, be-qereb.
BEA (בעה) בעא
ask 3
desire 3
make [petition] 1
pray 1
request 1
seek 3.
BEAD בְּעַד
about
for
out at
over
through
upon, etc.
†*See* mi[2].
BEAH = *BEA.*
BEATHAH בְּעָתָה *f.*
trouble 2.
BECHURIM בְּחֻרִים *pl.*
young men 1.
BECHUROTH בְּחוּרוֹת *f. pl.*
youth 2.
BEDAR בדר
PAEL scatter 1.
BEDEQ בֶּדֶק
breach 8.
†*See* chazaq[1].
BEDIL בְּדִיל
tin 5.
†*See* eben.
BEDOLACH בְּדֹלַח
bdellium 2
BEEL בְּעֵל
†chancellor (with *teem*) 3.
BEER בְּאֵר *f.*
pit 4
well 32

* Inexact translations, *e.g.*, of a noun by a verb or adjective, of an active by a passive.
† Cases where two or more words in the original are translated by one word or by a phrase.

BEERAH בְּעֵרָה *f.*
fire 1.
BEESH באשׁ
be displeased 1.
BEGADIM *pl. of* **BEGED** [1].
BEGED [1] בֶּגֶד
apparel 4
cloth 13
clothes (*pl.*) 69
clothing 1
garment 107
lap 1
rag 1
raiment 12
robe 4
vesture 1
wardrobe (*pl.*) 2.
BEGED [2] בֶּגֶד
[treachery]
*very 2.
BEHAL בהל
trouble 7
Hithpe. inf. in haste 3
HITHPA. be troubled 1.
BEHALAH בֶּהָלָה *f.*
terror 2
trouble 2.
BEHEMAH בְּהֵמָה *f.*
beast 136
behemoth (*pl.*) 1
cattle 52.
†*See* nephesh.
BEHILU בְּהִילוּ *f.*
in haste 1.
BEI בְּעִי
grave 1.
BEIR בְּעִיר
beast 4
cattle 2.
BEKEH בֶּכֶה
[weeping]
*sore 1.
BEKER בֶּכֶר *f.*
dromedary 1.
BEKI בְּכִי
overflowing 1
weeping 19
*weep 1.
†continual weeping (beki bab-beki) 1; sore (*with* gadol) 4. *See* marar, nathan, yarad.
BEKIRAH בְּכִירָה *f.*
firstborn 6.
BEKITH בְּכִית *f.*
mourning 1.
BEKOR בְּכוֹר
eldest 3
eldest son 2
firstborn 98
firstling 9.
†*See* ben[2].
BEKORAH בְּכוֹרָה *f.*
birthright 9
firstborn 1
firstling 1.
BELA בֶּלַע
devouring 1
that which he hath swallowed up 1.
BELA בלא
PAEL wear out 1.
BELI בְּלִי
corruption
none
not
where no . . . is
without, etc.
†base (*with* shem) 1; none (*with* ish[1]) 1. *See* be, le, min.
BELIL בְּלִיל
corn 1
fodder 1
provender 1.
BELIMAH בְּלִימָה *f.*
nothing 1.
BELIYAAL בְּלִיַּעַל
Belial 16
evil 1
naughty 1
ungodly 2
ungodly men 2
wicked 5.
BELO בְּלוֹא
old 3.

BELO בְּלוֹ
tribute 3.
BEMO בְּמוֹ
for 1
in 2
into 1
through 1
with 2
[*once untranslated.*]
†*See* ophel.
BEN [1] בֵּין
among
between
betwixt
with
within, etc.
†*When repeated generally left once untranslated, the other time rendered* between, betwixt, from, etc. *See* arbayim, be, le, min.
BEN [2] בֵּן
appointed to 3
arrow 1
bough 2
branch 1
breed 1
calf 2
children (*pl.*) *freq.*
colt 2
foal 1
man 21
meet for 1
one born 2
people (*pl.*) 1
son *freq.*
them of (*pl.*) 1
whelp 2
worthy 3
young (one) 52
youth 1
*age 3
*came up in 1
*common 1
*corn 1
*in 2
*of first 51
*old 132
*servant born 1
*soldier 1
*surely 1.
†afflicted (*with* oni) 1; anointed one (*with* yitshar) 1; arrow (*with* qesheth) 1; bullock (*with* baqar[2]) 8; calf (*with* baqar[2]) 3; firstborn (*with* bekor) 1; high (*with* ish) 1; hostage (*with* taaruboth) 2; kid (*with* ez) 1; lamb (*with* tson) 2; low (*with* adam) 1; man (*with* adam) 4; man of high degree (*with* ish) 1; man of low degree (*with* adam) 1; mighty (*with* elim) 1; nephew (*with* banim) 1; people (*pl. with* am) 5; rebel (*with* meri) 1; robber (*with* parits) 1; spark (*with* resheph) 1; steward (*with* mesheq) 1; stranger (*with* nekar) 12; tumultuous one (*with* shaon) 1; valiant (*with* chayil) 6; valiantest (*with* chayil) 1; very fruitful (*with* shemen) 1; whose father (*lit.* son of) 1. *See* arbayim, egel, par.
BEN [1] בֵּין
among 1
between 1.
BEN [2] בֵּן
child 6
son 3
young 1.
†captive (with *galutha*) 1.
BENA (בנה) בנא
build 14
make 1
HITHP. be builded 7.
BENAH = *BENA*.
BENAS בנס
be angry 1.
BENAYIM בֵּנַיִם *du.*
†*See* ish[1].
BENE *pl. of* **BEN** [2].

BENOTH בֵּינוֹת
among
between
betwixt, etc.
BEOSH באשׁ
stink 3.
BEQA בֶּקַע
bekah 1
half a shekel 1.
BEQAR בקר
PAEL enquire 1
*search be made 3.
HITHP. search be made 1.
BE-QEREB בְּקֶרֶב
among 48
before 1
in 8
through 5
unto charge [of] 1
within 25
†*With pron. suff.*: inwardly 1, therein 2.
BEQIA בְּקִיעַ
breach 1
cleft 1.
BERAK ברך
bless 1
kneel 1.
PAEL bless 3.
BERAKAH בְּרָכָה *f.*
blessing 60
pool 1
present 3
*liberal 1.
†blessed (li-berakah) 3.
BERAM בְּרַם
but 2
nevertheless 1
yet 2.
BEREK בֶּרֶךְ *f.*
knee 25.
BEREK בְּרַךְ *f.*
knee 1.
BEREKAH בְּרֵכָה *f.*
fishpool 1
pool 16.
BERI בָּרִי
fat 1.
BERIACH בְּרִיחַ
bar 40
fugitive 2.
BERIAH בְּרִיאָה *f.*
new thing 1.
BERITH בְּרִית *f.*
confederacy 2
covenant 260
league 15
*be in league 2.
†*See* baal[2], karath.
BEROMIM בְּרֹמִים
rich apparel 1.
BEROSH בְּרוֹשׁ
fir 7
fir tree 13.
BEROTHIM בְּרוֹתִים
fir 1.
BESAR בְּשַׂר
flesh 3.
BESEM בֶּשֶׂם
spice 18
sweet odours 2
*sweet 1.
BESER בֶּסֶר
unripe grape 1.
BESORAH בְּשׂוֹרָה *f.*
good tidings 1
reward for tidings 1
tidings 4.
BETACH בֶּטַח
assurance 1.
As adv. (*with or without* le)
boldly 1
careless 5
carelessly 3
in hope 1
in safety 9
safe 2
safely 17
secure 3
securely 2
surely 1.
with confidence 1
without care 1.

BETEL בטל
cease 2.
PAIL cause to cease 2
make to cease 2
*be hindered 1.
BETEN בֶּטֶן *f.*
belly 30
body 8
womb 30
*within 1.
†as they be born (mib-beten) 1; within (be-beten) 1.
BETH = **BAYITH.**
BETHER בֶּתֶר
part 2
piece 1.
BETHULAH בְּתוּלָה *f.*
maid 7
maiden 5
virgin 38.
BETHULIM בְּתוּלִים *pl.*
maid 2
virginity 8.
BETSA בֶּצַע
covetousness 10
dishonest gain 2
gain 7
lucre 1
profit 3.
BETSAR בֶּצֶר
gold 1.
BETSEL בָּצָל
onion 1.
BETSER בֶּצֶר
defence 1
gold 1.
BETSIM בֵּיצִים *f. pl.*
eggs 6.
BEUSHIM בְּאֻשִׁים
wild grapes 2.
BI [1] בִּי
alas 1
O 7
oh 4.
BI [2] = **BE.**
BIAH בִּאָה *f.*
entry 1.
BI-BELI בִּבְלִי
without, etc.
+ *See* daath.
BI-GELAL בִּגְלַל
See galal.[3]
BIKKUR בִּכּוּר
first fruit 14
first ripe 2
first ripe fig 1
hasty fruit 1.
BIKKURAH בִּכּוּרָה *f.*
first ripe 1
first ripe fruit 1.
BIKRAH בִּכְרָה *f.*
dromedary 1.
BILADE = **BALADE.**
BILTI בִּלְתִּי
beside
but
except
not
save
without, etc.
†continual (*with* sarah); unsatiable (*with* sobah). *See* le-bilti, mib-bilti.
BIN בִּין
consider 3
understand 5
Partic. prudent 1
Adv. inf. diligently 1.
NIPH. be prudent 1
have understanding 1
understand 1
Partic. discreet 2
eloquent 1
him that hath understanding 3
him that understandeth 1
man of understanding 3
one that hath understanding 1
prudent 6
understanding 3.
POLEL instruct 1.

HIPH. be cunning 1
can skill 1
cause to understand 2
consider 4
deal wisely 1
discern 3
feel 1
give understanding 6
have intelligence 1
have understanding 6
inform 1
instruct 1
know 1
look well 1
make to understand 2
mark 1
perceive 6
regard 5
teach 2
understand 48
view 1.
Partic. skilful 1
teacher 1
understanding 7
wise 2
wise man 1.
HITHP. attend 1
consider 14
consider diligently 1
get understanding 1
perceive 1
regard 1
think 1
understand 3.
BINAH בִּינָה *f.*
knowledge 1
meaning 1
understanding 31
wisdom 1
*perfectly 1
*understand 1.
†*See* yada.
BINAH בִּינָה *f.*
understanding 1.
BINYAH בִּנְיָה *f.*
building 1.
BINYAN בִּנְיָן
building 7.
BINYAN בִּנְיָן
building 1.
BIQA בִּקְעָא *f.*
plain 1.
BIQAH בִּקְעָה *f.*
plain 7
open valley 1
valley 12.
BIQQORETH בִּקֹּרֶת *f.*
*be scourged 1.
BIRAH בִּירָה *f.*
palace 16.
BIRAH בִּירָה *f.*
palace 1.
BIRANIYOTH בִּירָנִיּוֹת *f. pl.*
castles 2.
BIRYAH בִּרְיָה *f.*
meat 3.
BITCHAH בִּטְחָה *f.*
confidence 1.
BITHAN בִּיתָן
palace 3.
BITSTSAH בִּצָּה *f.*
fen 1
mire 1
miry place 1.
BITSTSARON בִּצָּרוֹן
stronghold 1.
BITTACHON בִּטָּחוֹן
confidence 2
hope 1.
BIUSH בְּאִישׁ
bad 1.
BIUTHIM בִּעוּתִים *pl.*
terrors 2.
BIZZAH בִּזָּה
prey 4
spoil 6.
BIZZAYON בִּזָּיוֹן
contempt 1.
BO בּוֹא
abide 2
attain 4
be brought 5
be come *freq.*
be down 4
be entered 3
befall 1
be fallen 1
be gone 4
be gone down 1
be laid 1
be mentioned 1
be set 1
be well stricken 7
come *freq.*
come against *freq.*
come in *freq.*
come out *freq.*
come to pass 14
come upon *freq.*
depart 1
enter 102
enter in 25
enter into 10
get 6
get in 1
get into 1
go 160
go down 15
go in 120
go into 4
go to 3
go to war 1
resort 1
run 1
run down 1
Partic. things for to come 1
Inf. entrance 2
going down 2
way 1
Adv. inf. certainly 3
doubtless again 1
indeed 1
surely 2.
HIPH. apply 2
bring 441
bring forth 1
bring in 44
bring into 6
bring to 6
bring to pass 3
bring up 1
call 1
carry 15
carry into 1
carry to 1
cause go down 1
cause to come 1
cause to enter 2
let come in 1
fetch 1
get 1
give 1
grant 1
lead 2
pull in 2
put 9
send 1
take 3
take in 1.
*be brought 3
*be brought in 1
HOPH. be brought 11
be brought in 2
be brought into 8
be carried 1
be put 2
†be besieged (*with* be-matsor) 3; be sold (*with* be-mechir) 1; *eat (*with* el qereb) 1; *eat up (*with* el qereb) 1; employ (*with* min *and* panim) 1; follow (*with* achar[2]) 3; invade (*with* be) 2. HIPH. lift up (*with* maalah) 1.
BOCHAN בֹּחַן
tried 1.
BOGEDOTH בֹּגְדוֹת *f. pl.*
*treacherous 1.
BOHAQ בֹּהַק
freckled spot 1.
BOHEN בֹּהֶן
great toe 7
thumb 7.
†great toe (*with* regel) 2
thumb (*with* yad) 2.
BOHU בֹּהוּ
emptiness 1
void 2.
BOQER [1] בּוֹקֵר
herdman 1.

* Inexact translations, *e.g.*, of a noun by a verb or adjective, of an active by a passive.
† Cases where two or more words in the original are translated by one word or by a phrase.

BOQER[2] בֹּקֶר
day 3
early 2
morning 189
morrow 7.
†*See* ereb, panah.

BOR[1] בֹּר
cleanness 4
pureness 1
*purely 1.
†never so (be-bor) 1.

BOR[2] בּוֹר (*twice* בֹּר)
cistern 6
dungeon 10
pit 42
well 9.
†*See* bayith.

BORITH בֹּרִית *f.*
sope 2.

BOSEM בֹּשֶׂם
smell 1
spice 6
*sweet 1.

BOSER בֹּסֶר
sour grape 4.

BOSH בּוֹשׁ
be ashamed 71
be confounded 21
become dry 1
put to confusion 1
*with shame 1.
Adv. inf. at all 1
PIEL be long 1
delay 1.
HIPH. be ashamed 1
bring to shame 1
cause shame 4
make ashamed 2
put to shame 1
shame 1.
HITHP. be ashamed 1.

BOSHAH בָּאְשָׁה *f.*
cockle 1.

BOSHETH בֹּשֶׁת
confusion 7
shame 19
shameful thing 1
*be ashamed 1
*greatly 1
†(*with pron.*) where they have been put to shame 1.

BOSHNAH בָּשְׁנָה *f.*
shame 1.

BOTNIM בָּטְנִים *pl.*
nuts 1.

BOTS בֹּץ
mire 1.

BUK בּוּךְ
NIPH. be entangled 1
be perplexed 2.

BUL בּוּל
food 1
stock 1.

BUQAH בּוּקָה *f.*
*empty 1.

BUR בּוּר
declare 1.

BUS בּוּס
loathe 1
tread (down) 4
tread under 1
tread under foot 1.
POLEL tread down 1
tread under foot 1.
HOPH. be trodden under foot 1.
HITHP. be polluted 2.

BUSHAH בּוּשָׁה *f.*
shame 4.

BUTH בּוּת
pass the night 1.

BUTS בּוּץ
fine linen 7
white linen 1.

BUZ[1] בּוּז
contemn 1
despise 10.
Adv. inf. utterly 1.

BUZ[2] בּוּז
contempt 7
*contemptuously 1
*despised 2
*shamed 1.

BUZAH בּוּזָה
*despised 1.

C

CHABA חבא
NIPH. be hid 2
do secretly 1
hide self 11.
PUAL hide selves 1.
HIPH. hide 6.
HOPH. be hid 1.
HITHP. be hid 4
hide selves 6.
†NIPH. *See* qol.

CHABAB חבב
love 1.

CHABAH חבה
hide self 1.
NIPH. hide selves 4.

CHABAL חבל
deal corruptly 1
offend 1
lay to pledge 1
take a pledge 2
take a pledge of 2
take for a pledge 1
take to pledge 4
withhold 1
Partic. bands 2.
Adv. inf. at all 1
very 1.
NIPH. be destroyed 1.
PIEL bring forth 2
destroy 5
spoil 1
travail with 1.
PUAL be corrupt 1
be destroyed 1.

CHABAL[1] חבל
PAEL destroy 2
hurt 1.
HITHPA. be destroyed 3.

CHABAL[2] חֲבַל
hurt 1.

CHABAL[3] חֲבָל
damage 1
hurt 1.

CHABAQ חבק
embrace 2
fold 1.
PIEL embrace 10.

CHABAR חבר
be coupled 1
be coupled together 1
be joined together 1
be joined 3
*couple together (*tr.*) 1.
Pass. pt. joined 1.
PIEL couple 8
join self 1.
PUAL be compact 1
be coupled together 1
be joined 1
be joined together 1
have fellowship with 1.
HIPH. heap up 1.
HITHP. join self 2
join selves together 1.
Inf. league 1.
†KAL *partic.* charmer (*with* cheber) 1; charming (*with* cheber) 1.

CHABAR חַבַר
companion 1
fellow 2.

CHABARBUROTH חֲבַרְבֻּרוֹת *f. pl.*
spots 1.

CHABASH חבש
be wrapped about 1
bind 4
bind up 6
gird about 1
govern 1
put 2
saddle 13
Partic. healer 1.
PIEL bind 1
bind up 1.
PUAL be bound up 2.

CHABAT חבט
beat 1
beat off 1
beat out 1
thresh 1
NIPH. be beaten out 1.

CHABATSTSELETH חֲבַצֶּלֶת *f.*
rose 2.

CHABBAR חַבָּר
companion 1.

CHABBURAH חַבּוּרָה (חַבֻּרָה) *f.*
blueness 1
bruise 1
hurt 1
stripe 2
wound 1.

CHABER חָבֵר
companion 7
fellow 4
knit together 1.

CHABERETH חֲבֶרֶת *f.*
companion 1.

CHABITTIM חֲבִתִּים
pans 1.

CHABOL חֲבֹל
pledge 3.

CHABOLAH חֲבֹלָה *f.*
pledge 1.

CHABRAH חַבְרָה *f.*
fellow 1.

CHABULAH חֲבוּלָה *f.*
hurt 1

CHABURAH = CHABBURAH.

CHACH חָח
bracelet 1
chain 2
hook 4.

CHAD[1] חַד
sharp 4.

CHAD[2] חַד
one 1.

CHAD חַד
a 4
first 4
one 5
together 1.

CHADAD חדד
be fierce 1
sharpen 1.
HIPH. sharpen 1.
HOPH. be sharpened 3.

CHADAH חָדָה
be joined 1
rejoice 1.
PIEL make glad 1.

CHADAL חדל
be ceased 1
be unoccupied 1
cease 20
end 1
fail 1
forbear 19
forsake 1
leave 5
leave off 5
let alone 2
rest 1
want 1.

CHADAR חדר
enter a privy chamber 1.

CHADASH[1] חדש
PIEL renew 6
repair 3.
HITHP. be renewed 1.

CHADASH[2] חָדָשׁ
fresh 1
new *freq.*
new thing *freq.*

CHADATH חֲדַת
new 1.

CHADDUDIM חַדּוּדִים *pl.*
*sharp 1.

CHADEL חָדֵל
frail 1
he that forbeareth 1
rejected 1.

CHADIN חֲדִין
breast 1.

CHAG חַג (חָג)
feast 52
feast day 2
sacrifice 3
solemn feast 3
solemnity 1.

CHAGAB חָגָב
grasshopper 4
locust 1

CHAGAG חגג
celebrate 1
dance 1
hold a feast 1
keep 8
keep a feast 1
keep a solemn feast 1
keep holyday 1
reel to and fro 1.

CHAGAR חגר
be able to put on 1
be afraid 1
gird 19
gird on 5
gird self 10
gird up 2
restrain 1
Pass. pt. appointed 3
†rejoice on every side (*with* gil) 1.

CHAGAVIM חֲגָוִים *pl.*
clefts 3.

CHAGOR חֲגוֹר
girded with 1
girdle 3.

CHAGORAH חֲגוֹרָה *f.*
apron 1
armour 1
girdle 3
*gird sackcloth 1.

CHAI[1] חַי
alive 29
live (*adj.*) 3
lively 1
living 73
living thing 4
man living 1
quick 3
raw 6
running 7
springing 1
thing living 1
*life 2
*of life 4.

CHAI[2] חַי
live 104.

CHAIYAH חַיָּה
appetite 1
beast 76
company 1
congregation 2
life 8
living creature 15
living thing 2
multitude of the wicked 1
troop 2
wild beast 1
*living 2
†*See* nephesh.

CHAIYIM חַיִּים *pl.*
life 132
lifetime 1
maintenance 1
*old 1
†*See* raah[1], sameach, yom.

CHAIYUTH חַיּוּת *f.*
*living 1.

CHAKAH חכה
wait 1.
PIEL long 1
tarry 2
wait 10.

CHAKAM חָכָם
cunning 6
cunning man 4
subtil 1
wise 102
wise man 15
†unwise (lo chakam) 2; wise-hearted (*with* leb) 1.

CHAKKAH חַכָּה *f.*
angle 2
hook 1.

CHAKKIM חַכִּים
wise 14.

CHAKLILI חַכְלִילִי
red 1.

CHAKLILUTH חַכְלִלוּת *f.*
redness 2.

CHAKMOTH חַכְמוֹת *f.*
*wise 1.

CHALA חלא
be diseased 1.

CHALAB חָלָב
milk 42
*sucking 1.
†*See* charits.

CHALAH חלה
be diseased 1
be grieved 1
be sick 23
be sorry 1
be (*or* become) weak 3
fall sick 4.
Partic. woman in travail 1.
NIPH. be grieved 4
be sick 1
put selves to pain 1.
Partic. diseased 2
grief 1
grievous 4.
PIEL beseech 6
entreat 3
lay 1
make prayer 1
make suit 1
make supplication 1
pray 3.
Infin. infirmity 1.
PUAL become weak 1.
HIPH. make sick 3
put to grief 1.
HOPH. be wounded 3.
HITHP. fall sick 1
make self sick 2.

CHALAL[1] חלל
be wounded 1.
Partic. players on instruments 1.
NIPH. be defiled 1
be polluted 4
be profaned 2
profane self 2.
PIEL break 3
cast as profane 1
defile 8
eat as common things 1
eat of 1
gather the grapes thereof 1
pipe 1
pollute 18
profane 30
prostitute 1
slay 1
stain 1.
PUAL be profaned 1
be slain 1.
POEL wound 1.
Poal partic. wounded 1.
HIPH. begin 52
break 1
pollute 1
sorrow 1
*first 1.
HOPH. *men began 1.

CHALAL[2] חָלָל
deadly wounded 1
profane 2
slain 79
whom he slew 1
wounded 9
*kill 2
*slay 1.
†*See* rabah.

CHALAM[1] חלם
dream 26.
HIPH. cause to be dreamed 1.

CHALAM[2] חלם
be in good liking 1.
HIPH. recover 1.

CHALAPH חלף
abolish 1
be changed 1
be over 2
change 2
cut off 1
go on forward 1
grow up 2
pass 2
pass away 1
pass on 1
pass through 1
strike through 2.
PIEL change 2.
HIPH. alter 1
be renewed 1
change 5
renew 2
sprout 1.

CHALAPH חֲלַף
pass 4.

CHALAQ[1] חלק
distribute 2
divide 6
give 1
have part 1
impart 1
part 1
take away a portion 1
receive 1
*be divided 3.
Partic. partner 1.
NIPH. be divided 4
be parted 1
divide self 1
*distribute 1
*divide 1.
PIEL deal 2
distribute 1
divide 21
part 2.
PUAL be divided 3.
HIPH. separate self 1.
HITHP. divide 1.

CHALAQ[2] חלק
be smoother 1.
HIPH. flatter 6
smooth 1.

CHALAQ[3] חָלָק
flattering 2
smooth 2.

CHALAQ חֲלָק
portion 3.

CHALAQLAQQOTH חֲלַקְלַקּוֹת *f. pl.*
flatteries 2
*slippery 2.

CHALAQQOTH חֲלַקּוֹת *f. pl.*
flatteries 1.

CHALASH חלש
discomfit 1
waste away 1
weaken 1.

CHALAT חלט
HIPH. catch 1.

CHALATS חלץ
draw out 1
loose 2
put off 1
withdraw self 1
Pass. pt. armed 8
armed man 3
ready armed 2
armed soldier 1
army 1
prepared 2.
NIPH. arm selves 1
be delivered 4
go armed 2.
PIEL deliver 12
take away 2.
HIPH. make fat 1.

CHALATSAYIM חֲלָצַיִם *f. du.*
loins 9
reins 1.

CHALCHALAH חַלְחָלָה *f.*
great pain 2
much pain 1
pain 1.

CHALI חֲלִי
jewel 1
ornament 1.

CHALIL חָלִיל
pipe 6.

CHALILAH חָלִילָה *f*
be (it) far 9
forbid 4
*God forbid 3.

CHALIPHAH חֲלִיפָה *f.*
change 11
course 1.

CHALITSAH חֲלִיצָה *f.*
armour 1
spoil 1.

CHALLAH חַלָּה *f.*
cake 14.

* Inexact translations, *e.g.*, of a noun by a verb or adjective, of an active by a passive.
† Cases where two or more words in the original are translated by one word or by a phrase.

CHALLAMISH חַלָּמִישׁ
flint 3
rock 1
*flinty 1.
CHALLAMUTH חַלָּמוּת *f.*
egg 1.
CHALLASH חַלָּשׁ
weak 1.
CHALLON חַלּוֹן
window 31.
CHALLUQ חַלֻּק
smooth 1.
CHALOM חֲלוֹם
dream 63
*dreamer 1.
†*See* baal[2].
CHALOPH חֲלוֹף
destruction 1.
CHALUQQAH חֲלֻקָּה *f.*
division 1.
CHALUSHAH חֲלוּשָׁה *f.*
*being overcome 1.
CHALUTS *pass. partic. of* **CHALATS.**
CHAM[1] חָם
father-in-law 4.
CHAM[2] חָם
hot 1
warm 1.
CHAMA חֵמָא (חֶמְאָ) *f.*
fury 2.
CHAMAD חמד
covet 4
delight in 1
desire 8
lust after 1.
Pass. pt. beauty 1
delectable thing 1.
NIPH. *pt.* pleasant 1
to be desired 3.
PIEL *with great delight 1.
CHAMAL חמל
have compassion 5
have pity 10
pity 8
spare 18.
CHAMAM חמם
be hot 1
be warm 1
get heat 1
have heat 1
warm at 1
warm self 2
wax hot 1
wax warm 1.
NIPH. be hot 1
enflame selves 1.
PIEL warm 1.
HITHP. be warmed.
CHAMAQ חמק
withdraw self 1.
HITHP. go about 1.
CHAMAR[1] חמר
be red 1.
CHAMAR[2] חמר
daub 1.
CHAMAR[3] חמר
be troubled 1.
POALAL be foul 1
be troubled 2.
CHAMAR חֲמַר
wine 6.
CHAMAS[1] חמס
do violence 1
imagine wrongfully 1
take away violently 1
shake off 1
violate 1
wrong 1.
NIPH. make bare 1.
CHAMAS[2] חָמָס
cruelty 4
damage 1
injustice 1
violence 38
violent dealing 1
wrong 3
*cruel 1
*false 1
*unrighteous 1
*violent 6.
†*See* ish.[1]

CHAMASH חמש
PIEL take up fifth part 1.
CHAMESH חָמֵשׁ
fifth 6
five *freq.*
†fifteen (*with* asar) 20; fifteenth (*with* asar) 17.
Repeated; five apiece 1.
CHAMETS[1] חָמֵץ
be leavened 3.
Partic. cruel man 1.
HIPH. be leavened 2.
HITHP. be grieved 1.
CHAMETS[2] חָמֵץ
leavened 1.
As noun leaven 5
leavened bread 5.
CHAMETS[3] חָמֵץ
Pass. pt. dyed 1.
CHAMISHI חֲמִישִׁי (חֲמִשִׁי)
fifth 40
fifth part 3
fifth time 1.
CHAMISHSHAH = CHAMESH.
CHAMISHSHIM חֲמִשִּׁים
fifties 6
fiftieth 4
fifty 148.
†by fifty (*with* ish) 2; fifty every where (*with* bachamishshim) 1.
CHAMITS חָמִיץ
clean 1.
CHAMMAH חַמָּה *f.*
heat 1
sun 5.
CHAMMANIM חַמָּנִים *pl.*
idols 1
images 7.
CHAMMUQ חַמּוּק
joint 1.
CHAMOR חֲמוֹר
ass 95
he ass 1
heaps (*pl.*) 1.
CHAMORATHAYIM חֲמֹרָתַיִם *f. du.*
heaps 2.
CHAMOTH חָמוֹת *f.*
mother-in-law 11.
CHAMUDOTH חֲמוּדוֹת *f. pl.*
pleasant things 1
precious things 1
*greatly beloved 3
*goodly 1
*pleasant 1
*precious 2.
CHAMUSHIM חֲמֻשִׁים *pl.*
armed 2
harnessed 2
As noun armed men 1.
CHANAH חנה
abide 1
abide in tents 3
camp 4
dwell 2
encamp 47
grow to an end 1
pitch 76
pitch tent 1
rest in tent 1.
Partic. that lie 2.
CHANAK חנך
dedicate 4
train up 1.
CHANAMAL חֲנָמַל
frost 1.
CHANAN חנן
be favourable 1
be gracious 13
be merciful 12
deal graciously 1
favour 3
graciously give 1
grant graciously 1
have mercy on 1
have mercy upon 13
have pity upon 3
intreat 1
shew favour 3
shew mercy 2
pity 1.
Adv. inf. very.
NIPH. be gracious 1.
PIEL be gracious to 1.
POEL favour 1
have mercy on 1.
HOPH. be shewed favour 1
find favour 1.
HITHP. beseech 4
intreat 1
make 1
make supplication 11
pray 1.
†PIEL speak fair (*with* qol) 1.
CHANAN חנן
shew mercy 1.
HITHP. make supplication 1.
CHANAQ חנק
NIPH. hang self 1.
PIEL strangle 1.
CHANAT חנט
embalm 4
put forth 1.
CHANEPH[1] חָנֵף
be defiled 2
be polluted 2
be profane 1
defile 1.
Adv. inf. greatly 1
HIPH. corrupt 1
defile 1
pollute 2.
CHANEPH[2] חָנֵף
hypocrite 10
hypocritical 2.
†*See* adam.
CHANIK חָנִיךְ
trained 1.
CHANINAH חֲנִינָה *f.*
favour 1.
CHANITH חֲנִית *f.*
javelin 6
spear 41.
CHANNUN חַנּוּן
gracious 13.
CHANUKKAH חֲנֻכָּה *f.*
dedicating 2
dedication 6.
CHANNUKKAH חֲנֻכָּה *f.*
dedication 4.
CHANUPPAH חֲנֻפָּה *f.*
profaneness 1.
CHANUTH חָנוּת *f.*
cabin 1.
CHAPH חַף
innocent 1.
CHAPHA חפא
PIEL do secretly 1.
CHAPHAH חפה
cover 6.
NIPH. be covered 1.
PIEL ceil 1
overlay 4.
CHAPHAPH חפף
cover 1.
CHAPHAR חפר
dig 16
dig for 1
paw 1
search out 3
seek 1.
CHAPHARPERAH חֲפַרְפֵּרָה
mole 1.
CHAPHAS חפש
search 2
search for 1
search out 1.
NIPH. be searched out 1
PIEL make diligent search 1
search 6
search out 1.
PUAL be hidden 1.
Partic. diligent 1.
HITHP. be changed 1
disguise self 7.
CHAPHASH חפש
PUAL be free 1.
CHAPHAZ חפז
haste 4
make haste 1
tremble 1.
NIPH. haste away 2
make haste 1.

CHAPHER חפר
be ashamed 3
be confounded 6
be brought to confusion 2
be brought unto shame 1
be put to shame 1
HIPH. be ashamed 1
be put to shame 1
bring reproach 1
come to shame 1.
CHAPHETS[1] חפץ
be pleased 3
be well pleased 1
delight 32
desire 9
favour 2
have delight 6
have pleasure 3
like 2
move 1
please 10
take delight 1
will 4.
Adv. inf. any at all 1.
CHAPHETS[2] חָפֵץ
he that desireth 1
that desire 1
that favour 1
that hath pleasure in 1
that wish 1
which hath pleasure 1
who desire 1
whosoever would 1
willing 1
*delight in 1
*please 1.
CHAQAH חקה
PUAL *pt.* carved work 1
pourtrayed 2.
HITHP. set a print 1.
CHAQAQ חקק
appoint 1
decree 1
grave 2
note 1
pourtray 2
set 1.
Partic. governor 1.
POEL *pt.* decree 1
governor 1
lawgiver 6.
PUAL *pt.* law 1.
HOPH. be printed 1.
CHAQAR חקר
make search 1
search 11
search out 7
seek 1
sound 1
try 1.
NIPH. be found out 2
be searched 1
be searched out 1.
PIEL seek out 1.
CHARAB חרב (חָרֵב)
be desolate 2
be dried up 4
be dry 12
be laid waste 4
be wasted 2
decay 1
lie waste 1
slay 1
waste 1.
Adv. inf. utterly 1.
NIPH. be desolate 1
be slain 1
be wasted 1.
PUAL be dried 2.
HIPH. destroy 1
dry up 6
lay waste 2
make waste 3.
Partic. destroyer 1.
HOPH. be laid waste 2.
Adv. inf. surely 1.
CHARAB חרב
HOPH. be destroyed 1.
CHARABAH חָרָבָה *f.*
dry 1
dry ground 3
dry land 4.
CHARABON חַרְבוֹן
drought 1.

CHARAD חרד
be afraid 8
be careful 1
quake 1
tremble 13.
HIPH. discomfit 1
fray 1
fray away 2
make afraid 12.
CHARADAH חֲרָדָה *f.*
care 1
fear 2
quaking 1
trembling 5
*exceedingly 1.
CHARAG חרג
be afraid 1.
CHARAH חרה
be angry 9
be displeased 4
be hot 5
be kindled 43
be wroth 14
burn 1
grieve 1
wax hot 5
Adv. inf. very 1.
NIPH. be incensed 2.
HIPH. close self 1.
[TIPHEL] contend 1.
HIPH. kindle 1
*earnestly 1.
HITHP. fret self 4.
CHARAIM חֲרָאִים (V.L.) *pl.*
dung 1.
CHARAK חרך
roast 1.
CHARAK חרך
HITHP. singe 1.
CHARAKKIM חֲרַכִּים *pl.*
lattice 1.
CHARAM[1] חרם
have flat nose 1.
CHARAM[2] חרם
HIPH. consecrate 1
destroy 2
devote 1
make accursed 1
utterly destroy 40
utterly make away 1
utterly slay 1.
Adv. inf. utterly 1.
HOPH. be devoted 1
be forfeited 1
be utterly destroyed 1.
CHARAPH חרף
reproach 4
winter 1.
NIPH. *pt.* betrothed 1.
PIEL blaspheme 1
defy 8
jeopard 1
rail 1
reproach 23
upbraid 1.
CHARAQ חרק
gnash 5.
CHARAR חרר
be burned 2
burn 1.
NIPH. be angry 1
be burned 5
be dried 1.
PILP. kindle 1.
CHARASH[1] חרש
be deaf 1
be silent 1
hold peace 3
keep silence 2.
HIPH. be still 1
cease 1
conceal 1
hold tongue 4
hold peace 23
keep silence 3
leave off speaking 1
rest 1
speak not a word 1
Adv. inf. altogether 3.
HITHP. be quiet 1.
CHARASH[2] חרש
devise 5
ear 1
imagine 1
plow 11.
Partic. plower 1
plowman 2
worker 1.
Pass. pt. graven 1.
NIPH. be plowed 2.
HIPH. secretly practise 1.
CHARASH[3] חָרָשׁ
artificer 2
carpenter 8
craftsman 4
engraver 3
maker 1
smith 3
worker 1
workman 6
such as wrought 1
*skilful 1.
†carpenter (*with* ets) 4; mason (*with* eben, qir) 2; smith (*with* barzel) 1.
CHARATH חרת
Pass. pt. graven 1.
CHARATS חרץ
bestir self 1
decide 1
decree 1
determine 1
maim 1
move 2.
Niph. pt. determined 5.
CHARATS חֲרַץ *f.*
loin 1.
CHARCHUR חַרְחֻר
extreme burning 5.
CHAREB[1] **= CHARAB.**
CHAREB[2] חָרֵב
desolate 2
dry 2
waste 6.
CHARED חָרֵד
afraid 1
that tremble 2
those that tremble 1
*tremble 2.
CHARERIM חֲרֵרִים *pl.*
parched places 1.
CHARGOL חַרְגֹּל
beetle 1.
CHARIM חֲרִים (V.L.) *pl.*
dung 2.
CHARISH חָרִישׁ
earing 1
earing time 1
ground 1.
CHARISHI חֲרִישִׁי
vehement 1.
CHARITIM חֲרִיטִים *pl.*
bags 1
crisping pins 1.
CHARITS חָרִיץ
harrow 2.
†cheese (*with* chalab) 1.
CHARON חָרוֹן
fierce wrath 1
fierceness 9
fury 1
sore displeasure 1
wrath 5
*fierce 23
*wrathful 1.
CHAROSHETH חֲרֹשֶׁת *f.*
carving 2
cutting 2.
CHARSITH חַרְסִית *f.*
east 1.
CHARTOM חַרְטֹם
magician 5.
CHARTSANNIM חַרְצַנִּים *pl.*
kernels 1.
CHARTSUBBOTH חַרְצֻבּוֹת *f. pl.*
bands 2.
CHARTUMMIM חַרְטֻמִּים *pl.*
magicians 11.
CHARUL חָרוּל
nettle 3.

* Inexact translations, *e.g.*, of a noun by a verb or adjective, of an active by a passive.
† Cases where two or more words in the original are translated by one word or by a phrase.

CHARUTS[1] חָרוּץ
diligent 5
sharp 1
decision 2.
As noun sharp pointed thing 1
threshing instrument 2
wall 1.

CHARUTS[2] חָרוּץ
fine gold 1
gold 6.

CHARUZIM חֲרוּזִים *pl.*
chains 1.

CHASAD חסד
PIEL put to shame 1.
HITHP. shew self merciful 2.

CHASAH חסה
have hope 1
make refuge 1
put trust 15
trust 19
*my trust is 1.

CHASAK חשׂך
assuage 1
forbear 1
hinder 1
hold back 1
keep 1
keep back 3
punish 1
refrain 3
reserve 1
spare 8
withhold 4.
NIPH. be asswaged 1
be reserved 1.

CHASAL חסל
consume 1.

CHASAM חסם
muzzle 1
stop 1.

CHASAN חסן
NIPH. be laid up 1.

CHASAN חסן
HAPH. possess 2.

CHASAPH חשׂף
clean 1
discover 2
draw out 1
make bare 4
take 1
uncover 2.

CHASAPH חֲסַף
clay 9.

CHASER[1] חסר
be abated 1
decrease 1
fail 2
have need 1
lack 5
want 7.
PIEL bereave 1
make lower 1.
HIPH. cause to fail 1
have lack 1.

CHASER[2] חָסֵר
he that is destitute of 1
he that is void of 2
he that wanteth 2
that lacketh 1
that wanteth 1
void of 4
*fail 2
*have need 1
*lack 3
*want 1
*want (*n.*) 1.

CHASHAB חשׁב
conceive 1
count 4
devise 20
esteem 2
find out 1
forecast 1
hold 1
imagine 7
impute 2
invent 1
mean 1
purpose 6
regard 2
think 16.
Partic. cunning 8
cunning man 1
cunning workman 2.
NIPH. be accounted 5
be counted 17
be esteemed 3
be imputed 2
be reckoned 2
reckoning to be made 1.
PIEL be like 1
make account of 1
consider 1
count 2
devise 2
forecast 1
imagine 2
reckon 4
think 1
think on 1.
HITHP. be reckoned 1.

CHASHAB חשׁב
repute 1.

CHASHACH חשׁח
be careful 1
have need of 1.

CHASHAH חשׁה
be silent 1
be still 1
hold peace 3
keep silence 2.
HIPH. be still 2
hold peace 6
still 1.

CHASHAK חשׁךְ
be black 1
be dark 3
be darkened 7
be dim 1.
HIPH. cause darkness 1
darken 2
hide 1
make dark 2.

CHASHAL חשׁל
Niph. pt. feeble 1.

CHASHAL חשׁל
subdue 1.

CHASHAQ חשׁק
desire 2
have a delight [in] 1
have a desire 1
long 1
set love [on] 2
*in love to 1.
PIEL fillet 1.
PUAL *pt.* filleted 2.

CHASHASH חֲשַׁשׁ
chaff 2.

CHASHCHUTH חַשְׁחוּת *f.*
*be needful 1.

CHASHEKAH חֲשֵׁכָה *f.*
darkness 5.

CHASHMAL חַשְׁמַל
amber 3.

CHASHMANNIM חַשְׁמַנִּים *pl.*
princes 1.

CHASHOK חָשֹׁךְ
mean man 1.

CHASHOK חֲשׁוֹךְ
darkness 1.

CHASHRAH חַשְׁרָה *f.*
*dark 1.

CHASHUQIM חִשֻּׁקִים *pl.*
fillets 8.

CHASID חָסִיד
godly man 1
good 1
holy 4
Holy One 1
merciful 3
saint 19
that is godly 2.
†ungodly (lo chasid) 1.

CHASIDAH חֲסִידָה *f.*
ostrich 1
stork 5.

CHASIL חָסִיל
caterpillar 6.

CHASIN חָסִין
strong 1.

CHASIPH חֲשִׂף
little flock 1.

CHASON חָסֹן
strong 2.

CHASPAS חַסְפַּס
round thing 1.

CHASSIR חַסִּיר
wanting 1.

CHASUTH חָסוּת *f.*
trust 1.

CHATA חטא
be in fault 1
bear blame 2
commit [sin] 6
do sin 2
have done harm 1
offend 4
sin 165
trespass 1.
PIEL bear loss 1
cleanse 8
make reconciliation 1
offer for sin 2
purge 1
purify (self) 2.
HIPH. miss 1
make an offender 1
cause to sin 2
make to sin 29.
HITHP be purified 2
purify 2
purify self 1.

CHATAAH חֲטָאָה *f.*
sin 7
sin offering 1.

CHATAB חטב
cut down 1
hew 7.
PUAL be polished 1.

CHATAI חֲטָי
sin 1.

CHATAM חטם
refrain 4.

CHATAPH חטף
catch 3.

CHATH חַת
broken 1
dismayed 1
dread 1
fear 1.

CHATHAH חתה
heap 1
take 2
take away 1.

CHATHAK חתך
NIPH. be determined 1.

CHATHAL חתל
PUAL be swaddled 1.
Hoph. adv. inf. at all 1.

CHATHAM חתם
seal 16
seal up 6.
NIPH. be sealed 2.
PIEL mark 1.
HIPH. be stopped 1.

CHATHAM חתם
seal 1.

CHATHAN[1] חתן
Partic. father in law 21
mother in law 1.
HITHP. be son in law 5
join in affinity 2
make affinity 1
make marriages 3.

CHATHAN[2] חָתָן
bridegroom 8
husband 2
son in law 10.

CHATHAPH חתף
take away 1.

CHATHAR חתר
dig 7
dig through 1
row 1.

CHATATH[1] חתת
be afraid 2
be amazed 1
be broken down 2
be broken in pieces 5
be chapt 1
be dismayed 6.
NIPH. be abolished 1
be affrighted 1
be afraid 3
be beaten down 1
be broken 1
be broken to pieces 1
be discouraged 1
be dismayed 20
go down 1.
PIEL be broken 1
scare 1.
HIPH. break 1
confound 1
cause to be dismayed 1
make afraid 1
terrify 1.

CHATHATH[2] חֲתַת
casting down 1.

CHATHCHATTIM חַתְחַתִּים *pl.*
fears 1.

CHATHULLAH חֲתֻלָּה *f.*
swaddling band 1.

CHATHUNNAH חֲתֻנָּה *f.*
espousal 1.

CHATSAB חצב (חָצַב)
dig 5
divide 1
hew 4
hew out 4
make 1.
Partic. hewer 4
mason 3.
NIPH. be graven 1.
PUAL be hewn 1.
HIPH. cut 1.

CHATSAH חצה
divide 8
live out half 1
reach to the midst 1
part 1.
NIPH. be divided 3
part 1.

CHATSAPH חצף
Haph. pt. hasty 2
urgent 1.

CHATSATS[1] חצץ
Partic. *by bands 1.
PIEL *pt.* archer 1.
PUAL be cut off in the midst 1.

CHATSATS[2] חָצָץ
arrow 1
gravel 1
gravel stone 1.

CHATSEB = **CHATSAB.**

CHATSER חָצֵר
court 140
town 1
village 45.

CHATSI חֲצִי (חֵצִי)
half 105
middle 1
midst 8
part 13
two parts 1.
†midnight (*with* layelah) 4.

CHATSIR[1] חָצִיר
court 1.

CHATSIR[2] חָצִיר
grass 17
hay 2
herb 1
leek 1.

CHATSOTH חֲצוֹת *f.*
†midnight (*with* layelah) 4.

CHATSOTSER חֲצֹצֵר
blow 1
sound 4.
Partic. trumpeter 1.

CHATSOTSERAH חֲצֹצְרָה *f.*
trumpet 28
trumpeter 1.

CHATTA חַטָּא
offender 1
sinful 1
sinner 16.

CHATTAAH חַטָּאָה *f.*
sin 2
*sinful 1.

CHATTAAH חַטָּאָה *f.*
sin offering 1.

CHATTATH חַטָּאת *f.*
punishment 2
punishment of sin 1
purification for sin 2
purifying 1
sin 169
sin offering 116
sinner 1.

CHATUBOTH חֲטֻבוֹת *f. pl.*
carved works 1.

CHAVAH חוה
PIEL shew 6.

CHAVAH חוה (חוא)
PAEL shew 4.
HAPH. shew 10.

CHAVAR חָוַר
wax pale 1.

CHAVVOTH חַוּוֹת *f. pl.*
small towns 1
towns 3.

CHAYA חֲיָא (חֲיָה)
live 5.
HAPH. keep alive 1.

CHAYAH חיה
be whole 1
live 148
recover 10
revive 4
*God save 8.
Adv. inf. certainly 1
surely 10.
PIEL give life 2
keep alive 5
leave alive 1
let live 1
make alive 2
nourish (up) 2
preserve 4
preserve alive 2
preserve life 1
quicken 14
repair 1
revive 6
save 1
save alive 13
save life 1
suffer to live 1.
HIPH. keep alive 3
let live 1
make alive 1
make to live 1
promise life 1
restore to life 4
revive 2
save 1
save alive 6
save lives 2.

CHAYAI חַיֵּי
live 22
save life 1.

CHAYEH חָיֶה
lively 1.

CHAYIL חַיִל
activity 1
army 54
band of men 1
band of soldiers 1
company 1
forces 13
great forces 1
goods 2
host 29
might 7
power 9
riches 11
strength 12
substance 8
train 1
valour 37
war 2
wealth 10
*able 3
*mighty 1
*strong 5
*valiant 14
*valiantly 5
*very 1
*virtuous 3
*virtuously 1
*worthily 1
*worthy 1.
†army (*with* tsaba). *See* ben[2].

CHAYITS חַיִץ
wall 1.

CHAYYAH = **CHAIYAH.**

CHAZA חזא (חזה)
behold 6
have [a dream] 1
see 23.
Pass. pt. wont 1.

CHAZAH חזה
behold 7
look 3
prophesy 2
provide 1
see 41.
Partic. [*See* chozeh].

CHAZAQ[1] חזק
be confirmed 1
be constant 1
be of good courage 6
be courageous 2
be encouraged 1
be established 1
be hardened 1
be made strong 1
be recovered 1
be sore 3
be stout 1
be strengthened 2
be strong 40
be waxen strong 1
be stronger 1
be sure 1
be urgent 1
catch hold 1
harden 1
make strong 2
prevail 8
strengthen 1
wax sore 1
*courageously 1.
PIEL amend 1
encourage 6
fasten 2
fortify 3
give strength 1
harden 9
help 1
maintain 1
make hard 1
make strong 2
mend 1
repair 13
strengthen 21.
HIPH. be strong 1
catch 4
catch hold
cleave 1
confirm 2
constrain 1
continue 1
force 1
hold 11
hold fast 5
lay hold 8
lean 2
make strong 4
obtain 1
prevail 2
receive 1
relieve 1
repair 34
retain 4
seize 1
strengthen 3
take 9
take hold 15
take fast hold 1.
HITHP. become mighty 1
behave selves valiantly 1
be of good courage 1
be strengthened 3
be strong 1
encourage self 2
hold 1
make self strong 1
play the man 2
shew self strong 1
strengthen self 9
take courage 1
wax mighty 1
withstand 1
†PIEL aid (*with du. of* yad) 1. HIPH. help (*with* beyad) 1. HITHP. *pt.* calker (*with* bedeq) 2.

CHAZAQ[2] חָזָק
hard 1
hot 1
loud 1
mighty 20
sore 3
strong 28.
†impudent (*with* metsach) 1; stiffhearted (*with* leb) 1.

CHAZEH חָזֶה
breast 13.

CHAZEK חָזֵק
strong 1.
†louder and louder (*with* meod) 1.

CHAZIR חֲזִיר
boar 1
swine 6.

* Inexact translations, *e.g.*, of a noun by a verb or adjective, of an active by a passive.
† Cases where two or more words in the original are translated by one word or by a phrase.

CHAZIZ חָזִיז
bright cloud 1
lightning 2.

CHAZON חָזוֹן
vision 35.

CHAZOTH חָזוֹת *f.*
vision 1.

CHAZOTH חָזוּת *f.*
sight 2.

CHAZUTH חָזוּת *f.*
agreement 1
vision 2
*notable 1
*notable one 1.

CHEBEL חֶבֶל (חֵבֶל) *c.*
band 1
coast 4
company 2
cord 16
country 1
destruction 1
line 7
lot 3
pain 1
pang 2
portion 4
region 3
rope 3
snare 1
sorrow 10
tackling 1.

CHEBER חֶבֶר
company 1
enchantment 2
*wide 2
[Ps. 58. 5 *untranslated*].

†*See* chabar.

CHEBRAH חֶבְרָה *f.*
company 1.

CHEBYON חֶבְיוֹן
hiding 1.

CHEDEL חֶדֶל
world 1.

CHEDEQ חֵדֶק
brier 1
thorn 1.

CHEDER חֶדֶר
chamber 17
innermost part 2
inward part 2
parlour 1
south 1.

†bedchamber (*with* mishkab 4, *with* mittah 2) 6; inner chamber (cheder be-cheder) 4; within (min chedarim) 1.

CHEDVAH חֶדְוָה *f.*
gladness 1
joy 1.

CHEDVAH חֶדְוָה *f.*
joy 1.

CHEK חֵךְ
mouth 9
roof of mouth 5
taste 4.

CHEL חֵיל
army 1
bulwark 1
host 2
rampart 2
trench 1
wall 2.

CHELAH [1] חֵילָה *f.*
bulwark 1.

CHELAH [2] חֶלְאָה *f.*
scum 5.

CHELBENAH חֶלְבְּנָה *f.*
galbanum 1.

CHELEB חֵלֶב
fat 75
fatness 4
grease 1
marrow 1
*best 5
*finest 2.

CHELED חֶלֶד
age 2
short time 1
world 2.

CHELEKAH חֵלְכָה
poor 2.

CHELEM חֵלֶם
dream 22.

CHELEPH חֵלֶף
for 2.

CHELEQ [1] חֵלֶק
inheritance 1
part 22
portion 40
*be partaker 1.

CHELEQ [2] חֵלֶק
flattering 1
flattery 1
*smooth *stone* 1.

CHELKAIM חֶלְכָּאִים
(V.L.)
poor 1.

CHELQAH [1] חֶלְקָה *f.*
field 3
ground 1
parcel 5
part 2
piece 3
piece of land 2
plat 2
portion 6.

CHELQAH [2] חֲלָקָה *f.*
flattery 1
slippery place 1
smooth 1
smooth thing 1
*flattering 2.

CHELYAH חֶלְיָה *f.*
jewel 1.

CHEMA חֵמָא *f.*
fury 1.

CHEMA = CHAMA.

CHEMAH [1] חֶמְאָה *f.*
butter 9.

CHEMAH [2] חֵמָה *f.*
butter 1.

CHEMAH [3] חֵמָה *f.*
anger 1
bottle 1
fury 64
heat 1
hot displeasure 3
indignation 1
poison 6
rage 2
wrath 33
*be wroth 1
*furious 4
*wrathful 1.

†furiously (be-chemah) 1. *See* baal[2].

CHEMAR חֵמָר
slime 2
*slime (*adj.*) 1.

CHEMDAH חֶמְדָּה *f.*
desire 4
*goodly 1
*pleasant 11
*precious 1.

CHEMED חֶמֶד
*desirable 3
*pleasant 2.

CHEMER חֶמֶר
red wine 1
*pure 1.

CHEMETH חֵמֶת
bottle 4.

CHEMLAH חֶמְלָה *f.*
pity 1
*merciful 1.

CHEN חֵן
favour 26
grace 38
*gracious 2
*pleasant 1
*precious 1.

†*See* tob.

CHEPHES חֵפֶשׂ
search 1.

CHEPHETS חֵפֶץ
delight 3
desire 8
matter 1
pleasure 15
purpose 3
thing to be desired 1
thing to desire 1
*acceptable 1
*delightsome 1
*desire (*vb.*) 1
*pleasant 1.

†willingly (be-chephets) 1.

CHEQ חֵיק
bosom 32
bottom 3
lap 1
midst 1
*within 1.

CHEQEQ חֵקֶק
decree 1
thought 1.

CHEQER חֵקֶר
finding out 1
number 1
search 2
searching 3
to search 1
*search out 1.

†unsearchable (en[1] cheqer) 3.

CHEREB חֶרֶב *f.*
axe 1
dagger 1
knife 5
mattock 1
sword 402
tool 1.

CHEREM [1] חֵרֶם
net 9.

CHEREM [2] חֵרֶם
accursed 3
accursed thing 10
curse 4
cursed thing 3
dedicated thing 1
devoted 2
devoted thing 3
things which should have been utterly destroyed 1
utter destruction 1
*appoint utter destruction 1.

CHERES [1] חֶרֶס
sun 3.

CHERES [2] חֶרֶס
itch 1.

CHERES [3] חֶרֶשׂ
earth 1
potsherd 5
sherd 2
stone 1
*earthen 8.

CHERESH [1] חֵרֵשׁ
deaf 9.

CHERESH [2] חָרָשׁ
artificer 1
craftsman 2
*secretly 1.

CHERET חֶרֶט
graving tool 1
pen 1.

CHERMESH חֶרְמֵשׁ
sickle 2.

CHERPAH חֶרְפָּה *f.*
rebuke 2
reproach 66
shame 3
*reproachfully 1.

†to reproach (*with* min) 1.

CHESED [1] חֶסֶד
favour 3
good deed 1
goodliness 1
goodness 12
kindness 38
loving kindness 30
merciful kindness 2
mercy *freq.*
pity 1
*kindly 5
*merciful 1.

CHESED [2] חֶסֶד
reproach 1
wicked thing 1.

CHESEN חֱסֵן
power 2.

CHESER חֶסֶר
poverty 1
want 1.

CHESHBON חֶשְׁבּוֹן
account 1
device 1
reason 1.

CHESHEB חֵשֶׁב
curious girdle 8.

CHESHEQ חֵשֶׁק
desire 3
pleasure 1.

CHESHKAH חֶשְׁכָה *f.*
*dark 1.

CHESRON חֶסְרוֹן
that which is wanting 1.

CHET חֵטְא
fault 1
offence 1
punishment of sin 1
sin 30
*grievously 1.

CHETHEPH חֶתֶף
prey 1.

CHETS חֵץ
arrow 48
dart 1
shaft 1
staff 1
wound 1.

†*See* baal[2].

CHETSEN חֵצֶן
bosom 1.

CHETSI [1] חֵצִי
arrow 5.

CHETSI [2] = **CHATSI.**

CHEVA חֵיוָא *f.*
beast 20.

CHEZEQ חֵזֶק
strength 1.

CHEZEV חֵזֵו
look 1
vision 11.

CHEZQAH חֶזְקָה *f.*
strength 1
*be strong 1
*strengthen self 1
*strong 1.

CHIBBEL חִבֵּל
mast 1.

CHIBBUQ חִבֻּק
folding 2.

CHIDAH חִידָה *f.*
dark saying 3
dark sentence 1
dark speech 1
hard question 2
proverb 1
riddle 9.

CHIL [1] חִיל (חוּל)
be afraid 1
be grievous 1
be in anguish 1
be in pain 4
be much pained 1
be pained 2
be sore pained 1
be sorrowful 1
be wounded 1
bring forth 1
dance 1
fall grievously 1
fall with pain 1
fear 2
grieve 1
have pain 2
sorrow 1
travail 3
travail with child 1
tremble 1.

POLEL
bear 1
be formed 1
calve 1
dance 1
drive away 1
form 5
make to calve 1.

PULAL
be brought forth 2
be made 1
be shapen 1.

HIPH.
shake (*tr.*) 2.

HOPH.
be made to bring forth 1.

HITHPO.
travail with pain 1.

Partic.
grievous 1.

HITHPAL.
be grieved 1.

CHIL [2] חִיל (חוּל)
abide 1
look for 1
rest 1
stay 2
tarry 1
wait carefully 1.

POLEL
trust 1.

HITHPO.
wait patiently 1.

CHIL [3] חִיל
pain 3
pang 2
sorrow 1.

CHILAH חִילָה *f.*
sorrow 1.

CHIN חִין
comely 1.

CHINNAM חִנָּם
causeless 2
free 1
freely 1
innocent 1
for nothing 1
for nought 6
in vain 2
that which did cost me nothing 1
without a cause 15
without cost 1
without wages 1.

CHINTIN חִנְטִין *pl.*
wheat 2.

CHIPPAZON חִפָּזוֹן
haste 3.

CHISH חִישׁ
soon 1.

CHISHSHEBONOTH
חִשְּׁבֹנוֹת *f. pl.*
engines 1
inventions 1.

CHISHSHUQIM חִשֻּׁקִים
felloes 1.

CHISHSHURIM חִשֻּׁרִים
spokes 1.

CHITSON חִיצוֹן
outer 1
outward 7
utter 12
without 5.

CHITTAH [1] חִטָּה *f.*
wheat 30.

CHITTAH [2] חִתָּה *f.*
terror 1.

CHITTITH חִתִּית *f.*
terror 8.

CHITTUL חִתּוּל
roller 1.

CHIVVAR חִוָּר
white 1.

CHIZZAYON חִזָּיוֹן
vision 9.

CHOACH חוֹחַ
bramble 1
thicket 1
thistle 5
thorn 5.

CHOB [1] חֹב
bosom 1.

CHOB [2] חוֹב
debtor 1.

CHOBEL חֹבֵל
pilot 4.

†*See* rab.

CHOBERETH חֹבֶרֶת *f.*
coupling 2
which coupleth 2.

CHODESH חֹדֶשׁ
month 220
new moon 20
*another 1
*monthly 1.

CHOGGA חָגָּא *f.*
terror 1.

CHOKMAH חָכְמָה *f.*
wisdom 146
wit 1
*skilful 1
*wisely 2.

CHOKMAH חָכְמָה *f.*
wisdom 8.

CHOKMOTH חָכְמוֹת *f.*
wisdom 4.

CHOL [1] חוֹל
sand 23.

CHOL [2] חֹל
common 2
profane 2
profane place 1
unholy 1.

CHOLED חֹלֶד
weasel 1.

CHOLI חֳלִי
disease 7
grief 4
sickness 12
*be sick 1.

CHOM חֹם
heat 9
*be hot 4
*warm 1.

CHOMAH חוֹמָה *f.*
wall 127
*walled 1.

CHOMER חֹמֶר
clay 11
heap 2
homer 11
mire 2
mortar 4.

CHOMESH [1] חֹמֶשׁ
fifth part 1.

CHOMESH [2] חֹמֶשׁ
fifth *rib* 4.

CHOMET חֹמֶט
snail 1.

CHOMETS חֹמֶץ
vinegar 6.

CHONEPH חֹנֶף
hypocrisy 1.

CHOPH חוֹף
coast 2
haven 2
shore 2
side 1.

CHOPHESH חֹפֶשׁ
precious 1.

CHOPHNAYIM חָפְנַיִם *du.*
fists 1
hands 3
both hands 1.

†*See* melo.

CHOPHSHI חָפְשִׁי
at liberty 1
free 16.

CHOPHSHITH חָפְשִׁית *f.*
several 2.

CHOQ [1] חֹק
bound 1
commandment 1
custom 2
decree 7
decreed place 1
due 4
law 4
measure 1
necessary food 1
ordinance 9
ordinary food 1
portion 3
set time 1
statute 87
task 1
*appointed for 1
*convenient for 1.

CHOQ [2] חוֹק
[V.L. for cheq.]

CHOR [1] חֹר
network 1.

CHOR [2] חוֹר
cave 1
hole 6.

CHORBAH חָרְבָּה *f.*
decayed place 1
desert 3
desolate place 5
desolation 8
destruction 1
waste 7
waste place 5
*desolate 1
*laid waste 1
*waste (*adj.*) 6.

†desolate (le-chorbah) 1; laid waste (le-chorbah) 1; utterly waste (*with* choreb) 1; wasted (le-chorbah) 1.

CHOREB חֹרֶב
desolation 1
drought 3
heat 6
waste 1
*dry 3
*waste (*adj.*) 1.

†*See* chorbah.

CHOREPH חֹרֶף
cold 1
winter 3
youth 1
*winter (*adj.*) 2.

CHORESH [1] חֹרֵשׁ
artificer 1.

CHORESH [2] חֹרֶשׁ
bough 1
forest 1
shroud 1
wood 4.

CHORI [1] חֳרִי
heat 1
*fierce 3
*great 2.

CHORI [2] חֹרִי
white 1

* Inexact translations, *e.g.*, of a noun by a verb or adjective, of an active by a passive.
† Cases where two or more words in the original are translated by one word or by a phrase.

CHORIM חֹרִים *pl.*
nobles 13.
CHOSEN חֹסֶן
riches 1
strength 2
treasure 2.
CHOSER חֹסֶר
want of 3.
CHOSHEK חֹשֶׁךְ
dark 5
darkness 69
night 1
obscurity 1
*dark (*adj.*) 2.
CHOSHEN חֹשֶׁן
breastplate 25.
CHOSHKAH חֲשֵׁכָה *f.*
*dark 1.
CHOTER חֹטֶר
rod 2.
CHOTHAM חוֹתָם
seal 5
signet 9.
CHOTHEMETH חֹתֶמֶת *f.*
signet 1.
CHOTSEN חֹצֶן
arm 1
lap 1.
CHOZEH חֹזֶה
[*Partic. of* chazah]
prophet 1
seer 18.
†stargazer (*with* ba-kokabim) 1. *See* asah.
CHOZEQ חֹזֶק
strength 5.
CHOZQAH חָזְקָה *f.*
force 2
*mightily 2
*repair 1
*sharply 1.
CHUB חב
PIEL make endanger 1.
CHUD חוד
put forth 4.
CHUG 1 חוג
†compass (*with* al2 pene) 1.
CHUG 2 חוג
circle 1
circuit 1
compass 1.
CHUL = CHIL.
CHUM חוּם
brown 4.
CHUPHSHAH חֻפְשָׁה *f.*
freedom 1.
CHUPPAH חֻפָּה *f.*
chamber 1
closet 1
defence 1.
CHUQQAH חֻקָּה *f.*
custom 2
manner 1
ordinance 22
rite 1
statute 77
*appointed 1.
CHUR 1 חוּר
white 2.
CHUR 2 חוּר
hole 2.
CHUS חוּס
have pity 2
pity 5
spare 16.
†*See* ayin.3
CHUSH חוּשׁ
haste 4
hasten 1
make haste 8.
Pt. pass. ready 1.
HIPH. haste 1
hasten 3
make haste 1.
CHUT חוּט
cord 1
fillet 1
line 1
thread 4.
CHUT חוּט
HAPH. join 1.
CHUTS חוּץ
abroad 10
field 2
forth 1
highway 1
out 6
outward 1
street 44
utter 1
without 9.
†abroad (ba-chuts 3, la-chuts 1) 4; more than (*with* min) 1; without (ba-chuts 12, el1 chuts 1, la-chuts 3) 16. Min chuts (le): abroad 6, abroad out of 1, forth 1, from without 2, on the outside 2, out from 2, out of 9, without 46.

D

DA דָּא
another 2
one 2
this 2.
DAAB דאב
mourn 1
sorrow 1
*sorrowful 1.
DAAG דאג
be afraid 3
be careful 1
be sorry 1
sorrow 1
take thought 1.
DAAH 1 דאה
fly 4.
DAAH 2 דָּאָה *f.*
vulture 1.
DAAK דעך
be extinct 1
be put out 6.
NIPH. be consumed 1.
PUAL be quenched 1.
DAATH דַּעַת *f.*
cunning 1
knowledge 82
*know 6.
†ignorantly (bi-beli daath) 1; unawares (bi-beli daath) 1; unwittingly (bi-beli daath) 2.
DABAB דבב
cause to speak 1.
DABAQ דבק (דָּבַק)
abide fast 1
be joined together 1
cleave 28
follow close 1
follow hard 1
keep fast 2
keep self 2
stick 2
take 1.
PUAL be joined 1
cleave fast together 1.
HIPH. cause to cleave 1
cause to stick 1
follow hard after 4
make cleave 2
overtake 3
pursue hard 1.
HOPH. cleave 1.
DABAR 1 דבר
Partic. bid 1
commune 1
promise 1
say 3
speak 21
talk 10
tell 1
utter 1.
Pt. pass. spoken 1.
Infin. speak 1.
NIPH. speak 3
talk 1.
PIEL answer 1
appoint 1
be spokesman 1
bid 3
command 4
commune 19
declare 2
destroy 1
give [judgment *or* sentence] 4
name 1
promise 29
pronounce 14
publish 1
rehearse 1
say 119
speak 814
talk 34
teach 2
tell 24
think 1
use [intreaties] 1
utter 6.
Adv. inf. well 1.
PUAL be spoken 1
be spoken for 1.
HIPH. subdue 2.
HITHP. speak 4.
†PIEL wont to speak (*with adv. inf.*) 1.
DABAR 2 דָּבָר
act 52
advice 2
affair 2
answer 15
any such 2
any thing 2
book (*pl.*) 7
business 8
care 1
case 1
cause 8
commandment 20
communication 2
counsel 1
dealing 1
decree 1
deed 5
disease 1
due 1
duty 2
effect 1
errand 3
hurt 1
language 1
manner 1
matter 63
message 3
oracle 1
ought 2
part 1
portion 1
promise 6
provision 1
purpose 1
question 2
rate 5
reason 1
report 2
request 2
sake 3
saying 34
sentence 3
somewhat to say 1
sort 1
speech 10
talk 2
task 2
thing 215
thought 1
tidings 4
whit 1
word 770
work 2
*commune 2
*done 1
*it 1
*say 5
*speak 2
*there 1
*what (*pl.*) 1
*wherewith 1.
†certain rate (*with* yom) 2; chronicles (*pl. with* yamin) 38; confer (*with* hayah) 1; iniquity (*with* avon) 1; judgment (*with* mispat) 1; lies (*with* kazab 1, sheqer 1) 2; lying (*with* sheqer) 1; power (*with* geburah) 1; sign (*with* oth) 1; song (*with* shir2) 1; that (*with* zeh) 1; thus (*with* zeh) 1; whatsoever (*with* mah) 1. *See* al2, asah, ervah, ish1, ke, lo, ra, shub.
DABBEROTH דִּבְּרוֹת *f. pl.*
words 1.
DABBESHETH דַּבֶּשֶׁת *f.*
bunch 1.
DABEQ 1 = **DABAQ.**
DABEQ 2 דָּבֵק
joining 1
that did cleave 1
that sticketh close [r] 1.
DACHAH דָּחָה
chase 1
overthrow 1
thrust 2
totter 1.
Adv. inf. sore 2.
NIPH. be driven away 1
be driven on 1
be outcast 3.
PUAL be cast down 1.
DACHAPH דָּחַף
Pass. pt. being hastened 1
being pressed on 1.
NIPH. haste 2.
DACHAQ דָּחַק
thrust 1
vex 1.
DACHAVAN דַּחֲוָן *f. pl.*
instruments of musick 1.
DAD דַּד
breast 2
teat 2.
DADAH דָּדָה
HITHP. go softly 1
go with 1.
DAG דָּג
fish 19.
DAGAH 1 דָּגָה *f.*
fish 15.
DAGAH 2 דָּגָה
grow 1.
DAGAL דָּגַל
set up banners 1.
Pass. pt. chiefest 1.
NIPH. *pt.* with banners 1.
DAGAN דָּגָן
corn 37
wheat 2.
†*See* goren.
DAGAR דָּגַר
gather 1
sit 1.
DAHAM דָּהַם
NIPH. *pt.* astonied 1.
DAHAR דָּהַר
Partic. prancing 1.
DAHARAH דַּהֲרָה *f.*
prancing 2.
DAI (DE) דַּי
ability 1
enough 5
so much as is sufficient 1
sufficient 4
very 2.
†sufficiently (le-mad-dai); too much (ke-dai). *See* be, ke, le, matsa, midde, naga.
DAK דַּךְ
afflicted 1
oppressed 3.
DAK = DEK.
DAKA דכא
NIPH. *pt.* contrite one 1.
PIEL beat to pieces 1
break 1
break in pieces 3
bruise 1
crush 1
destroy 1
oppress 1
smite 1
*be crushed 1.
PUAL be broken 2
be bruised 1
be humbled 1.
HITHP. be crushed 1
be destroyed 1.
DAKAH דָּכָה
crouch 1.
NIPH. be sore broken 1
be contrite 1.
PIEL break 1
break sore 1.
DAKKA דַּכָּא
contrite 2
destruction 1.
DAKKAH דַּכָּה *f.*
*in the stones 1.
DAL 1 דַּל
door 1.
DAL 2 דַּל
lean 1
needy 2
poor 43
poor man 1
weak [er] 1.
DALACH דלח
trouble 2.
DALAG דלג
leap 1.
PIEL leap 4.
DALAH 1 דלה
draw water 2
draw out 1.
Adv. inf. enough 1.
PIEL lift up 1.
DALAH 2 דַּלָּה *f.*
door 1.
DALAL דלל
be emptied 1
be not equal 1
bring low 3
dry up 1
fail 1.
NIPH. be impoverished 1
be made thin 1.
DALAPH דלף
drop through 1
melt 1
pour out 1.
DALAQ דלק
chase 1
hotly pursue 1
kindle 2
persecute 1.
Partic. burning 1
persecutor 1.
HIPH. inflame 1
kindle 1.
DALIYOTH *f. pl.*
branches 8.
DALLAH דַּלָּה *f.*
hair 1
pining sickness 1
poor 5
poorest sort 1.
DALLEQETH דַּלֶּקֶת *f.*
inflammation 1.
DAM דָּם
blood 213
blood guiltiness (*pl.*) 1
*bloody 14.
†*See* anashim, nakah.
DAMA דמע
weep 1.
Adv. inf. sore 1.
DAMAH 1 דמה
be like 13
be likened 1
liken 1.
NIPH. be like 1.
PIEL compare 1
devise 1
liken 4
mean 1
think 6
uses militudes 1.
HITHP. be like 1.
DAMAH 2 דמה
cease 2
destroy 1.
NIPH. be cut down 1
be cut off 4
be destroyed 1
be brought to silence 1
be undone 1
perish 2.
Adv. inf. utterly 1.
DAMAM דמם
be silent 2
be still 4
cease 2
forbear 1
hold peace 1
keep silence 5
rest 2
stand still 2
tarry 1
wait 1.
NIPH. be cut down 2
be cut off 3
be silent 2.
POAL quiet self 1.
HIPH. put to silence 1.
DAPHAQ דפק
knock 1
overdrive 1.
HITHP. beat 1.
DAQ דַּק
dwarf 1
small 5
thin 5
very little thing 1.
†leanfleshed (*with* basar2) 2.
DAQAQ דקק
be small 1
beat small 1
bruise 1.
HIPH. beat in pieces 1
make dust 1
stamp small 2
stamp 2.
Inf. into powder 1
very small 1.
HOPH. be bruised 1.
†to powder (ad1 asher daq) 1.
DAQAR דקר
pierce 1
thrust through 6.
NIPH. be thrust through 1.
PUAL *pt.* stricken through 1
thrust through 1
wounded 1.
DAR דַּר
white marble 1.
DAR דָּר
generation 4.
DARAK דרך
bend 14
come 1
draw 1
go 1
shoot 1
tread (down, on, out) 28
walk 1.
Partic. archer 1.
HIPH. bend 1
guide 1
lead 4
lead forth 1
make go over 1
make to go 1
make to walk 1
thresh 1
tread 1
tread down 1.
†KAL *partic.* archer (*with* qesheth) 1.
DARASH דרש
ask 1
care for 1
enquire 38
examine 1
make inquisition 2
question 1
regard 1
require 13
search 7
seek 88
seek out 1.
Adv. inf. diligently 1
surely 1.
NIPH. be required 1
be inquired 5
be sought 1
be sought for 1.
Adv. inf. at all 1.
†KAL care for (*with* achare) 1. *Partic.* necromancer (*with* el1 meth) 1.
DARDAR דַּרְדַּר
thistle 2.
DARKEMONIM דַּרְכְּמֹנִים *pl.*
drams 4.
DAROM דָּרוֹם
south 17.
DASHA 1 דשא
spring 1.
HIPH. bring forth 1.
DASHA 2 דֶּשֶׁא
at grass 1.
DASHEN 1 דָּשֵׁן
wax fat 1.
PIEL accept 1
anoint 1
make fat 1
receive ashes 1
take away the ashes from 1.
PUAL be made fat 4.
HOTHP. be made fat 1.
DASHEN 2 דָּשֵׁן
fat 3.
DATH דָּת *f.*
commandment 1
commission 1
decree 9
law 9
manner 1.
DATH דָּת *f.*
decree 3
law 11.
DAVAH דָּוָה
Inf. infirmity 1.

* Inexact translations, *e.g.*, of a noun by a verb or adjective, of an active by a passive
† Cases where two or more words in the original are translated by one word or by a phrase.

DAVEH דָּוֶה
faint 2
having sickness 1
menstruous cloth 1
she that is sick 1.

DAVVAG דַּוָּג
fisher 1.

DAVVAI דַּוָּי
faint 3.

DAYEQ דָּיֵק
fort 6.

DAYISH דַּיִשׁ
threshing 1.

DAYYAG דַּיָּג
fisher 2.

DAYYAH דַּיָּה *f.*
vulture 2.

DAYYAN דַּיָּן
judge 2.

DAYYAN דַּיָּן
judge 1.

DE = DAI.

DEA דֵּעַ
knowledge 2
opinion 3.

DEABAH דְּאָבָה *f.*
sorrow 1.

DEABON דְּאָבוֹן
sorrow 1.

DEAGAH דְּאָגָה *f.*
care 1
carefulness 2
fear 1
heaviness 1
sorrow 1.

DEAH דֵּעָה *f.*
knowledge 6.

DEBACH [1] דבח
offer [sacrifice] 1.

DEBACH [2] דְּבַח
sacrifice 1.

DEBAQ דבק
cleave 1.

DEBASH דְּבַשׁ
honey 52.
†*See* tsuph, sarath.

DEBELAH דְּבֵלָה *f.*
cake of figs 3
lump [of figs] 1.

DEBEQ דֶּבֶק
joint 2
sodering 1.

DEBER דֶּבֶר
murrain 1
pestilence 47
plague 1.

DEBIR דְּבִיר
oracle 16.

DEBORAH דְּבוֹרָה *f.*
bee 4.

DECHAL דחל
fear 2.
Pass. pt. dreadful 2
terrible 1.
PAEL make afraid 1.

DECHI דְּחִי
falling 2.

DEGEL דֶּגֶל
banner 1
standard 13.

DEHAB דְּהַב
gold 14
*golden 9.

DEK דֵּךְ
the same 1
this 11.

DEKAR דְּכַר
ram 3.

DELAQ דלק
Partic. burning 1.

DELEPH דֶּלֶף
dropping 2.

DELETH דֶּלֶת *f.*
door 68
gate 13
leaf 4
lid 1
two leaved gate 1.

DELI דְּלִי
bucket 1.

DEMA דֶּמַע
liquor 1.

DEMAH דמה
Partic. like 2.

DEMAMAH דְּמָמָה *f.*
calm 1
silence 1
*still 1.

DEMI דֳּמִי
cutting off 1.

DEMUTH דְּמוּת *f.*
fashion 1
likeness 19
manner 1
similitude 2
*like 1
*like as 1.

DENAH דְּנָה
one another 1
that 1
these 3
this 38
this matter 1
this sort 1
which 1.
†See *achare, al,*[2] *ke, kol, min.*

DEQAQ דקק
HAPH. break in (*or* to) pieces 9.

DERA דְּרָע *f.*
arm 1.

DERAON דֵּרָאוֹן
abhorring 1
contempt 1.

DEREK דֶּרֶךְ *c.*
conversation 2
custom 1
highway 1
journey 23
manner 8
way 1692
*by 1
*through 1
*toward 31.
†along (mid-derek) 1; away be-derek) 1; eastward (*with* qadim) 1; pathway (*with* nethibah) 1. *See* abar[2], asah, halak, yad.

DEROR [1] דְּרוֹר
liberty 7
*pure 1.

DEROR [2] דְּרוֹר
swallow 2.

DESHE דֶּשֶׁא
grass 5
herb 4
tender grass 2
tender herb 2
*green 1.

DESHEN [1] דֶּשֶׁן
fatness 7.

DESHEN [2] דֶּשֶׁן
ashes 8.

DETHABAR דְּתָבַר
counsellor 2.

DETHE דֶּתֶא
tender grass 2.

DEVAI דְּוַי
languishing 1
sorrowful 1.

DEYO דְּיוֹ
ink 1.

DI דִּי
but
for
seeing
that
therefore
until
when
which
whom
whose etc.
†without (with *la*) 1. See *ke, kol, la, mah, man.*[1]

DIBBAH דִּבָּה *f.*
defaming 1
evil report 3
infamy 2
slander 3.

DIBRAH דִּבְרָה *f.*
cause 1
end 1
estate 1
order 1
regard 1.

DIBRAH דִּבְרָה *f.*
intent 1
sake 1.

DIBYONIM דִּבְיֹנִים *pl.*
dove's dung 1.

DIG דִּיג
fish (*vb.*) 1.

DIKKEN דִּכֵּן
same 1
that 1
this 1.

DIKRON דִּכְרוֹן
record 1.

DIMAH דִּמְעָה *f.*
tears 23.

DIMYON דִּמְיוֹן
*like 1.

DIN [1] דִּין
contend 1
execute [judgment] 1
judge 17
minister judgment 1
plead 1
plead the cause 1.
Niph. pt. at strife 1.

DIN [2] דִּין
cause 8
judgment 9
plea 2
strife 1.

DIN [1] דִּין
judge 1.

DIN [2] דִּין
judgment 5.

DISH = DUSH.

DISHON דִּישֹׁן
pygarg 1.

DOB דֹּב (דּוֹב)
bear 12.

DOB דֹּב
bear 1.

DOBE דֹּבֶא
strength 1.

DOBER דֹּבֶר
fold 1
manner 1.

DOBEROTH דֹּבְרוֹת *f. pl.*
floats 1.

DOCHAN דֹּחַן
millet 1.

DOD דּוֹד
beloved 33
father's brother 2
love 8
uncle 16
wellbeloved 1.

DODAH דּוֹדָה *f.*
aunt 1
father's sister 1
uncle's wife 1.

DOKI דֳּכִי
wave 1.

DOKRAN דָּכְרָן
record 2.

DOLI דֳּלִי
bucket 1.

DOMEN דֹּמֶן
dung 6.

DOMI דֳּמִי
rest 1
silence 2.

DONAG דּוֹנַג
wax 4.

DOPHI דֳּפִי
†*See* nathan.

DOQ דֹּק
curtain 1.

DOR דּוֹר
age 2
generation 123
posterity 1
*another 1.
†evermore (le-dor va-dor) 1; never (lo le-dor va-dor) 1.

DOREBAN דָּרְבָן
goad 1.

DOREBONOTH דָּרְבֹנוֹת *f. pl.*
goads 1.

DUACH דּוּחַ
HIPH. cast out 1
purge 1
wash 1.

DUB דּוּב
HIPH. cause sorrow 1.

DUD דּוּד
basket 3
caldron 1
kettle 1
pot 2.

DUDAI דּוּדַי
baskets 1
mandrakes 6.

DUGAH דּוּגָה *f.*
†*See* sir.

DUK דּוּךְ
beat 1.

DUKIPHATH דּוּכִיפַת
lapwing 2.

DUMAH דּוּמָה *f.*
silence 2.

DUMIYYAH דּוּמִיָּה *f.*
silence 1
*silent 1
*wait 2.

DUMAM דּוּמָם
*dumb 1
*silent 1
*wait quietly 1.

DUMMAH דֻּמָּה *f.*
the destroyed 1.

DUN [1] דּוּן
strive 1.

DUN [2] דּוּן
judgment 1.

DUQ דּוּק (= *DEQAQ*)
be broken to pieces 1.

DUR [1] דּוּר
burn 1.

DUR [2] דּוּר
dwell 1.

DUR [3] דּוּר
ball 1
†round about (kad-dur) 1.

DUR דּוּר
dwell 5.
Partic. inhabitant 2.

DUSH דּוּשׁ
break 1
tear 1
thresh 8
tread out 2.
NIPH. be trodden down 1.
HOPH. be threshed 1.

DUSH דּוּשׁ
tread down 1.

DUTS דּוּץ
be turned into joy 1.

E

E אִי
where? etc.
†*With* zeh: where, which way, etc.; *with* miz-zeh: whence etc.

EB אֵב
fruit 1
greenness 1.

EB אֵב
fruit 3.

EBAH אֵיבָה *f.*
enmity 3
hatred 2.

EBED עֶבֶד
bondman 20
manservant 23
servant 716
*bondage (*pl.*) 10.
†*See* abodah.

EBEH אֵבֶה
swift 1.

EBEL אֵבֶל
mourning 24.

EBEN אֶבֶן *f.*
stone *freq.*
weight 4
*stony 1.
†carbuncle (*with* eqdach) 1; chalkstone (*with* gir) 1; great hailstone (*with* elgabish) 3; hailstone (*with* barad) 2; headstone (*with* roshah) 1; plummet (*with* bedil) 1; slingstone (*with* qela) 2. *Repeated*: divers weights 3. *See* charash.[3]

EBEN אֶבֶן *f.*
stone 8.

EBER [1] אֵבֶר
wing 2.
†*See* erek.

EBER [2] עֵבֶר
beyond 19
by 1
other side 24
over 1
passage 2
quarter 1
side 10
this side 27.
†other side (*with* hallaz) 1; over against (al[2] eber panim) 1. †*See* el, min.

EBRAH [1] אֶבְרָה *f.*
feather 2
wing 2.

EBRAH [2] עֶבְרָה *f.*
anger 1
rage 2
wrath 31.

EBUS אֵבוּס
crib 3.

EBYON אֶבְיוֹן
beggar 1
needy 35
poor 24
poor man 1.

ECHAD אֶחָד
a (an) 56
a certain 9
alike 1
alone 1
altogether 1
another 31
any 17
anything 1
a portion 11
each 7
each man 1
each one 2
every 4
everyone 6
few (*pl.*) 3
first 36
man 1
once (*fem.*) 10
one *freq.*
only 4
other 30
some 5.
†at once (be-echath); with one consent (ke-ish echad) 1. *See* ammud, asar[2], ke, lo, naqam,[2] paam, yom.

ED [1] אֵד
mist 1
vapour 1.

ED [2] אֵיד
calamity 17
destruction 7.

ED [3] עֵד
witness 69.

EDAH [1] עֵדָה *f.*
assembly 9
company 13
congregation 124
multitude 1
people 1
swarm 1.

EDAH [2] עֵדָה *f.*
testimony 22
witness 4.

EDAYIN אֱדַיִן
now 1
that time 1
then 55.

EDEN [1] אֶדֶן
foundation 1
socket 53.

EDEN. [2] *Only pl.* **ADANIM.**

EDER [1] אֶדֶר
robe 1
*goodly 1.

EDER [2] עֵדֶר
drove 4
flock 32
herd 2.

EDNAH עֶדְנָה *f.*
pleasure 1.

EDRA אֶדְרָע
force 1.

EDUTH עֵדוּת *f.*
testimony 55
witness 4.

EGEL עֵגֶל
bullock 2
calf 33.
†young calf (*with* ben[2] baqar) 1.

EGLAH עֶגְלָה *f.*
calf 1
heifer 10.
†heifer (*with* baqar) 2; young cow (*with* baqar) 1.

EGOZ אֱגוֹז
nut 1.

EGROPH אֶגְרֹף
fist 2.

EK אֵיךְ
how
what, etc.

EKAH אֵיכָה
how, etc.

EKAKAH אֵיכָכָה
how 4.

EKEPH אֶכֶף
hand 1.

EKES עֶכֶס
stocks 1
tinkling ornament 1.

EKO(H) אֵיכֹה (אֵיכוֹ)
where 1.

EL [1] אֶל־
against
as for
at
beside
concerning
in
into
near
to
toward
unto, etc.
†directly (*with* nokach) 1; forth of (*with* mib-beth 1; forth without (*with* mib-beth) 1; straight forward (*with* eber[2] panim) 3; near (*with* yad) 1; over against (*with* mul[2]) 2; toward (*with* mul[2]) 1. *See* min tachath.

EL [2] אֵל
God 212
god 15
idol 1
might 1
mighty one 1
power 3
*goodly 1
*great 1
*mighty 4
*strong 1.
†power (*with* yad) 1.

EL [3] אֵל
these 7
those 2.

EL אֵל
these 1.

ELA עֵלָּא
†over (with *min*) 1.

ELAH אֵלָה *f.*
elm 1
oak 11
teil tree 1.

ELAH אֱלָהּ
God 78
god 16.

ELAMMIM אֵילַמִּים (אֵלַמִּים) *pl.*
arches 13.

ELAMMOTH אֵלַמּוֹת *f. pl.*
arches 2.

ELEH אֵלֶּה
other
these
they
those
some, etc.

ELEH אֵלֶּה
these 1.

ELEM [1] אֵלֶם
congregation 1.

ELEM [2] עֶלֶם
stripling 1
young man 2.

* Inexact translations, *e.g.*, of a noun by a verb or adjective, of an active by a passive.
† Cases where two or more words in the original are translated by one word or by a phrase.

ELEPH אֶלֶף
family 1
kine (*pl.*) 4
oxen (*pl.*) 3
thousand *freq.*

ELEPH = ALAPH.

ELGABISH אֶלְגָּבִישׁ
†*See* eben.

ELI עֱלִי
pestle 1.

ELIL אֱלִיל
idol 17
image 1
no value 1
thing of nought 1.

ELIM אֵילִים *pl.*
might 4
mighty men 1
oaks 1
trees 2.

ELOAH אֱלוֹהַּ
God 52
god 5.

ELOHIM אֱלֹהִים *pl.*
angels 1
God *freq.*
goddess 2
gods 240
judges 5
*great 1
*mighty 2
*very great 1.
†exceeding (*lit.* to God) 1.

ELON אֵלוֹן
plain 9.

ELOM עֵילוֹם
ever 1.

ELYON עֶלְיוֹן
high 9
higher 4
highest 3
most high 27
on high 1
upper(most) 9.

ELYON עֶלְיוֹן
most High 4.

EM אֵם *f.*
dam 5
mother *freq.*
parting 1.

EMAH אֵימָה *f.*
dread 1
fear 5
horror 1
idol 1
terror 7
*terrible 2

EMDAH עֶמְדָּה *f.*
standing 1.

EMEQ עֵמֶק
dale 2
vale 4
valley 63.

EMER אֵמֶר
answer 1
saying 2
speech 2
word 42
*appointed 1.

EMESH אֶמֶשׁ
in former time 1
yesterday 3
yesternight 1.

EMETH אֱמֶת *f.*
establishment 1
right 1
truth 90
verity 1
*assured 1
*assuredly 1
*faithful 1
*faithfully 1
*of a truth 1
*right 2
*sure 1
*true (truly) 25.

EMRAH אִמְרָה *f.*
word 1.

EMTHANI אֵמְתָנִי
terrible 1.

EMUN אֵמֻן
faith 1
truth 1
*faithful 3.

EMUNAH אֱמוּנָה (אֱמֻנָה) *f.*
faith 1
faithfulness 18
set office 5
stability 1
truth 13
*faithful 3
*faithfully 5
*steady 1
*truly 1
*verily 1.

EMUNNAH = EMUNAH.

EN 1 **= AYIN.**1

EN 2 **= AYIN.**3

ENAB עֵנָב
grapes 17
ripe grapes 1
wine 1.

ENASH אֱנָשׁ (אֱנַשׁ)
man 23
†See *kol.*

ENAYIM (ENE). *Dual of* **AYIN.**3

ENOSH אֱנוֹשׁ [*pl.* **ANASHIM**].
another [man] 1
man 31
men 7
mortal man 1.
†familiar (*with* shalom) 1; stranger (*with* ger) 1.

ENUTH עֱנוּת *f.*
affliction 1.

EPHA אֶפַע
of nought 1.

EPHAH 1 אֵיפָה *f.*
ephah 34
measure 2.
†*Repeated:* divers measures 2.

EPHAH 2 עֵיפָה *f.*
darkness 2.

EPHEH אֶפְעֶה
viper 3.

EPHER אֵפֶר
ashes 22.

EPHES אֶפֶס
ankle 1
end 13
less than nothing 1
none 6
not any 1
nothing 3
thing of nought 1
uttermost part 1
want 1
*no 3
*not 2
As prep. and adv.
but 1
but only 1
howbeit 1
nevertheless 1
notwithstanding 1
save 1
saving 1
without 2
without cause 1.
†nor any (ve-ephes) 1.

EPHO אֵפוֹא (אֵפוֹ)
here 1
now 1
where? 4.

EPHOD אֵפוֹד (אֵפֹד)
ephod 49.

EPHO אֵיפֹה
what manner 1
where 9.

EPHROCHIM אֶפְרֹחִים *pl.*
young 2
young ones 2.

EQDACH אֶקְדָּח
†*See* eben.

EQEB עֵקֶב
reward 3.
Adv. unto the end 2
Prep. by 1
for 1
Conj. because 2
if 1
†because (*with* asher 2, *with* ki 2) 4; because that (*with* asher) 1.

EQED עֵקֶד
†*See* bayith.

EQER עֵקֶר
stock 1.

ERABON עֵרָבוֹן
pledge 3.

EREB 1 אֶרֶב
den 1.
†to lie in wait (lemo ereb) 1.

EREB 2 עֶרֶב
even 62
evening 46
eventide 1
night 4.
†day (*with* boqer) 1; evening (*with* yom) 1. Ben1 ha-arbayim: at even 8, in the evening 1. *See* eth2, panah.

EREB 3 עֵרֶב
mingled people 4.

EREB 4 עֵרֶב
mixed multitude 1
woof 9
*mixed 1.

EREG אֶרֶג
beam 1
weaver's shuttle 1.

EREK 1 אֶרֶךְ
patient 1
slow 9.
†longsuffering (*with* aph2) 4; long-winged (with eber1) 1.

EREK 2 עֵרֶךְ
estimation 24
price 1
taxation 1
things that are to be set in order 1
*be set at 1
*value (*vb.*) 1.
†equal (ke-erek) 1. *See* arak.2

EREK 3 עֵרֶךְ
proportion 1
suit 1.

EREL אֶרְאֵל
valiant one 1.

ERES עֶרֶשׂ
bed 5
bedstead 2
couch 3.
†bed (*with* yatsua) 1.

ERETS אֶרֶץ *c.*
country 140
earth *freq.*
field 1
ground 96
land *freq.*
nation 1
way 3
world 4
*common
*them that dwell in a country 1.
†wilderness (*with* midbar) 1.

EREZ אֶרֶז
cedar 66
cedar tree 6.

EROM עֵירֹם
naked 9
nakedness 1.

ERVAH עֶרְוָה *f.*
nakedness 51
shame 1.
†*With* dabar: some uncleanness 1, unclean thing 1. *See* basar2.

ERYAH עֶרְיָה *f.*
bare 4
naked 1
*quite 1.

ESAR = ISSAR.

ESAR אֱסָר
decree 7.

ESEB עֵשֶׂב
grass 16
herb 17.

ESH אֵשׁ *c.*
fire *freq.*
*burning 1
*fiery 2
*flaming 1
*hot 1.

ESHED אֶשֶׁד
stream 1.

ESHEK אֶשֶׁךְ
stones 1.

ESHEL אֵשֶׁל
grove 1
tree 2.

ESHETH 1 עֶשֶׁת
*bright 1.

ESHETH 2 **= ISHSHAH**

ESHKAR אֶשְׁכָּר
gift 1
present 1.

ESHKOL אֶשְׁכֹּל (אֶשְׁכּוֹל)
cluster 9
cluster of grapes 1.

ESHNAB אֶשְׁנָב
casement 1
lattice 1.

ESHPAR אֶשְׁפָּר
good piece 1
good piece of flesh 1.

ESHSHA אֶשָּׁא
flame 1.

ESHSHAH אֶשָּׁה *f.*
fire 1.

ESHTADDUR אֶשְׁתַּדּוּר
sedition 2.

ESHTONOTH עֶשְׁתֹּנֹת *f. pl.*
thoughts 1.

ESHUN אֱשׁוּן
*obscure 1.

ESRA = ASAR.

ESREH = ASAR.

ESRIM עֶשְׂרִים
twenty
twentieth.
†*See* meah.

ESRIN עֶשְׂרִין
twenty 1.

ESUR אֵסוּר
band 2.
†*See* bayith.

ESUR אֱסוּר
band 2
imprisonment 1.

ET עֵט
pen 4.

ETA עֵטָא
counsel 1.

ETH 1 אֵת
coulter 2
plowshare 3.

ETH 2 עֵת *c.*
season 15
time 257.
†after (le-eth 1, ke-eth *with inf. of* yatsa 1) 2; always (be-kol eth) 3; certain years (*pl. with pl. of* shanah) 1; continually (be-kol eth) 1; evening (*with* ereb2) 1; evening-tide (*with* ereb2) 2; eventide (*with* ereb2) 1; meal time (*with* okel) 1; noon-tide (*with* tsohorayim) 1; so long as (be-kol eth asher) 1; what time (be-eth) 1; when (le-eth 1, be-eth 5) 6; when at the first (ka-eth *with* rishon) 1. *See* panah.

ETHAN אֵיתָן (אֵתָן) *n.* and *adj.*
hard 1
mighty 4
rough 1
strength 2
strong 5.

ETHMOL אֶתְמוֹל (אִתְמוֹל, אֶתְמוּל)
of late 1.
†before that time (ke-ethmol shilshom) 1; beforetime (me ethmol shilshom) 1; heretofore (*with* shilshom) 1; in time past (*with* shilshom) 1; in times past (*with* shilshom) 1; of old (me-ethmol) 1. *See* yom.

ETHMUL = ETHMOL.

ETHNAH אֶתְנָה *f.*
reward 1.

ETHNAN אֶתְנַן
hire 8
reward 3.

ETS עֵץ
gallows 8
helve 1
plank 1
staff 4
stalk 1
stick 14
stock 4
timber 23
tree 162
wood 103.
†pine (*with* shemen) 1. *See* charash.

ETSADAH אֶצְעָדָה *f.*
bracelet 1
chain 1.

ETSAH 1 עֵצָה *f.*
tree 1.

ETSAH 2 עֵצָה *f.*
advice 1
advisement 1
counsel 82
purpose 2.
†*See* anashim, ish.

ETSBA אֶצְבַּע *f.*
finger 30
toe 2.

ETSBEAN אֶצְבְּעָן *pl.*
fingers 1
toes 2.

ETSEB 1 עֶצֶב
labour 2
sorrow 3
*grievous 1.

ETSEB 2 עֶצֶב
idol 1.

ETSEL אֵצֶל
at 2
beside 13
by 31
hard by 1
near 2
near unto 1
to 1
toward 1
unto 3
with 3.
†*See* me.

ETSEM עֶצֶם *f.*
body 2
bone 104
life (*pl.*) 1
*full 1
*same (selfsame) 16
*very 2.

ETSER עֵצֶר
†*See* yarash.

ETUN אֵטוּן
fine linen 1.

EVEL = AVEL.

EVIL אֱוִיל
fool 20
foolish 5
foolish man 1.

EVILI אֱוִלִי
foolish 1.

EYAL אֱיָל
strength 1.

EYALUTH אֱיָלוּת *f.*
strength 1.

EZ עֵז *f.*
goat 55
she goat 5
*kid 1.
†*See* ben2, gedi, seh, tsaphir.

EZ עֵז *f.*
†See *tsaphirim.*

EZER עֵזֶר
help 21.

EZOB אֵזוֹב
hyssop 10.

EZOR אֵזוֹר
girdle 14.

EZRACH אֶזְרָח
any of your own nation 1
bay tree 1
born 1
born [in the land] 3
born in the land 1
born in (of) the country 2
he that is born (in the land) 2
he that was born among them 1
homeborn 1
one born 1
one of your own country 3.

EZRAH עֶזְרָה (עֶזְרַת) *f.*
help 19
*help (*vb.*) 6
*helpers 1.

EZROA אֶזְרוֹעַ
arm 2.

EZUZ עִזּוּז
might 1
strength 1.

G

GAAH 1 גָּאָה
be risen 1
grow up 1
increase 1
triumph 2
Adv. inf. gloriously 1.

GAAH 2 גְּאָה
low 2.

GAAL 1 גָּעַל
abhor 5
loathe 3
NIPH. be vilely cast away 1
HIPH. fail 1.

GAAL 2 גָּאַל
deliver 1
do part of a kinsman 3
perform the part of a kinsman 1
purchase 1
ransom 2
redeem 43
stain 1
Partic. avenger 6
kinsfolk 1
kinsman 7
near kinsman
next kinsman
redeemer 14
revenger 7
Adv. inf. at all 2
in any wise 1
NIPH. be redeemed 7
redeem self 1.

GAAL 3 גָּאַל
NIPH. be defiled 1
be polluted 1
pollute selves 1
PIEL pollute 1
PUAL be polluted 2
put from as polluted 2
HIPH. stain 1
HITHP. defile self 1.

GAAR גָּעַר
corrupt 1
rebuke 12
reprove 1.

GAASH גָּעַשׁ
shake 2
PUAL be troubled 1
HITHP. be moved 1
shake 2
toss selves 1
HITHPO. be moved 2.

GAAVAH גַּאֲוָה *f.*
excellency 3
haughtiness 2
highness 1
pride 10
swelling 1
the proud 1
*proudly 1.

GAAYONIM גַּאֲיוֹנִים (V. L.) *pl.*
proud 1.

GAB גַּב
back 2
body 2
boss 1
eminent place 3
higher place 1
nave 1
ring 2.
†eyebrows (*pl. with* enayim) 1.

GAB גַּב
back 1.

* Inexact translations, *e.g.*, of a noun by a verb or adjective, of an active by a passive.
† Cases where two or more words in the original are translated by one word or by a phrase.

GABAH גָּבַהּ
be exalted 4
be haughty 5
be high 2
be higher 4
be lifted up 6
be proud 1
exalt self 1
lift self up 1
HIPH. exalt 4
make high 1
mount up 1
raise up a great height 1.
*height 2
*on high 1
*upward 1.

GABAH[2] גָּבָהּ
high 2
proud 2.

GABAL גָּבַל
be border 1
border 1
set 1
HIPH. set bounds 1
set bounds about 1.

GABAR גָּבַר
be great 2
be mighty 1
be stronger 1
be valiant 1
prevail 12
PIEL put to [strength] 1
strengthen 2
HIPH. confirm 1
prevail 1
HITHP. exceed 1
prevail 1
strengthen self 1

GABBACHATH גַּבַּחַת *f.*
bald forehead 3
*without 1.

GABHUTH גַּבְהוּת *f.*
loftiness 1
*lofty 1.

GABIA גָּבִיעַ
bowl 8
cup 5
pot 1.

GABISH גָּבִישׁ
pearl 1.

GABLUTH גַּבְלוּת *f.*
end 2.

GABNUNNIM גַּבְנֻנִּים *pl.*
high 2.

GABOAH גָּבֹהַּ (גָּבוֹהַּ)
haughty 1
height 1
high (higher, highest) 30
lofty 2
proud 1.
†exceeding proudly (*repeated*) 1.

GACHELETH גַּחֶלֶת *f.*
burning coal 3
coal 13
coals of fire 1
hot coals 1.

GACHON גָּחוֹן
belly 2.

GAD[1] גַּד
coriander 2.

GAD[2] גָּד
troop 2.

GADA גָּדַע
cut asunder 2
cut off 3
hew down 1
NIPH. be cut asunder 1
be cut down 3
be cut off 3
PIEL cut down 5
cut in sunder 1
cut off 1
hew down 1
PUAL be cut down 1.

GADAD גָּדַד
gather selves together 1
HITHP. assemble selves by troops 2
cut selves 5
gather self in troops 1.

GADAH גִּדָּה *f.*
bank 4.

GADAL גָּדַל
be brought up 3
be great 9
be greater 3
be grown 6
be grown up 2
be magnified 7
be much set by 2
become great 3
exceed 1
grow 8
grow up 2
wax great 5
PIEL advance 1
bring up 4
make great 5
make grow 2
magnify 7
nourish 3
nourish up 1
promote 1
PUAL be grown up 1
HIPH. be excellent 1
be come to great estate 1
be magnifical 1
become great 1
boast 1
do great things 1
exceed 1
give great 1
increase 1
lift up 1
magnify 14
make great 2
wax great 1
HITHP. magnify self 4
†KAL pass (*with* min) 1.
HIPH. speak proudly (*with* peh) 1. *See* asah, halak.

GADAPH גָּדַף
PIEL blaspheme 6
reproach 1.

GADAR גָּדַר
close up 1
fence up 1
hedge 1
inclose 1
make [a wall] 1
make up 2
Partic. mason 2
repairer 1.

GADEL גָּדֵל
great 1.

GADER גָּדֵר
fence 1
hedge 4
wall 7.

GADISH גָּדִישׁ
shock 1
shock of corn 1
stack of corn 1
tomb 1.

GADOL גָּדוֹל
elder 8
eldest 6
great 399
great man 7
great matter 1
great thing 7
greater 19
greatest 9
greatness 1
high 18
long 1
loud 19
mighty 7
more 4
much 1
noble 1
proud thing 1
*very 2.
†man of great wrath (*with* chemah[3]) 1; more abundant (*with* yether) 1 *See* osher, qol, raah, simchah, sinah, yirah.

GAG גָּג
house top 9
roof 11
roof of the house 2
top 4
top of the house 4.

GAHAH גהה
cure (*vb.*) 1

GAHAR גהר
cast self down 1
stretch self 1.

GAL גַּל
billow 1
heap 18
spring 1
wave 14.

GALA גָּלַע
HITHP. intermeddle 1
meddle 1
*be meddled with 1.

GALACH גָּלַח
PIEL poll 3
shave 10
shave off 5
PUAL be shaven 3
HITHP. be shaven 2.

GALAH גלה
appear 1
be carried away 2
be departed 4
be gone 1
be led away captive 1
be open 2
carry away captive 2
go captive 2
go into captivity 7
have open 1
open 4
publish 2
remove 2
reveal 2
tell 1
Partic. captive 2
exile 1
Infin. captivity 1.
Adv. inf. surely 2.
NIPH. appear 3
be discovered 12
be opened 1
be removed 1
be revealed 8
be shewed 1
be uncovered 1
discover selves 1
reveal self 1
shew self 1
uncover self 2
Adv. inf. plainly 1
shamelessly 1.
PIEL bewray 1
disclose 1
discover 16
open 3
reveal 4
shew openly 1
uncover 30.
PUAL be led away captive 1
Partic. open 1.
HIPH. bring 1
carry away 15
carry away captive 10
carry away into captivity 1
carry captive 3
cause to be carried away 1
cause to be carried away captive 2
cause to be led into captivity 1
cause to go into captivity 1
lead captive 1
remove 3.
HOPH. be carried away 3
be carried away captive 3.
HITHP. be uncovered 1
discover self 1.
†KAL advertise (*with* ozen) 1; reveal (*with* ozen) 1; shew (*with* ozen) 6; tell (*with* ozen) 1.

GALAL[1] גָּלַל
commit 2
remove 1
roll 5
roll away 1
trust 1.
NIPH. be rolled together 1
run down 1.
POAL be rolled 1.
HIPH. roll 1.
HITHP. seek occasion 1
wallow 1.
PILP. roll down 1.
HITHPAL. roll selves 1.

GALAL[2] גָּלָל
dung 1.

GALAL[3] גָּלָל
†bi-gelal: because of 4, because that for 1, for 1, for . . . sake 4.

GALAM גלם
wrap together 1.

GALASH גלשׁ
appear 2.

GALGAL גַּלְגַּל
heaven 1
rolling thing 1
wheel 9.

GALGAL גַּלְגַּל
wheel 1.

GALIL גָּלִיל
folding (*adj.*) 2
ring (*n.*) 2.

GALLAB גַּלָּב
barber 1.

GALMUD גַּלְמוּד
desolate 2
solitary 2.

GALUTH גָּלוּת *f.*
captives 3
captivity 10
they that are carried away captive 2.

GALUTH גָּלוּת *f.*
captivity 4.
†See *ben.*[2]

GAM גַּם
again
alike
also
as
but
even
likewise
in like manner
so much as
then
though
with
yea etc.
†*Repeated*: both . . . and; either . . . or; nay . . . neither; so . . . and etc.

GAMA גָּמָא
PIEL swallow 1.
HIPH. drink 1.

GAMAL[1] גָּמַל
bestow on 2
deal bountifully 4
do (unto) 5
do good 1
recompense 2
requite 1
reward 8
ripen 1
wean 5
serve 1
yield 1
Pass. pt. child that is weaned 1
weaned 1
weaned child 2
NIPH. be weaned.

GAMAL[2] גָּמָל
camel 54.

GAMAR גָּמַר
cease 1
come to an end 1
fail 1
perfect 1
perform 1.

GAN גַּן
garden 42.

GANAB גָּנַב
carry away 1
steal 25
steal away 3.
NIPH. be stolen 1.
PIEL steal 2
PUAL be secretly brought 1
be stolen 1
be stolen away 1.
HITHP. get by stealth 1
steal away 2
Adv. inf. indeed 1
†KAL steal away unawares to (*with* leb 1, *with* lebab 1) 2.

GANAN גָּנַן
defend 5.
HIPH. defend 3.

GANNAB גַּנָּב
thief 17.

GANNAH גַּנָּה *f.*
garden 12.

GANZAK גַּנְזַךְ
treasury 1.

GAON גָּאוֹן
arrogancy 3
excellency 10
majesty 7
pomp 5
pride 19
swelling 3
*proud 1.
†excellent (le-gaon) 1.

GAPH גַּף
†by himself (be-gaph *and suff*) 2; highest place (*with* marom) 1.

GAPH גַּף
wing 3.

GARA גָּרַע
clip 1
diminish 7
minish 1
restrain 2
take from 1
withdraw 1.
NIPH. be abated 1
be diminished 1
be done away 1
be kept back 1
be taken 2
be taken away 1.
PIEL make small 1

GARAB גָּרָב
PIEL. scab 1
scurvy 1.

GARAD גָּרַד
HITHP. scrape self 1

GARAH גָּרָה
PIEL stir up 3
HITHP. be stirred up 3
contend 3
meddle 4
strive 1.

GARAM גָּרַם
gnaw the bone 1.
PIEL break 2.

GARAPH גָּרַף
sweep away 1.

GARAR גָּרַר
catch 1
destroy 1.
NIPH. chew 1
POAL saw 1.

GARAS גָּרַס
break 1.
HIPH. break 1.

GARASH גָּרַשׁ
cast up 1
drive out 1
Pass. pt. divorced 1
divorced woman 1
her that is divorced 1
her that is put away 1
put away 1
NIPH. be cast out 2
Partic. troubled 1.
PIEL cast out 6
drive away 2
drive out 20
expel 1
thrust out 6
Adv. inf. surely 1.
PUAL be driven forth 1
be thrust out 1.

GARAZ גרז
NIPH. be cut off 1.

GARGAR גַּרְגַּר
berry 1.

GARGEROTH גַּרְגְּרוֹת *f. pl.*
neck 4.

GARON גָּרוֹן
mouth 1
neck 2
throat 4.
†aloud (be-garon) 1.

GARZEN גַּרְזֶן
ax 4.

GASHAM גשם
HIPH. cause rain 1
PUAL be rained upon 1.

GASHASH גָּשַׁשׁ
PIEL grope 2

GATH גַּת *f.*
press 1
winefat 1
winepress 3.

GAV גַּו
back 3.

GAV גַּו
midst 7
†*With prep. and suff*: therein 1
wherein 1
within the same 1.

GAVA גָּוַע
be dead 1
die 11
give up the ghost 8
perish 2
yield up ghost 1
Partic. ready to die 1.

GAY גַּיְא *c.*
valley 60.

GAZAL גָּזַל
catch 1
consume 1
exercise [robbery] 1
pluck (off) 4
rob 4
spoil 8
take away 2
take away violently 5
take by force 1
tear 1
take by violence 1.
NIPH. be taken away 1.

GAZAM גָּזָם
palmerworm 3.

GAZAR גָּזַר
be cut off 1
cut down 1
decree 1
divide 3
snatch 1.
NIPH. be cut off 5
be decreed 1

GAZAZ גָּזַז
cut off 1
poll 1
shave 1
shear 4
Partic. shearer 3
sheepshearer 2
NIPH. be cut down 1.
†KAL *part.* sheepshearer (with tson) 1.

GAZEL גָּזֵל
robbery 3
thing taken away by violence 1.

GAZITH גָּזִית *f.*
hewed stone(s) 4
hewn stone (s) 5
*hewed 1
*wrought 1.

GE גֵּא
proud 1.

GEAH גֵּאָה *f.*
pride 1.

GEARAH גְּעָרָה *f.*
rebuke 12.
rebuking 1
reproof 2.

GEB[1] גֵּב
pit 1.
†*Repeated*: full of ditches 1.

GEB[2] גֵּב
locust 1.

GEB[3] גֵּב
beam 1.

GEBAR גְּבַר
man 1.

GEBAR גְּבַר
certain 2
man 19.

GEBE גֶּבֶא
marish 1
pit 1.

GEBER גֶּבֶר
every one 1
man 67
manchild 1
*mighty 2.

* Inexact translations, *e.g.*, of a noun by a verb or adjective, of an active by a passive.
† Cases where two or more words in the original are translated by one word or by a phrase.

GEBERETH גְּבֶרֶת *f.*
lady 2
mistress 7.

GEBINAH גְּבִינָה *f.*
cheese 1.

GEBIR גְּבִיר
lord 2.

GEBIRAH גְּבִירָה *f.*
queen 6.

GEBUL גְּבוּל
border 157
bound 5
coast 69
landmark 4
limit 1
quarter 1
space 2.

GEBULAH גְּבוּלָה *f.*
border 1
bound 2
coast 5
landmark 1
place 1.

GEBURAH גְּבוּרָה *f.*
force 1
mastery 1
might 27
mighty act 4
mighty power 1
power 8
strength 17.
*mighty 1
†mighty (im[2] geburah) 1.

GEBURAH גְּבוּרָה *f.*
might 2.

GEDABERIN גְּדָבְרִין *pl.*
treasurers 2.

GEDAD גדד
hew down 2.

GEDER גָּדֵר
wall 2.

GEDERAH גְּדֵרָה *f.*
fold 4
hedge 4
wall 1.
†sheepcote (*with* tson) 1;
sheepfold (*with* tson) 1.

GEDI גְּדִי
kid 9.
†kid (*with pl. of* ez) 7.

GEDILIM גְּדִלִים *pl.*
fringes 1
wreaths 1.

GEDIYYAH גְּדִיָּה *f.*
kid 1.

GEDUD [1] גְּדוּד
army 4
band 13
band of men 1
company 4
troop 8
troop of robbers 2.

GEDUD [2] גְּדוּד
cutting 1
furrow 1.

GEDULAH (גְּדוּלָּה) גְּדוּלָה *f.*
dignity 1
great things 3
greatness 7
majesty 1.

GEDUPHAH גְּדוּפָה *f.*
taunt 1.

GEEH גֵּאֶה
proud 8.

[**GEH** גֵּה
this 1.]

GEHAH גֵּהָה *f.*
medicine 1.

GELAH גְּלָה
reveal 6.
Partic. revealer 1.
HAPH. bring over 1
carry away 1.

GELAL גְּלָל
great 2.

GELED גֶּלֶד
skin 1.

GELEL גֵּלֶל
dung 4.

GELILAH גְּלִילָה *f.*
border 3
coast 1
country 1.

GELOM גְּלוֹם
clothes 1.

GEMAR גמר
Part. pass. perfect 1.

GEMUL גְּמוּל
benefit 2
desert 1
deserving 1
that which he hath given 1
recompense 10
reward 3.
†as (*with* she) 1.

GEMULAH גְּמוּלָה
deed 1
recompense 1
reward 1.

GENAZIM גְּנָזִים *pl.*
chests 1
treasuries 2.

GENEBAH גְּנֵבָה *f.*
theft 2.

GEPHEN גֶּפֶן
vine 50.
†vine (*with* yayin) 1; vine tree (ets hag-gephen 2; *with* yayin) 3.

GER (גֵּיר) גֵּר
alien 1
sojourner 1
stranger 86.
†See enosh, ish.

GERAH [1] גֵּרָה *f.*
cud 11.

GERAH [2] גֵּרָה *f.*
gerah 5.

GEREM גֶּרֶם
bone 3
top 1
*strong 1.

GEREM גְּרֶם
bone 1.

GERES גֶּרֶשׂ
beaten corn 1
corn beaten 1.

GERESH גֶּרֶשׁ
*put forth 1.

GERUSHAH גְּרֻשָׁה *f.*
exaction 1.

GERUTH גֵּרוּת *f.*
habitation 1.

GESHEM גֶּשֶׁם
great rain 1
much rain 1
rain 26
shower 5.

GESHEM גְּשֶׁם
body 5.

GEULLAH גְּאֻלָּה *f.*
kindred 1
price of redemption 2
redeeming 1
redemption 3
right 1
*redeem 5.

GEUTH גֵּאוּת *f.*
excellent things 1
lifting up 1
majesty 2
pride 2
raging 1.
†proudly (be-geuth) 1.

GEV גֵּו
among 1
back 5
body 1.

GEVAH [1] גֵּוָה *f.*
body 1.

GEVAH [2] גֵּוָה *f.*
lifting up 1
pride 2.

GEVAH גֵּוָה *f.*
pride 1.

GEVIYYAH גְּוִיָּה *f.*
body 9
carcase 2
corpse 2
dead body 1.

GEZ גֵּז
fleece 2
mowing 1
mown grass 1.

GEZA גֶּזַע
stem 1
stock 2.

GEZAR גְּזַר
Partic. soothsayer 4.
ITHP. be cut out 2.

GEZEL גֵּזֶל
violence 1
violent perverting 1.

GEZELAH גְּזֵלָה *f.*
that he had robbed 1
spoil 1
violence 3
*that 1.

GEZER גֶּזֶר
part 1
piece 1.

GEZERAH גְּזֵרָה *f.*
*not inhabited 1.

GEZERAH גְּזֵרָה *f.*
decree 2.

GIACH (גּוּחַ) גִּיחַ
break forth 1
come forth 1
draw up 1
labour to bring forth 1
take out 1.
HIPH. come forth 1.

GIACH (גּוּחַ) גִּיחַ
HAPH. strive 1.

GIBAH גִּבְעָה *f.*
hill 65
little hill 4.

GIBBAR גִּבָּר
mighty 1.

GIBBEACH גִּבֵּחַ
forehead bald 1.

GIBBEN גִּבֵּן
crookbackt 1.

GIBBOR גִּבּוֹר
able man 1
champion 1
chief 1
giant 1
man 4
mighty (man, one) 139
strong 4
strongest 1
strong man 1
that excel 1
valiant 4
valiant man 1.

GIBLI גִּבְלִי
stonesquarer 1.

GIBOL גִּבְעֹל
bolled 1.

GID גִּיד
sinew 7.

GIDDUPH גִּדּוּף
reproach 1
reviling 2.

GIL [1] (גּוּל) גִּיל
be glad 10
be joyful 4
delight in 1
joy 2
rejoice 27.

GIL [2] גִּיל
gladness 2
joy 3
rejoicing 1
*greatly 1.
†exceedingly (ele gil) 1.
See chagar.

GIL [3] גִּיל
sort 1.

GILAH גִּילָה *f.*
joy 1
rejoicing 1.

GILGAL גִּלְגָּל
wheel 1.

GILLAYON גִּלָּיוֹן
glass 1
roll 1.

GILLULIM גִּלּוּלִים *pl.*
idols 47
images 1.

GINNAH גִּנָּה *f.*
garden 4.

GINZIN גִּנְזִין *pl.*
treasures 1
*treasure (*adj.*) 2.

GIR גִּיר
†*See* eben.

GIR גִּיר
plaister 1.

GIZBAR גִּזְבָּר
treasurer 1.

GIZBAR גִּזְבָּר
treasurer 1.

GIZRAH גִּזְרָה *f.*
polishing 1
separate place 7.

GIZZAH גִּזָּה *f.*
fleece 3.

GOAL גֹּעַל
loathing 1.

GOB גּוֹב
grasshopper 1.
†*Repeated*: great grasshopper 1.

GOB גֹּב
den 10.

GOBAH גֹּבַהּ
excellency 1
height 9
loftiness 1
pride 2
*haughty 1
*high 3.

GODEL גֹּדֶל
greatness 11
stoutness 1
*stout 1.

GOEL גֹּאַל
*defile 1.

GOI גּוֹי
Gentile 30
heathen 142
nation 373
people 11
*another 1.

GOL גֹּל
bowl 1.

GOLAH גּוֹלָה *f.*
captive 1
captives 1
captivity 21
that is carried away captive 3
them of the captivity 5
those(them) that (which) had been carried away 6
removing 2
ye of the captivity 1.
†carried away (lag-golah) 1; remove (bag-golah) 1.

GOLEM גֹּלֶם
substance yet unperfect 1.

GOME גֹּמֶא
bulrush 2
rush 2.

GOMED גֹּמֶד
cubit 1.

GOPHER גֹּפֶר
gopher 1.

GOPHRITH גָּפְרִית *f.*
brimstone 7.

GOR גּוֹר
whelp 2.

GORAL גּוֹרָל
lot 77.

GOREN גֹּרֶן
barn 1
barnfloor 1
corn 1
floor 11
threshingfloor 19
threshingplace 1
void place 2.
†cornfloor (*with* dagan) 1.

GOZAL גּוֹזָל
young pigeon 1
young 1.

GUACH = GIACH

GUD גּוּד
invade 1
overcome 2.

GUL = GIL

GULGOLETH גֻּלְגֹּלֶת *f.*
every man 1
head 1
poll 7
skull 2.

GULLAH גֻּלָּה *f.*
bowl 5
pommel 3
spring 6.

GUMMATS גּוּמָּץ
pit 1.

GUPH גּוּף
HIPH. shut 1.

GUPHAH גּוּפָה *f.*
body 2.

GUR [1] גּוּר
abide 2
be gathered 2
be stranger 6
dwell (in, with) 12
gather selves together 1
gather together 1
remain 1
sojourn 57.
Partic. inhabitant 1
sojourner 1.
Adv. inf. surely 1.
HITHP. assemble selves 1
sojourn 1.
Partic. continuing 1.

GUR [2] גּוּר
be afraid 6
fear 3
stand in awe 1.

GUR [3] גּוּר
whelp 6
young one 1.

GUSH גּוּשׁ
clod 1.

GUZ גּוּז
be cut off 1
bring 1.

H

HA [1] הַ, הָ
[*The Hebrew def. article. It has many forms which vary according to the consonant of the word it precedes, e.g.* hab, had, hag, hak, etc.]

HA [2] הֲ, הַ
[*Interrogative particle*].

HA הָא
lo 1.

HABAL הבל
become vain 3
be vain 1.
HIPH. make vain 1.

HABAR הבר
†*Partic.* astrologers (*with* shamayim) 1.

HABEL הֶבֶל [= HEBEL].
vanity 3.

HABHABIM הַבְהָבִים *pl.*
offerings 1.

HADAH הדה
put 1.

HADAK הדך
tread down 1.

HADAPH הדף
cast away 1
cast out 2
drive 3
expel 1
thrust 3
thrust away 1.

HADAR [1] הדר
countenance 1
honour 2.
Partic. crooked place 1
glorious 1.
NIPH. be honoured 1.
HITHP. put forth self 1.

HADAR [2] הָדָר
beauty 4
comeliness 2
excellency 2
glory 6
honour 5
majesty 7
*glorious 1
*goodly 1.

HADAR [1] הדר
PAEL glorify 1
honour 2.

HADAR [2] הֲדַר
honour 2
majesty 1.

HADARAH הֲדָרָה *f.*
beauty 4
honour 1.

HADAS (הֲדַס) הֲדַס
myrtle 2
myrtle tree 4.

HADDABERIN הַדָּבְרִין
counsellors 2.

HADDAMIN הַדָּמִין *pl.*
pieces 2.

HADOM הֲדֹם
†footstool (*with* regel) 6.

HAGAH [1] הָגָה
imagine 2
meditate 6
mourn 4
mutter 1
roar 1
speak 4
study 2
talk 1
utter 1.
Adv. inf. sore 1.
POAL utter 1.
HIPH. mutter 1.

HAGAH [2] הָגָה
stay 1
take away 2.

HAGIG הָגִיג
meditation 1
musing 1.

HAGIN הָגִין
directly 2.

HAGUTH הָגוּת *f.*
meditation 1.

HAH הָהּ
woe worth 1.

HAKAR הָכַר
HIPH. make selves strange 1.

HAKKARAH הַכָּרָה *f.*
shew 1.

HALA הָלָא
NIPH. be cast far off 1.

HALEAH הָלְאָה
back 1
forward 5
henceforward 1
hitherto 1
thenceforth 1
yonder 1.
†beyond (mi-haleah le 3, min . . . wa-haleah 2) 5.

HALAK הלך. *See* YALAK.
be at the point 1
be conversant 1
be gone 14
be gone up 1
come 16
depart 3
enter 1
go 217
go about 1
go along 1
go away 3
go forward 1
go on 3
go out 2
march 1
pass 1
pass away 4
run 3
run along 1
take [journey] 1
walk (along) 110
wander 2
whirl 1
work 2.
The adv. inf. and partic. are freq. used before the adv. inf. and partic. of other verbs to express continuance or the gradual progress of an action; translated along, apace, continually, forth, forward, on, etc. *Adv. inf.* quite surely, etc.
NIPH. be gone 1.
PIEL cause to go 1
exercise self 1
go 8
lead 1

* Inexact translations, *e.g.*, of a noun by a verb or adjective, of an active by a passive.
† Cases where two or more words in the original are translated by one word or by a phrase.

run 1
travel 1
walk 1
HIPH. *pt.* places to walk 1.
HITHP. be conversant 1
behave self 1
be wont to haunt 1
depart 1
go 8
go abroad 1
go on still 1
go up and down 2
move self 1
run 1
travel 1
walk 32
walk abroad 1
walk on 1
walk to and fro 5
walk up and down 4.

†KAL, be eased (*with* min *and pron. suff.*) 1; follow (*with* achar²) 7; need be gone (*with adv. inf.*) 1; prosper (*with adv. inf.*) 1. *Partic.* tale-bearer (with rakil) 1; traveller (*with* nethibah) 1; unto (*with* al²) 1; wayfaring man (*with* derek) 1. HITHP. follow (*with* achar² 1, *with* be *and dual of* regel 1) 2.

***HALAK*[1]** הֲלַךְ
come 1
go 1
go up 1
*be brought again 1.
PAEL walk 1.
HAPH. walk 2.

***HALAK*[2]** הֲלָךְ
custom 3.

HALAL הָלַל
deal foolishly 1
shine 1.
Partic. fool 1
foolish 2.
PIEL boast 2
celebrate 1
commend 1
praise 105
sing praise 4.
POEL make fools 1
make mad 2.
Pass. pt. mad 1
they that are mad 1.
PUAL be commended 1
be given to marriage 1
be praised 5.
Partic. renowned 1
worthy to be praised 2.
HIPH. give [light] 1
shine 2.
HITHP. be praised 1
boast 2
boast selves 5
glory 14
make boast 1.
HITHPO. be mad 3
feign self mad 1
rage 2.

HALAM הלם
be broken 2
beat 1
beat down 1
break down 2
smite 1
smite with the hammer 1.
Pass. pt. they that are overcome 1.

HALIK הָלִיךְ
step 1

HALIKAH הֲלִיכָה
company 1
going 2
walk 1
way 2.

HALLAZ הַלָּז *c.*
that 2
this 4.
†*See* eber.

HALLAZEH הַלָּזֶה
this 2.

HALLEZU הַלֵּזוּ *f.*
this 1.

HALMUTH הַלְמוּת *f.*
hammer 1.

HALOM הֲלֹם
here 2
hither 6
thither 1.
†*See* ad³.

HAMAH המה
be clamorous 1
be disquieted 4
be in an uproar 1
be loud 1
be moved 1
be troubled 2
cry aloud 1
make a noise 6
make a tumult 1
mourn 1
rage 2
roar 8
sound 3.
Partic. concourse 1
tumultuous 1.

HAMAM הכם
break 1
consume 1
crush 1
destroy 4
discomfit 5
trouble 1
vex 1.

HAMAN המן
multiply 1.

HAMASIM הֲמָסִים *pl.*
*melting 1.

HAMNIK הַמְנִיךְ
chain 3.

HAMON הָמוֹן
abundance 3
company 1
many 3
multitude 62
noise 4
riches 1
rumbling 1
sounding 1
store 2
tumult 4.

HAMULLAH הֲמֻלָּה *f.*
speech 1
tumult 1.

HANACHAH הֲנָחָה *f.*
release 1.

HAPHAK הפך
be turned 4
change 2
give 1
make [a bed] 1
overthrow 12
overturn 4
pervert 1
retire 1
turn 24
turn again 2
turn back 1.
Pass. pt. turned 1.
Infin. turning of things upside down 1.
NIPH. be changed 1
become 1
be converted 1
be overthrown 1
be turned 25
be turned aside 1
be turned to the contrary 1
be turned up 1
come 1.
HOPH. be turned 1.
HITHP. be turned 2
tumble 1
turn every way 1

†KAL overturn (*with* le-malah) 1. NIPH. have a perverse tongue (*with* bi-lashon) 1.

HAPHAKPAK הֲפַכְפַּךְ
froward 1.

HAPHEKAH הֲפֵכָה *f.*
overthrow 1.

HAPHUGAH הֲפוּגָה *f.*
intermission 1.

HAR הַר
hill 61
hill country 1
mount *or* mountain 486.

HARAG הָרַג
destroy 1
kill 25
murder 3
slay 132.
Partic. murderer 2
slayer 1.
Adv. inf. out of hand 1
surely 1.
NIPH. be slain 2
[slaughter] be made 1.
PUAL be killed 1
be slain 1.

†KAL *part. pass.* put to death (*with* maveth) 1.

HARAH[1] הרה
bear 1
be with child 3
conceive 39.
Partic. progenitor 1.
PUAL be conceived 1.
POEL conceive 1.

HARAH[2] הָרָה *f.*
great 1
with child 9
woman with child 1.

HARAR = HAR.

HARAS הרס
beat down 1
break 1
break down 6
break through 2
destroy 3
overthrow 3
pluck down 1
pull down 3
throw down 10.
NIPH. be broken down 3
be overthrown 1
be thrown down 2.
Partic. ruined 2.
PIEL overthrow 1.
Partic, destroyer 1.
Adv. inf. utterly 1.

HARBEH הַרְבֵּה (*adv. from* רבה).
great 5
great store 1
in abundance 1
many 10
more 1
much 19
much more 1
overmuch 2
plenty 1
plenteous 1
sore 1
store 1
very 1
*be multiplied 1.

†exceeding (le-harbeh meod) 1; exceedingly (*with* meod) 1; many (le-harbeh) 1.

HAREGAH הֲרֵגָה *f.*
slaughter 5.

HAREL הַרְאֵל
altar 1.

HARHOR הַרְהֹר
thought 1.

HARISAH הֲרִיסָה *f.*
ruin 1.

HARISUTH הֲרִיסוּת *f.*
destruction 1.

HARIYYAH הָרִיָּה
woman with child 1.

HARMON הַרְמוֹן
palace 1.

HAS הַס
be silent 1
hold thy peace 1
hold thy tongue 1
keep silence 1
let [the earth] keep silence 1
with silence 1.

HASAH הסה. (*See* HAS.)
Piel imper. hold peace 1.
Hiph. still 1.

HASHMAUTH הַשְׁמָעוּת
*cause to hear 1.

HATHAL התל
PIEL deal deceitfully 1
deceive 2
mock 6.
Pual pt. deceived 1.

HATHATH התת
POEL imagine mischief 1.

HATHULLIM הֲתֻלִּים *pl.*
mockers 1.

HATSTSALAH הַצָּלָה *f.*
deliverance 1.

HAVA(H) הָוָה (הָוָא)
be 5.
†have (*with* le) 1.

HAVA(H) הֲוָה (הֲוָא)
be 26
become 2
*have 1.

HAVVAH הַוָּה *f.*
calamity 4
iniquity 1
mischief 1
mischievous thing 1
naughtiness 1
perverse thing 1
substance 1
very wickedness 1
wickedness 2
*mischievous 1
*naughty 1
*noisome 1.

HAYAH היה
be
become
be done
come
come to pass
fall
happen
last
pertain
quit selves, etc.
NIPH. be 7
be accomplished 1
be brought to pass 1
be committed 1
be done 6
break 1
deed be done 1
faint 1.

†KAL be besieged (*with* be-matsor) 1; be burnt up (*with* le-serephah) 1; be put apart (*with* le-niddah) 1; be left (*with* sheerith) 1; be mentioned (*with* le-shemuah) 1; be removed (*with* le-niddah) 1; cause (*with* le) 1; cause to fall (*with* le-mikshol le) 1; commit (*with* be) 1; escape (*with* le-peletah 2, *with* peletah 1, *with* peletah le 2) 5; follow (*with* achar²) 5; have (*with* le) 1; help (*with* zeroa le) 1; howsoever (*impf. with* mah) 1; marry (*with* le-nashim) 2; require haste (*with* nachuts) 1; seem (*with* be-enayim) 2; seem to (*with* be-enayim) 7; seem unto (*with* be-enayim) 17; [thy servants'] trade hath been about (*with* anashim) 1; [their] trade hath been to feed (*with* anashim) 1; HIPH. become (*with* le) 1. *See* makkah.

HAZAH הזה
sleep 1.

HE[1] **= HA.**[1]

HE[2] הֵא
behold 1
lo 1.

HE הָא
even 1.

HEACH הֶאָח
ah! 1
aha 11
ha 2.

HEBEL הֶבֶל *c.*
in vain 7
vanity 58
*altogether 1
*vain 4.

HED הֵד
*sounding again 1.

HEDAD הֵידָד
shout 1
shouting 8.

HEDER הֶדֶר
glory 1.

HEGEH הֶגֶה
mourning 1
sound 1
tale 1.

HEK הֵיךְ
how 2.

HEKAL הֵיכָל *c.*
palace 10
temple 70.

HEKAL הֵיכַל *c.*
palace 5
temple 8.

HELEK הֵלֶךְ
traveller 1
*drop 1.

HEM (HEMAH) הֵם (הֵמָּה) *pl.*
them
themselves
these
they
those, etc.

HEMYAH הֶמְיָה *f.*
noise 1.

HEN[1] **(HENAH)** הֵן (הֵנָּה) *f. pl.*
them
these
those, etc.

HEN[2] הֵן
behold
if
lo
though, etc.

HEN הֵן
if 10
or 2
that if 1
whether 2.

HENAH[1] **= HEN.**[1]

HENAH[2] הֵנָּה
here
hither
now
thitherward, etc.
†*Repeated:* on this side . . . on that side; this way . . . or that way; to . . . fro. *See* ad³.

HEPHEK הֶפֶךְ (הֵפֶךְ)
contrary 2.

HERAYON הֵרָיוֹן
conception 2.

HEREG הֶרֶג
slaughter 4.
†to be slain (la-hereg) 1.

HERER = HAR.

HERES הֶרֶס
destruction 1.

HERON הֵרוֹן
conception 1.

HI[1] הִי
woe 1.

HI[2] הִיא *f.*
it
the same
she
she herself
that
this, etc.

HI הִיא
it
this, etc.

HIGGAYON הִגָּיוֹן
device 1
meditation 1
solemn sound 1.

HILLULIM הִלּוּלִים *pl.*
*merry 1
*to praise 1.

HIMMO הִמּוֹ (הִמּוֹן)
them 8
those 2.

HIN הִין
hin 22.

HINNEH הִנֵּה
behold
lo
see, etc.

HITTUK הִתּוּךְ
*be melted 1.

HO הֹו
alas 2.

HOBNIM הָבְנִים *pl.*
ebony 1.

HOD הוֹד
beauty 1
comeliness 1
glory 9
honour 6
majesty 4
*glorious 1
*goodly 1
*honourable 1.

HOI הוֹי
ah! 7
alas! 2
ho! 3
O! 3
woe! 36.

HOLELAH הוֹלֵלָה *f.*
madness 4.

HOLELUTH הוֹלֵלוּת *f.*
madness 1.

HON הוֹן
enough 2
riches 10
substance 7
wealth 5.
†to be rich (la-hon) 1. *See* lo.

HOTSEN הֹצֶן
chariot 1.

HOVAH הֹוָה *f.*
mischief 3.

HU הוא
he
him
himself
it
the same
that
this, etc.

HUM הום
destroy 1.
NIPH. be moved 1
ring again 2.
HIPH. make a noise 1
make great noise 1.

HUN הון
HIPH. be ready 1.

HUYYEDOTH הֻיְּדוֹת *f. pl.*
thanksgiving 1.

I

I[1] אִי
country 1
island 6
isle 30.

I[2] אִי
woe 2.

I[3] עִי
heap 4.

IBCHAH אִבְחָה *f.*
point 1.

IDDAN עִדָּן
time 13.

IDDERIN אִדְּרִין *pl.*
threshing-floors 1.

IDDIM עִדִּים *pl.*
filthy 1.

IGGERA אִגְּרָא *f.*
letter 3.

IGGERETH אִגֶּרֶת *f.*
letter 10.

IKKAR אִכָּר
husbandman 5
plowman 2.

ILAN אִילָן
tree 6.

ILLAH עִלָּה *f.*
occasion 3.

ILLAI עִלַּי
high 1
most high 8.

* Inexact translations, *e.g.*, of a noun by a verb or adjective, of an active by a passive.
† Cases where two or more words in the original are translated by one word or by a phrase.

ILLEG עִלֵּג
stammerer 1.

ILLEK אִלֵּךְ
these 10
those 3.

ILLEM אִלֵּם
dumb 5
dumb man 1.

ILLEN אִלֵּין
the 1
these 4.

ILLI עִלִּי
upper 2.

ILLITH עִלִּית *f.*
chamber 1.

ILLU אִלּוּ
but if 1
yea though 1.

IM[1] אִם
if
oh that
or
surely
whether, etc., etc.
†*With* lo: as truly as, except, of a truth, surely, whether, etc. *See* ki[2].

IM[2] עִם
accompanying
among
before
beside
by
by reason of
in
to
unto
with, etc.
†as long as . . . endure (im . . . ve-li-phene) 1.

IM עִם
by 1
like 1
to (unto) 3
toward 1
with 13.
†from . . . to (im . . . ve) 2.

IMMAD עִמָּד = IM.[2]

IMMERIN אִמְּרִין *pl.*
lambs 3.

IMRAH אִמְרָה *f.*
commandment 1
speech 7
word 28.

IN[1] אִין
not 1.

IN[2] עִין
eye (*vb.*) 1.

INNUN (INNIN) אִנּוּן (אִנִּין) *pl.*
them
these, etc.

INYAN עִנְיָן
business 2
travail 6.

IQQAR עִקַּר
stump 3.

IQQESH עִקֵּשׁ
crooked 1
froward 6
perverse 4.

IQQESHUTH עִקְּשׁוּת *f.*
*froward 2.

IR[1] עִיר
awake 1
raise 1.

IR[2] עִיר *f.*
city 1071
town 7.
†*Repeated*: several city 2.

IR עִיר
watcher 3.

ISH[1] אִישׁ
[*freq. untranslated*].
a certain 4
another 5
any 26
any man 24
each 5
each man 7
each one 1
either of them 2
every 1
every man 177
every one 119
fellow 1
goodman 1
great man 1
husband 69
male 2
man *freq.*
mighty man 2
one 70
one man 1
person 12
whoso 1
whosoever 4
*he 4
*he that receiveth 1
*him that giveth 1
*him that is 1
*worthy of 1.
†adversary (*with* rib) 1; champion (*with* benayim) 2; counsellor (*with* etsah[2]) 1; destroyer (*with* mashchith) 1; eloquent (*with pl. of* dabar[2]) 3; evil speaker (*with* lashon) 1; footman (*with* ragli) 4; he that being often reproved (*with pl. of* tokachath) 1; husbandman (*with* adamah 1, *with* obed adamah 1) 2; liar (*with* kazab[2]) 1; none (*with* lo) 17; oppressor (*with* chamas[2]) 1; reprover (*with* mokiach) 1; spiritual man (*with* ruach[2]) 1; steward (*with* asher al[2]) 1; stranger (*with* ger 1, *with* nokri 2, *with* zur *partic.* 3) 6; violent man (*with* chamas[2] ra) 1; whosoever (*with* asher) 4. *Repeated*: any man 3, every man 3, every one 4, what man soever 2, whatsoever 1, whatsoever man 3, whosoever 2. *See* basar[2], ben[2], beli, chamishshim, echad, ishshah, kol, nephesh.

ISH[2] אִישׁ
Hithp. shew selves men 1.

ISH[3] אִשׁ
are there? 1.
†can (*with* le) 1.

ISHON אִישׁוֹן
apple [of the eye] 2
*black 1.
†apple (*with* bath) 1.

ISHSHAH אִשָּׁה *f.*
each 2
every one 3
female 2
one 6
wife *freq.*
woman *freq.*
*every cow 1.
†adulteress (*with* ish) 1; together (*with* el achoth 1); none (*with* lo) 1. *See* zanah.

ISHSHEH אִשֶּׁה *f.*
offering by fire 2
offering made by fire 50
sacrifice made by fire 12.

ISSAR אִסָּר (אֱסָר)
bond 10
*binding 1.

ISSARON עִשָּׂרוֹן
tenth deal 28.

IT עִיט
fly [upon] 2
rail 1.

ITHAI אִיתַי
there are
there is, etc.
†cannot (*la ithai di*).

ITHON אִיתוֹן
entrance 1.

ITSTSABON עִצָּבוֹן
sorrow 2
toil 1.

ITTER עִטֵּר
†left-handed (*with* yad yamin) 2.

ITTI[1] אִטִּי
softly 1.

ITTI עִתִּי
fit 1.

ITTIM אִטִּים *pl.*
charmers 1.

IVIM עִוְעִים *pl.*
*perverse 1.

IVVARON עִוָּרוֹן
blindness 2.

IVVELETH אִוֶּלֶת *f.*
folly 13
foolishness 10
*foolish 1
*foolishly 1.

IVVER עִוֵּר
blind 24
blind men 1
blind people 1.

IYYIM אִיִּים *pl.*
wild beasts of the islands 3.

IZQA עִזְקָא *f.*
signet 2.

IZZABON עִזָּבוֹן
fairs (*pl.*) 6
wares (*pl.*) 1.

IZZIM *pl. of* EZ.

IZZUZ עִזּוּז
power 1
strong 1.

K

KA = KE.

KAAB כָּאַב
be sore 1
be sorrowful 2
have pain 1.
Hiph. make sad 1
make sore 1
mar 1.
Partic. grieving 1.

KAAH כָּאָה
Niph. be grieved 1
be viler 1.
Partic. broken 1.
Hiph. make sad 1.

KAAS[1] כָּעַס
be angry 2
be grieved 1
be wroth 1
have sorrow 1
take indignation 1.
Piel provoke 1
provoke to anger 1.
Hiph. provoke 2
provoke to anger 43
provoke unto wrath 1
vex 1.

KAAS[2] כַּעַס
anger 2
grief 6
provocation 4
provoking 1
sorrow 2
spite 1
wrath 3
*angry 1
*sore 1.

KAAS[3] כַּעַשׂ
grief 1
indignation 1
sorrow 1
wrath 1.

KA-ASHER כַּאֲשֶׁר
according as
after
alike
as
as if
as soon as
as though
as when
because
even
even as
like as
so with
when
whilst, etc.

KABAD כָּבַד (כָּבֵד)
be chargeable 1
be dim 1
be glorified 1
be grievous 1
be hardened 1
be heavier 2
be heavy 10
be laid more 1
be rich 1
be sore 1
come to honour 1
go sore 2
make glorious 1
prevail 1.
Niph. be glorified 5
be glorious 3
be had in honour 1
be honourable 12
be honoured 1
get honour 2
glory 1.
Partic. abounding with 1
glorious things 1
honourable man 1.
Piel bring to honour 1
do honour 1
glorify 7
harden 2
honour 21
make glorious 1
promote 3
promote to honour 1
promote unto honour 1.
Inf. great 1
very great 1.
Pual be honoured 1.
Partic. honourable 1.
Hiph. afflict more grievously 1
be chargeable 1
boast 1
glorify 1
harden 4
lade 1
lay heavily 1
make heavy 7
stop 1.
Hithp. honour self 1
make self many 1.

KABAH כָּבָה
be put out 1
be quenched 9
go out 4.
Piel put out 2
quench 8.

KABAR כבר
Hiph. multiply 1.
Partic. in abundance 1.

KABAS כָּבַס
Partic. fuller 3.
Piel wash 43.
Partic. fuller 1.
Pual be washed 2.
Hithp. be washed 1.
Inf. washing 1.

KABASH כָּבַשׁ
bring into bondage 1
bring into subjection 1
force 1
keep under 1
subdue 3.
Niph. be brought unto bondage 1
be subdued 4.
Piel subdue 1.
Hiph. bring into subjection 1 (V.L.).

KABBIR כַּבִּיר
mighty 5
most 1
strong 1
valiant 1.
†feeble (lo kabbir) 1; much older (*with* yamim) 1.

KABED[1] = KABAD.

KABED[2] כָּבֵד
great 8
grievous 8
hard 2
hardened 1
heavier 1
heavy 8
laden 1
much 2
slow 2
so great 1
sore 4
thick 1
too heavy 1.

KABED[3] כָּבֵד
liver 14.

KABOD כָּבוֹד
glorious 10
gloriously 1
glory 155
honour 29
honourable 1.

KABSAH כַּבְשָׂה (כִּבְשָׂה) *f.*
ewe lamb 6
lamb 2.

KACHAD כָּחַד
Niph. be cut down 1
be cut off 5
be hid 4.
Partic. desolate 1.
Piel conceal 4
hide 11.
Hiph. cut off 5
hide 1.

KACHAL כָּחַל
paint 1.

KACHASH[1] כָּחַשׁ
fail 1.
Niph. be found liars 1.
Piel belie 1
deal falsely 1
deceive 1
deny 5
dissemble 1
fail 2
lie 5
submit selves 3.
Hithp. submit selves 1.

KACHASH[2] כַּחַשׁ
leanness 1
lies (*pl.* 1) 4
lying 1.

KAD כַּד
barrel 4
pitcher 14.

KADKOD כַּדְכֹּד
agate 2.

KAH כָּה
†See *ad.*

KAHAH כָּהָה
be darkened 1
be dim 3
fail 1.
Adv. inf. utterly 1.
Piel faint 1
restrain 1.

KAHAN כָּהַן
Piel be priest 1
deck 1
do the office of a priest 1
execute the priest's office 3
minister in the priest's office 17.

KAHEN כָּהֵן
priest 8.

KAIM כָּאִים *pl.* (V.L.)
†*See* chayil.

KAKAH כָּכָה
after that manner
after this manner
so
in such a case
thus, etc.

KAKKERIN כַּכְּרִין *f. pl.*
talents 2.

KALA כָּלָא
forbid 1
keep 1
keep back 1
refrain 2
retain 1
shut up 4
withhold 2
*be stayed 2.
Niph. be restrained 2
be stayed 1.
Piel finish 1.

KALAH[1] כלה
be accomplished 3
be an end of 1
be consumed 16
be determined 5
be done 1
be ended 3
be finished 5
be fulfilled 1
be spent 3
cease 2
consume 1
consume away 2
end 1
fail
faint 2
finish 1
waste 2.
Piel accomplish 9
bring to pass 1
cause to fail 1
consume 41
destroy 1
destroy utterly 2
end 3
finish 7
fulfil 2
have done 7
leave 2
leave off 1
long 1
make an end 6
make clean d[ance] 1
pluck 1
quite take away 1
spend 5
wholly reap 1
*be done 1
*be expired 1
*fully 1.
Pual be ended 1
be finished 1.
†Kal. finish (*with inf.* of asah) 1.

KALAH[2] כָּלָה *f.*
consummation 1
consumption 2
end 1
full end 8
riddance 1
utter end 2.
*altogether 2.
†le-kalah: altogether 1, to consume 1. *See* asah.

KALAL כלל
make perfect 1
perfect 1.

KALAM כָּלַם
Niph. be ashamed 11
be confounded 10
be put to confusion 1
be put to shame 2
blush 2.
Hiph. blush 1
do shame 1
hurt 1
make ashamed 1
put to shame 3
reproach 2
shame 1.
Hoph. be confounded 1
be hurt 1.

KALEH כָּלֶה
*fail 1.

KALIL כָּלִיל
all 2
every whit 1
flame 1
perfect 3
perfection 1
utterly 1
whole bu[rnt] offering 1
whole bu[rnt] sacrifice 1
wholly 4.

KALLAH כַּלָּה *f.*
bride 9
daughter in [law] 17
spouse 8.

KAMAH כמה
long (*vb.*) 1.

KAMAR כמר
Niph. be black 1
be kindled 1
yearn 2.

KAMAS כמס
be laid up in store 1.

KAMMON כַּמֹּן
cummin 3.

KANA כנע
Niph. be brought in[to] subjection 1
be brought under 1
be humbled 1
be subdued 5
humble self 16.
Hiph. bring down 3
bring low 2
subdue 6.

* Inexact translations, *e.g.*, of a noun by a verb or adjective, of an active by a passive.
† Cases where two or more words in the original are translated by one word or by a phrase.

KANAH כנה
PIEL. give flattering titles 2
surname 1
surname himself 1.

KANAPH[1] כנף
NIPH. be removed into a corner 1.

KANAPH[2] כָּנָף c.
border 2
corner 2
end 2
overspreading 1
quarter 1
skirt 14
uttermost part 1
wing 70
*feathered 2
*flying 1
*other 1
*sort 1
*winged 1.
†*See* baal[2].

KANAS כָּנַס
gather 3
gather together 1
heap up 1.
PIEL gather 2
gather together 1.
HITHP. wrap self 1.

KANNAH כַּנָּה *f.*
vineyard 1.

KAPH כַּף *f.*
branch 1
cloud 1
hand 124
handle 1
hollow 4
middle 1
palm 6
paw 1
power 1
sole 18
spoon 23
*apiece 1.
†*See* male, melo, midrak, taphas.

KAPHAH כפה
pacify 1.

KAPHAL כפל
double 4.
NIPH. be doubled 1.

KAPHAN[1] כפן
bend 1.

KAPHAN[2] כָּפָן
famine 2.

KAPHAPH כפף
be bowed down 2
bow down 1.
NIPH. bow self 1.

KAPHAR[1] כָּפַר
pitch 1.
PIEL appease 1
be merciful 2
be pacified 1
forgive 2
make atonement 70
make reconciliation 4
pacify 1
pardon 1
purge 2
purge away 2
put off 1
reconcile 3
*atonement be made 1.
PAUL atonement be made 1
be cleansed 1
be disannulled 1
be purged 4.
NITHP. be forgiven 1.
HITHP. be purged 1.

KAPHAR[2] כְּפָר
village 2.

KAPHASH כפש
HIPH. cover 1.

KAPHIS כָּפִיס
beam 1.

KAPHTOR כַּפְתּוֹר
knop 16
lintel 1
upper lintel 1.

KAPPORETH כַּפֹּרֶת *f.*
mercy seat 27.

KAR כַּר
captain 1
furniture 1
lamb 10
large pasture 1
pasture 1
ram 2.

KARA כרע
be brought down 1
bow 10
bow down 8
bow selves 4
couch 1
fall 2
sink down 1
stoop down 1.
Partic. feeble 1.
Infin. kneeling 1.
HIPH. bring low 1
bring very low 1
cast down 1
smite down 1
subdue 2.

KARAH[1] כרה
dig 11
make 2
open 1
pierce 1.
NIPH. be digged 1.

KARAH[2] כרה
buy 2.

KARAH[3] כרה
make a banquet 1
prepare 1.

KARAR כרר
PILPEL dance 2.

KARATH כָּרַת
covenant 2
cut 6
cut down 18
cut off 15
destroy 1
hew 2
hew down 2
make [a covenant] 84
make a league 1.
Partic. feller 1.
NIPH. be chewed 1
be cut down 1
be cut off 58
be freed 1
fail 6
perish 1
*want 3.
Adv. inf. utterly 1.
PUAL be cut 1
be cut down 1.
HIPH. cut down 1
cut off 73
destroy 3
lose 1.
HOPH. be cut off 1.
†KAL be confederate (*with* berith) 1.

KARBELA כַּרְבְּלָא
hat 1.

KARI כָּרִי
captains 1.

KARKOB כַּרְכֹּב
compass 2.

KARKOM כַּרְכֹּם
saffron 1.

KARMEL כַּרְמֶל
fruitful field 6
fruitful place 1
full ears 1
full ears of corn 1
green ears 1
plentiful field 2
*plentiful 1.

KARMIL כַּרְמִיל
crimson 3.

KAROZ כָּרוֹז
herald 1.

KARPAS כַּרְפַּס
green 1.

KASACH כסח
Pass pt. cut down 1
cut up 1.

KASAH[1] כסה
conceal 1
cover 2.
NIPH. be covered 2.
PIEL close 1
conceal 3
cover 119
flee to hide 1
hide 5
overwhelm 2.
PUAL be clothed 1
be covered 5
*cover 1.
HITHP. be covered 4
clad self 1
cover self 4.

KASAH[2] כשה
be covered 1.

KASAL כסל
be foolish 1.

KASAM כסם
poll 1.
Adv. inf. only 1.

KASAPH כסף
be greedy 1
have desire 1.
NIPH. long 2.
Partic. desired 1.
Adv. inf. sore 1.

KASAS כסס
make count 1.

KASHAL כָּשַׁל
be decayed 1
be fallen 1
be ruined 1
be weak 1
fail 1
fall 12
fall down 1
stumble 8.
Partic. feeble 3.
Adv. inf. utterly 1.
NIPH. be cast down 2
be feeble 1
be overthrown 1
fall 10
stumble 10.
PIEL bereave 1.
HIPH. be the ruin of 1
cast down 1
cause to fall 2
cause to stumble 2
make to fall 3.
HOPH. be overthrown 1.

KASHAPH כשף
PIEL use witchcraft 1.
Part. sorcerers 3
witch 2.

KASHER כשר
be right 1
prosper 1.
HIPH. direct 1.

KASHSHAPH כַּשָּׁף
sorcerer 1.

KASHSHIL כַּשִּׁיל
axe 1.

KASIN כְּסוּי
covering 2.

KATHAB כָּתַב
describe 6
record 1
subscribe 4
write 193.
NIPH be written 17.
PIEL prescribe 1
write 1.

KATHAM כתם
NIPH. be marked 1.

KATHAR כתר
PIEL beset round 1
inclose round 1
suffer 1.
HIPH. be crowned 1
compass about 2.

KATHASH כתשׁ
bray [in a mortar] 1.

KATHATH כתת
beat 1
beat down 1
stamp 1.
Pass pt. crushed 1
broken in pieces 1.
PIEL beat 3
break in pieces 1
smite 1.
PUAL be destroyed 1.
HIPH. destroy 1
discomfit 1.
HOPH. be beaten down 1
be beaten to pieces 1
be destroyed 1
be smitten 1.

KATHEPH כָּתֵף
arm 1
corner 2
shoulder 22
shoulderpiece 4
side 35
undersetter 4.

KATHITH כָּתִית
beaten 4
pure 1.

KAVAH כוה
NIPH. be burned 2.

KAVVANIM כַּוָּנִים *pl.*
cakes 2.

KAVVIN כַּוִּין *pl.*
windows 1.

KAZAB[1] כָּזַב
Part. liar 1.
NIPH. be found a liar 1
be in vain 1.
PIEL fail 1
lie 11.
HIPH. make a liar 1.

KAZAB[2] כָּזָב
deceitful 1
false 1
leasing 2
lie 23
lying 2.
†*See* ish[1].

KE כְּ (כָּ, *etc.*)
as
like, etc.
†ke-de: according to, after, sufficient for. Ke-phi: according as. *See* dai.

KE כְּ
as
like, etc.
†*ke-dena*: thus, such, etc.; *ke-di*: as, when, etc.

KEAN כְּעַן
now 13.

KEBAR כְּבָר
already 5
now 3
seeing that which now 1.

KEBARAH כְּבָרָה *f.*
sieve 1.

KEBEDUTH כְּבֵדֻת *f.*
*heavily 1.

KEBEL כֶּבֶל
fetters 2.

KEBES כֶּבֶשׂ
lamb 102
sheep 2.
†*See* seh.

KEBESH כֶּבֶשׁ
footstool 1.

KEBIR כְּבִיר
pillow 2.

KEBUDDAH כְּבוּדָּה *f.*
carriage 1
*all glorious 1
*stately 1.

KECHASHIM כְּחָשִׁים *pl.*
lying 1.

KEDAB כְּדַב
lying 1.

KEEB כְּאֵב
grief 2
pain 1
sorrow 3.

KEENETH כְּעֶנֶת
at such a time 1.

KEETH כְּעֶת
at such a time 1.

KEHAH[1] כֵּהָה *f.*
darkish 1
of heaviness 1
smoking 1
somewhat dark 4
*wax dim 1.

KEHAH[2] כֵּהָה *f.*
healing 1.

KEHAL כהל
be able 2
could 2.

KEHUNNAH כְּהֻנָּה *f.*
priesthood 9
priest's office 5.

KELACH כֶּלַח
full age 1
old age 1.

KELAI = **KILAI**.

KELAL כְּלַל
SHAPH. finish 1
make up 2
set up 2.
ISHTAPH. set up 2.

KELAPPOTH כֵּילַפּוֹת *f. pl.*
hammers 1.

KELAYOTH כְּלָיוֹת *f.pl.*
kidneys 18
reins 13.

KELE כֶּלֶא
prison 4.
†*See* bayith.

KELEB כֶּלֶב
dog 32.

KELI כְּלִי
armour 10
artillery 1
bag 2
carriage 3
furniture 8
instrument 39
jewel 20
pot 1
sack 1
stuff 14
thing 12
tool 1
vessel 146
wares (*pl.*) 1
weapon 20
*another 1
*one 1
*that is made of 1
*that which pertaineth 1.
†psaltery (*with* nebel) 2. *See* asah, kol, nose.

KELIMMAH כְּלִמָּה *f.*
confusion 6
dishonour 3
reproach 1
shame 20.

KELIMMUTH כְּלִמּוּת *f.*
shame 1.

KELU כְּלוּא
†*See* bayith.

KELUB כְּלוּב
basket 2
cage 1.

KELULOTH כְּלוּלֹת *f. pl.*
espousals 1.

KEMARIM כְּמָרִים *pl.*
idolatrous priests 1
priests 1.

KEMO כְּמוֹ
as
as it were
like
like as
thus, etc.
†in like manner (*with* ken[3]) 1.

KEN[1] כֵּן
base 2
estate 4
foot 8
office 1
place 1
*well 1.

KEN[2] כֵּן
lice (*pl.*) 4.

KEN[3] כֵּן
as yet
even so
howbeit
in like manner
likewise
so
straightway
such
such thing
surely
this
thus, etc.
†*See* achare, ad[1], al[2], kemo, la.

KEN[4] כֵּן
aright
right
true men (*pl.*) 5
well.

KEN כֵּן
thus 8.

KENAAN כְּנַעַן
merchant 2
traffick 1
trafficker 1.

KENAANI כְּנַעֲנִי
merchant 2.

KENASH כְּנַשׁ
gather together 1.
HITHP. be gathered together 2.

KENATH כְּנָת
companion 1.

KENATH כְּנָת
companion 7.

KENEMA כְּנֵמָא
so 1
in this sort 1
this manner 1
thus 2.

KEPHATH כפת
be bound 1.
PAEL bind 3.

KEPHEL כֶּפֶל
double 2.

KEPHIM כֵּפִים *pl.*
rocks 2.

KEPHIR[1] כְּפִיר
lion 6
young lion 24.
†young lion (*with gen. pl. of* ari) 1.

KEPHIR[2] כְּפִיר
villages (*pl.*) 1.

KEPHOR כְּפוֹר
bason 6
hoarfrost 2
hoary frost 1.

KERA כרא
ITHP. be grieved 1.

KERAAYIM כְּרָעַיִם *du.*
legs 9.

KERAH כֵּרָה *f.*
provision 1

KERAZ כרז
HAPH. make a proclamation 1.

KEREM כֶּרֶם
increase of the vineyards 1
vines 3
vineyard 84
vintage 1.

KERES כְּרֵשׂ
belly 1.

KERITHUTH כְּרִיתוּת
divorce 1
divorcement 3.

KEROTH כְּרֹת *pl. f.*
cottages 1

KERUB כְּרוּב
cherub 28
cherubim (*pl.*) 64.

KERUTHOTH כְּרֻתוֹת *pl. f.*
beams 3.

KES כֵּס (?*error* = nes).
†*See* yad.

KESAPH כְּסַף
money 1
silver 12.

KESATHOTH כְּסָתוֹת *f. pl.*
pillows 2.

KESE כֶּסֶא
appointed 1.

KESEB כֶּשֶׂב
lamb 4
sheep 8.
†*See* seh.

KESEH כֶּסֶה
time appointed 1.

KESEL[1] כֶּסֶל
confidence 1
folly 2
hope 3.

KESEL[2] כֶּסֶל
flanks (*pl.* 5) 6
loins 1.

KESEPH כֶּסֶף
money 112
price
silver 287
silverlings 1

* Inexact translations, *e.g.*, of a noun by a verb or adjective, of an active by a passive.
† Cases where two or more words in the original are translated by one word or by a phrase.

KESHAPHIM כְּשָׁפִים *pl.*
sorceries 2
witchcrafts 4.

KESIL כְּסִיל
constellation 1
fool 61
foolish 8
Orion 3.

KESILUTH כְּסִילוּת *f.*
*foolish 1.

KESUTH כְּסוּת *f.*
covering 5
raiment 1
vesture 1.

KETHAB כְּתָב
register 2
scripture 1
writing 14.

***KETHAB*[1]** כְּתָב
writing 10
*be written 1
*prescribe 1.

***KETHAB*[2]** כְּתַב
write 8.

KETHAL כְּתַל
wall 2.

KETHEM כֶּתֶם
fine gold 3
gold 2
golden wedge 1
pure gold 1.
†most fine gold (*with* paz 1, *with* tob[2] 1) 2.

KETHER כֶּתֶר
crown 3.

KETHOBETH כְּתֹבֶת *f.*
†any marks (*with* qaaqa) 1.

KETHONETH כְּתֹנֶת (כֻּתֹּנֶת) *f.*
coat 23
garment 5
robe 1.

KEVIYYAH כְּוִיָּה *f.*
burning 2.

KI[1] כִּי
burning 1.

KI[2] כִּי
although
because that
but
certainly
else
even
except
for
forasmuch as
how
if
in that
inasmuch as
nevertheless
seeing
since
so that
surely
that
though
truly
when
whereas
while
yea
yet, etc.
†wherefore (with ak) 1. *With* im[1]: except, save, save only, saving, unless, yet, etc. *See* ad[1], ephes, yaan.

KIBRAH כִּבְרָה *f.*
*little 3.

KIBSAH = KABSAH.

KIBSHAN כִּבְשָׁן
furnace 4.

KID כִּיד
destruction 1.

KIDOD כִּידוֹד
sparks (*pl.*) 1

KIDON כִּידוֹן
lance 1
shield 2
spear 5
target 1.

KIDOR כִּידוֹר
battle 1.

KIKKAR כִּכָּר *f.*
loaf 4
morsel 1
piece 2
plain 12
talent 48.

KILAI כִּלַי (כִּילַי)
churl 2.

KILAYIM כִּלְאַיִם *du.*
divers seeds 1
diverse kind 1
mingled 1
mingled seed 1.

KILLAYON כִּלָּיוֹן
consumption 1
failing 1.

KIMAH כִּימָה *f.*
Pleiades 2
seven stars 1.

KIMRIRIM כִּמְרִירִים *pl.*
blackness 1.

KINAH כִּנְעָה *f.*
wares 1.

KINNAM כִּנָּם *f.*
lice 2.

KINNOR כִּנּוֹר
harp 42.

KIPPAH כִּפָּה *f.*
branch 3.

KIPPURIM כִּפֻּרִים *pl.*
atonement 8.

KIRAYIM כִּירַיִם *du.*
ranges for pots 1.

KIRBEL כִּרְבֵּל
clothed 1.

KIRKAROTH כִּרְכָּרוֹת *pl. f.*
swift-beasts 1.

KIRSEM כִּרְסֵם
waste (*vb.*) 1.

KIS כִּיס
bag 4
purse 1.

KISBAH כִּשְׂבָּה
lamb 1.

KISHOR כִּישׁוֹר
spindle 1.

KISHRON כִּשְׁרוֹן
equity 1
good 1
*right 1.

KISHSHALON כִּשָּׁלוֹן
fall 1.

KISLAH כִּסְלָה *f.*
confidence 1
folly 1.

KISSE כִּסֵּא
seat 7
stool 1
throne 124.

KISSEH כִּסֵּה
throne 3.

KIYYOR כִּיּוֹר
hearth 1
laver 20
pan 1
scaffold 1

KOACH[1] כֹּחַ
ability 2
force 3
fruits 1
might 7
power 47
strength 59
substance 1
wealth 1.
†not be able (en[1] koach) 1; powerful (bak-koach) 1. *See* atsar[2], yagia.

KOACH[2] כֹּחַ
chameleon 1.

KOBA כּוֹבַע
helmet 6

KOBED כֹּבֶד
great number 1
grievousness 1
*heavy 2.

KOH כֹּה
here
on the other side
on this wise
so
such
that manner
this
this manner
thus, etc.
† *See* ad[3]

KOHEN כֹּהֵן
chief ruler 2
priest 725
prince 1
principal officer 1
*own 1.
†high priest (*with* rosh[1]) 1.

KOKAB כּוֹכָב
star 36.

KOL כֹּל
all
all manner of
any
any manner of
as many as
enough
every
every one
every place
every thing
whole
whoso
whosoever, etc.
†all the people (*with* ish); in all points as (*with* ummath she) 1; whatsoever (*with* keli); whosoever (*with* ish asher). *See* lo.

KOL כֹּל
all.
any
every
whole, etc.
†whosoever (*with* enash di) 1. *With* gebel denah: for this cause, that, therefore, wherefore. *With* gebel di: as, because, forasmuch as, therefore, though. See *lo.*

KOPHER[1] כֹּפֶר
bribe 2
ransom 8
satisfaction 2
sum of money 1.

KOPHER[2] כפר
camphire 2.

KOPHER[3] כפר
pitch 1.

KOPHER[4] כפר
village 1.

KOR כֹּר
cor 1
measure 7.

KOR כּוֹר
measure 1.

KOREMIN כֹּרְמִים *pl.*
vinedressers 5.

KORSE כָּרְסֵא
throne 3.

KOS[1] כּוֹס *f.*
cup 31.

KOS[2] כּוֹס
little owl 2
owl 1.

KOSHAROTH כּוֹשָׁרוֹת *f. pl.*
chains 1.

KOTHEL כֹּתֶל
wall 1.

KOTHERETH כֹּתֶרֶת
chapiter 24.

KUL כּוּל
comprehend 1.
PILPEL. abide 1
contain 3
feed 6
forbear 1
guide 1
make provision 1
nourish 4
provide sustenance 1
provide victuals 2
sustain 3.
POLPAL be present 1.
HIPH. abide 2
bear 1
contain 3
hold 2
hold in 1
receive 2

KUMAZ כּוּמָז
tablets 2.

KUN כּוּן
NIPH. be certain 2
be directed 1
be established 27
be fashioned 1
be fitted 1
be fixed 4
be meet 2
be perfect 1
be prepared 7
be ready 8
be right 3
be set forth 1
be set in order 1
be stable 2
prepare 1
prepare self 1
stand 2
tarry 1.
Partic. certainty 1
faithfulness 1
in very deed 1
right 1.
POLEL be ready 1
confirm 2
establish 14
fashion 2
make ready 3
ordain 1
prepare 2
prepare self 1
stablish 3.
PULAL be ordered 1
be prepared 1.
HIPH. confirm 1
direct 3
establish 13
frame 1
make preparation 1
make provision 1
make ready 5
order 1
prepare 68
provide 4
set 3
set aright 1
set fast 1
stablish 1.
HOPH. be established 2
be prepared 3.
Partic. fastened 1.
HITHPO. be established 2
be prepared 1
prepare selves 1.

KUR כּוּר
furnace 9

KUSSEMETH כֻּסֶּמֶת *f.*
fitches 1
rie 2.

KUTTONETH = KETHONETH.

L

LA לָא
not, etc.
†See *alam, di, ithai,* etc.

LAAB לָעַב
HIPH. mock 1.

LAAG[1] לָעַג
have in derision 2
laugh 2
laugh to scorn 3
mock 5.
NIPH. *pt.* stammering 1.
HIPH. laugh to scorn 2
mock 2
mock on 1.

LAAG[2] לַעַג
derision 3
scorn 2
scorning 2.

LAAH לָאָה
be grieved 1
faint 1
weary selves 1
NIPH. be wearied 1
be weary 6
grieve 1
loathe 1
weary selves 1.
HIPH. make weary 1
weary 5.

LAANAH לַעֲנָה *f.*
hemlock 1
wormwood 7.

LAAT[1] לאט
cover 1.

LAAT[2] לעט
HIPH. feed 1.

LAAZ לעז
Partic. of strange language 1.

LABAB לָבַב
NIPH. be wise 1.
PIEL make [cakes] 1
make cakes 1
ravish the heart 1.

LABAN לָבָן
white 29.

LABASH לָבַשׁ (לָבֵשׁ)
array self 1
be apparelled 1
be armed 1
be clothed 26
clothe 3
clothe self 3
come upon 3
put on 32
wear 4.
PUAL be arrayed 1
be clothed 1
put on 1.
Partic. in apparel 1.
HIPH. arm 2
array 4
clothe 3
clothe in 1
clothe with 13
put 7
put upon 2.

LABAT לבט
NIPH. fall 3.

LABBAH לַבָּה *f.*
flame 1.

LABEN לבן
make [brick] 2
make brick 1.
HIPH. be white 2
be made white 1
be whiter 1
make white 1.
HITHP. be made white 1.

LABESH = LABASH.

LABI לָבִיא
great lion 3
lion 4
old lion 2
stout lion 1
young [lion] 1.

LACH לַח
green 6
moist 1.

LACHAK לחך
lick up 1.
PIEL lick 2
lick up 3.

LACHAM לחם
devour 1
eat 5
fight 3
fight against 1.
NIPH. fight 145
make war 8
overcome 2
prevail 1
war 10.
Adv. inf. ever 1

LACHASH[1] לחשׁ
PIEL *pt.* charmer 1.
HITHP. whisper 1
whisper together 1.

LACHASH[2] לַחַשׁ
charmed 1
earring 1
enchantment 1
orator 1
prayer 1.

LACHATS[1] לָחַץ
afflict 1
crush 1
force 1
hold fast 1
oppress 13.
Partic. oppressor 1.
NIPH. thrust self 1.

LACHATS[2] לַחַץ
affliction 5
oppression 7.

LACHEM לָחֶם
war 1.

LAEG לָעֵג
mocker 1
stammering 1.

LAH לָה (לָא =)
nothing 1.

LAHAB לַהַב
blade 2
flame 8
*bright 1
*glittering 1.

LAHAG לַהַג
study 1.

LAHAH להה
faint (*vb.*) 1.
Hithp. pt. mad 1.

LAHAM להם
Hithp. pt. *wounds 2.

LAHAQAH לַהֲקָה *f.*
company 1

LAHAT[1] להט
be set on fire 1.
Partic. flaming 1.
PIEL burn 2
burn up 3
kindle 1
set on fire 3.

LAHAT[2] לַהַט
*flaming 1.

LAHEBETH לַהֶבֶת *f.*
flame 1
head [of a spear] 1.

LAHEN לָהֵן
but 2
except 3
save 2
therefore 2
wherefore 1.

LAKAD לכד
catch 4
catch self 1
take 77.
Adv. inf. at all 1.
NIPH. be holden 1
be taken 35.
HITHP. be frozen 1
stick together 1.

LAMAD לָמַד
learn 22.
Partic. skilful 1.
Adv. inf. diligently 1.
PIEL instruct 2
teach 55.
PUAL be instructed 1
be taught 2.
Partic. expert 1.
†*Pual part.* unaccustomed (*with* lo *prefixed*) 1.

LAPHATH לפת
take hold 1.
NIPH. be turned aside 1
turn self 1.

LAPPID לַפִּיד
brand 1
burning lamp 1
firebrand 2
lamp 8
lightning 1
torch 2.

LAQACH לקח
accept 1
bring 25
buy 3
carry away 5
fetch 30
get 6
have 2
marry 4
place 1
put 1
receive 62
reserve 1
seize upon 1
send for 1
take (away) 793
use 1
win 1.
Pass. pt. drawn 1.
NIPH. be brought 1
be taken 6
be taken away 3.
PUAL be taken 7
be taken away 1
be taken up 1.
HOPH. be fetched 1
be taken 4
be taken away 1.
HITHP. *pt.* infolding itself 1
mingled 1.

* Inexact translations, *e.g.*, of a noun by a verb or adjective, of an active by a passive.
† Cases where two or more words in the original are translated by one word or by a phrase.

LAQAQ לקק
lap 2
lick 3.
PIEL lap 2.

LAQASH לקשׁ
PIEL gather 1.

LAQAT לקט
gather 13
glean 1.
PIEL gather 8
gather up 2
glean 11.
PUAL be gathered 1.
HITHP. be gathered 1.

LASHAN לשׁן
PIEL (POEL) slander 1.
HIPH. accuse 1.

LASHON לָשׁוֹן *c.*
bay 3
language 10
tongue 98
wedge 2
*talkers 1.
†*See* baal[2], ish[1].

LAT לט
enchantments (*pl.*) 3.
†Bal-lat: privily 1, secretly 1, softly 1.

LATASH לטשׁ
sharpen 2
whet 1.
Partic. instructor 1.
Pual pt. sharp 1.

LATSATS לצץ
scorn (*vb.*) 1.

LATSON לָצוֹן
scorning 1
*scornful 2.

LAVAH לוה
abide with 1
borrow 5.
NIPH. be joined 6
cleave 1
join self 4.
HIPH. lend 8.
Partic. lender 1.

LAYELAH (LAYIL) לַיְלָה
night 222
night-season 2.
†*See* chatsi, chatsoth, tayek.

LAYISH לַיִשׁ
lion 1
old lion 2.

LE (LI, LA, etc.) לְ
at
for
to, etc.
†li-beli: for lack of, without, etc.; le-yad: at 2, beside 3; *wait on 1; le-phi: according to 23, after 1, in 1, to 1, when 1. *See* dai, li-phene, lemaan, etc.

LEACH לֵחַ
natural force 1.

LEB לֵב
consent 1
heart 494
midst 12
mind 11
understanding 20
wisdom 6.
†hardhearted, wisehearted, etc. (*for*: hard of heart, etc.) 14; be minded (be-leb) 1; comfortably (al[2] leb) 4; friendly (al[2] leb) 2; I (*with pron. suff.*) 1; kindly (al[2] leb) 2; willingly (min leb) 1. *Repeated*: double heart 2. *See* ganab, min, sameach[2], shabar[1], shith, sum.

LEB לֵב
heart 1.

LEBAB לֵבָב
breast 1
courage 1
heart 224
midst 2
mind 4
understanding 3.
†comfortably (al[2] lebab) 1. *See* ganab, rak, shub, sum.

LEBAB לְבַב
heart 7.

LEBAIM לְבָאִים *pl.*
lions 1.

LEBANAH לְבָנָה *f.*
moon 3.

LEBAOTH לְבָאוֹת *f. pl.*
lionesses 1.

LEBASH לבשׁ
be clothed 2.
HAPH. clothe 1.

LE-BEN לְבֵן
*and 1.

LEBENAH לְבֵנָה *f.*
altar of brick 1
brick 9
tile 1.

LEBIBOTH לְבִבוֹת *f. pl.*
cakes 3.

LE-BILTI לְבִלְתִּי
from
lest
lest that
that no
that not
without, etc.

LEBIYAH לְבִיָּא *f.*
lioness 1.

LEBONAH לְבֹנָה *f.*
frankincense 15
incense 6.

LEBUSH לְבוּשׁ
apparel 8
clothing 9
garment 9
raiment 1
vestment 1
vesture 2.
†clothed (be-lebush) 1; that he had put on (*with pron.=his*) 1.

LEBUSH לְבוּשׁ
garment 2.

LECHEM לֶחֶם
bread 238
feast 1
food 21
fruit 1
loaf 5
meat 18
provision 1
victuals 2
*eat 1.
†shewbread (*with* maareketh 4, *with* panim 6) 10.

LECHEM לְחֶם
feast 1.

LECHENAH לְחֵנָה *f.*
concubine 3.

LECHI לְחִי
cheek 10
cheek bone 1
jaw 1
jawbone 3.

LECHUM לְחוּם
flesh 1
*while he is eating 1.

LEHABAH לֶהָבָה *f.*
flame 12
*flaming 4.

LEHATIM לְהָטִים *pl.*
enchantments 1.

LEKED לֶכֶד
*being taken 1.

LELYA לֵילְיָא *f.*
night 4.

LE-MAAN לְמַעַן
because of
for
for to
for sake of
to the end
to the intent that, etc.
†lest (*with* lo); that (*with* asher).

LEMO לְמוֹ
at 1
for 1
to 1
upon 1.

LEOM לְאֹם (לְאוֹם)
nation 10
people 25.

LEQACH לֶקַח
doctrine 4
fair speech 1
learning 4.

LEQESH לֶקֶשׁ
latter growth 2.

LEQET לֶקֶט
gleaning 2.

LESHAD לְשַׁד
moisture 1
*fresh 1.

LESHEM לֶשֶׁם
ligure 1.

LETAAH לְטָאָה *f.*
lizard 1.

LETHEK לֶתֶךְ
half homer 1.

LEVATH לְוָת
[untranslated] 1.

LEZUTH לְזוּת *f.*
*perverse 1.

LIBBAH לִבָּה *f.*
heart 8.

LI-BELI לִבְלִי
for lack of
without, etc.

LIBNAH לִבְנָה *f.*
*paved 1.

LIBNEH לִבְנֶה
poplar 2.

LILITH לִילִית *f.*
screech owl 1.

LIMMUD לִמּוּד
accustomed 1
disciple 1
learned 2
taught 1
used 1.

LIN[1] לִין (לוּן)
abide 4
abide all night 6
be left 1
continue 1
dwell 1
endure 1
grudge 1
lie all night 3
lodge 30
lodge all night 1
lodge in 2
lodge this night 1
remain 7
tarry 1
tarry all night 6
tarry that night 3.
Infin. lodging 1.
HIPH. cause to lodge 1.
HITHP. abide 2.

LIN[2] לִין
NIPH. murmur 7 (V.L. 2).
HIPH. murmur 8 (V.L. 2)
make murmur 1.

LIPHENAI לְפָנַי
*before it 1.

LI-PHENE לִפְנֵי
afore 2
against 2
before *freq.*
by reason of 5
more than 1
on 1
to 1
with 5
*to meet 2.
†right forth (*with pron.=him*) 1, with (ve-li-phene-hem) 1.

LISHKAH לִשְׁכָּה *f.*
chamber 46
parlour 1.

LISHSHAN לִשָּׁן *c.*
language 7.

LIVYAH לִוְיָה *f.*
ornament 2.

LIVYATHAN לִוְיָתָן
leviathan 5
mourning 1.

LO[1] לֹא (לוֹא)
nay
never
no
not, etc.
†never (*with* la-netsach 5, *with* le-olam 15, *with* tamid 1) 21; none (*with* echad) 2; nor (ve-lo); nothing (*with* dabar 2, *with* kol asher 1) 3; nought (*with* hon) 1. *See* aman, atsum, kabbir, lamad, meumah, sakan, yada, etc.

LOA לֹעַ
throat 1.

LOG לֹג
log [of oil] 5.

LOH לֹה
not 1.

LOT[1] לוֹט
covering 1.

LOT[2] לֹט
myrrh 2.

LOYOTH לֹיוֹת *f. pl.*
additions 3.

LU לוּ (לֻא, לוּא)
I pray thee 1
I would 2
if 6
if haply 1
oh that 4
O that 2
peradventure 1
though 1
would God 1
would God that 2
would to God 1.

LUA לוּעַ
be swallowed up 1
swallow down 1.

LUACH לוּחַ
board 4
plate 1
table 38.

LULAOTH לֻלָאֹת *f. pl.*
loops 13.

LULE לוּלֵי (לוּלֵא)
except 4
had not 1
if . . . not 2
unless 4
were it not that 2.

LULIM לוּלִים *pl.*
winding stairs 1.

LUN=LIN.

LUSH לוּשׁ
knead 5.

LUT לוּט
Pass. pt. wrapped 1.
HIPH. wrap 1.
†*Kal pt.* cast over (*with* all[2]) 1.

LUTS לוּץ
scorn 1.
Partic. mocker 1
scorner 14
scornful 1.
HIPH. have in derision 1
make a mock 1
scorn 3.
Partic. ambassador 1
interpreter 2
teacher 1.
HITHPAL. be mocker 1.

LUZ[1] לוּז
depart 1.
NIPH. *pt.* froward 2
perverse 1
perverseness 1.
HIPH. depart 1.

LUZ[2] לוּז
hazel [tree] 1.

M

MA מָא
†what (with *di*) 1.

MAABAR מַעֲבָר
ford 1
passage 1
place where . . . . shall pass 1.

MAABEH מַעֲבֶה
clay 1.

MAABUS מַאֲבוּס
storehouse 1.

MAAD מעד
slide 2
slip 3.
HIPH. make to shake 1.
PUAL *part.* out of joint 1.

MAADAN מַעֲדָן
dainty 1
delight 1
*delicately 2.

MAADANOTH מַעֲדַנּוֹת *f. pl.*
sweet influences 1.

MAAH מָעָה *f.*
gravel 1.

MAAK מעך
Pass. pt. bruised 1
stuck 1.
PUAL be pressed 1.

MAAKAL מַאֲכָל
food 5
fruit 1
meat 22
victual 1.
†bakemeats (*with* maaseh opheh) 1.

MAAKELETH מַאֲכֶלֶת *f.*
knife 4.

MAAKOLETH מַאֲכֹלֶת *f.*
fuel 2.

MAAL[1] מעל
commit [trespass] 9
commit [transgression] 1
do [a trespass] 2.
transgress 10
trespass 14.
Partic. trespassing 1.

MAAL[2] מַעַל
falsehood 1
transgression 7
trespass 19
*grievously 1
*sore 1
*very 1.

MAAL[3] מַעַל
above
forward
upward, etc.
†*With prefix* le: above, exceeding, exceedingly, on high, over, up, upward, very. *With pref.* min: above, from above, upon. *With pref.* min-le: above, from above, on high, over, upward. *See* bo.

MAALAH מַעֲלָה *f.*
degrees (*pl.*) 24
dial (*pl.*) 2
high degree 1
stairs (*pl.*) 5
steps (*pl.*) 11
stories (*pl.*) 1.
things that come (*pl.*) 1

MAALAL מַעֲלָל
doing 35
endeavour 1
invention 2
work 3.

MAALEH מַעֲלֶה
ascent 2
chiefest 1
cliff 1
going up 9
hill 1
mounting up 1
stairs 1
that goeth up 1
*be up 1.

MAAMAD מַעֲמָד
attendance 2
office 1
place 1
state 1.

MAAMAQQIM מַעֲמַקִּים *pl.*
deep 2
depths 3.

MAAMAR מַאֲמָר
commandment 2
decree 1.

MAAMASAH מַעֲמָסָה *f.*
*burdensome 1.

MAAMATSTSIM מַאֲמַצִּים *pl.*
forces 1.

MAAN. *See* **LE MAAN.**

MAANAH מַעֲנָה *f.*
furrow (V.L.) 1.
†acre (*with* tsemeth) 1.

MAANEH מַעֲנֶה
answer 7
*himself 1.

MAANITH מַעֲנִית (V.L.)
furrow 1.

MAAPHEH מַאֲפֶה
*baken 1.

MAAPHEL מַאֲפֵל
darkness 1.

MAAQASHSHIM מַעֲקַשִּׁים *pl.*
crooked things 1.

MAAQEH מַעֲקֶה
battlement 1.

MAAR[1] מאר
HIPH. *pt.* fretting 3
pricking 1.

MAAR[2] מַעַר
nakedness 1
proportion 1.

MAARAB[1] מַאֲרָב
ambushment 2
lurking place 1
lying in wait 1
*lie in ambush 1.

MAARAB[2] מַעֲרָב
market 4
merchandise 5.

MAARAB[3] מַעֲרָב
west 7
west side 2
westward 4.

MAARABAH מַעֲרָבָה *f.*
west 1.

MAARAK מַעֲרָךְ
preparation 4.

MAARAKAH מַעֲרָכָה *f.*
army 15
fight 1
ordered place 1
rank 1
row 1
*to be set in order 1.

MAARATSAH מַעֲרָצָה *f.*
terror 1.

MAAREH מַעֲרֶה
meadow 1.

MAAREKETH מַעֲרֶכֶת
row 2
shewbread 3.
†*See* lechem.

MAAROTH מַעֲרוֹת *f. pl.*
armies 1.

MAARUMMIM מַעֲרֻמִּים *pl.*
naked 1.

MAAS[1] מָאַס
abhor 4
cast away 7
cast off 3
contemn 2
despise 24
disdain 1
loathe 1
refuse 9
reject 21.
Adv. inf. utterly 1.
NIPH. be refused 1
become loathsome 1.
Partic. reprobate 1
vile person 1.

MAAS[2] מָאַס
NIPH. melt away 1.

* Inexact translations, *e.g.*, of a noun by a verb or adjective, of an active by a passive.
† Cases where two or more words in the original are translated by one word or by a phrase.

MAASEH מַעֲשֶׂה
act 4
art 3
business 1
deed 3
doing 3
labour 4
occupation 2
operation 2
possession 1
purpose 1
thing made 2
thing offered 1
wares of . . . making (*pl.*) 2
work 190
working 1
workmanship 1
*do 1
*wrought 1.
†handywork (*with* yad) 1; needlework (*with partic. of* ragam) 4; network (*with* resheth) 2; well set hair (*with* miqsheh) 1; wrought with needlework (*with pt. of* ragam) 2.

MAASER מַעֲשֵׂר
tenth 2
tenth part 3
tithe 26
tithing 1.

MAASHAQQOTH מַעֲשַׁקּוֹת *f. pl.*
oppressions 1
*oppressors 1.

MAAT מעט
be diminished 3
be few 1
be little 1
be minished 1
seem little 1.
Infin. fewness 1.
PIEL be few 1.
HIPH. borrow a few 1
bring to nothing 1
diminish 2
gather least 1
[gather] less 1
gather little 1
give few 1
give less 1
give the less 2
make few in number 1
suffer to decrease 1.

MAATAPHOTH מַעֲטָפוֹת *f. pl.*
mantles 1.

MAATEH מַעֲטֶה
garment 1.

MAATSAD מַעֲצָד
ax 1
tongs 1.

MAATSEBAH מַעֲצֵבָה *f.*
sorrow 1.

MAATSOR מַעְצוֹר
restraint 1.

MAAVAYYIM מַאֲוַיִּים *pl.*
desires 1.

MABAD מַעֲבָד
works (*pl.*) 1.

MABAD מַעְבָד
works (*pl.*) 1.

MABARAH מַעְבָּרָה *f.*
ford 3
passage 5.

MABBAT מַבָּט
expectation 2.

MABBUA מַבּוּעַ
fountain 1
spring 2.

MABBUL מַבּוּל
flood 13.

MABLIGITH מַבְלִיגִית *f.*
*comfort self 1.

MABO מָבוֹא *c.*
by which . . . came 1
coming in 2
entering (in) 3
entrance 3
entry 6
going down 5
where . . goeth down 1
*come 1
*enter 1.
†west (*with* shemesh) 1; westward (*with* shemesh) 1.

MACHA מחא
clap 2.
PIEL clap 1.

MACHABATH מַחֲבַת *f.*
pan 5.

MACHABE מַחֲבֵא
hiding place 1.

MACHABOIM מַחֲבֹאִים *pl.*
lurking places 1.

MACHAGORETH מַחֲגֹרֶת *f.*
girding 1.

MACHAH [1] מחה
blot 9
blot out 2
destroy 2
put out 2
wipe 4
wipe away 1.
Adv. inf. utterly 1.
NIPH. be abolished 1
be blotted out 2
be destroyed 3
be put out 1
be wiped away 1.
HIPH. blot out 1
destroy 1
wipe out 1.

MACHAH [2] מחה
Pual partic. full of marrow 1.

MACHAH [3] מחה
reach 1.

MACHALAH מַחֲלָה *f.*
disease 1
sickness 3.

MACHALAPHIM מַחֲלָפִים *pl.*
knives 1.

MACHALATSOTH מַחֲלָצוֹת *f. pl.*
changeable suits of apparel 1
change of raiment 1.

MACHALEH מַחֲלֶה
disease 1
infirmity 1.

MACHALOQETH מַחֲלֹקֶת *f.*
company 1
course 33
division 8
portion 1.

MACHALUYIM מַחֲלֻיִים *pl.*
diseases 1.

MACHAMAOTH מַחֲמָאוֹת *f. pl.*
*butter 1.

MACHAMUDDIM מַחֲמֻדִּים *pl.*
pleasant things 2.

MACHANAQ מַחֲנָק
strangling 1.

MACHANEH מַחֲנֶה *c.*
army 4
band 2
battle 1
camp 134
company 6
drove 1
host 61
tents (*pl.* 4) 5.

MACHAQ מחק
smite off 1.

MACHAR מָחָר
time to come 7
to-morrow 44.
†*See* yom.

MACHARAOTH מַחֲרָאוֹת *pl.* (V. L.)
draught house 1.

MACHARESHAH מַחֲרֵשָׁה *f.*
mattock 2.

MACHARESHETH מַחֲרֶשֶׁת *f.*
share 1.

MACHASHABAH (MACHASHEBETH) (מַחֲשֶׁבֶת) מַחֲשָׁבָה *f.*
cunning work 2
curious work 1
device 12
imagination 3
means (*pl.*) 1
purpose 6
thought 28
*cunning 1
*devised by 1
*invented by 1.

MACHATS [1] מחץ
be dipped 1
pierce 1
pierce through 1
smite 1
smite through 2
strike through 1
wound 7.

MACHATS [2] מַחַץ
stroke 1.

MACHATSITH מַחֲצִית *f.*
half 14
half so much 1.
†midday (*with* yom) 1.

MACHAZEH מַחֲזֶה
vision 3

MACHBERETH מַחְבֶּרֶת *f.*
coupling 8.

MACHLAPHOTH מַחְלָפוֹת *f. pl.*
locks 2.

MACHLEQAH מַחְלְקָה *f.*
course 1.

MACHMAD מַחְמָד
beloved fruit (*pl.*) 1
desire 5
pleasant place 1
pleasant thing 4
*goodly 1
*lovely 1
*pleasant 2.

MACHMAL מַחְמָל
*that which . . . pitieth 1.

MACHOL מָחוֹל
dance 5
dancing 1.

MACHOZ מָחוֹז
haven 1.

MACHSEH מַחֲסֶה
hope 2
place of refuge 2
refuge 13
shelter 2
trust 1.

MACHSHAK מַחְשָׁךְ
dark 1
darkness 4
dark place 2.

MACHSOM מַחְסוֹם
bridle 1.

MACHSOPH מַחְשֹׂף
*make appear 1.

MACHSOR מַחְסוֹר
lack 1
need 1
penury 1
poverty 1
want 8
*poor 1.

MACHTAH מַחְתָּה *f.*
censer 15
firepan 4
snuff-dish 3.

MACHTERETH מַחְתֶּרֶת *f.*
secret search 1.
†breaking up (ba-machtereth) 1.

MACHTSEB מַחְצֵב
*hewed 1
*hewn 3.

MAD מַד
armour (*pl.* 1) 2
clothes (*pl.*) 1
garment 4
measure 2
raiment 1.

MADAD מדד
measure 42
mete 1.
NIPH. be measured 3.
PIEL be gone 1
measure 2
mete out 2.
POL. measure 1.
HITHP. stretch self 1.

MADBACH מַדְבַּח
altar 1.

MADCHEPHOTH מַדְחֵפוֹת *f. pl.*
*overthrow 1.

MADDA (מַדָּע) מַדַּע
knowledge 4
science 1
thought 1.

MADDAI מַדַּי = **MAH-DAI** *See* **DAI.**

MADDUA מַדּוּעַ
how?
wherefore?
why? etc.

MADDUCHIM מַדּוּחִים *pl.*
causes of banishment 1.

MADER מַעְדֵּר
mattock 1.

MADHEBAH מַדְהֵבָה *f.*
golden city 1.

MADMENAH מַדְמֵנָה *f.*
dunghill 1.

MADON מָדוֹן
contention 5
discord 1
strife 7
*brawling 2
*contentious 3.

MADQAROTH מַדְקָרוֹת *f. pl.*
piercings 1.

MADREGAH מַדְרֵגָה *f.*
stairs 1
steep place 1.

MADVEH מַדְוֶה
disease 2.

MAEN [1] מאן
PIEL refuse 40.
Adv. inf. utterly 1.

MAEN [2] מָאֵן
*refuse 4.

MAGAL [1] מַעְגָּל
path 6
trench 2.
†*See* yad.

MAGALAH מַעְגָּלָה *f.*
going 2
path 3
trench 1
way 1.

MAGAN מגן
PIEL deliver 3.

MAGAR מגר
Pass. pt. terrors 1.
PIEL cast down 1.

MAGEN מָגֵן
buckler 8
defence 2
ruler 1
shield 47
*armed 2.
†*See* aphiq.

MAGGAL מַגָּל
sickle 2.

MAGGEPHAH מַגֵּפָה *f.*
plague 21
slaughter 3
stroke 1.
†that they should be plagued (le-maggephah) 1.

MAGOR מָגוֹר
fear 6
terror 2.

MAGUR מָגוּר
dwelling 2
pilgrimage 4
where they sojourn 1
wherein [thou art, etc.] a stranger 4.

MAGZERAH מַגְזֵרָה *f.*
ax 1.

MAH מה
how
what
what thing
why, etc.
†bam-mah: whereby, wherein, wherewith, etc.; kam-mah: how long, how oft, what, etc.; la-mah: what good, wherefore, why, to what end, etc.

MAH מָה
how great 1
how mighty 1
that which 1
what 6
why 3.
†whatsoever (with *di*) 1.

MAHAH מהה
HITHP. delay 1
linger 2
stay selves 1
tarry 5

MAHAL מהל
Partic. mixed 1.

MAHALAK מַהֲלָךְ
journey (*n.*) 3
walk (*n.*) 1.

MAHALAL מַהֲלָל
praise 1.

MAHALUMMOTH מַהֲלֻמוֹת *f. pl.*
stripes 1
strokes 1.

MAHAMOROTH מַהֲמֹרוֹת *f. pl.*
deep pits 1.

MAHAR [1] מהר
hasten 1.
NIPH. be carried headlong 1.
Partic. fearful 1
hasty 1
rash 1.
PIEL be as swift 1
be hasty 1
be ready 1
be swift 2
cause to make haste 1
fetch quickly 1
haste 23
hasten 5
make haste 13
make ready quickly 1
make speed 2
*hastily 2
*in haste 2
*quickly 2
*shortly 1
*soon 1
*so soon 1
*speedily 1
*straightway 1
*suddenly 1.
Inf. [*See* maher [2]].

MAHAR [2] מהר
endow 1.
Adv. inf. surely 1.

MAHATHALLOTH מַהֲתַלּוֹת *f. pl.*
deceits 1.

MAHER [1] מַהֵר
*haste (*vb.*) 1.

MAHER [2] מַהֵר
at once 1
hastily 2
quickly 8
soon 1
speedily 4
suddenly 1.

MAHIR מָהִיר
diligent 1
hasting 1
ready 2.

MAHPEKAH מַהְפֵּכָה *f.*
overthrow 2
*overthrow (*vb.*) 3
*overthrown by 1.

MAHPEKETH מַהְפֶּכֶת *f.*
prison 2
stocks 2.

MAKAK מכך
be brought low 1.
NIPH. decay 1.
HOPH. be brought low 1.

MAKAR מכר
sell 56
sell away 1.
Adv. inf. at all 1
NIPH. be sold 16
sell self 3.
HITHP. be sold 1
sell self 3.

MAKBER מַכְבֵּר
thick cloth 1.

MAKKAH מַכָּה *f.*
blow 1
plague 11
slaughter 14
sore 1
stripe 2
stroke 2
wound 14
*beaten 1
smite 1
†be wounded (*with* hayah) 1.

MAKKAR מַכָּר
acquaintance 2.

MAKKOLETH מַכֹּלֶת *f.*
food 1.

MAKLULIM מַכְלֻלִים *pl.*
all sorts of things 1.

MAKMOR מַכְמֹר
net 1.

MAKOB מַכְאוֹב
grief 2
pain 2
sorrow 12.

MAKON מָכוֹן
dwelling place 2
foundation 1
habitation 2
place 11
settled place 1.

MAKSHELAH מַכְשֵׁלָה *f.*
ruin 1
stumbling-block 1.

MAKTESH מַכְתֵּשׁ
hollow place 1
mortar 1.

MALA = **MALE** [1]

MALACH [1] מלח
season 1.
PUAL be tempered together 1.
HOPH. be salted 1.
Adv. inf. at all 1.

MALACH [2] מלח
NIPH. vanish away 1.

MALAH. *See* **MAAL** [3]

MALAK [1] מַלְאָךְ
ambassador 4
angel 111
messenger 98.

MALAK [2] מלך
be king 5
be queen 1
reign (begin to) 284
rule 1.
Adv. inf. indeed 1
surely 1.
HIPH. make [king] 6
make king 39
make queen 1
make to reign 1
set [king] 1
set up [king] 1
set up king 1.
HOPH. be made king 1.

MALAK [3] מלך
NIPH. consult 1.

MALAK מַלְאַךְ
angel 2.

MALAKUTH מַלְאָכוּת *f.*
message 1.

MALAL [1] מלל
speak 1.
PIEL say 1
speak 1
utter 2.

* Inexact translations, *e.g.*, of a noun by a verb or adjective, of an active by a passive.
† Cases where two or more words in the original are translated by one word or by a phrase.

MALAL [2] מלל
NIPH. be cut down 2
be cut off 1
branch be cut off 1
*circumcise 1.

MALAQ מלק
wring off 2.

MALAT מלט
NIPH. be delivered 11
be escaped 8
deliver self 1
escape 42
let get away 1.
Adv. inf. speedily 1.
PIEL deliver 20
lay 1
let alone 1
save 5.
Adv. inf. surely 1.
HIPH. be delivered of 1
preserve 1.
HITHP. be escaped 1
leap out 1.

MALATS מלץ
NIPH. be sweet 1.

MALBEN מַלְבֵּן
brick kiln 3.

MALBUSH מַלְבּוּשׁ
apparel 4
raiment 3
vestment 1

MALE [1] מלא
be accomplished 5
be at an end 1
become full 1
be expired 3
be filled 4
be fulfilled 12
be full (of) 44
be fully set 1
be replenished 1
be satisfied 1
fill 11
gather 1
presume 1
replenish 2.
Infin. fulness 1
space 1.
NIPH. be accomplished 1
be fenced 1
be filled (with) 21
be fulfilled 1
be full (of) 10
be replenished 2.
PIEL accomplish 1
confirm 1
fill (with) 56
fulfill 14
furnish 1
gather together 1
give in full tale 1
go fully 1
have full of 1
replenish 2.
satisfy 1
set 4
*be filled with 1
*fully 1
*wholly 7.
PUAL *pt.* set 1.
HITHP. gather selves 1.
†KAL consecrate (*with* yad) 1; overflow (*with* al[2]) 1. PIEL *be consecrated (*with* yad) 2; consecrate (*with* yad) 14; draw with full strength (*with* yad be) 1; overflow (*with* al [2]) 1; take a handful (*with* kaph) 1.

MALE [2] מְלֹא
as much as it is worth 1
filled with 1
full 57
fully 1
that is with child 1
*fill 2
*multitude 1.

MALEKU (***MALEKUTH***) מַלְכוּ *f.*
kingdom 46
realm 3
reign 4
*kingly 1.

MALEKUTH מַלְכוּת *f.*
empire 1
kingdom 49
realm 4
reign 21
*royal 14.

MALKAH מַלְכָּה *f.*
queen 35.

MALKAH מַלְכָּה *f.*
queen 2.

MALKODETH מַלְכֹּדֶת *f.*
trap 1.

MALLACH מַלָּח
mariner 4.

MALLUACH מַלּוּחַ
mallows 1.

MALMAD מַלְמָד
goad 1.

MALON מָלוֹן
inn 3
lodging 2
lodging place 1
place where . . . lodge 1.

MALQACHAYIM = **MELQACHAYIM**.

MALQOACH מַלְקוֹחַ
booty 1
jaw 1
prey 6.

MALQOSH מַלְקוֹשׁ
latter rain 8.

MALTAOTH מַלְתָּעוֹת *pl.*
great teeth 1.

MAMLAKAH מַמְלָכָה *f.*
kingdom 108
reign 2
*king's 1
*royal 4.

MAMLAKUTH מַמְלָכוּת *f.*
kingdom 8
reign 1.

MAMMEGUROTH מַמְּגֻרוֹת *f. pl.*
barns 1.

MAMMERORIM מַמְּרֹרִים *pl.*
bitterness 1.

MAMOTH מָמוֹת
death 2.

MAMTAQQIM מַמְתַּקִּים *pl.*
most sweet 1.
sweet 1

MAMZER מַמְזֵר
bastard 2.

MAN מָן
manna 14.

MAN [1] מָן
what 1
who 3
whosoever 13.
†whosoever (with *di*) 1; whoso (with *di*) 2.

MAN [2] מָאן
vessel 7.

MANA מנע
deny 2
keep 1
keep back 4
refrain 2
restrain 1
withhold 14.
NIPH. be withholden 3
let hinder 1.

MANAH [1] מנה
count 1
number 8
tell 3.
NIPH. be numbered 7.
PIEL appoint 2
prepare 5
set 1
*be appointed 1.
PUAL be appointed 1.

MANAH [2] מְנָה *f.*
part 3
portion 10
such things as belonged to (*pl.*) 1.

MANAMMIM מַנְעַמִּים *pl.*
dainties 1.

MANDAH מַנְדַּע
knowledge 2
reason 1
understanding 1.

MANEH מָנֶה
maneh 1
pound 4.

MANGINAH מַנְגִּינָה *f.*
musick 1.

MANOACH מָנוֹחַ
place of rest 1
rest 6.

MANOD מָנוֹד
shaking 1.

MANON מָנוֹן
son 1.

MANOR מָנוֹר
beam 4.

MANOS מָנוֹס
flight 1
refuge 4
way to flee 1
*apace 1.
†not escape (*with* abad[1]) 1.

MANUL מַנְעוּל
lock 6.

MAOG מָעוֹג
cake 1
feast 1.

MAON מָעוֹן
den 2
dwelling 3.
dwelling place 4
habitation 10.

MAOR [1] מָאוֹר
light 18
*bright 1.

MAOR [2] מָעוֹר
nakedness 1.

MAOT מְעַט
wrapped up 1.

MAOZ מָעוֹז
forces (*pl.*) 1
fort 1
fortress 3
rock 1
strength 24
stronghold 2
*most strong 1
*strengthen 1
*strong 3.

MAPELYAH מַאְפֵּלְיָה *f.*
darkness 1.

MAPHREQETH מַפְרֶקֶת *f.*
neck 1.

MAPHTEACH מַפְתֵּחַ
key 2
opening 1.

MAPPACH מַפָּח
*giving up 1.

MAPPAL מַפָּל
flake 1
refuse 1.

MAPPALAH מַפָּלָה *f.*
*ruinous 1.

MAPPATS מַפָּץ
*slaughter (*adj.*) 1.

MAPPELAH מַפֵּלָה *f.*
ruin 2.

MAPPELETH מַפֶּלֶת *f.*
carcase 1
fall 1
ruin 2.

MAPPETS מַפֵּץ
battle ax 1.

MAPPUACH מַפֻּחַ
bellows 1.

MAQ מַק
rottenness 1
stink 1.

MAQAQ מקק
NIPH. be corrupt 1
be dissolved 1
consume away 3
pine away 4.
HIPH. consume away 1.

MAQHELIM מַקְהֵלִים *pl.*
congregations 1.

MAQHELOTH מַקְהֵלוֹת *f. pl.*
congregations 1.

MAQOM מָקוֹם *c.*
country 1
home 3
place 390
room 3
space 1.
†open sight of others (*with part. of* raah [1]) 1; whithersoever (*with* asher) 1.

MAQOR מָקוֹר
fountain 11
issue 1
spring 3
well 1
wellspring 2.

MAQQABAH מַקָּבָה *f.*
hammer 3.

MAQQACHOTH מַקָּחוֹת *f. pl.*
ware 1.

MAQQEBETH מַקֶּבֶת *f.*
hammer 1
hole 1.

MAQQEL מַקֵּל
rod 7
staff 10.
†handstaff (*with* yad) 1.

MAQTSUOTH מַקְצֻעוֹת *f. pl.*
planes 1.

MAR [1] מַר
bitter 22
bitterly 3
bitterness 9
chafed 1
great 1
those that be heavy 1.
†angry (*with* nephesh) 1; discontented (*with* nephesh) 1.

MAR [2] מַר
drop 1.

MARA מרא
be filthy 1.
HIPH. lift up self 1.

MARACH מרח
lay for a plaister 1.

MARAD מרד
rebel (*vb.*) 22.
Partic. rebel 1
rebellious 1.

MARAD מְרַד
rebellious 2.

MARAH [1] מַרְאָה *f.*
looking-glass 1
vision 11.

MARAH [2] מרה
be disobedient 1
be rebellious 2
disobey 1
rebel 12.
Partic. rebel 1
rebellious 4
*bitter 1.
Adv. inf. grievously 1.
HIPH. be disobedient 1
change 1
provoke 7
rebel 7
rebel against 1.
Partic. rebellious 3.
Infin. provocation 1.

MARAQ [1] מרק
furbish 1.
Partic. bright 1.
PUAL be scoured 1.

MARAQ [2] מְרַק
broth 3.

MARAR מרר
be bitter 1
be grieved 1
be vexed 1
have bitterness 1.
PIEL have sorely grieved 1
make bitter 1.
HIPH. be in bitterness 2
deal bitterly 1
provoke 1
vex 1.
HITHP. be moved with choler 2.
†KAL be in bitterness (*with* le) 1; it grieveth (*with* le) 1. PIEL weep bitterly (*with* be-beki) 1.

MARASHOTH מַרְאֲשֹׁת *f. pl.*
principalities 1.

MARAT מרט
be furbished 3
be peeled 1
pluck off 1
pluck off hair 2.
NIPH. hair be fallen off 1
have his hair fallen off 1.
PUAL be furbished 2.
Partic. bright 1
peeled 2.

MARATS מרץ
NIPH. be forcible 1.
Partic. grievous 1
sore 1.
HIPH. embolden 1.

MARBADDIM מַרְבַדִּים *pl.*
coverings of tapestry 2.

MARBEH מַרְבֶּה
increase 1
*great 1.

MARBEQ מַרְבֵּק
stall 2
*fat 1
*fatted 1.

MARBETS מַרְבֵּץ
place to lie down in 1.

MARBITH מַרְבִּית *f.*
greatest part 1
greatness 1
increase 2
multitude 1.

MARCHESHETH מַרְחֶשֶׁת *f.*
frying pan 2.

MARDUTH מַרְדּוּת *f.*
*rebellious 1.

MARE מָרֵא
Lord 2
lord 2.

MAREH מַרְאֶה
appearance 37
beauty 1
countenance 11
form 1
pattern 1
sight 18
visage 1
vision 11
*apparently 1
*appear 1
*goodly 1
*seem 1
*to look on 1
*to look to 1
*to look upon 4.
†as soon as (*with* enayim) 1; look (*with* enayim) 1; to see to (le-mareh) 1. *See* ra, tob[2], yapheh.

MARGEAH מַרְגֵּעָה *f.*
refreshing 1.

MARGELOTH מַרְגְּלוֹת *f. pl.*
feet 5.

MARGEMAH מַרְגֵּמָה *f.*
sling 1.

MARGOA מַרְגּוֹעַ
rest 1.

MARITH מַרְעִית *f.*
flocks 1
pasture 10.

MARKOLETH מַרְכֹּלֶת *f.*
merchandise 1.

MAROACH מָרוֹחַ
broken 1.

MAROM מָרוֹם
above 5
dignity 1
far above 1
height 10
high one 1
high place 4
*haughty 1
*high 27
*loftily 1
*most high 1
*upward 1.
†*See* gaph.

MARPE מַרְפֵּא (מַרְפֵּה)
cure 1
healing 3
health 5
remedy 3
yielding 1
*sound 1
*wholesome 1.
†incurable (en[1] marpe) 1.

MARTSEA מַרְצֵעַ
aul 2.

MARTSEPHETH מַרְצֶפֶת *f.*
pavement 1.

MARUD מָרוּד
cast out 1
misery 2.

MARZEACH מַרְזֵחַ
mourning 1.

MAS [1] מָס
him that is afflicted 1.

MAS [2] מַס
levy 4
tributary 5
tribute 12.
†discomfited (le-mas) 1.
See sar.

MASAH מסה
HIPH. make melt 1
make to consume away 1
melt 1
water 1.

MASAK [1] מסך
mingle 5.

MASAK [2] מָסָךְ
covering 7
curtain 1
hanging 17.

MASAR מסר
commit 1.
NIPH. be delivered 1.

MASAS מסס
faint 1.
NIPH. be loosed 1
be melted 2
be molten 1
be refuse 1
faint 1
melt 11
melt away 1.
Adv. inf. utterly 1.
HIPH. discourage 1.

MASETH מַשְׂאֵת *f.*
burden 3
collection 2
flame 1
great flame 1
gifts 1
lifting up 1
mess 3
oblation 1
reward 1
sign of fire 1.

MASGER מַסְגֵּר
prison 3
smith 4.

MASHABBIM מַשְׁאַבִּים *pl.*
places of drawing water 1.

MASHACH משח
anoint 62
paint 1
*be anointed 1.
NIPH. be anointed 5.

MASHAH משה
draw 1.
HIPH. draw 2.

MASHAK משך
continue 1
draw 17
draw along 1
draw out 3
extend 1
forbear 1
give 1
handle 1
make long 1
sound long 1
sow 1
stretch out 1

***** **Inexact translations, *e.g.*, of a noun by a verb or adjective, of an active by a passive.**
† Cases where two or more words in the original are translated by one word or by a phrase.

NIPH. be prolonged 3.
PUAL *pt.* deferred 1
scattered 2.

MASHAL [1] משל
bear rule 4
have dominion 5
have power 2
have rule 2
reign 8
rule 51.
Partic. governor 4
ruler 19.
Adv. inf. indeed 1.
HIPH. cause to rule 1
make to have dominion 1.
Infin. dominion 1.

MASHAL [2] מָשַׁל
speak 1
speak in proverbs 1
use [a proverb] 2
use as a proverb 1
use proverb 2
utter 1.
NIPH. become like 2
be like 3.
PIEL speak 1.
HIPH. compare 1.
HITHP. become like 1.

MASHAL [3] מָשָׁל
byword 1
parable 18
proverb 19
*like 1.

MASHASH מִשֵּׁשׁ
feel 2.
PIEL grope 4
search 2.
HIPH. *be felt 1.

MASHBER מַשְׁבֵּר
birth 2
breaking forth 1.

MASHCHETH מַשְׁחֵת
*destroying 1.

MASHCHITH [1] מַשְׁחִית *f.*
corruption 2
destruction 1
trap 1
*destroy 4
*destroying 1.
†utterly (le-mashchith) 1.

MASHCHITH [2]
Hiph. part. of shachath.

MASHEN מַשְׁעֵן
stay 1.

MASHENAH מַשְׁעֵנָה *f.*
staff 1.

MASHIACH מָשִׁיחַ
anointed 37
Messiah 2.

MASHMAN = MISHMAN.

MASHOT מָשׁוֹט
oar 1.

MASHQEH מַשְׁקֶה
butlership 1
drink 2
fat pasture 1
well watered 1
*drinking 2.

MASHQOPH מַשְׁקוֹף
lintel 2
upper doorpost 1.

MASHROQITHA מַשְׁרוֹקִיתָא *f.*
flute 4.

MASHSHA מַשָּׁא
usury 2.

MASHSHAAH מַשָּׁאָה *f.*
debt 1.
[Deut. 24·10 *untrans.*]

MASHSHAON מַשָּׁאוֹן
deceit 1.

MASHSHAQ מַשָּׁק
running to and fro 1.

MASHSHEH מַשֶּׁה [*cf.* MASHSHA.]
†*See* baal[2].

MASHSHUOTH מַשּׁוּאוֹת *f. pl.*
desolations 1
destruction 1.

MASKITH מַשְׂכִּית *f.*
conceit 1
image 2
imagery 1
picture 2
*wish 1.

MASKORETH מַשְׂכֹּרֶת *f.*
reward 1
wages 3.

MASLUL מַסְלוּל
highway 1.

MASMER מַסְמֵר
nail 4.

MASMEROTH מַשְׂמְרוֹת *f. pl.*
nails 1.

MASORETH מָסֹרֶת *f.*
bond 1.

MASOS מָשׂוֹשׂ
joy 12
mirth 3
*rejoice 2.

MASRETH מַשְׂרֵת
pan 2.

MASSA [1] מַסָּע
dart 1.

MASSA [2] מַסָּע
*before it was brought thither 1.

MASSA [3] מַסָּע
journey 10
journeying 2.

MASSA [4] מַשָּׂא
burden 57
exaction 1
prophecy 2
song 3
that whereupon they set 1
tribute 1
*carry away 1.

MASSAAH מַשָּׂאָה *f.*
burden 1.

MASSACH מַסָּח
broken down 1.

MASSAD מַסָּד
foundation 1.

MASSAH מַסָּה *f.*
temptation 4
trial 1.

MASSEKAH [1] מַסֵּכָה *f.*
molten image 18
*molten 7.

MASSEKAH [2] מַסֵּכָה *f.*
covering 3
vail 1.

MASSEKETH מַסֶּכֶת *f.*
web 2.

MASSO מַשּׂא
respect 1.

MASSOR מַשּׂוֹר
saw 1.

MASTEMAH מַשְׂטֵמָה *f.*
hatred 2.

MASVEH מַסְוֶה
vail 3.

MATAMMIM מַטְעַמִּים *pl.*
savoury meat 6.

MATAMMOTH מַטְעַמּוֹת *f. pl.*
dainties 1
dainty meats 1.

MATAR [1] מטר
NIPH. be rained upon 1.
HIPH. cause to rain 6
rain 10.

MATAR [2] מָטָר
rain 38
showers 1.

MATATE מַטְאֲטֵא
besom 1.

MATBEACH מַטְבֵּחַ
slaughter 1.

MATHACH מתח
spread out 1.

MATHAI מָתַי
when? etc.
†*See* ad[3].

MATHAQ מתק
be sweet 2
feed sweetly 1
make sweet 1.
HIPH. be sweet 1
*take sweet 1.

MATHBEN מַתְבֵּן
straw 1.

MATHKONETH מַתְכֹּנֶת *f.*
composition 2
measure 1
state 1
tale 1.

MATHOQ מָתוֹק
sweet 8
sweeter 2
*sweetness 2.

MATMON מַטְמוֹן
hidden riches 1
hid treasures 1
treasure 1.

MATSA מצא
befall 5
catch 1
come on 1
come to 1
come unto 1
come upon 5
find 245
find out 18
get 5
get hold upon 1
hit 2
light on 1
light upon 1
meet 4
meet with 1
receive 1
speed 1
take hold on 1
*be found 4.
Partic. ready 1.
NIPH. be enough 1
be found 115
be here 1
be left 2
be present 17
come to 1
come to hand 1
*have 1
*have here 1.
Partic. present 2.
Adv. inf. certainly 1.
HIPH. cause to come 1
cause to find 1
deliver 2
present 3.
†KAL be able (*with* ke-de) 1; be able to bring (*with* de) 1; suffice (*with* le) 3.
See nasag, yad.

MATSAH מצה
suck 1
wring 1
wring out 1.
NIPH. be wrung out 3.

MATSAR מֵצַר
rule (*n.*) 1.

MATSATS מצץ
milk out 1.

MATSOD מָצוֹד
bulwark 1
net 1
snare 1.

MATSOQ מָצוֹק
anguish 1
distress 1
straitness 4.

MATSOR מָצוֹר
besieged place 2
bulwark 1
defence 2
fortress 2
siege 13
stronghold 1
tower 1
*fenced 1
*fortified 1
*strong 2.
†*See* bo, hayah.

MATSPUNIM מַצְפֻּנִים *pl.*
hidden things 1.

MATSREPH מַצְרֵף
fining pot 2.

MATSTSA מַצָּע
bed 1.

MATSTSAB מַצָּב
garrison 7
place . . where stood 1
station 1.

MATSTSABAH מַצָּבָה *f.*
garrison 1.

MATSTSAH [1] מַצָּה *f.*
unleavened bread 35
unleavened cake 5
*unleavened 12
*without leaven 1.

MATSTSAH [2] מַצָּה *f.*
contention 1
debate 1
strife 1.

MATSTSEBAH מַצֵּבָה *f.*
garrison 1
image 19
pillar 12
standing image 1.

MATSTSEBETH מַצֶּבֶת *f.*
pillar 4
substance 2.

MATSTSUTH מַצּוּת *f.*
*contend 1.

MATSUD מָצוּד
net 1.

MATSUQ מָצוּק
pillar 1
situate 1.

MATTA מַטָּע
plantation 1
planting 3
plant 2.

MATTAH מַטָּה [למטה†, מִלְמַטָּה]
beneath 7
down 1
downward 5
less 1
under 1
underneath 2
very low 1.

MATTAN מַתָּן
gift 4
gifts 1.

MATTANAH מַתָּנָה *f.*
gift 16.
†be able (*with* yad) 1.

MATTARA מַטָּרָא *f.*
mark 1.

MATTARAH מַטָּרָה *f.*
mark 2
prison 13.

MATTATH מַתָּת *f.*
gift 3
reward 1.
†able to give (*with* yad) 2.

MATTEH מַטֶּה
rod 49
staff 16
tribe 182.

MATTELAAH = MAH TELAAH.

MATTENA מַתְּנָא *f.*
gift 3.

MATVEH מַטְוֶה
that which they had spun 1.

MAUPH מָעוּף
dimness 1.

MAVETH מָוֶת
death 128
*be dead 3
*dead 2
*deadly 1
*die 22.
†slay (le-maveth) 1.

MAYAN מַעְיָן
fountain 16
spring 2
well 5.

MAYIM מַיִם *du.*
washing 1
water 570
*watering 1.
†piss (*with du. of* regel) 2.
See motsa, shibboleth, yabal.

MAZEH מָזֶה
burnt with 1.

MAZLEG מַזְלֵג
flesh-hook 2.

MAZMEROTH מַזְמֵרוֹת *f. pl.*
pruning hooks 4.

MAZON מָזוֹן
meat 1
victual 1.

MAZON מָזוֹן
meat 2.

MAZOR מָזוֹר
wound 3
*be bound up 1.

MAZZALOTH מַזָּלוֹת *f. pl.*
planets 1.

ME = MIN.
†*with* achare: away from, away from after, back from, from; *with* al: above, forth of, from above, from beside, from off, from over, from out, from out of, off, out of, upon, *etc.*; *with* al-pene: from off 2; *with* asher: for that, such as, where, *etc.*; *with* attah: from henceforth, from this time, straightway, *etc.*; *with* ayin: whence? 17, where? 1; *with* az: even from, even since, from the beginning, from that time, from this time, hitherto, of old, since, since that time, when once, *etc.*; *with* etsel: from; *with* im[2]: according as 1.

MEAH מֵאָה *f.*
hundred 575
hundredth 3.
†hundredfold (*with pl. of* paam) 1; hundredfold (*with pl. of* shaar) 1; six score (*with* ve-esrim) 1.

MEAH מְאָה *f.*
hundred 8.

MEAL מֵעַל
going down 1.

MEANIM מֵאֲנִים *pl.*
which refuse 1.

MEARAH מְעָרָה *f.*
cave 36
den 2
hole 1.

MEAT (מְעַט) מְעָט
but a little 1
few 18
fewer 1
fewest 1
little 51
little while 3
small 2
small matter 2
small thing 4
some few 1
too few 1
too little 2
very few 1
very small 2
*very 2.
†ke-meat: almost 4, lightly 1, some 1, soon 2. *See* methim, od.

MEBASHSHELOTH מְבַשְּׁלוֹת *f. pl.*
boiling places 1.

MEBBAT מַבָּט
expectation 1.

MEBO = MABO.

MEBUKAH מְבוּכָה *f.*
perplexity 2.

MEBUQAH מְבוּקָה *f.*
void 1.

MEBUSAH מְבוּסָה *f.*
treading down 1
*trodden down 1
*trodden under foot 1.

MEBUSHIM מְבֻשִׁים *pl.*
secrets 1.

MECHA מחא
smite 2.
PAEL stay 1.
HITHP. be hanged 1.

MECHABBEROTH מְחַבְּרוֹת *f. pl.*
couplings 1
joinings 1.

MECHETSAH מֶחֱצָה *f.*
half 2.

MECHEZAH מֶחֱזָה *f.*
light 4.

MECHI מְחִי
engines 1.

MECHILLOTH מְחִלּוֹת *f. pl.*
caves 1.

MECHIM מֵחִים *pl.*
fatlings 1
fat ones 1.

MECHIR מְחִיר
gain 1
hire 1
price 11
worth 1.
†*See* bo.

MECHITTAH מְחִתָּה *f.*
destruction 7
dismaying 1
ruin 1
terror 2.

MECHOLAH מְחוֹלָה *f.*
company 1
dance 5
dancing 2.

MECHQAR מֶחְקָר
deep place 1.

MECHUGAH מְחוּגָה *f.*
compass 1.

MEDANIM מְדָנִים *pl.*
discord 2
strifes 1.

MEDAR מְדָר
dwelling 1.

MEDEV מַדֶו
garment 2.

MEDINAH מְדִינָה *f.*
province 44.
†*Repeated*: every province 5, province 4.

MEDINAH מְדִינָה *f.*
province 10.

MEDOKAH מְדֹכָה *f.*
mortar 1.

MEDOR מְדוֹר
dwelling 3.

MEDURAH מְדוּרָה *f.*
pile 1
pile for fire 1.

MEDUSHAH מְדֻשָׁה *f.*
threshing 1.

MEERAH מְאֵרָה *f.*
curse 4
cursing 1.

MEGAMMAH מְגַמָּה *f.*
*sup up 1.

MEGAR מגר
PAEL destroy 1.

MEGED מֶגֶד
pleasant fruits 1
precious fruits 1
precious things 4
*pleasant 2.

MEGERAH מְגֵרָה *f.*
axe 1
saw 3.

MEGILLAH מְגִלָּה *f.*
roll 20
volume 1.

MEGILLAH מְגִלָּה *f.*
roll 1.

MEGINNAH מְגִנָּה *f.*
sorrow 1.

MEGORAH מְגוֹרָה *f.*
fear 1.

MEGRAPHAH מֶגְרָפָה *f.*
clod 1.

MEGURAH [1] מְגוּרָה *f.*
fear 2.

MEGURAH [2] מְגוּרָה *f.*
barn 1.

MEH = MAH.

* Inexact translations, *e.g.*, of a noun by a verb or adjective, of an active by a passive.
† Cases where two or more words in the original are translated by one word or by a phrase.

MEHERAH מְהֵרָה *f.*
As adv. hastily 1
make speed 1
quickly 8
shortly 1
soon 1
speedily 4
swiftly 1
with speed 1.
†quickly (be-meherah) 1.

MEHUMAH מְהוּמָה *f.*
destruction 3
discomfiture 1
trouble 3
tumult 2
vexation 2
*vexed 1.

MEI מְעִי
heap 1.

MEIL מְעִיל
cloke 1
coat 1
mantle 7
robe 19.

MEIM מֵעִים *pl.*
belly 3
bowels 27
womb 1
*heart 1.

MEIN מְעִין *pl.*
belly 1.

MEKASSEH מְכַסֶּה
clothing 1
that which covereth (covered) 2
*cover (*vb.*) 1.

MEKER מֶכֶר
price 1
ware 1.
†*See* nathan.

MEKERAH מְכֵרָה *f.*
habitation 1.

MEKES מֶכֶס
tribute 6.

MEKITTAH מְכִתָּה *f.*
bursting 1.

MEKONAH מְכוֹנָה *f.*
base 22.

MEKUNAH מְכֻנָה *f.*
base 1.

MEKURAH מְכוּרָה *f.*
birth 2
habitation 1
nativity 1.

MELA מלא
fill 1.
HITHP. be full 1.

MELACH מֶלַח
salt 18
*salt (*adj.*) 9
†*See* mikreh.

MELACH [1] מלח
†have maintenance (with *melach*[2]) 1.

MELACH [2] מְלַח
*salt 2.
†See *melach*[1].

MELACHIM מְלָחִים *pl.*
rotten rags 2.

MELAK מְלַךְ
counsel (*n.*) 1.

MELAKAH מְלָאכָה *f.*
business 12
cattle 1
goods 2
labour 1
manner of work 1
manner of workmanship 5
occupation 1
stuff 1
thing 2
thing made 1
use 1
work 126
workmanship 1.
†*See* anashim, asah, oseh.

MELAL מלל
PAEL say 1
speak 4.

MELEAH מְלֵאָה *f.*
first of ripe fruit 1
fruit 1
fulness 1.

MELECHAH מְלֵחָה *f.*
barren land 1
barrenness 1.
†*See* erets.

MELEK מֶלֶךְ
king 2518
*royal 2.

MELEK מֶלֶךְ
king 164
*royal 1.

MELEKETH מְלֶכֶת *f.*
queen[ofheaven] 5.

MELET מֶלֶט
clay 1.

MELILAH מְלִילָה *f.*
ear 1.

MELITSAH מְלִיצָה *f.*
interpretation 1
taunting 1.

MELO מְלֹא
all that is in . . 9
fulness 7
multitude 2
that [where]of it was full 1
*fill 2
*full 12.
†all along (*with* qomah) 1; handful (*with* chophnayim 1, *with* kaph 2, *with* qomets 2) 5.

MELQACHAYIM מֶלְקָחַיִם *du.*
snuffers 1
tongs 5.

MELTACHAH מֶלְתָּחָה *f.*
vestry 1.

MELUKAH מְלוּכָה *f.*
kingdom 18
*king's 2
*royal 4.

MELUNAH מְלוּנָה *f.*
cottage 1
lodge 1.

MEMADDIM מְמַדִּים *pl.*
measures 1.

MEMAR מֵאמַר
appointment 1
word 1.

MEMER מֶמֶר
bitterness 1.

MEMSHALAH מֶמְשָׁלָה *f.*
dominion 11
government 1
power 1
*rule (*vb.*) 4.

MENA מנא
mene 2
number (*vb.*) 1.
PAEL ordain 1
set 3.

MENAANIM מְנַעַנְעִים *pl.*
cornets 1.

MENAH = *MENA*.

MENAQQIYYOTH מְנַקִּיּוֹת *f. pl.*
bowls 3
cups 2.

MENATH מְנָת *f.*
portion 7.

MENI מְנִי
number 1.

MENORAH מְנוֹרָה *f.*
candlestick 43.

MENUCHAH מְנוּחָה *f.*
ease 1
rest 17
resting place 2
*quiet 1
*still 1.
†comfortable (le-menuchah) 1.

MENUSAH מְנוּסָה *f.*
fleeing 1
flight 1.

MEOD מְאֹד
might 2.
As adv. diligently 4
especially 1
exceeding 14
exceedingly 8
far 3
fast 1
great 1
greatly 49
mightily 2
mighty 1
much 10
quickly 1
right well 1
so much 2
so sore 1
sore 23
utterly 2
very 137
very sore 2
well 1
*diligent 1
*good 3
*great 11.
†*Repeated*: exceeding 3, exceedingly 3; be-meod meod: exceeding 2, exceedingly 1. *See* ad, chazeh, rabah.

MEONAH מְעוֹנָה *f.*
den 5
dwelling place 1
habitation 1
place 1
refuge 1.

MEPHITS מֵפִיץ
maul 1.

MEQAREH מְקָרֶה
building 1.

MEQATTEROTH מְקַטְּרוֹת *f. pl.*
altars for incense 1.

MEQERAH מְקֵרָה *f.*
*summer (*adj.*) 2.

MEQUTSOTH מְקֻצְעֹת *f. pl.*
corners 2.

MERAASHOTH מְרַאֲשֹׁת *f. pl.*
bolster 6
head 1
pillows 2.

MERAD מְרַד
rebellion 1.

MERAT מרט
be plucked 1.

MERCHAB מֶרְחָב
breadth 1
large place 4
large room 1.

MEROHAQ מֶרְחָק
far 7
far country 1
*that was far off 1
*that is very far off (*pl.*) 1.
†*With prefix min*: afar off 2, far off 1, from afar 1, from far 4.

MEREA מֵרֵעַ
companion 4
friend 3.

MERED מֶרֶד
rebellion 1.

MERERAH מְרֵרָה *f.*
gall 1.

MERI [1] מְרִי
rebellion 4
*bitter 1
*most rebellious 1
*rebellious 1.

MERI [2] מְרִיא
fat beast 1
fat cattle 3
fatling 3
fed beast 1.

MERIBAH מְרִיבָה *f.*
provocation 1
strife 3.

MERIRI מְרִירִי
bitter 1.

MERIRUTH מְרִירוּת *f*
bitterness 1.

MERKAB מֶרְכָּב
chariot 1
covering 1
saddle 1.

MERKABAH מֶרְכָּבָה *f.*
chariot 44.

MERORAH מְרֹרָה *f.*
bitter thing 1
gall 2
*bitter 1.

MERORIM מְרֹרִים *pl.*
bitter 2
bitterness 1.

MEROTS מֵרוֹץ
race 1.

MERQACHAH מֶרְקָחָה *f.*
pot of ointment 1
*well 1.

MERQACHIM מֶרְקָחִים *pl.*
†*See* migdal.

MERUQIM מְרוּקִים *pl.*
purifications 1.

MERUTSAH מְרוּצָה *f.*
course 2
running 2
violence 1.

MESAB מֵסַב
places round about (*pl.*) 1
round about 2
table 1.

MESAK מֵיסַךְ (V.L.)
covert 1.

MESEK מֶסֶךְ
mixture 1.

MESHACH מְשַׁח
oil 2.

MESHAMMAH מְשַׁמָּה
astonishment 1
*desolate 3.
†*Repeated*: desolate 3.

MESHARIM מֵישָׁרִים *pl.*
agreement 1
equity 3
right things 3
things that are equal 1
things that are right 1
upright 1
uprightness 3.
As adv. aright 1
righteously 1
sweetly 1
uprightly 1
with equity 1.

MESHEK מֶשֶׁךְ
price 1
*precious 1.

MESHEQ מֶשֶׁק
†*See* ben[2].

MESHI מֶשִׁי
silk 2.

MESHISSAH מְשִׁסָּה *f.*
booty 2
spoil 4.

MESHOAH מְשׁוֹאָה *f.*
desolation 1
waste ground 1
*waste 1.

MESHOL מָשׁוֹל
byword 1.

MESHUBAH מְשׁוּבָה *f.*
backsliding 11
turning away 1.

MESHUGAH מְשׁוּגָה *f.*
error 1.

MESHUSSAH מְשׁוּסָּה *f.*
(V.L.) spoil 1.

MESILLAH מְסִלָּה *f.*
causeway 2
course 1
highway 20
path 2
terrace 1
way 1.

MESUKAH [1] מְסוּכָה *f.*
thorn hedge 1.

MESUKAH [2] מְשׂוּכָה *f.*
hedge 2.

MESUKKAH מְסֻכָּה *f.*
covering 1.

MESURAH מְשׂוּרָה *f.*
measure 4.

META מטא (מְטָה)
come 5
reach 3.

METAB מֵיטָב
best 6.

METACHAVE מְטַחֲוֵי
†bow shot (*with* qesheth) 1.

METAH = *META*.

METH. *Partic. of* MUTH.

METHALLEOTH מְתַלְּעוֹת *f. pl.*
cheek teeth 1
jaws 1
jaw teeth 1.

METHAR מֵיתָר
cord 8
string 1.

METHEG מֶתֶג
bit 1
bridle 3.

METHEQ מֶתֶק
sweetness 2.

METHIM מְתִים *pl.*
few 2
few men 1
men 13
persons 1.
†few (*with* meat 1, *with* mispar 1) 2; few in number (*with* meat) 1; friend (*with* sod) 1; small number (*with* mispar) 1.

METHOM מְתֹם
soundness 3
*men 1.

METIL מְטִיל
bar 1.

METSACH מֵצַח
brow 1
forehead 10.
†*See* chazaq.

METSAD מְצָד (מְצַד)
castle 1
fort 2
hold 3
munition 1
stronghold 1.

METSAR מֵצַר
distress 1
pain 1
strait 1.

METSILLOTH מְצִלּוֹת *f. pl.*
bells 1.

METSILTAYIM מְצִלְתַּיִם *du.*
cymbals 13.

METSODAH מְצוֹדָה *f.*
hold 1
munition 1
net 1.

METSOLAH מְצוֹלָה *f.*
bottom (*pl.*) 1
deeps 2.

METSUDAH מְצוּדָה *f.*
castle 1
defence 1
fort 1
fortress 6
hold 6
net 1
snare 2
strong hold 1
strong place 1.
†to be hunted (le-metsudah) 1.

METSULAH מְצוּלָה *f.*
deep 5
depth 2
*deep (*adj.*) 1.

METSULLAH מְצֻלָּה *f.*
bottom 1.

METSUQAH מְצוּקָה
anguish 1
distress 6.

METSURAH מְצוּרָה
fort 1
munition 1
stronghold 1
*fenced (*adj.*) 5.

MEUM = **MUM**.

MEUMAH מְאוּמָה *f.*
anything 14
ought 5
somewhat 1
*fault 1.
†no (al-meumah) 1; nothing (lo-meumah) 9; nought (lo-meumah) 1.

MEURAH מְאוּרָה *f.*
den 1.

MEZACH מֵזַח (מְזִיחַ)
girdle 1
strength 2.

MEZAMMEROTH מְזַמְּרוֹת *f. pl.*
snuffers 5.

MEZARIM מְזָרִים *pl.*
north 1.

MEZEG מֶזֶג
liquor 1.

MEZEV מֶזֶו
garner 1.

MEZIACH = **MEZACH.**

MEZIMMAH מְזִמָּה *f.*
device 3
discretion 4
intent 1
lewdness 1
mischievous device 1
thought 1
wicked device 3
witty invention 1
*mischievous 1.
†wickedly (le-mezimmah) 1.

MEZUZAH מְזוּזָה *f.*
door post 2
post 14
side post 3.

MI [1] מִי
any
if any man
who? etc.
†O that (*with* yitten); would to God (*with* yitten).

MI [2]. [*Also* **MIB, MID, MIG**, *etc., etc.*] = **MIN.**

MIBCHAR מִבְחָר
choice 3
*choice (*adj.*) 4
*choicest 1
*chosen 4.

MIBCHOR מִבְחוֹר
*choice 2.

MIBDALOTH מִבְדָּלוֹת *f. pl.*
separate cities 1.

MIBNEH מִבְנֶה
frame 1.

MIBRACH מִבְרָח
fugitive 1.

MIBTA מִבְטָא
that which she uttered 1.
†utter (*with* hayah *understood*) 1.

MIBTACH מִבְטָח
confidence 9
hope 1
trust 4
*sure 1.

MIBTSAR מִבְצָר
fortress 6
stronghold 12
*defenced 4
*fenced 11
*most fenced 1
*most strong 1
*strong 2.

MICHYAH מִחְיָה *f.*
quick flesh 1
reviving 2
sustenance 1
victuals 1
*quick 1.
†to preserve life (le-michyah) 1. *See* ayin[1].

MIDBAR [1] מִדְבָּר
desert 13
south 1
wilderness 253.
†*See* erets.

MIDBAR [2] מִדְבָּר
speech 1.

* Inexact translations, *e.g.*, of a noun by a verb or adjective, of an active by a passive.
† Cases where two or more words in the original are translated by one word or by a phrase.

MIDCHEH מִדְחֶה
ruin 1.

MIDDAH[1] מִדָּה *f.*
great stature (*pl.* middoth) 1
(great) stature 2
(great) stature (*pl.* middin) 1
measure 27
measuring 1
meteyard 1
piece 7
size 3
stature 3
*measuring (*adj.*) 19
*wide 1.

MIDDAH[2] מִדָּה *f.*
toll 1
tribute 3.

MIDDAH[3] מַדָּה *f.*
garment 1.

MID-DE מִדֵּי (= MIN DAI).
after 1
as oft as 1
from 5
from the time that 1
since 3
when 3.

MIDDIN מִדִּין
judgment 1.

MIDRAK מִדְרָךְ
†foot-breadth (*with* kaph regel) 1.

MIDRASH מִדְרָשׁ
story 2.

MIDYANIM מִדְיָנִים *pl.* [= MADON].
contentions 2.

MIGBALOTH מִגְבָּלֹת *f. pl.*
ends 1.

MIGBAOTH מִגְבָּעוֹת *f. pl.*
bonnets 4.

MIGDAL מִגְדָּל
castle 1
pulpit 2
tower 47.
†sweet flowers (*pl. with* merqachim) 1.

MIGDANOTH מִגְדָּנוֹת *f. pl.*
precious things 4
presents 1.

MIGDOL מִגְדֹּל
tower 3

MIGERETH מִגְעֶרֶת *f.*
rebuke 1.

MIGRAOTH מִגְרָעוֹת *f. pl.*
narrowed rests 1.

MIGRASH מִגְרָשׁ
suburb 110
*cast out 1.

MIKAL מִיכַל
brook 1.

MIKBAR מִכְבָּר
grate 6.

MIKLAH מִכְלָה *f.*
fold 2.
†sheepfold (*with* tson) 1.

MIKLAL מִכְלָל
perfection 1.

MIKLOL מִכְלוֹל
all sorts 1
most gorgeously 1.

MIKLOTH מִכְלוֹת *f. pl.*
*perfect 1.

MIKMANNIM מִכְמַנִּים *pl.*
treasures 1.

MIKMAR מִכְמָר
net 1.

MIKMERETH מִכְמֶרֶת *f.*
drag 2.

MIKMORETH מִכְמֹרֶת *f.*
nets 1.

MIKNESAYIM מִכְנָסַיִם *du.*
breeches 5.

MIKREH מִכְרֶה
†saltpit (*with* melach[1]) 1.

MIKSAH מִכְסָה *f.*
number 1
worth 1.

MIKSEH מִכְסֶה
covering 16.

MIKSHOL מִכְשׁוֹל
offence 2
ruin 2
stumbling-block 8.
†*See* ayin[1], hayah.

MIKTAB מִכְתָּב
writing 9.

MIKVAH מִכְוָה *f.*
burning 4
*that burneth 1.

MILCHAMAH מִלְחָמָה *f.*
battle 150
fight 4
fighting 1
war 158.
†*See* asah, panim, tsaba.

MILLAH מִלָּה *f.*
any thing to say 1
byword 1
matter 1
speaking 2
speech 5
talking 1
that I have yet to speak 1
what to say 1
word 23.
†*See* shub.

MILLAH מִלָּה *f.*
commandment 1
matter 5
thing 11
word 7.

MILLETH מִלֵּאת *f.*
†fitly (al[2] milleth) 1.

MILLUAH מִלֻּאָה *f.*
inclosing 2
setting 1.

MILLUIM מִלֻּאִים *pl.*
consecration 11
stones to be set 1
*to be set 3.

MIMKAR מִמְכָּר
sale 2
that was sold 1
that which cometh of the sale 1
that which is sold 2
that which [he] sold 1
ware 1
*ought 1
*be sold 1.

MIMKERETH מִמְכֶּרֶת *f.*
*as 1.

MIMSAK מִמְסָךְ
drink offering 1
mixed wine 1.

MIMSHACH מִמְשַׁח
anointed 1.

MIMSHAL מִמְשָׁל
dominion 2
that ruled 1.

MIMSHAQ מִמְשָׁק
breeding 1.

MIN[1] מִין
kind 31.

MIN[2] מִן
at
because of
from
from among
of
out of
than, etc.
†or ever . . . was (*with pl. of* qedem) 1. *With* yad: from 2, of 1.
Note.—This word takes many forms in combination with other words. It is frequently prefixed to other words to form compound prepositions, e.g., mi-li-phene (of 2), mim-maal, mip-pene (because of 53, for fear of 9, from *freq.*, through 1), mip-pene asher (because 2), mip-pi (out of 1), mits-tsad (beside 3), etc., etc. *See* me, mi[2], mid-de, etc.

MIN מִן
because of
from
more than
of
out of, etc.
†aforetime (*with qadmath denah*) 1; ago (with *qadmath denah*) 1; because (with *di*); before (with *qodam*); from (with *qodam*) 2; I (with *qodam* and suff = me) 1; of (with *qodam*) 3; when (with *di*), etc. *See note under* min[2].

MINAL מִנְעָל
shoe 1.

MINCHAH מִנְחָה *f.*
gift 7
meat offering 131
oblation 5
offering 33
present 28
sacrifice 5.

MINCHAH מִנְחָה *f.*
meat offering 1
oblation 1.

MINDAH מִנְדָּה *f.*
toll 2.

MINHAG מִנְהָג
driving 2.

MINHAROTH מִנְהָרוֹת *f. pl.*
dens 1.

MINLEH מִנְלֶה
perfection 1.

MINNEZARIM מִנְּזָרִים *pl.*
crowned 1.

MINNI[1] = MIN.

MINNI[2] מִנִּי
whereby 1.

MINNIM מִנִּים *pl.*
stringed instruments 1.

MINYAN מִנְיָן
number 1.

MIPHAL מִפְעָל
work 1.

MIPHALAH מִפְעָלָה *f.*
work 2.

MIPHGA מִפְגָּע
mark 1.

MIPHLAAH מִפְלָאָה *f.*
wondrous work 1.

MIPHLAGGOTH מִפְלַגּוֹת *f. pl.*
divisions 1.

MIPHLAS מִפְלָשׂ
balancing 1.

MIPHLAT מִפְלָט
escape 1.

MIPHLETSETH מִפְלֶצֶת *f.*
idol 4.

MIPHQAD מִפְקָד
appointed place 1
commandment 1
number 2.

MIPHRAS מִפְרָשׂ
that which thou spreadest forth 1
spreading 1.

MIPHRATS מִפְרָץ
breach 1.

MIPHSAAH מִפְשָׂעָה *f.*
buttock 1.

MIPHTACH מִפְתָּח
opening 1.

MIPHTAN מִפְתָּן
threshhold 8.

MIQDASH מִקְדָּשׁ
chapel 1
hallowed part 1
holy place 2
sanctuary 69.

MIQLAATH מִקְלַעַת *f.*
carving 1
figure 1
graving 1
*carved 1.

MIQLAT מִקְלָט
refuge 2.

MIQNAH מִקְנָה *f.*
he that is bought 2
possession 1
price 2
purchase 5
*buy (bought) 8.

MIQNEH מִקְנֶה
cattle 63
flock 3
herd 1
possession 5
purchase 1
substance 2.
†flock (*with* tson) 1.

MIQQACH מִקָּח
taking 1.

MIQRA מִקְרָא
assembly 1
calling 1
convocation 19
reading 1.

MIQREH מִקְרֶה
chance 1
event 3
hap 1
that which befalleth 1
*befall 3
*happen 1.

MIQSAM מִקְסָם
divination 2.

MIQSHAH[1] מִקְשָׁה *f.*
beaten out of one piece 1
beaten work 6
whole piece 1
*beaten 1
*upright 1.

MIQSHAH[2] מִקְשָׁה *f.*
garden of cucumbers 1.

MIQSHEH מִקְשֶׁה
†*See* maaseh.

MIQTAR מִקְטָר
*to burn 1.

MIQTERETH מִקְטֶרֶת *f.*
censer 2.

MIQTSOA מִקְצוֹעַ
corner 6
turning 5.

MIQVAH מִקְוָה *f.*
ditch 1.

MIQVE מִקְוֵא
linen yarn 4.

MIQVEH מִקְוֶה
abiding 1
gathering together 1
hope 4
plenty 1
pool 1.

MIRBAH מִרְבָּה *f.*
much 1.

MIRBETS מִרְבָּץ
couching place 1.

MIREH מִרְעֶה
feeding place 1
pasture 12.

MIRMAH מִרְמָה *f.*
craft 1
deceit 20
guile 2
subtilty 1
treachery 1
*deceitful 8
*deceitfully 1
*false 2
*feigned 1.
†deceitfully (*be-mirmah* 1, *le-mirmah* 1) 2.

MIRMAS מִרְמָס
that which ye have trodden 1
treading 1
*be trodden down 3
*be trodden under foot 1.
†*See* sim.

MIRPAS מִרְפָּשׂ
that which ye have fouled 1.

MIRQACHATH מִרְקַחַת *f.*
ointment 2.
†*See* raqach.

MIRSHAATH מִרְשַׁעַת *f.*
wicked woman 1.

MIRZACH מִרְזַח
banquet 1.

MISAD מִסְעָד
pillar 1.

MISCHAQ מִשְׂחָק
scorn 1.

MISCHAR מִסְחָר
traffick 1.

MISDERON מִסְדְּרוֹן
porch 1.

MISGAB מִשְׂגָּב
defence 6
high fort 1
high tower 3
place of defence 1
refuge 5.

MISGERETH מִסְגֶּרֶת *f.*
border 14
close place 2
hole 1.

MISHALAH מִשְׁאָלָה *f.*
desire 1
petition 1.

MISHAN מִשְׁעָן
stay 4.

MISHBAR מִשְׁבָּרִים *pl.*
billows 1
waves 4.

MISHBATTIM מִשְׁבַּתִּים *pl.*
sabbaths 1.

MISHBETSOTH מִשְׁבְּצוֹת *f. pl.*
ouches 8
*wrought 1.

MISHCHAH מִשְׁחָה *f.*
anointing 22
ointment 1.

MISHCHAR מִשְׁחָר
morning 1.

MISHCHATH מִשְׁחַת
*marred 1.

MISHENETH מִשְׁעֶנֶת *f.*
staff 11.

MISHERETH מִשְׁאֶרֶת *f.*
kneading trough 2
store 2.

MISHGEH מִשְׁגֶּה
oversight 1.

MISHI מִשְׁעִי
*to supple 1.

MISHKAB מִשְׁכָּב
bed 34
couch 1
lying with 4
*lie with 1
*with 1.
†*See* cheder.

MISHKAB מִשְׁכַּב
bed 6.

MISHKAN מִשְׁכָּן
dwelling 6
dwelling place 6
habitation 5
tabernacle 119
tent 1
*dwell 1.

MISHKAN מִשְׁכַּן
habitation 1.

MISHLACH מִשְׁלָח
sending forth 1
*put 3
*set 3.

MISHLACHATH מִשְׁלַחַת *f.*
discharge 1
sending 1.

MISHLOACH מִשְׁלוֹחַ
sending 2
*lay 1.

MISHMA מִשְׁמָע
hearing 1.

MISHMAATH מִשְׁמַעַת *f.*
bidding 1
guard 2
*obey 1.

MISHMAN מִשְׁמָן
fat one 1
fatness 3
fattest 1
fattest place 1.

MISHMAR מִשְׁמָר
diligence 1
guard 3
office 1
prison 1
ward 12
watch 4.

MISHMERETH מִשְׁמֶרֶת *f.*
charge 50
office 1
ordinance 3
safeguard 1
ward 9
watch 7
*keep 1
*to be kept 6.

MISHNEH מִשְׁנֶה
college 2
copy 2
double 8
fatling 1
next 7
second 11
second order 1
twice as much 3.

MISHOL מִשְׁעוֹל
path 1.

MISHOR מִישׁוֹר
equity 2
even place 1
plain 13
uprightness 1
*made straight 1
*plain (*adj.*) 2
*right 1
*righteously 1
*straight 1.

MISHPACHAH מִשְׁפָּחָה *f.*
family 286
kind 1
kindred 9.
†*Repeated*: every family 3.

MISHPAT מִשְׁפָּט
cause 12
ceremony 1
charge 1
crime 1
custom 2
desert 1
determination 1
discretion 2
disposing 1
due 1
due order 1
fashion 3
form 1
judgment 294
justice 1
law 1
manner 39
manner of law 1
measure 2
order 3
ordinance 11
right 18
sentence 2
*be judged 1
*just 1
*justly 1
*lawful 7
*use to do 1
*worthy 1.
†wrong (be-lo mishpat) 1, wrongfully (be-lo mishpat) 1. *See* baal.[2]

MISHPETHAYIM מִשְׁפְּתַיִם *du.*
burdens 1
sheepfolds 1.

MISHQA מִשְׁקָע
*deep 1.

* Inexact translations, *e.g.*, of a noun by a verb or adjective, of an active by a passive.
† Cases where two or more words in the original are translated by one word or by a phrase.

MISHQAL מִשְׁקָל
full weight 1
weight 47.

MISHQELETH מִשְׁקֶלֶת *f.*
plummet 1.

MISHQOL מִשְׁקוֹל
weight 1.

MISHQOLETH מִשְׁקֹלֶת *f.*
plummet 1.

MISHRAH מִשְׁרָה *f.*
liquor 1.

MISHSHOT מִשּׁוֹט
oar 1.

MISHTACH מִשְׁטָח
spreading 1
*spread upon 1.

MISHTAR מִשְׁטָר
dominion 1.

MISHTEH מִשְׁתֶּה
banquet 10
drink 2
feast 24
feasting 6
*drink (*vb.*) 3.
†*See* asah.

MISHTEH מִשְׁתֵּה
banquet 1.

MISHTOACH מִשְׁטוֹחַ
a place to spread forth 1.

MISKEN מִסְכֵּן
poor 3
poor man 1.

MISKENOTH מִסְכְּנוֹת *f. pl.*
store 5
storehouses 1
treasure 1.

MISKENUTH מִסְכֵּנֻת *f.*
scarceness 1.

MISPACH מִשְׂפָּח
oppression 1.

MISPACHATH מִסְפַּחַת *f.*
scab 3.

MISPACHOTH מִסְפָּחוֹת *f. pl.*
kerchiefs 2.

MISPAR מִסְפָּר
account 1
certain number 1
number 109
sum 2
tale 1
telling 1
*all 3
*few 5
*numbered 1.
†in abundance (le-en¹ mispar) 1; infinite (en¹ mispar) 1; innumerable (en¹ mispar) 4; time (*with* yamin) 2.

MISPED מִסְפֵּד
lamentation 3
mourning 6
wailing 6
*mourn 1.

MISPO מִסְפּוֹא
provender 5.

MISRAH מִשְׂרָה *f.*
government 2.

MISRAPHOTH מִשְׂרְפוֹת *f. pl.*
burnings 2.

MISSAH מִסַּת *f.*
tribute 1.

MISTAR מִסְתָּר
secret place 7.
†in secret (*with pref.* be) 1; secretly (*with pref.* be) 2.

MISTOR מִסְתּוֹר
covert 1.

MITPACHATH מִטְפַּחַת *f.*
vail 1
wimple 1.

MITS מִיץ
churning 1
forcing 1
wringing 1.

MITSAD מִצְעָד
going 1
step 2.

MITSAR מִצְעָר
little one 2
little while 1
small company 1
*small 1.

MITSCHAH מִצְחָה *f.*
greaves 1.

MITSHALOTH מִצְהָלוֹת *f. pl.*
neighing 2.

MITSNEPHETH מִצְנֶפֶת *f.*
diadem 1
mitre 11.

MITSPEH מִצְפֶּה
watch tower 2.

MITSVAH מִצְוָה *f.*
commandment 173
law 1
ordinance 1
precept 4
*be commanded 1
*command 1

MITTAH מִטָּה *f.*
bed 28
bier 1.
†bedchamber (*with* cheder) 2.

MIZAR מִזְעָר
few 1
very 3.

MIZBEACH מִזְבֵּחַ
altar 401.

MIZLAGOTH מִזְלָגוֹת *f. pl.*
flesh hooks 5.

MIZMOR מִזְמוֹר
psalm 57.

MIZRA מִזְרָע
thing sown 1.

MIZRACH מִזְרָח
east 30
east end 1
east side 3
eastward 20
rising [of the sun] 7
rising of the sun 1
sun rising 1.
†east side (*with* shemesh) 2; eastward (*with* shemesh) 1; sun rising (*with* shemesh) 9.

MIZRAQ מִזְרָק
bason 11
bowl 21.

MIZREH מִזְרֶה
fan 2.

MOACH מֹחַ
marrow 1.

MOAD מוֹעָד
appointed time 1.

MOADOTH מוֹעָדוֹת *f. pl.*
solemn feast 1.

MOAL מֹעַל
lifting up 1.

MOBA מוֹבָא
coming in 2.

MOCHORATH מָחֳרָת *f.*
morrow 23
morrow after 6
next [day] 1
next day 2.

MODA מוֹדַע (מוֹדָע)
kinsman 1
kinswoman 1.

MODAATH מוֹדַעַת *f.*
kindred 1.

MOED מוֹעֵד
appointed feast 1
appointed season 4
appointed sign 1
appointed time 2
assembly 2
congregation 149
due season 1
feast 6
place of assembly 1
season 8
set feast 5
set time 6
solemn assembly 1.
solemn day 1
solemn feast 9
solemnity 4
synagogue 1
time 4
time appointed 9
*appointed 3
*solemn 1.

MOETSOTH מוֹעֵצוֹת *f. pl.*
counsels 6
devices 1.

MOHAR מֹהַר
dowry 3.

MOKIACH
Hiph. partic. of yakach.

MOL מוּל
over against 1.
†over against (le-mol) 1.

MOLEDETH מוֹלֶדֶת *f.*
issue 1
kindred 11
native 1
nativity 6
*begotten 1
*born 2.

MONIM מֹנִים *pl.*
times 2.

MOOMAD מָעֳמָד
standing 1.

MOPHETH מוֹפֵת
miracle 2
sign 8
wonder 23
*wondered at 1.

MOQED מוֹקֵד
burning 1
hearth 1.

MOQEDAH מוֹקְדָה *f.*
burning 1.

MOQESH מוֹקֵשׁ
gin 3
snare 20
trap 2
*be ensnared 1
*be snared 1.

MOR מֹר
myrrh 12.

MORA מוֹרָא
dread 1
fear 6
terribleness 1
terror 3
that ought to be feared 1.

MORAD מוֹרָד
going down 3
steep place 1
*thin 1.

MORAG מוֹרַג
threshing instrument 3.

MORAH¹ מֹרָה *f.*
grief 1.

MORAH² מוֹרָה
razor 3.

MORAH³ מוֹרָה
fear 1.

MORASH מוֹרָשׁ
possession 2
thought 1.

MORASHAH מוֹרָשָׁה *f.*
heritage 1
inheritance 2
possession 6.

MOREH מוֹרֶה
former rain 2
rain 1.

MOREK מֹרֶךְ
faintness 1.

MORRAH מָרָּה *f.*
bitterness 1.

MOSADOTH מוֹסָדוֹת *f. pl.*
foundations 13.

MOSAR מֹסָר
instruction 1.

MOSER מוֹסֵר
band 6
bond 5.

MOSHAB מוֹשָׁב
assembly 1
dwelling 12
dwellingplace 4
habitation 12
inhabited place 1
seat 7
sitting 2
situation 1
sojourning 1
*dwelt in 3.

MOSHAOTH מוֹשָׁעוֹת *f. pl.*
salvation 1.

MOSHCHAH מָשְׁחָה *f.*
anointing 2
*be anointed 1.

MOSHCHATH מָשְׁחָת
corruption 1.

MOSHEKOTH מוֹשְׁכוֹת *f. pl.*
bands 1.

MOSHEL¹ מֹשֶׁל
dominion 2.

MOSHEL² מֹשֶׁל
like 1.

MOT¹ מוֹט
be carried 1
be fallen in decay 1
be moved 4
be removed 2
shake 1
slide 1
slip 2.
Partic. falling down 1
ready 1.
Adv. inf. exceedingly 1.
NIPH. be moved 17
be out of course 1
be removed 1
fall 1
slip 1.
HIPH. cast 1.
HITHP. be moved 1.

MOT² מוֹט
bar 2
staff 1
yoke 1.

MOTAH מוֹטָה *f.*
band 2
staff 1
yoke 8
*heavy 1.

MOTH מוֹת
death 1.

MOTHAR מוֹתָר
plenteousness 1
pre-eminence 1
profit 1.

MOTHEQ מֹתֶק
sweetness 1.

MOTHNAYIM מָתְנַיִם *du.*
loins 42
side 3.
†*See* zarzir.

MOTS מֹץ
chaff 8.

MOTSA מוֹצָא
bud 1
east 1
going forth 4
going out 5
outgoing 1
spring 3
that which came out 1
that which is gone out 1
they that go forth into 1
thing that is gone out 1
vein 1
whatsoever proceeded out 1
word that proceedeth out 1
*brought out 2.
†watercourse (*with* mayim) 1; watersprings (*with* mayim) 2.

MOTSAOTH מוֹצָאוֹת *f. pl.*
draught house 1
goings forth 1.

MOZNAYIM מֹאזְנַיִם *du.*
balances 15.

MOZNAYIM מֹאזְנַיִם *du.*
balances 1.

MUADAH מוּעָדָה *f.*
*appointed 1.

MUAPH מוּעָף
dimness 1.

MUAQAH מוּעָקָה *f.*
affliction 1.

MUG מוּג
consume 1
faint 1
melt 2.
NIPH. be dissolved 3
be fainthearted 1
faint 2
melt away 2.
POL. dissolve 1
make soft 1.
HITHPOL. be melted 1
melt 2.

MUK מוּךְ
be poorer 1
be waxen poor 4.

MUL¹ מוּל
circumcise 13.
NIPH. be circumcised 16
circumcise selves 1
*circumcising 1.
Adv. inf. must needs 1.
POL. be cut down 1.
HIPH. destroy 3.
HITHPOL. be cut in pieces 1.

MUL² מוּל
against 6
before 2
from 1
over against 15
toward 2
to . . . ward 1
with 1.
†before (*with* panim) 2; forefront (*with* panim) 4. *See* el¹.

MULOTH מוּלוֹת *f. pl.*
circumcision 1.

MUM מוּם (מְאוּם)
blemish 16
blot 2
spot 3.

MUQ מוּק
HIPH. be corrupt 1.

MUR מוּר
NIPH. be changed 1.
HIPH. change 11
exchange 1
*be removed 1.
Adv. inf. at all 2.

MURAH מֻרְאָה *f.*
crop 1.

MURDAPH מֻרְדָּף
persecuted 1.

MUSAB מוּסַב
winding about 1.

MUSAD מוּסָד
foundation 2.

MUSADAH מוּסָדָה *f.*
foundation 1
*grounded 1.

MUSAK מוּסָךְ (V. L.)
covert 1.

MUSAR מוּסָר
bond 1
chastening 3
chastisement 3
check 1
correction 8
discipline 1
doctrine 1
instruction 30
rebuker 1.
†*See* shachar².

MUSH¹ מוּשׁ
be removed 1
depart 8
remove 2.
HIPH. cease 1
depart 3
go back 1
remove 3
take away 1.

MUSH² מוּשׁ
feel 1.
HIPH. feel 1
handle 1.

MUTH¹ מוּת
be dead 60
be like to be slain 1
die 420.
Partic. dead 62
dead body
dead man 2
one dead 3
very suddenly 1
worthy of death 1.
Infin. death 8.
Adv. inf. must needs 1
surely 48.
POL. slay 9.
HIPH. cause to die 1
destroy 2
kill 32
put to death 19
slay 81.
Partic. destroyer 1.
Infin. *crying 1.
Adv. inf. at all 1
in [no] wise 2
surely 2.
HOPH. be put to death 57
be slain 10
die 1.
†*See* darash.

MUTH² מוּת
death 1.

MUTS מוּץ
Partic. extortioner 1.

MUTSAQ¹ מוּצָק
casting 1
hardness 1.

MUTSAQ² מוּצָק (מוּעָק)
straitness 1
vexation 1
be straightened 1.

MUTSEQETH מוּצֶקֶת *f.*
pipe 1
*when it was cast 1.

MUTSTSAB מֻצָּב
mount 1.

MUTTEH מֻטֶּה
perverseness 1.

MUTTOTH מֻטּוֹת *f. pl.*
stretching out 1.

N

NA¹ נָא
raw 1.

NA² נָא
go to
I beseech thee
I pray
I pray thee
I pray you
now
oh, etc.

NAAH¹ נאה
PIL. be beautiful 1
become 1
be comely 1.

NAAH² נָאָה *f.*
habitation 5
house 1
pasture 5
pleasant place 1.

NAAL¹ נעל
bolt 2
lock 2
shoe 1.
Partic. inclosed 1
shut up 1.
HIPH. shoe 1.

NAAL² נַעַל *f.*
pair of shoes 2
shoe 18.
†dryshod (be-naalayim) 1.
See serok.

NAAM נאם [*See* NEUM].
say 1.

NAAMANIM נַעֲמָנִים *pl.*
*pleasant 1.

NAAPH נאף
commit adultery 10.

* Inexact translations, *e.g.*, of a noun by a verb or adjective, of an active by a passive.
† Cases where two or more words in the original are translated by one word or by a phrase.

Partic. adulterer 2
adulteress 3
women that break wedlock 1.
PIEL commit adultery 1.
Partic. adulterer 6
adulteress 1
adulterous 1.

NAAPHUPHIM נַאֲפוּפִים *pl.*
adulteries 1.

NAAQ נאק
groan 2.

NAAR [1] נאר
PIEL abhor 1
make void 1.

NAAR [2] נער
shake 2
shake off 1
yell 1.
Pass. pt. shaken out 1.
NIPH. be shaken 1
be tossed up and down 1
shake self 1.
PIEL overthrow 2
shake 1.
HITHP. shake self 1.

NAAR [3] נַעַר
babe 1
boy 1
child 51
lad 32
servant 54
young (man) 90
youth 4.

NAARAH נַעֲרָה *f.*
damsel 34
maid 7
maiden 15
young 4
young maiden 1
young woman 1.

NAATS נאץ
abhor 2
contemn 1
despise 5.
Piel abhor 2
contemn 1
despise 3
give great occasion to blaspheme 1
give occasion to blaspheme 4
provoke 5.
HIPH. flourish 1.
HITHPOL. *partic.* blasphemed 1.

NAATSUTS נַעֲצוּץ
thorn 2.

NABA [1] נבא
NIPH. prophesy 87.
HITHP. make self a prophet 2
prophesy 26.

NABA [2] נבע
Partic. flowing 1.
HIPH. abundantly utter 1
belch out 1
pour out 3
send forth 1
utter 4.

NABAB נבב
Partic. hollow 3
vain 1.

NABACH נבח
bark 1.

NABAL נָבָל
fool 9
foolish 5
foolish man 1
foolish woman 1
vile person 2.

NABAT נבט
PIEL look 1.
HIPH. behold 12
cause to behold 1
consider 5
have respect 3
look 36
look about 1
look down 1
look upon 1
regard 4
see 4.

NABEL נבל
come to nought 1
do foolishly 1
fade 5
fade away 4
fall down 1
fall off 1
wear away 1
wither 2.
Partic. fading 2
falling 1.
Adv. inf. surely 1.
PIEL disgrace 1
dishonour 1
lightly esteem 1
make vile 1.

NABI נָבִיא
prophet 313
them that prophesy 1
*prophecy 1.

NABLUTH נַבְלוּת *f.*
lewdness 1.

NACHAH נחה
guide 1
lead 9
lead forth 1.
HIPH. bestow 1
bring 4
govern 1
guide 5
lead 15
put 1
straiten 1.

NACHAL [1] נחל
divide 1
divide by inheritance 2
divide for inheritance 1
have [inheritance] 3
have inheritance 2
have in possession 1
inherit 16
possess 2
take as an heritage 1
take for inheritance 1
take inheritance 1.
PIEL distribute for inheritance 2
divide for inheritance 1
divide inheritance 1
take inheritance 1.
HIPH. cause to inherit 6
cause to possess 1
divide for an inheritance 1
divide inheritance 1
give for inheritance 2
give to inherit 2
leave for inheritance 2
make to inherit 2.
HOPH. be made to possess 1.
HITHP. divide for an inheritance 1
inherit 4
possess 1
take as an inheritance 1.

NACHAL [2] נַחַל
brook 46
flood 5
river 54
stream 10
valley 23.

NACHALAH נַחֲלָה *f.*
heritage 26
inheritance 192
possession 1
river 2
*inherit 2.

NACHALATH נַחֲלַת *f.*
heritage 1.

NACHAM נחם
NIPH. be comforted 8
ease [one's self] 1
receive comfort 1
repent 38.
PIEL comfort 41.
Infin. comfort 1.
Partic. comforter 8.
PUAL be comforted 2.
HITHP. be comforted 3
comfort self 2
repent 1
repent self 2.

NACHAR נַחַר
nostrils 1.

NACHARAH נַחֲרָה *f.*
snorting 1.

NACHASH [1] נחשׁ
PIEL divine 2
learn by experience 1
observe diligently 1
use enchantment 3
[use] enchantment 1.
Partic. enchanter 1.
Adv. inf. certainly 1
indeed 1.

NACHASH [2] נַחַשׁ
enchantment 2.

NACHASH [3] נָחָשׁ
serpent 31.

NACHATH [1] נחת
come down 1
enter 1
go down 1
press sore 1.
NIPH. stick fast 1.
PIEL be broken 2
settle 1.
HIPH. cause to come down 1.

NACHATH [2] נַחַת
lighting down 1
quiet 1
quietness 1
rest 4
that which should be set on 1.

NACHETH נָחֵת
*come down 1.

NACHLAH נַחְלָה
stream 1.

NACHNU נַחְנוּ
we 5.

NACHUSH נָחוּשׁ
brass 1.

NACHUTS נָחוּץ (*pas. pt.*)
†*See* hayah.

NADAB נדב
give willingly 1
make willing 2.
HITHPA. be offered willingly 1
be willing 1
offer freely 1
offer selves willingly 4
offer willingly 7.

NADACH נדח
be expelled 1.
Inf. forcing 1.
NIPH. be drawn away 1
be driven 3
be driven away 2
be driven out 4
be driven quite 1
fetch a stroke 1
go astray 1.
Partic. banished 2
cast out 1
outcast 5.
PUAL be driven 1.
HIPH. bring 1
cast down 1
cast out 2
compel 1
drive 14
drive away 2
drive out 2
force 1
thrust away 1
thrust out 1
withdraw 1.
HOPH. *part.* chased 1.

NADAD נדד
be removed 1
depart 1
flee 9
move 1
wander 7
wander abroad 1.
POAL flee away 1.
HIPH. be chased 1.
HOPH. be chased away 1.
Partic. thrust away 1.
HITHPOL. flee away 1.
†KAL *repeated*: flee apace 1. *See* shenah.

NADAH נדה
PIEL cast out 1
put far away 1.

NADAN [1] נָדָן
gift 1.

NADAN [2] נָדָן
sheath 1.

NADAPH נדף
drive away 2
thrust down 1.
NIPH. be driven away 2.
Partic. driven 1
driven to and fro 1
shaken 1
tossed to and fro 1.

NADAR נדר
make [a vow] 1
vow 31.

NADIB נָדִיב
free 2
liberal 4
liberal things (*pl.*) 2
noble 4
prince 14
willing 2.
†willing hearted (*with* leb) 1.

NAEM נעם
be delight 1
be pleasant 5
be sweet 1.
†pass in beauty (*with* min) 1.

NAGA נגע
be come 5
be near 1
come 1
get up 1
reach 4
smite 2
touch 91.
Pass. pt. plagued 1
stricken 1.
NIPH. be beaten 1.
PIEL plague 1
smite 2.
PUAL be plagued 1.
HIPH. be come 4
bring 3
bring down 2
cast 1
come 9
come nigh 1
draw near 3
draw nigh 2
happen 2
join 1
lay 1
reach 7
reach up 1
strike 1
touch 1.
†HIPH. be able to bring (*with* de) 1.

NAGACH נגח
gore 3
push 1.
PIEL push 6
push down 1.
HITHP. push 1.

NAGAD נגד
HIPH. bewray 1
certify 1
declare 62
denounce 1
expound 2
profess 1
rehearse 1
report 2
show (forth) 60
speak 1
tell 189
utter 5
*be told 2.
Partic. messenger 2
another [messenger] 1
Adv. inf. certainly 1
plainly 1
surely 2.
HOPH. be declared 1
be showed 1
be told 32.
Adv. inf. certainly 1
fully 1.

NAGAH נגה
shine 3.
HIPH. cause to shine 1
enlighten 1
lighten 1.

NAGAN נגן
Partic. players on instruments 1.
PIEL play 9
sing to the stringed instrument 1.
Partic. minstrel 2
player 1.
Inf. melody 1.

NAGAPH נגף
dash 1
hurt 2
plague 3
smite 16
strike 2
stumble 1.
NIPH. be beaten 1
be put to the worse 5
be slain 2
be smitten 12
be smitten down 3.
Adv. inf. surely 1.
HITHP. stumble 1.

NAGAR נגר
NIPH. flow away 1
run 1
trickle down 1.
Partic. spilt 1.
HIPH. fall 1
pour down 1
pour out 2
shed 1.
HOPH. be poured down 1.

NAGAS נגשׂ
exact 5.
Partic. driver 1
exactor 1
oppressor 7
taskmaster 6.
NIPH. be distressed 2
be oppressed 2.
†*See* abar.

NAGASH נגשׁ
approach 2
be near 1
come 13
come hither 1
come near 34
come nigh 8
draw near 6
draw nigh 4
give place 1
go hard 1
go near 4
go up 5
stand 1.
NIPH. approach 2
approach nigh 1
come 4
come near 3
come nigh 1
draw near 3
go nigh 1
overtake 2.
HIPH. bring 13
bring forth 3
bring hither 6
bring near 5
cause to come near 1
make to approach 1
offer 6
overtake 1
present 1.
HOPH. be offered 1
be put 1.
HITHP. draw near 1.

NAGGACH נַגָּח
used to push 1
wont to push 1.

NAGID נָגִיד
captain 2
chief 3
chief governor 1
chief ruler 1
excellent thing 1
governor 1
leader 4
noble 1
prince 9
ruler 19.

NAHAG נהג
bring 1
bring away 1
carry away 2
drive 5
drive away 1
lead 5
lead away 2
lead forth 2.
Partic. acquainting 1.
PIEL be guide 1
bring 2
carry away 1
drive 1
guide 1
lead 5.

NAHAH נהה
lament 1
wail 1.
NIPH. lament 1.

NAHAL נהל
PIEL carry 1
feed 1
guide 5
lead 1
lead gently 1.
HITHP. lead on 1.

NAHALOLIM נַהֲלֹלִים *pl.*
bushes 1.

NAHAM [1] נהם
mourn 2
roar 3.

NAHAM [2] נַהַם
roaring 2.

NAHAQ נהק
bray 2.

NAHAR [1] נָהַר
be lightened 1
flow 2
flow together 3.

NAHAR [2] נָהָר
flood 18
river 97
stream 2.

NAHIRU נְהִירוּ *f.*
light 2.

NAIM נָעִים
pleasant 9
pleasures (*pl.*) 2
sweet 2.

NAKA נָכָא
stricken 1.

NAKAH נכה
NIPH. be smitten 1
PUAL be smitten 2
HIPH. beat 5
cast forth 1
[cause] to be beaten 1
clap 1
give [wounds] 2
give stripes 1
kill 20
make [slaughter] 1
punish 1
slay 90
smite 340
strike 4
wound 2
*[wounds] be given 1
Partic. murderer 1
Infin. to be beaten 1
slaughter 5
stripes 1.
Adv. inf. forward 1
indeed 1
surely 1.
HOPH. be beaten 2
be slain 5
be smitten 7
be stricken 1
be wounded 1.
†HIPH. slay (*with* nephesh 1; *with* nephesh, dam 1) 2.

* Inexact translations, *e.g.*, of a noun by a verb or adjective, of an active by a passive.
† Cases where two or more words in the original are translated by one word or by a phrase.

NAKAL נכל
Partic. deceiver 1.
PIEL beguile 1.
HITHP. conspire 1
deal subtilly 4.

NAKAR נכר
NIPH. be known 2
dissemble 1.
PIEL behave selves strangely 1
deliver 1
estrange 1
know 1
regard 1.
HIPH. acknowledge 7
could 1
discern 6
have respect 2
know 16
perceive 1
respect 2
take knowledge 2
take notice 1.
HITHP. be known 1
feign self to be another 2
makeself strange 1.

NAKE נָכֵא
broken 2
wounded 1.

NAKEH נָכֶה
contrite 1
lame 2.

NAKOACH נָכֹחַ
in uprightness 1
plain 1
right 2.
[*Compare* nekochah.]

NALAH נלה
HIPH. make an end 1.

NAMER נָמֵר
leopard 6.

NAPHACH נפח
blow 4
breathe 2
give up 1.
Partic. seething 2.
PUAL be blown 1.
HIPH. cause to lose [life] 1
snuff 1.

NAPHAH[1] נָפָה *f.*
border 1
coast 1
region 1.

NAPHAH[2] נָפָה *f.*
sieve 1

NAPHAL נפל
be accepted 2
be cast down 1
be fallen 39
be fallen down 1
be lost 2
be overthrown 3
die 1
fail 5
fall 262
fall away 5
fall down 23
lay along 2
lie 1
lie down 1
light 2
light down 1
perish 1
rot 1
*present 1.
Partic. fugitive 1
inferior 2
ready to fall 1.
Adv. inf. surely 1.
HIPH. cast 15
cast down 7
cast in 1
cast lots 1
cast out 1
cease 1
cause to fall 9
cause to lie down 1
divide 1
divide by lot 5
fell 3
let be cast 1
let fail 4
let fall 1
make fall 1
make to rot 1
overthrow 2
overwhelm 1
present 4
slay 1
smite out 1
throw down 1.
HITHP. cast self down 1
fall 1
fall down 1.
†KAL have [inheritance] (*with* be) 1; keep [bed] (*with* le) 1; lose (*with* min) 1.

NAPHASH נפשׁ
NIPH. be refreshed 2
refresh selves 1.

NAPHATS נפץ
be overspread 1
be scattered 2
break 1.
Partic. broken 1
dispersed 1.
PIEL break 1
break in pieces 9
cause to be discharged 1
dash 3
dash in pieces 1
scatter 1.
PUAL be beaten in sunder 1.

NAPHTULIM נַפְתּוּלִים *pl.*
wrestlings 1.

NAQA נקע
be alienated 3.

NAQAB נקב
appoint 1
blaspheme 3
bore 1
curse 6
name 2
pierce 3
strike through 1.
Partic. with holes 1.
NIPH. be expressed 6.

NAQAH נקה
Adv. inf. altogether 1.
NIPH. be blameless 1
be clear 1
be cut off 1
be desolate 1
be free 2
be guiltless 2
be innocent 4
be quit 1
be unpunished 10.
Adv. inf. utterly 1.
PIEL acquit 3
cleanse 3
clear 2
hold guiltless 3
hold innocent 1
leave unpunished 4.
Adv. inf. altogether 1
at all 1
by no means 2
wholly 1.

NAQAM[1] נקם
avenge 5
avenge selves 1
revenge 2
take [vengeance] 2
take vengeance 2.
Adv. inf. surely 1.
NIPH. avenge self 3
be avenged 4
be punished 1
revenge 1
revenge self 1
take [vengeance] 1
take vengeance 1.
PIEL avenge 1
take [vengeance] 1.
HOPH. be avenged 1
be punished 1
vengeance be taken 1.
HITHP. be avenged 3.
Partic. avenger 2.
†KAL avenge (*with* neqamah) 1.

NAQAM[2] נָקָם
quarrel 1
vengeance 15.
†at once (*with* achath) 1.

NAQAPH נקף
kill 1.
PIEL cut down 1
destroy 1.
HIPH. compass 6
compass about 3
go about 1
go round 1
go round about 1
inclose 1
round 1
*be gone about 1
*be gone round about 1

NAQAR נקר
pick out 1
thrust out 1.
PIEL put out 1
*be pierced 1.
PUAL be digged 1.

NAQASH נקשׁ
be snared 1.
NIPH. be snared 1.
PIEL catch 1
lay snares 1.
HITHP. lay a snare 1.

NAQAT נקט
be weary 1.

NAQI[1] נָקִי
blameless 2
clean 1
clear 1
exempted 1
free 1
guiltless 4
innocent 30
quit 2.

NAQI[2] נָקִיא
innocent 2.

NAQOD נָקֹד
speckled 9.

NASA[1] נסע
be departed 4
be journeying 1
be on his way 1
be removed 1
depart 25
get 1
go 4
go away 2
go forth 2
go forward 3
go on 1
go onward 1
go out 1
go their way 1
journey 29
march 1
remove 25
set forth 2
set forward 14
take [journey] 1
take journey 12.
NIPH. be departed 1
go away 1.
HIPH. bring 3
cause to blow 1
make go forth 1
remove 2
set aside 1.
†journey (*with* regel) 1.

NASA[2] נשׂא
accept 11
arise 1
be able to bear 2
be burned 1
be partial 1
bear 156
bear up 2
bring 21
bring forth 3
burn 1
can bear 1
carry 25
carry away 7
cast 1
contain 1
ease 1
exalt 1
fetch 2
forgive 16
hold up 1
lay 1
lift up 137
lift up again 1
obtain 4
offer 1
pardon 4
pluck up 1
raise 1
raise up 1
receive 3
regard 4
respect 3
set (up) 10
spare 3
stir up 3
suffer 5
swear 1
take (away, up) 116
wear 3
yield 1
*be accepted 1
*be borne 1
*be carried 1
*be laid 3
*be taken away 1.
Inf. *See* seeth.
Adv. inf. needs 1
utterly 1.
NIPH. be borne 3
be carried 3
be exalted 3
be extolled 1
be lifted up 14
be magnified 1
lift up self 3
*take away 1.
PIEL advance 2
carry 1
exalt 1
furnish 1
further 1
give 1
help 2
lift up 1
take away 1.
HIPH. bring 1
suffer to bear 1.
HITHP. be exalted 2
exalt self 3
lift self up 2
lift up self 2.
†KAL accept (*with* panim) 1; armour bearer (*partic.* *with* keli) 18; be partial (*with* panim) 1; go on journey (*with* regel) 1; honourable (*partic. with* panim) 3; honourable man (*partic. with* panim) 1; lade (*with* al[2]) 1; laden (*part. with* min) 1; marry (*with* le *and pron. suff.*) 1; regard (*with* panim) 1; swear (*with* yad) 3. PIEL desire (*with* nephesh) 1; have a desire (*with* nephesh) 1.

NASACH נסח
be rooted out 1
destroy 1
pluck 1.
NIPH. be plucked 1.

NASAG[1] נשׂג
HIPH. attain 1
attain unto 1
be able 2
be able to bring 1
be able to get 3
can get 2
get 1
lay at 1
obtain 2
overtake 23
put 1
reach 2
take 1
take hold 1
take hold of 2
take hold on 1
take hold upon 1
wax rich 1.
†be able (*with* matsa ke-de) 1. *See* yad.

NASAG[2] נסג (נשׂג)
HIPH. (= *Hiph.* of sug).

NASAH נסה
PIEL adventure 1
assay 2
prove 20
tempt 12
try 1.

NASAK[1] נסך
cover 1
melt 2
offer 1
pour 1
pour out 1
set 1.
NIPH. be set up 1.
PIEL pour out 1.
HIPH. cause to be poured 1
offer 1
pour 2
pour out 10.
HOPH. cover 2.

NASAK[2] נְסַךְ
Pass. pt. that is spread 1.

NASAQ[1] נסק
ascend up 1.

NASAQ[2] נשׂק
NIPH. be kindled 1.
HIPH. burn 1
kindle 1.

NASAS[1] נסס
Partic. standard bearer 1.
Hithp. pt. lifted up as an ensign 1.

NASHA[1] נשׁא
Adv. inf. utterly 1.
NIPH. be deceived 1.
HIPH. beguile 1
deceive 10
seize 1.

NASHA[2] נשׁא
Adv. inf. exact 1.
Partic. giver of usury 1.
HIPH. exact 1.
†KAL be in debt (le *with suff. and partic.*) 1.

NASHAB נשׁב
blow 1.
HIPH. cause to blow 1
drive away 1.

NASHAH[1] נשׁה
forget 2.
NIPH. be forgotten 1.
PIEL make forget 1.
HIPH. deprive 1
†exact less (*with* min) 1.

NASHAH[2] נָשָׁה
exact 3
lend 1
lend on usury 2.
Partic. creditor 2
extortioner 1
taker of usury 1
usurer 1.
HIPH. lend 2.

NASHAK נשׁך
be lent upon usury 1
bite 10.
PIEL bite 2.
HIPH. lend upon usury 3.

NASHAL נשׁל
cast 1
cast out 1
loose 1
put off 1
put out 1
slip 1.
PIEL drive 1.

NASHAM נשׁם
destroy 1.

NASHAPH נשׁף
blow 2.

NASHAQ[1] נשׁק
be ruled 1
kiss 25.
PIEL kiss 5.
HIPH. touch 1.

NASHAQ[2] נשׁק
Partic. armed 1
armed men 1
being armed 1.

NASHATH נשׁת
fail 2.
NIPH. fail 1.

NASHEH נָשֶׁה
which shrank 2.

NASHIM נָשִׁים *f. pl.*
wives 114
women 93
*married 3.
†*See* hayah.

NASHIN נְשִׁין *f. pl.*
wives 1.

NASI[1] נָשִׂיא
captain 12
chief 9
governor 1
prince 95
ruler 6.

NASI[2] נָשִׂיא
clouds (*pl.*) 1
vapours (*pl.*) 3.

NASIK נָסִיךְ
drink offering 1
duke 1
prince 3
principal 1.

NATA נטע
fasten 1
plant 56.
NIPH. be planted 1

NATAH נטה
be gone 1
be turned 1
bow 2
bow self 1
decline 7
extend 1
go down 2
incline 3
intend 1
pitch 8
prolong 1
show 1
spread 3
spread out 1
stretch 2
stretch forth 13
stretch out 64
turn 13
turn aside 3
turn away 1
turn in to 1.
Partic. bowing 1
outstretched 3.
Infin. bowing down 1.
NIPH. be spread forth 1
be stretched forth 1
be stretched out 1.
HIPH. apply 1
bow 3
bow down 4
carry aside 2
cause to yield 1
decline 1
deliver 1
extend 2
incline 25
lay 2
lay self down 1
let down 1
overthrow 1
pervert 4
put away 1
spread 2
stretch forth 1
stretch out 2
take aside 1
turn 3
turn aside 9
turn away 4
wrest 3.
†KAL afternoon (*infin. with* yom) 1; offer (*with* al[2]) 1.

NATAL נטל
bear 1
take up 1.
PIEL bear 1.
†KAL offer (*with* al[2]) 1.

NATAL נְטַל
lift up 1.
Pass. pt. lifted up 1

NATAPH[1] נטף
drop 9.
HIPH. drop 4
prophesy 4.
Partic. prophet 1.

NATAPH[2] נָטָף
drops 1
stacte 1.

NATAR נטר
bear grudge 1
keep 6
reserve 2.

NATASH נטשׁ
cast off 1
forsake 13
join [battle] 1
leave 12
leave off 1
let fall 1
lie still 1
spread abroad 1
suffer 1.
Partic pass. drawn 1.
NIPH. be forsaken 1
be loosed 1
be stretched out 1
spread selves 3.
PUAL be forsaken 1.

NATHA נתע
NIPH. be broken 1.

NATHACH נתח
PIEL cut 4
cut in pieces 4
divide 1
hew in pieces 1.

* Inexact translations, *e.g.*, of a noun by a verb or adjective, of an active by a passive.
† Cases where two or more words in the original are translated by one word or by a phrase.

NATHAK נָתַךְ
be poured 2
be poured forth 2
be poured out 3.
NIPH. be melted 1
be molten 1
be poured 1
be poured forth 1
be poured out 3
drop 1.
HIPH. gather 1
gather together 1
melt 2
pour out 1.
HOPH. be melted 1.

NATHAN נָתַן
add 2
apply 2
appoint 11
ascribe 4
assign 2
bestow 5
bring 13
bring forth 2
bring hither 1
cast 4
cause 10
commit 5
count 1
deliver 156
deliver up 3
direct 1
distribute 1
fasten 5
frame 1
give 1023
give forth 1
give leave 1
give over 1
give up 6
grant 15
hang 1
hang up 2
lay 31
lay up 3
leave 2
lend 1
let 5
let out 1
lift up 2
make 108
occupy 3
offer 2
ordain 2
pay 3
perform 1
place 4
plant 2
pour 1
present 1
print 1
put 191
put forth 1
recompense 11
render 1
requite 1
restore 1
send (out, forth) 13
set (forth) 101
shew 7
shoot (forth, up) 3
strike 1
suffer 18
thrust 1
tie 1
trade 4
turn 2
utter 11
yield 14
*be bestowed 1
*be given 11
*be granted 2
*be made 1
*be put 1
*come 1.
Adv. inf. doubtless 1
indeed 1
surely 1
willingly 1
without fail 1.
Pass. pt. gift 1.
NIPH. be cast 1
be caused 1
be committed 1
be delivered 18
be done 1
be given 45
be given up 1
be granted 4
be laid 1
be made 1
be put 1
be set 1
be uttered 1.
Adv. inf. surely 2.
HOPH. be delivered 1
be given 2
be gotten 1
be put 1
be taken up 1.
†KAL avenge (*with* neqamah) 4; be healed (*with* rephuoth) 1; cause to multiply (*with* rebabah) 1; charge (*with* al[2] 1, *with* le 1) 2; consider (*with* el) 1; cry (*with* qol) 2; cry out (*with* qol) 1; have oversight (*p.p. with* be) 1; lay to charge of (*with* be-qereb) 1; lie (*with* shekobeth) 4; make sit (*with* maqom le) 1; make to be pitied (*with* le-rachamim) 1; pay (*with* meker) 1; pull away (*with part. of* sarar) 1; sing (*with* qol) 1; slander (*with* dophi) 1; submit (*with* yad) 1; take heed (*with* leb) 1; weep aloud (*with* qol be-beki) 1; withdraw (*with* katheph sorereth) 1; yell (*with* qol) 1; yield (*with* yad) 1. *See* mi.

NATHAQ נתק
draw 1
pluck 1.
Partic. broken 1.
NIPH. be broken 5
be broken off 1
be drawn away 1
be lifted up 1
be plucked away 1
be rooted out 1.
PIEL break 3
break in sunder 4
burst 4
pluck off 1
pull 1.
HIPH. draw 1
pull out 1.
HOPH. be drawn away 1.

NATHAR נתר
be moved 1.
PIEL leap 1.
HIPH. drive asunder 1
let loose 1
loose 2
make 1
undo 1.

NATHAS נתס
mar 1.

NATHASH נתשׁ
destroy 1
pluck 1
pluck out 2
pluck up 7
pluck up by the roots 1
root out 2
root up 1.
Adv. inf. utterly 1.
NIPH. be forsaken 1
be plucked up 2
be pulled up 1.
HOPH. be plucked up 1.

NATHATS נתץ
beat down 3
break down 15
break out 1
cast down 2
destroy 5
pull down 2
throw down 2.
Pass. pt. which are thrown down 1.
NIPH. be broken down 1
be thrown down 1.
PIEL break down 5
overthrow 1
throw down 1.
PUAL be cast down 1
HOPH. be broken down 1.

NATHIB נָתִיב
path 3
way 2.

NATIL נָטִיל
they that bear (*pl.*) 1.

NATSA נצא
flee 1.

NATSAB נצב
NIPH. be set over 4
be settled 1
present self 1
stand 28
stand still 1
stand up 1
stand upright 2.
Partic. appointed 1
at his best state 1
deputy 1
officer 6
standing 1.
HIPH. erect 1
establish 1
lay 1
make to stand 1
rear up 1
set 9
set up 3
sharpen 1
stablish 1.
HOPH. *pt.* pillar 1
set up 1.

NATSACH נצח
NIPH. *pt.* perpetual 1.
PIEL excel 1
oversee 1
set forward 4.
Partic. chief musician 56
chief singer 1
overseer 2.

NATSAH[1] נצה
NIPH. strive 1
strive together 4.
HIPH. strive 1.

NATSAH[2] נצה
be laid waste 1.
NIPH. *pt.* ruinous 2.

NATSAL נצל
NIPH. be delivered 12
be escaped 1
be preserved 1
be taken out 1
deliver self 2.
PIEL deliver 1
spoil 1
strip off 1.
HIPH. defend 1
deliver 168
recover 6
rescue 2
rid 3
save 1
take 3
take away 1
*escape 1.
Adv. inf. at all 2
surely 2
without fail 1.
HOPH. *pt.* plucked 2.
HITHP. strip self 1.
†HIPH. part (*with* ben[1]) 1.

NATSAR נצר
keep 37
observe 1
preserve 12.
Partic. keeper 1
preserver 1
watcher 1
watchman 3.
Pass. pt. besieged 2
hidden thing 1
monument 1
subtil 1.

NATSATS נצץ
sparkle 1.

NATSIR נָצִיר
preserved 1.

NAVAH[1] נוה
keep at home 1.
HIPH. prepare an habitation 1.

NAVAH[2] נָוָה
dwelling 1
habitation 1
she that tarried 1.

NAVEH[1] נָאוֶה (נָוֶה)
comely 7
seemly 2
*become 1.

NAVEH[2] נָוֶה
dwelling 2
dwelling place 1
fold 4
habitation 21
pleasant place 1
sheepcote 2
stable 1.

NAZAH נזה
be sprinkled 4.
HIPH. sprinkle 20.

NAZAL נזל
distil 1
drop 1
flow 5
flow out 1
gush out 1
melt 1
pour 1
pour down 1.
Partic. flood 3
running water 1
stream 2.
HIPH. cause to flow 1.

NAZAR נזר
NIPH. separate selves 4.
HIPH. consecrate 1
separate 5.

NAZID נָזִיד
pottage 6.

NAZIR נָזִיר
Nazarite 12
separate 1
separated 1
vine undressed 2.

NEAQAH נְאָקָה
groaning 4.

NEATSAH נְאָצָה *f.*
blasphemy 2.

NEATSOTH נְאָצוֹת *f. pl.*
blasphemies 1
provocations 2.

NEBA נבא
HITHP. prophesy 1.

NEBALAH נְבָלָה *f.*
folly 10
villany 2
*vile 1.

NEBEK נֶבֶךְ
spring 1.

NEBEL נֵבֶל (נֶבֶל)
bottle 8
flagon 1
pitcher 1
psaltery 23
vessel 1
viol 4.

NEBELAH נְבֵלָה *f.*
beast that dieth of itself 1
body 1
carcase 35
dead body 5
dead carcase 1
*dead of itself 1
*which died 1
*which dieth of itself 1.

NEBI נְבִיא
prophet 4.

NEBIAH נְבִיאָה *f.*
prophetess 6.

NEBIZBAH נְבִזְבָּה *f.*
rewards (*pl.* 1) 2.

NEBRASHTA נֶבְרַשְׁתָּא *f.*
candlestick 1.

NEBUAH נְבוּאָה *f.*
prophecy 3.

NEBUAH נְבוּאָה *f.*
prophesying 1.

NECHAMAH נֶחָמָה *f.*
comfort 2.

NECHASH נְחָשׁ
brass 9.

NECHATH נְחַת
come down 2.
APH. carry 1
lay up 1
place 1.
HOPH. be deposed 1.

NECHIRIM נְחִירַיִם *pl.*
nostrils 1.

NECHOSHETH נְחֹשֶׁת *c.*
brass 100
chain 3
copper 1
fetter 3
fetter of brass 2
filthiness 1
steel 1
*brasen 28.

NECHUSHAH נְחוּשָׁה *f.*
brass 7
steel 3.

NED נֵד
heap 6.

NEDAB נדב
ITHP. be minded of own freewill 1
offer freely 1
offer willingly 1.
Infin. freewill offering 1.

NEDABAH נְדָבָה *f.*
free offering 2
freewill offering 15
voluntary offering 1
willing offering 1
*freely 2
*voluntarily 1
*voluntary 1
*willing 1
*willingly 1.

NEDAD נדד
go from 1.

NEDEH נֵדֶה
gift 1.

NEDER נֶדֶר (נֵדֶר)
vow 59.
†vowed (*with* hayah *understd. and* al[2]) 1.

NEDIBAH נְדִיבָה *f.*
soul 1.

NEDUDIM נְדֻדִים *pl.*
tossings to and fro 1.

NEGA נֶגַע
plague 65
sore 5
stripe 2
stroke 4
wound 1
†be stricken (*with* le) 1.

NEGAD נגד
issue 1.

NEGEB נֶגֶב
south (ward) 105
south country 2
south side 5.

NEGED נֶגֶד
against
before
in the presence of
in the sight of
over against, etc.
†*Similarly* le-neged, minneged.

NEGED נֶגֶד
toward 1.

NEGEPH נֶגֶף
plague 6
stumbling 1.

NEGINAH נְגִינָה *f.*
music 1
song 5
stringed instrument 1.

NEGOHOTH נְגֹהוֹת *f. pl.*
brightness 1.

NEHAMAH נְהָמָה *f.*
disquietness 1
roaring 1.

NEHAR נְהַר
river 14
stream 1.

NEHARAH נְהָרָה *f.*
light 1.

NEHI נְהִי
lamentation 3
wailing 4.

NEHIR נְהִיר (V.L.)
light 1.

NEHOR נְהוֹר (V.L.)
light 1.

NEKACH נֹכַח
before 1
over against 1.

NEKAR נֵכָר
alien 1
strange 17.
stranger 6.
†*See* ben[2].

NEKASIM נְכָסִים *pl.*
riches 1
wealth 4.

NEKED נֶכֶד
nephew 2
son's son 1.

NEKEH נָכֶה
abject 1.

NEKEL נֵכֶל
wile 2.

NEKER נֵכֶר
*strange punishment 1.

NEKOCHAH נְכֹחָה *f.*
equity 1
right 1
right thing 1
uprightness 1.

NEKOTH[1] נְכֹאת *f.*
spicery 1
spices 1.

NEKOTH[2] נְכֹת
precious things 2.

NEMALAH נְמָלָה *f.*
ant 2.

NEMAR נְמַר
leopard 1.

NEMIBZAH נְמִבְזָה
vile 1.

NEORETH נְעֹרֶת *f.*
tow 2.

NEPHAL נפל
fall 3
fall down 7
have occasion 1.

NEPHAQ נפק
be gone forth 1
come forth 4
go forth 1.
HAPH. take forth 1
take out 4
*be taken out 1.

NEPHEL נֵפֶל (נֶפֶל)
untimely birth 3.

NEPHESH נֶפֶשׁ *c.*
any 4
appetite 2
beast 2
body 7
breath 1
creature 9
dead (body) 8
desire 5
ghost 2
heart 15
life 119
lust 2
man 3
mind 15
one 1
own 1
person 30
pleasure 4
self 19
soul 428
thing 2
will 4
*fish 1
*hearty 1
*mortal 1
*will (*vb.*) 1
*would have it 1.
†anyone (*with* achath) 1; beast (*with* behemah) 1; deadly (be-nephesh) 1; life (*with* chaiyah) 1; person (*with* adam 3, *with* ish 1) 4; that hath life (*with* chaiyah) 1. *With pron. suff.* = *Eng. pron.* 24. *See* az,[2] bayith, mar, nakah, ratsach.

NEPHETH נֶפֶת *f.*
country 1.

NEPHETS נֶפֶץ
scattering 1.

NEPHILIM נְפִלִים *pl.*
giants 3.

NEQAMAH נְקָמָה *f.*
revenge 2
revenging 1
vengeance 19.
†*See* naqam, nathan.

NEQARAH נְקָרָה *f.*
cleft 1
clift 1.

* Inexact translations, *e.g.*, of a noun by a verb or adjective, of an active by a passive.
† Cases where two or more words in the original are translated by one word or by a phrase.

NEQASH נקשׁ
smite 1.

NEQE נְקֵא
pure 1.

NEQEB נֶקֶב
pipe 1.

NEQEBAH נְקֵבָה *f.*
female 18
maid child 1
woman 3.

NEQIQ נָקִיק
hole 3.

NEQUDDOTH נְקֻדּוֹת *f. pl.*
studs 1.

NER (נִיר) נֵר
candle 9
lamp 33
light 1.

NERD נֵרְדְּ
spikenard 3.

NES נֵס
banner 2
ensign 6
pole 2
sail 2
sign 1
standard 7.

NESA נשׂא
carry away 1
take 1.
HITHP. make insurrection 1.

NESACH נסח
ITHP. be pulled down 1.

NESAK[1] נסך
PAEL offer 1.

NESAK[2] נְסַךְ
drink-offering 1.

NESAQ נסק
HAPH. take up 2.
HOPH. be taken up 1.

NESEK נֶסֶךְ (נֵסֶךְ)
drink-offering 59
molten image 3
*to cover withal 1.

NESHAMAH נְשָׁמָה *f.*
blast 3
breath 11
inspiration 1
soul 1.
spirit 2
*that breatheth 1
*that breathed 2.
†*See* ruach.[2]

NESHAR נְשַׁר
eagle 2.

NESHEK נֶשֶׁךְ
usury 12.

NESHEPH נֶשֶׁף
dark 1
dawning of the day 1
dawning of the morning 1
night 3
twilight 6.

NESHEQ (נֵשֶׁק) נֶשֶׁק
armed men 1
armour 3
armoury 1
battle 1
harness 1
weapon 3.

NESHER נֶשֶׁר
eagle 26.

NESHI נְשִׁי
debt 1.

NESHIQAH נְשִׁיקָה *f.*
kiss 2.

NESHIYYAH נְשִׁיָּה *f.*
forgetfulness 1.

NESIBBAH נְסִבָּה *f.*
cause 1.

NESUAH נְשׂוּאָה *f.*
carriage 1.

NETA נֶטַע
plant 5.

NETAR נטר
keep 1.

NETEL נֵטֶל
*weighty 1.

NETHACH נֵתַח
parts (*pl.*) 1
pieces (*pl.*) 12.

NETHAN נתן
bestow 2
give 4
pay 1.

NETHAR נתר
APH. shake off 1.

NETHEQ נֶתֶק
dry scall 1
scall 13.

NETHER נֶתֶר
nitre 2.

NETHIBAH נְתִיבָה *f.*
path 19.
†*See* derek, halak.

NETIIM נְטָעִים *pl.*
plants 1.

NETIPHOTH נְטִיפוֹת *f. pl.*
chains 1
collars 1.

NETISHOTH נְטִישׁוֹת *f. pl.*
battlements 1
branches 1
plants 1.

NETOTH
Inf. of. natah.

NETS[1] נֵץ
hawk 3.

NETS[2] נֵץ
blossom 1.

NETSACH[1] (נֵצַח) נֶצַח
alway 1
always 2
constantly 1
ever 24
evermore 1
perpetual 3.
†to the end (ad netsach) 1; unto the end (la-netsach) 1. *See* lo.

NETSACH[2] נֵצַח
blood 1
strength 3
victory 2.

NETSACH נצח
HITHP. *pt.* preferred 1.

NETSAL נצל
HAPH. deliver 2
rescue 1.

NETSER נֵצֶר
branch 1.

NETSIB נְצִיב
garrison 9
officer 2
pillar 1.

NEUM נְאֻם (*from* naam)
*say 374
*speak 1.

NEURIM נְעוּרִים *pl.*
childhood 1.
youth 45.

NEUROTH נְעוּרוֹת *f. pl.*
youth 1.

NEVALI נְוָלִי *f.*
dunghill 2.

NEVALU נְוָלוּ *f.*
dunghill 1.

NEZAQ נזק
have damage 1.
HAPH. endamage 1.
Partic. hurtful 1.
Infin. to the hurt of 1.

NEZEM נֶזֶם
ear-ring 12
jewel 3.

NEZEQ נֵזֶק
damage 1.

NEZER נֵזֶר
consecration 1
crown 11
hair 1
separation 10.

NI נִי
wailing 1.

NIB נִיב
fruit 2.

NICHOACH נִיחֹחַ
sweet odour 1
sweet 42.

NICHOACH נִיחֹחַ
sweet odour 1
sweet savour 1.

NICHUMIM נִחוּמִים *pl.*
comforts 1
repentings 1
*comfortable 1.

NID נִיד
moving 1.

NIDAH נִידָה *f.*
†*See* hayah.

NIDBAK נִדְבָּךְ
row 2.

NIDDAH נִדָּה *f.*
filthiness 2
flowers 2
menstruous woman 1
removed woman 2
separation 14
unclean thing 1
unclean with filthiness 1
uncleanness 1
*be put apart 1
*menstruous 1.
†far (le-niddah) 1. *See* hayah, tame.

NIDNEH נִדְנֶה
*body 1.

NIHYAH נִהְיָה *f.*
*doleful 1.

NIKSIN נִכְסִין *pl.*
goods 2.

NIN נִין
son 3.

NIPHQA נִפְקָא *f.*
expenses 2.

NIQPAH נִקְפָּה *f.*
rent 1.

NIQQAYON נִקָּיוֹן
cleanness 1
innocency 4.

NIQQUDDIM נִקֻּדִּים *pl.*
cracknels 1
mouldy 2.

NIR[1] ניר
break up 2.

NIR[2] נִיר
fallow ground 2
tillage 1.

NIR[3] נִיר
lamp 1
light 3.

NIR[4] נִר
plowing 1.

NIRGAN נִרְגָּן
talebearer 3
whisperer 1.

NISHBAR
Niph. partic. of shabar.

NISHKAH נִשְׁכָּה *f.*
chamber 3.

NISHMA נִשְׁמָא *f.*
breath 1.

NISHTEVAN נִשְׁתְּוָן
letter 2.

NISHTEVAN נִשְׁתְּוָן
letter 3.

NISSETH נִשֵּׂאת *f.*
gift 1.

NITSBAH נִצְבָּה *f.*
strength 1.

NITSOTS נִיצוֹץ
spark 1.

NITSTSAB נִצָּב
haft 1.

NITSTSAH נִצָּה *f.*
flower 2.

NITSTSAN נִצָּן
flower 1.

NIUPHIM נִאֻפִים *pl.*
adulteries 2.

NO נוא
HIPH. break 1
disallow 4
discourage 2
make of none effect 1.

NOAH נֹהַּ
wailing 1.

NOAM נֹעַם
beauty 4
pleasantness 1
*pleasant 2.

NOAR נֹעַר
child 2
youth 2.

NOCHAM נֹחַם
repentance 1.

NOD[1] נֹאד
bottle 6.

NOD[2] נֹד
wandering 1.

NOGAH נֹגַהּ *f.*
brightness 11
clear shining 1
light 1
shining 5
*bright 1
*shining (*adj.*) 1.

NOGAH נֹגַהּ *f.*
morning 1.

NOKACH נֹכַח
against 2
before 6
over against 8
right 1.
†le-nokach: before 1, for 1, right on 1. ad[3] nokach le-bo: over against 1. *el nokach pene* directly before 1.

NOKER נֵכָר
*become a stranger 1.

NOKRI נָכְרִי
alien 4
foreigner 2
outlandish 1
strange 16
stranger 19
strange woman 3.

NOPH נוֹף
situation 2.

NOPHEK נֹפֶךְ
emerald 4.

NOPHETH נֹפֶת
honeycomb 4
†honeycomb (*with* tsuph) 1.

NOQED נֹקֵד
herdman 1
sheepmaster 1.

NOQEPH נֹקֶף
shaking 2.

NOTSAH (נֹצָה) נוֹצָה
feather 4.

NUA נוּעַ
be gone away 1
be moveable 1
be moved 3
be promoted 3
be vagabond 1
move 2
reel 1
remove 1
stagger 2
wander 5
wander up and down 1.
Partic. fugitive 2.
Adv. inf. continually 1
to and fro 1.
NIPH. be shaken 1
be sifted 1.
HIPH. let wander up and down 1
move 1
scatter 1
set 1
shake 5
sift 1
wag 2.
†HIPH. make go up and down (*with inf. of* bo) 1.

NUACH נוּחַ
be at rest 3
be confederate 1
be quiet 1
cease 1
have rest 3
remain 1
rest 23.
Inf. resting place 1.
HIPH. bestow 1
cast down 1
cause to rest 7
give rest 20
lay 9
lay down 1
lay up 10
leave 21
leave off 1
let alone 4
let down 1
let remain 1
make to rest 1
pacify 1
place 3
put 5
quiet 1
set 6
set down 3
suffer 3
withdraw 1
withhold 1.
HOPH. be left 3
be set 1
have rest 1.

NUB נוּב
bring forth 1
bring forth fruit 1
increase 1.
PIL. make cheerful 1.

NUD נוּד
bemoan 6
be shaken 1
be sorry 1
flee 1
mourn 1
remove 3
take pity 1.
Partic. vagabond 2.
Infin. wandering 1.
Imper. get you 1.
HIPH. make move 1
remove 1
wag 1.
HITHPOL. bemoan self 1
be removed 1
skip for joy 1.

NUD נוּד
get away 1.

NUM נוּם
sleep 1
slumber 1.

NUMAH נוּמָה *f.*
drowsiness 1.

NUN נוּן
NIPH. be continued 1.

NUPH נוּף
perfume 1.
POL. shake 1.
HIPH. lift up 4
move 1
offer 4
send 1
shake 6
sift 2
strike 1
wave 14
*be waved 1.
HOPH. be waved 1.

NUQ נוּק
HIPH. nurse 1.

NUR נוּר
fire 7
*fiery 8.

NUS נוּס
abate 1
be fled 12
flee 131
flee away 11.
Adv. inf. away 1.
POL. lift up a standard 1.
HIPH. make flee 1
put to flight 1
hide (*tr.*) 1.
HITHPOL. be displayed 1.

NUSH נוּשׁ
be full of heaviness 1.

NUT נוּט
be moved 1.

NUTS נוּץ
flee away 1.
HIPH. bud 1
bud forth 1.

O

OB[1] אוֹב
bottle 1.

OB[2] אוֹב
familiar spirit 7
that hath (have, etc.) a fam. spirit 8.

OB[3] עָב
thick plank 1.

OBED[1] אֹבֵד
†to perish (ade obed) 2.

OBED[2]
Partic. of abad.[3]

OBI עֳבִי
thickness 3
*thick 1.

OBNAYIM אָבְנַיִם *du.*
stools 1
wheels 1.

OCHIM אֹחִים *pl.*
doleful creatures 1.

OCHORAN אָחֳרָן
another 2
other 3.
†at last (ad ochoran) 1.

OCHORI אָחֳרִי
another 5
other 1.

OD עוֹד
again
any longer
any more
as yet
besides
else
further
furthermore
henceforth
longer
more
moreover
still
the while
when
while yet
yet, etc.
†be almost ready (*with* meat) 1.

OD עוֹד
while 1.

ODEM אֹדֶם
sardius 3.

ODOTH (אוֹדָה) אוֹדוֹת *pl.*
cause 1
causes 1
sake 1.
†*See* al.[2]

OHABIM אֲהָבִים *pl.*
loves 1.

OHEL אֹהֶל
covering 1
dwelling 1
dwelling place 2
home 1
tabernacle *freq.*
tent *freq.*
†dwelling place (*with* mishkan) 1.

OKEL אֹכֶל
eating 4
food 16
meat 18
prey 2
victuals 3.
†*See* eth.

OKLAH אָכְלָה *f.*
food 1
fuel 3
meat 8
*consume 1
*devour 3
*eat 2.

OL עֹל
yoke 39.

OLAH[1] עֹלָה *f.*
ascent 1
burnt offering 266
burnt sacrifice 18
*to go up to 1.

OLAH[2] עֹלָה *f.*
iniquity 2
wickedness 1.

OLAL (עוֹלֵל) עֹלָל
babe 2
child 14
infant 3
little one 1
young child 1.

OLAM עוֹלָם
ancient time 1
beginning of the world 1
continuance 1
ever 267
everlasting 11
evermore 15
old 7
old time 1
world 2.

* Inexact translations, *e.g.*, of a noun by a verb or adjective, of an active by a passive.
† Cases where two or more words in the original are translated by one word or by a phrase.

Genitive always 1, ancient 5, at any time 1, eternal 1, everlasting 53, for ever 3, lasting 1, long 2, old 6, perpetual 20.
Plur. old 2.
†any more (ad olam) 2; alway (le-olam) 2; always (le-olam) 2; of old time (le-olamim) 1. Me-olam: ever of old 1, long time 1, of old 6, of old time 2. *See* ad[1], lo, yom.

OLEL = **OLAL.**

OLELOTH עֹלֵלוֹת *f. pl.* gleaning grapes 3, gleaning of the grapes 1, grapegleanings 1, grapes 1.

OMED עֹמֶד place 6, where [I] stood 1, *stand 1.
†upright (al[2] omdi) 2.

OMEN אֹמֶן truth 1.

OMEQ עֹמֶק depth 1.

OMER אֹמֶר promise 1, speech 2, thing 1, word 2.

OMER עֹמֶר omer 6, sheaf 8.

OMETS אֹמֶץ †*See* yasaph.

OMNAH[1] אָמְנָה *f.* †brought up (be-omnah) 1.

OMNAH[2] אָמְנָה indeed 2.

OMNAM אָמְנָם indeed 2, it is true 1, no doubt 1, of a truth 1, surely 1, truly 2.

OMNOTH אֹמְנוֹת *f. pl.* pillars 1.

ON אוֹן force 1, goods 1, might 2, strength 7, substance 1.

ONAH עוֹנָה *f.* duty of marriage 1, furrow 1.

ONEG עֹנֶג delight 1, *pleasant 1.

ONESH עֹנֶשׁ punishment 1, tribute 1.

ONI[1] אֳנִי *c.* galley 1, navy 5, navy of ships 1.

ONI[2] עֳנִי affliction 33, trouble 3.
†*See* ben.

ONIYYAH אֳנִיָּה *f.* ship 30.
†*See* anashim.

ONIYYOTH אוֹנִיּוֹת *f. pl.* ships 1.

OPH עוֹף bird 9, fowl 59, *flying 2, *that flieth 1.

OPH עוֹף fowl 2.

OPHAIM עֳפָאִים *pl.* branches 1.

OPHAN אוֹפָן wheel 33.

OPHEL[1] אֹפֶל darkness 7, obscurity 1.
†privily (bemo ophel) 1.

OPHEL[2] עֹפֶל emerods (*pl.*) 6, fort 1, strong hold 1, tower 1.

OPHEN אֹפֶן †*See* al[2].

OPHER עֹפֶר †young hart (*with* pl. of ayyal) 3; young roe (*with* tsebiyyah) 2.

OPHERETH עוֹפֶרֶת *f.* lead 6.

OPHI עֳפִי leaves 3.

OQBAH עָקְבָּה *f.* subtilty 1.

OR[1] אוֹר be enlightened 2, be light 1, have light 1, shine 2.
NIPH. be enlightened 1, *break of day 1.
Partic. glorious 1.
HIPH. cause to shine 5, enlighten 2, give light 10, give [light] 1, kindle 1, light 3, lighten 4, make to shine 5, set on fire 1, show light 2, shine 2.

OR[2] אוֹר day 2, light 114, lightning 1, morning 1, sun 1, *bright 2, *clear 2, *herbs 1.

OR[3] אֹר (=יְאֹר) flood 1.

OR[4] עוֹר hide 2, leather 1, skin 96.

ORACH אֹרַח *c.* highway 1, manner 1, path 23, race 1, rank 1, traveller 1, troop 1, way 30.
†byway (*with* aqalqal) 1. *See* abar[2].

ORAH אוֹרָה *f.* herb 2, light 2.

ORBOTH אָרְבּוֹת *f. pl.* spoils 1.

ORCHA אָרְחָא *f.* way 2.

OREB אֹרֶב wait 1.

OREB עֹרֵב raven 10.

OREK אֹרֶךְ length 67, *high 1, *long 22.
†for ever (le-orek yamim) 2; forbearing (*with du. of* aph) 1.

OREM עֹרֶם craftiness 1.

OREN אֹרֶן ash 1.

OREPH עֹרֶף back 8, neck 17.
†*See* qashah, qasheh.

ORLAH עָרְלָה *f.* foreskin 13, the uncircumcised 1.
†be uncircumcised (lo[2] orlah) 1. *See* arel.

ORMAH עָרְמָה *f.* guile 1, prudence 1, subtilty 1, wisdom 1.
†wilily (be-ormah) 1.

OSEH *Partic. of* asah.

OSEPH אֹסֶף *f.* gathering 2, *when they have gathered 1.

OSHEQ עֹשֶׁק extortion 1, oppression 12, *cruelly 1, *thing 1.

OSHER[1] אֹשֶׁר *happy 1.

OSHER[2] עֹשֶׁר riches 36.
†far richer (*with* gadol) 1.

OSHQAH עָשְׁקָה *f.* †I am oppressed (*with* li) 1.

OSHYOTH אֻשִּׁיּוֹת *f. pl.* foundations 1.

OSPARNA אָסְפַּרְנָא fast 1, forthwith 1, speedily 4, with speed 2.

OTH[1] אוֹת *c.* ensign 2, mark 1, miracle 2, sign 60, token 14.

OTH[2] אות NIPH. consent 4.

OTSAR אוֹצָר armoury 1, cellar 2, garner 1, store 1, storehouse 2, treasure 61, treasury 10.
†*See* bayith.

OTSEB עֹצֶב idol 1, sorrow 2, *wicked 1.

OTSEM עֹצֶם might 1, substance 1, *strong 1.

OTSER עֹצֶר oppression 1, prison 1, *barren 1.

OTSMAH עָצְמָה *f.* abundance 1, strength 2.

OY אוֹי alas 1, woe 23.

OYAH אוֹיָה woe 1.

OZ עֹז boldness 1, might 3, power 11, strength 60, *loud 1, *mighty 1, *strong 17.

OZEN אֹזֶן audience 7, ear *freq.*, hearing 5.
†hear (*with* shama) 1. *See* galah, raa, shema.

OZNIYYAH עָזְנִיָּה *f.* ospray 2.

P

PAAH[1] פאה HIPH. scatter into corners 1.

PAAH[2] פעה cry 1.

PAAL פעל commit 1, do 10, make 4, ordain 1, work 19.
Partic. doer 1, maker 2, worker 19.

PAAM[1] פעם move 1.
NIPH. be troubled 3.
HITHP. be troubled 1.

PAAM[2] פַּעַם *c.* anvil 1, corner 3, foot 7, footstep 1, going 1, now (*with art. pref.*) 9, once 5, order 1, rank 1, step 4, time 59, twice (*du.*) 5, wheel 1.
†at once (be-paam 1, *with* echad 2) 3; oftentimes (*with* rab 1, *with* shalosh 1) 2; once (*with* echad) 3. *See* meah, shalosh.

PAAMON פַּעֲמוֹן bell 7.

PAAR[1] פאר PIEL beautify 3, glorify 3.
HITHP. be glorified 3, boast self 1, glorify self 1, glory 1, vaunt selves 1.

PAAR[2] פאר PIEL go over the boughs 1.

PAAR[3] פער gape 1, open 2, open wide 1.

PACH[1] פַּח gin 2, snare 23.

PACH[2] פַּח plates (*pl.*) 1, thin plates (*pl.*) 1.

PACHACH פחח HIPH. *be snared 1.

PACHAD[1] פחד be afraid 9, be in fear 2, fear 12, stand in awe 1.
PIEL fear 2.
HIPH. make to shake 1.
†*See* pachad[2].

PACHAD[2] פַּחַד dread 3, fear 41, terror 2, *dreadful 1, *great 2.
†thing greatly feared (*with* pachad[1]) 1.

PACHAD[3] פַּחַד stones (*pl.*) 1.

PACHATH פַּחַת hole 1, pit 8, snare 1.

PACHAZ[1] פחז *Partic.* light 2.

PACHAZ[2] פַּחַז *unstable 1.

PACHAZUTH פַּחֲזוּת *f.* lightness 1.

PACHDAH פַּחְדָּה *f.* fear 1.

PADA פדע deliver 1.

PADAH פדה deliver 5, ransom 1, redeem 44, rescue 1.
Pass. pt. ransomed 1, redeemed 1, that were redeemed 2, those that are to be redeemed 2.
Adv. inf. by any means 1, surely 1.
NIPH. be redeemed 3.
HIPH. let be redeemed 1.
HOPH. *Adv. inf.* at all 1.

PAG פַּג green fig 1.

PAGA פגע come 1, fall 11, fall upon 2, intreat 2, light upon 1, make intercession 2, meet 11, meet together 1, pray 1, reach 7, run 1.
HIPH. cause to entreat 1, come betwixt 1, lay 1, make intercession 2.
Partic. intercessor 1.

PAGAR פגר PIEL be faint 2.

PAGASH פגש meet 9, meet together 1.
NIPH. be met 1, meet 1, meet together 1.
PIEL meet with 1.

PAK פַּךְ box 2, vial 1.

PAKAH פכה PIEL run out 1.

PALA פלא NIPH. arise too hard 1, be hidden 1, be marvellous 4, be too hard 3, be wonderful 3.
Partic. marvellously 1, marvellous things 4, marvellous works 4, marvels 1, miracles 1, wonderful things 1, wonderful works 7, wonderfully 1, wonders 9, wondrous things 3, wondrous works 11.
PIEL accomplish 1, perform 1.
HIPH. be wonderful 2, do a marvellous work 2, make wonderful 1, make singular 1, separate 1, show . . . marvellous 2, *marvellously 1, *wondrously 2.
HITHP. show self marvellous 1.
†HIPH. do wonderously (*with inf. of* asah).

PALACH פלח cut 1.
PIEL bring forth 1, cleave 1, shred 1, strike through 1.

PALAG פלג NIPH. be divided 2.
PIEL divide 2.

PALAH פלה NIPH. be separated 1, be wonderfully made 1.
HIPH. put a difference 1, set apart 1, sever 2, show . . . marvellous 1.

PALAL פלל execute judgment 1, judge 2, think 1.
NIPHLAL be judged 1.
HITHP intreat 1, make [prayer] 1, make [supplication] 1, make prayer 1, make supplication 1, pray 74, *prayer be made 1.

PALAS פלס PIEL make 1, ponder 3, weigh 2.

PALASH פלש HITHP. roll self 1, wallow self 3.

PALAT פלט escape 1.
PIEL calve 1, cause to escape 1, deliver 19, *be delivered 1.
Inf. deliverance 1, *escape 1.
HIPH. carry away safe 1, deliver 1.

PALATS פלץ HITHP. tremble 1.

PALDAH פַּלְדָּה *f.* torch 1.

PALET פֶּלֶט (פְּלֵיט) *escape 5.

PALI פִּלְאִי wonderful 1.

PALIL פָּלִיל judge 3.

PALIT פָּלִיט fugitive 1, that (which, etc.) escape (escaped, etc.) *escape 3.
†*See* shaar[1].

PALLATSUTH פַּלָּצוּת *f.* fearfulness 1, horror 2, trembling 1.

PALLET *Inf. piel of* palat.

PALMONI פַּלְמוֹנִי certain 1.

PANAH פנה appear 1, behold 1, be passed away 1, come on 1, go away 1, have respect, look 43, mark 1, regard 4, respect 2, return 1, turn (aside, away, face, self, be turned) 53.
Partic. *corner.
Infin. dawning 1.
PIEL cast out 1, empty 1, prepare 6.
HIPH. be turned back 1, look back 3, turn 3, turn self 1.

* Inexact translations, *e.g.*, of a noun by a verb or adjective, of an active by a passive.
† Cases where two or more words in the original are translated by one word or by a phrase.

HOPH. lie 1
turn back 1.
*KAL *infin.* eventide (*with* ereb[2]) 1; right early (*with* boqer) 1.

PANAQ פנק
PIEL delicately bring up 1.

PANIM פָּנִים *pl.*
anger 3
countenance 30
edge 1
face 356
favour 4
forefront 4
forepart 4
form 1
former time 1
front 2
heaviness 1
looks 2
mouth 1
old time 1
person 20
presence 75
prospect 6
sight 40
state 1
time past 1
times past 1
upside 2
*be purposed 1
*look 4
*open 13
*shewbread 1
*within 1.
†battle (*with* milchamah) 1; before (al[2] pene) 1; over against (al[2]-pene 7, el-pene 2) 9; to meet (el-pene) 1. Le-phanim: aforetime 2, beforetime 1, forward 2, of old 2. *With pron. suffix freq. translated by Eng. pronoun. See* al[2], amad, avah[2], bo, chug, im[1], lechem, li-phene, me, min[2], mul, nasa, qasheh, tob[1], shaar[1], shub.

PAQACH פקח
open 17.
NIPH. be opened 3.

PAQAD פקד
appoint 6
avenge 1
bestow 2
call to remembrance 1
charge 4
count 2
do judgment 2
enjoin 1
give a charge 1
go see 1
hurt 1
look 1
make 1
miss 2
number 110
punish 7
reckon 1
remember 1
set 1
sum 1
visit 57
want 1
*be numbered 1.
Pass. pt. officer 3
that were set over 1.
Adv. inf. at all 1
surely 4.
NIPH. be appointed 2
be empty 3
be lacking 2
be missed 2
be missing 2
be visited 5
be wanting 2
lack 2.
Adv. inf. by any means 1
PIEL muster 1.
PUAL be counted 1
be deprived 1.
HIPH. appoint 6
appoint to have the charge 1
commit 6
lay up 2
make governor 5
make overseer 3
make ruler 3
set 4.

HOPH. be delivered 1
have the oversight 4
is to be visited 1.
Partic. overseer 2.
HITHP. be numbered 4.
HOTHP. be numbered 4.
†punish (*with* al[2]) 24.

PAQID פָּקִיד
governor 1
officer 5
overseer 5
which had the charge 1
*set over 1.

PAQQUOTH פַּקֻּעֹת *f. pl.*
gourds 1.

PAR פַּר
bull 2
bullock 92
calf 1
ox 2.
†young bullock (*with* ben baqar 33, *with* shor 1) 34.

PARA[1] פרא
HIPH. be fruitful 1.

PARA[2] פרע
avoid 1
be naked 1
go back 1
make naked 1
refuse 3
set at nought 1
uncover 3.
Partic. bare 1.
NIPH. perish 1.
HIPH. let 1
make naked 1.
†*Kal infin.* avenging (*with* peraoth) 1.

PARACH פָּרַח
be broken out 2
be budded 1
blossom 5
break forth 2
break out 3
bud 3
flourish 6
grow 3
make fly 2
spread 1
spring 1
spring up 2.
Adv. inf. abroad 1
abundantly 1.
HIPH. bud 1
flourish 2
make to flourish 2.

PARAD פרד
be stretched 1.
NIPH. be divided 3
be parted 1
be separated 4
separate self 3
sever self 1.
PIEL be separated 1.
PUAL be dispersed 1.
HIPH. part 3
separate 4.
HITHP. be out of joint 1
be scattered 1
be scattered abroad 1
be sundered 1.

PARAH[1] פרה
bear 1
be fruitful 15
be increased 1
bring forth 1
bring fruit 1
grow 2
increase 1.
HIPH. cause to be fruitful 1
increase 1
make fruitful 1.

PARAH[2] פָּרָה *f.*
cow 2
heifer 6
kine 18.

PARAM פרם
rend 3.

PARAQ פָּרַק
break 1
deliver 1
redeem 1
rend in pieces 1.
PIEL break off 1
rend 1
tear in pieces 1.
HITHP. be broken 1
break off 2.

PARAQ פֶּרֶק
[V.L. ? = fragment].

PARAR פרר
Adv. inf. clean 1.
POEL divide 1.
PILP. break asunder 1.
HIPH. break 23
bring to nought 1
cast off 1
cause to cease 1
defeat 2
disannul 2
disappoint 1
fail 1
frustrate 2
make of none effect 1
make void 7
*be disappointed 1.
Adv. inf. any way 1
utterly 1.
HOPH. be broken 2
come to nought 1.
HITHP. be dissolved 1.

PARAS[1] פרס
deal 1
tear 1.
HIPH. divide 9
have hoofs 1
part 2.

PARAS[2] פרש
break 1
chop in pieces 1
lay open 1
spread 32
spread abroad 4
spread forth 6
spread out 5
spread selves forth 1
stretch 2
stretch forth 2
stretch out 2.
NIPH. be scattered 1.
PIEL scatter 1
spread 2
spread abroad 1
spread forth 4
spread out 1
stretch forth 1.

PARASH[1] פרש
*be showed 1.
NIPH. be scattered 1.
PUAL be declared 1.
Partic. distinctly 1.
HIPH. sting 1.

PARASH[2] פָּרָשׁ
horseman 55.
†*See* baal[2].

PARASHAH פָּרָשָׁה *f.*
declaration 1
sum 1.

PARAT פרט
chant 1.

PARATS פרץ
be increased 2
break 5
break down 8
break forth 5
break in 2
break out 1
break up 2
burst out 1
come abroad 1
disperse 1
grow 1
increase 3
make [a breach] 2
make a breach 1
scatter 1
spread abroad 1
*abroad 1
Part. pass. breach 1.
NIPH. *pt.* open 1.
PUAL be broken down 1.
HITHP. break away 1.
†KAL *with* be; break down 2, compel 1, press 2, urge 1.

PARAZ פְּרָז
village 1.

PARDES פַּרְדֵּס
forest 1
orchard 2.

PARITS פָּרִיץ
destroyer 1
robber 2
*ravenous 1.

PAROKETH פָּרֹכֶת *f.*
vail 24.

PAROSH פַּרְעֹשׁ
flea 2.

PARSAH פַּרְסָה *f.*
claw 2
hoof 17.
†*See* shosa.

PARSHEDONAH פַּרְשְׁדֹנָה
dirt 1.

PARSHEGEN פַּרְשֶׁגֶן
copy 1.

PARSHEGEN פַּרְשֶׁגֶן
copy 3.

PARSHEZ פַּרְשֵׁז
spread 1.

PARTEMIM פַּרְתְּמִים *pl.*
most noble 1
nobles 1
princes 1.

PARUR[1] פָּארוּר
blackness 1.

PARUR[2] פָּרוּר
pan 1
pot 2.

PARVAR פַּרְוָר
suburb 1.

PARZEL פַּרְזֶל
iron 20.

PAS פַּס
part 2.

PASA פשע
go 1.

PASACH פסח
halt 1
pass over 4.
NIPH. become lame 1.
PIEL leap 1.

PASAG פסג
PIEL consider 1.

PASAH פָּשָׂה
be spread 8
spread 8.
Adv. inf. much 1
much abroad 3.

PASAL פסל
grave 1
hew 5.

PASAQ פשק
open wide 1.
PIEL open 1.

PASAS פסס
fail 1.

PASH פַּשׁ
extremity 1.

PASHA פשע
rebel 6
revolt 6
transgress 16
trespass 1.
Partic. transgressors 9.
Infin. transgressing 1
transgression 1.
NIPH. *pt.* offended 1.

PASHACH פשח
PIEL pull in pieces 1.

PASHAT פשט
fall upon 2
invade 4
make an invasion 1
make a road 1
put off 6
run upon 1
rush 2
set [upon] 1
spoil 2
spread selves 1
spread selves abroad 1
strip 2
strip off 1.
PIEL spoil 1
strip 2.
HIPH. flay 4
pull off 1
strip 9
strip off 1.
HITHP. strip self 1.

PASSIM פַּסִּים *pl.*
divers colours 2
many colours 3.

PATAR פטר
dismiss 1
let out 1
slip away 1.
Pass. pt. free (V.L.) 1
open 4.
HIPH. shoot out 1.

PATH פַּת *f.*
meat 1
morsel 9
piece 4.

PATHACH פתח
draw out 1
open 81
set forth 1
spread out 1
*be opened 2.
Pass. pt. drawn 1
open 10.
Adv. inf. wide 1.
NIPH. be loosed 2
be open 1
be opened 10
be opening 1
be set open 1
be unstopped 1
break forth 1
have vent 1.
PIEL appear 1
be open 1
be opened 1
engrave 2
grave 5
let go free 1
loose 12
open 2
put off 2
ungird 1.
PUAL *pt.* graven 1.
HITHP. loose self 1.
†PIEL grave (*with* pittuach) 1.

PATHAH פתה
be deceived 1
be enticed 1.
Partic. him that flattereth 1
silly 1
silly one 1.
NIPH. be deceived 2.
PIEL allure 1
deceive 4
entice 8
flatter 1
persuade 3.
PUAL be deceived 1
be enticed 1
be persuaded 1.
HIPH. enlarge 1.

PATHAL פתל
NIPH. wrestle 1.
Partic. froward 2.
HITHP. show self froward 1
show self unsavoury 1.

PATHAR פתר
interpret 8
*interpretation 1.
Partic. interpreter 1.

PATHATH פתת
part 1.

PATHBAG פַּתְבַּג
portion of meat 5
provision of meat 1.

PATHIL פָּתִיל
bound 1
bracelet 2
lace 4
line 1
ribband 1
thread 1
wire 1.

PATHSHEGEN פַּתְשֶׁגֶן
copy 3.

PATIR פָּטִיר (V.L.)
free 1.

PATSA פצע
wound 2.
Pass. pt. wounded 1.

PATSACH פצח
break forth 5
break forth into joy 1
make a loud noise 1.
PIEL break 1.

PATSAH פצה
deliver 1
gape 1
open 10
rid 2
utter 1.

PATSAL פצל
PIEL pill (*vb*) 2.

PATSAM פצם
break 1.

PATSAR פצר
press 2
urge 4.
HIPH. *infin.* stubbornness 1.

PATTISH פַּטִּישׁ
hammer 3.

PAZ פַּז
fine gold 8
pure gold 1.

PAZAR פזר
Partic. scattered 1.
NIPH. be scattered 1.
PIEL disperse 1
scatter 6.
PUAL be scattered abroad 1.

PAZAZ[1] פזז
HOPH. *pt.* best 1.

PAZAZ[2] פזז
be made strong 1.
PIEL *pt.* leaping 1.

PEAH פֵּאָה *f.*
corner 16
end 1
part 1
quarter 4
side 64.

PECHAH פֶּחָה
captain 9
deputy 2
governor 17.

PECHAH פֶּחָה
captain 4
governor 6.

PECHAM פֶּחָם
coals 3.

PECHAR פֶּחָר
potter 1.

PECHETHETH פְּחֶתֶת *f.*
*fret inward 1.

PEDER פֶּדֶר
fat 3.

PEDUTH פְּדוּת *f.*
division 1
redemption 2
*redeem 1.

PEDUYIM פְּדוּיִם *pl.*
*wherewith..is to be redeemed 1.
[*See* padah *pass. partic.*]

PEER פְּאֵר
beauty 1
bonnet 2
ornament 1
tire 2
*goodly 1.

PEGA פֶּגַע
chance 1
*occurent 1.

PEGER פֶּגֶר
carcase 14
corpse 2
dead body 6.

PEH פֶּה
accord 1
appointment 2
assent 1
collar 1
command 1
commandment 37
edge 34
end 3
entry 1
hole 6
mind 1
mouth 341
part 1
portion 2
saying 2
sentence 1
skirt 1
sound 1
speech 2
talk 1
tenor 2
wish 1
word 16

* Inexact translations, *e.g.*, of a noun by a verb or adjective, of an active by a passive.
† Cases where two or more words in the original are translated by one word or by a phrase.

*another 3
*two-edged 1.
†eat of ([hayah] *be-phi-u*) 1; say (*be-phi-u*) 1. *See* al², gadal, ke, le, min, petsirah.

PELACH פֶּלַח
piece 6.

PELACH פלח
serve 9.
Partic. minister 1.

PELAG [1] פְּלַג
Partic. divided 1.

PELAG [2] פְּלַג
dividing 1.

PELAGGAH פְּלַגָּה *f.*
division 2
river 1.

PELE פֶּלֶא
marvellous thing 1
wonder 8
*wonderful 3
*wonderfully 1.

PELEG פֶּלֶג
river 9
stream 1.

PELEK פֶּלֶךְ
distaff 1
part 8
staff 1.

PELES פֶּלֶס
scales 1
weight 1.

PELETAH פְּלֵיטָה *f.*
deliverance 5
escaping 1
him that escapeth 1
remnant 1
that had escaped 1
that is (be, etc.) escaped 8
they that escape 2
*escaped 1
*to escape 2.
†*See* ayin¹, hayah.

PELI פְּלִי
secret 1.

PELILAH פְּלִילָה *f.*
judgment 1.

PELILI פְּלִילִי
judge 1
judgment 1.

PELONI פְּלֹנִי
†such and such (*with* almoni) 2; such a one (*with* almoni) 1.

PELUGGAH פְּלֻגָּה *f.*
division 1.

PELUGGAH פְּלֻגָּה *f.*
division 1.

PEN [1] פֵּן
corner 2.

PEN [2] פֶּן
lest
lest peradventure
peradventure
that . . . not.

PENE = PANIM.

PENIM פְּנִים
†within (mil-li-phenim) 1. [*Comp.* penimah.]

PENIMAH פְּנִימָה
in 1
inward 1
within 4.
†Le-phenimah: into the inner part 1, inward 1, within 8. Mip-penimah: within 3.

PENIMI פְּנִימִי
inner 30
inward 1.
†within (bap-penimi) 1.

PENINIM פְּנִינִים *pl.*
rubies 6.

PEQACH-QOACH
פְּקַח־קוֹחַ
opening of the prison 1.

PEQAIM פְּקָעִים *pl.*
knops 3.

PEQIDUTH פְּקִדֻת *f.*
ward 1.

PEQUDDAH פְּקֻדָּה *f.*
account 1
charge 1
custody 1
numbers 1
office 5
officer 3
ordering 1
oversight 2
reckoning 1
that have the charge 1
that which . . . laid up 1
visitation 13.
†*See* bayith.

PERA פֶּרַע
locks 2.

PERACH פֶּרַח
blossom 1
bud 2
flower 14.

PERAH פֵּרָה
[*See* chapharperah.]

PERAOTH פְּרָעוֹת *f. pl.*
revenges 1.
†*See* para².

PERAQ פרק
break off 1.

PERAS פרס
be divided 1.

PERASH פרש
PAEL *pt.* plainly 1.

PERAZI פְּרָזִי
*country 1
*of the villages 1
*unwalled 1.

PERAZON פְּרָזוֹן
inhabitants of villages 2.

PERAZOTH פְּרָזוֹת *f. pl.*
towns without walls 1
unwalled towns 1
unwalled villages 1.

PERE פֶּרֶא
wild ass 9
*wild 1.

PERED פֶּרֶד
mule 15.

PEREK פֶּרֶךְ
cruelty 1
rigour 5.

PEREQ פֶּרֶק
crossway 1
robbery 1.

PERES פֶּרֶס
ossifrage 2.

PERESH פֶּרֶשׁ
dung 7.

PERET פֶּרֶט
grape 1.

PERETS פֶּרֶץ
breach 14
breaking forth 1
breaking in 2
gap 2.

PERI פְּרִי
bough 1
fruit 113
reward for 1
*fruitful 2.
†*See* reshith.

PERUDOTH פְּרֻדוֹת *f. pl.*
seed 1.

PESA פֶּשַׂע
step 1.

PESACH פֶּסַח
passover 46
passover offering 3.

PESANTERIN פְּסַנְתֵּרִין (פְּסַנְטֵרִין) *pl.*
psaltery 4.

PESEL פֶּסֶל
carved image 2
graven image 29.

PESHA פֶּשַׁע
rebellion 1
sin 3
transgression 84
trespass 5.

PESHAR [1] פשר
make [interpretations] 1.
PAEL interpret 1.

PESHAR [2] פְּשַׁר
interpretation 31.

PESHER פֵּשֶׁר
interpretation 1.

PESILIM פְּסִילִים *pl.*
carved images 3
graven images 18
quarries 2.

PETER פֶּטֶר
firstling 4
that openeth 7.

PETESH פַּטֵּשׁ
hosen (*pl.*) 1.

PETHA פֶּתַע
suddenly 4
*very 1.
†at an instant (le-petha) 2; suddenly (be-petha) 1.

PETHACH [1] פֶּתַח
door 127
entering 10
entering in 7
entrance 3
entry 8
gate 8
opening 1
†open place (*with* enayim) 1.

PETHACH [2] פֵּתַח
entrance 1.

PETHACH פתח
PEIL be open 1
be opened 1.

PETHAI פְּתַי
breadth 2.

PETHALTOL פְּתַלְתֹּל
crooked 1.

PETHAYYUTH פְּתַיּוּת *f.*
*simple 1.

PETHEN פֶּתֶן
adder 2
asp 4.

PETHI פֶּתִי
foolish 1
simple 15
simplicity 1
simple one 2.

PETHICHOTH פְּתִחוֹת *f. pl.*
drawn swords 1.

PETHIGIL פְּתִיגִיל
stomacher 1.

PETHOTH פְּתוֹת
piece 1.

PETSA פֶּצַע
wound 7
wounding 1.

PETSALOTH פְּצָלוֹת *f. pl.*
strakes 1.

PETSIRAH פְּצִירָה *f.*
†file (*with pl. of* peh) 1.

PEULLAH פְּעֻלָּה *f.*
labour 2
reward 1
wages 1
work 10.

PEYAH פֵּיָה *f.*
edge 1.

PHANIM = PANIM.

PHI = PEH.

PI = PEH.

PIACH פִּיחַ
ashes 2.

PID פִּיד
destruction 2
ruin 1.

PIDYOM פִּדְיֹם
redemption 1.

PIDYON פִּדְיוֹן
ransom 1
redemption 1.

PIGGUL פִּגּוּל
abominable 2
abominable thing 1
abomination 1.

PILEGESH פִּילֶגֶשׁ *f.*
concubine 36
paramour 1.

PILI פִּלְאִי
wonderful 1.

PIM. *Pl. of* **PEH.**

PIMAH פִּימָה *f.*
collops of fat 1.

PINNAH פִּנָּה *f.*
bulwark 1
corner 22
stay 1
tower 2
*chief 2.

PIPHIYYOTH פִּיפִיּוֹת *f. pl.*
teeth 1
*two-edged 1.

PIQ פִּיק
*smite together 1.

PIQQADON פִּקָּדוֹן
store 1
that which was delivered him to keep 1
*that 1.

PIQQEACH פִּקֵּחַ
seeing 1
wise 1.

PIQQUDIM פִּקּוּדִים *pl.*
commandments 2
precepts 21
statutes 1.

PIRCHAH פִּרְחָה *f.*
youth 1.

PIRDAH פִּרְדָּה *f.*
mule 3.

PISHTAH פִּשְׁתָּה *f.*
flax 3
tow 1.

PISHTEH פִּשְׁתֶּה
flax 6
linen 9.

PISSAH פִּסָּה *f.*
handful 1.

PISSEACH פִּסֵּחַ
lame 14.

PITEDAH פִּטְדָה *f.*
topaz 4.

PITHECHON פִּתְחוֹן (= פִּתְחוֹן)
open 1
opening 1.

PITHGAM פִּתְגָּם
decree 1
sentence 1.

PITHGAM פִּתְגָם
answer 2
letter 1
matter 1
word 1.
†See *tub.*

PITHOM פִּתְאֹם
straightway 1
sudden 2
suddenly 22.

PITHRON פִּתְרוֹן
interpretation 5.

PITRAH פִּטְרָה *f.*
*such as open 1.

PITTUACH פִּתּוּחַ
carved work 1
engraving 5
graving 2
*be graven 1
*carved 1.
†*See* pathach.

PITTACHON פִּתָּחוֹן
[*See* pithechon].

PO פֹּה (פֹּא, פּוֹ)
here
hither
that side
the one side
the other side
this side.

POAL פֹּעַל
act 3
deed 2
getting 1
work 30
*to do 1.

POH = PO.

POL פּוֹל
beans 2.

POLCHAN פָּלְחָן
service 1.

PORAH פֹּארָה *f.*
bough 1
branch 4
sprig 1.

POTH פֹּת
hinge 1
secret part 1.

PUACH פּוּחַ
break 2.
HIPH. blow 1
blow upon 1
bring into a snare 1
puff 2
speak 6
utter 1.

PUG פּוּג
be slacked 1
cease 1
faint 1.
NIPH. be feeble 1.

PUGAH פּוּגָה *f.*
rest 1.

PUK פּוּךְ
fair colours 1
glistering 1
painting 1.
†*See* sum.

PUM פֻּם
mouth 6.

PUN פּוּן
be distracted 1.

PUQ [1] פּוּק
stumble 1.
HIPH. move 1.

PUQ [2] פּוּק
HIPH. afford 1
draw out 1
further 1
get 1
obtain 3.

PUQAH פּוּקָה *f.*
grief 1.

PUR פּוּר
HIPH. break 1
bring to nought 1
utterly take 1.

PURAH [1] פּוּרָה *f.*
press 1
wine press 1.

PURAH [2] פֻּארָה *f.*
bough 1.

PUSH פּוּשׁ
be grown fat 1
grow up 1
spread selves 1.
NIPH. be scattered 1.

PUTS פּוּץ
be dispersed 2
be scattered 8
be spread abroad 1
disperse selves 1
retire 1.
NIPH. be scattered 14
be spread abroad 1.
POL. break in pieces 1.
PILP. shake to pieces 1.
HIPH. be scattered 1
be scattered abroad 1
cast abroad 2
drive 1
scatter 29
scatter abroad 1.
Partic. he that dasheth in pieces 1.
HITHP. be scattered 1.

Q

QAAQA קַעֲקַע
†*See* kethobeth.

QAATH קָאַת *f.*
cormorant 2
pelican 3.

QAB קַב
cab 1.

QABA קבע
rob 4
spoil 2.

QABAB קבב
curse 7.
Adv. inf. at all 1.

QABAL קבל
PIEL choose 1
receive 6
take 3
undertake 1.
HIPH. hold 1
take hold 1.

QABAR קבר
bury 85
*be buried 2.
Adv. inf in any wise 1.
NIPH. be buried 39.
PIEL bury 6.
PUAL be buried 1.

QABATS קבץ
assemble 2
gather 15
gather together 17
gather up 1
heap 1.
NIPH. assemble 1
assemble selves 3
be gathered 5
be gathered together 9
gather selves 2
gather selves together 7
gather together 1
resort 1.
PIEL bring together 1
gather 42
gather together 4
gather up 2
take up 1.
Adv. inf. surely 1.
PUAL be gathered 1.
HITHP. be gathered together 3
gather selves 2
gather selves together 2
gather together 1.

QADACH קדח
be kindled 2
burn 1
kindle 2.

QADAD קדד
bow 2
bow down head 5
bow head 6
stoop 2.

QADAM קדם
PIEL come before 5
disappoint 1
go before 2
meet 2
prevent 13
*before 1.
HIPH. prevent 2.

QADAR קדר
be black 3
be blackish 1
be dark 2
be darkened 1
mourn 5.
Partic heavily 1.
HIPH. cause to mourn 1
make dark 2.
HITHP be black 1.

QADASH [1] קָדֵשׁ (קָדַשׁ)
be defiled 1
be hallowed 3
be holier 1
be holy 5
be sanctified 1.
NIPH. be hallowed 1
be sanctified 10.

* Inexact translations, *e.g.*, of a noun by a verb or adjective, of an active by a passive.
† Cases where two or more words in the original are translated by one word or by a phrase.

PIEL consecrate 2
hallow 14
keep holy 1
prepare 6
proclaim 1
sanctify 51.
Partic. holy place 1.
PUAL be consecrated 3.
Partic. sanctified one 1.
that are sanctified 1.
HIPH. appoint 1
bid 1
dedicate 9
hallow 7
prepare 1
sanctify 24.
Adv. inf. wholly 1.
HITHP. be kept 1
be purified 1
be sanctified 2
sanctify selves 20.

QADDACHATH קַדַּחַת *f.*
burning ague 1
fever 1.

QADDISH קַדִּישׁ
holy 4
Holy one 3
saint 7.

QADESH[1] = **QADASH**[1]

QADESH[2] קָדֵשׁ
sodomite 5
unclean 1.

QADIM קָדִים
east 50
east side 1
eastward 7
east wind 10.
†*See* derek.

QADMAH קַדְמָה *f.*
antiquity 1
former estate 3
old estate 1.
*afore 1

QADMAH (***QADMATH***) קַדְמָה *f.*
†See *min.*

QADMAI קַדְמַי
first 3.

QADMON קַדְמוֹן
east 1.

QADMONI קַדְמֹנִי
ancient 1
east 4
former 2
old 1
they that went before (*pl.*) 1
things of old 1.

QADOSH קָדוֹשׁ
Holy 1
holy 62
Holy one 41
saint 12.

QADRUTH קַדְרוּת *f.*
blackness 1.

QAHAH קהה
be set on edge 3.
PIEL be blunt 1.

QAHAL[1] קהל
NIPH. assemble selves 3
assemble together 2
be assembled 1
be gathered 2
be gathered together 3
gather selves together 8.
HIPH. assemble 5
gather 4
gather together 10
*be to be gathered together 1

QAHAL[2] קָהָל
assembly 17
company 17
congregation 86
multitude 3.

QAL קַל
light 1
swift 9
swifter 1
swiftly 2.

QAL קָל
sound 4
voice 3.

QALA קלע
carve 3
sling 1
sling out 1.
PIEL sling 1
sling out 1.

QALAH[1] קלה
roast 1.
Pass. pt. dried 1
parched 1.

QALAH[2] קלה
NIPH. be contemned 1
be despised 1
be lightly esteemed 1
seem vile 1.
Partic. base 1
loathsome 1.
HIPH. set light [by one] 1.

QALAL[1] קלל
be abated 1
be despised 2
be lightly esteemed 2
be swifter 4
be vile 2.
NIPH. be a light thing 5
be easy 1
be more vile 1
be swift 1
seem a light thing 1.
PIEL curse 39
make vile 1
revile 1.
PILP. make bright 1
whet 1.
PUAL be accursed 1
be cursed 2.
HIPH. be easier 1
bring into contempt 1
despise 1
ease 2
lighten 2
lightly afflict 1
make lighter 3
make somewhat lighter 1
set light 1.
HITHPAL. move lightly 1.
†NIPH. slightly (al[2] *with partic.*) 2.

QALAL[2] קָלָל
burnished 1
polished 1.

QALAS קלס
PIEL scorn 1.
HITHP. mock 2
scoff 1.

QALAT קלט
Pass. pt. lacking in his parts 1.

QALI (קָלִי) קָלִיא
parched corn 6.

QALLA קַלָּע
slinger 1.

QALLACHATH קַלַּחַת *f.*
caldron 2.

QALLASAH קַלָּסָה *f.*
mocking 1.

QALON קָלוֹן
confusion 1
dishonour 1
ignominy 1
reproach 1
shame 13.

QAMAH קָמָה *f.*
corn 2
grown up 2
stalk 1
standing corn 5.

QAMAL קמל
be hewn down 1
wither 1.

QAMAT קמט
fill with wrinkles 1.
PUAL be cut down 1.

QAMATS קמץ
take [a handful] 2
take an handful 1.

QANA קנא
PIEL be envious 4
be jealous 10
be zealous 2
envy 9
move to jealousy 1
provoke to jealousy 1
Infin. zeal 1
Adv. inf. very 1.
HIPH. move to jealousy 2
provoke to jealousy 1.

QANAH[1] קנה
attain 1
buy 48
get 16
possess 2
purchase 5
recover 1
redeem 1.
Partic. buyer 3
owner 1
possessor 3.
Adv. inf. surely 1
verily 1.
NIPH. be bought 1
be possessed 1.
HIPH. teach to keep cattle 1.

QANAH[2] קנה
HIPH. provoke to jealousy 1.

QANAN קנן
PIEL make nest 4.
PUAL *pt.* that makest thy nest 1.

QANEH קָנֶה
balance 1
bone 1
branch 24
calamus 3
cane 2
reed 28
stalk 2
*spearman 1.

QANNA קַנָּא
jealous 6.

QANNO קַנּוֹא
jealous 2.

QAPHA קפא
be congealed 1.
Partic. that are settled 1.
HIPH. curdle 1.

QAPHAD קפד
PIEL cut off 1.

QAPHATS קפץ
shut 2
shut up 1
stop 2.
NIPH. be taken out of the way 1.
PIEL *pt.* skipping 1.

QAR קַר
cold 2.

QARA[1] קרא
bewray self 1
call 425
call for 1
call upon 16
cry 90
cry unto 4
give [names] 1
invite 3
make proclamation 1
name 1
preach 2
proclaim 36
pronounce 1
publish 1
read 36
say 1
*be called 26
*be mentioned 1.
Pass. pt. guest 4
renowned 2
that are bidden 2.
NIPH. be called 51
be called forth 1
be cried 1
be famous 1
be named 4
be read 1
be renowned 1
call selves 1
*read 1.
PUAL be called 6
be cried 1.
†KAL be famous (*with* shem) 1; be named (*with* shem) 1; give a name (*with* shem le) 1; give names (*with* be-shemoth) 1. NIPH. *See* shem.

QARA[2] קרא
be come 1
befall 5
come 1
come upon 2
fall out 1
happen 1
help 1
meet 73
meet with 1
seek 1.
Inf. against 41
against be come 1
in the way 1.
NIPH. chance 1
happen to be 1
meet 2.
Adv. inf. by chance 1.
HIPH. cause to come 1.

QARA[3] קרע
cut 1
cut out 1
rend 52
tear 4.
Adv. inf. surely 1.
NIPH. be rent 3
rend (*intrans.*) 2.

QARAB (קָרֵב) קרב
approach 8
be at hand 3
be joined 1
be near 1
come 9
come near 32
come nigh 10
come together 1
draw near 11
draw nigh 7
go 4
go near 2
offer 1
stand by 1.
NIPH. be brought 2.
PIEL be at hand 1
bring near 1
cause to approach 1
go near 1
join 1
make ready 1
produce 1.
HIPH. be come near 1
be presented 1
bring 56
bring forth 1
bring near 4
cause to be brought 1
cause to come near 5
cause to draw near 2
draw near 1
draw nigh 1
lay 1
offer 104
present 1
take 1.

QARACH קרח
make bald (*intrans.*) 1
make [baldness] 1.
NIPH. make self bald 1.
HIPH. make self bald 1.
HOPH. be made bald 1.

QARACHATH קָרַחַת *f.*
bald head 3
bare within 1.

QARAH[1] קָרָה *f.*
cold 5.

QARAH[2] קרה
befall 4
come to pass unto 1
happen 4
happen to 1
happen unto 1
light on 1
meet 1.
NIPH. come 1
happen 1
meet 4.
HIPH. appoint 1
bring 1
send good speed 1.

QARAH[3] קרה
PIEL floor 1
lay beams 3
make beams 1.

QARAM קרם
cover 2.

QARAN קרן
shine 3.
HIPH. have horns 1.

QARAS קרס
stoop 2.

QARATS קרץ
move 1
wink 3.
PUAL be formed 1.

QARDOM קַרְדֹּם
ax 5.

QAREB[1] = **QARAB.**

QAREB[2] קָרֵב
that came 1
that cometh nigh 2
which come near 1
which shall come near 1
*approach 1
*drew near 2.
†come anything near (*repeated*) 1.

QAREH קָרֶה
uncleanness that chanceth 1.

QARETSIN קַרְצִין *pl.*
†See *akal.*

QARI קְרִיא
famous 2.

QAROB קָרוֹב
allied 1
any kin 1
at hand 6
kinsfolk 1
kinsman 1
more ready 1
near 35
near of kin 2
neighbour 5
next 3
nigh 12
nigh at hand 1
short 2
that is near 1
that is next 2
them that come nigh 1
†newly (miq-qarob) 1; shortly (miq-qarob) 1.

QARQA קַרְקַע
bottom 1
floor 5
one side of the floor 1
*other 1.

QARSULLAYIM קַרְסֻלַּיִם *du.*
feet 2.

QASAH קְשׂוֹת (*pl.*)
cover 3
cup 1.

QASAM קסם
divine 7
use [divination] 3.
Partic. diviner 7
prudent 1
soothsayer 1.
Infin. divination 1.

QASAS קסס
POEL cut off 1.

QASH קַשׁ
stubble 16.

QASHAB קשב
hearken 1.
HIPH. attend 10
cause to hear 1
cause to be heard 1
give heed 3
hearken 26
incline 1
mark 2
mark well 1
regard 1.

QASHACH קשח
HIPH. be hardened 1
harden 1.

QASHAH קשה
be cruel 1
be fiercer 1
be hard 1
be sore 1
seem hard 1.
NIPH. *pt.* hardly bestead 1.
PIEL have hard [labour] 1.
HIPH. be in hard [labour] 1
harden 12
make grievous 2
make stiff 1
stiffen 1
would hardly 1.
†HIPH. ask a hard thing (*with infin. of* shaal) 1; be stiff-necked (*with* oreph) 2.

QASHAR קשר
bind 11
conspire 15
work [treason] 1.
Partic. conspirator 1.
Pass. pt. bound 1
bound up 1
stronger 1.
NIPH. be joined together 1
be knit 1.
PIEL bind 2.
PUAL *pt.* stronger 1.
HITHP. conspire 3.
†KAL make a conspiracy (*with* qesher) 5.

QASHASH קשש
gather together 1.
POEL gather 6.
HITHP. gather selves together 1.

QASHEH קָשֶׁה
churlish 1
cruel 3
grievous 3
hard 4
hard things (*pl.*) 1
heavy 1
obstinate 1
prevailed 1
rough 1
roughly 5
sore 2
sorrowful 1
stiff 2
stubborn 1
too hard 1.
†hard hearted (*with* leb) 1; him that is in trouble (*with* yom) 1; impudent (*with* panim) 1; stiff-necked (*with* oreph) 6.

QASHSHAB קַשָּׁב
attentive 2.

QASHSHATH קַשָּׁת
†*See* rabah.

QASHSHUB קַשֻּׁב
attent 2
attentive 1.

QASQESETH קַשְׂקֶשֶׂת *f*
mail 1
scale 7.

QASVAH = **QASAH.**

QAT קַט
very 1.

QATAL קטל
kill 1
slay 2.

QATAN קָטָן
least 6
less 2
little 11
little one 1
small 11
small quantity 1
small things 1
smallest 1
young 1
younger 10
youngest 2.

QATAPH קטף
crop off 2
cut up 1
pluck 1.
NIPH. be cut down 1

* Inexact translations, *e.g.*, of a noun by a verb or adjective, of an active by a passive.
† Cases where two or more words in the original are translated by one word or by a phrase.

QATAR[1] קטר
PIEL burn 2
burn incense 36
offer a sacrifice 1
offer incense 3.
Adv. inf. not fail 1.
PUAL *pt.* perfumed 1.
HIPH. burn 48
burn incense 17
burn incense upon 2
burn sacrifice 1
kindle 1
offer 2.
HOPH. be burnt 1.
Partic. incense 1.

QATAR[2] קטר
Partic. pass. joined 1.

QATHROS קִתְרוֹס
harp 4.

QATON[1] קָטֹן
be a small thing 2
be not worthy 1.
HIPH. make small 1.

QATON[2] קָטֹן
least 4
less 3
lesser 1
little (one) 11
small 19
younger 4
youngest 13.

QATSA קצע
HIPH. cause to be scraped 1.
HOPH. *pt.* corner 1.

QATSAB קצב
cut down 1.
Pass. pt. shorn 1.

QATSAH[1] קצה
Inf. cutting off 1.
PIEL cut off 1
cut short 1.
HIPH scrape 1
scrape off 1.

QATSAH[2] קְצָה *f.*
coast 1
corner 1
edge 2
end 22
part 1
quarter 1
selvedge 2
uttermost part 2
*lowest 3.

QATSAPH קצף
be angry 3
be displeased 3
be wroth 22
wrath come 1.
HIPH. anger 1
provoke to wrath 1.
HITHP. fret selves 1.

QATSAR קצר
be grieved 1
be much discouraged 1
be shortened 6
be shorter 1
be straitened 1
be troubled 1
be vexed 1
be waxed short 1
cut down 1
loathe 1
reap 22.
Partic. harvestman 1
mower 1
reaper 9.
Adv. inf. at all 1.
Pass. pt. shorter 1.
PIEL shorten 1.
HIPH. shorten 1.

QATSATS קצץ
cut off 1.
Pass. pt. that are in utmost 3.
PIEL cut 1
cut asunder 1
cut in pieces 2
cut in sunder 1
cut off 4.
PUAL *pt.* cut off 1.

QATSEH קָצֶה
border 3
brim 1
brink 1
coast 1
edge 6
end 52
frontier 1
outmost coast 1
outside 3
quarter 2
shore 1
side 1
utmost 5
utmost part 2
uttermost 2
uttermost part 7
*other 3.
†after (miq-qatseh) 1; some (miq-qatseh) 1.

QATSER קָצֵר
few 1
hasty 1
small 2
soon 1.

QATSIN קָצִין
captain 3
guide 1
prince 4
ruler 4.

QATSIR קָצִיר
bough 3
branch 2
harvest 47
harvestman 1
harvest time 1

QAV (קָו) קַו
line 20
rule 1.
†meted out (*repeated*) 1.

QAVAH קוה
wait for 2
wait on 2
wait upon 2
NIPH. be gathered 1
be gathered together 1.
PIEL look 14
tarry 1
wait 22
wait for 2
wait on 2.
Adv. inf. patiently 1.

QAYAH קיה
spue 1.

QAYIN קַיִן
spear 1.

QAYIT קַיִט
summer 1.

QAYITS קַיִץ
summer 10
summer fruit 9
summer house 1.

QAYYAM קַיָּם
steadfast 1
sure 1.

QE קֵא
vomit 1.

QEARAH קְעָרָה *f.*
charger 14
dish 3.

QEBAH קֵבָה *f.*
maw 1.

QEBAL קבל
PAEL receive 1
take 2.

QEBEL (קֳבֵל) קֳבֵל
before 3
by reason of 1
over against 1.
†*lo qobel di* (*denah*) according to, by this means. See *kol*.

QEBER קֶבֶר
burying place 6
grave 35
sepulchre 26.

QEBURAH קְבוּרָה *f.*
burial 4
burying place 1
grave 4
sepulchre 5.

QEBUTSAH קְבֻצָה *f.*
*gather 1.

QEDEM קֶדֶם (*cf.* QEDEMAH)
aforetime 1
ancient 6
ancient time 2
before 2
east 21
east side 1
eternal 2
everlasting 1
forward 1
old 11
past 1.
†miq-qedem: before 1, east 1, eastward 1, from of old 1, of old 5. *See* min.

QEDEMAH קֵדְמָה
east 12
east end 1
east part 2
east side 1
eastward 10.

QEDESHAH קְדֵשָׁה *f.*
harlot 4
whore 1.

QEDORANNITH קְדֹרַנִּית
mournfully 1.

QEDUMIM קְדוּמִים *pl.*
ancient 1.

QEHILLAH קְהִלָּה *f.*
assembly 1
congregation 1.

QELA קלע
sling 4.
†*See* eben.

QELAIM קְלָעִים *pl.*
hangings 15
leaves [of a door] 1.

QELALAH קְלָלָה *f.*
curse 27
cursing 15
*accursed 1.

QELES קֶלֶס
derision 3.

QELOQEL קְלֹקֵל
light 1.

QEMACH קֶמַח
flour 4
meal 9.
†fine meal (*with* soleth) 1.

QEN קֵן
nest 12
room 1.

QENA קנא
buy 1.

QEPHADAH קְפָדָה
destruction 1.

QERA קרא
cry 3
read 7.
HITHP. be called 1.

QERAB קְרָב
battle 5
war 4.

QERAB קְרָב
war 1.

QERABAH קִרְבָה *f.*
*approach 1
*draw near 1.

QERACH קֶרַח
crystal 1
frost 3
ice 2.

QERAIM קְרָעִים *pl.*
pieces 3
rags 1.

QERASIM קְרָסִים *pl.*
taches 10.

QEREACH קֵרֵחַ
bald 1
bald head 2.

QEREB קרב
come 5
come near 4.
PAEL offer 1.
HAPH. bring near 1
offer 1.

QEREB קֶרֶב
bowels 1
heart 1
inward part 1
inward parts 2
inward thought 2
inwards 19
midst 73
purtenance 1.
Plur. that is within 1.
†*With pron. suff.*: him 2. miq-qedem: from among 27, out of 3. *See* be-qereb, bo.

QEREN קֶרֶן *f.*
hill 1
horn 75.

QEREN קֶרֶן *f.*
cornet 4
horn 10.

QERESH קֶרֶשׁ
bench 1
board 50.

QERETH קֶרֶת *f.*
city 5.

QERETS קֶרֶץ
destruction 1.

QERI קְרִי
contrary 7.

QERIAH קְרִיאָה *f.*
preaching 1

QESEM קֶסֶם
divination 8
divine sentence 1
reward of divination 1
witchcraft 1.

QESETH קֶסֶת *f.*
inkhorn 3.

QESHEB קֶשֶׁב
hearing 1
heed 1
*diligently 1
*that regarded 1.

QESHER קֶשֶׁר
confederacy 2
conspiracy 4
treason 5.
†*See* qashar.

QESHETH קֶשֶׁת *c.*
bow 67
*archer 2.
†*See* ben, darak, metachave, ramah, yarah.

QESHI קְשִׁי
stubbornness 1.

QESHOT קְשֹׁט
truth 2.

QESITAH קְשִׂיטָה *f.*
piece of money 2
piece of silver 1.

QETAL קטל
slay 1
Pass. pt. slain 2.
PAEL slay 2.
HITHP. be slain 1.
HITHPA. be slain 1.

QETAR קְטַר
doubt 2
joint 1.

QETEB קֶטֶב
destruction 2
*destroying 1.

QETEL קֶטֶל
slaughter 1.

QETORAH קְטוֹרָה *f.*
incense 1.

QETORETH קְטֹרֶת *f.*
incense 54
perfume 3
sweet incense 2.

QETS קֵץ
border 3
end 51
utmost border 1
*process 1
*very 1.
†after (miq-qets) 10; infinite (en[1] qets) 1.

QETSACH קֶצַח
fitches 3.

QETSAPH[1] קצף
be furious 1.

QETSAPH[2] קְצַף
wrath 1.

QETSAPHAH קְצָפָה
†*See* sim.

QETSATH קְצָת *f.*
end 4
part 1
uttermost part 1
*some 1.

QETSATH קְצָת *f.*
end 3.
†partly (*min qetsath*) 1.

QETSATS קצץ
PAEL cut off 1

QETSEB קֶצֶב
bottom 1
size 2.

QETSEH קָצֶה
end 4.
†infinite (en[1] qetseh) 1.

QETSEPH קֶצֶף
foam 1
indignation 3
wrath 23
*sore 2.

QETSEV קְצֵו
end 3.

QETSIOTH קְצִיעוֹת *f. pl.*
cassia 1.

QEVUTSTSOTH קְוֻצּוֹת *f. pl.*
locks 2.

QEYAM קְיָם
decree 1
statute 1.

QI קִיא
vomit 3.

QIBBUTS קִבּוּץ
company 1.

QIDDAH קִדָּה *f.*
cassia 2.

QIDMAH קִדְמָה *f.*
east 3
eastward 1.

QILLESHON קִלְּשׁוֹן
†*See* shalosh.

QIM קִים
substance 1.

QIMAH קִימָה *f.*
rising up 1.

QIMMASHON קִמָּשׁוֹן
thorns (*pl.*) 1.

QIMMOSH (קִימוֹשׂ) קִמּוֹשׂ
nettles 2.

QINAH[1] קִינָה
lamentation 18.

QINAH[2] קִנְאָה *f.*
envy 7
jealousy 25
zeal 9
*envied 1
*for sake [of] 1.

QINNAMON קִנָּמוֹן
cinnamon 3.

QINYAN קִנְיָן
getting 2
goods 2
riches 1
substance 4
*with 1.

QIPPAON קִפָּאוֹן
*dark 1.

QIPPOD קִפֹּד
bittern 3.

QIPPOZ קִפּוֹז
great owl 1.

QIQALON קִיקָלוֹן
shameful spewing 1.

QIQAYON קִיקָיוֹן
gourd 5.

QIR קִיר
side 4
town [wall] 1
wall 65
*very 1.
†*See* charash.

QIRYA קִרְיָה *f.*
city 29.

QIRYA (קִרְיָה) קִרְיָא *f.*
city 9.

QIRYAH = QIRYA.

QISHSHUIM קִשֻּׁאִים *pl.*
cucumbers 1.

QISHSHURIM קִשֻּׁרִים *pl.*
attire 1
headbands 1.

QITOR קִיטוֹר
smoke 3
vapour 1.

QITSON קִיצוֹן
outmost 1
uttermost 3.

QITSVAH = QETSATH.

QITTER קִטֵּר
incense 1.

QO קוֹא
spue 1.
HIPH. spue out 2
vomit 1
vomit out 2
vomit up 1
vomit up again 1.

QOBA קוֹבַע
helmet 2.

QOBAH קֹבָה *f.*
belly 1.

QOBAL קֳבָל
before 1.

QOBEL קֹבֶל
war 1.

QOBEL = QEBEL.

QODAM קֳדָם
before 30
in the presence of 1.
†See *min*, *shephar*.

QODESH קֹדֶשׁ
consecrated thing 1
dedicated thing 12
hallowed thing 7
holiness 29
holy day 1
holy portion 1
holy thing 29
saint 1
sanctuary 68
*consecrated 1
*hallowed 2
*holy 219.
†*With pl.*: most holy place 11, most holy thing 11, *most holy 25.

QODQOD קָדְקֹד
crown 1
crown of head 6
pate 1
scalp 1
top of head 1.

QOHELETH קֹהֶלֶת
preacher 7.

QOL[1] (קֹל) קוֹל
bleating 1
crackling 1
cry 1
fame 1
lowing 1
noise 48
proclamation 5
sound 39
thunder 12
thundering 2
voice 383.
†aloud (be-qol gadol) 2 held their peace (*with Niph. of* chabe) 1. *See* abar[2], chanan, nathan, rum[1].

QOL[2] קַל
lightness 1.

QOMAH קוֹמָה *f.*
height 30
stature 7
*high 5
*tall 2.
†*See* melo.

QOMEMIYYUTH קוֹמְמִיּוּת
*upright 1.

QOMETS קֹמֶץ
handful 2.
†*See* melo.

QOPH קוֹף
ape 2.

QOR קֹר
cold 1.

QORACH קֶרַח
ice 1.

QORAH קוֹרָה *f.*
beam 4
roof 1.

QORBAN קָרְבָּן
oblation 12
offering 66
sacrifice 1
*offered 1.

QORCHAH קָרְחָה *f.*
baldness 9
*bald 1
*utterly 1.

* **Inexact translations, *e.g.*, of a noun by a verb or adjective, of an active by a passive.**
† **Cases where two or more words in the original are translated by one word or by a phrase.**

QORE קֹרֵא
partridge 2.

QOSH קוֹשׁ
lay a snare 1.

QOSHET קֹשֶׁט
truth 1.

QOSHT קֹשְׁטְ
certainty 1.

QOTEB קֹטֶב
destruction 1.

QOTS קוֹץ
thorn 12.

QOTSER קֹצֶר
anguish 1.

QUBBAATH קֻבַּעַת *f.*
dregs 2.

QUBBAH קֻבָּה *f.*
tent 1.

QUM קוּם
abide 1
arise 211
arise up 3
be assured 1
be clearer 1
be dim 1
be established 5
be made sure 2
be performed 1
be risen 4
be risen up 10
be set 1
be up 1
continue 2
endure 1
get up 2
hold 1
remain 1
rise 38
rise against 1
rise up 105
rise up again 1
rise up against 7
stand 27
stand up 19
succeed 1.
Imperat. up 9.
Partic. enemy 1.
Infin. uprising 1.
Adv. inf. surely 1.
PIEL confirm 5
decree 1
enjoin 1
ordain 1
perform 1
stablish 1
strengthen 1.
POL. be risen up 1
raise up 3.
HIPH. accomplish 1
confirm 4
continue 1
establish 22
help up 1
help to lift up again 1
lift up 3
make 1
make good 1
make to arise up 1
make to stand 1
perform 22
pitch 1
raise 6
raise up 32
rear 2
rear up 8
rouse up 1
set 4
set up 23
stablish 2
stir up 4
uphold 1
*be reared up 1.
Adv. inf. but newly 1
surely 2.
HOPH. be performed 1
be raised up 1
be reared up 1.
HITHP. rise up 2
rise up against 2.

QUM קוּם
arise 5
rise 1
rise up 2
stand 5.
PAEL establish 1.
APH. appoint 1
establish 2
make 1
raise up self 1
set 3
set up 10.
HOPH. be made to stand 1.

QUN קוּן
POL. lament 1.
Partic. mourning woman 1.

QUR קוּר
dig 2.
HIPH. cast out 2.
PIL. break down 1
destroy 1.

QURBAN קֻרְבָּן
offering 2.

QURIM קוּרִים *pl.*
web 2.

QUT [1] קוּט
be grieved 1.
NIPH. loathe selves 2.
HITHPOL. be grieved 2.
†NIPH. loathe selves (*with* be) 1.

QUT [2] קוּט
be cut off 1.

QUTS [1] קוּץ
HIPH. arise 1
awake 17
be awake 1
wake 1
watch 1.

QUTS [2] קוּץ
summer (*vb.*) 1.

QUTS [3] קוּץ
abhor 3
be distressed 1
be grieved 1
be weary 2
loathe 1.
HIPH. vex 1.

R

RA רַע (רָעָה)
adversity 4
affliction 6
bad 13
calamity 1
displeasure 4
distress 1
evil (man, thing) 444
grief 1
grievous 2
harm 4
heavy 1
hurt 20
hurtful 1
ill 2
ill favoured 2
mischief 22
mischievous 1
misery 1
naught 3
naughty 1
noisome 2
sad 2
sore 9
sorrow 1
trouble 10
wicked 31
wickedness 54
worse 1
worst 1
wretchedness 1
wrong 1
*wickedly 1.
†evil (*with* dabar[2]) 1; evil-favouredness (*with* dabar[2]) 1; exceedingly (*with* gadol) 2; great wickedness (*with* ra) 1; harm (*with* dabar[2]) 1; ill-favoured (*with* mareh 2, *with* toar 1) 3; not please (*with* be-enayim) 1; wickedness (*with* dabar[2]) 1. *See* asah, mareh, panim, raa[1].

RAA[1] רעע
be evil 3
be grieved 2
be grievous 2
be sad 1
be worse 1
go ill 2
seem ill 1.
NIPH. afflict 5
behave self ill 1
bring evil 2
deal ill 1
deal worse 1
do evil 14
do harm 3
do hurt 1
do mischief 1
do wickedly 5
do worse 3
entreat evil 2
hurt 7
punish 1
vex 1.
Partic. evil doer 12
evil man 1
wicked 4
wicked doer 1.
Adv. inf. indeed 1
still 1.
†KAL; be displeased (*with* be-enayim) 2; displease (*with* be-enayim 9, *with* be-oznayim 1, *with* el 1) 11; do harm (*with* le) 1; grieve (*with* le) 2; not please (*with* be-enayim) 1; seem evil (*with* be-enayim) 1. NIPH. smart (*with* ra) 1.

RAA [2] רעע
be broken 1
break 3
break in pieces 1.
Adv. inf. utterly 1.
NIPH. be destroyed 1.
HITHP. be broken down 1.

RAA [3] רעע
associate self 1.
HITHP. shew self friendly 1.

RAAB רָעֵב
dearth 5
famine 86
hunger 8.
†*See* anashim.

RAAD [1] רעד
tremble 1.
HIPH. tremble 2.

RAAD [2] רַעַד
trembling 2.

RAAH [1] ראה
advise self 1
approve 1
behold 83
be near 1
consider 22
discern 1
enjoy 3
espy 1
foresee 2
gaze 1
have experience of 1
have respect to 1
have respect unto 2
look 88
look on 10
look out 2
look up 1
look upon 9
mark 1
perceive 5
provide 4
regard 4
respect 2
see 871
spy 6
stare 1
think 1
view 1
*shew 1.
Imper. lo 3.
Inf. vision 1.
Adv. inf. certainly 1
indeed 2
surely 1.
Part. pass. meet 1.
NIPH. appear 66
be looked upon 1
be seen 27
be shewed 1
be spied 1
present self 1
seem 1.
PUAL be seen 1.
HITHP. look one another 1
look one upon another 1
see one another 2.
HIPH. cause to see 1
let see 2
make to enjoy 1
shew 57
*be shewed 1.
HOPH. be shewed 4.
†KAL be in presence of (*with* panim) 1; live joyfully (*with* chaiyim) 1. *See* maqom.

RAAH [2] רָאָה *f.*
glede 1.

RAAH [3] רעה
be fed 1
devour 1
eat 1
eat up 1
fed 71
fed flock 2
keep [sheep] 5
wander 1
waste 1
*evil entreat 1.
Partic. herdman 7
pastor 8
shepherd 62
HIPH. feed 1.
†*Kal partic.* shepherd (*with* tson) 3. *See* bayith.

RAAH [4] רעה
keep company with 1.
Part. companion 2.
PIEL use as friend 1.
HITHP. make friendship with 1.

RAAH [5] = **RA.**

RAAL [1] רעל
HOPH. be terribly shaken 1.

RAAL [2] רַעַל
trembling 1.

RAAM [1] ראם
be lifted up 1.

RAAM [2] רעם
be troubled 1
roar 3.
HIPH. make to fret 1
thunder 8.

RAAM [3] רַעַם
thunder 6.

RAANAN רַעֲנָן
flourishing 1
fresh 1
green 18.

RAANAN רַעֲנַן
flourishing 1.

RAAPH רָעַף
distil 1
drop 2
drop down 1.
HIPH. drop down 1.

RAASH [1] רעשׁ
be moved 1
quake 1
remove (*intr.*) 1
shake 11
tremble 8.
NIPH. be moved 1.
HIPH. make afraid 1
make to shake 1
make to tremble 1
shake (*tr.*) 4.

RAASH [2] רַעַשׁ
commotion 1
confused noise 1
earthquake 6
fierceness 1
quaking 1
rattling 1
rushing 3
shaking 3.

RAASHOTH רַאֲשֹׁת *f. pl.*
bolster 2.

RAATS רָעַץ
dash in pieces 1
vex 1.

RAB [1] רַב
abundant 2
abundantly 2
common 1
elder 1
enough 8
exceedingly 2
full 1
great (man, one), greatly 128
long 10
long enough 2
manifold 3
many 190
many a time 1
many things 1
mighty 5
more 12
much 30
multitude 7
often 1
plenteous 3
populous 1
she that hath many 1
sufficient 1
too much 4
very much 1
who had done many 2
*abound 2
*in abundance 1
*increase 2
*suffice 3.
As noun captain 24
master 1
officer 1
prince 2.
†shipmaster (*with* chobel) 1. *See* yom.

RAB [2] רַבִּים *pl.*
archers 2.

RAB רַב
captain 1
chief 1
great 9
lord 1
master 2
stout 1

RABA [1] רבע
lie down to 2.
HIPH. let gender 1.

RABA [2] רבע
Pass. pt. four square 6
square 1
squared 1.
PUAL *pt.* four square 2
square 1.

RABAB [1] רבב
be increased 3
be manifold 1
be many 7
be more 2
be multiplied 3
multiply (*int.*) 2.
PUAL *pt.* ten thousand 1.

RABAB [2] רבב
shoot 2.

RABAD רבד
deck 1.

RABAH [1] רָבָה
be greater 1
be in authority 1
be increased 5
be long 3
be many 2
be more in number 1
be much greater 1
be multiplied 12
be so much 1
excel 1
grow up 1
increase (*intr.*) 12
multiply (*intr.*) 16.
PIEL bring up 1
increase (*tr.*) 2
nourish 1.
HIPH. ask much 1
be full of 1
be many 1
continue 1
enlarge 1
gather much 1
give many 2
give more 1
give the more
have many 3
have more 1
heap 1
increase (*tr.*) 21
make great 3
make many 5
make to multiply 1
multiply (*tr.*) 42
take much 1
use many 1
yield much 1
*abundantly 1
*any more 1
*many 1
*many a time 1
*more 2
*much 4
*much more 1
*throughly 1
*very much 1.
Partic. some more 1.
Adv. inf. exceedingly 1
greatly 1
in multiplying 1
[*See* harbeh].
†*KAL part.* archer (*with* qashshath) 1. HIPH. send many (*with pt. of* halak) 1; slay many (*with pl. of* chalal[2]) 1; trespass more and more (*with* ashmah) 1. *See* yom.

RABAK רבך
HOPH. *pt.* baken 1
fried 1
that which is fried 1.

RABATS רָבַץ
couch 2
couch down 1
fall down 1
lie 8
lie down 11
sit 1.
HIPH. cause to lie down 1
lay 1
make a fold 1
make to lie down 1
make to rest 1.

RABID רָבִיד
chain 2.

RABRAB רַבְרַב
great 7
great thing 1
very great thing 1.

RABREBAN רַבְרְבָן *pl.*
lords 6
princes 2.

RACHAB [1] רחב
be enlarged 2
*be an enlarging 1.
NIPH. *pt.* large 1.
HIPH. enlarge 14
make large 1
make room 2
make wide 1
open wide 2
*be enlarged 1.

RACHAB [2] רָחָב
broad 5
large 5
proud 3
wide 3
*liberty 1.
†broad (*with* yadayim) 1, large (*with* yadayim) 3, wide (*with* yadayim) 2.

RACHAB [3] רַחַב
breadth 1
broad place 1.

RACHAM [1] רחם
love 1.
PIEL have compassion 1
have compassion on 4
have compassion upon 3
have mercy 3
have mercy on 11
have mercy upon 12.
Inf. mercy 1.
Adv. inf. surely 1.
Part. merciful 1.
PUAL find mercy 1
have mercy (*int.*) 1
obtain mercy 1.
†PIEL: have pity on (*with* al[2]) 1; pity (*with* al[2]) 2.

RACHAM [2] רָחָם
gier-eagle 2.

RACHAM [3] רַחַם *f.*
damsel 3
womb 4.

RACHAMAH רָחָמָה *f.*
gier-eagle 1.

RACHAMIM רַחֲמִים *pl.*
bowels 2
compassion 4
great mercies 1
mercies 14
mercy 4
tender love 1
tender mercies 11
pity 1.
†*See* nathan.

RACHAMIN רַחֲמִין *pl.*
mercies 1.

* Inexact translations, *e.g.*, of a noun by a verb or adjective, of an active by a passive.
† Cases where two or more words in the original are translated by one word or by a phrase.

RACHAPH רחף
shake 1.
PIEL flutter 1
move 1.

RACHAQ רחק
be far 14
be far away 1
be far off 2
be far removed 1
be too far 2
flee far 1
get self far 1
go away far 1
go far 2
go far off 1
keep self far 1
refrain 1.
PIEL put away far 1
remove far 2
remove far away 1.
HIPH. be a good way 1
be far off 1
cast far off 1
drive far 1
go far 1
go far away 1
put away 1
put away far 1
put far 3
put far away 3
remove far 3
remove far off 1
withdraw far 1
*far off 1.
Adv. inf. afar off 1
a good way off 1
far 1
very 1.

RACHASH רחש
indite 1.

RACHATH רַחַת *f.*
shovel 1.

RACHATS [1] רָחַץ
bathe 6
bathe self 12
wash 46
wash self 5.
PUAL be washed 2.
HITHP. wash self 1.

RACHATS [2] רַחַץ
†*See* sir.

RACHEL רָחֵל *f.*
ewe 2
sheep 2.

RACHEQ רָחֵק
he that is far from 1.

RACHIQ רָחִיק
far 1.

RACHMANI רַחְמָנִי
pitiful 1.

RACHOQ רָחוֹק
afar off 28
far 31
far abroad 1
far off 14
long 1
*space 1.
†le-me-rachoq: for a great while to come 2, long ago 3; me-rachoq: of old 1.

RACHTSAH רַחְצָה *f.*
washing 2.

RACHUM רַחוּם
full of compassion 5
merciful 8.

RADAD רדד
subdue 2
*be spent 1.
HIPH. spread 1.

RADAH [1] רָדָה
bear rule 3
come to have dominion 1
have dominion 6
prevail against 1
reign 1
rule 9
rule over 1.
PIEL make to have dominion 1.
HIPH. make to rule 1.

RADAH [2] רָדָה
take 2.

RADAM רדם
NIPH. be cast into a deep sleep 1
be fast asleep 2
be in a deep sleep 2
sleep 1.
Partic. sleeper 1.

RADAPH רָדַף
chase 10
follow 9
follow after 8
follow on 1
hunt 1
persecute 18
pursue 76
put to flight 1.
Partic. persecutor 7.
NIPH. be past 1
be under persecution 1.
PIEL follow 1
follow after 3
persecute 1
pursue 4.
PUAL be chased 1.
HIPH. chase 1.
†KAL: persecute (*with* achar[2]) 1.

RADID רָדִיד
vail 1
veil 1.

RAEB [1] רעב
be famished 1
be hungry 4
have hunger 1
hunger 1
suffer hunger 2.
HIPH. suffer to famish 1
suffer to hunger 1.

RAEB [2] רָעֵב
hunger-bitten 1
hungry 21.

RAGA רגע
be broken 1
divide 3.
NIPH. rest 1.
HIPH. cause to rest 1
find ease 1
give rest 1
make to rest 1
rest 1
*for a moment 1
*suddenly 2.

RAGAL רגל
backbite 1.
PIEL espy out 1
search 1
slander 1
spy 12
spy out 8
view 2.
TIPHEL teach to go.

RAGAM רגם
stone 16.
Adv. inf. certainly 1.

RAGAN רגן
murmur 1.
NIPH. murmur 2.

RAGASH רגש
rage 1.

RAGAZ רגז
be afraid 1
be disquieted 1
be moved 3
be troubled 3
be wroth 1
fall out 1
fret 1
move (*intr.*) 4
quake 1
rage 1
tremble 10.
HIPH. disquiet 2
make to tremble 1
provoke 1
shake 3.
HITHP. rage 1.

RAGEA רָגֵעַ
he that is quiet 1.

RAGGAZ רַגָּז
trembling 1.

RAGLAYIM. *dual of* **REGEL.**

RAGLI רַגְלִי
footman 7
on foot 1.
†*See* ish.

RAHAB [1] רהב
behave self proudly 1
make sure 1.
HIPH. overcome 1
strengthen 1.

RAHAB [2] רָהָב
proud 1.

RAHAB [3] רַהַב
strength 1
*proud 2.

RAHAH רהה
be afraid 1.

RAHAT רַהַט
gallery 1
gutter 2
trough 1.

RAHIT רָהִיט
rafter 1.

RAK רַךְ
soft 3
tender 9
tender one 1
weak 1.
†faint-hearted (*with* lebab) 1, tender-hearted (*with* lebab) 1.

RAKAB רכב
get self up 1
ride 43.
Partic. rider 11.
Inf. riding 1.
HIPH. bring 1
bring on horseback 1
carry 3
cause to ride 7
make to ride 3
put 3
set 2.
†KAL *part.* (*with* sus) on horseback 2.

RAKAK רכך
be softer 1
be tender 2.
NIPH. faint 2.
PUAL be mollified 1.
HIPH. make soft 1.
†NIPH. be faint-hearted (*with* lebab) 1.

RAKAL רכל
Partic. merchant 17
spice merchant 1.

RAKAS רכס
bind 2.

RAKASH רכש
gather 1
get 4.

RAKIL רָכִיל
talebearer 2
that carries tales 1
*with slanders 1.
†*See* halak.

RAKKAB רַכָּב
chariot man 1
driver of a chariot 1
horseman 1.

RAMAH [1] רָמָה
carry 1
throw 2.
PIEL beguile 2
betray 1
deceive 5.
†KAL *partic.* bowman (*with* qesheth) 1.

RAMAH [2] רָמָה *f.*
high place 4.

RAMAH [3] רַעְמָה *f.*
thunder 1.

RAMAM רמם
be exalted 2.
NIPH. be lifted up 1
get (self) up 1
lift up selves 1
mount up 1.

RAMAS [1] רמס
stamp upon 2
trample 1
trample under foot 1
tread 4
tread down 7
tread upon 2.
Partic. oppressor 1.
NIPH. be trodden 1.

RAMAS [2] רמשׂ
creep 11
move 6.

RAMMAK רַמָּךְ *f.*
dromedary 1.

RAMOTH רָאמוֹת *f. pl.*
coral 2.

RAMUTH רָמוּת *f.*
height 1.

RANAH רנה
rattle 1.

RANAN רנן
cry 2
cry out 1
rejoice 1
shout 2
shout for joy 1
sing 12.
PIEL be joyful 1
cry out 1
greatly rejoice 1
rejoice 7
shout for joy 3
sing 6
sing aloud 3
sing for joy 1
sing out 1
triumph 1.
Infin. singing 1.
Adv. inf. aloud for joy 1.
PUAL be singing 1.
HIPH. cause to sing for joy 1
make to rejoice 1
rejoice 1
shout for joy 1
sing aloud 1.
HITHPOL. shout 1.

RAPHA [1] רפא
cure 1
heal 30
make whole 1.
Partic. physician 5.
NIPH. be healed 16
be made whole 1.
PIEL cause to be healed 1
heal 6
repair 1.
Adv. inf. thoroughly 1.
HITHP. be healed 3.
†KAL be healed (*with* le) 1.

RAPHA [2] רָפָא
giant 13
Rephaim (*pl.*) 4
Rephaims (*pl.*) 4.

RAPHAD רָפַד
spread 1.
PIEL comfort 1
make [a bed] 1.

RAPHAH [1] רָפָה
be abated 1
be faint 1
be feeble 3
be slack 1
be weak 1
be weakened 1
consume 1
draw [toward evening] 1
let go 1
wax feeble 1.
NIPH. *pt.* idle 3.
PIEL let down 2
weaken 3.
HIPH. be still 1
cease 1
fail 3
forsake 2
give respite 1
leave 1
let alone 4
let go 3
slack 1
stay 3.
HITHP. be slack 1
be slothful 1
faint 1.

RAPHAH [2] רָפָה
giant 4.

RAPHAQ רפק
HITHP. lean 1.

RAPHAS [1] רפס
HITHP. humble self 1
submit self 1.

RAPHAS [2] רפשׂ
foul 2.
NIPH. *pt.* troubled 1.

RAPHEH רָפֶה
weak 4.

RAPHSODOTH רַפְסֹדוֹת *f. pl.*
flotes 1.

RAQ [1] רַק
lean 1
thin 1.
†leanfleshed (*with* basar[2]) 1.

RAQ [2] רַק
at the least
but
even
except
howbeit
howsoever
in any wise
nevertheless
nothing but
notwithstanding
only
save
yet
yet so, etc.

RAQA רקע
spread abroad 2
spread forth 1
stamp 2
stretch out 1.
PIEL beat 1
spread over 1
*be made broad 1.
PUAL *pt.* spread into plates 1.
HIPH. spread out 1.

RAQAB [1] רקב
rot 2.

RAQAB [2] רָקָב
rotten thing 1
rottenness 4.

RAQACH רקח
compound 1
make [ointment] 1.
Partic. apothecary 4.
PUAL *pt.* prepared 1.
HIPH. spice 1.

RAQAD רקד
dance 1
skip 2.
PIEL dance 3
jump 1
leap 1.
HIPH. make to skip 1.

RAQAM רקם
Partic. embroiderer 2.
PUAL be curiously wrought.
†*See* maaseh.

RAQAQ רקק
spit 1.

RAQIA רָקִיעַ
firmament 17.

RAQIQ רָקִיק
cake 1
wafer 7.

RAQQACH רַקָּח
apothecary 1.

RAQQACHAH רַקָּחָה *f.*
confectionery 1.

RAQQAH רַקָּה *f.*
temples 5.

RASAS רסס
temper 1.

RASHA [1] רשע
be wicked 4
commit wickedness 1.
deal wickedly 1
do wickedly 1
wickedly depart 2
HIPH. condemn 15
do wickedly 7
do wickedly against 1
make trouble 1
vex 1.

RASHA [2] רָשָׁע
guilty 1
that did wrong 1
ungodly 8
wicked (man) 252.
†*See* yatsa.

RASHAM רשם
Pass. pt. noted 1.

RASHASH רשש
POEL impoverish 1.
PUAL be impoverished 1.

RATAB רטב
be wet 1.

RATASH רטש
PIEL dash 1
dash to pieces 2.
PUAL be dashed in pieces 3
be dashed to pieces 1.

RATHACH רתח
PIEL make to boil 1.
PUAL boil 1.
HIPH. make to boil 1.

RATHAM רתם
bind 1.

RATHAQ רתק
NIPH. be loosed 1.
PUAL be bound 1.

RATOB רָטֹב
green 1.

RATS רַץ
piece 1.

RATSA [1] רצא
run 1.

RATSA [2] רצע
bore 1.

RATSACH רצח
kill 6
murder 1
*be put to death 1.
Partic. manslayer 2
murderer 12
slayer 17.
NIPH. be slain 2.
PIEL murder 2.
Partic. murderer 2.
PUAL be slain 1.
†KAL *partic.* slayer (*with* nephesh) 1.

RATSAD רצד
PIEL leap 1.

RATSAH רצה
accept 17
accomplish 1
approve 1
be acceptable 1
be favourable 3
be pleased with 4
consent with 1
delight 4
delight self 1
enjoy 3
have a favour 1
have pleasure 1
like 1
please 2
set affection 1
take pleasure 5.
NIPH. be accepted 6
be pardoned 1.
PIEL seek to please 1.
HIPH. enjoy 1.
HITHP. reconcile self 1.

RATSAPH רצף
Partic. being paved 1.

RATSATS רצץ
be broken 3
be bruised 2
be discouraged 1
crush 2
oppress 3.
NIPH. be broken 1
break 1.
PIEL break 1
oppress 2.
POEL oppress 1.
HIPH. break 1.
HITHP. struggle together 1.

RATSON רָצוֹן
acceptance 1
delight 5
desire 3
favour 15
good pleasure
good will 2
pleasure 4
self will 1
voluntary will 1
will 8
*acceptable 8
*be accepted 4
*would 2.

* Inexact translations, *e.g.*, of a noun by a verb or adjective, of an active by a passive.
† Cases where two or more words in the original are translated by one word or by a phrase

RATTOQ רַתּוֹק (v. l. רַתּיק)
chain 1.

RATTUQOTH רַתּוּקוֹת *f. pl.*
chains 1.

RAVACH רָוַח
be refreshed 2.
Pual pt. large 1.

RAVAH רוה
be abundantly satisfied 1
be made drunk 1
take fill of 1.
Piel be bathed 1
be soaked 1
satiate 1
satisfy 1
water 1
water abundantly 1.
Hiph. fill 1
make drunken 1
satiate 1
water 1.

RAVEH רָוֶה
drunkenness 1
watered 2.

RAYAH רַעְיָה *f.*
love 9.

RAYON רַעְיוֹן
vexation 3.

RAYON רַעְיוֹן
cogitation 1
thought 5.

RAZ רָז
secret 9.

RAZAH רזה
famish 1.
Niph. wax lean 1.

RAZAM רזם
wink at 1.

RAZAN רָזַן
Partic. prince 5
ruler 1.

RAZEH רָזֶה
lean 2.

RAZI רָזִי
leanness 2.

RAZON[1] רָזוֹן
leanness 2
*scant 1.

RAZON[2] רָזוֹן
prince 1.

REA[1] רֵעַ
noise 1
*aloud 1
*shouted 1.

REA[2] רֵעַ (רֵיעַ)
brother 1
companion 5
fellow 10
friend 42
husband 1
lover 1
neighbour 104
*another 23
*other 2.

REA[3] רֵעַ
thought 2.

REA רְעַע
bruise 1.
Pael break 1.

REABON רְעָבוֹן
famine 3.

REACH רֵיחַ
savour 45
scent 2
smell 11.

REACH רֵיחַ
smell 1.

READAH רְעָדָה *f.*
fear 1
fearfulness 1
trembling 2.

REAH רֵעָה *f.*
companion 2
fellow 1.

REBA[1] רֶבַע
lying down 1

REBA[2] רֶבַע
fourth part 2
side 3
square 2.

REBABAH רְבָבָה *f.*
many 1
millions 1
ten thousand 13.
†*See* nathan.

REBAH רְבָה
be grown 3
grow 2.
Pael make a great man 1.

REBETS רֵבֶץ
place to lie down in 1
resting place 2
where . . . lay 1.

REBIBIM רְבִיבִים *pl.*
showers 6.

REBII רְבִיעִי
foursquare 1
fourth (part) 55.

REBII רְבִיעִי
fourth 5.

REBU רְבוּ *f.*
greatness 2
majesty 2.

RECHATS רחץ
Hithp. trust 1.

RECHAYIM רֵחַיִם *du.*
mill 2
millstones 2
nether millstone 1.

RECHEM רֶחֶם
matrix 5
womb 21.

RECHOB רְחוֹב *f.*
broad place 1
broad way 2
street 40.

REEH רֵעֶה
friend 3.

REEM רְאֵם
unicorn 9.

REGA רֶגַע
instant 2
moment 18
space 1
*suddenly 1.

REGAL רְגַל *c.*
foot 7.

REGASH רגש
Haph. assemble 2
assemble together 1.

REGAZ[1] רְגַז
Haph. provoke unto wrath 1.

REGAZ[2] רְגַז
rage 1.

REGEB רֶגֶב
clods 2.

REGEL רֶגֶל
foot (feet) 216
haunt 1
leg 1
times (*pl.*) 4
*be able to endure 1
*coming 4.
†be-regel (*or dual*): after 4, follow 4, in possession 1. *See* bohen, hadom, halak, mayim, nasa, sheber.

REGESH רֶגֶשׁ
company 1.

REI[1] רְאִי
looking glass 1.

REI[2] רְעִי
pasture 1.

REISHON = **RISHON.**

REKASIM רְכָסִים *pl.*
rough places 1.

REKEB רֶכֶב *c.*
chariot 114
millstone 2
upper millstone 1
wagon 1.

REKESH רֶכֶשׁ
dromedary 1
mule 2
swift beast 1

REKUB רְכוּב
chariot 1.

REKULLAH רְכֻלָּה *f.*
merchandise 2
traffick 2.

REKUSH רְכוּשׁ
goods 12
riches 5
substance 11.

REMAH רְמָה
be cast 1
be cast down 1
cast 4
impose 1.
Ithp. be cast 5.

REMES רֶמֶשׂ
creeping thing 15
moving thing 1
that creepeth 1.

REMIYYAH רְמִיָּה *f.*
deceit 2
guile 1
*deceitful 4
*deceitfully 3
*false 1
*idle 1
*slack 1
*slothful 2.

RENANAH רְנָנָה *f.*
joyful voice 1
singing 1
triumphing 1
*joyful 1.

RENANIM רְנָנִים *pl.*
*goodly 1.

REPHAIM רְפָאִים *pl.*
dead 7
deceased 1.

REPHAS רפס
stamp 2.

REPHATHIM רְפָתִים *pl.*
stalls 1.

REPHESH רֶפֶשׁ
mire 1.

REPHIDAH רְפִידָה *f.*
bottom 1.

REPHUOTH רְפֻאוֹת *f. pl.*
medicines 2.
†*See* nathan.

REQ רֵיק (רֵק)
emptied 1
empty 5
vain 5
vain fellow 1
vain man 1.

REQACH רֶקַח
*spiced 1.

REQAM רֵיקָם
empty 12
in vain 1
void 1
without cause 2.

RESEN רֶסֶן
bridle 4.

RESH (רֵאשׁ) רֵישׁ
poverty 5.

RESH רֵאשׁ
chief 1
head 12
sum 1.

RESHA רֶשַׁע
iniquity 1
wickedness 25
*wicked 4.

RESHAM רשם
sign 4.
Peil be signed 1
be written 2.

RESHEPH רֶשֶׁף
arrows (*pl.*) 1
burning coals 1
burning heat 1
coals (*pl.*) 3
hot thunderbolts (*pl.*) 1.
†*See* ben[2].

RESHETH רֶשֶׁת *f.*
net 20.
†*See* maaseh.

RESHITH רֵאשִׁית *f.*
beginning 18
chief 8
chiefest 1
first 9
firstfruits 11
first part 1
first time 1
principal thing 1.
†firstfruits (*with* peri) 1.

RESISIM רְסִיסִים *pl.*
breaches 1
drops 1.

RETEB רֶטֶב
fear 1.

RETHACH רֶתַח
*well (*adv.*) 1.

RETHETH רֶתֶת
trembling 1.

RETHUQOTH רְתֻקוֹת *f. pl.*
chains 1.

RETSACH רֶצַח
slaughter 1
sword 1.

RETSAPHIM (**RETSEPH**) רְצָפִים *pl.*
*baken on coals 1.

REUTH[1] רְאוּת *f.*
beholding 1.

REUTH[2] רְעוּת *f.*
mate 2
neighbour 2
*another 2.

REUTH[3] רְעוּת *f.*
vexation 7.

REUTH רְעוּת *f.*
pleasure 1
will 1.

REV רֵו
form 2.

REVACH רֶוַח
enlargement 1
space 1.

REVACHAH רְוָחָה *f.*
breathing 1
respite 1.

REVAYAH רְוָיָה *f.*
wealthy place 1
*runneth over 1.

RI רִי
watering 1.

RIB[1] רִיב
chide 6
complain 1
contend 12
debate 1
debate with 1
plead 27
rebuke 1
strive 13.
Adv. inf. ever 1
throughly 1.
Hiph. strive 1.
Partic. adversary 1

RIB[2] רִיב
cause 24
chiding 1
contention 2
controversy 13
pleading 1
strife 14
striving 2
suit 1
*contend 1
*strive 1.
†*See* ish[1].

RIBBEIM רִבֵּעִים *pl.*
fourth generation 4.

RIBBO רִבּוֹ (רִבּוֹא) *f.*
ten thousand 2.
Dual twenty thousand 1.
†*In combination with other numbers rendered by English* 18,000, 20,000 sixscore thousand, etc.

RIBBO רִבּוֹ *f.*
ten thousand 1
ten thousand times 1.

RIBBOTH. *Pl. of* **RIBBO.**

RIGMAH רִגְמָה *f.*
council 1.

RIGSHAH רִגְשָׁה *f.*
insurrection 1.

RIKBAH רִכְבָּה *f.*
chariots 1.

RIMMAH רִמָּה *f.*
worm 7.

RIMMON רִמּוֹן
pomegranate 30
pomegranate tree 2.

RINNAH רִנָּה *f.*
cry 12
gladness 1
joy 3
proclamation 1
rejoicing 3
shouting 1
singing 9
song 1
triumph 1
*sing 1.

RIPHOTH רִיפוֹת *f. pl.*
ground corn 1
wheat 1.

RIPHUTH רִפְאוּת *f.*
health 1.

RIPHYON רִפְיוֹן
feebleness 1.

RIQ רִיק
empty 1
in vain 6
to no purpose 1
vain thing 1
vanity 2.

RIQMAH רִקְמָה *f.*
broidered work 5
divers colours 2
needlework 1
raiment of needlework 1
*broidered 2.
Dual needlework on both sides 1.

RIQQABON רִקָּבוֹן
rotten 1.

RIQQUCHIM רִקֻּחִים *pl.*
perfumes 1.

RIQQUIM רִקֻּעִים *pl.*
*broad 1.

RIR רִיר
spittle 1
white [of an egg] 1.

RISH רִישׁ
poverty 2.

RISHAH[1] רֵאשָׁה *f.*
beginning 1.

RISHAH[2] רִשְׁעָה *f.*
fault 1
wickedness 13
*wickedly 1.

RISHON רִאשׁוֹן
aforetime 1
ancestor 1
before 4
beforetime 1
beginning 4
chief 3
eldest 1
first 130
foremost 3
former 26
former things (*pl.*) 6
of old time 1
old time 1
past 1.
†*See* ab[1], eth[2].

RISHONI רִאשֹׁנִי
first 1.

RISHYON רִשְׁיוֹן
grant 1.

RITSPAH רִצְפָּה *f.*
live coal 1
pavement 7.

ROA רֹעַ
badness 2
evil 11
naughtiness 1
sadness 1
sorrow 1
wickedness 3.
†me-roa: they are so evil 3, they were so bad 1.

ROAH רֹעָה *f.*
*broken 1.

ROB רֹב
abundance 39
great number 1
greatness 9
great things (*pl.*) 1
long time 1
multitude 69
plenty 3
*all 1
*be increased 1
*be many 1
*be more in number 1
*excellent 1
*great 8
*huge 1
*long 1
*many 2
*most 1
*much 7
*very 1.
†common sort (*with* adam) 1. la-rob: abundantly 4, greatly 1, plentifully 1.

ROBA רֹבַע
fourth part 2.

ROCHAB רֹחַב
breadth 72
largeness 1
thickness 2
wideness 1
*broad 22
*thick 1.

ROEH רֹאֶה
vision 1.

ROGEZ רֹגֶז
fear 1
noise 1
rage 1
trouble 3
troubling 1
wrath 1.

ROGZAH רָגְזָה *f.*
trembling 1.

ROHAB רֹהַב
strength 1.

ROI רֳאִי
gazingstock 1
*be seen 1
*see 1
*to look to 1.

ROK רֹךְ
tenderness 1.

ROKES רֹכֶס
pride 1.

ROM רוֹם
on high 1.

ROMACH רֹמַח
buckler 1
javelin 1
lancet 1
spear 12.

ROMAH רוֹמָה
*haughtily 1.

ROMAM רוֹמָם
high praises (*pl.*) 1.

ROMEMUTH רוֹמֵמוּת *f.*
lifting up of self 1.

RON רֹן
song 1.

ROQ רֹק
spitting
spittle 1
*to spit 1.

ROQACH רֹקַח
compound 1
confection 1.

ROSH[1] רֹאשׁ
band 2
beginning 14
captain 10
chapiter 4
chief 90
chiefest place 1
chief man 4
chief place 1
chief things 1
company 12
end [of staves]
forefront 1
head 349
height 1
highest part 1
ruler 2
sum 9
top 75
*every 1
*excellent 1
*first 6
*principal 5.
†be-rosh: on high 2, to lead 1. *See* kohen, sur.

ROSH[2] רֹאשׁ (רוֹשׁ)
gall 9
hemlock 1
poison 1
venom 1.

* Inexact translations, *e.g.*, of a noun by a verb or adjective, of an active by a passive.
† Cases where two or more words in the original are translated by one word or by a phrase.

ROSHAH ראשה
†*See* eben.

ROTHEM רתם *c.*
juniper 2
juniper tree 2.

RUA רוע
POL. be shouting 1.
HIPH. blow an alarm 1
cry 3
cry alarm 1
cry aloud 1
cry out 2
give a shout 1
make a joyful noise 7
shout 18
shout for joy 1
sound an alarm 2
triumph 1.
HITHPOL. shout for joy 1
triumph 2.

RUACH[1] רוח
HIPH. accept 1
make of quick understanding 1
smell 8
touch 1.

RUACH[2] רוח *c.*
air 1
anger 1
blast 4
breath 28
cool (*n.*) 1
courage 1
mind 5
quarters (*pl.*) 1
side 6
spirit 232
tempest 1
wind 90
*vain 2
*windy 1.
†breath (*with* neshamah) 1; whirlwind (*with* searah[1]) 1. *See* ish[1].

RUACH רוח *c.*
mind 1
spirit 8
wind 2.

RUD[1] רוד
be lord 1
rule 1.
HIPH. have the dominion 1.

RUD[2] רוד
HIPH. mourn 1.

RUM רום
be exalted 20
be high 4
be higher 2
be lifted up 9
be lift up 1
be lofty 2
breed 1
exalt self 2
go up 1
mount up 1.
Partic. haughty 1
high 17
high ones 1
lofty 1
loud 1
proud 1
tall 4
too high 1.
POLEL bring up 2
exalt 11
extol 2
lift up 4
lift up on high 1
promote 1
set up 3
set up on high 1.
POLAL be exalted 1
be extolled 2.
HIPH. exalt 12
give 5
heave 3
hold up 2
levy 1
lift 1
lift up 26
make on high 1
offer 12
offer up 4
set up 5
take 3
take away 1
take off 3
take up 7
*be promotion of 1.
Partic. lifter up 1.
Infin. promotion 1.
HOPH. be heaved up 1
be taken away 1
be taken off 1.
HITHPOL. be exalted 1
exalt self 1.
†HIPH. aloud (*with* qol) 1. *See* yad.

RUM[2] רום
haughtiness 3
height 1
*high 2.

RUM[1] רום
be lifted up 1
extol 1.
HAPH. set up 1.
HITHPOL. lift up self 1.

RUM[2] רום
height 5.

RUPH רוף
POL. tremble 1.

RUQ רוק
HIPH. arm 1
cast out 1
draw 3
draw out 5
empty 5
make empty 1
pour out 6
HOPH. be emptied 1
be poured forth 1.

RUR רור
run 1.

RUSH רוש
lack 1.
Partic. needy 1
poor 18
poor man 3.
HITHPOL. make self poor 1.

RUTAPHASH רטפש
be fresh 1.

RUTS רוץ
break down 1
run 69
run through 1.
Partic. footman 1
guard 14
post 8
*another 1.
POL. run 1.
HIPH. bring hastily 1
divide speedily 1
make run away 2
run 1
soon stretch out 1.

S

SAAD סעד
comfort 3
establish 1
hold up 3
refresh self 1
strengthen 3
*be upholden 1.

SAAH סעה
Partic. *storm 1.

SAAN סאן
Partic. warrior 1.

SAAPH סעף
PIEL lop 1.

SAAR[1] סער
be tempestuous 2
come out as a whirlwind 1.
Partic. tossed with tempest 1.
NIPH. be sore troubled 1.
PIEL scatter with a whirlwind 1.
POAL be driven with the whirlwind 1.

SAAR[2] סער
tempest 5
whirlwind 3.

SAAR[3] שער
be afraid 2
be horribly afraid 1
fear 1
take away as with a whirlwind 1.
NIPH. be tempestuous 1.
PIEL hurl as a storm 1.
HITHP. come like a whirlwind 1.

SAAR[4] שער
storm 1
*horribly 1
*sore 1.
†*See* achaz.

SAAR[5] שער
hair 1.

SAARAH שערה *f.*
hair 7.

SAB. *Partic of* **SIB.**

SABA[1] סבא
be drunken 1
fill selves 1.
Partic. drunkard 2.
Pass. pt. drunkard 1.
†*Partic.* winebibber (*with* yayin) 1.

SABA[2] שבע (שבע)
be filled 10
be filled full 1
be filled with 9
be full 7
be full of 6
be satiate 1
be satisfied 30
be satisfied with 7
be sufficed 1
be weary of 1
fill selves 1
have enough 3
have plenty of 2.
Infin. to the full 1.
PIEL satisfy 2.
HIPH. feed to the full 1
fill 5
satisfy 8
satisfy with 2.

SABA[3] שבע
abundance 1
plenteousness 1
plenty 4
*plenteous 2.

SABAB סבב
apply 1
be about on every side 2
beset 1
beset about 1
besiege 1
cast about 1
come round about 1
compass 27
compass about 10
compass in 1
compass round about 1
fetch a compass 1
go about 8
occasion 1
sit down 1
stand round about 1
turn 5
turn about 2
turn aside 1
walk about 1
*in circuit 1.
NIPH. avoid 1
be carried about 1
be driven 2
be set round about 1
be turned 4
compass 3
compass about 1
compass round 1
environ 1
fetch a compass 2
go about 1
remove 1
return 2
turn 11
turn about 2
turn aside 1
turn self about 1
*on every side 1
*winding about 1.
PIEL fetch about 1.
POEL close round about 1
compass 2
compass about 4
go about 2
go round about 1
lead about 1.
HIPH. bring about 2
bring again 1
carry 1
carry about 1
change 1
compass 1
compass about 1
fetch a compass 1
lead about 1
remove 1
turn 13
turn away 4
turn back 1.
HOPH. be changed 1
be inclosed 1
be set 1
be turned about 1.
Partic. inclosed 1
turning 1.
†KAL whirl about (*with* halak) 1. HIPH. cause to come about (*with* bo) 1.

SABAK[1] סבך
Pass. pt. folden together 1.

SABAK[2] שבך
net 1.

SABAL סבל
bear 3
carry 4.
PUAL *pt.* strong to labour 1.
HITHP. be a burden 1.

SABAR שבר
PIEL hope 3
tarry 1
wait 2.
†KAL view (*with* be) 1.

SABBAL סבל
bearer of burdens 3
burden 1
*to bear burdens 1.

SABBEKA שבכא (סבכא) *f.*
sackbut 4.

SABEA[1] = **SABA**[2].

SABEA[2] שבע
full 2
full of 6
satisfied 1
satisfied with 1.

SABIB סביב (סביבות)
about 22
all about 1
circuit 1
compass 2
on every side 7
places about 3
round about 248.
†*Repeated*: on every side 1, round about 27. Missabib: on every side 18, round about (*incl. above*). Sabib le: round about (*incl. above*).

SACHAB סחב
draw 2
draw out 2
tear 1.

SACHAH[1] סחה
PIEL scrape 1.

SACHAH[2] שחה
swim 2.
HIPH. make to swim 1.

SACHAPH סחף
Partic. sweeping 1.
NIPH. be swept away 1.

SACHAQ שחק
deride 1
have in derision 1
laugh 10
make sport 1
mock 2
rejoice 1
scorn 2.
PIEL be in sport 1
make sport 1
play 10
rejoice 1.
Partic. mocker 1
them that make merry 2.
HIPH. laugh to scorn 1.

SACHAR[1] סחר
go about 1
occupy with 1
trade 2
traffick 1.
Partic. merchant 14
merchantman 1.
PILP. pant 1.

SACHAR[2] סחר
mart 1
merchandise 2.

SACHAR[3] סחר
merchandise 4.

SACHAT שחט
press 1.

SACHISH סחיש
which springeth of the same 1.

SACHU שחו *f.*
*to swim in 1.

SAD סד
stocks 2.

SADAD שדד
PIEL break the clods 2
harrow 1.

SADAI שדי
field 13.

SADEH שדה
country 17
field 275
ground 4
land 10
soil 1
*wild 8.

SADIN סדין
fine linen 2
sheet 2.

SAGA שגא
HIPH. increase 1
magnify 1.

SAGAB שגב
be exalted 1
be too strong 1.
NIPH. be exalted 4
be excellent 1
be safe 1.
Partic. high 3
lofty 1.
PIEL defend 2
set on high 2
set up 1
set up on high 1.
PUAL be safe 1.
HIPH. exalt 1.

SAGAD סגד
fall down 4.

SAGAH שגה
grow 2
increase 1.
HIPH. increase 1.

SAGAR סגר
be inclosed 1
close 1
close up 1
repair 1
shut 26
shut up 3
shut up together 1
stop 1.
Partic. *straitly 1.
Pass. pt. *pure 8.
NIPH. be shut 4
be shut in 1
be shut out 2
shut self 1.
PIEL deliver 4.
PUAL be shut 1
be shut up 4.
HIPH. deliver 5
deliver up 7
give over 2
give up 2
shut up 13
*be shut up 1.

SAGGI שגיא
excellent 1
great 1.

SAGGI שגיא
exceeding 1
great 3
greatly 1
many 2
much 4
sore 1
very 1.

SAGRIR סגריר
*very rainy 1.

SAHAR סהר
*round 1.

SAHARONIM שהרנים *pl.*
ornaments 2
round tires like the moon 1.

SAHED שהד
record 1.

SAIR שעיר
devil 2
goat 23
he goat 1
kid 28
satyr 2
*hairy 2
*rough 1.

SAK סך
multitude 1.

SAKAK סכך (*once* שכך)
cover 13.
Partic. defence 1.
HIPH. cover 4
defend 1
hedge in 1
shut up 1.
PILP. join together 1
set 1.

SAKAL[1] סכל
NIPH. do foolishly 4.
PIEL make foolish 1
turn into foolishness 1.
HIPH. do foolishly 1
play the fool 1.

SAKAL[2] סכל
fool 4
foolish 2
sottish 1.

SAKAL[3] שכל
behave self wisely 1.
PIEL guide wittingly 1.
HIPH. behave self wisely 4
be instructed 1
be wise 3
consider 2
consider wisely 2
deal prudently 1
give skill 1
have good success 1
have understanding 2
instruct 3
make to understand 1
make wise 1
prosper 8
teach 2
understand 14.
Partic. expert 1
maschil 13
prudent 2
skilful 1
understanding 2
wise 8
wisely 1.
Infin. skill 1
understanding 2
wisdom 2.

SAKAN[1] סכן
be advantage 1
be profitable 2
cherish 2
profit 1.
Partic. treasurer 1.
HIPH. acquaint self 1
be acquainted 1
be wont 1.
Adv. inf. ever 1.
†KAL be unprofitable (lo sakan) 1.

SAKAN[2] סכן
NIPH. be endangered 1.
PUAL *pt.* impoverished 1.

SAKAR[1] סכר
NIPH. be stopped 1.
PIEL give over 1.

SAKAR[2] שכר (*once* סכר)
hire 15
reward 2.
Adv. inf. surely 1.
NIPH. hire out selves 1.
HITHP. earn wages 2.

* Inexact translations, *e.g.*, of a noun by a verb or adjective, of an active by a passive.
† Cases where two or more words in the original are translated by one word or by a phrase.

SAKAR[3] שָׂכָר
fare 1
hire 9
price 2
reward 7
wages 6
worth 1.
†be rewarded (yesh sakar le) 2.

SAKATH סכת
HIPH. take heed 1.

SAKIR שָׂכִיר
hired 2
hired men 1
hired servant 8
hireling 6.

SAKKIN שַׂכִּין
knife 1.

SAL סַל
basket 15.

SALA סלא
PUAL *pt.* comparable 1.

SALACH סלח
forgive 19
pardon 13
spare 1.
NIPH. be forgiven 13.

SALAD סלד
PIEL harden self 1.

SALAH סלה
tread down 1.
PIEL tread under foot 1.
PUAL be valued 2.

SALAL סלל
cast up 6
extol 1
make plain 1
raise up 2.
PILP. exalt 1.
HITHPO. exalt self 1.

SALAPH סלף
PIEL overthrow 4
pervert 3.

SALLACH סַלָּח
ready to forgive 1.

SALLONIM סַלּוֹנִים *pl.*
thorns 1.

SALMAH שַׂלְמָה *f.*
clothes 3
garment 8
raiment 5.

SALSILLOTH סַלְסִלּוֹת *f. pl.*
baskets 1.

SAMACH = **SAMEACH**[1].

SAMAK סמך
be established 1
be stayed 1
lay 18
lean 1
lie hard 1
put 5
set self 1
stand fast 1
sustain 3
uphold 9.
NIPH. be borne up 1
be holden up 1
lean 2
rest selves 1
stay self 1.
PIEL stay 1.

SAMAL שמאל
HIPH. [go] on the left 1
go to the left 1
turn to the left 1
[turn] to the left 1
[use] the left 1.

SAMAN סמן
NIPH. *pt.* appointed 1.

SAMAR[1] סמר
tremble 1.
PIEL stand up 1.

SAMAR[2] סָמָר
rough 1.

SAMEACH[1] שָׂמַח (שָׂמֵחַ)
be glad 34
be merry 1
have joy 3
joy 2
rejoice 84.
PIEL cause to rejoice 1
cheer 1
cheer up 1
make glad 11
make joyful 2
make to rejoice 1
rejoice 5.
Adv. inf. very 1.
HIPH. make to rejoice 1
†PIEL make merry (*with* chaiyim) 1.

SAMEACH[2] שָׂמֵחַ
glad 2
joyful 3
merry 2
making merry 1
rejoicing 1
*be glad 2
*merrily 1
*rejoice 10.
†merryhearted (*with* leb) 1.

SAMMIM סַמִּים *pl.*
sweet spices 2
*sweet 14.

SANE שׂנא
be hateful 1
hate 119.
Partic. enemy 3
foe 1.
Pass. pt. odious 1.
Adv. inf. utterly 1.
NIPH. be hated 2.
PIEL hate 15.

SANI שָׂנִיא
hated 1.

SANSINNIM סַנְסִנִּים *pl.*
boughs 1.

SANVERIM סַנְוֵרִים *pl.*
blindness 3.

SAPH[1] סַף
bason 4
bowl 2
cup 1.

SAPH[2] סַף
door 13
door post 1
gate 2
post 2
threshold 8.

SAPHACH[1] שפח
PIEL smite with the scab 1.

SAPHACH[2] ספח
put 1.
NIPH. cleave 1.
PIEL put 1.
PUAL be gathered together 1.
HITHP. *infin.* abiding 1.

SAPHAD ספד
lament 11
mourn 15
wail 1.
Partic. mourner 1.
NIPH. be lamented 2.

SAPHAH[1] ספה
be consumed 1
consume 1
destroy 3.
NIPH. be consumed 4
be destroyed 2
perish 2.

SAPHAH[2] ספה
add 3
augment 1
put 1.
NIPH. be joined 1.
HIPH. heap 1.

SAPHAH[3] שָׂפָה *f.*
band 1
bank 10
binding 1
border 3
brim 8
brink 5
edge 8
language 7
lip 112
prating 2
shore 6
side 3
speech 6
talk 1
*other 1
*vain (*pl.*) 2.

SAPHAM שָׂפָם
beard 1
lips 3
upper lip 1.

SAPHAN[1] ספן
cover 3.
Pass. pt. cieled 2
seated 1.

SAPHAN[2] שׂפן
Pass. pt. treasures 1.

SAPHAPH ספף
HITHPO. be doorkeeper 1.

SAPHAQ[1] ספק (*once* שפק)
clap 3
smite 3
strike 1
wallow 1.

SAPHAQ[2] שׂפק
HIPH. please selves 1.

SAPHAQ[3] שׂפק
suffice 1.

SAPHAR ספר
count 5
number 16
reckon 1
tell 3
tell out 1.
Partic. scribe 50
writer 4.
NIPH. be counted 1
be numbered 5
be told 2.
PIEL commune 1
declare 22
number 1
show forth 6
speak 2
talk 1
tell 31
tell of 1
*be declared 1
*be numbered 1.
PUAL be accounted 1
be declared 1
be told 3.
†*See* taar.

SAPHER סָפֵר
scribe 6.

SAPHIACH סָפִיחַ
such as groweth of itself 1
such things as grow of themselves 1
things which grow 1
which groweth of its own accord 1
which groweth of itself 1.

SAPPACHATH סַפַּחַת *f.*
scab 2.

SAPPIR סַפִּיר
sapphire 11.

SAQ שַׂק
sack 6
sackcloth (sackclothes) 42.

SAQAD שׂקד
NIPH. be bound 1.

SAQAL סקל
stone 10.
Adv. inf. surely 2.
NIPH. be stoned 4.
PIEL cast [stones] 1
gather [out stones] 2
throw [stones] 1.
PUAL be stoned 2.

SAQAR שׂקר
PIEL *pt.* wanton 1.

SAR[1] סַר
heavy 1
sad 1.

SAR[2] שַׂר
captain 125
captain that had rule 1
chief 33
chief captain 3
general 1
governor 6
keeper 3
lord 1
master 1
prince 208
principal 2
ruler 33
steward 1.
†taskmaster (*with* mas) 1.

SARA שׂרע
have anything superfluous 1.
Partic. thing superfluous 1.
HITHP. stretch out self 1.

SARABIM סָרָבִים *pl.*
briers 1.

SARACH סרח
hang 2
stretch selves 2.
Partic. spreading 1.
Pass. pt. exceeding in 1.
NIPH. be vanished 1.

SARAD שׂרד
remain 1.

SARAG שׂרג
PUAL be wrapped together 1.
HITHP. be wreathed 1.

SARAH[1] סָרָה *f.*
rebellion 2
revolt 1
that which is wrong 1.
†to turn you away from (*with* al[2]) 1. *See* amaq, bilti, yasaph.

SARAH[2] שׂרה
have power 1
have power as a prince 1.

SARAH[3] שָׂרָה *f.*
lady 2
princess 2
queen 1.

SARAK שׂרך
PIEL *pt.* traversing 1.

SARAPH[1] סרף
PIEL burn 1.

SARAPH[2] שׂרף
burn 92
burn up 2
cause to be burned 1
kindle 1
make [a burning] 1
*be burnt 1.
Pass. pt. burned 4
that were burnt 1.
Adv. inf. utterly 1.
NIPH. be burnt 14.
PUAL be burnt 1.

SARAPH[3] שָׂרָף
fiery 3
fiery serpent 3
seraphims (*pl.*) 2.

SARAPPAH סַרְעַפָּה *f.*
bough 1.

SARAPPIM שַׂרְעַפִּים *pl.*
thoughts 2.

SARAR[1] סרר
slide back 1
withdraw 1.
Partic. away 1
backsliding 1
rebellious 6
revolter 2
revolting 1
stubborn 4.

SARAR[2] שׂרר
bear rule 1
rule 2.
HITHP. make self a prince 1.
Adv. inf. altogether 1.

SARAT שׂרט
make [cuttings] 1.
Adv. inf. in pieces 1.
NIPH. be cut 1.

SARBALIN סַרְבָּלִין *pl.*
coats 2.

SAREKIN סָרְכִין *pl.*
presidents 5.

SARETETH שָׂרֶטֶת *f.*
cuttings 1.

SARID שָׂרִיד
alive 1
him that is left 1
left 2
remaining 9
remnant 2
rest 1
that remain (did remain, etc.) 5
*remain 7.

SARIGIM שָׂרִיגִים *pl.*
branches 3.

SARIQ שָׂרִיק
fine 1.

SARIS סָרִיס
chamberlain 13
eunuch 17
officer 12.

SAROQ שָׂרֹק
speckled 1.

SAS סָס
worm 1.

SASON שָׂשׂוֹן
gladness 3
joy 15
mirth 3
rejoicing 1.

SASSEAH סַאסְּאָה *f.*
measure 1.

SATAH שׂטה
decline 1
go aside 4
turn 1.

SATAM שׂטם
hate 5
oppose self against 1.

SATAN[1] שׂטן
be an adversary 5
resist 1.

SATAN[2] שָׂטָן
adversary 7
Satan 19.
†to withstand (le-satan) 1.

SATHAM[1] סתם (*once* שתם)
shut out 1.
shut up 2
stop 5.
Pass. pt. closed up 1
hidden 1
secret 1.
NIPH. be stopped 1.
PIEL stop 2.

SATHAR[1] סָתַר
NIPH. be absent 1
be hid 10
be kept close 2
hide self 16.
Partic. secret 2.
PIEL hide 1.
PUAL *pt.* secret 1.
HIPH. conceal 1
hide 42
keep secret 1.
Adv. inf. surely 1.
HITHP. be hid 1
hide self 4.

SATHAR[2] שׂתר
NIPH. have in (one's) secret parts 1.

SEACH שֵׂחַ
thought 1.

SEAD סעד
PAEL *pt.* helping 1.

SEAH סְאָה *f.*
measure 9.

SEAPHIM סְעִפִּים *pl.*
vain thoughts 1.

SEAPPAH סְעַפָּה *f.*
bough 2.

SEAR שֵׂעָר
hair 24
*hairy 2
*rough 1.

SEAR שְׂעַר
hair 3.

SEARAH[1] סְעָרָה *f.*
storm 1
tempest 1
whirlwind 9
*stormy 4.
†*See* ruach[2].

SEARAH[2] שְׂעָרָה *f.*
storm 1
tempest 1.

SEB שֵׂיב
age 1.

SEBAH שֵׂיבָה *f.*
gray hairs 5
grey head 1
hoar hairs 1
hoar head 2
hoary head 2
old age 6
*gray-headed 1
*hoary 1.

SEBAK סְבָךְ (*or* סְבֹךְ)
thicket 3.

SEBAKAH שְׂבָכָה *f.*
lattice 1
network 7
snare 1
wreath 3
wreathenwork 2
*checker 1.

SEBAL סבל
POAL *pt.* strongly laid 1.

SEBALAH סְבָלָה *f.*
burden 6.

SEBAR סבר
think 1.

SEBEL סֵבֶל
burden 2
charge 1.

SEBER שֵׂבֶר
hope 2

SEBOK סְבֹךְ
thicket 1
*thick 1.

SECHABOTH סְחָבוֹת *f. pl.*
cast clouts 2.

SECHI סְחִי
offscouring 1.

SECHOQ שְׂחוֹק
derision 5
laughing 1
laughter 6
sport 1
*laughed to scorn 1
*mocked 1.

SECHORAH סְחֹרָה *f.*
merchandise 1.

SEDARIM סְדָרִים *pl.*
order 1.

SEDERAH שְׂדֵרָה *f.*
board 1
range 3.

SEETH שְׂאֵת *f.* (*inf. of* NASA)
be accepted 1
dignity 1
excellency 2
highness 1
rising 7.

SEGA שְׂגָא
be multiplied 2
grow 1.

SEGANIM סְגָנִים *pl.*
princes 1
rulers 16.

SEGAR סגר
shut 1.

SEGID סְגִד
worship 12.

SEGOR סְגוֹר
caul 1
gold 1.

SEGULLAH סְגֻלָּה *f.*
jewel 1
peculiar treasure 3
proper good 1
*peculiar 2
*special 1.

SEH שֶׂה *c.*
cattle 8
ewe 1
lamb 16
lesser cattle 1
sheep 17
small cattle 1.
†goat (*with pl. of* ez) 1; lamb (*with pl. of* kebes) 1; kid (*with* be *and pl. of* ez) 1; sheep (*with pl. of* keseb) 1.

SEIPH סְעִף
branch 1
clift 1
outmost branch 1
top 3.

SEIPPIM[1] סְעִפִּים *pl.*
opinions 1.

SEIPPIM[2] שְׂעִפִּים *pl.*
thoughts 2.

SEIRAH שְׂעִירָה *f.*
kid 2.

* Inexact translations, *e.g.*, of a noun by a verb or adjective, of an active by a passive.
† Cases where two or more words in the original are translated by one word or by a phrase.

SEIRIM שְׂעִרִים *pl.*
small rain 1.

SEK שִׂכִּים *pl.*
pricks 1.

SEKAL שְׂכַל
ITHPAEL consider 1.

SEKEL סֶכֶל
folly 1.

SEKEL (שֶׂכֶל) שֵׂכֶל
discretion 1
knowledge 1
policy 1
prudence 1
sense 1
understanding 7
wisdom 3
*wise 1.

SEKER שֶׂכֶר
reward 1
sluice 1.

SEKIRAH שְׂכִירָה *f.*
that is hired 1.

SEKIYYAH שְׂכִיָּה *f.*
picture 1.

SEKVI שֶׂכְוִי
heart 1.

SELA סֶלַע
ragged rock 1
rock 56
stone 1
strong hold 1
*stony 1.

SELAH סֶלָה
Selah 76.

SELAQ סלק
come up 3.
PEIL come 1
come up 1.

SELAV (שְׂלָיו) שְׂלָו
quails 4.

SELEPH סֶלֶף
perverseness 2.

SELICHAH סְלִיחָה *f.*
forgiveness 2
pardon 1.

SEMADAR סְמָדַר
tender grape 3.

SEMALI שְׂמָאלִי
left 9.

SEMAMITH שְׂמָמִית *f.*
spider 1.

SEMEL (סֶמֶל) סֵמֶל
figure 1
idol 2
image 2.

SEMIKAH שְׂמִיכָה *f.*
mantle 1.

SEMOL (שְׂמֹאול) שְׂמֹאל
left 35
left hand 18
left side 1.

SENAPPIR סְנַפִּיר
fins 5.

SENE שְׂנֵא
hate (*vb.*) 1.

SENEH סְנֶה
bush 6.

SEON סְאוֹן
battle 1.

SEOR שְׂאֹר
leaven 4
leavened bread 1.

SEORAH שְׂעֹרָה *f.*
barley 34.

SEPHAR סְפָר
numbering 1.

SEPHAR סְפַר
book 4
roll 1.

SEPHEL סֵפֶל
bowl 1
dish 1.

SEPHEQ (שֶׂפֶק) סֵפֶק
stroke 1
sufficiency 2.

SEPHER סֵפֶר
bill 4
book 137
evidence 8
learning 2
letter 28
register 1
scroll 1.
†*See* yada.

SEPHINAH סְפִינָה *f.*
ship 1.

SEPHORAH סְפֹרָה *f.*
number 1.

SERACH סֶרַח
remnant 1.

SERAD שְׂרָד
service 4.

SERED שֶׂרֶד
line 1.

SEREN סֶרֶן
lord 21
plate 1.

SEREPHAH שְׂרֵפָה *f.*
burning 9
*burnt 2.
†thoroughly (li-serephah) 1. *See* hayah.

SERET שֶׂרֶט
cuttings 1.

SEROK שְׂרוֹךְ
latchet 1.
†shoe latchet (*with* naal) 1.

SERUQQIM שְׂרוּקִּים *pl.*
principal plants 1.

SETH = SEETH.

SETHAR סְתַר
PAEL destroy 1.
Partic. secret things 1.

SETHAV סְתָיו (V.L. סתו)
winter 1.

SETHER סֵתֶר
covering 5
covert 5
hiding place 3
secret 7
secret place 6
*backbiting 1
*secret (*adj.*) 1
†bas-sether: privily 1, secretly 9. *See* sum.

SETIM [1] סֵטִים *pl.*
that turn aside 1.

SETIM [2] שֵׂטִים *pl.*
revolters 1.

SHA = SHE.

SHAA שעע
cry 1.
PILP. delight 2
play.
PALP. be dandled 1.
HIPH. shut 1.
HITHPALP. cry out 1
delight self 2.

SHAAB שאב
draw [water] 13.
Partic. drawer 2
woman to draw 1.

SHAAG שאג
roar 21.
Adv. inf. mightily 1.

SHAAH [1] שאה
be wasted 1.
NIPH. be desolate 1
make a rushing 1
rush 1.
HIPH. lay waste 2.
HITHP. *pt.* wondering 1.

SHAAH [2] שעה
be dim 1
depart 1
have respect 3
look 4
look away 1
regard 1
turn 1.
HIPH. spare 1.
HITHP. be dismayed 1.

SHAAH שָׁעָה *f.*
hour 5.

SHAAL שאל
ask 87
ask counsel 8
ask on 1
beg 1
be lent 1
borrow 6
consult 2
demand 4
desire 9
enquire 22
lay to charge 1
pray 1
request 3
require 7
wish 1.
Inf. wishing 1.
Adv. inf. straitly 1
surely 1.
NIPH. ask leave 2
obtain leave 1.
Adv. inf. earnestly 2.
PIEL ask counsel 1
beg 1.
HIPH. lend 1.
†KAL greet (*with* le-shalom) 1; salute (*with* le-shalom) 5. *See* qashah.

SHAAN [1] שאן
PILEL be at ease 2
be quiet 2
rest 1.

SHAAN [2] שען
NIPH. lean 9
lie 1
rely 4
rest 1
rest on 1
rest selves 1
stay 5.

SHAANAN שַׁאֲנָן
quiet 2
that is at ease 6
tumult 2.

SHAAPH שאף
desire 1
devour 1
earnestly desire 1
haste 1
pant 2
snuff up 2
swallow up 6.

SHAAR [1] שאר
remain 1.
NIPH. be left 43
remain 45.
Partic. remnant 4
the rest 2.
HIPH. leave 33
reserve 1
*be left 1.
†let escape (*with* palit) 1; let remain (*with* sarid) 1.

SHAAR [2] שער
think 1.

SHAAR [3] שַׁעַר
†*See* meah.

SHAAR [4] שַׁעַר
city 3
door 2
gate 361
port 2.
†every gate (shaar shaar) 3, porters (lash-shaar) 1.

SHAARAH שַׁאֲרָה *f.*
near kinswoman 1.

SHAARUR שַׁעֲרוּר
horrible thing 1.

SHAARURI שַׁעֲרוּרִי
horrible thing 2.

SHAASHUIM שַׁעֲשֻׁעִים *pl.*
delight 7
*pleasant 2.

SHAATNEZ שַׁעַטְנֵז
garment of divers sorts 1
linen and woollen 1.

SHAAVAH שאוה
[V.L. *for* shoah].

SHABA שבע
Pass. pt. sworn 1.
NIPH. swear 154.
HIPH. adjure 3
cause to swear 2
charge 5
charge by an oath 1
charge with an oath 1
make to swear 10
swear (*trans.*) 2
take an oath of 4.
Adv. inf. straitly 2.

SHABACH שבח
PIEL commend 1
keep in 1
praise 5
still 1.
HIPH. still 1.
HITHP. glory 1
triumph 1.

SHABAH שבה
bring away captive 1
carry away 2
carry away [captives] 1
carry away captive 12
carry captive 4
lead away captive 1
lead captive 3
take [captive] 1
take [prisoners] 1
take away 1
take captive 7.
Pass. pt. captive 2.
NIPH. be carried away captive 1
be carried captives 3
be driven away 1
be taken captive 3.
†*Kal partic.* they (*lit.* their captors) 2.

SHABAR [1] שבר
break 46
break up 1
crush 1
destroy 2
quench 1
tear 2.
NIPH. be broken 45
be broken off 1
be destroyed 7
be hurt 2
break 2.
PIEL break 27
break down 4
break in pieces 5.
Adv. inf. quite 1.
HIPH. bring to the birth 1.
HOPH. be hurt 1.
†*Niph. partic.* broken-hearted (*with* leb) 1.

SHABAR [2] שבר
buy 14
sell 1.
HIPH. sell 5.

SHABATH שבת
cease 14
celebrate 1
keep 1
keep sabbath 1
rest 10.
NIPH. cease 4.
HIPH. cause to cease 18
cause to fail 1
leave 1
let cease 1
make to cease 10
make to fail 1
make to rest 1
put away 2
put down 1
rid 1
still 1
suffer to be lacking 1
take away 1.

SHABATS [1] שבץ
PIEL embroider 1.
PUAL be set 1.

SHABATS [2] שָׁבָץ
anguish 1.

SHABBATH שַׁבָּת *c.*
sabbath 110
*another 1.

SHABBATHON שַׁבָּתוֹן
rest 8
sabbath 3.

SHABIB שְׁבִיב
spark 1.

SHABLUL שַׁבְּלוּל
snail 1.

SHABUA שָׁבוּעַ *c.*
seven (*pl.*) 1
week 19.

SHACH שַׁח
†humble (*with* enayim) 1.

SHACHACH שחח
be bowed down 3
be brought low 1
bow 2
bow down 1
couch 1
humble self 1
stoop 1.
Inf. bending 1.
NIPH. be brought down 1
be brought low 1
be low 1
bow down 1.
HIPH. bring down 2.
HITHP. be cast down 4
reverence 1.

SHACHAD שחד
give reward 1
hire 1.

SHACHAH שחה
bow down 1.
HIPH. make to stoop 1.
HITHPAL. bow down 8
bow down selves 8
bow selves 35
crouch 1
do obeisance 5
do reverence 5
fall down 3
fall flat 1
humbly beseech 1
make obeisance 4
worship 99.

SHACHAL שַׁחַל
fierce lion 3
lion 4.

SHACHAPH שַׁחַף
cuckoo 2.

SHACHAQ [1] שחק
beat 3
wear 1.

SHACHAQ [2] שַׁחַק
cloud 11
heaven 2
sky 7
small dust 1.

SHACHAR [1] שחר
be black 1.

SHACHAR [2] שחר
diligently seek 1.
PIEL diligently seek 1
enquire early 1
rise betimes 1
seek betimes 1
seek early 4
seek in the morning 1.
†chasten betimes (*with* musar) 1.

SHACHAR [3] שַׁחַר
day 6
dayspring 1
light 1
morning 12
*rise 1.
Accus. early 2.

SHACHARUTH שַׁחֲרוּת *f.*
youth 1.

SHACHAT שחט
kill 40
make slaughter 1
offer 1
slay 36.
Pass. pt. beaten 5
shot out 1.
NIPH. be killed 2
be slain 1.

SHACHATH [1] שחת
NIPH. be corrupt 3
be corrupted 1
be marred 2.
PIEL cast off 1
corrupt 6
destroy 27
destroy self 1
lose 1
mar 1
perish 1
spill 1.
HIPH. batter 1
be corrupt 5
be corrupted 1
corrupt 6
destroy 70
do corruptly 1
mar 4
waste 1.
Partic. corrupter 2
destroyer 3
spoiler 2
waster 2.
Inf. destruction 1.
Adv. inf. utterly 1.
HOPH. *pt.* corrupt 1
corrupt thing 1.
†*See* ish.[1]

SHACHATH [2] שַׁחַת *f.*
corruption 4
destruction 2
ditch 2
grave 1
pit 14.

SHACHATS שַׁחַץ
pride 1
*lion 1.

SHACHEPHETH שַׁחֶפֶת *f.*
consumption 2.

SHACHIS שָׁחִיס
that which springeth of the same 1.

SHACHOR שָׁחֹר
black 6.

SHAD שַׁד
breast 18
pap 1
teat 1.

SHADAD שדד
be destroyed 1
be spoiled 2
destroy 1
oppress 1
spoil 10.
Partic. destroyer 1
robber 2
spoiler 11.
Adv. inf. utterly 1.
NIPH. be spoiled 1.
PIEL spoil 1
waste 1.
PUAL be laid waste 5
be spoiled 13
be wasted 2.
POEL spoil 1.
HOPH. be spoiled 2.

SHADAPH שדף
Pass. pt. blasted 3.

SHADDAI שַׁדַּי
Almighty 48.

SHAGA שגע
PUAL *pt.* mad 4
madman 1.
HITHP. be mad 1
play the mad man 1.

SHAGACH שגח
HIPH. look 2
look narrowly 1.

SHAGAG שגג
err 1
go astray 1
sin ignorantly 1.
Partic. deceived 1.

SHAGAH שגה
be deceived 1
be ravished 2
err 11
go astray 1
sin through ignorance 1
wander 1.
HIPH. cause to go astray 1
let wander 1
make to wander 1.
Partic. deceiver 1.

SHAGAL שגל (V.L. *for* SHAKAB)
lie with 1.
NIPH. be ravished 2.
PUAL be lien with 1.

SHAI שַׁי
present 3.

* Inexact translations, *e.g.*, of a noun by a verb or adjective, of an active by a passive.
† Cases where two or more words in the original are translated by one word or by a phrase.

SHAKAB שׁכב
be laid down 5
lay self down 7
lie 98
lie down 30
lie down to sleep 1
lie still 1
lie with (V.L.) 2
lodge 1
sleep 48
take rest 3.
Adv. inf. at all 1.
NIPH. be ravished (V.L.) 2.
PUAL be lien with (V.L.) 1.
HIPH. lay 5
make to lie down 1
stay 1.
Inf. casting down 1.
HOPH. be laid 3.
†KAL overlay (*with* al[2]) 1.

SHAKACH שׁכח
forget 85.
Adv. inf. at all 1.
NIPH. be forgotten 13.
PIEL cause to be forgotten 1.
HIPH. cause to forget 1.
HITHP. be forgotten 1.

SHAKAH שׁכה
HIPH. *pt.* in the morning 1.

SHAKAK שׁכך
asswage 1
be appeased 1
be pacified 1
set 1.
HIPH. make to cease 1.

SHAKAM שׁכם
HIPH. arise early 8
be risen early 1
be up early 1
get self early 1
get up early 2
rise early 10
rise up betimes 1
rise up early 23.
Partic. early 3.
Inf. morning 1
rising early 6
rising up betimes 1
rising up early 6.

SHAKAN = **SHAKEN.**

SHAKAR שׁכר
be drunken 7
be filled with drink 1
be merry 1
drink abundantly 1.
PIEL make drunk 2
make drunken 2.
HIPH. make drunk 2
make drunken 2.
HITHP. be drunken 1.

SHAKEACH שָׁכֵחַ
that forget 2.

SHAKEN[1] שָׁכֵן (שָׁכַן)
abide 8
be dwelt in 2
be inhabited 1
continue 1
dwell 83
dwell in 1
have habitation 1
inhabit 3
remain 4
rest 3.
Partic. dweller 1
inhabitant 1.
PIEL cause to dwell 3
make to dwell 1
place 6
set 2.
HIPH. cause to remain 1
dwell 1
lay 1
make to dwell 1
place 1
set up 1.

SHAKEN[2] שָׁכֵן
inhabitant 2
neighbour 17
nigh 1.

SHAKKUL שַׁכּוּל
barren 2
bereaved of children 1
bereaved of whelps 1
robbed of whelps 2.

SHAKOL שָׁכֹל
be bereaved 2
be childless 1
be deprived 1
lose children 1.
PIEL bereave 7
bereave of children 1
cast calf 1
cast fruit 1
cast young 2
destroy 1
make childless 1
rob of children 1
spoil 1.
Partic. barren 2.
HIPH. *pt.* miscarrying 1.

SHAL שַׁל
error 1.

SHALAB שׁלב
PUAL *pt.* equally distant 1
set in order 1.

SHALACH שׁלח
appoint 1
give 1
lay 13
let go 1
let loose 1
put (forth, in, out) 37
send (again, away, forth, out) 493
shoot out 1
stretch (forth, out) 13.
Adv. inf. earnestly 1.
NIPH. be sent 1.
PIEL bring 1
bring on the way 1
cast 5
cast away 1
cast out 6
conduct 1
give up 1
lay 1
let depart 2
let down 2
let go 74
let go away 2
let loose 2
push away 1
put (away, in, out) 11
reach forth 1
send (away, forth, out) 137
set 5
shoot (forth) 4
sow 3
spread out 1
suffer to grow long 1.
Adv. inf. any wise 1.
PUAL be cast 1
be put away 1
be sent 4
be sent away 1.
Partic. cast out 1
forsaken 1
left 1.
HIPH. send 5.

SHALAG שׁלג
HIPH. be as snow 1.

SHALAH[1] שָׁלָה (שָׁלוּ)
be happy 1
be in safety 1
prosper 3.

SHALAH[2] שׁלה
take away 1.
NIPH. be negligent 1.
HIPH. deceive 1.

SHALAK[1] שׁלך
HIPH. adventure 1
cast 72
cast [lots] 2
cast away 10
cast down 9
cast forth 4
cast off 2
cast out 9
hurl 1
pluck 1
throw 1.
HOPH. be cast 4
be cast down 2
be cast out 4
be thrown 1.
Partic. cast 2.

SHALAK[2] שָׁלָךְ
cormorant 2.

SHALAL[1] שׁלל
let fall 1
make a spoil 1
spoil 6
take [spoil] 5.
Adv. inf. of purpose 1.
HITHPO. be spoiled 1
make self a prey 1.

SHALAL[2] שָׁלָל
prey 10
spoil 63.

SHALAM שׁלם
be at peace 1
be at peace with 1
be ended 2
be finished 2
prosper 1.
Pass. pt. peaceable 1.
PIEL finish 1
give again 1
make amends 1
make good 6
make prosperous 1
make restitution 6
pay 20
pay again 1
perform 3
recompense 9
render 9
repay 6
requite 5
restore 8
reward 9
*be repayed 2.
Adv. inf. full 1
surely 4.
PUAL be performed 1
be recompensed 2
be rewarded 1.
Partic. that is perfect 1.
HIPH. make an end 2
make peace 7
make to be at peace 1
perform 3.
HOPH. be at peace 1.

SHALANAN שַׁלְאֲנָן
being at ease 1.

SHALAPH שׁלף
draw 17
draw off 1
grow up 1
pluck off 1
*be drawn 1.
Pass. pt. drawn 4.

SHALASH שׁלשׁ
PIEL do the third time 2
divide into three parts 1
stay three days 1.
PUAL *pt.* three 1
threefold 1
three years old 3.

SHALAT שׁלט
bear rule 1
have power 1
have rule 2
rule 1.
HIPH. have dominion 1
give power 2.

SHALAV = **SHALAH[1].**

SHALEM שָׁלֵם
full 2
just 1
made ready 1
peaceable 1
perfect 16
perfected 1
quiet 1
whole 4.

SHALEV שָׁלֵו (שָׁלֵיו)
at ease 1
being at ease 1
in prosperity 1
peaceable 1
quiet 1
quietness 1
wealthy 1.
†who prosper (ve-shalev) 1.

SHALHEBETH שַׁלְהֶבֶת *f.*
flame 2
*flaming 1.

SHALISH שָׁלִישׁ
captain 11
excellent thing 1
great lord 1
great measure 1
instrument of musick 1
lord 3
measure 2
prince 1.

SHALLEKETH שַׁלֶּכֶת *f.*
*cast 1.

SHALLETETH שַׁלֶּטֶת
imperious 1.

SHALLIT שַׁלִּיט
governor 1
mighty 1
ruler 1
that hath power 1.

SHALLIT שַׁלִּיט
captain 1
lawful 1
ruler 2.
*rule (*vb.*) 6.

SHALMONIM שַׁלְמֹנִים *pl.*
rewards 1.

SHALOM שָׁלוֹם
favour 1
good health 1
health 1
peace 172
prosperity 4
rest 1
welfare 4
*all is well 4
*familiar 1
*how . . . did 1
*peaceable 2
*prosperous 1
*safe 1
*salute 1
*well 8
*whether it be well with 1
*[whether it be] well with 1.
Accus. peaceably 6
safely 1.
Plur. such as be at peace 1
welfare 1
*wholly 1.
†be safe (*with* le) 2; peaceably (be-shalom) 1; perfect peace (shalom shalom). Le-shalom: how . . . did 2 how . . . fare 1, how . . . prospered 1, peaceably 2. *See* anashim, enosh, shaal.

SHALOSH שָׁלוֹשׁ
third 9
three 390.
†fork (*with* qilleshon) 1; thirteen (*with* asar) 13; thirteenth (*with* asar) 11; thrice (*with* paam[2]) 4. *See* paam[2].

SHALU שָׁלוּ *f.*
error 1
fail 1
thing amiss 1
*that ye fail not 1.

SHALVAH שַׁלְוָה *f.*
abundance 1
peace 1
prosperity 3
quietness 1.
†peaceably (be-shalvah) 2.

SHAM שָׁם
in it
there
therein
thither, etc.
†Mish-sham: thence, thereof, thereout.

SHAMA שָׁמַע (שָׁמַע)
be content 1
be obedient 5
consent 1
consider 1
discern 2
give ear 1
hear 730
hearken 196
hear tell 1
listen 1
obey 81
perceive 1
regard 1
understand 8.
Partic. hearing 1
obedient 1
understanding 1
witness 1
*whosoever 2.
Adv. inf. attentively 1
carefully 1
certainly 1
diligently 8
indeed 3
surely 2.
NIPH. be heard 36
be obedient 1
be perceived 1
be published 1
be reported 2
obey 1.
PIEL call together 1
gather together 1.
HIPH. call together 2
cause to be heard 6
cause to hear 5
declare 3
hear 2
let be heard 1
let hear 1
make [noise] 1
make a noise 1
make a proclamation 1
make a sound 2
make to be heard 3
make to hear 4
proclaim 1
publish 16
shew 6
shew forth 7
sound 2
tell 4
*sing loud 1.
†*See* ozen.

SHAMAD שׁמד
NIPH. be destroyed 19
be overthrown 1
perish 1.
Adv. inf. utterly 1.
HIPH. bring to nought 1
destroy 66
pluck down 1.
Inf. destruction 1.
Adv. inf. utterly 1.

SHAMAN שׁמן
be waxen fat 2
wax fat 1.
HIPH. become fat 1
make fat 1.

SHAMAR שׁמר
beware 1
keep 284
look narrowly 1
mark 8
observe 45
preserve 19
regard 5
reserve 1
save 1
spy 1
take heed 12
wait for 7
watch 4
Partic. keeper 26
they that lay wait for 1
they that watch 2
watch 1
watchman 8.
Pass. pt. sure 1.
Adv. inf. diligently 2.
NIPH. beware 8
be circumspect 1
be preserved 2
keep selves 2
save self 1
take heed 21
take heed to self 2.
PIEL observe 1.
HITHP. be kept 1
keep self 2.

SHAMAT שׁמט
discontinue 1
let rest 1
release 1
shake 1
stumble 1
throw down 1.
NIPH. be overthrown 1.
HIPH. release 1.

SHAMAYIM שָׁמַיִם
air 21
heaven 398.
†*See* habar.

SHAMEA = **SHAMA.**

SHAMEM[1] שׁמם
be an astonishment 1
be astonied 1
be astonished 11
be desolate 6
be laid desolate 1
destroy 1
make desolate 2.
Partic. desolate 7
desolate places 1
desolation 5.
NIPH. be astonied 1
be astonished 1
be desolate 14
be destitute 1
be laid desolate 1
be made desolate 1
lie waste 1.
Partic. desolate 3
waste 1.
POL. make desolate 2.
Partic. astonied 2.
HIPH. bring into desolation 1
bring unto desolation 1
destroy 1
lay waste 2
make 1
make amazed 1
make astonished 1
make desolate 7
make waste 1.
HOPH. be astonished 1
lie desolate 4.
HITHPOL. be astonished 1
be desolate 1
destroy self 1
wonder 2.

SHAMEM[2] שָׁמֵם
desolate 2.

SHAMEN שָׁמֵן
fat 8
lusty 1
plenteous 1.

SHAMIR שָׁמִיר
adamant 1
adamant stone 1
briers 8
diamond 1.

SHAMMAH שַׁמָּה *f.*
astonishment 13
desolation 12
wonderful thing 1
*desolate 10
*waste 3.

SHANA שְׁנָא
be changed 1.
PIEL change 1.
PUAL be changed 1.

SHANAH[1] שׁנה
be diverse 2
be given to change 1
do again 1
do the second time 1
repeat 1
return 1
speak again 1
strike again 1
*the 2nd time 1

* Inexact translations, *e.g.*, of a noun by a verb or adjective, of an active by a passive.
† Cases where two or more words in the original are translated by one word or by a phrase.

NIPH. be doubled 1.
PIEL alter 1
change 5
pervert 1
prefer 1.
HITHP. disguise self 1.

SHANAH [2] שָׁנָה *f.*
year 799
*yearly 3.
†yearly (sh. be-sh. 1, bash-sh. 1, be-kol-sh. 1) 3.
See yom.

SHANAN שנן
sharpen 1
whet 2.
Partic. sharp 4.
PIEL teach diligently 1.
HITHP. be pricked 1.

SHANAS שנס
PIEL gird up 1.

SHANI שָׁנִי
crimson 1
scarlet 5
scarlet thread 3.
†scarlet (*with* tolaath) 6.
See tolaath.

SHAON שָׁאוֹן
noise 8
pomp 1
rushing 3
tumult 4
*horrible 1
*tumultuous 1.
†*See* ben[2].

SHAPHAH [1] שפה
NIPH. *pt.* high 1.
PUAL stick out 1.

SHAPHAH [2] שְׁפָה *f.*
cheese 1.

SHAPHAK שפך
cast 6
cast up 3
gush out 1
pour 17
pour out 39
shed 33
shed out 1.
Partic. shedder 1.
NIPH. be poured 1
be poured out 5
be shed 2.
PUAL be poured out 1
be shed 1
slip 1.
HITHP. be poured 1
be poured out 2.

SHAPHAL שָׁפָל
base 4
basest 1
humble 4
low 5
lower 4
lowly 1.

SHAPHAN שָׁפָן
coney 4.

SHAPHAR שפר
*goodly 1.
PIEL garnish 1.

SHAPHAT שפט
avenge 2
be a judge 1
defend 2
deliver 1
execute 2
judge 117
rule 1.
Partic. judge 58
*those that condemn 1.
Adv. inf. needs 1.
NIPH. be judged 3
contend 1
execute judgment 1
plead 11
reason 1.
POEL *pt.* judge 1.

SHAPHATH שפת
bring 1
ordain 1
set on 3.

SHAPHEL שפל
be brought down 1
be brought low 1
be humbled 5
be low 1
be made low 2
humble self 1.
HIPH. abase 1
be cast down 1
be put lower 1
bring down 4
bring low 2
cast down 1
debase 1
humble 1
humble selves 1
lay low 4
put down 2.

SHAPHRIR שַׁפְרִיר
royal pavilion 1.

SHAPPIR שַׁפִּיר
fair 2.

SHAQ שָׁק
leg 1.

SHAQA שקע
be drowned 1
be quenched 1
sink 1.
NIPH. be drowned 1.
HIPH. let down 1
make deep 1.

SHAQAD [1] שקד
hasten 1
remain 1
wake 1
watch 7
watch for 1.
Infin. watching 1.

SHAQAD [2] שקד
PUAL *pt.* made after the fashion of almonds 1
made like almonds 3
made like unto almonds 2.

SHAQAH שָׁקָה
PUAL be moistened 1.
HIPH. cause to drink 4
give drink 14
give to drink 12
let drink 1
make drink 9
make to drink 3
water 17.
Partic. butler 9
cupbearer 3.

SHAQAL שקל
be weighed 1
pay 4
receive 1
spend 1
weigh 10.
Partic. receiver 1.
Adv. inf. throughly 1.
NIPH. be weighed 3.

SHAQAPH שקף
NIPH. appear 1
look 7
look down 1
look forth 1.
HIPH. look 4
look down 5
look out 3.

SHAQAQ שקק
have appetite 1
long 1
range 1
run 1
run to and fro 1.
HITHPAL. justle one against another 1.

SHAQAR שקר
deal falsely 1.
PIEL deal falsely 1
fail 1
lie 3.

SHAQAT שקט
be at rest 2
be in quiet 1
be in quietness 1
be in rest 3
be quiet 9
be still 2
have rest 6
rest 2
settle 1
take rest 1.
Partic. at quiet 1
quiet 2.
HIPH. appease 1
be quiet 2
give quietness 1
give rest 1
quiet 1
rest 1.
Inf. idleness 1
quietness 2.

SHAQATS שקץ
PIEL abhor 1
detest 1
have in abomination 2
make abominable 2.
Adv. inf. utterly 1.

SHAQED שָׁקֵד
almond 2
almond tree 2.

SHARAB שָׁרָב
heat 1
parched ground 1.

SHARAH שרה
direct 1.

SHARAQ שרק
hiss 12.

SHARAR שֹׁרֵ־
Partic. enemy 4.

SHARASH שרש
PIEL root out 2.
PUAL be rooted out 1.
POEL take root 1.
POAL take root 1.
HIPH. cause to take root 2
take root 1.

SHARATH שרת
PIEL do service 3
minister (unto) 63
serve 8
wait on 1.
Partic. minister 17
servant 5
servitor 1

SHARATS שרץ
breed abundantly 1
bring forth abundantly 1
bring forth in abundance 1
creep 6
increase abundantly 1
move 1.

SHAREBIT שַׁרְבִיט
sceptre 4.

SHARETH שָׁרֵת
ministry 1
*to minister 1.

SHARIR שָׁרִיר
navel 1.

SHAROTH שָׁרוֹת *f. pl.*
walls 1.

SHARSHAH שַׁרְשָׁה *f.*
chain 1.

SHARSHERAH שַׁרְשְׁרָה *f.*
chain 7.

SHASA שסע
Partic. that cleaveth 1.
Pass. pt. cloven 1.
PIEL cleave 1
rend 2
stay 1.
†KAL *part.* clovenfooted (*with* shesa parsah 2, *with* shesa 1) 3.

SHASAH שסה
rob 1
spoil 7.
Partic. destroyer 1
spoiler 2.
POEL rob 1.

SHASAPH שסף
PIEL hew in pieces 1.

SHASAS שסס
spoil 4.
NIPH. be rifled 1
be spoiled 1.

SHASHA שׁשׁא
PIEL leave but the sixth part 1.

SHASHAH שׁשׁה
PIEL give the sixth part 1.

SHASHAR שָׁשַׁר
vermilion 2.

SHATACH שטח
enlarge 1
spread 1.
Inf. all abroad 1.
PIEL stretch out 1.

SHATAPH שטף
drown 1
flow 1
overflow 19
overwhelm 1
rinse 1
run 1
rush 1
throughly wash away 1.
wash 1
wash away 1
NIPH. be overflown 1
be rinsed 1.
PUAL be rinsed 1.

SHATAR שטר
Partic. officer 23
overseer 1
ruler 1.

SHATH שָׁת
foundation 1
purpose 1.

SHATHAH שתה
banquet 1
drink 210.
Adv. inf. assuredly 1
certainly 1
surely 1.
NIPH. be drunk 1.
†*Kal partic.* drunkard (*with* shekar) 1.

SHATHAL שתל
plant (*vb.*) 10.

SHATHAM שתם
Pass. pt. be open 2.

SHATHAN שתן
HIPH. piss 6.

SHATHAQ שתק
be calm 2
be quiet 1
cease 1.

SHATHATH שתת
be laid 1
set 1.

SHAV שָׁוְא (שׁוּ)
lies 1
vanity 22.
*false 5
*falsely 1
*lying 2
*vain 22.

SHAVA שוע
PIEL cry 17
cry aloud 1
cry out 2
shout 1.

SHAVAH [1] שוה
avail 1
be compared 2
be equal 1
be like 1
countervail 1
profit 1.
Partic. profit 1.
PIEL behave 1
bring forth 1
lay 3
make like 2
make plain 1
reckon 1
set 1.
HIPH. equal 1
make equal 1.
NITHP. be alike 1.

SHAVAH [2] שַׁוְעָה *f.*
cry 11.

SHAYAH שיה
be unmindful 1.

SHAYISH שַׁיִשׁ
marble 1.

SHAYIT שַׁיִת
oar 1.

SHAYITH שַׁיִת
thorn 7.

SHAZAPH שזף
look upon 1
see 2.

SHAZAR שזר
HOPH. *pt.* twined 21.

SHE שֶׁ
that
which, etc.

SHEAGAH שְׁאָגָה *f.*
roaring 7.

SHEAR שְׁאָר
other 1
remnant 11
residue 4
rest 10.

SHEAR שְׁאָר
residue 2
rest 9
whatsoever more 1.

SHEAT שְׁאָט
despite 1
*despiteful 2.

SHEATAH שְׁעָטָה *f.*
stamping 1.

SHEBA שֶׁבַע
seven
seven times
seventh
†seventeen, seventeenth.

SHEBABIM שְׁבָבִים *pl.*
*broken in pieces 1.

SHEBACH שבח
PAEL praise 5.

SHEBAQ שבק
leave 3
let alone 1.
HITHPE. be left 1.

SHEBASH שְׁבַשׁ
HITHPA. be astonied 1.

SHEBAT שְׁבַט *c.*
tribe 1.

SHEBER [1] (שֶׁבֶר) שֵׁבֶר
affliction 2
breach 7
breaking 3
bruise 2
crashing 1
destruction 21
hurt 4
interpretation 1
vexation 1.
†brokenfooted (*with* regel) 1; brokenhanded (*with* yad) 1.

SHEBER [2] שֶׁבֶר
corn 8
victuals 1.

SHEBET שֵׁבֶט *c.*
dart 1
pen 1
rod 34
sceptre 10
staff 2
tribe 141
*correction 1.

SHEBETH. *Inf. of* **YASHAB.**

SHEBI שְׁבִי
captive 10
captivity 35
prisoners 2
that was taken 1
*take away 1.

SHEBIB שְׁבִיב
flame 2.

SHEBII שְׁבִיעִי
seventh (time) 96.

SHEBIL שְׁבִיל
path 2.

SHEBISIM שְׁבִיסִים *pl.*
cauls 1.

SHEBITH שְׁבִית *f.*
captives 1
captivity 5.

SHEBO שְׁבוֹ
agate 2.

SHEBUAH שְׁבוּעָה *f.*
curse 1
oath 28.
†*See* baal[2].

SHEBUTH שְׁבוּת
captivity 26.

SHECHARCHORETH שְׁחַרְחֹרֶת
black 1.

SHECHATH שחת
Partic. corrupt 1
fault 2.

SHECHELETH שְׁחֵלֶת *f.*
onycha 1.

SHECHIN שְׁחִין
boil 11
botch 2.

SHECHIPH שְׂחִיף
cieled with 1.

SHECHITAH שְׁחִיטָה *f.*
killing 1.

SHECHITH שְׁחִית *f.*
destruction 1
pit 1.

SHECHOR שְׁחוֹר
coal 1.

SHECHUTH שְׁחוּת *f.*
pit 1.

SHED שֵׁד
devil 2.

SHEDAR שדר
HITHPAEL labour 1.

SHEDEMAH [1] שְׁדֵמָה *f.*
*blasted 1.

SHEDEMAH [2] שְׁדֵמָה *f.*
field 5.

SHEDEPHAH שְׁדֵפָה *f.*
*blasted 1.

SHEEL שְׁאֵל
ask 3
demand 1
require 2.

SHEELA שְׁאֵלָא *f.*
demand 1.

SHEELAH שְׁאֵלָה *f.*
loan 1
petition 10
request 3.

SHEER שְׁאֵר
body 1
flesh 7
food 1
kin 1
kinsman 1
near kin 1
near kinswoman 2.
†near of kin (*with* basar[2]) 1; nigh of kin (*with* basar[2]) 1.

SHEERITH שְׁאֵרִית *f.*
posterity 1
remainder 2
remnant 43
residue 13
rest 3
that had escaped 1
*to remain 3.
†*See* hayah.

SHEGAGAH שְׁגָגָה *f.*
error 2
ignorance 12.
†be-shegagah: at unawares 2; unawares 2; unwittingly 1.

SHEGAL שֵׁגָל *f.*
queen 2.

SHEGAL שֵׁגַל *f.*
wife 2.

SHEGER שֶׁגֶר
increase 4
that cometh of 1.

SHEGIOTH שְׁגִיאוֹת *f. pl.*
errors 1.

SHEIYYAH שְׁאִיָּה *f.*
destruction 1.

SHEKABAH שְׁכָבָה *f.*
copulation 3
*lie 1
*that lay 1.
†carnally (*with* zera) 2
seed (*with* zera) 2.

SHEKACH שכח
HITHPE. be found 9.
HAPH. find 8
*be found 1.

SHEKAN שכן
have habitation 1.
PAEL cause to dwell 1.

SHEKAR שֵׁכָר
strong drink 21
strong wine 1.
†*See* shathah.

SHEKEM שְׁכֶם
back 2
consent 2
portion 1
shoulder 17.

SHEKEN שֶׁכֶן
habitation 1.

* Inexact translations, *e.g.*, of a noun by a verb or adjective, of an active by a passive.
† Cases where two or more words in the original are translated by one word or by a phrase.

SHEKOBETH שְׁכֹבֶת *f.*
†*See* nathan.

SHEKOL שְׁכוֹל
loss of children 2
spoiling 1.

SHEL שֶׁל
cause 1
sake 1.

SHELABBIM שְׁלַבִּים *pl.*
ledges 3.

SHELACH שְׁלַח
dart 1
plant 1
sword 3
weapon 2
*put off 1.

SHELACH שְׁלַח
put 1
send 12
*be sent 1.

SHELAH שְׁלָה
Partic. at rest 1.

SHELAM[1] שְׁלַם
be finished 1.
HAPH. deliver 1
finish 1.

SHELAM[2] שְׁלָם
peace 4.

SHELEG שֶׁלֶג
snow 19
*snowy 1.

SHELEM שֶׁלֶם
peace offering 84.
†*See* zebach.

SHELET שֶׁלֶט
shield 7.

SHELET שְׁלֵט
bear rule 1
be ruler 2
have power 1
have the mastery 1.
HAPH. make ruler 2.

SHELEV שְׁלֵו
prosperity 1.

SHELEVAH שְׁלֵוָה *f.*
tranquillity 1.

SHELI שֶׁלִי
†quietly (bash-sheli) 1.

SHELISHI שְׁלִישִׁי
third (part, rank, time), 90
three years old 4.

SHELOSHAH = SHALOSH.

SHELOSHIM שְׁלוֹשִׁים *pl.*
thirtieth 9
thirty 166.

SHELUCHOTH שְׁלֻחוֹת *f. pl.*
branches 1.

SHEM שֵׁם
fame 4
name 837
renown 7
report 1
*famous 2.
†be named (*with pron. suf.* 3, *with Niph.* qara[1] 1) 4, *See* anashim, beli, qara[1], sim, tame.

SHEMA שֶׁמַע
bruit 1
fame 5
hearing 1
report 5
speech 1
tidings 2
*hear 1
*loud 1.
†hear (*with* ozen) 1.

SHEMA שְׁמַע
hear 8.
HITHPA. obey 1.

SHEMAD שְׁמַד
HAPH. consume 1.

SHEMAM שְׁמַם
ETHPO. be astonied 1.

SHEMAMAH שְׁמָמָה *f.*
desolation 13
*desolate 40
*utterly 1
*waste 1.
†*See* shimamah.

SHEMARIM שְׁמָרִים *pl.*
dregs 1
lees 2
wines on the lees 2.

SHEMASH שְׁמַשׁ
PAEL minister 1.

SHEMAYIM שְׁמַיִם *du.*
heaven 38.

SHEMEN שֶׁמֶן *c.*
anointing 1
fatness 1
oil 165
ointment 13
olive 4
precious ointment 1
*fat 2
*fruitful 1
*oiled 2.
Plur. fat things 2.
†*See* ets.

SHEMESH שֶׁמֶשׁ *c.*
sun 117
windows (*pl.*) 1.
†*See* mabo, mizrach.

SHEMESH שְׁמֶשׁ *c.*
sun 1.

SHEMETS שֶׁמֶץ
a little 2.

SHEMINI שְׁמִינִי
eighth 27.

SHEMITTAH שְׁמִטָּה *f.*
release 5.

SHEMONEH שְׁמֹנֶה (שְׁמֹנָה)
eight 74
eighth 5.
†*With* asar: eighteen 18, eighteenth 11.

SHEMONIM שְׁמֹנִים *pl.*
eightieth 1
eighty 3
fourscore 33.

SHEMUAH שְׁמוּעָה *f.*
bruit 1
doctrine 1
fame 2
news 1
report 4
rumour 9
tidings 8.
†*See* hayah.

SHEMUROTH שְׁמֻרוֹת *f. pl.*
waking 1.

SHEN שֵׁן *c.*
crag 1
forefront 1
ivory 10
tooth 41
*sharp 2.

SHEN שֵׁן
tooth 3.

SHENA שֵׁנָא *f.*
sleep 1.

SHENA שְׁנָא
be changed 4
be diverse 4.
PAEL be changed 1
be diverse 1
change 1.
ITHPA. be changed 3
change 1.
HAPH. alter 2
be changed 2
change 2.

SHENAH שֵׁנָה *f.*
sleep 21.
†could not sleep (*with* nadad) 1.

SHENAH[1] שְׁנָה *f.*
year 7.

SHENAH[2] שְׁנָה *f.*
sleep 1.

SHENATH שְׁנַת *f.*
sleep 1.

SHENAYIM שְׁנַיִם *du.*
both 72
both parties 1
both twain 1
couple 1
double 5
second 9
twain 6
twice 6
two 528.
†sixscore thousand, twelfth, twelve, twenty thousand.

SHENE (SHENEM) שְׁנֵי, שְׁנֵים **= SHENAYIM.**

SHENHABBIM שֶׁנְהַבִּים *pl.*
ivory 2.

SHENI שֵׁנִי
again 8
another 7
more 3
other 37
second 84
second rank 1
second time 15.
†*See* ammud.

SHENIM שְׁנִים (V.L.) *pl.*
piss 2.

SHENINAH שְׁנִינָה *f.*
byword 3
taunt 1.

SHENITH = SHENI.

SHEOL שְׁאוֹל (שְׁאֹל) *c.*
grave 31
hell 31
pit 3.

SHEPHA שֶׁפַע
abundance 1.

SHEPHAL[1] שְׁפַל
HAPH. abase 1
humble 1
put down 1
subdue 1.

SHEPHAL[2] שְׁפַל
basest 1.

SHEPHAR שְׁפַר
be acceptable 1.
†it pleased (with *qodam*) 1; think good (with *qodam*) 1.

SHEPHARPARA שְׁפַרְפָּרָא
very early in the morning 1.

SHEPHAT שְׁפַט
Partic. magistrate 1.

SHEPHATIM שְׁפָטִים *pl.*
judgments 16.

SHEPHATTAYIM שְׁפַתַּיִם *du.*
hooks 1
pots 1.

SHEPHEK שֶׁפֶךְ
*where . . . are poured out 2.

SHEPHEL שֵׁפֶל
low estate 1
low place 1.

SHEPHELAH שְׁפֵלָה *f.*
low country 2
low plain 2
plain 3
vale 5
valley 7.

SHEPHER שֶׁפֶר
*goodly 1.

SHEPHI שְׁפִי
high place 9.

SHEPHIPHON שְׁפִיפֹן
adder 1.

SHEPHOT שְׁפוֹט
judgment 2.

SHEQAARUROTH שְׁקַעֲרוּרֹת *f. pl.*
hollow strakes 1.

SHEQEL שֶׁקֶל
shekel 88.

SHEQEPH שֶׁקֶף
windows 1.

SHEQER שֶׁקֶר
deceit 1
falsehood 12
liar 1
lie 28
vain thing 1
*deceitful 2
*false 21
*falsely 12
*in vain 1
*lying 22
*vain 1
*without a cause 1
*wrongfully 4.
†falsely (al[2] sheqer) 1; feignedly (be-sheqer) 1; in vain (lash-sheqer) 3. *See* dabar[2].

SHEQET שֶׁקֶט
quietness 1.

SHEQETS שֶׁקֶץ
abomination 9
*abominable 2.

SHEQUPHIM שְׁקֻפִים *pl.*
lights 1
windows 1.

SHERE שְׁרֵא
dissolve 1
dwell 1
loose 1.
PAEL begin 1
dissolve 1.
HITHPA. be loosed 1.

SHEREQAH שְׁרֵקָה *f.*
hissing 7.

SHERETS שֶׁרֶץ
creeping thing 11
moving creature 1
*creep 1
*move 1.

SHERIQOTH שְׁרִיקוֹת *f. pl.*
bleatings 1
hissing 1.

SHERIRUTH שְׁרִירוּת *f.*
imagination 9
lust 1.

SHEROSHI שְׁרֹשִׁי *f.*
banishment 1.

SHEROTH שֵׁרוֹת *f. pl.*
bracelets 5.

SHERUTH שֵׁרוּת (?)
remnant 1.

SHESA שֶׁסַע
cleft 1.
†*See* shasa.

SHESH[1] שֵׁשׁ
blue marble 1
fine linen 37
marble 2
silk 1.

SHESH[2] שֵׁשׁ
six (sixth) 189.
†*With* asar: sixteen (sixteenth) 25.

SHETAR שְׁטַר
side 1

SHETE = SHENAYIM.

SHETEPH שֶׁטֶף (שֵׁטֶף)
flood 4
overflowing of waters 1
*outrageous 1.

SHETH[1] שֵׁאת *f.*
desolation 1

SHETH[2] שֵׁת
buttocks 2.

SHETH שֵׁת (שִׁת)
six 1
sixth 1.

SHETHAH שְׁתָה
drink 5.

SHETHI שְׁתִי
drunkenness 1
warp 9.

SHETHIL שְׁתִיל
plant 1.

SHETHIYYAH שְׁתִיָּה *f.*
drinking 1.

SHETSEPH שֶׁצֶף
a little 1.

SHEVA שֶׁוַע
cry 1.

SHEVAH שְׁוָה
PAEL be made like 1.
HITHPA. be made 1.

SHEZAB שֵׁיזִב
PEEL (PEIL) deliver 9.

SHIBAH[1] **= SHEBA.**

SHIBAH[2] שִׁבָה *f.*
captivity 1.

SHIBAH[3] שִׁיבָה *f.*
*lay 1.

SHIBAH שִׁבְעָה
seven 1
seven times 4.

SHIBANAH שִׁבְעָנָה
seven 1.

SHIBATHAYIM שִׁבְעָתַיִם *du.*
seven times 1
sevenfold 5.

SHIBBARON שִׁבָּרוֹן
breaking 1
destruction 1.

SHIBBOLETH שִׁבֹּלֶת *f.*
branch 1
channel 1
ear 11
ear of corn 3
flood 2
Shibboleth 1.
†waterflood (*with* mayim) 1.

SHIBIM שִׁבְעִים *pl.*
seventy
threescore and ten.
†threescore and fifteen, etc.

SHIBYAH שִׁבְיָה *f.*
captives 8
captivity 1.

SHICHAH שִׁיחָה *f.*
pit 2.

SHIDDAH שִׁדָּה *f.*
musical instruments 1.
Plur. of all sorts 1.

SHIDDAPHON שִׁדָּפוֹן
blasting 5.

SHIGGAON שִׁגָּעוֹן
madness 2.
†furiously (be-shiggaon) 1.

SHIGGAYON שִׁגָּיוֹן
shiggaion 1.
Plur. shigionoth 1.

SHIKKARON שִׁכָּרוֹן
drunkenness 2
*be drunken 1.

SHIKKOR שִׁכּוֹר
drunk 2
drunkard 2
drunken 4
drunken man 1.

SHIKKULIM שִׁכֻּלִים *pl.*
*which [thou] shalt have after [thou] hast lost the other 1.

SHIKMAH שִׁכְמָה *f.*
shoulder blade 1.

SHILLEM שִׁלֵּם
recompence 1.

SHILLESHIM שִׁלֵּשִׁים *pl.*
(of) third generation 5.

SHILLUCHIM שִׁלּוּחִים *pl.*
presents 2
*send back 1.

SHILLUM שִׁלּוּם
recompence 2
reward 1.

SHILLUMAH שִׁלֻּמָה *f.*
reward 1.

SHILSHOM שִׁלְשׁוֹם
†*See* temol.

SHILTON שִׁלְטוֹן
power 2.

SHILTON שִׁלְטוֹן
ruler 2.

SHILYAH שִׁלְיָה *f.*
young one 1.

SHIMAMAH שִׁמָמָה *f.*
desolation 1.
†most desolate (*with* shemamah[2]) 1.

SHIMMAMON שִׁמָּמוֹן
astonishment 2.

SHIMMURIM שִׁמֻּרִים
*to be observed 1
*to be much observed 1.

SHIMTSAH שִׁמְצָה *f.*
shame 1.

SHINAN שִׁנְאָן
angels 1.

SHIPHAH שִׁפְעָה *f.*
abundance 3
company 2
multitude 1.

SHIPHCHAH שִׁפְחָה *f.*
bondmaid 1
bondwoman 3
handmaid 31
maid 12
maiden 3
maidservant 8
servant 1
wench 1
womanservant 1.

SHIPHLAH שִׁפְלָה *f.*
low place 1.

SHIPHLUTH שִׁפְלוּת *f.*
idleness 1.

SHIQMAH שִׁקְמָה *f.*
sycomore 1
sycomore fruit 1
sycomore tree 1.

SHIQQUI שִׁקּוּי
drink 1
marrow 1.

SHIQQUTS שִׁקּוּץ
abominable filth 1
abominable idol 1
abomination 20
detestable thing 5
*detestable 1.

SHIQQUV שִׁקּוּ
drink 1.

SHIR[1] שִׁיר
sing 37.
Partic. singer 5
singing men 3
singing women 3.
Infin. singing 1.
POL. behold
sing 2.
Partic. singer 30
singing men 2
singing women 2.
HOPH. be sung 1.

SHIR[2] שִׁיר
musick 8
singing
song 64
*musical 1
*singer 1.
†*See* dabar[2].

SHIRAH שִׁירָה *f.*
song 12
*sing 1.

SHIRYAH שִׁרְיָה *f.*
habergeon 1.

SHIRYAN שִׁרְיָן
breastplate 1
harness 2.

SHIRYON שִׁרְיוֹן
coat 1
coat [of mail] 1
coat of mail 1
habergeon 2.

SHISHSHAH = SHESH.

SHISHSHI שִׁשִּׁי
sixth 25
sixth part 3.

SHISHSHIM שִׁשִּׁים *pl.*
sixty 16
threescore 46.

* Inexact translations, *e.g.*, of a noun by a verb or adjective, of an active by a passive.
† Cases where two or more words in the original are translated by one word or by a phrase

SHITH [1] שִׁית
apply 1
appoint 3
be stayed 1
bring 1
lay 10
lay up 2
let alone 1
make 19
put 10
put on 1
set 23
shew 1
take 1.
Adv. inf. in array 1.
HOPH. be laid 2.
†consider well (*with* leb) 1; look well (*with* leb) 1; mark well (*with* leb) 1; regard (*with* leb) 2.

SHITH [2] שִׁית
attire 1
garment 1.

SHITH = SHETH.

SHITTAH שִׁטָּה *f.*
shittah tree 1
shittim (*pl.*) 26.

SHITTIN שִׁתִּין *pl.*
threescore 5.

SHO שׁוֹא
destruction 1.

SHOA [1] שׁוֹעַ
bountiful 1
rich 1.

SHOA [2] שׁוֹעַ
crying 1.

SHOAH שׁוֹאָה *f.*
desolate ground 1
desolation 7
destruction 2
storm 1
wasteness 1
*desolate 1
*destroy 1.

SHOAL שֹׁעַל
handful 2
hollow of the hand 1.

SHOAR שֹׁעָר
vile 1.

SHOBAB שׁוֹבָב
backsliding 2
frowardly 1.

SHOBEB שׁוֹבֵב
backsliding 2

SHOBEL שֹׁבֶל
leg 1.

SHOCHAD שֹׁחַד
bribe 3
bribery 1
gift 10
present 2
reward 7.

SHOD [1] שַׁד
breast 3.

SHOD [2] שֹׁד
desolation 2
destruction 7
oppression 1
robbery 2
spoil 4
spoiled 2
spoiler 1
spoiling 3
wasting 2
*spoil (*vb.*) 1.

SHOER שֹׁעֵר
doorkeeper 2
porter 35.

SHOHAM שֹׁהַם
onyx 11.

SHOLAL שׁוֹלָל
spoiled 2
stripped 1.

SHOLTAN שָׁלְטָן
dominion 14.

SHOMA שֹׁמַע
fame 4.

SHOMRAH שָׁמְרָה *f.*
watch 1.

SHOPHAR שׁוֹפָר
cornet 4
trumpet 68.

SHOPHEKAH שָׁפְכָה *f.*
privy member 1.

SHOQ שׁוֹק
hip 1
leg 4
shoulder 13
thigh 1.

SHOQETH שֹׁקֶת *f.*
trough 2.

SHOR [1] שׁוֹר
bull 1
bullock 11
cow 2
ox 61
wall 1.
†*See* par.

SHOR [2] שֹׁר
navel 2.

SHORER שֹׁרֶר
navel 1.

SHORESH שֹׁרֶשׁ
bottom 1
heel 1
root 31
*deep 1

SHORESH שֹׁרֶשׁ
roots 3.

SHOSHAN שׁוֹשַׁן
lily 8.

SHOSHANNAH שׁוֹשַׁנָּה *f.*
lily 4.

SHOT שׁוֹט
scourge 5
whip 6.

SHOTET שֹׁטֵט
scourge 1.

SHUA [1] שׁוּעַ
riches 1.

SHUA [2] שֶׁוַע
*cry (*vb.*) 1.

SHUACH שׁוּחַ
be bowed down 1
be humbled 1
incline 1.

SHUAL שׁוּעָל
fox 7.

SHUB שׁוּב
be come again 5
be converted 1
be gone back 2
be past 1
be restored 2
be restored again 2
be returned 1
be turned 5
be turned away 10
be turned back 5
bring again 10
bring back 3
come again 43
come back 1
convert 1
get self again 1
get self back again 1
go again 13
go back 8
go home 1
go out 1
repent 3
retire 1
return again 369
turn 185
turn again 40
turn away 22
turn back 13
turn backward 1
turn from 1
*again 29
*more 1.
Partic. converts 1.
Pass. pt. averse 1.
Infin. turning 1
Adv. inf. at all 2
certainly 2
in any wise 1
still 1.
POL. bring again 3
pervert 1
restore 1
slide back 1
turn away 1
turn back 2
turn self again 1.
Partic. restorer 1.
Infin. turning away 1.
PIEL be brought back 1.

HIPH. answer 13
bring 9
bring again 66
bring back 15
bring home 1
bring home again 2
call [to mind] 1
carry again 3
carry back 3
cause to answer 1
cause to return 15
cause to turn 1
consider 2
convert 1
deliver 1
deliver again 1
draw [back] 1
draw back 2
fetch home again 1
give 2
give again 2
hinder 2
let 1
make to return 1
make to turn 1
pay 1
pull in again 1
put 1
put again 4
put up again 1
recall 1
recompense 7
recover 6
refresh 1
relieve 3
render 18
render again 1
report 1
requite 5
rescue 1
restore 36
restore again 2
retrieve 1
return 16
reverse 3
reward 3
send back 1
set again 1
take 1
take back 1
take off 1
turn 25
turn again 3
turn away 24
turn back 4
withdraw 4
*be rendered 1.
Partic. restorer 1.
Adv. inf. certainly 1
in any case 2
in any wise 1
needs 1
surely 1.
HOPH. be brought again 3
be recompensed 1
be restored 1.
†KAL cease (*with* min) 1; continually (*adv. inf. with adv. inf. of* halak) 1; return again (*with infin. of* yalak) 1. HIPH. answer (*with* dabar[2] 6, *with* millah 1) 7; answer again (*with* dabar[2]) 1; bethink self (*with* el leb 1, *with* el lebab 1) 2; deny (*with* panim) 1; give answer (*with* dabar[2]) 1; say nay (*with* panim) 3. *See* yatsa.

SHUBAH שׁוּבָה *f.*
returning 1.

SHUCHAH שׁוּחָה *f.*
ditch 1
pit 4.

SHUD שׁוּד
waste 1.

SHUL שׁוּל
hem 6
skirt 4
train 1.

SHULCHAN שֻׁלְחָן
table 70.

SHUM שׁוּם
garlick 1.

SHUM שֻׁם
name 11.
†See *sim.*

SHUPH שׁוּף
break 1
bruise 2
cover 1.

SHUQ [1] שׁוּק
POL. water 1.
HIPH. overflow 2.

SHUQ [2] שׁוּק
street 4.

SHUR [1] שׁוּר
go 1.

SHUR [2] שׁוּר
behold 5
lay wait 1
look 2
observe 2
perceive 1
regard 1
see 4.

SHUR [3] שׁוּר
sing 1.
[*See* shir].

SHUR [4] שׁוּר
enemies (*pl.*) 1.

SHUR [5] שׁוּר
wall 4.

SHUR שׁוּר
wall 3.

SHUSHAN שׁוּשַׁן
lily 1.

SHUT [1] שׁוּט
despise 3.

SHUT [2] שׁוּט
go 1
go about 1
go through 1.
Partic. mariner 1
rower 1.
Infin. going to and fro 2.
POL. run to and fro 1.
HITHPOL. run to and fro 1.

SI שִׂיא
excellency 1.

SIACH [1] שִׂיחַ
commune 1
complain 2
meditate 5
pray 1
speak 4
talk 4
talk with 1.
POL. declare 1
muse 1.

SIACH [2] שִׂיחַ
babbling 1
communication 1
complaint 9
meditation 1
prayer 1.
†be talking (*with* le) 1.

SIACH [3] שִׂיחַ
bush 2
plant 1
shrubs 1.

SIB שִׂיב
be grayheaded 1.
Partic. grayheaded 1.

SIB שִׂיב
Partic. elders 5.

SIBAH שִׂבְעָה *f.*
fulness 1.

SIBBAH סִבָּה *f.*
cause 1.

SIBBOLETH סִבֹּלֶת *f.*
sibboleth 1.

SICHAH שִׂיחָה *f.*
meditation 2
prayer 1.

SID [1] שִׂיד
plaister (*vb.*) 2.

SID [2] שִׂיד
lime 2
plaister 2.

SIG [1] סִיג
dross 8.

SIG [2] שִׂיג
†be pursuing (*with* le) 1.

SIGENIN סִגְנִין *pl.*
governors 5.

SIKKUTH סִכּוּת *f.*
tabernacle 1.

SIKLUTH סִכְלוּת (שִׂכְלוּת) *f.*
folly 5
foolishness 2.

SILLON סִלּוֹן
brier 1.

SIM שִׂים, שׂוּם
appoint 19
bring 5
call [a name] 1
cast in 1
change 1
charge 1
commit 1
consider 2
convey 1
dispose 2
do 2
get 1
give 1
heap up 1
hold 1
impute 1
lay 64
lay down 1
lay up 3
leave 1
make 122
make out 1
ordain 3
order 2
place 2
preserve 1
purpose 1
put (in, on, to) 157
rehearse 1
reward 1
set (on, up, cause to be) 130
shed 1
shew 2
take 3
turn 5
work 1
*be laid 2
*be made 1
*be placed 1
*have 1
*stedfastly 1.
Pass. pt. determined 1.
Adv. inf. any wise 1
wholly 1.
HIPH. regard 1.
HOPH. be set 1.
†KAL barked (*with* li-qetsaphah) 1; care for (*with* leb el) 2; consider (*with* leb 3, *with* lebab 5) 8; disguise (*with* sether) 1; look well (*with* ayin) 2; mark well (*with* leb) 2; name (*with* shem) 1; overturn (*with* avvah) 3; painted (*with* bap-puk) 1; regard (*with* leb) 2; tell (*with* be-phi) 1; tread down (*with* mirmas) 1.

SIM שִׂים, שׂוּם
give 1
lay 1
make 14
set 1.
HITHP. be given 1
be laid 1
be made 1.
†command (with *teem*) 3; name (with *shum*) 1; regard (with *teem*) 2.

SIMCHAH שִׂמְחָה *f.*
gladness 32
joy 44
joyfulness 1
mirth 8
pleasure 1
rejoicing 2
*rejoice 3.
†exceeding (be-simchah 2; *with* gadol 1) 3; exceedingly (be-simchah) 1.

SIMLAH שִׂמְלָה *f.*
apparel 2
cloth 2
clothes 6
clothing 2
garment 6
raiment 11.

SINAH שִׂנְאָה *f.*
hatred 13
*hatefully 1
*to hate 1.
†exceedingly (*with* gadol meod) 1.

SIPHRAH סִפְרָה *f.*
book 1.

SIPPUN סִפֻּן
cieling 1.

SIR [1] סִיר *c.*
caldron 5
pan 1
pot 22.
†washpot (*with* rachats[2]) 2.

SIR [2] סִיר *c.*
thorn 4.
†fishhook (*with* dugah) 1.

SIRPAD סִרְפָּד
brier 1.

SIRYON סִרְיֹן
brigandine 2.

SIS [1] סִיס (V.L.)
crane 2.

SIS [2] שִׂישׂ (שׂוּשׂ)
be glad 4
joy 1
make mirth 1
rejoice 21.
Adv. inf. greatly 1.

SITHRAH סִתְרָה *f.*
protection 1.

SITNAH שִׂטְנָה *f.*
accusation 1.

SOBA שֹׂבַע
fill 2
full 3
fulness 1
satisfying 1
*be sufficed 1.

SOBAH שָׂבְעָה *f.*
enough 2
that which satisfieth 1
*be full 1
*sufficiently 1.
†*See* bilti.

SOBE סֹבֶא
drink 1
wine 1.

SOBEK שׂוֹבֶךְ
thick boughs 1.

SOBEL סֹבֶל
burden 3.

SOCHERAH סֹחֵרָה *f.*
buckler 1.

SOCHERETH סֹחֶרֶת *f.*
black marble 1.

SOD סוֹד
assembly 5
counsel 5
secret 9
secret counsel 1
*inward 1.

SOHAR סֹהַר
†*See* bayith.

SOK [1] סֹךְ (שֹׂךְ)
covert 1
den 1
pavilion 1
tabernacle 2.

SOK [2] שׂוֹךְ
bough 1.

SOKAH שׂוֹכָה *f.*
bough 1.

SOKLETHANU שָׂכְלְתָנוּ *f.*
understanding 3

SOLAM סָלְעָם
bald locust 1.

SOLELAH סֹלְלָה *f.*
bank 3
mount 8.

SOLETH סֹלֶת
†*See* qemach.

SOPH סוֹף
conclusion 1
end 3
hinder part 1.

SOPH סוֹף
end 5.

SORAH שׂוֹרָה *f.*
*principal 1.

SOREQ שֹׂרֵק
choicest vine 1
noble vine 1.

SOREQAH שֹׂרֵקָה *f.*
choice vine 1.

SUACH שׂוּחַ (*cf.* siach)
meditate 1.

SUCHAH סוּחָה *f.*
†torn (kas-suchah) 1.

* Inexact translations, *e.g.*, of a noun by a verb or adjective, of an active by a passive.
† Cases where two or more words in the original are translated by one word or by a phrase.

SUG[1] סוּג (שׂוּג)
be gone back 1
go back 1.
Pass. pt. backslider 1.
NIPH. be driven 1
be turned 4
be turned away 2
be turned back 2
depart away 1
turn away 1
turn back 2
*take 1.
HIPH. remove 6
*take hold 1.
HOPH. be turned away 1.

SUG[2] סוּג
Pass. pt. set about 1.

SUG[3] שׂוּג
PILP. make to grow 1.

SUGAR סוּגַר
ward 1.

SUK[1] סוּךְ
anoint 6
anoint self 2.
Adv. inf. at all 1.
HIPH. anoint 1.

SUK[2] שׂוּךְ
hedge up 1
make an hedge 1.
POLEL fence 1.

SUKKAH[1] סֻכָּה *f.*
booth 11
cottage 1
covert 1
pavilion 5
tabernacle 12
tent 1.

SUKKAH[2] שֻׂכָּה *f.*
barbed iron 1.

SULLAM סֻלָּם
ladder 1.

SUM = SIM.

SUM = SIM.

SUMPONEYAH סוּמְפֹּנְיָה *f.*
dulcimer 2.

SUPH[1] סוּף
be consumed 1
have an end 1
perish 1
*utterly 1.
HIPH. consume 4.

SUPH[2] סוּף
flags 3
weeds 1.
†See yam.

SUPH סוּף
be fulfilled 1.
HAPH. consume 1.

SUPHAH סוּפָה *f.*
storm 3
tempest 1
whirlwind 11.

SUPPONEYAH סוּפֹּנְיָה *f.*
dulcimer 1.

SUR[1] סוּר (*once* שׂוּר)
be departed 4
be gone aside 1
be gone away 1
be past 1
be removed 5
be revolted 1
be taken 1
be taken away 7
be without 1
decline 2
depart 73
depart away 1
depart from 1
eschew 3
go 3
go aside 2
go away 1
rebel 1
turn (aside, away, back, in) *freq.*
*be sour 1.
Imperat. get you 1.
Partic. grievous 1.
Pass. pt. removing to and fro 1.
POL. turn aside 2.
HIPH. bring 1
call back 1
lay away 1
lay by 1
leave undone 1
pluck away 1
put 2
put away 19
put down 1
put off 1
remove 31
take 8
take away 58
take off 6
turn away 2
withdraw 1.
HOPH. be taken away 4
be taken from 1.
†HIPH. behead (*with* rosh) 1.

SUR[2] סוּר
degenerate plant 1.

SUR[3] שׂוּר
have power 1
reign 1.
HIPH. make princes 1.

SUR[4] שׂוּר
cut 1.

SURIM סוּרִים
[*as if partic. pass. of* asar.]
†*See* bayith.

SUS[1] סוּס
horse 133.
†*See* aqeb, rakab.

SUS[2] סוּס
crane 2.

SUSAH סוּסָה *f.*
company of horses 1.

SUT שׂוּט
turn aside 1.

SUTH[1] סוּת
HIPH. entice 1
move 5
persuade 5
provoke 1
remove 1
set on 2
stir up 2
take away 1.

SUTH[2] סוּת
clothes 1.

T

TA תָּא
chamber 2
little chamber 10.

TAA תעע
PILP. *pt.* deceiver 1.
HITHPALP. misuse 1.

TAAB[1] תאב
long (*vb.*) 2.

TAAB[2] תעב (*once* תאב)
NIPH. be abominable 3.
PIEL abhor 14
make to be abhorred 1.
Adv. inf. utterly 1.
HIPH. commit more abominable 1
do abominable 2
do abominably 1.

TAABAH תַּאֲבָה *f.*
longing 1.

TAAH[1] תעה
HIPH. seduce 1.

TAAH[2] תאה
PIEL point out 3.

TAAH[3] תעה
be out of the way 1
err 5
go astray 12
pant 1
wander 7.
NIPH. be deceived 1
stagger 1.
HIPH. cause to err 8
cause to go astray 1
cause to wander 1
dissemble 1
err 1
make to err 3
make to stagger 1
seduce 3.

TAALAH תַּאֲלָה *f.*
curse 1.

TAALULIM תַּעֲלוּלִים *pl.*
babes 1
delusions 1.

TAALUMAH תַּעֲלֻמָה *f.*
secret 2
thing that is hid 1.

TAAM[1] טעם
perceive 1
taste 10.
Adv. inf. but 1.

TAAM[2] טַעַם
advice 1
behaviour 2
decree 1
discretion 1
judgment 1
reason 1
taste 5
understanding 1.

TAAM[3] תאם
Pass. pt. coupled 1
coupled together 1.
HIPH. bear twins 2.

TAAM טְעֵם
account 1
commandment 2
matter 1
*be commanded 1.

TAAN[1] טען
lade 1.

TAAN[2] טען
PUAL. *pt.* thrust through 1.

TAANAH תַּאֲנָה *f.*
occasion 1.

TAANITH תַּעֲנִית *f.*
heaviness 1.

TAANIYYAH תַּאֲנִיָּה *f.*
heaviness 1
mourning 1.

TAANUG תַּעֲנוּג
delight 3
*delicate 1
*pleasant 1.

TAAR[1] תאר
be drawn 5.
PIEL mark out 2.

TAAR[2] תַּעַר
rasor 4
scabbard 1
sheath 6.
†penknife (*with partic. of* saphar) 1. *See* abar.

TAARUBOTH תַּעֲרוּבוֹת
† *See* ben[2].

TAATSUMOTH תַּעֲצֻמוֹת *f. pl.*
power 1.

TAAVAH[1] תַּאֲוָה *f.*
dainty 1
desire 14
lust 1
*exceedingly 1
*greedily 1
*lusting 1
*pleasant 1.

TAAVAH[2] תַּאֲוָה *f.*
utmost bound 1.

TAB טָב
fine 1
good 1.

TABA טבע
be sunk 2
sink 4.
PUAL be drowned 1.
HOPH. be fastened 1
be settled 1
be sunk 1.

TABAATH טַבַּעַת *f.*
ring 45.

TABACH טבח
kill 4
make slaughter 1
slay 2.
Infin. slaughter 3.
†slay (*with* tebech) 1.

TABAL טבל
dip 15
plunge 1.
NIPH. be dipped 1.

TABBACH טַבָּח
cook 2
guard 30.

TABBACH טַבָּח
guard 1.

TABBACHOTH טַבָּחוֹת *f. pl.*
cooks 1.

TABBUR טַבּוּר
middle 1
midst 1.

TABLITH תַּבְלִית *f.*
destruction 1.

TABNITH תַּבְנִית *f.*
figure 1
form 3
likeness 5
pattern 9
similitude 2.

TABUN תָּבוּן
understanding 1.

TACHALUIM תַּחֲלֻאִים *pl.*
diseases 2
sicknesses 1
*grievous 1
*them that are sick 1.

TACHAN טחן
grind 8.

TACHANAH טַחֲנָה *f.*
grinding 1.

TACHANOTH תַּחֲנֹת *f. pl.*
camp 1.

TACHANUNIM תַּחֲנוּנִים *pl.*
intreaties 1
supplications 16.

TACHANUNOTH תַּחֲנוּנוֹת *f. pl.*
supplications 1.

TACHARA תַּחְרָא
habergeon 2.

TACHASH תַּחַשׁ
badger 14
badger's skin 2.

TACHATH תַּחַת
beneath
for
for sake of
in the place of
in the room of
in the stead of
under, etc.
†because (*with* asher) 2; wherefore (*with* meh) 1.
With obj. pron.: flat, in the same place, etc.
Mit-tachath (le-mit-tachath): beneath, from under, under, etc.

TACHBULOTH תַּחְבֻּלוֹת *f. pl.*
counsels 3
good advice 1
wise counsels 2.

TACHMAS תַּחְמָס
nighthawk 2.

TACHTI תַּחְתִּי
low 1
low parts 1
lower 2
lower parts 2
lowest 3
lowest parts 1
nether 3
nether part 6.

TACHTON תַּחְתּוֹן
lower 5
lowest 2
nether 4
nethermost 1.

TAGMUL תַּגְמוּל
benefit 1.

TAHALUKAH תַּהֲלֻכָה *f.*
*go 1.

TAHAR טהר
be clean 25
be cleansed 4
be made clean 1
be pure 2
be purged 2.
PIEL cleanse 21
make clean 1
pronounce clean 10
purge 3
purify 3.
Partic. purifier 1.
PUAL be cleansed 1.
HITHP. be clean 1
be cleansed 12
be made clean 1
be purified 1
cleanse selves 2
make selves clean 1
purify selves 2.

TAHOR טָהוֹר
clean 50
fair 2
pure 41
pureness 1
*he that hath clean 1.

TAHPUKOTH תַּהְפֻּכוֹת *f. pl.*
frowardness 3
froward things 2
perverse things 1
*froward 3
*very froward 1.

TAKAH תכה
PUAL sit down 1.

TAKAN תכן
ponder 2
weigh 1.
NIPH. be equal 8
be weighed 1.
PIEL bear up 1
direct 1
mete 1
weigh 1.
PUAL be told 1.
†be unequal (*with* lo *prefixed*) 2.

TAKLITH תַּכְלִית *f.*
end 2
perfection 2
*perfect 1.

TAKRIK תַּכְרִיךְ
garment 1.

TAL טַל
dew 31.

TAL טַל
dew 5.

TALA[1] טלא
Partic. spotted 6
with divers colours 1
PUAL *pt.* clouted 1.

TALA[2] תלא
be bent 1
hang 1
hang in doubt 1.

TALA[3] תלע
PUAL *pt.* in scarlet 1.

TALAH תלה
be hanged 4
hang 20.
NIPH. be hanged 1
be hanged up 1.
PIEL hang 2.

TALAL[1] טלל
PIEL cover 1.

TALAL[2] תָּלַל
Partic. eminent 1.

TALEH טָלֶה
lamb 2.

TALMID תַּלְמִיד
scholar 1.

TALPIYYOTH תַּלְפִּיּוֹת *f. pl.*
armoury 1.

TALTALLIM תַּלְתַּלִּים *pl.*
bushy 1.

TALTELAH טַלְטֵלָה *f.*
captivity 1.

TALTI תְּלָתִי
third 1.

TALUBOTH תַּלְאוּבֹת *f. pl.*
great drought 1.

TAM תָּם
perfect 9
plain 1
undefiled 2
upright 1.

TAM תַּם
thence 1
there 2
where 1.

TAMAH[1] טמה
NIPH. be defiled 1
be reputed vile 2.

TAMAH[2] תמה
be amazed 1
be astonished 1
marvel 3
wonder 2
*marvellously 1.
HITHP. wonder 1.

TAMAK תמך
hold 4
hold up 2
maintain 1
retain 4
stay 1
stay up 1
take hold 2
uphold 5.
NIPH. be holden 1.

TAMAM תמם
be accomplished 1
be all gone 1
be all here 1
be consumed 20
be ended 4
be finished 3
be perfect 1
be spent 3
be upright 1
be wasted 1
come to an end 1
end 1
fail 2
have done 2
*accomplish 1
*clean 3
*finish 1.
Infin. whole 1.
NIPH. be consumed 4
have an end 1.
HIPH. consume 2
end 1
make an end of 1
make perfect 1
sum 1
*be come to the full 1
*cease 1.
HITHP. show self upright 2.

TAMAN טָמַן
hide 23
lay privily 4.
Pass. pt. in secret 1.
NIPH. hide 1.
HIPH. hide 2.

TAMAR תָּמָר
palm 1
palm tree 11.

TAME[1] טמא
be defiled 8
be made unclean 1
be polluted 2
be unclean 60
defile self 6
take uncleanness 1.
NIPH. be defiled 12
be polluted 3
defile self 1
pollute selves 1.
PIEL defile 31
pollute 5
pronounce unclean 12
*be defiled 1.
Adv. inf. utterly 1.
PUAL be polluted 1.
HITHP. be defiled 2
be polluted 2
be unclean 1
defile selves 8
make selves unclean 2.
HOTHP. be defiled 1.

TAME[2] טָמֵא
defiled 5
polluted 1
unclean 80.
†infamous (*with* shem) 1; set apart for pollution (*with* niddah) 1.

* Inexact translations, *e.g.*, of a noun by a verb or adjective, of an active by a passive.
† Cases where two or more words in the original are translated by one word or by a phrase.

TAMID תָּמִיד
alway (always) 10
continual 26
continually 53
daily 7
ever 3
evermore 1
of continual employment 1
perpetual 2.
†*See* lo.

TAMIM תָּמִים
complete 1
full 1
perfect 14
sincerely 2
sincerity 1
sound 1
undefiled 1
upright 8
uprightly 4
whole 4
without blemish 44
without spot 6.

TAMMIM תַּמִּים *pl.*
coupled together 2.

TAMRUQ תַּמְרוּק
purifying 1
thing for purification 2
*cleanse 1.

TAMRURIM[1] תַּמְרוּרִים *pl.*
*bitter 2
*most bitterly 1.

TAMRURIM[2] תַּמְרוּרִים *pl.*
high heaps 1.

TANAH[1] תנה
hire 1.
HIPH. hire 1.

TANAH[2] תנה
PIEL lament 1
rehearse 1

TANAPH טנף
PIEL defile 1.

TANCHUMIM תַּנְחוּמִים *pl.*
comforts 1
consolations 2.

TANCHUMOTH תַּנְחוּמוֹת *f. pl.*
consolations 2.

TANNIM תַּנִּים
dragon 1
dragons 12
whale 1.

TANNIN תַּנִּין
dragon 8
sea monster 1
serpent 3
whale 2.

TANNOTH תַּנּוֹת *f. pl.*
dragons 1.

TANNUR תַּנּוּר
furnace 4
oven 11.

TAPH טַף
children 9
families 1
little children 3
little ones 25.

TAPHACH טפח
PIEL span 1
swaddle 1

TAPHAL טפל
forge 1
sew up 1
Partic. forger 1.

TAPHAPH[1] טפף
mince 1.

TAPHAPH[2] תפף
play with timbrels 1
POEL taber 1

TAPHAR תפר
sew 2
sew together 1.
PIEL *pt.* women that sew 1.

TAPHAS תפשׂ
catch 3
handle 8
hold 1
lay hold 1
lay hold on 1
take 29
take hold 2.
Pass. pt. laid over 1.
Adv. inf. surely 1.
NIPH. be caught 1
be stopped 1
be surprised 2
be taken 11
*taking 1.
PIEL take hold 1.
†KAL be handled (*with* kaph) 1.

TAPHASH טפשׁ
be fat 1.

TAPHEL תָּפֵל
foolish things 1
unsavoury 1
untempered 5.

TAPPUACH תַּפּוּחַ
apple 3
apple tree 3.

TAQA תקע
blow 46
cast 1
clap 2
fasten 5
pitch [tent] 3
smite 1
sound 2
strike 3
thrust 2.
Partic. *suretiship 1.
NIPH. be blown 2
strike 1.

TAQAN תקן
be made straight 1.
PIEL make straight 1
set in order 1.

TAQAPH תקף
prevail against 3.

TAQOA תָּקוֹעַ
trumpet 1.

TAQQIPH תַּקִּיף
mightier 1

TAQQIPH תַּקִּיף
mighty 2
strong 3.

TARA תָּרַע
porter 1

TARACH טרח
HIPH. weary 1

TARAD טרד
Partic. continual 2

TARAPH[1] טרף
catch 2
prey 1
ravin 4
tear 8
tear in pieces 2.
Adv. inf. surely 1
without doubt 1.
NIPH. be torn in pieces 2.
POAL be rent in pieces 1
be torn in pieces 1.
HIPH. feed 1.

TARAPH[2] טָרָף
pluckt off 1.

TARBITH תַּרְבִּית *f.*
increase 5
unjust gain 1.

TARBUTH תַּרְבּוּת *f.*
increase 1.

TARDEMAH תַּרְדֵּמָה *f.*
deep sleep 7.

TARELAH תַּרְעֵלָה *f.*
astonishment 1
trembling 2.

TARGEM תַּרְגֵּם
Pass. pt. interpreted 1

TARI טְרִי
new 1
putrifying 1.

TARMITH תַּרְמִית *f*
deceit 4
*deceitful 1.

TARSHISH תַּרְשִׁישׁ
beryl 7.

TASHBETS תַּשְׁבֵּץ
broidered 1.

TATUIM תַּעְתֻּעִים *pl.*
errors 2.

TAV תָּו
desire 1
mark 2.

TAVAH טוה
spin 2.

TAVAH תוה
PIEL scrabble 1.
HIPH. limit 1
set [a mark] 1.

TAVEK תָּוֶךְ
half 1
middle 7
midst 208
†midnight (*with* layelah) 1; therein (be-tok *with pron.*) 1; wherein (be-tavek *with* asher) 1; whereinto (el tavek *with* asher) 1. Be-thok: among (amongst) 138, between 3, in 19, through 1, through the midst of 4, with 1, within 19. El-tok: into 1, in the midst among 1. Mittok: out 1, out of 3.

TAYISH תַּיִשׁ
he goat 4.

TAZAZ תזז
HIPH. cut down 1.

TAZNUTH תַּזְנוּת *f.*
fornication 2
whoredom 18.

TEALAH תְּעָלָה *f.*
conduit 4
little river 1
trench 3
watercourse 1.
*healing 1
†be cured (*with* en[1] le) 1.

TEAM טעם
PAEL feed 1
make to eat 1.

TEASHSHUR תְּאַשּׁוּר
box 1
box tree 1.

TEBACH טֶבַח
slaughter 9
*beast 1
*sore 1.
†*See* tabach.

TEBAH תֵּבָה *f.*
ark 28.

TEBALLUL תְּבַלֻּל
blemish 1.

TEBAR תבר
Partic. broken 1.

TEBEL[1] תֵּבֵל *f.*
habitable part 1
world 35.

TEBEL[2] תֶּבֶל
confusion 2

TEBEN תֶּבֶן
chaff 1
straw 15
stubble 1.

TEBUAH תְּבוּאָה *f.*
fruit 13
gain 1
increase 23
revenue 5.

TEBULIM טְבוּלִים *pl.*
dyed attire 1.

TEBUNAH תְּבוּנָה *f.*
discretion 1
reason 1
skilfulness 1
understanding 37
wisdom 1.

TEBUSAH תְּבוּסָה *f.*
destruction 1.

TECHILLAH תְּחִלָּה *f.*
beginning 14
first 5
first time 2
*begin 1.

TECHINNAH תְּחִנָּה *f.*
favour 1
grace 1
supplication 23.

TECHON טְחוֹן
*grind 1.

TECHORIM טְחֹרִים *pl.*
emerods 8.

TECHOTH תְּחוֹת
under 4.

TEDIRA תְּדִירָא *f.*
†continually (*bi-tedira*) 2.

TEEB טאב
be glad 1.

TEEM טְעֵם
commandment 2
decree 13
taste 1
wisdom 1.
†See *beel, sum.*

TEENAH תְּאֵנָה *f.*
fig 15
fig tree 23.

TEHILLAH תְּהִלָּה *f.*
praise 56.

TEHOM תְּהוֹם
deep 20
deep place 1
depth 15.

TEKAKIM תְּכָכִים *pl.*
*deceitful 1.

TEKELETH תְּכֵלֶת *f.*
blue 49.

TEKUNAH[1] תְּכוּנָה *f.*
seat 1.

TEKUNAH[2] תְּכוּנָה *f.*
fashion 1
store 1.

TEL תֵּל
heap 4
strength 1.

TELAAH תְּלָאָה *f.*
travail 1
travel 2
trouble 1
weariness 1

TELAG תְּלַג
snow 1.

TELAIM טְלָאִים *pl.*
lambs 1.

TELAL טלל
HAPH. have shadow 1

TELATH תְּלָת (תְּלָת)
third 3
three 10.

TELATHIN תְּלָתִין *pl.*
thirty 2.

TELEM תֶּלֶם
furrow 4
ridge 1.

TELI תְּלִי
quiver 1.

TELITHAI תְּלִיתָי
third 1.

TELUNNOTH תְּלֻנּוֹת *f. pl.*
murmurings 8.

TEMAH תמה
wonder 3.

TEMAN תֵּימָן *c.*
south 12
south side 2
south wind 1
southward 8.

TEMES תֶּמֶס
*melt 1.

TEMOL תְּמוֹל
yesterday 4.
†*With* shilshom: before 3, beforetime 4, heretofore 6, that time 2, time(s) past 9, *these three days 1.

TEMUNAH תְּמוּנָה *f.*
image 1
likeness 5
similitude 4.

TEMURAH תְּמוּרָה *f.*
change 1
changing 1
exchange 2
recompence 1
restitution 1.

TEMUTHAH תְּמוּתָה *f.*
death 1
*die 1.

TENE טֶנֶא
basket 4.

TENUAH תְּנוּאָה *f.*
breach of promise 1
occasion 1.

TENUBAH תְּנוּבָה *f.*
fruit 3
increase 2.

TENUK תְּנוּךְ
tip 8.

TENUMAH תְּנוּמָה *f.*
slumber 4
slumbering 1.

TENUPHAH תְּנוּפָה *f.*
offering 7
shaking 2
wave offering 14
*be waved 1
*wave 6.

TEO תְּאוֹ
wild ox 1.

TEOMIM תְּאוֹמִים *pl.*
twins 4.

TEPHACH טֶפַח
coping 1
hand breadth 3.

TEPHAR טְפַר
nail 2.

TEPHILLAH תְּפִלָּה *f.*
prayer 76.

TEPHOTSAH תְּפוֹצָה *f.*
dispersion 1.

TEQA תֶּקַע
sound 1.

TEQAL תקל
Partic. Tekel 2.
PEIL be weighed 1.

TEQAN תקן
HOPH. be established 1.

TEQEPH תקף
become strong 1
be hardened 1
be strong 2.
PAEL make firm 1.

TEQOMEM תְּקוֹמֵם
those that rise up against (*pl.*) 1.

TEQOPH תְּקֹף
might 1
strength 1.

TEQUMAH תְּקוּמָה *f.*
power to stand 1.

TEQUPHAH תְּקוּפָה *f.*
circuit 1
end 2
*come about 1

TERA תְּרַע
gate 1
mouth 1.

TERAD טרד
drive 4.

TERAPHIM תְּרָפִים *pl.*
idolatry 1
idols 1
images 7
teraphim 6.

TEREM טֶרֶם
before
ere
not yet, etc.

TEREN תְּרֵין
second 1
two 1.
†twelve (with *asar*) 2.

TEREPH טֶרֶף
leaf 1
meat 3
prey 18
spoil 1.

TEREPHAH טְרֵפָה *f.*
ravin 1
that is torn 1
that which is torn in pieces 1
that which was (is) torn of (with) beasts 7.

TERUAH תְּרוּעָה *f.*
alarm 6
blowing of trumpets 1
blowing the trumpets 1
joy 2
joyful sound 1
jubilee 1
loud noise 1
rejoicing 1
shout 10
shouting 8
*high sounding 1
*sounding 1
*to blow 1
†*See* rum[1].

TERUMAH תְּרוּמָה *f.*
gift 1
heave offering 24
oblation 18
offering 28
*heave (*adj.*) 4
*that is offered 1.

TERUMIYYAH תְּרוּמִיָּה *f.*
oblation 1.

TERUPHAH תְּרוּפָה *f.*
medicine 1.

TESHA תֵּשַׁע (תִּשְׁעָה)
nine 44
ninth 6.
†*With* asar *or* esreh: nineteen 3, nineteenth 4.

TESHII תְּשִׁיעִי
ninth 17.

TESHUAH תְּשׁוּעָה *f.*
deliverance 5
help 5
safety 4
salvation 17
victory 2.

TESHUBAH תְּשׁוּבָה *f*
answer 2
return 3
*be expired 3.

TESHUOTH תְּשֻׁאוֹת *f. pl.*
crying 1
noise 1
shoutings 1
stirs 1.

TESHUQAH תְּשׁוּקָה *f.*
desire 3.

TESHURAH תְּשׁוּרָה *f.*
present 1.

TESUMETH תְּשׂוּמֶת *f.*
†fellowship (*with* yad) 1.

TEUDAH תְּעוּדָה *f.*
testimony 3.

TEUNIM תְּאֻנִים *pl.*
lies 1.

TEVAH תוה
be astonied 1.

TEVATH טְוָת *f.*
fasting 1.

THOK = TAVEK.

TIACH טִיחַ
daubing 1.

TIBCHAH טִבְחָה *f.*
flesh 1
slaughter 2.

TIDHAR תִּדְהָר
pine 1
pine tree 1

TIGRAH תִּגְרָה *f.*
blow 1.

TIKLAH תִּכְלָה *f.*
perfection 1

TIKON תִּיכוֹן
middle 8
middlemost 2
midst 1.

TILBOSHETH תִּלְבֹּשֶׁת *f.*
clothing 1.

TIMMAHON תִּמָּהוֹן
astonishment 2.

TIMMORAH תִּמֹּרָה *f.*
palm tree 19.

TIMROTH תִּימְרוֹת *f. pl.*
pillars 2.

TIN טִין
*miry 2.

TINSHEMETH תִּנְשֶׁמֶת *f.*
mole 1
swan 2.

TINYAN תִּנְיָן
second 1

TINYANUTH תִּנְיָנוּת
again 1

* Inexact translations, *e.g.*, of a noun by a verb or adjective, of an active by a passive.
† Cases where two or more words in the original are translated by one word or by a phrase

TIPHARAH (TIPHERETH) תִּפְאָרָה (תִּפְאֶרֶת) *f.*
beauty 10
bravery 1
glory 22
honour 4
*beautiful 6
*comely 1
*excellent 1
*fair 2
*glorious 3.

TIPHLAH תִּפְלָה *f.*
folly 2
*foolishly 1.

TIPHLETSETH תִּפְלֶצֶת *f.*
terribleness 1.

TIPHSAR טִפְסַר
captain 2.

TIPHTAYE תִּפְתָּיֵא *pl.*
sheriffs 2.

TIPPUCHIM טִפֻּחִים *pl.*
*span long 1.

TIQVAH תִּקְוָה *f.*
expectation 7
hope 23
line 2
thing that I long for 1
*expected 1.

TIRAH טִירָה *f.*
castle 3
goodly castle 1
habitation 1
palace 2
row 1.

TIROSH תִּירוֹשׁ
new wine 11
sweet wine 1
wine 26.

TIRZAH תִּרְזָה *f.*
cypress 1.

TISHAH = **TESHA.**

TISHIM תִּשְׁעִים *pl.*
ninety 20.

TIT טִיט
clay 3
dirt 2
mire 8.

TO תְּאוֹ
wild bull 1.

TOAH תּוֹעָה *f.*
error 1.
†*See* asah.

TOANAH תֹּאֲנָה *f.*
occasion 1.

TOAPHOTH תּוֹעָפוֹת *f. pl.*
plenty 1
strength 2.

TOAR תֹּאַר
countenance 1
form 3
visage 1
*comely 1
*goodly 1.
†resemble (ke-toar) 1. *See* ra, tob, yapheh.

TOB [1] טוֹב
be better 1
be good 3
be goodly 1
be well 5
go well 1
seem good 2.
HIPH. cheer 1
do [goodness] 1
do better 1
do good 4
do well 4
make goodly 1
play well on 1.
Partic. well 1.
†KAL be in favour (*with* be-ene) 1; favour (*with* be-ene) 1; it liketh (*with* be-ene 1, *with* le 1) 2; please (*with* al[2] 8, *with* be-ene 4, *with* li-phene 1) 13.

TOB [2] טוֹב
best 8
better 71
bountiful 1
cheerful 1
fair 8
fine 2
glad 2
good 356
goodly 11
graciously 1
joyful 1
kind 1
kindly 1
loving 1
merry 7
pleasant 2
pleasing 1
precious 3
ready 1
sweet 1
well 20.
As noun ease 1
fair word 1
good deed 1
goodness 16
goods 2
kindness 1
pleasure 2
prosperity 6
wealth 3
welfare 1.
†beautiful (*with* mareh) 2; fair (*with* mareh) 2; well-favoured (*with* chen 1, *with* mareh[1]) 2; goodly (*with* toar) 1. *See* kethen, tsahab.

TOCHELETH תּוֹחֶלֶת *f.*
hope 6.

TODAH תּוֹדָה *f.*
company of them that gave thanks 3
confession 2
praise 4
sacrifice of praise 2
thank offering 3
thanksgiving 18.

TOEBAH תּוֹעֵבָה *f.*
abominable thing 2
abomination 111
*abominable 1.

TOHAR [1] טֹהַר
clearness 1
purifying 2.

TOHAR [2] טְהָר
glory 1.

TOHOLAH תָּהֳלָה *f.*
folly 1.

TOHORAH טָהֳרָה *f.*
cleansing 7
purification 2
purifying 3
*be cleansed 1.

TOHU תֹּהוּ
confusion 3
empty place 1
nothing 1
nought 1
thing of nought 1
vanity 4
waste 1
wilderness 2
*vain 4
*without form 2.

TOK [1] = **TAVEK.**

TOK [2] תֹּךְ
deceit 2
fraud 1.

TOKACHATH תּוֹכַחַת *f.*
argument 1
correction 1
reasoning 1
rebuke 3
reproof 16
*be chastened 1
*be reproved 1.
†*See* ish.

TOKECHAH תּוֹכֵחָה *f.*
punishment 1
rebuke 4.

TOKEN תֹּכֶן
measure 1
tale 1.

TOKNITH תָּכְנִית *f.*
pattern 1
sum 1.

TOLA תּוֹלָע
crimson 1
scarlet 1
worm 1.

TOLAATH תּוֹלַעַת *f.*
worm 4
worms 2.
†scarlet (*with* shani) 27. *See* shani.

TOLAL תּוֹלָל
that wasted 1.

TOLEAH תּוֹלֵעָה *f.*
worm 1
worms 1.

TOLEDOTH תּוֹלְדוֹת *f. pl.*
birth 1
generations 38.

TOM תֹּם
integrity 11
perfection 1
simplicity 1
strength 1
uprightness 2
*him that is upright 1
*perfect 1
*upright 1
*uprightly 1.
†at a venture (le-tom *with pron. suff.*) 12, uprightly (bat-tom) 1.

TOMER תֹּמֶר
palm tree 2.

TOPH תֹּף
tabret 8
timbrel 9.

TOPHACH טֹפַח
handbreadth 4
*hand broad 1.

TOPHETH תֹּפֶת
tabret 1.

TOQEPH תֹּקֶף
authority 1
power 1
strength 1.

TOR [1] תּוֹר
turtle 5
turtle dove 9.

TOR [2] תּוֹר
border 1
row 1
turn 2.

TOR [3] תּוֹר
estate 1.

TOR תּוֹר
bullock 3
ox 4.

TORACH טֹרַח
cumbrance 1
trouble 1.

TORAH תּוֹרָה *f.*
law 216
manner 1.

TOREN תֹּרֶן
beacon 1
mast 2.

TORMAH תַּרְמָה *f.*
†privily (be-tormah) 1.

TOSHAB תּוֹשָׁב
foreigner 1
inhabitant 1
sojourner 9
stranger 3.

TOTAPHOTH טוֹטָפוֹת *f. pl.*
frontlets 3.

TOTHACH תּוֹתָח
darts 1.

TOTSAOTH תּוֹצָאוֹת *f. pl.*
border 1
going forth 2
going out 11
issue 2
outgoing 7.

TSAAD [1] צָעַד
go 3
march 2
march through 1
run over 1.
HIPH. bring 1.

TSAAD [2] צַעַד
going 1
pace 1
step 11
*go 1.

TSAAH צָעָה
wander 1.
Partic. captive exile 1
travelling 1
wanderer 1.
PIEL cause to wander 1.

TSAAN צָעַן
be taken down 1.

TSAAQ צָעַק
cry 43
cry out 3.
Adv. inf. at all 1.
NIPH. be called together 1
be gathered together 1
gather 1
gather selves together 3.
PIEL cry 1.
HIPH. call together 1.

TSAAR צָעַר
be brought low 1
be small 1.
Partic. little one 1.

TSAATSUIM צַעֲצֻעִים *pl.*
*image 1.

TSAB [1] צָב
litter 1
*covered 1.

TSAB [2] צָב
tortoise 1.

TSABA [1] צָבָא
assemble 3
fight 4
perform 1
wait upon 1
war 2.
HIPH. muster 2.

TSABA [2] צָבָא
appointed time 3
army 29
battle 6
company 1
host 394
service 6
soldiers 1
time appointed 2
waiting upon 1
war (warfare) 42.
†battle (*with* milchamah) 1. *See* chayil.

TSABAH [1] צָבָה
fight 1
swell 1.
HIPH. make to swell 1.

TSABAH [2] צָבָה
army 1.

TSABAR צָבַר
gather 1
gather together 1
heap 1
heap up 3
lay up 1.

TSABAT צָבַט
reach 1.

TSABEH צָבֶה
*to swell 1.

TSABUA צָבוּעַ
speckled 1.

TSACH צַח
clear 1
dry 1
plainly 1
white 1.

TSACHACH צָחַח
be whiter 1.

TSACHANAH צַחֲנָה *f.*
ill savour 1.

TSACHAQ צָחַק
laugh 6.
PIEL make sport 1
mock 4
play 2
sport 1.

TSACHAR צַחַר
white 1.

TSACHOR צָחֹר
white 1.

TSACHTSACHOTH צַחְצָחוֹת *f. pl.*
drought 1.

TSAD צַד
one side 1
side 32
*another 1.
†*See* min[2].

TSAD צַד
against 1
concerning 1.

TSADAH צָדָה
hunt 1
lie in wait 1.
NIPH. be destroyed 1.

TSADAQ צָדַק
be just 3
be justified 8
be righteous 10
justify self 1.
NIPH. be cleansed 1.
PIEL justify 5.
HIPH. do justice 2
justify 9
turn to righteouness 1.
HITHP. clear selves 1.

TSADDIQ צַדִּיק
just 41
lawful 1
righteous (man) 164.

TSAHAB צָהַב
†HOPH. *partic.* (*with* tob) fine 1.

TSAHAL צָהַל
bellow 1
cry aloud 1
neigh 1
rejoice 1.
PIEL cry aloud 1
cry out 1
lift up 1
shout 1.
HIPH. make to shine 1.

TSAHAR צָהַר
HIPH. make oil 1.

TSAHOB צָהֹב
yellow 3.

TSAIPH צָעִיף
vail 3.

TSAIR צָעִיר
least 4
little 3
little one 2
small 1
small one 1
younger 6
youngest 3.
†young (*with* le-yamim) 1; younger (*with* le-yamim) 1.

TSALA צָלַע
halt 4.

TSALAH צָלָה
roast 3.

TSALAL [1] צָלַל
quiver 1
tingle 3.

TSALAL [2] צָלַל
sink 1.

TSALAL [3] צָלַל
begin to be dark 1.
HIPH. *pt.* shadowing 1.

TSALEACH צָלֵחַ
be good 1
be meet 1
be profitable 1
break out 1
come 6
come mightily 2
go over 1
prosper 11
*prosperously 1.
HIPH. cause to prosper 1
make prosperous 1
make to prosper 2
prosper 29
prosperously effect 1
send prosperity 1.
Partic. prosperous 1.

TSALI צָלִי
roast 3.

TSALLACHATH צַלַּחַת *f.*
bosom 2
dish 1.

TSALMAVETH צַלְמָוֶת *f.*
shadow of death 18.

TSAMA צָמָא
thirst 15
*thirsty 1.

TSAMACH צָמַח
be grown up 1
bring forth 1
grow 4
grow up 1
spring 2
spring forth 3
spring up 2.
PIEL be grown 2
grow again 1.
HIPH. bear 1
bring forth 1
bud 1
cause to bud forth 1
cause to grow 1
cause to grow up 1
cause to spring forth 3
make to bud 2
make to grow 3
spring up 1.

TSAMAD צָמַד
NIPH. be joined 1
join self 2.
PUAL *pt.* fastened 1.
HIPH. frame 1.

TSAMAH צַמָּה *f.*
thirst 1.

TSAMAQ צָמַק
Partic. dry 1.

TSAMATH צָמַת
cut off 1.
NIPH. be cut off 1
vanish 1.
PIEL consume 1.
PIL. cut off 1.
HIPH. cut off 5
destroy 5.

TSAME [1] צָמֵא
be athirst 2
be thirsty 2
suffer thirst 1
thirst 5.

TSAME [2] צָמֵא
that thirsteth 1
thirsty 7
*thirst 1.

TSAMID צָמִיד
bracelet 6
covering 1.

TSAMMAH צַמָּה *f.*
locks 4.

TSAMMIM צַמִּים
robber 2.

TSAMMERETH צַמֶּרֶת *f.*
highest branch 2
top 3.

TSANA צָנַע
Pass pt. lowly 1.
HIPH. *humbly 1.

TSANACH צָנַח
fasten 1
light 2.

TSANAM צָנַם
Pass. pt. withered 1.

TSANAPH צָנַף
violently turn 1
*be attired 1.
Adv. inf. surely 1.

TSANIPH צָנִיף
diadem 2
hood 1
mitre 1.

TSANTAROTH צַנְתָּרוֹת *f. pl.*
pipes 1.

TSAPHAD צָפַד
cleave 1.

TSAPHAH [1] צָפָה
behold 2
keep the watch 1
look 1
look well 1
wait for 1
watch 3.
Partic. watchman 17.
PIEL cover 4
espy 1
garnish 1
look 1
look up 1
overlay 39
watch 3.
Partic. watchman 2.
PUAL *pt.* covered 1
overlaid 1.

* Inexact translations, *e.g.*, of a noun by a verb or adjective, of an active by a passive.
† Cases where two or more words in the original are translated by one word or by a phrase.

TSAPHAH 2 צָפָה *f.*
*swim 1.
TSAPHAN צפן
be privily set 1
esteem 1
hide 9
hide selves 1
keep secretly 1
lay up 8
lurk privily 2.
Pass. pt. hid 1
hid treasure 1
hidden one 1
secret 1
secret place 1
Niph be hid 1
be hidden 2.
Hiph hide 2.
TSAPHAPH צפף
Pilp chatter 1
peep 2
whisper 1.
TSAPHAR צפר
depart early 1.
TSAPHIA צְפִיעַ
dung 1.
TSAPHIR צָפִיר
goat 2
he goat 1.
†the goat (*with pl. of* ez) 4.
TSAPHITH צָפִית *f.*
watchtower 1.
TSAPHON צָפוֹן *c.*
north 113
north side 12
north wind 1
northward 24.
†northern (mits-tsaphon) 1.
TSAPHTSAPHAH צַפְצָפָה *f.*
willow tree 1.
TSAPPACHATH צַפַּחַת *f.*
cruse 7.
TSAPPICHITH צַפִּיחִת *f.*
wafers 1.
TSAR 1 צַר (צָר)
close 1
narrow 2
small 1
strait 3.
As noun adversity 1
affliction 3
anguish 1
distress 5
sorrow 1
tribulation 1
trouble 15.
†be afflicted (*with* le) 1
TSAR 2 צַר (צָר)
adversary 28
enemy 38
foe 2
they that trouble 1
those that trouble 1.
TSAR 3 צַר
flint 1.
TSARA צרע
Partic. leper 4
leprous 1.
Pual pt. leper 10
leprous 5.
TSARAATH צָרַעַת *f.*
leprosy 35.
TSARAB צרב
Niph. be burned 1.
TSARACH צרח
cry 1.
Hiph. roar 1.
TSARAH 1 צָרָה *f.*
adversity 5
affliction 7
anguish 5
distress 7
tribulation 3
trouble 44.
TSARAH 2 = TSAR 2
TSARAPH צרף
cast 1
melt 2
purge away 1
refine 2
try 4
*be refined 1
*be tried 1.
Partic. finer 1
founder 5
goldsmith 5.
Pass. pt. pure 2.
Niph. be tried 1.
Piel pt. refiner 1.
TSARAR צרר
afflict 3
be distressed 2
be in a strait 3
be in distress 2
be in trouble 2
bind 2
bind up 3
oppress 1
vex 5
*narrower 1
Partic. enemy 14.
Pass. pt. being bound up 1
bound 1
bound up 1
shut up 1.
Pual pt. bound up 1.
Hiph. be in affliction 1
besiege 4
bring distress 1
distress 1
vex 1.
Partic. pangs 2.
Inf. distress 1
TSAREBETH צָרֶבֶת *f.*
burning 2
inflammation 1.
TSARIACH צְרִיחַ
high place 1
hold 3.
TSAV צַו (צָו)
commandment 1
precept 8.
TSAVACH צוח
shout 1.
TSAVAH צוה
Piel appoint 6
bid 3
charge 24
command 422
forbid 2
give (a) charge 14
give a commandment 6
give in commandment 2
put in order 1
send a messenger 1
send with commandment 1
set in order 2
*be appointed 1
*be charged 1.
Pual be commanded 9.
TSAVVAR צַוָּאר (*once* צַוָּר)
neck 41.
TSAVVAR צַוַּר
neck 3.
TSAVVARONIM צַוְּרֹנִים *pl.*
neck 1.
TSAYAR ציר
Hithp. make as if were ambassadors 1.
TSAYID צַיִד
food 1
hunting 5
provision 2
that which he took in hunting 1
venison 8
victuals 2
*and catcheth 1
*hunter 3.
TSAYON צִיּוֹן
dry place 2.
TSAYYAD צַיָּד
hunter 1.
TSEADAH צְעָדָה *f.*
going 2
ornament of the legs 1.
TSEAH צֵאָה *f.*
that which cometh from 1
that cometh out 1.
TSEAQAH צְעָקָה *f.*
cry 19
crying 2
TSEBA 1 צבא
will (*vb.*) 9.
Inf. will (*n.*) 1.
TSEBA 2 צבע
Pael wet 1.
Hithp. be wet 4.
TSEBA צֶבַע
divers colours 3.
TSEBATHIM צְבָתִים *pl.*
handfuls 1.
TSEBI 1 צְבִי
beauty 2
glory 8
*beautiful 1
*glorious 5
*goodly 1
*pleasant 1.
TSEBI 2 צְבִי
roe 9
roebuck 5.
TSEBIYYAH צְבִיָּה *f.*
†*See* opher.
TSEBU צְבוּ *f.*
purpose 1.
TSECHIACH צְחִיחַ
higher place 1
top 4.
TSECHICHAH צְחִיחָה *f.*
dry land 1.
TSECHOQ צְחֹק
*laughed to scorn 1
*to laugh 1
TSEDA צְדָא
true 1.
TSEDAH צֵידָה *f.*
meat 1
provision 2
victuals 6.
TSEDAQAH צְדָקָה *f.*
justice 15
right 2
righteous act 3
righteousness 128
that which is right 7
*righteously (*pl.*) 1.
†moderately (li-tsedaqah) 1.
TSEDEQ צֶדֶק
justice 10
right (*n.*) 2
righteous cause 1
righteousness 79
that which is altogether just 1
*even 1.
*just 10
*righteous 7
*righteous man 1
*righteously 3.
†unrighteousness (lo tsedeq) 1.
TSEDIYYAH צְדִיָּה *f.*
lying of wait 2.
TSEELIM צֶאֱלִים *pl.*
shady trees 2.
TSEETSAIM צֶאֱצָאִים *pl.*
offspring 9
that come forth 1
that which cometh out 1.
TSEIRAH צְעִירָה *f*
youth 1.
TSEL צֵל
defence 3
shade 1
shadow 45.
TSELA צלא
Pael pray 2.
TSELA 1 צֵלָע *f*
beam 1
board 2
chamber 2
corner 2
halting 1
leaf 1
plank 1
rib 2
side 19
side chamber 9
*another 1
*one 1.
TSELA 2 צֶלַע
adversity 1
halting 1
*halt 1.
TSELACH צלח
Haph. promote 1
prosper 3.
TSELACHAH צְלָחָה *f.*
pan 1.
TSELATSAL צְלָצַל
locust 1
shadowing 1
spear 1.
TSELEL צְלָל
shadow 4.
TSELEM צֶלֶם
image 16
vain shew 1.
TSELEM צְלֵם (צְלֶם)
form 1
image 16.
TSELIL צְלִיל (V.L.)
cake 1.
TSELOCHITH צְלֹחִית *f.*
cruse 1.
TSELTSELIM צֶלְצְלִים *pl.*
cymbals 3.
TSELUL צְלוּל (V.L.)
cake 1.
TSEMACH צֶמַח
branch 1
Branch 4
bud 3
spring 1
springing 1
that which grew upon 1
where grew 1.
TSEMED צֶמֶד
acre 1
couple 4
two 2
yoke 5
yoke of oxen 2
*together (*pl.*) 1.
TSEMER צֶמֶר
wool 11
*woollen 5.
TSEMITHUTH צְמִיתֻת *f.*
ever 2.
TSEN צֵן
thorn 2.
TSENEPHAH צְנֵפָה *f.*
*and toss 1.
TSENINIM צְנִינִים *pl.*
thorns 2.
TSEPHA צֶפַע
cockatrice 1.
TSEPHARDEA צְפַרְדֵּעַ
frog 13.
TSEPHETH צֶפֶת *f.*
chapiter 1.
TSEPHIOTH צְפִעוֹת *f. pl.*
issue 1.
TSEPHIRIM צְפִירִים *pl.*
†he goats (with pl. of *ez*) 1.
TSEPHIRAH צְפִירָה *f.*
diadem 1
morning 2.
TSEPHONI צְפוֹנִי
northern 1.
TSERI = **TSORI.**
TSEROR 1 צְרוֹר
bag 3
bundle 4.
TSEROR 2 צְרוֹר
least grain 1
small stone 1.
TSEVACHAH צְוָחָה *f.*
complaining 1
cry 2
crying 1
TSI צִי
ship 4.
TSIBBURIM צִבֻּרִים *pl.*
heaps 1.
TSICHEH צִחֵה
dried up 1.
TSIDQAH צִדְקָה *f.*
righteousness 1.
TSIMAH צִמְאָה *f.*
thirst 1.
TSIMMAON צִמָּאוֹן
drought 1
dry ground 1
thirsty land 1.
TSIMMUQIM צִמּוּקִים *pl.*
bunches of raisins 2
clusters of raisins 2.
TSINNAH 1 צִנָּה *f.*
hook 1.
TSINNAH 2 צִנָּה *f.*
buckler 5
shield 10
target 5.
TSINNAH 3 צִנָּה *f.*
cold 1.
TSINNOR צִנּוֹר
gutter 1
waterspout 1.
TSINOQ צִינֹק
stocks 2.
TSINTSENETH צִנְצֶנֶת *f.*
pot 1.
TSIPHONI צִפְעוֹנִי
adder 1
cockatrice 3.
TSIPPAR צִפַּר
bird 1
fowl 3.
TSIPPIYYAH צְפִיָּה *f.*
watching 1.
TSIPPOR צִפּוֹר *c.*
bird 32
fowl 6
sparrow 2.
TSIPPOREN צִפֹּרֶן
nail 1
point 1.
TSIPPUI צִפּוּי
covering 3
overlaying 2.
TSIQLON צִקְלוֹן
husk 1.
TSIR 1 צִיר
beauty 1
idol 1.
TSIR 2 צִיר
ambassador 4
hinge 1
messenger 2.
TSIR 3 צִירִים *pl.*
pains 1
pangs 3
sorrows 1.
TSIRAH צִרְעָה *f.*
hornet 3.
TSITS צִיץ
blossom 1
flower 10
plate 3
wing 1.
TSITSAH צִיצָה *f.*
flower 1.
TSITSITH צִיצִת *f.*
fringe 3
lock 1.
TSIYYAH צִיָּה *f*
drought 1
dry land 1
dry place 4
solitary place 1
wilderness 2
*barren 1
*dry 8.
TSIYYIM צִיִּים *pl.*
inhabiting the wilderness 1
that dwell in the wilderness 2
wild beasts of the desert 3.
TSIYYUN צִיּוּן
sign 1
title 1
waymark 1
TSO צוֹא
filthy 2.
TSOAH צוֹאָה *f.*
dung 2
filth 1
filthiness 2
TSOHAR צֹהַר
midday 1
noon 11
noonday 10
window 1.
†*See* eth2.
TSOM צוֹם
fast 16
fasting 9.
†*See* tsum.
TSON צֹאן *c.*
cattle 14
flocks 137
lamb 1
sheep 108
small cattle 1.
†*See* ben2, gazaz, gederah, miklah, miqneh, raah3.
TSONE צֹנֶא (?)
sheep 1.
TSONEH צֹנֶה
sheep 1.
TSOQ צוֹק
*troublous 1
TSOR צֹר
flint 1
sharp stone 1.
TSOREK צֹרֶךְ
need 1.
TSOREPHI צֹרְפִי
goldsmith 1
TSORI צֳרִי (צְרִי)
balm 6.
TSUD צוד
chase 1
hunt 9
take 2.
Adv. inf. sore 1.
Poel hunt 4.
Hithp. take provision 1.
TSULAH צוּלָה *f.*
deep 1.
TSUM צוּם
fast 19.
Adv. inf. at all 1.
†fast (*with* tsom) 1.
TSUPH 1 צוּף
flow 1.
Hiph. make to overflow 1
swim 1.
TSUPH 2 צוּף
†honeycomb (*with* debash) 1. *See* nopheth.
TSUQ 1 צוּק
Hiph. constrain 1
distress 5
lie sore 1
press 1
straiten 1.
Partic. oppressor 2.
TSUQ 2 צוּק
pour out 2
*be molten 1
TSUQAH צוּקָה *f.*
anguish 3.
TSUR 1 צוּר
assault 1
beset 1
besiege 21
lay siege 3
*adversary 1
TSUR 2 צוּר
cast 1
fashion 1.
TSUR 3 צוּר (= TSARAR)
bind 2
bind up 2
distress 3
fortify 1
inclose 1
put up in bags 1.
TSUR 4 צוּר
edge 1
mighty one 1
rock 62
stone 1
strength 5
*God 1
*mighty God 1
*sharp 2
*strong 1
TSURAH צוּרָה
form 4.

* Inexact translations, *e.g.*, of a noun by a verb or adjective, of an active by a passive.
† Cases where two or more words in the original are translated by one word or by a phrase.

TSUTH צות
HIPH. burn 1.
TSUTS צוץ
blossom 1.
HIPH. bloom 1
blossom 1
flourish 5
*show self 1.
TU טוא
PILP. sweep 1.
TUACH טוּח
daub 7
overlay 1
plaister 1
shut 1.
NIPH. be plaistered 2.
TUB טוּב
gladness 1
good 7
good thing 1
good things 2
goodness 14
goods 3
joy 1
*fair 1
*go well with 1
*good (*adj.*) 1.
TUB תּוּב
return 3.
HAPH. answer 1
return 2
return answer 1
*be restored 1.
†HAPH. answer (*with* pithgam) 1.
TUCHOTH טֻחוֹת *f. pl.*
inward parts 2.
TUGAH תּוּגָה *f.*
heaviness 3
sorrow 1.
TUKKIYYIM תֻּכִּיִּים *pl.*
peacocks 2.
TUL טוּל
PILP. carry away 1.
HIPH. cast 2
cast forth 4
cast out 2
send out 1.
HOPH. be cast 1
be cast down 1
be cast out 1
be utterly cast out 1.
TUMAH טֻמְאָה *f.*
filthiness 7
uncleanness 26
*unclean 2.
TUMMAH תֻּמָּה *f.*
integrity 5.
TUPHINIM תֻּפִינִים *pl.*
†baken pieces (*with pl. of* path) 1.
TUR[1] טוּר
row 26.
TUR[2] תּוּר
espy 1
search 12
search out 3
seek 2
spy out 3.
HIPH. be excellent 1
send to descry 1.
†*See* anashim.
TUR טוּר
mountain 2.
TUS טוּשׂ
haste 1.
TUSHIYYAH תּוּשִׁיָּה *f.*
enterprise 1
sound wisdom 3
substance 1
that which is 1
thing as it is 1
wisdom 4
working 1.

U

U
and *freq.*
UB עוּב
HIPH. cover with a cloud 1.
UBAL אוּבַל (אֻבַל)
river 3.
UD[1] אוּד
brand 1
firebrand 2.
UD[2] עוּד
take to witness 1.
PIEL rob 1.
HIPH. admonish 1
bear witness against 1
be witness 1
call to record 2
call to witness 1
charge 2
give warning 1
give witness to 1
protest 5
take [witness] 1
take to record 1
take to witness for 1
testify 14
witness 1.
Adv. inf. earnestly 1
solemnly 2.
HOPH. be testified 1.
PIL. lift up 1
relieve 1.
HITHPAL. stand upright 1.
UG עוּג
bake 1.
UGAB עוּגָב (עֻגָב)
organ 4.
UGAH עֻגָה (עֻגָּה) *f.*
cake 6
cake upon the hearth 1.
UGGAB = UGAB.
UGGAH = UGAH.
UL[1] אוּל
mighty 1
strength 1.
UL[2] עוּל
Partic. ewes great with young 1
milch 2
with young 2.
UL[3] עוּל
infant 1
sucking child 1.
ULAI אוּלַי (אֻלַי)
if so be
may be
peradventure
unless.
ULAM[1] אוּלָם (אֻלָם)
porch 34.
ULAM[2] אוּלָם
as for 1
but 7
but truly 4
howbeit 1
in very deed 2
surely 2
wherefore 1.
ULPEH עֻלְפֶּה
fainted 1.
UMLAL אֻמְלַל
weak 1.
UMMAH אֻמָּה *f.*
nation 8.
UMMATH עֻמָּה *f.*
†le-ummath: against 5, answerable to 1, at 1, beside 2, hard by 1, over against 19. mil-le-ummath: over against 1. *See* kol.
UMMIM אֻמִּים (אֻמּוֹת) *pl.*
nations 1
people 2.
UMMOTH = UMMIM.
UMNAM אָמְנָם
indeed 3
in very deed 1
of a surety 1.
UPH עוּף
be faint 2
be weary 1
flee away 1
fly 14
fly away 4
shine forth 1
wax faint 1.
POL. brandish 1
fly 4.
HIPH. set 1.
HITHPOL. fly away 1.
UQ עוּק
HIPH. be pressed 2.
UR[1] אוּר
fire 5
light 1
urim (*pl.*) 7.
UR[2] עוּר
arise 1
awake 16
awake up 1
dare stir up 1
wake 1.
Partic. *master 1.
NIPH. be raised 2
be raised up 3
be wakened 2.
POL. awake 3
lift up 3
raise up 4
stir up 4.
HIPH. awake 3
raise 3
raise up 6
stir up 15
stir up self 1
wake 2
wake up 1
waken 2.
HITHPOL. awake 2
lift up self 1
stir up self 2.
UR[3] עוּר
NIPH. be made naked 1.
UR עוּר
chaff 1.
URAVOTH אֻרָוֹת (אֻרְיוֹת) *f. pl.*
stalls 3.
URAYOTH = URAVOTH.
USH עוּשׁ
assemble selves 1.
USHSHARNA אֻשַּׁרְנָא
wall 2.
USHSHIN אֻשִּׁין *pl.*
foundations 3.
UTH עוּת
speak in season 1.
UTS[1] אוּץ
be narrow 1
haste 3
hasten 1
make haste 1.
Partic. hasty 2.
HIPH. hasten 1
labour 1.
UTS[2] עוּץ
take advice 1.
†take counsel together (*with* etsah) 1.
UZ עוּז
HIPH. gather 1
gather selves 1
gather selves to flee 1
retire 1.

V

VA וְ
and *freq.*, etc.
VAHEB אֶת־וָהֵב
*what he did 1.
VALAD וָלָד
child 1.
VAV וָו
hook 13.
VAZAR וָזָר
strange 1.
VE וְ
and *freq.*, etc.
VELED וֶלֶד
child 1.

Y

YAAB יָאַב
long 1.
YAAD יָעַד
appoint 3
betroth 2.
NIPH. assemble selves 1
be agreed 1
be assembled 3
be gathered together 2
be met together 1
gather selves 1
gather selves together 1
make an appointment 1
meet 9.
HIPH. appoint a time 2
set a time 1.
HOPH. be set 1.
YAAH[1] יָאָה
appertain 1.
YAAH[2] יָעָה
sweep away 1.
YAAL[1] יָאַל
NIPH. become fools 1
be foolish 1
do foolishly 1
dote 1.
YAAL[2] יָאַל
HIPH. assay 1
be content 7
begin 1
please 4
take upon 2
would 3
*willingly 4.
YAAL[3] יָעַל
HIPH. be profitable 1
can do good 1
have profit 2
profit 17
set forward 1.
Adv. inf. at all 1.
YAALAH יַעֲלָה *f.*
roe 1.
YAAN יַעַן
because
because that
forasmuch
seeing then, etc.
†because (*with* asher 2, *with* ki 2) 4; forasmuch as (*with* asher 1, *with* ki 3) 4; that (*with* asher) 1; whereas (*with* asher) 1; why (*with* meh) 1.
YAANAH יַעֲנָה *f.*
†*See* bath[1].
YAAPH יָעֵף
be weary 2
faint 4
weary self 2.
HOPH. be caused to fly 1.
YAAR[1] יַעַר
forest 38
wood 19.
YAAR[2] יַעַר
honeycomb 1.
YAARAH[1] יַעְרָה
forest 1.
YAARAH[2] יַעֲרָה *f.*
†honeycomb (*with* debash) 1.
YAASH יָאַשׁ
NIPH. be no hope 3
despair 1.
Partic. one that is desperate 1.
PIEL cause to despair 1.
YAAT יָעַט
cover 1.
YAATS יָעַץ
advertise 1
consult 3
counsel 6
determine 2
devise 2
give [counsel] 6
give counsel 3
guide 1
purpose 5
take counsel 5.
Partic. counsel 1
counsellor 22.
NIPH. advise 1
consult 5
give advice 1
give counsel 2
take advice 1
take counsel 9.
Partic. well advised 1.
HITHP. consult 1.
YAAZ יָעַז
Niph. pt. fierce 1.
YABAB יָבַב
PIEL cry 1.
YABAL[1] יָבַל
HIPH. bring 1
carry 1
lead 1.
HOPH. be brought 6
be brought forth 1
be carried 3
be led forth 1.
YABAL[2] יָבָל
stream 1.
†watercourse (*with* mayim) 1.
YABAM[1] יָבָם
husband's brother 2.
YABAM[2] יָבַם
PIEL marry 1
perform the duty of a husband's brother 2.
YABASH יָבֵשׁ
HIPH. be ashamed 7
be confounded 9
do shamefully 1
shame 1.
YABBAL יַבָּל
having a wen 1.
YABBASHAH יַבָּשָׁה *f.*
dry ground 1
dry land 2
land 1
*dry 10.
YABBESHETH יַבֶּשֶׁת *f.*
dry land 2.
YABBESHETH יַבֶּשֶׁת *f.*
earth 1.
YABESH[1] יָבֵשׁ
be dried 2
be dried up 10
be withered 3
be withered away 1
dry 2
dry up 4
wither 16.
Adv. inf. clean 1
utterly 1.
PIEL dry 1
dry up 1
make dry 1.
HIPH. be dried up 2
be withered 1
be withered away 1
dry up 11
make dry 1.
YABESH[2] יָבֵשׁ
dried 1
dried away 1
dry 7.
YACHAD[1] יָחַד
be joined 2
be united 1.
PIEL unite 1.
YACHAD[2] יַחַד (יַחְדָּו, יַחְדָּיו)
alike 5
altogether 5
at all 1
at once 2
both 1
knit 1
likewise 1
only 1
together 120
withal 2.
YACHAL יָחַל
NIPH. stay 1
wait 1.
PIEL cause to hope 1
hope 13
make to hope 1
trust 2
wait 7.
HIPH. hope 6
have hope 1
tarry 3
wait 4
*be pained 1.
YACHAM יָחַם
be hot 2
be warm 1
conceive 2
get heat 1.
PIEL conceive 4.
YACHAS[1] יָחַשׂ
HITHP. be reckoned by genealogies 5
be reckoned by genealogy 5
genealogy is reckoned 2.
Infin. genealogy 6
number after [their] genealogy 1
number throughout the genealogy 1.
YACHAS[2] יַחַשׂ
genealogy 1.
YACHDAV = YACHAD[2]
YACHEPH יָחֵף
barefoot 4
being unshod 1.
YACHID יָחִיד
darling 2
desolate 1
only 6
only child 1
only son 1
solitary 1.
YACHIL יָחִיל
should hope 1.
YACHMUR יַחְמוּר
fallow deer 2.
YAD יָד *c.*
axletree 2
border 2
charge 1
coast 6
custody 4
debt 1
dominion 2
force 2
hand *freq.*
labour 1
ledge 2
means 4
mess (*pl.*) 1
ministry 2
order 2
ordinance 1
parts 4
paw 2
place 8
power 13
service (*du*) 2
side 11
sore 1
state 2
stay 4
stroke 1
tenon 6
times 2
work 1
*throwing 1
*where 1.
†ability (*with Hiph. of* nasag) 1; be fallen in decay (*with* mut) 1; find occasion (*with* matsa) 1; occasion serves (*with* matsa) 1; of [his] bounty (ke-yad) 1; presumptuously (be-yad ramah) 1; the Lord hath sworn (yad al[2] kes Yah) 1; wayside (*with* derek 1, with magal 1) 2; with (al[2] yede) 1. *See* al[2], atstsil, baal, be, bohen, chazaq, el, itter, le, maaseh, male, maqqah, mattanah, mattath, min, nasa, nathaq, rachab, sheber, tesumeth. *Freq. translated by Eng. pronoun alone when a poss. adj. qualifies it* (he, him, she, us, them, etc.).
YAD יַד
hand 16
power 1.
YADA יָדַע
acknowledge 5
advise 1
be aware 2
be privy to 1
be sure 5
can [not] 2
can discern 3
can have 1
can skill 3
can tell 6
comprehend 1
consider 7
could 2
discern 4
feel 3
have [knowledge] 2

* Inexact translations, *e.g.*, of a noun by a verb or adjective, of an active by a passive.
† Cases where two or more words in the original are translated by one word or by a phrase.

have [understanding] 2
have knowledge 10
have respect 1
know 662
mark 3
perceive 18
regard 1
take knowledge 3
understand 7
will 1
wist 7
wit 2
wot 6
*be known 1
*knowledge 1.
Partic. acquaintance 2
cunning 4
endued with 2
man of skill 1
of knowledge 1
skilful 1
such as are skilful 1.
Pass. pt. acquainted with 1
known 2.
Inf. knowledge 1.
Adv inf. assuredly 1
certainly 6
diligent 1
for a certain 1
for a certainty 1
for certain 1.
NIPH. be discovered 1
be famous 1
be instructed 1
be known 34
make self known 4.
PIEL cause to know 1.
POAL appoint 1.
PUAL *pt.* acquaintance 4
familiar friend 1
kinsfolk 1.
HIPH. acknowledge 1
answer 1
cause to discern 1
cause to know 5
declare 6
give knowledge 1
let know 2
make know 8
make known 17
make to be known 1
shew 17
teach 8
tell 2.
Partic. prognosticator 1.
HOPH. be known 1
come to knowledge 1.
HITHP make self known 2
†KAL *at unawares (lo yada) 1; be ignorant (lo yada) 3; be learned (*with* sepher) 3; come to understanding (*with* binah) 1; lie by man (*with* mishkab) 1.

YADAH 1 ידה
shoot 1.
PIEL cast 1
cast out 1

YADAH 2 ידה
HIPH be thankful 1
confess 7
give thanks 32
praise 53
thank 5.
Inf. thanksgiving 2.
HITHP. confess 9
make confession 2.

YADID יָדִיד
amiable 1
beloved 7
loves 1
wellbeloved 2.

YAEPH יָעֵף
faint 2
weary 2.

YAGA 1 יגע
be wearied 1
be weary 7
faint 1
labour 11
PIEL make to labour 1
weary 1.
HIPH. weary 4.

YAGA 2 יָגָע
*which he laboured for 1.

YAGAB יגב
Partic. husbandman 2.

YAGAH 1 יגה
NIPH. be afflicted 1
be sorrowful 1
PIEL grieve 1
HIPH. afflict 3
cause grief 1
vex 1.

YAGAH 2 יגה
HIPH. be removed 1

YAGEA יָגֵעַ
full of labour 1
weary 2.

YAGIA יְגִיעַ
weary 1.

YAGON יָגוֹן
grief 2
sorrow 12.

YAGOR יגר
be afraid 5
fear 2.

YAHAB יהב
ascribe 1
bring 2
come on 1
give 24
go to 4
set 1
take 1
*burden 1

YAHAD יהד
HITHP. become Jews 1.

YAHALOM יַהֲלֹם
diamond 3.

YAHIR יָהִיר
haughty 1
proud 2.

YAIM יָעִים *pl.*
shovels 9.

YAKACH יכח
NIPH. be reproved 1
dispute 1
reason together 1.
HIPH. appoint 2
argue 1
chasten 1
convince 1
correct 3
judge 1
maintain 1
plead 2
reason 2
rebuke 13
reprove 23
Partic daysman 1
reprover 2.
Infin. correction 1.
Adv. inf. in any wise 1
surely 1.
HOPH. be chastened 1.
HITHP. plead 1

YAKOL יכל
attain 2
be able 44
can 53
can away with 1
could 47
endure 3
have power 1
may 18
overcome 1
prevail 22
suffer 1.
Adv. inf. any at all 1
any ways 1
still 1.

YALA ילע
devour 1

YALAD ילד
be delivered 5
be delivered of a child 1
bear 153
beget 28
bring forth 19
bring forth children 1
bring forth young 1
bring up 1
calve 1
gender 1
hatch 1
travail 4
travail with child 2
*be born 1
Partic. travailing woman 2
woman in travail 8
woman that travaileth 2.
Pass. pt. born of 3
child 2
children 1
Infin birth 1
labour 2
time of delivery 1
travail 2.
NIPH. be begotten 1
be born 33
be brought forth 1
be the son of 1
come 1.
Infin. one's birth 1.
PIEL do the office of a midwife 1.
Partic. midwife 9.
PUAL be born 26
be brought forth 1
be brought up 1.
HIPH. beget 181
bring forth 1
cause to bring forth 1
make to bring forth 1.
HOPH. be born 1.
HITHP. declare pedigrees 1.
†*See* yom.

YALAK ילך (= **HALAK**)
be gone 10
be let down 1
come 80
come away 2
depart 66
flow 3
gain 1
get (thee, him, etc.) 28
get away 3
get hence 1
go 630
go away 12
go (one's) way 9
go on 2
go out 1
go to 1
go up 1
go up and down 1
grow 1
march 2
prosper 1
run 1
spread 2
take [journey] 1
vanish 1
walk 123
wax 1
*be weak 2.
Imperat. away 1.
HIPH. bear 1
bring 12
carry 5
carry away 1
cause to go 2
cause to run 1
cause to walk 2
go 1
lead 17
lead forth 1
make go 1
take away 1.
†KAL follow (*with* achar) 20; pursue (*with* achare) 1. *Infin.* following (*with* achar) 2. *See* shub.

YALAL ילל
HIPH. be howlings 1
howl 28
make to howl 1.

YALDAH יַלְדָּה *f.*
damsel 1
girl 2.

YALEDUTH יַלְדוּת *f.*
childhood 1
youth 2.

YALID יָלִיד
born 6
child 4
son 3.
†homeborn (*with* bayith) 1.

YALLEPHETH יַלֶּפֶת *f.*
scabbed 2.

YALQUT יַלְקוּט
scrip 1.

YAM יָם
sea 280
south 1
west 69
west side 1
western 1
westward 3
*seafaring man 1.
†Red Sea (*with* suph) 25.

YAM יָם
sea 3

YAMAN ימן
go on the right hand 1
go to the right 1
turn to the right hand 1
use the right hand 1

YAMAR ימר
HIPH. change 1.
HITHP. boast selves 1.

YAMIM = *pl. of* **YOM.**

YAMIMAH = *accus. of* **YAMIM.**

YAMIN יָמִין
right (hand, side) 134
south 3
†*See* itter.

YANAH ינה
destroy 1.
Partic. oppressing 3
oppressor 1
proud 1.
HIPH. do wrong 1
oppress 8
thrust out by oppression 1
vex 4.

YANAQ ינק
suck 9.
Partic. sucking child 3
suckling 6.
HIPH. give suck 4
make to suck 1
nurse 32.
Partic. milch 1
nurse 5
nursing mother 1.

YANSHUPH יַנְשׁוּף
great owl 2
owl 1.

YAPHA יפע
HIPH. be light 1
cause to shine 2
shew self 1
shine 2
shine forth 2.

YAPHACH יפח
HITHP. bewail self 1

YAPHAH יפה
be beautiful 1
be fair 3.
PIEL deck 1.
PUAL be fairer 1.
HITHP. make self fair 1.

YAPHEACH יָפֵחַ
such as breathe out 1.

YAPHEH יָפֶה
beautiful 5
comely 1
fair 21
fair one 2
fairest 2
pleasant 1.
†beautiful (*with* toar) 2; fair (*with* toar) 1; for his beauty (*with* ish) 1; goodly (*with* toar) 2; well favoured (*with* mareh 4, *with* toar 1) 5.

YAQA יקע
be alienated 2
be out of joint 1
depart 1.
HIPH. hang 1
hang up 2.
HOPH. be hanged 1

YAQAD יקד
burn 2
kindle 1
Pass. pt. hearth 1.
HOPH. be burning 3
burn 2.

YAQAR 1 יקר
be precious 7
be prized 1
be set by 1.
HIPH make precious 1
withdraw 1

YAQAR 2 יָקָר
clear 1
costly 4
excellent 2
honourable woman 1
in brightness 1
in reputation 1
precious 25.

YAQATS יקץ
awake 10
be awaked 1

YAQOSH 1 יָקוֹשׁ
fowler 1

YAQOSH 2 יקשׁ
lay [a snare] 1
lay a snare 1.
Partic. fowler 1.
NIPH. be snared 4
HOPH. *pt.* snared 1.

YAQQIR יַקִּיר
dear 1.

YAQQIR יַקִּיר
noble 1
rare 1.

YAQUSH יָקוּשׁ
fowler 2
snare 1.

YARA 1 = **YARAH.**

YARA 2 ירע
be grievous 1

YARAD ירד
be gone down 12
be subdued 1
come down 103
descend 19
fall 2
get down 5
go down 148
go downward 1
light 1
light down 1
run down 7
sink 1.
Adv. inf. indeed 1.
HIPH. bring down 39
carry down 2
cast down 4
cause run down 1
cause to come down 2
hang down 1
let down 1
let fall down 1
let go down 2
let run down 1
put down 1
put off 1
take down 7.
HOPH. be brought down 4
be taken down 1.
†KAL weep abundantly (*with* bi-beki), 1.

YARAH יָרָה
cast 4
lay 1
shoot 8.
Partic. archer 2
shooter 1
[*See* yoreh].
Adv. inf. through 1.
NIPH. be shot 1.
HIPH. cast 1
direct 1
inform 1
instruct 1
rain 1
shew 1
shoot 10
teach 46.
HOPH. be watered 1.
†*Hiph. partic.* archers (*with* baq-qesheth 1, *with* anashim baq-qesheth 1) 2.

YARAQ 1 ירק
spit 2
Adv. inf. but 1

YARAQ 2 יָרָק
green 2
herbs 3.

YARASH ירשׁ
be heir 5
enjoy 2
get in possession 1
have in possession 1
inherit 21
possess 112
succeed 4
take 1
take possession 2.
Partic heir 5
inheritor 1
NIPH. be poor 1
come to poverty 1.
PIEL consume 1
HIPH. cast out 11
destroy 1
disinherit 1
dispossess 4
drive out 37
expel 2
give to inherit 1
give to possess 1
leave for an inheritance 1
make poor 1
make to possess 1
possess 1
seize upon 1
Adv. inf. utterly 2
without fail 1.
†KAL, *partic.* magistrate (*with* etser) 1

YARAT ירט
be perverse 1
turn over 1

YARE ירא
be afraid 76
dread 1
fear 242
reverence 2
*see 1.
Partic. afraid 3
fearful 2.
NIPH. be feared 4
be had in reverence 1.
Partic. dreadful 5
fearful 2
fearfully 1
reverend 1
terrible 24
terrible acts 1
terribleness 1
terrible things 4.
PIEL affright 1
make afraid 2
put in fear 2.

YAREACH יָרֵחַ
moon 26.

YAREK יָרֵךְ *f.*
body 1
loins 2
shaft 3
side 7
thigh 21.

YAREKAH יַרְכָה *f.*
border 1.
Dual coasts 3
parts 2
quarters 1
sides 21.

YAREKAH יַרְכָה *f.*
thigh 1.

YARIB יָרִיב
that contend 1
that contendeth 1
that strive 1

YAROQ יָרוֹק
green thing 1.

YASAD יסד
establish 2
found 7
lay the foundation 10.
NIPH. foundation be laid 1
take counsel 2

* Inexact translations, *e.g.*, of a noun by a verb or adjective, of an active by a passive.
† Cases where two or more words in the original are translated by one word or by a phrase.

PIEL appoint 1
found 1
lay for a foundation 1
lay the foundation 5
ordain 2.
PUAL foundation be laid 1.
Partic foundation 1
set 1.
HOPH be instructed 1
foundation be laid 1.
Partic. *sure 1.
†*See* yom.

YASAK יסך
be poured 1.

YASAM ישם
be put 1.

YASAPH יסף
add 9
bring more 1
come more 1
exceed 1
increase 3
proceed 1
put 1
*again 6
*any more 1
*cease 1
*further 1
*more 9.
NIPH be added 1
be put 1
increase 1
join 1.
Partic. more 1.
HIPH. add 29
bring more 1
do again 1
do more 2
exceed 2
get more 1
give again 1
give moreover 1
increase 10
increase more and more 1
make more 2
proceed 1
proceed further 1
prolong 1
put more 1
*again 48
*again conceive 1
*any more 10
*be done 1
*be increased 1
*be put 1
*exceed (*intr.*) 1
*further 2
*give 1
*henceforth 2
*longer 1
*make 1
*more 39
*more again 1
*more and more 2
*more henceforth 1
*the more 1
*yet more 2
*yet the more 1
*yield 1.
†HIPH. be stronger and stronger (*with* omets) 1; continue (*with* seeth) 2; prolong (*with* yamim al[2]) 1.

YASAR יסר
chastise 2
instruct 1
reprove 1.
NIPH. be chastised 1
be corrected 1
be instructed 2
be reformed 1.
NITHP. be taught 1.
PIEL bind 1
chasten 8
chastise 6
correct 6
instruct 5
punish 1
teach 1.
Adv. inf. sore 1.
HIPH. chastise 1.

YASHA ישע
NIPH. be safe 1
be saved 19.
Partic. having salvation 1.

HIPH. avenge 3
bring salvation 2
defend 1
deliver 11
get victory 1
help 12
preserve 5
rescue 1
save 131.
Partic. deliverer 2
saviour 15.
Adv. inf. at all 1.

YASHAB ישב
abide 69
be inhabited 13
be set 3
be situate 2
cease 1
continue 5
dwell 434
ease self 1
endure 2
fail [to sit] 1
haunt 1
inhabit 18
remain 23
sit (down) 25
sit still 4
sit up 1
tarry 20.
Partic. dwelling 3
inhabitant 31
lurking 1.
Infin. downsitting 1
dwelling 11
habitation 3
loss of time 1
place 1
seat 2
sitting [place] 1
sitting down 1.
NIPH. be inhabited 9.
PIEL set 1.
HIPH. bring again to place 1
cause to dwell 3
establish 1
make to be inhabited 1
make to dwell 7
make to keep [house] 1
place 6
set 10
settle 1
*marry 2
*take 5.
HOPH. be inhabited 1
be placed 1.

YASHAM ישם
be desolate 4.

YASHAN [1] ישן
NIPH. remain long 1.
Partic. old 1
old store 1.

YASHAN [2] יָשָׁן
old 8.

YASHAR [1] ישר
be right 3
be upright 1
seem good 1
seem meet 1
take the straight way 1.
PIEL bring straight 1
direct 4
esteem right 1
go right on 1
make straight 2
*uprightly 1.
PUAL *pt.* fitted 1.
HIPH. look straight 1
make straight 1.
†KAL please (*with* be-ene) 4; please well (*with* be-ene) 4.

YASHAR [2] יָשָׁר
convenient 1
just 1
meet 1
meetest 1
most upright 1
right 53
righteous 9
straight 3
upright 40
*equity 1
*uprightly 1
*uprightness 1.
†pleased well (*with* be-ene) 1.

YASHAT ישט
HIPH. hold out 3.

YASHEN [1] ישן
sleep 15.
PIEL make to sleep 1.

YASHEN [2] יָשֵׁן
asleep 2
one out of sleep 1
sleeping 1
*sleep (*vb.*) 5.

YASHEPHEH יָשְׁפֵה
jasper 3.

YASHESH ישש
stoop for age 1.

YASHISH יָשִׁישׁ
aged 1
ancient 1
very aged man 1
very old 1.

YATAB יטב
be accepted 2
be glad 1
be good 2
be made better 1
be merry 4
be well 12
find favour 1
go well 4
please 2
seem best 1.
HIPH. amend 4
be better 2
be comely 1
benefit 1
deal well 3
do [goodness] 1
do good 18
do well 8
dress 1
entreat well 1
give [wealth] 1
make better 1
make cheerful 1
make good 1
make merry 1
make sweet 1
please 1
shew [kindness] 1
tire 1
trim 1
*speak well 1
*well 3.
Infin. diligent 1
diligently 2
earnestly 1
skilfully 1
thoroughly 1
very 1
very small 1.
Adv. inf. surely 1
throughly 1.
†KAL be content (*with* be-enayim) 1; please (*with* be-ene) 9; please better (*with* le) 1; please well (*with* be-ene) 2.

YATH ית
[*Accus. prefix.*]

YATHAR יתר
Partic. [*See* yother.]
NIPH. be left 39
be left behind 1
be remaining 2
remain 20.
Partic. remainder 1.
remnant 3
residue 3
rest 11.
HIPH. excel 1
leave 13
leave a remnant 1
let remain 2
make plenteous 2
preserve 1
reserve 3.
Inf. too much 1.

YATHED יָתֵד *f.*
nail 8
paddle 1
pin 13
stake 2.

YATHOM יָתוֹם
fatherless 38
fatherless child 3
orphan 1.

YATSA יצא
appear 1
be come forth 6
be come out 10
be departed 3
be gone forth 11
be gone out 17
be laid out 1
be risen 1
break out 1
come 10
come abroad 1
come forth 78
come out 108
come there out 1
come without 2
depart 12
escape 2
fail 2
fall 2
fall out 2
get away 1
get forth 1
get hence 1
get (out) 6
go abroad 1
go (away) 4
go forth 147
go on 3
go (out) 298
grow 1
issue (out) 7
lie out 3
proceed 16
shoot forth 1
spread 1
spring out 2
stand out 1
*bring forth 1
*do 1.
Partic. able to go 1
able to go forth 14
begotten 1
fit to go out 1.
Infin. departure 1
in the end of 1
still 1.
Adv. inf. assuredly 1
at any time 1
scarce 1
surely 2.
HIPH. bear out 1
bring forth 122
bring in and out 1
bring out 95
bring up 5
carry (forth) 12
carry out 8
cause to go forth 1
cause to go out 1
draw forth 3
exact 1
fetch forth 1
fetch out 1
have forth 2
have out 1
lay out 1
lead out 3
let go out 1
pluck out 2
pull out 1
pull away 2
take forth 1
take out 1
utter 6.
HOPH. be brought forth 5.
†KAL be condemned (*with* rasha) 1; follow (*with* achare) 1. *Adv. inf.* to and fro (*with infin. of* shub) 1. *See* eth.

YATSAB יצב
HITHP. be able to stand 3
can stand 1
present selves 9
resort 1
set 1
set selves 5
stand 21
stand fast 1
stand forth 1
stand still 2
stand up 2.
Infin. remaining 1.
†withstand (*with* im) 1.

YATSAG יצג
HIPH. establish 1
leave 1
make 2
present 1
put 2
set 8.
HOPH. be stayed 1.

YATSAQ יצק
cast 11
pour 19
pour out 4
run out 1
*grow 1.
Pass. pt. firm 2
hard 1
molten 1
*cleaveth fast 1.
HIPH. lay out 1
pour out 1
set down 1.
HOPH. be overflown 1
be poured 2.
Partic. molten 5
steadfast 1.

YATSAR [1] יצר
fashion 4
form 26
frame 3
make 3
purpose 1.
Partic. maker 4
potter 17
*earthen 1.
NIPH. be formed 1.
PUAL be fashioned 1.
HOPH. be formed 1.

YATSAR [2] יָצַר
be distressed 4
be in straits 1
be narrow 1
be straitened 2
be vexed 1.

YATSATH יצת
be burned 3
kindle 1.
NIPH. be burned 4
be burned up 1
be desolate 1
be kindled 2.
HIPH. burn 1
kindle 9
set [on fire] 6
set fire 1.

YATSI יְצִיא
*come forth 1.

YATSIA יָצִיעַ *c.*
chamber 3.

YATSTSIB יַצִּיב
certain 1
certainty 1
true 2
truth 1.

YATSUA יָצוּעַ
bed 3
couch 1.
†*See* eres.

YATTIR יַתִּיר
exceeding 2
exceedingly 1
excellent 5.

YAVEN יָוֵן
mire 1
*miry 1.

YAYIN יַיִן
wine 133
*banqueting 1.
†*See* gephen, saba.

YEAPH יְעָף
swiftly 1.

YEAT יעט
Partic. counsellors 2.
HITHP. consult together 1.

YEBAL יבל
HAPH. bring 2
carry 1.

YEBEMETH יְבֶמֶת *f.*
brother's wife 3
sister-in-law 2.

YEBUL יְבוּל
fruit 3
increase 10.

YEDA [1] ידא
HAPH. give thanks 1
thank 1.

YEDA [2] ידע
know 22.
HAPH. certify 4
make known 19
teach 1.

YEDE. *du. of* **YAD.**

YEDIDUTH יְדִידוּת *f.*
dearly beloved 1.

YEELIM יְעֵלִים *pl.*
wild goats 3.

YEENIM יְעֵנִים *pl.*
ostriches 1.

YEGEBIM יְגֵבִים *pl.*
fields 1.

YEGIA יְגִיעַ
labour 15
work 1.

YEGIAH יְגִעָה *f.*
weariness 1.

YEHAB יהב
deliver 1
give 17
lay 1
yield 1.
HITHP. be given 6
be paid 1.
†See *arkah.*

YEKIL יְכִל
be able 4
can 5
couldest 2
prevail 1.

YELALAH יְלָלָה *f.*
howling 5.

YELED יֶלֶד
boy 2
child 72
fruit 1
son 3
young man 7
young one 3.

YELEL יְלֵל
howling 1.

YELEQ יֶלֶק
cankerworm 6
caterpillar 3.

YELID = YALID.

YEMANI יְמָנִי
on the right hand 1
right 32.

YEMIM יֵמִם *pl.*
mules 1.

YEMINI ימיני [V. L.]
on the right hand 1
right 1.

YENIQOTH יְנִיקוֹת *f. pl.*
young twigs 1.

YEOR יְאוֹר
brook 5
flood 6
river 53
stream 1.

YEPHATH = YAPHEH.

YEPHEH-PHIYYAH יְפֵה־פִיָּה
very beautiful 1.

YEPHI יְפִי
beauty 1.

YEQAD יקד
Partic. burning 8.

YEQAR יְקָר
fat 1
honour 7
precious thing 1
precious things 2
price 1
*honour (*vb.*) 4
*precious 1.

YEQAR יְקָר
glory 5
honour 2.

YEQEB יֶקֶב
fat 2
press 2
pressfat 1
wine 1
winepress 10.

YEQEDAH יְקֵדָה *f.*
burning 1.

YEQOD יְקוֹד
burning 2.

YEQUM יְקוּם
living substance 1
substance 1.

YERA. *Imperf. of* **RAA** [1].

YERACH יֶרַח
month 11
moon 2.

YERACH יְרַח
month 2.

YERAQON יֵרָקוֹן
mildew 5
paleness 1.

YERAQRAQ יְרַקְרַק
greenish 2
yellow 1.

* Inexact translations, *e.g.*, of a noun by a verb or adjective, of an active by a passive.
† Cases where two or more words in the original are translated by one word or by a phrase.

YEREQ יֶרֶק
grass 1
green 3
green thing 2.
YERESHAH יְרֵשָׁה *f.*
possession 2.
YERIAH יְרִיעָה *f.*
curtain 53.
YERUSHSHAH יְרֻשָּׁה *f.*
heritage 1
inheritance 2
possession 11
YESAPH יסף
Hoph. be added 1.
YESH יֵשׁ
are
be
is
shall be
substance 1
there is
there shall be
there was
there were
was
were, etc. etc.
YESHA יֶשַׁע (יֵשַׁע)
safety 3
salvation 32
saving 1.
YESHACH יֶשַׁח
casting down 1.
YESHIMON יְשִׁימוֹן
desert 4
solitary 1
wilderness 2.
YESHUAH יְשׁוּעָה *f.*
deliverance 3
health 2
help 3
helping 1
salvation 63
saving health 1
welfare 1
*save 3.
YESOD יְסוֹד
bottom 3
foundation 10
repairing 1.
YESUD יְסֻד
*began 1.
YESUDAH יְסוּדָה *f.*
foundation 1.
YETAB יטב
seem good 1.
YETHER[1] יֶתֶר
excellency 3
remnant 14
residue 8
rest 63
that . . . hath left 3
what they leave 1
*excellent 1.
As adv. exceeding 1.
†plentifully (al[2] yether) 1. *See* gadol.
YETHER[2] יֶתֶר
cord 1
string 1
withs (*pl.*) 3.
YETHIB יְתִב
be set 1
dwell 1
sit 2.
Haph. set 1.
YETHUR יְתוּר
range 1
YETSA יצא
Shaph. be finished 1
YETSEB יצב
Pael *inf.* truth 1
YETSER יֵצֶר
frame 1
imagination 5
mind 1
thing framed 1
work 1.
YETSUQAH יְצֻקָה *f.*
*be cast 1
YETSURIM יְצֻרִים *pl.*
members 1.
YEZA יֶזַע
anything that causeth sweat 1.

YIDDEONI יִדְּעֹנִי
wizard 11.
YILLOD יִלּוֹד
born 7.
YIPHAH יִפְעָה *f.*
brightness 2.
YIQQEHAH יִקְּהָה *f.*
gathering 1
*to obey 1.
YIRAH יִרְאָה *f.*
fear 42
fearfulness 1
*dreadful 1.
†exceedingly (*with* gadol) 2.
YISHRAH יִשְׁרָה *f.*
uprightness 1.
YISSOR יִסּוֹר
*instruct 1.
YITHRAH יִתְרָה *f.*
abundance 1
riches 1.
YITHRON יִתְרוֹן *f.*
excellency 1
profit 6
*excel 2
*profitable 1.
†not be better (en yithron le) 1.
YITSHAR יִצְהָר
oil 22.
†*See* ben.
YITTEN = NATHAN.
YOBEL יוֹבֵל *c.*
jubilee 21
ram's [horn] 1
rams' horn 4
trumpet 1.
YOM יוֹם
day 1167.
time (*s. and pl.*) 65
weather 1
*daily 2
*remain 1
*when 1.
Plur. age 6
full year 1
life 4
season 3
space 3
while (a, the) 3
year 5
years 4
*full 9
*in continuance 1
*whole 4
*yearly 2.
Hay-yom (*article* + yom).
ago 1
agone 1
even now 1
now 3
nowadays 1
presently 1
then 1
to-day 30.
†as at other times (ke-yom be-yom) 1; as [it] required (be-yom) 3; as [it] shall require (be-yom) 1; as long as (kol hay-yamim 5, kol hay-yamim asher 4, bime (= bi-yeme) 1) 10; birthday (*with Hiph. inf. of* yalad) 1; continually (kol hay-yom) 10; daily (yom yom 7, yom be-yom 5, kol yamim 1, kol yom (*or* hay-yom) 10, le-yom echad 1, lay-yom 4, be-kol yom 1) 29; each day (yom yom) 2; everlasting (*pl. with* olam) 1; for ever (le-orek yamim) 2; foundation (*with inf. Niph. of* yasad) 1; of old (miy-yamim) 1; old (*with pl. of* shanah *and* chaiyim) 1; process of time (*pl. with* rab *and* hu 1, *pl. with* rabah 1) 2; since (miy-yom) 1; so long (miy-yom 1, miy-yamim 1, kol hay-yamim 1) 3; time to come (*with* machar) 1; to live (*pl. with pl. of* shanah *and* chaiyim) 1; when (be-yom) 5; while (miy-yom) 1; whole age (*with pl. of* shanah *and* chaiyim) 1; yearly (miy-yamim yamimah) 4; yesterday (*with* ethmol) 1. Kol hay-yamim: alway 4, always 4, ever 3, evermore 1, for ever 18, perpetually 2. *See* arak, dabar[2], kabbir, natah, qasheh, tsair, zaqen[2].
YOM יוֹם
day 14.
Plur. time 2.
YOMAM יוֹמָם
by day 18
by daytime 1
daily 2
day 20
in the day 1
in the daytime 7.
YONAH יוֹנָה *f.*
dove 21
pigeon 10.
YONEQ יוֹנֵק
tender plant 1.
YONEQETH יוֹנֶקֶת *f.*
branch 4
tender branch 1
young twig 1.
YOPHI יֳפִי
beauty 18.
YOREH יוֹרֶה [*as pt. of* **YARAH**].
first rain 1
former [rain] 1
former rain 1.
YOSHER יֹשֶׁר
equity 1
uprightness 9
*be meet 1
*right 2
*upright 1.
YOTHER יוֹתֵר
better 1
further 1
more 3
moreover 1
over 2
profit 1
rest 1
[*See* yathar].
YOTHERETH יֹתֶרֶת
caul 11.
YUBAL יוּבַל
river 1.

Z

ZAAK זעך
Niph. be extinct 1
ZAAM[1] זעם
abhor 2
be angry 1
defy 3
have indignation 3
*indignation 1.
Pass. pt. abominable 1.
Niph. be angry 1.
ZAAM[2] זַעַם
anger 1
indignation 20
rage 1.
ZAAPH[1] זעף
be wroth 2
fret 1
Partic. sad 1
worse liking 1.
ZAAPH[2] זַעַף
indignation 2
rage 2
raging 1
wrath 1.
ZAAQ זעק
call 1
cry 47
cry out 11.
Niph. assemble selves 1
be called together 1
be gathered 2
be gathered together 1
come with such a company 1.
Hiph. assemble 2
call 1
cause to be proclaimed 1
cry 1
gather together 1
make to cry 1.
ZAAVAH זַעֲוָה *f.*
*removed 6.
ZABACH זבח
do sacrifice 6
kill 5
offer 37
sacrifice 65
slay 5.
Piel offer 2
sacrifice 20.
ZABAD זבד
endue 1.
ZABAL זבל
dwell with 1.
ZACHACH זחח
Niph. be loosed 2.
ZACHAL זחל
be afraid 1
Partic. serpent 1
worm 1.
ZADON זָדוֹן
pride 6
*most proud 1
*proud 1
*thou most proud 1.
†presumptuously (be-zadon) 1.
ZAEPH זָעֵף
displeased 2
ZAG זָג
husk 1.
ZAHAB זָהָב
fair weather 1
gold 330
*golden 36.
ZAHAM זהם
Piel abhor 1
ZAHAR זהר
Niph be admonished 2
be warned 3
take warning 1.
Hiph. give warning 3
shine 1
teach 1
warn 9.
ZAK זַךְ
clean 2
pure 9.
ZAKAH זכה
be clean 2
be clear 1
count pure 1.
Piel cleanse 2
make clean 1.
Hithp. make clean 1.
ZAKAK זכך
be clean 1
be pure 2.
Hiph. make clean 1.
ZAKAR[1] זכר
be mindful 6
call to remembrance 1
have in remembrance 1
make mention 1
mention 1
recount 1
remember 158
think on 3.
Adv. inf. earnestly 1
still 1
well 1.
Niph. be in remembrance 1
be mentioned 3
be remembered 13
come to remembrance 1
mention be made 1.
Hiph. bring to remembrance 3
burn 1
call to remembrance 2
keep in remembrance 1
make mention of 15
make to be remembered 2
mention 1
put in remembrance 1
record 2
remember 4.
Partic. recorder 9.
ZAKAR[2] זָכָר
male 67
man 7
man child 5
mankind 2
*him 1.
ZAKAR[3] זכר
Niph. be male 1.
ZAKU זָכוּ *f.*
innocency 1.
ZAKUR זְכוּר
male 3
men children 1.
ZALAL זלל
Partic. glutton 2
riotous 1
riotous eater 1
vile 2.
Niph. flow down 2.
ZALAPHAH זַלְעָפָה *f.*
horror 1
*horrible 1
*terrible 1.
ZALZALLIM זַלְזַלִּים *pl.*
sprigs 5.
ZAMAM[1] זמם
consider 1
devise 3
imagine 1
plot 1
purpose 2
think 4
think evil 1.
ZAMAM[2] זָמָם
wicked device 1.
ZAMAN זמן
Pual *pt.* appointed 3.
ZAMAR זמר
prune 2.
Niph. be pruned 1.
Piel give praise 2
sing 12
sing forth 1
sing praises 29
sing psalms 2.
ZAMIR זָמִיר
singing 1.
ZAMMAR זַמָּר
singer 1
ZAN זַן
divers kinds (*pl.*) 1.
†all manner of store (miz-zan el zan) 1.
ZAN זַן
kind 4.
ZANAB[1] זָנָב
tail 11.
ZANAB[2] זנב
Piel smite the hindmost 2.
ZANACH זנח
cast off 15
remove far off 1.
Hiph. cast away 1.
cast off 2
turn far away 1.
ZANAH זנה
be an harlot 3
commit [whoredom] 1
commit fornication 2
commit whoredom 9
fall to whoredom 1
go a whoring 19
play the harlot 15
play the whore 3
*whore 1.
Partic harlot 16
whore 4
whorish 2.
Adv. inf. great 1.
Pual commit whoredom 1.
Hiph. cause to be a whore 1
cause to commit fornication 1
commit whoredom 3
make to go a whoring 2.
Infin. whoredom 1.
Adv. inf. continually 1.
†Kal go to commit whoredom with (*with* achare) 1. *Partic.* harlot (*with* ishshah) 4; whore (*with* ishshah) 1.
ZANAQ זנק
Piel leap 1.
ZAQAN זָקָן *c.*
beard 10.
ZAQAPH זקף
raise 1
raise up 1.
ZAQAQ זקק
fine 1
pour down 1
Piel purge 1.
Pual *pt.* purified 1
refined 3.
ZAQEN[1] זָקֵן
be aged man 1
be old 21
be old man 1
wax old 2.
Hiph. be old 1
wax old 1
ZAQEN[2] זָקֵן
aged 3
ancient 14
ancient man 1
elder 115
eldest 1
old 24
old man 19
old men and old women (*pl.*) 1
senator 1.
†elder (*with* le-yamim) 1
ZARA[1] זָרָא
loathsome 1
ZARA[2] זרע
set 1
sow 41.
Partic. sower 2
*bearing 1
*yielding 1.
Niph. be sown 5
conceive 1.
Pual be sown 1.
Hiph. conceive seed 1
yield 2.
ZARAB זרב
Pual wax warm 1
ZARACH זרח
arise 8
be risen 2
be up 1
rise 4
rise up 2
shine 1.
ZARAH זרה
cast away 1
fan 3
scatter 2
strew 1
winnow 2.
Niph be dispersed 1
be scattered 1
Piel compass 1
disperse 7
fan 1
scatter 15
scatter away 1
spread 1.
Pual be scattered 1
be spread 1.
ZARAM זרם
carry away as with a flood 1.
Poal pour out 1.
ZARAQ זרק
be here and there 1
scatter 2
sprinkle 29
strow 1.
Pual be sprinkled 2.
ZARAR זרר
Poel sneeze 1.
ZARZIPH זַרְזִיף
water 1.
ZARZIR זַרְזִיר
†greyhound (*with* mothnayim) 1.

* Inexact translations, *e.g.*, of a noun by a verb or adjective, of an active by a passive.
† Cases where two or more words in the original are translated by one word or by a phrase.

ZAVIYYOTH זָוִיּוֹת *f. pl.*
corners 1
corner stones 1.

ZAYITH זַיִת
olive 16
olive tree 14
oliveyard 6.

ZEAH זֵעָה *f.*
sweat 1.

ZEAQAH זְעָקָה *f.*
cry 17
crying 1.

ZEBACH זֶבַח
offering 6
sacrifice 155
*offer 1.
†peace offerings (*with pl. of* shelem) 2.

ZEBAN זבן
gain 1.

ZEBED זֶבֶד
dowry 1.

ZEBUB זְבוּב
fly 2.

ZEBUL (זְבֻל) זְבוּל
dwelling 1
habitation 3
*dwell in 1.

ZED זֵד
presumptuous 1
proud 12.

ZEDON זֵידוֹן
proud 1.

ZEEB זְאֵב
wolf 7.

ZEER זְעֵר
little 5.

ZEER זְעֵיר
little 1.

ZEH זֶה
he
it
now
this
this man, etc.

ZEHAR זהר
take heed 1.

ZEIQ זְעִק
cry 2.

ZEKER (זֶכֶר) זֵכֶר
memorial 5
memory 5
remembrance 12
scent 1.

ZEKUKITH זְכוּכִית *f.*
crystal 1.

ZEMAN זְמָן
season 1
time 3.

ZEMAN[1] זמן
HITHPA. prepare 1.

ZEMAN[2] זְמָן
season 2
time 9.

ZEMAR זְמָר
musick 4.

ZEMER זֶמֶר
chamois 1.

ZEMIR זָמִיר
branch 1
psalm 2
song 3
*psalmist 1.

ZEMORAH זְמוֹרָה *f.*
branch 3
slip 1
vine branch 1.

ZENUNIM זְנוּנִים *pl.*
whoredom 11.

ZENUTH זְנוּת *f.*
whoredom 9.

ZEPHETH זֶפֶת *f.*
pitch 3.

ZEQAPH זקף
Pass. pt. being set up 1.

ZEQUNIM זְקֻנִים *pl.*
old age 4.

ZER זֵר
crown 11.

ZERA זֶרַע
child 2
seed *freq.*
seedtime 1
sowing time 1
*fruitful 1.
†carnally (la-zera) 1. *See* shekabah.

ZERA זְרַע
seed 1.

ZERACH זֶרַח
rising 1.

ZEREM זֶרֶם
flood 1
overflowing 1
shower 1
storm 3
tempest 3.

ZERONIM זֵרְעֹנִים *pl.*
pulse 1.

ZERETH זֶרֶת *f.*
span 7.

ZEROA זְרוֹעַ *c.*
arm 82
power 3
shoulder 2
strength 1
*mighty 1.
†*See* hayah.

ZEROIM זֵרֹעִים *pl.*
pulse 1.

ZERUA זֵרוּעַ
sowing 1
things that are sown 1.

ZEVAAH זַעֲוָה *f.*
trouble 1
vexation 1.

ZID = ZUD.

ZIKKARON זִכָּרוֹן
memorial 17
record 1
remembrance 6.

ZIMMAH זִמָּה *f.*
heinous crime 1
lewdness 14
mischief 3
purpose 1
thought 1
wicked device 1
wicked mind 1
wickedness 4
*lewd 2.
†lewdly (be-zimmah) 1.

ZIMRAH זִמְרָה *f.*
best fruit 1
melody 2
psalm 2.

ZIMRATH זִמְרָת *f.*
song 3.

ZIQNAH זִקְנָה *f.*
old age 3
*old 3.

ZIQOTH זִיקוֹת *f. pl.*
sparks 2.

ZIQQIM זִקִּים *pl.*
chains 3
fetters 1
firebrands 1.

ZIRMAH זִרְמָה *f.*
issue 2.

ZIV זִיו
brightness 2
countenance 4.

ZIZ זִיז
abundance 1
wild beast 1
wild beasts 1.

ZO = ZEH.

ZOB זוֹב
issue 13.

ZOH = ZEH.

ZOHAR זֹהַר
brightness 2.

ZONOTH זוֹנוֹת *f. pl.*
armour 1.

ZOQEN זֹקֶן
age 1.

ZOTH זֹאת [*fem. of* ZEH].
it
she
that
this
this thing, etc.

ZU = ZEH.

ZUA זוּעַ
move 1
tremble 1.
PILP. vex 1.

ZUA זוּעַ
tremble 2.

ZUB זוּב
flow 22
gush out 3
have an issue 14
have a running issue 1
pine away 1
run 1.

ZUD זוּד
be proud 1
deal proudly 1.
HIPH. come presumptuously 1
deal proudly 3
do presumptuously 1
presume 1
seathe (sod) 1
*presumptuously 1.

ZUD זוּד
Haph. inf. pride 1.

ZUL זוּל
lavish 1.
HIPH. despise 1.

ZULAH זוּלָה *f.*
beside 7
but 2
only 1
save 5
save that 1.

ZULLUTH זֻלּוּת *f.*
*vilest 1.

ZUN זוּן
HOPH. be fed 1.

ZUN זוּן
HITHP. be fed 1.

ZUR[1] זוּר
be closed 1
crush 1
thrust together 1.

ZUR[2] זוּר
be estranged 3
be strange 1
come from another place 1.
Partic. another 1
another man 1
strange 14
stranger 44
strange thing 1
strange woman 4
*fanners (*j. l.*) 1.
NIPH. be estranged 1
be gone away 2.
HOPH. *pt.* stranger 1.
†*See* ish.

ZUREH זוּרֶה
that which is crushed 1.

* Inexact translations, *e.g.*, of a noun by a verb or adjective, of an active by a passive.
† Cases where two or more words in the original are translated by one word or by a phrase.

INDEX-LEXICON TO THE NEW TESTAMENT.

NOTE.—The system followed in this Lexicon is similar to that which precedes, except that marginal renderings are included. They are added in brackets and preceded by a capital M. Under verbs MID. stands for Middle, a form generally reflexive or reciprocal. PASS. stands for Passive.

ABARĒS ἀβαρής
*from being burdensome 1.

ABBA ἀββᾶ (ἀββά)
abba 3.

ABUSSOS ἄβυσσος *f.*
bottomless pit 5
deep 2
*bottomless 2.

ACHARISTOS ἀχάριστος
unthankful 2.

ACHEIROPOIĒTOS ἀχειροποίητος
made without hands 2
not made with hands 1.

ACHLUS ἀχλύς
mist 1.

ACHREIOOMAI ἀχρειόομαι
become unprofitable 1.

ACHREIOS ἀχρεῖος
unprofitable 2.

ACHRĒSTOS ἄχρηστος
unprofitable 1.

ACHRI(S) ἄχρι *or* ἄχρις
as far as 1
as far as to 1
even to 2
for 2
in 1
into 1
till 3
until 14
unto 13.
†*With* hou: till 4, until 2, while 2. *With* hou an: till 2. *See* deuro.

ACHURON ἄχυρον *n.*
chaff 2.

ADAPANOS ἀδάπανος
without charge 2.

ADĒLOS ἄδηλος
uncertain 1
which appears not 1.

ADĒLŌS ἀδήλως
uncertainly 1.

ADĒLOTĒS ἀδηλότης *f.*
*uncertain (M. uncertainty) 1.

ADELPHĒ ἀδελφή *f.*
sister 24.

ADELPHOS ἀδελφός
brother 346.

ADELPHOTĒS ἀδελφότης *f.*
brethren 1
brotherhood 1.

ADĒMONEŌ ἀδημονέω
be full of heaviness 1
be very heavy 2.

ADIAKRITOS ἀδιάκριτος
without partiality (M. without wrangling) 1.

ADIALEIPTOS ἀδιάλειπτος
continual 1.
without ceasing 1.

ADIALEIPTŌS ἀδιαλείπτως
without ceasing 4.

ADIAPHTHORIA ἀδιαφθορία *f.*
uncorruptness 1.

ADIKĒMA ἀδίκημα *n.*
evil doing 1
iniquity 1
matter of wrong 1.

ADIKEŌ ἀδικέω
be an offender 1
be unjust 2
do wrong 8
hurt 10
injure 1
wrong 2.
PASS. suffer wrong 2.
MID. take wrong 1.

ADIKIA ἀδικία *f.*
iniquity 6
unrighteousness 16
wrong 1
unjust 2.

ADIKOS ἄδικος
unjust 8
unrighteous 4.

ADIKŌS ἀδίκως
wrongfully 1.

ADŌ ᾄδω
sing 5.

ADOKIMOS ἀδόκιμος
castaway 1
rejected 1
reprobate 6 (M. of no judgment 1, void of judgment 2).

ADOLOS ἄδολος
sincere 1.

ADUNATEŌ ἀδυνατέω
be impossible 2.

ADUNATOS ἀδύνατος
impossible 6
impotent 1
not possible 1
weak 1.
*what . . . could not do 1

AEI ἀεί
alway 4
always 3
ever 1.

AĒR ἀήρ
air 7.

AETOS ἀετός
eagle 4.

AGALLIAŌ ἀγαλλιάω
rejoice 1.
MID. be exceeding glad 1
be glad 1
greatly rejoice 1
rejoice 6.
Partic. with exceeding joy 1.

AGALLIASIS ἀγαλλίασις *f.*
exceeding joy 1
gladness 3
joy 1.

AGAMOS ἄγαμος
unmarried 4.

AGANAKTEŌ ἀγανακτέω
be moved with indignation 1
be much displeased 2
be sore displeased 1
have indignation 2.
Partic with indignation 1.

AGANAKTĒSIS ἀγανάκτησις *f.*
indignation 1.

AGAPAŌ ἀγαπάω
love 135
Pass. pt. beloved 7.

AGAPĒ ἀγάπη *f.*
charity 27
feast of charity 1
love 86
*dear 1
†charitably (kata *with acc.*) 1.

AGAPĒTOS ἀγαπητός
beloved 47
dear 3
dearly beloved 9
well beloved 3.

AGATHOERGEO ἀγαθοεργέω
do good 1

AGATHOPOIEŌ ἀγαθοποιέω
do good 7
do well 2.
Partic. for well doing 1
with well doing 1.

AGATHOPOIIA ἀγαθοποιΐα *f.*
well doing 1.

AGATHOPOIOS ἀγαθοποιός
that doeth well 1.

AGATHOS ἀγαθός
good 63.
As noun benefit 1
good 12
good thing 14
goods 2
that which is good 9
the thing which is good 1.

AGATHŌSUNĒ ἀγαθωσύνη *f.*
goodness 4.

AGE ἄγε (*imper. of* AGŌ)
go to 2.

AGELĒ ἀγέλη *f.*
herd 8.

AGENEALOGĒTOS ἀγενεαλόγητος
without descent (M. w. pedigree) 1.

AGENĒS ἀγενής
As noun base things 1.

AĞGAREUŌ ἀγγαρεύω
compel 2
compel to go 1.

AĞGEION ἀγγεῖον *n.*
vessel 2.

AĞGELIA ἀγγελία
message (M. commandment) 1.

AĞGELOS ἄγγελος
angel 181
messenger 7.

AĞKALAI ἀγκάλαι *pl. f.*
arms 1.

AĞKISTRON ἄγκιστρον *n.*
hook 1.

AĞKURA ἄγκυρα *f.*
anchor 4.

AGNAPHOS ἄγναφος
new (M. raw *or* unwrought) 2.

AGNOĒMA ἀγνόημα *n.*
error 1.

AGNOEŌ ἀγνοέω
be ignorant 7
know not 4
understand not 3.
Partic. ignorant 1
unknown 2
*ignorantly 2.
Infin. *ignorant 3.

AGNOIA ἄγνοια *f.*
ignorance 4.

AGNŌSIA ἀγνωσία *f.*
ignorance 1.
†*See* echō.

AGNŌSTOS ἄγνωστος
unknown 1.

AGŌ ἄγω
bring 45
bring forth 2
carry 1
go (*always 1 pers. pl.*) 7
lead 12
lead away 1.
*be 1.
PASS. be kept 1
be open (M. be kept) 1.

AGŌGĒ ἀγωγή *f.*
manner of life 1.

AGŌN ἀγών
conflict 2 (M. fear *or* care 1).
contention 1
fight 2
race 1.

AGŌNIA ἀγωνία *f.*
agony 1.

AGŌNIZOMAI ἀγωνίζομαι
fight 3
labour fervently (M. strive) 1.
strive 3.

AGORA ἀγορά *f*
market 6
market-place 4 (M. court 1).
street 1.

AGORAIOS ἀγοραῖος
of the baser sort 1.
As noun law (M. court days) 1.

AGORAZŌ ἀγοράζω
buy 28
redeem 3.

AGRA ἄγρα *f.*
drought 2.

AGRAMMATOS ἀγράμματος
unlearned 1.

AGRAULEŌ ἀγραυλέω
abide in the field 1.

AGREUŌ ἀγρεύω
catch 1.

AGRIELAIOS ἀγριέλαιος *f.*
olive tree which is wild 1.
wild olive tree 1.

AGRIOS ἄγριος
raging 1
wild 2.

AGROS ἀγρός
country 8
farm 1
field 22
land 4
piece of ground 1.

AGRUPNEŌ ἀγρυπνέω
watch 4.

AGRUPNIA ἀγρυπνία *f.*
watching 2.

AICHMALŌSIA αἰχμαλωσία
captivity 2 (M. multitude of captives 1).

AICHAMALŌTEUŌ αἰχμαλωτεύω
lead captive 2.

AICHMALŌTIZŌ αἰχμαλωτίζω
bring into captivity 2
lead away captive 1.

AICHMALŌTOS αἰχμάλωτος
captive 1.

AÏDIOS ἀΐδιος
eternal 1
everlasting 1.

AIDŌS αἰδώς *f.*
reverence 1
shamefacedness 1.

AIGEIOS αἴγειος (*adj.*)
goat 1.

AIGIALOS αἰγιαλός
shore 6.

AINEŌ αἰνέω
praise 9.

AINESIS αἴνεσις *f*
praise 1.

AINIGMA αἴνιγμα *n.*
†darkly (en *with dat.*; M. in a riddle) 1.

AINOS αἶνος
praise 3.

AIŌN αἰών
age 2
beginning of the world 2
course 1
world 32
*eternal 2
*world began 1.
†Eis *with acc.*: for ever 27, for evermore 2, ever 1, while the world standeth 1. Eis *with acc. folld. by gen.*: for ever and ever 1. Eis *with acc. pl. and gen. pl.*: for ever and ever 20, for evermore 1. Ever (pas *with pl.*) 1; never (oute eis (ou mē eis) *with acc.*) 7; world without end (*with gen. pl.*) 1. *See* hēmera.

AIŌNIOS αἰώνιος
eternal 42
everlasting 25
*for ever 1.
†*See* chronos.

AIPHNIDIOS αἰφνίδιος
sudden 1.
*unawares 1.

AIRŌ αἴρω
bear 3
bear up 2
carry 1
lift up 4
loose 1
put away 1
remove 2
take 25
take away 25 (M. bear 1)
take up 32.
Imper. away with 5.
†*With* psuchē: make to doubt (M. hold in suspense) 1.

AISCHROKERDĒS αἰσχροκερδής
given to filthy lucre 1
greedy of filthy lucre 2.

AISCHROKERDŌS αἰσχροκερδῶς
for filthy lucre 1.

AISCHROLOGIA αἰσχρολογία *f.*
filthy communication 1.

AISCHROS αἰσχρός
filthy 1
*a shame 3.

AISCHROTĒS αἰσχρότης *f.*
filthiness 1.

AISCHUNĒ αἰσχύνη *f.*
dishonesty (M. shame) 1.
shame 5.

AISCHUNOMAI αἰσχύνομαι
be ashamed 5.

AISTHANOMAI αἰσθάνομαι
perceive 1.

AISTHĒSIS αἴσθησις *f.*
judgment (M. sense) 1.

AISTHĒTĒRION αἰσθητήριον *n.*
senses (*pl.*) 1.

AITĒMA αἴτημα *n.*
petition 1
request 1.
*require 1.

AITEŌ αἰτέω
ask 48
beg 2
call for 1
crave 1
desire 17
require 2.

AITIA αἰτία *f.*
accusation 3
case 1
cause 9
crime 1
fault 3.
†*See* dia.

AITIAMA αἰτίαμα *n.*
complaint 1.

AITION αἴτιον
cause 2
fault 2.

AITIOS αἴτιος (*adj.*)
*author 1.

AKAIREOMAI ἀκαιρέομαι
lack opportunity 1.

AKAIRŌS ἀκαίρως
out of season 1

AKAKOS ἄκακος
harmless 1
simple 1.

AKANTHA ἄκανθα *f.*
thorn(s) 14.

AKANTHINOS ἀκάνθινος
of thorns 2.

AKARPOS ἄκαρπος
unfruitful 6
without fruit 1

* Inexact translations, *e.g.*, of a noun by a verb or adjective, of an active by a passive.
† Cases where two or more words in the original are translated by one word or by a phrase.

AKATAGNŌSTOS ἀκατάγνωστος
that cannot be condemned 1.

AKATAKALUPTOS ἀκατακάλυπτος
uncovered 2.

AKATAKRITOS ἀκατάκριτος
uncondemned 2.

AKATALUTOS ἀκατάλυτος
endless 1.

AKATAPAUSTOS ἀκατάπαυστος
that cannot cease 1.

AKATASCHETOS ἀκατάσχετος
unruly 1.

AKATASTASIA ἀκαταστασία *f.*
commotion 1
confusion (M. tumult *or* unquietness) 1
tumult 2 (M. tossing to and fro 1).

AKATASTATOS ἀκατάστατος
unstable 1.

AKATHARSIA ἀκαθαρσία *f.*
uncleanness 10.

AKATHARTĒS ἀκαθάρτης *f.*
filthiness 1.

AKATHARTOS ἀκάθαρτος
foul 2
unclean 28.

AKERAIOS ἀκέραιος
harmless 2 (M. simple 1, sincere 1)
simple (M. harmless) 1.

AKLINĒS ἀκλινής
without wavering 1.

AKMAZŌ ἀκμάζω
be fully ripe 1.

AKMĒN ἀκμήν
yet 1.

AKOĒ ἀκοή *f.*
audience 1
ears 4
fame 3
hearing 10
report (M. preaching *or* hearing) 1
rumour 1
*preached (M. of hearing) 1
*which ye heard 1.

AKOLOUTHEŌ ἀκολουθέω
follow 90 (M. go with 1)
reach 1.

AKŌLUTŌS ἀκωλύτως
*no man forbidding 1.

AKŌN ἄκων
*against my will 1.

AKOUŌ ἀκούω
give audience 3
hear 415
hearken 6
understand (M. hear) 1.
Partic. hearer 2
*in the audience of (*gen.*) 1.
PASS. be noised 1
be reported 1
come to 1
come to ears of 1.
†be dull of hearing (*with* bareōs) 1.

AKRASIA ἀκρασία *f.*
excess 1
incontinency 1.

AKRATĒS ἀκρατής
incontinent 1.

AKRATOS ἄκρατος
without mixture 1.

AKRIBEIA ἀκρίβεια *f.*
perfect manner 1.

AKRIBĒS ἀκριβής
most straitest (*super.*) 1.

AKRIBOŌ ἀκριβόω
inquire diligently 2.

AKRIBŌS ἀκριβῶς
circumspectly 1
diligently 2
perfectly 4
*perfect 2.

AKRIS ἀκρίς *f.*
locust 4.

AKROATĒRION ἀκροατήριον *n.*
place of hearing 1.

AKROATĒS ἀκροατής
hearer 4.

AKROBUSTIA ἀκροβυστία *f.*
uncircumcision 16.
†uncircumcised (en *with dat.*) 2; though not circumcised (dia *with gen.*) 1. *See* echō.

AKROGŌNIAIOS ἀκρογωνιαῖος (*adj.*)
chief corner 2.

AKRON ἄκρον *n.*
end 1
tip 1
top 1
uttermost part 2
*other 1.

AKROTHINION ἀκροθίνιον *n.*
spoils (*pl.*) 1.

AKUROŌ ἀκυρόω
disannul 1
make of none effect 2.

ALABASTRON ἀλάβαστρον *n.*
alabaster box 3
box 1.

ALALĒTOS ἀλάλητος
which cannot be uttered 1.

ALALOS ἄλαλος
dumb 3.

ALALAZŌ ἀλαλάζω
tinkle 1
wail 1.

ALAZŌN ἀλαζών
boaster 2.

ALAZONEIA ἀλαζονεία *f.*
boasting 1
pride 1.

ALEIPHŌ ἀλείφω
anoint 9.

ALEKTŌR ἀλέκτωρ
cock 12.

ALEKTOROPHŌNIA ἀλεκτοροφωνία *f.*
cock crowing 1.

ALĒTHEIA ἀλήθεια *f.*
truth 107 (M. *with* en, truly 1)
verity 1
*true(M. of truth) 1.
†truly (epi *with gen.*; M. of a truth) 1.

ALĒTHĒS ἀληθής
true 23
*truth 1
*truly 1.

ALĒTHEUŌ ἀληθεύω
speak the truth 1
tell the truth 1.

ALĒTHINOS ἀληθινός
true 27.

ALĒTHŌ ἀλήθω
grind 2.

ALĒTHŌS ἀληθῶς
indeed 6
in truth 1
of a surety 1
of a truth 6
surely 3
truly 2
verily 1
very 1.

ALEURON ἄλευρον *n.*
meal 2.

ALISGĒMA ἀλίσγημα *n.*
pollution 1.

ALLA ἀλλά
and rather 1
but 572
howbeit 8
indeed 1
nay 4
nevertheless 10
no 1
notwithstanding 1
save 2
therefore 3
yea 15
yet 11, etc.

ALLACHOTHEN ἀλλαχόθεν
some other way 1.

ALLASSŌ ἀλλάσσω
change 6.

ALLĒGOREŌ ἀλληγορέω
Pass. partic. *allegory 1.

ALLĒLŌN, etc. ἀλλήλων
each other 2
one another 76 (M. themselves 1)
one the other 3
themselves 12
yourselves 3
yourselves together 1.
†mutual (en *with dat.*) 1; together (meta *with gen.* 1, pros *with acc.* 1) 2.

ALLĒLOUIA ἀλληλουϊά (*Heb.*).
alleluia 4.

ALLOGENĒS ἀλλογενής
stranger 1.

ALLOPHULOS ἀλλόφυλος
one of another nation 1.

ALLOS ἄλλος
another 62
more 1
one 4
other 74
other man 4
other things 3
some 11
*another man's (*gen.*) 1.
*otherwise 1
†another (*with* tis) 1.

ALLŌS ἄλλως
otherwise 1.

ALLOTRIOEPISKOPOS ἀλλοτριοεπίσκοπος
busybody in other men's matters 1.

ALLOTRIOS ἀλλότριος
alien 1
another man's 6
of others 1
strange 2.
As noun stranger 4

ALOAŌ ἀλοάω
thresh 1
tread out the corn 2.

ALOĒ ἀλόη *f.*
aloes 1.

ALOGOS ἄλογος (*adj.*)
brute 2
unreasonable 1.

ALŌPĒX ἀλώπηξ
fox 3.

ALPHA ἄλφα
Alpha 4.

ALUPOTEROS ἀλυπότερος
less sorrowful 1.

ALUSITELĒS ἀλυσιτελής
unprofitable 1.

AMACHOS ἄμαχος
no brawler 1
not a brawler 1.

AMAŌ ἀμάω
reap down 1.

AMARANTINOS ἀμαράντινος
that fadeth not away 1.

AMARANTOS ἀμάραντος
that fadeth not away 1.

AMARTUROS ἀμάρτυρος
without witness 1.

AMATHĒS ἀμαθής
unlearned 1.

AMELEŌ ἀμελέω
be negligent 1
make light of 1
neglect 2
regard not 1.

AMEMPTOS ἄμεμπτος
blameless 3
faultless 1
unblameable 1.

AMEMPTŌS ἀμέμπτως
blameless 1
unblameably 1.

AMĒN ἀμήν
amen 50.
verily 100.

AMERIMNOS ἀμέριμνος
without carefulness 1.
†*See* poieō.

AMETAKINĒTOS ἀμετακίνητος
unmovable 1.

AMETAMELĒTOS ἀμεταμέλητος
not to be repented of 1
without repentance 1.

AMETANOĒTOS ἀμετανόητος
impenitent 1.

AMETATHETOS ἀμετάθετος
immutable 1
As noun immutability 1.

AMETHUSTOS ἀμέθυστος
amethyst 1.

AMĒTŌR ἀμήτωρ
without mother 1.

AMETROS ἄμετρος
As noun things without measure 2.

AMIANTOS ἀμίαντος
undefiled 4.

AMMOS ἄμμος
sand 5.

AMNOS ἀμνός
lamb 4.

AMOIBĒ ἀμοιβή *f.*
†*See* apodidōmi.

AMŌMĒTOS ἀμώμητος
blameless 1
without rebuke 1.

AMŌMOS ἄμωμος
faultless 1
unblameable 1
without blame 1
without blemish 2
without fault 1
without spot (M. without fault) 1.

AMPELŌN ἀμπελών
vineyard 23.

AMPELOS ἄμπελος *f.*
vine 9.

AMPELOURGOS ἀμπελουργός
dresser of one's vineyard 1.

AMPHIBLĒSTRON ἀμφίβληστρον *n.*
net 2.

AMPHIENNUMI ἀμφιέννυμι
clothe 4.

AMPHODON ἄμφοδον *n.*
place where two ways meet 1.

AMPHOTEROI ἀμφότεροι
both 14.

AMUNOMAI ἀμύνομαι
defend 1.

AN ἄν
Conditional and indef. particle, not translated by a special word. See hos, etc.

ANA ἀνά
in 1
through 4.
Followed by numeral: apiece 2
by 3
each 1
every 1
every man 2, etc.
†*See* meros, meson.

ANABAINŌ ἀναβαίνω
arise 2
ascend 10
ascend up 8
climb up 2
come 2
come up 10
come up again 1
enter 2
go up 37
grow up 2
rise up 2
spring up 2.
†go upon (*with* epi) 1.

ANABALLOMAI ἀναβάλλομαι
defer 1.

ANABATHMOS ἀναβαθμός
stair 2.

ANABIBAZŌ ἀναβιβάζω
draw 1.

ANABLEPŌ ἀναβλέπω
look 1
look up 9
receive sight 15
see 1.

ANABLEPSIS ἀνάβλεψις *f.*
recovering of sight 1.

ANABOAŌ ἀναβοάω
cry 1
cry aloud 1
cry out 1.

ANABOLĒ ἀναβολή *f.*
delay 1.

ANACHŌREŌ ἀναχωρέω
depart 8
give place 1.
go aside 2
turn aside 1.
withdraw one's self 2.

ANACHUSIS ἀνάχυσις *f.*
excess 1.

ANADECHOMAI ἀναδέχομαι
receive 2.

ANADEIKNUMI ἀναδείκνυμι
appoint 1
show 1.

ANADEIXIS ἀνάδειξις *f.*
showing 1.

ANADIDŌMI ἀναδίδωμι
deliver 1.

ANAGAION = ANŌGEON.

ANAĞGELLŌ ἀναγγέλλω
declare 3
rehearse 1
report 1
show 6
speak of 1
tell 6.

ANAGENNAŌ ἀναγεννάω
beget again 1.
PASS. be born again 1.

ANAGINŌSKŌ ἀναγινώσκω
read 33.

ANAĞKAIOS ἀναγκαῖος
near 1
necessary 5
needful 1
*of necessity 1.

ANAĞKASTŌS ἀναγκαστῶς
by constraint 1.

ANAĞKAZŌ ἀναγκάζω
compel 5
constrain 4.

ANAĞKĒ ἀνάγκη *f.*
distress 3 (M. necessity 1)
necessity 7
*must needs 1
*necessary 1
*there must of necessity 1.
†*See* echō, eimi.

ANAGNŌRIZOMAI ἀναγνωρίζομαι
be made known 1.

ANAGNŌSIS ἀνάγνωσις *f.*
reading 3.

ANAGŌ ἀνάγω
bring 3
bring again 1
bring forth 1
bring up again 1
lead 1
lead up 1
offer 1
take up 1.
MID. (PASS.) depart 3
launch 3
launch forth 1
loose 3
sail 3
set forth 1.

ANAIDEIA ἀναίδεια *f.*
importunity 1.

ANAIREŌ ἀναιρέω
kill 11
put to death 2
slay 8
take away 1
take up 1.

ANAIRESIS ἀναίρεσις *f.*
death 2.

ANAITIOS ἀναίτιος
blameless 1
guiltless 1.

ANAKAINIZŌ ἀνακαινίζω
renew 1.

ANAKAINOŌ ἀνακαινόω
renew 2.

* Inexact translations, *e.g.*, of a noun by a verb or adjective, of an active by a passive.
† Cases where two or more words in the original are translated by one word or by a phrase.

ANAKAINŌSIS ἀνακαίνωσις *f.*
renewing 2.

ANAKALUPTŌ ἀνακαλύπτω
Pass pt. open 1.
†untaken away (*with negative*) 1.

ANAKAMPTŌ ἀνακάμπτω
return 3
turn again 1.

ANAKATHIZŌ ἀνακαθίζω
sit up 2.

ANAKEIMAI ἀνάκειμαι
be set down 1
lean 1
lie 1
sit 2
sit at meat 5 (M. sit together 1)
sit down 1.
Partic. at the table 1
guest 1.

ANAKEPHALAIOOMAI ἀνακεφαλαιόομαι
be briefly comprehended 1
gather together in one 1.

ANAKLINŌ ἀνακλίνω
lay 1
make sit down 3.
MID. sit down 4.

ANAKOPTŌ ἀνακόπτω
hinder (M. drive back) 1.

ANAKRAZŌ ἀνακράζω
cry out 5.

ANAKRINŌ ἀνακρίνω
ask question 2
discern 1
examine 6
judge 6 (M. discern 1)
search 1.

ANAKRISIS ἀνάκρισις *f.*
examination 1.

ANAKUPTŌ ἀνακύπτω
lift one's self up 3
look up 1.

ANALAMBANŌ ἀναλαμβάνω
receive up 3
take 3
take in 2
take unto 1
take up 4.

ANALĒPSIS ἀνάληψις *f.*
*that [he] should be received up 1.

ANALISKŌ ἀναλίσκω
consume 3.

ANALOGIA ἀναλογία *f.*
proportion 1.

ANALOGIZOMAI ἀναλογίζομαι
consider 1.

ANALOS ἄναλος
†lose saltness (ginomai analos) 1.

ANALUŌ ἀναλύω
depart 1
return 1.

ANALUSIS ἀνάλυσις *f.*
departure 1.

ANAMARTĒTOS ἀναμάρτητος
without sin 1.

ANAMENŌ ἀναμένω
wait for 1.

ANAMIMNĒSKŌ ἀναμιμνήσκω
bring into remembrance 1
call to mind 1
call to remembrance 1
put in remembrance 1
remember 1.

ANAMNĒSIS ἀνάμνησις *f.*
remembrance 3
remembrance again 1.

ANANEOOMAI ἀνανεόομαι
be renewed 1.

ANANĒPHŌ ἀνανήφω
recover one's self (M. awake) 1.

ANANTIRRHĒTOS ἀναντίῤῥητος
not to be spoken against 1.

ANANTIRRHĒTŌS ἀναντιῤῥήτως
without gainsaying 1.

ANAPAUŌ ἀναπαύω
give rest 1
refresh 4.
MID. rest 4
take ease 1
take rest 2.

ANAPAUSIS ἀνάπαυσις *f.*
rest 4.
†to rest (echō *with acc.*; M. have rest) 1.

ANAPEITHŌ ἀναπείθω
persuade 1.

ANAPEMPŌ ἀναπέμπω
send 2
send again 2.

ANAPĒROS ἀνάπηρος
maimed 2.

ANAPHAINOMAI ἀναφαίνομαι
appear 1.
PASS. discover 1.

ANAPHERŌ ἀναφέρω
bear 2
bring up 1
carry up 1
lead up 1
offer 2
offer up 3.

ANAPHŌNEŌ ἀναφωνέω
speak out 1.

ANAPIPTŌ ἀναπίπτω
be set down 1
lean 1
sit down 7
sit down to meat 2.

ANAPLĒROŌ ἀναπληρόω
fill up 1
fulfil 2
occupy 1
supply 2.

ANAPOLOGĒTOS ἀναπολόγητος
inexcusable 1
without excuse 1.

ANAPSUCHŌ ἀναψύχω
refresh 1.

ANAPSUXIS ἀνάψυξις *f.*
refreshing 1.

ANAPTŌ ἀνάπτω
kindle 3.

ANAPTUSSŌ ἀναπτύσσω
open 1.

ANARITHMĒTOS ἀναρίθμητος
innumerable 1.

ANASEIŌ ἀνασείω
move 1
stir up 1.

ANASKEUAZŌ ἀνασκευάζω
subvert 1.

ANASPAŌ ἀνασπάω
draw up 1
pull out 1.

ANASTASIS ἀνάστασις *f.*
resurrection 39
rising again 1.
†ek *with gen.*: raised to life again 1, that should rise 1.

ANASTATOŌ ἀναστατόω
make an uproar 1
trouble 1
turn upside down 1.

ANASTAUROŌ ἀνασταυρόω
crucify afresh 1.

ANASTENAZŌ ἀναστενάζω
sigh deeply 1.

ANASTREPHŌ ἀναστρέφω
overthrow 1
return 2.
MID. (PASS.) abide 1
be used 1
behave self 1
have one's conversation 2
live 2
pass 1.

ANASTROPHĒ ἀναστροφή *f.*
conversation 13.

ANATASSOMAI ἀνατάσσομαι
set forth in order 1.

ANATELLŌ ἀνατέλλω
arise 1
be up 2
make to rise 1
rise 2
spring 1
spring up 1.
Partic. *at the rising 1.

ANATHALLŌ ἀναθάλλω
to flourish again M. (be revived) 1.

ANATHEMA ἀνάθεμα *n.*
accursed 4 (M. separated 1, anathema 2)
anathema 1
*great 1.

ANATHĒMA ἀνάθημα *n.*
gift 1.

ANATHEMATIZŌ ἀναθεματίζω
bind under a curse 2 (M. bind with an oath of execration 1)
bind with an oath 1
curse 1.

ANATHEŌREŌ ἀναθεωρέω
behold 1
consider 1.

ANATITHEMAI ἀνατίθεμαι
communicate 1
declare 1.

ANATOLĒ ἀνατολή *f.*
dayspring 1 (M. sun-rising or branch 1)
east 7.
†east (*with gen. of* hēlios) 2.

ANATREPHŌ ἀνατρέφω
bring up 1
nourish 1
nourish up 1.

ANATREPŌ ἀνατρέπω
overthrow 1
subvert 1.

ANAXIOS ἀνάξιος
unworthy 1.

ANAXIŌS ἀναξίως
unworthily 2.

ANAZAŌ ἀναζάω
be alive again 2
live again 1
revive 2.

ANAZĒTEŌ ἀναζητέω
seek 2.

ANAZŌNNUMI ἀναζώννυμι
MID. gird up 1.

ANAZŌPUREŌ ἀναζωπυρέω
stir up 1.

ANDRAPODISTĒS ἀνδραποδιστής
manstealer 1.

ANDRIZOMAI ἀνδρίζομαι
Imper. quit you like men 1.

ANDROPHONOS ἀνδροφόνος
manslayer 1.

ANECHOMAI ἀνέχομαι
bear with 4
endure 2
forbear 2
suffer 7.

ANEGKLĒTOS ἀνέγκλητος
blameless 4
unreprovable 1

ANEKDIĒGĒTOS ἀνεκδιήγητος
unspeakable 1.

ANEKLALĒTOS ἀνεκλάλητος
unspeakable 1.

ANEKLEIPTOS ἀνέκλειπτος
that faileth not 1.

ANĒKŌ ἀνήκω
be convenient 2
be fit 1.

ANELEĒMŌN ἀνελεήμων
unmerciful 1.

ANEKTOS ἀνεκτός
tolerable 6.

ANĒMEROS ἀνήμερος
fierce 1.

ANEMIZOMAI ἀνεμίζομαι
be driven with the wind 1.

ANEMOS ἄνεμος
wind 31.

ANENDEKTOS ἀνένδεκτος
impossible 1.

ANEPAISCHUNTOS ἀνεπαίσχυντος
that needeth not to be ashamed 1.

ANEPILĒPTOS ἀνεπίληπτος
blameless 2
unrebukable 1.

ANEPSIOS ἀνεψιός
sister's son 1.

ANĒR ἀνήρ
fellow 1
husband 50
man 156
sir 6.
†a prophet(*with* prophētēs) 1; a murderer (*with* phoneus) 1.

ANERCHOMAI ἀνέρχομαι
go up 3
(M. return 1).

ANESIS ἄνεσις *f.*
liberty 1
rest 3
*be eased 1.

ANETAZŌ ἀνετάζω
examine 2 (M. torture 1).

ANĒTHON ἄνηθον *n.*
anise 1.

ANEU ἄνευ
without 3.

ANEURISKŌ ἀνευρίσκω
find 2.

ANEUTHETOS ἀνεύθετος
not commodious 1.

ANEXEREUNĒTOS ἀνεξερεύνητος
unsearchable 1.

ANEXICHNIASTOS ἀνεξιχνίαστος
past finding out 1
unsearchable 1.

ANEXIKAKOS ἀνεξίκακος
patient (M. forbearing) 1.

ANIĒMI ἀνίημι
forbear (M. moderate) 1
leave 1
loose 2.

ANILEŌS ἀνίλεως
without mercy 1.

ANIPTOS ἄνιπτος
unwashen 3.

ANISTĒMI ἀνίστημι
arise 38
arise up 1
lift up 1
raise 1
raise up 11
raise up again 2
rise 19
rise again 13
rise up 16
stand up 8
stand upright 1.
Infin. rising 1.

ANŌ ἄνω
above 5
high 1
up 2
*the brim 1.

ANOCHĒ ἀνοχή *f.*
forbearance 2.

ANOĒTOS ἀνόητος
foolish 4
unwise 1.
As noun fool 1.

ANŌGEON ἀνώγεον *n.*
upper room 2.

ANOIA ἄνοια *f.*
folly 1
madness 1.

ANOIGŌ ἀνοίγω
open (*vb.*) 70.
Partic. open 6.

ANOIKODOMEŌ ἀνοικοδομέω
build again 2.

ANOIXIS ἄνοιξις *f.*
†that I may open (en *with dat.*) 1.

ANOMIA ἀνομία *f.*
iniquity 12
transgression of the law 1
unrighteousness 1.
†*See* poieō.

ANOMOS ἄνομος
lawless 1
unlawful 1
wicked 2
without law 4.
As noun transgressor 2.

ANOMŌS ἀνόμως
without law 2.

ANŌPHELĒS ἀνωφελής
unprofitable 1.
As noun unprofitableness 1.

ANORTHOŌ ἀνορθόω
lift up 1
make straight 1
set up 1.

ANOSIOS ἀνόσιος
unholy 2.

ANŌTERIKOS ἀνωτερικός
upper 1.

ANŌTERON ἀνώτερον
above 1.
higher 1.

ANŌTHEN ἄνωθεν
again (M. from above) 1.
from above 5
from the beginning 1
from the very first 1
*the top 3.
†*See* palin.

ANTAGŌNIZOMAI ἀνταγωνίζομαι
strive against 1.

ANTALLAGMA ἀντάλλαγμα *n.*
exchange 2.

ANTANAPLĒROŌ ἀνταναπληρόω
fill up 1.

ANTAPODIDŌMI ἀνταποδίδωμι
recompense 6
recompense again 1
render 1
repay 1.

ANTAPODOMA ἀνταπόδομα *n.*
recompense 2.

ANTAPODOSIS ἀνταπόδοσις *f.*
reward 1.

ANTAPOKRINOMAI ἀνταποκρίνομαι
answer again 1
reply against(M. answer again or dispute with) 1.

ANTECHOMAI ἀντέχομαι
hold fast 1
hold to 2
support 1.

ANTEIPON ἀντεῖπον
gainsay 1
say against 1.

ANTHISTĒMI ἀνθίστημι
resist 9
withstand 5.

ANTHOMOLOGEOMAI ἀνθομολογέομαι
give thanks 1.

ANTHOS ἄνθος *n.*
flower 4.

ANTHRAKIA ἀνθρακία *f.*
fire of coals 2.

ANTHRAX ἄνθραξ
coal 1.

ANTHRŌPARESKOS ἀνθρωπάρεσκος
manpleaser 2.

ANTHRŌPINOS ἀνθρώπινος
after the manner of men 1
common to man (M. moderate) 1
man's 3
of man 1.
†mankind (*with* phusis; M. nature of man) 1.

* Inexact translations, *e.g.*, of a noun by a verb or adjective, of an active by a passive.
† Cases where two or more words in the original are translated by one word or by a phrase.

ANTHRŌPOKTONOS ἀνθρωποκτόνος
murderer 3.

ANTHRŌPOS ἄνθρωπος
a certain 3
man 551.
†enemy (*with* echthros) 1; nobleman (*with* eugenēs) 1; Romans (*with* rhōmaioi) 1; shepherds (*with pl. of* poimēn) 1.

ANTHUPATEUŌ ἀνθυπατεύω
be deputy 1.

ANTHUPATOS ἀνθύπατος
deputy 4.

ANTI ἀντί
for 15
in the room of 1
*for that [ye] ought 1.
†*With gen. pl of* hos: because 4, therefore 1.

ANTIBALLŌ ἀντιβάλλω
have 1.

ANTICHRISTOS ἀντίχριστος
antichrist 5.

ANTIDIATITHEMAI ἀντιδιατίθεμαι
oppose one's self 1.

ANTIDIKOS ἀντίδικος
adversary 5.

ANTIKALEŌ ἀντικαλέω
bid again 1.

ANTIKATHISTĒMI ἀντικαθίστημι
resist 1.

ANTIKEIMAI ἀντίκειμαι
be contrary 2
oppose 1.
Partic. adversary 5.

ANTIKRU ἀντικρύ
over against 1.

ANTILAMBANOMAI ἀντιλαμβάνομαι
help 1
support 1.
Partic. partaker 1.

ANTILEGŌ ἀντιλέγω
answer again (M. gainsay) 1
contradict 1
gainsay 1
speak against 5.
Partic. gainsayer 1.
†deny (*with negative*) 1.

ANTILĒPSIS ἀντίληψις *f.*
help 1.

ANTILOGIA ἀντιλογία *f.*
contradiction 2
gainsaying 1
strife 1.

ANTILOIDOREŌ ἀντιλοιδορέω
revile again 1.

ANTILUTRON ἀντίλυτρον *n.*
ransom 1.

ANTIMETREŌ ἀντιμετρέω
measure again 2.

ANTIMISTHIA ἀντιμισθία *f.*
recompense 2.

ANTIPARERCHOMAI ἀντιπαρέρχομαι
pass by on the other side 2.

ANTIPERAN ἀντιπέραν
over against 1.

ANTIPIPTŌ ἀντιπίπτω
resist 1.

ANTISTRATEUOMAI ἀντιστρατεύομαι
war against 1.

ANTITASSOMAI ἀντιτάσσομαι
oppose one's self 1
resist 4.

ANTITHESIS ἀντίθεσις *f.*
opposition 1.

ANTITUPON ἀντίτυπον *n.*
like figure 1.

ANTLĒMA ἄντλημα
†*See* oute.

ANTLEŌ ἀντλέω
draw 3
draw out 1.

ANTOPHTHALMEŌ ἀντοφθαλμέω
bear up 1.

ANUDROS ἄνυδρος
dry 2
without water 2.

ANUPOKRITOS ἀνυπόκριτος
unfeigned 4
without dissimulation 1
without hypocrisy 1.

ANUPOTAKTOS ἀνυπότακτος
disobedient 1
that is not put under 1
unruly 1.

AORATOS ἀόρατος
invisible 4.
As noun invisible things 1.

APAG̃CHOMAI ἀπάγχομαι
hang one's self 1.

APAG̃GELLŌ ἀπαγγέλλω
bring word 1
bring word again 1
declare 3
report 2
show 10
show again 1
tell 26.

APAGŌ ἀπάγω
bring 1
carry away 1
lead 2
lead away 10
put to death 1
take away 1.

APAIDEUTOS ἀπαίδευτος
unlearned 1.

APAIRŌ ἀπαίρω
take 1
take away 2.

APAITEŌ ἀπαιτέω
ask again 1
*be required (M. require) 1.

APALGEŌ ἀπαλγέω
be past feeling 1.

APALLASSŌ ἀπαλλάσσω
Mid. deliver 2
depart 1.

APALLOTRIOOMAI ἀπαλλοτριόομαι
be alienated 1.
Partic. alien 1
alienated 1.

APANTAŌ ἀπαντάω
meet 7.

APANTĒSIS ἀπάντησις *f.*
†to meet (eis *with acc.*) 4.

APARABATOS ἀπαράβατος
unchangeable (M. not passing from one to another) 1.

APARASKEUASTOS ἀπαρασκεύαστος
unprepared 1.

APARCHĒ ἀπαρχή *f.*
first fruit 1
first fruits 7.

APARNEOMAI ἀπαρνέομαι
deny 13.

APARTI ἀπάρτι
from henceforth 1.

APARTISMOS ἀπαρτισμός
†to finish it (pros *with acc.*) 1.

APATAŌ ἀπατάω
deceive 4.

APATĒ ἀπάτη *f.*
deceit 1
deceitfulness 3
deceivableness 1
deceiving 1
*deceitful 1.

APATŌR ἀπάτωρ
without father 1.

APAUGASMA ἀπαύγασμα *n.*
brightness 1.

APECHŌ ἀπέχω
be 5
be enough 1
have 4 (M. have received 1)
receive 2.
Mid. abstain 6.

APEIDON = APHORAŌ.

APEILĒ ἀπειλή *f.*
threatening 3
*straitly 1.

APEILEŌ ἀπειλέω
threaten 2.

APEIMI[1] ἄπειμι
be absent 6.
Partic. absent 1.

APEIMI[2] ἄπειμι
go 1.

APEIPON ἀπεῖπον
renounce 1.

APEIRASTOS ἀπείραστος
†cannot be tempted (eimi apeirastos) 1.

APEIROS ἄπειρος
unskilful (M. having no experience) 1.

APEITHEIA ἀπείθεια *f.*
disobedience 3 (M. unbelief 1)
unbelief 4 (M. disobedience 1).

APEITHEŌ ἀπειθέω
be disobedient 3
believe not 8 (M. obey not 1, be disobedient 2)
obey not 3.
Partic. disobedient 1
unbelieving 1.

APEITHĒS ἀπειθής
disobedient 6.

APEKDECHOMAI ἀπεκδέχομαι
look for 2
wait for 5.

APEKDUOMAI ἀπεκδύομαι *f.*
put off 1
spoil 1.

APEKDUSIS ἀπέκδυσις
puting off 1.

APELAUNŌ ἀπελαύνω
drive 1.

APELEGMOS ἀπελεγμός
†at nought (eis *with acc.*) 1.

APELEUTHEROS ἀπελεύθερος
freeman (M. made free) 1.

APELPIZŌ ἀπελπίζω
hope for again 1.

APENANTI ἀπέναντι
before 2
contrary to 1
in the presence of 1
over against 2.

APERANTOS ἀπέραντος
endless 1.

APERCHOMAI ἀπέρχομαι
come 4
depart 27
go 54
go aside 1
go away 14
go one's way 16
go out 1
pass 1
pass away 1.

APERISPASTŌS ἀπερισπάστως
without distraction 1.

APERITMĒTOS ἀπερίτμητος
uncircumcised 1.

APHAIREŌ ἀφαιρέω
cut off 2
smite off 1
take away 7.

APHANĒS ἀφανής
that is not manifest 1.

APHANISMOS ἀφανισμός
*to vanish away 1.

APHANIZŌ ἀφανίζω
corrupt 2
disfigure 1.
Pass. perish 1
vanish away 1.

APHANTOS ἄφαντος
†vanish out of sight (ginomai aphantos; M. cease to be seen) 1.

APHEDRŌN ἀφεδρών
draught 2.

APHEIDIA ἀφειδία *f.*
neglecting (M. punishing or not sparing) 1.

APHELOTĒS ἀφελότης *f.*
singleness 1.

APHEŌ = APHIĒMI.

APHESIS ἄφεσις *f.*
deliverance 1
forgiveness 6
liberty 1
remission 9.

APHIĒMI ἀφίημι (ἀφέω or ἀφίω)
cry 1
forgive 47
forsake 6
lay aside 1
leave 52
let 8
let alone 6
let be 1
let go 1
let have 1
omit 1
put away 2
remit 2
send away 2
suffer 13
suffer it to be so 1
yield up 1.

APHIKNEOMAI ἀφικνέομαι
come abroad 1.

APHILAGATHOS ἀφιλάγαθος
despiser of those that are good 1.

APHILARGUROS ἀφιλάργυρος
not greedy of filthy lucre 1
without covetousness 1.

APHIŌ = APHIĒMI.

APHISTĒMI ἀφίστημι
depart from 8
draw away 1
fall away 1
refrain from 1.
Mid. depart from 3
withdraw one's self 1.

APHIXIS ἄφιξις
departing 1.

APHNŌ ἄφνω
suddenly 3.

APHOBŌS ἀφόβως
without fear 4.

APHOMOIOOMAI ἀφομοιόομαι
be made like 1.

APHŌNOS ἄφωνος
dumb 3
without signification 1.

APHORAŌ ἀφοράω (ἀπεῖδον)
look 1
see 1.

APHORIZŌ ἀφορίζω
divide 1
separate 7
sever 1.
Pass. be separate 1.

APHORMĒ ἀφορμή *f.*
occasion 7.

APHRIZŌ ἀφρίζω
foam (*vb.*) 2.

APHRŌN ἄφρων
foolish 2
unwise 1.
As noun fool 8.

APHROS ἀφρός
†that he foameth again (meta *with gen.*) 1.

APHROSUNĒ ἀφροσύνη *f.*
folly 1
foolishness 1.
†foolishly (en *with dat.*) 2.

APHTHARSIA ἀφθαρσία *f.*
immortality 2
incorruption 4
sincerity (M. incorruption) 1.

APHTHARTOS ἄφθαρτος
immortal 1
incorruptible 4
not corruptible 1
uncorruptible 1.

APHUPNOŌ ἀφυπνόω
fall asleep 1.

APISTEŌ ἀπιστέω
believe not 7.

APISTIA ἀπιστία *f.*
unbelief 12.

APISTOS ἄπιστος
faithless 4
that believeth not 6
unbelieving 5
which believe not 1.
As noun infidel 2
thing incredible 1
unbeliever 4.

APO ἀπό
at 10
because of 1
before 2
by 9 (M. of 1)
for 10
from 372
from among 1
in 5
of 147 (M. from 1)
on 5
out of 27
since 7
upon 1
with 3
*they of 1.
†*With gen. of* hos: since 3, since the time 1, that 1. *With* makrothen: afar off 9.

APOBAINŌ ἀποβαίνω
come 1
go out 1
turn 2.

APOBALLŌ ἀποβάλλω
cast away 2.

APOBLEPŌ ἀποβλέπω
have respect 1.

APOBLĒTOS ἀπόβλητος
*to be refused 1.

APOBOLĒ ἀποβολή *f.*
casting away 1
loss 1.

APOCHŌREŌ ἀποχωρέω
depart 3.

APOCHŌRIZOMAI ἀποχωρίζομαι
depart 1
depart asunder 1.

APOCHRĒSIS ἀπόχρησις *f.*
using 1.

APODECHOMAI ἀποδέχομαι
Mid. accept 1
gladly receive 2
receive 2.
Pass. be received 1.

APODEIKNUMI ἀποδείκνυμι
approve 1
prove 1
set forth 1
show 1.

APODEIXIS ἀπόδειξις *f.*
demonstration 1.

APODEKATOŌ ἀποδεκατόω
give tithes 1
pay tithe 1
take tithes 1
tithe 1.

APODEKTOS ἀπόδεκτος
acceptable 2.

APODĒMEŌ ἀποδημέω
go into a far country 3
take one's journey 2
travel into a far country 1.

APODĒMOS ἀπόδημος
taking a far journey 1.

APODIDŌMI ἀποδίδωμι
deliver 1
deliver again 1
give 9
give again 1
make payment 1
pay 9
perform 1
recompense 1
render 9
repay 1
restore 1
reward 6
sell 3
yield 2.
†*With pl. of* amoibē, requite 1.

APODIORIZŌ ἀποδιορίζω
separate 1.

APODOCHĒ ἀποδοχή *f.*
acceptation 2.

APODOKIMAZŌ ἀποδοκιμάζω
disallow 2
reject 7.

APOGINOMAI ἀπογίνομαι
Partic. being dead 1.

* Inexact translations, *e.g.*, of a noun by a verb or adjective, of an active by a passive.
† Cases where two or more words in the original are translated by one word or by a phrase.

APOGRAPHĒ ἀπογραφή *f.*
taxing 2.

APOGRAPHŌ ἀπογράφω
PASS. be taxed 3 (M. be enrolled 1)
be written (M. be enrolled) 1.

APOKALUPSIS ἀποκάλυψις
appearing 1
coming. (M. revelation) 1
manifestation 1
revelation 12
*be revealed 2.
†to lighten (eis *with acc.*) 1.

APOKALUPTŌ ἀποκαλύπτω
reveal 26.

APOKARADOKIA ἀποκαραδοκία *f.*
earnest expectation 2.

APOKATALLATTŌ ἀποκαταλλάττω
reconcile 3.

APOKASTATASIS ἀποκατάστασις *f.*
restitution 1.

APOKATHISTANŌ ἀποκαθιστάνω
restore again 1.

APOKATHISTĒMI ἀποκαθίστημι (ἀποκαθιστάω)
restore 7.

APOKEIMAI ἀπόκειμαι
be appointed 1
be laid up 3.

APOKEPHALIZŌ ἀποκεφαλίζω
behead 4.

APOKLEIŌ ἀποκλείω
shut 1.

APOKOPTŌ ἀποκόπτω
cut off 6.

APOKRIMA ἀπόκριμα *n.*
sentence (M. answer) 1.

APOKRINOMAI ἀποκρίνομαι
answer 250.

APOKRISIS ἀπόκρισις *f.*
answer 4.

APOKRUPHOS ἀπόκρυφος
hid 2.
†*See* ginomai.

APOKRUPTŌ ἀποκρύπτω
hide 6.

APOKTEINŌ ἀποκτείνω
kill 55
put to death 6
slay 14.

APOKUEŌ ἀποκυέω
beget 1
bring forth 1.

APOKULIŌ ἀποκυλίω
roll away 3
roll back 1.

APOLAMBANŌ ἀπολαμβάνω
receive 10
receive again 1
take 1.

APOLAUSIS ἀπόλαυσις *f.*
†to enjoy (eis *with acc.*) 1.
See echō.

APŌLEIA ἀπώλεια *f.*
damnation 1
destruction 5
perdition 8
pernicious way (M. lascivious way) 1
waste 2
*damnable 1.
†die (eis *with acc.*) 1; perish (eimi eis *with acc.*) 1.

APOLEICHŌ ἀπολείχω
lick 1.

APOLEIPŌ ἀπολείπω
leave 3
PASS. remain 3.

APOLLUMI ἀπόλλυμι
destroy 23
lose 28.
MID. be destroyed 3
be lost 3
be marred 1
die 1
perish 33.

APOLOGEOMAI ἀπολογέομαι
answer 3
answer for one's self 3
excuse 1
excuse one's self 1
make defence 1
speak for one's self 1

APOLOGIA ἀπολογία *f.*
answer 3
answer for one's self 1
clearing of one's self 1
defence 3.

APOLOUŌ ἀπολούω
wash 1
wash away 1.

APOLUŌ ἀπολύω
dismiss 2
divorce 1
forgive 2
let depart 2
let go 13
loose 2
put away 14
release 17
send away 13
set at liberty 2.
MID. depart 1.

APOLUTRŌSIS ἀπολύτρωσις *f.*
deliverance 1
redemption 9.

APOMASSOMAI ἀπομάσσομαι
wipe off 1.

APONEMŌ ἀπονέμω
give 1.

APONIPTOMAI ἀπονίπτομαι
wash 1.

APOPHERŌ ἀποφέρω
bring 1
carry 1
carry away 3.

APOPHEUGŌ ἀποφεύγω
escape 3.

APOPHORTIZOMAI ἀποφορτίζομαι
unlade 1.

APOPHTHEĞGOMAI ἀποφθέγγομαι
say 1
speak forth 1.
*utterance 1.

APOPIPTŌ ἀποπίπτω
fall from 1.

APOPLANAŌ ἀποπλανάω
seduce 1.
PASS. err (M. be seduced) 1.

APŌPLEŌ ἀποπλέω
sail 4.

APOPLUNŌ ἀποπλύνω
wash 1.

APOPNIGŌ ἀποπνίγω
choke 3.

APOPSUCHŌ ἀποψύχω
Partic. hearts failing them 1.

APOREOMAI ἀπορέομαι
doubt 2 (M. be doubtful 1)
be perplexed 1
stand in doubt (M. be perplexed) 1.

APOSKEUAZOMAI ἀποσκευάζομαι
take up one's carriage 1.

APORIA ἀπορία *f.*
perplexity 1.

APORPHANIZOMAI ἀπορφανίζομαι
be taken from 1.

APORRHIPTŌ ἀποῤῥίπτω
cast one's self 1.

APOSKIASMA ἀποσκίασμα *n.*
shadow 1.

APOSPAŌ ἀποσπάω
draw 1
draw away 1
withdraw 1.
PASS. be gotten from 1.

APOSTASIA ἀποστασία *f.*
falling away 1.
†to forsake (*with* apo) 1.

APOSTASION ἀποστάσιον *n.*
divorcement 2
writing of divorcement 1.

APOSTEGAZŌ ἀποστεγάζω
uncover 1.

APOSTELLŌ ἀποστέλλω
put in 1
send 111
send away 3
send forth 15
send out 2
set 1.

APOSTEREŌ ἀποστερέω
defraud 4
keep back by fraud 1.
Pass. pt. destitute 1.

APOSTOLĒ ἀποστολή *f.*
apostleship 4.

APOSTOLOS ἀπόστολος
apostle 78
he that is sent 1
messenger 2.

APOSTOMATIZŌ ἀποστοματίζω
provoke to speak 1.

APOSTREPHŌ ἀποστρέφω
bring again 1
pervert 1
put up again 1
turn away 3.
MID. (PASS.) turn away from 4.

APOSTUGEŌ ἀποστυγέω
abhor 1.

APOSUNAGŌGOS ἀποσυνάγωγος
out of the synagogue 3.

APOTASSOMAI ἀποτάσσομαι
bid farewell 2
forsake 1
send away 1
take leave of 2.

APOTELEŌ ἀποτελέω
finish 1.

APOTHĒKĒ ἀποθήκη *f.*
barn 4
garner 2.

APŌTHEOMAI ἀπωθέομαι
cast away 2
put away 1
put from 1
thrust away 1
thrust from 1.

APOTHĒSAURIZŌ ἀποθησαυρίζω
lay up in store 1.

APOTHESIS ἀπόθεσις *f.*
putting away 1.
†I must put off (*with* esti) 1.

APOTHLIBŌ ἀποθλίβω
press 1.

APOTHNĒSKŌ ἀποθνήσκω
be a dying 1
be dead 28
die 76
lie a dying 1
perish 1
*death 1.
Partic. dead 1.
†be slain (*with dat. of* phonos) 1.

APOTINASSŌ ἀποτινάσσω
shake off 2.

APOTIŌ ἀποτίω
repay 1.

APOTITHEMAI ἀποτίθεμαι
MID. cast off 1
lay apart 1
lay aside 2
lay down 1
put away 1
put off 2.

APOTOLMAŌ ἀποτολμάω
be very bold 1.

APOTOMIA ἀποτομία *f.*
severity 2.

APOTOMŌS ἀποτόμως
sharply 1
*sharpness 1.

APOTREPOMAI ἀποτρέπομαι
turn away 1.

APOUSIA ἀπουσία *f.*
absence 1.

APROSITOS ἀπρόσιτος
which no man can approach unto 1.

APROSKOPOS ἀπρόσκοπος
void of offence 1
without offence 1.
†give none offence (ginomai aproskopos) 1.

APROSŌPOLĒPTŌS ἀπροσωπολήπτως
without respect of persons 1.

APSEUDĒS ἀψευδής
that cannot lie 1.

APSINTHOS ἄψινθος *f.*
wormwood 1.

APSUCHOS ἄψυχος
As noun things without life 1.

APTAISTOS ἄπταιστος
from falling 1.

ARA[1] ἀρά *f.*
cursing 1.

ARA[2] ἄρα
haply 2
no doubt 1
perhaps 1
so 4
so then 2
then 12
therefore 4
truly 1
wherefore 1.

ARA[3] ἆρα
therefore 1.
Untranslated in Luke xviii. 8, Acts viii. 30 (ἆρά γε).

ARCHAĞGELOS ἀρχάγγελος
archangel 2.

ARCHAIOS ἀρχαῖος
As noun of old time 2
old 7
old things 1.
†*See* hēmera.

ARCHĒ ἀρχή *f.*
beginning 40
corner 2
first 1
first estate (M. principality) 1
magistrate 1
power 1
principality 8
rule 1
*first (*adj.*) 1.
†*See* lambanō, logos.

ARCHĒGOS ἀρχηγός
author (M. beginner) 1
captain 1
prince 2 (M. author 1).

ARCHIERATIKOS ἀρχιερατικός
of the high priest 1.

ARCHIEREUS ἀρχιερεύς
chief of the priests 1
chief priest 64
high priest 59.

ARCHIPOIMĒN ἀρχιποίμην
chief shepherd 1.

ARCHISUNAGŌGOS ἀρχισυνάγωγος
chief ruler of the synagogue 2
ruler of the synagogue 7.

ARCHITEKTŌN ἀρχιτέκτων
master builder 1.

ARCHITELŌNĒS ἀρχιτελώνης
chief among the publicans 1.

ARCHITRIKLINOS ἀρχιτρίκλινος
governor of the feast 2
ruler of the feast 1.

ARCHŌ ἄρχω
reign over 1
rule over 1.
MID. begin 83.
Partic. from the beginning 1.

ARCHŌN ἄρχων
chief 2
chief ruler 1
magistrate 1
prince 11
ruler 22.

AREIOS PAGOS Ἄρειος πάγος
Areopagus (M. Mars' hill) 1
Mars' hill (M. Court of the Areopagites) 1.

ARĒN ἀρήν (= ἀρνός)
lamb 1.

ARESKEIA ἀρέσκεια *f.*
pleasing 1.

ARESKŌ ἀρέσκω
please 17.

ARESTOS ἀρεστός
As noun things that are pleasing 1
things that please 1.
†*With* eimi: be reason 1, please 1.

ARETĒ ἀρετή *f.*
praise (M. virtue) 1
virtue 4

ARGEŌ ἀργέω
linger 1.

ARGOS ἀργός
barren 1
idle 6
slow 1.

ARGURION ἀργύριον *n.*
money 11
piece of silver
silver 3
silver piece 1.

ARGUROKOPOS ἀργυροκόπος
silversmith 1.

ARGUROS ἄργυρος
silver 5.

ARGUROUS ἀργυροῦς
of silver 2
silver 1.

ARISTAŌ ἀριστάω
dine 3.

ARISTEROS ἀριστερός
left 2
on the left 1.

ARISTON ἄριστον *n.*
dinner 3.

ARITHMEŌ ἀριθμέω
number (*vb.*) 3.

ARITHMOS ἀριθμός
number 18.

ARKEŌ ἀρκέω
be enough 1
be sufficient 2
suffice 1.
MID. be content 3.
Partic. content 1.

ARKETOS ἀρκετός
enough 1
sufficient 1
*suffice 1.

ARKTOS ἄρκτος
bear 1.

ARNEOMAI ἀρνέομαι
deny 28
refuse 2.

ARNION ἀρνίον *n.*
lamb 1
Lamb 29.

ARŌMA ἄρωμα *n.*
spices 3
sweet spices 1.

AROTRIAŌ ἀροτριάω
plow 2.

AROTRON ἄροτρον *n.*
plow 1.

ARRHABŌN ἀῤῥαβών
earnest 3.

ARRHAPHOS ἄῤῥαφος
without seam 1.

ARRHĒN ἄῤῥην
man 2
man child 1.

ARRHĒTOS ἄῤῥητος
unspeakable 1.

ARRHŌSTOS ἄῤῥωστος
sick 2
sickly 1
that were sick 1.
Plur. sick folk 1.

* Inexact translations, *e.g.*, of a noun by a verb or adjective, of an active by a passive.
† Cases where two or more words in the original are translated by one word or by a phrase.

ARSĒN ἄρσην
male 4
man 2.

ARSENOKOITĒS ἀρσενοκοίτης
abuser of self with mankind 1
that defileth self with mankind 1.

ARTEMŌN ἀρτέμων
mainsail 1.

ARTI ἄρτι
even now 1
now this day 1
this hour 1
this present 2.
†Apo arti: henceforth 2, from henceforth 1, hereafter 2, now (M. from henceforth) 1. Heōs arti: hitherto 2.

ARTIGENNĒTOS ἀρτιγέννητος
new-born 1.

ARTIOS ἄρτιος
perfect 1.

ARTOS ἄρτος
bread 72
loaf 23.
†shew-bread (*with gen. of* prothesis) 3. *See* prothesis.

ARTUŌ ἀρτύω
season 3.

ASALEUTOS ἀσάλευτος
unmoveable 1
which can not be moved 1.

ASBESTOS ἄσβεστος
that never shall be quenched 2
unquenchable 2.

ASCHĒMŌN ἀσχήμων
uncomely 1.

ASCHĒMONEŌ ἀσχημονέω
behave self uncomely 1
behave self unseemly 1.

ASCHĒMOSUNĒ ἀσχημοσύνη *f.*
shame 1
that which is unseemly 1.

ASEBEIA ἀσέβεια *f.*
ungodliness 4
*ungodly 2.

ASEBEŌ ἀσεβέω
commit ungodly 1
live ungodly 1.

ASEBĒS ἀσεβής
ungodly 8.
As noun ungodly man 1.

ASELGEIA ἀσέλγεια *f.*
lasciviousness 6
wantonness 1.
Plur. much wantonness 1.
†filthy (en *with dat.*) 1.

ASĒMOS ἄσημος
mean 1.

ASITIA ἀσιτία *f.*
abstinence 1

ASITOS ἄσιτος
fasting 1.

ASKEŌ ἀσκέω
exercise 1.

ASKOS ἀσκός
bottle 12.

ASMENŌS ἀσμένως
gladly 2.

ASOPHOS ἄσοφος
fool 1.

ASŌTIA ἀσωτία
excess 1
riot 2.

ASŌTŌS ἀσώτως
*riotous 1.

ASPASMOS ἀσπασμός
greeting 3
salutation 7.

ASPAZOMAI ἀσπάζομαι
embrace 2
greet 15
salute 42
take leave of 1.

ASPHALEIA ἀσφάλεια *f.*
certainty 1.
safety 2.

ASPHALĒS ἀσφαλής
certain 1
safe 1
sure 1.
As noun certainty 2.

ASPHALIZŌ ἀσφαλίζω
make sure 1.
Mid. make fast 1
make sure 2.

ASPHALŌS ἀσφαλῶς
assuredly 1
safely 2.

ASPILOS ἄσπιλος
unspotted 1
without spot 3.

ASPIS ἀσπίς *f.*
asp 1.

ASPONDOS ἄσπονδος
implacable 1.
As noun truce-breaker 1.

ASSARION ἀσσάριον *n.*
farthing 2.

ASSON ἆσσον
close by 1.

ASTATEŌ ἀστατέω
have no certain dwelling-place 1.

ASTEIOS ἀστεῖος
fair 1
proper 1.

ASTĒR ἀστήρ
star 24.

ASTĒRIKTOS ἀστήρικτος
unstable 2.

ASTHENEIA ἀσθένεια *f.*
disease 1
infirmity 17
sickness 1
weakness 5.

ASTHENĒMA ἀσθένημα *n.*
infirmity 1.

ASTHENEŌ ἀσθενέω
be diseased 1
be made weak 1
be sick 10
be weak 12.
Partic. impotent man 1
impotent folk (*pl.*) 1
sick 7
weak 3.

ASTHENĒS ἀσθενής
feeble 1
impotent 1
sick 5
weak 13
without strength 1.
As noun sick folks (*pl.*) 1
weakness 2
weak thing 1.

ASTOCHEŌ ἀστοχέω
err 2.
swerve from (M. not aim at) 1.

ASTORGOS ἄστοργος
without natural affection 2 (M. unsociable 1).

ASTRAPĒ ἀστραπή *f.*
bright shining 1
lightning 8.

ASTRAPTŌ ἀστράπτω
lighten 1
shine 1.

ASTRON ἄστρον *n.*
star 4.

ASUMPHŌNOS ἀσύμφωνος
†*See* eimi.

ASUNETOS ἀσύνετος
foolish 2
without understanding 3.

ASUNTHETOS ἀσύνθετος
covenant breaker 1.

ATAKTEŌ ἀτακτέω
behave one's self disorderly 1.

ATAKTOS ἄτακτος
unruly (M. disorderly) 1.

ATAKTŌS ἀτάκτως
disorderly 1.

ATEKNOS ἄτεκνος
childless 1
without children 2.

ATENIZŌ ἀτενίζω
be fastened on 1
behold earnestly 1
behold steadfastly 1
look earnestly on 1
look earnestly upon 1
look on 1.
†*With* eis: behold steadfastly 1, fasten one's eyes upon 2, look steadfastly (toward, on, to) 3, look up steadfastly into 1, set one's eyes on 1.

ATER ἄτερ
in the absence of (M. without) 1.
without 1.

ATHANASIA ἀθανασία *f.*
immortality 3.

ATHEMITOS ἀθέμιτος
abominable 1.
As noun unlawful thing 1.

ATHEOS ἄθεος
without God 1.

ATHESMOS ἄθεσμος
wicked 2.

ATHETEŌ ἀθετέω
bring to nothing 1
cast off 1
despise 8 (M. reject 1)
disannul 1
frustrate 1
reject 4 (M. frustrate 2).

ATHETĒSIS ἀθέτησις
disannulling 1.
†to put away (eis *with acc.*) 1.

ATHLEŌ ἀθλέω
strive 2.

ATHLĒSIS ἄθλησις *f.*
fight 1.

ATHŌOS ἀθῷος
innocent 2.

ATHUMEŌ ἀθυμέω
be discouraged 1.

ATIMAO = ATIMOŌ.

ATIMAZŌ ἀτιμάζω
despise 1
dishonour 2
entreat shamefully 1.
Mid. dishonour 1.
Pass. suffer shame 1.

ATIMIA ἀτιμία *f.*
dishonour 4
reproach 1
shame 1
*vile 1.

ATIMOS ἄτιμος
despised 1
less honourable 1
without honour 2.

ATMIS ἀτμίς *f.*
vapour 2.

ATIMOŌ ἀτιμόω
handle shamefully 1.

ATOMOS ἄτομος
moment 1.

ATOPOS ἄτοπος
amiss 1
harm 1
unreasonable (M. absurd) 1.

AUCHMĒROS αὐχμηρός
dark 1.

AUGAZŌ αὐγάζω
shine 1.

AUGĒ αὐγή *f.*
break of day 1.

AULĒ αὐλή *f.*
court 1
fold 1
hall 2
palace 7.
†sheepfold (*with* probaton) 1.

AULEŌ αὐλέω
pipe 3.

AULĒTĒS αὐλητής
minstrel 1
piper 1.

AULIZOMAI αὐλίζομαι
abide 1
lodge 1.

AULOS αὐλός
pipe 1.

AURION αὔριον
morrow 5
next day 1
to-morrow 9.

AUSTĒROS αὐστηρός
austere 2.

AUTARKEIA αὐτάρκεια *f.*
contentment 1
sufficiency 1.

AUTARKĒS αὐτάρκης
content 1.

AUTHADĒS αὐθάδης
self-willed 2.

AUTHAIRETOS αὐθαίρετος
of one's own accord 1
willing of one's self 1.

AUTHENTEŌ αὐθεντέω
usurp authority over 1.

AUTOCHEIR αὐτόχειρ
with one's own hand 1.

AUTOKATAKRITOS αὐτοκατάκριτος
condemned of one's self 1.

AUTOMATOS αὐτόματος
of one's own accord 1
of one's self 1.

AUTOPHŌROS. *See* **EPAUTOPHŌRŌ.**

AUTOPTĒS αὐτόπτης
eyewitness 1.

AUTOS αὐτός (*freq. untranslated*).
A.
myself, thyself, himself, ourselves, yourselves, themselves — 94 (*pers. pron. prefixed* 29).
even . . . same, he 101, his own (*gen.*) 23, his own self 1, same 14, self same thing 2, that 3, that same 2, the said 1, the same 6, their own (*gen.*) 11, this 1, this man 1, very 3, very thing 2, etc.
B. *With article prefixed:*
like things 1
one place (*see* together) 10
the same 45
the same cause 1
the same matter 1
the same thing 6 (*pl.* 4)
the self-same 1
those 1, etc.
C. *As* 3 *pers. pron.* (*obl. cases*):
him, her, them, etc. — *freq.*
†*With prepos. freq. rendered* there (+*prepos.*) *e.g.* therein.

AUTOU αὐτοῦ
here 1
there 3.

AUXANŌ αὐξάνω (αὔξω)
give the increase 2
grow 10
grow up 1
increase (*tr.*) 1
increase (*intr.*) 3.
Pass. grow 2
increase 3.

AUXĒSIS αὔξησις *f.*
increase 2.

AXINĒ ἀξίνη *f.*
axe 2.

AXIOŌ ἀξιόω
count worthy 3 (M. vouchsafe 1)
desire 1
think good 1
think worthy 2.

AXIOS ἄξιος
meet 4 (M. answerable 1)
worthy 35 (M. meet 1).
As noun due reward 1.
†unworthy (ouk axios) 1.

AXIŌS ἀξίως
as becometh 2
worthy 3.
†*With gen. of* theos: after a godly sort 1.

AZUMOS ἄζυμος
unleavened 1.
As noun unleavened bread 8.

B

BAÏON βαΐον *n.*
branch 1.

BALANTION βαλάντιον *n.*
bag 1
purse 3.

BALLŌ βάλλω
arise (M. beat) 1
cast 86
cast out 4
lay 3
pour 2
put 13
put up 1
send 3
strike 1
throw 2
throw down 1
thrust 5.
Pass. lie 2.
†dung (*with* kopria) 1, strike with the palm of the hand (*with* rhapisma) 1.

BAPTISMA βάπτισμα *n.*
baptism 22.

BAPTISMOS βαπτισμός
baptism 1
washing 3.

BAPTISTĒS βαπτιστής
Baptist 14.

BAPTIZŌ βαπτίζω
baptise 74.
Partic. Baptist 1.
Mid. (Pass.) be baptised 2
wash 2.

BAPTŌ βάπτω
dip 3.

BAR βάρ
Bar 1.

BARBAROS βάρβαρος
barbarian 5
barbarous 1.

BAREOMAI βαρέομαι
be burdened 1
be charged 1
be heavy 3
be pressed 1.

BAREŌS βαρέως
†*See* akouō.

BAROS βάρος *n.*
burden 4
weight 1.
†eimi en *with dat.*: be burdensome (M. use authority) 1.

BARUNOMAI βαρύνομαι
be overcharged 1.

BARUS βαρύς
grievous 3
heavy 1
weighty 1.
As noun weighty matter 1.

BARUTIMOS βαρύτιμος
very precious 1.

BASANISMOS βασανισμός
torment 5.

BASANISTĒS βασανιστής
tormentor 1.

BASANIZŌ βασανίζω
pain 1
torment 8
toss 1
vex 1.
Pass. toil 1.

BASANOS βάσανος *f.*
torment 3.

BASILEIA βασιλεία *f.*
kingdom 161 (*in phrases* kingdom of God 72, kingdom of heaven 32).
†*See* echō.

BASILEIOS βασίλειος
royal 1.
As noun king's court 1.

BASILEUŌ βασιλεύω
reign 20.
Partic. king 1.

BASILEUS βασιλεύς
king 118.

BASILIKOS βασιλικός
royal 2.
As noun king's country 1
nobleman 2 (M. courtier or ruler 1).

BASILISSA βασίλισσα *f.*
queen 4.

BASIS βάσις *f.*
foot 1.

BASKAINŌ βασκαίνω
bewitch 1.

BASTAZŌ βαστάζω
bear 22
carry 3
take up 1.

BATHMOS βαθμός
degree 1.

BATHOS βάθος *n.*
deep 1
deepness 1
deep thing 1
depth 5.
†deep (kata bathos) 1.

BATHUNŌ βαθύνω
*deep 1.

BATHUS βαθύς
deep 2
very early 1.

BATOS[1] βάτος *f.*
bramble bush 1
bush 4.

* Inexact translations, *e.g.*, of a noun by a verb or adjective, of an active by a passive.
† Cases where two or more words in the original are translated by one word or by a phrase.

BATOS² βάτος *m.*
a measure 1.
BATRACHOS βάτραχος
frog 1.
BATTOLOGEŌ βαττολογέω
use vain repetitions 1.
BDELUGMA βδέλυγμα *n.*
abomination 6.
BDELUKTOS βδελυκτός
abominable 1.
BDELUSSOMAI βδελύσσομαι
abhor 1.
Partic. abominable 1.
BEBAIOŌ βεβαιόω
confirm 5
establish 1
stablish 2.
BEBAIOS βέβαιος
firm 1
of force 1
steadfast 4
sure 3.
BEBAIŌSIS βεβαίωσις *f.*
confirmation 2.
BEBĒLOŌ βεβηλόω
profane 2.
BEBĒLOS βέβηλος
profane 4.
As noun profane person 1.
BELOS βέλος *n*
dart 1.
BELTIŌN βελτίων *n.*
very well 1.
BĒMA βῆμα *n.*
judgment seat 10
throne 1
*to set . . . on 1.
BĒRULLOS βήρυλλος
beryl 1.
BIA βία *f.*
violence 4.
BIAIOS βίαιος
mighty 1.
BIASTĒS βιαστής
violent (M. they that thrust men) 1.
BIAZOMAI βιάζομαι
press 1
suffer violence (M. be gotten by force) 1.
BIBLARIDION βιβλαρίδιον *n.*
little book 4.
BIBLION βιβλίον *n*
bill 1
book 29
scroll 1
writing 1.
BIBLOS βίβλος
book 13.
BIBRŌSKŌ βιβρώσκω
eat 1.
BIOŌ βιόω
live 1.
BIOS βίος
good (*n.*) 1
life 5
living 5.
BIŌSIS βίωσις *f.*
manner of life 1.
BIŌTIKOS βιωτικός
of things pertaining to this life 1
of this life 1.
As noun things that pertain to this life 1.
BLABEROS βλαβερός
hurtful 1.
BLAPTŌ βλάπτω
hurt 2.
BLASPHĒMEŌ βλασφημέω
blaspheme 17
defame 1
rail on 2
report slanderously 1
revile 1
speak blasphemy 1
speak evil of 10.
Partic. blasphemer 1
*blasphemously 1.
BLASPHĒMIA βλασφημία *f.*
blasphemy 16
evil speaking 1
railing 2.
BLASPHĒMOS βλάσφημος
blasphemous 2
railing 1.
As noun blasphemer 2.
BLASTANŌ βλαστάνω
bring forth 1
bud 1
spring up 2.
BLEMMA βλέμμα *n.*
seeing 1.
BLEPŌ βλέπω
behold 10
beware 4
beware of 3
lie 1
look 3
look on 4
look to 1
perceive 1
see 90
take heed 12
take heed to 2.
Partic. sight 1.
Inf. sight 1.
†regard (*with* eis) 2.
BLĒTEOS βλητέος
must be put 2.
BOAŌ βοάω
cry 11.
BOĒ βοή *f.*
cry 1.
BOĒTHEIA βοήθεια *f.*
help 1.
†to help (eis *with acc.*) 1.
BOĒTHEŌ βοηθέω
help 6
succour 2.
BOĒTHOS βοηθός
helper 1.
BOLĒ βολή *f.*
cast 1.
BOLIS βολίς *f.*
dart 1.
BOLIZŌ βολίζω
sound 2.
BŌMOS βωμός
altar 1.
BORBOROS βόρβορος
mire 1.
BORRHAS βοῤῥᾶς
north 2.
BOSKŌ βόσκω
feed 5
keep 1.
MID. feed 3.
BOTANĒ βοτάνη *f.*
herbs 1.
BOTHUNOS βόθυνος
ditch 2
pit 1.
BOTRUS βότρυς
cluster 1.
BOULĒ βουλή *f.*
counsel 10
will 1.
†*See* tithēmi.
BOULĒMA βούλημα *n.*
purpose 1
will 1.
BOULEUTĒS βουλευτής
counsellor 2.
BOULEUOMAI βουλεύομαι
be minded 2
consult 2
determine 1
purpose 2
take counsel 1.
BOULOMAI βούλομαι
be disposed 1
be minded 2
be willing 1
intend 2
list 1
will 26 (would 11).
Partic. of one's own will 1.
BOUNOS βουνός
hill 2.
BOUS βοῦς
ox 8.
BRABEION βραβεῖον *n.*
prize 2.
BRABEUŌ βραβεύω
rule 1.
BRACHIŌN βραχίων
arm 3.
BRACHUS βραχύς
Neut. a little 1
a little while 1.
Plur. few words 1.
†*With* ti : a little 3 (M. a little while 1), a little space 1.
BRADUNŌ βραδύνω
be slack 1
tarry long 1.
BRADUPLOEŌ βραδυπλοέω
sail slowly 1.
BRADUS βραδύς
slow 3.
BRADUTĒS βραδυτής *f.*
slackness 1.
BRECHŌ βρέχω
rain (*tr.*) 1
rain (*intr.*) 2
send rain 1
wash 2.
†rain (*intr., with* huetos) 1.
BREPHOS βρέφος *n.*
babe 5
child 1
infant 1
young child 1.
BROCHĒ βροχή *f.*
rain 2.
BROCHOS βρόχος
snare 1.
BRŌMA βρῶμα *n.*
meat 16
victuals 1.
BRONTĒ βροντή *f.*
thunder 7
thundering 4.
†to thunder (*with* ginomai) 1.
BRŌSIMOS βρώσιμος *n.*
meat 1.
BRŌSIS βρῶσις *f.*
eating 1
food 1
meat 6 (M. eating 1)
morsel of meat 1
rust 2.
BRŌSKŌ = BIBRŌSKŌ
BRUCHŌ βρύχω
gnash 1.
BRUGMOS βρυγμός
gnashing 7.
BRUŌ βρύω
send forth 1.
BURSEUS βυρσεύς
tanner 3.
BUSSINOS βύσσινος
fine linen 4.
BUSSOS βύσσος *f.*
fine linen 2.
BUTHIZŌ βυθίζω
drown 1.
PASS. begin to sink 1.
BUTHOS βυθός
deep 1.

C

CHAIRŌ χαίρω
be glad 14
joy 5
rejoice 42.
Partic. joyfully 1.
Imper. all hail 1
farewell 1
hail 5.
Inf. God speed 2
greeting 1
send greeting 2.
CHALAŌ χαλάω
let down 5
strike 1.
CHALAZA χάλαζα *f.*
hail 4.
CHALEPOS χαλεπός
fierce 1
perilous 1.
CHALINAGŌGEŌ χαλιναγωγέω
bridle (*vb.*) 2.
CHALINOS χαλινός
bit 1
bridle 1.
CHALKĒDŌN χαλκηδών
chalcedony 1.
CHALKEOS χάλκεος (χαλκοῦς)
of brass 1.
CHALKEUS χαλκεύς
coppersmith 1.
CHALKION χαλκίον *n.*
brazen vessel 1.
CHALKOLIBANON χαλκολίβανον
fine brass 2.
CHALKOS χαλκός
brass 3
money 2.
CHALKOUS = CHALKEOS.
CHAMAI χαμαί
on the ground 1
to the ground 1.
CHARA χαρά *f.*
gladness 3
joy 53
joyfulness 1
*greatly (*dat.*) 1
*joyous (*gen.*) 1.
†joyfully (meta *with gen.*) 1
See huperperisseuō.
CHARAGMA χάραγμα
mark 8
*graven (*dat.*) 1.
CHARAKTĒR χαρακτήρ
express image 1.
CHARAX χάραξ
trench 1.
CHARIN χάριν
because of 2
for . . . cause 2
for the sake of 1
†wherefore (*with gen. of* hos 1, *gen. of* tis 1) 2.
CHARIS χάρις
benefit (M. grace) 1
favour 6
grace 129 (M. thanksgiving 1)
liberality (M. gift) 1
pleasure 2
thank 3
thanks 4
*acceptable (M. thank) 1
*gracious (*gen.*) 1
*thankworthy 1.
†God be thanked (*with dat. of* theos) 1. *See* echō.
CHARISMA χάρισμα *n.*
free gift 2
gift 15.
CHARITOŌ χαριτόω
make accepted 1.
PASS. *pt.* highly favoured (M. graciously accepted or much graced) 1.
CHARIZOMAI χαρίζομαι
deliver 2
forgive 11
forgive frankly 1
give 6
give freely 1
grant 1.
Partic. things that are freely given 1.
CHARTĒS χάρτης
paper 1.
CHASMA χάσμα *n*
gulf 1.
CHEILOS χεῖλος *n.*
lip 6
shore 1.
CHEIMARRHOS χείμαῤῥος
brook 1.
CHEIMAZŌ χειμάζω
toss with a tempest 1.
CHEIMŌN χειμών
foul weather 1
tempest 1
winter 4.
CHEIR χείρ *f.*
hand 178.
CHEIRAGŌGEŌ χειραγωγέω
lead by the hand 2.
CHEIRAGŌGOS χειραγωγός
some to lead by the hand (*pl.*) 1.
CHEIROGRAPHON χειρόγραφον *n.*
handwriting 1.
CHEIRŌN χείρων
sorer 1
worse 9.
†*With* ti : a worse thing 1.
CHEIROPOIĒTOS χειροποίητος
made by hands 1
made with hands 4.
As noun that is made with hands 1.
CHEIROTONEŌ χειροτονέω
choose 1
ordain 1.
CHEROUBIM χερουβίμ
cherubim 1.
CHĒRA χήρα *f.*
that was a widow 1
widow 26.
CHILIARCHOS χιλίαρχος
captain 2
chief captain 19
high captain 1.
CHILIAS χιλιάς *f.*
thousand 23.
CHILIOI χίλιοι
thousand 11.
CHIŌN χιών
snow 3.
CHITŌN χιτών
clothes (*pl.*) 1
coat 9
garment 1.
CHLAMUS χλαμύς *f.*
robe 2.
CHLEUAZŌ χλευάζω
mock 2.
CHLIAROS χλιαρός
lukewarm 1.
CHLŌROS χλωρός
green 2
pale 1
As noun green thing 1.
CHOÏKOS χοϊκός
earthy 3.
As noun that are earthy (*pl.*) 1.
CHOINIX χοῖνιξ *f.*
measure 1.
CHOIROS χοῖρος
swine 14.
CHOLAŌ χολάω
be angry 1.
CHOLĒ χολή *f.*
gall 2.
CHŌLOS χωλός
being a cripple 1
halt 4
lame 7
that is lame 1.
As noun lame man 1
that which is lame 1.
CHOOS χόος (χοῦς)
dust 2.
CHŌRA χώρα *f.*
coasts 1
country 14
field 2
ground 1
land 3
region 5.
CHORĒGEŌ χορηγέω
give 1
minister 1.
CHŌREŌ χωρέω
be room to receive 1
can contain 1
can receive 1
come 1
contain 1
go 1
have place 1
receive 1.
CHŌRION χωρίον *n.*
field 2
land 3
parcel of ground 1).
place 2
possession 1.
CHŌRIS χωρίς
beside 3
by itself 1
without 36 (M. severed from 1).
CHŌRIZŌ χωρίζω
put asunder 2
separate 1.
PASS. *pt.* separate 1.
MID. depart 8.
CHOROS χορός
dancing 1.
CHŌROS χῶρος
north-west 1.
CHORTASMA χόρτασμα *n.*
sustenance 1.
CHORTAZŌ χορτάζω
feed 1
fill 13
satisfy 1.
CHORTOS χόρτος
blade 2
grass 12
hay 1.
CHOUS = CHOOS
CHRAŌ χράω (κίχρημι)
lend 1.
MID. entreat 1
use 10.
CHRĒ χρή
ought 1.
CHREIA χρεία *f.*
business 1
lack 1
necessity 3
need 25
use 2
want 1
*necessary 1
*needful 1.
†to need (echō *with acc.*) 14.
CHRĒMA χρῆμα *n.*
money 1
money (*pl.*) 3
riches (*pl.*) 3

* Inexact translations, *e.g.*, of a noun by a verb or adjective, of an active by a passive.
† Cases where two or more words in the original are translated by one word or by a phrase.

CHRĒMATISMOS χρηματισμός
answer of God 1.

CHRĒMATIZŌ χρηματίζω
call 2
reveal 1
speak 1.
PASS. be admonished of God 1
be warned of (*or* from) God 4.

CHREŌPHEILETĒS χρεωφειλέτης
debtor 2.

CHRĒSIMOS χρήσιμος *n.*
profit 1.

CHRĒSIS χρῆσις *f.*
use 2.

CHRĒSTEUOMAI χρηστεύομαι
be kind 1.

CHRĒSTOLOGIA χρηστολογία *f.*
good words 1.

CHRĒSTOS χρηστός
easy 1
good 1
gracious 1
kind 2.
As noun goodness 1
Compar. better 1.

CHRĒSTOTĒS χρηστότης *f.*
gentleness 1
good 1
goodness 4
kindness 4.

CHRĒZŌ χρῄζω
have need of 3
need 2.

CHRIŌ χρίω
anoint 5.

CHRISMA χρίσμα *n.*
anointing 2
unction 1.

CHRONIZŌ χρονίζω
delay 2
tarry 3.

CHRONOS χρόνος
a long time (*pl.*) 1
a while 3
season 4
space 2
time 30.
†long time (ek *with gen.*) 1; oftentimes (*dat. pl. with* polus) 1; *the world began (*with* aiōnios) 3. *See* epi, hosos, posos, tessarakontaetēs.

CHRONOTRIBEŌ χρονοτριβέω
spend the time 1.

CHRŌS χρώς
body 1.

CHRUSEOS χρύσεος (χρυσοῦς)
golden 15
of gold 3.

CHRUSION χρυσίον *n.*
gold 9.

CHRUSODAKTULIOS χρυσοδακτύλιος
with a gold ring 1.

CHRUSOLITHOS χρυσόλιθος
chrysolite 1.

CHRUSOŌ χρυσόω
deck 2 (M. gild 1).

CHRUSOPRASOS χρυσόπρασος
chrysoprasus 1.

CHRUSOS χρυσός
gold 13.

CHRUSOUS = CHRUSEOS.

CHTHES χθές
yesterday 3.

D

DAIMŌN δαίμων
devil 5.

DAIMONIŌDĒS δαιμονιώδης
devilish 1.

DAIMONION δαιμόνιον *n.*
devil 59
god 1.

DAIMONIZOMAI δαιμονίζομαι
be possessed of the devils 2
be possessed with a devil 5
be possessed with devils 4
be vexed with a devil 1.
Partic. he that hath a devil 1.

DAKNŌ δάκνω
bite 1.

DAKRU δάκρυ (δάκρυον) *n.*
tear 11.

DAKRUŌ δακρύω
weep 1.

DAKRUON = DAKRU.

DAKTULIOS δακτύλιος
ring 1.

DAKTULOS δάκτυλος
finger 8.

DAMALIS δάμαλις *f.*
heifer 1.

DAMAZŌ δαμάζω
tame 4.

DANEION δάνειον *n.*
debt 1.

DANEISTĒS δανειστής
creditor 1.

DANEIZŌ δανείζω
lend 3.
MID. borrow 1

DAPANAŌ δαπανάω
be at charges 1
consume 1
spend 3.

DAPANĒ δαπάνη *f.*
cost 1.

DE δέ
and
but
even
for
further
howbeit
nevertheless
now
then
therefore, etc.

DĒ δή
also 1
and 1
doubtless 1
now 1
therefore 1.

DECHOMAI δέχομαι
accept 2
receive 52 (M. suffer 1)
take 5.

DEĒSIS δέησις *f.*
prayer 12
request 1
supplication 6.

DEI δεῖ
behove 1
be meet 2
be need 1
be needful 1
must 58
must needs 6
ought 30
should 4.
Partic. things which they ought (*pl.*) 1.

DEIGMA δεῖγμα *n.*
example 1.

DEIGMATIZO δειγματίζω
make a show of 1.

DEIKNUMI δείκνυμι (δεικνύω)
show 31.

DEILIA δειλία *f.*
fear 1.

DEILIAŌ δειλιάω
be afraid 1.

DEILOS δειλός
fearful 3.

DEINA δεῖνα
such a man 1.

DEINŌS δεινῶς
grievously 1
vehemently 1.

DEIPNEŌ δειπνέω
sup 3.
Infin. supper 1.

DEIPNON δεῖπνον *n.*
feast 3
supper 13.

DEISIDAIMŌN δεισιδαίμων
too superstitious 1.

DEISIDAIMONIA δεισιδαιμονία *f.*
superstition 1.

DEKA δέκα
ten 24.
†eighteen (*with* kai oktō) 3.

DEKADUO δεκαδύο
twelve 2.

DEKAPENTE δεκαπέντε
fifteen 3.

DEKATĒ δεκάτη *f.*
tenth 1
tenth part 1.
tithe 2.

DEKATESSARES δεκατέσσαρες
fourteen 5.

DEKATOŌ δεκατόω
receive tithes of 1.
PASS. pay tithes 1.

DEKATOS δέκατος
tenth 3.

DEKTOS δεκτός
acceptable 2
accepted 3.

DELEAZŌ δελεάζω
allure 1
beguile 1
entice 1.

DĒLOŌ δηλόω
declare 3
show 1
signify 3.

DĒLOS δῆλος
certain 1
evident 1
manifest 1.
†*See* poieō.

DĒMĒGOREŌ δημηγορέω
make an oration 1.

DĒMIOURGOS δημιουργός
maker 1.

DĒMOS δῆμος
people 4.

DĒMOSIOS δημόσιος
common 1.
Dat. publicly 2
openly 1.

DĒNARION δηνάριον *n.*
penny 14
*pennyworth (*gen. pl.*) 2.

DENDRON δένδρον *n.*
tree 26.

DEŌ δέω
bind 37
knit 1
tie 4
wind 1.
PASS. be in bonds 1.

DEOMAI δέομαι
beseech 9
make request 1
pray 12.

DĒPOTE δήποτε (δή ποτε)
†*See* hos.

DĒPOU δήπου (δήπου)
verily 1.

DERMA δέρμα *n.*
skin 1.

DERMATINOS δερμάτινος
leathern 1
of a skin 1.

DERŌ δέρω
beat 12
smite 3.

DESMĒ δέσμη *f.*
bundle 1.

DESMEŌ δεσμέω
bind 1.

DESMEUŌ δεσμεύω
bind 2.

DESMIOS δέσμιος
in bonds 1
prisoner 13
that is in bonds 1.

DESMOPHULAX δεσμοφύλαξ
jailor 1
keeper of the prison 2.

DESMOS δεσμός
band 3
bond 15
chain 1
string 1.

DESMŌTĒRION δεσμωτήριον *n.*
prison 4.

DESMŌTĒS δεσμώτης
prisoner 2.

DESPOTĒS δεσπότης
Lord 5
master 5.

DEURO δεῦρο
come 6
come hither 2.
†hitherto (achri deuro) 1.

DEUTE δεῦτε
come 12.
*follow (*with* opisō) 1.

DEUTERAIOS δευτεραῖος
the next day 1.

DEUTEROPRŌTOS δευτερόπρωτος
second after the first 1.

DEUTEROS δεύτερος
second 31.
Neut. afterward 1
again 1
secondarily 1
the second time 3.
†ek *with gen.*: again 2, the second time 4.

DEXIOLABOS δεξιολάβος
spearman 1.

DEXIOS δεξιός
right 12.
As noun right hand (*fem.* 17, *neut. pl.* 22) 39
right side (*neut. pl.*) 1.

DIA διά
Genit. after 3
among (M. by) 1
at 2
by 235 (M. because of 1, whereby 1)
by occasion of 1
for 1
for . . . sake 2
from 1
in 8
of 1
out of 1
through 87
throughout 4
to (M. by) 1
with 16
within 1, etc.
Accus. because of 29
by 8 (M. because of 1, for 1)
by reason of 4
for 58 (M. by 1)
for ——'s sake 45
of 2
through 6
with 1
*avoid 1
*because (*with infin.*) 24
*because that (*with infin.*) 2
*that (*with infin.*) 1, etc.
†*With* touto: for this cause 14, therefore 44, wherefore 8. *With* hos *and* aitia: wherefore 3.

DIABAINŌ διαβαίνω
come over 1
pass 1
pass through 1.

DIABALLŌ διαβάλλω
accuse 1.

DIABEBAIOOMAI διαβεβαιόομαι
affirm 1
affirm constantly 1.

DIABLEPŌ διαβλέπω
see clearly 2.

DIABOLOS διάβολος
devil 35
false accuser 2 (M. makebate 1)
slanderer 1.

DIACHEIRIZOMAI διαχειρίζομαι
kill 1
slay 1.

DIACHŌRIZOMAI διαχωρίζομαι
depart 1.

DIADECHOMAI διαδέχομαι
come after 1.

DIADĒMA διάδημα *n.*
crown 3.

DIADIDŌMI διαδίδωμι
distribute 2.
divide 1
give 1
make distribution 1.

DIADOCHOS διάδοχος
†*See* lambano.

DIAĞGELLŌ διαγγέλλω
declare 1
preach 1
signify 1.

DIAGINOMAI διαγίνομαι
be past 1
be spent 1
*after 1.

DIAGINŌSKŌ διαγινώσκω
inquire 1
know the uttermost 1.

DIAGNŌRIZŌ διαγνωρίζω
make known abroad 1.

DIAGNŌSIS διάγνωσις *f.*
hearing (M. judgment) 1.

DIAGŌ διάγω
lead a life 1
live 1.

DIAGOĞGUZO διαγογγύζω
murmur 2.

DIAGRĒGOREŌ διαγρηγορέω
be awake 1.

DIAIREŌ διαιρέω
divide 2.

DIAIRESIS διαίρεσις *f.*
difference 1
diversity 2.

DIAKATELEĞCHOMAI διακατελέγχομαι
convince 1.

DIAKATHARIZŌ διακαθαρίζω
purge thoroughly 2.

DIAKŌLUŌ διακωλύω
forbid 1.

DIAKONEŌ διακονέω
administer 2
minister 7
minister to 1
minister unto 15
serve 10
use the office of deacon 2 (M. minister 1).

DIAKONIA διακονία *f.*
administration 2
ministering 3
ministration 6
ministry 16 (M charge 1)
office 1
relief 1
service 2
serving 1
*do service 1
*minister (*vb.*) 1.

DIAKONOS διάκονος
deacon 3
minister 20
servant 7.

DIAKOSIOI διακόσιοι
two hundred 8.

DIAKOUŌ διακούω
hear 1.

DIAKRINŌ διακρίνω
discern 2
judge 3
make to differ (M. distinguish) 1
put a difference 1.
MID. (PASS.) be partial 1
contend 2
doubt 5 (M. discern and put a difference between meats 1)
make a difference 1
stagger 1
waver 2.

DIAKRISIS διάκρισις *f.*
discerning 1
*doubtful (M. *judge) 1.
†to discern (pros *with acc.*) 1.

DIALALEŌ διαλαλέω
commune 1
noise abroad 1.

DIALEGOMAI διαλέγομαι
dispute 6
preach 2
reason 2
reason with 2
speak 1.

DIALEIPŌ διαλείπω
cease 1.

DIALEKTOS διάλεκτος *f.*
language 1
tongue 5.

DIALLASSOMAI διαλλάσσομαι
be reconciled 1.

DIALOGISMOS διαλογισμός
disputation (M. his doubtful thoughts) 1
disputing 1
doubting 1
imagination 1
reasoning 1
thought 9.

* Inexact translations, *e.g.*, of a noun by a verb or adjective, of an active by a passive.
† Cases where two or more words in the original are translated by one word or by a phrase.

DIALOGIZOMAI διαλογίζομαι
cast in one's mind 1
consider 1
dispute 1
muse (M. reason *or* debate) 1
reason 11
think 1.

DIALUŌ διαλύω
scatter 1.

DIAMACHOMAI διαμάχομαι
strive 1.

DIAMARTUROMAI διαμαρτύρομαι
charge 3
testify 11
witness 1.

DIAMENŌ διαμένω
continue 1
remain 2.

DIAMERISMOS διαμερισμός
division 1.

DIAMERIZŌ διαμερίζω
divide 5
part 6.
Pass. pt. cloven 1.

DIANEMŌ διανέμω
spread 1.

DIANEUŌ διανεύω
beckon 1.

DIANOĒMA διανόημα *n.*
thought 1.

DIANOIA διάνοια *f.*
imagination 1
mind 9
understanding 3.

DIANOIGŌ διανοίγω
open 8.

DIANUKTEREUŌ διανυκτερεύω
continue all night 1.

DIANUŌ διανύω
finish 1.

DIAPANTOS διαπαντός
always (alway) 5
continually 2.

DIAPERAŌ διαπεράω
can pass 1
go over 1
pass over 3
sail over 1.

DIAPHANĒS διαφανής
transparent 1.

DIAPHĒMIZŌ διαφημίζω
blaze abroad 1
commonly report 1
spread abroad fame 1.

DIAPHERŌ διαφέρω
be better 3
be of more value 2
carry 1
differ from 2
drive up and down 1
make matter 1
publish 1.
Partic. things that are excellent (M. differ) 1
things that are more excellent (M. things that differ) 1.

DIAPHEUGŌ διαφεύγω
escape 1.

DIAPHOROS διάφορος
differing 1
diverse 1.
Comp. more excellent 2.

DIAPHTHEIRŌ διαφθείρω
corrupt 1
destroy 3 (M. corrupt 1).
PASS. perish 1.
Partic. corrupt 1

DIAPHTHORA διαφθορά *f.*
corruption 6.

DIAPHULASSŌ διαφυλάσσω
keep 1.

DIAPLEŌ διαπλέω
sail over 1.

DIAPONEOMAI διαπονέομαι
be grieved 2.

DIAPOREŌ διαπορέω
be in doubt 1
be perplexed 1
doubt 2.
PASS. be much perplexed 1.

DIAPOREUOMAI διαπορεύομαι
go through 3
pass by 1.
Partic. in one's journey 1.

DIAPRAGMATEUOMAI διαπραγματεύομαι
gain by trading 1.

DIAPRIOMAI διαπρίομαι
be cut 1
be cut to the heart 1.

DIARPAZŌ διαρπάζω
spoil 4.

DIARRHĒGNUMI (DIARRHĒSSŌ) (διαῤῥήσσω) διαῤῥήγνυμι
break 1
to rend 3.
MID. break 1.

DIASAPHEŌ διασαφέω
tell 1.

DIASEIŌ διασείω
do violence to (M. put in fear) 1.

DIASKORPIZŌ διασκορπίζω
disperse 1
scatter 2
scatter abroad 2
strew 2
waste 2.

DIASŌZŌ διασώζω
bring safe 1
heal 1
make perfectly whole 1
save 2.
PASS. escape 2
escape safe 1.

DIASPAŌ διασπάω
pluck asunder 1
pull in pieces 1.

DIASPEIRŌ διασπείρω
scatter abroad 3.

DIASPORA διασπορά *f.*
dispersed 1
scattered 1
which are scattered abroad 1.

DIASTELLOMAI διαστέλλομαι
MID. charge 6
give commandment 1.
PASS. be commanded 1.

DIASTĒMA διάστημα *n.*
space 1.

DIASTOLĒ διαστολή *f.*
difference 2
distinction 1.

DIASTREPHŌ διαστρέφω
pervert 2
turn away 1.
Pass. pt. perverse 4.

DIATAGĒ διαταγή *f.*
disposition 1
ordinance 1.

DIATAGMA διάταγμα *n.*
commandment 1.

DIATARASSŌ διαταράσσω
trouble 1.

DIATASSŌ διατάσσω
appoint 2
command 6
give order 1
ordain 2.
MID. appoint 2
command 1
ordain 1
set in order 1.

DIATELEŌ διατελέω
continue 1.

DIATĒREŌ διατηρέω
keep 2.

DIATHĒKĒ διαθήκη *f.*
covenant 20 (M. testament 6)
testament 13.

DIATI διατί
wherefore? 4
why? 23.

DIATITHEMAI διατίθεμαι
appoint 2
make 3.
Partic. testator 2.

DIATRIBŌ διατρίβω
abide 5
be 1
continue 2
tarry 2.

DIATROPHĒ διατροφή *f.*
food 1.

DIAUGAZŌ διαυγάζω
dawn 1.

DIAZŌNNUMI διαζώννυμι
gird 2
gird unto one's self 1.

DICHAZŌ διχάζω
set at variance 1.

DICHOSTASIA διχοστασία *f.*
division 2 (M. faction 1)
sedition 1.

DICHOTOMEŌ διχοτομέω
cut asunder (M. cut off) 1
cut in sunder (M. cut off) 1.

DIDACHĒ διδαχή *f.*
doctrine 29.
†as he hath been taught (kata *with acc.*; M. in teaching) 1.

DIDAKTIKOS διδακτικός
apt to teach 2.

DIDAKTOS διδακτός
taught 1
*which . . . teacheth 2.

DIDASKALIA διδασκαλία *f.*
doctrine 19
learning 1
teaching 1.

DIDASKALOS διδάσκαλος
doctor 1
master 5
Master 41
teacher 10.

DIDASKŌ διδάσκω
teach 97.

DIDŌMI δίδωμι
adventure 1
bestow 2
bring forth 1
commit 1
deliver 2
deliver up 1
give 367
give forth 1
give up 1
grant 10
make 2
minister 1
offer 2 (M. add 1)
put 5
set 1
show 1
suffer 2
take (M. yield) 1
utter 1
yield 2
†deliver (*with* sōtēria) 1; have power (*pass. with dat.*) 2; hinder (*with* egkopē) 1; receive (*with dat. of* autos; M. give 1; show openly (*with* ginomai *and* emphanēs) 1; smite with hand (*with* rhapisma) 1; strike with palm of hand (*with* rhapisma; M. strike with rod) 1.

DIDRACHMON δίδραχμον
tribute (*pl.*) 1
tribute money (*pl.*) 1.

DIEGEIRŌ διεγείρω
awake 2
raise 1
stir up 2.
PASS. arise 2.

DIĒGEOMAI διηγέομαι
declare 3
show 1
tell 4.

DIĒGĒSIS διήγησις *f.*
declaration 1.

DIĒNEKĒS διηνεκής
†Eis *with acc. neut.*: continually 2, for ever 2.

DIERCHOMAI διέρχομαι
come 1
depart 1
go 7
go about 1
go abroad 1
go everywhere 1
go over 2
go over all 1
go through 2
go throughout 1
pass 10
pass by 1
pass over 1
pass through 7
pass throughout 1
pierce through 1
travel 1
walk 2.

DIERMĒNEUŌ διερμηνεύω
expound 1
interpret 4.
Pass. pt. by interpretation 1.

DIERMĒNEUTĒS διερμηνευτής
interpreter 1.

DIERŌTAŌ διερωτάω
make enquiry for 1.

DIETĒS διετής
two years old 1.

DIETIA διετία *f.*
two years 2.

DIEXODOS διέξοδος *f.*
†highway (*with gen. pl. of* hodos) 1.

DIIKNEOMAI διϊκνέομαι
pierce 1.

DIISCHURIZOMAI διϊσχυρίζομαι
affirm confidently 1
affirm constantly 1.

DIISTĒMI διΐστημι
be parted 1
go further 1.
Partic. *the space of after 1.

DIKAIOKRISIA δικαιοκρισία *f.*
righteous judgment 1.

DIKAIŌMA δικαίωμα *n.*
judgment 2
justification 1
ordinance 3 (M. ceremony 1, rite or ceremony 1)
righteousness 4

DIKAIOŌ δικαιόω
free (M. justify) 1
justify 37.
Partic. justifier 1.
PASS. be righteous 1.

DIKAIOS δίκαιος
meet 2
just 33
right 5
righteous 41.

DIKAIŌS δικαίως
justly 2
righteously 2
*to righteousness 1.

DIKAIŌSIS δικαίωσις *f.*
justification 2.

DIKAIOSUNĒ δικαιοσύνη *f.*
righteousness 94.

DIKASTĒS δικαστής
judge 3.

DIKĒ δίκη *f.*
judgment 1
vengeance 2.
†See tio.

DIKTUON δίκτυον *n.*
net 12.

DILOGOS δίλογος
double-tongued 1.

DIO διό (*i.e.* δι' ὅ)
and therefore 1
for which cause 2
therefore 9
wherefore 40.

DIODEUŌ διοδεύω
go throughout 1
pass through 1.

DIŌGMOS διωγμός
persecution 10.

DIŌKŌ διώκω
ensue 1
follow 4
follow after 6
persecute 28
press toward 1.
Partic. given to 1.
PASS. suffer persecution 3.

DIŌKTĒS διώκτης
persecutor 1.

DIOPER διόπερ
wherefore 3.

DIOPETĒS Διοπετής
which fell down from Jupiter 1.

DIORTHŌSIS διόρθωσις *f.*
reformation 1.

DIORUSSŌ διορύσσω
break through 3
break up 1.

DIOTI διότι
because 10
because that 3
for 8 (M. for that 1)
therefore 1.

DIPLOŌ διπλόω
double 1.

DIPLOUS διπλοῦς
double 3
twofold more 1.

DIPSAŌ διψάω
be athirst 3
be thirsty 3
thirst 10.

DIPSOS δίψος *n.*
thirst 1.

DIPSUCHOS δίψυχος
double-minded 2.

DIS δίς
again 2
twice 4.

DISCHILIOI δισχίλιοι
two thousand 1.

DISTAZŌ διστάζω
doubt (*vb.*) 2.

DISTOMOS δίστομος
two-edged 2
with two edges 1.

DITHALASSOS διθάλασσος
where two seas meet 1.

DIULIZŌ διϋλίζω
strain at 1.

DOCHĒ δοχή *f.*
feast 2.

DŌDEKA δώδεκα
twelve 72.

DŌDEKAPHULON δωδεκάφυλον
twelve tribes 1.

DŌDEKATOS δωδέκατος
twelfth 1.

DOGMA δόγμα *n.*
decree 3
ordinance 2.

DOGMATIZOMAI δογματίζομαι
be subject to ordinances 1.

DOKEŌ δοκέω
be accounted 2 (M. think good 1)
be of reputation 1
seem 12 (M. think 1)
suppose 7
think 25
think (*with dat.*) 8
trow 1.
Impers. it pleaseth 2
it seemeth 1
it seemeth good 3.
Partic. pleasure 1.

DOKIMAZŌ δοκιμάζω
allow 2
approve 3 (M. try 2)
discern 2
examine 1
like 1
prove 10
try 4.

DOKIMĒ δοκιμή *f.*
experience 2
experiment 1
proof 3
trial 1.

DOKIMION δοκίμιον *n.*
trial 1
trying 1.

DOKIMOS δόκιμος
approved 5
tried 1
which is approved 1.

DOKOS δοκός *f.*
beam 6.

DOLIOŌ δολιόω
use deceit 1.

DOLIOS δόλιος
deceitful 1.

DOLOŌ δολόω
handle deceitfully 1.

* **Inexact translations,** *e.g.*, **of a noun by a verb or adjective, of an active by a passive.**
† **Cases where two or more words in the original are translated by one word or by a phrase.**

DOLOS δόλος
craft 1
deceit 2
guile 7
subtilty 2.

DOMA δόμα *n.*
gift 4.

DŌMA δῶμα *n.*
house-top 7.

DŌREA δωρεά *f.*
gift 11.

DŌREAN δωρεάν
for naught 1
freely 6
in vain 1
without a cause 1.

DŌRĒMA δώρημα *n.*
gift 2.

DŌREŌ δωρέω
give 3.

DŌRON δῶρον *n.*
gift 18
offering 1.

DOSIS δόσις *f.*
gift 1
giving 1.

DOTĒS δότης
giver 1.

DOULAGŌGEŌ δουλαγωγέω
bring into subjection 1.

DOULĒ δούλη *f.*
handmaid 1
handmaiden 2.

DOULEIA δουλεία *f.*
bondage 5.

DOULEUŌ δουλεύω
be in bondage 4
do service 3
serve 18.

DOULOŌ δουλόω
bring into bondage 1
make servant 1.
PASS. be brought in bondage 1
become servant 2
be under bondage 1.
Partic. given to 1
in bondage 1.

DOULOS δοῦλος
bond 6
bondman 1
servant 120.

DOXA δόξα *f.*
dignity 2
glory 144
honour 6
praise 4
worship 1
*glorious (*gen.*) 6.
†glorious (dia *and gen.*) 1; glorious (en *and dat.*) 3.

DOXAZŌ δοξάζω
glorify 54
honour 3
magnify 1.
PASS. be made glorious 1
have glory 2.
Partic. full of glory 1.

DRACHMĒ δραχμή *f.*
piece 2
piece of silver 1.

DRAKŌN δράκων
dragon 13.

DRASSOMAI δράσσομαι
take 1.

DREMŌ = TRECHŌ.

DREPANON δρέπανον *n.*
sickle 8.

DROMOS δρόμος
course 3.

DUMI = DUNŌ.

DUNAMAI δύναμαι
be able 37
be able to do 1
be possible 1
can 147
can do 2
may 18.
Partic. able 3
that is of power 1.

DUNAMIS δύναμις *f.*
ability 1
abundance (M. power) 1
meaning 1
might 4
mighty deed 1
mighty work 11
miracle 8
power 77
strength 7
violence 1
virtue 3
wonderful work 1
worker of miracles (M. power) 1.
*mighty (*gen.*) 2 (M. of power 1).
†mighty (en *with dat.*) 1.

DUNAMOŌ δυναμόω
strengthen 1.

DUNASTĒS δυνάστης
mighty 1
of great authority 1
Potentate 1.

DUNATEŌ δυνατέω
be mighty 1.

DUNATOS δυνατός
able 10
mighty 5
possible (*neut.*) 13
strong 3
that I could 1
that is mighty 1.
As noun mighty man 1
power 1.

DUNŌ δύνω (δῦμι)
be setting 1
set 1.

DUO δύο
both 2
twain 10
two 116
two men 1
two women 1.
†ana duo: two and two 1, two apiece 2. *Repeated* by two and two 1.

DUSBASTAKTOS δυσβάστακτος
grievous to be borne 2.

DUSENTERIA δυσεντερία *f.*
bloody flux 1.

DUSERMĒNEUTOS δυσερμήνευτος
hard to be uttered 1.

DUSKOLOS δύσκολος
hard 1.

DUSKOLŌS δυσκόλως
hardly 3.

DUSMĒ δυσμή *f.*
west (*pl.*) 5.

DUSNOĒTOS δυσνόητος
hard to be understood 1.

DUSPHĒMIA δυσφημία *f.*
evil report 1.

E

Ē[1] ἤ
and 3
either 8
except it be 1
neither 3
nor 5
or 257
or else 5
or if 1
what? 3.
†e kai: or else 1, yea and 1.

Ē[2] ἤ
but 1
but either 1
more than 1
rather than 3
save 1
than 35.
†all' e: but rather 1, but 1 than 1 *See* pleiōn.

Ē[3] ἦ
†surely (*with* mēn[1]) 1.

EAN ἐάν
and if 4
if 194
though 12
when 2.
†though (kai ean) 1. *With* kai: if (M. although) 1. *With* te: whether 3, or 3, though 1. *With* mē: if not 15, if no 1, except 33, but 3. *With* mē proteron: before 1, former 2, first 2, at the first 1.

EANPER ἐάνπερ
if 3.

EAŌ ἐάω
commit (M. leave) 1
leave 1
let 1
let alone 1
suffer 9.
Imper. let alone 2 (M. away 1).

ĒCHEŌ ἠχέω
roar 1
sound 1.

ECHIDNA ἔχιδνα *f.*
viper 5.

ECHŌ ἔχω
be able 1
be in that case 1
be old 1
be possessed with 2
can 4
could have 1
count 4
do 1
have 607 (M. hold fast 1)
hold 5
hold fast 1
keep 1
lie 1
retain 1
take for 1
use (M. have) 1.
Partic. with 1.
MID. accompany 1.
Partic. day following 1
next 2
next day 1.
†be bold (*with* parrhēsia) 1; be diseased (*with* kakōs) 2; be of age (*with* hēlikia) 2; be rebuked (*with* eleğxis) 1; be sick (*with* kakōs) 7; be with child (*with* en *and* gaster) 5; begin to amend (*with* kompsoteron) 1; conceive (*with* koitē) 1; eat (*with* nomē) 1; enjoy the pleasures (*with* apolausis) 1; fear (*with* phobos) 1; go to law (*with pl. of* krina) 1; have not knowledge (*with* agnōsia) 1; hold in reputation (M. in honour; *with* entimos) 1; lie at the point of death (*with* eschatōs) 1; recover (*with* kalōs) 1; reign (*with* basileia) 1; thank (*with* charis) 3; with child (*partic. with* en *and* gaster) 2. *With* anağkē: must needs 1, must of necessity 1, need 1, *be needful for 1. Mē echō: have not (M. be poor) 1, lack 1. *Partic.* sick people (*with* kakōs) 1. *See* ekstasis, tromos, etc.

ĒCHOS ἦχος
fame 1
sound 2.

ECHTHES = CHTHES.

ECHTHRA ἔχθρα *f.*
enmity 5
hatred 1.

ECHTHROS ἐχθρός
enemy 29
foe 2.
†*See* anthrōpos.

EDAPHIZŌ ἐδαφίζω
lay even with the ground 1.

EDAPHOS ἔδαφος *n.*
ground 1.

ĒDĒ ἤδη
already 18
by this time 1
even now 1
now 37
yet 2.

EĞCHRIŌ ἐγχρίω
anoint 1.

EGEIRŌ ἐγείρω
awake 1
lift up 3
lift out 1
raise 28
raise again 4
raise up 23
rear up 1
take up 1.
MID. (PASS.) arise 27
rise 36
rise again 5
rise up 8.
†stand forth (*with* eis to meson) 1.

EGERSIS ἔγερσις *f.*
resurrection 1.

EĞGIZŌ ἐγγίζω
approach 2
be at hand 9
be nigh 2
come near 5
come nigh 8
draw near 5
draw nigh 12.

EĞGRAPHO ἐγγράφω
write in 2.

EĞGUOS ἔγγυος
surety 1.

EĞGUS ἐγγύς
at hand 6
from 1
near 3
near to 2
nigh 7
nigh at hand 4
nigh to 3
nigh unto 4
ready 1.

EĞKAINIA ἐγκαίνια *n. pl.*
feast of the dedication 1.

EĞKAINIZŌ ἐγκαινίζω
consecrate (M. make new) 1
dedicate (M. purify) 1.

EĞKALEŌ ἐγκαλέω
accuse 4
call in question 1
implead 1.
†lay a thing to the charge of (*with* kata) 1.

EĞKATALEIPŌ ἐγκαταλείπω
forsake 7
leave 2.

EĞKATHETOS ἐγκάθετος
spy 1.

EĞKATOIKEŌ ἐγκατοικέω
dwell among 1.

EĞKENTRIZŌ ἐγκεντρίζω
graff in 4
graff into 2.

EĞKLĒMA ἔγκλημα *n.*
crime laid against one 1
*laid to one's charge 1.

EĞKOMBOOMAI ἐγκομβόομαι
be clothed with 1.

EĞKOPĒ ἐγκοπή
†*See* didōmi.

EĞKOPTŌ ἐγκόπτω
be tedious unto 1
hinder 2.

EĞKRATEIA ἐγκράτεια *f.*
temperance 4.

EĞKRATĒS ἐγκρατής
temperate 1.

EĞKRATEUOMAI ἐγκρατεύομαι
be temperate 1
can contain 1.

EĞKRINŌ ἐγκρίνω
make of the number 1.

EĞKRUPTŌ ἐγκρύπτω
hide 2.

EĞKUOS ἔγκυος
great with child 1.

EGŌ ἐγώ
I *freq.*

EI εἰ
if 325
that 5
whether 20.
†*With* de mē: else[2], or else 3. *With* de mēge: else 2, if otherwise 2, otherwise 1, or else 1, etc. *With* kai: else 2, if 3, though 14, etc. *With* mē: but 53, except 6, except that 1, if not 5, more than 1, save 16, saving 2, save that 1, save only that 1. *With* tis: whether any 1, whosoever 2, he that 2, that which 1.
Also combined with various other particles.

EIDEA = IDEA.

EIDŌ = EIDON = OIDA.

EIDŌLEION εἰδωλεῖον *n.*
idol's temple 1.

EIDŌLOLATREIA εἰδωλολατρεία *f.*
idolatry 4.

EIDŌLOLATRĒS εἰδωλολάτρης
idolater 7.

EIDŌLON εἴδωλον *n.*
idol 11.

EIDŌLOTHUTON εἰδωλόθυτον *n.*
meat offered to idols 1.
that which is offered in sacrifice to idols 1.
thing offered to idols 1
thing offered unto an idol 1.
thing offered unto idols 1
thing sacrificed unto idols 2
thing that is offered in sacrifice unto idols 1
thing which is offered to idols 1
*offered in sacrifice unto idols 1.

EIDON εἶδον. *Cf.* **HORAŌ.**
behold 16
consider 1
know 1
look 6
look on 2
perceive 5.
Imper. see 316 [ide *and* idou].

EIDOS εἶδος
appearance 1
fashion 1
shape 2
sight 1.

EIGE εἴγε (εἴ γε)
if 2
if so be that 2.
†if yet (*with* kai) 1.

EIKĒ εἰκῇ
in vain 5
vainly 1
without a cause 1.

EIKŌ[1] εἴκω
give place 1.

EIKŌ[2] εἴκω (ἔοικα)
be like 2.

EIKŌN εἰκών *f.*
image 23.

EIKOSI εἴκοσι
twenty 13.

EILIKRINEIA εἰλικρίνεια *f.*
sincerity 3.

EILIKRINĒS εἰλικρινής
pure 1
sincere 1.

EIMI εἰμί
to be.
Rendered also by become, begin to be, be made, come 3, come to pass, dure, endure, follow, have being, hold, is to say 6, make, mean 6, stand.
†agree (*with* isos) 2; agree in (*with* eis) 1; agree not (*with* asumphōnos) 1; be accepted of (*with* euarestōs) 1; be made (*with* eis) 1; belong unto (*with* ek) 1; fear exceedingly (*with* ekphobos) 1; follow (*with* meta) 1; give self wholly to (*with* en) 1; have (*with* en) 3; have the charge of (*with* epi) 1; live long (*with* makrochronios) 1; lust after (*with* epithumētēs) 1; must needs (*with* anağkē) 1; pass the flower of age (*with* huperakmos) 1; please well (*with* euarestos) 1; profit (*with* ōphelimos) 1; quake (*with* entromos) 1; sojourn (*with* paroikos) 1. *With genit. or dat.*: belong to 2, have 22, own 1.

EINAI. *Inf. of* **EIMI.**

EIŌTHA. *Perf. of* **ETHŌ.**

EIPER εἴπερ
if so be 1
if so be that 3
seeing 1
though 1

EIPON εἶπον
answer 1
bid 5
bring word 1
call 1
command 8
grant 1
say 865
say on 1
speak 55
speak of 1
tell 40
tell of 1.

EIPŌS εἴπως
if by any means 4.

EIRĒKA. *Perf. of* **ERŌ**

EIRĒNĒ εἰρήνη *f.*
peace 88
quietness 1
rest 1.
†at one again (eis *and acc.*) 1.

EIRĒNEUŌ εἰρηνεύω
be at peace 1
have peace 1
live in peace 1
live peaceably 1.

EIRĒNIKOS εἰρηνικός
peaceable 2.

EIRĒNOPOIEŌ εἰρηνοποιέω
make peace 1.

EIRĒNOPOIOS εἰρηνοποιός
peacemaker 1.

* Inexact translations, *e.g.*, of a noun by a verb or adjective, of an active by a passive.
† Cases where two or more words in the original are translated by one word or by a phrase.

EIRŌ = **ERŌ**.

EIS εἰς
against 25
among 16
at 20
for 91
in 131
into 571
that 30
on 57
to 282
toward 32
unto 208
upon 25, etc.
†*With pronouns freq. translated by the second part of* therein, thereunto, wherein, wherefore, etc. As concerning (*with* logos) 1.

EISAGŌ εἰσάγω
bring in 5.
†*With* eis: bring into 4, lead into 1.

EISAKOUŌ εἰσακούω
hear 5.

EISDECHOMAI εἰσδέχομαι
receive 1.

EISEIMI εἴσειμι
go in 1.
†*With* eis: enter 1, go into 2.

EISERCHOMAI εἰσέρχομαι
arise 1
come 2
come in 19
enter 107
enter in 17
go 4
go in 19.
†*With* eis: come into 9, come to 2, come unto 1, go into 17.

EISKALEŌ εἰσκαλέω
call in 1.

EISODOS εἴσοδος
coming 1
entering in 1
entrance 1
entrance in 1
*enter 1.

EISPĒDAŌ εἰσπηδάω
run 1
spring in 1.

EISPHERŌ εἰσφέρω
bring in 1.
†*With* eis: bring into 2, bring to 1, lead into 2.

EISPOREUOMAI εἰσπορεύομαι
come in 3
enter 8
enter in 5.
†*With* eis: go into 1.

EISTRECHŌ εἰστρέχω
run in 1.

EITA εἶτα
after that 3
afterward 1
furthermore 1
then 11.

EK ἐκ (ἐξ)
among 5
at 3
because of 3
between 1
betwixt 1
by 55
by reason of 3
by the means of 1
for 2
from 182
from among 3
from up 2
in 6 (M. out of 1)
of 402
off (A.V. 1611 of) 1
on 10
one of 8
out of 131
over 4
some of 6
them of 1
they of 1
through 2
unto 1
with 25.
†*With pronouns translated by second part of* thereof, etc.

EKBALLŌ ἐκβάλλω
bring forth 3
cast 2
cast forth 1
cast out 52 (M. excommunicate 1)
drive 1
drive out 1
expel 1
pluck out 1
pull out 3
put forth 3
put out 2
send away 1
send forth 3
send out 1
take out 1
thrust out 2.
MID. cast out 1.
†*With* exō: cast out 1, thrust out 1, leave out (M. cast out) 1.

EKBASIS ἔκβασις *f.*
end 1
way to escape 1.

EKBOLĒ ἐκβολή *f.*
†*With* poieomai: lighten the ship 1.

EKCHEŌ ἐκχέω
pour out 11
shed 4
shed forth 1
spill 1.
PASS. run out 1.

EKCHŌREŌ ἐκχωρέω
depart out 1.

EKCHUNŌ ἐκχύνω
pour out 1
shed 5
shed abroad 1
spill 1.
PASS. gush out 1
run greedily 1.

EKDAPANAOMAI ἐκδαπανάομαι
be spent 1.

EKDECHOMAI ἐκδέχομαι
expect 1
look for 2
tarry for 1
wait 1
wait for 3.

EKDĒLOS ἔκδηλος
manifest 1.

EKDĒMEŌ ἐκδημέω
be absent 2.
Partic. absent 1.

EKDIDŌMI ἐκδίδωμι
let forth 1
let out 3.

EKDIĒGEOMAI ἐκδιηγέομαι
declare 2.

EKDIKEŌ ἐκδικέω
avenge 5
revenge 1.

EKDIKĒSIS ἐκδίκησις *f.*
punishment 1
revenge 1
vengeance 4.
†*See* poieō.

EKDIKOS ἔκδικος
avenger 1
revenger 1.

EKDIŌKŌ ἐκδιώκω
persecute 2 (M. chase out 1).

EKDOCHĒ ἐκδοχή *f.*
looking for 1.

EKDOTOS ἔκδοτος
being delivered 1.

EKDUŌ ἐκδύω
strip 2
take off from 2
MID. be unclothed 1.

EKEI ἐκεῖ
there 96
thither 8
thitherward 1
to yonder place 1
yonder 1.
†*See* hopou.

EKEINOS ἐκεῖνος
he (she, it, they, etc.) 100
Peter 1
self-same 1
same 19
that 137
that same 4
that very 2
that way 1
the other 2
this 1.

EKEISE ἐκεῖσε
there 2.

EKEITHEN ἐκεῖθεν
afterward 1
from thence 14
from that place 1
thence 19
there 1.

EKGAMISKŌ ἐκγαμίσκω
give in marriage 2.

EKGAMIZŌ ἐκγαμίζω
give in marriage 5.

EKGONA ἔκγονα
nephews 1.

EKKAIOMAI ἐκκαίομαι
burn 1.

EKKAKEŌ ἐκκακέω
be weary 2 (M. faint 1)
faint 4.

EKKATHAIRŌ ἐκκαθαίρω
purge 1
purge out 1.

EKKENTEŌ ἐκκεντέω
pierce 2.

EKKLAŌ ἐκκλάω
break off 3.

EKKLEIŌ ἐκκλείω
exclude 2.

EKKLĒSIA ἐκκλησία *f.*
assembly 3
church 112.

EKKLINŌ ἐκκλίνω
avoid 1
eschew 1
go out of the way 1.

EKKOLUMBAŌ ἐκκολυμβάω
swim out 1.

EKKOMIZŌ ἐκκομίζω
carry out 1.

EKKOPTŌ ἐκκόπτω
cut down 2
cut off 4
cut out 1
hew down 3
hinder 1.

EKKREMAMAI ἐκκρέμαμαι
be very attentive (M. hang on) 1.

EKLALEŌ ἐκλαλέω
tell 1.

EKLAMPŌ ἐκλάμπω
shine forth 1.

EKLANTHANOMAI ἐκλανθάνομαι
forget 1.

EKLEGŌ ἐκλέγω
choose 2.
MID. choose 17
choose out 1
make choice 1.

EKLEIPŌ ἐκλείπω
fail 3.

EKLEKTOS ἐκλεκτός
chosen 7
elect 16.

EKLOGĒ ἐκλογή *f.*
election 6
*chosen 1.

EKLUŌ ἐκλύω
PASS. faint 5 (M. be tired and lie down 1).

EKMASSŌ ἐκμάσσω
wipe 5.

EKMUKTĒRIZŌ ἐκμυκτηρίζω
deride 2.

EKNĒPHŌ ἐκνήφω
awake 1.

EKNEUŌ ἐκνεύω
convey one's self away 1.

EKPALAI ἔκπαλαι
of a long time 1
of old 1.

EKPEIRAZŌ ἐκπειράζω
tempt 4.

EKPEMPŌ ἐκπέμπω
send away 1
send forth 1.

EKPETANNUMI ἐκπετάννυμι
stretch forth 1.

EKPHERŌ ἐκφέρω
bear 1
bring forth 2
carry forth 1
carry out 3.

EKPHEUGŌ ἐκφεύγω
escape 5
flee 2.

EKPHOBEŌ ἐκφοβέω
terrify 1.

EKPHOBOS ἔκφοβος
sore afraid 1.
†*See* eimi.

EKPHUŌ ἐκφύω
put forth 2.

EKPIPTŌ ἐκπίπτω
be cast 1
fail 1
fall 5
fall away 1
fall from 2
fall off 2
take none effect 1.

EKPLEŌ ἐκπλέω
sail 1
sail away 1
sail thence 1.

EKPLĒROŌ ἐκπληρόω
fulfil 1.

EKPLĒRŌSIS ἐκπλήρωσις *f.*
accomplishment 1.

EKPLĒSSOMAI ἐκπλήσσομαι
be amazed 3
be astonished 10.

EKPNEŌ ἐκπνέω
give up the ghost 3.

EKPOREUOMAI ἐκπορεύομαι
come forth 2
come from 1
come out 3
depart 3
go forth 2
go out 11
issue 2
proceed 10.

EKPORNEUŌ ἐκπορνεύω
give one's self over to fornication 1.

EKPSUCHŌ ἐκψύχω
give up the ghost 2
yield up the ghost 1.

EKPTUŌ ἐκπτύω
reject 1.

EKRIZOŌ ἐκριζόω
pluck up by the root 2
root up 2.

EKSTASIS ἔκστασις *f.*
amazement 1
astonishment 1
trance 3.
†be amazed (*with* echō 1, *with* lambanō 1) 2.

EKSTREPHŌ ἐκστρέφω
subvert 1.

EKTARASSŌ ἐκταράσσω
trouble exceedingly 1.

EKTEINŌ ἐκτείνω
cast out 1
put forth 3
stretch forth 10
stretch out 2.

EKTELEŌ ἐκτελέω
finish 2.

EKTENEIA ἐκτένεια
†instantly (en *with dat.*) 1.

EKTENĒS ἐκτενής
fervent 1
without ceasing (M. instant and earnest) 1.

EKTENESTERON ἐκτενέστερον
more earnestly 1.

EKTENŌS ἐκτενῶς
fervently 1.

EKTHAMBEOMAI ἐκθαμβέομαι
be affrighted 2
be greatly amazed 1
be sore amazed 1.

EKTHAMBOS ἔκθαμβος
greatly wondering 1.

EKTHETOS ἔκθετος
†*See* poieō.

EKTINASSŌ ἐκτινάσσω
shake 1
shake off 3.

EKTITHĒMI ἐκτίθημι
cast out 1
expound 3.

EKTOS ἐκτός
other than 1
out of 2
without 1
*he is excepted 1.
As noun the outside 1.
†*With* ei mē: but 1, except 1, unless 1.

EKTREPHŌ ἐκτρέφω
bring up 1
nourish 1.

EKTREPOMAI ἐκτρέπομαι
avoid 1
be turned 1
be turned out of the way 1
turn aside 2.

EKTRŌMA ἔκτρωμα *n.*
one born out of due time (M. an abortive) 1.

EKZĒTEŌ ἐκζητέω
inquire diligently 1
require 2
seek after 2
seek carefully 1
seek diligently 1.

ELACHISTOS ἐλάχιστος
least 7
smallest 1
very little 1
very small 1.
As noun that thing which is least 1
that which is least 1
very small thing 1.

ELACHISTOTEROS ἐλαχιστότερος
less than the least 1.

ELAIA ἐλαία *f.*
olive berry 1
Olives (*plur.*) 11
olive tree 3.

ELAION ἔλαιον *n.*
oil 11.

ELAIŌN ἐλαιών
Olivet 1.

ELAŌ = **ELAUNŌ**.

ELAPHRIA ἐλαφρία *f.*
lightness 1.

ELAPHROS ἐλαφρός
light 2.

ELASSŌN ἐλάσσων
less 1
under 1
younger (M. lesser) 1.
As noun that which is worse 1.

ELATTONEŌ ἐλαττονέω
have lack 1.

ELATTOŌ ἐλαττόω
make lower 2 (M. make inferior 1).
PASS. decrease 1.

ELAUNŌ ἐλαύνω (ἐλάω)
carry 1
drive 2
row 2.

ELEEINOS ἐλεεινός
miserable 2.

ELEĒMŌN ἐλεήμων
merciful 2.

ELEĒMOSUNĒ ἐλεημοσύνη *f.*
alms 13
almsdeed 1.

ELEEŌ ἐλεέω
have compassion of 1
have compassion on 2
have mercy on 15
have mercy upon 1
have pity on 1
show mercy 2.
PASS. obtain mercy 8
receive mercy 1.

ELEG̃CHŌ ἐλέγχω
convict 1
convince 4
rebuke 5
reprove 5 (M. convince 1, discover 1)
tell one's fault 1.

ELEG̃CHOS ἔλεγχος
evidence 1
reproof 1.

ELEG̃XIS ἔλεγξις
†*See* echō.

ELEOS ἔλεος
mercy 28.

ELEPHANTINOS ἐλεφάντινος
of ivory 1.

ELEUSIS ἔλευσις *f.*
coming 1.

ELEUTHERIA ἐλευθερία *f.*
liberty 11.

ELEUTHEROŌ ἐλευθερόω
deliver 1
make free 6.

* Inexact translations, *e.g.*, of a noun by a verb or adjective, of an active by a passive.
† Cases where two or more words in the original are translated by one word or by a phrase.

ELEUTHEROS ἐλεύθερος
free 18
at liberty 1.
As noun freeman 1
free woman 3.

ELI Ἡλί
Eli 2.

ELLOGEŌ ἐλλογέω
impute 1
put on one's account 1.

ELŌI Ἐλωΐ
Eloi 2.

ELPIS ἐλπίς *f.*
hope 53
faith 1.

ELPIZŌ ἐλπίζω
have hope 1
hope 9
hope for 2.
trust 18.
Partic. thing hoped for 1.

EMAUTOU ἐμαυτοῦ
I myself 1
me 4
mine own 1
mine own self 2
myself 29.

EMBAINŌ ἐμβαίνω
enter 8
step in 1.
†*With* eis: go into 2, go up into 1, come into 2, get into 2, take 2.

EMBALLŌ ἐμβάλλω
†*With* eis: cast into 1.

EMBAPTŌ ἐμβάπτω
dip 3.

EMBATEUŌ ἐμβατεύω
intrude into 1.

EMBIBAZŌ ἐμβιβάζω
put 1.

EMBLEPŌ ἐμβλέπω
behold 4
can see 1
gaze up 1
look upon 4
see 1.
†*With* eis: behold 1.

EMBRIMAOMAI ἐμβριμάομαι
charge straitly 2
groan 2
murmur against 1.

EME ἐμέ (*acc. of* EGŌ)
me *freq.*
myself 1.

EMEŌ ἐμέω
spue 1.

EMMAINOMAI ἐμμαίνομαι
be mad against 1.

EMMENŌ ἐμμένω
continue in 1.
†*With* en: continue in 2.

EMOI ἐμοί (*dat. of* EGŌ).
me *freq.*, etc.

EMOS ἐμός
mine own 11
my (mine) 62
of me 4
*that I have 1.

EMOU ἐμοῦ (*gen. of* EGŌ)
me *freq.*
my 9, etc.

EMPAIGMOS ἐμπαιγμός
mocking 1.

EMPAIKTĒS ἐμπαίκτης
mocker 1
scoffer 1.

EMPAIZŌ ἐμπαίζω
mock 13.

EMPERIPATEŌ ἐμπεριπατέω
walk in 1.

EMPHANĒS ἐμφανής
manifest 1.
†*See* didōmi.

EMPHANIZŌ ἐμφανίζω
declare plainly 1
inform 3
manifest 2
show 1
signify 1.
PASS. appear 2.

EMPHOBOS ἔμφοβος
affrighted 4
afraid 3.
†*See* gignomai.

EMPHUSAŌ ἐμφυσάω
breathe on 1.

EMPHUTOS ἔμφυτος
ingrafted 1.

EMPIPLAŌ = EMPIPLĒMI.

EMPIPLĒMI ἐμπίπλημι (ἐμπιπλάω)
fill 4.
PASS. be full 1.

EMPIPTŌ ἐμπίπτω
†*With* eis: fall among 1, fall into 6.

EMPLEKŌ ἐμπλέκω
entangle in 1.
MID. entangle one's self with 1.

EMPLOKĒ ἐμπλοκή *f.*
plaiting 1.

EMPNEŌ ἐμπνέω
breathe out 1.

EMPOREUOMAI ἐμπορεύομαι
buy and sell 1
make merchandise of 1.

EMPORIA ἐμπορία *f.*
merchandise 1.

EMPORION ἐμπόριον *n.*
merchandise 1.

EMPOROS ἔμπορος
merchant 5.

EMPRĒTHŌ ἐμπρήθω
burn up 1.

EMPROSTHEN ἔμπροσθεν
at 1
against 1
before 41
in one's sight 2
in the presence of 1
in the sight of 1
of 1.

EMPTUŌ ἐμπτύω
spit on 2
spit upon 2.
†*With* eis: spit in 1, spit upon 1.

EN ἐν
among 114
as 22
at 106
by 142
in 1863
into 11
on 45
through 37
to 15
unto 9
with 139
within 13, etc.
†always (*with dat. of* pas *and* kairos) 2. *With pronouns freq. translated by the second part of* hereby, herein, therein, thereon, whereby, wherein, etc.

ENAĞKALIZOMAI ἐναγκαλίζομαι
take in one's arms 1
take up in one's arms 1.

ENALIOS ἐνάλιος
As noun things in the sea 1.

ENANTI ἔναντι
before 1.

ENANTION ἐναντίον
before 4
in the sight of 1.

ENANTIOS ἐναντίος
against 1
contrary 6.
†over against (ex *with gen.*) 1.

ENARCHOMAI ἐνάρχομαι
begin 2.

ENATOS = ENNATOS.

ENDECHOMAI ἐνδέχομαι
can be 1.

ENDEĒS ἐνδεής
that lacketh 1.

ENDEIGMA ἔνδειγμα *n.*
manifest token 1.

ENDEIKNUMAI ἐνδείκνυμαι
do 1
show 9
show forth 1.

ENDEIXIS ἔνδειξις *f.*
evident token 1
proof 1
*declare 2.

ENDĒMEŌ ἐνδημέω
be at home 1
be present 1.
Partic. present 1.

ENDIDUSKŌ ἐνδιδύσκω
MID. be clothed in 1
wear 1.

ENDIKOS ἔνδικος
just 2.

ENDOMĒSIS ἐνδόμησις *f.*
building 1.

ENDOXAZOMAI ἐνδοξάζομαι
be glorified 2.

ENDOXOS ἔνδοξος
glorious 2
honourable 1
*gloriously 1.

ENDUMA ἔνδυμα *n.*
clothing 1
garment 2
raiment 5.

ENDUNAMOŌ ἐνδυναμόω
enable 1
strengthen 2.
MID. (PASS.) be made strong 1
be strong 3
increase in strength 1.

ENDUNŌ ἐνδύνω
†*With* eis: creep into 1.

ENDUŌ ἐνδύω
clothe with 1
put on 3.
MID. (PASS.) be arrayed in 1
be clothed 1
be clothed in 2
be clothed with 2
be endued with 1
have on 1
put on 16.

ENDUSIS ἔνδυσις *f.*
putting on 1.

ENECHŌ ἐνέχω
have a quarrel against (M. have an inward grudge, against) 1
urge 1.
PASS. be entangled with 1.

ENEDRA ἐνέδρα
†*See* poieō.

ENEDREUŌ ἐνεδρεύω
lay wait for 1
lie in wait for 1.

ENEDRON ἔνεδρον *n.*
lying in wait 1.

ENEĞKŌ. *Fut. of* PHERŌ.

ENEILEŌ ἐνειλέω
wrap in 1.

ENEIMI ἔνειμι
Partic. such things as ye have (M. as ye are able) 1.
[*See* eni.]

ENENĒKONTA ἐνενήκοντα
ninety 4

ENEOS = ENNEOS.

ENERGEIA ἐνέργεια *f.*
effectual working 2
operation 1
strong 1
working 4.

ENERGĒMA ἐνέργημα *n.*
operation 1
working 1.

ENERGEŌ ἐνεργέω
be mighty in 1
do 1
show forth one's self 2
work 7
work effectually in 1.
MID. be effectual (M. be wrought) 1.
work 5
work effectually 1.
Partic. effectual fervent 1.

ENERGĒS ἐνεργής
effectual 2
powerful 1.

ENEULOGEOMAI ἐνευλογέομαι
be blessed 2.

ENI ἔνι (*from* ENEIMI).
is 1
there is 4.

ENIAUTOS ἐνιαυτός
year 14.

ENISCHUŌ ἐνισχύω
be strengthened 1
strengthen 1.

ENISTĒMI ἐνίστημι
be at hand 1
come 1.
Partic. present 3
things present (*pl.*) 2.

ENNATOS ἔννατος (ἔνατος)
ninth 10.

ENNEA ἐννέα
nine 5.

ENNENĒKONTA = ENENĒKONTA

ENNEOS ἐννεός
speechless 1.

ENNEUŌ ἐννεύω
make signs to 1.

ENNOIA ἔννοια *f.*
intent 1
mind 1.

ENNOMOS ἔννομος
lawful (M. ordinary) 1
under the law 1.

ENNUCHON ἔννυχον
before day 1.

ENOCHLEŌ ἐνοχλέω
trouble 1.

ENOCHOS ἔνοχος
guilty of 4
in danger of 5
subject to 1.

ENOIKEŌ ἐνοικέω
dwell in 5.

ENŌPION ἐνώπιον
before 63
in one's presence 2
in one's sight 5
in the presence of 7
in the sight of 16
to 1.

ENŌTIZOMAI ἐνωτίζομαι
hearken to 1.

ENTALMA ἔνταλμα *n.*
commandment 3.

ENTAPHIASMOS ἐνταφιασμός
burying 2.

ENTAPHIAZŌ ἐνταφιάζω
bury 1.
Infin. burial 1.

ENTELLOMAI ἐντέλλομαι
charge 1
command 10
give charge 2
give commandment 3
enjoin 1.

ENTEUTHEN ἐντεῦθεν
from hence 3
hence 6.
†*With* kai enteuthen: on either side 1, of either side 1 (on either side *ed.* 1762, *etc.*).

ENTEUXIS ἔντευξις *f.*
intercession 1
prayer 1.

ENTHADE ἐνθάδε
here 3
hither 4
there 1.

ENTHUMEOMAI ἐνθυμέομαι
think 2
think on 1.

ENTHUMĒSIS ἐνθύμησις *f.*
device 1
thought 3.

ENTIMOS ἔντιμος
dear 1
honourable 1
precious 2.
†*See* echō.

ENTOLĒ ἐντολή *f.*
commandment 69
precept 2

ENTOPIOS ἐντόπιος
of that place 1.

ENTOS ἐντός
within 2 (M. among 1).

ENTREPHOMAI ἐντρέφομαι
be nourished up in 1.

ENTREPŌ ἐντρέπω
shame 1.
PASS. be ashamed 2.
MID. regard 2
reverence 4.

ENTROMOS ἔντρομος
trembling 1.
†tremble (eimi entr. 1, ginomai entr. 1) 2.

ENTROPĒ ἐντροπή *f.*
shame 2.

ENTRUPHAŌ ἐντρυφάω
sport one's self 1.

ENTUĞCHANŌ ἐντυγχάνω
deal with 1
make intercession 4.

ENTULITTŌ ἐντυλίττω
wrap in 2
wrap together 1.

ENTUPOŌ ἐντυπόω
engrave 1.

ENUBRIZŌ ἐνυβρίζω
do despite unto 1.

ENUPNIAZOMAI ἐνυπνιάζομαι
dream 1.
Partic. filthy dreamer 1.

ENUPNION ἐνύπνιον *n.*
dream 1.

EOIKA. *Perf. of* EIKŌ[2].

EPAĞGELIA ἐπαγγελία *f.*
message 1
promise 52.

EPAĞGELLOMAI ἐπαγγέλλομαι
MID. (PASS.) make promise 1
profess 2
promise 11
promise is made 1.

EPAĞGELMA ἐπάγγελμα *n.*
promise 2.

EPAGŌ ἐπάγω
bring in upon 1
bring upon 2.

EPAGŌNIZOMAI ἐπαγωνίζομαι
earnestly contend for 1.

EPAINEŌ ἐπαινέω
commend 1
laud 1
praise 4.

EPAINOS ἔπαινος
praise 11.

EPAIRŌ ἐπαίρω
hoist up 1
lift up 15
take up 1.
MID. exalt one's self 2.

EPAISCHUNOMAI ἐπαισχύνομαι
be ashamed 3
be ashamed of 8.

EPAITEŌ ἐπαιτέω
beg 1.

EPAKOLOUTHEŌ ἐπακολουθέω
follow 3
follow after 1.

EPAKOUŌ ἐπακούω
hear 1.

EPAKROAOMAI ἐπακροάομαι
hear 1.

EPAN ἐπάν
when 3

EPANAĞKES ἐπάναγκες
necessary 1.

EPANAGŌ ἐπανάγω
launch out 1
return 1
thrust out 1.

EPANAMIMNĒSKŌ ἐπαναμιμνήσκω
put in mind 1.

EPANAPAUOMAI ἐπαναπαύομαι
rest in 1.
†*With* epi: rest upon 1

EPANERCHOMAI ἐπανέρχομαι
come again 1
return 1.

EPANISTAMAI ἐπανίσταμαι
rise up against 2.

EPANŌ ἐπάνω
above 3
more than 1
on 4
over 6
upon 3.
†*With* autos: thereon 4.

* Inexact translations, *e.g.*, of a noun by a verb or adjective, of an active by a passive.
† Cases where two or more words in the original are translated by one word or by a phrase.

EPANORTHŌSIS ἐπανόρθωσις *f.*
correction 1.

EPAPHRIZŌ ἐπαφρίζω
foam out 1.

EPARCHIA ἐπαρχία *f.*
province 2.

EPARKEŌ ἐπαρκέω
relieve 3.

EPATHROIZOMAI ἐπαθροίζομαι
be gathered thick together 1.

EPAULIS ἔπαυλις *f.*
habitation 1.

EPAURION ἐπαύριον
day following 2
morrow 7
morrow after 1
next day 6
the next day after 1.

EPAUTOPHŌRŌ ἐπαυτοφώρῳ
in the very act 1.

EPECHŌ ἐπέχω
give heed unto 1
hold forth 1
mark 1
stay 1
take heed unto 1.

EPEGEIRŌ ἐπεγείρω
raise 1
stir up 1.

EPEI ἐπεί
because 7
else 3
forasmuch as 2
for that 1
for then 4
otherwise 4
seeing 3
seeing that 1
since 1
when 1.

EPEIDĒ ἐπειδή
after that 1
because 2
for 3
forasmuch as 1
for that 1
seeing 2
since 1.

EPEIDĒPER ἐπειδήπερ
forasmuch as 1.

EPEIDON ἐπεῖδον
look on 1.
†*With* epi: behold 1.

EPEIMI ἔπειμι
Partic. following 1
next 1
the day following 1
the next day 1.

EPEIPER ἐπείπερ
seeing 1.

EPEISAGŌGĒ ἐπεισαγωγή *f.*
bringing in 1.

EPEITA ἔπειτα
afterward 2
afterwards 1
after that 4
then 9.

EPEKEINA ἐπέκεινα
beyond 1.

EPEKTEINOMAI ἐπεκτείνομαι
reach forth unto 1.

EPENDUOMAI ἐπενδύομαι.
be clothed upon 2.

EPENDUTĒS ἐπενδύτης
fisher's coat 1.

ĒPER ἤπερ
than 1.

EPERCHOMAI ἐπέρχομαι
come 1
come on 1
come thither 1
come upon 6.
Partic. those things which are coming on 1.

EPĒREAZŌ ἐπηρεάζω
accuse falsely 1
use despitefully 2.

EPERŌTAŌ ἐπερωτάω
ask 50
ask after 1
ask a question 1
ask of 2
ask questions 1
demand 1
demand of 1
desire 1
question with 1.

EPERŌTĒMA ἐπερώτημα *n.*
answer 1.

EPH = EPI.

EPHALLOMAI ἐφάλλομαι
†*With* epi: leap on 1.

EPHAPAX ἐφάπαξ
at once 1
once 3
once for all 1.

EPHĒMERIA ἐφημερία *f.*
course 2.

EPHĒMEROS ἐφήμερος
daily 1.

EPHEURETĒS ἐφευρετής
inventor 1.

EPHIKNEOMAI ἐφικνέομαι
reach unto 2.

EPHISTĒMI ἐφίστημι
assault 1
be at hand 1
be instant 1
come 1
come in 1
come to 1
come upon 7
stand 1
stand by 3.
Partic. present 1.
†come unto (*with* epi) 1; stand before (*with* epi) 1; stand over (*with* epanō) 1.

EPHORAŌ = EPEIDON.

EPHPHATHA ἐφφαθά
ephphatha 1

EPI ἐπί
With gen. at 6
before 14
in 51
in the days of 2
in the time of 1
on 71
over 11
upon 37, etc.
With dat. against 6
at 29
by 8
for 19
in 52
on 10
over 11
upon 16
with 6, etc.
†*With* autos: whereon 1; *with* hos: whereon 1, wherein 3, wherefore 1, for that (M. in whom) 1, whereof 1; *with* houtos: wherewith 1.
With acc. against 33
for 9
for the space of 1
in 14
into 15
on 114
over 27
to 38
unto 41
upon 105, etc.
†*With* autos: thereon; *with* hos: whereon 2; *with* hosos chronos: as long as 3.

EPIBAINŌ ἐπιβαίνω
come into 2
enter into 1
go aboard 1
take ship 1.
†*With* epi: sit upon 1.

EPIBALLŌ ἐπιβάλλω
cast 1
cast upon 1
fall to 1
lay on 1
stretch forth (M. begin; †*with* cheir) 1.
Partic. when he thought thereon (M. abundantly *or* he began) 1.
†*With* epi: put upon 1, put unto 1, put to 1, lay on 8. *With* eis: beat into 1.

EPIBAREŌ ἐπιβαρέω
be chargeable to 1
be chargeable unto 1
overcharge 1.

EPIBIBAZŌ ἐπιβιβάζω
set on 3.

EPIBLĒMA ἐπίβλημα *n.*
piece 4.

EPIBLEPŌ ἐπιβλέπω
†*With* epi: have respect to 1, look upon 1, regard 1.

EPIBOAŌ ἐπιβοάω
cry 1.

EPIBOULĒ ἐπιβουλή *f.*
laying await 1
lying in wait 1.
†lay wait (with eimi hupo 1, *with* gignomai hupo 1) 2.

EPICHEIREŌ ἐπιχειρέω
go about 1
take in hand 1
take upon 1.

EPICHEŌ ἐπιχέω
pour in 1.

EPICHORĒGEŌ ἐπιχορηγέω
add 1
minister to 2
minister unto 1.
PASS. have nourishment ministered 1.

EPICHORĒGIA ἐπιχορηγία *f.*
supply 1
*to supply 1.

EPICHRIŌ ἐπιχρίω
†*With* epi: anoint (M. spread upon) 1.

EPIDECHOMAI ἐπιδέχομαι
receive 2.

EPIDEIKNUMI ἐπιδείκνυμι
show 8.
MID. show 1.

EPIDĒMEŌ ἐπιδημέω
be there 1.
Partic. stranger 1.

EPIDIATASSOMAI ἐπιδιατάσσομαι
add thereto 1.

EPIDIDŌMI ἐπιδίδωμι
deliver 2
give 7
offer 1.
†*Part. with pass. of* pherō: we let her drive 1.

EPIDIORTHOŌ ἐπιδιορθόω
MID. set in order 1.

EPIDUŌ ἐπιδύω
†*With* epi: go down upon 1.

EPIEIKEIA ἐπιείκεια *f.*
clemency 1
gentleness 1.

EPIEIKĒS ἐπιεικής
gentle 3
patient 1.
As noun moderation 1.

EPIGAMBREUŌ ἐπιγαμβρεύω
marry 1.

EPIGEIOS ἐπίγειος
earthly 2
terrestrial 2
*in earth 1.
As noun earthly things 2.

EPIGINOMAI ἐπιγίνομαι
blow 1.

EPIGINŌSKŌ ἐπιγινώσκω
acknowledge 5
have knowledge of 1
know 30
know well 1
perceive 3
take knowledge of 2.

EPIGNŌSIS ἐπίγνωσις *f.*
acknowledging 3
acknowledgment 1
knowledge 16 (M. acknowledge 1, acknowledgment 1).

EPIGRAPHĒ ἐπιγραφή *f.*
superscription 5 (M. inscription 1).

EPIGRAPHŌ ἐπιγράφω
write in 2
write over 1
write thereon 1
*this inscription 1.

EPIKALEŌ ἐπικαλέω
MID. appeal 1
appeal to 1
appeal unto 4
call 1
call on 7
call upon 4.
PASS. be called 1
be called by 1
be called upon 1
be one's surname 7
be surnamed 5.

EPIKALUMMA ἐπικάλυμμα *n.*
cloak 1.

EPIKALUPTŌ ἐπικαλύπτω
cover 1.

EPIKATARATOS ἐπικατάρατος
cursed 1.

EPIKATHIZŌ ἐπικαθίζω
set 1.

EPIKEIMAI ἐπίκειμαι
be imposed on 1
be instant 1
be laid thereon 1
be laid upon 1
lie on 1
lie upon 1
press upon 1.

EPIKOURIA ἐπικουρία *f.*
help 1.

EPIKRINŌ ἐπικρίνω
give sentence (M. assent) 1.

EPILAMBANOMAI ἐπιλαμβάνομαι
catch 2
lay hold on 2
lay hold upon 1
take 7
take by 5
take hold of 2
take on (M. take hold of) 2.

EPILANTHANOMAI ἐπιλανθάνομαι
be forgetful 1
forget 7.

EPILEGŌ ἐπιλέγω
call 1
MID. choose 1.

EPILEIPŌ ἐπιλείπω
fail 1.

EPILĒSMONĒ ἐπιλησμονή *f.*
forgetful 1.

EPILOIPOS ἐπίλοιπος
rest of 1.

EPILUŌ ἐπιλύω
determine 1
expound 1.

EPILUSIS ἐπίλυσις *f.*
interpretation 1.

EPIMARTUREŌ ἐπιμαρτυρέω
testify 1.

EPIMELEIA ἐπιμέλεια
†*See* tugchanō.

EPIMELEOMAI ἐπιμελέομαι
take care of 3.

EPIMELŌS ἐπιμελῶς
diligently 1.

EPIMENŌ ἐπιμένω
abide 1
abide in 1
abide still 1
abide still in 1
continue 2
continue in 5
tarry 7.

EPINEUŌ ἐπινεύω
consent 1

EPINOIA ἐπίνοια *f.*
thought 1.

EPIORKEŌ ἐπιορκέω
forswear one's self 1.

EPIORKOS ἐπίορκος
perjured person 1.

ĒPIOS ἤπιος
gentle 2.

EPIOUSA. *Partic. of* **EPEIMI.**

EPIOUSIOS ἐπιούσιος
daily 2.

EPIPHAINŌ ἐπιφαίνω
appear 1
give light to 1.
PASS. appear 2.

EPIPHANEIA ἐπιφάνεια *f.*
appearing 5
brightness 1.

EPIPHANĒS ἐπιφανής
notable 1.

EPIPHAUŌ ἐπιφαύω
give light 1.

EPIPHERŌ ἐπιφέρω
add 1
bring 2
bring against 1
take 1.

EPIPHŌNEŌ ἐπιφωνέω
cry 1
cry against 1
give a shout 1.

EPIPHŌSKŌ ἐπιφώσκω
begin to dawn 1
draw on 1.

EPIPIPTŌ ἐπιπίπτω
fall on 1
press upon (M. rush upon) 1.
†*With* epi: fall upon 2, fall on 7, fall into 1, lie on 1.

EPIPLĒSSŌ ἐπιπλήσσω
rebuke 1.

EPIPOREUOMAI ἐπιπορεύομαι
†*With* pros: come to 1.

EPIPOTHEŌ ἐπιποθέω
desire 1
desire earnestly 1
desire greatly 2
long 1
long after 2
long after greatly 1
lust 1.

EPIPOTHĒSIS ἐπιπόθησις *f.*
earnest desire
vehement desire 1.

EPIPOTHĒTOS ἐπιπόθητος
longed for 1.

EPIPOTHIA ἐπιποθία *f.*
great desire 1.

EPIRRHAPTŌ ἐπιῤῥάπτω
†*With* epi: sew on 1.

EPIRRHIPTŌ ἐπιῤῥίπτω
†*With* epi: cast upon

EPISCHUŌ ἐπισχύω
be the more fierce 1.

EPISĒMOS ἐπίσημος
notable 1
of note 1.

EPISITISMOS ἐπισιτισμός
victuals 1.

EPISKĒNOŌ ἐπισκηνόω
†*With* epi: rest upon 1.

EPISKEPTOMAI ἐπισκέπτομαι
look out 1
visit 10.

EPISKIAZŌ ἐπισκιάζω
overshadow 5.

EPISKOPĒ ἐπισκοπή *f.*
bishopric (M. office or charge) 1
office of bishop 1
visitation 2.

EPISKOPEŌ ἐπισκοπέω
look diligently 1
take the oversight 1.

EPISKOPOS ἐπίσκοπος
bishop 4
overseer 1.

EPISŌREUŌ ἐπισωρεύω
heap 1.

EPISPAOMAI ἐπισπάομαι
become uncircumcised 1.

EPISPHALĒS ἐπισφαλής
dangerous 1.

EPISTAMAI ἐπίσταμαι
know 13
understand 1.

EPISTATĒS ἐπιστάτης
Master 7.

EPISTELLŌ ἐπιστέλλω
write 1
write a letter unto 1
write unto 1.

EPISTĒMŌN ἐπιστήμων
endued with knowledge 1.

* Inexact translations, *e.g.*, of a noun by a verb or adjective, of an active by a passive.
† Cases where two or more words in the original are translated by one word or by a phrase.

EPISTĒRIZŌ ἐπιστηρίζω
confirm 3
strengthen 1.

EPISTOLĒ ἐπιστολή *f.*
epistle 15
letter 9.

EPISTOMIZŌ ἐπιστομίζω
stop the mouth of 1.

EPISTREPHŌ ἐπιστρέφω
be converted 5
come again 1
convert 2
go again 1
return 4
turn 15
turn again 4 (M. turn back) 1.
MID. (PASS.) be converted 1
return 2
turn about 4.

EPISTROPHĒ ἐπιστροφή *f.*
conversion 1.

EPISUNAGŌ ἐπισυνάγω
gather 1
gather together 6.

EPISUNAGŌGĒ ἐπισυναγωγή *f.*
assembling together 1
gathering together 1

EPISUNTRECHŌ ἐπισυντρέχω
come running together 1.

EPISUSTASIS ἐπισύστασις *f.*
that which cometh upon 1.
†*See* poieō.

EPITAGĒ ἐπιταγή *f.*
authority 1
commandment 6.

EPITASSŌ ἐπιτάσσω
charge 1
command 8
enjoin 1.

EPITĒDEIOS ἐπιτήδειος
As noun things which are needful to 1.

EPITELEŌ ἐπιτελέω
accomplish 2
do 1
finish 1
make 1
make perfect 1
perfect 1
perform 3 (M. finish 1).
Inf. performance 1.

EPITHANATIOS ἐπιθανάτιος
appointed (*ed.* 1611 *wrongly* approved) to death 1.

EPITHESIS ἐπίθεσις
laying on 3
putting on 1

EPITHUMEŌ ἐπιθυμέω
covet 3
desire 8
lust 3
lust after 1
would fain 1.

EPITHUMĒTĒS ἐπιθυμητής
†*See* eimi.

EPITHUMIA ἐπιθυμία *f.*
concupiscence 3
desire 3 (M. * heartily 1)
lust 31 (M. concupiscence 1)
*lust after 1.

EPITIMAŌ ἐπιτιμάω
charge 4
charge straitly 1
rebuke 24.

EPITIMIA ἐπιτιμία *f.*
punishment (M. censure) 1.

EPITITHĒMI ἐπιτίθημι
lay on 12
lay upon 4
put on 3
put upon 2
set on 1
set up 1.
MID. lade with 1.
†put on (*with* epanō) 1;
surname (*with* onoma) 1;
wound (*with* plēgē) 1.
†*With* epi: add unto 2, lay upon 2, lay on 4, put upon 4, put on 1, set on 2.

EPITREPŌ ἐπιτρέπω
give leave 2
give liberty 1
give license 1
let 1
permit 4
suffer 10.

EPITROPĒ ἐπιτροπή *f.*
commission 1.

EPITROPOS ἐπίτροπος
steward 2
tutor 1.

EPITUĞCHANŌ ἐπιτυγχάνω
obtain 5.

EPIZĒTEŌ ἐπιζητέω
desire 3
inquire 1
seek 3
seek after 5
seek for 2.

EPŌ = EIPON.

EPOIKODOMEŌ ἐποικοδομέω
build thereon 1
build thereupon 2
build up 1
build up on 1.
†*With* epi: build upon 2.

EPOKELLŌ ἐποκέλλω
run aground 1.

EPONOMAZŌ ἐπονομάζω
call 1.

EPOPTĒS ἐπόπτης
eye-witness 1.

EPOPTEUŌ ἐποπτεύω
behold 2.

EPOS ἔπος *n.*
[word]
*so 1.

EPOURANIOS ἐπουράνιος
celestial 2
heavenly 9
in heaven 1.
As noun heavenly places 3 (M. heavenly things 1)
heavenly things 3
high places (M. heavenly places) 1
they that are heavenly 1.

ERCHOMAI ἔρχομαι
appear 1
be brought 1
be coming 7
come 609
fall out 1
go 13
grow 1
light 1
pass by 1
resort 2.
Partic. next 1.
†accompany (*with* sun) 1;
enter into (*with* eis) 2.

EREIDŌ ἐρείδω
stick fast 1.

ERĒMIA ἐρημία *f.*
desert 1
wilderness 3.

ERĒMOŌ ἐρημόω
bring to desolation 2
make desolate 1.
Partic. desolate 1.
PASS. come to nought 1.

ERĒMOS ἔρημος
desert 10
desolate 4
solitary 1.
As noun desert 3
wilderness 32.

ĒREMOS ἤρεμος
quiet 1.

ERĒMŌSIS ἐρήμωσις *f.*
desolation 3.

EREŌ = ERŌ.

ERETHIZŌ ἐρεθίζω
provoke 1
provoke to anger 1.

EREUGOMAI ἐρεύγομαι
utter 1.

EREUNAŌ ἐρευνάω
search 6.

ERGASIA ἐργασία *f.*
craft 1
diligence 1
gain 2
gains 1
*work (*vb.*) 1.

ERGATĒS ἐργάτης
worker 3
workman 3
labourer 9.

ERGAZOMAI ἐργάζομαι
commit 1
do 3
labour 1
labour for 1
minister about 1
trade 1
trade by 1
work 28 (M. gain 1).
PASS. be wrought 1.
†forbear working (mē ergazomai) 1.

ERGON ἔργον *n.*
deed 22
doing 1
labour 1
work 152 (M. trade 1).

ERION ἔριον *n.*
wool 2.

ERIPHION ἐρίφιον *n.*
goat 1.

ERIPHOS ἔριφος
goat 1
kid 1.

ERIS ἔρις *f.*
contention 2
debate 2
strife 4
variance 1.

ERITHEIA ἐριθεία *f.*
contention 1
strife 5.
†that are contentious (ex *with gen.*) 1.

ERIZŌ ἐρίζω
strive 1.

ERŌ ἐρῶ (εἴρηκα)
call 1
say 57
speak 7
speak of 2
tell 4.

ERŌTAŌ ἐρωτάω
ask 23
beseech 14 (M. request 1)
desire 6
entreat 1
pray 14.

ERRHĒTHĒN ἐῤῥήθην (*aorist pass.*)
command 1
make 1
say 9.
Partic. he that was spoken of 1
it which was spoken 9
spoken of 2
that which was spoken 3.

ERUTHROS ἐρυθρός
red 2.

ESCHATOS ἔσχατος
last 46
lowest 2
uttermost 1
As noun ends 1
last state 2
latter end 1
uttermost part 1.

ESCHATŌS ἐσχάτως
†*See* echō.

ESŌ ἔσω
in 1
inner 1
into 2
inward 1
within 3.

ESOPTRON ἔσοπτρον *n.*
glass 2.

ESŌTEROS ἐσώτερος
inner 1
within 1.

ESŌTHEN ἔσωθεν
from within 3
inwardly 1
within 6.
As noun inward part 1
that which is within 1
the inward man 1.

ESTHĒS ἐσθής
apparel 3
clothing 2
raiment 1
robe 1.

ESTHĒSIS ἔσθησις *f.*
garment 1.

ESTHIŌ ἐσθίω
be eating 1
devour 1
eat 61
live of (M. feed of) 1.

ESTI ἐστι
is.

ETHELŌ = THELŌ.

ETHELOTHRĒSKEIA ἐθελοθρησκεία *f.*
will worship 1.

ETHIZŌ ἐθίζω
Pass. pt. custom 1.

ETHNARCHĒS ἐθνάρχης
governor 1.

ETHNIKŌS ἐθνικῶς
after the manner of Gentiles 1.

ETHNIKOS ἐθνικός
As noun heathen 1
heathen man 1.

ETHNOS ἔθνος
Gentiles (*plur.*) 93
heathen 5
nation 64
people 2.

ETHŌ ἔθω (εἴωθα)
be wont 2.
Partic. custom 1
manner 1.

ETHOS ἔθος *n.*
custom 7 (M. rite 1)
manner 4
*be wont 1.

ĒTHOS ἦθος *n.*
manner 1.

ETI ἔτι
also 1
any further 3
any longer 1
any more 5
even 1
further 3
longer 1
more 17
moreover 2
still 4
thenceforth 1
yet 51
yet more 2.

ĒTOI ἤτοι
whether 1.

ETOS ἔτος *n.*
year 49.

EU εὖ
good 1
well 3
well done 2.

EUAĞGELION εὐαγγέλιον *n.*
gospel 76

EUAĞGELISTES εὐαγγελιστής
evangelist 3.

EUAĞGELIZŌ εὐαγγελίζω
declare to 1
preach unto 1.
MID. bring glad tidings of 1
bring good tidings of 1
declare glad tidings unto 1
preach 17
preach any gospel 2
preach the gospel 11.
preach the gospel in 1
preach the gospel of 1
preach the gospel to 2
preach the gospel unto 2
preach unto 2.
PASS. be preached 2
be preached by the gospel 1
be preached to (M. the gospel is preached to) 1
have the gospel preached to one 1
the gospel is preached 1
the gospel is preached to 1
the gospel is preached unto 1.

EUARESTEŌ εὐαρεστέω
please 2.
PASS. be well pleased with 1.

EUARESTŌS εὐαρέστως
acceptably 1.

EUARESTOS εὐάρεστος
acceptable 4
well pleasing 2.
As noun that which is well pleasing 1.
†*See* eimi.

EUCHARISTEŌ εὐχαριστέω
be thankful 1
give thanks 25
thank 12.
PASS. thanks are given 1.

EUCHARISTIA εὐχαριστία *f.*
giving of thanks 3
thankfulness 1
thanks 2
thanksgiving 9.

EUCHARISTOS εὐχάριστος
thankful 1

EUCHĒ εὐχή *f.*
prayer 1
vow 2.

EUCHOMAI εὔχομαι
can wish 1
pray 2
wish 3 (M. pray 1)
would 1.

EUCHRĒSTOS εὔχρηστος
meet for use 1
profitable 2.

EUDIA εὐδία *f.*
fair weather 1.

EUDOKEŌ εὐδοκέω
be well pleased 7
be one's good pleasure 1
be willing 2
have pleasure 4
take pleasure 1.
Impers. it pleaseth 5
think good 1.

EUDOKIA εὐδοκία
desire 1
good pleasure 4
good will 2
†seem good (*with* gignomai) 2.

EUERGESIA εὐεργεσία *f.*
benefit 1
good deed done 1.

EUERGETEŌ εὐεργετέω
do good 1.

EUERGETĒS εὐεργέτης
benefactor 1.

EUGENĒS εὐγενής
noble 2.
†nobleman (*with* anthrōpos) 1.

EUKAIREŌ εὐκαιρέω
have convenient time 1
have leisure 1
spend one's time 1.

EUKAIRIA εὐκαιρία *f.*
opportunity 2.

EUKAIROS εὔκαιρος
convenient 1
in time of need 1.

EUKAIRŌS εὐκαίρως
conveniently 1
in season 1.

EUKOPŌTEROS εὐκοπώτερος
easier 7.

EULABEIA εὐλάβεια *f.*
godly fear 1
*he feared (M. his piety) 1.

EULABEOMAI εὐλαβέομαι
be moved with fear (M. be wary) 1
fear 1.

EULABĒS εὐλαβής
devout 3.

EULOGEŌ εὐλογέω
bless 43
praise 1.

EULOGĒTOS εὐλογητός
blessed 8.

EULOGIA εὐλογία *f.*
blessing 11
bounty (M. blessing) 1
fair speeches 1
matter of bounty 1
†bountifully (epi *with dat. pl.*) 2.

* Inexact translations, *e.g.*, of a noun by a verb or adjective, of an active by a passive.
† Cases where two or more words in the original are translated by one word or by a phrase.

EUMETADOTOS εὐμετάδοτος: ready to distribute 1.

EUNOEŌ εὐνοέω: agree 1.

EUNOIA εὔνοια *f.*: benevolence 1; good will 1.

EUNOUCHIZŌ εὐνουχίζω: make eunuch 2.

EUNOUCHOS εὐνοῦχος: eunuch 8.

EUŌDIA εὐωδία: sweet savour 1; sweet smell 1; *sweet smelling 1.

EUODOOMAI εὐοδόομαι: have a prosperous journey 1; prosper 3.

EUŌNUMOS εὐώνυμος: on the left hand 1.
As noun left 5; left foot (*pl.*) 1; left hand (*pl.*) 3.

EUPEITHĒS εὐπειθής: easy to be entreated 1.

EUPERISTATOS εὐπερίστατος: which doth so easily beset us 1.

EUPHĒMIA εὐφημία *f.*: good report 1.

EUPHĒMOS εὔφημος: of good report 1.

EUPHOREŌ εὐφορέω: bring forth plentifully 1.

EUPHRAINŌ εὐφραίνω: make glad 1.
MID. (PASS.) be merry 3; fare 1; make merry 3; rejoice 6.

EUPHROSUNĒ εὐφροσύνη *f.*: gladness 1; joy 1

EUPOIIA εὐποιΐα *f.*: *do good 1.

EUPOREOMAI εὐπορέομαι: *ability 1.

EUPORIA εὐπορία *f.*: wealth 1.

EUPREPEIA εὐπρέπεια *f.*: grace 1.

EUPROSDEKTOS εὐπρόσδεκτος: acceptable 2; accepted 3.

EUPROSEDROS εὐπρόσεδρος: that one may attend upon 1.

EUPROSŌPEŌ εὐπροσωπέω: make a fair show 1.

EUPSUCHEŌ εὐψυχέω: be of good comfort 1.

EURUCHŌROS εὐρύχωρος: broad 1.

EUSCHĒMŌN εὐσχήμων: comely 1; honourable 3.
As noun that which is comely 1.

EUSCHĒMONŌS εὐσχημόνως: decently 1; honestly 2 (M. decently 1).

EUSCHĒMOSUNĒ εὐσχημοσύνη *f.*: comeliness 1.

EUSEBEIA εὐσέβεια *f.*: godliness 14; holiness 1.

EUSEBEŌ εὐσεβέω: show piety at (M. show kindness at) 1; worship 1.

EUSEBĒS εὐσεβής: devout 3; godly 1.

EUSEBŌS εὐσεβῶς: godly 2.

EUSĒMOS εὔσημος: easy to be understood (M. significant) 1.

EUSPLAGCHNOS εὔσπλαγχνος: pitiful 1; tender-hearted 1.

EUTHEŌS εὐθέως: anon 1; as soon as 2; by and by 2; forthwith 7; immediately 35; shortly 1; straightway 32.

EUTHETOS εὔθετος: fit 2; meet 1.

EUTHUDROMEŌ εὐθυδρομέω: come with a straight course 1.
Partic. with a straight course 1.

EUTHUMEŌ εὐθυμέω: be merry 1; be of good cheer 2.

EUTHUMOS εὔθυμος: of good cheer 1.

EUTHUMOTERON εὐθυμότερον: more cheerfully 1.

EUTHUNŌ εὐθύνω: make straight 1.
Partic. governor 1.

EUTHUS[1] εὐθύς: right 3; straight 5.

EUTHUS[2] εὐθύς: anon 1; by and by 1; forthwith 1; immediately 3; straightway 2.

EUTHUTĒS εὐθύτης: righteousness (M. rightness or straightness) 1.

EUTONŌS εὐτόνως: mightily 1; vehemently 1.

EUTRAPELIA εὐτραπελία *f.*: jesting 1.

EX = **EK**.

EXAGGELLŌ ἐξαγγέλλω: shew forth 1.

EXAGŌ ἐξάγω: bring forth 1; bring out 5; fetch out 1; lead out 6.

EXAGORAZŌ ἐξαγοράζω: redeem 4.

EXAIPHNĒS ἐξαίφνης: suddenly 5.

EXAIREŌ ἐξαιρέω: pluck out 2.
MID. deliver 5; rescue 1.

EXAIRŌ ἐξαίρω: put away 1; take away 1

EXAITEOMAI ἐξαιτέομαι: desire 1.

EXAKOLOUTHEŌ ἐξακολουθέω: follow 3.

EXALEIPHŌ ἐξαλείφω: blot out 3; wipe away 2.

EXALLOMAI ἐξάλλομαι: leap up 1.

EXANASTASIS ἐξανάστασις *f.*: resurrection 1.

EXANATELLŌ ἐξανατέλλω: spring up 1.

EXANISTĒMI ἐξανίστημι: raise up 1; rise up 1.

EXAPATAŌ ἐξαπατάω: beguile 1; deceive 4.

EXAPINA ἐξάπινα: suddenly 1.

EXAPOREOMAI ἐξαπορέομαι: despair 1.
Partic. in despair (M. altogether without help *or* means) 1.

EXAPOSTELLŌ ἐξαποστέλλω: send 2; send away 4; send forth 4; send out 1.

EXARTIZŌ ἐξαρτίζω: accomplish 1; furnish thoroughly (M. perfect) 1.

EXASTRAPTŌ ἐξαστράπτω: glister 1.

EXAUTĒS ἐξαυτῆς: by and by 1; immediately 3; presently 1; straightway 1.

EXĒCHEOMAI ἐξηχέομαι: sound out 1.

EXEGEIRŌ ἐξεγείρω: raise up 2.

EXĒGEOMAI ἐξηγέομαι: declare 5; tell 1.

EXEIMI ἔξειμι: depart 2; get 1; go out 1.

EXELEGCHŌ ἐξελέγχω: convince 1.

EXELKOMAI ἐξέλκομαι: be drawn away 1.

EXERAMA ἐξέραμα *n.*: vomit 1.

EXERCHOMAI ἐξέρχομαι: come 4; come forth 9; come out 30; come thereout 1; depart 27; depart out 3; escape 1; get out 3; go 7; go abroad 2; go away 1; go forth 25; go out 82; proceed 2; proceed forth 1; spread abroad 2.
†*With* exō: come forth 1.*

EXEREUNAŌ ἐξερευνάω: search diligently 1.

EXESTI ἔξεστι: are lawful 5; is lawful 4; it is lawful 19 (M. it is possible 1); may I 1; thou mayest 1.
Partic. (*neut.*) lawful 1; let me (M. I may) 1.

EXETAZŌ ἐξετάζω: ask 1; enquire 1; search 1.

EXISCHUŌ ἐξισχύω: be able 1.

EXISTĒMI ἐξίστημι: bewitch 2; make astonished 1
MID. (*second aor. act.*) be amazed 6; be astonished 5; be beside one's self 2; wonder 1.

EXŌ ἔξω: away; forth 8; of 2; out 16; out of 13; outward 1; strange 1; without 18.
As noun one that is without 5.

EXOCHĒ ἐξοχή *f.*: †principal (kata *with acc.*) 1.

EXODOS ἔξοδος *f.*: decease 2; departing 1.

EXOLOTHREUŌ ἐξολοθρεύω: destroy 1.

EXOMOLOGEŌ ἐξομολογέω: promise 1.
MID. confess 8; thank 2.

EXON ἐξόν: *partic. of* exesti.

EXORKISTES ἐξορκιστής: exorcist 1.

EXORKIZŌ ἐξορκίζω: adjure 1.

EXORUSSŌ ἐξορύσσω: break up 1; pluck out 1.

EXŌTEROS ἐξώτερος: outer 3.

EXŌTHEN ἔξωθεν: from without 2; outward 2; outwardly 1; without 1.
As noun the outside 2; which is without 3.

EXŌTHEŌ ἐξωθέω: drive out 1; thrust in 1.

EXOUDENOŌ ἐξουδενόω: set at nought 1.

EXOUSIA ἐξουσία *f.*: authority 29; jurisdiction 1; liberty (M. power) 1; power 69 (M. right *or* privilege 1); right 2; strength 1.

EXOUSIAZŌ ἐξουσιάζω: bring under power 1; exercise authority upon 1; have power of 2.

EXOUTHENEŌ ἐξουθενέω: despise 6; set at nought 3.
PASS. be least esteemed 1.
Partic. contemptible 1.

EXUPNIZŌ ἐξυπνίζω: awake out of sleep 1.

EXUPNOS ἔξυπνος: †*See* ginomai.

G

GAGGRAINA γάγγραινα *f.*: canker (M. gangrene) 1.

GALA γάλα: milk 5.

GALĒNĒ γαλήνη *f.*: calm 3.

GAMEŌ γαμέω: marry 26; marry a wife 2.
Partic. married 1.

GAMISKŌ γαμίσκω: give in marriage 1

GAMŌ = **GAMEŌ**.

GAMOS γάμος: marriage 9; wedding 7.

GAR γάρ: and 4; because 3; because that 2; but 2; even 1; for 1006; indeed 2; no doubt 1; seeing 1; therefore 1; verily 2; what? 1; why 1; yet 1.
†because that (gar hoti) 1, for (kai gar) 23, yet (kai gar) 2.

GASTĒR γαστήρ *f.*: belly 1; womb 1.
†*See* echō.

GAZA γάζα *f.*: treasure 1.

GAZOPHULAKION γαζοφυλάκιον *n.*: treasury 5.

GE γέ: yet 2.
†*Freq. in combination with other particles.*

GĒ γῆ *f.*: country 2; earth 188 (M. land 1); ground 18; land 42; world 1.
†earthly (ek *with gen.*).

GEENNA γέεννα *f.*: hell 9; hell [fire] 3.

GEITŌN γείτων: neighbour 4.

GELAŌ γελάω: laugh 2.

GELŌS γέλως: laughter 1.

GEMIZŌ γεμίζω: fill 7; fill full 1.
PASS. be full 1.

GEMŌ γέμω: be full of 5.
Partic. full of 6.

GENEA γενεά *f.*: age 2; generation 36 (M. age 1); nation 1; time 2.

GENEALOGEOMAI γενεαλογέομαι
Partic. he whose descent is counted (M. pedigree is) 1.

GENEALOGIA γενεαλογία *f.*: genealogy 2.

GENESIA γενέσια *n. pl.*: birthday 2.

GENESIS γένεσις *f.*: generation 1; nature 1; *natural 1.

GENETĒ γενετή *f.*: birth 1.

GENNAŌ γεννάω: bear 2; be delivered of 1; beget 49; bring forth 1; conceive 1; gender 2.
PASS. be born 39; be made 1; spring 1.

GENNĒMA γέννημα *n.*: fruit 5; generation 4.

GENNĒSIS γέννησις *f.*: birth 2.

GENNĒTOS γεννητός: that is born 2.

GENOS γένος *n.*: diversity (M. kind) 1; generation 1; kind 5; kindred 3; nation 2; offspring 3; one's own countrymen 1; stock 2.
Dat. *born at 1; *born in 1; *of the country of 1.

GEŌRGEOMAI γεωργέομαι: be dressed 1.

GEŌRGION γεώργιον *n.*: husbandry (M. tillage) 1.

GEŌRGOS γεωργός: husbandman 19.

GĒRAS γῆρας *n.*: old age 1.

GĒRASKŌ γηράσκω: be old 1; wax old 1

GERŌN γέρων: old 1.

GEROUSIA γερουσία *f.*: senate 1.

GEUOMAI γεύομαι: eat 3; taste 12.

GIGNOMAI = **GINOMAI**.

GINOMAI γίνομαι: arise 16; be 249; be assembled 1; be brought 1; be brought to pass 1; be come 1; be divided 1; be done 62; be done to 1; be ended 1; be finished 1; be found 1; be fulfilled 3; be had 1; be kept 1; be made 69

* Inexact translations, *e.g.*, of a noun by a verb or adjective, of an active by a passive.
† Cases where two or more words in the original are translated by one word or by a phrase.

be married to 3
be ordained to be 1
be past 2
be performed 1
be preferred 3
be published 1
be put 2
be showed 1
be taken 1
be turned 1
be wrought 2
become 42
befall 1
behave self 1
come 53
come to pass 82
continue 1
fall 2
follow 1
grow 2
happen 1
wax 2
*be so 1
*have 3.
†awake out of sleep (*with* exupnos) 1; baptize (*with pt. of* baptizō) 1; be kept secret (*with* apokruphos) 1; be made (*with* eis) 1; be the doing of (*with* para) 1; become (*with* eis) 5; draw nigh (*with* eggus) 1; God forbid (*optative with negative*) 15; use (*with* en) 1; wax (*with* eis) 1. *See* analos, brontē, emphobos, entromos, epiboulē, heteros, hupēkoos, koinōnos, perikratēs, phaneros, etc., etc.

GINŌSKŌ γινώσκω
allow (M. know) 1
be aware 1 (ware; *ed.* 1611)
be aware of 1
be resolved 1
be sure 1
be sure of 1
can 1
can speak 1
feel 1
have knowledge 1
know 196
perceive 9
understand 8.

GLEUKOS γλεῦκος *n.*
new wine 1.

GLŌSSA γλῶσσα *f.*
tongue 50.

GLŌSSOKOMON γλωσσόκομον *n.*
bag 2.

GLUKUS γλυκύς
fresh 1
sweet 3.

GNAPHEUS γναφεύς
fuller 1.

GNĒSIOS γνήσιος
own 2
true 1.
As noun sincerity 1.

GNĒSIŌS γνησίως
naturally 1.

GNŌME γνώμη *f.*
advice 1
judgment 3
mind 2
will 1
purpose 1.
†*See* poieō.

GNOPHOS γνόφος
blackness 1.

GNŌRIZŌ γνωρίζω
certify 1
declare 4
do to wit 1
give to understand 1
make known 16
wot 1.

GNŌSIS γνῶσις *f.*
knowledge 28
science 1.

GNŌSTĒS γνώστης
expert 1.

GNŌSTOS γνωστός
known 10
notable 1.
As noun acquaintance (*pl.*) 2
that which may be known 1.
†know (*with* esti *and dat.*) 1.

GOĒS γόης
seducer 1.

GOGGUSMOS γογγυσμός
grudging 1
murmuring 3.

GOGGUSTĒS γογγυστής
murmurer 1.

GOGGUZŌ γογγύζω
murmur (*tr.* 1, *intr.* 7) 8.

GOMOS γόμος
burden 1
merchandise 2.

GONEUS γονεύς
parents (*pl.*) 19.

GŌNIA γωνία *f.*
corner 8
quarter 1.

GONU γόνυ *n.*
knee 7.
†*See* tithēmi.

GONUPETEŌ γονυπετέω
bow the knee 1
kneel down to 2
kneel to 1.

GRAMMA γράμμα *n.*
bill 1
learning 1
letter 9 (M. learning 1)
scripture 1
writing 1.

GRAMMATEUS γραμματεύς
scribe 66
townclerk 1.

GRAŌDĒS γραώδης
*old wives' 1.

GRAPHĒ γραφή
scripture 51.

GRAPHŌ γράφω
describe 1
write 189.
Pass. pt. it is written 1
writing 1.

GRAPTOS γραπτός
written 1.

GRĒGOREŌ γρηγορέω
be vigilant 1
wake 1
watch 20.
Partic. watchful 1.

GUMNASIA γυμνασία
exercise 1.

GUMNAZŌ γυμνάζω
exercise 4.

GUMNĒTEUŌ γυμνητεύω
be naked 1.

GUMNOS γυμνός
bare 1
naked 14.

GUMNOTĒS γυμνότης
nakedness 3.

GUNAIKARION γυναικάριον *n.*
silly woman 1.

GUNAIKEIOS γυναικεῖος
*wife 1.

GUNĒ γυνή
wife 92 (M. woman 1)
woman 129.

H

HADĒS ᾅδης
grave (M. hell) 1
hell 10 (M. grave 1).

HADROTĒS ἁδρότης *f.*
abundance 1.

HAGIASMOS ἁγιασμός
holiness 5
sanctification 5.

HAGIAZŌ ἁγιάζω
hallow 2
sanctify 26.
PASS. be holy 1.

HAGIOS ἅγιος
holy 161 (*with* pneuma 93).
As noun holiest 2
holiest of all 1
Holy One 4
holy place 3
holy thing 1
sanctuary 3 (M. holy one, holy things 1)
saint 62 (*plur.* 61)
*all 1.

HAGIŌSUNĒ ἁγιωσύνη *f.*
holiness 3.

HAGIOTĒS ἁγιότης *f.*
holiness 1.

HAGNEIA ἁγνεία *f.*
purity 2.

HAGNISMOS ἁγνισμός
purification 1.

HAGNIZŌ ἁγνίζω
purify 7.

HAGNOS ἁγνός
chaste 3
clear 1
pure 4.

HAGNŌS ἁγνῶς
sincerely 1.

HAGNOTĒS ἁγνότης *f.*
pureness 1.

HAIMA αἷμα *n.*
blood 99.

HAIMATEKCHUSIA αἱματεκχυσία *f.*
shedding of blood 1.

HAIMORRHOEŌ αἱμορρόεω
be diseased with an issue of blood 1.

HAIREOMAI αἱρέομαι
choose 3.

HAIRESIS αἵρεσις
heresy 4 (M. sect 1)
sect 5.

HAIRETIKOS αἱρετικός
that is an heretic 1.

HAIRETIZŌ αἱρετίζω
choose 1.

HALAS ἅλας *n.*
salt 8.

HALIEUŌ ἁλιεύω
go a fishing 1.

HALIEUS ἁλιεύς
fisher 4
fisherman 1.

HALIZŌ ἁλίζω
salt (*vb.*) 3.

HALLOMAI ἅλλομαι
leap 2
spring up 1.

HALŌN ἅλων *f.*
floor 2.

HALŌSIS ἅλωσις
†to be taken (eis *with acc.*) 1.

HALS ἅλς
salt 1.

HALUKOS ἁλυκός
salt (*adj.*) 1.

HALUSIS ἅλυσις *f.*
bonds (M. chain) 1
chain 10.

HAMA ἅμα
and 1
together 3
with 1
withal 3.
†also (*with* kai) 1. *See* prōi.

HAMARTANŌ ἁμαρτάνω
offend 1
sin 39
trespass 3.
Partic. for your faults 1.

HAMARTĒMA ἁμάρτημα *n.*
sin 4.

HAMARTIA ἁμαρτία *f.*
sin 172 (M. sacrifice for sin 1)
offence 1
*sinful 1.

HAMARTŌLOS ἁμαρτωλός
sinful 4.
As noun sinner 43.

HAPALOS ἁπαλός
tender 2.

HAPAS ἅπας
all 35 (*plur.* 31)
all things (*plur.*) 4
every man 1
every one 1
whole 3.

HAPAX ἅπαξ
once 15.

HAPHĒ ἁφή *f.*
joint 2.

HAPLOOS ἁπλόος
single 2.

HAPLŌS ἁπλῶς
liberally 1.

HAPLOTĒS ἁπλότης *f.*
bountifulness 1
liberality 1
simplicity 3 (M. liberally 1; en *with dat*)
singleness 2
*liberal 1.

HAPTŌ ἅπτω
kindle 1
light 3.
MID. touch 36.

HARMA ἅρμα *n.*
chariot 4.

HARMOS ἁρμός
joint 1.

HARMOZOMAI ἁρμόζομαι
espouse 1.

HARPAGĒ ἁρπαγή *f.*
extortion 1
ravening 1
spoiling 1.

HARPAGMOS ἁρπαγμός
robbery 1.

HARPAX ἅρπαξ
ravening 1.
As noun extortioner 4.

HARPAZŌ ἁρπάζω
catch 1
catch away 2
catch up 4
pluck 2
pull 1
take by force 3.

HEAUTOU ἑαυτοῦ
thyself
himself
herself
itself
ourselves
yourselves
themselves, etc.

HEBDOMĒKONTA ἑβδομήκοντα
seventy 2
three score and ten 1.
†*With* pente: three score and fifteen 1. *With* hex: three score and sixteen 1.

HEBDOMĒKONTAKIS ἑβδομηκοντάκις
seventy times 1.

HEBDOMOS ἕβδομος
seventh 9.

HEBRAÏSTI Ἑβραϊστί
in Hebrew 1
in the Hebrew 2
in the Hebrew tongue 3.

HĒDEŌS ἡδέως
gladly 3.
Superl. [hēdista]

HĒDISTA ἥδιστα
most gladly 1
very gladly 1.

HĒDONĒ ἡδονή *f.*
lust (M. pleasure) 2
pleasure 3.

HEDRAIŌMA ἑδραίωμα *n.*
ground (M. stay) 1.

HEDRAIOS ἑδραῖος
settled 1
steadfast 2.

HĒDUOSMON ἡδύοσμον *n.*
mint 2.

HĒGEMŌN ἡγεμών
governor 19
prince 1
*ruler 2

HĒGEMONEUŌ ἡγεμονεύω
be governor 2.

HĒGEMONIA ἡγεμονία *f.*
reign 1.

HĒGEOMAI ἡγέομαι
account 1
be chief 1
count 10
esteem 3
have the rule over 3 (M. be the guide 1, guide 1)
judge 1
suppose 1
think 4.
Partic. chief 1
governor 2.
†*Partic.* chief speaker (*with* logos) 1.

HEILISSŌ εἱλίσσω
roll together 1.

HEINEKEN = HENEKA.

HEIS εἷς (μία ἕν)
a (an) 15
a certain 6
another 2
any of them 1
any thing 1
first 2
one 283
one man (M. one) 1
one thing 5
only 1
other 7
some 6.
Fem. first day 6
one consent 1.
†each (*with* kata *and acc.*) 1; one by one (*ditto.*) 1. *With* hekastos: each 1, every 2, every man 2. Kata *with acc.*: every one 1, one by one 1, in particular 1. *In other combinations also.*

HEKASTOS ἕκαστος
any man 1
both 1
each one 1
every 14
every one 20
every man 39
every woman 1.
†particularly 1 (*with* kath' hen) 1. *See* heis.

HEKASTOTE ἑκάστοτε
always 1.

HEKATON ἑκατόν
hundred 14
hundredfold 2.

HEKATONTAETĒS ἑκατονταέτης
an hundred years old 1.

HEKATONTAPLASIŌN ἑκατονταπλασίων
hundredfold 3.

HEKATONTARCHĒS ἑκατοντάρχης
centurion 4.

HEKATONTARCHOS ἑκατόνταρχος
centurion 16.

HĒKŌ ἥκω
come 27.

HEKŌN ἑκών
willingly 2.

HEKOUSIOS ἑκούσιος
willingly (kata *with acc.*) 1.

HEKOUSIŌS ἑκουσίως
wilfully 1
willingly 1.

HEKTOS ἕκτος
sixth 14.

HĒLIKIA ἡλικία *f.*
age 1
stature 5 (M. age 2).
†*See* echō, kairos.

HĒLIKOS ἡλίκος
how great 1
what great 1.

HĒLIOS ἥλιος
sun 30.
†*See* anatolē.

HELISSŌ ἑλίσσω
fold up 1
roll together 1.

HELKŌ ἕλκω
draw 2.

HELKOŌ ἑλκόω
PASS. be full of sores.

HELKOS ἕλκος *n.*
sore 3.

HELKUŌ ἑλκύω
draw 6.

HĒLOS ἧλος
nail 2.

HĒMEIS ἡμεῖς
we
us
ourselves, etc.

HĒMERA ἡμέρα *f.*
day 355
judgment 1
time 3.
Plur. daytime 1
years 2.
†a good while ago (apo *with gen. and* archaios) 1; for ever (eis *with acc. and gen. of* aiōn) 1; sabbath (*with gen. pl. of* sabbaton) 1. *See* mesos, pas, probainō. Daily *freq. translates the acc. with* pas *or* hekastos (*often preceded by* kata).

HĒMETEROS ἡμέτερος
our 6
ours 2.

HĒMIŌRION ἡμιώριον *n.*
the space of half an hour 1.

HĒMISU ἥμισυ *n.*
half 5.

HĒMITHANĒS ἡμιθανής
half dead 1.

HEN = HEIS

HENDEKA ἕνδεκα
eleven 6.

HENDEKATOS ἑνδέκατος
eleventh 3.

HENEKA ἕνεκα (ἕνεκεν εἵνεκεν)
by reason of 1
for 2
for . . . cause 4
for . . . causes 1
for . . . sake 14
*that 1.
†because (*with* hos) 1; wherefore (*with* tis 1).

* Inexact translations, *e.g.*, of a noun by a verb or adjective, of an active by a passive.
† Cases where two or more words in the original are translated by one word or by a phrase

HENEKEN = HENEKA.

HĒNIKA ἡνίκα
†when (*with* an) 2.

HENOTĒS ἑνότης *f.*
unity 2.

HEORTAZŌ ἑορτάζω
keep the feast (M. k. holyday) 1.

HEORTĒ ἑορτή *f.*
feast 24
feast day 2
holyday 1.

HEŌS ἕως
as far as 3
even until 1
even unto 2
to 16
till 12
until 22
unto 28
up to 1
while 6.
†*With* an: till 15, until 5, until the time 1; *with* hou: till 11, until 5, while 1; *with* hotou: till 2, until 3, whiles 1. *In other combinations also.*

HEPTA ἑπτά
seven 86
seventh 1.

HEPTAKIS ἑπτάκις
seven times 4.

HEPTAKISCHILIOI ἑπτακισχίλιοι
seven thousand 1.

HERMĒNEIA ἑρμηνεία *f.*
interpretation 2.

HERMĒNEUŌ ἑρμηνεύω
interpret 1.
PASS. be by interpretation 3.

HERPETON ἑρπετόν *n.*
creeping thing 3
serpent 1.

HESPERA ἑσπέρα *f.*
evening 2
eventide 1.

HĒSUCHAZŌ ἡσυχάζω
be quiet 1
cease 1
hold one's peace 2
rest 1.

HĒSUCHIA ἡσυχία *f.*
quietness 1
silence 3.

HĒSUCHIOS ἡσύχιος
peaceable 1
quiet 1.

HETAIROS ἑταῖρος
fellow 1
friend 3.

HETERODIDASKALEŌ ἑτεροδιδασκαλέω
teach another doctrine 1
teach otherwise 1.

HETEROGLŌSSOS ἑτερόγλωσσος
of another tongue 1.

HETEROS ἕτερος
another 42
else 1
other 41
strange (M other) 1.
As noun another place 1
another psalm 1
next day 2
other matter 1
other thing 3.
†be altered (gignomai heteros). *Repeated*: one . . . another 1, some . . . other 3.

HETERŌS ἑτέρως
otherwise 1.

HETEROZUGEŌ ἑτεροζυγέω
be unequally yoked together with 1.

HETOIMASIA ἑτοιμασία *f.*
preparation 1.

HETOIMAZŌ ἑτοιμάζω
make ready 10
prepare 29
provide 1.

HETOIMOS ἕτοιμος
prepared 1
ready 14.
As noun readiness 1
things made ready to our hand 1.

HETOIMŌS ἑτοίμως
ready 3.

HĒTTAOMAI ἡττάομαι (ῶμαι)
be inferior 1
be overcome 2.

HĒTTĒMA ἥττημα *n.*
diminishing (M. decay or loss) 1
fault 1.

HĒTTŌN ἥττων (ἥσσων)
less 1
worse 1.

HEURISKŌ εὑρίσκω
can find 1
find 174
get 1
obtain 1.

HEX ἕξ
six 12.

HEXAKOSIOI ἑξακόσιοι
six hundred 2.

HEXĒKONTA ἑξήκοντα
sixty 3
sixty-fold 1
three-score 5.

HEXĒS ἑξῆς
next 1.
the morrow 1
the day after 1
the day following 1
the next day 1.

HEXIS ἕξις *f.*
use (M. habit or perfection) 1.

HIDRŌS ἱδρώς
sweat 1.

HIERATEIA ἱερατεία *f.*
office of the priesthood 1
priest's office 1.

HIERATEUMA ἱεράτευμα *n.*
priesthood 2.

HIERATEUŌ ἱερατεύω
execute the priest's office 1.

HIEREUS ἱερεύς
high priest 1
priest 31.

HIERON ἱερόν *n.*
temple 71.

HIEROPREPĒS ἱεροπρεπής
as becometh holiness (M. as becometh holy women) 1.

HIEROS ἱερός
holy 1.
As noun holy things (*pl.*) 1.

HIEROSULEŌ ἱεροσυλέω
commit sacrilege 1.

HIEROSULOS ἱερόσυλος
robber of churches 1.

HIERŌSUNĒ ἱερωσύνη *f.*
priesthood 4.

HIEROURGEŌ ἱερουργέω
minister 1.

HIKANOŌ ἱκανόω
make able 1
make meet 1

HIKANOS ἱκανός
able 1
enough 1
good 1
great 1
great number of 1
large 1
long 2
long season 1
long while 1
many (*pl.*) 10
many of (*pl.*) 1
meet 1
much 6
sufficient 3
worthy 5
*sore 1.
As noun security 1.
†*See* poieō.

HIKANOTĒS ἱκανότης *f.*
sufficiency 1.

HIKETĒRIA ἱκετηρία *f.*
supplication 1.

HILAROS ἱλαρός
cheerful 1.

HILAROTĒS ἱλαρότης *f.*
cheerfulness 1.

HILASKOMAI ἱλάσκομαι
make reconciliation for 1.
PASS. be merciful 1.

HILASMOS ἱλασμός
propitiation 2.

HILASTĒRION ἱλαστήριον *n.*
mercy-seat 1
propitiation 1.

HILEŌS ἵλεως
merciful 1
*be it far [from] 1.

HIMAS ἱμάς
latchet 3
thong 1.

HIMATION ἱμάτιον *n.*
apparel (*pl.*) 1
cloak 2
clothes 12 (*pl.* 11)
garment 31
raiment (*pl.*) 12
robe 2
vesture 2.

HIMATISMOS ἱματισμός
apparel 1
array 1
raiment 1
vesture 2
*apparelled 1.

HIMATIZŌ ἱματίζω
clothe 2.

HIMEIROMAI ἱμείρομαι
be affectionately desirous of 1.

HINA ἵνα
albeit 1
because 1
so as 1
so that 2
that 542
to the intent 1
to the intent that 1
†lest (*with* mē) 43; wherefore (*with* ti) 1; why (*with* ti) 5. *With following verb freq. translated by English infinitive* 78 (*preceded by* for to 8).

HIPPEUS ἱππεύς
horseman 2.

HIPPIKON ἱππικόν *n.*
horsemen 1.

HIPPOS ἵππος
horse 16.

HISTĒMI ἵστημι
Intrans. abide 1
continue 1
stand 99
stand by 3
stand forth 2
stand still 4
staunch 1.
Trans. appoint 2
covenant with for 1
establish 3
lay to one's charge 1
make stand 1
present 1
set 11
set up 1.
MID. (PASS.) be brought 1
be established 2
be holden up 1
stand 17
stand forth 1
stand up 2.

HISTOREŌ ἱστορέω
see 1.

HO[1] ὁ
the.
Freq. untranslated; often transl. by a pers. or demons. pron. by a noun supplied from the context, etc. The neut. pl. ta *is often rendered* the things (affairs, state), etc.

HO[2] ὅ
neut. of hos.

HODE ὅδε
he 1
she 1
such 1.
Plur. after this manner 1
these things 7
thus 1.

HŌDE ὧδε
here 45
hither 13
in this place 1
there 1
this place 1.

HODĒGEŌ ὁδηγέω
guide 2
lead 3.

HODĒGOS ὁδηγός
guide 4
leader 1.

HODEUŌ ὁδεύω
journey 1.

HODOIPOREŌ ὁδοιπορέω
go on one's journey 1.

HODOIPORIA ὁδοιπορία *f.*
journey 1
journeying 1.

HODOS ὁδός *f.*
highway 4 (*adj.* 1)
journey 6 (M. way 1)
way 83
way [side] 8.
†*See* poieō.

HOIOS οἷος
as 3
so as 1
such as 6
what 1
what manner 1
what manner of man 1
which 2.

HOLOKAUTŌMA ὁλοκαύτωμα *n.*
burnt offering 1
whole burnt offering 1.

HOLOKLĒRIA ὁλοκληρία *f.*
perfect soundness 1.

HOLOKLĒROS ὁλόκληρος
entire 1
whole 1.

HOLOS ὅλος
all 63
all [day] long 2
altogether 1
every whit 2
whole 43.

HOLŌS ὅλως
at all 2
commonly 1
utterly 1.

HOLOTELĒS ὁλοτελής
wholly 1.

HOMILEŌ ὁμιλέω
commune together 1
commune with 1
talk 2.

HOMILIA ὁμιλία *f.*
communication 1.

HOMILOS ὅμιλος
company 1.

HOMOIAZŌ ὁμοιάζω
agree thereto 1.

HOMOIŌMA ὁμοίωμα *n.*
likeness 3
shape 1
similitude 1.
*made like to 1.

HOMOIOŌ ὁμοιόω
liken 9
resemble 1.
PASS. be like 2
be made like 2.
Partic. in the likeness of 1.

HOMOIOPATHĒS ὁμοιοπαθής
of like passions 1
subject to like passions 1.

HOMOIOS ὅμοιος
like 47.

HOMOIŌS ὁμοίως
likewise 28
so 1.
†moreover (kai homoiōs) 1.

HOMOIŌSIS ὁμοίωσις *f.*
similitude 1.

HOMOIOTĒS ὁμοιότης *f.*
similitude 1.
†like as (kata *with acc.*) 1.

HOMOLOGEŌ ὁμολογέω
confess 13
give thanks (M. confess) 1
profess 3
promise 1.
PASS. confession is made 1.
†confess (*with* en) 4.

HOMOLOGIA ὁμολογία *f.*
confession (M. profession) 1
profession 4
*professed 1.

HOMOLOGOUMENŌS ὁμολογουμένως
without controversy 1.

HOMOPHRŌN ὁμόφρων
of one mind 1.

HOMŌS ὅμως)
and even 1
though it be but 1.
†nevertheless (*with* mentoi) 1.

HOMOTECHNOS ὁμότεχνος
of the same craft 1.

HOMOTHUMADON ὁμοθυμαδόν
with one accord 11
with one mind 1.

HOMOU ὁμοῦ
together 3.

HOPLIZŌ ὁπλίζω
MID. arm one's self with 1.

HOPLON ὅπλον *n.*
armour (*pl.*) 2
instrument 2 (M. arms or weapons 1)
weapon 2.

HOPOIOS ὁποῖος
of what sort 1
such as 1
what manner of 2.
†whatsoever (*with* pote) 1.

HOPŌS ὅπως
because 1
how 4
so that 1
that 41
to 4.
†*With* an: that 4, when 1.

HOPOTE ὁπότε
when 1.

HOPOU ὅπου
where 55
whereas 2
wheresoever 1
whither 9.
†*With* an *or* ean: in what place soever 1, wheresoever 5, whithersoever 5. *With* ekei: where 2.

HŌRA ὥρα *f.*
day 1
high time 1
hour 89
instant 1
season 3
time 11
*short 1.

HŌRAIOS ὡραῖος
beautiful 2
Beautiful 2.

HORAMA ὅραμα *n.*
sight 1
vision 11.

HORAŌ ὁράω
behold 1
look 1
look to 1
perceive 1
see 86
see to 2
take heed 5.
PASS. appear 17
shew one's self 1.

HORASIS ὅρασις *f.*
sight 1
vision 2
*look upon 1.

HORATOS ὁρατός
visible 1.

HORION ὅριον *n.*
border 1
coast 10.

HORIZŌ ὁρίζω
declare (M. determine) 1
determine 3
limit 1
ordain 2.
Pass. pt. determinate 1.

HORKIZŌ ὁρκίζω
adjure 2
charge (M. adjure) 1.

HORKŌMOSIA ὁρκωμοσία *f.*
oath 4 (M. swearing of an oath 1).

HORKOS ὅρκος
oath 10.

HORMAŌ ὁρμάω
run 1
run violently 3
rush 1.

HORMĒ ὁρμή *f.*
assault 1.

HORMĒMA ὅρμημα *n.*
violence 1.

HOROTHESIA ὁροθεσία *f.*
bound 1.

* Inexact translations, *e.g.*, of a noun by a verb or adjective, of an active by a passive.
† Cases where two or more words in the original are translated by one word or by a phrase.

HOS ὅς
that
who
which, etc.
†called (*with* ĕsti) 1; moreover (*with* loipon) 1; whatsoever (*with* dēpote) 1. *With* an (ean): whatsoever, whoso, whosoever, etc. *Preceded by prepos. often translated by where followed by preposition* (wherein, etc.).

HŌS ὡς
about 14
according as 3
after 3
after that 1
as 344
as it had been 2
as it were 20
as soon as 7
even as 6
even like 1
for 2
how 19
like 7
like as 1
like unto 3 (M. as 1)
since 1
so 1
so that 1
that 5
to wit 1
unto 1
when 41
while 4.
†*With* an (ean): as 2, as soon as 1, even as 1, when 1, whensoever 1; *with* kai: as well as 1.

HOSAKIS ὁσάκις
†*With* an (ean): as oft as 1, as often as 2.

HŌSANNA ὡσαννά
Hosanna 6.

HŌSAUTŌS ὡσαύτως
after the same manner 1
even so 1
in like manner 2
likewise 12.

HŌSEI ὡσεί
about 18
as 7
as it had been 2
as it were 1
like 4
like as 1.

HOSGE ὅσγε
he that 1.

HOSIŌS ὁσίως
holily 1.

HOSIOS ὅσιος
holy 4
Holy one 2.
As noun mercies 1 (M. holy or just things) 1.

HOSIOTĒS ὁσιότης *f.*
holiness 2.

HOSOS ὅσος
all 1
as many as 24
as much as 1
how much 3
that 9
what 3
whatsoever 9, etc.
†Eph'hoson: as long as 2; inasmuch as 3. Kath' hoson: as 1, inasmuch as 2. *With* an (ean): as many as 5, whatsoever 9, what things soever 1, wherewith soever 1, whosoever 2. *With* chronos: as long as 1.

HOSPER ὅσπερ
whosoever 1.

HŌSPER ὥσπερ
as 38
as when 1
even as 2
like as 1.

HŌSPEREI ὡσπερεί
as 1.

HŌSTE ὥστε
in so much that 16
so that 25
therefore 9
wherefore 17, etc.

HOSTIS ὅστις
he that
such as
that
which
who
whosoever, etc.
†*With* an: as 1, whatsoever 4, whosoever 5.

HOTAN ὅταν
(*With subj.*)
as long as 1
as soon as 2
that 1
when 114 (*indic.* 2)
whensoever 1
while 1.
†till (ei mē hotan) 1.

HOTE ὅτε
after 1
after that 2
as soon as 2
that 1
when 98
while 2.

HOTHEN ὅθεν
from thence 1
from whence 3
whence 1
where 2
whereby 1
wherefore 4
whereupon 3.

HOTI[1] ὅτι
as concerning that 1
as though 1
because 176 (M. that 2)
because that 4
for 265
for that 3
how 11
how that 20
in that 1
that 613 (M. as being 1)
why 2.

HOTI[2] = HOSTIS.

HOTOU ὅτου
†*See* heōs.

HOU οὗ
when 1
where 22
wherein 1
whither 1.
†from whence (ex hou) 1; since (aph' hou) 1; when once (aph' hou an) 1; whithersoever (*with* ean) 1.

HOUTŌ οὕτω (οὕτως)
after this manner 3
after that [manner] 1
as they were 1
even 1
even so 13
for all that 1
in like manner 1
in this manner 1
likewise 4
on this fashion 1
on this wise 6
so 158
thus 17
what! 1.
†like (*with* hōs) 1.

HOUTOS οὗτος
he 32
she 12
that 48
these (*pl.*) 158
these things (*pl.*) 175
this 590
this man 42, etc. etc.

HOUTŌS = HOUTŌ.

HUAKINTHINOS ὑακίνθινος
of jacinth 1.

HUAKINTHOS ὑάκινθος *f.*
jacinth 1.

HUALINOS ὑάλινος
of glass 3.

HUALOS ὕαλος *f.*
glass 2.

HUBRIS ὕβρις *f.*
harm 1
hurt (M. injury) 1
reproach 1.

HUBRISTĒS ὑβριστής
despiteful 1
injurious 1.

HUBRIZŌ ὑβρίζω
entreat shamefully 1
entreat spitefully 2
reproach 1
use despitefully 1.

HUDŌR ὕδωρ *n.*
water 79.

HUDRIA ὑδρία *f.*
water-pot 3.

HUDRŌPIKOS ὑδρωπικός
which had the dropsy 1.

HUDROPOTEŌ ὑδροποτέω
drink water 1.

HUETOS ὑετός
rain 5.
†*See* brechō.

HUGIAINŌ ὑγιαίνω
be in health 1
be sound 1
be whole 1.
Partic. safe and sound 1
sound 6
whole 1
wholesome 1.

HUGIĒS ὑγιής
sound 1
whole 13.

HUGROS ὑγρός
green 1.

HUIOS υἱός
child 50
foal 1
son 120
Son 210.

HUIOTHESIA υἱοθεσία *f.*
adoption 3
adoption of children 1
adoption of sons 1.

HULĒ ὕλη *f.*
matter (M. wood) 1.

HUMEIS ὑμεῖς
ye 304
you 1180
your 356 (*gen.* 352, *dat.* 4), etc.

HUMETEROS ὑμέτερος
your 7
yours 2.
As noun that which is your own 1.

HUMNEŌ ὑμνέω
sing an hymn (M. sing a psalm) 2
sing praises unto 1
sing praise unto 1.

HUMNOS ὕμνος
hymn 2.

HUPAGŌ ὑπάγω
depart 2
go 55
go away 3
go one's way 17.
Imper. get thee 3
get thee hence 1.

HUPAKOĒ ὑπακοή *f.*
obedience 11
obeying 1
*obedient 1.
†to obey (eis *with acc.*) 1, to make obedient (eis *with acc.*) 1.

HUPAKOUŌ ὑπακούω
be obedient to 2
hearken (M. ask who was there) 1
obey 18.

HUPANDROS ὕπανδρος *f.*
which hath an husband 1.

HUPANTAŌ ὑπαντάω
go and meet 1
meet 4.

HUPANTĒSIS ὑπάντησις *f.*
†to meet (eis *with acc.*) 1.

HUPARCHŌ ὑπάρχω
be 42
live 1
*after 1.
Partic. pl. goods 7
substance 1
that one hath 4
the things which one possesseth 2.
†have (*with dat.*) 2.

HUPARXIS ὕπαρξις *f.*
goods 1
substance 1.

HUPECHŌ ὑπέχω
suffer 1.

HUPEIKŌ ὑπείκω
submit one's self 1.

HUPĒKOOS ὑπήκοος
obedient 2.
†obey (ginomai hup.) 1.

HUPENANTIOS ὑπεναντίος
contrary 1.
As noun adversary 1.

HUPER ὑπέρ
With gen. by 1, concerning 1, for 105, for one's sake 8, in one's stead 2, in the behalf of 1, of 11, on one's behalf 3, on one's part 1, toward 1. *With acc.* above 12, beyond 1, more than 3, than 2, to 1. *As adv.* more 1.

HUPERAIRŌ ὑπεραίρω
MID. be exalted above measure 2
exalt one's self 1.

HUPERAKMOS ὑπέρακμος
†*See* eimi.

HUPERANŌ ὑπεράνω
far above 2
over 1.

HUPERAUXANŌ ὑπεραυξάνω
grow exceedingly 1.

HUPERBAINŌ ὑπερβαίνω
go beyond 1.

HUPERBALLŌ ὑπερβάλλω
exceed 3
excel 1
pass 1.

HUPERBALLONTŌS ὑπερβαλλόντως
above measure 1.

HUPERBOLĒ ὑπερβολή *f.*
abundance 1
excellency 1.
†Kata *with acc.*: beyond measure 1, exceeding 1, far more exceeding 1, more excellent 1, out of measure 1.

HUPERECHŌ ὑπερέχω
pass 1.
Partic. better 1
excellency 1
higher 1
supreme 1.

HUPEREIDON ὑπερεῖδον
wink at 1.

HUPEREKCHUNŌ ὑπερεκχύνω
PASS. run over 1.

HUPEREKEINA ὑπερέκεινα
beyond 1.

HUPEREKTEINŌ ὑπερεκτείνω
stretch beyond one's measure 1.

HUPERENTUGCHANŌ ὑπερεντυγχάνω
make intercession for 1.

HUPERĒPHANIA ὑπερηφανία *f.*
pride 1.

HUPERĒPHANOS ὑπερήφανος
proud 5.

HUPĒRETEŌ ὑπηρετέω
minister 2
serve 1.

HUPĒRETĒS ὑπηρέτης
minister 5
officer 11
servant 4.

HUPERLIAN ὑπερλίαν
very chiefest 2.

HUPERNIKAŌ ὑπερνικάω
be more than conqueror 1.

HUPEROCHĒ ὑπεροχή *f.*
authority (M. eminent place) 1
excellency 1.

HUPEROGKOS ὑπέρογκος *n. pl.*
great swelling words 2.

HUPERŌOS ὑπερῷος *n.*
upper chamber 3
upper room 1.

HUPERPERISSEUŌ ὑπερπερισσεύω
abound much more 1.
†be exceeding joyful (*pass. with dat. of* chara) 1.

HUPERPERISSŌS ὑπερπερισσῶς
beyond measure 1.

HUPERPHRONEŌ ὑπερφρονέω
think highly 1.

HUPERPLEONAZŌ ὑπερπλεονάζω
be exceeding abundant 1.

HUPERUPSOŌ ὑπερυψόω
exalt highly 1.

HUPHANTOS ὑφαντός
woven (M. wrought) 1.

HUPNOS ὕπνος
sleep 6.

HUPO ὑπό
With gen. among 1, by 42, from 2, of 116, with 14. *With acc.* in 1, into 1, under 48.

HUPOBALLŌ ὑποβάλλω
suborn 1.

HUPOCHŌREŌ ὑποχωρέω
go aside 1
withdraw one's self 1.

HUPODECHOMAI ὑποδέχομαι
receive 4.

HUPODEIGMA ὑπόδειγμα *n.*
ensample 1
example 4
pattern 1.

HUPODEIKNUMI ὑποδείκνυμι
forewarn 1
show 3
warn 2.

HUPODĒMA ὑπόδημα *n.*
shoe 10.

HUPODEŌ ὑποδέω
MID. be shod with 1
bind on 1
have shod 1.

HUPODIKOS ὑπόδικος
guilty (M. subject to judgment) 1.

HUPOGRAMMOS ὑπογραμμός
example 1.

HUPOKATŌ ὑποκάτω
under 9.

HUPOKRINOMAI ὑποκρίνομαι
feign 1.

HUPOKRISIS ὑπόκρισις *f.*
dissimulation 1
hypocrisy 5.

HUPOKRITĒS ὑποκριτής
hypocrite 20.

HUPOLAMBANŌ ὑπολαμβάνω
answer 1
receive 1
suppose 2.

HUPOLEIPŌ ὑπολείπω
leave 1.

HUPOLĒNION ὑπολήνιον *n.*
wine-fat 1.

HUPOLIMPANŌ ὑπολιμπάνω
leave 1.

HUPOMENŌ ὑπομένω
abide 1
endure 11
suffer 1
take patiently 2
tarry behind 1.
Partic. patient 1.

HUPOMIMNĒSKŌ ὑπομιμνήσκω
bring to remembrance 1
put in mind 1
put in remembrance 2
put in remembrance of 1
remember 1.
MID. remember 1.

HUPOMNĒSIS ὑπόμνησις *f.*
remembrance 3.

HUPOMONĒ ὑπομονή *f.*
enduring 1
patience 29
patient continuance 1
patient waiting (M. patience) 1.

HUPONOEŌ ὑπονοέω
deem 1
suppose 1
think 1.

HUPONOIA ὑπόνοια *f.*
surmising 1.

HUPOPHERŌ ὑποφέρω
bear 1
endure 2.

HUPŌPIAZŌ ὑπωπιάζω
keep under 1
weary 1.

* Inexact translations, *e.g.*, of a noun by a verb or adjective, of an active by a passive.
† Cases where two or more words in the original are translated by one word or by a phrase.

HUPOPLEŌ *ὑποπλέω*
sail under 2.

HUPOPNEŌ *ὑποπνέω*
blow softly 1.

HUPOPODION *ὑποπόδιον n.*
footstool 1
†footstool (*with gen. pl. of* pous) 8.

HUPOSTASIS *ὑπόστασις f.*
confidence 2
person 1
substance (M. ground or confidence) 1
*confident 1.

HUPOSTELLŌ *ὑποστέλλω*
withdraw 1.
MID. draw back 1
keep back 1
shun 1.

HUPOSTOLĒ *ὑποστολή f.*
*them who draw back 1.

HUPOSTREPHŌ *ὑποστρέφω*
come again 1
return 27
return again 4
return back again 1
turn back 1
turn back again 1.

HUPOSTRŌNNUMI *ὑποστρώννυμι*
spread 1.

HUPOTAGĒ *ὑποταγή f.*
subjection 4.

HUPOTASSŌ *ὑποτάσσω*
put in subjection 1
put in subjection under 1
put in subjection unto 1
put under 6
subdue unto 1
subject 1.
MID. (PASS.) be in subjection to 1
be in subjection unto 2
be made subject to 1
be made subject unto 1
be obedient unto 1
be subject 1
be subject to 5
be subject unto 6
be under obedience 1
submit one's self to 3
submit one's self unto 5.
Partic. obedient to 1.

HUPOTITHĒMI *ὑποτίθημι*
lay down 1.
MID. put in remembrance 1.

HUPOTRECHŌ *ὑποτρέχω*
run under 1.

HUPOTUPŌSIS *ὑποτύπωσις f.*
form 1
pattern 1.

HUPOZŌNNUMI *ὑποζώννυμι*
undergird 1.

HUPOZUGION *ὑποζύγιον n.*
ass 2.

HUPSĒLOPHRONEŌ *ὑψηλοφρονέω*
be high-minded 2.

HUPSĒLOS *ὑψηλός*
high 8.
As noun high 1
high things 1
that which is highly esteemed 1.

HUPSISTOS *ὕψιστος*
highest 4
Highest 4
most high 4
Most High 1.

HUPSŌMA *ὕψωμα*
height 1
high thing 1.

HUPSOŌ *ὑψόω*
exalt 14
lift up 6.

HUPSOS *ὕψος n.*
height 2
*be exalted 1
*high 1
*on high 1.

HUS *ὗς*
sow 1.

HUSSŌPOS *ὕσσωπος*
hyssop 2.

HUSTERĒMA *ὑστέρημα n.*
lack 1
penury 1
that which is behind (*pl.*) 1
that which is lacking (*pl.*) 1
want 3.

HUSTEREŌ *ὑστερέω*
be behind 2
come short 1
fail (M. fall) 1
lack 3
*want (*tr.*) 1.
Partic. part which lacked 1.
PASS. be destitute 1
be in want 1
be the worse (M. have the less) 1
come behind 1
come short of 1
suffer need 1
want 1.

HUSTERĒSIS *ὑστέρησις f.*
want 2.

HUSTERON *ὕστερον*
afterward 7
afterwards 1
at the last 1
last 2
last of all 1.

HUSTEROS *ὕστερος*
latter 1.

I

IAMA *ἴαμα n.*
healing 3.

IAOMAI *ἰάομαι*
heal 26
make whole 2.

IASIS *ἴασις f.*
cure 1
healing 1.
†to heal (eis *with acc.*) 1.

IASPIS *ἴασπις f.*
jasper 4.

IATROS *ἰατρός*
physician 7.

ICHNOS *ἴχνος n.*
step 3.

ICHTHUDION *ἰχθύδιον n.*
little fish 1
small fish 1.

ICHTHUS *ἰχθύς*
fish 20.

IDE *ἴδε*
behold 23
lo 3
look 1
see 1.

IDEA *ἰδέα f.*
countenance 1.

IDIOS *ἴδιος*
due 3
his 5
his several 1
one's own 72
one's proper 2
private 1
their 2
*severally (*dat.*) 1.
As noun home 1
one's acquaintance 1
one's own 2 (M. one's own home 1)
one's own business 1
one's own company 1
one's own home 1.
†home (*with* oikos) 1. Kata *with acc.*: apart 7, aside 1, privately 8 (M. severally 1), when they were alone 1.

IDIŌTĒS *ἰδιώτης*
ignorant 1
rude 1
unlearned 3.

IDOU *ἰδού*
behold 181
lo 29
see 3.

IKMAS *ἰκμάς f.*
moisture 1.

IOS *ἰός*
poison 2
rust 1.

IŌTA *ἰῶτα n.*
jot 1.

IOUDAÏSMOS *Ἰουδαϊσμός*
Jews' religion 2.

IOUDAÏZŌ *Ἰουδαΐζω*
live as do the Jews 1.

IRIS *ἶρις*
rainbow 2.

ISAGGELOS *ἰσάγγελος*
equal unto the angels 1.

ISCHUŌ *ἰσχύω*
avail 3
be able 6
be good 1
be of strength 1
be whole 2
can 10
can do 1
may 1
prevail 3.
†have much work (*with* molis) 1.

ISCHUROS *ἰσχυρός*
boisterous (M. strong) 1
mighty 10
powerful 1
strong 9
valiant 1.
As noun strong man 5.

ISCHUS *ἰσχύς*
ability 1
might 2
power 2
strength 4
*mighty (M. might) 1.
†mightily (en *with dat.*) 1.

ISOPSUCHOS *ἰσόψυχος*
like-minded (M. so dear unto me) 1.

ISOS *ἴσος (ἶσος)*
as much 1
equal 4
like 1.
†*See* eimi.

ISŌS *ἴσως*
it may be 1.

ISOTĒS *ἰσότης f.*
equality 2
that which is equal 1.

ISOTIMOS *ἰσότιμος*
like precious 1.

K

KAGŌ = KAI + EGŌ.

KAI *καί*
also
and
and also
and even
both
even
indeed
moreover
yea, etc., etc.

KAIGE *καίγε*
and 1
at least 1.

KAINOS *καινός*
new 44.
As noun new things 1.

KAINOTĒS *καινότης f.*
newness 2.

KAIŌ *καίω*
light 1.
PASS. be burned 2
burn 9.

KAIPER *καίπερ*
and yet 1
though 5.

KAIROS *καιρός*
certain season 1
convenient season 1
due season 2
due time 2 (M. time 1)
opportunity 2
season 11
time 63
while 1.
†age (*with gen. of* hēlikia) 1. *See* en.

KAITOI *καίτοι*
although 1.

KAITOIGE *καίτοιγε*
nevertheless 1
though 2.

KAKIA *κακία f.*
evil 1
malice 6
maliciousness 2
naughtiness 1
wickedness 1.

KAKOĒTHEIA *κακοήθεια f.*
malignity 1.

KAKOLOGEŌ *κακολογέω*
curse 2
speak evil of 2.

KAKOŌ *κακόω*
evil entreat 2
harm 1
hurt 1
make evil affected 1
vex 1.

KAKOPATHEIA *κακοπάθεια f.*
suffering affliction 1.

KAKOPATHEŌ *κακοπαθέω*
be afflicted 1
endure afflictions 1
endure hardness 1
suffer trouble 1.

KAKOPOIEŌ *κακοποιέω*
do evil 3.
Partic. for evil doing 1.

KAKOPOIOS *κακοποιός*
evil-doer 4
malefactor 1.

KAKOS *κακός*
bad 1
evil 8
noisome 1
wicked 1.
As noun evil 31 (M. evils 1)
evil things 3
harm 2
ill 1
that which is evil 2
they which are evil 1.

KAKŌS *κακῶς*
amiss 1
evil 2
grievously 1
miserably 1
sore 1.
†*See* echō.

KAKŌSIS *κάκωσις f.*
affliction 1.

KAKOUCHEŌ *κακουχέω*
PASS. be tormented 1
suffer adversity 1.

KAKOURGOS *κακοῦργος*
evil-doer 1
malefactor 3.

KALAMĒ *καλάμη f.*
stubble 1.

KALAMOS *κάλαμος*
pen 1
reed 11.

KALEŌ *καλέω*
bid 16
call 126
call forth 1
name 1
name so 1.
PASS. be one's name 1
be one's surname 1.

KALLIELAIOS *καλλιέλαιος*
good olive tree 1.

KALLION *κάλλιον*
very well 1.

KALODIDASKALOS *καλοδιδάσκαλος*
teacher of good things 1.

KALOPOIEŌ *καλοποιέω*
Partic. in well doing 1.

KALOS *καλός*
better 7
fair 1
good 76 (M. honest 1)
goodly 2
honest 2
meet 2
worthy 1
*well 1.
As noun good 3
good thing 2
honest thing 2
that which is good 2
that which is honest 1.

KALŌS *καλῶς*
full well 1
honestly 1
in a good place (M. well *or* seemly) 1
well 30.
†*See* echō, poieō.

KALUMMA *κάλυμμα n.*
veil 4.

KALUPTŌ *καλύπτω*
cover 5
hide 3.

KAME = KAI + EME.

KAMĒLOS *κάμηλος*
camel 6.

KAMINOS *κάμινος f.*
furnace 4.

KAMMUŌ *καμμύω*
close 2.

KAMNŌ *κάμνω*
be wearied 1
faint 1.
Partic. sick 1.

KAMOI = KAI + EMOI.

KAMPTŌ *κάμπτω*
bow 4.

KAN *κἄν* [= KAI AN]
also if 1
and if 3
and if so much as 1
at the least 1
if but 2
though 4
yet 1.

KANŌN *κανών*
line (M. rule) 1
rule (M. line) 1.

KAPĒLEUŌ *καπηλεύω*
corrupt (M. deal with deceitfully) 1.

KAPNOS *καπνός*
smoke 13.

KARDIA *καρδία f.*
heart 158.
†*See* suntribō.

KARDIOGNŌSTĒS *καρδιογνώστης*
which knoweth the hearts 2.

KARPHOS *κάρφος n.*
mote 6.

KARPOPHOROS *καρποφόρος*
fruitful 1.

KARPOPHOREŌ *καρποφορέω*
bear fruit 1
be fruitful 1
bring forth fruit 5.
MID. bring forth fruit 1.

KARPOS *καρπός*
fruit 66.

KARTEREŌ *καρτερέω*
endure 1.

KATA *κατά*
With genit. against 58
by 4
down 3
of 1
on 1
through 1
throughout 4
upon 1, etc.
With accus. according to 108
after 59
by 25
in 35, etc.

KATABAINŌ *καταβαίνω*
come down 41
descend 18
fall 1
fall down 1
get down 1
go down 17
step down 1.

KATABALLŌ *καταβάλλω*
cast down 2.
MID. lay 1.

KATABAREŌ *καταβαρέω*
burden 1.

KATABASIS *κατάβασις f.*
descent 1.

KATABIBAZŌ *καταβιβάζω*
bring down 1
thrust down 1.

KATABOLĒ *καταβολή f.*
foundation 10.
†to conceive (eis *with acc.*) 1.

KATABRABEUŌ *καταβραβεύω*
beguile of one's reward (M. judge against) 1.

KATACHEŌ *καταχέω*
pour 2.

KATACHRAOMAI *καταχράομαι*
abuse 2.

KATACHTHONIOS *καταχθόνιος*
under the earth 1.

KATADĒLOS *κατάδηλος*
evident 1.

* Inexact translations, *e.g.*, of a noun by a verb or adjective, of an active by a passive.
† Cases where two or more words in the original are translated by one word or by a phrase.

KATADEŌ καταδέω
bind up 1.

KATADIKAZŌ καταδικάζω
condemn 5.

KATADIŌKŌ καταδιώκω
follow after 1.

KATADOULOŌ καταδουλόω
bring into bondage 2.

KATADUNASTEŌ καταδυναστέω
oppress 2.

KATAGELAŌ καταγελάω
laugh to scorn 3.

KATAGGELEUS καταγγελεύς
setter forth 1.

KATAGGELLŌ καταγγέλλω
declare 2
preach 10
show 3
speak of 1
teach 1.

KATAGINŌSKŌ καταγινώσκω
condemn 2.
PASS. be blamed 1.

KATAGNUMI κατάγνυμι
break 4.

KATAGŌ κατάγω
bring 1
bring down 5
bring forth 1.
PASS. land 2
touch 1.

KATAGŌNIZOMAI καταγωνίζομαι
subdue 1.

KATAISCHUNŌ καταισχύνω
confound 3
dishonour 2
make ashamed 1
shame 1.
PASS. be ashamed 6 (M. be confounded 1).

KATAKAIŌ κατακαίω
burn 7
burn up 4
burn utterly 1.

KATAKALUPTŌ κατακαλύπτω
MID. be covered 2
cover 1.

KATAKAUCHAOMAI κατακαυχάομαι
boast 1
boast against 1
glory 1
rejoice against (M. glory against) 1.

KATAKEIMAI κατάκειμαι
lie 6
sit at meat 3
sit down 1.
†keep (*with* epi) 1.

KATAKLAŌ κατακλάω (κατακλάζω)
break 2.

KATAKLEIŌ κατακλείω
shut up 2.

KATAKLĒRODOTEŌ κατακληροδοτέω
divide by lot 1.

KATAKLINŌ κατακλίνω
make sit down 1.
MID. sit at meat 1
sit down 1.

KATAKLUSMOS κατακλυσμός
flood 4.

KATAKLUZŌ κατακλύζω
overflow 1.

KATAKOLOUTHEŌ κατακολουθέω
follow 1
follow after 1.

KATAKOPTŌ κατακόπτω
cut 1.

KATAKRĒMNIZŌ κατακρημνίζω
cast down headlong 1.

KATAKRIMA κατάκριμα *n.*
condemnation 3.

KATAKRINŌ κατακρίνω
condemn 17
damn 2.

KATAKRISIS κατάκρισις *f.*
condemnation 1.
†to condemn (pros *with acc.*) 1.

KATAKURIEUŌ κατακυριεύω
be lord over (M. overrule) 1
exercise dominion over 1
exercise lordship over 1
overcome 1.

KATALALEŌ καταλαλέω
speak against 1
speak evil of 4.

KATALALIA καταλαλία *f.*
backbiting 1
evil speaking 1.

KATALALOS κατάλαλος
backbiter 1.

KATALAMBANŌ καταλαμβάνω
apprehend 3
attain to 1
come upon 1
comprehend 1
obtain 1
overtake 1
take 3.
MID. comprehend 1
find 1
perceive 2.

KATALEGŌ καταλέγω
take into the number (M. choose) 1.

KATALEIMMA κατάλειμμα *n.*
remnant 1.

KATALEIPŌ καταλείπω
forsake 2
leave 22
reserve 1.

KATALITHAZŌ καταλιθάζω
stone 1.

KATALLAGĒ καταλλαγή *f.*
atonement 1
reconciliation 2
reconciling 1.

KATALLASSŌ καταλλάσσω
reconcile 6.

KATALOIPOS κατάλοιπος
As noun residue 1.

KATALUMA κατάλυμα *n.*
guestchamber 2
inn 1.

KATALUŌ καταλύω
be guest 1
destroy 9
dissolve 1
lodge 1
overthrow 1
throw down 3.
PASS. come to nought 1.

KATAMANTHANŌ καταμανθάνω
consider 1.

KATAMARTUREŌ καταμαρτυρέω
witness against 4.

KATAMENŌ καταμένω
abide 1.

KATAMONAS καταμόνας
alone 2.

KATANALISKŌ καταναλίσκω
consume 1.

KATANARKAŌ καταναρκάω
be burdensome to 2
be chargeable to 1.

KATANATHEMA κατανάθεμα *n.*
curse 1.

KATANATHEMATIZŌ καταναθεματίζω
curse 1.

KATANEUŌ κατανεύω
beckon unto 1.

KATANOEŌ κατανοέω
behold 4
consider 7
discover 1
perceive 2.

KATANTAŌ καταντάω
†*With* eis: attain to 1, attain unto 1, come to 5, come unto 4, come upon 1. *With* antikru: come over against 1.

KATANUSSŌ κατανύσσω
prick 1.

KATANUXIS κατάνυξις *f.*
slumber (M. remorse) 1.

KATAPATEŌ καταπατέω
trample 1
tread 1
tread down 1
tread under foot 2

KATAPAUŌ καταπαύω
cease 1
give rest 1
rest 1
restrain 1.

KATAPAUSIS κατάπαυσις *f.*
rest 9.

KATAPETASMA καταπέτασμα *n.*
veil 6.

KATAPHAGŌ = **KATESTHIŌ.**

KATAPHERŌ καταφέρω
give against 1.
PASS. fall 1
sink down 1.

KATAPHEUGŌ καταφεύγω
flee 2.

KATAPHILEŌ καταφιλέω
kiss 6.

KATAPHRONEŌ καταφρονέω
despise 9.

KATAPHRONĒTĒS καταφρονητής
despiser 1.

KATAPHTHEIRŌ καταφθείρω
PASS. perish utterly 1.
Partic. corrupt 1.

KATAPINŌ καταπίνω
devour 1
drown 1
swallow 1
swallow up 4.

KATAPIPTŌ καταπίπτω
fall 1
fall down 1.

KATAPLEŌ καταπλέω
arrive 1.

KATAPONEŌ καταπονέω
oppress 1
vex 1.

KATAPONTIZŌ καταποντίζω
MID. (PASS.) be drowned 1
sink 1.

KATAPSUCHŌ καταψύχω
cool 1.

KATARA κατάρα *f.*
curse 3
cursing 2
*cursed 1.

KATARAOMAI καταράομαι
curse 6.

KATARGEŌ καταργέω
abolish 3
bring to nought 1
cumber 1
deliver 1
destroy 5
do away 3
loose 1
make of none effect 2
make void 1
make without effect 1
put away 1
put down 1.
PASS. become of no effect 1
be to be done away 1
cease 1
come to nought 1
fail 1
vanish away 1.

KATARITHMEŌ καταριθμέω
number 1.

KATARTISIS κατάρτισις *f.*
perfection 1.

KATARTISMOS καταρτισμός
perfecting 1.

KATARTIZŌ καταρτίζω
fit (M. make up) 1
frame 1
make perfect 2
mend 2
perfect 2
prepare (M. fit) 1
restore 1.
PASS. be perfect (M. be perfected) 1
be perfectly joined together 1.

KATASCHESIS κατάσχεσις *f.*
possession 2.

KATASEIŌ κατασείω
beckon 4.

KATASKAPTŌ κατασκάπτω
dig down 1.
Pass. pt. ruins 1.

KATASKĒNOŌ κατασκηνόω
lodge 3
rest 1.

KATASKĒNŌSIS κατασκήνωσις *f.*
nest 2.

KATASKEUAZŌ κατασκευάζω
build 3
make 1
ordain 1
prepare 5.
PASS. be a preparing 1.

KATASKIAZŌ κατασκιάζω
shadow 1.

KATASKOPEŌ κατασκοπέω
spy out 1.

KATASKOPOS κατάσκοπος
spy 1.

KATASOPHIZOMAI κατασοφίζομαι
deal subtilely with 1.

KATASPHAZŌ κατασφάζω
slay 1.

KATASPHRAGIZŌ κατασφραγίζω
seal 1.

KATASTELLŌ καταστέλλω
appease 1.
Pass. pt. quiet 1.

KATASTĒMA κατάστημα *n.*
behaviour 1.

KATASTOLĒ καταστολή *f.*
apparel 1.

KATASTREPHŌ καταστρέφω
overthrow 2.

KATASTRĒNIAŌ καταστρηνιάω
begin to wax wanton against 1.

KATASTRŌNNUMI καταστρώννυμι
overthrow 1.

KATASTROPHĒ καταστροφή *f.*
overthrow 1
subverting 1.

KATASURŌ κατασύρω
hale 2.

KATATITHĒMI κατατίθημι
do 1
lay 1
show 1.

KATATOMĒ κατατομή *f.*
concision 1.

KATATOXEUŌ κατατοξεύω
thrust through 1.

KATATRECHŌ κατατρέχω
run down 1.

KATAXIOŌ καταξιόω
account worthy 2
count worthy 2.

KATĒCHEŌ κατηχέω
inform 2
instruct 3
teach 3.

KATECHŌ κατέχω
hold 3
hold fast 3
keep 2
keep in memory (M. hold fast) 1
let 1
make toward 1
possess 2
retain 1
seize on 1
stay 1
take 1
withhold 1.
PASS. *have 1.

KATĒGOREŌ κατηγορέω
accuse 21
object 1.

KATĒGORIA κατηγορία *f.*
accusation 3.
†accused (en *with dat.*) 1.

KATĒGOROS κατήγορος
accuser 7.

KATEIDŌLOS κατείδωλος
wholly given to idolatry (M. full of idols) 1.

KATENANTI κατέναντι
before (M. like unto) 1
over against 4.

KATENŌPION κατενώπιον
before 2
before the presence of 1
in one's sight 1
in the sight of 1.

KATĒPHEIA κατήφεια *f.*
heaviness 1.

KATEPHISTĒMI κατεφίστημι
make insurrection against 1.

KATERCHOMAI κατέρχομαι
come 3
come down 5
depart 1
descend 1
go down 2
land 1.

KATERGAZOMAI κατεργάζομαι
be wrought 1
cause 1
do 4 (M. overcome 1)
perform 1
work 14
work out 1.

KATESTHIŌ κατεσθίω
devour 10
devour up 2
eat up 3.

KATEUTHUNŌ κατευθύνω
direct 2 (M. guide 1)
guide 1.

KATEXOUSIAZŌ κατεξουσιάζω
exercise authority upon 2.

KATH' = **KATA.**

KATHA καθά
as 1.

KATHAIREŌ καθαιρέω
cast down 1
destroy 2
pull down 1
put down 1
take down 4.

KATHAIRESIS καθαίρεσις *f.*
destruction 2.
pulling down 1.

KATHAIRŌ καθαίρω
purge 2.

KATHAPER καθάπερ
as 7
as well as 1
even as 5.

KATHAPTŌ καθάπτω
fasten on 1.

KATHARISMOS καθαρισμός
cleansing 2
purification 1
purifying 2
*that one was purged 1.
†*See* poieō.

* Inexact translations, *e.g.*, of a noun by a verb or adjective, of an active by a passive.
† Cases where two or more words in the original are translated by one word or by a phrase.

KATHARIZŌ καθαρίζω
cleanse 16
make clean 5
purge 3
purify 3.
PASS. be clean 3.

KATHAROS καθαρός
clean 10
clear 1
pure 17.

KATHAROTĒS καθαρότης *f.*
purifying 1.

KATHEDRA καθέδρα *f.*
seat 3.

KATHĒGĒTĒS καθηγητής
master 3.

KATHĒKŌ καθήκω
fit 1.
Partic. things which are convenient 1.

KATHĒMAI κάθημαι
be set down 1
dwell 1
sit 82
sit by 2
sit down 3.

KATHĒMERINOS καθημερινός
daily 1.

KATHEUDŌ καθεύδω
be asleep 1
sleep 17.
Partic. asleep 4.

KATHEXĒS καθεξῆς
afterward 1
by order 1
in order 2.
As noun those that follow after 1.

KATHEZOMAI καθέζομαι
sit 6.

KATHIĒMI καθίημι
let down 4.

KATHISTĒMI καθίστημι
appoint 1
conduct 1
make 8
make ruler 6
ordain 3
set 1.
PASS. be 2.

KATHIZŌ καθίζω
be set 2
be set down 2
continue (M. sit) 1
set 2
sit 25
sit down 14
tarry 1.
MID. sit 1.

KATHO καθό
as 1
inasmuch as 1.
†according to that (*with* an) 1.

KATHOLOU καθόλου
at all 1.

KATHOPLIZŌ καθοπλίζω
arm 1.

KATHORAŌ καθοράω
see clearly 1.

KATHŌS καθώς
according as 4
as 151
even as 24
how 1
when 1.
†as well as (*with* kai) 1.

KATHOTI καθότι
because 1
because that 1
forsomuch as 1.
†*With* an: according as 1, as 1.

KATIOŌ κατιόω
canker 1.

KATISCHUŌ κατισχύω
prevail 1
prevail against 1.

KATŌ κάτω
beneath 2
down 5
*the bottom 2.
†beneath (ta katō) 1.

KATOIKEŌ κατοικέω
dwell 35
dwell at 4
dwell in 4.
Partic. dweller at 1
dweller in 1
inhabitant 1
inhabiter 1
inhabiter of 1.

KATOIKĒSIS κατοίκησις *f.*
dwelling 1.

KATOIKĒTĒRION κατοικητήριον *n.*
habitation 2.

KATOIKIA κατοικία *f.*
habitation 1.

KATOPTRIZŌ κατοπτρίζω
MID. behold as in a glass 1.

KATORTHŌMA κατόρθωμα *n.*
very worthy deed 1.

KATŌTERŌ κατωτέρω
under 1.

KATŌTEROS κατώτερος
lower 1.

KAUCHAOMAI καυχάομαι
boast 7
boast one's self 1
glory 22
joy 1
make one's boast 1
rejoice 4 (M. glory 1).
Partic. in glorying 1.

KAUCHĒMA καύχημα *n.*
boasting 1
glorying 2
rejoicing 4
*rejoice 1
*whereof to glory 1.
†nothing to glory of (ou kauchēma) 1.

KAUCHĒSIS καύχησις *f.*
boasting 6
glorying 1
rejoicing 4 (M. glorying 1)
whereof I may glory 1.

KAUMA καῦμα *n.*
heat 2

KAUMATIZŌ καυματίζω
scorch 4 (M. burn 1).

KAUSIS καῦσις *f.*
†to be burned (eis *with acc.*) 1.

KAUSŌN καύσων
burning heat 1
heat 2.

KAUSOŌ καυσόω
Pass. pt. with fervent heat 2.

KAUTĒRIAZŌ καυτηριάζω
scar with a hot iron 1.

KEIMAI κεῖμαι
be 1
be appointed 1
be laid 6
be laid up 1
be made 1
be set 6
lie 9.
Partic. *there 1.

KEIRIAI κειρίαι *f.*
grave-clothes 1.

KEIRŌ κείρω
shear 3.
Partic. shearer 1.

KELEUŌ κελεύω
bid 1
command 24
give commandment 1.
Partic. at one's commandment 1.

KELEUSMA κέλευσμα *n.*
shout 1.

KENODOXIA κενοδοξία *f.*
vainglory 1.

KENODOXOS κενόδοξος
desirous of vainglory 1.

KENOŌ κενόω
make of none effect 1
make of no reputation 1
make void 2.
PASS. be in vain 1.

KENOPHŌNIA κενοφωνία *f.*
*vain 2.

KENOS κενός
empty 4
vain 5
*in vain 3.
As noun vain things 1.
†in vain (eis *with acc.*) 5.

KENŌS κενῶς
in vain 1.

KĒNSOS κῆνσος
tribute 3
*tribute (*adj.*) 1.

KENTRON κέντρον *n.*
prick 2
sting 3.

KENTURIŌN κεντυρίων
centurion 3.

KEPHALAION κεφάλαιον *n.*
sum 2.

KEPHALAIOŌ κεφαλαιόω
wound in the head 1.

KEPHALĒ κεφαλή *f.*
head 75
Head 1.
†his head covered (kata *with gen.*) 1.

KEPHALIS κεφαλίς *f.*
volume 1.

KĒPOS κῆπος
garden 5.

KĒPOURGOS κηπουργός
gardener 1.

KERAIA κεραία *f.*
tittle 2.

KERAMEUS κεραμεύς
potter 3.

KERAMIKOS κεραμικός
of a potter 1.

KERAMION κεράμιον *n.*
pitcher 2.

KERAMOS κέραμος
tiling 1.

KERANNUMI κεράννυμι (κεραννύω)
fill 2
pour out 1.

KERAS κέρας *n.*
horn 11.

KERATION κεράτιον *n.*
husk 1.

KERDAINŌ κερδαίνω
gain 13
get gain 1
win 2.

KERDOS κέρδος *n.*
gain 2
lucre 1.

KĒRION κηρίον *n.*
comb 1.

KERMA κέρμα *n.*
money 1.

KERMATISTĒS κερματιστής
changer of money 1.

KĒRUGMA κήρυγμα *n.*
preaching 8.

KĒRUSSŌ κηρύσσω
preach 53
proclaim 2
publish 5.
Partic. preacher 1.

KĒRUX κήρυξ
preacher 3.

KĒTOS κῆτος *n.*
whale 1.

KIBŌTOS κιβωτός *f.*
ark 6.

KICHRĒMI = CHRAŌ.

KINAMŌMON κινάμωμον *n.*
cinnamon 1.

KINDUNEUŌ κινδυνεύω
be in danger 2
be in jeopardy 1
stand in jeopardy 1.

KINDUNOS κίνδυνος
peril 9.

KINEŌ κινέω
move 3
remove 1
wag 1.
Partic. mover 1.
MID. move 1.

KINĒSIS κίνησις *f.*
moving 1.

KITHARA κιθάρα *f.*
harp 4.

KITHARIZŌ κιθαρίζω
harp 2.

KITHARŌDOS κιθαρῳδός
harper 2.

KLADOS κλάδος
branch 11.

KLAIŌ κλαίω
bewail 1
weep 39.

KLAŌ κλάω
break 15.

KLASIS κλάσις *f.*
breaking 2.

KLASMA κλάσμα *n.*
broken meat (*pl.*) 2.
fragment 7.

KLAUTHMOS κλαυθμός
wailing 2
weeping 6.
†weep (*with* ginomai) 1.

KLEIŌ κλείω
shut 12
shut up 4.

KLEIS κλείς *f.*
key 6.

KLĒMA κλῆμα *n.*
branch 4.

KLEMMA κλέμμα *n.*
theft 1.

KLEOS κλέος *n.*
glory 1.

KLEPTĒS κλέπτης
thief 16.

KLEPTŌ κλέπτω
steal 13.

KLĒRONOMEŌ κληρονομέω
be heir 1
be heir of 1
inherit 15
obtain by inheritance 1.

KLĒRONOMIA κληρονομία *f.*
inheritance 14.

KLĒRONOMOS κληρονόμος
heir 15.

KLĒROŌ κληρόω
PASS. obtain an inheritance 1.

KLĒROS κλῆρος
heritage 1
inheritance 2
lot 3
lots 5
part 2.

KLĒSIS κλῆσις *f.*
calling 10
vocation 1.

KLĒTOS κλητός
called 10
which is called 1.

KLIBANOS κλίβανος
oven 2.

KLIMA κλίμα *n.*
part 1
region 2.

KLINĒ κλίνη *f.*
bed 9
table (M. bed) 1.

KLINIDION κλινίδιον *n.*
couch 2.

KLINŌ κλίνω
be far spent 1
bow 1
bow down 1
lay 2
turn to flight 1
wear away 1.

KLISIA κλισία *f.*
a company 1.

KLOPĒ κλοπή *f.*
theft 2.

KLUDŌN κλύδων
raging 1
wave 1.

KLUDŌNIZOMAI κλυδωνίζομαι
be tossed to and fro 1.

KNĒTHŌ κνήθω
PASS. have itching 1.

KODRANTĒS κοδράντης
farthing 2.

KOILIA κοιλία *f.*
belly 11
womb 12.

KOIMAŌ κοιμάω
MID. (PASS.) be asleep 2
be dead 1
fall asleep 4
fall on sleep 1
sleep 10.

KOIMĒSIS κοίμησις *f.*
taking of rest 1.

KOINŌNEŌ κοινωνέω
be made partaker of 1
be partaker of 4
communicate 2
distribute 1.

KOINŌNIA κοινωνία *f.*
communication 1
communion 4
contribution 1
distribution 1
fellowship 12
*to communicate 1.

KOINŌNIKOS κοινωνικός
willing to communicate (M. sociable) 1.

KOINŌNOS κοινωνός
companion 1
partaker 5
partner 3.
†have fellowship with (ginomai koinōnos) 1.

KOINOŌ κοινόω
call common 2
defile 11
pollute 1.
Pass. pt. unclean 1.

KOINOS κοινός
common 7
defiled (M. common) 1
unclean (M. common) 2.
As noun unholy thing 1.

KOITĒ κοίτη *f.*
bed 2
chambering (*pl.*) 1.
†*See* echō.

KOITŌN κοιτών
†chamberlain (ho epi *with gen.*; M. that was over the bedchamber) 1.

KOKKINOS κόκκινος
scarlet 2 (M. purple 1)
scarlet coloured 1.
As noun scarlet 2
scarlet colour 1.

KOKKOS κόκκος
corn 1
grain 6.

KOLAKEIA κολακεία *f.*
*flattering 1.

KOLAPHIZŌ κολαφίζω
buffet 5.

KOLASIS κόλασις *f.*
punishment 1
torment 1.

KOLAZŌ κολάζω
punish 2.

KOLLAOMAI κολλάομαι
be joined to (unto) 2
leave to 3
join one's self to 4
keep company with 1.

KOLLOURION κολλούριον *n.*
eye-salve 1.

KOLLUBISTĒS κολλυβιστής
changer 1
money-changer 2.

KOLOBOŌ κολοβόω
shorten 4.

KŌLON κῶλον *n.*
carcass 1.

KOLŌNIA κολωνία *f.*
colony 1.

KOLPOS κόλπος
bosom 5
creek 1.

KOLUMBAŌ κολυμβάω
swim 1.

KOLUMBĒTHRA κολυμβήθρα *f.*
pool 5.

KŌLUŌ κωλύω
forbid 16
hinder 2 (M. forbid 1)
keep from 1
let 1
suffer not 1
withstand 1.
†forbid to take (*with* apo) 1.

KOMAŌ κομάω
have long hair 2.

KŌMĒ κώμη *f.*
town 12
village 17.

KOMĒ κόμη *f.*
hair 1.

KOMIZŌ κομίζω
bring 1.
MID. receive 9
receive for 1.

KŌMOPOLIS κωμόπολις *f.*
town 1.

KŌMOS κῶμος
revelling 2
rioting 1.

* Inexact translations, *e.g.*, of a noun by a verb or adjective, of an active by a passive.
† Cases where two or more words in the original are translated by one word or by a phrase.

KOMPSOTERON κομψότερον
†*See* echō.

KONIAŌ κονιάω
white (*vb.*) 2.

KONIORTOS κονιορτός
dust 5.

KOPAZŌ κοπάζω
cease 3.

KŌNŌPS κώνωψ
gnat 1.

KOPĒ κοπή *f.*
slaughter 1.

KOPETOS κοπετός
lamentation 1.

KOPHINOS κόφινος
basket 6.

KŌPHOS κωφός
deaf 5
dumb 8
speechless 1.

KOPIAŌ κοπιάω
bestow labour 2
bestow labour on 1
be wearied 1
labour 16
toil 3.

KOPOS κόπος
labour 13
weariness 1.
†*See* parechō.

KOPRIA κοπρία *f.*
dunghill 1.
†*See* ballō.

KOPTŌ κόπτω
cut down 2.
MID. bewail 2
lament 2
mourn 1
wail 1.

KORASION κοράσιον *n.*
damsel 6
maid 2.

KORAX κόραξ
raven 1.

KORBAN κορβᾶν (κορβανᾶς)
Corban 1
treasury 1.

KORENNUMI κορέννυμι
MID. (PASS.) eat enough 1.
Partic. full 1.

KOROS κόρος (*Heb.*)
measure 1.

KOSMEŌ κοσμέω
adorn 5
garnish 4
trim 1.

KOSMIKOS κοσμικός
worldly 2.

KOSMIOS κόσμιος
modest 1
of good behaviour (M. modest) 1.

KOSMOKRATŌR κοσμοκράτωρ
ruler 1.

KOSMOS κόσμος
adorning 1
world 187.

KOUMI κοῦμι
cumi 1.

KOUPHIZŌ κουφίζω
lighten 1.

KOUSTŌDIA κουστωδία *f.* (*Lat.*)
watch 3.

KRABBATOS κράββατος (*Lat.*)
bed 11
couch 1.

KRAIPALĒ κραιπάλη *f.*
surfeiting 1.

KRANION κρανίον *n.*
Calvary(M. place of a skull) 1
skull 3.

KRASPEDON κράσπεδον *n.*
border 3
hem 2.

KRATAIOŌ κραταιόω
strengthen 1.
PASS be strong 1
wax strong 2.

KRATAIOS κραταιός
mighty 1.

KRATEŌ κρατέω
hold 12
hold by 1
hold fast 5
keep 1
lay hands on 2
lay hold on 8
lay hold upon 2
obtain 1
retain 2
take 8
take by 2.

KRATISTOS κράτιστος
most excellent 2
most noble 2.

KRATOS κράτος *n.*
dominion 4
power 6
strength 1.
†mightily (kata *with acc.*) 1.

KRAUGAZŌ κραυγάζω
cry 4
cry out 3.

KRAUGĒ κραυγή *f.*
clamour 1
cry 3
crying 2.

KRAZŌ κράζω
cry 40
cry out 19.

KREAS κρέας *n.*
flesh 2.

KREISSŌN (KREITTŌN) κρείσσων
best 1
better 13.
As noun better country 1
better thing 1.
Adv. better 1.
†*See* mallon.

KREMANNUMI κρεμάννυμι
hang 4.
MID. hang 3.

KRĒMNOS κρημνός
steep place 3

KRIMA κρίμα *n.*
condemnation 5 (M. judgment 2)
damnation 7 (M. judgment 1)
judgment 13.
†to be condemned (eis *with acc.*) 1. *See* echō, krinō.

KRINŌ κρίνω
call in question 2
conclude 1
condemn 5
damn 1
decree 1
determine 7
esteem 2
judge 87 (M. determine 1)
ordain 1
think 1
*[my] sentence is 1.
MID. (PASS) go to law 2
sue at the law 1.
†avenge (*with* krima) 1.

KRINON κρίνον
lily 2

KRISIS κρίσις *f.*
accusation 2
condemnation 3
damnation 3
judgment 41.

KRITĒRION κριτήριον *n.*
judgment 1
judgment-seat 1
*to judge 1.

KRITĒS κριτής
judge 17

KRITHĒ κριθή *f.*
barley 1

KRITHINOS κρίθινος
barley (*adj.*) 2.

KRITIKOS κριτικός
discerner 1.

KROUŌ κρούω
knock 9.

KRUPHĒ κρυφῆ
in secret 1.

KRUPTŌ κρύπτω
hide 12
keep secret 1.
Partic. secretly 1.
PASS. hide one's self 2.

KRUPTOS κρυπτός
hid 3
hidden 1
secret 1.
As noun hidden thing 2
secret 11
secret place 1.
†inwardly (en *with dat.*) 1.

KRUSTALLIZŌ κρυσταλλίζω
be clear as crystal 1.

KRUSTALLOS κρύσταλλος
crystal 2.

KTAOMAI κτάομαι
obtain 1
possess 3
provide (M. get) 1
purchase 2.

KTĒMA κτῆμα *n.*
possession 4.

KTĒNOS κτῆνος *n.*
beast 4.

KTĒTŌR κτήτωρ
possessor 1

KTISIS κτίσις *f.*
building 1
creation 6 (M. creature 1)
creature 11
ordinance 1.

KTISMA κτίσμα *n.*
creature 4.

KTISTĒS κτίστης
Creator 1.

KTIZŌ κτίζω
create 12
make 1.
Partic. Creator 1.

KUBEIA κυβεία *f.*
sleight 1.

KUBERNĒSIS κυβέρνησις *f.*
government 1.

KUBERNĒTĒS κυβερνήτης
master 1
ship-master 1.

KUKLOŌ κυκλόω
come round about 1
compass 1
compass about 2
stand round about 1.

KUKLOS κύκλος
round about (*dat.*) 7.

KUKLOTHEN κυκλόθεν
about 1
round about 3.

KULIŌ κυλίω
MID. wallow 1.

KULISMA κύλισμα *n.*
wallowing 1.

KULLOS κυλλός
maimed 4.

KUMA κῦμα *n.*
wave 5.

KUMBALON κύμβαλον *n.*
cymbal 1.

KUMINON κύμινον *n.*
cummin 1.

KUNARION κυνάριον *n.*
dog 4.

KUŌN κύων
dog 5.

KUPTŌ κύπτω
stoop 2
stoop down 1.

KURIA κυρία *f.*
lady 1.

KURIAKOS κυριακός
Lord's 2

KURIEUŌ κυριεύω
be lord of 1
exercise lordship over 1
have dominion over 4
Partic. lord 1.

KURIOS κύριος
lord 56
Lord 663
master 12
Master 2
owner 1
sir 13.

KURIOTĒS κυριότης *f.*
dominion 3
government (M. dominion) 1.

KUROŌ κυρόω
confirm 2.

L

LACHANON λάχανον *n.*
herb 4.

LAGCHANŌ λαγχάνω
be one's lot 1
cast lots 1
obtain 2

LAILAPS λαῖλαψ
storm 2
tempest 1.

LAKEŌ λακέω (λάσκω)
burst asunder 1.

LAKTIZŌ λακτίζω
kick 2.

LALEŌ λαλέω
preach 6
say 15
speak 241 (M. say 2, be spoken of 1)
speak of 2
speak with 2
talk 12
talk with 1
tell 11
utter 4
Fut. pt things which were to be spoken after 1.

LALIA λαλιά *f.*
saying 1
speech 3.

LAMA λαμά (λαμμᾶ)
lama 2.

LAMBANŌ λαμβάνω
accept 2
attain 1
bring 1
call to 1
catch 3
come on 1
have 3
hold (M. take)
obtain 2
receive 133 (M. take unto one's self 1)
take 104
take away 1
take to one's self 1
take up 2
take upon one's self 1.
†assay (*with* peira) 1; begin at the first (*with* archē) 1; *come into room [of] (*with* diadochos) 1; forget (*with* lēthē) 1. *See* ekstasis.

LAMPAS λαμπάς *f.*
lamp 7
light 1
torch 1

LAMPŌ λάμπω
give light 1
shine 6.

LAMPROS λαμπρός
bright 2
clear 1
gay 1
goodly 2
gorgeous 1
white 2.

LAMPRŌS λαμπρῶς
sumptuously 1

LAMPROTĒS λαμπρότης *f.*
brightness 1.

LANTHANŌ λανθάνω
be hid 2
be hidden 1
*be ignorant of 2
*unawares 1.

LAOS λαός
people 143.

LARUGX λάρυγξ
throat 1.

LATHRA λάθρα
privily 3
secretly 1.

LATOMEŌ λατομέω
hew 2.

LATREIA λατρεία *f.*
divine service 1
service 4.

LATREUŌ λατρεύω
do service 1
serve 16
worship 3.
Partic. worshipper 1.

LAXEUTOS λαξευτός
hewn in stone 1.

LEGEŌN λεγεών
legion 2
Legion 2.

LEGŌ λέγω
ask 1
bid 2
boast 1
call 47
describe 1
give out 1
name 2
put forth 1
say 1180
say on 1
show 1
speak 56
speak of 1
tell 33
utter 1.
PASS. is to say 3.
Partic things which were spoken 4
things which we have spoken 1
things which . . . spake 1.
†*Act. partic.* with these sayings (*with* tauta) 1

LEIMMA λεῖμμα *n.*
remnant 1

LEIOS λεῖος
smooth 1.

LEIPŌ λείπω
be wanting 2 (M. be left undone 1).
PASS. be destitute 1
lack 1.
†*Pass.* want (*with* en) 1.

LEITOURGIA λειτουργία *f.*
ministration 1
ministry 2
service 3.

LEITOURGEŌ λειτουργέω
minister (*vb.*) 3.

LEITOURGIKOS λειτουργικός
ministering 1.

LEITOURGOS λειτουργός
he that ministereth 1
minister 4.

LĒNOS ληνός
wine-press 5.

LENTION λέντιον *n.* (*Lat.*)
towel 2.

LEŌN λέων
lion 8
Lion 1.

LEPIS λεπίς *f.*
scale 1.

LEPRA λέπρα *f.*
leprosy 4.

LEPROS λεπρός
leper 9.

LĒPSIS λῆψις *f.*
receiving 1.

LEPTON λεπτόν *n.*
mite 3.

LĒROS λῆρος
idle tales 1

LĒSTĒS λῃστής
robber 4
thief 11

LĒTHĒ λήθη *f.*
†*See* lambanō.

LEUKAINŌ λευκαίνω
make white 1
white 1.

LEUKOS λευκός
white 25.

LIAN λίαν
a great while
exceeding 5
greatly 4
sore 1.
†*See* prōi.

LIBANOS λίβανος
frankincense 2

LIBANŌTOS λιβανωτός
censer 2.

LIKMAŌ λικμάω
grind to powder 2.

LIMĒN λιμήν
haven 3.

LIMNĒ λίμνη *f.*
lake 10.

LIMOS λιμός
dearth 2
famine 7
hunger 3.

LINON λίνον *n.*
flax 1
linen 1.

LIPAROS λιπαρός
dainty 1

LIPS λίψ
south-west 1.

LITHAZŌ λιθάζω
stone (*vb.*) 8

LITHINOS λίθινος
of stone 3

LITHOBOLEŌ λιθοβολέω
cast stones 1
stone 8.

LITHOS λίθος
stone 58
*another 6.

LITRA λίτρα *f.* (*Lat.*)
pound 2

LOGCHĒ λόγχη *f.*
spear 1.

LOGIA λογία *f.*
collection 1
gathering 1.

LOGIKOS λογικός
of the word 1
reasonable 1.

LOGION λόγιον *n.*
oracle 4.

LOGIOS λόγιος
eloquent 1.

LOGISMOS λογισμός
imagination (M. reasoning) 1
thought 1.

LOGIZOMAI λογίζομαι
account 3 (M. impute 1)
account of 1
conclude 1
count 5
esteem 1
impute 8
lay to one's charge 1

* Inexact translations, *e.g.*, of a noun by a verb or adjective, of an active by a passive.
† Cases where two or more words in the original are translated by one word or by a phrase.

number 1
reason 1
reckon 6
suppose 2
think 8 (M. reason 1)
think of (M. reckon) 1
think on 1.
†be despised (*with* eis ouden) 1.

LOGOMACHEŌ λογομαχέω
strive about words 1.

LOGOMACHIA λογομαχία *f.*
strife of words 1.

LOGOS λόγος
account 8
cause 1
communication 3
doctrine (M. word) 1
game 1
intent 1
matter 4
mouth 1
preaching 1
question (M. thing) 1
reason 2
rumour 1
saying 50 (M. thing 1)
shew 1
speech 8
talk 1
thing 4
things to say 1
tidings 1
treatise 1
utterance 4
word 208 (M. preaching 2)
Word 7
words 4 (M speech 1)
work (M. account) 2
*do 1.
†*See* eis, polus, sunairō, tis[2].

LOIDOREŌ λοιδορέω
revile 4.

LOIDORIA λοιδορία *f.*
railing 2
*speak reproachfully (M. railing) 1.

LOIDOROS λοίδορος
railer 1
reviler 1.

LOIMOS λοιμός
pestilence 2
pestilent fellow 1.

LOIPOS λοιπός
other 9.
As noun others 7
other grain 1
other places (M. others) 1
other things 1
other women 1
remnant 4
residue 1
rest 12
the other 1
things which remain 1.
As adv. besides 1
finally 5
from henceforth 2
furthermore 1
henceforth 1
now 2
then 1.
†remain (*with* esti) 1. *See* hos.

LOUŌ λούω
wash 6.

LOUTRON λουτρόν *n.*
washing 2.

LUCHNIA λυχνία *f.*
candlestick 12.

LUCHNOS λύχνος
light 6
candle 8.

LUKOS λύκος
wolf 6.

LUMAINOMAI λυμαίνομαι
make havoc of 1.

LUŌ λύω
break 6
break up 1
destroy 2
dissolve 2
loose 2
put off 1
unloose 3.
PASS. melt 1.

LUPĒ λύπη *f.*
grief 1
heaviness 2.
sorrow 11
*grievous 1.
†grudgingly (ek *with gen.*) 1.

LUPEŌ λυπέω
cause grief 1
grieve 2
make sorry 3
MID (PASS.) be grieved 4
be made sorry 3
be in heaviness 1
be sorrowful 4
be sorry 3
sorrow 3.
Partic. sorrowful 2.

LUSIS λύσις *f.*
*to be loosed 1.

LUSITELEŌ λυσιτελέω
be better 1.

LUTRON λύτρον *n.*
ransom 2.

LUTROŌ λυτρόω
redeem 1.
MID. redeem 2.

LUTRŌSIS λύτρωσις *f.*
redemption 2.
†*See* poieō.

LUTRŌTĒS λυτρωτής
deliverer 1.

M

MACHAIRA μάχαιρα *f.*
sword 29.

MACHĒ μάχη *f.*
fighting 2 (M. brawling 1)
strife 1
striving 1.

MACHOMAI μάχομαι
fight 1
strive 3.

MAGEIA μαγεία
sorcery 1.

MAGEUŌ μαγεύω
use sorcery 1.

MAGOS μάγος
wise man 4
sorcerer 2.

MAINOMAI μαίνομαι
be beside one's self 1
be mad 4.

MAKARIOS μακάριος
blessed 43
happy 6.

MAKARISMOS μακαρισμός
blessedness 3.

MAKARIZŌ μακαρίζω
call blessed 1
count happy 1.

MAKELLON μάκελλον *n.*
shambles 1.

MAKRAN μακράν
a good way off 1
a great way off 1
far 4
far hence 1
far off 1.
As noun that is afar off 1
which is afar off 1.

MAKROCHRONIOS μακροχρόνιος
†*See* eimi.

MAKROS μακρός
far 2.

MAKROTHEN μακρόθεν
afar off 4
from far 1.
†*See* apo.

MAKROTHUMEŌ μακροθυμέω
be long-suffering 1
bear long 1
be patient 3 (M. be long patient or suffer with long patience 1)
endure patiently 1
have long patience 1
have patience 2
suffer long 1.

MAKROTHUMIA μακροθυμία *f.*
long-suffering 11
patience 2.

MAKROTHUMŌS μακροθύμως
patiently 1.

MALAKIA μαλακία *f.*
disease 3.

MALAKOS μαλακός
effeminate 1
soft 2.
As noun soft clothing (*neut. pl.*) 1.

MALISTA μάλιστα
chiefly 2
especially 4
most of all 1
specially 6.

MALLON μᾶλλον
more 30
much 1
rather 32
the more 11
the rather 1
so much the more 1.
†so much the more a great deal (*with comp. of* perissos) 1; better (*with* kreissōn) 1. *See* perisseuō.

MAMMĒ μάμμη *f.*
grandmother 1.

MAMMŌNAS μαμμωνᾶς
mammon 4 (M. riches 2).

MANIA μανία *f.*
†*See* peritrepō.

MANNA μάννα *n.* (*Heb.*)
manna 5.

MANTEUOMAI μαντεύομαι
Partic. by soothsaying 1.

MANTHANŌ μανθάνω
learn 24
understand 1.

MARAINŌ μαραίνω
PASS. fade away 1.

MARAN ATHA μαρὰν ἀθά
maranatha 1.

MARGARITĒS μαργαρίτης
pearl 9.

MARMAROS μάρμαρος
marble 1.

MARTUREŌ μαρτυρέω
be witness 2
bear record 13
bear witness 25
give 1
give testimony 2
give witness 1
testify 19
witness 3.
MID. (PASS.) be witnessed 1
be well reported of 2
charge 1
have good report 2
have testimony 1
obtain good report 2
obtain witness 1
witness 1.
Partic. of good report 1
of honest report 1.

MARTURIA μαρτυρία *f.*
record 7
report 1
testimony 14
witness 15.

MARTURION μαρτύριον *n.*
testimony 15
witness 4
*to be testified (M. a testimony) 1.

MARTUROMAI μαρτύρομαι
take to record 1
testify 2.

MARTUS μάρτυς
martyr 3
record 2
witness 29.

MASSAOMAI μασσάομαι
gnaw 1.

MASTIGOŌ μαστιγόω
scourge 7.

MASTIZŌ μαστίζω
scourge 1.

MASTIX μάστιξ *f.*
plague 4
scourging 2.

MASTOS μαστός
pap 3.

MATAIOLOGIA ματαιολογία *f.*
vain jangling 1.

MATAIOLOGOS ματαιολόγος
vain talker 1.

MATAIOŌ ματαιόω
PASS. become vain 1.

MATAIOS μάταιος
vain 5.
As noun vanity 1.

MATAIOTĒS ματαιότης *f.*
vanity 3.

MATĒN μάτην
in vain 2.

MATHĒTĒS μαθητής
disciple 269.

MATHĒTEUŌ μαθητεύω
be a disciple 1
instruct 1
teach 2 (M. make disciples 2, or Christians of 1).

MATHĒTRIA μαθήτρια *f.*
disciple 1.

ME με (*acc. of* EGŌ).
me, etc.

MĒ μή
[*Very freq.* not; *also* lest 15, that not 8. *As an interrog. particle freq. not represented by a special word in English. Along with another word, e.g.,* tis *often translated by one English word* e.g., neither, no, none, nothing.]

MECHRI(S) μέχρι (μέχρις)
till 1
to 1
until 7
unto 8.
†till (*with* hou) 1.

MĒDAMŌS μηδαμῶς
not so 2.

MĒDE μηδέ
neither 32
no not 1
no not so much as 1
nor 17
not 3
not once 1
not yet 2.

MĒDEIS μηδείς
no 16
no man 32
no thing 1
none 5
not any 1
not at all 1
not a whit 1
nothing 27 (M. no man 1)
*not 1.
†*With neg*: any 2, any man 1, any thing 2. *See* poieō.

MĒDEPŌ μηδέπω
not as yet 1.

MĒDEPOTE μηδέποτε
never 1.

MEGALAUCHEŌ μεγαλαυχέω
boast great things 1.

MEGALEIOS μεγαλεῖος
As noun great thing 1
wonderful work 1.

MEGALEIOTĒS μεγαλειότης *f.*
magnificence 1
majesty 1
mighty power 1.

MEGALOPREPĒS μεγαλοπρεπής
excellent 1.

MEGALŌS μεγάλως
greatly 1.

MEGALŌSUNĒ μεγαλωσύνη *f.*
majesty 1
Majesty 2.

MEGALUNŌ μεγαλύνω
enlarge 2 (M. magnify 1)
magnify 5
shew great 1.

MEGAS μέγας
great 145
greatest 2
high 2
large 2
loud 33
mighty 1
strong 1
*to years 1.
As noun great ones 1
great thing 3
they that are great 1.
As adv. the more 1.
†*See* phobos.

MĒGE μήγε
not 3.
†*See* ei.

MEGETHOS μέγεθος *n.*
greatness 1.

MEGISTANES μεγιστᾶνες
great men 2
lords 1.

MEGISTOS μέγιστος
exceeding great 1.

MEIZON μείζων
elder (M. greater) 1
greater 32
greatest 9
more 1.
As noun greater thing 1
greater work 1.

MEIZOTEROS μειζότερος
greater 1.

MĒKETI μηκέτι
henceforth no more 1
henceforth not 2
no longer 4
no more 7
not any more 1
not henceforth 1
*no 1
*no . . . henceforward 1.
†*With neg.*: any longer 1, henceforth 1, hereafter 1.

MĒKOS μῆκος *n.*
length 3.

MĒKUNŌ μηκύνω
MID. grow up 1.

MELAN μέλαν *n.*
ink 3.

MELAS μέλας
black 3.

MELETAŌ μελετάω
imagine 1
meditate upon 1
premeditate 1.

MELI μέλι *n.*
honey 4.

MELISSIOS μελίσσιος
honey (*adj.*) 1.

MELLŌ μέλλω
be 4
be about 4
be almost 1
be at point of 1
be ready 3
be that should 1
be to come 3
be yet 1
begin 1
intend 2
mean 1
mind 1
shall 25
should 19
should after 2
should afterwards 1
should hereafter 1
tarry 1
will 8
would 8.
Partic. about 1
ready 2
thing to come 4
time to come 1
what things should 1
*to come 9.
†after that (eis to *with partic.*) 1; be coming on (*with* ginomai) 1.

MELŌ μέλω
care 9
take care 1.

MELOS μέλος *n.*
member 34.

MĒLŌTĒ μηλωτή *f.*
sheepskin 1.

MEMBRANA μεμβράνα *f.*
parchment 1.

MEMPHOMAI μέμφομαι
find fault 3.

MEMPSIMOIROS μεμψίμοιρος
complainer 1.

MEN μέν
even 1
indeed 22
truly 12
verily 14.
†*Freq. used to mark the 1st member of an antithesis (the 2nd being marked by* de) *and then gen. untranslated.*

MĒN[1] μήν
†*See* ē[3].

MĒN[2] μήν
month 18.

MENŌ μένω
abide 59 (M. wait for 1)
be 1
be present 1
continue 11

* Inexact translations, *e.g.*, of a noun by a verb or adjective, of an active by a passive.
† Cases where two or more words in the original are translated by one word or by a phrase.

dwell 15 (M. abide 1)
endure 3
remain 17
stand 1
tarry 9
tarry for 1.

MENOUNGE μενοῦνγε
nay but 1
yea doubtless 1
yea rather 1
yes verily 1.

MENTOI μέντοι
but 1
howbeit 1
nevertheless 1
yet 2.
†nevertheless (hopōs mentoi) 1.

MĒNUŌ μηνύω
show 3
tell 1.

MĒPŌ μήπω
not yet 2.

MĒPŌS μήπως
lest 5
lest by any means 3
lest by some means 1
lest haply 1
lest perhaps 1
lest that by any means 1.

MĒPOTE μήποτε
if peradventure 1
lest 12
lest at any time 7
lest haply 2
whether or not 1
*no . . . at all 1.

MERIMNA μέριμνα *f.*
care 6.

MERIMNAŌ μεριμνάω
be careful 2
care 5
have care 1
take thought 10.
Partic. with taking thought 1.

MERIS μερίς *f.*
part 4.
†to be partaker (eis *with acc.*) 1.

MERISMOS μερισμός
dividing asunder 1
gift (M. distribution) 1.

MERISTĒS μεριστής
divider 1.

MERIZŌ μερίζω
deal 1
distribute 2
divide 8
give part 1.
MID. divide 1.
PASS. be difference between 1.

MĒROS μηρός
thigh 1.

MEROS μέρος
behalf 2
coast 3
craft 1
part 24
piece 1
portion 3
respect 2 (M. part 1)
side 1
some sort 1.
†by course (ana meros) 1; in particular (ek *with gen.*) 1; particularly (kata m.) 1; partly (meros ti) 1; somewhat (apo *with gen.*) 1.

MESĒMBRIA μεσημβρία *f.*
noon 1
south 1.

MESITĒS μεσίτης
mediator 6.

MESITEUŌ μεσιτεύω
confirm (M. interpose one's self) 1.

MESONUKTION μεσονύκτιον *n.*
midnight 4.

MESOŌ μεσόω
be about the midst 1.

MESOS μέσος
among 6
in the midst 4
midst 37.
†among (ana *with acc.* 1, en *with dat.* 5) 6; before (en *with dat.*) 1; between (ana *with acc.*) 1; midday (*with* hēmera) 1; midnight (*with* nux) 2; out of the way (ek *with gen.*) 2.

MESOTOICHON μεσότοιχον *n.*
middle wall between 1.

MESOURANĒMA μεσουράνημα *n.*
midst of heaven 3.

MESTOŌ μεστόω
PASS. be full 1.

MESTOS μεστός
full 8.

META μετά
With gen. against 4
among 5
in 2
of 1
on 1
unto 1
upon 1
with 346
*and 1
*and setting 1
*promised to 1.
†without (ou meta) 1.
With acc. after 95
since 1
*hence 1
*when 2.
†that should follow (*with* tauta) 1.

METABAINŌ μεταβαίνω
depart 7
go 1
pass 2
remove 2.

METABALLŌ μεταβάλλω
MID. change one's mind 1.

METADIDŌMI μεταδίδωμι
give 2 (M. impart 1, distribute 1)
impart 3.

METAGŌ μετάγω
turn about 2.

METAIRŌ μεταίρω
depart 2.

METAKALEŌ μετακαλέω
MID. call 1
call for 1
call hither 1
call to one's self 1.

METAKINEŌ μετακινέω
move away 1.

METALAMBANŌ μεταλαμβάνω
be partaker of 2
eat 1
have 1
receive 1
take 1.

METALĒPSIS μετάληψις *f.*
†to be received (eis *with acc.*) 1.

METALLASSŌ μεταλλάσσω
change 2.

METAMELOMAI μεταμέλομαι
repent 5
repent one's self 1.

METAMORPHOŌ μεταμορφόω
MID. be changed 1
be transfigured 2
be transformed 1.

METANOEŌ μετανοέω
repent 34.

METANOIA μετάνοια *f.*
repentance 24 (M amendment of life 1, to change his mind 1).

METAPEMPŌ μεταπέμπω
call for 2
send for 6.

METASCHĒMATIZŌ μετασχηματίζω
MID. be transformed 2
change 1
transfer in a figure 1
transform one's self 1.

METASTREPHŌ μεταστρέφω
pervert 1
turn 2.

METATHESIS μετάθεσις
charge 1
removing 1
translation 1.

METATITHĒMI μετατίθημι
carry over 1
change 1
remove 1
translate 2
turn 1.

METAXU μεταξύ
between 6
meanwhile 2 (M. between 1)
next (M. between) 1.

MĒTE μήτε
neither 20
nor 14
or 1
so much as 1.

METECHŌ μετέχω
be partaker of 5
pertain to 1
take part of 1
use 1.

METEŌRIZŌ μετεωρίζω
MID. be of doubtful mind (M. live in careful suspense) 1.

METEPEITA μετέπειτα
afterward 1.

MĒTĒR μήτηρ *f.*
mother 85.

METHĒ μέθη *f.*
drunkenness 3.

METHERMĒNEUŌ μεθερμηνεύω
interpret 5.
PASS. be by interpretation 2.

METHISTĒMI μεθίστημι (μεθιστάνω)
can remove 1
put out of 1
remove 1
translate 1
turn away 1.

METHODEIA μεθοδεία *f.*
wile 1.
†whereby they lie in wait (pros *with acc.*) 1.

METHORIOS μεθόριος
borders (*pl.*) 1.

METHUŌ μεθύω
be drunken 5.
MID. be made drunk 1
have well drunk 1.

METHUSKŌ μεθύσκω
MID. be drunk 1
be drunken 2.

METHUSOS μέθυσος
drunkard 2.

MĒTI μήτι (μή τι)
any? 1
not? 2.
†how much more? (*with* ge) 1.

MĒTIS μήτις (μή τις)
any? 1
any man? 1.

METOCHĒ μετοχή *f.*
fellowship 2.

METOCHOS μέτοχος
fellow 1
partaker 4
partner 1.

METOIKESIA μετοικεσία *f.*
carrying away into 2
the time they were carried away to 1
*they were brought to 1.

METOIKIZŌ μετοικίζω
carry away 1
remove into 1.

METŌPON μέτωπον *n.*
forehead 8.

MĒTRA μήτρα *f.*
womb 2.

MĒTRALŌAS μητραλῴας
murderer of a mother 1.

METREŌ μετρέω
measure 7
mete 3.

METRĒTĒS μετρητής
firkin 1.

METRIOPATHEŌ μετριοπαθέω
have compassion on (M. reasonably bear with) 1.

METRIŌS μετρίως *adv.*
a little 1.

METRON μέτρον *n.*
measure 13.

MIA = HEIS.

MIAINŌ μιαίνω
defile 5.

MIASMA μίασμα *n.*
pollution 1.

MIASMOS μιασμός
uncleanness 1.

MIGMA μίγμα *n.*
mixture 1.

MIGNUMI μίγνυμι
mingle 4.

MIKROS μικρός
less 1
least 2
little 10
little one 6
small 6.
As adv. a little 5
a little while 10
a while 1.
†a little while (*with* hoson) 1.

MIKROTEROS μικρότερος
least 4
less 1.

MILION μίλιον *n.*
mile 1.

MIMEOMAI μιμέομαι
follow 4.

MIMĒTĒS μιμητής
follower 7.

MIMNĒSKOMAI μιμνήσκομαι
MID. (PASS.) be had in remembrance 1
be mindful of 3
come in remembrance 1
remember 17.

MISEŌ μισέω
hate 40.
Pass. pt. hateful 1.

MISTHAPODOSIA μισθαποδοσία *f.*
recompense of reward 3.

MISTHAPODOTĒS μισθαποδότης
rewarder 1.

MISTHIOS μίσθιος
hired servant 2.

MISTHŌMA μίσθωμα *n.*
hired house 1.

MISTHOŌ μισθόω
MID. hire 2.

MISTHOS μισθός
hire 3
reward 24
wages 2.

MISTHŌTOS μισθωτός
hired servant 1
hireling 3.

MNA μνᾶ *f.*
pound 9.

MNEIA μνεία *f.*
mention 4
remembrance 3 (M. mention) 1.

MNĒMA μνῆμα *n.*
grave 1
sepulchre 4
tomb 2.

MNĒMĒ μνήμη *f.*
remembrance 1.
†*See* poieō.

MNĒMEION μνημεῖον *n.*
grave 8
sepulchre 29
tomb 5.

MNĒMONEUŌ μνημονεύω
be mindful of 1
*make mention (M. remember) 1
remember 19.

MNĒMOSUNON μνημόσυνον *n.*
memorial 3.

MNĒSTEUŌ μνηστεύω
PASS. be espoused 3.

MOCHTHOS μόχθος
painfulness 1
travail 2.

MODIOS μόδιος
bushel 3.

MOGILALOS μογιλάλος
having an impediment in one's speech 1.

MOGIS μόγις
hardly 1.

MOI μοί (*dat. of* EGŌ)
me, etc.

MOICHALIS μοιχαλίς *f.*
adulteress 3
adulterous 3
adultery (M. adulteress) 1.

MOICHAŌ μοιχάω
MID. commit adultery 6.

MOICHEIA μοιχεία *f.*
adultery 4.

MOICHEUŌ μοιχεύω
commit adultery 12
commit adultery with 1.
MID. *pt.* in adultery 1.

MOICHOS μοιχός
adulterer 4.

MOLIS μόλις
hardly 1
scarce 2
scarcely 2.
†*See* ischuō.

MŌLŌPS μώλωψ
stripes 1.

MOLUNŌ μολύνω
defile 3.

MOLUSMOS μολυσμός
filthiness 1.

MŌMAOMAI μωμάομαι (μωμέομαι)
blame 2.

MŌMOS μῶμος
blemish 1.

MOMPHĒ μομφή *f.*
quarrel (M. complaint) 1.

MONĒ μονή *f.*
abode 1
mansion 1.

MONOGENĒS μονογενής
only 2
Only begotten 5
only begotten son 1
only child 1.

MONOŌ μονόω
Pass. pt. desolate 1.

MONOPHTHALMOS μονόφθαλμος
with one eye 2.

MONOS μόνος
alone 21
by one's self 2
only 24.
As adv. alone 3
but 1
only 62.

MŌRAINŌ μωραίνω
make foolish 1.
PASS. become a fool 1
lose savour 2.

MŌRIA μωρία *f.*
foolishness 5.

MŌROLOGIA μωρολογία *f.*
foolish talking 1.

MŌROS μωρός
foolish 6.
As noun fool 5
foolishness 1
foolish thing 1.

MORPHĒ μορφή *f.*
form 3.

MORPHOŌ μορφόω
form 1.

MORPHŌSIS μόρφωσις *f.*
form 2.

MOSCHOPOIEŌ μοσχοποιέω
make a calf 1.

MOSCHOS μόσχος
calf 6.

MOU μοῦ (*gen. of* EGO).
mine
my, etc.

MOUSIKOS μουσικός
musician 1.

MUELOS μυελός
marrow 1.

MUEŌ μυέω
instruct 1.

MUKAOMAI μυκάομαι
roar 1.

MUKTĒRIZŌ μυκτηρίζω
mock 1.

MULIKOS μυλικός
mill (*adj.*) 1.

MULŌN μύλων
mill 1.

MULOS μύλος
millstone 2.
†*With* onikos: millstone 2.

MUŌPAZŌ μυωπάζω
can not see afar off 1.

* Inexact translations, *e.g.*, of a noun by a verb or adjective, of an active by a passive.
† Cases where two or more words in the original are translated by one word or by a phrase.

MURIAS μυριάς *f.*
ten thousand 1.
Plur. an innumerable company 1
an innumerable multitude 1
ten thousand 1
ten thousand times 1
thousands 1.
†*Repeated*: hundred thousand thousand 1. *See* pente.

MURIOI μύριοι (μυρίοι)
ten thousand 3.

MURIZŌ μυρίζω
anoint 1.

MURON μύρον *n.*
ointment 14.

MUSTĒRION μυστήριον *n.*
mystery 27.

MUTHOS μῦθος
fable 5.

N

NAI ναί
even so 5
surely 1
truth 1
verily 1
yea 23
yes 3.

NAOS ναός
temple 45
shrine 1.

NARDOS νάρδος *f.*
†*With* pistikos: spikenard 2 (M. pure nard *or* liquid nard 1).

NAUAGEŌ ναυαγέω
make shipwreck 1
suffer shipwreck 1.

NAUKLĒROS ναύκληρος
owner of a ship 1.

NAUS ναῦς *f.*
ship 1.

NAUTĒS ναύτης
sailor 1
shipman 2.

NĒ νή
*I protest by 1.

NEANIAS νεανίας
young man 5.

NEANISKOS νεανίσκος
young man 10.

NEKROŌ νεκρόω
mortify 1.
Pass. pt. dead 2.

NEKROS νεκρός
dead 21.
As noun dead 105
dead man 3
he that is dead 2
one dead 1
*be dead 1.

NEKRŌSIS νέκρωσις *f.*
deadness 1
dying 1.

NEŌKOROS νεωκόρος
worshipper (M. temple-keeper) 1.

NEOPHUTOS νεόφυτος
novice (M. one newly come to the faith) 1.

NEOS νέος
new 11.
As noun new man 1
young woman 1.
[*See* neōteros].

NEOSSOS νεοσσός
young 1.

NEŌTERIKOS νεωτερικός
youthful 1.

NEŌTEROS νεώτερος
young 1
younger 7.
As noun young man 2
younger man 1.

NEOTĒS νεότης *f.*
youth 5.

NĒPHALIOS νηφάλιος (νηφάλεος)
sober 2 (M. vigilant 1)
vigilant 1.

NEPHELĒ νεφέλη *f.*
cloud 26.

NĒPHŌ νήφω
be sober 3
watch 2.
Partic. sober 1.

NEPHOS νέφος
cloud 1.

NEPHROS νεφρός
reins (*pl.*) 1.

NĒPIAZŌ νηπιάζω
be a child 1.

NĒPIOS νήπιος
babe 6
child 7
*childish 1.

NĒSION νησίον *n.*
island 1.

NĒSOS νῆσος *f.*
island 6
isle 3.

NĒSTEIA νηστεία *f.*
fast 1
fasting 7.

NĒSTEUŌ νηστεύω
fast 21.

NĒSTIS νῆστις
fasting 1.

NĒTHŌ νήθω
spin 2.

NEUŌ νεύω
beckon 2.

NIKAŌ νικάω
conquer 2
get the victory 1
overcome 24
prevail 1.

NIKĒ νίκη *f.*
victory 1.

NIKOS νῖκος *n.*
victory 4.

NIPTĒR νιπτήρ
basin 1.

NIPTŌ νίπτω
wash 17.

NOĒMA νόημα *n.*
device 1
mind 4
thought 1.

NOEŌ νοέω
consider 1
perceive 2
think 1
understand 10.

NOMĒ νομή *f.*
pasture 1.
†*See* echō.

NOMIKOS νομικός
about the law 1
lawyer 8.

NOMIMŌS νομίμως
lawfully 2.

NOMISMA νόμισμα *n.*
money 1.

NOMIZŌ νομίζω
think 5
suppose 9.
PASS. be wont 1.

NOMODIDASKALOS νομοδιδάσκαλος
doctor of the law 2
teacher of the law 1.

NOMOS νόμος
law 195.

NOMOTHESIA νομοθεσία *f.*
giving of the law 1.

NOMOTHETEŌ νομοθετέω
PASS. be established 1
receive the law 1.

NOMOTHETĒS νομοθέτης
lawgiver 1.

NOSĒMA νόσημα *n.*
disease 1.

NOSEŌ νοσέω
Partic. doting (M. sick) 1.

NOSOS νόσος *f.*
disease 6
infirmity 1
sickness 5.

NOSPHIZŌ νοσφίζω
MID. keep back 2
purloin 1.

NOSSIA νοσσιά *f.*
brood 1.

NOSSION νοσσίον *n.*
chicken 1.

NOTHOS νόθος
bastard 1.

NŌTHROS νωθρός
dull 1
slothful 1.

NOTOS νότος
south 4
south wind 3.

NŌTOS νῶτος
back 1.

NOUMĒNIA νουμηνία *f.*
new moon 1.

NOUNECHŌS νουνεχῶς
discreetly 1.

NOUS νοῦς
mind 15
minds 2
understanding 7.

NOUTHESIA νουθεσία *f.*
admonition 3.

NOUTHETEŌ νουθετέω
admonish 4
warn 4.

NUCHTHĒMERON νυχθήμερον *n.*
a night and a day 1.

NUMPHĒ νύμφη *f.*
bride 5
daughter-in-law 3.

NUMPHIOS νυμφίος
bridegroom 16.

NUMPHŌN νυμφών
bride-chamber 3

NUN νῦν
at this time 1
now 116
of late 1
this time 2.
†*Following artic.*: but now 1, now 4, that now is 1, this 2, this present 3; which I make now 1. apo tou nun: from henceforth 4, henceforth 1, hereafter 1.

NUNI νυνί
now 21.

NUSSŌ νύσσω
pierce 1.

NUSTAZŌ νυστάζω
slumber 2.

NUX νύξ *f.*
night 63.
†*See* mesos.

O

O [1] Ω
Omega 4.

O [2] ὦ
O 15.

OCHLEŌ ὀχλέω
vex 1.

OCHLOPOIEŌ ὀχλοποιέω
gather a company 1.

OCHLOS ὄχλος
company 7
multitude 79 (M. tumult 1)
number 1
number of people 1
people 82
press 5.

OCHURŌMA ὀχύρωμα *n.*
stronghold 1.

ŌDĒ ᾠδή *f.*
song 7.

ŌDIN ὠδίν *f.*
pain 1
travail 1
sorrow 2 (M. pain of a woman in travail) 1.

ŌDINŌ ὠδίνω
travail 1
travail in birth 1
travail in birth of 1.

ODOUS ὀδούς
tooth 11.

ODUNAŌ ὀδυνάω
MID. be tormented 2
sorrow 2.

ODUNĒ ὀδύνη *f.*
sorrow 2.

ODURMOS ὀδυρμός
mourning 2.

OGDOĒKONTA ὀγδοήκοντα
fourscore 2.

OGDOOS ὄγδοος
eighth 5.

OGKOS ὄγκος
weight 1.

OIDA οἶδα. *See* EIDON.

OIKEIOS οἰκεῖος
of one's own house (M. kindred) 1
of the household 2.

OIKĒMA οἴκημα *n.*
prison 1.

OIKEŌ οἰκέω
dwell 9.

OIKĒTĒRION οἰκητήριον *n.*
habitation 1
house 1.

OIKETĒS οἰκέτης
household servant 1
servant 3.

OIKIA οἰκία *f.*
home 1
house 93
household 1.

OIKIAKOS οἰκιακός
of one's household 2.

OIKODESPOTEŌ οἰκοδεσποτέω
guide the house 1.

OIKODESPOTĒS οἰκοδεσπότης
goodman 1
goodman of the house 4
householder 4
master of the house 3.

OIKODOMĒ οἰκοδομή *f.*
building 6
edification 4
edifying 6
*edify 1.
†*See* chreia.

OIKODOMEŌ οἰκοδομέω
build 24
build up 1
edify 7
embolden (M. edify) 1.
Partic. builder 5.
PASS. be in building 1.

OIKODOMIA οἰκοδομία *f.*
edifying 1.

OIKONOMEŌ οἰκονομέω
be steward 1.

OIKONOMIA οἰκονομία *f.*
dispensation 4
stewardship 3.

OIKONOMOS οἰκονόμος
chamberlain 1
governor 1
steward 8.

OIKOS οἶκος
home 4
house 102 (M. home 1)
household 3
temple 1.
†*See* idios.

OIKOUMENĒ οἰκουμένη *f.*
earth 1
world 14.

OIKOUROS οἰκουρός
keeper at home 1.

OIKTEIRŌ οἰκτείρω
have compassion on 2.

OIKTIRMŌN οἰκτίρμων
merciful 2
of tender mercy 1.

OIKTIRMOS οἰκτιρμός
mercy 5.

OINOPHLUGIA οἰνοφλυγία *f.*
excess of wine 1.

OINOPOTĒS οἰνοπότης
wine-bibber 2.

OINOS οἶνος
wine 32
*wine (*adj.*) 1.

OIOMAI οἴομαι
think 1
suppose 1.

OKNEŌ ὀκνέω
delay (M. be grieved) 1.

OKNĒROS ὀκνηρός
grievous 1
slothful 2.

OKTAĒMEROS ὀκταήμερος
the eighth day 1.

OKTŌ ὀκτώ
eight 6.

OLETHROS ὄλεθρος
destruction 4.

OLIGOPISTOS ὀλιγόπιστος
of little faith 5.

OLIGOPSUCHOS ὀλιγόψυχος
feeble-minded 1.

OLIGŌREŌ ὀλιγωρέω
despise 1.

OLIGOS ὀλίγος
few words (M. a little) 1
little 4
little time 2
short 1
small 5.
As. adv. a little 2
a short space 1
a while 1
for a season 1
little 1.
Plur. a few things 4
few 14
few stripes 1.
†almost (en *with dat.*) 2; briefly (dia *with gen. pl.*) 1; little (pros *with acc.*; M. for a little time) 1; long (ouk oligon) 1.

OLOLUZŌ ὀλολύζω
howl 1.

OLOTHREUŌ ὀλοθρεύω
destroy 1.

OLOTHREUTĒS ὀλοθρευτής
destroyer 1.

OLUNTHOS ὄλυνθος
untimely fig (M. green fig) 1

OMBROS ὄμβρος
shower 1.

OMMA ὄμμα
eye 1.

OMNUMI ὄμνυμι
swear 27.

ŌMOS ὦμος
shoulder 2.

ONAR ὄναρ *n.*
dream 6.

ONARION ὀνάριον *n.*
young ass 1.

ONEIDISMOS ὀνειδισμός
reproach 5.

ONEIDIZŌ ὀνειδίζω
cast in one's teeth 1
reproach 3
revile 2
upbraid 3.
PASS. suffer reproach 1.

ONEIDOS ὄνειδος
reproach 1.

ŌNEOMAI ὠνέομαι
buy 1.

ONIKOS ὀνικός
†*See* mulos.

ONINĒMI ὀνίνημι
MID. have joy 1.

ONOMA ὄνομα *n.*
name 193
*called (*dat.*) 3
*named (*dat.*) 24.
†*With dat. of rel. or* autos: named 4, called 1, named (to onoma), 1.

ONOMAZŌ ὀνομάζω
call 2
name 8.

ONOS ὄνος
ass 6.

ONTŌS ὄντως
certainly 1
clean 1
indeed 6
of a truth 1
verily 1.

ŌON ᾠόν *n.*
egg 1.

OPĒ ὀπή *f.*
cave 1
place (M. hole) 1.

OPHEILĒ ὀφειλή *f.*
debt 1
due 1.

OPHEILĒMA ὀφείλημα *n.*
debt 2.

OPHEILETĒS ὀφειλέτης
debtor 5
sinner (M. debtor) 1
which oweth 1.

OPHEILŌ ὀφείλω
be bound 2
be a debtor 1
be guilty (M. be a debtor *or* bound) 1
be indebted 1
must needs 1
ought 15
owe 7
should 1
*behove 1
*be one's duty 2.
PASS. be due 1.
Partic. debt 1
due 1.
†need require (*with* ginomai) 1.

ŌPHELEIA ὠφέλεια *f.*
advantage 1
profit 1.

ŌPHELEŌ ὠφελέω
prevail 2
profit 7.
MID. (PASS.) be advantaged 1
be bettered 1
be profited 3
profit 1.

* Inexact translations, *e.g.*, of a noun by a verb or adjective, of an active by a passive.
† Cases where two or more words in the original are translated by one word or by a phrase

ŌPHELIMOS ὠφέλιμος
profitable 3.
†*See* eimi.

OPHELON ὄφελον
I would 2
I would to God 1
would to God 1.

OPHELOS ὄφελος *n.*
*it advantageth 1
*it profiteth 2.

OPHIS ὄφις
serpent 14.

OPHRUS ὀφρύς *f.*
brow (M. edge) 1.

OPHTHALMODOULEIA ὀφθαλμοδουλεία *f.*
eye-service 2.

OPHTHALMOS ὀφθαλμός
eye 100
sight (*pl.*) 1.

OPISŌ ὀπίσω
after 22
back 1
behind 5
*which are behind 1.
†back (eis ta opisō) 5; backward (eis ta opisō) 1.

OPISTHEN ὄπισθεν
after 2
behind 4
on the backside 1.

OPŌRA ὀπώρα *f.*
fruits 1.

OPSARION ὀψάριον *n.*
fish 4
small fish 1.

OPSE ὀψέ
at even 1
in the end 1
*even 1.

OPSIMOS ὄψιμος
latter 1.

OPSIOS ὄψιος
even (*adj.*) 1.
As noun even 8
evening 3.
†*With partic. of* ginomai *or* eimi; at evening 1, at even 1, in the evening 1.

OPSIS ὄψις *f.*
appearance 1
countenance 1
face 1.

OPSŌNION ὀψώνιον *n.*
charges 1
wages 3 (M. allowance 1).

OPTANŌ ὀπτάνω
see 1.

OPTASIA ὀπτασία *f.*
vision 4.

OPTOS ὀπτός
broiled 1.

ORCHEŌ ὀρχέω
MID. dance 4.

OREGŌ ὀρέγω
MID. covet after 1
desire 2.

OREINOS ὀρεινός
hill (*adj.*) 2.

OREXIS ὄρεξις *f.*
lust 1.

ORGĒ ὀργή *f.*
anger 3
indignation 1
vengeance 1
wrath 31.

ORGILOS ὀργίλος
soon angry 1.

ORGIZŌ ὀργίζω
MID be angry 5
be wroth 3.

ORGUIA ὀργυιά *f.*
fathom 2.

ORNEON ὄρνεον *n.*
bird 1
fowl 2.

ORNIS ὄρνις
hen 2.

OROS ὄρος *n.*
hill 3
mount 21
mountain 41.

ORPHANOS ὀρφανός
comfortless (M. orphan) 1.
fatherless 1.

ORTHOPODEŌ ὀρθοποδέω
walk uprightly 1.

ORTHOS ὀρθός
straight (M. even) 1
upright 1.

ORTHŌS ὀρθῶς
plain 1
right 1
rightly 2.

ORTHOTOMEŌ ὀρθοτομέω
divide rightly 1.

ORTHRINOS ὀρθρινός
morning (*adj.*) 1.

ORTHRIOS ὄρθριος
early 1.

ORTHRIZŌ ὀρθρίζω
come early in the morning 1.

ORTHROS ὄρθρος
early in the morning (*gen.*) 1.
†early in the morning (hupo *with acc.*) 1. *See* bathus.

ŌRUOMAI ὠρύομαι
roar 1.

ORUSSŌ ὀρύσσω
dig 3.

OSMĒ ὀσμή *f.*
odour 2
savour 4.

OSPHRĒSIS ὄσφρησις *f.*
smelling 1.

OSPHUS ὀσφύς *f.*
loins 8.

OSTEON ὀστέον *n.*
bone 5.

OSTRAKINOS ὀστράκινος
earthen 1
of earth 1.

OTHONĒ ὀθόνη *f.*
sheet 2.

OTHONION ὀθόνιον *n.*
linen cloth 5.

ŌTION ὠτίον *n.*
ear 5.

OU οὐ (οὐκ, οὐχ)
at all 3
nay 11
no 8
not 1270.
†*With another word such as* tis *often translated by one English word, e.g.,* no, nothing, never, neither. *With* mē (ou mē) *rendered* not; by no means, in no wise, etc.

OUA οὐά
ah 1.

OUAI οὐαί
alas 6
woe 41.

OUCH=**OU.**

OUCHI οὐχί
nay 5
not 50
not so 1.

OUDAMŌS οὐδαμῶς
not 1.

OUDE οὐδέ
also not 1
even not 2
neither 68
neither indeed 1
never 1
no nor 1
no not 8
nor 31
nor yet 1
not 10
not so much as 3
etc.

OUDEIS οὐδείς
any (*with neg.*) 3
any man (*with neg.*) 3
aught (*with neg.*) 1
no 20
no man 95
none 26
not any 1
nothing 67
nought 1, etc.
†never man (*with gen. pl. of* anthrōpos) 1.

OUDEPŌ οὐδέπω
as yet . . . not 1
never before 1
never yet 1
not yet 1
yet (*with neg.*) 1.

OUDEPOTE οὐδέποτε
neither at any time 1
never 13
yet never 1.
†nothing at any time (*with* pas) 1.

OUK=**OU.**

OUKETI οὐκέτι
after that (*with neg.*) 2
any more (*with neg.*) 4
henceforth not 1
hereafter . . . not 1
no longer 1
no more 28
not as yet 1
not now 1
now . . . not 3
yet (*with neg.*) 1
yet not 1.
†no more at all (ou mē ouketi) 1.

OUKOUN οὐκοῦν
then? 1.

OUN οὖν
and 5
but 4
now 7
now then 1
so 11
then 192
therefore 245
wherefore 7.
†Men oun: and 6, and so 1, but 1, now 3, so 3, so then 1, then 5, therefore 11, truly 1, verily 1, wherefore 1.

OUPŌ οὔπω
as yet (*with neg.*) 1
hitherto. . . not 2
no . . . as yet 1
not yet 20.

OURA οὐρά
tail 4.

OURANIOS οὐράνιος
heavenly 6.

OURANOS οὐρανός
air 10
heaven 268 (M. heavens 1)
sky 5.
†heavenly (ek *with gen.*) 1.

OURANOTHEN οὐρανόθεν
from heaven 2.

OUS οὖς *n.*
ear 37

OUSIA οὐσία *f.*
goods 1
substance 1.

OUTE οὔτε
neither 46
no not 1
nor 39
nor yet 5
not 1
yet not 1
*none 1.
†neither (all' oute) 1; nothing to draw with (*with* antlēma) 1.

OUTHEN οὐθέν
nothing 1.

OXOS ὄξος *n.*
vinegar 7.

OXUS ὀξύς
sharp 7
swift 1.

OZŌ ὄζω
stink 1.

P

PACHUNŌ παχύνω
PASS. wax gross 2.

PAGIDEUŌ παγιδεύω
entangle 1.

PAGIS παγίς *f.*
snare 5.

PAGOS. *See* **AREIOS.**

PAIDAGŌGOS παιδαγωγός
instructor 1
schoolmaster 2.

PAIDARION παιδάριον *n.*
child 1
lad 1.

PAIDEIA παιδεία
chastening 3
chastisement 1
instruction 1
nurture 1.

PAIDEUŌ παιδεύω
chasten 6
chastise 2
instruct 1
teach 2.
PASS. be learned 1
learn 1.

PAIDEUTĒS παιδευτής
instructor 1
which correcteth 1.

PAIDION παιδίον *n.*
child 25 (M. sir 1)
damsel 4
little child 12
young child 10.

PAIDIOTHEN παιδιόθεν
of a child 1.

PAIDISKĒ παιδίσκη *f.*
bondmaid 1
bondwoman 4
damsel 4
maid 3
maiden 1.

PAIŌ παίω
smite 4
strike 1.

PAIS παῖς
child 7
maid 1
maiden 1
manservant 1
servant 10
son 1
Son 2
young man 1.

PAIZŌ παίζω
play 1.

PALAI πάλαι
a great while ago 1
any while 1
in time past 1
long ago 1
of old 1
old 1.

PALAIOŌ παλαιόω
make old 1.
PASS. decay 1
wax old 2.

PALAIOS παλαιός
old 17
*old wine 1.
As noun old things 1.

PALAIOTĒS παλαιότης *f.*
oldness 1.

PALĒ πάλη *f.*
*wrestle 1.

PALIGGENESIA παλιγγενεσία *f.*
regeneration 2.

PALIN πάλιν
again 140 (M. back 1)
†again (eis to palin 1, *with* anōthen 1) 2.

PAMPLĒTHEI παμπληθεί
all at once 1.

PAMPOLUS πάμπολυς
very great 1.

PANDOCHEION πανδοχεῖον *n.*
inn 1.

PANDOCHEUS πανδοχεύς
host 1.

PANĒGURIS πανήγυρις *f.*
general assembly 1.

PANOIKI πανοικί
with all one's house 1.

PANOPLIA πανοπλία *f.*
all . . . armour 1
whole armour 2.

PANOURGIA πανουργία *f.*
craftiness 3
cunning craftiness 1
subtilty 1.

PANOURGOS πανοῦργος
crafty 1.

PANTACHOTHEN πανταχόθεν
from every quarter 1.

PANTACHOU πανταχοῦ
everywhere 6
in all places 1.

PANTELĒS παντελής
†to the uttermost (eis to p.; M. evermore) 1; in no wise (mē eis to p.) 1.

PANTĒ πάντη
always 1.

PANTOKRATŌR παντοκράτωρ
Almighty 9
omnipotent 1.

PANTŌS πάντως
altogether 2
at all 1
by all means 2
no doubt 1
surely 1.
†in no wise (ou pantōs) 1.

PANTOTE πάντοτε
alway 5
always 29
ever 6
evermore 2.

PANTOTHEN πάντοθεν
on every side 1
round about 1.

PARA παρά
Gen. from 24
of 50
out of 1, etc.
Acc. above 4
against 2
at 12
by 5
by . . . side 15
contrary to 3
more than 2
nigh unto 2
past 1
save 1
than 11 (M. to 1), etc.
†therefore (*with* touto) 2.
Dat. among 3
before 3
by 3
in the sight of 1
of 2 (M. with 1)
with 42, etc.

PARABAINŌ παραβαίνω
fall by transgression 1
transgress 3.

PARABALLŌ παραβάλλω
arrive 1
compare 1.

PARABASIS παράβασις *f.*
breaking 1
transgression 6.

PARABATĒS παραβάτης
breaker 1
transgressor 3
who doth transgress 1.

PARABIAZOMAI παραβιάζομαι
constrain 2.

PARABOLĒ παραβολή *f.*
comparison 1
figure 2
parable 46
proverb 1.

PARABOULEUOMAI παραβουλεύομαι
regard not 1.

PARACHEIMASIA παραχειμασία *f.*
†to winter in (pros *with acc.*) 1.

PARACHEIMAZŌ παραχειμάζω
winter (*vb.*) 4.

PARACHRĒMA παραχρῆμα
forthwith 1
immediately 13
presently 1
soon 1
straightway 3.

PARADECHOMAI παραδέχομαι
receive 5.

PARADEIGMATIZŌ παραδειγματίζω
make a public example 1
put to an open shame 1.

PARADEISOS παράδεισος
paradise 3.

PARADIATRIBĒ παραδιατριβή *f.*
perverse disputings (M. gallings one of another) (*pl.*) 1.

PARADIDŌMI παραδίδωμι
be brought forth (M. be ripe) 1
betray 40
cast into prison (M. deliver up) 1
commit 1
deliver 54
deliver up 9
give 4
give over 2
give up 4
hazard 1
put in prison 1
recommend 2.
MID. commit one's self (M. commit one's cause) 1.

PARADOSIS παράδοσις *f.*
ordinance (M. tradition) 1.
tradition 12.

PARADOXOS παράδοξος *n.*
strange thing 1.

PARAGGELIA παραγγελία *f.*
charge 2
commandment 2
*straitly (*dat.*) 1.

* Inexact translations, *e.g.*, of a noun by a verb or adjective, of an active by a passive.
† Cases where two or more words in the original are translated by one word or by a phrase.

PARAGGELLŌ παραγγέλλω
charge 6
command 20
declare 1
give charge 1
give commandment 1
give in charge 1.

PARAGINOMAI παραγίνομαι
be present 1
come 34
come thither 1
go 1.

PARAGŌ παράγω
depart 1
pass away 1
pass by 5
pass forth 1.
MID. pass 1
pass away 1.

PARAINEŌ παραινέω
admonish 1
exhort 1.

PARAITEOMAI παραιτέομαι
MID. avoid 1
entreat 1
make excuse 1
refuse 5
reject 1.
PASS. be excused 2.

PARAKALEŌ παρακαλέω
beseech 43
call for 1
comfort 23 (M. exhort 1)
desire 8
entreat 3
exhort 19 (M. beseech 1, desire 1)
exhort one another 1
give exhortation 1
pray 6.
Partic. in his exhortation.
PASS. be of good comfort 1.

PARAKALUPTŌ παρακαλύπτω
hide 1.

PARAKATATHĒKĒ παρακαταθήκη *f.*
thing which is committed unto one 1
which is committed to one's trust 1.

PARAKATHIZŌ παρακαθίζω
†sit at (*with* para) 1.

PARAKEIMAI παράκειμαι
be present with 2.

PARAKLĒSIS παράκλησις *f.*
comfort 6
consolation 14
entreaty 1
exhortation 8.

PARAKLĒTOS παράκλητος
advocate 1
Comforter 4.

PARAKOĒ παρακοή *f.*
disobedience 3.

PARAKOLOUTHEŌ παρακολουθέω
attain 1
follow 1
have perfect understanding of 1
know fully (M. be a diligent follower of) 1.

PARAKOUŌ παρακούω
neglect to hear 2.

PARAKUPTŌ παρακύπτω
stoop down 3.
†*With* eis: look into 2.

PARALAMBANŌ παραλαμβάνω
receive 15
take 32
take unto 2
take with 1.

PARALEGŌ παραλέγω
MID. pass 1
sail by 1.

PARALIOS παράλιος
sea coast 1.

PARALLAGĒ παραλλαγή *f.*
variableness 1.

PARALOGIZOMAI παραλογίζομαι
beguile 1
deceive 1.

PARALUŌ παραλύω
Pass. pt. feeble 1
sick of the palsy 2.
taken with a palsy 2.

PARALUTIKOS παραλυτικός
sick of the palsy 9
that hath the palsy 1.

PARAMENŌ παραμένω
abide 1
continue 2.

PARAMUTHEOMAI παραμυθέομαι
comfort (*vb.*) 4.

PARAMUTHIA παραμυθία *f.*
comfort 1.

PARAMUTHION παραμύθιον *n.*
comfort 1.

PARANOMEŌ παρανομέω
be contrary to the law 1.

PARANOMIA παρανομία *f.*
iniquity 1.

PARAPHERŌ παραφέρω
remove 1
take away 1.

PARAPHRONEŌ παραφρονέω
be as a fool 1.

PARAPHRONIA παραφρονία *f.*
madness 1.

PARAPIKRAINŌ παραπικραίνω
provoke 1.

PARAPIKRASMOS παραπικρασμός
provocation 2.

PARAPIPTŌ παραπίπτω
fall away 1.

PARAPLEŌ παραπλέω
sail by 1.

PARAPLĒSION παραπλήσιον
nigh unto 1.

PARAPLĒSIŌS παραπλησίως
likewise 1.

PARAPOREUOMAI παραπορεύομαι
go 1
pass 1
pass by 3.

PARAPTŌMA παράπτωμα *n.*
fall 2
fault 2
offence 7
sin 3
trespass 9.

PARARRHEŌ παραρρέω
let slip (M. run out, as leaking vessels) 1

PARASĒMOS παράσημος
whose sign was 1.

PARASKEUAZŌ παρασκευάζω
make ready 1.
MID. be ready 1
prepare one's self 1.
Partic. ready 1.

PARASKEUĒ παρασκευή *f.*
preparation 6.

PARATEINŌ παρατείνω
continue 1.

PARATĒREŌ παρατηρέω
observe 1
watch 5.

PARATĒRĒSIS παρατήρησις *f.*
observation (M. outward show) 1.

PARATHALASSIOS παραθαλάσσιος
which is upon the sea coast 1.

PARATHĒKĒ παραθήκη *f.*
*which I have committed 1.

PARATHEŌREŌ παραθεωρέω
neglect 1.

PARATITHĒMI παρατίθημι
allege 1
put forth 2
set before 8.
Pass. pt. such things as are set before 1.
MID. commend 3
commit 3
commit the keeping of 1.

PARATUGCHANŌ παρατυγχάνω
meet with 1.

PARAUTIKA παραυτίκα
but for a moment 1.

PARAZĒLOŌ παραζηλόω
provoke to emulation 1
provoke to jealousy 3.

PARDALIS πάρδαλις *f.*
leopard 1.

PARECHŌ παρέχω
bring 1
do for 1
give 2 (M. offer 1)
keep 1
minister 1
offer 1
shew 1.
MID. bring 1
give 1
shew 1.
†ACT. trouble (*with pl. of* kopos) 5.

PARĒGORIA παρηγορία *f.*
comfort 1.

PAREIMI πάρειμι
be here 1
be here present 1
be present 9
come 10.
Partic. present 3
such things as ye have 1.
†lack (mē p. *and dat.*) 1.

PAREISAGŌ παρεισάγω
bring in privily 1.

PAREISAKTOS παρείσακτος
brought in unawares 1.

PAREISDUNŌ παρεισδύνω
creep in unawares 1.

PAREISERCHOMAI παρεισέρχομαι
come in privily 1
enter 1.

PAREISPHERŌ παρεισφέρω
give 1.

PAREKTOS παρεκτός
except 1
saving 1
*that are without 1.

PAREMBOLĒ παρεμβολή *f.*
army 1
camp 3
castle 6.

PARENOCHLEŌ παρενοχλέω
trouble 1.

PAREPIDĒMOS παρεπίδημος
pilgrim 2
stranger 1.

PARERCHOMAI παρέρχομαι
come 1
come forth 1
go 1
pass 10
pass away 12
pass by 3
pass over 1
transgress 1.
Partic. past 1.

PARESIS πάρεσις *f.*
remission (M. passing over) 1.

PARIĒMI παρίημι
PASS. hang down 1.

PARISTANŌ παριστάνω
yield 2.

PARISTĒMI παρίστημι
Trans. (*pres.*, 1 *aor.*, *fut.*)
commend 1
give presently 1
present 9
prove 1
provide 1
shew 2
yield 3.
Intrans. (*pf.*, *plupf.*, 2 *aor.*, *and mid.*)
assist 1
be brought before 1
come 1
stand 2
stand before (*mid.*) 1
stand by 12
stand here 1
stand up 1
stand with 1.

PARODOS πάροδος *f.*
way 1.

PAROICHOMAI παροίχομαι
be past 1.

PAROIKEŌ παροικέω
be a stranger 1
sojourn 1.

PAROIKIA παροικία *f.*
sojourning here 1
*dwell as strangers 1.

PAROIKOS πάροικος
foreigner 1
stranger 2.
†*See* eimi.

PAROIMIA παροιμία *f.*
parable 1
proverb 4 (M. parable) 1.

PAROINOS πάροινος
given to wine 2 (M. ready to quarrel and offer wrong, as one in wine) 1.

PAROMOIAZŌ παρομοιάζω
be like unto 1.

PAROMOIOS παρόμοιος
As noun like things 2.

PAROPSIS παροψίς *f.*
platter 2.

PARORGISMOS παροργισμός
wrath 1.

PARORGIZŌ παροργίζω
anger 1
provoke to wrath 1.

PAROTRUNŌ παροτρύνω
stir up 1.

PAROUSIA παρουσία *f.*
coming 22
presence 2.

PAROXUNŌ παροξύνω
MID. (PASS.) be easily provoked 1
be stirred 1.

PAROXUSMOS παροξυσμός
contention 1.
†*With* eis: provoke unto 1.

PARRHĒSIA παρρησία
boldness 8 (M. liberty 1)
boldness of speech 1
confidence 6
plainness (M. boldness) of speech 1.
Dat. boldly 1
openly 4
plainly 4.
†boldly (en *with dat.* 1, meta *with gen.* 1) 2; freely (meta *with gen.*) 1; openly (en *with dat.*) 1. *See* echō.

PARRHĒSIAZOMAI παρρησιάζομαι
be bold 1
preach boldly 1
speak boldly 4
wax bold 1.
Partic. boldly 1
freely 1.

PARTHENIA παρθενία *f.*
virginity 1.

PARTHENOS παρθένος
virgin 14.

PAS πᾶς
all 195
all manner 2
all manner of 10
all things 4
any 7
any one 1
any thing 2
every 113
every branch 1
every man 10
every one 24
everything 6
whatsoever 6
whatsoever thing 1
whole 12
whosoever 30.
Plur. all 541 (M. all things 1)
all manner of 1
all men 36
all points 1
all quarters 1
all they 1
all things 150 (M. all 1)
as many as 1
every 1
every man 1
every one 3
every one of you 1
every thing 1.
†En *with dat.*: on every side 2, every where 1, throughly 1. *With* hos *or* hostis: as many as 1, every 1, every one 1, whosoever 5, whatsoever 1. *Pl. with* hos *or* nosos: all 13, all things 17. Alway (*with* hēmera) 1; no (ou pas 10, mē pas 2) 12; nothing (ou pan rhēma) 1.

PASCHA πάσχα *n.*
Easter 1
passover 28.

PASCHŌ πάσχω
be vexed 1
feel 1
suffer 39.
Infin. passion 1.

PATASSŌ πατάσσω
smite 9
strike 1.

PATEŌ πατέω
tread 3
tread down 1
tread under foot 1.

PATĒR πατήρ
father 151
Father 265
parent 1.

PATHĒMA πάθημα *n.*
affection (M. passion) 1
affliction 3
motion (M. passion) 1
suffering 11.

PATHĒTOS παθητός
*should suffer 1.

PATHOS πάθος *n.*
affection 1
inordinate affection 1
lust 1.

PATRALŌAS πατραλῴας
murderer of a father 1.

PATRIA πατριά *f.*
family 1
kindred 1
lineage 1.

PATRIARCHĒS πατριάρχης
patriarch 4.

PATRIKOS πατρικός
of my fathers 1.

PATRIS πατρίς *f.*
country 3
one's own country 5.

PATRŌOS πατρῷος
of my fathers 1
of our fathers 1
of the fathers 1.

PATROPARADOTOS πατροπαράδοτος
received by tradition from your fathers 1.

PAUŌ παύω
MID. cease 12
leave 2
refrain 1.

PĒCHUS πῆχυς
cubit 4.

PĒDALION πηδάλιον *n.*
helm 1
rudder 1.

* Inexact translations, *e.g.*, of a noun by a verb or adjective, of an active by a passive.
† Cases where two or more words in the original are translated by one word or by a phrase.

PEDĒ πέδη *f.*
fetter 3.

PEDINOS πεδινός
†plain (*with* topos) 1.

PĒGANON πήγανον *n.*
rue 1.

PĒGĒ πηγή *f.*
fountain 8
well 4.

PĒGNUMI πήγνυμι
pitch 1.

PEINAŌ πεινάω
be an hungered 9
be hungry 3
hunger 10.
Partic. hungry 1.

PEIRA πεῖρα *f.*
trial 1.
†*See* lambanō.

PEIRAŌ πειράω
assay 1
go about 1.

PEIRASMOS πειρασμός
temptation 19
temptations 1.
†which is to try (pros *with acc.*) 1.

PEIRAZŌ πειράζω
assay 1
examine 1
go about 1
prove 1
tempt 29
try 4.
Partic. tempter 1.

PEISMONĒ πεισμονή *f.*
persuasion 1.

PEITHARCHEŌ πειθαρχέω
hearken unto 1
obey 2
obey a magistrate 1.

PEITHŌ πείθω
assure (M. persuade) 1
be confident 2
have confidence 6
have whereof one might trust 1
make one's friend 1
persuade 10
put one's trust 1
trust 8
wax confident 1.
MID. (PASS.) agree to 1
believe 3
be persuaded 11
obey 7 (M. believe 1)
yield unto 1.

PEITHOS πειθός
enticing (M. persuasible) 1.

PELAGOS πέλαγος *n.*
depth 1
sea 1.

PELEKIZŌ πελεκίζω
behead 1.

PĒLIKOS πηλίκος
how great 1
how large 1.

PĒLOS πηλός
clay 6.

PEMPŌ πέμπω
send 79
thrust in 2.

PEMPTOS πέμπτος
fifth 4.

PENĒS πένης
poor 1.

PENICHROS πενιχρός
poor 1.

PENTAKIS πεντάκις
five times 1.

PENTAKISCHILIOI πεντακισχίλιοι
five thousand 6.

PENTAKOSIOI πεντακόσιοι
five hundred 2.

PENTE πέντε
five 36.
†fifty thousand (*with pl. of* murias) 1.

PENTEKAIDEKATOS πεντεκαιδέκατος
fifteenth 1.

PENTĒKONTA πεντήκοντα
fifty 5.

PENTĒKOSTĒ πεντηκοστή *f.*
Pentecost 3.

PENTHEŌ πενθέω
bewail 1
mourn 7
wail 2.

PENTHERA πενθερά *f.*
mother-in-law 3
wife's mother 3.

PENTHEROS πενθερός
father-in-law 1.

PENTHOS πένθος *n.*
mourning 2
sorrow 3.

PEPOITHESIS πεποίθησις *f.*
confidence 5
trust 1.

PER περ
[*Particle attached to other words for emphasis. See* ean, epei, kai, etc.]

PERA πήρα *f.*
scrip 6.

PERAN πέραν
beyond 7
on the other side of 2
over 2.
As noun farther side 1
other side 10 (M. over 1).

PERAS πέρας *n.*
end 2
utmost part 1
uttermost part 1.

PERI περί
Gen. about 6
above 1
against 2
as concerning 2
as touching 8
at 3
concerning 35
for 59 (M. by a sacrifice for 1)
for . . . sake 1
for the sins of 1
of 145
on 2
on behalf 1
over 2
pertaining to 1
touching 3
with 1
*which concern 1, etc.
Acc. about 25
concerning 4
in 1
of 1
with 1, etc.

PERIAGŌ περιάγω
compass 1
go about 3
go round about 1
lead about 1.

PERIAIREŌ περιαιρέω
take away 3
take up (M. cut) 1.

PERIASTRAPTŌ περιαστράπτω
shine round 1
shine round about 1.

PERIBALLŌ περιβάλλω
array in 1
cast about 1
clothe 3
put on 1.
MID. (PASS.) be arrayed 3
be arrayed in 2
be clothed 11 (in 3, with 5)
cast about 1
have . . . cast about 1.

PERIBLEPŌ περιβλέπω
MID. look about on 1
look round about 3
look round about on 1
look round about upon 2.

PERIBOLAION περιβόλαιον *n.*
covering (M. veil) 1
vesture 1.

PERICHŌROS περίχωρος
country about 1
country round about 3
region round about 5
region that lieth round about 1.

PERIDEŌ περιδέω
bind about 1.

PERIECHŌ περιέχω
*be contained 1.
Partic. *after 1.
†*See* thambos.

PERIERCHOMAI περιέρχομαι
fetch a compass 1
wander about 1.
Partic. vagabond 1.
†wandering about from house to house (*with pl. of* oikia) 1.

PERIERGAZOMAI περιεργάζομαι
be a busy body 1.

PERIERGOS περίεργος
As noun busy body 1
curious arts (*pl.*) 1.

PERIISTĒMI περιΐστημι
stand by 1
stand round about 1.
MID avoid 1
shun 1.

PERIKALUPTŌ περικαλύπτω
blindfold 1
cover 1
overlay 1.

PERIKATHARMA περικάθαρμα *n.*
filth 1.

PERIKEIMAI περίκειμαι
be bound with 1
be compassed with 1
be hanged about 2.
†be compassed about with (echō *with partic.*) 1.

PERIKEPHALAIA περικεφαλαία *f.*
helmet 2.

PERIKRATĒS περικρατής
†come by (ginomai perikratēs) 1.

PERIKRUPTŌ περικρύπτω
hide 1.

PERIKUKLOŌ περικυκλόω
compass round 1.

PERILAMPŌ περιλάμπω
shine round about 2.

PERILEIPŌ περιλείπω
PASS. remain 2.

PERILUPOS περίλυπος
exceeding sorrowful 2
exceeding sorry 1
very sorrowful 2.

PERIMENŌ περιμένω
wait for 1.

PERIOCHĒ περιοχή *f.*
place 1.

PERIOIKEŌ περιοικέω
dwell round about 1.

PERIOIKOS περίοικος
neighbour 1.

PERIOUSIOS περιούσιος
peculiar 1.

PERIPATEŌ περιπατέω
be occupied 1
be walking 1
go 1
walk 92
walk about 1.

PERIPEIRŌ περιπείρω
pierce through 1.

PERIPHERŌ περιφέρω
bear about 1
carry about 4.

PERIPHRONEŌ περιφρονέω
despise 1.

PERIPIPTŌ περιπίπτω
fall among 1
fall into 2.

PERIPOIEŌ περιποιέω
MID. purchase 2.

PERIPOIĒSIS περιποίησις *f.*
obtaining 1
purchased possession 1
saving 1.
†Eis *with acc.*: peculiar (M. purchased) 1, to obtain 1.

PERIPSĒMA περίψημα *n.*
offscouring 1.

PERIRRHĒGNUMI περιρρήγνυμι
rend off 1.

PERISPAŌ περισπάω
cumber 1.

PERISSEIA περισσεία *f.*
abundance 2
superfluity 1.
†abundantly (eis *with acc.*) 1.

PERISSEUMA περίσσευμα *n.*
abundance 4
that was left 1.

PERISSEUŌ περισσεύω
abound 15
abound more 1
be left 1
be more abundant 1
be the better (M. have the more) 1
exceed 2
excel 1
have enough and to spare 1
increase 1
make abound 2
redound 1
remain 3
remain over and above 1.
Partic. abundance 3
abundant 1.
PASS. have abundance 1
have more abundance 1.
†*With* mallon: abound more and more 1, increase more and more 1.

PERISSOS περισσός
more 2
more abundantly 1
superfluous 1
*advantage 1.
Compar. far more 1
greater 1
more 3
more abundant 3
more abundantly 3
much more 1
overmuch 1
the more 1.
†Ek *with gen.*: beyond measure 1, vehemently 1. Huper ek *with gen.*: exceeding abundantly above 1, exceedingly 1, very highly 1. *See* mallon.

PERISSŌS περισσῶς
exceedingly 1
out of measure 1
the more 1.
Compar. exceedingly 1
more abundant 2
more exceedingly 1
more frequent 1
much more 1
the more abundantly 2
the more earnest 1
the more exceedingly 1
the rather 1.

PERISTERA περιστερά *f.*
dove 9
pigeon 1.

PERITEMNŌ περιτέμνω
circumcise 16.
Infin. circumcising 1.
PASS. *have circumcised 1.

PERITHESIS περίθεσις *f.*
wearing 1.

PERITITHĒMI περιτίθημι
bestow upon (M. put on) 1
put about 1
put on 3
put upon 1
set about 1.
†hedge round about (*with* phragmos) 1.

PERITOMĒ περιτομή *f.*
circumcision 35
*circumcised 1.

PERITRECHŌ περιτρέχω
run through 1.

PERITREPŌ περιτρέπω
†make mad (*with* eis *and acc. of* mania) 1.

PERIX πέριξ
round about 1.

PERIZŌNNUMI περιζώννυμι
MID. (PASS.) be girded about 1
be girt 1
gird one's self 3
have . . . girt about 1.
†have . . . girded (*with* peri) 1.

PERPEREUOMAI περπερεύομαι
vaunt one's self (M. be rash) 1.

PERUSI πέρυσι
†a year ago (apo perusi) 2.

PETAOMAI πετάομαι
fly 4.

PETEINON πετεινόν *n.*
bird 5
fowl 9.

PETOMAI πέτομαι
fly 1.

PETRA πέτρα *f.*
rock 14
Rock 2.

PETRŌDĒS πετρώδης
As noun stony ground 2
stony place 2.

PETROS Πέτρος
stone (M. Peter) 1

PEZEUŌ πεζεύω
go afoot 1.

PEZĒ πεζῇ
afoot 1
on foot 1.

PHAGŌ φάγω
eat 92.
Infin. aught to eat 1
eating 1
meat 3.

PHAGOS φάγος
glutton 2.

PHAILONĒS φαιλόνης
cloak 1.

PHAINŌ φαίνω
shine 7.
MID. (PASS.) appear 16
be seen 2
seem 1
shine 3
think 1.
Partic. things which do appear 1.

PHANEROŌ φανερόω
declare manifestly 1
make manifest 19
manifest 9
manifest forth 1
shew 3.
MID. (PASS.) appear 12
be manifest 2
shew one's self 2.

PHANEROS φανερός
known 3
manifest 9.
†appear (eimi phaneros) 1; be spread abroad (ginomai ph.) 1. En *with dat.*: openly 2, outwardly 1, outward 1. Eis *with acc.*: abroad 2.

PHANERŌS φανερῶς
evidently 1
openly 2.

PHANERŌSIS φανέρωσις *f.*
manifestation 2.

PHANOS φανός
lantern 1.

PHANTASIA φαντασία *f.*
pomp 1.

PHANTASMA φάντασμα *n.*
spirit 2.

PHANTAZŌ φαντάζω
Pass. pt. sight 1.

PHARANX φάραγξ *f.*
valley 1.

PHARMAKEIA φαρμακεία *f.*
sorcery 2
witchcraft 1.

PHARMAKEUS φαρμακεύς
sorcerer 1.

PHARMAKOS φαρμακός
sorcerer 1.

PHASIS φάσις *f.*
tidings 1.

PHASKŌ φάσκω
affirm 1
profess 1
say 2.

PHATNĒ φάτνη *f.*
manger 3
stall 1.

PHAULOS φαῦλος
evil 1.
As noun evil 2
evil thing 1.

PHEGGOS φέγγος *n.*
light 3.

* Inexact translations, *e.g.*, of a noun by a verb or adjective, of an active by a passive.
† Cases where two or more words in the original are translated by one word or by a phrase.

PHEIDOMAI φείδομαι
forbear 1
spare 9.

PHEIDOMENŌS φειδομένως
sparingly 2.

PHĒMĒ φήμη f.
fame 2.

PHĒMI φημί
affirm 1
say 57.

PHERŌ φέρω
bear 8
bring 33
bring forth 5
carry 1
endure 2
lay 1
lead 1
move 1
reach 1
reach hither 1
uphold 1.
MID. go on 1
rush 1.
PASS. be (M. be brought in) 1
be driven 1
be to,be brought 1
come 3
*let drive 1.

PHEUGŌ φεύγω
can escape 1
escape 2
flee 26
flee away 2.

PHIALĒ φιάλη f.
vial 12.

PHILADELPHIA φιλαδελφία f.
brotherly kindness 2
brotherly love 3 (M. love of the brethren) 1
love of the brethren 1.

PHILADELPHOS φιλάδελφος
*love as brethren (M. loving to the brethren) 1.

PHILAGATHOS φιλάγαθος
lover of good men (M. lover of good things) 1.

PHILANDROS φίλανδρος
†love their husbands (eimi philandros) 1.

PHILANTHRŌPIA φιλανθρωπία f.
kindness 1
love toward man (M. pity toward man) 1

PHILANTHRŌPŌS φιλανθρώπως
courteously 1.

PHILARGURIA φιλαργυρία f.
love of money 1.

PHILARGUROS φιλάργυρος
covetous 2.

PHILAUTOS φίλαυτος
lover of one's own self 1.

PHILĒ φίλη f.
friend 1.

PHILĒDONOS φιλήδονος
lover of pleasures 1.

PHILĒMA φίλημα n.
kiss 7.

PHILEŌ φιλέω
kiss 3
love 22.

PHILIA φιλία f.
friendship 1.

PHILONEIKIA φιλονεικία f.
strife 1.

PHILONEIKOS φιλόνεικος
contentious 1.

PHILOPHRŌN φιλόφρων
courteous 1.

PHILOPHRONŌS φιλοφρόνως
courteously 1.

PHILOPRŌTEUŌ φιλοπρωτεύω
love to have the pre-eminence 1.

PHILOS φίλος
friend 29.

PHILOSOPHIA φιλοσοφία f.
philosophy 1.

PHILOSOPHOS φιλόσοφος
philosopher 1.

PHILOSTORGOS φιλόστοργος
kindly affectioned 1.

PHILOTEKNOS φιλότεκνος
†to love their children (eimi philoteknos) 1.

PHILOTHEOS φιλόθεος
lover of God 1.

PHILOTIMEOMAI φιλοτιμέομαι
labour (M. endeavour) 1
strive 1
study 1.

PHILOXENIA φιλοξενία f.
hospitality 1
*to entertain strangers 1.

PHILOXENOS φιλόξενος
given to hospitality 1
lover of hospitality 1.
*use hospitality 1.

PHIMOŌ φιμόω
muzzle 2
put to silence 2.
PASS. be speechless 1
be still 1
hold one's peace 2.

PHLOGIZŌ φλογίζω
set on fire 2.

PHLOX φλόξ f.
flame 6
*flaming (gen.) 1.

PHLUAREŌ φλυαρέω
prate against 1.

PHLUAROS φλύαρος
tattler 1.

PHOBEOMAI φοβέομαι
be afraid 25
be afraid of 4
fear 63
reverence 1.

PHOBEROS φοβερός
fearful 1
terrible 1.
As noun fearful thing 1.

PHOBĒTRON φόβητρον n.
fearful sight 1.

PHOBOS φόβος
fear 41 (M. reverence) 1
terror 3.
†*With* megas: exceedingly 1, sore 1. *See* echō.

PHOINIX φοίνιξ
palm 1
palm-tree 1.

PHŌLEOS φωλεός
hole 2.

PHŌNĒ φωνή f.
noise 1
sound 8(M. voice 1)
voice 128
voices 3
†be noised abroad (*with* ginomai; M. voice be made) 1.

PHŌNEŌ φωνέω
call 23
call for 2
crow 12
cry 5.

PHONEUŌ φονεύω
do murder 1
kill 10
slay 1.

PHONEUS φονεύς
murderer 7.
†*See* anēr.

PHONOS φόνος
murder 8
slaughter 1.
†*See* apothnēskō.

PHOREŌ φορέω
bear 3
wear 3.

PHOROS φόρος
tribute 5.

PHORTION φορτίον n.
burden 5.

PHORTIZŌ φορτίζω
lade 1.
Pass. pt. heavy laden 1.

PHORTOS φόρτος
lading 1.

PHŌS φῶς n.
fire 2
light 66
Light 4.

PHŌSPHOROS φωσφόρος
day-star 1.

PHŌSTĒR φωστήρ
light 2.

PHŌTEINOS φωτεινός
bright 1
full of light 4.

PHŌTISMOS φωτισμός
light 1.
†to give light (pros *with acc.*) 1.

PHŌTIZŌ φωτίζω
bring to light 2
enlighten 2
give light 2
illuminate 1
light 1
lighten 2
make see 1.

PHRAGELLION φραγέλλιον n.
scourge 1.

PHRAGELLOŌ φραγελλόω
scourge (*vb.*) 2.

PHRAGMOS φραγμός
hedge 2
partition 1.
†*See* peritithēmi.

PHRASSŌ φράσσω
stop 3.

PHRAZŌ φράζω
declare 2.

PHREAR φρέαρ n.
pit 5
well 2.

PHRĒN φρήν f.
understanding (*pl.*) 2.

PHRENAPATAŌ φρεναπατάω
deceive 1.

PHRENAPATĒS φρεναπάτης
deceiver 1.

PHRISSŌ φρίσσω
tremble 1.

PHRONĒMA φρόνημα n.
mind 2 (M minding) 1
*to be minded (M. minding) 2.

PHRONEŌ φρονέω
be careful 1
be minded 3
mind 4
regard 3 (M. observe 1)
savour 2
set one's affection on (M. set one's mind on) 1
think 5
understand 1.
Infin. care 1.
†be of one mind (*with* to hen) 1; let this mind be (*imper. with* touto) 1. *With* to auto: be like-minded 2, be of one mind 1, be of the same mind 2.

PHRONĒSIS φρόνησις f.
prudence 1
wisdom 1.

PHRONIMOS φρόνιμος
wise 13.
As noun wise man 1.

PHRONIMŌS φρονίμως
wisely 1.

PHRONTIZŌ φροντίζω
be careful 1.

PHROUREŌ φρουρέω
keep 3
keep with a garrison 1.

PHRUASSŌ φρυάσσω
rage 1.

PHRUGANON φρύγανον n.
stick 1.

PHTHANŌ φθάνω
attain 1
attain already (*aor.*) 1
come 4
prevent 1.

PHTHARTOS φθαρτός
corruptible 5.
As noun corruptible things 1.

PHTHEGGOMAI φθέγγομαι
speak 3.

PHTHEIRŌ φθείρω
corrupt 4
defile (M. destroy) 1
destroy
MID. corrupt one's self 1.
PASS. be corrupt 1.

PHTHINOPŌRINOS φθινοπωρινός
whose fruit withereth 1.

PHTHOGGOS φθόγγος
sound 2 (M. tune) 1.

PHTHONEŌ φθονέω
envy (*vb.*) 1.

PHTHONOS φθόνος
envy 8 (M. enviously 1)
envying 1.

PHTHORA φθορά f.
corruption 7.
†eis *with acc.*: to perish 1, to be destroyed 1.

PHUGĒ φυγή f.
flight 2.

PHULAKĒ φυλακή f.
cage 1
hold 1
imprisonment 2
prison 35
ward 1
watch 6 (M. night-watches 1; *pl.*).

PHULAKIZŌ φυλακίζω
imprison 1.

PHULAKTĒRION φυλακτήριον n.
phylactery 1.

PHULASSŌ φυλάσσω
keep 21
observe 1
save 1.
MID. beware 2
beware of 1
keep 2
keep one's self 1
observe 1.

PHULAX φύλαξ
keeper 3.

PHULĒ φυλή f.
kindred 6
tribe 25.

PHULLON φύλλον n.
leaf 6.

PHUŌ φύω
spring up 3.

PHURAMA φύραμα n.
lump 5.

PHUSIKOS φυσικός
natural 3.

PHUSIKŌS φυσικῶς
naturally 1.

PHUSIOŌ φυσιόω
puff up 1.
MID. (PASS.) be puffed up 6.

PHUSIŌSIS φυσίωσις f.
swelling 1.

PHUSIS φύσις f.
kind (M. nature) 1
nature 10.
†natural (kata *with acc.*) 2.
See anthrōpinos.

PHUTEIA φυτεία f.
plant 1.

PHUTEUŌ φυτεύω
plant (*vb.*) 11.

PIAZŌ πιάζω
apprehend 2
catch 2
lay hands on 1
take 7.

PIEZŌ πιέζω
press down 1.

PIKRAINŌ πικραίνω
make bitter 2.
PASS. be bitter 2.

PIKRIA πικρία f.
bitterness 4.

PIKROS πικρός
bitter 2.

PIKRŌS πικρῶς
bitterly 2

PIMPLĒMI πίμπλημι (πλήθω)
accomplish 4
fill 18
furnish 1.
PASS. come full 1.

PIMPRĒMI πίμπρημι
PASS. swell 1.

PINAKIDION πινακίδιον n.
writing table 1.

PINAX πίναξ
charger 4
platter 1.

PINŌ πίνω
drink 68
drink of 7.

PIOTĒS πιότης f.
fatness 1.

PIPRASKŌ πιπράσκω
sell 9.

PIPTŌ πίπτω
fail 1
fall 68
fall down 19
light 1.

PISTEUŌ πιστεύω
believe 233 (M. trust 1)
commit to one's trust 1
commit unto 4.
Partic. believer 1.
Infin. believing 1.
PASS. be committed to one's trust 1
be committed unto 1
be put in trust with 1.
†ACT. believe (*with* eis 1, en 1, epi 1) 3.

PISTIKOS πιστικός
†*See* nardos.

PISTIS πίστις f.
assurance (M. faith) 1
belief 1
faith 239
fidelity 1
*them that believe 1.
†he which believeth (ho ek *with gen.*) 1.

PISTOŌ πιστόω
PASS. be assured of 1.

PISTOS πιστός
believing 2
faithful 52 (M. believing 1)
Faithful 1
sure 1
that believeth 3
true 2
which believeth 3.
As noun believer 1.
As adv. faithfully 1.

PITHANOLOGIA πιθανολογία f.
enticing words 1.

PLANAŌ πλανάω
be out of the way 1
deceive 24
err 6
go astray 5
seduce 2
wander 1.

PLANĒ πλάνη f.
deceit 1
delusion 1
error 7
*deceive 1.

PLANĒTĒS πλανήτης
wandering 1.

PLANOS πλάνος
deceiver 4
seducing 1.

PLASMA πλάσμα n.
thing formed 1.

PLASSŌ πλάσσω
form 2.

PLASTOS πλαστός
feigned 1.

PLATEIA πλατεῖα f.
street 10.

PLATOS πλάτος n.
breadth 4.

PLATUNŌ πλατύνω
enlarge 2
make broad 1.

PLATUS πλατύς
wide 1.

PLAX πλάξ f.
table 3.

PLĒGĒ πληγή f.
plague 12
stripe 5
wound 3.
†*See* epitithēmi.

PLEGMA πλέγμα n.
braided hair (M. plaited hair) 1.

PLEIŌN πλείων
above 1
greater 5
greater part 1
longer 1
many 12
many things 1
more 23
more excellent 1
more part 2
most 2
very many 2.
†epi pleion: further 3, long 1. Yet but (ou pleion e[2]) 1.

* Inexact translations, *e.g.*, of a noun by a verb or adjective, of an active by a passive.
† Cases where two or more words in the original are translated by one word or by a phrase.

PLEISTOS πλεῖστος
most 1
very great 1.
As adv. at the most 1.

PLEKŌ πλέκω
plait 3.

PLĒKTĒS πλήκτης
striker 2.

PLĒMMURA πλημμύρα *f.*
flood 1.

PLĒN πλήν
but 14
but rather 2
except 1
nevertheless 8
notwithstanding 4
save 1
than 1.

PLEŌ πλέω
sail 4
sail by 1.

PLEONAZŌ πλεονάζω
abound 6
make to increase 1.
Partic. abundant 1.
†have nothing over (ou pleonazō) 1.

PLEONEKTEŌ πλεονεκτέω
defraud 2 (M. oppress or overreach) 1
get an advantage of 1
make a gain of 2.

PLEONEKTĒS πλεονέκτης
covetous 3
covetous man 1.

PLEONEXIA πλεονεξία *f.*
covetousness 8
covetous practice 1
greediness 1.

PLĒRŌMA πλήρωμα
fulfilling 1
fulness 13
piece that filleth up 1
which is put in to fill up 1
*full 1.

PLĒROŌ πληρόω
accomplish 1
end 2
fill 17 (M. fulfil 1)
fill up 1
fulfil 51 (M. preach fully 1)
make full 1
preach fully 1
supply 1.
Pass. be filled with 1
be full 5
be full come 1
expire 1
fill 1
*after 1.
Partic. complete 2 (M. filled 1)
full 3
perfect 1.

PLĒROPHOREŌ πληροφορέω
make full proof of (M. fulfil) 1.
Pass. be fully known 1
be fully persuaded 2 (M. be fully assured 1).
Partic. things which are most surely believed 1.

PLĒROPHORIA πληροφορία *f.*
assurance 1
full assurance 3.

PLĒSION πλησίον
near 1.
As noun neighbour 16.

PLĒSMONĒ πλησμονή *f.*
satisfying 1.

PLĒSSŌ πλήσσω
smite 1.

PLĒTHŌ = **PIMPLĒMI**

PLĒTHOS πλῆθος *n.*
bundle 1
company 1
multitude 30.

PLĒTHUNŌ πληθύνω
be multiplied 1
multiply 7.
Pass. abound 1
multiply 3.

PLEURA πλευρά *f.*
side 5.

PLOIARION πλοιάριον *n.*
boat 3
little ship 2
small ship 1.

PLOION πλοῖον *n.*
ship 66
shipping (*pl.*) 1.

PLOOS πλόος
course 1
sailing 1
voyage 1.

PLOUSIOS πλούσιος
rich 17.
As noun rich man 11.

PLOUSIŌS πλουσίως
abundantly 2 (M. richly 1)
richly 2.

PLOUTEŌ πλουτέω
be increased with goods 1
be made rich 2
be rich 7
wax rich 1.
Partic. rich 1.

PLOUTIZŌ πλουτίζω
enrich 2
make rich 1.

PLOUTOS πλοῦτος
riches 22.

PLUNŌ πλύνω
wash 1.

PNEŌ πνέω
blow 6.

PNEUMA πνεῦμα
ghost 2
Ghost (*with* Holy) 89
life (M. breath) 1
spirit 151 (M. breath 1)
Spirit 137 (*with* Holy 4)
spiritual gift (M. spirit) 1
wind 1
*spiritually (*gen.*; M. of the Spirit) 1.

PNEUMATIKOS πνευματικός
spiritual 18 (M. spirit 1).
As noun he that is spiritual 1
he which is spiritual 1
spiritual gifts 1
spiritual things 3
that which is spiritual 2.

PNEUMATIKŌS πνευματικῶς
spiritually 2.

PNIGŌ πνίγω
choke 1
take by the throat 1.

PNIKTOS πνικτός
strangled 1.
As noun things strangled 1.

PNOĒ πνοή *f.*
breath 1
wind 1.

PODĒRĒS ποδήρης
garment down to the foot 1.

POIĒMA ποίημα *n.*
thing that is made 1
workmanship 1.

POIEŌ ποιέω
abide there 1
appoint (M. make) 1
be 1
bear 4
bring 1
bring forth 14
can do 1
cause 8
cause to be 1
commit 9
continue 2
deal with (*dat.*) 2
do 353
execute 2
exercise 1
fulfil 3
gain 1
give 1
hold 1
keep 4
make 102
mean 1
observe 1
ordain 1
perform 2
provide 1
purpose 1
put 2
shoot out 1
show 5
spend 1
take 1
tarry 1
work 8 (M. continue 1, do 1)
yield 1.
Partic. in doing 2.
Infin. doing 1.
Mid. give 1
make 12.
†Act. agree (*with acc. of* mia gnōmē) 1; avenge (*with* ekdikēsis) 3; band together (*with* sustrophē) 1; bewray (*with* dēlos) 1; cast out (*with* ekthetos) 1; content (*with* hikanos *and dat.*) 1; do good to (*with* kalōs) 2; go (*with* hodos) 1; lay wait (*with* enedra) 1; purge (*with* katharismos) 1; raise up (*with* episustasis) 1; redeem (*with* lutrōsis) 1; secure (*with* amerimnos) 1; transgress the law (*with* anomia) 1. Mid. have in remembrance (*with* mnēmē) 1; journey (*with* poreia) 1. *move (*with* logos) 1. *Partic.* without (*with* mēdeis) 1.

POIĒSIS ποίησις *f.*
deed (M. doing) 1.

POIĒTĒS ποιητής
doer 5
poet 1.

POIKILOS ποικίλος
divers 8
manifold 2.

POIMAINŌ ποιμαίνω
feed 6
feed cattle 1
rule 4 (M. feed) 1.

POIMĒN ποιμήν
pastor 1
shepherd 15
Shepherd 2.
†*See* anthrōpos.

POIMNĒ ποίμνη *f.*
flock 4
fold 1.

POIMNION ποίμνιον *n.*
flock 5.

POIOS ποῖος
what 27
what manner of 1
what things 1
what way 1
which 4.

POLEMEŌ πολεμέω
fight 3
make war 3
war 1.

POLEMOS πόλεμος
battle 5
fight 1
war 12.

PŌLEŌ πωλέω
sell 21.
Pass. pt. whatsoever is sold 1

POLIS πόλις *f.*
city 159.

POLITARCHĒS πολιτάρχης
ruler of the city 2.

POLITEIA πολιτεία *f.*
commonwealth 1
freedom 1.

POLITĒS πολίτης
citizen 3.

POLITEUMA πολίτευμα *n.*
conversation 1.

POLITEUŌ πολιτεύω
Mid. live 1
Imper. let your conversation be 1.

POLLAKIS πολλάκις
oft 4
often 7
oftentimes 3
ofttimes 3.

POLLAPLASIŌN πολλαπλασίων
manifold more 1.

PŌLOS πῶλος
colt 12.

POLULOGIA πολυλογία *f.*
much speaking 1.

POLUMERŌS πολυμερῶς
at sundry times 1.

POLUPOIKILOS πολυποίκιλος
manifold 1.

POLUS πολύς
abundant (M. much) 1
common 1
far passed 1
far spent 1
great 59
long 3
many 185 (*sing.* 2)
many stripes 1
many things 23
much 71 (*adj. and adv.*; *pl.* 17; M. many ways *or* oftentimes 1)
plenteous 1.
As adv. a great deal (*dat.*) 1
far (*dat.*) 1
greatly 4
oft 1
so much (*dat.*) 1
sore 1
straitly 2.
†a great while (epi polu) 1; altogether (en *with dat.*) 1; long after (meta polu) 1; much (*with* logos) 1.

POLUSPLAGCHNOS πολύσπλαγχνος
very pitiful 1.

POLUTELĒS πολυτελής
costly 1
of great price 1
very precious 1.

POLUTIMOS πολύτιμος
of great price 1
very costly 1.

POLUTROPŌS πολυτρόπως
in divers manners 1.

POMA πόμα *n.*
drink 2.

PONĒRIA πονηρία *f.*
iniquity 1
wickedness 6 (M. wicked) 1.

PONĒROS πονηρός
bad 1
evil 38
grievous 1
lewd 1
malicious 1
which is evil 2
wicked 11.
As noun evil 10
evil things 2
harm 1
wicked 1
wickedness 1
wicked one 6
wicked person 1.
†evil (*with* rhēma) 1.

PONOS πόνος
pain 3.

PŌPOTE πώποτε
at any time 3.
†never (*with negative*) 3.

POREIA πορεία *f.*
way 1.
†*See* poieō.

POREUOMAI πορεύομαι
be going 1
depart 11
go 119
go away 1
go forth 1
go one's way 7
go up 1
journey 2
make one's journey 1
take one's journey 1
walk 9.

PORISMOS πορισμός
gain 2.

PORNĒ πόρνη *f.*
harlot 8 (M. fornication) 1
whore 4.

PORNEIA πορνεία *f.*
fornication 26.

PORNEUŌ πορνεύω
commit fornication 7
commit [fornication] 1.

PORNOS πόρνος
fornicator 5
whoremonger 5.

PŌROŌ πωρόω
blind 2 (M. harden 1)
harden 3.

PŌRŌSIS πώρωσις *f.*
blindness (M. hardness) 2
hardness (M. blindness) 1.

PORPHURA πορφύρα *f.*
purple 5.

PORPHUREOS πορφύρεος
purple 2.
As noun purple 1.

PORPHUROPŌLIS πορφυρόπωλις *f.*
seller of purple 1.

PORRHŌ πόῤῥω
a great way off 1
far 2.
Comp. further 1.

PORRHŌTHEN πόῤῥωθεν
afar off 2.

PORTHEŌ πορθέω
destroy 2
waste 1.

PŌS[1] πως
by any means 8
by some means 1
haply 1
perhaps 1.

PŌS[2] πῶς
after what manner 1
by what means 2
how? 52
how 38
how is it that? 6
that 1.

POSAKIS ποσάκις
how oft? 1
how often? 2.

POSIS πόσις *f.*
drink 3 (M. drinking) 1.

POSOS πόσος
how great? 1
how many? 9
how many things? 2
how much? 13
what? 1.
†how long ago? (*with* chronos) 1.

POTAMOPHORĒTOS ποταμοφόρητος
carried away of the flood 1.

POTAMOS ποταμός
flood 4
river 9
stream 2
water 1.

POTAPOS ποταπός
what 1
what manner of? 5
what manner of person 1.

POTE[1] ποτέ
aforetime 1
any time 1
at any time 4
at length 1
at the last 1
ever yet 1
in old time (M. at any time) 1
in the old time 1
in time past 5
in times past 3
once 2
some time 1
sometime 1
sometimes 3
when 1.
†never (ou mē pote) 1.

POTE[2] πότε
when 12.
†how long? (heōs pote) 7.

POTĒRION ποτήριον *n.*
cup 33.

POTEROS πότερος
whether 1.

POTHEN πόθεν
from whence 8
whence 20.

POTIZŌ ποτίζω
feed 1
give drink 4
give to drink 4
make . . . drink 1
make to drink 1
water 3
*watering 1.

POTOS πότος
banqueting 1.

POU[1] που
about 1
in a certain place 2.

POU[2] ποῦ
where? 37
whither? 10.

POUS πούς
foot 85.
†*See* hupopodion.

PRAGMA πρᾶγμα *n.*
business 1
matter 3
thing 6
work 1.

PRAGMATEIA πραγματεία *f.*
affair 1.

PRAGMATEUOMAI πραγματεύομαι
occupy 1.

PRAITŌRION πραιτώριον *n.*
common hall (M. governor's house) 1
hall of judgment (M. Pilate's house) 1

* Inexact translations, *e.g.*, of a noun by a verb or adjective, of an active by a passive.
† Cases where two or more words in the original are translated by one word or by a phrase.

judgment hall 4
palace (M. Cæsar's court) 1
Prætorium 1.

PRAKTŌR πράκτωρ
officer 2.

PRAOS πρᾶος
meek 1.

PRAOTĒS πραότης *f.*
meekness 9.

PRASIA πρασιά *f.*
ranks (*pl.*) 1.

PRASSŌ πράσσω
commit 5
do 28
exact 1
keep 1
require 1
use 1.
†deeds (*pl. of rel. with* prassō) 1.

PRAUS πραΰς
meek 3.

PRAUTĒS πραΰτης *f.*
meekness 3.

PRAXIS πρᾶξις *f.*
deed 4
office 1
works 1.

PRĒNĒS πρηνής
headlong 1.

PREPŌ πρέπω
be comely 1
become 6.

PRESBEIA πρεσβεία *f.*
ambassage 1
message 1.

PRESBEUŌ πρεσβεύω
be an ambassador 2.

PRESBUTERION πρεσβυτέριον *n.*
elders 1
estate of elders 1
presbytery 1.

PRESBUTEROS πρεσβύτερος
elder 2
eldest 1.
As noun elder 62
elder woman 1
old man 1.

PRESBUTĒS πρεσβύτης
aged 1
aged man 1
old man 1.

PRESBUTIS πρεσβῦτις *f.*
aged woman 1.

PRIN πρίν
before 6.
†*With* ē: before 5, before that 2, ere 1.

PRIZŌ πρίζω (πρίω)
saw asunder 1.

PRO πρό
above 1
above . . . ago 1
before 45 (*adv.* 9)
or ever 1.

PROAGŌ προάγω
bring forth 2
bring out 1
go before 15.

PROAIREŌ προαιρέω
MID. purpose 1.

PROAITIAOMAI προαιτιάομαι
prove before (M. charge) 1.

PROAKOUŌ προακούω
hear before 1.

PROAMARTANŌ προαμαρτάνω
sin already 1
sin heretofore 1.

PROAULION προαύλιον *n.*
porch 1.

PROBAINŌ προβαίνω
go farther 1
go on 1.
Partic. well stricken 2.
†*Partic. with* en *and dat. of* hemera *and* pas: of a great age 1.

PROBALLŌ προβάλλω
put forward 1
shoot forth 1.

PROBATIKOS προβατικός
Fem. sheep market (M. sheep gate) 1.

PROBATON πρόβατον *n.*
sheep 40.

PROBIBAZŌ προβιβάζω
instruct before 1.
†draw out of (*with* ek) 1.

PROBLEPŌ προβλέπω
MID. provide (M. foresee) 1.

PROCHEIRIZOMAI προχειρίζομαι
choose 1
make 1.

PROCHEIROTONEŌ προχειροτονέω
choose before 1.

PROECHŌ προέχω
MID. be better 1.

PRODĒLOS πρόδηλος
evident 1
manifest beforehand 1
open beforehand 1.

PRODIDŌMI προδίδωμι
give first 1.

PRODOTĒS προδότης
betrayer 1
traitor 2.

PRODROMOS πρόδρομος
forerunner 1.

PROĒGEOMAI προηγέομαι
prefer 1.

PROEIDON προεῖδον
foresee 1
see before 1.

PROEIPON προεῖπον
foretell 1
forewarn 1
say before 4
speak before 3
tell before 2
tell in time past 1.

PROELPIZŌ προελπίζω
trust first (M. hope) 1.

PROENARCHOMAI προενάρχομαι
begin 1
begin before 1.

PROEPAĞGELŌ προεπαγγέλλω
MID. promise afore 1.

PROERCHOMAI προέρχομαι
go before 5
go farther 1
go forward 1
outgo 1
pass on 1.

PROETOIMAZŌ προετοιμάζω
ordain before (M. prepare) 1
prepare afore 1.

PROEUAĞGELIZOMAI προευαγγελίζομαι
preach the gospel before 1.

PROGINOMAI προγίνομαι
be past 1.

PROGINŌSKŌ προγινώσκω
foreknow 2
foreordain 1
know 1
know before 1.

PROGNŌSIS πρόγνωσις *f.*
foreknowledge 2.

PROGONOS πρόγονος
forefathers (*pl.*) 1
parents (*pl.*) 1.

PROGRAPHŌ προγράφω
ordain before 1
set forth evidently 1
write 1
write afore 1
write aforetime 1.

PRŌI πρωΐ
early 2
in the morning 4
morning 2.
†early in the morning (hama prōi) 1, very early in the morning (lian prōi) 1.

PRŌÏMOS πρώϊμος
early 1.

PRŌÏNOS πρωϊνός
morning 1.

PRŌÏOS πρωΐος
early 1
in the morning 1
morning 2.

PROÏSTĒMI προΐστημι
be over 1
maintain (M. profess) 1
rule 5.

PROKALEŌ προκαλέω
MID. provoke 1.

PROKATAĞGELŌ προκαταγγέλλω
foretell 1
show before 2.
Pass. pt. whereof ye had notice before (M. which hath been so much spoken of before) 1.

PROKATARTIZŌ προκαταρτίζω
make up beforehand 1.

PROKEIMAI πρόκειμαι
be first 1
be set before 3
be set forth 1.

PROKĒRUSSŌ προκηρύσσω
preach before 1
preach first 1.

PROKOPĒ προκοπή *f.*
furtherance 2
profiting 1.

PROKOPTŌ προκόπτω
be far spent 1
increase 2
proceed 1
profit 1
wax 1.

PROKRIMA πρόκριμα *n.*
preferring one before another (M. prejudice) 1.

PROKUROŌ προκυρόω
confirm before 1.

PROLAMBANŌ προλαμβάνω
come aforehand 1
overtake 1
take before 1.

PROLEGŌ προλέγω
foretell 1
tell before 2.

PROMARTUROMAI προμαρτύρομαι
testify beforehand 1.

PROMELETAŌ προμελετάω
meditate before 1.

PROMERIMNAŌ προμεριμνάω
take thought beforehand 1.

PRONOEŌ προνοέω
provide for 1.
MID. provide 1
provide for 1.

PRONOIA πρόνοια *f.*
providence 1
provision for 1.

PROORAŌ προοράω
see before 1.
MID. foresee 1.

PROORIZŌ προορίζω
determine before 1
ordain 1
predestinate 4.

PROPASCHŌ προπάσχω
suffer before 1.

PROPEMPŌ προπέμπω
accompany 1.
bring forward on one's journey 1
bring on one's journey 2
bring on one's way 4
conduct forth 1.

PROPETĒS προπετής
heady 1
*rashly 1.

PROPHASIS πρόφασις *f.*
cloak 2 (M. excuse) 1
colour 1
pretence 3
show 1.

PROPHERŌ προφέρω
bring forth 2.

PROPHĒTEIA προφητεία *f.*
prophecy 15
prophesying 3
the gift of prophecy 1.

PROPHĒTĒS προφήτης
prophet 149.
†*See* anēr.

PROPHĒTEUŌ προφητεύω
prophesy 28.

PROPHĒTIKOS προφητικός
of prophecy 1
of the prophets 1.

PROPHĒTIS προφῆτις *f.*
prophetess 2.

PROPHTHANŌ προφθάνω
prevent 1.

PROPOREUOMAI προπορεύομαι
go before 2.

PRŌRA πρῷρα *f.*
forepart 1
foreship 1.

PROS πρός
With gen. for 1.
With dat. about 1
at 1.
With acc. according to 3
against 24
among 20
at 11
for 24
to 176
toward 10
unto 338
with 42
*to answer 1
*to be compared with 1
*to give [answer] 1
*which belong unto 1
*which pertain to 1, etc., etc.

PROSABBATON προσάββατον *n.*
the day before the sabbath 1.

PROSAGŌ προσάγω
bring 3
draw near 1.

PROSAGŌGĒ προσαγωγή *f.*
access 3.

PROSAGOREUŌ προσαγορεύω
call 1.

PROSAITEŌ προσαιτέω
beg 3.

PROSANABAINŌ προσαναβαίνω
go up 1.

PROSANALISKŌ προσαναλίσκω
spend 1.

PROSANAPLĒROŌ προσαναπληρόω
supply 2.

PROSANATITHĒMI προσανατίθημι
MID. add in conference 1
confer 1.

PROSAPEILEŌ προσαπειλέω
MID. threaten further 1.

PROSCHUSIS πρόσχυσις *f.*
sprinkling 1.

PROSDAPANAŌ προσδαπανάω
spend more 1.

PROSDECHOMAI προσδέχομαι
accept 1
allow 1
look for 4
receive 3
take 1
wait for 4.

PROSDEOMAI προσδέομαι
need 1.

PROSDOKAŌ προσδοκάω
be in expectation (M. be in suspense) 1
expect 1
look 2
look for 8
tarry 1
wait for 3.

PROSDOKIA προσδοκία *f.*
expectation 1
looking after 1.

PROSEAŌ προσεάω
suffer 1.

PROSECHŌ προσέχω
attend unto 1
be given to 1
beware 7
give attendance at 1
give attendance to 1
give heed to 5
give heed unto 1
have regard to 1
take heed 1
take heed to 3
take heed unto 2.

PROSEDREUŌ προσεδρεύω
wait at 1.

PROSEĞGIZŌ προσεγγίζω
come nigh unto 1.

PROSĒLOŌ προσηλόω
nail to 1.

PROSĒLUTOS προσήλυτος
proselyte 4.

PROSERCHOMAI προσέρχομαι
be a coming 1
come 32
come to 24
come unto 19
consent to 1
draw near 2
go 1
go near 1
go to 2
go unto 2.
Partic. comer thereunto 1.

PROSERGAZOMAI προσεργάζομαι
gain 1.

PROSEUCHĒ προσευχή *f.*
prayer 36
*earnestly (M. in his prayer) 1.

PROSEUCHOMAI προσεύχομαι
make prayer 1
make prayers 2
pray 83
pray for 1.

PROSKAIROS πρόσκαιρος
but for a time 1
for a season 1
for a while 1
temporal 1.

PROSKALEŌ προσκαλέω
MID. call 6
call for 2
call to 1
call unto 21.

PROSKARTEREŌ προσκαρτερέω
attend continually upon 1
continue in 3
continue instant in 1
continue steadfastly in 1
continue with 1
give one's self continually to 1
wait on 1
wait on continually 1.

PROSKARTERĒSIS προσκαρτέρησις *f.*
perseverance 1.

PROSKEPHALAION προσκεφάλαιον *n.*
pillow 1.

PROSKLĒROŌ προσκληρόω
PASS. consort with 1.

PROSKLISIS πρόσκλισις *f.*
partiality 1.

PROSKOLLAOMAI προσκολλάομαι
be joined unto 1
cleave to 2
join one's self to 1.

PROSKOMMA πρόσκομμα *n.*
offence 1
stumbling 1
stumbling-block 2
*stumbling (*adj.*) 2.

PROSKOPĒ προσκοπή *f.*
offence 1.

PROSKOPTŌ προσκόπτω
beat upon 1
stumble 3
stumble at 2.
†dash against (*with* pros) 2.

* Inexact translations, *e.g.*, of a noun by a verb or adjective, of an active by a passive.
† Cases where two or more words in the original are translated by one word or by a phrase.

PROSKULIŌ προσκυλίω
roll to 1
roll unto 1.

PROSKUNEŌ προσκυνέω
worship 59 (M. beseech) 1.
†*With* enōpion: worship (M. fall down before) 1.

PROSKUNĒTĒS προσκυνητής
worshipper 1.

PROSLALEŌ προσλαλέω
speak to 1
speak with 1.

PROSLAMBANŌ προσλαμβάνω
MID. receive 7
take 5
take unto them 2.

PROSLĒPSIS πρόσληψις *f.*
receiving 1.

PROSMENŌ προσμένω
abide still 1
be with 1
cleave unto 1
continue in 1
continue with 1
tarry there 1.

PROSOCHTHIZŌ προσοχθίζω
be grieved with 2.

PROSŌPOLĒPSIA προσωποληψία *f.*
respect of persons 4.

PROSŌPOLĒPTEŌ προσωποληπτέω
have respect to persons 1.

PROSŌPOLĒPTĒS προσωπολήπτης
respecter of persons 1.

PROSŌPON πρόσωπον
appearance (M. the face) 1
countenance 3
face 55
fashion 1
man's person 1
outward appearance 1
person 6 (M. sight 1)
presence 7 (M. outward appearance 1).
†before (pro *with gen.* 1, eis *with acc.* 1) 2.

PROSORMIZŌ προσορμίζω
MID. draw to the shore 1.

PROSOPHEILŌ προσοφείλω
owe besides 1.

PROSPĒGNUMI προσπήγνυμι
crucify 1.

PROSPEINOS πρόσπεινος
very hungry 1.

PROSPHAGION προσφάγιον *n.*
meat 1.

PROSPHATOS πρόσφατος
new 1.

PROSPHATŌS προσφάτως
lately 1.

PROSPHERŌ προσφέρω
bring 2
bring to 5
bring unto 10
deal with 1
do 1
offer 24
offer up 3
present unto (M. offer) 1
put to 1.

PROSPHILĒS προσφιλής
lovely 1.

PROSPHŌNEŌ προσφωνέω
call to 2
call unto 2
speak to 2
speak unto 1.

PROSPHORA προσφορά *f.*
offering 8
offering up 1 (M. sacrificing) 1.

PROSPIPTŌ προσπίπτω
fall at 1
fall down at 1
fall down before 5
beat upon 1.

PROSPOIEŌ προσποιέω
MID. make as though 1.

PROSPOREUOMAI προσπορεύομαι
come unto 1.

PROSPSAUŌ προσψαύω
touch 1.

PROSRĒGNUMI προσρήγνυμι
beat vehemently against 1
beat vehemently upon 1.

PROSTASSŌ προστάσσω
bid 1
command 6.

PROSTATIS προστάτις *f.*
succourer 1.

PROSTITHĒMI προστίθημι
add 11
give more 1
increase 1
lay unto 1
proceed further 1
speak any more 1
*again 2.

PROSTRECHŌ προστρέχω
run 1
run thither to 1
run to 1.

PROTASSŌ προτάσσω
appoint before 1.

PROTEINŌ προτείνω
bind 1.

PROTEROS πρότερος
before 2
former 1.
As adv. at the first 1
before 4
first 2
former 2.
†before (ean mē pr.) 1.

PRŌTEUŌ πρωτεύω
have the preeminence 1.

PROTHESIS πρόθεσις *f.*
purpose 8.
†shew-bread (*with gen. pl. of* artos) 1. *See* artos.

PROTHESMIOS προθέσμιος
time appointed 1.

PROTHUMIA προθυμία *f.*
forwardness of mind 1
readiness 1
readiness of mind 1
ready mind 1
willing mind 1.

PROTHUMOS πρόθυμος
ready 2
willing 1.

PROTHUMŌS προθύμως
of a ready mind 1

PROTITHĒMI προτίθημι
MID. purpose 2
set forth (M. foreordain) 1.

PRŌTOKATHEDRIA πρωτοκαθεδρία
chief seat 2
highest seat 1
uppermost seats 1.

PRŌTOKLISIA πρωτοκλισία *f.*
chief room 2
highest room 1
uppermost room 1
uppermost rooms 1.

PRŌTOS πρῶτος
before 2
best 1
chief 7 (M. first 1)
chiefest 1
first 78
former 2
that are first 1.
As noun beginning 1
chief estate 1
chief man 2
first day 2.
As adv. at first 1
at the beginning 1
at the first 3
before 1
chiefly 1
first 52
first of all 2.
†first of all (en *with dat. pl.*) 1.

PRŌTOSTATĒS πρωτοστάτης
ringleader 1.

PRŌTOTOKIA πρωτοτόκια *n.*
birthright 1.

PRŌTOTOKOS πρωτότοκος
first-begotten 2
firstborn 7.

PROTRECHŌ προτρέχω
run before 1.
†outrun (*with* tachion) 1.

PROTREPŌ προτρέπω
MID. exhort 1.

PROÜPARCHŌ προϋπάρχω
be before 1
be beforetime 1.

PRUMNA πρύμνα *f.*
hinder part 1
hinder part of the ship 1
stern 1.

PSALLŌ ψάλλω
make melody 1
sing 3
sing psalms 1.

PSALMOS ψαλμός
psalm 5
Psalms (*pl.*) 2.

PSĒLAPHAŌ ψηλαφάω
feel after 1
handle 2.
Pass pt. that might be touched 1.

PSĒPHIZŌ ψηφίζω
count 2.

PSĒPHOS ψῆφος *f.*
stone 2
voice 1.

PSEUDADELPHOS ψευδάδελφος
false brethren (*pl.*) 2.

PSEUDAPOSTOLOS ψευδαπόστολος
false apostle 1.

PSEUDĒS ψευδής
false 1.
As noun liar 2.

PSEUDOCHRISTOS ψευδόχριστος
false Christs (*pl.*) 2.

PSEUDODIDASKALOS ψευδοδιδάσκαλος
false teacher 1.

PSEUDOLOGOS ψευδολόγος
speaking lies 1.

PSEUDOMAI ψεύδομαι
lie 10
lie to (M. deceive) 1
Partic. falsely (M. lying) 1.

PSEUDOMARTUR ψευδομάρτυρ
false witness 3.

PSEUDOMARTUREŌ ψευδομαρτυρέω
bear false witness 6.

PSEUDOMARTURIA ψευδομαρτυρία *f.*
false witness 2.

PSEUDŌNUMOS ψευδώνυμος
falsely so called 1.

PSEUDOPROPHĒTĒS ψευδοπροφήτης
false prophet 11.

PSEUDOS ψεῦδος *n.*
lie 7
lying 1
*lying (*gen.*) 1.

PSEUSMA ψεῦσμα *n.*
lie 1.

PSEUSTĒS ψεύστης
liar 10.

PSICHION ψιχίον *n.*
crumb 3.

PSITHURISMOS ψιθυρισμός
whispering 1.

PSITHURISTĒS ψιθυριστής
whisperer 1.

PSŌCHŌ ψώχω
rub 1.

PSŌMION ψωμίον *n.*
sop 4 (M. morsel) 1.

PSŌMIZŌ ψωμίζω
bestow to feed 1
feed 1.

PSUCHĒ ψυχή *f.*
heart 1
life 40
mind 3
soul 58.
†heartily (ek *with gen.*) 1.

PSUCHIKOS ψυχικός
natural 3
sensual (M. natural) 1.
As noun that which is natural 1.

PSUCHŌ ψύχω
PASS. wax cold 1.

PSUCHOS ψῦχος *n.*
cold 3.

PSUCHROS ψυχρός
cold 3.
As noun cold water 1.

PTAIŌ πταίω
fall 1
offend 3
stumble 1.

PTĒNON πτηνόν *n.*
bird 1.

PTERNA πτέρνα *f.*
heel 1.

PTERUGION πτερύγιον *n.*
pinnacle 2.

PTERUX πτέρυξ *f.*
wing 5.

PTŌCHEIA πτωχεία *f.*
poverty 3.

PTŌCHEUŌ πτωχεύω
become poor 3.

PTŌCHOS πτωχός
poor 30.
beggarly 1.
As noun beggar 2
poor man 1.

PTOEŌ πτοέω
terrify 2.

PTOĒSIS πτόησις *f.*
amazement 1.

PTŌMA πτῶμα *n.*
carcase 1
corpse 1
dead body 3.

PTŌSIS πτῶσις *f.*
fall 2.

PTUŌ πτύω
spit 3.

PTUON πτύον *n.*
fan 2.

PTURŌ πτύρω
terrify 1.

PTUSMA πτύσμα *n.*
spittle 1.

PTUSSŌ πτύσσω
close 1.

PUGMĒ πυγμῇ (*dat.*)
oft (M. diligently) 1.

PUKNOS πυκνός
often 1.
As adv. often 1.
Comp. the oftener 1.

PUKTEUŌ πυκτεύω
fight 1.

PULĒ πύλη *f.*
gate 10.

PULŌN πυλών
gate 17
porch 1.

PUNTHANOMAI πυνθάνομαι
ask 7
demand 2
inquire 2
understand 1.

PUR πῦρ *n.*
fire 73
*fiery (*gen.*) 1.

PURA πυρά *f.*
fire 2.

PURESSŌ πυρέσσω
be sick of a fever 2.

PURETOS πυρετός
fever 6.

PURGOS πύργος
tower 4.

PURINOS πύρινος
of fire 1.

PUROŌ πυρόω
PASS. be on fire 1
be tried 1
burn 3.
Partic. fiery 1.

PURŌSIS πύρωσις *f.*
burning 2
fiery trial 1.

PURRHAZŌ πυρράζω
be red 2.

PURRHOS πυῤῥός
red 1
that is red 1.

R

RHABBI Ῥαββί
master 9
Rabbi 8.

RHABBONI ῥαββονί (ῥαββουνί)
lord 1
Rabboni 1.

RHABDIZŌ ῥαβδίζω
beat 1
beat with rods 1.

RHABDOS ῥάβδος *f.*
rod 6
sceptre 2
staff 4.

RHABDOUCHOS ῥαβδοῦχος
serjeant 2.

RHADIOURGĒMA ῥαδιούργημα *n.*
lewdness 1.

RHADIOURGIA ῥαδιουργία *f.*
mischief 1.

RHAKA ῥακά
racha (*ed.* 1611; raca 1638) 1.

RHAKOS ῥάκος *n.*
cloth 2.

RHANTISMOS ῥαντισμός
sprinkling 2.

RHANTIZŌ ῥαντίζω
sprinkle 4.

RHAPHIS ῥαφίς *f.*
needle 3.

RHAPISMA ῥάπισμα *n.*
†*See* ballō, didōmi.

RHAPIZŌ ῥαπίζω
smite 1
smite with the palm of one's hand (M. smite w. a rod) 1.

RHEDA ῥέδα *f.*
chariot 1.

RHĒGMA ῥῆγμα *n.*
ruin 1.

RHĒGNUMI ῥήγνυμι (ῥήσσω)
break forth 1
burst 2
rend 1
tear 2 (M. dash) 1.
PASS. break 1.

RHĒMA ῥῆμα *n.*
saying 9 (M. thing 1)
thing 3
word 56.
†*See* pas, ponēros.

RHEŌ[1] ῥέω
flow 1.

RHEŌ[2] ῥέω
[*See* errhēthēn.]

RHĒTŌR ῥήτωρ
orator 1.

RHĒTŌS ῥητῶς
expressly 1.

RHIPĒ ῥιπή *f.*
twinkling 1.

RHIPIZŌ ῥιπίζω
toss 1.

RHIPTEŌ ῥιπτέω
cast off 1.

RHIPTŌ ῥίπτω
cast 2
cast down 2
cast out 1
throw 1.
PASS. be scattered abroad (M. lie down) 1.

RHIZA ῥίζα *f.*
root 16
Root 1.

RHIZOŌ ῥιζόω
MID. (PASS.) be rooted 2.

RHOIZĒDON ῥοιζηδόν
with a great noise 1.

RHOMPHAIA ῥομφαία *f.*
sword 7.

RHŌNNUMI ῥώννυμι
Pass. imper. farewell 2.

RHUMĒ ῥύμη *f.*
lane 1
street 3.

RHUOMAI ῥύομαι
deliver 13.
Partic. Deliverer 1.
PASS. be delivered 4.

RHUPARIA ῥυπαρία *f.*
filthiness 1.

* Inexact translations, *e.g.*, of a noun by a verb or adjective, of an active by a passive.
† Cases where two or more words in the original are translated by one word or by a phrase.

RHUPAROS ῥυπαρός
vile 1.

RHUPOŌ ῥυπόω
be filthy 2.

RHUPOS ῥύπος
filth 1.

RHUSIS ῥύσις *f.*
issue 3.

RHUTIS ῥυτίς *f.*
wrinkle 1.

S

SABACHTHANI σαβαχθανί
sabachthani 2.

SABAŌTH σαβαώθ
Sabaoth 1
sabaoth 1.

SABBATISMOS σαββατισμός
rest (M. keeping of a sabbath) 1.

SABBATON σάββατον
sabbath 16 (M. week 1)
sabbath day 34
week 9
*sabbath (*adj.*) 7.
†*See* hēmera.

SAGĒNĒ σαγήνη *f.*
net 1.

SAINŌ σαίνω
move 1.

SAKKOS σάκκος
sackcloth 4.

SALEUŌ σαλεύω
move 1
shake 10
shake together 1
stir up 1.
Pass. pt. things that are shaken (M. th. t. may be sh.) 1.
†*Pass. pt. with negative*: things which cannot be shaken 1.

SALOS σάλος
waves 1.

SALPIG̃X σάλπιγξ *f.*
trump 2
trumpet 9.

SALPISTĒS σαλπιστής
trumpeter 1.

SALPIZŌ σαλπίζω
sound 10
sound a trumpet (M. cause a trumpet to be sounded) 1
the trumpet sounds 1.

SANDALION σανδάλιον *n.*
sandal 2.

SANIS σανίς *f.*
board 1.

SAPPHEIROS σάπφειρος *f.*
sapphire 1.

SAPROS σαπρός
bad 1
corrupt 7.

SARDINOS σάρδινος
sardine 1.

SARDIOS σάρδιος
sardius 1.

SARDONUX σαρδόνυξ *f.*
sardonyx 1.

SARGANĒ σαργάνη *f.*
basket 1.

SARKIKOS σαρκικός
carnal 7
fleshly 2.
As noun carnal things 2.

SARKINOS σάρκινος
fleshly 1.

SAROŌ σαρόω
sweep 3.

SARX σάρξ *f.*
flesh 147
*carnal 2
*carnally (M. of the flesh) 1
*fleshly 1.

SATON σάτον *n.*
measure 2.

SAUTOU = SEAUTOU.

SBENNUMI σβέννυμι
quench 7.
PASS. go out (M. be going out) 1.

SCHEDON σχεδόν
almost 3.

SCHĒMA σχῆμα *n.*
fashion 2.

SCHISMA σχίσμα
division 5 (M. schism 1)
rent 2
schism (M. division) 1.

SCHIZŌ σχίζω
break 1
divide 2
make a rent 1
open (M. cleave or rend) 1
rend 5.

SCHOINION σχοινίον *n.*
rope 1
small cord 1

SCHOLAZŌ σχολάζω
give one's self to 1.
Partic. empty 1.

SCHOLĒ σχολή *f.*
school 1.

SEAUTOU σεαυτοῦ
thee 1
thine own self 2
thou thyself 1
thy 1
thyself 35.

SEBASMA σέβασμα *n.*
devotion (M. god that one worshippeth) 1.
that is worshipped 1.

SEBASTOS σεβαστός
Augustus' 1.

SEBAZOMAI σεβάζομαι
worship 1.

SEBŌ σέβω
PASS. worship 6.
Partic. devout 2
devout person 1
religious 1.

SEIŌ σείω
move 1
shake 2.
PASS. quake 1
shake 1.

SEIRA σειρά *f.*
chain 1.

SEISMOS σεισμός
earthquake 13
tempest 1.

SELĒNĒ σελήνη *f.*
moon 9.

SELĒNIAZOMAI σεληνιάζομαι
be lunatic 2.

SĒMAINŌ σημαίνω
signify 6.

SĒMEION σημεῖον *n.*
miracle 22
sign 51
token 1
wonder 3 (M. sign 2).

SĒMEIOŌ σημειόω
MID. note (M. signify) 1.

SĒMERON σήμερον
this day 22
to-day 18.
†this day (*with* hēmera) 1.

SEMIDALIS σεμίδαλις *f.*
fine flour 1.

SEMNOS σεμνός
grave 3
honest (M. venerable) 1.

SEMNOTĒS σεμνότης *f.*
gravity 2
honesty 1.

SĒPŌ σήπω
corrupt 1.

SĒRIKON σηρικόν *n.*
silk 1.

SĒS σής
moth 3.

SĒTOBRŌTOS σητόβρωτος
moth-eaten 1.

SIAGŌN σιαγών *f.*
cheek 2.

SIDĒREOS σιδήρεος
iron (*adj.*) 1
of iron 4.

SIDĒROS σίδηρος
iron 1.

SIGAŌ σιγάω
hold one's peace 4
keep close 1
keep secret 1
keep silence 3.

SIGĒ σιγή *f.*
silence 2.

SIKARIOS σικάριος
that is a murderer 1.

SIKERA σίκερα *n.*
strong drink 1.

SIMIKINTHION σιμικίνθιον *n.*
apron 1.

SINAPI σίναπι *n.*
mustard seed 5.

SINDŌN σινδών *f.*
fine linen 1
linen 2
linen cloth 3.

SINIAZŌ σινιάζω
sift 1.

SIŌPAŌ σιωπάω
hold one's peace 9.
Partic. dumb 1.
Imper. peace 1.

SITEUTOS σιτευτός
fatted 3.

SITISTOS σιτιστός *n.*
fatling 1.

SITOMETRION σιτομέτριον *n.*
portion of meat 1.

SITOS σῖτος
corn 2
wheat 12.

SKANDALIZŌ σκανδαλίζω
make to offend 2
offend 28 (M. cause to offend 2).

SKANDALON σκάνδαλον *n.*
occasion of stumbling (M. scandal) 1
occasion to fall 1
offence 9
stumbling block 3
thing that offendeth (M. scandal) 1.

SKAPHĒ σκάφη *f.*
boat 3.

SKAPTŌ σκάπτω
dig 3.

SKELOS σκέλος *n.*
leg 3.

SKĒNĒ σκηνή *f.*
habitation 1
tabernacle 19.

SKĒNŌMA σκήνωμα *n.*
tabernacle 3.

SKĒNOŌ σκηνόω
dwell 5.

SKĒNOPĒGIA σκηνοπηγία *f.*
*of tabernacles 1.

SKĒNOPOIOS σκηνοποιός
tent-maker 1.

SKĒNOS σκῆνος *n.*
tabernacle 1.

SKEPASMA σκέπασμα *n.*
raiment (*pl.*) 1.

SKEUĒ σκευή *f.*
tackling 1.

SKEUOS σκεῦος *n.*
goods (*pl.*) 2
sail 1
stuff (*pl.*) 1
vessel 19.

SKIA σκιά *f.*
shadow 7.

SKIRTAŌ σκιρτάω
leap 2
leap for joy 1.

SKLĒROKARDIA σκληροκαρδία *f.*
hardness of heart 3.

SKLĒROS σκληρός
fierce 1
hard 5.

SKLĒROTĒS σκληρότης *f.*
hardness 1.

SKLĒROTRACHĒLOS σκληροτράχηλος
stiff-necked 1.

SKLĒRUNŌ σκληρύνω
harden 4.
PASS. be hardened 2.

SKŌLĒKOBRŌTOS σκωληκόβρωτος
eaten of worms 1.

SKŌLĒX σκώληξ
worm 3.

SKOLIOS σκολιός
crooked 2
froward 1
untoward 1.

SKOLOPS σκόλοψ
thorn 1.

SKOPEŌ σκοπέω
consider 1
look at 1
look on 1
mark 2
take heed 1.

SKOPOS σκοπός
mark 1.

SKORPIOS σκορπίος
scorpion 5.

SKORPIZŌ σκορπίζω
disperse abroad 1
scatter 3
scatter abroad 1.

SKOTEINOS σκοτεινός
dark 1
full of darkness 2.

SKOTIA σκοτία *f.*
dark 2
darkness 14.

SKOTIZŌ σκοτίζω
darken 8.

SKOTOŌ σκοτόω
PASS. be full of darkness 1.

SKOTOS σκότος
darkness 32.

SKUBALON σκύβαλον *n.*
dung (*pl.*) 1.

SKULLŌ σκύλλω
trouble 2.
MID. trouble one's self 1.

SKULON σκῦλον *n.*
spoil 1.

SKUTHRŌPOS σκυθρωπός
of a sad countenance 1
sad 1.

SMARAGDINOS σμαράγδινος
emerald 1.

SMARAGDOS σμάραγδος
emerald 1.

SMURNA σμύρνα *f.*
myrrh 2.

SMURNIZŌ σμυρνίζω
mingle with myrrh 1.

SŌMA σῶμα *n.*
body 145
slave (M. body) 1
*bodily (*gen.*) 1.

SŌMATIKOS σωματικός
bodily 2.

SŌMATIKŌS σωματικῶς
bodily 1.

SOPHIA σοφία *f.*
wisdom 51.

SOPHIZŌ σοφίζω
make wise 1.
MID. devise cunningly 1.

SOPHOS σοφός
wise 19.
As noun wise man 3.

SŌPHRŌN σώφρων
discreet 1
sober 2
temperate 1.

SŌPHRONEŌ σωφρονέω
be in one's right mind 2
be sober 2
be sober-minded (M. be discreet) 1.
†soberly (eis *with infin.*; M. to sobriety) 1.

SŌPHRONISMOS σωφρονισμός
sound mind 1.

SŌPHRONIZŌ σωφρονίζω
teach to be sober (M. t. to be wise) 1.

SŌPHRONŌS σωφρόνως
soberly 1.

SŌPHROSUNĒ σωφροσύνη *f.*
soberness 1.
sobriety 2.

SŌREUŌ σωρεύω
heap 1
lade 1.

SOROS σορός *f.*
bier (M. coffin) 1.

SOS σός
thine own 3
thy (thine) 18.
As noun that is thine 2
thy friends 1
thy goods 1.

SŌTĒR σωτήρ
saviour 1
Saviour 23.

SŌTĒRIA σωτηρία *f.*
health 1
salvation 40
saving 1
*that we should be saved 1.
†that they might be saved (eis *with acc.*) 1. *See* didōmi.

SŌTĒRIOS σωτήριος
that bringeth salvation 1.
As noun salvation 4.

SOUDARION σουδάριον *n.*
handkerchief 1
napkin 3.

SŌZŌ σώζω
heal 3
make whole 9 (M. save) 1
preserve 1
save 92.
PASS. be whole 2
do well 1
save one's self 1.
Partic. such as should be saved 1.

SPAŌ σπάω
MID. draw 1
draw out 1.

SPARASSŌ σπαράσσω
rend 1
tear 3.

SPARGANOŌ σπαργανόω
wrap in swaddling clothes 2.

SPATALAŌ σπαταλάω
live in pleasure (M. live delicately) 1.

SPEIRA σπεῖρα *f.*
band 6
band of men 1.

SPEIRŌ σπείρω
sow 43.
Partic. sower 6.
PASS. receive seed 4.

SPEKOULATŌR σπεκουλάτωρ
executioner (M. one of his guard) 1.

SPĒLAION σπήλαιον
cave 1
den 5.

SPENDŌ σπένδω
MID. be offered (M. poured forth) 1.
be ready to be offered 1.

SPERMA σπέρμα *n.*
issue 1
seed 43.

SPERMOLOGOS σπερμολόγος
babbler (M. base fellow) 1.

SPEUDŌ σπεύδω
haste 1
haste unto (M. haste) 1
make haste 3.
Partic. with haste 1.

SPHAGĒ σφαγή *f.*
slaughter 3.

SPHAGION σφάγιον *n.*
slain beast 1.

SPHAZŌ σφάζω (σφάττω)
kill 1
slay 8
wound (M. slay) 1.

SPHODRA σφόδρα
exceeding 4
exceedingly 1
greatly 2
sore 1
very 3.

SPHODRŌS σφοδρῶς
exceedingly 1.

SPHRAGIS σφραγίς *f.*
seal 16.

SPHRAGIZŌ σφραγίζω
seal 22
seal up 1
set a seal 1
set to one's seal 1.

SPHURON σφυρόν *n.*
ankle-bone 1.

SPILAS σπιλάς *f.*
spot 1.

SPILOŌ σπιλόω
defile 1
spot 1.

SPILOS σπῖλος
spot 2.

SPLAG̃CHNA σπλάγχνα *n. pl.*
bowels 7
bowels of compassion 1
inward affection (M. bowels) 1.
*tender (M. bowels) 1.

* Inexact translations, *e.g.*, of a noun by a verb or adjective, of an active by a passive.
† Cases where two or more words in the original are translated by one word or by a phrase.

SPLAĞCHNIZOMAI σπλαγχνίζομαι
be moved with compassion 5
have compassion 7.

SPODOS σποδός *f.*
ashes 3.

SPOĞGOS σπόγγος
sponge 3.

SPORA σπορά *f.*
seed 1.

SPORIMOS σπόριμος
Neut. pl. corn 1
corn fields 2.

SPOROS σπόρος
seed 4
seed sown 1.

SPOUDAIOS σπουδαῖος
diligent 2
forward 1.

SPOUDAIŌS σπουδαίως
diligently 1
instantly 1.
Compar. the more carefully 1
very diligently 1.

SPOUDAZŌ σπουδάζω
be diligent 2
be forward 1
do diligence 2
endeavour 3
give diligence 1
labour 1
study 1.

SPOUDĒ σπουδή *f.*
business 1
care 1
carefulness 1
diligence 5
earnest care 1
forwardness 1
haste 2.

SPURIS σπυρίς *f.*
basket 5.

STACHUS στάχυς
ear 1
ear of corn 3.

STADION στάδιον *n.*
race 1.

STADIOS στάδιος
furlong 5.

STAMNOS στάμνος
pot 1.

STAPHULĒ σταφυλή *f.*
grapes 3.

STASIS στάσις *f.*
dissension 3
insurrection 1
sedition 3
uproar 1.
†be standing (echō stasis) 1.

STATĒR στατήρ
piece of money (M. stater) 1.

STAUROŌ σταυρόω
crucify 46.

STAUROS σταυρός
cross 28.

STEGĒ στέγη *f.*
roof 3.

STEGŌ στέγω
bear 1
can forbear 2
suffer 1.

STEIROS στεῖρος
barren 4.

STĒKŌ στήκω
stand 2
stand fast 6.

STELLŌ στέλλω
MID. avoid 1
withdraw one's self 1.

STEMMA στέμμα *n.*
garland 1.

STENAGMOS στεναγμός
groaning 2.

STENAZŌ στενάζω
groan 3
grudge (M. groan or grieve) 1
sigh 1.
Partic. with grief 1.

STENOCHŌREŌ στενοχωρέω
distress 1
straiten 2.

STENOCHŌRIA στενοχωρία *f*
anguish 1
distress 3.

STENOS στενός
strait 3.

STEPHANOŌ στεφανόω
crown 4.

STEPHANOS στέφανος
crown 18.

STEREŌMA στερέωμα *n.*
steadfastness 1.

STEREOŌ στερεόω
establish 1
make strong 1.
PASS. receive strength 1.

STEREOS στερεός
steadfast 1
strong 2
sure (M. steady) 1.

STĒRIGMOS στηριγμός
steadfastness 1.

STĒRIZŌ στηρίζω
establish 3
fix 1
set steadfastly 1
stablish 6
strengthen 2.

STĒTHOS στῆθος *n.*
breast 5.

STHENOŌ σθενόω
strengthen 1.

STIGMA στίγμα *n.*
mark 1.

STIGMĒ στιγμή *f.*
moment 1.

STILBŌ στίλβω
shine 1.

STOA στοά *f.*
porch 4.

STOIBAS στοιβάς *f.*
branch 1.

STOICHEION στοιχεῖον *n.*
element 4 (M. rudiment 2)
principle 1
rudiment 2 (M. element 1).

STOICHEŌ στοιχέω
walk 4
walk orderly 1.

STOLĒ στολή *f.*
long clothing 1
long garment 1
long robe 1
robe 5.

STOMA στόμα *n.*
edge 2
face (M. mouth) 2
mouth 72.

STOMACHOS στόμαχος
stomach 1.

STRATĒGOS στρατηγός
captain 5 (M. ruler 1)
magistrate 5.

STRATEIA στρατεία *f.*
warfare 2.

STRATEUMA στράτευμα *n.*
army 6
men of war 1
soldiers 1.

STRATEUŌ στρατεύω
MID. go a warfare 1
war 5.
Partic. soldier 1.

STRATIA στρατιά *f.*
host 2.

STRATIŌTĒS στρατιώτης
soldier 26.

STRATOLOGEŌ στρατολογέω
choose . . . to be a soldier 1.

STRATOPEDARCHĒS στρατοπεδάρχης
captain of the guard 1.

STRATOPEDON στρατόπεδον *n.*
army 1.

STREBLOŌ στρεβλόω
wrest 1.

STRĒNIAŌ στρηνιάω
live deliciously 2.

STRĒNOS στρῆνος *n.*
delicacy 1.

STREPHŌ στρέφω
turn 3.
MID. be converted 1
turn 8
turn about 1
turn again 1
turn back again 1
turn one's self 3.

STRŌNNUMI στρώννυμι (στρωννύω)
make . . . bed 1
spread 2
strew 2.

STROUTHION στρουθίον *n.*
sparrow 4.

STUGĒTOS στυγητός
hateful 1.

STUGNAZŌ στυγνάζω
be sad 1
lower 1.

STULOS στύλος
pillar 4.

SU σύ
thou
thee
thine (*gen.*) etc.

SUĞCHAIRŌ συγχαίρω
rejoice in (M. rejoice with) 1
rejoice with 6.

SUĞCHEŌ συγχέω (συγχύνω)
confound 2 (M. trouble in mind 1)
confuse 1
stir up 1.
PASS. be in an uproar 1.

SUĞCHRAOMAI συγχράομαι
have dealings with 1.

SUĞCHUNŌ = **SUĞCHEŌ.**

SUĞCHUSIS σύγχυσις *f.*
confusion 1.

SUĞGENEIA συγγένεια *f.*
kindred 3.

SUĞGENĒS συγγενής
cousin 2
kin 1
kinsfolk (*pl.*) 1
kinsfolks (*pl.*) 1
kinsman 7.

SUĞGNŌMĒ συγγνώμη *f.*
permission 1.

SUĞKAKOPATHEŌ συγκακοπαθέω
be partaker of afflictions 1.

SUĞKAKOUCHEŌ συγκακουχέω
PASS. suffer affliction with 1.

SUĞKALEŌ συγκαλέω
call together 2.
MID. call together 6.

SUĞKALUPTŌ συγκαλύπτω
cover 1.

SUĞKAMPTŌ συγκάμπτω
bow down 1.

SUĞKATABAINŌ συγκαταβαίνω
go down with 1.

SUĞKATAPSĒPHIZŌ συγκαταψηφίζω
number with 1.

SUĞKATATHESIS συγκατάθεσις *f.*
agreement 1.

SUĞKATATITHEMAI συγκατατίθεμαι
consent to 1.

SUĞKATHĒMAI συγκάθημαι
sit with 2.

SUĞKATHIZŌ συγκαθίζω
be set down together 1
make sit together 1.

SUĞKERANNUMI συγκεράννυμι
temper together 1.
PASS. be mixed with (M. be united with) 1.

SUĞKINEŌ συγκινέω
stir up 1.

SUĞKLEIŌ συγκλείω
conclude 2 (M. shut up together 1)
inclose 1
shut up 1.

SUĞKLĒRONOMOS συγκληρονόμος
fellow heir 1
heir together 1
heir with 1
joint heir 1.

SUĞKOINŌNEŌ συγκοινωνέω
be partaker of 1
communicate with 1
have fellowship with 1.

SUĞKOINŌNOS συγκοινωνός
companion 1
partaker 1.
†partake with (ginomai suğkoinōnos) 2.

SUĞKOMIZŌ συγκομίζω
carry to one's burial 1.

SUĞKRINŌ συγκρίνω
compare among 1
compare with 2.

SUĞKUPTŌ συγκύπτω
be bowed together 1.

SUĞKURIA συγκυρία *f.*
chance 1.

SUKAMINOS συκάμινος *f.*
sycamine tree 1.

SUKEA συκέα (συκῆ) *f.*
fig-tree 16.

SUKOMŌRAIA συκομωραία *f.*
sycamore tree 1.

SUKON σῦκον *n.*
fig 4.

SUKOPHANTEŌ συκοφαντέω
accuse falsely 1
take by false accusation 1.

SULAGŌGEŌ συλαγωγέω
spoil 1.

SULAŌ συλάω
rob 1.

SULLALEŌ συλλαλέω
commune with 1
confer with 1
talk with 3.
†speak among (*with* pros) 1.

SULLAMBANŌ συλλαμβάνω
catch 1
conceive 5
take 8.
MID. help 2.

SULLEGŌ συλλέγω
gather 5
gather together 1
gather up 2.

SULLOGIZOMAI συλλογίζομαι
†reason with (*with* pros) 1.

SULLUPEŌ συλλυπέω
grieve 1.

SUMBAINŌ συμβαίνω
be so 1
befal 1
happen 6.

SUMBALLŌ συμβάλλω
confer 1
encounter 1
meet with 1
ponder 1.
MID. help 1.
†ACT. make (*with* eis) 1.

SUMBASILEUŌ συμβασιλεύω
reign with 2.

SUMBIBAZŌ συμβιβάζω
gather assuredly 1
instruct 1
knit together 1
prove 1.
PASS. be compacted 1.

SUMBOULEUŌ συμβουλεύω
counsel 1
give counsel 1.
MID. consult 1
take counsel together 1
take counsel 1.

SUMBOULION συμβούλιον *n.*
consultation 1
council 2
counsel 5.

SUMBOULOS σύμβουλος
counsellor 1.

SUMMARTUREŌ συμμαρτυρέω
bear witness 1
bear witness also (M. witness with) 1
bear witness with 1.
MID. testify unto 1.

SUMMATHĒTĒS συμμαθητής
fellow disciple 1.

SUMMERIZŌ συμμερίζω
MID. be partaker with 1.

SUMMETOCHOS συμμέτοχος
partaker 1.
partaker with 1.

SUMMIMĒTĒS συμμιμητής
follower together 1.

SUMMORPHOŌ συμμορφόω
make conformable unto 1.

SUMMORPHOS σύμμορφος
conformed to 1
fashioned like unto 1.

SUMPARAGINOMAI συμπαραγίνομαι
come together 1
stand with 1.

SUMPARAKALEŌ συμπαρακαλέω
PASS. be comforted together 1.

SUMPARALAMBANŌ συμπαραλαμβάνω
take with one 4.

SUMPARAMENŌ συμπαραμένω
continue with 1.

SUMPAREIMI συμπάρειμι
be here present with 1.

SUMPASCHŌ συμπάσχω
suffer with 2.

SUMPATHEŌ συμπαθέω
be touched with the feeling of 1
have compassion of 1.

SUMPATHĒS συμπαθής
having compassion one of another (*pl.*) 1.

SUMPEMPŌ συμπέμπω
send with 2.

SUMPERILAMBANŌ συμπεριλαμβάνω
embrace 1.

SUMPHĒMI σύμφημι
consent unto 1.

SUMPHERŌ συμφέρω
Trans. bring together 1.
Intrans. be better 1
be expedient 7 (M. be profitable 1)
be good 1
be profitable 3.
Partic. profit 3.

SUMPHŌNEŌ συμφωνέω
agree 3
agree together 1
agree with 2.

SUMPHŌNĒSIS συμφώνησις *f.*
concord 1.

SUMPHŌNIA συμφωνία *f.*
music 1.

SUMPHŌNOS σύμφωνος
consent 1.

SUMPHULETĒS συμφυλέτης
countryman 1.

SUMPHUŌ συμφύω
PASS. spring up with 1.

SUMPHUTOS σύμφυτος
planted together 1.

SUMPINŌ συμπίνω
drink with 1.

SUMPLĒROŌ συμπληρόω
fill 1.
PASS. be fully come 1
come 1.

SUMPNIGŌ συμπνίγω
choke 4
throng 1.

SUMPOLITĒS συμπολίτης
fellow-citizen 1.

* Inexact translations, *e.g.*, of a noun by a verb or adjective, of an active by a passive.
† Cases where two or more words in the original are translated by one word or by a phrase.

SUMPOREUOMAI *συμπορεύομαι*
go with 3
resort 1.

SUMPOSION *συμπόσιον n.*
company 1.

SUMPRESBUTEROS *συμπρεσβύτερος*
also an elder 1.

SUMPSĒPHIZŌ *συμψηφίζω*
count 1.

SUMPSUCHOS *σύμψυχος*
of one accord 1.

SUN *σύν*
beside 1
with 123.

SUNAGŌ *συνάγω*
bestow 2
gather 15
gather together 8
gather up 1
lead into 1
take in 3.
MID. (PASS.) assemble themselves 1
assemble together 1
be assembled 3
be assembled together 1
be gathered 4
be gathered together 12
come together 6
gather 1
gather . . . selves together 2
resort 1.

SUNAGŌGĒ *συναγωγή f.*
assembly (M. synagogue) 1
congregation 1
synagogue 55.

SUNAGŌNIZOMAI *συναγωνίζομαι*
strive together with 1.

SUNAICHMALŌTOS *συναιχμάλωτος*
fellow prisoner 3.

SUNAIRŌ *συναίρω*
reckon 2
take 1.
†reckon (*with* logos) 1.

SUNAKOLOUTHEŌ *συνακολουθέω*
follow 2.

SUNALIZŌ *συναλίζω*
MID. (PASS.) be assembled together with (M. eat together with) 1.

SUNANABAINŌ *συναναβαίνω*
come up with 2.

SUNANAKEIMAI *συνανάκειμαι*
sit at meat with 4
sit at the table with 1
sit down with 1
sit together with 1
sit with 2.

SUNANAMIGNUMI *συναναμίγνυμι*
MID. (PASS.) company with 1
have company with 1
keep company 1.

SUNANAPAUŌ *συναναπαύω*
MID. be refreshed 1.

SUNANTAŌ *συναντάω*
meet 5.
Partic. things that shall befal 1.

SUNANTĒSIS *συνάντησις f.*
†to meet (eis *with acc.*) 1.

SUNANTILAMBANŌ *συναντιλαμβάνω*
MID. help 2.

SUNAPAGŌ *συναπάγω*
carry away with 1
lead away with 1
PASS. condescend to (M. be contented with) 1.

SUNAPOLLUMI *συναπόλλυμι*
MID. (PASS.) perish with 1.

SUNAPOSTELLŌ *συναποστέλλω*
send with 1.

SUNAPOTHNĒSKŌ *συναποθνήσκω*
be dead with (*aor.*) 1
die with 2.

SUNARMOLOGEŌ *συναρμολογέω*
frame fitly together 1
join fitly together 1.

SUNARPAZŌ *συναρπάζω*
catch 4.

SUNATHLEŌ *συναθλέω*
labour with 1
strive together for 1.

SUNATHROIZŌ *συναθροίζω*
call together 1
gather together 2.

SUNAUXANŌ *συναυξάνω*
MID. grow together 1.

SUNDEŌ *συνδέω*
bind with 1.

SUNDESMOS *σύνδεσμος*
band 1
bond 3.

SUNDOULOS *σύνδουλος*
fellow - servant 10.

SUNDOXAZŌ *συνδοξάζω*
glorify together 1.

SUNDROMĒ *συνδρομή f.*
†run together (*with* ginomai) 1.

SUNECHŌ *συνέχω*
constrain 1
keep in 1
press 1
stop 1
throng 1.
Partic. man that holdeth 1.
PASS. be in a strait 1
be straitened (M. be pained) 1
be taken with 3
lie sick of 1.

SUNĒDOMAI *συνήδομαι*
delight in 1.

SUNEDRION *συνέδριον n.*
council 22.

SUNEGEIRŌ *συνεγείρω*
raise up together 1.
PASS. rise with 2.

SUNEIDĒSIS *συνείδησις f.*
conscience 32.

SUNEIDON *συνεῖδον*
be privy to 1
be ware of 1
consider 1
know by 1.

SUNEIMI[1] *σύνειμι*
be with 2.

SUNEIMI[2] *σύνειμι*
be gathered together 1.

SUNEISERCHOMAI *συνεισέρχομαι*
go into with 1
go in with 1.

SUNEKDĒMOS *συνέκδημος*
companion in travel 1
*to travel with 1.

SUNEKLEKTOS *συνεκλεκτός*
elected together with 1.

SUNELAUNŌ *συνελαύνω*
†set at one again (*with* eis *and acc. of* eirēnē) 1.

SUNĒLIKIŌTĒS *συνηλικιώτης*
equal (M. equal in years) 1.

SUNEPHISTĒMI *συνεφίστημι*
rise up together 1.

SUNEPIMARTUREŌ *συνεπιμαρτυρέω*
bear witness also 1.

SUNEPOMAI *συνέπομαι*
accompany 1.

SUNERCHOMAI *συνέρχομαι*
accompany 1
assemble with 1
come 2
come together 18
come with 5
company with 1
go with 4
resort 2.

SUNERGEŌ *συνεργέω*
help with 1
work together 1
work with 2.
Partic. worker together 1.

SUNERGOS *συνεργός*
companion in labour 1
fellow helper 2
fellow labourer 3
fellow worker 1
helper 3
labourer together with 1
work fellow 1.

SUNESIS *σύνεσις f.*
knowledge 1
understanding 6.

SUNESTHIŌ *συνεσθίω*
eat with 5.

SUNĒTHEIA *συνήθεια f.*
custom 2.

SUNETOS *συνετός*
prudent 4.

SUNEUDOKEŌ *συνευδοκέω*
allow 1
be pleased 2
consent unto 2
have pleasure in (M. consent with) 1.

SUNEUŌCHEŌ *συνευωχέω*
MID. feast with 2.

SUNIĒMI *συνίημι*
be wise (M. understand) 1
consider 1
understand 24.

SUNISTĒMI *συνίστημι*
approve 2 (M. commend 1)
commend 10
consist 1
make 1
stand (M. consist) 1
stand with 1.

SUNOCHĒ *συνοχή f.*
anguish 1
distress 1.

SUNODEUŌ *συνοδεύω*
journey with 1.

SUNODIA *συνοδία f.*
company 1.

SUNŌDINŌ *συνωδίνω*
travail in pain together 1.

SUNOIDA = SUNEIDŌN.

SUNOIKEŌ *συνοικέω*
dwell with 1.

SUNOIKODOMEŌ *συνοικοδομέω*
build together 1.

SUNOMILEŌ *συνομιλέω*
talk with 1.

SUNOMOREŌ *συνομορέω*
join hard to 1.

SUNŌMOSIA *συνωμοσία f.*
conspiracy 1.

SUNTASSŌ *συντάσσω*
appoint 2.

SUNTELEIA *συντέλεια f.*
end 6.

SUNTELEŌ *συντελέω*
end 4
finish 1
fulfil 1
make 1.

SUNTEMNŌ *συντέμνω*
cut short 1.
Pass. pt. short 1.

SUNTĒREŌ *συντηρέω*
keep 1
observe (M. keep or save) 1
preserve 2.

SUNTHAPTŌ *συνθάπτω*
bury with 2.

SUNTHLAŌ *συνθλάω*
break 2.

SUNTHLIBŌ *συνθλίβω*
throng 2.

SUNTHRUPTŌ *συνθρύπτω*
break 1.

SUNTITHĒMI *συντίθημι*
MID. agree 2
assent 1
covenant 1.

SUNTOMŌS *συντόμως*
*a few words 1.

SUNTRECHŌ *συντρέχω*
run 1
run together 1
run with 1.

SUNTRIBŌ *συντρίβω*
break 2
break in pieces 1
break to shivers 1
bruise 3 (M. tread 1).
†broken-hearted (*pass. pt. with acc. of* kardia) 1.

SUNTRIMMA *σύντριμμα n.*
destruction 1.

SUNTROPHOS *σύντροφος*
which had been brought up with (M. foster-brother) 1.

SUNTUGCHANŌ *συντυγχάνω*
come at 1.

SUNUPOKRINOMAI *συνυποκρίνομαι*
dissemble with 1.

SUNUPOURGEŌ *συνυπουργέω*
help together 1.

SURŌ *σύρω*
drag 1
draw 3
hale 1.

SURTIS *σύρτις f.*
quicksands 1.

SUSCHĒMATIZŌ *συσχηματίζω*
MID. (PASS.) be conformed to 1
fashion one's self according to 1.

SUSPARASSŌ *συσπαράσσω*
tear 1.

SUSSĒMON *σύσσημον n.*
token 1.

SUSSŌMOS *σύσσωμος*
of the same body 1.

SUSTASIASTĒS *συστασιαστής*
that had made insurrection with 1.

SUSTATIKOS *συστατικός*
of commendation 2.

SUSTAUROŌ *συσταυρόω*
crucify with 5.

SUSTELLŌ *συστέλλω*
wind up 1.
Pass. pt. short 1.

SUSTENAZŌ *συστενάζω*
groan together 1.

SUSTOICHEŌ *συστοιχέω*
answer to (M. be in the same rank with) 1.

SUSTRATIŌTĒS *συστρατιώτης*
fellow-soldier 2.

SUSTREPHŌ *συστρέφω*
gather 1.

SUSTROPHĒ *συστροφή f.*
concourse 1.
†*See* poieō.

SUZAŌ *συζάω*
live with 3.

SUZĒTEŌ *συζητέω*
dispute 1
dispute with 1
inquire 1
question 2
question one with another 1
question with 2
reason 1
reason together 1.

SUZĒTĒSIS *συζήτησις f.*
disputation 1
disputing 1
reasoning 1.

SUZĒTĒTĒS *συζητητής*
disputer 1.

SUZEUGNUMI *συζεύγνυμι*
join together 2.

SUZŌOPOIEŌ *συζωοποιέω*
quicken together with 2.

SUZUGOS *σύζυγος*
yokefellow 1.

T

TA *τά. Neut. pl. of* **HO**[1].
†ta peri: affairs 2, concerning 1, estate 1, for 1, of 1, state 2, etc.

TABERNAI *ταβέρναι f. pl.*
taverns 1.

TACHA *τάχα*
peradventure 1
perhaps 1.

TACHEŌS *ταχέως*
hastily 1
quickly 2
shortly 4
soon 2
suddenly 1.

TACHINOS *ταχινός*
shortly 1
swift 1.

TACHION *τάχιον*
quickly 1
shortly 2
the sooner 1.
†*See* protrechō.

TACHISTA *τάχιστα*
†hōs tachista: with all speed 1.

TACHOS *τάχος n.*
quickly (*dat.*) 1.
†en *with dat.*: quickly 2, shortly 4, speedily 4.

TACHUS *ταχύς*
swift 1.
As adv. quickly 11
lightly 1.

TAGMA *τάγμα n.*
order 1.

TAKTOS *τακτός*
set 1

TALAIPŌREŌ *ταλαιπωρέω*
be afflicted 1.

TALAIPŌRIA *ταλαιπωρία f.*
misery 2.

TALAIPŌROS *ταλαίπωρος*
wretched 2.

TALANTIAIOS *ταλαντιαῖος*
the weight of a talent 1.

TALANTON *τάλαντον n.*
talent 15.

TALITHA *ταλιθά f.*
talitha 1.

TAMEION *ταμεῖον n.*
closet 2
secret chamber 1
store house 1

TAPEINOŌ *ταπεινόω*
abase 5
bring low 1
humble 6.
MID. humble one's self 2.

TAPEINOPHROSUNĒ *ταπεινοφροσύνη f.*
humbleness of mind 1
humility 3
humility of mind 1
lowliness 1
lowliness of mind 1.

* Inexact translations, *e.g.*, of a noun by a verb or adjective, of an active by a passive.
† Cases where two or more words in the original are translated by one word or by a phrase.

TAPEINOS ταπεινός
base 1
cast down 1
humble 2
lowly 1
of low degree 2.
As noun men of low estate (M. mean things) 1.

TAPEINŌSIS ταπείνωσις *f.*
humiliation 1
low estate 1
*be made low 1
*vile (*gen.*) 1.

TAPHĒ ταφή *f.*
†to bury in (eis *with acc.*) 1.

TAPHOS τάφος
sepulchre 6
tomb 1.

TARACHĒ ταραχή *f.*
trouble 1
troubling 1.

TARACHOS τάραχος
stir 2.

TARASSŌ ταράσσω
trouble (*vb.*) 16.
†be troubled (*with acc. of pron.*; M. troubled himself) 1.

TARTAROŌ ταρταρόω
cast down to hell 1.

TASSŌ τάσσω
addict 1
appoint 1
determine 1
ordain 2 (M. order 1)
set 1.
MID. appoint 2.

TAUROS ταῦρος
bull 2
ox 2.

TAUTA ταῦτα [*pl. neut. of* **HOUTOS**].

TAXIS τάξις *f.*
order 10.

TE τε
and 128
both 1
then 2, etc.

TECHNĒ τέχνη *f.*
art 1
craft 1
occupation 1.

TECHNITĒS τεχνίτης
builder 1
craftsman 3.

TEICHOS τεῖχος *n.*
wall 9.

TEKMĒRION τεκμήριον *n.*
infallible proof 1.

TEKNION τεκνίον *n.*
little child 9.

TEKNOGONEŌ τεκνογονέω
bear children 1.

TEKNOGONIA τεκνογονία *f.*
child-bearing 1.

TEKNON τέκνον *n.*
child 77
daughter (M. child) 1
son 21.

TEKNOTROPHEŌ τεκνοτροφέω
bring up children 1.

TĒKŌ τήκω
PASS. melt 1.

TEKTŌN τέκτων
carpenter 2.

TĒLAUGŌS τηλαυγῶς
clearly 1.

TELEIOŌ τελειόω
consecrate (M. perfect) 1
finish 4
fulfil 2
make perfect 12
perfect 4.
PASS. be perfect 1.

TELEIOS τέλειος
of full age (M. perfect) 1
perfect 15.
As noun man (M. perfect *or* of a ripe age) 1
that which is perfect 1
they that are perfect 1.

TELEIŌS τελείως
to the end (M. perfectly) 1.

TELEIŌSIS τελείωσις *f.*
perfection 1
performance 1.

TELEIOTĒS τελειότης *f.*
perfection 1
perfectness 1.

TELEIŌTĒS τελειωτής
finisher 1.

TELEŌ τελέω
accomplish 4
fill up 1
finish 8
fulfil 7
make an end 1
pay 2
perform 1.
PASS. expire 1
go over (M. end or finish) 1.

TELESPHOREŌ τελεσφορέω
bring fruit to perfection 1.

TELEUTAŌ τελευτάω
be dead 3
decease 1
die 8.

TELEUTĒ τελευτή *f.*
death 1.

TĒLIKOUTOS τηλικοῦτος
so great 3
so mighty 1.

TELŌNĒS τελώνης
publican 21.

TELŌNION τελώνιον *n.*
receipt of custom 3 (M. place where custom was received) 1.

TELOS τέλος *n.*
custom 3
end 35
ending 1
the uttermost 1
*finally 1.
†continual (eis *with acc.*) 1.

TEPHROŌ τεφρόω
turn into ashes 1.

TERAS τέρας *n.*
wonder 16.

TĒREŌ τηρέω
hold fast 1
keep 57
observe 4
preserve 2
reserve 8
watch 2.
Partic. keeper 1.

TĒRĒSIS τήρησις *f.*
hold 1
keeping 1
prison 1.

TESSARAKONTA τεσσαράκοντα
forty 21.

TESSARAKONTAETĒS τεσσαρακονταετής
of forty years 1.
†forty years old (*with* chronos) 1.

TESSARES τέσσαρες
four 43.

TESSARESKAIDEKATOS τεσσαρεσκαιδέκατος
fourteenth 2.

TETARTAIOS τεταρταῖος
dead four days 1.

TETARTOS τέταρτος
fourth 8
fourth part 1
*four 1.

TETRADION τετράδιον *n.*
quaternion 1.

TETRAGŌNOS τετράγωνος
foursquare 1.

TETRAKISCHILIOI τετρακισχίλιοι
four thousand 5.

TETRAKOSIOI τετρακόσιοι
four hundred 4.

TETRAMĒNOS τετράμηνος
four months 1.

TETRAPLOOS τετραπλόος
fourfold 1.

TETRAPOUS τετράπους *n.*
four-footed beast 3.

TETRARCHEŌ τετραρχέω
be tetrarch 1.
Partic. tetrarch 2.

TETRARCHĒS τετράρχης
tetrarch 4.

THALASSA θάλασσα *f.*
sea 91.

THALPŌ θάλπω
cherish 2.

THAMBEŌ θαμβέω
be astonished 1.
PASS. be amazed 2
be astonished 1.

THAMBOS θάμβος *n.*
wonder 1.
†be amazed (*with* gignomi epi) 1; be astonished (*with* periechō *and acc.*) 1.

THANASIMOS θανάσιμος
deadly thing 1.

THANATĒPHOROS θανατηφόρος
deadly 1.

THANATOŌ θανατόω
cause to be put to death 3
kill 2
mortify 1
put to death 4.
PASS. become dead 1.

THANATOS θάνατος
death 116
Death 1
*deadly 2.

THAPTŌ θάπτω
bury 11.

THARRHEŌ θαρρέω
be bold 2
be confident 1
have confidence 1.
Partic. boldly 1
confident 1.

THARSEŌ θαρσέω
be of good cheer 5
be of good comfort 3.

THARSOS θάρσος *n.*
courage 1.

THAUMA θαῦμα *n.*
admiration 1.

THAUMASIOS θαυμάσιος
As noun wonderful thing 1.

THAUMASTOS θαυμαστός
marvellous 5.
As noun marvel 1.
marvellous thing 1.

THAUMAZŌ θαυμάζω
admire 1
have in admiration 1
marvel 28
marvel at 2
wonder 12
wonder at 1.
MID. wonder 1.

THEA θεά *f.*
goddess 3.

THEAOMAI θεάομαι
behold 2
look on 1
look upon 1
see 17.
PASS. be seen 3.

THEATRIZŌ θεατρίζω
make a gazing stock 1.

THEATRON θέατρον *n.*
spectacle (M. theatre) 1
theatre 1.

THEIŌDĒS θειώδης
of brimstone 1.

THEION θεῖον *n.*
brimstone 7.

THEIOS θεῖος
divine 2.
As noun the Godhead 1.

THEIOTĒS θειότης *f.*
Godhead 1.

THĒKĒ θήκη *f.*
sheath 1.

THĒLAZŌ θηλάζω
give suck 4
suck 1
Partic. suckling 1.

THELĒMA θέλημα *n.*
desire (M. will) 1
pleasure 1
will 62 (*pl.* 1).

THELĒSIS θέλησις *f.*
will 1.

THELŌ θέλω
be desirous 1
be disposed 1
be forward (M. be willing) 1
be so 1
be willing 1
desire 13
had rather 1
intend 1
list 3
love 1
mean 2
will 98
will have 5
would 70
would have 5
*it pleased 2.
Partic. desirous 2
voluntary (M. being a voluntary) 1
willingly 2.

THĒLUS θῆλυς
female 3
woman 2.

THEMELIOŌ θεμελιόω
found 2
ground 2
lay the foundation of 1
settle 1.

THEMELIOS θεμέλιος (θεμέλιον)
foundation 16.

THEODIDAKTOS θεοδίδακτος
taught of God 1.

THEOMACHEŌ θεομαχέω
fight against God 1.

THEOMACHOS θεομάχος
*to fight against God 1.

THEOPNEUSTOS θεόπνευστος
given by inspiration of God 1.

THEŌREŌ θεωρέω
behold 11
consider 1
look on 1
perceive 4
see 40.

THEŌRIA θεωρία *f.*
sight 1.

THEOS Θεός
God 1326
god 12
*godly 3
*exceeding (*dat.*) (M. to God) 1.
†Kata *with acc.*: after a godly manner (M. according to God) 1, after a godly sort 1, godly 1. *See* axiōs.

THEOSEBEIA θεοσέβεια *f.*
godliness 1.

THEOSEBĒS θεοσεβής
worshipper of God 1.

THEOSTUGĒS θεοστυγής
hater of God 1.

THEOTĒS θεότης *f.*
Godhead 1.

THĒRA θήρα *f.*
trap 1.

THERAPEIA θεραπεία *f.*
healing 2
household 2.

THERAPEUŌ θεραπεύω
cure 5
heal 38
worship 1.

THERAPŌN θεράπων
servant 1.

THĒREUŌ θηρεύω
catch 1.

THĒRIOMACHEŌ θηριομαχέω
fight with beasts 1.

THĒRION θηρίον *n.*
beast 42
venomous beast 1
wild beast 3.

THERISMOS θερισμός
harvest 13.

THERISTĒS θεριστής
reaper 2.

THERIZŌ θερίζω
reap 21.

THERMAINŌ θερμαίνω
MID. be warmed 1
warm one's self 5.

THERMĒ θέρμη *f.*
heat 1.

THEROS θέρος *n.*
summer 3.

THĒSAURIZŌ θησαυρίζω
heap treasure together 1
keep in store 1
lay up 3
lay up treasure 1
treasure up 1.
Partic. in store 1.

THĒSAUROS θησαυρός
treasure 18.

THIGGANŌ θιγγάνω
handle 1
touch 2.

THLIBŌ θλίβω
afflict 3
throng 1
trouble 4.
PASS. narrow 1
suffer tribulation 1.

THLIPSIS θλῖψις *f.*
affliction 17
anguish 1
persecution 1
tribulation 21
trouble 3
*burdened 1
*dead 9
*die 1.
†to be afflicted (eis *with acc.*) 1.

THNĒSKŌ θνήσκω
be dead 9
die 1.
Partic. dead 3.

THNĒTOS θνητός
mortal 5.
As noun mortality 1.

THŌRAX θώραξ
breastplate 5.

THORUBEŌ θορυβέω
set on an uproar 1.
MID. make a noise 1
make this ado 1
trouble one's self 1.

THORUBOS θόρυβος
tumult 4
uproar 3.

THRAUŌ θραύω
bruise 1.

THREMMA θρέμμα *n.*
cattle 1.

THRĒNEŌ θρηνέω
lament 2
mourn 2.

THRĒNOS θρῆνος
lamentation 1.

THRĒSKEIA θρησκεία *f.*
religion 3
worshipping 1.

THRĒSKOS θρῆσκος
religious 1.

THRIAMBEUŌ θριαμβεύω
cause to triumph 1
triumph over 1.

THRIX θρίξ *f.*
hair 15.

THROEŌ θροέω
PASS. be troubled 3.

THROMBOS θρόμβος
great drop 1.

THRONOS θρόνος
seat 7
throne 54.

THUELLA θύελλα *f.*
tempest 1.

THUGATĒR θυγάτηρ *f.*
daughter 29.

THUGATRION θυγάτριον *n.*
little daughter 1
young daughter 1.

THUINOS θύϊνος
thyine (M. sweet) 1

THUMIAMA θυμίαμα *n.*
incense 4
odour 2 (M. incense) 1.

THUMIAŌ θυμιάω
burn incense 1.

THUMIATĒRION θυμιατήριον *n.*
censer 1.

THUMOMACHEŌ θυμομαχέω
be highly displeased with (M. bear an hostile mind, intending war with) 1.

THUMOS θυμός
fierceness 2
indignation 1
wrath 15.

* Inexact translations, *e.g.*, of a noun by a verb or adjective, of an active by a passive.
† Cases where two or more words in the original are translated by one word or by a phrase.

THUMOŌ θυμόω
Pass. be wroth 1.
THUŌ θύω
do sacrifice 2
kill 8 (M. sacrifice 1)
sacrifice 3 (M. slay) 1
slay 1.
THURA θύρα *f.*
door 38
gate 1.
THUREOS θυρεός
shield 1.
THURIS θυρίς *f.*
window 2.
THURŌROS θυρωρός
porter 2
that keepeth the door 2.
THUSIA θυσία *f.*
sacrifice 29.
THUSIASTĒRION θυσιαστήριον *n.*
altar 23.
TI = TIS.
TIKTŌ τίκτω
bear 1
be born 1
be delivered 4
be delivered of 1
be in travail 1
bring forth 9.
Pass. be born 2.
TILLŌ τίλλω
pluck 3.
TIMAŌ τιμάω
honour 19 (M. esteem 1)
value 2 (M. buy 1).
TIMĒ τιμή *f.*
honour 32
precious (M. honour) 1
price 8
sum 1.
TIMIOS τίμιος
dear 1
had in reputation 1
honourable 1
precious 11.
TIMIOTĒS τιμιότης *f.*
costliness 1.
TIMŌREŌ τιμωρέω
punish 2.
TIMŌRIA τιμωρία *f.*
punishment 1.
TINŌ (TIŌ) τίνω (τίω)
†be punished (*with* dikē) 1.
TIS[1] τις
a 11
a certain man 7
a kind of 1
a man 30
any 39
any man 55
anything 24
certain 104
one 34
some 75
somebody 2
something 5
somewhat 6, etc.
TIS[2] τίς
how is it? 4
what? 253
whether? 8
which? 17
who? (whose? whom?) 135
why? 66, etc.
†what (*with* logos; M. what speech) 1.
TITHĒMI τίθημι
appoint 5
bow 1
give 1
lay 28
lay aside 1
lay down 12
make 10
ordain 2
put 11
set 2
set forth 1.
Mid. appoint 1
commit (M. put) 1
conceive 1
lay up 1
let sink down 1
purpose 1
put 7
set 2
settle 1.
†Act. kneel (*with pl. of* gonu) 5. Mid. advise (*with* boulē) 1.
TITLOS τίτλος
title 2.
TO. *Neut. of* **HO**[1].
TOICHOS τοῖχος
wall 1.
TOIGAROUN τοιγαροῦν
therefore 1
wherefore 1.
TOINUN τοίνυν
then 1
therefore 3.
TOIOSDE τοιόσδε
such 1.
TOIOUTOS τοιοῦτος
such 41
such a fellow 1
such a man 1
such an one 8
such thing 9.
†of like occupation (peri *with neut. pl.*) 1.
TOKOS τόκος
usury 2.
TOLMAŌ τολμάω
be bold 4
dare 11.
Partic. boldly 1.
TOLMĒROTERON τολμηρότερον
the more boldly 1.
TOLMĒTĒS τολμητής
presumptuous 1.
TOMŌTEROS τομώτερος
sharper 1.
TOPAZION τοπάζιον *n.*
topaz 1.
TOPOS τόπος
coast 1
license 1
place 77
quarter 1
room 5.
†every where (ta peri ton topon ekeinon) 1; the same quarters (en *with* pas *and* topos) 1. *See* pedinos, trachus.
TOSOUTOS τοσοῦτος
as large 1
so great 5
so long 2
so much 7.
Plur. so many 4
so many things (M. so great things) 1
these many 1.
TOTE τότε
that time 4
then 149
when 1.
TOUNANTION τοὐναντίον
contrariwise 3.

TOUTO τοῦτο [*neut. sing. of* **HOUTOS**].
TOXON τόξον *n.*
bow 1.
TRACHĒLIZŌ τραχηλίζω
open 1.
TRACHĒLOS τράχηλος
neck 7.
TRACHUS τραχύς
rough 1.
†rocks (*with* topos) 1.
TRAGOS τράγος
goat 4.
TRAPEZA τράπεζα *f.*
bank 1
meat 1
table 13.
TRAPEZITĒS τραπεζίτης
exchanger 1.
TRAUMA τραῦμα *n.*
wound 1.
TRAUMATIZŌ τραυματίζω
wound (*vb.*) 2.
TRECHŌ τρέχω
have course (M. run) 1
run 18.
TREIS τρεῖς
three 68.
TREMŌ τρέμω
be afraid 1
tremble 3.
TREPHŌ τρέφω
bring up 1
feed 4
nourish 3.
TRIAKONTA τριάκοντα
thirty 9
thirty-fold 2.
TRIAKOSIOI τριακόσιοι
three hundred 2.
TRIBOLOS τρίβολος
brier 1
thistle 1.
TRIBOS τρίβος *f.*
path 3.
TRICHINOS τρίχινος
of hair 1.
TRIETIA τριετία *f.*
space of three years 1.
TRIMĒNON τρίμηνον *n.*
three months 1.
TRIS τρίς
thrice 10.
†Epi tris: thrice 1, three times 1.
TRISCHILIOI τρισχίλιοι
three thousand 1.
TRISTEGON τρίστεγον *n.*
third loft 1.
TRITOS τρίτος
third 32.
As noun the third day 2
the third part 15.
As adv. the third time 7
thirdly 1.
†the third time (ek *with gen.*) 1.
TRIZŌ τρίζω
gnash with 1.
TROCHIA τροχιά *f.*
path 1.

TROCHOS τροχός
course 1.
TRŌGŌ τρώγω
eat 6.
TROMOS τρόμος
trembling 4.
†tremble (*with* echō) 1.
TROPĒ τροπή *f.*
turning 1.
TROPHĒ τροφή *f.*
food 2
meat 11
some meat (*gen.*) 2.
TROPHOS τροφός *f.*
nurse 1.
TROPOPHOREŌ τροποφορέω
suffer one's manners (M. bear, or feed one, as a nurse beareth or feedeth her child) 1.
TROPOS τρόπος
conversation 1
manner 1
means 2
way 2.
†hos tropos: as 3, even as 1, in like manner as. Even as (kata *with acc.*) 2.
TRUBLION τρύβλιον *n.*
dish 2.
TRUGAŌ τρυγάω
gather 3.
TRUGŌN τρυγών *f.*
turtle-dove 1.
TRUMALIA τρυμαλιά *f.*
eye 2.
TRUPHAŌ τρυφάω
live in pleasure 1.
TRUPHĒ τρυφή *f.*
*to riot 1.
†delicately (en *with dat.*) 1.
TRUPĒMA τρύπημα *n.*
eye 1.
TUGCHANŌ τυγχάνω
be 2
chance 1
enjoy 1
obtain 5.
†no little (ou *with partic.*) 1; refresh self (*with* epimeleia) 1; special (ou *with partic.*) 1.
TUMPANIZŌ τυμπανίζω
torture 1.
TUPHLOS τυφλός
blind 40
that was blind 1
which was blind 1.
As noun blind man 10
he that was blind 1.
TUPHŌ τύφω
Pass. smoke 1.
TUPHŌNIKOS τυφωνικός
tempestuous 1.
TUPHOŌ τυφόω
Pass. be high-minded 1
be lifted up with pride 1
be proud (M. be a fool) 1.

TUPOS τύπος
ensample 5 (M. type 1)
example 2 (M. figure 1)
fashion 1
figure 2
form 1
manner 1
pattern 2
print 2.
TUPTŌ τύπτω
beat 3
smite 9
strike 1
wound 1.
TURBAZŌ τυρβάζω
Mid. (Pass.) be troubled 1.

X

XENIA ξενία *f.*
lodging 2.
XENIZŌ ξενίζω
entertain 1
lodge 4.
Partic. strange thing 1.
Pass. lodge 2.
Mid. think strange 2.
XENODOCHEŌ ξενοδοχέω
lodge strangers 1.
XENOS ξένος
host 1
strange 2.
As noun stranger 10
strange thing 1.
XĒRAINŌ ξηραίνω
dry up 3
wither 1.
Pass. be ripe (M. be dried) 1
be withered 3
pine away 1
wither 1
wither away 6.
XĒROS ξηρός
dry 1
withered 4.
As noun dry land 1
land 1.
XESTĒS ξέστης
pot 2.
XULINOS ξύλινος
of wood 2.
XULON ξύλον *n.*
staff 5
stocks 1
tree 10
wood 3.
XURAŌ ξυράω
shave 2.
Mid. shave 1.

Z

ZAŌ ζάω
be alive 9
live 118.
Partic. alive 7
lively 3
quick 4.
Infin. life 1
life-time 1.
ZĒLOŌ ζηλόω
affect 1
be jealous over 1
be moved with envy 1
be zealous 1
covet 1
covet earnestly 1
desire 1
desire to have 1
envy 1
zealously affect 2.

ZĒLOS ζῆλος
emulation 1
envy 1
envying 5
fervent mind 1
indignation 2 (M. envy 1)
jealousy 1
zeal 6.
ZĒLŌTĒS ζηλωτής
zealous 5.
ZĒMIA ζημία *f.*
damage 1
loss 3.
ZĒMIOŌ ζημιόω
Mid. (Pass.) be cast away 1
lose 2
receive damage 1
suffer loss 1
suffer the loss of 1.
ZEŌ ζέω
be fervent 1
Partic. fervent 1.
ZESTOS ζεστός
hot 3.
ZĒTĒMA ζήτημα *n.*
question 5.
ZĒTEŌ ζητέω
be about 1
desire 3
endeavour 1
go about 4
inquire 1
inquire for 1
require 2
seek 98
seek after 1
seek for 6
seek means 1.
ZĒTĒSIS ζήτησις *f.*
question 6 (M. how to enquire = eis *with acc.*) 1.
ZEUGOS ζεῦγος *n.*
pair 1
yoke 1.
ZEUKTĒRIA ζευκτηρία *f.*
band 1.
ZIZANION ζιζάνιον *n.*
tares (*pl.*) 8.
ZŌĒ ζωή *f.*
life 133
life-time 1.
ZŌGREŌ ζωγρέω
catch 1
take captive (M. take alive) 1.
ZŌNĒ ζώνη *f.*
girdle 6
purse 2.
ZŌNNUMI ζώννυμι (ζωννύω)
gird 2.
ZŌOGONEŌ ζωογονέω
preserve 1.
Pass. live 1.
ZŌON ζῷον *n.*
beast 23.
ZŌOPOIEŌ ζωοποιέω
give life 2 (M. quicken) 1
make alive 1
quicken 9.
ZOPHOS ζόφος
blackness 1
darkness 2
mist 1.
ZUGOS ζυγός
pair of balances 1
yoke 5.
ZUMĒ ζύμη *f.*
leaven 13.
ZUMOŌ ζυμόω
leaven (*vb.*) 4.

* Inexact translations, *e.g.*, of a noun by a verb or adjective, of an active by a passive.
† Cases where two or more words in the original are translated by one word or by a phrase.

SCRIPTURE PROPER NAMES.

INTRODUCTION.

THE following list of Scripture proper names is intended to be a guide to their "correct" pronunciation. It does not offer an absolute standard, for no such standard exists. The supreme authority in pronunciation is prevalent usage (among educated people). But the weakness of such an authority is specially clear in the case of Scripture names. Even names not uncommon are variously pronounced, and many are so unfamiliar that there is no "usage" by which to decide. In such cases people naturally pronounce according to the analogy of other words which are familiar, and the practice supplies a rule of treatment. Doubtful or unfamiliar words should be pronounced in harmony with the general tendencies of the language, or in a way similar to other words which strikingly resemble them. Scripture names are borrowed from the foreign languages Greek and Hebrew. They are, therefore, to be compared specially with words of similar origin, such as the names of classical antiquity. The original pronunciation exerts a certain influence which must be determined.

In actual speech unfamiliar words are pronounced as analogy suggests, unconsciously it may be. In the following list an attempt is made to apply this principle of analogy systematically to those words which have no definite customary pronunciation. In accordance with the preceding statement three influences or analogies must affect the treatment of Scripture names. These are, (1) the original pronunciation, (2) the characteristic tendencies of purely English speech, (3) the fixed customary pronunciation of certain words resembling others less common. There is no single court of appeal. In particular, the original pronunciation is not the only nor, perhaps, the chief influence. If it were better understood how impossible it is to pronounce Hebrew names as the ancient Hebrews did, there would be less temptation to lay stress on the original as the best guide. On the other hand, the closer the incorporation of Scripture names into English, the better; and this also is a consideration entitled to influence. Conflict of analogies cannot be wholly avoided. If one is not in itself stronger than another, the most "desirable" result in each case should be preferred. Ease of pronunciation is one test of desirability. The principle of pronunciation according to sense has also been used by the writer.

The presence in this list, as in all such lists, of words whose pronunciation is "theoretically" determined, and the constant disagreement of authorities, make it desirable to prefix a statement of principles. The principles here adopted are those which seem to express the English treatment of ancient foreign names which have become common property in the language. Almost every case has been noted in which customary pronunciation departs from and, of course, overrides general tendency. The reader is accordingly provided with an *explanation* of the pronunciations of the list. He may reject or modify the latter according as he judges the former.

Three subjects have to be considered:—1st, the sounds of the letters; 2nd, the position of the tone or stress of voice—the "accent"; 3rd, the length of the vowel sounds.

1. The Sounds of the Letters.

The general usage in current English is to pronounce ancient foreign names as if their spelling represented English sounds. In Biblical names the following limitations may be observed:—

1. Vowels.—(*a*) Final *e* is generally sounded (as Beth′phagë, Chlo′ë, Gethsem′anë), except in the (English) adjective terminations *ite* and *ene* (Am′orite, Nazare′ne), and in some completely anglicised words, generally not exclusively Scriptural (Crete, Rome). Magdale′në has also an anglicised form, Mag′dalen (*cf.* Ur′bane, best pronounced Ur′ban). In Acts xxvii. 12 the final *e* of Phœnice is not justified, as elsewhere, by the Greek, and may therefore be silent.

(*b*) Final *es* is similarly sounded (Sos′thenës), unless it is an (English) plural termination (Cretes, Aphar′sachites).

(*c*) *U* may be pronounced *oo* more often than in purely English words. It is pedantic, however, to make the usage very general.

(*d*) Two vowels, particularly in Hebrew names, are generally each pronounced (Bezal′ëel). But a long vowel, especially if accented, tends to absorb another preceding or following (A′aron, Ja′akan, Beu′lah, Deu′ël). *Ai* regularly becomes *ā* (Cain, Ja′irus, Ab′igail, and all names in final *ail*; *cf.* Mi′chael) or *ī* (Benai′ah, Si′nai). When *ai* ends a word, or when the *i* is the initially accented element, the pronunciation *i* is usual; but *a* is also permissible (Isai′ah, Si′nai). Jehal′eleel may be pronounced as Jehal′elel by analogy (in other words, also, there is a tendency to pronounce *ee* = *ē*). Saul is completely anglicised (*cf.* Paul). In Pharaoh, *a* in the last syllable is silent (see below). In Balaam, Canaan, and Zaph′nath-paan′eah, *aa* = *ă*. In New Testament names, *æ* and *œ* in the middle of a word = *ē* (Berœ′a). Final *ia* and *ius* tend to become *ya* and *yus*, less so after a long vowel (Apu′lia). In Zeb′edee, *ee* = *e*.

2. Consonants.—(*a*) *C* and *g* are generally "hard," even before *e* and *i* (Gergese′ne). But the "soft" pronunciation occurs in New Testament words (Beth′phagë, Can′dacë, Hermog′enës).

(*b*) *Ch* = *k*, except in Ra′chel.

(*c*) *T*, *p*, and *s* before *th*, *ph*, and *sh* are written for *th*, *ph*, and *sh* respectively, and are pronounced accordingly (Ap′phia, Mat′thew).

(*d*) If the analogy of the originals be followed, *h* should be pronounced except, in general, at the end of a word. But at the end of any syllable it is unnatural in English (Ah'lai, Ah'lab), and between two vowels is apt to be elided (Beth'lehem).

2. Stress of Voice ("Accentuation").

The English stress accent in ancient foreign names is determined, with limitations, by the original length of the vowels, not by the original stress.

1. Words of two syllables are accented on the penult (Ad'am, Pa'ran). Haura'n (*a* as in psalm) is a possible exception, by analogy of the modern name; and compounds like Ben-hur have no stress accent (level stress).

2. Words with a long penultimate vowel in the original accent this in English (Aba'na, Abi'hur).

Exceptions.—(*a*) Nouns in *iel* and *ael* are generally accented according to the analogy of Dan'iel, Is'rael, and Methu'sael (*cf.* also Be'lial). Pen'iel is therefore preferable to Peni'el, unless the analogy of Penu'el decide otherwise. Nouns in *uel* have the same tendency (Sam'uel, Lem'uel, Imman'uel). Beth'uel, Kem'uel, Pen'uel are thus common for Bethu'el, Kemu'el, Penu'el. In the case of rare names it may be regarded as more natural (in accordance with analogy) to put the accent on the third last syllable (Ham'uel, etc.). Difficulty of pronunciation may suggest Jehi'el rather than Jeh'iel.

(*b*) Words which have been given the English termination *ite* are naturally anglicised completely by placing the accent on the third last syllable (Ar'elite, Che'rethite (Cher'ethite), De'havite). It may be suggested that Hebrew forms in *i*, when *i* is equivalent to *ite*, should be uniformly accented in the same way (Jeb'usi = Jeb'usite, Gesh'uri = Gesh'urite; so Ha-ahash'tari). Even somewhat uncertain cases might be treated so (Ar'eli, Be'eri, for Are'li, Bee'ri). In some words the influence of the noun to which the termination is attached throws the accent still further back (Gib'eonite; Am'alekite for Amal'ekite seems cumbrous). The blocked syllable (see No. 3) in Mor'asthite suggests Moras'thite as an alternative. Shuth'alhite is easy if the *h* be made silent.

(*c*) Words ending in the adjective termination *ene* have, at least, an approach to a final accent (Nazare'ne, Damasce'ne). The ante-penultimate syllable has then also a certain stress (Dam'asce'ne).

(*d*) Plurals in *im* and *oth* are felt to be plurals only if the accent is thrown back according to English analogy: Ash'eroth, Ba'alim, De'danim, Caph'torim, Per'azim. This accentuation may, therefore, be preferred in designations of peoples or groups of persons. In place names, and in names of individuals that are not really nations, the plural accentuation is less appropriate (Ab'arim or Aba'rim, At'aroth or Ata'roth, etc.; Be'eroth, "wells," may be pronounced a plural). The long *a* of the plural Saba'oth (see 3. 1) attracts the accent (Leb'aoth would, similarly, be Leba'oth). Behe'moth, if a plural, will be accented Be'hemoth. For other plurals compare No. 3.

(*e*) The favourite English ante-penultimate accent is sanctioned by usage in a number of well-known names. *Examples*:—A'braham, Ab'salom, Aj'alon, Am'alek, An'athoth (a plural), Ar'arat, Areop'agus, As'ahel, Bethab'ara, Deb'orah, El'iphaz, Hav'ilah, Heph'zibah, I'chabod, Ith'amar, Jer'icho, Ka'desh Bar'nea, Leb'anon, Naph'tali, Pot'iphar, [Shib'boleth], Thad'deus, Zeb'ulun. But usage fluctuates even in these (Debo'rah, etc.), and others also are heard. *Examples*:—Am'raphel, El'ihu, Eph'ratah, Esh'taol, E'vil Mer'odach, Kez'ia, Mer'ibah, for Amra'phel, Eli'hu, etc. Where a speaker is uncertain of the length of the penultimate vowel an antepenultimate accent is likely to be preferred (Ar'abah, Ar'eli, Hag'abah, for Ara'bah, Are'li, Haga'bah).

(*f*) See compound words, No. 5.

3. The penultimate syllable is accented also if it be "shut," *i.e.*, if its vowel is "blocked" or followed by two consonants (Artaxer'xes). A doubled consonant has the same effect (Agrip'pa, Drusil'la). Akrab'bim, Asup'pim, Chesul'loth, Leum'mim, etc., though plurals (see No. 2*d*), may follow this analogy. Phil'ippi, when used for Philip'pi, is due to the analogy of Phil'ip. Hab'akkuk may be heard for Habak'kuk. Words in which an original double consonant is written once in English can scarcely be joined to this class (Am'ashai, Mach'benai, Mat'tathah, Ger'izim; Geri'zim has no good support though it is in use).

Exceptions:—*Tr*, *pr*, *br*, etc., are not held to block a syllable (Antip'atris, Ep'aphras).

4. Other words, in accordance with general English usage, are accented on the third last syllable.

Exceptions:—(*a*) *A* of the termination *aim* being long (see 3. 1) tends to attract the accent. It does so in all words of more than three syllables (Diblatha'im), and even in some trisyllabic words (Karna'im or Kar'naim, Gitta'im or Git'taim; but Eph'raim). En-eg'laim is a compound (see No. 5).

(*b*) Nouns in final *ezer* (*eser*) accent on the penult (Pile'ser, Shalmane'ser). This seems in accordance with No. 5 (Ab'i-e'zer). Jo'ezer may follow 5*a*.

(*c*) Penultimate *i*, even where it represents the Hebrew consonant *y*, has a strong tendency to attract the accent (Goli'ath); it absorbs a preceding *a* or *e* (Benai'ah, Hashabnei'ah; see 1. 1*d*). The usage is invariable in the case of nouns in *iah* = *yah* (Hezeki'ah), and this analogy may be allowed to determine the case of other Hebrew names in which *i* is followed by *a* (Adali'a, Ahi'an, Ali'ah, Ali'an, Casiphi'a). On grounds of etymology it would be preferable to treat the *i* as a consonant, not only in A'rieh, A'rioch, He'zion, etc., but also in Adal'ia, Ah'ian, etc. (for Adali'a, Ahi'an). Where *u* represents Hebrew *w* it has never been accented (Ish'uah). New Testament names in *ia* do not accent the *i* unless it represents an original diphthong (Ap'phia, Attali'a). Old Testament Ahi'o seems easier than Ah'io (or A'hio).

(*d*) The accent of Ene'as is due to the analogy of Vergil's hero. The original *a* of Geha'zi is also short. It seems an entirely isolated case.

(*e*) See compound words, No. 5.

5. Easily recognisable compounds are best treated as such, by giving to each element a separate accent. Beth'-she'mesh (temple of the sun), not Beth'shemesh. Examples are compounds with *abi* (father), *ahi* (brother), *baal* (lord, Baal),

bath (daughter), *beer* (well), *ben* (son), *beth* (house, temple), *el* (God), *en* (fountain). *E.g.*, Ab'i-a'thar, Ab'i-e'zer, Ba'al-ha'zor, El'i-a'thah. On the same principle the Hebrew article (*hâ*, etc.) may be treated as a separate element (Ham-me'lech, Beth-hac-ce'rem). If the second element of the compound is a monosyllable, the whole is always treated as one word (Abi'hur, Adoni'ram, Hak'koz, Ker'en-hap'puch for Ker'en-hap-pu'ch).

Exceptions:—(*a*) Compounds in which the first element is *Jo* or *Jeho* (*Jehoi*) = *Jehovah*, are given a single accent (Jo'ahaz, Jo'hanan, Josh'ua, Jehon'adab, Jehoi'akim, for Jo-a'haz, Jeho-na'dab, Jehoi-a'kim, etc.). Although the penult is long, the accent rests on this first element (against No. 2).

(*b*) Usage decides for Abim'elech, not Ab'i-me'lech, and this analogy determines Elim'elech, etc. Other exceptions to be admitted are (Beel'zebub), Beth'lehem, Ben'jamin, and En'gedi. Ahith'ophel and Mephib'osheth may also be recognised, and perhaps Abed'nego. Many others are usual (Abi'athar, Eli'a-thah, even Bath'sheba, Ammin'adab), though not to be preferred. The Concordance list carries out the principle more uniformly than is done in present practice. Ab'igail (for Ab'i-ga'il) is a partial exception, since *ail* coalesces into one syllable and has at most a secondary accent (so Ab'ihail). Zerub'babel, if treated as a compound, would be Zer'ub-ba'bel.

3. Length of Vowels.

1. Unaccented vowels are usually short. At the beginning of a word *i* (*y*) in an open syllable is long (Isai'ah, Phile'mon, Shilo'ah, Idume'a, Hymene'us). So are all vowels immediately preceding another (Is'räel, Mōadi'ah, Jāazi'ah). These long vowels have really a secondary accent (I'dume'a). *U* in any open syllable seems to be long (Uri'ah), and *o* has a similar tendency (Obadi'ah).

2. The vowel of an accented open penult is long (Aba'na).

Exceptions:—(*a*) In the first member of a compound there is a tendency to shorten (and make the accent secondary). *Examples*:—Ben'e-be'rak, Eb'en-e'zer, Had'ad-e'zer, Pad'an-a'ram (for Pa'dan-a'ram, etc.).

(*b*) Numerous familiar dissyllables have a short vowel. *Examples*:—Ad'am, Am'on, Ash'er, Beth'el (by this analogy, Beth'ul), Clem'ent, Cor'inth, Her'od. Gesh'ur, Gesh'em, Gesh'am seem easier than Ge'shur, etc. Hash'ub is uniform with Has'shub. Tab-rim'on is by analogy of Rim'mon.

(*c*) Ellas'ar is frequent for Ella'sar. Comp. Dian'a.

3. The vowel of an accented "shut" penult is short.

Exceptions:—*Tr*, *br*, *dr* may be regarded as leaving the syllable open (*cf.* above, 2. 3). Hence Ce'dron, E'phrath, E'phron, He'brew, He'bron, Sha'drach, for Eph'ron, Heb'ron, etc. The original short vowel is in favour of Heb'ron, Shad'-rach, etc., and influences the pronunciation of those acquainted with the original.

4. The vowel of an accented ante-penultimate syllable is generally short (Bal'adan, Ith'amar, Sim'eon, Syr'ia).

Exceptions:—(*a*) If followed immediately by another vowel it is long (Ma'achah, Na'aman). Also if separated from a vowel only by *h* (Ana'harath, De'havite, Jo'hanan, O'holah), unless perhaps in the case of initial *a* (Ah'ara).

(*b*) *A*, *e*, *o*, and *u* in an open syllable are long when the last syllable commences with a vowel which is preceded by *i* (A'riel, A'sia, Eze'kiel, Gama'liel, Ico'nium, Ju'lius, Lysa'nias, Pu'tiel, Sama'ria). In these words the penultimate and final syllables merge into one, so that they approximate to the class of words in No. 2. A'dria (for Ad'ria), Ga'briel, etc., also belong to this class (see No. 3 and 2. 3). A'braham seems to be an extension of it (along with a possible E'phraim). Excepting A'riel, Pu'tiel, U'riel, and Zu'riel, trisyllables in final *iel* follow the analogy of Dan'iel and Pen'iel. Some other words also tend to receive a short vowel (Ar'ioch, Hez'ion, Jahaz'iel, Ker'ioth, etc.). But in the Concordance list the vowel of such words is made uniformly long, except in the case of Iscar'iot.

(*c*) An original long vowel may be retained (Epe'netus, O'mega, I'chabod (is Ich'abod also less emphatic ?), Me'deba, So'pater).

(*d*) In adjectives and plurals a long vowel may be due to the root word (even if hypothetical): E'domite, Sha'ronite, De'danim. But usage fluctuates, *e.g.*, Ag'agite (A'gagite), Ar'elite, Jez'erite.

(*e*) Sy'racuse is in accordance with the modern tendency to pronounce Greek *y* as *ī*.

Transliteration of Hebrew Names.—Hebrew names, with the exception of some adjective forms, are followed by what may be regarded as an exact transliteration of their originals. Every reader may thus use the original to influence his English pronunciation. It has not been considered necessary to supplement the Greek names in this way, because the English spelling already sufficiently represents the original. Those acquainted with Hebrew will readily recognise the system of transliteration adopted. The following general description contains all that can be of interest or value to the general reader. There are three *s* sounds in Hebrew (*s*, *ṣ*, *ś*), two *t*'s, two *k*'s, and two *h*'s (*t*, *ṭ*, *k*, *ḳ*, *h*, *ḥ*). *ḥ* frequently has a *ch* sound (Welsh rather than Scotch or German). There are two consonants for which there is no sign in English. ʾ was a very slight sound, generally in the end becoming silent. It is sometimes represented in the English Bible by *e* (Abdeel). ʿ is represented by a variety of letters (by *g* in Gaza, *e* in Gilead, *a* in Balaam and Pharaoh—the silenced *a* in these two words seems thus accounted for). The name Shimʿî has three representatives in the English Bible (Shimei, Shimi, Shimhi). This sign had probably two different sounds. ᵃ ᵉ ᵒ and ᵉ represent very slight vowel sounds ("shevas"). *Kh*, *bh*, *dh*, *gh* are sounds which have the same relation to *k*, *b*, *d*, *g* that *ph* and *th* have to *p* and *t* (*kh* and *gh* roughly = Scotch or German *ch*, *bh* = *v*, *dh* = *th* in "thee"). Short vowels are unmarked, long vowels have a circumflex. Final *ah* = *â* (*h* silent). It may be observed that the divergence of English names from the Hebrew is sometimes due to the influence of the Vulgate or Septuagint, which may contain forms older than the present Hebrew text offers.

Note.—An asterisk marks words which depart from some principle and receive special mention in what precedes. When the accent ' comes immediately after a vowel the vowel is long, if a consonant intervenes it is short (Aba'na, Abad'don).

A COMPLETE LIST OF SCRIPTURE PROPER NAMES

AS IN THE

AUTHORISED AND REVISED VERSIONS,

SHOWING THEIR MODERN PRONUNCIATION AND THE EXACT FORM OF THE ORIGINAL HEBREW.

A′aron.
'ah^{a}rôn.
A′aronite.
Abad′don.
Abag′tha.
'^{a}bhagh^{e}thâ.
Aba′na.
'^{a}bhâna*h*.
*Aba′rim (Ab′arim).
'^{a}bhârîm.
[Ab′ba.]
Ab′da.
'abhdâ.
Ab′deel.
'abhd'êl.
Ab′di.
'abhdî.
Ab′diel.
'abhdî'êl.
Ab′don.
'abhdôn.
*Abed′nego (Ab′ed-ne′go).
'^{a}bhêdh n^{e}ghô.
A′bel.
'âbhêl;hebhel(hâbhel).
A′bel-beth-ma′achah.
'âbhêl bêth ham-ma'^{a}kha*h*.
A′bel-cher′amim(R.V.).
'âbhêl k^{e}râmîm.
A′bel-ma′im.
'âbhêl mayim.
A′bel-meho′lah.
'abhêl m^{e}ḥôla*h*.
A′bel-miz′raim.
'âbhêl miṣrayim.
A′bel-shit′tim.
'âbhêl hash-shiṭṭîm.
A′bez.
'ebheṣ ('âbheṣ).
A′bi.
'^{a}bhî.
Abi′a (Abi′ah).
'^{a}bhîya*h*.
Ab′i-al′bon.
'^{a}bhî 'al^{e}bhôn.
Ab′i-a′saph.
'^{a}bhî 'âsâph.
Ab′i-a′thar.
'ebhyâthâr.
A′bib.
'âbhîbh.
Abi′da (Abi′dah).
'^{a}bhîdhâ'.
Abi′dan.
'^{a}bhîdhân.
*Ab′iel.
'^{a}bhî'êl.
Ab′i-e′zer.
'^{a}bhî'ezer.
Ab′i-ez′rite.
Ab′igail.
^{a}bhîghayil ; '^{a}bhîghal.

Ab′igal (R.V.).
'^{a}bhîghal.
*Ab′ihail.
'^{a}bhîḥayil.
Abi′hu.
'^{a}bhîhû'.
Abi′hud.
'^{a}bhîhûdh.
Abi′jah.
'^{a}bhîya*h*.
Abi′jam.
'^{a}bhîyâm.
Abile′ne.
Ab′i-ma′el.
'^{a}bhîmâ'êl.
*Abim′elech.
'^{a}bhîmelekh.
Ab′i-na′dab.
'^{a}bhînâdhâbh.
Abi′ner.
'^{a}bhînêr.
Ab′i-no′am.
'^{a}bhîno'am.
Abi′ram.
'^{a}bhîrâm.
Abi′shag.
'^{a}bhîshagh.
Abi′-shai.
'^{a}bhîshai.
Ab′i-sha′lom.
'^{a}bhîshâlôm.
Ab′i-shu′a.
'^{a}bhîshûa'
Abi′shur.
'^{a}bhîshûr.
Abi′tal.
'^{a}bhîṭal.
Abi′tub.
'^{a}bhîṭûbh
Abi′ud.
Ab′ner.
'abhnêr.
A′braham.
'abhrâhâm.
A′bram.
'abhrâm.
Abro′nah (R.V.).
'abhrôna*h*.
Ab′salom.
'abhshâlôm.
Ac′cad.
'akkadh.
Ac′cho.
'akkô.
Acel′dama.
Acha′ia.
Acha′icus.
A′chan.
'âkhân.
A′char.
'âkhâr.
A′chaz.
Ach′bor.
'akhbôr.

A′chim.
A′chish.
'âkhîsh.
Ach′metha.
'aḥm^{e}thâ.
A′chor.
'âkhôr.
Ach′sa (Ach′sah).
'akhsa*h*.
Ach′shaph.
'akhshâph.
Ach′zib.
'akhzîbh.
Ada′dah.
'adh'âdha*h*.
A′dah.
'âdha*h*.
Adai′ah.
'^{a}dhâya*h*.
*Adali′a.
'^{a}dhalyâ.
Ad′am.
'âdhâm.
Ada′mah.
'^{a}dhâma*h*.
Ada′mi.
'^{a}dhâmî.
Ada′mi-ne′keb (R.V.).
'^{a}dhâmî han-nekebh.
A′dar.
'^{a}dhâr ; 'addâr.
Ad′beel.
'adhb^{e}'êl.
Ad′dan.
'addân.
Ad′dar.
'addâr.
Ad′di
Ad′don.
'addôn.
A′der.
'edher ('âdher).
*Ad′iel.
'^{a}dhî'êl.
A′din.
'âdhîn
Adi′na.
'^{a}dhînâ.
Adi′no.
'^{a}dhînô.
Aditha′im.
'^{a}dhîthayim.
Ad′lai.
'adhlâi.
Ad′mah.
'adhma*h*.
Adma′tha.
'adhmâthâ.
Ad′na.
'adhnâ
Ad′nah.
'adhna*h*.
Ado′ni-be′zek.
'^{a}dhônî bhezek.

Adoni′jah.
'^{a}dhônîya*h*.
Adoni′kam.
'^{a}dhônîkâm
Adoni′ram.
'^{a}dhônîrâm.
Ado′ni-ze′dek.
'^{a}dhônî ṣedhek.
Adora′im.
'^{a}dhôrayim.
Ado′ram.
'^{a}dhôrâm.
Adram′melech.
'adhrammelekh.
Adramyt′tium.
*A′dria.
*Ad′riel.
'adhrî'êl.
Adul′lam.
'^{a}dhullâm.
Adul′lamite.
Adum′mim.
'^{a}dhummîm.
*Aene′as.
Ae′non.
Ag′abus.
A′gag.
'^{a}ghagh.
*A′gagite.
A′gar.
A′gee (ee = e).
'âghê'.
Agrip′pa.
A′gur.
'âghûr.
A′hab.
'aḥ'âbh
Ah′arah.
'aḥrah.
Ahar′hel.
'^{a}ḥarḥêl.
Ah′asai.
'aḥzai.
Ahas′bai.
'^{a}ḥasbai.
Ahas′uérus.
'^{a}ḥashwêrôsh.
Ah′ava.
'aḥ^{a}wâ.
A′haz.
'âḥâz.
Ahazi′ah.
'^{a}ḥazya*h* ; '^{a}ḥazyâhû.
Ah′ban.
'aḥbân.
A′her.
'aḥêr.
A′hi.
'^{a}ḥî.
Ahi′ah.
'^{a}ḥîyə
Ahi′am.
'^{a}ḥî'âm.

*Ahi′an.
'^{a}ḥyân.
Ah′i-e′zer.
'^{a}ḥî'ezer.
Ahi′hud.
'^{a}ḥîhûdh ; '^{a}ḥîḥûdh.
Ahi′jah.
'^{a}ḥîya*h*.
Ahi′kam.
'^{a}ḥikâm.
Ahi′lud.
'^{a}ḥîlûdh.
Ah′i-ma′az.
'^{a}ḥîma'aṣ.
Ahi′man.
'^{a}ḥîman.
*Ahim′elech.
'^{a}ḥîmelekh.
Ahi′moth.
'^{a}ḥîmôth.
Ah′i-na′dab.
'^{a}ḥînâdhâbh.
Ah′i-no′am.
'^{a}ḥînô'am.
*Ahi′o.
'aḥyô.
Ahi′ra.
'^{a}ḥîra'.
Ahi′ram.
'^{a}ḥîrâm.
Ahi′ramite.
Ah′i-sa′mach.
'^{a}ḥîsâmâkh.
Ah′i-sha′har.
'^{a}ḥîshaḥar.
Ahi′shar.
'^{a}ḥîshâr.
*Ahith′ophel.
'^{a}ḥîthôphel.
Ahi′tub.
'^{a}ḥîṭûbh.
*Ah′lab.
'aḥlâbh.
*Ah′lai.
'aḥlai.
Aho′ah.
'^{a}ḥôa*h*.
Aho′hite.
Ah′olah.
'oh^{o}la*h*.
Aholi′ab.
'oh^{o}lî'âbh.
Aholi′bah.
'oh^{o}lîbhah..
Ah′oliba′mah.
'oh^{o}lîbhâma*h*.
Ahu′mai.
'^{a}ḥûmai.
Ah′uzam (Ahuzzam R.V.).
'^{a}ḥuzzâm.
Ahuz′zath.
'^{a}ḥuzzath.

Ah'zai (R.V.).
'ahzai.
A'i.
hâ-'ai.
Ai'ah (A'jah).
'aiyah.
Ai'ath.
'aiyâth.
Ai'ja.
'aiyâ.
*Ai'jalon.
'aiyâlôn.
Ai'jeleth sha'har.
'aiyeleth shaḥar.
A'in.
'ayin.
*Aj'alon.
'aiyâlôn.
A'kan.
'^{a}kân.
Ak'kub.
'akkûbh.
*Akrab'bim.
akrabbîm.
Al'ameth.
'âlemeth ('âlâmeth).
Alam'melech (R.V. Allam'melech).
'allammelekh.
[Al'amoth.
'^{a}lâmôth.]
Al'emeth.
'allemeth ('âlemeth).
Alexan'der.
Alexan'dria.
*Ali'ah.
'alyah.
*Ali'an.
'alyân.
Al'lemeth (R.V.).
'allemeth ('âlemeth).
Al'lon.
'allôn.
Al'lon-ba'chuth.
'allôn bâkhûth.
Almo'dad.
'almôdhâdh.
Al'mon.
'almôn.
Al'mon-diblatha'im.
'almôn dibhlatháy^{e}mah.
A'loth.
'âlôth.
Al'pha.
Alphe'us.
[Al-tas'chith.
'al tashḥêth.
A'lush.
'âlûsh.
Al'vah.
'alwah.
Al'van.
'alwân.
A'mad.
'am'âdh.
A'mal.
'âmâl.
*Am'alek.
'^{a}mâlêk.
*Amal'ekite.

A'mam.
'^{a}mâm.
Ama'na.
'^{a}mânah.
Amari'ah.
'^{a}maryah ; '^{a}maryâhû.
Ama'sa.
'^{a}mâśâ.
Ama'sai.
'^{a}mâśai.
Am'ashai (R.V. Amash'sai).
'^{a}mashśai.
Amasi'ah.
'^{a}masyah.
Amazi'ah.
'^{a}maṣyah ; '^{a}maṣyâhû.
A'mi.
'âmî.
Amina'dab.
Amit'tai.
'^{a}mittai.
Am'mah.
'ammah.
Am'mi.
'ammî.
Am'miel.
'ammî'êl.
Ammi'hud.
'ammîhûdh.
Ammi'hur (R.V.).
'ammîḥûr.
*Am'mi-na'dab.
'ammînâdhâbh.
Am'mi-na'dib.
'ammî nâdhîbh.
Am'mi-shad'dai.
'ammîshaddai.
Am'mi-za'bad.
'ammîzâbhâdh.
Am'mon.
'ammôn.
Am'monite.
Am'non.
'amnôn ; 'amînôn.
A'mok.
'âmôk.
*A'mon (Am'on).
'âmôn.
Am'orite.
'^{e}môrî.
A'mos.
'âmôs.
A'moz.
'âmôṣ.
Amphip'olis.
Am'plias.
Amplia'tus.
Am'ram.
'amrâm ; ḥamrân.
Am'ramite.
Amra'phel.
'amrâphel.
Am'zi.
'amṣî.
A'nab.
'^{a}nâbh.
A'nah.
'^{a}nah.

Ana'harath.
'^{a}nâḥarâth.
Anai'ah.
'^{a}nâyah.
A'nak.
'^{a}nâk ; '^{a}nôk.
An'akim.
'^{a}nâkîm.
An'amim.
'^{a}nâmîm.
Anam'melech.
'^{a}nammelekh.
A'nan.
'ânân.
Ana'ni.
'^{a}nânî.
Anani'ah.
'^{a}nanyah.
Anani'as.
A'nath.
'^{a}nâth.
*An'athoth.
'^{a}nâthôth.
An'athothite (R.V.).
An'drew.
Androni'cus.
A'nem.
'ânêm.
A'ner.
'ânêr.
An'ethothite (An'etothite).
Ani'am.
'^{a}nî'âm.
A'nim.
'ânîm.
An'na.
An'nas.
Anthothi'jah (R.V.).
'anthôthîyah.
An'tioch.
An'tipas.
*Antipat'ris.
Antothi'jah.
'anthôthîyah.
An'tothite.
A'nub.
'ânûbh.
Apel'les.
Aphar'sachites.
'^{a}phars^{e}khâyê.
Apharsath'chites.
'^{a}pharsath^{e}khâyê.
Aphar'sites.
'^{a}phâr^{e}sâyê.
A'phek.
'^{a}phêk ('^{a}phêkah).
Aphe'kah.
'^{a}phêkah.
Aphi'ah.
'^{a}phîaḥ.
A'phik.
'^{a}phîk.
Aph'rah.
'aphrah.
Aph'ses.
hap-piṣṣêṣ.
Apollo'nia.
Apol'los.

Apoll'yon.
Ap'paim.
'appayim.
Ap'phia.
Ap'pii Fo'rum.
Aq'uila.
Ar.
'âr.
A'ra.
'^{a}râ.
A'rab.
'^{a}râbh.
*Ara'bah.
'^{a}râbhah.
Ara'bia.
Ara'bian.
A'rad.
'^{a}râdh.
A'rah.
'âraḥ.
A'ram.
'^{a}râm.
Ar'amitess.
A'ram Ma'acah (R.V.).
'^{a}ram ma'^{a}khah.
A'ram Nahara'im.
'^{a}ram nah^{a}rayim.
A'ram Zo'bah.
'^{a}ram ṣôbhah.
A'ran.
'^{a}rân.
*Ar'arat.
'^{a}râraṭ.
Ar'arite (R.V.).
'^{a}rârî.
Arau'nah.
'^{a}raunah.
Ar'ba.
'arba'.
Ar'bathite.
Ar'bite.
Archela'us.
Ar'chevites.
'ark^{e}wâyê.
Ar'chi.
hâ-'arkî.
Archip'pus.
Ar'chite.
hâ-'arkî.
Arctu'rus.
Ard.
'ard.
Ar'dite.
Ar'don.
'ardôn.
*Are'li.
'ar'êlî.
*Ar'elite.
Areop'agite.
Areop'agus.
Ar'etas.
Ar'gob.
'argôbh.
Ari'dai.
'^{a}rîdhai.
*Arida'tha.
'^{a}rîdhâthâ.
A'rieh.
hâ-'aryê.

*A'riel.
'^{a}rî'êl.
Arimathe'a.
A'rioch.
'aryôkh.
Ari'sai.
'^{a}rîsai.
Aristar'chus.
Aristobu'lus.
Ar'kite.
'arkî.
Armaged'don.
Arme'nia.
Armo'ni.
'armônî.
Ar'nan.
'arnân.
Ar'ni (R.V.).
Ar'non.
'arnôn.
A'rod.
'^{a}rôdh.
Aro'di.
'^{a}rôdhî.
Ar'odite.
hâ-'^{a}rôdhî.
Aro'er.
'^{a}rô'êr.
Aro'erite.
Ar'pad (Ar'phad).
'arpâdh.
Arphax'ad (R.V. Arpach'shad).
'arpakhshadh.
Artaxer'xes.
'artaḥshast(â).
Ar'temas.
Ar'uboth (R.V. Ar'ubboth).
'^{a}rubbôth.
Aru'mah.
'^{a}rûmah.
Ar'vad.
'arwadh.
Ar'vadites.
Ar'za.
'arṣâ.
A'sa.
'âsâ.
*As'ahel.
'^{a}śah'êl.
Asahi'ah (Asai'ah).
'^{a}śâyah.
A'saph.
'âsâph.
Asar'eel (R.V. As'arel).
'^{a}śar'êl.
Asare'lah.
'^{a}śarêlah.
As'enath.
'âs^{e}nath.
A'ser.
A'shan.
'âshân.
Ashbe'a.
'ashbêa'.
Ash'bel.
'ashbêl.
Ash'belite.

Ash'chenaz.
’ashk^{e}naz.

Ash'dod.
’ashdōdh.

Ash'dodite.

Ash'doth Pis'gah.
’ashdôth hap-pisgah.

Ash'er.
’âshêr.

Ashe'rah (R.V.)
’^{a}shêrah.

Ash'erim (R.V.).
’^{a}shêrîm.

Ash'erite.

Ash'eroth (R.V.).
’^{a}shêrôth.

Ashi'ma.
’^{a}shîmâ.

Ash'kelon.
’ashk^{e}lôn.

Ash'kelonite (R.V.).

Ash'kenaz.
’ashk^{e}naz.

Ash'nah.
’ashnah.

Ash'penaz.
’ashp^{e}naz.

Ash'riel.
’aśrî’êl.

Ash'taroth.
‘ashtârôth.

Ashter'athite.

Ash'teroth Kar'naim.
‘asht^{e}rôth karnayim.

Ashto'reth.
‘ashtôreth.

As'hur.
’ashḥûr.

Ash'urite.
’^{a}shûrî.

Ash'vath.
‘ashwâth.

A'sia.

As'iel.
‘^{a}śî’êl.

As'kelon.
’ashk^{e}lôn.

As'nah.
’asnah.

Asnap'per.
’osnappar.

Aspa'tha.
’aspâthâ.

As'riel.
’aśrî’êl.

As'rielite.

As'shur.
’ashshûr.

As'shurim.
’ashshûrîm.

As'sir.
’assîr.

As'sos.

As'sur.
’ashshûr.

Assyr'ia.

Assyr'ian.

As'taroth.
‘ashtârôth.

*Asup'pim.
hâ ’^{a}suppîm

Asyn'critus.

A'tad.
’âṭâdh.

Ata'rah.
‘^{a}ṭârah.

*Ata'roth (At'roth).
‘^{a}ṭârôth.

A'ter.
’âṭêr.

A'thach.
‘^{a}thâkh.

Athai'ah.
‘^{a}thâyah.

Athali'ah.
‘^{a}thalyah ; ‘^{a}thalyâhû.

Atha'rim (R.V.).
hâ-’^{a}thârîm.

Athe'nian.

Ath'ens.

Ath'lai.
‘athlai.

At'roth.
‘aṭrôth.

At'roth-sho'phan.
‘aṭ^{e}rôth shôphân.

At'roth - beth - Jo'ab (R.V.).
‘aṭ^{e}rôth bêth yô’âbh.

At'tai.
‘attai.

Attali'a.

Augus'tus.

A'va (R.V. Av'va).
‘awwâ.

A'ven.
’âwen.

A'vim (R.V. Av'vim).
‘awwîm.

A'vite (R.V. Av'vite).

A'vith.
‘^{a}wîth.

A'zal.
’âṣêl.

Azali'ah.
’^{a}ṣalyâhû.

Azani'ah.
’^{a}zanyah.

Azar'ael (R.V. Az'arel.)
‘^{a}zar’êl.

Azar'eel (R.V. Az'arel).
‘^{a}zar’êl.

Azari'ah.
‘^{a}zaryah.

A'zaz.
‘âzâz.

Aza'zel (R.V.).
‘^{a}zâzêl.

Azazi'ah.
‘^{a}zazyâhû.

Az'buk.
‘azbûḳ.

Aze'kah.
‘^{a}zêḳah.

A'zel.
’âṣêl.

A'zem.
‘eṣem (‘âṣem).

Az'gad.
‘azgâdh.

Az'iel.
‘azî’êl.

Azi'za.
‘^{a}zîzâ.

Azma'veth.
‘azmâweth.

Az'mon.
‘aṣmôn.

Az'noth Ta'bor.
’az^{e}nôth tâbhôr.

A'zor.

Azo'tus.

Az'riel.
‘azrî’êl.

Azri'kam.
‘azrîḳâm.

Azu'bah.
‘^{a}zûbhah.

A'zur.
‘azzûr.

Az'zah.
‘azzah.

Az'zan.
‘azzân.

Az'zur.
‘azzûr.

B

Ba'al.
hab-ba‘al.

Ba'al-be'rith.
ba‘al b^{e}rîth.

Ba'al-gad.
ba‘al gâdh.

Ba'al-ha'mon.
ba‘al hâmôn.

Ba'al-ha'nan.
ba‘al ḥânân.

Ba'al-ha'zor.
ba‘al ḥâṣôr.

Ba'al-her'mon.
ba‘al ḥermôn.

Ba'al-me'on.
ba‘al m^e‘ôn.

Ba'al-pe'or.
ba‘al p^e‘ôr.

*Ba'al-per'azim.
ba‘al p^{e}râṣîm.

Ba'al-shali'sha.
ba‘al shâlîshah.

Ba'al-ta'mar.
ba‘al tâmâr.

Ba'al-ze'bub.
ba‘al z^{e}bhûbh.

Ba'al-ze'phon.
ba‘al ṣ^{e}phôn.

Ba'alah.
ba‘^{a}lah.

Ba'alath.
ba‘^{a}lath.

Ba'alath-be'er.
ba‘^{a}lath b^e’êr.

Ba'ale.
ba‘^{a}lê.

Ba'ale Ju'dah (R.V.).
ba‘^{a}lê y^{e}hûdhah.

Ba'ali.
ba‘^{a}lî.

Ba'alis.
ba‘^{a}lîs

Ba'ana.
ba‘^{a}nâ.

Ba'anah.
ba‘^{a}nah ; ba‘^{a}nâ.

Ba'ara.
ba‘^{a}râ.

Ba'asei'ah.
ba‘^{a}śêyah.

Ba'asha.
ba‘shâ.

Ba'bel.
bâbhel.

Bab'ylon.

Babylo'nian.

Babylo'nish.

Ba'ca.
bâkhâ.

Bach'rite.

Bah'arumite.

Bah'urim.
baḥûrîm.

Ba'jith.
hab-bayith.

Bakbak'kar.
baḳbaḳḳar

Bak'buk.
baḳbûḳ.

Bakbuki'ah.
baḳbûḳyah.

Ba'laam (aa = a).
bil‘âm.

Ba'lac.

Bal'adan.
bal’^{a}dhan.

Ba'lah.
bâlah.

Ba'lak.
bâlâḳ.

Ba'mah.
bâmah.

Ba'moth.
bâmôth.

Ba'moth-ba'al.
bâmôth ba‘al.

Ba'ni.
bânî.

Barab'bas.

Bar'achel.
barakh’êl.

Barachi'ah.
barakhyah.

Barachi'as.

Ba'rak.
bârâḳ.

Bar'humite.

Bari'ah.
bârîaḥ.

Bar-je'sus.

Bar-jo'na.

Bar'kos.
barḳôs.

Bar'nabas.

Bar'sabas (R.V. Bar-sab'bas).

Barthol'omew.

Bartime'us.

Ba'ruch.
bârûkh

Barzil'lai.
barzillai.

Bas'emath (R.V.).
bâś^{e}math.

Ba'shan.
hab-bâshân.

Ba'shan-hav'oth-ja'ir.
bâshân ḥawwôth yâ’îr.

Bash'emath.
bâś^{e}math.

Bas'math.
bâś^{e}math.

Bath-rab'bim.
bath rabbîm.

*Bath-she'ba.
bath sh^{e}bha‘.

Bath-shu'a.
bath shûa‘.

Ba'vai.
bawwai.

Baz'lith.
baṣlîth.

Baz'luth.
baṣlûth.

Beali'ah.
b^e‘alyah.

Be'aloth.
b^e‘âlôth.

Be'bai.
bêbhai.

Be'cher.
bekher.

Be'cherite (R.V.).

Becho'rath.
b^{e}khôrath.

Be'dad.
b^{e}dhadh.

Be'dan.
b^{e}dhân.

Bedei'ah.
bêdh^{e}yah.

*Be'eli'ada.
b^e‘elyâdhâ‘

*Beel'zebub.

Be'er.
b^e’êr.

Bee'ra.
b^e’êrâ.

Bee'rah.
b^e’êrah.

Be'er-e'lim.
b^e’êr ’êlîm.

Bee'ri.
b^e’êrî.

Be'er-lahairo'i.
b^e’êr lahai rô’î.

Be'eroth.
b^e’êrôth.

Be'erothite.

Be'eroth - ben'e - ja'a-kan (R.V.).
b^e’êrôth b^{e}nê ya‘^{a}ḳân.

Be'er-she'ba.
b^e’êr sheba‘.

Beesh'terah.
b^e‘esht^{e}rah.

[Behe'moth.
b^{e}hêmôth.]

Bel.
bêl.

Be'la (Be'lah).
bela‘.
Be'laite.
*Be'lial.
b^{e}lîya‘al.
Belshaz'zar.
bêlshaṣṣar.
Belteshaz'zar.
bêlt^{e}shaṣṣar.
Ben-ab'i-na'dab (R.V.).
ben ’^{a}bhînâdhâbh.
Benai'ah.
b^{e}nâyah; b^{e}nâyâhû.
Ben-am'mi.
ben ‘ammî.
Ben-de'ker (R.V.).
ben-deḳer.
Ben'e-be'rak.
b^{e}nê bh^{e}râḳ.
Ben'e-ja'akan.
b^{e}nê ya‘^{a}ḳân.
Ben-ge'ber (R.V.).
ben gebher.
Ben-ha'dad.
ben h^{a}dhadh.
Ben-ha'il.
ben ḥayil.
Ben-ha'nan.
ben ḥânân.
Ben-he'sed (R.V.).
ben ḥesedh.
Ben-hur (R.V.).
ben ḥûr.
Beni'nu.
b^{e}nînû.
*Ben'jamin.
binyâmîn.
Ben'jamite.
Be'no.
b^{e}nô.
Beno'ni.
ben ’ônî.
Benzo'heth.
ben zôḥêth.
Be'on.
b^e‘ôn.
Be'or.
b^e‘ôr.
Be'ra.
bera‘.
Bera'chah.
b^{e}râkhah.
Berachi'ah.
berekhyâhû.
Berai'ah.
b^{e}râyah.
Bere'a.
Berechi'ah.
berekhyah; berekhyâhû.
Be'red.
bered (bared).
Be'ri.
bêrî.
Beri'ah.
b^{e}rî‘ah.
Beri'ite.
Be'rite.
Be'rith.
b^{e}rîth.

Berni'ce.
Bero'dach Bal'adan.
b^{e}rôdhakh bal’^{a}dhân.
Beroe'a (R.V.).
Bero'thah.
bêrôthah.
Bero'thai.
bêrôthai.
Be'rothite.
Be'sai.
bêsâi.
Besodei'ah.
b^{e}sôdhyah.
Be'sor.
b^{e}śôr.
Be'tah.
beṭah.
Be'ten.
beṭen.
*Beth-ab'ara.
Beth-a'nath.
bêth‘^{a}nâth.
Beth-a'noth.
bêth‘^{a}nôth.
Beth'any.
*Beth-ara'bah.
bêth hâ-‘^{a}râbhah.
Beth-a'ram.
bêth hârâm.
Beth-ar'bel.
bêth ’arbêl.
Beth-a'ven.
bêth âwen.
Beth-azma'veth.
bêth ‘azmâweth.
Beth-ba'al-me'on.
bêth ba‘al m^e‘ôn.
Beth-ba'rah.
bêth bârah.
Beth-bir'ei (R.V. Beth-bi'ri).
bêth bir’î.
Beth-car.
bêth kâr.
Beth-da'gon.
bêth dâghôn.
Beth-diblatha'im.
bêth dibhlâthayim.
Beth'el.
bêth ’êl.
Beth'elite.
Beth-e'mek.
bêth hâ-‘êmeḳ.
Be'ther.
bether (bather).
Bethes'da.
Bethe'zel.
bêth hâ-’êṣel.
Beth-ga'der.
bêth gâdhêr.
Beth-ga'mul.
bêth gâmûl.
*Beth-hacce'rem.
bêth hak-kerem.
Beth-ha'ran.
bêth hârân.
Beth-hog'lah.
bêth ḥoghlah.
Beth-ho'ron.
bêth ḥôrôn.

Beth-jesh'imoth (Beth-jes'imoth).
bêth ha-y^{e}shîmôth.
Beth-le-Aph'rah (R.V.).
bêth le-‘aphrah.
Beth-leb'aoth.
bêth l^{e}bhâ’ôth.
*Beth'lehem.
bêth leḥem.
Beth'lehem Ephra'tah.
bêth lehem ’ephrâthah.
Beth'lehemite.
Beth-ma'achah.
bêth ma‘^{a}khah.
Beth-mar'caboth.
bêth ham-markâbhôth.
Beth-me'on.
bêth m^e‘ôn.
Beth-nim'rah.
bêth nimrah.
Beth-pa'let (Beth-phe'let, R.V. Beth-pe'let).
bêth pâleṭ (peleṭ).
Beth-paz'zez.
bêth paṣṣêṣ.
Beth-pe'or.
bêth p^e‘ôr.
*Beth'phage.
Beth-ra'pha.
bêth râphâ.
Beth-re'hob.
bêth r^{e}ḥôbh.
Bethsai'da.
Beth'shan.
bêth shân.
Beth-she'an.
bêth sh^e’ân.
Beth-she'mesh.
bêth shemesh.
Beth'shemite.
Beth-shit'tah.
bêth hash-shiṭṭah.
Beth-tappu'ah.
bêth tappûah.
*Bethu'el (Beth'uel).
b^{e}thû’êl.
Be'thul.
b^{e}thûl.
Beth-zur.
bêth ṣûr.
Beto'nim.
b^{e}ṭônîm.
Beu'lah.
b^e‘ûlah.
Be'zai.
bêṣai.
Bezal'eel (R.V. Bez'alel).
b^{e}ṣal’êl.
Be'zek.
bezeḳ.
Be'zer.
beṣer.
Bich'ri.
bikhrî.
Bid'kar.
bidhḳar.

Big'tha.
bigh^{e}tha.
Big'than.
bigh^{e}thân.
Bigtha'na.
bigh^{e}thânâ.
Big'vai.
bighwai.
Bil'dad.
bildadh.
Bil'eam.
bil‘âm.
Bil'gah.
bilgah.
Bil'gai.
bilgai.
Bil'hah.
bilhah.
Bil'han.
bilhân.
Bil'shan.
bilshân.
Bim'hal.
bimhâl.
Bin'ea.
bin‘â; bin‘ah.
Binnu'i.
binnûy.
Bir'sha.
birsha‘.
Birza'vith (R.V. Birza'ith).
birzawith; birzayith.
Bish'lam.
bishlâm.
Bithi'ah.
bithyah.
Bith'ron.
hab-bithrôn.
Bithyn'ia.
Biz'joth-jah (R.V. Biz'iothi'ah).
bizyôthyah.
Biz'tha.
biz^{e}thâ.
Blas'tus.
Boaner'ges
Bo'az.
bô‘az.
Boch'eru.
bôkh^{e}rû.
Bo'chim.
hab-bôkhîm.
Bo'han.
bôhan.
Bo'oz.
Bos'cath.
boṣkath.
Bo'sor.
Bo'zez.
bôṣêṣ.
Boz'kath.
boṣkath.
Boz'rah.
boṣrah.
Buk'ki.
buḳḳî.
Bukki'ah.
buḳḳîyâhû.

Bul.
bûl.
Bu'nah.
bûnah.
Bun'ni.
bunnî.
Buz.
bûz.
Bu'zi.
bûzî.
Buz'ite.

C

Cab'bon.
kabbôn.
Ca'bul.
kâbhûl.
Cae'sar.
Caesare'a.
*Caesare'a Philip'pi.
Cai'aphas.
Cain.
ḳayin.
Cai'nan.
ḳênân.
Ca'lah.
kâlaḥ.
Cal'col.
kalkôl.
Ca'leb.
kâlêbh.
Ca'leb Ephra'tah.
kâlêbh ’ephrâthah.
Cal'neh.
kalneh; kalnêh.
Cal'no.
kalnô.
Cal'vary.
Ca'mon.
ḳâmôn.
Ca'na.
Ca'naan (aa = a).
k^{e}na‘an.
Ca'naanite (aa = a).
Cananæ'an (R.V.).
*Can'dace.
Can'neh.
kannêh.
Caper'naum.
Caph'tor.
kaphtôr.
Caph'torim (Caphthorim).
kaphtôrîm.
Cappado'cia.
Car'cas.
karkas.
Car'chemish.
kark^{e}mîsh.
Care'ah.
ḳarêaḥ.
Ca'rite (R.V.).
Car'mel.
karmel.
Car'melite.
Car'mi.
karmî.
Car'mite.

Car'pus.
Car'shena.
karsh^{e}nâ.
*Casiphi'a.
kâsiphyâ.
Cas'luhim.
kaslûḥîm.
Cas'tor.
Cau'da (R.V.).
*Ce'dron.
Cen'chrea (R.V. Cen'chreae).
Ce'phas.
Chal'col.
kalkôl.
Chalde'a.
Chalde'an.
Chal'dee.
Cha'naan (aa = a).
Char'ashim.
ḥ^{a}râshîm.
Char'chemish.
kark^{e}mîsh.
Char'ran.
Che'bar.
k^{e}bhâr.
Che'dor-lao'mer.
k^{e}dhorlâ'ômer.
Che'lal.
k^{e}lâl.
Chel'luh (R.V. Chelu'hi, Chelu'hu).
k^{e}lûhû ; k^{e}lûhî.
Che'lub.
k^{e}lûbh.
Chelu'bai.
k^{e}lûbhâi.
Chem'arim(s).
k^{e}mârîm.
Che'mosh.
k^{e}môsh.
Chena'anah.
k^{e}na'^{a}nah.
Chena'ni.
k^{e}nânî.
Chenani'ah.
k^{e}nanyah.
Che'phar Ha-ammo'nai (R.V. Ammo'ni).
k^{e}phar hâ-'ammônai.
Chephi'rah.
k^{e}phîrah.
Che'ran.
k^{e}rân.
*Cher'ethites (Cher'ethims).
k^{e}rêthîm.
Che'rith.
k^{e}rîth.
Chesa'lon.
k^{e}sâlôn.
Che'sed.
keśedh.
Che'sil.
k^{e}sîl.
*Chesul'loth.
k^{e}sulloth.
Che'zib.
k^{e}zîbh.

Chi'don.
kîdhôn.
Chil'eab.
kil'âbh.
Chil'ion.
kilyôn.
Chil'mad.
kilmadh.
Chim'ham.
kimhâm.
Chin'nereth.
kinnereth.
Chin'neroth (Cin'neroth).
kinn^{e}rôth.
Chi'os.
Chis'leu.
kislêu.
Chis'lon.
kislôn.
Chis'loth-ta'bor.
kislôth tâbhôr.
Chit'tim.
kittîm.
Chi'un.
kîyûn.
Chlo'e.
Chora'shan.
kôr 'âshân.
Chora'zin.
Choze'ba.
kôzêbhâ.
Chub.
kûbh.
Chun.
kûn.
Chu'shan-rishatha'im.
kûshan rish'âthayim.
Chu'za.
Cilic'ia.
Cin'neroth.
kinn^{e}rôth.
Cis.
Clau'da.
Clau'dia.
Clau'dius.
Clem'ent.
Cle'opas.
Cle'ophas (R.V. Clo'pas).
Cni'dus.
Colho'zeh.
kol hôzeh.
Colos'se.
Conani'ah.
konanyâhû.
Coni'ah.
konyâhû.
Cononi'ah.
konanyâhû.
Co'os (R.V. Cos).
Cora'shan (R.V.).
kôr 'âshân.
Co're.
Cor'inth.
Corin'thian.
Corne'lius.
Co'sam.

Coz.
kôṣ.
Coz'bi.
kozbî.
Cres'cens.
*Crete.
*Cretes.
Cre'tians.
Cre'tans (R.V.).
Cris'pus.
Cush.
kûsh.
Cu'shan.
kûshân.
Cu'shi.
kûshî.
Cu'shite.
Cuth.
kûth.
Cu'thah.
kûthah.
Cy'prus.
Cyre'ne.
Cyre'nian.
Cyre'nius.
Cy'rus.
kôresh.

D

Dab'areh.
dâbh^{e}rath.
Dabba'sheth.
dabbâsheth.
Dab'erath.
dâbh^{e}rath.
Da'gon.
dâghôn.
Dalai'ah.
d^{e}lâyah.
Dalmanu'tha.
Dalma'tia.
Dal'phon.
dal^{e}phôn.
Dam'aris.
*Dam'asce'ne.
Damas'cus.
Dan.
dân.
Dan'iel.
dânîyêl.
Dan'ite.
Danja'an.
dân ya'an.
Dan'nah.
dannah.
Da'ra.
dâra'.
Dar'da.
dardâ'.
Dari'us.
dâr^{e}yâwesh.
Dar'kon.
darḳôn.
Da'than.
dâthân.
Da'vid.
dâwîdh.
De'bir.
d^{e}bhîr.

*Deb'orah.
d^{e}bhôrah.
Decap'olis.
De'dan.
d^{e}dhân.
*De'danim.
d^{e}dhînîm.
De'danite (R.V.).
De'havite.
dehâwê ; dehâyê.
De'kar.
deḳer.
Delai'ah.
d^{e}lâyah (d^{e}lâyâhû).
Deli'lah.
d^{e}lîlah.
De'mas.
Deme'trius.
Der'be.
*Deu'el.
d^{e}'û'êl.
*Dian'a.
Dib'lah (R.V.).
dibhlah.
Dibla'im.
dibhlayim.
Dib'lath.
dibhlah.
Di'bon.
dîbhôn.
Di'bon-gad.
dîbhôn gâdh.
Dib'ri.
dibhrî.
Did'ymus.
Dik'lah.
diḳlah.
Dil'ean.
dil'ân.
Dim'nah.
dimnah.
Di'mon.
dîmôn.
Dimo'nah.
dîmônah.
Di'nah.
dînah.
Di'naite.
dinâyê.
Dinha'bah.
dinhâbhah.
Dionys'ius.
Diot'rephes.
Di'phath (R.V.).
dîphath.
Di'shan.
dîshân.
Di'shon.
dîshôn ; dîshân.
Diza'hab.
dî zâhâbh.
Do'dai.
dôdhai.
Do'danim.
dôdhânîm.
Doda'vah.
dôdhâwâhû.
Do'do.
dôdhô.

Do'eg.
dô'êgh.
Doph'kah.
dophkah.
Dor.
dôr.
Dor'cas.
Do'than.
dôthân ; dôthayin.
Drusil'la.
Du'mah.
dûmah.
Du'ra.
dûrâ.

E

E'bal.
'êbhâl.
E'bed.
*Eb'ed-me'lech.
'ebhedh melekh.
*Eb'en-e'zer.
'ebhen hâ-'ezer.
E'ber.
'êbher.
Eb'i-a'saph.
'ebhîyâsâph.
Ebro'nah.
'abhrônah.
Ed.
['êdh].
E'dar.
'êdher.
E'den.
'êdhen.
E'der.
'êdher.
E'dom.
'^{e}dhôm.
E'domite.
Ed'rei.
'edhr^{e}'î.
Eg'lah.
'eghlah.
Egla'im.
'eghlayim.
Eg'lon.
'eghlôn.
E'gypt.
miṣrayim.
Egyp'tian.
E'hi.
'êhî.
E'hud.
'êhûdh.
E'ker.
'êḳer.
Ek'ron.
'eḳrôn.
Ek'ronite.
E'la (R.V.).
'êlâ.
El-a'dah.
'el'âdhah.
E'lah.
'êlah ; 'êlâ.
E'lam.
'êlâm.
E'lamite.
El-a'sah (El-ea'sah).
'el'âśah.

E'lath.
'êlath; 'êlôth.
El-beth'el.
'êl bêth 'êl.
El-da'ah.
'eldâ'ah.
El'dad.
'eldâdh.
El'ead.
'el'âdh.
El-ea'leh.
'el'âlêh; 'el'âlê.
·El-ea'sah (Ela'sah).
'el'âśah.
El-ea'zar.
'el'âzâr.
El'-elo'he-is'rael.
'êl 'elôhê yisrâ'êl.
E'leph.
'eleph.
El-ha'nan.
'elḥânân.
E'li.
'êlî.
Eli'ab.
'elî'âbh.
El-ia'da.
'elyâdhâ'.
E'l-ia'dah.
'elyâdhâ'.
Eli'ah.
'êlîyah.
El-iah'ba.
'elyaḥbâ.
El-ia'kim.
'elyâḳîm.
Eli'am.
'elî'âm.
Eli'as.
El-ia'saph.
'elyâsâph.
El-ia'shib.
'elyâshîbh.
*El'i-a'thah.
'elî'âthah.
Eli'dad.
'elîdhâdh.
El'iel.
'elî'êl.
El'i-e'nai.
'elî'ênai.
El'i-e'zer.
'elî'ezer.
El'i-hoe'nai.
'ely'hô'ênai.
El'i-ho'reph.
'elîḥôreph.
Eli'hu.
'elîhû.
Eli'jah.
'êlîyâhû.
Eli'ka.
'elîḳâ.
E'lim.
'êlîm.
*Elim'elech.
'elîmelekh.
El'ioe'nai.
'elyô'ênai; 'ely'hô'ênai.
Eli'phal.
'elîphâl.

El'i-pha'let (El'i-phe'let).
'elîphelet ('elîphâlet).
El'iphaz.
'elîphaz.
El'i-phe'leh (R.V. El'i-phele'hu).
'elîph'lêhû.
Elis'abeth.
Elise'us.
Eli'sha.
'elîshâ'.
Eli'shah.
'elîshah.
El'i-sha'ma.
'elîshâmâ'.
El'i-sha'phat.
'elîshâphâṭ.
El'i-she'ba.
'elîshebha'.
El'i-shu'a.
'elîshûa'.
Eli'ud.
El'i-za'phan.
'elîṣâphân.
Eli'zur.
'elîṣûr.
Elka'nah.
'elḳânah.
El'koshite.
*Ella'sar.
'ellâsâr.
Elmo'dam (R.V. El-ma'dam).
Elna'am.
'elna'am.
Elna'than.
'elnâthân.
[Elo'i.]
E'lon.
'êlôn.
E'lon-beth-ha'nan.
'êlôn bêth ḥânân.
E'lonite.
E'loth.
'êlôth.
El-pa'al.
'elpa'al.
El-pa'let (R.V. El-pe'let).
'elpâleṭ ('elpeleṭ).
El-pa'ran.
'êlpârân.
El-te'keh.
'elt'kê; 'elt'kêh.
El-te'kon.
'elt'kôn.
El-to'lad.
'eltôladh.
E'lul.
'elûl.
El-u'zai.
'el'ûzai.
El'ymas.
El-za'bad.
'elzâbhâdh.
El-za'phan.
'elṣâphân.
Em'ek-ke'ziz (R.V.).
'êmek ḳ'ṣîṣ.

E'mim.
'êmîm.
Emman'uel.
Emma'us.
Em'mor.
Ena'im (R.V.).
ênayim.
E'nam.
'ênâm.
E'nan.
'ênân
En'dor.
'ên dôr.
*Ene'as.
En-eg'laim.
'ên 'eghlayim.
En-gan'nim.
'ên gannîm.
*En'gedi.
En-had'dah.
'ên haddah.
En'-hakko're.
'ên hak-ḳôrê.
En-ha'zor.
'ên ḥâṣôr.
En-mish'pat.
'ên mishpâṭ.
E'noch.
ḥ'nôkh.
E'nos (E'nosh).
'enôsh.
En-rim'mon.
'ên rimmôn.
En-ro'gel.
'en rôghêl.
En-she'mesh.
'ên shemesh.
En-tappu'ah.
'ên tappûaḥ.
*Ep'aphras.
Epaph'rodi'tus.
*Epe'netus.
E'phah.
'êphah.
E'phai.
'êphai.
E'pher.
'êpher.
E'phes-dam'mim.
'ephes dammîm.
Ephe'sian.
Eph'esus.
Eph'lal.
'ephlâl.
[Ephpha'tha.]
E'phod.
'êphôdh.
Eph'raim.
'ephrayim.
Eph'raimite.
Eph'rain.
'ephrayin.
*Ephra'tah (R.V. Eph-ra'thah).
'ephrâthah.
*E'phrath.
'ephrâth.
Eph'rathite.
E'phron.
'ephrôn.

Ep'icure'an.
Er.
'êr.
E'ran.
'êrân.
E'ranite.
Eras'tus.
E'rech.
'erekh.
E'ri.
'êrî.
E'rite.
Esai'as.
E'sarhad'don.
'êsarḥaddôn.
E'sau.
'êśâw.
E'sek.
'êśek.
Esh-ba'al.
'eshba'al.
Esh'ban.
'eshbân.
Esh'col.
'eshkôl.
Esh'ean.
'esh'ân.
E'shek.
'êshek.
Esh'kalonite.
*Eshta'ol.
'eshtâ'ôl.
Eshta'ulite (R.V. Esh-ta'olite).
Eshtemo'a.
'esht'môa'.
Esh'temoh.
'esht'môh.
Esh'ton.
'eshtôn.
Es'li.
Es'rom.
Es'ther.
'estêr.
E'tam.
'êṭâm.
E'tham.
'êthâm.
E'than.
'êthân.
E'thanim.
hâ'êthânîm.
Eth-ba'al.
'ethba'al.
E'ther.
'ether.
Ethio'pia.
kûsh.
Ethio'pian.
Ethka'zin (R.V.).
'ittah ('êth) ḳâṣîn.
Eth'nan.
'ethnân.
Eth'ni.
'ethnî.
Eubu'lus.
Euni'ce.
Euo'dias (R.V. Euo'-dia).

Euphra'tes.
p'râth.
Euroc'lydon (R.V. Euraq'uilo).
Eu'tychus.
Eve.
ḥawwah.
E'vi.
'ewî.
*E'vil-mero'dach.
'ewîl m'rôdhâkh.
E'zar.
'êser.
Ez'bai.
'ezbai.
Ez'bon.
'eṣbôn.
Ezeki'as.
Eze'kiel.
y'ḥezkêl.
E'zel.
'ezel.
E'zem.
'eṣem.
E'zer.
'êzer; 'ezer ('âzer).
Ez'ion-ge'ber (Ez'ion-ga'ber).
'eṣyôn gebher (gâbher).
Ez'nite.
hâ 'eṣnî.
Ez'ra (R.V. *once* Ez'-rah).
'ezrâ; 'ezrah.
Ez'rahite.
hâ-'ezrâḥî.
Ez'ri.
'ezrî.

F

Fe'lix.
Fes'tus.
Fortuna'tus.

G

Ga'al.
ga'al.
Ga'ash.
ga'ash.
Ga'ba.
gebha' (gâbha').
Gab'bai.
gabbai.
Gab'batha.
Ga'briel.
gabhrî'êl.
Gad.
gâdh.
Gad'arene.
Gad'di.
gaddî.
Gad'diel.
gaddî'êl.
Ga'di.
gâdhî.
Gad'ite.
Ga'ham.
gaḥam.
Ga'har.
gaḥar

Gai′us.
Ga′lal.
gâlâl.
Gala′tia.
Gala′tian.
Gal′eed.
gal‘êdh.
Galile′an.
Gal′ilee.
Gal′lim.
gallîm.
Gal′lio.
Gama′liel.
gamlî′êl.
Gam′madim.
gammâdîm.
Ga′mul.
gâmûl.
Ga′reb.
gârêbh.
Gar′mite.
Gash′mu.
gashmû.
Ga′tam.
ga‘tâm.
Gath.
gath.
Gath-he′pher.
gath ḥêpher.
Gath-rim′mon.
gath rimmôn.
Ga′za.
‘azza*h*.
Gaz′zam.
gazzâm.
Ga′zathite.
Ga′zer.
gezer (gâzer).
Ga′zez.
gâzêz.
Ga′zite.
Ge′ba.
gebha‘ (gâbha‘).
Ge′bal.
g^{e}bhal.
Ge′balite (R.V.).
Ge′ber.
gebher
Ge′bim.
gêbhîm.
Gedali′ah.
gedhalya*h*; gedhalyâhû.
Ged′eon.
Ge′der.
gedher.
Gede′rah.
hag-g^{e}dhêra*h*.
Gede′rathite.
Ge′derite.
Ged′eroth.
g^{e}dhêrôth.
Ged′erotha′im.
g^{e}dhêrôthayim.
Ge′dor.
g^{e}dhôr.
Ge-har′ashim (R.V.).
gê′ ḥ^{a}râshîm.
*Geha′zi.
gêḥ^{a}zî.

Gel′iloth.
g^{e}lîlôth.
Gemal′li.
g^{e}mallî.
Gemari′ah.
g^{e}marya*h*; g^{e}maryâhû.
Gennes′aret.
Gen′tile.
Genu′bath.
g^{e}nûbhath.
Ge′ra.
gêrâ.
[Ge′rah.
gêra*h*].
Ge′rar.
g^{e}râr.
Ger ase′nes (R.V.).
Ger′gese′nes.
*Ger′izim.
g^{e}rizzîm.
Ger′shom.
gêrshôm.
Ger′shon.
gêrshôn.
Ger′shonite.
Ge′ruth-chim′ham (R.V.).
gêrûth kimhâm.
*Gesh′am (R.V. Gesh′an).
gêshân.
*Gesh′em.
geshem.
*Gesh′ur.
g^{e}shûr.
*Gesh′uri.
g^{e}shûrî.
Gesh′urite.
Ge′ther.
gether.
Gethsem′ane.
Geu′el.
g^{e}û′êl.
Ge′zer.
gezer.
Gez′rite.
Gi′ah.
gîaḥ.
Gib′bar.
gibbâr.
Gib′bethon.
gibb^{e}thôn.
Gib′ea.
gibh‘â.
Gib′eah.
gibh‘a*h*; gebha‘ (gâbha‘).
Gib′eath.
gibh‘ath.
Gib′eathite.
Gib′eath-ha-ar′aloth (R.V.).
gibh‘ath hâ-‘^{a}râlôth.
Gib′eon.
gibh‘ôn.
Gib′eonite.
Gib′lite.
Giddal′ti.
giddaltî.

Gid′del.
giddêl.
Gid′eon.
gidh‘ôn.
Gideo′ni.
gidh‘ônî.
Gi′dom.
gidh‘ôm.
Gi′hon.
gîḥôn.
Gil′alai.
gîl^{a}lai.
Gilbo′a.
gilbôa‘.
Gil′ead.
gil‘âdh.
Gil′eadite.
Gil′gal.
gilgâl.
Gi′loh.
gîlô*h*.
Gi′lonite.
Gim′zo.
gimzô.
Gi′nath.
gînath.
Gin′netho.
ginn^{e}thôy.
Gin′nethon.
ginn^{e}thôn.
Gir′gashite.
Gir′zite (R.V.).
Gis′pa (R.V. Gish′pa).
gishpâ.
Git′tah he′pher.
gitta*h* ḥêpher.
*Git′taim.
Git′tite.
[Git′tith.
hag-gittîth].
Gi′zonite.
Go′ath (R.V. Go′ah).
gô‘âth (gô‘â*h*).
Gob.
gôbh.
Gog.
gôgh.
Go′iim (R.V.).
gôyîm.
Go′lan.
gôlân.
Gol′gotha.
*Goli′ath.
golyâth.
Go′mer.
gômer.
Gomor′rah.
‘^{a}môra*h*.
Go′shen.
gôshen.
Go′zan.
gôzân.
Gre′cia.
Gre′cian.
Gudgo′dah.
gudhgôdha*h*.
Gu′ni.
gûnî.
Gu′nite.

Gur.
gûr.
Gur-ba′al.
gûr-ba‘al.

H

*Ha′ahash′tari.
hâ-^{a}ḥashtârî.
Habai′ah.
ḥ^{a}bhaiya*h*; ḥ^{o}bâya*h*.
Habak′kuk.
ḥ^{a}bhakkûk.
Habaz′ini′ah.
ḥ^{a}bhaṣṣinya*h*.
Ha′bor.
ḥâbhôr.
Hachali′ah.
ḥ^{a}khalya*h*.
Hachi′lah.
ḥ^{a}khîla*h*.
Hachmo′ni.
ḥ^{a}khmônî.
Hach′monite.
Ha′dad.
h^{a}dadh; ḥ^{a}dhadh.
*Had′ad-e′zer.
h^{a}dhadh‘ezer.
Had′ad-rim′mon.
h^{a}dhadhrimmôn.
Ha′dar.
h^{a}dhar; ḥ^{a}dhar.
Had′ar-e′zer.
h^{a}dhar‘ezer.
Hada′shah.
ḥ^{a}dhâsha*h*.
Hadas′sah.
h^{a}dhassa*h*.
Hadat′tah.
ḥ^{a}dhatta*h*.
Ha′did.
ḥâdhîdh.
Had′lai.
ḥadhlâi.
Hado′ram.
h^{a}dhôrâm.
Ha′drach.
ḥadhrakh.
Ha′gab.
ḥâghêbh.
Haga′ba.
ḥ^{a}ghâbhâ.
Haga′bah.
ḥ^{a}ghâbha*h*.
Ha′gar.
hâghâr.
Hagare′ne.
haghrîm.
Hag′arite (R.V. Hag′rite).
haghrî′îm.
Ha′gerite (R.V. Hag′rite).
haghrî.
Hag′gai.
ḥaggai.
Hag′geri (R.V. Hag′ri).
haghrî.
Hag′gi.
ḥaggî

Haggi′ah.
ḥaggîya*h*.
Hag′gite.
Hag′gith.
ḥaggîth.
Hag′ri (R.V.).
haghrî.
Hag′rite (R.V.).
haghrî.
Ha′i.
ha-‘ai.
Hakka′tan.
hak-kâṭân.
*Hak′koz.
hak-kôṣ.
Haku′pha.
ḥ^{a}kûphâ.
Ha′lah.
ḥ^{a}laḥ.
Ha′lak.
ḥâlâk.
Hal′hul.
ḥalḥûl.
Ha′li.
ḥ^{a}lî.
Hallo′hesh (Halo′hesh).
hal-lôḥêsh.
Ham.
hâm; ḥâm.
Ha′man.
hâmân.
Ha′math.
ḥ^{a}mâth.
Ha′mathite.
Ha′math-zo′bah.
ḥ^{a}math ṣôbha*h*.
Ham′math.
ḥammath.
Hamme′ah (R.V.).
ham-mê′a*h*.
Hammeda′tha.
hamm^{e}dhâthâ.
*Hamme′lech.
ham-melekh.
Hammo′leketh.
ham-môlekheth.
Ham′mon.
ḥammôn.
Ham′moth-dor.
ḥammôth dôr.
Ham′muel (R.V.).
ḥammû′êl.
Hamo′nah.
h^{a}môna*h*.
Ha′mon-gog.
h^{a}môn gôgh.
Ha′mor.
ḥ^{a}môr.
Ham′ran (R.V.).
ḥamrân.
Ham′uel.
ḥammû′el.
Ha′mul.
ḥâmûl.
Ha′mulite.
Hamu′tal.
ḥ^{a}mûṭal.
Hanam′eel.
ḥ^{a}nam′êl.

Ha'nan.
ḥânân.
Hanan'eel.
ḥ^a^nan'êl.
Hana'ni.
ḥ^a^nânî.
Hanani'ah.
ḥ^a^nanyah; ḥ^a^nanyâhû.
Ha'nes.
ḥânêṣ.
Han'iel (R.V. Han'-niel).
ḥannî'êl.
Han'nah.
ḥannah.
Hanna'thon.
ḥannâthôn.
Han'niel.
ḥannî'êl.
Ha'noch.
ḥ^a^nôkh.
Ha'nochite.
Ha'nun.
ḥânûn.
Haphra'im (*or* Haph-ara'im).
ḥ^a^phârayim.
Happiz'zez (R.V.).
hap-piṣṣêṣ.
Ha'ra.
hârâ.
Hara'dah.
ḥ^a^râdhah.
Ha'ran.
hârân ; ḥârân.
Ha'rarite.
h^a^rârî ; hârârî ; 'arârî.
Harbo'na.
ḥar^e^bhônâ.
Harbo'nah.
ḥar^e^bhônah.
Ha'reph.
ḥârêph.
Ha'reth.
ḥâreth.
Harhai'ah.
ḥarh^a^yah.
Har'has.
ḥarḥas.
Har'hur.
ḥarḥûr.
Ha'rim.
ḥârîm.
Ha'riph.
ḥârîph.
Harne'pher.
ḥarnepher.
Har-Maged'on (R.V.).
Ha'rod.
ḥ^a^rôdh.
Ha'rodite.
Haro'eh.
hâ-rô'eh.
Ha'rorite.
Haro'sheth.
ḥ^a^rôsheth.
Har'sha.
ḥarshâ.
Har'sith (R.V.).
ha-ḥarsîth.

Ha'rum.
hârûm.
Haru'maph.
ḥ^a^rûmaph.
Ha'ruphite.
ḥ^a^rûphî.
Ha'ruz.
hârûṣ.
Hasadi'ah.
ḥ^a^sadhyah.
Hasenu'ah (R.V. Has-senu'ah).
has-s^e^nû'ah.
Hashabi'ah.
ḥ^a^shabhyah ; ḥ^a^shabh-yâhû.
Hashab'nah.
ḥashabhnah.
Hashabni'ah (R.V. Hashabnei'ah).
ḥ^a^shabhn^e^yah.
Hashbada'na (R.V. Hashbadda'nah).
ḥashbaddânah.
Ha'shem.
hâshêm.
Hashmo'nah.
ḥashmônah.
*Hash'ub (Has'shub).
ḥashshûbh.
Hashu'bah.
ḥ^a^shûbhah.
Ha'shum.
ḥâshûm.
Has'rah.
ḥasrah.
Hassena'ah.
has-s^e^nâ'ah.
Hassenuah (R.V.).
has-s^e^nû'ah.
Has'shub.
ḥashshûbh.
Hasu'pha(Hashu'pha).
ḥ^a^śûphâ.
Ha'tach (R.V. Ha'-thach).
h^a^thâkh.
Ha'thath.
ḥ^a^thath.
Hati'pha.
ḥ^a^ṭîphâ.
Hati'ta.
ḥ^a^ṭîṭâ.
Hat'til.
ḥaṭṭil.
Hat'tush.
ḥaṭṭûsh.
*Hau'ran (Haura'n).
ḥaurân.
*Hav'ilah.
ḥ^a^wîlah.
Hav'oth-ja'ir (R.V. Hav'voth-ja'ir).
ḥawwôth yâ'îr.
Haz'ael.
ḥ^a^zâ'êl.
Hazai'ah.
ḥ^a^zâyah.
Ha'zar-ad'dar.
ḥ^a^ṣar 'addâr.

Ha'zar-e'nan.
ḥ^a^ṣar 'ênân.
Ha'zar-e'non (R.V.).
ḥ^a^ṣar 'ênôn.
Ha'zar-gad'dah.
ḥ^a^ṣar gaddah.
Ha'zar-hatti'con (R.V. Ha'zer-hatti'con).
ḥâṣêr hat-tîkhôn.
Ha'zar-ma'veth.
ḥ^a^ṣarmâweth.
Ha'zar-shu'al.
ḥ^a^ṣar shû'âl.
Ha'zar-su'sah.
ḥ^a^ṣar sûsah.
Ha'zar-su'sim.
ḥ^a^ṣar sûsîm.
Haz'azon-ta'mar (Haz'ezon-ta'mar).
ḥaṣ^a^ṣôn tâmâr.
Haz'elelpo'ni (R.V. Haz'zelelpo'ni).
haṣṣ^e^lelpônî.
Haz'erim.
ḥ^a^ṣêrîm.
Haz'eroth.
ḥ^a^ṣêrôth.
Haz'iel.
ḥ^a^zî'êl.
Ha'zo.
ḥ^a^zô.
Ha'zor.
ḥâṣôr.
Ha'zor-hadat'tah (R.V.).
ḥâṣôr h^a^dhattah.
He'ber.
ḥebher ; ḥêbher ; 'êbher.
He'berite.
He'brew.
*He'bron (Heb'ron).
ḥebhrôn ; 'ebhrôn.
Heb'ronite.
He'gai.
hêghai.
He'ge.
hêghê.
He'lah.
hel'ah.
He'lam.
ḥêlâm.
Hel'bah.
ḥelbah.
Hel'bon.
ḥelbôn.
Hel'dai.
ḥeldai.
He'leb.
ḥêlebh.
He'led.
ḥêledh.
He'lek.
ḥêleḳ.
He'lekite.
He'lem.
ḥêlem.
He'leph.
ḥeleph.

He'lez.
ḥeleṣ (ḥâleṣ) ; ḥêleṣ.
He'li.
Hel'kai.
ḥelḳai.
Hel'kath.
ḥelḳath ; ḥelḳâth.
Hel'kath-hazzu'rim.
ḥelḳath haṣ-ṣûrîm.
He'lon.
ḥêlôn.
He'mam.
hêmâm.
He'man.
hêmân.
He'math.
ḥ^a^mâth ; ḥammath.
Hem'dan.
ḥemdân.
Hen.
ḥên.
He'na.
hêna'.
Hena'dad.
ḥênâdhâdh.
He'noch.
ḥ^a^nôkh.
He'pher.
ḥêpher.
He'pherite.
*Heph'zibah.
ḥephṣî bhah.
He'res.
ḥeres.
He'resh.
ḥeresh.
He'reth (R.V.).
ḥereth (ḥâreth).
Her'mas.
Her'mes.
Hermog'enes.
Her'mon.
ḥermôn.
Her'monite.
Her'od.
Hero'dian.
Hero'dias.
Hero'dion.
He'sed.
ḥesedh.
Hesh'bon.
ḥeshbôn.
Hesh'mon.
ḥeshmôn.
Heth.
ḥêth.
Heth'lon.
ḥethlôn.
Hez'eki (R.V. Hiz'ki).
ḥizḳî.
Hezeki'ah.
ḥizḳîyah ; ḥizḳîyâhû.
*He'zion.
ḥezyôn.
He'zir.
ḥêzîr.
Hez'rai.
ḥeṣrai.
Hez'ro.
ḥeṣrô.

Hez'ron.
ḥeṣrôn.
Hez'ronite.
Hid'dai.
hiddai.
Hid'dekel.
ḥiddeḳel.
Hi'el.
ḥî'êl.
Hierap'olis.
[Higga'ion.
higgâyôn].
Hi'len.
ḥîlên.
Hilki'ah.
ḥilḳîyah ; ḥilḳîyâhû.
Hil'lel.
hillêl.
Hin'nom.
hinnôm.
Hi'rah.
ḥîrah.
Hi'ram.
ḥîrâm ; ḥîrôm.
Hit'tite.
ḥittî.
Hi'vite.
ḥiwwî.
Hiz'ki (R.V.).
ḥizḳî.
Hizki'ah.
ḥizḳîyah.
Hizki'jah.
ḥizḳîyah.
Ho'bab.
ḥôbhâbh.
Ho'bah.
ḥôbhah.
Hobai'ah (R.V.).
ḥ^o^bhâyah.
Hod.
hôdh.
Hodai'ah.
hôdhawyâhû (*or* ? hôdhaiwâhû).
Hodavi'ah.
hôdhawyah.
Ho'desh.
ḥôdhesh.
Ho'devah.
hôdhwah.
Hodi'ah (Hodi'jah).
hôdhîyah.
Hog'lah.
ḥoghlah.
Ho'ham.
hôhâm.
Ho'lon.
ḥôlôn.
Ho'mam.
hômâm.
Hoph'ni.
ḥophnî.
Hor.
hôr.
Ho'ram.
hôrâm.
Ho'reb.
ḥôrêbh.
Ho'rem.
ḥ^o^rêm.

Hor-hagid′gad (R.V. Hor-haggid′gad).
ḥôr hag-gidhgâdh.
Ho′ri.
ḥôrî.
Ho′rim.
ḥôrîm.
Ho′rite.
Hor′mah.
ḥorma*h*.
Horona′im.
ḥôrônayim.
Ho′ronite.
Ho′sah.
ḥôsa*h*.
Hose′a.
hôshêaʿ.
Hoshai′ah.
hôshaʿya*h*.
Hosha′ma.
hôshâmâʿ.
Hoshe′a.
hôshêaʿ.
Ho′tham.
ḥôthâm.
Ho′than.
ḥôthâm.
Ho′thir.
ḥôthîr.
Ho′zai (R.V.).
ḥôzâi.
Huk′kok.
ḥukkôḳ.
Hu′kok.
ḥûḳôḳ.
Hul.
ḥûl.
Hul′dah.
ḥulda*h*.
Hum′tah.
ḥumṭa*h*.
Hu′pham.
ḥûphâm.
Hu′phamite.
Hup′pah.
ḥuppa*h*.
Hup′pim.
ḥuppîm.
Hur.
ḥûr.
Hu′rai.
ḥûrai.
Hu′ram.
ḥûrâm.
Hu′ri.
ḥûrî.
Hu′shah.
ḥûsha*h*.
Hu′shai.
ḥûshai.
Hu′sham.
ḥûshâm.
Hu′shathite.
Hu′shim.
ḥûshîm.
Huz.
ʿûṣ.
Huz′zab.
huṣṣabh.
Hymene′us.

I

Ib′har.
yibhḥâr.
Ib′leam.
yibhl^{e}ʿâm.
Ibnei′ah.
yibhn^{e}ya*h*.
Ibni′jah.
yibhnîya*h*.
Ib′ri.
ʿibhrî.
Ib′zan.
ʾibhṣân.
*I′chabod.
ʾî khâbhôdh.
Ico′nium.
Id′alah.
yidhʾ^{a}la*h*.
Id′bash.
yidhbâsh.
Id′do.
ʿiddô ; yiddô ; yeʿdô ; ʾiddô.
I′dume′a.
Ie′zer (R.V.).
ʾîʿezer.
Iez′erites (R.V.).
I′gal (Ig′eal).
yighʾâl.
Igdali′ah.
yighdalyâhû.
I′im.
ʿîyîm.
I′je-ab′arim.
ʿîyê hâ-ʿ^{a}bhârîm.
I′jon.
ʿîyôn.
Ik′kesh.
ʿikkêsh.
I′lai.
ʿîlai.
Illyr′icum.
Im′la.
yimlâ.
Im′lah.
yimla*h*.
Imman′uel.
ʿimmânûʾêl.
Im′mer.
ʾimmêr.
Im′na.
yimnâʿ.
Im′nah.
yimna*h*.
Im′mite (R.V.).
Im′rah.
yimra*h*.
Im′ri.
ʾimrî.
In′dia.
Iphedei′ah (R.V. Iph-dei′ah).
yiphd^{e}ya*h*.
Iph′tah-el (R.V.).
yiphtaḥ ʾêl.
Ir.
ʿîr.
I′ra.
ʿîrâ.
I′rad.
ʿîrâdh.
I′ram.
ʿîrâm.
I′ri.
ʿîrî.
Iri′jah.
yirʾîya*h*.
Ir-na′hash.
ʿîr nâḥâsh.
I′ron.
yirʾôn.
Ir′peel.
yirp^{e}ʾêl.
Ir-she′mesh.
ʿîr shemesh.
I′ru.
ʿîrû.
I′saac.
yiṣḥâḳ ; yiśḥâḳ.
Isai′ah.
y^{e}shaʿyâhû.
Is′cah.
yiska*h*.
Iscar′iot.
Ish′bah.
yishbaḥ.
Ish′bak.
yishbâḳ.
Ishbi′benob (Ish′bi be′nob).
yishbî bh^{e}nôbh.
Ish-bo′sheth.
ʾîsh bôsheth.
Ish′hod (R.V.).
ʾîsh hôdh.
I′shi.
yishʿî ; ʾîshî.
Ishi′ah.
yishshîya*h*.
Ishi′jah.
yishshîya*h*.
Ish′ma.
yishmâ.
Ish′mael.
yishmâʿêl.
Ish′maelite.
Ishmai′ah.
yishmaʿyâhû.
Ish′merai.
yishm^{e}rai.
I′shod.
ʾîsh hôdh.
Ish′pah (R.V.).
yishpa*h*.
Ish′pan.
yispân.
Ish′tob.
ʾîsh ṭôbh.
*Ish′uah (R.V. Ish′vah).
yishwa*h*.
Ish′ui (Ish′uai; R.V. Ish′vi).
yishwî.
Ish′vite (R.V.).
Ismachi′ah.
yismakhyâhû.
Ismai′ah.
yishmaʿya*h*.
Is′pah.
yishpa*h*.
Is′rael.
yiśrâʾêl.
Is′raelite.
Is′sachar.
yiśśâkhâr.
Isshi′ah.
yishshîya*h*.
Isshi′jah (R.V.).
yishshîya*h*.
Is′uah.
yishwa*h*.
Is′ui.
yishwî.
It′aly.
I′thai.
ʾîthai.
*Ith′amar.
ʾîthâmâr.
Ith′iel.
ʾîthîʾêl.
Ith′lah (R.V.).
yithla*h*.
Ith′mah.
yithma*h*.
Ith′nan.
yithnân.
Ith′ra.
yithrâ.
Ith′ran.
yithrân.
Ith′ream.
yithr^{e}ʿâm.
Ith′rite.
It′tah-ka′zin.
ʿitta*h* ḳâṣîn.
It′tai.
ʾittai.
I′ture′a.
I′vah (R.V. Iv′vah).
ʿiwwa*h*.
Iye-ab′arim (R.V.).
ʿîyê hâ-ʿ^{a}bhârîm.
I′yim (R.V.).
ʿîyîm.
Iz′har (Iz′ehar).
yiṣhâr.
Iz′harite (Iz′eharite).
Izli′ah (R.V.).
yizlîʾa*h*.
Izrahi′ah.
yizraḥya*h*.
Iz′rahite.
yizrâḥ.
Iz′ri.
yiṣrî.
Izzi′ah (R.V.).
yizzîya*h*.

J

*Ja′akan.
yaʿ^{a}ḳân.
Ja′ako′bah.
yaʿ^{a}ḳôbha*h*.
Ja′ala.
yaʿ^{a}lâ.
Ja′alah.
yaʿ^{a}la*h*.
Ja′alam.
yaʿ^{a}lâm.
Ja′anai.
yaʿ^{a}nai.
Ja′are-o′regim.
yaʿ^{a}rê ʾôr^{e}ghîm.
Ja′areshi′ah (R.V.).
yaʿ^{a}reshya*h*.
Ja′asau (R.V. Ja′asu).
[Uncertain.]
Jaas′iel.
yaʿ^{a}śîʾêl.
Ja′azani′ah.
yaʾ^{a}zanya*h* ; yaʾ^{a}zan yâhû.
Ja′azer.
yaʿzêr.
Ja′azi′ah.
yaʿ^{a}zîyâhû.
Jaaz′iel.
yaʿ^{a}zîʾêl.
Ja′bal.
yâbhâl.
Jab′bok.
yabbôḳ.
Ja′besh.
yâbhêsh.
Ja′besh-gilead.
yâbhêsh gilʿâdh.
Ja′bez.
yaʿbêṣ.
Ja′bin.
yâbhîn.
Jab′neel.
yabhn^{e}ʾêl.
Jab′neh.
yabhne*h*.
Ja′chan (R.V. Ja′can).
yaʿkân.
Ja′chin.
yâkhîn.
Ja′chinite.
Ja′cob.
yaʿ^{a}ḳôbh.
Ja′da.
yâdhâʿ.
Ja′dau.
yaddau.
Jad′dua.
yaddûaʿ.
Ja′don.
yâdhôn.
Ja′el.
yâʿêl.
Ja′gur.
yâghûr.
Jah.
yâh.
Ja′hath.
yaḥath (yâḥath).
Ja′haz.
yahaṣ ; yâh^{e}ṣa*h*.
Jah′aza (Jah′azah).
yah^{e}ṣa*h*.
Jahazi′ah.
yaḥz^{e}ya*h*.
Jaha′ziel.
yaḥ^{a}zîʾêl.
Jah′dai.
yehdâi (yâhdâi).
Jah′diel.
yaḥdîʾêl.
Jah′do.
yaḥdô.

Jah'leel. yaḥl^e'êl.

Jah'leelite.

Jah'mai. yaḥmai.

Jah'zah. yah^{e}ṣa*h*.

Jah'zeel. yaḥṣ^e'êl.

Jah'zeelite.

Jahzei'ah (R.V.). yaḥz^{e}ya*h*.

Jahze'rah. yaḥzêra*h*.

Jah'ziel. yaḥṣî'êl.

Ja'ir. yâ'îr ; yâ'îr.

Ja'irite.

Ja'irus.

Ja'kan. ya'^{a}ḳân

Ja'keh. yâḳe*h*.

Ja'kim. yâḳîm.

Ja'lam (R.V.). ya'lâm.

Ja'lon. yâlôn.

Jam'bres.

James.

Ja'min. yâmîn.

Ja'minite.

Jam'lech. yamlêkh.

Ja'nai (R.V.). ya'nai.

Ja'nim (R.V.). yânîm (yânûm).

Jan'na.

Jan'nes.

Jano'ah. yânôaḥ.

Jano'hah. yânôḥa*h*.

Ja'num. yânûm (yânîm).

Ja'pheth. yepheth (yâpheth).

Japhi'a. yâphîa'.

Japh'let. yaphlêṭ.

Japhle'ti. yaphlêṭî.

Ja'pho. yâphô.

Ja'rah. ya'ra*h*.

Ja'reb. yârêbh.

Ja'red. yeredh (yâredh).

Jaresi'ah. ya'^{a}reshya*h*.

Jar'ha. yarḥâ'.

Ja'rib. yârîbh.

Jar'muth. yarmûth.

Jaro'ah. yârôaḥ.

Ja'shen. yâshên.

Ja'sher (R.V. Ja'shar). yâshâr.

Jashob'eam. yâshobh'âm.

Ja'shub yâshûbh.

Jashu'bi-le'hem. yâshûbhi leḥem.

Ja'shubite.

Jas'iel. ya'^{a}ṡî'êl.

Ja'son.

Jath'niel. yathnî'êl.

Jat'tir. yattîr.

Ja'van. yâwân.

Ja'zer. ya'zêr (ya'^{a}zêr).

Ja'ziz. yâzîz.

Je'arim. y^e'ârîm.

Jeat'erai. y^e'ath^{e}rai.

Jeber'echi'ah. y^{e}bherekhyâhû.

Je'bus. y^{e}bhûs.

*Jeb'usite (Jeb'usi). y^{e}bhûsî.

Jecami'ah. y^{e}ḳamya*h*.

Jecholi'ah. y^{e}kholyâhû.

Jechoni'as.

Jeconi'ah. y^{e}khonyah ; y^{e}khonyâhû.

Jedai'ah. y^{e}dha'ya*h*.

Jedi'ael. y^{e}dhî'^{a}'êl.

Jedi'dah. y^{e}dhîdha*h*.

Jedidi'ah. y^{e}dhîdhya*h*.

Jedu'thun. y^{e}dhûthûn.

Je'ezer. 'î'ezer.

Je'ezerite.

Je'gar-sahadu'tha. y^{e}ghar ṡah^{a}dhûthâ.

*Jehal'eleel (Jehal'elel; R.V. Jehal'lelel). y^{e}hallel'êl.

Jehdei'ah. yeḥd^{e}yâhû.

Jehez'ekel. y^{e}ḥez^{e}ḳêl.

Jehi'ah. y^{e}ḥîya*h*.

Jeh'iel. y^{e}ḥî'êl ; y^e'î'el.

*Jehi'eli. y^{e}ḥî'êlî.

Jehizki'ah. y^{e}ḥizḳîyâhû.

Jeho'adah (R.V. Jeho'addah). y^{e}hô'adda*h*.

Jeho'addan. y^{e}hô'addân ; y^{e}hô'addîn.

Jeho'addin (R.V.). y^{e}hô'addîn.

Jeho'ahaz. y^{e}hô'âḥâz ; yô'âḥâz.

Jeho'ash. y^{e}hô'âsh.

Jeho'hanan. y^{e}hôḥânân.

*Jehoi'ada. y^{e}hôyâdhâ' ; yôyâdhâ'.

*Jehoi'achin. y^{e}hôyâkhîn.

*Jehoi'akim. y^{e}hôyâḳîm.

*Jehoi'arib. y^{e}hôyârîbh.

*Jehon'adab. y^{e}hônâdhâbh.

Jehon'athan. y^{e}hônâthân.

Jeho'ram. y^{e}hôrâm.

Jehoshab'eath. y^{e}hôshabh'ath.

Jehosh'aphat. y^{e}hôshâphâṭ.

Jehosh'eba. y^{e}hôshebha'.

Jehosh'ua. y^{e}hôshûa'.

Jeho'vah. yahwe*h* (?).

Jeho'vah-ji'reh. yahwe*h* yir'e*h*.

Jeho'vah-nis'si. yahwe*h* nissî.

Jeho'vah-sha'lom. yahwe*h* shâlôm.

Jehoz'abad. y^{e}hôzâbhâdh.

Jehoz'adak. y^{e}hôṣâdhâḳ.

Je'hu. yêhû'.

Jehub'bah. y^{e}ḥubba*h*.

Jehu'cal. y^{e}hûkhal.

Je'hud. y^{e}hûdh.

Je'hudi. y^{e}hûdhî.

Jehudi'jah. y^{e}hûdîya*h*.

Jeh'uel (R.V.). y^{e}ḥû'êl (y^{e}ḥî'êl).

Je'hush. y^e'ûsh.

Jei'el. y^e'î'êl.

Jekab'zeel. y^{e}ḳabhṣ^e'êl.

Jekam'eam. y^{e}ḳam'âm.

Jekami'ah. y^{e}ḳamya*h*.

Jeku'thiel. y^{e}ḳûthî'êl.

Jemi'ma (R.V. Jemi'mah). y^{e}mîma*h*.

Jem'uel. y^{e}mû'êl.

Jeph'thae.

Jeph'thah. yiphtâḥ.

Jephun'neh. y^{e}phunne*h*.

Je'rah. yeraḥ.

Jerah'meel. y^{e}raḥm^e'êl.

Jerah'meelite.

Je'red. yeredh.

Jere'mai. y^{e}rêmai.

Jeremi'ah. yirm^{e}ya*h* ; yirm^{e}yâhû.

Jeremi'as.

Jere'moth. y^{e}rêmôth.

Jer'emy.

Jeri'ah. y^{e}rîyâhû.

Jeri'bai. y^{e}rîbhai.

Jer'icho. y^{e}rîḥô ; y^{e}rêḥô.

Jer'iel. y^{e}rî'êl.

Jeri'jah. y^{e}rîya*h*.

Jeri'moth. y^{e}rîmôth ; y^{e}rêmôth.

Jeri'oth. y^{e}rî'ôth.

Jerobo'am. yârobh'âm.

Jero'ham. y^{e}rôḥâm.

Jerubba'al. y^{e}rubba'al.

Jerubbe'sheth. y^{e}rubbesheth.

Jeru'el. y^{e}rû'êl.

Jeru'salem. y^{e}rûshâlêm ; y^{e}rûshalayim.

Jeru'sha. y^{e}rûshâ.

Jeru'shah. y^{e}rûsha*h*.

Jeshai'ah (Jesai'ah). y^{e}sha'ya*h* ; y^{e}sha'yâhû.

Jesha'nah. y^{e}shâna*h*.

Jeshare'lah. y^{e}shar'êla*h*.

Jesheb'eab. yeshebh'âbh.

Je'sher. yêsher.

Jeshi'mon. y^{e}shîmôn.

Jeshi'shai. y^{e}shîshai.

Jeshohai'ah. y^{e}shôḥâya*h*.

*Jeshu'a (Jeshu'ah). yêshûa'.

Jeshu'run (Jesu'run). yêshûrûn.

Jesi'ah. yishshîya*h* ; yishshîyâhû.

Jesim'iel. y^{e}ṡîmî'êl.

Jes'se. yîshai.

Jes'ui. yishwî.

Jes'uite.

Je'sus.

Je'ther. yether.

Je'theth. y^{e}thêth.

Jeth'lah. yithla*h*.

Jeth'ro. yithrô.

Je'tur. y^{e}ṭûr.

Jeu'el. y^e'û'êl.

Je'ush. y^e'ûsh.

Je'uz. y^e'ûṣ.

Jew.

Jew'ry.

Jezani'ah. y^{e}zanyâhû.

Jez'ebel. 'îzebhel.

Je'zer. yêṣer.

Jez'erite.

Jezi'ah. yizzîya*h*.

Jez'iel. y^{e}zî'êl.

Jezli'ah. yizlî'a*h*.

Jezo'ar. ṣôḥar (*or* ? yiṣḥâr).

Jezrahi'ah. yizraḥya*h*.

Jez'reel. yizr^e'el ; yizr^e'êl.

Jez'reelite.

Jib'sam. yibhṡâm.

Jid'laph. yidhlâph.

Jim'nah (Jim'na). yimna*h*.

Jim'nite.
Jiph'tah.
yiphtâḥ.
Jiph'thah-el.
yiphtaḥ'êl.
Jo'ab.
yô'âbh.
Jo'ah.
yô'âḥ.
*Jo'ahaz.
yô'âḥâz.
Joan'na (R.V. Joan'an).
Jo'ash.
yô'âsh ; yô'âsh.
Jo'atham.
Job
'îyôbh.
Jo'bab.
yôbhâbh.
Joch'ebed.
yôkhebhedh.
Jo'da (R.V.).
Jo'ed.
yô'êdh.
Jo'el.
yô'êl.
Joe'lah.
yô'êlah.
*Jo'ezer.
yô'ezer.
Jog'behah.
yoghb^{e}hah.
Jog'li.
yoghlî.
Jo'ha.
yôḥâ.
*Jo'hanan.
yôḥânân ; y^{e}hôḥânân.
John.
Joi'ada.
yôyâdhâ'.
Joi'akim.
yôyâḳîm.
Joi'arib.
yôyâribh.
Jok'deam.
yoḳdh^e'âm.
Jo'kim.
yôḳîm.
Jok'meam.
yoḳm^e'âm.
Jok'neam.
yoḳn^e'âm.
Jok'shan.
yoḳshân.
Jok'tan.
yoḳṭân.
Jok'theel.
yoḳth^e'êl.
Jon'adab.
yônâdhâbh ; y^{e}hônâdhâbh.
Jo'nah.
yônah.
Jo'nan (R.V. Jo'nam).
Jo'nas (Jo'na).
[Jo'nath-e'lem-recho'kim.
yônath 'êlem r^{e}ḥôḳîm.]

Jon'athan.
yônâthân; y^{e}hônâthân.
Jop'pa.
yâphô.
Jo'rah.
yôrah.
Jo'rai.
yôrai.
Jo'ram.
yôrâm ; y^{e}hôrâm.
Jor'dan.
hay-yardên.
Jo'rim.
Jor'koam (R.V. Jor'keam).
yorḳ^e'âm.
Jos'abad (R.V. Joz'abad).
yôzâbhâdh.
Jos'aphat.
Jo'se.
Jo'sech (R.V.).
Jos'edech.
y^{e}hôṣâdhâḳ.
Jo'seph.
yôsêph.
Jo'ses.
Jo'shah.
yôshah.
Josh'aphat.
yôshâphâṭ.
Joshavi'ah.
yôshawyah.
Joshbeka'shah.
yoshb^{e}ḳâshah.
Josh'ua.
y^{e}hôshûa'.
Josi'ah.
yôshîyah ; yôshîyâhû.
Josi'as.
Josibi'ah (R.V. Joshibi'ah).
yôshîbhyah.
Josiphi'ah.
yôsîphyah.
Jot'bah.
yoṭ^{e}bhah.
Jotba'thah (Jot'bath).
yoṭ^{e}bhâthah.
Jo'tham.
yôthâm.
Joz'abad.
yôzâbhâdh.
Joz'achar (R.V. Joz'acar).
yôzâkhâr.
Joz'adak.
yôṣâdhâḳ.
Ju'bal.
yûbhâl.
Ju'cal.
yûkhal.
Ju'da.
Ju'dah.
y^{e}hûdhah.
Ju'das.
Jude'a.
Ju'dith.
y^{e}hûdhîth.
Ju'lia.

Ju'lius.
Ju'nia (R.V. Ju'nias).
Ju'piter.
Ju'shab-he'sed.
yûshabh ḥesedh.
Jus'tus.
Ju'tah (R.V.)
yûṭah.
Jut'tah.
yuṭṭah ; yûṭah.

K

Kab'zeel.
ḳabhṣ^e'êl.
Ka'desh.
ḳâdhêsh.
*Ka'desh-bar'nea.
ḳâdhêsh barnêa'.
Kad'miel.
ḳadhmî'êl.
Kad'monite.
Ka'in (R.V.).
ḳayin.
Kal'lai.
ḳallai.
Ka'mon (R.V.).
ḳâmôn.
Ka'nah.
ḳânah.
Kare'ah.
ḳârêaḥ.
Karka'a (R.V. Kar'ka).
ḳarḳâ'.
Kar'kor.
ḳarḳôr.
Kar'tah.
ḳartah.
Kar'tan.
ḳartân.
Kat'tath.
ḳaṭṭâth.
Ke'dar.
ḳêdhâr.
Ked'emah.
ḳêdh^{e}mah.
Kede'moth.
ḳ^{e}dhêmôth.
Ke'desh.
ḳedhesh.
Kehela'thah.
ḳ^{e}hêlâthah.
Kei'lah.
ḳ^e'îlah.
Kelai'ah.
ḳêlâyah.
Keli'ta.
ḳ^{e}lîṭâ.
Kemu'el (Kem'uel)
ḳ^{e}mû'êl.
Ke'nan.
ḳênân.
Ke'nath.
ḳ^{e}nâth.
Ke'naz (Ke'nez).
ḳ^{e}naz.
Ken'ezite.
Ke'nite (Ken'ite)
Ken'izzite.

Ker'en-hap'puch.
ḳeren hap-pukh.
Ke'rioth.
ḳ^{e}rîyôth.
Ker'ioth-hez'ron (R.V.).
ḳ^{e}rîyôth ḥeṣrôn.
Ke'ros.
ḳêrôs.
Ketu'rah.
ḳ^{e}ṭûrah.
*Kezi'a (R.V. Kezi'ah).
ḳ^{e}ṣî'ah.
Ke'ziz.
ḳ^{e}ṣîṣ.
Kib'roth-hatta'avah.
ḳibh^{e}rôth hat-ta'^{a}wah.
Kibza'im.
ḳibhṣayim.
Kid'ron.
ḳidhrôn.
Ki'nah.
ḳînah.
Kir.
ḳîr.
Kir-har'eseth (-har'aseth).
ḳîr ḥ^{a}reśeth (ḥ^{a}râśeth).
Kir-he'res (-ha'resh).
ḳîr ḥereś (ḥâreś).
Kir'iath (R.V. *for* Kir'jath).
ḳiryath.
Kiriatha'im.
ḳiryâthayim.
Kiri'oth.
ḳ^{e}rîyôth.
Kir'jath.
ḳiryath.
Kirjatha'im.
ḳiryâthayim.
Kir'jath-ar'ba.
ḳiryath 'arba'.
Kir'jath-a'rim.
ḳiryath 'ârîm.
Kir'jath-ba'al.
ḳiryath ba'al.
Kir'jath-hu'zoth.
ḳiryath ḥûṣôth.
Kir'jath-je'arim.
ḳiryath y^e'ârîm.
Kir'jath-san'nah.
ḳiryath sannah.
Kir'jath-se'pher.
ḳiryath sêpher.
Kish.
ḳîsh.
Ki'shi.
ḳîshî.
Kish'ion.
ḳishyôn.
Ki'shon.
ḳishyôn ; ḳîshôn.
Kison.
ḳîshôn.
Kith'lish.
kithlîsh.
Kit'ron.
ḳitrôn.
Kit'tim.
kittîm.

Ko'a.
ḳôa'.
Ko'hath.
ḳ^{e}hâth ; ḳ^{o}hâth.
Ko'hathite.
Kolai'ah.
ḳôlâyah.
Ko'rah.
ḳôraḥ.
Ko'rahite (Ko'rathite and Kor'hite).
Ko're.
ḳôrê.
Koz.
haḳ-ḳôṣ.
Kushai'ah.
ḳûshâyâhû.

L

La'adah.
la'dah.
La'adan (R.V. La'dan).
la'dân.
La'ban.
lâbhân.
La'chish.
lâkhîsh.
La'el.
lâ'êl.
La'had.
lahadh.
Lahairo'i.
la-ḥai rô'î.
Lah'mam.
laḥmâs *or* laḥmâm.
Lah'mi.
laḥmî.
La'ish (R.V. once La'ishah).
layish (lâyish); lay^{e}shah.
La'kum (R.V. Lak'kum).
laḳḳûm.
La'mech.
lemekh (lâmekh)
La'odice'a.
La'odice'an.
Lap'idoth.
lappîdhôth.
Lase'a.
La'sha.
lâsha'.
Lasha'ron (R.V. Lassha'ron).
lashshârôn.
Laz'arus.
Le'ah.
lê'ah.
[Lean'noth.
l^{e}annôth.]
Leba'na.
l^{e}bhânâ.
Leba'nah.
l^{e}bhânah.
*Leb'anon.
l^{e}bhânôn.
*Leb'aoth.
l^{e}bhâ'ôth.
Lebbe'us.

Lebo'nah.
l^e bhônah.
Le'cah.
lêkhah.
Le'habim.
l^e hâbhîm.
Le'hi.
l^e ḥî (leḥî).
*Lem'uel.
l^e mû'êl.
Le'shem.
leshem.
*Let'ushim.
l^e ṭûshîm.
*Leum'mim.
l^e ummîm.
Le'vi.
lêwî.
Le'vite.
Lib'ertine.
Lib'nah.
libhnah.
Lib'ni.
libhnî.
Lib'nite.
Lib'ya.
pûṭ.
Lib'yan.
Lik'hi.
likhî.
Li'nus.
Loam'mi.
lô 'ammî.
Lod.
lôdh.
Lo-de'bar.
lô dh^e bhâr.
Lo'is.
Lo-ruha'mah.
lô ruḥâmah.
Lot.
lôṭ.
Lo'tan.
lôṭân.
Lu'bim(s)
lûbhîm.
Lu'cas.
Luc'ifer.
hêlêl.
Lu'cius.
Lud.
lûdh.
Lu'dim.
lûdhîm.
Lu'hith.
lûḥîth.
Luke.
Luz.
lûz.
Ly'cao'nia.
Lyc'ia.
Lyd'da.
Lyd'ia.
Lyd'ian.
Lysa'nias.
Lys'ias.
Lys'tra.

M

Ma'acathite (R.V.).
Ma'achah (Ma'acah).
ma'^a khah.
Ma'achathite (Ma'-achathi).
Ma'adai.
ma'^a dhî.
Maadi'ah.
ma'adhyah.
Ma'ai.
mâ'ai.
Ma'aleh - acrab'bim (R.V. -akrab'bim).
ma'^a lêh 'aḳrabbîm.
Ma'arath.
ma'^a râth.
Ma'areh-ge'ba (R.V.).
ma'^a rêh ghebha' (ghâbha').
Ma'asei'ah.
ma'^a śêyah (-yâhû); maḥsêyah.
Maasi'ai (R.V. Ma'asai).
ma'śai.
Ma'ath.
Ma'az.
ma'aṣ.
Maazi'ah.
ma'azyah; ma'azyâhû.
Macedo'nia.
*Mach'banai (R.V. Machban'nai).
makhbannai.
Machbe'nah (R.V. Machbe'na).
makhbênâ.
Ma'chi.
mâkhî.
Ma'chir.
mâkhîr.
Ma'chirite.
Machnad'ebai.
makhnadh^e bhai.
Machpe'lah.
makhpêlah.
Ma'dai.
mâdhai.
Ma'dian.
Madman'nah.
madhmannah.
Mad'men.
madhmên.
Madme'nah.
madhmênah.
Ma'don.
mâdhôn.
Mag'adan (R.V.).
Mag'bish.
maghbîsh.
Mag'dala.
*Magdale'ne (*or* Mag'-dalen).
Mag'diel.
maghdî'êl.
Ma'gog.
mâghôgh.
Ma'gor-missa'bib.
mâghôr mis-sâbhîbh.

Magpi'ash.
maghpî'âsh.
[Ma'gus.]
Mah'alah.
maḥlah.
Mahalal'eel (R.V. Mahal'alel).
mah^a lal'êl.
[Mah'alath lean'noth.
maḥ^a lath l^e annôth.]
Mah'ali.
maḥlî.
Mahana'im.
maḥ^a nayîm.
Mah'aneh-dan.
maḥ^a nêh dhân.
Mah'ari.
mah^a rai.
Ma'hath.
maḥath.
Mah'avite.
ham-maḥ^a wîm.
Maha'zioth.
maḥ^a zî'ôth.
Ma'her-sha'lal-hash-baz.
mahêr shâlâl ḥâsh baz.
Mah'lah.
maḥlah.
Mah'li.
maḥlî.
Mah'lite.
Mah'lon.
maḥlôn.
Ma'hol.
mâḥôl.
Ma'kaz.
mâkaṣ.
Mak'heloth.
makhêlôth.
Makke'dah.
makkêdhah.
Mak'tesh.
makhtêsh.
Mal'achi.
mal'âkhî.
Mal'cham (R.V. Mal'-cam).
malkâm.
Malchi'ah (Malchi'-jah).
malkîyah.
Mal'chiel.
malkî'êl.
Mal'chielite.
Malchi'ram.
malkîrâm.
Malchishu'a.
malkîshûa'.
Mal'chus.
Malel'eel.
Mallo'thi.
mallôthî.
Mal'luch.
mallûkh.
Mallu'chi (R.V.).
m^e lîkhû (*or* ? mallûkhî)
Mam're.
mamrê.

Man'aen.
Man'ahath.
mânaḥath (mânâḥath).
Man'ahethite (R.V. -athite; menuhoth.
mânaḥtî; M^e nûḥôth).
Manas'seh.
m^e nashsheh.
Manas'ses.
Manas'site.
Mano'ah.
mânôah.
Ma'och.
mâ'ôkh.
Ma'on.
mâ'ôn.
Ma'onite.
Ma'ra.
mârâ.
Ma'rah.
mârah.
Mar'alah.
mar'^a lah.
[Ma'ran a'tha.]
Mare'shah.
mârêshah.
Mar'cus.
Mark.
Ma'roth.
mârôth.
Mar'sena.
mars^e nâ.
Mar'tha.
Ma'ry.
[Mas'chil.
maśkîl.]
Mash.
mash.
Ma'shal.
mâshâl.
Masre'kah.
maśrêkah.
Mas'sa.
maśśâ.
Mas'sah.
massah.
Mathu'sala.
Mat'red.
maṭrêdh
Mat'ri.
maṭrî.
Mat'tan.
mattân.
Matta'nah.
mattânah.
Mattani'ah.
mattanyah; mattanyâhû.
Mat'tatha.
*Mat'tathah (R.V. Mattat'tah).
mattattah.
Mattathi'as.
Mat'tenai.
matt^e nai.
Mat'than.
Mat'that.
Mat'thew.

Matthi'as.
Mattithi'ah.
mattithyah; mattithyâhû.
Maz'zaroth.
mazzârôth.
Me'ah.
mê'ah.
Mea'rah.
m^e 'ârah.
Mebun'nai.
m^e bhunnai.
Meche'rathite.
Me'dad.
mêdhâdh.
Me'dan.
m^e dhân.
*Me'deba.
mêdh^e bhâ.
Mede.
mâdhai.
Me'dia.
mâdhai.
Me'dian.
Megid'do.
m^e ghiddô.
Megid'don.
m^e ghiddôn.
Mehet'abel (Mehetab'eel).
m^e hêṭâbh'êl.
Mehi'da.
m^e ḥîdhâ.
Me'hir.
m^e ḥîr.
Meho'lathite.
Mehu'jael.
m^e ḥûyâ'êl.
Mehu'man.
m^e hûmân.
Me'hunim(s) (Me'unim).
m^e 'ûnîm.
Me-jar'kon.
mê hay-yarkôn.
Meko'nah.
m^e khônah.
Melati'ah.
m^e laṭyah.
Mel'chi.
Melchi'ah.
malkîyah.
Melchis'edek.
Melchishu'a.
malkîshûa'.
Melchiz'edek.
malkî ṣedheḳ.
Me'lea.
Me'lech.
melekh.
Meli'cu.
m^e lîkhû.
Mel'ita.
Mel'zar.
ham-melṣar.
Mem'phis.
môph.
Memu'can.
m^e mûkhân.

Men'ahem.
m^{e}naḥêm.

Me'nan (R.V. Men'na).

[Me'ne.
m^{e}nê.]

Menuhoth (R.V.).
m^{e}nûḥôth.

Men'uim (R.V.).

Meo'nenim.
m$^{e'}$ôn^{e}nîm.

Meono'thai.
m$^{e'}$ônôthai.

Mepha'ath.
mêpha'ath (mêphâ-'ath).

*Mephib'osheth.
m^{e}phîbhôsheth.

Me'rab.
mêrabh.

Merai'ah.
m^{e}râyah.

Merai'oth.
m^{e}râyôth.

Mera'ri.
m^{e}rârî.

Mera'rite.

Mer'atha'im.
m^{e}râthayim.

Mercu'rius (R.V. Mer'cury).

Me'red.
meredh (mâredh).

Mere'moth.
m^{e}rêmôth.

Me'res.
meres.

*Meri'bah.
m^{e}rîbhah.

Me'rib-ba'al.
m^{e}rîbhba'al ; m^{e}rî-bha'al.

Meri'bath (R.V.).
m^{e}rîbhath.

Meri'both (R.V.).
m^{e}rîbhôth.

Mero'dach.
m^{e}rôdhakh.

Mero'dach-bal'adan.
m^{e}rôdhakh bal'^{a}dhân.

Me'rom.
mêrôm.

Meron'othite.

Me'roz.
mêrôz.

Me'sha.
mêsha' ; mêshâ'.

Me'shach.
mêshakh.

Me'shech (Me'sech).
meshekh.

Meshel'emi'ah.
m^{e}shelemyah ; -yâhû.

Meshezab'eel.
m^{e}shêzabh'êl.

Meshille'mith.
m^{e}shillêmîth.

Meshille'moth.
m^{e}shillêmôth.

Mesho'bab.
m^{e}shôbhâbh.

Meshul'lam.
m^{e}shullâm.

Meshul'lemeth.
m^{e}shullemeth.

Meso'baite.
m^{e}ṣôbhâyah.

Mes'opota'mia.
'aram nah^{a}rayim.

Messi'ah.

Messi'as.

Meth'eg-am'mah.
methegh hâ-'ammah.

Methu'sael.
m^{e}thûshâ'êl.

Methu'selah.
m^{e}thûshelaḥ.

Me'unim.
m$^{e'}$ûnîm.

Meza'hab.
mê zâhâbh.

Mezo'baite (R.V.).
m^{e}ṣôbhâyah.

Mia'min.
miy-yâmîn.

Mib'har.
mibhḥâr.

Mib'sam.
mibhśâm.

Mib'sar.
mibhṣâr.

Mi'cah (Mi'chah).
mîkhah ; mîkhâ.

Micai'ah.
mîkhây^{e}hû.

Mi'cha (R.V. Mi'ca).
mîkhâ.

*Mi'chael.
mîkhâ'êl.

Michai'ah.
mîkhâyah (-y^{e}hû, -yâhû).

Mi'chal.
mîkhâl.

Mich'mas.
mikhmâs.

Mich'mash.
mikhmâsh (mikh-mash).

Mich'methah.
mikhm^{e}thah.

Mich'ri.
mikhrî.

Mich'tam.
mikhtâm.

Mid'din.
middîn.

Mid'ian.
midhyân.

Mid'ianite.

Mid'iani'tish.

Mig'dal-el.
mighdal'êl.

Mig'dal-gad.
mighdal gâdh.

Mig'dol.
mighdôl.

Mig'ron.
mighrôn.

Mija'min.
miy-yâmîn.

Mik'loth.
miḳlôth.

Miknei'ah.
miḳnêyâhû.

Mil'alai.
mil^{a}lai.

Mil'cah.
milkah.

Mil'com.
milkôm.

Mile'tus (Mile'tum).

Mil'lo.
millô.

Minia'min.
minyâmîn.

Min'ni.
minnî.

Min'nith.
minnîth.

Miph'kad.
miphḳâdh.

Mir'iam.
miryâm.

Mir'ma.
mirmah.

Mis'gab.
ham-miśgâbh.

Mish'ael.
mîshâ'êl ; mish'âl.

Mi'sham.
mish'âm.

Mi'shal (Mish'eal).
mish'âl.

Mish'ma.
mishmâ'.

Mishman'nah.
mishmannah.

Mish'raite.
mishrâ'î.

*Mis'pereth.
mispereth.

Mis'rephoth-ma'im.
miśr^{e}phôth mayim.

Mith'cah.
mithkah.

Mith'nite.

Mith'redath.
mithr^{e}dhâth.

Mityle'ne.

Mi'zar.
miṣ'âr.

Miz'pah.
miṣpah.

Miz'peh.
miṣpeh ; miṣpah.

Miz'par (R.V. Mis'par).
mispâr.

Miz'raim.
miṣrayim.

Miz'zah.
mizzah.

Mna'son.

Mo'ab.
mô'âbh.

Mo'abite.

Moadi'ah.
mô'adhyah.

Mola'dah.
môlâdhah.

Mo'lech (Mo'loch).
môlekh.

Mo'lid.
môlîdh.

*Mor'asthite (R.V. Mor'ashtite).

Mor'decai.
mord^{e}khai.

Mo'reh.
môreh.

Mo'resheth-gath.
môresheth gath.

Mori'ah.
môrîyah.

Mose'ra (R.V. Mose'rah).
môsêrah.

Mo'seroth.
môsêrôth.

Mo'ses.
môsheh.

Mo'za.
môṣâ.

Mo'zah.
ham-môṣah.

Mup'pim.
muppîm.

Mu'shi.
mûshî.

Mu'shite.

[Muth-lab'ben.
mûth labbên.]

My'ra.

Mys'ia.

N

Na'am.
na'am.

Na'amah.
na'^{a}mah.

Na'aman.
na'^{a}mân.

Na'amathite.

Na'amite.

Na'arah.
na'^{a}rah.

Na'arai.
na'^{a}rai.

Na'aran.
na'^{a}rân.

Na'arath.
na'^{a}râth *or* na'^{a}rah.

Na'ashon.
naḥshôn.

Na'ason.

Na'bal.
nâbhâl.

Na'both.
nâbhôth.

Na'chon (R.V. Na'con).
nâkhôn.

Na'chor.

Na'dab.
nâdhâbh.

Nag'ge (R.V. Nag'gai).

Naha'liel.
naḥ^{a}lî'êl.

Nah'al(l)al.
nah^{a}lâl.

Nahalol.
nah^{a}lôl.

Na'ham.
naḥam.

Nahama'ni.
naḥ^{a}mânî.

Nah'arai.
naḥ^{a}rai.

Nah'ari.
naḥrai.

Na'hash.
nâḥâsh.

Na'hath.
naḥath.

Nah'bi.
naḥbî.

Na'hor.
nâḥôr.

Nah'shon.
naḥshôn.

Na'hum.
naḥûm.

Na'in.

Nai'oth.
nâyôth.

Na'omi.
no'^{o}mî.

Na'phish.
nâphîsh.

Naph'tali.
naphtâlî.

Naph'tuhim.
naphtûḥîm.

Narcis'sus.

Na'than.
nâthân.

Na'than-me'lech.
n^{e}than melekh.

Nathan'ael.

Na'um.

Nazare'ne.

Naz'areth.

Naz'arite (R.V. Naz'irite).
nâzîr.

Ne'ah.
han-nê'ah.

Neap'olis.

Neari'ah.
n$^{e'}$aryah.

Ne'bai.
nêbhai *or* nôbhai.

Nebai'oth (Neba'joth).
n^{e}bhâyôth.

Nebal'lat.
n^{e}bhallâṭ.

Ne'bat.
n^{e}bhâṭ.

Ne'bo.
n^{e}bhô

Neb'uchadnez'zar.
n^{e}bhûkhadhneṣṣar.

Neb'uchadrez'zar.
n^{e}bhûkhadhreṣṣar.

Nebushas'ban.
n^{e}bhûshazbân.

Nebuzar'adan.
n^{e}bhûzar'^{a}dhân.

Ne'cho (R.V. Ne'co).
n^{e}khô.

Nedabi'ah.
n^{e}dhabhyah.

[Negi'nah.
n^eghînah.]
[Negi'noth.
n^eghînôth.]
Neh'elamite.
Nehemi'ah.
n^eḥemyah.
[Nehi'loth.
n^eḥîlôth.]
Ne'hum.
n^eḥûm.
Nehush'ta.
n^eḥushtâ.
Nehush'tan.
n^eḥushtân.
Nei'el.
n^e'î'êl.
Ne'keb.
han-neḳebh.
Neko'da.
n^eḳôdhâ.
Nem'uel.
n^emû'êl.
Nem'uelite.
Ne'pheg.
nephegh.
Neph'ilim (R.V.).
n^ephîlîm.
Ne'phish.
nâphîsh.
Nephish'esim (R.V. Nephush'esim).
n^ephîsh^esîm (or ? n^eph-ûsh^esîm).
Neph'thalim.
Nephto'ah.
nephtôaḥ.
Neph'usim (R.V. Neph'isim).
n^ephûsîm (or ? nephîsîm).
Ner.
nêr.
Ne'reus.
Ner'gal.
nêr^eghal.
Ner'gal-share'zer.
nêr^eghal shar'eṣer.
Ne'ri.
Neri'ah.
nêrîyah ; nêrîyâhû.
Neta'im (R.V.).
n^eṭâ'îm.
Nethan'eel (R.V. Neth'anel).
n^ethan'êl.
Nethani'ah.
n^ethanyah ; n^ethanyâhû.
Neth'inims (R.V. -im).
n^ethînîm.
Neto'phah.
n^eṭôphah.
Neto'phathite (Neto'phathi).
Nezi'ah.
n^eṣîaḥ.
Ne'zib.
n^eṣîbh.
Nib'haz.
nibhḥaz.

Nib'shan.
han-nibhshân.
Nica'nor.
Nicode'mus.
Nicola'itane (R.V. -tan).
Nic'olas.
Nicop'olis.
Ni'ger.
Nim'rah.
nimrah.
Nim'rim.
nimrîm.
Nim'rod.
nimrôdh.
Nim'shi.
nimshî.
Nin'eve.
Nin'eveh.
nîn^ewêh.
Nin'evite.
Ni'san.
nîsân.
Nis'roch.
nisrôkh.
No.
nô.
Noadi'ah.
nô'adhyah.
No'ah.
nôaḥ ; nô'ah.
No-am'on (R.V.).
nô 'âmôn.
Nob.
nôbh.
No'bah.
nôbhaḥ.
No'bai (R.V.).
nôbhai or nêbhai.
Nod.
nôdh.
No'dab.
nôdhâbh.
No'e.
No'gah.
nôghah.
No'hah.
nôḥah.
Non.
nôn.
Noph.
nôph.
No'phah.
nôphah.
Nun.
nûn.
Nym'phas.

O

Obadi'ah.
'ôbhadhyah (-yâhû).
O'bal.
'ôbhâl.
O'bed.
'ôbhêdh.
O'bed-e'dom.
'ôbhêdh '^edhôm.
O'bil.
'ôbhîl.

O'both.
'ôbhôth.
Oc'ran (R.V. Och'ran).
'okhrân.
O'ded.
'ôdhêdh.
Og.
'ôgh.
O'had.
'ôhadh.
O'hel.
'ôhel.
Oh'olah (R.V.).
'oh^olah.
Oholi'ab (R.V.).
'oh^olî'âbh.
Oholi'bah (R.V.).
'oh^olîbhah.
Oh'oliba'mah (R.V.).
'oh^olîbhâmah.
Ol'ivet.
Olym'pas.
O'mar.
'ômâr.
O'mega.
Om'ri.
'omrî.
On.
'ôn.
O'nam.
'ônâm.
O'nan.
'ônân.
Ones'imus.
Onesiph'orus.
O'no.
'ônô.
O'phel.
hâ-'ôphel.
O'phir.
'ôphîr.
Oph'ni.
hâ-'ophnî.
Oph'rah.
'ophrah.
O'reb.
'ôrêbh.
O'ren.
'ôren.
Ori'on.
k^esîl.
Or'nan.
'ornân.
Or'pah.
'orpah.
O'see.
Oshe'a.
hôshêa'.
Osnap'par (R.V.).
'osnappar.
Oth'ni.
'othnî.
Oth'niel.
'othnî'êl.
O'zem.
'ôṣem.
Ozi'as.
Oz'ni.
'oznî.
Oz'nite.

P

Pa'arai.
pa'^arai.
Pad'an (R.V. Pad'dan).
paddân.
*Pad'an-a'ram (R.V. Pad'dan-a'ram).
Pà'don.
pâdhôn.
Pag'iel.
pagh'î'êl.
Pa'hath-mo'ab.
paḥath mô'âbh.
Pa'i.
pâ'î.
Pa'lal.
pâlâl.
Palesti'na (Pal'estine).
p^elesheth.
Pal'lu.
pallû'.
Pal'luite.
Pal'ti.
palṭî.
Pal'tiel.
palṭî'êl.
Pal'tite.
Pamphyl'ia.
Pan'nag.
pannagh.
Pa'phos.
Pa'rah.
hap-pârah.
Pa'ran.
pârân.
Par'bar.
parbâr.
Parmash'ta.
parmashtâ.
Par'menas.
Par'nach.
parnâkh.
Pa'rosh.
par'ôsh.
Parshanda'tha.
parshandâthâ.
Par'thian.
Paru'ah.
pârûaḥ.
Parva'im.
parwâyîm.
Pa'sach.
pâsakh.
Pas-dam'mim.
pas dammîm.
Pase'ah (Phase'ah).
pâsêaḥ.
Pash'ur (R.V. Pash'hur).
pashḥûr.
Pat'ara.
Path'ros.
pathrôs.
Path'rusim.
pathrûsîm.
Pat'mos.

Pat'robas.
Pa'u.
pâ'û.
Paul.
Paul'us.
Ped'ahel.
p^edhah'êl.
Pedah'zur.
p^edhâhṣûr.
Pedai'ah.
p^edhâyah ; p^edhâyâhû.
Pe'kah.
peḳaḥ.
Pekahi'ah.
p^eḳaḥyah.
Pe'kod.
p^eḳôdh.
Pelai'ah.
p^elâyah.
Pelali'ah.
p^elalyah.
Pelati'ah.
p^elaṭyah ; p^elaṭyâhû.
Pe'leg.
pelegh.
Pe'let.
peleṭ.
Pe'leth.
peleth.
Pe'lethite.
Pe'lonite.
*Pen'iel.
p^enî'êl.
Penin'nah.
p^eninnah.
*Penu'el (Pen'uel).
Pe'or.
p^e'ôr.
Pe'res.
p^erês.
Pe'resh.
peresh.
Pe'rez.
pereṣ.
Pe'rezite (R.V.).
Per'ez-uz'za (-uzzah).
pereṣ 'uzzâ ('uzzah).
Per'ga.
Per'gamos (R.V. Per'gamum).
Peri'da.
p^erîdhâ.
Per'izzite.
Per'sia.
pâras.
Per'sian.
Per'sis.
Peru'da.
p^erûdhâ.
Pe'ter.
Pethahi'ah.
p^ethaḥyah.
Pe'thor.
p^ethôr.
Peth'uel
p^ethû'êl.
Peul'thai (R.V. Peul'lethai).
p^e'ull^ethai.
Pha'lec.

Phal'lu.
pallû'.
Phal'ti.
palṭî.
Phal'tiel.
palṭî'êl.
Phanu'el (Phan'uel).
*Pha'raoh.
par'ôh.
Pha'raoh-hoph'ra.
par'ôh ḥophra'.
Pha'raoh-ne'cho.
par'ôh nekhô.
Pha'res.
Pha'rez.
pereṣ (pâreṣ)
Phar'isee.
Pha'rosh.
par'ôsh.
Phar'par.
parpar.
Phar'zite.
Phase'ah.
pâsêaḥ.
Phe'be.
*Pheni'ce.
Phenic'ia.
Phi'beseth.
pî bheseth.
Phi'chol (R.V. Phi'col).
pîkhôl.
Philadel'phia.
Phile'mon.
Phile'tus.
Phil'ip.
*Philip'pi.
Philip'pian.
Philis'tia.
pelesheth.
Phil'istim.
pelishtîm.
Phil'istines.
pelishtîm.
Philol'ogus.
Phin'ehas.
pînehâs.
Phle'gon.
Phœ'be (R.V.).
Phœnic'ia (R.V.).
Phœ'nix (R.V.).
Phryg'ia.
Phu'rah.
pûrah.
Phut.
pûṭ.
Phu'vah.
pûwah.
Phygel'lus (R.V. Phyg'-elus).
Pibeseth.
pî bheseth.
Pi'hahi'roth.
pî hahîrôth.
Pi'late.
Pil'dash.
pildâsh.
Pil'eha (R.V. Pil'ha).
pilḥâ.

Pil'tai.
pilṭai.
Pi'non.
pînôn.
Pi'ram.
pir'âm.
Pira'thon.
pir'âthôn.
Pira'thonite.
Pis'gah.
pisgah.
Pisid'ia.
Pi'son (R.V. Pi'shon).
pîshôn.
Pis'pah (R.V. Pis'pa).
pispah.
Pi'thom.
pîthôm.
Pi'thon.
pîthôn.
Plei'ades.
kîmah.
Poch'ereth.
pôkhereth.
Poch'ereth - hazze-ba'im (R.V.).
pôkhereth haṣ-ṣebhâ-yîm.
Pol'lux.
Pon'tius.
Pon'tus.
Pora'tha.
pôrâthâ.
Por'cius.
Pot'iphar.
pôṭîphar.
Potiph'erah (R.V. Potiph'era).
pôṭî phera'.
[Praeto'rium.]
Pris'ca.
Priscil'la.
Proch'orus.
Ptolema'is.
Pu'a.
pûwah.
Puah.
pû'ah.
Pub'lius.
Pu'dens.
Pu'hite.
hap-pûthî.
Pul.
pûl.
Pu'nite.
Pu'non.
pûnôn.
Pur.
pûr.
Pu'rah (R.V.).
pûrah.
Pu'rim.
pûrîm.
Put.
pûṭ.
Pute'oli.
Pu'thite (R.V.).
Pu'tiel.
pûṭî'êl.
Pyr'rhus (R.V.).

Q

Quar'tus.
Quirin'ius (R.V.).

R

Ra'ama (R.V.).
ra'mâ.
Ra'amah.
ra'mah ; ra'mâ.
Ra'ami'ah.
ra'amyah.
*Raam'ses.
ra'amsês.
Rab'bah.
rabbah (rabbath).
Rab'bath.
rabbah (rabbath).
[Rab'bi.]
Rab'bith.
hâ-rabbîth.
[Rabbo'ni.]
Rab-mag.
rabh mâgh.
Rab-sa'ris.
rabh sârîs.
Rab-sha'keh.
rabh shâkeh.
[Ra'ca.]
Ra'chab.
Ra'chal (R.V. Ra'cal).
râkhâl.
Ra'chel.
râḥêl.
Rad'dai.
raddai.
Ra'gau.
Ragu'el (Rag'uel).
re'û'êl.
Ra'hab.
râḥâbh ; rahabh.
Ra'ham.
raḥam.
Ra'hel.
râḥêl.
Ra'kem.
râkem.
Rak'kath.
rakkath.
Rak'kon.
hâ-rakkôn.
Ram.
râm.
Ra'ma.
Ra'mah.
hâ-râmah.
Ra'math.
râmath.
Ramatha'im-zo'phim.
hâ-râmâthayim ṣô-phîm.
Ra'mathite.
Ra'math-le'hi.
râmath leḥî.
Ra'math-miz'peh.
râmath ham-miṣpeh.
Ram'eses.
ra'mesês.

Rami'ah.
ramyah
Ra'moth.
râmôth.
Ra'moth-gil'ead.
râmôth gil'âdh.
Ra'pha.
râphâ ; râphah.
Ra'phah (R.V.).
râphah.
Ra'phu.
râphû'.
Reai'ah (Reai'a).
re'ayah.
Re'ba.
rebha'.
Rebec'ca.
Rebek'ah.
ribhkah.
Re'chab.
rêkhâbh.
Rech'abite.
Re'chah.
rêkhah.
Reelai'ah.
re'êlâyah.
Re'gem.
reghem.
Re'gem-me'lech.
reghem melekh.
Rehabi'ah.
reḥabhyah (-yâhû).
Re'hob.
reḥôbh.
Rehobo'am.
reḥabh'âm.
Re'hoboth.
reḥôbhôth.
Re'hum.
reḥûm.
Re'i.
rê'î.
Re'kem.
rekem.
Remali'ah.
remalyâhû.
Re'meth.
remeth.
Rem'mon.
rimmôn.
Rem'mon-metho'ar.
rimmôn ham-metho'âr.
Rem'phan.
Reph'ael.
rephâ'êl.
Re'phah.
rephaḥ.
Rephai'ah.
rephâyah.
Reph'aim(s).
rephâ'îm.
Re'phan (R.V.).
Reph'idim.
rephîdhîm.
Re'sen.
resen.
Re'sheph.
resheph.
Re'u.
re'û.

Reu'ben.
re'ûbhên.
Reu'benite.
Reu'el.
re'û'êl.
Reu'mah.
re'ûmah
Re'zeph.
reṣeph.
Rezi'a.
riṣyâ.
Re'zin.
reṣîn.
Re'zon.
rezôn.
Rhe'gium.
Rhe'sa.
Rho'da.
Rhodes.
Ri'bai.
rîbhai.
Rib'lah.
ribhlah.
Rim'mon.
rimmôn.
Rimmo'no (R.V.).
rimmônô.
Rim'mon-pa'rez (R.V. Rim'mon-pe'rez).
rimmôn pereṣ (pâreṣ).
Rin'nah.
rinnah.
Ri'phath.
rîphath.
Ris'sah.
rissah.
Rith'mah.
rithmah.
Rizi'a (R.V.).
riṣyâ.
Riz'pah.
riṣpah.
Robo'am (R.V. Reho-bo'am).
Ro'danim (R.V.).
rôdhânîm.
Ro'gelim.
rôghelîm.
Roh'gah.
rohgah.
Romam'tie'zer.
rômamtî 'ezer.
Ro'man.
Rome.
Rosh.
rôsh.
Ru'fus.
Ruha'mah.
ruḥâmah.
Ru'mah.
rûmah.
Ruth.
rûth.

S

[Sabach'thani.]
[Saba'oth.]
Sabe'an.
shebhâ'îm ; sebhâ'îm.

Sab'ta.
sabtâ.
Sab'tah.
sabtah.
Sab'techa(h) (R.V. (Sab'teca).
sabhtᵉkhâ.
Sa'car.
śâkhâr.
Sad'ducee.
Sa'doc.
Sa'la.
Sa'lah.
shelaḥ (shâlaḥ).
Sal'amis.
Sala'thiel.
shᵉ'altî'êl.
Sal'chah (Sal'cah; R.V. Sal'ecah).
salᵉkhah.
Sa'lem.
shâlêm.
Sa'lim.
Sal'lai.
sallai.
Sal'lu.
sallû; sallû'.
Sal'ma.
śalmâ.
Sal'mai (R.V.).
śalmai.
Sal'mon.
śalmôn; śalmah; ṣalmôn.
Salmo'ne.
Salo'me.
Sa'lu.
sâlû'.
Sama'ria.
shômᵉrôn.
Samar'itan.
Sam'gar-ne'bo.
samgar nᵉbhô.
Sam'lah.
śamlah.
Sa'mos.
Samothra'cia.
Sam'son.
shimshôn.
Sam'uel.
shᵉmû'êl.
Sanbal'lat.
sanballaṭ.
Sansan'nah.
sansannah.
Saph.
saph.
Sa'phir.
shâphîr.
Sapphi'ra.
Sa'rah (Sa'ra).
śârah; śâraḥ.
Sa'rai.
śârai.
Sa'raph.
śârâph.
Sar'dis.
Sar'dite.
Sarep'ta.

Sar'gon.
sarᵉghôn.
Sa'rid.
śârîdh.
Sa'ron.
Sar'sechim.
śarsᵉkhîm.
Sa'ruch.
Sa'tan.
Saul.
shâ'ûl.
Sce'va.
Scyth'ian.
Se'ba.
sᵉbhâ.
Se'bam (R.V.).
śᵉbhâm.
Se'bat.
shᵉbhâṭ.
Seca'cah.
sᵉkhâkhah.
Se'chu (R.V. Se'cu).
śêkhû.
Secun'dus.
Se'gub.
śᵉghûbh.
Se'ir.
śê'îr.
Sei'rath (R.V. Sei'rah).
haś-śᵉ'îrah.
Se'la (Selah).
sela'.
Se'lah.
selah.
Se'la-hammah'lekoth.
sela' ham-maḥlᵉkôth.
Se'led.
seledh.
Seleu'cia.
Sem.
Semachi'ah.
sᵉmakhyâhû.
Sem'ei (R.V. Sem'eïn).
Sena'ah.
has-sᵉnâ'ah.
Se'neh.
seneh.
Se'nir.
śᵉnîr.
Sennach'erib.
sanḥêrîbh.
Senu'ah.
has-sᵉnû'ah.
Seo'rim.
śᵉ'ôrîm.
Se'phar.
sᵉphâr.
Sepha'rad.
sᵉphârâdh.
Sepharva'im.
sᵉpharwayim.
Seph'arvite.
Se'rah.
śeraḥ (śâraḥ).
Serai'ah.
śᵉrâyah; śᵉrâyâhû.
[Ser'aphim.
śᵉrâphîm.]
Se'red.
seredh.

Ser'gius.
Se'rug.
śᵉrugh.
Seth.
shêth.
Se'thur.
sᵉthûr.
Seve'neh (R.V.).
sᵉwênêh.
Shaalab'bin.
sha'ᵃlabbîn.
Shaal'bim.
sha'alᵉbhîm.
Shaal'bonite.
Sha'aph.
sha'aph.
Shaara'im.
sha'ᵃrayim.
Shaash'gaz.
sha'ashgaz.
Shab'bethai.
shabbᵉthai.
Shachi'a.
shâkhᵉyah.
Shad'dai.
shaddai.
*Sha'drach.
shadhrakh.
Sha'ge.
shâghê'.
Sha'har.
shaḥar.
Shahara'im.
shaḥᵃrayim.
Shahazi'mah.
shaḥᵃṣîmah.
Sha'lem.
shâlêm.
Sha'lim.
sha'ᵃlîm.
Shali'sha.
shâlîshah.
Shal'lecheth.
shallekheth.
Shal'lum.
shallûm.
Shal'lun.
shallûn.
Shal'mai.
shalmai; śalmai.
Shal'man.
shalman.
*Shalmane'ser.
shalman'eser.
Sha'ma.
shâmâ'.
Shamari'ah.
shᵉmaryah.
Sha'med.
shemer (shâmer).
Sha'mer.
shemer (shâmer).
Sham'gar.
shamgar.
Sham'huth.
shamhûth.
Sha'mir.
shâmîr.
Sham'lai (R.V.).
shamlai *or* shalmai.

Sham'ma.
shammâ.
Sham'mah.
shammah.
Sham'mai.
shammai.
Sham'moth.
shammôth.
Shammu'a (Sham-mu'ah).
shammûa'.
Sham'sherai.
shamshᵉrai.
Sha'pham.
shâphâm.
Sha'phan.
shâphân.
Sha'phat.
shâphâṭ.
Sha'pher.
shepher (shâpher).
Sha'phir (R.V.).
shâphîr.
Sha'rai.
shârai.
Shara'im.
sha'ᵃrayim.
Sha'rar.
shârâr.
Share'zer.
shar'eṣer.
Sha'ron.
shârôn.
Sha'ronite.
Sharu'hen.
shârûhen.
Sha'shai.
shâshai.
Sha'shak.
shâshak.
Sha'ul.
shâ'ûl.
Sha'ulite.
Sha'veh.
shâwêh.
Sha'veh-kiriatha'im.
shâwêh ḳiryâthayim.
Shav'sha.
shawshâ.
She'al.
shᵉ'âl.
Sheal'tiel.
shᵉaltî'el; shaltî'êl.
Sheari'ah.
shᵉ'aryah.
She'ar-ja'shub.
shᵉ'âr yâshûbh.
She'ba.
shᵉbhâ; shebha'.
She'bah.
shibh'ah.
She'bam.
śᵉbhâm.
Shebani'ah.
shᵉbhanyah (-yâhû).
Sheba'rim.
shᵉbhârîm.
She'ber.
shebher.
Sheb'na.
shebhnâ; shebhnah.

Shebnah (R.V.).
shebhnah.
Sheb'uel.
shᵉbhû'êl.
Shechani'ah (She-cani'ah).
shᵉkhanyah (-yâhû).
She'chem.
shᵉkhem (shekhem).
She'chemite.
Shede'ur.
shᵉdhê'ûr.
She'erah (R.V.).
she'ᵉrah.
Shehari'ah.
shᵉḥaryah.
She'lah.
shêlah; shelaḥ.
She'lanite.
Shelemi'ah.
shelemyah (-yâhû).
She'leph.
sheleph.
She'lesh.
shêlesh.
Shelo'mi.
shᵉlômî.
Shelo'mith.
shᵉlômîth; shᵉlômôth.
Shelo'moth.
shᵉlômôth.
Shelu'miel.
shᵉlûmî'êl.
Shem.
shêm.
She'ma.
shema'; shᵉmâ'.
Shema'ah.
hash-shᵉmâ'ah.
Shemai'ah.
shᵉma'yah (-yâhû).
Shemari'ah.
shᵉmaryah (-yâhû).
Sheme'ber.
shem'êbher.
Shemed (R.V.).
shemer (shâmer).
She'mer.
shemer.
Shemi'dah(Shemi'da).
shᵉmîdhâ'.
[Shemi'nith.
hash-shᵉmînîth.]
Shemi'daite.
Shemira'moth.
shᵉmîrâmôth.
Shem'uel.
shᵉmû'êl.
Shen.
shên.
Shen'azar (R.V. Shen-az'zar).
shen'aṣṣar.
She'nir.
shᵉnîr.
She'pham.
shᵉphâm.
Shephati'ah (She-phathi'ah).
shᵉphaṭyah (-yâhû).

She'pher (R.V.).
shepher (shâpher).
She'phi.
sh^{e}phî.
She'pho.
sh^{e}phô.
Shephu'phan.
sh^{e}phûphân.
She'rah.
she'^{e}ra*h*.
Sherebi'ah.
shêrêbhya*h*.
She'resh.
sheresh.
Shere'zer.
shar'eṣer.
She'shach.
shêshakh.
She'shai.
shêshai.
She'shan.
shêshân.
Sheshbaz'zar.
shêshbaṣṣar.
Sheth.
shêth.
She'thar.
shêthâr.
She'thar-boz'nai (R.V. -boz'enai).
sh^{e}thar bôz^{e}nai.
She'va.
sh^{e}wâ.
Shi'bah (R.V.)
shibh'a*h*.
*[Shib'boleth.
shibbôleth.]
Shib'mah.
śibhma*h*.
Shic'ron.
shikk^{e}rôn(a*h*).
[Shiggai'on.
shiggâyôn.]
[Shig'ionoth.]
shigh^{e}yônôth.
Shi'hon (R.V. Shi'on).
shî'ôn.
Shi'hor.
shîḥôr.
Shi'hor-lib'nath.
shîḥôr libhnâth.
Shik'keron (R.V.).
shikk^{e}rôn(a*h*).
Shil'hi.
shilḥî.
Shil'him.
shilḥîm.
Shil'lem.
shillêm.
Shil'lemite.
Shilo'ah.
shîlôaḥ.
Shi'loh.
shîlô*h*.
Shi'loni.
Shi'lonite.
Shil'shah.
shilsha*h*
Shim'ea.
shim'â.
Shim'eah.
shim'a*h*; shim'â; shim'a*h*.
Shim'eam.
shim'âm.
Shim'eath.
shim'âth.
Shim'eathite.
Shim'ei (Shi'mi, Shim'hi).
shim'î.
Shim'eon.
shim'ôn.
Shi'mite (R.V. Shim'eite).
Shim'ma.
shim'â.
Shi'mon.
shîmôn.
Shim'rath.
shimrâth.
Shim'ri.
shimrî.
Shim'rith.
shimrîth.
Shim'rom.
shimrôn.
Shim'ron.
shimrôn.
Shim'ronite.
Shim'ron-me'ron.
shimrôn m^{e}rôn.
Shim'shai.
shimshai.
Shi'nab.
shin'âbh.
Shi'nar.
shin'âr.
Shi'phi.
shiph'î.
Shiph'mite.
Shiph'rah.
shiphra*h*.
Shiph'tan.
shiphṭân.
Shi'sha.
shîshâ.
Shi'shak.
shîshaḳ.
Shit'rai.
shiṭrai.
Shit'tim.
shiṭṭîm.
Shi'za.
shîzâ.
Sho'a.
shôa'.
Sho'bab.
shôbhâbh.
Sho'bach.
shôbhakh.
Sho'bai.
shôbhai.
Sho'bal.
shôbhâl.
Sho'bek.
shôbhêḳ.
Sho'bi.
shôbhî.
Sho'co (Sho'cho).
śôkhô.
Sho'choh.
śôkhô*h*.
Sho'ham.
shôham.
Sho'mer.
shômêr.
Sho'phach.
shôphakh.
Sho'phan.
shôphân.
[Shoshan'nim.
shôshannîm.]
[Shoshan'nim e'duth.
shôshannîm 'êdhûth.
Shu'a.
shû'â; shûa'
Shu'ah.
shû'a; shûaḥ; shûḥa*h*.
Shu'al.
shû'âl.
Shub'ael.
shûbhâ'êl.
Shu'hah (R.V.).
shûḥa*h*.
Shu'ham.
shûḥâm.
Shu'hamite.
Shu'hite.
Shu'lamite (R.V. Shu'lammite).
Shu'mathite.
Shu'nammite.
Shu'nem.
shûnêm.
Shu'ni.
shûnî.
Shu'nite.
Shu'pham.
sh^{e}phûphâm.
Shu'phamite.
hash-shûphâmî.
Shup'pim.
shuppîm.
Shur.
shûr.
Shu'shan.
shûshan.
Shu'shanchites (R.V.).
[Shu'shan e'duth.
shûshan 'êdhûth.]
*Shuth'alhite (R.V. Shuthel'ahite).
shûthalḥî.
Shuth'elah.
shûthèlaḥ.
Si'a.
sî'â.
Si'aha.
sî'^{a}hâ.
Sib'becai (Sib'bechai).
sibb^{e}khai.
[Sib'boleth.
sibbôleth.]
Sib'mah.
śibhma*h*.
Sib'raim.
sibhrayim.
Si'chem.
sh^{e}khem.
Sid'dim.
śiddîm.
Si'don.
ṣîdhôn.
Sido'nian.
Si'hon.
sîḥôn.
Si'hor.
shîḥôr.
Si'las.
Sil'la.
sillâ.
Silo'ah.
hash-shelaḥ.
Silo'am.
Silva'nus.
Sim'eon.
shim'ôn.
Sim'eonite.
Si'mon.
Sim'ri.
shimrî.
Sin.
sîn.
Si'na.
Si'nai.
sînai.
Si'nim.
sînîm.
Si'nite.
Si'on.
sî'ôn.
Siph'moth.
śiphmôth.
Sip'pai.
sippai.
Si'rah.
sîra*h*.
Sir'ion.
śiryôn.
Sis'amai (R.V. Sis'mai).
sismai.
Sis'era.
sîs^{e}râ.
Sith'ri (R.V.).
sithrî.
Sit'nah.
śiṭna*h*.
Si'van.
sîwân.
Smyr'na.
So.
sô'.
So'cho.
śôkhô.
So'coh (So'choh).
śôkhô*h*.
So'di.
sôdhî.
Sod'om.
s^{e}dhôm.
Sod'ome.
Sod'omite.
Sol'omon.
sh^{e}lômô*h*.
So'pater.
Soph'ereth.
has-sôphereth.
So'rek.
śôrêḳ.
Sosip'ater.
Sos'thenes.
So'tai.
sôṭai.
Sta'chys.
Steph'anas.
Ste'phen.
Sto'icks.
Su'ah.
sûaḥ.
Suc'coth.
sukkôth.
Suc'coth-be'noth.
sukkôth b^{e}nôth.
Such'athite (R.V. Suc'athite).
Suk'kiims (R.V. Suk'kiim).
sukkîyîm.
Suph (R.V.).
sûph.
Su'phah (R.V.).
sûpha*h*.
Sur.
sûr.
Su'sanchite.
Susan'na.
Su'si.
sûsî.
Sy'char.
Sy'chem.
Sye'ne.
s^{e}wênê*h*.
Sym'eon (R.V.).
Syn'tyche.
Sy'racuse.
Syr'ia.
'^{a}râm.
Syr'ian.
Syrophenic'ian.

T

Ta'anach.
ta'^{a}nâkh; ta'nâkh.
Ta'anath-shi'loh.
ta'^{a}nath shîlô*h*.
Tabba'oth.
ṭabbâ'ôth.
Tab'bath.
ṭabbâth.
Tab'eal.
ṭâbh^{e}'al.
Tab'eel.
ṭabh^{e}'êl.
Tabe'rah.
tabh'êra*h*.
Tab'itha.
Ta'bor.
tâbhôr.
Tab-rim'on (R.V. Tab-rim'mon).
ṭabhrimmôn.
Tach'monite (R.V. Tahchem'onite).
Tad'mor.
tadhmôr.
Ta'han.
taḥan.
Ta'hanite

Tahap'anes.
tahpanhês.
Ta'hash (R.V.).
tahash.
Ta'hath.
tahath.
Tahpan'hes.
tahpanhês.
Tah'penes.
tahp^{e}nês.
Tahre'a.
tahrêa'.
Tah'tim-hod'shi.
tahtîm hodhshî.
*[Tali'tha cu'mi.]
Tal'mai.
talmai.
Tal'mon.
ṭalmôn.
Ta'mah.
temah (tâmah).
Ta'mar.
tâmâr.
Tam'muz.
tammuz.
Ta'nach.
ta'nâkh.
Tanhu'meth.
tanhûmeth.
Ta'phath.
ṭâphath.
Tappu'ah.
tappûah.
Ta'rah.
terah (târah).
Tar'alah.
tar'^{a}lah.
Tare'a.
ta'rêa'.
Tar'pelite.
ṭarp^{e}lâyê.
Tar'shish.
tarshîsh.
Tar'sus.
Tar'tak.
tartak.
Tar'tan.
ṭartân.
Tat'nai (R.V. Tat'-tenai).
tatt^{e}nai.
Te'bah.
ṭebhah.
Tebali'ah.
ṭ^{e}bhalyâhû.
Te'beth.
têbhêth.
Tehaph'nehes.
t^{e}haphn^{e}hês.
Tehin'nah.
t^{e}hinnah.
[Te'kel.
t^{e}kêl.]
Teko'a (Teko'ah).
t^{e}kôa'.
Teko'ite.
Tel-a'bib.
têl 'âbhîbh

Tel-har'esha (Tel-har'sa; R.V. Tel-har'sha).
têl harshâ.
Tel-me'lah.
têl melah.
Te'lah.
telah.
Tela'im.
ṭ^{e}lâ'îm.
Telas'sar.
t^{e}laśśâr.
Te'lem.
ṭelem.
Te'ma.
têmâ.
Te'mah (R.V.).
temah (tâmah).
Te'man.
têmân.
Te'mani.
Te'manite.
Te'meni.
têm^{e}nî.
Te'rah.
terah.
[Ter'aphim.
t^{e}râphîm.]
Te'resh.
teresh.
Ter'tius.
Tertul'lus.
*Thad'deus.
Tha'hash.
tahash.
Tha'mah.
temah (tâmah).
Tha'mar.
Tha'ra.
Thar'shish.
tarshîsh.
The'bez.
têbhêṣ.
Thelas'ar.
t^{e}laśśar.
Theoph'ilus.
Thessalo'nian.
Thes'saloni'ca.
Theu'das.
Thimna'thah.
timnâthah.
Thom'as.
Thyati'ra.
Tibe'rias.
Tibe'rius.
Tib'hath.
ṭibhhath.
Tib'ni.
tibhnî.
Ti'dal.
tidh'âl.
*Tig'lath-pile'ser.
tighlath pil'eṣer (p^{e}le-ser).
Tik'vah.
tikwah.
Tik'vath.
tokhath.

Til'gath-pilne'ser.
tighlath piln^{e}'eser (pil-neser).
Ti'lon.
tîlôn.
Timæ'us.
Tim'na.
timna' (timnâ').
Tim'nah.
timnah; timnâ'.
Tim'nath.
timnâth.
Tim'nath-he'res.
timnath heres.
Tim'nath-se'rah.
timnath serah.
Tim'nite.
Ti'mon.
Timo'theus.
Tim'othy.
Tiph'sah.
tiphsah.
Ti'ras.
tîrâs.
Ti'rathite.
tir'âthî.
Tirha'kah.
tirhâkah.
Tir'hanah.
tirh^{a}nah.
Tiri'a.
tîr^{e}yâ.
Tirsha'tha
hat-tirshâthâ
Tir'zah.
tirṣah.
Tish'bite.
Ti'tus.
Ti'zite.
tîṣî.
To'ah.
tôah.
Tob.
ṭôbh.
Tob-adoni'jah.
ṭôbh '^{a}dhônîyah.
Tobi'ah.
ṭôbhîyah (-yâhû).
Tobi'jah.
ṭôbhîyâhû.
To'chen.
tôkhen.
Togar'mah.
tôgharmah.
To'hu.
tôhû.
To'i.
tô'î.
Tok'hath (R.V.).
tokhath.
To'la.
tôlâ'.
To'lad.
tôladh.
To'laite.
To'phel.
tôphel.
To'phet (To'pheth).
tôpheth.
To'u.
tô'û.

Trachoni'tis.
Tro'as.
Trogyl'lium.
Troph'imus.
Tryphe'na.
Trypho'sa.
Tu'bal.
tûbhal.
Tu'bal-cain.
tûbhal kayin.
Tych'icus.
Tyran'nus.
Tyre (Ty'rus).

U

U'cal.
'ûkhâl *or* 'ukkâl.
U'el.
'û'êl.
U'lai.
'ûlai.
U'lam.
'ûlâm.
Ul'la.
'ullâ.
Um'mah.
'ummah.
Un'ni.
'unnî.
Un'no (R.V.).
'unnî (*or* ? 'unnô).
[Uphar'sin.
ûpharsîn.]
U'phaz.
'ûphâz.
Ur.
'ûr.
*Ur'bane (R.V. Urba'-nus).
U'ri.
'ûrî.
Uri'ah.
'ûrîyah.
Uri'as.
U'riel.
'ûrî'êl.
Uri'jah.
'ûrîyah (-yâhû).
U'thai.
'ûthai.
Uz.
'ûṣ.
U'zai.
'ûzai.
U'zal.
'ûzâl.
Uz'za
'uzzâ; 'uzzah.
Uz'zah.
'uzzah.
Uz'zen-she'rah (R.V. -she'erah.
'uzzên she'^{e}rah.
Uz'zi.
'uzzî.
Uzzi'a.
'uzzîyâ.

Uzzi'ah.
'uzzîyah (-yâhû).
Uz'ziel.
'uzzî'êl.
Uz'zielite.

V

Va'heb (R.V.).
wâhêbh.
Vajeza'tha (R.V. Vai-za'tha).
waizâthâ.
Vani'ah.
wanyah.
Vash'ni.
washnî.
Vash'ti.
washtî.
Voph'si.
wophsî.

Z

Za'ana'im.
ṣa'^{a}nannîm.
Za'anan.
ṣa'^{a}nân.
Za'anan'nim.
ṣa'^{a}nannîm.
Za'avan.
za'^{a}wân.
Za'bad.
zâbhâdh.
Zab'bai.
zabbai.
Zab'bud.
zakkûr (*or* ? zâbhûdh).
Zab'di.
zabhdî.
Zab'diel.
zabhdî'êl.
Za'bud.
zâbhûdh.
Zab'ulon.
Zac'cai.
zakkai.
Zacchae'us.
Zac'cur (Zac'chur).
zakkûr.
Zachari'ah.
z^{e}kharyah (-yâhû).
Zachari'as,
Za'cher.
zekher (zâkher).
Za'dok.
ṣâdhôk.
Za'ham.
zaham.
Za'ir.
ṣâ'îr.
Za'laph.
ṣâlâph.
Zal'mon.
ṣalmôn.
Zalmo'nah.
ṣalmônah
Zalmun'na.
ṣalmunnâ

Zamzum'mim.
zamzummîm.
Zano'ah.
zânôah.
*Zaph'nath-paan'eah.
şâph^e^nath pa'nêah.
Zaphenath-pan'eah (R.V.).
şâph^e^nath pa'nêah.
Za'phon.
şaphôn.
Za'ra.
Za'rah.
zeraḥ (zâraḥ).
Zar'eah.
şor'*ah*.
Zar'eathite.
şor'âthî.
Za'red.
zeredh (zâredh).
Zar'ephath.
şar^e^phath.
Zar'etan (Zar'than).
şâr^e^thân.
Zar'ethan (R.V.).
şâr^e^thân.
Za'reth-sha'har.
şereth hash-shaḥar.
Zar'hite.
zarḥî.
Zar'tanah.
şâr^e^thân(*ah*).
Zat'tu (Zat'thu).
zattû'.
Za'van.
za'^a^wân.
Za'za.
zâzâ.
Zebadi'ah.
z^e^bhadhya*h* (-yâhû).
Ze'bah.
zebhaḥ.
Zeba'im.
ş^e^bhâyim.
Zeb'edee.
Zebi'dah (R.V.).
z^e^bhudda*h* (*or* ? z^e^bhîdha*h*).
Zebi'nà.
z^e^bhînâ.
Zebo'im (Zebo'iim).
ş^e^bhôyîm ; ş^e^bhô'îm.

Zeb'udah.
z^e^bhudda*h*.
Ze'bul.
z^e^bhûl.
Zeb'ulonite.
Zeb'ulun.
z^e^bhûlûn.
Zeb'ulunite.
Zechari'ah.
z^e^kharya*h* (-yâhû).
Ze'cher (R.V.).
zekher (zâkher).
Ze'dad.
ş^e^dhâdh (ş^e^dhâdha*h*).
Zedeki'ah.
şidh^e^kîya*h* (-yâhû).
Ze'eb.
z^e^êbh.
Ze'lah (R.V. *once* Ze'la).
şêla' ; şêlâ'.
Ze'lek.
şelek.
Zeloph'ehad.
ş^e^lophḥâdh.
Zelo'tes.
Zel'zah.
şelşaḥ.
Zemara'im.
ş^e^mârayim
Zem'arite.
ş^e^mârî.
Zemi'ra.
z^e^mîra*h*.
Ze'nan.
ş^e^nân.
Ze'nas.
Zephani'ah.
ş^e^phanya*h* (-yâhû).
Ze'phath.
ş^e^phath.
Zepha'thah.
ş^e^phâtha*h*.
Ze'phi.
ş^e^phî.
Ze'pho.
ş^e^phô.
Ze'phon.
ş^e^phôn.
Ze'phonite.
Zer.
şêr.

Ze'rah.
zeraḥ (zâraḥ).
Zerahi'ah.
z^e^raḥya*h*.
Ze'rahite (R.V.).
zarḥî.
Ze'red.
zeredh.
Zere'da (R.V. Zere'dah).
haş-ş^e^rêdha*h*.
Zereda'thah (R.V. Zere'dah).
ş^e^rêdhâtha*h*.
Zere'rath (R.V. Zere'rah).
ş^e^rêra*h* *or* ş^e^rêrâth.
Ze'resh.
zeresh.
Ze'reth.
şereth.
Zer'eth-sha'har (R.V.).
şereth hash-shaḥar.
Ze'ri.
ş^e^rî.
Ze'ror.
ş^e^rôr.
Zeru'ah.
ş^e^rû'a*h*.
*Zerub'babel.
z^e^rubbâbhel.
Zerui'ah.
ş^e^rûya*h*.
Ze'tham.
zêthâm.
Ze'than.
zêthân.
Ze'thar.
zêthar.
Zi'a.
zîa'.
Zi'ba.
şîbhâ'.
Zib'eon.
şibh'ôn.
Zibi'a.
şibhyâ.
Zibi'ah.
şibhya*h*.
Zich'ri.
zikhrî.

Zid'dim.
haş-şiddîm.
Zidki'jah.
şidhkîya*h*.
Zi'don.
şîdhôn.
Zido'nian.
Zif.
zîw.
Zi'ha.
şîḥâ.
Zik'lag.
şiklagh.
Zil'lah.
şilla*h*.
Zil'pah.
zilpa*h*.
Zil'thai (R.V. Zil'lethai).
şill^e^thai.
Zim'mah.
zimma*h*.
Zim'ran.
zimrân.
Zim'ri.
zimrî.
Zin.
şîn.
Zi'na.
zînâ.
Zi'on.
şîyôn.
Zi'or.
şî'ôr.
Ziph.
zîph.
Zi'phah.
zîpha*h*.
Zi'phims.
zîphîm.
Ziph'ion.
şiphyôn.
Zi'phites.
zîphîm.
Ziph'ron.
ziphrôn.
Zip'por.
şippôr.
Zippo'rah.
şippôra*h*.
Zith'ri.
sithrî.

Ziv (R.V.).
zîw.
Ziz.
şîş.
Zi'za.
zîzâ.
Zi'zah.
zîza*h*.
Zo'an.
şô'an.
Zo'ar.
şô'ar.
Zo'ba.
şôbhâ.
Zo'bah.
şôbha*h*.
Zobe'bah.
haş-şôbhêbha*h*.
Zo'har.
şôḥar.
Zo'heleth.
zôḥeleth.
Zo'heth.
zôḥêth.
Zo'phah.
şôphaḥ.
Zo'phai.
şôphai.
Zo'phar.
şôphar.
Zo'phim.
şôphîm.
Zo'rah (Zo'reah).
şor'a*h*.
Zo'rathite.
şor'âthî.
Zo'rite.
Zorob'abel.
Zu'ar.
şû'âr.
Zuph.
şûph.
Zur.
şûr.
Zu'riel.
şûrî'êl.
Zu'ri-shad'dai.
şûrî shaddai.
Zu'zims (R.V. Zuzim).
zûzîm.

THE CANON OF SCRIPTURE

BY R. K. HARRISON, PROFESSOR OF OLD TESTAMENT, WYCLIFFE COLLEGE, UNIVERSITY OF TORONTO
AND EVERETT F. HARRISON, PROFESSOR OF NEW TESTAMENT, FULLER THEOLOGICAL SEMINARY

THE CANON OF SCRIPTURE

All the major world religions have as their legacy a collection of writings that the devout regard to a greater or lesser extent as the word of God and therefore as containing authoritative norms for faith and practice. Not all adherents of the various religious faiths in the modern world maintain that their Scriptures are necessarily inspired, but in any event they normally regard them as enshrining the highest degree of religious authority.

The English word "canon" is derived from the Greek kanṓn, *which is related to Semitic cognates (Assyrian* qanû, *Ugaritic* qn, *Hebrew* qaneh*) borrowed from the Sumerian GI-NA, which originally meant "reed." A number of metaphorical applications of the word developed out of this literal meaning: in Greek it was used, among other things, to describe a rule, standard, paradigm, model, boundary, chronological table, and a tax assessment. The Greek and Latin Church Fathers applied it to the rule of faith or the standard of apostolic teaching handed down in the church. That teaching, when put into creedal form, was known as the "canon of truth." As time passed, the apostolic writings were designated as canonical to indicate their authoritative character and to distinguish them from other Christian literature. Ultimately the noun was employed for the corpus of writings that had gained general recognition in the church as Holy Scripture. The earliest evidence of the use of "canon" for the Bible is found in the* Decrees of the Synod of Nicea *(ca. A.D. 352).*[1]

[1]*For a more complete account of the history of the word, see Souter,* The Text and Canon of the New Testament *(1912), pp. 154-156; and H. W. Beyer's article in Kittel (ed.),* Theological Dictionary of the New Testament, *III, 596-602.*

I.
THE CANON OF THE OLD TESTAMENT

R. K. HARRISON

The earliest designation of the books of the Old Testament as the "holy books" or "holy writings" is found in the work of Josephus, *ca.* A.D. 100. For him the essential characteristic of canonical Scripture was that it constituted divine pronouncements of unquestioned authority that originated within the prophetic period and were therefore under divine inspiration. It was to be distinguished from every other form of literature because of its intrinsic holiness; the number of canonical writings was strictly limited, and its verbal form was inviolable (*Against Apion,* I, 38ff.). These views were completely in accord with the pronouncements of official Judaism as they were ultimately crystallized in the Talmud.

Although the Jews of the immediate pre-Christian period venerated their national literature, and in particular regarded the Torah as the authoritative guide to godly living, they were somewhat indiscriminate in their acceptance of material that could be considered as "holy writ." The nearest approach to the idea of canonicity was expressed in the Mishnah, where it was stated that those writings which accorded with such a concept "render the hands unclean" (*Yad.* III, 5). The meaning of this phrase is at best rather uncertain, and numerous explanations have been adduced for it. It may have been intended to insure greater caution against the profanation of the sacred scrolls by careless handling, but it seems more likely that, regarding the sacrosanct nature of the canonical writings, it described a situation whereby contact with such scrolls demanded ritual ablutions after handling in order that conditions of ceremonial purity might be maintained. The term was ultimately extended to include all the writings in the canonical list determined by the rabbinic authorities, thereby distinguishing such compositions from noncanonical works.

While there is a distinct sense in which it can be asserted that it was Christian theism that specifically related the ideas of inspiration and authority to the concept of biblical canonicity (using the latter term to embrace the writings of the New Testament as well as those compositions that were venerated by the Jews), it must never be forgotten that later Jewish tradition also adopted the view that every word of Holy Writ was inspired by the divine Spirit. In each instance this Spirit was believed to have rested upon a prophet, and in consequence every Old Testament book was attributed to the activity of a prophetic author. For the Christian the use of the term "Old Testament canon" signifies that the Old Testament is to be regarded as a closed collection of books, inspired by the Spirit of God (2 Tim. 3:15), having a normative authority, and valid as the rule for faith and life. The final provision is important for the Christian, since it serves to emphasize the unity of the revelation in both Testaments, and also witnesses that there are important aspects of the Old Testament self-disclosure of God in history that are binding upon both Christians and Jews for all time. This is in direct contravention of the view, popular in some quarters, which asserts that the Christian ethic can commence with the Sermon on the Mount rather than with the events on Mount Sinai and earlier phases of Hebrew covenantal history.

In any discussion of the Old Testament canon it is important to distinguish between that of the Hebrew Bible and its counterpart in other versions of Scripture. The degree of difference in the idea of a canon of sacred writings can be seen by reference on the one hand to the Samaritan version, in which only the Pentateuch was accorded canonicity, and on the other to the Septuagint, which included the writings known as the Apocrypha. Furthermore, while in many versions the books listed were generally the same as those of the Old Testament canon, the order and number were apt to differ considerably, as was the length of certain of the compositions. The Hebrew canon comprises twenty-four books arranged in three major divisions which are designated the Law, the Prophets, and the Writings respectively. By contrast, the various Christian Bibles, following the general pattern of the Greek and Latin versions, recognized thirty-nine books as canonical, dividing Samuel, Kings, Chronicles, and Ezra-Nehemiah into two books each, and regarding the Minor Prophets as twelve separate works.

The very fact that the canon exists at all in its present form is a striking testimony to human activity and thought under divine guidance. Unfortunately it is virtually impossible to be more specific than this about the processes by which the Old Testament canon, or parts of it, became acknowledged as authoritative. While the Bible legitimately ought to be allowed to define and describe canonicity, it has in fact almost nothing to say about the manner in which holy writings were assembled, or the personages who exercised an influence over the corpus during the diverse stages of its growth. Historical investigation is no more fruitful in uncovering significant information about the activities of synods or other authoritative bodies with regard to the formation of the Old Testament canon than any other form of study. For the Hebrew Scriptures, however, this circumstance need not occasion particular surprise, since they are of a self-authenticating character, and do not derive their authority either from individual human beings or from corporate ecclesiastical pronouncements. As N. H. Ridderbos has pointed out, the various books possessed and exercised divine authority long before men ever made pronouncements to that effect. Ecclesiastical councils did not give the books their divine authority, but merely recognized that they both had it and exercised it.

The concept of a divine norm or rule reaches far back into Hebrew history. Adam, Noah, and Abraham received specific commandments from God that served as their rule of faith and life, and which were enshrined in written form at an early period. During the Mosaic age specific collections of laws were put into writing, as indicated by the formulation of the Book of the Covenant (Exod. 24:4ff.) and the composition of the essentials of Deuteronomy (Deut. 31:9ff.). The latter was of particular importance, because it was placed in close proximity to the highly sacred Ark of the Covenant to constitute the divine witness to the people. Its position was an indication of the sacredness and divine authority attaching to this legal code, which was required to be read in the presence of the nation (Deut. 31:11). To insure equity in Israel, the king was to be given a copy of it, and he was to regulate his decisions according to its contents (Deut. 17:18ff.). Even a revered figure such as Joshua was commanded to adhere to its precepts (Josh. 1:8).

In subsequent periods of Hebrew history the Mosaic Torah was considered to be the divine rule for faith and life (1 Kgs. 2:3; 2 Kgs. 14:6), and the people were urged continually to obey its injunctions. In this connection the prophets played an important role, for they reminded their hearers that the misfortunes and calamities that overtook them were divine judgments for disobedience of the Law, and made it clear that further infractions could only result in drastic punishment. While the prophets urged deference to the Law, and frequently based their own utterances upon its doctrinal themes, they also regarded the words that they themselves spoke under the influence of the divine afflatus as of equal authority with the Torah, arising as they did from the same inspirational source. Popular disregard of their pronouncements was held to bring an equal measure of divine wrath upon the heads of the offenders as did disregard of the Law.

The exalted position that the Torah occupied in Hebrew national life as the standard for faith and practice is reflected in the attitude adopted by the Old Testament writers towards their sources. Unlike many authors in other nations and at different periods, the Hebrews treated their source material with profound respect, preferring to copy the sections that they needed as literally as possible rather than quoting them freely from memory. Because their sacred literature was an essentially vital and relevant corpus, and because it still had to attain to the degree of fixity that became a concomitant of canonicity, it was possible for the ancient Hebrews to interpolate additional material into their writings, to replace one law by another when altered circumstances made such a procedure necessary,[2] or to engage in whatever revisions were considered desirable and proper at the particular time.

The belief that God could reveal His will by means of a holy book was thus an early and indelible feature of Israelite religious life. This concept did not originate, as some scholars have imagined, from a belief in the word of an inspired person—the *torah* of the priest or the utterance of the prophet—so much as from the fact that what the inspired individual said constituted the *verba ipsissima* of God, and was accepted as such even though its implications were not always taken to heart. By uniform tradition the early normative communications of God to Israel took the form of laws, which were committed to writing by and large within the contemporary situation. On two

[2]For such modifications compare Num. 26:52-56 with 27:1-11; 36:1-9; Num. 15:22-31 with Lev. 4:1ff.

occasions Israel solemnly pledged herself to obey the Book of the Law that God had given through Moses, first during the reign of Josiah (2 Kgs. 23:2ff.; 2 Chron. 34:30ff.), subsequent to the discovery of an ancient legal code of unknown content, second during the period of Ezra and Nehemiah (Ez. 7:6, 14; Neh. 8:1ff.), when the "Book of the Law" comprised at the very least a part of the Pentateuch.

It is impossible in the light of present knowledge to state with any degree of certainty exactly when the Pentateuch was finished in its extant form, although there seem to be substantial grounds for thinking that it was virtually complete by the death of Samuel. What can be said, however, is that from the very beginning of its existence, high authority was attached to its contents, and as a result it is little wonder that it became the first major section of the Hebrew Scriptures to be accorded unquestioned acceptance prior to subsequent formal canonicity. It is evident that the Torah in general, and Deuteronomy in particular, goes back in principle to an early period of Israelite life from the presence of a formula of imprecation warning against adding anything to its contents or detracting from it in any way (Deut. 4:2; 12:32). So specific a command, which is reflected only once in other parts of the Old Testament (Prov. 30:6), was employed in a considerably more elaborate form at the end of the laws of Hammurabi, where imprecations were directed at any who would endeavor to alter the law. Hammurabi's law was codified under the stated patronage of the deity Shamash and mediated by a great leader of the state to the people, who were given due warning to pay careful heed to its contents. As far as Hebrew religious tradition was concerned, the fundamental precepts of the Mosaic Torah were manifested to Israel through the agency of a divinely appointed leader of the populace. Thus the idea of a revealed, authoritative, and mediated written code was by no means novel both before and during the Mosaic era. The fact and existence of the Mosaic Torah at an early period furnished the foundations for all subsequent religious writing in Israel, and as such supplied one element of the concept of canonicity.

It has been suggested that another germinal aspect relating to the formation of a canon of Scripture is what Gerhard von Rad has called the "historical *credo* of Israel" as it occurs in certain types of Old Testament literature.[3] Some caution should be urged in entertaining this idea, however, since it would be comparatively easy to assume that such a *credo* constituted the skeletal form that was subsequently clothed by the religious traditions of an Israelite "amphictyony" and enriched by the "laws of the state." It must be remembered, accordingly, that the *credo,* if it can be legitimately conceived of as such, was only one element in a tradition that was already rich in literary material and had as its authoritative written foundation the legislation given to Moses on Mount Sinai.

It is clear, therefore, that the Torah did not only mark the beginning of a body of national literature (a fact that, in the event, is rather incidental to more pressing spiritual considerations) but also constituted the normative expression of the divine will for the Hebrew people. By its very nature it established a basis for doctrine and life upon which subsequent expositors of revealed religion leaned heavily. So deeply rooted were the traditions as to the antiquity and sanctity of the Mosaic enactments that the term "Torah" was applied not only to the first five books of the developing canon, but also to the entire corpus of the Hebrew Scriptures at a later period. This designation, which occurs in 2 Esdras 19:21, and in John 10:34 under the form *nomos,* arose from the belief, popular in rabbinic circles, that the Prophets and the Writings were to be included in the Torah, since Holy Writ in its entirety constituted the Word of God. Since, however, "Torah" was the title of the first and principal section of the biblical writings, it is also conceivable that it was transferred to the entire collection as a means of indicating its inspiration and canonicity.

The second major section of the canon, the Prophets, was commonly subdivided into two parts, These were the "Former Prophets," consisting of the books of Joshua, Judges, Samuel, and Kings, and the "Latter Prophets," which comprised Isaiah, Jeremiah, Ezekiel, and the Twelve. The authority that the Former Prophets acquired is readily understandable when it is realized that these writings describe the manner in which the provisions of the Covenant agreement were applied to the conditions in the land of Canaan. As chronicles of the relationships between God and His people, these documents were without doubt drawn up by individuals of official standing in Israel, and so in many respects would have a secular as well as a religious authority.

By their very nature the compositions of the Latter Prophets were held to be authoritative from their earliest appearances, although initially, at least, the number of those who venerated them as writings whose tenor and spirit were akin to that of the Torah was probably quite small. Almost certainly their authority was enhanced greatly when the predictions of disaster that many of them contained found fulfillment in the exile, and the victims of that catastrophe were forced to think of other aspects of the prophetic message. That the individual prophets themselves felt that they stood in a firm and unified spiritual tradition can be seen from the manner in which they ascribed authority to their predecessors either by quoting from their utterances, alluding to incidents in the Torah (e.g. Jer. 4:4; 5:15, 17; 11:4), or rebuking the nation for not listening to previous prophecies (Zech. 1:4ff.; Hos. 6:5). Undoubtedly some of this material was set down in written form during the lifetime of most if not all of the individuals concerned, as were the prophecies of Jeremiah. If the reference in Daniel 9:2 to "the books" is to a collection of prophetic writings, as seems most probable, it would imply that these works were regarded as having divine authority, and were thus akin to the Pentateuchal compositions.

The third major division of the canon, known as the Writings or Hagiographa, comprised eleven compositions of diverse character emanating from various facets of He-

[3]Exod. 15:1ff.; Deut. 26:5-9 (cf. 6:20-24); Josh. 24:2-13; Ps. 136:1ff.

brew life. The collections of psalms that formed the basis of the Psalter were important both for private and public devotions and for their associations with the sanctuary and the cultus and the revered name of David, the traditional father of Hebrew psalmody. In the same manner, the connecting of the proverbs with Solomon and the growth of the Wisdom Literature from the utterances and traditions of the Hebrew sages led to the acceptance of important elements of this division of the canon as constituting authoritative moral and spiritual pronouncements that participated fully in the divine spirit expressed in the Torah. Historical and prophetic writings such as those attributed to Daniel, Ezra, and Nehemiah were also accepted as being in keeping with the religious tenor of other aspects of the national literature, as were the Chronicles, which were compiled from a specific theological standpoint. These and other books were regarded properly as holy writings because of their association with the cultus, the national history and tradition, and revered personages of the past. If the Prophets can be said to have derived some of their authority from their consonance with the teachings of the Torah, the Writings did also, springing as they did from the very warp and woof of the Hebrew spiritual fabric.

There are some grounds for assuming the antiquity of a twofold rather than a threefold division of the canon, in which the Writings were subsumed under the second major section because of their similarity to the works of the prophets. As a result, the canon was simply thought of in terms of the Law and the Prophets. References in certain of the Qumran scrolls indicate that the sectaries themselves thought in terms of a twofold division, as did some of the copyists of later Septuagint manuscripts.

The foregoing outline of the conjectured growth of a canonical corpus of Old Testament writings is, of course, general and is based in part upon the rather scanty internal information that the Old Testament furnishes with regard to the assembling and the relationships of the various canonical books. From the purely Jewish standpoint there is a distinct sense in which the concept of canonicity can only have been crystallized and implemented when there were sufficient works in the corpus of Hebrew literature from which a selection could be made, since not all Hebrew writings were accorded canonicity. As far as the historical books were concerned, the finished product alone rather than the underlying sources constituted the preferred choice. In the sense that they were incorporated in some manner into the final production the sources themselves could be considered canonical, but the most obvious reason for the overall attitude consisted in the comparative availability of the extant work as contrasted with that of the source material. Public acceptance was thus one important criterion of canonicity. The feelings of the readers regarding canonicity were governed, of course, by the considerations of essential consonance with the spirit of the Torah and the other factors referred to above.

Speculation About the Old Testament Canon

The completed Jewish canon consisted of twenty-four books as follows: five of the Pentateuch; eight books of the Prophets—Joshua, Judges, Samuel, Kings, Isaiah, Jeremiah, Ezekiel, the Minor Prophets; and eleven Writings—Psalms, Proverbs, Job, Song of Solomon, Ruth, Lamentations, Ecclesiastes, Esther, Daniel, Ezra, and Chronicles. From the Greek translation by Aquila it is seen that Samuel and Kings formed one book each; the Twelve were also known as a single work in the time of Ben Sira (Ecclus. 49:10). The division of the Prophets into "Former" and "Latter" was evidently introduced by the Massoretes. Later Jewish tradition gave great prominence to the activity of prophets in the formulation of the canon of Scripture, and held that every word of Holy Writ was inspired by the Spirit of God. Because this Spirit was believed to have rested in every case upon a prophet, it followed that the authorship of such biblical books ought to be attributed to prophetic functioning.

1. Baba Bathra. The classical passage for the sequence of the books is the *baraitha* (unauthorized gloss) in the Babylonian Talmudic tractate *Baba Bathra* 14b. This document proceeded on the assumption of prophetic authorship, discovering the prophetic author either in the titles or the sequence of the works themselves. Thus Moses, Joshua, Samuel, Ezra, and the Prophets were credited with having written the compositions attributed to them; in addition Moses was regarded as the author of Job, whose hero was held to have been his contemporary. The last eight verses of the Pentateuch were thought to have been composed by Joshua. Samuel was given credit for the authorship of Judges and Ruth. Jeremiah was believed to have written Kings and Lamentations, and Ezra the scribe was regarded as the author of Chronicles. There was thus an unbroken chain of prophets from Moses to Malachi, into which company David and Solomon were also placed. The Psalms were credited as a whole to David; Proverbs, Canticles, and Ecclesiastes to Solomon. Esther alone was not attributed a prophetic author, but this omission was more apparent than real since Jewish tradition venerated Mordecai as a prophet contemporary with Haggai, Zechariah, and Malachi and he was held to have prophesied at the time of Darius I. In any event, the position of Esther was safeguarded by the tradition that the Great Synagogue had numerous prophets among its members, who took upon themselves the right to have the Esther scroll written down. Quite clearly, then, one dominant criterion of canonicity for the ancient Jews was the attribution of a work to prophetic authorship, so that a composition such as Ecclesiasticus, in which the identity of the author was known to be non-prophetic, presented absolutely no problems as far as canonicity was concerned.

In summary, from the Jewish standpoint only those works which could properly claim prophetic authorship had a right to canonicity, and out of this corpus there was a decided preference for finished works rather than for source material of prophetic origin. The relationship of the particular author to the theocracy was also an important determining consideration. Moses was naturally a towering figure in the Old Testament generally, since he occupied a pre-eminent position as the faithful servant of God (cf. Num. 12:1ff.). In virtue of being assumed as the author of the Pentateuch as a whole, and the real contributor of a significant amount of its contents, his literary products formed the foundation on which the entire Old Testament corpus was based.

Although the second section of the Hebrew canon, the Prophets, comprised material written by men standing within the spiritual tradition of Moses, these individuals were nevertheless inferior in stature to the great lawgiver himself. In the theocracy, therefore, their position in the affections of the Jews is shown by the division that incorporated their writings into a second major group of sacred literature, different in content from the Torah but akin in moral and spiritual quality. Although there are some respects in which the attribution of prophetic stature to certain of the authors of compositions in the Hagiographa imposes a strain upon the concept of prophetism, it may well be that the writers concerned were thought of in the ancient Hebrew sense as mediators between God and the nation, or as representatives of God in their capacity as spokesmen to the people (cf. Exod. 4:16; 7:1; Deut. 18:15ff.). At all events they appear to have been accorded a position of considerable importance in the traditions of the Israelites, quite aside from being regarded as inspired by the Holy Spirit of God. Perhaps it was this that led to a twofold division of the canon into the Law of Moses and the Prophets, in which some, if not all, of the compositions subsequently designated by the technical term *K^e thubhim* or "Writings" were included.

Whatever the motivation governing the curious and sometimes rather uncritical kind of rabbinic speculation in matters of Scripture, the threefold division of the canon was well established in the early Christian era. The New Testament makes it clear that the canon familiar to Jesus Christ was identical with the one which exists today. None of the Apocrypha or Pseudepigrapha is ever cited by name, much less accorded the status of Scripture, whereas Daniel is specifically quoted as a prophetic composition in Matthew 24:15. The three chief divisions were enumerated in Luke 24:44 as the Law, the Prophets, and the Psalms. Usually the New Testament writers only mentioned the first two sections (cf. Matt. 5:17; Lk. 16:16), but quite obviously they included the Hagiographa with the Prophets just as the Talmudic teachers did (due perhaps to the lack of a current technical term for the Hagiographa).

From the words of Jesus in Matthew 23:35 and Luke 11:51, it can be inferred that Chronicles was regarded as the last book in the Hebrew canon at that time. The murder of Abel is recorded in the first canonical writing (Genesis); that of Zechariah is contained in the final book of the Hebrew Scriptures (2 Chronicles 24:20). Of course no chronological order is intended to be conveyed by the words of Jesus, since innocent blood was shed after the killing of Zechariah (Jer. 26:23). The reference in Matthew could possibly be to the prophet Zechariah, who was the son of Berechiah (Zech. 1:1), although there is no independent evidence to the effect that he was martyred. Alternatively, some have supposed that the reference is to the martyrdom of Zechariah the son of Jehoiada (2 Chron. 24:20-22), and that the error of the father's name was due either to the Evangelist himself, or, since it does not occur in the best manuscript of Luke, to the addition of a copyist.

Further evidence of a threefold division of the canon is provided by Josephus, who enumerated five books of Moses, thirteen prophetical writings, and four books of hymns to God and precepts for human behavior. Probably Josephus arrived at the number thirteen for the second division of the canon by including Ruth with Judges and Lamentations with Jeremiah, and regarding the Minor Prophets as a unified book in the manner current in the time of Ben Sira. A threefold canon of Scripture was also given attestation in the writings of Philo, particularly in his *Contemplative Life,* written about A.D. 40. Philo mentions by title the Law, the Prophets, the Psalms and other books, but does not refer to Ezekiel, Daniel, or the five Megilloth (Canticles, Ruth, Lamentations, Ecclesiastes, and Esther) in his extant works. But Philo's failure to name these books cannot be taken as proof that they were not in his canon of Scripture, for, as L. Blau has pointed out in the *Jewish Encyclopedia,* the silence of Philo concerning Ezekiel is most probably accidental, since even Ben Sira mentioned the book attributed to that prophet. Consequently, there seems no good ground for questioning the assertion that the canon known to Philo was essentially the same as that current at the present time.

An even earlier attestation of the threefold division is to be seen in the Prologue to Ecclesiasticus, dated about 132 B.C., in which specific mention was made of the Law and the Prophets (or prophecies) as well as "the others which follow after them." Since the author of the Prologue stated that his grandfather Jesus ben Sira, the compiler of Ecclesiasticus *ca.* 190 B.C., had long given himself to a careful study of the "law and the prophets and the other books of the fathers," it is legitimate to assume that this threefold division went back at least to the beginning of the second century B.C.

A reference in 2 Maccabees, which was extant by about the middle of the first century of the Christian era and may have been compiled as early as 100 B.C., spoke of the founding of a library by Nehemiah, who "gathered together the books concerning the kings and the prophets, and those of David, and the epistles of the kings concerning holy gifts" (2 Macc. 2:13f.). The Torah is not mentioned in this list, since its wide circulation made references to it unnecessary. However, there can be no doubt about the second part of the canon, which is unmistakably specified by "books concerning the kings," that is, Joshua, Judges, Samuel, and Kings, and by "the prophets," namely, Isaiah, Jeremiah, Ezekiel, and the Minor Prophets. Since the Hagiographa had not at that time received its technical designation, the contents were referred to as "those of David," that is, the Psalms, using as a title the first and most important book of the collection. But if the expression "the books of the kings concerning holy gifts" indicates the royal letters mentioned in Ezra and Nehemiah, then the Hagiographa as a whole would seem to be implied by reference to the Psalms and Ezra-Nehemiah-Chronicles as the first and last books respectively.

As mentioned above, the classical definition of the sequence of canonical Hebrew Scriptures was the *baraitha* in *Baba Bathra.* There are reasons for believing that the gloss is of second-century B.C. origin, for at that time there was considerable discussion as to which books of Scripture belonged to the same section, and therefore were to be written in one roll. With the exclusion of interpolated comments the *baraitha* is as follows:

> The order of the prophets is Joshua, Judges, Samuel, Kings, Jeremiah, Ezekiel, Isaiah, the Twelve [Minor Prophets]. That of the Kethubhim is Ruth, Psalms, Job, Proverbs, Ecclesiastes, Song of Solomon, Lamentations, Daniel, the roll of Esther, Ezra, Chronicles.
>
> Who wrote the books? Moses wrote his book, the section about Balaam, and Job; Joshua wrote his book and the last eight verses of the Torah; Samuel wrote his book, Judges, and Ruth. David wrote the Psalms at the direction of the Ten Ancients, namely through Adam [Ps. 139:16; Ps. 92?], Melchizedek [Ps. 110], Abraham [Ps. 89], Moses [Pss. 90-100], Heman [Ps. 88], Jeduthun [Ps. 62, Ps. 77?], Asaph [Pss. 50, 73-83], and the three sons of Korah [Pss. 42, 49, 78, 84, 85, 88]. Jeremiah wrote his book, the Book of Kings, and Lamentations; king Hezekiah and his council wrote Isaiah, Proverbs, Song of Solomon, and Ecclesiastes; the men of the Great Synagogue wrote Ezekiel, the Twelve Prophets, Daniel, and Esther. Ezra wrote his book and the genealogy of Chronicles down to his own period. Nehemiah completed it.

From the fact that Moses is mentioned as the author of the Torah it may be gathered that the five books of the Law were originally designated in the collection to which the gloss referred. However, because of the familiarity of the Jews with the Torah through contemporary synagogue usage, it could well have been regarded as comprising a single work whose component parts needed no specific enumeration. Since the gloss does not specify the books according to their origin, succession, and age, it can only have considered the order of the biblical writings insofar as they belonged to the same section of the canon. Yet it seems clear from the gloss that the "Former Prophets" had been credited with a fixed sequence of considerable antiquity concerning which there was no doubt in the minds of the rabbinical authorities. This was evidently occasioned by the way in which the writings from Joshua to Kings carried on the narrative of Hebrew history from post-Mosaic times (cf. 2 Macc. 2:13). The order of the "Latter Prophets" was irregular, and in the majority of manuscripts the only uniformity occurred in the placing of the Twelve Minor Prophets at the end of the list of books.

The *baraitha* is a curious piece of writing, containing in its complete form[4] some strange and occasionally impossible traditions regarding the composition of certain books of the Hebrew canon. While it has often been held to have had an important bearing upon the history of the canon, its contents demonstrate that it can throw no light at all upon the processes by which the canon achieved its final form. The unusual order of Jeremiah, Ezekiel, and Isaiah was explained by Talmudic authorities on the basis of a principle of internal consistency. Kings ended with destruction, and as such was appropriately succeeded by the prophecy of Jeremiah, which began and concluded with desolation also. Despite the fact that Ezekiel commenced with destruction, it ended with consolation, while all of Isaiah consisted of a consoling theme. In this way destruction appropriately followed upon destruction, and consolation upon consolation. This explanation is patently artificial, and it seems most probable that the prophetical books were actually arranged according to their size, a principle that appears to have been followed also in the accumulation of Mishnaic treatises.

2. Apocrypha, Septuagint, and patristic sources. It seems highly improbable that there was ever any specific enumeration of the books of the canon in Jewish literature generally. Early estimates were apt to vary somewhat; 2 Esdras 14:44ff. gives the number as twenty-four, whereas Josephus computed the number as twenty-two. In his preface to Samuel and Kings, Jerome mentions twenty-two books, but he finally arrived at a total of twenty-four, whereas Origen adhered to the number suggested by Josephus. Since both Origen and Jerome studied under Jewish teachers, it appears probable that the synagogue authorities themselves were somewhat undecided on the matter. The *baraitha* seems to favor twenty-four books, if Ruth formed one roll along with Judges or Psalms, and if Lamentations was included with Jeremiah on another roll, thus making twenty-two rolls but twenty-four books. The latter number was mentioned specifically in some Midrashic passages and was also known in antiquity in certain non-Jewish circles.

Scholars generally assume the arrangement of the books as given in *Baba Bathra* to be essentially the original one, and that of the Septuagint to be secondary. This view is by no means undisputed, however. Although the antiquity of the threefold division of the canon is never seriously questioned, it is obviously difficult to ascertain the order and contents of a section referred to as "the prophets" (Lk. 24:44), for example. Josephus enumerated the five books of Moses, thirteen compositions in which the prophets described Hebrew history from the immediate post-Mosaic period to the reign of the Persian monarch Artaxerxes I, and four books containing hymns of praise and regulations for social behavior. It seems reasonably certain that he combined Ruth and Lamentations with Judges and Jeremiah respectively in his computation, as suggested above, and that in so doing he was following a well-established Palestinian tradition.

Origen, who also held that the Jews accepted twenty-two books as their scriptural canon, showed considerably greater conformity to the order of the Septuagint in his enumeration of the canonical writings than did Josephus

[4]This complete text can be found in H. E. Ryle, *The Canon of the Old Testament,* pp. 284ff.

and some rabbinical authorities. However, he did not follow the Septuagint listing slavishly, and there are significant differences between the two. It is at least reasonable to conclude from Origen's testimony that the order of the canon in *Baba Bathra* did not command unquestioned assent in Palestine during that period. From the evidence presented by the Qumran texts it would seem probable that there were several different forms of the canon in existence by the first century of the Christian era, which is in harmony with the rather fluid picture of the pre-Massoretic text as indicated by the Qumran scrolls.

Any assessment of the Septuagint canon of the Old Testament must note that the Greek manuscripts exhibit significant differences, both in the number of the books that they contain and the order in which they are arranged. Such a situation would appear to reflect an earlier Palestinian Jewish tradition, and indicate the secondary nature of the Septuagint canon. It is significant that Philo followed the Jewish rather than the Alexandrian tradition in his estimate of the content of Scripture. It would seem that the differences between the Hebrew and the Septuagint canons lie not so much in a wider interpretation of the canon by the Alexandrian Jews because they thought in terms of a much broader view of inspiration, as in the fact that the Jews in Alexandria (and the Diaspora generally) did not distinguish as sharply between the canonical and non-canonical works as their Palestinian counterparts did. Had they done so it is highly probable that the early Christian Church would have looked a little more critically at the excess of the Hebrew canon that they used in the Septuagint version.

A criticism of the originality of the Hebrew order was made by P. Katz, who related the earliest attestation of the Hebrew selection of books to the period of the reconstitution of Judaism after the destruction of the Temple. He further claimed that the evidence for twenty-four as the number of Old Testament canonical books was scanty, and that twenty-two was the proper and correct total as known in Palestine. In order to disprove the originality of the Hebrew order of books, he maintained that the arrangement Ezra-Nehemiah-Chronicles was artificial, a position that, in the view of the present author, is extremely difficult to justify, even if the Chronicler is considered to be someone other than Ezra. As has been remarked above, it is quite likely that in early times several forms of the canon existed side by side, preserving the same threefold division but varying to some degree in content. The fact that the Old Testament books were written down on separate rolls would contribute to this diversity and indeed would serve as a hindrance to the appearance of a fixed order of books. The canon of the Septuagint evidently reflected this general state of affairs, and perpetuated it in some ways, thus showing its dependence upon the traditions of the Palestinian Jews.

Although neither the *baraitha* nor the Hellenistic Jews of Alexandria can furnish proper information relating to the compilation of the Hebrew canon, it is interesting to note that for many centuries the view was current that the canon of the Old Testament was formulated and completed within the lifetime of Ezra. This tradition drew for its biblical foundation upon Ezra and Nehemiah (cf. Ez. 7:10, 25; Neh. 8:1ff.; 9:3), and was given currency not merely by *Baba Bathra,* which credited Ezra with the compilation of his own book and the genealogy of Chronicles to his own time, but also to some extent by the opinions of Josephus. About A.D. 95 Josephus recorded that the history of the origin of the world up to the reign of Artaxerxes I had been described in the Jewish holy writings, and added that although the story had subsequently been carried towards his own time, this latter material did not deserve the same confidence on the part of the reader, since the succession of the prophets was not fixed accurately. From this statement it can be inferred with great probability that during the lifetime of Ezra the historical books of the Old Testament, and perhaps some portions of the Hagiographa as well, were circulating in their extant form.

Second Esdras, a Jewish apocalyptic composition whose central section seems to have been written by an unknown Jew at the end of the first century of the Christian era, preserved the tradition that in the thirtieth year after the destruction of Jerusalem (557 B.C.) Ezra was inspired to dictate ninety-four books to five scribes within a period of some forty days. Of this corpus twenty-four books were to be made available for general perusal, while the remaining seventy, evidently consisting of apocalyptic material, were to be restricted to the wise men (2 Esdr. 14:18ff.). Presumably the twenty-four books were the same as those mentioned by other writers—with Ruth and Lamentations as separate works which had been incorporated, for various reasons, with Judges, Psalms, or Jeremiah. Another apocryphal work, 2 Maccabees (ch. 2:13ff.), contains a letter purporting to have been written by Palestinian Jews to the Hellenistic Jews of Alexandria. This epistle mentions the nature of the library said to have been assembled by Nehemiah. If it is genuine, it would be dated 165 B.C., but many scholars have denied its authenticity and assigned it to the first century B.C. While these passages may be nothing more than attempts to project into the age of Ezra and Nehemiah certain tendencies that were only evident at a later period, it must not be forgotten that the middle of the fifth century B.C. was a time when considerable interest was shown in the codification of Hebrew sacred literature. On the other hand, neither the Talmud nor Josephus specifically credits Ezra with a special function in the formulation of the Old Testament canon, even though *Baba Bathra* mentions his literary activity. The tradition that ascribes to Ezra an important role in the creation of the Old Testament canon only appears to go back with certainty as far as the account in 2 Esdras, and the nature of this material is such that it is difficult to ascertain its historical value. Despite this fact it may well be that the narrative was based upon a genuine tradition of collection and assemblage of scriptural materials in the fifth century B.C., whether by Ezra, Nehemiah, or some of their followers. In the same way it is at least possible that an historically reliable tradition is at the root of the information furnished by 2 Maccabees. Whatever is the case, little is known about the development of the canon in the period immediately following the time of Ezra and Nehemiah. As has been observed previously, Ben Sira knew of the threefold division of the Old Testament canon, and attached high authority to the various sections. He was familiar with at least some of the Writings, though to what extent he was conversant with all of them is uncertain. In the narratives about the Maccabees there are numerous references to the sacred books of the Jews (e.g. 1 Macc. 1:56f.; 4:30; 7:41; 12:9), although it is impossible to be certain of the extent to which such a corpus corresponded to the Old Testament canon.

By the time of Christ, it would seem, the Old Testament existed as a complete collection. The evidence presented by the New Testament writers indicates that the Old Testament as a whole was referred to as "the Scriptures" (Matt. 26:54; John 5:39) or "the Scripture" (John 2:22; Acts 8:32) at that period to designate a familiar and unified group of inspired and authoritative writings. In particular, the specific designation of "Old Testament" was applied by the primitive Church to this corpus of Holy Writ to convey the sense of a completed assemblage of scriptural compositions (2 Cor. 3:14). New Testament authors commonly alluded to the Scriptures in terms of two categories—the Law and the Prophets. Support for this position has been provided by the discoveries from Qumran, where in four instances the Community Rule or Manual of Discipline (1QS, I:3; VIII:13ff.) and the Zadokite Fragment (CDC, V:21; VII:15ff.) referred to the Old Testament writings in precisely the same two categories. That this twofold canon included all the present works appears obvious from the fact that the Qumran community cited most of the Old Testament books, including those later classified in the third section of the canon. On this evidence alone there would seem to be considerable ground for a theory of the antiquity of a twofold division of the Old Testament canon.

Naturally it is impossible to determine in detail the contents of the canon in the time of Christ, although, as has been mentioned above, one reference (Matt. 23:35; Lk. 11:51) would imply that the canon terminated with Chronicles at that time. The fact that Esther, Ecclesiastes, Canticles, Ezra, Nehemiah, Obadiah, Nahum, and Zephaniah are not cited by New Testament authors does not in itself indicate that these compositions were not considered to constitute part of the Old Testament at that particular period, since being quoted in the New Testament is not a necessary condition of canonicity for an Old Testament book.

If this assemblage of sacred writings was substantially the same in the days of Jesus Christ as it is at the present, such a canon was "closed" more by common consent and popular acceptance than by formal decree on the part of the rabbinic or early Christian authorities. In connection with this latter concept an appeal has sometimes been made to the work of the "men of the Great Synagogue," who were referred to in the Talmud. Unfortunately it is far from clear as to precisely who these men were. According to some theories they belonged to a generation that included Haggai, Zechariah, Daniel, and Esther. In the view of Elias Levita (d. A.D. 1549), these men, along with Ezra, united in one volume the twenty-four books of the canon, which until that time had circulated separately, and classified them in three divisions, determining the order of the Prophets and the Sacred Writings.

Although Levita's arrangement differs from the order listed in *Baba Bathra,* his view gained currency in the sixteenth century, and for the next two hundred years was accepted as orthodox. From the middle of the seventeenth century, however, the nature of the "Great Synagogue" was disputed, and in the nineteenth century Kuenen argued strongly that the "Synagogue" was none other than the great assembly at Jerusalem described in Nehemiah 8:1ff., which pledged itself to the acceptance of those conditions enunciated by Ezra the scribe from the ancient Jewish law. On the basis of the available evidence it would seem that if such a body of men as was envisaged in *Baba Bathra* actually existed, its activity was confined to the period of Ezra and that it extended to only four books, not the entire Old Testament canon. When it is said that they "wrote" Ezekiel, the Twelve Prophets, Daniel, and Esther, what is meant is clearly that they were engaged in editing such works, probably with a view to incorporating them into a sacred canon.

3. The "Council of Jamnia." It has also been suggested that pronouncements that defined the limits of the Old Testament canon were made by a formal council of Jewish authorities held towards the end of the first century after Christ at Jamnia or Jabneh. Very little is known about this supposed Synod. After Jerusalem was destroyed by the forces of Titus in A.D. 70, Rabbi Johanan ben Zakkai obtained permission from the Romans to settle in Jamnia, where he proposed to carry on his literary activities. The location soon became an established center of scriptural study, and from time to time certain discussions took place relating to the canonicity of specific Old Testament books including Ezekiel, Esther, Canticles, Ecclesiastes, and Proverbs. There can be little doubt that such conversations took place both before and after this period, and it seems probable that nothing of a formal or binding nature was decided in these discussions, even though, as H. H. Rowley has indicated, the various debates helped to crystallize and establish the Jewish tradition in this regard more firmly than had been the case previously.

If it is questionable as to how far one can speak correctly of the Council of Jamnia, it is even more doubtful that the participants in the discussions were actually concerned with the problem as to whether certain books should be *included* in the canon of Scripture or not. Rather, the conversations seem to have centered upon the question of whether specific books should be *excluded* from what was to be regarded as the scriptural corpus. Certain compositions were generally accepted as inspired and authoritative, even though they reflected the Jewish tradition in a somewhat peculiar fashion: Esther did not mention the Divine Name; Ecclesiastes seemed partly Epicurean to some authorities and out of harmony with contemporary Jewish philosophy; and the Song of Songs, though credited to Solomon, appeared to be nothing more than a composition dealing with the vagaries of human passion and physical love.

The fact is that the works under discussion were already accorded canonical status in popular esteem, so that the "Council" was actually confirming public opinion, not forming it. The conversations that took place were strictly academic, and in consequence it is very questionable if the doubts that they raised in connection with certain compositions actually represented the general attitude of the populace as a whole to any significant extent. Certainly Ezekiel, to mention but one topic of dispute, must have been accepted as Scripture long before the rabbis of Jamnia undertook to examine its status. It ought to be concluded, therefore, that no formal pronouncement as to the limits of the Old Testament canon was ever made in rabbinic circles at Jamnia.

4. Modern theories. The manuscript discoveries at Qumran provide little information about the origin and limits of the Old Testament canon. The library of the sectaries included numerous religious compositions other than those normally accepted by the Jews, but as far as the content of the Hebrew canon is concerned, the only work missing in the early discoveries was Esther. One reason for this omission from the Qumran collection of scrolls may be that it was deliberately rejected by the sectaries. On the other hand, the absence of the manuscript could be entirely a matter of chance, and the book may yet be discovered in the fragments which have still to be examined and evaluated.

As far as the available evidence goes, it is clear that while the Old Testament does not furnish any significant information about the manner in which the canon arose, or the extent of the Prophets and the Writings at any given period of their history, it does bear testimony to the existence from early times of an authoritative literature to which appeal was made in varying ways and which, with subsequent additions, was venerated as Holy Writ. This vague internal testimony has been more than offset by the precision of modern critical scholarship, which has furnished a number of theories as to the growth and content of the Old Testament canon. These views have generally emphasized the concept of the biblical canon in terms of purely human acceptance of a national literature, taking no particular cognizance of the divine inspiration or authority of the canonical writings.

Such approaches are a product of their age in the sense that, for the most part, they are firmly wedded to the outlook and tenets of the Graf-Wellhausen school. In *The Canon of the Old Testament* Ryle maintained that a Hebrew national literature was in existence long before there was any canon as such. While the latter was assembled in three successive stages, due notice had to be taken of the literary antecedents of the various books, the redaction to their extant form, and finally the elevation of these works to a position in the national canon of Scripture. For Ryle, as for all liberal scholars, the Pentateuch in its finished form was the end-product of a prolonged period of growth during which various supposed documents were brought together and edited. When Ezra read what Ryle and others thought to be the Pentateuch in the presence of the assembled multitude, this Law was acknowledged as binding upon the people and was deemed canonical as a result. However, such a canon was inadequate, for considerable interest had been aroused during the time of Nehemiah in preserving the utterances of the prophets. These books were subsequently canonized perhaps between 300 and 200 B.C., possibly as a result of the threat that Hellenistic culture was posing to traditional Judaism. When the prophetic portion of the canon was closed, other writings such as Ecclesiastes were assembled, and their popularity during the Maccabean period led to their being recognized as authoritative. Ryle maintained that the entire collection was deemed canonical by about A.D. 100, and related this activity to the Council of Jamnia.

A modification of this view appeared in the work of G. Hölscher, who thought that one mark of canonicity consisted in the fact that the very holiness of the books distinguished them from every other form of literature, a suggestion made considerably earlier by Josephus. In his work *Kanonisch und Apokryph,* he rejected the idea of a threefold canonization of Scripture, suggesting instead that the concept of the canon arose because Greek culture and the growth of Greek literature presented a serious challenge to the religious traditions of Judaism. Equally pressing was the widespread dissemination of Jewish apocryphal material, so that in being compelled to separate the genuine from the spurious the Jewish religious authorities were forced to accept the idea of a canon of Scripture. The Torah was highly venerated from the seventh century B.C., but even when it had reached its final form about the end of the fourth century B.C. it was still not accorded canonicity. The same was true of the Prophets, which in the opinion of Hölscher were added periodically to the larger corpus up to the middle of the second century B.C. The testimony of Ben Sira could not be regarded as evidence that the prophetical canon was closed by that time, but instead served to indicate the particular works that had come to be regarded with special veneration by about 190 B.C. For Hölscher, proof that the idea of a canon had not arisen at that time was furnished by the fact that Ben Sira could speak of himself as the latest of all the biblical writers (Ecclus. 33:16), and deck out his utterances in the style of the ancient prophets. Plausible as the latter objection sounds, it does not explain precisely why Ecclesiasticus failed to gain acceptance into the Old Testament canon, nor does it recognize the fact that Ben Sira was not standing in the tradition of the prophets, but of the ancient Hebrew sages.

A similar view of the formation of the canon was adopted by Oesterley and Robinson, who acknowledged their indebtedness to Hölscher, and maintained that the concept of relative holiness provoked the idea of a canon of Scripture. The feeling that some books were more holy than others could not, in their view, have arisen all at once. Indeed, it was only gradually and by general consent that certain works came to have a special sanctity attached to them. In their *Introduction to the Books of the Old*

Testament, Oesterley and Robinson followed Hölscher in maintaining that there had never been three successive stages in which the principal collections of books were in turn recognized as canonical in the strictest sense. For them the fixing of the biblical canon was a piecemeal affair, governed in part by the spread of Hellenism and the impact of Jewish apocryphal literature upon the nation. The canon was supposed to have been formulated finally about A.D. 100, and when completed was recognized by the Jews as binding and authoritative. A theory of this sort seems to attribute too much to an assembly whose very existence has been questioned, and for which the evidence is neither precise nor complete. Any denial of a threefold stage in the organization of the canonical Hebrew Scriptures must take cognizance of the veneration associated with the Law on the part of both Jews and Samaritans, and the fact that, for the latter, the Torah alone was canonical. This is not to say, however, that a more detailed tripartite division of Holy Writ did not ultimately emerge from a clarification in definition and usage of a corpus of Scripture which was in general thought of in terms of two preponderant sections, the Law and a collection of prophetical writings.

According to A. Bentzen's *Introduction to the Old Testament,* the reading of the Law in the time of Ezra and Nehemiah probably signified the introduction of the form of the Torah that was current in Babylonian Jewish circles at that period. Basing his views upon the critical analysis of the Pentateuch, Bentzen maintained that even if the latter was not complete, comparatively little could have been lacking. In any event, the idea of a normative lawbook occurred as early as the reform of King Josiah in 621 B.C., a time of particular importance for the formation of the idea of a holy written law. Even earlier, however, was the ancient concept of law as given by a god, and also the ancient *credo* of Israel. Nevertheless, these ideas did not lead to the fixed concept of a canon, the oldest portion of which was established when the various alleged strata of the Pentateuch were unified in the post-exilic period. For Bentzen the prophetic section of the Old Testament canon commenced when Isaiah (8:16) imposed upon his disciples the obligation to be the bearers and preservers of his words, and when Jeremiah instructed his secretary Baruch to commit his prophecies to writing. The exile was of great importance in that it sealed the prophetic utterances with the stark confirmation of history. The post-exilic prophets, who stood in the tradition of their predecessors (cf. Zech. 1:4; 7:7), had their writings regarded as canonical somewhat before 200 B.C., while the Hagiographa, the most vaguely defined portion of the canon, was probably complete by the time the prologue to Ecclesiasticus was written. Plausible as this theory may appear, it unfortunately fails to take account of the fact that the Samaritans venerated the Torah as canonical from at least the time of Ezra and Nehemiah, if not indeed considerably earlier, and that it was the Jewish and not the Babylonian form of the Law that they accepted as authoritative. Again like many another liberal scholar, Bentzen assigns too late a date to many of the writings in the Prophets and the Hagiographa, and thus finds it necessary to consider the Synod of Jamnia important in the fixing of the Old Testament canon.

A modification of the views expressed by Ryle occurred in the *Introduction to the Old Testament* by R. H. Pfeiffer. He maintained that the first instance of canonization in human history occurred when Deuteronomy, discovered during the reign of King Josiah, was venerated as the Word of God and respected as a norm for human behavior. Apart from this, other literary works in Israel were being combined and edited about 650 B.C. to comprise a national epic. A century later the canonized Deuteronomy was interpolated into the corpus of this material, with the result that the latter also came to be regarded as canonical. About 200 B.C. the so-called "Priestly document" was inserted into this combined work, and it also attained to canonicity as a result. Unhappily this theory not merely reflects all the weaknesses associated with the developmental theory of Pentateuchal origins, but assumes quite gratuitously and without any evidence that the lawbook recovered from the Temple in the time of Josiah actually constituted the book of Deuteronomy, a position for which there is not the slightest factual justification. Even a casual reading of the text will be sufficient to indicate that the finding of the Temple scroll was in fact the rediscovery of an already authoritative book, of which both Josiah and Hilkiah had heard previously, but which had been lost. Pfeiffer maintained an inadequate view of the concept of canonicity, as would seem evident from his assertion that a book could apparently exist from 650 to 550 B.C. as a mere national epic, and then suddenly span the gap separating the secular from the sacred to become the Word of God. Furthermore, Pfeiffer's assumption that the Jewish scribes would incorporate non-canonical material with that which was deemed canonical reflects a fundamental misunderstanding of the entire Jewish attitude towards Scripture.

Critical authors have been apt to maintain that the Law, in part or whole, attained to canonical status through the activities of Ezra and Nehemiah. Since, however, Ezra was described as an "adept scribe in the Law of Moses" (Ez. 7:6), it is apparent that the Mosaic enactments had already become an object of professional study in their own right prior to his time. Furthermore, the whole purpose of Ezra in going up to Jerusalem with the permission of Artaxerxes was to insure that the precepts of the Law were carried out. Ezra 7:14, 23, 25, and 26 show clearly that the Law was already in existence, and that its commands required the wholehearted obedience of the people. There is consequently no evidence whatever that Ezra, in virtue of his position in the community, was about to impart to certain already existing religious writings of the Hebrews a degree of moral and spiritual authority that they had not possessed at an earlier time.

In the same way it is incorrect to see Nehemiah 8-10 as an account of the canonization of scriptural writings. The "book of the Law of Moses" that Ezra read at the request of the people, which resulted in a solemn act of religious renewal, owed its authority to the fact that it was an ancient document believed to have constituted material revealed by God to Moses. Rather than being an occasion on which the opinions of men were given in such a way as to assign canonical stature to a written composition by common resolve, it demonstrated that it was the inherent authority of the book itself that, when properly received, subjected the assembled throng to the judgment of God and recalled the populace to the observance of the ancient religious precepts.

If these considerations apply to Ezra and Nehemiah, they are of equal force for the "men of the Great Synagogue" and the Council of Jamnia—assuming that the latter was a properly constituted body. What these groups did, if anything, was to approve as canonical works that which had for long been venerated as authoritative. Even though doubts had arisen concerning Ecclesiastes and the Song of Solomon, the weight of tradition was such that they were included in the corpus of Scripture without undue difficulty.

The fundamental issue that divides liberal scholars from their more conservative counterparts appears to be their rejection of inspiration as the ultimate determining principle of the extent of the Old Testament canon. For liberal scholars the formation of the scriptural corpus was nothing more than a type of human activity in which certain books were regarded as canonical because they had demonstrated their pragmatic value in religious usage. However, such a theory has to face the fact that, although works such as Ecclesiasticus and 1 Maccabees had undoubted value for Judaism, they failed to secure a place in the canon of Scripture. Even if the concept of conformity to the spirit and ideals of the Torah is held to be the determining factor in the formation of the canon, as is commonly maintained by some writers, the problem still needs to be taken one stage further back by accounting for those principles which resulted in the canonization of the Law.

In contradistinction to the liberal outlook, the available evidence supports the position that the Old Testament writings, being divinely inspired, were consequently authoritative and were accepted as such from the period of their initial appearance. The Spirit of God that inspired these compositions also worked in the hearts and minds of the chosen people to testify to them that the writings were in fact the divine Word. It was this witness, in conjunction with the conscious human response, that was evidently the ultimate determining agent in the formulation of the canon. Had the question of canonicity merely rested upon purely academic decisions without an acknowledged concept of inspiration, it is impossible to see how the Jews could ever have come to accept the Old Testament books as being of divine authority. If considerations of positive affectivity had been dominant in the process of arriving at some form of canonical delineation it is very doubtful that more than a fraction of the extant canon would ultimately have proved to be acceptable, since the majority of the Old Testament compositions were severely critical of the ancient Hebrews in one way or another.

There is little doubt that matters relating to inspiration were responsible for furnishing at least some of the criteria by which certain compositions were assigned by the rabbinic authorities to the third division of the Hebrew canon. As has been noticed earlier, Jewish tradition maintained that all the Old Testament authors were prophets. Not all the contributors to the *K^{e}thubhim* or Sacred Writings could claim this distinction, however; for example, Daniel was a statesman rather than a classic mediator between God and a theocratic nation. His position in the third division of the canon was apparently justified by the fact that works in the *K^{e}thubhim* were deemed to have been written by individuals who were not prophets in the strictest sense of the word, but who nevertheless wrote under divine inspiration.

It has been already observed that numerous questions were raised at different times among rabbinic authorities concerning the canonicity of certain highly esteemed compositions. In particular, discussion centered upon Ezekiel, Esther, and the three works attributed popularly to Solomon—Proverbs, Ecclesiastes, and Canticles. The opposition to Ezekiel was only temporary, and apparently arose because the priestly nature of the program outlined in the concluding nine chapters of the prophecy was thought to be in conflict with the tenor of the Pentateuch. Those who questioned its suitability for inclusion in the canon wished to prevent its use as authoritative Scripture, but the work was ultimately rehabilitated by the labors of a certain Hananiah ben Hezekiah ben Garon, who "spent three hundred jars of oil to release it."

Tannaite scribes of the second century B.C. were eager to include the Esther scroll in the canon of Scripture, and in the end the issue turned upon the question as to whether or not the work actually constituted a revealed composition. If the book was found to have proceeded from other than divine inspiration, it could not properly be given a place in the list of scriptural writings. Despite considerable uncertainty on the matter, it was ultimately agreed, with Rabbi Simeon (150 B.C.), that Esther "defiled the hands," and as such it was deemed canonical. The opposition to Proverbs was comparatively slight, and was based for the most part upon apparent internal inconsistencies. Similar objections were levelled against Ecclesiastes, although in this case it was felt that the quasi-Epicurean tone of the book was out of harmony with the religious traditions of Judaism. The canonicity of Ecclesiastes was supported, among others, by the followers of Hillel, while the most vigorous opposition apparently came from the strict school of the Shammaites.

According to Rabbi Simon ben Menasya, the Song of Solomon "defiled the hands," since it was inspired by the Holy Spirit of God. Regarding this work it can be said in general that it does not appear to have evoked any specific statement to the contrary. That there was prolonged, and perhaps acrimonious, discussion concerning Canticles, however, is apparent from the drastic step taken by Rabbi Aqiba about A.D. 100 to rehabilitate the Song in his celebrated pronouncement that "he who, for the sake of entertainment, sings the Song as though it were a profane song, will have no share in the future world." There can be little doubt that the popularity of works such as Esther, Ecclesiastes, and Canticles in connection with Jewish feast days furnished powerful support for their claim to canonicity.

While certain books were the subject of periodic discussion in this regard, there was no controversy at all in connection with the books of the Apocrypha, for everyone was agreed that they were non-canonical. The reason appears to have been that the works themselves simply gave no evidence whatever of having been divinely inspired. As W. H. Green and others have pointed out, some of these writings contain egregious historical, chronological, and geographical errors, quite apart from justifying falsehood and deception and making salvation dependent upon deeds of merit. Although the books of the Apocrypha can quite obviously claim to possess much that is in harmony with the spirit of the canonical compositions, there are numerous instances in which they diverge sharply from the latter.

The lengthy processes by which the canon of the Old Testament arrived at its present form cannot be traced with anything approaching exactitude, and only the most general of principles can be enunciated reasonably satisfactorily. Without doubt the element of divine inspiration was a profoundly important consideration for the Jews, particularly in the immediate pre-Christian period. Equally true is the fact that, from its beginnings, the Pentateuch was considered authoritative because it contained the divine revelation to Moses, and as a direct result it was regarded as the standard to which other writings were to be related. The Torah must obviously have possessed what amounts to canonical authority long before it was accorded such by the Hebrews, otherwise the nation of Israel would have been under no obligation to accept its precepts as the norm for moral and spiritual behavior. The fact of this recognition was thus the effect rather than the cause of the "canonical" status associated with the Torah from early times. It is apparent from the evidence presented by the Samaritan Pentateuch that the Torah commanded a high degree of veneration even prior to the early post-exilic period, and that during the time of Ezra and Nehemiah its authority was accepted anew by the nation.

As far as the prophetic literature is concerned, the evidence is even more scanty, for there is no record in the Old Testament either of formal recognition or acceptance by the people of any of the works contained in the second and third divisions of the Hebrew canon. The fact that some portions of the Hagiographa are older than certain of the prophecies might imply that the second division of the canon remained "open" until much of the Hagiographa was in existence. Whether this was actually the case or not, the determining principle of canonicity for the Jewish religious authorities appeared to be that of divine inspiration. Even here there are certain difficulties in interpretation, however, for the medieval scholars were accustomed to assert that the three divisions of the canon corresponded to three degrees of inspiration. The highest of these was that of Moses, who communicated directly with God; the second was that attributed to the prophets, who wrote by the spirit of prophecy; while the lowest was that of the other writers, who were inspired by the Holy Spirit of God. Such a differentiation is, of course, completely unsupported by the Scriptures themselves. The prophets believed that they stood firmly in the Mosaic tradition and that their own words possessed equal moral and spiritual authority with the pronouncements of the great lawgiver. Furthermore, the alleged distinction between the spirit of prophecy and the Holy Spirit is purely imaginary.

While the "men of the Great Synagogue" and the Council of Jamnia may possibly have played some small part in the growth of the canon in its final stages, there is insufficient evidence to show that their disputations resulted in any significant fixing of its limits. If the views of those liberal writers who regard the canon as having been "closed" about A.D. 100 are unacceptable because their dating is far too late, the theories of those conservative scholars who would place the closing of the Old Testament canon about 400 B.C. are equally improbable, simply because such a date appears to be too early. In all its essentials the canon was most probably complete by about 300 B.C., and while discussion concerning certain component parts was continued well into the Christian era, the substance of the canon as it existed a century-and-a-half after the time of Ezra and Nehemiah remained unaffected by these controversies.

II.
THE CANON OF THE NEW TESTAMENT

EVERETT F. HARRISON

Any explanation for the church's acceptance of the books that now make up the New Testament as Scripture must begin with an examination of the use of these books in the early church and the occasional references to them found in the Church Fathers.

It is hardly reasonable to expect to find in the New Testament itself any definite information on the canon, at any rate on the limits of it. But at least two things are worth noting. Exhortations are given from time to time concerning the public reading of apostolic writings (1 Thess. 5:27; Col. 4:16; 1 Tim. 4:13; Rev. 1:3; 2:7, 11, 17, 29; 3:6, 13, 22). Of these, Colossians 4:16 has special interest in that it involves an additional feature, namely, the circulating of an epistle to at least one other church, and the admonition to obtain a second epistle from the other church (Laodicea) that it might be read in the church at Colossae. It is a reasonable inference that neither the writer nor the readers looked upon such documents as having only momentary value. A need for them might well arise elsewhere, warranting their preservation.

Further, the New Testament bears witness to something approaching a collection of books. In 2 Peter 3:15-16 attention is called to the writings of Paul ("in all his epistles") and the observation is made that the unlearned and unstable wrest these epistles, as they do *the other Scriptures,* to their own destruction. Since 2 Peter is written to a rather general audience, at least not to a single church, a widespread knowledge of Paul's writings is implied. It is impossible to know how many epistles of Paul the writer had in mind, but several are in view, and they are placed on a par with the Old Testament writings. The value of this testimony depends upon the estimate of the date of 2 Peter, which some put as late as the middle of the second century, thus eliminating it as a witness for the apostolic age. But there are serious difficulties involved in denying its authenticity.

In 1 Timothy 5:18 a statement quoted from Deuteronomy 25:4, "You shall not muzzle a threshing ox," is coupled with another, "The laborer is worthy of his hire" (Luke 10:7), and the term Scripture is applied to both. The most natural inference is that Luke is given the status of Scripture here and put on a level with the Old Testament. To be sure, the Pastoral Epistles have been challenged as to their Pauline authorship and as to a date within Paul's lifetime. But even if they are relegated to the following generation, this testimony to the standing of a Gospel as Scripture is extremely valuable.

1. The Post-apostolic Age. This is the period of the Apostolic Fathers and the Apologists, lasting until the last quarter of the second century, the time of the emergence of the Old Catholic Church and the testimonies of such men as Irenaeus, Clement of Alexandria, and Tertullian.

Writing to the Corinthian church (*ca.* 95), Clement of Rome makes copious use of the Old Testament, which he cites as Scripture, the work of the Holy Spirit. He makes explicit mention of Paul's First Epistle to the Corinthians (chap. 47) and shows familiarity with the teaching of Christ. The Epistle to the Hebrews is known, likewise several others. Clement is acquainted with "the words of the Lord Jesus" (chaps. 13 and 46), but the use of written Gospels at these points is debatable; however, it is clear that Clement, when referring to material emanating from Christ or the apostles, nowhere uses the term Scripture. His introduction of Christ's sayings by "The Lord spake," etc., may be called an archaic form of citation in contrast to the habit of later writers who did not hesitate to label such utterances as Scripture.

The Epistle of Barnabas bears the name of a New Testament figure, but it belongs to the early part of the second century. Generous use is made of the Old Testament in order to show how it points to Christ. Several times reference is made to the teaching of Jesus. Though the term Scripture is not used of these materials, the words "many [are] called but few chosen" (Matt. 22:14) appear, introduced by a formula that is common for the quotation of Old Testament Scripture—"as it stands written" (4:14).

Ignatius, Bishop of Antioch, was martyred at Rome during the reign of Trajan (98-117). As he journeyed through Asia Minor, a captive of the empire, he wrote seven epistles to various churches. In one of these he refers to some who say, "If I do not find it in the archives, I do not believe in the gospel" (*Philadelphians* 8:2). Though the archives could conceivably be taken to refer to Gospel records, they are more likely the Old Testament Scriptures of which the gospel is the fulfillment. While Ignatius is acquainted with Gospel materials, he nowhere alludes to such materials as Scripture or quotes an individual Gospel by name. He is aware that Paul wrote letters and is familiar with several of them (*Ephesians* 12:2), and carefully distinguishes his own position from that of the apostles (*Romans* 4:3).

Polycarp's *Epistle to the Philippians* (*ca.* 115) abounds with language drawn from the New Testament. More than once statements are attributed to Jesus, introduced by the words, "The Lord said." In citing Paul, Polycarp several times uses the introductory phrase, "knowing that," which J. B. Lightfoot takes to be a formula of citation (see 1:15; 5:1). Most striking is the quoting of Psalm 4:5, "Be angry and sin not," followed immediately by Ephesians 4:26, "Let not the sun go down upon your wrath," and the prefacing of the combined statements with the words, "as it is said in these Scriptures" (12:1).

The *Didache,* or *Teaching of the Twelve Apostles,* has been assigned to the close of the first century, but a date somewhere in the first quarter of the second century is a safer conclusion. Numerous citations from Matthew are used, but without naming the source. Twice the writer uses the expression, "As you have [it] in the gospel" (15:3, 4), which may well imply the use of written records, but the appeal is to the message, not to a particular Gospel. The word Scripture is not used in connection with these allusions. From the same general period, the *Shepherd of Hermas* shows acquaintance with the teaching of the Gospels and with several of the Epistles, but there is no citation of any of this material as Scripture.

From the title of *Exposition of the Oracles of the Lord* by Papias, Bishop of Hierapolis (130-140?), it is evident that the documents involved were considered Scripture (see the use of "oracles" in Rom. 3:2). Fragments of this work preserved in Eusebius mention Matthew and Mark by name, thus confirming the assumption that the canonical Gospels were used as the basis of this exposition. Incidentally, this is the first specific mention by name of any Gospel.

The attempt to maintain that the work of Papias was simply a narrative account of Jesus' discourses based on tradition has not been successful. His own statement, "but I will not scruple also to give a place along with my interpretations to all that I learned carefully and remembered carefully in time past from the elders," clearly implies a distinction, in view of the word *also,* between the material to be interpreted and the oral traditions that are looked upon as something additional.

From Eusebius' silence about any testimony of Papias to Luke and John it is precarious to assume that Papias had not included them with the others as the basis of his own exposition. Any failure to include them would likely have evoked comment from Eusebius.

It has sometimes been held that Papias disparaged books in favor of oral tradition and therefore cannot be a valid witness to canonical development in the church. This opinion is grounded on a misunderstanding of his meaning when he says, "I did not suppose that information from books would help me as much as the word of a living and surviving voice." In view of his high regard for Mark it seems clear that the books referred to are accounts of traditional material that Papias considered less helpful than immediate contact with the "elders." The books in question here, then, are not to be identified with our written Gospels, which Papias used in his *Exposition*.

The recently discovered *Gospel of Truth*, with observable Gnostic tendencies, is probably attributable to Valentinus around A.D. 140. It has an important contribution to make to the study of the New Testament canon, since its use of the canonical writings is so comprehensive as to warrant the conclusion that in Rome at this period a New Testament was in existence that corresponded very closely with what we have today. Furthermore, what is utilized, whether from the Gospels, the Acts, the letters of Paul, Hebrews, or the Revelation, is regarded as authoritative.

An early apologist, Justin Martyr, wrote around the middle of the second century two apologies and his *Dialogue with Trypho the Jew*. His *First Apology*, chapter 67, contains a famous passage descriptive of Christian worship. "On the day called Sunday, all Christians gather together to one place and the memoirs of the apostles or the writings of the prophets are read as long as time permits, and when the reader has ceased, the president verbally instructs and exhorts to the imitation of these good things. Then we all rise together and pray, and as we said before, when our prayer is ended, bread and wine and water are brought, and the president in like manner offers prayers and thanksgivings, according to his ability, and the people assent, saying 'Amen.' " Here Justin speaks of the memoirs of the apostles, which he explicitly says in the preceding chapter are also called Gospels.

The question is, Can these be identified with our canonical Gospels? This is rendered probable by the consideration that there is substantial agreement between Justin's allusions to items in the life of Christ and the corresponding material in our Gospels. Furthermore, when Justin refers to traditions not found in our Gospels, he does not cite Gospel authority for them. Six times he uses the formula "it is written" in connection with the Gospels, but not in connection with items derived from other sources.

It must be granted that there is often a lack of verbal agreement between Justin's quotations and our present text of the Gospels, but this disparity is relieved by the following observations: (1) like the early Fathers in general, he may be presumed to have quoted largely from memory, and (2) his quotations from pagan Greek writers and from the Septuagint show no less striking differences from those texts than his citations from the Gospels.

Justin's failure to refer to the Epistles as Scripture may well have been due to the apologetic character of his work. Jews and pagans would be less impressed by the testimony of such writings than by the Old Testament allusions and the utterances of Jesus of Nazareth.

Regarding the Apocalypse, Justin bears testimony that it was the work of "a certain man among us whose name was John, one of the apostles of Christ" (*Dial.* 81). It can hardly be doubted that he knew John's Gospel also, though the use he made of it was for doctrinal rather than historical data.

In describing the innovations of a heretical group known as Encratites, Eusebius mentions Tatian as their leader and goes on to state that "he composed in some way a combination and collection of the Gospels, and gave this the name of *The Diatessaron*, and this is still extant in some places." The presence of the four Gospels in this work is explicitly affirmed by Epiphanius (315-404). In the fifth century Theodoret reports having found over two hundred such books in the churches of Syria, which he ordered replaced by the Gospels of the Four Evangelists. Tatian's *Harmony* places the Gospel materials in a continuous narrative, beginning with John 1:1, omitting parallel passages, but it is not a Harmony in the modern sense of the word. Diatessaron means "through four," and assures us that shortly after the middle of the second century (170), in Syria at any rate, the four Gospels were accepted as canonical.

Of unknown authorship, the Muratorian Canon (170 or somewhat later) gets its name from Muratori, who discovered an eighth-century Latin manuscript of this document in a library at Milan, which was published in 1740. Unfortunately the manuscript is mutilated at the beginning and probably also at the end, but it is nevertheless of immense value as giving what is likely a fair consensus of the view of the canon held by the church in the West toward the end of the second century. It is reasonably certain that the list of New Testament books contained herein was drawn up in conscious opposition to the canon of the heretic Marcion, whose theological views were unacceptable to the church at Rome. Marcion's heresy is referred to by name, and the description of the Gospels as a whole — "all things in all [of them] are declared by the one sovereign Spirit" — suggests a side-glance at Marcion with his deliberate choice of Luke to the exclusion of the other three, and recalls Tertullian's outburst, "What Pontic mouse ever had such gnawing powers as he who has gnawed the Gospels to pieces?" Marcion published his own recension of Luke and ten epistles of Paul, not including the Pastorals in his list. These constituted his New Testament.

In the Muratorian Canon the opening words apparently have to do with Mark (the portion dealing with Matthew is lost). Then Luke and John are mentioned, followed by the Acts, then the thirteen epistles of Paul, beginning with 1 Corinthians and concluding with the two to Timothy. Pseudo-Pauline letters to the Laodiceans and to the Alexandrians are mentioned, but not as accepted. The list is rounded out by the Epistle of Jude, two of John, also his Apocalypse, with the indication that some accept that of Peter but others will not have it read in the church. Some scholars have felt that the text is corrupt here and originally indicated one epistle (rather than Apocalypse) of Peter as accepted, with doubt cast on the second epistle. If this critical emendation be accepted, only Hebrews, James, and one epistle of John are absent. The Muratorian Canon is not an individualistic document, the statement of a personal opinion or the expression of a novel theory, but a deliberate exposition of the views of the church universal so far as the writer is acquainted with its outlook and practice.

Before continuing the historical survey, it may be well to note that during the patristic period the earlier witnesses speak of Gospel and Apostle rather than of individual Gospels or Epistles. This terminology reflects a consciousness that special importance was to be attached to those documents that dealt with the historical unfolding of the gospel in the ministry of Jesus and to those in which Paul expounded that message in terms of the needs of the churches. The twofold division of Marcion's canon, however truncated, reflects this fundamental outlook. In addition, especially after the time of Marcion, the church recognized the Book of Acts as the needed "bridge" between the Gospels and the Epistles.

2. Later patristic writers. Toward the close of the second century Christian literature becomes more extensive, with prominent voices in various geographical areas speaking out in behalf of their local congregations, but also out of a conscious oneness with believers in the church universal. Such men are Irenaeus of Lyons in Gaul, Clement of Alexandria, and Tertullian of North Africa. If it is ascertained that the testimony of these leaders with respect to the canon is in agreement, it will follow that their verdict is the consensus of the widely separated sections of the church that they may be said to represent.

Irenaeus is of special importance for several reasons. He came originally from Asia Minor, where he sat at the feet of Polycarp, who was privileged to have personal contact with several "eyewitnesses of the Word of life." Later, when he was presbyter at Lyons, his bishop Pothinus had likewise been associated with Christians of apostolic days. Having spent some time at Rome, Irenaeus was in position to reflect the knowledge and judgment of this prominent center of the faith where leading apostles had ministered. Consequently his associations were both ancient and widely diffused. Furthermore, he was the first theologian of the Old Catholic Church.

In his Epistle to Florinus Irenaeus mentions the instruction he had received as a boy from Polycarp and states that this venerable figure "reported all things in agreement with the Scripture." He is familiar with the names of the Gospel writers and the traditions surrounding their work. "The Word," he says, ". . .gave to us the Gospel in a fourfold shape, but held together by one Spirit." Irenaeus gives several reasons why there are four Gospels, but these reasons, however fanciful and mystical — such as the existence of four directions and four winds — are not the actual grounds upon which he receives four Gospels and no more, but a justification for the existence of these only as given by God. In addition to the Gospels, Irenaeus makes reference to the Book of Acts, First Peter, First John, all the Epistles of Paul except Philemon, and the Revelation. Lack of mention of a few books does not constitute proof of their noncanonical standing in the eyes of Irenaeus, since he does not furnish a formal list of New Testament writings.

We have the testimony of Eusebius that Clement of Alexandria wrote explanations of all the canonical Scriptures, including the disputed writings, and even commented on the Epistle of Barnabas and the Apocalypse of Peter. He was clear, however, in his understanding of the line between canonical and apocryphal in respect to the Gospels. After quoting a saying of an apocryphal nature, he says, "we do not find this saying in the four Gospels that have been handed down to us, but in that according to the Egyptians."

Tertullian refused to use any other Gospels than those that the church acknowledges as inspired and authoritative. In a single passage he mentions Corinthians, Galatians, Philippians, Thessalonians, Ephesians, and Romans as samples of apostolic writings. Concerning some of the Catholic Epistles he is silent.

The testimony of Irenaeus, Clement, and Tertullian, coming from a period close to the end of the second century is sufficient to establish that there was a body of authoritative writings revered by the church as a whole. The only question that remains unsettled is the extent of the canon, which involves a discussion of the disputed books.

Origen of Alexandria was the great leader of the generation following. Speaking of the four Gospels "which alone are uncontroverted in the church of God spread under heaven," Origen then proceeds to name them. In his commentary on Joshua, translated into Latin probably by Rufinus, he takes occasion to say that Paul thundered with the fourteen "trumpets" of his epistles. It may be that Origen himself did not write "fourteen," thus assigning Hebrews to Paul, but that the figure was changed from thirteen to fourteen by the translator. This Father indicates some doubt in the church of his time about 2 Peter and 2 and 3 John. Little, if anything, of the complete New Testament is lacking in Origen and therefore in the Egyptian church of his time.

Either because of omission from patristic testimony in some quarters or because of being named with a degree of question, the following books lacked universal endorsement in the early centuries: Hebrews, James, 2 Peter, 2 and 3 John, Jude, and the Revelation. Hebrews, questioned in the West because of uncertainty as to apostolic authorship, gained acceptance in the East under the plea of the Alexandrians that it was Pauline in some sense, and in due time it was classified as one of Paul's letters. In the case of James, several factors may have operated: uncertainty as to the identity of the James in question, the problem as to the meaning of the Twelve Tribes scattered abroad, and the scarcity of distinctive Christian teaching on the doctrinal side. Doubt arose respecting 2 Peter because it differs so greatly in vocabulary and somewhat in style from the First Epistle. It seems to have had limited circulation also. Failure to include 2 and 3 John is understandable in view of their brevity, personal nature, and the relative unimportance of their contents. Jude was plagued with uncertainty as to the apostolic standing of the writer, who seems to set himself apart from the apostles (v.17). John's Apocalypse had a solid place in the canon in the earlier patristic period, being questioned only by the sect known as the Alogi, but generally received throughout the church. The failure of writers in the East during the fourth century to include it in the New Testament may be assigned to the influence of the criticism of Dionysius of Alexandria, who argued the great differences between the Revelation and the Fourth Gospel as ground for concluding that another John must have written the Apocalypse. Influenced by Dionysius, Eusebius felt that it was wise to put the book not only among the acknowledged writings *(Homologoumena)* but also with the non-genuine, saying that some reject it.

3. The testimony of the versions. In Syria the church was Syriac-speaking, and during the second century had the Gospels in this tongue, as attested by the Diatessaron and the *Old Syriac*. Manuscript evidence for the rest of the New Testament at this early period is lacking, but there is no reasonable ground for doubt that most of the books were translated. The Peshitta, the common version or official Bible of the Syriac Church, was rendered in the fifth century. It reflected the reluctance of the East to receive certain books, since 2 Peter, 2 and 3 John, Jude and Revelation were lacking. In the following century these deficiencies were made up in the Philoxenian Syriac.

Toward the end of the second century the Christians of Egypt had the New Testament in the native Coptic tongue, at least in the Sahidic, and a few decades later in the Bohairic. However, since the manuscripts that attest the text come from varying periods, especially for the Sahidic, it is precarious to insist on a complete New Testament from the beginning.

With respect to the Latin, it is well known that Jerome prepared the Vulgate shortly before 400 because the Old Latin stood in dire need of revision. The inclusion of the complete New Testament in the Vulgate may be regarded as presumptive evidence of its presence in the Old Latin. As early as 180 there is indication of a collection of Paul's letters in North Africa, and if this be true, the Gospels must surely have been in use also.

Concerning other versions it is unnecessary to make inquiry, since they pertain to more remote areas of the church and belong to somewhat later times.

4. The fourth century. During this period the church came more and more to a position of unanimity regarding the canon. Eusebius (260-340) lists only James, Jude, 2 Peter, 2 and 3 John as disputed books *(Antilegomena).* Cyril, Bishop of Jerusalem (315-386), accepts all but the Revelation. Athanasius, Bishop of Alexandria, in his 39th Festal Epistle (367), is the first to cite all 27 books.

During this era the church was free to engage in discussion at various councils, now that the threat of official Roman persecution was past. That it had been able to hold some gatherings, at least on a local scale, prior to this time, is indicated by Tertullian's broadside leveled at the *Shepherd of Hermas*. In his treatise on modesty (chap. 10) he states that this writing had been "habitually judged by every council of churches . . . among apocryphal and false [writings]." This suggests that discussions on the canon may have been fairly common in some areas, but this is only an inference. At the Council of Laodicea (363) the books of the Bible seem at first sight to have been made the subject of special study. This was a local gathering attended by only a few delegates. The 59th canon records the decision of the council regarding the contents of Scripture. With reference to the New Testament, all the books are present except the Revelation. However, since not all the sources have this final canon of the council, it is probable that the list of books was added at a later time. Firmer ground is reached with the Third Council of Carthage (397), which declared that these 27 books and these only were to be received as canonical.

It has sometimes been asserted that the canon derives both its form and authority from church councils, as though the church had no recognized Scripture prior to their action. Such is not the case. What the councils did was to certify the canon that was already widely acknowledged in the church. Conciliar action did not provide for the first time a rule of faith and practice, but rather gave public and united testimony to that which the church had long known and used and cherished as its authoritative guide. This is readily apparent from the testimonies of the Fathers that we have already noted, which are representative but by no means complete. Only in the case of disputed books could conciliar action be construed as legislative in any sense, and only as speaking in behalf of the majority who already received these books as Scripture.

If the church did not derive its notion of the uniqueness of these books from the action of councils, what then was the basis upon which it revered them above other Christian writings and carefully distinguished them as alone normative for the faith? This is the next subject for investigation.

Principles Governing Canonicity

1. The testimony of the ancients. This subject is seldom discussed by the early Fathers in a formal way, but enough information is available to enable us to know how they justified the reception of the New Testament books as authoritative to the exclusion of others.

First, these books had *apostolic origin.* It was clear from the New Testament that Jesus had chosen certain men and had conferred on them the dignity of apostles in order that they might be responsible and informed witnesses to himself and authoritative guides of the infant church. The teaching of these men was accepted by the church as possessing the authority of Christ. Consequently, when they wrote, their testimony had a unique place in the esteem of believers. Their writings were read in the churches. Even so early a figure as Clement of Rome recognized that Paul wrote to the Corinthians "with true inspiration," whereas he himself can claim neither apostolic rank nor inspiration. Ignatius sharply distinguished between himself (a bishop of the church) and the apostles Peter and Paul, though he was headed for martyrdom such as they had endured.

Even in the New Testament period apostles received communication from Christian groups (e.g. 1 Cor. 7:1), but such letters were not preserved and included with those of the apostles. This easily overlooked fact underscores the uniqueness of the writings of those who were qualified to declare Christian truth and its implications for the church because of designation by Christ himself.

The importance of apostolicity in the eyes of the early church may be seen by recalling the history of the Epistle to the Hebrews and the Apocalypse of John. The former was more widely received in the East than in the West for the reason that the name of Paul had become attached to it by the Alexandrians. In the West, Tertullian, because he ascribed the book to Barnabas, was not willing to receive it as Scripture in the full sense. As to the Apocalypse, Dionysius of Alexandria weakened its position in the East by the force of his literary criticism, pointing out certain differences between it and the Gospel of John and thereby bringing into question its apostolic origin. The reason for its ultimate reception in the East was the insistence upon its apostolic authorship by various leaders of the church, despite the contrary opinion of Dionysius.

Again, the readiness of some Church Fathers to give canonical rank to such works as the *Didache,* the *Epistle of Clement,* and the *Shepherd of Hermas,* can be explained when it is realized that the authors might be confused with genuinely apostolic figures. The full name of the *Didache* is the *Teaching of the Twelve Apostles*. Clement of Alexandria probably endorsed the *Epistle of Clement* (of Rome) on the same ground as his successor, Origen, who identified this writer with the person mentioned by Paul in Philippians 4:3. This would not make Clement an apostle in the narrower sense such as pertained to the Twelve and to Paul, but he might be regarded as an apostle in the somewhat looser sense in which the term is occasionally employed in the New Testament. The acceptance in some quarters of the *Shepherd of Hermas* as canonical is to be traced to the belief that the author was the one mentioned in Romans 16:14.

Apostolicity in the strict sense will not account for all the books of the New Testament, however. Some theory had to be devised to accredit Mark and Luke. Here the church fell back upon the consideration that these men wrote under the direction of Peter and Paul respectively, so that their work possessed the authority of these apostolic men. We may feel the need of caution in regarding this explanation as entirely valid, but again it reveals the strength of the hold that the test of apostolicity had on the church. Actually, when to Mark and Luke we add the writer to the Hebrews and Jude, the list of those who stand outside the apostolic circle is rather imposing. But all these men were close to the source of the stream of Christian tradition and the Spirit was free to use them as well as the more official representatives of the church.

Second, the Fathers stressed the *reception* of the New Testament writings by the original churches and the continued knowledge and use of these documents by later generations. This is a natural corollary to apostolicity. Readers of the New Testament have noted the care that Paul displayed on occasion to make certain his writings were accepted as genuine (writing his signature with his own hand and committing the documents to trustworthy messengers, 2 Thess. 3:17; cf. 2:2). Each local church would be able to vouch for any such communication that another group might wish to copy and use. The practice of reading should be noted in this connection. To make use of a writing in connection with Christian worship was not absolute evidence of its canonical standing (e.g., 1 Clement was read in the Corinthian church alongside Scripture late in the second century), but it was tantamount to this. For the most part such reading was confined to canonical books.

Third, *consistency of doctrine* with the standard already possessed in the Old Testament and in the teaching of the apostles was a useful requirement, enabling the church to expose and repudiate heretical writings, such as those of the Gnostics, and also many of the Apocrypha.

2. The Roman Catholic position. Scripture is independent of the church so far as its inspiration is concerned. This is of God only, so that when Scripture is viewed in isolation, it possesses its own canonical authority. Practically, however, as Scripture comes into contact with human lives, it requires the voice of the church to authenticate it as well as to interpret it. Another feature is the recognition of the validity of unwritten tradition alongside that of Scripture. The Council of Trent, at its fourth session, April 8, 1546, committed the church to honor along with the Scripture "the unwritten traditions which, received by the Apostles from the mouth of Christ himself, or from the Apostles themselves, the Holy Ghost dictating, have come down even unto us, transmitted as it were from hand to hand." In its extent, the Roman Catholic New Testament is identical with that agreed upon at the Third Council of Carthage.

3. The Reformers. Luther, with typical independence, singled out certain books as basic on the ground that they exhibit Christ. On the other hand, he relegated four books to a secondary position, putting Hebrews, James, Jude, and the Revelation at the end of his New Testament in a detached position. He did not deny to other Christians the right to consider these books on a par with the rest, but for himself found them inferior for various reasons.

Calvin commented on the New Testament in a comprehensive way, but he passed by 2 and 3 John and the Revelation. This does not mean he refused to honor them as Scripture, though he seems to have had reservations about them. Knowing the doubts of the ancients on other *Antile-*

gomena, he nevertheless was not particularly disturbed about these books, and received them.

Calvin's contribution to the doctrine of Scripture emerged in connection with his teaching on the believer's assurance concerning the word of God. This assurance is provided by the testimony of the Holy Spirit working with the word read or heard in preaching. Quite obviously this work of the Spirit is chiefly concerned with the central issue of the gospel message and cannot be relied upon to settle the limits of the canon. But it provides a measure of certification of the canon on the subjective side to supplement the objective factors centering in the reception of the New Testament documents by the early church. Logically the external testimony comes first, for internal testimony, owing to the fact that some material in the sacred record pertains to mundane matters of fact as distinct from spiritual instruction, is limited in its power to give confirmation. It is difficult to conceive of the Spirit as attesting one name in a genealogical list as opposed to a possible alternative. Furthermore, if internal testimony were sufficient for establishing the word of God, it should be possible on this basis to settle every disputed text of the New Testament, thus eliminating the necessity for textual criticism. No one conversant with the problems will affirm that the testimony of the Spirit can properly be appealed to in this realm.

4. Modern study. For the English-speaking world the work of B. F. Westcott has proved of abiding worth. In his *History of the Canon,* Westcott emphasized the importance of a superintending providence guiding the church from the beginning to an appreciation of the books that time and use confirmed. He writes regarding the canon: "Its limits were fixed in the earliest times by use rather than by criticism; and this use itself was based on immediate knowledge" (p. 496). Again, he affirms that it was under the influence of the Spirit that the church recognized in the New Testament the law of its constitution (p. 498). The formation of the canon was an act of the intuition of the church (p. 56).

The German scholar, Adolf Harnack, with a keen interest in Christian origins, included the canon in the scope of his studies. According to Harnack, the canon came into being rather suddenly, at about the beginning of the last quarter of the second century, as the conscious and deliberate creation of the Old Catholic Church, in order to meet the challenge of Gnosticism and Montanism. At first the church had only the Old Testament as Scripture in the strict sense of the word. Its need of instruction on an immediate basis was provided by the ministry of prophets, whose utterances were viewed as the word of God. This situation was changed by the emergence of the two movements mentioned above. The Gnostics (and for the immediate purpose Marcion may be classed with them) rejected the Old Testament and appealed to certain writings that the church had been using, notably the Epistles of Paul, in the case of Marcion. This obliged the church to declare itself. Marcion forced the hand of the church when he set up his canon.

Harnack undoubtedly overestimated the influence of Marcion on canonical developments within the church, primarily because he did not distinguish sufficiently between the principle of canonicity and the drawing up of a formal list of books. As Westcott states (p. 326), "The canon of Marcion may have been the first which was publicly proposed, but the general consent of earlier Catholic writers proves that within the Church there had been no need for pronouncing a judgment on a point which had not been brought into dispute." Our survey of the history of the canon has shown us that before Marcion's time there is reasonably clear evidence of the Gospel canon and a collection of Paul's writings. It is hazardous to conclude that Marcion must be credited with the idea of a canon embracing Gospel and Apostle. He was a competitor but not an innovator in the strictest sense of the word. Tertullian and other Fathers charge Marcion with rejecting books. This in itself presupposes in the minds of these men the acknowledged position of such books in what was in fact a canon, even though it had not been published as such. W. C. van Unnik makes the point that the generous use of the New Testament books in the *Gospel of Truth* implies the authoritative position of these books at Rome *before the condemnation of Marcion* (italics added).

Montanism began to be a menace to the church's life shortly after the time of Marcion. Montanus insisted that the prophetic gift was permanently granted to the church and that he himself was an authoritative prophet of the Lord. Harnack claimed that whereas the church up to this time had accepted the prophetic as the norm of authoritative divine utterance, it was now obliged by the pressure of Montanism with its vagaries to call upon the principle of apostolicity, which of course made revelation beyond the apostolic age impossible. But Harnack tended to exaggerate the importance of the prophetic element in the early church. Evidence points to the fact that even in the apostolic age it was necessary to examine critically the utterances of those who professed to have the gift (1 Cor. 12:10; 14:29). It is not clear that prophecy can be identified with revelation in the fullest sense. Certainly the case of Agabus points to a very limited and specific function (Acts 11:28; 21:10). There can be no doubt that the church from the beginning looked to apostles rather than prophets for its primary guidance. In Ephesians 4:11, for example, prophets are subordinated to apostles.

E. J. Goodspeed seems to share with Harnack the feeling that the dominance of the Spirit in the life of the church logically makes a written canon unnecessary. "That the early church should have made itself an authoritative scripture and placed it side by side with the Old Testament is from some points of view strange." Then he goes on to explain that the church "possessed an inner guide, the Spirit of God, the mind of Christ, far superior to written rules and records."[1] Yet it is certainly right to say that there is no conscious antinomy in the Scripture or in the early church, so far as can be detected, between a written rule and the guidance of the Spirit. One of the classic statements of inspiration, 2 Peter 1:20-21, makes this

[1] *Interpreter's Bible,* I, 63a.

apparent. Christianity is the religion of a book as well as of the Spirit. A written rule, while subject to the vicissitudes of copying and also of interpretation, had great advantage over occasional prophetic utterances that needed to be tried.

Goodspeed approaches the study of the canon largely from the standpoint of the historian, and his chief contribution is the emphasis upon the formation of collections that together make up the New Testament, especially the Epistles of Paul and then the Gospels. He tends to put the collection of Paul's letters later than necessary, however. In seeking to show that these had fallen into disuse shortly after being penned by pointing to the failure of the Synoptic Gospels and Acts to make use of them, he dubiously employs the precarious argument from silence. How can it be shown that the writers of the Gospels or of Acts felt under obligation to use epistolary material? The fact that they did not do so simply shows their fidelity to the task to which they had set themselves.

Zahn, who was a contemporary of Harnack, had considerable dispute with him over this subject of the canon. He maintained that a canon existed before the time of Marcion, and pointed to the lack of conciliar action in the latter part of the second century relative to this important matter. He insisted that the canon was not created by the church in the sense that bishops or councils formulated it. In his judgment the important factor in canonical development was the cultus, the use of the New Testament writings in the worship of the church. It was the suitability of the writings for this purpose that gave them a place in the canon. Zahn's view has a measure of truth, surely, but it would be hard to substantiate in the case of all the books of the New Testament, some of which are obviously less suited than others for ecclesiastical use because of their brevity and in some cases their rather private character.

Karl Barth's view of the canon moves along traditional lines. "In no sense of the concept could or can the Church give the Canon to itself. The Church cannot 'form' it, as historians have occasionally said without being aware of the theological implications. The Church can only confirm or establish it as something which has already been formed and given" (*Church Dogmatics,* I/2, p. 473). Again, "For the obvious core of the history of the Canon is this, that within the various churches, and with all kinds of vacillations, particular parts of the oldest tradition have gradually been distinguished and set apart from others in the appreciation and acceptance of Christendom, a process which proper and formal canonization by synodic resolutions and the like could only subsequently confirm. At some time and in some measure (with all the chance features which this appreciation and acceptance may have strengthened) these very writings, by the very fact that they were canonical, saw to it that they in particular were later recognized and proclaimed to be canonical" (p. 474).

W. G. Kümmel doubts the validity of apostolic authorship as a valid criterion for canonicity. In its place he proposes a chronological criterion. Writings composed after the first quarter of the second century cannot be regarded as original witnesses and hence must be excluded, since the canon means basically a testimony to the early Christian history. Any book lying outside the chronological limits of the apostolic kerygma can and ought to be excluded. H. Diem points out that the chronological test runs into some difficulty with *First Clement,* which clearly meets the demands of the time test but does not have canonical rank. To say that it was excluded because of its contents is hardly a sufficient answer, since it is not heretical.

Oscar Cullmann develops his view of the canon from within the framework of *Heilsgeschichte* (history of salvation, or saving history) and the importance of the apostolate as the authenticated medium of Christ for the teaching of the church. In *The Early Church,* he holds that "*the infant Church itself distinguished between apostolic tradition and ecclesiastical tradition,* clearly subordinating the latter to the former, in other words, subordinating itself to the apostolic tradition." Again, "The fixing of the Christian canon of scripture means that *the Church itself,* at a given time, traced a clear and definite line of demarcation between the period of the apostles and that of the Church, between the time of foundation and that of construction, between the apostolic community and the Church of the bishops, in other words, between apostolic tradition and ecclesiastical tradition. Otherwise the formation of the canon would be meaningless." It is not the difference between oral and written tradition that is of major importance, but that the tradition was fixed by the apostles. "By establishing the *principle* of a canon the Church recognized that *from that time* the tradition was no longer a criterion of truth." Its unreliability was already beginning to be apparent in the proliferation of apocryphal writings.

Seeking to meet the Roman Catholic objection that Scripture by itself is a dead thing, requiring the vital life of God flowing through the church to support and implement it, Cullmann insists on the truth that Scripture is not rightly used if it is not apprehended as the means of the risen Lord's continuing ministry in the church even as that ministry was manifest in the witness of the apostles during their lifetime.

A weakness in Cullmann's position is that it requires a degree of self-consciousness on the part of the early church in this matter of canonical development that the sources of the middle of the second century do not indicate. This is the perennial problem in dealing with the canon. The historical materials are too limited to satisfy the historian, so he must call upon theological theory to bridge the gap.

Conclusion

The principle of canonicity cannot be divorced from the idea of authority, in this case a divine authority, in spite of the obvious fact that the Scriptures were written by men. Back of the written word lies the oral tradition concerning Christ and his work, and back of the oral tradition lies the preaching of the apostles as authoritative spokesmen for Christ (cf. 2 Cor. 13:3), and back of this apostolic testimony lies Christ himself as the one whom the Father sent to accomplish redemption for the world. Christ both authenticated the Old Testament Scriptures and promised the activity of the Spirit of truth as making possible what became in fact the New Testament. So in the ultimate sense Christ is the key to canonicity.

The very character of New Testament revelation was bound to make the written record that enshrined it authoritative. If the church was conscious of the fulfillment of Old Testament prophecy in the life and mission of Christ and in its own beginnings, it was inevitable that the church should regard the record of these fulfillments as partaking of the same authoritative character as the Old Testament, which now for the first time spoke to men's hearts with fullness of meaning as seen in the light of the new and completed revelation.

Some people are disturbed because there was not complete agreement in the early church as to which books should stand in the New Testament canon. Some measure of discussion was no doubt necessary in order to satisfy as many minds as possible and lead to a consensus. The important fact to remember here, however, is this, that the very fact of discussion about the right of books to stand in the canon presupposes the idea of a canon, the idea of a body of writings sacred and authoritative in a unique sense. Passing disagreement on a few books should not be allowed to overshadow in importance the vastly greater measure of agreement on the majority of the books. Furthermore, basic agreement on the canon by various sections of the church on a voluntary basis (apart from and prior to action by church councils) is a noteworthy fact that should be given its full weight.

It is unrealistic to expect that the church at the end of the first century would be aware that it had a complete canon in its possession and would give united expression to the fact so as to close the issue of New Testament Scripture once for all. The church was extending itself territorially, with limited contact between its various segments, and had no pressure either from without or from within to make a definitive statement on the subject of the canon. To quote G. W. H. Lampe, "The early church did not possess the critical or historical equipment to define the canon quickly, uniformly, or exactly; but it gradually succeeded in isolating such early works, in addition to the gospels and the recognized apostolic epistles, as it believed to embody the general doctrinal position of the apostles. That there were loose ends here and there — an epistle or two not universally accepted which came to be acknowledged, and a sub-apostolic book or two which were very nearly accepted but which came to be rejected, did not seem to the early Church to be a matter of any great moment. Under the guidance of the Spirit in the Church at large the apostolic tradition handed down in the Churches came to take the form of defined Scriptures."[2]

[2]In *Scripture and Tradition*, ed. by F. W. Dillistone, p. 43.

The church's uncertainty regarding a few books may be a matter of some concern to us, but we see that on the whole it was irenically handled, and became dissolved as the books in question became more and more widely known and used. On the other hand, the violence of the church's reaction to the effort of Marcion to set up a restricted canon is a testimony to the fact that the church was aware of its larger riches, which it refused to deny to itself.

It is of some interest to observe that the books that raised most questions in the early church are grouped last in the order of our English Bible, from Hebrews to Revelation, although two which stand near the end, 1 Peter and 1 John, were rarely held in any doubt.

The indefiniteness of address common to the so-called Catholic Epistles may explain why they were late in gaining general acceptance, for there was no one church, in such cases, which received the letter and vouched for it to others. This may have counterbalanced the consideration that the very indefiniteness of destination presupposes a fairly wide original reception. In *Supreme Authority,* J. N. Geldenhuys deals with this problem of tardiness in acceptance of a few books and the related problem of a few non-canonical books being treated as canonical by a few men, by advancing the explanation that these conditions were largely due to the expansion of the church. This state of affairs did not exist at first nor did it last indefinitely, for the church gradually came to agreement.

Doubtless some questions remain unanswered. Because the term "Scripture" is applied to New Testament writings only occasionally in the sub-apostolic age, the student may conclude that the apostolic writers were themselves not aware of composing Scripture. This is quite possible, for to them Scripture meant the Old Testament. What is essential, however, is to approach the matter from the divine standpoint, from the standpoint of God's purpose to provide the finished revelation. Even from the human standpoint there was awareness on the part of the apostles that God was speaking and commanding through them. So the lack of awareness of composing Scripture is no more damaging to the cause of canonical authority than is a similar situation among Old Testament writers.

Another question pertains to the role of the church in relation to the canon. Is the canon dependent on the church or does it occupy a position apart from and above the church, in some fashion approximating the relation of Christ to the church? Much depends on how the matter is stated. In so far as men were needed to write the documents and secure their transmission and make known their contents, the canon is indeed dependent on the church. On the other hand, to maintain that the church "created" Scripture is a contradiction of what the church has always understood when it has described these writings as the word of God. As Barth has reminded us, the canon is something given to the church.